ARTPRICE INDICATOR®

"Chiner malin"

2002

D1601117

EHRMANN

Artprice.com & Server Group Chairman Président Fondateur	Thierry Ehrmann
Editorial Director - Directeur de Rédaction	Nadège Ehrmann
Marketing Director - Direction Marketing	Josette Mey
Administrative Management - Direction Administrative	Nabila Arify
Financial Management - Direction Financière	Alain Dutertre
Editor in Chief 17th , 18th, 19th C. Dept	Frank Van Wilder
Editor in Chief US	Peter H. Falk
R&D/Art market indices	Helga Unterlechner
Art Director - Directeur Artistique	Marc Del Piano
Infographist - Infographiste	Thibault Laplanche
Webmaster	Jean-Baptiste Hatté
Webmaster Assistants	Valérie Petit / Josie Gauthier
Coordination	Véronique Compagne-Louvet
Senior Editors - Rédacteurs	Jean-Michel Grillou / Astrid Llinas
Editorial Assistants - Assistants de Rédaction	Nicole Bernard / Madeleine Brotons / Latifa Boukraa / Dominique Delmas / Aleksandra Delrieu / Lucile Desgardins / Gaëlle Desmurs / Olivier Fagot / Ghislaine Fayolle / Nathalie Nanquette / Séverine Plantade / Maria Retamero / Carine Salini
Biography Dept. Assistants Assistantes de Rédaction Département Biographie	Claire Chappatte / Fabienne Despert / Caroline Fayolle / Véronique Hepp/ Anelore Leveau / Claire Morin / Laurence Sparfel / Frédérique Stenger / Karel Tarallo
Research Assistants - Documentalistes	Daniella Lienard / Stéphanie Milossi / Nathalie Tarrare
Computer Management D. G. Informatique-Internet	Christophe Vigny / Valérie Pigeon / Souad Idrissi / Thierry Matrat
Sales and Marketing Dept. Département Commercial et Marketing	Maud Bain / Amélie Bonin / Emilie Frochot / Maude Galliano / Sanna Gustafsson / Sandra Karoun / Pénélope Kergall / Cendrine Martin / Salima Neffar / Véronique Paluch / Laurent Tatford / Françoise Terraillon
Financial Assistant - Comptable	Sylvie Briel
Logistique	Eric Martel
Publishing Director Directeur de la publication	Thierry Ehrmann
Printing - Impression	Imprimerie NOAO Capital(e), Paris

server group

Sarl Capital 598 539 000 FRF
RCS LYON 408 309 270

email adresses : info@artprice.com / artist@artprice.com / catalog@artprice.com / marketing@artprice.com

2002 edition
Edition 2002

The Artprice Indicator 2002 gives for each artist, and for each category (paintings, drawings, sculptures….) and class of dimension selected, the most representative auction results to provide the best indication of possible value.

The choice of the artists listed remains independent of all judgements concerning the artist's importance and free of any arbitrary or even informed appreciation. This selection is based strictly according to the rules of supply and demand in the art market. All artists whose work was sold at auction in the preceeding three years are noted. Their results from June 1998 to June 2001 have been balanced in such way as to give greater weight to the more recent transactions.

Our procedure consists in identifying a transaction which is the

L'Artprice Indicator / Chiner Malin 2002 offre pour chaque artiste, et dans chaque genre et dimensions sélectionnés, les résultats de ventes aux enchères les plus significatifs, donnant ainsi la meilleure indication possible de la cote d'un artiste.

Le choix des artistes répertoriés est indépendant de tout jugement sur l'importance de l'artiste et de toute appréciation arbitraire ou même éclairée. Cette sélection est basée sur la façon dont le marché appréhende la production de l'artiste par les règles économiques de l'offre et de la demande. Tout artiste dont les œuvres sont passées en vente publiques durant les 3 années précédentes est pris en compte.

Leurs résultats pour la période de Juin 1998 à Juin 2001 sont pondérés, afin de donner plus d'importance aux transactions récentes.

Notre démarche consiste à identifier la

closest to the representative prices commanded by the artist, as evidenced in the Art Price Index.

The result is a volume whose apparent simplicity and handiness conceals a sophisticated work solidly founded on econometrics in which nothing has been left to chance or arbitrariness.

The Artprice Indicator is sourced from the **Artprice.com** data bank which gives full reliability to the results published. The exhaustiveness of our worldwide data bank guarantees your access to complete information for the whole art market. The systematic gathering of auction sales results throughout the world gives the **Artprice.com** data bank its unique character and this pocket guide draws the best from it.

The **Artprice.com** data bank grows each year by hundred of thousands of records and now totals 2,500,000 results and over 271,000 artists.

Collectors, art lovers and art market dealers who wish to find more details about the results can choose from four ways to consult the data bank:

• Internet: **www.artprice.com**

• CD-ROM:
  Fine Art or Works on Paper

• Books: Artprice Annual
  (14 editions from 1988 to 2001)

transaction dont le prix est le plus proche de la cote d'un artiste, telle que celle-ci nous est donnée par l'Art Price Index.

Il en résulte un volume qui, sous le couvert de sa simplicité apparente et de sa maniabilité, est de par sa méthodologie solidement fondée sur l'économétrie, un ouvrage sophistiqué où rien n'a été laissé au hasard et à l'arbitraire.

*Les résultats présentés dans l'Artprice Indicator sont extraits de la banque de données **Artprice.com**, dont la quasi exhaustivité garantit la fiabilité et la crédibilité mondiale.*

*La collecte systématique des résultats de ventes aux enchères dans le monde entier confère aux données **Artprice.com** leur caractère unique, dont le présent ouvrage tire le meilleur parti.*

*La banque de données **artprice.com** s'étoffe chaque année de plusieurs centaines de milliers de données et dénombre à ce jour 2 500 000 résultats et plus de 271 000 artistes.*

Ces informations détaillées sont accessibles pour tous collectionneurs, amateurs ou professionnels de l'art sur 4 supports :

• *Internet : www.artprice.com*

• *CD-ROM : Fine Art ou Works on Paper*

• *Publication papier : Artprice Annual (14 éditions de 1988 à 2001)*

• *Minitel : 3617ARTPRICE*

Artprice.com
Artprice.com

Artprice.com (formerly Art Price Annual SA) is a French limited company with a capital of 6,250,000 Euro, incorporated in February 1997 held at 60% by Group Server, founded in 1987 by Thierry Ehrmann.

Artprice.com owns and runs one of the world's biggest art price quotation data banks, spanning paintings, prints, drawings, miniatures, sculptures, posters, photographs, tapestries (4 million results dating back to 1700), available for consultation on its main website **www.artprice.com** and 900 others (secondary data banks hanging vertically from the parent). **Artprice.com** anchors its worldwide leadership position on an industrial process integrating the gathering, monitoring, keyboarding, processing and enrichment of data on practically all art transactions, sourced from over 2,900 auction houses in more than 40 countries.

In February 2001, Europ@web transferred its 17% of the company's shares to AGAFIN (Bernard Arnault group).

Artprice.com owns now the main art price guides and has purchased 100% of the Swiss company Xylogic, specialized in the development of indices and

Thierry Ehrmann

Artprice.com (anciennement nommée Art Price Annual SA) est une société anonyme au capital de 6 250 000 Euro, créée en février 1997 et détenue majoritairement (60%) par le Groupe Serveur fondé en 1987 par Thierry Ehrmann.

Artprice.com possède et exploite une des plus importantes banques de données de cotations d'œuvres d'art (peintures, estampes, dessins, miniatures, sculptures, affiches, photos, tapisseries) dans le monde (4 millions de résultats depuis 1700). A travers son site web principal www.artprice.com et ses 900 autres sites web (banques de données verticales provenant de la banque de données mère) Artprice.com bénéficie d'une position de leader mondial renforcée par un process industriel intégrant la collecte, la surveillance exhaustive, la saisie, le traitement et l'enrichissement de la quasi intégralité de toutes les ventes d'art en provenance de plus de 2 900 maisons de ventes dans plus de 40 pays.

En février 2001, Europ@web a amené sa participation (17% dans Artprice.com) à AGAFIN (groupe Bernard Arnault).

Artprice.com a racheté les principaux

software packages for the art market and auction houses.

Since then **Artprice.com** has acquired other art reference encyclopedias and well known publishers: Sound View Press (USA), Van Wilder publishing (France), the Caplan Monograms and Signatures, the dictionary of 18th and 19th C. auction records, the Rare books auction records and the Bayer data bank of English auction records (1700-1913).

Five departments to produce the art market reference data banks.

1. Auction Data banks Department: Gathering and processing current Fine Art auction catalogues. More than 450,000 artworks from worldwide auctions are recorded each year. The bought-in lots are also included.

2. Historical Data banks Department: Documenting the details and results of all of the world's art auctions, from the 17th Century until the mid 20th Century.

3. Artist's Biographies Department: A comprehensive biographical data bank of artists, ranging from Old Masters to modern and contemporary artists. (150,000 artists and 900,000 by the end of 2001), and data bank of signatures and monograms.

livres de cotes internationaux et la société Suisse Xylogic, SSII spécialisée dans les progiciels Intranet/Extranet utilisés par les auctioneers avec la production d'indices économétriques sur le marché de l'art et vient de réaliser successivement les acquisitions stratégiques :

1. Sound View Press (USA) : ensemble de 15 fonds éditoriaux sur l'art américain créé en 1975 (dont le célèbre Who was who in American Art).

2. Monogrammes et Signatures de Caplan (USA).

3. Un fonds éditorial unique des œuvres d'art du XVIIIᵉ et XIXᵉ siècles.

4. Les Editions Van Wilder (France).

5. L'Argus du Livre de Collection (France).

6. La banque de données Bayer sur le marché de l'art anglo-saxon de 1700 à 1913.

Cinq départements pour produire les banques de données de référence sur le marché de l'art.

1. Département collecte, saisie, traitement et enrichissement des données de l'année (intégralité des ventes aux enchères mondiales de Fine Art soit environ 450 000 données par an incluant les invendus).

2. Département reconstitution en banques de données des fonds édito-

4. Art Econometry Department: The art market indices are econometric tools providing practical information to the primary news agencies, the economic press, the banking/insurance sectors, and art investors.

5. Development of software for the auction industry (created by Xylogic Switzerland, now **artprice.com Suisse**). The focus is upon migration towards ASP/world intranet in order to provide high standards and conventions to assist auction houses.

The company expects to make a further ten major acquisitions of European works on art history and data.

riaux du XVIIᵉ au milieu du XXᵉ siècles relatifs au marché de l'art (Type dictionnaire Mireur).

3. Département biographies avec constitution d'une banque de données centralisant les biographies des artistes anciens, modernes et contemporains (à ce jour 150 000 – fin 2001 environ 900 000), ainsi que les signatures et monogrammes.

4. Département d'économétrie avec production d'indices spécifiques pour les agences d'information primaire, presse économique et secteurs banque / assurance.

5. Département Xylogic Suisse (**Artprice.com suisse**). SSII produisant depuis 1985 les logiciels pour les grandes maisons de ventes (avec de prestigieuses références) et une migration en ASP/intranet mondial en vue d'une normalisation des standards du marché de l'art.

Artprice.com projette de réaliser, en croissance externe, une dizaine d'acquisitions majeures d'ouvrages européens sur l'histoire et l'information de l'art.

THIERRY EHRMANN
Chairman
artprice.com
& Server Group

desa DESA
ANTIQUES & FINE ART

established 1950

The oldest and the most experienced antiqued firm in POLAND

AUCTION HOUSE
CRACOW

Floriańska Street 13
31–019 Cracow
Poland
phone: +48 (12) 422-19-66
fax: +48 (12) 422-98-91

http://www.desa.art.pl
e-mail: biuro@desa.art.pl

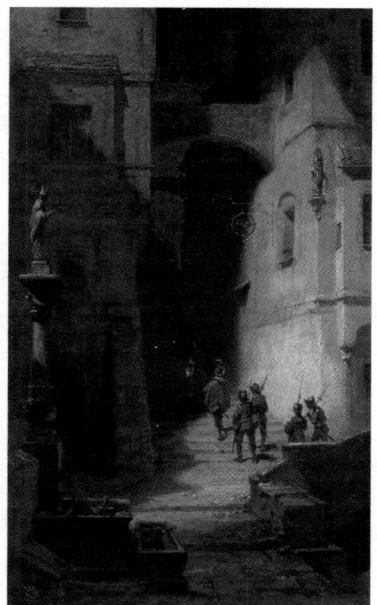

Signs and symbols
Signes et symboles

Paintings *Peinture*

Oil painting, acrylic, tempera, mixed media, miniature, etc.

Peinture à l'huile, acrylique, tempera, techniques mixtes, miniature, etc.

Drawings *Dessin*

Works on paper are usually classified under "drawing". Pen, chalk, pastel, ink, wash, watercolor, gouache, etc.

Les œuvres sur papier sont répertoriées le plus souvent en "dessin". Crayon, craies, pastel, encre, lavis, aquarelle, gouache, etc.

Prints *Estampe*

Images usually printed on paper after engraving on metal, wood, etc. Lithography, silkscreen, stencil, poster, tapestry, etc.

Images imprimées le plus souvent sur papier après gravure sur métal, bois, etc. Lithographie, sérigraphie, pochoir, poster, affiche, tapisserie, etc.

Sculptures *Sculpture*

Techniques resulting in three-dimentional works. Wooden and stone sculptures, assembly, compression, mobile, ceramic, etc.

Techniques de création en trois dimensions. Sculptures en bois, pierre, assemblage, compression, mobile, céramique, etc.

Photographs *Photographie*

Various techniques involving photographs and print runs, colour photograph, Polaroïd, silver prints, daguerreotype, etc.

Techniques diverses de prises de vues ou de tirage, photo couleur, Polaroïd, tirage argentique, daguerréotype, etc.

Genre / Category

AA van der Pieter Boudewyn XX [5]
$203 - €288 - £183 - FF691
Los grandes mandarines en la Corte de China
Grabado (27x35cm 10x13in) Madrid 1999

AAE Arvid 1877-1913 [4]
$4 812 - €5 366 - £3 292 - FF35 196
Interiör med lille pige, der syr Oil/canvas (70x53cm
27x20in) Viby J, Århus 2000

AAGAARD Carl Frederik 1833-1895 [183]
$1 834 - €2 012 - £1 246 - FF13 198
Juni i Skoven, Motiv fra Lellinge Oil/canvas
(67x54cm 26x21in) København 2000
$743 - €862 - £526 - FF5 655
Eveneing Landscape with Farm House and
Cows Oil/canvas (32.5x48cm 12x18in) Amsterdam

Technique / Medium

AALTO Ilmari 1891-1934 [54]
$1 632 - €1 429 - £990 - FF9 374
Hus invid parken Oil/panel (40x48.5cm 15x19in)
Helsinki 1998

AALTONEN Aarre 1889-1980 [20]
$171 - €202 - £119 - FF1 323
Mor och barn Plaster (H25cm H9in) Helsinki 2000

AALTONEN Wäinö 1894-1966 [101]
$1 524 - €1 430 - £941 - FF9 377
Regnbåge Oil/canvas (55x46cm 21x18in) Helsinki
1999
$547 - €605 - £379 - FF3 971
Pojken och stjärnan Bronze relief (37x36cm
14x14in) Helsinki 2001
$543 - €504 - £326 - FF3 309
Maija Akvarell/papper (46x38cm 18x14in) Helsinki
1999

AARON Joseph XX [10]
$750 - €805 - £501 - FF5 280
Big Sur Coastline Oil/canvas (27x35cm 11x14in)
Altadena CA 2000

AARON ... XX [...]
$3 750 - €4 483 - £2 586 - FF29 407
... Oil/... (... H20in)
Milford C... 2000

Dates de l'artiste
Artist's dates

AARTMAN Nicolaes Matthijs 1713-1793 [2]
$3 000 - €3 209 - £2 045 - FF21 050
Morning/Midday Wash (19x27.5cm 7x10in) New-
York 2001

AARTS Johannes J. 1871-1934 [37]
$61 - €68 - £41 - FF446
Perseus met het hoofd van Medusa Copper
engraving (21.2x29.8cm 8x11in) Haarlem 2000

Nombre d'œuvre
répertoriée dans artprice.com
Number of works
recorded by artprice.com

ABA-NOVAK Vilmos 1894-1941 [11]
$16 100 - €17 812 - £10 580 - FF116 840
Clowns Tempera/board (59x69cm 23x27in)
2000
$10 360 - €10 885 - £6 440 - FF71 400
Lacikonyha Huile/bois (27x34cm 10x13in) Budapest
2000
$1 850 - €1 944 - £1 150 - FF12 750
Paysage de collines Encre/papier (39x54cm
15x21in) Budapest 2000

ABADIAS J. [12]
$346 - €330 - £220 - FF2 167
Sanlucar de Barrameda Oleo/tabla (18x29cm
7x11in) Madrid 1999

ABADIE-LANDEL Pierre 1896-1972 [32]
$181 - €183 - £113 - FF1 200
Au bar à Montparnasse Monotype (30x24.5cm
11x9in) Quimper 2000

ABAKANOWICZ Magdalena 1930 [30]
$38 000 - €32 785 - £22 838 - FF215 053
Standing Figure ... (... 31x9c...
63x19x11in) New-York 1998
$10 000 - €9 629 - £6 251 - FF56 574
Dimensions / Size
Untitled Sculpture (62x16.5x21cm 24x6x8in) Beverly-
Hills CA 1999
$8 500 - €9 521 - £5 906 - FF62 454
Bull Face, 85A Charcoal/paper (100.5x75.5cm
39x29in) New-York 2001

ABATE Alberto 1946 [10]
$840 - €726 - £420 - FF4 760
«Orifica» Tecnica mista/carta (100x70cm 39x27in)
Prato 1999

ABATE de Goffredo 1849-1932 [1]
$2 000 - €2 073 - £1 200 - FF13 600
Meriggio sul Po, Torino Olio/tavola (20x33.5cm
7x13in) Vercelli 2001

ABATUCC... ...
$85... - €818 - £537 - FF5 366
B... Lee ... Oil/canvas (70x91cm
27x35in) Köln 1999

Prix de vente, cote
Hammer price

ARPAL André 1876-1953 [81]
$3 673 - €4 269 - £2 618 - FF28 000
P... Bronze (H13cm 11x3in) Paris 2001
$162 - €152 - £100 - FF1 000
Bretonne en coiffe à la fenêtre Aquarelle/papier
(17x10.4cm 6x4in) Paris 1999

ABBASSY Samira 1965 [2]
$3 600 - €3 344 - £2 165 - FF21 944
Annunciation Mixed media (78.5x117x6.5cm
30x51x2in) London 1998

Titre de l'œuvre
Title of work

ABBATE dell' Niccolo c.1509-1571 [9]
$18 368 - €114 057 - £80 000 - FF748 108
Portrait of a Young Man wearing a Plumed Hat
Oil/canvas (105x76.5cm 41x30in) London 1998

ABBATI Giuseppe 1836-1868 [5]
$39 500 - €40 948 - £23 700 - FF268 600
Caletta a Castiglioncello Olio/tavola (20x15cm
7x5in) Prato 1999

ABBATI Vincenzo 1803-1866 [4]
$47 500 - €47 028 - £28 560 - FF323 680
La casa del pescatore Huile/toile (86x106cm
33x41in) Milano 2000

ABBE Albert 1889-1966 [32]
$350 - €357 - £221 - FF2 495
... bei Glurns ... (... 59x56cm
23x34in) Mailand 1999

ABBÉ James 1883-1973 [11]
$1 713 - €2 061 - £1 200 - FF26 642
Lieu & date de la vente
Place & date of sale
... Vaterland Photograph
(35x27cm 13x9in) London 1999

ABBÉ Salomon 1693-1739 [22]
$201 - €223 - £140 - FF1 463
Courtyard Scene Etching (26x26cm 10x10in)
London 2001

METROPOLIS
Galerie d'Art Contemporain

Rudolf Wehrung,
Hymne au Printemps, 120 x 120 cm

19 rue Auguste Comte - 69002 Lyon, France
Tél. : +33 478 422 337   Fax : +33 478 383 206

email : galmetropolis@free.fr
site : http://galmetropolis.free.fr

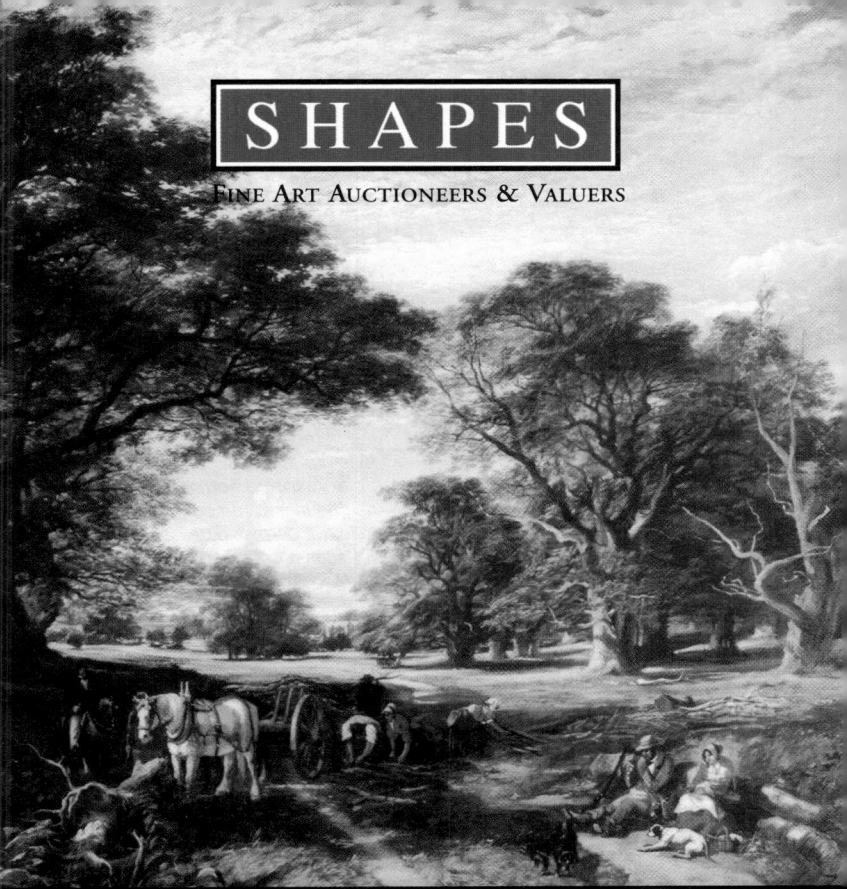

Multi-media distribution

Diffusion multi-support

of the information

de l'information

Publications

The **artprice.com** data bank has spawned a range of digital publications and products. The beauty of the **artprice.com** concept is that it uses high profile traditional media - the respected Artprice Annual - to promote the new generation of digital products that will ultimately make the paper version obsolete, due to their greater flexibility, more frequent updating, reliability and ease of use.

Artprice.com can thus access both professional users and the general public.

Publications

*Sur la base de cette méta-banque de données, **Artprice.com** décline une gamme de publications et produits numériques. La richesse du projet **Artprice.com** est liée à la maîtrise de la gamme complète des produits qui permet d'utiliser les supports les plus connus (livre de cotes Artprice Annual en version papier) pour promouvoir les supports multimédia qui s'imposent ensuite aux utilisateurs grâce à leur puissance d'information (mise à jour permanente, rapidité, fiabilité) et leur ergonomie.*

__Artprice.com__ est ainsi en mesure de répondre à la demande des utilisateurs à la fois professionnels et grand public.

(Egalement sur Minitel 3617 ARTPRICE) 0,843 EUR/min (TTC)

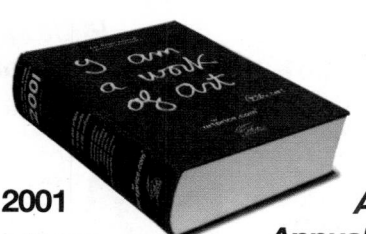

Artprice Annual® 2001

Auction price guide sold in 84 countries.

- The bible of the art world and essential reference aid;
- For professionals, aficionados and collectors worldwide;
- 170.000 representative art auction results selected from the 450,000 auction results recorded by **artprice.com** in 2000.

Artprice Annual ® 2001

Bible du marché de l'art distribuée dans 84 pays. Edition limitée

- *Véritable outil de référence incontournable.*
- *Livre destiné aux professionnels et aux amateurs-collectionneurs.*
- *Regroupe, pour l'année 2000, les 170 000 adjudications d'œuvres d'art les plus significatives en ventes publiques dans le monde.*

Fine Art Annual® 2001

By Van Wilder Edition

Auction results of the year 2000, more than 30,000 artists quoted.

3,000 catalogues raisonnés quoted.

Covering prints, drawings, pastels, watercolours, paintings, sculptures, tapestries, ceramics, photographs and multiples.

Annuel des Arts® 2001

Par les Editions Van Wilder.

Résultats de ventes aux enchères de l'année 2000. Plus de 30 000 artistes cités.

3 000 catalogues raisonnés cités.

Les techniques représentées sont les multiples, gravures, dessins, pastels, aquarelles, gouaches, peintures, sculptures, photos, tapisseries, céramiques.

Artprice Indicator® 2002

- A quick and easy reference handbook for the most significant auction results of an artist's works over the last 3 years.

"Chiner malin"® 2002

Véritable guide de poche pour la recherche simple et rapide des résultats de ventes les plus significatifs sur les 3 dernières années d'un artiste.

Photography Price Indicator ® 2001

This reference tool, covering 12 years (1988/2000) of photograph results at auctions, contains 50,000 results for 5,000 artists.

Photography Price Indicator ® 2001

Ouvrage de référence couvrant 12 années de résultats de ventes aux enchères d'œuvres photographiques du monde entier (1988/2000), soit 50 000 données pour 5 000 artistes.

Fine Art CD-ROM

Providing access to 2,450,000 auction results of catalogued fine art sales covering paintings, drawings, sculptures, ceramics, miniatures, tapestries, prints, posters and photographs (auctions held from 1987 to March 2001).

230,000 artists listed.

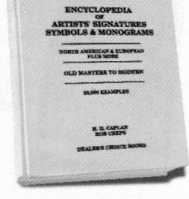

CD-ROM Fine Art

L'outil de référence le plus complet, couvrant neuf disciplines : peinture, dessin, sculpture, estampe, photographie, miniature, affiche, tapisserie, et céramique.

2 450 000 résultats de ventes aux enchères entre 1987 et mars 2001.

230 000 artistes répertoriés.

Works on Paper CD-ROM

Extacted from the Fine Art CD-ROM, a version specialising in photographs, prints, drawings and posters (auctions held from 1987 to March 2001).

1,000,000 auction results

90,000 artists listed.

CD-ROM Works on Paper

Une version extraite du CD-ROM Fine Art et spécialisée en photographie, dessin, estampe, affiche.

1 000 000 résultats de ventes aux enchères entre 1987 et mars 2001.

90 000 artistes répertoriés.

Encyclopedia of artists' signatures, symbols and monograms

By H. H.Caplan & B. Creps

It is the most comprehensive reference on the matter: 9,400 artists, old masters to contemporary artists, from Europe, America and Australia.

Encyclopédie des signatures, symboles et monogrammes d'artistes

Par Caplan & Creps.
Index simple et spécialisé de signatures, monogrammes et symboles de 9 400 artistes des Maîtres anciens aux artistes contemporains. d'Europe, d'Amérique du

25,000 signatures and hundreds of data never published.

This Encyclopedia is divided into four sections:
- signatures,
- monograms,
- symbols,
- illegible or misleading signatures.

nord et d'Australie. 25 000 exemples plus des centaines de nouvelles entrées jamais publiées auparavant.

L'ouvrage se compose de quatre sections : Les signatures, Les monogrammes, Les symboles, Les signatures illisibles ou trompeuses.

Signatures and Monograms of artists from the 19th and 20th C.

By Frank Van Wilder. Some 10,000 artists' signatures and 2,500 monograms.

Signatures et Monogrammes d'artistes des XIXᵉ et XXᵉ siècles

Par Frank Van Wilder.
Cet ouvrage recense 10 000 signatures et 2 500 monogrammes.

Who Was Who in American Art

By Sound View Press. Last publication 1999, 3,750 pages.

A three-volume prestigious art reference work containing 65,000 biographies of American artists from 1564 to 1975.

Who Was Who in American Art

Par les Editions Sound View Press.
Dernière édition 1999, 3 750 pages.

Un ouvrage répertoriant en 3 volumes plus de 65 000 biographies d'artistes américains de 1564 à 1975.
Contient plusieurs milliers d'exemples de signatures.

L' Argus de l'autographe et du manuscrit from 1982 to 1994

Yearly guide listing autographs and manuscripts sold at public auctions. Contains an index of themes and recipients.

L'Argus de l'autographe et du manuscrit de 1982 à 1994

Répertoire annuel des ventes publiques. Index des thèmes et des destinataires.

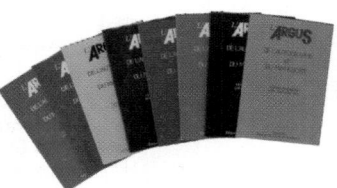

L'Argus du livre de collection

Since 1982.
Published yearly.

Bibliographic guide recording sales for books sold for more than FRF550 at auction.
Contains six indexes.

L'Argus du livre de collection

Depuis 1982.
Parution annuelle.

Répertoire bibliographique des livres adjugés à plus de 550 FRF en ventes publiques.

The "Mireur"

Dictionary of 18th and 19th C.

European art auctions. First edition published in 1911. The new edition in 7 volumes enriched with comments by Frank Van Wilder.

Covers:
- 150,000 works (paintings, prints, drawings, watercolours, miniatures, pastels, gouaches, sepias, charcoals, enamels, painted fans and stained-glass windows)

- 3,000 public auctions

- 30,000 artists.

Le "Mireur"

Réédition en 7 volumes avec commentaires de Frank Van Wilder du Dictionnaire des Ventes d'Art en France et à l'Etranger pendant les XVIIIe et XIXe siècles publié pour la première fois en 1911.

Tableaux, estampes, dessins, aquarelles, miniatures, pastels, gouaches, sépias, fusains, émaux, éventails peints et vitraux. Plus de 3 000 ventes publiques, 30 000 artistes, 150 000 œuvres.

Code des Ventes Volontaires et Judiciaires®

The "Code des ventes volontaires et judiciaires" analyses the genesis, impact and application of the law concerning the reform of public auctions with:
- a comparative study of the status of public sales in the Member States of the European Union;
- a chronological study of the Parliaments works and of the genesis of the reform;
- a historical presentation of French public auctions.
- Also includes Alain Quemin's latest work, "La Réforme des Ventes aux Enchères, des Commissaires-Priseurs aux sociétés de ventes publiques".

Le Code des Ventes Volontaires et Judiciaires"®

Ce code analyse la genèse, la portée et les conséquences de la loi relative à la réforme des ventes publiques.

- Etude comparative du statut des ventes publiques des Etats membres de l'Union Européenne.

- Etude chronologique des travaux parlementaires, genèse de la réforme et historique des ventes aux enchères en France.

- Inclut : Le nouvel ouvrage d'Alain Quemin, "La Réforme des Ventes aux Enchères, des Commissaires-Priseurs aux sociétés de ventes publiques".

POLAND
AUCTION HOUSE
Fine Art and Antiques

Veriera from Heinrich Graf von Brühl service, 1740-41
Lot 11: 20.09.2000; Rempex, Warsaw

REMPEX • WARSAW • CRACOW • POLAND

00-333 Warszawa,
Krakowskie PrzedmieÊcie 4/6 str
phone (48-22) 826 44 08,
fax (48-22) 826 26 25

31-010 Kraków
Jagiello*f*ska 6a str
phone (48-12) 421 88 62
fax (48-12) 421 88 62

http://www.rempex.com.pl
e-mail: rempex@rempex.com.pl

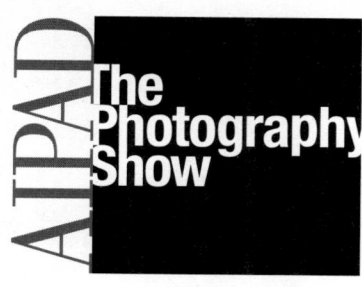

FEBRUARY 15-17, 2002
The Photography Show 2002
New York Hilton, New York City

Exhibitions Open
Friday, February 15th and
Saturday, February 16th, 12–8pm
Sunday, February 17th, 11am–6pm
(Thursday night preview by exhibitor invitation only)

Ticket Price
$20/One day pass,
$30/Three day pass
*(Ticket price includes AIPAD's Annual Membership
Directory and Illustrated Catalogue)*
Additional details and schedule of events to follow

*The Photography Show 2001 Membership Directory
and Illustrated Catalogue is available for
$25 US ($35 outside domestic US).
To purchase, please send check or
money order made payable to AIPAD.*

Special Hotel Rates
available at the New York Hilton.
Call 1-800-HILTONS and mention
The Photography Show 2002.

Sponsored by
**The Association of International
Photography Art Dealers**
1609 Connecticut Avenue, NW
Washington DC 20009
Tel: 202.986.0105   Fax: 202.986.0448
Web: www.photoshow.com
E-mail: aipad@aol.com

The World's Premier
Exposition Devoted
to Fine Art Photography

New York City

2002

A L'IMAGE DU GRENIER SUR L'EAU - PARIS
ACHAT DE PHOTOGRAPHIES XIX⁽ᵉ⁾ - XX⁽ᵉ⁾

Jeune femme tibétaine. Épreuve sur papier albuminé circa 1880. Ancienne collection Soustiel

45, rue des Francs-Bourgeois 75004 Paris
Tél.: +33 (0)1 42 71 02 31 - Fax +33 (0)1 42 71 89 66
Ouvert t.l.j.de 10h30 à 19h, dim. 14h - 19h

www.photos-site.com - email: image.di-maria@wanadoo.fr
Galerie Di Maria fondée en 1976

AA van der Pieter Boudewyn XVIII **[5]**
📖 $292 - €288 - £182 - FF1 891
Los grandes mandarines en la Corte de China
Grabado (27x35cm 10x13in) Madrid 1999

AAE Arvid 1877-1913 **[4]**
🖌 $4 812 - €5 366 - £3 292 - FF35 196
Interiör med lille pige, der syr Oil/canvas (70x53cm
27x20in) Viby J, Århus 2000

AAGAARD Carl Frederik 1833-1895 **[183]**
🖌 $1 834 - €2 012 - £1 246 - FF13 198
Juni i Skoven, Motiv fra Lellinge Oil/canvas
(67x54cm 26x21in) København 2000
🖌 $743 - €862 - £526 - FF5 655
**Eveneing Landscape with Farm House and
Cows** Oil/canvas (32.5x48cm 12x18in) Amsterdam
2000

AALTO Ilmari 1891-1916 **[54]**
🖌 $1 632 - €1 429 - £989 - FF9 374
Hus invid parken Oil/panel (40x49.5cm 15x19in)
Helsinki 1998

AALTONEN Aarre 1889-1980 **[20]**
🗿 $171 - €202 - £119 - FF1 323
Mor och barn Plaster (H25cm H9in) Helsinki 2000

AALTONEN Wäinö 1894-1966 **[101]**
🖌 $1 524 - €1 430 - £941 - FF9 374
Regnbåge Oil/canvas (55x46cm 21x18in) Helsinki
1999
🗿 $547 - €605 - £379 - FF3 971
Pojken och stjärnan Bronze relief (37x36cm
14x14in) Helsinki 2001
🖊 $543 - €504 - £326 - FF3 309
Maija Akvarell/papper (46x38cm 18x14in) Helsinki
1999

AARON Joseph XX **[10]**
🖌 $750 - €805 - £501 - FF5 280
Big Sur Coastline Oil/canvas (27x35cm 11x14in)
Altadena CA 2000

AARONS George 1896-1980 **[4]**
🗿 $3 750 - €4 483 - £2 586 - FF29 407
Old Testament Figure Bronze (H51cm H20in)
Milford CT 2000

AARTMAN Nicolaes Matthijsz. 1713-1793 **[12]**
🖊 $3 000 - €3 209 - £2 045 - FF21 050
Morning/Midday Wash (19x27.5cm 7x10in) New-
York 2001

AARTS Johannes J. 1871-1934 **[37]**
📖 $61 - €68 - £41 - FF446
Perseus met het hoofd van Medusa Copper
engraving (21.2x29.8cm 8x11in) Haarlem 2000

ABA-NOVAK Vilmos 1894-1941 **[11]**
🖌 $16 100 - €17 812 - £10 580 - FF116 840
Clowns Tempera/board (59x69cm 23x27in) Budapest
2000
🖌 $10 360 - €10 885 - £6 440 - FF71 400
Lacikonyha Huile/bois (27x34cm 10x13in) Budapest
2000
🖊 $1 850 - €1 944 - £1 150 - FF12 750
Paysage de collines Encre/papier (39x54cm
15x21in) Budapest 2000

ABADIAS J. **[12]**
🖌 $346 - €330 - £220 - FF2 167
Sanlucar de Barrameda Oleo/tabla (18x29cm
7x11in) Madrid 1999

ABADIE-LANDEL Pierre 1896-1972 **[32]**
📖 $181 - €183 - £113 - FF1 200
Au bar à Montparnasse Monotype (30x24.5cm
11x9in) Quimper 2000

ABAKANOWICZ Magdalena 1930 **[30]**
🗿 $38 000 - €32 785 - £22 838 - FF215 053
Standing Figure Bronze (162.5x49.5x29cm
63x19x11in) New-York 1998
🗿 $10 000 - €9 629 - £6 253 - FF63 163
Untitled Sculpture (62x16.5x21cm 24x6x8in) Beverly-
Hills CA 1999
🖊 $8 500 - €9 521 - £5 906 - FF62 454
Bull Face, 85A Charcoal/paper (100.5x75.5cm
39x29in) New-York 2001

ABATE Alberto 1946 **[10]**
🖊 $840 - €726 - £420 - FF4 760
«Orifica» Tecnica mista/carta (100x70cm 39x27in)
Prato 1999

ABATE de Goffredo 1849-1932 **[1]**
🖌 $2 000 - €2 073 - £1 200 - FF13 600
Meriggio sul Po, Torino Olio/tavola (20x33.5cm
7x13in) Vercelli 2001

ABATUCCI Pierre 1871-1942 **[44]**
🖌 $854 - €818 - £537 - FF5 366
Baumumsäumter See Öl/Leinwand (70x91cm
27x35in) Köln 1999

ABBAL André 1876-1953 **[81]**
🗿 $3 673 - €4 269 - £2 618 - FF28 000
Faucon Bronze (H34cm H13in) Paris 2001
🖊 $162 - €152 - £100 - FF1 000
Bretonne en coiffe à la fenêtre Aquarelle/papier
(17x10.4cm 6x4in) Paris 1999

ABBASSY Samira 1965 **[2]**
🖌 $3 600 - €3 818 - £2 440 - FF25 045
Annunciation Mixed media (78.5x132x6.5cm
30x51x2in) Tel Aviv 2001

ABBATE dell' Niccolo c.1509-1571 **[9]**
🖌 $133 968 - €114 057 - £80 000 - FF748 168
Portrait of a Young Man wearing a Plumed Hat
Oil/canvas (105x76.5cm 41x30in) London 1998

ABBATI Giuseppe 1836-1868 **[5]**
🖌 $39 500 - €40 948 - £23 700 - FF268 600
Caletta a Castiglioncello Olio/tavola (20x15cm
7x5in) Prato 1999

ABBATI Vincenzo 1803-1866 **[4]**
🖌 $47 600 - €49 345 - £28 560 - FF323 680
La casa del pescatore Huile/toile (86x106cm
33x41in) Milano 1999

ABBE Albert 1889-1966 **[32]**
🖌 $410 - €380 - £255 - FF2 495
Backarna vid Glumslöv Oil/canvas (56x88cm
22x34in) Malmö 1999

ABBÉ James 1883-1973 **[11]**
📷 $4 713 - €4 061 - £2 800 - FF26 641
Rudolph and Natasha Valentino Photograph
(35x27cm 13x10in) London 1998

ABBÉ van Salomon 1883-1955 **[28]**
📖 $201 - €223 - £140 - FF1 463
Courtroom Scene Etching (26x26cm 10x10in)
London 2001

ABBÉMA Louise 1853-1927 [115]

$20 000 - €20 154 - £12 468 - FF132 200
Portrait de Madame Duvelleroy Oil/canvas
(212.5x113cm 83x44in) New-York 2000

$2 956 - €3 201 - £2 024 - FF21 000
Femme au chapeau fleuri Huile/toile (60x41cm
23x16in) Paris 2001

$873 - €976 - £592 - FF6 400
Autoportrait Huile/panneau (24x19cm 9x7in) Pontoise
2000

$406 - €427 - £267 - FF2 800
Portrait de Sarah Bernard Aquarelle/papier
(15x12cm 5x4in) Paris 2000

$686 - €762 - £477 - FF5 000
**«Chemin de Fer du Midi et d'Orléans, Amélie-
les-Bains»** Affiche (106x76cm 41x29in) Paris 2001

ABBETT Robert Kennedy 1926 [12]

$3 300 - €3 747 - £2 292 - FF24 578
Mare and Colt Oil/board (60x76cm 24x30in) Dallas
TX 2001

ABBEY Edwin Austin 1852-1911 [30]

$485 - €544 - £336 - FF3 571
**Straatscene met groep hoornblazende mannen
in irientaalse kledij** Encre (47.5x35cm 18x13in) The
Hague 2000

ABBIATI Filippo 1640-1715 [3]

$14 400 - €12 440 - £9 600 - FF81 600
Giuda e Tamar Olio/tela (42.5x62.5cm 16x24in)
Milano 1998

ABBO Jussuf 1888-1953 [33]

$167 - €194 - £117 - FF1 274
Frauenbüste Radierung (20x15.5cm 7x6in) Berlin
2001

ABBOTT Arthur 1804-1843 [9]

$2 432 - €2 354 - £1 500 - FF15 438
**The Ponte Molle, Rome/The Temple of
Vesta/The Villa Mattei/Colonna** Watercolour/paper
(24x26cm 9x10in) London 1999

ABBOTT Berenice 1898-1991 [793]

$3 000 - €3 454 - £2 047 - FF22 656
First Ave and East 70 St Gelatin silver print
(23x18cm 9x7in) New-York 2000

ABBOTT Ernest Edwin 1888-1973 [16]

$94 - €88 - £58 - FF580
Coolabah and Billabong Etching (20x30cm 7x11in)
Sydney 1999

ABBOTT John White 1763-1851 [152]

$5 936 - €5 810 - £3 800 - FF38 109
A Horseman with Figures on a Path Oil/canvas
(60x80cm 23x31in) London 1999

$4 037 - €4 462 - £2 800 - FF29 268
Fishermen unloading their Boats on the Shore
Oil/canvas (26x35.5cm 10x13in) London 2001

$5 047 - €5 577 - £3 500 - FF36 585
«The Head of the Lake of Geneva from Vevay»
Ink (25.5x111.5cm 10x43in) London 2001

ABBOTT Lemuel Francis 1760-1803 [23]

$12 702 - €13 635 - £8 500 - FF89 438
**Edward Cotsford, Seated Three-Quarter-Length,
in a Dark Brown Jacket** Oil/canvas (127x101.5cm
50x39in) London 2000

$3 249 - €3 161 - £2 000 - FF20 737
**John Stuart, wearing a blue Coat and white
Stock** Oil/canvas (75x62cm 29x24in) London 1999

ABBOTT Yarnall 1870-1938 [19]

$2 600 - €2 702 - £1 638 - FF17 727
The procession Oil/canvas (76x91cm 30x36in)
Bethesda MD 2000

ABBOUD Chafik 1926 [70]

$9 940 - €10 671 - £6 650 - FF70 000
La 2e porte Huile/toile (81x200cm 31x78in) Paris
2000

$2 608 - €2 439 - £1 579 - FF16 000
Composition Huile/toile (116x73cm 45x28in) Paris
1999

$787 - €762 - £495 - FF5 000
Composition Tempera/carton (23.5x37.5cm 9x14in)
Paris 1999

ABDULLAH Frères Wichen/Kevork/Hovsep XIX-XX [8]

$401 - €457 - £275 - FF3 000
**Cortège du Sultan le jour de la Selamlick/Palais
de Tshéragan** Tirage albuminé (19.5x25.5cm 7x10in)
Paris 2000

ABDULLAH Raden Basoeki 1915-1993 [66]

$14 845 - €12 455 - £8 710 - FF81 700
Buffalo at Work Oil/canvas (100x150cm 39x59in)
Singapore 1998

$6 886 - €7 820 - £4 713 - FF51 295
Nude Oil/canvas (81x120cm 31x47in) Singapore 2000

$1 168 - €1 223 - £734 - FF8 025
Portrait of a Girl Pastel/paper (65x50cm 25x19in)
Singapore 2000

ABDULLAH Sudjono 1911-1991 [27]

$4 328 - €4 033 - £2 670 - FF26 457
Reclining Nude Oil/canvas (70x120cm 27x47in)
Singapore 1999

ABEDIN Zainul 1917-1976 [10]

$800 - €945 - £567 - FF6 200
Famine Series Ink (29x40.5cm 11x15in) New-York
2000

ABEELE van den Albijn Binus 1835-1918 [5]

$9 106 - €8 842 - £5 626 - FF58 000
La lisière de la forêt Huile/panneau (21x30cm
8x11in) Paris 1999

ABEILLÉ Jack 1873-? [24]

$734 - €701 - £459 - FF4 600
«Biscuit Pernot» Affiche (140.5x100cm 55x39in)
Orléans 1999

ABEILLE Jacques 1906-? [1]

$4 983 - €4 265 - £3 000 - FF27 975
Pears on a Plate with an Apple and a Jug
Oil/canvas (38.5x61.5cm 15x24in) London 1998

ABEL Carl Andreas 1907-1994 [5]

$839 - €791 - £506 - FF4 694
Arbeitslos, Wohnungslos Gelatin silver print
(40.3x30.4cm 15x11in) Köln 1998

ABEL Ernst Heinrich c.1737-? [1]

$3 417 - €3 835 - £2 369 - FF25 154
**Waldweg mit Jäger, Hunden, Bauer mit
Schubkarre und Knaben am Gatter** Öl/Leinwand
(70x55.5cm 27x21in) München 2000

ABEL Josef 1764-1818 [7]

$4 069 - €4 724 - £2 860 - FF30 985
Engel tragen Magdalena himmelwärts Oil/panel
(64x82cm 25x32in) Wien 2001

ABEL-TRUCHET Louis 1857-1918 [123]

$7 621 - €8 497 - £5 423 - FF58 000
Scène de marché en Bretagne Huile/panneau
(47x37.5cm 18x14in) Paris 2001

$1 422 - €1 372 - **£898** - FF9 000
Femmes causant au jardin Huile/panneau
(41x32.5cm 16x12in) Paris 1999
$1 045 - €915 - **£633** - FF6 000
La Salute Pastel/papier (75x101cm 29x39in) Versailles
1998
$961 - €1 067 - **£668** - FF7 000
**«Tunisie, Cie des chemins de Fer, Bone-
Guelma»** Affiche (107x72cm 42x28in) Paris 2001

ABELA Eduardo 1892-1966 [37]
$10 000 - €8 697 - **£6 029** - FF57 050
El niño y el hada Oil/panel (51x61cm 20x24in) New-
York 1998
$16 000 - €15 529 - **£9 961** - FF101 865
La vaca sedienta Oil/masonite (21.5x27.5cm 8x10in)
New-York 1999
$10 000 - €8 697 - **£6 029** - FF57 050
Vendedoras de flores Watercolour/paper
(58x49.5cm 22x19in) New-York 1998

ABELENDA ESCUDERO Alfonso 1931 [4]
$1 820 - €2 102 - **£1 260** - FF13 790
Composición Técnica mixta/lienzo (75x60cm
29x23in) Madrid 2000

ABELLO MARTIN Joan 1920 [32]
$2 133 - €2 373 - **£1 501** - FF15 563
«Peixos» Oleo/lienzo (65x81cm 25x31in) Barcelona
2001
$1 053 - €1 171 - **£721** - FF7 683
«Nota» Oleo/lienzo (35.5x27.5cm 13x10in) Barcelona
2001
$532 - €571 - **£361** - FF3 743
Desnudo femenino Craies/papier (32.5x43cm
12x16in) Madrid 2001

ABELLO Palmira 1934 [4]
$1 296 - €1 442 - **£912** - FF9 456
Vista urbana Pastel/papier (49x63cm 19x24in) Madrid
2001

ABELLO PRAT Joan 1922 [79]
$2 255 - €2 463 - **£1 476** - FF16 154
Flores Oleo/lienzo (66x111.5cm 25x43in) Barcelona
2000
$1 036 - €1 111 - **£684** - FF7 289
Yo (Autorretrato) Oleo/lienzo (41x33cm 16x12in)
Barcelona 2000
$477 - €541 - **£333** - FF3 546
Figura en el bosque Técnica mixta/papel (60x42cm
23x16in) Barcelona 2000

ABELMAN Ida York 1910 [2]
$1 100 - €1 227 - **£720** - FF8 050
Tenement Interior Lithograph (25x27cm 10x11in)
Chicago IL 2000

ABELS Jacobus Theodorus 1803-1866 [33]
$13 609 - €11 508 - **£8 138** - FF75 486
**A Moonlit Wooded River Landscape with a
Church in the Distance** Oil/panel (74x96cm
29x37in) Amsterdam 1998
$1 391 - €1 361 - **£891** - FF8 929
**A wooded Landscape with a Peasantwoman
driving Cows on a Country Road** Oil/canvas
(36x41cm 14x16in) Amsterdam 1999
$634 - €681 - **£424** - FF4 464
Moored Vessels on a moonlit river Watercolour
(15x21cm 5x8in) Amsterdam 2000

ABERCROMBIE Gertrude 1909-1977 [6]
$3 250 - €3 853 - **£2 367** - FF23 000
The Well Oil/masonite (13x16cm 5x6in) Chicago IL
2001

ABERDAM Alfred 1894-1963 [123]
$1 045 - €1 220 - **£733** - FF8 000
Personnages dans un paysage Huile/toile
(46x55cm 18x21in) Paris 2001
$420 - €446 - **£284** - FF2 924
Figure and a Goat Gouache/paper (36x26cm
14x10in) Tel Aviv 2001

ÅBERG Gunnar 1869-1894 [5]
$6 854 - €7 960 - **£4 816** - FF52 214
Sidensvansar Oil/canvas (37x30cm 14x11in)
Stockholm 2001

ÅBERG Pelle 1909-1964 [258]
$1 569 - €1 758 - **£1 091** - FF11 532
Frälsningssoldater Oil/panel (122x61cm 48x24in)
Stockholm 2001
$1 785 - €1 674 - **£1 104** - FF10 981
Flicka i grön hatt Oil/panel (27x22cm 10x8in)
Stockholm 1999
$735 - €824 - **£511** - FF5 406
«Stadsbild» Gouache/paper (20x35cm 7x13in)
Uppsala 2001

ABERLI Johann Ludwig 1723-1786 [125]
$7 866 - €9 170 - **£5 446** - FF60 148
Die Elfenau mit Aareschlaufe Watercolour
(29.7x49cm 11x19in) Bern 2000
$642 - €625 - **£395** - FF4 101
Vue prise aux environs de la Tour Eau-forte couleurs (39.4x59cm 15x23in) Bern 1999

ABIDINE Dino 1913-1993 [36]
$4 252 - €3 506 - **£2 504** - FF23 000
Le Fort d'Antibes Huile/toile (91x130cm 35x51in)
Paris 1998
$441 - €457 - **£279** - FF3 000
Sans titre Huile/toile (17x27cm 6x10in) Paris 2000
$2 647 - €2 744 - **£1 679** - FF18 000
La grande marche Encre Chine/papier (107x71cm
42x27in) Paris 2000

ABILDGAARD Nicolai Abraham 1743-1809 [36]
$40 460 - €45 566 - **£27 880** - FF298 894
Scene fra fjerde akt af Voltaire «Le triumvirat»
Oil/canvas (50x51cm 19x20in) Köbenhavn 2000
$542 - €538 - **£339** - FF3 527
Hoved af en mand med turban set skråt bagfra
Pencil/paper (18x12.5cm 7x4in) Köbenhavn 1999

ABLETT William Albert 1877-1937 [119]
$1 302 - €1 487 - **£906** - FF9 756
Elégante au théâtre Huile/toile (61x50cm 24x19in)
Bruxelles 2001
$593 - €640 - **£409** - FF4 200
Effets de nuit Huile/bois (35x27cm 13x10in) Paris
2001
$235 - €229 - **£149** - FF1 500
Fumeuse de cigarette Eau-forte, aquatinte (50x60cm
19x23in) Paris 1999

ABRAAMYAN Artashes 1921 [34]
$978 - €867 - **£600** - FF5 685
Blue House by the Mountains Oil/canvas
(57x80cm 22x31in) London 1999

ABRAHAMS Ivor 1935 [44]
$476 - €462 - **£300** - FF3 030
Pathways I-IV Color lithograph (60.5x60.5cm
23x23in) London 1999

ABRAHAMS Louis XIX-XX [2]
$3 361 - €3 780 - **£2 280** - FF24 794
Reflection Oil/canvas (29.5x25.5cm 11x10in)
Melbourne 2000

ABRAHAMSON Erik 1871-1907 **[30]**
- $1 361 - €1 167 - £818 - FF7 652
  Kustlandskap med båtar och figurer Oil/canvas (51x69cm 20x27in) Uppsala 1998

ABRAM Paul XX **[2]**
- $4 180 - €3 904 - £2 579 - FF25 606
  Day Raiders Oil/board (50x76cm 20x30in) Dallas TX 1999

ABRAM Paul 1854-1925 **[41]**
- $1 800 - €1 769 - £1 156 - FF11 606
  Farmer sharpening his Scythe Watercolour (54x36cm 21x14in) New-York 1999

ABRAMOVIC Marina 1946 **[5]**
- $70 000 - €67 731 - £43 169 - FF444 283
  Cleaning the Mirror I Installation (284.5x62x48.5cm 112x24x19in) New-York 1999
- $3 500 - €3 020 - £2 103 - FF19 807
  Role Exchange Photograph (76x100.5cm 29x39in) New-York 1998

ABRAMOVICH Pinchas 1909-1986 **[39]**
- $1 800 - €2 026 - £1 240 - FF13 288
  Landscape Oil/paper/canvas (49x64cm 19x25in) Herzelia-Pituah 2000

ABRAMOWICZ Léon, Leo 1889-1978 **[109]**
- $1 150 - €1 308 - £808 - FF8 580
  Sitzender Akt Öl/Karton (44x62cm 17x24in) Wien 2001
- $313 - €363 - £216 - FF2 383
  Liegender Akt Aquarell/Papier (29.5x43.5cm 11x17in) Graz 2000

ABRAMS Eleanor ?-1929 **[6]**
- $200 - €219 - £129 - FF1 439
  Sailboat in river Oil/canvas/board (34x44cm 13x17in) Wallkill NY 2000

ABRAMSON Larry 1954 **[2]**
- $6 000 - €5 561 - £3 730 - FF36 480
  Impression de soleil, III Oil/canvas (150.5x76cm 59x29in) Tel Aviv 1999

ABRATE Angelo 1900-1985 **[26]**
- $800 - €1 037 - £600 - FF6 800
  La Dora e il Monte Bianco Olio/tela (60x50cm 23x19in) Vercelli 2001
- $925 - €959 - £555 - FF6 290
  «Verso il ghiacciaio del Ruiter» (Courmayeur) Olio/tavola (23x34cm 9x13in) Vercelli 1999

ABREU Mario 1919-1993 **[32]**
- $255 - €220 - £150 - FF1 440
  Sin título Tinta/papel (24.5x19cm 9x7in) Caracas 1998

ABRIL Ben 1923-1995 **[16]**
- $1 300 - €1 395 - £870 - FF9 153
  Near the Panamint Range Oil/canvas (55x76cm 22x30in) Altadena CA 2000

ABRY Léon 1857-1905 **[17]**
- $3 300 - €3 099 - £2 037 - FF20 325
  Élégante à l'éventail Huile/toile (91x72cm 35x28in) Bruxelles 1999

ABSALON (Eshel Meir) 1964-1993 **[2]**
- $22 032 - €25 916 - £15 793 - FF170 000
  Disposition Construction (182x107x28cm 71x42x11in) Paris 2001
- $22 000 - €24 642 - £15 285 - FF161 638
  Proposition d'habitation Sculpture (29x54x74cm 11x21x29in) New-York 2001

ABSOLON John 1815-1895 **[78]**
- $747 - €803 - £500 - FF5 265
  A Cavalier in an Interior Watercolour (26.5x17.5cm 10x6in) London 2000

ABSOLON Kurt 1925-1958 **[24]**
- $2 049 - €2 035 - £1 279 - FF13 347
  Tierkopf Indian ink (30.5x46.5cm 12x18in) Wien 1999
- $1 042 - €871 - £618 - FF5 716
  Stadtrand Farblithographie (39x46cm 15x18in) Wien 1998

ABT Otto 1903-1982 **[40]**
- $437 - €488 - £305 - FF3 200
  Composition cubiste Huile/carton (46x38cm 18x14in) Entzheim 2001
- $1 363 - €1 252 - £837 - FF8 215
  Liegender weiblicher Akt mit Blumenstrauss Öl/Karton (27x35cm 10x13in) Zürich 1999
- $290 - €330 - £201 - FF2 165
  Stadt Felt pen (15.5x10cm 6x3in) Zofingen 2000

ABU SHAKRA Asim 1961-1990 **[3]**
- $38 000 - €42 437 - £24 335 - FF278 369
  Plane Mixed media (122x279cm 48x109in) Tel Aviv 2000

ABU'L HASAN GHAFFARI III (Yahia Khan) XIX **[1]**
- $30 126 - €31 437 - £19 000 - FF206 214
  Portrait of Nasir al-Din Shah Qajar Oil/canvas (90.5x62cm 35x24in) London 2000

ABULARACH Rodolfo 1933 **[4]**
- $10 000 - €9 730 - £6 155 - FF63 823
  Nocho-Nubes Oil/canvas (177x127cm 69x50in) New-York 1999

AC d' Rob XIX-XX **[4]**
- $1 694 - €1 448 - £1 017 - FF9 500
  «Au comptoir des Viandes Grenoble» Affiche (159x118cm 62x46in) Paris 1998

ACCARD Eugène 1824-1888 **[13]**
- $5 500 - €4 768 - £3 361 - FF31 277
  The Conversation Oil/panel (61x49.5cm 24x19in) New-York 1999
- $6 806 - €6 859 - £4 242 - FF44 991
  Junge Frau mit kleinem Hund Öl/Leinwand (40.5x33cm 15x12in) Zürich 2000

ACCARDI Carla 1924 **[103]**
- $11 000 - €11 403 - £6 600 - FF74 800
  Due cerchi Tempera (91.5x141cm 36x55in) Milano 2000
- $3 400 - €4 406 - £2 550 - FF28 900
  «Serie Parentesi, Rosso verde» Acrilico (70x55cm 27x21in) Vercelli 2001
- $600 - €777 - £450 - FF5 100
  «Rosso-verde» Gouache/carta (18x26cm 7x10in) Vercelli 2001

ACCONCI Vito 1940 **[39]**
- $13 000 - €12 206 - £8 054 - FF80 068
  Gands Up, Hands Down Acrylic (101.5x61cm 39x24in) New-York 1999
- $2 856 - €2 467 - £1 428 - FF16 184
  «Three Place Studies» Tecnica mista/carta (76x101cm 29x39in) Venezia 1999
- $1 400 - €1 241 - £858 - FF8 138
  Crash, Diptych Silkscreen (51.5x128cm 20x50in) New-York 1999
- $7 000 - €6 573 - £4 337 - FF43 113
  Memory Box I Gelatin silver print (23x16.5cm 9x6in) New-York 1999

ACERBI Ezechiele 1850-1920 [3]

$11 305 - €11 719 - **£6 783** - FF76 874
Strada di paese con figure Olio/tela (61x49cm 24x19in) Milano 1999

$3 213 - €2 776 - **£1 606** - FF18 207
In cerca di rane Olio/tela/cartone (24x33cm 9x12in) Milano 1999

ACEVEDO Manuel Hernández 1921-1989 [4]

$9 100 - €10 511 - **£6 300** - FF68 950
Inmaculada concepción Oleo/lienzo (170x116cm 66x45in) Seville 2000

ACEVES T. XIX-XX [9]

$4 385 - €5 032 - **£3 000** - FF33 006
The Courtyard of A Moorish Palace Oil/canvas (61x46cm 24x18in) London 2000

ACHARD Jean Alexis 1807-1884 [106]

$1 570 - €1 524 - **£970** - FF10 000
Sous-bois à Cernay Huile/toile (38x46cm 14x18in) Grenoble 1999

$2 168 - €1 982 - **£1 327** - FF13 000
Les arbres Huile/carton (35x27cm 13x10in) Grenoble 1999

ACHEFF William 1947 [20]

$23 000 - €20 908 - **£13 852** - FF137 149
Tranquility Oil/canvas (60x55cm 24x22in) Hayden ID 1998

$6 000 - €5 454 - **£3 613** - FF35 778
Rio Grande Drum Oil/canvas (17x12cm 7x5in) Hayden ID 1998

ACHEN Georg Nikolaj 1860-1912 [29]

$3 525 - €3 494 - **£2 139** - FF22 919
Portraet af kunstnerens hustru Ane, född Thiele Oil/canvas (112x75cm 44x29in) Vejle 2000

ACHENBACH Andreas 1815-1910 [265]

$27 510 - €30 678 - **£18 498** - FF201 234
Sturm an der Mole von Vlissingen Öl/Leinwand (124x170cm 48x66in) Köln 2000

$9 758 - €10 226 - **£6 180** - FF67 078
Blüchers Rheinübergang bei Kaub im Winter Öl/Leinwand (37x109cm 14x42in) Köln 2000

$4 094 - €4 090 - **£2 560** - FF26 831
Blick auf ein holländisches Städtchen Öl/Karton (37.5x42.5cm 14x16in) Köln 1999

$602 - €511 - **£363** - FF3 352
Genier ich Ihne? dann sagen se's, dann geb ich Ihne eins ins Gesicht Pencil/paper (14.5x22cm 5x8in) Köln 1998

$161 - €179 - **£109** - FF1 173
Genredarstellungen Radierung (19.6x13.1cm 7x5in) Hamburg 2000

ACHENBACH Oswald 1827-1905 [146]

$69 370 - €63 529 - **£42 280** - FF416 724
Montefiascone Oil/canvas (130x180cm 51x70in) Amsterdam 1999

$14 376 - €14 940 - **£9 055** - FF98 000
Baie de Capri Huile/toile (44.5x60.5cm 17x23in) Paris 2000

$4 215 - €3 937 - **£2 601** - FF25 825
Gewitterlandschaft mit Wanderern Oil/panel (32.5x44cm 12x17in) Köln 1999

ACHILLE Henri 1873-1933 [1]

$11 615 - €9 909 - **£7 007** - FF65 000
Scène animée à la Porte des Arènes Huile/toile (60x92cm 23x36in) Calais 1998

ACHILLE-FOULD Mlle. Georges 1865-1951 [5]

$5 500 - €4 700 - **£3 230** - FF30 829
Portrait of a Beauty Holding an Apple Oil/canvas (94x69cm 37x27in) New-Orleans LA 1998

ACHOFF William XX [2]

$31 900 - €29 791 - **£19 688** - FF195 419
Taos Charmer Oil/canvas (63x38cm 25x15in) Dallas TX 1999

ACHTERBERG van Gerard 1872-1953 [8]

$1 378 - €1 428 - **£873** - FF9 370
Paysage, Colonie hollandaise Fusain/papier (38x50cm 14x19in) Genève 2000

ACHTSCHELLINCK Lucas 1629-1699 [10]

$63 520 - €58 138 - **£38 720** - FF381 360
Erlegtes Wild mit Jagdgeräten in einer bewalde-ten Landschaft Öl/Leinwand (147x119cm 57x46in) Wien 1999

$11 823 - €10 671 - **£7 287** - FF70 000
Promeneurs à l'orée du bois Huile/toile (85x106cm 33x41in) Paris 1999

ACKE Johan Axel Gustaf 1859-1924 [29]

$2 964 - €2 585 - **£1 792** - FF16 958
Interiör (Rokoko) Oil/canvas (84x43cm 33x16in) Stockholm 1998

$540 - €586 - **£370** - FF3 841
Tallskog i vinterskrud Oil/canvas/panel (24x19.5cm 9x7in) Stockholm 2001

ACKE Marcelle 1882-1952 [10]

$1 871 - €1 815 - **£1 178** - FF11 906
Sonrai Woman, Tombouctou Pastel (33.5x26cm 13x10in) Amsterdam 1999

ACKER van Flori-Marie 1858-1940 [26]

$14 625 - €16 112 - **£9 555** - FF105 690
'S Zomers builten Huile/toile (115x152cm 45x59in) Bruxelles 2000

$1 400 - €1 633 - **£982** - FF10 710
«Station balnéaire» Poster (99x69cm 38x27in) New-York 2000

ACKERMAN Paul 1908-1981 [213]

$271 - €305 - **£176** - FF2 000
Alors avouez Madame, est-ce là l'oeuvre d'un juif? Huile/toile (100x50cm 39x19in) Paris 2000

$121 - €137 - **£85** - FF900
Femme nue allongée Fusain/papier (32x40cm 12x15in) Paris 2001

ACKERMANN Franz 1963 [4]

$29 298 - €28 515 - **£18 000** - FF187 048
Evasion 1 Acrylic/canvas (280x290cm 110x114in) London 1999

$9 806 - €10 836 - **£6 800** - FF71 080
Untitled (Mental Map) Collage (12.5x18.5cm 4x7in) London 2001

ACKERMANN Gerald 1876-1960 [126]

$980 - €1 140 - **£700** - FF7 481
View of Warwick Castle Watercolour (25x36cm 9x14in) London 2001

ACKERMANN Max 1887-1975 [547]

$48 465 - €47 039 - **£30 176** - FF308 558
Ohne Titel Tempera (120.5x100cm 47x39in) Berlin 1999

$9 851 - €11 248 - **£6 945** - FF73 785
Ohnetitel Oil/panel (65x50cm 25x19in) Stuttgart 2001

$3 806 - €4 346 - **£2 683** - FF28 508
Ohne Titel Oil/panel (19.5x18cm 7x7in) Stuttgart 2001

$1 868 - €2 147 - **£1 319** - FF14 086
Ohne Titel Graphit (22.4x19.5cm 8x7in) Dettelbach-Effeldorf 2001

$318 - €353 - **£220** - FF2 314
Komposition in Lachs, und Blautönen mit schwarz, Umbrabraun, Gelb... Farbserigraphie (32x48.5cm 12x19in) Heidelberg 2001

ACKERMANN Otto 1872-1953 [32]
$369 - €434 - **£264** - FF2 850
Sonniger Tag am Hofe Oil/panel (27x34.5cm 10x13in) Düsseldorf 2001

ACKERMANN Peter 1934 [62]
$71 - €77 - **£47** - FF503
Abgeschirmt unter Wolkenlicht Radierung (85.6x65.5cm 33x25in) Köln 2000

ACKROYD Norman 1938 [52]
$212 - €252 - **£150** - FF1 652
Evening Rain, Derwentwater Aquatint (47x42cm 18x16in) London 2000

ACOSTA LÉON Angel 1932-1964 [31]
$90 000 - €77 710 - **£54 900** - FF509 742
Quema del Cañaveral Oil/masonite (193x119cm 75x46in) Miami FL 1999
$40 000 - €34 789 - **£24 116** - FF228 200
Fragmento de guarapera Oil/canvas (91,5x91.5cm 36x36in) New-York 1998
$6 000 - €6 971 - **£4 216** - FF45 727
Cafetera Oil/board (25.5x20.5cm 10x8in) New-York 2001

ACQUA dall' Cristoforo 1734-1787 [9]
$800 - €829 - **£480** - FF5 440
Satyra Vestalis, da Felice Buscarati Acquaforte (70x47cm 27x18in) Milano 2000

ACQUA Dell' Cesare Felix Georges 1821-1905 [57]
$11 931 - €12 501 - **£7 552** - FF82 000
La Sérénade Huile/toile (82x166cm 32x65in) Paris 2000
$4 207 - €3 946 - **£2 600** - FF25 881
Portrait of a Young Lady with a Fan Oil/canvas (68x51cm 26x20in) London 1999
$631 - €595 - **£381** - FF3 902
Bon vin Huile/panneau (33x25cm 12x9in) Antwerpen 1999
$2 173 - €2 033 - **£1 320** - FF13 333
De zwempartij Watercolour/paper (33x48cm 12x18in) Lokeren 1999

ACTON Stewart XX [7]
$472 - €504 - **£320** - FF3 307
Blackcap on the Downs, near Lewes Watercolour/paper (33x45cm 13x18in) Lewes, Sussex 2001

ADAM Albert 1833-? [17]
$257 - €305 - **£181** - FF2 000
Chien d'arrêt et lièvre après le tiré Lithographie (48.5x64cm 19x25in) Paris 2000

ADAM Albrecht 1786-1862 [40]
$330 000 - €284 709 - **£199 089** - FF1 867 569
Napoleon at Ostrovno, July 26 1812/Prince Eugene de Beauharnais Oil/canvas (124x180cm 48x70in) New-York 1998
$6 886 - €7 994 - **£4 840** - FF52 437
Kornernte beim Tegernsee Oil/panel (41.5x52.5cm 16x20in) Wien 2001
$927 - €920 - **£579** - FF6 037
Szene aus den napoleonischen Kriegen Öl/Papier (19x33cm 7x12in) München 1999
$458 - €511 - **£320** - FF3 353
Blick auf den Garten der «Adamei» Pencil (21x33.5cm 8x13in) München 2001

ADAM Benno Raffael 1812-1892 [39]
$10 026 - €8 474 - **£6 000** - FF55 584
The Kill Oil/canvas (77.5x113cm 30x44in) London 1998
$783 - €818 - **£496** - FF5 366
Jäger mit Hunden Pencil/paper (43x57cm 16x22in) München 2000

ADAM Édmond, «Adam Fils» 1868-1938 [54]
$6 354 - €5 488 - **£3 837** - FF36 000
Le Ville de Saint-Nazaire Huile/toile (62x92cm 24x36in) Le Havre 1998

ADAM Édouard, A. du Havre 1847-1929 [88]
$4 681 - €4 878 - **£2 944** - FF32 000
«Burdigala» (1912), construit en 1897. Ex: «Kaiser Friedrich» Huile/toile (60x92cm 23x36in) Paris 2000

ADAM Elias XX [3]
$1 393 - €1 545 - **£926** - FF10 137
El espejo humeante Técnica mixta/papel (120x150cm 47x59in) México 2000

ADAM Emil 1843-1924 [54]
$7 992 - €7 318 - **£4 872** - FF48 000
«Gouvernant», né en 1901, par Flying Fox et Gouvernante Huile/toile (71x91cm 27x35in) Paris 1999
$1 282 - €1 491 - **£900** - FF9 778
The Racehorse, Missal, in a Stable Oil/panel (19x24.5cm 7x9in) London 2001
$1 078 - €1 067 - **£672** - FF7 000
Les commères Aquarelle/papier (38x55cm 14x21in) Paris 1999

ADAM Eugen 1817-1880 [20]
$983 - €1 125 - **£676** - FF7 378
Dalmatinisches Hirtenpaar mit Ziegen Watercolour (25x18.5cm 9x7in) München 2000

ADAM Franz 1815-1886 [21]
$14 606 - €13 294 - **£9 126** - FF87 201
Pferde auf einer Hochalp am Wiesenhang Öl/Leinwand (120.5x109.5cm 47x43in) München 1999
$12 280 - €14 316 - **£8 503** - FF93 909
Vor dem Ausritt Öl/Leinwand (76x58cm 29x22in) Magdeburg 2000
$16 041 - €15 339 - **£9 768** - FF100 617
Rast eines Provianttransportes, die Pferde sin abgesattelt Öl/Leinwand (26x36cm 10x14in) Stuttgart 1999

ADAM Heinrich 1787-1862 [13]
$37 459 - €42 129 - **£26 149** - FF276 347
Blick auf Como Öl/Leinwand (52x68.5cm 20x26in) Luzern 2001
$5 500 - €4 547 - **£3 227** - FF29 825
Blick ins Isartal mit Burg Schwaneck bei Pullach Öl/Leinwand (23.5x33.5cm 9x13in) Heidelberg 1998

ADAM Henri-Georges 1904-1967 [25]
$169 - €198 - **£121** - FF1 300
Mai - Femme cruche/Oiseau gris Burin (76x56cm 29x22in) Paris 2001

ADAM Joseph 1824-1895 [17]
$552 - €540 - **£350** - FF3 542
Malo Mill, near Trefriw, Wales Oil/canvas (40.5x61cm 15x24in) London 1999

ADAM Joseph Denovan 1842-1896 [65]
$2 988 - €3 208 - **£2 000** - FF21 043
Highland river landscape Oil/canvas (76x127cm 29x50in) Canterbury, Kent 2000

$893 - €853 - **£550** - FF5 597
Highland Cattle in a Byre Oil/panel (35.5x43.5cm 13x17in) Edinburgh 1999

$2 963 - €3 304 - **£2 000** - FF21 674
By the Cottage Door Watercolour/paper (100x65cm 39x25in) Edinburgh 2000

ADAM Julius I 1826-1874 **[10]**
$20 801 - €20 652 - **£13 000** - FF135 469
Mother and her Kittens Oil/canvas (43.5x70.5cm 17x27in) London 1999

ADAM Julius II 1852-1913 **[58]**
$9 491 - €9 203 - **£6 012** - FF60 370
Katze mit sechs Jungen auf der Wiese in Sonnenlicht Öl/Leinwand (41x75.5cm 16x29in) München 1999

$11 797 - €10 737 - **£7 371** - FF70 431
Drei spielende Kätzchen auf einer Schilfmatte bei einem Futternapf Oil/panel (13x18cm 5x7in) München 1999

ADAM Otto 1901-1973 **[33]**
$1 148 - €1 227 - **£764** - FF8 049
«Mädchen und Möwen» Oil/panel (58x45cm 22x17in) Konstanz 2000

$747 - €716 - **£470** - FF4 695
Landschaft in Südfrankreich, südliche Häuser an einer Strasse Aquarell/Papier (38x52cm 14x20in) Konstanz 1999

ADAM Patrick William 1854-1929 **[99]**
$17 539 - €19 556 - **£12 000** - FF128 276
By the Shore Oil/canvas (125x153cm 49x60in) Perthshire 2000

$5 115 - €5 704 - **£3 500** - FF37 413
Venice Oil/canvas/board (62x37.5cm 24x14in) Perthshire 2000

$1 835 - €1 642 - **£1 100** - FF10 773
Leuchars, Fifshire Watercolour (40x30cm 15x11in) Perthshire 2000

ADAM Richard Benno 1873-1937 **[33]**
$597 - €511 - **£351** - FF3 351
Polospiel in weiter Wiesenlandschaft Oil/panel (20.5x32cm 8x12in) Stuttgart 1998

ADAM Victor Jean 1801-1866 **[53]**
$317 - €305 - **£196** - FF2 000
Corrida de toros Lithographie (29.5x40cm 11x15in) Paris 1999

ADAM William 1846-1931 **[17]**
$400 - €375 - **£247** - FF2 461
Pt. Lobos Oil/canvas/board (25x34cm 10x13in) St. Petersburg FL 1999

ADAMA N. XVII **[1]**
$13 423 - €12 706 - **£8 346** - FF83 344
Still Life of Oysters, Shrimps and Bread, all on a Wooden Ledge Oil/panel (17x22.5cm 6x8in) Amsterdam 1999

ADAMI Franco 1933 **[14]**
$4 002 - €4 421 - **£2 775** - FF29 000
Le casque d'Alexandre Marbre (42x23x16.5cm 16x9x6in) Paris 2001

ADAMI Valerio 1935 **[607]**
$13 608 - €16 007 - **£9 754** - FF105 000
«Le mur des lamentations» Acrylique/toile (149x117cm 58x46in) Paris 2001

$7 500 - €775 - **£4 848** - FF51 000
Figure Olio/tavola (62x73cm 24x28in) Venezia 1999

$1 932 - €2 134 - **£1 339** - FF14 000
«La Specchio» Mine plomb (49x68cm 19x26in) Paris 2001

$155 - €183 - **£111** - FF1 200
Personnage Lithographie couleurs (65x50cm 25x19in) Paris 2001

ADAMS Ansel Easton 1902-1984 **[821]**
$8 500 - €7 255 - **£5 083** - FF47 592
Canyon de Chelly National Monument, Arizona Gelatin silver print (39.5x49cm 15x19in) San-Francisco CA 1998

ADAMS Charles James 1859-1931 **[86]**
$2 430 - €2 760 - **£1 700** - FF18 106
Cows resting in a Summer Landscape by a Stream Oil/canvas (36x54cm 14x21in) Send-Woking, Surrey 2001

$1 555 - €1 534 - **£1 000** - FF10 064
Cattle and Chickns before a Barn Watercolour (26.5x37cm 10x14in) London 1999

ADAMS Charles Partridge 1858-1942 **[63]**
$11 000 - €10 678 - **£6 793** - FF70 042
Estes Park Landscape Oil/canvas (56x61cm 22x24in) Cedar-Falls IA 1999

$3 750 - €3 451 - **£2 250** - FF22 639
17 Mile Drive near Carmel, Calif in Spring Oil/canvas (30x40cm 12x16in) Pasadena CA 1999

$2 000 - €1 711 - **£1 204** - FF11 226
Landscape with Snowcapped Mountains beyond Watercolour, gouache/paper (26x43cm 10x17in) New-York 1998

ADAMS Dacre 1864-1951 **[2]**
$957 - €915 - **£600** - FF6 003
«See Britain First on Shell, Shillingford Bridge, Oxfordshire» Poster (76x113cm 29x44in) London 1999

ADAMS Douglas 1853-1920 **[24]**
$115 - €135 - **£80** - FF883
The Putting Green Print in colors (66x85cm 26x33in) Church-Stretton, Shropshire 2000

ADAMS Frank XX **[7]**
$393 - €414 - **£260** - FF2 718
The Huntsman outside his Cottage Watercolour (25x20cm 9x7in) London 2000

ADAMS Herbert 1858-1945 **[5]**
$30 000 - €33 637 - **£20 373** - FF220 644
Girl with Water Lilies Bronze (H160cm H63in) Cleveland OH 1999

$4 000 - €4 294 - **£2 676** - FF28 164
Débutante Bronze (H38.5cm H15in) New-York 2000

ADAMS John Clayton 1840-1906 **[64]**
$3 639 - €3 511 - **£2 300** - FF23 028
Ewhurst Hill, near Guildford Oil/canvas (70x93cm 27x36in) London 1999

ADAMS John Ottis 1851-1927 **[2]**
$29 000 - €33 643 - **£20 630** - FF220 684
Bay Through the Trees Oil/canvas (45x60cm 18x24in) Carmel IN 2000

ADAMS John Quincy 1874-1933 **[18]**
$1 800 - €2 006 - **£1 211** - FF13 158
Half-Portrait of Child with clasped Hands Oil/canvas (48x38cm 19x15in) Portsmouth NH 2000

ADAMS Kenneth Miller 1897-1966 **[7]**
$120 000 - €102 526 - **£72 036** - FF672 528
A Street in Taos Oil/canvas (46.5x77cm 18x30in) New-York 1998

ADAMS Mark 1925 **[2]**
$2 000 - €1 690 - **£1 193** - FF11 086
Catherine Wheel Tapestry (137x137cm 53x53in) San-Francisco CA 1998

ADAMS Neal 1941 [3]
📖 $1 600 - €1 543 - **£1 011** - FF10 124
World's Finest No.203 Ink (38x25.5cm 14x10in)
New-York 1999

ADAMS Norman 1927 [65]
📖 $280 - €327 - **£200** - FF2 147
«Rocky Cliffs and a dark Sea, South Harris»
Watercolour/paper (22x25cm 8x9in) London 2001

ADAMS Robert 1917-1984 [30]
🖎 $1 761 - €1 503 - **£1 050** - FF9 859
Semaphore Bronze (H25cm H9in) London 1998
📇 $345 - €394 - **£240** - FF2 585
Standing Figures Lithograph (28x20cm 11x7in)
London 2000

ADAMS Robert 1937 [17]
📷 $2 000 - €1 877 - **£1 235** - FF12 313
The Pawnee Grasslands Gelatin silver print
(22.5x30cm 8x11in) New-York 1999

ADAMS Sarah 1958 [7]
🖌 $4 515 - €4 954 - **£3 000** - FF32 499
Hyacinth Macaws with Stanhopea Orchids
Oil/board (91x85cm 35x33in) London 2000
🖌 $3 066 - €2 550 - **£1 800** - FF16 728
Galah Cockatoos in Eucalyptus Acrylic/board
(38.5x38.5cm 15x15in) London 1998

ADAMS Stephen 1953 [7]
🖌 $4 258 - €3 542 - **£2 500** - FF23 234
Tigress with Cubs -Tiger's Pride Oil/board
(61x107cm 24x42in) London 1998

ADAMS Wayman Eldridge 1883-1959 [20]
🖌 $3 250 - €2 972 - **£1 988** - FF19 498
Table Top Still life with Apples and Open Book
Oil/canvas (68x81cm 27x32in) Boston MA 1998
🖌 $1 600 - €1 361 - **£954** - FF8 929
Mother and Child Oil/canvas (21x21cm 8x8in) New-
York 1998

ADAMS Willis Seaver 1844-1921 [10]
🖌 $4 250 - €4 719 - **£2 956** - FF30 953
Feather St., Suffield, Conn Oil/canvas (59x99cm
23x39in) Milford CT 2001

ADAMSKI Hans Peter 1947 [35]
🖌 $338 - €393 - **£237** - FF2 577
«Kuss mit Zungenschlag» Acrylic (39x53cm
15x20in) Luzern 2001
📖 $276 - €297 - **£184** - FF1 945
Mann in Betrachtung eines Tieres Watercolour
(34x45.2cm 13x17in) Hamburg 2000

ADAMSON Harry Curieux XX [3]
🖌 $10 000 - €11 553 - **£7 002** - FF75 781
Canvasbacks at dawn Oil/canvas (55x71cm
22x28in) New-York 2001

ADAMSON Robert 1821-1898 [57]
📷 $4 500 - €4 209 - **£2 720** - FF27 610
Portrait, Possibly Sheriff Gay Salt print (20x14cm
7x5in) New-York 1999

ADAMSSON Bo Åke 1941 [24]
🖌 $2 354 - €2 261 - **£1 464** - FF14 830
I maj månag Oil/canvas (80x64cm 31x25in)
Stockholm 1999

ADAN Louis Émile 1839-1937 [36]
🖌 $8 650 - €8 232 - **£5 378** - FF54 000
Elégante près de la coiffeuse Huile/toile
(51.5x36cm 20x14in) Chambéry 1999
📖 $18 716 - €15 678 - **£11 005** - FF102 843
Chemin de la cascade Watercolour/paper (54x37cm
21x14in) Amsterdam 1998

ADDAMS Charles Samuel 1912-1988 [39]
📖 $5 000 - €5 828 - **£3 462** - FF38 232
Thoughtful Uncle Fester in his Attic Study
Watercolour (24x36cm 9x14in) New-York 2000

ADDERTON Charles William 1866-1944 [22]
📖 $501 - €428 - **£300** - FF2 809
**Figures on a Beached Fishing Vessel at low
Tide** Watercolour (24x34.5cm 9x13in) London 1998

ADDEY Joseph Poole 1855-1922 [13]
$1 420 - €1 651 - **£998** - FF10 827
**Sailing off the Coast of Haulbowline Island/The
Quay at Kingstown** Watercolour/paper (17x24cm
6x9in) Dublin 2001

ADEMOLLO Carlo 1825-1911 [11]
🖌 $20 000 - €20 733 - **£12 000** - FF136 000
**Garibaldi con Garibaldini nella battaglia di
Mentana** Olio/tela (180x300cm 70x118in) Formigine,
Mo 2000
🖌 $8 961 - €8 156 - **£5 500** - FF53 498
Stolen Pleasures Oil/canvas (114x84cm 44x33in)
London 1999

ADEMOLLO Luigi 1764-1849 [18]
📖 $5 750 - €5 961 - **£3 450** - FF39 100
Composizione con scene delle storia antica
Tecnica mista/carta (63x97cm 24x38in) Roma 1999

ADIE Edith Helena act.1892-1930 [18]
📖 $604 - €533 - **£360** - FF3 495
The Garden Trellis Watercolour/paper (18x14cm
7x5in) London 1998

ADJUKIEWICZ von Thaddäus 1852-1916 [6]
🖌 $4 526 - €3 779 - **£2 654** - FF24 787
Portrait of Karola Stefana Habsburga Oil/panel
(25x20cm 9x7in) Warszawa 1998

ADLER Edmund 1876-1965 [108]
🖌 $8 374 - €7 669 - **£5 104** - FF50 308
Musikunterricht Öl/Leinwand (54x102cm 21x40in)
München 1999
🖌 $2 849 - €3 312 - **£2 000** - FF21 728
Let them all Come Oil/board (30x20cm 11x7in)
Billingshurst, West-Sussex 2001

ADLER Jankel 1895-1949 [214]
🖌 $101 623 - €94 079 - **£62 210** - FF617 117
Mann mit Pferd Mixed media/canvas (101x120cm
39x47in) München 1999
🖌 $12 000 - €13 164 - **£7 743** - FF86 350
Still Life with Fruit Oil/board (65x50cm 25x19in) Tel
Aviv 2000
🖌 $6 000 - €7 173 - **£4 138** - FF47 052
Figure Oil/board (28x22cm 11x8in) Tel Aviv 2000
📖 $934 - €818 - **£565** - FF5 365
Mädchen am Fenster Pencil (22.5x17.4cm 8x6in)
Berlin 1998

ADLER Jules 1865-1952 [122]
🖌 $2 549 - €2 897 - **£1 789** - FF19 000
Montigny-sur-Loing Huile/toile (46x38cm 18x14in)
Paris 2001
🖌 $583 - €656 - **£378** - FF4 300
Scène d'après l'Antiquité Huile/toile (40.5x32.5cm
15x12in) Paris 2000
📖 $261 - €305 - **£183** - FF2 000
Picpus Crayon/papier (13x10cm 5x3in) Paris 2000

ADLER Karol 1936 [5]
🖌 $1 789 - €2 104 - **£1 297** - FF13 800
Le coq du village Huile/toile (73x60cm 28x23in)
Provins 2001

ADLER Rose 1892-1969 **[36]**
🖋 **$13 104** - €14 635 - **£8 880** - FF96 000
　　Composition géométrique aux coquillages
　　Gouache/papier (23.5x28cm 9x11in) Paris 2000

ADLIVANKIN Samuel Jakovlevic 1897-1966 **[4]**
🖋 **$12 000** - €13 923 - **£8 284** - FF91 332
　　Untitled Watercolour/paper (31x22cm 12x8in) New-
　　York 2000

ADLOFF C. Act.1850 **[1]**
😊 **$5 499** - €6 647 - **£3 838** - FF43 600
　　Nächtlicher Fischfang bei Vollmond Öl/Leinwand
　　(69.5x114cm 27x44in) Düsseldorf 2000

ADMIRAL d' Jacob II 1700-1770 **[3]**
🗐 **$989** - €885 - **£592** - FF5 804
　　Naauwkeurige Waarneemingen Omtrent de
　　Veranderingen Insekten Etching in colors
　　(42.5x26.5cm 16x10in) Amsterdam 1998

ADNET Françoise 1924 **[66]**
😊 **$1 129** - €1 220 - **£780** - FF8 000
　　Le plein été devant chez moi Huile/toile (50x73cm
　　19x28in) Coulommiers 2001

ADNET Jacques 1900-1984 **[8]**
🖎 **$1 428** - €1 250 - **£865** - FF8 200
　　Tête de femme Sculpture (H40cm H15in) Paris 1998
🗐 **$12 089** - €11 739 - **£7 469** - FF77 000
　　Tapis à décor sur la bordure d'une frise de che-
　　vrons Tapisserie (545x261cm 214x102in) Paris 1999

ADOLFS Gerard Pieter, Ger 1897-1968 **[139]**
😊 **$3 265** - €2 740 - **£1 916** - FF17 974
　　«Padisnit» Oil/board (40x50cm 15x19in) Singapore
　　1998
😊 **$1 772** - €1 651 - **£1 071** - FF10 833
　　Blind Beggar Oil/canvas (40x30cm 15x11in)
　　Singapore 1999

ADOMEIT George Gustav 1879-1967 **[26]**
😊 **$3 350** - €3 518 - **£2 193** - FF23 077
　　New England Seacoast Oil/canvas/board (39x44cm
　　15x17in) Cleveland OH 2000
🗐 **$300** - €288 - **£183** - FF1 890
　　Provincetown Street Linocut (12x10cm 5x4in)
　　Provincetown MA 1999

ADRIAENSSEN Alexander 1587-1661 **[40]**
😊 **$8 579** - €8 395 - **£5 500** - FF55 067
　　Still Life of Fish, Lobster, Songbirds and a
　　English Partridge, a Cat Oil/panel (38x60cm
　　14x23in) London 2000
😊 **$7 250** - €7 211 - **£4 500** - FF47 300
　　Still Life of Finches on wooden Table/Still Life of
　　Pike, Fish Oil/panel (19.5x25cm 7x9in) London 1999

ADRIAENSSEN Vincent 1595-1675 **[5]**
😊 **$11 036** - €11 676 - **£7 000** - FF76 591
　　Daniel in the Lion's Den Oil/canvas (132x175cm
　　51x68in) London 2000

ADRIAN Marc 1930 **[8]**
😊 **$9 229** - €7 991 - **£5 599** - FF52 415
　　«AB2» Mixed media/panel (93x73cm 36x28in) Wien
　　1998

ADRIAN-NILSSON Gösta, dit Gan 1885-1965 **[329]**
😊 **$94 556** - €88 849 - **£56 980** - FF582 813
　　Sjömansvals Oil/canvas (143x192cm 56x75in)
　　Stockholm 1999
😊 **$24 560** - €23 078 - **£14 800** - FF151 380
　　Idrottsmän Oil/canvas (75x100cm 29x39in)
　　Stockholm 1999

😊 **$2 931** - €3 284 - **£2 043** - FF21 540
　　Komposition Mixed media (15.5x13cm 6x5in)
　　Stockholm 2001
🖋 **$2 955** - €2 499 - **£1 766** - FF16 394
　　«Eskimö», «Ishavsbaletten» Akvarell/papper
　　(33x22cm 12x8in) Stockholm 1998

ADRICHOM van Christian XVI **[1]**
🗐 **$1 064** - €976 - **£650** - FF6 399
　　Ierusalem et suburbia Engraving (51x74cm
　　20x29in) London 1999

ADRION Lucien 1889-1953 **[320]**
😊 **$4 274** - €3 659 - **£2 572** - FF24 000
　　Promeneurs dans le port Huile/toile (60x73cm
　　23x28in) Paris 1998
😊 **$1 134** - €1 143 - **£707** - FF7 500
　　La Plage de Deauville Huile/panneau (24x33cm
　　9x12in) Paris 2000

ADUATZ Fritz 1907-1994 **[16]**
😊 **$6 056** - €5 814 - **£3 800** - FF38 136
　　Ohne Titel Öl/Leinwand (55.5x68cm 21x26in) Wien
　　1999

ADVINENT Étienne Louis 1767-1831 **[5]**
😊 **$4 671** - €4 573 - **£2 874** - FF30 000
　　Portraits de deux révolutionnaires Huile/toile/car-
　　ton (19x14cm 7x5in) Paris 1999

ADZAK Roy 1927-1987 **[46]**
😊 **$752** - €758 - **£469** - FF4 975
　　Paris Mixed media (99x81cm 38x31in) Stockholm
　　2000

AECKERLIN Christian 1884-1943 **[3]**
🖎 **$2 070** - €2 382 - **£1 429** - FF15 627
　　Panter (Panther) Bronze (25x46.5cm 9x18in)
　　Maastricht 2000

AELST van Willem Jansz. 1627-1683/86 **[18]**
😊 **$552 891** - €593 483 - **£370 000** - FF3 892 992
　　Tulips, Roses, Lilies, Carnations, Morning Glory
　　and Other Flowers Oil/canvas (115.5x159.5cm
　　45x62in) London 2000
😊 **$100 000** - €95 457 - **£62 480** - FF626 160
　　Fish on a Pewter Platter, an Orpheus Salt Cellar,
　　a Roemer Oil/canvas (55.5x45cm 21x17in) New-York
　　1999

AEMISEGGER-GIEZENDANNER Anna Barbara
1831-1905 **[10]**
😊 **$5 224** - €5 031 - **£3 267** - FF32 999
　　Die Alpfahrt Tempera (16x25.5cm 6x10in) Zürich
　　1999
🖋 **$7 502** - €8 487 - **£5 248** - FF55 671
　　«Alpfahrt und Sennerei» Watercolour (25x41cm
　　9x16in) St. Gallen 2001

AEPLY Jeanine XX **[2]**
🗐 **$635** - €610 - **£398** - FF4 000
　　Composition, d'après Paul Klee
　　(réplique/papier/toile) Estampe (59.5x47cm 23x18in)
　　Vannes 1999

AEREBOE Albert 1889-1970 **[10]**
🖋 **$818** - €818 - **£512** - FF5 366
　　Dünenlandschaft Pastell/Papier (46.5x61cm 18x24in)
　　Hamburg 1999

AERNI Franz Theodor 1853-1918 **[20]**
😊 **$5 500** - €4 655 - **£3 292** - FF30 538
　　Desert Sandstorm Oil/canvas (71x124cm 27x48in)
　　New-York 1998

AERS Marguerite, Marg 1918-1995 [75]

$672 - €744 - £471 - FF4 878
Elégante allongée sur l'herbe Huile/toile (60x80cm 23x31in) Bruxelles 2001

$435 - €471 - £302 - FF3 089
Jeune fille et sa poupée Huile/panneau (40x21cm 15x8in) Bruxelles 2001

AERTS Hendrick ?-1575 [1]

$20 173 - €21 654 - £13 500 - FF142 041
The Interior of a Cathedral with a Procession Oil/copper (30x42cm 11x16in) London 2000

AERTSEN Pieter 1507/08-1575 [16]

$55 000 - €54 974 - £33 599 - FF360 607
The Nativity Oil/panel (139.5x108.5cm 54x42in) New-York 2000

$25 403 - €27 268 - £17 000 - FF178 867
Christ on the Mount of Olives Oil/panel (81.5x66cm 32x25in) London 2000

$100 007 - €86 377 - £60 286 - FF566 596
Christ driving the Money Changers from the Temple Oil/panel (28.7x34cm 11x13in) Amsterdam 1998

AERTTINGER Karl August 1803-1876 [6]

$15 000 - €16 083 - £9 924 - FF105 498
Great Stone Mill on a River with Mounted Tradesmen, Peasant Workers Oil/canvas (116x110cm 46x43in) New-Orleans LA 2000

AESCHBACHER Arthur 1923 [73]

$1 276 - €1 189 - £787 - FF7 800
Circassienne et tant d'autres Technique mixte/toile (46x38.5cm 18x15in) Paris 1999

$648 - €762 - £464 - FF5 000
Composition Technique mixte (31.5x22.5cm 12x8in) Paris 2001

$574 - €579 - £358 - FF3 800
Composition abstraite Collage (45x59.5cm 17x23in) Toulon 2000

AESCHBACHER Hans 1906-1980 [18]

$2 830 - €3 284 - £1 954 - FF21 539
Plastik Nr.VII Metal (H55cm H21in) Zürich 2000

AFFANDI Kusuma 1907-1990 [94]

$17 217 - €19 550 - £11 784 - FF128 238
Fishing Boats Oil/canvas (89.5x135cm 35x53in) Singapore 2000

$14 767 - €13 763 - £8 925 - FF90 282
Self Portrait Oil/canvas/board (91x81cm 35x31in) Singapore 1999

AFFLECK Andrew F. 1874-c.1935 [38]

$103 - €100 - £65 - FF657
Rheims Cathedral Etching (56x30cm 22x12in) Par, Cornwall 1999

AFFLECK William 1869-1909 [44]

$1 586 - €1 665 - £1 000 - FF10 924
English Rose Watercolour/paper (29x41.5cm 11x16in) London 2000

AFFORTUNATI Aldo 1906-? [26]

$1 700 - €1 437 - £1 010 - FF9 424
Singin in the Parlor Oil/canvas (60x49cm 24x19in) Philadelphia PA 1998

$650 - €674 - £390 - FF4 420
Scena galante Olio/cartone (27.5x34cm 10x13in) Prato 2000

AFONSO Nadir 1920 [5]

$7 740 - €8 973 - £5 400 - FF58 860
Sem título Gouache/papier (21.5x30.5cm 8x12in) Lisboa 2001

AFRICANO Nicholas 1948 [29]

$12 000 - €13 923 - £8 284 - FF91 332
Lost boy Sculpture (29.5x41.5cm 11x16in) New-York 2000

AFRO 1912-1976 [283]

$132 000 - €114 032 - £66 000 - FF748 000
Terra d'ombra Olio/tela (93x162cm 36x63in) Milano 1999

$31 200 - €40 429 - £23 400 - FF265 200
Composizione astratta Tempera (58x69cm 22x27in) Milano 2000

$9 500 - €9 848 - £5 700 - FF64 600
Composizione Olio/tela (45.5x30.5cm 17x12in) Milano 2000

$6 400 - €8 293 - £4 800 - FF54 400
Composizione Acquarello/carta (24x34cm 9x13in) Milano 2000

$700 - €726 - £420 - FF4 760
Senza titolo Litografia (48x66cm 18x25in) Prato 2001

AFSARY Cyrus 1941 [15]

$15 400 - €14 382 - £9 504 - FF94 340
Chrysantheum and Fruit Oil/canvas (66x233cm 26x92in) Dallas TX 1999

$8 000 - €9 084 - £5 558 - FF59 584
Ready to Move Oil/canvas (45x60cm 18x24in) Dallas TX 2001

$4 400 - €4 109 - £2 715 - FF26 954
Drum Beat Oil/canvas (27x35cm 11x14in) Dallas TX 1999

AGAM Yaacov 1928 [284]

$30 000 - €35 865 - £20 694 - FF235 260
Peinture Polimorphique Métamorphique Oil/wood (111x130cm 43x51in) Tel Aviv 2000

$7 776 - €9 147 - £5 574 - FF60 000
Composition abstraite Huile/panneau (48x39.5cm 18x15in) Paris 2001

$5 484 - €5 026 - £3 351 - FF32 969
Ligne métamorphose Technique mixte/panneau (28.5x30cm 11x11in) Zürich 1999

$650 - €726 - £425 - FF4 760
Infinity Sculpture, wood (26x26cm 10x10in) Chicago IL 2000

$800 - €865 - £548 - FF5 677
«Picture» Coloured pencils/paper (44x52cm 17x20in) Tel Aviv 2001

$260 - €298 - £177 - FF1 956
Star of David Serigraph (65x65cm 25x25in) New-York 2000

AGAR Eileen 1904-1991 [72]

$2 891 - €2 785 - £1 800 - FF18 266
Figures in a Garden Oil/canvas (61x51cm 24x20in) London 1999

$2 646 - €2 475 - £1 600 - FF16 236
Moonface Oil/canvas (40.5x30.5cm 15x12in) London 1999

$386 - €424 - £249 - FF2 780
Abstract in Green and Yellow Charcoal (29x20cm 11x7in) London 2000

AGARD Charles 1866-1950 [116]

$333 - €381 - £234 - FF2 500
Le battage Huile/toile (26.5x34.5cm 10x13in) Fontainebleau 2001

AGASSE Jacques Laurent 1767-1849 [50]

$65 000 - €69 417 - £44 291 - FF455 344
A grey Hunter in a wooded Landscape Oil/canvas (63.5x76cm 25x29in) New-York 2001

$29 000 - €29 337 - **£17 707** - FF192 441
Lady with a Hunting Dog in the Valley of l'Arve, Geneva Oil/canvas (38x34.5cm 14x13in) New-York 2000

$1 704 - €1 565 - **£1 046** - FF10 269
Landschaften Encre (13.5x14.5cm 5x5in) Zürich 1999

AGAZZI Rinaldo 1857-1939 **[12]**
$3 900 - €3 369 - **£1 950** - FF22 100
Ritratto di fanciulla Olio/tela (82x56cm 32x22in) Milano 1999

$2 520 - €2 177 - **£1 260** - FF14 280
Maternita Carboncino (60x40cm 23x15in) Milano 1999

AGERO XIX-XX **[1]**
$3 297 - €3 201 - **£2 037** - FF21 000
Le joueur de tambour Crayons couleurs/papier (21x37cm 8x14in) Paris 1999

AGERSNAP Hans 1857-1925 **[118]**
$289 - €269 - **£174** - FF1 766
Vinterlandskab med strätaekte huse Oil/canvas (60x89cm 23x35in) Köbenhavn 1999

AGGER Knud 1895-1973 **[82]**
$384 - €322 - **£225** - FF2 114
Interiör med laesende pige Oil/canvas (64x60cm 25x23in) Vejle 1998

AGHAIAN Alain XX **[5]**
$5 216 - €4 878 - **£3 216** - FF32 000
Hécate, d'après Georges Braque Tapisserie (170x140cm 66x55in) Paris 1999

AGHTE Curt 1862-1943 **[19]**
$410 - €460 - **£278** - FF3 018
Der Hofbrunnen in Rothenburg Öl/Karton (35x44cm 13x17in) München 2000

AGLIO Agostino 1777-1857 **[15]**
$2 988 - €3 208 - **£2 000** - FF21 043
Travellers Resting in an Extensive Wooded Landscape Oil/canvas (83.5x120cm 32x47in) London 2000

AGNATI Emilio 1876-1937 **[1]**
$30 000 - €33 260 - **£20 832** - FF218 169
Semi-nude Male and Female Bronze (H122cm H48in) New-York 2001

AGNEESSENS Edouard 1842-1885 **[27]**
$1 113 - €1 091 - **£686** - FF7 154
Vrouw in profiel Oil/canvas (46x38cm 18x14in) Lokeren 1999

$984 - €992 - **£612** - FF6 504
Elégante tenant des jumelles de spectacle Huile/panneau (30x23cm 11x9in) Bruxelles 2000

AGNETTI Vincenzo 1926-1981 **[38]**
$3 300 - €2 851 - **£2 200** - FF18 700
«Assioma n.4» Tecnica mista (68.5x70cm 26x27in) Milano 1998

$2 200 - €2 851 - **£1 650** - FF18 700
Elisabetta d'Inghilterra Photo (40x30cm 15x11in) Milano 2000

AGOSTINI Guido XIX **[51]**
$1 799 - €1 597 - **£1 100** - FF10 474
Firenze dal Villa Magna/Castello di Donoratico, Maremma, Pisana Oil/board (25.5x21.5cm 10x8in) London 2000

AGOSTINI Max 1914-1997 **[179]**
$818 - €808 - **£504** - FF5 300
Le jardin fleuri Huile/toile (46x61cm 18x24in) Paris 1999

$513 - €579 - **£361** - FF3 800
Nature morte Huile/toile (33x41cm 12x16in) Paris 2001

AGOSTINI Tony 1916-1990 **[224]**
$936 - €884 - **£582** - FF5 800
Nature morte orange Huile/toile (46x38cm 18x14in) Neuilly-sur-Seine 1999

$668 - €762 - **£464** - FF5 000
Nature morte aux fruits et au pichet Huile/toile (27x19cm 10x7in) Paris 2001

AGRASOT Y JUAN Joaquín 1837-1919 **[55]**
$16 200 - €18 019 - **£11 400** - FF118 200
Jugando a las cartas Oleo/lienzo (52x62cm 20x24in) Madrid 2001

$2 700 - €3 003 - **£1 900** - FF19 700
Pensativa Oleo/tabla (20x13.5cm 7x5in) Madrid 2001

$3 430 - €2 943 - **£2 127** - FF19 306
Italiana Acuarela/papel (32x21cm 12x8in) Madrid 1998

AGRESTI Rodolfo XIX **[3]**
$2 389 - €2 487 - **£1 500** - FF16 311
Grinding the Coffee Oil/canvas (40.5x30.5cm 15x12in) London 2000

AGRICOLA Carl Josef Alois 1779-1852 **[29]**
$11 685 - €10 901 - **£7 050** - FF71 505
Angebliches Bildnis der Tänzerin Fanny Elssler als Flora Öl/Leinwand (190.5x127.5cm 75x50in) Wien 1999

$5 264 - €5 814 - **£3 648** - FF38 136
Nereus und seine Töchter die Nereiden, im Sturm Öl/Karton (36x45cm 14x17in) Wien 2001

$2 621 - €2 543 - **£1 617** - FF16 684
Bildnis des Prinzen Friedrich Schwarzenberg in Uniform Miniature (7.5x6.5cm 2x2in) Wien 1999

$656 - €767 - **£461** - FF5 030
Junges Mädchen mit lockig hochgestecktem Haar/Offizier/Junge Dame Aquarell/Papier (17x13cm 6x5in) München 2000

AGRICOLA Christophe-Ludwig 1667-1719 **[52]**
$2 426 - €2 250 - **£1 500** - FF14 756
Birds sitting on Branches Gouache (26.5x18cm 10x7in) London 1999

AGRICOLA Eduard 1800-1874 **[16]**
$9 981 - €11 248 - **£6 912** - FF73 785
Die Wasserfälle von Tivoli bei Rom Öl/Leinwand (71x106cm 27x41in) Berlin 2000

AGTERBERG Chris 1883-1948 **[6]**
$1 571 - €1 724 - **£1 044** - FF11 311
Coromandel Figure of a Fish Sculpture (H29.5cm H11in) Amsterdam 2000

AGUADO Olympe, comte 1827-1894 **[23]**
$822 - €762 - **£511** - FF5 000
Allée bordée d'arbres Tirage albuminé (18.6x23.3cm 7x9in) Paris 1999

AGUADO Y GUERRA José ?-1905 **[3]**
$7 000 - €6 197 - **£4 279** - FF40 648
Vanguard crossing a River Oil/panel (44.5x65cm 17x25in) New-York 1999

AGUAYO Fermin 1926-1977 **[20]**
$1 025 - €1 220 - **£731** - FF8 000
Composition brune Huile/toile (76x61.5cm 29x24in) Paris 2000

$1 677 - €1 652 - **£1 045** - FF10 835
Composición Oleo/lienzo (42x32cm 16x12in) Madrid 1999

AGUÉLI Ivan 1869-1917 **[52]**
- $22 884 - €19 900 - **£13 801** - FF130 536
  Sydländskt landskap Oil/canvas/panel (18x23cm 7x9in) Stockholm 1998

AGUERREGARAY Charles-Jean XX **[26]**
- $1 106 - €915 - **£649** - FF6 000
  Le port de Lequeitio Huile/toile (54x73cm 21x28in) Biarritz 1998
- $331 - €274 - **£194** - FF1 800
  La Concha à Saint Sébastien Aquarelle/papier (18x31.5cm 7x12in) Biarritz 1998

AGUIAR GARCIA José 1898-1976 **[11]**
- $4 800 - €4 505 - **£3 000** - FF29 550
  Florero Oleo/cartón (78x61cm 30x24in) Madrid 1999

AGUILA Y ACOSTA Adolfo XIX-XX **[11]**
- $8 540 - €8 409 - **£5 460** - FF55 160
  La salida de misa Oleo/lienzo (45x72cm 17x28in) Madrid 1999

AGUILAR ALCUAZ Federico 1932 **[5]**
- $8 608 - €9 775 - **£5 892** - FF64 119
  Woman with a Cat Oil/canvas (83x83cm 32x32in) Singapore 2000

AGUILAR d' Michael 1924 **[39]**
- $651 - €558 - **£393** - FF3 663
  The Peasants Oil/masonite (89x119.5cm 35x47in) Toronto 1998
- $379 - €431 - **£260** - FF2 827
  La siesta Oil/canvas (20x41cm 7x16in) London 2000

AGUILAR MORE Ramón 1924 **[52]**
- $2 784 - €2 883 - **£1 728** - FF18 912
  Barcas amarradas Oleo/lienzo (60x92cm 23x36in) Barcelona 2000
- $1 276 - €1 321 - **£814** - FF8 668
  Joven de perfil Oleo/cartón (44x31cm 17x12in) Barcelona 2000
- $527 - €511 - **£323** - FF3 349
  Joven cantado Técnica mixta/papel (28x17.5cm 11x6in) Barcelona 1999

AGUJARI Tito 1834-1908 **[12]**
- $2 900 - €3 006 - **£1 740** - FF19 720
  Signora coi mughetti Olio/tela (62x52cm 24x20in) Trieste 1999

AGUSTIN Y GRANDE Francisco 1753-1800 **[4]**
- $83 200 - €78 084 - **£52 000** - FF512 200
  Don Juan Despuig y Zaforteza, de cuerpo entero, vestido de negro Oleo/lienzo (174.5x124.5cm 68x49in) Palma de Mallorca 1999

AGUTTE Georgette 1867-1922 **[38]**
- $2 614 - €3 049 - **£1 836** - FF20 000
  Le port de Bordeaux Huile/toile (81x100cm 31x39in) Versailles 2000

AGUZZI Fabio 1953 **[5]**
- $1 100 - €1 140 - **£660** - FF7 480
  «Cestino con michette» Olio/tela (40x70cm 15x27in) Vercelli 1999

AHL Henry Hammond 1869-1953 **[31]**
- $7 000 - €7 720 - **£4 740** - FF50 638
  Fall River Landscape Oil/canvas (63.5x76cm 25x29in) New-York 2000
- $440 - €461 - **£276** - FF3 021
  Autumn Scene Oil/canvas (16x20cm 6x8in) Hampton NH 2000

AHLBERG Arvid 1851-1932 **[14]**
- $978 - €922 - **£606** - FF6 048
  Månsskensseglats Oil/canvas (90x122.5cm 35x48in) Stockholm 1999

- $1 985 - €1 981 - **£1 239** - FF12 996
  Karlskrona sett från Kobebus Oil/canvas (37x5cm 14x1in) Uppsala 1998

AHLBERG Olof 1876-1956 **[11]**
- $924 - €884 - **£582** - FF5 798
  Sankt Göran och draken Plaster (H67cm H26in) Stockholm 1999

AHLBORN August Wilhelm J. 1796-1857 **[6]**
- $6 328 - €6 106 - **£4 000** - FF40 050
  The Roman Amphitheatre, Taormina Oil/canvas (84x112cm 33x44in) London 1999
- $1 734 - €1 588 - **£1 057** - FF10 418
  View of Gubbio, near Perugia, Italy Pencil/paper (37.5x49.5cm 14x19in) Amsterdam 1999

AHLERS-HESTERMANN Friedrich, Fritz 1883-1973 **[60]**
- $6 217 - €5 370 - **£3 754** - FF35 223
  Artaval Öl/Leinwand (55.4x46.4cm 21x18in) Köln 1998
- $2 200 - €2 556 - **£1 546** - FF16 769
  Selbstbildnis Oil/board/canvas (42.5x35.5cm 16x13in) Hamburg 2001

AHLGREN Lauris 1929 **[13]**
- $567 - €538 - **£345** - FF3 530
  I famnen på moder jord Gouache/paper (49x67cm 19x26in) Helsinki 1999

AHLGREN Olavi 1897-1966 **[21]**
- $171 - €202 - **£119** - FF1 323
  Hus Oil/canvas (51x61cm 20x24in) Helsinki 2000

AHLGRENSSON Björn 1872-1918 **[6]**
- $3 700 - €4 210 - **£2 584** - FF27 615
  Landskap från Rackstad Mixed media (38x54.5cm 14x21in) Stockholm 2000

AHLSTEDT Fredrik 1839-1901 **[31]**
- $12 699 - €14 295 - **£8 746** - FF93 772
  Favoritplatsen Oil/canvas (43x66cm 16x25in) Helsinki 2000
- $6 132 - €6 727 - **£3 948** - FF44 128
  Aftonljus Oil/panel (31.5x48cm 12x18in) Helsinki 2000

AHLSTEDT Nina 1853-1907 **[8]**
- $2 662 - €2 607 - **£1 638** - FF17 099
  Kesäidylli Oil/canvas (36.5x54cm 14x21in) Helsinki 2000

AHMAD Zakii Anwar 1955 **[2]**
- $9 608 - €10 617 - **£6 662** - FF69 642
  Contemplation in blue Acrylic/canvas (122x183cm 48x72in) Singapore 2001

AHRENDT L. XIX **[1]**
- $18 188 - €17 179 - **£11 000** - FF112 688
  Berlin, six studies (views of Street, square, River Spree...) Albumen print (16.5x21.5cm 6x8in) London 1999

AHRENDTS Carl Eduard 1822-1898 **[41]**
- $1 921 - €1 815 - **£1 198** - FF11 906
  The Arrival of the Fishing Fleet Oil/panel (16x22cm 6x8in) Amsterdam 1999

AHRLE Rene 1893-1976 **[5]**
- $1 352 - €1 175 - **£814** - FF7 709
  Odeon-Reklame Vintage gelatin silver print (19.2x15.7cm 7x6in) Berlin 1998

AHTELA H., Einar Reuter 1881-1968 **[5]**
- $1 359 - €1 261 - **£816** - FF8 274
  Blommor i vas Oil/canvas (64x78cm 25x30in) Helsinki 1999

AHTOLA Taisto 1917-2000 **[12]**
- **$1 051** - €1 177 - **£730** - FF7 722
  Födelsedag Oil/board (40x29cm 15x11in) Helsinki 2001

AHUATZI Armando 1950 **[9]**
- **$2 144** - €2 378 - **£1 426** - FF15 596
  Granadas Oleo/lienzo (81x61cm 31x24in) México 2000

AI XUAN 1947 **[25]**
- **$7 051** - €8 287 - **£4 889** - FF54 362
  February Oil/canvas (51x61cm 20x24in) Hong-Kong 2000

AICHELE Paul 1859-1910 **[29]**
- **$8 000** - €9 295 - **£5 622** - FF60 969
  Eagle Hunter Bronze (H104cm H40in) New-York 2001
- **$652** - €752 - **£450** - FF4 933
  Small Bust of a young Woman Bronze (10x4cm 3x1in) Billingshurst, West-Sussex 2000

AID George Charles 1872-1938 **[15]**
- **$5 000** - €5 367 - **£3 346** - FF35 205
  Le Point de Jour Oil/canvas (60.5x81.5cm 23x32in) New-York 2000

AIGEN Karl Joseph 1684-1762 **[5]**
- **$16 008** - €17 262 - **£10 744** - FF113 230
  Faraos dotter finner Moses/Hagar och Ismael lämnar Abraham Oil/canvas (34x58cm 13x22in) Stockholm 2000

AIGENS Christian 1870-1940 **[58]**
- **$459** - €496 - **£317** - FF3 254
  Pige med sytoj ved bord med blomsteri vase Oil/canvas (91x100cm 35x39in) København 2001
- **$645** - €697 - **£446** - FF4 574
  Portraet af Marie Kroyer Oil/canvas (34x31cm 13x12in) København 2001

AIGNER Joseph Mathäus 1818-1886 **[11]**
- **$1 200** - €1 122 - **£725** - FF7 362
  Portrait of a Lady with her dog Oil/canvas (69x55cm 27x21in) New-York 1999

AIGNER Lucien 1901-1999 **[15]**
- **$819** - €793 - **£505** - FF5 200
  Fiorello Laguardia, maire de New York, NY Tirage argentique (17.5x22.5cm 6x8in) Paris 1999

AIGNER Paul 1932 **[8]**
- **$481** - €436 - **£300** - FF2 858
  «Sports d'hiver en Autriche» Poster (94x64cm 37x25in) London 1999

AIKES Jan Hendrik 1790-1846 **[2]**
- **$3 200** - €3 071 - **£2 006** - FF20 145
  Basket of Fruit Oil/panel (21.5x27cm 8x10in) New-York 1999

AIKMAN William 1682-1731 **[9]**
- **$26 200** - €23 961 - **£16 000** - FF157 171
  Portrait of Colonel the Hon. Charles Leslie, 9th Earle of the Rothes Oil/canvas (127x101cm 50x39in) London 1998
- **$4 548** - €4 426 - **£2 800** - FF29 032
  Portrait of the Hon James Hamilton (1684-1732) Oil/canvas (73.5x61.5cm 28x24in) London 1999

AILLAUD Gilles 1928 **[27]**
- **$3 556** - €3 964 - **£2 392** - FF26 000
  Le serpent Huile/toile (81x100cm 31x39in) Lille 2000

AIRY Anna 1882-1964 **[45]**
- **$15 747** - €15 237 - **£9 710** - FF99 948
  The Lesson Oil/canvas (114.5x152cm 45x59in) Dublin 1999
- **$5 383** - €6 283 - **£3 800** - FF41 215
  Still Life, Roses in a Pewter Mug on a Table Oil/canvas (50x60cm 20x24in) Woodbridge, Suffolk 2000
- **$736** - €860 - **£520** - FF5 640
  Bird on a Branch eyeing a Spider in its web Watercolour (18x18cm 7x7in) Woodbridge, Suffolk 2000

AISTROP E. XIX **[17]**
- **$1 700** - €1 851 - **£1 170** - FF12 145
  Clumber Spaniel, «Bailie Friar» Oil/board (16.5x21cm 6x8in) New-York 2001

AITCHISON Craigie 1926 **[35]**
- **$24 865** - €21 213 - **£15 000** - FF139 146
  Crucifixion II Oil/canvas (173x145cm 68x57in) London 1998
- **$23 803** - €27 684 - **£17 000** - FF181 592
  Star, Tree and Sheepdog Oil/canvas (35.5x25.5cm 13x10in) London 2001
- **$3 829** - €4 373 - **£2 700** - FF28 682
  Christ Color lithograph (76x63cm 29x24in) London 2001

AITKEN Doug 1968 **[2]**
- **$10 000** - €11 201 - **£6 948** - FF73 472
  «Mirror #2» Photograph (51x63.5cm 20x25in) New-York 2001

AITKEN James act.1880-1935 **[14]**
- **$2 164** - €2 081 - **£1 350** - FF13 650
  Poolwash Bay, Isle of Man Oil/canvas (31x46cm 12x18in) West-Yorshire 1999
- **$714** - €695 - **£440** - FF4 562
  The Morning Sea Watercolour/paper (33x49cm 13x19in) Fernhurst, Haslemere, Surrey 1999

AITKEN James Alfred 1846-1897 **[48]**
- **$1 519** - €1 518 - **£950** - FF9 958
  Cottage near Kyleakin, Skye Oil/canvas (30x50cm 11x19in) Edinburgh 1999
- **$725** - €666 - **£449** - FF4 370
  Kelp gatherers at Dusk Watercolour (21.5x32.5cm 8x12in) London 1999

AITKEN John Ernest 1881-1957 **[84]**
- **$2 600** - €2 243 - **£1 562** - FF14 714
  «Home from the Fishing» Watercolour/paper (49x73.5cm 19x28in) Boston MA 1998

AITKEN Robert Ingersoll 1878-1949 **[9]**
- **$2 500** - €2 274 - **£1 533** - FF14 916
  Standing Female Nude Bronze (H63cm H25in) Bloomfield-Hills MI 1998

AITSINGER Michael XVI **[1]**
- **$1 964** - €1 800 - **£1 200** - FF11 806
  Terra promissionis Engraving (37x42cm 14x16in) London 1999

AIVAZIAN Suren 1958 **[3]**
- **$2 200** - €1 930 - **£1 335** - FF12 658
  Red Trees Oil/canvas (50x100cm 19x39in) Chicago IL 1999

AIVAZOVSKY Ivan Constantinovich 1817-1900 **[281]**
- **$270 351** - €314 106 - **£190 000** - FF2 060 398
  Rocky Coastal Landscape in the Aegean with Ships in the Distance Oil/canvas (115.5x152cm 45x59in) London 2001

$69 200 - €72 672 - **£43 600** - FF476 700
Segelschiffe bei ruhiger See Öl/Leinwand/Karton
(60x93cm 23x36in) Wien 2000

$17 118 - €16 253 - **£10 491** - FF106 613
Segelschiff auf bewegtem Meer Öl/Leinwand
(21x28cm 8x11in) Zürich 1999

$4 139 - €3 783 - **£2 532** - FF24 816
Port Watercolour, gouache/paper (24.8x33cm 9x12in)
Warszawa 1999

AIZELIN Eugène Antoine 1821-1902 [93]

$6 024 - €5 949 - **£3 720** - FF39 024
Mignon Bronze (H80cm H31in) Antwerpen 1999

$1 931 - €2 211 - **£1 328** - FF14 500
Raphaël Sanzio Bronze (H77cm H30in) Paris 2000

AIZENBERG Nina 1902-1974 [6]

$2 800 - €3 347 - **£1 931** - FF21 957
Pierrot Pastel (37x22cm 14x8in) Tel Aviv 2000

AIZENBERG Roberto 1928-1996 [4]

$15 000 - €13 046 - **£9 043** - FF85 575
Torre Oil/canvas (150.5x62cm 59x24in) New-York
1998

AÏZPIRI Paul Augustin 1919 [387]

$26 462 - €25 808 - **£16 200** - FF169 290
Girl with Flowers Oil/canvas (130x97cm 51x38in)
Tokyo 1999

$10 020 - €11 434 - **£6 960** - FF75 000
Vase de fleurs Huile/toile (65x55cm 25x21in) Paris
2000

$4 480 - €3 811 - **£2 672** - FF25 000
Bouquet de fleurs Huile/toile (46x27cm 18x10in)
Paris 1998

$1 968 - €1 829 - **£1 195** - FF12 000
Bateau pavoisé Aquarelle, gouache/papier (21x28cm
8x11in) Calais 1998

$289 - €305 - **£191** - FF2 000
L'oiseau Lithographie couleurs (76x56cm 29x22in)
Paris 2000

AJDUKIEWICZ Sigismund 1861-1917 [24]

$20 801 - €20 652 - **£13 000** - FF135 469
On the Right Track Oil/panel (54x76cm 21x29in)
London 1999

$3 367 - €3 595 - **£2 300** - FF23 582
Cossack on Horseback Oil/panel (25x15cm 9x5in)
Billingshurst, West-Sussex 2001

AJDUKIEWICZ Tadeusz 1852-1916 [20]

$67 408 - €77 608 - **£46 000** - FF509 077
An Arab Caravan in the Desert Oil/canvas
(122x194cm 48x76in) London 2000

AJMONE Giuseppe 1923 [97]

$8 000 - €8 293 - **£4 800** - FF54 400
Cielo di tempesta Olio/tela (130x160cm 51x62in)
Milano 1999

$1 920 - €2 488 - **£1 440** - FF16 320
Verdeacqua Olio/tela (61x50cm 24x19in) Prato 2000

$880 - €1 140 - **£660** - FF7 480
Nudo Olio/tela (33x41cm 12x16in) Milano 2000

$250 - €259 - **£150** - FF1 700
Nudino Acquarello/carta (50x35cm 19x13in) Vercelli
1999

AJMONE Lidio 1884-1945 [20]

$500 - €518 - **£300** - FF3 400
Ritratto Olio/tela (69x55cm 27x21in) Vercelli 2001

$1 500 - €1 555 - **£900** - FF10 200
Paesaggio montano Olio/tavola (22.5x27.5cm
8x10in) Vercelli 1999

AKDIK Seref 1909-1972 [6]

$10 225 - €8 454 - **£6 000** - FF55 452
Return from Market Oil/canvas (99x73.5cm 38x28in)
London 1998

AKEN van François c.1677-c.1714 [2]

$8 965 - €9 624 - **£6 000** - FF63 129
**Still life with various Spoils of War, a classical
City beyond** Oil/canvas (92x119cm 36x46in) London
2000

AKEN van Jan 1614-1661 [17]

$6 928 - €6 784 - **£4 263** - FF44 500
Scènes d'intérieur Huile/toile (51x59cm 20x23in)
Besançon 1999

$1 303 - €1 481 - **£900** - FF9 714
Travellers resting in a rocky Landscape Ink
(18x15.5cm 7x6in) London 2000

$322 - €307 - **£200** - FF2 012
**Rheinlandschaft mit ruhenden Wanderern, nach
H. Saftleven** Radierung (21.6x27.4cm 8x10in) Berlin
1999

AKEN van Josef 1709-1749 [14]

$12 670 - €10 671 - **£7 483** - FF70 000
Scène de marché près de la fontaine du village
Oil/canvas (64.5x81cm 25x31in) Paris 1998

ÅKERBLOM Rudolf 1849-1925 [34]

$525 - €589 - **£356** - FF3 861
Strandlandskap Oil/canvas (12x19cm 4x7in) Helsinki
2000

AKERS Vivian Milner 1886-1966 [30]

$2 800 - €2 536 - **£1 713** - FF16 637
Lily Pond Oil/canvas/board (74x63cm 29x25in)
Portland ME 2000

ÅKESSON Gerda 1909-1992 [24]

$414 - €469 - **£280** - FF3 076
Rullende galaxer Oil/canvas (30x100cm 28x39in)
Köbenhavn 2000

AKIN Louis B. 1868-1913 [1]

$6 000 - €6 585 - **£3 863** - FF43 192
Oraibi (Arizona) Oil/canvas (51.5x36cm 20x14in)
Beverly-Hills CA 2000

AKKERINGA Johannes Evert 1861-1942 [114]

$10 628 - €9 983 - **£6 406** - FF65 485
Children playing in the Dunes Oil/canvas
(51x60cm 20x23in) Amsterdam 1999

$11 229 - €11 316 - **£7 000** - FF74 225
Lunch Time Oil/canvas (33x47cm 12x18in) London
2000

$801 - €680 - **£483** - FF4 460
Drie spelende kinderen aan het strand Black
chalk (24x34cm 9x13in) Den Haag 1998

AKKERMAN Ben 1920 [7]

$4 016 - €4 311 - **£2 687** - FF28 277
Untitled Oil/canvas/panel (50x50cm 19x19in)
Amsterdam 2000

AKKERSDYK Jacob 1815-1862 [15]

$3 474 - €4 084 - **£2 409** - FF26 789
The Letter Oil/panel (39.5x52cm 15x20in) Amsterdam
2000

$3 000 - €3 282 - **£2 068** - FF21 531
**Genre Scene of a Family of Four in Front of a
Stoop** Oil/panel (43x36cm 17x14in) Downington PA
2000

AKOPOV Alexander XX [9]

$476 - €457 - **£300** - FF2 995
A Sunny Day Oil/canvas (30x50cm 11x19in)
Fernhurst, Haslemere, Surrey 1999

AL-HASHASHI Mohammad B. Mahmoud XIX [1]
$5 957 - €7 013 - £4 186 - FF46 000
Enluminures calligraphiées Gouache/papier
(53x73.5cm 20x28in) Paris 2000

ALAJALOV Constantin 1900-1987 [9]
$6 500 - €6 225 - £4 015 - FF40 832
**Backstage at the Opera Lohengrin, Magazine
Cover** Tempera drawing (34x23cm 13x9in) New-York
1999
$700 - €672 - £433 - FF4 409
«Morgana» Gouache/paper (35.5x43cm 13x16in)
Washington 1999

ALANEN Joseph 1885-1920 [3]
$2 319 - €2 523 - £1 528 - FF16.548
**Neidon ryöstö, aihe Kalevalasta, Jungfrus bor-
trövande** Tempera/canvas (50x60cm 19x23in) Helsinki
2000

ALANKO Aarne 1896-1968 [105]
$373 - €319 - £219 - FF2 093
Den stora tallen Oil/canvas (34x57cm 13x22in)
Helsinki 1998
$200 - €235 - £138 - FF1 544
Ensam tall Oil/panel (25x31.5cm 9x12in) Helsinki
2000

ALAPHILIPPE Camille 1873-c.1930 [1]
$2 608 - €3 049 - £1 862 - FF20 000
Le mendiant Bronze (H54cm H21in) Paris 2001

ALARCON Y CACERES José María ?-1904 [13]
$4 160 - €4 805 - £2 880 - FF31 520
Mujer con guitarra Oleo/lienzo (99x68cm 38x26in)
Madrid 2000

ALARCON-SUAREZ José XIX [7]
$2 125 - €2 553 - £1 487 - FF16 745
Modelo calentándose Oleo/lienzo (41x29cm
16x11in) Madrid 2000

ALASTAIR Hans H. Baron Voigt 1887-1969 [6]
$9 500 - €10 197 - £6 357 - FF66 889
Polaire/Self-Portrait Gouache (30x14cm 11x5in)
New-York 2000

ALAUX François 1878-1952 [6]
$2 308 - €2 409 - £1 455 - FF15 800
Le remorqueur Huile/toile (81.5x70cm 32x27in)
Toulouse 2000

ALAUX Guillaume 1852-1913 [11]
$1 937 - €2 211 - £1 345 - FF14 500
Romero le toréro Huile/panneau (36.5x27cm
14x10in) Paris 2000
$305 - €320 - £193 - FF2 100
Élégant Pastel/papier (41x33cm 16x13in) Paris 2000

ALAUX Gustave 1887-1965 [51]
$6 178 - €6 860 - £4 306 - FF45 000
Le départ Huile/toile (38x55cm 14x21in) Neuilly-sur-
Seine 2001
$1 312 - €1 220 - £796 - FF8 000
Vue de Venise Huile/panneau (27x35cm 10x13in)
Calais 1998

ALAUX Jean, le Romain 1786-1864 [14]
$131 894 - €129 188 - £85 000 - FF847 416
The Atelier of Ingres in Rome Oil/canvas (52x49cm
20x19in) London 1999

ALAUX Jean-Pierre 1925 [44]
$601 - €701 - £421 - FF4 600
L'oeuf et le sablier Huile/toile (33x22cm 12x8in)
Neuilly-sur-Seine 2000

ALBACETE Alfonso 1950 [5]
$5 940 - €6 607 - £4 070 - FF43 340
«Serie dos continentes No.10» Oleo/lienzo
(152x168cm 59x66in) Madrid 2001

ALBANI Francesco l'Albane 1578-1660 [18]
$1 019 094 - €966 186 - £620 000 - FF6 337 764
The Maritime Realm: Neptune and Amphitrite
Oil/copper (88.5x103cm 34x40in) London 1999
$270 000 - €273 142 - £164 862 - FF1 791 693
Rest on the Flight into Egypt Oil/copper
(35x26.5cm 13x10in) New-York 2000
$1 762 - €1 750 - £1 101 - FF11 479
Venus omgivet af nymfer og amoriner Ink
(17x25.5cm 6x10in) København 1999

ALBANIS DE BEAUMONT Jean-François 1755-
1812 [2]
$1 345 - €1 444 - £900 - FF9 473
**Views of the Antiquities and harbours in the
South of France** Aquatint (39.5x28cm 15x11in)
London 2000

ALBEE Grace Thurston 1890-1985 [14]
$225 - €251 - £144 - FF1 648
7 rue Campagne Première, Paris Woodcut
(60x11.5cm 23x4in) New-York 2000

ALBERICI Augusto 1846-? [4]
$4 548 - €4 426 - £2 800 - FF29 032
Corso Vittorio Emanuele Messina Oil/canvas
(55x36cm 21x14in) London 1999

ALBEROLA Jean-Michel 1953 [69]
$6 220 - €7 318 - £4 459 - FF48 000
Près du patio I Acrylique/toile (213x196cm 83x77in)
Paris 2001
$3 070 - €3 049 - £1 912 - FF20 000
Madeira Acrylique (91.5x64cm 36x25in) Paris 1999
$1 776 - €1 753 - £1 094 - FF11 500
Sans titre Pastel/papier (65x60cm 25x23in) Versailles
1999

ALBERS Anni 1899-1994 [13]
$8 500 - €9 049 - £5 790 - FF59 355
Epitaph Mixed media (150x57cm 59x22in) Miami FL
2000
$550 - €624 - £376 - FF4 096
Untitled Silkscreen (38x31cm 15x12in) Chicago IL
2000

ALBERS Antoine 1765-1844 [4]
$6 101 - €5 624 - £3 654 - FF36 888
Der Genfer See Öl/Leinwand (49x65.5cm 19x25in)
Dresden 1998

ALBERS Josef 1888-1976 [465]
$170 000 - €190 412 - £118 116 - FF1 249 024
«Homage to the Square: Obvious» Oil/masonite
(122x122cm 48x48in) New-York 2001
$32 554 - €31 684 - £20 000 - FF207 832
Study for Homage to the Square: Looking Deep
Oil/masonite (76x76cm 29x29in) London 1999
$12 409 - €10 644 - £7 500 - FF69 821
**Study for Homage to the Square «In Wide
Light»** Oil/cardboard (31x30.5cm 12x12in) London
1998
$2 400 - €2 798 - £1 661 - FF18 351
**Ink Drawing for Embossed Linear Construction
«B»** Ink (58.5x37cm 23x14in) New-York 2000
$800 - €891 - £523 - FF5 845
White Line Square XVII Color lithograph (40x40cm
15x15in) New-York 2000
$4 395 - €3 820 - £2 648 - FF25 056
Portrait of Walter Gropius Vintage gelatin silver
print (16.8x10.9cm 6x4in) Berlin 1998

ALBERT Adolphe 1869-1932 **[10]**
- **$1 116** – €1 313 – **£800** – FF8 610
  Sicht auf Paris bei Nacht Oil/canvas/panel
  (21x39.5cm 8x15in) Zürich 2001

ALBERT Ernest 1900-1976 **[36]**
- **$1 500** – €1 238 – **£880** – FF8 120
  Vue de plage Huile/toile (50x60cm 19x23in)
  Antwerpen 1998
- **$80** – €87 – **£53** – FF569
  Nu debout Aquarelle/papier (25x18cm 9x7in)
  Antwerpen 2000

ALBERT Ernest 1857-1946 **[56]**
- **$2 750** – €2 596 – **£1 709** – FF17 031
  Clouds Oil/canvas (40x50cm 16x20in) Milford CT
  1999
- **$1 350** – €1 253 – **£810** – FF8 218
  River Snowscene Oil/canvas/board (22x30cm
  9x12in) Milford CT 1999
- **$1 500** – €1 404 – **£932** – FF9 289
  Winter Landscape with Barn Watercolour/paper
  (49x59cm 19x23in) Milford CT 1999

ALBERT Gustave 1866-1905 **[20]**
- **$4 165** – €4 088 – **£2 583** – FF26 813
  Franskt kanallandskap Oil/canvas (46x55cm
  18x21in) Stockholm 1999

ALBERT Hermann 1937 **[18]**
- **$3 650** – €4 090 – **£2 542** – FF26 831
  Sieger Öl/Leinwand (190x155cm 74x61in) Berlin 2001
- **$372** – €381 – **£231** – FF2 500
  Champs d'honneur Huile/toile (95x85cm 37x33in)
  Paris 2000

ALBERT Joseph, Jos 1886-1981 **[124]**
- **$4 228** – €4 538 – **£2 829** – FF29 766
  Still Life with Apples and Pears Oil/canvas
  (55x68cm 21x26in) Amsterdam 2000
- **$995** – €942 – **£619** – FF6 178
  Nature morte à la pomme Huile/toile (38x18cm
  14x7in) Bruxelles 1999
- **$184** – €198 – **£123** – FF1 300
  Pinocchio Aquarelle/papier (27x23cm 10x9in)
  Antwerpen 2000
- **$334** – €286 – **£196** – FF1 876
  Hommage to the Square Farbserigraphie
  (49.5x49.8cm 19x19in) Bielefeld 1998

ALBERTI C. XIX **[5]**
- **$3 885** – €4 573 – **£2 730** – FF30 000
  Rue animé, au Maroc Huile/toile (55.5x46cm
  21x18in) Paris 2000

ALBERTI Cherubino 1553-1615 **[43]**
- **$5 070** – €5 946 – **£3 646** – FF39 000
  Saint Marc/David Encre (19.5x18cm 7x7in) Paris
  2001
- **$628** – €716 – **£438** – FF4 695
  Die drei Grazien, nach Raffael Radierung
  (31x57cm 12x22in) Berlin 2001

ALBERTI Rafael 1902-1999 **[55]**
- **$3 296** – €3 667 – **£2 197** – FF24 053
  Caja tabaquera musical decorada Construction
  (18x13cm 7x5in) Madrid 2000
- **$504** – €541 – **£333** – FF3 546
  Dama en el balcón Feutre/papier (34x23.5cm
  13x9in) Madrid 2000
- **$217** – €204 – **£129** – FF1 339
  Picasso (II) Delirio Litografía (65x50cm 25x19in)
  Madrid 1999

ALBERTIN André 1867-1933 **[33]**
- **$192** – €229 – **£137** – FF1 500
  Environs de fontaine Huile/carton (12x17cm 4x6in)
  Grenoble 2000

ALBERTINELLI Mariotto 1474-1515 **[4]**
- **$62 000** – €54 568 – **£37 745** – FF357 944
  The Madonna and Child in a Landscape
  Oil/panel (78.5x57cm 30x22in) New-York 1999

ALBERTINI Luciano 1910 **[2]**
- **$1 750** – €1 814 – **£1 050** – FF11 900
  Verona, Piazza delle Erbe Olio/tavola (29x39cm
  11x15in) Trieste 2001

ALBERTINI Oreste 1887-1953 **[47]**
- **$6 116** – €6 340 – **£3 669** – FF41 588
  Il lago di Antermola illuminato di luce dorata
  Olio/tela (70x90cm 27x35in) Milano 1999
- **$2 400** – €2 488 – **£1 440** – FF16 320
  Contadini sullo sfondo delle Dolomiti Olio/carto-
  ne (30x40cm 11x15in) Milano 1999

ALBERTIS de Sebastiano 1828-1897 **[23]**
- **$20 000** – €25 916 – **£15 000** – FF170 000
  Il ritorno dalla battaglia di Bezzecca Olio/tela
  (78x52cm 30x20in) Milano 2000
- **$3 668** – €4 090 – **£2 466** – FF26 831
  Auf dem Schlachtfeld Öl/Leinwand (37.5x25cm
  14x9in) Ahlden 2000
- **$10 500** – €10 885 – **£6 300** – FF71 400
  Lanceri a cavallo Acquarello/carta (17.5x25.5cm
  6x10in) Milano 2000

ALBERTO Pietro 1929 **[9]**
- **$1 800** – €1 866 – **£1 080** – FF12 240
  Senza titolo Acrilico/tela (60x50cm 23x19in) Vercelli
  2001
- **$800** – €1 037 – **£600** – FF6 800
  Senza titolo Acrilico/tavola (45x35cm 17x13in)
  Vercelli 2000

ALBERTOLLI Raffaello 1770-1812 **[3]**
- **$9 568** – €9 357 – **£5 909** – FF61 375
  Ansicht von Lugano und Luganersee Aquarell,
  Gouache/Papier (47x62.5cm 18x24in) Zürich 1999

ALBERTS Jacob 1860-1941 **[7]**
- **$8 708** – €7 538 – **£5 286** – FF49 448
  **Nordfrisisk marklandskab daekket med lyserö-
  de blomster** Oil/canvas (91x106cm 35x41in)
  Köbenhavn 1998

ALBERTS Tom 1962 **[3]**
- **$2 744** – €2 946 – **£1 837** – FF19 325
  The Clairvoyant Oil/board (35x41.5cm 13x16in)
  Sydney 2000

ALBERTS Willem Jacobus 1912-1990 **[13]**
- **$587** – €499 – **£354** – FF3 270
  Riviergezicht Oil/canvas (49x59cm 19x23in)
  Rotterdam 1998

ALBIGNAC d' François 1903-1958 **[209]**
- **$223** – €213 – **£139** – FF1 400
  Femme au sweater bleu Aquarelle, gouache/papier
  (27x22cm 10x8in) Paris 1999

ALBIN Charles XX **[1]**
- **$4 250** – €3 963 – **£2 565** – FF25 997
  **Actress Claire Eames as John Singer Sargent's
  Madame X** Photograph (34.5x19cm 13x7in) New-York
  1999

ALBIN Eleazar Weiss act.1713-1759 **[10]**
$6 416 - €6 466 - **£4 000** - FF42 414
Eyed Hawkmoth/Death's-Head Hawkmoth/Puss Moth/Buff-tip Watercolour, gouache/paper (47.5x34cm 18x13in) London 2000

ALBIN-GUILLOT Laure 1892-1962 **[150]**
$548 - €640 - **£385** - FF4 200
Nature morte, soupière carafe et raisins Tirage charbon (26x38cm 10x14in) Paris 2001

ALBINOWSKA-MINKIEWICZOWA Zofia 1886-1971 **[15]**
$2 187 - €2 046 - **£1 325** - FF13 422
Artist's Interior Oil/board (50x69cm 19x27in) Warszawa 1999

ALBITZ Richard 1876-1954 **[23]**
$716 - €613 - **£430** - FF4 024
Ein altes Felsennest am Rhein Öl/Karton (48x53cm 18x20in) Hamburg 1998

ALBIZU Olga 1924 **[6]**
$6 500 - €6 309 - **£4 046** - FF41 382
Untitled Oil/canvas (91.5x101.5cm 36x39in) New-York 1999

ALBOTTO Francesco 1721-1753 **[29]**
$38 000 - €33 445 - **£23 134** - FF219 385
Santa Maria della Salute, Venice, with the Entrance to the Grand Canal Oil/canvas (60.5x86cm 23x33in) New-York 1999

ALBRECHT Gretchen 1943 **[11]**
$4 965 - €5 832 - **£3 525** - FF38 256
Stratum, Red and Black Acrylic/canvas (133x180cm 52x70in) Auckland 2000
$4 232 - €4 742 - **£2 950** - FF31 108
«Study for Drift II» Acrylic (107x63cm 42x24in) Wellington 2001

ALBRECHT-SERVESTA Hermann 1871-c.1943 **[2]**
$3 171 - €3 403 - **£2 121** - FF22 324
Crowned Madonna Oil/canvas (70x60cm 27x23in) Amsterdam 2000

ALBRICCI Enrico 1714-1775 **[8]**
$2 000 - €2 073 - **£1 200** - FF13 600
Nani parrucchieri Inchiostro (12x20cm 4x7in) Milano 2001

ALBRIER Joseph 1791-1863 **[7]**
$27 064 - €29 118 - **£18 412** - FF191 000
La nymphe libérée Huile/toile (46.5x35.5cm 18x13in) Paris 2001

ALBRIGHT Adam Emory 1862-1957 **[57]**
$11 000 - €9 527 - **£6 746** - FF62 496
Two Children Walking with Pails Oil/canvas (45.5x61cm 17x24in) New-York 1999

ALBRIGHT Gertrude Partington 1883-1959 **[3]**
$7 000 - €8 271 - **£4 960** - FF54 255
Me in the Studio at 737 Oil/canvas (56x71cm 22x27in) Boston MA 2000

ALBRIGHT Ivan Le Lorraine 1897-1983 **[53]**
$3 750 - €4 483 - **£2 576** - FF29 407
California Coast Oil/board (30x40cm 12x16in) Chicago IL 2000
$850 - €994 - **£597** - FF6 521
«Fleeting Time, Thou Hast Left Me Old» Lithograph (34.5x24.5cm 13x9in) New-York 1999

ALBUQUERQUE Lita 1946 **[6]**
$1 200 - €1 155 - **£750** - FF7 579
Solar Pulse Coloured chalks/paper (91.5x114cm 36x44in) Beverly-Hills CA 1999

ALCANTARA Antonio 1898-? **[15]**
$2 585 - €3 047 - **£1 816** - FF19 986
Paisaje Oleo/lienzo (65x51cm 25x20in) Caracas ($) 2000
$1 723 - €2 031 - **£1 210** - FF13 321
Flores Huile/bois (46x33cm 18x12in) Caracas ($) 2000

ALCAYDE MONTOYA Julia 1865-1936 **[25]**
$185 - €192 - **£118** - FF1 260
Ramillete de rosas Carboncillo (35x29cm 13x11in) Madrid 2000

ALCAZAR TEJEDOR José 1850-? **[2]**
$31 500 - €27 029 - **£19 350** - FF177 300
Cual los mozos del Batan Oleo/lienzo (58x100cm 22x39in) Madrid 1998

ALCAZAR Y RUIZ Manuel 1858-1914 **[5]**
$4 410 - €4 205 - **£2 800** - FF27 580
Descansando en la fuente Oleo/lienzo (76x115cm 29x45in) Madrid 1999

ALCHIMOWICZ Kazimierz 1840-1916 **[11]**
$7 255 - €7 622 - **£4 785** - FF50 000
Soldat courtisant une jeune femme Huile/toile (99x70cm 38x27in) Louviers 2000

ALCIATI Ambrogio A. 1878-1929 **[18]**
$6 354 - €5 490 - **£3 177** - FF36 009
Il canale della Giudecca, La Salute Olio/tela (40x50cm 15x19in) Venezia 1999

ALCIATI Evangelina 1883-1959 **[13]**
$2 000 - €2 073 - **£1 200** - FF13 600
Natura morta Olio/tela (60x56cm 23x22in) Vercelli 2000

ALCOCK Edward c.1740-c.1790 **[3]**
$10 000 - €10 697 - **£6 818** - FF70 167
Portrait of Giles Bridges, Duke of Chandos Oil/canvas (76x63.5cm 29x25in) New-York 2001
$4 541 - €4 362 - **£2 800** - FF28 612
Gentleman, in academic Robes/Lady, mourning the death of Tancred Oil/copper (42x32cm 16x12in) London 1999

ALCOLEA Carlos 1949-1992 **[5]**
$22 100 - €25 528 - **£15 300** - FF167 450
Vicioso Acrílico/lienzo (73x100cm 28x39in) Seville 2000

ALCORLO BARRERA Manuel 1935 **[56]**
$1 400 - €1 502 - **£950** - FF9 850
Pupazzo Oleo/lienzo (95x70cm 37x27in) Madrid 2001
$335 - €330 - **£209** - FF2 167
Flora Lápiz/papel (49x34cm 19x13in) Madrid 1999
$132 - €120 - **£82** - FF788
Jóvenes en un jardin Grabado (55x47cm 21x18in) Madrid 2000

ALDE Yvette 1911-1967 **[86]**
$435 - €488 - **£305** - FF3 200
Paysage du midi Huile/toile (65x81cm 25x31in) Paris 2001
$435 - €488 - **£305** - FF3 200
Paysage montagneux Huile/toile (16x27cm 6x10in) Paris 2001
$171 - €183 - **£108** - FF1 200
Le chant Aquarelle/papier (27x16cm 10x6in) Paris 2000

ALDEGREVER Heinrich 1502-1561 **[265]**
$140 000 - €141 629 - **£88 487** - FF929 026
Lazarus begging for Crumbs from Dives's Table Ink (9x11cm 3x4in) New-York 2000

$441 - €383 - **£265** - FF2 514
Herkules kämpft gegen den Flussgott Achelus
Kupferstich (10.7x6.7cm 4x2in) Berlin 1998

ALDEMIRA Varela 1895-? **[2]**
$24 510 - €21 370 - **£14 620** - FF140 180
Feira de Barcelos Oleo/lienzo (95.5x129cm 37x50in)
Lisboa 1998

ALDERSON Dorothy & Elizabeth XX **[21]**
$545 - €550 - **£340** - FF3 605
**Trixie, a Portrait of a Horse in an Outdoor set-
ting** Watercolour/paper (32x45.5cm 12x17in) London
2000

ALDERSON James Simpson XIX-XX **[6]**
$150 - €161 - **£100** - FF1 056
Figures Before a Cottage Watercolour (14.5x21cm
5x8in) London 2000

ALDI Pietro 1852-1888 **[3]**
$14 654 - €16 871 - **£10 000** - FF110 669
The Connoisseur's Choice Oil/canvas (54.5x75cm
21x29in) London 2000

ALDIN Cecil Ch.Windsor 1870-1935 **[599]**
$1 120 - €1 303 - **£800** - FF8 545
Dachshund Running Ink (12x21cm 4x8in) London
2001
$400 - €366 - **£245** - FF2 400
The Cottesbrook Hunt: the Hunt Dinner Estampe
couleurs (57x83.5cm 22x32in) Dijon 1999

ALDRICH George Ames 1872-1941 **[54]**
$5 500 - €6 160 - **£3 821** - FF40 409
«Winter Stream» Oil/panel (50x63cm 20x25in)
Cincinnati OH 2001

ALDRIDGE Alan XX **[6]**
$3 424 - €3 992 - **£2 400** - FF26 184
Happy-Go-Lucky Grasshopper Acrylic (51.5x36cm
20x14in) London 2000
$8 369 - €7 225 - **£5 000** - FF47 393
There's a Place Drawing (40x43cm 15x16in) London
1998
$2 929 - €2 688 - **£1 800** - FF17 635
Chelsea Girls Poster (76x51cm 29x20in) London
1999

ALDRIDGE Frederick James 1850-1933 **[330]**
$1 738 - €1 920 - **£1 200** - FF12 595
Fishing Vessels in choppy Waters Oil/canvas
(43x29cm 16x11in) Hockley, Birmingham 2001
$811 - €779 - **£500** - FF5 109
Barges in a Stiff Breeze Pencil (25.5x35.5cm
10x13in) London 1999

ALDRIDGE John A. Malcolm 1905-1984 **[51]**
$1 517 - €1 547 - **£950** - FF10 149
The Grove, January Oil/canvas (48x74cm 19x29in)
Tunbridge-Wells, Kent 2000
$977 - €1 140 - **£680** - FF7 477
Deya, the Road up From the Sea Oil/board
(27x36cm 10x14in) London 2000
$650 - €758 - **£450** - FF4 971
The Theatre, Tusculum Watercolour (35.5x56cm
13x22in) London 2000

ALDRIDGE Peter 1947 **[1]**
$8 000 - €7 636 - **£4 999** - FF50 092
Untitled for the Steuben Project Sculpture, glass
(43x21x21cm 16x8x8in) New-York 1999

ALEBARDI Angiolo 1883-1969 **[4]**
$5 000 - €5 183 - **£3 000** - FF34 000
Palazzo Ducale e marina a Venezia Olio/tavola
(49.5x59.5cm 19x23in) Torino 2001

ALECHINSKY Pierre 1927 **[1635]**
$56 012 - €59 721 - **£38 000** - FF391 742
«Sur le terrain Olmèque» Acrylic/paper/canvas
(115x155cm 45x61in) London 2001
$20 153 - €22 863 - **£14 202** - FF149 971
De source Oil/canvas (81x65cm 31x25in) Köbenhavn
2001
$5 702 - €6 708 - **£4 131** - FF44 000
Terre retrouvée Huile/toile (31.5x13.5cm 12x5in)
Paris 2001
$2 325 - €2 496 - **£1 555** - FF16 371
Untitled Bronze (17.5x23.5cm 6x9in) Amsterdam 2000
$6 244 - €5 336 - **£3 780** - FF35 000
L'Empire d'Alexandre Encre Chine (40x50cm
15x19in) Paris 1998
$433 - €471 - **£285** - FF3 089
Arc-en-terre Etching in colors (56x45cm 22x17in)
Lokeren 2000

ALEGIANI Francesco XIX **[16]**
$4 066 - €4 710 - **£2 812** - FF30 894
**Trompe l'oeil représentant 2 gouaches et un
calendrier avec un timbre** Huile/toile (101x76cm
39x29in) Bruxelles 2000
$1 500 - €1 603 - **£1 021** - FF10 514
**Trompe l'Oeil: Nightgale Cock Canary, Live
Singing-Singing Died** Oil/canvas (33x18cm 13x7in)
New-Orleans LA 2001

ALEGRE MONFERRER Agustín 1936 **[10]**
$850 - €1 021 - **£595** - FF6 698
Caserío Oleo/tablex (46x38cm 18x14in) Madrid 2000

ALENZA Y NIETO Leonardo 1807-1845 **[52]**
$5 940 - €6 607 - **£4 180** - FF43 340
La sangría Oleo/lienzo (58x46cm 22x18in) Madrid
2001
$19 500 - €19 521 - **£12 025** - FF128 050
**Familia de mendigos calentándose en torno a
una hoguera** Oleo/lienzo (30.5x23cm 12x9in) Madrid
2000
$560 - €601 - **£380** - FF3 940
La pelea IV Carboncillo (24.5x41cm 9x16in) Madrid
2000

ALERS Rudolf 1812-c.1850 **[3]**
$2 745 - €2 812 - **£1 694** - FF18 446
**Burg mit weiter Landschaft, im Vordergrund ein
Jäger** Öl/Leinwand (31.5x42.5cm 12x16in) Düsseldorf
2000

ALES Nikolaus, Mikolas 1852-1913 **[34]**
$231 - €219 - **£144** - FF1 434
Recruitment in Jicin Ink/paper (19x15cm 7x5in)
Praha 2001

ALÉSI d' Hugo, Fred. Alexianu 1849-1906 **[231]**
$555 - €625 - **£382** - FF4 100
La charrette sur le pont Huile/toile (60.5x46cm
23x18in) Tarbes 2000
$446 - €381 - **£267** - FF2 500
«Port Marchand Marseille» Affiche (76x117cm
29x46in) Paris 1998

ALESSANDRI Innocente XVIII **[2]**
$1 611 - €1 582 - **£1 000** - FF10 379
Descrizioni degli Animali, Quadrupedi Engraving
(35.5x50cm 13x19in) London 1999

ALEXANDER Cosmo 1724-1772 **[9]**
$12 962 - €12 466 - **£8 000** - FF81 771
**Henry Stuart, Cardinal York (1725-1807), in
Cardinal's Robes, book** Oil/canvas (77.5x75cm
30x29in) London 1999

ALEXANDER Douglas 1871-1945 **[85]**
- **$1 967** - €2 286 - **£1 382** - FF14 992
  West of Ireland Lake and Mountains
  Oil/canvas/board (41x46cm 16x18in) Dublin 2001
- **$1 899** - €2 159 - **£1 311** - FF14 159
  Lake and Mountain Landscape Oil/board
  (25x35cm 10x14in) Dublin 2000
- **$992** - €1 143 - **£677** - FF7 496
  **Estuary Scene, with Thatched Cottages/Bridge
  and Thatched Cottage** Watercolour/paper (25x33cm
  10x13in) Blackrock, Co.Dublin 2000

ALEXANDER Edwin J. 1870-1926 **[27]**
- **$959** - €984 - **£600** - FF6 457
  White Crocuses in a Pewter Bowl Watercolour
  (31.5x17cm 12x6in) London 2000

ALEXANDER Francis 1800-1880 **[3]**
- **$9 000** - €7 710 - **£5 410** - FF50 577
  The Gilbert Children Of Boston Oil/canvas
  (76x63cm 30x25in) Cleveland OH 1998

ALEXANDER George 1832-1913 **[3]**
- **$635** - €736 - **£450** - FF4 831
  Forge Valley, Nr. Scarbro Oil/canvas (60x91cm
  24x36in) Carmarthen, Wales 2000

ALEXANDER Herbert 1874-1946 **[8]**
- **$973** - €941 - **£600** - FF6 175
  Willesley Forge, Wilts Watercolour/paper (28x38cm
  11x14in) London 1999

ALEXANDER John 1945 **[25]**
- **$3 750** - €3 913 - **£2 365** - FF25 668
  American Gothic II Oil/canvas (228.5x279.5cm
  89x110in) New-York 2000

ALEXANDER John White 1856-1915 **[31]**
- **$280 000** - €239 228 - **£168 084** - FF1 569 232
  A Meadow Flower Oil/canvas (128x103cm 50x40in)
  New-York 1998
- **$20 000** - €23 105 - **£14 004** - FF151 562
  The Garden Door Oil/canvas (56x35.5cm 22x13in)
  New-York 2001

ALEXANDER Lena L. Duncan XIX-XX **[11]**
- **$1 505** - €1 564 - **£950** - FF10 261
  Roses and Books Pastel (49x39.5cm 19x15in)
  London 2000

ALEXANDER Peter 1939 **[11]**
- **$6 500** - €6 259 - **£4 064** - FF41 055
  Untitled Sculpture (15.5x31x14cm 6x12x5in) Beverly-
  Hills CA 1999

ALEXANDER Richard Dykes 1788-1865 **[5]**
- **$1 500** - €1 573 - **£939** - FF10 316
  **Catherine Smart, her sister Eleza King and ele-
  ven Pupils** Albumen print (17x14cm 7x5in) New-York
  2000

ALEXANDER Robert L. 1840-1923 **[18]**
- **$19 764** - €18 798 - **£12 000** - FF123 308
  The Setters: Gordon and Laverock Oil/canvas
  (93x127cm 36x50in) Edinburgh 1999
- **$963** - €1 074 - **£650** - FF7 044
  Study of a Dog Oil/board (19x12cm 7x4in)
  Edinburgh 2000

ALEXANDER William 1767-1816 **[18]**
- **$1 570** - €1 369 - **£949** - FF8 982
  **A Sheet of Figure Studies for «The Dinner in
  Mote Park, Maidstone»** Pencil (19x26cm 7x10in)
  London 1998

ALFARO HERNANDEZ Andreu 1929 **[6]**
- **$988** - €1 141 - **£684** - FF7 486
  Sin título Métal (H51.5cm H20in) Madrid 2001

ALFELT Else 1910-1974 **[79]**
- **$4 865** - €4 709 - **£2 999** - FF30 887
  Fjelde Oil/canvas (58x70cm 22x27in) København 1999
- **$960** - €1 073 - **£642** - FF7 039
  Vulkan Watercolour/paper (31x47cm 12x18in)
  København 2000

ALFIERI Attilio 1904-1992 **[42]**
- **$800** - €829 - **£480** - FF5 440
  Natura morta Olio/tela (40x50cm 15x19in) Vercelli
  1999

ALFONZO Carlos josé 1950-1991 **[49]**
- **$20 000** - €17 394 - **£12 058** - FF114 100
  Sin título Oil/canvas (137.5x203cm 54x79in) New-
  York 1998
- **$4 500** - €3 914 - **£2 713** - FF25 672
  Sin título Watercolour, gouache/paper (112x76.5cm
  44x30in) New-York 1998

ALFRED W.L. XIX **[3]**
- **$869** - €907 - **£550** - FF5 950
  Rhuddlan Castle leaving Dunkerque Oil/canvas
  (61x90cm 24x35in) London 2000

ALGARDI Alessandro 1595/1602-1654 **[13]**
- **$9 217** - €7 842 - **£5 500** - FF51 443
  Hercules and Iolaus with the Hydra Bronze
  (H31.5cm H12in) London 1998

ALHEIM d' Jean c.1840-1894 **[17]**
- **$2 780** - €3 049 - **£1 888** - FF20 000
  Vue de Venise Huile/toile (50x93cm 19x36in) Calais
  2000
- **$2 475** - €2 494 - **£1 542** - FF16 360
  **Küstenszene mit Ruder- Segelbooten und
  Dampfer** Öl/Karton (15.5x26.5cm 6x10in) Zürich 2000

ALI KHAN Ghulam XIX **[1]**
- **$1 571** - €1 470 - **£950** - FF9 644
  Carpenter at his work Watercolour (31x21cm
  12x8in) London 1999

ALI KHAN Mazhar XIX **[3]**
- **$4 630** - €4 332 - **£2 800** - FF28 413
  View of Humayun's Tomb, near Delhi Watercolour
  (20.5x30cm 8x11in) London 1999

ALI Shakir 1916-1975 **[2]**
- **$9 500** - €11 225 - **£6 732** - FF73 632
  The Masks Oil/board (52x52cm 20x20in) New-York
  2000

ALIANI d' Lorenzo 1825-1862 **[1]**
- **$11 257** - €12 782 - **£7 822** - FF83 847
  **Abendstimmung am Arno in Florenz, im
  Hintergrund San Frediano** Öl/Papier (25.5x37cm
  10x14in) Berlin 2001

ALIBERTI Dino 1935 **[29]**
- **$200** - €207 - **£120** - FF1 360
  Vaso di fiori Olio/tela (60x40cm 23x15in) Vercelli
  2001

ALINARI Fratelli Edizione, Firenze XIX-XX **[23]**
- **$1 295** - €1 451 - **£900** - FF9 516
  «Florence, Hall of the Uffizi» Albumen print
  (32x41.5cm 12x16in) London 2001

ALINARI Luca 1943 **[232]**
- **$2 100** - €2 177 - **£1 260** - FF14 280
  Ocarina Acrilico/tela (100x100cm 39x39in) Firenze
  2000
- **$800** - €829 - **£480** - FF5 440
  Di case disperse Olio/tela (19x24cm 7x9in) Vercelli
  1999

$375 - €389 - £225 - FF2 550
Paesaggio Acquarello/carta (11x28.5cm 4x11in) Prato 1999

$125 - €130 - £75 - FF850
Senza titolo Serigrafia (90x90cm 35x35in) Vercelli 1999

ALINOVI Guiseppe 1811-1848 **[1]**

$3 000 - €3 110 - £1 800 - FF20 400
Serra in un parco Acquarello/carta (190x210cm 74x82in) Firenze 2000

ALISON David 1882-1955 **[16]**

$4 105 - €4 425 - £2 800 - FF29 026
Margueritas and Scabia Oil/canvas/board (76x63cm 29x24in) London 2001

$442 - €463 - £280 - FF3 038
Rocks and Waves Oil/board (30x39cm 11x15in) Edinburgh 2000

ALISON Henry Young 1889-1972 **[10]**

$3 259 - €3 635 - £2 200 - FF23 841
Girl Raking Beneath Cherry Blossom, Dysart Oil/canvas (100x78.5cm 39x30in) Edinburgh 2000

ALIVEZ XX **[2]**

$3 937 - €3 811 - £2 495 - FF25 000
Entrée de la ville Huile/toile (40x52cm 15x20in) Paris 1999

ALIX Pierre Michel 1762-1817 **[15]**

$3 369 - €3 506 - £2 129 - FF23 000
Marie-Antoinette, Reine de France, d'après Mme Vigée-Lebrun Gravure (23.5x18cm 9x7in) Paris 2000

ALIX Yves 1890-1969 **[68]**

$2 351 - €2 058 - £1 424 - FF13 500
Le port de Toulon Huile/toile (71x92cm 27x36in) Paris 1998

ALIZARD Paul 1867-1948 **[2]**

$4 208 - €3 950 - £2 600 - FF25 910
«Ca ne va pas!» Oil/canvas (87.5x115cm 34x45in) London 1999

ALKARA Ovadia 1939 **[10]**

$3 200 - €3 435 - £2 141 - FF22 531
Landscapes and Figures Oil/canvas (64x60.5cm 25x23in) Tel Aviv 2000

ALKEMA Wobbe 1900-1984 **[14]**

$4 296 - €4 991 - £3 019 - FF32 742
«Composition no.11» Oil/board (81x61cm 31x24in) Amsterdam 2001

$1 813 - €1 684 - £1 106 - FF11 047
Abstract composition Ink (23x17.5cm 9x6in) Amsterdam 1998

ALKEN Henry Thomas I 1785-1850/51 **[194]**

$17 550 - €16 778 - £11 000 - FF110 055
Full Cry Oil/canvas (61x93.5cm 24x36in) London 2001

$9 101 - €10 585 - £6 500 - FF69 436
At the Start/The Final Furlong Oil/canvas (25.5x36cm 10x14in) London 2001

$1 450 - €1 353 - £900 - FF8 874
Turkish Cavalrymen engaging Watercolour (23.5x33cm 9x13in) London 1999

$174 - €183 - £110 - FF1 201
Unkenneling Aquatint in colors (22.5x30cm 8x11in) London 2000

ALKEN Samuel Henry G. II 1810-1894 **[110]**

$8 500 - €10 112 - £5 881 - FF66 333
Hunting Scene Oil/canvas (81x40cm 32x16in) Detroit MI 2000

$4 750 - €5 395 - £3 333 - FF35 389
Horse-drawn Coach Oil/panel (19.5x24cm 7x9in) New-York 2001

$1 474 - €1 473 - £900 - FF9 663
A Group of Hunting Scenes Watercolour (23.5x33.5cm 9x13in) London 2000

ALKEN Samuel Henry I 1750/56-1815 **[22]**

$3 750 - €3 823 - £2 349 - FF25 075
Hunting Pheasants Watercolour (26.5x70.5cm 10x27in) New-York 2000

ALKEN Samuel, Jr. 1784-c.1825 **[24]**

$6 000 - €6 440 - £4 015 - FF42 246
Out Shooting Oil/canvas (35.5x45.5cm 13x17in) New-York 2000

$6 000 - €6 971 - £4 216 - FF45 727
The Find/Nearing the Kill Oil/canvas (25.5x30.5cm 10x12in) New-York 2001

ALLAIN Patrick XX **[36]**

$627 - €717 - £442 - FF4 700
La perdrix au fusil cassé Bronze (H11cm H4in) Paris 2001

ALLAIS Pierre c.1700-1782 **[9]**

$29 673 - €32 014 - £19 803 - FF210 000
Portrait de Madame Geoffrin (1699-1777) Huile/toile (100x80cm 39x31in) Monaco 2000

$6 940 - €6 555 - £4 321 - FF43 000
Portrait d'une dame et son enfant Pastel/toile (60x74cm 23x29in) Paris 1999

ALLAN Andrew 1863-? **[3]**

$7 905 - €7 519 - £4 800 - FF49 323
Goldfinches on thistledown Oil/canvas (43x58.5cm 16x23in) Edinburgh 1999

ALLAN Archibald Russell W. 1878-1959 **[21]**

$12 846 - €12 219 - £7 800 - FF80 150
Farm above Millport Oil/canvas (114.5x107cm 45x42in) Edinburgh 1999

ALLAN David 1744-1796 **[8]**

$58 054 - €50 491 - £35 000 - FF331 201
Portrait of the Children of Henry Dundas, 1st Viscount Melville Oil/canvas (122x151cm 48x59in) London 1998

$7 411 - €7 049 - £4 500 - FF46 240
Catechising in the Church of Scotland Watercolour (35.5x48cm 13x18in) Edinburgh 1999

ALLAN Hugh 1862-1909 **[4]**

$6 258 - €5 953 - £3 800 - FF39 047
The Mill-Lade, Glen Farg near Abernethy Oil/canvas (77x122cm 30x48in) Edinburgh 1999

ALLAN Robert Weir 1851-1942 **[89]**

$3 507 - €3 911 - £2 400 - FF25 655
Fishing Village Oil/panel (37.5x53.5cm 14x21in) Perthshire 2000

$2 416 - €2 373 - £1 500 - FF15 569
Near Lockalsh - Gleaners in a Cornfield Oil/panel (26x35cm 10x13in) Penzance, Cornwall 1999

$2 046 - €1 879 - £1 250 - FF12 327
A French Harbour Scene with Numerous Figures and Boats Watercolour/paper (35x48cm 14x19in) Aylsham, Norfolk 1998

ALLAN Ugolin XIX-XX **[3]**

$4 046 - €3 798 - £2 500 - FF24 914
Portrait of a Lady, Head and Shoulders, holding a Fan Oil/canvas (39.5x29.5cm 15x11in) Billingshurst, West-Sussex 1999

ALLAN William 1782-1850 **[11]**
- $110 811 - €96 623 - **£67 000** - FF633 806
  The Celebration of the Birthday of James Hogg Oil/panel (61x82.5cm 24x32in) London 1998

ALLAND Alexander Sr. 1902 **[2]**
- $3 000 - €3 145 - **£1 879** - FF20 632
  The Normandie, New York City Silver print (18x21cm 7x8in) New-York 2000

ALLAR André Joseph 1845-1926 **[11]**
- $32 000 - €29 624 - **£19 318** - FF194 320
  Allegorical Female Figures Bronze (157x148.5cm 61x58in) New-York 1999
- $2 298 - €2 211 - **£1 416** - FF14 500
  Enfant des Abruzzes Bronze (H64cm H25in) Paris 1999

ALLARD Georges XX **[24]**
- $464 - €396 - **£280** - FF2 600
  «Le Mépris» Affiche couleur (80x60cm 31x23in) Paris 1998

ALLARD L'OLIVIER Fernand 1883-1933 **[171]**
- $2 743 - €3 222 - **£1 924** - FF21 138
  Vachers rwandais et leur troupeau Huile/toile (80x150cm 31x59in) Bruxelles 2000
- $2 420 - €2 324 - **£1 500** - FF15 247
  Jewish Market Scene Oil/canvas (81x100cm 31x39in) London 1999
- $1 437 - €1 677 - **£1 009** - FF11 000
  Scène de village Huile/panneau (27x34cm 10x13in) Paris 2000
- $192 - €177 - **£115** - FF1 161
  A view of a street in Stanleyville Pencil (19x24cm 7x9in) Amsterdam 1998

ALLASON Silvio 1843-1912 **[8]**
- $3 250 - €3 369 - **£1 950** - FF22 100
  Serenità alpestre Olio/tela (50x86.5cm 19x34in) Vercelli 1999
- $2 880 - €2 488 - **£1 440** - FF16 320
  Strada a mare Olio/tavola (24.5x59cm 9x23in) Vercelli 1999

ALLASON Thomas XVIII-XIX **[9]**
- $1 160 - €1 076 - **£700** - FF7 059
  Views on the Plain of Sparta Ink (20.5x47cm 8x18in) London 1999

ALLBON Charles Frederick 1856-1926 **[77]**
- $580 - €487 - **£343** - FF3 195
  Romney, Maron, Kent Watercolour/paper (16x48cm 6x19in) Stansted Mountfitchet, Essex 1998

ALLCOTT John Charles 1889-1973 **[140]**
- $1 802 - €1 694 - **£1 133** - FF11 115
  Timber Ship leaving Lauriton Oil/canvas/board (37x44cm 14x17in) Sydney 1999
- $1 052 - €1 014 - **£650** - FF6 651
  Siren Oil/canvas/board (24x29cm 9x11in) Sydney 1999
- $725 - €854 - **£509** - FF5 603
  The Cruiser Heading to Sea Watercolour, gouache/paper (17x25cm 6x9in) Sydney 2000

ALLDRIDGE Richard L. c.1840-c.1900 **[3]**
- $6 823 - €5 731 - **£4 000** - FF37 594
  And, thinking this will please him best, she takes a riband or a rose Oil/canvas (34x29cm 13x11in) Billingshurst, West-Sussex 1998

ALLEBÉ Augustus 1838-1927 **[22]**
- $1 183 - €1 221 - **£792** - FF8 334
  Breiende oude dame Gouache/paper (34x25cm 13x9in) Dordrecht 2000

ALLEGRAIN Étienne 1644-1736 **[18]**
- $16 024 - €15 550 - **£9 975** - FF102 000
  Paysage aux bergers près d'une rivière Huile/toile (64x81cm 25x31in) Paris 1999

ALLEGRE Raymond 1857-1933 **[42]**
- $15 700 - €15 245 - **£9 700** - FF100 000
  Diligence aux abords du village de Martigues sur l'étang de Berre Huile/toile (93x146cm 36x57in)
- $2 317 - €2 287 - **£1 428** - FF15 000
  Composition Huile/panneau (46x55cm 18x21in) Arles 1999
- $1 917 - €1 952 - **£1 227** - FF12 805
  Vista de un puerto Oleo/tabla (31x46cm 12x18in) Barcelona 2000

ALLEGRET Marc 1900-1973 **[14]**
- $517 - €610 - **£363** - FF4 000
  Jeunes garçons Tirage argentique (22x16cm 8x6in) Paris 2000

ALLEGRINI Flaminio 1587-c.1635 **[5]**
- $3 586 - €3 849 - **£2 400** - FF25 251
  Our Lady of Loretto Bodycolour (17x12cm 6x4in) London 2000

ALLEGRINI Francesco 1587-1663 **[36]**
- $15 000 - €15 550 - **£9 000** - FF102 000
  Combattimento di cavalieri Olio/tela (53x73cm 20x28in) Venezia 1999
- $1 320 - €1 140 - **£660** - FF7 480
  Scena di battaglia Inchiostro (30x23cm 11x9in) Milano 1999

ALLEN Albert Arthur XIX-XX **[20]**
- $2 400 - €2 242 - **£1 450** - FF14 705
  Day in Harem/Night in Harem Vintage gelatin silver print (25x20cm 10x8in) New-York 1999

ALLEN Charles Curtis 1886-1950 **[30]**
- $1 100 - €997 - **£677** - FF6 539
  Old Grey Barn Oil/board (40x50cm 16x20in) Mystic CT 1999
- $825 - €963 - **£571** - FF6 314
  «Gray Day» Oil/canvas/board (22x27cm 9x11in) South-Natick MA 2000

ALLEN Davida 1951 **[21]**
- $2 328 - €2 598 - **£1 619** - FF17 041
  Woman on Stove Oil/panel (77x78cm 30x30in) Sydney 2001
- $3 716 - €3 990 - **£2 487** - FF26 172
  Death of my Father (27 drawings) Coloured pencils (24.5x32cm 9x12in) Sydney 1999
- $2 008 - €2 255 - **£1 302** - FF14 791
  Close to the Bone, Images of Vicki Meyers Etching (28.5x39cm 11x15in) Malvern, Victoria 2000

ALLEN Harry Epworth 1894-1958 **[68]**
- $9 742 - €9 611 - **£6 000** - FF63 044
  Hikers Tempera/board (49.5x34.5cm 19x13in) London 1999
- $1 268 - €1 460 - **£865** - FF9 578
  Dark Hills Tempera/board (24x33cm 9x12in) Dublin 2000
- $433 - €465 - **£290** - FF3 051
  The Ruins of Roche Abbey, Nr. Rotherham Watercolour, gouache/paper (21.5x29cm 8x11in) West-Yorkshire 2000

ALLEN James Edward 1894-1964 **[46]**
- $4 250 - €4 954 - **£2 942** - FF32 497
  Settlers in Wagon Train crossing Mountainous Pass Oil/canvas (71x121cm 28x48in) New-York 2000

$1 400 - €1 318 - £864 - FF8 644
Teeming Ingots Etching (30x25cm 11x9in) New-York 1999

ALLEN Joseph William 1803-1852 [15]
$3 589 - €4 024 - £2 500 - FF26 393
The Vale of Clwyd Oil/canvas (53x99cm 20x38in) Leyburn, North Yorkshire 2001
$568 - €557 - £350 - FF3 651
Clwyd, Wales Watercolour/paper (17x27cm 7x11in) Aylsham, Norfolk 1999

ALLEN Junius 1898-1962 [10]
$4 000 - €4 294 - £2 676 - FF28 164
Fish Wharf #1 Oil/canvas (30x40cm 12x16in) Portland ME 2000

ALLEN Mary Cecil 1893-1962 [6]
$7 310 - €8 268 - £5 145 - FF54 234
Sorrento Hotel Oil/board (57.5x60.5cm 22x23in) Malvern, Victoria 2001

ALLEN Thomas B. 1928 [5]
$1 500 - €1 433 - £938 - FF9 397
Man with large fish on beach Watercolour/paper (100x76cm 39x30in) Cambridge MA 1999

ALLERT Henrik 1937 [49]
$537 - €602 - £374 - FF3 949
Huvud med sneda ögon Ceramic (H41cm H16in) Stockholm 2001

ALLEYNE Francis XVIII [21]
$2 947 - €2 695 - £1 800 - FF17 681
Portrait of Richard Wood, in Military Uniform/Portrait of Hutton Wood Oil/canvas (45x37.5cm 17x14in) London 1998
$1 658 - €1 435 - £1 000 - FF9 416
Mother and Child, Small Three-quarter length, Both with Dresses Oil/panel (25.5x20cm 10x7in) London 1998

ALLFREY Henry W. act.1842-1861 [1]
$9 724 - €10 900 - £6 800 - FF71 500
The Dorking and London Royal Mail leaving the Marquess of Granbury Oil/canvas (75x100cm 29x39in) London 2001

ALLINGHAM Helen, née Paterson 1848-1926 [295]
$4 569 - €5 307 - £3 211 - FF34 809
I trädgården Oil/canvas (50x76cm 19x29in) Stockholm 2001
$11 409 - €10 374 - £7 000 - FF68 046
Old Farm Buildings, Didcot, Berkshire Watercolour (37.5x27cm 14x10in) London 1999

ALLINGHAM William J. XIX-XX [8]
$283 - €305 - £190 - FF1 999
Untitled, After J.B.Pater Engraving (36x29cm 14x11in) London 2000

ALLINSON Adrian Paul 1890-1959 [95]
$1 970 - €2 044 - £1 250 - FF13 406
Road to the Sea (Elba) Oil/board (56x81cm 22x31in) Cheshire 2000
$718 - €771 - £480 - FF5 059
Costume Designs for Isadora Duncan Watercolour (24x31.5cm 9x12in) London 2000
$1 341 - €1 556 - £950 - FF10 205
«Jersey, SR & GWR, The Sunshine Island» Poster (102x127cm 40x50in) London 2000

ALLIOT Lucien 1877-1967 [57]
$965 - €1 037 - £646 - FF6 800
Le bonnet d'âne Chryséléphantine (H18.5cm H7in) Paris 2000

ALLIS C. Harry 1870-1938 [8]
$12 000 - €13 995 - £8 425 - FF91 804
Hillside View in Autumn Oil/canvas (101x127cm 40x50in) Dedham MA 2000

ALLISON John William 1866-1934 [3]
$2 105 - €2 335 - £1 400 - FF15 319
The Old Hand of Experience Watercolour (52x61cm 20x24in) London 2000

ALLOATI Giovanni Battista 1878/79-1964 [2]
$1 550 - €1 607 - £930 - FF10 540
«La discordia» Bronzo (10.5x13x22cm 4x5x8in) Torino 2000

ALLOM Thomas 1804-1872 [56]
$4 233 - €4 832 - £2 941 - FF31 698
En kinesisk afstraffelsesscene Oil/canvas (40x61cm 15x24in) København 2000
$567 - €609 - £380 - FF3 998
Sardis - Mountainous Landscape Watercolour/paper (23x35cm 9x13in) Bath 2000
$1 471 - €1 677 - £1 010 - FF11 000
Constantinople et ses environs Gravure (21x27cm 8x10in) Paris 2000

ALLONGÉ Auguste 1833-1898 [212]
$15 000 - €16 790 - £10 461 - FF110 137
View from Plougastel, Brittany Oil/canvas (127x203cm 50x79in) New-York 2001
$1 545 - €1 601 - £983 - FF10 500
Paysage au pont Huile/toile (30x55cm 11x21in) Neuilly-sur-Seine 2000
$2 597 - €2 592 - £1 621 - FF17 000
Paysanne sur le chemin Huile/toile (28.5x54cm 11x21in) Fontainebleau 1999
$847 - €838 - £528 - FF5 500
La Seine à Villenne, près de Poissy Fusain/papier (48.5x72cm 19x28in) Paris 1999

ALLORI Cristofano Bronzino 1577-1621 [13]
$4 014 - €4 726 - £2 821 - FF31 000
Religieux de face, les bras étendus, un genou à terre Pierre noire (38x25cm 14x9in) Paris 2000

ALLORI IL BRONZINO Agnolo di Cosimo All 1503-1572 [2]
$81 885 - €76 072 - £50 000 - FF499 000
Head of a Bearded Young Man, Seen in Profile Black chalk/paper (18.5x13.5cm 7x5in) London 1998

ALLORI IL BRONZINO Alessandro 1535-1607 [23]
$40 000 - €47 112 - £27 664 - FF309 036
Mercury and Argus Oil/panel (144.5x87.5cm 56x34in) New-York 2000
$72 500 - €69 207 - £45 298 - FF453 966
Portrait of an Elegant Lady Oil/panel (65.5x54.5cm 25x21in) New-York 1999
$290 000 - €293 375 - £177 074 - FF1 924 411
The flight into Egypt Oil/copper (34x37cm 13x14in) New-York 2001

ALLOU Gilles 1670-1751 [4]
$5 049 - €5 934 - £3 500 - FF38 924
Lady, Half-length, in a Yellow Dress with Flowers in her Lap Oil/canvas (91x72cm 35x28in) London 2000

ALLOUARD Henri 1844-1929 [31]
$7 645 - €8 385 - £5 192 - FF55 000
Vénus, dans un encadrement à motif de feuilles d'acanthe et fruit Bas-relief (195x180cm 76x70in) Paris 2000
$486 - €544 - £330 - FF3 571
«Taquinerie enfantine» Bronze (H35cm H13in) Amsterdam 2000

ALLPORT Henry Curzon 1788-1854 [2]
$1 549 - €1 616 - **£977** - FF10 603
Distant View of Sydney from the North Shore
Watercolour/paper (12x18cm 4x7in) Sydney 2000

ALLUAUD Eugène 1866-1947 [29]
$2 351 - €2 515 - £1 549 - FF16 500
Les ruines de Crozant Huile/toile (38x55cm
14x21in) Guéret 2000

ALLUSTANTE Y PALLARES Joaquin 1853-1935 [5]
$8 100 - €9 010 - **£5 700** - FF59 100
Semana Santa en Madrid (Calle de Alcalá)
Oleo/lienzo (45.5x55.5cm 17x21in) Madrid 2001
$4 860 - €5 406 - £3 420 - FF35 460
Place de l'Opera Oleo/lienzo (47.5x33cm 18x12in)
Madrid 2001

ALMA Peter 1886-1969 [12]
$10 120 - €9 983 - **£6 232** - FF65 485
Still Life Oil/canvas (45x38cm 17x14in) Amsterdam
1999
$123 - €136 - **£83** - FF893
Portrait of Lenin Woodcut (17.3x26cm 6x10in)
Haarlem 2000

ALMA-TADEMA Laura Theresa Epps 1852-1909
[20]
$224 145 - €240 601 - **£150 000** - FF1 578 240
Looking Out o'Window (Sunshine) Oil/canvas
(61.5x39.5cm 24x15in) London 2000
$10 543 - €10 164 - **£6 500** - FF66 671
A Carol Oil/panel (38x23cm 14x9in) London 1999
$6 403 - €7 440 - **£4 500** - FF48 803
May I come in? Watercolour (25x17cm 9x6in)
London 2001

ALMA-TADEMA Lawrence 1836-1912 [101]
$98 000 - €91 793 - **£60 250** - FF602 121
A Love Missile Oil/panel (69x46cm 27x18in) New-
York 1999
$20 000 - €23 716 - **£13 760** - FF155 566
Portrait of a Woman Mixed media (25x40cm 9x15in)
New-York 2000
$4 326 - €4 781 - **£3 000** - FF31 359
Fourteenth Century Interior Watercolour
(37x29.5cm 14x11in) London 2001
$440 - €425 - **£278** - FF2 789
The Roman Stadium Etching, aquatint (64.5x79cm
25x31in) London 1999

ALMADA NEGREIROS José Sobral 1893-1970 [17]
$4 515 - €5 234 - £3 150 - FF34 335
«Boa hora!» Tinta china/papel (24x11.5cm 9x4in)
Lisboa 2000
$13 500 - €14 955 - **£8 700** - FF98 100
O jogo das cinco pedrinhas Tapisserie (158x145cm
62x57in) Lisboa 2000

ALMAR Agustin XIX-XX [3]
$9 350 - €10 211 - **£6 460** - FF66 980
Conversando en el patio Oleo/lienzo (49x62cm
19x24in) Madrid 2001

ALMARAZ Carlos 1941-1989 [24]
$8 000 - €9 295 - **£5 622** - FF60 969
City Bridge Oil/board (30.5x23cm 12x9in) Beverly-
Hills CA 2001

ALMAVIVA Marco 1934 [6]
$1 100 - €1 140 - **£660** - FF7 480
Voldo Olio/tela (40x70cm 15x27in) Prato 2000

ALMBERG Thomas 1936 [9]
$484 - €576 - **£345** - FF3 779
Dansande Buddha Bronze (H50cm H19in)
Stockholm 2000

ALMEIDA de Alvaro Duarte 1909-1972 [18]
$2 070 - €2 293 - £1 334 - FF15 042
**Paisagem da Lagoa de Obidos - Foz do Arelho,
com pinheiros** Oleo/lienzo (60.5x50cm 23x19in)
Lisboa 2000
$1 260 - €1 396 - **£812** - FF9 156
Paisagem da Rascoia - Vale- Cháo de Couce
Oleo/tabla (24x33cm 9x12in) Lisboa 2000
$484 - €548 - **£341** - FF3 597
Toureio a cavalo, corrida à Portuguesa
Acuarela/papel (20.5x31cm 8x12in) Lisboa 2001

ALMEIDA E SILVA de José 1864-1945 [4]
$9 600 - €9 970 - **£6 200** - FF65 400
Composiçao com barros, cobre e vidros
Oleo/lienzo (70x112cm 27x44in) Lisboa 2000
$5 040 - €5 234 - £3 255 - FF34 335
Duas figuras femininas Tinta china/papel
(34x22.5cm 13x8in) Lisboa 2000

ALO Charles Hallo, dit 1882-1969 [166]
$281 - €320 - **£193** - FF2 100
P.O., Allez au Maroc» Affiche (102.5x71cm 40x27in)
Paris 2000

ALOISE Aloise Corbaz 1886-1964 [12]
$7 813 - €9 189 - **£5 602** - FF60 274
«Bonaparte au lit, marrons» Coloured chalks/paper
(67.5x50cm 26x19in) Bern 2001

ALOISI GALDANINI Baldassare 1577-1638 [2]
$24 156 - €27 441 - **£16 668** - FF180 000
Cupidon bandant son arc Huile/toile
(136.5x64.5cm 53x25in) Paris 2000

ALONSO Alonso 1930 [10]
$832 - €781 - **£520** - FF5 122
«Bodegón de los tulipanes rojos» Olio/tela
(73x92cm 28x36in) Madrid 1999

ALONSO Angel 1923-1994 [20]
$132 - €152 - **£90** - FF1 000
Je t'aime Gouache (66x78cm 25x30in) Paris 2000

ALONSO Carlos 1929 [29]
$800 - €881 - **£531** - FF5 781
Technos de la ciudad Técnica mixta (65x50cm
25x19in) Buenos-Aires 2000
$750 - €871 - **£527** - FF5 715
La abuela Técnica mixta/papel (25x16cm 9x6in)
Buenos-Aires 2001

ALONSO FERNANDEZ Rafael 1924 [5]
$1 560 - €1 802 - **£1 080** - FF11 820
Sanjenjo Acuarela/papel (49x69cm 19x27in) Madrid
2000

ALONSO PALACIOS Vicente 1955 [16]
$324 - €360 - **£216** - FF2 364
En la playa Oleo/lienzo (15x20cm 5x7in) Madrid 2000
$945 - €1 051 - **£630** - FF6 895
En la playa Acuarela/papel (34x50cm 13x19in)
Madrid 2000

ALONSO-PÉREZ Carlos XIX-XX [4]
$1 740 - €1 802 - **£1 110** - FF11 820
Sombrero al río Oleo/lienzo (80x120cm 31x47in)
Madrid 2000

ALONSO-PÉREZ Mariano 1857-1930 [95]
$6 800 - €6 777 - **£4 130** - FF44 457
The Fishing Party Oil/panel (64x53cm 25x21in)
Chicago IL 2000
$1 538 - €1 829 - **£1 096** - FF12 000
Le soulier défait Huile/panneau (21.5x13.5cm 8x5in)
Neuilly-sur-Seine 2000

$187 - €204 - **£129** - FF1 339
La gallinita ciega/El examen de retrato de la dama Tinta/papel (23.5x33cm 9x12in) Madrid 2001

ALONZO Dominique XX **[63]**

$1 745 - €1 982 - **£1 194** - FF13 000
Bretonne et son enfant Bronze (H51cm H20in) Senlis 2001

ALOTT Robert 1850-1910 **[53]**

$27 000 - €31 370 - **£18 975** - FF205 772
The Promenade Oil/canvas (139.5x117cm 54x46in) New-York 2001

$2 624 - €3 049 - **£1 870** - FF20 000
Campement Huile/panneau (37x63cm 14x24in) Paris 2001

$11 488 - €12 992 - **£8 085** - FF85 225
On the Beach Oil/board (25x51cm 9x20in) Melbourne 2001

ALPERIZ Nicolás 1865-1928 **[12]**

$9 000 - €10 091 - **£6 111** - FF66 193
Travellers on a Rainy Path Oil/canvas (121.5x152.5cm 47x60in) New-York 2000

$5 490 - €5 406 - **£3 510** - FF35 460
Dama ante el espejo Oleo/lienzo (96x66cm 37x25in) Madrid 1999

$2 593 - €2 820 - **£1 709** - FF18 500
Le garde Huile/toile (44x26cm 17x10in) Paris 2000

ALPERN Merry XX **[2]**

$2 400 - €2 664 - **£1 673** - FF17 475
«Dirty Windows» Gelatin silver print (45x30.5cm 17x12in) New-York 2001

ALPERT Max Vladimirovitch 1899-1980 **[21]**

$1 200 - €1 209 - **£748** - FF7 932
The Hunt Gelatin silver print (28x38cm 11x14in) New-York 2000

ALPUY Julio 1919 **[52]**

$9 369 - €7 618 - **£5 205** - FF49 969
Sin título Oleo/cartón (80.5x50.5cm 31x19in) Caracas 1998

$2 100 - €2 184 - **£1 326** - FF14 329
Naturaleza muerta Oleo/cartón (36x39cm 14x15in) Montevideo 2000

$45 000 - €52 283 - **£31 626** - FF342 954
Construcción de madera Sculpture, wood (H76cm H29in) New-York 2001

ALSINA Jacques XIX-XX **[16]**

$2 250 - €2 479 - **£1 520** - FF16 260
Oriëntallstiche scène (Scène orientaliste) Huile/toile (46x62cm 18x24in) Antwerpen 2000

$4 071 - €4 269 - **£2 550** - FF28 000
Le détente Huile/panneau (26.5x35cm 10x13in) Paris 2000

ALSLOOT van Denijs 1570-c.1628 **[14]**

$589 040 - €660 452 - **£400 000** - FF4 332 280
View of the Abbey of Groenendael near Brussels in Winter Oil/panel (45x85.5cm 17x33in) London 2000

ALSTON Charles Henry 1907-1977 **[3]**

$3 750 - €4 095 - **£2 414** - FF26 863
Abstract Watercolour/paper (66x53cm 26x21in) Mystic CT 2000

ALT Franz 1821-1914 **[159]**

$1 752 - €1 997 - **£1 211** - FF13 098
Innenansicht des Stephansdomes Oil/panel (17.5x13.5cm 6x5in) Zürich 2000

$1 373 - €1 257 - **£836** - FF8 247
Ansicht von Rotterdam Crayon (16.5x21cm 6x8in) Zürich 1999

ALT Jacob 1789-1872 **[52]**

$15 450 - €15 339 - **£9 654** - FF100 617
Ägyptische Ideallandschaft Öl/Leinwand (38x52cm 14x20in) München 1999

$11 978 - €12 271 - **£7 392** - FF80 493
Blick auf Florenz Öl/Leinwand (36x44cm 14x17in) Düsseldorf 2000

$1 756 - €1 994 - **£1 220** - FF13 080
Waldige Gebirgslandschaft mit einem Wasserfall Aquarell/Papier (21.5x15cm 8x5in) Berlin 2001

$1 095 - €929 - **£650** - FF6 091
View of Austrial Lithograph (26x35.5cm 10x13in) London 1998

ALT Otmar 1940 **[282]**

$12 229 - €11 760 - **£7 546** - FF77 139
Feuerblumenilse Acryl/Leinwand (140x110cm 55x43in) Köln 2000

$3 945 - €4 602 - **£2 770** - FF30 185
Der Tortenräuber Acryl/Leinwand (80x60cm 31x23in) Köln 2000

$3 588 - €3 426 - **£2 241** - FF22 471
Der Zauberlehrling I Öl/Leinwand (32.5x28.4cm 12x11in) Köln 2000

$438 - €511 - **£307** - FF3 353
Stier von der Osterinsel Bronze (H8.5cm H3in) München 2000

$603 - €562 - **£372** - FF3 689
Professor Grashops und der Zaubergarten Gouache/board (29.8x20.7cm 11x8in) Hamburg 1999

$132 - €153 - **£92** - FF1 006
«Grüne Piraten» Farbserigraphie (41.5x37cm 16x14in) Berlin 2001

ALT Theodor 1846-1937 **[18]**

$1 127 - €1 176 - **£709** - FF7 714
Mutter und Kind auf der Blumenwiese Öl/Leinwand (36x47cm 14x18in) Stuttgart 2000

$2 256 - €2 352 - **£1 482** - FF15 427
Mädchenkopf Oil/board (36.5x31.5cm 14x12in) München 2000

ALT von Rudolf 1812-1905 **[223]**

$34 937 - €35 791 - **£21 560** - FF234 773
Der Brunnen auf dem Monte Pincio, Rom Öl/Leinwand (39x50cm 15x19in) Düsseldorf 2000

$19 350 - €18 168 - **£12 000** - FF119 175
Im Hafen bei Rovinj Oil/panel (22x28.5cm 8x11in) Wien 1999

$25 170 - €21 793 - **£15 270** - FF142 950
Blick auf den Hochaltar der Franziskanerkirche in Salzburg Aquarell/Papier (42.5x29cm 16x11in) Wien 1998

$900 - €777 - **£450** - FF5 100
Das neue Opernhaus in Wien Acquaforte (26.5x37cm 10x14in) Milano 1999

ALTAMURA Alessandro 1855-1918 **[5]**

$1 600 - €1 659 - **£960** - FF10 880
Ritratto di giovane donna Matita/carta (44x33.5cm 17x13in) Milano 2000

ALTAMURA Ioannis, Jean 1852-1878 **[11]**

$20 801 - €20 652 - **£13 000** - FF135 469
The Shipwreck Oil/panel (41.5x61cm 16x24in) London 1999

$10 789 - €9 959 - **£6 719** - FF65 327
Graekenland Oil/canvas (34x47cm 13x18in) Viby J, Arhus 1999

ALTAMURA Saverio Francesco 1826-1897 **[10]**

$5 652 - €5 860 - **£3 391** - FF38 437
Scena orientale Olio/tela (65x52cm 25x20in) Milano 2000

$7 250 – €7 516 – **£4 350** – FF49 300
«Partenope dolente» Pastelli (40x24.5cm 15x9in)
Milano 2000

ALTDORFER Albrecht 1480-1538 **[128]**
$538 – €613 – **£375** – FF4 024
Die Auferstehung Christi Woodcut (7.5x4.5cm
2x1in) Berlin 2001

ALTEN Mathias Joseph 1871-1938 **[21]**
$4 250 – €4 562 – **£2 844** – FF29 924
Unloading Salt Hay at Old Lyme, Conn. Oil/can-
vas (45x55cm 18x22in) Altadena CA 2000
$2 250 – €2 674 – **£1 559** – FF17 543
Sailboat, Three Sailors and Two Oxen on a
Beach Oil/board (27x43cm 11x17in) Detroit MI 2000
$600 – €630 – **£378** – FF4 132
Interior Scene with an Old Man Reading
Pencil/paper (30x35cm 12x14in) Bloomfield-Hills MI
2000

ALTENBOURG Gerhard 1926-1989 **[248]**
$4 940 – €5 880 – **£3 530** – FF38 569
Kniende Berg-Kuppe Mixed media (33x19.8cm
12x7in) Berlin 2000
$3 184 – €3 579 – **£2 235** – FF23 477
«Viel Wirbel in einem Zwischenraum»
Watercolour (22.5x18cm 8x7in) Düsseldorf 2001
$593 – €665 – **£413** – FF4 360
«Neigende Darbringung» Farbradierung
(12.5x10cm 4x3in) Berlin 2001

ALTENKIRCH Otto 1875-1945 **[23]**
$979 – €1 022 – **£620** – FF6 707
Birkenweg im Mai Öl/Leinwand (103x86cm 40x33in)
München 2000

ALTHEIM Wilhelm 1871-1914 **[25]**
$2 191 – €2 352 – **£1 466** – FF15 427
Der Apfelweinwirt mit Gast in der
Gartenwirtschaft Pastel (19x15cm 7x5in) Frankfurt
2000
$213 – €204 – **£134** – FF1 341
Mann mit Pfeife/Mann mit Hund/Drei Bauern mit
Esel/Zahnzieher/Mann Radierung (12.5x19cm
4x7in) Hamburg 1999

ALTINK Jan 1885-1976 **[96]**
$7 812 – €9 076 – **£5 490** – FF59 532
Farmhouse in summer landscape Oil/canvas
(55x44cm 21x17in) Amsterdam 2001
$1 293 – €1 361 – **£854** – FF8 929
Still life with Sunflowers Oil/canvas (39.5x34.5cm
15x13in) Amsterdam 2000
$920 – €908 – **£566** – FF5 953
Farmhouses Watercolour (30x47cm 11x18in)
Amsterdam 1999
$246 – €272 – **£167** – FF1 786
Park View Etching, aquatint (18.5x25.1cm 7x9in)
Haarlem 2000

ALTMAN Harold 1924 **[41]**
$200 – €214 – **£136** – FF1 405
«November 1984, IV» Color lithograph (20x16cm
8x6in) Cleveland OH 2001

ALTMAN Howard XX **[11]**
$200 – €235 – **£142** – FF1 540
November 1984, I Color lithograph (21x16.5cm
8x6in) Philadelphia PA 2000

ALTMAN Natan Isaevich 1889-1970 **[19]**
$11 565 – €9 780 – **£6 912** – FF64 152
Nature morte Oil/canvas (75x68cm 29x26in)
Stockholm 1998

ALTMANN Alexandre 1885-1950 **[165]**
$2 518 – €2 997 – **£1 800** – FF19 661
Tree by the River Oil/canvas (81.5x60.5cm 32x23in)
London 2001

ALTMANN Anton II 1808-1871 **[23]**
$1 422 – €1 308 – **£853** – FF8 580
Am Heimweg Öl/Leinwand (25x35cm 9x13in) Wien
1999
$800 – €730 – **£486** – FF4 790
The Devotional Altar Wax crayon/paper (33x41cm
13x16in) Boston MA 1998

ALTMANN Gerhard 1877-1940 **[56]**
$1 049 – €975 – **£640** – FF6 393
Sheaves of Wheat in an extensive Summer
Landscape Oil/canvas (50x70cm 19x27in) Amsterdam
1998
$576 – €544 – **£359** – FF3 571
Cows in a Sunlit Meadow Oil/canvas (30x50cm
11x19in) Amsterdam 1999

ALTMANN Joseph 1795-1867 **[5]**
$500 – €6 382 – **£3 797** – FF41 860
The Uprising Oil/panel (31.5x38cm 12x14in) New-
York 2000

ALTMANN Karl 1800-1861 **[5]**
$4 452 – €4 090 – **£2 735** – FF26 831
Alpenländisches Volksleben Oil/panel (33x47cm
12x18in) Stuttgart 2001

ALTOBELLI Gioacchino XIX **[3]**
$686 – €818 – **£489** – FF5 366
Staatswagen des Kardinals von Hohenlohe
Albumen print (27.3x59.5cm 10x23in) München 2000

ALTOMONTE Bartholomäus 1702-1779 **[6]**
$10 127 – €9 447 – **£6 110** – FF61 971
Christus und die Samariterin am Brunnen
Öl/Leinwand (77.5x56cm 30x22in) Wien 1999

ALTOMONTE Martino Hohenberg 1657-1745 **[14]**
$720 – €818 – **£500** – FF5 366
Maria Immaculata Chalks (33x17cm 12x6in) Köln
2001

ALTON Lois Lupp 1894-1972 **[13]**
$1 116 – €1 090 – **£708** – FF7 150
Hafen von Malcesine am Gardasee Oil/panel
(49x49cm 19x19in) Salzburg 1999
$500 – €581 – **£352** – FF3 813
«Stilleben mit Primeln» Öl/Karton (30x30cm
11x11in) Salzburg 2001

ALTOON John 1925-1969 **[28]**
$2 750 – €2 324 – **£1 640** – FF15 246
Untitled ABS -83 Pastel (152.5x101.5cm 60x39in)
San-Francisco CA 1998

ALTORF Johan Coenraad 1876-1955 **[16]**
$9 032 – €8 622 – **£5 644** – FF56 555
A Parrot Sculpture (H14cm H5in) Amsterdam 1999

ALTORJAI Sandor 1933-1979 **[2]**
$1 610 – €1 781 – **£1 058** – FF11 684
Night Landscape Mixed media/paper (73x102cm
28x40in) Budapest 2000

ALTSCHULE Hilda 1900-1983 **[1]**
$4 000 – €4 549 – **£2 774** – FF29 840
Erie Canal Coal Docks-Pittsford Oil/canvas
(87x105cm 34x41in) Chicago IL 2000

ALTSON Abbey 1864-c.1950 **[30]**
$5 000 – €4 232 – **£2 993** – FF27 762
Romance Oil/canvas (92x72cm 36x28in) New-York
1998

$4 192 - €3 818 - £2 566 - FF25 044
Fantasy - Angel Drawing the Cloth of Night
Oil/board (44x31cm 17x12in) Malvern, Victoria 1998

ALTZAR Anders 1886-1939 [33]
$823 - €693 - £486 - FF4 548
Sol över vinterlandskap Oil/canvas (66x73cm
25x28in) Stockholm 1998

ALTZENBACH Gerhard XVII [1]
$932 - €1 022 - £633 - FF6 707
Vanitasallegorie (Skelett mit Sense und
Schädeln) Kupferstich (24.3x14.5cm 9x5in) Berlin
2000

ALUF Nic XX [2]
$22 120 - €21 343 - £13 986 - FF140 000
Sophie Taeuber Arp derrière sa tête Dada Photo
(22.5x16cm 8x6in) Paris 1999

ALUMA Jordi 1926 [17]
$1 677 - €1 652 - £1 072 - FF10 835
Bailarinas Oleo/tabla (95x40cm 37x15in) Barcelona
1999
$616 - €661 - £418 - FF4 334
Rostro Pastel/papier (82x71cm 32x27in) Barcelona
2001

ALVARD 1945 [2]
$1 092 - €1 189 - £751 - FF7 800
Le grand large Huile/toile (81x65cm 31x25in) Reze
2001

ALVAREZ ARMESTO Primitivo XIX [11]
$2 720 - €2 553 - £1 657 - FF16 745
Joven Oleo/lienzo (66x50cm 25x19in) Madrid 1999

ALVAREZ BRAVO Manuel 1902 [208]
$2 250 - €2 098 - £1 358 - FF13 764
Retrato de lo eterno Photograph (24x19cm 9x7in)
New-York 1999

ALVAREZ CATALA Luis 1836-1901 [43]
$30 500 - €30 032 - £19 000 - FF197 000
El paseo del cardenal Oil/canvas (31.4x58cm
12x22in) Madrid 1999
$14 000 - €13 303 - £8 517 - FF87 260
Elegant Melodies Oil/panel (32.5x25cm 12x9in)
New-York 1999

ALVAREZ DIAZ Emilio 1874-1952 [35]
$3 465 - €3 304 - £2 145 - FF21 670
Damas goyescas en el parque Oleo/tabla
(43x47.5cm 16x18in) Madrid 1999
$795 - €901 - £540 - FF5 910
Saliendo de la iglesia Oleo/tabla (20x13cm 7x5in)
Madrid 2000

ALVAREZ DUMONT César 1866-1945 [7]
$3 050 - €3 003 - £1 900 - FF19 700
Ajuste de cuentas Oleo/lienzo (54.5x66cm 21x25in)
Madrid 1999

ALVAREZ DUMONT Eugenio 1864-1927 [14]
$35 000 - €39 087 - £22 414 - FF256 392
At the Beach in Biarritz Oil/canvas (89x114.5cm
35x45in) New-York 2000
$5 035 - €5 706 - £3 420 - FF37 430
Caravana de gitanos Oleo/lienzo (25x50cm 9x19in)
Madrid 2000
$900 - €852 - £559 - FF5 588
«La Correspondencia de España» Poster
(49x24cm 19x9in) New-York 1999

ALVAREZ Luis 1932-1997 [26]
$942 - €884 - £582 - FF5 800
Portrait de femme Huile/toile (48x36cm 18x14in)
Avignon 1999

ALVAREZ Mabel 1891-1985 [40]
$5 250 - €4 977 - £3 279 - FF32 645
Woman Reading Oil/canvas (50x40cm 20x16in)
Mystic CT 1999
$3 575 - €3 644 - £2 240 - FF23 905
Still life-fruit and covered jar Oil/canvas/board
(30x40cm 12x16in) Altadena CA 2000
$750 - €641 - £454 - FF4 205
Seated Woman Looking at a Book Coloured pen-
cils/paper (28x21.5cm 11x8in) San-Francisco CA 1998

ALVAREZ Toribio 1668-1730 [2]
$17 940 - €15 617 - £10 920 - FF102 440
Festejo de caza en la Moraleja Oleo/lienzo
(165x278cm 64x109in) Madrid 1999

ALVERMANN Hans Peter 1931 [9]
$850 - €818 - £525 - FF5 366
Wüstenten Iron (49.5x110cm 19x43in) Köln 1999

ALVES CARDOSO Artur 1883-1930 [3]
$62 700 - €54 668 - £37 400 - FF358 600
«Namoro» Oleo/lienzo (54x65.5cm 21x25in) Lisboa
1998

ALVES Justino 1940 [1]
$3 300 - €3 739 - £2 325 - FF24 525
Naturalezas mortas Oleo/lienzo (41x33cm 16x12in)
Lisboa 2001

ALVIANI Getulio 1939 [79]
$1 800 - €1 555 - £1 200 - FF10 250
Superficie a testura vibratile Tecnica mista
(50x50cm 19x19in) Prato 1998
$2 148 - €2 496 - £1 509 - FF16 371
«Opera Programata N.6014» Mixed media
(28x28cm 11x11in) Amsterdam 2001
$2 520 - €2 177 - £1 260 - FF14 280
Superficie a testura vibratile Metal (70x70cm
27x27in) Milano 1999

ALVIN John 1948 [31]
$13 000 - €13 954 - £8 699 - FF91 533
E.T. The Extra-Terrestrial - Amblin
Entertainment Universal Pictures Acrylic
(101x60cm 40x24in) Beverly-Hills CA 2000
$1 200 - €1 288 - £803 - FF8 449
The Hunchback of Notre-Dame - Walt Disney
Studios Acrylic (45x31cm 18x12in) Beverly-Hills CA
2000
$1 057 - €769 - £363 - FF6 363
«Blade Runner» Poster (104x68.5cm 40x26in)
London 1999

AMABLE Amable Petit, dit 1846-c.1914 [39]
$470 - €488 - £310 - FF3 200
Projet de décor pour Hérodiade, du 2e tableau
Aquarelle/papier (36.5x61cm 14x24in) Versailles 1999

AMADEO XX [8]
$4 781 - €5 026 - £3 000 - FF32 968
A Turkish Water-Carrier - Saka Selling Water to
Children Watercolour (34.5x25.5cm 13x10in) London
2000

AMADO Manuel da Silva 1938 [2]
$4 500 - €4 985 - £2 900 - FF32 700
Pinhal de manhã Oleo/lienzo (65x92cm 25x36in)
Lisboa 2000

AMAN-JEAN Edmond 1860-1936 [111]
$3 500 - €3 807 - £2 307 - FF24 970
Le Quai de Bourbon à Paris Oil/canvas
(72.5x59.5cm 28x23in) Boston MA 2000
$509 - €488 - £320 - FF3 200
Femme nue de dos Crayon (19x27cm 7x10in) Paris
1999

▥ **$344** - €369 - **£230** - FF2 423
Portrait de Mlle Moréno de la Comédie-Française Farblithographie (34.2x37.7cm 13x14in) Bern 2000

AMAND Jean-François 1730-1769 **[4]**
✎ **$906** - €1 067 - **£637** - FF7 000
Scène de l'histoire ancienne Lavis (24x28cm 9x11in) Paris 2000

AMAND Roger 1931 **[23]**
😊 **$2 322** - €2 592 - **£1 615** - FF17 000
La vie de quartier Huile/toile (146x114cm 57x44in) Paris 2001
😊 **$1 912** - €2 134 - **£1 330** - FF14 000
Ebauche d'un récit Huile/toile (116x89cm 45x35in) Paris 2001

AMANS Jacques Guillaume L. 1801-1888 **[5]**
😊 **$17 000** - €14 263 - **£9 973** - FF93 561
Portrait of Col. Thomas Bryan Pugh Oil/canvas (106x81cm 42x32in) New-Orleans LA 1998

AMANTINI Tommaso XVII **[1]**
◈ **$110 000** - €109 757 - **£66 957** - FF719 961
Ecstasy of Theresa of Avila Relief (88.5x47.5cm 34x18in) New-York 2001

AMARASEKARA Abraham C.G.S. 1883-1959 **[1]**
😊 **$4 458** - €4 317 - **£2 800** - FF28 315
Sunset Oil/board (15x23cm 5x9in) London 1999

AMARELHE Américo ?-1947 **[3]**
✎ **$1 584** - €1 795 - **£1 080** - FF11 772
Figuras de revista Técnica mixta/papel (34x98cm 13x38in) Lisboa 2000

AMAT Frederic 1952 **[18]**
✎ **$2 145** - €1 952 - **£1 332** - FF12 805
Signos asociados Técnica mixta/papel (72x101cm 28x39in) Barcelona 1999
▥ **$272** - €264 - **£167** - FF1 733
Tinajas Grabado (77.5x93cm 30x36in) Barcelona 1999

AMAT José 1901-1991 **[4]**
😊 **$14 850** - €16 518 - **£10 450** - FF108 350
Paseo de Sant Feliu Oleo/lienzo (50x65cm 19x25in) Barcelona 2001

AMAT PAGES Gabriel 1899-1984 **[24]**
✎ **$235** - €228 - **£144** - FF1 497
Paseo de la garriga Acuarela/papel (38x56cm 14x22in) Barcelona 1999

AMAT PAGES José 1901-1991 **[35]**
😊 **$18 300** - €18 019 - **£11 400** - FF118 200
Paseo de Sant Feliu de Guíxols Oleo/lienzo (60x80.5cm 23x31in) Barcelona 1999
😊 **$1 500** - €1 502 - **£925** - FF9 850
Paisaje Oleo/lienzo (38.5x32cm 15x12in) Madrid 2000
$335 - €330 - **£209** - FF2 167
Carros y peatones en una calle Aguada/papel (19.5x25.5cm 7x10in) Barcelona 1999

AMATO Flip XX **[1]**
😊 **$7 000** - €6 671 - **£4 245** - FF43 756
Willie Mays, Mickey Mantle, and Duke Snider Acrylic/board (58.5x76cm 23x29in) New-York 1999

AMATO Francesco c.1590-? **[5]**
▥ **$807** - €920 - **£563** - FF6 037
Der Heilige Joseph mit dem Christkind Radierung (28.5x18.5cm 11x7in) Berlin 2001

AMATO Luigi XIX-XX **[9]**
😊 **$986** - €1 019 - **£620** - FF6 686
Kvinna med krus vid mur Oil/canvas (99x69cm 38x27in) Stockholm 2000

AMAURY-DUVAL Eugène Pineu-Duval 1808-1885 **[11]**
😊 **$10 000** - €10 077 - **£6 234** - FF66 100
The Bather Oil/canvas/panel (52x30cm 20x11in) New-York 2000

AMBERG Wilhelm A. Lebrecht 1822-1899 **[27]**
😊 **$8 000** - €8 794 - **£5 126** - FF57 683
The Secret Oil/canvas (64x51cm 25x20in) New-York 2000
😊 **$714** - €767 - **£478** - FF5 030
Junge Frau unter einer Pergola Öl/Karton (26.5x22cm 10x8in) Köln 2000

AMBILLE Paul 1930 **[77]**
😊 **$1 789** - €1 753 - **£1 153** - FF11 500
Le kiosque Huile/toile (97x130cm 38x51in) Avignon 1999
😊 **$1 060** - €1 220 - **£748** - FF8 000
La chambrière Huile/toile (46x38cm 18x14in) Barbizon 2001

AMBROGIANI Pierre 1907-1985 **[1138]**
😊 **$3 588** - €4 116 - **£2 454** - FF27 000
Sans titre Huile/toile (80x160cm 31x62in) Paris 2000
😊 **$939** - €3 887 - **£2 427** - FF25 500
Maison dans la crique Huile/toile (50x100cm 19x39in) Calais 1999
😊 **$1 665** - €1 982 - **£1 153** - FF13 000
Bouquet Huile/panneau (20.5x18cm 8x7in) Albi 2000
✎ **$358** - €381 - **£226** - FF2 500
Terrasse provençale Aquarelle/papier (47.5x62.5cm 18x24in) Paris 2000
▥ **$163** - €152 - **£100** - FF1 000
Le Haut Pays Lithographie couleurs (33x53cm 12x20in) Paris 1999

AMBROS von Raphael 1855-1895 **[11]**
😊 **$43 962** - €50 614 - **£30 000** - FF332 007
Blessing the Arms Oil/panel (62x43cm 24x16in) London 2000
😊 **$8 327** - €7 729 - **£5 000** - FF50 696
The Watermelon Seller Oil/panel (18.5x24cm 7x9in) London 1999

AMBROSE John 1931 **[176]**
😊 **$588** - €684 - **£420** - FF4 486
Old Boats, Polperro Oil/board (40x50cm 16x20in) Par, Cornwall 2001
😊 **$303** - €328 - **£210** - FF2 152
St.Michaels' Mount Oil/board (30x40cm 12x16in) Par, Cornwall 2001

AMBROSI Alfredo Gauro 1901-1945 **[1]**
😊 **$8 627** - €8 944 - **£5 176** - FF58 667
Aeropittura Olio/tavoletta (82x56cm 32x22in) Venezia 1999

AMBROSI-EISENSTADT Gustinus 1893-1975 **[28]**
◈ **$2 971** - €2 545 - **£1 739** - FF16 691
«Der Bücherwurm» Plaster (H51cm H20in) Wien 1998

AMBROZZI Josef Peter XVIII **[1]**
😊 **$3 757** - €3 553 - **£2 340** - FF23 309
Latona and Peasants Oil/metal (15.5x22cm 6x8in) Praha 1999

AMÉGLIO Mério 1897-1970 **[358]**
😊 **$1 151** - €1 372 - **£820** - FF9 000
Place du Tertre Huile/toile (46x55cm 18x21in) Paris 2000
😊 **$718** - €838 - **£504** - FF5 500
Vue de la côte italienne Huile/carton (32x40cm 12x15in) Versailles 2000

AMELIN Albin 1902-1975 **[220]**
- $3 451 - €3 236 - £2 134 - FF21 230
  Modell i röd interiör Oil/canvas (116x89cm 45x35in)
  Stockholm 1999
- $886 - €874 - £546 - FF5 736
  Mansportträtt Gouache/paper (68x54cm 26x21in)
  Stockholm 1999
- $267 - €254 - £162 - FF1 663
  Vattenkraftverk Color lithograph (55x71.5cm
  21x28in) Stockholm 1999

AMELL Y JORDA Manuel 1843-1902 **[7]**
- $9 500 - €9 243 - £5 847 - FF60 631
  André Étameur Fondeur Oleo/lienzo (83x115cm
  32x45in) Buenos-Aires 1999

AMEN Irving 1918-? **[44]**
- $90 - €104 - £62 - FF682
  «**Sabbath**» Etching in colors (44x28cm 17x11in)
  Cleveland OH 2000

AMEN Jeanne 1863-1923 **[2]**
- $3 205 - €3 811 - £2 207 - FF25 000
  Choisy-le-Roi Huile/toile (43x70cm 16x27in)
  Fontainebleau 2000

AMEN van Woody 1936 **[4]**
- $5 669 - €5 218 - £3 402 - FF34 230
  Gunung Matterhorn Bali Mixed media/paper
  (111x156cm 43x61in) Amsterdam 1999

AMENNECIER Mary Antoinette 1888-1960 **[38]**
- $183 - €213 - £129 - FF1 400
  Sans titre Huile/toile (41x33cm 16x12in) Paris 2001

AMERLING von Friedrich Ritter 1803-1887 **[61]**
- $6 267 - €6 135 - £3 856 - FF40 246
  **Porträt des Düsseldorfer Malers Eduard Julius
  Friedrich Bendemann** Oil/paper/canvas (52x37cm
  20x14in) Stuttgart 1999
- $101 166 - €99 445 - £65 000 - FF652 314
  **Portrait of the engraver Franz Xaver Stöber,
  Head-and-Shoulders** Oil/canvas (41x33cm 16x12in)
  London 1999

AMERSTORFER Siegfried 1920 **[11]**
- $249 - €291 - £176 - FF1 906
  Landschaft Aquarell/Papier (23x32cm 9x12in)
  Salzburg 2000

AMES Daniel F. act.1837-1858 **[1]**
- $4 500 - €3 780 - £2 645 - FF24 793
  **Gentleman in Striped Waistcoat/Lady in a Lace
  Trimmed Black Dress** Oil/canvas (76x63cm
  30x25in) Boston MA 1998

AMETLLER Blas 1768-1841 **[13]**
- $336 - €288 - £201 - FF1 891
  La caza del Avestruz Grabado (63x46cm 24x18in)
  Madrid 1998

AMICI Aurelio 1832-1889 **[4]**
- $4 500 - €4 665 - £2 700 - FF30 600
  Cannone alla cinta aureliana Olio/tela
  (30.5x43.5cm 12x17in) Roma 1999

AMICI Domenico 1808-? **[7]**
- $686 - €694 - £431 - FF4 552
  Raccolta delle principali vedute di Roma
  Estampe (17x23.5cm 6x9in) Bruxelles 2000

AMICIS de Cristoforo 1902-1987 **[36]**
- $2 760 - €2 384 - £1 840 - FF15 640
  «**Ortensie**» Olio/tela (60x50cm 23x19in) Milano 1998

AMICK Robert Wesley 1879-1969 **[24]**
- $1 200 - €1 408 - £847 - FF9 237
  Palomino in Landscape Oil/canvas (76x101.5cm
  29x39in) New-York 2000
- $700 - €799 - £493 - FF5 242
  At the Dock Watercolour/paper (55x69.5cm 21x27in)
  Boston MA 2001

AMIET Cuno 1868-1961 **[672]**
- $385 500 - €375 217 - £236 880 - FF2 461 260
  Grosse Obsternte Öl/Leinwand (149x129cm
  58x50in) Zürich 1999
- $31 399 - €35 851 - £22 137 - FF235 169
  **Die Frau des Künstlers mit Blumenstrauss im
  Garten** Öl/Karton (73.5x39cm 28x15in) Bern 2001
- $8 563 - €9 778 - £6 037 - FF64 137
  «**Der rote Apfel**» Öl/Leinwand/Karton (33x41cm
  12x16in) Bern 2001
- $2 714 - €2 610 - £1 672 - FF17 120
  Vallendar am Rhein, bei Koblenz Aquarell/Papier
  (22x28cm 8x11in) St. Gallen 1999
- $155 - €175 - £109 - FF1 150
  «**Heimat**» Lithographie (35x24cm 13x9in) Bern 2001

AMIGO Juan XVII **[1]**
- $12 000 - €14 134 - £8 299 - FF92 710
  Portrait of Doña Antonia de Eguillaz del Barco
  Oil/canvas (199x109cm 78x42in) New-York 2000

AMIGONI Jacopo 1675/82-1752 **[55]**
- $46 062 - €46 017 - £28 800 - FF301 851
  Das Urteil des Paris Öl/Leinwand (102x126cm
  40x49in) Köln 1999
- $25 000 - €26 742 - £17 045 - FF175 417
  Cupid holding a Broken Arrow Oil/canvas
  (77.5x104cm 30x40in) New-York 2001

AMIR OF KARRAYA Shaikh Muhammad c.1800-
c.1850 **[8]**
- $9 923 - €9 282 - £6 000 - FF60 885
  Calcutta Hackney Coach Watercolour (20x29.5cm
  7x11in) London 1999

AMISANI Giuseppe 1881-1941 **[44]**
- $3 000 - €3 110 - £1 800 - FF20 400
  Nudo di donna Olio/legno (58x43cm 22x16in) Roma
  1999
- $2 100 - €1 814 - £1 400 - FF11 900
  Nonna Bestetti Olio/tavola (49x30cm 19x11in) Roma
  1998

AMLING Franz 1853-1894 **[7]**
- $3 184 - €3 323 - £2 015 - FF21 800
  Jagdgesellschaft Öl/Leinwand (80x110cm 31x43in)
  München 2000

AMMAN Jost 1539-1591 **[46]**
- $125 - €130 - £75 - FF850
  Tito Manlio uccide il gallo sul ponte Stampa
  (14.5x16.5cm 5x6in) Firenze 2001

AMMAN Marguerite 1911-1962 **[7]**
- $3 263 - €3 503 - £2 183 - FF22 976
  Selbstbildnis Gouache/paper (46.7x31cm 18x12in)
  Bern 2000

AMMIRATO Domenico 1833-? **[15]**
- $4 911 - €4 869 - £3 075 - FF31 938
  Golf von Neapel Öl/Leinwand (54.5x92cm 21x36in)
  Wien 1999
- $1 146 - €1 089 - £697 - FF7 143
  Italiaans havenplaatsje Oil/panel (19.5x12.5cm
  7x4in) Den Haag 1999

AMMON Hans XVII **[1]**
$6 706 - €5 667 - **£4 000** - FF37 174
Juno and Argus Oil/panel (95x77cm 37x30in)
London 1998

AMOEDO Rodolpho XIX **[1]**
$7 747 - €6 364 - **£4 500** - FF41 743
A young Child gathering Sticks Oil/canvas
(54.5x45cm 21x17in) London 1998

AMON Rosalia 1825-c.1907 **[4]**
$2 562 - €2 543 - **£1 599** - FF16 684
Blumenkranz Öl/Leinwand (48x40cm 18x15in) Wien
1999

AMOR Rick 1948 **[32]**
$12 579 - €13 503 - **£8 419** - FF88 576
Dog Oil/canvas (128x161cm 50x63in) Sydney 2000
$3 157 - €3 685 - **£2 229** - FF24 174
«Hitch-hiker, Baxter» Oil/canvas (76x91.5cm
29x36in) Malvern, Victoria 2000
$3 501 - €3 926 - **£2 431** - FF25 756
«Pathway by the Gardens» Oil/canvas (39x39cm
15x15in) Melbourne 2001
$415 - €399 - **£256** - FF2 620
Metal Worker at the Bridge Ink (104x74cm
40x29in) Melbourne 1998
$649 - €715 - **£435** - FF4 692
A Town by The Sea Lithograph (56.5x76cm 22x29in)
Malvern, Victoria 2000

AMORGASTI Antonio 1880-1942 **[38]**
$516 - €496 - **£322** - FF3 252
Chien de chasse Bronze (33x65cm 12x25in)
Bruxelles 1999

AMOROSI Antonio Mercurio 1660-1738 **[50]**
$17 868 - €18 294 - **£11 220** - FF120 000
Bacchus Huile/toile (74x47cm 29x18in) Lille 2000
$5 750 - €5 961 - **£3 450** - FF39 100
Il suonatore di putipú Olio/tela (45x35cm 17x13in)
Roma 1999

AMORSOLO Y CUETO Fernando 1892-1972 **[99]**
$22 956 - €26 066 - **£15 712** - FF170 984
Resting under the Tree Oil/canvas (51x66cm
20x25in) Singapore 2000
$18 752 - €18 895 - **£11 689** - FF123 942
Woman in White Oil/board (35x24cm 13x9in)
Singapore 2000
$1 736 - €1 862 - **£1 147** - FF12 214
Desnudo femenino Lápiz/papel (23x16cm 9x6in)
Madrid 2000

AMOS Imre 1907-1944/45 **[12]**
$9 240 - €10 501 - **£6 440** - FF68 880
Femme se rechauffant près d'un poèle
Huile/toile (80x70cm 31x27in) Budapest 2001
$1 092 - €1 050 - **£686** - FF6 890
Walk in Szentendre Mixed media/paper (36x28.5cm
14x11in) Budapest 1999

AMPENBERGER Stefan 1908-1983 **[15]**
$438 - €491 - **£306** - FF3 224
Figures and Cart with Cottages beyond Oil/board
(50x59.5cm 19x23in) Cape Town 2001

AMRHEIN Wilhelm 1873-1926 **[6]**
$1 603 - €1 453 - **£102** - FF9 529
«Engelberg» Poster (94x66cm 37x25in) London 1999

AMSEL Richard 1947-1985 **[14]**
$4 200 - €4 508 - **£2 810** - FF29 572
The Shootist Pencil (28x45cm 11x18in) Beverly-Hills
CA 2000

$245 - €271 - **£170** - FF1 779
«Woodstock» Poster (61x43cm 24x16in) London
2001

AMSHEWITZ John Henry 1882-1942 **[37]**
$570 - €665 - **£400** - FF4 364
«Don Quixote!» Oil/canvas (47x39.5cm 18x15in)
Crewkerne, Somerset 2000

AMSLER Samuel 1791-1849 **[6]**
$225 - €256 - **£156** - FF1 676
**Der Triumph der Religion in den Künsten, nach
Friedrich Overbeck** Radierung (59.5x50cm 23x19in)
Berlin 2001

AMSTEL van Cornelis Ploos 1726-1798 **[35]**
$3 067 - €2 949 - **£1 889** - FF19 347
Roses, carnations/Grapes, Plums and Peaches
Watercolour/paper (29x22.5cm 11x8in) Amsterdam
1999
$279 - €307 - **£190** - FF2 012
**Der auf einem Stuhl sitzende junge Mann, nach
G.van Eeckhout** Etching, aquatint (29.8x22.8cm
11x8in) Berlin 2000

AMUCHASTEGUI Axel 1921 **[12]**
$2 140 - €2 495 - **£1 500** - FF16 369
Ringtailed Coati Watercolour/paper (71x53cm
27x20in) London 2000

AMUS Eugenio 1834-1899 **[2]**
$4 835 - €4 116 - **£2 878** - FF27 000
La gardienne de moutons Huile/toile (41x65cm
16x25in) Toulouse 1998

ANASTASI Auguste Paul Charles 1820-1889 **[62]**
$8 832 - €9 757 - **£6 124** - FF64 000
Relais de chasse en Sologne Huile/toile (39x65cm
15x25in) Paris 2001
$1 639 - €1 829 - **£1 072** - FF12 000
Ferme de Linetot en Normandie Huile/panneau
(27.5x47cm 10x18in) Fontainebleau 2000
$529 - €534 - **£330** - FF3 500
Paysage Fusain/papier (25x29.5cm 9x11in) Paris 2000

ANATOL Anatol Herzfeld 1931 **[64]**
$1 000 - €1 125 - **£702** - FF7 378
«Sonnenwiedergeburt» Mixed media (50x50x7cm
19x19x2in) Düsseldorf 2001
$308 - €358 - **£212** - FF2 347
Guten Tag Watercolour, gouache (23.5x28cm 9x11in)
Köln 2000

ANCELET Émile c.1865-? **[25]**
$1 233 - €1 220 - **£770** - FF8 000
Quinéville Huile/carton (24x33cm 9x12in) Cherbourg
1999
$2 988 - €2 744 - **£1 825** - FF18 000
Les meules en été, effet de soleil Pastel/papier
(50x65cm 19x25in) Deauville 1998

ANCELET Gabriel Auguste XIX **[5]**
$2 250 - €2 212 - **£1 445** - FF14 510
Romanesque Church Watercolour/paper (27.5x38cm
10x14in) New-York 1999

ANCHER Anna 1859-1935 **[106]**
$27 048 - €30 873 - **£18 791** - FF202 515
Fiskegarnene redes Oil/canvas (52x64cm 20x25in)
København 2000
$4 293 - €4 166 - **£2 607** - FF27 326
Portraet af en fiskerkone Oil/canvas/panel
(28x22cm 11x8in) Viby J, Århus 2000
$1 090 - €1 050 - **£678** - FF6 889
Efter gudstjenesten Pencil/paper (17.5x22.5cm
6x8in) København 1999

$186 - €201 - £128 - FF1 319
Interior med gammel laesende kone Etching
(12x11cm 4x4in) Köbenhavn 2001

ANCHER Helga 1883-1964 **[20]**
$3 353 - €3 621 - £2 316 - FF23 751
Interior med en gammel kone ved et vindue
Oil/canvas (50x43cm 19x16in) Köbenhavn 2001
$1 821 - €1 674 - £1 125 - FF10 983
Vinterlandskab Oil/canvas (33x43cm 12x16in) Vejle
1998

ANCHER Michael 1849-1927 **[446]**
$747 600 - €804 382 - £508 800 - FF5 276 400
Pigerne på stranden Oil/canvas (81x163cm 31x64in)
Köbenhavn 2001
$6 665 - €6 717 - £4 155 - FF44 060
Der hygges i dagligstuen på Kruseminde
Oil/canvas (68x60cm 26x23in) Köbenhavn 2000
$3 390 - €3 361 - £2 120 - FF22 047
Glade Elsie Oil/panel (40x32cm 15x12in) Köbenhavn
1999
$546 - €511 - £340 - FF3 353
Ung fiskerkone Pencil/paper (16x16cm 6x6in)
Köbenhavn 1999

ANCKERMANN Ricardo 1842-1907 **[6]**
$10 720 - €9 610 - £6 560 - FF63 040
Los concellers de Barcelona y Alfonso V
Oleo/lienzo (90x150cm 35x59in) Madrid 1999

ANCONA d'Vito 1825-1884 **[11]**
$27 500 - €28 508 - £16 500 - FF187 000
Le belle e la scimmia Olio/tela (35x49cm 13x19in)
Prato 1999
$21 500 - €22 288 - £12 900 - FF146 200
Figura femminile di profilo con ventaglio
Olio/tavola (34x26cm 13x10in) Milano 2000

ANDENMATTEN Leo 1922-1979 **[15]**
$3 212 - €3 097 - £1 980 - FF20 314
Nonnen vor einer Kirche Oil/canvas/panel
(51x59cm 20x23in) Bern 1999
$2 891 - €2 787 - £1 782 - FF18 283
Stilleben mit Äpfeln und blauer Vase Öl/Leinwand
(27x35cm 10x13in) Bern 1999

ANDER Ture 1881-1959 **[19]**
$1 020 - €1 131 - £692 - FF7 416
**Interiör med blomsterstilleben (Still Life with
Flowers)** Oil/canvas (59x48cm 23x18in) Stockholm
2000

ANDERBOUHR Paul Jean 1909 **[18]**
$1 760 - €1 982 - £1 225 - FF13 000
Kasba, Maroc Huile/toile (51x61cm 20x24in) Nice
1999

ANDERLE Jiri 1936 **[82]**
$1 011 - €957 - £630 - FF6 275
Adam a Eve Huile/toile (25x60cm 9x23in) Praha
2000
$140 - €132 - £87 - FF869
Versuch einer Annäherung Lithographie (52x63cm
20x24in) Praha 1999

ANDERLECHT van Engelbert 1918-1961 **[37]**
$552 - €545 - £343 - FF3 577
Composition No.474 Encre (50x65cm 19x25in)
Liège 1999

ANDERS Ernest 1845-1911 **[19]**
$7 964 - €8 289 - £5 000 - FF54 373
Motherly Affection Oil/canvas (87x55cm 34x21in)
London 2000

ANDERSEN Cilius 1865-1913 **[59]**
$9 408 - €10 739 - £6 536 - FF70 440
To skovnymfer, der driller en satyr Oil/canvas
(95x146cm 37x57in) Köbenhavn 2000
$2 622 - €2 411 - £1 620 - FF15 816
Interiör med rygvendt kvinde i sollys Oil/canvas
(38x45cm 14x17in) Vejle 1998

ANDERSEN Ib 1907-1969 **[32]**
$522 - €511 - £322 - FF3 350
«Politiken» Affiche (173x62cm 68x24in) Paris 1999

ANDERSEN Mogens Helge 1916 **[170]**
$6 971 - €7 775 - £4 843 - FF50 999
Komposition Oil/canvas (146x114cm 57x44in)
Köbenhavn 2001
$1 685 - €1 877 - £1 184 - FF12 310
Komposition Oil/canvas (65x54cm 25x21in) Vejle
2001
$555 - €538 - £349 - FF3 532
Komposition Oil/canvas (22x27cm 8x10in)
Köbenhavn 1999
$66 - €672 - £415 - FF4 406
Komposition Indian ink (58.5x53cm 23x20in)
Köbenhavn 1999

ANDERSEN Nils 1897-1972 **[39]**
$621 - €599 - £383 - FF3 926
Durban Harbour Oil/canvas/board (44.5x60cm
17x23in) Johannesburg 1999

ANDERSEN Robin Christian 1890-1969 **[78]**
$3 443 - €3 997 - £2 420 - FF26 218
Stilleben mit Orangen und Blauem Krug
Öl/Leinwand (51x65cm 20x25in) Wien 2001
$2 348 - €2 761 - £1 630 - FF18 114
Früchtestilleben Öl/Karton (40.5x34.5cm 15x13in)
Wien 2000
$685 - €654 - £417 - FF4 290
**Entwurf für ein Glasfenster der Austria Tabak
Linz** Charcoal (45.5x60cm 17x23in) Wien 1999

ANDERSEN Roy 1930 **[24]**
$42 500 - €38 635 - £25 597 - FF253 427
Pretty Shield Finds the Buffalo Sign Oil/canvas
(101x152cm 40x60in) Hayden ID 1998
$19 000 - €21 574 - £13 201 - FF141 513
Strong Heart Sings Oil/canvas (76x50cm 30x20in)
Dallas TX 2001
$8 000 - €9 084 - £5 558 - FF59 584
Strong Heart Oil/canvas (30x40cm 12x16in) Dallas
TX 2001
$10 000 - €11 355 - £6 948 - FF74 481
The Crooked Lance Watercolour (76x71cm 30x28in)
Dallas TX 2001

ANDERSEN Valdemar 1875-1928 **[23]**
$5 023 - €5 631 - £3 511 - FF36 939
Henri Nathansen siddende i en have Oil/canvas
(51x51cm 20x20in) Köbenhavn 2001
$179 - €204 - £125 - FF1 339
«Den Hollandske Udstilling» Poster (61x85.5cm
24x33in) Hoorn 2001

ANDERSEN-LUNDBY Anders 1840-1923 **[151]**
$12 275 - €14 465 - £8 625 - FF94 887
Winter in Oberbayern Oil/canvas (105x175cm
41x68in) Malmö 2000
$4 284 - €8 333 - £2 567 - FF25 142
Schnee liegt in der Luft Öl/Leinwand (75x73cm
29x28in) Hamburg 1998
$1 350 - €1 208 - £809 - FF7 922
**Stranden Vedbaek, Fiskere ved deres optrukne
både på stranden** Oil/canvas (25x34cm 9x13in)
Köbenhavn 1998

ANDERSON Abraham Archibald 1847-1940 [3]
$5 500 - €6 329 - **£3 791** - FF41 514
  Portrait of Louise Van Beuren Bond Oil/canvas (96x71cm 38x28in) New-Orleans LA 2000

ANDERSON Alfred Charles S. 1884-1966 [12]
$2 133 - €1 792 - **£1 250** - FF11 752
  Thatching the New Rick Watercolour/paper (22x31cm 8x12in) Billingshurst, West-Sussex 1998
$522 - €594 - **£360** - FF3 894
  Quai Duperré, La Rochelle Drypoint (20.5x33.5cm 8x13in) London 2000

ANDERSON Clayton 1964 [4]
$1 340 - €1 478 - **£886** - FF9 697
  Row and Be Damned Bluff Acrylic/canvas (38x76cm 14x29in) Vancouver, BC. 2000

ANDERSON Domenico 1854-1939 [6]
$600 - €716 - **£428** - FF4 695
  Rom und Neapel Albumen print (27x41cm 10x16in) München 2000

ANDERSON Gary XX [1]
$4 177 - €4 022 - **£2 600** - FF26 384
  Eleven Flowers Acrylic (15x15cm 5x5in) London 1999

ANDERSON Harry 1906-1996 [17]
$2 500 - €2 914 - **£1 731** - FF19 116
  Gardening Woman Interrupted by Man And Bull-Dog Gouache/paper (53x44cm 21x17in) New-York 2000

ANDERSON J.W., Captain XIX [4]
$5 642 - €6 585 - **£4 000** - FF43 196
  Royal Yacht Squadron's schooner rounding the Nab lighting Oil/canvas (45.5x66cm 17x25in) London 2001

ANDERSON James Isaac Atkinson 1813-1877 [8]
$3 218 - €3 125 - **£1 988** - FF20 500
  Le Colisée/Cloître de la Basilique San Paolo Fuori Le Mura Tirage albuminé (28.5x37cm 11x14in) Paris 1999

ANDERSON John MacVicar 1835-1915 [3]
$70 150 - €83 429 - **£50 000** - FF547 260
  View of Waterloo Bridge Oil/canvas (92.5x183cm 36x72in) London 2000
$112 273 - €111 060 - **£70 000** - FF728 504
  The Thames from Hungerford Bridge Oil/canvas (76x152.5cm 29x60in) London 1999

ANDERSON Karl J. 1874-1956 [9]
$5 500 - €4 695 - **£3 289** - FF30 795
  «Children at an Abandoned Well» Oil/canvas (73x68cm 29x27in) New-York 1998

ANDERSON Oscar 1873-1953 [14]
$1 800 - €1 670 - **£1 080** - FF10 957
  Late Autumn Oil/canvas (63x76cm 25x30in) Milford CT 1999

ANDERSON Robert 1842-1885 [18]
$581 - €505 - **£350** - FF3 314
  Haying Scene near Thatched Cottage Watercolour/paper (26.5x38cm 10x14in) Toronto 1998

ANDERSON Sophia Gengembre 1823-1903 [36]
$18 960 - €18 068 - **£11 500** - FF118 516
  Study of a Young Girl asleep in an Armchair Oil/canvas (53x43cm 21x17in) Stratford-upon-Avon, Warwickshire 1999
$14 890 - €13 969 - **£9 200** - FF91 631
  Shoulder Length Portrait of a young Lady holding bundle of Flowers Oil/canvas (34x28cm 13x11in) Dorking, Surrey 1999

ANDERSON Victor Coleman 1882-1973 [10]
$5 000 - €5 547 - **£3 325** - FF36 383
  The Young Patriot Oil/canvas/board (50x40cm 20x16in) Milford CT 2000

ANDERSON Walter Inglis 1903-1965 [14]
$3 800 - €3 602 - **£2 373** - FF23 628
  Toad Fish Watercolour/paper (21x27cm 8x11in) New-Orleans LA 1999
$900 - €868 - **£565** - FF5 696
  Old King Cole Woodcut (186x49cm 73x19in) New-Orleans LA 1999

ANDERSON Wayne 1946 [42]
$651 - €740 - **£450** - FF4 857
  Angry Man in the Moon Falling Towards a Child/Child at the Door Coloured crayons/paper (22.5x35cm 8x13in) London 2000

ANDERSON Will ?-c.1895 [6]
$271 - €294 - **£180** - FF1 928
  Farmyard Scene with Figures Resting in a Field Watercolour (18x46.5cm 7x18in) Billingshurst, West-Sussex 2000

ANDERSON William 1757-1837 [82]
$13 633 - €13 486 - **£8 500** - FF88 461
  View on the River Thames with Westminster Bridge Oil/canvas (52x67.5cm 20x26in) London 1999
$8 902 - €8 380 - **£5 500** - FF54 969
  An Offshore Anchorage with a Man-o'War firing a Salute Oil/panel (16.5x24cm 6x9in) London 1999
$3 928 - €4 672 - **£2 800** - FF30 646
  The Attack on Curacao on January 1st Watercolour (12x18cm 4x7in) London 2000

ANDERSSON Mårten 1934 [32]
$14 659 - €17 010 - **£10 121** - FF111 577
  Mannen som lyssnar på fågelsången Oil/canvas (111x162cm 43x63in) Stockholm 2000
$763 - €715 - **£458** - FF4 689
  Religiöst motiv Gouache/paper (38x28cm 14x11in) Stockholm 1999
$652 - €550 - **£387** - FF3 605
  Italienska trädgårdar Color lithograph (46x36cm 18x14in) Stockholm 1998

ANDERSSON Nils 1817-1865 [23]
$1 852 - €1 616 - **£1 120** - FF10 599
  Bergigt landskap med kor Oil/canvas (46x56cm 18x22in) Stockholm 1998

ANDERSSON Torsten 1926 [16]
$7 327 - €8 209 - **£5 107** - FF53 850
  Ansikte Oil/canvas/panel (48x38cm 18x14in) Stockholm 2001
$4 895 - €5 458 - **£3 400** - FF35 800
  Komposition Oil/canvas (42x33cm 16x12in) Stockholm 2001

ANDESSNER Irene 1954 [28]
$520 - €509 - **£330** - FF3 336
  Kopf Mischtechnik/Papier (55x43cm 21x16in) Salzburg 1999

ANDOE Joe 1955 [44]
$8 500 - €8 870 - **£5 361** - FF58 182
  Dog Oil/canvas (178x213.5cm 70x84in) New-York 2000
$2 000 - €2 230 - **£1 344** - FF14 628
  Tower Oil/canvas (91.5x117cm 36x46in) New-York 2000

ANDORFF Paul 1849-1920 [8]
$1 098 - €1 227 - **£744** - FF8 049
  Ohne Titel Oil/panel (19.5x27cm 7x10in) Saarbrücken 2000

ANDRADA de José XX [2]
- $33 120 – €30 490 – **£19 880** – FF200 000
  Le Salon Huile/toile (120x128cm 47x50in) Saint-Germain-en-Laye 1999

ANDRADA Elsa 1920 [9]
- $1 525 – €1 502 – **£950** – FF9 850
  La Casa del Reloj Oleo/lienzo (60x81cm 23x31in) Madrid 1999

ANDRADE BLASQUEZ Angel 1866-1932 [24]
- $4 560 – €4 805 – **£2 880** – FF31 520
  A la feria Oleo/lienzo (41x56cm 16x22in) Madrid 2000

ANDRAE Elisabeth 1876-1945 [7]
- $511 – €511 – **£320** – FF3 353
  Flusslandschaft mit Eisenbrücke Öl/Leinwand (63x75cm 24x29in) München 1999

ANDRAU XX [8]
- $6 115 – €6 403 – **£3 843** – FF42 000
  Femme nue Plâtre (H140cm H55in) Toulouse 2000
- $670 – €762 – **£460** – FF5 000
  Femme drapée Plâtre (H79cm H31in) Toulouse 2000

ANDRÉ Albert 1869-1954 [234]
- $13 717 – €12 806 – **£8 307** – FF84 000
  Bouquet de fleurs Huile/toile (55x46cm 21x18in) Besançon 1999
- $3 452 – €3 887 – **£2 404** – FF25 500
  Nature morte Huile/carton (25x31cm 9x12in) Nice 2001
- $905 – €991 – **£624** – FF6 500
  Femme au fauteuil Aquarelle/papier (22.5x21.5cm 8x8in) Paris 2001

ANDRE Carl 1935 [117]
- $14 000 – €15 681 – **£9 727** – FF102 860
  Door, a God Enamel (31.5x30.5cm 12x12in) New-York 2001
- $190 000 – €212 443 – **£128 079** – FF1 393 536
  Lead-Zine Plain Installation (183x183x5cm 72x72x1in) New-York 2000
- $48 831 – €47 526 – **£30 000** – FF311 748
  Venus Arc Installation (0.5x270x540cm x106x212in) London 1999
- $25 000 – €28 281 – **£17 490** – FF185 512
  Flags, an Opera for Three Voices Ink/paper (21.5x28cm 8x11in) New-York 1999

ANDRÉ Jean XX [5]
- $1 596 – €1 524 – **£1 005** – FF10 000
  L'éléphant Bronze (26x45x13cm 10x17x5in) Deauville 1999

ANDRÉ-SPITZ 1884-1977 [2]
- $67 440 – €76 695 – **£46 770** – FF503 085
  Versuchung Öl/Leinwand (29.2x36cm 11x14in) Hamburg 2000

ANDREA DI BARTOLO ?-1428 [6]
- $65 450 – €67 849 – **£39 270** – FF445 060
  Cristo benedicente Tempera/tavola (58.5x37cm 23x14in) Venezia 2000
- $164 373 – €176 441 – **£110 000** – FF1 157 376
  St Martin and the Beggar/St Benedict/St Stephen/St Lawrence/St Antony Tempera (51x20cm 20x7in) London 2000

ANDRÉA Kees 1914 [42]
- $1 292 – €1 271 – **£830** – FF8 334
  Kings in a hilly Landscape Oil/canvas (60.5x80cm 23x31in) Amsterdam 1999
- $823 – €908 – **£537** – FF5 953
  Ezels in de sneeuw in de Voorde Oil/panel (28x38cm 11x14in) Den Haag 1999

ANDREA Nicolaus c.1550-? [1]
- $1 475 – €1 431 – **£918** – FF9 390
  Bildnis des Juristen Stanislaus Sabinus von Stracza aus Wilna Kupferstich (42.4x32.6cm 16x12in) Berlin 1999

ANDREA Pat 1942 [59]
- $3 783 – €4 573 – **£2 643** – FF30 000
  El Latino Huile/toile (160x175cm 62x68in) Paris 2000
- $1 857 – €1 677 – **£1 145** – FF11 000
  «Nature and genlus» Technique mixte (34x38cm 13x14in) Paris 1999
- $968 – €892 – **£583** – FF5 853
  La dispute Technique mixte/papier (80x102cm 31x40in) Antwerpen 1999

ANDREAE Tobias 1823-1873 [2]
- $4 663 – €4 346 – **£2 877** – FF28 508
  Mondnacht am Chiemsee Oil/panel (35x69cm 13x27in) Köln 1999

ANDREANI Andrea c.1546-1623 [27]
- $1 420 – €1 374 – **£900** – FF9 014
  Virtue, after Ligozzi Woodcut (47x32.5cm 18x12in) London 1999

ANDREAS A. c.1864-1899 [3]
- $700 – €781 – **£458** – FF5 122
  «Exposition de Murer, les ciels de France» Poster (120x77cm 47x30in) New-York 2000

ANDRÉASSON Folke 1902-1948 [26]
- $1 976 – €1 723 – **£1 195** – FF11 305
  Blomsterstilleben Oil/panel (61x49.5cm 24x19in) Stockholm 1998

ANDREENKO Mikhail, Michel 1894-1982 [60]
- $1 262 – €1 067 – **£751** – FF7 000
  Composition abstraite Gouache/papier (33.5x42cm 13x16in) Vittel 1998

ANDREINI Ferdinando 1843-? [5]
- $40 000 – €37 030 – **£24 148** – FF242 900
  Psyche Marble (H229.5cm H90in) New-York 1999

ANDREIS de Alex XIX-XX [86]
- $1 965 – €2 059 – **£1 300** – FF13 507
  Study of a Cardinal, Reading in a Library Oil/panel (51.5x45cm 20x17in) Billingshurst, West-Sussex 2000
- $800 – €736 – **£480** – FF4 829
  Bust Length Portrait of a Cavalier Holding a Sword Oil/canvas (39x31cm 15x12in) Detroit MI 1999

ANDREONI Cesare 1903-1961 [11]
- $650 – €6 479 – **£3 750** – FF42 500
  Ricostruzione Olio/tela (73x52.5cm 28x20in) Milano 2000

ANDREOTTI Federico 1847-1930 [100]
- $103 896 – €104 693 – **£64 765** – FF686 743
  The Wedding Dance Oil/canvas (91.5x136.5cm 36x53in) London 2000
- $17 000 – €18 687 – **£10 893** – FF122 576
  The Flower Seller Oil/canvas (105.5x78.5cm 41x30in) New-York 2000
- $3 800 – €4 924 – **£2 850** – FF32 300
  L'oste Olio/tela (30x28cm 11x11in) Milano 2000

ANDREOTTI Libero 1875-1933 [9]
- $6 000 – €6 220 – **£3 600** – FF40 800
  Figura femminile con levriero Bronzo (46x26cm 18x10in) Milano 2000

ANDREU Mariano 1888-1977 [78]
- $6 080 – €5 706 – **£3 800** – FF37 430
  Descargando en el puerto Oleo/lienzo (73x82cm 28x32in) Madrid 1999

$4 357 - €4 116 - **£2 635** - FF27 000
Nus Huile/panneau (26x31.5cm 10x12in) Paris 1999

$1 220 - €1 201 - **£780** - FF7 880
Cabeza de mujer Acuarela/papel (13x10cm 5x3in) Madrid 1999

$65 - €76 - **£45** - FF500
Place Vendôme rue de la Paix, Paris Lithographie (75x105cm 29x41in) Paris 2000

ANDREWS Benny 1930 [12]

$1 700 - €1 758 - **£1 074** - FF11 533
Emil Arnold, Study Oil/canvas (42x37cm 16x14in) New-York 2000

ANDREWS Edith Alice Cubitt XIX-XX [25]

$462 - €539 - **£320** - FF3 533
Still Life Depicting Flowers in a Vase by a Window Watercolour/paper (42x31cm 16x12in) Loughton, Essex 2000

ANDREWS Edward William XIX-XX [4]

$8 509 - €9 879 - **£6 000** - FF64 799
Robert Lever of Great Bolton/James Lever, his son/His wife Elisabeth Oil/canvas (76x63.5cm 29x25in) London 2001

ANDREWS George Henry 1816-1898 [28]

$2 932 - €2 669 - **£1 800** - FF17 508
Travellers on a Hill before an Eastern City Oil/canvas (61x106.5cm 24x41in) London 1999

$1 648 - €1 509 - **£1 000** - FF9 901
Unloading the Day's Catch before Ambleteuse Castle, Normandy Watercolour (38x63.5cm 14x25in) London 1999

ANDREWS Henry 1794-1868 [32]

$13 039 - €11 856 - **£8 000** - FF77 767
Hunting Party Oil/canvas (112x173cm 44x68in) London 1999

$7 229 - €6 962 - **£4 500** - FF45 666
The Wedding Feadt Oil/canvas (66x81.5cm 25x32in) London 1999

$9 739 - €9 365 - **£6 000** - FF61 430
Proposal not present/The Bit of Scandal Oil/panel (38x31.5cm 14x12in) London 1999

ANDREWS John 1736-1809 [1]

$5 750 - €6 420 - **£3 843** - FF42 110
New and Accurate View of the Country Twenty-Five Miles Round London Engraving (125x137cm 49x54in) New-York 2000

ANDREWS Sybil 1898-1992 [279]

$6 491 - €7 340 - **£4 568** - FF48 150
Daniel Bran, Shipwright and Boat Builder Oil/canvas (56x68.5cm 22x26in) Vancouver, BC. 2001

$2 891 - €2 785 - **£1 800** - FF18 266
Design for Wembley Arena Ice Hockey Poster Watercolour (25.5x58.5cm 10x23in) London 1999

$1 088 - €1 041 - **£682** - FF6 826
Indian Dance Linocut in colors (26.5x25cm 10x9in) Vancouver, BC. 1999

ANDRI Ferdinand 1871-1956 [76]

$2 325 - €2 180 - **£1 437** - FF14 301
Motiv aus Lassing am Hochkar Öl/Karton (30.3x41cm 11x16in) Wien 2000

$397 - €436 - **£264** - FF2 860
Entwurf zur Sezessions-Ausstellung Pencil (21x43.5cm 8x17in) Wien 2000

$165 - €182 - **£106** - FF1 191
Henne mit Kühen beim Futternapf Woodcut in colors (15.8x16.6cm 6x6in) Wien 2000

ANDRIEN Mady 1941 [5]

$1 344 - €1 487 - **£936** - FF9 756
Saute-mouton Sculpture (H43cm H16in) Liège 2001

ANDRIES Jacob 1710-1788 [1]

$14 881 - €14 056 - **£9 000** - FF92 199
The Offering of Abigail/Solomon and the Queen of Sheba Oil/canvas (48x59.5cm 18x23in) London 1999

ANDRIESSE Emmy 1914-1953 [7]

$992 - €1 180 - **£707** - FF7 739
Aardbeziënverkoopster Silver print (34x31cm 13x12in) Amsterdam 2000

ANDRIESSE Erik 1957-1993 [3]

$7 069 - €6 807 - **£4 420** - FF44 649
Amaryllis Oil/canvas (70x55cm 27x21in) Amsterdam 1999

ANDRIESSEN Anthony 1746-1813 [17]

$446 - €386 - **£269** - FF2 829
Kneeling figure shooting in a forest Black chalk/paper (20.3x15.8cm 7x6in) Amsterdam 1998

ANDRIESSEN Juriaan 1742-1819 [19]

$18 000 - €19 749 - **£11 957** - FF129 542
The Contest of Minerva and Neptune Oil/canvas (61x159cm 24x62in) New-York 2000

ANDRIESSEN Mari 1897-1979 [45]

$1 367 - €1 588 - **£960** - FF10 418
Two figures with horse Bronze (H19cm H7in) Amsterdam 2001

ANDRIEUX Auguste Clément 1829-c.1890 [23]

$2 460 - €2 897 - **£1 729** - FF19 000
Autoportrait présumé de l'artiste à son chevalet Huile/papier/panneau (25x19cm 9x7in) Paris 2000

ANDRIUOLI Mimmo 1946 [40]

$500 - €518 - **£300** - FF3 400
«Piano Bar» Olio/tavola (50x50cm 19x19in) Vercelli 2001

$275 - €285 - **£165** - FF1 870
«Folla» Olio/tela (40x30cm 15x11in) Vercelli 2001

ANDRUS Vera Eugenia 1895-1979 [10]

$275 - €258 - **£169** - FF1 843
Spring/Cat-Walk/Girl from Guatemala/Lanterns Lithograph (29.5x21.5cm 11x8in) New-York 1999

ANELAY Henry 1817-1883 [2]

$20 000 - €17 255 - **£12 066** - FF113 186
Ferdinand and Miranda Watercolour, gouache (59x46cm 23x18in) New-York 1998

ANESI Paolo 1697-1773 [33]

$100 000 - €101 164 - **£61 060** - FF663 590
View of the Tiber, Rome, with the Ponte Rotto Oil/canvas (95.5x133cm 37x52in) New-York 2000

$15 767 - €16 681 - **£10 000** - FF109 417
Rome, a View of Tivoli with the Temple of the Tiburtine Sibyl Oil/canvas (48.5x63.5cm 19x25in) London 2000

$6 750 - €6 997 - **£4 050** - FF45 900
Paesaggio con acquedotto/Paesaggio con rovine Olio/tela (40x30cm 15x11in) Milano 1999

ANETHAN d' Alix 1848-1921 [1]

$1 902 - €2 134 - **£1 318** - FF14 000
La lettre Huile/panneau (31x27cm 12x10in) Paris 2000

ANFRIE Charles 1833-1905 [38]

$1 081 - €1 067 - **£666** - FF7 000
Le fantassin Bronze (H46cm H18in) Paris 1999

ANG KIUKOK 1931 [15]
$8 034 - €9 123 - £5 499 - FF59 844
Bananas Oil/board (30.5x81.5cm 12x32in) Singapore 2000

$3 751 - €3 496 - £2 314 - FF22 930
Scream Tempera/paper (44.5x30cm 17x11in) Singapore 1999

ANGAS George French 1822-1886 [18]
$17 700 - €19 502 - £11 883 - FF127 923
Images From The South Australian Great Northern Exploring Expedition Ink/paper (12.5x19cm 4x7in) Malvern, Victoria 2000

$172 - €200 - £119 - FF1 314
Malay Creale Boy, Malay Boy Of Cape Town/Hottentot Herdboys/Hottentot Color lithograph (25x16cm 9x6in) Johannesburg 2000

ANGELI d' Giovanni Battista XVI [3]
$516 - €613 - £357 - FF4 024
Die Madonna mit dem Christusknaben Kupferstich (24.5x32.8cm 9x12in) Köln 2000

ANGELI Eduard 1942 [50]
$1 344 - €1 599 - £959 - FF10 487
Stille Mischtechnik/Papier (61x93cm 24x36in) Wien 2000

ANGELI Filippo Napoletano 1587/91-c.1630 [14]
$7 020 - €7 808 - £4 680 - FF51 220
Paisaje fluvial con castillo y Leto convirtiendo a los campesinos Oleo/lienzo (93x91.5cm 36x36in) Madrid 2000

$1 538 - €1 829 - £1 066 - FF12 000
Navire dans une tempête Lavis (16x26cm 6x10in) Paris 2000

ANGELI Franco 1935-1988 [479]
$2 023 - €2 097 - £1 213 - FF13 756
Half dollar Acrilico/tela (150x100cm 59x39in) Venezia 1999

$1 150 - €1 192 - £690 - FF7 820
Simboli americani Smalto/tela (70x120cm 27x47in) Vercelli 2000

$750 - €777 - £450 - FF5 100
Il giovane al cinema Tecnica mista (35x25cm 13x9in) Roma 2000

$750 - €777 - £450 - FF5 100
Senza titolo Acquarello (101x71cm 39x27in) Prato 2000

ANGELI Giuseppe 1712-1798 [13]
$15 960 - €13 583 - £9 500 - FF89 099
The Madonna and Child with Saint Anthony of Padua Oil/canvas (55x65cm 21x25in) London 1998

ANGELI von Heinrich, Baron 1840-1925 [25]
$1 825 - €1 611 - £1 274 - FF10 566
Romeo and Juliet Oil/canvas (67x51cm 26x20in) London 1998

$1 260 - €1 483 - £903 - FF9 726
«Miss Bell» Oil/panel (30x24cm 11x9in) Hamburg 2001

ANGELIS de Pietro XVIII [6]
$1 813 - €2 134 - £1 274 - FF14 000
Le char de Bacchus, projet de plafond Aquarelle (17.5x24.5cm 6x9in) Paris 2000

ANGELL COLEMAN Helen Cordelia 1847-1884 [20]
$4 209 - €5 006 - £3 000 - FF32 835
Pink and White Peonies in a Bowl Watercolour (40.5x56cm 15x22in) London 2000

ANGELO Pal Funk / Paul 1894-1974 [9]
$795 - €915 - £547 - FF6 000
Étude de nu féminin Tirage argentique (23x16cm 9x6in) Chartres 2000

ANGELO Valenti XX [4]
$950 - €1 079 - £650 - FF7 079
Chemical Plant Lithograph (33x25.5cm 12x10in) New-York 2000

ANGELUCCIO c.1620-c.1650 [1]
$32 000 - €31 985 - £19 548 - FF209 808
Park Landscape with Elegant Figures Conversing Oil/canvas (64.5x66.5cm 25x26in) New-York 2000

ANGENENDT Erich 1894-1962 [4]
$398 - €470 - £282 - FF3 085
Fabrik-Werkstatt Vintage gelatin silver print (23x29cm 9x11in) Berlin 2001

ANGERER Ludwig 1827-1879 [10]
$636 - €534 - £373 - FF3 500
Bukarest, vue perspective Tirage papier salé (20.7x26.8cm 8x10in) Paris 1998

ANGERER Max 1877-1955 [6]
$2 031 - €2 180 - £1 386 - FF14 301
Das Karwendel von der Vomper Wiese Öl/Leinwand (42x57cm 16x22in) Wien 2001

ANGERMANN Peter 1945 [7]
$1 020 - €881 - £510 - FF5 780
«Sonnenuntergang» Olio/tela (40x50cm 15x19in) Prato 1999

ANGERMEYER Johann Adalbert 1674-1740 [7]
$20 188 - €20 348 - £12 600 - FF133 476
Zwei Füchse pflegen einen Hund Öl/Kupfer (18.5x29.5cm 7x11in) Wien 2000

ANGILLIS Pieter 1685-c.1734 [35]
$5 230 - €5 614 - £3 500 - FF36 825
Still Life of Vegetables with a Flower Girl Oil/canvas (52.5x46cm 20x18in) London 2000

ANGKARN KALAYANAPONGSA 1926 [16]
$10 146 - €9 425 - £6 270 - FF61 826
The Righteous Way Oil/canvas (103x74cm 40x29in) Bangkok 1999

$2 040 - €2 194 - £1 368 - FF14 302
The Best Face Crayon (68x50cm 26x19in) Bangkok 2000

ANGLADA CAMARASA Hermenegildo 1873-1959 [40]
$418 404 - €449 122 - £280 000 - FF2 946 048
Olivos, Valle de son March (Olive Trees) Oil/canvas (105x145cm 41x57in) London 2001

$26 000 - €30 032 - £18 000 - FF197 000
Desnudo Oleo/lienzo (58x43.5cm 22x17in) Madrid 2001

$19 425 - €20 852 - £13 000 - FF136 780
Troncs (Tree Trunk) Oil/panel (32x49.5cm 12x19in) London 2001

$7 810 - €6 607 - £4 620 - FF43 340
Jaleo Flamenco Lápiz (19.5x24cm 7x9in) Madrid 1998

ANGLADA PINTO Luis 1873-1946 [14]
$1 307 - €1 265 - £828 - FF8 300
Fillette au foulard vert Huile/toile (46x38cm 18x14in) Paris 1999

ANGLADA SARRIERA Lola 1892-1984 [5]
$870 - €901 - £555 - FF5 910
Vista de Gerona Acuarela/papel (23x31cm 9x12in) Barcelona 2000

ANGLADE Gaston 1854-1919 [164]

$955 - €915 - **£588** - FF6 000
Champ de bruyères dominant la vallée
Huile/toile (46x65cm 18x25in) Calais 1999
$995 - €915 - **£611** - FF6 000
Saint-Denis près de Matel Lot Huile/toile
(25x34cm 9x13in) Guéret 1999

ANGO Jean-Robert act.1759-c.1773 [52]

$994 - €1 067 - **£665** - FF7 000
**Vue intérieure de Saint-Pierre de Rome, d'après
Hubert Robert** Sanguine/papier (32x22.5cm 12x8in)
Paris 2000

ANGRAND Charles 1854-1926 [45]

$4 408 - €5 031 - **£3 062** - FF33 000
Scieurs et fillette près d'une maison Huile/toile
(50x65cm 19x25in) Paris 2000
$8 009 - €8 766 - **£5 525** - FF57 500
Petite ferme Huile/panneau (19x27cm 7x10in) Paris
2001
$5 084 - €5 793 - **£3 492** - FF38 000
Maternité Crayon/papier (59x34cm 23x16in) Paris
2000

ANGRAVE Bruce ?-1983 [2]

$1 341 - €1 556 - **£950** - FF10 205
**«South Wales for Bracing Holidays, GWR,
Atlantic Breezes,Golden Sands»** Poster
(100x62cm 39x24in) London 2000

ANGUIANO Raúl 1915 [56]

$4 320 - €4 355 - **£2 692** - FF28 564
Muchacha de Cuetzalan Oleo/lienzo (105x80cm
41x31in) México 2000
$2 000 - €1 690 - **£1 193** - FF11 086
La Pensiva Pastel/paper (65x51cm 26x20in) San-
Francisco CA 1998
$750 - €832 - **£499** - FF5 458
Dos mujeres platicando Litografía (72x95cm
28x37in) México 2000

ANGUIER Michel 1612/14-1686 [8]

$5 895 - €5 477 - **£3 600** - FF35 928
Bacchus and Amphirite Bronze (H37cm H14in)
London 1998

ANGUISCIOLA Lucia ?-1565 [1]

$35 884 - €33 562 - **£22 000** - FF220 154
**Sofonisba Anguisciola, half length, Wearing a
Red Doublet** Oil/panel (12x9cm 4x3in) London 1998

ANGUISCIOLA Sofonisba c.1527-1625/26 [6]

$14 000 - €14 513 - **£8 400** - FF95 200
Corteo di donne che escono da una città
Olio/tela (150x116cm 59x45in) Venezia 2000
$42 500 - €40 569 - **£26 554** - FF266 118
Portrait of a Nobleman Oil/canvas (123x95cm
48x37in) New-York 1999

ANGUS John 1821-? [4]

$5 760 - €5 949 - **£3 624** - FF39 024
Dame à la guitare Huile/panneau (43x38cm 16x14in)
Antwerpen 2000

ANGUS Maria L. XIX-XX [18]

$2 480 - €2 343 - **£1 500** - FF15 366
Hermia Watercolour/paper (24x16.5cm 9x6in)
Billingshurst, West-Sussex 1999

ANGUS Rita XX [5]

$14 108 - €15 814 - **£9 866** - FF103 733
Sunset, North Canterbury Oil/canvas (25.5x33cm
10x12in) Auckland 2001
$8 488 - €9 670 - **£5 866** - FF63 432
The Sawmill Site, Maungataniwha, Hawkes Bay
Watercolour/paper (27.5x38cm 10x14in) Auckland 2000

ANISFELD Boris Israelovich 1878-1973 [21]

$20 000 - €17 052 - **£12 066** - FF111 856
«Islamé, Design for the Decor» Oil/canvas
(61x84.5cm 24x33in) New-York 1998
$3 779 - €4 170 - **£2 500** - FF27 353
The Circus Watercolour (23x31cm 9x12in) London
2000

ANIVITTI Filippo 1876-1955 [61]

$2 056 - €2 339 - **£1 436** - FF15 342
Spanska Trappan, Rom Oil/canvas (40x48cm
15x18in) Stockholm 2000
$1 150 - €1 192 - **£690** - FF7 820
Terrazzo fiorito Acquarello/cartone (35x59cm
13x23in) Milano 1999

ANKARCRONA Alexis 1825-1901 [20]

$982 - €1 157 - **£690** - FF7 531
**Havsvik med bâtar, i förgrunden fiskare, sen
eftermiddag** Oil/canvas (72x107cm 28x42in) Malmö
2000

ANKARCRONA Gustav 1869-1933 [26]

$1 284 - €1 282 - **£801** - FF8 409
Flodlandskap med aftonstämning och lägereld
Oil/canvas (96x106cm 37x41in) Uppsala 1999
$675 - €780 - **£472** - FF5 116
**Rastande ryttare vid eld, skogslandskap i
skymning** Oil/panel (30x40cm 11x15in) Stockholm
2001

ANKARCRONA Henrik 1831-1917 [52]

$4 965 - €5 503 - **£3 440** - FF36 100
Pausande beduiner vid oasis Oil/canvas
(46.5x85cm 18x33in) Malmö 2001
$3 462 - €3 370 - **£2 131** - FF22 103
Kamelkaravan Oil/canvas (16x21cm 6x8in)
Stockholm 2000

ANKER Albert 1831-1910 [435]

$183 315 - €218 010 - **£130 647** - FF1 430 055
Der Abend Öl/Leinwand (54x90cm 21x35in) Zürich
2000
$13 701 - €15 644 - **£9 660** - FF102 619
Porträt einer Arlesierin Öl/Leinwand (24.5x21cm
9x8in) Bern 2001
$3 091 - €2 862 - **£1 892** - FF18 773
Bäuerin in Berner Tracht mit Apfel Charcoal/paper
(37.5x24cm 14x9in) Bern 1999

ANKER Annette 1851-1885 [1]

$7 637 - €8 824 - **£5 348** - FF57 883
Fra Hegdehaugen Oil/canvas (30x42cm 11x16in)
Oslo 2001

ANKER Johann Baptist 1760-? [4]

$2 382 - €2 034 - **£1 425** - FF13 344
**Bildnis einer Dame in blauem decolltiertem
Kleid und Haarband** Miniature (5.9x4.7cm 2x1in)
Wien 1998

ANNA d'Vito 1720-1769 [2]

$10 000 - €10 971 - **£6 643** - FF71 968
**Moses and the Fathers of the Latin Church with
Music-Making Angels** Oil/paper/canvas (76x50.5cm
29x19in) New-York 2000

ANNA Margit 1913-1991 [2]

$9 620 - €10 107 - **£5 980** - FF66 300
Cour Tempera/papier (63x45cm 24x17in) Budapest
2000

ANNALA Matti 1898-1958 [25]

$517 - €437 - **£308** - FF2 867
Landskap Oil/canvas (45x59cm 17x23in) Helsinki
1998

ANNAN James Craig 1864-1946 **[22]**

$686 - €818 - **£489** - FF5 366
Frau Mathasius Photogravure (20.8x15.7cm 8x6in)
München 2000

ANNAND Douglas Shenton 1903-1976 **[3]**
$1 200 - €1 308 - **£830** - FF8 577
«Sydney» Poster (100x63cm 39x25in) New-York 2001

ANNELER Karl 1886-1957 **[59]**
$563 - €605 - **£377** - FF3 968
Bei Blatten im Lötschental, Lötschen im Herbst
Öl/Leinwand (55x46cm 21x18in) Zofingen 2000
$222 - €262 - **£156** - FF1 720
Lötschental im Winter, im Vordergrund eine
Viehtränke Aquarell/Papier (26.5x32cm 10x12in) Bern
2000

ANNEN Anna Margrit 1951 **[2]**
$3 312 - €3 949 - **£2 361** - FF25 903
Ohne Titel Acrylic (65x75cm 25x29in) Luzern 2000

ANNENKOV Youri P. Georges 1889-1974 **[53]**
$5 754 - €5 336 - **£3 472** - FF35 000
Maisons rouges Huile/toile (81x100cm 31x39in)
Paris 1999
$806 - €865 - **£550** - FF5 675
Group of Figures Running Gouache/paper
(58.5x58.5cm 23x23in) London 2001

ANNESLEY Charles Francis 1787-1863 **[7]**
$547 - €515 - **£340** - FF3 375
Lago di Como Ink (19.5x33cm 7x12in) London 1999

ANNIGONI Pietro 1910-1988 **[205]**
$7 500 - €7 775 - **£4 500** - FF51 000
Studio per gli Angeli a desta dell'affresco di
Montecassino Tecnica mista (57x78cm 22x30in)
Prato 2000
$2 800 - €3 628 - **£2 100** - FF23 800
Uomo alal scrivania Olio/cartone (30x40cm
11x15in) Milano 2001
$1 440 - €1 244 - **£720** - FF8 160
Rissa Carboncino/carta (28.5x41cm 11x16in) Prato
1999
$120 - €155 - **£90** - FF1 020
Volto Litografia (70.5x49.5cm 27x19in) Prato 2000

ANNOIS Will. L. LLoyd, Len 1906-1966 **[21]**
$479 - €461 - **£295** - FF3 023
Church on Mykonos, Greece Watercolour/paper
(44x60cm 17x23in) Melbourne 1999

ANNUNCIACAO Toma José 1818-1879 **[5]**
$47 786 - €41 363 - **£29 000** - FF271 326
Fisherfolk on a Beach Before a Coastal Town
Oil/canvas (54.5x69cm 21x27in) London 1998

ANORO LLAGOSTERA Manuel 1943 **[7]**
$700 - €735 - **£441** - FF4 821
Flores amarillas Serigraph (53x64cm 21x25in)
Pittsburgh PA 2000

ANQUETIN Louis 1861-1932 **[129]**
$3 936 - €4 573 - **£2 766** - FF30 000
Promenade au bois Huile/toile (50x61cm 19x24in)
Paris 2001
$1 228 - €1 220 - **£788** - FF8 000
Nu dans un paysage Huile/panneau (34x42cm
13x16in) Paris 1999
$6 115 - €6 707 - **£4 155** - FF43 995
Dans la rue, Forskitse Watercolour/paper (44x56cm
17x22in) København 2000
$1 176 - €1 126 - **£740** - FF7 389
«Marguerite Dufay dans son Répertoire» Affiche
(91x125cm 35x49in) Bern 1999

ANRAEDT van Pieter c.1635-1678 **[5]**
$6 445 - €6 330 - **£4 000** - FF41 519
Portrait of Cornelis de Witt Oil/canvas (49x37cm
19x14in) London 1999

ANREITER von Alois 1803-1882 **[20]**
$1 850 - €2 179 - **£1 300** - FF14 293
A young Lady, facing right in black dress with
lace Collar Miniature (10x7.5cm 3x2in) London 2000
$1 645 - €1 817 - **£1 140** - FF11 917
Bildnis einer Dame in schwarzem Kleid und
einer weissen Rose im Haar Watercolour
(10x7.5cm 3x2in) Wien 2001

ANROOY van Anton 1870-1949 **[16]**
$1 800 - €2 088 - **£1 263** - FF13 699
«Edinburgh by East Coast Route» Poster
(101x127cm 40x50in) New-York 2000

ANSCHÜTZ Hermann 1802-1880 **[1]**
$19 106 - €18 500 - **£12 000** - FF121 350
The String of Pearls Oil/canvas (91x70.5cm
35x27in) London 1999

ANSDELL Charles XIX **[1]**
$4 856 - €4 558 - **£3 000** - FF29 896
The Log-Teams Lunch Oil/canvas (75x126cm
29x49in) Billingshurst, West-Sussex 1999

ANSDELL Richard 1815-1885 **[162]**
$46 417 - €44 310 - **£29 000** - FF290 652
The Shepherd's Revenge Oil/canvas (138x87.5cm
54x34in) London 1999
$18 000 - €17 871 - **£11 250** - FF117 226
Highland Folk, Two Lambs, a Ewe and a Fox
Oil/canvas (61x94.5cm 24x37in) New-York 1999
$12 000 - €13 942 - **£8 433** - FF91 454
At the Water Pump Oil/panel (28x41.5cm 11x16in)
New-York 2001

ANSELMI Michelangelo 1491-1554 **[3]**
$40 777 - €38 139 - **£25 000** - FF250 175
The Nativity and the Annunciation to the
Shepherds beyond Oil/canvas (59.5x48cm 23x18in)
London 1998

ANSHUTZ Thomas Pollock 1851-1912 **[38]**
$1 300 - €1 218 - **£799** - FF7 987
Impressionistic Landscape Watercolour
(16.5x12cm 6x4in) New-York 1999

ANSIEAU Roland 1901-1987 **[7]**
$962 - €872 - **£600** - FF5 717
«Picon Chaud» Poster (160x117cm 62x46in) London
1999

ANSINGH Lizzy 1875-1959 **[87]**
$23 970 - €27 227 - **£16 818** - FF178 596
«Het verzonken beeldje» Oil/canvas (115x161cm
45x63in) Amsterdam 2001
$2 058 - €2 269 - **£1 344** - FF14 883
Moederschap Oil/canvas (49x63.5cm 19x25in) Den
Haag 2000
$847 - €998 - **£586** - FF6 548
Wajang Pop Oil/panel (24.5x18.5cm 9x7in)
Amsterdam 2000
$374 - €408 - **£258** - FF2 678
«Poppenhuis, 3 Vrienden» Coloured chalks/paper
(34x27cm 13x10in) Amsterdam 2001

ANSLOO van Pieter Laurensz. 1623-c.1680 **[2]**
$5 000 - €5 183 - **£3 000** - FF14 800
Riposo durante la fuga in Egitto Olio/tavola
(59x83cm 23x32in) Milano 2000

ANSPACH Johannes 1752-1823 [5]
✎ **$716** - €613 - **£430** - FF4 024
Zwei Herrenbildnisse Pastell/Papier (13.5x11cm 5x4in) Köln 1998

ANTCHER Isaac 1899-1992 [78]
🖌 **$662** - €686 - **£419** - FF4 500
Paris, bords de Seine Huile/toile (38x55cm 14x21in) Paris 2000
🖌 **$470** - €488 - **£298** - FF3 200
Attablée de Rabbins Huile/panneau (23x47cm 9x18in) Paris 2000

ANTES Adam 1891-? [3]
🐾 **$1 168** - €1 380 - **£825** - FF9 055
Aufstrebender Mädchentorso Bronze (H51cm H20in) Köln 2001

ANTES Horst 1936 [817]
🖌 **$43 475** - €51 743 - **£31 068** - FF339 414
Paar, für Jean Genet Acryl/Leinwand (150.5x120cm 59x47in) Berlin 2000
🖌 **$24 278** - €27 610 - **£16 837** - FF181 110
Rote Figur für Friedrich Herlt Acrylic/canvas (60x39.5cm 23x15in) München 2000
🖌 **$4 240** - €4 116 - **£2 640** - FF26 998
Tagebild Mixed media/board (20.8x34.8cm 8x13in) Berlin 1999
🐾 **$4 551** - €5 368 - **£3 210** - FF35 215
Figur 1000 Iron (90x67cm 35x26in) Köln 2001
🐾 **$5 073** - €5 624 - **£3 522** - FF36 892
Der Kopf Metal (45x46x13.5cm 17x18x5in) Heidelberg 2001
✎ **$2 748** - €3 234 - **£1 940** - FF21 212
Zwei Figuren und ein Löffel Watercolour, gouache (37.5x32cm 14x12in) Berlin 2001
▥ **$290** - €276 - **£180** - FF1 811
Sitzende weibliche Figur, männliche Figur mit Vogel und Hase Radierung (39.2x52.5cm 15x20in) Hamburg 1999

ANTHONISSEN Louis Joseph 1849-1913 [13]
🖌 **$11 954** - €12 832 - **£8 000** - FF84 172
Au Sud de l'Algérie Oil/canvas (57.5x80.5cm 22x31in) London 2000

ANTHONISSEN van Arnoldus c.1630-1703 [4]
🖌 **$22 276** - €22 447 - **£13 885** - FF147 243
Marine, Fischerboote auf bewegter See Huile/panneau (30x43cm 11x16in) Zürich 2000

ANTHONISSEN van Hendrick c.1606-1654/60 [12]
🖌 **$4 728** - €5 624 - **£3 376** - FF36 892
Marine Oil/panel (40.5x71cm 15x27in) Köln 2000
🖌 **$32 140** - €31 880 - **£20 000** - FF209 116
Dutch men-o-war anchored off the Coat Oil/panel (33.5x44.5cm 13x17in) London 1999

ANTHONY Carol 1943 [2]
🖌 **$250** - €290 - **£175** - FF1 905
«Meadow Eventide» Pastel/paper (51x51cm 20x20in) Miami FL 2001

ANTHONY Henry Mark 1817-1886 [15]
🖌 **$1 930** - €1 959 - **£1 200** - FF12 850
The Severn Valley Oil/canvas (46x67.5cm 18x26in) London 2000

ANTIGA Agustín 1874-1942 [4]
🖌 **$1 240** - €1 201 - **£760** - FF7 880
Barceloneta antigua Oleo/tabla (50x59cm 19x23in) Barcelona 2000

ANTIGNA Alexandre 1817-1878 [21]
🖌 **$3 335** - €3 594 - **£2 233** - FF23 577
Une jolie petite main Huile/panneau (56x42cm 22x16in) Antwerpen 2000

ANTINO D' Nicola 1880-1966 [2]
🐾 **$700** - €726 - **£420** - FF4 760
Maternità Bronzo (H23cm H9in) Roma 1999

ANTOINE Jacques Denis 1733-1801 [1]
✎ **$1 495** - €1 753 - **£1 075** - FF11 500
Plan du rez-de-chaussée du premier projet de l'hôtel de la Monnaie Aquarelle (56x40cm 22x15in) Paris 2001

ANTOINE Marguerite 1907-1988 [20]
🖌 **$413** - €421 - **£258** - FF2 764
Les danseuses Huile/toile (46x36cm 18x14in) Bruxelles 2000

ANTOINE Otto 1865-1951 [57]
🖌 **$1 114** - €1 278 - **£762** - FF8 384
Berlin, Bahnhof Alexanderplatz mit Königsstrasse Öl/Leinwand (31x40cm 12x15in) Berlin 2000
✎ **$219** - €204 - **£132** - FF1 341
Berlin, Brandenburger Tor mit Spaziergängern am Pariser Platz Pencil/paper (20x27cm 7x10in) Berlin 1999
▥ **$191** - €179 - **£116** - FF1 173
Flusslandschaft mit Enten Radierung (23.7x29.4cm 9x11in) Berlin 1999

ANTOLINEZ José 1635-1675 [7]
🖌 **$4 595** - €5 336 - **£3 241** - FF35 000
La Visitation Huile/toile (62.5x84cm 24x33in) Paris 2001
🖌 **$20 000** - €17 543 - **£12 144** - FF115 076
Coronation of the Virgin Oil/canvas (44.5x32cm 17x12in) New-York 1999

ANTOLINEZ Y SARABIA Francisco 1644-1700 [32]
🖌 **$55 000** - €54 974 - **£33 599** - FF360 607
David Anointed by Samuel/David and Goliath Oil/canvas (122x186cm 48x73in) New-York 2000
🖌 **$7 410** - €7 808 - **£4 680** - FF51 220
El Nacimiento Oleo/lienzo (70x103.5cm 27x40in) Madrid 2001

ANTON Gus XX [2]
▥ **$639** - €738 - **£450** - FF4 840
«Macbeth» Poster (160x119.5cm 62x47in) London 2000

ANTON Ottomar 1895-1976 [22]
▥ **$382** - €374 - **£235** - FF2 450
«Antlantischen Inseln» Affiche (84x60cm 33x23in) Paris 1999

ANTONI Janine 1964 [8]
🐾 **$27 670** - €26 931 - **£17 000** - FF176 657
Posthuman Assemblage (174.5x38x44cm 68x14x17in) London 1999
🐾 **$67 760** - €57 894 - **£41 000** - FF379 762
Lick & Lather Sculpture (61x38x33cm 24x14x12in) London 1998
📷 **$97 129** - €104 260 - **£65 000** - FF683 904
Mom & Dad Cibachrome print (61x51cm 24x20in) London 2000

ANTONIANI Pietro 1740/50-1805 [22]
🖌 **$52 300** - €56 140 - **£35 000** - FF368 256
Naples, a View of the Bay with the Eruption of Vesuvius Oil/canvas (75x123cm 29x48in) London 2000
🖌 **$10 800** - €13 995 - **£8 100** - FF91 800
«Napoli, veduta dalla punta di posillipo del Lazzaretto, Nissita...» Olio/tela (31x41cm 12x16in) Milano 2001

ANTONIO DA TRENTO Antonio Fantuzzi c.1508-c.1560 **[25]**
- $1 000 - €944 - £621 - FF6 193
  St. John the Baptist Woodcut (14x14cm 5x5in) New-York 1999

ANTONIO de Cristobal 1870-? **[13]**
- $4 905 - €4 362 - £3 000 - FF28 611
  The Conversation Oil/canvas (38x45.5cm 14x17in) London 1999
- $2 994 - €2 536 - £1 800 - FF16 635
  Still Life of Flowers in a Vase Oil/board (35.5x27cm 13x10in) London 1998

ANTONIO Lino 1898-1974 **[4]**
- $3 168 - €3 589 - £2 160 - FF23 544
  Desenho alusivo ás obras públicas Aquarelle/papier (41.5x50.5cm 16x19in) Lisboa 2000

ANTONISSEN Henri Joseph 1737-1794 **[13]**
- $896 - €961 - £592 - FF6 304
  Paisaje con pastor y rebaño Tinta (28x40cm 11x15in) Madrid 2000

ANTOYAN Arès 1955 **[47]**
- $15 735 - €13 568 - £9 345 - FF89 000
  «Le deuxième cercle» Huile/toile (200x160cm 78x62in) Bourg-en-Bresse 1998

ANTRAL Louis Robert 1895-1940 **[135]**
- $1 338 - €1 448 - £927 - FF9 500
  Le port de Nantes Huile/toile (46x55cm 18x21in) Dijon 2001
- $715 - €610 - £426 - FF4 000
  Voiliers au port Huile/carton (33x41cm 12x16in) Paris 1998
- $375 - €442 - £269 - FF2 900
  Le gardien de moutons et son troupeau Aquarelle/papier (30.5x46.5cm 12x18in) Paris 2001
- $151 - €152 - £94 - FF1 000
  Le port de Brest Lithographie (42x35cm 16x13in) Quimper 2000

ANTRO van Alexandre XIX-XX **[7]**
- $6 636 - €6 941 - £4 396 - FF45 528
  Nature morte aux fleurs Huile/toile/carton (103x81cm 40x31in) Bruxelles 2000

ANTUNEZ Nemesio 1918-1993 **[5]**
- $6 000 - €5 838 - £3 693 - FF38 293
  Viaje al mar I Oil/canvas (64.5x92cm 25x36in) New-York 1999

ANTY d' Henry 1910-1998 **[698]**
- $509 - €579 - £353 - FF3 800
  Le village aux toits rouges Huile/toile (46x55.5cm 18x21in) Paris 2000
- $311 - €305 - £199 - FF2 000
  Vue de Venise Huile/toile (22x27cm 8x10in) L'Isle-Adam 1999
- $265 - €290 - £174 - FF1 900
  Scène d'intérieur Technique mixte/papier (52x51.5cm 20x20in) Douai 2000

ANUNCIAÇÃO de Tomá 1818-1879 **[6]**
- $21 600 - €23 928 - £13 920 - FF156 960
  Pinhal Oleo/lienzo (50x96.5cm 19x37in) Lisboa 2000
- $4 730 - €5 484 - £3 300 - FF35 970
  Varina na praia Oleo/papel (15.5x11cm 6x4in) Lisboa 2001

ANUSZKIEWICZ Richard Joseph 1930 **[75]**
- $6 000 - €5 667 - £3 628 - FF37 174
  Untitled Oil/canvas (230x230cm 90x90in) New-York 1999

$3 200 - €2 992 - **£1 972** - FF19 626
  Double red Acrylic/panel (58.5x78.5cm 23x30in) New-York 1999
- $4 000 - €4 641 - £2 761 - FF30 444
  Deep Red-Warm Center/Deep Red-Cool Center Acrylic/panel (43x30.5cm 16x12in) New-York 2000
- $90 - €104 - £61 - FF680
  No.7, William Blake Portfolio Silkscreen (64x49cm 25x19in) Cleveland OH 2000

ANWANDER Johann c.1715-c.1770 **[3]**
- $21 630 - €21 802 - £13 500 - FF143 010
  Himmelfahrt Mariens Öl/Leinwand (56x31.5cm 22x12in) Wien 2001

ANZIL Giovanni Toffolo 1911 **[14]**
- $2 340 - €2 021 - £1 560 - FF13 260
  «Neve a Tarcento» Tecnica mista/tavola (48x58cm 18x22in) Trieste 1998
- $2 000 - €2 073 - £1 200 - FF13 600
  Ragazza Olio/tela (42x35cm 16x13in) Trieste 2001

ANZINGER Siegfried 1952 **[453]**
- $1 813 - €1 587 - £1 098 - FF10 411
  Schrei Tempera/canvas (94x76.5cm 37x30in) Berlin 1998
- $693 - €818 - £489 - FF5 366
  Ohne Titel Gouache/paper (41.6x29.5cm 16x11in) Köln 2001

AOKI Shigeru 1882-1911 **[1]**
- $190 000 - €209 619 - £125 666 - FF1 375 011
  Landscape (Fukei) Oil/canvas (59.5x45.5cm 23x17in) New-York 2000

AOUAD Farid XX **[35]**
- $710 - €762 - £475 - FF5 000
  Scène de rue Pastel (25.5x33cm 10x12in) Paris 2000

AOYAMA Yoshio 1894-? **[10]**
- $723 - €686 - £440 - FF4 500
  Fleurs au pichet Huile/carton (65x52cm 25x20in) Paris 1999

APELLANIZ Jesús 1898-1969 **[36]**
- $9 180 - €10 211 - £6 460 - FF66 980
  Pueblo pesquero Oleo/lienzo (99x196cm 38x77in) Madrid 2001
- $3 200 - €3 003 - £2 000 - FF19 700
  «Pueblo de Aya, Guipúzcoa» Oleo/lienzo (46x55cm 18x21in) Madrid 1999
- $930 - €901 - £585 - FF5 910
  Puerto de Bilbao Oleo/tabla (15x15cm 5x5in) Madrid 1999

APFELBAUM Polly 1955 **[1]**
- $3 500 - €4 061 - £2 416 - FF26 638
  Untitled Watercolour (158.5x214.5cm 62x84in) New-York 2000

APHEL Fabio 1957 **[19]**
- $500 - €518 - £300 - FF3 400
  «L'isola del fuoco» Olio/tavola (60x60cm 23x23in) Vercelli 2001

APIN Mochtar 1923-1994 **[13]**
- $2 582 - €2 932 - £1 767 - FF19 235
  Face Oil/canvas (65x54cm 25x21in) Singapore 2000

APOL Adrianus 1870-1862 **[3]**
- $3 827 - €3 857 - £2 385 - FF25 301
  Still Life with Flowers on a stone Ledge Oil/panel (27x20.5cm 10x8in) Amsterdam 2000

APOL Armand 1879-1950 **[195]**
- $836 - €843 - £520 - FF5 528
  Village enneigé Huile/toile (60x70cm 23x27in) Bruxelles 2000

$361 - €347 - **£225** - FF2 276
Bateau sur l'Escaut Huile/panneau (24.5x34cm 9x13in) Bruxelles 1999

$80 - €87 - **£55** - FF569
Chaloupes au bord de la rive Eau-forte couleurs (50x54.5cm 19x21in) Antwerpen 2001

APOL Louis F.H. 1850-1936 [268]
$18 866 - €18 052 - **£11 720** - FF118 412
Winter Landscape Oil/canvas (54.5x74.5cm 21x29in) Toronto 1999

$4 469 - €3 857 - **£2 697** - FF25 301
Landweg te princenhage Oil/canvas (34x45cm 13x17in) Amsterdam 1999

$1 681 - €1 815 - **£1 149** - FF11 906
A Bridge in a Wooded Winter Landscape Watercolour, gouache/paper (24x33cm 9x12in) Amsterdam 2001

APOLLINAIRE Guillaume 1880-1918 [18]
$34 540 - €33 539 - **£21 340** - FF220 000
Femme nue sur un sopha Huile/toile (156x145cm 61x57in) Paris 1991

$7 413 - €6 403 - **£4 477** - FF42 000
Page de dessins originaux Encre/papier (24x30.5cm 9x12in) Paris 1998

APOLLONIO DI GIOVANNI 1415/17-1465 [1]
$270 000 - €288 816 - **£184 086** - FF1 894 509
The Continence of Scipio Tempera/panel (42x128cm 16x50in) New-York 2001

APONOVICH James XX [3]
$2 000 - €1 643 - **£1 116** - FF10 775
Study : Still Life with Teabags Charcoal/paper (81.5x101.5cm 32x39in) New-York 1998

APPEL Charles P. 1857-1928 [36]
$2 500 - €2 670 - **£1 703** - FF17 513
Mpressionist Landscape at Sunrise Oil/canvas (60x76cm 24x30in) St. Petersburg FL 2001

$950 - €1 108 - **£657** - FF7 265
Evening Oil/canvas (30x45cm 12x18in) South-Natick MA 2000

APPEL Jakob 1680-1751 [1]
$3 003 - €3 222 - **£2 015** - FF21 138
Halte des cavaliers dans un paysage montagneux Huile/panneau (30x33cm 11x12in) Antwerpen 2000

APPEL Karel 1921 [2737]
$44 000 - €37 961 - **£26 545** - FF249 009
Some Day Baby Oil/canvas (130x97cm 51x38in) New-York 1998

$13 196 - €12 706 - **£8 251** - FF83 344
Waiting Together Oil/paper/canvas (55x78cm 21x30in) Amsterdam 1999

$6 363 - €6 057 - **£3 982** - FF39 730
Fabeldyr Acrylic (29x33cm 11x12in) Köbenhavn 1999

$17 000 - €19 725 - **£11 736** - FF129 387
Amsterdam Clown Sculpture, wood (122x188x33cm 48x74x12in) New-York 2000

$8 360 - €7 052 - **£4 903** - FF46 261
Appel Circus Sculpture, wood (59x95.5x29.5cm 23x37x11in) Berlin 1998

$10 374 - €8 746 - **£6 155** - FF57 369
«Cobra...» Mixed media/paper (50x64cm 19x25in) Köbenhavn 1998

$382 - €434 - **£262** - FF2 850
Katze Farbserigraphie (59x82.5cm 23x32in) Hamburg 2000

APPELT Dieter 1935 [33]
$2 600 - €2 620 - **£1 620** - FF17 186
Bandaged Hands Gelatin silver print (29x38cm 11x14in) New-York 2000

APPENZELLER Charles Felix 1892-1964 [19]
$1 512 - €1 669 - **£1 000** - FF10 947
Nue couchée Öl/Leinwand (65x92cm 25x36in) St. Gallen 2000

APPERLEY George Owen Wynne 1884-1960 [90]
$2 430 - €2 703 - **£1 620** - FF17 730
Belleza granadina Oleo/cartón (41x32.5cm 16x12in) Madrid 2000

$1 395 - €1 351 - **£877** - FF8 865
Casa de Mondragón Acuarela/papel (25.5x35.5cm 10x13in) Madrid 1999

APPERT Georges XIX [20]
$743 - €762 - **£464** - FF5 000
Le marché aux fleurs Huile/toile (65x46cm 25x18in) Avignon 2000

$652 - €610 - **£394** - FF4 000
Les mousquetaires Huile/toile (35x19cm 13x7in) Lille 1999

APPIAN Adolphe 1818-1898 [274]
$4 253 - €3 964 - **£2 623** - FF26 000
Les bateaux Huile/toile (37x54cm 14x21in) Lyon 1999

$2 816 - €2 363 - **£1 652** - FF15 500
Le Furans Huile/toile (21x39.5cm 8x15in) Lyon 1998

$322 - €305 - **£200** - FF2 000
Paysage au petit pont Mine plomb (37x31cm 14x12in) Saint-Dié 1999

$133 - €143 - **£89** - FF939
Bords du Lac Bourget/Le champ de Blé/Marais de la Burbanche Radierung (15x20cm 5x7in) Königstein 2000

APPIAN Louis 1862-1896 [38]
$1 312 - €1 524 - **£922** - FF10 000
La basse-cour près du village Huile/toile (40x34cm 15x13in) Rennes 2001

APPIANI Andrea I 1754-1817 [29]
$49 603 - €49 247 - **£31 000** - FF323 041
Ritratto di Don Pascual Falca de Belaochaga y Pujades Oil/canvas (74.5x59cm 29x23in) London 1999

$2 250 - €2 332 - **£1 350** - FF15 300
Ritratto di uomo visto di profilo Matita/carta (38x28cm 14x11in) Milano 2000

APPLEBROOG Ida 1929 [8]
$4 000 - €3 841 - **£2 478** - FF25 197
Study for a small Bird is Dropping a Large Load Overhead Ink (122x127cm 48x50in) New-York 1999

APPLEGATE Delilah XIX [2]
$39 000 - €43 126 - **£26 083** - FF282 890
Fruit in Compotes Watercolour/paper (41x50cm 16x20in) Portsmouth NH 2000

APPLETON Honor Charlotte 1879-1951 [20]
$1 322 - €1 249 - **£800** - FF8 195
Up-Up-Up with my Gas Balloon Watercolour/paper (25x19cm 9x7in) Billingshurst, West-Sussex 1999

APPLETON Jean 1911 [14]
$805 - €901 - **£560** - FF5 907
Sunday Morning Oil/board (34x51.5cm 13x20in) Sydney 2001

APPLETON Thomas Gold 1812-1884 **[6]**
📖 $65 - €73 - £45 - FF482
New Lovesongs, Milk below Maids Mezzotint
(101x35cm 40x14in) Bury St. Edmunds, Suffolk 2000

APPLEYARD Frederick, Fred 1874-1963 **[20]**
😊 $54 355 - €59 652 - £35 000 - FF391 293
Moonrise and Memories Oil/canvas (89x134.5cm
35x52in) London 2001

APPLEYARD Joseph 1908-1960 **[10]**
😊 $2 430 - €2 588 - £1 600 - FF16 977
The Bramham Moor Hunt Oil/board (29.5x44.5cm
11x17in) Billingshurst, West-Sussex 2000

APPS Paul 1958 **[28]**
😊 $13 628 - €11 334 - £8 000 - FF74 349
«Waterhole Gang II» -Zebras watering Oil/canvas
(92x152cm 36x59in) London 1998
😊 $5 110 - €4 250 - £3 000 - FF27 881
The Spirit of Freedom -Elephant Oil/masonite
(56x82cm 22x32in) London 1998

APSHOVEN van Thomas 1622-1664 **[38]**
😊 $20 197 - €19 059 - £12 461 - FF125 017
The Preaching of Saint Ignatius of Loyol Oil/can-
vas (62.5x90cm 24x35in) Amsterdam 1999
😊 $5 922 - €6 541 - £4 140 - FF42 903
Drei Bauern mit einem Hund in einer
Landschaft Oil/panel (20x25.5cm 7x10in) Wien 2001

APVRIL d' Édouard 1843-1928 **[56]**
😊 $3 205 - €3 811 - £2 285 - FF25 000
Jeune fille au papillon Huile/toile (46x38cm
18x14in) Grenoble 2000
😊 $1 570 - €1 524 - £970 - FF10 000
Les couturières Huile/carton (19x13cm 7x5in)
Grenoble 1999

AQUILA Pietro 1650-1692 **[10]**
📖 $405 - €450 - £270 - FF2 955
Cúpulas del Vaticano Grabado (57x42cm 22x16in)
Madrid 2000

AQUINO Luis I. 1895-1968 **[3]**
😊 $5 000 - €5 509 - £3 335 - FF36 136
Paisaje otoñal, Córdoba Oleo/tabla (69x58cm
27x22in) Montevideo 2000

AR Giuseppe 1898-1956 **[1]**
😊 $3 250 - €3 369 - £1 950 - FF22 100
Natura morta con poponi/Natura morta con uva
e fiasco di vino Olio/tavola (25.5x55.5cm 10x21in)
Roma 2001

ARA Krishna Hawlaji 1914-1984 **[29]**
😊 $11 207 - €12 030 - £7 500 - FF78 912
Bharata Natya Oil/canvas (92x97cm 36x38in) London
2000
😊 $2 500 - €2 158 - £1 493 - FF14 156
Red Nude Gouache (74x54cm 29x21in) New-York
1998

ARAGO Peris 1907 **[4]**
😊 $720 - €721 - £444 - FF4 728
Almosaret Oleo/tabla (21.5x30cm 8x11in) Madrid
2000

ARAGON Louis 1897-1982 **[2]**
📖 $21 140 - €22 689 - £14 145 - FF148 830
Celui qui dit les choses sans rien dire Etching,
aquatint in colors (50x38.5cm 19x15in) Amsterdam
2000

ARAKAWA Shusaku 1936 **[105]**
😊 $19 497 - €19 087 - £12 000 - FF125 202
At N.T City Mixed media/canvas (180x120cm
70x47in) London 1999

ARAKI Nobuyoshi 1940 **[119]**
📷 $1 360 - €1 601 - £975 - FF10 500
Sans titre Polaroid (10.5x8.5cm 4x3in) Paris 2001

ARALOV Vladimir Nicolaevich 1893-1973 **[4]**
😊 $4 000 - €4 320 - £2 764 - FF28 335
Old Moscow Oil/paper (29.5x42cm 11x16in) Bethesda
MD 2001

ARAPOFF Alexis Pawlowitsch 1904-1948 **[22]**
😊 $745 - €838 - £513 - FF5 500
Deux élégantes Huile/toile (65x54cm 25x21in) Paris
2000

ARATA Francesco 1890-1956 **[1]**
😊 $4 368 - €4 528 - £2 621 - FF29 705
Portovenere Olio/tela (70x90cm 27x35in) Milano
1999

ARATYM Hubert 1936-2000 **[16]**
😊 $2 504 - €2 907 - £1 760 - FF19 068
«Fercite Murale II» Öl/Leinwand (60x73cm 23x28in)
Wien 2001
✏ $1 802 - €1 817 - £1 125 - FF11 917
Schwebende Mischtechnik/Papier (24.6x38.8cm
9x15in) Wien 2000

ARAUJO de Marceliano c.1690-1769 **[7]**
🗿 $61 540 - €51 833 - £36 346 - FF340 000
Paire de Statues Porte-Cierges Sculpture bois
(150x62x80cm 59x24x31in) Paris 1998

ARAUJO Y RUANO Joaquín 1851-1894 **[51]**
✏ $207 - €204 - £129 - FF1 339
Arbol Lápiz/papel (25.5x22cm 10x8in) Madrid 1999

ARBARELLO Luigi 1860-1923 **[8]**
😊 $1 000 - €1 037 - £600 - FF6 800
Laghetto alpino Olio/tavola (33x48cm 12x18in)
Torino 2000

ARBAS Avni 1919 **[3]**
😊 $5 004 - €5 488 - £3 398 - FF36 000
Joueurs de boule sur la plage Huile/toile
(60x80cm 23x31in) Cabestany 2000
😊 $540 000 - €612 845 - £360 000 - FF4 020 000
Paysage Aquarelle/papier (19x21cm 7x8in) Istanbul
2001

ARBESSER von Josef 1850-? **[2]**
😊 $1 607 - €1 817 - £1 085 - FF11 917
Die Kirche San Giovanni in Venedig
Aquarell/Papier (38x22cm 14x8in) Wien 2000

ARBO Per Nicolai 1831-1892 **[8]**
😊 $2 100 - €2 497 - £1 496 - FF16 380
Jaktlag i skoglysning Oil/canvas (33x52cm 12x20in)
Oslo 2000
😊 $3 075 - €2 675 - £1 853 - FF17 544
Ryttere og hunder Oil/canvas (23x32cm 9x12in)
Oslo 1998

ARBORELIUS Olof 1842-1915 **[136]**
😊 $2 730 - €2 911 - £1 851 - FF19 097
Korna vattnas vid insjÖ Oil/canvas (87x150cm
34x59in) Stockholm 2001
😊 $1 931 - €1 791 - £1 201 - FF11 745
Strandkant med uppdragen eka Oil/canvas
(70x106cm 27x41in) Malmö 1999

🐆 **$628** - €604 - **£382** - FF3 961
   Insjölandskap med man vid eka Oil/canvas (24x34cm 9x13in) Stockholm 1999

ARBOS Y AYERBE Manuel ?-1875 [1]
🐆 **$1 936** - €1 778 - **£1 200** - FF11 665
   The Artist/The Poet Watercolour/paper (36x51cm 14x20in) Devon 1999

ARBOTORI Bartolomeo c.1585-1676 [5]
🐆 **$22 500** - €23 325 - **£13 500** - FF153 000
   Natura morta ortaggi Olio/tela (75.5x93.5cm 29x36in) Imbersago (Lecco) 2001

ARBUCKLE George Franklin 1909 [35]
🐆 **$651** - €557 - **£391** - FF3 654
   «St. Lawrence River at Baie St. Paul» Oil/board (30.5x40.5cm 12x15in) Toronto 1998

ARBUS André 1903-1969 [31]
🐆 **$4 539** - €4 573 - **£2 829** - FF30 000
   Christ Plâtre (H147cm H57in) Paris 2000
🐆 **$2 343** - €2 515 - **£1 592** - FF16 500
   Tête d'enfant Bronze (H21cm H8in) Paris 2001

ARBUS Diane 1923-1971 [198]
📷 **$6 500** - €6 259 - **£4 064** - FF41 055
   Retired Man and his Wife at Home in a nudist camp Gelatin silver print (37x37cm 14x14in) New-York 1999

ARBUTHNOT Malcolm 1874-1967 [27]
✏ **$165** - €155 - **£100** - FF1 014
   Tree Study Watercolour/paper (37.5x28cm 14x11in) Bristol, Avon 1999

ARCANGELO 1956 [18]
🐆 **$375** - €389 - **£225** - FF2 550
   Composizione Pastel gras (28x40cm 11x15in) Vercelli 2001

ARCANGELO DI JACOPO SELLAJO 1478-1531 [2]
🐆 **$11 041** - €10 221 - **£6 665** - FF67 048
   The Blood of the Redeemer/Adoring Angel, Panels from a Ciborium Oil/panel (25x39.5cm 9x15in) Dublin 1999

ARCE Marco 1968 [1]
✏ **$8 000** - €9 295 - **£5 622** - FF60 969
   Stratification/Mouth/Over the Head/Reflection/Castle/Broken Watercolour/paper (12.5x18cm 4x7in) New-York 2001

ARCHER Charles 1855-1931 [20]
🐆 **$3 522** - €3 198 - **£2 200** - FF20 975
   Still Life of Apples and Grapes in a Woven Basket Oil/canvas (26x35.5cm 10x13in) London 1999

ARCHER Frank Joseph 1912 [11]
🐆 **$8 537** - €9 919 - **£6 000** - FF65 065
   Capriccio of a harvesting scene, Sussex Oil/board (75.5x57.5cm 29x22in) London 2001

ARCHER Frederick Scott 1813-1857 [5]
📷 **$1 134** - €1 341 - **£800** - FF8 794
   Rochester Cathedral & Castle & old Bridge Albumen print (17x22.5cm 6x8in) London 2001

ARCHER James 1823/24-1904 [18]
🐆 **$11 354** - €10 905 - **£7 000** - FF71 531
   Lady, in a blue Lace-trimmed Dress, holding a Fan, a Glass of Wine Oil/canvas (155x96.5cm 61x37in) London 1999

ARCHIPENKO Alexander 1887-1964 [386]
🐆 **$13 167** - €12 132 - **£8 132** - FF83 847
   Nackter Frauentorso Öl/Leinwand (76.3x50.8cm 30x20in) München 1999

🐆 **$460 000** - €515 234 - **£319 608** - FF3 379 712
   Vase de fleurs Oil/panel (30.5x22cm 12x8in) New-York 2001
🐆 **$220 000** - €241 439 - **£141 658** - FF1 583 736
   Hindu Princess Bronze (122x30.5x30.5cm 48x12x12in) New-York 2000
🐆 **$18 000** - €15 364 - **£10 764** - FF100 783
   Madonna Bronze (H72.5cm H28in) New-York 1998
✏ **$6 500** - €7 542 - **£4 487** - FF49 471
   Seated Female Nude Pencil/paper (50x33cm 19x12in) New-York 2001
▥ **$1 352** - €1 588 - **£954** - FF10 415
   Les formes vivantes Lithographie (76x56cm 29x22in) St. Gallen 2000

ARCHIPOV Abram Iefimovich 1862-1930 [1]
🐆 **$5 780** - €5 467 - **£3 600** - FF35 860
   Seated Woman Oil/canvas (60x50cm 23x19in) Praha 2001

ARCIERI Charles F. 1885-1945 [12]
🐆 **$2 800** - €2 616 - **£1 744** - FF17 160
   Seated Woman with Dog Oil/canvas (35x40cm 14x16in) Mystic CT 1999

ARCIMBOLDO Giuseppe c.1527-1593 [2]
🐆 **$1 300 000** - €1 315 127 - **£793 780** - FF8 626 670
   A Reversible Anthropomorphic Portrait of a Man Composed of Fruit Oil/panel (56x41.5cm 22x16in) New-York 2000

ARCOS Y MEGALDE Santiago 1865-1912 [8]
🐆 **$1 993** - €2 134 - **£1 356** - FF14 000
   Abords de ferme Huile/panneau (24x16cm 9x6in) Lyon 2001

ARDEN Henri 1858-1917 [46]
🐆 **$688** - €694 - **£428** - FF4 552
   Le séchage des voiles Huile/toile (60x40cm 23x15in) Bruxelles 2000
🐆 **$577** - €547 - **£360** - FF3 585
   Figures on the Lane in a Snow Covered Village Oil/panel (26.5x40cm 10x15in) London 1999

ARDEN-QUIN Carmelo 1913 [41]
🐆 **$4 479** - €4 116 - **£2 751** - FF27 000
   «E-O» Huile/carton (65x52cm 25x20in) Paris 1999
🐆 **$6 805** - €7 622 - **£4 730** - FF50 000
   Composition Huile/carton (32x43cm 12x16in) Paris 2001

ARDIA CARACCIOLO D' Niccolo 1941-1989 [18]
🐆 **$4 724** - €4 571 - **£2 913** - FF29 984
   Portrait of a Young Girl Oil/canvas 50.5x39.5cm 19x15in) Dublin 1999
🐆 **$5 760** - €5 587 - **£3 625** - FF36 647
   Francis Street, Dublin Oil/board (24x37cm 9x14in) Dublin 1999
✏ **$670** - €762 - **£463** - FF4 997
   Portrait Sutdy of the Head of a Boy Charcoal/paper (38x26cm 15x10in) Dublin 2000

ARDIN Johann Friedrich XVII-XVIII [7]
🐆 **$2 195** - €2 556 - **£1 533** - FF16 769
   Profilporträt der Kurfürstin Anna Maria Luisa von der Pfalz Miniature (4.5x3.5cm 1x1in) München 2000

ARDISSONE Louis XIX-XX [1]
🐆 **$12 000** - €11 240 - **£7 377** - FF73 729
   Venus and Vulcan and the Abduction of Europa Relief (52x41.5cm 20x16in) New-York 1999

ARDISSONE Yolande 1927 [80]
🐆 **$1 989** - €2 287 - **£1 404** - FF15 000
   Le Pont Neuf Huile/toile (65x54cm 25x21in) Barbizon 2001

$435 - €457 - **£288** - FF3 000
Bretagne, les filets bleus Huile/toile (27x35cm 10x13in) Quimper 2000

ARDITI Georges 1914 [48]
$289 - €320 - **£201** - FF2 100
Composition Huile/toile (46x66cm 18x25in) Neuilly-sur-Seine 2001

ARDITTI Judith 1951 [2]
$1 621 - €1 829 - **£1 140** - FF12 000
Videoclip Technique mixte/papier (50x70cm 19x27in) Paris 2001

ARDIZZONE Edward 1900-1978 [147]
$6 873 - €7 378 - **£4 600** - FF48 399
Hampstead Fun fair Oil/board (51x61cm 20x24in) London 2000
$1 984 - €2 352 - **£1 400** - FF15 425
The Waiting Room at the Chiropodist Watercolour/paper (16x25.5cm 6x10in) London 2000
$269 - €288 - **£180** - FF1 887
The Old Charterhouse Lithograph (50x65cm 19x25in) London 2000

ARDON Mordechaï 1896-1992 [143]
$120 000 - €135 466 - **£83 580** - FF888 600
Jerusalem in Twilight Oil/canvas (130x162cm 51x63in) Tel Aviv 2001
$60 000 - €64 910 - **£41 106** - FF425 784
«Yellow Landscape» Oil/canvas (61x50cm 24x19in) Tel Aviv 2001
$10 434 - €9 604 - **£6 263** - FF62 997
Composition Mixed media/board (25x34cm 9x13in) Tel Aviv 1999
$3 500 - €2 875 - **£2 032** - FF18 857
Composition Watercolour/paper (22.5x27cm 8x10in) Tel Aviv 1998
$410 - €457 - **£285** - FF3 000
Composition Aquatinte couleurs (69.5x57cm 27x22in) Paris 2001

AREE SOOTHIPUNT 1930 [9]
$2 136 - €1 984 - **£1 320** - FF13 016
Floating Market Watercolour/paper (36x65cm 14x25in) Bangkok 1999

ARELLANO XVII-XVIII [6]
$27 200 - €24 026 - **£16 800** - FF157 600
Florero Oleo/lienzo (65x50cm 25x19in) Madrid 1999

ARELLANO Juan 1881-1960 [1]
$8 860 - €8 258 - **£5 355** - FF54 169
Landscape Oil/panel (34x47cm 13x18in) Singapore 1999

ARELLANO Y FRANCISCO CAMILO de Juan 1614-1676 [30]
$16 800 - €18 019 - **£11 400** - FF118 200
Virgen amamantando al niño Oleo/lienzo (158x107cm 62x42in) Madrid 2001
$145 800 - €162 175 - **£97 200** - FF1 063 800
Cesto de flores Oleo/lienzo (51.5x65.5cm 20x25in) Madrid 2000
$51 300 - €57 062 - **£34 704** - FF374 300
Florero con lirios y tulipanes Oleo/lienzo (40x28.5cm 15x11in) Madrid 2000

ARENBURG von Mark XX [3]
$650 - €705 - **£433** - FF4 623
«Fly to Bermuda by Clipper, Pan American World Airways» Poster (106x71cm 42x28in) New-York 2000

ARENDS Jan 1738-1805 [8]
$1 870 - €2 178 - **£1 306** - FF14 287
View of a Formal Garden with an Avenue, and a Couple Playing with Dog Ink (17.5x30.5cm 6x12in) Amsterdam 2000

ARENIUS Olof 1700-1766 [7]
$42 148 - €47 947 - **£29 438** - FF314 511
Konung Adolf Fredrik/Lovisa Ulrika Oil/canvas (142x113cm 55x44in) Stockholm 2000

ARENTSZ. Arent Cabel 1586-1635 [15]
$231 680 - €263 278 - **£160 000** - FF1 726 992
A River Landscape with Two Fishermen Pulling in their Nets Oil/panel (31x58cm 12x22in) London 2000
$12 401 - €11 713 - **£7 500** - FF76 833
River Landscape with Fisherboy mending a Net seated on a Punt Oil/panel (42x36cm 16x14in) London 1999

ARENYS GALDON Ricardo 1914-1977 [33]
$1 235 - €1 141 - **£779** - FF7 486
«Yegua y potro» Oleo/lienzo (50x65cm 19x25in) Madrid 1999

ARGELES ESCRICHE Rafael 1894-1979 [9]
$1 332 - €1 114 - **£795** - FF7 307
Jardín Oleo/cartón (52.5x45cm 20x17in) Madrid 1998

ARGENCE d' Eugène 1853-1920 [18]
$652 - €610 - **£406** - FF4 000
Chemin près de Fermanville Huile/toile (45x81cm 17x31in) Cherbourg 1999
$1 170 - €999 - **£700** - FF6 554
«Compagnie Générale Transatlantique» Poster (80x154cm 31x60in) London 1998

ARGENT d'Yan 1824-1899 [25]
$11 362 - €9 909 - **£6 870** - FF65 000
Le repos des promeneurs sous les futaies Huile/toile (54x120cm 21x47in) Paris 1998
$1 629 - €1 372 - **£962** - FF9 000
Études de bergers Crayon (30x26cm 11x10in) Paris 1998

ARGENTI Antonio 1845-1916 [8]
$15 029 - €12 844 - **£8 828** - FF84 248
A Child with a Cat Marble (H97cm H38in) Amsterdam 1998
$2 839 - €3 048 - **£1 900** - FF19 991
Girl in a Scarf with Plaits Marble (H67cm H26in) Billingshurst, West-Sussex 2000

ARGOV Michael 1920-1982 [22]
$8 200 - €9 257 - **£5 711** - FF60 721
Bateaux Oil/canvas (113x89cm 44x35in) Tel Aviv 2001
$2 500 - €2 822 - **£1 741** - FF18 512
Woman with Flowers Gouache/paper (65x50cm 25x19in) Tel Aviv 2001

ARGY-ROUSSEAU Gabriel 1885-1953 [29]
$4 422 - €5 031 - **£3 069** - FF33 000
Rayon de soleil Sculpture verre (H15cm H5in) Royan 2000

ARGYROS Oumbertos 1882-1967 [32]
$22 969 - €21 035 - **£14 000** - FF137 978
La chanson de Pierrot Oil/canvas (148x109cm 58x42in) London 1999
$3 241 - €3 020 - **£2 000** - FF19 813
Port Scene, Nothern Greece Oil/canvas (35.5x51cm 13x20in) London 1999
$5 554 - €6 373 - **£3 800** - FF41 807
Jenny Lieber-Argyros, The Artist's Wife in her Boudoir Oil/panel (34x26cm 13x10in) London 2000

ARHARDT Johann Jakob 1613-1674 **[4]**
$1 861 - €1 738 - £1 148 - FF11 403
Das Fundament des Strassburger Münsters
Indian ink/paper (24.5x34.4cm 9x13in) Köln 1999

ARIAS ALVAREZ Francisco 1911-1977 **[65]**
$2 790 - €2 703 - £1 710 - FF17 730
Bodegón Oleo/lienzo (65x80cm 25x31in) Barcelona 1999
$616 - €661 - £418 - FF4 334
Paisaje montañoso Oleo/cartón (30x40cm 11x15in) Madrid 2001
$216 - €240 - £144 - FF1 576
Barco en la costa Craies/papier (15.5x21.5cm 6x8in) Madrid 2000

ARIAS RAMIREZ José XIX-XX **[4]**
$2 573 - €2 923 - £1 800 - FF19 171
Interior de Los Reales Alcazares de Sevilla
Oil/panel (29x18cm 11x7in) London 2001

ARICKX Lydie 1954 **[19]**
$275 - €290 - £173 - FF1 900
Autoportrait Gouache/papier (18x22cm 7x8in) Fontainebleau 2000

ARICO Rodolfo 1930 **[47]**
$750 - €777 - £450 - FF5 100
Composizione Olio/tela (100x80cm 39x31in) Milano 1999

ARIELI Mordechai 1909-1993 **[10]**
$3 000 - €3 350 - £1 921 - FF21 976
Landscape Oil/canvas (60x73cm 23x28in) Tel Aviv 2000

ARIENTI Stefano 1961 **[4]**
$4 000 - €5 183 - £3 000 - FF34 000
Senza titolo Tecnica mista (85x120cm 33x47in) Milano 2000

ARIFF Abdullah 1904-1965 **[2]**
$12 995 - €12 112 - £7 854 - FF79 448
Rhapsody in green Watercolour/paper (40x57cm 15x22in) Singapore 1999

ARIFIEN Neif 1955 **[26]**
$10 173 - €11 241 - £7 054 - FF73 738
Interior Oil/canvas (190x144cm 74x56in) Singapore 2001
$3 839 - €4 326 - £2 320 - FF23 473
Penyesalan: Regret Oil/canvas (70x60cm 27x23in) Singapore 1999
$2 362 - €2 202 - £1 428 - FF14 445
The Chamber Oil/canvas (40x36cm 15x14in) Singapore 1999

ARIKHA Avigdor 1929 **[226]**
$60 000 - €49 283 - £34 848 - FF323 274
The old Tuxedo Oil/canvas (146x114cm 57x44in) Tel Aviv 1998
$25 000 - €26 835 - £16 730 - FF176 025
Offrande Oil/canvas (100x50cm 39x19in) Tel Aviv 2000
$7 000 - €6 488 - £4 352 - FF42 560
Untitled Oil/canvas (18x14cm 7x5in) Tel Aviv 1999
$3 000 - €3 220 - £2 007 - FF21 123
Interior with Bottles Ink/paper (24x32.5cm 9x12in) Tel Aviv 2000
$650 - €698 - £435 - FF4 579
Olive Tree in the Israel Museum, Jerusalem Lithograph (56x36cm 22x14in) Tel Aviv 2000

ARIOLA Fortunato 1827-1872 **[2]**
$10 000 - €10 734 - £6 692 - FF70 410
Nancy Nellie Hall Bacon, Thomas Jefferson's Niece Oil/canvas (117x91.5cm 46x36in) San-Francisco CA 2000

ARKAY Lidi 1896-? **[1]**
$2 200 - €2 566 - £1 544 - FF16 830
«Ifjusagi Kiallitasa» Poster (63.5x95cm 25x37in) New-York 2001

ARKHIPOV Abram Efimovich 1862-1930 **[8]**
$76 575 - €85 859 - £52 000 - FF563 196
Peasant Women on the Banks of the Volga Oil/canvas (100.5x189cm 39x74in) London 2000
$7 114 - €8 266 - £5 000 - FF54 221
Young Peasant Boy Oil/canvas (46.5x38.5cm 18x15in) London 2001

ARKHIPOV Sergei Nikolaevich 1881-c.1938 **[1]**
$3 918 - €4 663 - £2 800 - FF30 585
Music by the Well Oil/canvas (60x74cm 23x29in) London 2000

ARKLEY Howard 1951-1999 **[79]**
$38 480 - €42 976 - £24 641 - FF281 905
The Cacci Succulents Acrylic (120x200cm 47x78in) Malvern, Victoria 2000
$6 315 - €7 371 - £4 458 - FF48 349
Theatrical Facade Acrylic (73.5x55.5cm 28x21in) Malvern, Victoria 2000
$1 457 - €1 633 - £1 019 - FF10 715
Spots Acrylic (45x34.5cm 17x13in) Melbourne 2001
$2 619 - €2 886 - £1 738 - FF18 928
Study for Floriated Residence Ink (29x21.5cm 11x8in) Woollahra, Sydney 2000
$3 307 - €3 714 - £2 144 - FF24 362
The Triffids Offset (68.5x56.5cm 26x22in) Malvern, Victoria 2000

ARLDT C.W. XIX **[6]**
$155 - €164 - £98 - FF1 073
Leuchtturm Lithographie (14.8x23.6cm 5x9in) Braunschweig 2000

ÄRLINGSSON Erling 1904-1982 **[120]**
$1 403 - €1 524 - £887 - FF9 996
Fiskehamnen Oil/panel (41x54cm 16x21in) Stockholm 2000

ARLT Fritz 1887-1972 **[40]**
$303 - €307 - £185 - FF2 012
Mädchen mit Hund Indian ink (25x20cm 9x7in) Stuttgart 2000

ARMAGNAC d' Marie-Claire XX **[14]**
$2 254 - €2 134 - £1 404 - FF14 000
Symphonie bleue Huile/toile (60x60cm 23x23in) Saint-Malo 1999

ARMAN (Armand Fernandez) 1928 **[2412]**
$18 751 - €22 038 - £13 000 - FF144 560
Coulée de boîtes de peinture Mixed media (165x120cm 64x47in) London 2000
$5 754 - €5 336 - £3 472 - FF35 000
Allure d'objet Huile/papier (75x108cm 29x42in) Paris 1999
$1 834 - €2 088 - £1 289 - FF13 698
Sans Titre Öl/Papier (37.5x23cm 14x9in) Zürich 2001
$15 881 - €14 801 - £9 800 - FF97 086
Accumulation brisée Accumulation (160x120x12cm 62x47x4in) London 1999
$3 177 - €3 201 - £1 980 - FF21 000
Inclusion de roses Assemblage (H53cm H20in) Paris 2000

$1 261 - €1 524 - £881 - FF10 000
Sans titre Crayon gras/papier (24x19.5cm 9x7in) Paris 2000

$247 - €213 - £149 - FF1 400
Violent Violins Sérigraphie (76.5x56.5cm 30x22in) Paris 1998

ARMAND Aristide XX [3]
$7 500 - €7 775 - £4 500 - FF51 000
Violino scomposto Tecnica mista (46x33cm 18x12in) Vercelli 2001

ARMAND-DUMARESQ Édouard 1826-1895 [28]
$2 521 - €2 363 - £1 515 - FF15 500
La promenade Huile/panneau (28x22.5cm 11x8in) Paris 1999

$2 902 - €3 201 - £1 919 - FF21 000
Les chevaux à l'écurie Aquarelle/papier (26.5x45cm 10x17in) Paris 2000

ARMANDO Herman van Dodeveert 1929 [70]
$10 718 - €12 706 - £7 809 - FF83 344
«Schwarzes Gestrüp» Oil/canvas (210x244cm 82x96in) Amsterdam 2001

$3 515 - €4 084 - £2 470 - FF26 789
Fahne Oil/canvas (100x40cm 39x15in) Amsterdam 2001

$1 274 - €1 452 - £881 - FF9 525
Untitled Mixed media/paper (40x52cm 15x20in) Amsterdam 2000

$390 - €454 - £274 - FF2 976
Schwartze Fahne Lithograph (78x59cm 30x23in) Amsterdam 2001

ARMENISE Raffaele 1852-1925 [14]
$11 000 - €11 403 - £6 600 - FF74 800
Il vino del convento Olio/tela (62x51.5cm 24x20in) Milano 1999

$2 500 - €2 592 - £1 500 - FF17 000
Mendicante arabo China/carta (38x27.5cm 14x10in) Napoli 1999

ARMES Thomas W., Tom XX [29]
$309 - €347 - £210 - FF2 274
Village Beneath a Mountain with Castle Watercolour/paper (25x35cm 10x14in) Aylsham, Norfolk 2000

ARMET Josep 1843-1911 [3]
$30 800 - €33 036 - £20 350 - FF216 700
Paisaje con yunta de bueyes y riachuelo Oleo/lienzo (99x132cm 38x51in) Barcelona 2000

ARMET Y PORTANELL José 1843-1911 [15]
$31 900 - €34 036 - £20 350 - FF216 700
Pastora y rebaño junto al mar Oleo/lienzo (183.5x115.5cm 72x45in) Barcelona 2000

$18 720 - €21 623 - £12 960 - FF141 840
Paisaje con figuras Oleo/lienzo (70.5x100.5cm 27x39in) Madrid 2000

ARMFIELD Diana Maxwell 1920 [41]
$2 381 - €2 783 - £1 700 - FF18 256
Aonited and Snowdrops Oil/board (28x21.5cm 11x8in) London 2001

$694 - €750 - £480 - FF4 920
San Marco in the Mist Pastel/paper (17.5x17.5cm 6x6in) London 2001

ARMFIELD Edward 1817-1896 [183]
$1 905 - €2 193 - £1 300 - FF14 387
Terriers Ratting Oil/canvas (42x52cm 16x20in) Billingshurst, West-Sussex 2001

$1 400 - €1 550 - £970 - FF10 169
Scenes of terriers in a barn Oil/canvas (40x30cm 16x12in) Downington PA 2001

ARMFIELD Edwin ?-c.1875 [10]
$12 000 - €13 942 - £8 433 - FF91 454
Approaching Footsteps/The Game Keeper's Kitchen Oil/canvas (127x101.5cm 50x39in) New-York 2001

$2 222 - €2 478 - £1 500 - FF16 255
Otter Hounds Hunting Oil/canvas (60x121cm 24x48in) Aylsham, Norfolk 2001

ARMFIELD George Smith c.1808-1893 [266]
$3 080 - €3 583 - £2 200 - FF23 500
Pheasants and Rabbits on a wooded Track Oil/canvas (51x61cm 20x24in) London 2001

$2 108 - €2 040 - £1 300 - FF13 379
Study of a Fox with a Bird, a Terrier looking down from a Bank Oil/canvas (25x35cm 9x13in) West-Midlands 1999

ARMFIELD Maxwell Ashby 1882-1972 [106]
$2 839 - €3 048 - £1 900 - FF19 991
Window Ledge Still Life Oil/board (52x33cm 20x12in) London 2000

$3 041 - €2 762 - £1 900 - FF18 115
Cagnes-sur-Mer Oil/panel (32.5x24.5cm 12x9in) London 1999

$1 190 - €1 114 - £720 - FF7 306
Hips in a Air Watercolour (31.5x25.5cm 12x10in) London 1999

ARMFIELD Stuart Maxwell 1916 [68]
$921 - €1 081 - £650 - FF7 090
Jonquils and Flower Pots Oil/panel (36x60.5cm 14x23in) London 2000

ARMINGTON Caroline Helena 1875-1939 [71]
$3 062 - €2 856 - £1 900 - FF18 734
Notre-Dame, Paris Oil/canvas/board (89x71cm 35x27in) London 1999

$761 - €884 - £537 - FF5 800
La Seine à Paris Huile/panneau (21x27cm 8x10in) Paris 2001

$119 - €132 - £80 - FF866
Le Grand Canal, Venise Etching (22.5x31.5cm 8x12in) Toronto 2000

ARMINGTON Frank Milton 1876-1941 [69]
$1 934 - €1 804 - £1 200 - FF11 832
Danseuse à la barre/Le Repos/Après la répétition/Ballerina Oil/canvas (59.5x49.5cm 23x19in) London 1999

$1 101 - €1 067 - £693 - FF7 000
Bords de Seine à Bercy Huile/panneau (32.5x41cm 12x16in) Paris 1999

$455 - €390 - £274 - FF2 557
«Wood Billies, Stockholm»/«Lancieux» Watercolour (23x30.5cm 9x12in) Toronto 1998

$98 - €114 - £67 - FF750
The American Church of Paris Lithograph (24x22cm 9x9in) Calgary, Alberta 2000

ARMITAGE Alfred c.1860-c.1900 [10]
$2 680 - €2 620 - £1 700 - FF17 183
The Toy Yacht Oil/panel (40.5x31cm 15x12in) London 1999

ARMITAGE Kenneth 1916 [61]
$10 000 - €10 974 - £6 439 - FF71 988
Triarchy (model) Bronze (26x37x13cm 10x14x5in) New-York 2001

$1 045 - €1 006 - £650 - FF6 600
Two Figures Charcoal (39.5x40cm 15x15in) London 1999

ARMLEDER John Michael 1948 **[64]**
- $7 932 - €8 765 - **£5 500** - FF57 495
  Untitled Mixed media (203.5x73.5cm 80x28in)
  London 2001
- $7 933 - €9 324 - **£5 500** - FF61 160
  Untitled Oil/canvas (100.4x100.4cm 39x39in) London
  2000
- $756 - €654 - **£458** - FF4 292
  Pour Painting Mixed media/canvas (28x29.5cm
  11x11in) Amsterdam 1998
- $3 465 - €3 492 - **£2 159** - FF22 904
  Chest with Circular Mirror Objet (177x52x111cm
  69x20x43in) Zürich 2000
- $1 485 - €1 496 - **£925** - FF9 816
  Ohne Titel Collage (45x39cm 17x15in) Zürich 2000
- $937 - €1 036 - **£650** - FF6 796
  Untitled Screenprint (182x71cm 71x27in) London
  2001

ARMODIO (Vilmore Schenardi) 1938 **[19]**
- $4 250 - €4 406 - **£2 550** - FF28 900
  Serva di scena Tempera/tavola (100x70cm 39x27in)
  Vercelli 2000
- $424 - €397 - **£257** - FF2 601
  Il rettore Tempera/panel (34x24cm 13x9in) Lokeren
  1999
- $1 600 - €1 659 - **£960** - FF10 880
  Ritratto femminile Acquarello/carta (52x34cm
  20x13in) Milano 1999

ARMOR Charles 1844-1911 **[8]**
- $525 - €599 - **£365** - FF3 931
  Still Life with Peaches Oil/canvas (35x48cm
  14x19in) Cleveland OH 1999

ARMOUR George Denholm 1864-1949 **[119]**
- $17 584 - €20 246 - **£12 000** - FF132 802
  Powder Play Oil/canvas (96x140cm 37x55in) London
  2000
- $7 406 - €6 856 - **£4 600** - FF44 972
  Old English Sheepdog, with a Pointer Oil/canvas
  (54x74cm 21x18in) Cheshire 1999
- $405 - €470 - **£280** - FF3 086
  Addressing the Chief de Gare Ink (23x18cm
  9x7in) London 2000

ARMOUR Mary Nicol Neil 1902-2000 **[108]**
- $8 606 - €9 554 - **£6 000** - FF62 669
  Still Life with a Glass Oil/panel (37x52cm 14x20in)
  London 2001
- $4 438 - €4 611 - **£2 800** - FF30 244
  Tulips and Spring Flowers Oil/canvas (45.5x30.5cm
  17x12in) London 2000
- $1 008 - €1 129 - **£700** - FF7 406
  Cleggan, Connemara Pastel/paper (26x41cm
  10x16in) London 2001

ARMOUR William 1903-1979 **[14]**
- $311 - €347 - **£210** - FF2 275
  Loch Morar Watercolour/paper (28x47cm 11x18in)
  Edinburgh 2000

ARMS John Taylor 1887-1953 **[268]**
- $650 - €625 - **£403** - FF4 097
  Segovia Etching (34.5x44cm 13x17in) New-York 1999

ARMSHEIMER XX **[1]**
- $2 200 - €1 930 - **£1 335** - FF12 658
  «Dartmouth Winter Carnival» Poster (86x54cm
  34x21in) New-York 1999

ARMSTRONG Arthur 1924-1996 **[50]**
- $9 132 - €8 888 - **£5 610** - FF58 303
  Abstract I Oil/board (121x106cm 48x42in) Dublin
  1999

- $3 188 - €3 428 - **£2 172** - FF22 488
  Landscape, West Cork Oil/board (61x76cm
  24x29in) Dublin 2001
- $1 963 - €1 905 - **£1 236** - FF12 493
  Connnemara Coast Oil/board (30.5x40.5cm
  12x15in) Dublin 1999
- $1 208 - €1 270 - **£757** - FF8 329
  Men Waiting Collage (37x51cm 14x20in) Dublin 2000

ARMSTRONG David Maitland 1836-1918 **[6]**
- $4 750 - €4 542 - **£2 893** - FF29 796
  Venetian Fishing Boats Oil/canvas (28.5x45.5cm
  11x17in) Boston MA 1999

ARMSTRONG Elizabeth 1859-1912 **[1]**
- $9 750 - €9 242 - **£6 090** - FF60 626
  Young Girl Peeling Onions Oil/canvas (38x27cm
  15x11in) Mystic CT 1999

ARMSTRONG Francis Abel William 1849-1920 **[34]**
- $454 - €385 - **£269** - FF2 526
  A Highland Torrent Oil/canvas (61x92cm 24x36in)
  Billingshurst, West-Sussex 1998

ARMSTRONG Ian 1923 **[40]**
- $7 294 - €8 674 - **£5 198** - FF56 900
  Mount Korong Oil/canvas (128x161cm 50x63in)
  Melbourne 2000
- $1 473 - €1 720 - **£1 040** - FF11 281
  Three Figures at a Table Oil/canvas (61x50.5cm
  24x19in) Malvern, Victoria 2000
- $521 - €620 - **£371** - FF4 064
  Playing in the Yard Gouache/paper (58x48cm
  22x18in) Melbourne 2000
- $216 - €210 - **£133** - FF1 379
  The Italian Model Woodcut (32.5x21.5cm 12x8in)
  Malvern, Victoria 1999

ARMSTRONG John 1893-1973 **[123]**
- $4 751 - €4 941 - **£3 000** - FF32 409
  The Seer Oil/canvas (61x41cm 24x16in) London 2000
- $1 894 - €1 837 - **£1 200** - FF12 049
  Still Life with Pots, Apples and Orange Oil/canvas
  (30.5x45.5cm 12x17in) London 1999
- $7 718 - €6 585 - **£4 600** - FF43 192
  The Three Philosophers Tempera/paper (50x71cm
  19x27in) London 1998

ARMSTRONG Rolf 1890-1960 **[13]**
- $7 500 - €8 743 - **£5 193** - FF57 348
  Smiling Film Actress Agnes Ayers Pastel/paper
  (45x34cm 18x13in) New-York 2000

ARMSTRONG Thomas 1835-1911 **[1]**
- $8 876 - €8 568 - **£5 500** - FF56 200
  The Olive Pickers Oil/canvas (80x122.5cm 31x48in)
  London 1999

ARMSTRONG William 1822-1914 **[52]**
- $1 617 - €1 547 - **£1 004** - FF10 149
  **Ontario Battalion Camp, Hudson Bay Grounds,
  Sault Ste. Marie** Watercolour/paper (18x31cm 7x12in)
  Calgary, Alberta 1999

ARNAC Marcel XX **[2]**
- $800 - €757 - **£496** - FF4 967
  «Le Merle Blanc» Poster (118x156.5cm 46x61in)
  New-York 1999

ARNAL François 1924 **[204]**
- $1 716 - €1 906 - **£1 196** - FF12 500
  «Le paysan» Huile/toile (60x72.5cm 23x28in) Paris
  2001
- $384 - €427 - **£268** - FF2 800
  «Bombardement 104 Cosmos de clous»
  Huile/toile (22x14cm 8x5in) Douai 2001

🖊 $275 - €305 - £186 - FF2 000
La vie est un tango (texte de Bernard Lenteric)
Technique mixte/papier (30x21cm 11x8in) Paris 2000

ARNALD George 1763-1841 **[22]**
😊 $16 000 - €15 259 - £9 739 - FF100 094
The Wood Gatherers with a View of Siddon Hill, Highclere Park Oil/canvas (105x137cm 41x53in) New-York 1999
😊 $10 863 - €12 605 - £7 500 - FF82 685
A Traveller on Horseback Surveying an Extensive Landscape Oil/canvas (86.5x112.5cm 34x44in) London 2000

ARNAUD Marcel 1877-1956 **[63]**
😊 $2 141 - €1 799 - £1 259 - FF11 800
Nature morte à la coupe Huile/carton (38x46cm 14x18in) Aubagne 1998
😊 $3 266 - €3 506 - £2 185 - FF23 000
L'entrée du village Huile/toile (22x25cm 8x9in) Marseille 2000

ARNAUD-DURBEC Jean-Baptiste F. 1827-1910 **[2]**
😊 $2 646 - €2 965 - £1 851 - FF19 452
Die Vier Jahreszeiten Aquarell/Papier (43x57cm 16x22in) München 2001

ARNDT Axel 1941-1998 **[13]**
🖊 $348 - €409 - £241 - FF2 683
Winterlandschaft Indian ink/paper (24x32cm 9x12in) Stuttgart 2000
📽 $81 - €77 - £50 - FF503
Stadtlandschaften Radierung (8.7x15cm 3x5in) Stuttgart 1999

ARNDT Franz Gustav 1842-1905 **[10]**
😊 $1 625 - €1 687 - £1 031 - FF11 067
Die Edmundsklamm in der böhmischen Schweiz Öl/Leinwand (58x44cm 22x17in) Leipzig 2000

ARNEGGER Aloïs 1879-1967 **[280]**
😊 $1 800 - €2 008 - £1 178 - FF13 172
Mountain Lake Oil/canvas (60x91cm 24x36in) Chicago IL 2000

ARNEGGER Alwin 1883-1916 **[29]**
😊 $1 261 - €1 176 - £787 - FF7 714
Alpenglühen Öl/Leinwand (62x92cm 24x36in) Köln 1999

ARNEGGER Gottfried 1905 **[22]**
😊 $1 000 - €1 167 - £705 - FF7 655
Canal Scene at Dusk Oil/canvas (60x78cm 24x31in) Cedar-Falls IA 2000
😊 $4 281 - €4 175 - £2 600 - FF27 386
Villa Before a Mountainous Italianate Landscape Oil/canvas (35x40.5cm 13x15in) London 2000

ARNESEN Vilhelm Karl Ferd. 1865-1948 **[240]**
😊 $7 200 - €7 149 - £4 500 - FF46 893
Calm Day off the Danish Coast Oil/canvas (114.5x152.5cm 45x60in) London 1999
😊 $1 364 - €1 146 - £800 - FF7 518
Ship in Full Sail Oil/canvas (68.5x100.5cm 26x39in) Billingshurst, West-Sussex 1998
😊 $424 - €482 - £290 - FF3 164
Marine Oil/canvas (30x44.5cm 11x17in) Vejle 2000
🖊 $2 095 - €1 749 - £1 228 - FF11 473
Skibsportraet af «Flora, af Aalborg» Gouache/paper (54x72cm 21x28in) København 1998

ARNESON Robert Carston 1930-1992 **[44]**
🗿 $40 000 - €41 437 - £25 460 - FF271 812
High Noon at Mission Beach Glazed ceramic (33.5x33x15cm 13x12x5in) New-York 2000

📽 $2 250 - €2 125 - £1 399 - FF13 937
Up Against It Color lithograph (101.5x76.5cm 39x30in) San-Francisco CA 1999

ARNHARDT-DEININGER Gabriele 1855-? **[11]**
😊 $4 187 - €3 835 - £2 552 - FF25 154
Im Dachauer Moos Oil/panel (24x41cm 9x16in) München 1999

ARNING Eddie 1898-1993 **[18]**
🖊 $1 000 - €835 - £586 - FF5 476
Three Gentlemen in a Parlor with Fishbowl Crayon (40.5x56cm 15x22in) New-York 1998

ARNO Peter 1904-1968 **[19]**
🖊 $2 200 - €2 564 - £1 523 - FF16 822
Woman Walking out on Angry Man Charcoal (44x36cm 17x14in) New-York 2000

ARNOLD Christian 1889-1960 **[146]**
😊 $4 000 - €3 719 - £2 469 - FF24 398
Figure in a Landscape Oil/canvas (100x60cm 39x24in) Portland ME 1999
🖊 $507 - €613 - £354 - FF4 024
Um Stephani (Ruinenlandschaft am Abend) Aquarell/Papier (39.8x54.5cm 15x21in) Berlin 2000

ARNOLD Clara 1879-1959 **[6]**
🖊 $1 900 - €2 216 - £1 334 - FF14 535
Rhode Island Doorway Watercolour, gouache/paper (24x19cm 9x7in) Boston MA 2000

ARNOLD Edward Everard 1824/26-1866 **[4]**
🖊 $850 - €932 - £548 - FF6 116
The sail ship Great Republic in open seas Watercolour/paper (38x64cm 15x25in) Wallkill NY 2000

ARNOLD Eve 1913 **[35]**
📷 $1 200 - €1 346 - £831 - FF8 830
Bar Girl in a Brothel, Havana, Cuba Gelatin silver print (23x34cm 9x13in) New-York 2000

ARNOLD Karl 1883-1953 **[16]**
🖊 $1 650 - €1 636 - £1 032 - FF10 732
Das Auge des Gesetzes schläft/Der Schleichhandel blüht Indian ink (30x20cm 11x7in) München 1999

ARNOLD Reginald Ernest 1853-1938 **[8]**
😊 $5 000 - €5 361 - £3 308 - FF35 166
Skaters on Frozen River Oil/canvas (50x76cm 20x30in) New-Orleans LA 2000

ARNOLD-GRABONÉ Georg 1898-1981 **[290]**
🖊 $584 - €613 - £386 - FF4 024
Raureif am Karpfensee Öl/Leinwand (70x80cm 27x31in) München 2000

ARNOLDI Charles 1946 **[50]**
😊 $7 500 - €8 530 - £5 240 - FF55 953
Untitled Mixed media (122x117cm 48x46in) Beverly-Hills CA 2000
😊 $2 250 - €2 279 - £1 399 - FF14 950
Dudley Acrylic/canvas (101x81cm 40x32in) Bloomfield-Hills MI 2000
📽 $275 - €266 - £173 - FF1 744
Untitled, Sticks Serigraph (68x101cm 27x40in) Chicago IL 1999

ARNOLDI Chuck XX **[4]**
😊 $4 500 - €4 523 - £2 684 - FF24 944
Second Unit, a diptych Acrylic (80x131.5cm 31x51in) San-Francisco CA 1998

ARNOLDI Nag 1928 **[14]**
🗿 $1 443 - €1 380 - £879 - FF9 055
Il Gattino Bronze (H33cm H12in) Bielefeld 1999

$542 - €619 - **£382** - FF4 062
«**Les Bohêmes**» Soft pencil/paper (25x15.5cm 9x6in)
Bern 2001

ARNOLDI Per 1941 [90]
$422 - €404 - **£264** - FF2 649
Rödt serielt maskineri Oil/canvas (86x82cm
33x32in) København 1999

ARNOTT Graeme 1941 [13]
$1 043 - €1 032 - **£650** - FF6 769
**Cock and Hen Pheasants in a Winter
Landscape** Watercolour (53.5x71cm 21x27in) London
1999

ARNOUD GERKENS d' Johannes Christiaan 1823-
1892 [3]
$242 - €272 - **£168** - FF1 786
Spelen in het park Aquarelle/papier (13.5x10.5cm
5x4in) The Hague 2000

ARNOULD Reynold 1919-1980 [43]
$393 - €457 - **£276** - FF3 000
La veillée Huile/toile (50x65cm 19x25in) Paris 2001
$341 - €381 - **£238** - FF2 500
Visage Gouache/papier (43x30cm 16x11in) Évreux
2001

ARNOUT Jean-Baptiste 1788-? [11]
$505 - €435 - **£300** - FF2 854
Fleet Street, from Ludgate Hill Color lithograph
(42x28cm 16x11in) London 1998

ARNOUT Jules 1814-1868 [6]
$252 - €270 - **£166** - FF1 773
Vue du Palais des Tuileries Litografía (28.5x41.5cm
11x16in) Madrid 2000

ARNOUX Guy 1890-1951 [24]
$178 - €152 - **£107** - FF1 000
«**Vins de Bourgogne**» Affiche (78x119cm 30x46in)
Paris 1998

ARNOUX Michel 1833-1877 [5]
$5 311 - €4 686 - **£3 200** - FF30 739
The New Toy Oil/panel (22x15.5cm 8x6in) London
1998

ARNTZ Gerd 1900-1989 [84]
$127 - €143 - **£88** - FF939
Hotel Woodcut (25x16cm 9x6in) Berlin 2001

ARNTZENIUS Floris 1864-1925 [135]
$13 848 - €12 389 - **£8 296** - FF81 269
The Hoofdtoren, Hoorn Oil/canvas (50x36cm
19x14in) Amsterdam 1998
$4 105 - €4 311 - **£2 597** - FF28 277
A Self Portrait Oil/canvas (40.5x34cm 15x13in)
Amsterdam 2000
$12 098 - €12 706 - **£7 655** - FF83 344
Figures in a Street, The Hague Watercolour,
gouache/paper (18x11.5cm 7x4in) Amsterdam 2000

ARNTZENIUS Paul 1883-1965 [45]
$854 - €998 - **£609** - FF6 548
«**Veer Eck en Wiel**» Oil/canvas (36x50cm 14x19in)
Amsterdam 2001
$624 - €681 - **£430** - FF4 464
Bird hanging Oil/panel (27.5x38cm 10x14in)
Amsterdam 2001

ARNULL Georges, Géo ?-c.1938 [4]
$6 000 - €6 236 - **£3 781** - FF40 908
Bay Racehorse with Jockey Up Oil/canvas
(49.5x64.5cm 19x25in) New-York 2000

ARNZ Albert 1832-1914 [20]
$27 450 - €28 121 - **£16 940** - FF184 464
Küste von Sorrent Öl/Leinwand (99x148cm
38x58in) Düsseldorf 2000
$4 393 - €4 346 - **£2 739** - FF28 508
Gänseherde am Dorfrand Öl/Leinwand
(75.5x51.5cm 29x20in) Ahlden 1999

AROCH Arie 1908-1974 [47]
$30 000 - €33 503 - **£19 212** - FF219 765
Still Life with Flowers Oil/board (50x65cm 19x25in)
Tel Aviv 2000
$12 500 - €12 960 - **£8 237** - FF85 012
Composition Mixed media/paper (22x30cm 8x11in)
Herzelia-Pituah 2000
$1 600 - €1 698 - **£1 082** - FF11 140
Boat Color lithograph (53.5x58.5cm 21x23in) Tel Aviv
2001

ARONSON Naum Lvovich 1872-1943 [5]
$8 293 - €7 213 - **£5 000** - FF47 314
Beethoven, a bust Bronze (H33cm H12in) London
1998

AROSENIUS Ivar 1878-1909 [125]
$54 990 - €52 348 - **£34 404** - FF343 382
Prinsessan Oil/canvas (89x119cm 35x46in)
Stockholm 1999
$1 976 - €1 723 - **£1 195** - FF11 305
«**Utsikt från Elfängen**» Oil/canvas (20.5x50cm
8x19in) Stockholm 1998
$1 084 - €1 164 - **£725** - FF7 636
Toffelhjälten Indian ink/paper (19x12cm 7x4in)
Stockholm 2000

AROU Georges XX [7]
$617 - €686 - **£429** - FF4 500
«**Plm, Sports d'hiver**» Affiche (99x62cm 38x24in)
Paris 2001

ARP Carl 1867-1913 [37]
$1 717 - €1 485 - **£1 019** - FF9 738
Schneelandschaft mit Dorf Öl/Leinwand (43x54cm
16x21in) Rudolstadt-Thüringen 1998
$1 782 - €1 817 - **£1 115** - FF11 917
Taormina auf Sizilien Oil/panel (24x40cm 9x15in)
Wien 2000

ARP Hans 1887-1966 [879]
$22 698 - €27 441 - **£15 858** - FF180 000
Configuration Technique mixte (38x45cm 14x17in)
Paris 2000
$8 827 - €10 671 - **£6 167** - FF70 000
Composition Technique mixte/carton (33x25cm
12x9in) Paris 2000
$141 903 - €138 686 - **£90 000** - FF909 720
Coupe chimérique Polished bronze (H80cm H31in)
London 1999
$9 143 - €8 804 - **£5 717** - FF57 748
Noeud de Meudon Bronze (8x13x7cm 3x5x2in)
Zürich 1999
$7 000 - €7 682 - **£4 507** - FF50 391
Untitled Collage (37x37cm 14x14in) New-York 2000
$522 - €589 - **£360** - FF3 861
Composition Color lithograph (54.5x38.5cm 21x15in)
Helsinki 2000

ARPA Y PEREA José 1860-1952 [32]
$3 840 - €3 604 - **£2 400** - FF23 640
Barco en el Puerto de Sevilla Oleo/lienzo
(30x41cm 11x16in) Madrid 1999

ARPKE Otto 1886-1943 [3]
$225 - €236 - **£150** - FF1 568
«**Hapag Mittlemeer und Orientfahrten**» Poster
(84x59cm 33x23in) New-York 2001

A

ARPS

ARPS Bernardus 1865-1938 **[18]**
- $444 - €398 - £266 - FF2 610
  A Still Life with Sunflowers in an Earthen Ware Jug Oil/canvas (82x55cm 32x21in) Amsterdam 1998
- $405 - €454 - £281 - FF2 976
  Bloemstilleven Oil/panel (42x29cm 16x11in) Rotterdam 2001

ARRANZ BRAVO Eduardo 1941 **[41]**
- $224 - €228 - £140 - FF1 497
  Anciana Feutre/papier (43x31cm 16x12in) Barcelona 2000

ARREDONDO AVENDANO Eduardo 1872-1910 **[1]**
- $4 728 - €5 624 - £3 370 - FF36 892
  Der Innenhof eines Bauernhofs in Toledo Oil/panel (26x50.5cm 10x19in) Köln 2000

ARREDONDO Y CALMACHE Ricardo 1850-1911 **[9]**
- $18 900 - €21 023 - £13 300 - FF137 900
  Patio toledano Oleo/tabla (26x50cm 10x19in) Madrid 2001

ARRIDE Louis 1936 **[8]**
- $662 - €762 - £456 - FF5 000
  Le port de Sanary Huile/toile (54.5x65cm 21x25in) Toulon 2000

ARRIETA José Agustín 1802-1879 **[7]**
- $120 000 - €115 592 - £74 508 - FF758 232
  Al Excelentísimo Señor General Don Felipe Oil/canvas (79x99cm 31x38in) New-York 1999

ARRIGO FIAMMINGO (Henricus malinis) 1523-1601 **[7]**
- $17 000 - €16 962 - £10 347 - FF111 266
  Design for a Stained Glass Window: St. Bernardino Preaching Ink (41x16.5cm 16x6in) New-York 2000

ARRIGONI-NERI Jean-François 1937 **[16]**
- $1 826 - €1 753 - £1 145 - FF11 500
  Verba volant scripta manent Huile/toile (24x33cm 9x12in) Angers 1999

ARROWSMITH Aaron 1750-1823 **[3]**
- $100 - €112 - £69 - FF734
  Map of Europe Engraving (127x147cm 50x58in) St. Louis MO 2001

ARROYO Eduardo 1937 **[471]**
- $16 471 - €15 311 - £10 000 - FF100 432
  Napoleon descending into Hell Oil/canvas (162x114cm 63x44in) London 1998
- $8 206 - €7 013 - £4 968 - FF46 000
  Deux hommes en chapeau Technique mixte/toile (38x46cm 14x18in) Paris 1998
- $3 920 - €4 205 - £2 660 - FF27 580
  Fausto Acrílico (39x29.5cm 15x11in) Madrid 2001
- $2 028 - €1 677 - £1 190 - FF11 000
  Carmen Amaya Bronze (65x32x25cm 25x12x9in) Paris 1998
- $1 911 - €2 134 - £1 278 - FF14 000
  Ramoneur Crayon (71x50cm 27x19in) Paris 2000
- $196 - €210 - £133 - FF1 379
  Personaje Litografía (76x55.5cm 29x21in) Barcelona 2001

ARROYO Y LORENZO Manuel 1854-1902 **[5]**
- $1 280 - €1 201 - £800 - FF7 880
  Balcón en Granada Oleo/tabla (13x21.5cm 5x8in) Madrid 1999

ARRUE Ramiro 1892-1971 **[322]**
- $6 958 - €7 470 - £4 655 - FF49 000
  Le matin dans la vallée Huile/toile (60x73cm 23x28in) Pau 2000

- $3 138 - €3 369 - £2 099 - FF22 100
  Portrait de femme nue Email (21x8cm 8x3in) Paris 2000
- $2 208 - €1 906 - £1 327 - FF12 500
  «Le Pelotari» Gouache/papier (24x21cm 9x8in) Pau 1998
- $552 - €610 - £382 - FF4 000
  Le joueur de pelote basque Lithographie (39x31cm 15x12in) Bordeaux 2001

ARRUE Y VALLE José 1885-1977 **[9]**
- $3 510 - €3 904 - £2 405 - FF25 610
  Personajes vascos Acuarela/papel (35x49cm 13x19in) Madrid 2000
- $2 682 - €2 897 - £1 854 - FF19 000
  Scènes basques Gravure (27.5x42cm 10x16in) Biarritz 2001

ARSENIUS Carl Georg 1855-1908 **[29]**
- $407 - €469 - £280 - FF3 076
  Hästporträtt Oil/panel (24.5x31cm 9x12in) Stockholm 1999

ARSENIUS John 1818-1903 **[48]**
- $1 731 - €1 506 - £1 044 - FF9 878
  Hästen belönas Oil/canvas (53x81cm 20x31in) Stockholm 1998
- $660 - €616 - £407 - FF4 038
  Slädåkare på is Oil/copper (24x17.5cm 9x6in) Stockholm 1999

ARSON Alphonse Alexandre 1822-1882 **[32]**
- $1 598 - €1 753 - £1 085 - FF11 500
  Chevaux effrayés par un chien Bronze (17.5x22cm 6x8in) Pontoise 2000

ART & LANGUAGE 1966 **[12]**
- $66 000 - €56 942 - £39 666 - FF373 513
  Hostage Series (XXXI, XXXII, XXVII, XXVIII) Oil/canvas/panel (183.5x498cm 72x196in) New-York 1998

ART Berthe 1857-1934 **[69]**
- $754 - €644 - £457 - FF4 227
  Attelage de boeufs Pastel/papier (74x107cm 29x42in) Bruxelles 1998

ARTAN (DE SAINT-MARTIN) Louis 1837-1890 **[122]**
- $1 924 - €1 760 - £1 178 - FF11 544
  Marine Huile/toile (34.5x60cm 13x23in) Bruxelles 1999
- $725 - €762 - £477 - FF5 000
  L'atelier Huile/toile/panneau (35.5x41.5cm 13x16in) Lyon 2000

ARTARIA Ferdinand II XIX **[1]**
- $3 170 - €2 965 - £1 920 - FF19 452
  Der Mailänder Dom mit Piazza Etching, aquatint (58x74cm 22x29in) Bremen 1999

ARTARIA Mathias 1814-1885 **[3]**
- $1 981 - €2 250 - £1 376 - FF14 757
  Campagnalandschaft mit Bauern Watercolour (26.5x29.5cm 10x11in) Berlin 2001

ARTAUD Antonin 1896-1948 **[3]**
- $41 275 - €38 112 - £25 700 - FF250 000
  Autoportrait Crayon/papier (19x15cm 7x5in) Paris 1999

ARTEMOFF Georges 1892-1965 **[26]**
- $2 845 - €2 820 - £1 779 - FF18 500
  La dame de trèfle Huile/toile (80x52cm 31x20in) Toulouse 1999

48

ARTENS von Peter 1937 [13]
- $16 000 - €18 589 - £11 244 - FF121 939
  Still life in red box Oil/canvas (74x67cm 29x26in)
  New-York 2001

ARTER John Charles 1860-1923 [10]
- $3 500 - €3 975 - £2 395 - FF26 072
  Japanese Street Vendor Oil/canvas (89x58.5cm
  35x23in) New-York 2000

ARTETA Y ERRASTI Aurelio 1879-1940 [24]
- $19 125 - €22 524 - £13 875 - FF147 750
  Arrantzale Oleo/lienzo (55x41cm 21x16in) Madrid
  2001
- $1 575 - €1 351 - £945 - FF8 865
  Campesinos Carboncillo (22x31.5cm 8x12in) Madrid
  1998

ARTEZ Raoul XIX-XX [4]
- $3 992 - €3 811 - £2 495 - FF25 000
  «**Le Rêve de Charlot soldat**» Affiche couleur
  (160x120cm 62x47in) Paris 1999

ARTHOIS d' Jacques 1613-c.1690 [60]
- $24 466 - €22 883 - £15 000 - FF150 105
  **Rudolf of Hapsburg Lending his Horse to a
  Priest Carrying the Holy** Oil/canvas (206.5x284cm
  81x111in) London 1998
- $13 833 - €13 014 - £8 703 - FF88 000
  **Paysage boisé avec personnages et troupeaux
  près d'un village** Huile/toile (80x100cm 31x39in)
  Neuilly-sur-Seine 1999
- $6 232 - €5 814 - £3 760 - FF38 136
  Bewaldete Landschaft mit Figuren Oil/panel
  (13x17cm 5x6in) Wien 1999
- $367 - €409 - £240 - FF2 683
  **Flämische Landschaft mit Tempel auf einer
  Anhöhe** Ink (19.5x32cm 7x12in) München 2000

ARTHUR-BERTRAND Huguette 1922 [69]
- $633 - €686 - £433 - FF4 550
  Composition Huile/toile (61x50cm 24x19in) Paris
  2001

ARTHUS-BERTRAND Yann XX [4]
- $1 166 - €1 372 - £836 - FF9 000
  **Elépahnts dans le delta de l'Okavango,
  Bostwana** Photo couleurs (120x180cm 47x70in) Paris
  2001

ARTIGAS Josep Llorens 1898-1980 [2]
- $58 680 - €60 980 - £36 800 - FF400 000
  Plaque double face Céramique (17.5x14cm 6x5in)
  Paris 2000

ARTIGAU SEGUI Francesc 1940 [22]
- $1 220 - €1 201 - £740 - FF7 880
  Zoco Técnica mixta/tabla (81x100cm 31x39in)
  Barcelona 2000

ARTIGUE Albert Émile XIX-XX [12]
- $3 966 - €4 083 - £2 500 - FF26 782
  The Dance Watercolour (27x42cm 10x16in)
  Cambridge 2000

ARTIGUE Bernard Joseph XIX-XX [7]
- $1 300 - €1 250 - £802 - FF8 200
  «**Feuillantine**» Poster (74.5x34cm 29x13in) New-York
  1999

ARTIOLI Bruno 1943 [27]
- $520 - €674 - £390 - FF4 420
  Gli ombrelloni Tecnica mista (60x90cm 23x35in)
  Vercelli 2000

ARTS Dorus 1901-1961 [20]
- $850 - €893 - £536 - FF5 857
  Scheveningen Beach, Holland Oil/canvas
  (30.5x40.5cm 12x15in) Washington 2000

ARTSCHWAGER Richard Ernst 1923 [178]
- $46 000 - €39 243 - £27 747 - FF257 416
  Two Diners Acrylic (233x201x13cm 91x79x5in) New-
  York 1998
- $65 000 - €72 571 - £43 446 - FF476 034
  George Washington Mixed media (41x52cm
  16x20in) New-York 2000
- $11 207 - €12 030 - £7 500 - FF78 912
  All Over Patter Acrylic (42x34cm 16x13in) London
  2000
- $8 500 - €9 180 - £5 874 - FF60 216
  Booktable II Plastic (100.5x106.5x56cm 39x41x22in)
  New-York 2001
- $4 500 - €4 854 - £2 704 - FF25 466
  Time Piece Sculpture, wood (65x59.5x13cm
  25x23x5in) New-York 1998
- $4 000 - €4 031 - £2 493 - FF26 440
  Volcano V Charcoal/paper (63x47.5cm 24x18in) New-
  York 2000
- $1 500 - €1 445 - £926 - FF9 478
  Surveillance Etching (51x58cm 20x23in) Chicago IL
  1999

ARTUS Charles 1897-1978 [7]
- $2 954 - €3 354 - £2 052 - FF22 000
  Une sterne Bronze (16.5x23.5x8.5cm 6x9x3in)
  Pontoise 2001

ARTZ Constant 1870-1951 [259]
- $3 992 - €4 311 - £2 730 - FF28 277
  Ducks and Ducklings on a Riverbank Oil/canvas
  (40x50cm 15x19in) Amsterdam 2001
- $3 225 - €2 719 - £1 914 - FF17 836
  Ducks on a Riverbank Oil/panel (25x45cm 9x17in)
  Amsterdam 1998
- $1 698 - €1 970 - £1 172 - FF12 923
  Enten in einem Teich Pastell/Papier (50x65cm
  19x25in) Luzern 2000

ARTZ David Adolf Constant 1837-1890 [66]
- $19 304 - €18 151 - £11 952 - FF119 064
  **Voor vader's thuikomst: awaiting father's home-
  coming** Oil/canvas (81x117cm 31x46in) Amsterdam
  1999
- $2 453 - €2 408 - £1 520 - FF15 793
  Preparing for School Oil/canvas (43x27.5cm
  16x10in) Toronto 1999
- $1 427 - €1 499 - £900 - FF9 832
  Feral Ducks by a Pond Watercolour (25x30.5cm
  9x12in) London 2000

ARTZYBASHEFF Boris 1900-1965 [10]
- $600 - €526 - £364 - FF3 452
  «**Bermuda by Clipper**» Poster (106x68cm 42x27in)
  New-York 1999

ARUNDALE Francis Vyvyan Jago 1807-1853 [5]
- $2 896 - €3 361 - £2 000 - FF22 048
  Reconstruction of the Roman Forum
  Watercolour/paper (64.5x100cm 25x39in) London 2000

ARUS Raoul 1848-1921 [16]
- $5 055 - €5 903 - £3 568 - FF38 720
  Kavaleriets ankomst Oil/canvas/panel (80x140cm
  31x55in) København 2000
- $676 - €593 - £420 - FF4 547
  L'Attente Du Cortège Oil/panel (10.5x16.5cm 4x6in)
  Billingshurst, West-Sussex 2000

ARVEN Florence 1952 [14]
$700 - €751 - £468 - FF4 928
Le passage aux Bougainville'es Oil/canvas
(26x21cm 10x8in) New-York 2000

ARYA Badri Nath XX [9]
$4 034 - €4 331 - £2 700 - FF28 408
Philosopher Wash (97x61cm 38x24in) London 2000

ARZADUN de Carmelo 1888-1968 [58]
$2 000 - €2 147 - £1 338 - FF14 086
Paisaje de Piriapolis Oleo/tabla (39x48cm 15x18in)
Montevideo 2000
$2 135 - €2 102 - £1 330 - FF13 790
Constructivo Oleo/cartón (32x40cm 12x15in) Madrid
1999

ASAF Halé 1903-1937 [2]
$12 249 - €13 720 - £8 514 - FF90 000
Jeune fille assise Huile/toile (55x39cm 21x15in) Le
Touquet 2001

ASAI Chu 1856-1907 [1]
$20 000 - €19 374 - £12 474 - FF127 084
Shinobazu Pond, Tokyo Oil/canvas/panel (19x28cm
7x11in) New-York 1999

ASAM Franz Erasmus 1730-1795 [1]
$4 257 - €3 948 - £2 600 - FF25 896
The Miracle of the Eucharist Appearing from a
Tree Wash (25.5x16cm 10x6in) London 1998

ASARTA Inocencio Garcia 1862-1921 [4]
$4 575 - €4 505 - £2 850 - FF29 550
Pescadores Oleo/lienzo (45.5x59cm 17x23in) Madrid
1999

ASCENZI Ettore XIX [10]
$400 - €518 - £300 - FF3 400
Alla fonte Acquarello/cartone (54x36cm 21x14in)
Roma 2000

ASCH van Pieter Jansz. 1603-1678 [22]
$5 893 - €5 096 - £3 503 - FF33 426
Weite Landschaft mit heimkommenden Jägern
und Spaziergängern Huile/panneau (38x60cm
14x23in) Zürich 1998
$8 394 - €9 452 - £5 846 - FF62 000
Cavalier dans un paysage Huile/panneau (33x43cm
12x16in) Toulouse 2001

ASCHENBRENNER Lennart 1943 [73]
$1 740 - €1 689 - £1 074 - FF11 082
Komposition Oil/canvas (114x146cm 44x57in)
Stockholm 1999

ASCHMANN Johann Jakob 1747-1809 [17]
$12 702 - €13 635 - £8 500 - FF89 438
Falls of the Rhine at Schaffhausen/View of the
village Küsnacht Black chalk (27x43cm 10x16in)
London 2000
$833 - €991 - £593 - FF6 500
Vue de Thalwil près du lac de Zurich Print in
colors (31.5x46.5cm 12x18in) Zürich 2000

ASCIONE Aniello 1680-1708 [8]
$12 070 - €12 958 - £8 075 - FF85 000
Nature morte aux poires et aux figues/Nature
morte aux poires Huile/toile (30.5x46cm 12x18in)
Paris 2000

ASENSIO MARINE Joaquín 1890-1961 [35]
$702 - €781 - £494 - FF5 122
Pueblo Oleo/tablex (38x46cm 14x18in) Madrid 2001
$490 - €420 - £301 - FF2 758
Vista del Tibidabo desde el Guinardo Oleo/tabla
(16x22cm 6x8in) Madrid 1999

ASH Thomas Morris XIX-XX [17]
$1 077 - €1 203 - £720 - FF7 889
Figures on a Mountain Path, with Cattle nearby
Oil/canvas (38.5x58cm 15x22in) West-Midlands 2000

ASHBURNER William F. XIX-XX [23]
$1 233 - €1 168 - £750 - FF7 662
Returning from Church/Steps to l'Eglise,
Brittany Watercolour/paper (26.5x18.5cm 10x7in)
London 1999

ASHEVAK Karoo 1940-1974 [5]
$11 979 - €10 852 - £7 470 - FF71 184
E4-196, Spence Bay Sculpture (H24.5cm H9in)
Toronto 1999

ASHEVAK Kenojuak 1927 [42]
$397 - €426 - £269 - FF2 794
Days on the Coast Color lithograph (17.5x24.5cm
6x9in) Calgary, Alberta 2001

ASHFORD William c.1746-1824 [14]
$28 233 - €27 567 - £18 000 - FF180 828
Pastoral Scene, said to be in County Sligo, with
View of Cumming House Oil/canvas (42.5x61cm
16x24in) London 1999
$1 785 - €1 522 - £1 077 - FF9 986
A Mill near Bantry Watercolour (23x36cm 9x14in)
Dublin 1998

ASHLEY Clifford Warren 1881-1947 [4]
$11 500 - €10 795 - £7 126 - FF70 810
Whales and Surf Oil/canvas (86x121cm 34x48in)
Portsmouth NH 1999

ASHMORE Charles 1851-1925 [13]
$317 - €330 - £200 - FF2 163
Landscape Hemsworth Norton Watercolour/paper
(25x36cm 9x14in) Doncaster, South-Yorkshire 2000

ASHMORE Peter J. XX [3]
$3 849 - €3 808 - £2 400 - FF24 977
St.Mary-Le Bow, Cheapside Watercolour
(28.5x21cm 11x8in) London 1999

ASHOONA Pitseolak 1904-1983 [26]
$258 - €220 - £153 - FF1 445
Family with Walrus Engraving (43x87cm 17x34in)
Vancouver, BC. 1998

ASHTON Ethel V. 1896-1975 [6]
$1 600 - €1 612 - £997 - FF10 576
Summer Boardwalk Pastel (22x30cm 8x11in) New-
York 2000

ASHTON Fédérico 1836-? [6]
$7 500 - €7 775 - £4 500 - FF51 000
Bosco con figure Olio/tela (64x100cm 25x39in)
Milano 2000

ASHTON James 1859-1935 [27]
$233 - €218 - £143 - FF1 427
Ships between the HEads Oil/board (27.5x39cm
10x15in) Sydney 1999
$3 674 - €4 312 - £2 592 - FF28 283
Swimming at the Foot of Mount Eliza
Watercolour/paper (22.5x34cm 8x13in) Nedlands 2000

ASHTON John William 1881-1963 [191]
$8 299 - €9 307 - £5 763 - FF61 052
Morning Light, Sospel, France Oil/canvas
(102x127cm 40x50in) Melbourne 2001
$2 639 - €2 824 - £1 738 - FF18 524
Berry's Bay, Sydney Harbour Oil/canvas (44x60cm
17x23in) Sydney 2000
$2 170 - €1 893 - £1 312 - FF12 416
Morning Light, Sospel, France Oil/canvas
(36x43cm 14x16in) Melbourne 1998

ASHTON Julian Howard 1877-1964 **[13]**
🖝 **$1 079** - €1 011 - **£667** - FF6 633
   Off de Coast Oil/panel (10x23cm 3x9in) Melbourne 1999

ASHTON Julian Rossi 1851-1942 **[50]**
🖝 **$12 327** - €11 719 - **£7 693** - FF76 874
   Mrs Julian Ashton Oil/canvas (58x43cm 22x16in) Melbourne 1999
🖝 **$2 922** - €3 212 - **£1 872** - FF21 068
   Portrait of Alice Muskett Oil/wood (35x13cm 13x5in) Melbourne 2000
✎ **$1 984** - €2 187 - **£1 319** - FF14 344
   Looking at Bondi Watercolour/paper (21.5x34.5cm 8x13in) Melbourne 2000

ASHTON William 1853-1927 **[8]**
🖝 **$4 348** - €3 711 - **£2 600** - FF24 344
   «The Empire, Shepherds Bush» Oil/canvas (51x61cm 20x24in) Leeds 1998
🖝 **$469** - €505 - **£320** - FF3 312
   An Evening Landscape with Ducks beside a Stream Oil/panel (20x24cm 7x9in) West-Yorkshire 2001
✎ **$1 247** - €1 341 - **£850** - FF8 798
   A River Landscape with a Windmill and Cottages Watercolour (26.5x43cm 10x16in) West-Yorkshire 2001

ASIS Antonio 1932 **[200]**
✎ **$519** - €504 - **£323** - FF3 308
   Sans titre Gouache/papier (16.5x16.5cm 6x6in) Luzern 1999

ASKENAZY Mischa, Maurice 1888-1961 **[39]**
🖝 **$2 750** - €2 970 - **£1 900** - FF19 480
   Seated Nude in Interior Oil/board (76x60cm 30x24in) Altadena CA 2001

ASKEVOLD Anders Monsen 1834-1900 **[85]**
🖝 **$5 865** - €6 118 - **£3 700** - FF40 130
   På vei til beite Oil/canvas (60x87cm 23x34in) Oslo 2000
🖝 **$2 005** - €2 222 - **£1 360** - FF14 574
   Landskap med gårdstun Oil/panel (33x43cm 12x16in) Oslo 2000

ASKEW Julie G. XX **[4]**
✎ **$3 064** - €2 784 - **£1 900** - FF18 265
   Morning Watch Gouache/paper (62x45cm 24x17in) Billingshurst, West-Sussex 1999

ASKNASY Isaac Lvovich 1856-1902 **[2]**
🖝 **$14 000** - €15 028 - **£9 368** - FF98 574
   Moses and Aaron in Front of Paroh Oil/board (12.5x20.5cm 4x8in) Tel Aviv 2000

ÅSLUND Acke 1881-1958 **[115]**
🖝 **$1 065** - €1 170 - **£687** - FF7 673
   Fäbod, Elgesandsbodarna i Jämtland Oil/canvas (50x60cm 19x23in) Lund 2000
🖝 **$752** - €817 - **£475** - FF5 358
   Travhäst Mixed media (31x46cm 12x18in) Stockholm 2000
✎ **$509** - €483 - **£317** - FF3 166
   Hästskjuts Black chalk/paper (28.5x46cm 11x18in) Stockholm 1999

ASMUS Dieter 1939 **[12]**
🖝 **$7 152** - €8 436 - **£5 045** - FF55 339
   «Landschaft mit zwei Düsenjägern» Acryl/Leinwand (100x90cm 39x35in) Köln 2001

ASOMA Tadashi 1923 **[11]**
🖝 **$4 500** - €5 285 - **£3 195** - FF34 668
   After the Bath/Reclining Woman in Autumn Oil/canvas (105x92cm 41x36in) New-York 2000

ASPARI Domenico 1745-1831 **[9]**
▥ **$1 600** - €1 659 - **£960** - FF10 880
   Veduta del Cortile di Brera Acquaforte (47x66cm 18x25in) Milano 2001

ASPDEN David 1935 **[26]**
🖝 **$457** - €491 - **£306** - FF3 221
   Castle Hill Summer Acrylic/paper (98x67cm 38x26in) Melbourne 2000

ASPE Renée 1929-1969 **[161]**
🖝 **$955** - €991 - **£629** - FF6 500
   Nature morte aux poires Huile/carton (46x38cm 18x14in) Lavaur 2000
🖝 **$646** - €671 - **£426** - FF4 400
   Le kiosque vert Huile/carton (33x41cm 12x16in) Lavaur 2000
✎ **$315** - €381 - **£220** - FF2 500
   Orchestre du Capitole la Loge Crayon/papier (35x47cm 13x18in) Lavaur 2000

ASPERTINI Amico 1475-1552 **[5]**
🖝 **$17 920** - €20 348 - **£12 264** - FF133 476
   Die Heilige Familie, im Hintergrund die Flucht nach Ägypten Oil/panel (45x42cm 17x16in) Wien 2000

ASPETTI Tiziano c.1565-1607 **[4]**
🖎 **$23 000** - €23 843 - **£13 800** - FF156 400
   Marte Bronzo (H48cm H18in) Firenze 2001

ASPEVIG Clyde 1951 **[11]**
🖝 **$37 500** - €34 089 - **£22 586** - FF223 612
   Alpine Lake Oil/canvas (101x121cm 40x48in) Hayden ID 1998
🖝 **$16 000** - €14 545 - **£9 636** - FF95 408
   St. Mary's Storm - Glacier National Park Oil/canvas (91x101cm 36x40in) Hayden ID 1998

ASPINWALL Reginald 1858-1921 **[51]**
🖝 **$5 300** - €4 907 - **£3 200** - FF32 188
   River Landscape Oil/canvas (77x62cm 30x24in) Leicestershire 1999
🖝 **$1 518** - €1 768 - **£1 050** - FF11 595
   North Country River Landscape with Woman Before a Stone Bridge Oil/panel (23x35cm 9x13in) Cheshire 2000
✎ **$1 297** - €1 255 - **£800** - FF8 233
   Sheep Grazing in a Watermeadow Watercolour/paper (25.5x35cm 10x13in) London 1999

ASPLUND Erik Gunnard 1885-1940 **[6]**
✎ **$740** - €706 - **£450** - FF4 629
   Woodland Cemetery, Stockholm, Chapel Arcade Pencil (25x25cm 9x11in) London 1999

ASSCHE van Henri 1774-1841 **[14]**
🖝 **$2 896** - €3 291 - **£2 000** - FF21 587
   River Landscape with Travellers Below a Hilltop Church Oil/panel (25.5x34.5cm 10x13in) London 2000

ASSCHER Henriette 1848-1933 **[2]**
✎ **$1 688** - €1 815 - **£1 150** - FF11 906
   Joodse tabakkervers Pastel/paper (35x56cm 13x22in) Maastricht 2001

ASSE Geneviève 1923 **[61]**
🖝 **$2 259** - €2 439 - **£1 561** - FF16 000
   Composition Huile/toile (92x74cm 36x29in) Paris 2001

ASSELBERGS Jan 1937 **[28]**
✎ **$1 012** - €998 - **£623** - FF6 548
   Christel Pastel/paper (48x31cm 18x12in) Amsterdam 1999

ASSELIJN Jan c.1610-1652 **[38]**
- $50 000 - €53 484 - **£34 090** - FF350 835
  Peasants Merrymaking in a Ruined Building, an Italianate Landscape Oil/canvas (61x51cm 24x20in) New-York 2001
- $9 790 - €9 101 - **£6 000** - FF59 701
  Peasants and Cattle beside a Tower in an extensive Landscape Oil/panel (29x26cm 11x10in) London 1998

ASSELIN Maurice 1882-1947 **[195]**
- $677 - €762 - **£471** - FF5 000
  Matin à Marseille Huile/panneau (37x46cm 14x18in) Paris 2001
- $322 - €274 - **£191** - FF1 800
  Jeune femme recueillie Huile/toile (22x19.5cm 8x7in) Paris 1998
- $303 - €335 - **£210** - FF2 200
  Scène de pêche à Concarneau Aquarelle/papier (19x26cm 7x10in) Paris 2001

ASSELINEAU Léon Auguste 1808-1889 **[19]**
- $422 - €442 - **£280** - FF2 900
  Orléans, vue prise de la Colonne Commemorative de Jeanne d'Arc Lithographie (57x75cm 22x29in) Orléans 2000

ASSENDELFT van Cornelis Albert 1870-1945 **[35]**
- $992 - €920 - **£617** - FF6 037
  Bauer bei der Feldarbeit Öl/Leinwand (38x49cm 14x19in) Kempten 1999
- $708 - €771 - **£487** - FF5 060
  «Vrouwen met korenschoven» Pastel/paper (60x71cm 23x27in) Amsterdam 2001

ASSERETO Gioacchino 1600-1649 **[13]**
- $21 000 - €21 770 - **£12 600** - FF142 800
  Prometeo Olio/tela (217x143cm 85x56in) Milano 2000
- $43 000 - €44 576 - **£25 800** - FF292 400
  Suicidio di Catone l'uticense Olio/tela (120x98cm 47x38in) Genova 2001

ASSEZAT DE BOUTEYRE Eugène 1864-1942 **[5]**
- $4 918 - €4 878 - **£3 059** - FF32 000
  Les débuts du modèle Huile/toile (66x100cm 25x39in) Enghien 1999

ASSFALG Siegfried 1925 **[17]**
- $142 - €153 - **£95** - FF1 006
  Organische Komposition Woodcut in colors (54x36cm 21x14in) Kempten 2000

ASSTEYN Bartholomeus 1607-1668 **[15]**
- $21 376 - €24 279 - **£15 000** - FF159 262
  Still Life of Peaches, Grapes and a Pear in a Blue and White Bowl Oil/canvas (54.5x70cm 21x27in) London 2001
- $4 704 - €4 003 - **£2 800** - FF26 260
  Peaches on a Porcelain dish, on a partially draped ledge Oil/panel (34x47cm 13x18in) London 1998

ASSUS Armand J. 1892-1977 **[12]**
- $6 123 - €5 946 - **£3 783** - FF39 000
  Rue de Bou-Saâda, Algérie Huile/toile (100x81cm 39x31in) Paris 1999

ASSUS Maurice 1880-1955 **[4]**
- $3 949 - €4 421 - **£2 679** - FF29 000
  Paysage d'Algérie Huile/panneau (50x60cm 19x23in) Paris 2000

AST van der Balthasar 1593/94-1657 **[43]**
- $144 800 - €164 549 - **£100 000** - FF1 079 370
  Lillies, Roses, Irises, Tulips, Narcissi, Carnations, Other Flowers Oil/panel (127.5x81cm 50x31in) London 2000

- $451 864 - €422 977 - **£280 000** - FF2 774 548
  Apricots on a Stalk, Cherries, a Wild Strawberry, Redcurrants, Shells Oil/panel (19x33.5cm 7x13in) London 1997

ASTANIERES d' Clément, comte 1841-1917 **[5]**
- $9 908 - €11 490 - **£7 000** - FF75 368
  L'enfant à la falaise Bronze (H101cm H39in) London 2001
- $4 250 - €4 454 - **£2 692** - FF29 216
  Seated Imp Bronze (H51cm H20in) Boston MA 2000

ASTÉ d' Joseph, Giuseppe XIX-XX **[58]**
- $1 400 - €1 199 - **£841** - FF7 867
  La fête au village Gilded bronze (39x50cm 15x20in) Chicago IL 1998

ASTI Angelo 1847-1903 **[29]**
- $5 033 - €4 294 - **£3 000** - FF28 169
  Elegant Lady Oil/canvas (61x48cm 24x18in) London 1998
- $1 878 - €2 180 - **£1 320** - FF14 301
  Damenportrait Öl/Leinwand (46x32cm 18x12in) Wien 2001

ASTLER Erhard Theodor 1914-1998 **[351]**
- $226 - €220 - **£143** - FF1 442
  Blick auf Limburg mit steinerner Bogenbrücke und Dom, Wintertag Mixed media (41.5x56cm 16x22in) Lindau 1998
- $200 - €194 - **£126** - FF1 274
  Winterliche Flusslandschaft Öl/Leinwand (38x31cm 14x12in) Lindau 1999
- $120 - €112 - **£72** - FF737
  Zigeunerkind, Portrait eines jungen Mädchens Red chalk/paper (41x29cm 16x11in) Lindau 1999
- $79 - €77 - **£50** - FF503
  Hessische Bauernhäuser Linocut (45.5x65cm 17x25in) Lindau 1999

ASTOIN Marie 1923 **[149]**
- $2 046 - €1 982 - **£1 287** - FF13 000
  La brocante dans le Midi Huile/toile (80.5x59.5cm 31x23in) Paris 1999
- $829 - €762 - **£509** - FF5 000
  Le pichet blanc Huile/toile (46x33cm 18x12in) Paris 1999

ASTON Charles Reginald 1832-1908 **[16]**
- $407 - €371 - **£250** - FF2 431
  «Barmouth» Watercolour/paper (18.5x24.5cm 7x9in) Devon 1998

ASTRANNE Leon XX **[1]**
- $849 - €745 - **£515** - FF4 888
  «Maria del Villar» Poster (102x77cm 40x30in) New-York 1999

ÅSTRÖM Werner 1885-1979 **[45]**
- $872 - €992 - **£598** - FF6 508
  Vindala kyrkby i södra österbotten Oil/canvas (64x77cm 25x30in) Helsinki 2000

ASTRUC Monique 1953 **[14]**
- $444 - €457 - **£282** - FF3 000
  L'homme d'actions Technique mixte/papier (51x54cm 20x21in) Paris 2000

ASTRUC Zacharie 1835-1907 **[5]**
- $2 637 - €2 744 - **£1 666** - FF18 000
  Femme sur son balcon Aquarelle/papier (30x22cm 11x8in) Paris 2000

ASTRUP Nikolai 1880-1928 **[27]**
- $526 473 - €611 679 - **£370 000** - FF4 012 354
  Soleier og regnbue (buttercups and rainbow) Oil/canvas (72x98cm 28x38in) London 2001

$2 053 - €2 370 - **£1 445** - FF15 547
Fra Sandalstrand Woodcut (25x53cm 9x20in) Oslo 2000

ASTUDIN von Nicolai 1848-1925 [28]
$1 761 - €1 687 - **£1 108** - FF11 067
Der alte Marktplatz in Erpel am Rhein Öl/Leinwand (42x59cm 16x23in) Köln 1999
$1 103 - €1 064 - **£692** - FF6 981
Die Maxburg Öl/Leinwand (28x45cm 11x17in) St. Gallen 1999

ASTURI Antonio 1905 [16]
$340 - €441 - **£255** - FF2 890
Paesaggio campano Olio/tavola (13x20.5cm 5x8in) Napoli 2000
$700 - €726 - **£420** - FF4 760
Maternità Tecnica mista/carta (24.5x18.5cm 9x7in) Napoli 1999

ATALAYA Enrique 1851-1914 [109]
$7 200 - €6 222 - **£4 273** - FF40 816
Group picknicking at lake's edge Oil/board (61x43cm 24x17in) Asheville NC 1998
$1 000 - €915 - **£612** - FF6 000
Paris, les quais de Seine à Passy Huile/papier (11x7cm 4x2in) Calais 1999
$800 - €811 - **£496** - FF5 321
Gentleman Rides into Town Watercolour/paper (23x15cm 9x6in) New-York 2000

ATAMIAN Charles Garabed 1872-1947 [60]
$11 000 - €9 311 - **£6 584** - FF61 077
Enfants à la plage Oil/canvas (54x65cm 21x25in) New-York 1998
$491 - €549 - **£333** - FF3 600
Bord de mer Huile/toile (32x40cm 12x15in) Paris 2000
$1 500 - €1 673 - **£981** - FF10 977
«Trois jeunes filles nues» Poster (155x115cm 61x45in) New-York 2000

ATCHÉ Jane 1880-? [19]
$1 368 - €1 524 - **£920** - FF10 000
«Chocolat Vincent, au miel de Provence, Avignon» Affiche (149x109.5cm 58x43in) Orléans 1999

ATCHERLEY Ethel XIX-XX [4]
$2 363 - €2 294 - **£1 500** - FF15 046
The Sculptors Studio Watercolour/paper (40.5x58cm 15x22in) London 1999

ATENCIO Gilbert 1930 [5]
$3 500 - €4 085 - **£2 470** - FF26 795
Untitled Watercolour/paper (54.5x37cm 21x14in) New-York 2000

ATGET Eugène 1857-1927 [627]
$3 273 - €3 037 - **£2 000** - FF19 924
Rue de l'Ave-Maria Salt print (22x18cm 8x7in) London 1999

ATHERTON John Carlton 1900-1952 [25]
$13 000 - €14 227 - **£8 967** - FF93 324
The Bass Season Oil/canvas (66x51cm 25x20in) New-York 2001
$4 675 - €3 988 - **£2 820** - FF26 161
Still life of a boy's room, for Saturday Evening Post, June 30 Gouache/paper (66x50cm 26x20in) New-York 1998
$850 - €921 - **£566** - FF6 044
«Hawaii by Clipper, Pan American World Airways» Poster (105x71cm 41x28in) New-York 2000

ATKINS Albert Henry 1875-1951 [1]
$7 500 - €8 306 - **£5 086** - FF54 483
Dieu marin Bronze (H40cm H16in) New-York 2000

ATKINS Anna 1799-1871 [4]
$10 794 - €12 090 - **£7 500** - FF79 305
«Palipodium Muscoscum, Jamaica» Photograph (32x22cm 12x8in) London 2001

ATKINS Fred XX [3]
$710 - €820 - **£500** - FF5 380
«The Deer Hunter» Poster (101.5x68.5cm 39x26in) London 2000

ATKINS Peter M. Thomas 1963 [4]
$3 886 - €4 356 - **£2 717** - FF28 573
«Flask» Enamel (215x206cm 84x81in) Melbourne 2001

ATKINS Samuel c.1787-1808 [63]
$2 792 - €2 787 - **£1 700** - FF18 279
Panorama with Shipping in the lower Thames Estuary Watercolour (10x30.5cm 3x12in) London 2000

ATKINS William Edward 1842-1910 [41]
$794 - €679 - **£480** - FF4 453
Entering Harbour Watercolour/paper (15x23cm 5x9in) London 1999

ATKINSON George Mounsey Wh. 1806-1884 [10]
$21 356 - €21 310 - **£13 000** - FF139 783
«H.M.S Inconstant, 36 Guns, Captain Owen, leaving Cork Harbour, 1811» Oil/canvas (86.5x132.5cm 34x52in) London 2000
$2 247 - €2 413 - **£1 504** - FF15 825
Portrait of Young Lady Oil/canvas (41x28cm 16x11in) Dublin 2000

ATKINSON Herbert D. XIX [2]
$1 141 - €1 331 - **£800** - FF8 728
Cape Bufalo and Gaur Oil/board (35.5x25cm 13x9in) London 2000

ATKINSON John 1863-1924 [98]
$3 086 - €3 671 - **£2 200** - FF24 079
Saddled Bay Hunter in a Stable with a Terrier Oil/canvas (40.5x56cm 15x22in) London 2000
$1 697 - €1 400 - **£1 000** - FF9 182
View of a Bay with a Man Horse and Cart in the Foregrounded Watercolour/paper (34.5x50cm 13x19in) Tyne & Wear 1998

ATKINSON John Augustus 1775-1833 [14]
$809 - €759 - **£500** - FF4 977
A French Drummer Watercolour (22x16.5cm 8x6in) London 1999

ATKINSON John Gunson c.1820-c.1890 [19]
$1 400 - €1 359 - **£864** - FF8 914
On the River Llugwy Oil/canvas (40x60cm 16x24in) New-Orleans LA 1999
$577 - €647 - **£400** - FF4 247
«Near Woodford, Essex» Oil/canvas (19x29cm 7x11in) Penrith, Cumbria 2000

ATKINSON Thomas Lewis 1817-? [3]
$253 - €244 - **£160** - FF1 603
Windsor Castle in the Present Time after Edwin Landseer Engraving (56x71cm 22x27in) Ipswich 1999

ATKYNS Lee 1913-1987 [12]
$900 - €771 - **£541** - FF5 057
Rural Oil/canvas (76x63cm 30x25in) Cincinnati OH 1998

ATL Doctor 1875-1964 **[69]**
- **$35 000** - €33 702 - **£21 784** - FF221 070
  Dama con volcanes Mixed media/canvas
  (119.5x119.5cm 47x47in) New-York 1999
- **$50 000** - €48 649 - **£30 775** - FF319 115
  Tepozteco Oil/masonite (48.5x52cm 19x20in) New-York 1999
- **$5 500** - €4 796 - **£3 325** - FF31 458
  Paisaje con volcanes Charcoal (30x47cm 11x18in) New-York 1998

ATLAN Jean Michel 1913-1960 **[427]**
- **$33 217** - €32 777 - **£20 468** - FF215 000
  La Fête du Maïs Huile/toile (50x73cm 19x28in) Versailles 1999
- **$3 456** - €3 354 - **£2 151** - FF22 000
  Composition Huile/toile (32x25cm 12x9in) Paris 1999
- **$7 757** - €6 555 - **£4 613** - FF43 000
  Composition Pastel/papier (24x33cm 9x12in) Versailles 1998
- **$596** - €511 - **£358** - FF3 353
  Sagittaire Farblithographie (55x49cm 21x19in) Berlin 1998

ATLAS Paul 1910 **[2]**
- **$10 648** - €10 367 - **£6 541** - FF68 000
  Composition Huile/papier (24.5x31.5cm 9x12in) Paris 1999

ATOCHE Louis Jean Marie 1785-1832 **[4]**
- **$452** - €381 - **£267** - FF2 500
  Paysage au château fort Aquarelle (31.5x49cm 12x19in) Paris 1998

ATOYAN Armen 1922 **[36]**
- **$437** - €498 - **£300** - FF3 266
  Portrait of a Girl in Red Oil/board (57x37cm 22x14in) London 2000

ATSUKO Tanaka 1932 **[1]**
- **$13 000** - €13 382 - **£8 193** - FF87 779
  Untitled Enamel (159x129cm 62x50in) New-York 2000

ATTANASIO Dino 1925 **[45]**
- **$262** - €259 - **£160** - FF1 700
  Spaghetti, pl.4 de Club de vacances Encre Chine/papier (41x30cm 16x11in) Neuilly-sur-Seine 2000

ATTANASIO Natale 1845-1923 **[12]**
- **$15 778** - €17 515 - **£11 000** - FF114 893
  The Child Prodigy Oil/canvas (59x99.5cm 23x39in) London 2001
- **$2 250** - €2 332 - **£1 350** - FF15 300
  Figura femminile seduta, che allatta une bambino Inchiostro (31.5x21cm 12x8in) Milano 2000

ATTAR Suad 1942 **[2]**
- **$12 890** - €14 498 - **£9 000** - FF95 103
  Dream City Oil/canvas (30x60cm 11x23in) London 2001
- **$2 434** - €2 738 - **£1 700** - FF17 963
  Inspiration from Love Poem by Mahmoud Darwish Oil/board (29x39cm 11x15in) London 2001

ATTARDI Ugo 1923 **[124]**
- **$6 000** - €6 220 - **£3 600** - FF40 800
  La chiara luna Olio/tela (130x150cm 51x59in) Milano 1999
- **$3 720** - €3 214 - **£2 480** - FF21 080
  Lungotevere Olio/tela (50x69cm 19x27in) Roma 1998

- **$1 450** - €1 503 - **£870** - FF9 860
  Ponte su Tevere Olio/tavola (30x40cm 11x15in) Vercelli 2000
- **$1 120** - €1 451 - **£840** - FF9 520
  Nudo seduto con bastone Bronzo (63.5x26x35cm 25x10x13in) Milano 2001
- **$700** - €726 - **£420** - FF4 760
  Figura Tecnica mista/carta (70x50cm 27x19in) Torino 2001

ATTENDU Antoine Ferdinand c.1845-? **[16]**
- **$5 253** - €4 991 - **£3 196** - FF32 742
  Culinair stilleven van diverse kaassoorten Oil/canvas (80x116cm 31x45in) Rotterdam 1999

ATTERSEE Christian Ludwig 1941 **[265]**
- **$14 564** - €15 988 - **£9 680** - FF104 874
  Wanderlust Acrylic (112x224cm 44x88in) Wien 2000
- **$3 901** - €4 602 - **£2 752** - FF30 185
  «Essball» Acrylic (107x87cm 42x34in) Köln 2001
- **$1 682** - €1 817 - **£1 162** - FF11 917
  Eiblume Mischtechnik/Karton (31x21,7cm 12x8in) Wien 2001
- **$1 948** - €1 891 - **£1 213** - FF12 405
  Backmordstütze Mischtechnik/Papier (62x43.5cm 24x17in) Luzern 1999
- **$247** - €281 - **£171** - FF1 844
  Schinkenhöschen/Rückenschmuck für Schwäne und Foxeln Farbserigraphie (70.5x96.1cm 27x37in) Hamburg 2000

ATTIRET Jean-Denis 1702-1768 **[1]**
- **$1 800** - €2 088 - **£1 280** - FF13 697
  The Victory of Khorgos Engraving (51x89cm 20x35in) St. Louis MO 2001

ATTWELL Mabel Lucie 1879-1964 **[36]**
- **$2 320** - €2 002 - **£1 400** - FF13 133
  Oh How Lovely! Aunt Clotida, I Have Been so Petted Before Watercolour (22x15cm 8x5in) London 1998

ATTWOOD Judith Mason 1938 **[13]**
- **$132** - €154 - **£91** - FF1 010
  Beethoven Screenprint in colors (50.5x70.5cm 19x27in) Johannesburg 2000

ATTWOOD Thomas Reginald c.1865-1926 **[7]**
- **$594** - €677 - **£410** - FF4 440
  Native Bush Scene Oil/canvas (59.5x90cm 23x35in) Auckland 2000

AUBÉ Jean Paul 1837-1916/20 **[15]**
- **$2 238** - €2 130 - **£1 400** - FF13 972
  «La Peinture» Gilded bronze (H62.5cm H24in) London 1999

AUBERJONOIS René 1872-1957 **[215]**
- **$15 028** - €14 394 - **£9 457** - FF94 417
  L'homme au manteau jaune - Clément Matthiessen Öl/Leinwand (99x65.5cm 38x25in) Bern 2001
- **$3 067** - €2 818 - **£1 884** - FF18 485
  Paysage au mulet Öl/Leinwand/Karton (17.5x24cm 6x9in) Zürich 1999
- **$618** - €720 - **£427** - FF4 725
  Weidende Pferde Pencil/paper (18.5x22cm 7x8in) Bern 2000

AUBERT Antoine c.1783-? **[1]**
- **$2 725** - €2 496 - **£1 661** - FF16 371
  Napoleon le Grand, Astre brillant, immense, after A.Tardieu Etching (53x40.5cm 20x15in) Amsterdam 1999

AUBERT Jean Ernest 1824-1906 **[7]**
- $2 670 - €2 668 - £1 669 - FF17 500
  Jeune femme et ange Huile/toile (54x44cm 21x17in) Pontoise 1999
- $2 400 - €2 785 - £1 657 - FF18 266
  Concert Oil/canvas (31x20.5cm 12x8in) New-York 2000

AUBERT Louis c.1720-c.1790 **[5]**
- $8 626 - €8 423 - £5 500 - FF55 253
  Lady seated in profile to the right reading a Book Black chalk (23x21cm 9x8in) London 1999

AUBERT René 1894-1977 **[19]**
- $700 - €758 - £466 - FF4 975
  «Versailles, Séjour idéal à 20 minutes de Paris» Poster (99x61cm 39x24in) New-York 2000

AUBERTIN Bernard 1934 **[168]**
- $756 - €915 - £528 - FF6 000
  Tableau Feu Technique mixte (50x65cm 19x25in) Paris 2001
- $474 - €534 - £326 - FF3 500
  «Mono Rosso» Acrylique/métal (30x30cm 11x11in) Paris 2001
- $775 - €838 - £530 - FF5 500
  Dessin de feu Assemblage (71x101cm 27x39in) Paris 2001
- $386 - €427 - £268 - FF2 800
  Empreinte noire Encre/papier (37x53cm 14x20in) Paris 2001

AUBLET Albert 1851-1938 **[88]**
- $13 719 - €12 958 - £8 542 - FF85 000
  Bouquet de pivoines sur un entablement Huile/toile (242x135cm 95x53in) Paris 1999
- $11 438 - €12 990 - £8 000 - FF85 207
  Pureté Oil/canvas (78x56.5cm 30x22in) London 2001
- $2 836 - €2 744 - £1 749 - FF18 000
  Souk à Tunis Huile/panneau (35x26.5cm 13x10in) Paris 1999
- $2 556 - €2 744 - £1 710 - FF18 000
  La Marsa Aquarelle/papier (30x46cm 11x18in) Paris 2000

AUBREY Charles XIX **[2]**
- $1 944 - €2 171 - £1 300 - FF14 244
  Shipping on the Thames at Tower Bridge Oil/canvas (24x34cm 9x13in) West-Midlands 2000

AUBRIET Claude 1651/65-1742 **[6]**
- $2 242 - €2 407 - £1 500 - FF15 786
  Hocco à pierre - Nothern Helmeted Curassow - Pauxi pauxi Watercolour (40.5x30.5cm 15x12in) London 2000

AUBROECK Karel 1894-1986 **[10]**
- $1 135 - €1 091 - £708 - FF7 154
  Nu agenouillé Sculpture bois (H43cm H16in) Bruxelles 1999

AUBRY Charles Hippolyte 1811-1877 **[19]**
- $1 147 - €1 278 - £750 - FF8 384
  Blossom Albumen print (36x25cm 14x10in) London 2000

AUBRY Émile 1880-1964 **[191]**
- $3 520 - €3 659 - £2 208 - FF24 000
  Jeune berger Huile/toile (50x60cm 19x23in) Paris 2000
- $484 - €488 - £301 - FF3 300
  Souk Huile/carton (27x35cm 10x13in) Paris 2000
- $368 - €305 - £216 - FF2 000
  Étude de femme nue à la cruche Fusain/papier (42x28cm 16x11in) Paris 1998

AUBRY Étienne 1745-1781 **[21]**
- $56 800 - €60 980 - £38 000 - FF400 000
  Le déjeuner des enfants/La lecture Huile/toile (46x54.5cm 18x21in) Paris 2000

AUBRY Louis François 1767-1851 **[20]**
- $805 - €915 - £555 - FF6 000
  Jeune homme en redingote bleue, gilet et cravate blancs Miniature (8.5x6.5cm 3x2in) Paris 2000

AUBURTIN Jean-Francis 1866-1930 **[14]**
- $1 028 - €1 037 - £641 - FF6 800
  Paysage de Bretagne Aquarelle/papier (29x43cm 11x16in) Rennes 2000

AUCHENTHALLER Josef Maria 1865-1949 **[1]**
- $1 917 - €2 180 - £1 347 - FF14 301
  Motiv bei Leobersdorf mit Burg Kreuzenstein Pastell/Papier (69x132.5cm 27x52in) Wien 2001

AUCHERE Henri 1908-2000 **[62]**
- $564 - €610 - £390 - FF4 000
  Martinique Huile/toile (50x60cm 19x23in) Paris 2001
- $141 - €152 - £97 - FF1 000
  Arbres en fleurs en Artois Aquarelle/papier (33.5x53.5cm 13x21in) Paris 2001

AUDEBERT Jean-Baptiste 1759-1800 **[3]**
- $1 000 - €937 - £614 - FF6 144
  Monkeys Engraving (51.5x33cm 20x12in) New-York 1999

AUDETTE Yvonne 1930 **[3]**
- $26 245 - €30 799 - £18 520 - FF202 025
  Into the Wild Blue (Cantana no.9) Oil/board (95.5x130.5cm 37x51in) Melbourne 2000

AUDOUIN Louis 1883-1968 **[1]**
- $2 590 - €3 049 - £1 820 - FF20 000
  Un matin devant une vielle porte à Fès, Maroc Huile/panneau (33x41.5cm 12x16in) Paris 2000

AUDRAN Benoît I 1661-1721 **[3]**
- $975 - €897 - £585 - FF5 887
  Vie de Catherine de Medicis, d'après Rubens Gravure (51x35cm 20x13in) Montréal 1999

AUDRAN Gérard 1640-1703 **[9]**
- $486 - €541 - £333 - FF3 546
  «Pareja de escenas biblicas» Grabado (49x36cm 19x14in) Madrid 2001

AUDUBON John James 1785-1851 **[370]**
- $230 000 - €265 713 - £161 046 - FF1 742 963
  White breasted Hawk Pastel (51.5x42cm 20x16in) New-York 2001
- $650 - €557 - £381 - FF3 655
  White Headed Eagle Lithograph (67x100cm 26x39in) Baltimore MD 1998

AUDUBON John Woodhouse 1812-1868 **[11]**
- $6 500 - €6 440 - £3 943 - FF42 244
  Grizzly Bear Color lithograph (54x68.5cm 21x26in) New-York 2000

AUDY Jonny XIX **[42]**
- $3 927 - €3 811 - £2 445 - FF25 000
  Portrait de «Mon étoile» Huile/toile (54x65cm 21x25in) Montfort L'Amaury 1999
- $584 - €549 - £362 - FF3 600
  Portrait du cheval, Shotovel Gouache/papier (31x42cm 12x16in) Deauville 1999

AUER Grigor 1882-1967 **[34]**
- $342 - €370 - £236 - FF2 427
  Stugor Oil/canvas (43x58cm 16x22in) Helsinki 2001

AUERBACH Arnold 1898-1978 **[29]**
- $352 - €356 - **£220** - FF2 332
  Paddington Tube Station Sérigraphie/toile (75x60cm 29x23in) London 2000
- $5 677 - €5 473 - **£3 500** - FF35 899
  Swans Watercolour (38x25cm 14x9in) London 1999

AUERBACH Ellen Rosenberg 1906 **[9]**
- $2 028 - €1 763 - **£1 222** - FF11 564
  Schaufenster, New York Gelatin silver print (25.2x18.8cm 9x7in) Berlin 1998

AUERBACH Frank 1931 **[152]**
- $281 520 - €262 338 - **£170 000** - FF1 720 825
  «Rebuilding Empire Cinema, Leicester Square» Oil/board (152.5x152.5cm 60x60in) London 1998
- $124 320 - €105 995 - **£75 000** - FF695 280
  J.Y.M. Seated VI Oil/canvas (66.5x72cm 26x28in) London 1998
- $23 946 - €28 276 - **£17 000** - FF185 478
  Figure on a Bed IV Oil/board (30x33cm 11x12in) London 2001
- $3 469 - €4 040 - **£2 400** - FF26 503
  Bacchus & Ariadne Pencil/paper (23x27cm 9x10in) Loughton, Essex 2000
- $699 - €729 - **£440** - FF4 783
  Seated Figure Silkscreen in colors (10x7cm 3x2in) London 2000

AUERBACH Johann Gottfried 1697-1753 **[6]**
- $31 128 - €30 598 - **£20 000** - FF200 712
  Emperor Franz I (1708-1765), Imperial Regalia on the Table Oil/canvas (161x128.5cm 63x50in) London 1998

AUFDENBLATTEN Emil ?-1959 **[10]**
- $6 678 - €5 609 - **£3 925** - FF36 794
  Matterhorn im Hochnebel Huile/panneau (81x100cm 31x39in) Bern 1998
- $836 - €984 - **£606** - FF6 452
  «Zematt» Affiche couleur (102x65cm 40x25in) Sion 2001

AUFRAY Joseph Athanase 1836-? **[22]**
- $2 750 - €2 952 - **£1 840** - FF19 362
  Little Mother Oil/panel (40x30cm 16x12in) Morris-Plains NJ 2000

AUGÉ Étienne XIX **[1]**
- $2 041 - €1 982 - **£1 261** - FF13 000
  Les enfants de la ferme Huile/toile (21.5x16.5cm 8x6in) Grenoble 1999

AUGÉ Philippe 1935 **[40]**
- $1 317 - €1 220 - **£813** - FF8 000
  La fleur rose Huile/toile (46x55cm 18x21in) Arcachon 1999

AUGENSTEIN Kaethe 1899-1981 **[1]**
- $2 362 - €2 812 - **£1 688** - FF18 446
  Die Berliner Bildhauerin Renée Sintenis Vintage gelatin silver print (21x17.8cm 9x7in) Berlin 2000

AUGER Lucas 1685-1765 **[7]**
- $4 250 - €4 178 - **£2 730** - FF27 406
  Putti frolicking Oil/panel (53.5x38cm 21x14in) New-York 1999

AUGUIN Louis Auguste 1824-1904 **[16]**
- $1 360 - €1 524 - **£923** - FF10 000
  Paysage à l'arche d'aqueduc/Paysage de colline Pastel/papier (30x47cm 11x18in) Paris 2000

AUGUSTIN Edgar 1936-1996 **[31]**
- $869 - €1 022 - **£629** - FF6 707
  Sitzende Figur Bronze (21.8x4.5x9.4cm 8x1x3in) Hamburg 2001

- $571 - €613 - **£382** - FF4 024
  Gliederpuppe Pencil (21.5x40.5cm 8x15in) Hamburg 2000

AUGUSTIN Jean-Baptiste 1759-1832 **[52]**
- $7 674 - €9 147 - **£5 472** - FF60 000
  Portrait d'une jeune fille dans un paysage forestier Miniature (17x11.5cm 6x4in) Nice 2000
- $1 444 - €1 435 - **£900** - FF9 412
  Baron Dominique Vivant-Denon, wearing a Fur Hat Black & white chalks/paper (24.5x19.5cm 9x7in) London 1999

AUGUSTIN Ludwig 1882-1960 **[17]**
- $1 100 - €1 272 - **£778** - FF8 347
  Curiosity Oil/masonite (43x38cm 17x15in) Cleveland OH 2000
- $2 000 - €1 941 - **£1 260** - FF12 732
  The Connoisseur Oil/panel (31x25cm 12x10in) New-York 1999

AUGUSTINER Werner 1922-1986 **[32]**
- $1 195 - €1 163 - **£736** - FF7 627
  Liebespaar Öl/Leinwand (149x64cm 58x25in) Linz 1999
- $330 - €363 - **£210** - FF2 383
  Anneliese Charcoal (48.5x25cm 19x9in) Graz 2000

AUGUSTINUS Paul 1952 **[21]**
- $10 551 - €10 140 - **£6 500** - FF66 516
  Lion Evening Oil/canvas (80.5x121.5cm 31x47in) London 1999

AUGUSTO Mario 1895-1941 **[3]**
- $17 200 - €19 940 - **£12 000** - FF130 800
  Vista de Barcarena Oleo/tabla (41x33cm 16x12in) Lisboa 2001

AUGUSTSON Göran 1936 **[85]**
- $2 988 - €3 364 - **£2 058** - FF22 064
  I skogen Oil/canvas (120x110cm 47x43in) Helsinki 2000
- $2 253 - €2 523 - **£1 564** - FF16 548
  Önskan Acrylic (124x63.5cm 48x25in) Helsinki 2001
- $504 - €471 - **£311** - FF3 089
  Det regnar Gouache/paper (33x38cm 12x14in) Helsinki 1999
- $258 - €218 - **£154** - FF1 433
  Lido Serigraph (87x67cm 34x26in) Helsinki 1998

AUGUSTYNOWICZ Aleksander 1865-1944 **[19]**
- $1 161 - €1 091 - **£720** - FF7 156
  Portrait d'un jeune montagnard Watercolour/board (68x48cm 26x18in) Warszawa 1999

AUJAME Jean 1905-1965 **[146]**
- $1 760 - €1 829 - **£1 108** - FF12 000
  Bord de rivière Huile/toile (60x73cm 23x28in) Le Havre 2000
- $597 - €579 - **£378** - FF3 800
  Dans le jardin Huile/toile (24x33cm 9x12in) Paris 1999
- $272 - €320 - **£195** - FF2 100
  Paysage Gouache/papier (41.5x57.5cm 16x22in) Paris 2001

AULD James Muir 1879-1942 **[32]**
- $543 - €473 - **£328** - FF3 105
  Horse and Cart Oil/board (22.5x28.5cm 8x11in) Melbourne 1998

AULIE Reidar 1904-1977 **[67]**
- $2 682 - €3 129 - **£1 867** - FF20 522
  Havneby Oil/canvas (63x100cm 24x39in) Oslo 2000
- $216 - €249 - **£152** - FF1 636
  Gutt og sommerfugl Color lithograph (46x55cm 18x21in) Oslo 2000

AULT George Copeland 1891-1948 **[33]**
- $18 000 - €20 161 - **£12 506** - FF132 249
  Desert Landscape Oil/canvas (71.5x46cm 28x18in) New-York 2001
- $3 400 - €4 043 - **£2 423** - FF26 523
  A Newark Home Oil/panel (35x25cm 13x9in) New-York 2000
- $6 250 - €5 664 - **£3 848** - FF37 155
  Oranges Watercolour/paper (51x69cm 20x27in) Mystic CT 1999

AUMONIER James 1832-1911 **[76]**
- $1 218 - €1 125 - **£749** - FF7 380
  South Cove Common, Suffolk Oil/canvas (44.5x91cm 17x35in) London 1999
- $573 - €637 - **£400** - FF4 178
  Coverack Watercolour/paper (16.5x26cm 6x10in) London 2001

AURELI Giuseppe 1858-1929 **[76]**
- $800 - €829 - **£480** - FF5 440
  Pastorello Olio/tavola (34x24cm 13x9in) Roma 1999
- $1 518 - €1 505 - **£950** - FF9 874
  Farm Workers Returning Home Watercolour (80x135.5cm 31x53in) London 1999

AURILI Richard XIX-XX **[23]**
- $25 000 - €27 919 - **£16 010** - FF183 137
  The Water Carrier Marble (H193cm H75in) New-York 2000

AURIOUST Gabrielle XIX **[1]**
- $1 960 - €2 287 - **£1 363** - FF15 000
  Animation Faubourg Bab-Azoun Gouache/papier (37x59cm 14x23in) Paris 2000

AURRENS Henry 1873-? **[24]**
- $3 736 - €3 659 - **£2 299** - FF24 000
  Matin d'été à Montredon Huile/toile (130x88cm 51x34in) Aix-en-Provence 1999
- $3 742 - €4 192 - **£2 604** - FF27 500
  Notre-Dame de Paris Huile/toile (41x33cm 16x12in) Clamecy 2000

AUSLEGER Rudolf 1897-1974 **[38]**
- $4 498 - €5 292 - **£3 175** - FF34 711
  Stilleben Öl/Karton (23x62cm 9x24in) Berlin 2001
- $1 315 - €1 534 - **£923** - FF10 061
  Abstrakte Komposition Pastel (43.3x38cm 17x14in) Köln 2000

AUSTEN Alexander XIX-XX **[19]**
- $2 904 - €2 789 - **£1 800** - FF18 296
  The Duet/The Recital Oil/canvas (45.5x61cm 17x24in) London 1999
- $641 - €647 - **£400** - FF4 241
  The Connoisseur Oil/canvas (46x30.5cm 18x12in) London 2000

AUSTEN Winifred Marie L. 1876-1964 **[134]**
- $681 - €657 - **£420** - FF4 308
  Young Robin Watercolour/paper (15.5x20.5cm 6x8in) West-Sussex 1999
- $224 - €211 - **£140** - FF1 384
  Group of Sparrows/Lesser Whitethroat Etching (15x23cm 5x9in) Stansted Mountfitchet, Essex 1999

AUSTIN Darrel 1907 **[17]**
- $1 500 - €1 604 - **£1 021** - FF10 520
  Woman with Raven Oil/canvas (76x60cm 30x24in) New-Orleans LA 2001

AUSTIN Robert S. act.1875-1881 **[6]**
- $3 250 - €3 077 - **£2 023** - FF20 184
  Schooner at Sea Oil/canvas (81x106cm 32x42in) Bolton MA 1999

- $1 730 - €1 912 - **£1 200** - FF12 543
  Figure on Rocks Etching (18.5x16cm 7x6in) London 2001

AUSTIN Robert Sargent 1895-1973 **[45]**
- $386 - €432 - **£261** - FF2 831
  Summer Flowers Watercolour/paper (26x22cm 10x8in) Dublin 2000
- $392 - €366 - **£243** - FF2 400
  Scythes Engraving (13x9.5cm 5x3in) London 1999

AUSTIN Samuel 1796-1834 **[42]**
- $2 118 - €1 926 - **£1 300** - FF12 637
  Busy Country Lane Watercolour/paper (20x27.5cm 7x10in) London 1999

AUSTIN William Frederick 1833-1899 **[29]**
- $222 - €248 - **£150** - FF1 625
  Cow Tower and Riverside, Norwich Watercolour/paper (30x48cm 12x19in) Aylsham, Norfolk 2000

AUSTIN-CARTER Mathilde XIX-XX **[2]**
- $3 362 - €3 858 - **£2 300** - FF25 304
  Male and Female Portraits Miniature (6x5cm 2x2in) Little-Lane, Ilkley 2000

AUSTRIAN Ben 1870-1921 **[31]**
- $40 000 - €47 570 - **£28 508** - FF312 040
  From Old Virginia Oil/canvas (157.5x107.5cm 62x42in) New-York 2000
- $11 698 - €13 639 - **£8 200** - FF89 463
  The Proud Mother Oil/canvas (50x65cm 19x25in) Crewkerne, Somerset 2000
- $9 000 - €7 551 - **£5 280** - FF49 532
  Chicks in a Basket Oil/canvas (35x40cm 14x16in) Philadelphia PA 1998

AUTERE Hannes 1888-1967 **[37]**
- $365 - €404 - **£253** - FF2 647
  Vårvinter Oil/panel (25x21cm 9x8in) Helsinki 2001
- $717 - €807 - **£493** - FF5 295
  Lucifer Sculpture, wood (H34.5cm H13in) Helsinki 2000

AUTERI Lodovico XIX-XX **[6]**
- $5 539 - €5 729 - **£3 500** - FF37 579
  Lady riding side-saddle with her greyhound Bronze (43x44.5cm 16x17in) London 2000

AUTHOUART Daniel 1943 **[31]**
- $968 - €945 - **£613** - FF6 200
  Violoncelles Pastel/papier (28x30cm 11x11in) Dieppe 1999
- $142 - €153 - **£95** - FF1 006
  Map Collector Farblithographie (65x50cm 25x19in) Königstein 2000

AUTIO Rudy 1926 **[14]**
- $4 000 - €4 144 - **£2 546** - FF27 181
  Figure Vessel R-21 Ceramic (34x40x21cm 13x15x8in) New-York 2000
- $4 000 - €4 144 - **£2 546** - FF27 181
  Untitled Drawing Pencil (146x124.5cm 57x49in) New-York 2000

AUTISSIER Louis Marie 1772-1830 **[21]**
- $4 553 - €5 362 - **£3 200** - FF35 172
  Equerry to Louis, King of Holland, facing right in blue Coat Miniature (5.5x4.5cm 2x1in) London 2000

AUTRIQUE Édouard J. Fr. 1799-1876 **[3]**
- $70 752 - €67 078 - **£44 220** - FF440 000
  Bouquets de fleurs sur un entablement Huile/toile (114x93cm 44x36in) Vichy 1999

$8 683 - €8 232 - £5 427 - FF54 000
Bouquet de fleurs sur un entablement Huile/toile (41x32.5cm 16x12in) Vichy 1999

AUVIGNÉ Jan XX **[4]**
$1 400 - €1 517 - **£933** - FF9 951
«Algerie, Tunisie, Maroc, CIE, GLE Transatlantique» Poster (99x62cm 39x24in) New-York 2000

AUVREST XVIII-XIX **[8]**
$645 - €762 - **£458** - FF5 000
Napoléon à cheval/Frédéric II Roi de Prusse à cheval Encre (35.5x25.5cm 13x10in) Paris 2001

AUZOLLE Marcellin 1862-1942 **[63]**
$615 - €686 - **£414** - FF4 500
«Exposition internationale automobiles, aviation, cycles, Lyon» Affiche (160x120cm 62x47in) Orléans 2000

AUZOU Pauline Desmarquêts 1775-1835 **[28]**
$2 209 - €2 477 - **£1 500** - FF16 250
Girl in Profile to the Right, Bust-Length, Wearing a Hat/Study Oil/paper (45x33cm 17x12in) London 2000
$2 356 - €2 642 - **£1 600** - FF17 329
Portrait of a Girl, Bust Length, Yurned Three-Quarters to the Left Black & white chalks (42x38.5cm 16x15in) London 2000

AVANZI Vittorio 1850-1913 **[9]**
$7 600 - €9 848 - **£5 700** - FF64 600
Paesaggio Olio/tela (86x147cm 33x57in) Prato 2001

AVATI James 1912 **[11]**
$2 000 - €1 851 - **£1 224** - FF12 145
Smiling Girl seated on bed of modest Shack, cover for Lilly Crackell Oil/board (45x39cm 18x15in) New-York 1999

AVATI Mario 1921 **[257]**
$240 - €244 - **£151** - FF1 600
Les artichauts Gouache (18x27cm 7x10in) Saint-Dié 2000
$177 - €198 - **£123** - FF1 300
«Les trois petits pains» Gravure (37.5x47.5cm 14x18in) Paris 2001

AVED Jacques A. le Batave 1702-1766 **[8]**
$5 946 - €5 445 - **£3 624** - FF35 719
Young Nobleman, Bust Length, Wearing a Gold Embroidered Waistcoat Oil/canvas (54.5x45cm 21x17in) Amsterdam 1999

AVEDON Richard 1923 **[188]**
$1 283 - €1 457 - **£900** - FF9 560
«The Beatles» Poster (67.5x49.5cm 26x19in) London 2001
$6 000 - €6 583 - **£3 985** - FF43 180
Billy Wilder and Marilyn Monroe Photo (25.5x20cm 10x7in) Beverly-Hills CA 2000

AVELINE Pierre Alexandre 1702-1760 **[1]**
$1 760 - €1 652 - **£1 100** - FF10 835
«Le toucher» «Le gout» «L'odorat» «L'ouie» Grabado (26x18cm 10x7in) Madrid 1999

AVELLI Tino XX **[5]**
$192 - €229 - **£133** - FF1 500
«Baci Rubati, baisers volés, François Truffaut avec J.P. Leaud...» Affiche (140x200cm 55x78in) Paris 2000

AVENALI Marcello 1912-1981 **[28]**
$6 000 - €6 220 - **£3 600** - FF40 800
Modella Tecnica mista (60x82cm 23x32in) Prato 1999

$500 - €518 - **£300** - FF3 400
Innamorati Gouache (42x34cm 16x13in) Roma 2000

AVENDAÑO Donato 1840-? **[2]**
$3 510 - €3 904 - **£2 340** - FF25 610
Vista del Palacio Real de Madrid Oleo/lienzo (88x60cm 34x23in) Madrid 2000

AVENDAÑO Serafín 1838-? **[8]**
$15 680 - €16 818 - **£10 640** - FF110 320
Marina Oleo/lienzo (80x125cm 31x49in) Madrid 2001

AVERCAMP Hendrick 1585-1634 **[10]**
$2 983 - €2 556 - **£1 793** - FF16 766
Eisvergnügen Oil/panel (30x40cm 11x15in) Köln 1998
$148 048 - €172 436 - **£103 436** - FF1 131 108
Haaerlemmerpoort, Amsterdam/Haarlemmerpoort, Seen from Within the City Ink (11.5x31cm 4x12in) Amsterdam 2000

AVERINE Alexandre 1952 **[215]**
$660 - €617 - **£400** - FF4 044
By the Birch Trees Oil/canvas (50x61cm 19x24in) Fernhurst, Haslemere, Surrey 1999
$363 - €351 - **£228** - FF2 300
Leçon de piano Huile/toile (33x24cm 12x9in) L'Isle-Adam 1999

AVERY Milton 1885-1965 **[410]**
$80 000 - €95 140 - **£57 016** - FF624 080
Nude on Blue Settee Oil/canvas/board (51x40.5cm 20x15in) New-York 2000
$14 000 - €11 990 - **£8 265** - FF78 652
Standing Nude Oil/board (38x12.5cm 14x4in) New-York 1998
$12 000 - €13 133 - **£8 277** - FF86 145
Pasture Gouache (37x56cm 14x22in) New-York 2001
$2 200 - €2 452 - **£1 528** - FF16 086
Birds and Sea Woodcut (24.5x61cm 9x24in) New-York 2001

AVERY Ralph Hillyer 1906-1976 **[4]**
$1 500 - €1 559 - **£945** - FF10 227
Fitzhurgh St.Rochester, HY Watercolour/paper (21x28cm 8x11in) Batavia NY 2000

AVIA PEÑA Amalia 1930 **[40]**
$2 295 - €2 553 - **£1 530** - FF16 745
Rincón de ácido Oleo/tabla (50x73cm 19x28in) Madrid 2000
$170 - €144 - **£100** - FF945
Calle nevada Grabado (24.5x32cm 9x12in) Madrid 1998

AVIBUS Gaspar ab Osello c.1536-? **[1]**
$1 794 - €2 045 - **£1 252** - FF13 415
Die Allegorie der Jagd, nach Luca Penni Kupferstich (36x25cm 14x9in) Berlin 2001

AVNER Hervé 1954 **[112]**
$990 - €1 143 - **£693** - FF7 500
Retour de pêche Pastel/papier (38x63cm 14x24in) Paris 2001

AVNI Aharon 1906-1951 **[41]**
$2 700 - €2 898 - **£1 806** - FF19 010
Landscape Oil/canvas (52x43cm 20x16in) Tel Aviv 2000
$375 - €399 - **£248** - FF2 616
Still life Gouache/paper (34x49cm 13x19in) Tel Aviv 2000

AVNI Shimon 1932 **[24]**
$900 - €966 - **£602** - FF6 336
Trees Oil/canvas (70x100cm 27x39in) Tel Aviv 2000

AVONDO Vittorio 1836-1910 **[17]**
- $37 500 - €38 874 - **£22 500** - FF255 000
  Quiete Olio/tela (69.5x135cm 27x53in) Milano 1999
- $8 000 - €8 293 - **£4 800** - FF54 400
  Paesaggio Olio/tela (26.5x34cm 10x13in) Vercelli 1999

AVONT van Pieter 1600-1632 **[27]**
- $42 500 - €37 279 - **£25 806** - FF244 536
  The Holy Family with Putti in a Landscape Oil/panel (57x85cm 22x33in) New-York 1999
- $7 226 - €7 013 - **£4 488** - FF46 000
  Personnages Huile/panneau (43.5x33cm 17x12in) Marseille 1999

AVRAMIDIS Joannis 1922 **[35]**
- $5 635 - €6 647 - **£3 975** - FF43 600
  Zweiformenkopf Bronze (H32.3cm H12in) Köln 2001

AVRILLAUD XIX-XX **[1]**
- $2 151 - €2 134 - **£1 338** - FF14 000
  La Goélette La Gratitude entrant tout d'sus dans l'estuaire la Garonne Aquarelle/papier (48x60cm 18x23in) Paris 1999

AWAD Farid 1924-1982 **[1]**
- $9 310 - €10 471 - **£6 500** - FF68 685
  Seated Man Oil/canvas (72x48cm 28x18in) London 2001

AXENTOWICZ Teodor 1859-1938 **[135]**
- $4 950 - €4 133 - **£2 903** - FF27 111
  Portrait of a Young Woman Oil/panel (67x50cm 26x19in) Warszawa 1998
- $3 760 - €3 520 - **£2 331** - FF23 091
  Peasant Woman holding a Plate Oil/board (31.5x24cm 12x9in) Warszawa 1999
- $5 255 - €5 221 - **£3 273** - FF34 247
  Madame Ewa Pastel/paper (60x45.5cm 23x17in) Warszawa 1999
- $3 432 - €3 684 - **£2 296** - FF24 165
  Fille avec un vase Gravure (35.5x21cm 13x8in) Warszawa 2000

AXER Otto 1906-1983 **[6]**
- $4 749 - €5 450 - **£3 249** - FF35 750
  Deux femmes Huile/toile (70x57cm 27x22in) Katowice 2000

AXTMANN Léopold 1700-1748 **[1]**
- $25 000 - €23 173 - **£15 545** - FF152 002
  Horse portraits: a white and a black lipizzaner stallions Oil/canvas (48.5x61cm 19x24in) New-York 1999

AYERS Dick XX **[3]**
- $1 800 - €1 736 - **£1 137** - FF11 390
  Sgt. Fury and his Howling Commandos No.108 Ink (38x25.5cm 14x10in) New-York 1999

AYLING George 1887-1960 **[76]**
- $1 903 - €1 824 - **£1 200** - FF11 963
  The Gateway to the Empire's Commerce' Oil/canvas/board (49x60cm 19x23in) Billingshurst, West-Sussex 1999
- $439 - €401 - **£275** - FF2 651
  Departure at Dusk Watercolour/paper (28x43cm 11x17in) Fernhurst, Haslemere, Surrey 1999
- $327 - €314 - **£200** - FF2 061
  «The Matlocks» Poster (84x64cm 33x25in) London 1999

AYLWARD James DeVine ?-1917 **[15]**
- $2 080 - €1 986 - **£1 300** - FF13 026
  The Master of Defence Oil/panel (28.5x18.5cm 11x7in) London 1999

AYLWARD William James 1875-1956 **[11]**
- $1 700 - €1 574 - **£1 040** - FF10 323
  Sketch of a boating scene on Hudson river Watercolour, gouache (28x44cm 11x17in) New-York 1999
- $600 - €526 - **£364** - FF3 452
  «Majestic» Poster (74x49cm 29x19in) New-York 1999

AYMÉ FAUTEREAU Alix 1894-1989 **[29]**
- $3 405 - €3 735 - **£2 312** - FF24 500
  La Vietnamienne et ses filles Huile/panneau (50.5x37.5cm 19x14in) Soissons 2000
- $914 - €1 067 - **£642** - FF7 000
  Fillette au fichu noir Huile/toile (36.5x27.5cm 14x10in) Bayeux 2000
- $1 808 - €1 998 - **£1 254** - FF13 109
  La jeune Tonkinoise nue (the Naked Tonkinese Girl) Gouache (57x89cm 22x35in) Singapore 2001

AYOTTE Léo 1909-1979 **[138]**
- $1 488 - €1 469 - **£916** - FF9 633
  Nature morte au pain Huile/toile (46x61cm 18x24in) Montréal 1999
- $751 - €826 - **£520** - FF5 420
  Pointe à mire, St-Jacques des Pils Huile/panneau (20.5x25.5cm 8x10in) Montréal 2001

AYRAULT Christian 1950 **[2]**
- $2 639 - €2 820 - **£1 794** - FF18 500
  Un castor Bronze (27x45.5cm 10x17in) Pontoise 2001

AYRES Frederico 1887-1963 **[9]**
- $8 600 - €9 970 - **£6 000** - FF65 400
  Mocímboa da praia Oleo/lienzo (48x76cm 18x29in) Lisboa 2001
- $3 870 - €4 487 - **£2 700** - FF29 430
  Palhota da Beira Indígena Oleo/tabla (24x29.5cm 9x11in) Lisboa 2001

AYRES George B. XIX-XX **[5]**
- $2 750 - €2 565 - **£1 660** - FF16 823
  Abraham Lincoln Photograph (21x17cm 8x6in) New-York 1999

AYRES Gillian 1930 **[69]**
- $4 116 - €3 868 - **£2 500** - FF25 374
  Untitled Oil/board (70.5x66cm 27x25in) London 1999
- $1 316 - €1 444 - **£849** - FF9 471
  Abstract Composition Watercolour (76x75cm 29x29in) London 2000
- $280 - €261 - **£173** - FF1 714
  Phoebus'Blaze Silkscreen in colors (92x92cm 36x36in) London 1999

AYRTON Michael 1921-1975 **[280]**
- $7 744 - €7 113 - **£4 800** - FF46 661
  Figures in a red Room Oil/canvas (88.5x113.5cm 34x44in) London 1999
- $2 887 - €2 910 - **£1 800** - FF19 086
  Harvest Oil/board (21x31cm 8x12in) London 2000
- $5 678 - €6 095 - **£3 800** - FF39 982
  Figure in Balance V Bronze (H82cm H32in) London 2000
- $3 896 - €3 844 - **£2 400** - FF25 217
  Minotaur Crouching Bronze (H15cm H5in) London 1999
- $1 403 - €1 220 - **£849** - FF8 005
  Portrait of Christopher Isherwood Ink (33x23.5cm 12x9in) London 1999
- $224 - €212 - **£140** - FF1 390
  The Shepherd at Night Lithograph (34x45cm 13x18in) Fernhurst, Haslemere, Surrey 1999

AZACETA Luis Cruz 1942 [13]
- $32 500 - €28 339 - £19 649 - FF185 890
  The Exiled (Man with two Flags) Acrylic/canvas (267x208.5cm 105x82in) New-York 1998
- $9 000 - €7 827 - £5 426 - FF51 345
  Innocence Acrylic/canvas (77x62cm 30x24in) New-York 1998

AZAMBRE Etienne 1859-1935 [3]
- $1 959 - €2 331 - £1 400 - FF15 292
  A Young Beauty Standing Beside a Jug of Lilies Oil/canvas (73.5x55.5cm 28x21in) London 2000

AZE Adolphe 1823-1884 [4]
- $5 112 - €4 269 - £2 998 - FF28 000
  Dans le port d'Alger Huile/toile (40x56cm 15x22in) Paris 1998

AZEGLIO d' Massimo 1798-1866 [21]
- $10 710 - €11 103 - £6 426 - FF72 828
  Sosta di contadini nella boscaglia Olio/tela (104x145cm 40x57in) Milano 1999
- $8 330 - €8 635 - £4 998 - FF56 644
  Veduta lacustre con figure Olio/tavola (34.5x53.5cm 13x21in) Milano 1999
- $4 250 - €4 406 - £2 550 - FF28 900
  Agguato nel bosco Olio/cartone (32x41cm 12x16in) Vercelli 1999

AZEMA Jacques XX [2]
- $11 670 - €12 958 - £8 117 - FF85 000
  Jeune arabe à la coupe d'eau Gouache/papier (45x36.5cm 17x14in) Paris 2001

AZÉMA Louis 1876-1963 [35]
- $548 - €640 - £375 - FF4 200
  Dentelière provençale Huile/toile (55x46cm 21x18in) Troyes 2000
- $404 - €389 - £254 - FF2 550
  Noces Bretonnes Gouache/papier (35x44.5cm 13x17in) Angers 1999

AZÉNE Arie 1934 [6]
- $7 130 - €6 644 - £4 437 - FF43 580
  Composition Oil/canvas (130x162cm 51x63in) Tel Aviv 1999

AZIZ & CUCHER 1961/1958 [4]
- $1 297 - €1 512 - £898 - FF9 917
  Interior #4 Type C color print (127x101cm 50x39in) Caracas ($) 2000

AZIZ Abdul 1928 [18]
- $6 636 - €6 185 - £4 095 - FF40 568
  Mother and Child Oil/canvas (50x39cm 19x15in) Singapore 1999
- $4 591 - €5 213 - £3 142 - FF34 196
  Ladies by the Window Oil/canvas (40.5x30cm 15x11in) Singapore 2000

AZUELOS Samuel 1930 [1]
- $3 572 - €3 811 - £2 262 - FF25 000
  Jérusalem Huile/toile (78x100cm 30x39in) Garches 1998

AZUMA Kenjiro 1926 [4]
- $2 800 - €3 628 - £2 100 - FF23 800
  Senza titolo Bronzo (50x60x5cm 19x23x1in) Milano 2000

AZZAWI Dia 1939 [2]
- $20 768 - €23 358 - £14 500 - FF153 221
  Oriental Window Acrylic/canvas (114x108cm 44x42in) London 2001
- $6 445 - €7 249 - £4 500 - FF47 551
  What Al-Niffari sait to Abdullah Gouache/paper (158x53cm 62x20in) London 2001

AZZINARI Franco 1949 [7]
- $1 550 - €1 607 - £930 - FF10 540
  Pesco in fiore Olio/tela (40x60cm 15x23in) Vercelli 2000

B

BAADE Knud Andreassen 1808-1879 [21]
- $22 414 - €24 060 - £15 000 - FF157 824
  Norwegian Fjord by Moonlight Oil/canvas (159.5x132cm 62x51in) London 2000
- $7 905 - €9 404 - £5 467 - FF61 687
  Nattstemning Oil/canvas (55x60cm 21x23in) Oslo 2000
- $2 310 - €2 747 - £1 645 - FF18 018
  Måneskin over elven Oil/panel (17x25cm 6x9in) Oslo 2000

BAADER Amalie 1763-c.1840 [3]
- $407 - €486 - £290 - FF3 186
  Die Frau des Künstlers Georg Friedrich Schmidt, nach G.Fr.Schmidt Radierung (9.4x8cm 3x3in) Berlin 2000

BAADER Louis 1828-c.1919 [13]
- $10 368 - €12 196 - £7 512 - FF80 000
  La présentation au salon Huile/toile (65x93cm 25x36in) Lorient 2001

BAADSGAARD Alfrida V. Ludovica 1839-1912 [29]
- $879 - €808 - £540 - FF5 299
  Opstilling med blomster i krukker Oil/canvas (45x35cm 17x13in) Vejle 1999

BAAGØE Carl Erik 1829-1902 [114]
- $4 275 - €4 037 - £2 667 - FF26 484
  Stille dag med sejl- og dampskibe i Sundet Oil/canvas (43x70cm 16x27in) København 1999
- $1 244 - €1 077 - £755 - FF7 064
  Et fiskerleje Oil/canvas (28x40cm 11x15in) København 1998
- $257 - €242 - £159 - FF1 589
  Pumpestationen, Nissum Fjord Pencil/paper (24x35cm 9x13in) Viby J, Århus 1999

BAAKE Boleslaw 1905-1963 [2]
- $3 540 - €3 679 - £2 246 - FF24 132
  Vue sur Kazimierz Huile/toile (66x78cm 25x30in) Warszawa 2000

BAAR Hugo 1873-1912 [12]
- $7 225 - €6 834 - £4 500 - FF44 825
  Winter Oil/canvas (160x60cm 62x23in) Praha 2000

BABBERGER August 1885-1936 [19]
- $2 367 - €2 750 - £1 663 - FF18 040
  «Blick auf den Pilatus» Öl/Karton (50x70cm 19x27in) Luzern 2001

BABCOCK Richard Fayerweather 1887-1954 [2]
- $650 - €605 - £401 - FF3 967
  «Join the Navy» Poster (105x72cm 41x28in) New-York 1999

BABCOCK William Perkins 1826-1899 [8]
- $10 213 - €8 728 - £6 000 - FF57 252
  Roses and Pansies in White Vase Oil/canvas (32x24cm 12x9in) Glasgow 1998

BABOULENE Eugène 1905-1994 [348]
- $3 596 - €4 040 - £2 504 - FF26 500
  L'auberge de Sainte-Anne d'Avenos Huile/toile (38x46cm 14x18in) Cannes 2001

🍷 **$1 680** - €1 982 - **£1 181** - FF13 000
La blonde Huile/toile (22x27cm 8x10in)
Fontainebleau 2000

✎ **$897** - €1 067 - **£639** - FF7 000
Le port Aquarelle/papier (32x49.5cm 12x19in) Paris 2000

📖 **$110** - €130 - **£77** - FF850
Intérieur Lithographie couleurs (45.5x54cm 17x21in) Paris 2000

BABUREN van Dirck c.1594-1624 [9]
🍷 **$62 500** - €64 791 - **£37 500** - FF425 000
Giacatori di carte Olio/tela (94x111cm 37x43in)
Imbersago (Lecco) 2001
🍷 **$6 426** - €5 551 - **£4 284** - FF36 414
La cattura di Cristo Olio/tela (26x37cm 10x14in)
Venezia 1998

BAC (Ferdinand Bach) 1859-1952 [138]
✎ **$146** - €137 - **£88** - FF900
Désespoir poétique Encre (27x21cm 10x8in) Paris 1999
📖 **$1 104** - €1 211 - **£733** - FF7 943
«Yvette Guilbert, tous les soirs à l'horloge»
Poster (200x74cm 78x29in) Stockholm 2000

BACARISAS PODESTA Gustavo 1873-1971 [14]
🍷 **$590** - €601 - **£370** - FF3 940
Montañas nevadas de Suecia Oleo/lienzo (59x49cm 23x19in) Madrid 2000
🍷 **$1 760** - €1 652 - **£1 100** - FF10 835
Gallinas Oleo/lienzo (22x29cm 8x11in) Madrid 1999

BACCALARIO Angelo 1852-? [1]
🍷 **$4 384** - €4 116 - **£2 708** - FF27 000
Rue animée Huile/toile (50x35.5cm 19x13in) Paris 1999

BACCANI Attilio XIX-XX [9]
🍷 **$2 800** - €3 180 - **£1 964** - FF20 861
Portrait of Two Sisters Oil/canvas (111.5x86.5cm 43x34in) New-York 2001

BACCI Aris 1894-1948 [3]
✎ **$500** - €518 - **£300** - FF3 400
Composizione Pastelli/carta (44x33cm 17x12in) Roma 1999

BACCI Baccio Maria 1888-1974 [36]
🍷 **$3 200** - €4 147 - **£2 400** - FF27 200
Il popone Olio/cartone (37x52cm 14x20in) Prato 2000
🍷 **$2 040** - €1 762 - **£1 360** - FF11 560
Nudo femminile con maschera Olio/tavoletta (30x19cm 11x7in) Firenze 1998

BACCI Edmondo 1913-1989 [29]
🍷 **$8 000** - €10 367 - **£6 000** - FF68 000
«Avvenimento 345» Olio/tela (140x140cm 55x55in) Milano 2000
🍷 **$1 700** - €1 750 - **£1 080** - FF11 480
Avvenimento #101/Avvenimento #102 Oil/canvas (39x83cm 15x33in) Plainville CT 2000

BACCIARELLI Marcello 1731-1818 [6]
🍷 **$9 869** - €10 824 - **£6 368** - FF71 000
Portrait de Ursula Zakoyska Huile/toile (66x54cm 25x21in) Paris 2000
✎ **$1 642** - €1 534 - **£1 013** - FF10 061
Stanislaus Poniatowski, König van Polen (1732-1798) Coloured chalks/paper (25x19.3cm 9x7in) Köln 1999

BACCUET Prosper 1798-1854 [2]
🍷 **$12 164** - €14 178 - **£8 425** - FF93 000
L'Arc de Triomphe de Djémila Huile/toile (65x100cm 25x39in) Auxerre 2000

BACH Alois 1809-1893 [18]
🍷 **$10 448** - €11 760 - **£7 199** - FF77 139
Fuhrwerk am Steinbruch Öl/Leinwand (47x64cm 18x25in) München 2000
🍷 **$1 563** - €1 431 - **£952** - FF9 390
Rastende Bauern neben den Pferden am Feldrain Öl/Leinwand/Karton (17.5x25cm 6x9in) München 1999

BACH Elvira 1951 [150]
🍷 **$8 787** - €8 692 - **£5 479** - FF57 016
Schlangenhochzeit III Acryl/Leinwand (200x180cm 78x70in) Berlin 1999
🍷 **$2 423** - €2 352 - **£1 508** - FF15 427
Weibliche Figur Acryl/Papier (104.3x77.6cm 41x30in) Berlin 1999
🍷 **$2 649** - €2 470 - **£1 601** - FF16 199
Grüne Erdbeere Acryl/Leinwand (40x30cm 15x11in) München 1999
🍷 **$1 017** - €971 - **£635** - FF6 372
Weibliche Figur Gouache/paper (29.5x20.8cm 11x8in) Köln 1999
📖 **$533** - €460 - **£320** - FF3 017
Drei Frauen Serigraph in colors (70x100cm 27x39in) Köln 1998

BACH Guido 1828-1905 [45]
🍷 **$1 191** - €1 321 - **£825** - FF8 664
Ung kvinna med turkossmycken Oil/canvas (45.5x35.5cm 17x13in) Malmö 2000
✎ **$696** - €785 - **£480** - FF5 148
Mother and Child and Other Figures Seated on a Church Steps Watercolour/paper (65.5x43cm 25x16in) Newbury, Berkshire 2000

BACH Marcel 1879-1950 [16]
🍷 **$581** - €610 - **£385** - FF4 000
Les vendanges Huile/toile (45x55cm 17x21in) Quimper 2000

BACHE Otto 1839-1927 [177]
🍷 **$3 007** - €3 352 - **£2 102** - FF21 985
Tangkörsel på stranden Oil/canvas (68x93cm 26x36in) Köbenhavn 2001
🍷 **$819** - €780 - **£512** - FF5 114
Vildsvinsjägare Oil/canvas (30x43cm 11x16in) Stockholm 1999

BACHELET Emile Just 1892-1981 [10]
🗿 **$1 675** - €1 799 - **£1 121** - FF11 800
Baigneuse Bronze (H29cm H11in) Paris 2000

BACHELIER Jean-Jacques 1724-1806 [15]
🍷 **$35 370** - €34 334 - **£21 846** - FF225 214
La Justice et la Verité Öl/Leinwand (94x138cm 37x54in) Luzern 1999

BACHELIN Auguste 1830-1890 [56]
🍷 **$4 828** - €5 183 - **£3 230** - FF34 000
La chasse aux canards Huile/toile (60x132cm 23x51in) Soissons 2000
🍷 **$563** - €657 - **£395** - FF4 311
Italienisches Trachtenmädchen in Landschaft Öl/Leinwand (40x32cm 15x12in) Luzern 2000

BACHEM Bele 1916-1996 [10]
✎ **$300** - €307 - **£188** - FF2 012
Insel der Seligen Indian ink (19x33.5cm 7x13in) Hamburg 2000
📖 **$105** - €112 - **£71** - FF737
Meeresidylle Lithographie (51x42cm 20x16in) Bamberg 2001

BACHER Otto Henry 1856-1909 **[15]**
- $28 000 - €31 794 - **£19 163** - FF208 555
  The Waiting Room Oil/canvas (46x53cm 18x20in)
  New-York 2000
- $300 - €250 - **£175** - FF1 642
  Venetian Scene Etching (16x24cm 6x9in) Shaker-
  Heights OH 1998

BACHER Sebastian 1876-1961 **[80]**
- $523 - €562 - **£350** - FF3 689
  Ruhende Venus mit Spiegel haltendem Amor
  Öl/Leinwand (69x101cm 27x39in) Kempten 2000

BACHINSKI Walter Joseph Gerard 1939 **[15]**
- $192 - €194 - **£120** - FF1 273
  **Seated Figure, from Twentieth Anniversary
  Portfolio** Color lithograph (56x39cm 22x15in) Toronto
  2000

BÄCHLI Silvia 1956 **[9]**
- $450 - €524 - **£311** - FF3 440
  Frauen mit gestreckten Armen Ink/paper
  (11.5x20cm 4x7in) Bern 2000

BACHMANN Adolphe c.1880-? **[22]**
- $1 876 - €1 753 - **£1 158** - FF11 500
  Le départ pour la fête Huile/toile (65x54cm
  25x21in) Melun 1999
- $2 388 - €2 211 - **£1 461** - FF14 500
  Venise Huile/panneau (22x40cm 8x15in) Aubagne
  1999

BACHMANN Alfred August Felix 1863-1956 **[64]**
- $3 099 - €3 601 - **£2 178** - FF23 624
  «Ansicht von Venedig mit dem Dogenpalast»
  Öl/Leinwand (35x55cm 13x21in) Luzern 2001

BACHMANN Hans 1852-1917 **[55]**
- $1 127 - €1 210 - **£754** - FF7 937
  Bauernmädchen mit heller Schürze
  Öl/Leinwand/Karton (58.5x31cm 23x12in) Zürich 2000
- $638 - €726 - **£442** - FF4 764
  **Sommerlicher Parkeinblick mit
  Zwetschgenbäumchen** Öl/Karton (32x48cm
  12x18in) Zofingen 2000

BACHMANN Jacob Edwin 1873-1957 **[21]**
- $501 - €500 - **£313** - FF3 283
  **Zürichsee mit Ufenau von Hurden
  aus/Zürichsee bei Pfäffikon** Öl/Leinwand
  (44x49cm 17x19in) Zofingen 1999

BACHMANN John act.1850-1884 **[10]**
- $1 400 - €1 634 - **£988** - FF10 718
  Bird's Eye View of New York and Brooklyn
  Lithograph (54x81cm 21x32in) New-York 2000

BACHMANN Karoly, Karl 1874-1924 **[21]**
- $356 - €332 - **£220** - FF2 180
  Blick auf Frauenchiemsee Oil/panel (11x22cm
  4x8in) Bremen 1999

BACHMANN Max 1862-1921 **[5]**
- $18 000 - €16 618 - **£11 070** - FF109 006
  Bust of Abraham Lincoln Bronze (H76cm H29in)
  New-York 1999

BACHMANN Otto 1915-1996 **[170]**
- $1 499 - €1 378 - **£921** - FF9 037
  Amazonenschlacht Huile/panneau (79.5x79.5cm
  31x31in) Zürich 1999
- $201 - €187 - **£123** - FF1 225
  Der Gehenkte Crayon/papier (34.5x24.8cm 13x9in)
  Bern 1999
- $154 - €150 - **£95** - FF981
  Zirkus/Am Hafen Farblithographie (54x73.5cm
  21x28in) Zürich 1999

BACHRACH David, Jnr. 1845-1921 **[1]**
- $14 000 - €13 219 - **£8 694** - FF86 714
  **The Gettysburg Battlefield Dedication
  Ceremony, November 19** Albumen print
  (10.5x10.5cm 4x4in) New-York 1999

BACHSTROM Sigismond XVIII **[1]**
- $65 000 - €71 617 - **£43 361** - FF469 774
  View of the Hongs at Canton Watercolour,
  gouache/paper (43x71cm 17x28in) Portsmouth NH
  1999

BACK George, Admiral 1786-1878 **[4]**
- $12 908 - €12 397 - **£8 000** - FF81 317
  «Point Griffin, West of the McKenzie River»
  Watercolour/paper (13x23.5cm 5x9in) London 1999

BACK Robert Trenaman 1922 **[3]**
- $8 271 - €9 176 - **£5 500** - FF60 188
  **The Battle of Trafalgar: H.M.Ships Victory,
  temeraire and Neptune** Oil/canvas (81.5x117cm
  32x46in) London 2000

BÄCK Yngve 1904-1990 **[42]**
- $864 - €739 - **£507** - FF4 847
  Vid fönstret Oil/canvas (82x100cm 32x39in) Helsinki
  1998

BACKER Adriaen 1635-1684 **[5]**
- $14 377 - €12 418 - **£8 666** - FF81 454
  The Rape of the Sabine Women Oil/canvas
  (105.5x160cm 41x62in) Amsterdam 1998

BACKER de François J. 1812-1872 **[3]**
- $4 122 - €4 462 - **£2 862** - FF29 268
  L'artiste peintre et son apprenti Huile/panneau
  (34x42cm 13x16in) Bruxelles 2001

BACKER de Jacob I 1560-c.1590/91 **[21]**
- $26 000 - €25 988 - **£15 883** - FF170 469
  Justice Embracing peace Oil/canvas (160x110cm
  62x43in) New-York 2000

BACKER de Philips XVII **[1]**
- $9 460 - €10 008 - **£6 000** - FF65 650
  Wooded Landscape with a Hermit Praying
  Oil/canvas (191x100.5cm 75x39in) London 2000

BACKER Jacob Adriaensz 1608-1651 **[17]**
- $7 051 - €8 385 - **£5 027** - FF55 500
  Saint Jean-Baptiste Huile/toile (48.5x42cm 19x16in)
  Monte-Carlo 2000
- $2 241 - €2 406 - **£1 500** - FF15 782
  Seated Woman Black & white chalks (34x24.5cm
  13x9in) London 2000

BACKLER Joseph 1815-1897 **[4]**
- $5 722 - €5 567 - **£3 521** - FF36 520
  **Portrait of Robert MacPhillamy/Portrait of
  Catherine MacPhillamy** Oil/canvas (91x75cm
  35x29in) Melbourne 1999

BACKMANSSON Hugo 1860-1953 **[142]**
- $1 074 - €908 - **£641** - FF5 956
  Tanger Oil/canvas (34x51cm 13x20in) Helsinki 1998
- $936 - €874 - **£577** - FF5 736
  Tanger Oil/canvas (35x30cm 13x11in) Helsinki 1999
- $228 - €219 - **£139** - FF1 434
  Marockan Akvarell/papper (22x13cm 8x5in) Helsinki
  1999

BÄCKSTRÖM Barbro 1939-1990 **[66]**
- $17 940 - €16 869 - **£11 115** - FF110 655
  Ydra Sculpture (160x130cm 62x51in) Stockholm 1999
- $2 023 - €1 897 - **£1 251** - FF12 445
  Vågform II Sculpture (H33.5cm H13in) Stockholm
  1999

BACKSTRÖM Miriam 1967 **[3]**
$1 409 - €1 646 - £966 - FF10 794
Scenografier, Set Constructions Cibachrome print
(50x64cm 19x25in) Stockholm 2000

BACKUS Albert E. 1916-1996 **[10]**
$6 138 - €5 972 - £3 778 - FF39 173
Clouds Blowing In Oil/canvas (63x76cm 25x30in)
Nepean, Ont. 1999

BACKVIS Frans 1857-1926 **[19]**
$1 096 - €1 264 - £765 - FF8 292
Bergère et ses moutons Huile/toile (85x64cm
33x25in) Bruxelles 2001
$884 - €818 - £551 - FF5 365
Schapenhoedster Oil/canvas (42x30cm 16x11in)
Lokeren 1999

BACLER D'ALBE Louis, baron 1761-1824 **[27]**
$197 - €213 - £136 - FF1 400
Le pont de Graille à Grenoble Lavis (12x23.5cm
4x9in) Paris 2001
$590 - €671 - £410 - FF4 400
Sans titre Gravure (25x34cm 9x13in) Entzheim 2001

BACON Cecil Walter 1905 **[2]**
$1 200 - €1 154 - £740 - FF7 569
Opening of the Piccadilly Line Extension» Poster
(101.5x63.5cm 39x25in) New-York 1999

BACON Francis 1909-1992 **[436]**
$4 043 760 - €4 406 362 - £2 800 000 -
FF28 903 840
«3 Studies for a Portrait of John Edwards»
Oil/canvas (198x148cm 77x58in) London 2001
$4 034 610 - €4 330 820 - £2 700 000 -
FF28 408 320
Study for a Portrait (Man Screaming) Oil/canvas
(61x51cm 24x20in) London 2000
$1 790 470 - €1 742 608 - £1 100 000 -
FF11 430 760
Three Studies for a Self-Portrait Oil/canvas
(35.5x30.5cm 13x12in) London 1999
$3 219 - €3 532 - £2 072 - FF23 167
Serigrafier Serigraph (62x46cm 24x18in) Helsinki
2000

BACON Henry 1839-1912 **[72]**
$8 000 - €6 712 - £4 715 - FF44 028
Sleeping Gypsy Girl Oil/canvas (49x71cm 19x28in)
Greenwich CT 1998
$700 - €650 - £436 - FF4 261
Woman Riding a Donkey Through a Rocky
Landscape Oil/canvas (33x40cm 13x16in) East-
Dennis MA 1999
$450 - €430 - £281 - FF2 820
«Sacred Lake» Watercolour/paper (28x48cm
11x19in) Dedham MA 1999

BACON Irving Lewis 1853-1910 **[5]**
$3 750 - €4 374 - £2 633 - FF28 692
Still Life with Grapes, Melon, Pears and
Peaches Oil/canvas (61x91cm 24x35in) Boston MA
2000

BACON John Henry Fred. 1865-1914 **[17]**
$47 787 - €49 735 - £30 000 - FF326 238
The Interval Oil/canvas (96.5x133cm 37x52in)
London 2000
$627 - €674 - £420 - FF4 419
Barristers Eating their Dinners in the Temple
Watercolour/paper (25x21.5cm 9x8in) London 2000

BACON Peggy (M. Frances) 1895-1987 **[120]**
$550 - €515 - £338 - FF3 381
Page of Cats #2 Ink (23x27cm 9x10in) New-York
1999
$800 - €749 - £491 - FF4 915
Low Tide/Short Voyage/Terribly Heavy Drypoint
(16.5x19cm 6x7in) New-York 1999

BACOT Edmond 1814-1875 **[6]**
$2 615 - €2 211 - £1 555 - FF14 500
Caen, Eglise St-Pierre et vue sur l'Odon Tirage
papier salé (20.8x14.8cm 8x5in) Chartres 1998

BACQUÉ Daniel J. 1874-1947 **[8]**
$3 088 - €3 506 - £2 145 - FF23 000
Diane et biche Bronze (70x72cm 27x28in) Pontoise
2001

BADA SHANREN 1626-1705 **[18]**
$150 000 - €129 486 - £89 610 - FF849 375
Crab and Reeds Ink/paper (95x33.5cm 37x13in)
New-York 1998

BADALOCCHIO Sisto 1585-1647 **[9]**
$78 000 - €67 382 - £52 000 - FF442 000
Rinaldo che abbandona Armida Olio/tela
(106x155cm 41x61in) Milano 1998
$28 960 - €32 910 - £20 000 - FF215 874
St.Mary Magdalene Oil/canvas (95.5x78.5cm
37x30in) London 2000
$36 000 - €31 297 - £21 787 - FF205 293
Madonna and Child in Glory with the Infant
Baptist Oil/panel (36.5x26.5cm 14x10in) New-York
1999
$1 317 - €1 278 - £820 - FF8 384
Laokoon Radierung (38.2x30.2cm 15x11in) Berlin
1999

BADAROCCO Giovanni Raffaelo 1648-1726 **[3]**
$60 000 - €52 630 - £36 432 - FF345 228
The Holy Family with Saints Anne and the
Infant John the Baptist Oil/canvas (126.5x171cm
49x67in) New-York 1999

BADEN van Hans Jurriaensz. c.1604-1663 **[13]**
$7 799 - €7 632 - £5 000 - FF50 061
The Presentation of Christ Oil/panel (39x52.5cm
15x20in) London 1999
$4 080 - €4 573 - £2 841 - FF30 000
Intérieur d'église animé de personnages
Huile/panneau (33x33cm 13x17in) Paris 2001

BADGER Francis 1904 **[2]**
$1 900 - €2 233 - £1 317 - FF14 647
Old Superior Street Oil/canvas (76x60cm 30x24in)
Cincinnati OH 2000

BADGER Samuel Finley Morse 1873-1919 **[16]**
$8 000 - €8 814 - £5 336 - FF57 818
The American Three-Masted Schooner,
E.I.Morrison Oil/canvas (55x91cm 22x36in)
Portsmouth NH 2000

BADHAM Herbert Edward 1899-1961 **[11]**
$15 666 - €17 717 - £11 025 - FF116 217
London Pub Oil/board (49.5x60cm 19x23in) Malvern,
Victoria 2001
$9 793 - €9 187 - £6 051 - FF60 265
Haymarket, Sydney Oil/board (31.5x24cm 12x9in)
Melbourne 1999

BADI Aquiles 1894-1976 **[3]**
$2 400 - €2 788 - £1 686 - FF18 290
«Canal grande con San Jeremias, Venecia»
Oleo/tabla (34x44cm 13x17in) Buenos-Aires 2001

BADIA CAMPS Angel 1929 **[20]**
🖼 **$364** - €390 - **£247** - FF2 561
Playa de Saint Feliu Oleo/tablex (23x31cm 9x12in)
Madrid 2000

BADIALE Alessandro 1623-1668 **[2]**
〰 **$2 144** - €2 556 - **£1 529** - FF16 769
Die Heilige Familie Radierung (30.3x23.4cm 11x9in)
Berlin 2000

BADIALI Carla 1907-1992 **[6]**
🖼 **$26 400** - €22 806 - **£13 200** - FF149 600
Composizione 40 Olio/cartone/tela (49.5x39.5cm
19x15in) Milano 1999
🖼 **$12 000** - €12 440 - **£7 200** - FF81 600
Composizione Olio/tavola (43x31cm 16x12in)
Milano 2000

BADILE Antonio 1518-1560 **[2]**
🖼 **$8 000** - €9 422 - **£5 532** - FF61 807
Madonna and Child Oil/canvas (61.5x51.5cm
24x20in) New-York 2000

BADIN Jean Jules 1843-? **[2]**
🖼 **$10 460** - €11 228 - **£7 000** - FF73 651
The Offering Oil/canvas (130x98cm 51x38in) London
2000

BADMIN Stanley Roy 1906-1989 **[39]**
✏ **$2 245** - €2 263 - **£1 400** - FF14 845
Autumn Afternoon, near Petersfield, Hants
Watercolour (25x40cm 9x15in) London 2000
〰 **$2 887** - €2 910 - **£1 800** - FF19 086
Addington Kent/Dulwich Village/Tanyard Farm
Etching (6x27.5cm 2x10in) London 2000

BADODI Arnaldo 1913-1943 **[3]**
🖼 **$18 500** - €19 178 - **£11 100** - FF125 800
Il circo Olio/tavola (71x91cm 27x35in) Torino 2000

BADURA Ben, Bernard XX **[5]**
✏ **$350** - €394 - **£242** - FF2 587
Quarry Scene Graphite (43x56cm 17x22in) Hatfield
PA 2000

BADURA Faye Swengel 1904 **[7]**
✏ **$275** - €296 - **£184** - FF1 939
Hibiscus #2 Watercolour/paper (25x31cm 10x12in)
Hatfield PA 2000

BAECHLER Donald 1956 **[164]**
🖼 **$26 000** - €29 122 - **£18 064** - FF191 027
«Flowers» Oil/canvas (152.5x152.5cm 60x60in) New-
York 2001
🖼 **$5 769** - €6 781 - **£4 000** - FF44 480
Abstract Painting With Clown Mixed media
(35.5x45.5cm 13x17in) London 2000
🖼 **$1 382** - €1 724 - **£853** - FF8 720
Untitled Mixed media/canvas (20x15cm 7x5in) Köln
1999
✏ **$3 749** - €3 579 - **£2 342** - FF23 477
Ohne Titel (Crowd Painting) Indian ink/paper
(58.5x45.2cm 23x17in) Köln 1999
〰 **$1 324** - €1 453 - **£880** - FF9 534
Family Radierung (22x20cm 8x7in) Wien 2000

BAECK Johan c.1600-1655 **[4]**
🖼 **$8 196** - €9 909 - **£5 726** - FF65 000
Une joueuse de viole dans un estaminet
Huile/panneau (37x54.5cm 14x21in) Paris 2000

BAEDER John 1938 **[17]**
✏ **$15 000** - €17 404 - **£10 356** - FF114 165
Kings Chef, Colorado Springs, Colorado
Watercolour/paper (55x75.5cm 21x29in) New-York
2000

〰 **$175** - €182 - **£111** - FF1 195
Open, Yellow Diner Screenprint (40.5x63.5cm
15x25in) Boston MA 2000

BAEGERT Jan, Derick c.1440-c.1515 **[4]**
〰 **$16 047** - €17 895 - **£10 790** - FF117 386
Fragment einer Kalvarienbergtafel Oil/panel
(30.5x27.2cm 12x10in) Köln 2000

BAELLIEUR de Cornelis I 1607-1671 **[16]**
🖼 **$45 390** - €45 735 - **£28 290** - FF300 000
**Scène de la vie de la Vierge entourées d'une
guirlande de fleurs** Huile/toile/panneau (123x92cm
48x36in) Paris 2000
🖼 **$8 185** - €7 070 - **£4 934** - FF46 376
A Couple embracing in an Interior Oil/copper
(25.3x20.4cm 9x8in) Amsterdam 1998

BAEN de Jan 1633-1702 **[15]**
🖼 **$8 710** - €7 523 - **£5 250** - FF49 349
**Portrait of a Lady, standing half length on a
Terrace** Oil/canvas (99.7x82.8cm 39x32in) Amsterdam
1998
〰 **$4 289** - €5 113 - **£3 058** - FF33 539
**Der Brand des alten Rathauses von Amsterdam
am 9.Juni 1652** Radierung (27x33.8cm 10x13in)
Berlin 2000

BAER George 1895-1971 **[5]**
🖼 **$470** - €520 - **£326** - FF3 411
Jardin fleuri Huile/panneau (55x38cm 21x14in)
Genève 2001

BAER Howard 1906 **[2]**
🖼 **$1 800** - €1 724 - **£1 112** - FF11 307
Busy Night on Times Square, Illustration
Gouache/paper (39x25cm 15x10in) New-York 1999

BAER Jo 1929 **[13]**
🖼 **$15 000** - €17 071 - **£10 540** - FF111 978
Pale blue Oil/canvas (122x122cm 48x48in) New-York
2001

BAER Morley 1916 **[6]**
📷 **$2 800** - €3 079 - **£1 941** - FF20 199
**Carriage Malaga/Winter Storm/House in
Mijas/Casares/Cortijo/Antequera** Silver print
(23x18cm 9x7in) New-York 2001

BAERDEMAECKER de Felix 1836-1878 **[10]**
🖼 **$1 562** - €1 785 - **£1 087** - FF11 707
Paysage montagneux avec rivière Huile/toile
(72.5x114cm 28x44in) Bruxelles 2001

BAERENTZEN Emilius 1799-1868 **[332]**
🖼 **$2 887** - €3 219 - **£1 975** - FF21 117
**Portraet af Frederik VII i admiralsuniform, ståen-
de på broen** Oil/panel (36x30cm 14x11in) Viby J,
Århus 2000

BAERTLING Olle 1911-1981 **[332]**
🖼 **$20 220** - €23 462 - **£13 960** - FF153 900
Karak Oil/canvas (195x97cm 76x38in) Stockholm 2000
🖼 **$6 643** - €7 443 - **£4 630** - FF48 824
Noir, Rouge, Blanc Oil/canvas (92x60cm 36x23in)
Stockholm 2001
🔨 **$9 089** - €8 547 - **£5 631** - FF56 065
Xuy Iron (H255cm H100in) Stockholm 1999
〰 **$417** - €432 - **£262** - FF2 831
Diagonalkomposition Serigraph in colors (32x17cm
12x6in) Stockholm 2000

BAERWIND Rudolf 1910-1982 **[100]**
🖼 **$1 009** - €941 - **£610** - FF6 171
Komposition in Rot Mixed media (54.3x73.3cm
21x28in) München 1999

B

BAES Émile 1879-1954 **[249]**
- $1 863 - €2 231 - £1 278 - FF14 634
  Olympia Huile/toile (129x194cm 50x76in) Bruxelles 2000
- $714 - €694 - £436 - FF4 552
  Modèle penchée Huile/toile (65x50cm 25x19in) Bruxelles 1999
- $542 - €540 - £332 - FF3 252
  Nu assis Huile/toile (41x33cm 16x12in) Bruxelles 1999

BAES Firmin 1874-1945 **[164]**
- $1 050 - €1 250 - £750 - FF8 199
  Laundry Drying by River, Figures Harvesting Beyond,Pastoral Landscape Oil/canvas (56x100.5cm 22x39in) London 2000
- $1 519 - €1 735 - £1 057 - FF11 382
  Jeune femme au châle bleu Pastel/toile (79x59cm 31x23in) Bruxelles 2001

BAES Lionel 1839-1913 **[11]**
- $836 - €843 - £520 - FF5 528
  Le flûtiste Huile/toile (42x31cm 16x12in) Liège 2000

BAES Rachel 1912-1983 **[84]**
- $666 - €744 - £462 - FF4 878
  L'escalier Huile/toile (65x54cm 25x21in) Antwerpen 2001

BAETS de Angelus 1793-1855 **[2]**
- $5 327 - €4 431 - £3 248 - FF29 067
  The Interior of the Sint Baafs-Cathedral, Ghent Oil/panel (75x54.5cm 29x21in) Amsterdam 1998

BAETS Marc XVII-XVIII **[3]**
- $19 850 - €18 168 - £12 100 - FF119 175
  Flusslandschaft mit vielen Figuren und Booten Öl/Leinwand (50x59cm 19x23in) Wien 1999
- $8 647 - €8 168 - £5 394 - FF53 578
  Peasants and travellers on roads by villages in river landscapes Oil/panel (22.5x34cm 8x13in) Amsterdam 1999

BAEZA Manuel Gomez 1915-1986 **[44]**
- $594 - €661 - £396 - FF4 334
  Paisaje con cielo azul Gouache/papier (50x65cm 19x25in) Madrid 2001

BAFFIER Jean Eugène 1851-1921 **[13]**
- $392 - €381 - £242 - FF2 500
  Le goûter de veau Bas-relief (40x26.5cm 15x10in) Paris 1999

BAGARIA Luis 1882-1940 **[8]**
- $702 - €781 - £494 - FF5 122
  Los evacuados Tinta/papel (30.5x30.5cm 12x12in) Madrid 2001

BAGDATOPULOS William Spencer 1888-1965 **[29]**
- $1 411 - €1 219 - £850 - FF7 949
  «A California Barn» Watercolour/paper (52.5x74.5cm 20x29in) Billingshurst, West-Sussex 1999
- $1 914 - €1 830 - £1 200 - FF12 006
  «Bombay-Delhi, Bombay Baroda and Central India RLY» Poster (102x127cm 40x50in) London 1999

BAGEL Moses Bahelfer 1908-1995 **[5]**
- $2 091 - €2 439 - £1 467 - FF16 000
  A la gloire du travail Huile/toile (143x75cm 56x29in) Paris 2001

BAGER Johann Daniel 1734-1815 **[8]**
- $50 052 - €45 553 - £30 722 - FF298 806
  Früchtestilleben mit Vogelnest, Eidechse und Schmetterling Öl/Kupfer (37.5x43.5cm 14x17in) Zürich 1999

BAGETTI Giuseppe Pietro 1764-1831 **[9]**
- $78 456 - €71 700 - £48 000 - FF470 318
  Turin: The City from the surrounding Campagna with the River Po Watercolour/paper (60x90.5cm 23x35in) London 1999

BAGGE Eva 1871-1964 **[68]**
- $772 - €891 - £540 - FF5 847
  Stilleben med luta, Michelangelo Oil/canvas (73x62cm 28x24in) Stockholm 2001
- $988 - €862 - £597 - FF5 652
  «Gröna äpplen i träskål» Oil/canvas (41x33cm 16x12in) Stockholm 1998
- $912 - €769 - £541 - FF5 047
  Flickporträtt Pastel/paper (39x32cm 15x12in) Stockholm 1998

BAGGE Magnus Thulstrup 1825-1894 **[12]**
- $3 167 - €3 304 - £1 998 - FF21 670
  Skoglandskap i måneskinn Oil/canvas (55x79cm 21x31in) Oslo 2000
- $346 - €403 - £247 - FF2 641
  Strandparti med robåd Oil/canvas (10x14cm 3x5in) Aarhus 2001

BAGLIONE Giovanni 1566/71-1643/44 **[23]**
- $32 000 - €41 466 - £24 000 - FF272 000
  Danae Olio/tela (75x99cm 29x38in) Milano 2001
- $1 190 - €1 234 - £714 - FF8 092
  Studi di volto e di mani Sanguina/carta (23.5x41cm 9x16in) Venezia 2001

BAGSHAWE Joseph Richard 1870-1909 **[13]**
- $1 945 - €1 883 - £1 200 - FF12 350
  Whitby Fishing Boats off a Coastline Oil/canvas (61x91.5cm 24x36in) West-Yorshire 1999
- $7 337 - €7 890 - £5 000 - FF51 754
  Unloading the Catch Oil/canvas (35x45cm 13x17in) West-Yorshire 2001
- $986 - €1 158 - £700 - FF7 595
  Fishing Vessels in Whitby Harbour Watercolour/paper (23x33cm 9x13in) Whitby, Yorks 2000

BAHIEU Jules 1860-? **[49]**
- $1 836 - €1 687 - £1 128 - FF11 067
  Ein Schäfer weidet seine Herde im Schatten mächtiger Laubbäume Öl/Leinwand (63x53cm 24x20in) Stuttgart 1999
- $1 153 - €1 372 - £822 - FF9 000
  Le poulailler Huile/panneau (24x30cm 9x11in) Calais 2000

BAHUET Louis Alfred 1862-1910 **[3]**
- $3 668 - €4 335 - £2 600 - FF28 435
  L'atelier du peintre Oil/canvas (72.5x54cm 28x21in) London 2000
- $1 100 - €1 041 - £683 - FF6 830
  «Royal Muscat» Poster (140x99cm 55x38in) New-York 1999

BAI MING 1965 **[3]**
- $2 952 - €3 143 - £1 872 - FF20 619
  The Silent World No.10 Mixed media/canvas (100x100cm 39x39in) Taipei 2000

BAI YIEFU (Cao Jingmao) 1963 **[2]**
- $2 100 - €2 177 - £1 260 - FF14 280
  Moutain with Snow China (96x177cm 37x69in) Prato 1999

BAIER Jean 1932 **[61]**
- $524 - €625 - £373 - FF4 101
  Ohne Titel Watercolour (23x23cm 9x9in) Luzern 2000

$115 - €128 - £78 - FF841
Ohne Titel Farberigraphie (66x59cm 25x23in) Zürich
2000

BAIERL Theodor 1881-1932 [24]
$1 030 - €1 022 - £643 - FF6 707
Schleiertanz dreier Mädchen auf einer von ioni-
schen Säulen Oil/panel (53x45.5cm 20x17in)
München 1999
$1 291 - €1 434 - £900 - FF9 404
The Story of a Maiden's flight Coloured chalks
(66.5x139.5cm 26x54in) London 2001

BAIG Ramkinkar XX [2]
$8 000 - €7 574 - £4 989 - FF49 685
Woman bathing a Child Watercolour (40x30cm
15x11in) New-York 1999

BAIGAI Totoki 1749-1804 [3]
$1 667 - €1 789 - £1 115 - FF11 738
Gedichtzeilen über Seelandschaft mit Tempel
Indian ink/paper (119.1x10.8cm 46x4in) Köln 2000

BAIJ Ramkinkar 1910-1980 [32]
$3 592 - €4 191 - £2 500 - FF27 490
Bengal Village Oil/board (36.5x52cm 14x20in)
London 2000
$4 630 - €4 332 - £2 800 - FF28 413
Horse and Cart Oil/canvas (18x32.5cm 7x12in)
London 1999
$3 000 - €2 590 - £1 792 - FF16 987
Man and Tree Watercolour (18.5x24cm 7x9in) New-
York 1998

BAIJOT-GOMARD Marie-Ange XX [11]
$1 093 - €1 220 - £738 - FF8 000
Études de bécasses et de griffons cortal
Gouache (48.5x59cm 19x23in) Deauville 2000

BAïKOV Leonid Petrovich 1918-1994 [33]
$420 - €398 - £260 - FF2 608
Fishing Trawler/Unloading the Cargo Oil/canvas
(33x20cm 12x7in) London 1999

BAIL Franck 1858-1924 [17]
$4 806 - €5 488 - £3 380 - FF36 000
Le partage de pain, fermière coupant une miche
Huile/toile (66x46cm 25x18in) Fontainebleau 2001

BAIL Jean-Antoine 1830-1919 [15]
$5 677 - €6 095 - £3 799 - FF39 979
Kitchen Interior with Young Woman Knitting
Oil/canvas (76x53.5cm 29x21in) Dublin 2000
$5 996 - €5 031 - £3 517 - FF33 000
«La trempée» Huile/toile (46x32cm 18x12in) Orléans
1998

BAIL Joseph 1862-1921 [134]
$11 180 - €9 909 - £6 857 - FF65 000
Jeune fille à son ouvrage de tapisserie
Huile/toile (101x85cm 39x33in) Cannes 1999
$2 454 - €2 134 - £1 479 - FF14 000
Portrait de jeune femme en buste Huile/toile
(24x19cm 9x7in) Paris 1998
$3 088 - €2 668 - £1 865 - FF17 500
La jeune dentellière Gouache/carton (26x21cm
10x8in) Barbizon 1998

BAILEY David Royston 1938 [28]
[📷] $775 - €767 - £484 - FF5 030
Mrs.David Bailey Photograph (29.3x35cm 11x13in)
München 1999

BAILEY Frederick Victor ?-1997 [48]
$1 313 - €1 191 - £800 - FF7 812
Poppies, Lilac, Anemonies and other Summer
Flowers in a Basket Oil/panel (44.5x39cm 17x15in)
London 1998

BAILEY William H. 1930 [39]
$90 000 - €101 812 - £62 964 - FF667 845
K Oil/canvas (152.5x127cm 60x50in) New-York 2001
$2 100 - €2 254 - £1 430 - FF14 787
Seated female Nude Graphite (36x28cm 14x11in)
Boston MA 2001
$1 200 - €1 129 - £741 - FF7 409
Still Life Color lithograph (76.5x56cm 30x22in) New-
York 1999

BAILIE Samuel Colville 1879-1926 [2]
$577 - €592 - £360 - FF3 883
«Visitez Heyst-Duinbergen» Poster (102x62cm
40x24in) London 2000

BAILLÉ Hervé 1896-1974 [22]
$254 - €290 - £174 - FF1 900
«S.N.C.F., pour vos vacances, billets touris-
tiques: fer/autocar» Affiche (100x61cm 39x24in)
Paris 2000

BAILLET Ernest 1853-1902 [14]
$587 - €656 - £397 - FF4 300
Bateaux en mer Huile/panneau (23.5x32.5cm 9x12in)
Dieppe 2000

BAILLY Alice 1872-1938 [51]
$2 069 - €2 004 - £1 300 - FF13 146
Place Pigalle Oil/canvas (53.5x72.5cm 21x28in)
London 1999
$2 240 - €2 618 - £1 599 - FF17 173
Sitzende Frau Oil/Leinwand (24x19cm 9x7in) Zürich
2001
$6 460 - €7 280 - £4 473 - FF47 752
Concert au jardin Gouache/paper (84x96cm 33x37in)
Zürich 2000
$236 - €275 - £163 - FF1 806
Platz in einem Walliser Bergdorf Print in colors
(38x24.5cm 14x9in) Bern 2000

BAILLY David 1584-1657 [3]
$56 783 - €60 952 - £38 000 - FF399 820
Boy Playing a Lute, After Frans Hals Black chalk
(20.5x16.5cm 8x6in) London 2000

BAILY Edward Hodges 1788-1867 [18]
$19 185 - €18 258 - £12 000 - FF119 764
Figure of Psyche Marble (H131cm H51in) London
1999
$2 185 - €2 498 - £1 500 - FF16 389
Bust of Richard Hart Davis (1766-1842) Marble
(H69cm H27in) London 2000

BAIN Donald 1904-1979 [35]
$3 155 - €3 503 - £2 200 - FF22 978
Boat House, Jetty, Loch Lomond Oil/canvas/board
(48x60.5cm 18x23in) London 2001
$1 502 - €1 346 - £900 - FF8 814
«Puffer and Yachts, Arran» Oil/canvas (23.5x28cm
9x11in) Perthshire 1998
$609 - €552 - £380 - FF3 621
Summer Scene, Largs Watercolour/paper (25x28cm
9x11in) Glasgow 1999

BAIN Marcel Adolphe 1878-1937 [20]
$21 110 - €20.594 - £13 000 - FF135 090
In the Garden Oil/canvas (100.5x124.5cm 39x49in)
London 1999

BAIN Walter XIX-XX **[1]**
🖉 **$1 426** - €1 482 - **£900** - FF9 721
Distant View, said to be Stirling Watercolour/paper (42x52.5cm 16x20in) London 2000

BAINE Mila XX **[1]**
🖉 **$1 600** - €1 481 - **£979** - FF9 716
Naval officer saluting young woman, movie magazine cover Pastel/paper (53x45cm 21x18in) New-York 1999

BAINES Henry 1823-1894 **[11]**
☞ **$2 100** - €2 443 - **£1 500** - FF16 022
Figures below the High Bridges kings Lynn Oil/canvas (41.4x31.5cm 16x12in) Norfolk 2001

BAINES Thomas John 1822-1875 **[53]**
☞ **$32 975** - €38 836 - **£22 800** - FF254 750
«Trek Ox Seized by a Crocodile While Drinking in the Limpopo» Oil/canvas (46x61cm 18x24in) Cape Town 2000
☞ **$16 136** - €15 496 - **£10 000** - FF101 647
Kraal, Eastern Cape Oil/canvas/board (30.5x43cm 12x16in) London 1999
☞ **$19 363** - €18 595 - **£12 000** - FF121 976
One of the largest kind of canoes used on the Zambesi river Watercolour/paper (23x35.5cm 9x13in) London 1999

BAIRD Nathaniel Hughes J. 1865-1936 **[48]**
🖉 **$1 804** - €1 542 - **£1 092** - FF10 114
Working in the Fields Watercolour/paper (41.5x41.5cm 16x16in) Edinburgh 1998

BAIRD William Baptiste 1847-1899 **[85]**
☞ **$3 564** - €3 735 - **£2 256** - FF24 500
Cerf près d'un lac Huile/toile (54x81cm 21x31in) Paris 2000
☞ **$2 255** - €1 906 - **£1 341** - FF12 500
Moulin dans la campagne Huile/toile (33x46cm 12x18in) Senlis 1998

BAIREI Kono 1844-1895 **[20]**
▥ **$181** - €169 - **£112** - FF1 106
Adler/Hahn und Henne Woodcut in colors (22x30cm 8x11in) Kempten 1999

BAIRNSFATHER Bruce 1888-1959 **[9]**
🖉 **$302** - €319 - **£200** - FF2 541
If yer knows of a better 'ole than - go to it Pencil/paper (20x12.5cm 7x4in) London 2000

BAISCH Hermann 1846-1894 **[62]**
☞ **$10 148** - €10 226 - **£6 326** - FF67 078
Morgen auf der Hochalm Öl/Leinwand (186x151cm 73x59in) Stuttgart 2000
☞ **$2 619** - €2 812 - **£1 753** - FF18 446
Weite miederländische Landschaft mit Kuhkerde Öl/Leinwand/Karton (53x40cm 20x15in) Stuttgart 2000
☞ **$1 286** - €1 534 - **£917** - FF10 061
See im Alpenvorland Oil/panel (30.5x39cm 12x15in) Berlin 2000

BAITLER Zoma 1908-1994 **[93]**
☞ **$1 500** - €1 293 - **£891** - FF8 479
Parque Rodó Oleo/lienzo (60x50cm 23x19in) Montevideo 1998
☞ **$600** - €537 - **£358** - FF3 525
«Molino» Oleo/lienzo (26x31cm 10x12in) Montevideo 1998

BAIXAS CARRETE Juan Manuel 1863-1925 **[13]**
☞ **$798** - €841 - **£532** - FF5 516
Paisaje con río Oleo/lienzo (53x65cm 20x25in) Madrid 2000

BAIXERAS Dionis Verdaguer 1862-1943 **[122]**
🖉 **$1 674** - €1 862 - **£1 178** - FF12 214
Oleaje y rompientes Oleo/lienzo (61x100cm 24x39in) Barcelona 2001
☞ **$265** - €300 - **£185** - FF1 970
Marina Oleo/lienzo (9x16.5cm 3x6in) Barcelona 2000
☞ **$239** - €228 - **£148** - FF1 497
Pescador con barretina Lápiz/papel (19.5x26cm 7x10in) Madrid 1999

BAIXERAS Ramon XX **[1]**
▨ **$1 120** - €1 129 - **£700** - FF7 405
«Esports d'hivern à la molina, centre excursionista de Cataluña» Poster (51x37cm 20x14in) London 2000

BAIZE Wayne 1943 **[5]**
🖉 **$2 300** - €2 611 - **£1 598** - FF17 130
Mister Rocky Coloured pencils/paper (28x58cm 11x23in) Dallas TX 2001

BAJ Enrico 1924 **[681]**
☞ **$29 000** - €30 063 - **£17 400** - FF197 200
Personaggi Tecnica mista/tela (163x125cm 64x49in) Prato 1999
☞ **$6 000** - €6 220 - **£3 600** - FF40 800
Giuseppe Verdi Tecnica mista/tela (45x55cm 17x21in) Milano 1999
☞ **$3 692** - €3 964 - **£2 470** - FF26 000
Visage Technique mixte (23x17cm 9x6in) Paris 2000
🗿 **$425** - €441 - **£255** - FF2 890
Libro per costruzione Scultura (34x26x7cm 13x10x2in) Prato 1999
🖉 **$1 485** - €1 239 - **£870** - FF8 130
Baj chez baj Mixed media/paper (69x100cm 27x39in) Lokeren 1998
▨ **$240** - €207 - **£120** - FF1 400
Il Generale Serigrafia (81.5x54.5cm 32x21in) Firenze 1999

BAK Samuel 1933 **[142]**
☞ **$34 500** - €32 147 - **£21 472** - FF210 870
Group Portrait with Blue Angel Oil/canvas (190x170cm 74x66in) Tel Aviv 1999
☞ **$15 000** - €16 455 - **£9 679** - FF107 938
Still Life with Tree Oil/canvas (97x80.5cm 38x31in) Tel Aviv 2000
☞ **$3 600** - €4 052 - **£2 480** - FF26 577
Bird a Chick Oil/paper/canvas (28x26cm 11x10in) Herzelia-Pituah 2000
☞ **$2 457** - €2 744 - **£1 643** - FF18 000
Nature morte à la bouteille et la poire Pastel (72.5x52.5cm 28x20in) Paris 2000

BAKALOWICZ Ladislaus 1833-1903 **[74]**
☞ **$90 000** - €85 834 - **£54 783** - FF563 031
Henri III, his Favourites, and Bussy d'Ambroise Attending the Wedding Oil/canvas (111x163cm 43x64in) New-York 1999
☞ **$7 878** - €6 703 - **£4 699** - FF43 972
Provocation Oil/canvas (55.5x32.5cm 21x12in) Warszawa 1998
☞ **$3 301** - €3 828 - **£2 332** - FF25 111
Jeune fille à la cage Huile/panneau (32.5x24cm 12x9in) Montréal 2001
☞ **$2 253** - €1 930 - **£1 354** - FF12 663
Dziewczyna w rozowej koszulce Pastel/paper (63x32.3cm 24x12in) Warszawa 1998

BAKALOWICZ Stefan W. 1857-1947 **[13]**
☞ **$12 782** - €10 567 - **£7 500** - FF69 315
Reading in an Interior Oil/canvas (36.5x50cm 14x19in) London 1998

BAKER Alan Douglas 1914-1987 **[119]**
- $1 931 - €2 190 - **£1 360** - FF14 366
  Jean Lynne camellias Oil/board (44.5x36.5cm 17x14in) Sydney 2001
- $1 594 - €1 536 - **£985** - FF10 074
  Camelias Oil/board (29x37cm 11x14in) Sydney 1999

BAKER Dennis 1951 **[8]**
- $12 426 - €11 645 - **£7 687** - FF76 385
  Artist's Camp Northern Territory Oil/canvas (90x165cm 35x64in) Sydney 1999

BAKER Elisha Taylor 1827-1890 **[14]**
- $10 000 - €10 264 - **£6 277** - FF67 326
  The Schooner «Madawaska Maid» Oil/canvas (55x86cm 22x34in) Bolton MA 2000

BAKER George Herbert 1878-1943 **[18]**
- $7 000 - €8 007 - **£4 867** - FF52 524
  Red Barn in Winter Oil/canvas (45x55cm 18x22in) Cincinnati OH 2000
- $170 - €184 - **£117** - FF1 204
  Sugar Creek/Baden, Ohio Drawing (27x35cm 11x14in) Cincinnati OH 2001

BAKER Gladys 1889-? **[1]**
- $3 500 - €3 753 - **£2 315** - FF24 616
  The Birthday Party Oil/canvas (50x60cm 20x24in) New-Orleans LA 2000

BAKER Jan 1939 **[8]**
- $162 - €187 - **£114** - FF1 227
  Narren Etching (50x33cm 19x12in) Oslo 2000

BAKER Normand Henry 1908-1955 **[34]**
- $1 816 - €2 034 - **£1 261** - FF13 345
  Washing Day Oil/board (37x28.5cm 14x11in) Melbourne 2001

BAKER OF LEAMINGTON Thomas 1809-1869 **[66]**
- $5 250 - €5 237 - **£3 277** - FF34 355
  Fisherman Beneath the Aquaduct Oil/canvas (53x40cm 21x16in) Dedham MA 1999
- $6 615 - €5 769 - **£4 000** - FF37 839
  Cattle Watering beneath Goodwich Castle on the Wye Oil/canvas (51x76.5cm 20x30in) London 1998
- $7 201 - €6 874 - **£4 500** - FF45 091
  Cattle Watering in a Tranquil River Oil/canvas (33x48cm 12x18in) London 1999
- $3 399 - €3 190 - **£2 100** - FF20 927
  Anglers on a Rocky Riverbank Oil/canvas (29x44.5cm 11x17in) Billingshurst, West-Sussex 1999
- $1 003 - €856 - **£600** - FF5 618
  Harvesters at Tachbrook Watercolour (22x33.5cm 8x13in) London 1998

BAKER Richard 1959 **[1]**
- $4 200 - €4 177 - **£2 606** - FF27 402
  Stone Oil/panel (25.5x25.5x3cm 10x10x1in) Beverly-Hills CA 1999

BAKER Samuel Burtis 1882-1967 **[1]**
- $19 000 - €18 272 - **£11 726** - FF119 855
  Old Taffeta Oil/canvas (132x109cm 51x42in) Boston MA 1999

BAKER Samuel Henry 1824-1909 **[28]**
- $518 - €581 - **£360** - FF3 810
  Pengwern, Festiniog Oil/canvas (20x30cm 8x12in) Little-Lane, Ilkley 2001
- $549 - €594 - **£380** - FF3 895
  By the Cross, CHester Watercolour/paper (28x34cm 11x13in) Cheshire 2001

BAKER Walter 1859-1912 **[31]**
- $178 - €208 - **£124** - FF1 363
  «Habitant -Prov. Of Quebec»/«Chateau de Ramesay, Montreal» Watercolour/paper (12.5x9cm 4x3in) Toronto 2000

BAKER William George 1864-1929 **[12]**
- $1 269 - €1 423 - **£885** - FF9 332
  «Rai Falls, Marlborough» Oil/canvas (89x59cm 35x23in) Wellington 2001

BAKER-CLACK Arthur 1887-1955 **[27]**
- $3 716 - €3 990 - **£2 487** - FF26 172
  French Farmhouses, Decorative Landscape Oil/canvas (54x80cm 21x31in) Melbourne 2000
- $3 353 - €2 834 - **£2 000** - FF18 587
  Mediterranean Reflections Oil/cardboard (26.5x34cm 10x13in) Glasgow 1998

BAKHUIJZEN Alexander Hieronymus 1826-1878 **[22]**
- $2 847 - €3 057 - **£1 905** - FF20 052
  Abendlandschaft mit Figurenstaffage Oil/panel (29.5x44cm 11x17in) Zürich 2000

BAKHUIJZEN VAN DE SANDE Geraldine Jacoba 1826-1895 **[31]**
- $23 164 - €21 781 - **£14 342** - FF142 876
  Still Life with Gladioli and Roses Oil/canvas (64x48.5cm 25x19in) Amsterdam 1999
- $5 791 - €5 445 - **£3 585** - FF35 719
  Autumn treasures: Grapes in a Wicker Basket Oil/panel (33.5x43.5cm 13x17in) Amsterdam 1999
- $3 667 - €4 311 - **£2 543** - FF28 277
  A Still Life with Roses Watercolour/paper (50x33cm 19x12in) Amsterdam 2000

BAKHUIJZEN VAN DE SANDE Hendrik 1795-1860 **[46]**
- $51 864 - €54 454 - **£32 700** - FF357 192
  Pastoral Peace Oil/canvas (107.5x150cm 42x59in) Amsterdam 2000
- $19 516 - €20 452 - **£12 360** - FF134 156
  Kühe und Schafe in weiter holländischer Weidelandschaft Oil/panel (71x91cm 27x35in) Köln 2000
- $772 - €908 - **£535** - FF5 953
  Cowherd with Cattle Wash (17x23cm 6x9in) Amsterdam 2000

BAKHUIJZEN VAN DE SANDE Julius Jacobus 1835-1925 **[64]**
- $6 987 - €5 891 - **£4 147** - FF38 645
  Cows on a Forest Path Oil/canvas (75x106cm 29x41in) Amsterdam 1998
- $1 930 - €1 815 - **£1 195** - FF11 906
  Woodland with Ducks in a pond Oil/canvas (45x35cm 17x13in) Amsterdam 1999

BAKHUYSEN Ludolf 1631-1708 **[76]**
- $194 259 - €208 521 - **£130 000** - FF1 367 808
  Christ in the Storm on Lake Galilee Oil/canvas (119.5x174.5cm 47x68in) London 2000
- $37 215 - €40 840 - **£23 958** - FF267 894
  Storm off Hoorn with a wijdschip going about and a pink Oil/canvas (77.5x102cm 30x40in) Amsterdam 2000
- $4 955 - €4 765 - **£3 052** - FF31 254
  Shipping in a Breeze Ink (14.5x19cm 5x7in) Amsterdam 1999
- $400 - €354 - **£241** - FF2 319
  Ships on the IJ at Amsterdam Etching (18x24cm 7x9in) Amsterdam 1998

BAKKER Corneille 1771-1849 [1]
$16 332 - €18 294 - £11 448 - FF120 000
La promenade des enfants Huile/panneau
(55x72cm 21x28in) Paris 2001

BAKOF Julius 1819-1857 [6]
$4 012 - €3 886 - £2 520 - FF25 489
**Nächtliche Froschhochzeit an Waldsee,
Froschpaar unter Fliegenpilz** Öl/Leinwand
(121x91cm 47x35in) Berlin 1999

BAKOS Jozef G. 1891-1976 [10]
$17 500 - €15 098 - £10 517 - FF99 037
Sunmount Oil/canvas (50x60cm 20x24in) Santa-Fe
NM 1998
$1 500 - €1 294 - £901 - FF13 982
Corner Fish Market Watercolour (43x58cm 17x23in)
Santa-Fe NM 1998

BAKSHEEV Vassily N. 1878-1971 [4]
$4 078 - €4 634 - £2 864 - FF30 399
Parkscen Oil/canvas (97x74cm 38x29in) Stockholm
2001

BAKST Léon 1866-1924 [181]
$3 498 - €4 163 - £2 500 - FF27 308
Stage Design for the Ballet Sleeping Beauty
Watercolour (19.5x25.5cm 7x10in) London 2000
$2 500 - €2 132 - £1 508 - FF13 982
Nijinsky in «l'Après-midi d'un faune» Silkscreen
(63.5x48cm 25x18in) New-York 1998

BAKSTEEN Dirk 1886-1971 [148]
$3 103 - €3 594 - £2 189 - FF23 577
Le chemin du village Huile/toile (40x54cm 15x21in)
Bruxelles 2000
$1 397 - €1 611 - £962 - FF10 569
Kempische hoeve Oil/panel (16.8x26.4cm 6x10in)
Lokeren 2000
$133 - €124 - £82 - FF813
**Kempense Dorpstraat II, Kempische Dorpstraat
II** Eau-forte (9x15.5cm 3x6in) Bruxelles 1999

BALABENE Rudolf Raimund 1890-1968 [11]
$1 898 - €2 035 - £1 296 - FF13 347
Reiter Öl/Leinwand (101x80cm 39x31in) Wien 2001

BALACA Y CANSECO Ricardo 1844-1880 [15]
$2 120 - €2 403 - £1 440 - FF15 760
Retrato de niña Oleo/lienzo (51x42cm 20x16in)
Madrid 2001

BALACA Y CARRION Ricardo 1810-1869 [3]
$3 920 - €4 205 - £2 660 - FF27 580
Dama con abanico Oleo/lienzo (112x88cm 44x34in)
Madrid 2001

BALACA Y OREJAS-CANSECO Eduardo 1840-
1914 [5]
$7 320 - €7 208 - £4 560 - FF47 280
Retrato de la duquesa de San Carlos Oleo/lienzo
(110x84.5cm 43x33in) Madrid 1999

BALAKSHIN Yevgeny 1961 [113]
$448 - €481 - £304 - FF3 152
Jardín soleado Oleo/lienzo (44x38cm 17x14in)
Madrid 2001
$189 - €210 - £129 - FF1 379
Vino y queso Oleo/lienzo (22x27cm 8x10in) Madrid
2001

BALANDE Gaston 1880-1971 [627]
$5 116 - €6 098 - £3 648 - FF40 000
Vue de Chauvigny Huile/toile (101x152cm 39x59in)
Poitiers 2000

$2 420 - €2 439 - £1 508 - FF16 000
Voiliers et bateaux de pêche sur une rivière
Huile/carton (48x64cm 18x25in) Pontoise 2000
$1 142 - €1 067 - £704 - FF7 000
Pont suspendu Huile/toile (21x34.5cm 8x13in) Metz
1999
$279 - €259 - £173 - FF1 700
Vers Larchant Aquarelle/papier (23.5x30cm 9x11in)
Paris 1999

BALANYA MOIX Ismael 1921 [10]
$737 - €661 - £451 - FF4 334
Las vías del tren Oleo/tablex (70.5x81cm 27x31in)
Madrid 1999

BALASCH MATEU Mateo 1870-1936 [15]
$1 260 - €1 081 - £756 - FF7 092
Paisaje Oleo/lienzo (32x52cm 12x20in) Madrid 1998

BALASSI Mario 1604-1667 [4]
$5 634 - €6 541 - £3 960 - FF42 903
Samson und Delila Öl/Leinwand (70x56.5cm
27x22in) Wien 2001

BALAY Charles L. M. 1861-1943 [3]
$4 500 - €4 115 - £2 748 - FF26 994
Two women at a spinning wheel Oil/canvas
(81x64cm 32x25in) New-York 1998
$3 000 - €2 997 - £1 875 - FF19 657
French Soldier smoking Pipe and drinking Wine
Oil/canvas (31x26cm 12x10in) Wethersfield CT 1999

BALBI Filippo 1806-1890 [1]
$23 650 - €22 121 - £14 500 - FF145 101
**A Glass Jug of Water, Glasses, a Fried Egg and
Other Ustensils** Oil/canvas (47x37cm 18x14in)
London 1998

BALCAR Jiri 1929-1968 [8]
$200 - €185 - £122 - FF1 214
Afternoon Tea Engraving (32x49cm 12x19in)
Chicago IL 1999

BALCERA Juan XX [3]
$1 700 - €1 983 - £1 193 - FF13 005
**«Sevilla, feria de abril, fiestas primaverales
1935»** Poster (106.5x162cm 41x63in) New-York 2000

BALDASSINI Guglielmo 1885-1952 [11]
$4 000 - €4 147 - £2 400 - FF27 200
Scogliera ligure Olio/tela (62x77cm 24x30in) Vercelli
2001
$6 000 - €5 183 - £3 000 - FF34 000
Venezia Olio/cartone/tela (35x44.5cm 13x17in)
Vercelli 1999

BALDENBACH Herrmann 1949 [8]
$655 - €613 - £397 - FF4 024
Farbraum-Himmel III Acrylic/canvas (90x103cm
35x40in) Stuttgart 1999

BALDERO Giorgio XIX-XX [5]
$500 - €569 - £352 - FF3 730
Cavalier wearing a Red Cape Oil/board (60x38cm
24x15in) Philadelphia PA 2001

BALDERO Luigi G. XIX-XX [17]
$723 - €842 - £516 - FF5 520
The Campaign Oil/canvas (52x71cm 20x27in)
Toronto 2001

BALDESSARI John Anthony 1931 [104]
$25 000 - €23 348 - £15 430 - FF153 150
A Healty Life (with Jogger) Acrylic (159x214.5cm
62x84in) New-York 1999
$42 000 - €39 224 - £25 922 - FF257 292
Palm Trees in the Wind (4 Shots per Second)
Mixed media (90x109cm 35x42in) New-York 1999

BALDESSARI

$24 000 - €22 535 - **£14 870** - FF147 818
Couple (With Observer) Watercolour (135.5x152.5cm 53x60in) New-York 1999

$750 - €823 - **£484** - FF5 401
Falling Star Lithograph (163.5x58cm 64x22in) New-York 2000

$11 500 - €12 858 - **£7 752** - FF84 345
This Cloud That Ship Photograph (56x77.5cm 22x30in) New-York 1998

BALDESSARI Roberto Iras 1894-1965 **[38]**

$13 000 - €13 476 - **£7 800** - FF88 400
Senza titolo Olio/tavola (55x43cm 21x16in) Milano 2000

$973 - €1 022 - **£614** - FF6 707
Cap S.Antonio (Spanien) Öl/Karton (35x45cm 13x17in) Stuttgart 2000

$3 750 - €3 887 - **£2 250** - FF25 500
Natura morta Carboncino/carta (26x35cm 10x13in) Milano 2001

BALDESSIN George Joseph Victor 1939-1978 **[62]**

$17 816 - €16 843 - **£11 057** - FF110 482
Trapeze Bronze (H172cm H67in) Malvern, Victoria 1999

$1 244 - €1 396 - **£864** - FF9 157
«Personnage and Entrances» Screenprint (100x106cm 39x41in) Melbourne 2001

BALDI Lazzaro c.1623-1703 **[12]**

$20 000 - €20 733 - **£12 000** - FF136 000
Il ritrovamento di Mosè Olio/tela (173x246cm 68x96in) Milano 1999

$7 000 - €7 179 - **£4 375** - FF47 089
The Vision of St John the Evangelist on Patmos Ink (45.5x24.5cm 17x9in) New-York 2000

BALDOCK Charles Edwin XIX-XX **[6]**

$1 543 - €1 836 - **£1 100** - FF12 044
Two Rufford Hounds Watercolour (33.5x23cm 13x9in) London 2000

BALDOCK James Walsham 1825-1898 **[31]**

$4 911 - €5 841 - **£3 500** - FF38 312
Black prince, a Dark Brown Racehorce in a Stable Oil/canvas (71x91.5cm 27x36in) London 2000

$360 - €424 - **£250** - FF2 780
Cattle Watering Watercolour/paper (17x25cm 7x10in) Lewes, Sussex 2000

BALDRIGHI Giuseppe 1723-1802 **[3]**

$20 706 - €17 887 - **£13 804** - FF117 334
Ritratto di nobiluomo Olio/tela (132x104cm 51x40in) Venezia 1999

BALDUCCI IL COSCI Giovanni c.1560-1603/31 **[16]**

$5 680 - €6 098 - **£3 800** - FF40 000
La prédication de Saint Jean-Baptiste Encre (36x22.5cm 14x8in) Paris 2000

BALDUNG GRIEN Hans Gmünd 1484/85-1545 **[50]**

$1 300 - €1 442 - **£864** - FF9 459
St.Catherine Woodcut (23.5x16cm 9x6in) New-York 2000

BALDUS Édouard Denis 1813-1882 **[198]**

$1 761 - €1 982 - **£1 212** - FF13 000
Caen, le chevet de l'église Saint-Pierre Tirage albuminé (44x33cm 17x12in) Bayeux 2000

BALDWIN Frederick William 1899-1962 **[13]**

$230 - €208 - **£140** - FF1 367
Barn Interior Watercolour (28x38cm 11x14in) Godalming, Surrey 1998

BALDWYN Charles Henry C. 1859-1943 **[28]**

$2 749 - €2 969 - **£1 900** - FF19 474
Three Sparrows Oil/canvas (20x37cm 7x14in) London 2001

$729 - €867 - **£519** - FF5 690
Country Scene Watercolour/paper (29x45cm 11x17in) Woollahra, Sydney 2000

BALE Alice Marian Ellen 1875-1955 **[36]**

$1 653 - €1 608 - **£1 017** - FF10 550
Chrysanthemums Oil/canvas/board (47.5x53.5cm 18x21in) Malvern, Victoria 1999

$605 - €630 - **£382** - FF4 131
Old Fashioned Roses Oil/board (17x20.5cm 6x8in) Melbourne 2000

BALE Charles Thomas ?-1878 **[223]**

$2 080 - €1 986 - **£1 300** - FF13 026
Grapes, Plums, Apples, a Gourd, Partridge, and Ceramic Pots Oil/canvas (50.5x76cm 19x29in) London 1999

$1 122 - €1 335 - **£800** - FF8 756
Still Life of Fruit, a Bird's Nest and Flagon on a Table Oil/canvas (36x31cm 14x12in) Bath 2000

BALE Edwin 1842-1923 **[16]**

$661 - €565 - **£400** - FF3 705
Portrait of a Woman in a White Dress, Seated and holding a Pink Fan Watercolour/paper (57x45cm 22x18in) London 1998

BALE John Edward XIX **[1]**

$4 033 - €3 958 - **£2 500** - FF25 966
The Interior of Etchingham Church, Sussex Watercolour (48.5x48.5cm 19x19in) London 1999

BALE T.C. XIX **[1]**

$2 260 - €2 368 - **£1 500** - FF15 535
The Village Festival Oil/canvas (23x35.5cm 9x13in) London 2000

BALEN van Hendrik I 1575-1632 **[56]**

$272 340 - €274 408 - **£169 740** - FF1 800 000
Adam et Eve/Création Adam/Caïn et Abel/Paradis/L'arche Noë/Vie après Huile/toile (116x166.5cm 45x65in) Paris 2000

$117 313 - €99 814 - **£70 000** - FF654 738
Venus at the Forge of Vulcan Oil/panel (63.5x108.5cm 25x42in) London 1998

$14 292 - €13 081 - **£8 712** - FF85 806
Bacchanal von Putten in einer bewaldeten Flusslandschaft Oil/panel (32.5x41cm 12x16in) Wien 1999

BALEN van Hendrik II 1623-1661 **[2]**

$46 566 - €45 317 - **£28 665** - FF297 258
Venus och Aeneas i Vulcani Grotta Oil/copper (66x89cm 25x35in) Stockholm 1999

BALEN van Jan 1611-1654 **[18]**

$7 335 - €6 860 - **£4 441** - FF45 000
Scène mythologique: 9 muses, Mercure, Minerve, Mars, scène de bataille Huile/toile/panneau (72.5x91cm 28x35in) Saint-Dié 1999

$5 782 - €4 989 - **£3 489** - FF32 728
Pan and Syrinx Oil/copper (18x14cm 7x5in) Amsterdam 1998

BALESTRA Angelo 1803-1881 **[1]**

$18 156 - €18 294 - **£11 316** - FF120 000
Vue d'un arc romain animé de personnages auprès d'une fontaine Huile/toile (81x65cm 31x25in) Paris 2000

BALESTRA Antonio 1666-1740 [35]
- $65 000 - €61 154 - **£40 560** - FF401 141
  Juno and the Peacock Oil/canvas (184x155cm 72x61in) New-York 1999
- $12 250 - €12 699 - **£7 350** - FF83 300
  Riposo durante la fuga in Egitto Olio/tela (42x53cm 16x20in) Milano 2001
- $1 900 - €1 970 - **£1 140** - FF12 920
  San Luigi Gonzaga Olio/tela (42x33cm 16x12in) Roma 2001
- $15 685 - €15 315 - **£10 000** - FF100 460
  The Madonna and Child with Saint Luigi Gonzaga and Angels Black chalk (29x17.5cm 11x6in) London 2001

BALESTRIERI Lionello 1874-1958 [98]
- $3 200 - €4 147 - **£2 400** - FF27 200
  Popolana Olio/tela (100x70cm 39x27in) Roma 2000
- $1 000 - €1 296 - **£750** - FF8 500
  Paesaggio Olio/cartone/tela (12.5x21.5cm 4x8in) Milano 2000
- $1 583 - €1 764 - **£1 036** - FF11 571
  Futuristische Komposition Gouache/Karton (29.7x39.8cm 11x15in) München 2000

BALET Jan 1913 [29]
- $1 666 - €1 943 - **£1 169** - FF12 744
  Sommernacht Öl/Leinwand/Karton (40x50cm 15x19in) Köln 2001

BALFOUR James Lawson 1870-1966 [11]
- $5 823 - €6 359 - **£3 748** - FF41 712
  Beach Scene Oil/canvas/board (25x33.5cm 9x13in) Melbourne 2000

BALINK Henry C. 1882-1963 [13]
- $9 350 - €8 732 - **£5 770** - FF57 278
  Chieftain Oil/board (41x43cm 16x17in) Dallas TX 1999
- $7 500 - €7 133 - **£4 554** - FF46 792
  Teseque Chief Oil/canvas (29x24cm 11x9in) Beverly-Hills CA 1999
- $12 000 - €13 169 - **£7 726** - FF86 385
  Ted-su-on-ja (Yellow Bird) Crayon (61x51cm 24x20in) Beverly-Hills CA 2000

BALINT Endre 1914-1986 [18]
- $1 428 - €1 374 - **£884** - FF9 010
  Our Father, our King Oil/canvas (32.5x122cm 12x48in) Budapest 1999
- $555 - €583 - **£345** - FF3 825
  Cavalier égaré Encre (17x21cm 6x8in) Budapest 2000
- $262 - €290 - **£172** - FF1 905
  Composition Monotype (27x21cm 10x8in) Budapest 2000

BALJEU Joost 1925-1991 [11]
- $16 066 - €17 244 - **£10 750** - FF113 110
  Untitled Oil/canvas (96x60cm 37x23in) Amsterdam 2000
- $10 684 - €12 706 - **£7 616** - FF83 344
  Reliëf constructie Relief (22.5x90x12cm 8x35x4in) Amsterdam 2000
- $233 - €272 - **£166** - FF1 786
  Composition Screenprint in colors (47.5x148cm 18x58in) Amsterdam 2001

BALKA Miroslaw 1958 [2]
- $12 702 - €13 635 - **£8 500** - FF89 438
  Untitled Sculpture, wood (48x190.5x86.5cm 18x75x34in) London 2000

BALKE Peder 1804-1887 [15]
- $9 384 - €9 788 - **£5 920** - FF64 208
  Vinter i Finnmark Oil/canvas (35x52cm 13x20in) Oslo 2001
- $2 184 - €2 419 - **£1 482** - FF15 870
  Seilskuter Oil/panel (8x10cm 3x3in) Oslo 2000

BALKÉ Théodore Charles 1875-1951 [11]
- $2 492 - €2 897 - **£1 776** - FF19 000
  Sidi Bou Saïd Huile/toile (45x60.5cm 17x23in) Paris 2001
- $2 331 - €2 744 - **£1 638** - FF18 000
  Souk à Tunis Huile/panneau (27x35cm 10x13in) Paris 2000

BALKENHOL Stephan 1957 [66]
- $29 480 - €31 432 - **£20 000** - FF206 180
  Large Male Head Relief Mixed media (142x116x14cm 55x45x5in) London 2001
- $65 000 - €75 419 - **£44 876** - FF494 715
  Relief Heads 1-6 Painting (70x55cm 27x21in) New-York 2000
- $35 000 - €38 400 - **£23 250** - FF251 888
  Harlequin Sculpture, wood (170x56x28cm 66x22x11in) New-York 2000
- $4 043 - €4 406 - **£2 800** - FF28 903
  Stehender Nacker Mann Bronze (H41cm H16in) London 2001
- $222 - €204 - **£136** - FF1 341
  Acht Steindrucke Lithographie (29.8x20cm 11x7in) Bielefeld 1999

BALL Adam Gustavus 1821-1882 [1]
- $2 395 - €2 182 - **£1 466** - FF14 311
  Aboriginal family group Pencil/paper (46x60cm 18x23in) Malvern, Victoria 1998

BALL Sydney 1933 [16]
- $4 151 - €4 650 - **£2 884** - FF30 500
  «Painting No 7» Acrylic/canvas (183x176cm 72x69in) Melbourne 2001

BALL Thomas 1819-1911 [17]
- $75 000 - €87 138 - **£52 710** - FF571 590
  Liberty Bronze (H85cm H33in) New-York 2001
- $4 250 - €4 938 - **£2 986** - FF32 390
  Daniel Webster Bronze (H76cm H29in) New-York 2001

BALL Wilfred Williams 1853-1917 [96]
- $508 - €545 - **£340** - FF3 577
  Continental Village Scene Watercolour/paper (23.5x19.5cm 9x7in) London 2000

BALLA Béla 1882-1965 [30]
- $980 - €1 084 - **£644** - FF7 112
  Riverside of River Zazar Oil/cardboard (39x50cm 15x19in) Budapest 2000

BALLA Giacomo 1871-1958 [401]
- $113 673 - €110 893 - **£70 000** - FF727 412
  Donna che cuce Oil/canvas (159x113cm 62x44in) London 1999
- $57 500 - €59 608 - **£34 500** - FF393 500
  Forme rumore Olio/tela (77.5x34cm 30x13in) Prato 2000
- $12 500 - €12 958 - **£7 500** - FF85 000
  Compenetrazione iridescente Smalto/tavola (33x30.5cm 12x12in) Milano 1999
- $23 000 - €23 843 - **£13 800** - FF156 400
  «Feu d'artifice» Ricostruzione di Elio Marcheggiani in scala 1.13,333 Sculpture (90x90x69cm 35x35x27in) Prato 1999
- $1 080 - €1 399 - **£810** - FF9 180
  Fiore futurista Sculpture bois (33x20x20cm 12x7x7in) Milano 2001

B

✏ **$10 088** - €12 196 - **£7 048** - FF80 000
Composition Lavis (9x13.5cm 3x5in) Paris 2000

BALLABENE Rudolf Raimund 1890-1968 **[51]**
⛳ **$1 136** - €1 109 - **£700** - FF7 274
At the Races Oil/canvas (79x70cm 31x27in) London 1999

BALLAGH Robert 1943 **[25]**
⛳ **$7 611** - €7 365 - **£4 693** - FF48 308
Ingres - The Turkish Bath Acrylic/canvas (168x168cm 66x66in) Dublin 1999
⛳ **$2 049** - €2 413 - **£1 439** - FF15 825
The Atomic Theory Oil/canvas (57x46cm 22x18in) Dublin 2000
⛳ **$3 450** - €4 063 - **£2 425** - FF26 652
Figure with an Ellsworth Kelly Oil/canvas (25x33cm 9x12in) Dublin 2000
✏ **$2 833** - €3 047 - **£1 931** - FF19 989
Study for the 3rd May Gouache/paper (65x76cm 25x29in) Dublin 2001
▣ **$401** - €432 - **£273** - FF2 831
Liberty leading the People, after Delacroix Print (48x62cm 18x24in) Dublin 2001

BALLARD Brian 1943 **[39]**
⛳ **$3 024** - €3 047 - **£1 885** - FF19 989
Still Life Oil/canvas (41x51cm 16x20in) Dublin 2000
⛳ **$1 442** - €1 651 - **£992** - FF10 827
Orchids in Grey Vase Oil/board (40x30cm 16x12in) Dublin 2000

BALLAVOINE Jules Frédéric c.1855-1901 **[71]**
⛳ **$6 434** - €7 307 - **£4 500** - FF47 929
Au jardin Oil/canvas (54x36cm 21x14in) London 2001
⛳ **$4 518** - €4 339 - **£2 800** - FF28 461
Portrait of a young lady Oil/canvas (40x30cm 15x11in) London 1999

BALLE Mogens 1921-1988 **[458]**
⛳ **$4 788** - €4 037 - **£2 841** - FF26 478
«Forårets komme» Oil/canvas (98x130cm 38x51in) København 1998
⛳ **$1 623** - €1 742 - **£1 086** - FF11 430
Figurkomposition Oil/canvas (65x81cm 25x31in) København 2000
⛳ **$837** - €938 - **£583** - FF6 155
Komposition Acrylic/canvas (24x33cm 9x12in) København 2001
✏ **$710** - €673 - **£432** - FF4 414
Komposition Watercolour, gouache (21x29cm 8x11in) København 1999
▣ **$157** - €134 - £92 - FF881
Ansigtskomposition Lithograph (26x33cm 10x12in) Viby J, Århus 1998

BALLE Otto Petersen 1865-1916 **[43]**
⛳ **$481** - €536 - **£329** - FF3 519
En passiar i en have Oil/canvas (45x64cm 17x25in) Viby J, Århus 2000
⛳ **$228** - €255 - **£160** - FF1 670
Landskab ved solnedgang Oil/canvas (28.5x43cm 11x16in) Vejle 2001

BALLENBERGER Karl 1801-1860 **[7]**
⛳ **$2 448** - €2 301 - **£1 486** - FF15 092
Albertus Magnus in der Studierstube Oil/panel (41.5x32.5cm 16x12in) München 1999

BALLERIO Osvaldo 1870-1942 **[1]**
▣ **$1 332** - €1 381 - **£799** - FF9 057
«Cicli Dei Gomme Pirelli» Affiche couleur (95x65cm 37x25in) Torino 2000

BALLESIO Federico XIX **[15]**
⛳ **$5 500** - €5 940 - **£3 801** - FF38 961
A New Trick Oil/canvas (47x31cm 18x12in) Bethesda MD 2001
⛳ **$1 700** - €1 665 - **£1 095** - FF10 922
Man and Woman seated in a Courtyard Watercolour (52.5x37cm 20x14in) New-York 1999

BALLESIO Francesco 1860-1923 **[34]**
✏ **$12 000** - €10 353 - **£7 239** - FF67 911
The Carpet seller Watercolour/paper (36x53cm 14x20in) New-York 1998

BALLESIO Giuseppe XIX-XX **[2]**
✏ **$2 000** - €1 869 - **£1 246** - FF12 257
Interior Watercolour/paper (71x50cm 28x20in) Mystic CT 1999

BALLESTER Anselmo 1897-1974 **[35]**
▣ **$894** - €821 - **£549** - FF5 384
Stagecoach -Ombre Rosse Poster (200x140cm 78x55in) London 1999

BALLESTER MONTESOL Javier 1952 **[31]**
✏ **$201** - €180 - **£123** - FF1 182
El chico del colmado/Plaza Técnica mixta/papel (37.5x55cm 14x21in) Madrid 1999

BALLESTER Rosalie 1949 **[73]**
⛳ **$732** - €625 - **£442** - FF4 100
Le continent de l'ombre Technique mixte/toile (81x65cm 31x25in) Paris 1998

BALLIN Claude 1615-1678 **[1]**
⚔ **$4 191** - €3 542 - **£2 500** - FF23 234
Urn, the cylindrical body cast depicting Apollo Chasing Daphne Gilded bronze (H66.5cm H26in) London 1998

BALLINGALL Alexander 1870-1910 **[40]**
✏ **$960** - €950 - **£600** - FF6 230
Fishing Boat, Pell Harbour Watercolour (48x73cm 18x28in) Glasgow 1999

BALLINGER Harry Russell 1892-1994 **[20]**
⛳ **$600** - €706 - **£431** - FF4 628
Landscape with barn Oil/canvas (50x60cm 20x24in) Hatfield PA 2001

BALLMER Theo XIX-XX **[4]**
▣ **$835** - €716 - **£502** - FF4 694
Vii.Kantonal-Schützenfest beider Basel Poster (106x72cm 41x28in) Hamburg 1998

BALLOT Clémentine XIX-XX **[8]**
⛳ **$997** - €1 289 - **£711** - FF7 800
Barques de pêches aux Andelys Huile/toile (54x73cm 21x28in) Paris 2000

BALLUE Pierre Ernest 1855-1928 **[80]**
⛳ **$2 343** - €2 287 - **£1 483** - FF15 000
Pêcheur en bord de rivière Huile/toile (49x65cm 19x25in) Calais 1999
⛳ **$828** - €915 - **£574** - FF6 000
Les environs de Clisson Huile/toile (16x23cm 6x9in) Paris 2001

BALLUF Ernst 1921 **[13]**
✏ **$611** - €727 - **£436** - FF4 767
Winterlandschaft Aquarell/Karton (30x49cm 11x19in) Linz 2000

BALLURIAU Paul 1860-1917 **[34]**
▣ **$236** - €198 - **£138** - FF1 300
«L'Eclair de Paris» Affiche (119x77.5cm 46x30in) Paris 1998

BALMER George 1806-1846 **[11]**
- $8 760 - €8 181 - **£5 406** - FF53 662
  Blick auf Köln Öl/Leinwand (61x86.5cm 24x34in)
  Köln 1999
- $1 955 - €2 169 - **£1 300** - FF14 229
  Barge on a River by Moonlight Oil/canvas
  (15x20cm 5x7in) London 2000
- $1 260 - €1 465 - **£900** - FF9 613
  Fishing Beach with Figures Watercolour/paper
  (15x25cm 6x10in) Par, Cornwall 2001

BALMER Paul Friedr. Wilhelm 1865-1922 **[54]**
- $407 - €407 - **£254** - FF2 668
  **Zwei Segelschiffe in sonnenbeschienenem
  Hafen** Öl/Leinwand (61x45cm 24x17in) Zofingen 1999

BALOUZET Armand Auguste 1858-1905 **[13]**
- $3 184 - €3 049 - **£2 004** - FF20 000
  Bords du Caron Huile/toile (105x70cm 41x27in)
  Joigny 1999

BALSAMO Vincenzo 1935 **[28]**
- $1 120 - €1 451 - **£840** - FF9 520
  Campagna Olio/tavola (47x47cm 18x18in) Vercelli
  2001
- $750 - €777 - **£450** - FF5 100
  Da Le Evocazioni Olio/faesite (40x30cm 15x11in)
  Vercelli 2000

BALSGAARD Carl Vilhelm 1812-1893 **[38]**
- $6 604 - €5 780 - **£4 000** - FF37 916
  Still Life of Flowers and Fruit on a Windowsill
  Oil/canvas (69x57.5cm 27x22in) London 1998
- $1 666 - €1 876 - **£1 148** - FF12 307
  Opstilling med smykkeskrin, frugter på et fad
  Oil/canvas (44x35cm 17x13in) København 2000

BALSON Ralph 1890-1964 **[26]**
- $14 523 - €16 288 - **£10 085** - FF106 842
  Non abjective Oil/board (122x137cm 48x53in)
  Melbourne 2001
- $14 025 - €15 417 - **£8 988** - FF101 126
  Non-Objective Painting Oil/board (64.5x90cm
  25x35in) Melbourne 2000
- $6 363 - €6 015 - **£3 949** - FF39 458
  Abstract Pastel/paper (49x75cm 19x29in) Malvern,
  Victoria 1999

BALTARD Louis Pierre 1764-1846 **[12]**
- $2 145 - €2 287 - **£1 360** - FF15 000
  Paysage au temple Huile/toile (23.5x31.5cm 9x12in)
  Paris 2000

BALTEN Pieter c.1525-1598 **[14]**
- $326 844 - €321 283 - **£210 000** - FF2 107 476
  **Performance of the Farce Een Cluyte van
  Plaeyerwater, Flemish Village** Oil/panel
  (122x170.5cm 48x67in) London 1999
- $1 351 - €1 483 - **£918** - FF9 726
  **Der Heilige Johannes der Täufer in einer
  Landschaft** Kupferstich (28.5x22.7cm 11x8in) Berlin
  2000

BALTERMANTS Dmitri 1912-1990 **[84]**
- $2 200 - €1 839 - **£1 302** - FF12 061
  Ataka Silver print (19x28cm 7x11in) New-York 1998

BALTHUS (B. Klossowski) 1908-2001 **[289]**
- $2 800 000 - €3 089 123 - **£1 851 920** -
  FF20 263 320
  Nu aux bras levés Oil/canvas (150.5x82.5cm
  59x32in) New-York 2000
- $92 646 - €99 448 - **£62 000** - FF652 339
  Enfants au Luxembourg Oil/canvas (55x46cm
  21x18in) London 2000

- $202 840 - €167 694 - **£119 020** - FF1 100 000
  Portrait d'enfant Huile/carton (38.5x28.5cm 15x11in)
  Paris 1998
- $8 500 - €7 723 - **£5 269** - FF50 657
  Fleurs et pomme Watercolour (25.5x35.5cm
  10x13in) New-York 1999
- $790 - €762 - **£499** - FF5 000
  Jeune fille endormie Lithographie couleurs
  (56x76cm 22x29in) Paris 1999

BALTZ Lewis 1945 **[7]**
- $8 000 - €8 319 - **£5 051** - FF54 566
  Near Reno Gelatin silver print (16x24cm 6x9in) New-
  York 2000

BALUGANI Luigi 1737-1770 **[1]**
- $4 019 - €3 422 - **£2 400** - FF22 445
  **The temple of juno at Paestum / The Basilica at
  Paestum** Watercolour, gouache/paper (31.9x39.4cm
  12x15in) London 1998

BALUNIN Mikhail Abramovich 1875-? **[8]**
- $7 257 - €8 006 - **£4 800** - FF52 519
  The Merry Maker's Return Oil/canvas (58x89cm
  22x35in) London 2000
- $1 600 - €1 784 - **£1 075** - FF11 703
  After the Work Watercolour/paper (25x34cm 9x13in)
  Kiev 2000

BALUSCHEK Hans 1870-1935 **[77]**
- $2 082 - €2 301 - **£1 444** - FF15 092
  Im Eisenbahn-Depot Öl/Karton (32x41cm 12x16in)
  München 2001
- $2 242 - €1 842 - **£1 302** - FF12 080
  **Weinselig eingeschlafener Student in
  Gartenlokal** Watercolour (18x24cm 7x9in) Berlin
  1998
- $232 - €230 - **£145** - FF1 510
  Bei Mutter grün Lithographie (27x20cm 10x7in)
  Berlin 1999

BALWÉ Arnold 1898-1983 **[110]**
- $9 415 - €9 203 - **£5 972** - FF60 370
  Goldender Strauss Öl/Leinwand (93x61cm 36x24in)
  München 1999

BALZE Raymond 1818-1909 **[71]**
- $3 859 - €3 659 - **£2 347** - FF24 000
  Vierge à l'enfant Huile/toile (98x77.5cm 38x30in)
  Aubagne 1999
- $1 875 - €2 011 - **£1 278** - FF13 194
  Udisgt ved Liguria La Spezzia Oil/wood (31x25cm
  12x9in) København 2000
- $616 - €610 - **£384** - FF4 000
  Vue de Tivoli Fusain (28x45cm 11x17in) Paris 1999

BALZER Anton 1771-1807 **[7]**
- $182 - €172 - **£113** - FF1 130
  Einganstor in Adrspach Etching, aquatint in colors
  (37x43cm 14x16in) Praha 1999

BALZER Gerd 1909-1986 **[8]**
- $1 922 - €1 789 - **£1 182** - FF11 738
  Entwurf für einen Teewagen Ink (34.8x49.5cm
  13x19in) München 1999

BALZER Johann 1738-1799 **[11]**
- $128 - €153 - **£91** - FF1 006
  **Elternfreuden: ein junges Paar betrachtet sein
  schlafendes Kind** Radierung (12.7x17.2cm 5x6in)
  Paris 1999

BAMA James Elliott 1926 **[24]**
- $4 500 - €5 012 - **£2 943** - FF32 878
  **Paperback book cover: Elegante couple, he
  seated** Oil/board (53x36cm 21x14in) New-York 2000

$20 000 - €22 797 - **£13 954** - FF149 538
Blizzard Oil/panel (30x43cm 12x17in) Dallas TX 2001

$20 000 - €18 181 - **£12 046** - FF119 260
Pre-Columbian Indian Watercolour/paper (38x48cm 15x19in) Hayden ID 1998

BAMBER Bessie, Betsie XIX-XX [48]

$4 795 - €4 529 - **£2 900** - FF29 708
Kittens Oil/wood (28.5x75cm 11x29in) Billingshurst, West-Sussex 1999

$1 942 - €1 886 - **£1 200** - FF12 370
Portrait of a Pekinese Dog seated on a green Cushion Oil/board (24x17cm 9x6in) Manchester 1999

BAMBERGER Fritz 1814-1873 [43]

$16 000 - €14 847 - **£9 776** - FF97 392
Extensive River Landscape with the Escorial and the Sierra Guadarrama Oil/canvas (131.5x176.5cm 51x69in) New-York 1999

$5 466 - €6 391 - **£3 841** - FF41 923
Felslandschaft im Abendglühen Öl/Leinwand (32x50cm 12x19in) München 2000

$9 414 - €8 692 - **£5 790** - FF57 016
Romantische Gebirgslandschaft Öl/Leinwand (36x44cm 14x17in) München 1999

$440 - €511 - **£309** - FF3 353
Rheinlandschaft mit dem Drachenfels bei Oberwinter Pencil/paper (18.5x28.5cm 7x11in) Berlin 2001

BAMBERGER Gustav 1860-1936 [28]

$1 565 - €1 817 - **£1 100** - FF11 917
Kartause Gaming Aquarell/Papier (41x54.5cm 16x21in) Wien 2001

BAMBINI Nicolo 1651-c.1736 [7]

$9 975 - €11 330 - **£7 000** - FF74 322
The Annunciation Oil/canvas (88x67.5cm 34x26in) London 2001

$16 000 - €18 168 - **£10 950** - FF119 175
Die Vision des Heiligen Antonius von Padua Öl/Leinwand (44x35.5cm 17x13in) Wien 2000

BAMFYLDE Copplestone Warre 1720-1791 [11]

$34 610 - €38 245 - **£24 000** - FF250 872
Claudian Landscape with a Castle, Abbey, Bridge and Mountains Oil/canvas (107x157cm 42x61in) London 2001

$12 404 - €10 816 - **£7 500** - FF70 948
Wooded River Landscape with figures by a bridge beneath a castle Oil/canvas (71x91.5cm 27x36in) London 1998

BAMRAH Dharbinder Singh 1956 [27]

$5 110 - €4 250 - **£3 000** - FF27 881
India Night -Tiger Oil/canvas (51x91.5cm 20x36in) London 1998

$482 - €494 - **£300** - FF3 241
Giraffe Oil/canvas (30x50cm 11x19in) Billingshurst, West-Sussex 2000

BAN Gerbrand 1613-1652 [4]

$15 861 - €16 655 - **£10 000** - FF109 247
Gentleman and his Wife, Full-Length, their Four Children on a Terrace Oil/panel (67x86.5cm 26x34in) London 2000

BANANA Charly 1953 [19]

$957 - €920 - **£590** - FF6 037
New York Indian ink (45.5x60.7cm 17x23in) Köln 1999

BANC Joseph, Jef 1930 [39]

$1 351 - €1 524 - **£950** - FF10 000
«Dc 1896» Technique mixte/papier (38x52cm 14x20in) Paris 2001

BANCHIERI Giuseppe 1927-1994 [61]

$1 750 - €1 814 - **£1 050** - FF11 900
Letto e luce Olio/tela (100x70cm 39x27in) Milano 1999

$750 - €777 - **£450** - FF5 100
Paesaggio Olio/carta (23x23cm 9x9in) Vercelli 1999

BANCO del Alma 1878-1943 [9]

$2 088 - €1 789 - **£1 255** - FF11 736
Fischerboote Öl/Leinwand (70.5x79.5cm 27x31in) Hamburg 1998

BANCROFT Elias ?-1924 [25]

$1 026 - €1 182 - **£700** - FF7 751
A Gatehouse, Bayern/A Courtyard, Bayern Oil/board (35.5x25.5cm 13x10in) London 2000

$896 - €962 - **£600** - FF6 313
Clovelly Watercolour (26.5x18.5cm 10x7in) London 2000

BANCROFT Milton Herbert 1867-1947 [6]

$4 000 - €3 776 - **£2 486** - FF24 772
Bad News Oil/canvas (60x45cm 24x18in) Milford CT 1999

BAND Max 1900-1974 [28]

$11 326 - €12 127 - **£7 708** - FF79 551
Paysage après l'orage Huile/toile (81x100cm 31x39in) Warszawa 2001

$1 100 - €1 181 - **£736** - FF7 745
Field of Tulips Oil/canvas/board (33x40cm 13x16in) New-York 2000

BANDEIRA Antonio 1922-1967 [45]

$25 530 - €28 203 - **£17 704** - FF185 000
«Eclipse» Huile/toile (46x55cm 18x21in) Paris 2001

$4 035 - €4 878 - **£2 819** - FF32 000
Composition Huile/toile (30x25.5cm 11x10in) Paris 2000

$14 000 - €11 930 - **£8 342** - FF78 255
«La bataille des arbres en noir et blanc» Ink (39x57cm 15x22in) New-York 1998

BANDEIRA Benedetto 1557/64-1634 [1]

$16 100 - €16 690 - **£9 660** - FF109 480
Il matrimonio mistico di Santa Caterina d'Alessandria Olio/tavola (72x61cm 28x24in) Roma 1999

BANDINELLI Baccio 1493-1560 [23]

$14 900 - €14 549 - **£9 500** - FF95 437
The Deposition Black chalk (20x28cm 7x11in) London 1999

BANDINI Giovanni 1540-1599 [5]

$620 000 - €663 207 - **£422 716** - FF4 350 354
Adonis and his Hound Marble (H180cm H70in) New-York 2001

$18 824 - €21 391 - **£13 000** - FF140 318
Evangelist Ink (40x19.5cm 15x7in) London 2000

BANDO Toshio 1890-1973 [80]

$6 272 - €5 336 - **£3 741** - FF35 000
Fillette aux poupées russes Huile/toile (54x65cm 21x25in) Paris 1998

$1 465 - €1 239 - **£875** - FF8 130
Les poissons Huile/toile (24x19cm 9x7in) Bruxelles 1998

$478 - €534 - **£334** - FF3 500
Femme endormie Pastel/papier (26.5x43cm 10x16in) Paris 2001

BANG Christian 1868-1950 [6]

$32 000 - €35 109 - **£21 257** - FF230 297
The Visit to the Studio of Thorvaldsen Oil/canvas (141.5x165.5cm 55x65in) New-York 2000

BANG Vilhelmine Maria 1848-1932 [11]
- $1 891 - €2 010 - £1 267 - FF13 186
  En tjenestepige på trappen Oil/canvas (51x38cm 20x14in) Viby J, Århus 2001

BANKHARDT Alois XX [5]
- $515 - €613 - £368 - FF4 024
  Heinz Trökes Vintage gelatin silver print (22.7x29.2cm 8x11in) Berlin 2000

BANKS J.O. XIX [1]
- $4 250 - €3 998 - £2 652 - FF26 228
  The Young Harvesters Oil/panel (31x41.5cm 12x16in) New-York 1999

BANKS Thomas John 1828-1896 [17]
- $3 609 - €3 305 - £2 200 - FF21 682
  Sunlit Scottish Valley with Children and Dog to the foreground Oil/canvas (57x91cm 22x35in) Cambridge 1999
- $414 - €360 - £249 - FF2 361
  Ellerbeck Bridge on the old Mail Coach Road Oil/board (30.5x47cm 12x18in) London 1998

BANNATYNE John James 1835-1911 [40]
- $950 - €812 - £575 - FF5 325
  Saithe Fishing - Sound of Kilbraman Oil/canvas (35.5x61cm 13x24in) Edinburgh 1998
- $575 - €554 - £360 - FF3 636
  The firth of Clyde, with Arran in the Distance Watercolour (26x56cm 10x22in) Billingshurst, West-Sussex 1999

BANNER Alfred XIX-XX [20]
- $1 344 - €1 444 - £900 - FF9 469
  Good Morning Oil/canvas (46x35.5cm 18x13in) London 2000
- $1 604 - €1 616 - £1 000 - FF10 603
  Feeding the Ducks, Arley-on-Severn Oil/canvas (25.5x35.5cm 10x13in) London 2000

BÄNNINGER Otto Charles 1897-1976 [29]
- $708 - €686 - £437 - FF4 498
  Zwei Frauen Bronze (15x7.5x3.5cm 5x2x1in) Zürich

BANNISTER Edward Mitchell 1828-1901 [13]
- $22 000 - €20 835 - £13 376 - FF136 666
  Farmer Pushing a Wheelbarrow Oil/canvas (76x56cm 29x22in) New-York 1999
- $20 000 - €17 275 - £12 080 - FF113 314
  Landscape Oil/canvas (28x35cm 11x14in) Watertown MA 1998

BANSAGI Vincze 1881-1960 [7]
- $1 476 - €1 677 - £1 036 - FF11 000
  Hiver Huile/toile (66x77cm 25x30in) Paris 2001

BANTI Cristiano 1824-1904 [13]
- $20 000 - €20 733 - £12 000 - FF136 000
  La Castellana Olio/tela (81x57.5cm 31x22in) Milano 1999
- $19 800 - €17 105 - £13 200 - FF112 200
  La fienaiole Olio/tavoletta (38x20cm 14x7in) Milano 1998

BANTING Frederick Grant 1891-1941 [17]
- $3 096 - €3 121 - £1 935 - FF20 472
  Mouth of French River Oil/panel (21x26cm 8x10in) Toronto 2000
- $4 355 - €4 804 - £2 880 - FF31 515
  The Artist's paint Box and Palette Object (36.5x27x14cm 14x10x5in) Vancouver, BC. 2000

BANTING John 1902-1972 [122]
- $1 178 - €1 143 - £733 - FF7 500
  Composition surréaliste Huile/panneau (51x40cm 20x15in) Paris 1999
- $482 - €464 - £300 - FF3 044
  Tray full of Autumn Leaves Oil/cardboard (30x36cm 11x14in) London 1999
- $406 - €371 - £250 - FF2 432
  Aux Folies Atomiques Watercolour (74x53.5cm 29x21in) London 1999
- $1 179 - €1 087 - £720 - FF7 128
  Figures in a Room/Figures in a Landscape Print (33x19.5cm 12x7in) London 1998

BANTLI Leonhard 1810-1880 [6]
- $743 - €749 - £463 - FF4 911
  Blick in ein Tal Aquarell/Papier (14.5x19.5cm 5x7in) Zürich 2000
- $748 - €844 - £526 - FF5 538
  «Berne prise sur la route de Thoune» Aquatinta (17x25cm 6x9in) Bern 2001

BANTZER Carl 1857-1941 [16]
- $10 948 - €10 226 - £6 616 - FF67 078
  Die vier Kinder des Künstlers im Spiel auf blühender Sommerwiese Öl/Leinwand (168x151cm 66x59in) Berlin 1999
- $5 267 - €5 113 - £3 253 - FF33 539
  Der Leinenweber Rupp Öl/Leinwand (44.5x58cm 17x22in) Frankfurt 1999
- $2 981 - €2 812 - £1 858 - FF18 446
  Schwälmer Kinder Öl/Leinwand (20x43cm 7x16in) Frankfurt 1999

BARABAS Miklós 1810-1898 [9]
- $22 200 - €23 325 - £13 800 - FF153 000
  Petite fille jouant avec une poupée Huile/toile (142x105cm 55x41in) Budapest 2000
- $2 370 - €2 180 - £1 422 - FF14 301
  Portrait eines Herren vor einem Landschaftshintergrund Öl/Leinwand (80x63cm 31x24in) Wien 1999
- $2 625 - €2 904 - £1 725 - FF19 050
  Portrait of a young Man Oil/board (26.5x21.5cm 10x8in) Budapest 2000

BARABINO Angelo 1883-1950 [15]
- $27 000 - €23 325 - £18 000 - FF153 000
  La rapina, studio Olio/cartone (41x47cm 16x18in) Milano 1998
- $3 000 - €3 110 - £1 800 - FF20 400
  Gelsi Olio/cartone (21.5x31.5cm 8x12in) Milano 1999

BARABINO Nicoló 1832-1891 [14]
- $2 975 - €3 084 - £1 785 - FF20 230
  Paesaggio Olio/tavoletta (33x24cm 12x9in) Milano 1999

BARABINO Simone 1585-? [5]
- $20 400 - €17 623 - £10 200 - FF115 600
  Madonna col Bambino Olio/tela (148x118cm 58x46in) Milano 1999
- $18 937 - €22 105 - £13 398 - FF145 000
  Le repos pendant la fuite en Egypte Huile/toile (91.5x70cm 36x27in) Paris 2001

BARACUDTS Max 1869-1927 [1]
- $3 944 - €3 630 - £2 367 - FF23 812
  Drei Krokodile in historischem Interieur Oil/panel (31x39cm 12x15in) Augsburg 1999

BARAJAS DIAZ Andres 1941 [12]
- $2 437 - €2 252 - £1 500 - FF14 775
  Mujer frente a la ventana Oleo/lienzo (116x81cm 45x31in) Madrid 1999

B

BARAK William King Billy c.1824-1903 **[2]**
- **$23 680** - €22 844 - **£14 965** - FF149 846
  Ceremony Charcoal (46.5x62cm 18x24in) Melbourne 1999

BARALIS Louis 1862-1940 **[4]**
- **$2 743** - €2 561 - **£1 661** - FF16 800
  Bacchus entouré de danseuses Bronze (H66cm H25in) Auxerre 1999

BARANOFF-ROSSINÉ Vladimir 1888-1944 **[61]**
- **$8 065** - €7 927 - **£5 179** - FF52 000
  Les baigneuses Huile/toile (50x73cm 19x28in) Paris 1999

BARASCUDTS Max 1869-1927 **[29]**
- **$685** - €665 - **£434** - FF4 360
  Kardinals-Triumvirat in einem historischen Interieur Oil/panel (32.5x39cm 12x15in) München 1999
- **$2 239** - €2 601 - **£1 573** - FF17 062
  Confuse Gouache (43x33.5cm 16x13in) Warszawa 2001

BARAT Pierre Martin c.1730-c.1790 **[5]**
- **$4 576** - €4 878 - **£3 104** - FF32 000
  Portrait de Lekain en empereur romain Pastel/papier (64x51cm 25x20in) Argenteuil 2001

BARATTA Carlo Alberto 1754-1815 **[3]**
- **$4 200** - €4 485 - **£2 861** - FF29 422
  The Adoration of the Magi Black chalk (43.5x33cm 17x12in) New-York 2001

BARATTI Filippo XIX-XX **[16]**
- **$5 678** - €6 095 - **£3 800** - FF39 982
  The Morning Ride, a Hunt Beyond Oil/canvas (33.5x41cm 13x16in) London 2000

BARAU Émile Barau-Bacou 1851-c.1930 **[8]**
- **$2 974** - €2 820 - **£1 809** - FF18 500
  Chemin après la pluie Huile/panneau (52x45cm 20x17in) Paris 1999

BARBAGLIA Giuseppe 1841-1910 **[18]**
- **$41 772** - €36 086 - **£20 886** - FF236 708
  Gli incoscenti Olio/tela (102x157cm 40x61in) Milano 1999
- **$600** - €777 - **£450** - FF5 100
  Pesce Olio/tela (27.5x52cm 10x20in) Vercelli 2001
- **$8 925** - €9 252 - **£5 355** - FF60 690
  L'edera Acquarello/carta (45x35cm 17x13in) Milano 1999

BARBANÇON Christian 1940-1993 **[42]**
- **$948** - €884 - **£585** - FF5 800
  Composition abstraite Acrylique/toile (73x100cm 28x39in) Paris 1999

BARBARIN de Thomas 1821-1892 **[1]**
- **$2 250** - €2 363 - **£1 422** - FF15 500
  Orphée Pastel/papier (120x93cm 47x36in) Paris 2000

BARBARINI Emil 1855-1930 **[135]**
- **$5 057** - €4 857 - **£3 135** - FF31 862
  Die Rückkehr des Vaters Öl/Leinwand (32x66.5cm 12x26in) Ahlden 1999
- **$4 516** - €5 368 - **£3 129** - FF35 215
  Gemüse-markt in Wien nach dem Regen Oil/panel (21x15.5cm 8x6in) Bremen 2000

BARBARINI Franz 1804-1873 **[85]**
- **$2 208** - €2 543 - **£1 508** - FF16 684
  Stadt am Flussufer Öl/Leinwand (73.5x99.5cm 28x39in) Wien 2001
- **$2 153** - €2 325 - **£1 488** - FF15 254
  Idylle am Weiher Öl/Leinwand (32x45cm 12x17in) Wien 2001

$1 222 - €1 453 - **£872** - FF9 534
  Rast des Wanderer im Gebirge Watercolour (15x15cm 5x5in) Wien 2000

BARBARINI Gustav 1840-1909 **[75]**
- **$1 952** - €2 045 - **£1 291** - FF13 415
  Haus am Gebirgsbach mit konversierendem Landvolk und der Brücke Öl/Leinwand (68x105cm 26x41in) München 2000
- **$2 395** - €2 301 - **£1 485** - FF15 092
  Gebirgslandschaft mit Bauernhaus und Personenstaffage Öl/Leinwand (31.5x47cm 12x18in) Hildrizhausen 1999

BARBARITE James Peter 1912-1990 **[2]**
- **$3 800** - €3 206 - **£2 229** - FF21 029
  Franklin and Fulton Station, Brooklyn, New York Oil/canvas (61x81cm 24x31in) New-York 1998

BARBARO Giovanni XIX-XX **[146]**
- **$466** - €530 - **£320** - FF3 479
  Still Life of Fruit Watercolour/paper (31x75cm 12x29in) London 2000

BARBASAN LAGUERUELA Mariano 1864-1924 **[66]**
- **$25 000** - €30 032 - **£17 500** - FF197 000
  Pastora en el monte Oleo/lienzo (65x90cm 25x35in) Madrid 2000
- **$2 000** - €2 073 - **£1 200** - FF13 600
  Anatre nel lago Olio/tavoletta (12.5x22cm 4x8in) Milano 2000

BARBAUD-KOCH Marthe Élisabeth 1862-c.1928 **[22]**
- **$1 156** - €1 372 - **£841** - FF9 000
  Cerises dans une coupe en cuivre Huile/toile (50x61cm 19x24in) Lyon 2001

BARBAULT Jean 1718-1766 **[11]**
- **$132 331** - €123 872 - **£82 000** - FF812 546
  Ambassadeur de la Chine, an Oriental Gentleman, full-length Oil/canvas (61.5x50.5cm 24x19in) London 1999
- **$720** - €622 - **£360** - FF4 080
  Vedute dell'antica Roma Acquaforte (50.5x36cm 19x14in) Firenze 1999

BARBAZZA Francesco XVIII **[4]**
- **$137** - €162 - **£97** - FF1 063
  «Veduta di Castel e Ponte S.Angelo» Grabado (43x60cm 16x23in) Madrid 2001

BARBE Pascal XX **[1]**
- **$2 024** - €1 982 - **£1 245** - FF13 000
  La terre s'évapore Pastel gras (14x10x7cm 5x3x2in) Paris 1999

BARBEAU Marcel Christian 1925 **[46]**
- **$846** - €724 - **£509** - FF4 750
  Untitled Indian ink/paper (16.5x20.5cm 6x8in) Toronto 1998

BARBEAU Marius Charles 1883-1969 **[8]**
- **$977** - €1 135 - **£675** - FF7 442
  Thomas Cooke/Frank Gollan/Child with Mask/Mr&Mrs Frank/Indians/F.Bolta Vintage gelatin silver print (8x14cm 3x5in) Vancouver, BC. 2000

BARBEDIENNE Ferdinand 1810-1892 **[41]**
- **$2 024** - €1 650 - **£1 085** - FF11 095
  Vase with a Fairy with Flowing Hair, from Model by E.Barrjas Bronze (H14cm H5in) London 2000

BARBELLA Constantino 1852-1925 **[8]**
- **$14 000** - €16 601 - **£9 632** - FF108 896
  A Reclining Nude Marble (37x65cm 14x25in) New-York 2000

BARBELLI Giangiacomo 1590-1656 [2]
$45 000 - €38 874 - **£22 500** - FF255 000
Scena di genere Olio/tela (117x172cm 46x67in)
Milano 1999

BARBER Alfred Richardson 1841-1925 [22]
$7 376 - €7 091 - **£4 600** - FF46 513
Family of Rabbits, Cauliflowers and a Wicker Basket Oil/canvas (43x58cm 17x23in) Guildford, Surrey 1999
$2 849 - €3 312 - **£2 000** - FF21 728
Rabbits Oil/canvas (30.5x35.5cm 12x13in) London 2001

BARBER Charles Burton 1845-1894 [27]
$60 000 - €51 765 - **£36 198** - FF339 558
The Hiding Place Oil/canvas (72x92cm 28x36in) New-York 1998
$2 250 - €2 430 - **£1 555** - FF15 593
Young Girl and her Dogs Pencil/paper (45.5x59cm 17x23in) Bethesda MD 2001

BARBER Elizabeth Blair 1909 [6]
$1 574 - €1 848 - **£1 111** - FF12 121
Freshwater Bay Oil/canvas (29x39cm 11x15in) Nedlands 2000
$3 674 - €4 312 - **£2 592** - FF28 283
Freshwater Bay Yacht Club Watercolour (37.5x44.5cm 14x17in) Nedlands 2000

BARBER Reginald 1851-1928 [7]
$2 013 - €2 235 - **£1 400** - FF14 659
Portrait of a young Lady Watercolour/paper (58x48cm 22x18in) Crewkerne, Somerset 2001

BARBER Sam XX [3]
$3 500 - €3 726 - **£2 384** - FF24 440
«Iris Accents (Chipping Camden, England)» Oil/canvas (76x101cm 30x40in) Delray-Beach FL 2001

BARBER Thomas Stanley XIX-XX [24]
$1 996 - €1 710 - **£1 200** - FF11 216
Figure on a Riverside Path Oil/canvas (30x53cm 12x21in) Aylsham, Norfolk 1998
$897 - €969 - **£620** - FF6 354
River Landscape with Ferry Boat/Woodland Cottage Oil/canvas (25x46cm 9x18in) Cheshire 2001

BARBERI Giuseppe 1746-1809 [4]
$5 230 - €5 615 - **£3 500** - FF36 830
The Interior of a Circular Temple Ink (43x57.5cm 16x22in) London 2000

BARBERI Michelangelo XIX [1]
$49 500 - €48 923 - **£30 294** - FF320 916
Luminous Arrangement of Flowers in a Vase Mixed media (40x50cm 16x20in) Wellesley MA 2000

BARBERIIS de Eugène 1851-1937 [10]
$813 - €762 - **£489** - FF5 000
Bords du Rhône Huile/panneau (24x32.5cm 9x12in) Paris 1999

BARBERIS Franco 1905-1992 [8]
$900 - €1 050 - **£631** - FF6 885
«Berner Oberland» Poster (70x101cm 27x39in) New-York 2000

BARBERO Ernesto 1887-1936 [9]
$2 350 - €2 592 - **£1 500** - FF17 000
Festa su Po (carnevale del Bogo) Olio/cartone (19x24cm 7x9in) Vercelli 1999

BARBETTE Josias N. 1645-1730 [3]
$4 390 - €5 113 - **£3 067** - FF33 539
Brustporträt eines Fürsten in Rüstung Miniature (5x4cm 1x1in) München 2000

BARBEY Bruno 1941 [1]
$4 000 - €4 543 - **£2 806** - FF29 801
«Morocco»/«Fez» Dye-transfer print (37x55.5cm 14x21in) New-York 2001

BARBEY Maurice XIX-XX [11]
$268 - €305 - **£186** - FF2 000
«Simplon orient express», d'après Felix Ziem Affiche (108x77cm 42x30in) Paris 2000

BARBIER André Georges 1883-1970 [227]
$1 149 - €1 311 - **£798** - FF8 600
Venise Huile/toile (39x57cm 15x22in) Paris 2000

BARBIER Antoine 1859-1948 [15]
$367 - €396 - **£253** - FF2 600
Morte fontaine en été Aquarelle/papier (36x55cm 14x21in) Lyon 2001

BARBIER Georges 1882-1932 [295]
$800 - €682 - **£482** - FF4 474
Costum Design for a Woman in 18th Century Dress Watercolour (26.5x22.5cm 10x8in) New-York 1998
$250 - €262 - **£167** - FF1 721
Celui qui monte un cheval noir Lithograph (29x29cm 11x11in) New-York 2001

BARBIER Nicolas Alexandre 1789-1864 [1]
$28 000 - €26 343 - **£17 472** - FF172 799
A Château in a Landscape Oil/canvas (75.5x97cm 29x38in) New-York 1999

BARBIER S. XIX [1]
$30 077 - €28 965 - **£18 715** - FF190 000
Vue du port d'Assem Kalasi / Vue de Santorin Gouache/papier (22.8x32.9cm 8x12in) Montfort L'Amaury 1999

BARBIERE (del) Domenico 1501-1565 [3]
$672 - €767 - **£469** - FF5 030
Schlachtszene Kupferstich (29x43.5cm 11x17in) Berlin 2001

BARBIERI Contardo 1900-1966 [22]
$2 750 - €2 851 - **£1 650** - FF18 700
Alberi sul Lago Maggiore Olio/tela (60x80cm 23x31in) Milano 1999

BARBIERI IL GUERCINO Giovan Francesco 1591-1666 [185]
$80 000 - €70 173 - **£48 576** - FF460 304
Christ in the Garden of Gethsemane Oil/canvas (215x141cm 84x55in) New-York 1999
$130 000 - €114 417 - **£79 144** - FF750 529
Saint Jerome in the Wilderness Oil/canvas (118x96.5cm 46x37in) New-York 1999
$57 920 - €65 820 - **£40 000** - FF431 748
The Vision of Saint Jerome Oil/copper (34x26.5cm 13x10in) London 2000
$13 448 - €14 436 - **£9 000** - FF94 694
Saint Barbara Ink (18.5x24.5cm 7x9in) London 2000

BARBIERS Pieter II 1798-1848 [7]
$5 640 - €6 353 - **£3 887** - FF41 672
Travellers Resting on a Sandy Track in a Mountainous Landscape Oil/panel (78x92.5cm 30x36in) Amsterdam 2001

BARBIERS Pieter III Pietersz. 1749-1842 [17]
$3 000 - €3 360 - **£2 084** - FF22 041
Summer/Winter Watercolour/paper (42.5x55cm 16x21in) New-York 2001

BARBINI Alfredo 1912 [7]
$3 182 - €3 278 - **£1 969** - FF21 500
Tigre rugissant Sculpture verre (32x60cm 12x23in) Caen 2000

BARBISAN Giovanni 1914-1988 **[18]**
- $7 497 - €6 476 - £3 748 - FF42 483
  Giardino Olio/tela (55x85cm 21x33in) Venezia 1999
- $4 400 - €5 702 - £3 300 - FF37 400
  Natura morta con le zucche, i cachi e l'uva
  Olio/tela (30x40cm 11x15in) Milano 2001
- $1 350 - €1 399 - £810 - FF9 180
  Vigneto Acquaforte (33x45cm 12x17in) Venezia 2000

BARBOT Prosper 1798-1878 **[3]**
- $2 614 - €3 049 - £1 818 - FF20 000
  Le café derrière le Mosquée Aquarelle,
  gouache/papier (48x34cm 18x13in) Paris 2000

BARBOZA Diego 1945 **[15]**
- $595 - €539 - £385 - FF3 535
  Homenaje a Zurbarán Pastel (40x50.5cm 15x19in)
  Caracas 1999

BARBUT-DAVRAY Luc 1863-? **[8]**
- $3 423 - €3 201 - £2 072 - FF21 000
  **Jeune femme en déshabillé près de la chemi-
  née** Huile/toile (55x38cm 21x14in) Lille 1999
- $2 184 - €2 287 - £1 372 - FF15 000
  Scène d'intérieur Huile/toile (41x33cm 16x12in)
  Saint-Dié 2000

BARCAGLIA Donato 1849-1930 **[11]**
- $60 000 - €55 677 - £36 660 - FF365 220
  Amore Accieca Marble (H142cm H55in) New-York
  1999

BARCELO ALBALADEJO José 1923 **[7]**
- $10 580 - €10 297 - £6 500 - FF67 545
  Untitled Watercolour, gouache/paper (50x65.5cm
  19x25in) London 1999

BARCELO Miquel 1957 **[173]**
- $167 364 - €196 817 - £120 000 - FF1 291 032
  «Le chien chinois» Mixed media/canvas (195x300cm
  76x118in) London 2001
- $28 000 - €30 032 - £19 000 - FF197 000
  «34 anys» Técnica mixta (50x65cm 19x25in) Madrid
  2001
- $9 000 - €7 678 - £5 364 - FF50 364
  Verre Mixed media (33x24cm 12x9in) New-York 1998
- $7 713 - €6 708 - £4 650 - FF44 000
  Sans titre No.5 Gouache/papier (57x77cm 22x30in)
  Paris 1998
- $864 - €961 - £608 - FF6 304
  Frutas Grabado (9.5x21cm 3x8in) Madrid 2001

BARCHUS Eliza R. 1857-1959 **[57]**
- $2 200 - €2 037 - £1 346 - FF13 360
  Mont Shasta Oil/canvas (55x91cm 22x36in) San
  Rafael CA 1999
- $1 100 - €1 283 - £785 - FF8 416
  Mt.Hood Seen from Hood River Oil/panel
  (24x28cm 9x11in) Portland OR 2000

BARCLAY John 1876-1923 **[1]**
- $1 112 - €1 044 - £700 - FF6 851
  The Golfer Etching (21x20cm 8x7in) Manchester 1999

BARCLAY John Rankin 1884-1962 **[34]**
- $467 - €537 - £320 - FF3 520
  Zennor Oil/canvas (76x91cm 30x36in) Par, Cornwall
  2000
- $292 - €281 - £180 - FF1 846
  The Reader Etching (24.5x20cm 9x7in) Edinburgh
  1999

BARCLAY McClelland 1891-1943 **[76]**
- $2 900 - €3 230 - £1 896 - FF21 188
  Profile of blond, short-haired woman Oil/canvas
  (45x43cm 18x17in) New-York 2000

- $400 - €411 - £253 - FF2 698
  Rocky Shore Scene Oil/board (30x40cm 12x16in)
  Columbia SC 2000
- $450 - €426 - £279 - FF2 794
  World War II Scene Watercolour/paper (48x48cm
  19x19in) Wallkill NY 1999
- $2 249 - €1 901 - £1 337 - FF12 470
  «Hotel for Women» Poster (104x68.5cm 40x26in)
  New-York 1998

BARCSAY Jenö 1900-1968 **[9]**
- $2 600 - €2 557 - £1 625 - FF16 770
  Sitting at the Table Oil/canvas (61x101cm 24x39in)
  Budapest 1999

BARD James 1815-1897 **[16]**
- $180 000 - €153 789 - £108 054 - FF1 008 792
  Steamboat James W. Baldwin Oil/canvas
  (87.5x151cm 34x59in) New-York 1998
- $220 000 - €234 949 - £149 908 - FF1 541 166
  The Schooner Norma Oil/canvas (76x132cm
  29x51in) New-York 2001

BARDASANO Y BAOS José 1910-1979 **[55]**
- $1 600 - €1 505 - £1 000 - FF9 875
  Tentación Oleo/tablex (38x46cm 14x18in) Madrid
  1998
- $3 853 - €4 519 - £2 772 - FF29 645
  Palacio de Buckingham Oleo/lienzo (24x31cm
  9x12in) México 2001

BARDELLINO Pietro 1728-1810 **[29]**
- $9 750 - €10 107 - £5 850 - FF66 300
  Sacra Famiglia con San Giovannino Olio/tela
  (75x64cm 29x25in) Roma 2000
- $3 250 - €3 369 - £1 950 - FF22 100
  S. Giuseppe col Bambino Gesù Olio/rame
  (13.5x10cm 5x3in) Venezia 1999

BARDI Luigi XIX **[3]**
- $3 774 - €4 346 - £2 576 - FF28 508
  Selbstbildnis der Elisabeth Vigée-Lebrun
  Öl/Leinwand (82.3x101cm 32x39in) München 2000

BARDILL Ralph William 1876-1935 **[13]**
- $1 043 - €1 051 - £650 - FF6 894
  Figures and Geese Before Thatched Cottages
  Watercolour (44.5x59cm 17x23in) London 2000

BARDIN Jean 1732-1809 **[4]**
- $15 759 - €15 550 - £9 710 - FF102 000
  **Alexandre le Grand, médecin Philippe
  d'Arcanie/Antiochus, Stratonice** Encre
  (18.5x30.5cm 7x12in) Avallon 1999

BARDINERO Dario 1868-1908 **[2]**
- $2 000 - €2 592 - £1 500 - FF17 000
  Vino, cipolla e aringhe Olio/cartone (27x35cm
  10x13in) Torino 2000

BARDONE Guy 1927 **[152]**
- $1 376 - €1 524 - £923 - FF10 000
  L'olivier du nouvel an, Bandol Huile/toile
  (50x65cm 19x25in) Paris 2000
- $355 - €381 - £237 - FF2 500
  Paysage du Jura Gouache/papier (64x49.5cm
  25x19in) Paris 2001

BARDWELL Thomas 1704-1767 **[23]**
- $12 464 - €11 628 - £7 520 - FF76 272
  Bildnis von Anne, Countess of Strattford
  Öl/Leinwand (234x141cm 92x55in) Wien 1999
- $9 563 - €10 266 - £6 400 - FF67 338
  **Young Boy Possibly Master Money, Half-Length,
  with His Dog** Oil/canvas (73.5x63.5cm 28x25in)
  Suffolk 2000

BAREAU Georges Marie 1866-1931 **[21]**
- $9 500 - €8 041 - **£5 686** - FF52 748
  Figural Group Bronze (H80cm H31in) New-York 1998
- $1 143 - €1 227 - **£765** - FF8 049
  Sänger Bronze (H76.5cm H30in) Stuttgart 2000

BAREFORD David XX **[4]**
- $2 400 - €2 418 - **£1 496** - FF15 864
  Winter Landscape Oil/canvas (60x91cm 24x36in) Chicago IL 2000

BARELA Patrocinio 1908-1964 **[9]**
- $2 600 - €2 952 - **£1 806** - FF19 365
  Rooster in Relief Sculpture, wood (H38cm H15in) Dallas TX 2001

BARENGER James II 1780-1831 **[13]**
- $28 600 - €31 378 - **£19 000** - FF205 827
  Unkenneling/Going to drawn/Gone away/The Kill Oil/canvas (63x76cm 24x29in) London 2000
- $3 249 - €3 161 - **£2 000** - FF20 737
  Dark Day Hunter in a Landscape Oil/canvas (19x24cm 7x9in) London 1999

BARET Guisti 1883-1935 **[1]**
- $3 905 - €4 192 - **£2 612** - FF27 500
  Vue du palais, Italie, deux chiens devant l'escalier Huile/panneau (65x54cm 25x21in) Bayeux 2000

BARETTA Michele 1916-1987 **[33]**
- $2 000 - €2 073 - **£1 200** - FF13 600
  Il cappelino della nonna Olio/masonite (70x50cm 27x19in) Vercelli 1999
- $1 200 - €1 244 - **£720** - FF8 160
  Il molo Olio/masonite (30x40cm 11x15in) Vercelli 2000
- $750 - €777 - **£450** - FF5 100
  Caschetto biondo Tempera/carta (70x50cm 27x19in) Vercelli 1999

BARFUSS Ina 1949 **[45]**
- $400 - €341 - **£239** - FF2 240
  Ohne Titel Gouache/paper (38x46cm 14x18in) Zürich 1998

BARGAS A.-F. XVII-XVIII **[4]**
- $2 395 - €2 659 - **£1 669** - FF17 440
  «Weite Flusslandschaft mit Personen und Häusern» Öl/Leinwand (20x26cm 7x10in) Stuttgart 2001

BARGHEER Eduard 1901-1979 **[981]**
- $8 020 - €7 669 - **£4 884** - FF50 308
  Südliche Stadt, Forio d'Ischia Öl/Leinwand (42x55cm 16x21in) Bielefeld 1999
- $3 147 - €3 579 - **£2 182** - FF23 477
  Prozession für den toten Fischer/Männerkopf Öl/Karton (43.3x32.1cm 17x12in) Hamburg 2000
- $1 967 - €2 250 - **£1 350** - FF14 757
  Fischer bei der Arbeit Aquarell/Papier (32.2x43.3cm 12x17in) Lindau 2000
- $150 - €179 - **£107** - FF1 175
  Selbstbildnis Drypoint (42.2x30.6cm 16x12in) Berlin 2000

BARGUE Charles 1825-1883 **[30]**
- $16 000 - €14 987 - **£9 836** - FF98 305
  The Smoker Oil/panel (13.5x9cm 5x3in) New-York 1999

BARIGGI Galli XIX **[1]**
- $2 924 - €2 845 - **£1 800** - FF18 663
  The Mouse, after Giacomo Favretto (1849-1887) Watercolour/paper (29x45cm 11x17in) London 1999

BARIL Tom XX **[2]**
- $2 000 - €1 880 - **£1 238** - FF12 335
  Sunflowers Silver print (86x66cm 34x26in) New-York 1999

BARILE Xavier J. 1891-1981 **[53]**
- $475 - €472 - **£291** - FF3 093
  Artist Painting Model Oil/canvas (50x40cm 20x16in) Mystic CT 2000
- $350 - €353 - **£218** - FF2 313
  September Afternoon Oil/board (30x40cm 12x16in) Hatfield PA 2000

BARILLI Aristide 1913 **[4]**
- $2 000 - €2 073 - **£1 200** - FF13 600
  S.O.S Olio/cartone (16x27cm 6x10in) Milano 2000

BARILLOT Léon 1844-1929 **[27]**
- $1 836 - €1 707 - **£1 115** - FF11 200
  Cour de village Huile/panneau (35x27cm 13x10in) Paris 1998

BARISON Giuseppe 1853-1930 **[29]**
- $12 250 - €12 699 - **£7 350** - FF83 300
  Porto di Trieste Olio/tela (39x64.5cm 15x25in) Torino 2000
- $1 750 - €1 814 - **£1 050** - FF11 900
  Dichiarazione Olio/tavola (25x20cm 9x7in) Trieste 1999

BARJOLA Juan 1919 **[70]**
- $35 840 - €33 636 - **£22 400** - FF220 640
  Tauromaquia Oleo/lienzo (97x130cm 38x51in) Madrid 1999
- $14 280 - €16 818 - **£9 800** - FF110 320
  Cabeza Oleo/lienzo (100x81cm 39x31in) Madrid 2000
- $12 600 - €13 515 - **£8 325** - FF88 650
  Tauromaquia Oleo/tablex (27x35cm 10x13in) Madrid 2000
- $1 600 - €1 502 - **£950** - FF9 850
  Figura Gouache/papier (54x36cm 21x14in) Madrid 1999
- $616 - €661 - **£418** - FF4 334
  Sin título Litografía (58x46cm 22x18in) Madrid 2000

BARKER Albert Winslow 1874-1947 **[20]**
- $130 - €140 - **£87** - FF918
  Valley Road/The Island Lithograph (22x17cm 9x7in) Cleveland OH 2000

BARKER Anthony Raine 1880-1963 **[11]**
- $869 - €1 002 - **£600** - FF6 571
  «Teddington» Poster (104x152cm 40x59in) London 2000

BARKER Clive 1940 **[37]**
- $3 220 - €2 981 - **£2 000** - FF19 553
  A Lovely Shape Bronze (H38cm H14in) London 1999
- $791 - €879 - **£550** - FF5 765
  Zip I/Zip II Screenprint (76x49.5cm 29x19in) London 2001

BARKER Edmund 1940 **[12]**
- $1 935 - €1 759 - **£1 200** - FF11 536
  Mtoto Sheltering Under Mama Oil/canvas (44x54cm 17x21in) Billingshurst, West-Sussex 1999

BARKER George act.c.1856 **[3]**
- $489 - €545 - **£320** - FF3 534
  Burleigh, North Front Albumen print (22.5x19cm 8x7in) Devon 2000

BARKER Kathleen Frances 1901-? **[5]**
- $1 232 - €1 323 - **£825** - FF8 680
  Otter Hunting Yoi Over Now Etching (23x30cm 9x12in) Little-Lane, Ilkley 2000

B

BARKER OF BATH Benjamin 1776-1838 **[25]**
- **$1 006** - €859 - **£600** - FF5 633
  Country Landscapes Oil/board (13.5x18.5cm 5x7in)
  London 1998

BARKER OF BATH John Joseph XIX **[40]**
- **$3 000** - €2 597 - **£1 809** - FF17 035
  Stable interior with a Horse and a Donkey with two Stable Boys behind Oil/canvas (91.5x71cm 36x27in) San-Francisco CA 1998

BARKER Thomas 1769-1847 **[58]**
- **$4 253** - €4 584 - **£2 900** - FF30 067
  Figures and Cattle Resting Before a River Estuary at Sunset Oil/canvas (63.5x98.5cm 25x38in) London 2001
- **$693** - €808 - **£480** - FF5 300
  Country Lane with Two Figures and a Cottage, near Bath Oil/panel (34x24cm 13x9in) Cheshire 2000

BARKER Thomas Jones 1815-1882 **[27]**
- **$35 122** - €40 745 - **£25 000** - FF267 272
  Nelson on the captured San Josef after the Battle of Cape St.Vincent Oil/canvas (155x277cm 61x109in) London 2001
- **$5 500** - €5 387 - **£3 544** - FF35 336
  Margaret in the Cathedral Oil/canvas (105.5x76cm 41x29in) New-York 1999

BARKER Wright 1864-1941 **[92]**
- **$10 764** - €10 031 - **£6 500** - FF65 796
  Won't You Play Oil/canvas (61x91.5cm 24x36in) London 1998
- **$963** - €935 - **£600** - FF6 135
  «Marechal», a bay Hunter in a Loosebox Oil/canvas (30.5x45.5cm 12x17in) London 1999

BARKOFF Alexis ?-1942 **[2]**
- **$2 160** - €2 403 - **£1 440** - FF15 760
  Thissio Watercolour/paper (40x50cm 15x19in) Athens 2000

BARKS Carl 1901 **[37]**
- **$1 188** - €1 115 - **£733** - FF7 317
  Donald Duck Pistolero Huile/toile (47x26cm 18x10in) Antwerpen 1999
- **$8 500** - €8 200 - **£5 372** - FF53 788
  Uncle Scrooge Cover Watercolour (25.5x21.5cm 10x8in) New-York 1999
- **$1 600** - €1 772 - **£1 085** - FF11 623
  Untitled Color lithograph (39x49cm 15x19in) New-York 2000

BARLACH Ernst 1870-1938 **[723]**
- **$11 398** - €13 294 - **£8 002** - FF87 201
  Maske (Kopf eines Mönches) Bronze (H13.7cm H5in) Köln 2000
- **$2 595** - €2 952 - **£1 800** - FF19 363
  Prometheus Charcoal/paper (35.5x25.5cm 13x10in) London 2000
- **$428** - €511 - **£305** - FF3 353
  Der Zauberlehrling I Lithographie (16.5x20.2cm 6x7in) Berlin 2000

BARLAG Isaak Ph.Hartvig Kee 1840-1913 **[30]**
- **$1 470** - €1 748 - **£1 047** - FF11 466
  Vadestedet Oil/canvas (68x90cm 26x35in) Oslo 2000
- **$1 111** - €969 - **£672** - FF6 359
  Berglandskap med fors Oil/canvas (35x28cm 13x11in) Stockholm 1998

BARLAND Adam c.1843-c.1875 **[30]**
- **$2 385** - €2 778 - **£1 650** - FF18 221
  Tranquil River Landscape with Cattle before a Cottage & Figures Oil/canvas (51x76cm 20x29in) Cheshire 2000

BARKER OF BATH

- **$1 133** - €1 344 - **£800** - FF8 814
  Figures Rowing on a River with Cattle Grazing on the Banks Oil/canvas (21x39cm 8x15in) Eastbourne, Sussex 2000

BARLE Maurice 1903-1961 **[23]**
- **$1 240** - €1 361 - **£824** - FF8 929
  Scène en Mauritanie Oil/panel (27x35cm 10x13in) Amsterdam 1999

BARLIER André 1920 **[4]**
- **$2 614** - €2 211 - **£1 563** - FF14 500
  Paysage des Pyrénées Huile/toile (33x41.5cm 12x16in) Toulouse 1998

BARLOW Francis 1626-1702 **[18]**
- **$3 586** - €3 849 - **£2 400** - FF25 251
  A Hound by a Stream in a Landscape Oil/canvas (37.5x63.5cm 14x25in) London 2000
- **$4 037** - €4 462 - **£2 800** - FF29 268
  Deer by a Wood Watercolour (15x11cm 5x4in) London 2001

BARLOW Gordon Clifford 1913 **[27]**
- **$258** - €290 - **£180** - FF1 900
  Wycaller Dene Oil/canvas/board (29x39cm 11x15in) Leyburn, North Yorkshire 2001

BARLOW John Noble 1861-1917 **[39]**
- **$6 500** - €7 856 - **£4 538** - FF51 535
  Mounts Bay from near Penzance Oil/canvas (99x127cm 39x50in) Philadelphia PA 2000
- **$836** - €898 - **£560** - FF5 892
  Lamorna Valley Oil/canvas (35.5x45.5cm 13x17in) Devon 2000
- **$680** - €734 - **£460** - FF5 235
  «The Mount's Bay, Cornwall» Oil/canvas (29x44.5cm 11x17in) London 2000

BARLOW Lou XX **[2]**
- **$1 200** - €1 293 - **£818** - FF8 483
  «Orchard Street» Woodcut in colors (28x20.5cm 11x8in) New-York 2001

BARLOW Myron G. 1873-1937 **[44]**
- **$13 000** - €11 945 - **£7 985** - FF78 351
  Untitled Oil/canvas (88x88cm 35x35in) Detroit MI 1999

BARNABÉ Duilio 1914-1961 **[133]**
- **$1 557** - €1 524 - **£995** - FF10 000
  Paysage italien Huile/toile (75x93cm 29x36in) L'Isle-Adam 1999
- **$1 048** - €1 098 - **£693** - FF7 200
  La religieuse Huile/toile (29.5x19cm 11x7in) Paris 2000

BARNADAS Ramón 1909-1981 **[16]**
- **$2 040** - €2 403 - **£1 440** - FF15 760
  Paisaje Oleo/lienzo (65x81cm 25x31in) Barcelona 2000

BARNARD Edward Herbert 1855-1909 **[11]**
- **$2 600** - €2 791 - **£1 771** - FF18 307
  Summer Woodland Scene Oil/canvas (36x46cm 14x18in) Boston MA 2001

BARNARD Frederick 1846-1896 **[10]**
- **$4 073** - €3 707 - **£2 500** - FF24 317
  Scrumping Oil/canvas (51x69cm 20x27in) London 1999
- **$328** - €289 - **£200** - FF1 896
  Hole in the Pocket Watercolour/paper (32.5x22cm 12x8in) London 1999

BARNARD George 1832-1890 **[16]**
🖝 **$1 226** - €1 355 - **£850** - FF8 887
   Goat Herders Resting in a Mountainous Lakeland Landscape Watercolour (44.5x73cm 17x28in) London 2001

BARNARD George Grey 1863-1938 **[3]**
🕭 **€4 250** - €3 637 - **£2 558** - FF23 859
   The Builder Bronze (H44cm H17in) New-York 1998

BARNARD George N. 1819-1902 **[18]**
📷 **$2 400** - €2 250 - **£1 483** - FF14 762
   General Sherman and Staff Albumen print (26x36cm 10x14in) New-York 1999

BARNARD Lady Anne 1750-1825 **[1]**
🖝 **$2 003** - €2 247 - **£1 401** - FF14 739
   Portrait of the Tutor at the Farm Onverwatcht Watercolour (26x21cm 10x8in) Cape Town 2001

BARNARD Mary B. 1870-1946 **[15]**
🕭 **$8 859** - €8 325 - **£5 500** - FF54 610
   Arranging Flowers before Tea Mixed media/canvas (127x89.5cm 50x35in) London 1999
🕭 **$2 016** - €2 235 - **£1 400** - FF14 661
   The artist's sister, Elizabeth Barnard Oil/canvas (34x39cm 13x15in) Mere, Wiltshire 2001
🖝 **$460** - €511 - **£320** - FF3 351
   The artist's mother Pastel/canvas (61x45cm 24x18in) Mere, Wiltshire 2001

BARNBAUM Bruce 1943 **[9]**
📷 **$425** - €364 - **£255** - FF2 389
   Dune Ridges at Sunrise, death Valley Gelatin silver print (27.5x33cm 10x12in) San-Francisco CA 1998

BARNEDA [2]
🖝 **$2 116** - €2 470 - **£1 500** - FF16 203
   The brigantine-schooner Costa Brava Ink (42x61cm 16x24in) London 2001

BARNEKOW Brita 1868-1936 **[13]**
🕭 **$1 217** - €1 342 - **£824** - FF8 801
   Börn i skoven en septemberdag Oil/canvas (62x85cm 24x33in) Vejle 2000

BARNES Archibald George 1887-1972 **[26]**
🕭 **$5 678** - €6 095 - **£3 800** - FF39 982
   The Shawl Oil/canvas (83.5x63cm 32x24in) London 2000

BARNES Edward Charles c.1830-c.1890 **[60]**
🕭 **$4 781** - €5 133 - **£3 200** - FF33 669
   Lunch Time Oil/canvas (38x48cm 14x18in) London 2000
🕭 **$789** - €827 - **£500** - FF5 426
   The Spanish Fan Oil/canvas (38.5x34.5cm 15x13in) Edinburgh 2000

BARNES Ernie XX **[2]**
🕭 **$7 500** - €7 300 - **£4 608** - FF47 883
   Dance Hall Oil/canvas (60x91cm 24x36in) San-Francisco CA 1999

BARNES Frank ?-c.1940 **[11]**
🕭 **$1 554** - €1 543 - **£953** - FF10 119
   The S.S. Rotomahana The Black Painted Hull If This Famous Oil/board (36x61cm 14x24in) Auckland 2000
🕭 **$1 813** - €1 800 - **£1 111** - FF11 805
   The S.S.Murray of the Anchor line Fleet Watercolour/paper (33x46cm 12x18in) Auckland 2000

BARNES Hiram Putnam 1857-? **[4]**
🖝 **$350** - €379 - **£239** - FF2 483
   Stream with Cattails Watercolour/paper (31x42cm 12x16in) Thomaston ME 2001

BARNES James ?-c.1923 **[10]**
🖝 **$1 180** - €1 322 - **£820** - FF8 670
   The Riverside Galde, a young Country Girl gathering Wood by a Stream Watercolour (50x36cm 19x14in) Newbury, Berkshire 2001

BARNES John Pierce 1895-1952 **[10]**
🕭 **$3 000** - €3 381 - **£2 077** - FF22 176
   «Head and Life» Oil/canvas (50x60cm 20x24in) Hatfield PA 2000
🕭 **$9 500** - €9 825 - **£6 003** - FF64 448
   Pointillist Landscape with Stream Oil/panel (33x40cm 13x16in) Hatfield PA 2000

BARNES Joseph H. act.c.1867-c.1887 **[14]**
🖝 **$676** - €636 - **£420** - FF4 170
   Lunch on the Deck Watercolour/paper (27.5x20.5cm 10x8in) London 1999

BARNES Robert 1840-1895 **[5]**
🖝 **$4 403** - €3 771 - **£2 600** - FF24 738
   «Not very Well» Watercolour (27x31cm 10x12in) Ipswich 1998

BARNET Will 1911 **[87]**
🗔 **$425** - €363 - **£249** - FF2 383
   «Winter» Lithograph (66x51cm 25x20in) Boston MA 1998

BARNETT G. William XIX **[1]**
🕭 **$9 096** - €8 508 - **£5 500** - FF55 811
   Moghul Tomb by a Banyan Tree Oil/canvas (51x61.5cm 20x24in) London 1999

BARNETT Thomas P. 1870-1929 **[6]**
🕭 **$1 000** - €1 175 - **£693** - FF7 709
   Venice Oil/canvas/board (35x40cm 14x16in) Cincinnati OH 2000

BARNEY Frank A. 1862-1954 **[18]**
🕭 **$2 000** - €1 869 - **£1 246** - FF12 257
   Landscape Oil/canvas (40x60cm 16x24in) Mystic CT 1999
🕭 **$500** - €571 - **£352** - FF3 746
   Autumnal Forest Interior, upstate NY Oil/board (30x40cm 12x16in) Pittsfield MA 2001

BARNEY Joseph XVIII **[3]**
🗔 **$1 000** - €1 037 - **£600** - FF6 800
   The Happy Cottagers Stampa (48x37.5cm 18x14in) Milano 2001

BARNEY Matthew 1967 **[32]**
🕭 **$20 000** - €22 301 - **£13 448** - FF146 288
   Cover-Cadence Mixed media (44x38x2cm 17x14xin) New-York 2000
🕭 **$350 000** - €328 499 - **£216 230** - FF2 154 810
   Cremaster 4 Construction (120x120x90cm 47x47x35in) New-York 1999
🕭 **$24 000** - €23 222 - **£14 800** - FF152 325
   Cover-Cadence Construction (45.5x36x6cm 17x14x2in) New-York 1999
🗔 **$756** - €915 - **£528** - FF6 000
   Cremaster 5 Lithographie (85x60cm 33x23in) Paris 2000
📷 **$65 000** - €71 314 - **£43 179** - FF467 792
   Cremaster 4: The Loughton Candidate Photograph in colors (49.5x45.5cm 19x17in) New-York 1999

BARNEY Tina 1945 **[17]**
📷 **$6 000** - €5 766 - **£3 696** - FF37 823
   «#4754» Photograph in colour (121x152.5cm 47x60in) New-York 1999

B

BARNI Roberto 1939 **[76]**
🖐 **$2 250** – €2 332 – **£1 350** – FF15 300
　　Senza titolo Olio/tela (120x100cm 47x39in) Prato
　　2001
🖐 **$720** – €933 – **£540** – FF6 120
　　«**Dispersione**» Olio/tela (120x99cm 47x38in) Prato
　　2000
✏ **$1 020** – €881 – **£680** – FF5 780
　　Senza titolo Pastelli/carta (46x36.5cm 18x14in) Prato
　　1998

BARNOIN Camille 1841-1881 **[2]**
🖐 **$4 604** – €5 488 – **£3 283** – FF36 000
　　Les lavandières Huile/toile (56x40cm 22x15in) Riom
　　2000

BARNOIN Henri Alphonse 1882-? **[435]**
🖐 **$16 666** – €19 818 – **£11 882** – FF130 000
　　**Thoniers au mouillage sous la ville Close,
　　Concarneau** Huile/toile (100x140cm 39x55in) Brest
　　2000
🖐 **$6 033** – €6 632 – **£3 836** – FF43 500
　　Marché près de Concarneau Huile/toile (48x40cm
　　18x15in) Paris 2000
🖐 **$4 106** – €3 781 – **£2 465** – FF24 800
　　Port de Concarneau Huile/panneau (21x27cm
　　8x10in) Laval 1999
✏ **$2 149** – €2 058 – **£1 324** – FF13 500
　　Marché en Bretagne Pastel (22x31cm 8x12in) Calais
　　1999
▭ **$248** – €282 – **£174** – FF1 850
　　Marché Place Terre-aux-Ducs à Quimper
　　Lithographie (22x28cm 8x11in) Quimper 2001

BARNS-GRAHAM Wilhelmina 1912 **[35]**
🖐 **$1 459** – €1 402 – **£900** – FF9 196
　　Grey Line, Porthmear Acrylic (27.5x40cm 10x15in)
　　London 1999
🖐 **$4 014** – €3 707 – **£2 500** – FF24 314
　　Farm Track Watercolour (20x27.5cm 7x10in) London
　　1999

BARNSLEY James Macdonald 1861-1929 **[28]**
🖐 **$1 656** – €1 834 – **£1 123** – FF12 031
　　Rural Landscape Oil/canvas (76x111.5cm 29x43in)
　　Toronto 2000
🖐 **$1 228** – €1 321 – **£845** – FF8 662
　　Cattle Grazing, Saint Vaast Oil/panel (23.5x33.5cm
　　9x13in) Toronto 2001

BAROCCI Federico 1526/35-1612 **[40]**
✏ **$38 997** – €38 159 – **£25 000** – FF250 305
　　Study for a Holy Family St John Ink (16x14.5cm
　　6x5in) London 1999
▭ **$4 448** – €4 314 – **£2 800** – FF28 301
　　The Annunciation Etching (44x31cm 17x12in)
　　London 1999

BAROJA NESSI Ricardo 1871-1953 **[58]**
🖐 **$13 040** – €12 013 – **£7 800** – FF78 800
　　Varadero Oleo/lienzo (38x46cm 14x18in) Madrid
　　1999
✏ **$2 280** – €2 403 – **£1 440** – FF15 760
　　Catedral de Segovia Pastel/carton (30x38cm
　　11x14in) Madrid 2000
▭ **$246** – €264 – **£162** – FF1 733
　　Barco en el puerto Aguafuerte (20x29cm 7x11in)
　　Madrid 2000

BARON Christian 1948 **[36]**
🖐 **$1 475** – €1 220 – **£865** – FF8 000
　　Nu Huile/toile (50x61cm 19x24in) L'Isle-Adam 1998

BARON Henri Charles A. 1816-1885 **[67]**
🖐 **$9 788** – €8 537 – **£5 919** – FF56 000
　　Jeunes enfants jouant près d'un bassin
　　Huile/panneau (68x46cm 26x18in) Paris 1998
🖐 **$892** – €1 050 – **£646** – FF6 887
　　Néréide Huile/toile (16.5x22cm 6x8in) Sion 2001
✏ **$1 900** – €1 823 – **£1 191** – FF11 961
　　Afternoon of Song Watercolour, gouache/paper
　　(22x28cm 8x11in) New-York 1999

BARON Marie Céline XIX **[3]**
🖐 **$6 240** – €5 391 – **£3 120** – FF35 360
　　Vaso di fiori Olio/tela (64x81cm 25x31in) Genova
　　1999

BARON Théodore 1840-1899 **[98]**
🖐 **$1 161** – €1 091 – **£717** – FF7 154
　　Arrière de ferme Huile/bois (47x65cm 18x25in)
　　Bruxelles 1999
🖐 **$627** – €694 – **£436** – FF4 552
　　«**Vue de Modave**» Huile/toile (32.5x40.5cm 12x15in)
　　Liège 2001

BARONE Antonio 1889-1971 **[37]**
🖐 **$750** – €857 – **£529** – FF5 620
　　Farm View in Summer Oil/canvas/board (50x65.5cm
　　19x25in) Boston MA 2001

BARONE Carlo Adolfo 1861-? **[3]**
🖐 **$4 800** – €6 220 – **£3 600** – FF40 800
　　La guardiana dei tacchini Olio/tela (51x71cm
　　20x27in) Roma 2000

BARONI Paolo 1871-? **[15]**
🖐 **$1 800** – €2 332 – **£1 350** – FF15 300
　　Paesaggio con rovine antiche Olio/tavola
　　(75x65cm 29x25in) Prato 2001
🖐 **$905** – €991 – **£624** – FF6 500
　　Le boxeur Pastel/papier (51x50cm 20x19in) Paris
　　2001

BAROOSHIAN Martin 1929 **[7]**
▭ **$250** – €234 – **£154** – FF1 538
　　«**Creatures of Prometheus**» Etching, aquatint in
　　colors (39.5x45.5cm 15x17in) New-York 1999

BAROTTE Léon 1866-1933 **[27]**
🖐 **$407** – €381 – **£246** – FF2 500
　　Bord de rivière Huile/toile (44x65cm 17x25in) Lons-
　　Le-Saunier 2000

BAROVIER Angelo XX **[3]**
🏺 **$3 256** – €3 783 – **£2 288** – FF24 818
　　Nudo Sculpture, glass (H40cm H15in) München 2001

BAROVIER Ercole 1898-1974 **[4]**
🏺 **$80 000** – €93 371 – **£56 472** – FF612 472
　　Primavera Sculpture, glass (H31cm H12in) New-York
　　2000

BARR William 1867-1933 **[34]**
🖐 **$2 156** – €1 875 – **£1 300** – FF12 301
　　Stable Companions Oil/canvas (35.5x45.5cm
　　13x17in) Glasgow 1998
🖐 **$359** – €419 – **£250** – FF2 749
　　The Smithy Oil/canvas (30.5x41cm 12x16in) London
　　2000

BARRA, MONSU DESIDERIO Didier 1590-1650 **[4]**
🖐 **$108 000** – €93 299 – **£72 000** – FF612 000
　　Veduta del porto di Napoli Olio/tela (129x230cm
　　50x90in) Prato 1998

BARRABAND Jacques 1767/8-1809 **[179]**
✏ **$22 219** – €25 916 – **£15 606** – FF170 000
　　Le Barbu de la Guyane mâle Aquarelle, gouache
　　(52x38cm 20x14in) Paris 2000

🗒️ $200 - €199 - £121 - FF1 307
Le Tocan #3 Engraving (52x35cm 20x14in) St. Petersburg FL 2000

BARRABLE George Hamilton XIX **[5]**
🖼️ $12 749 - €11 651 - £7 800 - FF76 426
Five Classical Ladies Seated on Steps to Coliseum Oil/canvas (165x114cm 65x45in) Dorking, Surrey 1999

BARRADAS Jorge Nicholson 1894-1971 **[9]**
🖋️ $1 408 - €1 595 - £902 - FF10 464
Boémios Tinta china/papel (25x17cm 9x6in) Lisboa 2001

BARRAL Ch. **[1]**
🖼️ $8 158 - €7 927 - £5 101 - FF52 000
Roses et framboises sur fond de paysage Huile/toile (82x62cm 32x24in) Lyon 1999

BARRALET John James c.1747-1815 **[5]**
🖋️ $9 492 - €10 096 - £6 000 - FF66 228
Portrait of John Meheux, half-Length, Reading Black chalk (26.5x21cm 10x8in) London 2000

BARRATT Watson 1884-1964 **[3]**
🖋️ $1 000 - €1 059 - £661 - FF6 945
Bitter Sweet: Design for the Decor Gouache (30.5x51cm 12x20in) New-York 1999

BARRAU BUÑOL Laureano 1864-1957 **[82]**
🖼️ $31 200 - €36 039 - £21 600 - FF236 400
Idilio en el columpio Oleo/lienzo (184x136cm 72x53in) Madrid 2000
🖼️ $12 200 - €12 013 - £7 600 - FF78 800
Ibicenca tendiendo la ropa Oleo/lienzo (68x55cm 26x21in) Madrid 1999
🖼️ $896 - €841 - £560 - FF5 516
Niño en la playa Oleo/lienzo (29x13cm 11x5in) Madrid 1999
🖋️ $196 - €222 - £136 - FF1 457
Estudio de mujer tejiendo/Estudio de hombres pescando Lápiz/papel (15x23.5cm 5x9in) Madrid 2001

BARRAUD Aimé 1902-1954 **[74]**
🖼️ $1 598 - €1 825 - £1 127 - FF11 972
Stilleben mit roten und violetten Dahlien Öl/Leinwand (50.5x42.5cm 19x16in) Bern 2001
🖼️ $913 - €1 043 - £644 - FF6 841
Nature morte aux pêches Öl/Leinwand (22x27cm 8x10in) Bern 2001

BARRAUD Charles Decimus 1822-1897 **[17]**
🖋️ $500 - €520 - £314 - FF3 413
Cheltenham beach, Auckland Watercolour/paper (24x34cm 9x13in) Auckland 1999

BARRAUD Francis James 1856-1924 **[3]**
🖼️ $15 846 - €16 294 - £10 000 - FF106 883
The Little Milkmaid Oil/canvas (91x60cm 35x23in) Devon 2000

BARRAUD Francis Philip 1824-1901 **[15]**
🖋️ $347 - €331 - £220 - FF2 171
St Giles Caen Watercolour (17.5x12.5cm 6x4in) London 1999

BARRAUD François Émile 1899-1934 **[52]**
🖼️ $3 113 - €3 612 - £2 149 - FF23 692
Stilleben mit Büchern, chinesischem Dachreiter und Aloe Öl/Leinwand (38x46cm 14x18in) Luzern 2000
🖼️ $2 113 - €1 941 - £1 298 - FF12 734
Nature morte aux roses de Noël Öl/Leinwand (41x32cm 16x12in) Zürich 1999

BARRAUD Gustave François 1883-1964 **[65]**
🖼️ $642 - €619 - £396 - FF4 062
Sitzende junge Frau in einer Laube Öl/Karton (53x68cm 20x26in) Bern 1999

BARRAUD Henry 1811-1874 **[39]**
🖼️ $9 000 - €10 456 - £6 325 - FF68 590
Knight of Downe, with J.Salmon up Oil/canvas (71x91.5cm 27x36in) New-York 2001
🖼️ $1 624 - €1 581 - £1 000 - FF10 368
Portrait of a Girl, in a Landscape holding a Rose Oil/panel (37.5x28cm 14x11in) London 1999

BARRAUD Maurice 1889-1955 **[372]**
🖼️ $22 300 - €26 231 - £16 160 - FF172 064
«La robe à fleurs» Öl/Leinwand (130x96cm 51x37in) Zofingen 2001
🖼️ $6 720 - €7 854 - £4 797 - FF51 519
Sous le figuier Oil/panel (76x85.5cm 29x33in) Zürich 2001
🖼️ $3 102 - €3 239 - £1 963 - FF21 245
Portrait de jeune fille Huile/panneau (35x28cm 13x11in) Genève 2000
🖋️ $534 - €499 - £330 - FF3 275
Atelierszene Crayon/papier (37x52.5cm 14x20in) Luzern 1999
🗒️ $268 - €249 - £164 - FF1 634
Europe Lithographie (33.5x25.5cm 13x10in) Bern 1999

BARRAUD William 1810-1850 **[34]**
🖼️ $68 606 - €65 586 - £43 000 - FF430 215
Richard Crawshay, on a black Pony, talking to a Gamekeeper and a Man Oil/canvas (107x138.5cm 42x54in) London 1999
🖼️ $4 632 - €4 972 - £3 100 - FF32 617
Bay Hunter in a Landscape Oil/canvas (58x74.5cm 22x29in) Billingshurst, West-Sussex 2000

BARRAUD William & Henry 1810/11-1850/74 **[7]**
🖼️ $41 483 - €39 657 - £26 000 - FF260 130
Sam.Richard Block, of Greenhill,Barnet, later High Sheriff and his Son Oil/canvas (72.5x102cm 28x40in) London 1999

BARRE Albert Désiré 1818-1878 **[2]**
🔨 $4 485 - €3 838 - £2 700 - FF25 177
Ballerinas Bronze (H44cm H17in) London 1998

BARRE Auguste Jean 1811-1896 **[26]**
🔨 $8 614 - €9 657 - £6 000 - FF63 343
«Rachel» Bronze (H43.5cm H17in) London 2001

BARRÉ Martin 1924-1993 **[68]**
🖼️ $8 164 - €7 927 - £5 044 - FF52 000
Composition Huile/toile (100x81cm 39x31in) Versailles 1999
🖼️ $3 264 - €3 064 - £2 022 - FF20 100
Composition Huile/toile (22x16cm 8x6in) Paris 1999
🖼️ $1 618 - €1 601 - £1 009 - FF10 500
Sans titre Encre/papier (46x50cm 18x19in) Paris 1999

BARRE Raoul Vital Achille 1874-1932 **[2]**
🖼️ $4 817 - €4 116 - £2 914 - FF27 000
«Hommage de Roses» Huile/panneau (20x15cm 7x5in) Montréal 1998

BARREDA Ignacio Maria XVIII **[1]**
🖼️ $9 000 - €8 757 - £5 539 - FF57 440
Retrato de Maria Ysabel Antonia Galves y Estrada Oil/canvas (53x40.5cm 20x15in) New-York 1999

BARRERA Francisco ?-c.1657 **[5]**
🖼️ $10 260 - €11 412 - £7 030 - FF74 860
Alegoria del gusto Oleo/lienzo (122x102cm 48x40in) Madrid 2000

BARRERE Adrien 1877-1931 **[63]**
🎬 **$1 159** - €1 067 - **£695** - FF7 000
«Little Moritz est trop petit» Affiche (120x160cm
47x62in) Paris 1999

BARRET Gaston 1910-1991 **[46]**
✒ **$201** - €229 - **£141** - FF1 500
Barques et brume Aquarelle/papier (43.5x52cm
17x20in) Quimper 2001
🎬 **$39** - €43 - **£27** - FF280
Le chien Gravure (29.5x21cm 11x8in) Quimper 2001

BARRET George I 1728/32-1784 **[48]**
🖼 **$21 870** - €21 404 - **£14 000** - FF140 401
River Landscape with Figures before a Waterfall
Oil/canvas (98x124cm 38x48in) London 1999
🖼 **$59 772** - €64 160 - **£40 000** - FF420 864
View of Lord Hamilton's Landscape Garden at
Painthill, Surrey Oil/canvas (66x96.5cm 25x37in)
London 2000
✒ **$1 290** - €1 240 - **£800** - FF8 131
Wooded Landscape Black & white chalks (50x67cm
19x26in) London 1999

BARRET George II c.1767-1842 **[70]**
✒ **$645** - €620 - **£400** - FF4 065
Figure on a Bridge over a River at Dusk/River in
a Landscape Watercolour (30x22cm 11x8in) London
1999

BARRET Marius 1865-? **[17]**
🖼 **$2 840** - €3 049 - **£1 900** - FF20 000
Une restauratrice de Kilims Huile/toile (43x30cm
16x11in) Paris 2000

BARRETO Pedro 1935 **[11]**
🗿 **$975** - €1 021 - **£585** - FF6 695
Sin título Sculpture bois (H44.5cm H17in) Caracas
2000

BARRETT Ranelagh ?-1768 **[2]**
🖼 **$70 000** - €81 329 - **£49 196** - FF533 484
Four of Sir Robert Walpole's Hounds in a
Landscape Oil/canvas (152.5x239cm 60x94in) New-
York 2001

BARRETT William S. 1854-1927 **[8]**
🖼 **$7 000** - €7 092 - **£4 393** - FF46 519
New England Coastal Scene Oil/canvas (35x55cm
14x22in) Cincinnati OH 2000

BARRIAS Félix Joseph 1822-1907 **[26]**
🖼 **$6 153** - €7 318 - **£4 267** - FF48 000
Esquisse de la femme de droite dans «La
Conspiration des concubines» Huile/toile
(31x39.5cm 12x15in) Paris 2000
✒ **$427** - €396 - **£266** - FF2 600
Trois personnages orientaux en buste Aquarelle
(22x27.5cm 8x10in) Paris 1999

BARRIAS Louis Ernest 1841-1905 **[161]**
🗿 **$10 925** - €12 493 - **£7 500** - FF81 947
La renommée (An Allegory of Fame) Gilded bron-
ze (H84.5cm H33in) London 2000
🗿 **$5 112** - €5 488 - **£3 420** - FF36 000
La source Chryséléphantine (H25.5cm H10in)
Clermont-Ferrand 2000

BARRIBAL William H. act.1919-1938 **[38]**
✒ **$882** - €1 031 - **£620** - FF6 766
Study of a Young Lady Watercolour (34x27.5cm
13x10in) Oxfordshire 2000
🎬 **$3 811** - €4 420 - **£2 700** - FF28 991
«Scarborough, LNER, New Guide from Town
Clerk or Any LNER Agency» Poster (107x184cm
42x72in) London 2000

BARRIERE Georges 1881-1944 **[19]**
✒ **$419** - €396 - **£261** - FF2 600
La Pagode de Confucius, Hué Aquarelle/papier
(18x26cm 7x10in) Paris 1999

BARRIERE-PRÉVOST Marguerite XX **[14]**
✒ **$760** - €884 - **£533** - FF5 800
Femme arabe dans un riad Gouache/papier
(30.5x23cm 12x9in) Paris 2001

BARRINGER Gwendoline l'Avance 1883-1960 **[8]**
✒ **$605** - €630 - **£380** - FF4 132
The Thames Watercolour/paper (26x46cm 10x18in)
Melbourne 2000

BARRINGTON-BROWNE William E. 1908-1985 **[20]**
🖼 **$701** - €805 - **£480** - FF5 281
The Naver Oil/board (21.5x29cm 8x11in) Edinburgh
2000

BARRIOS Armando 1920 **[17]**
🖼 **$27 000** - €25 154 - **£16 500** - FF165 000
Rithmes, París Oleo/lienzo (162.5x113cm 63x44in)
Caracas 1998
🖼 **$45 360** - €47 484 - **£27 216** - FF311 472
Persistente recuerdo Oleo/lienzo (107x61cm
42x24in) Caracas 2000
🖼 **$5 600** - €5 336 - **£3 500** - FF35 000
Paisaje Oleo/lienzo (40x30cm 15x11in) Caracas 1999

BARRIOS Rafael 1947 **[15]**
🗿 **$1 902** - €2 242 - **£1 336** - FF14 705
Levitación Obtusa Fer (33x33x8cm 12x12x3in)
Caracas ($) 2000

BARRIVIERA Lino Bianchi 1906-1985 **[3]**
🎬 **$400** - €415 - **£240** - FF2 720
Pianura lombarda Gravure (38x46cm 14x18in) Prato
2001

BARRON Y CARRILLO Manuel 1814-1884 **[29]**
🖼 **$28 000** - €30 032 - **£19 000** - FF197 000
Los Reales Alcázares de Sevilla Oleo/lienzo
(135x105cm 53x41in) Madrid 2001
🖼 **$22 000** - €24 026 - **£15 200** - FF157 600
La despedida del soldado a la orilla del
Guadalquivir Oleo/lienzo (56x72cm 22x28in) Madrid
2001

BARROS Augusto Ferreira 1929-1998 **[9]**
✒ **$2 376** - €2 692 - **£1 674** - FF17 713
Sem título Gouache/papier (16.5x12cm 6x4in) Lisboa
2001

BARROS de Geraldo 1923-1998 **[5]**
📷 **$2 135** - €2 045 - **£1 319** - FF13 415
Pamulha, Belo horizonte, Brasilien Gelatin silver
print (30.2x40cm 11x15in) Köln 1999

BARROW Edith Isabel ?-1930 **[15]**
✒ **$2 388** - €2 324 - **£1 470** - FF15 244
Stilleben med blommor Akvarell/papper (55x36cm
21x14in) Stockholm 1999

BARROW Jane XIX **[1]**
🖼 **$4 933** - €5 556 - **£3 400** - FF36 442
Ironing Day Oil/panel (28x37cm 11x14in) London
2000

BARROW Joseph Charles XVIII-XIX **[7]**
✒ **$5 243** - €4 830 - **£3 200** - FF31 683
A bay in Jamaica Ink (35.5x47cm 13x18in) London
1998

BARROW Julian 1939 **[24]**
🖼 **$320** - €365 - **£220** - FF2 392
Easton Neston Oil/canvas (30.5x40.5cm 12x15in)
London 2000

B

BARRY Anne Meredith 1932 **[24]**
- $529 – €568 - **£359** - FF3 726
  Early Snow Mixed media/paper (29.5x22cm 11x8in) Calgary, Alberta 2001
- $130 – €152 - **£90** - FF997
  Road Across the Pond No.2 Woodcut in colors (42x49cm 16x19in) Calgary, Alberta 2000

BARRY Charles 1795-1860 **[8]**
- $5 122 – €5 951 - **£3 600** - FF39 039
  Design for the East, West and North Elevations of the House of Lords Pencil/paper (54.5x74.5cm 21x29in) London 2001

BARRY Claude Francis 1883-1970 **[30]**
- $57 684 – €63 742 - **£40 000** - FF418 120
  Victory celebrations Oil/canvas (160x172.5cm 62x67in) London 2001
- $1 538 – €1 332 - **£933** - FF8 736
  A beached fishing boat Oil/canvas (65x80cm 25x31in) Amsterdam 1998

BARRY David F. 1854-1934 **[21]**
- $1 600 – €1 494 - **£967** - FF9 803
  John Sitting Bull/Wild Horse/Chief Goose Silver print (20x15cm 8x6in) New-York 1999

BARRY Edith M. XIX **[1]**
- $2 841 – €2 755 - **£1 800** - FF18 073
  Thorpe Abbotts, Norfolk Watercolour (44x59cm 17x23in) London 1999

BARRY François Pierre 1813-1905 **[27]**
- $13 138 – €14 483 - **£8 740** - FF95 000
  Bataille navale Huile/toile (90x136cm 35x53in) Biarritz 2000
- $12 780 – €13 720 - **£8 550** - FF90 000
  Vue du Bosphore animé au premier plan de personnages Huile/toile (66x90cm 25x35in) Marseille 2000
- $627 – €732 - **£436** - FF4 800
  Le bassin de carénage Huile/panneau (13.5x22cm 5x8in) Nice 2000

BARRY Moyra 1886-1960 **[19]**
- $1 121 – €1 204 - **£750** - FF7 897
  Roses in Sunlight Oil/canvas (45.5x35.5cm 17x13in) London 2000
- $978 – €1 041 - **£618** - FF6 829
  Still life of flowers Oil/canvas (32x41cm 12x16in) Dublin 2000

BARRY Robert 1936 **[44]**
- $5 048 – €5 933 - **£3 500** - FF38 920
  Untitled Acrylic/canvas (122x122cm 48x48in) London 2000
- $1 380 – €1 524 - **£957** - FF10 000
  Sans titre Acrylique (66x66cm 25x25in) Paris 2001
- $1 228 – €1 372 - **£832** - FF9 000
  Sans titre Peinture (37x37cm 14x14in) Paris 2000
- $1 794 – €1 982 - **£1 244** - FF13 000
  Sans titre Encre (57x76.5cm 22x30in) Paris 2001

BARTA Ernö 1878-1956 **[9]**
- $1 000 – €853 - **£603** - FF5 596
  «Pestinapló» Poster (91x123cm 35x48in) New-York 1998

BARTELLETTI Aldo XX **[2]**
- $10 460 – €11 228 - **£7 000** - FF73 651
  Bust of Beethoven Marble (H63cm H24in) London 2000

BARTELS Hermann 1928-1989 **[12]**
- $3 710 – €4 311 - **£2 607** - FF28 277
  Untitled Oil/canvas (42.5x34cm 16x13in) Amsterdam 2001

BARTELS Rudolf 1872-1946 **[7]**
- $3 453 – €3 579 - **£2 188** - FF23 477
  Alpenveilchen (mit Äpfeln und Büchern Öl/Karton (47x67cm 18x26in) Buxtehude 2000

BARTELS von Hans 1856-1913 **[99]**
- $1 512 – €1 278 - **£899** - FF8 383
  Fischerfrauen am Strand Oil/panel (39x45cm 15x17in) Bremen 1998
- $789 – €920 - **£546** - FF6 037
  Binz Öl/Karton (21x27cm 8x10in) Buxtehude 2000
- $1 079 – €1 022 - **£656** - FF6 707
  Holländisches Fischerpaar am Kamin Gouache/paper (80x100cm 31x39in) München 1999

BARTEZAGO Luigi 1829-1905 **[4]**
- $4 000 – €4 147 - **£2 400** - FF27 200
  Idillio Olio/tela (18x41cm 7x16in) Milano 2000
- $1 650 – €1 710 - **£990** - FF11 220
  Milano, Porta Romana Tempera/carta (16.5x21cm 6x8in) Venezia 2000

BARTH Carl 1896-1976 **[39]**
- $1 382 – €1 329 - **£853** - FF8 720
  Rotterdam Oil/panel (79.5x60.2cm 31x23in) Köln 1999

BARTH Carl Wilhelm 1847-1919 **[20]**
- $325 – €378 - **£232** - FF2 482
  Til rors Oil/canvas (16x22cm 6x8in) Oslo 2001

BARTH Ferdinand 1902-1979 **[25]**
- $307 – €358 - **£216** - FF2 347
  Hamburger Hafenansichten Watercolour (34.5x26cm 13x10in) Hamburg 2001

BARTH Paul Basilius 1881-1955 **[138]**
- $1 761 – €1 985 - **£1 220** - FF13 023
  Mädchenbildnis Öl/Leinwand (82x60cm 32x23in) Zürich 2000
- $791 – €683 - **£475** - FF4 477
  Selbstbildnis Öl/Karton (42x34cm 16x13in) Bern 1998

BARTH Uta 1958 **[11]**
- $14 000 – €13 546 - **£8 633** - FF88 856
  Field #24 Acrylic/canvas (228.5x335cm 89x131in) New-York 1999
- $7 000 – €6 773 - **£4 316** - FF44 428
  Ground #46 Photograph in colors (49.5x53.5cm 19x21in) New-York 1999

BARTH Wolf 1926 **[21]**
- $1 642 – €1 625 - **£1 024** - FF10 657
  Ohne Titel Tempera (52x40cm 20x15in) Luzern 1999

BARTHA Laszlo 1902-1998 **[3]**
- $4 000 – €3 933 - **£2 500** - FF25 800
  In the Studio Tempera/paper (59x79.5cm 23x31in) Budapest 1999

BARTHALOT Marius 1861-? **[11]**
- $3 637 – €3 811 - **£2 302** - FF25 000
  La jeune cuisinière provençale Huile/toile (65x81cm 25x31in) Paris 2000

BARTHEL Paul 1862-1933 **[7]**
- $87 000 – €75 060 - **£52 487** - FF492 359
  Happy Children Oil/canvas (107.5x209.5cm 42x82in) New-York 1998

BARTHELEMY Camille 1890-1961 **[71]**
- $1 950 – €1 202 - **£1 202** - FF12 805
  Entrada a la Kasba Oleo/lienzo (91x140cm 35x55in) Madrid 2000
- $11 298 – €10 411 - **£6 804** - FF68 292
  Vue de Latour (près de Virton) Huile/toile (50x60cm 19x23in) Bruxelles 1999

$2 080 - €2 479 - £1 490 - FF16 260
Nature morte Huile/panneau (33x41cm 12x16in)
Liège 2000

$770 - €892 - £532 - FF5 853
Jardin printanier Pastel/carton (44x56cm 17x22in)
Bruxelles 2000

$428 - €446 - £282 - FF2 926
Clochers Eau-forte (22x18cm 8x7in) Bruxelles 2000

BARTHÉLÉMY Gérard 1927 [49]

$394 - €427 - £266 - FF2 800
Péniches à quai Huile/toile (46x55cm 18x21in)
Provins 2000

$497 - €534 - £332 - FF3 500
Environ du Touquet Huile/toile (27x46cm 10x18in)
La Varenne-Saint-Hilaire 2000

BARTHELEMY L. XX [5]

$1 729 - €1 845 - £1 154 - FF12 100
Danseuse aux cimbales Chryséléphantine
(H28.5cm H11in) Paris 2000

BARTHOLD Manuel 1874-1947 [5]

$3 244 - €3 131 - £2 038 - FF20 535
Portrait du Prince Georges de Grèce Huile/toile
(35.5x27cm 13x10in) Genève 1999

BARTHOLDI Frédéric Auguste 1834-1904 [46]

$6 604 - €7 775 - £4 641 - FF51 000
Les gamins sont partout les mêmes Huile/pan-
neau (40.5x30.5cm 15x12in) Paris 2000

$1 695 - €1 753 - £1 067 - FF11 500
**Le ramassage des vendanges: coupe à socle
polylobé** Bronze (22x25cm 8x9in) Paris 2000

BARTHOLOMÉ Albert 1848-1928 [41]

$1 096 - €1 278 - £769 - FF8 384
Trauernder Frauenakt Bronze (H45cm H17in)
München 2000

BARTHOLOMEW James H. 1962 [3]

$9 128 - €9 798 - £6 200 - FF64 271
**«J-Class Yachts racing off Cowes with
Velsheda, Britannia, Canada...»** Oil/canvas
(76x102cm 29x40in) London 2001

BARTHOLOMEW Valentine 1799-1879 [23]

$1 443 - €1 455 - £900 - FF9 543
**A Still Life of Rodedendron, Peonies and other
Flowers** Watercolour/paper (42.5x52cm 16x20in)
London 2000

BARTLETT Charles William 1860-1940 [47]

$3 000 - €2 593 - £1 780 - FF17 006
Chinese Bridge and Pagoda Pastel (91x60.5cm
35x23in) New-York 1998

$700 - €600 - £420 - FF3 933
Kyoto Print in colors (23x36cm 9x14in) Dedham MA
1998

BARTLETT Dana 1878/82-1957 [44]

$4 500 - €3 845 - £2 722 - FF25 219
«Towers of Notre Dame, Paris» (No. 355) Oil/can-
vas (63.5x76cm 25x29in) San-Francisco CA 1998

$3 100 - €2 870 - £1 897 - FF18 825
Cypress Point, Monterey County Oil/canvas/board
(45x30cm 18x12in) San Rafael CA 1999

BARTLETT Jennifer Losch 1941 [85]

$38 000 - €42 563 - £26 402 - FF279 193
«At Sands Point #25» Oil/canvas (122x122cm
48x48in) New-York 2001

$18 000 - €15 530 - £10 818 - FF101 867
At Sands Point No.5 Oil/canvas (30.5x152.5cm
12x60in) New-York 1998

$5 500 - €6 036 - £3 541 - FF39 596
Aspen Six Weeks: Pastel #12 Pastel/paper
(76x76cm 29x29in) New-York 2000

$3 200 - €3 003 - £1 977 - FF19 701
Rhapsody House, Trees, Beach, Birds Etching in
colors (29.5x29.5cm 11x11in) New-York 1999

BARTLETT Paul Wayland 1865-1925 [21]

$4 686 - €4 193 - £2 800 - FF27 505
Deep Water Fish Bronze (12x23cm 4x9in) Perthshire
1998

BARTLETT William Henry 1809-1854 [46]

$600 - €661 - £400 - FF4 336
**Man and Child standing on a Road near a Body
of Water** Wash/paper (7x10cm 3x4in) Portsmouth NH
2000

BARTLETT William Henry 1858-1932 [27]

$39 841 - €46 289 - £28 000 - FF303 637
Sea Wrack Oil/canvas (84x127cm 33x50in) London
2001

$9 722 - €10 216 - £6 400 - FF67 013
Oyster Catchers at Sunrise, Co.Donegal Oil/can-
vas (25x35.5cm 9x13in) Cheltenham, Gloucestershire
2000

BARTNING Ludwig 1876-1956 [12]

$1 499 - €1 687 - £1 032 - FF11 067
**Bunter Blumenstrauss vor Tiefer Landschaft
mit Schmeterling** Oil/panel (36x45cm 14x17in)
München 2000

BARTOLDY J. XVII [1]

$29 003 - €28 483 - £18 000 - FF186 838
Architectural Capriccio of a Lakeside Palace
Oil/panel (84x110cm 33x43in) London 1999

BARTOLENA Cesare 1830-1903 [3]

$15 600 - €13 476 - £10 400 - FF88 400
La partenza del soldato Olio/tela (70x50cm
27x19in) Milano 1998

BARTOLENA Giovanni 1866-1942 [111]

$8 400 - €7 257 - £4 200 - FF47 600
Due asinelli Olio/tela (49x63.5cm 19x25in) Firenze
1999

$4 500 - €4 665 - £2 700 - FF30 600
Natura morta con boccale e castagne Olio/tavola
(34x44cm 13x17in) Roma 1999

BARTOLI Jacques 1920-1997 [17]

$359 - €427 - £255 - FF2 800
Jeune fille dans un intérieur Huile/toile (22x27cm
8x10in) Toulon 2000

BARTOLI NATINGUERRA Amerigo 1890-1971 [36]

$1 200 - €1 555 - £900 - FF10 200
Isola farnese Olio/tavola (33.5x48cm 13x18in)
Milano 2001

$1 200 - €1 555 - £900 - FF10 200
«Paesaggio romano» Olio/cartone (38x42cm
14x16in) Milano 2001

BARTOLI Pietro Santi 1635-1700 [9]

$1 926 - €1 913 - £1 200 - FF12 550
Frieze of Bacchantes, after the Antique Ink
(6x18.5cm 2x7in) London 1999

$802 - €808 - £500 - FF5 301
**Eminentissimo Ac Reverendissimo Principi
Camillo Maximo** Engraving (33.5x23cm 13x9in)
London 2000

BARTOLINI Federico act.1861-1908 [29]

$4 099 - €4 377 - £2 800 - FF28 708
Arab Traders Watercolour/paper (52.5x36cm 20x14in)
Billingshurst, West-Sussex 2001

BARTOLINI

BARTOLINI Luciano 1948-1994 **[30]**
- $2 000 - €2 073 - £1 200 - FF13 600
  Iconostasi Tecnica mista/carta (150x100cm 59x39in)
  Prato 1999

BARTOLINI Luigi 1892-1963 **[297]**
- $2 760 - €2 384 - £1 840 - FF15 640
  «Fruttiera» Olio/cartone (40.5x47.5cm 15x18in)
  Milano 1998
- $950 - €985 - £570 - FF6 460
  Cacciatore all'albeggiare Olio/tavola (17x24cm
  6x9in) Roma 1999
- $550 - €570 - £330 - FF3 740
  San Valentino Matita (30x40cm 11x15in) Vercelli
  2000
- $900 - €933 - £540 - FF6 120
  Genziane in boccio Acquaforte (18x21.5cm 7x8in)
  Milano 1999

BARTOLINI Ubaldo 1944 **[16]**
- $880 - €1 140 - £660 - FF7 480
  Paesaggio Olio/tavola (41.5x93.5cm 16x36in) Milano
  2000
- $700 - €726 - £420 - FF4 760
  Paesaggio con rovine Olio/tela (30x25cm 11x9in)
  Prato 1999

BARTOLO di Taddeo 1362/63-1422 **[6]**
- $135 000 - €116 623 - £90 000 - FF765 000
  San Galgano e San Nicola Tempera/tavola
  (139x81cm 54x31in) Milano 1998
- $89 776 - €102 020 - £62 000 - FF669 209
  **Saint Mary Magdalene: a Fragement from an
  Altarpiece** Tempera (28x16cm 11x6in) London 2000

**BARTOLOMMEO DELLA PORTA Fra Baccio della
P.** 1472-1517 **[12]**
- $900 000 - €961 156 - £613 260 - FF6 304 770
  Study of Trees and Two Saplings Black chalk
  (40.5x27.5cm 15x10in) New-York 2001

BARTOLOZZI Francesco 1727-1815 **[282]**
- $663 - €708 - £420 - FF4 641
  **Portrait of William Warham, archbishop of
  Canterbury** Black chalk (43x31.5cm 16x12in) London
  2000
- $281 - €279 - £175 - FF1 832
  **Bacchanalian Putti in mountainous Landscape,
  after M.A.Franchesehini** Engraving (27x40cm
  11x16in) Dublin 1999

BARTOLUZZI Millo XX **[3]**
- $4 250 - €3 971 - £2 647 - FF26 047
  Vegetable Seller Oil/canvas (26x36cm 10x14in)
  Mystic CT 1999

BARTON Donald Blagge 1903-1990 **[74]**
- $700 - €654 - £432 - FF4 288
  Clothes on the Line Oil/canvas (40.5x51cm 15x20in)
  Boston MA 1999
- $425 - €380 - £260 - FF2 491
  «Gloucester Scene» Oil/canvas/board (20x25cm
  8x10in) Boston MA 1999
- $225 - €242 - £150 - FF1 585
  Cioggia, Italy Watercolour/paper (21x26cm 8x10in)
  Bolton MA 2000

BARTON Mary Georgina 1861-1929 **[9]**
- $730 - €702 - £450 - FF4 607
  The Diana Fountain, Hyde Park Watercolour
  (63x45cm 24x17in) London 1999

BARTON Rose Maynard 1856-1929 **[64]**
- $5 737 - €6 369 - £4 000 - FF41 779
  The water Babies Watercolour (26x24.5cm 10x9in)
  London 2001

BARTONEK Vojtech, Adalbert 1859-1908 **[8]**
- $22 000 - €20 119 - £13 435 - FF131 973
  After School Oil/canvas (72.5x53cm 28x20in) New-
  York 1998

BARTSCH Carl Frederick 1829-1908 **[68]**
- $1 749 - €1 480 - £1 046 - FF9 708
  En flok hjorte på en eng Oil/canvas (45x57cm
  17x22in) Viby J, Århus 1998
- $527 - €603 - £366 - FF3 957
  Køer på en skovvej Oil/canvas (34x46cm 13x18in)
  København 2000

BARTSCH Gustav 1821-? **[6]**
- $1 056 - €1 022 - £663 - FF6 707
  **Junge Lautenspielerin in rosa-schwarz-gestreif-
  tem Ballkleid** Öl/Leinwand (58x44cm 22x17in) Berlin
  1999

BARTSCH Reinhold 1925 **[8]**
- $1 039 - €1 125 - £712 - FF7 378
  Am Brandenburger Tor Öl/Leinwand (70x90cm
  27x35in) Stuttgart 2001

BARTSCH von Adam 1757-1821 **[22]**
- $897 - €1 022 - £626 - FF6 707
  Selbstbildnis en Face mit wildem Haar Radierung
  (17x12.5cm 6x4in) Berlin 2001

BARTSCH Wilhelm 1871-1953 **[24]**
- $523 - €562 - £350 - FF3 689
  Meeresstrand Öl/Karton (18.5x23cm 7x9in) Bremen
  2000

BARTTENBACH Hans 1908-? **[6]**
- $500 - €480 - £309 - FF3 149
  Tyrol Peasant with his Wife Oil/panel (17x13cm
  7x5in) Chicago IL 1999

BARUCCI Pietro 1845-1917 **[117]**
- $21 960 - €21 802 - £13 710 - FF143 010
  Blumenverkäuferinnen im Forum Romanum
  Öl/Leinwand (88x165cm 34x64in) Wien 1999
- $7 475 - €6 397 - £4 500 - FF41 962
  The Long Journey Home Oil/canvas (61x109.5cm
  24x43in) London 1998
- $1 680 - €1 451 - £1 120 - FF9 520
  Paesaggio romano con rovine Olio/tavola
  (32x22cm 12x8in) Milano 1998
- $1 756 - €1 951 - £1 176 - FF12 795
  Kvinna vid brunn Pastel/paper (54x37cm 21x14in)
  Stockholm 2000

BARUCHELLO Gianfranco 1924 **[46]**
- $953 - €1 125 - £672 - FF7 378
  «Comfort noir» Mixed media (36x50.5cm 14x19in)
  Köln 2001

BARVITIUS Victor 1834-1902 **[9]**
- $11 560 - €10 934 - £7 200 - FF71 720
  Vor einer Schmiede Öl/Leinwand (66x81cm
  25x31in) Praha 2001

BARWE Prabhakar 1936 **[8]**
- $4 300 - €4 022 - £2 600 - FF26 383
  Blown Hourglass Enamel/canvas (91.5x106.5cm
  36x41in) London 1999

BARWELL Frederick Bacon act.1855-1897 **[10]**
- $80 210 - €80 825 - £50 000 - FF530 180
  Return of the Missing crew Oil/canvas (105x153cm
  41x60in) London 2001

BARWIG Franz 1868-1931 **[34]**
- $403 - €436 - £279 - FF2 860
  Bär mit Ball Ceramic (H32cm H12in) Wien 2001

B

BARYE Alfred 1839-1882 **[164]**
- $2 500 - €2 861 - **£1 719** - FF18 767
  Arab Hunter Metal (H81cm H32in) New-York 2000
- $1 199 - €1 296 - **£830** - FF8 500
  Saute-mouton Bronze (10x12cm 3x4in) Le Havre 2001

BARYE Antoine-Louis 1796-1875 **[2182]**
- $11 410 - €11 281 - **£7 126** - FF74 000
  Rochers en forêt de Fontainbleau
  Huile/papier/toile (13x31.5cm 5x12in) Cherbourg 1999
- $1 198 - €1 372 - **£824** - FF9 000
  Bouquetin Bronze (95x12cm 37x4in) Paris 2000
- $3 790 - €4 421 - **£2 662** - FF29 000
  Panthère attaquant un cerf Bronze (39x57cm 15x22in) Paris 2000
- $2 484 - €2 744 - **£1 722** - FF18 000
  Deux études de tigre et trois reprises de la tête
  Crayon/papier (14x22cm 5x8in) Paris 2001
- $400 - €384 - **£246** - FF2 519
  Une lionne et ses petits Lithograph (12.5x21cm 4x8in) New-York 1999

BARZAGHI Francesco 1839-1892 **[14]**
- $57 500 - €66 806 - **£40 411** - FF438 219
  Young Girl Marble (H119cm H46in) New-York 2001

BARZAGHI-CATTANEO Antonio 1835-1922 **[10]**
- $50 000 - €55 838 - **£32 020** - FF366 275
  Lady Jane Grey Oil/canvas (186.5x68.5cm 73x26in) New-York 2000
- $852 - €915 - **£570** - FF6 000
  L'artiste présentant son oeuvre au pape
  Huile/toile (27.5x35cm 10x13in) Lyon 2000

BARZAGLI Massimo 1960 **[28]**
- $5 500 - €5 702 - **£3 300** - FF37 400
  Fiorile Olio/tela (160x140cm 62x55in) Prato 2000
- $640 - €829 - **£480** - FF5 440
  Fiorile Olio/tela (30x24cm 11x9in) Prato 2000

BARZANTI Licinio 1857-1944 **[11]**
- $5 750 - €5 961 - **£3 450** - FF39 100
  Peonie Olio/tela (70x100cm 27x39in) Firenze 2001

BARZANTI Pietro XIX-XX **[21]**
- $4 860 - €4 539 - **£3 000** - FF29 777
  Leda and the Swan Marble (H86cm H33in) Billingshurst, West-Sussex 2001
- $1 286 - €1 448 - **£895** - FF9 500
  Buste antique Marble (H61.5cm H24in) Toulouse 2001

BARZOTTI Biagio XVIII-XIX **[2]**
- $10 870 - €10 034 - **£6 500** - FF65 820
  Pope Leo XIII with Cardinals Rampolla, Parochi, Bonaparte and Sacconi Mixed media (30.5x42.5cm 12x16in) London 1999

BAS 1963 **[4]**
- $8 065 - €7 328 - **£5 000** - FF48 067
  Sumatran Sovereignty Oil/canvas (75x100cm 29x39in) Billingshurst, West-Sussex 1999

BASAGNI Adriano 1941 **[11]**
- $720 - €933 - **£540** - FF6 120
  «L'Arno a S.Niccoló» Olio/tela (35x50cm 13x19in) Prato 2001
- $350 - €363 - **£210** - FF2 380
  Imbarcadero a S. Niccoló Olio/tavola (20x30cm 7x11in) Prato 2000

BASAN Pierre François 1723-1797 **[12]**
- $130 - €119 - **£80** - FF778
  La lecture diabolique, after Teniers Etching (31.5x22cm 12x8in) London 1999

BASCH Edith 1895-1980 **[5]**
- $3 150 - €3 485 - **£2 070** - FF22 860
  Lilianne, Nude Oil/canvas (100x72.5cm 39x28in) Budapest 1999

BASCHANT Rudolf 1897-1955 **[12]**
- $2 032 - €1 892 - **£1 250** - FF12 409
  Abstrakte Komposition aus Linien, Quadrat-, Rund- und Dreieckformen Lithographie (15x10.5cm 5x4in) München 1999

BASCHENIS Evaristo 1617-1677 **[6]**
- $22 958 - €19 818 - **£13 715** - FF130 000
  Canards et pièces de volailles plumées sur un entablement de pierre Huile/toile (91x126cm 35x49in) Paris 1998

BASCHNY Emanuel 1873-1932 **[10]**
- $3 294 - €3 270 - **£2 056** - FF21 451
  Blick auf Klagenfurt Öl/Karton (19x26.5cm 7x10in) Wien 1999

BASCOM Ruth Henshaw 1772-1848 **[7]**
- $130 000 - €118 306 - **£81 224** - FF776 035
  Dr Caleb Chapin/D.S.W Chapin/M.S Chapin/S.W Chapin Jr/D.C Chapin Pastel (46x33cm 18x13in) Bolton MA 1999

BASCOULES Jean-Désiré 1886-1976 **[39]**
- $4 837 - €4 421 - **£2 960** - FF29 000
  Place du Gouvernement, Alger Huile/toile/panneau (27x45cm 10x17in) Paris 1999

BASELEER Richard 1867-1951 **[68]**
- $745 - €892 - **£511** - FF5 853
  Paard en kar in de duinen (cheval et charrette dans les dunes) Huile/panneau (31x48cm 12x18in) Antwerpen 2000

BASELITZ Georg 1938 **[569]**
- $223 776 - €190 791 - **£135 000** - FF1 251 504
  «Die musikstunde» Oil/canvas (250x200cm 98x78in) London 1998
- $95 000 - €91 920 - **£58 586** - FF602 955
  Ralfkopf Oil/panel (118x96cm 46x37in) New-York 1999
- $21 913 - €18 405 - **£12 880** - FF120 726
  Adler/Adler Sculpture, wax (53x41.5cm 20x16in) Stuttgart 1998
- $10 500 - €10 885 - **£6 300** - FF71 400
  Senza titolo Gouache/carta (61x43cm 24x16in) Milano 2000
- $1 195 - €1 283 - **£800** - FF8 417
  Adler Woodcut (64.5x49.5cm 25x19in) London 2000

BASER Robert 1908-1998 **[15]**
- $480 - €569 - **£349** - FF3 732
  In Port Watercolour/paper (20.5x29.5cm 8x11in) Tel Aviv 2001

BASHILOV Yakov Stepanovich 1839-1896 **[1]**
- $2 233 - €2 186 - **£1 374** - FF14 341
  Lukuhetki Oil/canvas (39x31.5cm 15x12in) Helsinki 1999

BASHINDJIAGAN Georgii Zakharovich 1857-1925 **[2]**
- $5 597 - €6 661 - **£4 000** - FF43 692
  Boating on the Lake Oil/canvas (50x85cm 19x33in) London 2000

BASHKIRTSEVA Maria Konstantinovna 1860-1884 **[3]**
- $1 206 - €1 372 - **£837** - FF9 000
  Jeune femme lisant Encre (15x10.5cm 5x4in) Paris 2000

BASIANO MARTINEZ PEREZ Jesús 1889-1966 **[12]**
- $12 540 - €11 412 - £7 600 - FF74 860
  Paisaje Oleo/lienzo (79x91cm 31x35in) Madrid 1999
- $1 620 - €1 802 - £1 080 - FF11 820
  Paisaje de Aralar Oleo/cartón (41.5x32cm 16x12in)
  Madrid 2000

BASIRE Isaac 1704-1768 **[22]**
- $268 - €252 - £168 - FF1 654
  Plano de Tarragona en el siglo XVIII Grabado
  (39x48cm 15x18in) Madrid 1999

BASIRE James I, II or III XVIII-XIX **[3]**
- $313 - €337 - £210 - FF2 209
  **The Embarkation of King Henry VIII at
  Dover/The Interview, after Grimm** Print (66x125cm
  25x49in) Devon 2000

BASKE Yamada ?-1934 **[12]**
- $425 - €476 - £295 - FF3 123
  Cherry Tree in Yomenite Stream, Japan
  Watercolour/paper (26x38cm 10x15in) Watertown MA
  2001

BASKERVILLE Charles 1896-1994 **[24]**
- $750 - €641 - £440 - FF4 206
  Siri Watercolour/paper (19.5x25cm 7x9in) New-York
  1998

BASKIN Leonard 1922-2000 **[253]**
- $6 000 - €6 440 - £4 015 - FF42 246
  Marsyas Bronze (H118cm H46in) New-York 2000
- $5 000 - €4 683 - £3 074 - FF30 720
  Bird Man Bronze (H42cm H16in) New-York 1999
- $500 - €557 - £336 - FF3 655
  Bust Portrait of William Morris Ink (27x35cm
  11x14in) Portsmouth NH 2000
- $160 - €176 - £101 - FF1 153
  Spread Eagle Etching (21x30cm 8x12in) Bethesda
  MD 2000

BASQUIAT Jean-Michel 1960-1988 **[806]**
- $350 000 - €338 653 - £225 845 - FF2 221 415
  Sacred Ape Acrylic (213.5x152.5cm 84x60in) New-
  York 1999
- $94 230 - €112 653 - £65 000 - FF738 952
  Untitled Acrylic (91.5x91.5cm 36x36in) London 2000
- $21 745 - €25 997 - £15 000 - FF170 527
  Top Tee Mixed media (30.5x23cm 12x9in) London
  2000
- $300 000 - €298 392 - £186 210 - FF1 957 320
  Untitled Construction (260.5x126x30.5cm
  102x49x12in) Beverly-Hills CA 1999
- $26 000 - €29 122 - £18 064 - FF191 027
  Untitled Watercolour (45.5x61cm 17x24in) New-York
  2001
- $34 000 - €36 495 - £22 752 - FF239 394
  Back of the Neck Screenprint in colors (127x256.5cm
  50x100in) Beverly-Hills CA 2000

BASS Saul 1920-1996 **[59]**
- $693 - €766 - £480 - FF5 026
  «Love in the Afternoon» Poster (104x68.5cm
  40x26in) London 2001

BASSANO Francesco il Giovane 1549-1592 **[30]**
- $45 603 - €51 796 - £32 500 - FF339 760
  The Annunciation to the Shepherds Oil/canvas
  (99.5x136cm 39x53in) London 2001
- $15 887 - €18 519 - £11 000 - FF121 478
  The Birth of the Virgin Oil/panel (47x36cm 18x14in)
  London 2000
- $7 242 - €7 775 - £4 845 - FF51 000
  Jeune garçon accroupi Pierre noire (23x21cm
  9x8in) Paris 2000

BASSANO Francesco il Vecchio c.1470/75-
c.1530/40 **[4]**
- $16 000 - €15 053 - £9 984 - FF98 742
  The Annunciation to the Shepherds Oil/canvas
  (127x178cm 50x70in) New-York 1999

BASSANO Gerolamo da Ponte 1566-1621 **[14]**
- $101 360 - €115 184 - £70 000 - FF755 559
  Lazarus at the Feast of Dives Oil/canvas
  (159x250cm 62x98in) London 2000
- $6 607 - €5 449 - £3 892 - FF35 745
  Noli me tangere Öl/Leinwand (73x84.5cm 28x33in)
  Wien 1998

BASSANO Giambattista 1553-1613 **[3]**
- $10 096 - €11 867 - £7 000 - FF77 840
  The Annunciation to the Shepherds Oil/canvas
  (80x64.5cm 31x25in) London 2000

BASSANO Jacopo da Ponte 1510/18-1592 **[22]**
- $184 805 - €183 307 - £115 000 - FF1 202 417
  Dives and Lazarus Oil/canvas (117.5x164.5cm
  46x64in) London 1999
- $47 500 - €49 241 - £28 500 - FF323 000
  L'annuncio ai pastori Olio/tela (110x90.5cm
  43x35in) Venezia 2000
- $7 140 - €7 402 - £4 284 - FF48 552
  Studio di bambino coricato Black & white
  chalks/paper (18.5x30cm 7x11in) Venezia 2000

BASSANO Leandro da Ponte 1557-1622 **[41]**
- $40 777 - €38 139 - £25 000 - FF250 175
  Orpheus Charming the Animals Oil/canvas
  (98x141cm 38x55in) London 1998
- $11 102 - €11 658 - £7 000 - FF76 472
  Diana and Callisto Oil/canvas (61x75cm 24x29in)
  London 2000
- $7 125 - €8 093 - £5 000 - FF53 087
  The Madonna and child Oil/panel (26.5x21cm
  10x8in) London 2001

BASSEN van Bartolomeus c.1590-1652 **[21]**
- $21 411 - €20 365 - £13 000 - FF133 584
  The Interior of Antwerp Cathedral Oil/canvas
  (75.5x101.5cm 29x39in) London 1999
- $12 972 - €11 281 - £7 821 - FF74 000
  Intérieur d'église Huile/panneau (45x35cm 17x13in)
  Paris 1998

BASSETT Reveau Mott 1897-1981 **[5]**
- $6 600 - €6 164 - £4 073 - FF40 431
  Trepid Lake Mallards Oil/board (60x76cm 24x30in)
  Dallas TX 1999

BASSETTI Marcantonio 1586-1630 **[14]**
- $46 740 - €43 603 - £28 200 - FF286 020
  **Compianto sul Cristo morto (Die Beweinung
  Christi)** Oil/panel (38x29cm 14x11in) Wien 1999
- $1 200 - €1 555 - £900 - FF10 200
  Strage degli innocenti China (13.5x11cm 5x4in)
  Milano 2000

BASSFORD Wallace 1900-? **[31]**
- $550 - €516 - £339 - FF3 383
  «Beginning of Summer» Oil/canvas (60x50cm
  24x20in) Delray-Beach FL 1999

BASSI Gian Battista 1784-1852 **[2]**
- $9 344 - €8 179 - £5 659 - FF53 649
  Waldlandschaft mit zeichnendem Künstler
  Oil/paper/canvas (43.5x30cm 17x11in) Berlin 1998

BASSI Javier 1964 **[3]**
- $3 600 - €3 483 - £2 220 - FF22 848
  Segundo crepúsculo Graphite (62x195cm 24x76in)
  Montevideo 1999

BASSMAN Lillian 1917 [7]
- $4 500 - €4 209 - £2 720 - FF27 610
  Lingerie Model Gelatin silver print (31x26cm 12x10in) New-York 1999

BASSOT Ferdinand XIX [6]
- $2 900 - €3 049 - £1 914 - FF20 000
  Jeune femme de qualité assise Huile/toile (117x89.5cm 46x35in) Paris 2000

BAST de Dominique 1781-1842 [6]
- $4 644 - €4 462 - £2 862 - FF29 268
  Scène de naufrage Huile/panneau (46.5x59cm 18x23in) Bruxelles 1999

BAST Karl Heinz 1937 [14]
- $514 - €613 - £367 - FF4 024
  Rudolf Hausner Photograph (29.9x39.7cm 11x15in) München 2000

BAST Pieter c.1570-1605 [2]
- $3 200 - €3 582 - £2 231 - FF23 496
  View of Amsterdam from the West Etching (26x76cm 10x29in) New-York 2001

BASTARD Marc Auguste 1863-1926 [12]
- $1 400 - €1 346 - £864 - FF8 831
  «Bières de la Meuse» Poster (150.5x94.5cm 59x37in) New-York 1999

BASTERRETXEA ARZADUN Néstor 1924 [9]
- $11 360 - €9 610 - £6 720 - FF63 040
  Composición en un plano cóncavo ideal Oleo/tablex (121x265cm 47x104in) Madrid 1998

BASTERT Nicolaas 1854-1939 [72]
- $1 902 - €2 042 - £1 273 - FF13 394
  Evening Falling Oil/canvas (62.5x95.5cm 24x37in) Amsterdam 2000
- $631 - €544 - £380 - FF3 571
  Fence and willow-tree Oil/canvas (28x48cm 11x18in) Amsterdam 1999
- $749 - €817 - £516 - FF5 357
  Shepherd with his Flock at the Border of a Village Watercolour/paper (40.5x55.5cm 15x21in) Amsterdam 2001

BASTET Jean, dit Tancrède 1858-1942 [30]
- $1 962 - €1 906 - £1 212 - FF12 500
  L'heure du café Huile/toile (55x38cm 21x14in) Paris 1999

BASTET Victorien Antoine 1853-1905 [7]
- $18 004 - €18 141 - £11 221 - FF119 000
  Jeune femme nue debout Marbre Carrare (H112cm H44in) Tours 2000

BASTIEN Alfred Theod. Joseph 1873-1955 [373]
- $1 218 - €1 040 - £726 - FF6 825
  Chemin vers la source de l'Empereur Huile/toile (90x70cm 35x27in) Bruxelles 1998
- $360 - €397 - £249 - FF2 601
  Couple dans la forêt Huile/panneau (18x22cm 7x8in) Bruxelles 2001
- $157 - €149 - £95 - FF975
  Souvenir à Criquet Fusain/papier (24x33cm 9x12in) Antwerpen 1999

BASTIEN-LEPAGE Jules 1848-1884 [46]
- $7 902 - €8 080 - £4 976 - FF53 000
  Portrait de Mr Andrieux Louis, Préfet de Paris Huile/toile (46x38cm 18x14in) Toulouse 2000
- $1 200 - €1 450 - £837 - FF9 514
  Barnyard Chickens Oil/canvas (21x35cm 8x14in) Thomaston ME 2000

- $376 - €427 - £257 - FF2 800
  Portrait d'homme barbu Crayon gras/papier (27x21.5cm 10x8in) Paris 2000

BASTIN Henri 1896-1979 [49]
- $7 815 - €9 294 - £5 569 - FF60 964
  Central Australian Landscape with Partially Submerged Forest Oil/board (122x245cm 48x96in) Woollahra, Sydney 2000
- $526 - €594 - £370 - FF3 894
  Three Musicians Acrylic (54.5x74.5cm 21x29in) Malvern, Victoria 2001
- $2 001 - €2 148 - £1 339 - FF14 091
  Star of the Morning station Gouache/paper (49x63.5cm 19x25in) Melbourne 2000

BASTOW Michael 1943 [9]
- $442 - €427 - £279 - FF2 800
  Sans titre Aquarelle (64.5x50cm 25x19in) Paris 1999

BATAILLE Henry 1872-1922 [7]
- $1 384 - €1 524 - £923 - FF10 000
  Yvone Debray au fume-cigarette Huile/carton (50x65cm 19x25in) Deauville 2000

BATARDA Eduardo 1943 [2]
- $10 560 - €11 964 - £7 440 - FF78 480
  Turvo (imitação) Acrílico/lienzo (100x73cm 39x28in) Lisboa 2001

BATCHELDER Stephen John 1849-1932 [235]
- $1 050 - €1 221 - £750 - FF8 011
  Sunset near Salhouse Watercolour/paper (34.5x51cm 13x20in) Norfolk 2001

BATCHELLER Frederick Stone 1837-1889 [18]
- $3 000 - €3 526 - £2 173 - FF23 127
  The Cornucopia, Genre Scene with Squirrel Oil/canvas (91x60cm 36x24in) Bolton MA 2001
- $2 900 - €2 650 - £1 774 - FF17 384
  Still Life with Grapes Oil/canvas (30.5x45.5cm 12x17in) Boston MA 1999

BATCHELOR Roland 1889-1989 [37]
- $1 020 - €1 160 - £700 - FF7 611
  In the Bar, Jersey Watercolour (16x20cm 6x7in) London 2000

BATELLI Ferdinando XIX [1]
- $17 000 - €14 667 - £10 256 - FF96 208
  Diana Marble (H107cm H42in) New-York 1998

BATEMAN Henry Mayo 1887-1970 [62]
- $5 119 - €5 250 - £3 200 - FF34 438
  An Income Tax Official Tracking a Halfpenny Ink (39.5x26.5cm 15x10in) London 2000

BATEMAN James 1893-1959 [4]
- $35 432 - €41 992 - £25 000 - FF275 450
  Westmoreland Farm Oil/canvas (89x106.5cm 35x41in) London 2000
- $6 803 - €8 062 - £4 800 - FF52 886
  The Argument Watercolour (22x22cm 8x8in) London 2000

BATEMAN John Yunge XX [1]
- $8 000 - €7 683 - £4 957 - FF50 395
  Untitled Watercolour, gouache (50x40cm 19x15in) New-York 1999

BATEMAN Robert 1842-1922 [3]
- $21 045 - €25 029 - £15 000 - FF164 178
  Reading of Love, He being by Watercolour (25.5x34.5cm 10x13in) London 2000

BATEMAN Robert McLellan 1930 [38]
- $11 925 - €13 206 - £8 087 - FF86 625
  Rough-Legged Hawk Mixed media/board (61x105.5cm 24x41in) Toronto 2000
- $1 341 - €1 496 - £875 - FF9 811
  Summer Landscape Oil/masonite (20x25cm 7x9in) Calgary, Alberta 2000
- $2 343 - €2 293 - £1 500 - FF15 043
  Study of a Long-eared Owl Ink (36x49cm 14x19in) Perth 1999

BATES David 1840-1921 [285]
- $3 386 - €4 027 - £2 413 - FF26 417
  River valley with Figures and Cattle Oil/canvas (39.5x58.5cm 15x23in) Woollahra, Sydney 2000
- $2 894 - €2 683 - £1 800 - FF17 600
  A Couple watching a Fisherman, Mountain River Landscape Oil/canvas (29x43cm 11x16in) London 1999
- $1 381 - €1 364 - £840 - FF8 944
  Bridge near the Hammocks, Ecklington Watercolour/paper (26x36cm 10x14in) Kirkby-Lonsdale, Cumbria 2000

BATES Frederick Davenport 1867-1930 [19]
- $597 - €642 - £400 - FF4 208
  A Lakeland Landscape with Sheep grazing in a Sunlit Meadow Oil/canvas (51x76cm 20x29in) West-Yorkshire 2000

BATES Harry 1850-1899 [6]
- $10 197 - €9 657 - £6 200 - FF63 346
  «Then indeed aeneas weeps» Plaster (23.5x23cm 9x9in) London 1999

BATES Maxwell Bennett 1906-1980 [152]
- $4 882 - €4 178 - £2 939 - FF27 405
  Portrait of Eleanor Friedman Oil/canvas (76x61cm 29x24in) Toronto 1998
- $1 105 - €1 294 - £779 - FF8 487
  «Women» Oil/board (40.5x30.5cm 15x12in) Calgary, Alberta 2001
- $306 - €295 - £188 - FF1 932
  Portrait Ink/paper (28x33.5cm 11x13in) Vancouver, BC. 1999
- $266 - €253 - £162 - FF1 659
  Figures at a Table Color lithograph (56x41cm 22x16in) Calgary, Alberta 1999

BATET François 1921 [107]
- $14 420 - €16 400 - £10 000 - FF107 574
  Charleston Oil/canvas (97x131cm 38x51in) London 2000
- $2 481 - €2 129 - £1 500 - FF13 964
  Pensive Oil/canvas (91.5x74cm 36x29in) London 1998
- $1 323 - €1 135 - £800 - FF7 447
  Sur fond rouge Oil/canvas (33x41cm 12x16in) London 1998

BATHA Gerhard 1937 [13]
- $597 - €693 - £412 - FF4 548
  Grand Canal, Venice Oil/canvas (54.5x74.5cm 21x29in) Johannesburg 2000
- $4 974 - €4 664 - £3 073 - FF30 593
  View of the Sea from a House Gouache/paper (66.5x93.5cm 26x36in) Johannesburg 1999

BATHIEU Jules XIX [3]
- $6 750 - €6 257 - £4 197 - FF41 040
  Shepherd and his Flock Oil/canvas (65x92cm 25x36in) New-Orleans LA 1999

BATLEY Walter Daniel 1850-? [7]
- $13 000 - €11 225 - £7 930 - FF73 629
  Sisters Oil/canvas (157x119cm 62x47in) Detroit MI 1999

BATONI Pompeo Girolamo 1708-1787 [59]
- $16 437 - €15 584 - £10 000 - FF102 222
  Gentleman, in a Fur-lined blue Coat, letter in his left Hand Oil/canvas (99x74cm 38x29in) London 1999
- $8 500 - €7 390 - £5 144 - FF48 472
  Sheet of Studies, Central Female Nude, a Separate Study of her Head Red chalk/paper (24.5x25cm 9x9in) New-York 1999

BATOWSKI-KACZOR Stanislaw 1866-1946 [43]
- $3 464 - €3 441 - £2 157 - FF22 572
  Devant le palais Oil/canvas (71x92.5cm 27x36in) Warszawa 1999
- $1 184 - €1 181 - £739 - FF7 747
  Fern Gathering Watercolour, gouache/board (41x31cm 16x12in) Warszawa 1999

BATT Arthur 1846-1911 [32]
- $2 079 - €2 178 - £1 315 - FF14 284
  Gårdsinteriör med vilande hund och kycklingar Oil/canvas (25x35cm 9x13in) Malmö 2000

BATTAGLIA Alessandro 1870-1940 [19]
- $8 400 - €10 885 - £6 300 - FF71 400
  Contadina seduta Olio/tela (87x55.5cm 34x21in) Milano 2001

BATTAGLIA Clelia Bompiani 1847-1927 [19]
- $1 222 - €1 111 - £750 - FF7 290
  The Sisters Watercolour/paper (54.5x37.5cm 21x14in) London 1999

BATTAGLIA Xante 1943 [37]
- $550 - €570 - £330 - FF3 740
  «Arcaico» Olio/tela (50x40cm 19x15in) Vercelli 2001

BATTAGLIOLI Francesco c.1722-c.1790 [6]
- $50 806 - €54 536 - £34 000 - FF357 734
  Capriccio View of a Town with elegant Figures on a Terrace Oil/canvas (51x78cm 20x30in) London 2000

BATTAILLE Irène 1913 [42]
- $390 - €397 - £244 - FF2 601
  Nature morte aux fleurs Huile/toile (46x35cm 18x13in) Antwerpen 2000

BATTARBEE Rex 1893-1969 [21]
- $454 - €472 - £286 - FF3 098
  Twisted Gum Watercolour/paper (30.5x31.5cm 12x12in) Melbourne 2000

BATTELLI R. XIX-XX [3]
- $4 750 - €5 598 - £3 273 - FF36 719
  Bust of a Young Girl Marble (H61cm H24in) New-York 2000

BATTEM Gerrit, Gerard c.1636-1684 [13]
- $15 120 - €12 868 - £9 000 - FF84 410
  Rhenish Landscape with Peasants resting by a Table Oil/panel (46x61.5cm 18x24in) London 1998

BATTERSBY Martin 1916-1982 [28]
- $375 - €439 - £266 - FF2 880
  Helping with the War Effort Oil/canvas (35x30cm 14x12in) Cedar-Falls IA 2001

BATTHYANY Gyula, Count 1887-1959 [10]
- $56 000 - €55 065 - £35 000 - FF361 200
  In a Turkish Style, Rococo Ladies Oil/canvas (200x150cm 78x59in) Budapest 1999
- $9 600 - €9 440 - £6 000 - FF61 920
  Woman, smoking a little dog Oil/canvas (130x90cm 51x35in) Budapest 1999
- $1 386 - €1 575 - £966 - FF10 332
  Femme de harem Crayon/papier (49x64cm 19x25in) Budapest 2001

BATTI Léon XIX-XX [2]
- 🖎 **$1 814** - €2 134 - **£1 300** - FF14 000
  Napoléon à cheval Bronze (43x34x12cm 16x13x4in)
  Paris 2001

BATTIGLIO Eugenio XIX-XX [2]
- 🖎 **$20 000** - €19 074 - **£12 174** - FF125 118
  Classical Maiden Marble (H175.5cm H69in) New-York 1999

BATTISS Walter Whall 1906-1982 [168]
- ☞ **$31 872** - €36 983 - **£22 008** - FF242 592
  African Paradise Oil/board (122x248cm 48x97in)
  Johannesburg 2000
- ☞ **$5 734** - €6 394 - **£3 739** - FF41 944
  Interior with Birds and Figures Oil/canvas
  (45x55cm 17x21in) Johannesburg 2000
- ☞ **$2 003** - €2 247 - **£1 401** - FF14 739
  Morning Coffee Oil/board (25x34cm 9x13in) Cape
  Town 2001
- ✏ **$396** - €444 - **£275** - FF2 911
  «Creation Myth» Ink (37.5x51cm 14x20in)
  Johannesburg 2001
- 🎞 **$300** - €337 - **£210** - FF2 210
  Seated Male Nude Monotype (28x22cm 11x8in)
  Cape Town 2001

BATTISTA Eric 1933 [145]
- ☞ **$699** - €762 - **£458** - FF5 000
  Marée basse Huile/toile (54x65cm 21x25in) Brest
  2000
- ☞ **$334** - €305 - **£203** - FF2 000
  Au port - Barques de pêche Huile/toile (10x24cm
  3x9in) Douarnenez 1998

BATTISTA Giovanni 1858-1925 [92]
- ✏ **$950** - €861 - **£584** - FF5 647
  Coastal Scene Gouache/papier (49x78cm 19x31in)
  Mystic CT 1999
- 🎞 **$710** - €601 - **£430** - FF3 940
  «Carcere oscura» Grabado (38.5x23.5cm 15x9in)
  Madrid 2001

BATTISTINI Leopoldo 1865-1936 [3]
- ✏ **$1 320** - €1 496 - **£870** - FF9 810
  Figura feminina Pastel/carton (65.5x47cm 25x18in)
  Lisboa 2000

BATTUT Michèle 1946 [36]
- ☞ **$2 400** - €2 287 - **£1 521** - FF15 000
  Paysage Huile/toile (41x33cm 16x12in) Provins 1999

BATTY Robert 1789-1848 [10]
- ☞ **$2 667** - €2 974 - **£1 800** - FF19 506
  Edinburgh from Calton Hill Oil/board (23x34cm
  9x13in) Edinburgh 2000

BATURIN Viktor Pavlovich 1863-1938 [8]
- ☞ **$3 569** - €3 997 - **£2 480** - FF26 218
  Park mit blühenden Sträuchern
  Öl/Leinwand/Karton (49x34cm 19x13in) Wien 2001

BATZ Eugen 1905-1984 [23]
- ☞ **$1 303** - €1 124 - **£783** - FF7 375
  «Auf Saturnrot» Oil/canvas/panel (30x40cm 11x15in)
  Köln 1998
- ✏ **$693** - €818 - **£489** - FF5 366
  Ohne Titel Gouache (30.3x35.2cm 11x13in) Köln
  2001

BAUCH Emil 1830-1898 [1]
- ☞ **$6 920** - €7 267 - **£4 360** - FF47 670
  Kaiser Franz Joseph I. von Österreich
  Öl/Leinwand (97x71cm 38x27in) Wien 2000

BAUCH Jan 1898-1995 [82]
- ☞ **$5 202** - €4 920 - **£3 240** - FF32 274
  Ein Mädchenakt Öl/Leinwand (41x51cm 16x20in)
  Praha 2000
- ☞ **$469** - €545 - **£330** - FF3 575
  «Bildnis» Oil/panel (38x28cm 14x11in) Salzburg 2001
- ✏ **$346** - €328 - **£216** - FF2 151
  Still Life with Fruit Watercolour/paper (43x64cm
  16x25in) Praha 2000

BAUCHANT André 1873-1958 [415]
- ☞ **$21 300** - €22 867 - **£14 250** - FF150 000
  Le chèvrefeuille devant le château de Lavardin
  Huile/toile (146x101cm 57x39in) Paris 2000
- ☞ **$6 686** - €6 403 - **£4 120** - FF42 000
  Table de fruits Huile/toile (50x65cm 19x25in) Calais
  1999
- ☞ **$2 491** - €2 675 - **£1 667** - FF17 545
  Baumkrone mit Vögeln Öl/Leinwand (19.5x26cm
  7x10in) Zürich 2000

BAUCK Jeanna Maria Ch. 1840-1926 [11]
- ☞ **$1 546** - €1 345 - **£932** - FF8 820
  Vinterlandskap med vedsamlerska Oil/canvas
  (60x48cm 23x18in) Stockholm 1998

BAUD-BOVY Auguste 1848-1899 [17]
- ☞ **$2 604** - €3 022 - **£1 827** - FF19 821
  Recueillement, La Witte Huile/toile (53.5x43cm
  21x16in) Genève 2000
- ☞ **$667** - €787 - **£469** - FF5 160
  Kampfszene Oil/panel (32.5x24cm 12x9in) Bern 2000

BAUDART P. XIX [7]
- ✏ **$475** - €492 - **£285** - FF3 230
  Studi di teste dall'antico Matita (58x45cm 22x17in)
  Formigine, Mo 1999

BAUDERON Louis 1809-? [2]
- ☞ **$340** - €376 - **£230** - FF2 464
  Sydlandsk kystparti med mandolinspiller
  Oil/canvas (36x28cm 14x11in) Vejle 2000

BAUDESSON Nicolas 1611-1680 [53]
- ☞ **$12 367** - €12 958 - **£7 828** - FF85 000
  Bouquet de fleurs Huile/toile (57x45cm 22x17in)
  Paris 2000
- ☞ **$14 490** - €16 007 - **£10 048** - FF105 000
  Fleurs dans un panier Huile/panneau (28x35cm
  11x13in) Lille 2001

BAUDET Étienne 1638-1711 [13]
- 🎞 **$338** - €316 - **£204** - FF2 070
  **Bearbed Man/Roman Consul/Greek
  Woman/Roman Woman/Philosopher/Young Man**
  Engraving (58.5x43cm 23x16in) Toronto 1999

BAUDIN Eugène 1843-1907 [40]
- ☞ **$19 758** - €16 922 - **£11 577** - FF111 000
  Vase d'oeillets Huile/carton (39.5x51cm 15x20in)
  Paris 1998
- ☞ **$898** - €991 - **£608** - FF6 500
  Autoportrait Huile/toile (31.5x23.5cm 12x9in) Paris
  2000

BAUDISCH Gudrun 1907-1982 [21]
- 🖎 **$2 197** - €2 045 - **£1 351** - FF13 415
  Mädchenkopf Ceramic (H13.5cm H5in) München
  1999

BAUDISSIN Ulrik 1816-1893 [4]
- ☞ **$9 844** - €9 015 - **£6 000** - FF59 133
  Frederiksborg Slot Oil/canvas (62x89.5cm 24x35in)
  London 1999

BAUDIT Amédée 1825-1890 [37]
- $13 000 - €15 279 - **£9 012** - FF100 222
  Au bord de l'étang Lacanau Oil/canvas
  (196x311cm 77x122in) New-York 2000
- $3 319 - €2 744 - **£1 947** - FF18 000
  Composition au jeté de roses et vase de Nankin
  Huile/toile (63.5x38.5cm 25x15in) Pau 1998

BAUDIT Louis Amédée 1870-1960 [39]
- $1 943 - €2 086 - **£1 300** - FF13 682
  Chasse aux canards Oil/canvas (40x50cm 15x19in)
  London 2000
- $401 - €416 - **£254** - FF2 729
  Bateau à vapeur sur le lac Fusain/papier (32x48cm
  12x18in) Genève 2000

BAUDOIN Jean-Franck 1870-1961 [132]
- $1 922 - €1 829 - **£1 195** - FF12 000
  L'atelier de l'artiste, Montparnasse, Paris
  Huile/toile (81x60cm 31x23in) Le Bois-Plage-en-Ré
  1999
- $192 - €183 - **£119** - FF1 200
  La mosquée Huile/panneau (13.5x22cm 5x8in) Le
  Bois-Plage-en-Ré 1999
- $400 - €381 - **£249** - FF2 500
  Rouen Aquarelle/papier (16.5x24cm 6x9in) Le Bois-
  Plage-en-Ré 1999

BAUDOIN Pierre Antoine 1723-1769 [20]
- $24 466 - €22 883 - **£15 000** - FF150 105
  Young Lovers in a Landscape Oil/canvas
  (41.5x34.5cm 16x13in) London 1998
- $8 000 - €8 093 - **£4 884** - FF53 087
  Le Coucher de la Mariée Black & white
  chalks/paper (41x33cm 16x12in) New-York 2000

BAUDOUIN Paul A. 1844-1931 [7]
- $30 000 - €34 855 - **£21 084** - FF228 636
  The Harvesters Oil/canvas (99.5x171cm 39x67in)
  New-York 2001

BAUDRY A. XIX-XX [18]
- $802 - €915 - **£551** - FF6 000
  **Monument élevé à la mémoire de Soliman
  Pacha** Aquarelle (52x35.5cm 20x13in) Paris 2000
- $802 - €915 - **£551** - FF6 000
  **Ville d'Alexandrie, Monument à la mémoire de
  Nubar Pacha** Estampe (75.5x57.5cm 29x22in) Paris
  2000

BAUDRY Léon Georges 1898-1978 [3]
- $1 491 - €1 753 - **£1 033** - FF11 500
  Deux femmes au lévrier Terracotta (H65cm H25in)
  Brest 2000

BAUDRY Paul 1828-1886 [48]
- $2 395 - €2 303 - **£1 478** - FF15 109
  Venus and Amor Öl/Leinwand (38x54.5cm 14x21in)
  Bern 1999
- $396 - €366 - **£237** - FF2 400
  **Les Trois Grâces, Étude pour «Le Parnasse» à
  l'Opéra de Paris** Crayon/papier (41x19.5cm 16x7in)
  Paris 1999

BAUDUIN Raphael 1870-1956 [5]
- $2 794 - €3 346 - **£1 917** - FF21 951
  Bord de Meuse Huile/toile (70x90cm 27x35in)
  Antwerpen 2000

BAUER August 1828-1913 [2]
- $2 690 - €2 299 - **£1 580** - FF15 080
  **Blick vom Tüllinger Berg nach Altweil und die
  Rheinebene** Öl/Leinwand (30x40cm 11x15in) Staufen
  1998

BAUER Carl Franz 1879-1954 [93]
- $2 122 - €1 817 - **£1 242** - FF11 922
  Ausfahrt von Kaiser Franz Josef Öl/Karton
  (34x49cm 13x19in) Wien 1998
- $1 166 - €1 252 - **£780** - FF8 211
  The Polo Match Huile/papier (31x26.5cm 12x10in)
  London 2000
- $689 - €595 - **£414** - FF3 900
  Trotteurs Aquarelle/papier (10x25cm 3x9in) Tours
  1998

BAUER Ferdinand 1760-1826 [3]
- $47 664 - €46 227 - **£30 000** - FF303 228
  Passion Flowers Oil/canvas (34.5x25cm 13x9in)
  London 1999

BAUER Gérard 1947 [76]
- $502 - €488 - **£313** - FF3 200
  Arlequin en Bugatti Acrylique/toile (46x55cm
  18x21in) Paris 1999

BAUER Gustav 1874-c.1933 [16]
- $652 - €752 - **£450** - FF4 930
  «Reichardt Pralinen, schokolade» Poster
  (178x84cm 70x33in) London 2000

BAUER Herbert R. XIX [1]
- $2 500 - €2 609 - **£1 581** - FF17 114
  Images of Iris Alberto Photograph (23x16.5cm
  9x6in) New-York 2000

BAUER Jean-Wilhelm 1600-1642 [2]
- $1 600 - €1 791 - **£1 115** - FF11 748
  **Bortreffichen Komischen Poetens Publii Ovidii
  Nasonis Metamorphoseon** Etching (34x21cm
  13x8in) New-York 2001

BAUER John 1882-1918 [104]
- $9 329 - €10 950 - **£6 583** - FF71 829
  Konstnären med modell i ateljén Oil/canvas
  (84.5x85cm 33x33in) Stockholm 2000
- $5 902 - €6 854 - **£4 147** - FF44 962
  Prinsessa i snöyra Mixed media (22x16.5cm 8x6in)
  Stockholm 2000
- $3 092 - €2 689 - **£1 865** - FF17 640
  «Humpe» Bronze (H11cm H4in) Stockholm 1998
- $2 570 - €2 924 - **£1 795** - FF19 177
  Harpspelaren Indian ink (28x24cm 11x9in)
  Stockholm 2000
- $311 - €366 - **£225** - FF2 400
  Drottning och troll Woodcut (22.5x23cm 8x9in)
  Stockholm 2001

BAUER Karl 1905-1993 [7]
- $4 904 - €5 814 - **£3 464** - FF38 136
  Begegnung Öl/Leinwand (100x70cm 39x27in)
  Klagenfurt 1999
- $1 298 - €1 453 - **£902** - FF9 534
  Beweinung Christi Pastell/Papier (71.5x47.5cm
  28x18in) Klagenfurt 2001

BAUER Marius Alexander J. 1867-1932 [486]
- $31 226 - €29 496 - **£18 889** - FF193 479
  Witte Pauw Oil/canvas (117x177cm 46x69in)
  Amsterdam 1999
- $6 791 - €7 714 - **£4 765** - FF50 602
  **Blinde bedelaar (Blinde Beggar on a Hill Top, a
  Town beyond)** Oil/canvas (49x58.5cm 19x23in)
  Amsterdam 2001
- $2 030 - €1 723 - **£1 224** - FF11 299
  Havengezicht Rotterdam 30 mei Oil/canvas/panel
  (20x26.5cm 7x10in) Rotterdam 1998
- $1 359 - €1 588 - **£970** - FF10 418
  Oosterse vrouwen Watercolour/paper (25x18cm
  9x7in) Amsterdam 2001

BAUER Rudolf 1889-1953 **[139]**
- $156 - €163 - **£99** - FF1 071
  Egyptische tempelwachters Etching (17.2x23.3cm 6x9in) Maastricht 2000
- $50 000 - €54 872 - **£32 195** - FF359 940
  Sinfonie Oil/canvas (100x123cm 39x48in) New-York 2000
- $18 174 - €17 640 - **£11 316** - FF115 709
  Larghetto III Tempera (61x85.8cm 24x33in) Berlin 1999
- $283 - €307 - **£194** - FF2 012
  Auf der Terrasse Watercolour (35.5x28cm 13x11in) Stuttgart 2001
- $400 - €403 - **£249** - FF2 644
  Kubiste Frauen Akt Lithograph (33.5x22.5cm 13x8in) New-York 2000

BAUERLE Amelia M. ?-1916 **[4]**
- $1 600 - €1 567 - **£1 031** - FF10 279
  Mermaid Watercolour (34.5x24cm 13x9in) New-York 1999

BAUERLE Karl Wilhelm Friedr. 1831-1912 **[16]**
- $10 000 - €11 212 - **£6 791** - FF73 548
  Young Girl with Flowers Pot Oil/canvas (94x66cm 37x25in) New-York 2000
- $3 956 - €4 115 - **£2 500** - FF26 995
  Two Young Boys Oil/canvas (42x38cm 16x14in) Billingshurst, West-Sussex 2000

BAUERMEISTER Mary Hilde Ruth 1934 **[29]**
- $1 350 - €1 534 - **£924** - FF10 061
  Studio Fetish Assemblage (50x25x7cm 19x9x2in) Berlin 2000

BAUERNFEIND Gustav 1848-1904 **[43]**
- $640 000 - €599 464 - **£393 472** - FF3 932 224
  Market Day in old Jaffa Oil/canvas (87x145cm 34x57in) New-York 1999
- $23 317 - €21 640 - **£14 000** - FF141 948
  Orientalische Strassenszene Oil/canvas (102x70cm 40x27in) London 1999
- $8 500 - €8 779 - **£5 285** - FF51 680
  Abendstimmung bei Jerusalem (Evening Mood near Jerusalem) Oil/board (23x31cm 9x12in) Tel Aviv 1999

BAUERNFREUND Jakub 1904-1976 **[2]**
- $1 734 - €1 640 - **£1 080** - FF10 758
  Bildnis eines Jungen Öl/Leinwand (82x53cm 32x20in) Praha 2000

BAUFFE Victor 1849-1921 **[40]**
- $1 840 - €1 588 - **£1 110** - FF10 418
  The hit Oil/canvas (70.5x100.5cm 27x39in) Amsterdam 1999
- $1 677 - €1 906 - **£1 177** - FF12 501
  A Still Life of Apples Oil/canvas/board (18x25.5cm 7x10in) Amsterdam 2001
- $1 731 - €1 588 - **£1 066** - FF10 418
  Woman Strolling Along a Canal Watercolour (28.5x38.5cm 11x15in) Amsterdam 1999

BAUGNIES de René 1869-1962 **[118]**
- $631 - €545 - **£376** - FF3 575
  Paysage montagneux Huile/toile (46x61cm 18x24in) Bruxelles 1998
- $333 - €399 - **£230** - FF2 617
  Cattle in a Landscape Oil/canvas (32x45cm 12x17in) Penzance, Cornwall 2000

BAUGNIET Charles 1814-1886 **[16]**
- $29 385 - €34 970 - **£21 000** - FF229 387
  La guirlande Oil/panel (80x107cm 31x42in) London 2000

BAUGNIET Marcel Louis 1896-1995 **[148]**
- $1 908 - €2 269 - **£1 360** - FF14 883
  La maret verte (le soleil rouge...) Oil/canvas (96x94cm 37x37in) Amsterdam 2000
- $3 507 - €4 090 - **£2 462** - FF26 831
  Ohne Titel Oil/panel (25.3x20.3cm 9x7in) Köln 2000
- $4 322 - €3 924 - **£2 700** - FF25 742
  Lamp Sculpture, glass (22.5x29x6.5cm 8x11x2in) London 1999
- $566 - €595 - **£357** - FF3 902
  L'Homme Feuille Technique mixte/papier (54x41cm 21x16in) Bruxelles 2000
- $156 - €161 - **£99** - FF1 056
  «Le groupe l'assaut de Bruxelles expose du 9 au 25 juin» Affiche (59x41.5cm 23x16in) Bruxelles 2000

BAUKNECHT Philipp 1884-1933 **[46]**
- $32 991 - €31 765 - **£20 629** - FF208 362
  Farmers in ther Field near Davos Oil/canvas (70x81.5cm 27x32in) Amsterdam 1999
- $329 - €307 - **£203** - FF2 012
  Das einsame Gefährt Woodcut (27x35.5cm 10x13in) Hamburg 1999

BAUM Charles / Carl 1812-1878 **[7]**
- $23 000 - €23 837 - **£14 572** - FF156 358
  Still life with Fruit and Bird's Nest Oil/canvas (73x60cm 29x24in) Portsmouth NH 2000

BAUM Otto 1900-1977 **[2]**
- $6 090 - €7 158 - **£4 222** - FF46 954
  Kämmende Metal (H40cm H15in) Stuttgart 2000

BAUM Paul 1859-1932 **[64]**
- $48 916 - €47 039 - **£30 185** - FF308 558
  Dorfstrasse Öl/Leinwand (57.5x69.5cm 22x27in) Köln 2000
- $4 289 - €5 113 - **£3 058** - FF33 539
  Dorfrstrasse Öl/Leinwand (38x27cm 14x10in) Ahlden 2000
- $2 628 - €2 659 - **£1 604** - FF17 440
  Boote am Steg Watercolour (36.5x50.5cm 14x19in) Stuttgart 2000
- $87 - €82 - **£54** - FF536
  Blick über eine Wiese auf ein Gehöft und das Rathaustürmchen Etching (14x17.4cm 5x6in) Heidelberg 1999

BAUM Walter Emerson 1884-1956 **[283]**
- $14 000 - €13 626 - **£8 601** - FF89 381
  Easton Oil/canvas (101x127cm 40x50in) Hatfield PA 1999
- $6 000 - €6 440 - **£4 015** - FF42 246
  Bucks County Village Oil/masonite (40.5x50.5cm 15x19in) New-York 2000
- $2 600 - €2 531 - **£1 597** - FF16 599
  Springtime Landscape with Houses along River and Trees in blossom Oil/board (25x20cm 10x8in) Hatfield PA 1999
- $600 - €644 - **£401** - FF4 224
  Spring day landscape Gouache/board (38x49cm 15x19in) Hatfield PA 2000
- $100 - €116 - **£70** - FF758
  Country Village Landscape Lithograph (20x25cm 8x10in) Hatfield PA 2000

BAUMANN Gustave 1881-1971 **[133]**
- $3 500 - €3 902 - **£2 432** - FF25 595
  «Monterey Cypress» Woodcut in colors (20.5x21cm 8x8in) New-York 2001

BAUMANN Ida 1864-? **[4]**

$7 000 - €8 227 - £4 853 - FF53 965
Feeding the Rabbits Oil/canvas (102x76cm 40x29in)
New-York 2000

BAUMANN Marc 1921 **[150]**

$438 - €488 - £307 - FF3 200
Espace Technique mixte/toile (81x65cm 31x25in)
Paris 2001

BAUMBERGER Otto 1889-1961 **[105]**

$1 784 - €2 098 - £1 292 - FF13 765
«Stilleben mit Goldfischglas» Öl/Leinwand
(46x38cm 18x14in) Zofingen 2001

$1 000 - €1 121 - £694 - FF7 356
«Faco» Poster (124x89cm 49x35in) New-York 2001

BAUMEISTER Willi 1889-1955 **[600]**

$331 360 - €308 981 - £200 000 - FF2 026 780
Dialogue in Red-Blue Oil/board (100x130cm
39x51in) London 2000

$90 997 - €84 998 - £55 000 - FF557 551
Eidos Schwebend Oil/canvas (49.5x36cm 19x14in)
London 1999

$77 476 - €63 638 - £45 000 - FF417 438
Eidos Amö Mixed media/board (45x33cm 17x12in)
London 1998

$8 965 - €9 624 - £6 000 - FF63 129
Collage mit Phantom Collage/paper (23.5x18.5cm
9x7in) London 2000

$1 529 - €1 431 - £947 - FF9 390
Schwarzes Tier Lithographie (36x45.5cm 14x17in)
Heidelberg 1999

BÄUMER Eduard 1892-1977 **[15]**

$5 024 - €4 724 - £3 042 - FF30 985
Blumenstilleben Mischtechnik/Papier (54x78.5cm
21x30in) Wien 1999

BAUMER Lewis Christ. Edward 1870-1963 **[33]**

$2 238 - €2 522 - £1 550 - FF16 544
The Party Dress Oil/board (28x35.5cm 11x13in)
Ipswich 2000

$672 - €637 - £420 - FF4 180
The Lunchen Interval, Portrait of a Gentleman
Pencil (32x20.5cm 12x8in) London 1999

BAUMGARTL Moritz 1934 **[18]**

$2 274 - €2 301 - £1 388 - FF15 092
Le gardien de l'aigle Oil/panel (25x30cm 9x11in)
Stuttgart 2000

$68 - €77 - £47 - FF503
«Arbeitsniederlegung» Farbserigraphie (55x39cm
21x15in) Stuttgart 2001

BAUMGARTNER Adolf 1850-1924 **[177]**

$6 000 - €5 034 - £3 509 - FF33 021
Horse-Drawn Coach and Rider Carrying Torch
Oil/canvas (104x139cm 41x55in) Cutchogue NY 1998

$2 144 - €2 454 - £1 475 - FF16 098
**Zwei Reiter in weiter Winterlandschaft am Ufer
eines Flüsschens** Öl/Leinwand (77x100cm 30x39in)
München 2000

$1 558 - €1 624 - £980 - FF10 653
Snowy Landscape with Horses Oil/canvas
(20x30cm 7x11in) North-Lincolnshire 2000

BAUMGARTNER Christian 1855-1942 **[55]**

$84 - €98 - £58 - FF644
**Seeufer mit Schilffeldern in hügeliger
Landschaft** Aquarell, Gouache/Papier (26.5x41cm
10x16in) Bern 2000

BAUMGARTNER E. XIX-XX **[2]**

$2 600 - €2 495 - £1 629 - FF16 368
Interior of the Pavlosk Palace Watercolour/paper
(46x35.5cm 18x13in) New-York 1999

BAUMGARTNER Fritz 1929 **[18]**

$2 600 - €2 695 - £1 560 - FF17 680
La morte di Odisseus Olio/tela (70x100cm 27x39in)
Torino 2001

$1 600 - €2 073 - £1 200 - FF13 600
Madonna con Bambino Olio/tavola (40x30cm
15x11in) Torino 2000

BAUMGÄRTNER Heiner 1891-? **[5]**

$1 064 - €1 022 - £660 - FF6 707
Canna indica Öl/Karton (70x53cm 27x20in)
Hildrizhausen 1999

BAUMGARTNER Johann Wolfgang 1712-1761 **[24]**

$8 960 - €10 174 - £6 132 - FF66 738
Die Marter der Heiligen Symphorosa
Öl/Leinwand (31.5x23cm 12x9in) Wien 2000

$2 018 - €2 301 - £1 408 - FF15 092
**Reliquienbüste eines Klerikers, von Engeln auf
einer Säule gehalten** Ink (20x14cm 7x5in) Berlin
2001

BAUMGARTNER John Jay 1865-1946 **[4]**

$6 500 - €6 182 - £3 946 - FF40 553
Silver and Green Gouache (35.5x25.5cm 13x10in)
Beverly-Hills CA 1999

BAUMGARTNER Peter 1834-1911 **[28]**

$15 000 - €13 279 - £9 171 - FF87 103
An Offer Declined Oil/canvas (76x95.5cm 29x37in)
New-York 1999

$4 048 - €4 346 - £2 709 - FF28 508
**Richter, Mönch und Wächter stehen fassungs-
slos im leeren Kerker** Öl/Leinwand (30x24.5cm
11x9in) Kempten 2000

BAUMGARTNER Thomas 1892-1962 **[5]**

$1 470 - €1 534 - £925 - FF10 061
Muttergottes Öl/Leinwand (60x49cm 23x19in)
München 2000

BAUMGARTNER Warren W. 1894-1963 **[10]**

$2 000 - €1 851 - £1 224 - FF12 145
**Frontiermen in horseback battle with Indians,
ill. for True Magazine** Watercolour/paper (28x58cm
11x23in) New-York 1999

BAUMGRAS Peter 1827-1904 **[6]**

$3 750 - €4 164 - £2 608 - FF27 312
Picnic by the Waterfall Oil/board (54x38cm
21x15in) Milford CT 2001

$4 000 - €3 778 - £2 419 - FF24 782
On the Wings of a Butterfly Oil/panel (25.4x14.5cm
10x5in) New-York 1999

BAUMHOFER Walter Martin 1904-1986 **[12]**

$3 000 - €3 360 - £2 084 - FF22 041
Artist and Model in Rooftop Studio Oil/canvas
(49x80cm 19x31in) New-York 2001

BAUQUIER Georges 1910-1997 **[4]**

$6 910 - €7 775 - £4 824 - FF51 000
«Nature morte à la cruche» Huile/toile (53.7x65cm
21x25in) Paris 2001

BAUR Johann Wilhelm 1607-1641 **[29]**

$28 000 - €24 644 - £17 046 - FF161 652
**Italian Landscape with an Imaginary View of a
Grand Staircase** Oil/canvas (40x71cm 15x27in) New-
York 1999

$19 000 - €19 221 - **£11 601** - FF126 082
**Cavalry Skirmish in an Extensive Mountainous
Landscape** Bodycolour (13x18.5cm 5x7in) New-York
2000

$596 - €669 - **£415** - FF4 390
**«Dem Hoch Edlen unnd Gestrengen Herren
Jonae von Heyssperg Auff...»** Eau-forte
(13x20.5cm 5x8in) Bruxelles 2001

BAUR Max 1898-1988 **[57]**
$695 - €818 - **£498** - FF5 366
«Postdam» Vintage gelatin silver print (23x17cm
9x6in) Berlin 2001

BAUR Nicolaus Bauer 1767-1820 **[7]**
$8 463 - €9 878 - **£6 000** - FF64 794
Dutch warship announcing its arrival offshore
Oil/canvas (43x36cm 16x22in) London 2001

BAURIEDL Otto 1881-1961 **[41]**
$261 - €297 - **£181** - FF1 949
Ausblick auf See und Gebirge Gouache/paper
(47x36cm 18x14in) Zofingen 2000

BAURSCHEIT van Jan Pierer 1669-1728 **[2]**
$17 184 - €18 446 - **£11 500** - FF120 998
Two Children Stone (H98cm H38in) London 2000

BAUSCHERT Heiner 1928-1986 **[33]**
$79 - €66 - **£46** - FF436
«Schwäbisch Gmünd» Woodcut in colors (50x49cm
19x19in) Stuttgart 1998

BAUSE Johann Friedrich 1738-1814 **[14]**
$1 286 - €1 534 - **£917** - FF10 061
**Der Totenkopf eines Kindes, nach Adam
Friedrich Oeser** Radierung (12.5x18.7cm 4x7in)
Berlin 2000

BAUTERS Sonja 1938 **[9]**
$828 - €992 - **£568** - FF6 504
**Stilleven met kruiken en flessen (Nature morte
aux cruches, bouteille)** Huile/panneau (62x100cm
24x39in) Antwerpen 2000

BAUTZER Carl Ludwig 1857-1941 **[1]**
$8 428 - €8 181 - **£5 248** - FF53 662
Portrait eines Schwälmer Bauern Öl/Leinwand
(43x35cm 16x13in) Frankfurt 1999

BAUZIL Jean 1766-1820 **[5]**
$943 - €884 - **£582** - FF5 800
**Dignitaire espagnol, portant la décoration de
l'Ordre de la Toison d'Or** Miniature (7.5x7cm 2x2in)
Bordeaux 1999

BAVOUX Charles J. Nestor 1824-c.1885 **[4]**
$6 500 - €6 389 - **£4 176** - FF41 910
Still Life with Grapes and Newspaper Oil/canvas
(56x61.5cm 22x24in) New-York 1999

BAWA Manjit 1941 **[16]**
$20 000 - €22 746 - **£13 974** - FF149 202
Untitled Acrylic/canvas (137x114.5cm 53x45in) New-
York 2000
$4 443 - €4 312 - **£2 800** - FF28 287
Man with Pipe Acrylic/canvas (55x50cm 21x19in)
London 1999
$1 494 - €1 604 - **£1 000** - FF10 521
Man with Fish Pencil/paper (76x56cm 29x22in)
London 1999

BAWDEN Edward 1903-1989 **[137]**
$2 520 - €2 931 - **£1 800** - FF19 227
Two Ashbins Gouache/paper (45.5x55cm 17x21in)
Norfolk 2001

$862 - €958 - **£600** - FF6 282
The Changing of the Guards Linocut in colors
(43.5x30.5cm 17x12in) London 2001

BAWDEN Richard 1936 **[9]**
$190 - €183 - **£120** - FF1 202
The Birdwatcher Aquatint (57x45cm 22x17in)
Ipswich 1999

BAXTER Adeline XIX-XX **[2]**
$8 000 - €9 453 - **£5 669** - FF62 006
Twilight on Columbus Avenue Oil/canvas
(56x46cm 22x18in) Boston MA 2000

BAXTER Charles 1809-1879 **[49]**
$2 400 - €2 125 - **£1 467** - FF13 936
Nap Time Oil/canvas (47x62.5cm 18x24in) New-York
1999
$883 - €890 - **£550** - FF5 836
**Portrait of a Young Woman, Small Three-Quater-
Length, in a Black Dress** Oil/canvas (31.5x26cm
12x10in) London 2000

BAXTER Evelyn Monette 1925 **[15]**
$321 - €354 - **£213** - FF2 322
Still Life Oil/canvas (24.5x37.5cm 9x14in) Melbourne
2000

BAXTER George 1804-1867 **[241]**
$105 - €99 - **£65** - FF648
Australia News for Home/News for Australia
Print (10x14cm 4x5in) Little-Lane, Ilkley 1999

BAXTER Glen 1944 **[9]**
$561 - €667 - **£400** - FF4 378
**It Became Apparent That Brenda Would Not Be
Sharing Her Meatball** Crayon (78.5x57cm 30x22in)
London 2000
$30 - €31 - **£19** - FF205
**«How It's Done, The Wonder Book of Sex,
Galleria del Cavalino»** Poster (68x48cm 26x18in)
Sydney 2000

BAXTER Thomas 1782-1821 **[3]**
$1 416 - €1 304 - **£850** - FF8 553
Six Views taken in and near Swansea Etching
(24x30cm 9x11in) Glamorgan 1999

BAYA Fatima Haddad, dite 1931-1998 **[4]**
$2 611 - €2 439 - **£1 577** - FF16 000
Joueuse de Mandore Aquarelle, gouache/papier
(100x100cm 39x39in) Paris 1999

BAYARD Hippolyte 1801-1887 **[20]**
$85 982 - €81 211 - **£52 000** - FF532 708
Autoportrait avec appareil sur pied Albumen print
(34.5x27.5cm 13x10in) London 1999

BAYENS Han 1876-1945 **[5]**
$1 642 - €1 815 - **£1 139** - FF11 906
Strolling along a river in Richmond, England
Oil/board (21x26.5cm 8x10in) Amsterdam 2001

BAYENS Hans 1924 **[21]**
$1 231 - €1 361 - **£854** - FF8 929
A hilly Belgian landscape Oil/board (28x35cm
11x13in) Amsterdam 2001
$1 649 - €1 588 - **£1 031** - FF10 418
Girl on a Horse Bronze (H26cm H10in) Amsterdam
1999
$2 325 - €2 496 - **£1 555** - FF16 371
Mother and Child Charcoal (44x57cm 17x22in)
Amsterdam 2000

BAYER Herbert 1900-1985 **[188]**
$4 500 - €5 222 - **£3 107** - FF34 252
Larger Anthology Acrylic (203x203cm 79x79in)
New-York 2000

$639 - €716 - **£444** - FF4 695
Star of the Desert Öl/Leinwand (41x51cm 16x20in)
Berlin 2001

$3 600 - €3 880 - **£2 455** - FF25 450
Youth and Old Age Oil/canvas/board (22.5x16.5cm
8x6in) New-York 2001

$4 000 - €3 427 - **£2 404** - FF22 478
Weitere der SS Werbung Collage/paper (24x19cm
9x7in) Cincinnati OH 1998

$326 - €369 - **£220** - FF2 418
«Bauhaus» Poster (58x42.5cm 22x16in) London 2000

$4 000 - €4 293 - **£2 716** - FF28 162
Selected images Gelatin silver print (18.5x29.5cm
7x11in) Beverly-Hills CA 2001

BAYER Johann Christoph 1738-1812 **[2]**
$5 131 - €4 442 - **£3 115** - FF29 139
**Opstillinger med roser, nelliker og latyvisi
vaser på en karm** Gouache/paper (42x33cm 16x12in)
Köbenhavn 1998

BAYER Julius 1840-1883 **[6]**
$4 400 - €4 154 - **£2 735** - FF27 249
Village Waterway Oil/canvas (58x86cm 23x34in)
Cleveland OH 1999

BAYER-WECH Heidi 1943 **[3]**
$4 646 - €4 346 - **£2 814** - FF28 508
Komposition Öl/Leinwand (60x70cm 23x27in)
Stuttgart 1999

$2 733 - €2 556 - **£1 655** - FF16 769
Meditationswand Mixed media (17x18.5cm 6x7in)
Stuttgart 1999

BAYERLEIN Fritz 1872-1955 **[42]**
$1 128 - €997 - **£689** - FF6 540
«Bachlandschaft mit Birken» Öl/Leinwand
(110x80cm 43x31in) München 1999

BAYERN von Pilar, Prinzessin 1891-1983 **[66]**
$879 - €869 - **£538** - FF5 701
Magnolienbaum im Nymphenburger Park
Öl/Leinwand (50x60cm 19x23in) Kempten 2000

$439 - €434 - **£269** - FF2 850
Blumengeschmückter Torbogen Aquarell/Papier
(41x29cm 16x11in) Kempten 2000

$284 - €281 - **£174** - FF1 844
Strasse in weiter Landschaft mit Person
Lithographie (42x32cm 16x12in) Kempten 2000

BAYES Alfred Walter 1832-1909 **[20]**
$667 - €752 - **£460** - FF4 930
Morning Rise before Battle Oil/canvas (29.5x50cm
11x19in) Bristol, Avon 2000

BAYES Gilbert William 1872-1953 **[11]**
$5 493 - €6 397 - **£3 800** - FF41 964
Custodo Bronze (H53cm H20in) London 2000

BAYES Jessie 1890-1939 **[12]**
$983 - €942 - **£620** - FF6 181
Fons Amoris Tempera/paper (45x23cm 17x9in)
Billingshurst, West-Sussex 1999

BAYES Walter John 1869-1956 **[57]**
$2 551 - €3 023 - **£1 800** - FF19 832
Casino, Boulogne Oil/canvas (39.5x53.5cm 15x21in)
London 2001

$401 - €347 - **£240** - FF2 274
Cafe de Tunis Watercolour (17.5x21.5cm 6x8in)
London 1998

BAYEU Y SUBIAS Francisco 1734-1795 **[17]**
$58 300 - €66 071 - **£39 600** - FF433 400
Ascensión del Señor Oleo/lienzo (65x64.5cm
25x25in) Madrid 2000

$14 250 - €15 016 - **£9 000** - FF98 500
**Aparición de la Virgen a San Julián, Obispo de
Cuenca** Oleo/lienzo (30x18cm 11x7in) Madrid 2000

$525 - €450 - **£322** - FF2 955
La Inmaculada Grabado (35x23cm 13x9in) Madrid
1998

BAYLAC Lucien 1851-1913 **[26]**
$1 500 - €1 280 - **£904** - FF8 394
«Electricine» Poster (87x123.5cm 34x48in) New-York
1998

BAYLINSON Abraham Solomon 1882-1950 **[14]**
$1 000 - €853 - **£596** - FF5 596
Reclining Nude Oil/canvas (61.5x86.5cm 24x34in)
New-York 1998

BAYLISS Margaret E. XIX-XX **[2]**
$2 806 - €3 337 - **£2 000** - FF21 890
Gossamer Fairy/A Friendly Elf Watercolour
(28x18.5cm 11x7in) London 2000

BAYNARD Ed 1940 **[33]**
$2 000 - €1 915 - **£1 235** - FF12 563
Tulips Aquatint in colors (106x74.5cm 41x29in) New-
York 1999

BAYNES Frederick Thomas 1824-1874 **[12]**
$1 229 - €1 062 - **£750** - FF6 964
Finch and Grapes Watercolour/paper (30x21cm
12x8in) Birmingham 1999

BAYNES Keith Stuart 1887-1977 **[33]**
$920 - €1 075 - **£650** - FF7 050
Landscape near Toulon Oil/canvas (49x74cm
19x29in) Guernsey 2000

BAYNES Pauline Diana 1922 **[6]**
$1 263 - €1 502 - **£900** - FF9 855
Snow White and the Seven Dwarves Bodycolour
(23x15cm 9x5in) London 2000

BAYON SALADO Juan 1912-1995 **[18]**
$1 830 - €1 502 - **£900** - FF7 880
Notre-Dame Oleo/tabla (57x44cm 22x17in) Madrid
1999

$1 100 - €1 201 - **£700** - FF7 880
Una calle de pasajes Oleo/tablex (41x33cm
16x12in) Madrid 2000

BAYROS von Franz 1866-1924 **[65]**
$1 227 - €1 431 - **£864** - FF9 390
**Bunter Papagei auf blauer Vase vor einer
Tänzerin als Porzellanfigur** Watercolour (52x64cm
20x25in) Königstein 2001

$100 - €116 - **£70** - FF762
Amorous Drawing Lithograph (16x23cm 6x9in)
Thomaston ME 2001

BAZAINE Jean 1904-2001 **[283]**
$2 089 - €2 287 - **£1 441** - FF15 000
Litanies de la Vierge Huile/toile (35x62cm 13x24in)
Paris 2001

$5 749 - €6 781 - **£4 000** - FF44 480
Paysage Oil/panel (24x18.5cm 9x7in) London 2000

$2 007 - €2 287 - **£1 378** - FF15 000
Sans titre Aquarelle/papier (47.5x62.5cm 18x24in)
Paris 2000

$97 - €107 - **£64** - FF700
Hollande III Lithographie (38x28.5cm 14x11in) Douai
2000

BAZÉ Paul Robert 1901-1985 **[53]**
$1 440 - €1 372 - **£912** - FF9 000
Flamenco Huile/panneau (46x55cm 18x21in) Biarritz
1999

B

> $705 - €838 - £485 - FF5 500
> **Danseuse espagnole** Huile/panneau (27x22cm
> 10x8in) Biarritz 2000

> $4 610 - €3 811 - £2 705 - FF25 000
> **Pelote à Bassussary** Gouache/papier (47x64cm
> 18x25in) Biarritz 1998

BAZILLE Frédéric 1841-1870 [6]

> $9 795 - €11 434 - £6 915 - FF75 000
> **Études d'après Delacroix** Crayon (18.5x13.5cm
> 7x5in) Paris 2000

BAZIN Charles L. 1802-1859 [6]

> $8 690 - €10 084 - £6 000 - FF66 144
> **Henry Edward Surtees of Redworth (1819-
> 1885)/Mrs Elizabeth Surtees** Oil/canvas
> (127x101.5cm 50x39in) London 2000

> $6 678 - €6 135 - £4 102 - FF40 246
> **Porträt des französischen Kaisers Napoleon III
> (1852-1870)** Öl/Leinwand (81x64.5cm 31x25in)
> Stuttgart 1999

BAZIOTES William 1912-1963 [56]

> $30 000 - €28 051 - £18 495 - FF184 002
> **Two Puppets** Oil/canvas (96x73cm 37x28in) New-
> York 1999

> $1 800 - €1 510 - £1 056 - FF9 906
> **Untitled** Indian ink/paper (21.5x28cm 8x11in) New-
> York 1999

BAZIRAY XVIII [4]

> $26 980 - €28 965 - £18 050 - FF190 000
> **Portrait de jeune femme en Cérès** Huile/toile
> (215x92cm 84x36in) Paris 2000

BAZZANI Giuseppe 1690-1769 [7]

> $21 204 - €19 832 - £13 000 - FF130 091
> **Saint Helena Finding the True Cross**
> Oil/paper/panel (49x35cm 19x13in) London 1998

BAZZANI Luigi 1836-1927 [22]

> $10 390 - €10 300 - £6 500 - FF67 561
> **Maidens in a Classical Interior** Oil/panel (67x47cm
> 26x18in) London 1999

> $1 286 - €1 453 - £868 - FF9 534
> **Der Constantinsbogen in Rom** Aquarell/Papier
> (55x36cm 21x14in) Wien 2000

BAZZANTI Pietro XIX [31]

> $5 637 - €6 250 - £3 903 - FF41 000
> **La source** Marbre Carrare (H90cm H35in) Nîmes
> 2001

> $1 500 - €1 749 - £1 053 - FF11 475
> **Bust of a Lady** Marble (H55cm H22in) Dedham MA
> 2000

BAZZARO Ernesto 1859-1937 [21]

> $4 000 - €3 658 - £2 442 - FF23 995
> **In the caravan** Bronze (H51cm H20in) New-York
> 1998

BAZZARO Leonardo 1853-1937 [70]

> $18 000 - €23 325 - £13 500 - FF153 000
> **Il cervino da valtournenche** Olio/tela (110x160cm
> 43x62in) Milano 2001

> $7 500 - €7 775 - £4 500 - FF51 000
> **Figure maschili** Olio/tela (90x60cm 35x23in) Milano
> 2000

> $912 - €984 - £576 - FF6 304
> **Venecia** Oleo/cartón (26x21cm 10x8in) Madrid 2000

BEA Manuel Cervera 1934-1997 [50]

> $487 - €452 - £300 - FF2 962
> **Sin título** Oleo/lienzo (101x81.5cm 39x32in) Madrid
> 1998

BEACH Ernest George 1865-? [14]

> $654 - €749 - £450 - FF4 911
> **Ploughing the Field** Watercolour/paper (23x34.5cm
> 9x13in) West-Midlands 2000

BEACH Thomas 1738-1806 [37]

> $1 877 - €2 035 - £1 300 - FF13 347
> **Portrait of a young girl** Oil/canvas (125x100cm
> 49x39in) Billingshurst, West-Sussex 2001

> $2 245 - €2 263 - £1 400 - FF14 845
> **Lady, half-length, in a White Dress and Green
> Sash** Oil/canvas (75.5x63.5cm 29x25in) London 2000

BEADLE James Prinsep Barnes 1863-1947 [13]

> $10 627 - €9 451 - £6 500 - FF61 992
> **Life Guards and the King's Troop in Hyde Park**
> Oil/canvas (69x130cm 27x51in) London 1999

BEAL Gifford 1879-1956 [77]

> $2 700 - €3 151 - £1 909 - FF20 671
> **Bouquet in Japanese Vase** Oil/canvas (45x60cm
> 18x24in) Boston MA 2001

> $500 - €6 246 - £3 764 - FF40 969
> **By the Pier** Oil/board (30.5x38cm 12x14in) New-York
> 2000

> $1 800 - €2 044 - £1 231 - FF13 407
> **Dark Sky, Cape Ann** Watercolour, gouache/paper
> (34x50cm 13x19in) New-York 2000

> $200 - €236 - £141 - FF1 550
> **Miraculous Draught of Fishes** Etching (24x35cm
> 9x14in) Provincetown MA 2000

BEAL Jack 1931 [35]

> $6 500 - €5 454 - £3 813 - FF35 773
> **Self-Portrait as Envy** Oil/canvas (66x56cm 25x22in)
> New-York 1998

BEAL Reynolds 1867-1951 [158]

> $22 000 - €20 607 - £13 525 - FF135 170
> **Cold Spring on Hudson, N.Y** Oil/canvas
> (45.5x61cm 17x24in) New-York 1999

> $3 250 - €3 031 - £2 016 - FF19 881
> **My Skiff** Oil/canvas/board (16x23.5cm 6x9in) New-
> York 1999

> $2 000 - €1 888 - £1 243 - FF12 386
> **Santa Maria** Watercolour (35x53cm 14x21in) Milford
> CT 1999

> $440 - €490 - £287 - FF3 214
> **New England Whaler** Etching (27x35cm 11x14in)
> Rockport MA 2000

BEALE Charles 1660-c.1714 [9]

> $4 221 - €4 165 - £2 600 - FF27 319
> **Young Lady, Half-Length, Wearing a Brown
> Dress with a Blue Shaw** Oil/canvas (76.5x63.5cm
> 30x25in) London 1999

BEALE Mary, née Cradock 1632-1697 [20]

> $6 878 - €6 390 - £4 200 - FF41 916
> **Portrait of the King Charles II** Oil/canvas (76x63cm
> 29x24in) London 1998

> $15 654 - €18 432 - £11 000 - FF120 905
> **Young Lady called Nell Gwynne in a Lansdcape**
> Miniature (12x10.5cm 4x4in) London 2000

> $3 750 - €3 541 - £2 331 - FF23 226
> **Portrait of Van Dyck/Portrait of a Lady** Red
> chalk/paper (22x16cm 8x6in) New-York 1999

BEALL Lester Thomas 1903-1969 [6]

> $4 000 - €4 486 - £2 777 - FF29 427
> **«Cross out Slums»** Poster (101x76cm 40x30in)
> New-York 2001

BEALS Jessie Tarbox 1870-1942 **[33]**
- 📷 **$1 600** - €1 494 - **£969** - FF9 799
  Sheridan Square Platinum print (23x17.5cm 9x6in)
  New-York 1999

BEAM Carl 1943 **[9]**
- 🎨 **$100** - €113 - **£66** - FF738
  Family Lithograph (60x50cm 23x19in) Calgary, Alberta
  2000

BEAMENT Thomas Harold 1898-1984 **[61]**
- 🖼 **$1 484** - €1 267 - **£885** - FF8 309
  Eskimo Berry Pickers Oil/canvas/board (61x76cm
  24x29in) Vancouver, BC. 1998
- 🖼 **$330** - €285 - **£199** - FF1 872
  Ste Rose/Village en hiver Huile/panneau
  (30.5x40.5cm 12x15in) Montréal 1999

BEAN Bennett 1941 **[1]**
- 🏺 **$4 500** - €4 662 - **£2 864** - FF30 578
  Vessel Ceramic (20.5x21cm 8x8in) New-York 2000

BEAN Caroline Van Hook 1880-1970 **[2]**
- 🖼 **$4 600** - €5 470 - **£3 278** - FF35 884
  Geraniums Oil/canvas (36x30.5cm 14x12in) New-
  York 2000

BEANLAND Frank 1936 **[20]**
- 🖼 **$431** - €484 - **£300** - FF3 172
  Porthleven Oil/board (122x61cm 48x24in) London
  2001

BEARD James Henry 1812-1893 **[10]**
- 🖼 **$1 500** - €1 688 - **£1 033** - FF11 074
  Comforting Shoulder Oil/canvas (54x43cm 21x16in)
  Washington 2000

BEARD Peter 1938 **[18]**
- 📷 **$3 981** - €4 492 - **£2 800** - FF29 463
  **Blue Portrait of Francis Bacon, Narrow Street,
  London** Photograph in colors (35x23.5cm 13x9in)
  London 2001

BEARD William Holdbrook 1823-1900 **[34]**
- 🖼 **$15 000** - €12 816 - **£9 004** - FF84 066
  Discovery of Adam Oil/canvas (46x61cm 18x24in)
  New-York 1998
- 🖼 **$11 000** - €10 686 - **£6 712** - FF70 098
  **Squirrel in a Woodland Setting With Ferns and
  Leaves** Oil/canvas (35x30cm 14x12in) Asheville NC
  2000
- 🖼 **$2 800** - €2 362 - **£1 642** - FF15 495
  Susannah and the Elders Charcoal/paper
  (87.5x117cm 34x46in) New-York 1998

BEARDEN Romare Howard 1914-1988 **[302]**
- 🖼 **$25 000** - €28 432 - **£17 467** - FF186 502
  In the Garden Mixed media (55x40cm 22x16in)
  Chicago IL 2000
- 🖼 **$9 000** - €8 619 - **£5 560** - FF56 537
  Ritual Bayou Collage (44x52.5cm 17x20in) New-York
  1999
- 🎨 **$2 200** - €2 071 - **£1 359** - FF13 584
  Two Women Screenprint in colors (58.5x36cm
  23x14in) New-York 1999

BEARDSLEY Aubrey 1872-1898 **[54]**
- 🖼 **$3 249** - €2 815 - **£1 993** - FF18 462
  «Sandro Botticelli» Pencil/paper (35x19.5cm 13x7in)
  New-York 1999
- 🎨 **$411** - €490 - **£293** - FF3 213
  The Lady with the Rose Radierung (9.5x16cm
  3x6in) Hamburg 2000

BEARE George XVIII **[9]**
- 🖼 **$16 660** - €17 271 - **£9 996** - FF113 288
  **Ritratto di gentiluomo appoggiato ad una
  balaustra** Olio/tela (124x102cm 48x40in) Roma 1999
- 🖼 **$2 639** - €2 845 - **£1 800** - FF18 659
  Portrait on a Lady, Half-length, in a White Dress
  Oil/canvas (76.5x63.5cm 30x25in) London 2001

BEARNE Edward H. XIX-XX **[15]**
- 🖼 **$413** - €357 - **£250** - FF2 342
  Figures on a Horse and Cart on a Beach
  Watercolour (21.5x34cm 8x13in) London 1999

BEARS Orlando Hand 1811-1851 **[2]**
- 🖼 **$10 000** - €10 680 - **£6 814** - FF70 053
  Portrait of a Man/Portrait of a Woman Oil/canvas
  (76x63cm 30x25in) New-York 2001

BEASTALL W.E. XVIII-XIX **[1]**
- 🎨 **$1 290** - €1 240 - **£800** - FF8 131
  Negroes Sunday Market of Antigua Lithograph
  (28.5x41cm 11x16in) London 1999

BEATO A. / Felice 1830-1906 **[84]**
- 📷 **$1 092** - €1 143 - **£686** - FF7 500
  Vue de Lucknow Tirage albuminé (25x29.5cm
  9x11in) Paris 2000

BEATO Antonio / Antoine c.1825-c.1903 **[12]**
- 📷 **$1 233** - €1 385 - **£800** - FF9 088
  Egypt, Studies Photograph (36x26cm 14x10in)
  London 2000

BEATON Cecil 1904-1980 **[390]**
- 🖼 **$753** - €868 - **£520** - FF5 695
  **Portrait of Nancy, Lady Smiley, Seated in a
  Burnt Umber Dress** Oil/canvas/board (76x55.5cm
  29x21in) Newbury, Berkshire 2000
- 🖼 **$800** - €860 - **£545** - FF5 642
  Portrait of Ina Claire Gouache (12.5x10cm 4x3in)
  Beverly-Hills CA 2001
- 📷 **$1 047** - €1 125 - **£708** - FF7 378
  Josephine und Victoria Chaplin Photograph
  (23.7x24.1cm 9x9in) München 2000

BEATON Penelope 1886-1963 **[19]**
- 🖼 **$3 326** - €2 850 - **£2 000** - FF18 694
  Mixed Bunch of Flowers Oil/board (53x68cm
  20x26in) Edinburgh 1998
- 🖼 **$922** - €779 - **£550** - FF5 111
  Autumn Flowers Watercolour (56.5x44cm 22x17in)
  Glasgow 1998

BEATRIZET Nicolaus Beatricius 1515-c.1570 **[27]**
- 🎨 **$943** - €1 125 - **£672** - FF7 378
  Der Flussgott Oceanus Kupferstich (42x31cm
  16x12in) Berlin 2000

BEATTY John William 1869-1941 **[67]**
- 🖼 **$2 271** - €1 921 - **£1 358** - FF12 591
  Landscape with River and Sailing Vessel Oil/can-
  vas (44x56.5cm 17x22in) Toronto 1998
- 🖼 **$1 360** - €1 301 - **£852** - FF8 532
  Sunlit Houses Oil/board (25x32cm 9x12in)
  Vancouver, BC. 1999

BEAU Henri 1865-1949 **[42]**
- 🖼 **$1 502** - €1 442 - **£942** - FF9 460
  Blanche Beau, soeur de Henri Beau Oil/canvas
  (29x23cm 11x9in) Montréal 1999
- 🖼 **$304** - €297 - **£187** - FF1 949
  Jaujac Watercolour/paper (16x24cm 6x9in) Montréal
  1999

BEAUBRUN Charles Bobrun 1604-1692 **[12]**
- $23 175 - €22 867 - **£14 280** - FF150 000
  Portrait de Claire-Clémence de Maillé, princesse de Condé Huile/toile (129x103cm 50x40in) Neuilly-sur-Seine 1999

BEAUBRUN Henri 1603-1677 **[6]**
- $23 175 - €22 867 - **£14 280** - FF150 000
  Portrait de Claire-Clémence de Maillé, princesse de Condé Huile/toile (129x103cm 50x40in) Neuilly-sur-Seine 1999

BEAUCÉ Jean-Adolphe 1818-1875 **[8]**
- $13 590 - €15 245 - **£9 420** - FF100 000
  Napoléon et son État-Major à la bataille de Montmirail Huile/toile (82x105cm 32x41in) Paris 2000
- $3 367 - €3 964 - **£2 366** - FF26 000
  Scène animée avec cavalier Huile/toile (34x26cm 13x10in) Valenciennes 2000

BEAUCHAMP Robert 1923-1995 **[24]**
- $400 - €473 - **£283** - FF3 100
  Becket Graphite (26x21cm 10x8in) Provincetown MA 2000

BEAUCLERK Diana 1734-1808 **[11]**
- $2 845 - €3 306 - **£2 000** - FF21 688
  The Infant Pan Pencil (32x21.5cm 12x8in) London 2001

BEAUCORPS de Gustave 1825-1906 **[52]**
- $571 - €610 - **£380** - FF4 000
  Rome: Vue de la fontaine Pauline Tirage albuminé (26.5x38cm 10x14in) Paris 2000

BEAUCOURT de François 1740-1794 **[2]**
- $2 219 - €2 043 - **£1 332** - FF13 398
  Têtes d'anges Huile/toile (28x40cm 11x15in) Montréal 2000

BEAUDIN André 1895-1979 **[267]**
- $10 628 - €11 129 - **£6 690** - FF73 000
  Les trois ponts Huile/toile (195x114cm 76x44in) Versailles 2000
- $2 334 - €2 592 - **£1 626** - FF17 000
  La porte vitrée Huile/toile (33x55cm 12x21in) Paris 1999
- $3 013 - €3 544 - **£2 161** - FF23 248
  Abstraction Öl/Leinwand (27x35.5cm 10x13in) Bern 2001
- $588 - €686 - **£413** - FF4 500
  Composition abstraite Aquarelle/papier (31x47.5cm 12x18in) Paris 2000
- $100 - €107 - **£68** - FF700
  Abstract composition Lithograph (54x47cm 21x18in) St. Petersburg FL 2001

BEAUDUIN Jean 1851-1916 **[52]**
- $2 784 - €2 975 - **£1 896** - FF19 512
  Les baigneuses Huile/toile (61x73cm 24x28in) Lokeren 2001

BEAUFOND de Inès XIX-XX **[1]**
- $35 000 - €30 196 - **£21 115** - FF198 075
  A young Girl playing a piano Oil/canvas/board (194.5x129.5cm 76x50in) New-York 1998

BEAUFORT Jacques-Antoine 1721-1784 **[1]**
- $8 349 - €7 013 - **£4 908** - FF46 000
  La présentation au temple Huile/toile (78x51cm 30x20in) Lille 1998

BEAUFRERE Adolphe-Marie 1876-1960 **[637]**
- $7 834 - €8 537 - **£5 135** - FF56 000
  Portrait de Job, marin-pêcheur sur fond de Sinagot Huile/panneau (41x43cm 16x16in) Brest 2000
- $1 661 - €1 906 - **£1 136** - FF12 500
  Bord de côte Huile/papier/toile (21x22.5cm 8x8in) Paris 2000
- $168 - €198 - **£118** - FF1 300
  L'église de Quimperlé dans la ville haute Encre/papier (10.5x8.5cm 4x3in) Brest 2000
- $141 - €152 - **£97** - FF1 000
  La chaumière au bout du chemin Eau-forte (20x11.5cm 7x4in) Quimper 2001

BEAUGUREAU Francis Henry 1920 **[7]**
- $2 100 - €2 254 - **£1 405** - FF14 786
  Little Woman of klagetoh Oil/canvas (98x74cm 38x29in) Chicago IL 2000

BEAULIEU de Anatole Henri 1819-1884 **[13]**
- $17 000 - €19 029 - **£11 855** - FF124 822
  Allegory Oil/canvas (207.5x107.5cm 81x42in) New-York 2001
- $5 954 - €6 403 - **£3 990** - FF42 000
  Guerrier combattant un serpent Huile/toile (133x85.5cm 52x33in) Paris 2000

BEAULIEU Paul-Vanier 1910-1995 **[139]**
- $2 643 - €3 085 - **£1 811** - FF20 237
  Nature morte au poisson vert Huile/toile (38x46cm 14x18in) Montréal 2000
- $1 288 - €1 513 - **£774** - FF7 294
  Winter Landscape Oil/masonite (26x30cm 10x11in) Nepean, Ont. 1998
- $912 - €788 - **£550** - FF5 169
  Nature morte aux fruits Encre (48x63.5cm 18x25in) Montréal 1998

BEAUME Émile Marie 1888-1967 **[23]**
- $3 669 - €3 354 - **£2 246** - FF22 000
  Porte de souk Gouache/papier (49x60cm 19x23in) Paris 1999

BEAUME Joseph 1796-1885 **[18]**
- $2 304 - €2 188 - **£1 412** - FF14 351
  Mädchen mit Vogelnest Öl/Leinwand (33x24.5cm 12x9in) Zürich 1999
- $1 123 - €1 323 - **£777** - FF8 679
  Le maître d'école Watercolour/paper (19.5x23cm 7x9in) Amsterdam 2000

BEAUMONT Arthur Edwaine 1890-1978 **[11]**
- $1 700 - €1 983 - **£1 183** - FF13 010
  «Shag Harbor» Watercolour/paper (40x50cm 16x20in) Altadena CA 2000

BEAUMONT Arthur J. 1877-1956 **[11]**
- $1 400 - €1 339 - **£852** - FF8 781
  Low Tide in the harbor Oil/board (27x34cm 10x13in) Boston MA 1999

BEAUMONT Claudio Francesco 1694-1766 **[16]**
- $45 000 - €46 649 - **£27 000** - FF306 000
  Caccia al cervo Tecnica mista (300x217cm 118x85in) Venezia 1999
- $40 000 - €42 718 - **£27 256** - FF280 212
  Armida enchanting Rinaldo/The Warriors in Armida's Garden Oil/canvas (87x82cm 34x32in) New-York 2001
- $750 - €777 - **£450** - FF5 100
  Studio di uomo seduto Matita/carta (23.5x33cm 9x12in) Milano 2001

BEAUMONT de Edouard Charles 1812-1888 **[41]**
- $30 000 - €31 100 - **£18 000** - FF204 000
  Allegoria delal verità svelata Olio/tela (135x185cm 53x72in) Roma 1999
- $4 448 - €4 818 - **£2 953** - FF32 000
  Le petit chaperon rouge Huile/toile (36x27cm 14x10in) Melun 2000

BEAUPUY Louis Jean 1896-1974 **[9]**
$2 339 - €2 269 - £1 472 - FF14 883
Portrait of a Girl Charcoal (61x46cm 24x18in)
Amsterdam 1999

BEAUQUESNE Wilfred Constant 1847-1913 **[75]**
$2 228 - €2 439 - £1 540 - FF16 000
Paysage orientaliste Huile/toile (38x87cm 14x34in)
Aurillac 2001
$929 - €1 037 - £648 - FF6 800
Cuirassier aux aguets Huile/panneau (25x19cm
9x7in) Versailles 2001

BEAUVAIS Walter 1942 **[34]**
$368 - €432 - £260 - FF2 836
Lady on the Balcony Oil/board (24x16cm 9x6in)
London 2000

BEAUVARLET Jacques Firmin 1731-1797 **[19]**
$187 - €183 - £118 - FF1 200
**La lecture espagnole/La conversation espagno-
le** Eau-forte (58x42cm 22x16in) Paris 1999

BEAUVERIE Charles 1839-1924 **[57]**
$14 200 - €15 245 - £9 500 - FF100 000
Tanagra Huile/toile (146x114cm 57x44in) Blangy-sur-
Bresle 2000
$2 948 - €2 515 - £1 778 - FF16 500
Gardien de troupeau Huile/toile (64x79cm 25x31in)
Saint-Étienne 1998
$536 - €579 - £370 - FF3 800
Paysage de printemps Huile/toile (19x27cm
7x10in) Lyon 2001

BEAUX Cecilia 1855-1942 **[16]**
$6 500 - €7 509 - £4 551 - FF49 257
Road in the Country Oil/board (14x21.5cm 5x8in)
New-York 2001
$3 000 - €3 345 - £2 094 - FF21 940
Marquis Cusani Confalonieri Charcoal (43x35cm
17x14in) Detroit MI 2001

BEAVIS Richard 1824-1896 **[87]**
$12 095 - €14 053 - £8 500 - FF92 180
«Incident at Waterloo» Oil/canvas (111.5x183cm
43x72in) London 2001
$1 738 - €1 920 - £1 200 - FF12 595
Bullocks on Sea Shore Oil/canvas (45.5x61cm
17x24in) Hockley, Birmingham 2001
$1 604 - €1 616 - £1 000 - FF10 603
The Charge/The Recall Oil/canvas (16x19.5cm
6x7in) London 2000
$964 - €988 - £600 - FF6 482
Horse and Donkey Grazing in a Landscape
Watercolour (44x69cm 17x27in) Billingshurst, West-
Sussex 2000

BECAN Bernard Kahn 1890-1943 **[27]**
$2 808 - €3 346 - £2 011 - FF21 951
La danseuse aux anges (Spinelly) Huile/toile
(122x84cm 48x33in) Bruxelles 2000
$1 244 - €1 190 - £780 - FF7 803
«Lucie Caffaret» Poster (76x118cm 29x46in) London
1999

BÉCAT Paul-Émile 1885-1960 **[43]**
$2 018 - €1 860 - £1 209 - FF12 203
Forest track, Ayeme, Gabon Gouache/paper
(52.5x32.5cm 20x12in) Amsterdam 1998
$69 - €76 - £47 - FF500
Poèmes d'amour Pointe sèche couleurs (25x16.5cm
9x6in) Orléans 2000

BECCAFUMI IL MECARINO Domenico 1486-1551
[19]
$670 360 - €570 367 - £400 000 - FF3 741 360
**The Holy Family with the Enfant Saint John the
Baptist, Ste Catherine** Oil/panel (61x51cm 24x20in)
London 1998
$1 305 - €1 431 - £886 - FF9 390
Der Alchemist und Vulkan Woodcut (17.5x11.5cm
6x4in) Berlin 2000

BECERRA German 1928 **[5]**
$1 666 - €1 943 - £1 216 - FF12 744
Lagernder Frauenakt Gouache/paper (24x33cm
9x12in) Köln 2001

BECHARD XX [3]
$4 602 - €4 497 - £2 917 - FF29 500
Place de Tunis Huile/toile (45x90.5cm 17x35in) Paris
1999

BÉCHARD Henri XIX **[19]**
$1 165 - €1 279 - £750 - FF8 392
No 11 Temple de Dakkeh (Nubie) Albumen print
(26x37cm 10x14in) London 2000

BECHER Hilla W. & Bernd 1934/1931 **[152]**
$156 - €174 - £108 - FF1 140
**Duisburg Meiderich/Greencastle/Kerkhangate
bei Leeds** Offset (40.5x31cm 15x12in) Heidelberg
2001
$2 397 - €2 045 - £1 446 - FF13 414
**Hochofenwerk Ilsede:
Gichtgaseinigung/Kokerei** Vintage gelatin silver
print (40.4x30.9cm 15x12in) Köln 1998

BECHI Luigi 1830-1919 **[48]**
$57 500 - €59 608 - £34 500 - FF391 000
Bambini con il gatto Olio/tela (100.5x130cm
39x51in) Milano 2000
$28 000 - €26 704 - £17 043 - FF175 165
The Apple of his Eye Oil/canvas (100.5x73.5cm
39x28in) New-York 2001

BECHSTEDT Johann Caspar 1735-1801 **[2]**
$2 289 - €2 556 - £1 466 - FF16 769
Der erlegte Bär Öl/Leinwand (43x35.5cm 16x13in)
Lindau 2001

BECHSTEIN Lothar 1884-1936 **[6]**
$1 828 - €1 815 - £1 142 - FF11 906
Still Life Oil/canvas (70x80cm 27x31in) Amsterdam
1999

BECHTEJEFF von Wladimir Georgiew. 1878-1971
[8]
$99 613 - €117 595 - £70 748 - FF771 374
Nach dem Bade Öl/Leinwand (74.5x88.5cm 29x34in)
Berlin 2001

BECHTLE Robert Alan 1932 **[27]**
$26 000 - €24 413 - £16 109 - FF160 136
67 Chrysler Oil/canvas (122x175.5cm 48x69in) New-
York 1999
$7 000 - €6 962 - £4 344 - FF45 670
Zenith Oil/canvas (91.4x101.6cm 35x40in) Beverly-
Hills CA 1999
$50 - €53 - £34 - FF349
The Artist Mugging Lithograph (41.5x51cm 16x20in)
Miami FL 2001

BECHTOLD Erwin 1925 **[13]**
$10 962 - €13 038 - £7 813 - FF85 524
Bild 89-29-Winkel Öl/Leinwand (191x168cm
75x66in) München 2000
$2 631 - €3 068 - £1 846 - FF20 123
«87-13» Acrylic (110x98cm 43x38in) Köln 2001

▥ **$216** - €240 - **£148** - FF1 576
«**Be-4**» Aguafuerte (67x49cm 26x19in) Barcelona 2001

BECHTOLSHEIM von Gustav Freiherr 1842-1924 [25]
↝ **$4 114** - €3 835 - **£2 538** - FF25 154
Am Wasser Öl/Leinwand (71x60cm 27x23in) Köln 1999
↝ **$771** - €869 - **£542** - FF5 701
Zwei Hütebuben Öl/Karton (27x40cm 10x15in) München 2001

BECK & JUNG Beckström/Ljungberg 1939/1939 [45]
↝ **$366** - €431 - **£265** - FF2 824
«**Med åtta monoliter**» Acrylic/canvas (115x98cm 45x38in) Stockholm 2001

BECK Christian Frederick 1876-1954 [34]
↝ **$650** - €563 - **£394** - FF3 690
Farm Scene Oil/canvas (48x68cm 19x27in) Mystic CT 1998

BECK Gustav Kurt 1902-1983 [7]
↝ **$6 057** - €6 541 - **£4 185** - FF42 903
«**Die Grenze**» Öl/Leinwand (60x100cm 23x39in) Wien 2001

BECK Heinrich XIX [5]
◉ **$582** - €610 - **£366** - FF4 000
Daphné temple d'Apollon Tirage albuminé (25x33.5cm 9x13in) Paris 2000

BECK Jacob Samuel 1715-1778 [20]
↝ **$7 473** - €7 158 - **£4 702** - FF46 954
Stilleben mit Blumenkohl, Möhren und einem Hasen Öl/Leinwand (45x58cm 17x22in) Köln 1999
↝ **$12 701** - €13 634 - **£8 500** - FF89 433
Crabapples in a basket, together with apples and pears Oil/canvas (26x36cm 10x14in) London 2000

BECK Julia 1853-1935 [29]
↝ **$23 936** - €26 398 - **£16 214** - FF173 162
Franskt landskap Oil/canvas (181x140cm 71x55in) Stockholm 2000
↝ **$3 108** - €3 356 - **£2 148** - FF22 011
Självporträtt Oil/canvas (50x35cm 19x13in) Stockholm 2001
↝ **$2 305** - €2 560 - **£1 543** - FF16 793
Interiörer från Gripsholms slott Oil/canvas (42x32cm 16x12in) Stockholm 2000

BECK Lucy Boyd 1916 [19]
⬍ **$1 007** - €944 - **£623** - FF6 191
Sisters Ceramic (70x121cm 27x47in) Melbourne 1999

BECK Maurice 1886-1960 [2]
▥ **$1 300** - €1 458 - **£902** - FF9 564
«**Always in Touch, London Underground**» Poster (101x62cm 40x24in) New-York 2001

BECK Otto Walter 1864-1954 [22]
✑ **$2 200** - €2 085 - **£1 374** - FF13 679
The Old Guard of New York, Third Group Pastel/paper (150x179.5cm 59x70in) Washington 1999

BECK Richard 1912-1985 [33]
▥ **$650** - €725 - **£424** - FF4 757
«**Orient Line Cruises**» Poster (97x59cm 38x23in) New-York 2000

BECK Wilhelm XIX [4]
↝ **$8 235** - €7 050 - **£4 846** - FF46 244
Berlin Scene Oil/canvas (101x152cm 40x60in) Citra FL 1998

✑ **$1 490** - €1 534 - **£939** - FF10 061
Belagerung von Strassburg Gouache/paper (100x148cm 39x58in) Berlin 2000

BECKEN van der Ignace 1689-1774 [6]
↝ **$7 000** - €6 022 - **£4 100** - FF39 500
Escena palaciega Oleo/lienzo (48.5x58cm 19x22in) Madrid 1998

BECKENKAMP Gaspar Benedikt 1747-1828 [3]
↝ **$30 620** - €34 768 - **£21 277** - FF228 065
Bildnis einer Familie im Freien Öl/Leinwand (51.5x71cm 20x27in) Köln 2001
↝ **$2 358** - €2 812 - **£1 681** - FF18 446
Prinzessin Kunigunde von Sachsen, Fürstäbtissin von Essen, zu Pferde Öl/Leinwand (35.7x43.5cm 14x17in) Köln 2000

BECKER Albert 1830-1896 [6]
↝ **$10 007** - €11 248 - **£7 026** - FF73 785
Eine kleine Attraktion Öl/Leinwand (87x148cm 34x58in) Düsseldorf 2001
↝ **$4 278** - €4 360 - **£2 676** - FF28 602
Waidmanns Töchterlein Öl/Leinwand (80x107cm 31x42in) Wien 2000

BECKER August 1822-1887 [24]
↝ **$14 021** - €13 294 - **£8 530** - FF87 201
Blick ins Inntal Öl/Leinwand (107x188.5cm 42x74in) Köln 1999
↝ **$2 678** - €2 249 - **£1 574** - FF14 755
Heroische Alpenlandschaft im Schein der Abendsonne Öl/Leinwand (79x94cm 31x37in) Köln 1998

BECKER Boris 1961 [11]
◉ **$545** - €511 - **£336** - FF3 353
Hochbunker, München Gelatin silver print (38.7x29.4cm 15x11in) Köln 1999

BECKER Carl Ludwig Fried. 1820-1900 [33]
↝ **$65 000** - €61 763 - **£39 546** - FF405 138
Othello relating his Adventures to Desdemona Oil/canvas (188x218.5cm 74x86in) New-York 1999
↝ **$2 928** - €2 907 - **£1 828** - FF19 068
Freundliche Bewirtung Oil/canvas/panel (73x49cm 28x19in) Wien 1999
↝ **$750** - €777 - **£450** - FF5 100
La raccolta della legna Olio/tela (20.5x26cm 8x10in) Vercelli 1999

BECKER Curt Georg 1904-1972 [32]
↝ **$2 966** - €2 491 - **£1 740** - FF16 085
«**Häuser in Montagnola**» Öl/Karton (47x65cm 18x25in) Radolfzell 1998
▥ **$173** - €143 - **£101** - FF938
«**Abstrakter Frauenakt**» Lithographie (75.5x54cm 29x21in) Radolfzell 1998

BECKER Edmund XVIII-XIX [4]
✎ **$569** - €503 - **£350** - FF3 297
«**Near Dolgelly**» Wash (23.5x28.5cm 9x11in) Godalming, Surrey 1999

BECKER Emelle XX [1]
↝ **$5 000** - €5 509 - **£3 335** - FF36 136
U.S.S. Constitution Oil/canvas (51x81cm 20x32in) Portsmouth NH 2000

BECKER Frederick William 1888-1974 [19]
↝ **$800** - €864 - **£552** - FF5 667
«**Aspens in Winter**» Oil/masonite (50x40cm 20x16in) Altadena CA 2001
↝ **$850** - €918 - **£587** - FF6 021
Winter Landscape- «**Taos**» Oil/canvas/board (40x30cm 16x12in) Altadena CA 2001

B

BECKER Harry 1865-1928 **[45]**
- $3 214 - €3 650 - **£2 200** - FF23 942
  Plough Horses Oil/board (38.5x48cm 15x18in) Bury St. Edmunds, Suffolk 2000
- $3 798 - €4 314 - **£2 600** - FF28 296
  Between the Shafts Oil/board (25.5x34.5cm 10x13in) Bury St. Edmunds, Suffolk 2000
- $699 - €799 - **£480** - FF5 244
  Landscape with Lane Crayon (36x55cm 14x21in) Sudbury, Suffolk 2000
- $364 - €416 - **£250** - FF2 731
  The Lane Etching (18x15cm 7x5in) Sudbury, Suffolk 2000

BECKER Johann Wilhelm 1744-1782 **[1]**
- $3 878 - €3 323 - **£2 331** - FF21 796
  Flusslandschaft Oil/panel (23.5x31cm 9x12in) Köln 1998

BECKER Ludwig 1808-1861 **[1]**
- $35 400 - €39 003 - **£23 766** - FF255 846
  First Camp from Duraodoo (Mud Plain Camp, the Search for Water) Ink (14x22.5cm 5x8in) Malvern, Victoria 2000

BECKER Peter 1828-1904 **[23]**
- $516 - €613 - **£357** - FF4 024
  Blick auf Boppard und Höhenburg Watercolour (32.3x42.8cm 12x16in) Köln 2000

BECKER von Adolf 1831-1909 **[12]**
- $5 500 - €5 279 - **£3 447** - FF34 625
  The Cobbler and his Apprentice Oil/canvas (116x90cm 45x35in) New-York 1999
- $3 805 - €4 205 - **£2 637** - FF27 580
  Nervi Oil/canvas (33x46cm 12x18in) Helsinki 2001

BECKER VON WORMS Jakob 1810-1872 **[2]**
- $27 273 - €25 609 - **£16 900** - FF167 985
  Nach dem Kirchgang, Mädchen in Schwälmer Tracht Öl/Leinwand (88.5x65cm 34x25in) Luzern 1999

BECKER Walter 1893-1984 **[25]**
- $3 990 - €3 732 - **£2 417** - FF24 483
  Drei Frauen Öl/Leinwand (71x91cm 27x35in) Stuttgart 1999

BECKERT Fritz 1877-1962 **[50]**
- $1 330 - €1 124 - **£796** - FF7 376
  Eissen Oil/panel (74x50cm 29x19in) Berlin 1998
- $109 - €102 - **£67** - FF670
  In einem alten Städtchen Farblithographie (55.3x75.7cm 21x29in) Heidelberg 1999

BECKETT Clarice Marjoribanks 1887-1935 **[67]**
- $15 630 - €18 588 - **£11 139** - FF121 929
  Out Strolling Oil/canvas/board (49.5x50cm 19x19in) Melbourne 2000
- $8 766 - €9 635 - **£5 617** - FF63 204
  Foggy Morn Oil/board (40.5x30.5cm 15x12in) Melbourne 2000

BECKMAN Ford 1952 **[18]**
- $5 000 - €4 805 - **£3 080** - FF31 519
  White Painting, mon jardinet #4 Mixed media/panel (162.5x128.5cm 63x50in) New-York 1999

BECKMANN Anders 1907-1967 **[5]**
- $167 - €191 - **£116** - FF1 102
  «Zweden» Poster (61x100cm 24x39in) Hoorn 2001

BECKMANN Hannes 1909-1977 **[8]**
- $8 494 - €9 983 - **£5 889** - FF65 485
  Summer Landscape with Figures in a Boat Oil/canvas (65x98cm 25x38in) Amsterdam 2000

BECKMANN Max 1884-1950 **[1132]**
- $3 500 000 - €3 920 257 - **£2 431 800** - FF25 715 200
  Perseus', Herkule's Letzte Aufgabe, Perseus's Hercules' Last Duty Oil/canvas (89.5x142cm 35x55in) New-York 2001
- $530 176 - €494 369 - **£320 000** - FF3 242 848
  Still Life with Violin and Flute Oil/canvas (50x75cm 19x29in) London 2001
- $20 420 - €24 107 - **£14 503** - FF158 131
  Portrait einer jungen Frau Öl/Metall (25x19.5cm 9x7in) Berlin 2001
- $230 000 - €257 617 - **£159 804** - FF1 689 856
  Adam und Eve Bronze (H86.5cm H34in) New-York 2001
- $20 920 - €24 602 - **£15 000** - FF161 379
  Kopf Bronze (H13cm H5in) London 2001
- $20 368 - €22 344 - **£13 835** - FF146 565
  Frauenportrait Pencil/paper (33x23.7cm 12x9in) Berlin 2000
- $2 576 - €2 930 - **£1 800** - FF19 219
  Stephan Lackner, Der Mensch ist kein Haustier Lithograph (23x14.5cm 9x5in) London 2000

BECKMANN Wilhelm 1852-1942 **[5]**
- $26 504 - €24 535 - **£16 000** - FF160 942
  The Surrender of the City Oil/canvas (206x267cm 81x105in) London 1999

BECKMANN-TUBE Minna 1881-1964 **[2]**
- $1 972 - €2 301 - **£1 385** - FF15 092
  Jünglingsporträt Oil/panel (40x30cm 15x11in) Köln 2000

BECKWITH James Carroll 1852-1917 **[44]**
- $2 200 - €2 579 - **£1 582** - FF16 920
  Portrait of the Artist's Mother Oil/canvas (54.5x48.5cm 21x19in) New-York 2001
- $15 000 - €15 548 - **£9 511** - FF101 991
  Brunette combing her Hair Oil/canvas (40.5x25.5cm 15x10in) New-York 2000
- $9 500 - €8 771 - **£5 842** - FF57 531
  Peasant against Hay Watercolour, gouache/paper (51x35cm 20x13in) New-York 1999

BECQUER Joaquín 1805-1841 **[4]**
- $9 758 - €8 428 - **£5 882** - FF55 284
  Jour de fête à Séville Huile/toile (50.5x65cm 19x25in) Bruxelles 1999

BECQUEREL André Vincent XIX-XX **[76]**
- $1 541 - €1 403 - **£963** - FF9 200
  Couple de vieux Bronze (H37cm H14in) Toulouse 1999

BECX Johannes c.1630-c.1700 **[2]**
- $11 988 - €13 613 - **£8 205** - FF89 298
  Naval Engagement Oil/panel (90.5x125.5cm 35x49in) Amsterdam 2000

BEDA Francesco 1840-1900 **[21]**
- $20 000 - €17 255 - **£12 066** - FF113 186
  The Ring Oil/canvas (63.5x92.5cm 25x36in) New-York 1998

BEDA Giulio 1879-1954 **[11]**
- $1 361 - €1 534 - **£957** - FF10 061
  Fischerboote in der Lagune Öl/Leinwand (66x132cm 25x51in) München 2001

BEDARD Jean-Claude 1928 **[58]**
- $341 - €381 - **£238** - FF2 500
  Composition ocre, brun, noir Huile/toile (60x81cm 23x31in) Evreux 2001

BEDDINGTON Maud XIX-XX **[2]**
$7 959 - €6 890 - £4 800 - FF45 197
The Song of the Wind Oil/canvas (44x242cm 17x95in) London 1998

BEDEL Marie-Augustin XIX-XX **[2]**
$666 - €747 - £464 - FF4 900
Visite à la jument et son poulain Aquarelle, gouache/papier (27x37.5cm 10x14in) Soissons 2001

BEDFORD Ella M. XIX-XX **[2]**
$3 580 - €4 328 - £2 500 - FF28 389
The Village Gossips Oil/canvas (83x62.5cm 32x24in) Cirencester, Gloucesterhire 2000

BEDFORD Francis 1816-1894 **[16]**
$437 - €381 - £264 - FF2 500
Le yacht «Osborne» à Ithica et vue du Parthénon Tirage albuminé (18x27cm 7x10in) Paris 1998

BEDFORD Francis Donkin 1864-1954 **[5]**
$773 - €730 - £480 - FF4 787
A Corner of the Artist's Studio, Ladbroke Square Watercolour (20.5x13cm 8x5in) Billingshurst, West-Sussex 1999

BEDFORD Paddy c.1922 **[5]**
$2 463 - €2 636 - £1 622 - FF17 289
Untitled Mixed media (91x183.5cm 35x72in) Woollahra, Sydney 2001

BEDIA VALDÉS José 1959 **[47]**
$20 000 - €23 548 - £14 054 - FF154 468
Ixtli Yolotl Acrylic/canvas (256.5x175.5cm 100x69in) New-York 2000
$19 000 - €18 295 - £11 825 - FF120 009
Las cosas que hacen falta Oil/canvas (59.5x177.5cm 23x69in) New-York 1999
$6 000 - €5 823 - £3 735 - FF38 199
Mayimbe Tempera/paper (69x100cm 27x39in) New-York 1999

BEDIL Dewil Putu 1921 **[15]**
$7 460 - €8 471 - £5 106 - FF55 569
Fruit market Tempera (136x101cm 53x39in) Singapore 2000
$1 800 - €1 728 - £1 115 - FF11 338
Market Scene Mixed media (127x88cm 50x35in) Chicago IL 1999

BEDINI Paolo 1844-1924 **[12]**
$14 989 - €13 911 - £9 000 - FF91 252
A Cardinal in his Study Oil/canvas (40x43cm 15x16in) London 1999
$17 601 - €17 475 - £11 000 - FF114 627
Winding the Skein Oil/panel (32.5x23.5cm 12x9in) London 1999
$804 - €922 - £550 - FF6 051
At her Leisure Watercolour/paper (25x13cm 9x5in) Edinburgh 2000

BEE John Francis 1895-? **[2]**
$2 258 - €2 619 - £1 600 - FF17 177
«Cornwall, GWR, Monthly Return Tickets, Any Day, Any Train, Anywhere» Poster (102x64cm 40x25in) London 2000

BEECHEY Richard Brydges 1808-1895 **[19]**
$8 876 - €10 158 - £6 104 - FF66 632
A Wooded River Landscape with Figures and Cattle Oil/canvas (50x76cm 20x30in) Dublin 2000
$22 000 - €22 162 - £13 714 - FF145 420
The H.M.S Defense engaging the San. Ildefonso Oil/canvas (27x39.5cm 10x15in) New-York 2000

BEECHEY William 1753-1839 **[75]**
$324 920 - €316 143 - £200 000 - FF2 073 760
Archdeacon Strachey and his Family (his Wife seated,6 children around) Oil/canvas (140x183cm 55x72in) London 1999
$10 427 - €10 507 - £6 500 - FF68 923
Portrait of a Young Girl, Three-Quarter Length Oil/canvas (60.5x50.5cm 23x19in) London 2000
$6 173 - €6 007 - £3 800 - FF39 401
Lady Frances Herbert, Lady Ducie (1775-1830), wearing a white Dress Oil/canvas (29x23.5cm 11x9in) London 1999

BEECQ van Jan Karel Donatus 1638-1722 **[4]**
$6 246 - €6 975 - £4 400 - FF45 755
The Morning Gun Oil/canvas (56x84cm 22x33in) London 2000

BEECROFT Vanessa 1969 **[59]**
$12 000 - €13 923 - £8 284 - FF91 332
Blue Acrylic (150x99.5cm 59x39in) New-York 2000
$8 000 - €8 945 - £5 392 - FF58 675
Portrait of a Woman Oil/canvas (101.5x101.5cm 39x39in) New-York 2000
$2 800 - €3 628 - £2 100 - FF23 800
Senza titolo Collage (80x60cm 31x23in) Milano 2001
$12 981 - €15 257 - £9 000 - FF100 080
V.B 35, Performance Detail-Solomon R.Guggenheim Museum, New York Photograph in colour (95x125cm 37x49in) London 2000

BEEK van Bernard Antoine 1875-1941 **[40]**
$1 367 - €1 168 - £827 - FF7 662
On the Maas Huile/toile (40.5x73.5cm 15x28in) Montréal 1998
$675 - €726 - £460 - FF4 762
In den Polder Oil/board (28x21cm 11x8in) Amsterdam 2001
$427 - €363 - £257 - FF2 378
Rivierlandschap met afgemeerd vissersschip Watercolour/paper (46.5x65cm 18x25in) Den Haag 1998

BEEK van der Harmsen XX **[116]**
$989 - €862 - £598 - FF5 657
Noddy Pulled it on his Head, and it Fitted! Watercolour (8x12cm 3x4in) London 1998

BEEK van der Theodor 1838-1921 **[8]**
$688 - €818 - £476 - FF5 366
Italienerin, auf dem Heimweg ausruhend Öl/Leinwand (61.5x50cm 24x19in) Bremen 2000
$3 070 - €3 068 - £1 920 - FF20 123
Die Brautschuhe Öl/Leinwand (35.5x43cm 13x16in) Köln 2000

BEEK van Juriaen Marinus 1879-1965 **[45]**
$1 057 - €1 134 - £707 - FF7 441
Fishingboat on a rough sea Oil/canvas (61.5x100cm 24x39in) Amsterdam 2000
$148 - €172 - £102 - FF1 131
Bloemstilleven Oil/panel (17x23cm 6x9in) Rotterdam 2000

BEEK van Sam 1878-1957 **[9]**
$327 - €318 - £204 - FF2 083
Heron Watercolour/paper (32x24cm 12x9in) Amsterdam 1999

BEEKE Anthon 1940 **[16]**
$71 - €82 - £50 - FF55
«Holland Festival» Poster (59x82cm 23x32in) Hoorn 2001

BEEKMAN Chris Hendrik 1887-1964 **[28]**
$164 - €145 - £99 - FF951
Milkmaid Etching (143x253cm 56x99in) Amsterdam 1998

BEELDEMAKER Adriaen Cornelisz. 1618-1709 **[48]**
$2 400 - €2 788 - £1 686 - FF18 290
A Man, a Boy and two Dogs returning from the Hunt Oil/canvas (45.5x59.5cm 17x23in) New-York 2001

BEELER Joe Neil 1931 **[31]**
$9 000 - €10 219 - £6 253 - FF67 032
Hill Country Cowboys Oil/canvas (60x91cm 24x36in) Dallas TX 2001
$2 500 - €2 839 - £1 737 - FF18 620
The Storytellers Bronze (H17cm H7in) Dallas TX 2001
$1 800 - €2 112 - £1 270 - FF13 856
Seated cowboy Charcoal/paper (40x30cm 15x11in) New-York 2000
$2 000 - €2 350 - £1 386 - FF15 418
Two Cowboys Etching (20.5x24.5cm 8x9in) Beverly-Hills CA 2000

BEELT Cornelis c.1660-c.1700 **[18]**
$15 071 - €12 831 - £9 000 - FF84 168
The Beach at Scheveningen Oil/canvas (97x143cm 38x56in) London 1998
$10 906 - €10 174 - £6 580 - FF66 738
Holländische Strandlandschaft mit vielen Figuren und einem Turm Oil/panel (40x61cm 15x24in) Wien 1999

BEENFELDT Ulrik Ferdinand 1714-1782 **[6]**
$35 140 - €37 521 - £23 940 - FF246 120
Det Fengerske familieportraet Oil/canvas (185x232cm 72x91in) Vejle 2001

BEER Andrew 1862-1954 **[16]**
$581 - €641 - £380 - FF4 206
No Wonder/No Fluke Oil/canvas (26.5x39cm 10x15in) London 2000

BEER de Jan c.1480-c.1536 **[2]**
$41 840 - €44 912 - £28 000 - FF294 604
The Emperor Heraclius Beheading the Persian King Chosroe Oil/panel (24x42.5cm 9x16in) London 2000

BEER Dick 1893-1938 **[32]**
$529 - €610 - £365 - FF3 999
Gränd i Sydfrankrike Oil/canvas/panel (44x38cm 17x14in) Stockholm 2000
$897 - €843 - £555 - FF5 532
Franskt landskap Oil/panel (30.5x39.5cm 12x15in) Stockholm 1999

BEER J.D. XVIII **[1]**
$14 382 - €13 613 - £8 943 - FF89 298
Dutch Whalers hunting a Polar Bear in Greenland Oil/panel (69.5x92.5cm 27x36in) Amsterdam 1999

BEER John act.1885-1915 **[61]**
$772 - €919 - £550 - FF6 026
Ard Patrick wins the Princess of Wales Stakes by 3 lengths, Newmarket Watercolour (26.5x37cm 10x14in) London 2000

BEER Sidney James 1875-1952 **[44]**
$74 - €80 - £50 - FF526
Falmouth Harbour Watercolour/paper (12x25cm 5x10in) Par, Cornwall 2000

BEER Wilhelm Amandeus 1837-1907 **[21]**
$542 - €511 - £337 - FF3 353
Olga in russischer Tracht Aquarell/Papier (23x17cm 9x6in) Frankfurt 1999

BEERBOHM Max 1872-1956 **[112]**
$1 811 - €1 702 - £1 100 - FF11 164
Mr Benjamin Ink (29.5x18cm 11x7in) London 1999

BEERENDONK Theo 1905-1979 **[23]**
$53 - €59 - £36 - FF387
Woman sitting on a Chair Etching (31x26cm 12x10in) Haarlem 2000

BEERNAERT Euphrosine 1831-1901 **[16]**
$1 664 - €1 983 - £1 192 - FF13 008
Femme se promenant Huile/toile (92x96cm 36x37in) Antwerpen 2000

BEERNAERT Jacques XVIII **[4]**
$17 040 - €18 294 - £11 400 - FF120 000
Le passage des fortifications/Le camp devant la ville assiégée Huile/toile (65x81.5cm 25x32in) Paris 2000

BEERS Julie Hart 1835-1913 **[5]**
$21 000 - €24 814 - £14 882 - FF162 766
A Walk in the Mountains Oil/canvas (32x51.5cm 12x20in) Boston MA 2000
$2 400 - €2 801 - £1 694 - FF18 374
Birch Study Oil/paper (20x13cm 8x5in) New-York 2000

BEERS van Jan 1852-1927 **[91]**
$4 480 - €4 958 - £3 120 - FF32 520
De droom - De eenzaamheid (Le rêve - La solitude) Huile/toile (55x100cm 21x39in) Antwerpen 2001
$784 - €665 - £468 - FF4 362
Badevergnügen Oil/panel (9.8x14cm 3x5in) Bremen 1998

BEERSTRATEN Abraham 1639-c.1665 **[8]**
$22 234 - €21 148 - £13 500 - FF138 722
Italianate Harbour Scene with Figures on the Shore Oil/canvas (63x76.5cm 24x30in) London 1999

BEERSTRATEN Anthonie 1637-c.1665 **[6]**
$45 603 - €51 796 - £32 000 - FF339 760
Village in Winter, with Villagers on a frozen waterway Oil/panel (76x110cm 29x43in) London 2001

BEERSTRATEN Jan Abrahamsz. 1622-1666 **[34]**
$32 226 - €31 648 - £20 000 - FF207 598
The Battle of Scheveningen (Ter Heide), 10 August Oil/canvas (127x196.5cm 50x77in) London 1999
$20 932 - €17 821 - £12 500 - FF116 901
A Rocky Coastal Landscape with a Fortified Town and Figures Oil/panel (86x100.5cm 33x39in) London 1998
$5 230 - €5 614 - £3 500 - FF36 825
View of the Fortified Gate and Walls of a Riverside Town Wash (11.5x14cm 4x5in) London 2000

BEERT Osias I c.1570-1623/24 **[20]**
$368 520 - €412 782 - £250 000 - FF2 707 675
Apples, Peaches and Pears in a Wan-li Porcelain Dish, Red Grapes Oil/panel (51.5x66cm 20x25in) London 2000

BEERTS Albert XX **[7]**
$220 - €251 - £153 - FF1 646
«Une entrée sensationnelle» Affiche couleur (40x60cm 15x23in) Sion 2000

B

BEEST van Albert 1820-1860 **[23]**
- $13 000 - €14 773 - **£8 977** - FF96 903
  Dutch fishing Vessels bringing in the Catch
  Oil/canvas (127x183cm 50x72in) New-York 2000
- $5 000 - €5 038 - **£3 117** - FF33 050
  Dutch Ship Sailing Out Oil/canvas (56x75cm
  22x29in) New-York 2001
- $592 - €544 - **£366** - FF3 571
  A boat heading for the Coast of Malta Pencil
  (51x63cm 20x24in) Amsterdam 1999

BEEST van Sybrand 1610-1674 **[7]**
- $15 000 - €13 040 - **£9 078** - FF85 539
  Fish Market Oil/canvas (72.5x96.5cm 28x37in) New-
  York 1999
- $10 607 - €10 379 - **£6 800** - FF68 083
  Market Scene Oil/panel (32.5x45cm 12x17in) London
  1999

BEETHAM William c.1810-c.1860 **[3]**
- $4 257 - €3 894 - **£2 600** - FF25 540
  **Portrait of Jane Bell (1816-1888),in a White
  Dress, a Landscape beyond** Oil/canvas (76x63.5cm
  29x25in) London 1998

BEETZ-CHARPENTIER Elisa XIX-XX **[5]**
- $1 500 - €1 534 - **£940** - FF10 061
  Child Wearing a Hooded Cloak Bronze (H45cm
  H17in) Washington 2000

BEEVER van Emanuelus Samson 1876-1912 **[18]**
- $775 - €726 - **£482** - FF4 762
  Little Girl Playing with a Cat Oil/panel (16x21cm
  6x8in) Amsterdam 1999

BEFANIO Gennaro 1866-? **[10]**
- $7 500 - €6 496 - **£4 599** - FF42 611
  Little Girl in White Oil/canvas (115.5x89.5cm
  45x35in) New-York 1999
- $6 957 - €6 441 - **£4 200** - FF42 247
  The Parasol Oil/canvas (41.5x33.5cm 16x13in)
  London 1999

BEGA Cornelis Pietersz. 1631-1664 **[88]**
- $6 254 - €5 938 - **£3 833** - FF38 954
  Interieur einer Taverne Huile/panneau (48x40cm
  18x15in) Zürich 1999
- $8 000 - €9 422 - **£5 532** - FF61 807
  Peasants in a Tavern Oil/panel (37x30.5cm 14x12in)
  New-York 2000
- $3 154 - €2 721 - **£1 903** - FF17 851
  Standing woman Red chalk/paper (25.1x12.2cm
  9x4in) Amsterdam 1998
- $279 - €307 - **£190** - FF2 012
  Der Mann mit der Hand im Mantel Radierung
  (5.7x5.8cm 2x2in) Berlin 2000

BEGARAT Eugène 1943 **[241]**
- $1 270 - €1 067 - **£746** - FF7 000
  Lumières du soir Huile/toile (46x55cm 18x21in)
  Thonon-les-Bains 1998
- $406 - €457 - **£279** - FF3 000
  Lumières du matin Huile/toile (46x27cm 18x10in)
  Albi 2000

BEGAS Adalbert Franz Eugen 1836-1888 **[14]**
- $6 525 - €7 158 - **£4 432** - FF46 954
  Flötespielender Hirtenjunge Öl/Leinwand
  (51x87.5cm 20x34in) Düsseldorf 2000

BEGAS Karl Joseph 1794-1854 **[12]**
- $14 409 - €16 361 - **£10 012** - FF107 324
  Die Kinder der Bonner Familie Simrock
  Öl/Leinwand (81x104cm 31x40in) Köln 2001

BEGAS Oskar 1828-1883 **[10]**
- $9 622 - €11 164 - **£6 643** - FF73 232
  Mutterglück (Caritas) Öl/Leinwand (111x90.5cm
  43x35in) Luzern 2000

BEGAS Reinhold 1831-1911 **[14]**
- $1 966 - €1 841 - **£1 218** - FF12 074
  Stehender weiblicher Akt Bronze (24x11x6cm
  9x4x2in) Heidelberg 1999

BEGAS-PARMENTIER von Luise 1850-1920 **[16]**
- $1 823 - €1 789 - **£1 130** - FF11 738
  Bergdorf, wohl in Südtirol Oil/panel (60x47cm
  23x18in) München 1999
- $2 817 - €3 270 - **£1 944** - FF21 451
  Strandansicht von Venedig Oil/panel (26x46cm
  10x18in) Wien 2000

BÉGAUD Albert Pierre XIX-XX **[13]**
- $7 360 - €7 013 - **£4 664** - FF46 000
  Jeune fille à la rose Huile/toile (55x46cm 21x18in)
  Biarritz 1999

BEGAY Harrison 1917 **[39]**
- $700 - €748 - **£476** - FF4 906
  Navajo Fire Dance Ceremony Painting (56x48cm
  22x19in) Cloudcroft NM 2001
- $400 - €427 - **£272** - FF2 803
  Navajo Boy, Colt & Dog Acrylic (34x25cm 13x10in)
  Cloudcroft NM 2001
- $475 - €523 - **£317** - FF3 433
  Girls on Horseback with a Dog Watercolour/paper
  (43x39cm 17x15in) St. Ignatius MT 2000

BEGEER Piet 1890-1955 **[6]**
- $520 - €545 - **£399** - FF35 719
  Paaschstemming Oil/board (18.5x23.5cm 7x9in)
  Amsterdam 1999

BEGEYN Abraham Jansz. 1637-1697 **[52]**
- $7 193 - €8 181 - **£5 025** - FF53 662
  Südliche Landschaft mit Hirten und Herde
  Öl/Leinwand (80x96cm 31x37in) München 2000
- $3 215 - €3 018 - **£1 985** - FF19 800
  Troupeau dans un paysage Huile/toile (35x40.5cm
  13x15in) Paris 1999

BEGGARSTAFF BROTHERS J. Pryde/W.Nicholson
XIX-XX **[9]**
- $4 495 - €4 726 - **£2 821** - FF31 000
  «Rowntrees Elect Cocoa» Affiche (101x75cm
  39x29in) Lyon 2000

BEGGROV Alexander Pavlovich 1841-1914 **[17]**
- $178 563 - €171 606 - **£110 000** - FF1 125 663
  **The Official Visit of the President of France,
  Emile Loubet, 7th May** Oil/canvas (93x132.5cm
  36x52in) London 1999
- $57 452 - €63 385 - **£38 000** - FF415 777
  **View of the Stock Exchange, The Rostral
  Columns and the Admiralty** Oil/canvas
  (75.5x134cm 29x52in) London 2000
- $1 849 - €2 149 - **£1 300** - FF14 097
  View of Treport Oil/canvas (25x41cm 9x16in) London
  2001
- $5 684 - €6 647 - **£3 994** - FF43 600
  Ansicht von St.Petersburg Aquarell/Papier
  (42x61cm 16x24in) München 2000

BEGHIN Gabrielle XIX-XX **[1]**
- $2 480 - €2 403 - **£1 560** - FF15 760
  Retrato de Anne Charlotte Corday D. Armont
  Pintura (44.5x30cm 17x11in) Madrid 1999

BEGLIA Charles 1887-1963 **[8]**
📖 **$305** - €335 - **£207** - FF2 200
«Menton» Affiche couleur (98x61cm 38x24in) Paris 2000

BÉGO Charles 1918-1983 **[87]**
✏ **$77** - €84 - **£53** - FF550
Montparnasse Aquarelle, gouache/papier (32x42cm 12x16in) Melun 2001

BEGOU Alain 1945 **[7]**
🔨 **$2 016** - €1 707 - **£1 211** - FF11 200
Vase méplat à panse rectangulaire Sculpture verre (H39cm H15in) Paris 1998

BEGROW Alexander 1841-1914 **[2]**
🔨 **$4 506** - €5 045 - **£3 129** - FF33 096
Low tide Oil/board (15.5x23.5cm 6x9in) Helsinki 2001

BÉGUYER DE CHANCOURTOIS René Louis Maurice 1757-1817 **[12]**
✏ **$2 331** - €2 211 - **£1 418** - FF14 500
Sans titre Aquarelle, gouache (49x69cm 19x27in) La Baule 1999

BEHAM Barthel 1502-1540 **[36]**
📖 **$343** - €409 - **£244** - FF2 683
Judith Kupferstich (8.5x6.6cm 3x2in) Berlin 2000

BEHAM Hans Sebald 1500-1550 **[300]**
📖 **$381** - €434 - **£266** - FF2 850
Lichas bringt Herkules das Nesseusgewand Kupferstich (5x7.5cm 1x2in) Berlin 2001

BEHAN John 1938 **[10]**
🔨 **$3 010** - €3 303 - **£2 000** - FF21 666
Torah Scholar Bronze (H48cm H18in) London 2000
📖 **$136** - €152 - **£92** - FF999
Seated Woman Screenprint (56x36cm 22x14in) Dublin 2000

BEHEIM Johann XVIII **[1]**
📖 **$3 055** - €2 965 - **£1 902** - FF19 452
Die heiligen Franziskus, Sebastian und Katharina von Siena Radierung (44.6x28.9cm 17x11in) Berlin 1999

BEHEL Henri XIX-XX **[3]**
🔨 **$2 594** - €2 592 - **£1 621** - FF17 000
«Automobiles & Cycles Georges Richard» Affiche (190x122cm 74x48in) Orléans 1999

BEHLER Will XX **[5]**
🔨 **$475** - €510 - **£318** - FF3 347
View of Farm Landscape Oil/canvas (50x76cm 20x30in) Hatfield PA 2000

BEHM Karl 1858-1905 **[10]**
🔨 **$4 700** - €4 602 - **£2 892** - FF30 185
Holländische Vergnügungen, auf einem zuge-frorenen Kanal Öl/Leinwand (83x107cm 32x42in) Stuttgart 1999

BEHM Wilhelm 1859-1934 **[76]**
🔨 **$585** - €689 - **£424** - FF4 518
Vinterlandskap med faluröd stuga Oil/canvas (92x105cm 36x41in) Stockholm 2001
🔨 **$272** - €279 - **£168** - FF1 828
Landskap i månsken Oil/panel (15x22cm 5x8in) Stockholm 2000

BEHMER Marcus 1879-1958 **[40]**
✏ **$136** - €153 - **£95** - FF1 006
«Der Zweifel» Ink (13.5x13cm 5x5in) Berlin 2001

BEHN Fritz 1878-1972 **[32]**
🔨 **$1 920** - €1 789 - **£1 160** - FF11 738
Sitzender Panther Bronze (H29cm H11in) Zwiesel 1999

BEHN von Andreas Norvagus 1650-c.1713 **[3]**
✏ **$1 755** - €1 671 - **£1 098** - FF10 959
Sovande Venus vid Cupido och Satyr Mixed media/paper (10x14cm 3x5in) Stockholm 1999

BEHNES William 1795-1864 **[8]**
🔨 **$1 350** - €1 441 - **£900** - FF9 452
Bust of Gentleman with Short Curly Hair and Furrowed Brow Marble (H77cm H30in) Leyburn, North Yorkshire 2000

BEHR Carel Jacobus 1812-1895 **[11]**
🔨 **$2 400** - €2 237 - **£1 450** - FF14 673
A Part of a Dutch Port Oil/board (39x49cm 15x19in) New-Orleans LA 1999
🔨 **$4 103** - €4 724 - **£2 800** - FF30 987
Morning on the Canal Oil/canvas (34x42cm 13x16in) London 2000

BEHREND-CORINTH Charlotte 1880-1967 **[7]**
✏ **$809** - €920 - **£561** - FF6 037
Narzissen und Tulpen in einer Vase Watercolour (52.5x33.5cm 20x13in) Berlin 2000

BEHRENS Peter 1868-1940 **[42]**
📖 **$423** - €511 - **£295** - FF3 353
Der Kuss Woodcut in colors (19x15cm 7x5in) Köln 2000

BEHRMAN Adolf, Abraham 1876-1942 **[26]**
🔨 **$1 467** - €1 585 - **£1 014** - FF10 398
Barques au bord Huile/carton (34.5x62.5cm 13x24in) Warszawa 2001

BEICH Joachim Franz 1665-1748 **[66]**
🔨 **$6 706** - €5 667 - **£4 000** - FF37 174
Mountainous, River Landscape with Fishermen and Cattle Beneath Falls Oil/canvas (140.5x134.5cm 55x52in) London 1998
🔨 **$2 723** - €2 744 - **£1 697** - FF18 000
Christus mit Schülern in einer Landschaft Öl/Leinwand (61x50cm 24x19in) Zürich 2000
🔨 **$1 661** - €1 789 - **£1 122** - FF11 738
Gebirgslandschaft Öl/Leinwand (32.5x40cm 12x15in) München 2001
📖 **$226** - €204 - **£139** - FF1 341
Hirte mit Herde/Wassertträgerin/Zwei Fischer unter Bäumen/Badende Radierung (17.5x15cm 6x5in) Lindau 1999

BEIGEL John XIX **[1]**
🔨 **$100 000** - €85 439 - **£60 030** - FF560 440
Field flowers Oil/canvas (61x51cm 24x20in) New-York 1998

BEINASCHI Giovan Battista 1636-1688 **[31]**
🔨 **$7 951** - €9 259 - **£5 500** - FF60 738
Saint Peter Repentant Oil/canvas (171x121.5cm 67x47in) London 2000
✏ **$1 500** - €1 555 - **£900** - FF10 200
Re Saul lancia uno strale a Davide Inchiostro (28.5x41cm 11x16in) Milano 2001

BEINKE Fritz 1842-1907 **[43]**
🔨 **$3 925** - €4 397 - **£2 727** - FF28 843
Schäfer und Herde beim Aufbruch vom Hof Öl/Leinwand (40x50cm 15x19in) Oersberg-bei Kappeln 2001
🔨 **$2 536** - €2 812 - **£1 761** - FF18 446
Kammerdiener mit einem Probierglas am Buffet Öl/Leinwand (44x33.5cm 17x13in) Köln 2001

BEISCHLÄGER Emil 1897-c.1976 **[39]**
🔨 **$996** - €1 163 - **£704** - FF7 627
Stilleben mit Krug und Äpfel Öl/Leinwand (55x60cm 21x23in) Salzburg 2000

$1 153 - €1 163 - £720 - FF7 627
Blumen Öl/Leinwand (40x36cm 15x14in) Wien 2000

BEITHAN Emil 1878-1955 **[8]**
$2 538 - €3 068 - £1 771 - FF20 123
Schwälmer Mädchen auf einer Truhe sitzend beim Stricken Watercolour (30.5x24.5cm 12x9in) Bad-Vilbel 2000

BEJAR NOVELLA Pablo Antonio 1869-1920 **[2]**
$12 200 - €12 013 - £7 490 - FF78 800
Full-length portrait of woman in white wearing large plumed hat Oil/canvas (197x112cm 77x44in) Madrid 1999

BEJEMARK Karl Göte 1922-2000 **[7]**
$773 - €651 - £456 - FF4 273
Nils Ferlin Bronze (H20.5cm H8in) Stockholm 1998

BÉJOT Eugène 1867-1931 **[60]**
$2 284 - €2 134 - £1 409 - FF14 000
Paris, la Place Vendôme Huile/panneau (23x30cm 9x11in) Le Touquet 1999
$137 - €118 - £82 - FF771
«Quai de Béthune, Paris» Radierung (18x20.5cm 7x8in) München 1998

BEKHTEYEV Vladimir Georgievich 1878-1971 **[3]**
$7 365 - €7 036 - £4 637 - FF46 156
The Picnic Oil/panel (55x66cm 22x26in) Vancouver, BC. 1999

BEKLEMISCHEFF Sergei Vasilevich 1870-1920 **[1]**
$8 644 - €9 076 - £5 450 - FF59 532
The People's Revolt Oil/canvas (40.5x50.5cm 15x19in) Amsterdam 2000

BEKSINSKI Zdzislaw 1929 **[18]**
$4 994 - €5 525 - £3 470 - FF36 244
«Qz» Huile/panneau (132.5x98cm 52x38in) Warszawa 2001
$11 556 - €9 900 - £6 948 - FF64 940
Sans titre Oil/panel (72.5x60.2cm 28x23in) Warszawa 1998
$1 993 - €2 313 - £1 376 - FF15 173
Visage Crayon/papier (97.5x67.5cm 38x26in) Warszawa 2000

BÉLAIR de Pierre Mitiffiot 1892-1956 **[9]**
$5 568 - €6 411 - £3 800 - FF42 054
The surprise Meeting Oil/canvas (120.5x84.5cm 47x33in) London 2000

BELANGER Louis 1736-1816 **[56]**
$15 536 - €17 655 - £10 912 - FF115 808
Landskap med figurer Oil/canvas (117x167cm 46x65in) Stockholm 2001
$3 506 - €3 049 - £2 114 - FF20 000
Paysage avec torrent Aquarelle, gouache (34.5x49cm 13x19in) Paris 1998

BELANYI Victor 1877-1955 **[24]**
$5 469 - €5 164 - £3 400 - FF33 871
Portrait of a Boy, standing half-Length, in a white Shirt and Shorts Oil/canvas (120x99cm 47x38in) London 1999

BELARSKI Rudolph 1900-1983 **[2]**
$3 750 - €4 371 - £2 596 - FF28 674
Señorita Doing Mexican Hat Dance as Admiring Cowboy Lights Up Oil/canvas (86x60cm 34x24in) New-York 2000

BELAY de Pierre 1890-1947 **[1034]**
$13 472 - €12 501 - £8 232 - FF82 000
Port en Bretagne Huile/toile (95x159cm 37x62in) Paris 1999

$5 538 - €5 946 - £3 705 - FF39 000
Saint-Tropez, le vieux port Huile/toile (50x61cm 19x24in) Cheverny 2000
$3 360 - €3 201 - £2 129 - FF21 000
Au Jardin du Luxembourg Huile/carton (27x35cm 10x13in) Douarnenez 1999
$602 - €717 - £429 - FF4 700
La lecture, Hélène Aquarelle (36x22cm 14x8in) Brest 2000
$217 - €259 - £155 - FF1 700
Marins au café Eau-forte (15x20cm 5x7in) Brest 2000

BELCAMP van Jan c.1620-c.1660 **[1]**
$4 482 - €4 812 - £3 000 - FF31 564
Portrait of a Lady, said to be Lady Halifax, wearing a white Dress Oil/canvas (66x52.5cm 25x20in) London 2000

BELCHER George Frederick A. 1875-1947 **[39]**
$237 - €245 - £150 - FF1 610
Christmas comes by Once a Year Crayon (38x34cm 15x13in) Dorchester, Dorset 2000

BELDER de Jozef, Jef 1871-1927 **[28]**
$1 201 - €1 289 - £816 - FF8 455
Nature morte aux pêches et aux fleurs Huile/toile (63x86cm 24x33in) Bruxelles 2001

BELEYS Colette 1911-1998 **[497]**
$216 - €244 - £152 - FF1 610
Les dunes et les fleurs à Noordwijk Huile/panneau (38x55cm 14x21in) Paris 2001
$184 - €183 - £115 - FF1 200
Coin de jardin: Tyrol Huile/toile (22x27cm 8x10in) Paris 1999

BELGRANO José Denis 1844-1917 **[21]**
$3 200 - €3 399 - £2 110 - FF22 296
Maiden and Cavalier in a Garden Oil/canvas (49x34cm 19x13in) Cleveland OH 2001
$5 400 - €4 516 - £3 225 - FF29 625
Al paseo/Galanteo en la plaza Oleo/tabla (43.5x19.5cm 17x7in) Madrid 1998

BELIMBAU Adolfo 1845-1938 **[26]**
$9 000 - €8 413 - £5 555 - FF55 186
The letter Oil/canvas (98x62cm 38x24in) Bethesda MD 1999
$2 000 - €2 592 - £1 500 - FF17 000
Scorcio di casolari Olio/tavola (23x8cm 9x3in) Roma 2000

BELIN Claude XX **[7]**
$414 - €381 - £248 - FF2 500
«Vers sa destinée» Affiche (120x160cm 47x62in) Paris 1999

BELIN Jean-Baptiste, fils 1688-1730 **[1]**
$13 000 - €12 035 - £7 848 - FF78 942
Still Life of a Bouquet of Flowers Oil/canvas (45.5x37.5cm 17x14in) New-York 1999

BELINSKY Claude XX **[16]**
$124 - €122 - £75 - FF800
«Minuit Champs-Elysées» de Roger Blanc, avec Robert Berri, J.Pierreux Affiche (120x160cm 47x62in) Paris 2000

BELKIN Arnold 1930-1992 **[10]**
$4 240 - €4 980 - £3 012 - FF32 664
Sin título Oleo/lienzo (95x105cm 37x41in) México 2000

BELKNAP Zedekiah 1781-1858 **[12]**
☞ **$3 800** - €4 058 - **£2 589** - FF26 620
    Woman with Gold Beads and Lace Fichu Holding Bible Oil/canvas (71x60cm 28x24in) New-York 2001

BELL A.D. XIX-XX **[89]**
✎ **$351** - €339 - **£220** - FF2 222
    Our Village Watercolour (17x25cm 6x9in) Billingshurst, West-Sussex 1999

BELL Arthur George 1849-1916 **[27]**
✎ **$516** - €584 - **£360** - FF3 832
    Sheep grazing near a church Watercolour/paper (34x52cm 13x20in) Billingshurst, West-Sussex 2001

BELL Cecil Crosley 1906-1970 **[30]**
☞ **$1 700** - €1 633 - **£1 053** - FF10 709
    Sledding in Central Park Watercolour, gouache (24x34.5cm 9x13in) New-York 1999

BELL David C. 1950 **[32]**
✎ **$372** - €361 - **£230** - FF2 371
    Fishing Boat at Anchor Watercolour/paper (30x44cm 12x17in) Driffield, East Yorkshire 1999

BELL Edward ?-c.1847 **[1]**
☞ **$32 012** - €30 558 - **£20 000** - FF200 450
    Fishing : A Scene at Magpie Island, Henley-on-Thames Oil/board (37.5x45.5cm 14x17in) London 1999

BELL George Henry Fred. 1878-1966 **[63]**
☞ **$3 496** - €3 402 - **£2 152** - FF22 317
    Madam VIP Makes an Entrance Oil/board (61.5x45.5cm 24x17in) Malvern, Victoria 1999
☞ **$1 915** - €1 670 - **£1 158** - FF10 956
    Australian Native Wildflowers Oil/board (44.5x34.5cm 17x13in) Melbourne 1998
▥ **$496** - €547 - **£330** - FF3 588
    The Departure Linocut in colors (17x13cm 6x5in) Melbourne 2000

BELL Graham 1910-1943 **[6]**
☞ **$2 452** - €2 752 - **£1 700** - FF18 050
    In the Fields Oil/board (53x67.5cm 20x26in) London 2000

BELL Hesketh Davis XIX **[6]**
✎ **$1 203** - €1 190 - **£750** - FF7 809
    Shooting on the Moors Watercolour/paper (43x67.5cm 16x26in) London 1999

BELL John 1811-1895 **[17]**
▥ **$34 960** - €39 977 - **£24 000** - FF222 231
    The American Slave Bronze (H156.5cm H61in) London 2000
▥ **$1 300** - €1 488 - **£894** - FF9 758
    Miranda/Lalage Seated on a Rock by the Ocean Sculpture (H39cm H15in) New-York 2000

BELL John c.1830-c.1890 **[5]**
☞ **$31 776** - €30 818 - **£20 000** - FF202 152
    Celebrating the Grape Harvest, Lake Orta, North Italy Oil/canvas (120x185.5cm 47x73in) London 1999

BELL John Christopher act.1841-1892 **[11]**
☞ **$20 000** - €19 956 - **£12 174** - FF130 902
    Grouse in the Snow Oil/canvas (57x77cm 22x30in) New-York 2000

BELL Larry Stuart 1939 **[25]**
✎ **$5 000** - €5 686 - **£3 493** - FF37 300
    United from Elin Series Drawing (134.5x91.5cm 52x36in) Beverly-Hills CA 2000

BELL Laura Anning 1867-1950 **[3]**
▥ **$4 640** - €4 878 - **£2 912** - FF32 000
    «University College» Affiche (180x80cm 70x31in) Lyon 2000

BELL Lillian Russell XIX-XX **[14]**
✎ **$860** - €955 - **£600** - FF6 266
    At Castletown, Isle of Man Watercolour/paper (19x29cm 7x11in) Godalming, Surrey 2001

BELL Robert Anning 1863-1933 **[44]**
✎ **$418** - €449 - **£280** - FF2 946
    Head of a Girl Pencil/paper (18x18cm 7x7in) Par, Cornwall 2000

BELL Rodolphe XIX **[4]**
☞ **$3 130** - €3 686 - **£2 200** - FF24 181
    Young Lady, full Face in white Dress with lace-bordered Underdress Miniature (11.5x9cm 4x3in) London 2000

BELL Sandra XX **[10]**
▧ **$2 432** - €2 539 - **£1 539** - FF16 658
    Princess paulowna Bronze (56x23x18cm 22x9x7in) Dublin 2000

BELL Stuart Henry 1823-1896 **[16]**
☞ **$1 511** - €1 584 - **£1 000** - FF10 390
    Sunderland Harbour Oil/canvas (39x59cm 15x23in) Billingshurst, West-Sussex 2000

BELL Vanessa 1879-1961 **[94]**
☞ **$9 732** - €9 382 - **£6 000** - FF61 542
    Still Life with classical Head Oil/canvas (58.5x48cm 23x18in) London 1999
☞ **$4 726** - €4 499 - **£3 000** - FF29 511
    Still Life of Mixed Flowers in Vase Oil/canvas (27x22cm 10x8in) Billingshurst, West-Sussex 1999

BELL-SMITH Frederic Marlett 1846-1923 **[227]**
☞ **$3 906** - €3 342 - **£2 351** - FF21 924
    Low Tide, Bay of Fundy Oil/canvas (38x63.5cm 14x25in) Toronto 1998
☞ **$2 043** - €1 964 - **£1 258** - FF12 882
    Village on the River Oil/board (31x47cm 12x18in) Vancouver, BC. 1999
✎ **$1 633** - €1 561 - **£1 023** - FF10 239
    Train coming through the Selkirk Mountains, BC Watercolour/paper (34.5x51cm 13x20in) Vancouver, BC. 1999

BELLAMY John Haley 1836-1914 **[3]**
☞ **$18 000** - €16 305 - **£11 016** - FF106 952
    American Eagle Oil/wood (22x124cm 9x49in) Portland ME 1998

BELLANGÉ Hippolyte 1800-1866 **[90]**
☞ **$2 863** - €2 897 - **£1 748** - FF19 000
    La halte des dragons en Bourgogne Huile/toile (46x55cm 18x21in) Corbeil-Essonnes 2000
☞ **$3 461** - €4 116 - **£2 467** - FF27 000
    La charge des cavaliers Huile/panneau (24x32cm 9x12in) Neuilly-sur-Seine 2000
✎ **$518** - €579 - **£332** - FF3 800
    Militaires houspillant la Veuve Lajoye devant son auberge Aquarelle/papier (17x20cm 6x7in) Paris 2000

BELLANGE Jacques c.1580-1616/38 **[21]**
▥ **$1 777** - €8 181 - **£5 008** - FF53 662
    Drei Heilige Frauen Radierung (31.5x19.5cm 12x7in) Berlin 2001

BELLANGE Michel Bruno 1726-1793 **[6]**
- **$8 321** - €8 385 - **£5 186** - FF55 000
  **Nature morte au panier de fleurs et pommes
  sur un entablement** Huile/toile (48x71cm 18x27in)
  Paris 2000

BELLANGER Camille 1853-1923 **[11]**
- **$34 000** - €38 058 - **£23 711** - FF249 645
  Daphnis and Chloe Oil/canvas (146x110cm 57x43in)
  New-York 2001
- **$8 000** - €9 086 - **£5 613** - FF59 603
  Watering the Garden Oil/canvas (89x63cm 35x24in)
  New-York 2001

BELLANGER-ADHÉMAR Paul 1868-1948 **[13]**
- **$1 793** - €1 925 - **£1 200** - FF12 625
  Still Life of roses in an Oriental Vase Oil/canvas
  (79.5x58.5cm 31x23in) London 2000

BELLANY John 1942 **[111]**
- **$8 297** - €9 252 - **£5 600** - FF60 687
  Aberdeen Fisherman Oil/canvas (161x99cm
  63x38in) Edinburgh 2000
- **$2 740** - €3 028 - **£1 900** - FF19 860
  «Pitten Ween» Oil/canvas (50.5x61cm 19x24in)
  London 2001
- **$1 263** - €1 421 - **£880** - FF9 318
  Man with Razor Shell Ink (79.5x58.5cm 31x23in)
  Edinburgh 2001
- **$373** - €420 - **£260** - FF2 753
  Moonlight Etching in colors (75x55cm 29x21in)
  Edinburgh 2001

BELLASIS John B., Colonel XIX **[1]**
- **$2 722** - €2 685 - **£1 750** - FF17 612
  **Album of drawings of Views in India, Malta,
  Madeira, Italy** Drawing (37.5x27.5cm 14x10in)
  London 1999

BELLAVIA Marcantonio XVII **[11]**
- **$235** - €204 - **£141** - FF1 340
  Flussgott, ein Ruder in der Rechten Radierung
  (11.7x17.3cm 4x6in) Berlin 1998

BELLE Alexis Simon 1674-1734 **[9]**
- **$16 189** - €16 312 - **£10 090** - FF107 000
  **Mademoiselle de Presteseille-Adnet et sa soeur
  cadete Mlle.de Blois** Huile/toile (137x106cm
  53x41in) Paris 2000
- **$12 104** - €12 196 - **£7 544** - FF80 000
  **Portrait présumé de Louis-Philippe d'Orléans
  Duc de Chartres enfant** Pastel/papier (40x33cm
  15x12in) Paris 2000

BELLE Clément L. 1722-1806 **[2]**
- **$4 275** - €4 856 - **£3 000** - FF31 852
  **Three Theological Virtues: Faith, Hope and
  Charity** Oil/canvas (87x123.5cm 34x48in) London
  2001

BELLE Marcel 1871-1948 **[160]**
- **$150 000** - €166 397 - **£99 750** - FF1 091 490
  Jeune fille et enfant à la Ferté Gaucher Oil/can-
  vas (160x190cm 62x74in) New-York 2000
- **$725** - €762 - **£455** - FF5 000
  Bords de Seine à Javel Huile/toile (38x46cm
  14x18in) Paris 2000

BELLE van Karel, Charles 1884-1959 **[48]**
- **$861** - €744 - **£519** - FF4 878
  Femme endormie sur le sofa Huile/toile (50x65cm
  19x25in) Bruxelles 1999

BELLEFLEUR Léon 1910 **[104]**
- **$3 906** - €3 342 - **£2 351** - FF21 924
  «Portrait d'ancêtre» Oil/canvas (81.5x65.5cm
  32x25in) Toronto 1998

- **$1 029** - €1 150 - **£717** - FF7 541
  A flanc de montagne Huile/toile (22x26.5cm
  8x10in) Montréal 2001
- **$388** - €451 - **£272** - FF2 961
  Sans titre Encre/papier (47x63cm 18x24in) Montréal
  2001
- **$214** - €230 - **£143** - FF1 511
  Pyramide baroque Eau-forte (25.5x19.5cm 10x7in)
  Montréal 2000

BELLEFROID Guillaume M. Edmond 1893-? **[8]**
- **$1 261** - €1 497 - **£918** - FF9 822
  Korenschoven in heuvellandschap Oil/panel
  (36x48cm 14x18in) Maastricht 2001

BELLEGARDE Claude 1927 **[74]**
- **$4 147** - €3 811 - **£2 547** - FF25 000
  **Temps F - Sans titre (achrome de la période
  blanche)** Technique mixte/carton (20x33cm 7x12in)
  Paris 1999

BELLEI Gaetano 1857-1922 **[35]**
- **$19 000** - €18 054 - **£11 559** - FF118 425
  Cheers Oil/canvas (58.5x86.5cm 23x34in) New-York
  1999
- **$3 339** - €2 805 - **£1 962** - FF18 397
  Tuba spielender Mönch Öl/Leinwand (35x28cm
  13x11in) Bern 1998

BELLENGER Jacques & Pierre 1909 **[16]**
- **$500** - €537 - **£334** - FF3 520
  «Quinquina Bourin» Poster (102.5x125.5cm
  40x49in) Los-Angeles CA 2000

BELLENGER Pierre XX **[5]**
- **$475** - €499 - **£317** - FF3 270
  «Sud» Poster (155x114cm 61x45in) New-York 2001

BELLERMANN Ferdinand Konrad 1814-1889 **[17]**
- **$5 500** - €5 030 - **£3 358** - FF32 993
  A wooded mountain path Oil/canvas/board
  (68x38cm 27x15in) New-York 1998

BELLEROCHE de Albert 1864-1944 **[75]**
- **$2 843** - €2 624 - **£1 700** - FF17 214
  **Portrait of Lily Grenier in the Forest of Villier-
  Catteret/Landscape** Oil/canvas (73x54cm 28x21in)
  London 1999
- **$650** - €655 - **£405** - FF4 299
  Pirette Lithograph (41.5x32cm 16x12in) New-York
  2000

BELLERY-DESFONTAINES Henri Jules Ferd. 1867-
1910 **[20]**
- **$5 000** - €5 831 - **£3 510** - FF38 252
  «Automobiles Georges Richard» Poster
  (150x88cm 59x34in) New-York 2000

BELLESIA Bruno 1923 **[2]**
- **$350** - €380 - **£233** - FF2 490
  «Durban's» Poster (100x69cm 39x27in) New-York
  2000

BELLET DU POISAT Jean-Pierre J.Alfred 1823-
1883 **[7]**
- **$6 279** - €6 327 - **£3 913** - FF41 500
  Le sculpteur Pastel (114x92cm 44x36in) Lyon 2001

BELLETESTE Jean Antoine 1718-1811 **[2]**
- **$25 096** - €24 504 - **£16 000** - FF160 736
  Crucifixion Sculpture (H37cm H14in) London 1999

BELLETTE Jean Mary 1909-1991 **[37]**
- **$1 070** - €1 112 - **£675** - FF7 294
  Rift Valley Oil/canvas (89x120cm 35x47in) Sydney
  2000

$2 032 - €2 396 - £1 433 - FF15 720
The Encounter Oil/board (29x38.5cm 11x15in)
Woollahra, Sydney 2001
$89 - €94 - £56 - FF615
Hill End Landscape Charcoal (37x50cm 14x19in)
Sydney 2000

BELLEVOIS Jacob Adriaensz 1621-1675 [23]
$13 407 - €11 407 - £8 000 - FF74 827
**Dutch Merchantman, a Pink and other shipping
in rough Seas** Oil/canvas (59.5x72cm 23x28in)
London 1998

BELLI Benito XIX-XX [7]
$1 680 - €1 802 - £1 140 - FF11 820
Caballero con sombrero Oleo/tabla (23x17cm
9x6in) Madrid 2000

BELLI Carlo 1903-1991 [11]
$2 400 - €2 073 - £1 600 - FF13 600
L'ombra Olio/tela (34x24cm 13x9in) Firenze 1998

BELLI Filippo XIX [3]
$1 601 - €1 677 - £1 006 - FF11 000
Étude de campagnards Tirage albuminé
(25.5x19cm 10x7in) Paris 2000

BELLI Luigi 1848-? [2]
$17 000 - €20 158 - £11 696 - FF132 231
A Roman Soldier Gilded bronze (73.5x15cm 28x5in)
New-York 2000

BELLIER Charles 1796-? [7]
$5 337 - €4 878 - £3 267 - FF32 000
**Scène de combat entre Grecs et Turcs lors de
la guerre d'Indépendance** Huile/toile (65x80cm
25x31in) Paris 1999
$27 201 - €27 006 - £17 000 - FF177 151
Scenes from the Greek War of Independence
Oil/canvas (32x40cm 12x15in) London 1999

BELLIN Jacques-Nicolas 1703-1772 [12]
$457 - €491 - £306 - FF3 220
Carte réduite de la presque iles de l'Inde
Engraving (59.5x84.5cm 23x33in) London 2000

BELLING Rudolf 1886-1972 [31]
$11 252 - €13 294 - £7 948 - FF87 201
Tänzerin Bronze (H44.5cm H17in) Köln 2001
$819 - €767 - £496 - FF5 030
Reliefentwurf Charcoal (35x47cm 13x18in) Stuttgart
1999

BELLINGHAM-SMITH Elinor 1906-1988 [43]
$986 - €1 059 - £660 - FF6 944
Essex Field in Summer Oil/board (50x76cm
20x30in) Birmingham 2000
$439 - €470 - £300 - FF3 086
Summer thoughts Watercolour/paper (49x32.5cm
19x12in) London 2001

BELLINI Emmanuel 1904-1989 [66]
$1 943 - €2 211 - £1 348 - FF14 500
Le port de Cannes Huile/toile (60x73cm 23x28in)
Paris 2000
$467 - €457 - £287 - FF3 000
Le fiacre/Le sulky Aquarelle/papier (18x25.5cm
7x10in) Soissons 1999

BELLINI Filippo 1550/55-1604 [7]
$2 509 - €2 454 - £1 600 - FF16 073
The Resurrection Black chalk (28.5x15.5cm 11x6in)
London 1999

BELLINI Giovanni 1430-1516 [4]
$567 834 - €609 523 - £380 000 - FF3 998 208
**Saint-Jérôme: Fragment from the Altarpiece of
S.Cristoforo della Pace** Oil/panel (86x35.5cm
33x13in) London 2000

BELLINI Jacopo c.1400-c.1470 [1]
$68 400 - €59 089 - £45 600 - FF387 600
Santa Lucia Tempera/tavola (39x26.5cm 15x10in)
Milano 1998

BELLIS de Antonio ?-1656 [15]
$101 166 - €99 445 - £65 000 - FF652 314
The Liberation of Saint Peter Oil/canvas
(178.5x260.5cm 70x102in) London 1999
$4 989 - €5 793 - £3 518 - FF38 000
Caïn tuant Abel Huile/toile (113x98.5cm 44x38in)
Paris 2001

BELLIS Hubert 1831-1902 [155]
$2 379 - €2 180 - £1 455 - FF14 301
Blumenstrauss in einer Vase Öl/Karton
(42.5x61cm 16x24in) Wien 1999
$825 - €917 - £551 - FF6 016
Nature morte aux fraises Huile/panneau
(20.5x26.5cm 8x10in) Bruxelles 2000

BELLMER Hans 1902-1975 [843]
$17 946 - €19 992 - £11 741 - FF131 137
La marionnette Öl/Leinwand (65x65cm 25x25in)
München 2000
$18 960 - €18 294 - £11 976 - FF120 000
La demi-poupée Sculpture bois (H110cm H43in)
Paris 1999
$10 725 - €11 434 - £6 802 - FF75 000
Les doigts immobiles Bronze (30x32x20cm
11x12x7in) Paris 1999
$1 296 - €1 524 - £929 - FF10 000
Femme à la colonne Crayon (19x15cm 7x5in) Paris
2001
$265 - €223 - £155 - FF1 462
Danseuse Eau-forte (65x51cm 25x20in) Liège 1998
$6 500 - €5 427 - £3 862 - FF35 597
La poupée Gelatin silver print (14.5x14cm 5x5in)
New-York 1998

BELLOC Auguste c.1815-c.1870 [23]
$3 813 - €4 269 - £2 654 - FF28 000
Nu féminin sur canapé Tirage papier salé (16x21cm
6x8in) Paris 2001

BELLOCQ Ernest James 1873-1949 [25]
$1 400 - €1 468 - £877 - FF9 628
New Orleans prostitute Photograph (49x39cm
19x15in) New-York 2001

BELLOLI Andrei 1821-1881 [7]
$747 - €802 - £500 - FF5 260
A Half Length Portrait of Richard Amos
Watercolour/paper (45x36.5cm 17x14in) London 2000

BELLON Denise 1902-1999 [29]
$582 - €640 - £373 - FF4 200
**Paris, Péniche et remorqueurs au Pont des Arts
15 mars** Tirage argentique (17x20.5cm 6x8in) Paris
2000

BELLON Jean 1941 [10]
$1 100 - €1 218 - £746 - FF7 991
Le petit déjeuner Oil/canvas (46x38cm 18x14in)
New-York 2000

BELLONI Giorgio 1861-1944 [63]
$11 200 - €9 539 - £6 751 - FF62 569
Estación de trenes Oleo/lienzo (33x60cm 12x23in)
Buenos-Aires 1998

$4 500 - €4 665 - **£2 700** - FF30 600
Porto Olio/cartone (29.5x39cm 11x15in) Milano 1999

BELLONI José 1882-1965 **[7]**
$1 700 - €1 465 - **£1 010** - FF9 611
El Palenque Bronze (H29cm H11in) Montevideo 1998

BELLONI Serge 1925 **[67]**
$1 296 - €1 524 - **£929** - FF10 000
L'île de la cité, les quais Huile/panneau (40x50cm 15x19in) Paris 2001
$850 - €851 - **£510** - FF5 780
La Senna a Parigi Olio/cartone (30x40cm 11x15in) Torino 2000

BELLOTTI Pietro di Canaletti XVIII-XIX **[4]**
$21 000 - €20 046 - **£13 120** - FF131 493
View on the Venetian Lagoon Oil/canvas (57x119cm 22x46in) New-York 1999

BELLOTTO Bernardo 1721-1780 **[94]**
$1 793 160 - €1 924 809 - **£1 200 000** - FF12 625 920
The Castelvecchio and the Ponte Scaligero, Verona Oil/canvas (84.5x137.5cm 33x54in) London 2000
$15 599 - €15 264 - **£10 000** - FF100 122
An architectural Capriccio, with Palaces by an ornamental Bridge Ink (29.5x47cm 11x18in) London 1999
$5 000 - €7 257 - **£4 200** - FF47 600
Vue de la ville de Pirne devant le port nommé Ober Thor Gravure (42x54cm 16x21in) Imbersago (Lecco) 2001

BELLOWS Albert Fitch 1829-1883 **[34]**
$10 000 - €8 567 - **£6 012** - FF56 197
Picnic in the Forest Oil/canvas (38x60cm 15x24in) Cleveland OH 1998
$4 750 - €5 167 - **£3 131** - FF33 891
Figures on a Wooded Path Oil/canvas (42x25.5cm 16x10in) Boston MA 2000
$7 000 - €8 325 - **£4 988** - FF54 607
Safely Landed Watercolour, gouache/paper (46.5x31.5cm 18x12in) New-York 2000

BELLOWS George Wesley 1882-1925 **[306]**
$160 000 - €186 734 - **£113 424** - FF1 224 896
Portrait of Elizabeth Alexander Oil/canvas (134.5x109cm 52x42in) New-York 2001
$260 000 - €285 258 - **£172 718** - FF1 871 168
Summer Fantasy Oil/canvas (91.5x122cm 36x48in) New-York 2000
$24 000 - €24 877 - **£15 218** - FF163 185
Evening Hills Oil/board (29x38cm 11x14in) New-York 2000
$5 500 - €5 904 - **£3 680** - FF38 728
Nude Standing Charcoal/paper (31.5x26cm 12x10in) New-York 2000
$3 117 - €2 855 - **£1 900** - FF18 725
Artists judging Works of Art Lithograph (45x61.5cm 17x24in) London 1999

BELLUCCI Antonio 1654-1726 **[22]**
$26 000 - €26 953 - **£15 600** - FF176 800
Betsabea al bagno Olio/tela (145x110.5cm 57x43in) Napoli 2000
$8 000 - €10 367 - **£6 000** - FF68 000
Madonna con bambino Olio/tela (93x73cm 36x28in) Milano 2000

BELMON Gaston 1907-1995 **[62]**
$392 - €457 - **£274** - FF3 000
Vieux Puit à Hammamet Huile/toile (50x65cm 19x25in) Paris 2000

$340 - €396 - **£237** - FF2 600
Anier Aquarelle/papier (64x50cm 25x19in) Paris 2000

BELMONDO Paul 1898-1982 **[70]**
$4 669 - €5 488 - **£3 384** - FF36 000
Enfant et chamois Bronze (H21cm H8in) Calais 2001
$2 205 - €2 363 - **£1 501** - FF15 500
Le modèle assis Mine plomb (18x19cm 7x7in) Calais 2001

BELOFF Angelina 1879-1969 **[9]**
$32 647 - €34 301 - **£21 487** - FF225 000
Le village Huile/toile (61x50cm 24x19in) Paris 2000
$3 750 - €3 147 - **£2 200** - FF20 640
Femme s'habillant Oil/canvas (27.5x22cm 10x8in) New-York 1998

BELON José c.1875-1927 **[12]**
$1 000 - €1 116 - **£654** - FF7 318
«Moulin Rouge, tous les soirs, Spectacle-Concert-Bal» Poster (81.5x60.5cm 32x23in) New-York 2000

BELONOG Anatoli 1946 **[82]**
$2 380 - €2 232 - **£1 472** - FF14 642
By the Lake Oil/canvas (65x92cm 25x36in) Stockholm 1999

BELSKY Wladimir 1959 **[111]**
$561 - €555 - **£350** - FF3 642
Still Life on the Seashore Oil/canvas (46x55cm 18x21in) Fernhurst, Haslemere, Surrey 1999
$212 - €250 - **£150** - FF1 643
Fishing Boats at Low Tide Oil/canvas/board (33x45.5cm 12x17in) London 2001

BELTRAN José 1952 **[14]**
$2 950 - €2 744 - **£1 827** - FF18 000
Le port de Sanary Huile/toile (65x50cm 25x19in) Barjols 1999
$2 850 - €2 897 - **£1 791** - FF19 000
Isle-sur-Sorgue Huile/toile (41x27cm 16x10in) Barjols 2000

BELTRAN-MASSES Federico 1885-1949 **[92]**
$5 073 - €5 445 - **£3 394** - FF35 719
Corrida Oil/canvas (170x206cm 66x81in) Amsterdam 2000
$4 000 - €4 805 - **£2 800** - FF31 520
Elegancia y señorio Oleo/lienzo (100x81cm 39x31in) Madrid 2001
$1 026 - €1 067 - **£646** - FF7 000
Femmes espagnoles et musiciens Huile/panneau (28.5x24.5cm 11x9in) Paris 2000

BELTRAND Jacques 1874-1977 **[23]**
$302 - €305 - **£188** - FF2 000
La Côte à Belle Ile Gravure bois couleurs (28.5x36cm 11x14in) Quimper 2000

BELTRANO Agostino 1607-c.1665 **[10]**
$38 400 - €36 588 - **£24 336** - FF240 000
Le retour triomphal de David Huile/toile (116x156cm 45x61in) Clermont-Ferrand 1999

BELVEDERE Abate Andrea 1642-1732 **[12]**
$36 075 - €35 225 - **£23 000** - FF231 058
Ornamental garden with Muscovy Ducks, Bee Eather, Stone Fountain Oil/canvas (125.5x168.5cm 49x66in) London 1999
$43 440 - €49 365 - **£30 000** - FF323 811
Carnations and Irises in a Glass Vase/Carnations in a Glass Vase Oil/canvas (48x36cm 18x14in) London 2000

BELY Alexander Fedorovich 1874-1934 [3]
🖼 **$3 699** - €4 298 - **£2 600** - FF28 194
 Dusk over the Harbour Oil/board (30.5x42cm
 12x16in) London 2001

BEMELMANS Fons 1938 [2]
🖼 **$13 356** - €15 882 - **£9 520** - FF104 181
 Suzanna Bronze (H74cm H29in) Amsterdam 2000

BEMELMANS Ludwig 1898-1962 [74]
🖼 **$16 000** - €19 028 - **£11 403** - FF124 816
 At the Bank Oil/board (76x54cm 29x21in) New-York
 2000
✏ **$7 000** - €7 840 - **£4 863** - FF51 430
 «East Hampton» Watercolour/paper (55x73cm
 22x29in) Cincinnati OH 2001

BEMIS William Otis 1819-1883 [3]
🖼 **$750** - €823 - **£519** - FF5 396
 Marblehead sailboats Oil/canvas (22x31cm 9x12in)
 Cambridge MA 2000

BEMMEL van J. XVII [1]
🖼 **$9 930** - €11 434 - **£6 780** - FF75 000
 Le repas des bergers Huile/toile (89.5x117cm
 35x46in) Amiens 2000

BEMMEL van Willem 1630-1708 [24]
🖼 **$12 000** - €14 134 - **£8 299** - FF92 710
 River Landscape with a Fortress Beyond
 Oil/canvas (112x145.5cm 44x57in) New-York 2000
🖼 **$4 809** - €4 538 - **£2 967** - FF29 766
 **Travellers on a Road Passing an Inn Among
 Classical Ruins** Oil/canvas (68x92.5cm 26x36in)
 Amsterdam 1999
✏ **$896** - €962 - **£600** - FF6 313
 Landscape with Roman Ruins Wash (29.5x39.5cm
 11x15in) London 2000

BEMMEL von Georg Christoph Got. 1738-1794 [4]
🖼 **$7 074** - €6 860 - **£4 482** - FF45 000
 Paysage de neige au lac et forêt de pins
 Huile/toile (52x71.5cm 20x28in) Paris 1999

BEMMEL von Johann Christoph c.1707-1778 [9]
🖼 **$5 654** - €5 793 - **£3 488** - FF38 000
 Paysage à la tour/Paysage aux arbres croisés
 Huile/toile (93.5x119cm 36x46in) Vendôme 2000

BEMMEL von Karl Sebastian 1743-1796 [8]
🖼 **$4 914** - €5 624 - **£3 380** - FF36 892
 **Hügellandschaft mit zwei Reitern auf dem Weg
 vor einem Dorf** Oil/paper/panel (13x9.5cm 5x3in)
 München 2000
🖼 **$3 119** - €3 579 - **£2 133** - FF23 477
 **Felsige Landschaft mit Wasserfall und
 Holzbrücke/Flusslandschaft** Gouache
 (17.3x22.8cm 6x8in) Heidelberg 2000

BEMMEL von Peter 1685-1754 [40]
🖼 **$1 905** - €2 045 - **£1 275** - FF13 415
 **Südländische Ideallandschaft mit einem künst-
 lich angelegten Wasserfall** Öl/Kupfer (15x19cm
 5x7in) Stuttgart 2000
🖼 **$585** - €665 - **£406** - FF4 360
 In der Schwäbischen Alb Chalks (14x20cm 5x7in)
 Köln 2001
🖼 **$131** - €153 - **£92** - FF1 006
 Die bergigen und waldigen Landschaften
 Radierung (13.5x18.2cm 5x7in) München 2000

BEN 1935 [392]
🖼 **$4 500** - €4 665 - **£2 700** - FF30 600
 L'arte è un discorso sull'arte Olio/tela (170x190cm
 66x74in) Prato 2000
🖼 **$2 381** - €2 556 - **£1 594** - FF16 769
 Tue es Acryl/Leinwand (50x60cm 19x23in) Köln 2000

🖼 **$1 035** - €1 143 - **£717** - FF7 500
 La punition Acrylique/carton (30.5x21.5cm 12x8in)
 Paris 2001
🖼 **$1 242** - €1 372 - **£861** - FF9 000
 «Je leur crève les yeux» Construction
 (22x31.5x13cm 8x12x5in) Paris 2001
✏ **$354** - €412 - **£249** - FF2 700
 J'aime le pain Feutre (10x50cm 3x19in) Paris 2001
🖼 **$196** - €229 - **£138** - FF1 500
 L'art ne tient qu'à un fil Sérigraphie (30x21cm
 11x8in) Paris 2001

BEN BELLA Mahdjoub 1946 [17]
🖼 **$1 640** - €1 601 - **£1 038** - FF10 500
 Composition Huile/toile (92x73cm 36x28in) Douai
 1999

BEN TRÉ Howard 1949 [15]
🖼 **$23 000** - €21 955 - **£14 372** - FF144 014
 Untitled Sculpture, glass (81x30.5x12cm 31x12x4in)
 New-York 2000
🖼 **$2 750** - €2 849 - **£1 750** - FF18 690
 Burial Box Sculpture, glass (9x12x8cm 3x4x3in) New-
 York 2000

BEN ZVI Asaf 1953 [1]
🖼 **$8 000** - €9 564 - **£5 518** - FF62 736
 Waiting for the Ride Oil/canvas (175x175cm
 68x68in) Tel Aviv 2000

BEN ZVI Zeev 1904-1952 [10]
🖼 **$3 200** - €3 435 - **£2 141** - FF22 531
 Mask Bronze (H23cm H9in) Tel Aviv 2000

BENAIM Ricardo 1949 [26]
✏ **$223** - €188 - **£131** - FF1 231
 **Collage mit alten Buchseiten und verschiede-
 nen Papiersorten** Mischtechnik/Papier (70x50.5cm
 27x19in) Bern 1998

BÉNARD Hubert Eugène 1834-? [11]
🖼 **$8 321** - €8 385 - **£5 186** - FF55 000
 Déchargement d'un bâteau échoué Huile/toile
 (82x145cm 32x57in) Évreux 2000

BÉNARD Jean-Baptiste ?-c.1790 [26]
🖼 **$12 000** - €14 103 - **£8 319** - FF92 512
 Amaryllis Oil/canvas (56.5x46.5cm 22x18in) New-
 York 2000
🖼 **$6 695** - €6 555 - **£4 119** - FF43 000
 Les dénicheurs d'oiseaux Huile/toile (33x41cm
 12x16in) Le Mans 1999

BENASCHI Giovanni Battista 1636-1688 [4]
✏ **$8 246** - €9 246 - **£5 600** - FF60 651
 Male Nude Pulling a Rope Black & white chalks
 (33.5x22.5cm 13x8in) London 2000

BENASSIT Louis Émile 1833-1902 [13]
🖼 **$1 775** - €1 982 - **£1 162** - FF13 000
 Scène pendant la guerre de Vendée Huile/pan-
 neau (26x40.5cm 10x15in) Fontainebleau 2000

BENATOV 1942 [4]
🖼 **$5 610** - €5 336 - **£3 503** - FF35 000
 Icare éclaté Bronze (45x29x31cm 17x11x12in)
 Deauville 1999

BENAVENT CALATAYUD José 1858-? [7]
🖼 **$8 000** - €8 970 - **£5 432** - FF58 838
 Assistance required Oil/canvas (54.5x38cm
 21x14in) New-York 2000
🖼 **$2 000** - €1 871 - **£1 209** - FF12 271
 At the Well Oil/panel (32x19.5cm 12x7in) New-York
 1999

BENAVIDES Pablo 1918 **[37]**
$1 156 - €1 047 - £748 - FF6 868
Mi jardín Oleo/lienzo (50x40cm 19x15in) Caracas 1999
$1 020 - €960 - £660 - FF6 300
Paisaje de San Luis Oleo/lienzo (30x40cm 11x15in) Caracas 1999

BENAZECH Peter c.1730-c.1795 **[2]**
$900 - €962 - £612 - FF6 308
The Calm/The Storm Engraving (43x50cm 17x20in) New-Orleans LA 2001

BENAZZI Raffael 1933 **[15]**
$4 113 - €3 770 - £2 513 - FF24 727
Wandskulptur Sculpture bois (H73cm H28in) Zürich 1999

BENBRIDGE Henry 1743-1812 **[3]**
$5 000 - €4 629 - £3 018 - FF30 362
Mrs. Samuel Wilson, facing right in salmon dress Oil/canvas (17x13cm 7x5in) New-York 1999

BENCE Jacques Martin c.1770-? **[2]**
$4 115 - €4 878 - £2 998 - FF32 000
Vue d'Italie Aquarelle/papier (35.5x55.5cm 13x21in) Neuilly-sur-Seine 2001

BENCOVICH Federico c.1660-c.1745 **[7]**
$32 500 - €33 691 - £19 500 - FF221 000
Sacrificio di Isacco Olio/tela (90x122cm 35x48in) Genova 2000
$7 770 - €8 341 - £5 200 - FF54 712
The Immaculate Madonna/The Nurture of Jupiter Black chalk (37.5x26cm 14x10in) London 2000

BENCZUR von Gyula 1844-1920 **[9]**
$22 000 - €20 871 - £13 365 - FF136 903
A Peacock in a classical Landscape with Lilies and Roses Oil/canvas (180.5x92cm 71x36in) New-York 1999
$20 000 - €19 666 - £12 500 - FF129 000
Hypnos, Dream Oil/canvas (43x68cm 16x26in) Budapest 1999

BENDA Arthur 1885-1969 **[18]**
$414 - €472 - £286 - FF3 098
Knieender Akt Vintage gelatin silver print (6x18cm 2x7in) Wien 2000

BENDA G.K., Georges Kugel. XIX-XX **[35]**
$1 900 - €1 767 - £1 172 - FF11 589
«Mistinguett» Poster (160x117cm 63x46in) New-York 1999

BENDA Jan 1897-1967 **[11]**
$303 - €287 - £189 - FF1 882
Nature morte à la coupe et aux pommes Huile/toile (25x30cm 9x11in) Praha 2001
$1 734 - €1 640 - £1 080 - FF10 758
Maler und sein Modell Indian ink (30x40cm 11x15in) Praha 2001

BENDA Wladyslaw Theodor 1873-1948 **[13]**
$3 500 - €3 352 - £2 162 - FF21 986
Mask: Placid Woman, Golden Hair Sculpture (18x13x10cm 7x5x4in) New-York 1999
$5 500 - €5 092 - £3 366 - FF33 400
Peasant army crossing field of snow, story ill. Pastel (58x91cm 23x36in) New-York 1999

BENDALL Claude D. 1891-1970 **[22]**
$962 - €970 - £600 - FF6 362
Studio in Paris Watercolour, gouache/paper (66x51cm 25x20in) London 2000

BENDALL Mildred 1891-1977 **[30]**
$4 812 - €4 849 - £3 000 - FF31 810
Tabletop Still Life Oil/canvas (65.5x81cm 25x31in) London 2001

BENDEMANN Eduard Julius Fr. 1811-1889 **[18]**
$13 974 - €14 316 - £8 624 - FF93 909
Jeremias auf den Trümmern Jerusalems Oil/canvas/panel (41x61cm 16x24in) Düsseldorf 2000
$4 106 - €3 835 - £2 534 - FF25 154
Wo Barthel den Most holt Öl/Leinwand (28.5x28.5cm 11x11in) Köln 1999
$2 500 - €2 370 - £1 562 - FF15 549
Die Weinlese Mischtechnik/Papier (16x29cm 6x11in) Luzern 1999

BENDEMANN Rudolf Christ. Eugen 1851-1884 **[3]**
$2 472 - €2 832 - £1 714 - FF18 446
Weite Wüstenlandschaft mit vorbeiziehender Karawane Öl/Leinwand (60x80cm 23x31in) Staufen 2000

BENDIEN Jacob 1890-1933 **[15]**
$770 - €679 - £464 - FF4 457
Het Muzikantje/Hoek van Een Gracht Lithograph (58.5x29.5cm 23x11in) Amsterdam 1998

BENDINER Alfred 1899-? **[1]**
$100 - €107 - £66 - FF704
Joseph Szigeti & Eugene Ormandy Lithograph (26.5x24.5cm 10x9in) Philadelphia PA 2000

BENDRAT Arthur 1899-? **[7]**
$204 - €215 - £129 - FF1 409
Figurkompositioner Indian ink (73x57cm 28x22in) Köbenhavn 2000

BENDIXEN Siegfried Detlev 1786-1864 **[18]**
$4 987 - €5 665 - £3 500 - FF37 161
Swans in a River Landscape encircle with Roses Oil/canvas (50.5x40.5cm 19x15in) London 2001
$426 - €496 - £300 - FF3 253
View near Baden Baden Oil/canvas (36x30cm 14x11in) Stansted Mountfitchet, Essex 2001

BENDRAT Arthur 1899-? **[7]**
$580 - €610 - £364 - FF4 000
«Deutsche Bav Ausstellung» Affiche (94x65cm 37x25in) Lyon 2000

BENDRE Narayan Shridhar 1910-1992 **[25]**
$16 000 - €15 590 - £11 334 - FF121 681
Landscape Oil/canvas (106.5x120cm 41x47in) New-York 2000
$14 695 - €16 237 - £10 189 - FF106 511
Untitled Oil/canvas (54.5x91.5cm 21x36in) Singapore 2001
$2 388 - €2 312 - £1 500 - FF15 168
Woman Oil/cardboard (46.5x28cm 18x11in) London 1999
$3 000 - €3 545 - £2 126 - FF23 252
Lessons in Walking Watercolour (28x32.5cm 11x12in) New-York 2000

BENDTSEN Folmer 1907-1993 **[141]**
$2 392 - €2 682 - £1 672 - FF17 590
Europaeisk morgen Oil/canvas (128x146cm 50x57in) Köbenhavn 2001
$1 255 - €1 340 - £855 - FF8 790
Sneklaedt byparti, Köbenhavn Oil/canvas (66x82cm 25x32in) Vejle 2001

BENDZ Wilhelm Ferdinand 1804-1832 **[30]**
$15 210 - €13 420 - £9 160 - FF88 030
Portraet af stiftamtmand i Odense/Antoinette Margrethe, f. Gersdorf Oil/canvas (34.5x29cm 13x11in) Köbenhavn 1998

✏ $5 220 - €5 634 - **£3 502** - FF36 955
Kunstnerens selvportraet med kalot Pencil/paper
(10.5x8.3cm 4x3in) Köbenhavn 2000

BENE Géza 1900-1960 [2]
✏ $1 470 - €1 620 - **£966** - FF10 626
Sun, House, Tree Watercolour/paper (44x51cm
17x20in) Budapest 2000

BENECKE Ernest XIX [5]
📷 $1 293 - €1 524 - **£909** - FF10 000
Chamelier et chameaux Tirage papier salé
(15.5x21cm 6x8in) Paris 2000

BENEDETTI Andries, Andrea 1620-? [4]
☞ $61 229 - €60 131 - **£38 000** - FF394 436
**Melons, Grapes, Oysters, Crabs and Lemons on
Pewter Plates** Oil/panel (73.5x101cm 28x39in)
London 1999

BENEDETTO Enzo 1905-1993 [2]
☞ $10 000 - €12 763 - **£6 000** - FF68 000
Esplosiione della primavera Olio/tela (73x62cm
28x24in) Milano 2000

BENEDICTUS Edouard 1878-1930 [12]
▥ $85 - €89 - **£56** - FF585
«Relais-6» Pochoir (44x35cm 17x14in) Cleveland OH
2001

BENEDIT Luis Fernando 1937 [24]
☞ $6 000 - €5 838 - **£3 693** - FF38 293
Toreros en el jardín Oil/canvas (100x114.5cm
39x45in) New-York 1999
✏ $5 000 - €4 865 - **£3 077** - FF31 911
**Proyecto juguete NRO, 62 (Barco de guerra
según tomás)** Watercolour (72.5x54.5cm 28x21in)
New-York 1999

BENEDITO VIVES Manuel 1875-1963 [53]
☞ $2 295 - €2 553 - **£1 530** - FF16 745
Escena madrileña: el cochero Oleo/lienzo
(26x37cm 10x14in) Madrid 2000
✏ $780 - €781 - **£481** - FF5 122
Mujer Acuarela/papel (14x16cm 5x6in) Madrid 2000
▥ $176 - €168 - **£109** - FF1 103
Anciano Aguafuerte (51x38cm 20x14in) Madrid 1999

BENEKER Gerrit A. 1882-1934 [30]
☞ $2 800 - €2 837 - **£1 757** - FF18 607
Helen Oil/canvas (76x63cm 30x25in) Cincinnati OH
2000
☞ $2 500 - €2 684 - **£1 703** - FF17 603
New York Street Scene Oil/canvas (26.5x40.5cm
10x15in) Boston MA 2001

BENES Vincenc 1883-1979 [81]
☞ $3 757 - €3 553 - **£2 340** - FF23 309
Prague seen from the Petrin Hill Oil/canvas
(75.5x101cm 29x39in) Praha 2000
☞ $1 120 - €1 060 - **£700** - FF6 956
Hinter einer Tenne Oil/board (43.5x32.5cm 17x12in)
Praha 1999

BENESCH Josef Ferdinand 1875-1954 [13]
☞ $2 397 - €2 761 - **£1 637** - FF18 114
**Bick auf eine Parklandschaft mit Kirche im
Hintergrund** Öl/Leinwand (74x100cm 29x39in) Wien
2000

BENET VANCELLS Rafael 1889-1979 [18]
☞ $4 880 - €4 805 - **£2 960** - FF31 520
Niños posando Oleo/lienzo (116x88cm 45x34in)
Barcelona 2000

BENEZIT Emmanuel Charles 1887-1975 [166]
☞ $494 - €427 - **£298** - FF2 800
L'aurore, deux danseuses Huile/toile (24x33cm
9x12in) Saint-Dié 1998

BENFATTO Luigi 1559-1611 [7]
☞ $10 906 - €10 174 - **£6 580** - FF66 738
Scena dalla storia romana Öl/Leinwand (84x161cm
33x63in) Wien 1999

BENGER Berenger 1868-1935 [36]
✏ $425 - €395 - **£260** - FF2 589
Horses Watering at a Pool Watercolour/paper
(26x42cm 10x16in) London 1998

BENGER William Edmund 1841-1915 [7]
✏ $503 - €564 - **£350** - FF3 700
Estuary Scene Watercolour/paper (76x127cm
29x50in) London 2001

BENGLIS Lynda 1941 [46]
⚒ $11 000 - €12 763 - **£7 594** - FF83 721
Shady Grove Plaster (89x61x8cm 35x24x3in) New-
York 2000
⚒ $13 000 - €14 706 - **£9 094** - FF96 466
«Kajal» Bronze (73.5x45.5x45.5cm 28x17x17in) New-
York 2001

BENGSTON Billy Al 1934 [24]
☞ $4 500 - €3 778 - **£2 639** - FF24 779
Tom Mixed media (66x63.5cm 25x25in) Beverly-Hills
CA 1998
☞ $3 500 - €3 481 - **£2 172** - FF22 835
Kim Oil/canvas (26x26cm 10x10in) Beverly-Hills CA
1999
✏ $2 600 - €2 586 - **£1 613** - FF16 963
Venice Watercolour/paper (33.5x33.5cm 13x13in)
Beverly-Hills CA 1999

BENGTS Carl 1876-1934 [10]
☞ $1 502 - €1 766 - **£1 041** - FF11 583
Interiör Oil/canvas (21x34cm 8x13in) Helsinki 2000

BENGTSSON Dick 1936-1989 [22]
☞ $48 850 - €54 729 - **£34 050** - FF359 000
Turister på Hawaii Oil/panel (145.5x122cm 57x48in)
Stockholm 2001
☞ $1 660 - €1 861 - **£1 157** - FF12 206
Utan titel Oil/panel (48x57cm 18x22in) Stockholm
2001
☞ $2 313 - €1 956 - **£1 382** - FF12 830
Collage Mixed media (27x35cm 10x13in) Stockholm
1998
✏ $439 - €493 - **£306** - FF3 231
Formation Pencil/paper (29x19cm 11x7in) Stockholm
2001

BENGTZ Ture 1907 [4]
▥ $600 - €549 - **£366** - FF3 599
Children Looking at the Moon Lithograph
(34x23cm 13x9in) Boston MA 1998

BENIGNI Léon 1892-? [9]
▥ $2 943 - €2 617 - **£1 800** - FF17 167
«Brides Les Bains» Affiche couleur (99x62cm
38x24in) London 1999

BENISTI Louis 1903-1995 [1]
☞ $3 283 - €3 659 - **£2 301** - FF24 000
Famille algérienne devant la porte verte
Huile/toile (55x46cm 21x18in) Paris 2001

BENITO Domingo 1927 [55]
✏ $73 - €72 - **£46** - FF472
Paisaje Acuarela/papel (17x23cm 6x9in) Madrid 1999

B

BENITO Edouard Garcia 1891-1981 **[18]**
- **$161** - €183 - **£112** - FF1 200
  La danse persane et la danse hindoue Pochoir (32x49.5cm 12x19in) Pontoise 2001

BENJUMEA Rafael XIX **[8]**
- **$3 640** - €4 234 - **£2 600** - FF27 772
  Spanish Dancer in an Interior Oil/canvas (34x29.5cm 13x11in) Oxfordshire 2001

BENK Johannes 1844-1914 **[6]**
- **$4 498** - €4 724 - **£2 834** - FF30 985
  Kaiser Franz Joseph I.von Österreich Ceramic (H62cm H24in) Wien 2000

BENKA Martin 1888-1971 **[26]**
- **$3 179** - €3 007 - **£1 980** - FF19 723
  Landscape Oil/canvas (50x56cm 19x22in) Praha 2000
- **$1 156** - €1 093 - **£720** - FF7 172
  Heuernte Oil/Karton (24x16cm 9x6in) Praha 1999

BENLLIURE Y GIL Blas 1852-1936 **[6]**
- **$793** - €781 - **£507** - FF5 122
  Bodegón de rosas Oleo/tabla (20x33cm 7x12in) Madrid 1999

BENLLIURE Y GIL José 1855-1937 **[73]**
- **$13 000** - €12 013 - **£8 000** - FF78 800
  Anciano Oleo/lienzo (54x37cm 21x14in) Madrid 1999
- **$23 800** - €20 344 - **£14 280** - FF133 448
  Rückkehr vom Felde Oil/panel (22x32cm 8x12in) Wien 1998
- **$1 008** - €1 081 - **£666** - FF7 092
  Arabe Lápiz/papel (31x23cm 12x9in) Madrid 2000

BENLLIURE Y GIL Mariano 1862-1947 **[109]**
- **$119 544** - €128 321 - **£80 000** - FF841 728
  Buzo de playa (The Young Diver) Marble (H210cm H82in) London 2000
- **$3 737** - €3 454 - **£2 300** - FF22 655
  Busto del nieto del artista Ceramic (H24cm H9in) Madrid 1999
- **$464** - €481 - **£296** - FF3 152
  Toro Tinta/papel (50x69cm 19x27in) Barcelona 2000

BENLLIURE Y ORTIZ José 1884-1916 **[6]**
- **$16 250** - €15 016 - **£10 250** - FF98 500
  Verano y Otoño Oleo/lienzo (110x157cm 43x61in) Madrid 1999

BENN Ben 1884-1983 **[19]**
- **$1 000** - €1 073 - **£669** - FF7 041
  View of the Outskirts of a Village Oil/canvas (36.5x44cm 14x17in) Tel Aviv 2000
- **$1 300** - €1 271 - **£824** - FF8 334
  The Calico Cat Oil/board (39x30cm 15x12in) Bolton MA 1999

BENN Benejou R., dit 1905-1989 **[93]**
- **$816** - €793 - **£504** - FF5 200
  Portrait de Madame Bordeaux Le Pecq Huile/toile (55x46cm 21x18in) Évreux 1999

BENNEKENSTEIN Hermann c.1830-c.1890 **[6]**
- **$2 739** - €3 068 - **£1 903** - FF20 123
  Wallfahrtskapelle bei Beil-Stein an der Mosel Öl/Leinwand (63x89cm 24x35in) Staufen 2001

BENNER Emmanuel 1836-1896 **[50]**
- **$21 000** - €23 989 - **£14 784** - FF157 357
  The Fall of Alsace Lorraine Oil/canvas (130x97cm 51x38in) Pittsfield MA 2001
- **$2 957** - €2 744 - **£1 845** - FF18 000
  Portrait d'un Oriental Huile/toile (54x65cm 21x25in) Biarritz 1999

- **$2 234** - €2 134 - **£1 393** - FF14 000
  Jeune espagnole Huile/toile (22x16cm 8x6in) Paris 1999

BENNER Emmanuel, dit Many 1873-1965 **[24]**
- **$10 938** - €11 428 - **£7 178** - FF74 961
  Female Nude by an Empire Cheval Mirror Oil/canvas (195x130cm 76x51in) Dublin 2000
- **$2 573** - €2 923 - **£1 800** - FF19 171
  Nu à genoux Oil/canvas (55x46.5cm 21x18in) London 2001
- **$1 792** - €1 631 - **£1 100** - FF10 699
  The Artist's Model Oil/canvas (41x33.5cm 16x13in) London 1999

BENNER Gerrit 1897-1981 **[165]**
- **$20 294** - €21 781 - **£13 579** - FF142 876
  Lanschap Oil/canvas (80x100cm 31x39in) Amsterdam 2000
- **$6 067** - €6 807 - **£4 204** - FF44 649
  Bloemen Gouache/paper (65x50cm 25x19in) Amsterdam 2000

BENNER Jean 1796-1849 **[5]**
- **$17 308** - €20 343 - **£12 000** - FF133 440
  Still Life with Flowers on a Ledge Oil/canvas (85x68.5cm 33x26in) London 2000

BENNER Jean 1836-1909 **[37]**
- **$3 919** - €3 887 - **£2 437** - FF25 500
  Les trois enfants Huile/toile (65x81cm 25x31in) Enghien 1999

BENNER Jean Henri 1776-1829 **[3]**
- **$3 454** - €3 354 - **£2 134** - FF22 000
  Jeune femme rousse au buste nu Huile/toile (27.5x35cm 10x13in) Entzheim 1999

BENNETT Alfred 1861-1916 **[20]**
- **$1 648** - €1 709 - **£1 045** - FF11 210
  Henley on Thames Oil/canvas (39x60cm 15x23in) Manchester 2000

BENNETT Andrew XX **[19]**
- **$494** - €577 - **£350** - FF3 786
  Endeavour, Yankee and Velsheda racing off the Royal Yacht Squadron Oil/canvas (61x91.5cm 24x36in) London 2001

BENNETT Charles S. 1869-1930 **[10]**
- **$303** - €292 - **£187** - FF1 916
  Mornington Watercolour/paper (24.5x33.5cm 9x13in) Melbourne 1999

BENNETT Compton XX **[2]**
- **$353** - €409 - **£250** - FF2 686
  «To The Theatre in Comfort, London Underground, Putney Bridge» Poster (99x62cm 38x24in) London 2000

BENNETT Elton 1911-1974 **[12]**
- **$275** - €300 - **£177** - FF1 970
  Seagulls on Pilings/Birds on Floating Logs/Mountain Landscape Silkscreen (39x54cm 15x21in) Portland OR 2000

BENNETT Frank Moss 1874-1953 **[291]**
- **$5 294** - €4 945 - **£3 200** - FF32 439
  The last Wood/the New Fly Oil/canvas (35.5x51cm 13x20in) London 1999
- **$2 840** - €2 958 - **£1 800** - FF19 403
  The Cardinal Oil/canvas (36x26cm 14x10in) London 1999
- **$768** - €645 - **£450** - FF4 233
  Harbour Scene with H.M.S. Implacable in the Foreground Watercolour/paper (25x34.5cm 9x13in) Billingshurst, West-Sussex 1998

BENNETT Gordon 1955 **[8]**
🖌 **$8 291** - €8 900 - **£5 549** - FF58 381
The shooting Gallery Acrylic (80.5x201cm 31x79in)
Sydney 2000
🖌 **$2 401** - €2 578 - **£1 607** - FF16 910
Course of Empire Mixed media (30x110.5cm
11x43in) Sydney 2000

BENNETT Newton 1854-1922 **[4]**
✏ **$4 373** - €4 973 - **£3 097** - FF32 619
Days Lock and the Wittenham Clumps
Watercolour (26.5x34cm 10x13in) Oxfordshire 2000

BENNETT William 1811-1871 **[52]**
✏ **$572** - €644 - **£400** - FF4 226
Near Longleat Watercolour (33x53.5cm 12x21in)
London 2001

BENNETT William James 1787-1844 **[14]**
▥ **$500** - €472 - **£311** - FF3 098
West Point, from Phillipstown Aquatint
(47.5x60.5cm 18x23in) San-Francisco CA 1999

BENNETT William Rubery 1893-1987 **[116]**
🖌 **$8 309** - €7 990 - **£5 119** - FF52 412
The Hawkesbury River Oil/canvas (58.5x74cm
23x29in) Melbourne 1999
🖌 **$2 598** - €2 437 - **£1 606** - FF15 987
Serene Idyll Oil/board (25x29cm 9x11in) Sydney
1999

BENNETTER Johan Jacob 1822-1904 **[27]**
🖌 **$27 408** - €23 839 - **£16 523** - FF156 374
Skibbrudd Oil/canvas (95x137cm 37x53in) Oslo 1998
🖌 **$6 670** - €7 472 - **£4 637** - FF49 014
Segelfartyg i storm vid hamninlopp Oil/canvas
(85x130cm 33x51in) Uppsala 2001
🖌 **$1 354** - €1 271 - **£837** - FF8 334
Threemasted Barque in a Scandinavian Port
Oil/panel (19.5x27cm 7x10in) Amsterdam 1999

BENNEWITZ VON LÖFEN Karl 1826-1895 **[10]**
🖌 **$5 238** - €5 399 - **£3 084** - FF28 596
Herbstliche Waldlandschaft Öl/Leinwand
(90x55cm 35x25in) Wien 1998
🖌 **$1 238** - €1 380 - **£865** - FF9 055
**Kühe an der Tränke an einem Wasser vor einem
Sandhang mit Bäumen** Öl/Karton (27x46cm
10x18in) München 2001

BENOIS Albert Nikolaïevich 1852-1936 **[35]**
🖌 **$2 356** - €2 642 - **£1 600** - FF17 329
Silver Birches by the Marshes Oil/cardboard
(20.5x29.5cm 8x11in) London 2000
✏ **$2 061** - €2 018 - **£1 268** - FF13 238
Maisema krimiltä Akvarell/papper (34x55cm
13x21in) Helsinki 1999

BENOIS Alexander Nikolaïev. 1870-1960 **[273]**
🖌 **$1 054** - €883 - **£620** - FF5 794
Costume of the Moor in Petrouchka for Orloff
Mixed media (32x21cm 12x8in) London 1998
✏ **$3 220** - €3 041 - **£2 000** - FF19 949
**Bourgeois couple taking a Stroll in the
«Summer Gardens»** Pencil (37x50.5cm 14x19in)
London 1999

BENOIS DI STETTO Alexandre A. 1888-? **[9]**
▥ **$1 371** - €1 518 - **£950** - FF9 958
«Grindelwald» Poster (100x70cm 39x27in) London
2001

BENOIS Nadia 1896-1975 **[41]**
🖌 **$942** - €981 - **£600** - FF6 433
Pompom Dahlias Oil/canvas (56x40.5cm 22x15in)
London 2000

BENOIS Nikolaï Alexandrov. 1901-1988 **[8]**
✏ **$1 323** - €1 135 - **£800** - FF7 447
Three Costume designs Watercolour, gouache
(46x30.5cm 18x12in) London 1998

BENOIST J.L. XVIII-XIX **[2]**
▥ **$3 125** - €2 897 - **£1 943** - FF19 000
L'Histoire de Télémaque Eau-forte couleurs
(39x46cm 15x18in) Paris 1999

BENOIST Philippe 1813-c.1880 **[13]**
▥ **$153** - €183 - **£109** - FF1 200
Allicante, vue prise de la rade, par A.Rouargue
Lithographie (35.5x58.5cm 13x23in) Paris 2000

**BENOIST, née DELAVILLE-LEROULX Marie
Guilhelmine** 1768-1826 **[2]**
🖌 **$54 200** - €60 980 - **£37 320** - FF400 000
L'Innocence entre le Vice et la Vertu Huile/toile
(87x115cm 34x45in) Paris 2000

BENOIST-GIRONIERE Yvan 1930 **[43]**
✏ **$375** - €427 - **£260** - FF2 800
La carriole Aquarelle/papier (48.5x32.5cm 19x12in)
Senlis 2000

BENOIT Jacqueline 1928 **[23]**
🖌 **$2 118** - €2 134 - **£1 320** - FF14 000
Le chat noir Huile/toile (55x46cm 21x18in) Orléans
2000

BENOIT Paul XIX-XX **[23]**
✏ **$128** - €152 - **£91** - FF1 000
Madagascar Aquarelle/papier (10.5x15.5cm 4x6in)
Nantes 2000

BENOIT-LÉVY Jules 1866-1952 **[23]**
🖌 **$487** - €544 - **£326** - FF3 571
Street in Katwijk Oil/panel (24x18cm 9x7in)
Amsterdam 2000

BENOUVILLE Achille 1815-1891 **[53]**
🖌 **$16 500** - €17 105 - **£9 900** - FF112 200
Il Tevere a Tor di Quinto Olio/tela (103x160cm
40x62in) Roma 1999
🖌 **$5 187** - €5 793 - **£3 515** - FF38 000
Femme Italienne Huile/toile (55x34cm 21x13in)
Pontoise 2000
🖌 **$6 445** - €6 541 - **£3 903** - FF37 000
Vue des jardins de la villa d'Este à Tivoli
Huile/toile (40x32.5cm 15x12in) Paris 1998
✏ **$10 447** - €11 434 - **£7 222** - FF75 000
Rome vue du Forum du Capitole Gouache/papier
(30x58cm 11x22in) Vendôme 2001

BENOUVILLE Léon François 1821-1859 **[26]**
🖌 **$3 000** - €3 298 - **£1 922** - FF21 631
Poussin Finding the Subject for his Moses
Oil/canvas/board (58.5x98cm 23x38in) New-York 2000
✏ **$1 437** - €1 448 - **£895** - FF9 500
Jeune éphèbe Crayon (34.5x23.5cm 13x9in) Neuilly-
sur-Seine 2000

BENRATH Frédéric 1930 **[87]**
🖌 **$1 071** - €1 220 - **£756** - FF8 000
Composition Huile/toile (50x65cm 19x25in)
Versailles 2001

BENSA Ernesto XIX-XX **[17]**
🖌 **$2 269** - €2 556 - **£1 596** - FF16 769
Dame beim Rosenpflücken im Garten Öl/Karton
(28x20.5cm 11x8in) München 2001

✍ **$1 500** - €1 412 - **£932** - FF9 260
The Bargello Watercolour/paper (78x50cm 31x20in)
East-Dennis MA 1999

BENSA von Alexander Franz 1794-c.1846 **[2]**

🖎 **$4 094** - €4 602 - **£2 874** - FF30 185
Reiter-Umtrunk vor dem Gutshof/Beim Hufschmied Oil/panel (20.5x31.5cm 8x12in)
Hamburg 2001

BENSA von Alexander Ritter 1820-1902 **[77]**

🖎 **$1 925** - €2 130 - **£1 265** - FF13 970
Bear-Hunters Oil/board (36.5x57.5cm 14x22in)
Budapest 2000

🖎 **$2 588** - €2 710 - **£1 626** - FF17 775
Die Einquartierung Öl/Karton (20.5x32cm 8x12in)
Bremen 2000

BENSELL George Frederick 1837-1879 **[15]**

🖎 **$2 000** - €2 320 - **£1 422** - FF15 219
Boaters in a Western Autumnal River Landscape Oil/canvas (76x127cm 29x50in)
Washington 2000

BENSO Giulio 1592-1668 **[13]**

✍ **$7 000** - €6 140 - **£4 250** - FF40 276
The Martyrdom of Saint Catherine Ink (33.5x24cm 13x9in) New-York 1999

BENSON Ambrosius c.1495-1550 **[18]**

🖎 **$20 000** - €21 359 - **£13 628** - FF140 106
Saint Mary Magdalen reading Oil/panel (52.5x41.5cm 20x16in) New-York 2001

🖎 **$37 500** - €37 936 - **£22 897** - FF248 846
The Virgin and Child Oil/panel (37x28.5cm 14x11in)
New-York 2000

BENSON Eugene 1839-1908 **[8]**

🖎 **$16 000** - €14 771 - **£9 840** - FF96 894
A Vestal of the Spring Oil/canvas (30x87.5cm 11x34in) New-York 1999

BENSON Frank Weston 1862-1951 **[345]**

🖎 **$440 000** - €487 285 - **£298 408** - FF3 196 380
Indian Guide Oil/canvas (81.5x101.5cm 32x39in)
New-York 2000

✍ **$30 000** - €25 632 - **£18 153** - FF168 132
Birds in Winter Watercolour/paper (61x50cm 24x19in) San-Francisco CA 1998

🗒 **$700** - €656 - **£430** - FF4 300
Mallard Drake Etching (15x20cm 5x7in) New-York 1999

BENT van der Johannes c.1650-1690 **[21]**

🖎 **$23 908** - €25 664 - **£16 000** - FF168 345
Capriccio of a Mediterranean Harbour with Elegant Travellers, a Moor Oil/canvas (106x145.5cm 41x57in) London 2000

🖎 **$9 618** - €9 076 - **£5 934** - FF59 532
Shepherdess and Milkmaid by a Fountain Mounted by a Sculpture Oil/canvas (67x90.5cm 26x35in) Amsterdam 1999

BENTABOLE Louis 1820-1880 **[22]**

🖎 **$3 208** - €3 201 - **£2 003** - FF21 000
L'embarquement en Bretagne Huile/toile (43.5x59cm 17x23in) Fontainebleau 1999

🖎 **$1 609** - €1 622 - **£1 003** - FF10 637
Marine mit Fischern und Booten Huile/panneau (23.5x36cm 9x14in) Zürich 2000

BENTELE Fidelis 1905-1987 **[4]**

🪶 **$2 104** - €1 968 - **£1 272** - FF12 912
Flöte blasendes Kind Sculpture (H58.5cm H23in)
Lindau 1999

BENTELE Fidelis 1830-1901 **[6]**

🖎 **$885** - €1 012 - **£607** - FF6 640
Blick auf Schloss Heiligenberg Öl/Leinwand (32x30cm 12x11in) Lindau 2000

BENTES Manuel 1885-1961 **[2]**

🖎 **$9 000** - €9 970 - **£6 590** - FF65 400
Paisagem de montanha Oleo/lienzo (64x53cm 25x20in) Lisboa 2000

🖎 **$3 520** - €3 988 - **£2 400** - FF26 160
Jarra com flores Huile/papier (46x33cm 18x12in)
Lisboa 2000

BENTIVOGLIO C. 1882-1943 **[4]**

✍ **$3 648** - €3 496 - **£2 300** - FF22 930
Lady with Parasol strolling on the Beach Watercolour/paper (49.5x100cm 19x39in) Billingshurst, West-Sussex 1998

BENTIVOGLIO Cesare 1900-1972 **[21]**

🖎 **$2 280** - €1 970 - **£1 520** - FF12 920
Stagno nel bosco Olio/tela (57x115cm 22x45in)
Milano 1998

🖎 **$780** - €674 - **£520** - FF4 420
Casa ligure Olio/cartone (33x35cm 12x13in) Milano 1998

BENTLEY Charles 1806-1854 **[74]**

✍ **$2 006** - €1 713 - **£1 200** - FF11 236
Fishermen unloading a Beached Vessel Watercolour (26x37cm 10x14in) London 1998

BENTLEY John William 1880-1951 **[54]**

🖎 **$5 000** - €4 671 - **£3 115** - FF30 643
Winter Day Oil/canvas (81x101cm 32x40in) Mystic CT 1999

🖎 **$1 000** - €1 127 - **£692** - FF7 392
Beach Scene with Sailboat, Key West, FL Oil/board (20x25cm 8x10in) Hatfield PA 2000

BENTLEY Joseph Clayton 1809-1851 **[6]**

✍ **$360** - €424 - **£250** - FF2 782
Passing the Lock Watercolour (29.5x61.5cm 11x24in) London 2000

BENTON Thomas Hart 1889-1975 **[735]**

🖎 **$200 000** - €191 192 - **£125 360** - FF1 254 140
Design for Mural «Jacques Cartier and the St.Lawrence» Oil/board (49.5x82.5cm 19x32in) New-York 1999

✍ **$30 000** - €35 013 - **£21 267** - FF229 668
Smugglers Oil/board (25.5x21cm 10x8in) New-York 2001

✍ **$5 500** - €5 838 - **£3 721** - FF38 296
Investigation, The Flood of 37 Watercolour (22x30cm 9x12in) Delray-Beach FL 2001

🗒 **$1 700** - €1 956 - **£1 171** - FF12 831
Shallow Creek Lithograph (36x23cm 14x9in)
Cleveland OH 1999

BENTZEN Axel 1893-1952 **[104]**

🖎 **$450** - €470 - **£283** - FF3 083
Parti fra Gilleleje Oil/canvas (56x83cm 22x32in)
Köbenhavn 2000

BENVENUTI Benvenuto 1881-1959 **[36]**

🖎 **$4 500** - €4 587 - **£2 250** - FF25 500
Paesaggio con carro e pagliaio Olio/cartone (22.5x35cm 8x13in) Prato 1999

🖎 **$1 800** - €1 866 - **£1 080** - FF12 240
Paesaggio Matita/carta (70x100cm 27x39in) Prato 2000

BENVENUTI Eugenio 1881-1959 **[51]**

🖎 **$550** - €479 - **£327** - FF3 141
Venice Canal Watercolour/paper (38x23cm 15x9in)
St. Louis MO 1998

BENVENUTI L'ORTOLANO Giovanni Battista c.1487-c.1530 **[6]**
- $32 000 – €31 985 – **£19 548** – FF209 808
  The Birth of the Virgin Oil/panel (33.5x48.5cm 13x19in) New-York 2000

BENVENUTI Pietro 1769-1844 **[8]**
- $43 989 – €44 332 – **£27 423** – FF290 796
  Allegorisk sceneri med lystigt selskab med Bacchus i spidsen Oil/canvas (143x100cm 56x39in) København 2000
- $650 – €696 – **£443** – FF4 563
  Nymphs and a drunken Satyr Ink (12x25.5cm 4x10in) New-York 2001

BENVENUTO DI GIOVANNI di Meo di Guasta 1436-c.1517 **[2]**
- $226 246 – €192 499 – **£135 000** – FF1 262 709
  Assumption of the Virgin wit St Thomas receiving the Girdle Tempera/canvas (294x219cm 115x86in) London 1998

BENVENUTO di Girolamo 1470-1524 **[3]**
- $48 933 – €45 767 – **£30 000** – FF300 210
  The Presentation of the Virgin Tempera/panel (33x44.5cm 12x17in) London 1998

BENWELL Joseph Austin c.1830-1890 **[28]**
- $4 260 – €3 924 – **£2 600** – FF25 742
  Praying to Mecca Watercolour (48x35.5cm 18x13in) London 1998

BENZ Achilles 1766-1843 **[9]**
- $2 570 – €2 501 – **£1 582** – FF16 406
  Lugano Aquarelle (16.5x26.8cm 6x10in) Bern 1999

BENZONI Giovanni Maria 1809-1873 **[23]**
- $17 695 – €19 596 – **£12 000** – FF128 544
  Achilles and Penthesilea Marble (H124cm H48in) London 2000
- $35 000 – €39 087 – **£22 414** – FF256 392
  A Young Girl and Her Dog Marble (H78.5cm H30in) New-York 2000

BEÖTHY Étienne 1897-1961 **[41]**
- $2 412 – €2 287 – **£1 467** – FF15 000
  Opus 17, Femme I Bronze (41.5x20.5x3.5cm 16x8x1in) Paris 1999
- $2 970 – €3 375 – **£2 070** – FF22 140
  Composition Tempera/papier (38.5x33cm 15x12in) Budapest 2001

BERALDO Franco 1944 **[21]**
- $1 400 – €1 451 – **£840** – FF9 520
  Natura morta nel paesaggio Olio/tela (50x60cm 19x23in) Vercelli 2001
- $760 – €985 – **£570** – FF6 460
  «Natura morta» Olio/tela (40x30cm 15x11in) Vercelli 2000

BERANGER Antoine 1785-1867 **[5]**
- $38 287 – €42 929 – **£26 000** – FF281 598
  A blind Beggar accompanied by a small Boy outside a House Oil/canvas (74x92.5cm 29x36in) London 2000

BERANGER Charles 1816-1853 **[3]**
- $2 029 – €2 250 – **£1 408** – FF14 757
  Stilleben mit Kupferkanne und erlegten Rebhühnern Oil/panel (18x13.5cm 7x5in) Köln 2001

BERANGER Gabriel 1729-1817 **[1]**
- $3 308 – €3 809 – **£2 277** – FF24 987
  Simmon's Court Castle Watercolour/paper (14x14cm 5x5in) Dublin 2000

BERANGER Jean Baptiste Emile 1814-1883 **[1]**
- $6 481 – €6 053 – **£4 000** – FF39 702
  Morning Oil/panel (22x17cm 9x7in) Fernhurst, Haslemere, Surrey 1999

BERANN Heinrich 1915 **[13]**
- $297 – €276 – **£184** – FF1 811
  «125 Jahre Befreiung Tirols» Poster (95x126cm 37x49in) Wien 1999

BÉRARD Christian 1902-1949 **[468]**
- $16 026 – €14 025 – **£9 706** – FF92 000
  Les musiciens Huile/panneau (150x137cm 59x53in) Paris 1998
- $4 950 – €5 488 – **£3 427** – FF36 000
  Portrait d'homme à la chemise rouge Huile/toile (81x65cm 31x25in) Paris 2001
- $5 099 – €4 726 – **£3 044** – FF31 100
  Portrait de femme Huile/toile (41x33cm 16x12in) Paris 1999
- $710 – €762 – **£475** – FF5 000
  Étude d'une danseuse Encre (50.5x32.5cm 19x12in) Paris 2000

BERARDI Fabio 1728-? **[11]**
- $400 – €415 – **£240** – FF2 720
  Paesaggio con pescatori Gravure (45.5x59.5cm 17x23in) Milano 2000

BÉRAUD Jean 1849-1936 **[144]**
- $1 450 000 – €1 250 994 – **£874 785** – FF8 205 985
  The Casino at Monte Carlo Oil/canvas (103x131cm 40x51in) New-York 1998
- $54 950 – €53 357 – **£33 950** – FF350 000
  Portrait d'une jeune parisienne Huile/toile (55.5x38.5cm 21x15in) Paris 1999
- $15 318 – €14 025 – **£9 338** – FF92 000
  Jeune élégante Huile/panneau (19x15cm 7x5in) Paris 1999
- $4 000 – €3 932 – **£2 570** – FF25 791
  The Can-Can Watercolour (45x32.5cm 17x12in) New-York 1999

BERBERIAN Ovanes 1951 **[13]**
- $2 750 – €2 350 – **£1 664** – FF15 414
  «Arroyo Seco Bridge, Pasadena, California» Oil/canvas (45.5x61cm 17x24in) San-Francisco CA 1998
- $850 – €912 – **£568** – FF5 984
  Near Sedona Oil/masonite (30x40cm 12x16in) Altadena CA 2000

BERCHEM Claes Nicolas P. 1620-1683 **[109]**
- $35 060 – €40 390 – **£21 140** – FF200 000
  Vue d'un port méditerranéen Huile/toile (47.5x58.5cm 18x23in) Paris 1998
- $13 448 – €14 436 – **£9 000** – FF94 694
  Peasant with her livestock in a Landscape, Ruins and Moutains beyond Oil/panel (31.5x24cm 12x9in) London 2000
- $1 779 – €1 910 – **£1 191** – FF12 532
  Hirte mit Tieren und Transportwagen Black chalk/paper (12.9x20.9cm 5x8in) Bern 2000
- $695 – €818 – **£500** – FF5 366
  Der Flötespielende Hirt auf dem Brunnen und das Mädchen Radierung (26.5x21cm 10x8in) Hamburg 2001

BERCHERE Narcisse 1819-1891 **[97]**
- $7 490 – €6 555 – **£4 536** – FF43 000
  L'oasis à Memphis Huile/toile (58x78cm 22x30in) Paris 1998
- $5 180 – €6 098 – **£3 640** – FF40 000
  Campement Huile/toile (25.5x44.5cm 10x17in) Paris 2000

✏ **$1 348** - €1 250 - **£838** - FF8 200
Paysage d'Égypte avec les pyramides Crayon (18.5x27cm 7x10in) Paris 1999

BERCHMANS Emile 1867-1947 **[74]**
✏ **$395** - €471 - **£283** - FF3 089
Allégorie de l'automne Encre Chine/papier (20x14cm 7x5in) Liège 2000
▥ **$170** - €198 - **£117** - FF1 300
Les trois huit Lithographie couleurs (44x84cm 17x33in) Liège 2000

BERCHMANS Emile Edouard 1843-1914 **[10]**
🖼 **$248** - €273 - **£160** - FF1 788
Plage Huile/toile (28x42.5cm 11x16in) Liège 2000

BERCHMANS Henri 1856-1911 **[1]**
✏ **$1 278** - €1 487 - **£882** - FF9 756
La repasseuse Pastel/carton (68x50cm 26x19in) Liège 2000

BERCHTOLD Hubert 1922 **[3]**
✏ **$4 200** - €4 039 - **£2 587** - FF26 495
Komposition Gouache (47x63cm 18x24in) St. Gallen 2000

BERCK (Arthur Berckmans) 1929 **[4]**
✏ **$730** - €701 - **£452** - FF4 600
Couverture «Sammy, bons vieux pour les gorilles» Encre Chine/papier (37x25.5cm 14x10in) Paris 1999

BERCKHEYDE Gerrit Adriaensz 1638-1698 **[27]**
🖼 **$16 000** - €18 845 - **£11 065** - FF123 614
Italianate Landscape with a Peasant Family Fording a Stream Oil/panel (48.5x69cm 19x27in) New-York 2000
✏ **$38 960** - €45 378 - **£27 220** - FF297 660
The Dam Square, Amsterdam, with the Royal Palace to the Left Black chalk (14x19cm 5x7in) Amsterdam 2000

BERCKHEYDE Job Adriaensz. 1630-1693 **[18]**
🖼 **$135 384** - €153 770 - **£95 000** - FF1 008 662
The Interior of the St.Bavokerk, Haarlem, looking south-west Oil/panel (44.5x37cm 17x14in) London 2001
🖼 **$9 862** - €9 350 - **£6 000** - FF61 333
Peasants playing backgammon beneath the Arbour of a Tavern Oil/panel (34.5x29cm 13x11in) London 1999

BERCKHOLTZ von Alexandra 1821-1899 **[5]**
🖼 **$1 993** - €1 841 - **£1 241** - FF12 074
Damenportrait vor heiterem Himmel Öl/Leinwand (72x62cm 28x24in) Frankfurt 1999

BERCKMANS Matheus c.1635-c.1675 **[2]**
🖼 **$19 560** - €18 294 - **£11 988** - FF120 000
La Cène Huile/panneau (75.5x106cm 29x41in) Paris 1998

BERCOVITCH Alexandre 1891-1951 **[12]**
✏ **$2 706** - €2 670 - **£1 666** - FF17 515
Nue assise Pastel (126x74.5cm 49x29in) Montréal 1999

BERCZY William 1748-1813 **[1]**
🖼 **$39 711** - €33 981 - **£23 905** - FF222 900
Flowers in a creamware vase Oil/canvas (35x24cm 13x9in) Toronto 1998

BERDANIER Paul Frederick 1879-? **[6]**
▥ **$900** - €907 - **£561** - FF5 949
Inevitability - Death and Taxes Etching (30x20cm 11x7in) New-York 2000

BERDOT XVII **[2]**
🖼 **$1 744** - €1 982 - **£1 220** - FF13 000
Caprice architectural dans un port Huile/cuivre (12x16cm 4x6in) Paris 2001

BERECHEL Claudine 1925 **[24]**
🗿 **$429** - €366 - **£255** - FF2 400
Grande Prétresse Bronze (30x6x4cm 11x2x1in) Paris 1998

BEREKETOGLU Vecihi 1895-1973 **[5]**
🖼 **$36 000 000** - €40 856 337 - **£24 000 000** - FF268 000 000
Barques sur l'eau Huile/toile (60x81cm 23x31in) Istanbul 2001
🖼 **$5 850 000** - €6 639 155 - **£3 899 999** - FF43 550 000
Nature morte Huile/panneau (33x41cm 12x16in) Istanbul 2001

BEREND-CORINTH Charlotte 1880-1967 **[39]**
🖼 **$1 033** - €1 022 - **£644** - FF6 707
An der Ostseeküste Öl/Leinwand (56.1x76.1cm 22x29in) Berlin 1999
✏ **$558** - €511 - **£340** - FF3 353
Bunter Blumenstrauss aus Tulpen, Narzissen und Stiefmütterchen Watercolour, gouache/paper (50.5x42.5cm 19x16in) Berlin 1999
▥ **$175** - €184 - **£110** - FF1 207
Akt mit Boa und Hut Lithographie (58x47cm 22x18in) Stuttgart 2000

BERENTS Jacob act.1663-1723 **[4]**
✏ **$5 084** - €5 899 - **£3 510** - FF38 695
Cleopatra with the Asp, in an Elegant Interior Bodycolour (20x14cm 7x5in) Amsterdam 2000

BERENTZ Christian 1658-1722 **[18]**
🖼 **$54 869** - €51 361 - **£34 000** - FF336 909
Figs and Peaches on a Pewter Platter, Glasses of Wine on a Gold Dish Oil/canvas (63.5x47.5cm 25x18in) London 1999

BERENY Cacio 1951 **[31]**
✏ **$193** - €198 - **£121** - FF1 300
Troyes, la Ruelle des Chats Gouache (38x26cm 14x10in) Troyes 2000

BERENY Robert 1887-1953 **[10]**
🖼 **$1 092** - €1 050 - **£676** - FF6 890
Village Street with Geese Oil/canvas (50x60cm 19x23in) Budapest 1999
✏ **$17 600** - €17 306 - **£11 000** - FF113 520
Lido Pastel/paper (46x67cm 18x26in) Budapest 1999

BERESTEYN van Claes 1627-1684 **[1]**
✏ **$89 608** - €104 369 - **£62 606** - FF684 618
Dune Landscape with Trees to the Left, and an Overgrown Ruin Ink (14x19cm 5x7in) Amsterdam 2000

BERETTA Petrus Augustus 1805-1866 **[11]**
🖼 **$113** - €131 - **£79** - FF861
Intérieur Huile/toile (64x53cm 25x20in) Genève 2000

BEREZOWSKA Maja 1898-1978 **[38]**
✏ **$308** - €362 - **£220** - FF2 372
Scène de genre: en route Aquarelle (27x30cm 10x11in) Warszawa 2000

BERG Adolf Julius 1820-1873 **[3]**
🖼 **$1 985** - €1 896 - **£1 237** - FF12 437
Landskapsav Oil/canvas (71x93cm 27x36in) Stockholm 1999

BERG Albert 1825-1884 **[15]**
- **$7 000** - €7 509 - **£4 771** - FF49 257
  Parti fra en havn ved Palermo Oil/canvas (60x87cm 23x34in) Köbenhavn 2001

BERG Christian 1893-1976 **[71]**
- **$661** - €653 - **£407** - FF4 283
  Gatumotiv från Paris Oil/canvas (32x25cm 12x9in) Stockholm 1999
- **$5 371** - €5 895 - **£3 460** - FF38 668
  Spjutbörd II Bronze (H34.5cm H13in) Stockholm 2000

BERG Else 1877-1942 **[51]**
- **$5 355** - €4 636 - **£3 249** - FF30 408
  A Garden with Lambs Oil/canvas (61.5x71cm 24x27in) Amsterdam 1998
- **$3 816** - €4 538 - **£2 720** - FF29 766
  A mining district near Tilleur, Belgium Oil/board (30x36cm 11x14in) Amsterdam 2000
- **$1 007** - €1 134 - **£694** - FF7 441
  Autumn Landscape in the South of France Watercolour (26x37cm 10x14in) Amsterdam 2000

BERG Frans 1892-1949 **[15]**
- **$2 023** - €1 897 - **£1 251** - FF12 445
  Kvinnan i allén Oil/panel (54.5x50cm 21x19in) Stockholm 1999

BERG Gunnar 1864-1894 **[9]**
- **$1 782** - €1 975 - **£1 209** - FF12 955
  Fra Svolvaer Oil/canvas/panel (28x45cm 11x17in) Oslo 2000

BERG Julius 1820-1873 **[4]**
- **$4 134** - €4 560 - **£2 800** - FF29 909
  Sommarlandskap Oil/canvas (73x92cm 28x36in) Stockholm 2000

BERG van den Ans 1873-1942 **[39]**
- **$1 472** - €1 271 - **£888** - FF8 334
  Still Life with Tulips in a Vase Oil/canvas/board (37x46cm 14x18in) Amsterdam 1999
- **$1 051** - €908 - **£634** - FF5 953
  Flowers in a bowl Watercolour/paper (32x43.5cm 12x17in) Amsterdam 1999

BERG van den Freek 1918-2000 **[28]**
- **$2 760** - €2 723 - **£1 699** - FF17 859
  Portret Van Anke Brokstra Oil/canvas (100x70cm 39x27in) Amsterdam 1999

BERG van den Josna Michiel 1905-1978 **[10]**
- **$1 536** - €1 586 - **£966** - FF10 406
  Dame assise Huile/toile (99x74cm 38x29in) Antwerpen 2000

BERG van den Siep 1913-1998 **[7]**
- **$976** - €1 134 - **£686** - FF7 441
  Untitled Oil/canvas (80x120cm 31x47in) Amsterdam 2001

BERG van den Simon 1812-1891 **[28]**
- **$2 600** - €3 066 - **£1 834** - FF20 114
  Shepherd with his flock in a landscape Oil/canvas (49x83cm 19x33in) New-Orleans LA 2001
- **$2 003** - €1 897 - **£1 222** - FF12 206
  Poultry in a sunlit yard Oil/panel (21.5x33cm 8x12in) Amsterdam 1999
- **$872** - €908 - **£547** - FF5 953
  Breiend schapenhoedstertje achter de duinen Ink/paper (24x35cm 9x13in) Dordrecht 2000

BERG van den Willem 1886-1970 **[117]**
- **$2 100** - €2 343 - **£1 374** - FF15 368
  Scheveningen Oil/board (91x63cm 36x25in) Chicago IL 2000

- **$1 011** - €998 - **£614** - FF6 548
  Farmer Oil/panel (22x17cm 8x6in) Amsterdam 2000
- **$399** - €363 - **£245** - FF2 381
  Heron Watercolour (55x43cm 21x16in) Amsterdam 1999

BERG Werner 1904-1981 **[54]**
- **$26 670** - €30 522 - **£18 816** - FF200 214
  Frau mit Kopftuch Öl/Leinwand (35x55cm 13x21in) Wien 2001
- **$1 851** - €2 180 - **£1 302** - FF14 301
  Haus in der Nacht Woodcut (28.5x50.5cm 11x19in) Wien 2000

BERGAGNA Vittorio 1884-1965 **[8]**
- **$1 150** - €1 192 - **£690** - FF7 820
  La spagnola Tecnica mista (37x25cm 14x9in) Trieste 1998

BERGAIGNÉ Pierre 1652-1708 **[4]**
- **$29 808** - €35 063 - **£21 367** - FF230 000
  Gitans et des pèlerins dans un paysage vallonné Huile/cuivre (14x25cm 5x9in) Lille 2001

BERGAMINI Francesco XIX **[62]**
- **$5 000** - €4 331 - **£3 066** - FF28 407
  Caught in Mischief Oil/canvas (45.5x68.5cm 17x26in) New-York 1999
- **$3 244** - €3 114 - **£2 034** - FF20 426
  Listening carefully to the Teacher's Instructions Oil/canvas (26.5x39.5cm 10x15in) Montréal 1999

BERGANDER Rudolf 1909-1970 **[9]**
- **$125** - €143 - **£87** - FF939
  Mutter und Sohn Etching, aquatint (20.5x13.8cm 8x5in) Berlin 2000

BERGE Edward 1876-1924 **[40]**
- **$5 000** - €4 545 - **£3 011** - FF29 815
  Young Girl sitting next to a Fish Pond Bronze (H60cm H24in) Amesbury MA 1998

BERGE ten Bernardus Gerardus 1835-1875 **[16]**
- **$3 944** - €4 214 - **£2 686** - FF27 642
  Schapen in een landschap Huile/toile (42.5x66cm 16x25in) Lokeren 2001
- **$1 147** - €1 115 - **£702** - FF7 317
  Coin de rue avec personnage assis Huile/toile (40x33.5cm 15x13in) Bruxelles 1999

BERGEN 1954 **[11]**
- **$2 525** - €2 820 - **£1 711** - FF18 500
  Le 24 août Technique mixte (40x50cm 15x19in) Rambouillet 2000
- **$778** - €762 - **£497** - FF5 000
  Mozart Technique mixte (30x25cm 11x9in) Rambouillet 1999

BERGEN Claus 1885-1964 **[37]**
- **$4 018** - €4 857 - **£2 805** - FF31 862
  Vorstoss nach Norwegen (Minensuchboote) Öl/Leinwand (91x150.5cm 35x59in) Düsseldorf 2000
- **$830** - €920 - **£574** - FF6 037
  «Ertrinkender Matrose mit Kriegsflagge vor Sinkendem Kriegsschiff» Gouache/paper (15x10cm 5x3in) Kempten 2001

BERGEN Fritz 1857-1941 **[15]**
- **$496** - €511 - **£313** - FF3 353
  Bismarck, vor Kaiser Wilhelm I/Bismarck... Aquarell/Papier (26x20cm 10x7in) Berlin 2000

BERGEN van Dirck 1645-1690 **[31]**
- **$3 800** - €4 375 - **£2 593** - FF28 697
  Famyard Landscape with Drovers Oil/canvas (40.5x49cm 15x19in) New-York 2000

BERGEN von Carl 1853-1930 **[10]**
- $2 283 - €2 301 - £1 423 - FF15 092
  Junge, strahlende Mutter in ländlicher Kleidung
  Öl/Leinwand (64x46cm 25x18in) Staufen 2000

BERGER Anthony XIX **[4]**
- $14 000 - €16 231 - £9 917 - FF106 471
  Lincoln Abraham, Seated Portrait of President Lincoln Albumen print (22x16.5cm 8x6in) New-York 2000

BERGER Edith 1900-1994 **[30]**
- $2 355 - €2 287 - £1 455 - FF15 000
  Le jardin d'Édith vu de sa fenêtre Huile/panneau (68x138cm 26x54in) Grenoble 1999
- $5 680 - €6 098 - £3 800 - FF40 000
  Le clocher de Lalley Huile/carton (30x40cm 11x15in) Grenoble 2000
- $542 - €610 - £380 - FF4 000
  Les blés Pastel/papier (31x48cm 12x18in) Grenoble 2001

BERGER Einar 1890-1961 **[21]**
- $905 - €839 - £563 - FF5 505
  Sommarnatt i Finnmarken Oil/canvas (57x74cm 22x29in) Malmö 1999

BERGER Georges 1908-1976 **[57]**
- $245 - €274 - £164 - FF1 800
  Saint-Germain-des-Prés, Paris Huile/toile (55x46cm 21x18in) Paris 2000

BERGER Hans 1882-1977 **[94]**
- $1 712 - €1 955 - £1 207 - FF12 827
  Maisons au soleil Öl/Leinwand (46x61.5cm 18x24in) Bern 2001
- $1 363 - €1 252 - £837 - FF8 215
  Le Break Huile/panneau (39x36cm 15x14in) Zürich 1999
- $835 - €813 - £513 - FF5 332
  Tisch mit Geschirr Aquarell/Papier (29x35cm 11x13in) Zürich 1999

BERGER Jacques 1902-1977 **[8]**
- $1 451 - €1 651 - £1 006 - FF10 828
  Composition abstraite Gouache/panneau (46.5x56cm 18x22in) Sion 2000

BERGER Joe 1939-1991 **[41]**
- $224 - €254 - £157 - FF1 668
  «Das kritiklose Herumstehen» Mischtechnik/Papier (42x56cm 16x22in) Wien 2001

BERGER Johan 1842-? **[2]**
- $4 000 - €4 583 - £3 000 - FF34 000
  Una sala di Palazzo Pitti Acquarello/carta (43x61cm 16x24in) Venezia 2000

BERGER Johan Christian 1803-1871 **[13]**
- $4 179 - €4 067 - £2 572 - FF26 677
  Fridhem Oil/canvas (35x50cm 13x19in) Stockholm 1999
- $4 314 - €4 125 - £2 704 - FF27 058
  Utsilt över Fridhem, Gotland Oil/canvas (30x41cm 11x16in) Stockholm 1999

BERGER Julius Victor 1850-1902 **[6]**
- $45 000 - €42 690 - £27 337 - FF280 030
  Entertaining the Pasha Oil/panel (63.5x49.5cm 25x19in) New-York 1999

BERGER Mathieu 1807-? **[1]**
- $11 000 - €12 182 - £7 460 - FF79 909
  Still Life of Flowers in a Vase Resting on a Table Oil/canvas (64x53cm 25x20in) New-York 2000

BERGER-BERGNER Paul 1904-1978 **[7]**
- $136 - €153 - £95 - FF1 006
  «Geburt» Woodcut in colors (28.5x44cm 11x17in) Berlin 2001

BERGER-REVAL E. XIX-XX **[1]**
- $5 212 - €6 126 - £3 613 - FF40 184
  Young Girl Reading Oil/canvas (72.5x81cm 28x31in) Amsterdam 2000

BERGERE Richard 1912 **[3]**
- $400 - €384 - £247 - FF2 519
  Twilight over Brooklyn Bridge Lithograph (23x32cm 9x12in) New-York 1999

BERGERET Denis Pierre 1846-1910 **[37]**
- $43 000 - €47 687 - £28 612 - FF312 807
  Nature morte Oleo/lienzo (202x282cm 79x111in) Buenos-Aires 2000
- $3 362 - €3 630 - £2 299 - FF23 812
  A Still Life with Poppies and Daisies Oil/panel (67x47.5cm 26x18in) Amsterdam 2001
- $900 - €1 024 - £628 - FF6 714
  Ostras y marsicos Oleo/lienzo (24.5x32.5cm 9x12in) Buenos-Aires 2000

BERGERET Pierre Nolasque 1782-1863 **[14]**
- $2 000 - €2 324 - £1 405 - FF15 242
  The Meeting of King Francis I of France and King Henry VIII of England Ink (17.5x25.5cm 6x10in) New-York 2001

BERGES Ernest Georges 1870-1934 **[8]**
- $4 760 - €5 336 - £3 332 - FF35 000
  Un après-midi sur la plage Huile/toile (50x61cm 19x24in) Paris 2001

BERGES Werner 1941 **[29]**
- $2 026 - €2 301 - £1 408 - FF15 092
  «Mitte Juni» Acryl/Leinwand (100x80cm 39x31in) München 2001
- $164 - €153 - £101 - FF1 006
  Figürliche Darstellungen Farbserigraphie (61x43cm 24x16in) Hamburg 1999

BERGEVIN Albert J.-P. 1887-1974 **[28]**
- $1 846 - €2 058 - £1 242 - FF13 500
  «Baie du Mont St.Michel, Avranches, St.Jean-le-Thomas» Affiche (119x80cm 46x31in) Orléans 2000

BERGEY Earle K. 1901-1952 **[6]**
- $7 500 - €8 401 - £5 211 - FF55 104
  Strutting Showgirl with Tophat and Cane Oil/canvas (58x48cm 23x19in) New-York 2001

BERGGREN Guillaume Gustave 1835-1920 **[3]**
- $3 345 - €3 811 - £2 297 - FF25 000
  Vues de Constantinople: dames turques, der-niche antiquaire, marchands Tirage albuminé (13.5x10cm 5x3in) Paris 2000

BERGH Anton 1828-1907 **[2]**
- $4 586 - €5 081 - £3 112 - FF33 327
  To jegere Oil/canvas (41x59cm 16x23in) Oslo 2000

BERGH de Gillis Gillisz. c.1600-1669 **[6]**
- $66 066 - €63 529 - £40 698 - FF416 724
  «Pronk» Violin, a Silver Salt cellar, Peaches, Prunes, and Pears Oil/canvas (108x138cm 42x54in) Amsterdam 1999
- $10 089 - €11 920 - £7 149 - FF78 193
  Stilleben mit Flechtkorb und Trauben Öl/Leinwand (39.5x47.2cm 15x18in) Zürich 2000

BERGH Edvard 1828-1880 **[51]**
- $2 613 - €2 444 - £1 616 - FF16 029
  Landskap med gård och figurer Oil/canvas (88x130cm 34x51in) Stockholm 1999

BERGH Richard 1858-1919 **[36]**
- $3 326 - €3 110 - £2 049 - FF20 400
  Vitklädd kvinna, studie till Riddaren och Jungfrun Oil/panel (63x49cm 24x19in) Stockholm 1999
- $1 428 - €1 658 - £1 003 - FF10 878
  «Dam läsande tidning» Oil/panel (24.5x24cm 9x9in) Stockholm 2001
- $291 - €352 - £203 - FF2 312
  Modellstudie Pencil/paper (70x52cm 27x20in) Stockholm 2000

BERGH Svante 1885-1946 **[63]**
- $714 - €670 - £441 - FF4 392
  Italiensk gård i bergslandskap Oil/canvas (66.5x54.5cm 26x21in) Stockholm 1999

BERGH van den Jan 1587/88-c.1650 **[1]**
- $13 448 - €14 436 - £9 000 - FF94 694
  Profile Study Seated Old Man, Resting his Forehead on his Left Hand Red chalk (20.5x13.5cm 8x5in) London 2001

BERGH van den Nicolaes 1725-1774 **[1]**
- $25 421 - €29 496 - £17 550 - FF193 479
  The Seven Acts of Mercy Oil/panel (59x81cm 23x31in) Amsterdam 2000

BERGHE van den Charles Auguste 1798-1853 **[6]**
- $3 926 - €4 421 - £2 734 - FF29 000
  Femme à la robe bleue/Homme au col de fourrure Oil/canvas (92x73cm 36x28in) Paris 2001

BERGHE van den Christoffel 1590-1642 **[13]**
- $23 508 - €27 441 - £16 596 - FF180 000
  Paysage fluvial avec hallebardier sur un chemin creux et soldats Huile/cuivre (22x31cm 8x12in) Paris 2000

BERGHE van den Frits 1883-1939 **[87]**
- $14 421 - €14 129 - £8 892 - FF92 682
  Hoeve te laren Oil/canvas (45.5x56.5cm 17x22in) Lokeren 1999
- $3 180 - €2 975 - £1 968 - FF19 512
  Jeune femme nue étendue les bras levés Huile/toile (23.5x55cm 9x21in) Lokeren 1999
- $2 278 - €2 107 - £1 419 - FF13 821
  De metgezellen II Pencil (14x11.5cm 5x4in) Lokeren 1999

BERGHE van der Ignatius-Joseph 1752-1824 **[2]**
- $17 318 - €15 060 - £10 444 - FF98 784
  Flamländsk byscen Oil/panel (54x71cm 21x27in) Stockholm 1998
- $1 657 - €1 406 - £1 000 - FF9 225
  Nymphs bathing/Diana and Shepherdess Engraving (55x72cm 21x28in) London 1998

BERGIER Alfred 1881-1971 **[12]**
- $178 - €206 - £122 - FF1 350
  Bord de mer Aquarelle/papier (55x37cm 21x14in) Avignon 2000

BERGLER Joseph II 1753-1829 **[38]**
- $180 - €215 - £128 - FF1 408
  Die göttliche Weisheit siegt über die Unwissenheit Ink (18.1x13.4cm 7x5in) Berlin 2000

BERGMAN Anna-Eva 1909-1987 **[64]**
- $1 196 - €1 372 - £818 - FF9 000
  Sans titre Huile/papier (50x65cm 19x25in) Paris 2000
- $661 - €734 - £460 - FF4 813
  Grasse, Frankrike Oil/panel (12.5x27cm 4x10in) Oslo 2001
- $128 - €152 - £91 - FF1 000
  Composition Gravure bois (50.5x65.5cm 19x25in) Paris 2000

BERGMAN Franz XIX-XX **[81]**
- $1 160 - €1 134 - £716 - FF7 441
  Erotic Group Bronze (H13cm H5in) Amsterdam 1999

BERGMAN Henry Eric 1893-1958 **[38]**
- $260 - €304 - £183 - FF1 991
  Lone Tree with Forest in Distance, Winter Woodcut (16x9cm 6x3in) Calgary, Alberta 2000

BERGMAN Karl 1891-1965 **[79]**
- $656 - €618 - £406 - FF4 056
  Skärgårdslandskap med solbelysta tallar Oil/canvas (57x97cm 22x38in) Stockholm 1999

BERGMAN Oskar 1879-1963 **[437]**
- $1 142 - €1 327 - £802 - FF8 702
  «Vinter vid baggensfjärden» Oil/panel (37x62cm 14x24in) Stockholm 2001
- $981 - €1 099 - £682 - FF7 208
  Skogsdunge i solnedgång Miniature (5.5x4cm 2x1in) Uppsala 2001
- $1 094 - €1 271 - £769 - FF8 339
  Våren kommer Akvarell/papper (13.5x9cm 5x3in) Stockholm 2001

BERGMANN Max 1884-1955 **[95]**
- $2 206 - €2 045 - £1 372 - FF13 415
  Ruhende Kühe und Kälbchen vor weiter Landschaft Oil/panel (40x60.5cm 15x23in) Kempten 1999

BERGMANN-MICHEL Ella 1895-1971 **[10]**
- $2 386 - €2 045 - £1 434 - FF13 413
  E. Bemmonshorn Mixed media (34.5x35.5cm 13x13in) Hamburg 1998
- $1 350 - €1 534 - £938 - FF10 061
  Innenansicht eines roten Raumes von unten mit Grundriss Gouache (24x30.5cm 9x12in) Berlin 2001

BERGMANS Emile Edouard 1843-1914 **[1]**
- $3 762 - €4 338 - £2 625 - FF28 455
  Dimanche à la plage Huile/toile (27.5x42cm 10x16in) Bruxelles 2001

BERGMÜLLER Johann Georg 1688-1762 **[22]**
- $1 072 - €1 278 - £764 - FF8 384
  Das Dankopfer Noahs Indian ink (17.8x20.6cm 7x8in) Köln 2000
- $343 - €409 - £244 - FF2 683
  Der Sommer Radierung (22x18.5cm 8x7in) Berlin 2000

BERGNER Vladimir Jossif Josl 1920 **[332]**
- $8 000 - €9 004 - £5 511 - FF59 061
  Miracle No.2 Oil/canvas (162x130cm 63x51in) Herzelia-Pituah 2000
- $7 000 - €8 299 - £5 099 - FF54 436
  Klezmer Musicians Oil/canvas (80x69.5cm 31x27in) Tel Aviv 2001
- $2 400 - €2 488 - £1 581 - FF16 322
  Flowers Oil/canvas (40x30cm 15x11in) Herzelia-Pituah 2000
- $600 - €711 - £437 - FF4 666
  Landscape Watercolour, gouache/paper (23x47.5cm 9x18in) Tel Aviv 2001
- $212 - €220 - £133 - FF1 446
  The Bridesmaid Serigraph in colors (40x51.5cm 15x20in) Melbourne 2000

BERGOLLI Aldo 1916-1972 **[28]**
- $1 100 - €1 140 - £660 - FF7 480
  Paesaggio nella stanza 2 Olio/tela (79.5x69.5cm 31x27in) Milano 2000

BERGOUGNAN Raoul 1900-1982 **[15]**
- $2 352 - €2 439 - **£1 550** - FF16 000
  Le canal du Midi Huile/papier (44x59cm 17x23in)
  Lavaur 2000
- $1 204 - €1 372 - **£832** - FF9 000
  La place Saint-Pierre à Toulouse Aquarelle,
  gouache/papier (22.5x30.5cm 8x12in) Toulouse 2000

BERGSLIEN Knud Larsen 1827-1908 **[6]**
- $65 880 - €74 566 - **£46 080** - FF489 120
  «St.Hansaften paa Landet» Oil/canvas (66x83cm
  25x32in) Oslo 2001

BERGSLIEN Nils Nilsen 1853-1928 **[23]**
- $4 541 - €5 400 - **£3 235** - FF35 424
  Fra Håkon Håkonsens historie Oil/canvas
  (233x140cm 91x55in) Oslo 2000
- $8 797 - €9 177 - **£5 550** - FF60 195
  Lorden og romjekolla Oil/canvas (69x55cm 27x21in)
  Oslo 2000
- $5 865 - €6 118 - **£3 700** - FF40 130
  Nissen og gröten Akvarell/papper (26x20cm 10x7in)
  Oslo 2000

BERGSTAD Terje 1938 **[4]**
- $2 865 - €3 180 - **£1 996** - FF20 859
  «Fra Leningrad skisse» Oil/panel (60x73cm
  23x28in) Oslo 2001
- $2 534 - €2 813 - **£1 766** - FF18 452
  «Luraasovnen» Oil/panel (27x35cm 10x13in) Oslo
  2001

BERGSTEDT Amanda 1841-1918 **[2]**
- $8 960 - €10 174 - **£6 286** - FF66 738
  Kaiserin Elisabeth Öl/Leinwand (71x57cm 27x22in)
  Wien 2001

BERGSTRÖM Alfred 1869-1930 **[40]**
- $2 760 - €2 976 - **£1 852** - FF19 522
  Humlegården, Stockholm Oil/canvas (46x59cm
  18x23in) Stockholm 2000
- $317 - €351 - **£220** - FF2 300
  Strandparti från Havre Oil/panel (23.5x32.5cm
  9x12in) Stockholm 2001

BERGUE de Tony 1820-1890 **[33]**
- $4 600 - €4 287 - **£2 838** - FF28 120
  Bathers being observed over the Garden Wall
  Oil/panel (64x47cm 25x18in) New-Orleans LA 1999
- $4 260 - €4 573 - **£2 850** - FF30 000
  Honfleur - La Côte de Grâce vue de la mer
  Huile/panneau (27x45cm 10x17in) Nantes 2000

BÉRIC XX **[3]**
- $182 - €189 - **£109** - FF1 241
  «Diques, radio-télé» Affiche couleur (160x118cm
  62x46in) Torino 2000

BÉRILLE Francis XX **[33]**
- $934 - €1 067 - **£658** - FF7 000
  Bécasse Bronze (15.5x13.5cm 6x5in) Paris 2001

BERJON Antoine 1754-1843 **[36]**
- $20 535 - €22 867 - **£14 430** - FF150 000
  **Nature morte à la grappe de raisins et aux
  fleurs** Huile/toile (46x55.5cm 18x21in) Paris 2001
- $59 772 - €64 160 - **£40 000** - FF420 864
  **Portrait of a Gentleman, Half-Length, Wearing a
  Hat and a Stock** Pencil (25x19cm 9x7in) London
  2000

BERJONNEAU Jehan 1890-1972 **[64]**
- $314 - €305 - **£194** - FF2 000
  Moulins Huile/toile (33x46cm 12x18in) Châtellerault
  1999

BERKE Hubert 1908-1979 **[149]**
- $1 734 - €2 045 - **£1 223** - FF13 415
  November Öl/Leinwand (100.2x70.4cm 39x27in)
  Köln 2001
- $476 - €511 - **£318** - FF3 353
  **Komposition mit Grün, Orange, Pink und
  Schwarz** Watercolour (62x48cm 24x18in) Köln 2000
- $278 - €281 - **£169** - FF1 844
  «Hubert Berke - Zehn Holzschnitte» Woodcut
  (40x30cm 15x11in) Stuttgart 2000

BERKES Antal 1874-1938 **[222]**
- $1 249 - €1 189 - **£776** - FF7 800
  Place animée Huile/toile (58x76cm 22x29in) Mâcon
  1999
- $465 - €460 - **£290** - FF3 018
  **Verschneiter Boulevard mit reicher
  Personenstaffage** Öl/Karton (21x34cm 8x13in)
  Hildrizhausen 1999

BERKHOLZ Gustav act.c.1860-c.1872 **[1]**
- $8 118 - €9 076 - **£5 650** - FF59 532
  **Bouquet with orange Blossom, indian Cress,
  Roses, Irises and Violets** Oil/canvas (63x52.5cm
  24x20in) Amsterdam 2001

BERKO Ferenc 1928 **[19]**
- $220 - €236 - **£149** - FF1 551
  Zoë Dye-transfer print (48x33cm 18x12in) Beverly-
  Hills CA 2001

BERLAGE Hendrik Petrus 1856-1934 **[3]**
- $1 007 - €1 143 - **£699** - FF7 500
  «Harwich van Hoek Holland» Affiche (99x65cm
  38x25in) Paris 2001

BERLAND Rubén 1955 **[2]**
- $12 000 - €13 923 - **£8 284** - FF91 332
  Mogote sobre las rocas doradas Oil/canvas
  (149x121cm 58x47in) New-York 2000

BERLANT Tony 1941 **[18]**
- $28 000 - €30 055 - **£18 737** - FF197 148
  The Letter Mixed media (183.5x183.5cm 72x72in)
  Beverly-Hills CA 2000
- $8 000 - €7 957 - **£4 965** - FF52 195
  Yang Na Metal (71x71x71cm 27x27x27in) Beverly-
  Hills CA 1999

BERLEWI Henryk 1894-1967 **[45]**
- $20 136 - €21 560 - **£13 704** - FF141 424
  Nature morte Huile/toile (40x64.5cm 15x25in)
  Warszawa 2001
- $4 385 - €3 661 - **£2 571** - FF24 012
  Portrait of a young Woman with a Hat Oil/panel
  (33x23.7cm 12x9in) Warszawa 1998
- $2 069 - €1 982 - **£1 275** - FF13 000
  Femme Pastel (28x22cm 11x8in) Douai 1999
- $204 - €204 - **£128** - FF1 341
  Ohne Titel Farbserigraphie (60.8x50cm 23x19in)
  Hamburg 1999

BERLIN Dis 1959 **[8]**
- $1 088 - €1 021 - **£680** - FF6 698
  La gacela Técnica mixta (58x79cm 22x31in) Madrid
  1999

BERLIN Sven 1911 **[62]**
- $181 - €157 - **£109** - FF1 032
  Venus Watercolour/paper (24x28cm 9x11in) London
  1999

BERLINGIERI F. **[4]**
- $2 148 - €2 439 - **£1 492** - FF16 000
  Réunion sur le port Huile/toile/carton (20x40cm
  7x15in) Pontoise 2001

BERLIT Rüdiger 1883-1939 **[54]**

✏ $367 - €409 - **£240** - FF2 683
Damenkopf im Profil Charcoal/paper (44.4x32.7cm 17x12in) Leipzig 2000

▭ $87 - €102 - **£61** - FF670
Dörfliche Landschaft Radierung (19.8x25cm 7x9in) Berlin 2000

BERLOT Jean-Baptiste 1775-1836 **[7]**

◉ $9 001 - €7 775 - **£5 436** - FF51 000
Vue du Panthéon à Rome Huile/toile (82x101cm 32x39in) Granville 1998

◉ $6 039 - €6 860 - **£4 167** - FF45 000
Scène prise sur la terrasse d'un palais dans la campagne romaine Huile/toile (40x33cm 15x12in) Paris 2000

BERLY DE VLAMINCK Madeleine 1896-1953 **[17]**

✏ $2 684 - €3 049 - **£1 884** - FF20 000
Portrait de femme Gouache (29x23cm 11x9in) Paris 2001

BERMAN Eugene 1899-1972 **[189]**

◉ $3 600 - €3 757 - **£2 270** - FF24 642
L'orage sur la mer Oil/canvas (73x91cm 28x35in) New-York 2000

◉ $2 500 - €2 232 - **£1 531** - FF14 640
The Stairs, Rome/The Old Roman Raod with Bridge Oil/paper (40x30cm 15x11in) New-York 1999

✏ $1 400 - €1 194 - **£844** - FF7 829
«Le Bourgeois Gentilhomme» Costume Design Watercolour/paper (31x25cm 12x9in) New-York 1998

BERMAN Leonid 1898-1976 **[28]**

✏ $497 - €579 - **£348** - FF3 800
Parc à huîtres, Marennes d'Oléron Huile/toile (66x126cm 25x49in) Neuilly-sur-Seine 2000

BERMAN Marietta 1917-1990 **[1]**

◉ $11 000 - €11 807 - **£7 361** - FF77 451
Cellista Acrylic/canvas (199.5x151cm 78x59in) New-York 2000

BERMAN Mieczyslaw 1903-1975 **[4]**

◉ $8 000 - €7 473 - **£4 835** - FF49 017
Untitled Photograph (40x50cm 16x20in) New-York 1999

BERMAN Saul 1899-1972 **[4]**

◉ $23 000 - €22 386 - **£14 131** - FF146 841
Eighth and Vermont Oil/canvas (45x71cm 18x28in) San-Francisco CA 1999

BERMAN Wallace 1926-1976 **[17]**

◉ $18 000 - €15 110 - **£10 557** - FF99 118
Untitled Mixed media (122x116cm 48x45in) Beverly-Hills CA 1998

◉ $9 000 - €8 666 - **£5 627** - FF56 846
Untitled Mixed media/panel (94x83cm 37x32in) Beverly-Hills CA 1999

◉ $4 000 - €3 978 - **£2 482** - FF26 097
Untitled Collage/board (32.5x35.5cm 12x13in) Beverly-Hills CA 1999

✏ $7 000 - €7 840 - **£4 863** - FF51 430
Untitled Collage (61x66cm 24x25in) New-York 2001

BERMOND André 1903-1983 **[13]**

▭ $561 - €621 - **£380** - FF4 075
«Agadir Maroc» Poster (100x62cm 39x24in) London 2000

BERMUDEZ Cundo 1914 **[94]**

◉ $42 000 - €40 865 - **£25 851** - FF268 056
Mujer sentada con guitarra Oil/panel (88x72cm 34x28in) New-York 1999

◉ $11 000 - €12 780 - **£7 730** - FF83 833
«El mundo secreto de Beatriz» Oil/canvas/board (68x22.5cm 26x8in) New-York 2001

◉ $7 000 - €6 044 - **£4 270** - FF39 646
Saltimbancos Tempera/paper (40.5x91.5cm 15x36in) Miami FL 1999

BERMUDEZ Jorge 1883-1926 **[2]**

◉ $25 000 - €29 046 - **£17 570** - FF190 530
Camino el mercado Oleo/lienzo (126x96cm 49x37in) Buenos-Aires 2001

BERNADSKY Guennadi 1956 **[33]**

◉ $375 - €440 - **£267** - FF2 884
Young Lady in a Garden with Umbrella Oil/canvas (78x57cm 31x22in) Delray-Beach FL 2000

BERNAERTS Nicasius 1620-1678 **[5]**

◉ $11 169 - €12 958 - **£7 947** - FF85 000
Présentation de gibiers et de volailles dans un intérieur de cuisine Huile/toile (121x152cm 47x59in) Paris 2001

BERNALDO Allan Thomas 1900-1988 **[98]**

✏ $935 - €876 - **£578** - FF5 749
Still Life Watercolour/paper (50x40cm 19x15in) Melbourne 1999

BERNARD Édouard Alexandre 1879-1950 **[20]**

▭ $400 - €411 - **£253** - FF2 698
«Edouard, un lavois sec, à l'eau, ou au cassis?» Poster (78x119cm 31x47in) Cincinnati OH 2000

BERNARD Émile 1868-1941 **[738]**

◉ $11 360 - €12 196 - **£7 600** - FF80 000
Les Trois Grâces Huile/toile (119x120cm 46x47in) Paris 2000

◉ $6 390 - €6 860 - **£4 275** - FF45 000
Nature morte à la bouteille Huile/carton (60x80cm 23x31in) Paris 2000

◉ $3 026 - €2 820 - **£1 872** - FF18 500
La cascade Huile/toile (41x27cm 16x10in) Paris 1999

✏ $802 - €686 - **£482** - FF4 500
Femme debout de profil Fusain/papier (13.5x8.5cm 5x3in) Paris 1998

▭ $105 - €107 - **£66** - FF700
Portrait de Toulouse-Lautrec Gravure (49.5x31.5cm 19x12in) Rennes 2000

BERNARD Francis 1900-1979 **[18]**

▭ $1 200 - €1 346 - **£833** - FF8 828
«Black and Decker» Poster (160x118cm 63x46in) New-York 2001

BERNARD François 1812-c.1875 **[7]**

◉ $38 000 - €35 418 - **£22 967** - FF232 328
Portrait of Creole Children Oil/canvas (142x112cm 56x44in) New-Orleans LA 1999

◉ $57 045 - €65 642 - **£39 321** - FF430 584
Portrait of Two Chitimacha Indians Oil/panel (59x38cm 23x15in) New-Orleans LA 2000

BERNARD Jacques Samuel XVII **[9]**

◉ $5 696 - €6 353 - **£3 717** - FF41 672
Still Life of Flowers in an Ormolu mounted Copper Vessel Oil/canvas (48.5x39cm 19x15in) Amsterdam 2000

BERNARD Jean-Joseph 1740-1809 **[10]**

✏ $2 250 - €2 646 - **£1 613** - FF17 356
Portrait of Marie Antoinette, Head and Shoulders, in Profile Watercolour (44.5x36cm 17x14in) New-York 2001

BERNARD Joseph 1864-1933 **[45]**
- $4 776 - €4 625 - **£3 000** - FF30 337
  The Artist's Atelier Oil/panel (81.5x63.5cm 32x25in)
  London 1999
- $6 763 - €6 353 - **£4 076** - FF41 672
  Ein Störenfried/Die ersten Früchte Oil/paper/panel
  (53x26cm 20x10in) Amsterdam 1999

BERNARD Joseph Antoine 1866-1931 **[53]**
- $129 760 - €125 095 - **£80 000** - FF820 568
  **Jeune fille à sa toilette, an impressive Art Deco
  Figure** Bronze (H158cm H62in) London 1999
- $10 627 - €12 501 - **£7 617** - FF82 000
  Les voix Bronze (H39cm H15in) Paris 2001

BERNARD Louis Michel 1885-1962 **[172]**
- $1 101 - €960 - **£665** - FF6 300
  Maison en bord de mer Huile/carton (57x107cm
  22x42in) Toulouse 1998
- $2 202 - €1 921 - **£1 331** - FF12 600
  Le port d'Alger Gouache/papier (53x100cm 20x39in)
  Toulouse 1998

BERNARDI de Domenico 1892-1963 **[10]**
- $4 000 - €4 147 - **£2 400** - FF27 200
  Borgo in riva al lago Olio/masonite (50x60cm
  19x23in) Milano 1999
- $1 280 - €1 659 - **£960** - FF10 880
  «Pomeriggio di fine novembre» Olio/tavola
  (18.5x24cm 7x9in) Milano 2001

BERNARDI Joseph 1826-1907 **[25]**
- $1 982 - €1 815 - **£1 208** - FF11 906
  «Waldlandschaft» Oil/canvas (104x90cm 40x35in)
  Amsterdam 1999

BERNARDI Romolo 1876-1956 **[10]**
- $125 - €130 - **£75** - FF850
  Montagne Olio/cartone (19x26cm 7x10in) Vercelli
  2001

BERNARDINO DI LORENZO DI CECCO XV-XVI **[1]**
- $31 625 - €32 784 - **£18 975** - FF215 050
  **Madonna con Bambino ed I Santi Pietro e Paolo
  con un donatore** Tempera/tavola (87x54cm 34x21in)
  Roma 1999

BERNARDO Montsu 1624-1687 **[3]**
- $3 412 - €3 811 - **£2 312** - FF25 000
  Portrait d'une vieille femme lisant un livre
  Huile/toile (64x47.5cm 25x18in) Paris 2000

BERNARDS Laureys act.1644-1676 **[1]**
- $11 342 - €12 706 - **£7 882** - FF83 344
  **View of a Store-Room with Servants, Poultry, a
  Dog and a Cat** Oil/panel (53.5x74.5cm 21x29in)
  Amsterdam 2001

BERNARTZ Hans Willy 1912-1989 **[7]**
- $208 - €204 - **£128** - FF1 341
  Rad-Fregatte «Hansa» Chalks (33x48cm 12x18in)
  Bremen 1999

BERNASCONI George H. act.1861-1881 **[1]**
- $9 532 - €10 273 - **£6 500** - FF67 386
  A Walk in the Zoo/A Conversation on the Beach
  Oil/canvas (15.5x21.5cm 6x8in) London 2001

BERNASCONI Ugo 1874-1960 **[20]**
- $2 975 - €3 084 - **£1 785** - FF20 230
  Giacinti nel vaso Olio/cartone/tela (46x36cm
  18x14in) Milano 2000
- $800 - €829 - **£480** - FF5 440
  Vaso viole Olio/tavoletta (33x25cm 12x9in) Firenze
  2000

BERNATH Aurél 1895-1982 **[16]**
- $1 122 - €1 275 - **£782** - FF8 364
  Rêveuse Pastel/papier (68.5x47.5cm 26x18in)
  Budapest 2001

BERNATH Sandor 1892-1984 **[19]**
- $850 - €796 - **£526** - FF5 219
  Provincetown Houses Watercolour/paper (30x40cm
  12x16in) Norwalk CT 1999

BERNATZIK Wilhelm 1853-1906 **[7]**
- $21 981 - €25 307 - **£15 000** - FF166 003
  Winternachmittag Oil/canvas (163.5x100cm 64x39in)
  London 2000

BERNAUS Jordi 1929 **[43]**
- $627 - €571 - **£380** - FF3 743
  Muchacha con una pecera Oleo/lienzo (73x60cm
  28x23in) Barcelona 1999

BERNDT Siegfried 1880-1946 **[26]**
- $152 - €164 - **£102** - FF1 073
  Fischer am Kanal Woodcut in colors (14.7x24.7cm
  5x9in) Berlin 2000

BERNDTSON Gunnar 1854-1895 **[30]**
- $14 344 - €13 455 - **£8 864** - FF88 256
  Dam i festdräkt Oil/canvas (120x90cm 47x35in)
  Helsinki 1999
- $11 240 - €12 782 - **£7 797** - FF83 843
  Antonia Bonjean Oil/panel (24x19cm 9x7in) Helsinki
  2000
- $1 623 - €1 766 - **£1 069** - FF11 583
  Flicka Pencil/paper (37x24cm 14x9in) Helsinki 2000

BERNE-BELLECOUR Étienne 1838-1910 **[109]**
- $90 000 - €79 673 - **£55 026** - FF522 621
  On the Dueling Ground Oil/canvas (131x99cm
  51x38in) New-York 1999
- $5 331 - €6 341 - **£3 800** - FF41 591
  Quick Escape Oil/panel (50x34cm 19x13in) London
  2000
- $1 700 - €1 886 - **£1 130** - FF12 370
  Soldiers Conversing Oil/panel (25x29cm 10x11in)
  Milford CT 2000
- $1 100 - €1 097 - **£686** - FF7 197
  Soldier Lighting his Pipe Watercolour/paper
  (25x15cm 10x6in) Dedham MA 1999

BERNE-BELLECOUR Jean-Jacques 1874-? **[24]**
- $2 300 - €2 727 - **£1 675** - FF17 886
  Officer in Landscape with Windmill Oil/canvas
  (64x53cm 25x21in) Chicago IL 2001
- $2 500 - €2 286 - **£1 526** - FF14 997
  A moments rest Oil/panel (40x31cm 16x12in) New-
  York 1998
- $1 428 - €1 524 - **£975** - FF10 000
  L'EmpereurNapoléon 1er à cheval Aquarelle,
  gouache/papier (31x39cm 12x15in) Paris 2001

BERNEKER Louis Frederick 1872-1937 **[23]**
- $2 700 - €2 333 - **£1 602** - FF15 306
  Proserpine Oil/canvas (68.5x56cm 26x22in)
  Washington 1998

BERNER Bernd 1930 **[28]**
- $954 - €1 125 - **£670** - FF7 378
  Ohne Titel Mischtechnik/Papier (63x48.9cm 24x19in)
  Düsseldorf 2000

BERNERT Alfred 1893-1991 **[62]**
- $383 - €358 - **£231** - FF2 347
  **Doppelportrait der Gebrüder Jacob und
  Wilhelm Grimm** Öl/Leinwand (70x50cm 27x19in)
  Lindau 1999

BERNHARD Franz 1934 **[27]**
- $13 390 - €12 782 - **£8 365** - FF83 847
  Figur Brücke Sculpture, wood (80x200x140cm 31x78x55in) Köln 1999
- $772 - €920 - **£550** - FF6 037
  Ohne Titel Ink/paper (45x63cm 17x24in) Berlin 2000

BERNHARD Lucian 1883-1972 **[42]**
- $1 500 - €1 359 - **£918** - FF8 912
  «REM» Poster (116x150cm 46x59in) New-York 1998

BERNHARD Pieter Gerardus 1813-1880 **[3]**
- $4 920 - €4 958 - **£3 060** - FF32 520
  La leçon de danse Huile/panneau (50.5x40.5cm 19x15in) Bruxelles 2000

BERNHARD Ruth 1905 **[113]**
- $2 400 - €2 763 - **£1 637** - FF18 124
  Two Leaves Gelatin silver print (50x40cm 19x15in) New-York 2000

BERNHARDT Sarah 1844-1923 **[32]**
- $320 - €381 - **£221** - FF2 500
  L'oncle incarné Huile/panneau (37x20.5cm 14x8in) Paris 2000
- $960 - €1 143 - **£665** - FF7 500
  Buste d' Emile Girardin Bronze (H32cm H12in) Sceaux 2000

BERNI Antonio 1905-1981 **[50]**
- $400 000 - €385 306 - **£248 360** - FF2 527 440
  Chelsea Hotel Mixed media/canvas (201x163cm 79x64in) New-York 1999
- $20 000 - €19 412 - **£12 452** - FF127 332
  Paisaje de Barracas Oil/canvas (49.5x73.5cm 19x28in) New-York 1999
- $5 000 - €5 809 - **£3 514** - FF38 106
  El santiagueñito Oleo/lienzo (45x35cm 17x13in) Buenos-Aires 2001
- $1 100 - €1 278 - **£773** - FF8 383
  Perfil Grabado (32x26cm 12x10in) Buenos-Aires 2001

BERNI G. XIX-XX **[1]**
- $1 600 - €1 785 - **£1 047** - FF11 709
  «Bazar de l'Hôtel de Ville, Paris 1900 , Etrennes» Poster (112x155.5cm 44x61in) New-York 2000

BERNIER Camille 1823-1903 **[13]**
- $5 494 - €6 250 - **£3 813** - FF41 000
  Pâturage sous les arbres Huile/toile (81x120.5cm 31x47in) Fontainebleau 2000
- $1 003 - €1 139 - **£686** - FF7 470
  Landskab med kvinde med krukke Oil/canvas (35x25cm 13x9in) Vejle 2000

BERNIER Georges, Géo 1862-1918 **[80]**
- $803 - €695 - **£484** - FF4 557
  Landskab med hästar vid vatten Oil/canvas (58x79cm 22x31in) Stockholm 1999
- $398 - €397 - **£248** - FF2 601
  Attelages dans les champs Huile/toile (18x40cm 7x15in) Bruxelles 1999

BERNIER Pascal 1960 **[2]**
- $7 172 - €7 699 - **£4 800** - FF50 503
  Accident de chasse Sculpture (77x37x50cm 30x14x19in) London 2000

BERNIGEROTH Johann Martin 1713-1767 **[3]**
- $762 - €869 - **£532** - FF5 701
  Abriss der Illumination und des Feuerwerks Radierung (52.5x72.5cm 20x28in) Berlin 2001

BERNIK Janez 1933 **[5]**
- $352 - €383 - **£232** - FF2 515
  Kreuzabnahme Etching, aquatint (48.5x64cm 19x25in) Hamburg 2000

BERNINGER Edmund 1843-1909 **[49]**
- $30 000 - €28 100 - **£18 444** - FF184 323
  An Arab Caravan above Tunis Oil/canvas (95x163cm 37x64in) New-York 1999
- $6 165 - €7 285 - **£4 369** - FF47 785
  Landschaft bei Sorrent Öl/Leinwand (55x81.5cm 21x32in) Zürich 2000
- $893 - €869 - **£548** - FF5 701
  Sahara, Hügelkette und Wolken Öl/Leinwand/Karton (18x23cm 7x9in) Berlin 1999
- $198 - €204 - **£125** - FF1 341
  Torbole, Olivenhain und Hangpartie unter Gewitterhimmel Aquarell/Papier (33x42cm 12x16in) Berlin 2000

BERNINGER John E. XX **[12]**
- $1 700 - €1 655 - **£1 044** - FF10 853
  Farm Landscape with River and cloudy Sky Oil/board (40x50cm 16x20in) Hatfield PA 1999

BERNINGHAUS Oscar Edmund 1874-1952 **[76]**
- $40 000 - €36 362 - **£24 092** - FF238 520
  Indian Encampment Oil/board (71x175cm 28x69in) Hayden ID 1998
- $65 000 - €60 177 - **£39 786** - FF394 732
  A New Mexico Desert Landscape, three Native Americans on Horseback Oil/canvas (76x101cm 30x40in) St. Louis MO 1999
- $22 000 - €18 981 - **£13 222** - FF124 504
  Indian in a White Robe Oil/board (33x22cm 13x9in) Santa-Fe NM 1998
- $800 - €741 - **£489** - FF4 858
  The Incas Watercolour/paper (39x48cm 15x19in) St. Louis MO 1999

BERNINI Giovanni Lorenzo 1598-1680 **[8]**
- $26 000 - €22 432 - **£15 480** - FF147 141
  Busto of Gregory XV Ludovisi Sculpture (H72.5cm H28in) New-York 1998

BERNOUD Alphonse 1820-1875 **[7]**
- $1 696 - €1 905 - **£1 100** - FF12 496
  Lathyrus Latifoluis (Gesse & Lange Feuille) Albumen print (26.5x20.5cm 10x8in) London 2000

BERNOUD E. XIX-XX **[7]**
- $2 103 - €2 119 - **£1 310** - FF13 900
  Statuette Chryséléphantine (H36cm H14in) Biarritz 2000

BERNSTEIN Theresa Ferber 1890-? **[61]**
- $3 500 - €2 991 - **£2 055** - FF19 618
  A Busy Harbor, Possibly Gloucester, Mass. Oil/board (66x87cm 26x34in) Downington PA 1998
- $5 000 - €5 547 - **£3 325** - FF36 383
  Afterglow Oil/board (30x25cm 12x10in) Milford CT 1999

BERNT Rudolf 1844-1914 **[26]**
- $723 - €799 - **£501** - FF5 243
  «Letzte Rosen» Aquarell/Papier (24x17cm 9x6in) Wien 2001

BERNY D'OUVILLÉ Claude Charles Ant. 1775-1842 **[19]**
- $1 049 - €1 220 - **£737** - FF8 000
  Portrait présumé de Jacques Lefebure (1769-1830) Miniature (14x10.5cm 5x4in) Paris 2001

B

B

BERONNEAU André 1886-1973 **[52]**
- $680 - €798 - £480 - FF5 235
  «St.Marine, Finistère» Oil/canvas (45.5x54.5cm 17x21in) London 2000

BÉROUD Louis 1852-1930 **[43]**
- $55 000 - €61 565 - £38 357 - FF403 837
  Mona Lisa at the Louvre Oil/canvas (130x161.5cm 51x63in) New-York 2001
- $10 000 - €11 858 - £6 880 - FF77 783
  Le Palais des Champs-Élysées, Paris Oil/panel (95.5x67cm 37x26in) New-York 2000
- $1 633 - €1 829 - £1 135 - FF12 000
  Intérieur à la statue Voltaire Huile/toile (35x24.5cm 13x9in) Paris 2001

BERQUE Jean 1896-1954 **[12]**
- $690 - €762 - £478 - FF5 000
  Portrait de garçonne Huile/toile (55x46cm 21x18in) Paris 2001

BERQUET Gilles 1956 **[22]**
- $896 - €838 - £542 - FF5 500
  Autoportrait en Francis Bacon Tirage argentique (12x12cm 4x4in) Paris 1999

BERRÉ Jean-Baptiste 1777-1838 **[14]**
- $1 934 - €1 982 - £1 193 - FF13 000
  Animaux au repos Huile/panneau (23x30cm 9x11in) Vendôme 2000

BERRESFORD Virginia 1902-1994 **[9]**
- $5 000 - €5 719 - £3 477 - FF37 517
  Dunes and Shells Oil/canvas (53x91cm 21x36in) Cincinnati OH 2000
- $2 100 - €2 352 - £1 459 - FF15 429
  «Gravestones» Oil/canvas (33x40cm 13x16in) Cincinnati OH 2000
- $350 - €335 - £213 - FF2 198
  Block of Houses Lithograph (48x38.5cm 18x15in) Boston MA 1999

BERRETTONI Niccolo 1637-1682 **[4]**
- $12 500 - €12 958 - £7 500 - FF85 000
  Madonna Olio/tavola (52x41cm 20x16in) Roma 2000

BERRI Peter Robert 1864-1942 **[3]**
- $14 417 - €17 109 - £10 496 - FF112 226
  Winterliche Gebirgslandschaft Engadin Öl/Leinwand/Karton (20x29cm 7x11in) Zürich 2001

BERRIE John Archibald Alex. 1887-1962 **[4]**
- $22 863 - €21 048 - £14 000 - FF138 066
  Portrait of Sir Winston Churchill Oil/canvas (76x64cm 29x25in) London 1998

BERROCAL Miguel Ortiz 1933 **[565]**
- $833 - €971 - £584 - FF6 372
  Ohne Titel Tempera (60.2x42cm 23x16in) Köln 2000
- $9 750 - €9 010 - £6 000 - FF59 100
  Alfa e Romeo Fer (94x54cm 37x21in) Madrid 1999
- $1 070 - €1 220 - £735 - FF8 000
  Membres Métal (H14cm H5in) Paris 2000
- $183 - €188 - £111 - FF1 182
  Figuras femeninas Litografía (62x87cm 24x34in) Barcelona 2000

BERROETA de Pierre 1914 **[145]**
- $638 - €610 - £398 - FF4 000
  Composition Huile/toile (65x100cm 25x39in) Paris 1999
- $319 - €335 - £211 - FF2 200
  Montmartre Gouache/papier (50x64.5cm 19x25in) Paris 2000

BERRUER Pierre François 1733-1793 **[2]**
- $8 740 - €9 994 - £6 000 - FF65 557
  Figure of a Nymph, Sincérité Terracotta (H74.5cm H29in) London 2000

BERRUETA Vicente 1867-1909 **[2]**
- $1 995 - €2 102 - £1 330 - FF13 790
  Trabajando en el Caserío Oleo/lienzo (46x57.5cm 18x22in) Madrid 2000

BERRY Carroll Thayer 1886-1978 **[42]**
- $175 - €192 - £112 - FF1 259
  Old Fort Edgecomb-Maine/Booth Tarkington's Schooner-Kennebunkport Woodcut (17x22cm 7x9in) South-Natick MA 2000

BERRY John 1920 **[10]**
- $7 500 - €7 025 - £4 611 - FF46 080
  Palace Guards Oil/canvas (58.5x91.5cm 23x36in) New-York 1999

BERRY Patrick Vincent 1843-1913 **[24]**
- $1 100 - €1 025 - £664 - FF6 725
  Country Landscape with Deer Grazing at Sunset Oil/canvas (29x25cm 11x10in) New-Orleans LA 1999

BERSANI Stefano 1872-1914 **[8]**
- $4 000 - €4 147 - £2 400 - FF27 200
  Paesaggio con alberi Olio/tela (76x124cm 29x48in) Milano 2000

BERSERIK Herman 1921 **[65]**
- $9 749 - €8 440 - £5 916 - FF55 361
  Ontmoeting in Lixhe Acrylic (80x40cm 31x15in) Amsterdam 1998
- $352 - €408 - £249 - FF2 678
  Modellen Ink (24.5x21cm 9x8in) Amsterdam 2000
- $154 - €170 - £104 - FF1 116
  Three Trees and two Kites Etching (21x25.6cm 8x10in) Haarlem 2000

BERSSENBRUGGE Henri 1873-1959 **[14]**
- $3 236 - €3 630 - £2 242 - FF23 812
  Portrait of a Laughing Clown Photograph (39x28.5cm 15x11in) Amsterdam 2000

BERT A. XIX-XX **[4]**
- $439 - €488 - £306 - FF3 200
  Nijinsky dans le Spectre de la Rose Tirage argentique (13x8cm 5x3in) Paris 2001

BERT-HÅGE Karl Olof 1923 **[8]**
- $1 074 - €1 190 - £729 - FF7 807
  Middag på stadshotellet (Diner at the Village Hotell) Oil/canvas (45x54cm 17x21in) Stockholm 2000

BERTA Edoardo 1867-1931 **[5]**
- $8 332 - €9 909 - £5 938 - FF65 002
  Waldbach Oil/panel (49x37cm 19x14in) Zürich 2000
- $3 505 - €3 845 - £2 380 - FF25 222
  Landschaft im Tessin Oil/panel (27x21.5cm 10x8in) Luzern 2000

BERTAUX Jacques c.1745-1818 **[9]**
- $13 120 - €15 245 - £9 220 - FF100 000
  Combat contre les Turcs/Scène de bataille Huile/toile (45.5x55cm 17x21in) Paris 2001
- $6 840 - €7 769 - £4 800 - FF50 964
  Stag Hunt Oil/canvas (32.5x40.5cm 12x15in) London 2000

BERTEAULT Jules Louis XIX-XX **[8]**
- $2 622 - €2 897 - £1 818 - FF19 000
  Les arbres en fleurs Huile/toile (33x46cm 12x18in) Paris 2001

BERTEL-NORDSTRÖM Engelbert 1884-1967 **[56]**
  $504 - €559 - £342 - FF3 669
    **Nattstycke, Stockholm mot Södermalm
    (Stockholm by Södermalm at Night)** Oil/canvas
    (54x65cm 21x25in) Stockholm 2000

BERTELLI Ferdinando XVI **[3]**
  $1 398 - €1 534 - £949 - FF10 061
    Perseus und Andromeda Kupferstich (38.5x51cm
    15x20in) Berlin 2000

BERTELLI Flavio 1865-1941 **[10]**
  $3 480 - €3 006 - £2 320 - FF19 720
    Roccaccia di Modigliana Olio/tavola (31x50.5cm
    12x19in) Roma 1998

BERTELLI Luca XVI **[2]**
  $772 - €920 - £550 - FF6 037
    **Der Zinsgroschen, nach Domenico
    Campagnola** Kupferstich (34.4x43.3cm 13x17in)
    Berlin 2000

BERTELLI Luigi 1833-1916 **[18]**
  $4 750 - €4 924 - £2 850 - FF32 300
    Pascolo Olio/tela (63x82cm 24x32in) Prato 1999

BERTELLI Renato Giuseppe 1900-1974 **[6]**
  $28 095 - €24 005 - £17 000 - FF157 462
    Profilo continuato di Mussolini Terracotta
    (H29.5cm H11in) London 1998

BERTELSEN Albert 1921 **[59]**
  $2 210 - €2 478 - £1 539 - FF16 254
    Clochard/Gare du Nord Oil/canvas (116x104cm
    45x40in) Viby J, Århus 2001
  $1 989 - €1 884 - £1 209 - FF12 360
    Komposition med figur og fuglebure Oil/panel
    (127x48cm 50x18in) København 1999

BERTELSMANN Walter 1877-1963 **[30]**
  $819 - €767 - £496 - FF5 030
    Weser und Hafen bei Dedesdorf Öl/Karton
    (39x56.5cm 15x22in) Bremen 1999

BERTEN Hugo 1894-1954 **[17]**
  $310 - €363 - £221 - FF2 381
    Flower Still Life Oil/canvas (80x70cm 31x27in)
    Amsterdam 2001

BERTHÉLEMY Jean Simon 1742/43-1811 **[17]**
  $30 127 - €29 728 - £18 720 - FF195 000
    Jupiter et Antiope Huile/toile (49.5x59cm 19x23in)
    Paris 1999

BERTHELEMY Pierre Émile 1818-1890 **[5]**
  $1 597 - €1 789 - £1 100 - FF11 738
    Segelschiff im Hafen von Conquet Oil/panel
    (13x26.5cm 5x10in) Hamburg 2000

BERTHELON Eugène 1829-1924 **[41]**
  $1 570 - €1 677 - £1 072 - FF11 000
    Village au bord du lac Huile/toile (50x73cm
    19x28in) Paris 2001
  $446 - €417 - £270 - FF2 737
    Study of a River with Bridge Oil/wood (8x15cm
    3x5in) West-Sussex 1999

BERTHELSEN Christian 1839-1909 **[87]**
  $706 - €804 - £496 - FF5 275
    Landskab med hollehavn Oil/canvas (44x69cm
    17x27in) Vejle 2001

BERTHELSEN Johann 1883-1969 **[158]**
  $5 000 - €5 687 - £3 467 - FF37 301
    5th Ave in Winter Oil/board (50x40cm 20x16in)
    Cincinnati OH 2000

  $2 800 - €3 151 - £1 928 - FF20 671
    Winter in New York Oil/canvas (40x30cm 16x12in)
    Chicago IL 2000
  $700 - €751 - £476 - FF4 929
    The Approaching Storm Pastel/paper (22x30.5cm
    8x12in) Boston MA 2001

BERTHET Philippe 1956 **[14]**
  $392 - €412 - £248 - FF2 700
    **Pin Up: héroïne en tenue légère sur un lit (pour
    un ex-libris)** Mine plomb (17x9cm 6x3in) Paris 2000

BERTHILS Birger 1891-1967 **[4]**
  $599 - €701 - £427 - FF4 595
    Kveldslys Oil/canvas (30x47cm 11x18in) Oslo 2001

BERTHOLLE Jean 1909-1996 **[102]**
  $1 512 - €1 448 - £932 - FF9 500
    Composition Huile/papier/toile (42x75cm 16x29in)
    Douai 1999
  $964 - €915 - £586 - FF6 000
    Composition Peinture (12x58.5cm 4x23in) Paris 1999
  $477 - €457 - £294 - FF3 000
    Petit intérieur Pastel/papier (33.5x15cm 13x5in)
    Douai 1999

BERTHOLO René 1935 **[19]**
  $2 280 - €1 988 - £1 360 - FF13 040
    Près, loin, très loin Acuarela/papel (56x37.5cm
    22x14in) Lisboa 1998

BERTHOMMÉ-SAINT-ANDRÉ Louis 1905-1977
[237]
  $942 - €915 - £586 - FF6 000
    La coquette Huile/toile (50x41cm 19x16in) Troyes
    1999
  $211 - €229 - £146 - FF1 500
    Une vie Aquarelle/papier (24x16cm 9x6in) La Varenne-
    Saint-Hilaire 2001

BERTHON Auguste 1858-? **[2]**
  $2 800 - €2 752 - £1 799 - FF18 053
    La lectrice du gil blas Oil/panel (33.5x26cm
    13x10in) New-York 1999

BERTHON Maurice 1888-1914 **[5]**
  $4 728 - €4 573 - £2 916 - FF30 000
    Promenade sous les balcons de bois Huile/toile
    (54x65cm 21x25in) Paris 1999

BERTHON Paul 1872-1909 **[124]**
  $852 - €915 - £579 - FF6 000
    «La lyre» Lithographie (50x64cm 19x25in) Paris 2001

BERTHOUD Alfred Henri 1848-1906 **[10]**
  $1 127 - €1 210 - £754 - FF7 937
    Seelandschaft mit Blick auf Murten Öl/Karton
    (22x28cm 8x11in) Zürich 2000

BERTHOUD Léon Rodolphe 1822-1892 **[25]**
  $2 296 - €2 668 - £1 613 - FF17 500
    Paysage à la fontaine près de Tivoli Huile/toile
    (72x58cm 28x22in) Paris 2001

BERTHOUD Paul François 1870-1939 **[14]**
  $1 329 - €1 418 - £843 - FF9 300
    Jeune fille au collier et coiffée Marbre (H55cm
    H21in) Bar-le-Duc 2000

BERTI Antonio 1904-1990 **[4]**
  $1 800 - €2 332 - £1 350 - FF15 300
    Maternità Bas-relief (48x36cm 18x14in) Prato 2000

BERTI Renato XX **[2]**
  $5 310 - €4 587 - £2 655 - FF30 090
    Ritratto di signora con le zinnie Olio/tavola
    (76x55cm 29x21in) Milano 1999

B

BERTI Vinicio 1921-1991 **[87]**
- $750 - €777 - **£450** - FF5 100
«Guardare in alto (Materialmente)» Idropittura (99.5x69cm 39x27in) Prato 2001
- $375 - €389 - **£225** - FF2 550
Costruzione positiva AH Idropittura/tela (40x30cm 15x11in) Prato 2000
- $660 - €570 - **£330** - FF3 740
Senza titolo Tecnica mista/carta (38.5x48cm 15x18in) Prato 1999

BERTIER Charles Alexandre 1860-1924 **[80]**
- $3 124 - €3 354 - **£2 090** - FF22 000
Les trois pics de Belledone, le matin Huile/toile (55x46cm 21x18in) Grenoble 2000
- $1 538 - €1 829 - **£1 096** - FF12 000
Le pont Saint-Bruno en Chartreuse Huile/carton (27x16cm 10x6in) Grenoble 2000

BERTIN Édouard François 1797-1871 **[29]**
- $13 516 - €13 416 - **£8 386** - FF88 000
L'église de Montmorency Huile/toile (36.5x53cm 14x20in) Paris 1999
- $2 331 - €2 744 - **£1 638** - FF18 000
La citadelle Huile/toile (34x44cm 13x17in) Toulouse 2000
- $197 - €213 - **£136** - FF1 400
Monastère dans la montagne Pierre noire (18.5x27.5cm 7x10in) Paris 2001

BERTIN Jean Victor 1767/75-1842 **[65]**
- $62 034 - €52 422 - **£37 000** - FF343 866
Classical Landscape Oil/canvas (205x214cm 80x84in) London 1998
- $17 343 - €18 348 - **£11 000** - FF120 358
Wooded River Landscape with Fishermen and Bathers Oil/canvas (48x59cm 18x23in) London 2000
- $7 000 - €6 140 - **£4 250** - FF40 276
Landscape with a Young Fisherman Oil/canvas (40.5x32cm 15x12in) New-York 1999

BERTIN Nicolas 1668-1736 **[22]**
- $109 554 - €94 518 - **£65 844** - FF620 000
Joseph reconnu par ses Frères/L'Adoration des Mages Huile/toile (106x138cm 41x54in) Tours 1998
- $13 253 - €14 860 - **£9 000** - FF97 476
The Education of Love Oil/canvas (79.5x64.5cm 31x25in) London 2000
- $3 223 - €2 985 - **£2 000** - FF19 578
Peace and Concorde Oil/canvas (36x32cm 14x12in) London 1999

BERTIN Roger 1915 **[124]**
- $604 - €686 - **£419** - FF4 500
Paysage au château Huile/toile (54x65cm 21x25in) Orléans 2001
- $257 - €305 - **£187** - FF2 000
Cannes Aquarelle/papier (46x63cm 18x24in) Paris 2001

BERTINI Gianni 1922 **[385]**
- $960 - €1 244 - **£720** - FF8 160
«Le amiche» Tela (55x48cm 21x18in) Milano 2001
- $570 - €492 - **£285** - FF3 230
Repertoriale, Nudo Olio/tela (12x9cm 4x3in) Prato 1999
- $850 - €881 - **£510** - FF5 780
Tantare caskrr Tecnica mista/carta (55x46cm 21x18in) Milano 2001
- $1 205 - €1 372 - **£850** - FF9 000
«Le naufrage d'Uranie» Sérigraphie (80x58cm 31x22in) Versailles 2001

BERTINI Giuseppe 1825-1898 **[17]**
- $2 800 - €3 628 - **£2 100** - FF23 800
Fuga in Egitto Olio/tela (81x55cm 31x21in) Milano 2001

BERTLE Hans 1880-1943 **[14]**
- $2 535 - €2 181 - **£1 503** - FF14 307
Selbstbildnis als K.und K.Offizier Öl/Leinwand (47x35cm 18x13in) Wien 1998

BERTOIA Harry 1915-1978 **[202]**
- $13 000 - €11 216 - **£7 842** - FF73 570
Spray Sculpture (106.5x25.5x25.5cm 41x10x10in) New-York 1998
- $8 600 - €8 591 - **£5 375** - FF56 351
Bush Bronze (20x35cm 8x14in) Chicago IL 1999
- $1 700 - €2 022 - **£1 176** - FF13 266
Sculptural forms Print (30x99cm 12x39in) Lambertville NJ 2000

BERTOIN Marcel 1897-1983 **[30]**
- $214 - €244 - **£148** - FF1 600
La lavandière Huile/toile (54x65cm 21x25in) Toulouse 2000
- $1 460 - €1 524 - **£924** - FF10 000
Le Tage à Tolède Huile/panneau (27x22cm 10x8in) Toulouse 2000

BERTOJA Jacopo Zanguidi 1544-1574 **[12]**
- $86 669 - €93 032 - **£58 000** - FF610 252
Landscape with Scenes from the Legend of Apollo and Marsyas Oil/panel (34.5x38.5cm 13x15in) London 2000
- $75 000 - €75 873 - **£45 795** - FF497 692
Soldiers on Horseback pursued by Foot-soldiers Ink (19x27.5cm 7x10in) New-York 2000

BERTOLLA Cesare 1845-1920 **[11]**
- $480 - €622 - **£360** - FF4 080
L'Aniene Acquarello/carta (13.5x21.5cm 5x8in) Roma 2001

BERTOLO Alejandro 1954 **[12]**
- $1 873 - €1 558 - **£1 100** - FF10 223
Jaguar Watercolour (59x92cm 23x36in) London 1998

BERTOLOTTI Cesare 1854-1932 **[4]**
- $10 000 - €10 367 - **£6 000** - FF68 000
Paesaggio bresciano Olio/tela (43x88cm 16x34in) Milano 2000

BERTONI Wander 1925 **[7]**
- $4 758 - €4 724 - **£2 970** - FF30 985
Wir und der Mond, aus dem Zyklus «Der Spiegel» Bronze (H76cm H29in) Wien 1999

BERTOS Francesco XVII-XVIII **[7]**
- $31 800 - €36 039 - **£21 600** - FF236 400
Agua Marbre (80.5x56x37cm 31x22x14in) Madrid 2000
- $31 800 - €36 039 - **£21 600** - FF236 400
El Aire Marbre (68x45x36cm 26x17x14in) Madrid 2000

BERTRAM Abel 1871-1954 **[311]**
- $1 794 - €2 134 - **£1 279** - FF14 000
Couple de promeneurs devant la chaumière normande Huile/toile (50x65cm 19x25in) Calais 2000
- $961 - €1 143 - **£685** - FF7 500
Bateaux Huile/panneau (16x27cm 6x10in) Paris 2000
- $284 - €320 - **£195** - FF2 100
Voiliers à quai Aquarelle (21x31cm 8x12in) Barbizon 2000

BERTRAM Paul XIX-XX **[15]**

✏️ **$361** - €415 - **£250** - FF2 721
Sheep in Snow near a Copse Watercolour/paper (18x25.5cm 7x10in) Harrogate, North Yorkshire 2000

BERTRAN 1929 **[46]**

🖼️ **$907** - €762 - **£533** - FF5 000
Le Tricorne rouge Huile/toile (40x60cm 15x23in) Paris 1998

BERTRAND Alexander 1877-1947 **[9]**

🖼️ **$7 458** - €7 394 - **£4 664** - FF48 504
Munke samler blomster i en klosterhave Oil/canvas (80x134cm 31x44in) Köbenhavn 1999

BERTRAND Élise XIX **[5]**

🖼️ **$9 000** - €9 650 - **£5 954** - FF63 298
Still Life of Roses, Lilacs, Pansies and Decorated Vase Oil/panel (38x49cm 15x19in) New-Orleans LA 2000

🖼️ **$1 265** - €1 253 - **£767** - FF8 221
Cat at the Piano Oil/canvas (34x23cm 13x9in) New-Orleans LA 2000

BERTRAND Émile XIX-XX **[6]**

📜 **$1 400** - €1 562 - **£916** - FF10 245
«Cendrillon, conte de fées (d'après Perrault) par Henri Cain» Poster (79.5x59.5cm 31x23in) New-York 2000

BERTRAND Eugène 1858-1934 **[9]**

🖼️ **$3 689** - €3 842 - **£2 340** - FF25 203
L'atelier du peintre Huile/toile (50x67cm 19x26in) Bruxelles 1999

BERTRAND Gaston 1910-1994 **[83]**

🖼️ **$5 852** - €5 453 - **£3 608** - FF35 772
«Duroc» Huile/toile (55x46cm 21x18in) Bruxelles 1999

✏️ **$820** - €892 - **£540** - FF5 853
Huizen op de dijk Gouache/paper (27x32.5cm 10x12in) Lokeren 2000

BERTRAND Jean-Bapt., James 1823-1887 **[18]**

🖼️ **$10 000** - €10 367 - **£6 000** - FF68 000
Verso il santuario Olio/tela (90x150cm 35x59in) Roma 1999

🖼️ **$8 500** - €7 525 - **£5 196** - FF49 358
Day of the Regata Oil/canvas (63.5x99cm 25x38in) New-York 1999

🖼️ **$2 420** - €2 324 - **£1 500** - FF15 247
Harvesting Grapes Oil/canvas (50x30cm 19x11in) London 1999

BERTRAND Noël François 1785-1852 **[2]**

📜 **$732** - €721 - **£456** - FF4 728
Napoléon Le Grand, sobre un dibujo de Eugène Bourgeois Grabado (73x54cm 28x21in) Madrid 1999

BERTRAND Paulin 1852-1940 **[23]**

🖼️ **$3 131** - €3 201 - **£1 963** - FF21 000
La pointe de Carqueiranne Huile/toile (46x65cm 18x25in) Toulon 2000

BERTRAND Philippe 1663-1724 **[3]**

🗿 **$120 888** - €111 288 - **£72 562** - FF730 000
Démocrite/Héraclite Terracotta (H35cm H13in) Paris 1999

BERTSCH Auguste Adolphe ?-1871 **[3]**

📷 **$10 362** - €11 606 - **£7 200** - FF76 133
Interior View of the Palais de l'Industrie under Construction Salt print (18.5x16.5cm 7x6in) London 2001

BERTUCHI NIETO Mariano 1885-1955 **[60]**

🖼️ **$7 680** - €7 208 - **£4 800** - FF47 280
«Casa de comidas, Tetuan» Oleo/lienzo (63x81cm 24x31in) Madrid 1999

🖼️ **$1 512** - €1 652 - **£1 045** - FF10 835
Calle árabe Oleo/cartón (18x26cm 7x10in) Madrid 2001

✏️ **$488** - €481 - **£304** - FF3 152
Monje y árabe en el claustro Tinta/papel (15x9cm 5x3in) Madrid 1999

BERTUZZI L'ANCONITANO Nicolas 1710-1777 **[12]**

🖼️ **$9 000** - €7 775 - **£4 500** - FF51 000
Adorazione dei Magi Olio/tela (45x60cm 17x23in) Milano 1999

BERUETE Y MORET Aureliano 1845-1912 **[24]**

🖼️ **$10 675** - €10 511 - **£6 825** - FF68 950
«Paisaje de la Sierra de Guadarrama» Oleo/lienzo (38x57cm 14x22in) Madrid 1999

🖼️ **$17 280** - €19 221 - **£11 840** - FF126 080
Toledo Oleo/lienzo (33.5x30.5cm 13x12in) Madrid 2001

BERVOETS Fred 1942 **[249]**

🖼️ **$7 392** - €6 941 - **£4 564** - FF45 528
Autoportrait Acrylique (200x240cm 78x94in) Antwerpen 1999

🖼️ **$618** - €694 - **£431** - FF4 552
Autoportrait comme suisse Huile/toile (73x62cm 28x24in) Antwerpen 2001

✏️ **$820** - €694 - **£490** - FF4 552
Den artist Pauwels Encre/papier (25.5x16cm 10x6in) Antwerpen 1998

📜 **$131** - €118 - **£78** - FF731
Nu à l'atelier Eau-forte (12x13.5cm 4x5in) Antwerpen 1998

BERZEVICZY-PALLAVICINI Friedrich 1909-1989 **[16]**

✏️ **$1 738** - €1 453 - **£1 030** - FF9 528
Zwei Katzen Tempera/paper (46.5x59cm 18x23in) Wien 1998

BESCHEY Balthasar 1708-1776 **[77]**

🖼️ **$10 528** - €11 628 - **£7 296** - FF76 272
Diana und Acteon Öl/Kupfer (41x50.5cm 16x19in) Wien 2001

🖼️ **$8 188** - €7 607 - **£5 000** - FF49 900
Diana and Her Nymphs Resting After the Chase Oil/panel (31x45cm 12x17in) London 1999

✏️ **$5 285** - €5 087 - **£3 304** - FF33 369
Die heilige Familie mit Engeln in ihrem Heim Gouache/paper (25.5x34cm 10x13in) Wien 1999

BESCHEY Jacob Andries 1710-1786 **[14]**

🖼️ **$6 400** - €6 006 - **£4 000** - FF39 400
La educación de la Virgen Oleo/tabla (53x39cm 20x15in) Madrid 1999

🖼️ **$9 671** - €8 954 - **£6 000** - FF58 734
The Holy Family Oil/panel (32x24.5cm 12x9in) London 1999

BESCHEY Karel, Charles 1706-c.1770 **[38]**

🖼️ **$27 500** - €25 458 - **£16 601** - FF166 993
Extensive Winter Landscape with a Town and Figures Oil/panel (37x48.5cm 14x19in) New-York 1999

🖼️ **$22 558** - €22 154 - **£14 000** - FF145 318
Bosky Landscape with a Fruit Seller and other Figures on a Track Oil/panel (31.5x43.5cm 12x17in) London 1999

BESCO Donald, Don 1941 **[10]**
- $1 227 - €1 159 - £762 - FF7 602
«Rainy Day, Front St Toronto» Oil/canvas
(76x91cm 29x35in) Nepean, Ont. 1999

BESKOW Bo 1906-1989 **[49]**
- $727 - €689 - £453 - FF4 522
Fiskeläge i Portugal Oil/canvas (63x81cm 24x31in)
Stockholm 1999

BESKOW Elsa 1874-1953 **[25]**
- $1 484 - €1 291 - £895 - FF8 467
Trädgård i vårgrönska Akvarell/papper (10.5x16cm
4x6in) Stockholm 1998

BESLER Basilius 1561-1629 **[53]**
- $1 150 - €1 351 - £816 - FF8 859
Piper Indictum from Hortus Eystettensis
Eicstatt Engraving (48x39.5cm 18x15in) Philadelphia
PA 2000

BESLI G., Prof. XIX **[3]**
- $1 315 - €1 239 - £795 - FF8 130
Jeanne d'Arc Marbre Carrare (H53cm H20in)
Antwerpen 1999

BESNARD Jean 1889-1958 **[1]**
- $6 552 - €6 936 - £4 336 - FF45 500
Vase cylindrique, décor d'épaisses coulées
d'émaux crispés beige Céramique (H30cm H11in)
Neuilly-sur-Seine 2000

BESNARD Paul Albert 1849-1934 **[228]**
- $3 623 - €3 354 - £2 244 - FF22 000
Portrait de femme au balcon Huile/panneau
(54x45cm 21x17in) Paris 1999
- $5 196 - €4 573 - £3 165 - FF30 000
Femme dans un intérieur Huile/panneau (35x20cm
13x7in) Vendôme 1999
- $501 - €427 - £299 - FF2 800
Un jeune curé Pastel (55x44cm 21x17in) Paris 1998
- $250 - €256 - £157 - FF1 679
Interior Scene Etching (31x24cm 12x9in) Cleveland
OH 2000

BESNARD-FORTIN Jeanne 1892-1978 **[184]**
- $64 - €73 - £44 - FF48
Transparence Aquarelle/papier (27x21cm 10x8in)
Orléans 2000

BESNUS Amédée 1831-1909 **[10]**
- $2 448 - €2 287 - £1 510 - FF15 000
Scène de la vie champêtre Huile/toile (36x54cm
14x21in) Melun 1999

BESNYÖ Eva 1910 **[16]**
- $1 606 - €1 724 - £1 075 - FF11 311
Kratten Gelatin silver print (35x30.5cm 13x12in)
Amsterdam 2000

BESS Forrest Clemenger 1911-1977 **[7]**
- $19 000 - €19 146 - £11 844 - FF125 590
Untitled No.5 Oil/canvas (30.5x31cm 12x12in) New-
York 2000

BESSA Pancrace 1772-1835 **[34]**
- $1 073 - €1 220 - £740 - FF8 000
Étude d'iris Gouache/papier (27x20.5cm 10x8in) Paris
2000
- $124 - €143 - £85 - FF939
Pfirsiche Farblithographique (50x38cm 19x14in) Leipzig
2000

BESSE Raymond 1899-1969 **[203]**
- $362 - €412 - £248 - FF2 700
Rue de la monnaie Huile/toile (61x50cm 24x19in)
Orléans 2000

BESSELIEVRE Claude-Jean c.1779-c.1830 **[3]**
- $2 613 - €2 287 - £1 582 - FF15 000
Charles V et son fils Huile/toile (32.5x24cm 12x9in)
Paris 1998

BESSERVE René 1883-1959 **[75]**
- $774 - €640 - £454 - FF4 200
«Chamonix, Mont-Blanc» Affiche (100x62cm
39x24in) Paris 1998

BESSIRE Dale Phillip 1892-1974 **[7]**
- $4 000 - €4 480 - £2 779 - FF29 388
«Road in Brown County» Oil/canvas (63x76cm
25x30in) Cincinnati OH 2001
- $2 200 - €2 377 - £1 523 - FF15 589
October Color Oil/board (25x30cm 10x12in)
Cincinnati OH 2001

BESSON Faustin 1821-1882 **[10]**
- $5 233 - €5 946 - £3 673 - FF39 000
La conversation galante auprès de l'auberge
Huile/toile (61x96cm 24x37in) La Varenne-Saint-Hilaire
2001

BESSONOF Boris XX **[9]**
- $2 261 - €2 103 - £1 400 - FF13 793
Woodland Stream Oil/canvas (64x81cm 25x32in)
Birmingham 1999

BEST Arthur William 1859-1935 **[12]**
- $1 900 - €1 628 - £1 142 - FF10 677
Lupines and Poppies Oil/paper/board (25x35cm
10x14in) Cincinnati OH 1998

BEST Hans 1874-1942 **[91]**
- $826 - €971 - £592 - FF6 372
Mann mit Hut Oil/panel (68x50cm 26x19in) München
2001
- $917 - €869 - £558 - FF5 701
Lachender Bauer, Brustbild, nach links gewen-
der, vor Flusslandschaft Oil/panel (32.4x24.1cm
12x9in) München 1999

BEST Harry Cassie 1863-1936 **[16]**
- $1 600 - €1 717 - £1 070 - FF11 265
Yosemite Valley, indians and lake Oil/canvas
(50x76cm 20x30in) Altadena CA 2000
- $350 - €3 488 - £2 174 - FF22 883
Long boats in sunset seas Oil/canvas/board
(25x40cm 10x16in) Altadena CA 2000

BEST John c.1720-c.1795 **[7]**
- $11 487 - €10 982 - £7 200 - FF72 036
A saddled Bay Hunter with a Groom and
Hounds, in a Lake Landscape Oil/canvas
(72x91.5cm 28x36in) London 1999

BESTALL Alfred Edmeades 1892-? **[5]**
- $3 424 - €3 992 - £2 400 - FF26 184
Rupert and Friends Pencil (27x35cm 10x13in)
London 2000

BESTER Willie 1956 **[5]**
- $11 339 - €10 437 - £6 805 - FF68 461
Election Mixed media (152x137cm 59x53in)
Amsterdam 1999
- $3 872 - €3 719 - £2 400 - FF24 395
Migrant Miseries Mixed media (70x122cm 27x48in)
London 1999

BETHKE Hermann 1825-1895 **[7]**
- $6 000 - €6 824 - £4 230 - FF44 762
Untitled Oil/canvas (69x84cm 27x33in) MT. Morris
NY 2001

$2 143 - €2 301 - £1 434 - FF15 092
Mittagsruh, eine Bäuerin sitzt in ihrer Kammer
Öl/Leinwand (29x36cm 11x14in) Stuttgart 2000

BETHUNE Gaston 1857-1897 **[11]**
$560 - €534 - £348 - FF3 500
La route de Roquebrune Aquarelle/papier
(37x54cm 14x21in) Paris 1999

BETIGNY Ernest 1873-1960 **[74]**
$288 - €322 - £201 - FF2 113
Dimanche à la campagne Huile/toile (36x50cm
14x19in) Bruxelles 2001
$180 - €173 - £112 - FF1 138
Petit chemin Huile/toile (23x27cm 9x10in) Bruxelles
1999

BETTELHEIM Jolan Gross 1900-1972 **[19]**
$1 100 - €1 018 - £683 - FF6 678
Church Lithograph (36x26cm 14x10in) New-York
1999

BETTELINI Pietro 1763-1829 **[4]**
$424 - €481 - £296 - FF3 152
**Vista del lateral de Mediodia, según Anibal
Carracci (1560-1609)** Grabado (50x84cm 19x33in)
Madrid 2001

BETTENCOURT Pierre 1917 **[55]**
$4 262 - €4 726 - £2 951 - FF31 000
Les nus de Babylone Technique mixte/panneau
(122x159cm 48x62in) Paris 2001
$3 879 - €4 573 - £2 727 - FF30 000
Portrait de Léon X Technique mixte/panneau
(60x52cm 23x20in) Paris 2000

BETTERA Bartolomeo 1639-1690/1700 **[9]**
$89 110 - €92 376 - £53 466 - FF605 949
Natura morta Olio/tela (162x222cm 63x87in) Milano
1999
$29 580 - €34 838 - £20 880 - FF228 520
Bodegón con reloj y frutas escarchadas
Oleo/lienzo (74x98cm 29x38in) Madrid 2000

BETTERMANN Gerhard 1910-1992 **[17]**
$198 - €220 - £137 - FF1 442
«Selbstbild» Woodcut (41.5x34.5cm 16x13in)
Heidelberg 2001

BETTS Anna Whelan XIX **[2]**
$4 500 - €5 040 - £3 126 - FF33 062
**Magazine cover, Standing Woman with green
Parasol** Oil/board (48x27cm 19x11in) New-York 2001

BETTS Louis 1873-1961 **[26]**
$4 000 - €4 350 - £2 636 - FF28 537
Still Life with Daffodils and Figure Oil/canvas
(51x40.5cm 20x15in) Boston MA 2000

BETZLER Emil 1892-1974 **[17]**
$129 - €155 - £92 - FF1 014
«Liebespaare» Woodcut (29x20cm 11x7in) Hamburg
2000

BEUCHOT Jean-Baptiste 1821-? **[3]**
$6 000 - €6 727 - £4 074 - FF44 128
An early Start Oil/canvas (73.5x60cm 28x23in) New-
York 2000

BEUCKER de Pascal 1861-1945 **[16]**
$1 139 - €1 339 - £788 - FF8 780
Nature morte aux oeillets dans un panier tressé
Huile/toile (46x71cm 18x27in) Antwerpen 2000

BEUL de Frans 1849-1919 **[52]**
$1 989 - €2 231 - £1 395 - FF14 634
Vaches attaquées par les loups Huile/toile
(45x66cm 17x25in) Maisieres-Mons 2001

$1 007 - €1 134 - £694 - FF7 441
A Still Life with Peonies Oil/canvas (35.5x31cm
13x12in) Amsterdam 2000

BEUL de Henri 1845-1900 **[39]**
$3 660 - €3 908 - £2 500 - FF25 632
The Young Herdsman Oil/canvas (81x59.5cm
31x23in) Billingshurst, West-Sussex 2001
$670 - €638 - £416 - FF4 185
Farmyard Friends Oil/panel (21x15cm 8x5in)
Toronto 1999

BEUL de Laurent 1821-1876 **[13]**
$1 600 - €1 848 - £1 120 - FF12 125
Tending the Flock Oil/canvas (56x86cm 22x34in)
New-York 1999

BEUL de Oscar 1881-? **[10]**
$766 - €892 - £547 - FF5 853
Le vendeur de harengs Bronze (H48cm H18in)
Bruxelles 2001

BEULAS RECASENS José 1921 **[170]**
$9 720 - €10 812 - £6 480 - FF70 920
Chopera junto al Isuela (Huesca) Oleo/lienzo
(100x159cm 39x62in) Madrid 2000
$3 520 - €3 304 - £2 200 - FF21 670
Paisaje Oleo/lienzo (46x65cm 18x25in) Madrid 1999
$1 540 - €1 652 - £1 045 - FF10 835
Paisaje Oleo/tabla (30x40cm 11x15in) Madrid 2001
$759 - €661 - £473 - FF4 334
Paisaje Dibujo (17x24.5cm 6x9in) Madrid 1999

BEURDEN van Alfons, Jnr. 1878-1962 **[80]**
$8 897 - €7 689 - £5 363 - FF50 437
Baigneuses Huile/toile (101x131cm 39x51in)
Bruxelles 1998
$919 - €1 041 - £621 - FF6 829
La ferme ensoleillée Huile/toile (70.5x101cm
27x39in) Bruxelles 2000

BEURDEN van Alfons, Snr. 1854-1938 **[50]**
$1 331 - €1 586 - £953 - FF10 406
Le jeune chanteur Bronze (H54cm H21in)
Antwerpen 2000

BEURMANN Emil 1862-1951 **[44]**
$854 - €816 - £534 - FF5 352
Mohnblumenzauber in Vase Oil/panel (72x55cm
28x21in) Zofingen 1999
$261 - €297 - £181 - FF1 949
Sitzende Frau in Négligé Pencil (30x23cm 11x9in)
Zofingen 2000

BEUVILLE Georges 1902-1982 **[11]**
$502 - €457 - £308 - FF3 000
**«Le feu prend mal, la cendre tombe dans la
soupe»** Affiche (100x74.5cm 39x29in) Saint-Cloud
1999

BEUYS Joseph 1921-1986 **[1549]**
$9 713 - €10 427 - £6 500 - FF68 394
Vacuum - Mass Mixed media (125x175cm 49x68in)
London 2000
$4 313 - €5 079 - £3 031 - FF33 316
**«How the Dictatorship of the Parties can be
Overcome»** Mixed media (75x51cm 29x20in) Dublin
2000
$1 150 - €1 277 - £800 - FF8 377
Sonne statt Reagan Mixed media (17.5x17.5cm
6x6in) London 2001
$17 416 - €16 809 - £11 000 - FF110 261
Filzanzug Object (170x60cm 66x23in) London 1999
$1 874 - €1 789 - £1 171 - FF11 738
Hasenblut Object (62.5x45cm 24x17in) Köln 1999

B

🖊 **$2 022** - €2 269 - **£1 401** - FF14 883
Fett Zeichnung Drawing (29.5x21cm 11x8in)
Amsterdam 2000

▥ **$400** - €459 - **£273** - FF3 010
Self-Portrait Print (30x23.5cm 11x9in) New-York 2000

📷 **$945** - €1 143 - **£660** - FF7 500
Paris Photo (60x50cm 23x19in) Paris 2000

BEVAN Irwin J. XIX-XX [6]

🖊 **$3 287** - €3 529 - **£2 200** - FF23 147
Submarines Heading Out to Sea Past H.M.S. Victory Watercolour/paper (30.5x48cm 12x18in) London 2000

BEVAN Robert Polhill 1865-1925 [56]

👝 **$21 086** - €20 328 - **£13 000** - FF133 342
Farm Buildings, Luppitt Common Oil/canvas (63.5x81.5cm 25x32in) London 1999

👝 **$5 620** - €5 189 - **£3 500** - FF34 039
The Gate Lodge Oil/canvas/board (20.5x25.5cm 8x10in) London 1999

🖊 **$3 117** - €2 855 - **£1 900** - FF18 725
In the Upper Culme Balley Crayon (25.5x35.5cm 10x13in) London 1999

▥ **$483** - €534 - **£335** - FF3 500
The plongh, le charme Lithographie (24.5x34.5cm 9x13in) Nantes 2001

BEVAN Tony 1951 [12]

👝 **$46 214** - €50 358 - **£32 000** - FF330 329
Corridor, Red Acrylic (268x200cm 105x78in) London 2001

👝 **$17 330** - €18 884 - **£12 000** - FF123 873
Head Oil/canvas (88x68cm 34x26in) London 2001

🖊 **$391** - €460 - **£271** - FF3 018
Hand Mischtechnik/Papier (34x25cm 13x9in) Stuttgart 2000

BEVERLEY William Roxby c.1811/24-1889 [63]

🖊 **$488** - €475 - **£300** - FF3 117
Twilight in Harbour Watercolour/paper (9.5x21cm 3x8in) London 1999

BEWICK Pauline 1935 [33]

👝 **$909** - €1 041 - **£625** - FF6 829
Reflections Mixed media (76x55cm 30x22in) Dublin 2000

🖊 **$2 156** - €2 539 - **£1 515** - FF16 658
Man & Woman on the World Watercolour/paper (68.5x101.5cm 26x39in) Dublin 2000

BEWICK William 1795-1866 [1]

🖊 **$3 750** - €4 408 - **£2 600** - FF28 912
The Libican Sybil, after Michelangelo Buonarotti (1475-1564) Bodycolour (298x214cm 117x84in) London 2000

BEYER de Jan 1703-c.1785 [26]

🖊 **$1 651** - €1 588 - **£1 017** - FF10 418
Westerkerke on the Prinsengracht, Amsterdam Ink (14x18.5cm 5x7in) Amsterdam 1999

BEYER Hans Joachim XX [6]

🖊 **$1 253** - €1 176 - **£774** - FF7 714
Marschlandschaft Gouache/paper (80x53cm 31x20in) Stuttgart 1999

BEYER Max Otto XIX-XX [10]

👝 **$600** - €644 - **£403** - FF4 227
Nature morte à l'écrevisse Huile/toile (60x110cm 23x43in) Bruxelles 2000

BEYER Otto 1885-1962 [37]

👝 **$907** - €767 - **£542** - FF5 029
Berlin-Reinickendorf im Winter Öl/Leinwand (60x69cm 23x27in) Berlin 1998

BEYEREN van Abraham Hendricksz c.1620-1690 [30]

👝 **$60 000** - €52 630 - **£36 432** - FF345 228
Fish on a Table Oil/canvas (71x58.5cm 27x23in) New-York 1999

BEYFUSS Ludwig c.1805-c.1866 [8]

👝 **$3 853** - €4 538 - **£2 665** - FF29 766
Portrait of a Lady Oil/canvas (79.5x63cm 31x24in) Amsterdam 2000

BEYLE Pierre Marie 1838-1902 [20]

👝 **$4 194** - €4 726 - **£2 904** - FF31 000
Femmes pêchant des crevette Huile/toile (65x48.5cm 25x19in) Bordeaux 2000

BEYNON Jan Daniël 1830-1877 [12]

👝 **$118 140** - €110 108 - **£71 400** - FF722 260
Tropical Fruits Oil/canvas (112x147cm 44x57in) Singapore 1999

👝 **$18 532** - €21 781 - **£12 849** - FF142 876
Portrait of Seima Oil/canvas (65.5x47.5cm 25x18in) Amsterdam 2000

👝 **$10 618** - €9 895 - **£6 552** - FF64 909
Bathers Oil/panel (35x29cm 13x11in) Singapore 1999

BEYSCHLAG Robert 1838-1903 [28]

👝 **$3 288** - €3 835 - **£2 308** - FF25 154
Psyche mit der Urne Öl/Leinwand (65x40cm 25x15in) Kempten 2000

BEYSSON Louis 1856-1912 [4]

👝 **$10 764** - €9 909 - **£6 461** - FF65 000
Locomotive traversant le pont la nuit Huile/toile (87x113cm 34x44in) Lyon 1999

BEZ Michel XX [9]

👝 **$4 207** - €3 811 - **£2 517** - FF25 000
Hector Protector Huile/toile (81x100cm 31x39in) Deauville 1998

BEZAAN Johan, Jo 1894-1952 [30]

▥ **$86** - €95 - **£58** - FF625
Three Cows Drypoint (19.6x24cm 7x9in) Haarlem 2000

BEZARD Philippe 1947 [4]

👝 **$34 325** - €38 112 - **£23 925** - FF250 000
La salle de bain Acrylique/toile (100x81cm 39x31in) Paris 2001

BEZEM Naftali 1924 [122]

👝 **$15 000** - €16 228 - **£10 276** - FF106 446
Ladder & Figures Oil/canvas (100x130cm 39x51in) Tel Aviv 2001

👝 **$5 000** - €4 464 - **£3 062** - FF29 281
Fish Legend Oil/canvas (50x61cm 19x24in) New-York 1999

👝 **$2 200** - €2 174 - **£1 346** - FF14 262
Man flying Oil/canvas (30.5x40.5cm 12x15in) Tel Aviv 2000

🖊 **$700** - €751 - **£468** - FF4 843
Figure in a Boat Gouache/paper (18x22cm 7x8in) Tel Aviv 2000

BEZOMBES Roger 1913-1994 [108]

👝 **$68 635** - €80 798 - **£48 230** - FF530 000
Le roi du Maroc Huile/toile (162x150cm 63x59in) Paris 2000

👝 **$1 500** - €1 651 - **£1 041** - FF10 827
«Le vase noir» Oil/board (60x49cm 24x19in) Delray-Beach FL 2001

🖊 **$392** - €457 - **£275** - FF3 000
Les chasseurs Gouache/papier (43x55.5cm 16x21in) Versailles 2000

$1 200 - €1 116 - £740 - FF7 319
«Air France, vie du monde» Poster (99x59cm 39x23in) New-York 1999

BEZZI Bartolomeo 1851-1923 [16]
$21 000 - €21 770 - £12 600 - FF142 800
Fantasia dell'Aria Olio/tela (120x160cm 47x62in) Milano 2000
$7 500 - €7 775 - £4 500 - FF51 000
Sulle rive del fiume Olio/cartone (34x49.5cm 13x19in) Milano 2000
$3 750 - €3 887 - £2 250 - FF25 500
Paesaggio di Val di Sole Olio/tavola (15x23.5cm 5x9in) Milano 1999

BEZZI IL NOSADELLA Giovanni Francesco 1530-1571 [3]
$3 275 - €3 043 - £2 000 - FF19 960
Samson and Delilah Ink (15.5x18.5cm 6x7in) London 1998

BEZZUOLI Giuseppe 1784-1855 [48]
$2 160 - €1 866 - £1 440 - FF12 240
Ritratto di Gianfilippo Saladini giovinetto Olio/tavoletta (24x18cm 9x7in) Firenze 1998
$390 - €337 - £260 - FF2 210
Madonna con bambino in tabernacolo China/carta (29x17cm 11x6in) Firenze 1998

BHATTACHARJEE Bikash 1940 [21]
$7 500 - €8 530 - £5 240 - FF55 950
Visit Acrylic/canvas (172.5x132cm 67x51in) New-York 2000

BHATTACHARYA Chittoprasad 1915-1978 [3]
$2 988 - €3 208 - £2 000 - FF21 043
Nude/Nude Pastel/paper (26x37.5cm 10x14in) London 2000

BHENGU Gerard 1910-1990 [72]
$7 968 - €9 246 - £5 502 - FF60 648
Woman Carrying Water Outside a Hut Oil/canvas/board (48x68cm 18x26in) Johannesburg 2000
$396 - €444 - £275 - FF2 911
Portrait of a Woman with a Headpiece Watercolour/paper (36x26.5cm 14x10in) Johannesburg 2001

BIAGINI Alfredo 1886-1952 [8]
$760 - €985 - £570 - FF6 460
L'orso Bronzo (H15cm H5in) Roma 2000

BIAIS Maurice c.1875-1926 [15]
$2 200 - €1 877 - £1 327 - FF12 311
«Quinquina Vouvray». Poster (99.5x136.5cm 39x53in) New-York 1998

BIALYNICKI-BIRULA Witold Kaetanovitch 1872-1957 [16]
$4 500 - €4 464 - £2 800 - FF29 279
Early Spring Oil/canvas (72x54cm 28x21in) Kiev 1999

BIAN SHOUMIN 1684-1752 [11]
$11 538 - €13 107 - £8 100 - FF85 977
Flowers, Birds and Insects Ink/paper (24x32cm 9x12in) Hong-Kong 2001

BIAN WENYU c.1611-1671 [6]
$33 384 - €36 454 - £21 476 - FF239 122
Views of West Lake Ink (23x15.5cm 9x6in) Hong-Kong 2000

BIANCHI Alberto 1882-1969 [35]
$900 - €933 - £540 - FF6 120
La vendemmia Olio/tela/cartone (59.5x50cm 23x19in) Milano 1999

$550 - €570 - £330 - FF3 740
Venezia Olio/legno (35x30cm 13x11in) Roma 1999

BIANCHI BARRIVIERA Lino 1906-1985 [21]
$285 - €247 - £142 - FF1 618
Il canneto Acquaforte (19x14cm 7x5in) Venezia 1999

BIANCHI Domenico 1955 [16]
$3 750 - €3 887 - £2 250 - FF25 500
Senza titolo Tecnica mista (80x60cm 31x23in) Prato 2000

BIANCHI Isidoro 1581-1662 [4]
$4 000 - €4 279 - £2 727 - FF28 066
Job Tormented by his Wife Black chalk (23.5x19.5cm 9x7in) New-York 1999

BIANCHI Luigi 1827-1914 [9]
$21 000 - €19 670 - £12 910 - FF129 026
Convincing the Client Oil/canvas (82.5x113cm 32x44in) New-York 1999

BIANCHI Mosè di Giosuè 1840-1904 [101]
$30 000 - €25 916 - £15 000 - FF170 000
Crocifissione Olio/tela (160x105cm 62x41in) Prato 1999
$32 084 - €32 330 - £20 000 - FF212 072
An Afternoon Stroll Oil/canvas (59x47cm 23x18in) London 2000
$29 000 - €30 063 - £17 400 - FF197 200
La Darsena di Porta Ticinese Olio/tela (43x33cm 16x12in) Venezia 2000
$1 800 - €1 555 - £1 200 - FF10 200
Coppia di contadini lungo le rive del Lago Maggiore Pastelli (27.5x19cm 10x7in) Milano 1998

BIANCHI Mosè di Giuseppe 1836-1893 [6]
$2 000 - €2 592 - £1 500 - FF17 000
Signora con cuffia/Gentiluomo Olio/tela (70x51.5cm 27x20in) Vercelli 2000

BIANCHI Tom 1945 [7]
$700 - €813 - £492 - FF5 334
Larry surrounded Gelatin silver print (27x42cm 11x16in) New-Orleans LA 2001

BIANCHINI Artur 1869-1955 [51]
$10 591 - €10 394 - £6 568 - FF68 182
Tallen och havet Oil/canvas (120x184cm 47x72in) Stockholm 1999
$812 - €839 - £511 - FF5 506
Gårdsplan i solljus Oil/panel (70x60cm 27x23in) Stockholm 2000
$347 - €315 - £213 - FF2 064
Järnvägsspår på Liljeholmen Oil/panel (44x31cm 17x12in) Stockholm 1999

BIANCINI Angelo 1911-1988 [10]
$520 - €674 - £390 - FF4 420
Angioletto Relief (48x45x6.5cm 18x17x2in) Roma 2000

BIANCO del Baccio 1604-1656 [6]
$9 600 - €10 901 - £6 570 - FF71 505
Trinkender Bacchus in einer Landschaft Öl/Leinwand (68x50cm 26x19in) Wien 2000

BIANCO Pieretto Bortoluzzi 1875-1937 [35]
$1 400 - €1 451 - £840 - FF9 520
Canale a Burano Olio/tela (37x50cm 14x19in) Trieste 2000
$750 - €777 - £450 - FF5 100
Scorcio di Venezia Olio/tavola (24.5x36cm 9x14in) Torino 1999
$475 - €492 - £285 - FF3 230
Venezia Acquarello/carta (39x18cm 15x7in) Trieste 2000

B

BIANCO Remo 1922-1990 **[34]**
👉 **$1 600** - €1 659 - **£960** - FF10 880
    Senza titolo Tecnica mista (70x50cm 27x19in) Milano 1999
👉 **$1 100** - €1 140 - **£660** - FF7 480
    Tableau doré Tecnica mista/cartone (29.5x24cm 11x9in) Milano 1999

BIANCONI Carlo 1732-1803 **[2]**
✎ **$3 181** - €2 709 - **£1 900** - FF17 769
    Relief of the Poetess Corilla in profile, with the attributes Theatre Black chalk (35x22.5cm 13x8in) London 1998

BIANCONI Fulvio 1915 **[19]**
🏺 **$4 800** - €5 602 - **£3 388** - FF36 748
    Figural applied Vase Sculpture, glass (H24cm H9in) New-York 2000

BIARD François-Auguste 1798-1882 **[43]**
👉 **$2 780** - €3 049 - **£1 888** - FF20 000
    Campement en Laponie Huile/toile (61x46cm 24x18in) Lille 2000

BIASI DA TEULADA Giuseppe 1885-1945 **[9]**
👉 **$25 000** - €25 916 - **£15 000** - FF170 000
    La sposa sarda Olio/tela (101x145cm 39x57in) Milano 2000
👉 **$8 000** - €10 367 - **£6 000** - FF68 000
    Teresita, donna sarda in costume Olio/tela (83x56cm 32x22in) Milano 2000
👉 **$10 000** - €10 367 - **£6 000** - FF68 000
    Alla fonte Acquarello/cartone (65x120cm 25x47in) Milano 2000

BIASI Guido 1933-1982 **[55]**
👉 **$649** - €610 - **£402** - FF4 000
    Monument à l'insomnie Huile/toile (92x72cm 36x28in) Paris 1999

BIB Georges Breitel, dit 1888-? **[8]**
📜 **$269** - €244 - **£161** - FF1 600
    Personnalités aux courses Lithographie couleurs (26x18cm 10x7in) Deauville 1998

BIBBER von M. XX **[2]**
✎ **$1 800** - €1 932 - **£1 204** - FF12 673
    Winnie Winkle Sunday Pages Ink (43x63.5cm 16x25in) New-York 2000

BIBEL Léon XX **[1]**
📜 **$1 700** - €1 633 - **£1 053** - FF10 709
    Brooklyn Bridge Screenprint in colors (36x28.5cm 14x11in) New-York 1999

BIBIENA Antonio Galli 1700-1774 **[8]**
👉 **$9 691** - €7 992 - **£5 709** - FF52 426
    Phantastische Palastarchitektur mit Figuren Öl/Leinwand (67x85cm 26x33in) Wien 1998
✎ **$26 000** - €27 851 - **£17 755** - FF182 691
    Stage Design for a Fantastical Royal Bedroom Ink (35.5x39.5cm 13x15in) New-York 2001

BIBIENA Ferdinando Galli 1657-1743 **[9]**
👉 **$120 000** - €119 944 - **£73 308** - FF786 780
    Architectural Fantasy with Classical Figures Conversing Oil/canvas (197x290cm 77x114in) New-York 2000
✎ **$11 000** - €11 783 - **£7 511** - FF77 292
    Architectural Fantasy, with Numerous Arches and Barley-Sugar Columns Ink (24x34.5cm 9x13in) New-York 2001

BIBIENA Giuseppe Galli 1696-1757 **[18]**
✎ **$14 000** - €14 997 - **£9 560** - FF98 372
    Architectural Fantasy with a Series of Receding Arches Leading to Door Ink (39x45cm 15x17in) New-York 2001

BICCHI Silvio 1874-1948 **[19]**
✎ **$750** - €777 - **£450** - FF5 100
    Carro con botte Pastelli/carta (17x24.5cm 6x9in) Prato 2000

BICCHIERARI Antonio XVII **[1]**
✎ **$3 600** - €3 110 - **£1 800** - FF20 400
    Isituzione della Biblioteca Evoriana Inchiostro (28x43cm 11x16in) Milano 1999

BICCI DI LORENZO c.1368/73-1452 **[7]**
👉 **$38 106** - €44 210 - **£27 115** - FF290 000
    Madone et l'enfant en trône entre deux anges Tempera (158x68.5cm 62x26in) Paris 2001
👉 **$34 000** - €44 058 - **£25 500** - FF289 000
    Madonna col Bambino tra i Santi G.Battista e Caterina d'Alessandria Tempera/tavola (47.5x24.5cm 18x9in) Prato 2000

BICHET Charles Théodore 1863-1929 **[38]**
✎ **$492** - €457 - **£308** - FF3 000
    La Vienne à l'Isle Pastel/papier (30.5x23cm 12x9in) Paris 1999

BICHET Pierre 1922 **[5]**
👉 **$3 216** - €3 735 - **£2 290** - FF24 500
    Chemin enneigé Huile/toile (60x92cm 23x36in) Besançon 2001

BICKEL Karl 1886-1982 **[20]**
📜 **$197** - €200 - **£122** - FF1 309
    «Schweizer Mustermesse Basel» Poster (128.5x90.5cm 50x35in) Haarlem 2000

BICKEL V. XVIII **[1]**
👉 **$3 228** - €2 994 - **£2 000** - FF19 641
    Church Interior with a King and his Court making Offerings Oil/copper (18.5x25.5cm 7x10in) London 1999

BICKERSTAFF George Sanders 1893-1954 **[25]**
👉 **$650** - €702 - **£449** - FF4 604
    Stream in Mountain Landscape Oil/canvas (60x76cm 24x30in) Altadena CA 2001

BICKERTON Ashley 1959 **[22]**
🏺 **$13 000** - €12 578 - **£8 017** - FF82 509
    Atmosphere #1 Metal (203x193x107cm 79x75x42in) New-York 1999

BICKFORD Nelson Norris 1846-1943 **[2]**
👉 **$3 000** - €3 267 - **£2 066** - FF21 432
    Seated Monkey scratching Head Bronze (28x22x17cm 11x9x7in) Altadena CA 2001

BICKFORD Sid 1862-1947 **[3]**
👉 **$3 850** - €3 580 - **£2 376** - FF23 483
    Seven trouts Oil/canvas (91x53cm 36x21in) Gray ME 1999

BICKHAM Georges I c.1684-1758 **[1]**
📜 **$1 121** - €1 315 - **£800** - FF8 623
    View of the House of Stowe in Buckinghamshire Engraving (26x40cm 10x15in) London 2000

BICKNELL Albion Harris 1837-1915 **[21]**
👉 **$1 500** - €1 712 - **£1 042** - FF11 227
    Cows grazing Oil/canvas (63x76cm 25x30in) Dedham MA 2001

BICKNELL Evelyn 1857-1936 **[11]**
- 🔨 **$4 000** - €3 878 - **£2 476** - FF25 437
  Ship Off The Coast Oil/canvas (30x71cm 12x28in) Mystic CT 1999

BICKNELL Frank Alfred 1866-1943 **[34]**
- 🔨 **$6 000** - €7 173 - **£4 138** - FF47 052
  A Bend in the River Oil/canvas (60x76cm 24x30in) Milford CT 2000
- 🔨 **$2 400** - €2 635 - **£1 634** - FF16 759
  «A Bit of Coast Monhegan Island-Me.» Oil/board (20x25.5cm 7x10in) New-York 2001

BICKNELL William Henry Warren 1860-1947 **[28]**
- 🔨 **$9 500** - €10 197 - **£6 357** - FF66 889
  Salem Road, Woburn Oil/canvas (91x127cm 36x50in) Portland ME 2000
- 🏛 **$225** - €216 - **£137** - FF1 418
  Backyard Shadows Etching (25x17cm 10x7in) Provincetown MA 1999

BIDA Alexandre 1813-1895 **[39]**
- ✏ **$1 308** - €1 189 - **£787** - FF7 800
  Les bédouins Mine plomb (41x58cm 16x22in) Soissons 1998

BIDAU Eugène XIX-XX **[9]**
- 🔨 **$110 000** - €122 844 - **£70 444** - FF805 805
  A Peacock and Doves in a garden Oil/canvas (250.5x160cm 98x62in) New-York 1999
- 🔨 **$47 500** - €40 981 - **£28 656** - FF268 816
  Still Life with Chicks and Plate of Eggs Oil/canvas (91.5x119.5cm 36x47in) New-York 1998

BIDAULD Jean Pierre Xavier 1743-1813 **[6]**
- 🔨 **$41 782** - €41 443 - **£26 000** - FF271 850
  Roses, Stocks, Jasmine and other Flowers in a Vase, Peaches, Grapes Oil/panel (51x40cm 20x15in) London 1999
- 🔨 **$19 000** - €21 875 - **£12 965** - FF143 488
  Trompe l'oeil of Dead Songbirds Oil/panel (32x24cm 12x9in) New-York 2000

BIDAULD Joseph J. Xavier 1758-1846 **[35]**
- 🔨 **$66 108** - €64 029 - **£41 580** - FF420 000
  Vue du parc d'Ermenonville prise au midi Huile/toile (48.5x82cm 19x32in) Paris 1999
- 🔨 **$60 258** - €50 308 - **£35 343** - FF330 000
  Vue du bord et d'une partie de la ville de la Vava, Royaume de Naples Huile/papier/toile (20.5x27.5cm 8x10in) Tours 1998
- ✏ **$423** - €457 - **£292** - FF2 800
  Vue du Sapey. une des entrées de la Grande-Chartreuse en 1803 Encre/papier (54x42cm 21x16in) Grenoble 2001

BIDAUX Patrick 1969 **[4]**
- 🔨 **$1 086** - €1 067 - **£674** - FF7 000
  Port du Sud Huile/toile (73x60cm 28x23in) Lyon 1999

BIDDLE George 1885-1973 **[25]**
- 🔨 **$9 000** - €10 236 - **£6 241** - FF67 141
  Tropical Village Scene Oil/canvas (50x60cm 20x24in) Chicago IL 2000
- ✏ **$1 400** - €1 590 - **£958** - FF10 427
  House in the Hills Watercolour/paper (35.5x56cm 13x22in) New-York 2000

BIDDLE Laurence 1888-? **[66]**
- 🔨 **$1 505** - €1 681 - **£1 050** - FF11 029
  A Bowl of Geraniums Oil/canvas (34.5x52cm 13x20in) Bath 2001
- 🔨 **$932** - €1 079 - **£660** - FF7 076
  Flower Subject Oil/board (33x47cm 12x18in) Glasgow 2000

BIDLO Mike 1953 **[30]**
- 🔨 **$28 000** - €32 488 - **£19 331** - FF213 108
  Not Pollock Enamel/canvas (106.5x193cm 41x75in) New-York 2000
- 🔨 **$3 750** - €3 604 - **£2 310** - FF23 642
  Not Picasso (Nude with raised Arms, 1907) Oil/canvas (63x42.5cm 24x16in) New-York 1999

BIE de Eugène 1914-1983 **[10]**
- 🔨 **$2 441** - €2 355 - **£1 510** - FF15 447
  Le port de Guilvinec Huile/panneau (53x80cm 20x31in) Bruxelles 1999

BIEBER Armin 1892-1970 **[26]**
- ✏ **$174** - €162 - **£107** - FF1 061
  Sonnenbeschienene Kirche in winterlicher Landschaft Aquarelle (40.5x29cm 15x11in) Bern 1999

BIEDERMANN Johann Jakob 1763-1830 **[59]**
- 🔨 **$22 089** - €24 767 - **£15 000** - FF162 460
  River Landscape with a young Girl standing on a Terrace Oil/copper (45.5x56.5cm 17x22in) London 2000
- 🔨 **$9 796** - €9 432 - **£6 126** - FF61 873
  Blick auf den Pilatus Öl/Leinwand (25x33cm 9x12in) Zürich 1999
- ✏ **$2 264** - €2 627 - **£1 563** - FF17 231
  Blick von Wipkingen gegen die Stadt Watercolour (32.3x49.4cm 12x19in) Zürich 2000
- 🏛 **$979** - €943 - **£612** - FF6 187
  Les Cataractes du Rhin près de Schaffousen Radierung (31.5x48cm 12x18in) Zürich 1999

BIEGAS Boleslas 1877-1954 **[152]**
- 🔨 **$3 172** - €2 777 - **£1 921** - FF18 213
  Composition symbolique Oil/panel (56.8x41cm 22x16in) Warszawa 1998
- 🔨 **$1 800** - €2 134 - **£1 271** - FF14 000
  Tête de femme penchée, profil droit sur fond de rosaces Huile/toile (48x33cm 18x12in) Paris 2000
- ⚒ **$1 876** - €2 087 - **£1 210** - FF13 500
  Le roi de l'espace Terracotta (55.5x15cm 21x5in) Paris 2000

BIEGEL Peter 1913-1988 **[99]**
- 🔨 **$4 747** - €4 910 - **£3 000** - FF32 210
  The Workingham Stakes, Royal Ascot Oil/canvas (35.5x50.5cm 13x19in) London 2000
- ✏ **$1 000** - €1 127 - **£692** - FF7 392
  «Goodnight» Watercolour/paper (23x34cm 9x13in) Hatfield PA 2000

BIELECKY Stanley 1903-1985 **[7]**
- ✏ **$500** - €569 - **£346** - FF3 730
  Untitled Crayon (21x14cm 8x5in) Chicago IL 2000

BIELEFELD Bruno 1879-1973 **[22]**
- 🔨 **$476** - €511 - **£318** - FF3 353
  Am Stadttor Öl/Karton (50x39cm 19x15in) Berlin 2000

BIELER André Charles 1896-1989 **[56]**
- 🔨 **$711** - €696 - **£437** - FF4 568
  Les vieux Oil/board (26.5x21.5cm 10x8in) Toronto 1999
- ✏ **$324** - €367 - **£228** - FF2 407
  Burial Palce, kitwanga, BC Coloured inks/paper (29x39cm 11x15in) Vancouver, BC. 2001
- 🏛 **$246** - €212 - **£146** - FF1 391
  «Sur le St Laurent» Woodcut in colors (26x32cm 10x12in) Toronto 1998

BIÉLER Ernest 1863-1948 **[114]**

$44 800 - €52 361 - **£31 984** - FF343 464
Dame mit Windhund Öl/Leinwand (200x119cm 78x46in) Zürich 2001

$12 221 - €14 534 - **£8 709** - FF95 337
Paysage valaisan Öl/Leinwand (52.5x72.5cm 20x28in) Zürich 2000

$35 040 - €33 810 - **£22 010** - FF221 778
Bildnis einer Mädchens mit Trachtenhäubchen Tempera/canvas (23.5x28cm 9x11in) Zürich 1999

$5 664 - €4 957 - **£3 430** - FF32 518
Automne en Valais Pastel/papier (57x77.5cm 22x30in) Genève 1998

$1 003 - €1 180 - **£727** - FF7 742
«Illustrations pour la Fête des Vignerons» Affiche (16x25cm 6x9in) Sion 2001

BIELER Nathalie XIX-XX **[2]**

$2 852 - €2 907 - **£1 784** - FF19 068
Stilleben mit Muscheln und Krautkopf Öl/Leinwand (64x80cm 25x31in) Wien 2000

BIELING Herman Frederik 1887-1964 **[168]**

$2 030 - €1 723 - **£1 224** - FF11 299
Bergse Plas in de winter met rechts de uitkijktoren van Plaswijk Oil/canvas (56x77cm 22x30in) Rotterdam 1998

$532 - €499 - **£328** - FF3 274
Stilleven Oil/canvas (31x39cm 12x15in) Rotterdam 1999

$11 340 - €9 917 - **£6 881** - FF64 393
Lichtende Wachter Bronze (H47cm H18in) Amsterdam 1998

$859 - €998 - **£603** - FF6 548
Dancers Gouache/paper (38x50cm 14x19in) Amsterdam 2001

$155 - €133 - **£93** - FF871
«Paar» Linocut (28.3x21.5cm 11x8in) Berlin 1998

BIEN Julius 1826-1909 **[2]**

$4 000 - €3 963 - **£2 426** - FF25 996
Wild Turkey (Plate 287), After J.J Audubon Color lithograph (91.5x63cm 36x24in) New-York 2000

BIENABE ARTIA Bernardino 1899-1987 **[13]**

$1 485 - €1 652 - **£990** - FF10 835
Caserío Olazabal, Irún Oleo/tabla (63x49cm 24x19in) Madrid 2000

BIENAIMÉ Luigi 1795-1878 **[5]**

$11 000 - €10 976 - **£6 695** - FF71 996
Busts of W.J. and Caroline Lysley Marble (H75cm H29in) New-York 2000

BIENVETU Gustave act.c.1875-c.1914 **[23]**

$1 724 - €1 906 - **£1 196** - FF12 501
A Still Life of roses in a Vase Oil/canvas (55x36.5cm 21x14in) Amsterdam 2001

BIERENBROODSPOT Gerti 1940 **[46]**

$630 - €681 - **£431** - FF4 464
Tribal Dance Watercolour (101x67cm 39x26in) Amsterdam 2001

BIERGE Roland 1922-1991 **[81]**

$612 - €686 - **£426** - FF4 500
«Cherchez les jonquilles» Huile/toile (55x46cm 21x18in) Versailles 2001

BIERMANN Aenne Sternefeld 1898-1933 **[18]**

$2 013 - €1 943 - **£1 265** - FF12 744
Magdalene Engels Photograph (17.7x23.3cm 6x9in) München 1999

BIERMANN Eduard 1803-1892 **[6]**

$1 211 - €1 329 - **£823** - FF8 720
Der Königssee mit St.Bartholomae Aquarell/Papier (23.3x31.3cm 9x12in) Berlin 2000

BIERMANN Gottlieb 1824-1908 **[2]**

$4 812 - €4 849 - **£3 000** - FF31 810
An Amazon Oil/canvas (75x42.5cm 29x16in) London 2000

BIERSTADT Albert 1830-1902 **[237]**

$975 000 - €968 018 - **£609 375** - FF6 349 785
Lake Louise Oil/canvas (96.5x152.5cm 37x60in) New-York 1999

$95 909 - €91 272 - **£59 991** - FF598 702
A View from Sacramento Oil/paper/canvas (45.5x66cm 17x25in) New-York 1999

$30 000 - €29 199 - **£18 432** - FF191 532
A Laska Sunset Oil/panel (13x20cm 5x8in) San-Francisco CA 1999

$10 100 - €9 187 - **£6 183** - FF60 262
Butterfly Watercolour, gouache/paper (11x18cm 4x7in) Portsmouth NH 1998

$4 100 - €4 200 - **£2 549** - FF27 547
Mountainscape with Lake and Native American Camp with Many Animals Engraving (50x76cm 20x30in) Hatfield PA 2000

BIERUMA-OOSTING Jeanne 1898-1995 **[139]**

$1 310 - €1 134 - **£796** - FF7 441
Grapes on a Table Oil/canvas (50x63.5cm 19x25in) Amsterdam 1999

$573 - €544 - **£348** - FF3 571
De Amstel Watercolour/paper (38x48cm 14x18in) Den Haag 1999

$154 - €170 - **£104** - FF1 116
Etende modellen Etching (28x19.4cm 11x7in) Haarlem 2000

BIESBROECK van Jules Pierre 1873-1965 **[74]**

$59 888 - €57 931 - **£36 936** - FF380 000
Le grand marché Huile/toile (120x200cm 47x78in) Paris 1999

$3 505 - €3 811 - **£2 310** - FF25 000
Algéroise et son enfant Huile/toile (60x50cm 23x19in) Paris 2000

$1 455 - €1 438 - **£899** - FF9 430
Femme nue Bronze (H30cm H11in) Antwerpen 1999

$2 912 - €3 470 - **£2 086** - FF22 764
De opschik Pastel/paper (60x45cm 23x17in) Lokeren 2000

BIESE Gerth 1901-1980 **[22]**

$190 - €194 - **£119** - FF1 274
Zwei rufende Frauen Linocut in colors (45.7x60cm 17x23in) Hamburg 2000

BIESE Helmi 1867-1933 **[36]**

$13 831 - €12 106 - **£8 380** - FF79 408
Stormklipporna på villinge Oil/canvas (94x138cm 37x54in) Helsinki 1998

$2 759 - €3 027 - **£1 776** - FF19 857
Sandäs Oil/canvas (54x31cm 21x12in) Helsinki 2000

BIESE Karl 1863-1926 **[37]**

$1 336 - €1 534 - **£914** - FF10 061
Verschneites Bauerngehöft Watercolour (44x60cm 17x23in) Heidelberg 2000

$124 - €143 - **£85** - FF939
Letzter Schnee Farblithographie (26.5x37cm 10x14in) Heidelberg 2000

BIESSY Gabriel Marie 1854-1935 **[12]**

$3 800 - €4 277 - **£2 617** - FF28 524
Two Children walking through a Snowscape Oil/canvas (81.5x116cm 32x45in) Washington 2000

BIESTER Anton, Anthony 1837-1917 **[2]**
🖼 **$2 018** - €2 250 - **£1 411** - FF14 757
   Waldlandschaft mit Jäger und Reisigsammlerin auf dem Weg vorne links Oil/panel (32.5x42.5cm 12x16in) München 2001

BIESZCZAD Seweryn 1852-1923 **[19]**
🖼 **$3 832** - €3 168 - **£2 248** - FF20 780
   Pejzaz letni Oil/panel (53x67.8cm 20x26in) Warszawa 1998
✎ **$2 227** - €2 599 - **£1 572** - FF17 051
   Scène de pardon devant une figure Aquarelle/carton (53x28cm 20x11in) Warszawa 2000

BIEVRE de Marie 1865-1940 **[32]**
🖼 **$2 730** - €2 603 - **£1 701** - FF17 073
   Nature morte, parapluie et coupe de roses sur une table de salon Huile/toile (74x61cm 29x24in) Antwerpen 1999
🖼 **$484** - €499 - **£300** - FF3 274
   Silver Birches Oil/canvas/board (25x16cm 9x6in) London 2001

BIGAND Auguste 1803-? **[3]**
🖼 **$4 000** - €3 741 - **£2 418** - FF24 542
   Cloaked figur Oil/canvas (58.5x48cm 23x18in) New-York 1999

BIGARI Vittorio Maria 1692-1776 **[17]**
🖼 **$42 658** - €39 064 - **£26 000** - FF256 245
   A Capriccio of architectural Ruins and buildings on a Lagoon Tempera/canvas (114.5x202.5cm 45x79in) London 1999
✎ **$4 749** - €4 412 - **£2 900** - FF28 942
   The Celebration of the Eucharist Red chalk (18x28.5cm 7x11in) London 1998

BIGAUD Wilson 1931 **[45]**
🖼 **$1 200** - €1 014 - **£715** - FF6 651
   Family at Home, Making Casava Oil/board (61x75.5cm 24x29in) San-Francisco CA 1998

BIGAZZI Luigi 1814-? **[3]**
🖼 **$3 800** - €4 924 - **£2 850** - FF32 300
   Autoritratti di celebri pittori: Rubens, Rembrandt, Michelangelo Miniature (14x12cm 5x4in) Prato 2000

BIGELOW Daniel Folger 1823-1910 **[12]**
🖼 **$6 000** - €5 595 - **£3 721** - FF36 699
   Autumn Landscape Oil/canvas (61x112cm 24x44in) New-York 1999

BIGG William Redmore 1755-1828 **[22]**
▥ **$1 737** - €1 625 - **£1 050** - FF10 659
   Saturday Evening the Husband Returns from Labour/Sun-day Morning Engraving (46x57cm 18x22in) London 1999

BIGGI DEI FIORI Felice Fortunato c.1680-c.1750 **[12]**
🖼 **$46 000** - €47 686 - **£27 600** - FF312 800
   Putto con vaso di fiori, anguria, fichi, funghi, conigli e uccelli Olio/tela (94x131.5cm 37x51in) Milano 2000
🖼 **$17 000** - €17 623 - **£10 200** - FF115 600
   Vaso di fiori Olio/tela (93x73cm 36x28in) Milano 2001

BIGGI Fausto XIX **[4]**
🗿 **$38 000** - €35 593 - **£23 362** - FF233 475
   Summer Marble (H107cm H42in) New-York 1999

BIGGS Electra Waggoner 1912-2001 **[1]**
🗿 **$5 600** - €6 383 - **£3 907** - FF41 870
   Riding Into the Sunset, Will Rogers Bronze (H28cm H11in) Dallas TX 2001

BIGGS Walter 1886-1968 **[13]**
🖼 **$4 500** - €5 292 - **£3 226** - FF34 712
   Going Home Oil/canvas (63.5x76cm 25x29in) Philadelphia PA 2001
🖼 **$2 500** - €2 314 - **£1 530** - FF15 182
   Southern snowfall Oil/canvas (30x40cm 12x16in) New-York 1999
🖼 **$3 250** - €3 640 - **£2 258** - FF23 878
   Man in Wheelchair relaxing in Garden Watercolour (76x67cm 30x26in) New-York 2001

BIGLIONE Annibale 1923-1981 **[7]**
🖼 **$4 750** - €4 924 - **£2 850** - FF32 300
   Senza titolo Olio/tela (75x60cm 29x23in) Torino 2000

BIGNAMI Vespasiano 1841-1929 **[7]**
🖼 **$2 330** - €2 415 - **£1 398** - FF15 844
   Ragazza seduta con gatto Olio/tela (35.5x28cm 13x11in) Milano 1999

BIGNOLI Antonio 1812-1886 **[14]**
✎ **$1 200** - €1 037 - **£600** - FF6 800
   Popolana/Ritratto di gentiluomo Acquarello/carta (35.5x25cm 13x9in) Milano 1999

BIGOT Georges Ferdinand 1860-1927 **[25]**
🖼 **$5 961** - €5 488 - **£3 578** - FF36 000
   Nature morte japoniste Huile/toile (45x81cm 17x31in) Pontoise 1999

BIGOT Raymond 1872-1953 **[142]**
🗿 **$2 415** - €2 744 - **£1 690** - FF18 000
   Chouette Sculpture (H29cm H11in) Neuilly-sur-Seine 2000
✎ **$245** - €252 - **£153** - FF1 650
   Les Dindons Aquarelle (24x29cm 9x11in) Deauville 2000
▥ **$51** - €61 - **£36** - FF400
   Dindes et dindon Lithographie (33x51cm 12x20in) Ourville-en-Caux 2000

BIJL Aarts 1885-1962 **[12]**
✎ **$371** - €431 - **£263** - FF2 827
   Cargo Ships in the Drydocks of the Rotterdam Harbour Pencil (50x79.5cm 19x31in) Amsterdam 2000

BIJLARD Cornelis 1813-1855 **[3]**
🖼 **$8 631** - €9 715 - **£5 947** - FF63 724
   Winterlandschaft Öl/Leinwand (59.7x72.3cm 23x28in) München 2000

BILAL Enki 1951 **[21]**
✎ **$1 056** - €992 - **£652** - FF6 504
   Exterminateur, pl.11 Encre/papier (44x33cm 17x12in) Antwerpen 1999
▥ **$174** - €168 - **£108** - FF1 100
   Un quai de gare, du Dernier train supplémentaire Sérigraphie (73x50cm 28x19in) Paris 1999

BILAN Richard 1946 **[1]**
🖼 **$6 500** - €7 338 - **£4 527** - FF48 132
   Figure Oil/board (63x48cm 24x18in) Tel Aviv 2001

BILAS Peter 1952 **[5]**
🖼 **$21 080** - €23 542 - **£13 500** - FF154 425
   The Battle of Trafalgar Oil/canvas (95x145cm 37x57in) London 2000

BILBAO MARTINEZ Gonzalo 1860-1938 **[42]**
🖼 **$3 640** - €3 904 - **£2 405** - FF25 610
   Paisaje Oleo/cartón (43x50cm 16x19in) Madrid 2000
🖼 **$2 992** - €3 153 - **£1 995** - FF20 685
   Fuenterrabía Oleo/cartón (34x42cm 13x16in) Madrid 2000

B

BILCOQ Marc-Antoine 1755-1838 **[25]**
- $1 441 - €1 601 - **£1 004** - FF10 500
  La visite de la jeune fille Huile/cuivre (11x15cm
  4x5in) Paris 2001
- $2 244 - €2 592 - **£1 570** - FF17 000
  L'escamoteur Encre (19x26cm 7x10in) Paris 2001

BILDERS Albertus Gerardus 1838-1865 **[10]**
- $613 - €644 - **£387** - FF4 227
  Bergère sur un petit pont Huile/panneau
  (42.5x34cm 16x13in) Bruxelles 2000
- $1 500 - €1 570 - **£991** - FF10 301
  Cows Drinking from Stream in Pasture
  Watercolour/paper (63x78cm 25x31in) Thomaston ME
  2000

BILDERS Johannes Wernardus 1811-1890 **[51]**
- $6 394 - €6 338 - **£4 000** - FF41 576
  Figures in a Landscape before a Coastal Town
  Oil/canvas (101.5x136cm 39x53in) London 1999
- $4 447 - €3 761 - **£2 659** - FF24 668
  **A Wooded Landscape with Travellers on a
  Sandy Track at Dusk** Oil/canvas/panel (40x50cm
  15x19in) Amsterdam 1999
- $4 083 - €3 857 - **£2 470** - FF25 301
  Figures on a Country Road Oil/panel (32x39.5cm
  12x15in) Amsterdam 1999
- $566 - €544 - **£353** - FF3 571
  Landscape near Oosterbeek Wash/paper
  (17.5x25cm 6x9in) Amsterdam 1999

BILDERS VAN BOSSE Maria Philippina 1837-1900
[15]
- $2 074 - €2 178 - **£1 312** - FF14 287
  Children by a Stream in a Wooded Landscape
  Oil/panel (33x44.5cm 12x17in) Amsterdam 2000

BILEK Aloïs 1887-1960 **[31]**
- $867 - €820 - **£540** - FF5 379
  «In Park» Oil/canvas (81x66cm 31x25in) Praha 2001

BILEK Frantisek 1872-1941 **[25]**
- $622 - €578 - **£387** - FF3 790
  Oh, my Lord Black chalk (70x99cm 27x38in) Praha
  1999

BILGER Margret 1904-1971 **[7]**
- $549 - €654 - **£392** - FF4 290
  «Frau Bereht» Woodcut (50x40cm 19x15in) Linz
  2000

BILGERI Flora 1900-1985 **[7]**
- $3 443 - €3 997 - **£2 420** - FF26 218
  «Pferderennen» Öl/Leinwand (58.5x48.5cm 23x19in)
  Salzburg 2001
- $2 191 - €2 543 - **£1 540** - FF16 684
  Stilleben Oil/canvas/panel (42x24.5cm 16x9in) Wien
  2001
- $2 191 - €2 543 - **£1 540** - FF16 684
  «Memento Mori» Tempera/paper (59x43.5cm
  23x17in) Wien 2001

BILIBINE Ivan Iakovlevich 1876-1942 **[22]**
- $11 363 - €10 920 - **£7 000** - FF71 633
  Illustration for Russian Skazka Watercolour
  (25.5x20.5cm 10x8in) London 1999

BILINSKA-BOHDANOWICZ Anna 1857-1893 **[3]**
- $5 806 - €4 800 - **£3 406** - FF31 486
  Zaglowki w Pourville Oil/panel (41x33cm 16x12in)
  Warszawa 1998
- $1 590 - €1 603 - **£991** - FF10 515
  Paysage estival Watercolour/paper (25x34.7cm
  9x13in) Warszawa 2000

BILIVERTI Giovanni 1576-1644 **[22]**
- $174 460 - €198 184 - **£120 380** - FF1 300 000
  Carlo et Ubaldo allant déliver Renaud Huile/toile
  (269x235.5cm 105x92in) Paris 2000
- $7 896 - €8 721 - **£5 472** - FF57 204
  Ecce Homo Oil/panel (27x20cm 10x7in) Wien 2001
- $1 256 - €1 069 - **£750** - FF7 015
  Study for a Putto, and various hand studies
  Black chalk (21x21.5cm 8x8in) London 1998

BILL Jakob 1942 **[24]**
- $2 536 - €2 947 - **£1 782** - FF19 328
  Ohne Titel Öl/Leinwand (90x90cm 35x35in) Luzern
  2001

BILL Lina, Louis Bonnot 1855-1936 **[16]**
- $1 766 - €1 951 - **£1 225** - FF12 800
  **Bord de mer, effets de lumière sur l'eau au
  Lavandou** Huile/toile (38x56cm 14x22in) Nantes 2001

BILL Max 1908-1994 **[396]**
- $23 749 - €22 922 - **£15 000** - FF150 357
  **Rhythmus Mit Gleichen Quanten (A Steady
  Rhythm)** Oil/canvas (113x113cm 44x44in) London
  1999
- $14 156 - €13 139 - **£8 500** - FF86 183
  **Zerstrahlung von rot zu blau (Radiation from
  red to blue)** Oil/canvas (88x88cm 34x34in) London
  1999
- $9 570 - €9 203 - **£5 905** - FF60 370
  Blau, grün, braun Öl/Leinwand (33.5x33.5cm
  13x13in) Köln 1999
- $44 220 - €47 148 - **£30 000** - FF309 270
  Fläche im Raum mit Zwei Ecken Gilded bronze
  (H124.5cm H49in) London 2001
- $31 902 - €33 148 - **£20 000** - FF217 434
  Unendliche Schleife Metal (13x42x21.5cm
  5x16x8in) London 2000
- $2 078 - €2 017 - **£1 294** - FF13 232
  **Vorstudie zu Oelbild: Horizontal-Vertikal
  Rhytmus** Crayon gras/papier (21x29.5cm 8x11in)
  Luzern 1999
- $333 - €395 - **£235** - FF2 589
  Komposition Farbserigraphie (67.5x67.5cm 26x26in)
  Zürich 2000

BILLAUD Eugène 1888-1964 **[40]**
- $414 - €457 - **£287** - FF3 000
  La baie de Tunis Huile/panneau (23x32.5cm 9x12in)
  Paris 2001
- $348 - €396 - **£240** - FF2 600
  Canal de la goulette Aquarelle/papier (22.5x30.5cm
  8x12in) Paris 2001

BILLE Carl Ludvig 1815-1898 **[172]**
- $4 990 - €4 227 - **£3 000** - FF27 726
  The Fishing Fleet by Moonlight Oil/canvas
  (58.5x84cm 23x33in) London 1998
- $866 - €873 - **£540** - FF5 727
  Kystparti med sejlskib ad stranden, Italien
  Oil/canvas (39x33cm 15x12in) København 2000
- $1 666 - €1 679 - **£1 038** - FF11 015
  Sejlskib på havet Indian ink (49x63cm 19x24in)
  København 2000

BILLE Edmond 1878-1959 **[61]**
- $3 774 - €3 230 - **£2 271** - FF21 186
  Ferme de montagne Huile/carton (36x49.5cm
  14x19in) Zürich 1998
- $2 341 - €2 754 - **£1 696** - FF18 066
  Alpage à Chandolin Huile/carton (28x47.5cm
  11x18in) Sion 2001
- $1 116 - €1 313 - **£800** - FF8 610
  Idylle au Mazot Indian ink (19.5x27.5cm 7x10in)
  Bern 2001

BILLE Ejler 1910 [185]

$14 220 - €16 082 - **£9 612** - FF105 492
Billedornament Oil/canvas (46x40cm 18x15in)
Köbenhavn 2000

$5 399 - €5 115 - **£3 283** - FF33 550
Maske Bronze (28x30x38cm 11x11x14in) Köbenhavn
1999

$434 - €469 - **£300** - FF3 078
Abstrakt komposition med fabeldyr Coloured
chalks (23x18.5cm 9x7in) Köbenhavn 2001

$188 - €161 - **£110** - FF1 057
Farvekomposition Lithograph (20x22cm 7x8in) Viby
J, Århus 1998

BILLE Vilhelm 1864-1908 [143]

$1 450 - €1 211 - **£850** - FF7 943
Det havarerede skib forlades Oil/canvas (44x64cm
17x25in) Köbenhavn 1998

$678 - €672 - **£411** - FF4 407
Marine med sejlskibe Oil/canvas (30x47cm 11x18in)
Vejle 2000

BILLET Étienne 1821-1888 [16]

$2 805 - €3 188 - **£1 955** - FF20 910
Scène d'intérieur Huile/bois (43x69.5cm 16x27in)
Budapest 2000

BILLET Pierre 1837-1922 [21]

$2 898 - €2 723 - **£1 747** - FF17 859
La petite gardeuse Oil/canvas (73.5x54.5cm
28x21in) Amsterdam 1999

BILLGREN Ernst 1957 [101]

$8 575 - €7 915 - **£5 271** - FF51 919
Regnskogen vid juletid Oil/panel (115x140cm
45x55in) Stockholm 1999

$2 990 - €2 811 - **£1 852** - FF18 442
Utan titel Mixed media/panel (72x73cm 28x28in)
Stockholm 1999

$23 465 - €20 467 - **£14 193** - FF134 254
Räv Sculpture (108x128cm 42x50in) Stockholm 1998

$2 907 - €3 457 - **£2 073** - FF22 677
Anka Sculpture, glass (H25cm H9in) Stockholm 2000

BILLGREN Ola 1940 [135]

$29 798 - €33 385 - **£20 770** - FF218 990
Cityscape, Rondpoint de l'Étoile Oil/canvas
(125x194cm 49x76in) Stockholm 2001

$5 459 - €6 335 - **£3 769** - FF41 553
Melankolisk scen Oil/canvas (58x65cm 22x25in)
Stockholm 2000

$5 874 - €6 549 - **£4 080** - FF42 960
Grekland Oil/canvas (30x30cm 11x11in) Stockholm
2001

$1 172 - €1 314 - **£817** - FF8 616
Smygande leopard Akvarell/papper (40x33cm
15x12in) Stockholm 2001

$147 - €173 - **£103** - FF1 138
Anita Color lithograph (42x35cm 16x13in) Stockholm
2000

BILLIARD Louis Victor Marie 1864-1952 [215]

$237 - €244 - **£149** - FF1 600
Prison St-Lazare - Les Bains Huile/toile (40x33cm
15x12in) Deauville 2000

$249 - €221 - **£153** - FF1 450
Hôtel Orléans à Pétropolis Aquarelle/papier
(15x23.5cm 5x9in) Bayeux 1999

BILLING Anna Svenborg 1849-1927 [15]

$419 - €460 - **£278** - FF3 018
Midsommar Akvarell/papper (26x38cm 10x14in)
Stockholm 2000

BILLING Frederick W. 1835-1914 [8]

$4 500 - €4 830 - **£3 011** - FF31 684
A Bear near the Grand Tetons Oil/canvas
(61x45.5cm 24x17in) San-Francisco CA 2000

BILLING Lars Teodor 1817-1892 [40]

$765 - €735 - **£475** - FF4 819
Bergslandskap med kvarn Oil/canvas (66x97cm
25x38in) Stockholm 1999

$456 - €504 - **£316** - FF3 306
Inslölandskap med hus på udde Oil/canvas
(29.5x45cm 11x17in) Stockholm 2001

BILLINGHAM Richard 1970 [12]

$5 000 - €4 805 - **£3 080** - FF31 519
Untitled Photograph in colour (80x119.5cm 31x47in)
New-York 2001

BILLINGHURST Alfred John 1880-1963 [66]

$656 - €764 - **£450** - FF4 862
Street Scene Oil/canvas/board (32.5x49.5cm 12x19in)
London 2000

BILLOIN Charles 1813-1869 [10]

$2 220 - €2 479 - **£1 450** - FF16 260
Mère et enfant au repos dans les dunes
Huile/toile (52x44cm 20x17in) Antwerpen 2000

BILLOTTE L. XIX [1]

$2 450 - €2 425 - **£1 500** - FF15 906
The Young Sculptor Oil/panel (44.5x34cm 17x13in)
London 2000

BILLOTTE René 1846-1915 [45]

$16 546 - €16 056 - **£10 500** - FF105 323
Scène de crépuscule Oil/canvas (99x130.5cm
38x51in) London 1999

$1 500 - €1 658 - **£1 040** - FF10 873
French snowy mountain Landscape Oil/canvas
(81x60cm 32x24in) Felton CA 2001

$3 658 - €3 201 - **£2 215** - FF21 000
**Paysage de Scandinavie: Campement au bord
de la rivière** Pastel/toile (46x65.5cm 18x25in) Paris
1998

BILS Claude 1884-1968 [170]

$968 - €884 - **£589** - FF5 800
Le port de Douarnenez Huile/toile (46x54cm
18x21in) Douarnenez 1998

BILTIUS Jacobus 1633-1681 [6]

$16 204 - €18 151 - **£11 260** - FF119 064
**Partridge/Pigeons suspended by Ropes atta-
ched to Nails** Oil/canvas (55.5x40cm 21x15in)
Amsterdam 2001

BIMBI Bartolomeo 1648-1725 [6]

$28 000 - €29 026 - **£16 800** - FF190 400
Natura morta con cedri ed uccellino Olio/tela
(41x55cm 16x21in) Venezia 2000

BIMMERMANN Caesar XIX [28]

$4 314 - €4 090 - **£2 624** - FF26 831
**Winterabend, Bauer und zwei Packesel auf ver-
schneitem Waldweg** Öl/Leinwand (51x44.5cm
20x17in) Köln 1999

BINCK Jakob c.1500-1569 [13]

$395 - €383 - **£246** - FF2 515
Der hl. Antonius Kupferstich (7.6x5.2cm 2x2in)
Berlin 1999

BINDER Alois 1857-1933 [38]

$2 313 - €2 556 - **£1 604** - FF16 769
Männer mit Pfeife Öl/Leinwand (47x40cm 18x15in)
München 2001

B

$707 - €713 - **£440** - FF4 674
A Fine Vintage Oil/canvas (44.5x30cm 17x11in)
London 2000

BINDER Joseph 1898-1972 **[20]**
$802 - €686 - **£482** - FF4 500
«Autriche» Affiche (61x95cm 24x37in) Paris 1998

BINDER Tony 1868-1944 **[50]**
$889 - €1 022 - **£628** - FF6 707
Wassermühle im Orient Öl/Leinwand (35x50cm 13x19in) Bremen 2001
$1 625 - €1 585 - **£1 000** - FF10 398
Cairo, El Moyad Oil/canvas (48x32cm 18x12in) Montréal 1999
$464 - €434 - **£281** - FF2 850
Orientalische Gasse bei Nacht Aquarell/Papier (20.7x15.3cm 8x6in) Stuttgart 1999

BINDESBØLL Thorvald 1846-1908 **[30]**
$419 - €483 - **£289** - FF3 169
Udkast til dekoration af keramik Watercolour/paper (28x71cm 11x27in) København 2000

BINDL Andreas 1926 **[11]**
$2 038 - €1 765 - **£1 237** - FF11 578
Kopf Bronze (35x26x14.5cm 13x10x5in) München 1998

BINDLEY Frank XIX **[9]**
$2 464 - €2 895 - **£1 750** - FF18 989
The Shellfish Gatherers Oil/canvas (47x89cm 18x35in) Whitby, Yorks 2000

BINDON Steve 1960 **[4]**
$4 032 - €3 664 - **£2 500** - FF24 033
Serval Oil/canvas (86x66cm 33x25in) Billingshurst, West-Sussex 1999

BINET Adolphe 1854-1897 **[13]**
$13 000 - €11 508 - **£7 948** - FF75 489
The Break Oil/canvas (61.5x65.5cm 24x25in) New-York 1999
$6 228 - €6 098 - **£3 832** - FF40 000
Chevaux se rendant au départ Pastel/papier (60x81cm 23x31in) Paris 1999

BINET Georges 1865-1949 **[233]**
$2 407 - €2 425 - **£1 500** - FF15 909
Cavalry Soldiers on Guard Oil/panel (65x81.5cm 25x32in) London 2000
$2 616 - €3 049 - **£1 812** - FF20 000
Scène de marché Huile/carton (40x32cm 15x12in) Le Havre 2000
$307 - €305 - **£191** - FF2 000
La plage et le casino de Trouville Aquarelle (8x13.5cm 3x5in) Paris 1999

BINET Louis 1744-1800 **[12]**
$12 820 - €15 245 - **£8 830** - FF100 000
Scènes Historiques ou la formation des Royaumes Encre (31.5x24.5cm 12x9in) Paris 2000

BINET Victor Jean-Baptiste 1849-1924 **[41]**
$3 177 - €3 201 - **£1 980** - FF21 000
Berger et son troupeau de moutons Huile/toile (66x92cm 25x36in) Calais 2000
$2 608 - €2 897 - **£1 818** - FF19 000
La Seine près de Rouen Huile/panneau (41x33cm 16x12in) Douai 2001

BING Ilse 1899-1998 **[73]**
$3 500 - €4 030 - **£2 388** - FF26 432
Chrysler Building Gelatin silver print (28.5x18.5cm 11x7in) New-York 2000

BINGHAM George Caleb 1811-1879 **[10]**
$14 000 - €15 322 - **£9 657** - FF100 503
Eliza Thomas Bingham Oil/canvas (90x70cm 35x27in) New-York 2001

BINGLEY James Georges c.1841-1920 **[33]**
$4 758 - €5 259 - **£3 300** - FF34 494
Flower Seller Oil/canvas (40x28.5cm 15x11in) Manchester 2001
$1 203 - €1 212 - **£750** - FF7 952
A Cottage at Plaistow, Surrey Watercolour/paper (30.5x25.5cm 12x10in) London 2000

BINJÉ François, Frantz 1835-1900 **[67]**
$574 - €496 - **£346** - FF3 254
Vue de village Huile/toile (35.5x50.5cm 13x19in) Bruxelles 1998
$391 - €421 - **£270** - FF2 764
Le moulin avant l'orage Huile/panneau (26x36.5cm 10x14in) Bruxelles 2001

BINKS Reuben Ward 1860-c.1950 **[187]**
$5 163 - €4 792 - **£3 100** - FF31 431
Pointer and Black Retriever Waiting for their Master Oil/canvas (69x89cm 27x35in) Carlisle, Cumbria 1999
$1 800 - €1 835 - **£1 127** - FF12 036
At Point Oil/canvas/board (23x29cm 9x11in) New-York 2000
$1 100 - €1 121 - **£689** - FF7 355
An English Setter Working a Wood Gouache/paper (24x31.5cm 9x12in) New-York 2000
$130 - €150 - **£90** - FF982
Tense Moments Aquatint (21.5x32cm 8x12in) Penrith, Cumbria 2000

BINKS Thomas A. 1799-1852 **[5]**
$4 305 - €4 643 - **£2 889** - FF30 455
Marin med ångbåt och segelfartyg Oil/panel (38x57cm 14x22in) Stockholm 2000

BINNEY Don 1940 **[10]**
$13 705 - €15 362 - **£9 584** - FF100 769
Pipiwhararoa, late summer Oil/board (91.5x61cm 36x24in) Auckland 2001
$2 938 - €2 756 - **£1 815** - FF18 079
Bird and Landscape Gouache (38.5x30.5cm 15x12in) Melbourne 1999
$844 - €887 - **£555** - FF5 819
Swoop of the Kotare, Wainamu Screenprint (65x47cm 25x18in) Auckland 2000

BINNING Bertram Charles 1909-1976 **[15]**
$13 608 - €13 008 - **£8 528** - FF85 328
Comment on Horseshoe Bay Oil/board (45.5x61cm 17x24in) Vancouver, BC. 1999
$2 596 - €2 504 - **£1 827** - FF19 260
Head Oil/board (45.5x30.5cm 17x12in) Vancouver, BC. 2001
$1 839 - €1 767 - **£1 132** - FF11 593
Floats, Boats and Bicycle, Vancouver Ink/paper (45.5x61cm 17x24in) Vancouver, BC. 1999

BINOIT Peter c.1590/93-1632 **[14]**
$51 912 - €52 324 - **£32 400** - FF343 224
Stilleben von Weintrauben und Nüssen sowie Äpfeln und Birnen Oil/panel (40x55cm 15x21in) Wien 2000
$752 960 - €855 654 - **£520 000** - FF5 612 724
Tulips, Roses, Cornflower, Lily of the Valley/Iris, Narcissi,Butterfly Oil/copper (24x19cm 9x7in) London 2000

BINYINYUWUY 1928-1982 **[9]**
$855 - €825 - **£540** - FF5 411
Murrayanna Mixed media (62x31cm 24x12in)
Melbourne 1999

BINYON Edward c.1830-1876 **[6]**
$607 - €715 - **£420** - FF4 691
The Arch of Titus Watercolour/paper (27x38cm
10x14in) Devon 2000

BINZ Oskar 1895-1957 **[14]**
$177 - €193 - **£117** - FF1 266
Blick auf den Bielersee mit St.Petersinsel
Aquarell/Papier (17.5x11cm 6x4in) Bern 2000

BINZER von Carl 1824-1912 **[5]**
$5 704 - €5 814 - **£3 568** - FF38 136
Auf der Alm Öl/Leinwand (87.5x117.5cm 34x46in)
Wien 2000

BIONDA Mario 1913-1985 **[50]**
$1 400 - €1 451 - **£840** - FF9 520
«Immagine murale» Tecnica mista (100x80cm
39x31in) Milano 2001

BIONDO del Giovanni c.1340-c.1400 **[3]**
$40 000 - €42 788 - **£27 272** - FF280 668
**Saint Francis receiving the Stigmata and Saint
Catherine of Siena** Tempera/panel (41.5x32cm
16x12in) New-York 2001

BIOT Charles 1754-1838 **[8]**
$9 834 - €9 909 - **£6 129** - FF65 000
**Bord de rivière, Temple de Vesta/Ponts, archi-
tecture et personnages** Huile/toile (25x32cm
9x12in) Paris 2000

BIOT Michel 1936 **[57]**
$1 304 - €1 220 - **£789** - FF8 000
Ciel de désert Huile/toile (116x73cm 45x28in) Paris
1999

BIOULES Vincent 1938 **[49]**
$2 840 - €3 049 - **£1 900** - FF20 000
Jardin IV Huile/toile (130x160cm 51x62in) Paris 2000

BIR Rosette 1926 **[18]**
$432 - €488 - **£304** - FF3 200
Sans titre Métal (25x25x10cm 9x9x3in) Paris 2001

BIRCH Lionel XIX-XX **[15]**
$449 - €534 - **£320** - FF3 502
Study of a Collie Dog Oil/canvas (59x48cm 23x18in)
Bath 2000
$326 - €292 - **£200** - FF1 915
Valley River with Cattle Oil/canvas (45x30cm
18x12in) Par, Cornwall 1999

BIRCH Samuel John Lamorna 1869-1955 **[550]**
$21 683 - €21 045 - **£13 500** - FF138 049
**The old Quarry near Roseland Peninsula,
Cornwall** Oil/canvas (94x141cm 37x55in) London
1999
$7 393 - €7 050 - **£4 500** - FF46 248
Cattle Drinking From A Stream Oil/canvas
(61x76cm 24x29in) London 2000
$2 525 - €3 010 - **£1 800** - FF19 743
The Pixie Pool, Evening on the Lamorna Stream
Oil/board (26x36cm 10x14in) Leyburn, North Yorkshire
2000
$1 068 - €1 015 - **£650** - FF6 658
River Landscape with Cattle Watercolour/paper
(13x22cm 5x8in) London 1999
$115 - €128 - **£80** - FF839
St.Ives Print (48x58cm 19x23in) Par, Cornwall 2001

BIRCH Thomas 1779-1851 **[33]**
$30 000 - €35 013 - **£21 267** - FF229 668
Ships at Sea Oil/canvas (63.5x101.5cm 25x39in)
New-York 2001

BIRCHALL William Minshall 1884-1941 **[202]**
$724 - €706 - **£440** - FF4 634
On Active Service Watercolour (20.5x30.5cm
8x12in) London 2000

BIRCHE Henry XVIII **[3]**
$989 - €1 028 - **£620** - FF6 740
Game Keepers Mezzotint (44.5x66cm 17x25in)
Suffolk 2000

BIRCK Alphonse 1859-? **[62]**
$1 428 - €1 220 - **£854** - FF8 000
Jeune femme aux mimosas Aquarelle,
gouache/papier (56x41cm 22x16in) Paris 1998
$1 072 - €1 220 - **£744** - FF8 000
**«Cie Internationale des Wagons-lits, fêtes de
Ghezireh au Caire»** Affiche (150x115cm 59x45in)
Orléans 2000

BIRD Clarance Arthur XIX-XX **[1]**
$2 266 - €2 127 - **£1 400** - FF13 951
Collecting the fallen Apples Oil/canvas (33x24cm
12x9in) Billingshurst, West-Sussex 1999

BIRD Edward 1772-1819 **[15]**
$25 667 - €25 864 - **£16 000** - FF169 657
The Departure to London Oil/panel (61x91.5cm
24x36in) London 2000

BIRD Esther Brock XX **[4]**
$125 - €134 - **£83** - FF881
Washington Square Etching (14x12cm 5x5in)
Cleveland OH 2000

BIRD Jean 1936 **[3]**
$730 - €702 - **£450** - FF4 607
Mrs Swinburn's Pigs Gouache/paper (28x30.5cm
11x12in) London 1999

BIRD John Alex. Harington 1846-1936 **[44]**
$6 500 - €6 756 - **£4 096** - FF44 317
Racehorse with Jockey Up Oil/canvas (38x50.5cm
14x19in) New-York 2000
$994 - €984 - **£620** - FF6 452
The Chestnut Hunter Exile in a Stable
Watercolour (28x34cm 11x13in) Leyburn, North
Yorkshire 1999

BIRD Mary Holden ?-1978 **[16]**
$681 - €583 - **£410** - FF3 823
Cyprus/Etra from an Orange Grove
Watercolour/paper (24x34cm 9x13in) St. Helier, Jersey
1998

BIRGER Birger Ericson 1904-1994 **[145]**
$1 883 - €1 787 - **£1 143** - FF11 722
Parkbänken Oil/panel (122x122cm 48x48in)
Stockholm 1999
$449 - €503 - **£313** - FF3 302
Tv rummet Oil/panel (48.5x63.5cm 19x25in)
Stockholm 2001

BIRGER Hugo 1854-1887 **[35]**
$7 856 - €9 221 - **£5 544** - FF60 488
Dam med spåkvinna Oil/canvas (87x77cm 34x30in)
Stockholm 2000

BIRKEMOSE Jens 1943 **[182]**
$2 799 - €2 821 - **£1 745** - FF18 505
Komposition Oil/masonite (141x122cm 55x48in)
Köbenhavn 2000

B

$826 - €833 - £515 - FF5 463
Komposition Oil/canvas (65x54cm 25x21in)
København 2000

$397 - €336 - £237 - FF2 206
Bröndums forlags Jubilaeumsmappe Graphite
(50x40cm 19x15in) København 1998

$1 864 - €2 078 - £1 306 - FF13 630
Utan titel Color lithograph (100x70cm 39x27in)
København 2000

BIRKHAMMER Axel 1874-1936 **[58]**

$312 - €335 - £213 - FF2 199
Dollerup Bakker Oil/canvas (70x100cm 27x39in)
København 2001

BIRKHOLM Jens 1869-1915 **[24]**

$1 820 - €1 723 - £1 132 - FF11 301
**Kniplerske på balkonen i baggrunden udsigt
mod havet** Oil/canvas (46x58cm 18x22in) Vejle 1999

BIRKINGER Franz Xaver 1822-1906 **[5]**

$4 303 - €4 724 - £2 860 - FF30 985
Orchideenstilleben Öl/Leinwand (82x51.5cm
32x20in) Wien 2000

BIRKLE Albert 1900-1986 **[67]**

$80 597 - €92 793 - £55 000 - FF608 679
Mr. Spindler Oil/canvas (48x40.5cm 18x15in) London
2000

$1 867 - €1 599 - £1 124 - FF10 487
Wanderer Charcoal (31.5x42.5cm 12x16in) Wien 1998

BIRLEY Oswald Hornby J. 1880-1952 **[29]**

$1 364 - €1 327 - £839 - FF8 705
Landscape with Coastal View Oil/canvas (63x76cm
25x30in) Nepean, Ont. 1999

BIRMANN Peter 1758-1844 **[44]**

$15 508 - €13 410 - £9 219 - FF87 965
**Arkadische Landschaft mit Hirten und Ziegen
im Vordergrund** Öl/Leinwand (67x94cm 26x37in)
Zürich 1998

$2 716 - €3 152 - £1 875 - FF20 677
Ansicht von Schloss Münchenstein
Aquarell/Papier (34.5x39.5cm 13x15in) Luzern 2000

$1 361 - €1 372 - £848 - FF9 001
**Vue des Environs de Sursee prise à Knutwil,
Canton de Lucerne** Farbradierung (37.8x58.7cm
14x23in) Zürich 2000

BIRNBAUM Uriel 1894-1956 **[13]**

$432 - €509 - £300 - FF3 336
Hochsommer, Illustration zu Leben in Liebe
Indian ink (22.5x18.2cm 8x7in) Wien 2000

BIRNEY William Verplanck 1858-1909 **[18]**

$4 482 - €4 812 - £3 000 - FF31 564
After the Hunt Oil/canvas (40.5x30.5cm 15x12in)
London 2000

BIRO Antal 1907 **[38]**

$255 - €274 - £171 - FF1 800
Composition Technique mixte/papier (23x18cm
9x7in) Douai 2000

BIRO Mihaly 1886-1948 **[15]**

$391 - €363 - £242 - FF2 383
«A Tarsasag» Poster (63x94cm 24x37in) Wien 1999

BIROLLI Renato 1905-1959 **[116]**

$27 500 - €28 508 - £16 500 - FF187 000
Momento della natura Olio/tela (105x128cm
41x50in) Milano 1999

$19 200 - €16 586 - £12 800 - FF108 800
Ragazza con sedia Olio/tela (65x54cm 25x21in)
Prato 1998

$7 000 - €7 257 - £4 200 - FF47 600
Lume Olio/tela (40x33cm 15x12in) Milano 2000

$1 126 - €945 - £664 - FF6 200
Femme Fusain (65x48cm 25x18in) Paris 1998

BIRREN Joseph Pierre 1864-1933 **[11]**

$3 000 - €3 276 - £1 931 - FF21 490
The Fish House Oil/canvas (40x50cm 16x20in)
Mystic CT 2000

BIRRIKIDJI Gumana 1898-1982 **[3]**

$1 673 - €1 446 - £1 010 - FF9 482
Barama Sculpture, wood (H53cm H20in) Malvern,
Victoria 1998

BIRT John Orlando XX **[38]**

$228 - €245 - £153 - FF1 610
Italian Challenge Watercolour/paper (35x51cm
13x20in) Sydney 2000

BIRTLES Henry, Harry 1838-1907 **[24]**

$884 - €857 - £560 - FF5 622
Farmyard Scene at Harvest Time
Watercolour/paper (24x33cm 9x13in) Little-Lane, Ilkley
1999

BIRTWHISTLE Cecil H. 1910-1990 **[10]**

$878 - €941 - £600 - FF6 173
Artist's Daughter, Mandy Oil/canvas (62x85cm
24x33in) London 2001

BISBING Henry Singlewood 1849-1933 **[10]**

$2 090 - €1 996 - £1 286 - FF13 092
The Expatriate Artist's Sunny Dunes Oil/canvas
(30x45cm 12x18in) Portsmouth NH 1999

BISCAINO Bartolommeo 1632-1657 **[33]**

$92 174 - €78 425 - £55 000 - FF514 437
**The Denial of Saint Peter/The Offering of
Abigail** Oil/canvas (126x173.5cm 49x68in) London
1998

$15 685 - €15 315 - £10 000 - FF100 460
The Holy Family with the Infant Baptist Red chalk
(11x17.5cm 4x6in) London 1999

$545 - €617 - £383 - FF4 044
Die Anbetung der Könige Radierung (21x14.5cm
8x5in) Bern 2001

BISCARETTI DI RUFFIA Carlo 1879-1959 **[23]**

$958 - €1 062 - £650 - FF6 965
«Anisetta Evangelisti» Poster (140x100cm 55x39in)
London 2000

BISCARRA Carlo Felice 1823-1894 **[3]**

$2 200 - €2 851 - £1 650 - FF18 700
Giovane pastore Olio/tela (80x65cm 31x25in)
Vercelli 2000

BISCARRA Cesare 1866-1943 **[16]**

$600 - €518 - £300 - FF3 400
Paesaggio Olio/tavola (11.5x18.5cm 4x7in) Vercelli
1999

$44 520 - €4 406 - £2 550 - FF28 900
Giovane donna Bronze (57x61x36cm 22x24x14in)
Torino 2000

BISCHOF Werner 1916-1954 **[45]**

$962 - €970 - £600 - FF6 362
«St.Moritz» Poster (102x65cm 40x25in) London 2000

$821 - €920 - £571 - FF6 037
Pressephotographen Gelatin silver print
(31.5x46.5cm 12x18in) Köln 2001

BISCHOFF Elmer Nelson 1916-1991 **[14]**

$190 000 - €159 500 - £111 435 - FF1 046 254
«Woman with Yellow Flowers» Oil/canvas
(143x144cm 56x56in) Beverly-Hills CA 1998

$6 000 - €6 962 - **£4 142** - FF45 666
«#57» Acrylic/canvas (104x96.5cm 40x37in) New-York 2000

$5 500 - €5 296 - **£3 439** - FF34 739
Seated Nude Ink/paper (42.5x35cm 16x13in) Beverly-Hills CA 1999

BISCHOFF Franz Arthur 1864-1929 **[124]**

$26 000 - €30 557 - **£18 025** - FF200 444
Point Lobos, Monterey Coast Oil/board (76x101.5cm 29x39in) Beverly-Hills CA 2000

$5 500 - €6 464 - **£3 813** - FF42 401
Mountain Landscape Oil/board (33x48cm 13x19in) Cincinnati OH 2000

$6 500 - €5 553 - **£3 933** - FF36 428
Vase with Roses Glazed ceramic (H40.5cm H15in) San-Francisco CA 1998

$45 000 - €43 798 - **£27 648** - FF287 298
Red, Pink and White Roses in a Pot Watercolour/paper (51x71cm 20x28in) San-Francisco CA 1999

BISCHOFF Friedrich 1819-1873 **[6]**

$1 139 - €1 278 - **£789** - FF8 384
Dorf am Flussufer Öl/Leinwand (47x56.5cm 18x22in) München 2000

BISCHOFFSHAUSEN Hans 1927-1987 **[59]**

$3 124 - €3 630 - **£2 196** - FF23 812
Untitled Acrylic/board (35.5x46cm 13x18in) Amsterdam 2001

$3 294 - €3 270 - **£2 056** - FF21 451
Sturm 2 Mixed media/panel (42x32cm 16x12in) Wien 1999

$2 485 - €2 949 - **£1 809** - FF19 347
Untitled Drawing (60x65cm 23x25in) Amsterdam 2001

BISEO Cesare 1843-1909 **[13]**

$2 400 - €2 488 - **£1 440** - FF16 320
Disegno per la copertina di Costantinopoli di Edmondo de Amicis Matita (43.5x33cm 17x12in) Milano 2000

BISHOP Alfred S. XIX-XX **[3]**

$20 000 - €18 538 - **£12 436** - FF121 602
The Puckeridge Pack Oil/canvas (101.5x127cm 39x50in) New-York 1999

BISHOP Isabel 1902-1988 **[125]**

$42 000 - €45 083 - **£28 106** - FF295 722
Nude by Stream Tempera (66.5x50.5cm 26x19in) New-York 2000

$650 - €647 - **£403** - FF3 949
Soda Counter Ink (22.5x11cm 8x4in) New-York 1999

$600 - €647 - **£409** - FF4 241
In the Bus Etching (25x8cm 4x3in) New-York 2001

BISHOP Richard Evett 1887-1975 **[27]**

$190 - €222 - **£135** - FF1 453
Greenheads Etching (25x34cm 10x13in) St. Louis MO 2000

BISHOP Walter Follen 1856-1936 **[31]**

$2 341 - €1 998 - **£1 400** - FF13 108
A Picnic in the Meadows Watercolour (29x44.5cm 11x17in) London 1998

BISI Giuseppe 1787-1869 **[7]**

$2 596 - €3 068 - **£1 840** - FF20 123
Blick auf Castel Gandolfo Öl/Leinwand (60x40cm 23x15in) Stuttgart 2000

$3 319 - €2 929 - **£2 000** - FF19 212
Italian Battle Scene Oil/canvas (34x45cm 13x17in) London 1998

BISI Luigi 1814-1886 **[12]**

$1 300 - €1 348 - **£780** - FF8 840
Venezia Acquarello/carta (21x28cm 8x11in) Roma 2000

BISMOUTH Maurice 1891-1965 **[66]**

$2 908 - €3 049 - **£1 822** - FF20 000
Les rabbins de l'ancienne Synagogue Huile/toile (55.5x46cm 21x18in) Paris 2000

$1 071 - €915 - **£640** - FF6 000
Rabbin en prière Huile/panneau (18x13cm 7x5in) Paris 1998

BISOGNO Vicenzo 1866-? **[1]**

$1 200 - €1 435 - **£824** - FF9 410
Putti at Play: Pompeiian Themes Watercolour, gouache/paper (63.5x17cm 25x6in) New-York 2000

BISON Giuseppe Bernardino 1762-1844 **[229]**

$32 226 - €31 648 - **£20 000** - FF207 598
Capriccio View of the Interior of the Church of Santa Maria Oil/canvas (165x123cm 64x48in) London 1999

$14 022 - €13 081 - **£8 460** - FF85 806
Paesaggio fluviale con figure Öl/Leinwand (60x50cm 23x19in) Wien 1999

$28 549 - €29 978 - **£18 000** - FF196 644
The Nave of the Duomo, Milan, Looking East Oil/canvas (36x28cm 14x11in) London 2000

$2 400 - €2 073 - **£1 200** - FF13 600
Il caffè Acquarello/carta (11.5x15.5cm 4x6in) Milano 1999

BISPHAM Henry Collins 1841-1882 **[13]**

$3 070 - €3 049 - **£1 912** - FF20 000
Troupeau de vaches traversant un pont Huile/toile (65x101cm 25x39in) Paris 1999

BISSCHOP Abraham 1670-1730 **[15]**

$85 000 - €90 923 - **£57 953** - FF596 419
Two Swans on a Lake Oil/canvas (119.5x164cm 47x64in) New-York 2001

BISSCHOP Christoffel 1828-1904 **[22]**

$25 932 - €27 227 - **£16 350** - FF178 596
Sunlit Hindeloopen Interior with Parents proudly admiring Oil/canvas (152x123cm 59x48in) Amsterdam 2000

$2 956 - €2 492 - **£1 754** - FF16 349
A Lady in a Church Oil/panel (23x18.5cm 9x7in) Amsterdam 1998

$3 196 - €3 630 - **£2 242** - FF23 812
Avondmaal der Mennonieten Watercolour (79x55cm 31x21in) Amsterdam 2001

BISSCHOP Cornelis 1630-1674 **[9]**

$12 825 - €14 568 - **£9 000** - FF95 557
Infant Bacchanal Oil/canvas (84x65.5cm 33x25in) London 2001

$36 190 - €33 539 - **£22 506** - FF220 000
La bataille du Pont Milvio dite bataille de Constantin,d'après Raphaël Encre (39x108.8cm 15x42in) Paris 1999

BISSCHOP Suze Robertson 1856-1922 **[90]**

$8 494 - €9 983 - **£5 889** - FF65 485
Melk voor de poes Oil/panel (56.5x45.5cm 22x17in) Amsterdam 2000

$1 743 - €1 815 - **£1 104** - FF11 906
Mandje rozen Oil/panel (39x29cm 15x11in) Den Haag 2000

$1 866 - €2 178 - **£1 299** - FF14 287
Seated Woman in an Interior Pastel/paper (30x26cm 11x10in) Amsterdam 1999

B

BISSCHOPS Charles 1894-1975 **[132]**
- $846 - €719 - £504 - FF4 715
  «Vue de ville animée, Martigues en Provence»
  Huile/toile (65x100cm 25x39in) Bruxelles 1998
- $465 - €397 - £280 - FF2 601
  «Relève des filets» Huile/panneau (19x19cm 7x7in)
  Bruxelles 1998
- $246 - €273 - £171 - FF1 788
  Jeune fille au chapeau Pastel/papier (58x44cm
  22x17in) Bruxelles 2001

BISSELL George Edwin 1839-1920 **[11]**
- $3 500 - €4 066 - £2 459 - FF26 674
  Abraham Lincoln Bronze (H42cm H16in) New-York
  2001

BISSEN Rudolf 1846-1911 **[37]**
- $415 - €390 - £259 - FF2 560
  Kystparti med traeklaedte skraenter Oil/canvas
  (68x93cm 26x36in) Vejle 1999

BISSEN Vilhelm Christian.G 1836-1913 **[8]**
- $1 171 - €1 048 - £700 - FF6 876
  Squirrel Eating a Nut Bronze (17x17cm 6x6in)
  Perthshire 1998

BISSI Sergio Cirno 1902-? **[7]**
- $1 200 - €1 037 - £600 - FF6 800
  Scena galante Olio/tela (50x70cm 19x27in) Firenze
  1999

BISSIER Julius 1893-1965 **[267]**
- $49 105 - €48 573 - £30 618 - FF318 620
  Familienbild der Karamasow Öl/Leinwand
  (100x144.5cm 39x56in) Berlin 1999
- $18 751 - €22 038 - £13 000 - FF144 560
  Untitled Tempera (45x59cm 17x23in) London 2000
- $12 000 - €10 671 - £7 339 - FF69 999
  «10 April 61 M» Tempera (18x21.5cm 7x8in) New-
  York 1999
- $4 950 - €4 988 - £3 085 - FF32 720
  Komposition Encre Chine/papier (24x30cm 9x11in)
  Zürich 2000
- $605 - €588 - £377 - FF3 857
  Stehende männliche Figur Radierung (26.9x12.3cm
  10x4in) Berlin 1999

BISSIERE Roger 1886-1964 **[207]**
- $17 745 - €19 818 - £12 025 - FF130 000
  Hiroshima Technique mixte (142x177cm 55x69in)
  Paris 2000
- $4 675 - €5 183 - £3 236 - FF34 000
  Femme accoudée sous les arbres Huile/toile
  (55x37.5cm 21x14in) Paris 2001
- $6 588 - €6 124 - £4 000 - FF40 172
  Untitled Oil/canvas (24x41cm 9x16in) London 1998
- $2 311 - €2 287 - £1 441 - FF15 000
  Bucolique Aquarelle (57x58.5cm 22x23in) Paris 1999
- $218 - €186 - £130 - FF1 222
  Composition Etching in colors (50.5x66cm 19x25in)
  Zürich 1998

BISSILL George W. 1896-1973 **[52]**
- $414 - €384 - £250 - FF2 519
  Snowy Winter Landscape Oil/canvas (29x39.5cm
  11x15in) Billingshurst, West-Sussex 1999

BISSINGER Louis 1899-1978 **[157]**
- $134 - €152 - £91 - FF1 000
  Ciel crépusculaire Huile/toile (22x27cm 8x10in)
  Lons-Le-Saunier 2000

BISSON Édouard 1856-? **[17]**
- $4 800 - €5 565 - £3 400 - FF36 504
  The Mandolin Player Oil/canvas (100.5x74cm
  39x29in) New-York 2000

- $2 000 - €1 706 - £1 206 - FF11 192
  «B. Sirven» Poster (44x74cm 17x29in) New-York
  1998

BISSON Frères Louis & Auguste 1814/26-
1876/1900 **[116]**
- $1 225 - €1 372 - £853 - FF9 000
  Cour du Palais Ducal, Venise Tirage albuminé
  (37x45cm 14x17in) Paris 2001

BISSON JEUNE Auguste Rosalie 1826-1900 **[9]**
- $942 - €915 - £582 - FF6 000
  Vues de Rome/Arc de Titus/Arc de Titus, détail
  Tirage albuminé (26x38cm 10x14in) Paris 1999

BISSON Lucienne 1880-? **[6]**
- $11 993 - €14 172 - £8 500 - FF92 961
  La terrasse au bord de l'eau Oil/canvas (81x100cm
  31x39in) London 2000

BISTAGNÉ Paul 1850-1886 **[26]**
- $2 777 - €3 303 - £1 979 - FF21 667
  Italienische Küstenlandschaft Öl/Leinwand
  (34x64cm 13x25in) Zürich 2000

BISTOLFI Leonardo 1859-1933 **[26]**
- $1 850 - €1 918 - £1 110 - FF12 580
  Paesaggio di montagna Olio/tavoletta (13.5x18cm
  5x7in) Torino 2000
- $2 700 - €2 332 - £1 800 - FF15 300
  Fanciulla Plâtre (H54cm H21in) Milano 1998

BISTTRAM Emil James 1895-1976 **[65]**
- $7 000 - €7 514 - £4 684 - FF49 287
  Light (Morning) Oil/canvas (81.5x91.5cm 32x36in)
  New-York 2000
- $2 000 - €2 271 - £1 389 - FF14 896
  The Archangle Michael Pencil/paper (48x34cm
  19x13in) Dallas TX 2001

BISWAS Nikhil XX **[3]**
- $1 077 - €1 257 - £750 - FF8 247
  The Performance Gouache (36x30cm 14x11in)
  London 2000

BITRAN Albert 1929 **[178]**
- $938 - €1 067 - £661 - FF7 000
  «Linéaire» Huile/toile (61x50cm 24x19in) Paris 2001
- $718 - €686 - £447 - FF4 500
  Composition Gouache/papier (58x76cm 22x29in)
  Paris 1999

BITTAR Antoine 1957 **[33]**
- $408 - €393 - £251 - FF2 576
  Thai Market, Thailand Oil/panel (15x20.5cm 5x8in)
  Vancouver, BC. 1999

BITTAR Pierre 1934 **[14]**
- $2 539 - €2 963 - £1 800 - FF19 438
  Saint-Paul de Vence Oil/canvas (89x116cm 35x45in)
  London 2001

BITTER Ary Jean Léon 1883-1973 **[127]**
- $1 201 - €1 372 - £845 - FF9 000
  Le chat Bronze (17x11cm 6x4in) Marseille 2001

BITTER Karl Theodore F. 1867-1915 **[4]**
- $2 500 - €2 448 - £1 597 - FF16 056
  Nude Study Ink/paper (45x21cm 18x8in) Asheville
  NC 1999

BITTER Theo 1916-1994 **[42]**
- $2 070 - €2 042 - £1 274 - FF13 394
  Interieur met Tafeltje en Luit Oil/canvas (50x40cm
  19x15in) Amsterdam 1999

BITTNER Norbert 1786-1851 **[4]**
✏ **$674** - €767 - **£467** - FF5 030
Ansicht aus Mödling Ink (31.5x45cm 12x17in)
Hamburg 2000

BIVA Henri 1848-1928 **[73]**
☞ **$26 000** - €22 432 - **£15 685** - FF147 141
From the Water's Edge Oil/canvas (151x125cm 59x49in) New-York 1998
☞ **$5 094** - €4 878 - **£3 206** - FF32 000
Les Nénuphars Huile/toile (65.5x81cm 25x31in) Paris 1999
✏ **$1 870** - €2 226 - **£1 295** - FF14 600
Bouquet de fleurs Aquarelle/papier (50x60cm 19x23in) Nancy 2000

BIVA Paul 1851-1900 **[18]**
☞ **$13 500** - €14 808 - **£9 169** - FF97 132
Life of Peonies in a Basket Oil/canvas (111x142cm 44x56in) New-Orleans LA 2000
☞ **$6 500** - €7 130 - **£4 414** - FF46 767
Still Life of Wisteria Oil/canvas (49x66cm 19x26in) New-Orleans LA 2000

BIVEL Fernand 1888-1950 **[31]**
☞ **$257** - €274 - **£163** - FF1 800
Vase de roses Huile/toile (41x33cm 16x12in) La Baule 2000

BIXBEE William Johnson 1850-1921 **[16]**
✏ **$300** - €293 - **£190** - FF1 923
Rocky Landscape Gouache/paper (33x43cm 13x17in) Bolton MA 1999

BIXLER David XIX **[3]**
✏ **$4 750** - €5 252 - **£3 176** - FF34 454
A Stag Watercolour/paper (13x10cm 5x4in) Portsmouth NH 2000

BIZAMANUS Angelus 1467/70-? **[1]**
☞ **$11 000** - €12 182 - **£7 460** - FF79 909
Madonna and Child Tempera/panel (14x11.5cm 5x4in) New-York 2000

BIZARD Suzanne 1873-1963 **[12]**
🗝 **$2 185** - €2 498 - **£1 500** - FF16 389
A Greyhound Bronze (40x48.5cm 15x19in) London 2000

BIZER Emil 1881-1957 **[46]**
☞ **$3 423** - €3 835 - **£2 379** - FF25 154
Dorf im Winter Öl/Leinwand (74x100cm 29x39in) Staufen 2001
✏ **$157** - €179 - **£109** - FF1 173
Blick ins Markgräflerland Chalks/paper (18x24cm 7x9in) Staufen 2000

BJERG Johannes C. 1886-1955 **[23]**
🗝 **$3 262** - €3 744 - **£2 251** - FF24 648
Eva Bronze (H48.5cm H19in) Köbenhavn 2000

BJERKE-PETERSEN Wilhelm 1909-1957 **[253]**
☞ **$932** - €1 044 - **£647** - FF6 847
Surreal Composition Oil/panel (65x81cm 25x31in) Stockholm 2001
☞ **$760** - €869 - **£535** - FF5 699
Motgående rörelse Oil/canvas (35x27cm 13x10in) Stockholm 2001
✏ **$312** - €349 - **£214** - FF2 287
Komposition Oil chalks/paper (27x72cm 10x28in) Köbenhavn 2000

BJERRE Niels 1864-1942 **[59]**
☞ **$874** - €968 - **£523** - FF5 297
Udsigt mod stor gård Oil/canvas (56x74cm 22x29in) Köbenhavn 1999

✏ **$251** - €215 - **£147** - FF1 409
Parti fra Vesterhavet Watercolour/paper (33x42cm 12x16in) Viby J, Århus 1998

BJÖRCK Gustav Oscar 1860-1929 **[59]**
☞ **$8 092** - €9 113 - **£5 576** - FF59 778
Skål, munter skålende mand med guitar Oil/canvas (134x99cm 52x38in) Köbenhavn 2000
☞ **$2 283** - €2 532 - **£1 582** - FF16 606
Brygga vid havet, Skagen Oil/canvas (43x65cm 16x25in) Malmö 2001
☞ **$1 791** - €1 943 - **£1 102** - FF11 433
Stilleben med äpplen och druvor Oil/canvas (35x32cm 13x12in) Stockholm 1999
☞ **$1 088** - €1 200 - **£737** - FF7 871
Djurgårdsekar Coloured chalks/paper (45x60cm 17x23in) Stockholm 2000

BJÖRK Jakob 1726-1793 **[10]**
☞ **$4 615** - €5 417 - **£3 257** - FF35 536
Drottning Sofia Magdalena iklädd röd klänning, violett hermelinmantel Oil/canvas (71x54cm 27x21in) Stockholm 2000
☞ **$3 803** - €4 327 - **£2 656** - FF28 382
Landskap med jakthund och fasantupp Oil/canvas (24.5x36.5cm 9x14in) Stockholm 2000

BJØRKLUND Poul Rasmussen 1909-1984 **[63]**
✏ **$89** - €94 - **£56** - FF616
Tre modelstudier Indian ink/paper (34x21cm 13x8in) Köbenhavn 2000

BJORLO Per Inge 1952 **[2]**
▦ **$1 600** - €1 782 - **£1 046** - FF11 690
Ride Linocut (228.5x256.5cm 89x100in) New-York 2000

BJØRN Christian Aleth 1859-1945 **[12]**
☞ **$3 765** - €4 020 - **£2 565** - FF26 370
Parti fra Köbenhavns Havn en vinterdag Oil/canvas (84x131cm 33x51in) Vejle 2001

BJULF Søren Christian 1890-1958 **[287]**
☞ **$959** - €828 - **£577** - FF5 431
Fiskförsäljerskor, Gammelstrand Oil/canvas (66x60cm 25x23in) Malmö 1998

BJURSTRÖM Tor 1888-1966 **[177]**
☞ **$2 359** - €2 120 - **£1 407** - FF13 909
Landskap med röda hustak Oil/panel (61x72cm 24x28in) Stockholm 1998
☞ **$719** - €743 - **£452** - FF4 876
Abstraktion Oil/canvas (34x44cm 13x17in) Stockholm 2000
✏ **$1 709** - €1 916 - **£1 191** - FF12 565
Stilleben i glasvas Gouache/paper (55x47cm 21x18in) Stockholm 2001

BLAADEREN van Gerrit Willem 1873-1935 **[22]**
☞ **$3 591** - €3 109 - **£2 179** - FF20 393
A farmer in a field, a church beyond Oil/canvas (55.5x65cm 21x25in) Amsterdam 1998
✏ **$2 052** - €1 777 - **£1 245** - FF11 657
A canal in a village Watercolour (59.5x47cm 23x18in) Amsterdam 1998

BLAAS de Eugenio 1843-1931 **[154]**
☞ **$400 000** - €381 482 - **£243 480** - FF2 502 360
The Appointment Oil/canvas (155x100cm 61x39in) New-York 1998
☞ **$125 000** - €118 775 - **£76 050** - FF779 112
The Fruit Vendor Oil/panel (78.5x52cm 30x20in) New-York 1999
☞ **$6 111** - €5 086 - **£3 598** - FF33 362
Auf der Holzveranda Oil/panel (24x18cm 9x7in) Wien 1998

B

🖋 **$3 987** - €4 143 - **£2 500** - FF27 179
Portrait of a Young Lady with a Blue Shawl
Watercolour/paper (37x29.5cm 14x11in) Oxfordshire
2000

BLAAS von Carl 1815-1894 [34]

🖼 **$8 138** - €9 447 - **£5 720** - FF61 971
Die heilige Katharina wird von Engel nach
ihrem Märtyrertod getragen Öl/Karton
(37.5x50.5cm 14x19in) Wien 2001

🖼 **$733** - €716 - **£464** - FF4 695
Frau mit Korallenschmuck im Profil Öl/Leinwand
(29.5x24cm 11x9in) Bremen 1999

BLAAS von Julius 1845-1922 [114]

🖼 **$33 350** - €34 572 - **£20 010** - FF226 780
Passeggiata in calesse Olio/tela (93x150cm
36x59in) Roma 1999

🖼 **$3 289** - €3 068 - **£1 986** - FF20 123
Eskadron Dragoner bei der Parade Öl/Leinwand
(42x64cm 16x25in) Lindau 1999

🖼 **$1 580** - €1 453 - **£948** - FF9 534
Wilder Heimritt vor dem Gewitter Öl/panel
(23.5x30cm 9x11in) Wien 1999

BLAAUW Pieter Aartsz. 1744-1808 [7]

🖼 **$21 065** - €23 597 - **£14 638** - FF154 783
The Sailing vessel T Huys Te spyk and other
Ships on T lj Oil/canvas (74x107.5cm 29x42in)
Amsterdam 1999

BLACHE Christian Vigilius 1838-1920 [254]

🖼 **$5 628** - €5 387 - **£3 496** - FF35 336
På nordsiden af stranden ved Kronborg Oil/can-
vas (105x155cm 41x61in) Köbenhavn 1999

🖼 **$1 380** - €1 474 - **£940** - FF9 669
Sommerstemning ved en bådebro, i baggrun-
den sejlskibe Oil/canvas (33x55cm 12x21in) Vejle
2001

🖼 **$623** - €618 - **£378** - FF4 054
Marstrandsfiskere på vej ud i deres båd Oil/can-
vas (37x25cm 14x9in) Vejle 2000

🖋 **$369** - €387 - **£233** - FF2 539
Marin med segel och ångfartyg Grisaille
(63x95cm 24x37in) Malmö 2000

BLACK Andrew 1850-1916 [41]

🖼 **$2 312** - €2 548 - **£1 542** - FF16 712
Fiskere på stranden Oil/canvas (77x128cm 30x50in)
Vejle 2000

🖼 **$644** - €601 - **£400** - FF3 944
Fishermen Mending nets on the Shore Oil/canvas
(30x45cm 11x17in) Billingshurst, West-Sussex 1999

BLACK Dorothea F., Dorrit 1891-1951 [22]

🖼 **$16 010** - €17 186 - **£10 715** - FF112 733
Hills, Brickyard Oil/cardboard (56x38cm 22x14in)
Melbourne 2000

🖼 **$1 299** - €1 459 - **£842** - FF9 571
Still Life Gouache/paper (18.5x14cm 7x5in) Malvern,
Victoria 2000

🖼 **$1 230** - €1 160 - **£762** - FF7 608
Harbour, Veere Linocut (27.5x20.5cm 10x8in)
Malvern, Victoria 1999

BLACK James Wallace 1825-1896 [6]

📷 **$16 000** - €16 698 - **£10 123** - FF109 531
Boston, as the Eagle and Wild Goose see it
Albumen print (24x19.5cm 9x7in) New-York 1999

BLACK LaVerne Nelson 1887-1938 [20]

🖼 **$55 000** - €52 578 - **£34 474** - FF344 888
Apache Land Oil/canvas (82x102cm 32x40in) New-
York 1999

🖼 **$17 000** - €19 050 - **£11 849** - FF124 963
Night Scene at the Mission Oil/board (19.5x25.5cm
7x10in) Beverly-Hills CA 2001

🗿 **$4 750** - €4 537 - **£2 990** - FF29 763
Indian on Horseback Bronze (39x39cm 15x15in)
Fairfield ME 1999

BLACK Montague Birrell 1889-? [8]

🗞 **$564** - €655 - **£400** - FF4 294
«Colwyn Bay, British Railways, London Midland
Region, North Wales» Poster (102x64cm 40x25in)
London 2000

BLACK Olive Parker 1868-1948 [60]

🖼 **$4 250** - €4 562 - **£2 844** - FF29 927
A Summer Stream Oil/canvas (40.5x61cm 15x24in)
San-Francisco CA 2000

🖼 **$1 300** - €1 478 - **£908** - FF9 698
Landscape Oil/board (17x22cm 7x9in) Mystic CT
2000

BLACKADDER Elizabeth Violet 1931 [145]

🖼 **$8 288** - €7 071 - **£5 000** - FF46 382
Jug of Flowers on a Grey Table Oil/canvas
(63x75.5cm 24x29in) London 1998

🖼 **$2 141** - €2 036 - **£1 300** - FF13 358
Heart and yo-yo Oil/canvas (20.5x25.5cm 8x10in)
Edinburgh 1999

🖼 **$3 750** - €4 408 - **£2 600** - FF28 912
Les Grandes Dalles, Normandy Watercolour
(52x77.5cm 20x30in) Edinburgh 2000

🗞 **$325** - €297 - **£200** - FF1 946
Winter Landscape Color lithograph (47x67.5cm
18x26in) London 1999

BLACKBERD C. XVIII-XIX [2]

🖼 **$11 436** - €12 276 - **£7 654** - FF80 524
Young Girl in the Forest Oil/paper (162x114cm
63x44in) Melbourne 1999

BLACKBURN Arthur 1853-1925 [20]

🖼 **$4 025** - €3 926 - **£2 478** - FF25 756
Riverside Town Oil/canvas (50x76cm 20x30in)
Chicago IL 1999

🖼 **$1 591** - €1 719 - **£1 100** - FF11 274
The Sandpit, Bluebberhouses/The Strid, Bolton
Abbey Oil/canvas (23x34cm 9x13in) Scarborough,
North-Yorshire 2001

BLACKBURN Joseph 1700/30-c.1778 [2]

🖼 **$5 000** - €5 367 - **£3 346** - FF35 205
Boy with a Drum Oil/canvas (76x63.5cm 29x25in)
New-York 2000

BLACKBURN Morris Atkinson 1902-1979 [21]

🖼 **$1 900** - €2 128 - **£1 320** - FF13 959
«Backyard, Taos, Sangra de Cristos Mountains»
Oil/board (45x60cm 18x24in) Cincinnati OH 2001

🖋 **$500** - €442 - **£305** - FF2 898
Taos Watercolour/paper (55x74cm 21x29in) New-York
1999

🗞 **$2 200** - €2 371 - **£1 500** - FF15 552
«Landscape Forms» Screenprint in colors
(23.5x30.5cm 9x12in) New-York 2001

BLACKBURN Vera B. 1911 [7]

🗞 **$237** - €205 - **£142** - FF1 345
Angling in Tasmania Linocut (25x20cm 9x7in)
Sydney 1998

BLACKHAM Dorothy Isobel 1896-1975 [15]

🖼 **$2 867** - €3 301 - **£1 956** - FF21 655
The Old Bridge, Buncrana, Co.Donegal Oil/can-
vas (50x66cm 19x25in) Dublin 2000

BLACKHAM G. Warren act.1888-1906 **[13]**
$2 611 - €2 941 - **£1 800** - FF19 292
Crossing the Ford Oil/canvas (51x76cm 20x29in) London 2000
$266 - €309 - **£190** - FF2 029
Showery Weather Flor Waterfall Farm Nr Witton Norfolk Watercolour/paper (36x53cm 14x20in) Norfolk 2001

BLACKLOCK Thomas Bromley 1863-1903 **[29]**
$5 049 - €5 934 - **£3 500** - FF38 924
The Picnic Oil/canvas (46x61cm 18x24in) Edinburgh 2000
$2 595 - €2 952 - **£1 800** - FF19 363
The Brook Oil/board (24.5x35cm 9x13in) Edinburgh 2000

BLACKLOCK William Kay 1872-1924 **[121]**
$7 797 - €8 787 - **£5 400** - FF57 638
Apple Picking Oil/canvas (74x54cm 29x21in) Little-Lane, Ilkley 2000
$3 222 - €2 780 - **£1 936** - FF18 235
A Dutch Idyll Oil/canvas/panel (26x34cm 10x13in) Nepean, Ont. 1998
$1 283 - €1 269 - **£800** - FF8 325
Richmond, Yorkshire Watercolour/paper (29x22cm 11x8in) Leyburn, North Yorkshire 1999

BLACKMAN Charles 1928 **[932]**
$23 376 - €25 694 - **£14 980** - FF168 544
Autumn Garden no.3 Oil/board (136x211.5cm 53x83in) Melbourne 2000
$12 976 - €12 336 - **£8 000** - FF80 920
Lovers Oil/paper/board (74x48cm 29x18in) Melbourne 1999
$5 920 - €6 612 - **£3 791** - FF43 370
Girl and Boat Oil/panel (29x34cm 11x13in) Malvern, Victoria 2000
$3 112 - €3 490 - **£2 161** - FF22 894
Alice and the Cane Train Ink/paper (48.5x72cm 19x28in) Melbourne 2001
$302 - €338 - **£210** - FF2 215
Alice in Wonderland Series: untitled Etching (37x45cm 14x17in) Sydney 2001

BLACKMAN Walter 1847-1928 **[16]**
$3 250 - €3 791 - **£2 282** - FF24 867
«Fisherfolk in a Harbor» Oil/canvas (58x95cm 22x37in) Boston MA 2000
$1 300 - €1 508 - **£924** - FF9 892
Portrait of a Young Woman with a White Scarf Oil/panel (23x16.5cm 9x6in) Washington 2000

BLACKOWL Archie 1911-1992 **[3]**
$2 200 - €2 181 - **£1 376** - FF14 304
Prayer for the Mother Gouache/paper (33x54.5cm 12x21in) New-York 1999

BLACKSHAW Basil 1932 **[34]**
$77 165 - €91 772 - **£55 000** - FF601 986
Race Horses on Beach Oil/board (121x121cm 48x48in) Belfast 2000
$16 715 - €19 681 - **£11 745** - FF129 099
Horse and Cart Oil/canvas (45.5x61cm 17x24in) Dublin 2000
$4 971 - €5 333 - **£3 389** - FF34 981
Budore Landscape Oil/board (20.5x30.5cm 8x12in) Dublin 2001
$4 605 - €5 158 - **£3 200** - FF33 837
River Landscape Watercolour/paper (18.5x20cm 7x7in) London 2001

BLACKSHEAR Kathleen 1897-1988 **[3]**
$325 - €370 - **£225** - FF2 424
Baptism Linocut (14x13cm 5x5in) Chicago IL 2000

BLACKWELL Elizabeth 1710-1774 **[12]**
$60 - €70 - **£42** - FF462
Night Shade, Plate 107 from A.Curious Herbal, London Engraving (30.5x20cm 12x7in) Philadelphia PA 2000

BLACKWOOD David Lloyd 1941 **[154]**
$5 192 - €5 872 - **£3 654** - FF38 520
«August Door'59» Oil/board (66x122cm 25x48in) Vancouver, BC. 2001
$681 - €655 - **£419** - FF4 294
Watercolour Bird, from the Beach Object Series, Georgian Bay Watercolour/paper (45.5x61cm 17x24in) Vancouver, BC. 1999
$1 099 - €1 181 - **£756** - FF7 750
«Northern Patrol» Etching, aquatint (50x80cm 19x31in) Toronto 2001

BLADEL van Ida 1931 **[1]**
$2 200 - €2 454 - **£1 440** - FF16 100
«Levi's» Poster (61.5x90cm 24x35in) New-York 2000

BLAESER Johann Carl 1821-? **[1]**
$3 154 - €3 630 - **£2 174** - FF23 812
General von Bonin Marble (H59cm H23in) Saarbrücken 2000

BLAEU Joan 1596-1673 **[55]**
$287 - €329 - **£200** - FF2 158
Staffordiensis comitatus Engraving (41x50cm 16x19in) London 2000

BLAEU Willem 1571-1638 **[50]**
$310 - €360 - **£220** - FF2 361
Regiones Inundatae in finibus comitatus Engraving (43.5x54cm 17x21in) London 2000

BLAGOVESHCHENSKY Nikolai Dmitrievich 1868-? **[1]**
$6 296 - €7 493 - **£4 500** - FF49 154
The Train Passes Through Oil/canvas (52.5x85.5cm 20x33in) London 2000

BLAHOVE Marcos 1928 **[1]**
$16 836 - €20 023 - **£12 000** - FF131 342
Portrait of Aaron Copland Oil/paper (58.5x68.5cm 23x26in) London 2000

BLAIKLEY Alexander 1816-1903 **[6]**
$10 781 - €9 377 - **£6 500** - FF61 508
Interior of the Crystal Palace with the Stand of the Mysterious Gypsy Oil/canvas (49x75.5cm 19x29in) London 1998

BLAIN DE FONTENAY Jean-Baptiste 1653-1715 **[25]**
$22 500 - €26 501 - **£15 561** - FF173 832
Flowers in a Vase and Fruit on a Partly Draped Pedestal Oil/canvas (131x136cm 51x53in) New-York 2000
$24 150 - €20 164 - **£14 355** - FF132 270
Et par opstillinger med blomster, fugle og frugter på en karm Oil/canvas (74x50cm 29x19in) København 1998
$8 156 - €7 964 - **£5 200** - FF52 239
Still Life of a variegated Carnation, Convolvulus in a Glass Vase Oil/canvas (42x32.5cm 16x12in) London 1999

BLAINE Mahlon 1894-1969 **[6]**
$1 600 - €1 792 - **£1 111** - FF11 755
Allegory, Figure grasped by the Hands of Time Tempera (73x48cm 29x19in) New-York 2001

BLAIR Charles Henry XIX-XX **[6]**
- $6 545 - €5 794 - **£4 001** - FF38 007
Pride of Place Oil/canvas (37.5x47.5cm 14x18in)
New-York 1999

BLAIR John 1850-1934 **[60]**
- $747 - €802 - **£500** - FF5 260
Tantallon Castle Watercolour/paper (12.5x18cm
4x7in) St. Boswells 2000

BLAIR Lee Everett 1911-1993 **[12]**
- $4 750 - €4 241 - **£2 908** - FF27 816
Picnic in Park Oil/canvas (76x86cm 30x34in)
Altadena CA 1999

BLAIR Mary Robinson 1911-1978 **[2]**
- $1 200 - €1 400 - **£835** - FF9 183
Coastal, Point Sur Watercolour/paper (37x54cm
14x21in) Altadena CA 2000

BLAIRAT Marcel 1849-? **[36]**
- $5 180 - €6 098 - **£3 640** - FF40 000
Rue animée Huile/toile (31x38.5cm 12x15in) Paris
2000
- $487 - €579 - **£347** - FF3 800
L'arrivée au campement Aquarelle (38x60cm
14x23in) Lyon 2000

BLAIS Jean-Charles 1956 **[331]**
- $12 357 - €13 720 - **£8 613** - FF90 000
Homme Technique mixte (160x82cm 62x32in) Douai
2001
- $4 877 - €4 269 - **£2 954** - FF28 000
Sans titre Acrylique/papier (63x122cm 24x48in) Paris
1998
- $3 783 - €4 573 - **£2 643** - FF30 000
Personnage aux bras levés Huile/papier (39x29cm
15x11in) Lille 2000
- $2 647 - €2 744 - **£1 679** - FF18 000
Attention Crayon gras/papier (41.5x29.5cm 16x11in)
Paris 2000
- $159 - €191 - **£114** - FF1 250
Sans titre Sérigraphie (26x16cm 10x6in) Paris 2000

BLAISE Barthélémy 1738-1819 **[1]**
- $81 885 - €76 072 - **£50 000** - FF499 000
Actaeon Marble (H81cm H31in) London 1998

BLAISE Saint-Louis 1945-1993 **[16]**
- $5 883 - €7 013 - **£4 195** - FF46 000
Lucie Huile/panneau (25x20cm 9x7in) Paris 2000

BLAIZE Candide 1795-1855 **[13]**
- $493 - €467 - **£300** - FF3 065
**Mrs Richard Samuel Guinness/Lady Nugent,
née G.E Jenkinson** Watercolour (25.5x21cm 10x8in)
London 1999

BLAKE Benjamin 1757-1831 **[45]**
- $807 - €870 - **£550** - FF5 708
Game in a Larder Oil/canvas (61x51cm 24x20in)
London 2001
- $1 635 - €1 575 - **£1 010** - FF10 334
Gamebirds and a Hare in the Larder Oil/panel
(29x37cm 11x14in) Johannesburg 1999

BLAKE Frederick Donald 1908-1997 **[32]**
- $269 - €254 - **£170** - FF1 669
Suburbia Mixed media/paper (47x34cm 18x13in)
London 1999

BLAKE Peter 1932 **[135]**
- $16 437 - €17 644 - **£11 000** - FF115 737
Wall Mixed media (175x105.5cm 68x41in) London
2000

- $12 212 - €13 682 - **£8 512** - FF89 750
Portrait of the artist's Mother Oil/panel (48x38cm
18x14in) Stockholm 2001
- $9 661 - €8 943 - **£6 000** - FF58 659
Dog Act Mixed media (28x35cm 11x13in) London
1999
- $14 919 - €12 728 - **£9 000** - FF83 487
Drum Majorette Sculpture (H155cm H61in) London
1998
- $5 967 - €5 091 - **£3 600** - FF33 395
Pair of Painted Shoes, détail from «Locker»
Sculpture, wood (27.5x32cm 10x9in) London 1998
- $8 834 - €8 574 - **£5 500** - FF56 242
Hollywood Blondes versus the Gilded Sluts
Watercolour (13.5x46.5cm 5x18in) London 1999
- $539 - €524 - **£340** - FF3 434
French Postcards Screenprint in colors (42.5x27cm
16x10in) London 1999
- $4 641 - €3 960 - **£2 800** - FF25 973
White MM Photograph (21.5x17cm 8x6in) London
1998

BLAKE Quentin 1932 **[6]**
- $1 448 - €1 681 - **£1 000** - FF11 024
Mr.Joe Felt pen/paper (50x37cm 19x14in) London
2000

BLAKE T. XIX **[1]**
- $34 000 - €32 455 - **£21 243** - FF212 894
**Benefit with Randall and Turner Sparring, the
Fives Court, London** Oil/canvas (59x72cm 23x28in)
New-York 1999

BLAKE William 1757-1827 **[61]**
- $26 217 - €24 150 - **£16 000** - FF158 416
**The Elders of Israel receiving the Ten
Commandments (?)/Seated Woman..** Ink
(31x33cm 12x12in) London 1998
- $1 100 - €1 188 - **£760** - FF7 795
**And When they lifted up their eyes afar off, pl.7
from The Book of Job** Engraving (22x17cm 8x6in)
New-York 2001

BLAKELOCK Ralph Albert 1847-1919 **[95]**
- $3 200 000 - €3 543 891 - **£2 170 240** -
FF23 246 400
Indian Encampment Along the Snake River
Oil/canvas (120.5x213.5cm 47x84in) New-York 2000
- $3 500 - €3 757 - **£2 342** - FF24 643
Moonlight Oil/panel (37.5x53cm 14x20in) San-
Francisco CA 2000
- $3 750 - €3 581 - **£2 308** - FF23 491
Autumn Landscape Oil/panel (17x21cm 7x8in)
Cincinnati OH 1999

BLAKESLEE Frederick XX **[6]**
- $7 700 - €6 569 - **£4 644** - FF43 089
**Dogfight over the city of Shanghai, cover of
Dare-Devil Aces** Oil/canvas/board (66x49cm 26x19in)
New-York 1998

BLAMEY Norman 1914 **[7]**
- $5 750 - €5 484 - **£3 500** - FF35 971
Breton Ferry Oil/canvas (51x61cm 20x24in) London
1999

BLAMPIED Clifford George 1875-? **[31]**
- $244 - €222 - **£150** - FF1 459
St. Brelade's Bay looking towards La Cote
Watercolour/paper (32x43cm 12x16in) Channel-Islands
1999

BLAMPIED Edmund 1886-1966 **[507]**
- $5 821 - €4 987 - **£3 500** - FF32 715
On the banks of the Odet, Brittany Oil/board
(46x56cm 18x22in) Edinburgh 1998

$4 840 - €4 446 - **£3 000** - FF29 163
Vraic Carts, Jersey Oil/board (20x29cm 7x11in)
London 1999

$1 275 - €1 069 - **£750** - FF7 009
«Karl Schnabel» Pencil/paper (18x24.5cm 7x9in)
London 1998

$639 - €616 - **£400** - FF4 040
The Thunderstorm Drypoint (27x34.5cm 10x13in)
Billingshurst, West-Sussex 1999

BLANC & DEMILLY Théo & Antoine 1898/92-1985/64 **[127]**
$1 099 - €1 296 - **£772** - FF8 500
Enseigne de chapelier Tirage argentique
(29.5x29.5cm 11x11in) Paris 2000

BLANC Célestin Joseph 1818-1888 **[3]**
$4 695 - €5 450 - **£3 300** - FF29 750
Mittagsrast einer neapolitanischen Bauernfamilie Öl/Leinwand (45x55cm 17x21in) Wien 2001

$3 140 - €3 049 - **£1 940** - FF20 000
Italienne donnant la soupe à son enfant
Huile/panneau (32x24cm 12x9in) Grenoble 1999

BLANC Louis Ammy 1810-1885 **[8]**
$12 492 - €13 805 - **£8 664** - FF90 555
Mädchen am Herd mit Vögeln Öl/Leinwand
(95x76cm 37x29in) München 2001

$1 050 - €1 134 - **£718** - FF7 441
An Italian Girl in Local Dress Oil/canvas
(36x30.5cm 14x12in) Amsterdam 2001

BLANC Pierre 1902-1986 **[6]**
$2 913 - €2 743 - **£1 800** - FF17 990
Stylised Parakeet Bronze (H40.5cm H15in) London 1999

BLANC-DUMONT Michel 1948 **[7]**
$496 - €457 - **£298** - FF3 000
Jonathan Cartland, pl.30 de l'album Silver Canyon Encre Chine/papier (38.5x30cm 15x11in) Paris 1999

BLANC-FONTAINE Henri 1819-1897 **[16]**
$5 128 - €6 098 - **£3 656** - FF40 000
Stella Matutina Huile/toile (92x67cm 36x26in)
Grenoble 2000

$615 - €732 - **£438** - FF4 800
La terrasse au bord de la mer Huile/carton
(24x37.5cm 9x14in) Grenoble 2000

BLANCA Paul 1954 **[33]**
$338 - €363 - **£226** - FF2 381
Flowers Silver print (28.5x28cm 11x11in) Amsterdam 2000

BLANCH Arnold 1896-1968 **[19]**
$6 500 - €6 977 - **£4 349** - FF45 766
Some Place in Georgia Oil/canvas (30.5x40.5cm 12x15in) New-York 2000

BLANCH PLA Xavier 1918-1999 **[98]**
$522 - €541 - **£333** - FF3 546
Muchacha descansado en un sillón Oleo/lienzo
(81x65cm 31x25in) Barcelona 2000

$159 - €180 - **£108** - FF1 182
Figura femenina sentada Gouache/papier (64x49cm 25x19in) Barcelona 2000

BLANCHARD Antoine 1910-1988 **[265]**
$7 127 - €6 803 - **£4 453** - FF44 628
Paris Street Scene Oil/canvas (53x43cm 21x17in)
Cedar-Falls IA 1999

$5 856 - €6 252 - **£4 000** - FF41 012
Place de la Concorde, Paris Oil/canvas (32x44.5cm 12x17in) Billingshurst, West-Sussex 2001

BLANCHARD Auguste I c.1766-c.1835 **[1]**
$9 796 - €9 432 - **£6 126** - FF61 873
Napoleon au Col du Simplon Aquarell,
Gouache/Papier (50x70cm 19x27in) Zürich 1999

BLANCHARD Blanche Virginia 1866-1959 **[5]**
$25 000 - €27 626 - **£17 337** - FF181 217
«Gathering Clouds, Louisiana Scene» Oil/canvas
(35x60cm 14x24in) New-Orleans LA 2001

BLANCHARD Émile Théophile 1795-? **[7]**
$3 915 - €3 811 - **£2 405** - FF25 000
Bouquet de fleurs sur fond de paysage
Huile/toile (32.5x24.5cm 12x9in) Paris 1999

$1 494 - €1 604 - **£1 000** - FF10 521
Pangolin - Giant anteater - Mymecophaga pentadactyla - Encoubert Watercolour (16x9.5cm 6x3in) London 2000

BLANCHARD Henri Pierre L. 1805-1873 **[7]**
$31 000 - €33 160 - **£21 135** - FF217 517
A Reception for the Prince de Joinville at Veracruz, Mexico Oil/canvas (49x73cm 19x28in)
New-York 2001

$615 - €732 - **£423** - FF4 800
Vue d'une église Aquarelle/papier (21x28cm 8x11in)
Paris 2000

BLANCHARD Jacques 1912-1992 **[40]**
$564 - €551 - **£360** - FF3 616
Abricots et cerises Oil/board (21x26cm 8x10in)
Billingshurst, West-Sussex 1999

BLANCHARD María 1881-1932 **[58]**
$54 000 - €60 065 - **£36 000** - FF394 000
Dolor d emuelas Oleo/lienzo (55x38cm 21x14in)
Madrid 2000

$15 395 - €14 940 - **£9 584** - FF98 000
Étude d'enfant, la Clownesse Huile/toile (35x24cm 13x9in) Paris 1999

$20 250 - €22 524 - **£13 875** - FF147 750
Le journal Tinta (31x27.5cm 12x10in) Madrid 2001

$640 - €601 - **£400** - FF3 940
Mujer con una cesta Litografía (28.5x22.5cm 11x8in) Madrid 1999

BLANCHARD Maurice 1903 **[44]**
$236 - €252 - **£160** - FF1 654
Sacré Coeur Gouache/paper (33x25cm 12x9in)
Helsinki 2001

BLANCHARD Pharamond 1805-1875 **[12]**
$24 000 - €22 547 - **£15 000** - FF117 350
La procesión del Corpus Christ Oleo/lienzo
(100x150cm 39x59in) Madrid 1999

$983 - €945 - **£610** - FF6 200
Les banderilleros Lithographie (46.5x62.5cm 18x24in) Paris 1999

BLANCHARD Rémy 1958-1993 **[84]**
$1 100 - €1 140 - **£660** - FF7 480
Panthère Acrilico/tavola (152x102cm 59x40in) Milano 1999

$780 - €762 - **£497** - FF5 000
La mer comme un cheval au galop Acrylique/toile
(80.5x99.5cm 31x39in) Paris 1999

BLANCHE Jacques-Émile 1861-1942 **[232]**
$111 760 - €121 959 - **£75 840** - FF800 000
Désirée Manfred Huile/toile (157x118cm 61x46in)
Paris 2000

$4 942 - €5 488 - **£3 445** - FF36 000
Vase de fleurs Huile/toile (49x60cm 19x23in) Paris 2001

$2 397 - €2 377 - **£1 500** - FF15 591
La Porte St Martin Oil/canvas/board (26.5x35cm 10x13in) London 1999

$1 525 - €1 601 - **£1 011** - FF10 500
Personnage au bistrot Encre (26.5x21cm 10x8in) Ourville-en-Caux 2000

BLANCHER Ernest XX [1]

$6 228 - €6 098 - **£3 832** - FF40 000
Crucifixion Email (53x47cm 20x18in) Limoges 1999

BLANCHET Alexandre 1882-1961 [78]

$1 315 - €1 127 - **£790** - FF7 393
Marktfrau, auf dem Boden sitzend Öl/Leinwand (60x50cm 23x19in) St. Gallen 1998

$618 - €720 - **£427** - FF4 725
Plateau de fruits Öl/Leinwand (30x52cm 11x20in) Bern 2000

BLANCHET Louis Gabriel 1705-1772 [23]

$6 390 - €6 860 - **£4 275** - FF45 000
Jeune femme à la draperie jaune - Portrait de la marquise d'Hautpaul Huile/toile (73.5x56cm 28x22in) Bayeux 2000

$650 - €762 - **£467** - FF5 000
Ruines romaines Crayon (24x38.5cm 9x15in) Paris 2001

BLANCHET Thomas 1614/17-1689 [15]

$7 500 - €8 023 - **£5 113** - FF52 625
Italianate Landscape Oil/canvas (73.5x97cm 28x38in) New-York 2001

$2 356 - €2 642 - **£1 640** - FF17 329
Doctor of the Church and Baptism of Clovis/An Angel Supporting a Cloud Black chalk (26x20.5cm 10x8in) London 2000

BLANCHON Émile 1845-? [1]

$35 000 - €38 411 - **£22 536** - FF251 958
Un fort de la vallée - Halles centrales Oil/canvas (275x148.5cm 108x58in) New-York 2000

BLANCO Antonio Maria 1927-1999 [28]

$20 086 - €22 808 - **£13 748** - FF149 611
Reclining Nude Oil/canvas/board (40x50cm 15x19in) Singapore 2000

$3 208 - €3 233 - **£2 000** - FF21 207
The Portrait of my Balinese Father-in-Law Oil/canvas (33x24cm 12x9in) London 2000

$7 719 - €6 477 - **£4 529** - FF42 484
Balinese Dancer Charcoal (54x36cm 21x14in) Singapore 1998

BLANCPAIN Jules 1860-1914 [11]

$3 544 - €3 256 - **£2 177** - FF21 361
Strasse in Algier Öl/Leinwand (82x61cm 32x24in) Zürich 1999

BLAND Emily Beatrice 1864-1951 [48]

$1 301 - €1 516 - **£900** - FF9 943
Summer Bouquet Oil/board (51x61cm 20x24in) London 2000

BLANES Juan Manuel 1830-1901 [14]

$15 500 - €16 118 - **£9 787** - FF105 726
La Casta Susana Oleo/lienzo (50x40cm 19x15in) Montevideo 2000

$6 000 - €6 239 - **£3 788** - FF40 927
Ensayo de encausto Acuarela/papel (48.5x37.5cm 19x14in) Montevideo 2000

BLANES VIALE Pedro 1879-1926 [25]

$70 000 - €72 788 - **£44 198** - FF477 456
Parque de la Quinta de Carlos Castro (Prado) Oleo/lienzo (126x151cm 49x59in) Montevideo 2000

$55 000 - €63 816 - **£37 972** - FF418 605
Cerro Arequita, Sierras de Minas Oil/canvas (64x80cm 25x31in) New-York 2000

BLANKE Wilhelm 1873-1943 [39]

$738 - €818 - **£501** - FF5 366
Am Dorfteich Öl/Karton (48.5x58cm 19x22in) Hamburg 2000

BLANKERHOFF Jan Theunisz. 1628-1669 [6]

$47 160 - €45 735 - **£29 670** - FF300 000
Navires hollandais aux abords du rivage avec un palais baroque Huile/toile (44x67.5cm 17x26in) Paris 1999

BLANPAIN Jean-Marie Luc 1947 [41]

$413 - €381 - **£252** - FF2 500
Vieux gréements à marée basse Huile/toile (22x27cm 8x10in) Bayeux 1998

BLANQUART-EVRARD Louis Désiré 1802-1872 [11]

$1 500 - €1 254 - **£888** - FF8 223
Detail of the Facade of the Palace of Justice (pl.33) Salt print (23x18cm 9x7in) New-York 1998

BLANVILLAIN Paul 1891-1965 [5]

$2 958 - €3 201 - **£2 026** - FF21 000
Le port de Barfleur Huile/toile (33x46cm 12x18in) Granville 2001

BLARENBERGHE van Henri Désiré 1734-1812 [4]

$3 936 - €4 573 - **£2 766** - FF30 000
Scène pastorale Gouache/papier (18x28cm 7x11in) Paris 2001

BLARENBERGHE van Henri Joseph 1741-1826 [14]

$8 977 - €10 202 - **£6 200** - FF66 920
Village Scene with Figures by a Country House Watercolour, gouache/paper (38x64cm 14x25in) London 2000

BLARENBERGHE van Jacques Willem c.1679-1742 [12]

$16 450 - €18 168 - **£11 400** - FF119 175
Fest in einem Dorf mit vielen Figuren und einem Planwagen Öl/Kupfer (25x30cm 9x11in) Wien 2001

BLARENBERGHE van Louis-Nicolas 1716-1794 [44]

$25 859 - €28 965 - **£17 974** - FF190 000
L'arsenal et le château de Brest vus de Recouvrance Huile/toile (48.5x81.5cm 19x32in) Paris 2001

$14 622 - €14 166 - **£9 200** - FF92 926
Figures walkings and riding along the banks/Musicians and Figures Miniature (3x7.5cm 1x2in) London 1999

$4 750 - €5 088 - **£3 243** - FF33 376
Military Encampment, with a Gentleman Receiving Two Ladies Gouache/paper (17x22.5cm 6x8in) New-York 2001

BLASCHNIK Arthur 1823-c.1910 [10]

$6 862 - €8 181 - **£4 892** - FF53 662
Florentiner Skizzenbuch Pencil/paper (23.1x15cm 9x5in) Berlin 2000

BLASCO Francisco XIX-XX [3]

$5 643 - €4 979 - **£3 400** - FF32 660
Barcelona Harbour Scene Oil/canvas (70x120cm 27x47in) London 1998

BLASCO-FERRER Eleuterio 1907 **[21]**
$297 - €330 - £209 - FF2 167
Figura masculina Carbón/papel (59x39cm 23x15in)
Madrid 2001

BLASHFIELD Edwin Howland 1848-1936 **[22]**
$18 000 - €20 107 - £12 198 - FF131 895
Spring Scattering Stars Oil/canvas (127x106cm 50x42in) Detroit MI 2000
$4 000 - €4 542 - £2 779 - FF29 792
Temple of Isis at Philae in Nubia Oil/canvas (68x99cm 27x39in) Detroit MI 2001
$13 000 - €13 475 - £8 243 - FF88 392
The Roman Pose Oil/canvas (40.5x21.5cm 15x8in) New-York 2000
$2 800 - €3 283 - £2 014 - FF21 535
Study of a Head Pencil (61x47.5cm 24x18in) New-York 2001

BLASHKO Abe 1920 **[1]**
$3 000 - €2 881 - £1 859 - FF18 898
«**The Pillars**» Lithograph (49x31cm 19x12in) New-York 1999

BLAT Ismael 1901-1976 **[18]**
$1 690 - €1 952 - £1 170 - FF12 805
Gitana Oleo/lienzo (81x64cm 31x25in) Madrid 2001

BLATAS Arbit 1909-1999 **[59]**
$2 400 - €2 592 - £1 658 - FF17 001
Ourdoor restaurant Oil/canvas (73x92.5cm 28x36in) Bethesda MD 2001

BLATTER Robert 1899-1998 **[8]**
$236 - €227 - £147 - FF1 488
Projet pour de nouvelles vitrines au théâtre Capitole de Québec Graphite (26.5x26.5cm 10x10in) Montréal 1999

BLATTER Vincent 1843-1913 **[17]**
$446 - €525 - £323 - FF3 441
Sion vu de Châteauneuf Huile/papier/toile (18x26cm 7x10in) Sion 2001

BLÄTTERBAUER Theodor 1823-1906 **[10]**
$2 730 - €2 626 - £1 690 - FF17 225
Under the spreading Oak Oil/canvas (42x57cm 16x22in) Budapest 1999

BLAU-LANG Tina 1845-1937 **[90]**
$18 300 - €18 168 - £11 425 - FF119 175
St.Anton am Arlberg Oil/panel (24x36cm 9x14in) Wien 1999
$1 711 - €1 622 - £1 068 - FF10 638
Promenade am Bach Encre Chine/papier (25x28cm 9x11in) Luzern 1999

BLAUENSTEINER Leopold 1880-1947 **[25]**
$9 229 - €7 991 - £5 599 - FF52 415
«**Die Donau mit Schloss Schönbühel**» Oil/panel (52x67cm 20x26in) Wien 1998

BLAUTH Birthe 1959 **[1]**
$652 - €727 - £425 - FF4 767
Zwölf Herzen Farbradierung (39x29cm 15x11in) Wien 2000

BLAUUW Pieter Aartsz. 1744-1808 **[1]**
$21 204 - €19 832 - £13 000 - FF130 091
Shipping Scenes on Choppy Seas Oil/panel (22x33cm 8x12in) London 1998

BLAVIER G. XIX-XX **[1]**
$3 335 - €3 506 - £2 093 - FF23 000
Buste de jeune femme tenant deux colombes entre ses mains Terracotta (65x35cm 25x13in) Paris 2000

BLAY Y FABREGA Miguel 1866-1936 **[15]**
$300 - €280 - £181 - FF1 837
Parisian Bust of a Woman Sculpture (H28cm H11in) Philadelphia PA 1999

BLAYNEY William Alvin, Rev. 1917-1986 **[1]**
$8 500 - €7 333 - £5 146 - FF48 104
Daniel Revelation Mural Mixed media/board (61x86.5cm 24x34in) New-York 1999

BLAZEDY James (Blazeby?) XIX **[2]**
$5 977 - €6 416 - £4 000 - FF42 086
Two Prize Bulls in Landscapes Oil/canvas (46.5x59.5cm 18x23in) London 2000

BLAZER Carel 1911-1980 **[9]**
$419 - €499 - £299 - FF3 274
Ijsbreker bij de Moerdijk Silver print (22.5x20cm 8x7in) Amsterdam 2000

BLAZEY Lawrence Edwin 1902-1999 **[7]**
$1 500 - €1 706 - £1 040 - FF11 190
Switching Yard in Pittsburgh Watercolour/paper (24x35cm 9x14in) Chicago IL 2000

BLAZICEK Oldrich 1887-1953 **[43]**
$2 312 - €2 187 - £1 440 - FF14 344
Skiers Oil/cardboard (50x60cm 19x23in) Praha 2000
$1 040 - €984 - £648 - FF6 454
Wayside cross in Winter Oil/cardboard (33.5x43cm 13x16in) Praha 2000

BLECHEN Karl 1798-1840 **[22]**
$19 964 - €20 452 - £12 320 - FF134 156
Landschaft mit Kapelle Oil/panel (10.1x27.5cm 3x10in) Düsseldorf 2000
$1 580 - €1 534 - £984 - FF10 061
Romantische Ruine mit Kuh am Wasser Radierung (20.1x23.8cm 7x9in) Berlin 1999

BLECKMANN Wilhelm Ch. Constant 1853-1942 **[11]**
$1 502 - €1 421 - £936 - FF9 323
Sacristie de l'église Huile/panneau (37x49cm 14x19in) Praha 2000

BLECKNER Ross 1949 **[177]**
$36 000 - €41 770 - £24 854 - FF273 996
Deceased Mixed media (222.5x221cm 87x87in) New-York 2000
$10 460 - €11 228 - £7 000 - FF73 651
Study: Brother's Swords Oil/canvas (67x67cm 26x26in) London 2000
$7 000 - €7 682 - £4 507 - FF50 391
Bird Oil/canvas (45.5x35cm 17x13in) New-York 2000
$4 000 - €4 320 - £2 764 - FF28 335
Untitled Watercolour/paper (76x56cm 29x22in) New-York 2001
$475 - €445 - £292 - FF2 922
Sphere and Moulding Silkscreen in colors (89x73.5cm 35x28in) New-York 1999

BLEECK van Richard c.1670-1733 **[5]**
$10 094 - €11 155 - £7 000 - FF73 171
Portrait of Mrs Mytton of Halston née Letitia Owen (1696-1755) Oil/canvas (236x146cm 92x57in) London 2001

BLÉGER Paul Léon 1889-1981 **[16]**
$13 000 - €12 986 - £8 126 - FF85 182
Trois grâces Oil/canvas (166x149cm 65x58in) New-York 1999
$509 - €591 - £357 - FF3 878
Portrait de dame Huile/panneau (41x32cm 16x12in) Genève 2000

B

BLEKEN Håkon 1929 **[13]**
$1 322 - €1 468 - **£921** - FF9 627
«Befriene III» Oil/panel (60x90cm 23x35in) Oslo 2001
$1 105 - €1 238 - **£768** - FF8 119
I et rom Charcoal/paper (40x64cm 15x25in) Oslo 2001
$221 - €247 - **£153** - FF1 623
Fata morgana Color lithograph (50x70cm 19x27in)
Oslo 2001

BLEKER Gerrit Claesz 1610-1656 **[12]**
$3 285 - €3 811 - **£2 337** - FF25 000
Scène de bataille Huile/panneau (34.5x47cm
13x18in) Paris 2001

BLENNER Carle Joan 1864-1952 **[41]**
$5 250 - €4 497 - **£3 099** - FF29 496
Still Life with Gladiolus Oils/canvas (76x63.5cm
29x25in) New-York 1998

BLÉRY Eugène S. 1805-1886 **[17]**
$209 - €230 - **£142** - FF1 509
Pflanzen- und Kräuterstudien Etching
(20.2x28.3cm 7x11in) Berlin 2000

BLES David Joseph 1821-1899 **[78]**
$6 240 - €5 949 - **£3 912** - FF39 024
Dans l'étable Huile/panneau (55x45cm 21x17in)
Antwerpen 1999
$4 106 - €3 857 - **£2 475** - FF25 301
Près du berceau Oil/panel (28x21cm 11x8in)
Amsterdam 1999

BLES Herri met de 1485/90-c.1560 **[15]**
$51 561 - €50 637 - **£32 000** - FF332 156
The Conversion of St Paul Oil/panel (111x142cm
43x55in) London 1999
$217 867 - €185 369 - **£130 000** - FF1 215 942
Panoramic Mountain Landscape with Town
River, Christ with Cleopas Oil/panel (57x86.5cm
22x34in) London 1998
$61 849 - €69 347 - **£42 000** - FF454 889
Landscape with the Parable of the Good
Samaritan Oil/panel (33.5x46.5cm 13x18in) London
2000

BLES Joseph 1792-1883 **[3]**
$5 315 - €4 549 - **£3 200** - FF29 840
Figures promenading beside a River Oil/panel
(25.5x35cm 10x13in) London 1998

BLES Joseph 1825-1875 **[24]**
$4 659 - €5 445 - **£3 326** - FF35 719
Elegant Figures on a Sunday Morning having a
Pick-nick Oil/panel (37x50cm 14x19in) Amsterdam
2001
$5 485 - €6 403 - **£3 872** - FF42 000
Parade dans une ville du nord Huile/panneau
(28x37cm 11x14in) Paris 2000

BLESS Johann Peter 1825-1880 **[5]**
$4 066 - €4 563 - **£2 818** - FF29 930
Udsigt over Århus Oil/canvas (85x120cm 33x47in)
Köbenhavn 2000

BLEULAND VAN OORDT Johanna 1864-1948 **[1]**
$4 883 - €4 710 - **£3 021** - FF30 894
La première leçon de tricot Pastel/papier (50x60cm
19x23in) Bruxelles 1999

BLEULER Johann Heinrich 1758-1823 **[58]**
$3 001 - €3 323 - **£2 080** - FF21 800
«Die grosse Fontäne auf Wilhelmshöhe (bei
Cassel)» Gouache/paper (48x67.5cm 18x26in) Berlin
2001

$504 - €541 - **£337** - FF3 551
Château de Greiffensee auf Canton de Zurich à
Zurich chez H.Bleuler Radierung (19.3x30.2cm
7x11in) Zürich 2000

BLEULER Johann Heinrich, Jr. 1787-1857 **[11]**
$4 437 - €4 782 - **£2 975** - FF31 368
Aussicht von der Promenade bey Vevay nach
dem Genfersee Gouache/papier (44.5x66cm 17x25in)
Zürich 2000

BLEULER Johann Ludwig, Louis 1792-1850 **[107]**
$3 722 - €3 218 - **£2 212** - FF21 111
Teufelsbrücke Gouache/papier (34x50cm 13x19in)
Zürich 1998
$321 - €313 - **£197** - FF2 050
Vue de Genève Aquatinte couleurs (19.5x29.5cm
7x11in) Bern 1999

BLEUMNER Oscar Florianus 1867-1938 **[3]**
$1 300 - €1 516 - **£912** - FF9 945
Landscape with Mountainous Watercolour
(27x39cm 10x15in) Boston MA 2000

BLEYL Fritz 1880-1966 **[58]**
$460 - €537 - **£323** - FF3 521
Bauernhof im Erzgebirge Chalks (32.4x43.3cm
12x17in) Köln 2000
$244 - €204 - **£144** - FF1 340
Dammbauerboote auf der Elbe Woodcut
(11.9x17cm 4x6in) Hamburg 1998

BLEYNIE Claude 1923 **[4]**
$1 423 - €1 524 - **£969** - FF10 000
Les oiseaux Tapisserie (111x191cm 43x75in) Calais
2001

BLIECK de Daniel ?-1673 **[16]**
$110 000 - €117 475 - **£74 954** - FF770 583
Church Interior by Candlelight with Figures
conversing Oil/panel (85x115cm 33x45in) New-York
2001

BLIECK Maurice 1876-1922 **[64]**
$1 444 - €1 537 - **£985** - FF10 081
Vue de port Huile/toile (56x70cm 22x27in) Bruxelles
2001

BLIGH Jabez act.c.1860-1889 **[23]**
$749 - €826 - **£500** - FF5 417
Still Lifes with Blackberries/Wild Flowers
Watercolour/paper (16x20cm 6x8in) Little-Lane, Ilkley
2001

BLIGNY Albert 1849-1908 **[29]**
$4 445 - €4 421 - **£2 757** - FF29 000
La parade Huile/panneau (25x40.5cm 9x15in)
Neuilly-sur-Seine 1999
$205 - €229 - **£143** - FF1 500
La caserne Crayon (42.5x30.5cm 16x12in) Paris 2001

BLIJK van den Frans Jacobus 1806-1876 **[12]**
$6 392 - €7 260 - **£4 484** - FF47 625
A sailing Vessel at full Sail, approaching a
Harbour Oil/panel (51.5x72.5cm 20x28in) Amsterdam
2001

BLIN Francis, François 1827-1866 **[8]**
$1 492 - €1 433 - **£925** - FF9 403
Weite Flusslandschaft Öl/Leinwand (40.5x60cm
15x23in) Zürich 1999
$1 597 - €1 677 - **£1 006** - FF11 000
Baigneuses Huile/toile (27x21.5cm 10x8in) Besançon
2000

BLINKS Thomas 1860-1912 **[94]**

📷 **$110 000** - €93 982 - **£66 033** - FF616 484
Away! Away! Oil/canvas (114.5x183cm 45x72in)
New-York 1998

📷 **$36 000** - €30 758 - **£21 610** - FF201 758
The York and Ainsty Hounds on the Ferry at Newby Oil/canvas (51.5x76cm 20x29in) New-York 1998

📷 **$2 286** - €2 234 - **£1 450** - FF14 656
Gentleman on a Grey Hunter Taking a Fence and Stream Oil/canvas (17x22cm 7x9in) Leicester 1999

🖋 **$1 600** - €1 386 - **£981** - FF9 090
Fox Hunting Watercolour/board (30.5x51cm 12x20in) New-York 1999

BLISS Douglas Percy 1900-1984 **[19]**

📷 **$1 570** - €1 754 - **£1 050** - FF11 504
Gardeners in a London Square Oil/canvas (50x60cm 19x23in) West-Midlands 2000

BLOC André 1896-1966 **[103]**

🗿 **$2 766** - €2 287 - **£1 623** - FF15 000
Envol Bronze (78x98x40cm 30x38x15in) Paris 1998

BLOCH Albert 1882-1961 **[10]**

📷 **$165 450** - €154 542 - **£100 000** - FF1 013 730
Souvenir Oil/canvas (90.5x110cm 35x43in) London 1999

📷 **$11 000** - €11 879 - **£7 602** - FF77 922
Head of a Clown Oil/canvas (28.5x20.5cm 11x8in) New-York 2001

BLOCH Carl 1834-1890 **[63]**

📷 **$4 405** - €4 171 - **£2 740** - FF27 363
En fisker fra Sorrent Oil/canvas (65x49cm 25x19in) Köbenhavn 1999

📷 **$1 580** - €1 745 - **£1 046** - FF11 445
Skovparti med spadserende dreng Oil/panel (25x17cm 9x6in) Viby J, Århus 2000

🖋 **$266** - €269 - **£166** - FF1 762
Italienerinde med en lille dreng Indian ink/paper (29x17.5cm 11x6in) Köbenhavn 2000

BLOCH Julius Thlengen 1888-1966 **[44]**

📷 **$1 000** - €1 107 - **£678** - FF7 264
Petunias Oil/canvas (66x55cm 26x22in) New-York 2000

🖋 **$450** - €506 - **£310** - FF3 322
The Quarry Watercolour (29.5x46.5cm 11x18in) Philadelphia PA 2000

▦ **$130** - €140 - **£87** - FF918
Battle Casualty Lithograph (26x35cm 10x14in) Cleveland OH 2000

BLOCH Marcel 1884-? **[35]**

▦ **$389** - €442 - **£270** - FF2 900
«Demay Armurier, le Havre» Affiche (155x118cm 61x46in) Paris 2001

BLOCH Martin 1883-1954 **[10]**

📷 **$3 614** - €3 447 - **£2 200** - FF22 610
Figures by the Shore Oil/canvas (91.5x66cm 36x25in) London 1999

🖋 **$447** - €431 - **£280** - FF2 828
Portrait of Jupp Dernbach Charcoal/paper (39.5x30.5cm 15x12in) London 1999

BLOCK de Emiel 1941 **[11]**

🗿 **$3 094** - €3 222 - **£1 950** - FF21 138
Nu Bronze (H70cm H27in) Antwerpen 2000

BLOCK de Eugène 1812-1893 **[32]**

📷 **$434** - €504 - **£300** - FF3 307
Shepherd Going to Work Oil/canvas (64x44cm 25x17in) London 2000

📷 **$1 829** - €1 601 - **£1 107** - FF10 500
Personnages devant une chaumière Huile/panneau (29.5x39cm 11x15in) Paris 1998

🖋 **$366** - €372 - **£229** - FF2 439
Serieus nieuws Lavis/papier (19x14cm 7x5in) Antwerpen 2000

BLOCK Joseph 1863-1923 **[6]**

📷 **$1 097** - €1 180 - **£747** - FF7 739
Nude in Front of a Mirror Oil/canvas (73x103cm 28x40in) Amsterdam 2001

BLOCKHOUWER Herman Bartholoniesz XVII **[1]**

📷 **$25 000** - €25 565 - **£15 675** - FF167 695
Waldlandschaft mit Häusergruppe an einem Gewässer Ink (13.5x17.9cm 5x7in) Köln 2000

BLOCKLANDT van Anthonis 1532-1583 **[5]**

📷 **$36 190** - €39 970 - **£25 080** - FF262 185
Die Anbetung der Hirten Öl/Leinwand (199x147cm 78x57in) Wien 2001

BLOEMAERT Abraham 1564-1651 **[131]**

📷 **$10 000** - €10 367 - **£6 000** - FF68 000
Sacra Famiglia Olio/tela (83.5x67cm 32x26in) Milano 1999

📷 **$21 685** - €25 253 - **£15 000** - FF165 649
The Rest on the Flight into egypt Oil/panel (35.5x41.5cm 13x16in) London 2000

🖋 **$6 877** - €6 377 - **£4 200** - FF41 832
A Seated Bishop Holding a Crozier, a Sword, a Whip and a Book Ink (22x16cm 8x6in) London 1998

BLOEMAERT Adriaen 1609-1666 **[14]**

📷 **$10 815** - €10 901 - **£6 750** - FF71 505
Gebirgslandschaft mit Ruinen Oil/panel (51.5x64.5cm 20x25in) Wien 2000

BLOEMAERT Hendrick 1601/02-1672 **[23]**

📷 **$70 000** - €72 597 - **£47 698** - FF490 371
Virgin Annunciate/Angel of the Annunciation Oil/panel (63.5x55cm 25x21in) New-York 2001

BLOEMEN van Jan Franz Orizzonte 1662-1749 **[103]**

📷 **$25 000** - €25 916 - **£15 000** - FF170 000
Paesaggio fluviale con figure Olio/tela (146x221cm 57x87in) Milano 1999

📷 **$35 000** - €30 701 - **£21 252** - FF201 383
Italianate Landscape with Figures Oil/canvas (45.5x61cm 17x24in) New-York 1999

📷 **$32 874** - €35 288 - **£22 000** - FF231 475
Classical Landscape with Figures by Ruins Oil/canvas (27x35cm 10x13in) London 2000

BLOEMEN van Norbert il Bamboccio 1670-1746 **[7]**

📷 **$15 676** - €17 805 - **£11 000** - FF116 792
Roman Street Scene with a Vegetable Seller Oil/canvas (81x114.5cm 31x45in) London 2001

BLOEMEN van Pieter 1657-1720 **[95]**

📷 **$25 000** - €25 916 - **£15 000** - FF170 000
Paesaggio fluviale con figure Olio/tela (146x221cm 57x87in) Milano 1999

📷 **$6 800** - €8 812 - **£5 100** - FF57 800
Il maniscalco Olio/tavola (45.5x62cm 17x24in) Roma 2000

📷 **$4 530** - €4 360 - **£2 832** - FF28 602
Einschmähen wird vor der Schmiede beschlagen Öl/Leinwand (35.5x43.5cm 13x17in) Wien 1999

🖋 **$1 556** - €1 443 - **£950** - FF9 466
A Horse Lying Down, Seen From the Back Watercolour (18x22cm 7x8in) London 1998

BLOEMERS Arnoldus 1786-1844 **[25]**
- 🖼 $32 050 – €38 112 - **£22 850** – FF250 000
  Nature morte au faisan et à la perdrix sur un entablement de marbre Huile/toile (82x73.5cm 32x28in) Neuilly-sur-Seine 2000
- 🖼 $6 052 – €6 098 - **£3 772** – FF40 000
  Jeté de fleurs Huile/toile (35x28.5cm 13x11in) Paris 2000

BLOGG John 1851-1936 **[2]**
- 🖼 $4 450 – €4 330 - **£2 739** – FF28 404
  Gumleaf Decoration Bas-relief (43x24.5cm 16x9in) Malvern, Victoria 1999

BLOHM Roy 1922 **[4]**
- 🖼 $1 873 – €2 079 - **£1 305** – FF13 639
  «Potetskrellersken» Oil/canvas (74x61cm 29x24in) Oslo 2001

BLOM Gerhard Lichtenberg 1866-1930 **[51]**
- 🖼 $332 – €358 - **£228** – FF2 347
  Winterlandschaft mit Feldweg Öl/Leinwand (70x100cm 27x39in) München 2001

BLOM Gustav Vilhelm 1853-1942 **[20]**
- 🖼 $554 – €538 - **£342** – FF3 529
  Haveexteriör Oil/canvas (40x46cm 15x18in) Vejle 1999

BLOM Jan c.1622-1685 **[8]**
- 🖼 $2 504 – €2 907 - **£1 760** – FF19 068
  Ein elegantes Paar spaziert durch einen Schlosspark Öl/Leinwand (37x33cm 14x12in) Wien 2001

BLOMBERG Stig 1901-1970 **[67]**
- 🖼 $353 – €395 - **£245** – FF2 594
  Tidningspojken Bronze (H19.5cm H7in) Stockholm 2001

BLOME Richard XVII **[23]**
- 🖼 $144 – €136 - **£90** – FF894
  Haute Ecole Subjects Engraving (27x35cm 11x14in) Fernhurst, Haslemere, Surrey 1999

BLOMFIELD Charles 1848-1926 **[42]**
- 🖼 $2 345 – €2 464 - **£1 544** – FF16 166
  Cascade on the Nihotopu Oil/canvas (40x59cm 15x23in) Auckland 2000
- 🖼 $933 – €1 064 - **£645** – FF6 977
  «Southern Alps from th Bush, Westland» Oil/board (24x38.5cm 9x15in) Auckland 2000

BLOMFIELD James Jerris 1872-1951 **[25]**
- 🖼 $121 – €117 - **£75** – FF767
  At Highland Creek/Birchcliff Bay, Scarborough Etching (11x15cm 4x5in) Toronto 1999

BLOMMAERDT Maximilian XVII **[20]**
- 🖼 $7 936 – €7 496 - **£4 800** – FF49 173
  Elegant Company making Music and dining/Card Players fighting Oil/canvas (49x59cm 19x23in) London 1999
- 🖼 $11 736 – €9 918 - **£7 000** – FF65 055
  Riverside towns with Numerous Figures and Sailing Boats Oil/panel (26x39.5cm 10x15in) London 1998

BLOMMAERT Abraham 1626-c.1683 **[2]**
- 🖼 $48 612 – €54 454 - **£33 780** – FF357 192
  Architectural Capriccio of a Portico, with an Italianate Landscape Oil/panel (62.5x88.5cm 24x34in) Amsterdam 2001

BLOMME Alphonse Joseph 1889-1979 **[110]**
- 🖼 $631 – €545 - **£380** – FF3 577
  Jour de fête en Bretagne Huile/panneau (58x60cm 22x23in) Bruxelles 1999

BLOMMERS Bernardus Johannes 1845-1914 **[143]**
- 🖼 $30 000 – €27 839 - **£18 330** – FF182 610
  In the Garden Oil/canvas (46.5x62.5cm 18x24in) New-York 1998
- 🖼 $3 861 – €4 538 - **£2 677** – FF29 766
  Mother's Little Helper Oil/canvas (31x25cm 12x9in) Amsterdam 2000
- 🖼 $4 331 – €4 365 - **£2 699** – FF28 630
  Küstenlandschaft mit Krabbenfischern Aquarell/Papier (36x53cm 14x20in) Zürich 2000

BLOMSTEDT Juhanna 1937 **[16]**
- 🖼 $1 236 – €1 345 - **£815** – FF8 825
  Komposition Oil/canvas (50x100cm 19x39in) Helsinki 2000
- 🖼 $143 – €168 - **£99** – FF1 103
  Komposition Serigraph (16x32cm 6x12in) Helsinki 2000

BLOMSTEDT Väinö 1871-1947 **[23]**
- 🖼 $4 841 – €4 541 - **£2 991** – FF29 786
  Vårvinter Oil/canvas (81x116cm 31x45in) Helsinki 1999
- 🖼 $852 – €920 - **£589** – FF6 037
  Mondnacht über Pompeji Öl/Karton (18x24cm 7x9in) Frankfurt 2001

BLOND Maurice 1899-1974 **[120]**
- 🖼 $945 – €1 067 - **£658** – FF7 000
  Paysage animé Huile/toile (81x65cm 31x25in) Lons-Le-Saunier 2001
- 🖼 $504 – €427 - **£303** – FF2 800
  Cafetière et Théière Huile/isorel (16x20cm 6x7in) Paris 1998
- 🖼 $522 – €610 - **£366** – FF4 000
  Danseuse, projet pour les ballets russes Aquarelle (25.5x20cm 10x7in) Paris 2001

BLØNDAHL Gunnlaugur 1893-1962 **[16]**
- 🖼 $5 572 – €4 709 - **£3 325** – FF30 891
  Portraet af ung kvinde, der saetter sit hår Oil/canvas (84x70cm 33x27in) København 1998
- 🖼 $1 896 – €2 144 - **£1 281** – FF14 065
  Fiskekutter ved molen med fjelde i baggrunden Watercolour (59x47cm 23x18in) København 2000

BLONDAT Max 1879-1926 **[23]**
- 🖼 $1 761 – €1 524 - **£1 069** – FF10 000
  Peau d'âne Bronze (H15.5cm H6in) Lyon 1998

BLONDEAU Paul XIX-XX **[17]**
- 🖼 $5 500 – €5 940 - **£3 801** – FF38 964
  At the River Oil/canvas (46.5x55cm 18x21in) New-York 2000

BLONDEEL Lancelot 1496-1561 **[2]**
- 🖼 $29 835 – €25 560 - **£17 935** – FF167 665
  Maria mit Kind Oil/panel (70x46.5cm 27x18in) Köln 1998

BLONDEL André 1909-1949 **[9]**
- 🖼 $779 – €838 - **£531** – FF5 500
  Paysage Huile/carton (26.5x34.5cm 10x13in) Paris 2001

BLONDEL Jacques François 1705-1774 **[4]**
- 🖼 $5 500 – €5 892 - **£3 755** – FF38 165
  Design for a Fountain Ink (28x45.5cm 11x17in) New-York 2001

BLONDEL Jean-François 1705-1775 **[2]**
- 🖼 $897 – €1 022 - **£626** – FF6 707
  Vue générale des décorations et feux d'artifice par la ville de Paris Kupferstich (51.5x84cm 20x33in) Berlin 2001

BLONDEL Merry-Joseph 1781-1853 [22]
- $13 020 - €14 521 - **£8 496** - FF95 251
  The Penitent Magdalene Oil/canvas (124.5x173.5cm 49x68in) Amsterdam 2000
- $22 500 - €26 501 - **£15 561** - FF173 832
  Portrait of Two Children in an Empire Style Interior Oil/canvas (61x51cm 24x20in) New-York 2000
- $3 318 - €3 049 - **£2 038** - FF20 000
  La Sainte Famille avec saint Jean-Baptiste Huile/toile (30x24.5cm 11x9in) Paris 1999

BLONDIN Charles XX [41]
- $289 - €278 - **£178** - FF1 822
  Place de la Concorde, Paris Oil/canvas (27x35cm 10x13in) Malmö 1999

BLOOM Hyman 1913 [4]
- $550 - €506 - **£330** - FF3 320
  Wrestlers III Pencil/paper (41x27cm 16x11in) Detroit MI 1999

BLOOMER Hiram Reynolds 1845-1910 [18]
- $1 100 - €1 251 - **£768** - FF8 206
  Western Landscape Oil/board (45x35cm 18x14in) Mystic CT 2000

BLOOMFIELD Harry c.1870-? [30]
- $117 - €125 - **£80** - FF823
  Portrait of a Gentleman with a Bow Tie Gouache/paper (44.5x36cm 17x14in) London 2001

BLOOS Richard 1878-1956 [53]
- $41 145 - €38 347 - **£25 387** - FF251 542
  Blick über eine Pontonbrücke und die Seine auf den Gare d'Orsay Öl/Leinwand (130x162cm 51x63in) Köln 1999
- $6 581 - €6 749 - **£4 113** - FF44 271
  Burgruine im Herbst mit Figurenstaffage Oil/panel (60x45cm 23x17in) Saarbrücken 2000

BLOOT de Pieter 1601/02-1658 [36]
- $17 192 - €17 074 - **£10 752** - FF112 000
  Vue d'une rue de village avec un joueur de vielle devant l'auberge Huile/panneau (40x70cm 15x27in) Paris 1999
- $16 000 - €14 812 - **£9 659** - FF97 160
  Peasant Playing Cards in an Inn/ Peasant Drinking in an Inn Oil/panel (27.5x20.5cm 10x8in) New-York 2000

BLOOTELING Abraham Bloteling 1640-1690 [9]
- $337 - €383 - **£233** - FF2 515
  Löwenstudien, nach Peter Paul Rubens Radierung (13.8x17.8cm 5x7in) Berlin 2000

BLOSSFELDT Karl 1865-1932 [66]
- $6 636 - €7 350 - **£4 500** - FF48 212
  Ohne Titel (Pflanzenabguss) Bronze (29.7x10cm 11x3in) Berlin 2000
- $832 - €823 - **£518** - FF5 399
  Silene Conica (Kegelfrüchtiges Leimkraut) Gelatin silver print (30.3x24cm 11x9in) Berlin 1999

BLOSSOM Christopher 1956 [4]
- $13 500 - €12 404 - **£8 293** - FF81 364
  Henry B.Hyde Arriving in NYC Oil/canvas (60x101cm 24x40in) St. Petersburg FL 1999

BLOT Eugène 1830-1899 [4]
- $12 688 - €13 294 - **£8 392** - FF87 201
  Orientalische Tänzerin Metal (H92.5cm H36in) München 2000

BLOTT Géo XIX-XX [22]
- $580 - €640 - **£393** - FF4 200
  «Margarine Pellerin de Malaunay 60 dépôts dans Paris» Affiche couleur (90x185cm 35x72in) Nice 2000

BLOW Sandra 1925 [75]
- $2 516 - €2 147 - **£1 500** - FF14 084
  Blue Composition Oil/canvas (91.5x71cm 36x27in) London 1998
- $722 - €810 - **£500** - FF5 313
  Purple Abstract Oil/paper (26x33cm 10x12in) London 2000
- $517 - €603 - **£360** - FF3 958
  Abstract Studies Oil chalks (16x26.5cm 6x10in) London 2000

BLUCK John XVIII-XIX [10]
- $315 - €354 - **£220** - FF2 322
  University and Queen's Colleges, High Street/High Street looking West Aquatint in colors (24x29cm 9x11in) Leyburn, North Yorkshire 2001

BLUEMNER Oscar Florianus 1867-1938 [124]
- $1 400 - €1 562 - **£916** - FF10 245
  Untitled Crayon (10x15cm 4x6in) Chicago IL 2000

BLUHM H. Faber act.c.1875-1881 [1]
- $44 630 - €52 484 - **£32 000** - FF344 275
  Cross and Crescent Oil/canvas (71x91cm 27x35in) London 2001

BLUHM Norman 1920 [70]
- $5 599 - €5 593 - **£3 500** - FF36 688
  Black #2 Oil/canvas (129.5x162.5cm 50x63in) London 1999
- $950 - €1 037 - **£645** - FF6 805
  Untitled Oil/canvas (45.5x91.5cm 17x36in) New-York 1999
- $1 133 - €1 344 - **£800** - FF8 814
  «Green & Blue No.1» Watercolour/paper (75x56cm 29x22in) London 2000

BLUHM Oskar 1867-1912 [19]
- $1 272 - €1 431 - **£876** - FF9 390
  Das Geburtstagskind Ink (43x32cm 16x12in) Stuttgart 2000

BLUM Felix XIX-XX [3]
- $1 000 - €1 073 - **£669** - FF7 041
  Orientalist Scene Watercolour/paper (97x72cm 38x28in) Portland ME 2000

BLUM Günter 1949-1997 [9]
- $1 217 - €1 431 - **£872** - FF9 390
  «Patrizia» Gelatin silver print (39x48cm 15x18in) Berlin 2001

BLUM Hans 1858-1942 [3]
- $6 018 - €6 984 - **£4 155** - FF45 809
  A Fruit Seller Oil/board (37x54cm 14x21in) Co. Wicklow 2000

BLUM Ludwig 1891-1974 [98]
- $9 500 - €10 277 - **£6 508** - FF67 415
  Jerusalem, Har-Zion Oil/canvas (60x73cm 23x28in) Tel Aviv 2000
- $5 043 - €4 642 - **£3 027** - FF30 449
  Market Scene Oil/canvas (28x36cm 11x14in) Tel Aviv 1999
- $3 800 - €3 188 - **£2 229** - FF20 913
  Bird's Eye View of Jerusalem Watercolour/paper (44x58cm 17x23in) Philadelphia PA 1998

BLUM Maurice 1832-1909 **[33]**
- $4 988 - €5 107 - **£3 132** - FF33 500
  Un événement au château Huile/toile (55x46cm 21x18in) Lille 2000
- $544 - €549 - **£339** - FF3 600
  Place de village animé Huile/panneau (11x13cm 4x5in) Tours 2000

BLUM Robert Frederick 1857-1903 **[28]**
- $1 350 000 - €1 153 420 - **£810 405** - FF7 565 940
  Venetian Bead Stringers Oil/canvas (76x103.5cm 29x40in) New-York 1998
- $3 800 - €4 136 - **£2 611** - FF27 129
  Japanese Tea Party Oil/panel (20x12cm 8x5in) St. Louis MO 2001
- $5 500 - €6 354 - **£3 851** - FF41 679
  «Flora di Staphano» Pencil/paper (27.5x22.5cm 10x8in) New-York 2001

BLUMANN Sigismund 1872-1956 **[8]**
- $582 - €562 - **£366** - FF3 689
  Im Studio Photograph (24x18.9cm 9x7in) München 1999

BLUME Anna & Bernhard 1937/1937 **[9]**
- $1 055 - €1 176 - **£690** - FF7 714
  Mediumistische Szene Gelatin silver print (41.7x29.7cm 16x11in) Köln 2000

BLUME Bernhard Johannes 1937 **[72]**
- $314 - €337 - **£210** - FF2 213
  Junger Optimist mit libidinösen Punkten Oil chalks (29.7x21cm 11x8in) Hamburg 2000
- $545 - €501 - **£335** - FF3 286
  Memento Mori Photo (29.5x21cm 11x8in) Zürich 1999

BLUME Edmund 1844-1910 **[11]**
- $1 231 - €1 334 - **£820** - FF8 752
  Rosina/Ciccillo: Studies of Peasants Oil/panel (30.5x22.5cm 12x8in) Billingshurst, West-Sussex 2000

BLUME Peter 1906 **[8]**
- $13 500 - €12 338 - **£8 259** - FF80 929
  Weekend House Oil/canvas (20x30.5cm 7x12in) Boston MA 1999

BLUME-SIEBERT Ludwig 1853-1929 **[14]**
- $4 200 - €4 798 - **£2 956** - FF31 471
  Folling around at the Inn Oil/canvas (76x106cm 30x42in) Cambridge MA 2001

BLUMENFELD Erwin 1897-1969 **[68]**
- $8 000 - €8 319 - **£5 051** - FF54 566
  Die Augan (Ein Kuss mit Hindernissen) Collage (21x18.5cm 8x7in) New-York 2000
- $1 562 - €1 815 - **£1 098** - FF11 906
  Nude Silver print (30x24cm 11x9in) Amsterdam 2001

BLUMENSCHEIN Ernest L. 1874-1960 **[15]**
- $8 500 - €7 727 - **£5 119** - FF50 685
  The Long Trail Gouache/paper (10x12cm 4x5in) Hayden ID 1998

BLUMENSCHIEN Helen 1909-1989 **[3]**
- $2 000 - €2 147 - **£1 338** - FF14 082
  New Oceana Sunset Watercolour/paper (36x52cm 14x20in) San-Francisco CA 2000
- $400 - €409 - **£250** - FF2 682
  Trinity Church Lithograph (40x23cm 16x9in) Cleveland OH 2001

BLUMENTHAL Hermann 1905-1942 **[26]**
- $9 322 - €10 226 - **£6 332** - FF67 078
  Sitzender aufschauend (Sterngucker) Bronze (H27.5cm H10in) Düsseldorf 2000

BLUMER Lucien Charles 1871-1947 **[10]**
- $823 - €915 - **£573** - FF6 000
  «Chemins de Fer d'Alsace & de Lorraine, La vallée de Munster» Affiche (99.5x62cm 39x24in) Paris 2001

BLUNCK Ditlev Konrad 1798-1854 **[4]**
- $3 673 - €4 269 - **£2 581** - FF28 000
  Psyché et Adonis Huile/toile (72x58cm 28x22in) Paris 2001

BLUNT John Silvester 1798-1835/37 **[7]**
- $11 000 - €9 035 - **£6 388** - FF59 266
  View of a Harbor Oil/canvas (68x88cm 27x35in) New-York 1998

BLYHOOFT Zacharias act.1658-1682 **[9]**
- $4 500 - €4 806 - **£3 066** - FF31 526
  Villagers Rescuing Travellers Drowning in a Frozen River Black chalk (10x19.5cm 3x7in) New-York 2001

BLYTH Robert Henderson 1919-1970 **[13]**
- $1 280 - €1 266 - **£800** - FF8 307
  Angus Farm Oil/canvas/board (43.5x53.5cm 17x21in) Glasgow 1999

BLYTHE David Gilmore 1815-1865 **[8]**
- $18 000 - €17 871 - **£11 250** - FF117 226
  Tavern Scene Oil/canvas (63.5x76cm 25x29in) New-York 1999

BO Giacinto 1850-1912 **[48]**
- $3 360 - €2 903 - **£1 680** - FF19 040
  Sul canale Olio/cartone (89x33.5cm 35x13in) Torino 1999
- $1 200 - €1 555 - **£900** - FF10 200
  Mare in burrasca Olio/cartone (26.5x42.5cm 10x16in) Vercelli 2001

BOADEN John act.1812-1839 **[1]**
- $9 952 - €8 656 - **£6 000** - FF56 777
  Portrait of Fanny Kemble (1809-1893) Oil/canvas (74x62.5cm 29x24in) London 1998

BOBAK Bruno J. 1923 **[35]**
- $368 - €430 - **£260** - FF2 820
  Alice Maynell's Roses Oil/canvas (35x25cm 13x9in) London 2000

BOBAK Molly Joan Lamb 1922 **[44]**
- $1 878 - €1 817 - **£1 158** - FF11 920
  Anemones Oil/board (40.5x61cm 15x24in) Toronto 1999
- $808 - €943 - **£577** - FF6 185
  Young Canada Games Huile/panneau (15x30cm 5x11in) Montréal 2000
- $314 - €348 - **£213** - FF2 285
  Flower Garden Watercolour/paper (47x62cm 18x24in) Toronto 2000
- $818 - €861 - **£580** - FF6 304
  Beach Lithograph (73.5x99cm 28x38in) Toronto 2000

BOBELDIJK Felicien 1876-1964 **[26]**
- $576 - €499 - **£350** - FF3 274
  Moored boats in a harbour Oil/canvas (13.5x21cm 5x8in) Amsterdam 1999
- $263 - €295 - **£184** - FF1 934
  Jongen met aapje Watercolour/paper (46.5x26cm 18x10in) Dordrecht 2001

BOBERG Ferdinand 1860-1946 **[28]**
- $219 - €254 - **£155** - FF1 668
  «Grà läget» Indian ink (25x19cm 9x7in) Stockholm 2001

BOBERG Jörgen 1940 **[43]**
🖎 **$809** - €740 - **£507** - FF4 854
Prinsessen bliver vasket Oil/canvas (93x71cm
36x27in) Köbenhavn 1999

BOBOT Pierre 1902 **[4]**
🖎 **$15 000** - €17 839 - **£10 690** - FF117 015
**New York, New York, from «The Roseland
Ballroom»** Technique mixte (183x87cm 72x34in)
New-York 2000

BOBYCHEV Mikhail 1910 **[2]**
🖎 **$2 393** - €2 640 - **£1 621** - FF17 316
Eldkamrater Oil/canvas (39x27cm 15x10in)
Stockholm 2000

BOCANEGRA Pedro Anastasio 1638-1689 **[5]**
🖎 **$10 240** - €9 610 - **£6 400** - FF63 040
**La Virgen con el Niño, Isabel y San
Juanito** Oleo/lienzo (104x146cm 40x57in) Madrid
1999
✑ **$1 674** - €1 426 - **£1 000** - FF9 352
The Repentence of Saint Peter Ink (12x15cm
4x5in) London 1998

BOCCACCI Marcello 1914-1996 **[60]**
🖎 **$1 080** - €1 013 - **£667** - FF6 646
Girl with a Bowl of Citrons Oil/panel (79x44cm
31x17in) Cleveland OH 1999
🖎 **$600** - €622 - **£404** - FF4 080
Festa di cacciatori Olio/cartone (25x35cm 9x13in)
Prato 2000
✑ **$250** - €259 - **£150** - FF1 700
Fiori, pesci e figure China (20x8.5cm 7x3in) Firenze
2001

BOCCACCINO Boccaccio c.1467-1524/25 **[1]**
✑ **$4 584** - €4 251 - **£2 800** - FF27 888
Studies After Raphael Red chalk/paper (27x41cm
10x16in) London 1998

BOCCACCINO Camillo 1501-1546 **[5]**
✑ **$16 000** - €17 139 - **£10 926** - FF112 425
Design for a Spandrel: a Bishop and Angels Ink
(15x8.5cm 5x3in) New-York 2001

BOCCARDO Federico 1869-1912 **[1]**
✑ **$2 900** - €3 006 - **£1 740** - FF19 720
Testina Matita/carta (19x17.5cm 7x6in) Torino 2001

BOCCASILE Gino 1901-1952 **[53]**
🖎 **$5 526** - €5 488 - **£3 456** - FF36 000
Les Trois Grâces Huile/toile (116.5x81cm 45x31in)
Paris 1999
🞣 **$600** - €526 - **£364** - FF3 452
Gilera 125 Poster (46x33cm 18x13in) New-York 1999

BOCCHECIAMPE Vikentios 1856-1933 **[9]**
🖎 **$6 632** - €6 149 - **£4 000** - FF40 338
The Doge's Palace, Venice Oil/canvas (32x53cm
12x20in) London 1999
✑ **$1 922** - €2 134 - **£1 336** - FF13 997
Portrait of a girl Watercolour/paper (51x38cm
20x15in) Kingston, Ontario 2001

BOCCHETTI Gaetano 1888-1992 **[11]**
🖎 **$1 200** - €1 555 - **£900** - FF10 200
Paesaggio con pescatore Olio/tela (57x66cm
22x25in) Napoli 2000

BOCCHI Faustino 1659-1742 **[15]**
🖎 **$54 883** - €63 976 - **£38 000** - FF419 653
The Concert Oil/canvas (124.5x202cm 49x79in)
London 2000
🖎 **$44 829** - €48 120 - **£30 000** - FF315 648
Pygmies Fighting Over a Skull Oil/canvas
(61x73cm 24x28in) London 2000

🖎 **$5 000** - €5 183 - **£3 000** - FF34 000
Personaggi fantastici Olio/tavola (24x35cm 9x13in)
Milano 2000

BOCCHINO V. XIX-XX **[8]**
🞣 **$671** - €762 - **£466** - FF5 000
«Cognac J.Dupont» Affiche (130x90cm 51x35in)
Paris 2001

BOCCIARDO Clemente 1600-1658 **[1]**
🖎 **$30 000** - €26 315 - **£18 216** - FF172 614
**The Assumption of the Virgin with Saint
Jacobus, a Franciscan** Oil/canvas (246x174cm
96x68in) New-York 1999

BOCCIARDO Domenico 1686-1746 **[1]**
✑ **$2 160** - €1 866 - **£1 080** - FF12 240
La sepoltura di Tobia Acquarello (29x22cm 11x8in)
Milano 1999

BOCCIONI Umberto 1882-1916 **[117]**
🖎 **$248 000** - €321 363 - **£186 000** - FF2 108 000
Ritratto del dottor Tian Olio/tela (68.5x68.5cm
26x26in) Milano 2000
✑ **$22 500** - €25 202 - **£15 633** - FF165 312
Le Forze di Una Strada Ink (12.5x10cm 4x3in)
New-York 2001
🞣 **$4 000** - €4 147 - **£2 400** - FF27 200
I portatori Puntasecca (15x30cm 5x11in) Prato 1999

BOCH Anna 1848-1933 **[47]**
🖎 **$7 552** - €7 065 - **£4 645** - FF46 341
Le verger Huile/toile (39x47cm 15x18in) Bruxelles
1999
🖎 **$1 478** - €1 636 - **£1 029** - FF10 731
Paysage au bord de la mer Huile/carton (25x35cm
9x13in) Liège 2001

BOCHMANN Max XIX-XX **[2]**
🖎 **$1 544** - €1 841 - **£1 100** - FF12 074
Kinder mit Pudel Porcelain (H14.8cm H5in) Ahlden
2000

BOCHMANN von Gregor 1850-1930 **[81]**
🖎 **$7 308** - €8 692 - **£5 208** - FF57 016
**Estnische Bauern mit Pferdefuhrwerken vor
dem Gehöft des Schmiedes** Öl/Leinwand
(92x158cm 36x62in) Köln 2000
🖎 **$2 251** - €2 556 - **£1 564** - FF16 769
Beim Entladen des Fischfangs Öl/Leinwand
(76x100cm 29x39in) Köln 2001
🖎 **$2 200** - €2 198 - **£1 376** - FF14 421
Dünenlandschaft mit Pferdefuhrwerk Oil/panel
(13.5x18cm 5x7in) Köln 1999
✑ **$317** - €358 - **£219** - FF2 347
Mit Seetang beladener Karren am Strand
Aquarell/Papier (12.5x16cm 4x6in) Berlin 2000

BOCHNER Mel 1940 **[49]**
✑ **$4 000** - €4 472 - **£2 696** - FF29 337
Measurement Series: Degrees Ink (28x23cm
11x9in) New-York 2000
🞣 **$523** - €562 - **£350** - FF3 689
Ohne Titel (Würfel) Etching, aquatint in colors
(83x120cm 32x47in) Hamburg 2000

BOCHOUTT van Godfried act.1659-1666 **[1]**
🖎 **$3 848** - €4 311 - **£2 674** - FF28 277
**Hunting Still Life with a Wood-Pecker, a
Kingfisher** Oil/canvas (58.5x47cm 23x18in)
Amsterdam 2001

BOCION François Louis David 1828-1890 **[57]**
🖎 **$24 415** - €23 764 - **£15 002** - FF155 879
Château de Chillon Öl/Leinwand (48x76cm
18x29in) Zürich 1999

B

$6 132 - €7 213 - £4 444 - FF47 317
Le port de Meillerie Huile/carton (30x41cm 11x16in)
Sion 2001

$3 549 - €3 826 - £2 380 - FF25 095
**Chalet sur les hauteurs de Gryon près de
Villars-sur-Ollon** Aquarel/Papier (18.5x26cm 7x10in)
Zürich 2001

BOCK Adolf 1890-1968 [71]

$28 815 - €25 220 - £17 460 - FF165 435
I dimma Oil/canvas (160x120cm 62x47in) Helsinki
1998

$2 943 - €3 297 - £2 046 - FF21 624
Marin med fullriggare och människor i roddbåt
Oil/canvas (50x70cm 19x27in) Landskrona 2001

$2 868 - €2 691 - £1 772 - FF17 651
Till havs Oil/canvas (33x46cm 12x18in) Helsinki 1999

$1 214 - €1 076 - £745 - FF7 060
Villefranche Gouache/paper (33x56cm 12x22in)
Helsinki 1999

BOCK de Théophile Émile 1851-1904 [167]

$3 240 - €3 403 - £2 050 - FF22 324
A Sunlit Spot in the Woods Oil/canvas/board
(50x34.5cm 19x13in) Amsterdam 2000

$1 801 - €1 815 - £1 122 - FF11 906
Sandy Trail through a Heath Landscape Oil/canvas (25x36.5cm 9x14in) Amsterdam 2000

$549 - €590 - £367 - FF3 869
Bosrand met zandverstuiving Watercolour,
gouache/paper (16x10cm 6x3in) Dordrecht 2000

BOCK John 1965 [3]

$2 929 - €2 851 - £1 800 - FF18 704
Lord Byron-Stiefel Construction (75x20x42cm
29x7x16in) London 1999

BOCK Ludwig 1886-1971 [22]

$1 618 - €1 841 - £1 122 - FF12 074
Stilleben mit Äpfeln Öl/Karton (36x41.5cm 14x16in)
Lindau 2000

BÖCKER Hermann 1890-1978 [25]

$342 - €383 - £232 - FF2 515
Moorlandschaft/Baumlandschaft Aquarell/Papier
(10.5x15cm 4x5in) München 2000

BÖCKLI Carl 1889-1970 [22]

$189 - €204 - £127 - FF1 336
Karikatur, amtlicher Schweinejauche-Riecher
Encre Chine (16x11cm 6x4in) St. Gallen 2000

$606 - €579 - £380 - FF3 801
«Waibel & Maurer» Poster (127x90cm 50x35in)
London 1999

BÖCKLIN Arnold 1827-1901 [39]

$23 589 - €28 121 - £16 819 - FF184 464
Am Waldrand Öl/Leinwand (67.5x94.5cm 26x37in)
Berlin 2000

$5 046 - €5 624 - £3 527 - FF36 892
Waldlandschaft mit herbstlichen Bäumen
Öl/Leinwand (26.3x21.8cm 10x8in) München 2001

BÖCKSTIEGEL Peter August 1889-1951 [143]

$32 160 - €35 280 - £21 845 - FF231 419
Glockenblumen Öl/Leinwand (100x118cm 39x46in)
Berlin 2000

$1 905 - €2 045 - £1 275 - FF13 415
Pferde auf der Weide Indian ink (33x49cm 12x19in)
Königstein 2000

$964 - €1 125 - £678 - FF7 378
Der Mäher Lithographie (66x50cm 25x19in)
Königstein 2001

BOCQUET Paul 1868-1947 [46]

$4 292 - €3 964 - £2 672 - FF26 000
**Paysage d'automne, le Mont Joly à Villers-
Allerand** Huile/toile (46x55cm 18x21in) Reims 1999

$4 005 - €3 811 - £2 490 - FF25 000
Villers Allerand, Le Mont Joli Huile/toile (31x40cm
12x15in) Reims 1999

BODAREWSKY Nikolai Kornilievich 1850-1921 [3]

$14 229 - €16 532 - £10 000 - FF108 442
Fin de siècle Beauty Oil/canvas (98x135cm 38x53in)
London 2001

BODDINGTON Edwin H., Jnr. 1836-1905 [101]

$1 940 - €1 825 - £1 200 - FF11 974
Anglers fishing in a River Landscape Oil/canvas
(30.5x56cm 12x22in) London 1999

$896 - €962 - £600 - FF6 313
On the Thames Oil/canvas (20x40.5cm 7x15in)
London 2000

BODDINGTON Henry John 1811-1865 [70]

$13 000 - €14 494 - £9 074 - FF95 076
Anglers in River Landscape Oil/canvas (88x137cm
35x54in) Detroit MI 2001

$9 264 - €9 945 - £6 200 - FF65 233
The Way to the Mill, N.Wales Oil/canvas
(61x91.5cm 24x36in) London 2000

$3 070 - €2 579 - £1 800 - FF16 917
Figures by a Highland Stream Oil/canvas
(30x40cm 11x15in) Billingshurst, West-Sussex 1998

BODDY William James 1832-1911 [32]

$373 - €436 - £260 - FF2 859
At York Watercolour (10.5x22.5cm 4x8in) West-
Yorkshire 2000

BODE Vaughn XX [3]

$1 400 - €1 503 - £936 - FF9 857
Drawing strip «Rain Drop» Ink (48x35.5cm
18x13in) New-York 2000

BODE Wilhelm 1830-1893 [9]

$3 130 - €3 634 - £2 200 - FF23 835
**Mone Cristallo mit dem Dürrensee im
Ampezzotal** Öl/Leinwand (81x125cm 31x49in) Wien
2001

BODEMANN Willem 1806-1880 [23]

$5 755 - €5 704 - £3 600 - FF37 418
**Travellers on a Track in an Extensive
Landscape** Oil/panel (38x52cm 14x20in) London
1999

$21 440 - €19 831 - £13 360 - FF130 080
Winter Oil/panel (27.5x37cm 10x14in) Lokeren 1999

BODEN Samuel Standige 1826-1882 [4]

$675 - €680 - £420 - FF4 462
Cottage Scene with Figures Watercolour
(24.5x35cm 9x13in) Billingshurst, West-Sussex 2000

BODENEHR Gabriel 1664/69-1758/66 [31]

$65 - €61 - £40 - FF402
Gagliari in Sardinien Kupferstich (18x31cm 7x12in)
Staufen 1999

BODIFÉE Paul 1866-1939 [66]

$919 - €862 - £568 - FF5 655
Bosschages Oil/canvas (37x49.5cm 14x19in)
Rotterdam 1999

$378 - €408 - £258 - FF2 678
A Birch-Lane Oil/board (27.5x35.5cm 10x13in)
Amsterdam 2001

BODINE A. Aubrey 1906-1970 **[82]**
📷 $2 000 - €1 865 - **£1 207** - FF12 233
Cubist Design, Baltimore Steps Photograph
(50x39.5cm 19x15in) New-York 1999

BODINI Floriano 1933 **[26]**
🖎 $4 400 - €5 702 - **£3 300** - FF37 400
Spogliarello Bronzo (31x44.5cm 12x17in) Milano
2000

BODINIER Guillaume 1795-1872 **[12]**
☞ $8 327 - €7 729 - **£5 000** - FF50 696
A melancholy Ballad Oil/canvas (64.5x80.5cm
25x31in) London 1999

BODINIER Marie-Claire 1911-? **[2]**
✐ $1 670 - €1 610 - **£1 029** - FF10 563
Junge Frau in Walliser Tracht Pastell/Papier
(46x40.5cm 18x15in) Bern 1999

BODMER Karl 1809-1893 **[157]**
☞ $2 522 - €3 049 - **£1 762** - FF20 000
Le repos des sangliers Huile/toile (81x100cm
31x39in) Granville 2000
✐ $1 286 - €1 534 - **£917** - FF10 061
**Phantastische Rheinlandschaft mit der
Wernerskapelle in Bacharach** Aquarell/Papier
(60x74cm 23x29in) Köln 2000
▥ $500 - €554 - **£339** - FF3 632
Fac simile of an Indian Painting, tableau 22
Engraving (36.5x49cm 14x19in) New-York 2000

BODMER Walter 1903-1973 **[35]**
☞ $4 508 - €5 238 - **£3 168** - FF34 362
Komposition Öl/Leinwand (48x72cm 18x28in)
Luzern 2001
✐ $749 - €755 - **£466** - FF4 950
Katze Fusain (28x39cm 11x15in) Zürich 2000

BODOM Erik 1829-1879 **[18]**
☞ $3 822 - €4 234 - **£2 593** - FF27 772
Havneparti Oil/canvas (37x52cm 14x20in) Oslo 2000

BODOY Ernest Alexandre XIX **[14]**
☞ $4 233 - €5 002 - **£3 000** - FF32 809
**Edward VII Prince of Wales/The Princess of
Wales** Oil/board (38x25cm 14x9in) London 2000

BØE Frants Diderik 1820-1891 **[24]**
☞ $8 959 - €10 658 - **£6 196** - FF69 912
Conchylier, Smykker og Blomster Oil/canvas
(46x56cm 18x22in) Oslo 2000
☞ $3 382 - €3 908 - **£2 368** - FF25 633
Midnattsol ved Hestmanøy i Nordland Oil/canvas
(25x37cm 9x14in) Oslo 2001

BOECK de Félix 1898-1995 **[257]**
☞ $4 107 - €3 842 - **£2 495** - FF25 203
Gefusilleerde Oil/panel (73.5x59.5cm 28x23in)
Lokeren 1999
☞ $928 - €1 041 - **£646** - FF6 829
Portrait de Hans Meyer Huile/panneau (40.5x30cm
15x11in) Bruxelles 2001

BOECKHORST Johan, Lange Jan 1605-1668 **[20]**
☞ $11 750 - €12 181 - **£7 050** - FF79 900
Venere e Adone Olio/tela (90x135cm 35x53in) Roma
2001
☞ $19 573 - €18 307 - **£12 000** - FF120 084
The Punishment of Midas Oil/canvas (58.5x55.5cm
23x21in) London 1998
☞ $3 539 - €3 403 - **£2 180** - FF22 324
The Delivery of the Keys to St Peter Ink
(25.5x19cm 10x7in) Amsterdam 1999

BOECKL Herbert 1894-1966 **[112]**
☜ $47 390 - €50 871 - **£32 340** - FF333 690
«Sommerlicher Hochwald» Öl/Leinwand
(52.2x67.2cm 20x26in) Wien 2001
☜ $2 106 - €2 231 - **£1 341** - FF14 634
Vase garni de fleurs Huile/toile (42x33cm 16x12in)
Bruxelles 2000
✐ $10 010 - €9 447 - **£6 214** - FF61 971
Die Anatomie Indian ink (48.5x62cm 19x24in) Wien
1999
▥ $1 278 - €1 453 - **£898** - FF9 534
Dominikarner Etching, aquatint (49x34cm 19x13in)
Wien 2001

BOEHLE Fritz 1873-1916 **[32]**
▥ $175 - €184 - **£110** - FF1 207
Tierpredigt Radierung (30.2x39.8cm 11x15in)
Heidelberg 1999

BOEHM Joseph Edgar 1834-1890 **[27]**
🖎 $2 000 - €1 839 - **£1 389** - FF14 896
Suffolk Punch and Blacksmith Bronze (H53cm
H21in) St. Petersburg FL 2001

BOEHM von Thomas 1916-2000 **[34]**
☞ $1 546 - €1 514 - **£951** - FF9 928
Marbellasta Oil/panel (54x74cm 21x29in) Helsinki
1999
☞ $715 - €841 - **£496** - FF5 516
Stilleben Oil/panel (18x27cm 7x10in) Helsinki 2000

BOEHS Berthold 1877-? **[14]**
🖎 $471 - €509 - **£325** - FF3 336
Schlangentänzerin Porcelain (H20cm H7in) Wien
2001

BOEL Cornelis 1576-c.1621 **[1]**
▥ $729 - €869 - **£519** - FF5 701
**Madonna mit Kind und einem Engel mit dem
Kreuz, nach Cornelis Ketel** Kupferstich (18.4x14cm
7x5in) Berlin 2000

BOEL Coryn / Quirinus 1622-1688 **[2]**
▥ $372 - €434 - **£262** - FF2 850
Der Geigenspieler, nach D.Teniers Kupferstich
(23.5x33.5cm 9x13in) Berlin 2001

BOEL John Henry XIX-XX **[62]**
☞ $551 - €656 - **£380** - FF4 303
Kilehurn Castle Oil/canvas (50x75cm 19x29in)
Burton-on-Trent, Staffs 2000

BOEL Pieter 1622-1674 **[28]**
☞ $26 000 - €30 623 - **£17 981** - FF200 873
**Still Life of Gamebirds and a Rabbit with an
Embossed Platter** Oil/canvas (105.5x148cm
41x58in) New-York 2000
☞ $8 393 - €8 385 - **£5 247** - FF55 000
**Nature morte à la bécassine, perdreau gris,
caille et geai** Huile/toile (41.5x59.5cm 16x23in) Paris
1999
☞ $5 174 - €4 345 - **£3 041** - FF28 504
**Stilleben mit jagdbaren Vögeln und
Fayenceschalen** Öl/Leinwand (35.5x45cm 13x17in)
Köln 1998

BOELEN J. XIX **[2]**
✐ $9 155 - €10 753 - **£6 500** - FF70 536
Landing at Itaparica, Brazil Watercolour/paper
(42.5x53cm 16x20in) London 2000

BOEMM Ritta 1868-1948 **[33]**
☞ $612 - €622 - **£380** - FF4 078
**Interior Scene with a Vase of Flowers on a
Partly Draped Table** Oil/canvas (60.5x50cm 23x19in)
London 2000

BOER de Hessel 1921 **[9]**
🖼 **$1 548** - €1 543 - **£940** - FF10 120
Huis te Zorgvliet in de winter, Den Haag Oil/can-
vas (55x60cm 21x23in) Amsterdam 2000

BOER von Zoltan 1924 **[7]**
🖼 **$1 399** - €1 338 - **£877** - FF8 775
Porträtt Oil/panel (37x32cm 14x12in) Stockholm 1999

BOEREWAARD Isidoor / Door 1893-1972 **[43]**
🖼 **$387** - €446 - **£266** - FF2 926
Marine Oil/canvas (50x69cm 19x27in) Lokeren 2000

BOERO Nilda XIX-XX **[1]**
🗿 **$48 000** - €48 369 - **£29 923** - FF317 280
Figure of a Bathing Nude Marble (H137cm H53in)
New-York 2000

BOERS Frans Henri 1904-? **[21]**
🖼 **$2 835** - €2 454 - **£1 720** - FF16 098
«**Paris**» Oil/canvas (46x65.5cm 18x25in) Amsterdam
1998
🖼 **$3 199** - €3 176 - **£1 999** - FF20 836
Landscape Oil/canvas (26x40cm 10x15in) Amsterdam
1999

BOERS Willy 1905-1978 **[45]**
🖼 **$3 656** - €3 630 - **£2 284** - FF23 812
Untitled Oil/canvas (54x45cm 21x17in) Amsterdam
1999
🖼 **$1 426** - €1 361 - **£891** - FF8 929
Abstract Composition Oil/paper (31x48.5cm
12x19in) Amsterdam 1999
✏ **$1 057** - €1 143 - **£707** - FF7 441
Abstract composition Gouache/paper (28.5x37.5cm
11x14in) Amsterdam 2000

BOESE Henry 1824-c.1863 **[12]**
🖼 **$11 500** - €13 676 - **£8 196** - FF89 711
Scene near the Cherry Valley Mountains Oil/can-
vas (71x127cm 27x50in) New-York 2000

BOESE Wolfgang 1912 **[14]**
📷 **$500** - €468 - **£302** - FF3 067
Turbine Gelatin silver print (6x6cm 2x2in) New-York
1999

BOESEN August Vilhelm 1812-1875 **[17]**
🖼 **$3 923** - €4 560 - **£2 757** - FF29 913
Parti fra Capri, Italien Oil/paper/canvas (35x46cm
13x18in) København 2001
🖼 **$242** - €254 - **£153** - FF1 666
Kor vid vattendrag Oil/panel (25.5x38cm 10x14in)
Malmö 2000

BOESEN Johannes 1847-1916 **[82]**
🖼 **$825** - €738 - **£492** - FF4 841
Bistader i en bondegårdshave Oil/canvas
(41x64cm 16x25in) København 1998

BOESS Berthold 1877-? **[15]**
🗿 **$487** - €460 - **£300** - FF3 018
Schlangentänzerin Porcelain (H20cm H7in) Lindau
1999

BOET Johan Hans XVII **[3]**
🖼 **$35 000** - €30 701 - **£21 252** - FF201 383
Venus and Cupid in the Forge of Vulcan Oil/cop-
per (36x46.5cm 14x18in) New-York 1999

BOETTCHER Christian Eduard 1818-1889 **[16]**
🖼 **$78 000** - €74 116 - **£47 455** - FF486 166
**Setting out for the Grape Harvest, Oberwesel-
on-Rhine** Oil/canvas (92.5x156cm 36x61in) New-York
1999
🖼 **$8 187** - €9 508 - **£5 753** - FF62 367
Vid vaggan Oil/panel (49x39cm 19x15in) Stockholm
2001

$1 217 - €1 431 - **£872** - FF9 390
**Zwei kleine Mädchen haben unter einem
Strauch** Oil/panel (20x16.5cm 7x6in) Stuttgart 2001

BOETTI Alighiero 1940-1994 **[437]**
🖼 **$48 814** - €57 405 - **£35 000** - FF376 551
Ogni lettera un suono Acrylic (102x287.5cm
40x113in) London 2001
🖼 **$3 200** - €4 147 - **£2 400** - FF27 200
I vedenti Tecnica mista (70.5x50.5cm 27x19in) Vercelli
2001
🖼 **$200** - €2 073 - **£1 200** - FF13 600
I vedenti Tecnica mista (35x25cm 13x9in) Vercelli
2000
🖼 **$7 750** - €8 034 - **£4 650** - FF52 700
Metereinmoto Biro (100x70cm 39x27in) Milano 1999
📜 **$7 500** - €7 715 - **£4 500** - FF51 000
Senza titolo Tapisserie (118x26cm 46x10in) Prato
1999

BOETTO Giulio 1894-1967 **[26]**
🖼 **$1 040** - €1 348 - **£780** - FF8 840
Autunno nelal Valle di Fex Oil/tela (48x58cm
18x22in) Milano 2001
🖼 **$2 160** - €1 866 - **£1 080** - FF12 240
Paesaggio montano Olio/tavola (24.5x33cm 9x12in)
Torino 1999

BOEVER de Jan Frans 1872-1949 **[69]**
🖼 **$885** - €838 - **£550** - FF5 500
Les Questeurs Huile/carton (57x40cm 22x15in) Paris
1999
🖼 **$839** - €942 - **£585** - FF6 138
Le paon Huile/panneau (23x28cm 9x11in) Bruxelles
2001
✏ **$1 536** - €1 487 - **£966** - FF9 756
Arlequin déplorant sa femme morte Pastel
(60x70cm 23x27in) Antwerpen 1999

BOEYERMANS Theodore 1620-1678 **[11]**
🖼 **$39 520** - €47 098 - **£28 310** - FF308 940
Allégorie du Temps Huile/toile (193x144cm
75x56in) Antwerpen 2000
🖼 **$53 477** - €51 130 - **£32 560** - FF335 390
**Allegorie der Stadt Antwerpen als Patronin der
Künste** Öl/Leinwand (84x118cm 33x46in) Bielefeld
1999

BOFA Gus (Gustave Blanchot) 1883-1968 **[40]**
📜 **$505** - €579 - **£345** - FF3 800
«**Cinéma du nouveau théâtre du château d'eau,
ouverture samedi 11 juin**» Affiche (59x39cm
23x15in) Paris 2000

BOFFA TARLATTA Luigi 1889-1965 **[11]**
🖼 **$450** - €466 - **£270** - FF3 060
Verso il santuario Olio/tela (23x27cm 9x10in)
Vercelli 2001

BOFILL Antoine XIX-XX **[59]**
🗿 **$925** - €915 - **£577** - FF6 000
Chevalier en armure Chryséléphantine (H34cm
H13in) Lyon 1999

BOGAERT Emile XX **[1]**
📜 **$804** - €732 - **£493** - FF4 800
«**L'alcool empoisonne lentement**» Affiche
(100x120cm 39x47in) Saint-Cloud 1999

BOGAERT Gaston 1918 **[155]**
🖼 **$1 055** - €1 239 - **£760** - FF8 130
En sourdine Huile/panneau (60x75cm 23x29in)
Bruxelles 2001
🖼 **$667** - €719 - **£461** - FF4 715
Arcades Huile/panneau (24x19cm 9x7in) Bruxelles
2001

ꟷ $113 - €124 - **£73** - FF813
Nocturne Estampe couleurs (46.5x67.5cm 18x26in)
Liège 2000

BOGAERT Hendrick Hendriksz. 1626/27-c.1672 [10]

ꕯ $4 482 - €4 812 - **£3 000** - FF31 564
The Interior of a Barn, with a Slaughtered Jug
Oil/panel (48.5x63.5cm 19x25in) London 2000

BOGAERTS Jan 1878-1962 [23]

ꕯ $8 695 - €8 168 - **£241** - FF53 578
Anemones and Oriental Lacquer Box on a Marble Ledge Oil/canvas (33x57cm 12x22in)
Amsterdam 1999

BOGART Bram 1921 [513]

ꕯ $15 979 - €13 291 - **£9 382** - FF87 184
«Roddwitrood» Mixed media (210x210cm 82x82in)
Amsterdam 1998

ꕯ $6 618 - €5 677 - **£4 000** - FF37 238
Quatorze jaune Mixed media/board (39.5x44.5cm 15x17in) London 1998

ꕯ $896 - €992 - **£624** - FF6 504
Bleu-noir Technique mixte (23x17cm 9x6in) Bruxelles 2001

ꟷ $2 208 - €2 439 - **£1 531** - FF16 000
«Yellow» Plâtre (28x28cm 11x11in) Paris 2001

ꕯ $919 - €908 - **£559** - FF5 953
Untitled Ink (32.5x27.5cm 12x10in) Amsterdam 2000

ꟷ $466 - €545 - **£332** - FF3 577
Rectangle noir et blanc Estampe (83x110cm 32x43in) Bruxelles 2001

BOGATOV Nikolai Alekseevich 1854-1935 [3]

ꕯ $2 921 - €2 808 - **£1 800** - FF18 419
Provincial Courtyard with Hens Oil/canvas/board (16.5x23cm 6x9in) London 1999

BOGDANI Jacob 1660-1724 [41]

ꕯ $35 000 - €32 929 - **£21 840** - FF215 999
Salmon-crested Cockatoo, Lovebird, a Magpie, wooded landscape Oil/canvas (63.5x103cm 25x40in) New-York 1999

BOGDANOV-BELSKY Nikolai Petrovich 1868-1945 [56]

ꕯ $10 430 - €10 737 - **£6 575** - FF70 431
Vier Knaben, in ein Lagerfeuer blickend Öl/Leinwand (71x86cm 27x33in) Berlin 2000

ꕯ $2 303 - €2 301 - **£1 440** - FF15 092
Die Holzfuhre Öl/Leinwand (20x33cm 7x12in) München 1999

BOGDANOVE Abraham Jacobi 1888-1946 [14]

ꕯ $2 200 - €2 369 - **£1 514** - FF15 542
Rocky Coastline/Female Nude Study Oil/board (60x45cm 24x18in) New-York 2001

ꕯ $1 900 - €1 767 - **£1 172** - FF11 589
The Struggle Oil/canvas/board (33x40cm 13x16in) Portland ME 1999

BOGDANOVICH Borislav 1899-1970 [11]

ꕸ $945 - €1 022 - **£646** - FF6 707
Zwei männliche Akte Pastell/Papier (42x30cm 16x11in) Stuttgart 2001

BØGELUND-JENSEN Thor 1890-1959 [20]

ꟷ $950 - €950 - **£580** - FF6 231
«Politiken» Poster (106x78cm 42x31in) New-York 2000

BOGERT George Henry 1864-1944 [52]

ꕯ $1 000 - €1 144 - **£695** - FF7 503
Breezy Morning, Venice, Italy Oil/board (60x91cm 23x36in) Philadelphia PA 2000

BØGGILD Mogens 1901-1987 [20]

ꕸ $2 197 - €2 020 - **£1 350** - FF13 248
Leda og svanen Bronze (31x50cm 12x19in) København 1999

BOGGIO Emilio, Émile 1857-1920 [101]

ꕯ $39 051 - €45 924 - **£28 000** - FF301 240
«Le Moulin de Périgny» Oil/canvas (116x180cm 45x70in) London 2001

ꕯ $7 645 - €8 385 - **£5 192** - FF55 000
Chevaux s'abreuvant Huile/panneau (36x46cm 14x18in) Pontoise 2000

ꕯ $4 140 - €3 857 - **£2 530** - FF25 300
Marina Huile/masonite (22x27cm 8x10in) Caracas 1998

ꕸ $330 - €339 - **£220** - FF2 222
Desnudo Carboncillo (17x22cm 6x8in) Caracas 2000

BOGGIONE Enrico 1889-1985 [41]

ꕯ $260 - €337 - **£195** - FF2 210
«Lo stagno Crystal Palace Londra» Olio/cartone (24x29cm 9x11in) Vercelli 2001

BØGH Carl Henrik 1827-1893 [95]

ꕯ $1 930 - €1 838 - **£1 207** - FF12 054
Vilande getter vid rosenbuske Oil/canvas (37x58cm 14x22in) Stockholm 1999

ꕯ $640 - €716 - **£434** - FF4 695
Angepflocktes Schaf auf einem Weg in Wiesenlandschaft Öl/Leinwand (28.5x27.5cm 11x10in) Saarbrücken 2000

BOGLIANI Enrico XIX-XX [7]

ꕯ $1 320 - €1 420 - **£900** - FF9 315
Retrieved Oil/canvas (82x112cm 32x44in) Billingshurst, West-Sussex 2001

BOGLIARDI Oreste 1900-1968 [1]

ꕸ $1 400 - €1 451 - **£840** - FF9 520
Composizione Tecnica mista/carta (47x32cm 18x12in) Prato 1999

BOGLIONE Marcello 1891-1957 [18]

ꕯ $1 000 - €1 037 - **£600** - FF6 800
Luci e ombre nel paesaggio Olio/tavola (27x37cm 10x14in) Vercelli 2001

ꟷ $300 - €311 - **£180** - FF2 040
Solitudine Acquaforte (11.5x15cm 4x5in) Firenze 2000

BOGMAN Herman, Jnr. 1890-1975 [28]

ꕯ $2 225 - €2 087 - **£1 375** - FF13 692
Zonovergoten boerderij Oil/panel (37.5x46cm 14x18in) Rotterdam 1999

ꕯ $628 - €590 - **£388** - FF3 869
Koeien langs de waterkant Oil/canvas (20x31.5cm 7x12in) Rotterdam 1999

BOGMAN Hermanus Charles Ch. 1861-1921 [37]

ꕯ $1 174 - €1 316 - **£816** - FF8 632
Polderlandschap metvee Oil/canvas (38x58cm 14x22in) Rotterdam 2001

ꕯ $946 - €817 - **£571** - FF5 357
Cows watering in a polder Landscape Oil/canvas (29x50cm 11x19in) Amsterdam 1999

BOGO Christian 1882-1945 [34]

ꕯ $2 026 - €2 340 - **£1 417** - FF15 348
Marin med tremastad bark, kustvy med Kronoborgs slott i bakgrunden Oil/canvas (136x90cm 53x35in) Stockholm 2001

ꕯ $314 - €358 - **£218** - FF2 347
Dreimaster auf nächtlicher See Öl/Leinwand (80x80cm 31x31in) Hamburg 2000

BOGOLJUBOFF Alexei Petrovich 1824-1896 **[36]**
- $40 554 - €45 409 - **£28 161** - FF297 864
  Night in Venice Oil/canvas (35x55cm 13x21in)
  Helsinki 2001
- $8 304 - €8 721 - **£5 232** - FF57 204
  Ansicht eines südichen Hafens Öl/Leinwand
  (28.5x39cm 11x15in) Wien 2000

BOGOMAZOV Aleksandr Konstantin 1880-1930
[14]
- $4 545 - €4 368 - **£2 800** - FF28 653
  Girl dreaming in the Garden Oil/canvas/board
  (34x53cm 13x20in) London 1999
- $3 344 - €3 087 - **£2 200** - FF20 252
  Street Fight Oil/paper (26x32.5cm 10x12in) London
  1999
- $8 000 - €8 874 - **£5 320** - FF58 212
  Composition Crayon (28x23.5cm 11x9in) New-York
  2000

BOGUCKI Edwin Arnold 1932 **[1]**
- $7 500 - €8 714 - **£5 271** - FF57 162
  Head Study of Secretariat Bronze (28x32cm
  11x12in) New-York 2001

BOHATSCH Erwin 1951 **[84]**
- $698 - €665 - **£434** - FF4 360
  Fliegende Glocke Öl/Papier (38.3x56.5cm 15x22in)
  Hamburg 1999
- $474 - €436 - **£293** - FF2 860
  Ohne Titel Mischtechnik/Papier (26.5x21.5cm 10x8in)
  Wien 1999

BOHEMEN van Kees 1929-1986 **[146]**
- $8 593 - €9 983 - **£6 039** - FF65 485
  «Klaprozen» Oil/canvas (110x110cm 43x43in)
  Amsterdam 2001
- $1 618 - €1 815 - **£1 121** - FF11 906
  Informele Compositie Oil/canvas (85x78cm
  33x30in) Amsterdam 2001
- $798 - €862 - **£546** - FF5 655
  Interior Pencil (29x41cm 11x16in) Amsterdam 2001
- $239 - €272 - **£166** - FF1 786
  Female Nude II Silkscreen in colors (64.5x49.5cm
  25x19in) Haarlem 2000

BOHL Walter E. 1907 **[3]**
- $500 - €588 - **£346** - FF3 858
  Reflections Etching (30x24.5cm 11x9in) Beverly-Hills
  CA 2000

BÖHLER Hans 1884-1961 **[37]**
- $4 750 - €4 053 - **£2 831** - FF26 583
  Blummenstilleben Oil/canvas (39x46cm 15x18in)
  New-York 1998
- $1 236 - €1 453 - **£886** - FF9 534
  Dessous mit Stuhl Pencil/paper (45x31.4cm
  17x12in) Wien 2001

BÖHM Adolf 1861-1927 **[23]**
- $1 112 - €1 308 - **£772** - FF8 580
  October Indian ink (26x24.4cm 10x9in) Wien 2000
- $4 326 - €4 300 - **£2 700** - FF28 602
  «V.III.Ausstellung Secession» Poster (95x63cm
  37x24in) Wien 2000

BÖHM Alfred 1850-1885 **[7]**
- $1 127 - €1 329 - **£792** - FF8 720
  **Abendstimmung am Kanal mit Windmühlen
  und Staffagen** Oil/panel (24x32cm 9x12in) Frankfurt
  2000

BOHM C. Curry 1894-1971 **[7]**
- $8 500 - €9 483 - **£5 564** - FF62 204
  Spring Melody Oil/canvas (66x74cm 26x29in)
  Chicago IL 2000

BÖHM Eduard 1830-1890 **[107]**
- $1 589 - €1 503 - **£990** - FF9 861
  Alpenlandschaft mit einem Landstreicher
  Öl/Leinwand (53x42cm 20x16in) Praha 2000

BOHM Max 1868-1923 **[13]**
- $13 000 - €12 311 - **£7 904** - FF80 757
  Crossing the Bar Oil/canvas (126x181.5cm 49x71in)
  New-York 1999
- $9 500 - €10 397 - **£6 553** - FF68 198
  The Spirit of Transportation Oil/canvas (76x56cm
  29x22in) New-York 2000

BÖHM Pál, Paul 1839-1905 **[29]**
- $876 - €818 - **£530** - FF5 366
  Sitzender Akt Öl/Papier (72x50cm 28x19in) Berlin
  1999
- $1 674 - €1 534 - **£1 020** - FF10 061
  **Zigeunerfamilie bei einer Feuerstelle bei der
  Vorbereitung** Öl/Leinwand (26x45cm 10x17in)
  München 1999

BÖHME Gerd 1899-1978 **[21]**
- $194 - €204 - **£122** - FF1 341
  Freibergstrasse, Unterführung Pencil
  (35.3x42.2cm 13x16in) Heidelberg 2000

BÖHME Karl Theodor 1866-1939 **[36]**
- $907 - €869 - **£571** - FF5 701
  **Südliche Meeresküste mit bizarren
  Felsformationen** Öl/Leinwand (108x84cm 42x33in)
  Stuttgart 1999

BÖHMER Gunter 1911-1994 **[48]**
- $7 485 - €7 158 - **£4 558** - FF46 954
  Kirche in Ospedaletti Öl/Leinwand (60x73cm
  23x28in) Bielefeld 1999
- $427 - €409 - **£260** - FF2 683
  Der Idiot, Dostojewski Indian ink (31.5x42cm
  12x16in) Bielefeld 1999

BÖHMER Heinrich 1852-1930 **[31]**
- $1 298 - €1 457 - **£900** - FF9 556
  Woodland Pool Oil/canvas (60.5x80.5cm 23x31in)
  London 2000

BOHRDT Hans 1857-1945 **[37]**
- $1 438 - €1 636 - **£997** - FF10 732
  Küstenansicht vor Teneriffa Öl/Leinwand
  (55x81cm 21x31in) Hamburg 2000
- $1 515 - €1 738 - **£1 036** - FF11 403
  **Ahlbeck, Strand mit Badenden, Booten und
  Strandpavillon** Mixed media (23x33cm 9x12in)
  Berlin 2000
- $450 - €511 - **£308** - FF3 353
  «Hamburg-Südamerikanische...-Brasilien» Poster
  (94x68cm 37x26in) Hannover 2000

BOHRES Th. XVIII-XIX **[1]**
- $3 101 - €3 403 - **£1 996** - FF22 324
  **Frans Joseph.A de Nérée/Jan J.Aloysius de
  Nérée/J.Philip de Nérée** Pastel/paper (51x39cm
  20x15in) Amsterdam 2000

BÖHRINGER Volker 1912-1961 **[3]**
- $10 257 - €11 810 - **£7 000** - FF77 468
  Road to Waiblingen Tempera (40.5x33cm 15x12in)
  London 2000

BOHRMANN Karl Heinz 1928-1998 **[46]**
- $868 - €971 - **£585** - FF6 372
  Im Schlachthof Watercolour (50x50.5cm 19x19in)
  München 2000
- $218 - €204 - **£135** - FF1 341
  Strichkomposition Etching (24.2x23.5cm 9x9in)
  Heidelberg 1999

BOHROD Aaron 1907-1992 **[124]**
- $10 000 - €11 075 - **£6 782** - FF72 645
  Unstringing Tobacco Tempera (68.5x89cm 26x35in) New-York 2000
- $1 900 - €1 638 - **£1 128** - FF10 746
  Poverty Oil/board (30x22cm 12x9in) Cincinnati OH 1998
- $400 - €375 - **£245** - FF2 457
  Nude Bending/Street in Chicago Coloured inks (28x21cm 11x8in) New-York 1999
- $125 - €143 - **£86** - FF938
  Street Scene, Mexico City Lithograph (24x34cm 9x13in) Milwaukee WI 2000

BOHUSZ-SIESTRZENCEWICZ Stanislaw 1869-1927 **[9]**
- $8 595 - €7 313 - **£5 127** - FF47 970
  Carriage Oil/canvas (75x135cm 29x53in) Warszawa 1998

BOHUSZEWICZ Jan 1878-1935 **[9]**
- $609 - €680 - **£425** - FF4 463
  Novembre Huile/carton (44.5x35cm 17x13in) Warszawa 2001

BOICEAU Ernest 1881-1950 **[19]**
- $517 - €579 - **£351** - FF3 800
  Étude pour un fauteuil Aquarelle, gouache/papier (31x48.5cm 12x19in) Paris 2000

BOICHARD Henri Joseph 1783-c.1850 **[6]**
- $942 - €915 - **£582** - FF6 000
  La visite au Saint Hermite Huile/toile (38x46.5cm 14x18in) Paris 1999
- $6 188 - €6 941 - **£4 312** - FF45 528
  Le repos des voyageurs Huile/toile (32.5x41cm 12x16in) Bruxelles 2001

BOICHARD J. XIX-XX **[6]**
- $874 - €762 - **£528** - FF5 000
  «Cirque d'hiver. Dompteur soulevant un léopard» Affiche (125x91.5cm 49x36in) Paris 1998

BOIFFARD Jacques-André 1903-1961 **[2]**
- $12 796 - €14 438 - **£9 000** - FF94 705
  «Alberto Giacometti» Silver print (22.5x16.5cm 8x6in) London 2001

BOILLY Julien-L., Jules 1796-1874 **[60]**
- $10 110 - €11 731 - **£6 980** - FF76 950
  Le petit chapardeur Oil/canvas (97x128cm 38x50in) Stockholm 2000
- $36 000 - €31 578 - **£21 859** - FF207 136
  Trompe-l'oeil of a Bas Relief after Clodion depicting Galatea Oil/canvas (27x81cm 10x31in) New-York 1999
- $644 - €732 - **£447** - FF4 800
  Portrait de femme en buste Crayon/papier (22.5x18cm 8x7in) Clermont-Ferrand 2001

BOILLY Louis Léopold 1761-1845 **[292]**
- $133 968 - €114 057 - **£80 000** - FF748 168
  Young Couple at a Table: «La Moquerie» Oil/canvas (46x37cm 18x14in) London 1998
- $4 800 - €5 266 - **£3 188** - FF34 544
  Portrait of a Gentleman, in a black Jacket Oil/canvas (21.5x16.5cm 8x6in) New-York 2000
- $8 486 - €7 927 - **£5 236** - FF72 457
  Deux têtes de jeune fille et d'enfant pour l'Héroïne de Saint-Milhier Crayon (28x26cm 11x10in) Paris 1999
- $358 - €307 - **£215** - FF2 012
  Les Antiquaires Lithographie (22.5x19.5cm 8x7in) Hamburg 1998

BOILVIN Émile 1845-1899 **[5]**
- $8 960 - €9 610 - **£5 920** - FF63 040
  Sín título Tinta (27.5x17cm 10x6in) Madrid 2000

BOISROND François 1959 **[238]**
- $3 693 - €4 116 - **£2 484** - FF27 000
  Isseyb Miake à la Fondation Cartier Acrylique/toile (130x162cm 51x63in) Lille 2000
- $1 317 - €1 220 - **£813** - FF8 000
  Le pont du Gard Huile/toile (60x60cm 23x23in) Monte-Carlo 1999
- $286 - €274 - **£180** - FF1 800
  Aidez-nous Technique mixte/papier (30x20cm 11x7in) Versailles 1999

BOISSARD Robert c.1570-? **[2]**
- $1 278 - €1 372 - **£855** - FF9 000
  Mascarades: première suite Eau-forte (17.5x13.5cm 6x5in) Paris 2000

BOISSART Pierre 1878-1944 **[81]**
- $188 - €183 - **£118** - FF1 200
  Trois marins sur les quais Fusain/papier (47x60cm 18x23in) Nantes 1999

BOISSEAU Catherine 1952 **[36]**
- $634 - €579 - **£386** - FF3 800
  Chevreuil debout Bronze (H18cm H7in) Laon 1998

BOISSEAU Émile André 1842-1923 **[47]**
- $4 047 - €4 710 - **£2 850** - FF30 894
  «La défense du foyer» Bronze (H88cm H34in) Antwerpen 2001
- $2 693 - €2 830 - **£1 692** - FF18 500
  La Défense du Foyer Sculpture (H61cm H24in) La Flèche 2000

BOISSELIER Antoine Félix 1790-1857 **[15]**
- $5 593 - €5 183 - **£3 338** - FF34 000
  Les solitaires, souvenir d'Auvergne, environs de Clermont Huile/toile (81.5x100.5cm 32x39in) Paris 1999
- $4 830 - €5 336 - **£3 349** - FF35 000
  Paysage de cascade animé de pêcheurs Huile/toile (41x33cm 16x12in) Paris 2001

BOISSERE Frederick XIX **[6]**
- $504 - €523 - **£320** - FF3 432
  A Welsh River Valley Watercolour/paper (22x40cm 8x15in) Cheshire 2000

BOISSEVAIN William 1927 **[60]**
- $1 554 - €1 831 - **£1 092** - FF12 008
  Herons in the Swamp Oil/board (87x90cm 34x35in) Sydney 2000
- $1 667 - €1 983 - **£1 188** - FF13 005
  Brogas Watercolour/paper (60x85.5cm 23x33in) Melbourne 1999
- $2 742 - €2 574 - **£1 699** - FF16 885
  Fire in the Ranges Monotype (85x98cm 33x38in) Sydney 1999

BOISSIER André Claude 1760-1833 **[3]**
- $6 901 - €6 739 - **£400** - FF44 202
  Two Lovers in a Bedchamber Oil/panel (51x39cm 20x15in) London 2000

BOISSIEU de Claude Victor 1784-1869 **[3]**
- $1 231 - €1 448 - **£882** - FF9 500
  Paysage italien dominé par une ville fortifiée avec temple circulaire Encre (15x20.5cm 5x8in) Lyon 1999

BOISSIEU de Jean-Jacques 1736-1810 **[203]**
- $7 971 - €7 927 - **£4 945** - FF52 000
  La rentrée des foins Huile/panneau (31x26.5cm 12x10in) Lyon 1999

🖌 **$2 001** - €2 211 - **£1 387** - FF14 500
Paysage d'Italie Lavis (16.5x22.5cm 6x8in) Paris 2001

⚞ **$142** - €133 - **£86** - FF872
Zwei Männer mit einer Ziege am Fluss Radierung (18.5x24.8cm 7x9in) Basel 1999

BOISSONAS Frédéric 1858-1946 **[48]**

📷 **$873** - €915 - **£549** - FF6 000
Vue générale du Parthénon Tirage argentique (43x56.5cm 16x22in) Paris 2000

BOISSONNADE Henri Paul Marc XIX-XX **[2]**

🗿 **$6 724** - €7 218 - **£4 500** - FF47 347
Nude Washing Marble (34x50cm 13x19in) London 2000

BOIT Charles 1662-1727 **[16]**

🖌 **$2 195** - €2 556 - **£1 533** - FF16 769
Brustportrait des jungen Königs Georg II (1683-1760) von England Miniature (5x4.3cm 1x1in) München 2000

BOIT Edward Darley 1842-1916 **[15]**

🖌 **$2 000** - €2 203 - **£1 334** - FF14 454
Landscape with Stream Oil/board (15x25cm 6x10in) Portsmouth NH 2000

🖌 **$5 250** - €5 620 - **£3 572** - FF36 868
Terrace Gardens and Hillside, Cernitoio Watercolour/paper (49x69cm 19x27in) Portsmouth NH 2001

BOITARD François 1670-1715 **[53]**

🖌 **$577** - €529 - **£350** - FF3 469
Allegory of Envy and Heresy with Snakes and Scorpions Black chalk (33x44.5cm 12x17in) London 1998

BOITIAT Henri 1866-1944 **[4]**

🖌 **$1 900** - €2 119 - **£1 277** - FF13 897
Statue of Saint on a Cathedral Wall/Renaissance Portal in a Garden Oil/panel (26x21cm 10x8in) Portsmouth NH 2000

BOIVIN Émile 1846-1920 **[61]**

🖌 **$4 119** - €4 573 - **£2 871** - FF30 000
Enfants tunisiens sur la jetée Huile/toile (41x61cm 16x24in) Paris 2001

🖌 **$2 099** - €2 439 - **£1 496** - FF16 000
Halte à la fontaine, Maroc Huile/toile (24x35cm 9x13in) Paris 2001

🖌 **$2 326** - €2 439 - **£1 457** - FF16 000
Caravane dans le désert/Coup de vent Aquarelle/papier (17.5x28cm 6x11in) Paris 2000

BOIX-VIVES Anselme 1899-1969 **[44]**

🖌 **$3 499** - €4 116 - **£2 508** - FF27 000
Le clown Huile/carton/toile (68x37cm 26x14in) Paris 2001

🖌 **$1 277** - €1 453 - **£885** - FF9 529
Le paon Gouache/carton (65x46cm 25x18in) Sion 2000

BOIZOT Simon Louis 1743-1809 **[24]**

🗿 **$22 610** - €23 439 - **£13 566** - FF153 748
Busto di Racine Sculpture cire (H83cm H32in) Venezia 2000

🗿 **$3 997** - €3 857 - **£2 509** - FF25 300
L'Enlèvement de Proserpine Bronze (H48cm H18in) Monte-Carlo 2000

🖌 **$497** - €534 - **£332** - FF3 500
Portrait d'un homme vu de profil, en médaillon Pierre noire/papier (17.5x16.5cm 6x6in) Senlis 2000

BOK Hannes 1914-1964 **[4]**

🖼 **$6 000** - €6 994 - **£4 154** - FF45 879
Figure Riding Giant Kangaroo Rat Through Alien Landscape Oil/board (48x73cm 19x29in) New-York 2000

🖼 **$2 000** - €2 240 - **£1 389** - FF14 694
Standing stylized Nude in Springtime Landscape Oil/paper (42x34cm 16x13in) New-York 2001

BOKELBERG Werner 1937 **[12]**

📷 **$394** - €460 - **£273** - FF3 018
Dali Gelatin silver print (37.7x25.7cm 14x10in) Köln 2000

BOKKENHEUSER Børge 1910-1976 **[44]**

🖼 **$222** - €269 - **£155** - FF1 763
Kystparti Oil/canvas (61x77cm 24x30in) Viby J, Århus 2000

BÖKLIN Per Erik 1913 **[8]**

🖌 **$781** - €876 - **£544** - FF5 744
Komposition Gouache/paper (12.5x18cm 4x7in) Stockholm 2001

BOKLUND Johan Christoffer 1817-1880 **[28]**

🖼 **$868** - €875 - **£541** - FF5 740
Gårdsinteriörer från slottet Tratzburg Oil/canvas (54x45cm 21x17in) Stockholm 2000

🖼 **$463** - €467 - **£288** - FF3 061
Österrikisk rättfångare Oil/panel (31x18.5cm 12x7in) Stockholm 2000

BOKOR Miklos 1927 **[3]**

🖌 **$1 285** - €1 239 - **£792** - FF8 125
Ombres sur un mur Aquarell/Papier (51x69cm 20x27in) Bern 1999

BOKS Evert Jan 1838-1914 **[17]**

🖼 **$11 880** - €9 915 - **£6 960** - FF65 040
Surpris pendant une conversation confidentielle Huile/toile (108x76cm 42x29in) Antwerpen 1998

🖼 **$9 675** - €11 155 - **£6 615** - FF73 170
Les indiscrets surpris Huile/panneau (38.5x29.5cm 15x11in) Bruxelles 2000

BOL Ferdinand 1616-1680 **[72]**

🖌 **$39 408** - €39 370 - **£24 640** - FF258 250
Bildnis eines Gelehrten Öl/Leinwand (101x90cm 39x35in) Hamburg 1999

🖌 **$35 000** - €30 427 - **£21 182** - FF199 591
The Departure of the Young Tobias Ink (20x30cm 7x11in) New-York 1999

⚞ **$1 321** - €1 271 - **£824** - FF8 334
The Sacrifice of Isaac Etching (43.5x33cm 17x12in) Amsterdam 1999

BOL Hans 1534-1593 **[32]**

🖌 **$28 000** - €29 993 - **£19 121** - FF196 744
Panoramic Landscape with a Mill and Bridge in a Valley Ink (17x24cm 6x9in) New-York 2001

⚞ **$19 300** - €23 508 - **£13 761** - FF150 925
Weite Landschaft mit antiken Ruinen, im Hintergrund eine Stadt Radierung (21.7x31.7cm 8x12in) Berlin 2000

BOLANACHI Konstantinos 1837-? **[3]**

🖼 **$7 909** - €7 669 - **£5 010** - FF50 308
Burg Rheinfels bei St. Goar am Rhein Öl/Leinwand (54x41cm 21x16in) München 1999

BOLAND DE SPA Charles H.D. c.1850-? **[21]**

🖼 **$42 000** - €36 236 - **£25 338** - FF237 690
Home alone Oil/canvas (134.5x101cm 52x39in) New-York 1998

B

$2 166 - €2 355 - £1 491 - FF15 447
Souci maternel Huile/toile (51x62cm 20x24in)
Bruxelles 2001

BOLDINI Giovanni 1842-1931 **[276]**

$209 040 - €182 939 - £126 600 - FF1 200 000
Jeune femme lisant Huile/toile (73x57cm 28x22in)
Paris 1998

$18 800 - €24 361 - £14 100 - FF159 800
Ritratto della Marchesa Vettoria Olio/tela/tavola
(29x25.5cm 11x10in) Prato 2000

$6 132 - €6 098 - £3 804 - FF40 000
Femme aux draps Aquarelle/papier (26x34cm
10x13in) Neuilly-sur-Seine 1999

$300 - €259 - £150 - FF1 700
Autoritratto Acquaforte (12x8.5cm 4x3in) Vercelli
1999

BOLDIZSAR István 1897-1984 **[9]**

$910 - €1 007 - £598 - FF6 604
Park of Kenderes Oil/canvas (80x100cm 31x39in)
Budapest 2000

BOLDRINI Niccolo 1510-c.1570 **[12]**

$650 - €612 - £401 - FF4 016
Venus in Cupid in the Woods, after Titian
Woodcut (31x23cm 12x9in) New-York 1999

BOLDUC Blanche 1906-1998 **[21]**

$872 - €936 - £583 - FF6 141
Le Saint-Viatique d'autrefois Huile/panneau
(27.5x63.5cm 10x25in) Montréal 2000

$1 013 - €1 065 - £669 - FF6 984
Scène de village Huile/panneau (26.5x47.5cm
10x18in) Montréal 2000

BOLDUC David 1945 **[6]**

$3 308 - €3 551 - £2 247 - FF23 291
Night July Acrylic/canvas (36x48cm 14x18in) Calgary,
Alberta 2001

$1 124 - €1 207 - £764 - FF7 918
Summer Watercolour/paper (29.5x21.5cm 11x8in)
Calgary, Alberta 2001

BOLE Jeanne Toulza XIX **[8]**

$4 968 - €5 488 - £3 445 - FF36 000
La diseuse de bonne aventure Huile/toile
(101x73cm 39x28in) Paris 2001

BOLENS Ernest 1881-1959 **[29]**

$1 249 - €1 192 - £780 - FF7 822
**Herbststimmung in Paris, Seinebrücke mit
Passanten** Öl/Leinwand (65x80cm 25x31in) Zofingen
1999

BOLERADSZKY Beno 1885-? **[5]**

$1 800 - €2 091 - £1 265 - FF13 718
Cat in the Grass with Butterfly and Flowers
Oil/panel (25x35cm 10x14in) New-Orleans LA 2001

BOLIN Gustav 1920-1999 **[184]**

$1 815 - €1 829 - £1 131 - FF12 000
Grand nu beige Huile/toile (112x112cm 44x44in)
Paris 2000

$979 - €1 052 - £655 - FF6 900
Terrasse de café la nuit, IV Huile/toile
(80.5x99.5cm 31x39in) Paris 2000

$213 - €229 - £142 - FF1 500
Sans titre Encre Chine (43x51cm 16x20in) Paris 2000

BOLINK Bert Henri 1876-1950 **[5]**

$2 499 - €2 723 - £1 721 - FF17 859
Violets in a Vase Oil/panel (24x33cm 9x12in)
Amsterdam 2001

BOLL Reinholdt 1825-1897 **[6]**

$1 913 - €2 147 - £1 326 - FF14 084
Parti fra Ringerige Oil/wood (21x31cm 8x12in)
København 2000

BOLLÉ Martin 1912-1968 **[77]**

$817 - €694 - £487 - FF4 552
Fillette au Catogan Huile/toile (53x40cm 20x15in)
Bruxelles 1998

$699 - €644 - £421 - FF4 227
Nu couché Huile/panneau (29.5x40cm 11x15in)
Bruxelles 1999

BOLLER Louis, Ludwig 1862-1896 **[3]**

$1 473 - €1 534 - £933 - FF10 061
**Junger Angler am Flussufer nahe einem
Holzsteg** Öl/Leinwand (43x61cm 16x24in) München
2000

BOLLERY Nicolas 1560-1630 **[3]**

$29 886 - €32 080 - £20 000 - FF210 432
Wedding Procession Through a Town Oil/canvas
(106.5x150cm 41x59in) London 2000

BOLLES Enoch XX **[12]**

$10 000 - €9 299 - £6 173 - FF60 996
Making a Beau Peep Oil/canvas (71x53cm 28x21in)
Portland ME 1999

BOLLING Svein 1948 **[7]**

$1 983 - €2 202 - £1 382 - FF14 441
Kvinne mes stearinlys Tempera/canvas (90x60cm
35x23in) Oslo 2001

BOLLONGIER Hans c.1600-c.1650 **[9]**

$110 000 - €96 488 - £66 792 - FF632 918
Flowers in a Glass Vase on a Stone Ledge
Oil/panel (45x32cm 17x12in) New-York 1999

BOLLSCHWEILER Jacob Fried., Jack 1888-1938
[7]

$1 600 - €1 449 - £979 - FF9 506
«Sommer in Graubünden» Poster (102x72cm
40x28in) New-York 1998

BOLOTOWSKY Ilya 1907-1981 **[103]**

$6 500 - €5 780 - £3 975 - FF37 916
Opalescent Oil/canvas (122x122cm 48x48in) New-
York 1999

$6 000 - €5 770 - £3 696 - FF37 846
Untitled Oil/canvas (60.5x152cm 23x59in) New-York
1999

$1 984 - €2 352 - £1 400 - FF15 425
Miniature Small Vertical Acrylic/panel (32x13cm
12x5in) London 2000

$300 - €280 - £187 - FF1 836
Cream Back Ground, Blue and Yellow Screenprint
(76x101cm 30x40in) Norwalk CT 1999

BOLSWERT Boetius Adams 1580-1633 **[18]**

$318 - €272 - £191 - FF1 785
«A Peasant with Goats/A Peasant with Horses»
after A.Bloemaert Etching (11x14cm 4x5in) Haarlem
1998

BOLSWERT Schelte Adams 1586-1659 **[64]**

$268 - €256 - £166 - FF1 676
**Ein Bauer zu Pferd an einer Tränke/Weite hüge-
lige Landschaft** Kupferstich (33x45.7cm 12x17in)
Berlin 1999

BOLT Niels Peter 1886-1965 **[74]**

$556 - €512 - £342 - FF3 356
Parti fra Köbenhavns havn Oil/canvas (82x123cm
32x48in) Vejle 1999

B

$400 - €377 - £250 - FF2 472
Opstillinger med brogede blomster i vase
Pastel/paper (65x49cm 25x19in) Vejle 1999

BOLTANSKI Christian 1944 [116]
$6 323 - €7 165 - £4 418 - FF47 000
«Le blagueur» Mixed media (100x75cm 39x29in)
Zürich 2001
$40 000 - €44 803 - £27 792 - FF293 888
Monument Installation (195.5x150cm 76x59in) New-York 2001
$10 842 - €9 909 - £6 675 - FF65 000
Vitrine piégée Construction (40x64.5x12cm 15x25x4in) Paris 1999
$2 003 - €1 753 - £1 213 - FF11 500
«Christian Boltanski mort» Photo (32.5x23cm 12x9in) Paris 1999

BOLTON Gambier XIX [2]
$3 267 - €3 025 - £2 000 - FF19 842
Indian Rhinoceros Carbon print (25x30cm 10x12in)
London 1999

BOLTON James c.1740-1799 [3]
$2 173 - €2 522 - £1 500 - FF16 540
Lilium martagon albiflorum (White Martagon Lily) Watercolour (23x18cm 9x7in) London 2000

BOLTON John XX [2]
$2 000 - €1 929 - £1 264 - FF12 656
Bizarre Aventures No.26 Watercolour, gouache (45.5x37cm 17x14in) New-York 1999

BOLTON John Nunn 1869-1909 [3]
$12 000 - €13 942 - £8 433 - FF91 454
Country Landscape Oil/canvas (94x139.5cm 37x54in) New-York 2001

BOMBERG David 1890-1957 [240]
$19 920 - €23 145 - £14 000 - FF151 818
Purple Flowers Oil/canvas (58.5x58.5cm 23x23in) London 2001
$12 847 - €11 861 - £8 000 - FF77 804
Spring Flowers Oil/canvas (46x31cm 18x12in) London 1999
$4 762 - €4 065 - £2 800 - FF26 666
Mother and Child Watercolour (38x28cm 14x11in) London 1998
$3 580 - €3 485 - £2 200 - FF22 861
Russian Ballet Color lithograph (22x14cm 8x5in) London 1999

BOMBLED Karel Frederik 1822-1902 [16]
$4 781 - €5 133 - £3 200 - FF33 669
A Grey Hunter with a Dog in a stable Oil/canvas (50x70cm 19x27in) London 2000
$563 - €654 - £396 - FF4 290
Reiterin mit ihrem Hund am Waldweg Oil/panel (17.5x23cm 6x9in) Wien 2001

BOMBLED Louis-Charles 1862-1927 [64]
$5 540 - €5 336 - £3 440 - FF35 000
La promenade en calèche Huile/toile (60x120cm 23x47in) Paris 1999
$426 - €457 - £285 - FF3 500
Grenadier/Jeune paysanne Huile/toile (16x11cm 6x4in) Paris 2000
$540 - €534 - £333 - FF3 500
Scène d'équitation, le saut de la rivière
Aquarelle/papier (25.5x40cm 10x15in) Paris 1999

BOMBOIS Camille 1883-1970 [231]
$25 000 - €25 192 - £15 585 - FF165 250
Les enfants du châtelain Oil/canvas (55x46cm 21x18in) New-York 2000

$6 000 - €5 336 - £3 669 - FF34 999
Les Laumes-Fescia et le pont Romain Oil/canvas (16x24cm 6x9in) New-York 1999

BOMMEL van Elias Pieter 1819-1890 [88]
$20 000 - €23 520 - £14 338 - FF154 279
Grosse alte Hafenstadt Öl/Leinwand (102x133cm 40x52in) Hamburg 2000
$5 634 - €6 541 - £3 960 - FF42 903
Stadt am Meer mitsegelschiffen im Vordergrund
Öl/Leinwand (51x81cm 20x31in) Wien 2001
$3 805 - €4 084 - £2 546 - FF26 789
Skaters by a fortified mansion Oil/canvas (25x29cm 9x11in) Amsterdam 2000

BÖMMELS Pieter 1951 [29]
$2 953 - €3 170 - £1 976 - FF20 794
Es geht der Tod an Fahrt Mixed media/canvas (221.5x160cm 87x62in) Hamburg 2000

BOMPARD J.M. XX [2]
$722 - €728 - £450 - FF4 776
«Barcelonette, PLM» Poster (96x58cm 37x22in) London 2000

BOMPARD Maurice 1857-1936 [130]
$3 223 - €3 659 - £2 239 - FF24 000
Venise, Murano Huile/toile (38.5x55.5cm 15x21in) Pontoise 2001
$2 090 - €1 982 - £1 271 - FF13 000
Venise, le Grand Canal et la Salute Huile/toile (35x27cm 13x10in) Paris 1999

BOMPIANI Carlo XX [1]
$2 844 - €2 949 - £1 706 - FF19 342
«Grand Premio Pietro Cidonio, circuito di Collemaggio, l'Aquila» Affiche couleur (98x67cm 38x26in) Torino 2000

BOMPIANI Roberto 1821-1908 [14]
$4 500 - €4 665 - £2 700 - FF30 600
Disposizione dei fiori Olio/tavoletta (33.5x24cm 13x9in) Venezia 2000
$3 000 - €2 881 - £1 849 - FF18 899
Boy and Girl in a Landscape Watercolour/paper (53x35cm 21x14in) Bloomfield-Hills MI 1999

BONALUMI Agostino 1935 [150]
$4 500 - €3 887 - £3 000 - FF25 500
Rosso Tecnica mista (190x130.5cm 74x51in) Prato 1998
$3 057 - €2 608 - £1 822 - FF17 107
Ohne Titel Mixed media/canvas (49.5x40cm 19x15in) Zürich 1998
$650 - €674 - £390 - FF4 420
Il mondo azzurro Tecnica mista (38x35cm 14x13in) Vercelli 2001
$700 - €726 - £420 - FF4 760
Giallo Acquarello (32.5x34cm 12x13in) Vercelli 2001

BONAMICI Louis 1878-1966 [64]
$1 325 - €1 524 - £913 - FF10 000
Champ d'oliviers Huile/toile (50.5x61cm 19x24in) Toulon 2000

BONAPARTE Prince Roland Napoléon 1858-1924 [1]
$17 361 - €16 398 - £10 500 - FF107 566
Collection anthropologique du Prince Roland Bonaparte, Peaux Rouges Albumen print (22.5x17cm 8x6in) London 2000

BONAPARTE Princesse Mathilde 1820-1904 [6]
$2 073 - €2 287 - £1 404 - FF15 000
Autoportrait de profil Aquarelle (29x25cm 11x9in) Paris 2000

BONASONE Giulio di Antonio act.c.1531-c.1574 [63]
- 📖 **$400** - €415 - **£240** - FF2 720
L'infanzia di Giove Burin (28.5x43cm 11x16in)
Milano 2000

BONATO Victor 1934 [21]
- ✎ **$1 198** - €1 117 - **£724** - FF7 328
Objekt T-KX-69/70 Object (71x71x3cm 27x27x1in)
München 1999

BONATTI Giovanni c.1635-1681 [1]
- ✑ **$3 197** - €3 811 - **£2 280** - FF25 000
Les instruments de la Passion présentés à
Marie-Madeleine Huile/toile (42.5x34cm 16x13in)
Montluçon 2000

BONAVIA Carlo XVIII [26]
- ✑ **$151 651** - €176 775 - **£105 000** - FF1 159 567
An Extensive Italianate River with Travellers
and Soldiers Oil/canvas (99x136.5cm 38x53in)
London 2000
- ✑ **$62 800** - €65 102 - **£37 680** - FF427 040
Marina mediterranea con una grotta e pescatori
e con arco naturale Olio/tela (45x74.5cm 17x29in)
Roma 1999

BONCOMPAIN Pierre 1938 [15]
- ✑ **$2 015** - €2 211 - **£1 368** - FF14 500
Jeune femme sur le transat Huile/toile (55x46cm
21x18in) Calais 2000

BONCZA-TOMASZEWSKI Julian 1834-1920 [5]
- ✑ **$10 000** - €9 502 - **£6 084** - FF62 329
Springtime Oil/canvas (128.5x78cm 50x30in) New-
York 1999

BOND Henry 1966 [8]
- 📷 **$9 375** - €11 019 - **£6 500** - FF72 280
No.411 Type C color print (190x122cm 74x48in)
London 2000

BOND Simon 1947 [6]
- ✎ **$383** - €383 - **£240** - FF2 515
«101 Uses of a Dead Cat» Ink (15x21cm 5x8in)
London 1999

BOND Terence James 1946 [19]
- ✎ **$340** - €380 - **£230** - FF2 492
A Thrush on a Stump Watercolour/paper (30x22cm
12x9in) Aylsham, Norfolk 2000

BOND William Joseph J.C. 1833-1928 [115]
- ✑ **$1 659** - €1 554 - **£1 020** - FF10 194
Beach Scene with Figure on Horseback Oil/panel
(17x25cm 6x9in) West-Midlands 1999
- ✎ **$516** - €573 - **£360** - FF3 760
Boats in a West coast Harbour Watercolour
(13x28cm 5x11in) London 2001

BONDE Peter 1958 [50]
- ✑ **$2 666** - €2 687 - **£1 662** - FF17 624
Landskab, Kaempehöj Oil/canvas (170x180cm
66x70in) Köbenhavn 2000

BONDUEL Léon XIX-XX [3]
- ✎ **$2 762** - €2 592 - **£1 706** - FF17 000
L'alerte Bronze (55x78cm 21x30in) Fontainebleau
1999

BONDY Walter 1880-1940 [16]
- ✑ **$1 960** - €2 250 - **£1 341** - FF14 757
Blumen, Albarello, Tongefässe und Pfeife auf
Gartentisch vor Buschwerk Öl/Leinwand
(63x52cm 24x20in) Berlin 2000

BONE Charles Richard 1809-c.1880 [7]
- ✑ **$3 166** - €3 546 - **£2 200** - FF23 263
Young Gentleman believed to be the Brother of
the Artist Miniature (13x10.5cm 5x4in) London 2001

BONE Craig 1955 [15]
- ✑ **$4 769** - €3 967 - **£2 800** - FF26 022
Leopard on a Rock Oil/canvas (61x106.5cm
24x41in) London 1998
- ✑ **$2 903** - €2 638 - **£1 800** - FF17 304
Lion Oil/board (25x39cm 9x15in) Billingshurst, West-
Sussex 1999

BONE David Muirhead 1876-1953 [241]
- ✎ **$537** - €577 - **£360** - FF3 787
Bath Abbey Pencil/paper (25.5x17.5cm 10x6in)
London 2000
- 📖 **$445** - €464 - **£280** - FF3 043
Afternoon Sahagun, Spain Drypoint (30x18cm
11x7in) London 2000

BONE Henry 1755-1834 [47]
- ✑ **$11 931** - €10 011 - **£7 000** - FF65 666
Charles James Fox (1749-1806) Three Quarter
Length in a coloured Coat Miniature (16x12.5cm
6x4in) London 1998

BONE Henry Pierce 1779-1855 [45]
- ✑ **$3 984** - €4 692 - **£2 800** - FF30 775
Arthur Wellesley, 1st Duke of Wellington, full
face in blue Cloak Miniature (14.5x12cm 5x4in)
London 2000

BONE Robert Trewick 1790-1840 [3]
- ✑ **$2 121** - €2 014 - **£1 300** - FF13 212
Tobias/The Angel Oil/canvas (18x28cm 7x11in)
London 1999

BONE Stephen 1904-1958 [50]
- ✑ **$469** - €441 - **£290** - FF2 893
Stockholm Harbour Oil/panel (25.5x33cm 10x12in)
London 1999

BONECCHI Matteo c.1672-c.1755 [8]
- ✑ **$8 000** - €8 293 - **£4 800** - FF54 400
Nettuno e altre divinità marine Olio/tela
(62.5x77.5cm 24x30in) Venezia 2000

BONECHI Lorenzo 1955-1994 [8]
- ✑ **$4 500** - €3 887 - **£3 000** - FF25 500
Paesaggio Acrilico/tela (70x100cm 27x39in) Prato
1998
- ✑ **$952** - €1 022 - **£637** - FF6 707
Ohne Titel Pastell/Papier (107x120cm 42x47in) Köln
2000

BONEH Schmuel 1930-1999 [14]
- ✑ **$1 000** - €988 - **£612** - FF6 483
Figures Oil/canvas (54.5x65cm 21x25in) Tel Aviv
2000

BONELLI Giorgio 1941-1986 [2]
- ✑ **$4 680** - €4 043 - **£2 340** - FF26 520
Casa Hogarth Olio/tela (95x123cm 37x48in) Torino
1999

BONELLO Carmello XIX-XX [3]
- ✎ **$1 225** - €1 355 - **£850** - FF8 885
Vessels in the Grand Harbour, Valetta
Watercolour/paper (11x29cm 4x11in) London 2001

BONESI Gian Girolamo 1653-1725 [1]
- ✎ **$2 689** - €2 887 - **£1 800** - FF18 938
The Finding Moses Ink (17.5x27.5cm 6x10in)
London 2000

B

BONESTELL Chesley 1888-1986 **[2]**
📺 **$5 000** - €4 847 - **£3 096** - FF31 796
«New York Central Building» Poster (103x68cm 40x27in) New-York 1999

BONET Paul 1889-1971 **[98]**
✏️ **$436** - €457 - **£273** - FF3 000
«E.Hemingway, Romans N.R.F» Gouache/papier (23.5x23cm 9x9in) Paris 2000

BONEVARDI Marcelo 1929-1994 **[40]**
👉 **$13 000** - €15 084 - **£8 975** - FF98 943
Mesa del Astrólogo VII Mixed media (198x109cm 77x42in) New-York 2000
👉 **$10 000** - €11 618 - **£7 028** - FF76 212
«Construction #151, landscape» Oil/canvas (74x155cm 29x61in) New-York 2001
👉 **$550** - €614 - **£360** - FF4 028
Geometric Construction Mixed media (43x30cm 17x12in) Chicago IL 2000
🖐 **$7 000** - €8 242 - **£4 918** - FF54 063
Ritual Object Construction (122x77.5cm 48x30in) New-York 2000
🖐 **$7 000** - €6 732 - **£4 320** - FF44 157
Landscape Construction (71x152.5cm 27x60in) Washington 1999
✏️ **$1 800** - €2 088 - **£1 242** - FF13 699
The Door Watercolour (43x30.5cm 16x12in) New-York 2000

BONFANTI Angelo XX **[15]**
👉 **$353** - €381 - **£237** - FF2 500
Pique-nique Huile/isorel (58x63cm 22x24in) Grenoble 2000

BONFANTI Arturo 1905-1978 **[26]**
👉 **$3 570** - €3 701 - **£2 142** - FF24 276
Il ritrovamento della croce Olio/tela (65x49cm 25x19in) Venezia 2000
👉 **$3 152** - €3 017 - **£1 958** - FF19 787
Composizione A.45 Huile/panneau (37x35cm 14x13in) Zürich 1999

BONFANTINI Sergio 1910-1989 **[24]**
👉 **$1 800** - €1 866 - **£1 080** - FF12 240
«Quadro su quadro» Olio/tela (81x54cm 31x21in) Vercelli 2001

BONFILS Félix 1831-1885 **[76]**
📷 **$659** - €640 - **£407** - FF4 200
Cavas du consulat de Russie à Jérusalem Tirage albuminé (18x22cm 7x8in) Paris 1999

BONFILS Gaston 1855-1946 **[13]**
👉 **$1 514** - €1 789 - **£1 073** - FF11 738
Der Antiquitätenhändler Öl/Leinwand (45x54cm 17x21in) München 2000

BONFILS Robert 1886-1972 **[29]**
👉 **$5 422** - €5 793 - **£3 613** - FF38 000
Les deux baigneuses sur fond luxuriant Huile/toile (150x100cm 59x39in) Paris 2000
📺 **$195** - €229 - **£138** - FF1 500
«Cinquantenaire Paris» Affiche (80x30cm 31x11in) Neuilly-sur-Seine 2000

BONGART Sergei 1918-1985 **[33]**
👉 **$4 200** - €3 966 - **£2 608** - FF26 014
Still Life with Roses Oil/canvas (76x91.5cm 29x36in) Beverly-Hills CA 1999

BONHEUR Auguste 1824-1884 **[39]**
👉 **$1 991** - €1 757 - **£1 200** - FF11 527
Grazing Cattle Oil/canvas (25.5x32.5cm 10x12in) London 1998

BONHEUR Ferdinand XIX **[55]**
👉 **$2 250** - €2 414 - **£1 533** - FF15 832
Parti fra Napolibugten med Vesuv i baggrunden Oil/canvas (38x61cm 14x24in) København 2001
👉 **$2 013** - €2 287 - **£1 389** - FF15 000
Felouque dans le port Huile/panneau (21.5x41cm 8x16in) Paris 2000

BONHEUR Isidore Jules 1827-1901 **[372]**
🖐 **$2 900** - €2 812 - **£1 837** - FF18 446
Stier/Kuh Bronze (16x23x9.5cm 6x9x3in) München 1999

BONHEUR Rosa 1822-1899 **[375]**
👉 **$230 000** - €267 224 - **£161 644** - FF1 752 876
The Duel Oil/canvas (150x244cm 59x96in) New-York 2001
👉 **$8 872** - €9 909 - **£6 012** - FF65 000
L'attelage Huile/toile (33x60cm 12x23in) Saint-Germain-en-Laye 2000
👉 **$4 481** - €3 954 - **£2 700** - FF25 936
Two Grazing Sheep Oil/paper/canvas (32.5x39cm 12x15in) London 1998
👉 **$1 673** - €1 498 - **£1 000** - FF9 823
Taureau beuglant Bronze (15x21.5cm 5x8in) Perthshire 1998
✏️ **$704** - €838 - **£487** - FF5 500
Vaches et chèvres dans le pré Crayon (18x28cm 7x11in) Paris 2000
📺 **$715** - €797 - **£500** - FF5 229
Fighting Stallions Engraving (54.5x83cm 21x32in) Near NY 2001

BONHOMME Léon 1870-1924 **[84]**
👉 **$487** - €534 - **£336** - FF3 500
Couple Huile/panneau (23.5x15cm 9x5in) Paris 2001
👉 **$365** - €320 - **£221** - FF2 100
Portrait de femme au chapeau Aquarelle/papier (30x22cm 11x8in) La Varenne-Saint-Hilaire 1998

BONI A. XIX **[1]**
🖐 **$6 328** - €6 731 - **£4 000** - FF44 152
Bust of a Girl and her Cat Marble (H63.5cm H25in) London 2000

BONI Paolo 1926 **[23]**
📺 **$70** - €75 - **£47** - FF495
Abstract Etching in colors (20x14cm 8x5in) Cleveland OH 2000

BONICHI Claudio 1943 **[27]**
👉 **$2 160** - €1 866 - **£1 080** - FF12 240
Pere piagate Olio/tela (40x50cm 15x19in) Prato 1999
👉 **$3 600** - €3 110 - **£2 400** - FF20 400
«Rose sfatte» Olio/tavola (34x34cm 13x13in) Prato 1998
✏️ **$600** - €518 - **£400** - FF3 400
Garofano e conchiglia Acquarello/carta (27x42cm 10x16in) Prato 1998

BONIFACIO (B. Alfonso Gómez) 1934 **[31]**
👉 **$5 490** - €5 406 - **£3 510** - FF35 460
«Triana» Oleo/lienzo (186x200cm 73x78in) Madrid 1999
👉 **$1 530** - €1 802 - **£1 110** - FF11 820
«Cabeza y figuras» Oleo/lienzo (46x55cm 18x21in) Madrid 2001

BONIFACIO (Bonifacio Alfonso) 1903 **[32]**
👉 **$6 720** - €7 208 - **£4 560** - FF47 280
«Ingenio para lanzar proyectiles» Oleo/lienzo (162x212cm 63x83in) Madrid 2001
👉 **$3 960** - €3 604 - **£2 460** - FF23 640
Composición Oleo/lienzo (80x61cm 31x24in) Madrid 1999

$1 650 - €1 502 - **£1 025** - FF9 850
Composición Oleo/lienzo (40x30cm 15x11in) Madrid 1999

$290 - €264 - **£180** - FF1 733
Composición Litografía (64x47cm 25x18in) Madrid 1999

BONIFAS Y MASO Luis 1730-1786 **[1]**
$3 850 - €4 205 - **£2 660** - FF27 580
San Antonio de Pádua Sculpture bois (H64cm H25in) Barcelona 2001

BONIFAZI Adriano XIX **[31]**
$3 400 - €2 878 - **£2 035** - FF18 878
A Young Italian Peasant Girl Oil/panel (44.5x30.5cm 17x12in) New-York 1998

BONIFAZIO Natale 1537-1592 **[1]**
$1 715 - €2 045 - **£1 223** - FF13 415
Ecce Homo (die Schaustellung Christi) Kupferstich (33.6x25.9cm 13x10in) Berlin 2000

BONIFAZIO VERONESE Pitati de' 1487-1553 **[7]**
$22 400 - €25 435 - **£15 330** - FF166 845
Die Madonna mit den Kinde und den Heiligen Franziskus und Hieronymus Oil/panel (49x68cm 19x26in) Wien 2000
$14 758 - €16 361 - **£10 246** - FF107 324
Die Heldentat des Marcus Curtius Oil/panel (27x57cm 10x22in) Köln 2001

BONINGTON Richard Parkes 1801-1828 **[110]**
$4 770 - €4 486 - **£3 000** - FF29 425
The White Cliffs at Dover, with fisherfolk and boat on the beach Oil/canvas (39x53cm 15x20in) Co. Kilkenny 1999
$1 575 - €1 502 - **£975** - FF9 850
Mujer con cesto Oleo/papel (25x15.5cm 9x6in) Madrid 1999
$13 635 - €13 740 - **£8 500** - FF90 130
Fishermen with their Nets on the Beach, Le Havre Wash (11.5x19cm 4x7in) London 2000
$129 - €152 - **£92** - FF1 000
Rue du Gros-Horloge, Rouen Lithographie (24.5x25cm 9x9in) Paris 2001

BONIROTE Pierre 1811-1891 **[17]**
$21 840 - €18 587 - **£13 000** - FF121 925
In the Campagna Oil/canvas (117x157cm 46x61in) London 1998
$3 427 - €3 659 - **£2 340** - FF24 000
Nymphes dans un paysage Huile/toile (91x66cm 35x25in) Paris 2001
$1 727 - €1 677 - **£1 067** - FF11 000
Grecque assise dans les ruines Aquarelle/papier (21.5x29cm 8x11in) Paris 1999

BONITO Giuseppe 1707-1789 **[24]**
$86 880 - €98 729 - **£60 000** - FF647 622
Gentleman, Full-Length, in Ottoman Robes, a Page Beside Him Oil/canvas (198x150cm 77x59in) London 2000
$27 835 - €25 813 - **£17 000** - FF169 323
Portraits of Signora Palma Oil/canvas (99.5x74cm 39x29in) London 1998

BONIVENTO Eugenio 1880-1956 **[31]**
$1 200 - €1 244 - **£720** - FF8 160
Venezia, gondole sul Canal Grande Olio/tavola (20x24cm 7x9in) Milano 2000
$1 411 - €1 637 - **£1 000** - FF10 735
A Gondola before the Rialto Bridge/The Doges Palace from the Lagoon Watercolour (27x45cm 10x17in) London 2000

BONNAR James King 1885-1961 **[29]**
$1 600 - €1 828 - **£1 126** - FF11 989
«Dorset Farm» Oil/board (40x50cm 16x20in) Pittsfield MA 2001

BONNARD Pierre 1867-1947 **[1335]**
$240 000 - €278 469 - **£165 696** - FF1 826 640
Le jardin des tuileries Oil/canvas (50x66cm 19x25in) New-York 2000
$100 000 - €94 663 - **£62 110** - FF620 950
La dame en brun Oil/paper/panel (44x21.5cm 17x8in) New-York 1999
$3 091 - €3 333 - **£2 074** - FF21 865
Women leaning on a Rock Bronze (H18cm H7in) Stockholm 2000
$2 500 - €2 232 - **£1 531** - FF14 640
Sketch of a Woman Pencil/paper (16x17cm 6x6in) New-York 1999
$1 291 - €1 118 - **£783** - FF7 332
«Les peintres Graveurs» Farblithographie (64.7x47.7cm 25x18in) München 1998

BONNARDEL Alexandre-François 1867-1942 **[32]**
$1 176 - €991 - **£694** - FF6 500
Nature morte aux oranges et au pichet Huile/toile (41x32.5cm 16x12in) Grenoble 1998

BONNART Jean Baptiste Henri 1678-1726 **[4]**
$737 - €716 - **£459** - FF4 695
Die vier Jahreszeiten Radierung (19.8x30.1cm 7x11in) Berlin 1999

BONNAT Léon 1834-1922 **[67]**
$1 420 - €1 524 - **£950** - FF10 000
Portrait d'une élégance à la rose Huile/toile (73x60cm 28x23in) Paris 2000
$1 244 - €1 464 - **£891** - FF9 600
Tête d'homme barbu Huile/toile (40.5x36.5cm 15x14in) Besançon 2001

BONNEAUD Jacques 1898-1971 **[41]**
$438 - €547 - **£276** - FF3 000
«Les filles du Rhône» de Jean Paul Paulin avec Annie Ducaux Affiche (160x240cm 62x94in) Paris 2000

BONNEFOIT Alain 1937 **[229]**
$2 585 - €2 973 - **£1 825** - FF19 500
Catherine Huile/toile (46x38cm 18x14in) Barbizon 2001
$431 - €503 - **£299** - FF3 300
Laura Huile/papier (20x31cm 7x12in) Le Havre 2000
$539 - €579 - **£361** - FF3 800
Barbara Aquarelle/papier (35x27cm 13x10in) Coulommiers 2000
$149 - €145 - **£92** - FF950
Grand nu allongé Lithographie (61x82cm 24x32in) Orléans 1999

BONNEFOY Henri-Arthur 1839-1917 **[33]**
$1 502 - €1 677 - **£983** - FF11 000
Un dimanche en Ile-de-France Huile/toile (27.5x46.5cm 10x18in) Fontainebleau 2000

BONNEGRACE Charles Adolphe 1808-1882 **[7]**
$6 000 - €5 758 - **£3 761** - FF37 773
The Harvesters/The Musicians/Two Shepherds Oil/canvas (73x59.5cm 28x23in) New-York 1999

BONNEMAISON de Jules 1809-c.1865 **[15]**
$28 842 - €25 154 - **£17 440** - FF165 000
Halte gourmande d'un équipage devant un relais de chasse Huile/toile (167x135cm 65x53in) Paris 1998

$5 118 - €4 726 - £3 149 - FF31 000
La halte des cavaliers Huile/toile (90.5x72cm
35x28in) Paris 1999

BONNEMAISON Georges ?-1885 [8]
$3 200 - €2 993 - £1 934 - FF19 633
Harvesters in a Landscape Oil/canvas
(27.5x35.5cm 10x13in) New-York 1999

BONNET Anne 1908-1960 [33]
$812 - €793 - £499 - FF5 203
Nu assis et la cour d'école Huile/panneau
(38x46cm 14x18in) Bruxelles 1999
$786 - €942 - £539 - FF6 178
Compositie (composition) Lavis/papier (26x36cm
10x14in) Antwerpen 2000

BONNET Félix Alfred 1847-? [8]
$961 - €1 143 - £685 - FF7 500
Paysage soleil couchant Huile/toile (37x55cm
14x21in) Grenoble 2000

BONNET Léon 1868-1936 [5]
$1 000 - €1 142 - £704 - FF7 493
Sun, Surf and Rocks, Ogunquit, Maine Oil/board
(30x40cm 12x16in) Pittsfield MA 2001

BONNET Louis Marin, Tennob 1736-1793 [103]
$491 - €562 - £338 - FF3 689
Tulipe, rose jaune, fleur des champs Print in
colors (31.8x22cm 12x8in) München 2000

BONNET Rudolf 1895-1978 [149]
$8 790 - €8 857 - £5 479 - FF58 098
A Sawah with the Gunung Agung Oil/canvas
(64x53cm 25x20in) Singapore 2000
$7 125 - €5 978 - £4 180 - FF39 216
«Kairovan» Pastel (78x74cm 30x29in) Singapore 1998

BONNIER Eva 1857-1909 [14]
$1 638 - €1 559 - £1 024 - FF10 228
Orientalisk kvinna Oil/canvas (50x61cm 19x24in)
Stockholm 1999
$15 470 - €15 183 - £9 594 - FF99 593
Le jardin du Luxembourg Oil/panel (24x32.5cm
9x12in) Stockholm 1999

BONNIÉR Olle 1925 [195]
$62 682 - €72 732 - £43 276 - FF477 090
Big American Hot Oil/panel (122x122cm 48x48in)
Stockholm 2000
$2 354 - €2 637 - £1 636 - FF17 299
Komposition Oil/panel (42x123cm 16x48in)
Stockholm 2001
$208 - €236 - £142 - FF1 551
Komposition Mixed media (20x25cm 7x9in)
Stockholm 2000
$503 - €588 - £345 - FF3 855
Kosmisk komposition Mixed media/paper
(105x75cm 41x29in) Stockholm 2000
$169 - €181 - £115 - FF1 186
Figurkomposition Serigraph in colors (81x121cm
31x47in) Stockholm 2001

BONNIN GUERIN Francisco 1874-1963 [11]
$2 520 - €2 403 - £1 560 - FF15 760
Tenerife Acuarela/papel (47x38cm 18x14in) Madrid
1999

BONNIN MIRANDA Francisco 1911-1963 [2]
$513 - €571 - £342 - FF3 743
Marina Acuarela/papel (33x48cm 12x18in) Madrid
2000

BONNOTTE J. XX [2]
$3 840 - €3 871 - £2 400 - FF25 389
**Laissez moi, Madame, vous faire des skis sur
mesure** Watercolour/paper (13x19cm 5x7in) London
2000

BONO dal Eduardo 1841-1915 [3]
$2 616 - €2 521 - £1 616 - FF16 534
Waenhuiskrans, Visserhuisies Watercolour
(37.5x55cm 14x21in) Johannesburg 1999

BONO Primitif c.1890-? [18]
$1 017 - €1 067 - £637 - FF7 000
Le cortège royal à Fès Huile/panneau (34x25cm
13x9in) Paris 2000

BONOME Santiago Rodrigues 1901 [6]
$5 244 - €5 996 - £3 600 - FF39 334
A Guitarist and two Singers Bronze (61x36cm
24x14in) London 2000

BONOMI Alberto 1876-1914 [4]
$4 500 - €4 665 - £2 700 - FF30 600
Malinconia Olio/tela (82x138cm 32x54in) Milano
1999

BONOMI Joseph I 1739-1808 [7]
$13 448 - €14 436 - £9 000 - FF94 694
**Design of a Glass Frame and Commode for Mrs
Montagu's Bed Chamber** Watercolour (51.5x31cm
20x12in) London 2000

BONOMI Joseph II 1796-1878 [2]
$5 678 - €6 095 - £3 800 - FF39 982
Figure studies Pencil/paper (26x35cm 10x13in)
London 2000

BONONI Carlo 1569-1632 [14]
$616 - €571 - £380 - FF3 746
Ceiling Decoration: A Saint and Angels Ink
(19.5x28.5cm 7x11in) London 1999

BONQUART Adolphe Carbon 1864-1915 [4]
$2 431 - €2 211 - £1 464 - FF14 500
Paquebot «La Touraine» Aquarelle/papier
(147x228cm 58x90in) Marseille 1998

BONSI Giovanni XIV [2]
$90 300 - €101 741 - £63 560 - FF667 380
«Madonna con Bambino, angeli e Santi...»
Tempera (45x25cm 17x9in) Wien 2001

**BONSTETTEN-MESTRAL von Karl Gustav
Salomon** 1807-1886 [5]
$4 368 - €4 044 - £2 674 - FF26 527
Neapolitanische Landschaft mit Staffagefiguren
Öl/Leinwand (45.5x63cm 17x24in) Bern 1999

BONTECOU Lee 1931 [22]
$250 - €281 - £174 - FF1 840
Untitled Lithograph (104x70cm 40x27in) Washington
2001

BONTJES VAN BEEK Olga 1896-1995 [11]
$1 112 - €1 278 - £785 - FF8 384
Sommerabend an der Wümme Oil/panel (39x35cm
15x13in) Bremen 2001

BONVICINO MORETTO DA BRESCIA Alessandro
1498-1554 [3]
$425 000 - €440 578 - £255 000 - FF2 890 000
Venere e Amore Olio/tela (118x210cm 46x82in)
Milano 2000

BONVIN François 1817-1887 [93]
$9 333 - €10 214 - £6 452 - FF67 000
Nature morte au brie Huile/toile (55x66cm 21x25in)
Aubagne 2001

$2 029 - €2 269 - £1 412 - FF14 883
Stilleven met booking en citroen Oil/canvas
(21.5x26.5cm 8x10in) Amsterdam 2001
$33 286 - €33 539 - £20 746 - FF220 000
Intérieur de l'abbaye d'Aramont, à Verberie
Encre (31x28cm 12x11in) Paris 2000

BONVOISIN Catherine H. Lassare 1788-? [4]
$18 000 - €20 161 - £12 506 - FF132 249
**Portrait of a Man seated before a Chalk Board
and Desk** Oil/canvas (118x90cm 46x35in) New-York
2001

BONVOISIN Joseph 1896-1960 [53]
$442 - €446 - £275 - FF2 926
Vue de Callas, Var Huile/panneau (28.5x36cm
11x14in) Liège 2000
$116 - €111 - £72 - FF731
Adolescence anémiée Burin (27.5x19cm 10x7in)
Liège 1999

BONZAGNI Aroldo 1887-1918 [35]
$8 800 - €11 403 - £6 600 - FF74 800
Le suffragette non sono molte belle Tempera/car-
tone (50x42cm 19x16in) Torino 2000
$1 500 - €1 555 - £900 - FF10 200
La pace è stata firmata oggi Inchiostro (10x8cm
3x3in) Torino 2001

BONZI (IL GOBBO DA CORTONA) Pietro Paolo
c.1575-1636 [10]
$17 331 - €20 203 - £12 000 - FF132 522
**An Extensive River Landscape with the Finding
of Moses** Oil/canvas (53.5x71cm 21x27in) London
2000
$263 - €307 - £185 - FF2 012
Tobias und der Engel Radierung (15.5x23cm 6x9in)
Berlin 2001

BOODLE Walter XIX-XX [15]
$1 280 - €1 458 - £900 - FF9 561
Woods near Arundel Oil/panel (42x32cm 16x12in)
London 2001

BOOG Carle Michel 1877-1968 [6]
$1 900 - €2 207 - £1 335 - FF14 480
Garden Path Oil/canvas (41x30cm 16x12in) New-
York 2001

BOOGAARD Willem Jacobus 1842-1887 [40]
$6 725 - €6 197 - £4 050 - FF40 650
Attelage à la carrière Huile/toile (40x75cm 15x29in)
Antwerpen 1999
$2 788 - €3 176 - £1 927 - FF20 836
Stable Interior with Horses and a Dog Oil/panel
(16x21.5cm 6x8in) Amsterdam 2000

BOOGAERT Adriaen Geurtsz. 1586-c.1628 [1]
$8 044 - €6 844 - £4 800 - FF44 896
**An owl on a perch with dead birds in a landsca-
pe** Oil/canvas (72.5x103.5cm 28x40in) London 1998

BOOK Max Mikael 1953 [99]
$2 717 - €3 177 - £1 643 - FF15 545
«I Multan» Mixed media (120x126cm 47x49in)
Stockholm 1998
$1 104 - €1 211 - £733 - FF7 943
Medieval Mixed media (41.5x60cm 16x23in)
Stockholm 2000
$636 - €642 - £397 - FF4 209
Gedod Mixed media (24x36cm 9x14in) Stockholm
2000
$1 794 - €1 687 - £1 111 - FF11 065
Utan titel Mixed media/paper (120x138cm 47x54in)
Stockholm 1999

BOOK R. XX [1]
$4 000 - €4 576 - £2 781 - FF30 014
Peaceful Hour Oil/canvas (73x91cm 29x36in)
Cincinnati OH 2000

BOOM Charles 1858-1939 [50]
$566 - €544 - £353 - FF3 571
Scholar at his writing Desk Oil/canvas (39x47cm
15x18in) Amsterdam 1999

BOON Jan 1882-1975 [16]
$7 355 - €7 260 - £4 472 - FF47 625
Magnolias in Ginger Pot Oil/canvas (39x47cm
15x18in) Amsterdam 2000

BOONE Daniel van Boon c.1630-c.1700 [2]
$3 100 - €3 430 - £2 153 - FF22 500
Scène d'intérieur d'auberge Huile/toile (32x29cm
12x11in) Versailles 2001

BOONE Elmer L. 1881-1952 [2]
$4 100 - €4 662 - £2 812 - FF30 581
Crown Point, Colorado Oil/board (30x50cm
12x20in) Columbia SC 2000

BOONEN Arnold 1669-1729 [22]
$22 089 - €24 767 - £15 000 - FF162 460
**Young Boy taking fruit from a blue-and-white
porcelain bowl** Oil/canvas (55x42cm 21x16in)
London 2000
$6 653 - €6 647 - £4 160 - FF43 600
**Eine alte Frau beim Anzünden der Lanterne/Der
Leser** Öl/Leinwand (42x34cm 16x13in) Köln 1999

BOONEN Elias 1860-1931 [3]
$558 - €544 - £343 - FF3 571
Voorstraatshaven met Nieuwbrug Oil/board
(27x35cm 10x13in) Dordrecht 1999

BOONZAIER Gregoire 1909 [268]
$4 748 - €5 592 - £3 283 - FF36 684
Bo Kaap, Cape Town Oil/board (45x60cm 17x23in)
Cape Town 2000
$3 270 - €3 151 - £2 020 - FF20 668
Street Scene Oil/board (22x38cm 8x14in)
Johannesburg 1999
$1 146 - €1 019 - £702 - FF6 685
Figures on a Country Lane Pastel/paper
(28x42.5cm 11x16in) Johannesburg 1999
$178 - €210 - £123 - FF1 375
Moonflowers Linocut (35x24cm 13x9in) Cape Town
2000

BOOTH Edward C. 1821-? [27]
$481 - €425 - £290 - FF2 785
Low Tide Watercolour/paper (25x34cm 10x13in)
Whitby, Yorks 1998

BOOTH Franklin 1874-1948 [13]
$3 750 - €3 497 - £2 326 - FF22 939
Autumn Leaves Watercolour (39x28.5cm 15x11in)
New-York 1999

BOOTH James William 1867-1953 [50]
$2 430 - €2 749 - £1 700 - FF18 032
Three horse Team Oil/canvas (38x51cm 14x20in)
Kirkby-Lonsdale, Cumbria 2001
$631 - €682 - £420 - FF4 476
A Grey working Horse in Harness Oil/board
(23x30cm 9x11in) Scarborough, North-Yorshire 2000
$977 - €948 - £620 - FF6 219
The plough Team Watercolour (32.5x47.5cm
12x18in) West-Yorkshire 1999

BOOTH Kate E. XIX [12]
🖌 $814 - €909 - £550 - FF5 960
At Low Tide Watercolour/paper (33x48cm 13x19in)
Aylsham, Norfolk 2000

BOOTH Peter 1940 [62]
😊 $20 013 - €21 483 - £13 394 - FF140 917
Winter Landscape Oil/canvas (167x243cm 65x95in)
Sydney 2000
😊 $3 655 - €4 134 - £2 572 - FF27 117
Untitled Oil/canvas (50.5x76cm 19x29in) Malvern,
Victoria 2001
🖌 $582 - €641 - £386 - FF4 206
Man with Exploding Stomach Charcoal
(11.5x11.5cm 4x4in) Woollahra, Sydney 2000

BOOTH S. Lawson ?-1928 [26]
😊 $4 998 - €4 600 - £3 000 - FF30 174
Conway Castle from the Estuary Oil/canvas
(61x91.5cm 24x36in) Glamorgan 1999

BOOTH T. Dwight act.1830-1857 [1]
🖾 $1 400 - €1 387 - £849 - FF9 098
The Trappers Last Shot, After W.T Ranney
Engraving (45x60cm 17x23in) New-York 2000

BOOTY Frederick William 1840-1924 [55]
🖌 $1 046 - €1 123 - £700 - FF7 365
Runswick Bay Watercolour (31.5x81.5cm 12x32in)
West-Yorshire 2000

BOR Jan 1910-1994 [13]
😊 $4 113 - €4 084 - £2 570 - FF26 789
Still Life with a Bottle, Books and a Plate
Oil/canvas (70x65cm 27x25in) Amsterdam 1999
😊 $27 475 - €32 672 - £19 584 - FF214 315
Zelfportret in geel jasje Oil/canvas (41x31cm
16x12in) Amsterdam 2000

BOR Pál 1889-1982 [3]
😊 $1 815 - €2 063 - £1 265 - FF13 530
Femme et son enfant devant le lac Balaton
Huile/toile (100x79.5cm 39x31in) Budapest 2001

BORBOTTONI Fabio 1820-1901 [10]
😊 $450 - €466 - £270 - FF3 060
**Paesaggio di fiume con cascata/Paesagio con
tabernacolo** Olio/cartone (10x17cm 3x6in) Prato 1999

BORCHARD Edmond 1848-1922 [7]
😊 $8 295 - €7 165 - £5 010 - FF47 000
Chasse à courre au sanglier Huile/toile
(81x100.5cm 31x39in) Barbizon 1998

BORCHERT Erich 1907-1944 [19]
🖌 $775 - €767 - £483 - FF5 030
Häuser D.Industrie IX Watercolour (26.5x36cm
10x14in) Berlin 1999

BORCHT van der Lazarus XVII [3]
😊 $25 360 - €25 154 - £15 774 - FF165 000
Orphé charmant les animaux Huile/panneau
(67x60cm 26x23in) Lille 1999

BORCHT van der Pieter II 1545-1608 [12]
🖾 $1 115 - €1 329 - £795 - FF8 720
**Landschaft mit einem Schloss, nach Cornelis
Cort** Radierung (14.7x20.2cm 5x7in) Berlin 2000

BORDALLO Manuel 1920-1996 [4]
🖌 $549 - €541 - £333 - FF3 546
Sitges Acuarela/papel (50x71cm 19x27in) Barcelona
2000

BORDALO-PINHEIRO Columbano 1857-1929 [4]
😊 $266 600 - €309 075 - £186 000 - FF2 027 400
O Serão Oleo/tabla (29x45cm 11x17in) Lisboa 2001

🖌 $8 600 - €9 970 - £6 000 - FF65 400
Paisagem com duas figuras e cáes
Acuarela/papel (47.5x36cm 18x14in) Lisboa 2001

BORDALO-PINHERO Raphaël 1847-1905 [1]
😊 $9 900 - €10 967 - £6 380 - FF71 940
Menina sentada Oleo/cartón (37x24.5cm 14x9in)
Lisboa 2000

BORDE Henri 1888-1958 [21]
🖌 $151 - €152 - £94 - FF1 000
Femme endormie Crayons couleurs/papier
(20x25.5cm 7x10in) Tarbes 2000

BORDES Léonard 1898-1969 [261]
😊 $834 - €915 - £566 - FF6 000
Bord de rivière Huile/panneau (50x61cm 19x24in)
Calais 2000
🖌 $170 - €198 - £117 - FF1 300
Paysage Aquarelle/papier (24x36cm 9x14in) Le Havre
2000

BORDIGNON Noè 1841-1920 [13]
😊 $15 000 - €14 692 - £9 666 - FF96 372
Girl resting in a Field Oil/canvas (66x99.5cm
25x39in) New-York 1999
😊 $4 250 - €4 957 - £2 984 - FF32 517
Child mending Oil/panel (30x40cm 12x16in) Dedham
MA 2000

BORDONE Pâris 1500-1571 [13]
😊 $600 000 - €658 287 - £398 580 - FF4 318 080
**The Holy Family with Saint John the Baptist in
an Extensive Landscape** Oil/canvas/panel
(102x153.5cm 40x60in) New-York 2000
😊 $30 359 - €35 354 - £21 000 - FF231 909
Salvator Mundi Oil/canvas (61x50.5cm 24x19in)
London 2000

BORDUAS Paul Émile 1905-1960 [74]
😊 $51 210 - €49 552 - £31 582 - FF325 042
Noeuds et colonnes (knots and Columns)
Oil/canvas (81.5x99.5cm 32x39in) Toronto 1999
😊 $10 105 - €11 787 - £7 218 - FF77 320
Synthèse d'un paysage de St.Hilaire Huile/toile
(25x33cm 9x12in) Montréal 2000
🖌 $566 - €661 - £400 - FF4 338
Danse Irregulière Watercolour/paper (26x35cm
10x13in) Channel-Islands 2000

BOREIN John Edward 1872-1945 [483]
😊 $50 000 - €42 719 - £30 015 - FF280 220
Cutting Back a Steer Oil/canvas (49.5x76cm
19x29in) New-York 1998
🖌 $4 800 - €4 565 - £2 914 - FF29 947
Cowboy on Horseback Watercolour, gouache/paper
(18x13.5cm 7x5in) Beverly-Hills CA 1999
🖾 $3 000 - €2 727 - £1 806 - FF17 889
Little Trail Herd Etching (17x25cm 7x10in) Hayden
ID 1998

BORELY Charles 1817-1881 [1]
😊 $5 716 - €6 403 - £4 006 - FF42 000
Angélique et Médor Huile/toile (92.5x73.5cm
36x28in) Paris 2001

BOREN James 1921-1990 [29]
😊 $9 500 - €10 787 - £6 600 - FF70 757
Sms Ranch Yearlings Oil/canvas (60x91cm 24x36in)
Dallas 2001
😊 $2 200 - €2 586 - £1 525 - FF16 960
In the Horse Corral Oil/canvas (30.5x23cm 12x9in)
Beverly-Hills CA 2000
😊 $6 050 - €6 494 - £4 048 - FF42 598
Cowboys at Log Cabin Watercolour/paper (49x76cm
19x30in) Houston TX 2000

BORENSTEIN Samuel 1908-1969 [36]
🌀 **$4 054** - €3 906 - **£2 517** - FF25 620
Chrysanthemums Oil/canvas (61x51cm 24x20in)
Toronto 1999

BORER Albert, Al 1910 [7]
📜 **$424** - €372 - **£257** - FF2 441
Brunex Poster (127x89cm 50x35in) New-York 1999

BORES Francisco 1898-1972 [628]
🌀 **$52 086** - €50 694 - **£32 000** - FF332 531
Intérieur Inglés Oil/canvas (145x113cm 57x44in)
London 1999
🌀 **$21 000** - €18 019 - **£12 600** - FF118 200
Composition sur fond ocre Oleo/lienzo (65x81cm
25x31in) Madrid 1998
🌀 **$4 860** - €5 406 - **£3 420** - FF35 460
Figures Oleo/lienzo (22x27cm 8x10in) Madrid 2001
✏️ **$3 539** - €3 506 - **£2 145** - FF23 000
Enfant à la lecture Aquarelle/papier (26.5x34cm
10x13in) Paris 2000
📜 **$194** - €183 - **£133** - FF1 418
Carreta de bueyes Grabado (38x49cm 14x19in)
Madrid 2000

BORG Axel 1847-1916 [34]
🌀 **$3 706** - €3 958 - **£2 527** - FF25 963
Landskap med älg vid vattendrag Oil/canvas
(65x95cm 25x37in) Stockholm 2001
🌀 **$417** - €462 - **£289** - FF3 032
Hästhuvud i profil Oil/panel (22x13cm 8x5in)
Stockholm 2001

BORG Carl Oscar 1879-1947 [131]
🌀 **$15 000** - €17 629 - **£10 399** - FF115 641
The Painted Desert Oil/canvas/board (40.5x51cm
15x20in) Beverly-Hills CA 2000
🌀 **$8 000** - €9 402 - **£5 546** - FF61 675
San Miguel Island Oil/canvas (23x35.5cm 9x13in)
Beverly-Hills CA 2000
✏️ **$3 200** - €3 761 - **£2 218** - FF24 670
Hopi Shooyokos Katchina Graphite (25.5x20.5cm
10x8in) Beverly-Hills CA 2000
📜 **$1 900** - €2 234 - **£1 317** - FF14 651
Horace Se-I-Se-Ta Woodcut (25.5x22cm 10x8in)
Beverly-Hills CA 2000

BORGEAUD Georges 1913-1998 [61]
🌀 **$4 176** - €4 026 - **£2 574** - FF26 408
Griechische Strassenszene Öl/Leinwand
(65x54cm 25x21in) Bern 1999
🌀 **$2 570** - €2 477 - **£1 584** - FF16 251
Gasse in Rabat Öl/Leinwand (30x41cm 11x16in)
Bern 1999

BORGEAUD Marius 1861-1924 [27]
🌀 **$53 244** - €57 386 - **£35 703** - FF376 425
Homme au canotier dans un bistro Öl/Leinwand
(65x54cm 25x21in) Zürich 2000

BORGELLA Frédéric XIX-XX [57]
🌀 **$2 664** - €2 470 - **£1 657** - FF16 200
**Jeune fille jouant au ballon/La danseuse au
foulard** Huile/toile (60x72cm 23x28in) Paris 1999
🌀 **$1 815** - €1 829 - **£1 131** - FF12 000
La Lecture Huile/toile (38.5x31.5cm 15x12in) Paris
2000

BORGEN Fredrik 1852-1907 [18]
🌀 **$2 625** - €3 121 - **£1 870** - FF20 475
Tre mennesker i robåt Oil/canvas (110x86cm
43x33in) Oslo 2000

BORGES Jacobo 1931 [35]
🌀 **$3 400** - €3 171 - **£2 200** - FF20 800
Paisaje Oleo/lienzo (33.5x41cm 13x16in) Caracas
1999
✏️ **$660** - €677 - **£440** - FF4 444
J.V.Gómez Tinta china/papel (24.5x16.5cm 9x6in)
Caracas 2000

BORGES Phil 1950 [6]
📷 **$1 700** - €1 451 - **£1 016** - FF9 518
Lhasa, Tibet, Ahidha Gelatin silver print
(40.5x40.5cm 15x15in) San-Francisco CA 1998

BORGES SALAS Francisco 1901-1984 [5]
✏️ **$3 858** - €4 573 - **£2 724** - FF30 000
Trois personnages portant des cruches
Aquarelle (34.5x24cm 13x9in) Paris 2000

BORGET Auguste 1808-1877 [14]
🌀 **$71 680** - €60 980 - **£42 760** - FF400 000
**Pont chinois près d'Amoy, le jour de la fête des
lanternes** Huile/toile (55x45.5cm 21x17in) Paris 1998
🌀 **$6 072** - €5 183 - **£3 631** - FF34 000
**Mausolée au bord de l'eau/Palmeraie aux
abords de la cité** Huile/toile (15x21.5cm 5x8in) Paris
1998
✏️ **$3 041** - €3 529 - **£2 100** - FF23 150
Ships off the Faulkian Coast Wash (19.5x28cm
7x11in) London 2000

BORGHESE DI PIERO 1427-1463 [1]
🌀 **$140 000** - €133 640 - **£87 472** - FF876 624
**The Trinity with a Donor Figure and Saint John
the Baptist** Tempera/panel (30x21.5cm 11x8in) New-
York 1999

BORGHESE Franz 1941 [200]
🌀 **$2 100** - €2 177 - **£1 260** - FF14 280
Passeggiata con cagnolino Olio/tela (50x40cm
19x15in) Vercelli 1999
🌀 **$1 350** - €1 399 - **£810** - FF9 180
Il dottor Guarisciutto Olio/tela (35x25cm 13x9in)
Vercelli 1999
🗿 **$850** - €881 - **£510** - FF5 780
Cavaliere e dama Bronzo (H27.5cm H10in) Vercelli
2001
✏️ **$375** - €389 - **£225** - FF2 550
Il medico e la moglie Acquarello (35.5x25cm
13x9in) Vercelli 2001

BORGHESE Ippolito XVII [1]
🌀 **$9 217** - €7 842 - **£5 500** - FF51 443
The penitent Magdalen Oil/canvas (77.5x61cm
30x24in) London 1998

BORGHESI Giambattista 1790-1846 [2]
📜 **$2 796** - €3 068 - **£1 899** - FF20 123
Le principali Vedute di Venezia Lithographie
(28.5x40cm 11x15in) Berlin 2000

BORGHI Ambrogio c.1848-1887 [2]
🗿 **$11 207** - €12 030 - **£7 500** - FF78 912
Young Woman in Fashionable Costume Marble
(H195cm H76in) London 2000

BORGHT ven der Jan XVIII [1]
🌀 **$16 081** - €13 984 - **£9 698** - FF91 728
Blomsterstilleben Oil/canvas (100x77cm 39x30in)
Stockholm 1998

BORGIANNI Guido 1915 [63]
🌀 **$600** - €622 - **£360** - FF4 080
Sabato pomeriggio Olio/tela (50x70cm 19x27in)
Firenze 2001

BORGIANNI Orazio 1578-1616 **[5]**
- $59 772 - €64 160 - **£40 000** - FF420 864
  Saint John the Baptist in the Wilderness Oil/canvas (143.5x101cm 56x39in) London 2000
- $195 816 - €182 028 - **£120 000** - FF1 194 024
  The Holy Family with Saint Anne Oil/canvas (103x81.5cm 40x32in) London 1998

BORGIOTTI Mario 1906-1977 **[17]**
- $750 - €777 - **£450** - FF5 100
  Villaggio di pescatori a Punta Spina Olio/tela (40x80cm 15x31in) Milano 1999
- $1 400 - €1 451 - **£840** - FF9 520
  Paese sul mare Olio/tela (25x60cm 9x23in) Milano 1999

BORGLIND Stig 1892-1965 **[209]**
- $186 - €209 - **£129** - FF1 369
  «Akropolis» Etching (32x31.5cm 12x12in) Uppsala 2001

BORGLUM John Gutzon La Mothe 1867-1941 **[17]**
- $20 000 - €23 137 - **£14 056** - FF152 424
  Bust of Abraham Lincoln Bronze (H96.5cm H37in) New-York 2001
- $3 000 - €3 526 - **£2 079** - FF23 128
  Nude (Anna Enters) Bronze (H31.5cm H12in) Beverly-Hills CA 2000

BORGLUM Solon Hannibal 1868-1922 **[16]**
- $8 000 - €8 823 - **£5 417** - FF57 872
  Pioneer in a Storm Bronze (H28cm H11in) New-York 2000

BORGOÑA de Juan c.1470-c.1540 **[5]**
- $41 893 - €41 142 - **£26 000** - FF269 877
  Sainte Catherine before the Emperor Maxentius Oil/panel (83.5x61.5cm 32x24in) London 1999

BORGONI Mario 1869-1936 **[19]**
- $668 - €762 - **£464** - FF5 000
  «Capri» Affiche (62x100cm 24x39in) Paris 2001

BORGONUOVO Giovanni 1881-1975 **[4]**
- $12 500 - €12 958 - **£7 500** - FF85 000
  Tramonto decembrino nella campagna milanese Olio/tela (200x250cm 78x98in) Milano 2000
- $4 500 - €3 887 - **£3 000** - FF25 500
  Nel cortile di na cascina Olio/tavola (60x80cm 23x31in) Milano 1999

BORGRAVE Elie 1910-1992 **[29]**
- $418 - €421 - **£260** - FF2 764
  Composition abstraite Huile/toile (73x98cm 28x38in) Bruxelles 2000

BORIE Adolphe 1877-1934 **[10]**
- $3 500 - €3 757 - **£2 342** - FF24 643
  In a Cafe Oil/canvas (56x45.5cm 22x17in) New-York 2000
- $3 500 - €3 248 - **£2 101** - FF21 306
  Study of a Nude Oil/board (23x30cm 9x12in) Milford CT 1999

BORING Wayne 1916 **[4]**
- $700 - €751 - **£468** - FF4 928
  Original Artwork for Superman Daily Strips Ink (19x42cm 7x16in) New-York 2000

BORIONE Bernard 1865-? **[90]**
- $4 500 - €4 171 - **£2 798** - FF27 360
  The Duet Oil/panel (55x44cm 22x17in) New-Orleans LA 1999
- $664 - €762 - **£454** - FF5 000
  La lecture au coin du feu Huile/panneau (19x14cm 7x5in) Soissons 2000

- $662 - €732 - **£459** - FF4 800
  Scène d'intérieur au XVIIIe siècle Aquarelle/papier (46x37cm 18x14in) Paris 2001

BORISOV Gregory 1899-1942 **[3]**
- $2 386 - €2 013 - **£1 400** - FF13 207
  Two Worlds Poster (127x94cm 50x37in) London 1998

BORISSOW-MUSSATOW Viktor 1870-1905 **[4]**
- $14 508 - €15 369 - **£9 796** - FF100 812
  Le réservoir Tempera/toile (117x145cm 46x57in) Bruxelles 2001

BÖRJE Gideon 1891-1965 **[140]**
- $714 - €701 - **£442** - FF4 596
  Badande Olio/canvas (54x73cm 21x28in) Stockholm 1999
- $247 - €268 - **£156** - FF1 759
  Folkungagatan och Londonviadukten Pastel/paper (31x41cm 12x16in) Stockholm 2000

BÖRJESSON Agneta 1827-1900 **[9]**
- $2 000 - €2 592 - **£1 500** - FF17 000
  Figure in un interno Olio/tela (35x45cm 13x17in) Roma 2001

BORLA Hector 1937 **[4]**
- $4 650 - €4 505 - **£2 850** - FF29 550
  El príncipe Carlos, según Alonso Sánchez Coello Oleo/lienzo (60x70cm 23x27in) Madrid 1999
- $3 500 - €3 405 - **£2 154** - FF22 338
  Variación sobre la grande baigneuse Oil/canvas (45x35cm 17x13in) New-York 1999

BORLAND Christine 1965 **[1]**
- $11 083 - €10 697 - **£7 000** - FF70 166
  Extremities Mixed media (22x40cm 8x15in) London 1999

BORLASE Nancy 1914 **[12]**
- $2 163 - €2 045 - **£1 342** - FF13 415
  Pioneers Oil/board (24.5x36.5cm 9x14in) Malvern, Victoria 1999

BORM Abraham ?-1668 **[3]**
- $18 000 - €17 182 - **£11 246** - FF112 708
  Young Man with a Fortune Teller Oil/panel (43.5x33.5cm 17x13in) New-York 1999

BORMAN Johannes c.1630-c.1670 **[8]**
- $28 278 - €27 441 - **£17 820** - FF185 000
  Nature morte à la coupe de fruits Huile/panneau (40.5x50cm 15x19in) Paris 1999

BORMANN Emma 1887-1974 **[19]**
- $180 - €179 - **£112** - FF1 173
  München, Rodeln im Garten Woodcut (28.1x45cm 11x17in) Berlin 1999

BORN Adolf 1930 **[16]**
- $1 127 - €1 066 - **£702** - FF6 992
  Une gaie compagnie Aquarelle/papier (48x34cm 18x13in) Praha 2000
- $187 - €178 - **£117** - FF1 165
  Départ de vieux magicien Lithographie couleurs (32x43.5cm 12x17in) Praha 2001

BORNEMISZA Geza 1884-1966 **[6]**
- $17 640 - €16 968 - **£10 920** - FF111 300
  View of a Village Oil/canvas (63.5x70cm 25x27in) Budapest 1999

BÖRNER Franz August 1861-1929 **[2]**
- $973 - €1 022 - **£614** - FF6 707
  Flötenkonzert Friedrich des Grossen in Sanssouci, nach Ad.von Menzel Radierung (64.3x93.5cm 25x36in) Braunschweig 2000

B

BORNSCHLEGEL de Victor 1820-? **[3]**
🖼 **$9 600** - €9 532 - **£6 000** - FF62 524
Tea time in the artist's Studio Oil/panel (40x32.5cm 15x12in) London 1999

BORODULIN Lev 1923 **[36]**
📷 **$1 300** - €1 222 - **£805** - FF8 018
Ornament of Sport, Moscow Silver print (31x22cm 12x9in) New-York 1999

BOROFSKY Jonathan 1942 **[98]**
🗿 **$22 000** - €23 615 - **£14 722** - FF154 902
Man with a Briefcase Metal (226x90cm 88x35in) Beverly-Hills CA 2000
$2 784 - €2 806 - **£1 735** - FF18 405
The Moon in my Mind Mischtechnik/Papier (34x24.8cm 13x9in) Zürich 2000
🖼 **$2 100** - €2 011 - **£1 297** - FF13 192
Stickman Color lithograph (133x96cm 52x37in) New-York 1999

BOROMISZA Tibor 1880-1960 **[2]**
$2 220 - €2 332 - **£1 380** - FF15 300
Marché hebdomadaire de Nagybanya Technique mixte/papier (60x50cm 23x19in) Budapest 2000

BOROS Gyula 1951 **[18]**
🖼 **$2 032** - €1 753 - **£1 227** - FF11 500
Fruits sur un entablement Huile/panneau (40x50cm 15x19in) Marseille 1999

BOROWSKI Waclaw 1885-1954 **[18]**
🖼 **$6 897** - €7 566 - **£4 581** - FF49 632
Travail: hommes construisant une maison Oil/canvas (80x90.5cm 31x35in) Warszawa 2000
$3 425 - €3 453 - **£2 136** - FF22 649
Nature morte avec des pommes Oil/canvas (46.5x33.5cm 18x13in) Warszawa 2000
✏ **$1 135** - €1 067 - **£705** - FF7 001
Fille avec les yeux mi-clos Pastel/paper (44.5x50cm 17x19in) Warszawa 1999

BOROWSKY G. XVIII **[1]**
🖼 **$1 228** - €1 126 - **£750** - FF7 383
Prospeckt der heutigen Stadt Jerusalem Engraving (37x50cm 14x19in) London 1999

BORRA Pompeo 1898-1973 **[119]**
$1 600 - €2 073 - **£1 200** - FF13 600
Ritratto di donna Olio/tela (70x50cm 27x19in) Milano 2001
$440 - €570 - **£330** - FF5 000
Vaso di fiori Olio/masonite (32x23.5cm 12x9in) Milano 2001
✏ **$700** - €726 - **£420** - FF4 760
Figure sulla spiaggia Acquarello (25.5x40.5cm 10x15in) Prato 2001

BORRACK John Leo 1933 **[29]**
✏ **$559** - €520 - **£345** - FF3 410
The Long Valley, Strath Creek Watercolour/paper (53x73cm 20x28in) Melbourne 1999

BORRANI Odoardo 1833-1905 **[28]**
$7 600 - €9 848 - **£5 700** - FF64 600
Gentiluomo Olio/tela (42x34cm 16x13in) Prato 2001

BORRAS Jorge 1952 **[106]**
🖼 **$1 341** - €1 448 - **£927** - FF9 500
Papillon Bronze (H22cm H8in) La Varenne-Saint-Hilaire 2001

BORREL André 1912 **[23]**
$352 - €396 - **£245** - FF2 600
Scène de plage Huile/panneau (25x32cm 9x12in) Honfleur 2001

BORRELL PLA Ramon 1876-1963 **[5]**
$5 610 - €5 106 - **£3 400** - FF33 490
Caballos de tiro Oleo/lienzo (55x100.5cm 21x39in) Barcelona 1999
$145 - €156 - **£98** - FF1 024
«Retrato de Rembrandt» Oleo/cartón (25.5x19cm 10x7in) Madrid 2001

BORRELL Y PLA Julio 1877-1957 **[34]**
$3 290 - €2 823 - **£1 974** - FF18 518
El primer pitillo Oleo/lienzo (84x65cm 33x25in) Madrid 1998
✏ **$540** - €601 - **£380** - FF3 940
Paisaje de Zaragoza Pastel/papier (70x92cm 27x36in) Barcelona 2001

BORSA Emilio 1857-1931 **[8]**
$40 020 - €34 572 - **£26 680** - FF226 780
Contadinella nel pollaio Olio/tela (182x85cm 71x33in) Pavia 1998
$19 200 - €24 880 - **£14 400** - FF163 200
Figure a villa reale in Monza Olio/tavola (38x71cm 14x27in) Milano 2001

BORSATO Renato 1927 **[20]**
$450 - €466 - **£270** - FF3 060
Villa Mansi Olio/tela (50x75.5cm 19x29in) Prato 2001

BORSELEN van Helena Maria 1867-1947 **[3]**
$4 274 - €3 626 - **£2 578** - FF23 788
Fruitstilleven Oil/panel (27x38cm 10x14in) Den Haag 1998

BORSELEN van Jan Willem 1825-1892 **[63]**
$29 642 - €32 672 - **£19 360** - FF214 315
Landschap met boerenfamilie en hooiwagen Oil/canvas (44x69.5cm 17x27in) Den Haag 2000
$4 537 - €4 311 - **£2 760** - FF28 277
Houtsprokkelaarster op bospad Oil/panel (27x41cm 10x16in) Den Haag 1999
✏ **$161** - €181 - **£113** - FF1 190
Molens bij de Vliet en Boerderijen Pencil/paper (12.5x19.2cm 4x7in) Dordrecht 2001

BORSSOM van Anthonie c.1629-1677 **[22]**
$9 234 - €7 976 - **£5 566** - FF52 319
Cattle and Sheep by a Tree on a River Bank, Shipping beyond Oil/canvas (67x81cm 26x31in) Amsterdam 1999
$3 043 - €3 579 - **£2 181** - FF23 477
Kühe vor Tiefer Landschaft Öl/Leinwand (33x42cm 12x16in) München 2001
$2 200 - €2 357 - **£1 502** - FF15 458
Dog Chasing a Family of Ducks Ink (7x10cm 2x3in) New-York 2001

BORSTEL Reginald Arthur ?-c.1917/18 **[11]**
$894 - €988 - **£620** - FF6 480
The Square-rigged Wiscombe park at Sea Oil/canvas (51x76cm 20x29in) London 2001

BORSZÉKY Frigyes 1880-1955 **[1]**
$8 750 - €9 642 - **£5 750** - FF63 250
Celebration of Youth Oil/canvas (149x230.5cm 58x90in) Budapest 2000

BORTER Klara 1888-1948 **[17]**
🖼 **$866** - €944 - **£600** - FF6 193
«Palace Hotel Wengen» Poster (99x70cm 38x27in) London 2001

BORTIGNONI Giuseppe act.1883-1908 **[12]**
$13 887 - €11 894 - **£8 200** - FF78 020
The Ravenous Cavalier Oil/canvas (37.5x47cm 14x18in) London 1998

$3 200 - €3 071 - **£2 006** - FF20 145
Mending the Cloth Oil/canvas (38x28cm 14x11in)
New-York 1999

BORTNYIK Sándor 1893-1976 **[52]**
$1 020 - €1 153 - **£720** - FF7 560
Mère et son enfant sur le quai Tempera/papier
(58x38cm 22x14in) Budapest 2001
$954 - €818 - **£573** - FF5 365
Bortnyik Album MA/1921 Farbserigraphie
(47.5x39cm 18x15in) Hamburg 1999

BORTOLONI Mattia 1696-1750 **[2]**
$3 500 - €3 628 - **£2 100** - FF23 800
Diana ed Atteone Inchiostro (37.5x24cm 14x9in)
Milano 2000

BORTOLUZZI Camillo, Millo 1868-1933 **[21]**
$13 800 - €11 922 - **£6 900** - FF78 200
Chioggia con popolane Olio/tela (100x60cm
39x23in) Milano 1999
$6 250 - €6 479 - **£3 750** - FF42 500
Fruttivendola Olio/tela (26.5x36.5cm 10x14in)
Venezia 2000

BORTOLUZZI Patrice 1950 **[66]**
$609 - €564 - **£373** - FF3 700
Chalutier rentrant à Palais Belle Ile
Gouache/papier (76x57cm 29x22in) Versailles 1999

BÖRTSÖK Samu 1881-1931 **[13]**
$1 200 - €1 180 - **£750** - FF7 740
Landscape of Nagybánya with the Kereszthegy
Oil/canvas (65x72.5cm 25x28in) Budapest 1999

BORZINO Leopoldina XIX **[5]**
$3 000 - €3 536 - **£2 108** - FF23 195
Golden Child as Sculptor's Model Oil/canvas
(58x25cm 23x10in) New-Orleans LA 2000

BORZONE Luciano 1590-1645 **[3]**
$25 000 - €25 916 - **£15 000** - FF170 000
Giuditta con testa di Oloferne Olio/tela
(123.5x100cm 48x39in) Milano 1999

BOS Cornelis 1506-c.1564 **[3]**
$632 - €613 - **£393** - FF4 024
Der Kampf der Giganten Kupferstich (28.5x42cm
11x16in) Berlin 1999

BOS Henk 1901-1979 **[33]**
$1 300 - €1 508 - **£924** - FF9 892
Still Life Oil/canvas (50x60cm 20x24in) Chicago IL
2000
$1 093 - €1 066 - **£673** - FF6 994
Old Can and Saucer of Plums Oil/canvas
(30x40cm 12x16in) Chicago IL 1999

BOS Jacob act.1549-1580 **[3]**
$1 286 - €1 534 - **£917** - FF10 061
Die Statue des Pyrrhus Kupferstich (46.5x30.3cm
18x11in) Berlin 2000

BOS van den Casper 1634-? **[1]**
$4 525 - €5 336 - **£3 181** - FF35 000
Marine Huile/panneau (30.5x42.5cm 12x16in) Paris
2000

BOS van den Georges 1852-1916 **[22]**
$6 489 - €6 541 - **£4 050** - FF42 903
**Florence Nightingale mit Blick über den
Bosborus auf Konstantinopel** Öl/Leinwand
(92x73.5cm 36x28in) Wien 2000

BOS Willem, Wim 1906-1977 **[38]**
$458 - €499 - **£315** - FF3 274
View of the Rotterdam Harbour Oil/canvas
(50x70cm 19x27in) Amsterdam 2001

$401 - €431 - **£268** - FF2 827
Fishing smack Charcoal (49x69cm 19x27in)
Amsterdam 2000

BOSA Louis 1905-1981 **[63]**
$950 - €1 117 - **£683** - FF7 328
«The Good Samaritan» Oil/masonite (38x48cm
15x19in) Hatfield PA 2001
$550 - €620 - **£380** - FF4 065
«Nuns Skating» Mixed media (21x26cm 8x10in)
Hatfield PA 2000
$120 - €129 - **£81** - FF843
Fantasia, Fontastica Ink (27x35cm 11x14in)
Cleveland OH 2001

BOSAI Kameda 1752-1826 **[2]**
$2 100 - €1 780 - **£1 255** - FF11 673
Horizontal Calligraphy Ink/paper (44x28cm
17x11in) Boston MA 2001

BOSBOOM Herman 1920 **[7]**
$2 058 - €2 269 - **£1 344** - FF14 883
Overslag in een Rotterdamse haven
Watercolour/paper (32x47cm 12x18in) Rotterdam 2000

BOSBOOM Johannes 1817-1891 **[175]**
$17 600 - €16 518 - **£11 000** - FF108 350
Niños jugando delante de una iglesia Oleo/tabla
(55x68cm 21x26in) Madrid 1999
$7 942 - €8 950 - **£5 500** - FF58 709
Synagogue Interior Oil/panel (21.5x51cm 8x20in)
London 2000
$1 717 - €1 951 - **£1 205** - FF12 799
A View of a Town along a River Watercolour/paper
(18x27cm 7x10in) Amsterdam 2001

BOSCARATTI Felice 1721-1807 **[2]**
$22 848 - €19 738 - **£14 428** - FF129 472
**Arlecchino fa il ritratto di una
ragazza/Arlecchino mascherato** Olio/tela
(81x42.5cm 31x16in) Venezia 1999

BOSCH Ernst 1834-1917 **[12]**
$22 980 - €27 152 - **£16 285** - FF178 108
Jäger und Kinder am Lagerfeuer Oil/panel
(23.5x32cm 9x12in) Zürich 2000

BOSCH Florian 1900-1972 **[35]**
$166 - €179 - **£111** - FF1 173
Landschaft Watercolour (49.5x61.5cm 19x24in)
München 2000

BOSCH ROGER Emilio 1894-1980 **[69]**
$4 725 - €5 256 - **£3 237** - FF34 475
Puerto de Barcelona Oleo/lienzo (60x72.5cm
23x28in) Barcelona 2001
$390 - €330 - **£231** - FF2 167
Catedral de Barcelona Acuarela/papel (41x32cm
16x12in) Madrid 1999

BOSCH van den Edouard 1828-1878 **[10]**
$3 321 - €3 743 - **£2 300** - FF24 554
Herding Water Buffalo Oil/canvas (81x101.5cm
31x39in) London 2000

BOSCHAN Walter Josef, Prof. 1911-1984 **[33]**
$119 - €116 - **£75** - FF762
**Sigmund Haffnergasse mit dem Blick auf das
Rathaus** Felt pen/paper (48x34cm 18x13in) Salzburg
1999

BOSCHERI Maurizio 1955 **[4]**
$792 - €897 - **£558** - FF5 886
The Wind Oleo/lienzo (120x80cm 47x31in) Lisboa
2001

BOSCHI Fabrizio 1570-1642 **[2]**

🖋 **$1 674** - €1 426 - **£1 000** - FF9 352
Saints gathering water from a Fountain, Saint Paul and Saint Catherine Red chalk (16x26.5cm 6x10in) London 1998

BOSCOLI Andrea c.1560-1606 **[27]**

🖋 **$3 215** - €3 634 - **£2 170** - FF23 835
Entwurf zu einem Altar Ink (30x38cm 11x14in) Wien 2000

BOSCOVITS Fritz 1871-1965 **[3]**

📜 **$675** - €726 - **£460** - FF4 762
«Art Nouveau Exhibition» Poster (100x70cm 39x27in) Amsterdam 2001

BOSE Nandalal 1882-1966 **[23]**

🖋 **$3 502** - €3 392 - **£2 200** - FF22 247
I cling to this living Raft, my Body Watercolour/paper (20x13cm 7x5in) London 1999

BOSELLI Felice c.1651-1732 **[43]**

⌒ **$35 627** - €40 466 - **£25 000** - FF265 437
Two Turkeys and other dead Birds/Fish, a Seashell, a Crayfish Oil/canvas/board (95x136.5cm 37x53in) London 2001

⌒ **$9 519** - €11 248 - **£6 747** - FF73 785
Grosses Stilleben mit Lilien in einem Tonkrug, Pfirsichen und Birnen Öi/Leinwand (95x73cm 37x28in) Stuttgart 2000

BOSER Karl Friedrich 1809-1881 **[10]**

⌒ **$2 600** - €3 032 - **£1 825** - FF19 891
Portrait of a Girl with Flowers Oil/canvas (66x51cm 25x20in) Boston MA 2000

BOSHAMER Johan Hendrik 1775-1862 **[13]**

⌒ **$5 871** - €6 807 - **£4 159** - FF44 649
Fishing Pinks at a Rough Sea Oil/panel (37x48.5cm 14x19in) Amsterdam 2000

⌒ **$8 119** - €7 714 - **£4 940** - FF50 602
Zeilschepen op woelige zee bij havenhoofd Oil/panel (35x43cm 13x16in) Rotterdam 1999

🖋 **$2 166** - €2 450 - **£1 465** - FF16 073
De pont van Dordtrecht op Zwijndrecht Watercolour (40x50cm 15x19in) Dordrecht 2000

BOSHART Wilhelm 1815-1878 **[3]**

⌒ **$11 268** - €13 081 - **£7 920** - FF85 806
Heimtrieb der Herde am Seeufer Öl/Leinwand (68.5x116cm 26x45in) Wien 2001

BOSHIER Bowen 1964 **[12]**

🖋 **$1 623** - €1 560 - **£1 000** - FF10 233
Leo Pencil/paper (41.5x53cm 16x20in) London 1999

BOSHOFF Adriaan 1935 **[28]**

⌒ **$4 382** - €4 915 - **£3 066** - FF32 242
Figure on a quiet Street Oil/panel (59.5x90cm 23x35in) Cape Town 2001

⌒ **$533** - €500 - **£329** - FF3 277
Landscape with Buildings Oil/canvas/board (16x24cm 6x9in) Johannesburg 1999

BOSIA Agostino 1886-1962 **[8]**

⌒ **$3 200** - €3 611 - **£2 200** - FF27 200
Paesaggio di campagna Olio/tavola (49x59.5cm 19x23in) Torino 2000

⌒ **$2 250** - €2 332 - **£1 350** - FF15 300
Fiori con caraffa Olio/tela (24x33.5cm 9x13in) Torino 2000

BOSIERS René 1875-1927 **[70]**

⌒ **$182** - €173 - **£114** - FF1 138
Église dans un village Huile/toile (28x31cm 11x12in) Antwerpen 1999

BOSIN Francis Blackbear 1921-1980 **[2]**

⌒ **$3 000** - €2 855 - **£1 876** - FF18 727
Roders Mixed media/paper (47.5x32.5cm 18x12in) New-York 1999

BOSIO François Joseph 1768-1845 **[22]**

🗿 **$9 106** - €8 842 - **£5 626** - FF58 000
Henri IV enfant Bronze (217x109x129cm 85x42x50in) Paris 1999

🗿 **$375** - €454 - **£252** - FF2 978
King Henry IV Enfant Bronze (H38cm H14in) Bethesda MD 2000

BOSIO Jean-François 1764-1827 **[24]**

⌒ **$5 100** - €5 900 - **£3 609** - FF38 702
Girl Feeding a Canary Oil/canvas (34x38cm 13x15in) Cleveland OH 2001

🖋 **$6 670** - €7 013 - **£4 186** - FF46 000
Récital de piano Encre (21x30cm 8x11in) Paris 2000

📜 **$798** - €818 - **£504** - FF5 365
Bal de l'opéra, la bouillotte et bal de société Eau-forte (31x45cm 12x17in) Bruxelles 2000

BOSKERCK van Robert Ward 1855-1932 **[31]**

⌒ **$2 200** - €2 579 - **£1 582** - FF18 920
The Banks of the River Oil/canvas (51x66cm 20x25in) New-York 2001

⌒ **$1 500** - €1 399 - **£930** - FF9 174
Boy on a Riverboat Oil/canvas (18.5x22cm 7x8in) New-York 1999

BOSLEY Frederick Andrew 1882-1942 **[7]**

⌒ **$60 000** - €55 393 - **£36 900** - FF363 354
The Letter Oil/canvas (89x91.5cm 35x36in) New-York 1999

BOSMA Wim 1902-1985 **[24]**

⌒ **$2 536** - €2 723 - **£1 697** - FF17 859
The Portugese Istraelian cemetery in Ouderkerk aan de Amstel Oil/canvas (100x112cm 39x44in) Amsterdam 2000

BOSMAN Richard 1944 **[49]**

⌒ **$5 800** - €5 423 - **£3 575** - FF35 573
Night Fall Oil/canvas (137x106.5cm 53x41in) New-York 1999

📜 **$400** - €429 - **£267** - FF2 816
Falling Man Woodcut in colors (143x106cm 56x42in) Bolton MA 2000

BOSS Eduard 1873-1958 **[49]**

⌒ **$854** - €816 - **£534** - FF5 352
Bauernpaar mit Pferdeeinspänner beim Pflügen Öl/Leinwand (46x70cm 18x27in) Zofingen 1999

🖋 **$337** - €322 - **£213** - FF2 577
Frühlingslandschaft mit Bauer auf dem Acker Pastel (52x76cm 20x29in) Bern 2000

BOSS H. Wolcott 1827-1916 **[1]**

⌒ **$1 900** - €2 220 - **£1 356** - FF14 565
Two men in small boat, Hudson River landscape Oil/board (30x45cm 12x18in) Altadena CA 2001

BOSSCHAERT Abraham 1612/13-1643 **[5]**

⌒ **$41 097** - €41 423 - **£25 650** - FF271 719
Blumenstrauss von Rosen, Tulpen, Lilien und anderen Blüten Oil/panel (56x40cm 22x15in) Wien 2000

BOSSCHAERT Ambrosius I 1573-1621 **[14]**

⌒ **$2 615 025** - €2 807 013 - **£1 750 000** - FF18 412 800
Still Life of a Bouquet of Flowers, Including Variegated Tulips Oil/copper (30x20cm 11x7in) London 2000

BOSSCHAERT Jean-Baptiste 1667-1746 [38]
- $11 707 – €13 294 - **£8 135** - FF87 201
  Blumenstilleben Öl/Leinwand (180x117cm 70x46in)
  Köln 2001
- $13 467 – €13 111 - **£8 273** - FF86 000
  Nature morte au panier de fleurs, fruits et gibier dans un jardin Huile/toile (73x100cm 28x39in) Paris 1999

BOSSCHAERT Johannes 1610/11-c.1630 [6]
- $825 000 – €723 658 - **£500 940** - FF4 746 885
  Flowers in a Vase, a Branch of Cherries, a Wan-li Dish Full of Fruit Oil/panel (40.5x62cm 15x24in) New-York 1999

BOSSCHE van den Balthazar 1681-1715 [24]
- $27 864 – €24 697 - **£17 091** - FF162 000
  Abraham renvoyant Agar et ses fils Huile/toile (114.5x128cm 45x50in) Paris 1999
- $7 683 – €8 385 - **£5 214** - FF55 000
  L'atelier du peintre Huile/toile (51.5x61.5cm 20x24in) Paris 2000

BOSSCHE van den Dominique 1854-1906 [9]
- $756 – €694 - **£464** - FF4 552
  Buste d'une jeune Fille Terracotta (H53cm H20in) Antwerpen 1999

BOSSCHE van den Hubert 1874-1957 [14]
- $14 560 – €16 112 - **£10 205** - FF105 690
  Les faucheurs Huile/toile (102x83.5cm 40x32in) Bruxelles 1999

BOSSCHERE de Jean 1881-1953 [6]
- $800 – €891 - **£523** - FF5 845
  Fox approaching crowing cock (book illustration) Watercolour (20x13cm 8x5in) New-York 2000

BOSSCKE Lodewijk, Lode 1900-1980 [17]
- $452 – €421 - **£278** - FF2 764
  Nu Huile/toile (81x60cm 31x23in) Bruxelles 1999

BOSSE Abraham 1602-1676 [52]
- $1 974 – €2 211 - **£1 399** - FF14 500
  Salomé apportant à Hérodiade la tête de St Jean-baptiste sur plateau Encre (16.5x22cm 6x8in) Paris 2000
- $807 – €920 - **£563** - FF6 037
  Die Festtafel des Geizigen/Der Tod des Lazarus/Der Tod des Geizigen Radierung (26x33cm 10x12in) Berlin 2001

BOSSE Walter 1904-1979 [73]
- $211 – €245 - **£148** - FF1 609
  Elefant Ceramic (H13cm H5in) München 2001

BÖSSENROTH Carl 1869-1935 [16]
- $974 – €1 022 - **£658** - FF6 707
  Ruinen eines griechischen Amphitheaters Öl/Leinwand (72x96cm 28x37in) Kempten 2001
- $534 – €511 - **£335** - FF3 353
  Herbstlandschaft Öl/Karton (33x39cm 12x15in) Hamburg 1999

BOSSHARD Rodolphe Théophile 1889-1960 [183]
- $8 500 – €8 812 - **£5 100** - FF57 800
  Donna seduta Olio/tela (101x73.5cm 39x28in) Milano 1999
- $3 549 – €3 860 - **£2 339** - FF25 323
  Vase mit Tulpenstrauss Öl/Karton (33x45.5cm 12x17in) Bern 2000
- $671 – €563 - **£395** - FF3 693
  «Etude pour Nausicaa» Chalks (33.5x24.8cm 13x9in) Bern 1998

BOSSI Benigno 1727-1792 [11]
- $134 – €153 - **£93** - FF1 006
  Philosoph zwischen antiken Trümmern und einem Tierschädel Radierung (13x9.5cm 5x3in) Berlin 2001

BOSSI DA ESTE Francesco c.1770-c.1820 [3]
- $12 000 – €11 109 - **£7 244** - FF72 870
  Cat Holding Birds in its Mouth/Melons, a Pomegranite, a chocolate Oil/canvas (54x68.5cm 21x26in) New-York 1999

BOSSI Domenico 1765-1853 [24]
- $2 704 – €3 184 - **£1 900** - FF20 888
  Alexander I, Emperor of Russia, facing right in black Coat Miniature (7x4cm 2x1in) London 2000

BOSSI Giuseppe 1777-1815 [15]
- $1 100 – €1 140 - **£660** - FF7 480
  Studi per Madonna con Bambino e San Giovannino Inchiostro (19x13.5cm 7x5in) Milano 2000

BOSSO di Renato Righetti 1905-1983 [5]
- $3 400 – €3 525 - **£2 040** - FF23 120
  Piazza delle Erbe a Verona Olio/cartone (35x30cm 13x11in) Roma 1999
- $749 – €777 - **£449** - FF5 098
  Ciclismo (aerosilografia futurista)/Sci (aerosilografia futurista) Gravure bois (43x35cm 16x13in) Milano 2000

BOSSO Francesco 1864-1933 [10]
- $840 – €1 088 - **£630** - FF7 140
  Temporale imminente Olio/tavola (33x25cm 12x9in) Vercelli 2000
- $1 000 – €1 296 - **£750** - FF8 500
  Luci del sottobosco Pastelli/cartone (47x61cm 18x24in) Vercelli 2000

BOSSOLI Carlo 1815-1884 [113]
- $192 012 – €190 635 - **£120 000** - FF1 250 484
  Giochi d'acqua all'arena di Milano Tempera/canvas (130x160cm 51x62in) London 1999
- $4 800 – €6 220 - **£3 600** - FF40 800
  «Dintorni di Odessa d'inverno» Tempera/cartone (39x50cm 15x19in) Torino 2000
- $1 440 – €1 866 - **£1 080** - FF12 240
  Paesaggio di Crimea Tempera (16x23.5cm 6x9in) Torino 2000
- $2 242 – €2 407 - **£1 500** - FF15 786
  Fireworks Over Bridgewater House on the Occasion of Peace Celebrations Watercolour (18.5x28cm 7x11in) London 2000

BOSSON Ernest 1927-1991 [9]
- $284 – €309 - **£187** - FF2 025
  Asiatische Thronszene Gouache (25x18cm 9x7in) Bern 2000

BOSSUET François Antoine 1798-1889 [60]
- $17 014 – €14 483 - **£10 155** - FF95 000
  Mme. de Cordoue Huile/toile (92x64cm 36x25in) Paris 1998
- $1 935 – €2 231 - **£1 350** - FF14 634
  Chantier à la place Sainte Catherine Huile/panneau (32x24cm 12x9in) Bruxelles 2001
- $335 – €322 - **£209** - FF2 113
  Saint-Laurent à Rouen Crayon/papier (35x26cm 13x10in) Bruxelles 1999

BOSSUET van Francis 1635-1692 [2]
- $278 720 – €243 918 - **£168 800** - FF1 600 000
  Mars Sculpture (H44cm H17in) Paris 1998

BOSTIER DE BEZ Jean Joseph 1780-c.1845 **[2]**
🪑 **$4 348** - €4 878 - **£3 014** - FF32 000
Vue de Buscallion au Vigan, Gard Huile/toile
(38x57cm 14x22in) Paris 2000

BOSTIK Vaclav 1913 **[40]**
🪑 **$1 647** - €1 558 - **£1 026** - FF10 220
Jardin Huile/toile (40x33cm 15x12in) Praha 2001
✏️ **$346** - €328 - **£216** - FF2 151
Brouillard bleu Pastel/papier (20x15cm 7x5in) Praha
2000
▥ **$98** - €93 - **£61** - FF609
Ensemble Pointe sèche (15x12cm 5x4in) Praha 2000

BOSTON Joseph Henry 1859-1954 **[15]**
🪑 **$1 320** - €1 346 - **£827** - FF8 826
Figure in a Landscape Oil/canvas (40x30cm
16x12in) Altadena CA 2000

BOSTON Paul 1952 **[13]**
✏️ **$2 329** - €2 543 - **£1 499** - FF16 684
Red Forms Pastel/paper (55x75cm 21x29in)
Melbourne 2000

BOTELHO Carlos 1899-1982 **[9]**
🪑 **$59 400** - €67 299 - **£40 500** - FF441 450
Reportagem, restauradores Huile/toile (46x55cm
18x21in) Lisboa 2000
✏️ **$1 496** - €1 695 - **£1 054** - FF11 118
Sem título Gouache/papier (20.5x18cm 8x7in) Lisboa
2001

BOTELLO BARRO Angel 1913-1986 **[188]**
🪑 **$22 000** - €19 183 - **£13 301** - FF125 833
Les filles a l'ombrelle Oil/panel (122x107cm
48x42in) New-York 1998
🪑 **$13 000** - €13 954 - **£8 699** - FF91 533
Two Women Oil/canvas (66x57cm 25x22in) New-York
2000
🪑 **$7 000** - €5 997 - **£4 208** - FF39 337
Portrait Oil/masonite (41x34cm 16x13in) Dedham MA
1998
🗿 **$26 000** - €27 908 - **£17 399** - FF183 066
La coiffure Bronze (86.5x43x33.5cm 34x16x13in)
New-York 2000
🗿 **$17 000** - €16 500 - **£10 584** - FF108 232
Madre e Hijo Bronze (25x28x18cm 9x11x7in) New-
York 1999
▥ **$496** - €463 - **£300** - FF3 036
The Dance Linocut in colors (42.5x35.5cm 16x13in)
London 1998

BOTER Ramon 1954 **[11]**
🗿 **$240 000** - €231 183 - **£149 016** - FF1 516 464
Roman soldier Bronze (185x70x90cm 72x27x35in)
New-York 1999

BOTERO Fernando 1932 **[480]**
🪑 **$210 000** - €238 830 - **£146 727** - FF1 566 621
Antonio Chaves Chavito Oil/canvas (183x107cm
72x42in) Beverly-Hills CA 2000
🪑 **$90 000** - €86 662 - **£56 016** - FF568 467
Poodle Oil/canvas (101.5x81cm 39x31in) New-York
1999
🪑 **$60 000** - €70 645 - **£42 162** - FF463 404
The Thief on the Roof Oil/paper/board (34x40cm
13x15in) New-York 2000
🗿 **$230 000** - €266 867 - **£158 792** - FF1 750 530
Caballo Bronze (130x145x78cm 51x57x30in) New-
York 2000
🗿 **$130 000** - €153 065 - **£91 351** - FF1 004 042
Maternidad Bronze (50x28x32cm 19x11x14in) New-
York 2000

✏️ **$20 000** - €23 237 - **£14 056** - FF152 424
Bodegón con sandía Watercolour/paper (36x51cm
14x20in) New-York 2001
▥ **$2 200** - €2 371 - **£1 500** - FF15 552
To Amnesty International Print in colors (81x61cm
31x24in) New-York 2001

BOTH Andries Dirksz. c.1608-c.1641/49 **[29]**
🪑 **$13 480** - €11 429 - **£8 000** - FF74 968
The Adoration of the Shepherds Oil/canvas
(105x137cm 41x53in) London 1998
🪑 **$6 000** - €5 183 - **£4 000** - FF34 000
Scena di genere Olio/tavola (51.5x74cm 20x29in)
Milano 1998
🪑 **$37 688** - €36 302 - **£23 288** - FF238 128
**Vanitas: Old Man Seated on a Barrel Weighing
Gold, Old Peasant** Oil/panel (34.5x28.5cm 13x11in)
Amsterdam 1999
✏️ **$2 047** - €2 045 - **£1 280** - FF13 415
Eine Bettlerfamilie Red chalk (18.5x22cm 7x8in)
Köln 1999
▥ **$807** - €920 - **£563** - FF6 037
In der Dorfwirtschaft Radierung (17.5x22.5cm
6x8in) Berlin 2001

BOTH Jan Dirksz. 1618-1652 **[70]**
🪑 **$1 942 590** - €2 085 210 - **£1 300 000** -
FF13 678 080
**Italianate Evening Landscape with a Muleteer
and Goatherds on a Path** Oil/canvas
(138.5x172.5cm 54x67in) London 2000
🪑 **$46 551** - €45 596 - **£30 000** - FF299 088
Italianate Landscape with Bathers at a River
Oil/canvas (51.5x61cm 20x24in) London 1999
🪑 **$120 000** - €128 154 - **£81 768** - FF840 636
**Italinate Landscape with Travellers before the
Plompetoren, Utrecht** Oil/panel (32.5x40cm
12x15in) London 1999
▥ **$90** - €102 - **£63** - FF670
Die Frau auf dem Maulesel Radierung
(26.7x20.5cm 10x8in) München 2001

BOTHAMS Walter c.1850-1914 **[16]**
✏️ **$630** - €529 - **£370** - FF3 470
Drovers on a Country Road Watercolour/paper
(7x25cm 3x10in) London 1998

BOTKE Cornelis J. 1887-1954 **[23]**
🪑 **$2 250** - €1 923 - **£1 361** - FF12 612
«Shore at Elk» Oil/canvas/panel (45.5x61cm 17x24in)
San-Francisco CA 1998
🪑 **$3 750** - €4 050 - **£2 591** - FF26 564
Cabins in «Eucalyptus Grove» Oil/board (34x38cm
13x15in) Altadena CA 2001
▥ **$600** - €576 - **£376** - FF3 777
Landscape, old Tree Etching (30x34cm 12x13in)
Altadena CA 1999

BOTKE Jessie Arms 1883-1971 **[73]**
🪑 **$50 000** - €49 642 - **£31 250** - FF325 630
Blue Peacock Oil/masonite (101.5x81.5cm 39x32in)
New-York 1999
🪑 **$6 500** - €7 134 - **£4 185** - FF46 795
Still Life with Butterflies/Still Life with Birds
Oil/masonite (37x32cm 14x12in) Beverly-Hills CA
2000
✏️ **$2 200** - €2 586 - **£1 525** - FF16 960
Seashells Watercolour/paper (25.5x36cm 10x14in)
Beverly-Hills CA 2000
▥ **$1 700** - €1 998 - **£1 178** - FF13 109
Landscape Woodcut in colors (21x26.5cm 8x10in)
Beverly-Hills CA 2000

B

BOTLER Gaspar XVIII **[1]**
- $9 666 - €9 615 - £6 000 - FF63 067
  The Grotto at Pozzuoli Oil/copper (19.5x28.5cm 7x11in) London 1999

BOTMAN Machiel 1950 **[9]**
- $634 - €681 - £424 - FF4 464
  Elisabeth and Bert Vintage gelatin silver print (50x60cm 19x23in) Amsterdam 2000

BOTNEN Trond 1937 **[19]**
- $110 - €124 - £76 - FF811
  Jeg glemmer aldri ham du vet (II) Serigraph in colors (70x52cm 27x20in) Oslo 2001

BOTT Francis 1904-1998 **[229]**
- $2 849 - €3 323 - £2 000 - FF21 800
  Rigueur Öl/Leinwand (34.2x70.8cm 13x27in) Köln 2000
- $1 008 - €1 083 - £674 - FF7 101
  Komposition in verschiedenen Blau, Rot und Gelb Öl/Karton (19x14cm 7x5in) Bern 2000
- $661 - €456 - FF5 030
  Schwarz und Violett Oil chalks/paper (24x36cm 9x14in) Köln 2000
- $92 - €82 - £56 - FF536
  Komposition Farblithographie (60x42cm 23x16in) Stuttgart 1999

BOTTEMA Tjeerd 1884-1940 **[27]**
- $3 906 - €4 538 - £2 745 - FF29 766
  Picknick in the grass Oil/canvas (37.5x54cm 14x21in) Amsterdam 2001
- $185 - €204 - £125 - FF1 339
  Violinist Etching (27x21.8cm 10x8in) Haarlem 2000

BÖTTGER Herbert 1898-1954 **[24]**
- $6 059 - €6 647 - £4 115 - FF43 600
  Vorfrühling Öl/Leinwand (40.5x45.5cm 15x17in) Düsseldorf 2000
- $8 460 - €10 226 - £5 906 - FF67 078
  Sommerblumen Öl/Leinwand (40.5x30.5cm 15x12in) Düsseldorf 2000

BÖTTGER Klaus 1942-1992 **[66]**
- $68 - €77 - £47 - FF503
  «Überschwemmung» Etching, aquatint (20x35cm 7x13in) Köln 2001

BOTTI Italo 1889-1974 **[4]**
- $1 900 - €2 207 - £1 335 - FF14 480
  «Retiro (Gris), Buenos Aires» Oleo/tabla (24x30cm 9x11in) Buenos-Aires 2001

BOTTICELLI Sandro Filipepi 1444/45-1510 **[3]**
- $850 000 - €909 236 - £579 530 - FF5 964 195
  The Madonna and Child, a Landscape through a Window beyond Oil/panel (76x49.5cm 29x19in) New-York 2001

BOTTICINI Francesco 1446-1497 **[7]**
- $8 000 - €6 716 - £4 692 - FF44 052
  The Deposition Oil/panel (46.5x38cm 18x14in) New-York 1998
- $29 927 - €33 991 - £21 000 - FF222 967
  The Madonna and Child enthroned, flanked by two Angels Tempera/panel (43.5x33.5cm 17x13in) London 2001
- $90 000 - €91 047 - £54 954 - FF597 231
  Drapery Study for a Virgin Annunciate Black chalk (32x13cm 12x5in) New-York 2000

BOTTIGLIONI J. XIX **[2]**
- $36 896 - €37 180 - £23 000 - FF243 882
  Day and Night Gilded bronze (H100cm H39in) London 2000

BOTTINELLI Antonio 1827-1898 **[1]**
- $11 796 - €13 064 - £8 000 - FF85 696
  Figure of Vanity Marble (H155cm H61in) Billingshurst, West-Sussex 2000

BOTTINI Georges Alfred 1874-1907 **[74]**
- $3 397 - €2 897 - £2 050 - FF19 000
  Deux femmes dans un bal masqué Aquarelle/papier (36x23.5cm 14x9in) Paris 1998
- $3 516 - €3 486 - £2 200 - FF22 866
  Sagot's Gallery Color lithograph (38x28cm 14x11in) London 1999

BÖTTNER Wilhelm 1752-1805 **[13]**
- $5 618 - €5 113 - £3 510 - FF33 539
  Venus und Amor schlafend Öl/Leinwand (50x65cm 19x25in) München 1999
- $256 - €281 - £174 - FF1 844
  Kavalier überreicht seiner Dame einen Blumenstrauss Ink (13.8x19cm 5x7in) Berlin 2000

BOTTOLI Oskar 1921-1996 **[21]**
- $630 - €545 - £380 - FF3 573
  Don Quixote Bronze relief (25.5x39.5cm 10x15in) Wien 1998

BOTTOMLEY Albert Ernest 1873-1950 **[40]**
- $230 - €268 - £164 - FF1 756
  The Mackerel Nets Gouache/paper (21.5x32cm 8x12in) Toronto 2001

BOTTOMLEY Edwin 1865-1929 **[16]**
- $5 974 - €5 162 - £3 600 - FF33 861
  Chickens in a Barn Oil/canvas (49x74.5cm 19x29in) Billingshurst, West-Sussex 1999
- $746 - €837 - £520 - FF5 489
  Farmers Building a Haystack Watercolour (26x35cm 10x13in) Leyburn, North Yorkshire 2001

BOTTOMLEY Frederic 1883-1960 **[37]**
- $506 - €547 - £350 - FF3 587
  Trafalgar Square Oil/canvas (50x60cm 19x23in) London 2001
- $646 - €723 - £450 - FF4 741
  St.Ives Harbour and Quayside Oil/canvas/board (32x40.5cm 12x15in) Penzance, Cornwall 2001

BOTTOMLEY John William 1816-1900 **[11]**
- $8 606 - €9 554 - £6 000 - FF62 669
  Returning from the Moor Oil/canvas (64x102cm 25x40in) London 2001

BOTTON de Jean Isy 1898-1978 **[72]**
- $1 100 - €942 - £667 - FF6 181
  «Symphonie en blancs» Oil/canvas (63x76cm 25x30in) New-York 1999
- $400 - €464 - £284 - FF3 043
  Le char du soleil Oil/canvas (30.5x41.5cm 12x16in) Washington 2001

BOTTSCHILD Samuel 1640-1707 **[14]**
- $24 975 - €24 527 - £15 500 - FF160 888
  Orpheus and Eurydice Oil/canvas (172x161cm 67x63in) London 1999

BOTZARIS Sava 1894-1965 **[3]**
- $7 550 - €6 441 - £4 500 - FF42 253
  George Bernard Shaw Bronze (H52cm H20in) London 1998

BOUBAT Édouard 1923-1999 **[124]**
- $819 - €915 - £555 - FF6 000
  Vue de New York Photo (26x38cm 10x14in) Paris 2000

BOUCART Gaston 1878-1962 **[18]**
- $1 600 - €1 731 - **£1 096** - FF11 354
  Venetian canal Scene with Gondolas Oil/canvas (66x81cm 26x32in) Delaware OH 2001
- $1 278 - €1 372 - **£855** - FF9 000
  Les gondoliers à Venise Huile/toile (33x41cm 12x16in) Soissons 2000

BOUCHARD Edith Marie 1924 **[7]**
- $1 036 - €1 209 - **£721** - FF7 930
  Repas de noce de mon frère dans la demeure de l'artiste Oil/board (61x91.5cm 24x36in) Toronto 2000

BOUCHARD Henri Louis 1875-1960 **[38]**
- $3 880 - €3 354 - **£2 303** - FF22 000
  Cavalier oriental Bronze (19.5x40cm 7x15in) Dijon 1998

BOUCHARD Lorne Holland 1913-1978 **[108]**
- $1 226 - €1 178 - **£755** - FF7 729
  Lac Croche Oil/board (45.5x76cm 17x29in) Vancouver, BC. 1999
- $326 - €359 - **£226** - FF2 356
  «The Beach, April» Huile/masonite (20.5x30.5cm 8x12in) Montréal 2001

BOUCHARD Simone Mary 1912-1945 **[14]**
- $1 363 - €1 542 - **£953** - FF10 117
  La maison paternelle Oil/canvas (40x47cm 15x18in) Toronto 2001

BOUCHARDON Edmé 1698-1762 **[52]**
- $1 227 - €1 067 - **£739** - FF7 000
  Académie d'homme debout Pierre noire (58.2x44.4cm 22x17in) Paris 1998

BOUCHARDY Étienne 1797-c.1849 **[12]**
- $2 107 - €2 312 - **£1 400** - FF15 166
  Young Gentleman, facing right in black Coat Miniature (13.5x12cm 5x4in) London 2000
- $1 416 - €1 372 - **£891** - FF9 000
  Portrait du Duc de Bordeaux et sa soeur vue de profil Sanguine/papier (20.5x22.5cm 8x8in) Paris 1999

BOUCHAUD Jean 1891-1977 **[16]**
- $4 329 - €5 031 - **£3 085** - FF33 000
  Cavalier devant les remparts, Maroc Huile/carton (60x73cm 23x28in) Paris 2001
- $1 176 - €1 403 - **£839** - FF9 200
  Jeunes algériennes Fusain (46x29cm 18x11in) Châtellerault 2000

BOUCHAUD Michel XIX-XX **[1]**
- $3 000 - €3 499 - **£2 106** - FF22 951
  «La plage de Monte-Carlo» Poster (78x116cm 30x45in) New-York 2000

BOUCHÉ de Arnulf 1872-1945 **[19]**
- $2 092 - €2 045 - **£1 327** - FF13 415
  Liegender Frauenakt Öl/Leinwand (57x68cm 22x26in) München 1999

BOUCHE Georges 1874-1941 **[70]**
- $1 573 - €1 677 - **£997** - FF11 000
  Femme assise Huile/toile (46x38cm 18x14in) Paris 2000

BOUCHÉ Guillaume XIX **[2]**
- $4 000 - €4 289 - **£2 646** - FF28 132
  Still Life with Yellow and Pink Roses Oil/canvas (41x32cm 16x12in) New-Orleans LA 2000

BOUCHÉ Louis Alexandre 1838-1911 **[32]**
- $2 081 - €2 363 - **£1 446** - FF15 500
  Bergère et ses moutons Huile/toile (41.5x57.5cm 16x22in) Barbizon 2001

- $1 120 - €1 067 - **£709** - FF7 000
  Au bord de la rivière Huile/toile (33.5x41.5cm 13x16in) Soissons 1999

BOUCHE Louis George 1896-1969 **[19]**
- $2 000 - €1 680 - **£1 175** - FF11 019
  High Street Bus Barn Oil/canvas (50x60cm 20x24in) Saugerties NY 1998

BOUCHÉ René 1905-1963 **[5]**
- $1 400 - €1 316 - **£850** - FF8 630
  Fashion Sketch, Woman at Sotheby's looking though an auction catalogue Pencil/paper (63x50cm 25x20in) New-York 1999

BOUCHEIX François 1940 **[71]**
- $1 932 - €2 134 - **£1 339** - FF14 000
  Pleine lune sur la neige Huile/toile (55x46cm 21x18in) Armentières 2001
- $484 - €534 - **£323** - FF3 500
  Rêve en bleu Huile/toile (18x14cm 7x5in) Arcachon 2000

BOUCHENE Dimitri 1893-1993 **[41]**
- $3 200 - €3 100 - **£1 995** - FF20 333
  Le pavilion de Musique de la «Villa Trianon» Pastel/paper (66x51cm 25x20in) Beverly-Hills CA 1999

BOUCHER Alfred 1850-1934 **[125]**
- $6 634 - €5 770 - **£4 000** - FF37 851
  Psyche, l'Hirondelle blessée Bronze (H95cm H37in) London 1998
- $3 197 - €3 811 - **£2 280** - FF25 000
  Portrait de Charles Claudel Marbre (H70cm H27in) Tourcoing 2000

BOUCHER François 1703-1770 **[241]**
- $100 000 - €83 993 - **£58 790** - FF550 960
  An Extensive Mountainous Landscape with Peasants Resting Oil/canvas (129.5x97cm 50x38in) New-York 1998
- $180 000 - €192 544 - **£122 724** - FF1 263 006
  Young Woman with a Bouquet of Roses Oil/canvas (56x47cm 22x18in) New-York 2001
- $105 072 - €102 253 - **£64 680** - FF670 736
  Ceres Oil/canvas (40x31cm 15x12in) Stockholm 1999
- $12 627 - €15 017 - **£9 000** - FF98 506
  Group of Figures in Discussion Ink (21.5x30.5cm 8x12in) London 2000
- $374 - €324 - **£226** - FF2 128
  Les petits buveurs de lait Etching (19.5x13.5cm 7x5in) New-York 1998

BOUCHER Jean Marie 1870-1939 **[9]**
- $1 236 - €1 220 - **£761** - FF8 000
  Fra Angelico Bronze (H66cm H25in) Epinal 1999

BOUCHER Juste Nathan 1736-1781 **[1]**
- $2 454 - €2 134 - **£1 479** - FF14 000
  Vestiges antiques avec une statue et une fontaine Encre (36x23.2cm 14x9in) Paris 1998

BOUCHER Lucien 1889-1971 **[48]**
- $2 200 - €2 453 - **£1 435** - FF16 092
  Lipnitzki Gouache (25x17cm 10x7in) New-York 2000
- $225 - €193 - **£135** - FF1 264
  «Indochine Française» Poster (93x62cm 36x24in) London 1999

BOUCHER Pierre 1908-2000 **[80]**
- $338 - €381 - **£236** - FF2 500
  Nu féminin assis Tirage argentique (21x18cm 8x7in) Paris 2001

BOUCHERLE Pierre 1894-1988 **[16]**
🐎 **$3 149** - €3 583 - **£2 185** - FF23 500
Moulin de la Goulette, Tunisie Huile/toile (73x60cm 28x23in) Paris 2000

BOUCHET Auguste 1831-1889 **[7]**
🐎 **$9 000** - €10 672 - **£6 192** - FF70 004
The Open Market Oil/canvas (25x46.5cm 9x18in) New-York 2000

BOUCHET Jules Frédéric 1799-1860 **[7]**
🐎 **$2 200** - €2 556 - **£1 546** - FF16 766
Figures resting in the Courtyard of a Roman Villa Watercolour (21.5x27.5cm 8x10in) New-York 2001

BOUCHET Louis André G. 1759-1842 **[6]**
🐎 **$14 200** - €15 245 - **£9 500** - FF100 000
Jeune garçon étudiant une carte/Jeune fille étudiant une partition Huile/toile (92x73cm 36x28in) La Flèche 2000

BOUCHET-DOUMENG Henri XIX **[2]**
🐎 **$3 162** - €3 278 - **£2 003** - FF21 500
Portrait de jeune femme à l'ombrelle Huile/toile (41x32cm 16x12in) Abbeville 2000

BOUCHEZ Charles 1811-? **[10]**
🐎 **$1 321** - €1 271 - **£824** - FF8 334
In the Tavern Oil/canvas (20x28cm 7x11in) Amsterdam 1999

BOUCHOR Joseph-Félix 1853-1937 **[54]**
🐎 **$4 050** - €4 462 - **£2 646** - FF29 268
La fête des Aïssaouas Huile/toile (38.5x46cm 15x18in) Bruxelles 2000
🐎 **$1 100** - €938 - **£662** - FF6 156
Le marché aux volailles sur la Place Victor Emmanuel Oil/panel (23x33cm 9x13in) Norwalk CT 1999

BOUCLE van Peter c.1610-1673 **[26]**
🐎 **$25 352** - €23 020 - **£15 839** - FF151 000
Combat de coq Huile/toile (126x162cm 49x63in) Rennes 1999
🐎 **$14 823** - €14 099 - **£9 000** - FF92 481
Still Life of Pike, Eels, carp and Other Freshwater Fish, Vegetables Oil/canvas (65.5x103cm 25x40in) London 1999

BOUDA Cyril 1901-1984 **[39]**
✎ **$231** - €219 - **£144** - FF1 434
Seelandschaft Aquarell/Papier (23x32cm 9x12in) Praha 2000

BOUDET Pierre 1925 **[318]**
🐎 **$2 766** - €2 744 - **£1 720** - FF18 000
Honfleur: bateaux dans le grand bassin Huile/toile (38x46cm 14x18in) L'Isle-Adam 1999
🐎 **$643** - €686 - **£408** - FF4 500
Sculptures et bassin dans le parc du Château de Versailles Huile/isorel (35x27cm 13x10in) Paris 2000

BOUDEWIJNSE Adriaan Joh. Petrus 1862-1909 **[2]**
🐎 **$20 884** - €17 892 - **£12 554** - FF117 365
Markttreiben vor römischen Ruinen Öl/Leinwand (68.5x86.7cm 26x34in) Stuttgart 1998

BOUDEWYNS & BOUT Adriaen Fr. & Peeter 1644/58-1711/19 **[4]**
🐎 **$63 672** - €72 537 - **£44 000** - FF475 811
Townsfolk Gathering on the Shore of an Estuary/Townsfolk Gathering Oil/panel (34x48cm 13x18in) London 2000

BOUDEWYNS Adriaen Frans 1644-1711 **[97]**
🐎 **$8 861** - €8 813 - **£5 500** - FF57 811
Landscape with Elegant Compagny in a Horse-Drawn Carriage, Travellers Oil/canvas (71x94cm 27x37in) London 1999
🐎 **$6 097** - €5 336 - **£3 692** - FF35 000
Paysage animé Huile/cuivre (26x20cm 7x10in) Paris 1998
✎ **$950** - €975 - **£594** - FF6 393
Italianate Landscape with a Walled Farm House Red chalk/paper (14.5x19cm 5x7in) New-York 2000
📜 **$1 050** - €1 088 - **£630** - FF7 140
Vue de la ville d'Ardres/Vues du Château de Versailles Gravure (51x78cm 20x30in) Venezia 2000

BOUDIN Eugène 1824-1898 **[1138]**
🐎 **$154 938** - €149 400 - **£95 550** - FF980 000
Pêcheurs dans la baie d'Antibes Huile/toile (127x187cm 50x74in) Paris 1999
🐎 **$70 000** - €78 405 - **£48 636** - FF514 304
La Touques à Saint-Arnoult Oil/canvas (54x74.5cm 21x29in) New-York 2001
🐎 **$41 841** - €49 204 - **£30 000** - FF322 758
Bord de Seine à Caudebec en Caux Oil/panel (31x42cm 12x16in) London 2001
✎ **$6 000** - €5 770 - **£3 696** - FF37 846
Deux Bretonnes dans un intérieur Watercolour (17x22.5cm 6x8in) New-York 1999
📜 **$375** - €421 - **£261** - FF2 760
Le bord de la mer à Trouville Color lithograph (25x40cm 9x15in) Washington 2001

BOUDNIK Vladimír 1924-1968 **[7]**
📜 **$751** - €711 - **£448** - FF4 661
«Strukturalni grafika» Monotype (18x38cm 7x14in) Praha 2001

BOUDON André XX **[3]**
📜 **$508** - €579 - **£354** - FF3 800
«Chemin de fer du Médoc, Soulac-sur-Mer» Affiche (102.5x75cm 40x29in) Paris 2001

BOUDON Émile XIX-XX **[2]**
🪙 **$3 108** - €3 435 - **£2 155** - FF22 533
Young Tonkinese Girl Bronze (H23cm H9in) Singapore 2001

BOUDON Patrick 1944 **[27]**
🐎 **$500** - €605 - **£349** - FF3 967
En mand går på line Oil/canvas (100x80cm 39x31in) Viby J, Århus 2000

BOUDRY Aloïs 1851-1938 **[35]**
🐎 **$845** - €908 - **£565** - FF5 953
Meisje bij wasketel Oil/canvas (51x60cm 20x23in) Dordrecht 2000
🐎 **$374** - €446 - **£268** - FF2 926
De koperslager (le chaudronnier) Huile/bois (36x27cm 14x10in) Antwerpen 2000

BOUDRY Robert 1878-1965 **[45]**
🐎 **$291** - €347 - **£208** - FF2 276
Huisje te Brugge (maisonette à Bruges) Huile/panneau (80x65cm 31x25in) Antwerpen 2000

BOUGH Samuel, Sam 1822-1878 **[233]**
🐎 **$57 500** - €57 942 - **£35 845** - FF380 075
Aberdour Harbor Oil/canvas (99x137cm 39x54in) Oakland CA 2000
🐎 **$6 732** - €6 360 - **£4 200** - FF41 719
Haymaking Oil/canvas (46x77cm 18x30in) Perthshire 1999
🐎 **$965** - €816 - **£580** - FF5 350
Lakeland Scene with Cattle and Drover Oil/panel (25x38cm 10x15in) London 1998

✐ $703 - €791 - **£490** - FF5 188
   Returning from Hay Watercolour, gouache/paper
   (14x23cm 5x9in) Edinburgh 2001

BOUGHTON George Henry 1833-1905 **[67]**
⌒ $6 000 - €6 387 - **£4 087** - FF41 898
   The Jealous Suitor Oil/canvas/panel (66x117cm
   25x46in) New-York 2001
⌒ $6 500 - €5 454 - **£3 831** - FF35 773
   Winter Moonlight Oil/canvas (19x30cm 7x12in)
   Greenwich CT 1998
✐ $2 200 - €1 905 - **£1 349** - FF12 499
   Young Lady with Muff Gouache/paper (49x37cm
   19x14in) New-York 1999

BOUGHTON H. XIX **[2]**
✐ $36 696 - €35 081 - **£23 000** - FF230 115
   **The Defiance London-to-Plymouth Coach at
   Hyde Park Corner** Oil/canvas (71x91.5cm 27x36in)
   London 1999

BOUGUEREAU Elizabeth-Jeanne 1837-1922 **[19]**
⌒ $150 000 - €177 869 - **£103 200** - FF16 745
   L'Imprudente Oil/canvas (104x138.5cm 40x54in)
   New-York 2000
⌒ $120 000 - €131 694 - **£77 268** - FF863 856
   Young Girl holding a Basket of Grapes Oil/canvas
   (106x64cm 41x25in) New-York 2000

BOUGUEREAU William Adolphe 1825-1905 **[208]**
⌒ $650 000 - €616 639 - **£394 875** - FF4 044 885
   La vague Oil/canvas (121x160.5cm 47x63in) New-
   York 1999
⌒ $250 000 - €237 169 - **£151 875** - FF1 555 725
   Boucles d'oreilles Oil/canvas (121x77.5cm 47x30in)
   New-York 1999
⌒ $26 000 - €28 534 - **£16 741** - FF187 168
   Study for Sainte Famille Oil/board (25x16cm 9x6in)
   New-York 2000
⚒ $3 692 - €3 964 - **£2 470** - FF26 000
   L'amour vainqueur Bronze (61x17x17cm 24x6x6in)
   Lyon 2000
✐ $1 958 - €1 829 - **£1 208** - FF12 000
   Le mari, la femme et le voleur Crayon (23x27cm
   9x10in) Paris 1999

BOUHOT Étienne 1780-1862 **[16]**
⌒ $24 000 - €20 158 - **£14 109** - FF132 230
   The Bridge at Austerlitz, Paris Oil/canvas
   (47x68cm 18x26in) New-York 1998
⌒ $2 099 - €2 498 - **£1 500** - FF16 389
   Figures in the Side Chapel of Church Oil/canvas
   (32.5x24.5cm 12x9in) London 2000

BOUHUIJS Jacob 1902-1983 **[7]**
⌒ $1 380 - €1 361 - **£849** - FF8 929
   Don quichotte en Sanch Panches Oil/canvas
   (50x50cm 19x19in) Amsterdam 1999

BOUILLIAT J.-B. XVIII **[1]**
✐ $5 960 - €5 820 - **£3 800** - FF38 174
   **Vase of Poppies, Roses, other Flowers/Vase of
   Asters, Poppies, other** Watercolour (18.5x16cm
   7x6in) London 1999

BOUILLON Charles XVII-XVIII **[1]**
⌒ $44 324 - €42 686 - **£27 524** - FF280 000
   **Trompe-l'oeil aux gravures, dessin, lettres et
   partitions** Huile/toile (90x122cm 35x48in) Paris 1999

BOUILLON Michel XVII **[12]**
⌒ $12 104 - €12 196 - **£7 544** - FF80 000
   Nature morte au trophées de chasse Huile/toile
   (133x78.5cm 52x30in) Neuilly-sur-Seine 2000

BOUILLON-LANDAIS Paul Louis 1828-? **[1]**
⌒ $9 266 - €10 519 - **£6 437** - FF69 000
   Le port de Marseille Huile/toile (68x127cm 26x50in)
   Grasse 2001

BOUISSET Firmin Étienne 1859-1925 **[71]**
▥ $718 - €793 - **£486** - FF5 200
   «Manchon l'omnibus coiffe tous les becs»
   Affiche couleur (100x130cm 39x51in) Nice 2000

BOUKERCHE Miloud ?-1979 **[25]**
⌒ $3 454 - €3 354 - **£2 134** - FF22 000
   Les amoureux Huile/toile (73x60cm 28x23in) Paris
   1999
⌒ $320 - €349 - **£217** - FF2 290
   The Elder Oil/masonite (26.5x22cm 10x8in) New-
   York 2000

BOULANGER François Jean Louis 1819-1873 **[21]**
⌒ $77 229 - €64 236 - **£45 345** - FF421 362
   The Courthouse, Ghent Oil/canvas (117x171cm
   46x67in) Amsterdam 1998
⌒ $10 652 - €8 860 - **£6 254** - FF58 119
   «Papiermolens, Akkergem» Oil/panel (46x60.5cm
   18x23in) Amsterdam 1998
⌒ $4 320 - €3 966 - **£2 656** - FF26 016
   La Lys à Gand Huile/panneau (28.5x35.5cm 11x13in)
   Bruxelles 1999
✐ $406 - €471 - **£281** - FF3 089
   Petite fille aux poussins Crayon/papier (26x20cm
   10x7in) Bruxelles 2000

BOULANGER Gustave Clarence 1824-1888 **[31]**
⌒ $140 000 - €166 011 - **£96 320** - FF1 088 962
   The Bathers Oil/canvas (102x81cm 40x31in) New-
   York 2000

BOULANGER Louis 1806-1867 **[40]**
⌒ $3 635 - €3 811 - **£2 277** - FF25 000
   Animation dans la cour d'une maison Huile/toile
   (60x74cm 23x29in) Paris 2000
⌒ $3 000 - €3 315 - **£2 080** - FF21 746
   Feeding the Roosters Oil/panel (46x33cm 18x13in)
   New-Orleans LA 2001
✐ $691 - €762 - **£468** - FF5 000
   Autoportrait à l'âge de trente-six ans Crayons
   couleurs/papier (28x21cm 11x8in) Paris 2000

BOULANGER Louis-René 1860-1917 **[1]**
⌒ $4 689 - €5 399 - **£3 200** - FF35 414
   Pink Peonies in a Bowl Oil/canvas (57x87cm
   22x34in) London 2000

BOULARD Auguste fils 1852-1927 **[14]**
▥ $800 - €829 - **£480** - FF5 440
   La revue, da Françoise Flameng Acquaforte
   (48.5x89cm 19x35in) Firenze 2001

BOULARD Auguste père 1825-1897 **[37]**
⌒ $1 294 - €1 220 - **£784** - FF8 000
   Femme aux fleurs Huile/toile (70x59cm 27x23in)
   Paris 1999
⌒ $1 142 - €1 067 - **£704** - FF7 000
   Cour de ferme animée Huile/carton (40x32cm
   15x12in) Melun 1999

BOULARD Émile 1861-1943 **[26]**
⌒ $2 031 - €2 134 - **£1 337** - FF14 000
   Jeune femme lisant dans son intérieur Huile/toile
   (46x38cm 18x14in) Paris 2000
⌒ $412 - €427 - **£262** - FF2 800
   Les quais animés Huile/carton (25x30cm 9x11in)
   Neuilly-sur-Seine 2000

BOULARD Théodore 1887-1961 **[53]**
🖐 **$4 981** - €4 269 - **£2 996** - FF28 000
«**Autour du feu**» Huile/toile (33x41cm 12x16in) Le Mans 1998

BOULENGER Hippolyte 1837-1874 **[61]**
🖐 **$2 395** - €1 993 - **£1 406** - FF13 070
Autumn Lake, Tervueren Oil/canvas (35.5x46cm 13x18in) Amsterdam 1998
🖐 **$653** - €545 - **£382** - FF3 577
Landschap met beekje Oil/canvas/panel (36.5x28.5cm 14x11in) Lokeren 1998

BOULEZ Jules Jacques 1889-1960 **[42]**
🖐 **$860** - €892 - **£547** - FF5 853
Landschap Oil/canvas (60x73cm 23x28in) Lokeren 2000

BOULIER Lucien 1882-1963 **[133]**
🖐 **$453** - €457 - **£282** - FF3 000
Portrait de femme Huile/panneau (26x33.5cm 10x13in) La Varenne-Saint-Hilaire 2000

BOULINEAU Abel 1839-? **[11]**
🖐 **$1 947** - €2 211 - **£1 352** - FF14 500
Le moulin dans le village Huile/toile (103x65cm 40x25in) Dijon 2001

BOULLET Jean 1921-1970 **[17]**
🖐 **$7 123** - €8 281 - **£5 000** - FF54 322
Colette Oil/canvas (60x81cm 23x31in) London 2001

BOULLIER Robert XIX-XX **[7]**
🖐 **$641** - €762 - **£457** - FF5 000
«**Thonon-les-Bains**» Affiche (99x78cm 38x30in) Orléans 2000

BOULOGNE de Bon 1649-1717 **[7]**
🖐 **$6 534** - €6 860 - **£4 117** - FF45 000
Préparation du concert Huile/toile (26x33cm 10x12in) Tours 2000
🖐 **$1 632** - €1 524 - **£1 007** - FF10 000
Zéphyr couronnant Flore Pierre noire (21x24cm 8x9in) Paris 1999

BOULOGNE de Louis I 1609-1674 **[3]**
🖐 **$1 846** - €1 982 - **£1 235** - FF13 000
La Vierge et l'Enfant Crayon (32x26cm 12x10in) Paris 2000

BOULOGNE de Louis II 1654-1733 **[31]**
🖐 **$18 000** - €16 935 - **£11 232** - FF111 085
Zephyr crowning Flora Oil/canvas (67.5x56cm 26x22in) New-York 1999
🖐 **$5 000** - €5 340 - **£3 407** - FF35 026
The Madonna and Child Black & white chalks/paper (32x28cm 12x11in) New-York 2001

BOULOGNE de Valentin 1591-1631 **[7]**
🖐 **$26 500** - €27 471 - **£15 900** - FF180 200
La Buona Ventura Olio/tela (113x154cm 44x60in) Venezia 2000

BOULT Francis Cecil XIX-XX **[11]**
🖐 **$12 804** - €12 223 - **£8 000** - FF80 180
Polo: Preparing for the Game Oil/canvas (61x91.5cm 24x36in) London 1999

BOUMANN Johannes c.1600-c.1655 **[2]**
🖐 **$27 979** - €31 371 - **£19 000** - FF205 783
Apples and Pears in a Blue-and-White Porcelain Bowl Oil/panel (33x54.5cm 12x21in) London 2000

BOUMEESTER Christine 1904-1971 **[100]**
🖐 **$1 915** - €1 829 - **£1 194** - FF12 000
Composition Huile/toile (78x91cm 30x35in) Paris 1999

🖐 **$426** - €457 - **£285** - FF3 000
Sans titre Mine plomb (47.5x61.5cm 18x24in) Douai 2000

BOUNIEU Michel-Honoré 1740-1814 **[6]**
🖐 **$25 138** - €21 389 - **£15 000** - FF140 301
David and Bathsheba Oil/canvas (163x137.5cm 64x54in) London 1998
🖐 **$9 078** - €9 147 - **£5 658** - FF60 000
Nature morte au chaudron et légumes Huile/toile (62x79.5cm 24x31in) Paris 2000
🖐 **$4 784** - €5 641 - **£3 363** - FF37 000
La Vierge soutenue par deux anges Huile/toile/carton (46x21cm 18x8in) Paris 2000

BOUNIOL Lucie 1896-1988 **[1]**
🖐 **$1 576** - €1 906 - **£1 101** - FF12 500
Etude de nue Gouache/papier (159x111cm 62x43in) Lavaur 2000

BOUQUET Michel 1807-1890 **[22]**
🖐 **$1 468** - €1 677 - **£1 032** - FF11 000
Rivière animée Peinture (16x27cm 6x10in) Aubagne 2001

BOUQUILLON Robert 1923 **[70]**
🖐 **$522** - €457 - **£316** - FF3 000
L'inspiration Huile/toile (46x38cm 18x14in) Douai 1998

BOURAINE Marcel ?-1935 **[151]**
🖐 **$4 000** - €3 818 - **£2 499** - FF25 046
Figural Lamp Gilded bronze (H49cm H19in) New-York 1999

BOURBON ET BRAGANCE de Carlota Joaquina 1775-1830 **[1]**
🖐 **$6 600** - €7 478 - **£4 500** - FF49 050
Pescador Oleo/lienzo (52.5x45cm 20x17in) Lisboa 2000

BOURCE Henri 1826-1899 **[25]**
🖐 **$14 430** - €16 112 - **£9 425** - FF105 690
Les voyeuses Oil/canvas (160x120cm 62x47in) Antwerpen 2000
🖐 **$3 688** - €4 311 - **£2 633** - FF28 277
Mother and her Children returning Home Oil/canvas (80.5x60.5cm 31x23in) Amsterdam 2001

BOURDELLE Émile-Antoine 1861-1929 **[330]**
🖐 **$20 176** - €24 392 - **£14 096** - FF160 000
Bacchante Plâtre (H184cm H72in) Paris 2000
🖐 **$9 500** - €10 538 - **£6 317** - FF69 127
Danseur du 14 juillet Bronze (H26.5cm H10in) New-York 2000
🖐 **$1 529** - €1 677 - **£1 015** - FF11 000
Léda et le cygne Aquarelle (19.5x15cm 7x5in) Paris 2000

BOURDIN Guy 1933-1991 **[7]**
🖐 **$3 764** - €3 493 - **£2 300** - FF22 913
Le Néant Silver print (41.5x35cm 16x13in) London 2000

BOURDIN Joseph c.1810-1869 **[1]**
🖐 **$2 076** - €1 982 - **£1 297** - FF13 000
Brick danois et vapeur à aubes Aquarelle/papier (42x56cm 16x22in) Paris 1999

BOURDON Sébastien 1616-1671 **[40]**
🖐 **$13 040** - €15 245 - **£9 310** - FF100 000
Le sacrifice de la fille de Jephté Huile/toile (55x46cm 21x18in) Paris 2001
🖐 **$3 602** - €3 347 - **£2 200** - FF21 956
St John the Baptist Preaching Wash (18x25cm 7x9in) London 1998

$301 - €256 - £181 - FF1 676
Kleidung der nackten in Palastarchitektur
Etching (43.5x58.5cm 17x23in) Köln 1998

BOURDUGE Jouineau XX **[2]**
$750 - €831 - £509 - FF5 453
«Tirez sur le pianiste» Poster (119x160cm 47x63in)
New-York 2000

BOURET Eutrope 1833-1906 **[106]**
$1 300 - €1 159 - £801 - FF7 601
Au Clair de la Lune Bronze (H45cm H18in)
Bloomfield-Hills MI 1999

BOURET Germaine 1907-1953 **[499]**
$312 - €335 - £209 - FF2 200
Le marchand de bouquets Fusain/papier (48x35cm
18x13in) Douarnenez 2000
$134 - €145 - £92 - FF950
Ces bas de soie, quelle camelote!/La prière
Gravure (18x13cm 7x5in) Paris 2001

BOURGAIN Gustave 1855-1921 **[29]**
$2 994 - €2 536 - £1 800 - FF16 635
Wrestling Match/The Sailor's Haircut Watercolour,
gouache/paper (45.5x59cm 17x23in) London 1998

BOURGEOIS Amédée 1798-1837 **[4]**
$70 000 - €74 757 - £47 698 - FF490 371
**View of the Basilica of Maxentius and
Constantine** Oil/paper/canvas (38x52.5cm 14x20in)
New-York 2000

BOURGEOIS Charles Arthur 1838-1886 **[21]**
$14 000 - €15 922 - £9 781 - FF104 441
The Snake Charmer Sculpture (H112cm H44in)
Chicago IL 2000

BOURGEOIS DU CASTELET Constant Florent F.
1767-1836 **[16]**
$677 - €640 - £409 - FF4 200
Paysage avec églises et moine priant Pierre noire
(14.5x21.5cm 5x8in) Paris 1999

BOURGEOIS Eugène 1855-1909 **[52]**
$505 - €442 - £306 - FF2 900
Bord de mer dans la Hague Huile/toile
(24.2x34.7cm 9x13in) Cherbourg 1998
$957 - €915 - £600 - FF6 003
«Chamonix-Montenvers» Poster (108x76cm
42x29in) London 1999

BOURGEOIS Louis Maximilien 1839-1901 **[2]**
$4 091 - €4 421 - £2 833 - FF29 000
Le charmeur de serpent Bronze (H56cm H22in) Le
Havre 2001

BOURGEOIS Louise 1911 **[105]**
$5 776 - €6 295 - £4 000 - FF41 291
Untitled Mixed media (25.5x27cm 10x10in) London
2001
$240 000 - €268 818 - £166 752 - FF1 763 328
Mortise Bronze (152.5x45.5x38cm 60x17x14in) New-
York 2001
$11 553 - €12 590 - £8 000 - FF82 582
Give or Take II Bronze (7x23.5x24cm 2x9x9in)
London 2001
$16 000 - €18 565 - £11 046 - FF121 776
Untitled Pencil (21.5x33cm 8x12in) New-York 2000
$1 600 - €1 418 - £981 - FF9 300
Untitled, Safety Pins Drypoint (30x38cm 11x14in)
New-York 2000

BOURGEOIS Victor Ferdinand 1870-1957 **[23]**
$550 - €656 - £392 - FF4 300
Paris, le parc Monceau, hiver Pastel/papier
(40x31cm 15x12in) Paris 2000

BOURGEOIS-BORGEX Louis 1873-? **[26]**
$556 - €596 - £380 - FF3 909
Shepherd with His Flock at Dusk Oil/canvas
(45x81cm 17x31in) London 2001
$874 - €994 - £600 - FF6 523
Boats on the Siene Oil/board (15.5x21.5cm 6x8in)
London 2000
$3 000 - €3 499 - £2 106 - FF22 951
«Bounty of the Sea» Poster (40x100.5cm 15x39in)
New-York 2000

BOURGES Léonide P. Élise 1838-1910 **[12]**
$3 846 - €4 497 - £2 702 - FF29 500
Pommiers en fleurs Huile/toile (45x78cm 17x30in)
Paris 2000
$3 637 - €3 964 - £2 384 - FF26 000
Petite fille au chapeau de paille Huile/panneau
(27x22cm 10x8in) Dijon 2000

BOURGOGNE Pierre 1838-1904 **[10]**
$15 000 - €14 253 - £9 126 - FF93 493
Still Life of Flowers and fruit Oil/canvas
(194.5x124.5cm 76x49in) New-York 1999
$3 588 - €3 964 - £2 488 - FF26 000
Nature morte au chou Huile/toile (81x65cm
31x25in) Chartres 2001
$4 005 - €4 573 - £2 817 - FF30 000
Bouquet de roses et collier de perles Huile/toile
(41x33cm 16x12in) Fontainebleau 2001

BOURGOIN Marie Désiré 1839-1912 **[9]**
$2 777 - €3 125 - £1 912 - FF20 500
Pauline, l'amie de Sarah Bernhardt
Aquarelle/papier (68x50cm 26x19in) Beaune 2000

BOURHILL J.E. XIX **[17]**
$4 605 - €4 361 - £2 800 - FF28 608
Water Rat/Hedgehog with a Frog Oil/canvas
(28x38cm 11x14in) London 1999

BOURJINON J(ohanna?) XVII **[4]**
$10 460 - €11 228 - £7 000 - FF73 651
**Peaches and a Fig on a Pewter Dish, Grapes on
the Vine** Oil/canvas (54.5x76.5cm 21x30in) London
2000
$20 178 - €23 841 - £14 299 - FF156 387
Früchtestilleben Öl/Leinwand (27.7x38.9cm
10x15in) Zürich 2000

BOURKE Brian XX **[28]**
$1 608 - €1 778 - £1 115 - FF11 660
Polling Landscape Mixed media (73.5x51cm
28x20in) Dublin 2001
$1 904 - €2 032 - £1 268 - FF13 326
Portrait of JMcM Oil/canvas (34x29cm 13x11in)
Dublin 2001
$887 - €952 - £605 - FF6 246
Rehearsing Big Maggie Pencil/paper (35.5x53cm
13x20in) Dublin 2001

BOURKE-WHITE Margaret 1904-1971 **[308]**
$5 000 - €5 499 - £3 467 - FF36 070
Molten Metal, Aluminium Company of America
Silver print (33x23cm 13x9in) New-York 2001

BOURNE James, Rev. 1773-1854 **[50]**
$261 - €282 - £180 - FF1 853
«Pulverback Church from the Oaks» Watercolour
(18x25cm 7x9in) Billingshurst, West-Sussex 2001

BOURNE John Cooke XIX **[12]**
- $189 - €216 - £130 - FF11 418
  View from above Kilsby Tunnel Color lithograph (24.5x36cm 9x14in) West-Midlands 2000

BOURNE Samuel 1834-1912 **[48]**
- $2 849 - €3 312 - £2 000 - FF21 728
  Ulswater/Kilchurro Castle Watercolour/paper (51x73cm 20x28in) Billingshurst, West-Sussex 2001
- $628 - €610 - £388 - FF4 000
  Agra, The Fort/Gwalior, Ancient Brahminical Temple/Temple de Gwalior Tirage albuminé (29x23cm 11x9in) Paris 1999

BOURNICHON François Édouard 1816-1896 **[19]**
- $1 674 - €1 524 - £1 025 - FF10 000
  Pêcheur au bord de la rivière Huile/toile (41x66cm 16x25in) Cherbourg 1998

BOUROTTE Auguste 1853-1940 **[10]**
- $1 025 - €1 002 - £650 - FF6 574
  The Accused Oil/panel (40.5x54.5cm 15x21in) London 1999

BOURQUE Loretta 1963 **[2]**
- $9 500 - €8 198 - £5 749 - FF53 774
  Scream Oil/canvas (122x58.5cm 48x23in) Tel Aviv 1999

BOUSSEAU Jacques, Jacobo Buso 1681-1740 **[4]**
- $5 865 - €7 013 - £4 029 - FF46 000
  Soldat bandant son arc Bronze (H48cm H18in) Paris 2000

BOUT Peeter 1658-1702/19 **[111]**
- $41 840 - €44 912 - £28 000 - FF294 604
  Classical landscape with a Waggon Train and Pedestrians on a road Oil/canvas (128x178cm 50x70in) London 2000
- $17 369 - €16 319 - £10 326 - FF98 521
  Händler und Bauern be- und entladen Boote Öl/Leinwand (48x62cm 18x24in) Zürich 1998
- $10 153 - €9 433 - £6 200 - FF61 876
  A Wooded River Landscape with Woodmen and Travellers on a Track Oil/panel (33x45cm 12x17in) London 1998
- $732 - €767 - £484 - FF5 030
  Feldlager Ink (21x26.5cm 8x10in) München 2000
- $454 - €511 - £319 - FF3 353
  Fischmarkt an der Küste von Scheveningen Etching (19.4x28cm 7x11in) Köln 2001

BOUTAREL Simone act.c.1925-? **[2]**
- $2 418 - €2 255 - £1 500 - FF14 790
  Figure of a Hoop Dancer Bronze (H73cm H28in) London 1999

BOUTELLE DeWitt Clinton 1817/20-1884 **[19]**
- $3 500 - €4 043 - £2 450 - FF26 523
  Cattle watering by a Stream Oil/canvas (54x84cm 21x33in) New-York 2001
- $5 500 - €6 483 - £3 864 - FF42 524
  Stream in the Catskills Oil/canvas (30x45cm 12x18in) New-Orleans LA 2001

BOUTEN Armand 1893-1965 **[23]**
- $2 198 - €2 531 - £1 500 - FF16 600
  Two Lesbian Prostitutes Watercolour, gouache (34.5x26.5cm 13x10in) London 2000

BOUTER Cornelius Wouter 1888-1966 **[159]**
- $2 045 - €1 932 - £1 270 - FF12 671
  Mother and Children with Lamb Oil/canvas (41x51cm 16x20in) Nepean, Ont. 1999
- $1 606 - €1 724 - £1 075 - FF11 311
  Malle jan Oil/canvas (30x40cm 11x15in) Dordrecht 2000

BOUTER Pieter Adrianus 1887-1968 **[27]**
- $438 - €499 - £302 - FF3 274
  Shepherd and his Flock of Sheep Oil/canvas (50x91cm 19x35in) Amsterdam 2000

BOUTERWEK Frédérick 1806-1867 **[6]**
- $1 374 - €1 620 - £966 - FF10 627
  Musicerande herdepar Oil/canvas (39x47cm 15x18in) Malmö 2000

BOUTET DE MONVEL Bernard 1884-1949 **[61]**
- $12 950 - €15 245 - £9 100 - FF100 000
  Personnage assis Huile/toile (45.5x40.5cm 17x15in) Paris 2000
- $1 854 - €1 829 - £1 142 - FF12 000
  Au cinodrome Aquarelle/papier (24x24cm 9x9in) Neuilly-sur-Seine 1999
- $248 - €226 - £150 - FF1 485
  «Departing for the Chase» Print in colors (27x50cm 11x20in) London 1998

BOUTET DE MONVEL Louis-Maurice 1851-1913 **[14]**
- $401 - €457 - £279 - FF3 000
  «Société des aquarelles françaises, 19ème exposition, Champs-Elysées» Affiche (94x66.5cm 37x26in) Paris 2001

BOUTIBONNE Charles Edouard 1816-1897 **[23]**
- $3 255 - €3 718 - £2 265 - FF24 390
  Jeune femme en tenue néo-classique Huile/toile (118x73cm 46x28in) Moscou 2001
- $4 000 - €3 658 - £2 442 - FF23 995
  Jeune femme à la tapisserie Oil/panel (43x28cm 17x11in) New-York 1998
- $1 127 - €1 067 - £702 - FF7 000
  Le songe Pastel/papier (62x74cm 24x29in) Deauville 1999

BOUTIGNY Paul Émile 1854-1929 **[20]**
- $1 278 - €1 372 - £855 - FF9 000
  Le pousse-café Huile/panneau (46x38cm 18x14in) Cherbourg 2000

BOUTON Charles Marie 1781-1853 **[7]**
- $6 052 - €6 098 - £3 772 - FF40 000
  Moines dominicains dans un cloître/Un élégant dans une cage d'escalier Huile/toile (32.5x24.5cm 12x9in) Paris 2000

BOUTRY Paul 1936 **[51]**
- $256 - €274 - £169 - FF1 800
  Jeux de plage Huile/panneau (24x33cm 9x12in) Lons-Le-Saunier 2000

BOUTSHOORN Willem XX **[3]**
- $1 840 - €1 815 - £1 133 - FF11 906
  Untitled Gouache/paper (65x55cm 25x21in) Amsterdam 1999

BOUTTATS Frederick I 1612-1661 **[14]**
- $25 680 - €29 746 - £17 760 - FF195 120
  Le jardin d'Eden Huile/panneau (33.5x46cm 13x18in) Bruxelles 2000

BOUTTATS Jacob 1660-1718 **[18]**
- $21 888 - €24 392 - £14 896 - FF160 000
  Orphée charmant les animaux Huile/panneau (36x72cm 14x28in) Paris 2000
- $9 500 - €8 361 - £5 783 - FF54 846
  The Garden of Eden Oil/copper (11.5x18cm 4x7in) New-York 1999

BOUTTATS Johann Baptist act.1690-1735 **[3]**
- $48 960 - €57 502 - £34 762 - FF377 190
  Garde-manger Huile/toile (114.5x144.5cm 45x56in) Warszawa 2000

$17 671 - €19 813 - **£12 000** - FF129 968
River Landscape with an elegant Couple in a
Carriage on a Ferry Oil/canvas (70.5x109cm
27x42in) London 2000

BOUVAL Maurice 1860-1926 [53]
$2 514 - €2 820 - **£1 742** - FF18 500
Vase «le lierre» Bronze (H28.5cm H11in) Paris 2000

BOUVARD Antoine 1840-1920 [242]
$11 801 - €11 891 - **£7 355** - FF78 000
Gondoles à Venise Huile/toile (50x65cm 19x25in)
Calais 2000
$13 407 - €12 918 - **£8 282** - FF84 738
Rio San Marco, Venice Oil/canvas (23x32cm 9x12in)
Johannesburg 1999

BOUVARD Antoine 1870-1956 [211]
$16 000 - €15 727 - **£10 280** - FF103 164
Canal in the Afternoon Oil/canvas (54.5x81.5cm
21x32in) New-York 1999
$9 295 - €10 419 - **£6 500** - FF68 345
The Grand Canal, Venice Oil/canvas (33x46cm
12x18in) London 2001

BOUVARD Colette XIX-XX [6]
$6 328 - €6 106 - **£4 000** - FF40 050
The Waterfront, Venice Oil/canvas (38.5x54cm
15x21in) London 1999
$4 630 - €5 000 - **£3 200** - FF32 799
Deep Waters Oil/canvas (36x27cm 14x10in) Cheshire
2001

BOUVARD Noël Georges 1912-1975 [56]
$12 976 - €10 990 - **£7 800** - FF72 088
Le Zitelle alla Giudecca, Venice Oil/canvas
(54x81cm 21x31in) London 1998
$3 817 - €3 368 - **£2 300** - FF22 094
Le Grand Canal -Venise Oil/canvas (27x35cm
10x13in) London 1998

BOUVÉ Rosamond Ch. Smith 1876-1948 [7]
$80 000 - €88 597 - **£54 256** - FF581 160
Afternoon Reverie Oil/canvas (135x152cm 53x60in)
New-York 2000

BOUVET Henry 1859-1945 [85]
$324 - €305 - **£204** - FF2 000
Baigneuse dans les rochers Huile/toile (13x18cm
5x7in) Vannes 1999

BOUVIER Agnes Rose 1842-c.1892 [10]
$500 - €518 - **£300** - FF3 400
Ritratto femminile Acquarello/carta (16x12cm 6x4in)
Milano 2000

BOUVIER Armand 1913-1997 [265]
$632 - €610 - **£399** - FF4 000
Baie de Saint-Tropez Huile/toile (50x61cm 19x24in)
Paris 2000

BOUVIER Arthur 1837-1921 [15]
$1 120 - €1 239 - **£750** - FF8 130
Voiliers sur la plage Huile/toile (34x51cm 13x20in)
Antwerpen 2000
$145 - €173 - **£104** - FF1 138
Voiliers sur la rivière Huile/toile (27x39cm 10x15in)
Antwerpen 2000

BOUVIER Augustus Jules 1825-1881 [43]
$2 335 - €2 195 - **£1 450** - FF14 397
A Mother and her Daughter in an Interior
Watercolour/paper (34x26cm 13x10in) Salisbury,
Wiltshire 1999

BOUVIER Gustavus Arthur XIX [8]
$597 - €642 - **£400** - FF4 208
Searvant Girl Before Curtain Watercolour/paper
(33x20cm 12x7in) Edinburgh 2000

BOUVIER Joseph ?-1888 [11]
$7 114 - €8 266 - **£5 000** - FF54 221
Maidens Reclining/Maidens gathering Fruit
Oil/canvas (56x86cm 22x33in) London 2001
$1 992 - €2 314 - **£1 400** - FF15 181
«Field Flowers» Oil/panel (25.5x19.5cm 10x7in)
London 2001
$1 288 - €1 211 - **£800** - FF7 943
A Woman outside a Cottage offering Cherries to
two Children Watercolour/paper (20x14cm 7x5in)
Salisbury, Wiltshire 1999

BOUVIER Jules 1800-1867 [7]
$899 - €1 013 - **£620** - FF6 645
The Water Nymph Watercolour (49x33.5cm 19x13in)
London 2000

BOUVIER Pierre Louis 1766-1836 [18]
$14 012 - €16 556 - **£9 930** - FF108 602
Portrait der Kaiserin Joséphine Öl/Leinwand
(28.5x24.5cm 11x9in) Zürich 2000

BOUVIER Pietro 1839-1927 [6]
$3 000 - €3 110 - **£1 800** - FF20 400
Ritratto di giovane donna con rosa bianca
Olio/tavola (17x10cm 6x3in) Milano 2001

BOUVIOLLE Maurice 1893-1971 [77]
$2 622 - €2 897 - **£1 818** - FF19 000
Bou-Noura Huile/toile (53.5x65cm 21x25in) Paris
2001
$1 884 - €1 829 - **£1 164** - FF12 000
Halte devant les remparts Huile/toile/carton
(19x26.5cm 7x10in) Paris 1999
$423 - €427 - **£264** - FF2 800
Place du marché Aquarelle/papier (23.5x31cm
9x12in) Paris 2000

BOUY Gaston 1866-? [40]
$1 127 - €1 067 - **£685** - FF7 000
Élégantes Pastel/papier (45x35cm 17x13in) Paris 1999

BOUYS André 1656-1740 [11]
$11 000 - €12 956 - **£7 607** - FF84 984
Still Life of a Coffee Service, Milk Pot, Sucrier,
Mallet and Hatchet Oil/canvas (56x93.5cm 22x36in)
New-York 2000

BOUYSSOU Jacques 1926-1997 [370]
$2 454 - €2 287 - **£1 513** - FF15 000
Plage de Grandcamp Huile/toile (54x55cm 21x21in)
Le Havre 1999
$794 - €915 - **£542** - FF6 000
La boucherie Huile/toile (27x35cm 10x13in) Paris
2000
$314 - €351 - **£212** - FF2 300
Une rue à Caen Aquarelle/papier (30.5x43.5cm
12x17in) Paris 2000

BOUZIANIS Georgios 1885-1959 [7]
$135 000 - €150 162 - **£90 000** - FF985 000
Man with hat - Man mit melone Oil/canvas
(131x71cm 51x27in) Athens 2000
$94 500 - €105 114 - **£63 000** - FF689 500
Portrait of a Child - Kinderbild Watercolour
(54x35.5cm 21x13in) Athens 2000

BOUZONNET-STELLA Claudine 1636-1697 [3]
$2 459 - €2 439 - **£1 529** - FF16 000
L'adoration des Rois Mages Encre (38.5x28cm
15x11in) Paris 1999

BOVAR J. Ph. XVIII-XIX **[1]**

🖊 $7 842 - €9 147 - £5 508 - FF60 000
La Grand Grimpar mâle Aquarelle, gouache (50.2x39.3cm 19x15in) Paris 2000

BOVI Mariano 1758-? **[5]**

▥ $638 - €663 - £400 - FF4 348
Allegory of the Fine Arts, After Francesco Bartolozzi, R.A & Cipriani Engraving (19x47cm 7x18in) Suffolk 2000

BOVIN Karl 1907-1985 **[104]**

☺ $2 896 - €3 217 - £2 016 - FF21 103
Marklandskab Oil/canvas (76x103cm 29x40in) København 2001

☺ $615 - €565 - £378 - FF3 709
Ral àl Zalaét Oil/paper (26x36cm 10x14in) København 1999

🖊 $266 - €323 - £186 - FF2 116
Bronzealderhöjene, Bahrain Watercolour/paper (14x23cm 5x9in) Viby J, Arhus 2000

BOVINET Edme 1767-1832 **[8]**

▥ $134 - €153 - £93 - FF1 004
Carte du royaume polonais Gravure cuivre couleurs (34x42.5cm 13x16in) Lódz 2000

BOVIS Marcel 1904-1996 **[33]**

📷 $654 - €613 - £404 - FF4 024
Paris la nuit, Brasserie Dupont Vintage gelatin silver print (24x22.7cm 9x8in) Köln 2000

BOWDOIN Harriette ?-1947 **[14]**

☺ $3 000 - €2 784 - £1 801 - FF18 262
Garden Scene with Trellis Oil/canvas (68x55cm 27x22in) Milford CT 1999

BOWEN Emanuel XVIII **[48]**

▥ $218 - €190 - £130 - FF1 245
An Accurate Map of the County of York Divided Into Its Riding Print (45x51cm 17x20in) Bath 1998

BOWEN Greta 1880-1981 **[6]**

☺ $1 243 - €1 206 - £782 - FF7 912
Party Time along the River Oil/board (44.5x58.5cm 17x23in) Dublin 1999

🖊 $887 - €952 - £605 - FF6 246
Interior with Cat Gouache/paper (44.5x30.5cm 17x12in) Dublin 2001

BOWEN John T. 1801-c.1856 **[54]**

▥ $1 200 - €1 016 - £718 - FF6 663
Tah-Ro-Ho, an Iowan Warrior/A Musquakee Brave Lithograph (50.5x35cm 19x13in) San-Francisco CA 1998

BOWEN Owen 1873-1967 **[259]**

☺ $1 297 - €1 255 - £800 - FF8 233
Blue Bell Wood Oil/canvas (42x52cm 16x20in) West-Yorkshire 1999

☺ $945 - €917 - £600 - FF6 018
A Still Life of Anemones upon a Table Oil/canvas/board (34x39cm 13x15in) West-Yorshire 1999

🖊 $518 - €502 - £320 - FF3 293
A Yorkshire Coastal Scene, Possibly a Scene at Ravenscar Watercolour (26.5x38cm 10x14in) West-Yorshire 1999

BOWEN Thomas ?-1790 **[5]**

▥ $150 - €156 - £95 - FF1 026
Map of the British and French Settlements in North America Print (21x49cm 8x19in) Swindon, Wiltshire 2000

BOWER Edward c.1610-c.1670 **[5]**

⊙ $26 657 - €31 703 - £19 000 - FF207 958
Portrait of Richard Coffin, Three-quarter Length Oil/canvas (98x77cm 38x30in) London 2000

BOWER J.S. XIX **[4]**

🖊 $650 - €725 - £439 - FF4 757
Returning Home on a Winter Day Mixed media/paper (36x49cm 14x19in) Bolton MA 2000

BOWERS Edward 1822-1870 **[3]**

🖊 $12 000 - €13 270 - £8 025 - FF87 043
Still Life with Grapes, Orange, Apple, Strawberries Pastel/paper (31x39cm 12x15in) Portsmouth NH 2000

BOWERS Henry Robertson 1883-1912 **[5]**

📷 $7 747 - €9 099 - £5 500 - FF59 685
Forestalles. Amundsen's Tent at the South Pole, 18 Juanary Gelatin silver print (27.5x38.5cm 10x15in) London 2000

BOWERS Stephen J. XIX **[28]**

🖊 $553 - €630 - £380 - FF4 131
Fishing by Richmond Bridge Watercolour/paper (23.5x52cm 9x20in) London 2000

BOWIE David 1947 **[2]**

☺ $10 920 - €9 294 - £6 500 - FF60 962
The Heart's Filthy Lesson Oil/canvas (119.5x90cm 47x35in) London 1998

BOWKETT Jane Maria 1837-1891 **[22]**

🖊 $2 176 - €2 451 - £1 500 - FF16 078
Loves Swet Dream Oil/canvas (61x51cm 24x20in) London 2000

BOWLER Thomas William 1812-1869 **[32]**

☺ $34 894 - €36 640 - £22 000 - FF240 343
The Wreck of the Royalo Anbert, Table Bay Oil/canvas (47x63.5cm 18x25in) London 2000

🖊 $4 509 - €4 258 - £2 800 - FF27 928
Green Point Lighthouse Watercolour/paper (14x26cm 5x10in) London 1999

▥ $2 860 - €3 190 - £1 865 - FF20 924
Panoramic of Cape Town and Surrounding Scenery Color lithograph (23.5x116cm 9x45in) Johannesburg 2000

BOWLES Charles Oldfield XVIII-XIX **[7]**

🖊 $628 - €537 - £380 - FF3 525
In the Channel Watercolour/paper (24x33cm 9x12in) London 1999

BOWLES Ian XX **[18]**

🖊 $402 - €366 - £249 - FF2 399
Green Woodpecker and Bluebells Watercolour/paper (32x23cm 12x9in) Billingshurst, West-Sussex 1999

BOWLES-CARINGTON XVIII-XIX **[4]**

▥ $532 - €624 - £380 - FF4 096
The Battle of Culloden, April 16th Engraving (36x49cm 14x19in) London 2000

BOWMAN Jean Eleanor 1917 **[2]**

☺ $7 000 - €6 567 - £4 325 - FF43 077
«Late Bloome» with Jockey up at Belmont Park Oil/canvas (63.5x77cm 25x30in) New-York 1999

BOWNESS William 1809-1867 **[9]**

☺ $1 283 - €1 162 - £800 - FF7 623
The thunderstorm Oil/canvas (92x75.5cm 36x29in) Glasgow 1999

BOWYER William 1926 **[41]**
$1 601 - €1 453 - **£1 000** - FF9 534
The Conservatory Oil/canvas/board (53x53cm 20x20in) London 1999

BOXER Stanley Robert 1926 **[22]**
$650 - €614 - **£404** - FF4 028
Surgedrest Print (140x107cm 55x42in) San-Francisco CA 1999

BOYADJIEV Latchezar 1959 **[1]**
$5 500 - €5 026 - **£3 364** - FF32 971
Taking Flight Sculpture, glass (H28.5cm H11in) New-York 1999

BOYAL Davy XX **[3]**
$12 039 - €11 173 - **£7 500** - FF73 287
Anthropomorphic Skeletal Sofa Iron (114x252x125cm 44x99x49in) London 1999

BOYCE George Price 1826-1897 **[35]**
$5 941 - €5 899 - **£3 712** - FF38 694
Anstis Cove, South Devon Watercolour/paper (26.5x38cm 10x14in) Toronto 1999

BOYCE William Thomas N. 1858-1911 **[72]**
$464 - €410 - **£280** - FF2 689
Tug Pulling a Tall Ship at Sunset Watercolour/paper (50x35cm 19x13in) Retford, Nottinghamshire 1998

BOYD Arthur M. Bloomfield 1920-1999 **[697]**
$51 462 - €55 241 - **£34 443** - FF362 358
Nude with Beast V, Diana and Actaeon III Oil/board (182x159.5cm 71x62in) Melbourne 2000
$27 421 - €26 417 - **£16 946** - FF173 285
Shoalhaven Hillside with driving Black Bird Oil/canvas (90x120cm 35x47in) Sydney 1999
$10 426 - €10 880 - **£6 576** - FF71 370
Harvest & Heat Stubble Oil/board (20x29cm 7x11in) Sydney 2000
$1 167 - €1 286 - **£776** - FF8 438
Teapot with Teapot Face Ceramic (H23cm H9in) Melbourne 2000
$2 083 - €2 431 - **£1 450** - FF15 946
Nebuchadnezzar in Flight Watercolour/paper (49.5x62cm 19x24in) Melbourne 2000
$611 - €657 - **£416** - FF4 311
Bundanon Lithograph (30x45cm 11x17in) Sydney 2001

BOYD Arthur Merric 1862-1940 **[39]**
$622 - €698 - **£432** - FF4 579
Landscape at Yarra Glen Oil/canvas/board (21.5x29.5cm 8x11in) Melbourne 2001
$970 - €921 - **£605** - FF6 044
House in the Valley Watercolour/paper (17x24cm 6x9in) Sydney 1999
$480 - €477 - **£300** - FF3 126
Untitled Etching, aquatint (60x42cm 23x16in) London 1999

BOYD David 1924 **[422]**
$37 167 - €39 896 - **£24 875** - FF261 703
King Found Oil/board (122x137cm 48x53in) Melbourne 2000
$3 397 - €3 195 - **£2 103** - FF20 955
Goddess of Fruit Oil/board (44.5x50cm 17x19in) Melbourne 1999
$1 331 - €1 386 - **£836** - FF9 091
The Mystery of Wattle Oil/canvas (29.5x39.5cm 11x15in) Melbourne 2000
$442 - €516 - **£308** - FF3 388
Horse Decorated jug Glazed ceramic (H13cm H5in) Melbourne 2000

$898 - €1 069 - **£621** - FF7 012
The Chorister Ink (20x17.5cm 7x6in) Sydney 2000
$259 - €301 - **£182** - FF1 974
Red Angel Etching (22x22cm 8x8in) Sydney 2000

BOYD Emma Minnie 1858-1936 **[36]**
$1 697 - €1 592 - **£1 048** - FF10 446
Saplings Watercolour/paper (30.5x15cm 12x5in) Melbourne 1999

BOYD Guy Martin a'Beckett 1923-1988 **[51]**
$8 265 - €8 042 - **£5 086** - FF52 751
Three Bathers Bronze (83x96x12cm 32x37x4in) Malvern, Victoria 1999
$2 554 - €2 227 - **£1 544** - FF14 608
Adam's Rib Bronze (H75cm H29in) Melbourne 1998

BOYD John 1957 **[6]**
$3 247 - €3 204 - **£2 000** - FF21 014
Gramarye of the Sign, my Deceiver Liveth Oil/board (75x109cm 29x42in) London 1999

BOYD Theodore Penleigh 1890-1923 **[70]**
$11 688 - €12 847 - **£7 490** - FF84 272
Sydney Harbour Oil/canvas (39x54cm 15x21in) Melbourne 2000
$4 573 - €4 300 - **£2 831** - FF28 209
Road to the Farmhouse Oil/board (18x23cm 7x9in) Melbourne 1999
$1 829 - €1 964 - **£1 224** - FF12 883
Stand of Tree Watercolour/paper (26x36.5cm 10x14in) Melbourne 1999
$321 - €278 - **£194** - FF1 823
«The Jetty, Portsea Pier» Etching (21x25cm 8x9in) Malvern, Victoria 1998

BOYD Walter Scott 1834-1901 **[9]**
$3 572 - €3 835 - **£2 391** - FF25 154
Bildnis einer jungen Dame in durchsichtigem Gewand Öl/Leinwand (77x51cm 30x20in) Stuttgart 2000

BOYD William Merric 1888-1959 **[24]**
$214 - €222 - **£135** - FF1 454
Bird Pencil/paper (18x24cm 7x9in) Sydney 2000

BOYDELL Creswick XIX-XX **[25]**
$512 - €489 - **£320** - FF3 206
Children at Play Before a Thatched Cottage Watercolour/paper (23x38cm 9x14in) Cheshire 1999

BOYDELL John 1719-1804 **[28]**
$300 - €311 - **£180** - FF2 040
Paesaggio agreste con armenti, da Claude Gellée Le Lorrain Acquatinta (22.5x29cm 8x11in) Milano 2000

BOYDELL Josiah 1752-1817 **[5]**
$592 - €544 - **£366** - FF3 571
Fruit Piece, after Angelo Campidoglio Etching (30x35cm 11x13in) Amsterdam 1999

BOYÉ Abel Dominique 1864-1934 **[19]**
$4 458 - €4 317 - **£2 800** - FF28 315
Young Beauty in a Garden Oil/canvas (81x54cm 31x21in) London 1999

BOYENVAL Alexis François 1784-c.1855 **[2]**
$2 515 - €2 439 - **£1 593** - FF16 000
Gentilhomme soignant un moine dans la cour d'un monastère Huile/toile (41x33cm 16x12in) Paris 1999

BOYER Émile 1877-1948 **[130]**
$411 - €381 - **£254** - FF2 500
Vue de Paris Huile/carton (50x60cm 19x23in) Paris 1999

BOYER Michel 1668-1724 **[1]**
🖼 **$130 000** - €114 417 - **£79 144** - FF750 529
Trompe l'oeil of a Lute, a Violin and a Flute, with Books of Music Oil/canvas (130x97cm 51x38in)
New-York 1999

BOYER Otto 1874-1912 **[9]**
🖼 **$3 393** - €3 176 - **£2 111** - FF20 836
Lady in an Autumn Landscape near a Lake
Oil/canvas (73x85.5cm 28x33in) Amsterdam 1999

BOYER Trevor 1948 **[58]**
🖼 **$2 711** - €3 161 - **£1 900** - FF20 734
Tiger Acrylic/panel (50x64cm 19x25in) London 2000
🖼 **$1 045** - €1 071 - **£650** - FF7 027
Mallard Acrylic (38x29cm 14x11in) Billingshurst, West-Sussex 2000

BOYLE Alicia 1908-1996 **[18]**
🖼 **$3 276** - €2 795 - **£1 952** - FF18 333
Charlotte Oil/board (45x35cm 18x14in) Dublin 1998
🖼 **$496** - €584 - **£348** - FF3 831
Bar, Dun Laoghaire Oil/canvas (34.5x24cm 13x9in)
Dublin 2000

BOYLE Charles Wellington 1861-1925 **[11]**
🖼 **$20 000** - €19 978 - **£12 502** - FF131 050
On the Bayou Lacombe, La Oil/canvas (50x66cm 20x26in) New-Orleans LA 1999
🖼 **$2 000** - €2 217 - **£1 388** - FF14 544
Sketch, Louisiana Landscape Oil/canvas (22x30cm 9x12in) New-Orleans LA 2001

BOYLE Eleanore Vere 1825-1916 **[4]**
🖼 **$5 320** - €6 188 - **£3 800** - FF40 591
Death but a Sleep Watercolour (15x11.5cm 5x4in)
London 2001

BOYLE George A. 1826-1899 **[128]**
🖼 **$795** - €859 - **£550** - FF5 637
Country Landscape with Trees Oil/board (36.5x50cm 14x19in) London 2001
🖼 **$368** - €413 - **£250** - FF2 707
Verdant River Landscape Oil/canvas (25x20cm 10x8in) Aylsham, Norfolk 2000

BOYLE Neil 1931 **[1]**
🖼 **$4 000** - €4 542 - **£2 779** - FF29 792
The Water is Cold Oil/canvas (91x121cm 36x48in)
Dallas TX 2001

BOYLEY Errol 1918 **[22]**
🖼 **$981** - €945 - **£606** - FF6 200
The Herder Oil/board (59.5x75cm 23x29in)
Johannesburg 1999

BOYS du Paulus c.1620-c.1660 **[2]**
🖼 **$2 774** - €3 354 - **£1 938** - FF22 000
Le voile de sainte Véronique Huile/panneau (29x21cm 11x8in) Paris 2000

BOYS Thomas Shotter 1803-1874 **[144]**
🖼 **$6 584** - €6 431 - **£4 200** - FF42 186
Elizabeth Castle, Jersey Watercolour (17x25.5cm 6x10in) London 1999
🖼 **$257** - €240 - **£160** - FF1 577
St Fleet Street/The Strand Color lithograph (42x31cm 16x12in) London 1999

BOYVIN René c.1525-c.1580/98 **[4]**
🖼 **$1 704** - €1 829 - **£1 140** - FF12 000
Danse de Dryades d'après Le Rosso Eau-forte (28x40cm 11x15in) Paris 2000

BOZE Honoré 1830-1908 **[23]**
🖼 **$25 587** - €21 492 - **£15 000** - FF140 977
At the oasis Oil/canvas (107.5x166cm 42x65in)
London 1998

🖼 **$6 260** - €7 013 - **£4 356** - FF46 000
Paysage orientaliste animé Huile/toile (38x54.5cm 14x21in) Marseille 2001

BOZE Joseph 1744-1826 **[25]**
🖼 **$10 572** - €8 719 - **£6 228** - FF57 192
Bildnis des Schriftstellers Pierre Augustin Caron de Beaumarchais Pastell/Papier (63x50cm 24x19in) Wien 1998

BOZNANSKA Olga 1865-1940 **[49]**
🖼 **$276 375** - €303 164 - **£187 750** - FF1 988 625
A l'atelier Huile/toile (137x108cm 53x42in) Warszawa 2000
🖼 **$18 466** - €16 958 - **£11 277** - FF111 237
Still Life with Flowers Oil/panel (47.5x34cm 18x13in) Warszawa 1998
🖼 **$7 001** - €8 327 - **£4 992** - FF54 624
Vase bleu Huile/carton (33x24cm 12x9in) Warszawa 2000

BOZZACHI Louis XIX-XX **[1]**
🖼 **$31 464** - €35 063 - **£21 160** - FF230 000
Vénus, surgissant de l'eau s'appuie sur un dauphin, Mars et Neptune Pierre (39.5x20cm 15x7in)
Mayenne 2000

BOZZALLA Giuseppe 1874-1958 **[8]**
🖼 **$2 000** - €2 592 - **£1 500** - FF17 000
Torrente ad Oropa Olio/tavola (44x31cm 17x12in)
Vercelli 2001

BOZZOLINI Silvano 1911-1998 **[148]**
🖼 **$641** - €762 - **£457** - FF5 000
Rythmes dynamiques No 2 Huile/toile (100x100cm 39x39in) Calais 2000
🖼 **$203** - €229 - **£142** - FF1 500
Composition Collage/papier (24.5x24.5cm 9x9in)
Paris 2001

BRAAK van den Karel 1953 **[16]**
🖼 **$828** - €992 - **£568** - FF6 504
Torso (Torse) Bronze (H27cm H10in) Antwerpen 2000

BRABAZON Hercules Brabazon 1821-1906 **[576]**
🖼 **$2 072** - €1 788 - **£1 250** - FF11 726
St Catarena Mixed media (16x24cm 6x9in) London 1998
🖼 **$1 313** - €1 411 - **£900** - FF9 254
Fiesole Watercolour (12x15.5cm 4x6in) London 2001

BRABO Albert 1894-1964 **[7]**
🖼 **$1 300** - €1 465 - **£900** - FF9 610
Farm Buildings in an extensive Landscape
Oil/canvas (60.5x81cm 23x31in) London 2000

BRACCESCO Carlo act.1478-1501 **[1]**
🖼 **$60 000** - €64 910 - **£41 106** - FF425 784
Saint Andrew transforming the Seven Devils of Nicea into Dogs Tempera/panel (42.5x29.5cm 16x11in) New-York 2001

BRACCI Michele XVIII **[2]**
🖼 **$1 750** - €1 814 - **£1 050** - FF11 900
Trompe l'oeil Inchiostro (21x30cm 8x11in) Milano 2001

BRACHO Gabriel 1915-1995 **[41]**
🖼 **$850** - €770 - **£550** - FF5 050
Paisaje Oleo/cartón (32x54.5cm 12x21in) Caracas 1999

BRACHT Eugen Felix Prosper 1842-1921 **[129]**
🖼 **$12 417** - €12 782 - **£7 827** - FF83 847
Mächtige, Schatten spendende Eichen
Öl/Leinwand (127x169cm 50x66in) Berlin 2000

$3 866 - €4 346 - £2 714 - FF28 508
«Steinzaun bei Arkona» Öl/Karton (37x55cm
14x21in) Hamburg 2001
$1 289 - €1 278 - £806 - FF8 384
Räbener Spring (Heidelandschaft) Öl/Leinwand
(31.5x49.5cm 12x19in) München 1999

BRACK Cecil John 1920-1999 [110]
$104 440 - €118 114 - £73 500 - FF774 780
Double nude II Oil/canvas (153x127cm 60x50in)
Malvern, Victoria 2001
$64 760 - €60 891 - £40 100 - FF399 420
Still Life with Purple Scissors Oil/canvas
(81.5x115.5cm 32x45in) Melbourne 1999
$45 332 - €42 624 - £28 070 - FF279 594
Glass of Claret Oil/board (22x45cm 8x17in)
Melbourne 1999
$9 720 - €10 434 - £6 505 - FF68 445
Sketch for junior Latin American Crayon
(44x67cm 17x26in) Melbourne 2000
$1 417 - €1 592 - £919 - FF10 441
Adagio Lithograph (38.5x24cm 15x9in) Malvern,
Victoria 2000

BRACK Emil 1860-1905 [12]
$35 257 - €38 347 - £23 242 - FF251 542
Interieur mit Figurengruppe Öl/Leinwand
(82x108cm 32x42in) Heidelberg 2000

BRACKETT Sydney Lawrence 1852-1910 [22]
$1 125 - €1 307 - £801 - FF8 574
Four Kittens Oil/canvas (60x45cm 24x18in) Cleveland
OH 2001
$425 - €456 - £289 - FF2 994
Massachusetts Farm House Oil/canvas (30.5x46cm
12x18in) Boston MA 2001
$2 100 - €1 772 - £1 231 - FF11 621
Playtime Pastel/paper (45x60cm 18x24in) Mystic CT
1998

BRACKETT Walter M. 1823-1919 [8]
$16 000 - €14 942 - £9 875 - FF98 016
Trout, Rod and Reel on a Riverbank Oil/canvas
(51x81cm 20x31in) Boston MA 1999

BRÄCKLE Jakob 1897-1987 [44]
$2 239 - €2 556 - £1 578 - FF16 769
«Heuernte» Öl/Karton (17x18cm 6x7in) Stuttgart
2001
$169 - €158 - £104 - FF1 039
Holzfäller Woodcut (42x36cm 16x14in) Heidelberg
1999

BRACKMAN David 1932 [21]
$20 995 - €19 744 - £13 000 - FF129 509
«Britannia» at Hunter Quay during Clyde Week,
1923 Oil/canvas (69x101.5cm 27x39in) London 1999
$4 845 - €4 556 - £3 000 - FF29 886
«Suzanne» leaving Portsmouth, 1910
Watercolour, gouache/paper (49.5x74.5cm 19x29in)
London 1999

BRACKMAN Robert 1898-1980 [113]
$3 200 - €3 030 - £1 945 - FF19 878
Portrait in Studio Light Oil/canvas (92x72cm
36x28in) New-York 1999
$1 300 - €1 232 - £812 - FF8 083
Dish of Fruit Oil/canvas (20x25cm 8x10in) Mystic CT
1999
$700 - €808 - £492 - FF5 298
Two Female Nude models Pastel/paper (55x43cm
22x17in) Norwalk CT 2000

BRACONNIER Stéphane 1958 [13]
$347 - €381 - £230 - FF2 500
Sans titre Linogravure (85x85cm 33x33in) Paris 2000

BRACQUEMOND Félix 1833-1914 [191]
$19 000 - €16 218 - £11 362 - FF106 382
Portrait de Madame Calmas Pastel/paper (46x35cm
18x13in) New-York 1998
$541 - €457 - £323 - FF3 000
Alidor Delzant Eau-forte (41x33.5cm 16x13in) Paris
1998

BRADBERRY Georges 1878-1959 [74]
$11 500 - €13 079 - £7 975 - FF85 792
Bouquet de fleurs Huile/toile (68x44cm 26x17in)
Newport-Beach CA 2000
$1 558 - €1 753 - £1 072 - FF11 500
Bouquet de fleurs Pastel/papier (68x44cm 26x17in)
Rouen 2000

BRADBURY Arthur Royce 1892-1977 [54]
$244 - €222 - £150 - FF1 459
Guernsey Coastal Scene Watercolour/paper
(17x25cm 6x9in) Channel-Islands 1999

BRADBURY Bennett XX [11]
$700 - €751 - £468 - FF4 928
Point Vicente-Big Sur Oil/canvas (50x76cm 20x30in)
Altadena CA 2000

BRADDON Paul 1864-1938 [74]
$302 - €305 - £188 - FF2 000
Le gros Horloge Aquarelle, gouache/papier (75x53cm
29x20in) Rennes 2000

BRADFORD Lodowick H. XIX [1]
$1 300 - €1 262 - £809 - FF8 276
Lawrence Machine Shop, The Abbott Lawrence
Lithograph (59x34cm 23x33in) Bolton MA 1999

BRADFORD William 1823-1892 [81]
$50 000 - €54 857 - £33 215 - FF359 840
A Calm Afternoon, the Coast of Labrador
Oil/canvas (50.5x76cm 19x29in) New-York 2000
$18 000 - €17 046 - £10 944 - FF111 817
Sunset on the Labrador Coast Oil/board (23x38cm
9x14in) New-York 1999
$3 000 - €3 220 - £2 043 - FF21 124
Falmouth Harbour 7th May Graphite (10.5x21cm
4x8in) Boston MA 2001
$1 500 - €1 606 - £1 020 - FF10 533
Sloops in Artic Waters Etching (33x54cm 13x21in)
Portsmouth NH 2001

BRADLEY Ann Cary 1884-? [7]
$3 000 - €3 545 - £2 126 - FF23 252
St.Stephen's in Sunlight, Ashland, Maine
Oil/masonite (67x55cm 26x22in) Austinburg OH 2000

BRADLEY Basil 1842-1904 [55]
$5 578 - €6 560 - £4 000 - FF43 034
Mid-summers day on the Thames Oil/panel
(31x56cm 12x22in) Oxford 2001
$1 384 - €1 538 - £927 - FF10 089
Three Dogs in the Mountains Watercolour/paper
(26x36cm 10x14in) Melbourne 2000

BRADLEY Cuthbert 1861-1943 [27]
$11 000 - €12 780 - £7 730 - FF83 833
Foxhounds outside the Kennel Oil/canvas
(61x91.5cm 24x36in) New-York 2001
$882 - €873 - £550 - FF5 728
Over the Brook, the Cambridgeshire Hunt
Oil/canvas (30.5x51cm 12x20in) London 1999
$140 - €163 - £100 - FF1 072
«The Consolation Race» Watercolour (19.5x31cm
7x12in) London 2001

BRADLEY Helen Layfield 1900-1979 **[207]**
- $52 688 - €49 513 - **£33 924** FF324 787
  Oh, what a Pity it's starting to snow
  Oil/canvas/board (63.5x73.5cm 25x28in) London 1999
- $23 051 - €21 662 - **£14 000** - FF142 094
  On windy Days at Blackpool Oil/board (23x30.5cm
  9x12in) London 1999
- $12 528 - €12 160 - **£7 800** - FF79 762
  Blackpool Beach Watercolour (26.5x37cm 10x14in)
  London 1999
- $304 - €302 - **£190** - FF1 979
  Winter Street Color lithograph (37x55cm 14x21in)
  London 1999

BRADLEY John ?-1847 **[4]**
- $7 000 - €6 671 - **£4 437** - FF43 756
  Portrait of a gentleman holding a Scroll Oil/can-
  vas (84x41cm 33x16in) Cleveland OH 1999

BRADLEY Martin 1931 **[119]**
- $1 300 - €1 348 - **£780** - FF8 840
  Hell Olio/tela (100x50cm 39x19in) Prato 1999
- $275 - €285 - **£165** - FF1 870
  Autumn Hill Tempera/carta (42x56cm 16x22in) Prato
  2000

BRADLEY William act.1872-1889 **[13]**
- $7 966 - €6 883 - **£4 800** - FF45 148
  Ponies in a Woodland Glade Oil/canvas (82x108cm
  32x42in) Billingshurst, West-Sussex 1999
- $2 092 - €2 246 - **£1 400** - FF14 730
  The Bridge at Sonning, Berkshire
  Watercolour/paper (45.5x70cm 17x27in) London 2000

BRADLEY William H. 1868-1962 **[41]**
- $1 000 - €1 116 - **£624** - FF7 318
  «The Chap-Book Being a Miscellany» Poster
  (54x36cm 21x14in) New-York 2000

BRADSHAW Constance H. act.1898-1961 **[10]**
- $954 - €801 - **£560** - FF5 253
  «Flowers» Oil/board (50x41.5cm 19x16in) Bristol,
  Avon 1998

BRADSHAW George Fagan 1887-1960 **[34]**
- $298 - €321 - **£200** - FF2 104
  Moonlight in St.Ives Oil/board (53x63cm 21x25in)
  Par, Cornwall 2000
- $1 195 - €1 283 - **£800** - FF8 417
  View to Godrevy Watercolour (53x72cm 21x28in)
  Par, Cornwall 2000

BRADWAY Florence Dell 1897-? **[2]**
- $3 750 - €4 079 - **£2 472** - FF26 757
  **Edgartown Harbor looking towards
  Chappaquidick** Oil/canvas/board (51x60cm 20x23in)
  Boston MA 2000

BRADY Charles Michael 1926-1997 **[44]**
- $5 631 - €5 333 - **£3 423** - FF34 981
  Two Eye drop Boxes Oil/board (55x66cm 22x26in)
  Dublin 1999
- $3 447 - €3 809 - **£2 390** - FF24 987
  Palette with two Colours Oil/canvas (20x34cm
  7x13in) Dublin 2001

BRADY Mathew B. 1823-1896 **[75]**
- $1 200 - €1 391 - **£850** - FF9 126
  Lincoln Conspirators Photograph (13.5x10.5cm
  5x4in) New-York 1999

BRAEKELEER de Adrien Ferdinand 1818-1904 **[40]**
- $6 272 - €6 941 - **£4 396** - FF45 528
  L'atelier de menuiserie Huile/toile (64x86cm
  25x33in) Bruxelles 2001

- $2 562 - €2 659 - **£1 625** - FF17 440
  Küchenszene Oil/panel (27x23cm 10x9in) Leipzig
  2000

BRAEKELEER de Ferdinand Jr. 1828-1857 **[12]**
- $2 210 - €2 107 - **£1 343** - FF13 821
  Scène villageoise Huile/toile (39x55cm 15x21in)
  Bruxelles 1999

BRAEKELEER de Ferdinand Sr. 1792-1883 **[137]**
- $13 993 - €16 652 - **£10 000** - FF109 232
  Strijdtoneel Met Kenau Simons Hasselaar
  Oil/canvas (147.5x169.5cm 58x66in) London 2000
- $14 400 - €15 864 - **£9 408** - FF104 064
  Représentation gala Huile/panneau (36.5x48cm
  14x18in) Bruxelles 2000
- $3 626 - €4 116 - **£2 519** - FF27 000
  A votre santé Huile/panneau (30.5x23.5cm 12x9in)
  Barbizon 2001
- $310 - €322 - **£197** - FF2 113
  De spaanse furie Wash/paper (22x31cm 8x12in)
  Lokeren 2000

BRAEKELEER de Henri 1840-1888 **[105]**
- $1 576 - €1 588 - **£982** - FF10 418
  Interior of a Workshop Oil/canvas (36x51.5cm
  14x20in) Amsterdam 2000
- $1 295 - €1 239 - **£795** - FF8 130
  L'Aquarelliste Huile/panneau (30x20cm 11x7in)
  Bruxelles 1999
- $337 - €372 - **£220** - FF2 439
  Intérieurs - Maisons Crayon/papier (13.5x19.5cm
  5x7in) Bruxelles 2000

BRAGG Charles 1931 **[42]**
- $150 - €136 - **£91** - FF895
  «Bacchus»/Monk under a Tree Engraving
  (12x10cm 5x4in) New-Orleans LA 1998

BRAIN John XIX **[1]**
- $1 400 - €1 493 - **£950** - FF9 793
  English Cathedral Interior with Figures
  Watercolour/paper (47x38cm 18x14in) London 2001

BRAINARD Joe 1942 **[2]**
- $1 900 - €1 775 - **£1 148** - FF11 641
  Bruce Pencil (34.5x26.5cm 13x10in) New-York 1999

BRAITH Anton 1836-1905 **[125]**
- $12 025 - €11 248 - **£7 284** - FF73 785
  Junger Ziegenhirte bei seiner Herde Öl/Leinwand
  (52.5x96cm 20x37in) Düsseldorf 1999
- $4 715 - €4 345 - **£2 823** - FF28 504
  Zwei Ochsen an der Tränke Öl/Leinwand
  (22.5x39.5cm 8x15in) Dresden 1998
- $225 - €230 - **£141** - FF1 509
  Der Ziegenhirte mit seinen Tieren Pencil/paper
  (10x16cm 3x6in) Augsburg 2000

BRAKEN van den Peter 1896-1979 **[21]**
- $581 - €544 - **£362** - FF3 571
  «De Peelhut» Oil/canvas (47x67cm 18x26in)
  Amsterdam 1999

BRAKENBURGH Richard 1650-1702 **[35]**
- $11 177 - €13 294 - **£7 966** - FF87 201
  Bauernhochzeit Öl/Leinwand (101x127cm 39x50in)
  Köln 1999
- $11 216 - €12 196 - **£7 392** - FF80 000
  Réjouissances à l'auberge Huile/toile (50x63.5cm
  19x25in) Paris 2000
- $3 431 - €3 358 - **£2 200** - FF22 026
  Gentleman and Lady playing Backgammon
  Oil/panel (32x26cm 12x10in) London 1999

B

BRALEY Clarence E. XIX-XX **[17]**
$175 - €168 - **£109** - FF1 099
Seashore Watercolour/paper (20x27cm 8x11in)
Dedham MA 1999

BRAMANTI Bruno 1897-1957 **[2]**
$1 300 - €1 348 - **£780** - FF8 840
Case nel verde Olio/cartone (26x35.5cm 10x13in)
Firenze 2001

BRAMBILLA Ambrogio act.1582-1599 **[3]**
$300 - €311 - **£180** - FF2 040
Le sette etta dell'uomo Acquaforte (26x20cm 10x7in) Milano 2000

BRAMBILLA Fernando 1763-1834 **[20]**
$180 - €204 - **£122** - FF1 339
Vista de una parte del acueducto de Segovia
Grabado (36x51cm 14x20in) Madrid 2000

BRAMER Josef 1948 **[40]**
$5 439 - €5 087 - **£3 290** - FF33 369
Baum in der Dämmerung Öl/Leinwand (60x60cm 23x23in) Wien 1999
$371 - €436 - **£263** - FF2 860
Leopold Gratz Aquarell/Papier (15.5x15cm 6x5in) Wien 2000
$168 - €182 - **£116** - FF1 191
Vollmond Farblithographie (17.5x22cm 6x8in) Wien 2001

BRAMER Leonard 1596-1674 **[70]**
$9 600 - €10 901 - **£6 570** - FF71 505
Soldaten bei einem nächtlichen Lagerfeuer
Öl/Leinwand (92x72cm 36x28in) Wien 2000
$15 100 - €14 521 - **£9 302** - FF95 251
The Circumcision of Christ Oil/copper (13x16.5cm 5x6in) Amsterdam 1999
$1 424 - €1 220 - **£857** - FF8 000
Le Christ au jardin des Oliviers Crayon (36.5x29cm 14x11in) Paris 1998

BRAMLEY Frank 1857-1915 **[42]**
$10 673 - €12 567 - **£7 500** - FF82 435
Sunshine and Shadows Oil/canvas (39x44cm 15x17in) London 2000
$3 646 - €3 882 - **£2 400** - FF25 465
The Sleen Prison, Antwerp Oil/panel (23.5x14cm 9x5in).West-Midlands 2000

BRAMLEY William act.1900-1932 **[1]**
$2 843 - €3 208 - **£2 000** - FF21 045
Stroll in the Garden Oil/canvas (45.5x30.5cm 17x12in) London 2001

BRAMSON Stern J. 1912-1989 **[4]**
$2 600 - €2 898 - **£1 822** - FF19 010
Baron la Velle Lawrence Jones in his Home Theater, Louisville Silver print (36x46cm 14x18in) New-York 2001

BRANCA Giulio 1850-1926 **[5]**
$13 000 - €13 476 - **£7 800** - FF88 400
Rosmunda Marbre (H93cm H36in) Milano 2001

BRANCACCIO Carlo 1861-1920 **[208]**
$38 000 - €42 142 - **£25 285** - FF276 434
Bahia napolitana Oleo/lienzo (88x136.5cm 34x53in) Buenos-Aires 2001
$11 000 - €10 452 - **£6 692** - FF68 561
Along the Coast, Naples Oil/canvas (73x100.5cm 28x39in) New-York 1999
$3 200 - €4 147 - **£2 400** - FF27 200
Parigi Olio/cartone (15x23cm 5x9in) Milano 2001
$480 - €622 - **£360** - FF4 080
Scalinata a Napoli Acquarello/cartone (50x40cm 19x15in) Roma 2001

BRANCACCIO Giovanni 1903-1975 **[9]**
$3 893 - €3 739 - **£2 400** - FF24 525
Natura Morta Oil/canvas (63.5x83.5cm 25x32in) London 1999

BRANCUSI Constantin 1876-1957 **[99]**
$160 000 - €151 461 - **£99 376** - FF993 520
L'enfant endormi Bronze (H11cm H4in) New-York 1999
$200 000 - €192 321 - **£123 220** - FF1 261 540
Étude de Mademoiselle Pogany Gouache/board (64x49.5cm 25x19in) New-York 1999
$5 049 - €5 934 - **£3 500** - FF38 924
Projet d'architecture Gelatin silver print (28x21cm 11x8in) London 2001

BRAND Christian Hülfgott 1695-1756 **[28]**
$6 390 - €7 267 - **£4 400** - FF47 670
«Waldige Hügellandschaft mit Ruine und Staffage» Öl/Leinwand (65.5x79cm 25x31in) Wien 2001
$3 800 - €4 415 - **£2 670** - FF28 960
Italianate Landscape with Travellers and a Packmule on a River Bank Oil/panel (18.5x22cm 7x8in) New-York 2001

BRAND Friedrich August 1735-1806 **[3]**
$3 160 - €3 068 - **£1 968** - FF20 123
Landschaft mit Gebirgsbach Red chalk/paper (46.3x37cm 18x14in) Berlin 1999

BRAND Johann Christian 1722-1795 **[34]**
$13 404 - €14 330 - **£9 400** - FF94 000
Paysage animé au bord du lac l'incendie/Paysage animé de montagne
Huile/toile (80x106cm 31x41in) Lyon 2001
$2 303 - €2 543 - **£1 596** - FF16 684
Reisende in einer Landschaft Öl/Leinwand (26x35cm 10x13in) Wien 2001

BRANDANI Enrico 1914-1979 **[18]**
$604 - €560 - **£370** - FF3 673
Fillette à l'Herbier Huile/panneau (33x27.5cm 12x10in) Bern 1999

BRANDARD Robert 1805-1862 **[10]**
$4 766 - €4 623 - **£3 000** - FF30 322
Mother and Children in a Cottage Oil/panel (35.5x45.5cm 13x17in) London 1999

BRANDEIS Antonietta 1849-1920 **[220]**
$9 293 - €10 554 - **£6 500** - FF69 230
The interior of Santa Croce, Florence Oil/canvas (55.5x75.5cm 21x29in) London 2001
$7 498 - €8 286 - **£5 200** - FF54 355
Fishing Boats, Venice Oil/board (17x23cm 6x9in) London 2001
$2 303 - €2 543 - **£1 596** - FF16 684
Park in Rom mit Aussicht auf St.Peter Aquarell/Papier (15x27cm 5x10in) Wien 2001

BRANDELIUS Gustaf 1833-1884 **[30]**
$1 820 - €1 971 - **£1 246** - FF12 927
Vallflicka i sommarlandskap Oil/canvas (46.5x77cm 18x30in) Stockholm 2001
$2 331 - €2 538 - **£1 526** - FF16 650
Steeple chase Oil/canvas (25x35cm 9x13in) Uppsala 2000

BRANDEN van den Guy 1926 **[157]**
$455 - €446 - **£280** - FF2 926
Compositie Oil/canvas (90x90cm 35x35in) Lokeren 1999
$133 - €149 - **£92** - FF975
Composition Gouache/papier (52x38cm 20x14in) Antwerpen 2001

BRANDENBURG Cornelis 1884-1954 **[17]**
- **$74** - €82 - **£50** - FF535
  Lijnbaansgracht Etching in colors (31.4x20.5cm 12x8in) Haarlem 2000

BRANDENBURG Martin 1870-1919 **[5]**
- **$10 400** - €9 715 - **£6 285** - FF63 724
  Blühender Bauerngarten an der Ostseeküste Öl/Leinwand (74x95cm 29x37in) Berlin 1999

BRANDENBURG Wilhelm 1824-1901 **[23]**
- **$1 079** - €1 227 - **£748** - FF8 049
  Flusslandschaft mit Schafhirten Öl/Leinwand (48.5x69cm 19x27in) Hamburg 2000
- **$645** - €767 - **£447** - FF5 030
  Holsteinische Landschaft Oil/panel (21x27cm 8x10in) Bremen 2000

BRANDER Fredrik 1705-1779 **[2]**
- **$1 428** - €1 658 - **£1 003** - FF10 878
  Gustaf Adolf Gyllenborg Oil/canvas (71x56cm 27x22in) Stockholm 2001

BRANDES Hans Heinrich Jürgen 1803-1868 **[6]**
- **$5 054** - €5 696 - **£3 500** - FF37 362
  Bowl of Punch, with a Pineapple and a Carpet on a Table Oil/canvas (77x63.5cm 30x25in) London 2000
- **$5 024** - €4 602 - **£3 062** - FF30 185
  Im Harz, Sonniger Waldweg und Felsen mit zwei sichernden Rehen Oil/panel (32x48.5cm 12x19in) Berlin 1999

BRANDES Peter 1944 **[106]**
- **$2 600** - €2 950 - **£1 832** - FF19 351
  Figur med arm Oil/canvas (130x96cm 51x37in) Köbenhavn 2001
- **$155** - €134 - **£94** - FF882
  Komposition Lithograph (44x30cm 17x11in) Vejle 1999

BRANDES Willy 1876-1956 **[24]**
- **$837** - €767 - **£510** - FF5 030
  Herbstliche Allee Öl/Leinwand (80x135cm 31x53in) Berlin 1999
- **$682** - €665 - **£419** - FF4 360
  Kleinstadtstrasse mit an Raufe wartendem Pferdegespann und Gänseschar Öl/Leinwand (24x36cm 9x14in) Berlin 1999

BRANDI Domenico 1683-1736 **[46]**
- **$10 000** - €12 958 - **£7 500** - FF85 000
  Pastore con capre in un paesaggio montagnoso Olio/tela (100x150cm 39x59in) Roma 2000
- **$3 000** - €3 454 - **£2 047** - FF22 656
  Mountainous Landscape with a Herdsman in the Foreground Oil/canvas (95x117.5cm 37x46in) New-York 2000
- **$3 750** - €3 887 - **£2 250** - FF25 500
  Animali e pastorella Olio/tela (26.5x20cm 10x7in) Napoli 1999

BRANDI Giacinto 1623-1691 **[22]**
- **$5 674** - €6 860 - **£3 964** - FF45 000
  La Déploration du Christ Huile/toile (62x75cm 24x29in) Paris 2000

BRANDIMARTE Benedetto c.1550-c.1614 **[1]**
- **$7 000** - €7 257 - **£4 200** - FF47 600
  Natività Olio/tela (122x90cm 48x35in) Roma 2001

BRANDIS von August 1862-1947 **[45]**
- **$1 601** - €1 534 - **£1 007** - FF10 061
  Grüner Salon in einem Partizierhaus Öl/Leinwand (92x68cm 36x26in) Köln 1999

BRANDL Herbert 1959 **[38]**
- **$8 652** - €9 561 - **£6 000** - FF62 718
  Untitled Oil/canvas (140.5x90cm 55x35in) London 2001

BRANDNER Karl C. 1898-1961 **[11]**
- **$550** - €594 - **£380** - FF3 897
  Morning Light Oil/board (35x40cm 14x16in) Cincinnati OH 2001

BRANDOIN Michel Vincent 1733-1807 **[21]**
- **$3 448** - €3 369 - **£2 200** - FF22 097
  View of the Chateau of Gleyrolle, near Vevey on Lake Geneva Watercolour (25.5x38.5cm 10x15in) London 1999

BRANDON Édouard J. Émile 1831-1897 **[18]**
- **$24 150** - €22 503 - **£15 031** - FF147 609
  Rabbi with Children Oil/panel (24.5x41cm 9x16in) Tel Aviv 1999

BRANDON Frédéric 1943 **[5]**
- **$4 970** - €5 336 - **£3 325** - FF35 000
  Vanités Acrylique/toile (100x81cm 39x31in) Paris 2000

BRANDRIFF George Kennedy 1890-1936 **[22]**
- **$12 000** - €10 253 - **£7 261** - FF67 252
  «Blue and Gold» Oil/canvas (45.5x61cm 17x24in) San-Francisco CA 1998
- **$3 200** - €3 761 - **£2 218** - FF24 670
  Houses Among the Eucalyptus Oil/canvas (35.5x43cm 13x16in) Beverly-Hills CA 2000

BRANDS Eugene 1913 **[624]**
- **$10 684** - €12 706 - **£7 616** - FF83 344
  Abstrakt landschap Oil/canvas (106x145cm 41x57in) Amsterdam 2000
- **$3 399** - €3 176 - **£1 999** - FF20 836
  Vrouw - Woman Oil/paper (49x49cm 19x19in) Amsterdam 1999
- **$2 289** - €2 723 - **£1 632** - FF17 859
  Cat Oil/paper (23x50cm 9x19in) Amsterdam 2000
- **$1 840** - €1 682 - **£1 152** - FF11 032
  Portrait of a Woman Gouache/paper (65x55cm 25x21in) Köbenhavn 1999
- **$315** - €318 - **£196** - FF2 083
  Blauwe vaas Serigraph (83x63cm 32x24in) Amsterdam 2000

BRANDSTÄTTER Peter 1917 **[3]**
- **$1 652** - €1 599 - **£1 018** - FF10 487
  Teichlandschaft Aquarell/Papier (43.5x69cm 17x27in) Klagenfurt 1999

BRANDT Anthony XX **[9]**
- **$847** - €982 - **£600** - FF6 441
  «The Isle of Man, British Railways, L.M.Region» Poster (102x127cm 40x50in) London 2000

BRANDT Bill 1904-1983 **[406]**
- **$4 000** - €3 741 - **£2 418** - FF24 542
  Nude Gelatin silver print (23x20cm 9x7in) New-York 1999

BRANDT Carl 1852-1930 **[235]**
- **$1 571** - €1 844 - **£1 108** - FF12 097
  Norrländskt sjölandskap, solig vinterdag Oil/canvas (97x130cm 38x51in) Stockholm 2000
- **$1 051** - €1 049 - **£656** - FF6 880
  Solbelyst vinterlandskap med röd stuga Oil/canvas (59x94cm 23x37in) Uppsala 1999
- **$338** - €362 - **£231** - FF2 373
  Insjölandskap Pastel/paper (133x185cm 52x73in) Stockholm 2001

BRANDT Edgar 1880-1960 **[34]**
- 🔨 $260 800 - €304 898 - **£186 200** - FF2 000 000
  Olympie Bronze (H214cm H84in) Paris 2001
- 🔨 $2 037 - €1 982 - **£1 253** - FF13 000
  Pied de lampe «Coquillages» Fer (H30.5cm H12in) Paris 1999

BRANDT Federico 1879-1932 **[13]**
- 🖼 $10 720 - €10 214 - **£6 700** - FF67 000
  Rosas Oleo/lienzo (90x60cm 35x23in) Caracas 1999
- 🖼 $1 575 - €1 617 - **£1 050** - FF10 605
  Callejón de la Casona Oleo/lienzo (24.5x35.5cm 9x13in) Caracas 2000

BRANDT Johannes Herman 1850-1926 **[104]**
- 🖼 $1 306 - €1 408 - **£890** - FF9 234
  Solskinsdag ved den bornholmske kyst med udsigt tim Gudhjem Oil/canvas (52x77cm 20x30in) København 2001
- 🖼 $288 - €336 - **£206** - FF2 201
  Marine Oil/canvas (25x32cm 9x12in) Aarhus 2001

BRANDT Muriel 1882-1978 **[8]**
- 🖼 $1 775 - €2 032 - **£1 221** - FF13 326
  Birds Oil/board (31x30cm 12x12in) Dublin 2000
- ✏ $429 - €406 - **£260** - FF2 665
  Nun's Chapel, Clonmacnoise/St. Kevin's Kitchens Ink (20x27cm 8x11in) Dublin 1999

BRANDT Otto 1828-1892 **[16]**
- 🖼 $687 - €778 - **£480** - FF5 106
  Feeding the chickens Oil/panel (30.5x40cm 12x15in) Billingshurst, West-Sussex 2001

BRANDT Rexford Elson 1914-2000 **[30]**
- ✏ $2 300 - €2 148 - **£1 419** - FF14 089
  Fishing Watercolour (34x53cm 13x21in) Detroit MI 1999

BRANDT von Józef 1841-c.1915/28 **[65]**
- 🖼 $64 894 - €71 710 - **£45 000** - FF470 385
  The rendez vous Oil/canvas (40.5x64cm 15x25in) London 2001
- 🖼 $7 184 - €6 917 - **£4 492** - FF45 373
  Zwei Kosaken zu Pferd Huile/panneau (36x26cm 14x10in) Zürich 1999
- 🖼 $688 - €767 - **£463** - FF5 032
  Nu Crayon/papier (45x29cm 17x11in) Warszawa 2000

BRANDT Warren 1918 **[3]**
- 🖼 $1 600 - €1 856 - **£1 104** - FF12 177
  The Bentwood Rocker Oil/canvas (61x61cm 24x24in) New-York 2000

BRANDTNER Fritz 1896-1969 **[95]**
- 🖼 $1 359 - €1 581 - **£956** - FF10 370
  «The Changing Season» Oil/canvas (43x61cm 16x24in) Calgary, Alberta 2001
- 🖼 $682 - €663 - **£419** - FF4 352
  Harbour Front Activities Mixed media (25x36cm 10x14in) Nepean, Ont. 1999
- ✏ $855 - €856 - **£579** - FF6 269
  Basketball players Encres couleurs (37x22cm 14x8in) Montréal 2000

BRANDTSOEN Hendrick 1941 **[2]**
- 🖼 $2 291 - €2 496 - **£1 577** - FF16 371
  Still Life Oil/panel (22x28cm 8x11in) Amsterdam 2001

BRANEGAN John Francis 1843-1909 **[42]**
- ✏ $599 - €580 - **£380** - FF3 806
  Evening near Cromer/Near Grimsby Watercolour/paper (22x48cm 9x19in) Manchester 1999

BRANGWYN Frank 1867-1956 **[624]**
- 🖼 $15 748 - €13 435 - **£9 500** - FF88 125
  North African Coast Oil/board (39.5x51.5cm 15x20in) London 1998
- 🖼 $6 040 - €5 153 - **£3 600** - FF33 802
  In the Dock, Cape Town Oil/canvas/board (43x31.5cm 16x12in) London 1998
- ✏ $997 - €1 159 - **£705** - FF7 605
  Venetian Canal Scene Watercolour (25x19.5cm 9x7in) Billingshurst, West-Sussex 2001
- 🍴 $320 - €323 - **£200** - FF2 120
  Coffee Stall, Hammersmith Etching (30x23.5cm 11x9in) London 2000

BRANNER Martin M. 1888-1970 **[9]**
- ✏ $1 125 - €1 113 - **£689** - FF7 300
  Bicot Winnie Winkle, planche de 4 strips paru le 15 janvier Encre Chine/papier (66x48cm 25x18in) Neuilly-sur-Seine 2000

BRANSOM John Paul 1885-1979 **[11]**
- ✏ $1 760 - €1 501 - **£1 061** - FF9 849
  Bittern flying over pond, story illustration Charcoal (45x45cm 18x18in) New-York 1998

BRANWHITE Charles 1817-1880 **[28]**
- 🖼 $4 812 - €4 849 - **£3 000** - FF31 810
  Angler in a Wooded River Landscape Oil/canvas (46x68.5cm 18x26in) London 2000
- 🖼 $1 071 - €1 108 - **£675** - FF7 270
  Sunset over Avonmouth Watercolour (46x74cm 18x29in) London 2000

BRANWHITE Charles Brooke 1851-1929 **[63]**
- ✏ $514 - €521 - **£320** - FF3 418
  A Beach with Boats Aground Watercolour/paper (40x58cm 16x23in) Par, Cornwall 2000

BRAQUAVAL Louis 1853-1919 **[78]**
- 🖼 $2 548 - €2 668 - **£1 601** - FF17 500
  Vue de la Baie de Saint-Valery Huile/panneau (46x37cm 18x14in) Saint-Dié 2000
- 🖼 $649 - €610 - **£402** - FF4 000
  La Seine en hiver Huile/panneau (33x41cm 12x16in) Deauville 1999

BRAQUE Georges 1882-1963 **[1960]**
- 🖼 $150 000 - €164 617 - €96 585 - FF1 079 820
  Oiseau Mixed media (142.5x117.5cm 56x46in) New-York 2000
- 🖼 $240 000 - €263 388 - **£154 536** - FF1 727 712
  Vase d'anémones aux fruits Oil/canvas (50x61cm 19x24in) New-York 2000
- 🖼 $72 553 - €85 324 - **£52 026** - FF559 689
  Paysage aux coquelicots Oil/panel (16.5x41cm 6x16in) Bern 2001
- 🔨 $12 271 - €10 671 - **£7 399** - FF70 000
  Aegle Bronze (26.5x12.5x12cm 10x4x4in) Paris 1998
- 🖼 $13 000 - €13 800 - **£8 797** - FF90 519
  Hephaistos Gouache/paper (26x20cm 10x8in) Delray-Beach FL 2001
- 🍴 $2 649 - €2 469 - **£1 600** - FF16 196
  Phaéton, Char I Color lithograph (31x43.5cm 12x17in) London 1998
- 📷 $7 744 - €6 403 - **£4 544** - FF42 000
  Portrait de Picasso revêtu de l'uniforme militaire de Braque, Avril Tirage argentique (11x8cm 4x3in) Paris 1998

BRAQUEHAIS Bruno 1823-1875 **[8]**
- 📷 $2 149 - €2 030 - **£1 300** - FF13 317
  Étude de nu debout Albumen print (18x16cm 7x6in) London 1999

B

BRASCASSAT Jacques Raymond 1804-1867 **[58]**
- $47 123 - €52 836 - **£32 000** - FF346 582
  Hunting Still Life with a hound sniffing some dead game Oil/canvas (99x130.5cm 38x51in) London 2000
- $6 000 - €6 046 - **£3 740** - FF39 660
  Shepherd and his Flock Oil/canvas (73.5x92cm 28x36in) New-York 2000
- $1 866 - €1 753 - **£1 124** - FF11 500
  Tête de bélier Huile/toile (41x35cm 16x13in) Toulouse 1999

BRASCH August XIX **[2]**
- $4 905 - €4 362 - **£3 000** - FF28 611
  The Street Vendor Oil/canvas (75.5x59.5cm 29x23in) London 1999

BRASCH Hans 1882-1973 **[46]**
- $276 - €307 - **£192** - FF2 012
  «Selbstbildnis» Öl/Leinwand (86x43cm 33x16in) Stuttgart 2001

BRASCH Magnus 1731-1787 **[7]**
- $2 090 - €1 789 - **£1 258** - FF11 736
  «Rast von der Jagd», Jägern mit Hunden und erlegtem Wild Öl/Leinwand (40x30cm 15x11in) Stuttgart 1998

BRASCH Sven 1886-1970 **[16]**
- $324 - €348 - **£217** - FF2 286
  Höeberg & Victor Schiöler/H.C.Andersen og ukendt Pencil (23x21cm 9x8in) København 2000
- $1 200 - €1 339 - **£785** - FF8 781
  «Broken Blossoms, World Cinema» Poster (56.5x61.5cm 22x24in) New-York 2000

BRASCH Wenzel/Vaclav Ignaz ?-1761 **[30]**
- $4 636 - €4 857 - **£3 066** - FF31 862
  Hundemeute, einen Fuchs jagend/Hundemeute, ein Reh reissend Öl/Leinwand (35x47cm 13x18in) München 2000
- $3 258 - €2 744 - **£1 924** - FF18 000
  Le départ pour la chasse Huile/toile (32x42cm 12x16in) Paris 1998

BRASCHLER Otto 1909-1985 **[17]**
- $189 - €187 - **£118** - FF1 229
  Rheinlandschaft Aquarelle (46x59cm 18x23in) St. Gallen 1999

BRASEN Hans Ole 1849-1930 **[105]**
- $1 523 - €1 743 - **£1 059** - FF11 432
  Graessende köer ved en fjord Oil/canvas (72x60cm 28x23in) København 2000
- $507 - €604 - **£361** - FF3 959
  Afskeden Oil/wood (26x18cm 10x7in) København 2000

BRASILIER André 1929 **[493]**
- $13 947 - €16 401 - **£10 000** - FF107 586
  Loupeigne sous la neige Oil/canvas (130x161.5cm 51x63in) London 2001
- $13 230 - €11 162 - **£7 875** - FF73 215
  Sous-bois Huile/toile (73x116cm 28x45in) Antwerpen 1998
- $5 791 - €4 967 - **£3 500** - FF32 583
  Chevaux Oil/canvas/board (42x34.5cm 16x13in) London 1998
- $1 600 - €1 520 - **£973** - FF9 972
  Horses on a green Ground Glazed ceramic (H52cm H20in) New-York 1999
- $3 179 - €3 615 - **£2 180** - FF23 712
  Loufeigne en automne Watercolour (55.5x61cm 21x24in) Zürich 2000

- $385 - €381 - **£240** - FF2 500
  L'écharpe rose Lithographie couleurs (89.5x61cm 35x24in) Paris 1999

BRASS Hans 1885-1959 **[24]**
- $2 673 - €3 125 - **£1 877** - FF20 500
  Venise, gondoliers sur le Grand Canal devant un palais Huile/panneau (23.5x13.5cm 9x5in) Paris 2000

BRASS Italico 1870-1943 **[14]**
- $14 500 - €15 031 - **£8 700** - FF98 600
  Barche alla regata Olio/tela (50x61cm 19x24in) Milano 1999
- $5 475 - €6 135 - **£3 774** - FF40 246
  Blick auf die Piazzetta in Venedig Öl/Leinwand (30x34cm 11x13in) Hamburg 2000

BRASSAï (Gyula Halasz) 1899-1984 **[498]**
- $4 800 - €4 513 - **£2 972** - FF29 605
  Two Girls in a Cafe Silver print (30x23cm 12x9in) New-York 1999

BRASSAUW Melchior 1709-c.1760 **[11]**
- $4 602 - €4 363 - **£2 800** - FF28 622
  Two Women and a Man making Music in an Interior Oil/panel (38x31cm 14x12in) London 1999

BRASSEUR Georges 1880-1950 **[18]**
- $1 456 - €1 735 - **£1 043** - FF11 382
  Jeune femme nue se mirant Pastel/papier (63x26cm 24x10in) Bruxelles 2000

BRAT Vladimir 1965 **[42]**
- $1 305 - €1 351 - **£832** - FF8 865
  Bodegón de otoño frente a la ventana Oleo/lienzo (60x81cm 23x31in) Madrid 2000

BRATBY John Randall 1928-1992 **[373]**
- $1 446 - €1 562 - **£1 000** - FF10 249
  Sir David Frost Oil/canvas (152x91cm 59x35in) London 2001
- $852 - €917 - **£580** - FF6 012
  Rialto Bridge, Gondola, my Darling Patti twice Semi-nude Oil/canvas (121.5x91cm 47x35in) Billingshurst, West-Sussex 2001
- $344 - €402 - **£240** - FF2 639
  Auberon Waugh Oil/canvas (40.5x35cm 15x13in) London 2000
- $379 - €431 - **£260** - FF2 827
  Mercedes Parked in the Woods Pencil (38.5x55cm 15x21in) London 2000

BRATE Fanny 1861-1940 **[28]**
- $4 043 - €4 556 - **£2 800** - FF29 886
  The young Farmhands Oil/canvas (37.5x46cm 14x18in) London 2000
- $672 - €774 - **£463** - FF5 076
  Sommarlandskap med röda stugor Oil/canvas (28x43cm 11x16in) Stockholm 2000

BRATKOWSKI Roman 1869-1954 **[20]**
- $1 565 - €1 817 - **£1 100** - FF11 917
  Abendstimmung über einer Landschaft mit einem Bauernhof Öl/Leinwand (44x61cm 17x24in) Wien 2001

BRAU Casimir XIX-XX **[2]**
- $1 500 - €1 740 - **£1 067** - FF11 414
  «Labor» Poster (160x112cm 63x44in) Chicago IL 2000

BRAUER Erich, Arik 1929 **[247]**
- $17 160 - €18 294 - **£10 884** - FF120 000
  Idole d'or Huile/panneau (86x121cm 33x47in) Paris 2000

$8 074 – €7 925 – **£5 005** – FF51 985
Papageno/Papagena Oil/panel (24x20cm 9x7in)
München 1999

$3 820 – €3 272 – **£2 236** – FF21 460
«Ein warmer Wind» Aquarell/Papier (22.5x30cm
8x11in) Wien 1998

$175 – €179 – **£109** – FF1 173
Das Käppchen/Davids Harfe Etching, aquatint in
colors (21x26cm 8x10in) Hamburg 2000

BRAUER Marius 1867-1932 [2]
$12 963 – €13 613 – **£8 202** – FF89 298
Kameel Oil/canvas (53x41cm 20x16in) Amsterdam
2000

BRAUGHT Ross E. 1898-? [3]
$9 000 – €8 760 – **£5 529** – FF57 459
Snow covered Mountainside Oil/canvas (76x91cm
30x36in) Hatfield PA 1999

BRAUN Adam 1748-1827 [5]
$6 559 – €6 700 – **£4 609** – FF50 308
Maler in seinem Atelier Öl/Kupfer (50x36cm
19x14in) München 2000

BRAUN Adolphe 1811-1877 [111]
$1 300 – €1 214 – **£785** – FF7 965
Still Life Albumen print (36x43cm 14x17in) New-York
1999

BRAUN Augustin c.1570-c.1641 [1]
$12 000 – €12 854 – **£8 194** – FF84 319
Diana and Actaeon Wash (15x19cm 5x7in) New-
York 2001

BRAUN Georges 1541-1622 [26]
$353 – €344 – **£217** – FF2 255
Luxembourg Copper engraving in colors
(34.8x41.3cm 13x16in) Bern 1999

BRAUN Louis / Ludwig 1836-1916 [45]
$26 591 – €31 700 – **£18 959** – FF207 941
Dorfhochzeit Öl/Leinwand (110x185cm 43x72in)
Köln 2000

$2 090 – €1 789 – **£1 258** – FF11 736
Bauern mit Pferden bei der Heimkehr
Öl/Leinwand (40x50cm 15x19in) München 1998

$829 – €717 – **£492** – FF4 701
Bayerischer Bauer in Tracht Oil/panel (16x11.5cm
6x4in) Hildrizhausen 1998

$652 – €610 – **£394** – FF4 000
Halte à l'auberge Aquarelle/papier (19x26cm 7x10in)
Lille 1999

BRAUN Maurice 1877-1941 [158]
$22 500 – €24 151 – **£15 057** – FF158 422
Midsummer Oil/canvas (40.5x51cm 15x20in) San-
Francisco CA 2000

$6 000 – €6 440 – **£4 015** – FF42 246
Eucalyptus in a Mountainous Landscape
Oil/board (20x25cm 8x10in) Cedar-Falls IA 2000

BRAUN Reinhold 1821-1884 [13]
$2 794 – €3 323 – **£1 991** – FF21 800
**Stute mit ihrem Fohlen an der Tränke neben
dem Dorfwaschhaus** Oil/panel (22x28.5cm 8x11in)
Köln 2000

BRAUN Wilhelm Hans 1873-1938 [17]
$606 – €670 – **£420** – FF4 500
Kvinde med syrener Oil/canvas (69x55cm 27x21in)
Vejle 2001

BRAUND Dorothy Mary 1926 [62]
$3 179 – €3 093 – **£1 956** – FF20 289
Lovers Oil/board (81x55cm 31x21in) Melbourne 1999

$1 354 – €1 580 – **£942** – FF10 365
Boys with Sheet Acrylic/board (29.5x40cm 11x15in)
Melbourne 2000

$1 167 – €1 286 – **£776** – FF8 438
Tropical Montage Watercolour (17x43cm 6x16in)
Melbourne 2000

BRAUNER Victor 1903-1966 [494]
$55 233 – €53 444 – **£35 000** – FF350 570
L'acteur Oil/canvas (55x46cm 21x18in) London 1999

$9 000 – €9 330 – **£5 400** – FF61 200
Interlocking Figure Tecnica mista (24x18cm 9x7in)
Milano 1999

$3 783 – €4 573 – **£2 643** – FF30 000
Tête d'homme Dessin (7x5cm 2x1in) Paris 2000

$600 – €622 – **£360** – FF4 080
Figura Acquaforte, acquatinta (15x10cm 5x3in) Roma
2000

$19 000 – €19 757 – **£11 996** – FF129 595
Rire du Fleuve et mon Mystère Gelatin silver print
(39x29cm 15x11in) New-York 2000

BRAUNEROVA Zdenka 1858-1934 [9]
$6 358 – €6 014 – **£3 960** – FF39 446
Paris Öl/Leinwand (32x44.5cm 12x17in) Praha 2000

BRAUWER de Cyriel 1899-1988 [32]
$455 – €545 – **£312** – FF3 577
Vrouw met harp (femme à la harpe) Sculpture bois
(H53cm H20in) Antwerpen 2000

BRAVO Claudio 1936 [189]
$105 000 – €121 994 – **£73 794** – FF800 226
Messaoud et son fils Oil/canvas (130x97.5cm
51x38in) New-York 2001

$55 000 – €52 960 – **£34 232** – FF347 396
Sin título Oil/canvas (100x50cm 39x19in) New-York
1999

$55 000 – €58 663 – **£36 635** – FF384 802
Untitled Oil/canvas (33x41.5cm 12x16in) New-York
2000

$20 000 – €19 258 – **£12 448** – FF126 326
Retro de dama Graphite (101.5x73cm 39x28in) New-
York 1999

BRAWLEY Robert Julius 1937 [1]
$2 900 – €2 506 – **£1 721** – FF16 439
Still Life with Self Portrait Graphite (61x47cm
24x18in) Washington 1998

BRAY de Dirck c.1640-c.1690 [3]
$633 218 – €709 986 – **£430 000** – FF4 657 201
**Peonies, Columbine, Morning Glory and other
Flowers in a Vase** Oil/panel (62x44cm 24x17in)
London 2000

BRAY de Jan c.1627-1697 [17]
$4 800 – €5 007 – **£3 022** – FF32 842
Retrato de caballero Oleo/lienzo (73x57cm 28x22in)
Buenos-Aires 2000

$9 000 – €9 611 – **£6 132** – FF63 047
**Young Girl Looking at her Reflection in a Mirror
Held by a Page** Black chalk (16x14cm 6x5in) New-
York 2001

BRAY de Salomon 1597-1664 [11]
$40 221 – €34 222 – **£24 000** – FF224 481
The Banishment of Hagar and Ishmael Oil/panel
(59x50cm 23x19in) London 1998

BRAY James XIX [1]
$8 355 – €9 449 – **£5 880** – FF61 982
Dan kelly, carte de visite Albumen print (20.5x13cm
8x5in) Malvern, Victoria 2001

BRAY Phyllis 1911 [6]

📁 $670 - €789 - £480 - FF5 173
«Wimbledon Championships» Poster (26x32cm 10x12in) London 2001

BRAYER Paul 1905-1968 [2]

✏️ $2 626 - €2 515 - £1 618 - FF16 500
Cheval et petite maison en Camargue
Aquarelle/papier (28x22cm 11x8in) Calais 1999

BRAYER Yves 1907-1990 [1401]

🖼️ $20 726 - €19 361 - £12 788 - FF127 000
Nature morte au globe de mariage Huile/toile (114x162cm 44x63in) Le Touquet 1999

🖼️ $8 862 - €8 842 - £5 394 - FF58 000
La Camargue Huile/toile (65x81cm 25x31in) Paris 2000

🖼️ $4 706 - €3 964 - £2 779 - FF26 000
Les Baux de Provence Huile/toile (27x35cm 10x13in) Paris 1998

✏️ $1 768 - €1 982 - £1 199 - FF13 000
«Aux armées» Aquarelle, gouache/papier (31x42cm 12x16in) Paris 1999

📁 $189 - €183 - £119 - FF1 200
En Provence Lithographie couleurs (32x41.5cm 12x16in) Paris 1999

BRAZ Osip Emmanuelovich 1873-1936 [3]

🖼️ $4 058 - €3 900 - £2 500 - FF25 583
Tea-Time Oil/canvas (49x63cm 19x24in) London 1999

BRAZDA Oscar 1888-1977 [8]

🖼️ $115 - €109 - £72 - FF717
Nature morte aux fleurs Huile/toile (30x34cm 11x13in) Praha 2001

BRAZIER Marie-Caroline act.c.1833-c.1848 [1]

✏️ $5 368 - €6 098 - £3 756 - FF40 000
Cactus en fleur Aquarelle/papier (51x41cm 20x16in) Paris 2001

BRAZZA SAVORGNAN di Asciano 1793-1877 [3]

🖼️ $46 000 - €47 686 - £27 600 - FF312 800
Napoli, pescatori a Chiaia Olio/tela (200x260cm 78x102in) Roma 2000

🖼️ $38 000 - €39 393 - £22 800 - FF258 400
Veduta di Istambul Olio/carta (29x275cm 11x108in) Roma 2000

BREAKER Charles 1906-1985 [30]

✏️ $102 - €106 - £65 - FF698
Prawns Ink (26x37cm 10x14in) Penzance, Cornwall 2000

BREAKSPEARE William A. 1855-1914 [70]

🖼️ $5 117 - €4 298 - £3 000 - FF28 195
Lovelorn Oil/canvas (72x42cm 28x16in) Billingshurst, West-Sussex 1998

🖼️ $2 044 - €2 380 - £1 440 - FF15 609
La lettre Huile/panneau (34x14cm 13x5in) Antwerpen 2001

BREANSKI de Alfred, Jnr. 1877-1957 [376]

🖼️ $4 941 - €4 700 - £3 000 - FF30 827
Sunset in the Highlands, with Cattle watering and Mountains beyond Oil/canvas (61x91.5cm 24x36in) Edinburgh 1999

🖼️ $2 250 - €2 204 - £1 450 - FF14 458
Evening near Arundel Oil/canvas (31x46cm 12x18in) New-York 1999

✏️ $459 - €509 - £320 - FF3 342
Mill Pond Watercolour/paper (27.5x38cm 10x14in) Godalming, Surrey 2001

BRÉANSKI de Alfred, Snr. 1852-1928 [490]

🖼️ $27 500 - €30 394 - £19 263 - FF199 372
Burnham Beeches Oil/canvas (91x161cm 36x63in) Chicago IL 2001

🖼️ $19 428 - €19 000 - £12 000 - FF124 630
The Dee near Balmoral Oil/canvas (49.5x74.5cm 19x29in) Newcastle-upon-Tyne 1999

🖼️ $3 355 - €3 902 - £2 396 - FF25 595
«The Falls at Callander, NB» Oil/canvas (20.5x30.5cm 8x12in) Toronto 2001

BREANSKI de Alfred, Snr. or Jnr. XIX-XX [9]

🖼️ $1 586 - €1 865 - £1 100 - FF12 232
Returning to Harbour Oil/canvas (40x60cm 16x24in) Lewes, Sussex 2000

BREANSKI de Gustave c.1856-1898 [142]

🖼️ $1 610 - €1 728 - £1 077 - FF11 338
The Ebb Tide Oil/canvas (56x91.5cm 22x36in) Toronto 2000

🖼️ $537 - €561 - £340 - FF3 678
Street View in Guernsey Oil/board (31x23cm 12x9in) London 2000

BRÉBIETTE Pierre c.1598-c.1650 [17]

📁 $167 - €168 - £104 - FF1 100
La Sainte Vierge à genoux considérant l'enfant Jésus, par terre Eau-forte (24.5x17.5cm 9x6in) Paris 1999

BRECHALL Martin c.1757-1831 [6]

🖼️ $1 700 - €1 850 - £1 168 - FF12 136
Tiebert Family, Berne Township, Berks County, with Central Heart Watercolour (34x39cm 13x15in) Downington PA 2001

BRECHT George 1925 [26]

🖼️ $3 213 - €3 068 - £2 007 - FF20 123
Flag Mixed media (31x41x2cm 12x16xin) Köln 1999

🖼️ $3 213 - €3 068 - £2 007 - FF20 123
What Word Object (30x40x7cm 11x15x2in) Köln 1999

✏️ $13 152 - €15 339 - £9 234 - FF100 617
Appendix blue Felt pen (59.5x79.5cm 23x31in) Köln 2000

📁 $195 - €213 - £128 - FF1 400
Expérimental enlargement Estampe (119x114cm 46x44in) Douai 2000

BRECK John Leslie 1860-1899 [14]

🖼️ $75 000 - €89 194 - £53 452 - FF585 075
Study for Indian Summer Oil/canvas (39.5x50cm 15x19in) New-York 2000

🖼️ $22 000 - €25 658 - £15 446 - FF168 308
Monet's Backyard Oil/canvas (27.5x35.5cm 10x13in) Boston MA 2000

BRECKENRIDGE Hugh Henry 1870-1937 [6]

🖼️ $8 000 - €8 587 - £5 353 - FF56 328
Study for War Oil/canvas/board (36.5x46.5cm 14x18in) New-York 2000

🖼️ $11 000 - €12 788 - £7 720 - FF83 886
The tower series Oil/board (18.5x15cm 7x5in) New-York 2001

BREDA von Carl Fredrik 1759-1818 [18]

🖼️ $2 509 - €2 897 - £1 755 - FF19 003
Porträtt av okänd adelsdam klädd i blå klänning Oil/canvas (91x78cm 35x30in) Stockholm 2001

BREDA von Lukas 1676-1752 [2]

🖼️ $4 626 - €5 262 - £3 231 - FF34 519
Carl Oxenstierna af Eka och Lindö Oil/canvas (84.5x68cm 33x26in) Stockholm 2000

BREDAEL van Alexander 1663-1720 [25]
- $11 815 - €12 958 - £8 024 - FF85 000
  Villageois sur la place du marché Huile/toile (69.5x87.5cm 27x34in) Lille 2000
- $38 568 - €38 255 - £24 000 - FF250 939
  Peasants by a Mediterranean Harbour/Shepherds, Peasants and Merchants Oil/canvas (33x43cm 12x16in) London 1999

BREDAEL van Jan Frans I 1686-1750 [16]
- $4 680 - €4 462 - £2 844 - FF29 268
  Paysage fluvial avec combat de cavalerie Huile/panneau (66x51cm 25x20in) Bruxelles 1999
- $11 520 - €13 081 - £7 884 - FF85 806
  Flusslandschaft mit einem Bauernhaus und Figuren Öl/Kupfer (18x23cm 7x9in) Wien 2000

BREDAEL van Jan Peter II 1683-1735 [13]
- $17 014 - €19 059 - £11 823 - FF125 017
  Travellers and Peasants on Horse and Wagons ambushed on a country road Oil/copper (37.5x53.5cm 14x21in) Amsterdam 2001
- $13 215 - €10 899 - £7 785 - FF71 490
  Landschaft mit zwei Reitern Öl/Kupfer (19x23cm 7x9in) Wien 1998

BREDAEL van Joseph 1688-1739 [45]
- $17 343 - €18 348 - £11 000 - FF120 358
  River Landscape with Fishermen and Waggoners Oil/panel (38x48cm 14x18in) London 2000
- $26 910 - €29 728 - £18 661 - FF195 000
  Paysage à la charrette Huile/panneau (17.2x23.7cm 6x9in) Lille 2001

BREDAEL van Pieter 1629-1719 [32]
- $60 310 - €56 406 - £36 519 - FF370 000
  Scène villageoise Huile/toile (137.5x194cm 54x76in) Lille 1999
- $14 054 - €13 275 - £8 500 - FF87 077
  A Cavalry Skirmish Oil/canvas (55x65cm 21x25in) London 1999
- $10 210 - €10 288 - £6 364 - FF67 486
  Weite Flusslandschaft Öl/Kupfer (12.5x16cm 4x6in) Zürich 1999

BREDAL Niels 1841-1888 [14]
- $2 250 - €2 332 - £1 350 - FF15 300
  Paese laziale Olio/tela (77.5x55cm 30x21in) Venezia 2000
- $277 - €269 - £168 - FF1 763
  Parti fra Venedig Watercolour/paper (25x17cm 9x6in) Viby J, Århus 2000

BREDDO Gastone 1915-1991 [63]
- $500 - €518 - £300 - FF3 400
  Vaso con fiori: gli iris Olio/tela (70x50cm 27x19in) Prato 2000

BREDSDORFF Johan Ulrik 1845-1928 [55]
- $186 - €201 - £128 - FF1 319
  Aftenstemning ved havet Oil/canvas (26x50cm 10x19in) København 2001

BREDT Ferdinand Max 1860-1921 [23]
- $9 136 - €7 819 - £5 500 - FF51 288
  The Bather Oil/canvas (60x50cm 23x19in) London 1998

BREE de Anthony, Anton XIX-XX [10]
- $2 968 - €2 690 - £1 800 - FF17 647
  The Day's Bag Oil/canvas (24.5x32.5cm 9x12in) Billingshurst, West-Sussex 1998

BREE van Mathieu Ignace 1773-1839 [18]
- $9 500 - €8 333 - £5 768 - FF54 661
  Portrait of a Man, Possibly a Self-Portrait, Before a City Oil/canvas (82x68.5cm 32x26in) New-York 1999

BREE van Philippe 1786-1871 [16]
- $9 180 - €8 428 - £5 644 - FF55 284
  Trois femmes orientales et paôn Huile/panneau (105x180cm 41x70in) Antwerpen 1999
- $12 376 - €14 372 - £8 697 - FF94 276
  Mor och barn utanför ett bageri i Rom Oil/canvas (98x73cm 38x28in) Stockholm 2001

BREEDVELD Hendrik 1918 [10]
- $690 - €709 - £433 - FF4 649
  Mare with Foal Oil/canvas (88x58cm 35x23in) Vancouver, BC. 2000
- $1 342 - €1 440 - £898 - FF9 448
  Docks with Young on a River/Duckling Swimming in a Marshy Pond Oil/canvas (25.5x30.5cm 10x12in) Toronto 2000

BREEN van Adam c.1590-c.1650 [17]
- $358 632 - €384 962 - £240 000 - FF2 525 184
  Winter Landscape with elegant Figures skating and playing Kolf Oil/panel (74x105.5cm 29x41in) London 2000
- $642 224 - €694 769 - £440 000 - FF4 557 388
  A Winter Scene Oil/panel (25x39.5cm 9x15in) Lenton-Lane, Nottingham 2001

BREENBERGH Bartholomeus 1599-c.1657 [53]
- $18 000 - €14 970 - £10 566 - FF98 199
  Italianate Landscape with the Town of Acquapendente, near Rome Oil/copper (33x53.5cm 12x21in) New-York 1998
- $11 554 - €13 469 - £8 000 - FF88 348
  An Italianate Landscape with Goatherds Amongst Ruins Oil/copper (22x27.5cm 8x10in) London 2000
- $1 538 - €1 328 - £927 - FF8 714
  A Capriccio View of a Roman City, the cupola of a Church Wash (9x14.5cm 3x5in) Amsterdam 1998
- $421 - €409 - £262 - FF2 683
  Die Ruine des Aquädukts von Mezza Via zwischen Rom und Albano Radierung (10.3x6.5cm 4x2in) Berlin 1999

BREGNÖ Jens Jakob 1877-1946 [62]
- $955 - €807 - £570 - FF5 295
  Danserinde Bronze (H26.5cm H10in) København 1998

BREGOLI L. XIX-XX [27]
- $4 034 - €3 857 - £2 475 - FF25 301
  Cockerel with Chickens, Ducks and a Jay, after Melchior d'Hondecoeter Oil/canvas (90.5x104.5cm 35x41in) Amsterdam 1999
- $1 933 - €2 178 - £1 333 - FF14 287
  Portrait of a Lady, Small Half Length, After Hans Holbein II Oil/panel (44x33cm 17x12in) Amsterdam 2000

BREHM Worth 1883-1928 [5]
- $1 050 - €994 - £622 - FF6 520
  Illustration «The Challenge» Charcoal/paper (53x74cm 21x29in) Walkill NY 1999

BREHME Hugo 1882-1954 [17]
- $400 - €456 - £276 - FF2 989
  «India Zapoteca, Oaxaca»/«Indio de Xochimilco» Silver print (16x11cm 6x4in) New-York 2000

B

BREHMER Emil 1822-1895 **[2]**
- $1 986 - €2 180 - £1 320 - FF14 301
  Stilleben mit Weinflasche und Becher
  Öl/Leinwand/Karton (27x21cm 10x8in) Wien 2000

BREINLINGER Hans 1888-1963 **[65]**
- $1 125 - €1 329 - £797 - FF8 720
  Obsthändlerin Tempera (72x49cm 28x19in) Konstanz 2000
- $472 - €511 - £323 - FF3 353
  Das Kartenspiel Ink/paper (21x30cm 8x11in) Stuttgart 2001

BREITBACH Carl 1833-1904 **[25]**
- $3 439 - €4 090 - £2 451 - FF26 831
  Korallenmädchen auf Capri Öl/Leinwand (108x78cm 42x30in) Köln 2000

BREITENBACH Josef 1896-1984 **[93]**
- $1 723 - €1 705 - £1 074 - FF11 185
  Portrait Bertolt Brecht Gelatin silver print (35.4x27.9cm 13x10in) Berlin 1999

BREITER Herbert 1927-1999 **[32]**
- $3 727 - €4 346 - £2 615 - FF28 508
  Steirische Landschaft Öl/Leinwand (70x90cm 27x35in) Köln 2001
- $789 - €920 - £553 - FF6 037
  Fluss durch eine Hügellandschaft Aquarell/Papier (38x58cm 14x22in) Köln 2001
- $202 - €225 - £140 - FF1 475
  Südliche Landschaft am Meer/Südliche Berglandschaft/Weite Landschaft Farblithographie (33.5x56cm 13x22in) Heidelberg 2001

BREITMAYER M. Vern 1889-1966 **[8]**
- $260 - €281 - £180 - FF1 842
  California coastal Scene Watercolour/paper (33x45cm 13x18in) Cincinnati OH 2001

BREITNER Georg Hendrik 1857-1923 **[179]**
- $48 375 - €40 787 - £28 710 - FF267 543
  The Bridge over the Reguliersgracht, Amsterdam Oil/canvas (90x101cm 35x39in) Amsterdam 1998
- $6 763 - €6 353 - £4 076 - FF41 672
  Circus Horses - A Study Oil/paper/panel (16.5x32.5cm 6x12in) Amsterdam 1999
- $6 804 - €5 754 - £4 069 - FF37 741
  Donkeys on a Beach Watercolour/paper (28x45cm 11x17in) Amsterdam 1998
- $1 242 - €1 452 - £887 - FF9 525
  Reclining Nude Etching (17.5x28.5cm 6x11in) Amsterdam 2001

BREITWIESER Robert 1899-1975 **[28]**
- $2 164 - €1 829 - £1 287 - FF12 000
  Paysage du Sundgau Huile/toile (60x90cm 23x35in) Saint-Dié 1998
- $873 - €915 - £549 - FF6 000
  Paysage Huile/carton (23x32cm 9x12in) Saint-Dié 2000

BREITWIESER Theodor 1847-1930 **[10]**
- $2 975 - €2 543 - £1 785 - FF16 681
  Feldmesse unter Anwesenheit des Zaren Alexander II und seines Stabes Öl/Leinwand (63.5x89.7cm 25x35in) Wien 1998

BREKELENKAM van Quiringh Gerritsz c.1620-1668 **[57]**
- $8 835 - €9 907 - £6 000 - FF64 984
  Interior with a Woman reading by an open Window Oil/panel (50x37.5cm 19x14in) London 2000

BREKER Arno 1900-1991 **[263]**
- $1 767 - €1 636 - £1 066 - FF10 732
  Die Grazie, kniende, sicht mit der Hand aufstützend Bronze (26x22x18cm 10x8x7in) Heidelberg 1999
- $952 - €1 022 - £637 - FF6 707
  Sitzende weibliche Aktfigur mit untergeschlagenem Bein Indian ink (21.4x13.8cm 8x5in) Köln 2000
- $143 - €158 - £99 - FF1 039
  Verweilen Farblithographie (27.5x39cm 10x15in) Heidelberg 2001

BRELING Heinrich 1849-1914 **[42]**
- $4 099 - €3 835 - £2 483 - FF25 154
  Fischerhude, Kavalleristen halten Abends im Dorf Öl/Leinwand (66x50cm 25x19in) Bremen 1999
- $993 - €1 066 - £664 - FF6 992
  Das Rendezvous Oil/panel (16x21cm 6x8in) Hildrizhausen 2000
- $3 440 - €4 090 - £2 384 - FF26 831
  «Blick auf Schloss Linderhof» Gouache/paper (56x66cm 22x25in) München 2000

BREM Rolf 1926 **[18]**
- $1 402 - €1 538 - £952 - FF10 088
  Basset Bronze (13x23x9x5cm 5x11x3in) Luzern 2000

BREMAN Co 1865-1938 **[42]**
- $10 959 - €12 706 - £7 764 - FF83 344
  Warme Dag, View on the Ijssel with Deventer in the Background Oil/canvas (50x57cm 19x22in) Amsterdam 2000
- $774 - €771 - £470 - FF5 060
  Dode spreeuwen Oil/canvas (47x23.5cm 18x9in) Amsterdam 2000
- $6 764 - €7 260 - £4 526 - FF47 625
  Landscape in 't Gooi Watercolour, gouache/paper (46x70cm 18x27in) Amsterdam 2000

BREMER Edward P. XX **[2]**
- $1 200 - €1 116 - £740 - FF7 319
  «Rodeo Parade» Poster (101x76cm 40x30in) New-York 1999

BREMER Uwe 1940 **[90]**
- $117 - €128 - £77 - FF838
  Über das Befestigen von 1 Jungfrau/Der Abguss der Amazone Farbradierung (29.5x22cm 11x8in) Hamburg 2000

BREMMER Hendricus Petrus 1871-1956 **[22]**
- $10 261 - €8 883 - £6 227 - FF58 269
  Doorkijke-Kolenhok met bijkeuken Oil/canvas (36x26cm 14x10in) Amsterdam 1998

BRÉMOND Jean-François 1807-1868 **[3]**
- $1 443 - €1 677 - £1 014 - FF11 000
  Portrait de femme à l'ombrelle Huile/toile (92x73cm 36x28in) Paris 2001

BREMONTIER H. XIX **[10]**
- $1 364 - €1 534 - £958 - FF10 061
  Küste im Mondschein Öl/Leinwand (27x35.5cm 10x13in) Düsseldorf 2001

BRENAN James 1837-1907 **[2]**
- $2 295 - €2 666 - £1 613 - FF17 490
  The Lower Lake, Killarney Oil/panel (20x29cm 7x11in) Dublin 2001

BRENAN James Butler 1825-1889 **[9]**
- $4 731 - €5 079 - £3 166 - FF33 316
  Rev.H.J., Dean of Cork and Miss Newman, His Sister Oil/canvas (55x43cm 21x16in) Dublin 2000

$365 - €356 - £224 - FF2 332
Portrait of a young Lady Oil/canvas (35x30cm
14x12in) Dublin 1999

BRENDEKILDE Hans Andersen 1857-1942 [290]
$116 677 - €135 561 - £82 000 - FF889 224
Der plukkes anemoner (picking anemones)
Oil/canvas (127x153cm 50x60in) London 2001
$8 855 - €7 394 - £5 263 - FF48 499
**Interiör fra en bondestue med en kone, der kar-
ter uld og en pige** Oil/canvas (58x50cm 22x19in)
Köbenhavn 1998
$1 385 - €1 344 - £841 - FF8 815
Vandlöbs udlöb i Susaaen ved Herlufsholm
Oil/canvas (27x35cm 10x13in) Viby J, Århus 2000

BRENDEL Albert Heinrich 1827-1895 [52]
$3 476 - €3 579 - £2 191 - FF23 477
Schimmelstute im Stall Öl/Leinwand (35x46cm
13x18in) Berlin 2000

BRENDEL Karl Alexander 1877-1948 [20]
$105 - €97 - £65 - FF637
Drohendes Unwetter Woodcut in colors (21x29cm
8x11in) Rudolstadt-Thüringen 1999

BRENDEL Walter L. 1923 [31]
$372 - €409 - £253 - FF2 683
Komposition mit violettem Fleck Oil/panel
(18.5x28.5cm 7x11in) Berlin 2000
$692 - €825 - £493 - FF5 412
Figur Collage (35x28cm 13x11in) Hamburg 2000

BRENDERS Carl 1937 [11]
$2 272 - €2 184 - £1 400 - FF14 326
Musk oxen Gouache/paper (27x33cm 10x12in)
London 1999

BRENDSTRUP Thorald 1812-1883 [45]
$923 - €1 073 - £648 - FF7 038
Solnedgang over bugten ved Napoli Oil/canvas
(36x50cm 14x19in) Köbenhavn 2001
$768 - €740 - £477 - FF4 857
**Laesende munk i buegang i et kloster ved
Luganosöen** Oil/canvas (41x31cm 16x12in)
Köbenhavn 1999

BRENET Albert 1903-? [238]
$584 - €579 - £363 - FF3 800
Autriche, école et attelage Craies couleurs/papier
(42x25cm 16x9in) Brest 2000
$230 - €274 - £164 - FF1 800
**Les différents bâtiments ayant porté le nom de
«Cassard»** Pochoir (22x28cm 8x11in) Paris 2000

BRENET Nicolas-Guy 1728-1792 [9]
$18 540 - €18 294 - £11 424 - FF120 000
Rébecca présentant Jacob à Isaac Huile/toile
(54.5x65.5cm 21x25in) Mayenne 1999

BRENNA Vincenzo 1745-1820 [5]
$3 500 - €3 738 - £2 385 - FF24 521
**The Triumph of Titus and Vespasian, After
Giulio Romano** Bodycolour (19.5x28.5cm 7x11in)
New-York 2001

BRENNAN Alfred Laurens 1853-1921 [3]
$6 500 - €6 061 - £4 031 - FF39 757
Cale, Bravest of the Apaches Oil/canvas
(30.5x20.5cm 12x8in) New-York 1999

BRENNAN Angela 1960 [6]
$2 914 - €3 267 - £2 038 - FF21 430
«Untitled No.3» Oil/canvas (183x122cm 72x48in)
Melbourne 2001

BRENNER Art 1924 [1]
$6 067 - €6 807 - £4 204 - FF44 649
Still Life with Pitcher Oil/board (60x80cm 23x31in)
Amsterdam 2000

BRENNER Carl Christian 1833-1888 [11]
$1 300 - €1 536 - £921 - FF10 076
Woodland Interior Oil/panel (25x20cm 9x7in) Boston
MA 2000

BRENNER Franz 1873-1945 [15]
$312 - €327 - £207 - FF2 145
Kutschenfahrt im Park Aquarell/Papier
(24.5x24.5cm 9x9in) Graz 2000

BRENNER Frédéric 1959 [4]
$1 215 - €1 372 - £855 - FF9 000
Calcutta, Juif Irakien chez lui Photograph
(40x50cm 15x19in) Paris 2001

BRENNET Albert XX [1]
$4 831 - €5 488 - £3 380 - FF36 000
Croiseur et hydravion dans la rade de Toulon
Gouache (64x116cm 25x45in) Neuilly-sur-Seine 2001

BRENNIR Carl 1850-1920 [35]
$807 - €832 - £503 - FF5 457
Resting by the River Oil/canvas (40.5x61cm
15x24in) London 2000

BRENOT Pierre-Laurent 1913-1998 [37]
$1 076 - €1 005 - £650 - FF6 593
Hello Paradise Poster (173x121cm 68x47in) London
1999

BRENTANO DE GROOT F.L. XX [1]
$1 550 - €1 505 - £977 - FF9 870
Gestrandetes Schiff Aquarelle (27x44cm 10x17in)
Zürich 1999

BRENTEL Friedrich 1580-1651 [33]
$8 965 - €9 624 - £6 000 - FF63 129
The Sermon on the Mount Bodycolour (7x9cm
2x3in) London 2000

BRERETON James XX [20]
$2 108 - €2 025 - £1 300 - FF13 284
The Star of the East en Passage Oil/canvas
(51x101.5cm 20x39in) London 1999

BRESCIA da Giovanni Antonio XV-XVI [3]
$11 835 - €11 452 - £7 500 - FF75 122
**The risen Christ between St Andrew and
Longinus, after Mantegna** Engraving (28.5x25cm
11x9in) London 1999

BRESCIANI Antonio 1720-1817 [4]
$8 055 - €8 012 - £5 000 - FF52 556
Saint Margaret in Penitence Oil/canvas/board
(52x41cm 20x16in) London 1999

BRESCIANI Attilio 1879-? [1]
$4 600 - €4 769 - £2 760 - FF31 280
Verona, Piazza Erbe Olio/tavola (56x42cm 22x16in)
Trieste 1999

BRESCIANI DA GAZOLDO Archimede 1881-1939
[5]
$24 000 - €20 733 - £16 000 - FF136 000
Paesaggio dell'Alta Engadina Olio/tavola
(110x150cm 43x59in) Milano 1998
$5 533 - €5 736 - £3 330 - FF37 627
Vaso di zinnie Olio/tavola (83x77cm 32x30in) Milano
1999

BRESDIN Rodolphe 1822-1885 [205]
$29 110 - €31 252 - £19 475 - FF205 000
La sainte Famille Crayon (10x18cm 3x7in) Angers
2000

B

📖 **$1 589** – €1 494 - **£965** - FF9 800
Branchages Eau-forte (17x12cm 6x4in) Paris 1999

BRESLAU Marie-Louise 1856-1927 **[29]**
🎨 **$928** – €935 - **£578** - FF6 135
Blumenstrauss in Vase Öl/Leinwand (56x46cm 22x18in) Zürich 2000
🎨 **$5 000** – €5 606 - **£3 395** - FF36 774
A Good Book Oil/canvas (34x46cm 13x18in) New-York 2000
✏️ **$38 625** – €38 112 - **£23 800** - FF250 000
Les modistes Pastel/papier (57x74cm 22x29in) Paris 1999

BRESLAUER Marianne 1909-? **[31]**
📷 **$832** – €823 - **£518** - FF5 399
Zuschauer beim Fussball, Neapel Vintage gelatin silver print (17.9x24.1cm 7x9in) Berlin 1999

BRESLOW Louis 1908 **[2]**
📖 **$600** – €690 - **£413** - FF4 528
«Steeplechase» Woodcut (20x27cm 8x10in) Cleveland OH 2000

BRESOLIN Domenico 1814-1890 **[10]**
🎨 **$2 500** – €2 592 - **£1 500** - FF17 000
Lago di montagna/Valle montana Olio/cartone (18x35.5cm 7x13in) Milano 1999
📷 **$681** – €762 - **£474** - FF5 000
Façade de la Chartreuse de Pavie Tirage albuminé (24x32cm 9x12in) Paris 2001

BRESSANIN Vittorio Emanuele 1860-1941 **[16]**
🎨 **$56 168** – €59 965 - **£38 363** - FF393 346
The First Dance Oil/canvas (89x129cm 35x50in) Billingshurst, West-Sussex 2001
🎨 **$2 796** – €2 898 - **£1 677** - FF19 012
Partita a carte Olio/tavoletta (7.5x14cm 2x5in) Milano 1999

BRESSIN F. XIX **[7]**
🎨 **$3 246** – €2 973 - **£1 979** - FF19 500
«Union, ex Andrea», née en 1906, par Ajax et Andrée Huile/toile (61x73cm 24x28in) Paris 1999

BRESSLER Emile Alois L. 1886-1966 **[51]**
🎨 **$2 470** – €2 730 - **£1 713** - FF17 908
Paysage Huile/toile (44x59cm 17x23in) Genève 2001
🎨 **$783** – €919 - **£558** - FF6 025
Le travail dans les champs Huile/toile (12x23cm 4x9in) Genève 2000

BRESSLERN-ROTH von Norbertine 1891-1978 **[294]**
🎨 **$18 530** – €17 384 - **£11 447** - FF114 032
Flamingos Tempera (105x115cm 41x45in) Stuttgart 1999
🎨 **$21 960** – €21 802 - **£13 710** - FF143 010
Neues Leben Öl/Leinwand (70x70cm 27x27in) Wien 1999
✏️ **$2 817** – €3 270 - **£1 944** - FF21 451
Schattenspiel Oil chalks/paper (59x53cm 23x20in) Graz 2000
📖 **$563** – €654 - **£388** - FF4 290
Krebs und Octopus Linocut in colors (22x22cm 8x8in) Graz 2000

BRESSON René XX **[2]**
🎨 **$742** – €841 - **£504** - FF5 516
La bañista Oleo/lienzo (33x40cm 12x15in) Madrid 2000

BREST Fabius Germain 1823-1900 **[91]**
🎨 **$35 000** – €41 503 - **£24 080** - FF272 240
Constantinople Oil/canvas (80x59.5cm 31x23in) New-York 2000

🎨 **$32 538** – €35 388 - **£21 444** - FF232 127
Sonnenuntergang über dem Bosporus Öl/Karton (23x36.5cm 9x14in) Bern 2000

BRET-CHARBONNIER Claudia 1863-1950 **[19]**
🎨 **$18 000** – €18 138 - **£11 221** - FF118 980
Bouquets of Roses and Lilies of the Valley Oil/canvas (116x153cm 45x60in) New-York 2000

BRETHERTON James c.1750-c.1790 **[3]**
📖 **$1 081** – €1 127 - **£680** - FF7 391
City Hunt, After Henry Bunbury Etching (164x64.5cm 64x25in) London 2000

BRETLAND Thomas W. 1802-1874 **[26]**
🎨 **$4 134** – €3 605 - **£2 500** - FF23 649
Study of the Bay Racehorse «Lady Fane» with Jockey up Oil/canvas (57x70cm 22x27in) London 1998

BRETON André 1896-1966 **[8]**
🗿 **$248 940** – €205 806 - **£146 070** - FF1 350 000
Chanson-objet Objet (22.5x30x6cm 8x11x2in) Paris 1998
✏️ **$21 045** – €25 029 - **£15 000** - FF164 178
Cadavre exquis (Exquisite Corpse) Coloured crayons (30x24.5cm 11x9in) London 2000

BRETON Emile 1831-1902 **[24]**
🎨 **$220** – €244 - **£152** - FF1 600
Paysage au champ fleuri Huile/panneau (35x27cm 13x10in) Troyes 2001

BRETON Jules Adolphe 1827-1906 **[97]**
🎨 **$28 366** – €27 525 - **£18 000** - FF180 554
Jeune femme tricotant Oil/canvas (68x41cm 26x16in) London 1999
🎨 **$8 338** – €9 299 - **£5 605** - FF61 000
Enfants jouant sur la lande Huile/panneau (23x31cm 9x12in) Versailles 2000
✏️ **$8 000** – €8 970 - **£5 432** - FF58 838
The Gleaner Pencil/paper (28.5x16.5cm 11x6in) New-York 2000

BRETON Luc 1731-1800 **[1]**
🗿 **$5 826** – €6 663 - **£4 000** - FF43 705
Bust of Charles-Roger de Bauffremont (d.1795), Breast Plate Draped Terracotta (H66cm H25in) London 2000

BRETON Paul Eugène 1868-1933 **[2]**
🗿 **$4 180** – €3 659 - **£2 532** - FF24 000
Deux naïades surmontant deux vagues formant coquilles Bronze (48x63cm 18x24in) Paris 1998

BRETT Dorothy Eugenie 1883-1977 **[5]**
🎨 **$8 000** – €7 609 - **£4 857** - FF49 912
Winds of Spring Oil/canvas (45.5x30.5cm 17x12in) Beverly-Hills CA 1999

BRETT John 1830-1902 **[102]**
🎨 **$24 099** – €23 206 - **£15 000** - FF152 220
Coastal Landscape Oil/canvas (105x212cm 41x83in) London 1999
🎨 **$15 433** – €18 354 - **£11 000** - FF120 397
The Alter Rock, Sark Oil/canvas (70x51cm 27x20in) London 2000
🎨 **$2 849** – €3 312 - **£2 000** - FF21 728
Southerly on the Clyde/Cornish Coast/The Bristol Channel Oil/canvas (16.5x35cm 6x13in) Billingshurst, West-Sussex 2001
✏️ **$1 129** – €1 240 - **£750** - FF8 131
A Rocky Coastline Watercolour (17x33.5cm 6x13in) London 2000

B

BRETT Molly XX [3]
🖌 **$12 520** - €12 259 - **£8 000** - FF80 412
Fairy Dance Watercolour (43x54.5cm 16x21in)
London 1999

BRETT Oswald Longfield 1921 [13]
🖌 **$268** - €280 - **£170** - FF1 839
Two Sailing Vessels at Sea Gouache/paper
(25.5x43cm 10x16in) London 2000

BRETT Rosa XIX [10]
💬 **$12 900** - €12 519 - **£7 800** - FF73 786
«Catnap» Oil/canvas (28x35.5cm 11x13in) London
1998

BRETTE Pierre 1905-1961 [110]
💬 **$1 979** - €2 211 - **£1 341** - FF14 500
Bateaux à Cancale Huile/toile (27x37cm 10x14in)
Bayeux 2000
🖌 **$1 386** - €1 372 - **£864** - FF9 000
Bateau au mouillage aux Minquiers
Aquarelle/papier (24x30cm 9x11in) Coutances 1999

BREU M. XIX-XX [2]
💬 **$3 307** - €3 123 - **£2 000** - FF20 488
Off to the Pasture Oil/canvas (59x80.5cm 23x31in)
Billingshurst, West-Sussex 1999

BREUER Henry Joseph 1860-1932 [20]
💬 **$3 500** - €3 304 - **£2 175** - FF21 675
French Landscape Oil/canvas (50x66cm 20x26in)
Milford CT 1999

BREUER Leo 1893-1975 [20]
💬 **$4 385** - €5 113 - **£3 077** - FF33 539
«Gare de l'Est» Oil/panel (92x71cm 36x27in) Köln
2001
💬 **$192** - €213 - **£133** - FF1 400
Sans Famille Huile/panneau (41.5x32cm 16x12in)
Clermont-Ferrand 2001

BREUER Peter 1856-1930 [16]
🖎 **$2 130** - €1 789 - **£1 252** - FF11 737
Köln Venus und Amor Bronze (H40cm H15in) Köln
1998

BREUER-WIKMAN Frederika 1828-1896 [3]
💬 **$4 813** - €4 538 - **£2 983** - FF29 766
Yellow and Pink Roses Oil/canvas (101x66cm
39x25in) Amsterdam 1999

BREUHAUS DE GROOT Frans Arnold I 1796-1875
[13]
💬 **$2 725** - €3 068 - **£1 878** - FF20 123
Ausritt im Gehölz Oil/panel (52x43.5cm 20x17in)
Bremen 2000
💬 **$5 471** - €4 726 - **£3 304** - FF31 000
Sur la grève en Hollande Huile/toile (27x35cm
10x13in) Saint-Dié 1998

BREUHAUS DE GROOT Frans Arnold II 1824-1872
[10]
💬 **$19 252** - €18 151 - **£11 932** - FF119 064
Travellers Crossing a Forestpond Oil/canvas
(91x74cm 35x29in) Amsterdam 1999

BREUIL Georges 1904-1997 [19]
💬 **$817** - €854 - **£517** - FF5 600
Composition abstraite Huile/toile (92x73cm
36x28in) Toulouse 2000

BREUSTEDT Hans Joachim 1901-1984 [5]
🖌 **$1 001** - €1 163 - **£704** - FF7 627
«Köpfe» Indian ink (11x8cm 4x3in) Salzburg 2001

BREVEGLIERI Cesare 1902-1948 [23]
💬 **$6 800** - €8 812 - **£5 100** - FF57 800
Modella addormentata Olio/tela (41x87cm 16x34in)
Prato 2000
🖌 **$800** - €829 - **£480** - FF5 440
Paesaggio/Venezia Matita/carta (41x31cm 16x12in)
Milano 2000

BREVOORT James Renwick 1832-1918 [15]
💬 **$18 000** - €19 983 - **£12 519** - FF131 083
«Lake Maggiore, Italy» Oil/canvas (40x59cm 16x23in)
Milford CT 2001
💬 **$13 000** - €15 460 - **£9 265** - FF101 413
Sunset Oil/canvas (26.7x51cm 10x20in) New-York
2000

BREWER Adrian 1891-1956 [1]
💬 **$3 250** - €3 068 - **£2 020** - FF20 127
Texas Bluebonnets Oil/board (40x35cm 16x14in)
Milford CT 1999

BREWER Edward Vincent 1883-? [1]
🖵 **$1 200** - €1 339 - **£785** - FF8 781
«Rodeo Parade, Nothern Pacific» Poster
(76.5x101cm 30x39in) New-York 2000

BREWER Henry Charles 1866-1943 [57]
🖌 **$660** - €760 - **£450** - FF4 984
The Acropolis, Athens Watercolour (29x45.5cm
11x17in) Billingshurst, West-Sussex 2000

BREWER Henry William c.1830-1903 [10]
💬 **$13 289** - €11 373 - **£8 000** - FF74 600
Interior of the Cathedral of Bois-le-Duc Oil/can-
vas (91.5x71cm 36x27in) London 1998
🖵 **$1 344** - €1 403 - **£850** - FF9 200
Bird's Eye View of London seen from a Balloon
Woodcut (83x110cm 32x43in) London 2000

BREWER James Alphege XIX-XX [25]
🖌 **$1 614** - €1 664 - **£1 000** - FF10 914
San Giorgio Maggiore with Barges before
Watercolour (62x42.5cm 24x16in) London 2000

BREWER Nicholas Richard 1857-1949 [9]
💬 **$7 500** - €8 630 - **£5 169** - FF56 610
The Cotton Pickers Oil/canvas (81x101cm 32x40in)
New-Orleans LA 2000
💬 **$3 200** - €3 732 - **£2 246** - FF24 481
The Meadow Oil/board (18x26cm 7x10in) Portsmouth
NH 2000

BREWERTON George Douglas 1820-1901 [20]
💬 **$12 000** - €12 881 - **£8 030** - FF84 492
Tropical Sunrise Oil/canvas (66x91.5cm 25x36in)
San-Francisco CA 2000
🖌 **$1 250** - €1 191 - **£792** - FF7 813
Luminous River Landscape Pastel/paper (89x38cm
35x15in) St. Petersburg FL 1999

BREWSTER Anna Richards 1870-1952 [38]
💬 **$600** - €519 - **£364** - FF3 406
Old Boston Oil/board (15x20cm 6x8in) Mystic CT
1998

BREWSTER John, Jnr. 1766-1854 [12]
💬 **$16 000** - €17 087 - **£10 902** - FF112 084
John Cox of Bridgeton, Maine Oil/canvas
(76x63.5cm 29x25in) New-York 2001

BREWTNALL Edward Frederick 1846-1902 [14]
🖌 **$7 171** - €6 521 - **£4 400** - FF42 772
Gusty November Watercolour (51x35.5cm 20x13in)
London 1999

BREYDEL Frans 1679-1750 [6]
- $4 396 - €5 017 - £3 055 - FF32 908
  Eleganta sällskap i parkmiljö Oil/canvas (28x33cm 11x12in) Stockholm 2001

BREYDEL Karel 1678-1733 [63]
- $9 840 - €11 434 - £6 915 - FF75 000
  Chocs de cavalerie Huile/panneau (45x68cm 17x26in) Paris 2001
- $12 328 - €12 196 - £7 688 - FF80 000
  Scène de pillage près d'un village Huile/panneau (36x25cm 14x9in) Versailles 1999

BREYER Jan Hendrick 1818-1894 [3]
- $7 876 - €6 660 - £4 710 - FF43 688
  A Wooded Summer Landscape with Figures and Mules near a Wooden Bridge Oil/panel (23x27cm 9x10in) Amsterdam 1998

BREYER Robert 1866-1941 [19]
- $1 458 - €1 636 - £1 010 - FF10 732
  Hafen von Newport Öl/Leinwand (54x78cm 21x30in) Stuttgart 2000

BREYER von Josef XIX [1]
- $1 550 - €1 453 - £958 - FF9 534
  Ausfahrt der kaiserlichen Familie Aquarell, Gouache/Papier (43.2x61.2cm 17x24in) Wien 1999

BREYTENBACH Breyten 1939 [5]
- $1 149 - €1 134 - £698 - FF7 441
  Pink Dream Watercolour, gouache (64x49.5cm 25x19in) Amsterdam 2000

BRIAN Jean 1915 [35]
- $200 - €229 - £140 - FF1 500
  «Jeux Olympiques d'hiver Grenoble» Affiche (62x100cm 24x39in) Paris 2001

BRIANCHON Maurice 1899-1979 [311]
- $11 032 - €11 434 - £6 997 - FF75 000
  Nature morte Huile/toile (92x73cm 36x28in) Paris 2001
- $5 500 - €5 289 - £3 388 - FF34 692
  Sans titre Oil/board (24x38cm 9x14in) New-York 1999
- $3 405 - €3 811 - £2 310 - FF25 000
  Scène de théâtre Gouache/papier (45x34cm 17x13in) Paris 2000
- $103 - €118 - £71 - FF777
  Nature morte aux fruits Lithographie couleurs (30x43cm 11x16in) Genève 2000

BRIANTE Ezelino 1901-1971 [169]
- $1 040 - €1 348 - £780 - FF8 840
  Riflessi nel porto Olio/cartone (40x60cm 15x23in) Roma 2001
- $575 - €596 - £345 - FF3 910
  Lungo la via Olio/cartone (19x35cm 7x13in) Roma 1999

BRIAS Charles 1798-1884 [10]
- $4 854 - €4 553 - £3 000 - FF29 863
  The Cooper Oil/panel (23x18.5cm 9x7in) London 1999

BRIATA Georges 1933 [61]
- $1 057 - €1 006 - £657 - FF6 600
  Sans titre Huile/toile (54x66cm 21x25in) Marseille 1999
- $130 - €122 - £80 - FF800
  Les Toréadors Lithographie (54x37cm 21x14in) Marseille 1999

BRICHER Alfred Thompson 1837-1908 [282]
- $180 000 - €210 076 - £127 602 - FF1 378 008
  Low Tide Grand Manan Oil/canvas (76x160cm 29x62in) New-York 2001
- $53 000 - €62 625 - £37 561 - FF410 792
  Coastal View Oil/canvas (38x83cm 14x32in) Boston MA 2000
- $17 000 - €16 283 - £10 698 - FF106 807
  Summer scene of a pond with a young man fishing Oil/canvas (24x45cm 9x18in) Wallkill NY 1999
- $3 800 - €3 442 - £2 325 - FF22 578
  Rocks and Sea Watercolour/paper (27x43cm 11x17in) Portland ME 1998

BRICHERASIO di Sofia 1867-1950 [3]
- $750 - €777 - £450 - FF5 100
  Barca alla riva Olio/tavola (25.5x36.5cm 10x14in) Vercelli 2000

BRICKA A. XX [3]
- $1 982 - €2 363 - £1 413 - FF15 500
  Barques sur la grève Huile/toile (40x80cm 15x31in) Strasbourg 2000

BRICKDALE Eleanor Fortescue 1871-1945 [61]
- $24 099 - €23 206 - £15 000 - FF152 220
  Mary for all Generations Oil/canvas (76x193cm 29x75in) London 1999
- $994 560 - €858 065 - £600 000 - FF5 628 540
  The Deceitfulness of Riches Oil/canvas (85x110cm 33x43in) London 1998
- $12 174 - €11 706 - £7 500 - FF76 788
  The wounded Soldier Oil/board (45x27cm 17x10in) London 1999
- $7 229 - €6 962 - £4 500 - FF45 666
  Spring Bodycolour (25x51.5cm 9x20in) London 1999

BRICOUX Jules Charles XIX-XX [1]
- $4 080 - €3 811 - £2 540 - FF25 000
  La jeune fille et le cahier à dessin Huile/toile (89x70cm 35x27in) Cherbourg 1999

BRIDELL Frederick Lee 1831-1863 [22]
- $2 629 - €2 401 - £1 600 - FF15 748
  A Goatherder playing the Pipe Oil/paper/board (53.5x38cm 21x14in) London 1998

BRIDGE Elizabeth 1912-1996 [40]
- $407 - €361 - £250 - FF2 368
  «Suzy» a Black French Poodle, Seated Oil/canvas (59x49.5cm 23x19in) West-Midlands 1999

BRIDGE Joë 1886-1967 [14]
- $833 - €991 - £594 - FF6 500
  «Automobiles Vermorel» Affiche (120x78cm 47x30in) Orléans 2000

BRIDGEHOUSE Robert XIX [12]
- $2 545 - €2 668 - £1 700 - FF17 502
  Overlooking the Bay Oil/canvas (20.5x30.5cm 8x12in) London 1999

BRIDGEMAN George XIX-XX [4]
- $1 500 - €1 672 - £1 009 - FF10 965
  Anatomical Studies Charcoal/paper (10x20cm 4x8in) Chester NY 2000

BRIDGENS Richard XIX [1]
- $6 092 - €5 902 - £3 800 - FF38 715
  Sketches of West India Scenery Lithograph (37x26.5cm 14x10in) London 1999

BRIDGES Fidelia 1834-1923 [22]
- $10 000 - €8 390 - £5 894 - FF55 036
  Laura Brown in a Wing Chair Oil/canvas (53x45cm 21x18in) Greenwich CT 1998

$5 500 - €5 904 - £3 680 - FF38 728
Bird studies Oil/board (33x24cm 12x9in) New-York 2000

$2 000 - €2 345 - £1 438 - FF15 382
Lily Pads and barn Swallows Gouache/paper (25.5x34.5cm 10x13in) New-York 2001

BRIDGFORD Thomas 1812-1878 [2]
$5 273 - €5 525 - £3 500 - FF36 243
Happy Moments Oil/panel (25.5x43.5cm 10x17in) London 2000

BRIDGMAN Frederick Arthur 1847-1928 [223]
$75 068 - €74 309 - £46 530 - FF472 899
Odaliske und Dienerin Öl/Leinwand (110x170cm 43x66in) Ahlden 1999

$18 500 - €18 642 - £11 532 - FF122 285
By the City Gate Oil/canvas (57x45.5cm 22x17in) New-York 2000

$7 172 - €8 385 - £5 120 - FF55 000
Maternité Huile/panneau (27x21cm 10x8in) Paris 2001

$420 - €371 - £256 - FF2 435
Egyptian Morning Ink (23.5x30.5cm 9x12in) New-York 1999

BRIDGWATER Henry Scott 1864-1946 [7]
$456 - €481 - £304 - FF3 152
«**Paisaje con personajes**» Mezzotint (37x46cm 14x18in) Madrid 2000

BRIDT de Bernaert 1688-1722 [10]
$9 094 - €8 590 - £5 500 - FF56 344
A Hunting Still Life with a Hare, a Mallard and Songbirds in Landscape Oil/canvas (66x84cm 25x33in) London 1999

BRIEDÉ Johan 1885-1980 [30]
$2 758 - €2 723 - £1 677 - FF17 859
Sunlit Beach Oil/canvas (47x76cm 18x29in) Amsterdam 2000

BRIELMAN Jacques Alfred 1836-1892 [21]
$22 000 - €19 476 - £13 450 - FF127 751
Ducks bathing in a River Oil/canvas (163.5x260cm 64x102in) New-York 1999

$1 464 - €1 372 - £880 - FF9 000
Gitans dans la forêt Huile/toile (60.5x39.5cm 23x15in) Paris 1999

BRIERLY Oswald Walter 1817-1894 [45]
$1 210 - €1 260 - £760 - FF8 264
Shipping off Trieste Watercolour/paper (17x23cm 6x9in) Melbourne 2000

BRIëT Arthur 1867-1939 [41]
$1 973 - €1 815 - £1 220 - FF11 906
A kitchen Interior with a peasant Woman stirring in a cooking Pot Oil/canvas (42x60cm 16x23in) Amsterdam 1999

$1 606 - €1 724 - £1 075 - FF11 311
A farm interior Oil/canvas (42x32.5cm 16x12in) Amsterdam 2000

BRIGANTI Nicolas P. 1895-1989 [50]
$1 800 - €1 657 - £1 080 - FF10 867
Venetian Scene Oil/canvas (45x101cm 18x40in) Hampden MA 1999

BRIGDEN Frederick Henry 1871-1956 [58]
$948 - €929 - £583 - FF6 091
Sunlit Landscape Oil/board (40.5x51cm 15x20in) Toronto 2000

$291 - €313 - £200 - FF2 053
Morning on the Lake Watercolour/paper (30.5x35cm 12x13in) Toronto 2001

BRIGGS Austin 1908-1973 [13]
$4 500 - €4 309 - £2 780 - FF28 268
Grandmother Arrives for a Visit, Advertisement Oil/masonite (50x56cm 20x22in) New-York 1999

$2 900 - €3 230 - £1 896 - FF21 188
Advertisement: Family greeting father home from business trip Oil/panel (39x39cm 15x15in) New-York 2000

BRIGGS Lela Margaret 1896-1953 [12]
$225 - €218 - £139 - FF1 432
Red Wagon Watercolour/paper (48x60cm 19x24in) Cedar-Falls IA 1999

BRIGGS Raymond Redvers 1934 [1]
$2 540 - €2 727 - £1 700 - FF17 891
The snowman and boy dancing II Pencil/paper (17.5x16.5cm 6x6in) London 2000

BRIGHT Constance M. XX [3]
$1 496 - €1 745 - £1 050 - FF11 444
An old-fashioned Gown Oil/board (35x29.5cm 13x11in) Godalming, Surrey 2001

BRIGHT Harry 1846-1911 [84]
$905 - €878 - £570 - FF5 761
Last Years Nest Watercolour/paper (22.5x30cm 8x11in) Bristol, Avon 1999

BRIGHT Henry 1810/14-1873 [150]
$17 412 - €19 056 - £12 012 - FF125 000
The Land of Rob Roy Huile/toile (120x182cm 47x71in) Paris 1999

$6 087 - €7 013 - £4 200 - FF45 999
Scene in Holland, Cattle by a Windmill Oil/canvas (60.5x111.5cm 23x43in) Newbury, Berkshire 2000

$2 887 - €2 910 - £1 800 - FF19 086
Rustic Cottage with Figure by a pond Oil/canvas/panel (18x34cm 7x13in) Fernhurst, Haslemere, Surrey 2000

$410 - €391 - £260 - FF2 566
A Shepherd resting beneath a Tree Watercolour (19.5x18cm 7x7in) London 1999

BRIGHTWELL L. Robert XIX-XX [23]
$144 - €123 - £85 - FF809
«**Gentleman from China**» Etching (18x14cm 7x5in) Godalming, Surrey 1998

BRIGHTWELL Lucy XIX-XX [3]
$306 - €361 - £220 - FF2 366
«**The Babes in the Wood**» Etching (31x22cm 12x8in) London 2001

BRIGLIA Giovanni Francesco 1737-c.1794 [6]
$11 500 - €11 922 - £6 900 - FF78 200
Natura morta con gatto Olio/tela (52x60cm 20x23in) Milano 1999

BRIGMAN Annie Wardrope 1869-1950 [84]
$4 000 - €3 340 - £2 376 - FF21 906
Boy with Bubble Gelatin silver print (18x14.5cm 7x5in) New-York 1998

BRIGNOLI Alexandre XIX [10]
$2 198 - €2 134 - £1 358 - FF14 000
Homme et enfant Tirage albuminé (22x17.5cm 8x6in) Paris 1999

BRIGNONI Serge 1903 [159]
$368 - €4 044 - £2 674 - FF26 527
Les oiseaux Acrylic (47.5x64cm 18x25in) Bern 1999

$4 722 - €5 616 - £3 365 - FF36 836
Tessiner Landschaft Oil/panel (36x24.5cm 14x9in) Zürich 2000

$946 - €1 029 - £623 - FF6 752
Ohne Titel Aquarell, Gouache/Papier (29.5x41.5cm
11x16in) Bern 2000

$178 - €150 - £105 - FF984
Métamorphose Farblithographie (41.6x55.5cm
16x21in) Bern 1998

**BRIHUEGA GORROCHATEGUI Luis 1915-1981
[12]**

$228 - €240 - £152 - FF1 576
Desnudo femenino Grafite (49x32cm 19x12in)
Madrid 2000

BRIL Matthys II c.1550-1584 [4]
$13 332 - €13 018 - £8 500 - FF85 391
Piazza della Bocca della Verità, Church of
S.Maria in Cosmedin Black chalk (19x27cm 7x10in)
London 1999

BRIL Paul 1554-1626 [51]
$320 000 - €323 724 - £195 392 - FF2 123 488
Landscape with Villagers and ruins in the
Background Oil/canvas (111x159cm 43x62in) New-
York 2000

$45 603 - €51 796 - £32 000 - FF339 760
Stag Hunt in a Wooded Landscape Oil/canvas
(95.5x120.5cm 37x47in) London 2001

$75 600 - €84 091 - £50 400 - FF551 600
San Jerónimo en oración Oleo/tabla (26x45cm
10x17in) Madrid 2000

$5 700 - €4 924 - £2 850 - FF32 300
Veduta di rovine Matita/carta (22x30cm 8x11in)
Milano 1999

BRILL George Reiter 1867-1918 [1]
$2 200 - €2 116 - £1 357 - FF13 878
«Philadelphia Sunday Press» Poster (37x53.5cm
14x21in) New-York 1998

BRILL Reginald 1902-1974 [19]
$4 274 - €4 969 - £3 000 - FF32 593
Autumn Leaves Mixed media (75x52cm 29x20in)
Billingshurst, West-Sussex 2001

$2 988 - €3 208 - £2 000 - FF21 043
Study for Men in the Trench Watercolour
(29.5x68.5cm 11x26in) London 2001

BRILLOUIN Louis Georges 1817-1893 [26]
$5 500 - €5 030 - £3 358 - FF32 993
«Le Bourgeois Gentilhomme» Oil/panel (36x56cm
14x22in) New-York 1998

$700 - €797 - £494 - FF5 227
Cavalier Oil/panel (35x27cm 14x11in) Chicago IL
2001

BRINANT de Jules Ruinart 1839-1898 [14]
$2 655 - €2 230 - £1 557 - FF14 625
Village animé en bord de mer Huile/toile (25x34cm
9x13in) Bruxelles 1999

BRINCKMANN Enrique 1938 [6]
$476 - €511 - £323 - FF3 349
Sin título Tinta/papel (23.5x34cm 9x13in) Madrid
2000

BRINCKMANN Philipp Hieronymus 1709-1761 [11]
$7 720 - €9 203 - £5 504 - FF60 370
Landschaft mit Ruine Oil/panel (22.2x28.5cm
8x11in) Köln 2000

**BRINDEAU DE JARNY Louis Édouard 1867-1943
[20]**
$2 013 - €2 287 - £1 389 - FF15 000
«Marabout à Sidi M'Barak, aux portes de
Mekhnès» Huile/panneau (46x38cm 18x14in) Paris
2000

BRINDESI Giovanni, Jean XIX [5]
$4 532 - €5 336 - £3 185 - FF35 000
Personnages orientaux: Dames
Turques/Derviche/Bachi-Bazouk/Persan
Aquarelle (27.5x19cm 10x7in) Paris 2000

BRINDISI Remo 1918-1996 [355]
$4 000 - €4 147 - £2 400 - FF27 200
Pastorale Olio/tela (120x100cm 47x39in) Prato 2000

$1 750 - €1 814 - £1 050 - FF11 900
La trasfigurazione dell'uomo Olio/tela (60x40cm
23x15in) Milano 2000

$840 - €1 088 - £630 - FF7 140
Venezia Olio/tela (40x30cm 15x11in) Vercelli 2001

$425 - €441 - £255 - FF2 890
Pastorale China (25x34cm 9x13in) Prato 2000

$80 - €104 - £60 - FF680
Venezia Litografia a colori (56x48.5cm 22x19in)
Milano 2001

BRING Maj 1880-1971 [5]
$1 263 - €1 466 - £872 - FF9 618
Landskap Oil/panel (26x35cm 10x13in) Stockholm
2000

BRINI Ercole 1907-1989 [32]
$770 - €776 - £480 - FF5 089
«Brama di Vivere» Poster (99x68.5cm 38x26in)
London 2000

BRINKLEY Nell 1888-1944 [10]
$1 600 - €1 481 - £979 - FF9 716
Spring awakens as sprite and couple look on, a
newspaper feature Ink/paper (28x50cm 11x20in)
New-York 1999

BRINKS Kuno 1908-1972 [29]
$133 - €147 - £90 - FF967
Petrus vindt de stater in de bek van de vis
Copper engraving (21.2x15cm 8x5in) Haarlem 2000

BRION Gustave 1824-1877 [19]
$3 600 - €3 966 - £2 432 - FF26 016
Idylle bij de waterput (Scène idyllique au bord
du puits) Huile/toile (73x60cm 28x23in) Antwerpen
2000

BRIOSCHI Antonio, Anton 1855-1920 [23]
$500 - €518 - £300 - FF3 400
Scorcio di lago Olio/cartone (33.5x43.5cm 13x17in)
Vercelli 2001

BRIOSCHI Carlo 1826-1895 [7]
$4 069 - €4 724 - £2 860 - FF30 985
Blick vom Lido auf Venedig Öl/Leinwand (36x81cm
14x31in) Wien 2001

BRIOSCO Antonio c.1470-1532 [1]
$5 057 - €5 243 - £3 034 - FF34 391
Figure marine fantastiche Bronzo (H26cm H10in)
Venezia 2000

BRIOUX Lionel XIX [4]
$1 862 - €1 982 - £1 235 - FF13 000
Pêcheurs au bord du fleuve Huile/toile (33x46.5cm
12x18in) Paris 2000

BRIQUET A. c.1820-c.1900 [7]
$3 454 - €3 201 - £2 148 - FF21 000
Roches près Franchard/Longs
Rochers/Presqu'île au milieu d'un lac Tirage
albuminé (18x24cm 7x9in) Paris 1999

BRISBOIS Patrice 1945 [19]
$1 689 - €1 829 - £1 072 - FF12 000
Le chat sphinx Bronze (44x37cm 17x14in) Paris
2000

BRISCOE Arthur John Trevor 1873-1943 **[161]**
$6 246 – €6 975 – **£4 000** – FF45 755
Moonlight Oil/canvas (71x91.5cm 27x36in) London 2000
$1 069 – €1 012 – **£650** – FF6 641
Schooner under Sail Watercolour/paper (9x14cm 3x5in) Lymington 1999
$727 – €685 – **£449** – FF4 493
Re-Fitting Etching (35.5x25cm 13x9in) London 1999

BRISCOE Franklin Dullin 1844-1903 **[71]**
$5 000 – €5 367 – **£3 346** – FF35 205
Sunrise, Coast of Maine Oil/canvas (45x81cm 18x32in) Portland ME 2000
$2 200 – €2 046 – **£1 358** – FF13 419
On the Delaware Oil/canvas (20x35cm 8x14in) Portland ME 1999

BRISGAND Gustave ?-c.1950 **[28]**
$1 842 – €1 829 – **£1 147** – FF12 000
Jeune femme au voile Huile/panneau (31x23cm 12x9in) Paris 1999
$834 – €762 – **£510** – FF5 000
Jeune Orientale au voile rouge Pastel/papier (56x56cm 22x22in) Calais 1999

BRISIGHELLA Carlo c.1630-1718 **[1]**
$15 500 – €16 068 – **£9 300** – FF105 400
Battaglia Olio/tela (36x47cm 14x18in) Milano 2000

BRISPOT Henri 1846-1928 **[39]**
$1 682 – €1 896 – **£1 183** – FF12 435
Ein Mönch bemalt eine Marienskulptur mit Kind Öl/Leinwand (55.6x46.4cm 21x18in) Zürich 2001
$1 791 – €1 524 – **£1 066** – FF10 000
Paris, les bouquinistes devant Notre-Dame Huile/panneau (24x31cm 9x12in) Paris 1998

BRISSAUD Pierre 1885-? **[10]**
$150 – €169 – **£103** – FF1 107
Happy Holidays Ink (23x15cm 9x6in) Chicago IL 2000

BRISSET Émile ?-1904 **[6]**
$6 600 – €5 702 – **£4 400** – FF37 400
La visita Olio/tela (71.5x57.5cm 28x22in) Roma 1998

BRISSON Pierre Marie 1955 **[38]**
$203 – €231 – **£140** – FF1 516
Olympe Farbradierung (51x67cm 20x26in) Zofingen 2000

BRISSOT DE WARVILLE Félix Saturnin 1818-1892 **[150]**
$3 427 – €3 323 – **£2 171** – FF21 800
Schäfer mit seiner Herde in weiter Landschaft Öl/Leinwand (58.5x81.5cm 23x32in) München 1999
$1 988 – €2 134 – **£1 330** – FF14 000
Moutons sur un chemin de campagne Huile/panneau (15x25cm 5x9in) Paris 2000
$867 – €818 – **£540** – FF5 366
Schäfer mit seiner Herde am Stall Aquarell/Papier (25x35cm 9x13in) Frankfurt 1999

BRISTOL Horace 1909 **[19]**
$3 250 – €3 031 – **£1 962** – FF19 881
Industrial Study Photograph (22.5x18.5cm 8x7in) New-York 1999

BRISTOL John Bunyan 1826-1909 **[32]**
$4 200 – €3 638 – **£2 575** – FF23 862
Glimpse of the Lake Oil/canvas (56x86.5cm 22x34in) New-York 1999
$3 750 – €3 540 – **£2 331** – FF23 224
Housatonic River at Sheffield, Massachusetts Oil/board (30x50cm 12x20in) Milford CT 1999

BRISTOW Edmund 1787-1876 **[87]**
$5 762 – €5 501 – **£3 600** – FF36 081
A Girl on a grey Pony held by a Boy, by a Country Cottage Oil/panel (49x61cm 19x24in) London 1999
$2 877 – €2 852 – **£1 800** – FF18 709
The Day's Bag Oil/panel (22.5x30.5cm 8x12in) London 1999

BRITO de José 1855-1946 **[1]**
$2 400 – €2 493 – **£1 550** – FF16 350
Paisagem com rio Oleo/tabla (25.5x36cm 10x14in) Lisboa 2000

BRITO JORGE Jacqueline 1973 **[6]**
$1 700 – €1 653 – **£1 037** – FF10 843
Where the Bodies of Doubt Sleep Oil/canvas (32x32cm 12x12in) Tel Aviv 2000

BRITOV Kim 1925 **[115]**
$1 215 – €1 037 – **£733** – FF6 800
Le premier gel Huile/carton (50x64cm 19x25in) Enghien 1999
$693 – €640 – **£431** – FF4 200
Le Kremlin de Rostov le Grand Huile/carton (20x40cm 7x15in) Enghien 1999

BRITTAN Charles E., Sr or Jr XIX-XX **[10]**
$465 – €450 – **£295** – FF2 954
Dartmoor Landscape with Sheep Grazing beneath a Tor Watercolour/paper (18x26cm 7x10in) Devon 1999

BRITTAN Charles Edward, Jnr. 1870-1949 **[73]**
$559 – €613 – **£360** – FF4 024
Loch Eil near Port William, Weidelandschaft mit Schafen am Herbsttag Aquarell/Papier (36x53cm 14x20in) Lindau 2000

BRITTAN Charles Edward, Snr. 1837-1888 **[21]**
$883 – €890 – **£550** – FF5 838
Cattle Beside a River in a Mountainous Landscape Watercolour (30x50cm 11x19in) London 2000

BRITTEN Jack, Joolama 1921 **[17]**
$1 944 – €2 087 – **£1 301** – FF13 689
Gwali - Waali Mixed media/canvas (90x120cm 35x47in) Melbourne 2000

BRITTEN William Edward Frank 1848-1916 **[10]**
$551 – €603 – **£380** – FF3 958
A reclining dog Charcoal (50x130cm 19x51in) London 2001

BRITTON Alison 1949 **[5]**
$2 436 – €2 371 – **£1 500** – FF15 553
Brown Cleft Pot Ceramic (H35.5cm H13in) London 1999

BRITTON Harry 1878-1958 **[19]**
$681 – €655 – **£419** – FF4 294
Summer Field Oil/panel (23x33cm 9x12in) Vancouver, BC. 1999

BRIULLOV Alexander Pavlovich 1798-1877 **[6]**
$17 491 – €20 815 – **£12 500** – FF136 540
Warrior Accompanying a Young Maid on Horseback Watercolour (32x24.5cm 12x9in) London 2000

BRIZE Cornelis Brisé 1622-1670 **[3]**
$67 500 – €64 434 – **£42 174** – FF422 658
Letters, Seals and Documents Nailed to a Wooded Board Oil/canvas (73.5x62cm 28x24in) New-York 1999

BRIZIO Francesco c.1574-1623 **[18]**
- $2 900 - €3 006 - **£1 740** - FF19 720
  Martirio di San Lorenzo Olio/rame (33x27cm
  12x10in) Roma 2001
- $1 500 - €1 646 - **£996** - FF10 798
  **An Extensive Mountainous Landscape with Two
  Figures in the Foreground** Ink (25.5x38.5cm
  10x15in) New-York 2000
- $897 - €1 022 - **£626** - FF6 707
  **Madonna mit dem Kinde, unter einem Baum sit-
  zend,nach Agostino Carracci** Radierung
  (31.5x22.5cm 12x8in) Berlin 2001

BRO René Brault, dit 1930-1987 **[7]**
- $983 - €991 - **£613** - FF6 500
  Dallas Huile/toile (73x92cm 28x36in) Paris 2000

BROADHEAD W. Smithson 1888-1960 **[13]**
- $7 000 - €6 488 - **£4 352** - FF42 560
  «Oriole Lass» Oil/masonite (61x76cm 24x29in) New-
  York 1999

BROCA de Alexis Louis 1868-1948 **[24]**
- $3 267 - €3 811 - **£2 272** - FF25 000
  Vue de Fez Huile/toile (65x99cm 25x38in) Paris 2000

BROCAS Charles 1774-1835 **[3]**
- $12 406 - €10 728 - **£7 375** - FF70 372
  **Aeneas flieht mit Sohn und Vater Anchises aus
  dem brennenden Troja** Öl/Leinwand (144x113cm
  56x44in) Zürich 1998

BROCAS Henry, Jnr. XIX **[1]**
- $1 365 - €1 435 - **£856** - FF9 411
  **View of the Lying-in-Hospital/Nelson's Pillar,
  after S.Brocas** Aquatint in colors (28x42cm 11x16in)
  Dublin 2000

BROCAS Henry, Snr. 1766-1838 **[3]**
- $4 489 - €5 339 - **£3 200** - FF35 024
  Falmouth Harbour Watercolour (35.5x53cm 13x20in)
  London 2000

BROCHART Constant Joseph 1816-1899 **[26]**
- $3 759 - €3 436 - **£2 300** - FF22 536
  Portrait of Beautiful Young Women Pastel/paper
  (28x46cm 11x18in) Rotherham 1999

BROCHOCKI Walery 1847-1923 **[3]**
- $5 418 - €4 986 - **£3 251** - FF32 709
  Au bord de la rivière Wieprz Oil/canvas
  (39.5x69.5cm 15x27in) Warszawa 1999

BROCK Charles Edmund 1870-1938 **[36]**
- $3 230 - €3 037 - **£2 000** - FF19 921
  Portrait of a Girl Oil/canvas (103x70cm 40x27in)
  London 1999
- $52 300 - €56 140 - **£35 000** - FF368 256
  The Drive Oil/panel (35x45.5cm 13x17in) London
  2000
- $269 - €278 - **£170** - FF1 821
  Bank House, Trinity Street, Cambridge
  Watercolour/paper (39x20cm 15x7in) Cambridge 2000

BROCK Henry Matthew 1875-1960 **[17]**
- $273 - €318 - **£190** - FF2 089
  **Gentleman in Eighteen Century Dress Asleep in
  his Garden** Watercolour/paper (27x38cm 10x14in)
  Swindon, Wiltshire 2000

BROCK Richard Henry XIX-XX **[13]**
- $12 795 - €14 038 - **£8 500** - FF92 085
  Mares and Foals Oil/canvas (108x183cm 42x72in)
  London 2000
- $2 000 - €2 073 - **£1 200** - FF13 600
  Figura di cavallo con fantino Olio/tavoletta
  (28x39cm 11x15in) Milano 2000

BROCK William 1874-? **[8]**
- $4 250 - €5 137 - **£2 967** - FF33 696
  **A Wooded Landscape with Women and Rowing
  Boats on the River Bank** Oil/canvas (73x109cm
  29x43in) Philadelphia PA 2000

BROCKBANK Albert Ernest 1862-1958 **[22]**
- $300 - €343 - **£211** - FF2 247
  The Haystacks Watercolour/paper (27.5x38cm
  10x14in) Boston MA 2001

BROCKDORFF Victor 1911-1992 **[56]**
- $483 - €417 - **£292** - FF2 736
  Sommerblomster i haven Oil/canvas (73x55cm
  28x21in) Vejle 1999

BRÖCKER Ernst 1893-1963 **[54]**
- $678 - €665 - **£437** - FF4 360
  Bauernhaus am Gewässer Öl/Leinwand (60x70cm
  23x27in) Kempten 1999
- $526 - €613 - **£369** - FF4 024
  Gehöft mit Federvieh Öl/Leinwand (30x40cm
  11x15in) Kempten 2000

BROCKHURST Gerald Leslie 1890-1978 **[171]**
- $2 551 - €2 178 - **£1 500** - FF14 285
  Irish Landscape Oil/panel (47.5x61cm 18x24in)
  London 1998
- $3 287 - €3 529 - **£2 200** - FF23 147
  Portrait of a Lady Pencil/paper (33.5x27cm 13x10in)
  London 2000
- $403 - €396 - **£250** - FF2 599
  Clytie/Head of a Girl Etching (24x29cm 9x11in)
  London 1999

BROCKHUSEN von Theo 1882-1919 **[24]**
- $21 352 - €24 031 - **£14 711** - FF157 633
  Frühlingslandschaft Öl/Leinwand (108x135cm
  42x53in) München 2000
- $7 432 - €6 807 - **£4 530** - FF44 649
  Stormy Landscape with a Wind Mill Oil/canvas
  (65x81cm 25x31in) Amsterdam 1999

BROCKMAN Ann 1899-1943 **[8]**
- $800 - €820 - **£500** - FF5 381
  **Day at the Topsfield Fair/Afternoon in a Cape
  Ann Town** Watercolour/paper (36x54cm 14x21in)
  Bolton MA 2000

BROCKMANN Gottfried 1903-1983 **[24]**
- $7 790 - €9 203 - **£5 502** - FF60 370
  Das ausgekochte Huhn Oil/panel (44.5x36.5cm
  17x14in) Köln 2001
- $2 077 - €2 454 - **£1 467** - FF16 098
  Herr mit Melone Pencil/paper (20.5x12.5cm 8x4in)
  Köln 2001

BROCKTORFF von Charles Frederick 1775-1850
[8]
- $1 974 - €2 305 - **£1 400** - FF15 118
  **Admiral, Lord Collingwood, in naval uniform,
  wearing three medals** Watercolour (8x6.5cm 3x2in)
  London 2001

BROCQ Pierre Jules 1811-? **[4]**
- $8 278 - €7 927 - **£5 210** - FF52 000
  **Ananas, potiron, aubergines, abricots, raisins,
  pêches, artichauts** Aquarelle (108x76cm 42x29in)
  Paris 1999

BRODERICK Laurence 1935 **[19]**
- $1 141 - €1 331 - **£800** - FF8 728
  Lutra Lutra Maquette Bronze (H14cm H5in) London
  2000

BRODERS Roger 1883-1953 **[497]**
🖋 **$2 000** – €2 332 – **£1 404** – FF15 300
   Village at Water's Edge Gouache/paper (37.5x21cm
   14x8in) New-York 1999
📜 **$1 755** – €1 678 – **£1 100** – FF11 005
   «**Parcs de Grand Luxe**» Poster (122x82cm 48x32in)
   London 1999

BRODOVITCH Alexey 1898-1971 **[9]**
📜 **$2 800** – €3 140 – **£1 944** – FF20 599
   «**Libertad de Palabra**» Poster (101x70cm 40x27in)
   New-York 2000

BRODSKY Harry 1908-1997 **[4]**
📜 **$550** – €555 – **£343** – FF3 638
   Wine and Song Lithograph (25.5x20cm 10x7in)
   New-York 2000

BRODSKY N. XX **[2]**
📜 **$3 003** – €2 592 – **£1 813** – FF17 000
   «**La Grande Illusion**», de Jean Renoir Affiche
   couleur (240x160cm 94x62in) Argenteuil 1999

BRODSZKY Sandor 1819-1901 **[5]**
🖋 **$7 600** – €7 473 – **£4 750** – FF49 020
   Ruins of a Castle Oil/canvas (56x77.5cm 22x30in)
   Budapest 1999
🖋 **$1 320** – €1 500 – **£920** – FF9 840
   Ruisseau Huile/carton (30x39.5cm 11x15in) Budapest
   2001

BRODWOLF Jürgen 1932 **[147]**
🖋 **$2 598** – €2 522 – **£1 617** – FF16 540
   Zwei Figuren Technique mixte/carton (50x39cm
   19x15in) Luzern 1999
🖋 **$972** – €971 – **£608** – FF6 372
   Kleine rote und grosse weisse Figur Tempera
   (43.7x30.4cm 17x11in) Hamburg 1999
🖋 **$2 274** – €2 161 – **£1 388** – FF15 092
   Weiblicher Torso Sculpture (49x13.5x11cm
   19x5x4in) Stuttgart 2000
🖋 **$803** – €767 – **£501** – FF5 030
   Ohne Titel Mixed media/paper (34x21cm 13x8in)
   Köln 1999
📜 **$92** – €102 – **£64** – FF670
   «**Figurenscene**» Drypoint (22.5x28cm 8x11in)
   Heidelberg 2001

BRODZKY Horace Ascher 1885-1969 **[78]**
🖋 **$2 047** – €2 402 – **£1 444** – FF15 758
   The masked Ball Oil/board (24.5x30cm 9x11in)
   Nedlands 2000
🖋 **$201** – €225 – **£140** – FF1 476
   Mother & Child Ink (17x21.5cm 6x8in) Sydney 2001

BROE Vern 1930 **[26]**
🖋 **$700** – €649 – **£435** – FF4 256
   Summer harbor scene with sailboats Oil/board
   (45x60cm 18x24in) North-Harwich MA 1999

BROECK van den Clemence 1843-1922 **[25]**
🖋 **$986** – €1 148 – **£704** – FF7 528
   Kitchen Interior with Woman preparing a Meal
   Oil/canvas (38x55cm 14x21in) Toronto 2001

BROECK van den Crispiaen 1524-1588/91 **[15]**
🖋 **$141 165** – €137 835 – **£90 000** – FF904 140
   The Last judgment Oil/panel (142.5x115.5cm
   56x45in) London 1999
🖋 **$31 352** – €35 610 – **£22 000** – FF233 585
   **The Virgin and Child with the Infant Saint John
   the Baptist** Oil/panel (103.5x86.5cm 40x34in) London
   2001
🖋 **$7 535** – €6 416 – **£4 500** – FF42 084
   The Battle of Trasimene Ink (25.5x51cm 10x20in)
   London 1998

BROECK van den Elias 1657-1708 **[27]**
🖋 **$38 287** – €42 929 – **£26 000** – FF281 598
   **Lobster, a Conch Shell, a Tulip, Orange,
   Redcurrants, Bread, Cellar** Oil/canvas (49x40.5cm
   19x15in) London 2000
🖋 **$38 568** – €38 255 – **£24 000** – FF250 939
   **Forest Floor Still Life with a Bird's Nest,
   Toadstools, Snails** Oil/panel (31.5x26.5cm 12x10in)
   London 1999

BROECKAERT Herman 1878-1930 **[22]**
🖋 **$1 435** – €1 240 – **£865** – FF8 135
   De zonnebloemen Huile/toile (60.5x80.5cm 23x31in)
   Bruxelles 1998

BROEDELET Henriette, Hetty 1877-1966 **[11]**
🖋 **$435** – €454 – **£276** – FF2 976
   Stilleven met fruit en klepkan Oil/canvas (44x73cm
   17x28in) Den Haag 2000

BROEK ten Willem, Wim 1905-1993 **[20]**
📜 **$255** – €2 632 – **£1 545** – FF17 264
   «**Holland-America Line, New York, Exposition
   Mondiale**» Poster (96.5x62cm 37x24in) Hoorn 2000

BROEMEL Carl William 1891-1984 **[10]**
🖋 **$265** – €251 – **£165** – FF1 644
   Sailboats in Harbor Watercolour/paper (28x38cm
   11x15in) Cleveland OH 1999

BROGE Alfred K. Harald 1870-1955 **[102]**
🖋 **$639** – €606 – **£398** – FF3 973
   Exteriör med hus og figurer Oil/canvas (49x63cm
   19x24in) Vejle 1999
🖋 **$629** – €537 – **£376** – FF3 522
   Interiör med læsende pige Oil/canvas (33x26cm
   12x10in) Viby J, Århus 1998

BROGI Giacomo 1822-1881 **[17]**
📷 **$763** – €716 – **£471** – FF4 695
   Il perseo del Cellini Albumen print (37.2x28.4cm
   14x11in) Köln 1999

BROGI Gino 1902-1989 **[22]**
🖋 **$480** – €622 – **£360** – FF4 080
   Via Erbosa Olio/tavola (45x50cm 17x19in) Prato 2001

BROITMAN Yeuda 1956 **[4]**
🖋 **$9 521** – €10 301 – **£6 523** – FF67 570
   Arabian Nights, thousand and one Nights
   Oil/canvas (240x140cm 94x55in) Tel Aviv 2001
🖋 **$4 020** – €4 726 – **£2 786** – FF31 000
   Nature morte au flacon de cristal Huile/toile
   (74x74cm 29x29in) Paris 2000

BRÖKER Wilhelm 1848-1930 **[7]**
🖋 **$1 161** – €1 125 – **£729** – FF7 378
   Am Waldbach, Waldlandschaft mit Reh Oil/panel
   (13x16cm 5x6in) Berlin 1999

BROMBO Angelo 1893-1962 **[32]**
🖋 **$1 191** – €1 321 – **£825** – FF8 664
   Skördearbete Oil/canvas (70x99cm 27x38in) Malmö
   2001
🖋 **$709** – €772 – **£467** – FF5 064
   **Venezianischer Kanal mit Gondel im
   Sonnenschein** Öl/Leinwand (30x40cm 11x15in) Bern
   2000

BROMEIS Auguste 1813-1881 **[8]**
🖋 **$1 301** – €1 355 – **£824** – FF8 887
   Capri, Blick auf die Faraglioni-Felsen
   Öl/Leinwand (17x25cm 6x9in) München 2000

BROMLEY John Mallard ?-1940 **[36]**
🖋 **$349** – €398 – **£240** – FF2 609
   Chickens Watercolour/paper (24x34cm 9x13in)
   London 2000

B

BROMLEY William I 1769-1842 **[2]**
- $4 812 - €4 849 - **£3 000** - FF31 810
  The Penny Whistle Oil/canvas (46x61cm 18x24in)
  London 2000

BROMLEY William III ?-c.1888 **[52]**
- $14 732 - €17 521 - **£10 500** - FF114 929
  Fetching Water Oil/canvas (44.5x52cm 17x20in)
  London 2000
- $3 837 - €4 299 - **£2 666** - FF28 200
  Meeting in the Woods Oil/canvas (34.5x42cm
  13x16in) Durban 2001
- $3 586 - €3 849 - **£2 400** - FF25 251
  Quiet Read Watercolour (20.5x24cm 8x9in) London
  2000

BROMPTON Richard c.1734-1783 **[6]**
- $2 381 - €2 556 - **£1 594** - FF16 769
  Friedrich der Grosse Öl/Leinwand (45.5x35.5cm
  17x13in) Bremen 2000

BROMS Arvid 1910-1968 **[20]**
- $487 - €538 - **£337** - FF3 530
  Ansikte Oil/canvas (55x46cm 21x18in) Helsinki 2001

BROMS Birgit 1924 **[12]**
- $872 - €1 037 - **£621** - FF6 803
  Stilleben Oil/canvas (72x24cm 28x9in) Stockholm
  2000

BRONCKHORST Hendrick XVIII **[1]**
- $1 932 - €2 287 - **£1 428** - FF15 000
  Pie-grièche et moineau sur une branche
  Gouache/papier (30x24cm 11x9in) Paris 2001

BRONCKHORST Johannes 1648-1726/27 **[27]**
- $1 698 - €1 906 - **£1 177** - FF12 501
  Rode koningsparadijsvogel uit Nieuw Guinea
  Gouache/papier (24.5x19.5cm 9x7in) The Hague 2000

BRONCKORST van Jan Gerritsz. 1603-1677 **[6]**
- $163 800 - €155 931 - **£102 480** - FF1 022 840
  Musiken Oil/canvas (88x149cm 34x58in) Stockholm
  1999
- $26 814 - €22 815 - **£16 000** - FF149 654
  A Courtesan with a Lute Oil/canvas (77x64cm
  30x25in) London 1998
- $897 - €1 022 - **£626** - FF6 707
  **Ruinen eines römischen Tempels, nach
  Cornelis van Poelenburgh** Radierung (22x20cm
  8x7in) Berlin 2001

BRONDY Matteo 1866-1954 **[79]**
- $2 326 - €2 439 - **£1 457** - FF16 000
  Le thé sous la tente caïdale Huile/toile (46x61cm
  18x24in) Paris 2000
- $1 329 - €1 220 - **£826** - FF8 000
  Vue de Fez Huile/toile (33x46cm 12x18in) Paris 1999
- $1 235 - €1 296 - **£774** - FF8 500
  La grande caravane Crayon (52x76.5cm 20x30in)
  Paris 2000
- $451 - €385 - **£270** - FF2 528
  **«Meknès, ses remparts, ses cortèges maro-
  cains»** Poster (104x73.5cm 40x28in) London 1998

BRONGNIART Alexandre Théodore 1739-1813 **[4]**
- $1 256 - €1 220 - **£782** - FF8 000
  Profil de chastelet néogothique Aquarelle
  (28x22cm 11x8in) Montfort L'Amaury 1999

BRONNIKOV Fjodor Andrejevitj 1827-1902 **[4]**
- $2 032 - €2 287 - **£1 399** - FF15 000
  Moine riant Huile/toile (23x18cm 9x7in) Paris 2000

BRONT Luigi 1891-1978 **[4]**
- $2 100 - €2 177 - **£1 260** - FF14 280
  Rustico sul Natisone Olio/tela (35x45cm 13x17in)
  Trieste 2001

BRONTë Charlotte 1816-1855 **[1]**
- $1 920 - €1 935 - **£1 200** - FF12 694
  Cooking Pot - Storage Jar with a Lid Drawing
  (10x10cm 4x4in) London 2000

BROOD Herman 1946 **[76]**
- $2 394 - €2 072 - **£1 452** - FF13 594
  «Papa's Brand New Bas» Acrylic/canvas
  (130x99.5cm 51x39in) Amsterdam 1998
- $784 - €771 - **£504** - FF5 060
  Two Figures Acrylic (98x118.5cm 38x46in)
  Amsterdam 1999
- $271 - €318 - **£194** - FF2 083
  Untitled Lithograph (65x50cm 25x19in) Amsterdam
  2001

BROODTHAERS Marcel 1924-1976 **[127]**
- $110 683 - €107 725 - **£68 000** - FF706 628
  Signature de l'artiste Installation (100x50x28cm
  39x19x11in) London 2000
- $320 000 - €371 293 - **£220 928** - FF2 435 520
  Moules Sauce Blanche Sculpture (49x39.5x33cm
  19x15x12in) New-York 2000
- $3 360 - €3 927 - **£2 398** - FF25 759
  Ohne Titel Ballpoint pen (15x36cm 5x14in) Zürich
  2001
- $914 - €908 - **£571** - FF5 953
  Chère petite soeur Offset (63x43.5cm 24x17in)
  Amsterdam 1999

BROOK Alexander 1898-1980 **[30]**
- $2 500 - €2 683 - **£1 673** - FF17 602
  Stormy Skies Oil/canvas (68x96cm 27x38in) Portland
  ME 2000
- $1 200 - €1 028 - **£708** - FF6 741
  The Shawl Oil/canvas (40.5x28cm 15x11in) New-York
  1998

BROOK Peter 1927 **[13]**
- $916 - €843 - **£550** - FF5 532
  **Scotland Croft with Haystacks, Autumn
  Evening** Oil/canvas (50x76cm 19x29in) London 1999

BROOKE Leonard Leslie 1862-1940 **[23]**
- $2 089 - €2 072 - **£1 300** - FF13 592
  **Frontispiece design for The Nursery Rhyme
  Book** Watercolour (38x26.5cm 14x10in) London 1999

BROOKE Percy XIX-XX **[21]**
- $886 - €977 - **£600** - FF6 409
  **Study of Shepherd Driving Sheep Down a
  Country Path** Watercolour/paper (23x34cm 9x13in)
  Bourton-on-the-Water, Glos. 2000

BROOKER Bertram Richard 1888-1955 **[6]**
- $2 560 - €2 478 - **£1 579** - FF16 254
  Thick Stem Oil/board (38x30.5cm 14x12in) Toronto
  1999

BROOKER Harry 1848-1940 **[46]**
- $17 843 - €17 136 - **£11 000** - FF112 406
  The new Pupil Oil/canvas (71x91.5cm 27x36in)
  London 1999
- $4 950 - €5 749 - **£3 478** - FF37 710
  Interiör med syende kvinna Oil/canvas (34x28cm
  13x11in) Stockholm 2001

BROOKER William 1918-1983 **[42]**
- $4 572 - €4 210 - **£2 800** - FF27 613
  The Music Lesson Oil/board (40.5x51cm 15x20in)
  London 1998

BROOKES Samuel Marsden 1816-1892 **[10]**
$6 500 - €6 977 - **£4 349** - FF45 766
Mount Saint Helena Oil/canvas (81x101.5cm 31x39in) San-Francisco CA 2000

BROOKING Charles 1723-1759 **[14]**
$29 395 - €27 062 - **£18 000** - FF177 514
A Man of War Becalmed with Other Shipping off the Coast Oil/canvas (54x73cm 21x28in) London 1998

BROOKS Allan 1869-1946 **[32]**
$1 000 - €1 073 - **£681** - FF7 041
«**Sparrow**» Watercolour, gouache/paper (16.5x11cm 6x4in) Boston MA 2001

BROOKS Henry Jamyn c.1865-? **[9]**
$9 664 - €9 082 - **£6 000** - FF59 574
Eton College - The Entrance to School Yard Oil/canvas (61x91.5cm 24x36in) Salisbury, Wiltshire 1999

BROOKS James 1906-1992 **[32]**
$11 500 - €10 227 - **£7 033** - FF67 083
Tolen Acrylic/canvas (152.5x183cm 60x72in) New-York 1999
$5 000 - €5 487 - **£3 219** - FF35 994
Acton Acrylic/canvas (106.5x106.5cm 41x41in) New-York 2000
$1 600 - €1 631 - **£1 002** - FF10 698
Untitled Gouache (51x81.5cm 20x32in) New-York 2000

BROOKS Kim 1936 **[28]**
$20 442 - €17 002 - **£12 000** - FF111 524
Plight of the Silverbacks Oil/canvas (101.5x152.5cm 39x60in) London 1998
$19 973 - €23 285 - **£14 000** - FF152 742
On the Lookout, Black Maned Lion and Lioness Oil/canvas (93x73cm 36x28in) London 2000
$1 141 - €1 331 - **£800** - FF8 728
Black Maned Lion Pastel (58.5x47.5cm 23x18in) London 2000

BROOKS Leonard 1911-1993 **[55]**
$304 - €292 - **£188** - FF1 918
«**Late Sun**» Oil/panel (21.5x26.5cm 8x10in) Toronto 1999
$200 - €187 - **£123** - FF1 225
Town of San Andres Tuxtla Watercolour, gouache/paper (37x50cm 14x20in) Detroit MI 1999

BROOKS Mary Mason 1860-1915 **[1]**
$5 500 - €4 640 - **£3 226** - FF30 437
Garden Poppies, Isle of Shoals Watercolour/paper (35.5x51cm 13x20in) New-York 1998

BROOKS Mildred Bryant 1901-1995 **[13]**
$260 - €296 - **£180** - FF1 939
«**The Pines of Monterey**» Etching (31x15cm 12x6in) Cincinnati OH 2000

BROOKS Nicholas Alden 1849-c.1909 **[23]**
$3 800 - €3 291 - **£2 330** - FF21 589
Still Life with Carafe and Books Oil/canvas (35.5x45.5cm 13x17in) New-York 1999
$3 250 - €3 755 - **£2 275** - FF24 628
The Dollar Bill Ink (16x25.5cm 6x10in) New-York 2001

BROOKS Robin 1943 **[14]**
$639 - €616 - **£400** - FF4 040
A Clipper in full Sail Oil/canvas (60x90cm 23x35in) Billingshurst, West-Sussex 1999

BROOKS Thomas 1818-1891 **[33]**
$6 416 - €6 466 - **£4 000** - FF42 414
The Bridesmaid Oil/canvas (46x35.5cm 18x13in) London 2000

BROOKS Vincent 1814-1885 **[2]**
$2 596 - €3 051 - **£1 800** - FF20 016
The Floral Magazine: Figures and Descriptions of Popular Flowers Lithograph (25.5x17cm 10x6in) London 2000

BROOKSHAW George XVIII-XIX **[9]**
$1 900 - €1 780 - **£1 168** - FF11 673
Peaches Aquatint (51.5x42cm 20x16in) New-York 1999

BROOM Marion 1878-1962 **[194]**
$362 - €391 - **£250** - FF2 566
Still life of Blossom in a Tankard Oil/canvas (49.5x59.5cm 19x23in) Billinghurst, West-Sussex 2001
$358 - €398 - **£250** - FF2 611
Spray of Flowers Watercolour/paper (31x50cm 12x20in) Birmingham 2001

BROOME OF RAMSGATE William 1832-1892 **[17]**
$2 689 - €2 887 - **£1 800** - FF18 938
Fresh Breeze off The Needles Oil/canvas (51x76.5cm 20x30in) London 2000
$608 - €706 - **£420** - FF4 634
Running out the Harbour/Returning Home Oil/canvas (21.5x16.5cm 8x6in) London 2000

BROOTA Rameshwar 1941 **[8]**
$6 500 - €7 392 - **£4 541** - FF48 490
Silent Structures Acrylic/canvas (119.5x119.5cm 47x47in) New-York 2000

BROPHY Elizabeth / Liz XX **[9]**
$1 622 - €1 517 - **£1 000** - FF9 949
Beach Games Oil/board (30x41cm 11x16in) Co. Kilkenny 1999

BROSAMER Hans c.1500-1552 **[19]**
$24 466 - €22 883 - **£15 000** - FF150 105
Portrait of Jochum Wirman Oil/panel (49x34cm 19x13in) London 1998
$583 - €665 - **£406** - FF42 611
Samson wird von Dalila seiner Haare beraubt Kupferstich (8x9.5cm 3x3in) Berlin 2001

BROSCH Klemens 1894-1926 **[7]**
$6 588 - €6 541 - **£4 113** - FF42 903
Weg Indian ink (27.9x37.5cm 10x14in) Wien 1999

BROSS Simon XX **[2]**
$800 - €933 - **£560** - FF6 117
Traffic in a Busy Street Oil/canvas (55x71cm 22x28in) Cleveland OH 2000

BROSSA Joan 1919-1998 **[12]**
$162 - €180 - **£105** - FF1 182
Poema visual Litografía a color (50x38cm 19x15in) Madrid 2000

BROSSARD DE BEAULIEU François 1727-1810 **[3]**
$3 858 - €4 360 - **£2 604** - FF28 602
Bildnis des Jean-Baptiste Gabriel, capitaine du régiment de Brie Ol/Leinwand (80.5x64.5cm 31x25in) Wien 2000

BROSSARD Guillaume-Etienne-A. 1808-1890 **[2]**
$16 100 - €15 952 - **£9 767** - FF104 637
Portrait of Young Boy in Scottish Dress with Dog Oil/canvas (176x128cm 69x50in) New-Orleans LA 2000

BROSSE Charles Léonce 1871-? **[1]**
📖 **$4 400** - €5 132 - **£3 089** - FF33 661
«Meeting d'Aviation, Nice» Poster (78x108cm
30x42in) New-York 2000

BROTAT VILANOVA Joan 1920-1990 **[336]**
📷 **$1 620** - €1 355 - **£967** - FF8 887
Perfil Oleo/lienzo (55x46cm 21x18in) Madrid 1998
📷 **$434** - €420 - **£266** - FF2 758
Mujer y palomas Lápices de color/papel (30x25cm
11x9in) Madrid 1999
📷 **$179** - €192 - **£118** - FF1 260
Arabesca Pastel/papier (49x34cm 19x13in) Madrid
1998

BROTO José Manuel 1949 **[54]**
📷 **$15 000** - €14 550 - **£9 000** - FF102 000
«Infinito» Tecnica mista/tela (195x130cm 76x51in)
Milano 1999
📷 **$3 960** - €3 604 - **£2 400** - FF23 640
Sin título Oleo/papel (105x75cm 41x29in) Madrid
1999
📷 **$2 331** - €2 222 - **£1 406** - FF14 578
Sin título Técnica mixta/papel (63x46cm 24x18in)
Madrid 1999

BROUARD A. XIX-XX **[2]**
📷 **$1 368** - €1 524 - **£959** - FF10 000
Caravane près du marabout Aquarelle/papier
(25x33cm 9x12in) Paris 2001

BROUET Auguste 1872-1941 **[105]**
📷 **$6 053** - €5 153 - **£3 613** - FF33 800
Danseuse Fusain/papier (61x48cm 24x18in) Paris
1998
📖 **$241** - €259 - **£161** - FF1 700
Paysages de Paris Eau-forte (50.5x66cm 19x25in)
Paris 2000

BROUGH Robert 1872-1905 **[9]**
📷 **$4 615** - €5 425 - **£3 200** - FF35 584
Morrocan Scene Oil/canvas (51x61cm 20x24in)
Edinburgh 2000

BROUILLARD Eugène 1870-1950 **[37]**
📷 **$778** - €915 - **£564** - FF6 000
La Croix-Rousse Huile/carton (56x91cm 22x35in)
Lyon 2001
📷 **$551** - €656 - **£393** - FF4 300
Paysage au lac Huile/carton (23.5x39cm 9x15in)
Lyon 2000

BROUILLET Pierre André 1857-1914 **[31]**
📷 **$9 009** - €10 062 - **£6 105** - FF66 000
L'heure de la lecture Huile/toile (147x109cm
57x42in) Coulommiers 2000
📷 **$9 110** - €8 434 - **£5 500** - FF55 323
Picking Flowers Oil/canvas (73.5x60.5cm 28x23in)
London 1999
📷 **$4 199** - €4 075 - **£2 646** - FF26 732
Die Bootsfahrt auf einem Fluss Huile/panneau
(27x46.5cm 10x18in) Zürich 1999
📷 **$599** - €503 - **£352** - FF3 300
Femme en deuil Lavis (28x21cm 11x8in) Coutances
1998

BROUTIN Christian 1933 **[6]**
📖 **$357** - €305 - **£215** - FF2 000
«Jules et Jim» Affiche (60x80cm 23x31in) Paris 1998

BROUTY Charles 1897-1984 **[10]**
📷 **$1 613** - €1 677 - **£1 012** - FF11 000
El Oued Aquarelle (35x53cm 13x20in) Paris 2000

BROUWER Adriaen 1605/06-1638 **[9]**
📷 **$750** - €695 - **£459** - FF4 557
Exterior Scene with Figures Oil/panel (24x29cm
9x11in) Chicago IL 1999

BROUWER Berend Jan, Barand 1872-1936 **[28]**
📷 **$1 236** - €1 106 - **£740** - FF7 256
«De Kwakkenberg», Berg and Dal,Nijmegen
Oil/canvas (110x81cm 43x31in) Amsterdam 1998
📷 **$382** - €363 - **£232** - FF2 381
Polderlandschap met boerderij en ophaalbrug-
getje Oil/canvas (15x25cm 5x9in) Den Haag 1999

BROUWERS Jules 1869-1955 **[42]**
📷 **$358** - €397 - **£249** - FF2 601
Nature morte de fleurs et pommes Huile/panneau
(60x80cm 23x31in) Bruxelles 2001

BROWN & MURPHY Don & Stephen 1962/62 **[3]**
📷 **$3 942** - €4 654 - **£2 800** - FF30 529
Missile (No.4) Type C color print (181x230cm
71x90in) London 2001

BROWN Alexander Kellock 1849-1922 **[38]**
📷 **$1 422** - €1 653 - **£1 000** - FF10 844
Across the Loch Oil/canvas (56x91.5cm 22x36in)
London 2001
📷 **$1 100** - €1 029 - **£666** - FF6 749
Loch Oil/canvas (33x23cm 13x9in) Chicago IL 1999

BROWN Annora 1899-1987 **[22]**
📷 **$293** - €341 - **£202** - FF2 234
Untitled - Nasturtiums Watercolour/paper (21x14cm
8x5in) Calgary, Alberta 2000

BROWN Arthur William 1881-1966 **[5]**
📷 **$800** - €933 - **£553** - FF6 117
Young People relaxing At Elephant Shipboard
Party Pencil (38x46cm 15x18in) New-York 2000

BROWN Benjamin Chambers 1865-1942 **[47]**
📷 **$50 000** - €53 670 - **£33 460** - FF352 050
Mountainous Landscape Oil/canvas (101x127cm
40x50in) Bloomfield-Hills MI 2000
📷 **$10 000** - €9 204 - **£6 002** - FF60 373
Sierra Peaks, Big Pine Canyon Oil/canvas
(40x50cm 16x20in) Pasadena CA 1999
📷 **$1 500** - €1 768 - **£1 054** - FF11 597
California Seascape Oil/board (28x38cm 11x15in)
New-Orleans LA 2000
📖 **$1 200** - €1 104 - **£720** - FF7 244
Pasadena High-Bridge Lithograph (26x34cm
10x13in) Pasadena CA 1999

BROWN Cecil [2]
📷 **$3 617** - €3 906 - **£2 500** - FF25 624
Three Jockies racing together on a Square
Shaped Grassy Mound Bronze (H62cm H24in)
Edinburgh 2001

BROWN Cecily 1969 **[9]**
📷 **$75 000** - €87 022 - **£51 780** - FF570 825
Twenty Million Sweethearts Oil/canvas
(193x249cm 75x98in) New-York 2000
📷 **$1 100** - €1 276 - **£759** - FF8 372
Film Still From Cunning Stunts Watercolour
(12.5x14cm 4x5in) New-York 2000

BROWN Don 1962 **[3]**
📷 **$11 655** - €12 511 - **£7 800** - FF82 068
Submarine Type C color print (183x220cm 72x86in)
London 2000

BROWN E. c.1800-c.1877 **[8]**
📷 **$9 958** - €9 665 - **£6 200** - FF63 400
A Skewbald Hunter outside a Stable Oil/canvas
(51x66cm 20x25in) London 1999

BROWN

BROWN Eliphalet M. II 1816-1886 [1]
⊞ **$2 100** - €2 538 - **£1 466** - FF16 650
Clipper Ship Sovereign of the Seas Lithograph
(50x65cm 19x25in) Bolton MA 2000

BROWN F. Gregory 1887-1948 [22]
⊞ **$500** - €542 - **£333** - FF3 553
«**Saltburn**» Poster (100x63cm 39x25in) New-York
2000

BROWN Ford Madox 1821-1893 [20]
⊖ **$62 760** - €65 767 368 - **£42 000** - FF441 907
The Bromley Children Oil/canvas (127x101cm
50x39in) London 2000
⊘ **$56 732** - €65 857 - **£40 000** - FF431 996
**The supper at Emmaus and how it was known
of them by breaking of bread** Watercolour/paper
(53x48cm 20x18in) London 2001

BROWN Fred C. XIX-XX [5]
⊖ **$4 200** - €3 543 - **£2 463** - FF23 242
Apples, Grapes and Pear Oil/board (23.5x31cm
9x12in) New-York 1998

BROWN George Loring 1814-1889 [58]
⊖ **$5 000** - €5 709 - **£3 525** - FF37 449
«**Near Palermo, Clearing Away, View on the
Coast of Italy**» Oil/canvas (56x91cm 22x35in)
Boston MA 2001
⊖ **$950** - €849 - **£581** - FF5 569
«**Sand Embankment on the Pemigewasset
River**» Oil/canvas (26x36cm 10x14in) Boston MA
1999
⊘ **$700** - €799 - **£493** - FF5 242
«**Bay of Palermo from the Summit of Monte
Pelegrino...**» Graphite (20x35cm 7x13in) Boston MA
2001

BROWN Glenn 1966 [10]
⊖ **$28 391** - €30 476 - **£19 000** - FF199 910
You Take My Place in This Showdown Oil/canvas
(296.5x214.5cm 116x84in) London 2000
⊖ **$23 882** - €22 201 - **£14 500** - FF145 626
Telstar Oil/canvas/board (71x58.5cm 27x23in) London
1998
⊜ **$10 826** - €11 714 - **£7 500** - FF76 838
Never Forever Plaster (35.5x30.5x30.5cm
13x12x12in) London 2001

BROWN Grafton Tyler 1841-1918 [5]
⊖ **$42 500** - €45 619 - **£28 441** - FF299 242
A Canyon River with Pines and Figures Oil/can-
vas (91x142cm 35x55in) San-Francisco CA 2000

BROWN Harley W. 1939 [45]
⊘ **$1 047** - €1 246 - **£721** - FF8 173
Portrait walking Buffalo Pastel/paper (30x24cm
11x9in) Calgary, Alberta 2000

BROWN Harrison Bird 1831-1915 [70]
⊖ **$3 250** - €3 624 - **£2 193** - FF23 770
Grand Manan Shoreline Oil/canvas (31x56cm
12x22in) Thomaston ME 2000
⊖ **$2 200** - €2 355 - **£1 497** - FF15 449
**New England Landscape with Figures on a
Bridge** Oil/canvas (45x33cm 18x13in) Portsmouth NH
2001

BROWN Harry XX [1]
⊘ **$4 500** - €5 012 - **£2 943** - FF32 878
**Magazine cover: Singing boys choir approa-
ching pulpit** Gouache/paper (29x21cm 11x8in) New-
York 2000

BROWN Horace 1876-1949 [12]
⊖ **$880** - €820 - **£531** - FF5 380
Springfield, Vermont Oil/canvas (75x62cm 29x24in)
Plainfield NH 1999

BROWN Hugh Boycott 1909-1990 [294]
⊖ **$799** - €736 - **£480** - FF4 827
High Tide Across the Thames at Leigh-on-Sea
Oil/board (39x50cm 15x19in) London 1999
⊖ **$537** - €577 - **£360** - FF3 787
Bella Coola Harbour, British Columbia, Canada
Oil/board (20x25.5cm 7x10in) London 2000

BROWN James 1863-1943 [12]
⊖ **$5 620** - €5 189 - **£3 500** - FF34 039
Rye Sunset from factory Oil/canvas (43x51cm
16x20in) London 1999

BROWN James 1951 [242]
⊖ **$7 250** - €8 622 - **£5 168** - FF56 555
Untitled Acrylic/canvas (229x196cm 90x77in)
Amsterdam 2000
⊖ **$4 996** - €4 637 - **£3 000** - FF30 417
White Stabat Mater No.2 Mixed media (92x70.5cm
36x27in) London 1999
⊜ **$1 992** - €2 311 - **£1 375** - FF15 162
**Head of a Man with a Standing Figure on his
Head** Bronze (H63.5cm H25in) Johannesburg 2000
⊘ **$2 073** - €2 439 - **£1 486** - FF16 000
Têtes Mine plomb (66x51cm 25x20in) Paris 2001
⊞ **$763** - €908 - **£544** - FF5 953
The Maroccan Screenprint in colors (71x46cm
27x18in) Amsterdam 2000

BROWN James Michael 1854-1957 [6]
⊖ **$7 213** - €6 814 - **£4 500** - FF44 699
Lucy's Flittin Oil/canvas (128x85cm 50x33in)
Perthshire 1999
⊘ **$34 385** - €31 887 - **£21 000** - FF209 164
A Championship on the Course at Carnoustie
Watercolour/paper (26.5x38cm 10x14in) Glasgow 1998

BROWN Joan 1938-1990 [21]
⊖ **$9 000** - €7 605 - **£5 368** - FF49 888
A Toast to the Key of Life Oil/canvas (106.5x76cm
41x29in) San-Francisco CA 1998

BROWN Joe, Joseph 1909-1985 [14]
⊜ **$7 000** - €7 514 - **£4 684** - FF49 287
Jesse Owens Bronze (H62.5cm H24in) New-York
2000

BROWN John Alfred Arnesby 1866-1955 [72]
⊖ **$9 035** - €10 594 - **£6 500** - FF69 491
The Grange Farm Oil/canvas (41x51cm 16x20in)
London 2001
⊖ **$3 260** - €2 889 - **£2 000** - FF18 950
Cattle Resting in a Meadow Oil/canvas (20x27cm
8x11in) Aylsham, Norfolk 1999
⊘ **$567** - €645 - **£400** - FF4 233
Sheep grazing in Landscape Watercolour/paper
(7x12cm 3x5in) Aylsham, Norfolk 2001

BROWN John Appleton 1844-1902 [36]
⊖ **$2 000** - €1 912 - **£1 218** - FF12 544
The River in Autumn Oil/canvas (51x66cm 20x25in)
Boston MA 1999
⊘ **$1 300** - €1 227 - **£808** - FF8 051
River Landscape Watercolour/paper (25x35cm
10x14in) Milford CT 1999

BROWN John George 1831-1913 [163]
⊖ **$130 000** - €111 070 - **£78 039** - FF728 572
Deerhunter in the Woods Oil/canvas (107x147.5cm
42x58in) New-York 1998

Calendar & auction results : Internet www.artprice.com 3617 ARTPRICE 215

$25 000 - €25 914 - **£15 852** - FF169 985
Getting Acquainted Oil/canvas (64x51.5cm 25x20in)
New-York 2000

$6 000 - €5 701 - **£3 650** - FF37 397
Shovelling Snow Oil/canvas (30x22cm 11x8in) New-York 1999

$2 300 - €2 682 - **£1 614** - FF17 595
Girl amongst Queen Anne's Lace
Watercolour/paper (33x21cm 13x8in) Dedham MA 2000

BROWN John Henry 1818-1891 **[16]**
$800 - €909 - **£561** - FF5 960
Lady with brown Hair in a dark blue silk Dress
Miniature (11x8cm 4x3in) Philadelphia PA 2001

BROWN John Lewis 1829-1890 **[96]**
$1 947 - €1 873 - **£1 200** - FF12 286
Cavarly Officer on Horseback Oil/canvas
(72.5x63cm 28x24in) Billingshurst, West-Sussex 1999

$2 326 - €2 287 - **£1 494** - FF15 000
Visite cavalière Huile/toile (23.5x32.5cm 9x12in)
Paris 1999

$1 294 - €1 220 - **£784** - FF8 000
Après la bataille Pastel/papier (68x101cm 26x39in)
Paris 1999

BROWN Kellock 1856-1934 **[1]**
$4 144 - €3 535 - **£2 500** - FF23 191
Mother and Child Bronze (H53cm H20in) Glasgow 1998

BROWN Lancelot Capability 1716-1783 **[1]**
$4 170 - €4 203 - **£2 600** - FF27 569
The South Front for Croome, The Seat of the Right Honourable Ink (26.5x41.5cm 10x16in)
London 2000

BROWN Lilian S. XX **[2]**
$5 181 - €5 803 - **£3 600** - FF38 066
The Changing Room Oil/canvas (101.5x76.5cm 39x30in) London 2001

BROWN Lucy Madox 1843-1894 **[2]**
$9 821 - €11 680 - **£7 000** - FF76 616
Study for Romeo and Juliet in the Vault Black chalk (28x33.5cm 11x13in) London 2000

BROWN Manneville Elihu D. 1810-1896 **[6]**
$10 000 - €11 553 - **£7 002** - FF75 781
View of the Mohawk near Little Falls Oil/canvas
(100x125cm 39x49in) New-York 2001

$6 500 - €6 139 - **£3 931** - FF40 272
View of Mohawk, near Utica Oil/canvas (74x92cm 29x36in) New-York 1999

BROWN Mather 1761-1831 **[10]**
$7 748 - €7 173 - **£4 800** - FF47 049
Henry Blundell (1724-1810) Wearing a Black Coat and Waistcoat Oil/canvas (73.5x61cm 28x24in) London 1999

BROWN Matilda 1869-1954 **[1]**
$7 250 - €7 762 - **£4 933** - FF50 913
Oxen with blue Yoke Oil/board (30x40cm 12x16in)
Portsmouth NH 2001

BROWN May Marshall 1887-1968 **[19]**
$252 - €265 - **£160** - FF1 736
Village Square Watercolour/paper (26.5x37cm 10x14in) Edinburgh 2000

BROWN Nigel Roderick 1949 **[11]**
$1 862 - €2 087 - **£1 298** - FF13 687
Suburban Clothesline Acrylic (78x56cm 30x22in)
Wellington 2001

BROWN OF COVENTRY Edward 1823-1877 **[10]**
$11 825 - €13 067 - **£8 200** - FF85 714
Two Carriage Horse in a Stable Oil/canvas
(69x89cm 27x35in) London 2001

BROWN Paul 1893-1958 **[12]**
$1 900 - €1 886 - **£1 187** - FF12 373
Fishing, Shooting, and Golf Watercolour
(17.5x25.5cm 6x10in) New-York 1999

$900 - €1 071 - **£622** - FF7 023
Music Ahead/Hoik!Hoik!Hoik! Print in colors
(20x55cm 8x22in) Detroit MI 2000

BROWN Peter c.1730-c.1800 **[4]**
$8 927 - €8 585 - **£5 500** - FF56 311
Vase of Flowers Including Oriental Poppy, Peony, Rose, Bindweed Pencil (30x21cm 11x8in)
London 1999

BROWN Pieter Irwin 1903 **[5]**
$700 - €651 - **£432** - FF4 269
«Japan» Poster (100x63cm 39x25in) New-York 1999

BROWN Ralph 1928 **[25]**
$2 721 - €2 323 - **£1 600** - FF15 238
Girl Watching Bronze (H49cm H19in) London 1998

BROWN Reynold 1917-1991 **[29]**
$597 - €689 - **£420** - FF4 520
«The Time Machine» Poster (104x68.5cm 40x26in)
London 2000

BROWN Rodney, General XIX **[1]**
$1 344 - €1 444 - **£900** - FF9 469
Five Domed Mosque at Benares Watercolour
(42x56cm 16x22in) London 2000

BROWN Roger 1941-1997 **[36]**
$14 500 - €16 491 - **£10 131** - FF108 174
Twister from Disaster Series Oil/canvas
(122.5x153cm 48x60in) Beverly-Hills CA 2000

BROWN Roy H. 1879-1956 **[15]**
$16 000 - €17 174 - **£10 707** - FF112 656
Souhegan Valley Oil/canvas (101.5x127cm 39x50in)
Philadelphia PA 2000

BROWN Samuel John Milton 1873-1965 **[35]**
$653 - €736 - **£450** - FF4 830
Masted Ship at Sea Watercolour/paper (23x33cm 9x12in) Billingshurst, West-Sussex 2000

BROWN T. Bryant XIX-XX **[6]**
$7 172 - €7 699 - **£4 800** - FF50 503
Saint Marks Square, Venice Oil/canvas (61x92.5cm 24x36in) London 2000

BROWN Thomas Austen 1857-1924 **[30]**
$323 - €372 - **£220** - FF2 439
A Dog in an Interior Oil/board (52.5x43cm 20x16in)
London 2000

$4 167 - €3 937 - **£2 600** - FF25 826
The Threshing Mill Oil/canvas (21.5x32cm 8x12in)
Perthshire 1999

$384 - €435 - **£260** - FF2 853
Horses Driving the Plough at Sunset
Watercolour/paper (22x25cm 8x9in) London 2000

BROWN Vincent 1901-2001 **[78]**
$1 037 - €1 162 - **£721** - FF7 625
The Hay Yard, Coomera Oil/board (47.5x39.5cm 18x15in) Melbourne 1999

$6 358 - €6 186 - **£3 913** - FF40 578
Colonial Days Oil/board (34.5x39cm 13x15in)
Melbourne 1999

$511 - €492 - **£315** - FF3 225
The Bridge Watercolour/paper (26.5x36cm 10x14in)
Melbourne 1999

🎨 $81 - €77 - **£49** - FF504
Fisherman's House, Labrador Etching (15x20cm 5x7in) Sydney 1999

BROWN Walter Francis 1853-1929 **[17]**
🎨 **$1 400** - €1 344 - **£863** - FF8 819
Venezia Oil/canvas (39x51cm 15x20in) Cambridge MA 1999
🎨 **$750** - €819 - **£482** - FF5 372
Venetian Scene Oil/canvas (63x17cm 25x7in) Mystic CT 2000

BROWN William Beatty 1831-1909 **[51]**
🎨 **$2 295** - €2 548 - **£1 600** - FF16 711
On the Desk Oil/canvas/board (38.5x54.5cm 15x21in) London 2001

BROWN William Fulton 1873-1905 **[13]**
✏ **$373** - €420 - **£260** - FF2 753
Reading the Letter Watercolour/paper (32.5x23cm 12x9in) Edinburgh 2001

BROWN William Marshall 1863-1936 **[63]**
🎨 **$8 893** - €9 872 - **£6 200** - FF64 758
Concarneau boats Oil/canvas (35.5x46cm 13x18in) London 2001
🎨 **$1 555** - €1 735 - **£1 050** - FF11 378
Village of Kintillo, Pertshire Oil/canvas (24.5x35cm 9x13in) Edinburgh 2000
✏ **$1 950** - €2 277 - **£1 377** - FF14 935
«Boys Fishing» Watercolour/paper (25.5x35.5cm 10x13in) Toronto 2000

BROWN William Mason 1828-1898 **[37]**
🎨 **$17 000** - €19 932 - **£12 229** - FF130 748
Still Life with Melon, Peach, Fruit-filled Compote and Glass of Wine Oil/canvas (53.5x43cm 21x16in) New-York 2001
🎨 **$10 000** - €11 955 - **£6 898** - FF78 420
Luminist River landscape with Distant Mountains Oil/canvas (20x30cm 8x12in) Milford CT 2000

BROWN William Theophilus 1919 **[13]**
✏ **$1 500** - €1 267 - **£894** - FF8 314
Untitled Watercolour (11.5x19cm 4x7in) San-Francisco CA 1998

BROWNE Belmore 1880-1954 **[17]**
🎨 **$8 143** - €9 121 - **£5 658** - FF59 831
The Forest Ranger Oil/canvas (45x60cm 18x24in) Calgary, Alberta 2001
🎨 **$303** - €318 - **£191** - FF2 088
Vermillion Lakes Oil/board (30x40cm 12x16in) Victoria, B.C. 2000

BROWNE Byron 1907-1961 **[82]**
🎨 **$2 100** - €1 772 - **£1 231** - FF11 621
Objects Oil/canvas (50x66cm 20x26in) Mystic CT 1998
🎨 **$2 500** - €2 428 - **£1 562** - FF15 929
Young Woman with white Shirt and necklace Oil/canvas/board (36x30cm 14x11in) New-York 1999
✏ **$1 000** - €856 - **£590** - FF5 618
Clown Mixed media/paper (66x52cm 25x20in) New-York 1998

BROWNE Charles Francis 1859-1920 **[21]**
🎨 **$11 000** - €9 398 - **£6 656** - FF61 648
Pastoral Landscape with Figures Oil/canvas (66x99cm 25x38in) San-Francisco CA 1998
🎨 **$500** - €569 - **£346** - FF3 730
Coastal Scene Oil/board (25x34cm 10x13in) Cincinnati OH 2000

BROWNE George 1918-1958 **[4]**
🎨 **$10 209** - €10 095 - **£6 376** - FF66 220
Pheasants Rising Oil/canvas (40.5x51cm 15x20in) Calgary, Alberta 1999

BROWNE George Elmer 1871-1946 **[94]**
🎨 **$5 500** - €6 255 - **£3 842** - FF41 030
Marine Nocturne Oil/canvas (101x127cm 40x50in) New-York 2000
🎨 **$2 000** - €2 147 - **£1 338** - FF14 082
Allegorical Composition with Asian Themes Oil/canvas (100x100cm 39x39in) Bolton MA 2000
🎨 **$1 174** - €1 017 - **£720** - FF6 670
Meux Bois, Fontainbleu Oil/panel (33.5x25.5cm 13x10in) Billingshurst, West-Sussex 1999

BROWNE Hablot Knight,«Phiz» 1815-1882 **[49]**
✏ **$423** - €373 - **£260** - FF2 449
Mr Take it Easy Watercolour/paper (15x26cm 5x10in) Godalming, Surrey 1999

BROWNE Henriette 1829-1901 **[9]**
🎨 **$37 357** - €40 100 - **£25 000** - FF263 040
Un poète - Les Coptes dans la Haute Egypte Oil/canvas (62x72.5cm 24x28in) London 2000

BROWNE John 1741-1801 **[4]**
🎨 **$255** - €265 - **£160** - FF1 739
The Watering Place, After Rubens Engraving (42x56cm 16x22in) Suffolk 2000

BROWNE Joseph act.1765-1783 **[1]**
🎨 **$42 865** - €47 246 - **£28 000** - FF309 912
River Scene at Dusk with a Fisherman repairing his Nets, others Boats Oil/canvas (60.5x82.5cm 23x32in) London 2000

BROWNE Joseph Archibald 1862-1948 **[25]**
🎨 **$402** - €449 - **£262** - FF2 943
Patterson Bridge Oil/panel (14x18cm 5x7in) Calgary, Alberta 2000

BROWNE Matilda van Wyck 1869-1947 **[17]**
🎨 **$4 500** - €5 277 - **£3 237** - FF34 613
«Lobster Shacks, Noank» Oil/canvas (63.5x78.5cm 25x30in) New-York 2001
🎨 **$2 300** - €2 780 - **£1 605** - FF18 235
«Sunlight and Shadow» Oil/panel (30.5x40.5cm 12x15in) Bethesda MD 2000
✏ **$1 000** - €1 137 - **£698** - FF7 460
Sheep and Shepherd Watercolour/paper (25x35cm 10x14in) Mystic CT 2000

BROWNE Nassau Blair 1867-1940 **[7]**
🎨 **$1 168** - €1 327 - **£820** - FF8 706
Cattle resting by a Coastal Path Oil/canvas (35.5x50.5cm 13x19in) West-Midlands 2001

BROWNE Richard 1776-1824 **[12]**
✏ **$15 184** - €16 730 - **£10 080** - FF109 740
Burgun Watercolour, gouache/paper (30x24cm 11x9in) Woollahra, Sydney 2000

BROWNE Robert Ives 1865-1956 **[21]**
🎨 **$1 572** - €1 361 - **£955** - FF8 929
Sunlit polder landscape with cows grazing by a ditch Oil/canvas (38x55cm 14x21in) Amsterdam 1999

BROWNE Vincent R. Balfour 1880-1963 **[35]**
✏ **$2 612** - €2 521 - **£1 650** - FF16 539
Lights Down, Sights Down Watercolour/paper (23.5x35.5cm 9x13in) Ipswich 1999

BROWNE W.H., Lieut. XIX **[1]**
✏ **$2 220** - €2 332 - **£1 400** - FF15 294
The Expedition in Winter Harbour, Port Leopold, Oct 3th Watercolour/paper (8.5x19cm 3x7in) London 2000

B

BROWNELL Charles de Wolf 1822-1909 **[9]**
- **$64 000** - €70 237 - **£41 209** - FF460 723
  The Bay of Matanzas, Cuba Oil/canvas (76x112cm 29x44in) Beverly-Hills CA 2000

BROWNELL Peleg Franklin 1857-1946 **[41]**
- **$1 813** - €2 116 - **£1 262** - FF13 879
  Corner of the Farm Oil/canvas (35.5x45.5cm 13x17in) Toronto 2000
- **$8 785** - €8 462 - **£5 454** - FF55 510
  Canadian Winter Scene Oil/canvas (26x38cm 10x14in) Toronto 1999

BROWNING Amy Katherine 1882-1970 **[19]**
- **$1 925** - €1 940 - **£1 200** - FF12 724
  Nude Oil/board (37.5x44.5cm 14x17in) London 2000

BROWNING Mary XX **[7]**
- **$417** - €405 - **£260** - FF2 658
  Joint Meet of the Vale of Aylesbury and Bicester with Whaddon Chase Pastel/paper (53.5x71cm 21x27in) London 1999

BROWNJOHN Robert XX **[3]**
- **$1 546** - €1 448 - **£950** - FF9 498
  «Goldfinger» Poster (76x101.5cm 29x39in) London 1999

BROWNLOW Washington George 1835-1876 **[20]**
- **$10 014** - €8 959 - **£6 000** - FF58 765
  Edinburgh Castle from the Grassmarket Oil/canvas (46x59cm 18x23in) Perthshire 1998
- **$9 388** - €8 812 - **£5 800** - FF57 800
  The Moorhens Nest Oil/canvas (43x29cm 16x11in) Billingshurst, West-Sussex 1999

BROWNSCOMBE Jennie Augusta 1850-1936 **[33]**
- **$6 400** - €5 776 - **£3 944** - FF37 887
  Colonial Scene, figures entering church Oil/canvas (64x91cm 25x36in) Asheville NC 1999
- **$2 000** - €1 896 - **£1 249** - FF12 436
  Beach Scene Oil/canvas (17x25cm 7x10in) Mystic CT 1999
- **$1 000** - €956 - **£629** - FF6 271
  Greek Maiden at Wall Watercolour/paper (35x25cm 14x10in) Milwaukee WI 1999

BROZIK Václav 1913 **[2]**
- **$2 312** - €2 187 - **£1 440** - FF14 344
  Portrait de femme Huile/panneau (18.5x14cm 7x5in) Praha 2001

BROZIK von Wenceslas / Vaclaw 1851-1901 **[62]**
- **$38 000** - €38 292 - **£23 689** - FF251 180
  The Gossip Oil/panel (94x130cm 37x51in) New-York 2000
- **$9 000** - €8 655 - **£5 554** - FF56 773
  Jeune cavalier Oil/panel (52.5x30.5cm 20x12in) Boston MA 1999
- **$2 167** - €2 050 - **£1 350** - FF13 447
  Mère avec son enfant chez une tzigane Huile/toile/carton (41x33cm 16x12in) Praha 2000

BRU DE RAMON Juan Bautista XVIII **[16]**
- **$435** - €450 - **£277** - FF2 955
  Aligote/Locha/Jargo Aguafuerte (49x30cm 19x11in) Madrid 2000

BRU Georges 1933 **[14]**
- **$2 450** - €2 058 - **£1 440** - FF13 500
  Personnage à la flûte de pain Crayons couleurs (98x148cm 38x58in) Douai 1998

BRUANDET Lazare 1755-1804 **[43]**
- **$5 082** - €4 269 - **£2 987** - FF28 000
  Paysage pastoral Huile/toile (65x83.5cm 25x32in) Lille 1998

- **$1 957** - €2 102 - **£1 310** - FF13 786
  Ein Weg führt von einem kleinen See in den Wald hinein Huile/panneau (22.5x33cm 8x12in) Zürich 2000
- **$5 376** - €4 573 - **£3 207** - FF30 000
  Scène de chasse à courre Gouache/papier (62.5x101.5cm 24x39in) Paris 1998

BRUCE Edward 1879-1943 **[13]**
- **$2 600** - €2 593 - **£1 623** - FF17 012
  Peru, Vermont Oil/canvas (41x56cm 16x22in) Dedham MA 1999

BRUCE Patrick Henry 1881-1936 **[3]**
- **$1 100 000** - €1 308 180 - **£783 970** - FF8 581 100
  Still Life Oil/canvas (59.5x91.5cm 23x36in) New-York 2000

BRUCE Peter 1949 **[9]**
- **$1 712** - €1 996 - **£1 200** - FF13 092
  Gemsbok Fighting Gouache/board (40x49.5cm 15x19in) London 2000

BRUCHON Émile XIX-XX **[14]**
- **$1 250** - €1 342 - **£836** - FF8 801
  Hermes Bronze (H64cm H25in) St. Petersburg FL 2000

BRUCK Lajos, Ludwig 1846-1910 **[37]**
- **$15 000** - €16 818 - **£10 186** - FF110 322
  Allegory Oil/canvas (124x164cm 48x64in) New-York 2000
- **$5 686** - €5 532 - **£3 500** - FF36 290
  The Lovers' Quarrel Oil/canvas (58x77cm 22x30in) London 1999
- **$864** - €961 - **£576** - FF6 304
  Bodegón con pipa Oleo/lienzo (46x32.5cm 18x12in) Madrid 2000

BRÜCKE Wilhelm 1800-1874 **[12]**
- **$30 382** - €34 033 - **£21 112** - FF223 245
  The Forum Romanum, Rome, with Women and Children Staircase Oil/canvas (74.5x100cm 29x39in) Amsterdam 2001
- **$5 960** - €6 135 - **£3 757** - FF40 246
  Amalfi, arbeitende Fischer an ihren Booten am Strand Öl/Leinwand (26x37cm 10x14in) Berlin 2000

BRUCKMAN Lodewyk Karel, Loki 1903-1980 **[23]**
- **$900** - €769 - **£528** - FF5 044
  Give Us Our Daily Bread Oil/canvas (40.5x51cm 15x20in) Boston MA 1998

BRUCY Edmée XIX **[2]**
- **$24 215** - €22 105 - **£14 732** - FF145 000
  Portrait de Zénaïde Chapt de Rastignac, duchesse de la Rochefoucauld Huile/toile (130x97cm 51x38in) Clermont-Ferrand 1998

BRUDER Anton 1898-1983 **[2]**
- **$1 322** - €1 534 - **£912** - FF10 061
  Waldlandschaft Watercolour (35x36.5cm 13x14in) Köln 2000

BRUDO Yvonne XIX-XX **[5]**
- **$1 300** - €1 109 - **£784** - FF7 274
  «Pneus Gallus» Poster (57x79cm 22x31in) New-York 1998

BRUEGHEL Abraham 1631-1697 **[58]**
- **$209 469** - €205 713 - **£130 000** - FF1 349 387
  Watermelon, Melons, Figs, Grapes, Pomegranates, Peaches Oil/canvas (147x198cm 57x77in) London 1999
- **$29 127** - €32 014 - **£18 522** - FF210 000
  Nature morte aux fleurs et fruits Huile/toile (117x91cm 46x35in) Paris 2000

$28 952 - €31 976 - £20 064 - FF209 748
Stilleben von Blumen und Früchten Öl/Leinwand
(42x33cm 16x12in) Wien 2001

BRUEGHEL Ambrosius 1617-1675 [7]
$66 360 - €60 980 - £40 880 - FF400 000
Nature morte à la corbeille de fruits Huile/pan-
neau (49.5x64cm 19x25in) Deauville 1998

BRUEGHEL Jan I 1568-1625 [57]
$124 136 - €121 588 - £80 000 - FF797 568
**Peasants harvesting, an extensive Landscape
with a Church** Oil/canvas (131x101.5cm 51x39in)
London 1999
$82 560 - €79 322 - £50 880 - FF520 320
Le baptême du Christ Huile/cuivre (33x49cm
12x19in) Bruxelles 1999
$979 080 - €910 139 - £600 000 - FF5 970 120
**Wooded Landscape with Travellers and an
upset Cart on a wooded Track** Oil/copper
(16x23cm 6x9in) London 1998
$1 500 - €1 395 - £926 - FF9 149
Village Activity Watercolour/paper (16x49cm 6x19in)
Portland ME 1999
$928 - €869 - £575 - FF5 701
**Holländische Flusslandschaft mit
Dorf/Holländischer Küstenort** Kupferstich
(22.4x32cm 8x12in) Heidelberg 1999

BRUEGHEL Jan II 1601-1678 [167]
$218 400 - €234 253 - £148 200 - FF1 536 600
Eva ofrece el fruto prohibido Oleo/lienzo
(112x164cm 44x64in) Madrid 2001
$105 693 - €106 501 - £65 878 - FF698 603
Allegorie der verkehrten Welt Öl/Kupfer (70x87cm
27x34in) Zürich 2000
$32 000 - €34 174 - £21 804 - FF224 169
**Landscape, Travellers on a path overlooking a
Valley, City beyond** Oil/copper (25.6x33.5cm
10x13in) New-York 2001

BRUEGHEL Jan Peeter 1628-1664 [5]
$24 510 - €23 549 - £15 105 - FF154 470
Scène portuaire avec marché aux poissons
Huile/panneau (60x86cm 23x33in) Bruxelles 1999
$36 000 - €33 870 - £22 542 - FF222 170
**Tulips, Roses, Poppies, Anemones, Gardinia
and other Flowers** Oil/panel (34.5x28.5cm 13x11in)
New-York 1999

BRUEGHEL Pieter I 1525-1569 [7]
$2 450 - €2 479 - £1 540 - FF16 260
**Navire à trois mâts armé avec quatre hunes et
voiles de perroquet** Burin (22.5x28.5cm 8x11in)
Bruxelles 2000

BRUEGHEL Pieter II c.1564-1637/38 [103]
$1 850 000 - €1 622 748 - £1 123 320 -
FF10 644 530
The Triumph of the Death Oil/canvas (117x167cm
46x65in) New-York 1999
$775 000 - €679 800 - £470 580 - FF4 459 195
The Adoration of the Magi in the Snow Oil/panel
(38.5x56.5cm 15x22in) New-York 1999
$298 860 - €320 802 - £200 000 - FF2 104 320
**The Procession of the Bride/The Procession of
the Groom** Oil/panel (28x41cm 11x16in) London
2000

BRUEGHEL Pieter III 1589-c.1640 [15]
$138 643 - €129 672 - £85 000 - FF850 595
The Payment of Tithes Oil/panel (75x122cm
29x48in) London 1998

BRUEHL Anton 1900-1982 [24]
$5 000 - €4 733 - £3 109 - FF31 044
National Photographer's Magazine Photograph
(7x25cm 3x10in) New-York 1999

BRUELLE Gaston XIX-XX [7]
$2 069 - €2 147 - £1 312 - FF14 086
Im Hafen Öl/Leinwand (38x27cm 14x10in)
Magdeburg 2000

BRUESTLE Bertram G. 1902 [21]
$1 200 - €1 418 - £850 - FF9 301
Shed in Winter Oil/canvas (41x49cm 16x19in)
Austinburg OH 2000
$1 000 - €1 044 - £665 - FF6 846
Summer Landscape with Bridge Oil/canvas/board
(18x23cm 7x9in) Plainville CT 2001

BRUESTLE George Matthew 1872-1939 [38]
$1 400 - €1 601 - £973 - FF10 504
The Brook, Lyme, Connecticut Oil/board (22x30cm
9x12in) Cincinnati OH 2000

BRUGADA VILA de Antonio 1804-1863 [2]
$2 245 - €2 226 - £1 404 - FF14 600
**L'embouchure de Guadalquivir/Promenade en
bateau** Aquarelle/papier (28x45cm 11x17in) Toulouse
1999

BRUGADA Y PANIZO Ricardo 1867-1919 [20]
$9 960 - €11 572 - £7 000 - FF75 909
The Flower Garden Oil/canvas (48x76cm 18x29in)
London 2001
$495 - €541 - £315 - FF3 546
Manola Oleo/lienzo (35x27cm 13x10in) Madrid 2000

BRUGAIROLLES Victor 1869-1936 [64]
$15 710 - €15 245 - £9 780 - FF100 000
Le lampion Huile/toile (240x120cm 94x47in) Paris
1999
$810 - €700 - £489 - FF4 589
Flodlandskab i måneskin Oil/canvas (60x82cm
23x32in) Vejle 1999
$1 632 - €1 524 - £1 007 - FF10 000
Paysage aux moulins en Hollande Huile/panneau
(27x35cm 10x13in) Melun 1999

BRUGGEN van Coosje 1942 [3]
$11 000 - €12 072 - £7 082 - FF79 186
The Entropic Library in a Later Stage, #2
Charcoal (74.5x101.5cm 29x39in) New-York 2000

BRUGGEN van der Barend XX [5]
$675 - €686 - £424 - FF4 500
Les cabines de plage Huile/toile (50x61cm
19x24in) Armentières 2000

BRÜGGER Arnold 1888-1975 [43]
$3 533 - €3 406 - £2 178 - FF22 345
Im Gartenrestaurant Öl/Leinwand (65x70cm
25x27in) Bern 1999
$1 478 - €1 369 - £905 - FF8 978
Figurenpaar vor einem Tor Öl/Leinwand
(31.5x38cm 12x14in) Bern 1999

BRUGGHEN van der Guillaume Anne 1811-1891
[13]
$9 280 - €9 915 - £6 320 - FF65 040
De Jacht Huile/toile (84x114cm 33x44in) Lokeren
2001
$1 539 - €1 359 - £928 - FF8 915
Boy with his Dogs in a Landscape Oil/panel
(38x32.5cm 14x12in) Amsterdam 1998

BRÜGNER Cölestin 1824-1887 **[49]**
~ **$983** - €1 125 - **£676** - FF7 378
Mondscheinlandschaft mit Fischern im Boot am Seeufer Öl/Leinwand/Karton (15x22cm 5x8in) München 2000

BRUGNOLI Emanuele 1859-1944 **[40]**
~ **$3 200** - €4 147 - **£2 400** - FF27 200
Chiesa della Salute, Venezia Olio/tela (45x65cm 17x25in) Milano 2000
~ **$1 920** - €2 488 - **£1 440** - FF16 320
Venezia, il Bacino di S.Marco Olio/cartone (20x31cm 7x12in) Roma 2000
~ **$1 067** - €1 257 - **£750** - FF8 243
Grand Canal, Venice Watercolour/paper (34x47cm 13x18in) Suffolk 2000

BRUGUERAS PALLACH Felipe 1915 **[69]**
~ **$140** - €150 - **£92** - FF985
Rmabla de las flores Oleo/lienzo (27x35cm 10x13in) Barcelona 2000
~ **$157** - €150 - **£95** - FF985
Sagrada Familia, Barna Acuarela/papel (33x24cm 12x9in) Barcelona 2000

BRUGUIERE Francis Joseph 1879-1945 **[26]**
[◉] **$6 500** - €6 138 - **£4 036** - FF40 260
Solarization, Hands with Rose Gelatin silver print (14x21cm 5x8in) New-York 1999

BRUHL Louis Burleigh 1862-1942 **[29]**
⊘ **$269** - €225 - **£160** - FF1 474
Louvain Watercolour/paper (51x34.5cm 20x13in) Salisbury, Wiltshire 1998

BRÜHLMANN Hans 1878-1911 **[25]**
~ **$2 919** - €2 489 - **£1 761** - FF16 328
Weite hügelige Landschaft im Abendrot Öl/Leinwand (42x59cm 16x23in) Zürich 1998
~ **$12 920** - €14 559 - **£8 947** - FF95 504
Rosen im Dreieck Öl/Papier (35.5x42cm 13x16in) Zürich 2000
⊘ **$1 386** - €1 645 - **£1 009** - FF10 791
Sitzender Frauenakt Pencil (36.5x25.5cm 14x10in) Zürich 2001

BRUIJN OUBOTER de Rudolf 1894-1983 **[2]**
⊘ **$3 878** - €3 630 - **£2 413** - FF23 812
Still Life with a Doll, a Book and a Glass Vase Watercolour/paper (60x71cm 23x27in) Amsterdam 1999

BRUIN de Cornelis 1870-1940 **[46]**
~ **$494** - €454 - **£304** - FF2 976
Farmer Ploughing the Fields Oil/canvas/board (80.5x100.5cm 31x39in) Amsterdam 1999

BRUINE de Adrianus Hendrikus 1807-1870 **[3]**
~ **$1 814** - €1 534 - **£1 079** - FF10 060
Waldlandschaft mit Bach und Passanten am Wege Oil/panel (19.5x27cm 7x10in) Bremen 1998

BRULÉ AI XX **[1]**
~ **$3 750** - €4 371 - **£2 596** - FF28 674
Nude in Shell Floating Through Buble-Filled Sky Oil/board (50x60cm 20x24in) New-York 2000

BRULEY Claude André 1609-c.1660 **[2]**
~ **$7 263** - €6 860 - **£4 392** - FF45 000
La Crucifixion/L'Adoration des Rois Mages Huile/cuivre (38x28.5cm 14x11in) Paris 1999

BRULY BOUABRE Frédéric 1923 **[7]**
⊘ **$6 016** - €5 807 - **£3 800** - FF38 090
Connaissance du Monde: Sous le ciel/Signes relevés sur une orange Pencil (9.5x15cm 3x5in) London 1999

BRUMBACK Louise Upton 1872-1929 **[3]**
~ **$5 500** - €5 289 - **£3 394** - FF34 695
Harbor View Oil/canvas (61x71cm 24x27in) Boston MA 1999

BRUN Albert XIX-XX **[4]**
⊘ **$4 389** - €4 573 - **£2 760** - FF30 000
Amiral Gueydon Aquarelle, gouache/papier (54x66cm 21x25in) Paris 2000
▥ **$1 609** - €1 677 - **£1 012** - FF11 000
«De Paris au Transvaal et Madagascar, le paquebot est en mer» Affiche (89x66cm 35x25in) Paris 2000

BRUN Charles Guillaume 1825-1908 **[20]**
⊘ **$36 232** - €34 033 - **£21 840** - FF223 245
The Young Rag-gatherer Oil/canvas (118x80cm 46x31in) Amsterdam 1999
▥ **$2 000** - €2 231 - **£1 309** - FF14 636
«Cycles Buffalo, 5 rue Chantilly, Paris» Poster (97.5x136.5cm 38x53in) New-York 2000

BRUN DE VERSOIX Louis Auguste 1756-1815 **[4]**
⊘ **$1 959** - €1 886 - **£1 225** - FF12 374
Gesatteltes Pferd und Studie von Pferdeköpfen Fusain (29x40.6cm 11x15in) Zürich 1999

BRUN Donald 1909-1999 **[46]**
▥ **$330** - €309 - **£200** - FF2 027
F.F.S- Sempre al Vostro Servizio Poster (126x90cm 49x35in) Zürich 1999

BRUN E.M. XIX-XX **[5]**
▥ **$684** - €762 - **£460** - FF5 000
«Chemins de fer, PLM Cannes l'hiver» Affiche (97.5x72.5cm 38x28in) Orléans 2000

BRUN Édouard 1860-1935 **[54]**
~ **$529** - €610 - **£361** - FF4 000
L'Olan dans la Bérarde, Oisans Huile/toile/carton (26x34cm 10x13in) Lyon 2000
~ **$346** - €412 - **£246** - FF2 700
Devant le perron en été Aquarelle/papier (34x28cm 13x11in) Grenoble 2000

BRUN Frans Isaac 1535-c.1610/20 **[3]**
▥ **$353** - €327 - **£213** - FF2 146
Die Dame und der Tod Kupferstich (7x4.7cm 2x1in) Heidelberg 1999

BRUN Marguerite XIX-XX **[2]**
~ **$10 787** - €11 891 - **£7 176** - FF78 000
Bouquet de roses Huile/toile (115.5x89cm 45x35in) Biarritz 2000

BRUN Nicolas Antoine XVIII **[2]**
~ **$7 560** - €6 434 - **£4 500** - FF42 205
The Arrival at the INN/The Departure Oil/panel (51x38cm 20x14in) London 1998

BRUN Pierre 1915 **[18]**
⊷ **$621** - €686 - **£430** - FF4 500
Le chat Bronze (H31.5cm H12in) Neuilly-sur-Seine 2001

BRUN Raoul XIX-XX **[5]**
~ **$5 446** - €5 641 - **£3 466** - FF37 000
Brouillard en rade de Bordeaux Huile/toile (61x116cm 24x45in) Bordeaux 2000

BRUN-BUISSON Gabriel XX **[10]**
⊘ **$376** - €320 - **£224** - FF2 100
Cour de ferme Aquarelle/papier (37x56cm 14x22in) Grenoble 1998

BRUNA Dick 1927 **[13]**
▥ **$95** - €109 - **£66** - FF714
«P» Poster (45x65cm 17x25in) Hoorn 2001

BRUNATI Gabriele 1852-1925 **[3]**
🎨 **$9 000** - €10 578 - **£6 239** - FF69 384
Zingara, Gypsy Oil/canvas (120x85cm 47x33in) New-York 2000

BRUNBERG Håkan 1905-1978 **[63]**
🎨 **$3 092** - €3 027 - **£1 902** - FF19 857
Puistossa Oil/canvas (73x60cm 28x23in) Helsinki 1999
🎨 **$712** - €740 - **£446** - FF4 854
Dans Mixed media (32x23cm 12x9in) Helsinki 2000
✏️ **$494** - €420 - **£295** - FF2 758
Salutorget Gouache/paper (13x19cm 5x7in) Helsinki 1998

BRUNDRIT Reginald Grange 1883-1960 **[29]**
🎨 **$833** - €972 - **£580** - FF6 377
Grassington, Ripon, Yorks Oil/canvas (45.5x61cm 17x24in) West-Yorshire 2000
🎨 **$988** - €1 146 - **£700** - FF7 519
«Isle of Man, GWR, For Happy Holidays, Great Western Railway» Poster (102x127cm 40x50in) London 2000

BRUNE Pierre 1887-1956 **[10]**
🎨 **$706** - €686 - **£436** - FF4 500
Panier de pêches Huile/toile (27x35cm 10x13in) Paris 1999

BRUNEAU Odette 1891-1984 **[32]**
🎨 **$3 656** - €3 354 - **£2 272** - FF22 000
Jeune marocaine aux bijoux Huile/toile (65x54.5cm 25x21in) Paris 1999

BRUNEL DE NEUVILLE Alfred Arthur 1852-1941 **[510]**
🎨 **$2 981** - €3 354 - **£2 052** - FF22 000
Huîtres, crevettes, citrons et cuivre Huile/toile (46.5x55.5cm 18x21in) Barbizon 2000
🎨 **$2 394** - €2 363 - **£1 475** - FF15 500
Chatons jouant avec une pelote de laine Huile/toile (25x32.5cm 9x12in) Paris 1999

BRUNELLESCHI Umberto 1879-1949 **[90]**
🎨 **$6 500** - €6 738 - **£3 900** - FF44 200
Ritatto della moglie Camille sullo sfondo delle citta'di Firenze Olio/tela (138x62cm 54x24in) Firenze 2001
✏️ **$1 541** - €1 524 - **£961** - FF10 000
Danseuse de cabaret Aquarelle, gouache (32.5x24cm 12x9in) Paris 1999
🎨 **$700** - €726 - **£420** - FF4 760
Rasaura Pochoir (22x30cm 8x11in) Firenze 2001

BRUNERY François 1849-1926 **[163]**
🎨 **$14 499** - €12 179 - **£8 500** - FF79 887
Red to move Oil/canvas (60.5x74cm 23x29in) London 1998
🎨 **$2 420** - €2 324 - **£1 500** - FF15 247
Lady with Parrot Oil/canvas (30x23cm 11x8in) London 1999
✏️ **$737** - €610 - **£432** - FF4 000
Conversation galante Aquarelle/papier (60x78cm 23x30in) L'Isle-Adam 1998

BRUNERY Marcel 1893-1982 **[43]**
🎨 **$18 400** - €17 950 - **£11 330** - FF117 743
Surprise from the Kitchen Oil/canvas (48x58cm 19x23in) Chicago IL 1999
🎨 **$5 719** - €6 495 - **£4 000** - FF42 603
Une mélodie Watercolour, gouache/board (47x60cm 18x23in) London 2001

BRUNESSEAU Charles XVIII **[1]**
🖋️ **$1 437** - €1 448 - **£895** - FF9 500
Château et parcs animés Eau-forte (47x61.5cm 18x24in) Paris 2000

BRUNET Étienne XVIII-XIX **[1]**
🗿 **$5 451** - €5 259 - **£3 422** - FF34 500
Buste du Baron de Bourdieu Terracotta (H59cm H23in) Monte-Carlo 1999

BRUNET N.R. **[2]**
🗿 **$4 968** - €5 488 - **£3 445** - FF36 000
Panthère Bronze (45x75cm 17x29in) Autun 2001

BRUNET-DEBAINES Alfred Louis 1845-? **[18]**
🖋️ **$248** - €231 - **£150** - FF1 518
The Palace of Westminster from accross the Thames Etching (56x80cm 22x31in) London 1998

BRUNET-HOUARD Pierre Auguste 1829-1922 **[18]**
🎨 **$2 500** - €2 157 - **£1 502** - FF14 148
Cattle Beside the Stream at Sunset Oil/canvas (49x99cm 19x38in) Boston MA 1998

BRUNETTO Silvio 1932 **[18]**
🎨 **$400** - €518 - **£300** - FF3 400
«Venezia» Olio/tavola (43.5x28cm 17x11in) Vercelli 2001

BRUNI Bruno 1935 **[175]**
🗿 **$765** - €900 - **£530** - FF5 902
Zärtlichkeit Bronze (76.5x40.5cm 30x15in) Stuttgart 2000
✏️ **$1 316** - €1 278 - **£813** - FF8 384
Rückenakt Pencil (77.9x64.7cm 30x25in) München 1999
🖋️ **$134** - €153 - **£92** - FF1 006
Abbandonata Farblithographie (31x39.5cm 12x15in) Lindau 2000

BRUNI Umberto 1914 **[51]**
🎨 **$541** - €512 - **£337** - FF3 360
«Retour au village» Huile/carton/toile (30.5x40.5cm 12x15in) Montréal 1999

BRUNIAS Agostino c.1730-1796 **[18]**
🎨 **$163 000** - €152 449 - **£98 700** - FF1 000 000
Scènes de la vie quotidienne sur l'île de Saint-Domingue Huile/toile (29.5x23.5cm 11x9in) Nantes 1999
🎨 **$47 129** - €40 614 - **£28 000** - FF266 411
«A North View of the Buildings on the Sandy Point Estate...» Watercolour/paper (49.5x126cm 19x49in) London 1998
🖋️ **$577** - €647 - **£400** - FF4 247
Negroes Dance in the Island of Dominica Engraving (29x37cm 11x14in) London 2000

BRUNIN Charles 1841-1887 **[8]**
🗿 **$1 326** - €1 487 - **£900** - FF9 756
Allégorie Bronze (H61cm H24in) Bruxelles 2000

BRUNIN Léon de Meuter 1861-1949 **[65]**
🎨 **$2 583** - €2 232 - **£1 557** - FF14 643
Portrait de jeune fille aux boucles d'oreille Huile/toile (51x41cm 20x16in) Bruxelles 1998

BRÜNING Max 1887-1968 **[225]**
🎨 **$409** - €460 - **£285** - FF3 018
Blick über kleinen Weiher mit Birken auf das Säntis-Massiv Öl/Leinwand (45x45cm 17x17in) Lindau 2001
✏️ **$319** - €358 - **£222** - FF2 347
Liegende junge Frau, leicht frivol Charcoal (22x34cm 8x13in) Berlin 2001

BRÜNING Peter 1929-1970 **[170]**

🖼 $201 - €194 - £127 - FF1 274
Courtisane Radierung (44x34cm 17x13in) München 1999

🖼 $42 408 - €39 881 - £26 262 - FF261 604
Ohne Titel Öl/Leinwand (130x159cm 51x62in) Köln 1999

🖼 $24 276 - €28 633 - £17 124 - FF187 818
Komposition 114-62 Öl/Leinwand (80x60cm 31x23in) Köln 2001

✏ $4 288 - €4 704 - £2 912 - FF30 855
Ohne Titel Coloured chalks (36.1x48.5cm 14x19in) Berlin 2000

🖼 $386 - €358 - £233 - FF2 347
März Farbradierung (31.6x44.3cm 12x17in) Heidelberg 1999

BRUNINI Ettoré XIX-XX **[5]**

🖼 $3 394 - €4 040 - £2 350 - FF26 500
Scène d'intérieur Huile/toile (65x81cm 25x31in) Reims 2000

BRUNNER Ferdinand 1870-1945 **[51]**

🖼 $13 176 - €13 081 - £8 226 - FF85 806
Alte Nagelschmiede bei Persenbeug Öl/Leinwand (36x45cm 14x17in) Wien 1999

🖼 $8 490 - €7 270 - £4 970 - FF47 690
Motiv von der Adria Mischtechnik/Karton (39x28cm 15x11in) Wien 1998

BRUNNER Hans 1813-1888 **[10]**

🖼 $5 124 - €5 368 - £3 389 - FF35 215
Untersberger Gnomen Öl/Leinwand (46x36cm 18x14in) München 2000

BRUNNER Hansjörg 1942 **[16]**

🖼 $161 - €182 - £113 - FF1 192
Jean Tinguely Drypoint (24x31cm 9x12in) Bern 2001

BRUNNER Hattie K. 1890-1982 **[16]**

🖼 $2 400 - €2 241 - £1 481 - FF14 702
Winter Scene Oil/paper (15x20cm 6x8in) Hatfield PA 1999

✏ $4 000 - €4 460 - £2 689 - FF29 257
Country sale scene with Amish in horse drawn buggy, barn, house Watercolour/paper (26x36cm 10x14in) Delaware OH 2000

BRUNNER Josef 1826-1893 **[26]**

🖼 $720 - €818 - £500 - FF5 366
Die Peterskirche in Friesach, Kärnten Öl/Leinwand (52x42cm 20x16in) Köln 2001

🖼 $1 310 - €1 453 - £912 - FF9 534
Motiv vom Bodensee Oil/panel (18x34cm 7x13in) Wien 2001

BRUNNER Leopold I 1788-1866 **[10]**

🖼 $11 789 - €10 933 - £7 200 - FF71 713
A Still Life of Tulips and other Flowers in a Pottery Vase Oil/canvas (56x43cm 22x16in) London 1998

BRUNNER Leopold II 1822-1869 **[1]**

🖼 $2 191 - €2 543 - £1 540 - FF16 684
Der Zuchtbulle vor einer Meierei Oil/panel (31.5x41.5cm 12x16in) Wien 2001

BRUNNER Nils Göran 1923-1986 **[17]**

🖼 $242 - €254 - £153 - FF1 666
Landskap Oil/canvas (20x27cm 7x10in) Malmö 2000

BRUNNER Samuel 1858-1939 **[8]**

✏ $5 000 - €4 866 - £3 072 - FF31 922
The Street of the Synagogue, Nikolsburg Watercolour/paper (17.5x14.5cm 6x5in) Tel Aviv 1999

BRUNNER-LACOSTE Henri Émile 1838-1881 **[10]**

🖼 $1 887 - €2 165 - £1 290 - FF14 200
Les pivoines sur le banc Huile/panneau (38.5x56cm 15x22in) Soissons 2000

BRUNONI Serge 1938 **[48]**

🖼 $737 - €813 - £487 - FF5 333
Montreal, Place Jacques Cartier Acrylic/canvas (61x76cm 24x29in) Vancouver, BC. 2000

BRUNSDON John R. 1933 **[18]**

🖼 $81 - €95 - £56 - FF624
Stradbroke Church, England Etching in colors (59x44cm 23x17in) Calgary, Alberta 2000

BRUNTON Violet Angless 1878-1951 **[12]**

🖼 $2 677 - €2 812 - £1 688 - FF18 446
Mythologische Szene Öl/Leinwand (46x92cm 18x36in) Heidelberg 2000

🖼 $1 500 - €1 610 - £1 003 - FF10 561
Penelope Watercolour/paper (42.5x49cm 16x19in) New-York 2000

BRUNTON Winifred Mabel 1880-1959 **[9]**

🖼 $675 - €626 - £420 - FF4 106
A native Restaurant, Assint Watercolour (14x10cm 5x3in) London 1999

BRUS Günter 1938 **[159]**

🖼 $3 188 - €2 760 - £1 934 - FF18 107
«Es gibt eine Gefahr, die eine Gefahr so in sich birgt wie ein Mensch» Mischtechnik/Papier (64x49cm 25x19in) Wien 1998

🖼 $1 085 - €1 017 - £670 - FF6 673
Landläufiger Tod/Dorfchronik Radierung (57x45cm 22x17in) Wien 1999

📷 $1 285 - €1 431 - £840 - FF9 390
Aktion Silber Vintage gelatin silver print (29.2x23.7cm 11x9in) Köln 2000

BRUSAFERRO Gerolamo 1700-1760 **[13]**

🖼 $19 000 - €18 137 - £11 871 - FF118 970
The Young Alexander Oil/canvas (45x62cm 17x24in) New-York 1999

🖼 $3 000 - €3 887 - £2 250 - FF25 500
Crocifissione Matita (43x61.5cm 16x24in) Milano 2000

BRUSASORZI Felice Rizzo 1540-1605 **[11]**

🖼 $70 000 - €69 846 - £42 609 - FF458 157
Christ in Limbo Oil/panel (39x32cm 15x12in) New-York 2000

✏ $110 075 - €129 582 - £77 350 - FF850 000
Persée venant de couper la tête de Méduse Encre (30.5x23.5cm 12x9in) Paris 2000

BRUSENBAUCH Arthur 1881-1957 **[35]**

🖼 $3 046 - €2 370 - £2 079 - FF21 451
Ruine im Abendlicht Öl/Leinwand (57x73cm 22x28in) Wien 2001

✏ $311 - €358 - £219 - FF2 347
Kind mit Schnabeltasse Red chalk/paper (32x42cm 12x16in) Hamburg 2001

BRUSEWITZ Gunnar 1924 **[52]**

✏ $254 - €266 - £160 - FF1 745
Sjöfåglar på is Akvarell/papper (17x23cm 6x9in) Malmö 2000

🖼 $185 - €187 - £115 - FF1 224
Vaktlar Color lithograph (22x31cm 8x12in) Stockholm 2000

BRUSEWITZ Gustaf 1812-1899 **[14]**

🖼 $8 840 - €10 057 - £6 174 - FF65 970
Salongen på floda herrgård Oil/canvas (104x136cm 40x53in) Stockholm 2000

$2 412 - €2 786 - £1 687 - FF18 272
Efter badet Oil/canvas (81x100cm 31x39in)
Stockholm 2001

$1 155 - €1 210 - £731 - FF7 936
Familjeidyll Oil/canvas (19x25cm 7x9in) Malmö 2000

BRUSH George de Forest 1855-1941 **[15]**

$1 000 - €1 091 - £678 - FF7 158
Maiden with Flowers Oil/canvas (54.5x43cm
21x16in) New-York 2000

$26 000 - €28 534 - £16 741 - FF187 168
The Water Carrier Oil/panel (25.5x17.5cm 10x6in)
New-York 2000

BRUSKIN Grisha 1945 **[8]**

$380 000 - €440 910 - £262 352 - FF2 892 180
Logies, Part I Oil/canvas/panel (242x401cm 95x157in)
New-York 2000

BRUSSE Mark 1937 **[60]**

$870 - €915 - £575 - FF6 000
Sans titre Bronze (43x23.5x23cm 16x9x9in) Paris
2000

BRÜSSEL van Paul Theodor 1754-1795 **[10]**

$68 900 - €64 449 - £42 640 - FF422 760
**Nature morte aux iris, pivoines, pommes, rai-
sins, mûres, au panier** Huile/toile (55x45.5cm
21x17in) Antwerpen 1999

$37 453 - €32 777 - £22 682 - FF215 000
**Corbeille de fleurs et de fruits sur un entable-
ment** Huile/panneau (45x35.5cm 17x13in) Paris 1998

BRUSSEL-SMITH Bernard 1914-1989 **[12]**

$260 - €266 - £163 - FF1 743
One Meat Ball Woodcut in colors (11x7cm 4x3in)
Cleveland OH 2000

BRUSSELMANS Jean 1884-1953 **[139]**

$34 450 - €32 225 - £20 930 - FF211 380
La promenade de wandeling Oil/canvas
(128.5x124.5cm 50x49in) Lokeren 1999

$11 880 - €11 155 - £7 335 - FF73 170
Femme à la bouilloire Huile/toile (115x100cm
45x39in) Antwerpen 1999

$1 182 - €1 361 - £807 - FF8 929
Projet de décor Mixed media/paper (29x20cm
11x7in) Amsterdam 2000

BRUSSET Paul 1914-1985 **[13]**

$804 - €915 - £558 - FF6 000
«Mont-Genèvre Hautes-Alpes Sports d'Hiver»
Affiche (100x63cm 39x24in) Paris 2000

BRUSSILOVSKY Mikhaïl 1931 **[5]**

$2 971 - €2 799 - £1 800 - FF18 359
Judith and Holofernes Oil/board (69x86cm
27x33in) London 1999

BRUST Karl Friedrich 1897-1960 **[32]**

$589 - €665 - £414 - FF4 360
Ohne Titel Gouache/paper (80x58.5cm 31x23in)
Stuttgart 2000

BRUSTOLON Giovan Battista 1712/26-1796 **[24]**

$1 016 - €1 140 - £708 - FF7 479
Vues de venise, d'après J.B.Moretti Eau-forte
(39x50cm 15x19in) Bruxelles 2001

BRÜTT Ferdinand 1849-1936 **[15]**

$1 618 - €1 841 - £1 122 - FF12 074
Amoretten Öl/Leinwand (96x65cm 37x25in) Köln
2000

BRUYAS Marc Laurent 1821-1896 **[2]**

$18 500 - €17 328 - £11 373 - FF113 665
Still Life of Roses with a Basket Oil/canvas
(54x77.5cm 21x30in) New-York 1999

BRUYCKER de Frans Ant., François 1816-1882
[14]

$2 546 - €2 897 - £1 767 - FF19 000
Promenade au Luxembourg Huile/toile (65x54cm
25x21in) Fontainebleau 2000

$5 000 - €5 880 - £3 585 - FF38 569
The Happy Family Oil/panel (44x36cm 17x14in)
New-York 2001

BRUYCKER de Jules 1870-1945 **[518]**

$5 100 - €4 958 - £3 120 - FF32 520
L'idéaliste Technique mixte (43.5x41.5cm 17x16in)
Bruxelles 1999

$1 819 - €2 107 - £1 258 - FF13 821
Deux femmes assises, vues de dos Fusain/papier
(24.5x20.5cm 9x8in) Bruxelles 2000

$358 - €421 - £256 - FF2 764
Rue de la Horloge à Rouen, France Eau-
forte (57x43cm 22x16in) Bruxelles 2000

BRUYERE Élise Lebarbier 1776-1842 **[5]**

$4 257 - €4 504 - £2 700 - FF29 542
**Study of a Young Woman, half-length, in profile,
wearing a Robe** Oil/canvas (46x37.5cm 18x14in)
London 2000

$3 400 - €3 525 - £2 040 - FF23 120
Trionfo di fiori Olio/tela (35x26.5cm 13x10in) Milano
1999

BRUYN Bartholomaeus I 1493-1555 **[8]**

$20 587 - €24 542 - £14 678 - FF160 987
Bildnis eines kölner Handelsherrn Oil/panel
(34x24.2cm 13x9in) Köln 2000

BRUYN Bartholomaeus II c.1530-1606/10 **[5]**

$43 447 - €42 556 - £28 000 - FF279 148
**Gentleman in a black Coat, a letter in his
Hand/His Wife holding Rosary** Oil/panel
(49x34.5cm 19x13in) London 1999

BRUYN de Abraham 1540-1587 **[4]**

$894 - €818 - £547 - FF5 365
**Exhibemus hoc libello Romani Pontificis, epis-
corum, monachorum** Eau-forte (28x34cm 11x13in)
Bruxelles 1999

BRUYN de Cornelis 1652-1726 **[2]**

$1 228 - €1 126 - £750 - FF7 383
Jerusalem Engraving (28x123cm 11x48in) London
1999

BRUYN de Cornelis Johannes c.1763-c.1828 **[12]**

$5 177 - €4 799 - £3 200 - FF31 481
Flowers in a Vase on a Ledge Oil/panel
(43.5x33cm 17x12in) London 1999

BRUYN de Frans XIX-XX **[4]**

$1 646 - €1 815 - £1 075 - FF11 906
Hengelaars Oil/canvas (77x107.5cm 30x42in) Den
Haag 2000

BRUYN de Nicolaes 1571-1652 **[36]**

$349 - €332 - £217 - FF2 180
**Das Goldene Zeitalter, nach Abraham
Bleomaert** Kupferstich (43.5x67.8cm 17x26in) Berlin
1999

BRUYNE de Gustaaf 1914-1981 **[159]**

$18 550 - €17 352 - £11 270 - FF113 820
Tuin der illusie Oil/canvas (105.5x150.5cm 41x59in)
Lokeren 1999

$6 690 - €7 436 - £4 680 - FF48 780
**Jeune fille au voile sur fond de bocal avec pois-
sons rouges** Huile/panneau (50x40cm 19x15in)
Bruxelles 2001

🖊 $397 - €372 - **£246** - FF2 439
Baadsters Crayon gras (30x19cm 11x7in) Lokeren 1999

BRUYNEEL Victor XIX-XX **[4]**
🖼 $1 300 - €1 241 - **£800** - FF8 143
Bust of a Beauty Bronze (H60cm H24in) Norwalk CT 1999

BRUZZI Stefano 1835-1911 **[27]**
🖼 $31 369 - €27 457 - **£19 000** - FF180 104
On the Road to Market Oil/canvas (38x67.5cm 14x26in) London 1998
🖼 $8 800 - €11 403 - **£6 600** - FF74 800
Pecore in fuga Olio/tela (21x32cm 8x12in) Roma 2001

BRY de Johann Theodore 1561-1623 **[26]**
📖 $342 - €332 - **£213** - FF2 180
Herrestross mit Oberst, nach Sebald Beham Kupferstich (5.2x23.1cm 2x9in) Berlin 1999

BRY de Théodore 1528-1598 **[22]**
📖 $245 - €230 - **£152** - FF1 509
Serviles animus refugit/Quonam prolabor/Fallitur et fallit Venus Kupferstich (6.7x8.2cm 2x3in) Heidelberg 1999

BRYANS Lyna 1909-? **[16]**
🖼 $1 781 - €1 684 - **£1 105** - FF11 048
Lerderderg Gorge Oil/canvas/board (100x80cm 39x31in) Malvern, Victoria 1999

BRYANT Ambrose Moigniez XIX-XX **[1]**
🖼 $4 200 - €4 022 - **£2 588** - FF26 381
Horse and Foal Oil/canvas (43x66cm 17x26in) Portsmouth NH 1999

BRYANT Charles David Jones 1883-1937 **[39]**
🖼 $10 420 - €12 392 - **£7 426** - FF81 286
Fisherman Landing at St Ives Oil/canvas (100x125.5cm 39x49in) Melbourne 2000
🖼 $2 740 - €2 860 - **£1 728** - FF18 760
The King's Yacht, Tanya Oil/canvas/board (45x55cm 17x21in) Sydney 2000
🖼 $215 - €256 - **£152** - FF1 678
Mount Dorter from Nodup, New Guinea Oil/board (30x40.5cm 11x15in) Sydney 2000

BRYANT Everett Lloyd 1864-1945 **[15]**
🖼 $1 600 - €1 793 - **£1 114** - FF11 759
Still Life of Apple Blossoms in a chinese Jar Oil/canvas (61x51cm 24x20in) Washington 2001

BRYANT Henry 1812-1881 **[14]**
🖼 $4 250 - €4 049 - **£2 593** - FF26 557
Farmyard Scene with mother and child feeding a workhouse Oil/canvas (73x78cm 29x31in) Bloomfield-Hills MI 1999

BRYANT Henry Charles XIX **[25]**
🖼 $4 919 - €5 313 - **£3 400** - FF34 849
Market Scene Oil/canvas (38x48cm 14x18in) Newbury, Berkshire 2001
🖼 $2 252 - €2 126 - **£1 400** - FF13 947
The Farewell Oil/canvas (30.5x35.5cm 12x13in) London 1999

BRYCE Gordon 1943 **[8]**
🖼 $2 139 - €2 390 - **£1 450** - FF15 677
Apples and Black Teapot Acrylic/board (27x37cm 10x14in) Edinburgh 2000

BRYDER Mogens XX **[1]**
📖 $794 - €879 - **£550** - FF5 768
«Med Deds Til Norge» Poster (92x64cm 36x25in) London 2001

BRYEN Camille 1907-1977 **[376]**
🖼 $6 496 - €6 098 - **£4 024** - FF40 000
Composition nº103 Huile/toile (65x50cm 25x19in) Paris 1999
🖼 $3 384 - €3 125 - **£2 107** - FF20 500
Composition Huile/toile (41x33cm 16x12in) Douai 1999
🖊 $427 - €503 - **£306** - FF3 300
Composition Encre/papier (27x20.5cm 10x8in) Paris 2001
📖 $90 - €107 - **£65** - FF700
Composition Eau-forte couleurs (30x19.5cm 11x7in) Paris 2001

BRYER de Cornelis XVII **[2]**
🖼 $47 500 - €45 342 - **£29 678** - FF297 426
Grapes, Lemons and Oysters on a Platter and Glass Roemer Oil/canvas (39x44cm 15x17in) New-York 1999

BRYERS Duane 1911 **[8]**
🖼 $1 100 - €1 181 - **£736** - FF7 745
Broken Tether Oil/canvas (40x60cm 16x24in) Houston TX 2000

BRYK Rut 1916-1999 **[11]**
🖼 $843 - €925 - **£542** - FF6 067
Untitled Ceramic (H70cm H27in) Helsinki 2000

BRYMNER William 1855-1925 **[54]**
🖼 $2 921 - €3 305 - **£2 043** - FF21 680
Summer Landscape Oil/canvas (71x53.5cm 27x21in) Toronto 2001
🖼 $818 - €796 - **£503** - FF5 223
Portrait of a Young Woman Oil/board (23x33cm 9x13in) Nepean, Ont. 1999
🖊 $293 - €250 - **£177** - FF1 641
Studies of a Young Girl and Boy Fusain/papier (29x19cm 11x7in) Montréal 1998

BRYN Oscar M. XX **[1]**
📖 $800 - €928 - **£561** - FF6 088
«Pacific Northwest» Poster (104x68cm 41x27in) New-York 2000

BRYSON Hope Mercereau 1887-1944 **[3]**
🖊 $1 700 - €1 632 - **£1 065** - FF10 702
Portrait of Woman holding black Fan Pastel/paper (89x64cm 35x25in) Altadena CA 1999

BRYSON John XX **[1]**
📷 $24 000 - €22 827 - **£14 572** - FF149 736
Marilyn Monroe and Arthur Miller in Los Angeles Photograph (34x23cm 13x9in) New-York 1999

BRZOZOWSKI Tadeusz 1918-1987 **[14]**
🖼 $9 746 - €11 309 - **£6 727** - FF74 179
Estropié Huile/toile (61x30cm 24x11in) Warszawa 2000
🖊 $2 122 - €2 348 - **£1 474** - FF15 403
«Porteur d'eau et Exhaustor comique» Encre (64.5x47.5cm 25x18in) Warszawa 2001

BSOR C.G XIX-XX **[1]**
📖 $6 080 - €6 128 - **£3 800** - FF40 200
«Sports d'hiver, concours du ski club, Peira-Cava» Poster (66x46cm 25x18in) London 2000

BUABUSAYA Jit Prakit 1911 **[5]**
🖼 $4 845 - €5 211 - **£3 249** - FF34 181
Tabaybuya Tree, Samut Prakarn Oil/canvas (50x61cm 19x24in) Bangkok 2000
🖼 $4 590 - €4 937 - **£3 078** - FF32 382
Suburban Park, New York Acrylic/canvas (35x44cm 13x17in) Bangkok 2000

BUAL Artur 1926 [6]
- **$5 280** - €5 982 - **£3 720** - FF39 240
  Lady Godiva Oleo/lienzo (73x54cm 28x21in) Lisboa 2001
- **$2 288** - €2 592 - **£1 560** - FF17 004
  Composiçáo Huile/panneau (20x70cm 7x27in) Lisboa 2000

BUBAK Alois 1824-1870 [2]
- **$7 803** - €7 380 - **£4 860** - FF48 411
  View of a Landscape with architecture Oil/canvas (55x69cm 21x27in) Praha 2001

BUBARNIK Andreas Gyula 1936 [22]
- **$2 393** - €2 288 - **£1 500** - FF15 007
  Basket of Fruit with a Tankard, Champagne Bottle, Glass and Plate Oil/panel (51x60cm 20x23in) London 1999
- **$1 636** - €1 524 - **£1 009** - FF10 000
  La table du chimiste Huile/panneau (20x25cm 7x9in) Reze 1999

BUBENICEK Oto 1871-1962 [71]
- **$751** - €711 - **£468** - FF4 661
  Moulin à Dubine Huile/carton (35.5x50.5cm 13x19in) Praha 1999
- **$407** - €371 - **£254** - FF2 431
  From Stara Vozice Oil/cardboard (25x35cm 9x13in) Praha 1999

BUBLEY Esther 1921 [16]
- **$1 200** - €1 120 - **£726** - FF7 349
  Girl sitting alone Gelatin silver print (26.5x26.5cm 10x10in) New-York 1999

BUCAN Boris 1947 [3]
- **$4 200** - €4 039 - **£2 592** - FF26 494
  «Firebird & Petruska» Poster (204x195.5cm 80x76in) New-York 1999

BUCCHI Ermocrate 1842-1885 [4]
- **$2 592** - €2 723 - **£1 640** - FF17 859
  Yellow Roses in a Vase Watercolour/paper (32x54cm 12x21in) Amsterdam 2000

BUCCI Anselmo 1887-1955 [35]
- **$4 000** - €5 183 - **£3 000** - FF34 000
  Ritratto di nobildonna Olio/tela (60x50cm 23x19in) Milano 2001
- **$1 175** - €1 218 - **£705** - FF7 990
  Aurora sull'Adriatico III, Pesaro Olio/tavola (13x21cm 5x8in) Torino 2000
- **$288** - €249 - **£144** - FF1 632
  Rencontre Puntasecca (8.5x6cm 3x2in) Prato 1999

BUCCI Mario 1903-1970 [18]
- **$440** - €570 - **£330** - FF3 740
  Natura morta con pippa Olio/tela (45x65cm 17x25in) Firenze 2000

BUCCIARELLI Daniele 1839-1911 [24]
- **$362** - €426 - **£260** - FF2 797
  Fiesta in Rome Watercolour/paper (40x25cm 15x9in) Cheshire 2001

BUCHANAN George F. XIX [12]
- **$641** - €754 - **£460** - FF4 949
  Extensive Estuary View at Sunset Oil/canvas/board (55x91cm 21x35in) Cheshire 2001
- **$1 314** - €1 311 - **£800** - FF8 602
  Old Battersea Bridge Oil/panel (21x41cm 8x16in) London 2000

BUCHANAN Hugh 1958 [2]
- **$3 246** - €3 626 - **£2 200** - FF23 785
  Glamis II Watercolour/paper (37x28cm 14x11in) Edinburgh 2000

BUCHANAN William Cross XIX [1]
- **$1 600** - €1 511 - **£993** - FF9 910
  Lake Texcoco, with a Distant View of the City of Mexico Watercolour, gouache/paper (30.5x53cm 12x20in) Beverly-Hills CA 1999

BUCHBINDER Simeon 1853-? [9]
- **$2 484** - €2 300 - **£1 500** - FF15 088
  Study of a Girl Oil/panel (22x16cm 8x6in) Billingshurst, West-Sussex 1999

BÜCHE Josef 1848-1917 [71]
- **$1 367** - €1 534 - **£947** - FF10 061
  Brustbild eines Dirndls mit Stohhut und rotem Schal Öl/Leinwand (63x50cm 24x19in) München 2000
- **$1 229** - €1 308 - **£777** - FF8 580
  Bildnis eines bärtigen Tirolers Oil/panel (29x22cm 11x8in) Salzburg 2000

BUCHEL Emmanuel 1705-1775 [25]
- **$241** - €274 - **£167** - FF1 795
  «Grundriss der Gegend am Rhein bey...Basel» Kupferstich (26x45cm 10x17in) Basel 2001

BUCHET Gustave 1888-1963 [92]
- **$55 450** - €65 803 - **£40 370** - FF431 640
  Femme au drape rouge Öl/Leinwand (130x97cm 51x38in) Zürich 2001
- **$22 180** - €26 321 - **£16 148** - FF172 656
  Soleil en septembre, le reservoir à Vence Öl/Leinwand (83.5x61cm 32x24in) Zürich 2001
- **$16 635** - €19 741 - **£12 111** - FF129 492
  Nu couche de dos Oil/panel (33x41cm 12x16in) Zürich 2001
- **$5 600** - €6 545 - **£3 998** - FF42 933
  Voilier Aquarell/Papier (39.5x25.5cm 15x10in) Zürich 2001

BUCHHEISTER Carl 1890-1964 [118]
- **$10 790** - €12 271 - **£7 483** - FF80 493
  «Komposition Burma» Mixed media (57x80cm 22x31in) Hamburg 2000
- **$589** - €579 - **£378** - FF3 800
  Composition Gouache/papier (21x28cm 8x11in) Paris 1999
- **$272** - €256 - **£168** - FF1 676
  Komposition Desbu Lithographie (56x76.5cm 22x30in) Stuttgart 1999

BUCHHOLZ Erich 1891-1972 [37]
- **$35 246** - €37 836 - **£23 591** - FF248 188
  Geburt des Lichts Relief (36x27.3cm 14x10in) Köln 2000
- **$208** - €194 - **£126** - FF1 274
  Blitzform Woodcut in colors (57x39cm 22x15in) Hamburg 1999

BUCHHOLZ Karl 1849-1889 [29]
- **$7 765** - €7 157 - **£4 650** - FF46 949
  Gewitterlandschaft mit durchbrechender Sonne im Mittelgrund Öl/Leinwand (59x43.5cm 23x17in) Dresden 1998
- **$1 749** - €1 636 - **£1 059** - FF10 732
  Winter im Walde Öl/Karton (13x18cm 5x7in) Düsseldorf 1999

BUCHHOLZ Wolff 1935 [69]
- **$73** - €82 - **£51** - FF536
  Vulkanische Landschaft Farbradierung (20x15cm 7x5in) Heidelberg 2001

BUCHKA Karl 1868-1931 [5]
- **$637** - €558 - **£385** - FF3 658
  Vornehme Jagdgesellschaft vor Schloss Oil/panel (16x21cm 6x8in) Zofingen 1998

BÜCHLER Eduard 1861-1958 **[12]**
- $10 234 - €8 597 - £6 000 - FF56 391
  An Odalisque Oil/canvas (55x100.5cm 21x39in)
  London 1998

BÜCHNER Carl 1921 **[106]**
- $921 - €1 027 - £600 - FF6 736
  Two Boats Sailing Side By Side Oil/board
  (41x58cm 16x22in) Johannesburg 2000
- $527 - €621 - £364 - FF4 076
  Harlequin with Pastel Pink Suit Oil/board
  (28x21cm 11x8in) Cape Town 2000
- $201 - €224 - £131 - FF1 471
  Young Boy Wearing a Polo-Neck Shirt
  Charcoal/paper (32.5x24cm 12x9in) Johannesburg 2000

BUCHNER Georg 1858-1914 **[7]**
- $1 577 - €1 817 - £1 077 - FF11 917
  Dirndl im Profil Öl/Leinwand (21.5x17.5cm 8x6in)
  Wien 2000

BUCHNER Hans 1856-1941 **[5]**
- $2 406 - €2 301 - £1 465 - FF15 092
  **Stilleben mit Flieder, Narzissen und
  Schneeballen** Öl/Leinwand (106x82cm 41x32in)
  Stuttgart 1999

BUCHNER Rudolf 1894-1962 **[85]**
- $762 - €727 - £464 - FF4 767
  Im Hafen von Rotterdam Öl/Leinwand (56.5x65cm
  22x25in) Wien 1999
- $278 - €291 - £175 - FF1 906
  Weinberge Aquarell, Gouache/Papier (46x59.2cm
  18x23in) Wien 2000

BUCHS Raymond 1878-1958 **[13]**
- $5 324 - €5 791 - £3 509 - FF37 984
  La Hochmatt, vue de Bellegarde Öl/Leinwand
  (55x59.5cm 21x23in) Bern 2000

BÜCHSEL Elisabeth 1867-1957 **[33]**
- $2 872 - €3 068 - £1 957 - FF20 123
  Bauernkaten auf Hiddensee Öl/Leinwand/Karton
  (37x57cm 14x22in) Satow 2001
- $464 - €511 - £309 - FF3 353
  **Frühlingswald bei Behrenshagen mit
  Wasserlauf** Aquarell/Papier (35x23cm 13x9in) Satow
  2000

BUCHSER Frank 1828-1890 **[53]**
- $17 289 - €19 444 - £12 069 - FF127 545
  Die Netzflickerin in Fischerstube Öl/Leinwand
  (52x35cm 20x13in) Luzern 2001
- $9 465 - €10 202 - £6 347 - FF66 920
  Italienerin Öl/Karton (33x22.5cm 12x8in) Zürich 2001

BUCHTERKIRCH Armin 1859-? **[11]**
- $900 - €943 - £570 - FF6 186
  Goin' Home Watercolour/paper (17x22cm 7x9in)
  New-Orleans LA 2000

BUCHWALD-ZINNWALD Erich 1884-1972 **[16]**
- $157 - €179 - £109 - FF1 173
  «Nebeltag im Erzgebirge» Woodcut (30x40cm
  11x15in) Hamburg 2001

BUCK Adam 1759-1833 **[69]**
- $646 - €595 - £400 - FF3 903
  Young Gentleman Facing Right in Brown Coat
  Miniature (13.5x12cm 5x4in) London 1999
- $1 897 - €1 719 - £1 150 - FF11 278
  Portrait of Three Children Watercolour (35x24cm
  13x9in) Billingshurst, West-Sussex 1998

BUCK Claude 1890-1974 **[39]**
- $2 200 - €2 243 - £1 378 - FF14 710
  Orientalist Still Life Oil/board (50x40cm 20x16in)
  Altadena CA 2000
- $250 - €288 - £170 - FF1 891
  Audubon Park Oil/board (13x15cm 5x6in) New-
  Orleans LA 2000

BUCK de Evariste 1892-1974 **[25]**
- $2 654 - €2 496 - £1 607 - FF16 371
  Farms in a Winter Landscape Oil/canvas
  (44.5x51.5cm 17x20in) Amsterdam 1999

BUCK de Raphael 1902-1986 **[57]**
- $562 - €620 - £380 - FF4 065
  Bloemenstuk (Fleurs) Huile/toile (60x50cm
  23x19in) Antwerpen 2000

BUCK Frederick 1771-1839/40 **[108]**
- $932 - €872 - £575 - FF...
  Lady with Lace Bonnet Miniature (6.5x5cm 2x1in)
  Co. Kilkenny 1999

BUCK Nathaniel c.1695-c.1775 **[13]**
- $2 000 - €2 271 - £1 389 - FF14 896
  English Castles Engraving (20x38cm 8x15in) Detroit
  MI 2001

BUCK Samuel & Nathaniel XVII-XVIII **[76]**
- $410 - €429 - £260 - FF2 812
  The North East Prospect of the City of Hereford
  Engraving (30x80cm 11x31in) London 2000

BUCK William Henry 1840-1888 **[26]**
- $22 000 - €23 615 - £14 722 - FF154 902
  **Schooner at Sunset on Lake, Pontchartrain,
  Southeastern Louisiana** Oil/canvas (121x60cm
  48x24in) Portland ME 2000
- $17 000 - €18 248 - £11 376 - FF119 697
  Boys Fishing in the Bayou Oil/canvas (13x30cm
  5x12in) Portland ME 2000

BÜCKEN Peter 1831-1915 **[16]**
- $1 601 - €1 534 - £1 007 - FF10 061
  **Die Clemenskapelle bei Trechtingshausen am
  Rhein mit Burgruine** Öl/Leinwand (34.5x55cm
  13x21in) Köln 1999

BUCKHAM Alfred G. XIX-XX **[2]**
- $10 362 - €11 606 - £7 200 - FF76 133
  «The River Forth from above Stirling, Scotland»
  Silver print (51.5x40.5cm 20x15in) London 2001

BUCKLAND-WRIGHT John 1897-1954 **[9]**
- $256 - €297 - £177 - FF1 951
  L'enlèvement d'Europe Eau-forte (13.5x18cm 5x7in)
  Bruxelles 2000

BUCKLE Claude 1905-1973 **[39]**
- $543 - €448 - £320 - FF2 938
  The Fells Watercolour/paper (34x48cm 13x18in)
  Newbury, Berkshire 1998
- $900 - €865 - £550 - FF5 672
  «Edinburgh, British Railways, Scottish Region»
  Poster (102x64cm 40x25in) London 1999

BUCKLER John 1770-1851 **[22]**
- $653 - €736 - £450 - FF4 826
  **North View of Littlecote House, Wiltshire/South
  View of Littlecote** Drawing (18x24cm 7x9in)
  Newbury, Berkshire 2000

BUCKLER John Chessell 1793-1894 **[32]**
- $2 581 - €2 866 - £1 800 - FF18 800
  Wotton House, Buckinghamshire Watercolour
  (28x45cm 11x17in) London 2001

BUCKLER William 1814-1884 **[22]**
🖌 **\$2 540** - €2 727 - **£1 700** - FF17 886
    George Risdale as a Boy, Standing, Full-Length, Holding a Cricket Bat Watercolour/paper (42x33cm 16x12in) Suffolk 2000

BUCKLEY Charles Frederick XIX **[44]**
🖌 **\$1 233** - €1 168 - **£750** - FF7 662
    Loch Katrine, Morning/Loch Katrine, Evening Watercolour (36x50cm 14x19in) London 1999

BUCKLEY John Edmund 1820-1884 **[59]**
🖌 **\$1 321** - €1 141 - **£800** - FF7 482
    Cavaliers Seated Before a Half Timbered House Watercolour (33x52cm 12x20in) London 1999

BUCKLIN William Savery 1851-1928 **[6]**
🖌 **\$1 000** - €1 111 - **£669** - FF7 286
    Through the Woods to the Meadow Watercolour (73x52cm 29x20in) Delray-Beach FL 2000

BUCKLOW Christopher XX **[2]**
📷 **\$7 500** - €8 635 - **£5 118** - FF56 643
    Guest 10:51a.m, 18th March 1998 Cibachrome print (101.5x76.2cm 39x29in) New-York 2000

BUCKMAN Percy 1865-? **[4]**
🖌 **\$1 919** - €2 048 - **£1 300** - FF13 436
    Study in Clay Watercolour/paper (53x35cm 21x14in) Lewes, Sussex 2001

BUCKMASTER Ernest William 1897-1968 **[171]**
☞ **\$2 949** - €2 764 - **£1 824** - FF18 131
    River Nocturne Oil/canvas (47x75cm 18x29in) Melbourne 1999
☞ **\$1 007** - €944 - **£623** - FF6 191
    Fading Light Oil/canvas/board (35x45cm 13x17in) Melbourne 1999

BUCKNALL Ernest Pile 1861-? **[16]**
☞ **\$1 939** - €2 287 - **£1 363** - FF15 000
    «A Lime Kiln Road, Sunbridge Wells» Huile/toile (129x85cm 50x33in) Coulommiers 2000
☞ **\$394** - €347 - **£240** - FF2 275
    Watering the Horses Watercolour/paper (29.5x41cm 11x16in) London 1999

BUCKNER Richard 1812-1883 **[46]**
☞ **\$8 821** - €8 726 - **£5 500** - FF57 239
    Pet Rabbits Oil/canvas (127x102cm 50x40in) Leyburn, North Yorkshire 1999
☞ **\$6 453** - €7 195 - **£4 208** - FF47 199
    Portrait of an Elegant Lady, Seated, Half-length with her Dog Oil/canvas (124x87cm 48x34in) Johannesburg 2000
☞ **\$10 382** - €12 063 - **£7 297** - FF79 125
    Portrait of a young Man/Studies of Peasants and Fisherfolk Oil/canvas/board (45x29cm 17x11in) Dublin 2001

BUCKSTONE Frederick XIX **[7]**
☞ **\$3 798** - €3 559 - **£2 350** - FF23 348
    Clovelly Bideford Bay, North Devon/Mill Mouth Clovelly, North Devon Oil/canvas (28x44cm 11x17in) Penzance, Cornwall 1999

BUCOVITCH von Mario XIX-XX **[6]**
📷 **\$2 914** - €2 812 - **£1 830** - FF18 446
    Paris Photograph (15x22cm 5x8in) München 1999

BUDDENBERG Wilhelm 1890-1967 **[16]**
☞ **\$1 172** - €1 227 - **£736** - FF8 049
    Rehe im Schwarzwälder Hochwald Öl/Leinwand (40x55cm 15x21in) Bremen 2000

BUDELOT Philippe c.1770-1829 **[37]**
☞ **\$2 522** - €3 049 - **£1 762** - FF20 000
    Paysans et cavaliers sur les chemins dans la forêt Huile/toile (35x49cm 13x19in) Paris 2000
☞ **\$2 517** - €2 592 - **£1 599** - FF17 000
    Paysans cheminant dans un paysage de rivière Huile/toile (24.5x33cm 9x12in) Toulouse 2000

BUDKOW Joseph 1880-1940 **[23]**
🖌 **\$7 000** - €7 431 - **£4 736** - FF48 741
    Shtetel Tailor at the Entrance of his Shop Pastel/paper (50x40cm 19x15in) Tel Aviv 2001

BUDNICK Sydney Jonas 1921-1994 **[1]**
⚒ **\$11 000** - €12 272 - **£7 200** - FF80 500
    «De Stael Negative» Construction (60x60cm 24x24in) Chicago IL 2000

BUDNIK Dan 1933 **[1]**
📷 **\$2 548** - €2 822 - **£1 728** - FF18 513
    Georgia O'Keeffe, Abiquin, New Mexico Dye-transfer print (50.5x60.4cm 19x23in) Berlin 2000

BUDTZ-MØLLER Carl 1882-1953 **[142]**
☞ **\$655** - €603 - **£405** - FF3 954
    Parti fra Pompeji Oil/canvas (51x67cm 20x26in) Vejle 1998

BUECKELAER Joachim c.1530-c.1573 **[10]**
☞ **\$3 909 600** - €4 442 820 - **£2 700 000** - FF29 142 990
    The Four Elements: Air, Water, Earth & Fire Oil/canvas (157x215cm 61x84in) London 2000
☞ **\$6 770** - €7 267 - **£4 530** - FF47 670
    Die Köchin Oil/panel (109x76cm 42x29in) Wien 2000
☞ **\$35 000** - €37 492 - **£23 901** - FF245 931
    Execution of the Five Kings of the Amorites, Joshua XVI-XVII Oil/paper (26x19cm 10x7in) New-York 2001

BUEHLER Lytton Briggs 1888-? **[2]**
🖼 **\$849** - €745 - **£515** - FF4 888
    You Can be Sure of Shell Poster (83x147cm 33x58in) New-York 1999

BUEHR Karl Albert 1866-1952 **[27]**
☞ **\$5 000** - €4 824 - **£3 140** - FF31 645
    Western Landscape Oil/canvas (64x77cm 25x30in) Cambridge MA 1999

BUEL Herbert 1915-1984 **[2]**
🖌 **\$1 430** - €1 458 - **£896** - FF9 562
    Mendocino Coast Watercolour/paper (51x71cm 20x28in) Altadena CA 2000

BUELL Alfred Leslie 1910-1996 **[3]**
☞ **\$5 000** - €5 600 - **£3 474** - FF36 736
    Beautiful Woman seated at the Beach, Calendar Illustration Oil/canvas (76x60cm 30x24in) New-York 2001

BUENO Antonio 1918-1985 **[250]**
☞ **\$13 500** - €13 995 - **£8 100** - FF91 800
    Ragazza con viola Olio/masonite (50x35cm 19x13in) Vercelli 2000
☞ **\$9 500** - €9 848 - **£5 700** - FF64 600
    Stratonice Olio/faesite (30x30cm 11x11in) Vercelli 2000
🖌 **\$1 550** - €1 607 - **£930** - FF10 540
    Profilo Pastelli (21x15cm 8x5in) Vercelli 2001
🖼 **\$140** - €181 - **£105** - FF1 190
    Marinaio Litografia a colori (49.5x37cm 19x14in) Milano 2001

B

BUENO DE MESQUITA David Abraham 1889-1962 [14]

👐 **$4 053** - €3 765 - **£2 474** - FF24 697
Het Model Oil/canvas (83x93cm 32x36in) Amsterdam 1998

📖 **$154** - €170 - **£104** - FF1 116
Two Boys and a Dog on a landing, sailing Ships in the Background Etching (16.9x12cm 6x4in) Haarlem 2000

BUENO FERRER Pasqual 1930 [53]

👐 **$468** - €541 - **£324** - FF3 546
«Puerto Andratx, Palma de Mallorca» Oleo/lienzo (38x45.5cm 14x17in) Barcelona 2001

👐 **$212** - €228 - **£140** - FF1 497
Paisaje con camelleros Oleo/cartulina (31x40.5cm 12x15in) Barcelona 2000

BUENO Maria Lola 1970 [7]

👐 **$350** - €363 - **£210** - FF2 380
Aurora boreale Olio/tela (30x40cm 11x15in) Vercelli 2001

BUENO VILLAREJO Pedro 1910-1993 [37]

👐 **$2 450** - €2 102 - **£1 470** - FF13 790
Baile en el pueblo Oleo (60x73cm 23x28in) Madrid 1999

👐 **$1 440** - €1 351 - **£877** - FF8 865
Joven mujer Oleo/cartón (32x28cm 12x11in) Madrid 1999

BUENO Xavier 1915-1979 [146]

👐 **$10 400** - €13 476 - **£7 800** - FF88 400
«Ragazzo» Olio/tela (70x50cm 27x19in) Prato 2000

👐 **$9 000** - €9 330 - **£5 400** - FF61 200
Natura morta con pane Olio/tela (30x40cm 11x15in) Torino 2000

✏️ **$1 680** - €1 451 - **£840** - FF9 520
Pastorello Tecnica mista/carta (15.5x10cm 6x3in) Prato 1999

BUERGERNISS Carl 1877-1956 [32]

👐 **$475** - €536 - **£329** - FF3 514
Meadow Landscape with Purple Sky Oil/canvas (25x35cm 10x14in) Hatfield PA 2000

BUESEM Jan Jansz. c.1600-c.1649 [8]

👐 **$32 000** - €35 109 - **£21 257** - FF230 297
Couple Standing by Pots and Pans in a Stable, Boors Smoking Oil/panel (33x45.5cm 12x17in) New-York 2000

BUETTI Daniele 1955 [6]

📷 **$704** - €762 - **£482** - FF5 000
Good Fellows Photo couleurs (30x40cm 11x15in) Paris 2001

BUFALO del Claudia (?) XVI-XVII [1]

👐 **$20 662** - €17 850 - **£10 331** - FF117 088
Ritratto di Faustina Del Bufalo Olio/tela (105x88cm 41x34in) Roma 1999

BUFANO Benjiamico 1898-1970 [11]

🐚 **$1 680** - €2 113 - **£1 491** - FF13 858
Bust of a Child with a Ball Porcelain (H37cm H14in) San-Francisco CA 1998

BUFF Conrad 1886-1975 [45]

👐 **$3 000** - €2 761 - **£1 800** - FF18 111
Snowcapped Mountain Landscape Oil/board (60x91cm 24x36in) Pasadena CA 1999

👐 **$1 300** - €1 196 - **£780** - FF7 848
Southwest Landscape Oil/board (30x40cm 12x16in) Pasadena CA 1999

BUFF Sebastian 1829-1880 [3]

👐 **$4 784** - €4 678 - **£2 954** - FF30 687
Erinnerungen an Brienz Öl/Leinwand (42x69cm 16x27in) Zürich 1999

BUFFA G. XIX-XX [2]

📖 **$2 140** - €1 829 - **£1 285** - FF12 000
«Al Chiaro di Luna Teatro dal Verme, Ricordi Milano» Affiche (102x145cm 40x57in) Paris 1998

BUFFET Bernard 1928-1999 [2463]

👐 **$50 048** - €55 197 - **£33 902** - FF362 066
Le bouquet de tulipes Oil/canvas (95x130cm 37x51in) Stockholm 2000

👐 **$30 000** - €32 923 - **£19 317** - FF215 964
Bouquet de fleurs Oil/canvas (73x53.5cm 28x21in) New-York 2000

👐 **$13 000** - €14 561 - **£9 032** - FF95 513
Nature morte à la sole Oil/masonite (27x35cm 10x13in) New-York 2001

👐 **$9 598** - €9 588 - **£6 000** - FF62 893
Nature morte au pistolet Watercolour (49x63cm 19x24in) London 1999

👐 **$1 049** - €1 143 - **£726** - FF7 500
Nature morte aux poires Pointe sèche (36.5x25cm 14x9in) Paris 2001

BUFFON George Louis Leclerc 1707-1788 [20]

📖 **$29** - €31 - £19 - FF201
Quadrupeds Copper engraving (19x10cm 7x4in) Cleveland OH 2000

BUFFORD John H. XIX [9]

📖 **$2 900** - €3 505 - **£2 024** - FF22 992
Right Whaling in Behering Straits and Artic Ocean with its Varieties Color lithograph (51x89cm 20x35in) Bolton MA 2000

BUGALIMIAMIO MUNGATOPI Deaf Tommy XX [1]

🗿 **$3 289** - €3 173 - **£2 078** - FF20 812
Four Miniature Tiwi Pukamani Grave Posts Sculpture (35x25cm 13x9in) Melbourne 1999

BUGATTI Carlo 1856-1940 [22]

👐 **$5 871** - €5 793 - **£3 617** - FF38 000
Autoportrait Huile/panneau (49x38.2cm 19x15in) Paris 1999

BUGATTI Rembrandt 1884-1916 [327]

🗿 **$230 000** - €198 434 - **£138 759** - FF1 301 639
Mes Antilopes, La caresse Bronze (90x210x60cm 35x82x23in) New-York 1998

🗿 **$85 000** - €91 238 - **£56 882** - FF598 485
Petite panthère Bronze (18.5x37cm 7x14in) New-York 2000

✏️ **$2 624** - €3 049 - **£1 844** - FF20 000
Bison Crayon/papier (19.5x24cm 7x9in) Paris 2001

BUGIANI Pietro 1905 [5]

👐 **$5 100** - €4 406 - **£2 528** - FF28 900
Natura morta con conchiglia Olio/cartone (43x47cm 16x18in) Prato 1999

👐 **$2 250** - €2 332 - **£1 350** - FF15 300
Natura morta con candeliere Olio/cartone (28x22cm 11x8in) Prato 2000

BUGIARDINI Giuliano di Piero 1475-1554 [5]

👐 **$64 533** - €66 899 - **£38 720** - FF438 830
Madonna col Bambino e San Giovannino Olio/tavola (112x80cm 44x31in) Milano 1999

BUHLER Augustus W. 1853-1920 [8]

✏️ **$1 300** - €1 432 - **£867** - FF9 395
Gloucester fisherman with fishing Fleet in Background Watercolour/paper (38x50cm 15x20in) Portsmouth NH 2000

BUHLER Fritz 1909-1963 **[13]**
- $549 - €482 - £333 - FF3 162
  Metraux Sport Poster (127x89cm 50x35in) New-York 1999

BÜHLER Hans Adolf 1877-1951 **[14]**
- $1 674 - €1 430 - £983 - FF9 383
  Blick auf vier Burgen Oil/panel (79x98cm 31x38in) Staufen 1998

BUHLER Robert 1916-1989 **[63]**
- $2 085 - €2 101 - £1 300 - FF13 784
  Summer Landscape Oil/canvas/board (51x61cm 20x24in) London 2000

BÜHLMANN Rudolf Johan 1802-1890 **[28]**
- $4 022 - €4 053 - £2 507 - FF26 585
  Neapel mit Vesuv Öl/Leinwand (36x55cm 14x21in) Zürich 2000

BÜHLMAYER Conrad 1835-1883 **[14]**
- $7 716 - €8 692 - £5 426 - FF57 016
  Heimkehr von der Weide Öl/Leinwand (104x96cm 40x37in) Stuttgart 2001

BUHOT Charles Louis Hipp. 1815-1865 **[6]**
- $5 500 - €5 245 - £3 347 - FF34 407
  Hebe Seated on Jupiter's Eagle Bronze (H66cm H25in) New-York 1999

BUHOT Félix 1847-1898 **[346]**
- $7 791 - €9 094 - £5 500 - FF59 653
  Parisian Street, Winter Watercolour (30.5x45cm 12x17in) London 2000
- $1 000 - €1 013 - £622 - FF6 644
  Westminster Bridge Etching (29x40cm 11x15in) New-York 2000

BUI XUAN PHAÏ 1920-1988 **[69]**
- $9 955 - €9 277 - £6 142 - FF60 852
  Old Street of Hanoi Oil/canvas (55x65cm 21x25in) Singapore 1999
- $2 869 - €3 258 - £1 964 - FF21 373
  La Jeune Actrice du Cheo (The Young Cheo Actress) Oil/board (16x9cm 6x3in) Singapore 2000
- $2 969 - €2 491 - £1 742 - FF16 340
  Old Street Gouache/paper (34.5x45cm 13x17in) Singapore 1998

BUISSERET Louis 1888-1956 **[80]**
- $2 295 - €2 231 - £1 422 - FF14 634
  Recueillement Huile/panneau (48x38cm 18x14in) Bruxelles 1999
- $710 - €843 - £493 - FF5 528
  Marine Huile/panneau (16x26cm 6x10in) Maisieres-Mons 2000
- $516 - €496 - £324 - FF3 252
  Femme nue accroupie Crayon/papier (36x27cm 14x10in) Bruxelles 1999

BUKEN van Jan 1635-1694 **[5]**
- $4 266 - €3 681 - £2 540 - FF24 145
  Stilleben Oil/canvas/panel (41x29.5cm 16x11in) München 1998

BUKOVAC Vlaho 1855-1922 **[11]**
- $23 170 - €25 435 - £15 400 - FF166 845
  Gospodin Hugo von Berks Öl/Leinwand (165x85.5cm 64x33in) Wien 2000
- $18 536 - €20 348 - £12 320 - FF133 476
  Hugo Reichsritter von Berks Öl/Leinwand (85x63cm 33x24in) Wien 2000

BULAND Eugène 1852-1927 **[8]**
- $12 656 - €10 958 - £7 947 - FF85 000
  Lycerion et Daphnis Huile/toile (140x100cm 55x39in) Lille 2000

BULAS Jan 1878-1917 **[5]**
- $3 438 - €2 925 - £2 050 - FF19 188
  Pissenlits Oil/panel (49.5x69.5cm 19x27in) Warszawa 1998
- $1 541 - €1 554 - £961 - FF10 192
  Portrait d'homme Pastel/paper (47.5x62.5cm 18x24in) Warszawa 2000

BULATOV Eric 1933 **[3]**
- $4 634 - €5 087 - £3 080 - FF33 369
  New-York, New-York Coloured pencils/paper (29.5x42cm 11x16in) Wien 2000

BULCKE Emile 1875-1963 **[22]**
- $559 - €644 - £390 - FF4 227
  Allégorie du printemps Huile/toile (26x48cm 10x18in) Bruxelles 2001

BULFIELD Joseph 1850-1921 **[6]**
- $1 704 - €1 829 - £1 140 - FF12 000
  Fin de marché aux faïences le soir Pastel/papier (27x36cm 10x14in) Quimper 2000

BULGARINI Bartolomeo di Messer c.1345-1378 **[6]**
- $525 000 - €544 243 - £315 000 - FF3 570 000
  Madonna col Bambino, San Pietro Martire, San Giovanni Battista Tempera (147.5x217.5cm 58x85in) Firenze 2001

BULL Charles Livingston 1874-1932 **[40]**
- $20 000 - €19 100 - £12 312 - FF125 290
  The Chase Oil/canvas (109x140cm 43x55in) Cincinnati OH 1999
- $1 200 - €1 337 - £784 - FF8 767
  Bear cub chased by crows (book illustration) Ink (59x44cm 23x17in) New-York 2000

BULL Clarence Sinclair 1896-1979 **[52]**
- $612 - €513 - £368 - FF3 364
  Greta Garbo Hand to Forehead Photograph (35.5x28cm 13x11in) London 1998

BULL Knud Geelmuyden 1811-1889 **[5]**
- $25 296 - €30 093 - £17 496 - FF197 400
  Norsk elvelandskap Oil/canvas (35x51cm 13x20in) Oslo 2000
- $30 548 - €33 578 - £19 576 - FF220 256
  Wreck of the Waterloo Oil/board (29x39cm 11x15in) Melbourne 2000

BULL William Howell 1861-1940 **[8]**
- $1 100 - €1 023 - £679 - FF6 709
  «Crater Lake» Poster (58x40cm 23x16in) New-York 1999

BULLARD A., Amos? XIX **[1]**
- $26 000 - €22 432 - £15 743 - FF147 141
  Young Boy with Book Pastel/paper (68x51cm 27x20in) New-York 1999

BULLEID George Lawrence 1858-1933 **[19]**
- $5 977 - €6 416 - £4 000 - FF42 086
  The school Girl Watercolour/paper (36x29.5cm 14x11in) London 2000

BULLINGER Johann Balthasar I 1713-1793 **[16]**
- $3 654 - €3 131 - £2 197 - FF20 537
  Dekorative Landschaft mit Bach Öl/Leinwand (89x89.5cm 35x35in) Zürich 1998

BULLINGHAM Henry XIX **[2]**
- $2 845 - €3 306 - £2 000 - FF21 688
  Alice Carbon print (14.5x10cm 5x3in) London 2001

B

BULLIS Franklin Howard 1861-1937 **[1]**
$19 000 - €21 010 - **£12 707** - FF137 818
Port Kent, New York with Passenger Steamer «Vermont» on Lake Oil/canvas (40x50cm 16x20in) Portsmouth NH 2000

BULLOCK Wynn 1902-1975 **[98]**
$2 500 - €2 331 - **£1 509** - FF15 291
Mother and Child, Variant of Navigation without Numbers Photograph (20.5x25.5cm 8x10in) New-York 1999

BULMAN Job 1745-1818 **[7]**
$3 649 - €3 174 - **£2 200** - FF20 818
«Scarborough Sands» Pencil (31.5x52cm 12x20in) London 1998

BULMAN Orville XX **[23]**
$5 000 - €5 582 - **£3 342** - FF36 618
Le Larron Oil/canvas (63x76cm 25x30in) Delray-Beach FL 2000
$3 500 - €3 908 - **£2 339** - FF25 632
Pas possible Oil/canvas (40x35cm 16x14in) Delray-Beach FL 2000

BULOT Eugène XIX **[1]**
$3 613 - €3 506 - **£2 277** - FF23 000
Composition de diverses fleurs de printemps Aquarelle, gouache/papier (71x68.5cm 27x26in) Paris 1999

BUNBURY Henry William 1750-1811 **[39]**
$523 - €562 - **£350** - FF3 687
At the Barber's Watercolour (48x67.5cm 18x26in) Billingshurst, West-Sussex 2000
$260 - €254 - **£160** - FF1 662
The Country Club Engraving (39x50.5cm 15x19in) London 1999

BUNCHO Ippitsusai 1725-1794 **[11]**
$8 000 - €9 382 - **£5 708** - FF61 539
Actor Ichikawa Danjuro V as Samurai Breaking Through Screen with Baby Print in colors (32.5x14.5cm 12x5in) New-York 2000

BUNCHO Tani 1763-1840 **[11]**
$896 - €962 - **£600** - FF6 313
Sumi-e Landscape Ink/paper (124x50cm 48x19in) London 2000

BUNCOMBE John XVIII-XIX **[15]**
$3 664 - €4 219 - **£2 500** - FF27 672
Captain Clement William Whitby, of the 17th Regiment Silhouette (13.5x9.5cm 5x3in) London 2000

BUNDEL van den Willem c.1575-1655 **[10]**
$20 410 - €19 818 - **£12 610** - FF130 000
Promenade dans une allée d'arbres Huile/cuivre (25.5x35cm 10x13in) Paris 1999

BUNDSEN Jes 1766-1829 **[2]**
$1 142 - €1 022 - **£684** - FF6 704
Altona vom Stintfang aus Copper engraving (25.5x44cm 10x17in) Hamburg 1998

BUNDY Edgar 1862-1922 **[107]**
$37 881 - €45 052 - **£27 000** - FF295 520
The Doctor Forbids Oil/canvas (123x214.5cm 48x84in) London 2000
$4 254 - €4 529 - **£2 800** - FF29 710
The Tribunal Oil/canvas (49x75cm 19x29in) Billingshurst, West-Sussex 1999
$2 642 - €2 813 - **£1 800** - FF18 452
Game of Bowls Oil/panel (29.5x45cm 11x17in) Billingshurst, West-Sussex 2001

$2 876 - €2 932 - **£1 800** - FF19 231
Difference Watercolour (36x52.5cm 14x20in) London 2000

BUNDY Horace 1814-1883 **[9]**
$1 300 - €1 245 - **£801** - FF8 165
Portraits of Vermont Couple Oil/canvas (69x56cm 27x22in) Portsmouth NH 1999

BUNDY John Elwood 1853-1933 **[16]**
$3 250 - €3 104 - **£2 000** - FF20 359
Indiana Landscape Oil/canvas (60x81cm 24x32in) Cincinnati OH 1999
$1 200 - €1 087 - **£738** - FF7 133
Melting Snow Watercolour/paper (35x38cm 14x15in) Mystic CT 1999

BUNIN Hope Shipee 1908-1970 **[4]**
$4 000 - €4 480 - **£2 779** - FF29 388
«Lower Eastside Market» Oil/board (55x45cm 22x18in) Cincinnati OH 2001

BUNING Johan 1893-1963 **[30]**
$2 155 - €1 866 - **£1 307** - FF12 238
Still Life with a bottle and fruit Oil/canvas (50x40cm 19x15in) Amsterdam 1998
$201 - €227 - **£138** - FF1 488
Farmyard in Wooded Landscape Watercolour (66x87cm 25x34in) Amsterdam 2000

BUNKE Franz 1857-1939 **[47]**
$2 959 - €3 068 - **£1 875** - FF20 123
Schwaaner Landschaft Ol/Leinwand (77x102cm 30x40in) Satow 2000
$999 - €1 125 - **£688** - FF7 378
Mecklenburger Landschaft Oil/panel (26x38cm 10x14in) Satow 2000

BUNKER Dennis Miller 1861-1890 **[13]**
$470 000 - €520 509 - **£318 754** - FF3 414 315
Larmor Oil/canvas (45.5x64.5cm 17x25in) New-York 2000
$95 000 - €81 167 - **£57 484** - FF532 418
Two Beached Sailboats and a Dory Oil/canvas (30.5x48.5cm 12x19in) San-Francisco CA 1998

BUNNER Andrew Fisher 1841-1897 **[15]**
$3 750 - €3 746 - **£2 344** - FF24 571
Sylvan Glade with Children at Stream Oil/canvas (84x106cm 33x42in) New-Orleans LA 1999

BUNNEY John Wharlton 1826-1882 **[8]**
$10 594 - €9 632 - **£6 500** - FF63 185
La Porta della Carta nel Palazzo Ducale, Venezia Oil/canvas (82.5x61.5cm 32x24in) London 1999

BUNNY Rupert Ch. Wulsten 1864-1947 **[204]**
$85 833 - €83 512 - **£52 825** - FF547 803
Lees roses de Sainte Dorothée Oil/canvas (151x161.5cm 59x63in) Malvern, Victoria 1999
$23 524 - €22 888 - **£14 478** - FF150 138
Portrait of the Artist's Wife in the Garden Oil/canvas (72x59cm 28x23in) Melbourne 1999
$2 249 - €2 512 - **£1 440** - FF16 480
Landscape, South of France Oil/paper/board (16x24cm 6x9in) Melbourne 2000
$495 - €589 - **£352** - FF3 862
Seated Nude Ink (24.5x31.5cm 9x12in) Woollahra, Sydney 2000
$5 624 - €6 281 - **£3 601** - FF41 201
Poebus at Artemise Monotype (24.5x24.5cm 9x9in) Malvern, Victoria 2000

BUNSCH Adam 1896-1969 **[7]**
$4 365 - €4 905 - **£3 063** - FF32 176
Nature morte Huile/carton (34x39.5cm 13x15in) Katowice 2001

BÜNTING Heinrich XVI [1]
- $1 813 - €1 728 - £1 100 - FF11 336
  Die gantze Welt ein Kleeblat Woodcut (26x36cm 10x14in) London 1999

BUNTZEN Heinrich 1803-1892 [30]
- $3 384 - €4 024 - £2 412 - FF26 397
  Motiv fra Trieste Oil/canvas (46x62cm 18x24in) København 2000
- $497 - €471 - £310 - FF3 088
  Borgruin på klippetop Oil/paper/canvas (24x21.5cm 9x8in) København 1999

BUONAMICI Ferdinando 1820-1892 [1]
- $7 200 - €6 220 - £4 800 - FF40 800
  Una caserma di Modena Olio/tela (52x65cm 20x25in) Roma 1998

BUONO Leon Giuseppe 1888-1975 [34]
- $1 200 - €1 037 - £800 - FF6 800
  Riflessi sull'acqua Olio/legno (30x40cm 11x15in) Roma 1998

BUQUET Henri 1761-1833 [1]
- $13 000 - €12 035 - £7 848 - FF78 942
  Gentleman Seated at a Table with a Costal Landscape Beyond Oil/canvas (72x58.5cm 28x23in) New-York 1999

BURAGLIO Pierre 1939 [17]
- $6 968 - €7 927 - £4 836 - FF52 000
  Fenêtre Technique mixte (125x50cm 49x19in) Paris 2000
- $3 369 - €3 964 - £2 415 - FF26 000
  Angles de fenêtres Installation (25x25x5cm 9x9x1in) Paris 2001

BURAIMOH Jimoh 1943 [10]
- $630 - €734 - £450 - FF4 812
  Animals Gouache (51x137cm 20x54in) London 2001

BURBANK Elbridge Ayer 1858-1949 [33]
- $2 750 - €2 350 - £1 664 - FF15 414
  «Quin-Cha-Ke-Cha. Ute.» Oil/canvas (61x45.5cm 24x17in) San-Francisco CA 1998
- $325 - €363 - £220 - FF2 381
  Portrait of a Dog Oil/board (13x8cm 5x3in) Columbia SC 2000
- $425 - €402 - £265 - FF2 639
  Yaqui Man Pencil/paper (27x20cm 11x8in) St. Ignatius MT 1999

BURBURE de Louis, vicomte 1837-1911 [7]
- $4 992 - €5 949 - £3 576 - FF39 024
  Bateaux de pêche dans le canal d'Ostende Huile/toile (42x77cm 16x30in) Antwerpen 2000

BURCH van der Jacques A. Édouard 1756-1803 [3]
- $14 102 - €16 769 - £10 054 - FF110 000
  Chinoiserie Huile/toile (39.5x45.5cm 15x17in) Monte-Carlo 2000
- $7 413 - €7 470 - £4 620 - FF49 000
  Bergers dans un paysage montagneux Gouache/papier (55x76cm 21x29in) Neuilly-sur-Seine 2000

BURCHARTZ Max 1887-1961 [38]
- $238 - €204 - £143 - FF1 341
  Schlafende Frau Lithographie (26.4x35.5cm 10x13in) Berlin 1998

BURCHELL William John 1781-1869 [19]
- $4 509 - €4 258 - £2 800 - FF27 928
  Houses on the Waterfront, Rio de Janeiro Pencil (30.5x48.5cm 12x19in) London 1999

BURCHFIELD Charles Ephraim 1893-1967 [192]
- $19 000 - €16 233 - £11 405 - FF106 483
  Looking Westward Across Pine Hollow Watercolour/paper (45.5x56cm 17x22in) New-York 1998
- $2 600 - €2 497 - £1 602 - FF16 379
  Summer Benediction Lithograph (30.5x23.5cm 12x9in) New-York 1999

BURCKHARDT Heinrich 1853-1912 [5]
- $24 000 - €26 895 - £16 728 - FF176 419
  The Bridal Shower Oil/canvas (100.5x131cm 39x51in) New-York 2001

BURCKHARDT Rudy 1919 [4]
- $1 700 - €1 958 - £1 172 - FF12 845
  Paris Realization/Brooklyn Bridge/Flatiron Building Summer/Astor Place Silver print (27x22cm 11x9in) New-York 2000

BURD Clara Miller act.1900-1926 [1]
- $2 200 - €1 877 - £1 327 - FF12 311
  Cover of «The book of Golden Deeds», by charlotte Yonge Watercolour/paper (41x29cm 16x11in) New-York 1998

BÜRDE Paul 1819-1874 [7]
- $5 210 - €6 196 - £3 713 - FF40 643
  The Nursery Oil/canvas (53x37.5cm 20x14in) Melbourne 2000

BURDEN Chris 1946 [21]
- $15 000 - €16 457 - £9 964 - FF107 952
  Exploding Submarine Sculpture, wood (13x40.5x10cm 5x15x3in) New-York 2000
- $10 000 - €11 603 - £6 904 - FF76 110
  Full Financial Disclosure June and March Ballpoint pen (76x91.5cm 29x36in) New-York 2000
- $3 000 - €2 658 - £1 840 - FF17 438
  The Atomic Alphabet Etching (136x91cm 53x35in) New-York 1999

BURDICK Horace Robbins 1844-1942 [18]
- $400 - €471 - £281 - FF3 092
  Evening Scene with Woman Carrying a Basket Oil/board (26x35cm 10x14in) East-Dennis MA 2000

BUREAU Léon 1866-1906 [73]
- $1 500 - €1 529 - £939 - FF10 030
  Pointer Bronze (H33.5cm H13in) New-York 2000

BUREN Daniel 1938 [41]
- $12 864 - €12 196 - £7 824 - FF80 000
  Photo souvenir Acrylique (414x171cm 162x67in) Paris 1999
- $2 112 - €2 287 - £1 446 - FF15 000
  Les colonnes Feutre (22x30cm 8x11in) Paris 2001
- $2 000 - €1 725 - £1 202 - FF11 318
  The Rotating Square, In and Out of the Frame Lithograph (115.5x115.5cm 45x45in) New-York 1998

BURFIELD James M. c.1840-c.1895 [9]
- $7 787 - €8 605 - £5 400 - FF56 446
  Memories Oil/canvas (63.5x44.5cm 25x17in) London 2001

BURFORD Thomas c.1710-c.1780 [7]
- $79 775 - €76 263 - £50 000 - FF500 250
  Match at Newmarket, probably at The Turn of the Lands on Beacon Course Oil/canvas (89x138.5cm 35x54in) London 1999
- $397 - €461 - £280 - FF3 024
  Flora Mezzotint (35x25.5cm 13x10in) London 2001

B

BURGARITZKY Josef, Jacob 1836-1890 **[53]**
- $976 - €1 022 - £613 - FF6 707
  Wassermühle im Gebirgswald Öl/Leinwand
  (74x100cm 29x39in) Bremen 2000

BURGDORFF Ferdinand 1881-1975 **[36]**
- $1 100 - €940 - £665 - FF6 164
  «Christmas Night in a Redwood Canyon»
  Oil/masonite (61x91.5cm 24x36in) San-Francisco CA
  1998
- $750 - €694 - £459 - FF4 554
  Navaho riding Home Oil/board (30x40cm 12x16in)
  San Rafael CA 1999

BURGE Maude 1865-1957 **[2]**
- $3 174 - €3 557 - £2 212 - FF23 331
  St Ives Coast Watercolour/paper (39x45cm 15x17in)
  Wellington 2001

BURGER Anton 1824-1905 **[69]**
- $2 769 - €2 556 - £1 703 - FF16 769
  In der Schmiedewerkstatt Öl/Leinwand (37x51cm
  14x20in) München 1999
- $2 397 - €2 045 - £1 446 - FF13 414
  «Interieur einer Werkstatt» Oil/paper/board
  (42x31cm 16x12in) Kempten 1998
- $258 - €297 - £176 - FF1 945
  Apfelkelter Black chalk (20.4x19.6cm 8x7in)
  Heidelberg 2000

BURGER Gerhard XX **[1]**
- $2 329 - €2 486 - £1 576 - FF16 306
  Kraal in the Mountains Watercolour/paper (32x50cm
  12x19in) Cape Town 2001

BURGER Josef 1887-1966 **[98]**
- $625 - €716 - £429 - FF4 695
  **Altwasser an der Loisach an einem späten
  Herbsttag** Oil/panel (60.5x80cm 23x31in) Lindau
  2000

BÜRGER Lothar 1866-1943 **[22]**
- $683 - €727 - £432 - FF4 767
  Christbaumsuche Oil/panel (20.5x7.5cm 8x2in)
  Salzburg 2000

BURGER Willy Friedrich 1882-1964 **[46]**
- $1 400 - €1 562 - £916 - FF10 245
  «St.Moritz, Engadin» Poster (72.5x97cm 28x38in)
  New-York 2000

BURGER-WILLING Willi Hans 1882-1969 **[40]**
- $683 - €716 - £432 - FF4 695
  Ziegenherde in der Eifel Öl/Leinwand (70x80cm
  27x31in) Köln 2000

BÜRGERS Felix 1870-1934 **[19]**
- $1 044 - €1 022 - £672 - FF6 707
  Föntag im Hochgebirge Öl/Leinwand (66x88cm
  25x34in) Kempten 1999

BÜRGERS Hendricus Jacobus 1834-1899 **[22]**
- $9 866 - €9 076 - £6 100 - FF59 532
  Punch and Judy Oil/canvas (72x105cm 28x41in)
  Amsterdam 1999
- $1 175 - €1 098 - £725 - FF7 200
  Jeune femme à l'éventail et au petit chien
  Huile/panneau (33x21cm 12x8in) Brest 1999

BURGESS Arthur J. Wetherall 1879-1957 **[60]**
- $2 270 - €2 181 - £1 400 - FF14 306
  Vessels at the Quayside, probably Tilbury
  Oil/canvas (51x76cm 20x29in) London 1999
- $641 - €647 - £400 - FF4 241
  Warships at Sea Oil/canvas/board (29.5x50cm
  11x19in) Billingshurst, West-Sussex 2000

- $262 - €290 - £174 - FF1 900
  Through the Heads Watercolour (40.5x61cm
  15x24in) Melbourne 2000
- $1 449 - €1 223 - £850 - FF8 023
  «P&O and British India» Poster (72x48cm 28x18in)
  London 1998

BURGESS Eliza Mary 1873-? **[5]**
- $3 053 - €2 562 - £1 800 - FF16 806
  Portrait of a Young girl holding a Rose Oil/canvas
  (44x33cm 17x13in) Bransford, Worcester 1998
- $278 - €298 - £190 - FF1 955
  Still Life Study of sweet Peas in a Vase
  Watercolour/paper (25x27cm 10x11in) Cheltenham,
  Gloucestershire 2001

BURGESS James Howard 1817-1890 **[6]**
- $1 693 - €1 964 - £1 200 - FF12 882
  Herons in a Coastal Landscape Watercolour
  (37x68.5cm 14x26in) London 2000

BURGESS John 1815-1874 **[7]**
- $489 - €585 - £337 - FF3 840
  «Old Bridge Avignon» Watercolour/paper
  (37x54.5cm 14x21in) Penzance, Cornwall 2000

BURGESS John Bagnold 1830-1897 **[66]**
- $3 200 - €3 462 - £2 192 - FF22 708
  Priest Visit Oil/canvas/board (57x44cm 22x17in)
  Chicago IL 2001
- $959 - €896 - £580 - FF5 879
  Game of Cards Oil/panel (30.5x46cm 12x18in)
  London 1999

BURGESS John Cart 1798-1863 **[7]**
- $1 016 - €1 091 - £680 - FF7 154
  St.Michael's Mount, Cornwall/Mont St.Michel
  Watercolour (24x35cm 9x13in) London 2000

BURGESS William XVIII **[1]**
- $25 420 - €24 654 - £16 000 - FF161 721
  **View of Cave Castle, near Hull, with a Lady and
  Gentleman and Boats** Oil/canvas (97x143cm
  38x56in) London 1999

BURGESS William, of Dover 1805-1861 **[12]**
- $4 936 - €5 183 - £3 264 - FF34 000
  Pêcheurs sur la grève Huile/toile (36.5x49cm
  14x19in) Paris 2000

BURGGEIL de G. XIX-XX **[2]**
- $3 600 - €3 462 - £2 221 - FF22 709
  «Peugeot» Poster (157x116cm 61x45in) New-York
  1999

BURGH van der Cornelis Jacobz. 1640-? **[4]**
- $11 116 - €10 174 - £6 776 - FF66 738
  **Eine klassische Landschaft mit Figuren vor
  einem steinernen Brunnen** Öl/Leinwand
  (119.5x155cm 47x61in) Wien 1999

BURGH van der Hendrick 1769-1858 **[22]**
- $39 150 - €38 112 - £24 050 - FF250 000
  Un matin en Italie vue de la Cava Huile/toile
  (105x177cm 41x69in) Paris 1999
- $6 400 - €7 267 - £4 380 - FF47 670
  **Holländische Flusslandschaft mit einem
  Heuwagen** Oil/panel (36.5x45.5cm 14x17in) Wien
  2000

BURGH van der Hendrick Adam 1798-1877 **[11]**
- $1 976 - €2 178 - £1 290 - FF14 287
  Rustende koeien bij een stal Oil/panel (44x33cm
  17x12in) Den Haag 2001

B

BURGH van der Hendrik 1627-c.1666/69 [4]
🖼 $4 933 - €4 538 - **£3 050** - FF29 766
A maid seated by a table in a Kitchen Oil/panel (33x40.5cm 12x15in) Amsterdam 1999

BURGH van der Pieter Daniel 1805-1879 [9]
🖼 $2 439 - €2 556 - **£1 545** - FF16 769
Sommerliche Gracht mit herrschaftlichen Anwesen in Amsterdam Oil/panel (19x24.5cm 7x9in) Köln 2000

BURGHARDT Rezso 1884-1963 [6]
🖼 $1 360 - €1 337 - **£850** - FF8 772
Winter Sunshine Oil/canvas (56x69cm 22x27in) Budapest 1999

BURGI Jakob 1745-? [8]
✎ $1 500 - €1 304 - **£907** - FF8 553
Landscape with a Ruined Castle and a Waterfall Gouache/vellum (17.5x22cm 6x8in) New-York 1999

BURGIS William XVIII [2]
🗒 $1 200 - €1 388 - **£849** - FF9 106
New York Engraving (12x26cm 4x10in) New-York 2000

BURGKMAIR Hans I 1473-1531 [44]
🗒 $144 - €169 - **£101** - FF1 106
Die drei christlichen Heldinnen Woodcut (19x13cm 7x5in) Berlin 2001

BURGMEIER Max 1881-1947 [40]
🖼 $669 - €787 - **£484** - FF5 161
«Aareuferlandschaft bei Aarau» Öl/Leinwand (57x65cm 22x25in) Zofingen 2001

BURI Max Alfred 1868-1915 [24]
🖼 $28 396 - €30 884 - **£18 715** - FF202 584
Haus am Brienzersee Öl/Leinwand (57.5x72.5cm 22x28in) Bern 2000
🖼 $873 - €809 - **£534** - FF5 305
Ansicht von Algier Öl/Leinwand/Karton (21x37cm 8x14in) Bern 2000

BURI Samuel 1935 [154]
🖼 $3 037 - €3 332 - **£2 063** - FF21 859
Stilleben Acryl/Leinwand (47x60cm 18x23in) Luzern 2000
✎ $883 - €1 053 - **£629** - FF6 907
Ohne Titel Gouache/paper (21.5x20cm 8x7in) Luzern 2000
🗒 $167 - €161 - **£103** - FF1 056
Nach dem Essen Farblithographie (56.5x76cm 22x29in) Bern 1999

BURIAN Zdenek 1905-1981 [22]
✎ $419 - €396 - **£261** - FF2 599
Duel Technique mixte/papier (40x55cm 15x21in) Praha 2000

BURIDANT G. XX [3]
🗒 $265 - €305 - **£187** - FF2 000
«L'embuscade» Affiche (120x160cm 47x62in) Paris 2001

BURKE Augustus Nicolas 1838-1891 [13]
🖼 $5 602 - €5 311 - **£3 500** - FF34 835
Cattle on the Road Oil/canvas (61.5x92cm 24x36in) London 1999
🖼 $4 523 - €4 825 - **£3 013** - FF31 650
At the End of the Day - Farmer and Cattle Oil/canvas (30x25cm 12x10in) Dublin 2000

BURKE Keast 1896-1974 [9]
📷 $657 - €683 - **£423** - FF4 462
Young Man with Palm Dates Gelatin silver print (32x29cm 12x11in) Sydney 2000

BURKE Thomas 1749-1815 [19]
🗒 $246 - €256 - **£156** - FF1 676
Rest from Labour, nach G.Morland Mezzotint (45.1x35.5cm 17x13in) Leipzig 2000

BÜRKEL Heinrich 1802-1869 [145]
🖼 $38 767 - €38 347 - **£24 172** - FF251 542
Winterlandschaft mit heimkehrenden Jägern Öl/Leinwand (58x83cm 22x32in) Berlin 1999
🖼 $11 978 - €12 271 - **£7 392** - FF80 493
Viehhandel Oil/panel (14x14cm 5x5in) Düsseldorf 2000
✎ $241 - €281 - **£169** - FF1 844
Bayerische Landschaft mit Blick auf die Alpen Pencil (12.5x28cm 4x11in) Königstein 2001

BURKHALTER Jean 1895-1982 [81]
🖼 $494 - €534 - **£341** - FF3 500
Le repos du modèle Huile/toile (46x55cm 18x21in) Paris 2001

BURKHARD Kaspar 1810-? [3]
🗒 $928 - €935 - **£578** - FF6 135
Felsberg im Kanton Graubünden Aquatinta (29.7x43.5cm 11x17in) Zürich 2000

BURKHARDT Fritz 1900-1983 [39]
🖼 $783 - €920 - **£542** - FF6 037
Vorgebirgslandschaft Öl/Leinwand (59x79cm 23x31in) Stuttgart 2000
✎ $360 - €409 - **£246** - FF2 683
Bordellmotive Watercolour/paper (14.7x22.5cm 5x8in) Hamburg 2000

BURKHARDT Hans Gustav 1904-1994 [26]
✎ $1 100 - €1 251 - **£762** - FF8 206
Untitled, Three Figures Charcoal/paper (48x63cm 19x25in) Chicago IL 2000

BURKI Charles 1909-1994 [27]
🗒 $201 - €204 - **£125** - FF1 339
«D.A.F. Trucks/DH 825» Poster (84x119cm 33x46in) Haarlem 2000

BURLEIGH Averil Mary 1885-1949 [29]
✎ $912 - €790 - **£550** - FF5 183
And Soone the Spyde on the Moore so Broad- A Furious Night . Watercolour (26x18.5cm 10x7in) London 1998

BURLEIGH Charles H.H. 1869-1956 [49]
🖼 $646 - €693 - **£440** - FF4 545
Figures and cattle in a Farm Yard Oil/canvas (55x76cm 22x30in) Birmingham 2001
🖼 $583 - €627 - **£400** - FF4 113
Farmyard Scene Oil/board (23x30cm 9x11in) Stansted Mountfitchet, Essex 2001

BURLEIGH Sydney Richmond 1853-1931 [26]
🖼 $1 100 - €1 251 - **£768** - FF8 206
Fishing Village Mixed media (34x23cm 13x9in) Mystic CT 2000
✎ $600 - €582 - **£373** - FF3 820
Mediterranean Mountain Village with Girl Seated on a Wall Watercolour (27x38cm 11x15in) South-Natick MA 1999

BURLISON Clément XIX [8]
🖼 $2 254 - €2 286 - **£1 400** - FF14 998
Going to Church Oil/paper (41.5x25cm 16x9in) London 2000

BURLJUK David Davidovich 1882-1967 [283]
🖼 $4 417 - €4 953 - **£3 000** - FF32 492
View of a Shipyard on the Dniepr River Oil/canvas (33x51.5cm 12x20in) London 2000

$2 100 - €1 909 - £1 264 - FF12 522
Fishing Scene Oil/canvas (30x40cm 12x16in)
Bethesda MD 1998

$700 - €679 - £432 - FF4 457
Great Peconick Bay, L.I, N.Y Watercolour/paper
(27x38cm 11x15in) Cedar-Falls IA 1999

$856 - €866 - £541 - FF5 811
Femme et cheval Lithograph (18.5x12.3cm 7x4in)
Warszawa 2000

BURLJUK Vladimir Davidovich 1886/87-1917 **[7]**

$7 246 - €6 843 - £4 500 - FF44 885
Farmyard Landscape Oil/canvas (61.5x68cm
24x26in) London 1999

BURMAN Satki 1935 **[65]**

$7 442 - €6 961 - £4 500 - FF45 664
Ame toujours ravie Oil/canvas (116x89cm 45x35in)
London 1999

BURMANN Fritz 1892-1945 **[18]**

$5 317 - €5 113 - £3 281 - FF33 539
Winzerin Oil/panel (66.5x53.8cm 26x21in) Köln 1999

$70 339 - €80 983 - £48 000 - FF531 211
Frau Biene from Worpswede, 87 Years old
Tempera (44.5x34.5cm 17x13in) London 2000

BURMEISTER Paul 1847-1923 **[14]**

$2 677 - €2 812 - £1 771 - FF18 446
Canale Grande, Venedig Öl/Karton (25.5x34.5cm
10x13in) München 2000

BURMESTER Georg 1864-1939 **[42]**

$3 305 - €3 835 - £2 281 - FF25 154
Gewitterwolken über der Förde Öl/Leinwand
(61x75cm 24x29in) Köln 2000

BURN Gerald Maurice 1862-? **[14]**

$4 217 - €4 050 - £2 600 - FF26 568
Bassin Flamand, Anvers Oil/canvas (30.5x57cm
12x22in) London 1999

BURN Henry 1807-1884 **[13]**

$10 817 - €10 226 - £6 713 - FF67 078
Ferry on the Yarra at Studley Park
Watercolour/paper (30x42.5cm 11x16in) Malvern,
Victoria 1999

$2 590 - €2 442 - £1 605 - FF16 017
Panoramic View of the City of Melbourne
Lithograph (16x121cm 6x47in) Melbourne 1999

BURNAND Eugène 1850-1921 **[26]**

$1 474 - €1 705 - £1 043 - FF11 186
Ein braun-weisse Kuh im Freien Öl/Leinwand
(34x46cm 13x18in) Zürich 2000

$1 414 - €1 371 - £876 - FF8 996
**Saint François décrit à Frère Léon la joie parfai-
te** Pastel/papier (71.5x51.5cm 28x20in) Genève 1999

$1 254 - €1 290 - £795 - FF8 463
Soldaterportraetter af forskellig nationalitet
Color lithograph (22x17.5cm 8x6in) Vejle 2000

BURNAT-PROVINS Marguerite 1872-1950 **[28]**

$1 451 - €1 651 - £1 006 - FF10 828
Nature morte aux chrysanthèmes Huile/carton
(21.5x27cm 8x10in) Sion 2000

$348 - €396 - £241 - FF2 598
Maison dans le bois Gravure bois couleurs
(15.5x20.5cm 6x8in) Sion 2000

BURNE-JONES Edward Coley 1833-1898 **[302]**

$1 459 500 - €1 711 212 - £1 050 000 -
FF11 224 820
The Prince entering the Briar Wood Oil/canvas
(107x183cm 42x72in) London 2001

$358 632 - €384 962 - £240 000 - FF2 525 184
Katie Lewis Oil/canvas (61x127cm 24x50in) London
2000

$44 806 - €52 110 - £32 000 - FF341 820
Two seated Female Figures, in a Landscape
Oil/panel (26x36.5cm 10x14in) London 2001

$5 967 - €5 148 - £3 600 - FF33 771
**Sleeping Courtier, Study for «The Council
Chamber»** Ink (59.5x89.5cm 23x35in) London 1998

BURNELL Benjamin 1769-1828 **[4]**

$745 - €833 - £520 - FF5 462
**Portrait of a young Lady with an orange
Shawl/Portrait of a young Man** Pencil (22x16.5cm
8x6in) Bath 2001

BURNET John 1784-1868 **[13]**

$8 521 - €8 118 - £5 200 - FF53 250
Milking Oil/panel (38x53.5cm 14x21in) Bury St.
Edmunds, Suffolk 1999

BURNETT William Hickling c.1800-c.1870 **[4]**

$3 472 - €4 088 - £2 440 - FF26 818
The Church of San Giorgio Maggiore, Venice
Oil/canvas (36x54cm 14x21in) Sydney 2000

BURNEY Edward Francis 1760-1848 **[18]**

$736 - €679 - £449 - FF4 451
Q.Q.brought before the Chinese Emperor Ink
(16.5x20.5cm 6x8in) London 1998

BURNIER Richard 1826-1884 **[14]**

$2 748 - €2 949 - £1 838 - FF19 347
Shepherdess leading the cows home Oil/canvas
(63.5x98cm 25x38in) Amsterdam 2000

BURNITZ Karl Peter 1824-1886 **[34]**

$1 617 - €1 534 - £984 - FF10 061
Am Waldrand im Taunus Öl/Leinwand (34x52cm
13x20in) Köln 1999

$1 597 - €1 789 - £1 110 - FF11 738
**Grüne Flussniederung mit Kühen und einem
Angler im Boot** Öl/Leinwand (26.5x46cm 10x18in)
Oersberg-bei Kappeln 2001

BURNS Colin W. 1944 **[108]**

$17 000 - €19 751 - £11 947 - FF129 560
Pheasants in Woodland Oil/canvas (88.5x172.5cm
34x67in) New-York 2001

$7 000 - €6 950 - £4 375 - FF45 588
Phesants and Snowdrops Oil/canvas (69x96cm
27x37in) New-York 1999

$1 996 - €1 710 - £1 200 - FF11 216
«Pheasants» Oil/canvas (30x38cm 12x15in) Aylsham,
Norfolk 1998

$1 375 - €1 290 - £850 - FF8 465
Blackgame Amongst the Birches
Watercolour/paper (35x45cm 14x18in) Aylsham,
Norfolk 1999

$206 - €231 - £140 - FF1 516
The River Bure with Windmills and Boats Print in
colors (40x60cm 16x24in) Aylsham, Norfolk 2000

BURNS Milton J. 1853-1933 **[17]**

$42 500 - €40 628 - £26 639 - FF266 504
Waiting for the Fish to School Oil/canvas
(89x139.5cm 35x54in) New-York 1999

BURNS Robert 1869-1941 **[12]**

$328 - €312 - £200 - FF2 044
Study for a Scots Ballad Gouache/paper (30x19cm
11x7in) Edinburgh 1999

BURNS William Alexander 1921-1972 **[6]**

$2 470 - €2 350 - £1 500 - FF15 413
Harbour Image II Oil/board (31x41.5cm 12x16in)
Edinburgh 1999

B

BURON Henri 1880-1969 **[73]**
- $736 - €701 - **£466** - FF4 600
  Deux mâts à quai Huile/panneau (38x45.5cm 14x17in) Douarnenez 1999
- $912 - €869 - **£578** - FF5 700
  Animation sur la cale par temps de pluie Huile/panneau (27x22cm 10x8in) Douarnenez 1999
- $515 - €480 - **£317** - FF3 150
  Bouquet d'anémones Pastel/papier (45x37cm 17x14in) Nantes 1999

BURPEE William Partridge 1846-1940 **[10]**
- $3 700 - €4 222 - **£2 571** - FF27 693
  Haystacks Oil/canvas (46x61cm 18x24in) Cleveland OH 2001
- $950 - €1 020 - **£636** - FF6 692
  Winter Scene Pastel/paper (15x10cm 6x4in) Portland ME 2000

BURR Alexander Hohenlohe 1835-1899 **[15]**
- $20 394 - €23 718 - **£14 563** - FF155 579
  Teasing grandpa Oil/canvas (84x68.5cm 33x26in) Toronto 2001
- $8 537 - €9 919 - **£6 000** - FF65 065
  The Flower Sellers Oil/canvas (40.5x30.5cm 15x12in) London 2001

BURR David XIX **[4]**
- $373 - €424 - **£260** - FF2 778
  Map illustrating the Plan of the Defences of the Wetern Engraving (54.5x38.5cm 21x15in) London 2001

BURR George Brainerd 1876-1952 **[10]**
- $6 000 - €5 140 - **£3 607** - FF33 718
  Tooker Farm, Old Lyme Oil/canvas (50x63cm 20x25in) Cleveland OH 1998

BURR George Elbert 1859-1939 **[96]**
- $4 000 - €3 636 - **£2 409** - FF23 852
  Canyon Sunset Watercolour/paper (33x25cm 13x10in) Hayden ID 1998
- $425 - €435 - **£266** - FF2 852
  Evening Arizona Etching (11x16cm 4x6in) Cleveland OH 2000

BURR John P. 1831-1893 **[41]**
- $3 200 - €3 710 - **£2 266** - FF24 336
  The Litle Pipper Oil/canvas (92x71cm 36x27in) New-York 2000
- $2 238 - €2 218 - **£1 400** - FF14 551
  The Blackberry Thorn Oil/canvas (40x30cm 15x11in) London 1999

BURRA Edward 1905-1976 **[94]**
- $17 842 - €17 201 - **£11 000** - FF112 828
  Weald of Kent Watercolour (79x136cm 31x53in) London 1999
- $360 - €332 - **£220** - FF2 178
  The Bowl of Fruit Woodcut (34x25cm 13x9in) London 1999

BURRELL & KEARSLEY Kate M. & Bernard L. XX **[1]**
- $1 411 - €1 637 - **£1 000** - FF10 735
  «Boat Race, Putney Bridge, Hammersmith, Chiswick Park» Poster (32x44cm 12x17in) London 2000

BURRELL James XIX **[7]**
- $6 000 - €6 440 - **£4 015** - FF42 246
  Windy Day Along the Coast Oil/canvas (76x127cm 30x50in) Cedar-Falls IA 2000

BURRET Léonce 1866-1915 **[5]**
- $452 - €442 - **£279** - FF2 900
  «Lire le Chat Noir» Affiche (74.5x55cm 29x21in) Paris 1999

BURRI Alberto 1915-1995 **[224]**
- $140 000 - €156 810 - **£97 272** - FF1 028 608
  «Legno e nero 4» Acrylic (160x89.5x4.5cm 62x35x1in) New-York 2001
- $68 000 - €88 116 - **£51 000** - FF578 000
  Cellotex Tecnica mista (51x71cm 20x27in) Prato 2000
- $16 800 - €21 770 - **£12 600** - FF142 800
  Combustione Tecnica mista (33x20.5cm 12x8in) Prato 2000
- $12 000 - €12 440 - **£7 200** - FF81 600
  Senza titolo Ceramic (22.5x17cm 8x6in) Milano 1999
- $1 500 - €1 555 - **£900** - FF10 200
  Muffa, Prima Stampa (31.5x39.5cm 12x15in) Roma 1999

BURRI René 1933 **[33]**
- $946 - €1 117 - **£671** - FF7 328
  «Ernesto Che Guevara, Habana, Cuba» Gelatin silver print (24.5x36cm 9x14in) Berlin 2001

BURRILL Edward E. 1835-1913 **[7]**
- $750 - €826 - **£500** - FF5 420
  View of Ipswich Bluff Lithograph (38x48cm 15x19in) Portsmouth NH 2000

BURRINGTON Arthur Alfred 1856-1925 **[17]**
- $584 - €570 - **£360** - FF3 741
  Mother and Baby Watercolour/paper (41x22cm 16x8in) London 1999

BURRINI Giovanni Antonio 1656-1727/37 **[18]**
- $13 407 - €11 407 - **£8 000** - FF74 827
  Portrait of a gentleman in a Dark Red Coat holding an open book Oil/canvas (75x57cm 29x22in) London 1998

BURROUGHS Bryson 1869-1934 **[22]**
- $760 - €731 - **£480** - FF4 794
  Holy Women at the Sepulchre Oil/canvas (76x91cm 30x36in) Cleveland OH 1999
- $1 600 - €1 903 - **£1 140** - FF12 481
  A Sleeping Nude Pastel/paper (48.5x31.5cm 19x12in) New-York 2000

BURROUGHS Margaret Taylor Goss 1917 **[5]**
- $1 000 - €1 169 - **£702** - FF7 668
  «On the Beach» Woodcut (28x36.5cm 11x14in) New-York 2000

BURROUGHS William Seward 1914-1997 **[13]**
- $2 100 - €1 814 - **£1 400** - FF11 900
  Self Portrait of an Artist Tecnica mista (56.5x34.5x4cm 22x13x1in) Prato 1998
- $2 750 - €2 851 - **£1 650** - FF18 700
  Hot Star Tecnica mista (41x20.5cm 16x8in) Prato 2000
- $2 000 - €2 333 - **£1 392** - FF15 306
  Shot Sheriff, Secret Agent Ink (40x30.5cm 15x12in) New-York 2000

BURROW Edward S.J/J.(?) XIX **[6]**
- $769 - €745 - **£480** - FF4 890
  The Eton Portfolio Etching (43x33cm 16x12in) London 1999

BURROWS Hal 1889-1965 **[7]**
- $1 000 - €1 073 - **£669** - FF7 041
  Weekend Crowd Watercolour, gouache (38x50cm 15x20in) New-York 2000

BURROWS Robert 1810-1883 [38]

🖐 **$3 735** - €4 010 - **£2 500** - FF26 304
Peep at the Orwell Oil/canvas (61x91.5cm 24x36in)
Reepham, Norwich 2000

🖐 **$1 459** - €1 579 - **£1 000** - FF10 357
A Gipsy Encampment Oil/panel (19.5x26cm
7x10in) Lenton-Lane, Nottingham 2001

BURSSENS Jan 1925 [74]

🖐 **$999** - €1 115 - **£693** - FF7 317
Trois têtes Huile/panneau (60x122cm 23x48in)
Antwerpen 2001

🖐 **$132** - €124 - **£81** - FF813
Autoportrait avec personnages Technique
mixte/papier (35x25cm 13x10in) Antwerpen 1999

BURT Charles Thomas 1823-1902 [51]

🖐 **$2 608** - €2 880 - **£1 800** - FF18 893
The Harvest, near Burton Dassett, Warwickshire
Oil/canvas (40.5x61cm 15x24in) Hockley, Birmingham
2000

🖐 **$1 124** - €1 052 - **£680** - FF6 900
The Mawddach Estuary, N.Wales Oil/panel
(17x26cm 6x10in) London 1999

BURTE Herrmann 1879-1960 [11]

🖐 **$1 303** - €1 483 - **£904** - FF9 726
Feldweg im Schwarzwald Öl/Leinwand (61x82cm
24x32in) Staufen 2000

BURTON Arthur P. XIX-XX [2]

🖐 **$10 000** - €9 597 - **£6 269** - FF62 955
Sleeping Nymph Oil/canvas (36x107cm 14x42in)
New-York 1999

BURTON Charles W. c.1807-? [1]

🖐 **$3 385** - €3 157 - **£2 100** - FF20 706
Jersey City/New York Color lithograph (35x98cm
13x38in) Billingshurst, West-Sussex 1999

BURTON Claire Eva XX [15]

🖐 **$1 049** - €1 133 - **£725** - FF7 431
**Bula Hurdle, Cheltenham, Cruising Altitude
Leads Royal and Nomadie Way** Oil/canvas
(39x49cm 15x19in) Little-Lane, Ilkley 2001

BURTON Frederick William 1816-1900 [24]

🖐 **$11 687** - €11 238 - **£7 200** - FF73 716
The Lilac Seller Watercolour (50.5x28cm 19x11in)
London 1999

BURTON Jackson XX [1]

🖐 **$847** - €982 - **£600** - FF6 441
«Bristol, GWR & LMS» Poster (102x64cm 40x25in)
London 2000

BURTON Jeff 1963 [1]

📷 **$4 250** - €4 808 - **£2 973** - FF31 537
Untitled #77, Donnie Cibachrome print
(101.5x152.5cm 39x60in) New-York 2001

BURTON Ralph Wallace 1905-1983 [74]

🖐 **$306** - €298 - **£188** - FF1 958
Glen Tay River, Perth Ontario Oil/panel (26x34cm
10x13in) Nepean, Ont. 1999

BURTON Richmond 1960 [28]

🖐 **$8 000** - €9 050 - **£5 596** - FF59 364
Untitled Oil/canvas (152.5x127cm 60x50in) New-York
2001

🖐 **$2 400** - €2 688 - **£1 667** - FF17 633
«Boiled Like a Lobster» Acrylic (66.5x50cm
26x19in) New-York 2001

🖐 **$4 000** - €3 557 - **£2 446** - FF23 333
Untitled Oil/paper (28x21.5cm 11x8in) New-York
1999

🖐 **$1 300** - €1 527 - **£923** - FF10 018
Hart Woodcut (99x63.5cm 38x25in) New-York 2000

BURTON Scott 1939-1989 [20]

🖐 **$30 000** - €34 809 - **£20 712** - FF228 330
English Arm Chair and English Chair Sculpture,
wood (103.5x65x56cm 40x25x22in) New-York 2000

🖐 **$20 000** - €19 352 - **£12 334** - FF126 938
Plywood Cubes Sculpture, wood (51x51x51cm
20x20x20in) New-York 1999

BURTON William Paton 1828-1883 [7]

🖐 **$804** - €824 - **£500** - FF5 402
Old Monastery of the Dominics, Ghenet
Watercolour (29x46cm 11x18in) Billingshurst, West-
Sussex 2000

BURWOOD George Vempley XIX-XX [8]

🖐 **$163** - €182 - **£110** - FF1 192
Wooded Landscape Oil/canvas (38x45cm 15x18in)
Aylsham, Norfolk 2000

BURY Pol 1922 [126]

🖐 **$2 971** - €2 744 - **£1 850** - FF18 000
Empreintes de violon Acrylique/papier (60x47cm
23x18in) Douai 1999

🖐 **$680** - €686 - **£424** - FF4 500
Le Chemin de fer Technique mixte (17x25.5cm
6x10in) Paris 2000

🖐 **$4 200** - €3 816 - **£2 603** - FF25 030
Entite Erectile Red Relief (39.5x39.5cm 15x15in)
New-York 1999

🖐 **$105** - €124 - **£76** - FF813
Sans titre Lithographie couleurs (38x30cm 14x11in)
Bruxelles 2001

BURY Thomas Talbot XIX [5]

🖐 **$478** - €518 - **£320** - FF3 366
**Coloured Views on the Liverpool and
Manchester Railway** Aquatint in colors (24x29cm
9x11in) London 2000

BUSACK Friedrich 1899-1933 [2]

🖐 **$36 399** - €33 999 - **£22 000** - FF223 020
Dorfstrasse bei Liethe I Oil/canvas (33x43cm
12x16in) London 1999

BUSCAGLIONE Giuseppe 1868-1928 [47]

🖐 **$2 500** - €2 592 - **£1 500** - FF17 000
Alti pascoli Olio/tavola (41.5x57cm 16x22in) Vercelli
2000

🖐 **$1 400** - €1 451 - **£840** - FF9 520
Campagna con stagno e armenti Olio/tavola
(31x44.5cm 12x17in) Torino 2000

BUSCH Ernst XIX-XX [5]

🖐 **$100** - €962 - **£617** - FF6 308
«Curaçao Senglet» Poster (128.5x90cm 50x35in)
New-York 1999

BUSCH Wilhelm 1832-1908 [100]

🖐 **$16 436** - €19 403 - **£11 673** - FF127 276
«Blätter und Blütenzweige» Oil/board
(55.5x40.5cm 21x15in) Berlin 2001

🖐 **$9 707** - €8 947 - **£5 813** - FF58 686
Streitendes Bauernpaar Öl/Karton (15.5x20cm
6x7in) Dresden 1998

🖐 **$528** - €2 454 - **£1 574** - FF16 098
**Der Teufel sitzt dem Kellermeister, einem
Mönch im Nacken** Bronze (2x8.8x10.2cm x3x4in)
Berlin 1999

🖐 **$893** - €818 - **£544** - FF5 366
Landschaft mit Kirche Pencil/paper (10x15cm
3x5in) Berlin 1999

BÜSCHELBERGER Anton XX [16]
🔨 $619 - €665 - £414 - FF4 360
Gemsengruppe Bronze (H47cm H18in) Berlin 2000

BUSCIONI Umberto 1931 [13]
$4 500 - €4 665 - £2 700 - FF30 600
Caduta degli angeli ribelli Olio/tela (200x103cm 78x40in) Prato 2000

BUSH Harry 1883-1957 [31]
$12 000 - €14 226 - £8 742 - FF93 319
The Hurrying Year Oil/canvas (101x127cm 40x50in) Chicago IL 2001

BUSH Jack Hamilton 1909-1977 [61]
$14 000 - €14 665 - £9 781 - FF104 441
Down and Across Acrylic/canvas (147.5x124.5cm 58x49in) Beverly-Hills CA 2000
$5 400 - €5 505 - £3 383 - FF36 108
Mabel's Release #5 Acrylic/canvas (77x50cm 30x19in) New-York 2001
$2 041 - €1 951 - £1 279 - FF12 799
Country Church Oil/board (21x26cm 8x10in) Vancouver, BC. 1999
$689 - €652 - £428 - FF4 280
Green Loop Silkscreen (57x76cm 22x29in) Calgary, Alberta 1999

BUSH Norton 1834-1894 [26]
$30 000 - €28 534 - £18 216 - FF187 170
Lake Tahoe Oil/canvas (61x91.5cm 24x36in) Beverly-Hills CA 1999
$2 250 - €2 625 - £1 566 - FF17 219
Tropical Moonlit Landscape Oil/board (61x23cm 24x9in) Altadena CA 2000

BUSHBY Thomas 1861-1918 [7]
$1 016 - €1 091 - £680 - FF7 154
Kirkstall Abbey near Leeds Watercolour/paper (23x35cm 9x14in) Carlisle, Cumbria 2000

BUSHFIELD William XIX [1]
$11 500 - €11 219 - £7 081 - FF73 589
Pheasant Oil/canvas (72x92cm 28x36in) Chicago IL 1999

BUSI Luigi 1838-1884 [4]
$80 325 - €83 269 - £48 195 - FF546 210
Gioie materne Olio/tela (60x45cm 23x17in) Venezia 1999

BÜSINCK Ludolph c.1590-1669 [10]
$1 500 - €1 679 - £1 044 - FF11 015
Aeneas saving his Father Anchises from Burning Troy, After Lallemand Woodcut (34.5x22cm 13x8in) New-York 2001

BUSIRI Giovan Battista 1698-1757 [64]
$17 600 - €22 806 - £13 200 - FF149 600
Paesaggio con Villa Sacchetti del Pigneto/Sepolcro di Cecilia Metella Olio/tela (39x47cm 15x18in) Roma 2000
$10 400 - €13 476 - £7 800 - FF88 400
Paesaggio mediterraneo con un sentiero boschivo con edificio sul mare Tempera/carta (22x30.5cm 8x12in) Roma 2000

BUSIRI-VICI Andrea 1817-? [2]
$2 030 - €2 134 - £1 274 - FF14 000
Rue de village Encre (28.5x42.5cm 11x16in) Paris 2000

BUSOM GRAU Simon 1927 [58]
$732 - €721 - £444 - FF4 728
Teulades i balcons Oleo/lienzo (61x50cm 24x19in) Barcelona 2000

$280 - €300 - £190 - FF1 970
Bodegón Acuarela/papel (36x44cm 14x17in) Barcelona 2001

BUSS Robert William 1804-1875 [9]
$3 250 - €2 730 - £1 910 - FF17 908
Master's Out Oil/canvas (59.5x72.5cm 23x28in) New-York 1998

BUSSCHE van den Emmanuel 1837-1908 [32]
$2 050 - €1 906 - £1 245 - FF12 500
Port de Bastia Huile/toile (73x92cm 28x36in) Marseille 1998
$739 - €694 - £456 - FF4 552
Femme vêtue de rouge Huile/panneau (42x24cm 16x9in) Antwerpen 1999

BUSSCHE van den Jacques 1925 [20]
$634 - €681 - £424 - FF4 464
Moored fishing-boats in a mediterranean harbour Oil/panel (45x37.5cm 17x14in) Amsterdam 2000
$417 - €381 - £255 - FF2 500
Pêcheurs au mouillage Huile/carton (28x40cm 11x15in) Aubagne 1999

BUSSE Georg Heinrich 1810-1868 [25]
$171 - €204 - £122 - FF1 341
Ausbruch des Etnas im Jahr 1838 Radierung (16.8x24.5cm 6x9in) Berlin 2000

BUSSOLINO Vittorio 1853-1922 [13]
$720 - €933 - £540 - FF6 120
Paesaggio con cascinali Olio/cartone (24x33cm 9x12in) Firenze 2000

BUSSON Charles 1822-1908 [10]
$2 118 - €2 363 - £1 478 - FF15 500
Le troupeau s'abreuvant Huile/toile (61x74cm 24x29in) Versailles 2001

BUSSON DU MAURIER Georges L. Palmella 1834-1896 [35]
$805 - €687 - £480 - FF4 507
Young Girl Tearing Down a Poster/Tradesman and Maid at the Entrance Ink/paper (12x15cm 4x5in) London 1998

BUSSON Georges Louis Ch. 1859-1933 [95]
$5 426 - €5 183 - £3 417 - FF34 000
A l'écurie Huile/toile (65x81cm 25x31in) Deauville 1999
$533 - €488 - £326 - FF3 200
Le départ pour la chasse Gouache/papier (40x32cm 15x12in) Dijon 1999
$459 - €534 - £322 - FF3 500
Sanglier à la ferme Lithographie couleurs (51.5x72cm 20x28in) Blois 2001

BUSSON Marcel 1913 [30]
$1 956 - €2 287 - £1 396 - FF15 000
Menace d'orage sur le Djebel Sarhro, region d'El Kelãa M'Gouma Huile/toile (60x73cm 23x28in) Paris 2001

BUSSY Simon Albert 1869-1954 [70]
$3 319 - €3 724 - £2 300 - FF24 425
Swiss Landscape Pastel/paper (19.5x14.5cm 7x5in) London 2000
$1 273 - €1 358 - £850 - FF8 911
Bestiaire Pochoir (33x25.5cm 12x10in) London 2000

BUSTAMANTE Jean-Marc 1952 [6]
$24 000 - €23 222 - £14 800 - FF152 325
Lum 6.91 Silkscreen (140x185cm 55x72in) New-York 1999

BUSTARD William 1894-1973 **[7]**
🖌 **$2 922** - €3 212 - **£1 872** - FF21 068
Castle Hill, Townsville from the North Shore
Watercolour/paper (36.5x50cm 14x19in) Melbourne 2000

BUSTI Agostino il Bambaia 1483-1548 **[1]**
🗿 **$20 000** - €20 733 - **£12 000** - FF136 000
Pastore con capra che aillatta un cane Marbre (40x30x22cm 15x11x8in) Firenze 2001

BUTAKOV Maksim Kharitonovich 1916 **[2]**
🖼 **$4 542** - €4 789 - **£3 000** - FF31 413
Winter Sunlight in the Frozen Forest Oil/canvas (56x39.5cm 22x15in) London 2000

BUTHAUD René 1886-1986 **[116]**
🖼 **$37 080** - €36 588 - **£22 848** - FF240 000
Femme à la gazelle Technique mixte (110x178cm 43x70in) Paris 1999
🖼 **$3 090** - €3 049 - **£1 904** - FF20 000
Femme en buste à la couronne blanche
Technique mixte (52x37cm 20x14in) Paris 1999
🖼 **$1 944** - €2 058 - **£1 286** - FF13 500
Femme à la corne d'abondance Terracotta (68x20.5x16cm 26x8x6in) Neuilly-sur-Seine 2000
🖌 **$895** - €1 067 - **£638** - FF7 000
Le tapir, projet décoratif Gouache/papier (16.5x20.5cm 6x8in) Soissons 2000

BÜTHE Michael 1944-1994 **[116]**
🖼 **$8 854** - €9 715 - **£5 882** - FF63 724
Ohne Titel Mixed media (195x300cm 76x118in) München 2000
🖼 **$2 411** - €2 812 - **£1 692** - FF18 446
«Il Pittore» Öl/Leinwand (50x73.5cm 19x28in) Köln 2001
🖌 **$964** - €920 - **£602** - FF6 037
Ohne Titel Gouache (45x55x4.5cm 17x21x1in) Köln 1999
🗔 **$134** - €112 - **£79** - FF737
Ohne Titel Radierung (39.3x29.5cm 15x11in) Hamburg 1998

BUTI Camillo 1747-1808 **[2]**
🗔 **$737** - €767 - **£465** - FF5 030
Tanzende im blauen Schleiergewand mit winzigen Becken in den Händen Kupferstich (37.5x26cm 14x10in) Heidelberg 2000

BUTLER Charles Ernest 1864-? **[43]**
🖼 **$12 806** - €14 879 - **£9 000** - FF97 597
Britannia and her Allies Oil/canvas (229.5x154cm 90x60in) London 2001
🖼 **$260** - €288 - **£180** - FF1 886
Bluebells in Kew Gardens Oil/board (23x30.5cm 9x12in) London 2001

BUTLER David 1898-1997 **[20]**
🪨 **$200** - €219 - **£135** - FF1 439
3 Stars Metal (27x25cm 11x10in) New-Orleans LA 2000

BUTLER Elizabeth Southerd. 1846-1933 **[12]**
🖌 **$1 969** - €1 875 - **£1 250** - FF12 300
Escorting Wild Ponies into Glencar, Co. Kerry Watercolour/paper (24.5x35cm 9x13in) Billingshurst, West-Sussex 1999

BUTLER Fray Guillermo 1880-1961 **[4]**
🖼 **$18 000** - €17 466 - **£11 422** - FF114 571
Scène de Gisors Oil/hardboard (63x80cm 24x31in) Buenos-Aires 1999

BUTLER Herbert E. act.1881-1921 **[31]**
🖌 **$747** - €803 - **£500** - FF5 265
The Days Catch Watercolour (22.5x30.5cm 8x12in) London 2000

BUTLER Horacio 1897-1983 **[1]**
🖌 **$1 800** - €2 047 - **£1 257** - FF13 428
Calle de París Acuarela/papel (26x38cm 10x14in) Buenos-Aires 2000

BUTLER Howard Russel 1856-1934 **[50]**
🖼 **$1 100** - €1 256 - **£775** - FF8 238
Bald Head Cliff, Orgunquet Maine Oil/board (42x52cm 16x20in) Boston MA 2001
🖼 **$500** - €588 - **£358** - FF3 856
Montecito, California Oil/board (25x35cm 10x14in) Philadelphia PA 2001
🖌 **$325** - €370 - **£229** - FF2 424
Montecito, California, Entrance courtyard of Gillespie residence Watercolour/paper (27x33cm 11x13in) Philadelphia PA 2001

BUTLER James 1931 **[21]**
🖼 **$3 758** - €4 377 - **£2 600** - FF28 712
Standing Girl Bronze (H36.5cm H14in) London 2000

BUTLER James P. 1893-1976 **[21]**
🖼 **$1 700** - €1 456 - **£1 022** - FF9 553
Hillcrest, Candor NY Oil/canvas (64x74cm 25x29in) Cincinnati OH 1998

BÜTLER Joseph Niklaus 1822-1885 **[28]**
🖼 **$30 000** - €28 506 - **£18 252** - FF186 987
Alpine Vista Oil/canvas (136x188cm 53x74in) New-York 1999
🖼 **$8 204** - €6 941 - **£4 900** - FF45 528
Paysage Suisse Huile/toile (105x47cm 41x18in) Bruxelles 1998

BUTLER Mary 1865-1946 **[26]**
🖼 **$800** - €941 - **£575** - FF6 171
Western lansdcape with mountain range Oil/canvas (40x50cm 16x20in) Hatfield PA 2001

BUTLER Mildred Anne 1858-1941 **[132]**
🖼 **$12 658** - €10 798 - **£7 543** - FF70 833
Pigeons at the Pump, Kilmurry Oil/canvas (50.5x40.5cm 19x15in) Dublin 1998
🖼 **$3 409** - €2 860 - **£2 000** - FF18 761
Two Figures in a Garden Path Oil/canvas/board (17x12cm 7x5in) Co. Kilkenny 1998
🖌 **$3 772** - €4 317 - **£2 594** - FF28 318
Cattle Grazing in the Reeks, Co.Kerry Watercolour/paper (25x35cm 10x14in) Dublin 2000

BUTLER Reg, Reginald 1913-1981 **[73]**
🖼 **$60 014** - €57 856 - **£37 000** - FF379 512
Tall Woman Iron (H103cm H40in) London 1999
🖼 **$2 500** - €2 098 - **£1 466** - FF13 759
Standing female Nude Bronze (H54.5cm H21in) New-York 1998
🖌 **$1 606** - €1 534 - **£1 003** - FF10 061
Figure in Sling Graphite (94.2x68.4cm 37x26in) Köln 1999

BUTLER Theodore Earl 1861-1936 **[38]**
🖼 **$40 000** - €43 776 - **£27 592** - FF287 152
Suzanne and her Children Oil/canvas (190.5x110.5cm 75x43in) New-York 2001
🖼 **$30 000** - €29 736 - **£18 765** - FF195 057
The Epte, Giverny Oil/canvas (60.5x73cm 23x28in) New-York 1999

BUTLER Thomas c.1730-c.1760 **[8]**
🖼 **$68 051** - €70 384 - **£43 000** - FF461 686
The Godolphin Arabian Oil/canvas (81x124.5cm 31x49in) London 2000

B

BUTLER Tony 1959 **[8]**
- **$3 747** - €3 117 - **£2 200** - FF20 446
  Cheetah Cubs at Play Oil/canvas (72x130cm 28x51in) London 1998

BUTMAN Frederick A. 1820-1871 **[7]**
- **$6 500** - €6 182 - **£3 946** - FF40 553
  On Bear River Oil/canvas (71x101.5cm 27x39in) Beverly-Hills CA 1999
- **$2 900** - €2 502 - **£1 742** - FF16 412
  Deer in a River Landscape Oil/canvas (20.5x33cm 8x12in) Boston MA 1998

BUTRAGUEÑO Felipe XX **[52]**
- **$198** - €216 - **£136** - FF1 418
  Bodegón con pimiento rojo Oleo/tabla (38x46cm 14x18in) Madrid 2000

BUTTERFIELD Deborah 1949 **[18]**
- **$32 500** - €36 766 - **£22 737** - FF241 166
  Fractal Metal (86.5x274.5x152.5cm 34x108x60in) New-York 2001

BUTTERI Achille XIX-XX **[7]**
- **$3 800** - €4 239 - **£2 487** - FF27 809
  «Cycles Perfecta» Poster (153.5x115cm 60x45in) New-York 2000

BUTTERSACK Bernhard 1858-1925 **[50]**
- **$1 600** - €1 612 - **£997** - FF10 576
  Treed Landscape Oil/board (48x67cm 19x26in) Wilton NH 2000
- **$1 947** - €2 301 - **£1 309** - FF15 092
  Sommerlandschaft mit Wäscherin am Fluss Öl/Leinwand (35.5x28.5cm 13x11in) Stuttgart 2000

BUTTERSWORTH James Edward 1817-1894 **[93]**
- **$110 000** - €105 156 - **£68 948** - FF689 777
  American Shipping Displays the Flag Oil/canvas (45.5x61cm 17x24in) New-York 1999
- **$40 250** - €37 850 - **£25 313** - FF248 278
  Yacht race in Manhattan's upper bay Oil/canvas (23x30cm 9x12in) Fairfield ME 1999

BUTTERSWORTH Thomas 1768-1842 **[128]**
- **$12 913** - €11 954 - **£8 000** - FF78 415
  British Men of War under Way in the Straits of Messina Oil/canvas (44.5x60cm 17x23in) London 1999
- **$4 417** - €4 741 - **£3 100** - FF31 099
  British Frigate under Full Sail Oil/panel (25.5x31cm 10x12in) London 2001
- **$4 200** - €4 232 - **£2 618** - FF27 762
  Ships of the Line Watercolour/paper (48x66cm 18x25in) New-York 2000

BUTTERSWORTH Thomas, Jnr. XVIII-XIX **[6]**
- **$6 000** - €5 336 - **£3 669** - FF34 999
  Capture of a Barbary Corsair Oil/canvas (35x40.5cm 13x15in) New-York 1999

BUTTERY Edwin XIX **[35]**
- **$482** - €449 - **£300** - FF2 946
  Figures on a wooded Track Oil/canvas (20.5x40.5cm 8x15in) London 1999

BUTTI Argelia 1855-1924 **[1]**
- **$4 277** - €5 087 - **£3 052** - FF33 369
  Der Dank der Verliebten Öl/Leinwand (87x52cm 34x20in) Wien 2000

BUTTI Lorenzo 1805-1860 **[3]**
- **$1 825** - €2 045 - **£1 258** - FF13 415
  Schiffbruch auf stürmischer See Öl/Leinwand (29.4x41.5cm 11x16in) Hamburg 2000

BÜTTNER Erich 1889-1936 **[53]**
- **$1 589** - €1 503 - **£990** - FF9 861
  Porträt des Malers Emil Orlik Öl/Leinwand (90x66cm 35x25in) Praha 2000
- **$179** - €153 - **£107** - FF1 006
  Berlin, Kurfürstenstrasse Radierung (17.7x23.2cm 6x9in) Berlin 1998

BÜTTNER Hans / Gerhard Hans XIX **[11]**
- **$6 139** - €7 044 - **£4 200** - FF46 208
  Riders at a Cottage Door Oil/panel (16x25cm 6x9in) London 2000

BÜTTNER Werner 1954 **[18]**
- **$10 954** - €12 935 - **£7 777** - FF84 851
  «Mutwillig zerstörte Telefonzellen» Öl/Leinwand (189.5x149.5cm 74x58in) Berlin 2001

BUTTON Albert Prentice 1872-1934 **[34]**
- **$1 200** - €1 154 - **£740** - FF7 569
  Study, Beach Bluffs, Deveraux, Maas Oil/canvas (22x31cm 8x12in) Boston MA 1999
- **$950** - €986 - **£623** - FF6 469
  Corn Shocks Watercolour, gouache (14x10.5cm 5x4in) Boston MA 2000

BUTTRICK Charles Henry 1851-1927 **[7]**
- **$1 000** - €947 - **£622** - FF6 209
  Mill beside the River/Bridge over the River Oil/canvas (55x35cm 22x14in) Bolton MA 1999

BUTZMANN Manfred 1942 **[11]**
- **$82** - €92 - **£57** - FF603
  «Berliner Türme» Farblithographie (35x46cm 13x18in) Berlin 2001

BUUREN van Meeuwis 1902-1992 **[13]**
- **$725** - €681 - **£448** - FF4 464
  Woelige zee Oil/canvas (68x119cm 26x46in) Rotterdam 1999

BUVELOT Abraham Louis 1814-1888 **[54]**
- **$46 998** - €53 152 - **£33 075** - FF348 651
  Between Western Port bay and Dromana Oil/canvas (48x71cm 18x27in) Malvern, Victoria 2001
- **$5 900** - €6 501 - **£3 961** - FF42 641
  Towards Melbourne Oil/canvas/board (17x18cm 6x7in) Malvern, Victoria 2000
- **$2 083** - €2 431 - **£1 450** - FF15 946
  The Long Road Home Watercolour/paper (32x23.5cm 12x9in) Melbourne 2000

BUX Allah 1895-1978 **[9]**
- **$18 678** - €20 050 - **£12 500** - FF131 520
  The Moonlight Meeting Oil/canvas (75x103cm 29x40in) London 2000
- **$23 883** - €23 125 - **£15 000** - FF151 687
  Sohni Coloured chalks/paper (54.5x37cm 21x14in) London 1999

BUXIN Stephan 1909 **[2]**
- **$3 250** - €3 031 - **£2 016** - FF19 881
  Pierre on one Foot Bronze (H37cm H14in) New-York 1999

BUXTON Robert Hugh 1871-? **[9]**
- **$562** - €556 - **£350** - FF3 647
  The Berkley Hunt, Gloucestershire Pencil (26x36cm 10x14in) London 1999

BUYONG Dzukifli 1948 **[2]**
- **$7 032** - €7 086 - **£4 383** - FF46 478
  Patong-Patong - Dragonfly Oil/canvas/board (86x63cm 33x24in) Singapore 2000

BUYS Bob 1912-1970 **[25]**
🖼 $1 380 - €1 361 - **£849** - FF8 929
Het Anker Oil/canvas (47.5x65cm 18x25in)
Amsterdam 1999
🖋 $553 - €544 - **£355** - FF3 571
A Portrait of Maria Ruiz Watercolour/paper
(53x36cm 20x14in) Amsterdam 1999

BUYS Jacob 1724-1801 **[19]**
🖋 $2 559 - €2 556 - **£1 600** - FF16 769
Das Gefühl Gouache/papier (22.5x18.8cm 8x7in)
Köln 1999

BUYSSE Georges 1864-1916 **[16]**
🖼 $6 192 - €5 949 - **£3 816** - FF39 024
Le dock à Gand Huile/toile (47.5x76cm 18x29in)
Bruxelles 1999

BUYTEWECH Willem Pietersz. 1585-1625/27 **[5]**
🖋 $1 794 - €1 081 - **£1 081** - FF10 167
An Elegant Couple Ink (16x10.5cm 6x4in)
Amsterdam 1998
🗓 $6 000 - €6 738 - **£3 890** - FF44 196
**Landscape with a Ruined Tower, Ruins of
Brederode Castle near Haarlem** Etching
(8.5x12.5cm 3x4in) New-York 2000

BUZON de Frédéric Marius 1879-1958 **[39]**
🖼 $2 355 - €2 287 - **£1 455** - FF15 000
**La Tour de l'Horloge, place de France,
Casablanca** Huile/panneau (45x55cm 17x21in) Paris
1999

BUZZELLI Joseph Anthony 1907-1982 **[6]**
🖋 $5 000 - €4 683 - **£3 074** - FF30 720
In the Harem Watercolour/paper (82.5x61cm 32x24in)
New-York 1999

BUZZI Arturo XIX **[9]**
🖋 $1 059 - €1 228 - **£750** - FF8 058
The Love Letter Watercolour (37x54.5cm 14x21in)
London 2000

BUZZI Daniele, Dan 1890-1974 **[20]**
🗓 $155 - €181 - **£106** - FF1 190
«Tessin» Poster (101.5x64.5cm 39x25in) Hoorn 2000

BUZZI Tommaso 1900-1981 **[2]**
🔨 $6 821 - €7 925 - **£4 794** - FF51 985
Vogel Sculpture, glass (H26.5cm H10in) München
2001

BYARS James Lee 1932-1997 **[23]**
🖼 $16 000 - €16 123 - **£9 974** - FF105 760
Star Mixed media (166.5x157.5cm 65x62in) New-York
2000
🔨 $29 886 - €32 080 - **£20 000** - FF210 432
The Head of Plato Marble (175x48.5x48.5cm
68x19x19in) London 2000
🖋 $2 476 - €2 659 - **£1 657** - FF17 440
Tantnt, Things are neither this nor that Drawing
(67.5x49cm 26x19in) Köln 2000

BYATT Edwin 1888-1948 **[17]**
🗓 $988 - €1 146 - **£700** - FF7 519
«North East Dales, LNER» Poster (102x127cm
40x50in) London 2000

BYE de Marcus 1639-c.1690 **[14]**
🗓 $150 - €179 - **£107** - FF1 173
Schafe Radierung (11.9x14.7cm 4x5in) Königstein
2000

BYE Ranulph de Bayeux 1916 **[40]**
🖼 $1 100 - €1 272 - **£778** - FF8 347
Barn Interior Oil/canvas (35x53cm 14x21in) Hatfield
PA 2000

🖼 $1 800 - €2 082 - **£1 274** - FF13 659
Pond Reflections Oil/board (22x35cm 9x14in)
Hatfield PA 2000
🖋 $800 - €901 - **£554** - FF5 913
Winter Landscape with Old Cart
Watercolour/paper (36x26cm 14x10in) Hatfield PA 2000

BYLANDT de Alfred Edouard 1829-1890 **[29]**
🖼 $1 636 - €1 500 - **£1 000** - FF9 839
Travellers on an Alpine Pass Oil/panel (51.5x47cm
20x18in) London 1999
🖼 $4 288 - €4 878 - **£2 976** - FF32 000
Lac de Genève Huile/panneau (31x45cm 12x17in)
Fontainebleau 2000

BYLERT van Jan Harmensz. 1597/98-1671 **[33]**
🖼 $33 110 - €35 029 - **£21 000** - FF229 775
**Young Man, half-length, wearing a Breastplate
and Brooch** Oil/panel (50x40.5cm 19x15in) London
2000

BYLES William Hounsom 1872-? **[15]**
🖼 $2 801 - €3 103 - **£1 900** - FF20 352
Picking Flowers/Arranging Flowers Oil/board
(24.5x19.5cm 9x7in) Billingshurst, West-Sussex 2000
🖋 $3 711 - €3 408 - **£2 300** - FF22 358
Finish of St. Leger Stakes Watercolour (21x43.5cm
8x17in) West-Yorshire 1999

BYNG Robert 1666-1720 **[5]**
🖼 $15 622 - €15 289 - **£10 000** - FF100 287
Portrait of the Hon William and Fulwar Craven
Oil/canvas (124x99cm 48x38in) London 1999

BYRNE John / Patrick 1940 **[22]**
🖼 $1 392 - €1 408 - **£850** - FF9 237
Being and nothingness Acrylic (31x31cm 12x12in)
Sighthill 2000
🖋 $444 - €496 - **£300** - FF3 251
The Magi Gouache/paper (12x13cm 4x5in) Edinburgh
2000

BYRNE Samuel Michael, Sam 1883-1978 **[36]**
🖼 $2 178 - €2 443 - **£1 512** - FF16 026
«Dust Storm» Oil/board (58x89.5cm 22x35in)
Melbourne 2001

BYRON Frederick George c.1764-1792 **[4]**
🗓 $528 - €623 - **£364** - FF4 087
The Prince's Bow Aquatinta (21x190cm 8x74in)
Bern 2000

BYRON Michael 1954 **[38]**
🔨 $8 000 - €9 282 - **£5 523** - FF60 888
Bird Thief Installation (267x401x122cm
105x157x48in) New-York 2000

BYSS Johann Rudolf 1660-1738 **[11]**
🖼 $30 178 - €25 503 - **£18 000** - FF167 286
**A Hunting Scene with Lynwes attacking a Roe
Deer** Oil/canvas (110x137cm 43x53in) London 1998
🖼 $23 508 - €27 441 - **£16 596** - FF180 000
Bouquet de fleurs Huile/toile (86x79cm 33x31in)
Paris 2000
🖼 $101 258 - €87 557 - **£60 197** - FF574 339
**Gegenstücke : Riesenschnecke mit Blumen
und Fink/Grosse Jakobsmuschel** Öl/Leinwand
(44.5x35cm 17x13in) Zürich 1998
🖋 $5 894 - €5 466 - **£3 600** - FF35 856
A Large Leaf Watercolour (29x24cm 11x9in) London
1998

BYSTRÖM Johan Niklas 1783-1848 **[3]**
🔨 $35 685 - €33 971 - **£22 326** - FF222 833
Salamis Marble (H89cm H35in) Stockholm 1999

BYUN CHONGGON 1948 **[1]**
$4 000 - €4 691 - **£2 854** - FF30 769
Pablo de Sarasate Carmen fantasy, Op.25 Mixed media (76x25.5x9cm 29x10x3in) New-York 2000

BYUN KWAN-SHIK 1899-1976 **[1]**
$5 500 - €5 309 - **£3 407** - FF34 822
Landscapes Coloured inks/paper (127x31.5cm 50x12in) New-York 1999

BYWATER Katherine D.M. XIX-XX **[2]**
$6 528 - €6 198 - **£4 000** - FF40 653
The Girl at the Spinning Wheel Oil/canvas (95.5x74cm 37x29in) London 1999

BYZANTIOS Pericles 1893-1972 **[10]**
$11 275 - €10 454 - **£6 800** - FF68 576
Reclining Nude Oil/canvas (60x121cm 23x47in) London 1999

C

CABAILLOT-LASSALLE Camille Léopold 1839-? **[16]**
$7 593 - €7 775 - **£4 768** - FF51 000
Le bol de lait Huile/panneau (56x44.5cm 22x17in) Lille 2000

CABALLERO José 1916-1991 **[169]**
$1 982 - €1 952 - **£1 235** - FF12 805
Menina Técnica mixta/cartón (68x48cm 26x18in) Madrid 1999
$1 008 - €1 081 - **£684** - FF7 092
Puente del ferrocarril Oleo/lienzo (24x33cm 9x12in) Madrid 2001
$1 147 - €1 351 - **£810** - FF8 865
Boceto para decorado de la Suite Iberia, VII Triana Acuarela, gouache/papel (41x57cm 16x22in) Madrid 2000
$162 - €180 - **£111** - FF1 182
Composición Grabado (50x86cm 19x33in) Madrid 2001

CABALLERO Luis 1943-1995 **[81]**
$2 678 - €2 744 - **£1 666** - FF18 000
Dos d'homme nu assis Huile/papier (106x75.5cm 41x29in) Paris 2000
$1 538 - €1 332 - **£933** - FF8 736
A Nude Gouache (57x77cm 22x30in) Amsterdam 1998

CABALLERO Máximo Juderías 1867-1951 **[16]**
$11 400 - €11 412 - **£7 030** - FF74 860
Galantería Oleo/lienzo (54x65cm 21x25in) Madrid 2000

CABALLERO Y VILLAROEL José 1842-c.1905 **[3]**
$7 200 - €7 208 - **£4 440** - FF47 280
El rincón de la costura Oleo/tabla (42x32cm 16x12in) Madrid 2000

CABANAS OTEIZA Angel 1875-1964 **[22]**
$2 025 - €2 252 - **£1 350** - FF14 775
Paisaje Oleo/lienzo (49.5x60cm 19x23in) Madrid 2000
$1 336 - €1 220 - **£812** - FF8 000
Couple basque Aquarelle, gouache/papier (28.5x37cm 11x14in) Biarritz 1998

CABANE Edouard 1857-? **[5]**
$5 500 - €4 768 - **£3 361** - FF31 277
The Bather Oil/canvas (55.5x32.5cm 21x12in) New-York 1999

CABANEL Alexandre 1823-1889 **[54]**
$50 000 - €55 838 - **£32 020** - FF366 275
Queen Vashti Oil/canvas (130x99cm 51x38in) New-York 2000
$9 552 - €8 842 - **£5 916** - FF58 000
Portrait de femme Huile/toile (123x88cm 48x34in) Paris 1999
$789 - €884 - **£548** - FF5 800
Naissance de Louis XIII à Fontainebleau le 27/09/1601, d'après Rubens Huile/toile (40.5x32cm 15x12in) Argenteuil 2001
$1 105 - €1 239 - **£750** - FF8 129
Study of a Nude in Profile, the Left Leg Raised Black chalk (42x30cm 16x11in) London 2000

CABAÑES Feliú XVIII **[3]**
$12 600 - €13 515 - **£8 550** - FF88 650
Bodegón de caza Oleo/lienzo (63x76cm 24x29in) Madrid 2001

CABANYES de Alexandre 1877-1972 **[19]**
$9 600 - €9 010 - **£6 000** - FF59 100
Barcas de pesca en la playa de Vilanova Oleo/cartón (70x80cm 27x31in) Barcelona 1999

CABAT Louis 1812-1893 **[83]**
$5 237 - €5 946 - **£3 638** - FF39 000
Scène de la vie champêtre Huile/toile (60x100cm 23x39in) Barbizon 2001
$1 129 - €976 - **£682** - FF6 400
L'arbre Huile/panneau (15x22cm 5x8in) Barbizon 1998
$471 - €457 - **£293** - FF3 000
En forêt de Saint-Germain Aquarelle/papier (19x24cm 7x9in) Fontainebleau 1999

CABEL van der Adriaen c.1631-1705 **[43]**
$37 789 - €35 063 - **£22 678** - FF230 000
Port méditerranéen animé de marchands turcs Huile/toile (101x143.5cm 39x56in) Paris 1999
$11 044 - €12 383 - **£7 500** - FF81 230
Mediterranean Harbour Scene with Figures Oil/canvas (93x53.5cm 23x36in) London 2000
$15 989 - €17 989 - **£11 009** - FF118 000
Pêcheurs sur un lac Huile/toile (19.5x31cm 7x12in) Paris 2000
$1 651 - €1 588 - **£1 017** - FF10 418
Italianate Buildings on a Rocky Rise/Hersman with Cattle Wash (14.5x19.5cm 5x7in) Amsterdam 1999

CABIANCA Vincenzo 1827-1902 **[49]**
$7 000 - €7 257 - **£4 200** - FF47 600
Due giovani donne in un interno Olio/tela (67.5x54.5cm 26x21in) Milano 1999
$4 000 - €5 183 - **£3 000** - FF34 000
Paesaggio dei dintorni di Firenze Olio/cartone (16x24cm 6x9in) Roma 2001
$6 000 - €6 824 - **£4 192** - FF44 760
Nuns Conversing Watercolour/paper (49x28cm 19x11in) Mystic CT 2000

CABIÉ Louis Alexandre 1854-1939 **[206]**
$1 092 - €1 220 - **£760** - FF8 000
Vallée de la Veyzère Huile/panneau (37x52cm 14x20in) Paris 2001
$712 - €747 - **£471** - FF4 900
La Guichardière près de Thénac Huile/toile (31x40cm 12x15in) Royan 2000
$439 - €427 - **£273** - FF2 800
Le Sud-Ouest sous la neige Gouache/papier (40.5x50cm 15x19in) Fontainebleau 1999

C

CABOT William Channing 1868-1932 **[1]**
🖌 $4 500 - €4 185 - **£2 786** - FF27 452
  Red Dory Ashore Watercolour/paper (27x43cm
  11x17in) Nantucket MA 1999

CABRAL AGUADO Y BEJARANO Manuel 1827-1891 **[39]**
😊 $21 000 - €23 452 - **£13 448** - FF153 835
  In the Artist's Studio Oil/canvas (66.5x48.5cm
  26x19in) New-York 2000
😊 $151 - €168 - **£103** - FF1 103
  Semana Santa Tinta (30x20cm 11x7in) Madrid 2001

CABRÉ Manuel 1890-1984 **[17]**
😊 $52 500 - €51 081 - **£32 313** - FF335 070
  Paisaje Del Avila Oil/canvas (70.5x113cm 27x44in)
  New-York 1999
😊 $2 200 - €2 296 - **£1 387** - FF15 059
  Boy Pushing Wheelbarrow Oil/canvas/board
  (37x31.5cm 14x12in) New-York 2000

CABRERA Ben 1942 **[5]**
😊 $20 086 - €22 808 - **£13 748** - FF149 611
  Waiting for the Monsoon Oil/canvas (135x70cm
  53x27in) Singapore 2000

CABRERA Miguel 1695-1768 **[25]**
😊 $9 120 - €9 610 - **£5 760** - FF63 040
  La Coronación de la Virgen Oleo/lienzo
  (46.5x35cm 18x13in) Madrid 2000

CABRERA MORENO Servando 1923-1981 **[41]**
😊 $27 000 - €26 270 - **£16 618** - FF172 322
  Panorama de plenilunio Oil/canvas (91.5x152.5cm
  36x60in) New-York 1999
😊 $9 000 - €7 771 - **£5 490** - FF50 974
  Corolas Oil/canvas (81.5x81.5cm 32x32in) Miami FL
  1999
🖌 $192 - €180 - **£120** - FF1 182
  Composición Tinta/papel (45x61cm 17x24in) Madrid
  1999

CABRERA Ricardo Lopez 1864-1950 **[16]**
😊 $3 000 - €3 478 - **£2 125** - FF22 815
  The Comforts of the Kitchen Oil/canvas
  (56.5x66.5cm 22x26in) New-York 2000

CABUZEL Auguste Hector 1836-? **[3]**
😊 $7 000 - €8 232 - **£5 019** - FF53 997
  Training for Tea Oil/canvas/board (62x52cm 24x20in)
  New-York 2001

CACCAVELLO Annibale 1515-1570 **[1]**
🗿 $33 320 - €43 177 - **£24 990** - FF283 220
  La Carità Marbre (H125cm H49in) Napoli 2001

CACCIA IL MONCALVO Guglielmo 1568-1625 **[22]**
😊 $46 884 - €40 502 - **£31 256** - FF265 676
  La Madonna con Bambino e San Giorgio
  Olio/tela (278x174cm 109x68in) Pavia 1998
😊 $15 000 - €15 550 - **£9 000** - FF102 000
  Madonna col Bambino Olio/tavola (27x19.5cm
  10x7in) Milano 1999
🖌 $10 350 - €11 434 - **£7 177** - FF75 000
  Études de figures Encre (23x27.5cm 9x10in) Paris
  2001

CACCIA Orsola Maddalena 1596-1676 **[9]**
😊 $85 530 - €73 887 - **£57 020** - FF484 670
  Sibilla Libica Olio/tela (108x77cm 42x30in) Pavia
  1998

CACCIARELLI Umberto XIX **[5]**
🖌 $7 092 - €6 860 - **£4 374** - FF45 000
  Le brocanteur au caftan rose Aquarelle/papier
  (35x25.5cm 13x10in) Paris 1999

CACCIARELLI Victor XIX-XX **[12]**
😊 $14 440 - €16 272 - **£10 000** - FF106 737
  The Cardinal's first Visit Oil/canvas (46.5x82.5cm
  18x32in) London 2000
😊 $2 242 - €2 629 - **£1 600** - FF17 247
  Oriental Merchant Watercolour/paper (36x25cm
  14x9in) Manchester 2001

CACCIARINI Gianni 1941 **[4]**
😊 $480 - €622 - **£360** - FF4 080
  Natura morta Olio/carta (30x40cm 11x15in) Prato
  2000

CACHET Carel Adolph Lion 1864-1945 **[7]**
📜 $518 - €590 - **£359** - FF3 869
  «Kalender 1893» Woodcut (39.9x32.4cm 15x12in)
  Haarlem 2000

CACHOUD François Charles 1866-1943 **[158]**
😊 $543 - €2 973 - **£2 078** - FF19 500
  Bord de rivière Huile/toile (66x82cm 25x32in) Lyon
  1998
😊 $1 421 - €1 403 - **£875** - FF9 200
  Clair de lune Huile/panneau (22x27cm 8x10in)
  Aubagne 1999
🖌 $5 104 - €5 453 - **£3 476** - FF35 772
  Clair de lune Pastel (65.5x80.5cm 25x31in) Lokeren
  2001
📜 $600 - €644 - **£401** - FF4 224
  «Le Mont-Blanc» Poster (107x78cm 42x30in) Los-
  Angeles CA 2000

CADEL Eugène c.1860-1940 **[31]**
😊 $8 500 - €9 521 - **£5 906** - FF62 454
  La véranda Oil/canvas (131x174.5cm 51x68in) New-
  York 2001
😊 $2 487 - €2 134 - **£1 503** - FF14 000
  Le Picadore Huile/toile (80x98cm 31x38in)
  Valenciennes 1998

CADELL Florence St. John 1877-1966 **[13]**
😊 $4 328 - €4 089 - **£2 700** - FF26 819
  Dining in the Square Oil/canvas (51x84cm 20x33in)
  Perthshire 1999
😊 $814 - €909 - **£550** - FF5 960
  Study of an Infant in a Cot Oil/panel (24.5x31.5cm
  9x12in) Edinburgh 2000

CADELL Francis C. Boileau 1883-1937 **[161]**
😊 $53 225 - €45 599 - **£32 000** - FF299 110
  Still life of roses Oil/board (45x37cm 17x14in)
  Edinburgh 1998
😊 $42 519 - €50 390 - **£30 000** - FF330 540
  Iona Oil/panel (36x44cm 14x17in) London 2000
🖌 $8 038 - €8 963 - **£5 500** - FF58 793
  On the Clyde Watercolour (17x24cm 6x9in)
  Perthshire 2000

CADENASSO Giuseppe 1854-1918 **[28]**
😊 $4 100 - €4 782 - **£2 878** - FF31 366
  Figures in a Marin Co. Eucalyptus Landscape
  Oil/canvas (35x50cm 14x20in) San Rafael CA 2000
🖌 $2 750 - €2 803 - **£1 723** - FF18 388
  Landscape Pastel/board (17x22cm 7x9in) Altadena
  CA 2000

CADES Giuseppe 1750-1799 **[24]**
😊 $35 000 - €34 984 - **£21 381** - FF229 477
  **Saint Teresa Dictating her Memoirs in the
  Presence of Saint Gonzaga** Oil/canvas (229x135cm
  90x53in) New-York 1999
😊 $48 601 - €41 351 - **£29 000** - FF271 248
  The Adoration of the Shepherds Oil/canvas
  (90x67cm 35x26in) London 1998

C

🖊 **$9 000** - €9 641 - **£6 146** - FF63 239
Winged Victory Wash (42x12.5cm 16x4in) New-York 2001

CADMAN Dorothy A. act.1914-1927 **[5]**
🖼 **$650** - €758 - **£450** - FF4 971
The Picnic Oil/canvas (61x91.5cm 24x36in) London 2000

CADMUS Paul 1904-1999 **[169]**
🖊 **$5 500** - €6 449 - **£3 957** - FF42 304
Male Nude MN 137 Coloured crayons/paper (21x30cm 8x11in) New-York 2001
📃 **$2 400** - €2 662 - **£1 596** - FF17 463
Dancers Resting Color lithograph (56x39.5cm 22x15in) New-York 2000

CADORIN Guido 1892-1976 **[34]**
🖼 **$2 250** - €2 332 - **£1 350** - FF15 300
Vaso di fiori Olio/carta/tela (58x39cm 22x15in) Milano 2000

CADY Harrison 1877-1970 **[43]**
🖊 **$2 300** - €2 203 - **£1 420** - FF14 448
Santa Using a Car to Deliver presents Ink (46x57cm 18x22in) New-York 1999
📃 **$350** - €335 - **£213** - FF2 198
The Ladies of the Sideshow Etching (25.5x31.5cm 10x12in) Boston MA 1999

CAFFARO JAUME Pedro 1866-1959 **[1]**
🖼 **$13 800** - €12 043 - **£8 400** - FF79 000
«Estanque Deya» Oleo/lienzo (75x75.5cm 29x29in) Madrid 1998

CAFFASSI Alberto 1894-1973 **[16]**
🖼 **$900** - €933 - **£540** - FF6 120
Chiesa in collina Olio/tavola (30x30cm 11x11in) Vercelli 1999
🖼 **$275** - €285 - **£165** - FF1 870
La mietitura Pastelli/carta (31x110cm 12x43in) Vercelli 2000

CAFFÉ Nino 1909-1975 **[244]**
🖼 **$6 000** - €5 183 - **£4 000** - FF34 000
Sui gradini Olio/tela (70x50cm 27x19in) Milano 1998
🖼 **$3 000** - €3 110 - **£1 800** - FF20 400
Giochi d'inverno Olio/tela (30x35cm 11x13in) Roma 2001
🖊 **$360** - €311 - **£180** - FF2 040
Il vescovo Feutre/papier (29x23.5cm 11x9in) Prato 1999

CAFFERTY James Henry 1819-1869 **[9]**
🖼 **$2 600** - €2 455 - **£1 616** - FF16 102
Walking in the Woods Oil/canvas (68x54cm 27x22in) Milford CT 1999

CAFFI Cavaliere Ippolito 1809-1866 **[59]**
🖼 **$9 844** - €9 015 - **£6 000** - FF59 133
The Pantheon, Rome Oil/canvas (34x48cm 13x18in) London 1999
🖼 **$11 731** - €10 677 - **£7 200** - FF70 034
Fire at the Forum Oil/canvas (28x43cm 11x16in) London 1999
🖊 **$5 072** - €5 031 - **£3 154** - FF33 000
Vue du Panthéon à Rome Aquarelle/papier (21.7x28cm 8x11in) Paris 1999

CAFFI Margherita 1650-1710 **[35]**
🖼 **$28 060** - €27 630 - **£17 940** - FF181 240
Florero Oleo/lienzo (142x193cm 55x75in) Madrid 1999
🖼 **$22 414** - €24 060 - **£15 000** - FF157 824
Still life of Flowers in an Ornamental Urn Oil/canvas (121x89cm 47x35in) London 2000

CAFFIERI Hector 1847-1932 **[108]**
🖼 **$21 000** - €19 574 - **£12 994** - FF128 396
Peasants of St.Omer going to Market Oil/canvas (78x60cm 31x24in) Portland OR 1999
🖊 **$2 850** - €2 409 - **£1 700** - FF15 799
A Moment's Rest Watercolour (33.5x49cm 13x19in) Glasgow 1998

CAFFIERI Jean-Jacques 1725-1792 **[14]**
🗿 **$5 526** - €5 488 - **£3 441** - FF36 000
Figure allégorique d'un fleuve Bronze (H64cm H25in) Paris 1999

CAFFYN Walter Wallor 1845-1898 **[60]**
🖼 **$3 955** - €3 816 - **£2 500** - FF25 031
An old Sussex Mill Oil/canvas (71x91.5cm 27x36in) London 1999
🖼 **$2 800** - €3 101 - **£1 899** - FF20 340
Cows Passing Through a Stream/Canal at Dawn Oil/canvas (20.5x30.5cm 8x12in) New-York 2000

CAGE John 1912-1992 **[31]**
🖊 **$3 403** - €3 429 - **£2 121** - FF22 495
Buckminster Fuller Encre Chine (31x45cm 12x17in) Zürich 2000
📃 **$900** - €841 - **£544** - FF5 514
Design with Words Etching (64.5x47.5cm 25x18in) New-York 1999

CAGLI Corrado 1910-1976 **[132]**
🖼 **$2 640** - €2 281 - **£1 760** - FF14 960
Variazione Tecnica mista/cartone (48x66.5cm 18x26in) Prato 1998
🖼 **$1 320** - €1 710 - **£990** - FF11 220
Suonatore di flauto Olio/carta/tela (38.5x31cm 15x12in) Prato 2000
🖊 **$800** - €829 - **£480** - FF5 440
Composizione Tecnica mista/carta (50x34cm 19x13in) Roma 2000
📃 **$400** - €518 - **£300** - FF3 400
Pittore a cavalletto Monotype (47x38cm 18x14in) Milano 2001

CAGNACCI Guido Canlassi 1601-1681 **[5]**
🖼 **$52 000** - €45 767 - **£31 657** - FF300 211
The Magdalen Oil/canvas (75.5x65.5cm 29x25in) New-York 1999

CAGNACCIO DI SAN PIETRO 1897-1946 **[3]**
🖼 **$5 100** - €5 287 - **£3 060** - FF34 680
Paesaggio montano Olio/tavola (21.5x28cm 8x11in) Venezia 2000

CAGNEY James 1899-1986 **[9]**
🖼 **$1 900** - €2 174 - **£1 306** - FF14 262
Portraits of a Man Oil/canvas/board (48x38cm 19x15in) New-York 2000
🖼 **$2 000** - €2 289 - **£1 375** - FF15 013
Floral Still LIfe Oil/paper (20x12cm 8x5in) New-York 2000
🖊 **$5 500** - €6 294 - **£3 782** - FF41 287
Dancer Against Orange Ground, Possibly Self Portraits Watercolour (30x22cm 12x9in) New-York 2000

CAGNIART Émile 1851-1911 **[27]**
🖼 **$25 377** - €26 647 - **£16 000** - FF174 795
Rio de Janeiro Oil/canvas (46.5x61.5cm 18x24in) London 2000
🖼 **$1 050** - €1 028 - **£646** - FF6 742
View of a Lake Oil/canvas (31x46cm 12x18in) Columbia SC 1999

C

CAGNONE Angelo 1941 [67]
🖌 $1 120 - €1 451 - **£840** - FF9 520
Frammenti di teste su fondo blu Olio/tela (120x120cm 47x47in) Milano 2000
🖌 $500 - €518 - **£300** - FF3 400
Chiuso nel silenzio Tecnica mista (89x80cm 35x31in) Milano 1999

CAGNONI Amerino 1855-1923 [10]
🖌 $900 - €933 - **£540** - FF6 120
Mascherina Olio/tela (42x32cm 16x12in) Trieste 1999

CAHEN-MICHEL Lucien 1888-1979 [6]
🖌 $3 405 - €3 811 - **£2 310** - FF25 000
Environ Montigny sur Loing, personnage sortant du village Huile/panneau (55.2x46cm 21x18in) Paris 2000

CAHILL Richard Staunton XIX-XX [9]
🖌 $3 809 - €4 063 - **£2 507** - FF26 652
The Love Letter/Pensive Pose Oil/canvas (44x35cm 17x14in) Dublin 2000
✏ $2 011 - €2 286 - **£1 389** - FF14 992
Farmhand and the Piper Watercolour/paper (35x22cm 14x9in) Dublin 2000

CAHILL William 1878-1924 [4]
🖌 $5 500 - €5 941 - **£3 808** - FF38 973
Days Work Oil/canvas (91x60cm 36x24in) Cincinnati OH 2001

CAHN Marcelle 1895-1981 [99]
🖌 $8 280 - €9 147 - **£5 742** - FF60 000
Deux figures Huile/toile (46x56cm 18x22in) Paris 2001
🖌 $1 151 - €1 372 - **£820** - FF9 000
Nature morte Huile/toile (24x38cm 9x14in) Paris 2000
✏ $510 - €579 - **£349** - FF3 800
Composition Mine plomb (13x20cm 5x7in) Paris 2000

CAHN Miriam 1949 [15]
✏ $3 403 - €3 429 - **£2 121** - FF22 495
Erotische Zeichnungen Fusain/papier (30x20.5cm 11x8in) Zürich 2000

CAHOON Charles Drew 1861-1951 [45]
🖌 $4 000 - €3 720 - **£2 476** - FF24 402
Dune Scene Oil/canvas (38x50cm 15x20in) East-Dennis MA 1999
🖌 $3 300 - €2 850 - **£1 993** - FF18 696
Sailboats and Figures on a Beach Oil/board (22x30cm 9x12in) East-Dennis MA 1998

CAHOON Martha Farham 1905-1999 [27]
🖌 $6 400 - €5 818 - **£3 927** - FF38 163
Farm Scene with Figures and Train Oil/masonite (40x50cm 16x20in) East-Dennis MA 1998
🖌 $3 500 - €4 082 - **£2 457** - FF26 776
Guarding the Cove Oil/panel (35x30cm 14x12in) Dedham MA 2000
✏ $1 700 - €1 825 - **£1 137** - FF11 969
Sailor Beware, Depicting Two Sailors on a Beach Pencil/paper (38x50cm 15x20in) East-Dennis MA 2000

CAHOON Ralph Eugene 1910-1982 [80]
🖌 $30 000 - €27 900 - **£18 576** - FF183 018
A drunken Man in the Harborside being consoled by his Mermaid Wife Oil/masonite (42x55cm 16x22in) East-Dennis MA 1999
🖌 $16 000 - €17 174 - **£10 707** - FF112 656
Mermaid Sculling Oil/masonite (25x30cm 10x12in) East-Dennis MA 2000

🎞 $700 - €651 - **£433** - FF4 270
The Race Print in colors (73x102cm 29x40in) East-Dennis MA 1999

CAHOURS Henry Maurice 1889-1954 [88]
🖌 $667 - €640 - **£414** - FF4 200
En allant au marché aux cochons Huile/toile (55x38cm 21x14in) Paris 1999
🖌 $367 - €427 - **£254** - FF2 800
Bouquet Huile/toile (41x23cm 16x9in) Toulouse 2000
🖌 $322 - €366 - **£226** - FF2 400
Le carénage à Dournenez Aquarelle/papier (35x23cm 13x9in) Quimper 2001

CAHUN Claude 1894-1954 [8]
📷 $3 200 - €3 684 - **£2 183** - FF24 166
Surrealist Still-Life Gelatin silver print (10x7.5cm 3x2in) New-York 2000

CAI BAOYU 1958 [11]
🖌 $6 560 - €6 985 - **£4 160** - FF45 820
Still Life Oil/canvas (112x107cm 44x42in) Taipei 2000

CAI GUO-QIANG 1957 [2]
🖌 $137 700 - €156 344 - **£96 750** - FF1 025 550
Self Portrait Oil/canvas (167x118cm 65x46in) Taipei 2001

CAI HAN 1647-1686 [3]
🖌 $9 642 - €9 094 - **£5 980** - FF59 650
Chrysanthemums Ink (71x38cm 27x14in) Hong-Kong 1999

CAI JIA c.1720-1782 [3]
✏ $16 731 - €15 867 - **£10 179** - FF104 078
Various Subjects Ink (14.5x17cm 5x6in) Hong-Kong 1999

CAI YU SHUI 1963 [5]
🖌 $4 195 - €3 934 - **£2 608** - FF25 806
Marching Mixed media (80x100cm 31x39in) Taipei 1999
🖌 $3 174 - €2 958 - **£1 958** - FF19 402
Youthful Beauty Mixed media/paper (120x90cm 47x35in) Singapore 1999

CAILLARD Christian 1899-1985 [76]
🖌 $1 050 - €1 250 - **£748** - FF8 000
Maroc, Milouda en rose Huile/panneau (73x60cm 28x23in) Versailles 2001

CAILLAUD Aristide 1902-1990 [125]
🖌 $5 520 - €6 098 - **£3 828** - FF40 000
L'art Roman Huile/toile (162x130cm 63x51in) Paris 2001
🖌 $2 886 - €3 354 - **£2 028** - FF22 000
Village de Grèce Huile/toile (56x44cm 22x17in) Paris 2001
🖌 $1 238 - €1 143 - **£771** - FF7 500
La ville Huile/toile (29x29cm 11x11in) Douai 1999
🖌 $1 173 - €1 296 - **£813** - FF8 500
Le départ Gouache/papier (66x52cm 25x20in) Paris 2001

CAILLAUD Louis 1894-1960 [1]
🎞 $900 - €865 - **£555** - FF5 677
«Eaton's» Poster (120.5x79.5cm 47x31in) New-York 2000

CAILLAUX Rodolphe 1904-1989 [57]
🖌 $402 - €457 - **£282** - FF3 000
Le village au bord de l'eau Huile/toile (81x100cm 31x39in) Lyon 2001

CAILLE Léon Émile 1836-1907 [70]
🖌 $3 821 - €3 700 - **£2 400** - FF24 270
Mother nursing a Child in a Kitchen Interior Oil/canvas (33x41cm 12x16in) London 1999

CAILLEBOTTE Gustave 1848-1894 **[82]**
$900 000 - €766 930 - £536 310 - FF5 030 730
Voiliers sur la Seine à Argenteuil Oil/canvas
(65.5x82cm 25x32in) New-York 1998
$59 598 - €67 890 - £41 177 - FF445 332
Paysage avec maison au bout de la route
Öl/Leinwand (22x31cm 8x12in) Zürich 2000
$1 988 - €2 134 - £1 330 - FF14 000
L'arbre mort Trois crayons/papier (34x24cm 13x9in)
Besançon 2000

CAIN Auguste Nicolas 1821-1894 **[195]**
$1 169 - €1 329 - £820 - FF8 715
Model of a Vulture on a Spinx Head Bronze
(H50cm H19in) Billingshurst, West-Sussex 2001

CAIN Charles William 1893-1962 **[30]**
$80 - €93 - £56 - FF607
Middle Eastern Bazaar Etching (24x37cm 9x14in)
Cleveland OH 2000

CAIN Georges Jules A. 1856-1919 **[20]**
$24 000 - €22 089 - £14 404 - FF144 895
Heated Disagreement Between Commanders
Oil/canvas/board (112x160cm 44x63in) Chicago IL
1999
$980 - €843 - £574 - FF5 530
«Napoléon abandonando Fontainebleau des-
pués de su abdicación» Grabado (76x59cm
29x23in) Madrid 1998

CAIN Henri 1859-1937 **[11]**
$24 000 - €20 706 - £14 479 - FF135 823
The Toast Oil/canvas (133.5x168cm 52x66in) New-
York 1998
$5 299 - €5 488 - £3 373 - FF36 000
Fanfaron et Brillador Bronze (40x48cm 15x18in)
Bordeaux 2000

CAIN Peter 1959-1997 **[9]**
$11 000 - €11 085 - £6 857 - FF72 710
Untitled Oil/canvas (178x122cm 70x48in) New-York
2000
$2 400 - €2 785 - £1 657 - FF18 266
500 SL Number 4 Graphite (56x61cm 22x24in) New-
York 2000

CAIRATI Girolamo 1860-1943 **[16]**
$227 - €256 - £158 - FF1 676
«Frühlingstag an der Würm» Pastell/Papier
(47x58cm 18x22in) Lindau 2001

CAIRNS John XIX **[4]**
$873 - €823 - £550 - FF5 401
Figures in a Wheatfield near Blairgowrie Oil/can-
vas (20.5x33cm 8x12in) Godalming, Surrey 1999

CAIRO del Francesco Cavaliere 1607-1665 **[17]**
$18 000 - €18 660 - £10 800 - FF122 400
Cristo nell'orto Olio/tela (68x50cm 26x19in) Venezia
2000
$100 000 - €95 457 - £62 480 - FF626 160
Head of a Young Woman in Profile Oil/panel
(31x20cm 12x7in) New-York 1999

CALA Y MOYA de José 1856-1891 **[14]**
$21 432 - €18 294 - £12 816 - FF120 000
Divertissement au harem Huile/panneau (37x56cm
14x22in) Paris 1998

CALABRIA Ennio 1937 **[118]**
$9 000 - €7 775 - £6 000 - FF51 000
Fiera campionaria Olio/tela (130x165cm 51x64in)
Roma 1998
$1 800 - €2 332 - £1 350 - FF15 300
Studio per figura Olio/tela (70x48.5cm 27x19in)
Milano 2000

$1 650 - €1 710 - £990 - FF11 220
Figura al mare Olio/tela (30x40cm 11x15in) Vercelli
1999
$850 - €881 - £510 - FF5 780
Studio per un attore Pastelli (41.5x29.5cm 16x11in)
Roma 1999

CALAMATTA Luigi 1802-1869 **[5]**
$302 - €351 - £208 - FF2 300
Portrait de George Sand Burin (32x22.5cm 12x8in)
Paris 2000

CALAME Alexandre 1810-1864 **[266]**
$41 063 - €38 571 - £24 752 - FF253 011
Torrent running through an alpine landscape
with snow covered mountain Oil/canvas
(101x141cm 39x55in) Amsterdam 1999
$10 310 - €9 681 - £6 389 - FF63 506
Lit de ruisseau Öl/Leinwand/Karton (39x52.5cm
15x20in) Luzern 1999
$3 139 - €3 585 - £2 213 - FF23 516
Schwarzwald mit Reichenbach und Blick auf
das Wetterhorn Öl/Leinwand/Karton (38x27.5cm 14x10in) Bern
2001
$765 - €701 - £467 - FF4 600
Paysage Suisse Aquarelle, gouache/papier
(9.5x13cm 3x5in) Lyon 1999
$69 - €78 - £48 - FF510
Berglandschaft mit Ziegenhirten Lithographie
(24x39cm 9x15in) Luzern 2001

CALAME Arthur Jean Bapt. 1843-1919 **[89]**
$5 315 - €6 233 - £3 792 - FF40 885
Venise Huile/toile (45x61cm 17x24in) Genève 2000
$864 - €812 - £535 - FF5 326
Auf hoher See Öl/Leinwand/Karton (24x33cm
9x12in) Luzern 2000
$354 - €383 - £238 - FF2 511
Venis Crayon (13x37cm 5x14in) Genève 2000

CALAME Charles-Édouard 1815-1852 **[2]**
$4 026 - €4 497 - £2 728 - FF29 500
Vue d'Ischia Huile/panneau (52x69cm 20x27in)
Pontoise 2000

CALANDRA Davide 1856-1915 **[3]**
$2 900 - €3 006 - £1 740 - FF19 720
Minerva Bronzo (H48cm H18in) Milano 2000

CALANDRI Mario 1914-1993 **[5]**
$3 200 - €4 147 - £2 400 - FF27 200
Tre bambini in un paesaggio urbano Tecnica
mista (41x37cm 16x14in) Torino 2000
$600 - €777 - £450 - FF5 100
«Torrente» Gravure (16x23cm 6x9in) Torino 2000

CALANDRUCCI Giacinto 1646-1707 **[20]**
$1 915 - €2 147 - £1 300 - FF14 084
Apotheosis of a Bishop Saint Ink (40.5x33cm
15x12in) London 2000

CALAPAI Letterio 1904 **[25]**
$800 - €908 - £547 - FF5 958
Eight-Thirty Express Woodcut (13x21.5cm 5x8in)
New-York 2000

CALAU Benjamin 1724-1785 **[3]**
$1 764 - €2 013 - £1 225 - FF13 207
Portraet af en herre med skaeg Oil/canvas
(71x53cm 27x20in) Köbenhavn 2000

CALBET Antoine 1860-1944 **[288]**
$1 153 - €1 372 - £822 - FF9 000
Baigneuse aux branches fleuries Huile/toile
(61x50cm 24x19in) Neuilly-sur-Seine 2000

$1 404 - €1 494 - **£931** - FF9 800
Nu au drap blanc Huile/papier/toile (27x22cm 10x8in) Paris 2000
$575 - €534 - **£358** - FF3 500
Les deux amies Aquarelle, gouache/papier (49x31cm 19x12in) Le Raincy 1999

CALCAGNADORO Antonio 1876-1935 [12]
$2 100 - €2 177 - **£1 260** - FF14 280
Giochi infantili Olio/tela (43.5x59cm 17x23in) Roma 2000
$2 100 - €2 177 - **£1 260** - FF14 280
Bimbi sulla spiaggia Olio/tavola (29x43.5cm 11x17in) Roma 2000

CALCAR van Jan Stephan 1499-1546/50 [6]
$885 - €971 - **£601** - FF6 372
Der meditierende Tod, nach Tizian Woodcut (45.3x30cm 17x11in) Berlin 2000

CALDAS Waltercio 1946 [6]
$55 000 - €59 037 - **£36 806** - FF387 255
Los Velázquez Mixed media (130x95x6cm 51x37x2in) New-York 2000
$16 000 - €15 412 - **£9 934** - FF101 097
Untitled Sculpture, wood (30x100x25cm 11x39x9in) New-York 1999

CALDECOTT Randolph 1846-1886 [11]
$4 482 - €4 812 - **£3 000** - FF31 564
Over the Brook/Refusing the Brook/Over the Fence/Refusing the Fence Oil/board (20.5x24cm 8x9in) London 2000
$1 186 - €1 129 - **£750** - FF7 406
The Mad Dog Ink (21x18cm 8x7in) London 1999

CALDER Alexander 1898-1976 [2292]
$62 440 - €53 357 - **£37 800** - FF350 000
Formes bleu, rouge, noir Huile/toile (73x100cm 28x39in) Paris 1998
$440 000 - €510 527 - **£303 776** - FF3 348 840
Untitled Mobile (81x198x96.5cm 31x77x37in) New-York 2000
$137 683 - €138 729 - **£85 813** - FF910 000
Broc Métal (H65.5cm H25in) Tours 2000
$6 120 - €6 860 - **£4 153** - FF45 000
Personnages Gouache/papier (74x109cm 29x42in) Paris 2000
$507 - €574 - **£355** - FF3 768
Hommage au cinéma Farblithographie (50x38cm 19x14in) Zürich 2000

CALDERARA Antonio 1903-1978 [185]
$9 200 - €11 922 - **£6 900** - FF78 200
Bianco-rosso Olio/tela (200x62cm 78x24in) Milano 2000
$4 800 - €6 220 - **£3 600** - FF40 800
Paesaggio con Bison in Valle d'Aosta Olio/tavola (34.5x49.5cm 13x19in) Prato 2000
$3 867 - €4 009 - **£2 320** - FF26 299
Il cancello rosso Olio/masonite (9.5x17cm 3x6in) Milano 2000
$1 227 - €1 431 - **£861** - FF9 390
Ohne Titel Aquarell (20x24.8cm 7x9in) Köln 2000
$363 - €353 - **£226** - FF2 314
Ohne Titel Farbserigraphie (42.1x54.2cm 16x21in) Berlin 1999

CALDERINI Luigi 1880/81-1973 [13]
$4 000 - €4 147 - **£2 400** - FF27 200
Dalla Caravina - Lago di Lugano Olio/cartone (28.5x37.5cm 11x14in) Torino 2000
$700 - €816 - **£490** - FF5 353
German Pipe Smoker Watercolour/paper (35x20cm 14x8in) Cleveland OH 2000

CALDERINI Marco 1850-1941 [38]
$2 400 - €3 110 - **£1 800** - FF20 400
Laghetto nel bosco Olio/faesite (38x52cm 14x20in) Roma 2001
$1 600 - €2 073 - **£1 200** - FF13 600
Estate in montagna Olio/cartone/tela (27x36cm 10x14in) Vercelli 2001

CALDERON Celia 1921-1969 [4]
$7 172 - €7 961 - **£5 000** - FF52 224
Il bacino di San Marco, Venezia Oil/canvas (54.5x84cm 21x33in) London 2001
$2 752 - €3 228 - **£1 980** - FF21 175
Mujer en cuclillas Oleo/tabla (26x21cm 10x8in) México 2001

CALDERON Charles-Clément c.1870-1906 [75]
$6 387 - €7 194 - **£4 400** - FF47 190
Venice Oil/canvas (47x65cm 18x25in) Newbury, Berkshire 2000
$5 842 - €5 717 - **£3 738** - FF37 500
Venise: Grand Canal Huile/panneau (14x22cm 5x8in) Bayeux 1999

CALDERON Philip Hermogenes 1833-1898 [31]
$25 254 - €30 034 - **£18 000** - FF197 013
Mary Magdalene giving News of the Resurrection to the Disciples Oil/canvas (111x86.5cm 43x34in) London 2000

CALDERON William Frank 1865-1943 [26]
$63 304 - €60 872 - **£39 000** - FF399 297
How four Queens found Sir Lancelot sleeping Oil/canvas (122x183cm 48x72in) London 1999
$2 871 - €3 219 - **£2 000** - FF21 114
Hunter with a Pony in a Park Oil/canvas (64x92cm 25x36in) Leyburn, North Yorkshire 2001
$812 - €795 - **£500** - FF5 216
The Hunt Meet Oil/canvas (27x38cm 11x15in) Aylsham, Norfolk 1999

CALDWALL James 1739-c.1790 [4]
$1 173 - €1 264 - **£800** - FF8 293
The Nodding Renealmia Aquatint (55.5x43cm 21x16in) Bury St. Edmunds, Suffolk 2001

CALDWELL Edmund 1852-1930 [26]
$2 600 - €2 832 - **£1 790** - FF18 574
An Irish Waterspaniel Oil/canvas (40.5x30.5cm 15x12in) New-York 2001

CALDWELL John 1942 [9]
$1 473 - €1 746 - **£1 039** - FF11 454
Landscape Watercolour (99x149cm 38x58in) Sydney 2000

CALEGARI Giacomo 1848-1915 [1]
$14 500 - €15 031 - **£8 700** - FF98 600
Il ritorno del reduce d'Africa Olio/tela (88x134cm 34x52in) Trieste 2000

CALES Pierre, abbé 1870-1961 [172]
$345 - €2 683 - **£1 904** - FF17 600
Les Adrets sous la neige à Lyon Huile/carton (46x65cm 18x25in) Mâcon 1998
$2 570 - €2 165 - **£1 518** - FF14 200
La chantourne sous la neige Huile/carton (30x50cm 11x19in) Grenoble 1998

CALETTI IL CREMONESE Giuseppe c.1600-c.1660 [5]
$350 - €363 - **£210** - FF2 380
Sansone e Dalila Acquaforte (13.5x15cm 5x5in) Milano 2000

C

CALF Adolphe Félix 1810-1880 [1]
🖼 **$10 650** - €9 010 - **£6 450** - FF59 100
Campo de Honfleur Oleo/lienzo (60x119cm 23x46in) Madrid 1998

CALHOUN Frederic 1883 [3]
📖 **$8 000** - €7 662 - **£5 034** - FF50 262
Miss Baldwin, Modern Witch of Endeavour Lithograph (208x106cm 82x42in) Thomaston ME 1999

CALIARI Benedetto 1538-1598 [11]
🖼 **$13 407** - €11 407 - **£8 000** - FF74 827
Allegory of the Theological Virtues: Faith, Hope and Charity Oil/canvas (54.5x47cm 21x18in) London 1998
✏ **$1 430** - €1 677 - **£1 028** - FF11 000
Femme agenouillée au pied d'un arbre Crayon (20x12.5cm 7x4in) Paris 2001

CALIARI Carlo, Carletto 1570-1596 [15]
🖼 **$6 000** - €7 775 - **£4 500** - FF51 000
Pietà Olio/tela (110x85cm 43x33in) Milano 2001
✏ **$1 842** - €1 568 - **£1 100** - FF10 287
The Head of a young monk Black, red & white chalks (19.5x13cm 7x5in) London 1998

CALIFANO John, Giovanni 1862/64-1946 [67]
🖼 **$2 000** - €1 713 - **£1 202** - FF11 239
Boy Holding a Cat and a Civil War Kepi Oil/canvas (71x45cm 28x18in) Cleveland OH 1998

CALIGIANI Alberto 1894-1974 [15]
🖼 **$450** - €466 - **£270** - FF3 060
Paesaggio con fiume Idropittura (20x27cm 7x10in) Prato 1999
✏ **$800** - €829 - **£480** - FF5 440
Maternità Sanguina/carta (89x66cm 35x25in) Prato 2000

CALIGO Domenico XIX [3]
✏ **$15 392** - €18 318 - **£11 000** - FF120 155
Sala di giove con la statua delle Vittoria di Vincenzo Consani Watercolour (41.5x56cm 16x22in) London 2000

CALISCH Moritz 1819-1870 [8]
🖼 **$4 091** - €3 857 - **£2 535** - FF25 301
Elegant Lady Feeding a Parakeet Oil/canvas (70x64.5cm 27x25in) Amsterdam 1999

CALKIN Lance 1859-1936 [19]
🖼 **$42 090** - €50 058 - **£30 000** - FF328 356
Two Invalids Oil/canvas (141x113cm 55x44in) London 2000
🖼 **$829** - €718 - **£500** - FF4 708
Gentleman, half-length in a Tweed Jacket and Waistcoat Oil/canvas (76x63.5cm 29x25in) London 1998

CALLAHAN Harry 1912-1999 [249]
📷 **$3 500** - €3 976 - **£2 456** - FF26 079
Chicago Gelatin silver print (19x12.5cm 7x4in) New-York 2001

CALLANDER Adam XVIII-XIX [1]
✏ **$3 782** - €3 811 - **£2 357** - FF25 000
Promenade dans la montagne Aquarelle, gouache/papier (46x66cm 18x25in) Paris 2000

CALLCOTT Augustus Wall 1779-1844 [29]
🖼 **$5 163** - €4 959 - **£3 200** - FF32 527
Coastal Scene with Figures before an Approaching Storm Oil/canvas (38x54cm 14x21in) Suffolk 1999
🖼 **$1 800** - €1 944 - **£1 244** - FF12 751
Across the Moors Oil/panel (23x30.5cm 9x12in) Bethesda MD 2001

CALLCOTT William James XIX [19]
✏ **$2 635** - €2 569 - **£1 600** - FF16 853
Busy Harbour Watercolour (35x51.5cm 13x20in) London 2001

CALLÉ Denise 1915 [9]
🖼 **$779** - €732 - **£482** - FF4 800
Paysage de Saint-Rémy Huile/toile (46x61cm 18x24in) Les Andelys 1999

CALLE Paul 1928 [16]
🖼 **$55 000** - €62 450 - **£38 214** - FF409 645
The Trapper's Feast Oil/canvas (58x86cm 23x34in) Dallas TX 2001
🖼 **$12 100** - €12 988 - **£8 097** - FF85 196
They Call Me William Oil/board (30x22cm 12x9in) Houston TX 2000
🗿 **$3 850** - €3 596 - **£2 376** - FF23 585
Free Trapper Bronze (38x32cm 15x12in) Dallas TX 1999
✏ **$7 150** - €6 677 - **£4 413** - FF43 800
Gathering Storm on Circle B Ranch Pencil/paper (74x99cm 29x39in) Dallas TX 1999

CALLE Sophie 1953 [15]
📷 **$3 000** - €3 360 - **£2 084** - FF22 041
Les Tombes, Father, Mother Gelatin silver print (60x40cm 23x15in) New-York 2001

CALLERY Mary 1903-1977 [5]
🗿 **$3 200** - €3 713 - **£2 209** - FF24 355
Study for Equilibrist Bronze (61x40.5x30.5cm 24x15x12in) New-York 2000

CALLERY Simon 1960 [8]
✏ **$5 949** - €5 083 - **£3 600** - FF33 345
4G and Justice Pastel (173x243cm 68x95in) London 1998

CALLET Antoine François 1741-1823 [11]
🖼 **$31 108** - €33 539 - **£20 856** - FF220 000
Portrait du roi Louis XVI Huile/toile (72.5x59cm 28x23in) Paris 2001

CALLI Ibrahim 1882-1960 [4]
🖼 **$16 200 000** - €18 385 350 - **£10 800 000** - FF120 600 000
«Rumeli Hisari'nda Kis» Huile/panneau (23x30cm 9x11in) Istanbul 2001

CALLIAS de Horace 1847-1921 [7]
🖼 **$16 000** - €17 559 - **£10 302** - FF115 180
La Petite Soeur Oil/canvas (203x134.5cm 79x52in) New-York 2000
🖼 **$27 492** - €26 679 - **£17 115** - FF175 000
Une soirée chez la baronne double Huile/toile (79.5x98.5cm 31x38in) Montfort L'Amaury 1999
✏ **$2 991** - €2 744 - **£1 859** - FF18 000
Princesse au tigre Gouache (39x25.5cm 15x10in) Paris 2000

CALLOT Georges 1857-1903 [15]
✏ **$1 620** - €1 829 - **£1 129** - FF12 000
Portrait de jeune fille au ruban bleu Pastel/papier (46x38cm 18x14in) Bayeux 2001

CALLOT Henri 1875-1956 [28]
🖼 **$1 822** - €1 982 - **£1 201** - FF13 000
Port du Midi Huile/isorel (65x80cm 25x31in) Paris 2000

CALLOT Jacques 1592-1635 [577]
✏ **$164 373** - €176 441 - **£110 000** - FF1 157 376
The Martyrdom of Saint Sebastian Black chalk (12x22cm 4x8in) London 2000

C

🛢 $750 - €706 - **£463** - FF4 633
The Entombment, after Salimbeni Etching
(17x11.5cm 6x4in) New-York 1999

CALLOW George D. act.1858-1873 [48]
🖼 $1 302 - €1 406 - **£900** - FF9 224
The Ferry Oil/canvas (45.5x76cm 17x29in) London
2001
🖼 $978 - €947 - **£620** - FF6 210
**Tranquil Evening Coastal Scene and Other
Craft Offshore** Oil/canvas (31x41cm 12x16in) Devon
1999
✏ $385 - €433 - **£270** - FF2 839
Lifeboat off the Norfolk Coast, Scruby Sand
Watercolour/paper (36x48cm 14x18in) London 2001

CALLOW John 1822-1878 [134]
🖼 $6 971 - €6 151 - **£4 200** - FF40 345
Shipping off the Coast Oil/canvas (50x91.5cm
19x36in) London 1998
🖼 $610 - €577 - **£380** - FF3 784
At Full Sail Oil/canvas (20x30.5cm 7x12in) London
1999
✏ $1 065 - €1 015 - **£650** - FF6 656
Paddle Steamer leaving Dover Watercolour
(24x33cm 9x12in) Bury St. Edmunds, Suffolk 1999

CALLOW William 1812-1908 [369]
🖼 $2 370 - €2 108 - **£1 450** - FF13 829
The Kaufhaus on the Mosel Quay Oil/board
(34x24cm 13x9in) Newbury, Berkshire 1999
✏ $2 189 - €2 351 - **£1 500** - FF15 424
Cottage at Great Malvern Watercolour/paper
(24x34.5cm 9x13in) London 2001

CALLOWHILL T. Scott XIX [7]
🖼 $6 081 - €5 805 - **£3 800** - FF38 077
**Worcestershire Cottage/Figure by a Tranquil
River** Oil/board (18.5x26cm 7x10in) London 1999

CALMAN Mel 1931-1994 [5]
✏ $594 - €582 - **£380** - FF3 819
«In the Spring a Young Man's» Pencil
(28.5x19.5cm 11x7in) London 1999

CALMETTES Jean-Marie 1918 [48]
🖼 $583 - €686 - **£404** - FF4 502
Nature morte sur un entablement Huile/toile
(80x100cm 31x39in) Paris 2000

CALMETTES Pierre 1874-? [2]
🖼 $15 000 - €17 507 - **£10 588** - FF114 838
Le cabinet d'Anatole France Oleo/lienzo
(73x59.5cm 28x23in) Buenos-Aires 2000

CALOGERO Jean 1922 [94]
🖼 $1 004 - €1 115 - **£700** - FF7 315
Poupée au bouquet de fleurs Oil/canvas
(60.5x51cm 23x20in) London 2001
🖼 $400 - €388 - **£247** - FF2 543
Doll and Guitar Oil/canvas (40x33cm 16x13in)
Mystic CT 1999

CALOSCI Arturo 1855-1926 [7]
🖼 $4 760 - €4 934 - **£2 856** - FF32 368
Antignano Olio/tela (46x86cm 18x33in) Milano 1999
🖼 $1 600 - €2 073 - **£1 200** - FF13 600
Corteggiamento Olio/tela (38x30cm 14x11in) Roma
1999

CALRAET van Abraham 1643-1722 [22]
🖼 $50 277 - €42 777 - **£30 000** - FF280 602
A cavalry skirmish Oil/canvas (136x162cm 53x63in)
London 1998

🖼 $23 346 - €22 949 - **£15 000** - FF150 534
**Evening River Landscape with a cowherd and
Cows by the Edge of a Copse** Oil/canvas
(72x97.5cm 28x38in) London 1999
🖼 $24 000 - €24 279 - **£14 654** - FF159 261
**Peaches and Grapes with Butterflies on a
Ledge** Oil/copper (34x45cm 13x17in) New-York 2000

CALRAET van Barend 1649-1737 [6]
🖼 $6 616 - €7 260 - **£4 259** - FF47 625
**Riding Scholl by a wooded Outcrop/Travellers
watering their Horses** Oil/panel (40x48cm 15x18in)
Amsterdam 2000

CALS Adolphe Félix 1810-1880 [267]
🖼 $4 402 - €4 726 - **£2 945** - FF31 000
La veillée Huile/toile (46x38cm 18x14in) Paris 2000
🖼 $1 361 - €1 601 - **£987** - FF10 550
Ferme en Normandie Huile/toile (21x16cm 8x6in)
Calais 2001
✏ $242 - €229 - **£146** - FF1 500
Église de Bouillant près de Crépy en Valois
Encre (12x18cm 4x7in) Paris 1999

CALSINA BARO Ramón 1901-1992 [37]
🖼 $1 830 - €1 802 - **£1 140** - FF11 820
Visión Oleo/lienzo (46x55cm 18x21in) Barcelona 1999
✏ $459 - €541 - **£315** - FF3 546
Escena onírica Carboncillo (63x48cm 24x18in)
Barcelona 2000

CALTHROP Claude Andrew 1845-1893 [5]
🖼 $192 933 - €174 868 - **£117 000** - FF1 147 056
Tea-Time Oil/canvas (93x129cm 36x50in)
Billingshurst, West-Sussex 1998

CALVAERT Denys Fiammingo 1540-1619 [33]
🖼 $75 000 - €77 749 - **£45 000** - FF510 000
La caduta di San Paolo Olio/tela (92x133cm
36x52in) Venezia 1999
🖼 $100 000 - €106 969 - **£68 180** - FF701 670
Adoration of the Magi Oil/copper (49.5x38.5cm
19x15in) New-York 2001
🖼 $23 370 - €21 802 - **£14 100** - FF143 010
**Maria mit dem Kind, dem Johannesknaben und
der heiligen Elisabeth** Ol/Kupfer (31x24.5cm
12x9in) Wien 1999
✏ $6 004 - €7 158 - **£4 281** - FF46 954
**Die Heilige Familie mit der Mutter Anna und
dem Johannesknaben** Watercolour, gouache
(28.8x18.2cm 11x7in) Köln 2000

CALVERT Edward 1789-1883 [23]
🖼 $2 701 - €2 619 - **£1 700** - FF17 182
Rural Idyll Oil/canvas (20x38.5cm 7x15in) London
1999
✏ $427 - €498 - **£300** - FF3 269
**Wooded River Landscape with Figures by a
Boat** Watercolour/paper (16.5x23cm 6x9in) Godalming,
Surrey 2001
🛢 $568 - €610 - **£380** - FF4 002
The Cider Feast Woodcut (25.5x36cm 10x14in)
London 2000

CALVERT Frederick c.1785-1845 [53]
🖼 $4 166 - €3 961 - **£2 600** - FF25 982
Preparing to set out for the Fishing Grounds
Oil/canvas (58.5x81.5cm 23x32in) London 1999
🖼 $2 988 - €3 208 - **£2 000** - FF21 043
Unloading the Catch Oil/board (20x25cm 7x9in)
London 2000

CALVERT Henry 1798-1869 **[27]**
- $9 820 - €10 211 - **£6 200** - FF66 979
  Thomas Walker Stubbs, as a Boy on a Donkey Jumping a Log Oil/panel (51x61cm 20x24in) Newbury, Berkshire 2000
- $5 000 - €5 679 - **£3 508** - FF37 252
  Scenes from the Hunt Oil/canvas (20.5x40.5cm 8x15in) New-York 2001

CALVERT Samuel W., active XIX-XX **[10]**
- $2 134 - €2 516 - **£1 500** - FF16 503
  Off the Fishing Grounds Oil/canvas (48x53cm 19x21in) Altrincham 2000

CALVES Léon Georges 1848-1924 **[50]**
- $17 013 - €15 550 - **£10 414** - FF102 000
  Chevaux au débardage Huile/toile (150x242cm 59x95in) Dijon 1999
- $2 079 - €1 753 - **£1 233** - FF11 500
  Après la moisson Huile/toile (38x45.5cm 14x17in) Paris 1998
- $866 - €873 - **£540** - FF5 726
  Die Pferdetränke Öl/Leinwand (32.5x40.5cm 12x15in) Zürich 2000
- $1 472 - €1 524 - **£937** - FF10 000
  Labour avant l'orage Aquarelle/papier (64x52cm 25x20in) Bordeaux 2000

CALVES Marie-Didière 1883-1957 **[62]**
- $2 191 - €2 554 - **£1 517** - FF16 755
  Jagdhunde am Waldrand Öl/Leinwand (38x55cm 14x21in) Bern 2000
- $1 215 - €1 037 - **£733** - FF6 800
  Chiens de chasse Huile/toile (33x46cm 12x18in) Besançon 1998

CALVI DI BERGOLO Gregorio 1904-1994 **[4]**
- $1 900 - €1 970 - **£1 140** - FF12 920
  Palazzo di versailles Olio/tela (78x47cm 30x18in) Roma 2001

CALVI Ercole 1824-1900 **[25]**
- $9 600 - €12 440 - **£7 200** - FF81 600
  Giochi in riva al lago Olio/tela (44.5x80.5cm 17x31in) Milano 2000
- $1 000 - €1 037 - **£600** - FF6 800
  Cascinale Olio/tavola (21x30.5cm 8x12in) Milano 1999

CALVI Leopoldo [1]
- $3 450 - €3 576 - **£2 070** - FF23 460
  Napoli e Venezia Acquatinta (27x94cm 10x37in) Roma 1999

CALVI Pietro 1833-1884 **[25]**
- $99 522 - €86 557 - **£60 000** - FF567 774
  «Othello», a Bust Bronze (H90cm H35in) London 1998
- $30 186 - €34 998 - **£21 384** - FF229 570
  Othello, Bust modelled as the Shakespearian Moor with the Face cast Bronze (H73cm H28in) Melbourne 2000

CALVO Carmen 1950 **[14]**
- $8 665 - €9 442 - **£6 000** - FF61 936
  «L'Almoina» Mixed media (120x120cm 47x47in) London 2001
- $1 987 - €2 252 - **£1 387** - FF14 775
  Composición Oleo/cartón (76.5x56cm 30x22in) Madrid 2001
- $2 536 - €2 723 - **£1 697** - FF17 859
  Paisaje Tizas de Colores Coloured chalks (120x120cm 47x47in) Amsterdam 2000

CALVO Edmond François 1892-1958 **[26]**
- $7 617 - €7 013 - **£4 572** - FF46 000
  Le joyeux cow-boy Huile/panneau (55x45cm 21x17in) Paris 1999
- $695 - €640 - **£417** - FF4 200
  Le corbeau et le renard Gouache/papier (27x36cm 10x14in) Paris 1999

CALY Odette 1914 **[1]**
- $1 608 - €1 372 - **£970** - FF9 000
  Tapisserie Tapisserie (130x180cm 51x70in) Calais 1998

CALYO Niccolino V. 1799-1884 **[8]**
- $17 000 - €18 748 - **£11 512** - FF122 979
  Niagara Falls from Table Rock/View of Niagara Falls Oil/canvas (46x61cm 18x24in) New-York 2000
- $7 500 - €7 558 - **£4 985** - FF49 575
  The Bay of Naples with an American Frigate Gouache/paper (67.5x92cm 26x36in) New-York 2000

CALZA Antonio 1653-1725 **[26]**
- $22 000 - €28 508 - **£16 800** - FF187 000
  Battaglie Olio/tela (96x148cm 37x58in) Milano 2000
- $3 600 - €4 665 - **£2 700** - FF30 600
  Battaglie Olio/tela (73x99cm 28x38in) Milano 2001
- $20 390 - €19 910 - **£13 000** - FF130 598
  Cavalry Skirmish: outside a fortified Town/outside a Fortress... Oil/canvas (33.5x43cm 13x16in) London 1999

CALZADA Humberto 1944 **[7]**
- $12 000 - €10 437 - **£7 234** - FF68 460
  «Escher's Tropical House» Acrylic/canvas (122x183cm 48x72in) New-York 1998

CALZOLARI Pier Paolo 1943 **[38]**
- $10 000 - €10 367 - **£6 000** - FF68 000
  Composizione Tecnica mista/cartone (145x103cm 57x40in) Milano 2000
- $4 800 - €6 220 - **£3 600** - FF40 800
  Senza titolo Tecnica mista (70x100cm 27x39in) Milano 2001
- $44 896 - €53 395 - **£32 000** - FF350 246
  Io e miei 5 ami nell'angolo della mia reale reale predica Construction (250x180cm 98x71in) London 2000
- $1 600 - €2 073 - **£1 200** - FF13 600
  Senza titolo Matita (70x105cm 27x41in) Milano 2000

CAMACHO Jorge 1934 **[115]**
- $4 690 - €5 336 - **£3 255** - FF35 000
  «Le faiseur de pluie» Huile/toile (200x60cm 78x23in) Douai 2000
- $2 760 - €2 592 - **£1 710** - FF17 000
  Le regard brut Huile/toile (100x81cm 39x31in) Paris 1999
- $511 - €610 - **£364** - FF4 000
  Composition aux animaux fantastiques Mine plomb (50x65cm 19x25in) Paris 2000

CAMARA Victor 1921-1998 **[31]**
- $11 250 - €12 463 - **£7 250** - FF81 750
  Estrada de Azáleas Oleo/lienzo (100x140cm 39x55in) Lisboa 2000
- $4 050 - €4 349 - **£2 610** - FF29 430
  Paisagem açoreana com vacas a pastar Oleo/lienzo (70x100cm 27x39in) Lisboa 2000
- $308 - €349 - **£203** - FF2 289
  Retrato antigo Oil/wood (40x30.5cm 15x12in) Lisboa 2000

CAMARGO de Sergio 1930-1990 **[14]**
- $43 326 - €47 211 - **£30 000** - FF309 684
  «No.345» Mixed media (61x49.5cm 24x19in) London 2001

C

$9 598 - €8 796 - **£5 864** - FF57 696
Relief Nr.179 Sculpture bois (24.5x11.5cm 9x4in)
Zürich 1999

CAMARO Alexander 1901-1992 **[68]**
$188 - €179 - **£116** - FF1 173
Komposition Farbserigraphie (53x67.9cm 20x26in)
Hamburg 1999

CAMARON Y BORONAT José 1731-1803 **[8]**
$22 750 - €21 023 - **£14 000** - FF137 900
Alegoria del Comercio Oleo/lienzo (129x113.5cm
50x44in) Madrid 1999
$21 350 - €21 023 - **£13 650** - FF137 900
**Paisaje costero con puente y pastoras/Paisaje
fluvial con arquitectura** Oleo/lienzo (42x59cm
16x23in) Madrid 1999
$4 560 - €4 805 - **£2 880** - FF31 520
Alegoría Oleo/tabla (15.5x12cm 6x4in) Madrid 2000
$1 235 - €1 141 - **£741** - FF7 486
Sagrada Familia Tinta/papel (15x10cm 5x3in) Madrid
1999

CAMARON Y TORRA Vicente 1803-1864 **[4]**
$2 250 - €2 252 - **£1 387** - FF14 775
Escena de naufragio Oleo/lienzo (27x38cm
10x14in) Madrid 2000

CAMASSEI Andrea 1602-1649 **[4]**
$9 500 - €9 848 - **£5 700** - FF64 600
Strage degli Innocenti Olio/tela (75.5x123cm
29x48in) Formigine, Mo 2000
$842 - €818 - **£524** - FF5 366
Die heilige Familie mit Johannes der Täufer
Radierung (17x22.1cm 6x8in) Berlin 1999

CAMAUR Antonio 1875-1921 **[1]**
$4 800 - €5 304 - **£3 328** - FF34 793
Figure of a Reclining Infant Marble (48.5x65.5cm
19x25in) New-York 2001

CAMBELLOTTI Duilio 1876-1960 **[19]**
$2 322 - €2 641 - **£1 610** - FF17 326
Reiter zu Pferd Bronze (H35cm H13in) Zofingen
2000
$575 - €597 - **£345** - FF3 913
**«Feste commemorative della proclamazione del
regno d'Italia»** Affiche couleur (90x45cm 35x17in)
Torino 2000

CAMBI Andrei XIX-XX **[5]**
$26 000 - €30 575 - **£18 642** - FF200 561
The Toast Marble (H55cm H21in) New-York 2001

CAMBIASO Giovanni 1495-1579 **[1]**
$3 290 - €3 634 - **£2 280** - FF23 835
Kämpfende in antiker Rüstung Ink (19.3x27.9cm
7x10in) Wien 2001

CAMBIASO Luca 1527-1585 **[83]**
$20 500 - €21 251 - **£12 300** - FF139 400
Madonna con Bambino Olio/tela (88x74.5cm
34x29in) Imbersago (Lecco) 2001
$3 119 - €3 053 - **£2 000** - FF20 024
**St. Roch/Four Female Figures walking Hand in
Hand** Ink (27.5x30.5cm 10x12in) London 1999

CAMBIER Guy 1923 **[208]**
$639 - €616 - **£400** - FF4 040
Fille, Tête Bleue Oil/canvas (46x38cm 18x14in)
London 1999
$258 - €244 - **£160** - FF1 600
Travaux des champs Huile/isorel (22x27cm 8x10in)
Neuilly-sur-Seine 1999

CAMBIER Juliette 1879-1963 **[30]**
$733 - €694 - **£456** - FF4 552
Nature morte aux fleurs Huile/toile (60.5x73cm
23x28in) Bruxelles 1999

CAMBIER Nestor 1879-1957 **[36]**
$507 - €548 - **£350** - FF3 594
**Mixed Roses in Vases, Fruit and Brass Coffee-
Pot,Partilly Draped Table** Oil/canvas/board
(54x72.5cm 21x28in) London 2001

CAMBON Glauco 1875-1930 **[7]**
$3 800 - €3 939 - **£2 280** - FF25 840
**Pan insegue la Ninfa ai limiti del bosco/Alla
fonte** Olio/tavola (33x32cm 12x12in) Trieste 2001
$2 551 - €2 644 - **£1 530** - FF17 346
«Italia - Courmayeur» Affiche couleur (110x75cm
43x29in) Torino 2000

CAMBOUR Claude XX **[6]**
$1 200 - €1 260 - **£756** - FF8 265
Dock Scene at Honfleur Oil/canvas (80.5x80cm
31x31in) Washington 2000

CAMBRESIER Jean 1856-1928 **[18]**
$516 - €595 - **£355** - FF3 902
Coucher de soleil à Liège Aquarelle/papier
(34x53cm 13x20in) Liège 2000

CAMENISCH Paul 1893-1970 **[40]**
$777 - €869 - **£523** - FF5 701
Valle Muggio Coloured chalks/paper (34x50cm
13x19in) München 2000

CAMENZIND Balz 1907-1990 **[15]**
$1 465 - €1 702 - **£1 029** - FF11 167
Baumlandschaft Oil/panel (56x52cm 22x20in)
Luzern 2001

CAMERATAS Giuseppe II 1718-1803 **[3]**
$4 410 - €3 833 - **£2 657** - FF25 140
**Erzherzogin Maria von Oesterreich im Costüm
einer Dame von Galata** Radierung (30.8x24.8cm
12x9in) Berlin 1998

CAMERON David Young 1865-1945 **[313]**
$4 403 - €5 059 - **£3 048** - FF33 182
Loch Maree/Ben Slioch Oil/canvas (63x76cm
25x30in) Hamilton, Lanarkshire 2000
$6 091 - €5 754 - **£3 800** - FF37 746
The Giesha Girl Oil/canvas (46x34cm 18x13in)
Perthshire 1999
$859 - €967 - **£600** - FF6 340
View of a Loch with Mountains beyond
Watercolour (24x35.5cm 9x13in) London 2001
$153 - €153 - **£96** - FF1 006
Holyrood House Radierung (33.2x47cm 13x18in)
München 1999

CAMERON Douglas XIX-XX **[21]**
$1 242 - €1 400 - **£860** - FF9 184
Highland Cattle by a Loch Oil/canvas (47x61.5cm
18x24in) Toronto 2000

CAMERON Duncan 1837-1916 **[70]**
$1 562 - €1 529 - **£1 000** - FF10 028
Sunny Afternoon near Crail, Fife Oil/canvas
(49x74cm 19x29in) Perth 1999
$1 084 - €1 277 - **£750** - FF8 378
River Landscape with Cottages and Reepers
Oil/canvas (29x45cm 11x17in) Stansted Mounthitchet,
Essex 2000

CAMERON Hugh 1835-1918 **[26]**
$3 623 - €3 889 - **£2 424** - FF25 511
Preparing for the Journey Oil/canvas (37.5x50cm
14x19in) Toronto 2000

$1 600 - €1 583 - **£1 000** - FF10 384
The New Kitten Oil/canvas (25.5x35.5cm 10x13in)
Glasgow 1999

CAMERON John c.1828-1876 **[7]**
$1 600 - €1 934 - **£1 117** - FF12 685
The Celebrated Horse Dexter, The King of the Turf Lithograph (54x75cm 21x29in) Bolton MA 2000

CAMERON John XX **[1]**
$3 539 - €3 919 - **£2 400** - FF25 708
«Pavlova» Poster (188x102cm 74x40in) London 2000

CAMERON Julia Margaret 1815-1879 **[211]**
$7 915 - €8 866 - **£5 500** - FF58 157
Valentine Cameron Prinsep Albumen print (34.5x27cm 13x10in) London 2001

CAMERON Katherine 1874-1965 **[34]**
$1 026 - €1 075 - **£650** - FF7 054
Appin Head Watercolour (15x24cm 5x9in) Edinburgh 2000
$170 - €159 - **£105** - FF1 042
Wild Violets Etching (16x19cm 6x7in) Fernhurst, Haslemere, Surrey 1999

CAMERON Mary ?-1921 **[8]**
$28 600 - €31 378 - **£19 000** - FF25 827
Hurst Park races, Middlesex Oil/canvas (68.5x81.5cm 26x32in) London 2000

CAMERON Robert Hartley 1909 **[13]**
$3 200 - €2 704 - **£1 902** - FF17 739
Family at the Beach Oil/canvas (76x101cm 30x40in) Philadelphia PA 1998

CAMESI Gianfredo 1940 **[21]**
$306 - €283 - **£188** - FF1 854
Komposition Gouache/paper (34x34.5cm 13x13in) Stockholm 1999

CAMIN RUBIO Joaquin 1929 **[15]**
$15 000 - €15 016 - **£9 250** - FF98 500
Mujeres Oleo/lienzo (130x97cm 51x38in) Madrid 2000
$3 250 - €3 904 - **£2 275** - FF25 610
Paisaje urbano (Asturias) Oleo/lienzo (51x62cm 20x24in) Madrid 2000

CAMINADE Alexandre François 1789-1862 **[9]**
$5 787 - €6 860 - **£4 216** - FF45 000
Adèle de Maillé La Tour Landry, comtesse d'Hautefort Huile/toile (60x40cm 23x15in) Paris 2001

CAMM Robert 1847-1933 **[13]**
$1 664 - €1 530 - **£1 028** - FF10 035
Sheep in a Landscape Oil/canvas (51.5x89.5cm 20x35in) Melbourne 1998

CAMMARANO Michele 1835-1920 **[47]**
$34 000 - €44 058 - **£25 500** - FF289 000
Suonatori ambulanti Olio/tela (110x71.5cm 43x28in) Prato 2000
$4 800 - €4 147 - **£2 400** - FF27 200
Paesaggio roccioso di Cava Olio/tela (28.5x40cm 11x15in) Torino 1999

CAMMIDGE George XIX **[9]**
$1 500 - €1 440 - **£929** - FF9 449
A Quiet Afternoon on the Lake Oil/canvas (40x60cm 16x24in) Delray-Beach FL 1999

CAMMILLIERI OF MALTA Niccolo c.1800-c.1860 **[3]**
$3 075 - €2 895 - **£1 900** - FF18 989
Brig «Mary Winch» of Liverpool coming into Malta Watercolour (43.5x58.5cm 17x23in) London 1999

CAMMILLIERI OF MARSEILLES Nicholas c.1780-1855 **[16]**
$6 000 - €6 611 - **£4 002** - FF43 363
H.M.S.Rochfort, Off Malta Watercolour/paper (45x68cm 18x27in) Portsmouth NH 2000

CAMOCIO Giovanni Francesco XVI **[2]**
$2 787 - €3 323 - **£1 987** - FF21 800
Kämpfende Hengste im Wald, nach Baldung Grien Kupferstich (21.4x31.9cm 8x12in) Berlin 2000

CAMOIN Charles 1879-1965 **[687]**
$17 040 - €18 294 - **£11 400** - FF120 000
Paysage et coteaux près d'Aix-en-Provence Huile/toile (54x65cm 21x25in) Calais 2000
$5 291 - €5 641 - **£3 355** - FF37 500
Anémones et marguerites dans un vase Huile/carton (32.5x24cm 12x9in) Paris 2000
$3 369 - €2 897 - **£1 939** - FF19 000
Vue de la baie de Saint-Tropez Aquarelle/papier (20x24cm 7x9in) Calais 1999

CAMOREYT Jacques M. XIX-XX **[10]**
$11 498 - €11 586 - **£7 166** - FF76 000
Port méditerranéen animé Huile/toile (59x92cm 23x36in) Nice 2000

CAMOS Honoré 1906 **[13]**
$1 153 - €1 372 - **£822** - FF9 000
Pêcheurs dans un port méditerranéen Huile/panneau (60x73cm 23x28in) Lyon 2000

CAMP Jeffrey Bruce 1923 **[34]**
$1 195 - €1 283 - **£800** - FF8 417
Lovers On Pakefield Cliffs Oil/board (58.5x48cm 23x18in) London 2000

CAMP van Camille 1834-1891 **[26]**
$1 785 - €1 735 - **£1 092** - FF11 382
Bords de rivière Huile/toile (36x62cm 14x24in) Bruxelles 1999
$488 - €545 - **£341** - FF3 577
Dame au parasol Huile/toile (47x23cm 18x9in) Antwerpen 2001

CAMPABADAL PARDO José 1872-? **[4]**
$4 805 - €4 655 - **£3 022** - FF30 535
Oficial montano Oleo/lienzo (48.5x67cm 19x26in) Barcelona 1999

CAMPAGNA Girolamo 1550-c.1625 **[3]**
$14 400 - €18 660 - **£10 800** - FF122 000
Giunone Bronze (H36cm H14in) Firenze 2000

CAMPAGNARI Ottorino 1910-1987 **[50]**
$800 - €829 - **£480** - FF5 440
Lago del Frau, San Bernardo Olio/tavola (50x40cm 19x15in) Vercelli 2000
$240 - €311 - **£180** - FF2 040
Bimbe nel paesaggio Olio/tavola (29.5x39.5cm 11x15in) Torino 2000

CAMPAGNE Daniel P. Étienne 1851-1914 **[19]**
$2 000 - €2 301 - **£1 378** - FF15 096
Ondine, Woman by a Fountain Bronze (H75cm H29in) Boston MA 2000

CAMPAGNOLA Domenico 1494/1500-1564 **[25]**
$24 000 - €24 279 - **£14 654** - FF159 261
Extensive Mountainous Landscape with Cephalus and Procris Ink (36x48.5cm 14x19in) New-York 2000
$1 122 - €1 131 - **£700** - FF7 422
The Holy Family in an italianate Landscape, after Titian Woodcut in colors (44.5x30.5cm 17x12in) London 2000

CAMPAGNOLA Enrico 1911-1984 **[19]**
$1 069 - €915 - **£636** - FF6 000
La lampe Huile/toile (60x73cm 23x28in) Paris 1998

CAMPAGNOLI Adalberto 1905 **[2]**
$666 - €691 - **£399** - FF4 532
«**Torino, Italy**» Affiche couleur (99x62cm 38x24in)
Torino 2000

CAMPANA Tomaso XVII **[1]**
$11 973 - €11 243 - **£7 419** - FF73 749
Selbstbildnis Oil/panel (48.5x46.5cm 19x18in)
Luzern 1999

CAMPANELLA Angelo 1746-1811 **[6]**
$1 192 - €1 243 - **£750** - FF8 152
Fresco Designs, After Antonius Raphael Maron
Engraving (56x66cm 22x25in) London 2000

CAMPANELLA Vito 1932 **[2]**
$5 200 - €6 042 - **£3 654** - FF39 630
Elevación mística Oleo/lienzo (80x60cm 31x23in)
Buenos-Aires 2001

CAMPANO Miguel Angel 1948 **[11]**
$2 800 - €3 003 - **£1 900** - FF19 700
Composición Acrylique/carton (73x103cm 28x40in)
Barcelona 2001

CAMPBELL Christopher 1908-1972 **[5]**
$4 313 - €5 079 - **£3 031** - FF33 316
The Escort Oil/board (61x89cm 24x35in) Dublin 2000

CAMPBELL Cressida 1960 **[13]**
$516 - €500 - **£318** - FF3 278
Smoked mackerel Woodcut (28x68.5cm 11x26in)
Woollahra, Sydney 1999

CAMPBELL Edmund Simms 1881-1950 **[2]**
$1 600 - €1 865 - **£1 107** - FF12 234
**Tourists Photographing Topless Natives
Carrying Baskets** Watercolour/paper (44x29cm
17x11in) New-York 2000

CAMPBELL George F. 1917-1979 **[122]**
$6 096 - €6 143 - **£3 800** - FF40 293
Clown Writing Oil/board (51x40cm 20x15in) London
2000
$1 442 - €1 651 - **£992** - FF10 827
West of Ireland landscape Mixed media (27x41cm
11x16in) Dublin 2000
$1 311 - €1 524 - **£921** - FF9 994
Three Arabs, Tetuan Crayon (27x41cm 10x16in)
Dublin 2001

CAMPBELL Hugh XIX-XX **[23]**
$825 - €698 - **£494** - FF4 576
Lake House Oil/canvas (50x68cm 20x27in) Hatfield
PA 1998

CAMPBELL James 1828-1893 **[4]**
$49 047 - €56 996 - **£33 800** - FF373 866
Twilight, Trudging Homewards Oil/canvas
(56.5x45cm 22x17in) London 2001

CAMPBELL John Henry 1757-1828 **[17]**
$14 392 - €16 120 - **£10 000** - FF105 741
Extensive wooded Landscape, Co.Wicklow
Oil/canvas (74.5x100.5cm 29x39in) London 2001
$2 561 - €3 016 - **£1 800** - FF19 784
**Irish Views, Co.Wicklow/Dublin
Bay/Co.Down/Co.Fermanagh** Watercolour/paper
(15x20.5cm 5x8in) Suffolk 2000

CAMPBELL John Hodgson 1855-1927 **[13]**
$5 080 - €5 991 - **£3 583** - FF39 300
View of rose Bay Watercolour, gouache/paper
(38.5x64.5cm 15x25in) Woollahra, Sydney 2001

CAMPBELL John Reed XX **[17]**
$550 - €649 - **£386** - FF4 255
«**Nude Study for Discus Thrower, Tulane 75, Eric
Jim's Pal**» Oil/canvas (109x73cm 43x29in) New-
Orleans LA 2000
$500 - €589 - **£351** - FF3 865
Fall Evening Oil/canvas (27x35cm 11x14in) New-
Orleans LA 2000

CAMPBELL Marjorie Dunn 1910-1998 **[35]**
$150 - €146 - **£92** - FF955
Dancers Watercolour/paper (55x50cm 22x20in) Cedar-
Falls IA 2000

CAMPBELL Robert Richmond 1902-1972 **[84]**
$2 918 - €3 216 - **£1 941** - FF21 095
Kirribilli Point from Kurraba Oil/canvas (35.5x54cm
13x21in) Melbourne 2000
$1 672 - €1 585 - **£1 044** - FF10 399
«**Harbour, Early Morning**» Oil/board (12x19cm
4x7in) Woollahra, Sydney 1999

CAMPBELL Steven 1953 **[19]**
$330 - €371 - **£230** - FF2 435
Me Watercolour, gouache/paper (14.5x9.5cm 5x3in)
Edinburgh 2001

CAMPBELL Thomas, Tom 1865-1943 **[87]**
$1 095 - €1 205 - **£760** - FF7 906
Picnic by the River Oil/canvas (40.5x51cm 15x20in)
Glasgow 2001
$496 - €463 - **£300** - FF3 036
Sheep Grazing on a Spring Day Oil/board
(26.5x37cm 10x14in) Glasgow 1998
$345 - €332 - **£220** - FF2 176
«**The close of the Day, Garroch Head, Isles of
Bute**» Watercolour (25x34cm 9x13in) London 1999

CAMPECHE de José 1751-1809 **[4]**
$85 000 - €81 877 - **£52 776** - FF537 081
**Retrato de un oficial del regimento Fijo de
Puerto Rico** Oil/canvas (41x31.5cm 16x12in) New-
York 1999

CAMPECHE Miguel XVIII **[1]**
$43 200 - €48 052 - **£28 800** - FF315 200
Inmaculada Oleo/lienzo (85x61cm 33x24in) Madrid
2000

CAMPENDONCK Heinrich 1889-1957 **[208]**
$139 213 - €160 278 - **£95 000** - FF1 051 355
Interior with Nude and Figures Oil/canvas
(80x67.5cm 31x26in) London 2000
$52 587 - €59 903 - **£36 333** - FF392 940
Stilleben Öl/Leinwand (36.5x40cm 14x15in) Zürich
2000
$13 336 - €14 316 - **£8 926** - FF93 909
Springende Stiere Watercolour, gouache (9x14.1cm
3x5in) Hamburg 2000
$828 - €767 - **£507** - FF5 030
Frau mit Blume Woodcut (17.9x12.1cm 7x4in) Köln
1999

CAMPHAUSEN Wilhelm 1818-1885 **[30]**
$10 615 - €12 257 - **£7 425** - FF80 399
**Bataljscen med svenskar mot de kejserliga
arméerna,trettioåriga kriget** Oil/canvas (155x213cm
61x83in) Stockholm 2001
$3 055 - €3 634 - **£2 180** - FF23 835
Rendezvous im Wald Öl/Leinwand (40x47.5cm
15x18in) Wien 2000

CAMPHUIJSEN Jochem Govertsz. 1601-1659 **[15]**
$15 580 - €14 534 - **£9 400** - FF95 340
Bewaldete Landschaft mit einer Burgruine
Oil/panel (47.5x63cm 18x24in) Wien 1999

CAMPHUIJSEN Rafael Govertsz. 1598-1657 **[6]**
$43 579 - €42 838 - **£28 000** - FF280 996
Village Scene in the Dutch Countryside/Travellers, Dutch Landscape
Oil/panel (23.5x33.5cm 9x13in) London 1999

CAMPHUYSEN Govert Dircksz. 1623/24-1672 **[15]**
$6 643 - €6 555 - **£4 128** - FF43 000
Paysage aux promeneurs Huile/panneau (38x50cm 14x19in) Paris 1999

CAMPI Antonio c.1536-c.1591 **[5]**
$14 000 - €13 969 - **£8 521** - FF91 631
Man kneeling Black chalk (21x17.5cm 8x6in) New-York 2000

CAMPI Bernardino 1522-1592 **[12]**
$22 025 - €18 164 - **£12 975** - FF119 150
Ritratto di gentiluomo, Bildnis eines Edelmannes Öl/Leinwand (58.5x45.5cm 23x17in) Wien 1998

CAMPI Giacomo 1864-1921 **[26]**
$464 - €523 - **£320** - FF43 432
Vino Watercolour/paper (35x26cm 13x10in) Newbury, Berkshire 2000

CAMPI Giulio 1502-1572 **[12]**
$7 500 - €7 775 - **£4 500** - FF51 000
Crocifisso tra i Santi Domenico e Caterina da Siena Olio/tela (65x55cm 25x21in) Venezia 1999
$3 743 - €3 663 - **£2 400** - FF24 029
Putto Holding a Basket of Fruit Red chalk (17.5x10cm 6x3in) London 1999

CAMPI Vincenzo c.1532/36-1591 **[3]**
$18 500 - €19 178 - **£11 100** - FF125 800
Donna con piatto di frutta, a destra, paesaggio con agricoltori Olio/tela (93.5x73.5cm 36x28in) Venezia 2000

CAMPIGLI Massimo 1895-1971 **[598]**
$230 000 - €238 430 - **£138 000** - FF1 564 000
Gioco del diabolo Olio/tela (129x160cm 50x62in) Prato 2000
$68 000 - €88 116 - **£51 000** - FF578 000
Idoli Olio/tela (80x80cm 31x31in) Milano 2000
$26 000 - €26 953 - **£15 600** - FF176 800
Testina Olio/tela (38.5x32.5cm 15x12in) Milano 2000
$26 400 - €34 210 - **£19 800** - FF224 400
Donna con bambino Terracotta (34x30x4cm 13x11x1in) Milano 2001
$7 292 - €6 796 - **£4 500** - FF44 580
Due Figura Charcoal/paper (51x21cm 20x8in) London 1999
$1 200 - €1 070 - **£739** - FF7 016
Donna al balcone Color lithograph (59x49cm 23x19in) New-York 1999

CAMPION George Bryant 1796-1870 **[46]**
$634 - €666 - **£400** - FF4 369
Château de Chillion on Lake le Mans/Lake Geneva near Villeneuve Pencil (29x46.5cm 11x18in) London 2000

CAMPO del Federico 1837-1923 **[73]**
$65 628 - €60 099 - **£40 000** - FF394 224
Murano, Venice Oil/canvas (43.5x74cm 17x29in) London 1999
$29 000 - €25 020 - **£17 495** - FF164 119
A Busy Thoroughfare Oil/panel (28x18cm 11x7in) New-York 1998
$4 036 - €3 659 - **£2 447** - FF24 000
Gondola Beneath the Bridge of Sights, Venice Watercolour/paper (31.5x20cm 12x7in) Sydney 1998

CAMPOLO Placido 1693-1743 **[2]**
$10 500 - €10 885 - **£6 300** - FF71 400
Due vedute del porto di Messina Olio/tela (47.5x97cm 18x38in) Milano 1999

CAMPOREALE Sergio 1937 **[18]**
$1 000 - €973 - **£615** - FF6 382
El procurador Watercolour (59.5x79.5cm 23x31in) New-York 1999

CAMPOTOSTO Henri/y 1833-1910 **[31]**
$17 872 - €20 452 - **£12 292** - FF134 156
Zwei kleine Hirtinnen mit Hund, Ziegen, Schafen und Hühnern Oil/panel (35x47cm 13x18in) München 1999
$12 032 - €12 124 - **£7 500** - FF79 531
Feeding the Chickens Oil/panel (42x33.5cm 16x13in) London 2000

CAMPRIANI Alceste 1848-1923 **[61]**
$6 400 - €8 293 - **£4 800** - FF54 400
Il rientro della pesca Olio/tela (68x47cm 26x18in) Roma 2000
$2 900 - €3 006 - **£1 740** - FF19 720
L'acquaiolo Olio/tela (41x25cm 16x9in) Roma 2000
$3 000 - €3 887 - **£2 250** - FF25 500
Pecore Pastelli (63x100.5cm 24x39in) Prato 2000

CAMPRIANI Tullio XIX **[2]**
$4 000 - €3 719 - **£2 469** - FF24 398
Canal in Venice Oil/canvas (49x40cm 19x16in) Portland ME 1999

CAMPROBIN de Pedro 1605-1674 **[7]**
$130 000 - €114 031 - **£78 936** - FF747 994
Iris, Lilies, Roses and Carnations in Elaborate Urns Oil/canvas (94x73.5cm 37x28in) New-York 1999
$60 000 - €64 181 - **£40 908** - FF421 002
Plums and Apples in a Pewter Dish resting on a Ledge Oil/canvas (19.5x24cm 7x9in) New-York 2001

CAMPS Gaspar 1874-1931 **[8]**
$463 - €505 - **£320** - FF3 312
«Toulouse» Poster (105x74cm 41x29in) London 2001

CAMPS RIBERA Francisco 1895-1992 **[17]**
$371 - €420 - **£259** - FF2 758
Bodegón Oleo/lienzo (50x61cm 19x24in) Barcelona 2000

CAMPUZANO Y AGUIRRE Tomás 1857-1934 **[73]**
$1 820 - €1 952 - **£1 235** - FF12 805
Marina con trainera Oleo/tabla (19x35.5cm 7x13in) Madrid 2001
$420 - €420 - **£259** - FF2 758
Paisaje de montaña Acuarela/papel (36x27cm 14x10in) Madrid 2000
$145 - €168 - **£100** - FF1 103
Campesina Grabado (8.5x13.5cm 3x5in) Seville 2000

CAMRADT Frederik Christian 1762-1844 **[5]**
$3 697 - €3 499 - **£2 301** - FF22 955
Portraet af ung pige med törklaede bundet löst om halsen Oil/canvas (32.5x27.5cm 12x10in) Vejle 1999

CAMRADT Johannes Ludvig 1779-1849 **[19]**
$42 210 - €40 402 - **£26 220** - FF265 020
Syrener, roser, iris, paeoner og guldregen i en krukke på en melon Oil/canvas (80x68cm 31x26in) København 1999
$5 628 - €5 387 - **£3 496** - FF35 336
Opstilling med vindruer, melon, ferskner, valnöd, vinglas... Oil/canvas (35x42cm 13x16in) København 1999

C

CAMUCCINI Vincenzo 1771-1844 [17]
$2 464 - €2 287 - **£1 479** - FF15 000
Portrait d'un brigand italien Huile/toile (100x81cm 39x31in) Paris 1999

$550 - €570 - **£330** - FF3 740
Tolomeo Filadelfo nella Biblioteca di Alessandria Matita/carta (17x27cm 6x10in) Milano 2000

CAMUS Blanche Augustine 1884-1968 [27]
$3 199 - €3 196 - **£2 000** - FF20 964
Jeune fille à la campagne Oil/panel (46x38cm 18x14in) London 1999

CAMUS Gustave 1914-1984 [137]
$843 - €942 - **£585** - FF6 178
Le poisson bleu Huile/toile (69x30cm 27x11in) Antwerpen 2001

$468 - €545 - **£334** - FF3 577
«La dune ocrée» Huile/toile (22x49cm 8x19in) Bruxelles 2001

$279 - €309 - **£189** - FF2 029
Kustlandskap med bâtar vid strand (Coast View with Boats and Beach) Akvarell/papper (30x40cm 11x15in) Stockholm 2000

CAMUS Jacques 1937 [12]
$2 296 - €2 592 - **£1 615** - FF17 000
«Paris, Place de la Contrescarpe,hiver» Huile/panneau (46x55cm 18x21in) Paris 2001

CANA Louis Émile 1845-c.1895 [10]
$819 - €915 - **£555** - FF6 000
Couple de pluviers dorés Bronze (21x28x18cm 8x11x7in) Pontoise 2000

CANADÉ Vincent 1879-1961 [1]
$950 - €1 099 - **£672** - FF7 212
New York Roofs Lithograph (37x37cm 14x14in) New-York 2000

CANAL von Gilbert 1849-1927 [27]
$1 334 - €1 278 - **£839** - FF8 384
Holländische Flusslandschaft im Herbst, vorne am Ufer ein Mann Öl/Leinwand (45.5x65cm 17x25in) Köln 1999

CANALETTO Antonio Canal 1697-1768 [255]
$606 900 - €524 287 - **£404 600** - FF3 439 100
San Cristoforo, San Michele e Murano dalle Fondamente Nuove Olio/tela (141x155cm 55x61in) Venezia 1998

$1 500 000 - €1 499 298 - **£916 350** - FF9 834 750
The Church of St Giorgio Maggiore, Venice, with Sandalos and Gondolas Oil/canvas (47.5x77.5cm 18x30in) New-York 2000

$92 646 - €99 448 - **£62 000** - FF652 339
Convent by a River in the Veneto Wash (20.5x30.5cm 8x12in) London 2000

$3 200 - €3 029 - **£1 990** - FF19 868
The Portico with the Lantern Etching (30.5x43cm 12x16in) New-York 1999

CANALS Y LLAMBI Ricardo 1876-1931 [64]
$20 100 - €18 019 - **£12 300** - FF118 200
Escena de interior Oleo/lienzo (51.5x61.5cm 20x24in) Madrid 1999

$3 190 - €3 304 - **£2 035** - FF21 670
Ejercicio ecuestre en un círco Acuarela (35.5x26cm 13x10in) Barcelona 2000

$441 - €381 - **£261** - FF2 500
Danse espagnole Eau-forte, aquatinte (25x32.5cm 9x12in) Paris 1998

CAÑAS Benjamin 1933-1987 [20]
$50 000 - €53 330 - **£33 305** - FF349 820
El ilusionista Oil/panel (117x117cm 46x46in) New-York 2000

$15 000 - €14 595 - **£9 232** - FF95 734
Música Oil/wood (51x61cm 20x24in) New-York 1999

$6 000 - €5 181 - **£3 660** - FF33 982
Untitled Pastel/paper (113x82cm 44x32in) Miami FL 1999

CAÑAS Josep 1905-2001 [7]
$2 703 - €3 063 - **£1 836** - FF20 094
Mujer en jarras Pierre (H45cm H17in) Barcelona 2000

CAÑAVERAL Y PÉREZ Alfonso 1855-1932 [3]
$6 720 - €7 208 - **£4 440** - FF47 280
El brindis Oleo/lienzo (81x41cm 31x16in) Madrid 2000

CAÑAVERAL Y PÉREZ Enrique XIX-XX [2]
$3 780 - €3 265 - **£1 890** - FF21 420
Pastorella con tacchini Acquarello/cartone (57x80cm 22x31in) Milano 1999

CANCARET Jacques XIX-XX [3]
$6 500 - €7 552 - **£4 568** - FF49 537
Nude with a necklace Oil/canvas (110x82cm 43x32in) New-York 2001

CANCIANI Jacob c.1820-1891 [8]
$3 936 - €4 360 - **£2 670** - FF28 602
Friulanisches Tal Öl/Leinwand (48x64cm 18x25in) Klagenfurt 2000

CANDEE George E. 1837-1967 [1]
$4 250 - €4 012 - **£2 642** - FF26 320
Connecticut Homestead Oil/canvas (45x60cm 18x24in) Milford CT 1999

CANDIDO Salvatore XIX [20]
$28 420 - €29 781 - **£18 000** - FF195 352
Veduta di Napoli dal Carmine Oil/canvas (48x70cm 18x27in) London 1999

$16 000 - €16 586 - **£9 600** - FF108 800
Napoli Oil/tela (30x40cm 11x15in) Milano 1999

CANE du Ella c.1880-c.1940 [32]
$491 - €456 - **£300** - FF2 988
Flowers in Bloom on the Amalfi Coast Watercolour/paper (28.5x44.5cm 11x17in) London 1998

CANE Louis 1943 [467]
$2 562 - €3 049 - **£1 830** - FF20 000
Les Nymphéas Technique mixte (120x120cm 47x47in) Paris 2000

$1 242 - €1 372 - **£861** - FF9 000
Les Nymphéas Huile/papier (73x55cm 28x21in) Paris 2001

$13 272 - €12 196 - **£8 176** - FF80 000
Couple allongé Bronze (150x78x31cm 59x30x12in) Deauville 1998

$3 003 - €3 354 - **£2 035** - FF22 000
Menine Bronze (35x23x23cm 13x9x9in) Versailles 2000

$649 - €610 - **£402** - FF4 000
Mes ménines Gouache/papier (75.5x56.5cm 29x22in) Paris 1999

$69 - €76 - **£44** - FF500
Assemblée tribale Lithographie (69x59cm 27x23in) Bernay 2000

CANEGALLO Sexto 1892-1966 [5]
$12 800 - €16 586 - **£9 600** - FF108 800
Topazio Olio/tela (69.5x39cm 27x15in) Roma 2001

CANELLA Antonio XIX [17]
- 📧 **$419** - €385 - **£260** - FF2 527
  The Musical Recital Watercolour (17.5x23.5cm 6x9in) London 1999

CANELLA Carlo 1800-1879 [13]
- 🖎 **$22 848** - €19 738 - **£11 424** - FF129 472
  Castello del Valentino visto dall'eremo dei Capuccini a Torino Olio/tela (64x88.5cm 25x34in) Milano 1999
- 🖎 **$5 000** - €5 183 - **£3 000** - FF34 000
  Veduta del Coro della Chiesa dei frari a Venezia Olio/cartone (18x13cm 7x5in) Milano 2001

CANELLA Giuseppe 1788-1847 [66]
- 🖎 **$21 000** - €18 141 - **£10 500** - FF119 000
  Paesaggio lagunare al tramonto Olio/tela (55x91cm 21x35in) Milano 1999
- 🖎 **$19 000** - €19 696 - **£11 400** - FF129 200
  La chiesa conciliare a Trento Olio/tela (25x30cm 9x11in) Milano 2000
- 📧 **$1 200** - €1 555 - **£900** - FF10 200
  Studio di due figure/Vedute di Trieste Matita/carta (19x26cm 7x10in) Milano 2000

CANET Marcel 1875-1959 [27]
- 🖎 **$1 968** - €2 287 - **£1 402** - FF15 000
  Place animée Huile/toile/carton (37.5x46cm 14x18in) Paris 2001

CANEVA Giacomo 1810-1890 [28]
- 📷 **$2 777** - €2 571 - **£1 700** - FF16 865
  Mother breastfeeding her Baby, Rome Albumen print (16x20cm 6x8in) London 1999

CANGIULLO Francesco 1884-1977 [28]
- 📧 **$1 100** - €1 140 - **£660** - FF7 480
  Testa femminile Acquarello/carta (26.5x21cm 10x8in) Milano 1999

CANGIULLO Pascalino XIX-XX [3]
- 🖎 **$7 249** - €7 515 - **£4 349** - FF49 298
  Campane Acquarello/carta (52.5x36.5cm 20x14in) Milano 1999

CANIFF Milton 1907-1988 [25]
- 📧 **$452** - €412 - **£282** - FF2 700
  Strip Terry et les Pirates, Nibble about Nuptials Encre Chine/papier (18x57cm 7x22in) Paris 1999

CANINI Giovanni Angelo 1617-1666 [4]
- 📧 **$4 391** - €4 288 - **£2 800** - FF28 128
  The Annunciation Red chalk (19x15cm 7x5in) London 1999

CANINO Vincenzo 1892-? [20]
- 🖎 **$3 272** - €3 392 - **£1 963** - FF22 253
  Veduta napoletana con personaggi e carrozzelle Olio/tavoletta (36x51cm 14x20in) Roma 2001
- 🖎 **$1 000** - €1 037 - **£600** - FF6 800
  Venezia Olio/tavola (20x24.5cm 7x9in) Milano 2000

CANNAVACCIULO Maurizio 1954 [5]
- 🖎 **$1 600** - €2 073 - **£1 200** - FF13 600
  «Madonna paffuta con bambino anoressico» Acrilico/tela (70.5x50.5cm 27x19in) Prato 2000

CANNEEL Eugène 1882-1966 [35]
- 🖎 **$898** - €1 041 - **£643** - FF6 829
  Jeune femme se coiffant Bronze (H55cm H21in) Bruxelles 1999

CANNELL Ashton 1927-1994 [10]
- 📧 **$373** - €401 - **£250** - FF2 632
  St.Paul's From the Thames Watercolour/paper (50x66.5cm 19x26in) London 2000

CANNEY Michael 1923 [20]
- 🖎 **$703** - €689 - **£450** - FF4 517
  Sequence I Oil/board (30.5x30.5cm 12x12in) London 1999

CANNICCI Niccoló 1846-1906 [54]
- 🖎 **$20 000** - €20 733 - **£12 000** - FF136 000
  Pastore con il gregge all'alba Olio/tela (37.5x72cm 14x28in) Milano 2000
- 🖎 **$4 200** - €5 442 - **£3 150** - FF35 700
  Pastorella con gregge Acquarello/carta (36.5x26cm 14x10in) Milano 2000

CANNICIONI Léon Charles 1879-1957 [8]
- 🖎 **$18 427** - €20 581 - **£12 487** - FF135 000
  Allégorie Corse Oil/canvas (127x290cm 50x114in) Fontainebleau 2000
- 🖎 **$4 155** - €4 421 - **£2 627** - FF29 000
  Paysage de Corse: Calvi Huile/toile (54x65cm 21x25in) Paris 2000

CANNON William XIX-XX [5]
- 🖎 **$483** - €566 - **£340** - FF3 710
  Sailing Vessels in a Light Sea off a Harbour Town Watercolour/paper (13x28cm 5x11in) Oxfordshire 1999

CANO Alonso 1601-1667 [14]
- 🖎 **$27 500** - €30 032 - **£18 500** - FF197 000
  Cristo atado a la columna Oleo/lienzo (161x111cm 63x43in) Madrid 2000
- 🖎 **$16 269** - €19 161 - **£11 484** - FF125 686
  San Pedro Mártir/Santo Domingo Oleo/lienzo (76x41cm 29x16in) Madrid 2000
- 🖎 **$21 000** - €21 023 - **£12 950** - FF137 336
  Virgen de la Caridad Terracotta (H40.5cm H15in) Madrid 2000
- 📧 **$5 325** - €4 505 - **£3 150** - FF29 550
  Estudio de friso y capitel Tinta/papel (21x14cm 8x5in) Madrid 1998

CANOGAR Rafael García Gómez 1935 [156]
- 🖎 **$5 716** - €6 403 - **£3 973** - FF42 000
  Nocturno urbano Nº2 Acrylique/toile (200x200cm 78x78in) Paris 2001
- 🖎 **$6 890** - €7 808 - **£4 680** - FF51 220
  Sin título Oleo/tabla (100x64cm 39x25in) Madrid 2000
- 📧 **$2 816** - €2 643 - **£1 760** - FF17 336
  Composición Técnica mixta, dibujo (90x63cm 35x24in) Madrid 1999
- ▥ **$230** - €216 - **£144** - FF1 418
  Torso Litografía (64x49cm 25x19in) Madrid 1999

CANON Hans v.Straschiripka 1829-1885 [40]
- 🖎 **$8 554** - €10 174 - **£6 104** - FF66 738
  Türkischer Bazar Öl/Leinwand (144x104cm 56x40in) Wien 2000
- 🖎 **$2 744** - €2 352 - **£1 650** - FF15 425
  Selbstbildnis Öl/Leinwand (68x56cm 26x22in) Köln 1998

CANONICA Pietro 1869-1959 [4]
- ▧ **$4 750** - €4 924 - **£2 850** - FF32 300
  Ragazza in costume di Gressoney Bronzo (37x37x17cm 14x14x6in) Torino 2001

CANOT Pierre Ch. 1710-1777 [14]
- ▥ **$547** - €507 - **£340** - FF3 324
  Moderate Gale, after Backhuizen/Brisk Gale, after van der Velde Engraving (38x50cm 14x19in) Cheshire 1999

C

CANOVA Antonio 1757-1822 **[77]**

🐾 **$16 851** - €14 286 - **£10 000** - FF93 710
Busts of Napoleon and Canova Plaster (H228cm H90in) London 1998

🐾 **$4 748** - €4 403 - **£2 900** - FF28 884
Bust of a Lady Marble (H39cm H15in) London 1998

CANOVAS Fernando 1960 **[20]**

🖋 **$19 000** - €18 486 - **£11 694** - FF121 263
La Rueda-Gevurah Mixed media/canvas (200x200cm 78x78in) New-York 1999

CANT James Montgomery 1911-1982 **[47]**

☞ **$2 218** - €2 444 - **£1 475** - FF16 032
New Growth Oil/canvas (121x90cm 47x35in) Melbourne 2000

🖋 **$1 052** - €1 226 - **£743** - FF8 058
Still life with Roses Pastel/paper (26.5x22.5cm 10x8in) Malvern, Victoria 2000

CANTA de F. XIX **[1]**

☞ **$8 052** - €7 603 - **£5 000** - FF49 872
Humboldt on the Orinoco Oil/canvas/board (25.5x36.5cm 10x14in) London 1999

CANTA Johannes Antonius 1816-1888 **[7]**

☞ **$3 184** - €3 323 - **£2 015** - FF21 800
Jäger mit Weinglas, Flinte und allerlei Jagdutensilien Oil/panel (43x31cm 16x12in) München 2000

CANTAGALLINA Remigio c.1580-1656 **[29]**

🖋 **$1 770** - €1 982 - **£1 201** - FF13 000
Paysage boisé Encre (35.5x25.5cm 13x10in) Paris 2000

🗂 **$583** - €665 - **£406** - FF4 360
Evrito Echione et Etalide Radierung (19.5x26.5cm 7x10in) Berlin 2001

CANTARINI IL PESARESE Simone 1612-1648 **[86]**

☞ **$105 280** - €116 276 - **£72 960** - FF762 720
Madonna con bambino Öl/Leinwand (128x96.5cm 50x37in) Wien 2001

☞ **$58 904** - €66 045 - **£40 000** - FF433 228
Putti in Landscapes Oil/canvas (64x80cm 25x31in) London 2000

🖋 **$2 849** - €2 424 - **£1 740** - FF15 900
The Flaying of Marsyas/Partial Study of a Girl's Lower Face Red chalk (25.5x17.5cm 10x6in) London 1998

🗂 **$712** - €838 - **£511** - FF5 500
Mercure et Argus Eau-forte (25.5x30cm 10x11in) Paris 2001

CANTATORE Domenico 1906-1998 **[170]**

☞ **$7 000** - €7 257 - **£4 200** - FF47 600
Nudo Olio/tela (40x50cm 15x19in) Milano 1999

☞ **$5 100** - €4 406 - **£3 400** - FF28 900
Donna seduta Olio/cartone (35x28cm 13x11in) Roma 1998

🖋 **$1 400** - €1 451 - **£840** - FF9 520
Paesaggio Acquarello/carta (31x46cm 12x18in) Roma 2000

🗂 **$200** - €207 - **£120** - FF1 360
Gallo Litografia (25x18.5cm 9x7in) Firenze 2001

CANTI Giovanni 1653-1716 **[1]**

☞ **$18 000** - €18 660 - **£10 800** - FF122 400
Battaglia Olio/tela (94x139cm 37x54in) Prato 2000

CANTINEAU Virgile 1864-? **[6]**

☞ **$3 744** - €4 462 - **£2 682** - FF29 268
Les travaux ménagers Huile/panneau (29.5x37.5cm 11x14in) Bruxelles 2000

CANTO DA MAYA Ernesto 1890-1981 **[125]**

🐾 **$4 400** - €4 985 - **£3 000** - FF32 700
Toilette Terracotta (92x36x29cm 36x14x11in) Lisboa 2000

🐾 **$1 232** - €1 396 - **£840** - FF9 156
Rapariga com Pombas Terracotta (39x10.5cm 15x4in) Lisboa 2000

🖋 **$484** - €548 - **£330** - FF3 597
Nú, rapaz Dessin (63x28.5cm 24x11in) Lisboa 2000

CANTRÉ Jozef 1890-1957 **[85]**

🐾 **$845** - €908 - **£565** - FF5 953
Nude Boy (ash-tray) Bronze (H23cm H9in) Amsterdam 2000

CANU Yvonne 1921 **[180]**

☞ **$2 069** - €1 982 - **£1 275** - FF13 000
Saint-Tropez ensoleillé Huile/toile (50x65cm 19x25in) La Varenne-Saint-Hilaire 1999

☞ **$1 509** - €1 372 - **£926** - FF9 000
Le Cap Ferrat Huile/toile (35x27cm 13x10in) Biarritz 1998

CANUT Denis 1953 **[41]**

☞ **$294** - €274 - **£181** - FF1 800
Fruits sur un entablement Huile/toile (33x41cm 12x16in) Orléans 1999

CANUTI Domenico Maria 1620-1684 **[29]**

🖋 **$4 799** - €4 739 - **£2 891** - FF31 086
Study of a Faun Black, red & white chalks/paper (38x25.5cm 14x10in) New-York 2000

🗂 **$948** - €920 - **£590** - FF6 037
Die Madonna mit dem Rosenkranz über der Stadt Bologna Radierung (27.7x19cm 10x7in) Berlin 1999

CANZIANI Estella Louisa M. 1887-1964 **[9]**

🖋 **$1 490** - €1 399 - **£920** - FF9 177
The enchanted Pool Watercolour (32x24cm 12x9in) Billingshurst, West-Sussex 1999

CAO KEJIA 1906-1979 **[1]**

🖋 **$2 500** - €2 683 - **£1 673** - FF17 602
Amaranth and Cat Ink (108x35.5cm 42x13in) San-Francisco CA 2000

CAO LIWEI 1956 **[6]**

☞ **$4 494** - €4 932 - **£2 894** - FF32 350
Snowland in the Morning Oil/canvas (59.5x90cm 23x35in) Hong-Kong 2000

CAP Constant 1842-1915 **[25]**

☞ **$835** - €892 - **£568** - FF5 853
Ancienne porte à Anvers Huile/toile (43x52cm 16x20in) Antwerpen 2001

☞ **$207** - €223 - **£138** - FF1 463
Portrait de femme Huile/bois (22x17cm 8x6in) Antwerpen 2000

CAPA Cornell 1918 **[18]**

📷 **$1 100** - €1 221 - **£767** - FF8 012
«John F.Kennedy Campaigning in California» Gelatin silver print (34.5x48cm 13x18in) New-York 2001

CAPA Joaquím 1941 **[19]**

☞ **$2 560** - €2 403 - **£1 560** - FF15 760
Egyptian flower II Técnica mixta/tabla (103x83cm 40x32in) Madrid 1999

🖋 **$854** - €841 - **£546** - FF5 516
Sin título Técnica mixta/papel (28x34cm 11x13in) Madrid 1999

C

CAPA Robert (A.Friedmann) 1913-1954 **[59]**
📷 **$2 000** – €2 271 – **£1 403** – FF14 900
    Mothers of Naples lament their sons, Italy
    Gelatin silver print (18x24.5cm 7x9in) New-York 2001

CAPACCI Bruno 1906-1993 **[51]**
🖌 **$264** – €305 – **£180** – FF2 000
    Bord de mer Huile/toile (38x46cm 14x18in) Saint-Omer 2000
🖌 **$2 355** – €2 287 – **£1 455** – FF15 000
    Composition surréaliste Huile/bois (19x48cm 7x18in) Paris 1999

CAPARNE William John 1856-1940 **[49]**
✏ **$1 022** – €858 – **£600** – FF5 628
    Daffodil, Mrs H.J Elwes Watercolour/paper (22x16cm 9x6in) Tavistock, Devon 1998

CAPASSINI Nannoccio XVI **[1]**
🖌 **$19 350** – €21 802 – **£13 620** – FF143 010
    «La sacra famiglia con il Giovannino e la Santa Elisabetta» Oil/panel (98x119cm 38x46in) Wien 2001

CAPDEVIELLE Louis 1849-1905 **[5]**
🖌 **$920** – €945 – **£577** – FF6 200
    Femme plumant un poulet Huile/toile (46x38.5cm 18x15in) Biarritz 2000

CAPDEVILA MASSANA Manuel 1910 **[24]**
🖌 **$1 725** – €1 502 – **£1 075** – FF9 850
    Vista de pueblo Oleo/lienzo (61x50cm 24x19in) Madrid 1999

CAPDEVILA PUIG Genís 1860/72-? **[22]**
🖌 **$1 242** – €1 381 – **£851** – FF9 062
    Tertulia en una taberna Oleo/lienzo (84x139cm 33x54in) Barcelona 2001

CAPEINICK Jean 1838-1890 **[27]**
🖌 **$15 000** – €17 640 – **£10 755** – FF115 708
    Still Life with Roses in an Oriental Vase Oil/canvas (125.5x100cm 49x39in) New-York 2001
🖌 **$5 805** – €6 693 – **£3 969** – FF43 902
    Vase chinois fleuri de roses Huile/toile (88.5x65cm 34x25in) Bruxelles 2000

CAPEK Josef 1887-1945 **[44]**
🖌 **$37 570** – €35 534 – **£23 400** – FF233 090
    Vacances - enfants à la campagne Huile/toile (50x55cm 19x21in) Praha 2000
🖌 **$34 680** – €32 801 – **£21 600** – FF215 160
    Blooming Blackthorn in a Vase Oil/canvas (36x27cm 14x10in) Praha 2000
✏ **$1 156** – €1 093 – **£720** – FF7 172
    «Dialogue» Ink/paper (30x21cm 11x8in) Praha 2001
🗋 **$245** – €232 – **£153** – FF1 524
    Beggar Linocut (9.5x8cm 3x3in) Praha 2001

CAPEL-CURE Alfred 1826-1896 **[5]**
📷 **$3 166** – €3 546 – **£2 200** – FF23 263
    View of the East End of Wells Cathedral Albumen print (21.5x27cm 8x10in) London 2001

CAPELLAN Tony 1959 **[3]**
🗋 **$1 056** – €961 – **£640** – FF6 304
    Vista de los jardines del Belvedere según dibujo de F.Pannini Grabado (47x70.5cm 18x27in) Madrid 1999

CAPELLANI Antonio c.1740 **[1]**
🗋 **$1 700** – €1 886 – **£1 130** – FF12 370
    Del Giardino Vaticano de Belvedere, After Panini Etching (47x69.5cm 18x27in) New-York 2000

CAPELLE van de Jan c.1624-1679 **[3]**
🖌 **$20 328** – €17 370 – **£11 940** – FF113 940
    Zahlreiche Segelschiffe liegen in ruhiger See vor einer Hafenstadt Öl/Leinwand (52x64cm 20x25in) Stuttgart 1998

CAPET Marie-Gabrielle 1761-1818 **[18]**
🖌 **$9 342** – €9 147 – **£5 748** – FF60 000
    Autoportrait présumé Huile/toile (73x59cm 28x23in) Paris 1999

CAPITANI Alfredo 1895-1985 **[5]**
🗋 **$515** – €534 – **£309** – FF3 502
    «La Rosa Nera» Affiche couleur (195x140cm 76x55in) Torino 2000

CAPITELLI Bernardino 1589-1639 **[2]**
🗋 **$2 107** – €2 045 – **£1 312** – FF13 415
    Loth und seine Töchter, nach Rutilio Manetti Radierung (19.3x23.7cm 7x9in) Berlin 1999

CAPMANY Y MONTANER Ramón 1899-1992 **[34]**
🖌 **$3 040** – €2 853 – **£1 900** – FF18 715
    Masía y campesina Oleo/lienzo (50x65cm 19x25in) Barcelona 1999
🖌 **$810** – €901 – **£540** – FF5 910
    Paisaje Oleo/lienzo (33x46cm 12x18in) Madrid 2000

CAPMARTIN E. XIX **[2]**
✏ **$1 758** – €1 829 – **£1 111** – FF12 000
    El rancho del Salto avant d'arriver au Rio Grande (expédition Mexique) Fusain (50x63cm 19x24in) Paris 2000

CAPOBIANCHI Vincenzo 1817-1876 **[1]**
🖌 **$42 966** – €51 935 – **£30 000** – FF340 671
    The Mandolin Shop Oil/panel (51x65cm 20x25in) London 2000

CAPOBIANCHI Vitorio XIX **[5]**
🖌 **$55 000** – €47 451 – **£33 181** – FF311 261
    The Mandolin Shop Oil/panel (53x65cm 20x25in) New-York 1998

CAPOCCHINI Ugo 1901-1980 **[19]**
🖌 **$900** – €933 – **£540** – FF6 120
    Donna con parrucca Olio/tela (60x45cm 23x17in) Prato 2000

CAPOGROSSI Giuseppe 1900-1972 **[220]**
🖌 **$25 800** – €22 288 – **£17 200** – FF146 200
    Superficie 623 Tecnica mista/cartone (95x130cm 37x51in) Prato 1998
🖌 **$20 800** – €26 953 – **£15 600** – FF176 800
    «Superficie 410» Olio/tela (46x38cm 18x14in) Milano 2001
🖌 **$6 500** – €6 738 – **£3 900** – FF44 200
    Senza titolo Tempera/cartone (25x20.5cm 9x8in) Milano 1999
🏺 **$16 400** – €21 251 – **£12 300** – FF139 400
    «Nero - Superficie CP872/A» Céramique (20x20cm 7x7in) Roma 2000
✏ **$6 250** – €6 479 – **£3 750** – FF42 500
    Senza titolo Tempera/carta (33x23cm 12x9in) Milano 1999
🗋 **$420** – €363 – **£280** – FF2 380
    Superficie Acquaforte (25x21cm 9x8in) Prato 1998

CAPON Georges 1890-1980 **[94]**
🖌 **$1 383** – €1 143 – **£811** – FF7 500
    Le cirque Amar Huile/toile (46x55cm 18x21in) La Grand'Combe 1998
🖌 **$632** – €701 – **£439** – FF4 600
    L'offrande à Bacchus Huile/panneau (33x46cm 12x18in) Besançon 2001

CAPONE Gaetano 1845-1920/24 **[36]**
- $2 600 – €2 423 – **£1 604** – FF15 894
  Lake Landscape Oil/canvas (50x60cm 20x24in)
  New-Orleans LA 1999
- $525 – €497 – **£326** – FF3 262
  Native American Young Woman in Profile
  Oil/canvas (26x19cm 10x7in) Charlottesville VA 1999
- $1 000 – €1 028 – **£634** – FF6 745
  Kitchen Scene with Children Watercolour/paper
  (30x47cm 12x18in) Columbia SC 2000

CAPONIGRO Paul 1932 **[97]**
- $1 850 – €2 078 – **£1 200** – FF13 632
  Ice Abstraction Silver print (24.5x14.5cm 9x5in)
  London 2000

CAPOZZOLI Glauco 1929 **[15]**
- $1 220 – €1 201 – **£760** – FF7 880
  Composición con cabeza femenina tendida
  Crayon gras (80x100cm 31x39in) Barcelona 1999

CAPP Al 1909-1979 **[21]**
- $600 – €624 – **£401** – FF4 224
  Three Little Abner Daily Strip Ink (14.5x57cm
  5x22in) New-York 2000

CAPPA LEGORA Giovanni 1887-1970 **[13]**
- $3 000 – €3 110 – **£1 800** – FF20 400
  Bosco di betulle Olio/tela (85x65cm 33x25in)
  Vercelli 2001
- $1 200 – €1 555 – **£900** – FF10 200
  «Cortile rustico a Stroppino» Olio/cartone
  (35x45cm 13x17in) Vercelli 2000

CAPPELLE van de Jan 1626-1679 **[10]**
- $1 304 880 – €1 220 446 – **£800 000** – FF8 005 600
  A Calm Sea Oil/panel (45.5x65.5cm 17x25in) London
  1998
- $7 500 – €8 157 – **£4 944** – FF53 508
  Calm Sea with many Ships Oil/panel (19.5x26.5cm
  7x10in) Boston MA 2000

CAPPELLI Giovanni 1923-1994 **[30]**
- $1 500 – €1 555 – **£900** – FF10 200
  «Figura riversa» Olio/tela (50x60cm 19x23in)
  Vercelli 1999

CAPPELLI Pietro ?-1724 **[3]**
- $26 963 – €28 313 – **£17 000** – FF185 719
  Peasants Amongst Classical Ruins Oil/canvas
  (148.5x121.5cm 58x47in) London 1999

CAPPELLO Carmelo 1912-1996 **[22]**
- $10 500 – €10 885 – **£6 300** – FF71 400
  Vento di primavera Bronzo (165x90cm 64x35in)
  Roma 1999
- $3 000 – €2 592 – **£2 000** – FF17 000
  Senza titolo Bronzo (51x42.5cm 20x16in) Milano
  1998

CAPPER Chris 1951 **[5]**
- $2 099 – €2 464 – **£1 481** – FF16 162
  Backyard and Magpie Oil/board (56x76cm 22x29in)
  Nedlands 2000

CAPPIELLO Leonetto 1875-1942 **[727]**
- $2 264 – €1 982 – **£1 371** – FF13 000
  Yvette Guilbert Plâtre (34x21x11cm 13x8x4in) Paris
  1998
- $2 045 – €1 726 – **£1 200** – FF11 320
  Peroquet Watercolour (79x58cm 31x22in) London
  1998
- $2 110 – €2 287 – **£1 461** – FF15 000
  **«Cachou Lajaunie, Antinicotinico indispensable
  a los fumadores»** Affiche (135x97cm 53x38in) Paris
  2001

CAPPS Charles 1898-1981 **[5]**
- **«Winter's Here»** Etching (13x14cm 5x5in) Cleveland
  OH 2000

CAPRILE Vincenzo 1856-1936 **[142]**
- $6 500 – €6 738 – **£3 900** – FF44 200
  Barche a Venezia Olio/tela (30x55cm 11x21in) Roma
  1999
- $4 312 – €4 471 – **£2 587** – FF29 325
  Paese costiero con pescatori Olio/tela (35x18cm
  13x7in) Roma 1999
- $2 000 – €2 073 – **£1 200** – FF13 600
  Ritratto di giovane donna a mezzo busto
  Pastelli/carta (53x43cm 20x16in) Milano 2000

CAPRON Jean-Pierre 1921-1997 **[40]**
- $600 – €668 – **£419** – FF4 385
  Village en Provence Oil/canvas (72x91cm 28x36in)
  Delray-Beach FL 2001

CAPUANO Francesco 1854-? **[28]**
- $3 900 – €3 369 – **£1 950** – FF22 100
  Foresta Olio/tela (64x104cm 25x40in) Prato 1999

CAPULETTI José Manuel 1925-1975 **[46]**
- $2 805 – €2 423 – **£1 980** – FF21 670
  Retrato de Antonio Oleo/lienzo (61x51cm 24x20in)
  Madrid 2000
- $1 008 – €1 081 – **£684** – FF7 092
  Conduciendo los toros Acuarela/papel (50x72cm
  19x28in) Madrid 2001

CAPUTO Antonio, Tonino 1933 **[23]**
- $650 – €674 – **£390** – FF4 420
  Interno del Sud Olio/cartone/tela (70x55cm 27x21in)
  Vercelli 2000

CAPUTO Ulisse 1872-1948 **[139]**
- $6 300 – €5 442 – **£4 200** – FF35 700
  Fanciulla alla fontana Olio/tela (46x55cm 18x21in)
  Milano 1998
- $1 440 – €1 866 – **£1 080** – FF12 240
  Paesaggio con donna Olio/cartone (16x24cm 6x9in)
  Milano 2000

CAPUZZO Mario 1902-1972 **[8]**
- $2 564 – €3 049 – **£1 828** – FF20 000
  L'église de Sirmione Huile/toile (67x117cm 26x46in)
  Paris 2000

CARA F. XIX **[1]**
- $11 693 – €10 824 – **£7 156** – FF71 000
  Amour ailé au carquois Marbre (H77cm H30in)
  Reims 1999

CARA Ugo 1908 **[13]**
- $1 200 – €1 244 – **£720** – FF8 160
  Bagnante Bronzo (H34cm H13in) Trieste 2000

CARA-COSTEA Philippe 1925 **[50]**
- $419 – €457 – **£275** – FF3 000
  Nu assis Huile/toile (46x38cm 18x14in) Douai 2000

CARABAIN Jacques François 1834-1924/33 **[176]**
- $12 966 – €13 613 – **£8 175** – FF89 298
  View of a small fishing-port at Dusk Oil/panel
  (63x79cm 24x31in) Amsterdam 2000
- $4 312 – €4 857 – **£3 032** – FF31 862
  Kleines Dorf mit Backsteinhäuser am Fluss
  Oil/panel (24x34cm 9x13in) Stuttgart 2001

CARABAIN Victor ?-1942 **[43]**
- $1 205 – €1 091 – **£752** – FF7 154
  Mosquée Sainte Catherine à Tunis Huile/toile
  (90x60cm 35x23in) Bruxelles 1999

$675 - €793 - £486 - FF5 203
Accalmie sur l'Escaut Huile/toile (40x32cm 15x12in) Bruxelles 2001

CARABIN Rupert 1862-1932 **[39]**
$4 776 - €4 421 - £2 958 - FF29 000
Danseuse au voile Bronze (H23cm H9in) Paris 1999

CARACCIOLO IL BATTISTELLO Giovanni Battista c.1570-1637 **[9]**
$100 000 - €103 665 - £60 000 - FF680 000
Ecce Homo Olio/tela (74x97cm 29x38in) Venezia 1999
$2 250 - €2 332 - £1 350 - FF15 300
Putto visto di schiena Inchiostro (19x11cm 7x4in) Roma 2000

CARACCIOLO Niccola d'Arcia 1941-1989 **[4]**
$5 918 - €6 349 - £4 035 - FF41 645
Streetscape Oil/canvas (51x76cm 20x29in) Dublin 2001

CARADEC Louis 1802-1882 **[11]**
$1 513 - €1 524 - £943 - FF10 000
Les naufrageurs Huile/toile (38x55cm 14x21in) Paris 2000
$994 - €1 067 - £665 - FF7 000
Jeune bretonne filant la laine Huile/toile (24x19cm 9x7in) Douarnenez 2000

CARADOSSI Vittorio 1861-? **[17]**
$56 694 - €55 500 - £34 881 - FF364 056
Kolme nymfiä Marble (H101.5cm H39in) Helsinki 1999

CARAFFE Armand 1762-1822 **[4]**
$1 926 - €1 913 - £1 200 - FF12 550
Nude Holding a Sword and Kissing a Woman, in front of a Burning Altar Ink (18.5x21.5cm 7x8in) London 1999

CARAGLIO Gian Giacomo Karalis c.1505-1565 **[25]**
$1 578 - €1 841 - £1 111 - FF12 074
La Fureur, nach Rosso Fiorentino Kupferstich (25x18.5cm 9x7in) Berlin 2001

CARAN D'ACHE Emmanuel Poiré, dit 1858-1909 **[61]**
$483 - €534 - £335 - FF3 500
Scène de personnages Aquarelle/papier (17x27cm 6x10in) Paris 2001
$112 - €122 - £77 - FF800
«Exposition russe, Champ de Mars» Affiche (140x90cm 55x35in) Paris 2001

CARASSO Fred 1899-1969 **[23]**
$3 515 - €4 084 - £2 470 - FF26 789
Reclining Nude Sandstone (17.5x38cm 6x14in) Amsterdam 2001

CARAUD Joseph 1821-1905 **[44]**
$11 229 - €11 316 - £7 000 - FF74 225
In the Boudoir Oil/canvas (67x55.5cm 26x21in) London 2000

CARBAAT Jan 1866-1925 **[4]**
$1 562 - €1 815 - £1 098 - FF11 906
Still Life with a Jug and two Bottles Oil/canvas/panel (30.5x37.5cm 12x14in) Amsterdam 2001

CARBASIUS Françoise XX **[2]**
$15 590 - €18 477 - £11 000 - FF121 198
Dreigende uil Bronze (H30cm H11in) London 2000

CARBONE Giovanni Bernardo 1616-1683 **[11]**
$14 400 - €12 440 - £9 600 - FF81 600
Ritratto di un Doge della Repubblica di Genova Olio/tela (265x212cm 104x83in) Roma 1998
$5 500 - €4 783 - £3 315 - FF31 377
The Visitation Oil/canvas (78.5x68.5cm 30x26in) New-York 1998

CARBONELL Manuel 1918 **[12]**
$15 000 - €17 428 - £10 542 - FF114 318
Dos figuras con caballo Bronze (H171.5cm H67in) New-York 2001
$28 000 - €27 176 - £17 432 - FF178 264
Lovers Embracing Bronze (53.5x43cm 21x16in) New-York 2001

CARBONELL MASSABE Francesc 1928 **[111]**
$234 - €270 - £162 - FF1 773
«Carrer de Rupit, Can Banús» Oleo/lienzo (73x60cm 28x23in) Barcelona 2001

CARBONELL Santiago 1960 **[9]**
$32 500 - €31 622 - £20 003 - FF207 424
Revelación para un último momento Oil/canvas (100x120cm 39x47in) New-York 1999

CARBONELL Y SELVA Miguel 1855-1896 **[5]**
$260 - €240 - £156 - FF1 576
Cazador en el bosque Oleo/tabla (18.5x25.5cm 7x10in) Barcelona 1999

CARBONI Erberto 1899-1984 **[4]**
$1 200 - €1 136 - £745 - FF7 451
«Olio d'oliva Bertolli» Poster (137x98cm 53x38in) New-York 1999

CARBONNET Jean-Baptiste XVIII-XIX **[1]**
$5 898 - €6 532 - £4 000 - FF42 848
Emperor Napoleon I (1769-1821), facing right in coronation robes Miniature (12.5x9cm 4x3in) London 2000

CARCAN René 1925-1993 **[55]**
$59 - €66 - £40 - FF451
Les Arbres Etching in colors (15x13cm 6x5in) Calgary, Alberta 2000

CARCANO Filippo 1840-1914 **[24]**
$15 000 - €12 958 - £10 000 - FF85 000
La famiglia del congiurato Olio/tela (86.5x124cm 34x48in) Milano 1998
$1 800 - €1 555 - £1 200 - FF10 200
Portale di una villa Olio/tavola (18x10cm 7x3in) Milano 1998

CARDELLI Raimondo 1938 **[13]**
$600 - €622 - £360 - FF4 080
«Serenata» Olio/tela (50x60cm 19x23in) Vercelli 2001

CARDENAS Augustin 1927-2001 **[233]**
$14 000 - €12 088 - £8 540 - FF79 293
Totem Bronze (201x29x29cm 79x11x11in) Miami FL 1999
$6 268 - €6 098 - £3 856 - FF40 000
Forme sensible Marbre (56x36x30cm 22x14x11in) Paris 1999
$340 - €381 - £238 - FF2 500
Composition Encre/papier (30.5x24cm 12x9in) Paris 2001

CARDENAS Juan 1939 **[14]**
$12 000 - €11 647 - £7 471 - FF76 399
The Friend Oil/canvas (47x39cm 18x15in) New-York 1999

CARDENAS Santiago 1937 [10]
- $15 000 - €14 595 - **£9 232** - FF95 734
  Pizarra y flores Oil/canvas (85x96cm 33x37in) New-York 1999

CARDI IL CIGOLI Ludovico 1559-1613 [25]
- $11 360 - €12 196 - **£7 600** - FF80 000
  Pieta Huile/toile (190x143cm 74x56in) Paris 2000
- $45 000 - €46 649 - **£27 000** - FF306 000
  Compiando di Cristo con la Vergine e Giovanni Evangelista Olio/tavola (118x90cm 46x35in) Firenze 2000
- $44 829 - €48 120 - **£30 000** - FF315 648
  Figure of an Archer with right Arm outstretched whilst aiming at Sky Bronze (H34cm H13in) London 2000
- $5 000 - €4 989 - **£3 043** - FF32 725
  Statue of a King, possibly Albert I of Bavaria Ink (24x14.5cm 9x5in) New-York 2000

CARDIFF Jack XX [1]
- $30 000 - €28 534 - **£18 216** - FF187 170
  Marilyn Monroe Photograph (51x41cm 20x16in) New-York 1999

CARDINAL-SCHUBERT Joane 1942 [22]
- $600 - €648 - **£402** - FF4 249
  Medicine People Oil/paper (59.5x20.5cm 23x8in) Calgary, Alberta 2000
- $776 - €903 - **£546** - FF5 926
  «Sacred Birds Scroll» Mixed media/paper (59.5x19.5cm 23x7in) Calgary, Alberta 2001

CARDINAUX Emil 1877-1936 [152]
- $3 494 - €3 235 - **£2 139** - FF21 221
  Thunerseelandschaft bei Sonnenuntergang Öl/Leinwand (47.5x55.5cm 18x21in) Bern 1999
- $17 140 - €15 707 - **£10 472** - FF103 030
  Julierpass Gouache/papier (90x124cm 35x48in) Zürich 1999
- $2 165 - €2 396 - **£1 500** - FF15 717
  «Jungfrau-Railway» Poster (102x65cm 40x25in) London 2001

CARDON Antoine, Anthony 1772-1813 [6]
- $112 - €107 - **£70** - FF699
  La visite du Pasteur Copper engraving in colors (33.5x39cm 13x15in) Praha 2000

CARDON Claude act.1892-1920 [49]
- $4 026 - €4 606 - **£2 800** - FF30 212
  Sheep Grazing in a Turnip Field Oil/canvas (50x76cm 19x29in) Doncaster, South-Yorkshire 2000
- $2 314 - €2 186 - **£1 400** - FF14 342
  Cattle on a Riverbank Oil/canvas (29x49.5cm 11x19in) Billingshurst, West-Sussex 1999
- $1 268 - €1 188 - **£780** - FF7 795
  Changing Pastures Watercolour/paper (30.5x47.5cm 12x18in) West-Midlands 1999

CARDONA Joan 1877-1937 [32]
- $4 050 - €4 505 - **£2 850** - FF29 550
  «La gitana de las frutas» Oleo/lienzo (100x81cm 39x31in) Barcelona 2001
- $1 595 - €1 652 - **£1 017** - FF10 835
  Reunión festiva Tinta china (28.5x28.5cm 11x11in) Barcelona 2000

CARDONA José XIX-XX [9]
- $1 100 - €1 189 - **£762** - FF7 800
  Le terrassier Bronze (H28cm H11in) Deauville 2001

CARDONA LLADOS Juan 1877-1958 [12]
- $2 418 - €2 793 - **£1 674** - FF18 321
  Figuras de baile en el tablao Gouache/papier (43x34.5cm 16x13in) Madrid 2000

CARDONA TORRANDELL Armando 1928-1995 [26]
- $715 - €662 - **£440** - FF4 345
  Retrato imaginario Oleo/papel (64x46cm 25x18in) Madrid 1998

CARDOSO Abel 1877-1964 [4]
- $7 200 - €7 976 - **£4 640** - FF52 320
  Marinha Oleo/lienzo (64x105.5cm 25x41in) Lisboa 2000
- $2 610 - €2 891 - **£1 682** - FF18 966
  Perto do Corpo Santo - Guimarães Huile/bois (12x31.5cm 4x12in) Lisboa 2000

CARDOSO Maria Fernanda 1963 [2]
- $15 000 - €17 428 - **£10 542** - FF114 318
  Corona para una princesa Chibcha Sculpture (196x91.5x213.5cm 77x36x84in) New-York 2001

CARDUCHO Vicente 1576-1638 [6]
- $4 200 - €4 485 - **£2 861** - FF29 422
  The Flagellation Black chalk (25x18cm 9x7in) New-York 2001

CARDWELL Holme c.1815-? [7]
- $2 893 - €3 125 - **£2 000** - FF20 499
  A Woman standing and holding a Slipper and her right Foot on a Slipper Marble (H160cm H62in) Edinburgh 2001

CAREL Isidore-François XIX-XX [1]
- $1 955 - €2 193 - **£1 328** - FF14 385
  Rast auf der Sommerwiese Öl/Leinwand (33x46cm 12x18in) Zürich 2000

CAREL Johannes XIX-XX [93]
- $249 - €274 - **£165** - FF1 800
  Femme en rose appuyée à l'arbre Huile/panneau (24x17cm 9x6in) Morlaix 2000

CARELLI Achille 1852-? [5]
- $5 600 - €7 257 - **£4 200** - FF47 600
  Pescatori a Mergellina Olio/tela (38x63cm 14x24in) Roma 2001

CARELLI Conrad H.R. 1869-1950 [66]
- $360 - €399 - **£250** - FF2 615
  Ypres Watercolour (24.5x34.5cm 9x13in) London 2001

CARELLI Consalvo 1818-1900 [221]
- $9 288 - €8 721 - **£5 760** - FF57 204
  Bucht von Neapel mit Blick auf den Vesuv Öl/Leinwand (45x73.5cm 17x28in) Wien 1999
- $5 600 - €7 257 - **£4 200** - FF47 600
  Napoli, pescatori a Palazzo Donn'Anna Olio/tavola (42x25cm 16x9in) Roma 2000
- $2 160 - €1 866 - **£1 440** - FF12 240
  Paesaggio con figure Acquarello/carta (27x40cm 10x15in) Napoli 1998

CARELLI G. XIX-XX [6]
- $576 - €496 - **£342** - FF3 254
  Vue sur le Vésuve/Grotte à Naples Aquarelle/papier (20x25cm 7x9in) Antwerpen 1998

CARELLI Gabriele 1820-1880/1900 [153]
- $685 - €667 - **£420** - FF4 373
  Capri Pencil (14x24cm 5x9in) London 1999

CARELLI Giuseppe 1858-1921 [204]
- $3 893 - €4 589 - **£2 736** - FF30 104
  Meeresbucht mit Stadt Öl/Leinwand (38.5x65cm 15x25in) Bern 2000
- $3 200 - €3 456 - **£2 211** - FF22 668
  The Bay of Naples Oil/canvas (16x28cm 6x11in) New-York 2001

C

$481 - €486 - £300 - FF3 185
View of the Neapolitan Bay and Vesuvius
Watercolour (8x25.5cm 3x10in) London 2000

CARELLI Raffaele 1795-1864 [10]
$10 350 - €10 729 - £6 210 - FF70 380
Paesaggio costiero con figure Olio/cartone/tela (35x44cm 13x17in) Roma 1999

CARENA Antonio 1925 [11]
$500 - €518 - £300 - FF3 400
Fracti due Técnica mista/tela (100x100cm 39x39in) Vercelli 1999

CARENA Felice 1879-1966 [133]
$27 500 - €28 508 - £16 500 - FF187 000
Nudo di donna sdraiata Olio/tela (74x170cm 29x66in) Prato 2000
$10 000 - €12 958 - £7 500 - FF85 000
Natura morta con arance Olio/tela (40x50cm 15x19in) Torino 2000
$8 925 - €9 252 - £5 355 - FF60 690
Natura morta Olio/tavola (21x45cm 8x17in) Milano 1999
$440 - €570 - £330 - FF3 740
«Sul mare» China/carta (32x24cm 12x9in) Vercelli 2000

CARESME Jacques Philippe 1734-1796 [40]
$2 130 - €2 287 - £1 425 - FF15 000
Bacchante auprès de la statue de Priape Huile/panneau (32x18cm 12x7in) Paris 2000
$2 149 - €2 287 - £1 359 - FF15 000
L'Amour et les trois jeunes femmes Gouache/papier (29.5x23.5cm 11x9in) Paris 2000

CAREY Evelyn 1858-1932 [4]
$3 120 - €3 563 - £2 200 - FF23 371
The Forth Bridge, from the Hawes Pier Albumen print (37x29cm 14x11in) London 2001

CAREY Joseph William 1859-1937 [109]
$1 771 - €1 905 - £1 207 - FF12 493
Sailing off Gobbins Head, Islandbridge, County Antrim Watercolour/paper (20x51cm 7x20in) Dublin 2001

CAREY Peter, General 1774-1852 [7]
$30 669 - €28 391 - £19 000 - FF186 236
Indian Views Watercolour (18.5x29.5cm 7x11in) London 1999

CARGALEIRO Manuel 1927 [131]
$13 200 - €14 955 - £9 300 - FF98 100
Qui j'ose aimer Oleo/lienzo (91x72cm 35x28in) Lisboa 2001
$8 100 - €8 973 - £5 220 - FF58 860
Composiçáo abstracta Oleo/lienzo (27x19cm 10x7in) Lisboa 2000
$6 171 - €5 183 - £3 627 - FF34 000
Cathédrale Gouache/papier (33.5x25.5cm 13x10in) La Varenne-Saint-Hilaire 1998
$265 - €229 - £160 - FF1 500
Composition Lithographie (39x57cm 15x22in) Paris 2000

CARGNEL Vittore Antonio 1872-1931 [55]
$2 400 - €2 488 - £1 440 - FF16 320
Milano, corso indipendenza Olio/tela (49x57cm 19x22in) Milano 2000
$1 009 - €1 017 - £630 - FF6 673
Vorgebirgslandschaft Öl/Karton (18x32.5cm 7x12in) Wien 2000

CARIANI Valrado J. 1891-1969 [9]
$4 500 - €5 020 - £2 945 - FF32 931
The Autumn Sycamore Oil/board (60x50cm 24x20in) Chicago IL 2000

CARIFFA Francis 1890-1975 [27]
$2 221 - €2 592 - £1 545 - FF17 000
Vue de Mogador Huile/panneau (60x92cm 23x36in) Paris 2000

CARIGIET Alois 1902-1985 [496]
$15 674 - €15 092 - £9 801 - FF98 997
Die schwarze Madonna von Einsiedeln Öl/Leinwand (102x136cm 40x53in) Zürich 1999
$21 552 - €20 752 - £13 477 - FF136 121
Zirkus Öl/Leinwand (61x73cm 24x28in) Zürich 1999
$16 751 - €16 209 - £10 329 - FF106 327
Harlekin mit Laute Öl/Leinwand (44x31cm 17x12in) Zürich 1999
$1 424 - €1 370 - £878 - FF8 984
Stallszene Crayon/papier (30x43cm 11x16in) Bern 1999
$1 040 - €1 167 - £722 - FF7 654
Ziegenhirte Farblithographie (55.5x74cm 21x29in) Luzern 2001

CARILLO XV [1]
$84 045 - €82 615 - £54 000 - FF541 922
Virgin and Child Oil/panel (44x27.5cm 17x10in) London 1999

CARINI G. XIX-XX [1]
$11 109 - €12 958 - £7 726 - FF85 000
L'allumage des lampes de la mosquée Aquarelle, gouache/papier (45x34.5cm 17x13in) Paris 2000

CARIOT Gustave 1872-1950 [34]
$3 658 - €3 201 - £2 215 - FF21 000
Moisson Huile/toile (49x69cm 19x27in) Paris 1998
$2 318 - €2 134 - £1 391 - FF14 000
Les meules Huile/toile (22x33cm 8x12in) Lyon 1999

CARISS Henry T. 1850-1903 [2]
$28 000 - €30 055 - £18 737 - FF197 148
Contentment Oil/canvas (55x102cm 22x40in) New-York 2000

CARJAT Étienne 1828-1906 [49]
$734 - €640 - £443 - FF4 200
Portrait d'acteur en habit de bouffon du Roi Tirage albuminé (52x40cm 20x15in) Paris 1998

CARL-ROSA M. Cornilleau Raoul 1855-1913 [33]
$2 669 - €2 592 - £1 649 - FF17 000
Au pays de Jeanne d'Arc, la Meuse devant Domremy Huile/panneau (32x55cm 12x21in) Melun 1999
$1 618 - €1 387 - £973 - FF9 100
Le Doubs devant Pont de Roide Huile/toile (32x41cm 12x16in) Pontoise 1998

CARLANDI Onorato 1848-1939 [155]
$11 500 - €11 922 - £6 900 - FF78 200
Casa tra i cipressi Olio/tela (200x200cm 78x78in) Roma 1999
$9 900 - €8 552 - £6 600 - FF56 100
Ciliegi in fiori sullo sfondo di Tivoli Olio/tela (100x99cm 39x38in) Roma 1998
$1 295 - €1 215 - £800 - FF7 972
Villa d'Este Watercolour (51.5x51cm 20x20in) Billingshurst, West-Sussex 1999

CARLAW John 1850-1934 [6]
$333 - €309 - £200 - FF2 027
Sheep grazing beneath Trees in blossom Watercolour (48.5x33cm 19x12in) London 1999

CARLEBUR OF DORDRECHT François 1821-1893 **[16]**

$1 140 - €1 278 - £786 - FF8 384
Die Bark «Fortschritt» im Sturm von 1849
Watercolour (44x62.5cm 17x24in) Hamburg 2000

CARLES Arthur Beecher 1882-1952 **[68]**

$20 000 - €18 885 - £12 420 - FF123 878
Nude in Repose Oil/canvas (94x129.5cm 37x50in)
Beverly-Hills CA 1999

$40 000 - €45 019 - £27 556 - FF295 308
Nude with Mask Oil/canvas (101.5x92cm 39x36in)
Philadelphia PA 2000

$14 000 - €13 113 - £8 607 - FF86 071
Still Life with Flowers Oil/panel (33x40.5cm
12x15in) New-York 1999

$800 - €854 - £545 - FF5 604
Study of a Boy Wearing Blue Pastel (66x50cm
26x20in) Philadelphia PA 2001

CARLES Jean Antonin 1851-1919 **[19]**

$2 249 - €1 950 - £1 374 - FF12 792
«La Jeunesse» Bronze (H78.5cm H30in) New-York
1999

CARLES ROSICH Domingo 1888-1962 **[34]**

$540 - €601 - £360 - FF3 940
Bodegón de flores Oleo/lienzo (93x72cm 36x28in)
Madrid 2000

$780 - €901 - £540 - FF5 910
Marina Oleo/lienzo (24x34cm 9x13in) Madrid 2000

CARLEVARIS Luca 1665-1731 **[49]**

$300 466 - €317 474 - £180 279 - FF2 043 169
Veduta di porto con città fortificata Olio/tela
(98x130cm 38x51in) Milano 1999

$158 850 - €164 672 - £95 310 - FF1 080 180
**Venezia, La Piazzetta di San Marco verso le
colonne, la Libreria** Olio/tela (56.5x73cm 22x28in)
Roma 1999

$190 - €204 - £127 - FF1 341
Cortile del Palazzo Ducale Radierung (21x30cm
8x11in) Berlin 2000

CARLIER Émile Joseph N. 1849-1927 **[23]**

$670 - €789 - £480 - FF5 173
Labourer with a wheelbarrow Sculpture (H16cm
H6in) Billingshurst, West-Sussex 2001

CARLIER Max, Albert 1872-1938 **[114]**

$2 746 - €3 049 - £1 914 - FF20 000
Elégante au corsage fleuri Huile/toile (92x60cm
36x23in) Paris 2001

$1 283 - €1 308 - £802 - FF8 580
Rosenstück mit Obst Öl/Leinwand (27x35cm
10x13in) Wien 2000

CARLIER Modeste 1820-1878 **[43]**

$2 031 - €2 134 - £1 339 - FF14 000
Coupe de fleurs Huile/toile (40x50cm 15x19in)
Calais 2000

CARLIERI Alberto 1672-c.1720 **[15]**

$21 000 - €21 770 - £12 600 - FF142 800
Interno di palazzo con banchetto di Cleopatra
Olio/tela (120x149cm 47x58in) Milano 1999

$21 000 - €18 141 - £14 000 - FF119 000
Paesaggio con rovine e figure Olio/tela
(73.5x98.5cm 28x38in) Roma 1998

CARLIN James 1909/10 **[30]**

$3 200 - €3 718 - £2 249 - FF24 387
«Big Band» Oil/canvas (93x78cm 37x31in) Newark
OH 2001

CARLIN John 1813-1891 **[10]**

$6 100 - €6 639 - £4 192 - FF43 549
«Portrait of Minnie S.Mead» Oil/canvas (53x43cm
21x17in) St. Louis MO 2001

$3 000 - €2 905 - £1 884 - FF19 054
**Younf Boy with Drum seated on a blue Velvet
Cushions** Miniature (12x9cm 4x3in) New-York 1999

CARLINI Giulio 1830-1887 **[8]**

$45 000 - €53 361 - £30 960 - FF350 023
The Suez Canal Oil/canvas (155x160cm 61x62in)
New-York 2000

CARLISLE John XIX-XX **[14]**

$486 - €471 - £300 - FF3 087
Highland River Watercolour (43x66cm 16x25in)
Suffolk 1999

CARLO DA CAMERINO XIV **[1]**

$60 000 - €57 274 - £37 488 - FF375 696
The Decollation of Saint John the Baptist
Tempera/panel (38x29cm 14x11in) New-York 1999

CARLONE Carlo Innocenzo 1686/87-1775/76 **[42]**

$6 491 - €7 629 - £4 500 - FF50 044
**A Heron before the Muse of History - A model-
lo for a ceiling** Oil/paper/canvas (35.5x50cm 13x19in)
London 2000

$12 197 - €12 645 - £7 318 - FF82 943
Santo guerriero portato in cielo Olio/tela
(30x39cm 11x15in) Venezia 1999

$20 000 - €21 359 - £13 628 - FF140 106
**The Marriage of Hebe and Hercules: Design for
a Ceiling** Black chalk (33x24cm 12x9in) New-York
2001

$652 - €716 - £443 - FF4 695
**Die Madonna erscheint dem Heiligen Josef im
Traum** Radierung (18.5x11.8cm 7x4in) Berlin 2000

CARLONE Giovanni c.1590/91-1630 **[2]**

$41 312 - €48 784 - £29 344 - FF320 000
**La Vierge en gloire avec Saint Georges, Saint
Jean-Baptiste** Huile/toile (120x96cm 47x37in) Paris
2001

CARLONE Giovanni Battista 1592-1677 **[8]**

$16 000 - €15 053 - £9 984 - FF98 742
**Portrait of Gentleman in the guise of Paris
abducting Helen** Oil/canvas (164.5x207.5cm
64x81in) New-York 1999

$24 169 - €23 736 - £15 000 - FF155 698
The Fall of Phaethon Oil/canvas (90.5x120cm
35x47in) London 1999

$6 930 - €6 541 - £4 302 - FF42 903
**Die sterbende Amazone Clorinda/Skizzen zu
fliegenden Engeln** Black, red & white chalks/paper
(33.2x23.2cm 13x9in) Wien 1999

CARLONE Marco 1742-1796 **[5]**

$1 088 - €973 - £651 - FF6 385
**Three Classical Wall Decorations, after
Francesco Smagliewicz** Etching (49x51cm 19x20in)
Amsterdam 1999

CARLOS I de Bragança King of Portugal 1863-
1908 **[12]**

$2 475 - €2 742 - £1 595 - FF17 985
Pedras Salgadas Acuarela (21x14.5cm 8x5in) Lisboa
2000

CARLOS-REYMOND 1884-1970 **[54]**

$900 - €945 - £569 - FF6 200
Paysage de Provence Huile/toile (46x72cm
18x28in) Paris 2000

CARLSEN Bjørn 1945 **[12]**
- $17 081 - €18 958 - **£11 904** - FF124 356
  Overgansbilde Oil/canvas (140x100cm 55x39in) Oslo 2001
- $8 959 - €10 658 - **£6 196** - FF69 912
  Paradis Oil/canvas (96x117cm 37x46in) Oslo 2000
- $265 - €297 - **£184** - FF1 948
  Mykhorn med slöyfe Etching in colors (36x23cm 14x9in) Oslo 2001

CARLSEN Carl Christian E. 1855-1917 **[75]**
- $2 280 - €2 153 - **£1 422** - FF14 124
  En sommerdag ved Sundet Oil/canvas (37x55cm 14x21in) Köbenhavn 1999
- $150 - €174 - **£107** - FF1 144
  Kirkeinteriör Oil/canvas (29x34cm 11x13in) Aarhus 2001

CARLSEN Dines 1901-1966 **[37]**
- $15 000 - €14 542 - **£9 288** - FF95 389
  Samovar, Still Life Oil/canvas (109x83cm 43x33in) Englewood NJ 1999
- $425 - €506 - **£294** - FF3 318
  The Cascade Oil/board (30x38cm 12x15in) Chicago IL 2000

CARLSEN Sören Emil 1853-1932 **[130]**
- $20 000 - €19 857 - **£12 500** - FF130 252
  Roses in a Copper Jar Oil/canvas (49.5x40cm 19x15in) New-York 1999
- $2 500 - €2 770 - **£1 676** - FF18 168
  Sand Dunes Oil/board (21x26cm 8x10in) Dedham MA 2000
- $1 725 - €2 004 - **£1 229** - FF13 146
  Still Life with Stein Watercolour/paper (28x36cm 11x14in) Cleveland OH 2001

CARLSON George 1940 **[11]**
- $88 000 - €94 459 - **£58 889** - FF619 608
  Courtship Flight Bronze (H99cm H39in) Houston TX 2000
- $2 100 - €2 384 - **£1 459** - FF15 641
  Hopi Snake Gatherer Bronze (H28cm H11in) Dallas TX 2001

CARLSON John Fabian 1875-1945 **[68]**
- $56 000 - €64 695 - **£39 211** - FF424 373
  Forest Silence Oil/canvas (120.5x144.5cm 47x56in) New-York 2001
- $6 500 - €7 216 - **£4 520** - FF47 335
  Winter River Bed Oil/canvas (63x76cm 25x30in) Milford CT 2001
- $2 500 - €2 892 - **£1 769** - FF18 972
  Spring Melody Oil/canvas (25x20cm 10x8in) Hatfield PA 2000
- $650 - €737 - **£454** - FF4 834
  Snow Bound Watercolour (31x40.5cm 12x15in) New-York 2001

CARLSON Ken 1940 **[11]**
- $18 000 - €19 300 - **£11 908** - FF126 597
  Spirits of the Mountain Oil/board (55x38cm 22x15in) Hayden ID 2000

CARLSON William 1950 **[6]**
- $8 844 - €8 385 - **£5 379** - FF55 000
  Pyramide inversée, petit bouchon cylindrique Sculpture verre (21x35x10cm 8x13x3in) Paris 1999

CARLSSON Gustaf Herbert 1912 **[30]**
- $660 - €631 - **£415** - FF4 142
  Vita pioner Gouache/paper (47x59cm 18x23in) Stockholm 1999

CARLSSON Harry 1891-1968 **[26]**
- $3 513 - €4 020 - **£2 415** - FF26 370
  Teknisk landskab Oil/canvas (86x99cm 33x38in) Köbenhavn 2000

CARLSTEDT Birger 1907-1975 **[27]**
- $1 861 - €1 594 - **£1 098** - FF10 453
  Blomsterstilleben Oil/canvas (92x65cm 36x25in) Helsinki 1998
- $8 561 - €9 586 - **£5 945** - FF62 882
  Komposition Oil/board (33.5x24.5cm 13x9in) Helsinki 2001

CARLSTEDT Mikko 1892-1964 **[90]**
- $1 062 - €1 043 - **£659** - FF6 839
  Stilleben Oil/canvas (54x66cm 21x25in) Helsinki 1999

CARLSTRÖM Gustaf 1896-1964 **[49]**
- $1 930 - €2 228 - **£1 350** - FF14 618
  Flicka på sten vid vatten Oil/canvas (81x73cm 31x28in) Stockholm 2001

CARLSUND Otto Gustaf 1897-1948 **[43]**
- $42 000 - €40 781 - **£25 935** - FF267 505
  Fuga i blått, projekt för väggmålning för musik-krum Oil/canvas (95x50cm 37x19in) Stockholm 1999
- $2 393 - €2 640 - **£1 621** - FF17 316
  Komposition Coloured chalks/paper (24x18cm 9x7in) Stockholm 2000

CARLTON Frederick XIX **[12]**
- $1 851 - €2 159 - **£1 300** - FF14 165
  Surrey Meadows Oil/canvas (51x76cm 20x29in) Par, Cornwall 2000

CARLU Jean 1900-1997 **[112]**
- $1 800 - €1 724 - **£1 112** - FF11 307
  Head of Einstein Superimposed on Clock Face Unpublished Magazine Cover Gouache (32x24cm 12x9in) New-York 1999
- $537 - €610 - **£373** - FF4 000
  «Emprunt national» Affiche (80x120cm 31x47in) Paris 2001

CARLYLE Florence 1864-1923 **[5]**
- $7 207 - €6 211 - **£4 282** - FF40 740
  «The Heavenly Twins» Oil/canvas (92x76.5cm 36x30in) Toronto 1998

CARLYLE Robert 1775-1825 **[1]**
- $3 762 - €3 675 - **£2 400** - FF24 106
  Irish Gate/The Deanery from the City Walls/English Gate/Scotch Gate Watercolour (24.5x34cm 9x13in) London 1999

CARMASSI Arturo 1925 **[89]**
- $3 000 - €3 110 - **£1 800** - FF20 400
  Bagnante patafisica II Olio/tela (130x97cm 51x38in) Prato 2000
- $2 500 - €2 592 - **£1 500** - FF17 000
  Senza titolo Olio/tela (50x65cm 19x25in) Prato 2000
- $1 320 - €1 140 - **£660** - FF7 480
  Tempesta Olio/tela (45x35cm 17x13in) Firenze 1999
- $320 - €415 - **£240** - FF2 720
  Senza titolo Gouache/carta (65x46cm 25x18in) Milano 2001
- $600 - €622 - **£360** - FF4 080
  Grande archetipo Acquaforte, acquatinta (60.5x48.5cm 23x19in) Firenze 2001

CARME Félix XIX-XX **[8]**
- $6 500 - €5 635 - **£3 972** - FF36 964
  Still Life of Flowers Oil/canvas (117x73cm 46x28in) New-York 1999
- $1 390 - €1 540 - **£943** - FF10 100
  La table dressée Aquarelle/papier (39x32cm 15x12in) Bordeaux 2000

C

CARMI Eugenio 1920 [64]
- $800 - €1 037 - £600 - FF6 800
  «Piccolo incontro» Acrilico/tela (50x50cm 19x19in)
  Vercelli 2001
- $500 - €518 - £300 - FF3 400
  Tre piccole situazioni in fuga Olio/tela (35x30cm
  13x11in) Vercelli 2000

CARMICHAEL Franklin 1890-1945 [29]
- $25 908 - €30 226 - £18 032 - FF198 272
  «Barns and Elms, Southern Ontario» Oil/board
  (25.5x30.5cm 10x12in) Toronto 2000
- $25 545 - €24 548 - £15 735 - FF161 025
  La Cloche Hills Watercolour/paper (26.5x32cm
  10x12in) Vancouver, BC. 1999
- $356 - €416 - £247 - FF2 726
  The Spill Serigraph (8x9.5cm 3x3in) Toronto 2000

CARMICHAEL Ida Barbour 1884-? [2]
- $2 100 - €2 388 - £1 456 - FF15 666
  North Country Oil/board (76x63cm 30x25in) Chicago
  IL 2000

CARMICHAEL John (James) Wilson 1800-1868
[286]
- $11 587 - €13 445 - £8 000 - FF88 192
  Timely Rescue, View Holy Island,
  Northumberland Oil/canvas (101.5x174cm 39x68in)
  London 2000
- $8 690 - €10 084 - £6 000 - FF66 144
  Barges and Merchantmen off the Dutch Coast
  Oil/canvas (65x95cm 25x37in) London 2000
- $6 316 - €7 006 - £4 200 - FF45 958
  Ferrying Out To Greet the New Arrival Oil/canvas
  (26.5x30.5cm 10x12in) London 2000
- $1 528 - €1 443 - £950 - FF9 464
  Ripon Cathedral Watercolour/paper (30x46cm
  12x18in) Scarborough, North-Yorshire 1999

CARMIENCKE Johan Hermann 1810-1867 [43]
- $10 000 - €9 871 - £6 081 - FF64 750
  Langdon-Vanderbilt Mansion, Hyde Park Oil/can-
  vas (44.5x65.5cm 17x25in) New-York 1999
- $1 437 - €1 346 - £895 - FF8 826
  Skovparti ved sö, i baggrunden grusvej ind i
  skoven, Sommerdag Oil/canvas (32x40cm 12x15in)
  Köbenhavn 1999

CARMIGNANI Guido 1838-1909 [4]
- $22 950 - €25 477 - £16 000 - FF167 118
  Neatherds returning Home in a river Landscape
  Oil/canvas (104x148cm 40x58in) London 2001

CARMO Júlio Dinis XVI-XVII [1]
- $14 250 - €12 425 - £8 500 - FF81 500
  Martírio de S.Crispim e S.Crispiano Oleo/tabla
  (145x87cm 57x34in) Lisboa 1998

CARMONA Williams 1964 [3]
- $11 000 - €9 591 - £6 650 - FF62 916
  Entre tú y yo hay un muro de lamento
  Acrylic/canvas (56x160cm 22x62in) New-York 1998

CARMONTELLE Louis Carrogis, dit 1717-1806 [45]
- $6 370 - €7 470 - £4 581 - FF49 000
  Portrait de femme assise, tournée vers la
  gauche, avec un livre Pierre noire (22x16cm 8x6in)
  Paris 2001
- $2 692 - €3 201 - £1 854 - FF21 000
  Louis-Philippe, duc d'Orléans dit le Gros et son
  fils Eau-forte (29x19.5cm 11x7in) Paris 2000

CARNEIRO Antonio 1872-1930 [6]
- $792 - €897 - £540 - FF5 886
  Retrato de senhora Sanguine (31.5x30.5cm 12x12in)
  Lisboa 2000

CARNELLI Giuseppe 1838-1909 [2]
- $500 - €518 - £300 - FF3 400
  Autoritratto del pittore Olio/tela (38.5x29.5cm
  15x11in) Formigine, Mo 2000

CARNELLI J. XIX [1]
- $14 943 - €16 040 - £10 000 - FF105 216
  In the Souk Oil/canvas (100x74cm 39x29in) London
  2000

CARNEO Antonio 1637-1692 [18]
- $12 000 - €12 440 - £7 200 - FF81 600
  Susanna e i vecchioni Olio/tela (68.5x58.5cm
  26x23in) Milano 2000

CARNICERO Antonio 1748-1814 [11]
- $12 000 - €10 367 - £6 000 - FF68 000
  Ritratto di gentiluomo con cavalli e cani da cac-
  cia Olio/tela (82x62cm 32x24in) Firenze 1999
- $273 - €252 - £168 - FF1 654
  Vista de la Plaza y Corrida de Toros en Madrid
  Grabado (34x51cm 13x20in) Madrid 1999

CARNON Roy XX [10]
- $1 447 - €1 648 - £1 000 - FF10 813
  «2001 Aries Above Moonbase (Clavius)»/«2001
  Moonbase Landing Area» Watercolour, gouache
  (37x50.5cm 14x19in) London 2000

CARNOVALI IL PICCIO Giovanni 1804-1873 [12]
- $10 000 - €12 958 - £7 500 - FF85 000
  Morte di Virginia Olio/tela/cartone (16.5x23cm 6x9in)
  Milano 2001
- $693 - €571 - £4 002 - FF37 398
  Paysages italianisant animés de personnages
  Gouache/papier (42x56cm 16x22in) Bruxelles 1998

CARO Anthony 1924 [105]
- $36 000 - €40 252 - £24 267 - FF264 038
  Catalan Moment Metal (81.5x71x35.5cm
  32x27x13in) New-York 2000
- $15 000 - €12 592 - £8 797 - FF82 599
  «Stainless Piece L-L» Metal (14x59.5x38cm
  5x23x14in) Beverly-Hills CA 1998
- $2 200 - €1 944 - £1 344 - FF12 754
  «Valerice» Coloured crayons (67x72.5x9cm
  26x28x3in) New-York 1999

CARO de Baldassarre 1689-c.1750 [43]
- $7 000 - €7 752 - £4 747 - FF50 851
  Hunting Still Life with Game Birds, Dogs and a
  falcon in a Landscape Oil/canvas (123.5x177.5cm
  48x69in) New-York 2000
- $6 000 - €6 220 - £3 600 - FF40 800
  Cacciagione con cane Olio/tela (76x96.5cm
  29x37in) Venezia 2000

CARO de Lorenzo c.1700-c.1765 [18]
- $8 965 - €9 624 - £6 000 - FF63 129
  The Crucifixion Oil/canvas (76x51cm 29x20in)
  London 2000

CARO-DELVAILLE Henry 1876-1926 [28]
- $13 000 - €15 173 - £9 176 - FF99 526
  L'heure du thé Oleo/lienzo (60x72.5cm 23x28in)
  Buenos-Aires 2000

CAROLIS de Adolfo 1874-1928 [13]
- $37 500 - €38 874 - £22 500 - FF255 000
  Trittico: Allegoria del mare Tempera (73x308cm
  28x121in) Prato 2000
- $7 000 - €7 770 - £4 879 - FF50 970
  «The Struggle» Oil/board (68.5x99.5cm 26x39in)
  New-York 2000
- $1 618 - €2 097 - £1 213 - FF13 756
  Al pascolo Gouache/carta (29x50cm 11x19in) Napoli
  2001

🎨 **$630** - €716 - **£431** - FF4 695
«**Turin**» Poster (72x50cm 28x19in) Hannover 2000

CAROLUS Jean 1814-1897 **[47]**
🖼 **$9 457** - €11 248 - **£6 740** - FF73 785
Elegantes Paar im Interieur Öl/Leinwand (67x83cm 26x32in) Köln 2000

CAROLUS-DURAN Charles Émile 1837-1917 **[122]**
🖼 **$9 660** - €10 671 - **£6 699** - FF70 000
Grande étude de nu Huile/toile (175x160cm 68x62in) Paris 2001
🖼 **$4 236** - €3 855 - **£2 600** - FF25 290
The Opera Singer Oil/canvas (65x39cm 25x15in) London 1999
🖼 **$5 977** - €6 416 - **£4 097** - FF42 086
Portrait of a Bearded Gentleman Oil/canvas (29x25cm 11x9in) London 2000
🖼 **$950** - €1 017 - **£648** - FF6 668
Landscapewith Three Figures resting in the Shade of a Tree Ink (21.5x28cm 8x11in) New-York 2001

CARON Antoine c.1521-1599 **[6]**
🖼 **$48 000** - €51 262 - **£32 707** - FF336 254
Design for a Decorative Panel with a Triumph of Diana Black chalk (22x14cm 8x5in) New-York 2001

CARON Auguste 1806-? **[10]**
🖼 **$385** - €457 - **£281** - FF3 000
Portrait d'homme assis lisant Mine plomb (27.5x20cm 10x7in) Paris 2001

CARON Joseph 1866-1944 **[98]**
🖼 **$399** - €446 - **£261** - FF2 926
Déclin du jour Huile/toile (50x72cm 19x28in) Antwerpen 2000
🖼 **$264** - €248 - **£163** - FF1 626
Pommiers en fleurs Huile/panneau (28.5x40.5cm 11x15in) Bruxelles 1999

CARON Jules act.1860-1875 **[1]**
🖼 **$1 630** - €1 829 - **£1 141** - FF12 000
Panier de fruits avec perroquet Gouache/papier (34.5x50cm 13x19in) Paris 2001

CARON Marcel 1899-1966 **[49]**
🖼 **$3 223** - €2 725 - **£1 925** - FF17 875
«Plage» Huile/panneau (46x53cm 18x20in) Liège 1998
🖼 **$790** - €942 - **£566** - FF6 178
Paysage cubiste Huile/panneau (41x33.5cm 16x13in) Liège 2000
🖼 **$422** - €496 - **£296** - FF3 252
Boxeur et son entraîneur Dessin (21x26cm 8x10in) Liège 2000

CARON Paul Archibald 1874-1941 **[62]**
🖼 **$990** - €1 148 - **£699** - FF7 533
«Trail in the Woods, Murray Bay» Huile/panneau (13x18cm 5x7in) Montréal 2001
🖼 **$332** - €307 - **£209** - FF2 014
Eastern Townships Watercolour/paper (35x53cm 13x20in) Ottawa, Ontario 1999

CARONNI Paolo 1779-1842 **[1]**
🎨 **$800** - €829 - **£480** - FF5 440
Scena di storia romana antica, da Le Brun Gravure (59x102.5cm 23x40in) Milano 2000

CAROSELLI Angelo 1585-1652 **[7]**
🖼 **$100 000** - €101 164 - **£61 060** - FF663 590
Lesbia Mourning her Pet Sparrow Oil/canvas (97x134.5cm 38x52in) New-York 2000
🖼 **$14 875** - €15 420 - **£8 925** - FF101 150
Giuditta Olio/tela (73x61.5cm 28x24in) Venezia 2000

CAROSI Alberto 1891-1967 **[25]**
🖼 **$1 600** - €2 073 - **£1 200** - FF13 600
La vita Olio/legno (50x50cm 19x19in) Roma 2001

CAROTO Giovan Francesco c.1480-c.1555 **[3]**
🖼 **$12 800** - €16 586 - **£9 600** - FF108 800
Deposizione Olio/tavola (59.5x45cm 23x17in) Milano 2001

CARPACCIO Vittore 1450/54-1525/26 **[6]**
🖼 **$53 794** - €57 744 - **£36 000** - FF378 777
Seated Woman Black & white chalks (27.5x17.5cm 10x6in) London 2001

CARPANETTO Giovanni Battista 1863-1928 **[23]**
🖼 **$8 400** - €7 257 - **£4 200** - FF47 600
Prime case in montagna Olio/tela (43x56cm 16x22in) Genova 1999
🖼 **$12 600** - €10 885 - **£6 300** - FF71 400
Scena in costume direttorio (ai Giardini Reali di Torino) Acquarello/carta (80x120cm 31x47in) Torino 1999
🎨 **$2 939** - €3 354 - **£2 043** - FF22 000
«Guida di Torino» Affiche (97x175cm 38x68in) Paris 2001

CARPEAUX Jean-Baptiste 1827-1875 **[623]**
🖼 **$9 517** - €9 452 - **£5 927** - FF62 000
Scène présumée de la Commune Huile/toile (80x100cm 31x39in) Paris 1999
🖼 **$4 401** - €4 573 - **£2 772** - FF30 000
Jeune fille arabe Huile/carton (27.5x22.5cm 10x8in) Paris 2000
⚱ **$21 765** - €22 867 - **£14 355** - FF150 000
Génie de la danse avec l'Amour à la folie Bronze (H88cm H34in) Calais 2000
⚱ **$4 119** - €4 573 - **£2 871** - FF30 000
Le fumeur Bronze (59.5x32cm 23x12in) Paris 2001
🖼 **$1 537** - €1 524 - **£956** - FF10 000
Barque halée devant un fort Encre (18x28.5cm 7x11in) Paris 1999

CARPENTER Arthur Espenet 1920 **[1]**
⚱ **$14 000** - €13 364 - **£8 748** - FF87 661
Pedestal Table Sculpture (74x277x112cm 29x109x44in) New-York 1999

CARPENTER Fred Green 1882-1965 **[16]**
🖼 **$1 750** - €1 479 - **£1 040** - FF9 701
City scene Oil/canvas (52x44cm 20x17in) Mebane NC 1998
🖼 **$1 100** - €1 283 - **£785** - FF8 416
Jester on Green Background Oil/board (30x25cm 12x10in) St. Louis MO 2000

CARPENTER Margaret Sarah 1793-1872 **[20]**
🖼 **$9 119** - €10 846 - **£6 500** - FF71 143
Elza Boardman and her Son, Robert Oil/canvas (128x103cm 50x40in) London 2000
🖼 **$9 373** - €9 173 - **£6 000** - FF60 172
First Love Oil/panel (52.5x44cm 20x17in) London 1999

CARPENTER Mildred Bailey 1894-c.1984 **[6]**
🖼 **$5 687** - €5 047 - **£3 400** - FF33 106
Portrait of Isabela Horatia Seymour Daughter of Lord George Seymour Oil/canvas (91x71cm 36x28in) Cranbrook, Kent 1998
🖼 **$1 300** - €1 245 - **£803** - FF8 166
Sprites dancing Through Woods, Illustration Watercolour/paper (49x38cm 19x15in) New-York 1999

CARPENTER William 1818-1899 **[9]**
🖼 **$1 198** - €1 154 - **£749** - FF7 571
A Naples Market Watercolour/paper (17x24cm 6x9in) Billingshurst, West-Sussex 1999

C

CARPENTERO Henri Jos. Gommarus 1820-1874 **[28]**

➤ **$4 968 – €5 949 – £3 408** – FF39 024
Chez le cordonnier Huile/panneau (47x59cm 18x23in) Bruxelles 2000

➤ **$1 500 – €1 412 – £932** – FF9 260
Baby's First Steps Oil/panel (33x30cm 13x12in) East-Dennis MA 1999

CARPENTERO Jean Charles 1784-1823 **[4]**

➤ **$4 065 – €3 718 – £2 475** – FF24 390
Un jeu compliqué Huile/toile (50x80cm 19x31in) Antwerpen 1999

CARPENTIER Evariste 1845-1922 **[36]**

➤ **$15 096 – €16 856 – £10 540** – FF110 568
The sleeping Wife of the Carpenter Oil/canvas (100x125cm 39x49in) Bruxelles 2001

➤ **$18 161 – €15 896 – £11 000** – FF104 271
Les pigeons Oil/canvas (64x80cm 25x31in) London 1998

➤ **$1 758 – €1 486 – £1 050** – FF9 750
Sous-bois Pastel/carton (31x36cm 12x14in) Liège 1998

CARPENTIER Félix XX **[8]**

➤ **$5 250 – €6 100 – £3 690** – FF40 014
Garden Perspective with Azaleas, Rhododendron & Pansies Oil/canvas (83x111cm 33x44in) New-Orleans LA 2001

CARPENTIERS Adriaen c.1710-c.1790 **[5]**

➤ **$4 999 – €4 892 – £3 200** – FF32 091
Portrait of Master Wyche of Bedgbury, Kent, wearing a blue Coat Oil/canvas (74x62cm 29x24in) London 1999

CARPI Aldo 1886-1973 **[42]**

➤ **$2 250 – €2 332 – £1 350** – FF15 300
Marina Olio/tela (55x70cm 21x27in) Milano 1999

➤ **$225 – €233 – £135** – FF1 530
Fanciullo Matita/carta (27x17cm 10x6in) Vercelli 2001

CARPI da Girolamo 1501-1556 **[20]**

➤ **$90 354 – €100 616 – £63 492** – FF660 000
Le mariage mystique de Sainte-Catherine Huile/panneau (74.5x57cm 29x22in) Paris 2001

➤ **$1 617 – €1 500 – £1 000** – FF9 837
Figure, bearing Fruit in her Apron/Two Studies of Venus after antique Ink (22x7.5cm 8x2in) London 1999

CARPI da Ugo c.1450/80-1523 **[27]**

➤ **$1 007 – €998 – £630** – FF6 548
Diogenes, after Parmigianino Woodcut (46.3x35cm 18x13in) Haarlem 1999

CARPIONI Giulio 1613-1678 **[79]**

➤ **$129 104 – €120 851 – £80 000** – FF792 728
Eos and Tithonus Oil/canvas (147.5x226cm 58x88in) London 1999

➤ **$10 460 – €11 228 – £7 000** – FF73 651
The Deification of Aeneas Oil/canvas (63.5x82cm 25x32in) London 2000

➤ **$2 800 – €3 628 – £2 100** – FF23 800
Allegoria della fortuna Sanguina/carta (41.5x27.5cm 16x10in) Milano 2000

➤ **$400 – €468 – £281** – FF3 067
The Madonna of the Rosary Etching (22.5x15.5cm 8x6in) New-York 2000

CARQUEVILLE Will 1871-1946 **[12]**

➤ **$481 – €485 – £300** – FF3 181
«International December» Poster (47x32cm 18x12in) London 2000

CARR Emily M. 1871-1945 **[95]**

➤ **$48 885 – €56 726 – £33 750** – FF372 097
Along the Cliff, Beacon Hill, in the Distance Horseshoe Bay Oil/board (37.5x45cm 14x17in) Vancouver, BC. 2000

➤ **$19 212 – €21 276 – £13 029** – FF139 562
The Glade Oil/paper (50.5x31.5cm 19x12in) Toronto 2000

➤ **$2 272 – €2 571 – £1 589** – FF16 862
Klee Wyck Bowl Ceramic (5.5x6.5cm 2x2in) Toronto 2001

➤ **$32 659 – €31 220 – £20 467** – FF204 787
Totem D'Sonoqua Watercolour/paper (64x45.5cm 25x17in) Vancouver, BC. 1999

CARR Henry Marvell 1894-? **[12]**

➤ **$1 618 – €1 519 – £1 000** – FF9 965
Portrait of Aldous Huxley, half-Length, holding a Book Oil/canvas (91x71cm 35x27in) London 1999

CARR Leslie 1891-? **[10]**

➤ **$1 200 – €1 300 – £799** – FF8 529
«Navy Week, Visit the Dockyards, Chatham, Potsmouth, Devonport» Poster (100x125cm 39x49in) New-York 2000

CARR Samuel S. 1837-1908 **[35]**

➤ **$5 000 – €4 735 – £3 040** – FF31 060
Crossing the Stream Oil/canvas (56x91.5cm 22x36in) New-York 1999

➤ **$32 500 – €30 004 – £19 987** – FF196 816
Children at Beach Oil/canvas (23x30.5cm 9x12in) New-York 1999

CARR Thomas, Tom 1909-1999 **[73]**

➤ **$17 606 – €16 691 – £11 000** – FF109 483
The Front, Newcastle, Co. Down Oil/canvas (45.5x56cm 17x22in) London 1999

➤ **$3 586 – €3 849 – £2 400** – FF25 251
Duke of Buccleuch's Foxhounds Oil/canvas (32x49cm 12x19in) St. Boswells 2000

➤ **$2 175 – €2 032 – £1 342** – FF13 326
Washing Day Watercolour/paper (28x20cm 11x8in) Dublin 1999

➤ **$392 – €468 – £280** – FF3 071
The Shropshire Beagles Print in colors (31x48cm 12x18in) Leyburn, North Yorkshire 2000

CARRA Carlo 1881-1966 **[271]**

➤ **$62 500 – €64 791 – £37 500** – FF425 000
Venezia Punta della Dogana Olio/tela (40x60cm 15x23in) Prato 1999

➤ **$13 600 – €17 623 – £10 200** – FF115 600
Bozzetto di spaggia Olio/cartone (18.5x23.5cm 7x9in) Milano 2000

➤ **$6 000 – €6 220 – £3 600** – FF40 800
Paesaggio Matita/carta (24.5x16.5cm 9x6in) Prato 2000

➤ **$1 100 – €1 140 – £660** – FF7 480
Donna al lago, dalla cartella Segreti Litografia (36x23cm 14x9in) Milano 2001

CARRACCI Agostino 1557-1602 **[96]**

➤ **$12 500 – €12 958 – £7 500** – FF85 000
Cristo risorgente con i simboli della Passione Olio/tela (87.5x86cm 34x33in) Venezia 1999

➤ **$7 000 – €6 085 – £4 236** – FF39 918
Woman, Half-length, and a Separate Study of Another Head in Profile Ink (32.5x16.5cm 12x6in) New-York 1999

➤ **$500 – €486 – £311** – FF3 186
Die Hl. Familie mit den hl. Katharina, Johannes und Antonius Kupferstich (48.6x31.4cm 19x12in) Berlin 1999

CARRACCI Annibale 1560-1609 **[73]**
- $297 295 - €294 886 - **£185 000** - FF1 934 323
  Man as Bacchus drinking Wine, with two youths, a Magpie and an Ape Oil/canvas (132.5x97cm 52x38in) London 1999
- $130 000 - €124 095 - **£81 224** - FF814 008
  Madonna and Child, after Antonio Allegri da Correggio Oil/paper/panel (44x30cm 17x11in) New-York 1999
- $10 460 - €11 228 - **£7 000** - FF73 651
  Landscape with Mary Magdalene Ink (19.5x27cm 7x10in) London 2000
- $500 - €560 - **£348** - FF3 671
  The Adoration of the Shepherds Etching (10.5x13.5cm 4x5in) New-York 2001

CARRACCI Antonio 1583-1618 **[3]**
- $51 994 - €60 609 - **£36 000** - FF397 566
  The Baptism of Christ Oil/copper (52x39.5cm 20x15in) London 2000

CARRACCI Lodovico 1555-1619 **[28]**
- $4 750 000 - €4 747 777 - **£2 901 775** - FF31 143 380
  The Pietà Oil/canvas (95x173cm 37x68in) New-York 2000
- $100 000 - €106 969 - **£68 180** - FF701 670
  The Madonna and Child with Saints Catherine of Alexandria, Agnes Oil/copper (33x25.5cm 12x10in) New-York 2000
- $1 717 - €1 953 - **£1 200** - FF12 812
  Madonna and Child with Angels Etching (16.5x11.5cm 6x4in) London 2000

CARRAND Louis Hilaire 1821-1899 **[93]**
- $2 118 - €2 134 - **£1 320** - FF14 000
  Le rémouleur Huile/panneau (41x70cm 16x27in) Lyon 2000
- $1 101 - €1 220 - **£747** - FF8 000
  Paysage à la falaise Huile/carton (31.5x41cm 12x16in) Lyon 2000

CARRASCO Françoise 1944 **[9]**
- $798 - €762 - **£499** - FF5 000
  Personnage Sculpture (50x25x16cm 19x9x6in) Douai 1999

CARRASCO Humberto XX **[11]**
- $1 030 - €1 101 - **£702** - FF7 224
  Calle Juan de Tolosa Oleo/lienzo (45x60cm 17x23in) México 2001

CARRASSAN Marie Gabrielle XX **[2]**
- $1 971 - €2 287 - **£1 383** - FF15 000
  Le songe illumineuse Huile/toile (81x60cm 31x23in) Neuilly-sur-Seine 2000

CARRÉ Ketty, A.M. Lederer 1882-1964 **[5]**
- $4 396 - €4 269 - **£2 716** - FF28 000
  Les marchands Huile/toile/carton (46x55cm 18x21in) Paris 1999
- $1 108 - €1 296 - **£791** - FF8 500
  Le lever du rideau Huile/carton (34x26.5cm 13x10in) Paris 2000

CARRÉ Léon 1878-1942 **[56]**
- $1 678 - €1 906 - **£1 166** - FF12 500
  Matin de mars dans le Sahel algérois Huile/carton (38x46cm 14x18in) Orléans 2001
- $783 - €652 - **£460** - FF24 275
  «The Thought» Watercolour/paper (14.5x21cm 5x8in) London 1998
- $550 - €639 - **£386** - FF4 189
  «Tlemcen» Poster (99x61cm 39x24in) New-York 2000

CARRÉ Michiel 1657-1727/47 **[53]**
- $4 529 - €4 199 - **£2 800** - FF27 545
  Shepherds resting by a Stream Oil/canvas (40x48.5cm 15x19in) London 1999

CARRÉ Raoul ?-1934 **[10]**
- $952 - €915 - **£592** - FF6 000
  Procession à Fouesnan Huile/toile (26.5x35cm 10x13in) Paris 1999

CARRÉ-SOUBIRAN Victor ?-1897 **[2]**
- $3 929 - €4 421 - **£2 705** - FF29 000
  Le livre de comptes Huile/toile (56x46cm 22x18in) Barbizon 2002

CARRÉE Hendrik 1656-1721 **[4]**
- $4 617 - €3 988 - **£2 783** - FF26 162
  Portrait of a Lady, seated small three quarter length Oil/canvas (49x40cm 19x15in) Amsterdam 1998

CARREE Johannes 1698-1772 **[1]**
- $4 000 - €4 650 - **£2 807** - FF30 504
  Portrait of a Young Boy Oil/canvas (78x62cm 30x24in) New-York 2001

CARREÑO DE MIRANDA Juan 1614-1685 **[8]**
- $6 770 - €7 267 - **£4 530** - FF47 670
  Archimedes Öl/Leinwand (64x76cm 25x29in) Wien 2000

CARREÑO Mario 1913-1999 **[196]**
- $191 174 - €185 988 - **£117 608** - FF1 220 000
  Guajiras Huile/toile (100x151cm 39x59in) Paris 1999
- $32 450 - €33 036 - **£20 350** - FF216 700
  Composición con jarrón de flores Oleo/tabla (62x51cm 24x20in) Madrid 2000
- $18 000 - €17 513 - **£11 079** - FF114 881
  Mujeres Gouache/paper (57x72cm 22x28in) New-York 1999

CARRERA Augustin 1878-1952 **[41]**
- $396 - €457 - **£273** - FF3 000
  Le châle bleu Huile/toile (78x38cm 30x14in) Paris 2000

CARRICK Desmond 1928 **[17]**
- $1 420 - €1 651 - **£998** - FF10 827
  «Visitor at St.Gobnaits, Inishfree» Oil/board (61x81cm 24x31in) Dublin 2001
- $1 094 - €1 143 - **£692** - FF7 496
  Early Morning Departure on the Seine at Vernon Oil/canvas/board (30.5x39.5cm 12x15in) Dublin 2000
- $1 417 - €1 524 - **£965** - FF9 994
  Sailing on the Oise, France Gouache/board (34x44cm 13x17in) Dublin 2001

CARRICK John Mulcaster 1833-1896 **[36]**
- $16 836 - €20 023 - **£12 000** - FF131 342
  Boating at Richmond on Thames Oil/canvas (41x61cm 16x24in) London 2000
- $2 152 - €1 951 - **£1 305** - FF12 800
  Port Scene (possibly Villefranche) Oil/board (31x47.5cm 12x18in) London 2001

CARRICK William Arth. Laurie 1879-? **[19]**
- $1 464 - €1 722 - **£1 050** - FF11 296
  Stonehaven Harbour Oil/board (32x50cm 12x19in) Plymouth 2001

CARRICK-FOX Ethel 1872-1952 **[103]**
- $15 271 - €14 437 - **£9 477** - FF94 699
  Red Gum Blossom Oil/canvas/board (51x60.5cm 20x23in) Malvern, Victoria 1999
- $5 180 - €4 871 - **£3 208** - FF31 953
  In Morocco Oil/wood (14x19cm 5x7in) Melbourne 1999

C

$2 101 - €2 315 - £1 397 - FF15 188
Sunday Market Lithograph (27x37cm 10x14in) Melbourne 2000

CARRIER-BELLEUSE Albert Ernest 1824-1887 [600]

$65 000 - €72 758 - £45 331 - FF477 262
Mending the Pots Oil/canvas (65x98cm 25x38in) New-York 2001

$9 045 - €8 567 - £5 500 - FF56 194
La Mélodie Bronze (H80cm H31in) London 1999

$3 857 - €3 506 - £2 366 - FF23 000
La liseuse Bronze (H62cm H24in) Paris 1999

$1 136 - €1 220 - £760 - FF8 000
Nu féminin Pastel/toile (61x46cm 24x18in) Paris 2000

CARRIER-BELLEUSE Louis-Robert 1848-1913 [81]

$3 192 - €2 975 - £1 920 - FF19 512
L'élégante Huile/toile (74x60cm 29x23in) Liège 1999

$1 134 - €1 143 - £707 - FF7 500
Buste de femme au coffre Céramique (H38cm H14in) Paris 2000

$13 021 - €12 673 - £8 000 - FF83 132
La lettre Pastel/paper (100x81cm 39x31in) London 1999

CARRIER-BELLEUSE Pierre 1851-1933 [165]

$1 239 - €1 060 - £749 - FF6 954
Lady, half length, Wearing a Red Velvet Dress with a Lace Collar Oil/canvas (86x64.5cm 33x25in) London 1999

$1 982 - €1 952 - £1 267 - FF12 805
Liseuse Chryséléphantine (H26.5cm H10in) Madrid 1999

$2 414 - €2 592 - £1 615 - FF17 000
Élégante Pastel/paper (81x54cm 31x21in) Nice 2000

CARRIERA Rosalba 1675-1757 [46]

$14 392 - €16 120 - £10 000 - FF105 741
Girl, holding a Toy Spaniel wrapped in a blue Cloak Miniature (8x5.5cm 3x2in) London 2001

$23 527 - €22 973 - £15 000 - FF150 690
Portrait of a Woman, bust length Pastel/paper (57x43.5cm 22x17in) London 1999

CARRIERE Alphonse 1808-? [4]

$7 123 - €8 281 - £5 000 - FF54 322
Le papillon Oil/canvas (81x66cm 31x25in) London 2001

CARRIERE Eugène 1849-1906 [370]

$4 606 - €4 269 - £2 864 - FF28 000
Portrait de femme au turban rouge Huile/toile (48x38cm 18x14in) Paris 1999

$2 854 - €2 439 - £1 728 - FF16 000
Portrait de jeune fille Huile/toile (32.5x28.5cm 12x11in) Paris 1998

$332 - €381 - £227 - FF2 500
Femmes et enfants Crayon/papier (28x17cm 11x6in) Paris 2000

$324 - €274 - £194 - FF1 800
Buste de jeune fille Lithographie (30x24.4cm 11x9in) Paris 1998

CARRIES Jean Joseph Marie 1855-1894 [41]

$6 441 - €7 318 - £4 521 - FF48 000
La novice Grès (H44cm H17in) Paris 2001

CARRILLO Miguel 1947 [1]

$2 178 - €2 033 - £1 344 - FF13 338
Desnudo Lápiz/papel (62x87cm 24x34in) México 1999

CARRINGTON Dora 1893-1932 [16]

$49 792 - €48 327 - £31 000 - FF317 002
Watendlath Farm, Cumberland Oil/canvas (51x61cm 20x24in) London 1999

$8 503 - €10 078 - £6 000 - FF66 108
The Red Rose Oil/panel (29x24cm 11x9in) London 2000

$1 345 - €1 444 - £900 - FF9 473
Figures in a Landscape Pencil (29x28.5cm 11x11in) London 2000

CARRINGTON Leonora 1917 [153]

$120 000 - €116 757 - £73 860 - FF765 876
The Analyst Mixed media/panel (45x60.5cm 17x23in) New-York 1999

$3 743 - €4 390 - £2 692 - FF28 798
Sin título Tinta/papel (30x23cm 11x9in) México 2001

$1 500 - €1 456 - £933 - FF9 549
Tuesday Color lithograph (64.5x91cm 25x35in) New-York 1999

CARRODI Salomon XX [1]

$1 461 - €1 606 - £936 - FF10 534
Towards St.Marks Cathedral, Venice Watercolour/paper (38x25cm 14x9in) Melbourne 2000

CARROLL John 1892-1959 [34]

$1 100 - €942 - £649 - FF6 179
Huntsman Oil/canvas (63.5x102cm 25x40in) New-York 1998

$150 - €161 - £100 - FF1 059
Portrait of a Woman Lithograph (23x17cm 9x7in) Cleveland OH 2000

CARROLL Lawrence 1954 [19]

$10 000 - €11 603 - £6 904 - FF76 110
One Leaf Fell, Then Two, The Three Mixed media/canvas (274x122x30.5cm 107x48x12in) New-York 2000

CARROLL Lewis 1832-1898 [92]

$25 612 - €29 757 - £18 000 - FF195 195
Ina Liddell holding a Doll, seated, Summer Albumen print (15x12.5cm 5x4in) London 2001

CARROLL Patrick 1949 [22]

$454 - €429 - £274 - FF2 815
Galahs in the Bush Series, over the Maquarie, Bathurst Oil/paper (48x68cm 18x26in) Sydney 1999

CARROLL Robert 1934 [24]

$1 000 - €1 037 - £600 - FF6 800
Pomeriggio atemporale Olio/tela (54x65cm 21x25in) Vercelli 2000

CARROLL William Joseph XIX-XX [23]

$926 - €994 - £620 - FF6 523
Portrait of a Young Woman with baskets of fruit Oil/canvas (75.5x50cm 29x19in) Newcastle-upon-Tyne 2000

$2 251 - €1 910 - £1 357 - FF12 526
Contemplation Watercolour/paper (88.5x65cm 34x25in) Sydney 1998

CARS Laurent 1699/1702-1771 [8]

$2 980 - €2 910 - £1 900 - FF19 087
King Louis XV giving Peace to Europe, after François Le Moyne Red chalk/paper (57x43.5cm 22x17in) London 1999

CARSE Alexander 1770/79-1843 [10]

$4 832 - €4 541 - £3 000 - FF29 787
Eager for News Oil/canvas (38x48.5cm 14x19in) London 1999

CARSE James Howe 1818-1900 **[47]**
$1 275 - €1 229 - **£788** - FF8 059
View of an Estuary (said to be Middle Harbour)
Oil/canvas (49x75cm 19x29in) Sydney 1999
$971 - €913 - **£601** - FF5 991
The Valley Through the Hills Oil/wood
(10.5x26.5cm 4x10in) Melbourne 1999

CARSON Robert Taylor 1919 **[59]**
$1 780 - €1 991 - **£1 200** - FF13 057
Donegal Landscape Oil/canvas (51x63.5cm
20x25in) London 2000
$1 493 - €1 651 - **£1 035** - FF10 827
Atlantic Drive Oil/canvas (30.5x40.5cm 12x15in)
Dublin 2001
$1 553 - €1 778 - **£1 068** - FF11 660
Judging the Herd Pastel/paper (27x49cm 11x19in)
Dublin 2000

CARSTENS Julius Victor 1849-1908 **[11]**
$4 726 - €4 499 - **£3 000** - FF29 511
Guarding the Baby Oil/canvas (88.5x124.5cm
34x49in) Billingshurst, West-Sussex 1999

CARSTENSEN Claus 1957 **[53]**
$625 - €605 - **£385** - FF3 971
**Del af inventar, farveprøve 35, Worlds End, röd
orange og sort** Oil/masonite (50x60cm 19x23in)
København 1999

CARSTENSEN Ebba 1885-1967 **[97]**
$399 - €417 - **£251** - FF2 733
Skoven Oil/canvas (96x75cm 37x29in) Lingby 2000

CARSTENSEN Johannes 1924 **[18]**
$480 - €536 - **£334** - FF3 517
«Havn» Oil/canvas (56x74cm 22x29in) København
2001

CARTARO Mario ?-1620 **[2]**
$1 369 - €1 329 - **£852** - FF8 720
Admiranda beati aurelii Augustini Kupferstich
(39.3x50.7cm 15x19in) Berlin 1999

CARTE Anto 1886-1954 **[131]**
$56 580 - €57 013 - **£35 190** - FF373 980
Les archers Huile/toile (124.5x100cm 49x39in)
Bruxelles 2000
$7 722 - €6 445 - **£4 524** - FF42 276
Fresque Technique mixte/toile (75x108cm 29x42in)
Bruxelles 1998
$2 944 - €2 851 - **£1 817** - FF18 699
Vierge à l'enfant Technique mixte (20x12cm 7x4in)
Bruxelles 2001
$2 929 - €3 346 - **£2 038** - FF21 951
Jeune homme nu Technique mixte/papier
(118x76cm 46x29in) Bruxelles 2001
$158 - €173 - **£105** - FF1 138
Ange Estampe (40.5x41cm 15x16in) Bruxelles 2000

CARTELLIER Pierre 1757-1831 **[1]**
$8 304 - €7 165 - **£4 991** - FF47 004
Buste de Louis Bonaparte Plâtre (72.5x50x30cm
28x19x11in) Nice 1998

CARTER Allan 1909 **[6]**
$2 017 - €1 906 - **£1 220** - FF12 500
Lionne marchant Aquarelle (43x71.5cm 16x28in)
Paris 1999

CARTER Clarence Holbrook 1904-1985 **[42]**
$4 000 - €4 387 - **£2 716** - FF28 780
Cane Field Oil/canvas (71x58cm 28x23in) New-
Orleans LA 2000
$800 - €893 - **£556** - FF5 855
Woman in a Canoe Watercolour (23x30cm 9x12in)
Cleveland OH 2001

$325 - €349 - **£217** - FF2 289
Riderless Racers Etching (12x17cm 5x6in)
Cleveland OH 2000

CARTER Dennis Malone 1827-1881 **[2]**
$10 000 - €10 469 - **£6 283** - FF68 672
Oats, Peas, eans, and Barley Grow Oil/canvas
(40x50cm 16x20in) East-Dennis MA 2000

CARTER Gary 1939 **[16]**
$18 700 - €20 072 - **£12 514** - FF131 666
The Windshield Cowboys Oil/canvas (50x101cm
20x40in) Houston TX 2000
$6 600 - €7 084 - **£4 416** - FF46 470
Fat Cattle and Slim Rails Oil/canvas (30x50cm
12x20in) Houston TX 2000

CARTER George 1737-1796 **[1]**
$5 527 - €6 451 - **£3 901** - FF42 318
Portrait of an Officer Oil/canvas (76x63.5cm
29x25in) Toronto 2000

CARTER Henry Barlow 1803-1867 **[128]**
$884 - €835 - **£550** - FF5 479
Holy Island Watercolour/paper (21x30cm 8x12in)
Scarborough, North-Yorshire 1999

CARTER Henry William c.1840-c.1910 **[7]**
$875 - €847 - **£540** - FF5 557
Surprised! Oil/panel (24x31cm 9x12in) London 1999

CARTER Hugh 1837-1903 **[13]**
$273 - €306 - **£190** - FF2 009
Lady with her Poodle Watercolour/paper
(63.5x53.5cm 25x21in) London 2001

CARTER Jack XX **[20]**
$589 - €653 - **£400** - FF4 284
A Still Life of Pansies Watercolour (26x36cm
10x14in) Billingshurst, West-Sussex 2000

CARTER Joseph Newington 1835-1871 **[31]**
$344 - €402 - **£240** - FF2 639
Ship on a Stormy Sea off a Coastline Watercolour
(11.5x15.5cm 4x6in) West-Yorshire 2000

CARTER Keith 1948 **[45]**
$1 200 - €1 338 - **£841** - FF8 774
«Atlas Moth» Silver print (36x36cm 14x14in) New-
York 2001

CARTER Pruett 1891-1955 **[27]**
$3 750 - €3 300 - **£2 283** - FF21 649
«Worlds Wild Fire» Oil/canvas (89x99cm 35x39in)
Norwalk CT 1999

CARTER Richard Harry 1839-1911 **[41]**
$441 - €394 - **£270** - FF2 586
Cornish Coast Watercolour/paper (35x66cm 14x26in)
Par, Cornwall 1999

CARTER Samuel John 1835-1892 **[12]**
$10 501 - €12 213 - **£7 500** - FF80 114
The Rt.Hon.Jacob Astley Lord Hastings Oil/can-
vas (305x300cm 120x118in) Norfolk 2001
$22 342 - €24 765 - **£15 480** - FF162 450
Little Wanderers Oil/canvas (61.5x51.5cm 24x20in)
Malmö 2001

CARTER Sydney 1874-1945 **[108]**
$316 - €309 - **£200** - FF2 028
Woodland Scene Mixed media (26x38cm 10x14in)
Cape Town 1999
$199 - €231 - **£137** - FF1 516
View of a House with a Figure Nearby
Watercolour (30x42.5cm 11x16in) Johannesburg 2000

CARTER V.H.B. XIX [3]
- $6 571 - €6 557 - **£4 000** - FF43 010
  Glenara of Aberaeron, off Cork Hatbour Oil/canvas (61x88cm 24x34in) London 2000

CARTIER Edd 1914 [1]
- $4 500 - €5 040 - **£3 126** - FF33 062
  Bear Invaders arrive in Spaceship Ink (35x26cm 14x10in) New-York 2001

CARTIER Jacques XIX-XX [30]
- $17 631 - €20 581 - **£12 447** - FF135 000
  Panthère dans les ruines au Cambodge Huile/panneau (181x140cm 71x55in) Neuilly-sur-Seine 2000
- $2 427 - €2 820 - **£1 705** - FF18 500
  Cacatoès Huile/panneau (105x69cm 41x27in) Paris 2001

CARTIER Karl 1855-1925 [26]
- $1 676 - €1 906 - **£1 150** - FF12 500
  Les moutons Huile/toile (54x65cm 21x25in) Lyon 2000
- $741 - €781 - **£494** - FF5 122
  Calle de París Pastel/papier (36x44cm 14x17in) Madrid 2000

CARTIER Roger XX [14]
- $839 - €717 - **£506** - FF4 700
  «Ignace» Affiche couleur (240x160cm 94x62in) Paris 1998

CARTIER Thomas François 1879-1943 [158]
- $713 - €777 - **£467** - FF5 100
  Combat de cerfs Bronze (H13cm H5in) Montargis 2000

CARTIER-BRESSON Henri 1908 [569]
- $2 500 - €2 331 - **£1 509** - FF15 291
  Mexico, Santa Clara Photograph (24x36cm 9x14in) New-York 1999

CARTLIDGE Daniel XVIII [5]
- $2 000 - €1 966 - **£1 285** - FF12 895
  Botanical Studies Watercolour (36x23cm 14x9in) New-York 1999

CARTON Jean 1912-1988 [33]
- $5 495 - €6 479 - **£3 863** - FF42 500
  Femme en buste Bronze (H40cm H15in) Fontainebleau 2000
- $426 - €457 - **£290** - FF3 000
  Couple enlacé Sanguine (32x27cm 12x10in) Troyes 2001

CARTOTTO Ercole 1889-1946 [3]
- $5 500 - €5 904 - **£3 680** - FF38 725
  Portrait of Miss Marion Ryder Oil/canvas (81.5x63.5cm 32x25in) New-York 2000

CARTWRIGHT William P. 1864-1911 [25]
- $330 - €392 - **£240** - FF2 571
  «Cymmer Abbey, Vale of LLanelltyd/Looking towards Barmouth» Oil/canvas (39.5x65cm 15x25in) Billingshurst, West-Sussex 2001

CARUELLE D'ALIGNY Théodore 1798-1871 [49]
- $5 808 - €6 098 - **£3 660** - FF40 000
  Vue d'Italie Huile/toile (33x49cm 12x19in) Aubagne 2000
- $2 507 - €2 134 - **£1 492** - FF14 000
  Paysage Huile/toile (40x31cm 15x12in) Joigny 1998
- $1 000 - €1 641 - **£1 000** - FF10 763
  Landscape, Collonges Pencil/paper (27x17.5cm 10x6in) New-York 2000

CARUNCHO Luis 1929 [16]
- $1 710 - €1 802 - **£1 140** - FF11 820
  Composición Técnica mixta (90x128cm 35x50in) Madrid 2000

CARUS Carl Gustav 1789-1869 [9]
- $33 090 - €30 908 - **£20 000** - FF202 746
  Personen in altdeutscher Tracht in Betrachtung einer mittelalterlichen Oil/canvas (36.5x15.5cm 14x6in) London 1999
- $2 142 - €2 045 - **£1 338** - FF13 415
  Feldweg Pencil (18.4x27.6cm 7x10in) Hamburg 1999

CARUSO Bruno 1927 [46]
- $2 160 - €1 866 - **£1 440** - FF12 240
  La ricerca del tempo perduto Olio/tela (70x50cm 27x19in) Prato 1998
- $1 280 - €1 659 - **£960** - FF10 880
  Natura morta Olio/tavola (28x38cm 11x14in) Milano 2000
- $480 - €622 - **£360** - FF4 080
  Nudo Acquarello (55x35cm 21x13in) Milano 2000

CARUSO Enrico 1873-1921 [17]
- $1 000 - €1 109 - **£692** - FF7 273
  Smiling robed Caruso Ink (19x15cm 7x6in) St. Petersburg FL 2001

CARVALHAIS Stuart 1887-1961 [8]
- $946 - €1 097 - **£660** - FF7 194
  Mulher Carbón/papel (31.5x18cm 12x7in) Lisboa 2001

CARVALLO Feliciano 1920 [25]
- $1 020 - €951 - **£660** - FF6 240
  Sin título, jarrón de frutas Oleo/lienzo (46x55.5cm 18x21in) Caracas 1999

CARVER Robert 1730-1791 [5]
- $8 000 - €7 584 - **£4 867** - FF49 750
  Moonlit river Landscapes with Boatmen near a Waterfall, Ruins beyond Oil/panel (61x106.5cm 24x41in) New-York 1999

CARVIN Louis Albert 1860-1933 [28]
- $396 - €396 - **£248** - FF2 620
  Le chien et le lapin (encrier cynégétique) Bronze (H10cm H3in) Soissons 1999

CARY John XVIII-XIX [24]
- $118 - €132 - **£80** - FF867
  Map of Norfolk Print (40x50cm 16x20in) Aylsham, Norfolk 2000

CARY William La Montagne 1840-1922 [9]
- $2 500 - €2 109 - **£1 466** - FF13 835
  Deer Crossing the Stream Oil/panel (12.5x21cm 4x8in) New-York 1998
- $10 000 - €8 544 - **£6 003** - FF56 044
  Racing the Steam Train Watercolour/paper (41x56.5cm 16x22in) New-York 1998

CARZOU Jean 1907-2000 [594]
- $4 350 - €4 421 - **£2 734** - FF29 000
  Paysage marin Huile/toile (46x61cm 18x24in) Lyon 2000
- $681 - €762 - **£462** - FF5 000
  Villa d'Este Encre Chine/papier (21x27.5cm 8x10in) Paris 2000
- $105 - €107 - **£66** - FF700
  Sans titre Lithographie (44x55cm 17x21in) Saint-Dié 2000

CASAGEMAS Carlos 1880-1901 [4]
- $19 500 - €22 524 - **£13 500** - FF147 750
  Retrato de Picasso Oleo/lienzo (50x37cm 19x14in) Madrid 2000

⤢ $7 261 - €7 165 - **£4 474** - FF47 000
Femmes à l'éventail Pastel/papier (25x20cm 9x7in)
Paris 1999

CASAGRANDE Carla Maria XX **[2]**
📷 $4 500 - €4 680 - **£2 841** - FF30 690
**Darathy Peyton-Hill, gold Medal Diver,
Olympics, Berlin** Gelatin silver print (23x17cm 9x6in)
New-York 2000

CASAGRANDE Peter 1946 **[9]**
⤢ $1 786 - €1 917 - **£1 195** - FF12 577
Komposition mit Zeitungsausschnitten Collage
(70x60cm 27x23in) Kempten 2000

CASALI Andrea c.1720-1784 **[16]**
⤢ $20 000 - €17 543 - **£12 144** - FF115 076
**The Holy Family with Saint Oswald of
Northumbria** Oil/canvas (96x129cm 37x50in) New-
York 1999
⤢ $7 681 - €7 332 - **£4 800** - FF48 097
The Assassination of King Edward the Martyr
Oil/canvas (61x50cm 24x19in) London 1999

CASAMADA Albert Pacos XX **[3]**
⤢ $8 134 - €8 971 - **£5 509** - FF58 846
Pasaje Öl/Leinwand (100x81cm 39x31in) Zürich 2000

CASANOVA Carlo 1871-1950 **[1]**
⤢ $2 250 - €2 332 - **£1 350** - FF15 300
Paesaggio lacustre Olio/tela (60x80cm 23x31in)
Milano 2000

CASANOVA Enrique 1850-1913 **[4]**
⤢ $1 290 - €1 496 - **£900** - FF9 810
Mulher mourisca Acuarela/papel (28x16cm 11x6in)
Lisboa 2001

CASANOVA Francesco Giuseppe 1727-1802 **[68]**
⤢ $22 695 - €25 916 - **£15 963** - FF170 000
Réunion d'officiers devant le champ de bataille
Huile/toile (102x149cm 40x58in) Versailles 2001
⤢ $21 063 - €18 196 - **£14 042** - FF119 357
Ritratto di cavaliere Olio/tela (63x52cm 24x20in)
Venezia 1998
⤢ $8 295 - €7 622 - **£5 095** - FF50 000
La halte des cavaliers Huile/toile (31.5x40cm
12x15in) Nantes 1999
⤢ $1 326 - €1 487 - **£900** - FF9 757
Dragoons on a Road, a Town Beyond Black chalk
(22.5x28cm 8x11in) London 2000

CASANOVA José 1933 **[5]**
⤢ $2 560 - €2 403 - **£1 600** - FF15 760
Marina Oleo/lienzo (84x120cm 33x47in) Madrid 1999

CASANOVA Y ESTORACH Antonio Salvador 1847-
1896 **[44]**
⤢ $2 520 - €2 703 - **£1 710** - FF17 730
Burrito comiendo de un árbol Oleo/lienzo
(38x46cm 14x18in) Madrid 2000
⤢ $2 400 - €2 606 - **£1 662** - FF17 093
Naughty Monk Oil/canvas (40x33cm 16x13in)
Cleveland OH 2001

CASARI A. XIX-XX **[1]**
⤢ $21 000 - €19 749 - **£13 003** - FF129 544
Small Fishing Boat in the Surf Mixed media/panel
(37.5x54cm 14x21in) New-York 1999

CASARRUBIOS Gabriel 1953 **[34]**
⤢ $174 - €180 - **£111** - FF1 182
Playa con sombrillas Oleo/tabla (11.5x22.5cm
4x8in) Madrid 2000

CASAS ABARCA Pedro 1875-1958 **[15]**
⤢ $216 - €228 - **£144** - FF1 497
Mujeres en interior Oleo/lienzo (64x56cm 25x22in)
Madrid 2000

CASAS Victor 1936 **[6]**
⤢ $1 197 - €1 141 - **£741** - FF7 486
Maternidad Oleo/lienzo (90x66cm 35x25in) Madrid
1999

CASAS Y CARBO Ramón 1866-1932 **[43]**
⤢ $108 900 - €99 107 - **£66 000** - FF650 100
Mujer con loro Oleo/lienzo (80x100cm 31x39in)
Madrid 1999
⤢ $20 650 - €21 023 - **£12 950** - FF137 900
Guardias municipales Oleo/lienzo (46x33cm
18x12in) Barcelona 2000
⤢ $15 950 - €16 518 - **£10 175** - FF108 350
Dama elegante Pastel (31.5x23.5cm 12x9in)
Barcelona 2000
⤢ $1 300 - €1 231 - **£807** - FF8 072
«Anis del Mono» Poster (48x24cm 18x9in) New-
York 1999

CASAUS Jesús Mecko 1926 **[43]**
⤢ $700 - €659 - **£435** - FF4 321
Little Street - Cadaques Oil/canvas (64x86cm
25x34in) East-Dennis MA 2000

CASCELLA Andrea 1920-1990 **[33]**
⤢ $2 500 - €2 592 - **£1 500** - FF17 000
Senza titolo Marbre (16x21x13cm 6x8x5in) Milano
1999

CASCELLA Basilio 1860-1950 **[17]**
⤢ $2 220 - €1 918 - **£1 110** - FF12 580
Serenata al tramonto Olio/cartone (34x52.5cm
13x20in) Milano 1999
⤢ $750 - €805 - **£501** - FF5 280
Woman Smelling Flowers Oil/board (43x27cm
17x11in) Bloomfield-Hills MI 2000
⤢ $500 - €441 - **£307** - FF2 895
Nymphs and Satyrs Ink (30x22cm 12x9in) New-
York 1999

CASCELLA Michele 1892-1989 **[418]**
⤢ $23 000 - €24 688 - **£15 391** - FF161 943
Villa d'Esta Oil/canvas (152.5x101.5cm 60x39in)
New-York 1999
⤢ $9 500 - €9 848 - **£5 700** - FF64 600
Strada nel podere Olio/tela (50x70cm 19x27in)
Milano 1999
⤢ $2 600 - €3 369 - **£1 950** - FF22 100
Campo di papaveri Olio/tela (20x30cm 7x11in)
Milano 2001
⤢ $3 250 - €3 369 - **£1 950** - FF22 100
Paesaggio con alberi Pastelli/carta (47x56cm
18x22in) Roma 2001
⤢ $225 - €233 - **£135** - FF1 530
Portofino Serigrafia (50x70cm 19x27in) Vercelli 2001

CASCELLA Pietro 1921 **[20]**
⤢ $560 - €726 - **£420** - FF4 760
Senza titolo Fer (24x21x33cm 9x8x12in) Milano
2001

CASCELLA Tommaso 1890-1968 **[17]**
⤢ $2 100 - €1 814 - **£1 400** - FF11 900
Paesaggio della Maiella Olio/tavola (30x40cm
11x15in) Roma 1998
⤢ $1 700 - €1 762 - **£1 020** - FF11 560
Paesaggio fluviale Pastelli/carta (36x46cm 14x18in)
Roma 2000

CASCIARO Giuseppe 1863-1941 **[227]**
- **$3 000** - €3 887 - **£2 250** - FF25 500
  Giardino caprese Olio/tela (56x85cm 22x33in)
  Napoli 2000
- **$2 500** - €2 592 - **£1 500** - FF17 000
  Ischia Tecnica mista/cartone (20x29.5cm 7x11in)
  Vercelli 1999
- **$1 280** - €1 659 - **£960** - FF10 880
  Campagna al tramonto Pastelli/carta (23x31cm
  9x12in) Roma 2001

CASELLA Francesco XVI **[1]**
- **$14 400** - €18 660 - **£10 800** - FF122 400
  Martirio di San Sebastiano Olio/tela (84.5x61.5cm
  33x24in) Milano 2001

CASELLAS Juan 1957 **[72]**
- **$230** - €216 - **£140** - FF1 418
  Paisaje con riachuelo Oleo/lienzo (50x61cm
  19x24in) Barcelona 1999

CASELLI XX **[1]**
- **$4 487** - €5 336 - **£3 199** - FF35 000
  Portrait de Maria Callas/Vue de Portofino Fusain
  (60x70cm 23x27in) Paris 2000

CASEMBROODT Abraham c.1583-c.1658 **[2]**
- **$9 975** - €11 330 - **£7 000** - FF74 322
  Mediterranean Harbour, with an English Man-
  Of-War at Anchor Oil/canvas (97x130.5cm 38x51in)
  London 2001

CASENELLI Victor 1868-1961 **[11]**
- **$1 500** - €1 793 - **£1 034** - FF11 763
  Native american hunters Watercolour,
  gouache/paper (28x48cm 11x19in) Milford CT 2000

CASENTINO del Jacopo Landini 1297-1358 **[6]**
- **$24 000** - €22 910 - **£14 995** - FF150 278
  Madonna and Child Tempera/panel (101.5x66cm
  39x25in) New-York 1999
- **$132 000** - €171 048 - **£99 000** - FF1 122 000
  Madonna col Bambino, San Paolo, San
  Giovanni Battista, santo vescovo Tempera/tavola
  (31.5x24cm 12x9in) Firenze 2000

CASER Ettore 1880-1944 **[26]**
- **$1 500** - €1 680 - **£1 042** - FF11 020
  Satyr with Flute at Water's Edge Oil/board
  (60x60cm 24x24in) St. Louis MO 2001

CASERO SANZ Antonio 1898-1973 **[117]**
- **$122** - €144 - **£84** - FF945
  Citando al toro Stylo bille (15x11.5cm 5x4in) Madrid
  2000
- **$79** - €78 - **£49** - FF512
  Muerte del toro Grabado (60x44cm 23x17in) Madrid
  1999

CASILE Alfred 1848-1909 **[76]**
- **$4 899** - €5 259 - **£3 277** - FF34 500
  Lever de soleil Huile/toile (43x65cm 16x25in)
  Avignon 2000
- **$1 711** - €1 753 - **£1 055** - FF11 500
  Voilier en bord de côte Huile/toile (22x33cm
  8x12in) Aubagne 2000

CASILEAR John William 1811-1893 **[28]**
- **$150 000** - €178 388 - **£106 905** - FF1 170 150
  On the Path Oil/canvas (86.5x142cm 34x55in) New-
  York 2000
- **$17 000** - €18 605 - **£11 726** - FF122 039
  Landscape with Hunter Oil/canvas (39.5x63cm
  15x24in) New-York 2001
- **$21 000** - €24 509 - **£14 886** - FF160 767
  New England Beach Scene Oil/board (25.5x39.5cm
  10x15in) New-York 2001

$4 250 - €4 719 - **£2 956** - FF30 953
  Lake George Watercolour/paper (15x25cm 6x10in)
  Milford CT 2001

CASISSA Nicola ?-1730 **[30]**
- **$77 040** - €76 531 - **£48 000** - FF502 012
  Sculpted Lion on a Plinth Decorated/Sculpted
  Urn with Mixed Flowers Oil/canvas (156x128cm
  61x50in) London 1999
- **$25 403** - €27 268 - **£17 000** - FF178 867
  Still Lifes of Various Flowers in Gilt Vases
  Oil/canvas (63.5x36cm 25x14in) London 2000

CASLEY Leonard XX **[28]**
- **$280** - €300 - **£185** - FF1 970
  Paisajes de costa Acuarela/papel (24x34cm 9x13in)
  Madrid 2000

CASLEY William XIX-XX **[66]**
- **$358** - €385 - **£240** - FF2 525
  Waves Breaking on a Cornish Shore Watercolour
  (24x43.5cm 9x17in) London 2000

CASNELLI Victor 1867-1961 **[8]**
- **$2 600** - €3 072 - **£1 842** - FF20 152
  Indian Encampment Gouache/paper (21x39cm
  8x15in) Austinburg OH 2000

CASOLANI Alessandro 1552-1606 **[16]**
- **$847** - €838 - **£528** - FF5 500
  Etudes d'après un marbre antique de femme
  nue/Etude de tête Crayon (18x23cm 7x9in) Paris
  1999

CASORATI Dafne Maugham 1897-1984 **[36]**
- **$1 000** - €1 037 - **£600** - FF6 800
  Pavarolo Olio/tela (45x55cm 17x21in) Vercelli 2000
- **$275** - €285 - **£165** - FF1 870
  Scorcio del giardino Olio/tavola (31x22.5cm 12x8in)
  Vercelli 1999

CASORATI Felice 1883-1963 **[179]**
- **$96 000** - €82 932 - **£64 000** - FF544 000
  Figura nello studio Olio/tela (48x45cm 18x17in)
  Milano 1998
- **$13 000** - €13 476 - **£7 800** - FF88 400
  Nudino viola Tecnica mista (33x48cm 12x18in)
  Vercelli 2000
- **$13 000** - €13 476 - **£7 800** - FF88 400
  Menestrello Carboncino/carta (55x41cm 21x16in)
  Milano 1999
- **$900** - €777 - **£450** - FF5 100
  Notturno agli scogli Linogravure (24.5x15cm 9x5in)
  Firenze 1999

CASORATI PAVAROLO Francesco 1934 **[26]**
- **$225** - €233 - **£135** - FF1 530
  Tiro alla funa Tempera/carta (70x50cm 27x19in)
  Vercelli 1999

CASPAR Karl 1879-1956 **[49]**
- **$11 995** - €14 111 - **£8 467** - FF92 564
  Verkündigung an Abraham Öl/Leinwand
  (73.5x92.5cm 28x36in) Berlin 2001
- **$1 379** - €1 431 - **£875** - FF9 390
  Drei Frauen am Meer Aquarell/Papier (41.5x43cm
  16x16in) Zwiesel 2000
- **$95** - €107 - **£66** - FF704
  Anbetung Lithographie (40.5x28cm 15x11in) Berlin
  2001

CASPAR-FILSER Maria 1878-1968 **[51]**
- **$8 428** - €9 824 - **£5 835** - FF64 444
  Feldblumenstrauss Öl/Leinwand (95x65cm
  37x25in) Bern 2000

CASPEL van Johann Georg 1870-1928 **[16]**
📖 $179 - €204 - £125 - FF1 339
«Holland-Amerika Lijn» Poster (25x36.5cm 9x14in)
Hoorn 2001

CASPERS Pauline XIX-XX **[1]**
$31 000 - €27 443 - £18 953 - FF180 013
First Communion Oil/canvas (115.5x92cm 45x36in)
New-York 1999

CASS S. XIX **[1]**
$10 935 - €10 702 - £7 000 - FF70 200
A Tiger in an Indian Landscape Oil/canvas
(33x43cm 12x16in) London 1999

CASSAB Judy 1920 **[108]**
$467 - €515 - £310 - FF3 375
Grettan knitting Mixed media (48x59.5cm 18x23in)
Melbourne 2000
$442 - €643 - £308 - FF3 388
Street Scene Mixed media (30.5x37.5cm 12x14in)
Melbourne 2000
$182 - €207 - £127 - FF1 358
Seated Nude Wash (35.5x22cm 13x8in) Woollahra,
Sydney 2001

CASSANA Giovanni Agostino 1658-1720 **[21]**
$8 000 - €10 367 - £6 000 - FF68 000
Natura morta con tacchino, piccioni, gatto ed
un grande cesto Olio/tela (105x143cm 41x56in)
Milano 2001
$12 194 - €10 671 - £7 385 - FF70 000
Coqs, lapins, couvée de pigeons surpris par un
chat Huile/toile (99.5x111cm 39x43in) Paris 1998

CASSANA Niccolo 1659-1714 **[4]**
$5 927 - €5 800 - £3 800 - FF38 046
Portrait of an English Youth, half-length, wea-
ring an Ermine Hat Oil/canvas (72x55cm 28x21in)
London 1999

CASSANDRE A.M.(Adolphe Mouron) 1901-1968
[328]
$1 200 - €1 346 - £833 - FF8 828
«C.N.E.P.» Drawing (49x41cm 19x16in) New-York
2001
📖 $3 200 - €3 732 - £2 246 - FF24 481
«Colomba Motta» Poster (70x100.5cm 27x39in)
New-York 2001

CASSAS Louis-François 1756-1827 **[74]**
$6 300 - €5 842 - £3 800 - FF38 000
Retraite des Apôtres dans la vallée de
Josephat/Le tombeau d'Absalom Ink (39x24cm
15x9in) London 1999
$6 855 - €5 793 - £4 100 - FF38 000
Vue de la colonne dite de Pompée à Alexandrie
Gravure (55x78cm 21x30in) Paris 1998

CASSATT Mary 1844-1926 **[391]**
$49 170 - €41 923 - £29 672 - FF275 000
Mère et enfant Huile/toile (130x97cm 51x38in) Paris
1998
$900 000 - €892 087 - £562 950 - FF5 851 710
Two Young Girls with a Child Oil/canvas
(54.5x65.5cm 21x25in) New-York 1999
$750 000 - €830 599 - £508 650 - FF5 448 375
Sara Holding a cat Oil/canvas (40.5x33cm 15x12in)
New-York 2000
$13 000 - €14 397 - £8 816 - FF94 438
Jeune fille assise Pencil/paper (20.5x14.5cm 8x5in)
New-York 2000
📖 $2 200 - €2 572 - £1 545 - FF16 871
Margot Wearing a Bonnet (No.1) Drypoint in colors
(23.5x16.5cm 9x6in) New-York 2000

CASSE Germaine XIX-XX **[18]**
📖 $282 - €335 - £201 - FF2 200
«Société des Artistes Antillais» Affiche
(119x79cm 46x31in) Orléans 2000

CASSEL Pol (Paul) 1892-1945 **[7]**
$52 754 - €60 737 - £36 000 - FF398 408
Cemetery/Forest Interior Oil/canvas (110x129cm
43x50in) London 2000

CASSELL Frank XIX-XX **[15]**
$867 - €1 022 - £600 - FF6 702
Four Terriers Oil/canvas (43x53cm 16x20in) Stansted
Mountfitchet, Essex 2000
$600 - €700 - £421 - FF4 590
Two Dogs in Front of a Fireplace Oil/canvas
(30x25cm 12x10in) York PA 2000

CASSELLI Henry C. 1946 **[6]**
$600 - €643 - £397 - FF4 219
Tending to the Ballerina Pencil/paper (55x43cm
22x17in) New-Orleans LA 2000

CASSIDY Gerald Ira Diamond 1879-1934 **[24]**
$105 000 - €100 376 - £65 814 - FF658 423
The Priestesses Oil/canvas (101.5x76cm 39x29in)
New-York 1999
$17 600 - €18 892 - £11 777 - FF123 921
New Mexico Landscape with Adobe House
Oil/board (30x40cm 12x16in) Houston TX 2000
$3 200 - €3 761 - £2 218 - FF24 670
Ventura Mission Tower Watercolour, gouache/paper
(40x19.5cm 15x7in) Beverly-Hills CA 2000

CASSIE James 1819-1879 **[27]**
$2 825 - €3 344 - £2 000 - FF21 932
Scottish estuary scenes Oil/canvas (29x60cm
11x23in) Scarborough, North-Yorshire 2001
$3 338 - €2 986 - £2 000 - FF19 588
«The Firth of Tay» Oil/canvas (30.5x35.5cm 12x17in)
Perthshire 1999

CASSIEN Victor 1808-1893 **[119]**
📖 $75 - €84 - £50 - FF550
Valbonnais, l'église Lithographie couleurs (21x27cm
8x10in) Grenoble 2000

CASSIERS Hendrick, Henri 1858-1944 **[286]**
$2 425 - €2 603 - £1 627 - FF17 073
Le port de Hoorn Huile/carton (54x54cm 21x21in)
Antwerpen 2000
$796 - €908 - £550 - FF5 953
Quay in Gent Oil/cardboard (22x22cm 8x8in)
Amsterdam 2000
$840 - €693 - £492 - FF4 547
Bord de mer Gouache/carton (56x36cm 22x14in)
Liège 1998
📖 $294 - €335 - £204 - FF2 200
«Retour du marché»/«Ferme en Zélande»
Affiche (50x110cm 19x43in) Paris 2000

CASSIGNEUL Jean-Pierre 1935 **[315]**
$45 000 - €43 272 - £27 724 - FF283 846
Femme au bord de la mer Oil/canvas/board
(130x179cm 51x70in) New-York 1999
$17 000 - €18 657 - £10 946 - FF122 379
Portrait de femme Oil/canvas (92.5x65cm 36x25in)
New-York 2000
$8 330 - €8 125 - £5 100 - FF53 295
Sous bois Oil/canvas (27x22cm 10x8in) Tokyo 1999
$2 065 - €2 287 - £1 401 - FF15 000
Femme au chapeau devant un rosier en fleur
Gouache (60x47cm 23x18in) Paris 2001
📖 $594 - €709 - £424 - FF4 650
Femme à la toque et au manteau de fourrure
Lithographie couleurs (65x50cm 25x19in) Paris 2001

C

CASSINARI Bruno 1912-1992 **[275]**
- **$17 500** - €18 141 - **£10 500** - FF119 000
  Fondo marino Olio/tela (97x130cm 38x51in) Milano 1999
- **$7 600** - €9 848 - **£5 700** - FF64 600
  Natura morta Olio/tela (90x90cm 35x35in) Prato 2000
- **$3 000** - €3 110 - **£1 800** - FF20 400
  Natura morta sul tavolo Olio/tavola (20x30cm 7x11in) Vercelli 2000
- **$12 000** - €15 550 - **£9 000** - FF102 000
  Le carezze dell'amore Bronzo (H147cm H57in) Milano 2001
- **$1 650** - €1 710 - **£990** - FF11 220
  Due figure China (60x40cm 23x15in) Vercelli 1999
- **$250** - €259 - **£150** - FF1 700
  «Cavalli in Maremma»/«Cavalli in Liberia» Litografia (43x30cm 16x11in) Firenze 2001

CASSINELLI H. XIX **[5]**
- **$3 984** - €4 269 - **£2 713** - FF28 000
  Bateaux dans le port Huile/panneau (23x32cm 9x12in) Calais 2001

CASSINI Giovanni Maria XVIII **[3]**
- **$7 000** - €7 099 - **£4 347** - FF46 566
  Le isole di Sandwich/Isola O Taiti/Isole de gli amici/Isole Engraving (36.5x50cm 14x19in) Beverly-Hills CA 2000

CASSIOLI Amos 1832-1891 **[10]**
- **$47 052** - €54 882 - **£32 724** - FF360 000
  Sultane au collier de perles Huile/toile (102x84cm 40x33in) Paris 2000
- **$7 114** - €8 266 - **£5 000** - FF54 221
  La morte di Bianca Capella (the death of Bianca Capella) Oil/panel (26x33cm 10x12in) London 2001

CASSON Alfred Joseph 1898-1992 **[283]**
- **$26 428** - €24 824 - **£18 232** - FF189 727
  «India Village» Oil/canvas (76x91cm 30x36in) Vancouver, BC. 2001
- **$7 812** - €6 685 - **£4 702** - FF43 849
  «Lumbermen's Shacks, Lake Redstone» Oil/board (24x28.5cm 9x11in) Toronto 1998
- **$5 121** - €4 955 - **£3 158** - FF32 504
  Trilliums Watercolour/paper (40.5x30.5cm 15x12in) Toronto 1999
- **$235** - €262 - **£153** - FF1 720
  Red Head Silkscreen in colors (22x26cm 8x10in) Calgary, Alberta 2000

CASSON Hugh 1910 **[40]**
- **$811** - €780 - **£500** - FF5 119
  Exhibition Boats Arriving Seville Expo Watercolour (7.5x18.5cm 2x7in) London 1999

CASTAGNA Blas 1935 **[1]**
- **$9 000** - €7 848 - **£5 441** - FF51 477
  El Barquillero Mixed media (103x91cm 40x35in) New-York 1998

CASTAGNERI Mario 1892-1940 **[7]**
- **$5 000** - €5 756 - **£3 412** - FF37 760
  Termoil Photograph (42.5x30cm 16x11in) New-York 2000

CASTAGNINO Juan Carlos 1908-1972 **[11]**
- **$3 400** - €3 740 - **£2 269** - FF24 572
  Idilio en el parque Oleo/lienzo (48x60cm 18x23in) Buenos-Aires 2000

CASTAGNOLA Gabriele 1828-1883 **[11]**
- **$3 000** - €3 110 - **£1 800** - FF20 400
  Amor cortese Olio/tavola (61x38cm 24x14in) Prato 1999

CASTAIGNE Jean André 1861-1929 **[14]**
- **$1 600** - €1 792 - **£1 111** - FF11 755
  Market Day Oil/canvas/panel (78x53cm 31x21in) St. Louis MO 2001

CASTAN Gustave Eugène 1823-1892 **[168]**
- **$1 854** - €2 161 - **£1 283** - FF14 177
  Anglerin am Teich Öl/Papier (38x57cm 14x22in) Bern 2000
- **$1 478** - €1 369 - **£905** - FF8 978
  Landschaft mit Felsbrocken unter leicht bewölktem Himmel Öl/Leinwand/Karton (26.5x53.5cm 10x21in) Bern 1999

CASTAN Pierre Jean Edmond 1817-1892 **[25]**
- **$9 979** - €8 550 - **£6 000** - FF56 083
  The Billet-doux Oil/panel (34x26cm 13x10in) Edinburgh 1998

CASTAÑEDA Alfredo 1938 **[64]**
- **$45 000** - €48 303 - **£30 114** - FF316 845
  Self-Portrait with Calendar Oil/canvas (128.5x169cm 50x66in) Beverly-Hills CA 2000
- **$35 000** - €30 519 - **£21 161** - FF200 189
  Forasteros Oil/panel (80x80cm 31x31in) New-York 1998
- **$9 572** - €9 043 - **£5 970** - FF59 315
  Autoretrato Oleo/cartón (34x28cm 13x11in) Monterrey NL 2001

CASTAÑEDA Felipe 1933 **[64]**
- **$5 284** - €6 198 - **£3 801** - FF40 656
  Desnudo con alcatraces Bronze (50x25x33cm 19x9x12in) México 2001

CASTBERG Oskar 1846-1917 **[3]**
- **$4 200** - €4 994 - **£2 992** - FF32 760
  På ski i lange skjört Oil/canvas (29x46cm 11x18in) Oslo 2000

CASTEELS Gonzales Franciscus XVII **[2]**
- **$76 800** - €87 207 - **£52 560** - FF572 040
  Die Befreiungsschlacht von Gran in Ungarn Öl/Leinwand (169x244cm 66x96in) Wien 2000

CASTEELS Pauwel XVII **[6]**
- **$19 342** - €17 908 - **£12 000** - FF117 468
  Battle between King John Sobieski III and the Turks Oil/copper (88x109cm 34x42in) London 1999

CASTEELS Pieter I XVII **[21]**
- **$6 348** - €7 013 - **£4 402** - FF46 000
  Scène de port animé de nombreux personnages Huile/toile (39x57cm 15x22in) Lille 2001

CASTEELS Pieter II 1684-1749 **[114]**
- **$51 850** - €51 055 - **£32 300** - FF334 900
  Birds in a park with a fountain Oil/canvas (111x140cm 43x55in) Madrid 1999
- **$11 772** - €10 468 - **£7 200** - FF68 668
  Flowers in an Urn Oil/canvas (75x62cm 29x24in) Newbury, Berkshire 1999
- **$1 261** - €1 524 - **£881** - FF10 000
  Vues fantaisistes de ports méditerranéens animés de personnages Huile/toile (20x29cm 7x11in) Paris 2000

CASTEGNARO Felice 1872-1958 **[11]**
- **$2 856** - €2 467 - **£1 428** - FF16 184
  «Traghetti alla Salute» Olio/tavoletta (22.5x32.5cm 8x12in) Venezia 1999

CASTEL Éric 1915-? **[8]**
- **$302** - €335 - **£210** - FF2 200
  «Air France, Corse» Affiche (99.5x62cm 39x24in) Paris 2001

CASTEL Moshe 1909-1992 **[204]**
- **$23 000** - €25 531 - **£16 033** - FF167 474
  Hallelujah Oil/canvas (129x96.7cm 50x38in) Tel Aviv 2001
- **$15 652** - €14 406 - **£9 394** - FF94 496
  Village Scene Oil/board (61x44cm 24x17in) Tel Aviv 2000
- **$3 600** - €3 949 - **£2 323** - FF25 905
  Personnage Mixed media/canvas (35x24cm 13x9in) Tel Aviv 2000
- **$2 800** - €2 733 - **£1 773** - FF17 929
  Composition Gouache (40x29.5cm 15x11in) Tel Aviv 1999

CASTELBAJAC de Jean-Charles 1949 **[6]**
- **$826** - €915 - **£560** - FF6 000
  Un tout petit Paris, No.2 (texte de l'auteur) Pastel (33x42cm 12x16in) Paris 2000

CASTELEYN Vincent ?-1658 **[1]**
- **$4 314** - €4 084 - **£2 682** - FF26 789
  Moses striking Water from the Rock Oil/panel (55x70.5cm 21x27in) Amsterdam 1999

CASTELL Anton 1810-1864 **[12]**
- **$5 989** - €6 135 - **£3 696** - FF40 246
  Sächsische Landschaft Öl/Leinwand (52.5x81cm 20x31in) Düsseldorf 2000

CASTELLANAS GARRICH Josep 1896-1980 **[5]**
- **$2 762** - €2 553 - **£1 700** - FF16 745
  Cala en Mallorca Oleo/lienzo (74x64cm 29x25in) Madrid 1999

CASTELLANI Enrico 1930 **[109]**
- **$24 800** - €32 136 - **£18 600** - FF210 800
  Superficie bianca Tela (100x120cm 39x47in) Milano 2001
- **$11 000** - €11 403 - **£6 600** - FF74 800
  Superficie Oil/tela (100x81cm 39x31in) Roma 2000
- **$5 800** - €7 516 - **£4 350** - FF40 843
  Composizione Smalto (41x31.5cm 16x12in) Milano 2001
- **$3 124** - €3 630 - **£2 196** - FF23 812
  Untitled Drawing (88.5x117cm 34x46in) Amsterdam 2001
- **$625** - €726 - **£439** - FF4 762
  Untitled Print (42.5x53cm 16x20in) Amsterdam 2001

CASTELLANOS Antonio 1946 **[1]**
- **$9 000** - €7 848 - **£5 441** - FF51 477
  Madre e Hijo Polished bronze (44x76cm 17x29in) New-York 1998

CASTELLI DETTO SPADINO Bartolomeo Junior 1696-1738 **[4]**
- **$18 000** - €15 789 - **£10 929** - FF103 568
  Fruit Resting on Stone Ledges Oil/canvas (38x47cm 14x18in) New-York 1999

CASTELLI DETTO SPADINO Giovanni Paolo 1659-c.1730 **[26]**
- **$32 622** - €30 511 - **£20 000** - FF200 140
  Grapes, Cherries, Plums, Figs, Pomegranates, Melons and Other Fruits Oil/canvas (75.5x99cm 29x38in) London 1998
- **$5 500** - €5 702 - **£3 300** - FF37 400
  Melograni, pesche, uva e ciliege Olio/tela (32.5x46cm 12x18in) Milano 2000

CASTELLI Luciano 1951 **[107]**
- **$3 917** - €3 811 - **£2 410** - FF25 000
  Luciano et le cygne Acrylique/toile (160x200cm 62x78in) Paris 1999

$1 947 - €1 870 - **£1 206** - FF12 265
  Brigitt und Alida Öl/Papier (100x70cm 39x27in) Zürich 1999

- **$1 199** - €1 411 - **£846** - FF9 256
  Mit verbundenen Augen Gouache (100x70cm 39x27in) Berlin 2001
- **$209** - €250 - **£150** - FF1 638
  Toscana I/Toscana II Woodcut (47x63cm 18x24in) Zürich 2000

CASTELLINI DA BRESCIA Tommaso 1803-1869 **[2]**
- **$6 250** - €6 235 - **£3 902** - FF40 898
  Still Life of Flowers on a Ledge Oil/canvas (86x116cm 34x46in) Dedham MA 1999

CASTELLO Bernardo 1557-1629 **[8]**
- **$3 000** - €3 110 - **£1 800** - FF20 400
  Madonna col Bambino e Santi Craies couleurs (12x18cm 4x7in) Milano 2000

CASTELLO Félix 1595-1651 **[1]**
- **$28 500** - €30 032 - **£18 000** - FF197 000
  La Liberación de San Pedro por un ángel Oleo/lienzo (168x125.5cm 66x49in) Madrid 2000

CASTELLO Francesco 1540-? **[3]**
- **$14 915** - €14 483 - **£9 215** - FF95 000
  Vanité au sablier et au crâne Huile/panneau (57x47cm 22x18in) Paris 2000

CASTELLO IL BERGAMASCO Giovan Battista c.1500-1579 **[5]**
- **$2 241** - €2 406 - **£1 500** - FF15 782
  The Descent from the Cross Gouache/vellum (20.5x16.5cm 8x6in) London 2000

CASTELLO IL GENOVESE Giovan Battista 1547-1637 **[13]**
- **$11 461** - €10 629 - **£7 000** - FF69 721
  The Agony in the Garden, in a Decorative Frame Watercolour (23x29cm 9x11in) London 1998

CASTELLO Valerio 1624-1659 **[30]**
- **$45 603** - €51 796 - **£32 000** - FF339 760
  The Adoration of the Magi Oil/canvas (139x170.5cm 54x67in) London 2001
- **$37 052** - €42 084 - **£26 000** - FF276 055
  Hagar, Ismael and the Angel Oil/canvas (51x42cm 20x16in) London 2001
- **$26 000** - €27 767 - **£17 716** - FF182 137
  Adoration of the Shepherds Oil/copper (34x28.5cm 13x11in) New-York 2001
- **$8 965** - €9 624 - **£6 000** - FF63 129
  Christ and the Centurion: Design for a Lunette Black chalk (14x22cm 5x8in) London 2000

CASTELLON Federico 1914-1971 **[76]**
- **$8 500** - €9 632 - **£5 939** - FF63 179
  Bowling Night Oil/board (47x58.5cm 18x23in) New-York 2001
- **$2 698** - €2 897 - **£1 805** - FF19 000
  Grande baigneuse et son ombre Encre/papier (50x31.5cm 19x12in) Paris 2000
- **$275** - €238 - **£163** - FF1 558
  Six Etchings Etching (50x33cm 19x12in) New-York 1998

CASTEX-DÉGRANGE Adolphe L. Dégrange 1840-1918 **[15]**
- **$11 978** - €12 806 - **£8 156** - FF84 000
  Panier de fleurs Huile/toile (85x130cm 33x51in) Lyon 2001

CASTIGLIONE Francesco 1641/42-1716 **[11]**
- **$42 068** - €39 637 - **£25 480** - FF260 000
  Le départ pour la chasse au faucon Huile/toile (120x168cm 47x66in) Paris 1999

C

$50 000 - €54 092 - **£34 255** - FF354 820
Orpheus Charming the Animals Oil/canvas (73x98cm 28x38in) New-York 2001

$1 487 - €1 542 - **£892** - FF10 115
Scena mitologica Inchiostro (26.5x25.5cm 10x10in) Venezia 2000

CASTIGLIONE Giuseppe 1829-1908 **[29]**

$30 000 - €31 100 - **£18 000** - FF204 000
Di fronte al Vesuvio Olio/tela (90x162cm 35x63in) Milano 1999

$7 500 - €6 496 - **£4 599** - FF42 611
The Music Lesson Oil/panel (63x49.5cm 24x19in) New-York 1999

$1 400 - €1 451 - **£840** - FF9 520
Pescatorelli lungo il fiume Olio/tela (25x32cm 9x12in) Roma 1999

$2 000 - €2 015 - **£1 246** - FF13 220
Meeting the Cardinal Watercolour/paper (43.5x68cm 17x26in) New-York 2000

CASTIGLIONE IL GRECHETTO Giovanni Benedetto 1609-1664 **[227]**

$724 000 - €822 744 - **£500 000** - FF5 396 850
Jacob's Journey into Journey Oil/canvas (99.5x148.5cm 39x58in) London 2000

$1 314 984 - €1 411 527 - **£880 000** - FF9 259 008
Pagan Sacrifice Oil/canvas (43x75.5cm 16x29in) London 2000

$70 000 - €74 757 - **£47 698** - FF490 371
The Nativity Painting (41.5x27.5cm 16x10in) New-York 2001

$5 927 - €5 800 - **£3 800** - FF38 046
St. John the Baptist preaching Ink (20.5x30cm 8x11in) London 2001

$900 - €933 - **£540** - FF6 120
Satiro seduto ai piedi della statua di Priapo/Pan seduto Gravure (11x21cm 4x8in) Milano 2000

CASTIGLIONI Luigi 1936 **[12]**

$40 - €46 - **£28** - FF300
«Vélo pour tous» Affiche (70x48cm 27x18in) Paris 2001

CASTILLO del José 1737-1793 **[14]**

$10 000 - €8 694 - **£6 052** - FF57 026
Shepherd and Shepherderas/Peasant Girl/Girl on a Donkey Oil/paper/board (21.5x17cm 8x6in) New-York 1999

$1 064 - €1 141 - **£703** - FF7 486
Masacre de los Inocentes Lápiz/papel (19x13cm 7x5in) Madrid 2000

CASTILLO Fernando 1882-1940 **[1]**

$14 000 - €16 266 - **£9 839** - FF106 696
La familia Oil/canvas (49.5x60cm 19x23in) New-York 2001

CASTILLO Jorge 1933 **[689]**

$4 270 - €4 205 - **£2 730** - FF27 580
Militar y figura Oleo/lienzo (131x97cm 51x38in) Madrid 1999

$1 972 - €2 042 - **£1 258** - FF13 396
Niña dormida Oleo/lienzo (55x46cm 21x18in) Madrid 2000

$1 210 - €1 321 - **£836** - FF8 668
Personajes Técnica mixta/tabla (45x35cm 17x13in) Barcelona 2001

$647 - €640 - **£403** - FF4 200
Scène d'intérieur Gouache (16x29cm 6x11in) Paris 1999

$224 - €204 - **£136** - FF1 339
Personajes con perro Litografía a color (51x41cm 20x16in) Madrid 1999

CASTILLO Marcos 1897-1966 **[36]**

$9 000 - €8 385 - **£5 500** - FF55 000
Naturaleza muerta Oleo/tabla (66x52cm 25x20in) Caracas 1998

$3 300 - €3 454 - **£1 980** - FF22 660
Bodegón Oleo/lienzo (33x41cm 12x16in) Caracas 2000

CASTILLO Y SAAVEDRA del Antonio 1616-1668 **[18]**

$33 600 - €36 039 - **£22 200** - FF236 400
Adoración de los Pastores Oleo/lienzo (126x103.5cm 49x40in) Madrid 2000

CASTILVIEJO José Maria 1925 **[2]**

$2 240 - €2 102 - **£1 400** - FF13 790
Sembrado Oleo/lienzo (73x115.5cm 28x45in) Madrid 1999

CASTLE Philip 1942 **[3]**

$289 - €320 - **£200** - FF2 099
«Clockwork Orange» Poster (76x101.5cm 29x39in) London 2001

CASTLE Wendell 1932 **[8]**

$80 000 - €82 875 - **£50 920** - FF543 624
Illusions Coat Rack Sculpture, wood (H182cm H71in) New-York 2000

$18 000 - €19 321 - **£12 045** - FF126 738
Rocking Chair Sculpture, wood (H75cm H29in) New-York 2000

CASTLEDEN George Frederick 1861-1945 **[18]**

$350 - €349 - **£218** - FF2 290
«The St.Louis Old Cathedral» Watercolour (27x18cm 11x7in) New-Orleans LA 1999

CASTOLDI Guglielmo 1823-1882 **[4]**

$5 750 - €5 961 - **£3 450** - FF39 100
Nel convento Olio/tela (65x50cm 25x19in) Roma 1999

CASTONGUAY Gérard 1933 **[15]**

$582 - €559 - **£362** - FF3 667
Sentier ensoleillé Oil/canvas (50x40cm 20x16in) Calgary, Alberta 1999

CASTRES Édouard 1838-1902 **[64]**

$22 062 - €25 093 - **£15 298** - FF164 597
Magasin japonais Öl/Leinwand (55x73cm 21x28in) Zofingen 2000

$1 678 - €1 968 - **£1 197** - FF12 911
Paysage animé Huile/toile/panneau (30x45cm 11x17in) Genève 2000

CASTRES Edouard Gaspard 1881-1964 **[24]**

$2 489 - €2 171 - **£1 505** - FF14 238
Bord du lac Léman Huile/toile (64x92cm 25x36in) Genève 1998

CASTRO a Laureys XVII-XVIII **[5]**

$35 980 - €40 300 - **£25 000** - FF264 352
English fourth rate arriving off Genoa with another English Man-o'war Oil/canvas (103x121cm 40x47in) London 2001

CASTRO de Sergio 1922 **[41]**

$1 742 - €1 829 - **£1 098** - FF12 000
Nu Huile/toile (92x73cm 36x28in) Paris 2000

$450 - €534 - **£317** - FF3 500
Engadine Gouache/papier (105x39cm 41x15in) Paris 2000

CASTRO GIL Manuel 1891-1961 **[96]**

$123 - €132 - **£83** - FF866
«Castillo de Manzanares el Real» Aguafuerte (29x38cm 11x15in) Madrid 2001

CASTRO Humberto 1957 **[22]**
📖 **$1 570** - €1 462 - **£970** - FF10 000
El Che Sérigraphie (155x125cm 61x49in) Paris 1999

CASTRO ORTEGA Pedro 1956 **[8]**
🖼 **$2 325** - €2 252 - **£1 462** - FF14 775
«Campo circular» Oleo/lienzo (117x89cm 46x35in)
Madrid 1999

CASTRO PACHECO Fernando 1918 **[7]**
🖼 **$7 623** - €7 117 - **£4 704** - FF46 683
Mujeres sentadas Oleo/lienzo (80x113cm 31x44in)
México 1999

CATANO F. XIX-XX **[40]**
🖋 **$409** - €384 - **£253** - FF2 522
Sunset on Figures by Water's Edge with Mosque beyond Watercolour (31x51.5cm 12x20in)
Toronto 1999

CATARSINI Alfredo 1899-1993 **[119]**
🖼 **$10 000** - €12 958 - **£7 500** - FF85 000
Lavandaie Olio/masonite (102x151cm 40x59in)
Vercelli 2000
🖼 **$1 000** - €1 037 - **£600** - FF6 800
Congegno meccanico Olio/masonite (50x70cm 19x27in) Vercelli 2001
🖼 **$240** - €311 - **£180** - FF2 040
Oggetti in casa Olio/cartone (30x25cm 11x9in)
Vercelli 2000
🖋 **$175** - €181 - **£105** - FF1 190
Foce di un fiume Acquarelo/cartone (24x32cm 9x12in) Vercelli 2000

CATEL Franz Ludwig 1778-1856 **[19]**
🖼 **$40 926** - €41 926 - **£25 256** - FF275 019
Parklandschaft mit figürlicher Staffage Öl/Leinwand (44x66cm 17x25in) Düsseldorf 2000
🖼 **$10 032** - €9 715 - **£6 302** - FF63 724
Bei Pozzuoli, junger Fischer, zwei hübschen Landmädchen Öl/Leinwand (24x33.5cm 9x13in)
Berlin 1999

CATERINA Dario 1955 **[12]**
🖋 **$1 758** - €1 487 - **£1 044** - FF9 756
Femme et poupée Charcoal (150x150cm 59x59in)
Lokeren 1998

CATERINO VENEZIANO XIV **[1]**
🖼 **$72 000** - €93 299 - **£54 000** - FF612 000
Madonna in trono tra Giovanni Battista,Santa Caterina, Maria Maddelena Tempera/tavola
(50x29.5cm 19x11in) Milano 2001

CATESBY Mark 1679-1749 **[22]**
📖 **$500** - €466 - **£308** - FF3 056
Horned Caterpillar with Pigeon Plum, No.94
Engraving (36x26cm 14x10in) New-Orleans LA 1999

CATHELIN Bernard 1919 **[228]**
🖼 **$17 646** - €17 782 - **£11 000** - FF116 639
Maison de thé Oil/canvas (162x130cm 63x51in)
London 2000
🖼 **$11 954** - €12 832 - **£8 000** - FF84 172
Jardin aux maisons blanches Oil/canvas
(115x89cm 45x35in) London 2000
🖼 **$4 641** - €4 676 - **£2 892** - FF30 675
Figures in a Street Öl/Karton (35x27cm 13x10in)
Zürich 2000
🖋 **$1 618** - €1 840 - **£1 110** - FF12 071
Geishas Aquarell/Papier (46x72.5cm 18x28in) Zürich 2000
📖 **$439** - €427 - **£273** - FF2 800
Bouquet de fleurs Lithographie (66x51cm 25x20in)
Paris 1999

CATHERINE Norman Clive 1949 **[42]**
🖼 **$5 199** - €5 825 - **£3 612** - FF38 207
Dreamwalker Oil/canvas (90x160cm 35x62in)
Johannesburg 2001
🖼 **$396** - €444 - **£275** - FF2 911
«Microcosmic» Mixed media (35x31cm 13x12in)
Johannesburg 2001
🖋 **$398** - €462 - **£275** - FF3 032
Terminology of an Almost 1/2 Eaten Skeleton Ink (87x72.5cm 34x28in) Johannesburg 2000
📖 **$233** - €202 - **£140** - FF1 323
No Sugar Color lithograph (50x45.5cm 19x17in)
Johannesburg 1998

CATLETT Elizabeth 1915-1998 **[13]**
🖋 **$10 000** - €9 059 - **£6 236** - FF59 421
We Want Opportunity Crayon (44x59cm 17x23in)
New-York 1999
📖 **$1 500** - €1 703 - **£1 026** - FF11 172
Peonies Mexicanos/Confiterio Mexicano Linocut
(83x31.5cm 32x12in) New-York 2000

CATLIN George 1794-1872 **[50]**
🖼 **$230 000** - €218 760 - **£139 656** - FF1 434 970
Three Ponca Indians: Great Chief, Bending Willow, Pure Fountain Oil/board (44.5x60cm 17x23in) New-York 1999
🖋 **$30 000** - €33 494 - **£20 052** - FF219 708
Nee-Hee-O-Woo-Tis, Sheyenne Pencil/paper
(35.5x26.5cm 13x10in) New-York 2000
📖 **$1 600** - €1 786 - **£1 069** - FF11 717
Buffalo Hunt, approaching in a Ravine Color lithograph (42.5x58cm 16x22in) New-York 2000

CATOZZELLA Romeo XX **[1]**
🖼 **$20 000** - €19 023 - **£12 144** - FF124 780
Portrait of Marilyn Monroe Oil/canvas (71x55cm 28x22in) New-York 1999

CATS Jacob 1741-1799 **[53]**
🖋 **$2 831** - €2 723 - **£1 744** - FF17 859
Hersman with his Family and Cattle by a Stream Ink (17x24cm 6x9in) Amsterdam 1999

CATTANEO Achille 1872-1932 **[57]**
🖼 **$1 500** - €1 500 - **FF10 200**
Rose Olio/tela (60x45cm 23x17in) Vercelli 2001
🖼 **$400** - €518 - **£300** - FF3 400
Naviglio/Milano Olio/tavola (11x10cm 4x3in) Vercelli 2001

CATTAPAN Jon 1956 **[8]**
🖼 **$9 720** - €10 434 - **£6 505** - FF68 445
Grey Nocturne (The Pool) Oil/canvas (199x168cm 78x66in) Sydney 2000

CATTAPANE Luca XVI **[1]**
🖋 **$7 175** - €7 021 - **£4 600** - FF46 056
The Head of an old Man in Profile Red chalk/paper
(30.5x21.5cm 12x8in) London 1999

CATTELAN Maurizio 1960 **[20]**
🖼 **$100 000** - €112 007 - **£69 480** - FF734 720
Untitled Acrylic/canvas (101.5x75cm 39x29in) New-York 2001
🗿 **$781 032** - €918 477 - **£560 000** - FF6 024 816
La Ballata di Trotsky, (the Ballad of Trotsky) Sculpture (270x200x75cm 106x78x29in) London 2001
🗿 **$25 963** - €30 514 - **£18 000** - FF200 160
Strategies Construction (68x76x20.5cm 26x29x8in)
London 2000
🖋 **$8 665** - €9 442 - **£6 000** - FF61 936
Untitled Ink (34x42.5cm 13x16in) London 2001
📖 **$1 425** - €1 677 - **£1 021** - FF11 000
Gratis Gravure (17.5x25cm 6x9in) Paris 2001

C

CATTERMOLE Charles 1832-1900 **[101]**
$400 - €374 - **£246** - FF2 450
The Standard Bearer Watercolour, gouache
(53x37.5cm 20x14in) Boston MA 1999

CATTERMOLE George 1800-1868 **[75]**
$672 - €789 - **£480** - FF5 174
Harbour Scene with Fishing Vessels and Fisherfolk Oil/canvas (41x61cm 16x24in) Manchester 2000
$453 - €434 - **£278** - FF2 844
Queen Henrietta landing at Burlington Watercolour/paper (25.5x35.5cm 10x13in) London 1999

CATTERMOLE Lance Harry Mosse 1898-1992 **[7]**
$678 - €787 - **£480** - FF5 162
«Whitby, British Railways, North Eastern Region» Poster (102x64cm 40x25in) London 2000

CATTERMOLE Leonard F.G. XIX **[6]**
$3 308 - €3 670 - **£2 200** - FF24 073
Brisk Canter!/Playful Gambit Watercolour (52x78cm 20x30in) London 2000

CATTI Aurelio XIX-XX **[26]**
$17 000 - €17 623 - **£10 200** - FF115 600
Barche nel porto Olio/tela (100x140cm 39x55in) Roma 2000
$2 000 - €2 592 - **£1 500** - FF17 000
Mare e costa di Sicilia Olio/legno (60x50cm 23x19in) Roma 2001
$1 750 - €1 814 - **£1 050** - FF11 900
Marina con barche Olio/legno (20x35cm 7x13in) Roma 2000
$1 400 - €1 451 - **£840** - FF9 520
Roma, Trinità dei Monti Acquarello/cartone (51x36.5cm 20x14in) Roma 2000

CATTI Michèle 1855-1914 **[9]**
$4 613 - €3 994 - **£2 800** - FF26 197
After the Rain Oil/panel (37x24cm 14x9in) London 1998

CAUCHIE Paul 1875-1952 **[49]**
$442 - €496 - **£300** - FF3 252
Le béguinage à Bruges Technique mixte (50x62cm 19x24in) Bruxelles 2000
$473 - €545 - **£325** - FF3 577
Zomerlandschap Gouache/paper (54x73.5cm 21x28in) Lokeren 2000

CAUCHOIS Eugène Henri 1850-1911 **[481]**
$4 501 - €5 183 - **£3 073** - FF34 000
Corbeille de fleurs Huile/toile (37x53cm 14x20in) Lyon 2000
$3 126 - €2 936 - **£1 937** - FF19 256
Stilleben mit Sommerblumen Öl/Leinwand (32x40cm 12x15in) Luzern 1999

CAUCIG Franz 1755-1828 **[6]**
$1 286 - €1 453 - **£868** - FF9 534
Der Tod des Patroklos vor Troja Indian ink (25.5x36.7cm 10x14in) Wien 2000

CAUD Marcel 1883-? **[1]**
$5 213 - €4 745 - **£3 200** - FF31 126
Plate of Oysters with Lemons and Prauws, Bawl of Fruit and some Bread Oil/canvas (59.5x73cm 23x28in) London 1999

CAUER Robert, Snr. 1831-1893 **[7]**
$33 532 - €28 336 - **£20 000** - FF185 874
«Amor als Lehrer» Marble (H188.5cm H74in) London 1999
$7 288 - €8 288 - **£5 000** - FF54 365
Bust of a Girl with Garland of Lilies to her Hair Marble (H66cm H25in) London 2000

CAUKERCKEN van Cornelis 1626-1680 **[5]**
$106 - €99 - **£65** - FF650
Cimon en Pero, d'après Pieter-Paul Rubens Gravure bois (36x42cm 14x16in) Antwerpen 1999

CAULA Sigismondo 1637-1724 **[10]**
$1 300 - €1 390 - **£886** - FF9 121
St.Sebastian Ink (44x30cm 17x11in) New-York 2001

CAULA Y CONCEJO Antonio 1847-? **[2]**
$3 600 - €3 604 - **£2 220** - FF23 640
Llegada del rey Alfonso XII al puerto de El Ferrol Oleo/lienzo (32x49cm 12x19in) Madrid 2000

CAULAERT van Jean-Dominique 1897-1979 **[70]**
$193 - €211 - **£127** - FF1 382
Portret van een jonge vrouw Pastel/paper (49.5x40cm 19x15in) Lokeren 2000
$846 - €1 006 - **£603** - FF6 600
«Nouveau Casino, Nice Son Tabarin» Affiche (160x115cm 62x45in) Orléans 2000

CAULDWELL Leslie Giffen 1861-? **[8]**
$10 746 - €9 147 - **£6 396** - FF60 000
Jeune bretonne en costume de fête Huile/toile (56x33cm 22x12in) Brest 1998

CAULFIELD Patrick 1936 **[102]**
$12 432 - €10 606 - **£7 500** - FF69 573
Pipe and Blind Acrylic/canvas (76x61cm 29x24in) London 1998
$2 321 - €2 614 - **£1 600** - FF17 149
Party Game, Royal Ballet Acrylic/paper (29x42cm 11x16in) London 2000
$435 - €514 - **£300** - FF3 369
Coat Stand Screenprint (73x95cm 28x37in) London 2000

CAULITZ Peter 1650-1719 **[2]**
$9 631 - €10 891 - **£6 777** - FF71 438
Hound, a dead Fox, a dead Mallard, a grey Partridge Oil/canvas (161x149cm 63x58in) Amsterdam 2001

CAULLERY de Louis 1555/62-1621/22 **[93]**
$42 000 - €44 854 - **£28 618** - FF294 222
Carnival in a Town Square Oil/panel (100.5x134.5cm 39x52in) New-York 2001
$23 908 - €25 664 - **£16 000** - FF168 345
Carnival in the Piazzetta Looking Towards the Piazza San Marco, Venice Oil/panel (46x71cm 18x27in) London 2000
$4 743 - €5 641 - **£3 381** - FF37 000
Adoration des Mages Huile/cuivre (27x38cm 10x14in) Neuilly-sur-Seine 2000

CAULLET Albert 1875-1950 **[34]**
$490 - €584 - **£350** - FF3 830
Ponies in a Meadow Oil/canvas (76x100.5cm 29x39in) London 2000

CAUSÉ Emil 1867-? **[3]**
$1 100 - €1 058 - **£678** - FF6 939
«Expositions du Salon des Cent» Poster (59x39.5cm 23x15in) New-York 1999

CAUSSÉ Julien 1869-? **[18]**
$601 - €675 - **£420** - FF4 425
Figure of a Woman Bronze (H22cm H8in) Billingshurst, West-Sussex 2001

CAUTY Horace Henry 1846-1909 **[1]**
$5 865 - €5 338 - **£3 600** - FF35 017
Summer Idyll Oil/canvas (61x107cm 24x42in) London 1999

CAUVET Gilles Paul 1731-1788 **[8]**
- ✏ **$1 000** - €1 026 - **£625** - FF6 727
  Les Caractères du Génie des Beaux Arts Ink
  (40x26.5cm 15x10in) New-York 2000

CAUVIN Edouard Louis 1817-1900 **[18]**
- 🖎 **$2 572** - €2 592 - **£1 603** - FF17 000
  Paysage Huile/toile (30x45cm 11x17in) Nantes 2000

CAUVY Léon 1874-1933 **[105]**
- 🖎 **$26 080** - €30 490 - **£18 620** - FF200 000
  Le marché à l'Amirauté Huile/toile (132.5x147cm
  52x57in) Paris 2001
- 🖎 **$5 379** - €6 250 - **£3 833** - FF41 000
  Famille au clair de lune Huile/toile (38x46cm
  14x18in) Paris 2001
- 🖎 **$1 962** - €2 134 - **£1 293** - FF14 000
  Femmes au cimetière, Alger Huile/carton
  (27x21.5cm 10x8in) Paris 2000
- ✏ **$2 278** - €2 439 - **£1 550** - FF16 000
  Scène de marché Aquarelle, gouache/papier
  (22x27cm 8x10in) Avignon 2001
- ▥ **$691** - €762 - **£468** - FF5 000
  **«Centenaire De l'Algérie du 1er janvier au 30
  juin 1830-1940»** Affiche couleur (74x105cm 29x41in)
  Nice 2000

CAUWELAERT van Jean emil 1860-1907 **[4]**
- 🖎 **$8 440** - €9 915 - **£6 080** - FF65 040
  A la pompe Huile/toile (53x73.5cm 20x28in)
  Bruxelles 2001

CAUWER de Emile Pierre J. 1828-1873 **[13]**
- 🖎 **$10 246** - €11 798 - **£6 994** - FF77 391
  Numerous townfolk on a square, Gent Oil/panel
  (54.5x73cm 21x28in) Amsterdam 2000

CAUWER de Leopold c.1830-c.1891 **[9]**
- 🖎 **$1 661** - €1 534 - **£1 034** - FF10 061
  Hahn und Hennen am umgestürzten Apfelkorb
  Öl/Leinwand (20x31.5cm 7x12in) Frankfurt 1999

CAUWER-RONSSE de Joseph 1779-1854 **[3]**
- 🖎 **$4 008** - €3 735 - **£2 472** - FF24 500
  Le concert Huile/panneau (58.5x51cm 23x20in)
  Menton 1999

CAVADAS José XX **[4]**
- 🖎 **$2 376** - €2 692 - **£1 620** - FF17 658
  Paisagem Huile/bois (26.5x35cm 10x13in) Lisboa
  2000

CAVAEL Rolf 1898-1979 **[381]**
- 🖎 **$4 117** - €4 586 - **£2 693** - FF30 084
  63-N4 Öl/Karton (36x49.9cm 14x19in) München 2000
- 🖎 **$1 737** - €1 943 - **£1 171** - FF12 744
  Komposition Oil/panel (37.5x24.7cm 14x9in)
  München 2000
- ✏ **$780** - €920 - **£550** - FF6 037
  Komposition Coloured pencils/paper (28.6x20.6cm
  11x8in) Köln 2001
- ▥ **$276** - €266 - **£172** - FF1 744
  Lithofa 25 Farblithographie (44x29cm 17x11in)
  München 2001

CAVAGLIERI Mario 1887-1969 **[18]**
- 🖎 **$7 626** - €8 690 - **£5 272** - FF57 000
  Portrait d'élégante en costume XVIII Huile/toile
  (125x103cm 49x40in) Toulouse 2000
- 🖎 **$12 500** - €12 958 - **£7 500** - FF85 000
  Arcobaleno Olio/tela (50x61cm 19x24in) Milano
  1999
- ✏ **$1 800** - €1 555 - **£900** - FF10 200
  Piazza Santo Spirito Tempera/carta (31x46cm
  12x18in) Firenze 1999

CAVAGNA Giovanni Paolo 1556-1627 **[1]**
- 🖎 **$4 679** - €4 579 - **£3 000** - FF30 036
  **The Madonna and Child with Saints Francis
  and Lawrence** Mixed media/board (90.5x73.5cm
  35x28in) London 1999

CAVAILLES Jules 1901-1977 **[244]**
- 🖎 **$4 331** - €5 107 - **£3 045** - FF33 500
  Femme de dos se coiffant Huile/toile (46x38cm
  18x14in) Paris 2000
- 🖎 **$900** - €815 - **£550** - FF5 347
  Still Life Mixed media (39x28cm 15x11in) Portland
  ME 1999
- ✏ **$2 953** - €3 171 - **£1 976** - FF20 800
  Bouquet au vase bleu et coupe de fruits
  Aquarelle, gouache/papier (63x41cm 24x16in) Paris
  2000

CAVALCANTI di Emiliano 1897-1976 **[86]**
- 🖎 **$800 000** - €928 232 - **£552 320** - FF6 088 800
  Mulher deitada com peixes e frutas Oil/canvas
  (110x195cm 43x76in) New-York 2000
- 🖎 **$65 000** - €76 533 - **£45 675** - FF502 021
  Duas mulheres Oil/canvas (64x78.5cm 25x30in)
  New-York 2000
- 🖎 **$42 000** - €45 083 - **£28 106** - FF295 722
  Morro Oil/board (35x28.5cm 13x11in) New-York 2000
- ✏ **$17 000** - €16 500 - **£10 584** - FF108 232
  Capoeira Gouache/paper (34x48.5cm 13x19in) New-
  York 1999
- ▥ **$12 000** - €11 181 - **£7 406** - FF73 345
  Samba Tapestry (192x298cm 75x117in) New-York
  1999

CAVALERI Ludovico 1867-1942 **[31]**
- 🖎 **$2 750** - €2 851 - **£1 650** - FF18 700
  Notturno sulla spiaggia Olio/cartone (69.5x48cm
  27x18in) Milano 2000
- 🖎 **$1 600** - €2 073 - **£1 200** - FF13 600
  Collin a Fiesole Olio/cartone (18x18.5cm 7x7in)
  Milano 2001

CAVALIERE Alik 1926-1998 **[21]**
- 🗝 **$2 990** - €2 949 - **£1 841** - FF19 347
  Poirier et pomme Bronze (H54.5cm H21in)
  Amsterdam 1999

CAVALIERI Giovanni Battista 1525-1597 **[3]**
- ▥ **$1 300** - €1 483 - **£907** - FF9 726
  Studienblatt mit Frauenköpfen nach der Antike
  Kupferstich (30.5x21cm 12x8in) Berlin 2001

CAVALLA Mario 1902-1962 **[6]**
- 🖎 **$800** - €829 - **£480** - FF5 000
  Tramonto sul mare Olio/tavola (31x41.5cm 12x16in)
  Torino 2001

CAVALLERI Vittorio 1860-1938 **[83]**
- 🖎 **$5 000** - €5 183 - **£3 000** - FF34 000
  Pascolo in alta montagna Olio/cartone (56x71.5cm
  22x28in) Vercelli 2000
- 🖎 **$1 500** - €1 555 - **£900** - FF10 200
  Lungo il Po presso Torino Olio/tavola (35x44.5cm
  13x17in) Vercelli 1999

CAVALLI Emanuele 1904-1981 **[39]**
- 🖎 **$5 750** - €5 961 - **£3 450** - FF39 100
  Natura morta con cipolle rosse Olio/tavola
  (39.5x47cm 15x18in) Prato 2001
- 🖎 **$1 300** - €1 348 - **£780** - FF8 840
  Margherite Olio/tavola (26x23cm 10x9in) Prato 1999

CAVALLI Enrico 1849-1919 **[1]**
- 🖎 **$2 000** - €2 592 - **£1 500** - FF17 000
  Figure in un paesaggio Olio/tavola (18x23cm
  7x9in) Milano 2001

CAVALLI Nicolo 1730-1822 **[7]**

🎨 $86 - €82 - £54 - FF537
Seifenblase Kupferstich (40x31cm 15x12in) Praha 2000

CAVALLINO Bernardo 1616-1656/58 **[10]**

$347 520 - €394 917 - £240 000 - FF2 590 488
A Personification of Painting Oil/canvas (123.5x99.5cm 48x39in) London 2001

CAVALLO-PEDUZZI Emile Gustave 1851-1917 **[2]**

✏️ $1 271 - €1 448 - £873 - FF9 500
Lumière en sous-bois Aquarelle/papier (29x44cm 11x17in) Paris 2000

CAVALLON Giorgio 1904-1989 **[22]**

$20 000 - €22 401 - £13 896 - FF146 944
Untitled Oil/canvas (70x70cm 27x27in) New-York 2001

✏️ $2 400 - €2 331 - £1 500 - FF15 292
Untitled Watercolour/paper (38x55cm 14x21in) New-York 1999

CAVALLUCCI Antonio 1751-1798 **[8]**

$5 782 - €6 734 - £4 000 - FF44 173
Priest Holding a Rosary, Surrounded by Children/Priest Showing Picture Oil/canvas (14x31.5cm 5x12in) London 2000

CAVALORI Mirabello 1535-1572 **[1]**

$610 660 - €605 711 - £380 000 - FF3 973 204
Isaac blessing Jacob Oil/panel (58x43.5cm 22x17in) London 1999

CAVAROZZI Bartolomeo c.1590-1625 **[3]**

$800 000 - €809 309 - £488 480 - FF5 308 720
Still Life with a Basket of Fruit and two Children Oil/canvas (82x125.5cm 32x49in) New-York 2000

CAVÉ Jules C. 1859-c.1940 **[10]**

$3 899 - €3 794 - £2 400 - FF24 885
Girl with Lute Oil/canvas (63x42cm 24x16in) London 1999

$4 781 - €5 133 - £3 200 - FF33 669
Flora Oil/canvas (41x33cm 16x12in) London 2000

CAVÉ Lucien XX **[17]**

🎨 $467 - €457 - £288 - FF3 000
Meeting à Bussière-Poitevine Affiche (159x118cm 62x46in) Paris 1999

CAVE William XVIII-XIX **[2]**

$2 373 - €2 524 - £1 500 - FF16 557
White Dove Oil/panel (29x23cm 11x9in) London 2000

CAVEDONE Giacomo 1577-1660 **[31]**

$46 925 - €39 926 - £28 000 - FF261 895
The Madonna and Child Oil/canvas (124x98cm 48x38in) London 1998

$3 602 - €3 340 - £2 200 - FF21 912
A Left Hand Black chalk/paper (20.5x17cm 8x6in) London 1998

CAVELIER Jules 1814-1894 **[7]**

🖌️ $1 438 - €1 645 - £1 000 - FF10 790
Lion fighting Snake Bronze (18x36cm 7x14in) Doncaster, South-Yorkshire 2000

CAVENAGHI Emilio 1852-1876 **[1]**

$3 600 - €4 665 - £2 700 - FF30 600
Interno del Duomo di Milano Olio/tela (60x35.5cm 23x13in) Milano 2001

CAVERNE André XX **[5]**

$7 532 - €8 537 - £5 264 - FF56 000
Les moissons Huile/toile (97x130cm 38x51in) Bordeaux 2001

$3 757 - €4 269 - £2 629 - FF28 000
Femmes aux écrevisses Huile/toile (118x77cm 46x30in) Neuilly-sur-Seine 2001

CAVIN Marylin XX **[12]**

$642 - €686 - £437 - FF4 500
Parfum, souffle, couleurs Technique mixte/toile (81x60cm 31x23in) Paris 2001

CAVIOLI XIX-XX **[3]**

🖌️ $2 578 - €2 515 - £1 587 - FF16 500
Buste de Napoléon Bronze (H68cm H26in) Rennes 1999

CAW James Lewis 1864-1950 **[15]**

✏️ $262 - €251 - £160 - FF1 647
Lynam Moor/Lake of Lucerne/Loch Doich/Grey Sunset Watercolour/paper (18x25cm 7x9in) Sighthill 1999

CAWÉN Alvar 1886-1935 **[37]**

$4 771 - €5 382 - £3 353 - FF35 302
Stilleben Oil/canvas (61x65cm 24x25in) Helsinki 2001

$581 - €673 - £411 - FF4 412
Parisiska Oil/paper (41x33cm 16x12in) Helsinki 2000

✏️ $834 - €908 - £550 - FF5 957
Hustak vid ån Akvarell/papper (29x35cm 11x13in) Helsinki 2000

CAWSE John 1779-1862 **[9]**

$1 161 - €1 356 - £820 - FF8 893
«King Henry the Fifth Act 2, Scene 1st, Mrs.Quickly, Pistol, Nym...» Oil/canvas (70x82.5cm 27x32in) London 2000

CAWSTON Mick 1959 **[5]**

$1 043 - €1 032 - £650 - FF6 769
English Bull Terriers Oil/board (41x56cm 16x22in) London 1999

CAWTHORNE Neil 1936 **[143]**

$2 415 - €2 281 - £1 500 - FF14 961
Fernie Hunt, near Billesdon, in Full Cry Oil/canvas (51x76cm 20x29in) Suffolk 1999

CAY Jacob XVI **[1]**

$1 053 - €1 022 - £656 - FF6 707
Selbstbildnis mit den allegorischen Figuren der Malerei und Plastik Woodcut (22.4x17.9cm 8x7in) Berlin 1999

CAYLEY Neville, Jnr. Will. 1886-1950 **[42]**

✏️ $446 - €430 - £275 - FF2 820
Magpie/Kookaburra Watercolour/paper (30x21cm 11x8in) Sydney 1999

CAYLEY Neville, Snr. Henry 1853-1903 **[73]**

$421 - €491 - £297 - FF3 223
Kookaburra and Snake Watercolour/paper (57x44cm 22x17in) Malvern, Victoria 2000

🎨 $1 117 - €1 318 - £788 - FF8 646
Kookaburras Lithograph (62x50.5cm 24x19in) Woollahra, Sydney 2001

CAYLINA Paolo II 1485-c.1547 **[2]**

$6 180 - €5 339 - £3 090 - FF35 020
Preghiera nell'orto Olio/tavola (48x36.5cm 18x14in) Milano 1999

CAYON Henri 1878/79-? **[6]**

$2 590 - €3 049 - £1 820 - FF20 000
Femmes africaines Huile/toile (60x73cm 23x28in) Paris 2000

CAZABON Michel Jean 1813-1888 **[33]**

✏️ $19 363 - €18 595 - £12 000 - FF121 976
Grove in Trinidad Watercolour/paper (37x26.5cm 14x10in) London 1999

CAZANAVE Raymond 1893-1961 **[5]**

$319 - €305 - **£199** - FF2 000
Capitaine Fantôme, pl.45 Encre Chine/papier
(36x27cm 14x10in) Paris 1999

CAZAUBON Pierre Alfred Noël 1885-1979 **[3]**

$34 932 - €37 502 - **£23 370** - FF246 000
Fontaine de parc: Héraklès étouffant le serpent
Bronze (160x160cm 62x62in) Pau 2000

CAZAUX Édouard 1889-1974 **[126]**

$7 100 - €7 622 - **£4 750** - FF50 000
La femme nue Bronze (H90cm H35in) Paris 2000

$1 562 - €1 677 - **£1 045** - FF11 000
Femme à la fontaine Bronze (H33cm H12in) Paris
2000

$852 - €915 - **£570** - FF6 000
Shéhérazade Aquarelle/papier (30.5x33cm 12x12in)
Paris 2000

CAZES Pierre Jacques 1676-1754 **[18]**

$1 361 - €1 372 - **£848** - FF9 000
Sainte Cécile Huile/toile (54x46.5cm 21x18in) Paris
2000

CAZIEL Casimir Zielenkiewicz 1906-1988 **[5]**

$2 448 - €2 261 - **£1 524** - FF14 828
Le jardin du Luxembourg Oil/canvas (40x65cm
15x25in) Warszawa 1999

CAZIN Jean-Baptiste XVIII-XIX **[7]**

$52 304 - €47 800 - **£32 000** - FF313 545
**River Landscapes with Herdsmen, maids and
Travellers beside Waterfalls** Oil/canvas
(153.5x68cm 60x26in) London 2000

CAZIN Jean-Charles 1841-1901 **[103]**

$6 250 - €5 948 - **£3 909** - FF39 017
Village Street Oil/canvas/board (46x56cm 18x22in)
New-York 1999

$1 795 - €1 677 - **£1 107** - FF11 000
Paysage Huile/panneau (24x33cm 9x12in) Melun
2000

CAZNEAUX Harold Pierce 1878-1953 **[15]**

$448 - €466 - **£296** - FF3 058
River Gums Gelatin silver print (26.5x19.5cm 10x7in)
Sydney 2000

CAZZANIGA Giancarlo 1930 **[54]**

$1 800 - €1 555 - **£900** - FF10 200
«Jazz Man» Olio/carta/tela (50x70cm 19x27in) Milano
1999

$500 - €518 - **£300** - FF3 400
Girasoli Olio/tela (30x24cm 11x9in) Vercelli 2000

CECCANTI V. XIX-XX **[1]**

$12 000 - €11 360 - **£7 453** - FF74 514
«Caffé Espresso Servizio Istantaneo» Poster
(135.5x96cm 53x37in) New-York 1999

CECCARINI Sebastiano 1702-1783 **[7]**

$14 280 - €14 803 - **£8 568** - FF97 104
Ritratto di dama Olio/tela (76x63cm 29x24in) Roma
1999

CECCHI Adriano 1850-1936 **[28]**

$16 000 - €15 226 - **£10 008** - FF99 878
He Loves me, He Loves me not Oil/canvas
(37x46cm 14x18in) New-York 1999

$8 700 - €7 784 - **£5 214** - FF51 057
Et par kurtisaner i lyseblå/Lyseröd kjole Oil/can-
vas (35x26cm 13x10in) København 1998

CECCHI Sergio 1921-1986 **[34]**

$1 773 - €1 915 - **£1 189** - FF12 559
La Vieille-Ville Huile/toile (55x48cm 21x18in) Genève
2000

CECCHINI-PRICHARD Eugenio 1831-? **[9]**

$9 600 - €8 293 - **£4 800** - FF54 400
Marina Olio/tela (45x69.5cm 17x27in) Prato 1999

CECCOBELLI Bruno 1952 **[248]**

$1 250 - €1 296 - **£750** - FF8 500
Con l'alba sarai viandante Tecnica mista/cartone
(51x50cm 20x19in) Vercelli 2000

$500 - €518 - **£300** - FF3 400
«Bacio la bellezza» Tecnica mista/cartone (30x20cm
11x7in) Vercelli 2001

$1 270 - €1 364 - **£850** - FF8 945
Osco Assemblage (70x142x7cm 27x55x2in) London
2000

$437 - €427 - **£278** - FF2 800
Pied a Sal Gouache (60x40cm 23x15in) Paris 1999

CECCONI Alberto 1897-1973 **[58]**

$900 - €777 - **£450** - FF5 100
La vecchia porta di San Giovanni Olio/tela
(56x48cm 22x18in) Firenze 1999

$720 - €622 - **£360** - FF4 080
Veduta di campagna con chiesa sullo sfondo
Olio/tela (30x40cm 11x15in) Firenze 1999

CECCONI Eugenio 1842-1903 **[42]**

$45 000 - €46 649 - **£27 000** - FF306 000
Mezza festa Olio/tela (63.5x90cm 25x35in) Milano
1999

$6 000 - €6 220 - **£3 600** - FF40 800
Orto in una cascina Olio/tavoletta (20x12.5cm
7x4in) Milano 1999

CECCONI Nicoló 1835-? **[4]**

$5 330 - €4 554 - **£2 300** - FF29 874
«La Pregiera, woman with Children and Dog»
Oil/canvas (105x75cm 41x29in) St. Helier, Jersey 1998

CECIONI Adriano 1836-1886 **[44]**

$2 000 - €2 592 - **£1 500** - FF17 000
Cecioni nel suo studio Acquarello/carta
(21.5x28.5cm 8x11in) Milano 2000

CECOLI XIX **[2]**

$1 035 - €1 073 - **£621** - FF7 038
Ritratto di gentildonna Olio/tela (21x15cm 8x5in)
Roma 1999

CÉDANNE 1944 **[61]**

$512 - €610 - **£354** - FF4 000
Fin du jour au pied de la colline Huile/toile
(81x65cm 31x25in) Thonon-les-Bains 2000

$265 - €229 - **£157** - FF1 500
Marée basse en Bretagne Huile/toile (41x33cm
16x12in) Nantes 1998

CEDERBERG Eric 1897-1984 **[75]**

$196 - €231 - **£138** - FF1 518
Surrealistiskt strandlandskap Oil/panel
(17.5x25cm 6x9in) Stockholm 2000

CEDERGREN Per Wilhelm 1823-1896 **[35]**

$1 443 - €1 512 - **£913** - FF9 920
Vinterlandskap med figurer Oil/canvas (56x74cm
22x29in) Malmö 2000

$847 - €714 - **£503** - FF4 686
Segelfartyg vid borg Oil/canvas (24x35cm 9x13in)
Stockholm 1998

CEDERHOLM Axel Fredrik 1780-1828 **[7]**

$3 513 - €3 901 - **£2 352** - FF25 590
**Hemvändande soldater mottager lokalbefolk-
ningens hyllningar** Akvarell, gouache/papper
(62x88cm 24x34in) Stockholm 2000

C

CEDERSTRÖM Eva 1909-1995 [45]
🖉 $1 419 - €1 598 - £977 - FF10 480
  Vinterdag Oil/canvas (54x79cm 21x31in) Helsinki 2000
🖉 $315 - €336 - £214 - FF2 206
  Alpvy Akvarell/papper (24x33cm 9x12in) Helsinki 2001

CEDERSTRÖM Gustaf 1845-1933 [27]
🖉 $1 471 - €1 413 - £915 - FF9 268
  Kvinna i profil Oil/canvas (74x100cm 29x39in) Stockholm 1999
🖉 $980 - €1 104 - £675 - FF7 240
  Sydländska herdinnor Oil/panel (40x33cm 15x12in) Stockholm 2000

CEDERSTRÖM Thure Nikolaus F. 1843-1924 [25]
🖉 $3 192 - €2 905 - £1 959 - FF19 057
  Kardinal mit vorlesendem Benediktinerpater Öl/Leinwand (34x47.5cm 13x18in) Zürich 1999
🖉 $3 500 - €3 195 - £2 129 - FF20 958
  The Appreciating Monk Oil/panel (23x17cm 9x7in) New-Orleans LA 1998

CEESEPE Carlos Sánchez Pérez 1958 [29]
🖉 $1 567 - €1 652 - £990 - FF10 835
  Personajes Acrílico/papel (90x90cm 35x35in) Madrid 2000
🖉 $504 - €481 - £320 - FF3 152
  «Titiriterias» Técnica mixta/papel (48.5x33.5cm 19x13in) Madrid 1999

CEI Cipriano 1864-1922 [6]
🖉 $5 500 - €5 542 - £3 428 - FF36 355
  The Harvest Oil/canvas (86x60cm 34x24in) San Rafael CA 2000

CELADA DA VIRGILIO Ugo 1895-1995 [55]
🖉 $2 000 - €2 592 - £1 500 - FF17 000
  Ritratto in verde Olio/masonite (75x65cm 29x25in) Vercelli 2000
🖉 $2 750 - €2 851 - £1 650 - FF18 700
  Natura morta con uovo e bicchiere di vino Olio/faesite (40.5x29cm 15x11in) Roma 1999

CELEBI Ali 1904 [5]
🖉 $2 700 000 - €3 064 225 - £1 800 000 - FF20 100 000
  Paysage Huile/toile (32x40cm 12x15in) Istanbul 2001

CELEBRANO Francesco 1729-1814 [6]
🖉 $3 200 - €4 147 - £2 400 - FF27 200
  Cristo portacroce/Cristo cade sotto la croce Olio/tela (49x61.5cm 19x24in) Napoli 2000

CELENTANO Daniel Ralph 1902-1980 [15]
🖉 $20 000 - €21 888 - £13 796 - FF143 576
  Scene on the Lower East Side Oil/canvas (51x61cm 20x24in) New-York 2001
🖉 $4 000 - €4 549 - £2 774 - FF29 840
  Dice Playing Oil/board (27x22cm 11x9in) Chicago IL 2000
🖉 $1 500 - €1 706 - £1 040 - FF11 190
  Going to the Festival Watercolour/paper (36x25cm 14x10in) Chicago IL 2000

CELESTI Andrea 1637-1700/06 [7]
🖉 $10 000 - €11 618 - £7 028 - FF76 212
  Female Figure surrounded by desporting Putti Oil/canvas (89.5x120.5cm 35x47in) New-York 2001

CELIBERTI Giorgio 1929 [65]
🖉 $1 666 - €1 727 - £999 - FF11 328
  Il quadrato del muro Tecnica mista (70x29.5cm 27x11in) Milano 1999

CELIS de Agustín 1932 [13]
🖉 $660 - €721 - £420 - FF4 728
  La montaña y la luna Oleo/lienzo (60x80cm 23x31in) Madrid 2000

CELLO XX [1]
🖾 $827 - €773 - £500 - FF5 068
  Chambéry, Dolin Poster (121x161cm 47x63in) London 1999

CELLONY Joseph le Jeune 1730-1786 [6]
🖉 $1 540 - €1 448 - £932 - FF9 500
  La reddition Encre (20x26cm 7x10in) Lyon 1999

CELMINS Vija 1939 [53]
🖉 $300 000 - €334 943 - £200 520 - FF2 197 080
  Time Magazine Cover Oil/canvas (56x40.5cm 22x15in) New-York 2000
🖉 $360 000 - €348 328 - £222 012 - FF2 284 884
  Big Sea #2 Graphite (85x112cm 33x44in) New-York 1999
🖾 $3 250 - €3 789 - £2 250 - FF24 851
  Saturn Print (25.5x21.5cm 10x8in) New-York 2000

CELOMMI Pasquale 1851-1928 [16]
🖉 $4 500 - €4 670 - £2 854 - FF30 630
  Meeting along the Road - Genre Scene with Shepherdess and Mule Driver Oil/canvas (63x115.5cm 24x45in) Boston MA 2000
🖉 $1 920 - €1 659 - £1 280 - FF10 880
  Ritorno dai campi Olio/tavola (35x20cm 13x7in) Roma 1998

CELOMMI Raffaello 1883-? [12]
🖉 $4 000 - €4 147 - £2 400 - FF27 200
  Pescatori a riva Olio/tela (70x100cm 27x39in) Roma 2000

CÉLOS Julien 1884-1953 [89]
🖉 $1 254 - €1 487 - £912 - FF9 756
  Vue de ville en automne Huile/toile (70x80cm 27x31in) Antwerpen 2001

CEMIN Saint-Clair 1951 [53]
🖾 $15 000 - €14 449 - £9 313 - FF94 779
  Nova terra nova lua Installation (97.5x74.5cm 38x29in) New-York 1999
🖾 $4 028 - €4 702 - £2 760 - FF30 840
  Clasping Hands Bronze (H15.5cm H6in) Stockholm 2000

CENDALI Pietro 1893-? [2]
🖾 $25 000 - €25 916 - £15 000 - FF170 000
  Bambina con orsacchiotto Marbre (H107cm H42in) Milano 2000

CENNI DI FRANCESCO DI SER CENNI 1369-1415 [3]
🖉 $84 000 - €72 566 - £42 000 - FF476 000
  Natività e Crocifissione Tempera/tavola (77x43cm 30x16in) Milano 1999

CENTENO VALLENILLA Pedro 1904-1988 [50]
🖉 $2 040 - €1 903 - £1 320 - FF12 480
  Virgen de Coromoto Oleo/lienzo (44x49cm 17x19in) Caracas 1999
🖉 $238 - €222 - £154 - FF1 456
  Estudio para San Sebastián Graphite (75x54cm 29x21in) Caracas 1999

CERACCHI Giuseppe 1751-1802 [2]
🖾 $36 442 - €41 439 - £25 000 - FF271 825
  Portrait Profile Relief of a Young Boy Marble (H65cm H25in) Oxfordshire 2000

CERACCHINI Gisberto 1900-1982 **[11]**
🖙 **$9 250** - €9 589 - **£5 550** - FF62 900
    La famiglia del boscaiolo Olio/tavola
    (114.5x149.5cm 45x58in) Roma 2001

CERAMANO Charles-Ferdinand 1829-1909 **[154]**
🖙 **$6 177** - €7 013 - **£4 291** - FF46 000
    Berger et ses moutons près du bois Huile/toile
    (101.5x129.5cm 39x50in) Barbizon 2001
🖙 **$3 082** - €3 506 - **£2 139** - FF23 000
    **Cerf en forêt de Fontainebleau (La Mare aux
    fées)** Huile/toile (55x82cm 21x32in) Fontainebleau
    2000
🖙 **$2 559** - €2 211 - **£1 545** - FF14 500
    Meules dans la plaine de Chailly Huile/toile
    (27.5x32cm 10x12in) Barbizon 1998
✏ **$474** - €534 - **£325** - FF3 900
    Moutons sortant de la bergerie Crayon gras
    (54x65cm 21x25in) Barbizon 2000

CERCONE Ettore 1850-1896 **[11]**
🖙 **$7 500** - €7 775 - **£4 500** - FF51 000
    Odalisca in giardino Olio/tela (34.5x56cm 13x22in)
    Milano 1999

CERESA Carlo 1609-1679 **[14]**
🖙 **$8 500** - €8 812 - **£5 100** - FF57 800
    **Ritratto del comte Francesco
    Bolignini/Contessa Cornelia** Olio/tela (69x48cm
    27x18in) Imbersago (Lecco) 2001
🖙 **$1 900** - €1 970 - **£1 140** - FF12 920
    Ritratto di gentiluomo Olio/tela (44x34cm 17x13in)
    Milano 1999

CEREZO Mateo II 1635-1685 **[10]**
🖙 **$5 300** - €6 006 - **£3 600** - FF39 400
    Inmaculada Concepción Oleo/lienzo (102x82cm
    40x32in) Madrid 2001
🖙 **$8 099** - €9 081 - **£5 500** - FF59 568
    Mary Magdalene Oil/canvas/panel (41.5x32.5cm
    16x12in) London 2000

CÉRIA Edmond 1884-1955 **[256]**
🖙 **$1 152** - €1 067 - **£714** - FF7 000
    Le modèle allongé sur un lit Huile/toile (38x46cm
    14x18in) Paris 1999
🖙 **$1 132** - €991 - **£685** - FF6 500
    Le Pont des Arts Huile/panneau (27x41cm 10x16in)
    Saint-Christol-les-Alès 1998

CERIBELLI Cesar Costantino R. 1841-1818 **[12]**
🐾 **$4 000** - €3 468 - **£2 444** - FF22 747
    Bust of a Lady Gilded bronze (H61cm H24in) New-
    York 1999

CERIEZ Theodore 1832-1904 **[19]**
🖙 **$2 800** - €3 253 - **£1 967** - FF21 339
    Musical Discussion Oil/canvas (39x31cm 15x12in)
    New-Orleans LA 2001

CERMAK Frantisek 1822-1884 **[7]**
🖙 **$115** - €109 - **£72** - FF717
    Bosna Huile/panneau (26x32cm 10x12in) Praha 2000

CERMAK Jaroslav 1831-1878 **[24]**
🖙 **$4 335** - €4 100 - **£2 700** - FF26 895
    Bust-length Portrait of a Girl Oil/canvas (53x44cm
    20x17in) Praha 1999
🖙 **$1 734** - €1 640 - **£1 080** - FF10 758
    Coast in Montenegro Oil/panel (32x41cm 12x16in)
    Praha 1999
✏ **$346** - €328 - **£216** - FF2 151
    «Dancing Children» Wash/paper (22x21cm 8x8in)
    Praha 2001

CERNIGOI Augusto 1898-1985 **[16]**
🖙 **$3 250** - €3 369 - **£1 950** - FF22 100
    Mostra del Mare, Trieste Tempera (49x62cm
    19x24in) Trieste 2001

CERNOTZKY Ernst 1869-1939 **[4]**
🖙 **$1 179** - €1 308 - **£820** - FF8 580
    Stilleben mit Globus und alten Büchern Oil/panel
    (28x20cm 11x7in) Wien 2001

CERNY Charles 1892-1965 **[53]**
✏ **$285** - €335 - **£204** - FF2 200
    Balustrade à la vigne vierge Aquarelle/papier
    (29x39cm 11x15in) Paris 2001

CERNY Karel 1910-1960 **[25]**
🖙 **$13 005** - €12 300 - **£8 100** - FF80 685
    Paysage au cavalier Huile/toile (40x55cm 15x21in)
    Praha 2001
🗒 **$289** - €273 - **£180** - FF1 793
    Avant de s'endormir Lithographie (24x29.5cm
    9x11in) Praha 2001

CEROLI Mario 1938 **[64]**
🖙 **$1 300** - €1 348 - **£780** - FF8 840
    Autoritratto con Raffaella Collage/cartone
    (38.5x58cm 15x22in) Roma 2000
🗿 **$3 250** - €3 369 - **£1 950** - FF22 100
    Finestra e sole Sculpture bois (100x70x18cm
    39x27x7in) Roma 1999
🗿 **$2 000** - €2 073 - **£1 200** - FF13 600
    Profilo Sculpture bois (34.5x35.5cm 13x13in) Prato
    1999
🗒 **$840** - €726 - **£560** - FF4 760
    Twonbly Multiplo (100x70cm 39x27in) Prato 1998

CERQUOZZI Michelangelo 1602-1660 **[28]**
🖙 **$32 000** - €31 985 - **£19 548** - FF209 808
    **Park Landscape with Elegant Figures
    Conversing** Oil/canvas (64.5x66.5cm 25x26in) New-
    York 2000
🖙 **$9 000** - €10 456 - **£6 325** - FF68 590
    The Education of the Virgin Oil/panel (35.5x28cm
    13x11in) New-York 2001

**CERRINI IL CAVALIERE PERUGINO Gian
Domenico** 1609-1681 **[18]**
🖙 **$50 000** - €54 857 - **£33 215** - FF359 840
    The Denial of Saint Peter Oil/canvas (120x160cm
    47x62in) New-York 2000
🖙 **$10 000** - €10 971 - **£6 643** - FF71 968
    Saint Sebastian Oil/canvas (65x49cm 25x19in) New-
    York 2000

CERRUTI Michelangelo 1666-1748 **[2]**
🖙 **$6 232** - €5 814 - **£3 760** - FF38 136
    Noli me tangere Öl/Leinwand (37.5x24.5cm 14x9in)
    Wien 1999

CERRUTI-BEAUDUC Felice 1817-1896 **[2]**
🖙 **$23 640** - €22 867 - **£14 580** - FF150 000
    L'Abreuvoir Huile/toile (46x61cm 18x24in) Paris 1999

CERUTI IL PITOCCHETTO Giacomo Antonio 1698-
1767 **[22]**
🖙 **$14 000** - €18 141 - **£10 500** - FF119 000
    Ritratto di gentiluomo Olio/tela (93x63cm 36x24in)
    Milano 2001

CERUTTI H. XX **[3]**
🗒 **$958** - €915 - **£598** - FF6 000
    «Le Chaland qui passe» Affiche couleur
    (160x120cm 62x47in) Paris 1999

CERUTTI Peter XX [1]
- **$10 368** – €12 196 – **£7 432** – FF80 000
  Sans titre Acrylique/toile (73x92cm 28x36in) Paris 2001

CERVANTEZ Pedro 1915 [6]
- **$2 787** – €3 091 – **£1 853** – FF20 274
  Cabeza de caballo Bronze (35x25x55cm 13x9x21in) México 2000

CERVELLI Federico 1625-c.1700 [7]
- **$56 400** – €48 723 – **£37 600** – FF319 600
  Diana e Callisto Olio/tela (231x156cm 90x61in) Roma 1998

CÉSAR (César Baldaccini) 1921-1998 [1444]
- **$10 765** – €9 319 – **£6 534** – FF61 126
  Compression mit kleinen Medizinal-Schachteln Collage/panel (61x50cm 24x19in) Zürich 1998
- **$2 997** – €2 744 – **£1 827** – FF18 000
  Combustion de paquet de cigarettes Technique mixte/carton (46x31cm 18x12in) Paris 1999
- **$30 160** – €32 225 – **£20 540** – FF211 380
  Château magique Bronze (95x35cm 37x13in) Lokeren 2001
- **$4 580** – €4 443 – **£2 884** – FF29 142
  Plaque Bronze (H35cm H13in) Köbenhavn 1999
- **$1 160** – €1 296 – **£776** – FF8 500
  Poisson Feutre (11.5x30.5cm 4x12in) Paris 2000
- **$300** – €290 – **£189** – FF1 900
  Le Centaure Gravure (40x56cm 15x22in) Paris 1999
- **$928** – €1 037 – **£620** – FF6 800
  Portrait de Ricco Photo (34x45cm 13x17in) Paris 2000

CESARE de Ugo 1950 [6]
- **$680** – €881 – **£510** – FF5 780
  Piccolo pittore Olio/tela (50x40cm 19x15in) Napoli 2000

CESARI Bernardino ?-1614 [3]
- **$8 700** – €7 516 – **£5 800** – FF49 300
  Diana e Atteone Olio/tavola (26x37cm 10x14in) Prato 1998

CESARI IL CAVALIER D'ARPINO Giuseppe 1568-1640 [48]
- **$100 000** – €106 969 – **£68 180** – FF701 670
  Jupiter and Antiope Oil/panel (59.5x79cm 23x31in) New-York 2001
- **$127 015** – €136 341 – **£85 000** – FF894 336
  The Madonna and Child with Saint-Jérôme and an Attendant Angel Oil/panel (43x31cm 16x12in) London 2000
- **$4 099** – €4 337 – **£2 600** – FF28 448
  The Assumption of the Virgin Black chalk (35.5x24cm 13x9in) London 2000

CESARI Roberto 1949 [33]
- **$1 008** – €1 081 – **£684** – FF7 092
  Vista de Venecia Oleo/tabla (51.5x65cm 20x25in) Barcelona 2001
- **$560** – €601 – **£370** – FF3 940
  Venecia Oleo/tabla (29x40cm 11x15in) Madrid 2000

CESBRON Achille Théodore 1849-1915 [22]
- **$1 587** – €1 829 – **£1 095** – FF12 000
  Bouquet Huile/toile (86x45cm 33x17in) Paris 2000

CESBRON Charles XIX-XX [2]
- **$868** – €991 – **£603** – FF6 500
  «La Baule-les-Pins» Affiche (105x75cm 41x29in) Paris 2000

CESETTI Giuseppe 1902-1990 [211]
- **$15 000** – €12 958 – **£10 000** – FF85 000
  Paris, Saint-Germain, L'Auxerrois Olio/tela (119x109.5cm 46x43in) Prato 1998
- **$3 000** – €3 887 – **£2 250** – FF25 500
  Tre fantini a cavallo Olio/tela (60x81cm 23x31in) Milano 2000
- **$3 000** – €3 110 – **£1 800** – FF20 400
  Gondola Olio/tela (12.5x22cm 4x8in) Milano 2000
- **$960** – €1 244 – **£720** – FF8 160
  Fantini e cavalli Acquarello (27x35cm 10x13in) Milano 2001

CESI Bartolomeo 1556-1629 [14]
- **$7 205** – €6 694 – **£4 400** – FF43 912
  Study of a Man with his Hands Outstretched Red chalk (15x13.5cm 5x5in) London 1998

CESI Federico, Prince 1585-1630 [1]
- **$8 500** – €9 599 – **£5 190** – FF56 405
  The Curle of the Great Lady Ink (37.5x27cm 14x10in) New-York 2000

CESIO Carlo 1626-1686 [7]
- **$301** – €256 – **£181** – FF1 676
  Der heilige Andreas auf dem Ganz zur Richtstätte, nach Guido Reni Kupferstich (29.9x43.9cm 11x17in) Köln 1998

CESSELON Angelo 1922-1992 [8]
- **$424** – €440 – **£254** – FF2 886
  «Delitto Perfetto» Affiche couleur (198x139cm 77x54in) Torino 2000

CESTARO Giacomo, Jacopo c.1718-1778 [11]
- **$24 000** – €26 331 – **£15 943** – FF172 723
  Saint Dorothea Oil/canvas (80x62cm 31x24in) New-York 2000
- **$2 400** – €2 073 – **£1 200** – FF13 600
  Crocefissione Inchiostro (46.5x29cm 18x11in) Milano 1999

CESTERO Sebastian 1931-1998 [7]
- **$1 740** – €1 802 – **£1 110** – FF11 820
  Caballo en la cuadra Oleo/tabla (54x63cm 21x24in) Madrid 2000

CETTO Nikolaus Engelbert 1713-1746 [2]
- **$15 700** – €14 534 – **£9 720** – FF95 340
  Weihnachtskrippe Miniature (13x17cm 5x6in) Wien 1999

CEULEN van Cornelis I Janssens 1593-c.1664 [50]
- **$26 349** – €29 655 – **£18 154** – FF194 526
  Der Vater und das Kind Öl/Leinwand (124x100cm 48x39in) München 2000
- **$19 000** – €20 394 – **£12 714** – FF133 779
  Lu(?)Jue Cary Viscount Falkland Oil/canvas (74x64cm 29x25in) Chicago IL 2000

CEULEN van Cornelis II Janssens c.1622-c.1698 [2]
- **$4 800** – €5 577 – **£3 373** – FF36 581
  Young Woman in a white and gold Dress/Young Woman in red Dress Oil/canvas (51x44cm 20x17in) New-York 2000

CEYTAIRE Jean-Pierre 1946 [249]
- **$7 467** – €8 080 – **£5 114** – FF53 000
  «Femme jambe croisées, chausseur prévenant» Technique mixte (200x60cm 78x23in) Provins 2001
- **$2 890** – €3 354 – **£2 028** – FF22 000
  Femme offerte monsieur curieux Huile/bois (50x100cm 19x39in) Neuilly-sur-Seine 2000
- **$1 572** – €1 448 – **£959** – FF9 500
  «Il souffre encore d'avoir été un mauvais élève» Technique mixte (40.5x30cm 15x11in) Bayeux 1998

🖊 **$476** - €534 - **£331** - FF3 500
Sans titre Crayon/papier (23.5x31cm 9x12in)
Versailles 2001

CÉZANNE Paul 1839-1906 [474]

🔍 **$10 000 000** - €8 531 047 - **£6 032 000** -
FF55 960 000
L'estaque vu à travers les pins Oil/canvas
(73x92.5cm 28x36in) New-York 1998

🔍 **$347 182** - €335 935 - **£220 000** - FF2 203 586
Portrait de Madame Cézanne Oil/canvas
(20x14.5cm 7x5in) London 1999

🖊 **$105 000** - €89 576 - **£62 580** - FF587 580
Nature morte, objets de toilette Watercolour/paper
(31.5x47.5cm 12x18in) New-York 1998

▥ **$666** - €613 - **£400** - FF4 023
Tête de jeune fille Etching (13x10.5cm 5x4in)
London 1999

CHAB Victor 1930 [28]

🔍 **$1 400** - €1 626 - **£983** - FF10 669
«Sastre de tormenta» Oleo/lienzo (80x65cm
31x25in) Buenos-Aires 2001

▥ **$2 300** - €2 566 - **£1 599** - FF16 834
Homage to Marc Chagall Lithograph (31x23cm
12x9in) Cleveland OH 2001

CHABANIAN Arsène, Hemayack H-C 1864-1949 [86]

🔍 **$1 314** - €1 220 - **£820** - FF8 000
Bord de mer au clair de lune Huile/toile (60x81cm
23x31in) Deauville 1999

🖊 **$830** - €762 - **£510** - FF5 000
Effet de lumière sur la mer Pastel/toile (61x50cm
24x19in) Paris 1999

CHABAS Maurice 1862-1947 [154]

🔍 **$1 583** - €1 524 - **£978** - FF10 000
Campagne bord de rivière Huile/toile (86x116cm
33x45in) Paris 1999

🖊 **$670** - €762 - **£465** - FF5 000
Saint en Extase Aquarelle, gouache/papier (35x49cm
13x19in) Paris 2000

CHABAS Paul 1869-1937 [69]

🔍 **$5 961** - €7 013 - **£4 273** - FF46 000
Portrait de jeune femme Huile/toile (124x95cm
48x37in) Nice 2001

🔍 **$1 470** - €1 677 - **£1 026** - FF11 000
Les deux modèles Huile/toile (32x24cm 12x9in)
Paris 2001

CHABAUD Auguste 1882-1955 [460]

🔍 **$3 280** - €3 811 - **£2 305** - FF25 000
Homme assis Huile/papier/panneau (76x54cm
29x21in) Paris 2001

🔍 **$1 513** - €1 524 - **£943** - FF10 000
Fenêtre ouverte sur le jardin Huile/panneau
(17x12cm 6x4in) Calais 2000

🖊 **$707** - €656 - **£439** - FF4 300
Rue de village Aquarelle/papier (23.5x15cm 9x5in)
Arles 1999

CHABOT Hendrick 1894-1949 [18]

🔍 **$3 906** - €4 538 - **£2 745** - FF29 766
Selfportrait Oil/paper/panel (28x22cm 11x8in)
Amsterdam 2001

▥ **$493** - €544 - **£334** - FF3 571
Stal in Brabant Etching (24.5x35.5cm 9x13in)
Haarlem 2000

CHABRIER Gilles 1959 [6]

🔖 **$1 794** - €1 707 - **£1 115** - FF11 200
Déferlante Sculpture verre (51x23x19cm 20x9x7in)
Paris 1999

CHABROL Pierre 1920-1991 [76]

🔍 **$230** - €274 - **£164** - FF1 800
Arbres en hiver Huile/toile (60x60cm 23x23in)
Châtellerault 2000

🔍 **$140** - €168 - **£100** - FF1 100
Composition Gouache/papier (53x39cm 20x15in)
Châtellerault 2000

CHABRY Léonce 1832-1883 [18]

🔍 **$3 475** - €3 811 - **£2 360** - FF25 000
Paysage animé Huile/toile (94x123cm 37x48in)
Pontoise 2000

CHACÓN Sigfredo 1950 [6]

🖊 **$1 436** - €1 692 - **£1 009** - FF11 102
Act 1, Serie Pura Pintura Abstracta Collage
(170x170cm 66x66in) Caracas ($) 2000

CHADOURNE Georgette XX [31]

📷 **$297** - €259 - **£179** - FF1 700
Christian Bérard chez Boris Kochno Tirage argentique (17.8x23.7cm 7x9in) Saint-Germain-en-Laye 1998

CHADWICK Ernest Albert 1876-1955 [43]

🖊 **$1 491** - €1 443 - **£920** - FF9 468
Henley in Arden, Winter Watercolour/paper
(17.5x24.5cm 6x9in) West-Midlands 1999

CHADWICK Lynn 1914-1988 [489]

🔖 **$59 772** - €64 160 - **£40 000** - FF420 864
Second Girl Sitting on Bench Bronze (H96cm
H37in) London 2000

🔖 **$15 000** - €16 462 - **£9 658** - FF107 982
Maquette II Two Winged Figures Bronze
(26x13x11cm 10x5x4in) New-York 2000

🖊 **$994** - €1 067 - **£665** - FF7 000
Étude pour une sculpture Encre Chine (41x54cm
16x21in) Paris 2000

▥ **$151** - €180 - **£108** - FF1 184
Hommage à Picasso Farblithographie (77x56cm
30x22in) Hamburg 2000

CHADWICK Tom 1900-1950 [1]

🔍 **$23 847** - €28 427 - **£17 000** - FF186 469
The Proverbs Oil/canvas (102x127cm 40x50in)
London 2000

CHADWICK William 1879-1962 [33]

🔍 **$4 274** - €3 659 - **£2 572** - FF24 000
«Red roofs, Brandywine» Huile/toile (61x76cm
24x29in) Paris 1998

🔍 **$1 000** - €1 125 - **£688** - FF7 382
Early Autumn Oil/board (30x38cm 12x15in) Dedham
MA 2000

CHAFFANEL Eugène 1860-? [5]

🔍 **$1 768** - €1 982 - **£1 231** - FF13 000
Les joueurs de boules Huile/toile (64x80cm
25x31in) Paris 2001

CHAFFEE Oliver Newberry H.Jr 1881-1944 [25]

🖊 **$650** - €768 - **£460** - FF5 038
Autumn Watercolour (20x29cm 8x11in) Provincetown
MA 2000

CHAFFEE Samuel R. 1950-? [26]

🖊 **$400** - €345 - **£241** - FF2 266
River landscape Watercolour/paper (18x30cm
7x12in) Watertown MA 1998

CHAGALL Marc 1887-1985 [6530]

🔍 **$3 000 000** - €2 559 314 - **£1 809 600** -
FF16 788 000
Les trois cierges Oil/canvas (130x97.5cm 51x38in)
New-York 1998

C

$488 310 - €475 257 - **£300 000** - FF3 117 480
La promenade, personnages sur fond rouge et jaune Oil/canvas (81x65cm 31x25in) London 1999

$110 000 - €120 719 - **£70 829** - FF791 868
Peintre dans le Ciel du Village Mixed media (41.5x33cm 16x12in) New-York 2000

$19 425 - €20 852 - **£13 000** - FF136 780
Couple au coq Ceramic (27x23cm 10x9in) London 2000

$40 994 - €40 065 - **£26 000** - FF262 808
Le bouquet des amoureux Coloured pencils (42x32cm 16x12in) London 1999

$3 524 - €3 783 - **£2 359** - FF24 818
L'arbre vert aux amoureux Farblithographie (64.6x48cm 25x18in) Hamburg 2000

CHAGNIOT Alfred Jean 1905-1991 **[49]**

$1 254 - €1 098 - **£759** - FF7 200
L'église Saint-Vincent-de-Paul à Clichy Huile/iso-rel (54x65cm 21x25in) La Varenne-Saint-Hilaire 1998

CHAHINE Edgar 1874-1947 **[327]**

$1 622 - €1 558 - **£1 000** - FF10 218
Still Life Mixed media (66x51cm 25x20in) London 1999

$416 - €413 - **£260** - FF2 709
Louise France Etching (41x31cm 16x12in) London 1999

CHAHN SUTARAPONG 1938 **[9]**

$1 121 - €1 042 - **£693** - FF6 833
Strolling by the Canal Oil/canvas (49x60cm 19x23in) Bangkok 1999

CHAHNAZAR Kouyoumdjan 1897-1978 **[2]**

$1 550 - €1 647 - **£1 022** - FF10 802
Jardin du Luxembourg Oil/canvas (27x35cm 11x14in) Cleveland OH 2000

CHAIGNEAU Jean-Ferdinand 1830-1906 **[120]**

$30 681 - €28 660 - **£18 931** - FF188 000
Douceur de la vie pastorale Huile/toile (94.5x128cm 37x50in) Melun 1999

$9 928 - €8 600 - **£6 012** - FF57 002
Schafherde mit Schäfer bei Sonnenuntergang Öl/Leinwand (80x98cm 31x38in) Hildrizhausen 1998

$3 265 - €2 820 - **£1 972** - FF18 500
Bergères et leurs moutons près des arbres Huile/toile (27.5x35.5cm 10x13in) Barbizon 1998

$458 - €396 - **£277** - FF2 600
La rentrée du troupeau, le soir Pointe sèche (53x40.5cm 20x15in) Barbizon 1998

CHAIGNEAU Paul XIX-XX **[77]**

$5 103 - €5 793 - **£3 545** - FF38 000
Berger et ses moutons Huile/toile (46.5x55cm 18x21in) Barbizon 2001

$3 208 - €3 201 - **£2 003** - FF21 000
Berger et ses moutons Huile/panneau (22x27cm 8x10in) Fontainebleau 1999

CHAILLOUX Robert 1913 **[46]**

$1 307 - €1 195 - **£800** - FF7 838
Still Life with Bread, Grapes and a Wine Ewer Oil/canvas (55x45cm 22x18in) Oxford 1999

CHAISSAC Gaston 1910-1964 **[392]**

$23 328 - €27 441 - **£16 722** - FF180 000
Composition fond bleu nuit Huile/papier/toile (99x64cm 38x25in) Paris 2001

$2 204 - €2 592 - **£1 598** - FF17 000
Composition Peinture (30x30cm 11x11in) Vendôme 2001

$89 530 - €106 714 - **£63 840** - FF700 000
Totem Sculpture bois (135x29cm 53x11in) Lyon 2000

$3 146 - €3 583 - **£2 220** - FF23 500
Personnage jaune Crayons couleurs/papier (19x13cm 7x5in) Versailles 2001

$570 - €488 - **£342** - FF3 200
Personnages Lithographie (53.5x73cm 21x28in) Paris 1998

CHAIX Auguste 1860-1922 **[6]**

$1 326 - €1 143 - **£787** - FF7 500
Le lac à Évian-les-Bains Huile/toile (27x41cm 10x16in) Vernon 1998

CHAIX Louis c.1740-c.1811 **[11]**

$595 - €579 - **£366** - FF3 800
Ruine Romaine Pierre noire/papier (37x51cm 14x20in) Paris 1999

CHAIX Yves 1936 **[12]**

$900 - €872 - **£561** - FF5 718
«Navires au couchant» Oil/canvas (23x33cm 9x13in) Delray-Beach FL 1999

CHAKRABHAND POSAYAKRIT 1943 **[3]**

$122 400 - €131 643 - **£82 080** - FF863 520
The King's Mother Oil/canvas (112x85cm 44x33in) Bangkok 2000

$3 738 - €3 472 - **£2 310** - FF22 778
Mythological Tale Watercolour (28x37cm 11x14in) Bangkok 1999

CHAKRAVARTY Jayashree 1956 **[9]**

$730 - €702 - **£450** - FF4 605
Untitled Mixed media (36x48cm 14x18in) London 1999

$2 500 - €2 158 - **£1 493** - FF14 156
«Under the Red Sky» Tempera/paper (49x51.5cm 19x20in) New-York 1999

CHALAMBERT de Marie Alexandre 1838-c.1910 **[2]**

$2 670 - €2 564 - **£1 700** - FF16 818
St Martin and the Beggar Bronze (H78cm H30in) Billingshurst, West-Sussex 1999

CHALAND Yves 1957-1990 **[10]**

$1 344 - €1 487 - **£912** - FF9 756
Prince Riri, couverture de l'album Crayon/papier (19x19cm 7x7in) Bruxelles 2000

CHALDEJ Jewgeni 1916-1997 **[43]**

$688 - €665 - **£432** - FF4 360
Nürnberger Prozess Photograph (41x30cm 16x11in) München 1999

CHALEE Pop 1906-1993 **[5]**

$2 300 - €2 684 - **£1 623** - FF17 608
Untitled Tempera/paper (56x44.5cm 22x17in) New-York 2000

CHALERM NAKIRAKS 1917 **[10]**

$5 073 - €4 713 - **£3 135** - FF30 913
Songkran Festival Oil/canvas (60x74.5cm 23x29in) Bangkok 1999

$4 335 - €4 662 - **£2 907** - FF30 583
House by the River Oil/canvas (34x44cm 13x17in) Bangkok 2000

$2 269 - €2 108 - **£1 402** - FF13 829
Temple Among Trees Watercolour/paper (26x37cm 10x14in) Bangkok 1999

CHALERMCHAIT KOSITPIPAT 1955 **[8]**

$7 476 - €6 945 - **£4 620** - FF45 556
Released from Defilements Acrylic/canvas (60x60cm 23x23in) Bangkok 1999

$2 040 - €2 194 - **£1 368** - FF14 392
Stillness Under Golden Moonlight Pencil/paper (52x68cm 20x26in) Bangkok 2000

CHALEYÉ Jean 1878-1960 [35]
$1 000 - €1 073 - **£679** - FF7 040
Les femmes rentrant du jardin Oil/board (58x44cm 23x17in) Delray-Beach FL 2001

CHALFANT Jefferson David 1856-1931 [9]
$250 000 - €213 596 - **£150 075** - FF1 401 100
The Blacksmith Oil/canvas (65.5x85cm 25x33in) New-York 1998
$53 000 - €56 894 - **£36 108** - FF373 199
«In Hard Luck» Oil/copper (24.5x18.5cm 9x7in) Boston MA 2001
$3 800 - €4 191 - **£2 573** - FF27 489
Two Young Girls in a Decorated Interior Pencil/paper (48x39.5cm 18x15in) New-York 2000

CHALLE Charles Michel-Ange 1718-1778 [36]
$24 000 - €26 579 - **£16 276** - FF174 348
Diana Sleeping Oil/canvas (91x145.5cm 35x57in) New-York 2000
$1 060 - €991 - **£654** - FF6 500
Le Colisée Crayon (25x31.5cm 9x12in) Paris 1999

CHALLENER Frederick Sproston 1869-1959 [28]
$703 - €684 - **£440** - FF4 485
Corner of the Studio Oil/board (51x23cm 20x9in) Toronto 1999
$481 - €485 - **£301** - FF3 184
Laughing Eyes Coloured chalks/paper (51x37.5cm 20x14in) Toronto 2000

CHALLIÉ Jean Laurent 1880-1943 [26]
$3 266 - €3 659 - **£2 270** - FF24 000
Fenêtre ouverte sur la campagne Huile/toile (65x81cm 25x31in) Le Touquet 2001

CHALMERS George Paul 1833-1878 [24]
$2 526 - €2 647 - **£1 600** - FF17 364
The long Road Home Oil/canvas (40x55cm 15x21in) Edinburgh 2000
$2 850 - €2 436 - **£1 725** - FF15 977
A Young Girl Oil/panel (18x13.5cm 7x5in) Edinburgh 1998

CHALMERS George, Bt. c.1720-1791 [5]
$11 043 - €11 853 - **£7 500** - FF77 748
Sir John Knight of Jordanstone/His Wife Jean Hay of Ballindock Oil/canvas (126x101cm 49x39in) London 2001
$3 300 - €3 522 - **£2 200** - FF23 105
Colonel THomas Buck, Aide de Camp to the Duke of Cumberland Oil/canvas (76x64cm 29x25in) Leyburn, North Yorkshire 2000

CHALMERS Hector 1849-1943 [32]
$862 - €750 - **£520** - FF4 920
In Front of the Fire Oil/canvas (25.5x35.5cm 10x13in) Godalming, Surrey 1998

CHALON Alfred Edward 1780-1860 [74]
$376 - €406 - **£260** - FF2 665
Three quarter length portrait said to be Mrs.Whewell Miniature (17x13cm 6x5in) West-Midlands 2001
$1 000 - €840 - **£587** - FF5 509
Portrait of a Gentleman Said to be Carl Maria Von Weber Watercolour, gouache/paper (28.5x20.5cm 11x8in) New-York 1998

CHALON Henry Bernard 1771-1849 [53]
$11 227 - €11 106 - **£7 000** - FF72 850
«Sir David» Held by a Groom with Another Figure on a Pony Oil/canvas (86x114.5cm 33x45in) London 1999

$1 680 - €1 954 - **£1 200** - FF12 818
Pointers in a wooded Landscape Oil/canvas (23x40.5cm 9x15in) London 2001

CHALON Louis 1687-1741 [11]
$26 097 - €24 409 - **£16 000** - FF160 112
Dutch Men-O-War Off the Coast, with Fisherfolk Unloading their Catch Oil/panel (41x69.5cm 16x27in) London 1998
$2 850 - €3 237 - **£2 000** - FF21 235
A Rhenish River Landscape with Peasants loading a Barge Oil/panel (29.5x41cm 11x16in) London 2001

CHALON Louis 1866-? [29]
$18 000 - €21 344 - **£12 384** - FF140 009
Walkyrie Bronze (H96.5cm H37in) New-York 2000
$6 005 - €6 267 - **£3 800** - FF41 112
Sea Maidens Vase Bronze (H43.5cm H17in) London 2000

CHALOOD NIMSAMER 1929 [10]
$2 295 - €2 468 - **£1 539** - FF16 191
Religious Revelations of a Woman Watercolour/paper (76x52cm 29x20in) Bangkok 2000
$1 602 - €1 488 - **£990** - FF9 762
Barges Woodcut (44x52cm 17x20in) Bangkok 1999

CHALUREAU-PERRIN Madeleine XIX-XX [5]
$2 668 - €2 439 - **£1 633** - FF16 000
Portrait de Marocaine Pastel/papier (54x45cm 21x17in) Paris 1999

CHAMAILLARD de Ernest Ponthier 1862-1930 [49]
$2 448 - €2 287 - **£1 479** - FF15 000
Village breton Huile/toile (73x60cm 28x23in) Paris 1999
$615 - €671 - **£403** - FF4 400
Le château de Clisson Huile/toile (21x14cm 8x5in) Brest 2000

CHAMBAS Jean-Paul 1947 [69]
$1 339 - €1 524 - **£945** - FF10 000
«Dimanche dans un gymnase les majorettes» Pastel (150x225cm 59x88in) Versailles 2001

CHAMBAZ Marius André 1905-1988 [21]
$502 - €542 - **£337** - FF3 558
Soir sur le canal, Chioggia Huile/panneau (27x35cm 10x13in) Genève 2000

CHAMBERLAIN John 1927 [165]
$10 918 - €9 314 - **£6 507** - FF61 099
Untitled Collage/panel (30.5x30.5x7.6cm 12x12x2in) Zürich 1998
$75 000 - €84 844 - **£52 470** - FF556 537
Untitled Metal (152.5x61x53.5cm 60x24x21in) New-York 2001
$22 000 - €25 526 - **£15 188** - FF167 442
Untitled Sculpture (39.5x58.5x58.5cm 15x23x23in) New-York 2000
$3 500 - €4 080 - **£2 423** - FF26 762
Eau Awe Monotype (208.5x74cm 82x29in) New-York 2000

CHAMBERLAIN Norman Stiles 1887-1961 [7]
$5 000 - €5 400 - **£3 455** - FF35 419
Horses in atmospheric Landscape Watercolour/paper (50x60cm 20x24in) Altadena CA 2001

CHAMBERLAIN Samuel 1895-1975 [48]
$210 - €242 - **£145** - FF1 588
«The Château-Vitre» Lithograph (28x40cm 11x16in) Cleveland OH 2000

C

CHAMBERLIN Frank Tolles 1873-1961 **[8]**
🖌 **$2 000** - €2 241 - **£1 394** - FF14 701
  Late Afternoon Watercolour/paper (32.5x45.5cm
  12x17in) Beverly-Hills CA 2001

CHAMBERLIN Mason 1727-1787 **[5]**
😊 **$36 491** - €31 737 - **£22 000** - FF208 183
  Portrait of Francis Popham Oil/canvas (157x122cm
  61x48in) London 1998

CHAMBERS Charles Edward 1883-1941 **[23]**
😊 **$7 000** - €7 840 - **£4 863** - FF51 430
  Honeymoon Couple traveling under a full Moon
  Oil/canvas (53x119cm 21x47in) New-York 2001
📮 **$1 100** - €1 283 - **£772** - FF8 415
  «Grow White Corn, for Extra Profits» Poster
  (53.5x81cm 21x31in) New-York 2000

CHAMBERS George I 1803-1840 **[43]**
😊 **$22 666** - €21 312 - **£14 035** - FF139 797
  Ostend Pier Oil/canvas (111x140.5cm 43x55in)
  Melbourne 1999
😊 **$15 000** - €15 115 - **£9 351** - FF99 150
  Shipping Off Tynemouth Oil/canvas (83x122cm
  32x48in) New-York 2000
😊 **$4 231** - €4 939 - **£3 000** - FF32 397
  Drawing in the Net/Luggers off a jetty Oil/board
  (20x30cm 7x11in) London 2001
🖌 **$1 222** - €1 194 - **£780** - FF7 834
  Hulks moored in an Estuary Watercolour
  (20.5x29.5cm 8x11in) London 1999

CHAMBERS George II 1829-c.1874 **[38]**
😊 **$4 634** - €5 378 - **£3 200** - FF35 277
  Shipping at Anchor off the Boatyard Oil/canvas
  (46x61cm 18x24in) London 2000
😊 **$3 121** - €3 114 - **£1 900** - FF20 429
  **Fishing Boats off the Coast/Ship in Distress in
  a Storm off a Coast** Oil/canvas (25.5x35.5cm
  10x13in) London 2001
🖌 **$1 416** - €1 304 - **£850** - FF8 553
  Swansea from the Black Pill Watercolour (23x32cm
  9x12in) Glamorgan 1999

CHAMBERS George W. 1857-1897 **[6]**
😊 **$600** - €705 - **£416** - FF4 625
  Winter Oil/canvas/board (21x50cm 8x20in) Cincinnati
  OH 2000

CHAMBERS John Richard (Jack) 1931-1978 **[6]**
📮 **$884** - €845 - **£554** - FF5 546
  Figs Silkscreen in colors (49x49cm 19x19in) Toronto
  1999

CHAMBERS Thomas 1808-1866 **[17]**
😊 **$25 000** - €21 418 - **£15 030** - FF140 492
  Nex York Harbor with Castle Garden Oil/canvas
  (45x60cm 18x24in) Cleveland OH 1998
😊 **$1 643** - €1 500 - **£1 000** - FF9 842
  Mending the Nets Oil/canvas (30.5x40.5cm 12x15in)
  London 1998

CHAMBERT Erik 1902-1988 **[13]**
🖼 **$5 080** - €5 692 - **£3 541** - FF37 336
  Gaskamrar Relief (31.5x31.5x7.5cm 12x12x2in)
  Stockholm 2001
🖌 **$2 060** - €2 307 - **£1 432** - FF15 136
  Komposition I Gouache/paper (45x37cm 17x14in)
  Stockholm 2001

CHAMBI Martín 1891-1973 **[14]**
📷 **$650** - €741 - **£449** - FF4 860
  Man Playing a Traditional Horn, Cuzco, Peru
  Silver print (38x25cm 15x10in) New-York 2000

CHAMBON Émile François 1905-1993 **[36]**
😊 **$783** - €919 - **£558** - FF6 025
  Bord de Rhône à Genève Huile/panneau (17x25cm
  6x9in) Genève 2000

CHAMPAGNE Horace 1937 **[107]**
🖌 **$800** - €731 - **£489** - FF4 795
  Little Messanger Pastel/paper (53x73.5cm 20x28in)
  Boston MA 1999

CHAMPAIGNE de Jean-Baptiste 1631-1681 **[10]**
😊 **$5 379** - €5 336 - **£3 346** - FF35 000
  Portrait de Philippe de Champaigne Sanguine
  (38.5x27.5cm 15x10in) Paris 1999

CHAMPAIGNE de Philippe 1602-1674 **[29]**
😊 **$240 000** - €242 793 - **£146 544** - FF1 592 616
  Adam and Eve lamenting the Death of Abel
  Oil/canvas (97x132cm 38x51in) New-York 2000
😊 **$191 700** - €223 094 - **£135 000** - FF1 463 400
  Saint Jérôme Huile/toile (94x120.5cm 37x47in) Liège
  2001
🖌 **$81 885** - €76 072 - **£50 000** - FF499 000
  View of the City of Jerusalem Red chalk/paper
  (33x60cm 12x23in) London 1998

CHAMPEAUX DE LA BOULAYE de Octave 1827-1903 **[14]**
😊 **$2 857** - €2 515 - **£1 740** - FF16 500
  Enfants au parc Monceau en automne Huile/toile
  (62x50cm 24x19in) Vernon 1999

CHAMPEIL Jean-Baptiste 1866-1913 **[1]**
🗿 **$7 574** - €8 662 - **£5 200** - FF56 816
  Semi-Nude Standing Woman Marble (H73.5cm
  H28in) London 2000

CHAMPILLOU Jeanne 1897-1978 **[50]**
📮 **$67** - €76 - **£46** - FF500
  Ma mère reprisant Pointe sèche (18x13cm 7x5in)
  Orléans 2001

CHAMPIN Jean-Jacques 1796-1860 **[22]**
🖌 **$315** - €335 - **£199** - FF2 200
  Vues du jardin du Clos Saint-Marcel à Sceaux
  Pierre noire (23.5x31cm 9x12in) Paris 2000

CHAMPION DE CRESPIGNY Rose XIX-XX **[10]**
🖌 **$176** - €178 - **£110** - FF1 166
  Moored Boats at Dusk Watercolour (12x22.5cm
  4x8in) London 2000

CHAMPION Theo 1887-1952 **[75]**
😊 **$3 029** - €3 323 - **£2 057** - FF21 800
  Am Niederrhein Öl/Karton (40x50cm 15x19in)
  Düsseldorf 2000
😊 **$1 928** - €1 943 - **£1 201** - FF12 744
  Baum in winterlicher Landschaft Öl/Karton
  (38x23.5cm 14x9in) Düsseldorf 2000

CHAMPNEY Benjamin 1817-1907 **[68]**
😊 **$4 000** - €3 747 - **£2 459** - FF24 576
  Children at the Edge of the Forest Oil/canvas
  (40.5x61cm 15x24in) New-York 1999
😊 **$3 750** - €4 133 - **£2 494** - FF27 110
  Diana's Bath Oil/canvas (25x37cm 10x14in)
  Portsmouth NH 2000

CHAMPNEY James Wells 1843-1903 **[37]**
😊 **$38 000** - €37 728 - **£23 750** - FF247 478
  The lesson Oil/canvas (46.5x56cm 18x22in) New-
  York 1999
😊 **$2 800** - €3 006 - **£1 907** - FF19 716
  A Sunlit kitchen Oil/canvas (25.5x33cm 10x12in)
  Boston MA 2001

$2 160 - €2 536 - **£1 524** - FF16 634
Porträtt av Madame Pompadour efter Boucher
Pastel/paper (64x55cm 25x21in) Stockholm 2000

CHAMPSEIX E. Paul XX **[64]**
$232 - €259 - **£156** - FF1 700
«Sncf, Châteaux de la Loire, Cheverny» Affiche
(98.5x62cm 38x24in) Orléans 2000

CHAMRUANG VICHIENKET 1931 **[2]**
$1 785 - €1 920 - **£1 197** - FF12 593
Playing Golf Bronze (47x18x97cm 18x7x38in)
Bangkok 2000

CHAN ASOMSATTANA 1944 **[3]**
$22 695 - €21 083 - **£14 025** - FF138 295
Lazy Hills Oil/canvas (80x100cm 31x39in) Bangkok
1999

CHANCO Roland 1914 **[1167]**
$861 - €930 - **£595** - FF6 100
La nappe rouge Huile/toile (97x130cm 38x51in)
Paris 2001
$639 - €549 - **£386** - FF3 600
Trois chaises Huile/toile (92x73cm 36x28in) Paris
1998
$142 - €122 - **£85** - FF800
Simone et son chat Pastel/papier (65x50cm 25x19in)
Paris 1998

CHANCRIN René 1911-1981 **[23]**
$1 580 - €1 448 - **£965** - FF9 500
Nature morte au maïs Huile/toile (65x54cm
25x21in) Lyon 1999

CHANDLER Joseph Goodhue 1813-1884 **[12]**
$25 000 - €28 782 - **£17 060** - FF188 800
**Little Boy with Walking Stick & a Little Girl with
a Basket of Flowers** Oil/canvas (114x89cm 44x35in)
New-York 2000

CHANDRA Avinash 1931-1991 **[14]**
$14 885 - €13 923 - **£9 000** - FF91 328
Seven Moons Oil/board (121x183cm 47x72in)
London 1999
$2 646 - €2 475 - **£1 600** - FF16 236
Landscape Oil/canvas (81.5x100.5cm 32x39in)
London 1999
$1 344 - €1 444 - **£900** - FF9 469
Untitled Oil (45x32.5cm 17x12in) London 2000

CHANET Henri 1840-? **[1]**
$3 864 - €4 269 - **£2 679** - FF28 000
Le départ pour la chasse à courre Huile/toile
(38.5x56cm 15x22in) Lille 2001

CHANG FEE MING 1959 **[7]**
$13 773 - €15 640 - **£9 427** - FF102 590
Wind Song Watercolour/paper (55x76cm 21x29in)
Singapore 2000

CHANG JIN 1951 **[2]**
$1 155 - €1 262 - **£743** - FF8 277
Lakeside Scenery Ink (45.5x69cm 17x27in) Hong-
Kong 2000

CHANG SEATANG 1934-1990 **[3]**
$2 403 - €2 232 - **£1 485** - FF14 643
The Garden Path Watercolour/paper (38x53cm
14x20in) Bangkok 1999

CHANOU Jean-Baptiste 1779-1825 **[1]**
$9 411 - €9 189 - **£6 000** - FF60 276
Reclining Lions Terracotta (21.5x22cm 8x8in)
London 1999

CHANTERAC de François XIX-XX **[3]**
$2 196 - €2 058 - **£1 320** - FF13 500
Le port de Larmor Huile/toile (26x52.5cm 10x20in)
Paris 1999

CHANTEREAU Jérôme François 1710-1757 **[10]**
$1 036 - €1 120 - **£728** - FF8 000
**Femme au chapeau en buste, tournée vers la
gauche** Pierre noire (19x15.5cm 7x6in) Paris 2000

CHANTEREINE de Camille ?-1847 **[5]**
$1 796 - €1 586 - **£1 082** - FF10 401
Bouquet of Flowers with Peonies and Lilas
Watercolour/paper (34x24.5cm 13x9in) Amsterdam
1998

CHANTRELL Tom William XX **[4]**
$331 - €305 - **£198** - FF2 000
«Star Wars» Affiche (100x200cm 39x78in) Paris 1999

CHANTREY Francis Leggatt 1781-1842 **[10]**
$6 025 - €6 638 - **£4 000** - FF43 544
Seated Half Length Portrait of Chantrey Oil/can-
vas (81x101cm 32x40in) Grantham, Lincolnshire 2000
$9 498 - €9 147 - **£5 898** - FF60 000
**Francis Ingram Seymour-Conway, second
Marquis de Hertford (1743-1822)** Marble (H73cm
H28in) Paris 1999

CHANTRON Alexandre Jacques 1842-1918 **[16]**
$4 500 - €3 901 - **£2 749** - FF25 590
Still Life with Flowers Oil/canvas (44.5x54.5cm
17x21in) New-York 1999

CHAPELAIN-MIDY Roger 1904-1992 **[195]**
$2 176 - €2 439 - **£1 476** - FF16 000
La bicyclette Huile/toile (60x73cm 23x28in) Paris
2000
$1 271 - €1 448 - **£873** - FF9 500
Voiliers échoués Huile/toile (27x46cm 10x18in) Paris
2000
$887 - €991 - **£601** - FF6 500
Fortificataire au bord de mer Gouache/papier
(29.5x25.5cm 11x10in) Pontoise 2000

CHAPELET Roger 1902-1995 **[98]**
$897 - €1 067 - **£618** - FF7 000
Louis XIV et Colbert sur le pont d'un vaisseau
Huile/toile (116x90cm 45x35in) Paris 2000
$2 425 - €2 592 - **£1 654** - FF17 000
**Quatre-mâts barque par vent arrière au soleil
levant** Gouache/papier (44x38cm 17x14in) Paris 2001
$240 - €274 - **£165** - FF1 800
**«Cie de navigation mixte, l'Algérie, la Tunisie,
les Iles Baléares»** Affiche (96x60.5cm 37x23in) Paris
2000

CHAPELLIER Philippe XIX-XX **[28]**
$702 - €701 - **£438** - FF4 600
«Phare Alpha B.R.C» Affiche (160x120cm 62x47in)
Orléans 1999

CHAPERON Philippe-Marie 1823-1907 **[8]**
$562 - €640 - **£390** - FF4 200
Rue à Montigny-sur-Loing Lavis (21.5x25.5cm
8x10in) Fontainebleau 2000

CHAPI 1911-1949 **[1]**
$2 441 - €2 240 - **£1 500** - FF14 695
Cat People/La Mujet Pantera Poster (101.5x68.5cm
39x26in) London 1999

CHAPIN Bryant 1859-1927 **[39]**
$4 000 - €3 847 - **£2 468** - FF25 232
Still life Over Turned Bag of Raspberries Oil/can-
vas (38x61cm 15x24in) North-Harwich MA 1999

C

$1 800 – €1 704 – £1 120 – FF11 177
Still Life with Grapes, Peach and Plum Oil/canvas/board (21x26cm 8x10in) Detroit MI 1999

CHAPIN Deborah 1954 [1]
$4 106 – €4 602 – £2 830 – FF30 185
French Kiss Öl/Leinwand (9.5x13cm 3x5in) Hamburg 2000

CHAPIN Francis 1899-1965 [27]
$1 200 – €1 111 – £734 – FF7 287
View of Ansel Adams' Studio at North and Wells, Chicago Oil/canvas (40x50cm 16x20in) Chicago IL 1999
$1 500 – €1 740 – £1 067 – FF11 414
Ships at Portland Oil/board (26x44cm 10x17in) Chicago IL 2000
$300 – €284 – £182 – FF1 863
Boating Scene Watercolour (42.5x77.5cm 16x30in) New-York 1999

CHAPIN Sarah XIX [1]
$1 800 – €1 709 – £1 090 – FF11 208
Map of Kennebec County Watercolour (18x25cm 7x10in) New-York 2001

CHAPIRO Jacques 1887-1972 [351]
$1 093 – €1 037 – £665 – FF6 800
L'avenir du Monde Huile/toile (95x200cm 37x78in) L'Isle-Adam 1999
$605 – €610 – £377 – FF4 000
Paris, la Seine Huile/toile (81x116cm 31x45in) L'Isle-Adam 2000
$321 – €305 – £195 – FF2 000
Notre-Dame et la Seine Huile/carton (33x13cm 12x5in) L'Isle-Adam 1999
$336 – €396 – £236 – FF2 600
Port de Marseille Gouache/papier (38.5x52.5cm 15x20in) Garches 2000

CHAPLET Ernest 1835-1909 [37]
$832 – €762 – £507 – FF5 000
Vase à corps ovoïde et col droit Grès (H23.5cm H9in) Paris 1999

CHAPLIN Arthur 1869-? [14]
$1 200 – €1 418 – £850 – FF9 301
Floral Still Life in Archway Oil/canvas/board (40x87cm 16x34in) Austinburg OH 2000

CHAPLIN Charles Josua 1825-1891 [187]
$11 000 – €12 156 – £7 628 – FF79 735
Young Lady and sleeping Cat Oil/canvas (72x49cm 28x19in) New-Orleans LA 2001
$2 608 – €3 049 – £1 832 – FF20 000
Musicienne au King Charles Huile/toile (47x27cm 18x10in) Paris 2000
$675 – €762 – £470 – FF5 000
Femme au déshabillé vert Aquarelle (34.5x31cm 13x12in) Bayeux 2001

CHAPLIN Elisabeth 1890-1982 [41]
$880 – €1 140 – £660 – FF7 480
Fienile Olio/cartone (39x46cm 15x18in) Prato 2001

CHAPLIN Prescott 1897-1968 [3]
$550 – €590 – £368 – FF3 872
Peons Print in colors (42x55cm 16x22in) Altadena CA 2000

CHAPMAN Carlton Theodore 1860-1925 [38]
$750 – €887 – £531 – FF5 816
Battle at Sea Oil/canvas (35.5x51cm 13x20in) Boston MA 2000

CHAPMAN Charles Shepard 1879-1962 [22]
$7 500 – €6 496 – £4 599 – FF42 611
Ada the Vanity Oil/canvas (101.5x76cm 39x29in) New-York 1999
$250 – €227 – £153 – FF1 486
Western Landscape Oil/board (30x40cm 12x16in) Mystic CT 1999

CHAPMAN Conrad Wise 1842-1910 [54]
$182 240 – €202 096 – £121 210 – FF1 325 660
México desde la Hacienda de los Morales Oleo/lienzo (41x89cm 16x35in) México 2000
$22 500 – €21 838 – £14 008 – FF143 248
Valle de México Oil/panel (14x22cm 5x8in) New-York 1999

CHAPMAN Dinos & Jake 1962/1966 [25]
$17 745 – €19 818 – £12 025 – FF130 000
Cockroach Kid Sculpture verre (104x60x59cm 40x23x23in) Paris 2000
$5 523 – €5 344 – £3 500 – FF35 057
«Bring me the Head of...» Sculpture (25x33x18cm 9x12x7in) London 1999
$27 894 – €32 803 – £20 000 – FF215 000
Two Faced Cunt Pencil (168x135cm 66x53in) London 2001
$865 – €956 – £600 – FF6 271
All our Ideas for the next twenty Years Print (122x100cm 48x39in) London 2001
$3 139 – €3 506 – £2 127 – FF23 000
Wedding Ring Photo couleurs (33x47cm 13x18in) Paris 2000

CHAPMAN Dora Cecil 1911-1995 [10]
$247 – €289 – £172 – FF1 893
«The Girl with a Long Nose II» Serigraph in colors (38x28cm 14x11in) Melbourne 2000

CHAPMAN George 1908-1994 [20]
$1 030 – €1 154 – £720 – FF7 571
Up the Hill Oil/canvas (49.5x100cm 19x39in) Billingshurst, West-Sussex 2001

CHAPMAN George R. act.1863-1874 [2]
$8 652 – €9 561 – £6 000 – FF62 718
«Miss Ethel Mackenzie» Oil/canvas (117x122cm 46x48in) London 2001

CHAPMAN John Watkins c.1853-1903 [12]
$25 705 – €24 753 – £16 000 – FF162 368
The Old Curiosity Shop Oil/canvas (63.5x92cm 25x36in) London 1999

CHAPMAN Minerva Josephine 1858-1947 [21]
$1 065 – €1 074 – £664 – FF7 043
Figurale Strandszene Oil/panel (15x21cm 5x8in) Radolfzell 2000

CHAPMAN W.J. XIX [4]
$8 590 – €8 075 – £5 200 – FF52 971
Two prize Shorthorn Cows Oil/canvas (60x73cm 23x28in) London 1999

CHAPONNIER Alexandre 1753-1806 [12]
$250 – €280 – £174 – FF1 838
Prélude de Nina, after Boilly Engraving (51.5x39cm 20x15in) New-York 2001

CHAPOVAL Youla, Jules 1919-1951 [138]
$9 350 – €10 443 – £6 336 – FF68 500
Composition Huile/toile (114x146cm 44x57in) Versailles 2000
$2 880 – €3 732 – £2 160 – FF24 480
Peinture Olio/tela (73x60cm 28x23in) Torino 2000
$1 571 – €1 296 – £925 – FF8 500
Composition Huile/carton (23x50cm 9x19in) Paris 1998

🖋 **$566** - €549 - **£356** - FF3 600
Composition Pastel (35x23cm 13x9in) Paris 1999

CHAPPE Jean c.1660 [2]
🐾 **$4 034** - €4 331 - **£2 700** - FF28 408
Spaniel on an embroidered Red Cushion
Oil/canvas (38x46cm 14x18in) London 2000

CHAPPEL Alonzo 1828-1887 [5]
🐾 **$13 000** - €12 122 - **£8 063** - FF79 514
Captain John Smith Being Rescued by Pocahantas Oil/canvas (33x25.5cm 12x10in) New-York 1999

CHAPPEL Edward 1859-1944 [74]
🐾 **$444** - €496 - **£300** - FF3 251
La rivière Oil/canvas (68x86cm 27x34in) Aylsham, Norfolk 2000
🐾 **$640** - €533 - **£376** - FF3 495
Head of a Sheep, a Study Oil/canvas (28x41cm 11x16in) Amsterdam 1998

CHAPPELL OF POOLE Reuben 1870-1940 [67]
🐾 **$3 760** - €4 176 - **£2 500** - FF27 360
Gale off Bass Rock, Nothumberland Oil/canvas (53.5x87.5cm 21x34in) London 2000
🐾 **$1 064** - €998 - **£657** - FF6 548
«The M.S Oceaan of Groningen under Full Sail» Watercolour (36x53cm 14x20in) Amsterdam 1999

CHAPPELL Walter 1925-2000 [8]
📷 **$7 000** - €7 951 - **£4 911** - FF52 152
Waterlilies Gelatin silver print (19x24cm 7x9in) New-York 2000

CHAPPUIS Alberto XIX-XX [4]
🎨 **$2 800** - €2 650 - **£1 739** - FF17 386
«Liquore Strega» Poster (139x101cm 54x39in) New-York 1999

CHAPU Henri 1833-1891 [89]
🐾 **$9 045** - €8 374 - **£5 535** - FF54 930
Kvinna hållande bok och penna i friskulptur Bronze (125x79cm 49x31in) Uppsala 1999
🐾 **$1 177** - €1 131 - **£720** - FF7 420
Joan of Arc Bronze (H31cm H12in) Bristol, Avon 1999

CHAPUIS Pierre 1863-1942 [47]
🖋 **$211** - €198 - **£128** - FF1 300
Le port de la Trinité sur Mer Encre (17x20cm 6x7in) Rennes 1999

CHAPUROT Aristide XIX [1]
🖋 **$1 597** - €1 789 - **£1 100** - FF11 738
Hamburger Brigg Apollo vor französischer Mittelmeerküste Watercolour (38x62cm 14x24in) Hamburg 2000

CHAPUY Nicolas Marie Joseph 1790-1858 [12]
🎨 **$651** - €593 - **£400** - FF3 890
Genova veduta generale presa dal camino di San Rocco Lithograph (29x40cm 11x15in) London 1999

CHARAIRE XX [2]
🎨 **$452** - €534 - **£318** - FF3 500
«Le Petit Journal aux Gloires du Sport» Affiche (15x10cm 5x3in) Paris 1999

CHARASSE Jean 1941 [11]
🖋 **$297** - €305 - **£183** - FF2 000
Composition Pastel gras (40x26cm 15x10in) Paris 2000

CHARAVEL Paul 1877-1961 [84]
🐾 **$730** - €640 - **£443** - FF4 200
Bouquet de fleurs au vase vert Huile/panneau (81x60cm 31x23in) Paris 1999
🐾 **$415** - €406 - **£255** - FF2 666
Küstenlandschaft Huile/panneau (18.5x20cm 7x7in) Zürich 1999

CHARBONNEAU Georges XIX-XX [2]
🐾 **$3 129** - €3 659 - **£2 234** - FF24 000
Arabe, marchande d'oranges Huile/toile (64x47cm 25x18in) Angers 2001

CHARBONNET Marie Nathalie Loew 1845-1924 [1]
🐾 **$7 000** - €7 335 - **£4 433** - FF48 115
Lake Pontchartrain Shoreline with Fishing Camps, Live Oaks Oil/canvas (48x63cm 19x25in) New-Orleans LA 2000

CHARBONNIER Pierre 1897-1978 [19]
🐾 **$704** - €808 - **£481** - FF5 300
Nature morte Huile/panneau (27x32cm 10x12in) Paris 2000

CHARCHOUNE Serge 1888-1975 [510]
🐾 **$9 641** - €8 385 - **£5 813** - FF55 000
L'Abysse Huile/toile (130x195cm 51x76in) Paris 1998
🐾 **$4 460** - €3 811 - **£2 677** - FF25 000
Greig Huile/toile (52x73cm 20x28in) Paris 1998
🐾 **$1 806** - €1 724 - **£1 129** - FF11 311
Untitled Oil/canvas/board (10.5x42.5cm 4x16in) Amsterdam 1999
🖋 **$621** - €686 - **£430** - FF4 500
Composition Crayons couleurs/papier (22x14cm 8x5in) Paris 2001

CHARDERON Francine 1861-1928 [6]
🐾 **$4 191** - €4 573 - **£2 844** - FF30 000
Fillette tenant une poupée dans les bras Huile/toile (105.5x70.5cm 41x27in) Paris 2000
🖋 **$2 904** - €3 201 - **£1 932** - FF21 000
L'Innocence Pastel/papier (80x53cm 31x20in) Biarritz 2000

CHARDIET José 1956 [6]
🐾 **$3 500** - €3 749 - **£2 390** - FF24 593
«Building B-20» Sculpture, glass (H19cm H7in) Cleveland OH 2001

CHARDIGNY Jules ?-1892 [4]
🐾 **$2 755** - €2 897 - **£1 729** - FF19 000
Tête de chien Huile/panneau (22x15.5cm 8x6in) Paris 2000

CHARDIN Jean-Baptiste Siméon 1699-1779 [20]
🐾 **$104 601** - €112 281 - **£70 000** - FF736 512
Copper Cauldron, a Pestle Mortar, a Stoneware Jug, Eggs and an Onion Oil/canvas (37.5x47cm 14x18in) London 2000
🐾 **$800 000** - €877 716 - **£531 440** - FF5 757 440
Leeks, a Casserole with a Cloth, a Copper Pot and Cover, and Onion Oil/canvas (32x39.5cm 12x15in) New-York 2000
🖋 **$5 660** - €6 567 - **£3 908** - FF43 078
Le dessinateur Indian ink (13.5x15cm 5x5in) Luzern 2000

CHAREAU Pierre 1883-1950 [6]
🐾 **$21 086** - €20 328 - **£13 000** - FF133 342
Jardinière Iron (H96.5cm H37in) London 1999
🐾 **$25 096** - €22 814 - **£15 399** - FF149 650
Paire d'appliques Métal (39x20.5cm 15x8in) Paris 1999

C

CHARGESHEIMER Carl-Heinz Hargesh. 1924-1972 [47]

📷 **$958** – €818 – **£578** – FF5 365
Ohne Titel Vintage gelatin silver print (31.3x49.4cm 12x19in) Köln 1998

CHARIGNY André 1902 [67]

〜 **$3 003** – €2 668 – **£1 839** – FF17 500
Bouquet rouge et blanc Huile/toile (61x50cm 24x19in) Besançon 1999

〜 **$759** – €854 – **£533** – FF5 600
Nature morte aux tomates Huile/carton (22x27cm 8x10in) Belfort 2001

CHARLAMOFF Alexei Alexeivich 1842/49-1915/22 [131]

〜 **$250 000** – €279 191 – **£160 100** – FF1 831 375
The Flower Girls Oil/canvas (122x165cm 48x64in) New-York 2000

〜 **$18 589** – €22 105 – **£13 253** – FF145 000
Jeune femme à la robe rose Huile/toile (73x54cm 28x21in) Paris 2000

〜 **$2 100** – €2 413 – **£1 454** – FF15 831
Portrait af en ung pige med et sort törklaede om hovedet Oil/canvas (28x22cm 11x8in) Köbenhavn 2000

✎ **$11 344** – €10 572 – **£7 000** – FF69 347
A young Girl knitting Watercolour/paper (45.5x30.5cm 17x12in) London 1999

CHARLE-LUCAS E. XIX [15]

🎞 **$1 000** – €962 – **£617** – FF6 308
«Peugeot Cycles» Poster (139.5x108.5cm 54x42in) New-York 1999

CHARLEMAGNE XX [2]

🎞 **$1 154** – €1 278 – **£800** – FF8 380
«Megève» Poster (100x62cm 39x24in) London 2001

CHARLEMAGNE Iosif Adolfovich 1782-1861 [7]

✎ **$1 671** – €1 621 – **£1 029** – FF10 670
Preussisk officer vid Cardes de Corps Akvarell/papper (34x29cm 13x11in) Stockholm 1999

CHARLEMONT Eduard 1848-1906 [22]

〜 **$7 000** – €6 046 – **£4 219** – FF39 659
A Welcome Refreshment Oil/panel (51x39.5cm 20x15in) New-York 1998

〜 **$4 195** – €4 029 – **£2 600** – FF26 428
A Cup of Tea Oil/panel (40x30cm 15x11in) London 1999

CHARLEMONT Hugo 1850-1939 [92]

〜 **$2 031** – €2 180 – **£1 359** – FF14 301
Abendstimmung Öl/Leinwand (73x100cm 28x39in) Wien 2000

〜 **$5 000** – €4 677 – **£3 023** – FF30 678
Floral Still Life before a Print of Botticelli's Birth of Venus Oil/panel (40x34cm 15x13in) New-York 1999

CHARLES Hervé 1965 [2]

📷 **$3 550** – €3 811 – **£2 375** – FF25 000
Etna 1503 Photo couleur (153x152cm 60x59in) Paris 2000

CHARLES James 1851-1906 [47]

〜 **$6 074** – €6 021 – **£3 800** – FF39 497
Village Scene Oil/canvas (71x93.5cm 27x36in) London 2000

〜 **$1 738** – €2 017 – **£1 300** – FF13 228
Fisherman on the Shore with a Town Beyond Oil/canvas (25.5x19cm 10x7in) London 2000

CHARLES Sheila 1919 [4]

〜 **$3 059** – €2 832 – **£1 900** – FF18 575
The feathered Hat Oil/canvas (56x46cm 22x18in) London 1999

CHARLES William ?-1820 [7]

🎞 **$1 200** – €1 276 – **£758** – FF8 372
Johnny Bull and the Alexandrians Etching, aquatint (20x30cm 8x12in) New-York 2000

CHARLESWORTH Rod 1955 [30]

〜 **$603** – €665 – **£398** – FF4 363
Sky of Many Colours (BC Interior) Oil/board (45.75x61cm 17x24in) Vancouver, BC. 2000

〜 **$293** – €329 – **£203** – FF2 156
Distant Strait, West Coast Oil/board (20x25cm 8x10in) Calgary, Alberta 2001

CHARLESWORTH Sarah 1947 [14]

📷 **$4 250** – €4 808 – **£2 973** – FF31 578
Sphinx Cibachrome print (104x78.5cm 40x30in) New-York 2001

CHARLET Emile 1851-? [12]

〜 **$739** – €793 – **£496** – FF5 203
Jeune femme de profil Huile/toile (64.5x45.5cm 25x17in) Bruxelles 2000

CHARLET Frantz 1862-1928 [85]

〜 **$8 398** – €9 420 – **£5 852** – FF61 788
Le cake-walk Huile/toile (70x90cm 27x35in) Bruxelles 2001

〜 **$1 913** – €2 134 – **£1 286** – FF14 000
Scène d'Afrique du Nord Huile/panneau (17x26cm 6x10in) Versailles 2000

✎ **$2 500** – €2 917 – **£1 561** – FF15 545
Fisherman's Family Watercolour (51x66cm 20x25in) Chicago IL 1999

🎞 **$276** – €297 – **£190** – FF1 951
Trois enfants jouant dans un intérieur Eau-forte couleurs (50x60cm 19x23in) Bruxelles 2001

CHARLET Nicolas Toussaint 1792-1845 [108]

〜 **$1 942** – €2 287 – **£1 365** – FF15 000
Le départ de la Troupe Huile/toile (46x55.5cm 18x21in) Toulouse 2000

✎ **$497** – €534 – **£332** – FF3 500
Caporal de Grenadier de la Garde sous les armes devant l'Empereur Aquarelle, gouache/papier (27x20cm 10x7in) Paris 2000

🎞 **$196** – €229 – **£138** – FF1 500
Colonel d'infanterie, capitaine de grenadiers à pied Gravure (30x19cm 11x7in) Blois 2001

CHARLET Omer Pierre L. 1809-1882 [3]

〜 **$45 100** – €38 112 – **£26 825** – FF250 000
Le jeune conteur italien Huile/toile (135x183cm 53x72in) La Rochelle 1998

CHARLIER Jacques c.1720-1790 [15]

〜 **$5 782** – €5 336 – **£3 458** – FF35 000
Naïade Huile/panneau (15x20cm 5x7in) Paris 1999

CHARLOT Jean 1898-1979 [81]

〜 **$8 000** – €6 958 – **£4 823** – FF45 640
Ronda de indios Oil/canvas (102x76cm 40x29in) New-York 1998

〜 **$1 800** – €2 127 – **£1 275** – FF13 951
Figure with Drum Oil/canvas (40.5x30.5cm 15x12in) Boston MA 2000

✎ **$500** – €537 – **£340** – FF3 520
Temple of the Warriors, Chichen-Itza Watercolour (27x20.5cm 10x8in) Boston MA 2001

🎞 **$375** – €384 – **£235** – FF2 519
Mexican Kitchen Lithograph (34x25cm 13x10in) Cleveland OH 2000

CHARLOT Louis 1878-1951 **[75]**
- $987 - €945 - **£609** - FF6 200
  Ruines dans les champs Huile/carton (54x72cm 21x28in) Besançon 1999
- $2 115 - €1 982 - **£1 271** - FF13 000
  Accordéon et enfant Huile/carton (30x41cm 11x16in) Paris 1999

CHARLOT Paul 1906-1985 **[60]**
- $1 831 - €2 134 - **£1 268** - FF14 000
  Le boulevard Huile/toile (54x65cm 21x25in) Calais 2000
- $1 028 - €991 - **£635** - FF6 500
  Les Tourailles Huile/toile (27x41cm 10x16in) Paris 1999

CHARLOT Raymond 1879 **[31]**
- $633 - €744 - **£444** - FF4 878
  Portrait de bohémienne au violon Huile/toile (80x60cm 31x23in) Liège 2000

CHARLTON Alan 1948 **[7]**
- $11 954 - €12 832 - **£8 000** - FF84 172
  Untitled Acrylic/canvas (218.5x218.5cm 86x86in) London 2000
- $8 661 - €9 371 - **£6 000** - FF61 467
  Grey Panels Oil/canvas (90x27cm 35x10in) London 2001

CHARLTON Evan 1904-1984 **[10]**
- $805 - €745 - **£500** - FF4 888
  Interior Oil/board (40.5x5cm 15x20in) London 1999

CHARLTON George J. 1899-1979 **[23]**
- $1 143 - €1 281 - **£800** - FF8 403
  Welsh Chapel Oil/canvas (36x43.5cm 14x17in) Billingshurst, West-Sussex 2001

CHARLTON John 1849-1917 **[34]**
- $20 000 - €23 785 - **£14 254** - FF156 020
  Indomitable Oil/canvas (209.5x145cm 82x57in) New-York 2000
- $1 587 - €1 780 - **£1 100** - FF11 679
  Persian Cat Oil/canvas (20.5x25.5cm 8x10in) London 2000
- $1 077 - €1 156 - **£720** - FF7 584
  A Lion and Lioness Pastel/paper (69.5x90cm 27x35in) London 2000

CHARMAISON Raymond Louis 1876-1955 **[122]**
- $2 043 - €2 211 - **£1 399** - FF14 500
  Le café-concert Huile/toile (33x40cm 12x15in) Troyes 2001

CHARMAN Rodney John Keith 1844-? **[14]**
- $643 - €721 - **£450** - FF4 732
  Wind Jammer Awaiting a Pilot Oil/canvas (76.5x101.5cm 30x39in) London 2001

CHARMY Émilie 1878-1974 **[67]**
- $862 - €1 006 - **£605** - FF6 600
  Bouquet de fleurs sur fond bleu Huile/toile (81x60cm 31x23in) Versailles 2000
- $650 - €554 - **£391** - FF3 637
  Reclining Female nude in blue stockings Oil/board (18x23cm 7x9in) Norwalk CT 1999

CHARNAY Armand 1844-1916 **[4]**
- $14 924 - €12 898 - **£8 996** - FF84 604
  Dressage dans la cour du château Huile/toile (44.5x77cm 17x30in) Bruxelles 1998

CHARNAY Désiré 1828-1915 **[28]**
- $4 605 - €5 158 - **£3 200** - FF33 837
  «Baobab» Albumen print (28x22cm 11x8in) London 2001

CHAROL Dorothea 1889-1963 **[21]**
- $630 - €716 - **£438** - FF4 695
  Anita Porcelain (H25.5cm H10in) München 2001

CHARON Guy 1927 **[34]**
- $1 876 - €1 753 - **£1 158** - FF11 500
  Paysage des Alpilles Huile/toile (65x80cm 25x31in) Fontainebleau 1999

CHAROON BOONSUAN 1938 **[2]**
- $2 403 - €2 232 - **£1 485** - FF14 643
  Reflections in the Water Oil/canvas (82.5x113cm 32x44in) Bangkok 1999

CHARPENTIER Albert 1878-1916 **[35]**
- $1 712 - €1 677 - **£1 053** - FF11 000
  Scène de rue à Tunis Huile/toile (41x33.5cm 16x13in) Toulon 1999

CHARPENTIER Alexandre 1856-1909 **[41]**
- $658 - €610 - **£406** - FF4 000
  Ernest Laumann Relief (19x14cm 7x5in) Paris 1999

CHARPENTIER Auguste 1813-1860 **[2]**
- $9 309 - €10 976 - **£6 544** - FF72 000
  Portrait de Madame de B. Huile/toile (124x96cm 48x37in) Paris 2000

CHARPENTIER Félix M. 1858-1924 **[39]**
- $1 841 - €2 165 - **£1 276** - FF14 200
  Le jeune flûtiste Bronze (H79cm H31in) Brest 2000

CHARPENTIER Jean-Baptiste I 1728-1806 **[26]**
- $2 136 - €2 439 - **£1 502** - FF16 000
  Nostalgie Huile/toile (46x38cm 18x14in) Versailles 2001
- $7 440 - €7 028 - **£4 500** - FF46 099
  A Woman selling Sherbert Oil/panel (31.5x25.5cm 12x10in) London 1999

CHARPENTIER Michel 1927 **[25]**
- $221 - €183 - **£129** - FF1 200
  Homme Bronze (40x17x8cm 15x6x3in) Paris 1998

CHARPENTIER Philippe 1949 **[48]**
- $392 - €381 - **£242** - FF2 500
  Sans titre Technique mixte (100x81cm 39x31in) Paris 1999
- $275 - €305 - **£186** - FF2 000
  Sans titre (texte de Rogar Grenier) Technique mixte/papier (29x20cm 11x7in) Paris 2000

CHARPIN Albert 1842-1924 **[46]**
- $10 454 - €8 934 - **£6 141** - FF58 601
  Return of the Flock Oil/canvas (144x196cm 57x77in) New-Orleans LA 1998
- $2 224 - €2 439 - **£1 510** - FF16 000
  La rentrée du troupeau en fin de journée Huile/toile (73x100cm 28x39in) Lille 2001
- $795 - €915 - **£561** - FF6 000
  Scène pastorale Huile/bois (21x26cm 8x10in) Narbonne 2001

CHARRETON Victor 1864-1936 **[448]**
- $8 649 - €9 604 - **£6 029** - FF63 000
  La Couze et le Puy de Brissol Huile/carton (59.5x73cm 23x28in) Paris 2001
- $3 550 - €3 811 - **£2 375** - FF25 000
  Le champ de choux en hiver Huile/carton (22x35cm 8x13in) Lyon 2000

CHARTIER Henri G. 1859-1924 **[13]**
- $1 807 - €1 982 - **£1 227** - FF13 000
  La charge Huile/panneau (41x33cm 16x12in) Paris 2000

C

CHARTON Ernest 1813-1905 **[15]**
- $35 000 - €33 702 - **£21 784** - FF221 070
  Paisaje de Guayaquil Oil/canvas (41.5x60.5cm 16x23in) New-York 1999

CHARTRAN Théobald 1849-1907 **[29]**
- $14 000 - €12 079 - **£8 446** - FF79 230
  Portrait of Blanche Shoemaker Wagstaff Carr Oil/canvas (130x97cm 51x38in) New-York 1998
- $1 805 - €1 753 - **£1 115** - FF11 500
  Portrait de jeune file Huile/toile (66x56cm 25x22in) Châtellerault 1999
- $1 449 - €1 601 - **£1 004** - FF10 500
  Napoléon III et le Duc de Morny Lavis (23.5x33cm 9x12in) Paris 2001

CHARTRAND Esteban, Philippe 1824/25-1884/89 **[25]**
- $18 000 - €19 321 - **£12 045** - FF126 738
  Bahia de Matanzas Oil/canvas (43.5x74cm 17x29in) New-York 2000
- $8 000 - €9 419 - **£5 621** - FF61 787
  Bohío Oil/canvas (45.5x25.5cm 17x10in) New-York 2000

CHARVOLIN Félix 1832-? **[4]**
- $4 727 - €4 040 - **£2 777** - FF26 500
  Baie de Cassis Huile/toile (80x120cm 31x47in) Villeneuve-les-Avignon 1998

CHAS-LABORDE 1886-1941 **[47]**
- $496 - €488 - **£318** - FF3 200
  Promenade à Coney Island, New York Aquarelle/papier (27.5x38cm 10x14in) Paris 1999
- $74 - €69 - **£45** - FF450
  L'avenue du Bois Pointe sèche couleurs (31.2x40.7cm 12x16in) Paris 1999

CHASE Frank M. XIX-XX **[3]**
- $1 494 - €1 604 - **£1 000** - FF10 521
  Scene of a farmyard Watercolour/paper (39x25.5cm 15x10in) Woking, Surrey 2000

CHASE Frank Swift 1886-1958 **[24]**
- $1 700 - €1 557 - **£1 031** - FF10 210
  «Early Snow» Oil/canvas (45x60cm 18x24in) East-Dennis MA 1998
- $1 000 - €1 120 - **£694** - FF7 347
  «Early Autumn Landscape» Oil/board (27x33cm 11x13in) Cincinnati OH 2001

CHASE Harry 1853-1889 **[27]**
- $3 750 - €3 497 - **£2 326** - FF22 939
  Ships at Sea Oil/canvas (49x64cm 19x25in) New-York 1999
- $8 500 - €8 835 - **£5 356** - FF57 953
  Coastline Scene with Fishing Boats Oil/canvas (30x38cm 12x15in) Detroit MI 2000

CHASE Marian Emma 1844-1905 **[11]**
- $1 442 - €1 374 - **£880** - FF9 011
  Raspberries on a Mossy Bank Watercolor (17x24cm 6x9in) Bury St. Edmunds, Suffolk 1999

CHASE Richard A. 1892-1985 **[11]**
- $900 - €1 049 - **£589** - FF6 586
  Illinos Farm Oil/board (76x91cm 30x36in) Chicago IL 2000

CHASE William Merritt 1849-1916 **[129]**
- $47 500 - €49 237 - **£30 119** - FF322 971
  The Mandolin Player Oil/canvas (61.5x41.5cm 24x16in) New-York 2000
- $73 913 - €63 819 - **£45 087** - FF418 628
  Garden Scene with House Oil/panel (25x35cm 10x14in) Oakland CA 1999

- $19 000 - €21 042 - **£12 885** - FF138 025
  The Garden Wall Pastel/paper (19x31.5cm 7x12in) New-York 2000
- $300 - €253 - **£176** - FF1 660
  Portrait of D.M Treadwell Etching (16x10cm 6x4in) Mystic CT 1998

CHASHNIK Ilya Grigorevitch 1902-1929 **[13]**
- $11 393 - €11 089 - **£7 000** - FF72 741
  Suprematist Collage Collage/paper (11.5x11.5cm 4x4in) London 1999

CHASSAING J. XX **[6]**
- $2 010 - €2 287 - **£1 395** - FF15 000
  «La Ligne aurore est inimitable» Affiche couleur (158x117cm 62x46in) Paris 2000

CHASSÉRIAU Théodore 1819-1856 **[95]**
- $8 500 - €9 344 - **£5 447** - FF61 291
  Baigneuses Oil/canvas (54x53.5cm 25x21in) New-York 2000
- $11 275 - €13 263 - **£8 117** - FF87 000
  Maternité Mine plomb (20.5x17.5cm 8x6in) Bordeaux 2001
- $340 - €320 - **£206** - FF2 100
  Apollon et Daphné Lithographie (22.5x16cm 8x6in) Paris 1999

CHASSEVENT-BACQUES Gustave Adolphe 1818-1901 **[2]**
- $5 198 - €5 058 - **£3 200** - FF33 180
  Courtship/Rest by the Wayside Oil/canvas (33x25cm 12x9in) London 1999

CHASTEL Roger 1897-1981 **[84]**
- $1 152 - €1 067 - **£705** - FF7 000
  La tasse de café Huile/toile (46x55cm 18x21in) Soissons 1999
- $497 - €534 - **£332** - FF3 500
  Nature morte Huile/toile (20x32cm 7x12in) Paris 2000

CHATAUD Marc Alfred 1833-1908 **[74]**
- $1 972 - €1 859 - **£1 222** - FF12 195
  Paysage orientaliste animé de personnages dans les ruines Huile/toile (40x55cm 15x21in) Liège 1999
- $4 097 - €3 964 - **£2 527** - FF26 000
  Les belles du Harem Huile/panneau (29x18cm 11x7in) Paris 1999
- $570 - €579 - **£354** - FF3 800
  École coranique assemblée assise écoutant l'enseignement des écritures Mine plomb (25x32.5cm 9x12in) Paris 1999

CHATEIGNON Ernest c.1865-? **[22]**
- $3 484 - €3 964 - **£2 418** - FF26 000
  La fenaison Huile/toile (38x55cm 14x21in) Fontainebleau 2000
- $319 - €308 - **£200** - FF2 100
  Aux champs Oil/canvas (33x40cm 13x16in) Henley-on-Thames, Oxon 1999

CHATELAIN Jean-Baptiste Claude 1710-1771 **[9]**
- $400 - €410 - **£250** - FF2 690
  Landscape with Two Figures Coloured chalks/paper (22.5x41cm 8x16in) New-York 2000

CHATELET Claude Louis 1753-1794 **[78]**
- $140 000 - €153 600 - **£93 002** - FF1 007 552
  View of the Bay of Taormina Oil/canvas (87x171cm 34x67in) New-York 2000
- $22 414 - €24 060 - **£15 000** - FF157 824
  View of the Large Cascade at Terni outside Rome, near Foligno Oil/cardboard (92x60cm 36x23in) London 2000

$3 586 - €3 849 - £2 400 - FF25 251
Extensive Mediterranean Landscape with Peasants Baling Hay on Poles Watercolour (37x53cm 14x20in) London 2000

CHATELIN Ambroise N. c.1810-c.1860 [2]
$8 021 - €8 083 - £5 000 - FF53 018
By the Well/The Friary Washhouse Oil/canvas (38x48cm 14x18in) London 2000

CHATILLON de Charles 1777-1844 [5]
$4 887 - €4 449 - £3 000 - FF29 181
Portrait of the Emperor Napoleon Oil/canvas (74x60.5cm 29x23in) London 1999

CHATILLON Pierre 1885-1974 [52]
$502 - €547 - £331 - FF3 587
Stilleben mit Rotwein, Trauben und Buch Aquarelle (41x51cm 16x20in) Bern 2000

CHATROUSSE Émile Fr. 1829-1896 [6]
$4 928 - €5 453 - £3 830 - FF35 772
La lecture Bronze (H65cm H25in) Bruxelles 2001

CHATTAWAY William 1927 [14]
$5 371 - €6 403 - £3 830 - FF42 000
Femme debout Bronze (73x29.5x19.5cm 28x11x7in) Paris 2000

CHATTERTON Clarence Kerr 1880-1973 [30]
$1 750 - €1 951 - £1 181 - FF12 799
City Rooftops with Cooper Green Rooftops, Full Cityscape in Background Oil/canvas (48x64cm 19x25in) Thomaston ME 2000
$5 500 - €5 904 - £3 830 - FF38 728
Circus Scene Oil/canvas/board (23.5x28.5cm 9x11in) New-York 2000

CHAUDET Jeanne Elisabeth 1767-1832 [3]
$16 393 - €19 818 - £11 453 - FF130 000
Portrait de la comtesse de Vauréal Huile/toile (65x54.5cm 25x21in) Paris 2000

CHAUDIER Jean 1834-? [2]
$4 971 - €4 650 - £3 010 - FF30 500
Nature morte aux biscuits Huile/toile (66.5x92.5cm 26x36in) Saint-Étienne 1999

CHAUMAT Odette XX [1]
$3 600 - €3 462 - £2 221 - FF22 709
«Madrid, Exposition Française, Art et Luxe» Poster (104x74cm 40x29in) New-York 1999

CHAURAND-NAURAC Jean Raoul 1878-1948 [30]
$2 506 - €2 820 - £1 726 - FF18 500
Jockey au paddock, deuxième étude Huile/toile (55x46cm 21x18in) Dijon 2000
$1 371 - €1 518 - £950 - FF9 958
«Savoie et Dauphiné, PLM» Poster (100x62cm 39x24in) London 2001

CHAURAY Jean-Claude 1934-1996 [21]
$4 368 - €4 878 - £2 960 - FF32 000
Nature morte aux pêches, pot d'étain, pichet et verre Huile/toile (61x50cm 24x19in) La Rochelle 2000
$3 402 - €3 811 - £2 365 - FF25 000
Nature morte aux pommes/Nature morte aux poires Huile/toile (22x27cm 8x10in) Le Touquet 2001

CHAUVASSAIGNE F. XIX [14]
$1 373 - €1 524 - £957 - FF10 000
Bord de rivière/Linge séchant/Moulin/Arbre au milieu des ruines Tirage papier salé (16.5x21.5cm 6x8in) Paris 2001

CHAUVEAU Pascal 1962 [9]
$6 571 - €7 394 - £4 525 - FF48 500
Techniciens de l'impossible Acrylique/papier (46x61cm 18x24in) Paris 2000
$3 267 - €3 811 - £2 295 - FF25 000
«E = mc2» Acrylique (26.5x36.5cm 10x14in) Versailles 2000

CHAUVEL Georges 1886-1962 [14]
$1 700 - €1 832 - £1 159 - FF12 018
Nude female Form Bronze (H39cm H15in) Hatfield PA 2001

CHAUVELON Gabriel 1875-? [6]
$852 - €915 - £575 - FF6 000
Vue de Quimperlé Huile/toile (61x46cm 24x18in) Quimper 2000

CHAUVIN Jean, Louis 1889-1976 [54]
$6 921 - €6 860 - £4 329 - FF45 000
Les jumeaux Pierre (31x10cm 12x3in) Paris 1999
$307 - €305 - £192 - FF2 000
Composition Fusain/papier (49x31cm 19x12in) Paris 1999

CHAUVIN Pierre-Athanase 1774-1832 [13]
$30 000 - €33 224 - £20 346 - FF217 935
A Hilltop Town by a River, a Drover on a track in the Foreground Oil/canvas (70.5x97.5cm 27x38in) New-York 2000
$17 530 - €15 245 - £10 570 - FF100 000
Etude de paysage Huile/toile (45x30cm 17x11in) Paris 1998

CHAVANIS Stéphane XX [6]
$1 520 - €1 601 - £1 003 - FF10 500
Femme assise Pastel/papier (63x48cm 24x18in) Paris 2000

CHAVANNAZ B. XIX-XX [18]
$153 - €183 - £105 - FF1 200
«Ah! Quand supprimera-t-on l'alcool?» Affiche (119x80cm 46x31in) Paris 2000

CHAVANNES Alfred 1836-1894 [8]
$4 480 - €5 236 - £3 198 - FF34 346
Genfersee mit Schloss Chillon und Dents du Midi Öl/Leinwand (27x37cm 10x14in) Zürich 2001

CHAVAZ Albert 1907-1990 [79]
$10 752 - €9 954 - £6 582 - FF65 297
Sitzender weiblicher Akt Öl/Leinwand (91.5x65cm 36x25in) Bern 1999
$1 612 - €1 493 - £987 - FF9 794
Weisse Parkbank zwischen zwei Bäumen Öl/Karton (20x27cm 7x10in) Bern 1999
$445 - €374 - £261 - FF2 453
«Saviésanne de profil» Pencil/paper (27x21cm 10x8in) Bern 1998
$278 - €328 - £202 - FF2 150
La crique Aquatinte (22x30cm 8x11in) Sion 2001

CHAVDA Shiavax 1914-1990 [17]
$2 000 - €2 275 - £1 397 - FF14 920
Untitled Tempera (36x45.5cm 14x17in) New-York 2000

CHAVES ORTIZ José María 1839-1903 [67]
$2 700 - €3 003 - £1 900 - FF19 700
Picador Oleo/lienzo (42x28cm 16x11in) Madrid 2001
$128 - €120 - £80 - FF825
Mulos Aguada/papel (17x27cm 6x10in) Madrid 1999

CHAVET Victor 1822-1906 [31]
$2 400 - €2 782 - £1 700 - FF18 252
The Flute Player Oil/panel (21.5x15.5cm 8x6in) New-York 2000

C

CHAVEZ LOPEZ Gerardo 1937 **[36]**
- $1 438 - €1 677 - £1 008 - FF11 000
  Composition surréaliste Huile/toile (130x97cm 51x38in) Paris 2000
- $2 818 - €3 049 - £1 930 - FF20 000
  Scène surréaliste Technique mixte/toile (65x81cm 25x31in) Paris 2001
- $1 550 - €1 844 - £1 105 - FF12 094
  Bjornen og de Smukke Pastel/canvas (146x115cm 57x45in) Stockholm 2000

CHAVIGNAUD Georges 1865-1944 **[49]**
- $270 - €260 - £167 - FF1 705
  «Stormy Evening, Holland» Watercolour/paper (30x40cm 11x15in) Toronto 1999

CHAYE Simon 1930 **[3]**
- $1 056 - €1 143 - £678 - FF7 500
  Drakkar Tapisserie (74x52cm 29x20in) Paris 2000

CHAYKIN Howard XX **[1]**
- $1 800 - €2 176 - £1 256 - FF14 271
  «Star Wars» Poster (73.5x51cm 28x20in) New-York 2000

CHAZAL Antoine 1793-1854 **[17]**
- $3 586 - €3 849 - £2 400 - FF25 251
  Marmotte souslik - Marmot - Mangouste d'Egypte - Egyptian mongoose Watercolour (15.5x10cm 6x3in) London 2000

CHAZALY 1926 **[10]**
- $629 - €701 - £423 - FF4 600
  Boules de neige Huile/toile (24x38cm 9x14in) Castres 2000

CHAZAUD Georges XX **[1]**
- $2 664 - €2 515 - £1 656 - FF16 500
  Jardin suspendu Tapisserie (220x300cm 86x118in) Neuilly-sur-Seine 1999

CHEADLE Henry 1852-1910 **[39]**
- $1 819 - €1 755 - £1 150 - FF11 514
  Faggot Gatherers near Dolgelly, N.Wales Oil/canvas (44.5x36cm 17x14in) London 1999
- $672 - €722 - £450 - FF4 734
  The Avon from the Bridge at Fladbury Oil/canvas (25.5x40.5cm 10x15in) London 2000

CHECA José Luis 1950 **[93]**
- $1 060 - €1 201 - £720 - FF7 880
  Desgúace, Denia Oleo/lienzo (65x92cm 25x36in) Madrid 2000
- $357 - €420 - £259 - FF2 758
  «Cabañal, playa» Oleo/tabla (11x18cm 4x7in) Madrid 2001

CHECA Y DELICADO Felipe 1844-1907 **[24]**
- $972 - €1 081 - £666 - FF7 092
  Flores Oleo/lienzo (80x32cm 31x12in) Madrid 2001
- $1 080 - €1 201 - £720 - FF7 880
  Carrera de cuádrigas Oleo/lienzo (24x47cm 9x18in) Madrid 2000

CHECA Y SANZ Ulpiano 1860-1916 **[97]**
- $183 375 - €190 561 - £115 000 - FF1 250 000
  Le départ pour la fantasia Huile/carton (200x125cm 78x49in) Paris 2000
- $6 178 - €6 860 - £4 306 - FF45 000
  La conversation dans un jardin Huile/toile (73x50cm 28x19in) Paris 2000
- $4 611 - €4 573 - £2 868 - FF30 000
  Venise Huile/panneau (22.5x15cm 8x5in) Saint-Germain-en-Laye 1999
- $4 118 - €4 421 - £2 755 - FF29 000
  Indien à cheval Bronze (40x55x20cm 15x21x7in) Paris 2000

- $1 925 - €1 652 - £1 155 - FF10 835
  Inspiración Acuarela/papel (34x50cm 13x19in) Madrid 1999

CHECCHI Arturo 1886-1971 **[25]**
- $1 040 - €1 348 - £780 - FF8 840
  Figure nel parco Olio/tela (54x73cm 21x28in) Prato 2000
- $550 - €570 - £330 - FF3 740
  Natura morta Olio/tavola (32.5x43cm 12x16in) Prato 2000

CHEE Robert 1938-1971 **[10]**
- $400 - €441 - £267 - FF2 890
  Navajo Mother & Son in Corn Field Gouache/board (35x30cm 14x12in) St. Ignatius MT 2000

CHEEK Clifton Roy XX **[5]**
- $1 984 - €2 130 - £1 348 - FF13 974
  Eight Seconds Bronze (27x18cm 10x7in) Calgary, Alberta 2001

CHEESEMAN Thomas Gedge XIX-XX **[3]**
- $2 566 - €2 766 - £1 750 - FF18 141
  Unappreciated Vintage Oil/canvas (35.5x30.5cm 13x12in) Bury St. Edmunds, Suffolk 2001

CHEESMAN Arthur E. XX **[2]**
- $2 800 - €2 633 - £1 733 - FF17 269
  Elegants Silver print (26x22cm 10x9in) New-York 1999

CHEESMAN Harold 1915 **[32]**
- $155 - €165 - £98 - FF1 082
  Rowledge - Night approach Watercolour/paper (61x79cm 24x31in) Dublin 2000

CHEESMAN Thomas 1760-1834/35 **[4]**
- $6 500 - €6 440 - £3 943 - FF42 244
  General Washington, After John Trumbull Engraving (71x49cm 27x19in) New-York 2000

CHEESWRIGHT Ethel S. XIX-XX **[41]**
- $838 - €976 - £580 - FF6 405
  Creaux Harbour, Sark, C.I. Watercolour/paper (29x27cm 11x10in) Cheshire 2000

CHEFFER Henry 1880-1957 **[107]**
- $398 - €427 - £263 - FF2 800
  Le carré du capitaine Aquarelle/papier (16x13cm 6x5in) Douarnenez 2000
- $162 - €137 - £96 - FF900
  Animation dans un port du Nord Eau-forte (18x24cm 7x9in) Quimper 1998

CHEFFETZ Asa 1897-1965 **[43]**
- $150 - €125 - £88 - FF823
  «Covered Bridge» Woodcut (12x21cm 5x8in) Shaker-Heights OH 1998

CHEKHONIN Sergei Vasilevich 1878-1936 **[35]**
- $2 356 - €2 642 - £1 600 - FF17 329
  Costume Design for Snegurochka, Act 1 Watercolour (32x15.20.5cm 12x8in) London 2000

CHEKRYGIN Vassilii Nikolaevich 1897-1922 **[3]**
- $2 098 - €2 498 - £1 500 - FF16 384
  The Commencement of the Communal Liturgy Beyond the Church Walls Charcoal/paper (39x29.5cm 15x11in) London 2000

CHELI CAPELLA Giulia ?-1915 **[1]**
- $6 000 - €6 971 - £4 216 - FF45 727
  Portrait of the Artist, three-quarter length, in a black Dress Oil/canvas (100.5x80cm 39x31in) New-York 2001

CHELIUS Adolf 1856-1923 **[28]**

> $1 718 - €1 789 - **£1 088** - FF11 738
> **Hirtin und Hüterbub mit ihrer Schafherde am Seeufer** Öl/Leinwand (67x91cm 26x35in) München 2000

CHELMINSKI van Jan 1851-1925 **[46]**

> $12 510 - €14 543 - **£8 780** - FF95 395
> **Chevaux en fuite** Huile/toile (41x66cm 16x25in) Warszawa 2001

> $5 239 - €5 624 - **£3 506** - FF36 892
> **Preussische Kavalleristen** Oil/panel (30.7x40.3cm 12x15in) München 2000

CHELMONSKI Józef 1849-1914 **[68]**

> $27 456 - €29 471 - **£18 372** - FF193 320
> **Dans la soirée (Polesie)** Huile/toile (55x85cm 21x33in) Warszawa 2000

> $8 319 - €8 385 - **£5 188** - FF55 005
> **Les chaumières au crépuscule** Oil/canvas/board (25.3x38cm 9x14in) Warszawa 2000

> $3 284 - €3 189 - **£2 030** - FF20 920
> **Hérons** Indian ink/paper (17.5x22.5cm 6x8in) Warszawa 1999

CHEM XX **[2]**

> $1 200 - €1 136 - **£745** - FF7 451
> **«L'Aéronautique»** Poster (99.5x58cm 39x22in) New-York 1999

CHEMELLIER de Georges 1835-1907 **[5]**

> $3 550 - €3 811 - **£2 375** - FF25 000
> **Get Up!** Bronze (H60cm H23in) Soissons 2000

CHEMIAKIN Dorothée 1964 **[15]**

> $218 - €229 - **£137** - FF1 500
> **Sans titre** Lithographie couleurs (33x33cm 12x12in) Lille 2000

CHEMIAKIN Michael 1943 **[313]**

> $10 000 - €8 451 - **£5 965** - FF55 432
> **Carnival at St. Petersburg** Acrylic/canvas (132x132cm 51x51in) San-Francisco CA 1998

> $3 999 - €3 995 - **£2 500** - FF26 205
> **Le bouffon** Oil/canvas (115x89cm 45x35in) London 1999

> $2 075 - €2 439 - **£1 438** - FF16 000
> **Nature morte** Technique mixte (33x39cm 12x15in) Paris 2000

> $10 815 - €12 300 - **£7 500** - FF80 685
> **Carnaval de Saint-Petersbourg** Bronze (H119cm H46in) London 2000

> $3 749 - €4 264 - **£2 600** - FF27 969
> **Carnaval de Saint-Petersbourg** Bronze (H47cm H18in) London 2000

> $1 223 - €1 296 - **£815** - FF8 500
> **Sans titre** Encre (33x40cm 12x15in) Paris 2000

> $200 - €199 - **£121** - FF1 307
> **Saint Petersburg Carnival Suite** Lithograph (28x28cm 11x11in) Chester NY 2000

CHEMIAKIN Mikhaïl Fedorovitch 1875-1944 **[5]**

> $4 978 - €4 116 - **£2 921** - FF27 000
> **Carnaval de Saint-Petersbourg** Bronze (H50cm H19in) Paris 1998

CHEMIELINSKI W.T. XX **[8]**

> $2 800 - €3 024 - **£1 935** - FF19 834
> **Horse and carriageon City street** Oil/canvas (35.5x25.5cm 13x10in) Bethesda MD 2001

CHEMILINSKI van Jan 1851-1925 **[1]**

> $4 000 - €3 792 - **£2 498** - FF24 872
> **Polish Wedding** Oil/canvas (61x76cm 24x29in) Chicago IL 1999

CHEMIN Joseph Victor 1825-1901 **[62]**

> $1 032 - €915 - **£633** - FF6 000
> **Le chien savant** Bronze (H15cm H5in) Soissons 1999

CHEN BANDING 1877-1970 **[5]**

> $1 738 - €2 017 - **£1 200** - FF13 228
> **Jagged Mountainous Landscape Strew with Pine, Bamboo, Willow** Ink (135x52.5cm 53x20in) London 2001

CHEN CHENGBO Ch'en Ch'eng-po 1895-1947 **[8]**

> $131 200 - €139 704 - **£83 200** - FF916 400
> **Scenery of Si Hu Lake** Oil/canvas (37x44.5cm 14x17in) Taipei 2000

CHEN CHI 1912 **[15]**

> $700 - €654 - **£432** - FF4 288
> **Main Street, Houston, TX** Watercolour (38x68cm 15x27in) Detroit MI 1999

CHEN CHUN 1483-1544 **[9]**

> $44 505 - €41 971 - **£27 600** - FF275 310
> **Calligraphy in Cao Shu of the One Thousand Characters** Ink/paper (35x580cm 13x228in) Hong-Kong 1999

CHEN DA XX **[3]**

> $2 564 - €3 014 - **£1 778** - FF19 768
> **Landscape, after Wen Zhengming** Ink (106x32cm 41x12in) Hong-Kong 2000

CHEN DANQING 1953 **[5]**

> $7 078 - €6 717 - **£4 301** - FF44 060
> **Kissing** Oil/canvas (86.5x66cm 34x25in) Hong-Kong 1999

CHEN DEWANG Ch'en Te'-wang 1909-1984 **[7]**

> $65 056 - €60 289 - **£40 446** - FF395 472
> **Street Scent at Sanchong** Oil/canvas (45.5x53cm 17x20in) Taipei 1999

> $78 720 - €83 823 - **£49 920** - FF549 840
> **Still Life with Roses** Oil/canvas (31.5x41cm 12x16in) Taipei 2000

CHEN Georgette 1907-1992 **[12]**

> $22 956 - €26 066 - **£15 712** - FF170 984
> **Orchids** Oil/canvas (55x46cm 21x18in) Singapore 2000

> $9 756 - €11 078 - **£6 677** - FF72 668
> **Portrait of a Young Girl** Oil/canvas (35x27cm 13x10in) Singapore 2000

> $7 679 - €7 157 - **£4 641** - FF46 946
> **Still Life of tropical Fruits** Pastel/paper (48x33cm 18x12in) Singapore 1999

CHEN HENGKE 1876-1923 **[15]**

> $3 217 - €3 051 - **£1 957** - FF20 015
> **Flowers** Ink (19x56cm 7x22in) Hong-Kong 1999

CHEN HONGSHOU 1768-1822 **[6]**

> $2 820 - €3 315 - **£1 955** - FF21 744
> **Narcissus, Pine and Rock** Ink (114x33.5cm 44x13in) Hong-Kong 2000

CHEN HONGSHOU 1598-1652 **[10]**

> $15 384 - €18 082 - **£10 668** - FF118 608
> **Forest** Ink/paper (124.5x56.5cm 49x22in) Hong-Kong 2000

CHEN JIALING 1937 **[2]**

> $3 338 - €3 645 - **£2 147** - FF23 912
> **Lotus** Ink/paper (89x34.5cm 35x13in) Hong-Kong 2000

C

CHEN JIRU 1558-1639 **[3]**
🖌 **$4 871** - €5 534 - **£3 420** - FF36 301
Prunus in Ink Ink/paper (110.5x31cm 43x12in) Hong-Kong 2001

CHEN KEZHAN 1959 **[22]**
🖌 **$3 443** - €3 910 - **£2 356** - FF25 647
Lotus Indian ink (150x80.5cm 59x31in) Singapore 2000

CHEN MEI c.1726-1742 **[2]**
🖌 **$9 615** - €11 301 - **£6 667** - FF74 130
Hermitage Ink (100.5x51cm 39x20in) Hong-Kong 2001

CHEN PEIQIU 1922 **[8]**
🖌 **$13 461** - €15 170 - **£9 408** - FF99 508
Mandarin Duck and Spring Flowers Ink (91.5x54.5cm 36x21in) Hong-Kong 2001

CHEN QIKUAN Chen Chi-kwan 1921 **[18]**
🖌 **$8 974** - €10 113 - **£6 272** - FF66 339
Monkeys Ink/paper (59x81.5cm 23x32in) Hong-Kong 2001
🖼 **$1 677** - €1 409 - **£984** - FF9 240
Peaceful Coexistence Lithograph (62x62cm 24x24in) Taipei 1998

CHEN SHAOMEI 1909-1954 **[24]**
🖌 **$8 385** - €7 869 - **£5 180** - FF51 616
Staring afar on the Horse Ink (134x53cm 52x20in) Hong-Kong 1999

CHEN SHI XIX **[1]**
🖌 **$4 494** - €4 907 - **£2 891** - FF32 189
Landscapes Ink (12x8.5cm 4x3in) Hong-Kong 2000

CHEN SHUREN 1883-1948 **[12]**
🖌 **$4 871** - €5 490 - **£3 404** - FF36 012
Gibbons on a Cliff Ink (132x40.5cm 51x15in) Hong-Kong 2001

CHEN SHUZHONG 1960 **[1]**
🖌 **$6 153** - €7 318 - **£4 238** - FF48 004
Harvest Oil/canvas (80x100cm 31x39in) Hong-Kong 2000

CHEN TINGSHIH 1916 **[11]**
🖼 **$7 625** - €6 403 - **£4 475** - FF42 000
Day end Night Woodcut (120x120cm 47x47in) Taipei 1998

CHEN WENBO 1969 **[4]**
🖌 **$6 974** - €8 140 - **£4 774** - FF53 394
Vitamin Z no.8 Oil/canvas (163x150cm 64x59in) Taipei 2000

CHEN WENXI Chen Wenshi 1906-1991 **[27]**
🖌 **$57 390** - €65 166 - **£39 280** - FF427 460
Worker Oil/board (76.5x61cm 30x24in) Singapore 2000
🖌 **$5 938** - €4 982 - **£3 484** - FF32 680
Village Scene Ink/paper (58x56cm 22x22in) Singapore 1998

CHEN XIANGXUN 1956 **[2]**
🖌 **$4 487** - €5 274 - **£3 111** - FF34 594
Vase of Flowers Mixed media/paper (93x70cm 36x27in) Hong-Kong 2000

CHEN XIANZHANG 1428-1500 **[2]**
🖌 **$28 204** - €33 150 - **£19 558** - FF217 448
Poem in Cursive Script Calligraphy Ink/paper (30.5x480cm 12x188in) Hong-Kong 2000

CHEN YANNING 1945 **[22]**
🖌 **$77 220** - €73 276 - **£46 920** - FF480 660
Girls with Goldfish Oil/canvas (147.5x162.5cm 58x63in) Hong-Kong 1999

CHEN YIFEI 1946 **[32]**
🖌 **$167 310** - €158 765 - **£101 660** - FF1 041 430
Old Dreams of Shanghai #1: The Golden Age Oil/canvas (152.5x198cm 60x77in) Hong-Kong 1999
🖌 **$35 952** - €39 454 - **£23 156** - FF258 804
Tibetan Boy with red Scarf Oil/canvas (46x46cm 18x18in) Hong-Kong 2000

CHEN YIMING 1951 **[21]**
🖌 **$25 820** - €21 809 - **£15 500** - FF143 060
Secluded Beauty Oil/canvas (146x138cm 57x54in) Hong-Kong 1998
🖌 **$10 272** - €11 273 - **£6 616** - FF73 944
Two Fishermen Oil/canvas (55x80.5cm 21x31in) Hong-Kong 2000

CHEN YINPI (George Chann) 1913-1995 **[5]**
🖌 **$32 800** - €34 926 - **£20 800** - FF229 100
Lively and vigourous Flourishes in Calligraphy Oil/canvas (128x119cm 50x46in) Taipei 2000
🖌 **$9 510** - €11 100 - **£6 510** - FF72 810
Abstract Oil/canvas (50.5x121.5cm 19x47in) Taipei 2000

CHEN YONGMO Chen Yungmo 1961 **[4]**
🖌 **$2 820** - €3 315 - **£1 955** - FF21 744
Buddha Ink (89x34cm 35x13in) Hong-Kong 2000

CHEN YUANDU 1903-1967 **[1]**
🖌 **$4 902** - €4 600 - **£3 028** - FF30 175
Dancing Fairy Ink/paper (149.5x81cm 58x31in) Hong-Kong 1999

CHEN ZHUAN XVIII **[1]**
🖌 **$5 805** - €5 448 - **£3 586** - FF35 734
Flowers and Fruits Ink (25x31.5cm 9x12in) Hong-Kong 1999

CHEN ZONGCHEN 1959 **[1]**
🖌 **$2 696** - €2 944 - **£1 734** - FF19 313
Sutra in Kai Shu Ink/paper (72.5x24.5cm 28x9in) Hong-Kong 2000

CHENARD Christian 1918 **[354]**
🖌 **$299** - €320 - **£204** - FF2 100
Composition Huile/toile (92x73cm 36x28in) Abbeville 2001

CHENAVARD Paul M. Joseph 1807-1895 **[4]**
🖌 **$3 040** - €3 354 - **£2 059** - FF22 000
Autoportrait jeune Pastel/papier (31x19cm 12x7in) Paris 2000

CHENEY Russell 1881-1945 **[12]**
🖌 **$1 400** - €1 390 - **£858** - FF9 116
Cassis Oil/panel (38x45cm 15x18in) Mystic CT 2000

CHENG GONG XVII-XVIII **[2]**
🖌 **$37 087** - €34 976 - **£23 000** - FF229 425
Mount Huang Ink (48.5x571cm 19x224in) Hong-Kong 1999

CHENG Prince 1752-1823 **[3]**
🖌 **$10 296** - €9 764 - **£6 264** - FF64 048
Calligraph in Xing-Cao Shu Ink/paper (29x336cm 11x132in) Hong-Kong 1999

CHENG SHIFA 1921 **[66]**
🖌 **$5 180** - €4 916 - **£3 147** - FF32 244
Herding Ink (133x67cm 52x26in) Hong-Kong 1999

CHENG SUI 1605-1672 **[4]**
🖌 **$64 350** - €61 025 - **£39 150** - FF400 300
Autumn Mountains Ink/paper (26x195.5cm 10x76in) Hong-Kong 1999

CHENG TINGLU 1797-1859 **[1]**
$1 548 - €1 460 - **£960** - FF9 576
Traveling in the Mountain Ink (22x35cm 8x13in)
Hong-Kong 1999

CHENU Didier 1956 **[12]**
$2 447 - €2 134 - **£1 479** - FF14 000
Petite page d'inquisition Technique mixte/toile
(100x100cm 39x39in) Paris 1998

CHEONG SOO PIENG 1917-1983 **[37]**
$10 519 - €11 012 - **£6 607** - FF72 232
Family Gathering Oil/canvas (84x84cm 33x33in)
Singapore 2000
$3 389 - €3 548 - **£2 129** - FF23 274
Village Scene Watercolour (93.5x45cm 36x17in)
Singapore 2000

CHERBUIN Louis 1810-1875 **[1]**
$1 750 - €1 814 - **£1 050** - FF11 900
Lugo Acquatinta (34x105cm 13x41in) Milano 2000

CHEREMETEV Vassili V. 1829-? **[3]**
$1 454 - €1 524 - **£911** - FF10 000
Portrait de Khan Huile/toile (72x59cm 28x23in) Paris
1999

CHEREPOV George 1909-1987 **[13]**
$500 - €534 - **£340** - FF3 502
Woodland Stream Oil/canvas (91x76cm 36x30in)
Philadelphia PA 2001

CHERET Joseph Gustave 1838-1894 **[34]**
$4 402 - €4 726 - **£2 945** - FF31 000
Enfants aux paniers Céramique (H50cm H19in)
Toulouse 2000
$903 - €991 - **£600** - FF6 500
«Alcazar d'été - Revue fin de siècle» Affiche
(121x87cm 47x34in) Paris 2000

CHÉRET Jules 1836-1932 **[1303]**
$15 000 - €12 851 - **£9 018** - FF84 295
The Toast Oil/canvas (213x156cm 83x61in) New-York
1998
$50 000 - €48 084 - **£30 860** - FF315 410
Folies-Bergère, l'arc-en-ciel Oil/canvas
(128x79.5cm 50x31in) New-York 1999
$2 781 - €3 125 - **£1 937** - FF20 500
**Personnage en costume de bain sur une plage
Normande** Huile/panneau (23x18cm 9x7in) Cannes
2001
$1 200 - €1 303 - **£831** - FF8 546
«Le soir du mariage» Terracotta (H31cm H12in)
Cleveland OH 2001
$1 100 - €1 185 - **£750** - FF7 776
Femme assise Crayon (39x25.5cm 15x10in) New-
York 2001
$1 500 - €1 625 - **£999** - FF10 661
**«Exposition des arts incohérents, oeuvre de
protection de l'enfance»** Poster (121x86cm
48x34in) New-York 2000

CHERICI Angiolo XIX **[1]**
$7 245 - €6 205 - **£4 245** - FF40 703
**A Youth in a Cap and Gorget, after Rembrandt
Harmensz, Van Rijn (?)** Oil/canvas (67.5x56.5cm
26x22in) Amsterdam 1998

CHERINA Drago Marin 1949 **[135]**
$662 - €618 - **£410** - FF4 053
After Picasso Bronze (14x15x14cm 5x5x5in) Sydney
1999
$107 - €100 - **£66** - FF657
Study for Sculpture Pastel/paper (31x23cm 12x9in)
Sydney 1999

$176 - €165 - **£109** - FF1 080
Still Life with Flowers Lithograph (69x49cm
27x19in) Sydney 1999

CHERKI Sabine 1958 **[9]**
$795 - €915 - **£547** - FF6 000
Louloutte gestuelle Bronze (31x14x12cm 12x5x4in)
Paris 2000

CHERNETSOV Nikanor Grigorevich 1805-1879 **[8]**
$19 324 - €18 247 - **£12 000** - FF119 694
**«Dukhan» (Caucasian Inn) on the Descent from
Holy Kvishensky Mountain** Oil/canvas (43x61cm
16x24in) London 2000

CHERNIKHOV Iakov 1889-1951 **[6]**
$9 857 - €9 401 - **£6 000** - FF61 665
Architectural Study Pencil (23x30cm 9x11in)
London 1999

CHÉRON Louis 1660-1715 **[12]**
$21 073 - €24 447 - **£15 000** - FF160 363
Apollo in his Chariot & Apollo pursuing Daphne
Oil/canvas (73.5x50cm 28x19in) London 2001
$2 061 - €2 312 - **£1 400** - FF15 163
**Venus Landing on the Island of Paphos, in the
Presence of Jupiter** Black chalk (37x51.5cm
14x20in) London 2000

CHERRY Kathryn 1880-1931 **[11]**
$9 000 - €10 041 - **£5 891** - FF65 863
Floral Still Life in Vibrant Blues Oil/canvas
(63x76cm 25x30in) St. Louis MO 2000
$2 600 - €2 634 - **£1 632** - FF17 278
Gloucester Harbor Oil/canvas/board (27x35cm
11x14in) Cincinnati OH 2000

CHERRY-GARRARD Apsley 1886-1959 **[1]**
$3 806 - €3 997 - **£2 400** - FF26 219
Hut Point from Cape Evans Watercolour/paper
(14x22.5cm 5x8in) London 2000

CHERUBINI Andrea 1833-? **[19]**
$7 313 - €8 537 - **£5 012** - FF56 000
Baie de Naples Huile/toile (154x67cm 60x26in)
Laval 2000
$771 - €777 - **£480** - FF5 098
On the Neopolitan Coast Oil/panel (24x44.5cm
9x17in) London 2000

CHERUBINI Carlo 1897-1978 **[67]**
$12 078 - €13 720 - **£8 451** - FF90 000
Roger et Angélique Huile/toile (254x148cm
100x58in) Neuilly-sur-Seine 2001
$588 - €686 - **£413** - FF4 500
Bouquet de roses Huile/panneau (52x40cm 20x15in)
Versailles 2000
$500 - €495 - **£306** - FF3 245
La baigneuse Oil/board (12x9cm 5x3in) Delray-
Beach FL 2000
$1 300 - €1 395 - **£870** - FF9 153
«Lido» Poster (150x109.5cm 59x43in) Los-Angeles
CA 2000

CHERVIN Louis 1905-1969 **[33]**
$236 - €198 - **£138** - FF1 300
Paris Montmartre Aquarelle/papier (21x30cm 8x11in)
Lyon 1998

CHESSA Gigi 1898-1935 **[10]**
$22 500 - €23 325 - **£13 500** - FF153 000
Ragazza di Anticoli Olio/tela (66x60cm 25x23in)
Torino 2000
$9 600 - €8 293 - **£4 800** - FF54 400
I giocatori di carte Olio/cartone (32.5x26cm 13x10in)
Torino 1999

CHESTNUT Billy Dohlman XX [4]
$800 - €967 - £558 - FF6 342
«Happy Jake at the Age of 14 Years»
Watercolour/paper (38.5x36cm 15x14in) Bethesda MD
2000

CHESTRET de Caroline Levache XIX [1]
$2 307 - €2 509 - £1 520 - FF16 459
Üppiges Blumenbouquet in einer Prunkvase
Watercolour (52.5x40cm 20x15in) Bern 2000

CHEURET Albert 1884-1966 [23]
$195 000 - €209 312 - £130 494 - FF1 372 995
Heron Console Bronze (98.5x158.5x35.5cm
38x62x13in) New-York 2000
$5 000 - €5 367 - £3 346 - FF35 205
Table Lamps Bronze (H38.5cm H15in) New-York
2000

CHEVALIER Adolf 1831-? [29]
$1 597 - €1 534 - £990 - FF10 061
Wintertag an der Hufschmiede Öl/Leinwand
(44x72cm 17x28in) Ahlden 1999
$434 - €511 - £306 - FF3 353
«Ein Trunkenbold wird vor Augen der
Dorfgemeinde verwiesen» Öl/Leinwand
(18.5x28cm 7x11in) Köln 2001

CHEVALIER Eugène Adolphe XIX [6]
$40 000 - €34 510 - £24 132 - FF226 372
Still Life with Flowers and a Pineapple Oil/canvas
(114.5x85cm 45x33in) New-York 1998

CHEVALIER Gabriel XX [102]
$248 - €229 - £149 - FF1 500
Paris, le Pont-Neuf et le Vert Galand Huile/pan-
neau (54x65cm 21x25in) Grenoble 1999
$98 - €107 - £68 - FF700
Quais de l'Isère Aquarelle/papier (31x41cm 12x16in)
Grenoble 2001

CHEVALIER Henry 1886-1945 [1]
$3 237 - €3 811 - £2 275 - FF25 000
Environ d'Alger, lumière du soir Huile/carton/toile
(52x74cm 20x29in) Paris 2001

CHEVALIER Jean 1725-1790 [1]
$11 081 - €10 671 - £6 881 - FF70 000
Portrait équestre de Louis XV Huile/toile
(81x64cm 31x25in) Paris 1999

CHEVALIER Miguel 1959 [26]
$3 412 - €3 811 - £2 312 - FF25 000
Régate Photo (72x256x16.5cm 28x100x6in) Paris
2000

CHEVALIER Nicolas 1828-1902 [67]
$17 756 - €21 125 - £12 284 - FF138 569
The Sanctuary of Santa Rosalia Oil/canvas
(123x168cm 48x66in) Sydney 2000
$39 174 - €36 750 - £24 204 - FF241 062
Studley park at Sunrise/The Yarra above Yarra
Bend Oil/board (29.5x57.5cm 11x22in) Melbourne
1999
$1 618 - €1 556 - £998 - FF10 209
Segelschiffe auf hoher See/In einem Hafen
angelegte Zweimaster Oil/panel (23.5x33cm
9x12in) Bern 1999
$2 797 - €3 137 - £1 900 - FF20 578
Natives on the Shore of a south Sea Island
Watercolour (10x18.5cm 3x7in) London 2000

CHEVALIER Peter 1953 [27]
$3 281 - €2 812 - £1 972 - FF18 443
Haus und Hund Acryl/Leinwand (250x200cm
98x78in) Hamburg 1998

CHEVALIER Robert Magnus act.1876-1911 [3]
$5 612 - €6 674 - £4 000 - FF43 780
In an Eastern Street Oil/canvas (76x63.5cm 29x25in)
London 2000

CHEVILLIARD Vincent J.-Baptiste 1841-1904 [18]
$8 000 - €9 564 - £5 496 - FF62 736
The Lady and the Jester Oil/panel (50x35cm
20x14in) Chicago IL 2000
$839 - €915 - £550 - FF6 000
Le tronc pour les âmes du purgatoire Huile/pan-
neau (19.5x15cm 7x5in) Louviers 2000

CHEVIOT Lilian XIX-XX [62]
$4 673 - €5 520 - £3 300 - FF36 209
Study of three Scottie Dogs Oil/canvas (39x59cm
15x23in) Birmingham 2001
$712 - €828 - £500 - FF5 432
Kitten Oil/canvas (20x14.5cm 7x5in) Billinghurst,
West-Sussex 2001

CHEVOLLEAU Jean 1924-1996 [446]
$910 - €1 082 - £648 - FF7 100
Alcide maraîchin Huile/toile (55x46cm 21x18in)
Nantes 2001
$313 - €351 - £217 - FF2 300
«Route d'Auzay» Huile/toile (27x22cm 10x8in)
Versailles 2001
$171 - €191 - £119 - FF1 250
«L'entraînement» Crayons couleurs/papier (48x63cm
18x24in) Soissons 2001

CHEVRÉ Paul-Romain 1867-1914 [11]
$2 441 - €2 439 - £1 526 - FF16 000
Jeune garçon jouant avec des coqs Bronze
(H48.5cm H19in) Paris 2001

CHEVTSOV Igor XX [30]
$464 - €396 - £280 - FF2 600
Marché aux tapis Huile/toile (35x60cm 13x23in)
Enghien 1998
$300 - €300 - £185 - FF1 970
Veleros en el puerto Oleo/cartón (15x26cm 5x10in)
Madrid 2001

CHEYNEY S. Emma XIX-XX [1]
$1 538 - €1 444 - £950 - FF9 471
A Still Life of Wisteria in a Bowl Watercolour/paper
(50.5x72.5cm 19x28in) Billinghurst, West-Sussex 1999

CHHABDA Bal 1923 [3]
$3 000 - €3 412 - £2 096 - FF22 380
Graces face Women's Lib Acrylic/canvas
(182x91cm 71x35in) New-York 2000

CHIA Sandro 1946 [636]
$38 000 - €37 796 - £23 586 - FF247 927
Scherzoso Oil/panel (244x122cm 96x48in) Beverly-
Hills CA 1999
$5 200 - €6 738 - £3 900 - FF44 200
Senza titolo Tecnica mista (104x75cm 40x29in) Roma
2000
$2 000 - €2 073 - £1 200 - FF13 600
Figura con gallo Tempera (45x34cm 17x13in)
Vercelli 2000
$38 000 - €36 768 - £23 434 - FF241 182
Figure with Tear and Arrow Bronze
(127x183x81.5cm 50x72x32in) New-York 1999
$5 000 - €4 309 - £2 970 - FF28 264
Reclining Female Nude with a Bear Bronze
(41x20.5x30cm 16x8x11in) New-York 1998
$2 948 - €3 143 - £2 000 - FF20 618
Standing Figure Gouache/paper (75.5x57cm
29x22in) London 2001

$490 - €452 - **£301** - FF2 966
Colore Verte Etching in colors (91x59.5cm 35x23in)
Stockholm 1999

CHIALIVA Luigi 1842-c.1914 [134]
$40 000 - €44 774 - **£27 896** - FF293 700
Cows in a Landscape Oil/canvas (92.5x131cm 36x51in) New-York 2001
$20 000 - €18 973 - **£12 150** - FF124 458
Feeding Time Oil/canvas/board (58.5x82.5cm 23x32in) New-York 1999
$5 750 - €5 961 - **£3 450** - FF39 100
Ritorno al tramonto Olio/tela (33x46cm 12x18in) Milano 2000
$140 - €181 - **£105** - FF1 190
Paesaggio Matita/carta (22x28cm 8x11in) Vercelli 2000

CHIANESE Mario 1928 [7]
$1 440 - €1 866 - **£1 080** - FF12 240
«**Mattino grigio presso Nervi**» Olio/tela (45x65cm 17x25in) Torino 2000

CHIAPPELLI Francesco 1890-1947 [2]
$750 - €777 - **£450** - FF5 100
Le caravelle Acquaforte (69x58cm 27x22in) Firenze 2001

CHIARI Giuseppe 1926 [54]
$250 - €259 - **£150** - FF1 700
Claude Debussy Inchiostro/carta (30x22cm 11x8in) Vercelli 1999
$325 - €337 - **£195** - FF2 210
Gesti sulla chitarra Photo (40.5x30.5cm 15x12in) Prato 2001

CHIARI Giuseppe Bartolomeo 1654-1727 [15]
$47 817 - €51 328 - **£32 060** - FF336 691
Christ and the Woman Of Samaria Oil/canvas (134.5x98cm 52x38in) London 2000
$6 000 - €6 220 - **£3 600** - FF40 800
Cristo nell'orto Olio/tela (55x45cm 21x17in) Roma 1999

CHIBBARO José García 1949 [3]
$5 500 - €4 796 - **£3 325** - FF31 458
Cristóbal colón Oil/panel (47x33cm 18x12in) New-York 1998

CHICHARRO Eduardo 1873-1949 [6]
$4 320 - €4 805 - **£2 880** - FF31 520
Zíngara Oleo/lienzo (97x72cm 38x28in) Madrid 2000
$1 755 - €1 952 - **£1 202** - FF12 805
Blanco y negro Gouache/papier (51x38cm 20x14in) Madrid 2001

CHICHARRO Y AGÜERA Eduardo 1873-1949 [11]
$11 900 - €10 211 - **£7 140** - FF66 980
La verbena Oleo/lienzo (170x82cm 66x32in) Madrid 1999

CHICHESTER Cecil 1891-1963 [17]
$1 100 - €1 007 - **£667** - FF6 606
Landscape with Mountains and Lake in Distance Oil/canvas (76x91cm 30x36in) East-Dennis MA 1998
$900 - €771 - **£541** - FF5 057
Landscape Oil/board (20x25cm 8x10in) Cleveland OH 1998

CHICHKINE Vladimir 1959 [19]
$318 - €274 - **£192** - FF1 800
Nature morte aux chrysanthèmes Huile/toile (30x35cm 11x13in) Le Havre 1999

CHICKEN Edwin T. 1940 [21]
$1 022 - €850 - **£600** - FF5 576
Lapwing Watercolour/paper (22x28cm 8x11in) London 1998

CHIDZEY H.J. 1855-1926 [1]
$7 500 - €8 966 - **£5 153** - FF58 815
Coastal Schooner and Bridgwater Off the Lizard Oil/canvas (50x76cm 20x30in) Chicago IL 2000

CHIERICI Gaetano 1838-1920 [52]
$114 849 - €105 173 - **£70 000** - FF689 892
Feeding Baby Oil/canvas (56x80cm 22x31in) London 1999
$122 817 - €103 161 - **£72 000** - FF676 692
Farmyard Rascals Oil/canvas (31x40.5cm 12x15in) London 1998

CHIESA Pietro 1876-1959 [55]
$20 649 - €24 285 - **£14 807** - FF159 296
Mercato Oil/panel (127x97cm 50x38in) Bern 2001
$3 233 - €2 790 - **£1 950** - FF18 300
Abendfrieden Öl/Leinwand (50x65cm 19x25in) St. Gallen 1998
$643 - €624 - **£397** - FF4 094
Mutter mit Kind Pastel (43x27.5cm 16x10in) Luzern 1999

CHIESA Renato 1947 [14]
$550 - €570 - **£330** - FF3 740
Ombra Tecnica mista/tela (40x50cm 15x19in) Vercelli 2000

CHIESI Giorgio 1941 [77]
$300 - €311 - **£180** - FF2 040
Modernità Olio/tela (60x70cm 23x27in) Vercelli 2001

CHIEZO Taro 1962 [4]
$4 500 - €4 354 - **£2 775** - FF28 561
T.P.-557P Construction (61x46x46cm 24x18x18in) New-York 1999

CHIGHINE Alfredo 1914-1974 [75]
$7 200 - €9 330 - **£5 400** - FF61 200
Composizione Olio/tela (65x81cm 25x31in) Milano 2001
$1 320 - €1 140 - **£880** - FF7 480
Senza titolo Tecnica mista/carta (36.5x48.5cm 14x19in) Milano 1998

CHIGOT Eugène 1860-1923 [99]
$5 868 - €6 860 - **£4 122** - FF45 050
Femme et fille de pêcheur sur la grève Huile/toile/panneau (155x181.5cm 61x71in) Paris 2000
$2 243 - €2 668 - **£1 599** - FF17 500
Port au soleil couchant Huile/toile (46x61cm 18x24in) Calais 2000
$814 - €741 - **£500** - FF4 863
A Shepherdess tending her Flock Oil/canvas/board (33x46cm 12x18in) London 1999

CHIHULY Dale 1941 [65]
$78 000 - €74 456 - **£48 742** - FF488 397
Five-Part Wall Installation Sculpture, glass (203x254x30.5cm 79x100x12in) New-York 1999
$7 500 - €7 769 - **£4 773** - FF50 964
Sea Form Sculpture, glass (23.5x53.5x30.5cm 9x21x12in) New-York 2000

CHIKANOBU Yoshu / Toyoharu 1838-1912 [57]
$350 - €411 - **£253** - FF2 698
Garden by Moonlight Woodcut (34x72cm 13x28in) Chicago IL 2001

CHIKKEI Nakabayashi 1816-1867 **[3]**
- $3 000 - €2 747 - **£1 828** - FF18 020
  Waterfall Landscape Ink (125x30cm 49x11in) New-York 1999

CHIKUDEN Tanomura 1777-1835 **[1]**
- $14 000 - €14 411 - **£8 824** - FF94 532
  Village by a Stream Ink (182x96cm 71x37in) New-York 2000

CHIKUDO Kishi 1826-1897 **[2]**
- $359 - €409 - **£249** - FF2 683
  Herbstgräser und Rotkehlchen Indian ink (119.6x28cm 47x11in) Köln 2000

CHIKUTO 1776-1853 **[1]**
- $1 700 - €1 557 - **£1 036** - FF10 211
  Bamboo Ink (135x50cm 53x19in) New-York 1999

CHILD Jane Bridgham Curtis 1868-? **[1]**
- $9 792 - €11 416 - **£6 863** - FF74 882
  Beautiful young Woman as Muse of Epic Poetry Pastel/canvas (152x50cm 60x20in) Cleveland OH 2000

CHILDE Elias XVIII-XIX **[6]**
- $8 341 - €8 406 - **£5 200** - FF55 138
  Loading the Hay Wagon in a Farmyard Oil/canvas (61x74cm 24x29in) London 2000

CHILLIDA JUANTEGUI Eduardo 1924 **[502]**
- $7 930 - €7 808 - **£4 940** - FF51 220
  Homenaje a Picasso Acrilico/lienzo (42x56.5cm 16x22in) Madrid 1999
- $389 934 - €424 899 - **£270 000** - FF2 787 156
  Estela a José Antonio de Aguirre Iron (125.5x128.5x75.5cm 49x50x29in) London 2001
- $107 744 - €91 862 - **£65 000** - FF602 576
  Lotura I Metal (H33.5cm H13in) London 1998
- $17 931 - €19 248 - **£12 000** - FF126 259
  Untitled Ink (49x51.5cm 19x20in) London 2000
- $1 244 - €1 189 - **£776** - FF7 800
  Antzo VIII Eau-forte (53x75.5cm 20x29in) Paris 1999

CHILLIDA JUANTEGUI Gonzalo 1926 **[21]**
- $3 780 - €4 205 - **£2 660** - FF27 580
  Bosque Oleo/lienzo (92x73cm 36x28in) Madrid 2001

CHILLINGWORTH John 1928 **[5]**
- $899 - €832 - **£550** - FF5 460
  The Boy and the Distorting Mirror, Rotherham Gelatin silver print (30x25cm 12x10in) London 1999

CHILONE Vincenzo 1758-1839 **[15]**
- $21 376 - €24 279 - **£15 000** - FF159 262
  Venice, a View of the Piazzetta from the North, the Church beyond Oil/canvas (38x48cm 14x18in) London 2001

CHIM (David Szymin) 1911-1956 **[13]**
- $781 - €908 - **£549** - FF5 953
  Richard Avedon and Fred Astair Gelatin silver print (48x33.5cm 18x13in) Amsterdam 2001

CHIMAER VAN OUDENDORP Wilhelmus Cornelis 1822-1873 **[8]**
- $1 510 - €1 452 - **£930** - FF9 525
  Trompe l'oeil of Manuscript, Including an Almanac, Music Scores Ink (19.5x20cm 7x7in) Amsterdam 1999

CHIMCHDIAN Ovaneff XX **[10]**
- $4 870 - €4 116 - **£2 897** - FF27 000
  Femme allanguie Huile/toile/carton (42x54cm 16x21in) Paris 1998
- $251 - €295 - **£180** - FF1 937
  Sicht auf die Pyramiden von Giseh und den Nil Öl/Leinwand (31x44.5cm 12x17in) Zürich 2001

CHIMENTI Jacopo da Empoli c.1554-1640 **[27]**
- $14 080 - €15 988 - **£9 636** - FF104 874
  Die Heilige Familie mit dem Johannesknaben Öl/Leinwand (117x92cm 46x36in) Wien 2000
- $3 885 - €4 170 - **£2 600** - FF27 356
  Adam and Eve with their Sons Black chalk (29x23cm 11x9in) London 2000

CHIMOT Édouard 1880-1959 **[88]**
- $2 435 - €2 363 - **£1 545** - FF15 500
  Le modèle, Espagnole nue Huile/toile (73x103cm 28x40in) Paris 1999
- $130 - €122 - **£79** - FF800
  L'Hôpital Crayon (30x21cm 11x8in) Sainte-Geneviève-des-Bois 1999
- $81 - €76 - **£50** - FF500
  Bacchanale sur le bord de mer Pointe sèche (24.5x19cm 9x7in) Orléans 1999

CHIN Hsiao 1935 **[57]**
- $7 960 - €7 622 - **£5 010** - FF50 000
  Géométrie Huile/toile (130x195cm 51x76in) Paris 1999
- $1 249 - €1 452 - **£878** - FF9 525
  Untitled Acrylic/canvas (70x80cm 27x31in) Amsterdam 2001
- $958 - €1 113 - **£673** - FF7 302
  Composition NDA-9 Aquarell (57x40cm 22x15in) Luzern 2001

CHINAMI Nakajima 1945 **[3]**
- $90 000 - €99 293 - **£59 526** - FF651 321
  Kozan kitsuritsu (Soaring Mount Huang) Ink (165x339cm 64x133in) New-York 2000

CHINET Charles Louis 1891-1978 **[23]**
- $2 135 - €2 489 - **£1 478** - FF16 325
  Sommerlandschaft mit Dorf vor einer Hügelkette Öl/Leinwand (38x55.5cm 14x21in) Bern 2000
- $1 444 - €1 718 - **£1 029** - FF11 267
  Paysage Huile/toile (27x41cm 10x16in) Genève 2000

CHING Raymond Harris 1939 **[15]**
- $6 046 - €6 777 - **£4 228** - FF44 457
  North Island Chestnut Kiwi Oil/hardboard (50x41cm 19x16in) Auckland 2001
- $848 - €967 - **£586** - FF6 343
  Study of a reclining Nude Pencil/paper (44x72.5cm 17x28in) Auckland 2000

CHINI Galileo 1873-1956 **[120]**
- $15 200 - €19 696 - **£11 400** - FF129 200
  Danzatrice siamese Olio/tela (177x111cm 69x43in) Prato 2001
- $3 800 - €4 924 - **£2 850** - FF32 300
  La modella nello studio Olio/cartone (88x70cm 34x27in) Prato 2000
- $2 250 - €2 332 - **£1 350** - FF15 300
  Nevicata alla Merlaia Olio/cartone (26.5x35cm 10x13in) Prato 2000

CHINNERY George 1774-1852 **[230]**
- $26 771 - €29 851 - **£18 000** - FF195 811
  Young Lady, Three-Quarter Length, her Elbow Resting on a Pedestal Oil/canvas (124x99cm 49x39in) Leicester 2000
- $92 618 - €86 631 - **£56 000** - FF568 265
  Sherman Bird, Judge of the City Court of Dacca, seated, an Indian Oil/canvas (77x64.5cm 30x25in) London 1999
- $17 184 - €16 817 - **£11 000** - FF110 315
  Portrait of Miss Bennett, seated, wearing a green Dress and white Cap Oil/canvas (38.5x30.5cm 15x12in) London 1999

$1 801 - €1 647 - **£1 100** - FF10 805
Figures by a tomb Watercolour (9x15cm 3x6in)
London 1998

CHINTREUIL Antoine 1814-1873 [139]
$3 070 - €3 049 - **£1 912** - FF20 000
Lande aux genêts Huile/toile (35x72cm 13x28in)
Paris 1999
$2 524 - €2 428 - **£1 558** - FF15 926
Felsige Waldpartie Öl/Karton (23x30cm 9x11in)
Bern 1999
$1 664 - €1 640 - **£1 037** - FF11 000
Bord de rivière Pastel/papier (56x85.5cm 22x33in)
Cherbourg 2000

CHINZAN Tsubaki 1801-1854 [1]
$2 540 - €2 727 - **£1 700** - FF17 886
Three Friends Triptych Ink/paper (122x28cm
48x11in) London 2000

CHIOSTRI Carlo 1863-1939 [16]
$613 - €579 - **£380** - FF3 799
A Figure near ruined Roman Fortifications
Watercolour (19x24cm 7x9in) Billingshurst, West-
Sussex 1999

CHIPARUS Demeter H. 1888-1950 [651]
$7 246 - €7 349 - **£4 500** - FF48 209
**Naked Female Warrior, Reclining Backwards
with Length of Cloth** Bronze (H93.5cm H36in)
London 2000
$8 500 - €8 438 - **£5 213** - FF55 348
Starlight Bronze (H57cm H22in) Delray-Beach FL
2000

CHIRAC A. Désiré XIX [1]
$4 635 - €4 573 - **£2 856** - FF30 000
Amazone Huile/toile (60x81cm 23x31in) Neuilly-sur-
Seine 1999

CHIRIACKA Ernest 1920 [8]
$500 - €563 - **£344** - FF3 691
Ocean Mist Oil/panel (59x49cm 23x19in) Chicago IL
2000

CHIRICO de Giorgio 1888-1978 [1535]
$147 400 - €157 160 - **£100 000** - FF1 030 900
L'île de San Giorgio Oil/canvas (119x116cm
46x45in) London 2001
$66 000 - €85 524 - **£49 500** - FF561 000
Cavalli in riva al mare Olio/cartone (36x48cm
14x18in) Milano 2001
$27 500 - €28 508 - **£16 500** - FF187 000
Costume manzoniano Olio/tela (30x20cm 11x7in)
Venezia 1999
$132 000 - €114 032 - **£88 000** - FF748 000
Ettore e Andromaca Bronzo (230x118x91cm
90x46x35in) Prato 2000
$5 000 - €5 183 - **£3 000** - FF34 000
Il pittore Bronzo (H25.5cm H10in) Milano 1999
$8 000 - €6 902 - **£4 826** - FF45 274
Due Cavalli Ink (24x30cm 9x11in) New-York 1998
$721 - €858 - **£500** - FF5 626
Hebdomeros, from Metamorphosis Color lithogra-
ph (40.5x31cm 15x12in) London 2000

CHIRICO di Giacomo 1845-1891 [12]
$20 000 - €23 520 - **£14 340** - FF154 278
Proud parents Oil/panel (58.5x72cm 23x28in) New-
York 2001
$3 770 - €3 904 - **£2 405** - FF25 610
Niña leyendo Oleo/tabla (24x18cm 9x7in) Barcelona
2000

CHIRINO Martín 1925 [17]
$14 000 - €15 016 - **£9 500** - FF98 500
Sin título Fer (12x30cm 4x11in) Madrid 2001
$1 680 - €1 802 - **£1 110** - FF11 820
Vía láctea Técnica mixta/papel (60x45cm 23x17in)
Madrid 2001
$487 - €450 - **£292** - FF2 955
Abstracción con cruz Aguafuerte (74x110cm
29x43in) Madrid 1999

CHITTENDEN Alice Brown 1859-1945 [29]
$1 430 - €1 458 - **£896** - FF9 562
Floral Still Life Oil/canvas (66x60cm 26x24in)
Altadena CA 2000

CHITTUSSI Anton 1847-1891 [26]
$9 826 - €9 294 - **£6 120** - FF60 962
Paysage de France au coucher de soleil
Huile/toile (38x55cm 14x21in) Praha 2001
$1 878 - €1 777 - **£1 170** - FF11 654
Femme et paysage Huile/toile (21.5x25cm 8x9in)
Praha 2000
$1 734 - €1 640 - **£1 080** - FF10 758
Landscape with a Scarecrow Watercolour/paper
(27x38cm 10x14in) Praha 2000

CHLEBOWSKI Stanislaw 1835-1884 [34]
$92 500 - €86 641 - **£56 869** - FF568 329
A seated Bashi-Bazouk with a Rifle Oil/canvas
(52x38.5cm 20x15in) New-York 1998
$6 500 - €5 490 - **£3 903** - FF36 011
Arabs resting in a Portal Oil/canvas (33x26.5cm
12x10in) New-York 1998
$1 000 - €1 091 - **£678** - FF7 158
Portrait of a Sultan Pencil/paper (25.5x21cm 10x8in)
New-York 2000

CHMIELINSKI Wardek Vladislaw 1912-1979 [23]
$1 862 - €2 018 - **£1 289** - FF13 234
Course de traîneaux Huile/toile (50.5x71cm
19x27in) Warszawa 2001
$915 - €982 - **£606** - FF6 444
Vue de la rue Freta Aquarelle/papier (25x35cm
9x13in) Warszawa 2001

CHMIELINSKI Wladyslaw T. 1911 [49]
$1 565 - €1 505 - **£965** - FF9 872
Stadsmotiv med figurer Olio/canvas (35x50cm
13x19in) Malmö 1999
$984 - €849 - **£592** - FF5 571
Hästekipage med människor på byväg Oil/canvas
(18x25cm 7x9in) Malmö 1998
$689 - €607 - **£420** - FF3 982
Snow in Warsaw Watercolour (32.5x47cm 12x18in)
London 1999

CHOCARNE-MOREAU Paul-Charles 1855-1931 [96]
$80 000 - €69 020 - **£48 264** - FF452 744
Opportunity Makes the Thief Oil/canvas
(167x129cm 65x50in) New-York 1998
$13 000 - €11 216 - **£7 842** - FF73 570
Good Friends Oil/canvas (38x46cm 14x18in) New-
York 1998
$4 663 - €4 421 - **£2 836** - FF29 000
Le toréador Huile/toile (41x33cm 16x12in) Paris 1999
$3 912 - €3 659 - **£2 368** - FF24 000
Le ramoneur et le pâtissier Aquarelle/papier
(30x43cm 11x16in) Saint-Dié 1999

CHOCHON André 1910 [69]
$309 - €290 - **£187** - FF1 900
Paysage des îles Huile/panneau (19x24cm 7x9in)
Rennes 1999

CHODOWIECKI Daniel Nikolaus 1726-1801 **[447]**
- $6 188 - €6 235 - **£3 857** - FF40 901
  Bildnis der Manon Rahn Öl/Leinwand
  (89.4x70.3cm 35x27in) Zürich 2000
- $318 - €358 - **£219** - FF2 347
  Galante Gesellschaft Painting (9x11.2cm 3x4in)
  Heidelberg 2001
- $882 - €767 - **£531** - FF5 028
  Der Dorfschullehrer und seine Klasse vor dem Wanderausflug Ink/paper (6.1x6.7cm 2x2in) Berlin 1998
- $217 - €256 - **£156** - FF1 676
  Portrait von Johann Wolfgang von Goethe
  Radierung (17.5x10.5cm 6x4in) Hamburg 2001

CHOFFARD Pierre-Philippe 1730-1809 **[8]**
- $582 - €610 - **£386** - FF4 000
  Vue de la ville d'Orléans en 1761, d'après Desfriches A.T. Eau-forte (58x82cm 22x32in) Orléans 2000

CHOKAI Seiji 1902-1972 **[3]**
- $68 640 - €66 910 - **£42 000** - FF438 900
  Landscape in Hokkaido Oil/canvas (60x91cm 23x35in) Tokyo 1999
- $1 764 - €1 721 - **£1 080** - FF11 286
  Flamenco Pastel (27x24cm 10x9in) Tokyo 1999

CHONG SON 1676-1759 **[1]**
- $15 000 - €17 590 - **£10 704** - FF115 386
  Scholar in a Landscape Ink (31.5x21cm 12x8in)
  New-York 2000

CHOO KENG KWANG 1931 **[13]**
- $4 156 - €3 487 - **£2 438** - FF22 876
  Pigeon Oil/canvas (124x81cm 48x31in) Singapore 1998

CHOON Chew 1949 **[5]**
- $3 066 - €2 550 - **£1 800** - FF16 728
  The Approaching Storm -Elephants Watercolour (65x100cm 25x39in) London 1998

CHOPPING Richard W. XX **[1]**
- $2 620 - €2 396 - **£1 600** - FF15 717
  Proof design for the dust-jacket front panel of «Goldfinger» Print (51x42cm 20x16in) London 1998

CHOPPY R. XX **[7]**
- $410 - €457 - **£276** - FF3 000
  «La Houppa et son Fourtoutou» Affiche (118x77cm 46x30in) Orléans 2000

CHOQUET René-Maxime ?-c.1939 **[43]**
- $11 923 - €10 976 - **£7 156** - FF72 000
  Amazones à la chasse à courre Huile/toile (400x290cm 157x114in) Libourne 1999
- $1 280 - €1 220 - **£811** - FF8 000
  Le village de Ligas Huile/toile (50x61cm 19x24in) Biarritz 1999
- $2 332 - €2 744 - **£1 672** - FF18 000
  Le basque et son âne Huile/panneau (19x24cm 7x9in) Pau 2001

CHORNEY Steven 1951 **[17]**
- $15 000 - €16 101 - **£10 038** - FF105 615
  Labyrinth - Tri-Star Pictures Acrylic (127x76cm 50x30in) Beverly-Hills CA 2000
- $1 800 - €1 932 - **£1 204** - FF12 673
  Name of the Rose - Twentieth Century Fox
  Pencil (58x43cm 23x17in) Beverly-Hills CA 2000

CHOSHUN Miyagawa 1682-1752 **[2]**
- $9 000 - €9 363 - **£5 727** - FF61 419
  Courtesan Procession in The Snow Ink (98.5x40cm 38x15in) New-York 2000

CHOUBRAC Alfred 1853-1902 **[169]**
- $499 - €427 - **£299** - FF2 800
  «Trianon Concert Recensons» Affiche (57x79cm 22x31in) Paris 1998

CHOULTSÉ Ivan Fedorovitch 1874-1939 **[100]**
- $6 000 - €6 998 - **£4 212** - FF45 902
  The Moonlit Shore Oil/canvas (81.5x65cm 32x25in)
  Boston MA 2000
- $1 205 - €990 - **£700** - FF6 493
  Landscape on Artist's Palette Oil/panel (30x40cm 11x15in) London 1998

CHOUPPE Jean-Henri 1817-1894 **[64]**
- $533 - €488 - **£326** - FF3 200
  Le Chesnoy Aquarelle/papier (46x28cm 18x11in)
  Paris 1999

CHOW KWA c.1830-c.1890 **[3]**
- $275 000 - €263 338 - **£169 482** - FF1 727 385
  View of the Bund at Shanghai depicting American, English Shipping Oil/canvas (48x81cm 19x32in) Portsmouth NH 1999

CHOWDHURY Devi Prasad Roy XX **[11]**
- $4 500 - €4 261 - **£2 806** - FF27 948
  Day's End Oil/board (39x52.5cm 15x20in) New-York 1999
- $1 000 - €1 181 - **£708** - FF7 750
  Portrait of Rabindranath Tagore Watercolour/paper (37x24cm 14x9in) New-York 2000

CHOWDHURY Jogen 1939 **[42]**
- $10 000 - €11 373 - **£6 987** - FF74 601
  Untitled Acrylic/canvas (60.5x60.5cm 23x23in) New-York 2000
- $3 500 - €3 980 - **£2 445** - FF26 110
  Ganesh with crown Crayon (38x35.5cm 14x13in)
  New-York 2000

CHRÉTIEN René Louis 1867-1945 **[90]**
- $9 000 - €10 578 - **£6 239** - FF69 384
  Gourmandises Oil/canvas (126x157cm 49x61in)
  New-York 2000
- $2 963 - €3 501 - **£2 100** - FF22 966
  Nature morte aux raisins Oil/canvas (73x60cm 28x23in) London 2000
- $852 - €915 - **£570** - FF6 000
  Les vaches près du village Huile/carton (27x35cm 10x13in) Cherbourg 2000

CHRIST Martin Alfred 1900-1979 **[65]**
- $485 - €554 - **£342** - FF3 634
  Garten mit zugefrorenem Teich im Winter
  Öl/Leinwand (77x86cm 30x33in) Bern 2001

CHRIST Pieter Caspar 1822-1888 **[16]**
- $5 429 - €5 218 - **£3 385** - FF34 230
  Wooded Landscape with Grazing Sheep Oil/canvas (69x94cm 27x37in) Amsterdam 1999
- $1 149 - €1 271 - **£797** - FF8 334
  Peasantwomen doing Laundry in Front of a Farmhouse Oil/canvas/panel (40x35.5cm 15x13in)
  Amsterdam 2001

CHRISTENBERRY William 1936 **[24]**
- $2 000 - €1 877 - **£1 235** - FF12 313
  The Bar-B-Q Inn, Greensboro/Church, Sprott, Alabama Photograph in colors (8x12.5cm 3x4in) New-York 1999

CHRISTENSEN Anthonie, Anthonore 1849-1926 **[161]**
- $3 933 - €3 617 - **£2 430** - FF23 724
  Gule og blå iris Oil/canvas (81x50cm 31x19in) Vejle 1998

$937 - €1 072 - £652 - FF7 035
Tallerkensmaekkere Oil/canvas (16x35cm 6x13in)
Köbenhavn 2000

CHRISTENSEN Arent 1894-1982 **[5]**
$132 - €148 - £92 - FF974
Gutteportrett Etching (20x16cm 7x6in) Oslo 2001

CHRISTENSEN Flora XIX **[2]**
$2 250 - €2 013 - £1 348 - FF13 204
Roser og myrter Oil/canvas (26x33cm 10x12in)
Köbenhavn 2000

CHRISTENSEN Godfred B.W. 1845-1928 **[220]**
$2 424 - €2 680 - £1 682 - FF17 578
Kokkedal Mose Oil/canvas (126x185cm 49x72in)
Köbenhavn 2001
$699 - €673 - £434 - FF4 415
Udsigt over Vejledalen Oil/canvas (50x72cm
19x28in) Köbenhavn 1999
$542 - €538 - £329 - FF3 526
Sommerlandskab med figurer og hest Oil/canvas
(28x37cm 11x14in) Vejle 2000

CHRISTENSEN John Aksel 1896-1940 **[41]**
$273 - €295 - £188 - FF1 935
Opstilling med palet og flaske Pastel/paper
(36x47cm 14x18in) Köbenhavn 2001

CHRISTENSEN Kay 1899-1981 **[274]**
$1 113 - €941 - £665 - FF6 172
Lille pige i grönt landskab Oil/canvas (73x92cm
28x36in) Köbenhavn 1998
$258 - €282 - £178 - FF1 847
La mouche Watercolour/paper (46x29cm 18x11in)
Köbenhavn 2001

CHRISTIANSEN Hans 1866-1945 **[40]**
$2 095 - €2 250 - £1 402 - FF14 757
Südliche Landschaft Öl/Leinwand (50x65cm
19x25in) Köln 2000
$239 - €204 - £142 - FF1 341
**Mädchenköpfe mit ornamental gestalteten
Haaren** Farblithographie (14x9cm 5x3in) München
1998

CHRISTIANSEN Niels Hans act.1874-? **[98]**
$619 - €697 - £426 - FF4 572
Skridskoparti i vintersol Oil/canvas (51x76cm
20x29in) Uppsala 2000
$505 - €489 - £320 - FF3 205
Aldbrough Oil/board (21x13cm 8x5in) Guildford,
Surrey 1999

CHRISTIANSEN Nils H. 1850-1922 **[31]**
$1 197 - €1 145 - £750 - FF7 508
Log Cabins on the Banks of a Fjord Oil/canvas
(51x76cm 20x29in) London 1999
$750 - €694 - £459 - FF4 554
Church nestled in a snowy Landscape Oil/board
(26x34cm 10x13in) St. Louis MO 1999

CHRISTIANSEN Poul S. 1855-1933 **[39]**
$360 - €336 - £217 - FF2 207
Udsigt fra stakladen, Dyrnaes Oil/canvas
(48x61cm 18x24in) Köbenhavn 1999

CHRISTIANSEN Rasmus 1863-1940 **[132]**
$5 057 - €4 713 - £3 055 - FF30 915
Et möde på landevejen Oil/canvas (127x190cm
50x74in) Köbenhavn 1999
$499 - €484 - £316 - FF3 178
Raessende köer Oil/canvas (48x67cm 18x26in) Viby
J, Århus 1999

CHRISTIANSEN Søren 1858-1937 **[46]**
$542 - €538 - £338 - FF3 532
Interiör med passiarende damer Oil/canvas
(70x54cm 27x21in) Köbenhavn 1999

CHRISTIE James Elder 1847-1914 **[46]**
$7 925 - €8 233 - £5 000 - FF54 007
In Time of War Oil/canvas (139x88cm 54x34in)
London 2000
$2 853 - €2 964 - £1 800 - FF19 442
Gannets Eggs Oil/canvas (51x61cm 20x24in) London
2000
$1 183 - €1 156 - £750 - FF7 585
Children gathering Flowers Oil/canvas/panel
(24x34cm 9x13in) London 1999

CHRISTMANN Gunter Sylvester 1936 **[14]**
$2 859 - €3 069 - £1 913 - FF20 131
Now Oil/canvas (167x137cm 65x53in) Sydney 2000

CHRISTMAS Erwin S. 1885-1921 **[1]**
$4 000 - €3 375 - £2 346 - FF22 136
Galloping Horses Bronze (H57.5cm H22in) New-
York 1998

CHRISTO 1935 **[1155]**
$66 498 - €64 181 - £42 000 - FF420 999
Wrapped Pont-Neuf (Project for Paris) Mixed
media (147.5x166cm 58x65in) London 2001
$20 000 - €20 733 - £12 000 - FF136 000
Wrapped Monument to Cristobal Colon Tecnica
mista/cartone (71x55.5cm 27x21in) Prato 1999
$3 240 - €3 811 - £2 322 - FF25 000
Look Technique mixte (43x33cm 16x12in) Paris 2001
$55 000 - €61 604 - £38 214 - FF404 096
«Store Front Project» Relief (90x125x10cm
35x49x3in) New-York 2001
$12 000 - €11 539 - £7 393 - FF75 692
Wrapped Roses Object (14x41.5x89cm 5x16x35in)
New-York 1999
$25 890 - €29 006 - £18 046 - FF190 270
**The Umbrellas (Joint Projekct for Japan and
USA)** Coloured chalks (67x78cm 26x30in) Stockholm
2001
$671 - €737 - £432 - FF4 833
**10 Millions oil Drums Wall, Project for the Suez
Canal** Serigraph in colors (70.5x55.5cm 27x21in)
Stockholm 2000
$455 - €528 - £314 - FF3 462
**The Umbrellas, Project for Japan and Western
U.S.A.** Photograph in colors (42x30cm 16x11in)
Stockholm 2000

CHRISTOFFERSEN Frede 1919-1987 **[91]**
$1 016 - €1 140 - £710 - FF7 475
Sol Oil/canvas (45x52cm 17x20in) Köbenhavn 2001
$541 - €603 - £380 - FF3 956
Figurer ogsol Oil/canvas (30x42cm 11x16in) Vejle
2001
$199 - €201 - £124 - FF1 321
Hyben på et bord Watercolour/paper (11x24cm
4x9in) Köbenhavn 2000

CHRISTOFFERSEN Helge 1925-1965 **[4]**
$1 460 - €1 610 - £988 - FF10 561
Neptun, maske med fisk Ceramic (H33cm H12in)
Vejle 2000

CHRISTOFOROU John 1921 **[218]**
$2 553 - €2 439 - £1 592 - FF16 000
Le fou-savant Huile/toile (160x128cm 62x50in) Paris
1999
$1 199 - €1 209 - £747 - FF7 930
Seelandscape Oil/canvas (65x50cm 25x19in)
Köbenhavn 2000

$316 - €305 - **£199** - FF2 000
Sans titre Gouache/papier (22.5x20cm 8x7in) Paris 1999

CHRISTOL Frédéric XX [2]
$16 200 - €13 995 - **£10 800** - FF91 800
Mirror crapped Tecnica mista (124x75x3cm 48x29x1in) Prato 1998

CHRISTY F. Earl 1883-? [4]
$4 000 - €4 663 - **£2 769** - FF30 586
Woman Holding Powder Puff Pastel/paper (71x55cm 28x22in) New-York 2000

CHRISTY Howard Chandler 1873-1952 [143]
$42 000 - €38 883 - **£25 708** - FF255 057
«We invite you» Oil/canvas (139x106cm 55x42in) New-York 1999
$3 100 - €2 896 - **£1 931** - FF18 999
Landscape Oil/canvas (101x73cm 40x29in) Mystic CT 1999
$2 400 - €2 830 - **£1 693** - FF18 566
Landscape with houses Oil/canvas (23x33cm 9x13in) New-Orleans LA 2001
$1 400 - €1 641 - **£1 087** - FF10 767
«Doris Kenyon» Pencil/paper (44x31cm 17x12in) New-York 2001
$1 100 - €996 - **£673** - FF6 536
«I Want You for the Navy» Poster (104x68cm 41x27in) New-York 1998

CHU TEH-CHUN 1920 [215]
$42 660 - €41 161 - **£26 784** - FF270 000
Composition No.31 Huile/toile (147x115cm 57x45in) Paris 1999
$12 464 - €13 272 - **£7 904** - FF87 058
Le Mai 1979 Oil/canvas (60x60cm 23x23in) Taipei 2000
$5 308 - €4 878 - **£3 260** - FF32 000
Ouverture B Huile/toile (30x40cm 11x15in) Paris 1999
$1 923 - €2 287 - **£1 371** - FF15 000
Composition Encre (53x35cm 20x13in) Paris 2000

CHUA EK KAY 1947 [2]
$2 654 - €2 474 - **£1 638** - FF16 227
Morning View of Mount Annapurna, Purkara Indian ink (88x80cm 34x31in) Singapore 1999

CHUA MIA TEE 1931 [7]
$12 696 - €11 831 - **£7 834** - FF77 609
Koi (Beautiful Carps) Oil/canvas (130x194cm 51x76in) Singapore 1999
$5 938 - €4 982 - **£3 484** - FF32 680
Rabbits Oil/canvas (61x91.5cm 24x36in) Singapore 1998

CHUANG MOOLPINIT 1940 [3]
$3 204 - €2 976 - **£1 980** - FF19 524
Temple on the Lake Watercolour/paper (57x74cm 22x29in) Bangkok 1999

CHUGHTAI Abdur Rahman 1895-1975 [74]
$30 842 - €29 641 - **£19 000** - FF194 432
Young Couple in a Mughal Garden Watercolour (55.5x36cm 21x14in) London 1999
$2 500 - €2 954 - **£1 771** - FF19 377
The Fragrance Aquatint (30.5x31cm 12x12in) New-York 2000

CHUMAKOV Feodor Petrovich 1823-1911 [4]
$8 116 - €7 800 - **£5 000** - FF51 166
Reclining Nude Pastel (53x71cm 20x27in) London 1999

CHUN David Paul 1899-? [2]
$1 900 - €2 120 - **£1 243** - FF13 904
Picnic Lithograph (25x35cm 10x14in) Chicago IL 2000

CHUPIATOV Leonid T. 1890-1942 [1]
$19 479 - €18 721 - **£12 000** - FF122 799
The Moon over the Village Oil/canvas (163x102cm 64x40in) London 1999

CHURBERG Fanny 1845-1892 [21]
$22 950 - €22 705 - **£14 310** - FF148 932
Stilleben, fiskar och brännvin Oil/canvas (38x56cm 14x22in) Helsinki 1999
$6 723 - €5 885 - **£4 074** - FF38 601
Höstseglats Oil/panel (11.5x24.5cm 4x9in) Helsinki 1998

CHURBUCK Leander M. 1861-1940 [2]
$1 300 - €1 396 - **£885** - FF9 154
A Marblehead Street in Summer Watercolour, gouache (28x37cm 11x14in) Boston MA 2001

CHURCH Bernard W. XX [1]
$2 957 - €2 950 - **£1 800** - FF19 354
Ships Watercolour/paper (23x30cm 9x11in) London 2000

CHURCH Frederic Edwin 1826-1900 [20]
$950 000 - €811 666 - **£570 285** - FF5 324 180
View near Stockbridge Oil/canvas (69x101.5cm 27x39in) New-York 1998
$75 000 - €64 181 - **£45 150** - FF420 997
Moses Viewing the Promised Land Oil/board (23x30cm 9x12in) New-York 1998

CHURCH Frederick Stuart 1842-1923 [52]
$6 500 - €5 484 - **£3 823** - FF35 971
Orchids and White Leopards Oil/canvas (120x77cm 47x30in) New-York 1998
$2 750 - €2 952 - **£1 840** - FF19 362
Tourist and Eve Mixed media (31x16cm 12x6in) Bloomfield-Hills MI 2000
$8 500 - €8 140 - **£5 251** - FF53 396
Tiger Having Eaten Professor Smoking, Illustration Watercolour/paper (38x58cm 15x23in) New-York 1999

CHURCH Henry 1836-1908 [3]
$16 000 - €17 634 - **£10 644** - FF115 670
Compote of Fruit on Table-Top with Watermelon, Pineapple, Grapes Watercolour (25x36cm 10x14in) Portsmouth NH 2000

CHURCH William Worcester 1858-1926 [7]
$6 750 - €7 976 - **£4 784** - FF52 321
Elegant Interior with Mother and Daughter Oil/canvas (110x85cm 43x33in) Boston MA 2000

CHURCHILL Winston Spencer 1874-1965 [33]
$122 482 - €112 758 - **£75 000** - FF739 642
Blue Grass, La Capponcina Oil/canvas (63x76cm 24x29in) London 1998

CHURCHYARD Thomas 1798-1865 [71]
$1 659 - €1 421 - **£980** - FF9 324
Woodbridge Oil/panel (17.5x22.5cm 6x8in) Ipswich 1998
$898 - €1 042 - **£620** - FF6 834
Sunrise, Looking Towards St.Paul's and the City from Hampstead Heath Watercolour (10.5x17.5cm 4x6in) London 2000

CHUSAKU Ohyama 1922 [2]
$4 000 - €4 031 - **£2 493** - FF26 440
Tessenka (Clematis) Mixed media (43x51.5cm 16x20in) New-York 2000

$21 560 - €21 029 - **£13 200** - FF137 940
Carps Drawing (50x65cm 19x25in) Tokyo 1999

CHWALA Adolf 1836-1900 **[62]**
$1 914 - €1 994 - **£1 213** - FF13 080
Flusslandschaft bei Mondlicht (Mondnacht an der Schelde) Oil/panel (36.5x58cm 14x22in) München 2000

CHWALA Fritz 1872-1936 **[46]**
$842 - €810 - **£520** - FF5 315
Vattendrag i skogsglänta, höststämning Oil/canvas (41x51cm 16x20in) Malmö 1999

CIACELLI Arturo 1883-1966 **[37]**
$17 000 - €17 623 - **£10 200** - FF115 600
Ritratto di Corinne Maria Bach Olio/tela (176x127cm 69x50in) Prato 2000
$2 400 - €3 110 - **£1 800** - FF20 400
«Struttura ritmica» Olio/tela (74x48cm 29x18in) Vercelli 2001
$880 - €1 140 - **£660** - FF7 480
Danze ritmiche Tempera/carta (34.5x39cm 13x15in) Milano 2000
$1 035 - €894 - **£690** - FF5 865
Minne frau Paris Acquaforte (30x30cm 11x11in) Milano 1998

CIAMPI Alimondo 1876-1939 **[44]**
$19 500 - €20 215 - **£11 700** - FF132 600
La Fanciulla di Pompei Bronzo (150x43cm 59x16in) Firenze 2000
$1 500 - €1 555 - **£900** - FF10 200
Ritratto della moglie dell'artista Bronzo (34x27cm 13x10in) Firenze 2001

CIAN Fernand Ciancianaini XIX-XX **[7]**
$935 - €1 113 - **£644** - FF7 300
Jeune fille détachant sa sandale Terracotta (32x22.5cm 12x8in) Blois 2000

CIANI Cesare 1854-1925 **[48]**
$8 400 - €7 257 - **£4 200** - FF47 600
Contadino con buoi al carro e tacchini Olio/cartone (32x53.5cm 12x21in) Prato 1999
$1 860 - €1 607 - **£1 240** - FF10 540
Spiaggia con bagnanti Olio/cartone (21x31cm 8x12in) Firenze 1998

CIAPPA Federico XIX **[11]**
$850 - €770 - **£523** - FF5 053
Coastal Scene Oil/canvas (40x71cm 16x28in) Mystic CT 1999

CIAPPA Vincenzo 1766-1826 **[2]**
$2 515 - €2 287 - **£1 543** - FF15 000
Santa Lucia (Napoli) Huile/toile (31x40cm 12x15in) Biarritz 1998

CIARDI [1]
$3 100 - €2 737 - **£1 905** - FF17 951
Morning Prayer Oil/canvas (23x30cm 9x12in) New-York 1999

CIARDI Beppe 1875-1932 **[127]**
$13 710 - €11 586 - **£8 154** - FF76 000
Ruelle animée Huile/toile (271x50cm 106x19in) Neuilly-sur-Seine 1998
$16 660 - €17 271 - **£9 996** - FF113 288
Canale veneziano Olio/tela (53x41cm 20x16in) Milano 1999
$5 750 - €5 961 - **£3 450** - FF39 100
Tramonto in laguna Olio/tavola (30x50cm 11x19in) Roma 1999

CIARDI Emma 1879-1933 **[140]**
$12 000 - €14 179 - **£8 504** - FF93 009
Outdoor Festivities Oil/panel (38x48cm 15x19in) Austinburg OH 2000
$3 800 - €4 924 - **£2 850** - FF32 300
Scherzi in giardino Olio/tavola (27x37cm 10x14in) Milano 2001

CIARDI Guglielmo 1842/43-1917 **[100]**
$50 000 - €64 791 - **£37 500** - FF425 000
Cima delle Pale, Alpi Dolomitiche in Val di Fiemme Olio/tela (198x110cm 77x43in) Milano 2000
$33 000 - €34 210 - **£19 800** - FF224 400
Vita costiera con barche e pescatori Olio/tela (43x56cm 16x22in) Roma 1999
$8 100 - €6 997 - **£5 400** - FF45 900
Paesaggio al Comelico Olio/tela (19.5x36.5cm 7x14in) Trieste 1999
$2 720 - €3 525 - **£2 040** - FF23 120
Banchina di porto con peschereccio e figure Matita/carta (32x45cm 12x17in) Milano 2001

CIARDIELLO Carmine 1871-? **[15]**
$4 080 - €5 287 - **£3 060** - FF34 680
Pescatori Olio/tela (48.5x70cm 19x27in) Napoli 2000
$1 578 - €1 654 - **£1 000** - FF10 852
Pescatori Ai Faraglioni, Capri Oil/canvas (40x25cm 15x9in) London 2000

CIARDO Vincenzo 1894-1970 **[14]**
$3 712 - €3 207 - **£1 856** - FF21 039
Campagna estiva Olio/tela (78x104cm 30x40in) Venezia 1999
$850 - €881 - **£510** - FF5 780
Capri, monte Solaro Olio/cartone (30x32cm 11x12in) Vercelli 2000

CIARROCCHI Arnoldo 1916 **[12]**
$3 000 - €3 887 - **£2 250** - FF25 500
Paesaggio marino Olio/tela (60x70cm 23x27in) Prato 2000
$800 - €829 - **£480** - FF5 440
La stradina degli amanti Acquaforte (49x38cm 19x14in) Prato 2000

CIBO Gherardo 1512-1600 **[7]**
$5 615 - €5 495 - **£3 600** - FF36 043
View of a Monastery, with a separate Study of a Tree Watercolour (12.5x19.5cm 4x7in) London 1999

CIBOT Elisabeth 1960 **[4]**
$3 631 - €3 659 - **£2 263** - FF24 000
Maternité Bronze (H35cm H13in) Rennes 2000

CIBULKA Heinz 1943 **[9]**
$1 023 - €1 017 - **£635** - FF6 673
Reizbarkeit Weinviertel Photograph in colors (12.5x17.3cm 4x6in) Wien 1999

CICCIMARRA Richard Matthew 1924-1973 **[28]**
$329 - €390 - **£240** - FF2 561
View along a quayside Watercolour (35.5x49.5cm 13x19in) London 2001

CICCOTELLI Beniamino 1937 **[7]**
$1 000 - €1 037 - **£600** - FF6 800
Foglie di nespolo Olio/tela (80x100cm 31x39in) Vercelli 1999

CICERI Eugène 1813-1890 **[266]**
$4 633 - €3 887 - **£2 718** - FF25 500
Les pêcheurs Huile/panneau (35.5x55cm 13x21in) Saint-Dié 1998
$2 984 - €2 897 - **£1 858** - FF19 000
Promenade en forêt Huile/panneau (28x21cm 11x8in) Fontainebleau 1999

$814 - €686 - £481 - FF4 500
Paysage de bord de rivière Aquarelle/papier (19.5x30cm 7x11in) Paris 1998

$870 - €990 - £603 - FF6 497
St-Maurice Lithographie couleurs (27.5x38.5cm 10x15in) Sion 2000

CICERI Pierre Luc Charles 1782-1868 [33]
$652 - €716 - £443 - FF4 695
Ansicht von Venedig, Phantasievedute Gouache (14x18.8cm 5x7in) Berlin 2000

CICOGNA Giammaria 1813-1849 [1]
$2 600 - €3 369 - £1 950 - FF22 100
Scena d'interno Olio/tavola (33x28cm 12x11in) Milano 2000

CIDONCHA Rafael 1952 [7]
$1 540 - €1 652 - £1 045 - FF10 835
Pies sobre Manhattan Oleo/lienzo (38x38cm 14x14in) Madrid 2000

$1 960 - €2 102 - £1 330 - FF13 790
Perchero Lápiz/papel (102x76.5cm 40x30in) Madrid 2000

CIENFUEGOS Gonzalo 1949 [11]
$20 000 - €23 237 - £14 056 - FF152 424
«The Bishop and the Model #2» Oil/canvas (179.5x160cm 70x62in) New-York 2001

$12 000 - €10 437 - £7 234 - FF68 460
Sin título Charcoal (144x146cm 56x57in) New-York 1998

CIESLEWICZ Roman 1930-1996 [21]
$95 - €109 - £66 - FF714
«Movie: Noc Sylwestrova» Poster (59x86.5cm 23x34in) Hoorn 2001

CIESLEWSKI Tadeusz 1870-1956 [21]
$489 - €493 - £305 - FF3 235
L'entrée à Wawel Watercolour (29x27cm 11x10in) Warszawa 2001

CIFARIELLO Filippo 1864-1936 [2]
$273 - €256 - £165 - FF1 676
Nackter Athlet spielt Pelota Sculpture (H26cm H10in) Lindau 1999

CIGLER Vaclav 1929 [1]
$6 250 - €5 966 - £3 905 - FF39 137
Untitled Sculpture, glass (27x30.5x16.5cm 10x12x6in) New-York 1999

CIGNANI Carlo 1628-1719 [24]
$96 390 - €83 269 - £48 195 - FF546 210
Ercole e Onfale Olio/tela (230x155cm 90x61in) Venezia 1999

$96 150 - €114 337 - £66 225 - FF750 000
La Charité Huile/cuivre (53x71.5cm 20x28in) Blois 2000

$1 600 - €1 859 - £1 124 - FF12 193
Putto holding an Urn Black chalk/paper (19.5x14.5cm 7x5in) New-York 1998

CIGNAROLI Giambettino, Giov. B 1706-1770/72 [10]
$7 240 - €6 098 - £4 276 - FF40 000
La Vierge à l'Enfant entre Saint-François d'Assise et Ste-Christine Huile/toile (41.5x29cm 16x11in) Paris 1998

CIGNAROLI Martino 1649-1726 [3]
$40 000 - €35 086 - £24 288 - FF230 152
The Stag Hunt Oil/canvas (74x150cm 29x59in) New-York 1999

CIGNAROLI Pietro 1665-1720 [1]
$9 460 - €10 008 - £6 000 - FF65 650
River Landscape with Ducks and a Heron Eating an Eel Oil/canvas (106x128cm 41x50in) London 2000

CIGNAROLI Scipione c.1690-1753 [3]
$31 055 - €28 381 - £19 000 - FF186 167
The return of Tobias and the Angel/The finding of Moses Oil/canvas (151.5x100cm 59x39in) London 1999

CIGNAROLI Vittorio Amedeo 1730-1800 [24]
$84 994 - €77 674 - £52 000 - FF509 511
Landscape with a Boy Fishing, Figures/Landscape with Washermomen Oil/canvas (121x108cm 47x42in) London 1999

$26 152 - €23 900 - £16 000 - FF156 772
Wooded Landscape with Travellers crossing a Ford on Horseback Oil/canvas (70x88.5cm 27x34in) London 1999

CIGOLI Lodovico 1559-1613 [1]
$22 000 - €23 566 - £15 023 - FF154 585
Study of a Man Seated on the Ground, one Arm Raised Ink (22.5x54cm 8x21in) New-York 2001

CIKOVSKY Nicolai 1894-1984 [85]
$955 - €993 - £602 - FF6 515
Inlet with Docked Fishing Boats Oil/canvas (50.5x76cm 19x29in) Washington 2000

$700 - €648 - £428 - FF4 251
Near Fountain, Central Park Oil/board (30x40cm 12x16in) Chicago IL 1999

$400 - €339 - £241 - FF2 225
Figural Study of a Woman Black chalk (55x40cm 22x16in) New-York 1998

CILLA Francisco Ramón 1859-1937 [15]
$260 - €252 - £159 - FF1 654
Rateros Tinta/papel (11x8cm 4x3in) Madrid 1999

CIMA Luigi 1860-1938 [8]
$5 750 - €5 961 - £3 450 - FF39 100
Lavandaie al ruscello Olio/tela (32x50.5cm 12x19in) Milano 2000

CIMAROLI Giovan Battista 1687-c.1755 [21]
$108 849 - €92 672 - £65 000 - FF607 886
An Allegorical Monument to King George I Oil/canvas (182.5x241cm 71x94in) London 1998

$25 704 - €22 205 - £17 136 - FF145 656
Paesaggio fluviale con pastori e armenti Olio/tela (41x50.5cm 16x19in) Venezia 1998

CIMATORI IL VISACCI Antonio c.1550-1623 [3]
$3 249 - €2 825 - £1 966 - FF18 531
Study of a Sybil with Putti Among Coulds Black chalk (24.5x38cm 9x14in) New-York 1999

CIMETTA Guiseppe XIX [1]
$18 344 - €20 433 - £12 000 - FF134 034
The Architecture of Venice Albumen print (34x30cm 13x12in) London 2000

CIMIOTTI Emil 1927 [43]
$857 - €920 - £573 - FF6 037
Stehende IV Metal (25.5x8x6cm 10x3x2in) Köln 2000

CIMIOTTI Gustave 1875-1969 [68]
$800 - €749 - £495 - FF4 912
El Toro California Oil/board (40x50cm 16x20in) Detroit MI 1999

$350 - €349 - £218 - FF2 290
Rock and Sea Oil/masonite (30x40cm 12x16in) New-Orleans LA 1999

CINGRIA Alexandre 1879-1945 [43]
$396 - €460 - **£278** - FF3 016
Le ménétrier Gouache/papier (29x20cm 11x7in)
Genève 2000

CINI Alfredo 1887-1970 [47]
$1 074 - €1 121 - **£679** - FF7 354
Enfants à Lens, Valais Huile/toile (59x70cm
23x27in) Genève 2000

CINISELLI Giovanni 1832-1883 [1]
$11 324 - €13 131 - **£8 000** - FF86 135
Cupid on a Conche Marble (H60cm H23in) London
2001

CINOT Franck ?-1890 [5]
$5 500 - €5 897 - **£3 638** - FF38 682
Lovers Walking Along a Shaded Lane Oil/canvas
(66x48cm 26x19in) New-Orleans LA 2000

CINOTTI Guido 1870-1932 [10]
$1 920 - €2 488 - **£1 440** - FF16 320
Marina al tramonto Olio/tavola (43x59.5cm 16x23in)
Milano 2001

CIOCCHINI Cleto 1899-1974 [4]
$11 500 - €13 361 - **£8 082** - FF87 643
Regreso de la pesca Oleo/lienzo (124x112cm
48x44in) Buenos-Aires 2001
$3 000 - €3 306 - **£2 001** - FF21 688
Pescador Oleo/lienzo (100x80cm 39x31in)
Montevideo 2000

CIOLI Valerio di Simone 1529-1599 [1]
$10 504 - €12 196 - **£7 432** - FF80 000
Satyre femelle trayant une chèvre Marbre
(H105cm H41in) Paris 2001

CIOTTA C. XIX [5]
$2 709 - €2 973 - **£1 800** - FF19 499
On the Terrace/On The Beach Oil/panel
(15.5x26.5cm 6x10in) London 2000

CIOTTA F. XIX [5]
$1 801 - €2 147 - **£1 284** - FF14 086
Die Konzertprobe Oil/panel (44x34cm 17x13in) Köln
2000

CIOTTI Giuseppe, Bepi 1889-1991 [18]
$600 - €622 - **£360** - FF4 080
Dirigibles futurista, brezza del volo Tecnica
mista/cartone (30x40cm 11x15in) Vercelli 1999

CIPOLLA Fabio 1852-1935 [21]
$11 000 - €9 400 - **£6 461** - FF61 659
An Afternoon Read Oil/canvas (28x53cm 11x20in)
Boston MA 1998

CIPPER IL TODESCHINI Giacomo Francesco 1664-
1736 [66]
$40 000 - €35 246 - **£27 200** - FF231 200
Il mercato del pesce Olio/tela (125x159.5cm
49x62in) Roma 1998
$12 000 - €10 367 - **£8 000** - FF68 000
Contadino Olio/tela (76x65cm 25x21in) Milano 1998

CIPRIANI A. XIX-XX [54]
$1 712 - €1 983 - **£1 184** - FF13 008
Jeune femme assise sur un Sphinx Albâtre
(50x48.5x20cm 19x19x7in) Bruxelles 2000

CIPRIANI Giovanni Battista 1727-1785 [55]
$5 800 - €5 769 - **£3 600** - FF37 840
The Death of Dido Oil/copper (33.5x45cm 13x17in)
London 1999
$784 - €841 - **£518** - FF5 516
Hebe Acuarela (11.5x9cm 4x3in) Madrid 2000

$290 - €292 - **£180** - FF1 917
Sacrifice to Cupid Engraving (29x26cm 11x10in)
London 2000

CIPRIANI Giovanni Battista 1766-1839 [1]
$1 800 - €1 555 - **£900** - FF10 200
Disegni montati in un album di sei facciate
Inchiostro (18x25cm 7x9in) Milano 1999

CIPRIANI Giovanni Pinotti XIX-XX [13]
$4 532 - €5 336 - **£3 185** - FF35 000
Femme et enfant sur un dromadaire Bronze
(61x54cm 24x21in) Paris 2000

CIPRIANI Nazzareno 1843-1925 [32]
$650 - €645 - **£398** - FF4 232
Cardinal Reading Watercolour/paper (43x30cm
17x12in) Mystic CT 2000

CIRIA José Manuel 1960 [5]
$1 680 - €1 802 - **£1 140** - FF11 820
«Meeting II» Oleo/tabla (100x81cm 39x31in) Madrid
2001

CIRIELLO Averardo 1918 [25]
$463 - €427 - **£278** - FF2 800
«Divorzio all'italiana» Affiche (140x200cm 55x78in)
Paris 1999

CIRINO Antonio 1889-1983 [39]
$4 950 - €4 686 - **£3 074** - FF30 737
Autumn stroll Oil/canvas (63x76cm 25x30in)
Rockport MA 1999
$1 650 - €1 690 - **£1 026** - FF11 086
Church in Rockport Oil/canvas (20x27cm 8x11in)
Newport RI 2000

CIROU Paul 1869-1951 [25]
$381 - €446 - **£271** - FF2 926
Jeux d'enfants sur un pont Huile/panneau
(38x46cm 14x18in) Bruxelles 2001

CIRY Michel 1919 [271]
$1 626 - €1 829 - **£1 119** - FF12 000
Le port de Rotterdam Huile/toile (50x65cm
19x25in) Aix-en-Provence 2000
$1 462 - €1 601 - **£1 009** - FF10 500
«Stabat Mater» Huile/toile (46x33cm 18x12in) Paris
2001
$417 - €457 - **£288** - FF3 000
Couple endormi Encre (35x24.5cm 13x9in) Paris
2001
$111 - €94 - **£65** - FF615
«Hommage à Watteau» Radierung (36x29.5cm
14x11in) Bern 1998

CISNEROS José 1910 [3]
$1 700 - €1 518 - **£1 041** - FF9 955
Western and Mexican Horse and Rider Studies
Indian ink (30x23cm 12x9in) Altadena CA 1999

CITROEN Paul 1896-1983 [97]
$2 520 - €2 181 - **£1 529** - FF14 309
Still Life of Flowers Oil/canvas (57x45cm 22x17in)
Amsterdam 1998
$806 - €767 - **£500** - FF5 030
Interieur mit einer Frau im Sessel Indian ink
(38.6x51.5cm 15x20in) Hamburg 1999
$215 - €220 - **£134** - FF1 442
Park Lithographie (34x38.8cm 13x15in) Hamburg 2000
$1 479 - €1 588 - **£990** - FF10 418
Paulien Gelatin silver print (22x16.5cm 8x6in)
Amsterdam 2000

CITRON Minna Wright 1896-1991 **[26]**
$375 - €361 - £232 - FF2 366
Squid under Pier Etching in colors (37.5x45cm 14x17in) New-York 1999

CITTADINI IL MILANESE Pier Francesco 1616-1681 **[25]**
$18 424 - €20 348 - £12 768 - FF133 476
Jesusknabe in Blumenkranz Öl/Leinwand (52x42cm 20x16in) Wien 2001

CITTADINI Tito 1886-? **[11]**
$1 960 - €2 102 - £1 330 - FF13 790
Paisaje con palmeras Oleo/cartón (17x25.5cm 6x10in) Madrid 2001

CIVITALI Matteo di Giovanni 1436-1501 **[3]**
$140 000 - €181 414 - £105 000 - FF1 190 000
Giovane donna stante con libro Marbre (H113cm H44in) Firenze 2000

CIVITARESE Goffredo 1936 **[50]**
$850 - €881 - £510 - FF5 780
«Donna in rosso con cappello rosso» Olio/tela (70x50cm 27x19in) Vercelli 2001
$400 - €518 - £300 - FF3 400
«La mia brocca» Olio/tela (40x30cm 15x11in) Vercelli 2001

CIXI Dowager Empress 1835-1908 **[9]**
$15 408 - €16 909 - £9 924 - FF110 916
Peaches Ink (125x62cm 49x24in) Hong-Kong 2000

CLAASEN Hermann 1889-1987 **[26]**
$899 - €767 - £542 - FF5 030
Glockengasse Gelatin silver print (39.5x29.4cm 15x11in) Köln 1998

CLAEISSINS Antoon c.1536-1613 **[2]**
$34 202 - €38 847 - £24 000 - FF254 820
The Justice of Cambyses: an Allegorical group Portrait Oil/panel (110.5x123cm 43x48in) London 2001

CLAEISSINS Pieter II ?-1623 **[7]**
$18 011 - €16 703 - £11 000 - FF109 562
An Allegory of the Wars of Religion Oil/panel (62x73cm 24x28in) London 1998

CLAERHOUT Frans Martin 1919 **[79]**
$725 - €854 - £501 - FF5 604
Brown Cow Oil/board (50.5x61cm 19x24in) Cape Town 2000
$115 - €128 - £75 - FF840
Three Women Talking Pastel/paper (30.5x20cm 12x7in) Johannesburg 2000

CLAESZ Allaert 1508-c.1560 **[8]**
$1 100 - €1 220 - £731 - FF8 004
Vignette with a Sphinx and a Satyr Lithograph (51x14.5cm 20x5in) New-York 2000

CLAESZ Anthony I 1592-1635 **[4]**
$386 664 - €384 581 - £240 000 - FF2 522 688
Still Life of Flowers Oil/panel (104.5x77.5cm 41x30in) London 1999

CLAESZ Pieter 1597/98-1661 **[45]**
$16 000 - €18 845 - £11 065 - FF123 614
The Four Evangelists Oil/canvas (136x189cm 53x74in) New-York 2000
$149 430 - €160 401 - £100 000 - FF1 052 160
Giant Roemer, a Silver Tazza, a Pie and a partly Peeled Lemon Oil/panel (59.5x49cm 23x19in) London 2000

Lemon, a partly peeled Lemon, Grapes, a Roemer and Knife on a Ledge Oil/panel (21x25.5cm 8x10in) London 1999

CLAEUW de Jacques Grief c.1620-? **[9]**
$40 440 - €47 140 - £28 000 - FF309 218
A Vanitas Still Life with a Globe, Books, a Skull, a Violin, a Letter Oil/panel (37x47cm 14x18in) London 2000
$6 232 - €5 899 - £3 875 - FF38 695
Vanitas Still Life with Books, a Skull, a Violin, an Hourglass, a Globe Oil/panel (16x21cm 6x8in) Amsterdam 1999

CLAEYS Albert 1889-1967 **[22]**
$3 120 - €3 718 - £2 235 - FF24 390
De leie in de winter Oil/panel (47.5x60cm 18x23in) Lokeren 2000
$4 033 - €4 586 - £2 830 - FF30 081
Paysage de la Lys Huile/panneau (33x39cm 12x15in) Bruxelles 2001

CLAEYSEN Louise 1903-1997 **[145]**
$113 - €99 - £68 - FF650
Le bouquet sur la fenêtre Huile/toile (50x60cm 19x23in) Orléans 1998

CLAGETT Jean XX **[11]**
$3 212 - €3 583 - £2 169 - FF23 500
Al Capone Bronze (34x12.5x34cm 13x4x13in) Deauville 2000

CLAGHORN Joseph C. 1869-1947 **[14]**
$1 000 - €1 167 - £696 - FF7 653
«Twilight, Gloucester Harbor, Mass» Oil/board (35x43cm 14x17in) Altadena CA 2000
$100 - €1 155 - £743 - FF7 575
«On an old Turnpike» Watercolour/paper (48x74cm 19x29in) Fairfield ME 2001

CLAGUE Richard 1821-1873 **[7]**
$51 000 - €43 692 - £30 661 - FF286 604
Louisiana genre Scene Oil/canvas (40x30cm 16x12in) New-Orleans LA 1998

CLAIR Charles 1860-1947 **[118]**
$2 052 - €1 862 - £1 286 - FF12 211
A Figure on a Track at Sunset Oil/canvas (91.5x73cm 36x28in) London 1998
$1 700 - €1 467 - £1 021 - FF9 620
In the Sheep Barn Oil/panel (32.5x41cm 12x16in) Boston MA 1998

CLAIR-GUYOT E. XIX-XX **[5]**
$1 197 - €1 143 - £748 - FF7 500
«Bière Saint-Germain» Affiche (188.5x67.5cm 74x26in) Orléans 1999

CLAIRIN Georges Jules Victor 1843-1919 **[165]**
$20 864 - €24 392 - £14 896 - FF160 000
Les révoltés dans la forêt de Teniet el Haal, sic Had Huile/toile (400x300cm 157x118in) Paris 2001
$6 604 - €6 098 - £4 064 - FF40 000
Figure allégorique aux fruits Huile/toile (152x63.5cm 59x25in) Paris 1999
$898 - €991 - £608 - FF6 500
Autoportrait Crayon/papier (60x45cm 23x17in) Paris 2000
$1 748 - €1 524 - £1 057 - FF10 000
«Théâtre Sarah Bernhardt. Théodora» Affiche (205x74cm 80x29in) Paris 1999

CLAIRIN Pierre-Eugène 1897-1980 **[328]**
$710 - €762 - £475 - FF5 000
Sous la futaie en bordure du village Huile/toile (60x73cm 23x28in) Douarnenez 2000

📖 $248 - €274 - **£172** - FF1 800
Portrait de François Mauriac Crayon (21x18.5cm 8x7in) Paris 2001

📖 $108 - €99 - **£66** - FF650
Village sous la neige Lithographie (14x19cm 5x7in) Douarnenez 1998

CLAIRMONT Philip 1949-1984 **[22]**
🖼 $13 503 - €15 136 - **£9 443** - FF99 287
Mao Diptych Oil/canvas (97.5x186cm 38x73in) Auckland 2001

🖼 $5 924 - €6 639 - **£4 130** - FF43 551
Jesus in the Wardrobe Painting (47x38cm 18x14in) Wellington 2001

📖 $2 122 - €2 418 - **£1 466** - FF15 858
«Wardrobe» Watercolour (60x44.5cm 23x17in) Auckland 2000

📖 $886 - €994 - **£620** - FF6 520
«Sel Portrait» Linocut (31x19cm 12x7in) Auckland 2001

CLAISSE Geneviève 1935 **[99]**
🖼 $11 691 - €11 347 - **£7 279** - FF74 433
Composition Öl/Leinwand (130x97cm 51x38in) Luzern 1999

🖼 $3 043 - €3 536 - **£2 138** - FF23 194
Prélude Öl/Leinwand (65x54cm 25x21in) Luzern 2001

📖 $1 201 - €1 144 - **£752** - FF7 504
Concert Gouache/paper (56x45cm 22x17in) Köbenhavn 1999

CLANCY Michèle 1940 **[12]**
📖 $198 - €229 - **£136** - FF1 500
Terre d'ombre Pastel (16x21cm 6x8in) Paris 2000

CLAPERA ARGELAGUER Pere 1906-1984 **[32]**
📖 $240 - €222 - **£144** - FF1 457
Bailarines Técnica mixta/papel (42x29cm 16x11in) Barcelona 2001

CLAPP William Henry 1879-1954 **[55]**
🖼 $3 500 - €3 757 - **£2 342** - FF24 643
Nude Oil/masonite (45.5x38cm 17x14in) San-Francisco CA 2000

🖼 $3 300 - €3 364 - **£2 067** - FF22 066
Santa Cruz Beach Oil/board (18x22cm 7x9in) Altadena CA 2000

CLAPSADDLE Ellen H. 1865-1934 **[1]**
📖 $1 793 - €1 925 - **£1 200** - FF12 625
At the Net Lithograph (35x28cm 13x11in) London 2000

CLARA AYATS José 1878-1958 **[54]**
🖼 $12 070 - €14 025 - **£8 482** - FF92 000
L'esclave Bronze (H82cm H32in) Joigny 2001
🖼 $2 874 - €2 744 - **£1 796** - FF18 000
Modèle debout Bronze (H35cm H13in) Montpellier 1999
📖 $224 - €240 - **£152** - FF1 576
Paisaje rural con figura Acuarela/papel (20.5x30cm 8x11in) Madrid 2001

CLARA Juan 1875-1957 **[58]**
🖼 $772 - €667 - **£461** - FF4 374
Nenette Gilded bronze (H21cm H8in) Melbourne 1998

CLARAC de Charles O., comte 1777-1817 **[3]**
📖 $12 701 - €13 634 - **£8 500** - FF89 433
View of Jungle, Hunters Crossing a River, One About to Shoot an Arrow Gouache/paper (62.5x82.5cm 24x32in) London 2000

CLARASSO Enric 1857-1941 **[3]**
🖼 $3 825 - €4 505 - **£2 775** - FF29 550
Busto femenino Sculpture bois (H34.5cm H13in) Barcelona 2001

CLARE George 1835-1890 **[117]**
🖼 $5 500 - €6 078 - **£3 814** - FF39 867
English Still Life of Fruit Oil/canvas (45x60cm 18x23in) Felton CA 2001

🖼 $2 821 - €2 438 - **£1 700** - FF15 990
Violets, Blossom and Birds Nest Oil/canvas (17.5x25.5cm 6x10in) Billingshurst, West-Sussex 1999

📖 $108 - €4 668 - £3 200 - FF30 620
Plums, Grapes and Strawberries on a Mossy Bank/Flowers, Berries, Nest Watercolour/paper (22x30cm 9x12in) Fernhurst, Haslemere, Surrey 1999

CLARE Oliver 1853-1927 **[410]**
🖼 $2 958 - €2 701 - **£1 800** - FF17 716
Primulas and a Bird's Nest with Eggs, on a mossy Bank Oil/board (18x23cm 7x9in) London 1998

CLARE Vincent 1855-1930 **[217]**
🖼 $4 500 - €5 118 - **£3 144** - FF33 570
Still Life with Flowers in Basket Oil/canvas (49x58cm 19x23in) Chicago IL 2000

🖼 $2 321 - €2 614 - **£1 600** - FF17 149
Apple Blossom and a Bird's Nest with eggs, on a Mossy Bank Oil/canvas (22x30.5cm 8x12in) London 2000

📖 $1 012 - €1 178 - **£700** - FF7 730
Grapes, Peaches, and Plums Before a Mossy Bank Watercolour/paper (38x30cm 14x11in) Cheshire 2000

CLAREBOUDT Jean 1944-1997 **[106]**
✏ $627 - €579 - **£375** - FF3 800
Passage Bronze, Odense DK Bronze (H20cm H7in) Nantes 1999

✏ $231 - €213 - **£138** - FF1 400
Dessin note Sculptor's cloud's Mine plomb (66.5x51.5cm 26x20in) Nantes 1999

CLARENBACH Max 1880-1952 **[185]**
🖼 $11 565 - €11 256 - **£7 106** - FF73 837
Oberengadin im Winter vom Muottas-Muragl aus Öl/Leinwand (103x366cm 40x144in) Zürich 1999

🖼 $4 496 - €5 113 - **£3 118** - FF33 539
Letzter Schnee bei Kaiserswerth am Niederrhein Öl/Leinwand (60.5x81cm 23x31in) Köln 2000

🖼 $1 536 - €1 789 - **£1 073** - FF11 738
Baumbestandenes Seeufer, niederrheinische Landschaft Oil/panel (24x31.6cm 9x12in) Berlin 2000

📖 $238 - €256 - **£159** - FF1 676
Hafen zu Neuss im Winter Radierung (46.5x59cm 18x23in) Köln 2000

CLARET Jean-Luc 1968 **[7]**
✏ $1 432 - €1 220 - **£852** - FF8 000
Buste de kouros Bronze (40x30x15cm 15x11x5in) Corbeil-Essonnes 1998

CLARK Albert ?-c.1909 **[69]**
🖼 $2 085 - €2 062 - **£1 300** - FF13 529
Roan Before a Gate Oil/canvas (51x61cm 20x24in) London 1999

🖼 $987 - €956 - **£600** - FF6 271
Chesnut Mare in a Stable Oil/canvas (28x38cm 11x14in) London 2000

CLARK Allan 1898-1950 **[16]**
✏ $6 000 - €6 440 - **£4 015** - FF42 246
Head of an Oriental Woman Sculpture, wood (H21.5cm H8in) New-York 2001

CLARK Alson Skinner 1876-1949 **[85]**
🖼 $18 000 - €19 439 - **£12 439** - FF127 510
Sweet William Oil/board (54x64cm 21x25in) Altadena CA 2001

$3 000 – €2 833 – **£1 863** – FF18 581
To Sally, Portrait of a Young Woman
Oil/canvas/board (35.5x25.5cm 13x10in) Beverly-Hills
CA 1999
$1 500 – €1 440 – **£940** – FF9 443
Yacht Club, Point Loma Watercolour/paper
(44x54cm 17x21in) Altadena CA 1999

CLARK Benton H. 1895-1964 [17]
$2 600 – €2 791 – **£1 739** – FF18 306
Winfield Scott Treatying with the Indians Oil/canvas (60x91cm 24x36in) Chicago IL 2000
$600 – €576 – **£371** – FF3 779
Paymaster Oil/board (30x25cm 12x10in) Chicago IL 1999

CLARK C. Myron 1876-1925 [35]
$1 300 – €1 232 – **£812** – FF8 083
Lake Louise, Canadian Rockies Oil/canvas (55x86cm 22x34in) Cincinnati OH 1999
$375 – €416 – **£261** – FF2 726
«Old House at Siasconset, Nantucket»
Watercolour/paper (26x34cm 10x13in) New-Orleans LA 2001

CLARK Christopher 1875-1942 [24]
$1 059 – €1 228 – **£750** – FF8 058
«Trooping the Colour, British Railways, London, Midland Region» Poster (102x127cm 40x50in)
London 2000

CLARK Dixon XIX-XX [21]
$4 402 – €4 734 – **£3 000** – FF31 052
Scene of a Ploughman and Team of horses
Oil/canvas (54.5x75cm 21x29in) Newcastle-upon-Tyne 2001
$230 – €271 – **£160** – FF1 779
A Herdsman and Cattle beside a River
Watercolour (35x50cm 13x19in) London 2000

CLARK Edward, Ed XX [6]
$1 400 – €1 540 – **£970** – FF10 099
Monroe Marilyn Cibachrome print (81x58cm 32x23in) New-York 2001

CLARK Eleanor Arnold 1911-1982 [63]
$200 – €214 – **£136** – FF1 405
Adam and Eve Mixed media (116x76cm 46x30in)
Cleveland OH 2001

CLARK Elliot Candee 1883-1980 [93]
$1 200 – €1 025 – **£726** – FF6 725
«Across the Desert, Palm Springs»
Oil/canvas/board (45.5x61cm 17x24in) San-Francisco CA 1998
$500 – €588 – **£358** – FF3 856
Snow scene, Blue Ridge mountains Oil/canvas (30x25cm 12x10in) New-York 2001
$1 000 – €1 167 – **£705** – FF7 655
Shenandoah Valley Watercolour, gouache/paper (40x58cm 16x23in) Cedar-Falls IA 2000

CLARK James 1858-1943 [45]
$1 344 – €1 444 – **£900** – FF9 469
Runaway Horse Oil/canvas (39x60cm 15x23in)
Billingshurst, West-Sussex 2000
$2 400 – €2 644 – **£1 601** – FF17 345
Bay Hunter in a Stable Oil/canvas (30x40cm 12x16in) Detroit MI 2000

CLARK Joseph 1834-1926 [33]
$1 200 – €1 260 – **£756** – FF8 265
At The Village Gate Oil/canvas (45x35cm 18x14in)
Cleveland OH 2000

$1 424 – €1 656 – **£1 000** – FF10 864
The Goldfish Bowl Oil/canvas (39.5x29cm 15x11in)
Billingshurst, West-Sussex 2001

CLARK Larry 1943 [82]
$2 105 – €2 454 – **£1 457** – FF16 098
New York City Gelatin silver print (32x21cm 12x8in)
Köln 2000

CLARK Lygia 1920-1988 [11]
$54 774 – €64 677 – **£38 886** – FF424 255
«Superfície Modulada No.1» Painting (100x100cm 39x39in) Berlin 2001
$28 000 – €27 184 – **£17 298** – FF178 318
Unidade VI Oil/wood (30x30cm 11x11in) New-York 1999
$38 000 – €40 789 – **£25 429** – FF267 558
Bicho Metal (37x40x40cm 14x15x15in) New-York 2000

CLARK Matt 1903-1972 [20]
$1 900 – €1 825 – **£1 177** – FF11 968
Marshall Fields Christmas Window Mixed media (58x88cm 23x35in) Chicago IL 1999
$400 – €446 – **£261** – FF2 927
Cowboys Gouache/paper (38x68cm 15x27in) Chicago IL 2000

CLARK Norman 1913-1992 [15]
$423 – €373 – **£260** – FF2 449
In an Artist's Studio Watercolour (26x39.5cm 10x15in) Godalming, Surrey 1999

CLARK Octavius T. 1850-1921 [83]
$850 – €1 016 – **£584** – FF6 665
Landscape with Figures along the Path Oil/canvas (50x76cm 20x30in) Chicago IL 2000
$406 – €457 – **£280** – FF3 001
Country Landscapes Oil/board (30x26cm 11x10in)
London 2000
$967 – €902 – **£600** – FF5 915
A Figure driving Geese/A Faggot Gatherer on a rustic Path Watercolour/paper (39.5x59.5cm 15x23in)
Billingshurst, West-Sussex 1999

CLARK OF GREENOCK William 1803-1883 [22]
$10 781 – €9 377 – **£6 500** – FF61 508
Portrait of a Full rigged Ship Bombay in full Sail
Oil/canvas (76x110.5cm 29x43in) Glasgow 1998

CLARK Paraskeva Plistik 1898-1986 [13]
$11 683 – €13 213 – **£8 222** – FF86 670
Landscape on Thanksgiving Oil/canvas (81.5x101.5cm 32x39in) Vancouver, BC. 2001

CLARK Roland 1874-1957 [89]
$3 800 – €4 215 – **£2 527** – FF27 651
Black Ducks at Sunrise Oil/board (45x60cm 18x24in) Milford CT 2000
$7 500 – €8 114 – **£5 138** – FF53 223
Seven Mallard Ducks in Flight Watercolour/paper (60x45cm 24x18in) Thomaston ME 2001
$300 – €354 – **£210** – FF2 319
Duck Stamp Design Drypoint (16x26cm 6x10in)
Bolton MA 2000

CLARK Russell 1905 [14]
$49 656 – €58 321 – **£35 256** – FF382 560
An Argument, Otaki Oil/canvas (58.5x84cm 23x33in)
Auckland 2000
$6 046 – €6 777 – **£4 228** – FF44 457
Young Maori Woman seated Sculpture (H23cm H9in) Auckland 2001
$282 – €316 – **£197** – FF2 074
Cabbage Tree Study Ink/paper (24.5x28cm 9x11in)
Auckland 2001

CLARK Samuel Joseph 1834-c.1912 **[37]**
- $8 706 - €9 804 - **£6 000** - FF64 309
  The Lion Inn Oil/canvas (89x150cm 35x59in) London 2000
- $3 494 - €3 720 - **£2 300** - FF24 404
  The Log Cart Oil/canvas (74.5x126cm 29x49in) Billingshurst, West-Sussex 2000
- $1 846 - €1 746 - **£1 150** - FF11 453
  Landscape with Horses Oil/canvas (46x30cm 18x11in) Leicestershire 1999

CLARK Thomas 1814-1883 **[2]**
- $187 008 - €205 555 - **£119 840** - FF1 348 352
  Falls on the Wannon Oil/canvas (79.5x120cm 31x47in) Melbourne 2000

CLARK Walter 1848-1917 **[25]**
- $475 - €513 - **£328** - FF3 365
  Ducks on a Pond Oil/board (30x21cm 12x8in) Cincinnati OH 2001

CLARK Walter Appleton 1876-1906 **[4]**
- $2 700 - €3 024 - **£1 876** - FF19 837
  Gentleman watching Artist painting Woman's Portrait Oil/canvas (30x43cm 12x17in) New-York 2001

CLARK William Albert XX **[27]**
- $1 622 - €1 721 - **£1 100** - FF11 288
  Prize Bull Oil/canvas (42.5x52.5cm 16x20in) Crewkerne, Somerset 2001

CLARKE Carey 1938 **[4]**
- $6 100 - €5 202 - **£3 680** - FF34 121
  Promise of Summer Oil/canvas (53x92cm 21x36in) Dublin 1998

CLARKE David 1920 **[17]**
- $828 - €889 - **£565** - FF5 830
  Still life with Geraniums and fruit Oil/canvas (63.5x63.5cm 25x25in) Dublin 2001
- $1 006 - €1 079 - **£686** - FF7 079
  Evening 24th December Pastel/paper (49.5x63.5cm 19x25in) Dublin 2001

CLARKE Derek 1912 **[4]**
- $7 175 - €6 984 - **£4 408** - FF45 809
  The Goldfish Bowl Oil/canvas (76x63cm 30x25in) Dublin 1999

CLARKE F. XIX **[1]**
- $14 085 - €16 542 - **£10 000** - FF108 510
  An official Procession of Indians and Europeans with the Nizam's Watercolour (41x63.5cm 16x25in) London 2000

CLARKE Frederick 1834-1870 **[6]**
- $2 050 - €2 353 - **£1 402** - FF15 432
  Horse in a Stable Oil/canvas (50x66cm 20x26in) Cleveland OH 2000

CLARKE Geoffrey 1924 **[19]**
- $633 - €723 - **£440** - FF4 740
  Warrior Etching, aquatint in colors (91x55.5cm 35x21in) London 2000

CLARKE Graham 1941 **[131]**
- $639 - €634 - **£400** - FF4 157
  The Haymakers Etching, aquatint (33.5x53.5cm 13x21in) London 1999

CLARKE Harry 1889-1931 **[30]**
- $62 496 - €53 286 - **£37 703** - FF349 532
  Bluebeard's Last Wife Miniature (43x39x27cm 17x15x11in) Dublin 1998

CLARKE Joseph Clayton act.1883-1894 **[3]**
- $72 - €80 - **£50** - FF528
  Study of Bill Sykes Watercolour/paper (29x22cm 11x8in) Newbury, Berkshire 2001

CLARKE Margaret 1888-1961 **[13]**
- $15 053 - €16 515 - **£10 000** - FF108 330
  Ophelia Oil/panel (39x61cm 15x24in) London 2000
- $496 - €584 - **£348** - FF3 831
  The Sugar Loaf, Co.Wicklow Oil/board (32x42cm 12x16in) Dublin 2000

CLARKE William XVIII-XIX **[2]**
- $8 000 - €8 817 - **£5 322** - FF57 835
  Seated Woman with Fashionable Head-Dress, Holding Young Child & Bird Oil/canvas (97x87cm 38x34in) Portsmouth NH 2001

CLARKE William Hanna 1882-1924 **[15]**
- $4 969 - €5 600 - **£3 442** - FF36 736
  The Faggots Gatherers Oil/canvas (51x41cm 20x16in) Toronto 2000
- $1 406 - €1 582 - **£980** - FF10 377
  Head of a Farm Girl Charcoal/paper (30x24cm 11x9in) Edinburgh 2001

CLARKSON Edward XIX **[1]**
- $20 000 - €18 601 - **£12 384** - FF122 012
  Gentleman Chaise with Chestnut Trotter Oil/canvas (73x91cm 29x36in) Portsmouth NH 1999

CLAROT René 1882-1972 **[134]**
- $552 - €545 - **£336** - FF3 577
  Etangs en automne Huile/panneau (53x72cm 20x28in) Bruxelles 2000
- $259 - €248 - **£161** - FF1 626
  Voiliers au coucher du soleil Huile/toile/carton (17x23cm 6x9in) Antwerpen 1999

CLARY Eugène 1856-1930 **[31]**
- $2 220 - €2 058 - **£1 381** - FF13 500
  La Seine aux Andelys Huile/toile (45x81cm 17x31in) Rouen 1999

CLARY James XX **[1]**
- $5 000 - €5 943 - **£3 464** - FF38 986
  U.S.Michigan Acrylic/canvas (60x73cm 24x29in) Detroit MI 2000

CLARY-BAROUX Adolphe 1865-1933 **[88]**
- $1 191 - €1 156 - **£750** - FF7 580
  Fishing by a River Oil/canvas (38x46cm 14x18in) London 1999
- $556 - €610 - **£377** - FF4 000
  Vue de Rouen Pont Corneille et l'Ile Lacroix prise du Quai d'Elbeuf Huile/panneau (18x24cm 7x9in) Pontoise 2000

CLASEN Carl 1812-1886 **[25]**
- $405 - €409 - **£253** - FF2 683
  Findling am Bach Öl/Karton (23x29cm 9x11in) Düsseldorf 2000

CLAUDE Eugène 1841-1922 **[59]**
- $16 206 - €15 103 - **£10 000** - FF99 068
  Bouquet of Flowers, an Imari Bowl, a silver Ewer with Stand Oil/canvas (131x195.5cm 51x76in) London 1999
- $3 184 - €3 049 - **£1 967** - FF20 000
  Nature morte aux pêches et aux groseilles Huile/toile (60x73cm 23x28in) Calais 1999

C

$1 831 - €1 829 - **£1 144** - FF12 000
Nature morte aux prunes Huile/toile (27x40.5cm
10x15in) Pontoise 1999

CLAUDE Jean Maxime 1824-1904 **[15]**
$41 000 - €47 636 - **£28 814** - FF312 469
Morning, the Hunt at Chantilly Oil/canvas
(72.5x113cm 28x44in) New-York 2001
$5 838 - €6 403 - **£3 767** - FF42 000
La promenade au bois Huile/panneau (27x35.5cm
10x13in) Paris 2000
$1 182 - €1 372 - **£841** - FF9 000
Amazone sur la plage avec son chien
Aquarelle/papier (26.5x20.5cm 10x8in) Paris 2001

CLAUDEL Camille 1864-1943 **[97]**
$80 000 - €88 745 - **£53 200** - FF582 128
La petite châtelaine Bronze (H32cm H12in) New-
York 2000

CLAUDET Max 1840-1893 **[20]**
$366 - €381 - **£230** - FF2 500
Jeune fille tricotant Bronze (H32cm H12in) Paris
2000

CLAUDIUS Wilhelm Ludwig H. 1854-1942 **[26]**
$3 406 - €3 094 - **£2 111** - FF20 295
Aftenfred Oil/canvas (67x73cm 26x28in) Köbenhavn
1999
$491 - €460 - **£298** - FF3 018
Feierabend, Grossvater-Kindidyll Indian ink
(18x25.5cm 7x10in) Bremen 1999

CLAUDOT DE NANCY Jean-Baptiste 1733-1805
[39]
$9 212 - €10 174 - **£6 384** - FF66 738
Gebirgige Winterlandschaft mit einem
Wasserfall und Figuren Öl/Leinwand (63.5x79.5cm
25x31in) Wien 2001

CLAUS Carlfriedrich 1930-1998 **[73]**
$2 509 - €2 812 - **£1 747** - FF18 446
Ohne Titel Ink (9.5x14cm 3x5in) Berlin 2001
$319 - €358 - **£222** - FF2 347
«Annaberg-Buchholz: Denkgänge über unter
Tage» Lithographie (24.5x29.5cm 9x11in) Berlin 2001

CLAUS Emile 1849-1924 **[201]**
$236 660 - €272 268 - **£161 400** - FF1 785 960
Vue de la Lys, juin Oil/canvas (110x141cm 43x55in)
Amsterdam 2000
$23 908 - €25 664 - **£16 000** - FF168 345
Slepping Arab Musician Oil/canvas (48x35.5cm
18x13in) London 2000
$9 675 - €11 155 - **£6 660** - FF73 170
Park aan de leie Oil/panel (24.5x37cm 9x14in)
Lokeren 2000
$722 - €694 - **£445** - FF4 552
La terrasse, Marseille Crayon/papier (13.5x10.5cm
5x4in) Bruxelles 1999

CLAUS Hugo 1929 **[47]**
$1 206 - €1 289 - **£821** - FF8 455
Bollekop Encre/papier (70x59.5cm 27x23in) Lokeren
2001
$2 488 - €2 949 - **£1 812** - FF19 347
De Blijde en Onvoorziene Week Print in colors
(27x21cm 10x8in) Amsterdam 2001

CLAUSADE de Pierre 1902-1976 **[142]**
$925 - €898 - **£582** - FF5 888
Le coup de soleil Oil/canvas (58x66cm 22x25in)
London 1999

CLAUSELL Joaquín 1866-1935 **[43]**
$60 000 - €70 645 - **£42 162** - FF463 404
El mar Oil/canvas (89x146.5cm 35x57in) New-York
2000
$35 000 - €41 210 - **£24 594** - FF270 319
Paisaje con árboles Oil/canvas (47x60.5cm 18x23in)
New-York 2000

CLAUSEN Christian Valdemar 1862-1911 **[21]**
$1 568 - €1 675 - **£1 068** - FF10 987
Gadeparti med figurer i gadelys Oil/canvas
(90x98cm 35x38in) Vejle 2001

CLAUSEN Franciska 1899-1986 **[134]**
$543 - €603 - **£378** - FF3 957
Söskendepar Oil/panel (20x20cm 7x7in) Köbenhavn
2001
$1 631 - €1 344 - **£960** - FF8 818
Komposition Gouache/paper (28x22cm 11x8in)
Köbenhavn 1998

CLAUSEN George 1852-1944 **[177]**
$12 702 - €13 635 - **£8 590** - FF89 438
Still Life with Flowers in a Jug on a White Cloth
Oil/canvas (46.5x36cm 18x14in) London 2000
$10 886 - €9 884 - **£6 800** - FF64 832
November Morning Oil/canvas (21x39.5cm 8x15in)
London 1999
$519 - €591 - **£365** - FF3 877
Pollarded Trees by a Stream Watercolour
(36.5x26.5cm 14x10in) Woollahra, Sydney 2001

CLAUSEN Rosemarie 1907-1990 **[22]**
$434 - €511 - **£311** - FF3 353
Rollenporträt Elisabeth Flickenschildt Vintage
gelatin silver print (21.5x26.6cm 8x10in) Berlin 2001

CLAVÉ Antoni 1913 **[1422]**
$29 808 - €35 063 - **£21 367** - FF230 000
Nature morte Technique mixte (97x130cm 38x51in)
Paris 2001
$21 153 - €25 154 - **£15 081** - FF165 000
Nature morte sur fond rouge Huile/panneau
(60x81cm 23x31in) Calais 2000
$5 355 - €6 307 - **£3 675** - FF41 370
Guerrier Técnica mixta (35x41cm 13x16in) Barcelona
2000
$30 264 - €36 588 - **£21 144** - FF240 000
Guerrier au bouclier Bronze (250x200x60cm
98x78x23in) Paris 2000
$4 277 - €3 964 - **£2 659** - FF26 000
Forme nº4 Bronze (35x25x2.5cm 13x9xin) Paris 1999
$5 040 - €5 406 - **£3 330** - FF35 460
Plaza de Toros, Sevilla Collage (40x30cm 15x11in)
Barcelona 2000
$415 - €406 - **£255** - FF2 666
Reiter und Pferd Farblithographie (71x53cm
27x20in) Zürich 1999

CLAVÉ Y ROQUE Pelegrin 1811-1880 **[7]**
$1 877 - €2 116 - **£1 300** - FF13 880
Italian Gentleman Oil/canvas (40.5x30.5cm 15x12in)
London 2000

CLAVEL Ismaël Adolphe XIX **[1]**
$7 700 - €7 260 - **£4 772** - FF47 625
Elegant Lady in a Garden Oil/canvas (47x66cm
18x25in) Amsterdam 1999

CLAVIERE de Bernard 1934 **[8]**
$2 753 - €2 973 - **£1 903** - FF19 500
Portrait de cheval avec chemise d'écurie verte
Huile/toile (54.5x65.5cm 21x25in) Soissons 2001

CLAVO Javier 1918-1994 **[87]**
- **$2 560** - €2 403 - **£1 560** - FF15 760
  Oaxaca Oleo/lienzo (173x130cm 68x51in) Madrid 1999
- **$1 597** - €1 351 - **£945** - FF8 865
  Vista de Toledo Oleo/cartón (41x81cm 16x31in) Madrid 1998
- **$910** - €783 - **£533** - FF5 135
  Paisaje de Méjico Oleo/tablex (14x19cm 5x7in) Madrid 1998
- **$456** - €481 - **£304** - FF3 152
  Paisaje de montaña Acuarela/papel (23x31cm 9x12in) Madrid 2000
- **$214** - €192 - **£131** - FF1 260
  Escena surrealista Litografía (46x34cm 18x13in) Madrid 1999

CLAXTON Adelaide 1842-? **[8]**
- **$1 401** - €1 284 - **£850** - FF8 420
  Courting Watercolour (32.5x45cm 12x17in) London 1998

CLAXTON Marshall 1813-1881 **[8]**
- **$3 840** - €3 666 - **£2 400** - FF24 049
  Priscilla Frances Grabham (1833-1907) née Ingle, full-length Oil/canvas (76x63.5cm 29x25in) London 1999

CLAYES des Alice 1891-c.1971 **[22]**
- **$10 939** - €11 647 - **£7 200** - FF76 397
  Toilers of the Shore Oil/canvas (58.5x95cm 23x37in) Billingshurst, West-Sussex 2000
- **$393** - €448 - **£272** - FF2 941
  Plowing Time Watercolour/paper (16.5x24.5cm 6x9in) Montréal 2000

CLAYESEN Louise 1903-1997 **[210]**
- **$86** - €84 - **£53** - FF550
  Marche à Villeneuve-sur-Lot Huile/toile (73x60cm 28x23in) Orléans 1999

CLAYETTE Pierre XX **[27]**
- **$1 488** - €1 524 - **£918** - FF10 000
  L'attente au palais fantastique Gouache/papier (59x44cm 23x17in) Vendôme 2000

CLAYMAN Daniel 1957 **[3]**
- **$9 500** - €9 068 - **£5 936** - FF59 484
  Untitled Sculpture, glass (37.5x27x6cm 14x10x2in) New-York 1999

CLAYS Paul Jean 1819-1900 **[134]**
- **$29 532** - €27 044 - **£18 000** - FF177 400
  Marine Oil/canvas (147x103cm 57x40in) London 1999
- **$4 633** - €5 445 - **£3 212** - FF35 719
  Fishing Boats off a Jetty Oil/panel (64x51.5cm 25x20in) Amsterdam 2000
- **$1 544** - €1 815 - **£1 070** - FF11 906
  Shipping Near the Coast Oil/canvas (25.5x50.5cm 10x19in) Amsterdam 2000
- **$309** - €347 - **£210** - FF2 276
  Vue d'Anvers Crayon (33x23cm 12x9in) Bruxelles 2000

CLAYTON Harold 1896-1979 **[66]**
- **$15 961** - €17 974 - **£11 000** - FF117 901
  Summer Flowers in a Vase Oil/canvas (56x66cm 22x25in) London 2000
- **$4 353** - €4 902 - **£3 000** - FF32 154
  Spring Flowers in a White Vase Oil/canvas (30.5x40.5cm 12x15in) London 2000

CLAYTON Joseph Hughes ?-c.1929 **[108]**
- **$665** - €719 - **£460** - FF4 715
  Coastal Scene with Young Lady on a Coastal Path with Cottage Watercolour/paper (25x68cm 10x27in) Bristol, Avon 2001

CLAYTON William J.M. XX **[4]**
- **$4 500** - €4 830 - **£3 011** - FF31 684
  Souvenirs Oil/canvas (71x94cm 27x37in) San-Francisco CA 2000

CLEAVER Reginald Thomas 1870-1954 **[6]**
- **$215** - €200 - **£130** - FF1 311
  First Greetings: Entry into Pretoria Bodycolour (21x26cm 8x10in) London 1999

CLEELAND-HURA D.J. XX **[2]**
- **$4 994** - €5 822 - **£3 500** - FF38 190
  Lion Study Oil/board (30x44cm 11x17in) London 2000

CLEEMPUT van Jean 1881-? **[17]**
- **$578** - €595 - **£364** - FF3 902
  Vue de canal à Bruxelles Huile/toile (50x70cm 19x27in) Antwerpen 2000

CLEENEWERCK Henry 1818-1901 **[12]**
- **$5 500** - €5 128 - **£3 411** - FF33 640
  Indian Encampment Oil/canvas (87x46.5cm 34x18in) New-York 1999

CLEGG & GUTTMAN Michael & Martin 1957 **[17]**
- **$5 500** - €6 382 - **£3 797** - FF41 860
  The Board of Regents Cibachrome print (144x430cm 56x169in) New-York 2000

CLELAND-HURA D.J. XX **[2]**
- **$2 107** - €2 312 - **£1 400** - FF15 166
  Contemplation - Cougar Acrylic/board (29x36.5cm 11x14in) London 2000

CLEMANSIN DU MAINE Georges 1853-? **[1]**
- **$4 360** - €3 659 - **£2 558** - FF24 000
  Jeune femme à l'ombrelle Huile/toile (46x38cm 18x14in) Orléans 1998

CLEMENS Curt 1911-1947 **[53]**
- **$567** - €560 - **£349** - FF3 671
  Vägen fram Oil/panel (40.5x61.5cm 15x24in) Stockholm 1999

CLEMENS Gustaf Adolf 1870-1918 **[30]**
- **$825** - €713 - **£498** - FF4 677
  Solnedgang ved Skagen Strand Oil/canvas (48x75cm 18x29in) Vejle 1998
- **$441** - €404 - **£276** - FF2 647
  Hovede af et par pointere Oil/canvas (15x27cm 5x10in) København 1999

CLEMENS Johan Frederik 1749-1831 **[30]**
- **$387** - €429 - **£269** - FF2 812
  Portraet af Louise Augusta Copper engraving (34.5x24cm 13x9in) Vejle 2001

CLEMENS Martin XX **[5]**
- **$793** - €920 - **£547** - FF6 037
  «Zoologischer Garten Dresden» Poster (59x92cm 23x36in) München 2000

CLÉMENT Alain 1941 **[13]**
- **$529** - €534 - **£330** - FF3 500
  Sans titre Gouache/papier (79x73cm 31x28in) Paris 2000

CLÉMENT Charles 1889-1972 **[44]**
- **$389** - €341 - **£235** - FF2 235
  Rovéréaz Aquarelle/papier (41x50cm 16x19in) Genève 1998

CLEMENT Félix 1826-1888 **[6]**
- 🖼 **$2 136** - €2 439 - **£1 502** - FF16 000
  Egyptienne à la cruche Huile/toile (44x24cm 17x9in) Aubagne 2001

CLEMENT Gad Frederik 1867-1933 **[21]**
- 🖼 **$787** - €672 - **£472** - FF4 411
  Optrukne både ved Skagen Havn Oil/canvas (45x54cm 17x21in) København 1998
- 🖼 **$4 306** - €3 987 - **£2 600** - FF26 153
  The Breakfast Table Oil/canvas (35.5x43cm 13x16in) London 1999

CLÉMENT-SERVEAU 1886-1972 **[232]**
- 🖼 **$14 768** - €15 855 - **£9 880** - FF104 000
  Madame Clement-Serveau à l'atelier Huile/panneau (146x113cm 57x44in) Lyon 2000
- 🖼 **$1 562** - €1 677 - **£1 045** - FF11 000
  Nu assoupi Huile/panneau (45x65cm 17x25in) Lyon 2000
- 🖼 **$1 324** - €1 524 - **£904** - FF10 000
  Hommage à Matisse Peinture (42x33cm 16x12in) Lyon 2000
- 🖼 **$1 324** - €1 524 - **£904** - FF10 000
  Femme au guéridon Aquarelle/papier (45x33cm 17x12in) Lyon 2000

CLEMENTE Francesco 1952 **[296]**
- 🖼 **$95 000** - €106 223 - **£64 040** - FF696 774
  Untitled (C-1) (C-2) (C-3) (C-4) Enamel (101.5x137cm 39x53in) New-York 2000
- 🖼 **$31 500** - €32 655 - **£18 900** - FF214 200
  Senza titolo Tecnica mista/tavola (120x50cm 47x19in) Roma 2001
- 🖼 **$13 000** - €14 263 - **£8 635** - FF93 558
  Companion Coloured chalks/paper (67x48cm 26x18in) New-York 2000
- 🖼 **$1 700** - €1 596 - **£1 053** - FF10 470
  Untitled Print (50x71cm 19x27in) New-York 1999
- 📷 **$3 200** - €4 147 - **£2 400** - FF27 200
  «Le pazienze» Photo (49x53cm 19x20in) Prato 2000

CLEMENTS George Henry 1854-1935 **[28]**
- 🖼 **$1 200** - €1 122 - **£740** - FF7 358
  Portrait of J.B. Clements, Brother of George Henry Oil/canvas/board (27x20cm 11x8in) New-Orleans LA 1999
- 🖼 **$1 000** - €932 - **£604** - FF6 113
  Idyllic Landscape with Cows and Lake Watercolour/paper (26x36cm 10x14in) New-Orleans LA 1999

CLEMENTSCHITSCH Arnold 1887-1970 **[26]**
- 🖼 **$11 916** - €13 081 - **£7 920** - FF85 806
  Badehütten am Ossiachersee Öl/Karton (40x49.5cm 15x19in) Wien 2001

CLEMINSON Robert 1844-1888 **[170]**
- 🖼 **$2 000** - €2 015 - **£1 246** - FF13 220
  At Rest After the Hunt Oil/canvas (91x71cm 36x28in) New-York 2000
- 🖼 **$1 300** - €1 476 - **£903** - FF9 682
  Bird Dog on a Point Oil/canvas (22x38cm 9x15in) Portsmouth NH 2001

CLEMMENSEN Clemmen Jeppe 1885-1964 **[18]**
- 🖼 **$497** - €471 - **£302** - FF3 090
  Fra en dansk lystbådehavn Oil/canvas (34x49cm 13x19in) København 1999

CLENNELL Luke 1781-1840 **[7]**
- 🖼 **$5 117** - €4 928 - **£3 200** - FF32 324
  Figures and a waggon outside the Bell Inn Watercolour (34.5x41.5cm 13x16in) London 1999

CLERC de Oscar 1892-1968 **[4]**
- 🖼 **$936** - €1 041 - **£655** - FF6 829
  Profil de jeune femme Fusain/papier (24x19.5cm 9x7in) Bruxelles 2001

CLERC Jean XX **[1]**
- 🖼 **$1 764** - €1 778 - **£1 100** - FF11 664
  «Tignes» Poster (100x60cm 39x23in) London 2000

CLERC Sylvestre XX **[3]**
- 🖼 **$4 014** - €4 726 - **£2 821** - FF31 000
  Nu assis Marbre (H50cm H19in) Toulouse 2000

CLERC Yves 1947 **[1]**
- 🖼 **$28 000** - €30 238 - **£19 350** - FF198 349
  Jeune femme au chapeau Oil/canvas (161.5x114.5cm 63x45in) New-York 2001

CLERCK de Hendricx c.1570-1629 **[27]**
- 🖼 **$25 500** - €30 032 - **£18 000** - FF197 000
  Encuentro de Cristo con La Verónica camino del Calvario Oleo/lienzo (136x108cm 53x42in) Madrid 2001
- 🖼 **$17 942** - €16 781 - **£11 000** - FF110 077
  Mars and Venus Surprised by Vulcan Oil/panel (106x75cm 41x29in) London 1998
- 🖼 **$2 139** - €2 363 - **£1 483** - FF15 500
  Hector, Andromaque et Astynax Encre (18x12.5cm 7x4in) Paris 2001

CLERCK de Jan 1881-1962 **[19]**
- 🖼 **$1 664** - €1 983 - **£1 192** - FF13 008
  Het laatste schotje Huile/toile (34x44cm 13x17in) Antwerpen 2000

CLERCK de Oscar 1892-1968 **[19]**
- 🖼 **$792** - €744 - **£480** - FF4 878
  Christ aux outrages Céramique (H87cm H34in) Bruxelles 2001

CLERCQ de Alphonse 1868-1945 **[36]**
- 🖼 **$535** - €595 - **£374** - FF3 902
  Oude poort tr Schelle op Schelde Huile/toile (110x78cm 43x30in) Antwerpen 2001

CLERCQ de Louis 1836-1901 **[15]**
- 📷 **$2 400** - €2 266 - **£1 490** - FF14 865
  Kalaat-Esch-Schekif Albumen print (21.5x28.5cm 8x11in) New-York 1999

CLERCQ de Paul Jan 1891-1964 **[34]**
- 🖼 **$633** - €744 - **£438** - FF4 878
  Marine Huile/panneau (51x62cm 20x24in) Antwerpen 2000
- 🖼 **$285** - €297 - **£180** - FF1 951
  Orage sur l'Escaut Huile/panneau (35x43cm 13x16in) Antwerpen 2000

CLERGERIE Yvonne 1942 **[28]**
- 🖼 **$4 026** - €4 573 - **£2 817** - FF30 000
  La Lumière Bronze (H76cm H29in) Bordeaux 2001

CLERGET Alexandre 1856-1931 **[6]**
- 🖼 **$2 149** - €2 058 - **£1 352** - FF13 500
  Femme - Iris, bougeoir Bronze (H24.5cm H9in) Paris 1999

CLERGUE Lucien 1934 **[178]**
- 📷 **$1 000** - €934 - **£604** - FF6 127
  Nudes by the Sea Silver print (29x44cm 11x17in) New-York 1999

CLÉRICE François & Victor XIX-XX **[16]**
- 🖼 **$668** - €658 - **£327** - FF3 659
  «Les maris de Ginette, opérettes en 3 actes» Poster (111x77.5cm 43x30in) New-York 2000

CLERICI Fabrizio 1913-1993 **[88]**
- $5 808 - €4 878 - **£3 414** - FF32 000
  Bélier Huile/toile (70x90cm 27x35in) Douai 1998
- $1 000 - €1 037 - **£600** - FF6 800
  L'opera incompiuta Acquarello/carta (36x47.5cm 14x18in) Roma 2001

CLERICI Leone XIX **[5]**
- $5 476 - €6 403 - **£3 847** - FF42 000
  Diane au bain Marbre (H97cm H38in) Paris 2001
- $3 250 - €3 740 - **£2 240** - FF24 531
  A Grecian Woman Marble (H69cm H27in) Philadelphia PA 2000

CLERIGINO DA CAPODISTRIA XV **[1]**
- $131 274 - €112 466 - **£78 914** - FF737 726
  Die Anbetung der Könige Oil/panel (57x81.5cm 22x32in) Stuttgart 1998

CLERISSEAU Charles Louis 1721-1820 **[36]**
- $4 500 - €5 439 - **£3 141** - FF35 678
  Roman Capriccio with Figures Watercolour (61x81.5cm 24x32in) Bethesda MD 2000

CLERMONT DE GALLERANDE Adhémar Louis ?-1895 **[9]**
- $4 149 - €3 964 - **£2 613** - FF26 000
  Pique-nique au bois, arrivée en calèche Huile/panneau (30x49cm 11x19in) Deauville 1999

CLERMONT de M. XIX-XX **[7]**
- $602 - €656 - **£414** - FF4 300
  L'Oasis Huile/panneau (64x90cm 25x35in) Nîmes 2001

CLERMONT Jean-François, Ganif 1717-1807 **[15]**
- $1 051 - €915 - **£634** - FF6 000
  Esther devant Assuérus Encre (38.6x49.4cm 15x19in) Paris 1998

CLÉSINGER Jean-Bapt., Auguste 1814-1883 **[156]**
- $11 968 - €12 958 - **£7 599** - FF85 000
  La zingara, danseuse napolitaine Bronze (H102cm H40in) London 2000
- $3 207 - €2 905 - **£2 000** - FF19 058
  Bust of an Egyptian Maiden Bronze (H70.5cm H27in) London 1999
- $2 496 - €2 897 - **£1 723** - FF19 000
  Portrait de sa femme Solange Dudevant-Sand, assise dans un fauteuil Mine plomb (22x17cm 8x6in) Paris 2000

CLESSE Louis 1889-1961 **[246]**
- $11 128 - €12 890 - **£7 696** - FF84 552
  Paysage de neige ensoleillé Huile/toile (115x130.5cm 45x51in) Bruxelles 2000
- $1 505 - €1 735 - **£1 029** - FF11 382
  L'écluse en hiver Huile/panneau (40x50cm 15x19in) Bruxelles 2000
- $664 - €744 - **£453** - FF4 878
  Vue de Paris Huile/panneau (30x40cm 11x15in) Bruxelles 2000

CLEVE JON-AND Agnes 1876-1951 **[111]**
- $4 784 - €4 498 - **£2 964** - FF29 508
  Sydländskt landskap, Toledo Oil/panel (53x62cm 20x24in) Stockholm 1999
- $3 570 - €3 504 - **£2 214** - FF22 983
  Kanalmotiv med pråm Oil/panel (32x40cm 12x15in) Stockholm 1999
- $1 166 - €1 096 - **£703** - FF7 190
  Fiskebodar Gouache/paper (50x37cm 19x14in) Stockholm 1999
- $736 - €692 - **£444** - FF4 541
  Automobiler, Paris Woodcut in colors (18.5x28cm 7x11in) Stockholm 1999

CLEVE van Cornelis Sotte Cleef 1520-c.1569 **[5]**
- $34 164 - €39 637 - **£24 310** - FF260 000
  Vierge à l'Enfant sur fond de paysage Huile/panneau (63x53.5cm 24x21in) Paris 2001

CLEVE van Hendrik III c.1525-1589 **[19]**
- $41 728 - €48 784 - **£29 792** - FF320 000
  La construction de la Tour de Babel Huile/panneau (33x54cm 12x21in) Paris 2001

CLEVE van Joos van der Beke c.1484-c.1540 **[10]**
- $244 665 - €228 834 - **£150 000** - FF1 501 050
  A Young Prince, half length, Wearing a Red Doublet Oil/panel (56x38cm 22x14in) London 1998

CLEVE van Martin 1527-1581 **[24]**
- $48 563 - €41 346 - **£29 000** - FF271 210
  The Dismantling of the Citadel of Antwerp Oil/panel (71x118cm 27x46in) London 1998

CLEVELEY John I c.1712-1777 **[13]**
- $77 860 - €74 777 - **£48 000** - FF490 502
  The east Indiaman Northumberland in three Positions, with shipping Oil/canvas (76x136cm 29x53in) London 1998

CLEVELEY John II 1747-1786 **[25]**
- $3 930 - €3 594 - **£2 400** - FF23 575
  Shipping off the Coast in Calm Water Watercolour (22x36cm 9x14in) London 1998

CLEVELEY Robert 1747-1809 **[32]**
- $730 - €702 - **£450** - FF4 607
  Village Scene with Figure Climbing over a Fence Ink (26x35cm 10x13in) London 1999

CLEYN Francis c.1582-1658 **[7]**
- $342 - €360 - **£228** - FF2 364
  Eneas y la fundación de Troya/Batallas de Eneas Aguafuerte (20x30.5cm 7x12in) Madrid 2000

CLIFFE Henry 1919-1983 **[92]**
- $502 - €523 - **£320** - FF3 431
  Midnight Blue Abstract Oil/board (44x54.5cm 17x21in) London 2000
- $628 - €654 - **£400** - FF4 289
  Night City Oil/board (30x37.5cm 11x14in) London 2000
- $417 - €395 - **£260** - FF2 589
  Study of a Seated Female Nude Drawing (56x40.5cm 22x15in) London 1999
- $240 - €228 - **£150** - FF1 494
  Orange and Black Composition Lithograph (57x79.5cm 22x31in) London 1999

CLIFFORD Charles c.1819-1863 **[21]**
- $1 747 - €1 829 - **£1 098** - FF12 000
  Architecture hispano-mauresque Tirage albuminé (41x32.5cm 16x12in) Paris 2001

CLIFFORD Edward 1844-1907 **[22]**
- $1 478 - €1 458 - **£950** - FF9 561
  Mens Concia Recti Watercolour/paper (42x31cm 16x12in) London 1999

CLIFT William Brooks, III 1944 **[32]**
- $1 800 - €1 536 - **£1 076** - FF10 078
  White House Ruin, Canyon de Chelly, Arizona Gelatin silver print (34.5x49cm 13x19in) San-Francisco CA 1998

CLIME Winfield Scott 1881-1958 **[22]**
- $3 000 - €2 517 - **£1 768** - FF16 510
  The Parker House, Essex, CT Oil/canvas (63x76cm 25x30in) Greenwich CT 1998
- $1 200 - €1 025 - **£704** - FF6 726
  «Mt Byers, Colorado» Oil/panel (30x40cm 12x16in) Downington PA 1998

C

CLIMENT Elena 1955 [2]
 $15 000 – €10 101 – £10 038 – FF105 615
  Altar con muro y flores Acrylic/canvas (122x91.5cm 48x36in) New-York 2000

CLINCH Robert 1957 [2]
 $4 149 – €4 654 – £2 881 – FF30 526
  Parallax Gouache/paper (52x126cm 20x49in) Melbourne 2001

CLINT Alfred 1807-1883 [27]
 $941 – €919 – £600 – FF6 027
  Extensive Harbour Scene Oil/canvas (71x109cm 27x42in) Billingshurst, West-Sussex 1999
 $1 110 – €1 143 – £700 – FF7 499
  Fisherfolk and Their Boats Oil/panel (31x48cm 12x19in) Carlisle, Cumbria 2000

CLINT George 1770-1854 [13]
 $2 107 – €2 312 – £1 400 – FF15 166
  William Downton as Falstaff, Miss C.Jones as Mistress Quickly Oil/canvas/board (35x38cm 13x14in) Billingshurst, West-Sussex 2000

CLOAR Carroll 1913-1994 [9]
 $26 000 – €24 244 – £16 127 – FF159 029
  The red Haw Tree Oil/masonite (58.5x79cm 23x31in) New-York 1999

CLOCHARD William Marcel 1894-1990 [18]
 $1 058 – €915 – £628 – FF6 000
  Vase de fleurs Huile/toile (53x44cm 20x17in) Chartres 1998

CLODION Claude Michel, dit 1738-1814 [219]
 $13 000 – €12 427 – £8 148 – FF81 519
  Pair of Louis XVI Ormolu Foour Light Candelabra Bronze (82.5x28cm 32x11in) New-York 1999
 $1 367 – €1 250 – £837 – FF8 200
  Satyre à l'outre Bronze (H66cm H25in) Enghien 1999

CLOSE Chuck 1940 [79]
 $1 100 000 – €1 064 337 – £678 370 – FF6 981 590
  Cindy II Oil/canvas (183x152.5cm 72x60in) New-York 1999
 $70 000 – €67 731 – £43 169 – FF444 283
  Cindy II (Study) Mixed media (101.5x81.5cm 39x32in) New-York 1999
 $140 000 – €156 810 – £97 272 – FF1 028 608
  «Study for Joe» Mixed media (37x28cm 14x11in) New-York 2000
 $60 000 – €67 204 – £41 688 – FF440 832
  «Bob F. 2288» Graphite (54.5x43.5cm 21x17in) New-York 2001
 $6 000 – €6 994 – £4 154 – FF45 879
  Alex Katz Woodcut in colors (59x49cm 23x19in) New-York 2000
 $19 000 – €17 772 – £11 487 – FF116 576
  Susan, Five color States Dye-transfer print (49x40cm 19x15in) New-York 1999

CLOSS Gustav Paul 1840-1870 [4]
 $1 900 – €1 970 – £1 140 – FF12 920
  Pescatori sulla spiaggia di Sorrento Acquarello/carta (40x50cm 15x19in) Napoli 1999

CLOSTERMAN Johan Baptist 1660-1713 [10]
 $16 584 – €18 326 – £11 500 – FF120 209
  Portrait of David Papillon (c.1691-1762) Oil/canvas (124.5x99cm 49x38in) London 2001

CLOUARD Albert 1866-1952 [103]
 $3 475 – €3 811 – £2 360 – FF25 000
  La taverne aux lampions Huile/panneau (26x40cm 10x15in) Calais 2000

CLOUET Émile XIX-XX [18]
 $656 – €732 – £441 – FF4 800
  «Apéritif Bacchus Javilier & Sarrazin, Dijon» Affiche (155x116.5cm 61x45in) Orléans 2000

CLOUET Félix ?-1882 [3]
 $3 550 – €3 811 – £2 375 – FF25 000
  Nature morte au lièvre et colvert Huile/toile (81.5x62cm 32x24in) Paris 2000

CLOUGH George Lafayette 1824-1901 [29]
 $5 775 – €5 368 – £3 538 – FF35 213
  New York Scene Oil/canvas (40x76cm 16x30in) Portland ME 1998
 $2 750 – €2 596 – £1 709 – FF17 031
  Harvest Time, Upstate NY Oil/canvas (30x38cm 12x15in) Milford CT 1999

CLOUGH Peter XX [5]
 $2 315 – €2 166 – £1 400 – FF14 206
  Display Oil/board (34x28.5cm 13x11in) London 1999

CLOUGH Prunella 1919-1999 [59]
 $3 646 – €3 146 – £2 200 – FF20 638
  Still Life Oil/canvas (35.5x46cm 13x18in) London 1998
 $4 379 – €4 206 – £2 700 – FF27 590
  Wall and Brush Oil/canvas (40.5x30.5cm 15x12in) London 1999
 $391 – €386 – £240 – FF2 530
  Dead Flowers Ink (58.5x38.5cm 23x15in) London 1999
 $1 295 – €1 478 – £900 – FF9 695
  Geological Landscape Lithograph (18.5x23.5cm 7x9in) London 2000

CLOUGH Tom 1867-1943 [62]
 $1 495 – €1 550 – £897 – FF10 166
  Paesaggio con contadino al lavoro Acquarello/cartone (55x75cm 21x29in) Roma 1999

CLOVIO Giulio 1498-1578 [5]
 $23 000 – €19 995 – £13 919 – FF131 159
  Man Wearing a Cap and a Fur Collar Black chalk/paper (19.5x16.5cm 7x6in) New-York 1999

CLOWES Butler ?-1782 [1]
 $1 081 – €1 127 – £680 – FF7 391
  The Hen Peckt Husband Mezzotint (48x52.5cm 18x20in) London 2000

CLOWES Daniel 1774-1829 [25]
 $3 507 – €4 171 – £2 500 – FF27 363
  Chesnut Hunter in a Landscape Oil/canvas (46x62cm 18x24in) London 2000

CLOWES Henry 1799-1871 [2]
 $3 586 – €3 849 – £2 400 – FF25 251
  Two Cockfighting Scenes Oil/canvas (22x18cm 9x7in) Leominster, Herefordshire 2000

CLUSEAU-LANAUVE Jean 1914-1997 [44]
 $581 – €549 – £361 – FF3 600
  Reflets au matin sur le port, Honfleur Huile/toile (33x41cm 12x16in) Neuilly-sur-Seine 1999

CLUTTERBUCK Eugene, Colonel 1830-1904 [1]
 $4 500 – €4 196 – £2 716 – FF27 524
  Delhi, Agra and Rajpootana Albumen print (23x29cm 9x11in) May 1999

CLUYSENAAR Alfred Jean André 1837-1902 [20]
 $5 791 – €6 807 – £4 015 – FF44 649
  Sweet Memories Oil/canvas (97.5x68.5cm 38x26in) Amsterdam 2000

CLYMER John Ford 1907-1989 **[47]**
- $50 000 - €42 719 - **£30 015** - FF280 220
  Buffalo Hunt Oil/canvas (66x96.5cm 25x37in) New-York 1998
- $60 000 - €64 332 - **£39 696** - FF421 992
  Heading for Rendezvous Oil/board (25x50cm 10x20in) Hayden ID 2000
- $5 500 - €5 000 - **£3 312** - FF32 796
  An Old Timer Charcoal/paper (35x27cm 14x11in) Hayden ID 1998

COAST Oscar Regan 1851-1931 **[4]**
- $750 - €680 - **£461** - FF4 458
  Moonlight, Santa Barbara Oil/board (40x30cm 16x12in) Mystic CT 1999

COATES Edmund C. 1816-1871 **[14]**
- $3 000 - €3 220 - **£2 007** - FF21 123
  Ruins of Fort Ticonderoga with Lake George in the Background Oil/canvas (60x81cm 24x32in) Cedar-Falls IA 2000

COATES Tom 1941 **[33]**
- $867 - €1 010 - **£600** - FF6 626
  The Besom Maker Oil/canvas (40.5x50.5cm 15x19in) London 2000

COATS Randolph Lasalle 1891-1957 **[8]**
- $6 000 - €6 694 - **£3 927** - FF43 909
  Autumn Landscape Oil/canvas (63x162cm 25x64in) Chicago IL 2000

COBB Darius 1834-1919 **[6]**
- $7 000 - €6 527 - **£4 342** - FF42 815
  Dipper Missing Oil/canvas (79x58.5cm 31x23in) New-York 1999
- $2 250 - €2 571 - **£1 584** - FF16 863
  Figures along a Riverbank Oil/canvas (23x38cm 9x15in) Pittsfield MA 1999

COBB Victor Ernest 1876-1945 **[38]**
- $82 - €90 - **£54** - FF592
  Old red Gum, near the Yan Yean Etching (24.5x32cm 9x12in) Melbourne 2000

COBBAERT Jan 1909-1995 **[143]**
- $2 304 - €2 231 - **£1 422** - FF14 634
  Figures Huile/toile (80x70cm 31x27in) Bruxelles 1999
- $482 - €446 - **£300** - FF2 926
  Compositie Gouache (34x25cm 13x9in) Lokeren 1999

COBBE Bernard XIX **[4]**
- $6 000 - €5 311 - **£3 668** - FF34 841
  Chewing over the Accounts Oil/canvas (33x48cm 12x18in) New-York 1999

COBBETT Edward John 1815-1899 **[51]**
- $2 307 - €2 744 - **£1 645** - FF18 000
  La porteuse d'eau Huile/panneau (47x62cm 18x24in) Calais 2000
- $1 794 - €1 724 - **£1 118** - FF11 311
  The Little Harvest Girl Oil/panel (25x30.5cm 9x12in) Amsterdam 1999

COBELLE Charles 1902 **[64]**
- $600 - €596 - **£368** - FF3 907
  Brant Point Oil/canvas (50x60cm 20x24in) Delray-Beach FL 2000
- $200 - €191 - **£121** - FF1 254
  The Lutte Color lithograph (38x75cm 15x29in) Bolton MA 1999

COBO Chema 1952 **[32]**
- $478 - €499 - **£301** - FF3 274
  A Knowlestage Watercolour/paper (75x56cm 29x22in) Amsterdam 2000

COBURN Alvin Langdon 1882-1966 **[85]**
- $6 000 - €5 604 - **£3 626** - FF36 763
  Saltram's Seat Platinum print (27x17cm 11x7in) New-York 1999

COBURN Frank 1862-1938 **[40]**
- $7 000 - €6 443 - **£4 201** - FF42 261
  Houses, Figures, Tree lined Street Oil/canvas/board (40x50cm 16x20in) Pasadena CA 1999
- $3 750 - €4 382 - **£2 677** - FF28 747
  «Chief Calf child, Black Foot Tribe» Oil/board (35x25cm 14x10in) Altadena CA 2001
- $3 575 - €3 644 - **£2 240** - FF23 905
  Reflections, Street Scene Monotype (36x28cm 14x11in) Altadena CA 2000

COBURN Frederick Simpson 1871-1960 **[164]**
- $9 886 - €8 373 - **£5 943** - FF54 925
  A Trip to Town Oil/canvas (46x61cm 18x24in) Vancouver, BC. 1998
- $2 789 - €2 667 - **£1 748** - FF17 492
  Country Landscape Oil/board (30.5x38cm 12x14in) Vancouver, BC. 1999
- $322 - €275 - **£192** - FF1 806
  Near St Gregoire, Québec Charcoal (14.5x19cm 5x7in) Vancouver, BC. 1998

COBURN John 1925 **[228]**
- $11 640 - €12 825 - **£7 728** - FF84 126
  Earth Festival Oil/canvas (122x107cm 48x42in) Woollahra, Sydney 2000
- $6 040 - €5 877 - **£3 717** - FF38 549
  Blue of Memory, red as of Desire Oil/canvas/board (55x75.5cm 21x29in) Melbourne 1999
- $1 578 - €1 843 - **£1 114** - FF12 087
  «Study for Ah, What is Man?» Acrylic (27x24cm 10x9in) Malvern, Victoria 2000
- $1 556 - €1 744 - **£1 081** - FF11 437
  «Study for Nothern Sun» Gouache (35.5x52cm 13x20in) Melbourne 2001
- $416 - €486 - **£290** - FF3 189
  «Tree of Life» Serigraph in colors (60x54cm 23x21in) Melbourne 2000

COCCAPANI Sigismondo 1583-1642 **[7]**
- $36 000 - €31 100 - **£24 000** - FF204 000
  Sansone e Dalila Olio/tela (100x150cm 39x59in) Roma 1998

COCCETTI Napoleone c.1850-? **[1]**
- $2 251 - €2 087 - **£1 357** - FF13 692
  Dienstmeisje Oil/canvas (30x21.5cm 11x8in) Maastricht 2000

COCCORANTE Leonardo 1680-1750 **[45]**
- $37 357 - €40 100 - **£25 000** - FF263 040
  Classical Ruins with Banditti Oil/canvas (205x160cm 80x62in) London 2000
- $27 434 - €25 681 - **£17 000** - FF168 454
  Capriccio of Architectural Ruins with a Dutch Frigate Oil/canvas (73x127cm 28x50in) London 1999
- $9 030 - €8 842 - **£5 771** - FF58 000
  Scènes de port méditerranéen avec des portiques à l'antique Huile/toile (16x25cm 6x9in) Marseille 1999

COCEANI Antonio 1894-1983 **[14]**
- $1 800 - €1 866 - **£1 080** - FF12 240
  Laguna a Mofalcone Olio/tela (50x70cm 19x27in) Trieste 1999
- $1 100 - €1 140 - **£660** - FF7 480
  Nubi minacciose Olio/cartone (20x30cm 7x11in) Trieste 1999

COCHELET Louise XIX **[9]**
- $3 450 - €3 369 - **£2 200** - FF22 101
  View of Lake Constance Watercolour (19x15cm 7x5in) London 1999

COCHIN Charles-Nicolas I 1688-1754 **[19]**
- $1 807 - €1 982 - **£1 227** - FF13 000
  Portrait d'un homme et de sa femme dans un même encadrement Trois crayons/papier (17x25.5cm 6x10in) Paris 2000
- $650 - €722 - **£432** - FF4 733
  La Tentation de Saint-Antoine Etching (26x33cm 10x12in) New-York 2000

COCHIN Charles-Nicolas II 1715-1790 **[96]**
- $2 564 - €3 049 - **£1 778** - FF20 000
  Portrait de femme assise vue en buste tenant un éventail Crayon/papier (16x11.5cm 6x4in) Paris 2000
- $810 - €901 - **£540** - FF5 910
  Pompe funèbre de Philippe de Frances Roi d'Espagne, según Los Slodtz Grabado (49x75cm 19x29in) Madrid 2000

COCHIN Nicolas 1610-1686 **[16]**
- $132 - €153 - **£92** - FF1 006
  «Gesellschaft im Wald» Radierung (23x31cm 9x13in) Erlangén 2001

COCHRAN Allen Dean 1888-1935 **[26]**
- $1 100 - €1 015 - **£676** - FF6 661
  Woman Oil/canvas (76x63cm 30x25in) Hatfield PA 1999

COCHRANE Constance 1888-1962 **[8]**
- $1 000 - €1 125 - **£688** - FF7 382
  Sea at Monhegan Oil/canvas/board (39x50cm 15x20in) Philadelphia PA 2000

COCK de Camiel 1925 **[40]**
- $6 791 - €7 714 - **£4 765** - FF50 602
  Washerwomen at Work by a Windmill Oil/panel (24x38cm 9x14in) Amsterdam 2001

COCK de César 1823-1904 **[121]**
- $7 500 - €7 081 - **£4 662** - FF46 448
  Fisherman by a quiet Stream Oil/canvas (46x67cm 18x26in) Milford CT 1999
- $2 061 - €2 018 - **£1 268** - FF13 238
  Töissä pellolla Oil/panel (31x44cm 12x17in) Helsinki 1999
- $171 - €202 - **£119** - FF1 323
  I parken Watercolour/paper (26x16cm 10x6in) Helsinki 2000

COCK de Gilbert 1928 **[80]**
- $211 - €198 - **£130** - FF1 300
  Composition Gouache/papier (45x45cm 17x17in) Antwerpen 1999

COCK de Jan Claudius 1668-1735 **[16]**
- $896 - €862 - **£552** - FF5 655
  Putti Drawings Wine from a Decorative vat, drinking, washing cups Ink (15.5x19.5cm 6x7in) Amsterdam 1999

COCK de Jan Wellens act.1503-1527 **[7]**
- $26 000 - €28 128 - **£17 812** - FF184 506
  The Legend of Saint Jerome and the Animals Oil/panel (49.5x27cm 19x10in) New-York 2001

COCK de Xavier 1818-1896 **[40]**
- $7 567 - €7 013 - **£4 705** - FF46 000
  Vaches s'abreuvant Huile/panneau (31.5x27cm 12x10in) Paris 1999

- $284 - €297 - **£188** - FF1 951
  Deux petites filles Crayon/papier (19x15cm 7x5in) Bruxelles 2000

COCK Hieronymus 1510-1570 **[22]**
- $897 - €1 022 - **£626** - FF6 707
  Colossaei Ro Prospectus Radierung (26.5x20cm 10x7in) Berlin 2001

COCKBURN Edwin XIX **[9]**
- $4 141 - €4 310 - **£2 600** - FF28 274
  Music Oil/canvas (46x61cm 18x24in) London 2000
- $3 651 - €3 222 - **£2 200** - FF21 133
  Whitby Old Bridge and Detailed Harbourside Watercolour/paper (28x45cm 11x18in) Whitby, Yorks 1998

COCKBURN James Pattison 1778-1848 **[31]**
- $1 541 - €1 657 - **£1 050** - FF10 872
  View on the Ice Pond, Quebec City Watercolour (15x24cm 5x9in) Billingshurst, West-Sussex 2001
- $402 - €432 - **£269** - FF2 834
  Cape Diamond and Wolf's Cove Print (44x67cm 17x26in) Montréal 2000

COCKERELL Charles Robert 1788-1863 **[13]**
- $1 090 - €1 099 - **£680** - FF7 210
  The Interior of St Pauls Cathedral, London Watercolour/paper (21.5x18cm 8x7in) London 2000

COCKERELL Christabel Annie 1863-1951 **[5]**
- $3 892 - €3 753 - **£2 400** - FF24 617
  Portrait of Meredith Frampton Oil/canvas (102x37.5cm 40x14in) London 1999

COCKRAM George 1861-1950 **[38]**
- $708 - €782 - **£480** - FF5 127
  Gulls at the Sea Shore Watercolour/paper (29.5x50cm 11x19in) London 2000

COCKRILL Maurice 1936 **[103]**
- $4 437 - €4 217 - **£2 700** - FF27 659
  Manifold Landscape Oil/canvas (127x152cm 50x59in) London 1999
- $1 122 - €1 131 - **£700** - FF7 422
  Upward Oil/canvas (51x45.5cm 20x17in) London 2000
- $517 - €603 - **£360** - FF3 958
  Black and Tauape Oil/board (16.5x20.5cm 6x8in) London 2000

COCKS R. Sydney XIX-XX **[23]**
- $147 - €159 - **£102** - FF1 045
  The Bend Ti Tree Watercolour/paper (35.5x52.5cm 13x20in) Sydney 2001

COCKX Marcel 1930 **[63]**
- $227 - €273 - **£156** - FF1 788
  Kind met beertjes (enfants et ours en peluche) Huile/toile (70x60cm 27x23in) Antwerpen 2000

COCKX Philibert 1879-1949 **[64]**
- $1 128 - €942 - **£661** - FF6 178
  Nature morte Huile/toile (60x68cm 23x26in) Bruxelles 1998

COCONIS Ted C. 1927 **[2]**
- $3 750 - €4 200 - **£2 605** - FF27 552
  Montage of Marilyn Monroe Acrylic (40x46cm 16x18in) New-York 2001
- $1 600 - €1 792 - **£1 111** - FF11 755
  Nude withe red Necklace seated on Ornate Chair Gouache/paper (69x49cm 27x19in) New-York 2001

COCTEAU Jean 1889-1963 **[1668]**
- $26 484 - €24 544 - **£16 470** - FF161 000
  Eve Technique mixte/panneau (200x140cm 78x55in) Versailles 1999

  $1 400 - €1 509 - **£954** - FF9 897
Musiciens (Bowl) Ceramic (5x25cm 1x9in) New-York 2001

$1 617 - €1 877 - **£1 116** - FF12 312
Ansikte Coloured chalks/paper (29x24cm 11x9in) Stockholm 2000

$315 - €358 - **£219** - FF2 347
Auf einem Brunnen sitzender Knabe Farblithographie (44x26.5cm 17x10in) Berlin 2001

$480 - €534 - **£335** - FF3 500
Avec Picasso/Avec Simenon/Sur une échelle de bibliothèque Tirage argentique (24x18cm 9x7in) Paris 2001

CODAZZI Nicolo Viviani 1648-1693 [9]
$10 460 - €11 228 - **£7 000** - FF73 651
Classical Capriccio with a Hunting Party and Shepherds Oil/canvas (94x133.5cm 37x52in) London 2000

CODAZZI Viviano 1604-1670 [34]
$164 160 - €154 067 - **£102 600** - FF1 010 610
La Adoración de los Reyes Magos/Cristo expulsando a los mercaderes Oleo/lienzo (103x130cm 40x51in) Palma de Mallorca 1999

$30 400 - €39 393 - **£22 800** - FF258 400
Rovine romane con figure/Portico con la bottega di un maniscalco Olio/tela (67.5x50cm 26x19in) Milano 2000

CODDE Pieter Jacobsz. 1599-1678 [36]
$37 151 - €39 881 - **£24 866** - FF261 604
Holländisches Ehepaar mit geöffneter Tür stehend Oil/panel (53x43cm 20x16in) München 2000

$16 000 - €15 273 - **£9 996** - FF100 185
Card Game Oil/panel (28x28.5cm 11x11in) New-York 1999

CODDRON Oscar 1881-1960 [36]
$3 312 - €3 099 - **£2 050** - FF20 325
Zomer Huile/toile (108x143cm 42x56in) Lokeren 1999

$1 653 - €1 933 - **£1 177** - FF12 682
Fermette au bord d'un cours d'eau Huile/toile (100x100cm 39x39in) Bruxelles 2001

CODINA Y LANGLIN Victoriano 1844-1911 [21]
$5 000 - €6 006 - **£3 500** - FF39 400
La Presentación Oleo/lienzo (46x38cm 18x14in) Madrid 2000

$261 - €305 - **£183** - FF2 000
Napolitain au bonnet rouge Aquarelle/papier (24x15cm 9x5in) Neuilly-sur-Seine 2000

CODOGNATO Franco 1911-? [2]
$1 453 - €1 506 - **£871** - FF9 880
«2ºGran Premio dell'Autodromo» Affiche couleur (139x99cm 54x38in) Torino 2000

CODOGNATO Plinio 1878-1940 [12]
$259 - €295 - **£180** - FF1 934
«Dionis, Gran Spumante» Poster (33.5x47.5cm 13x18in) Hoorn 2001

CODY William F. 1846-1917 [1]
$3 065 - €3 556 - **£2 116** - FF23 329
Buffalo Bill Photograph (20x25cm 8x10in) Beverly-Hills CA 2001

COE Sue 1951 [5]
$13 000 - €15 084 - **£8 975** - FF98 943
Let Them Eat Cake Oil/canvas (152.5x213.5cm 60x84in) New-York 2000

$6 000 - €6 787 - **£4 197** - FF44 523
Pool Hall Graphite (148.5x106.5cm 58x41in) New-York 2001

COECKE VAN AELST Pieter I 1502/07-1550 [22]
$81 555 - €76 278 - **£50 000** - FF500 350
The Holy Family Oil/panel (88x56.5cm 34x22in) London 1998

$19 951 - €22 661 - **£14 000** - FF148 645
Three Elders Disputing Oil/canvas (26x25cm 10x9in) London 2001

$310 000 - €269 500 - **£187 612** - FF1 767 806
The Sacrifice at Lystra (Acts 14:13-15) Ink (29.5x46.5cm 11x18in) New-York 1999

COELENBIER Jan 1600-1677 [21]
$12 978 - €13 081 - **£8 100** - FF85 806
Dorf an einem Fluss mit einem Angler und Bauern Oil/panel (41x55cm 16x21in) Wien 2000

COELLO Claudio c.1632-1693 [5]
$25 920 - €28 831 - **£17 280** - FF189 120
Retrato de D.Fernando Valenzuela Oleo/lienzo (75x60cm 29x23in) Madrid 2000

COEN Margaret Agnes 1913-1994 [22]
$422 - €399 - **£255** - FF2 614
Still Life, Native Flowers Watercolour/paper (57x53cm 22x20in) Sydney 1999

COEN Constantinus Fidelio 1780-1841 [32]
$18 000 - €19 831 - **£12 160** - FF130 080
Feest in het dorp (Fête dans le village) Huile/bois (44x64cm 17x25in) Antwerpen 2000

$3 952 - €4 356 - **£2 581** - FF28 575
Interieur met personen Oil/panel (29x37cm 11x14in) Rotterdam 2000

COENE de Jean Henri 1798-1866 [12]
$4 784 - €5 701 - **£3 427** - FF37 398
De verpozing Oil/panel (47x36cm 18x14in) Lokeren 2000

COENE Jean-Baptiste 1805-c.1850 [11]
$851 - €818 - **£531** - FF5 365
Vaches et moutons dans un paysage Huile/panneau (30.5x41cm 12x16in) Bruxelles 1999

COENRAAD Jacob Jan 1837-1923 [2]
$5 435 - €5 387 - **£3 400** - FF35 339
Skaters on a Frozen River Oil/panel (27x21cm 10x8in) London 1999

COENRAETS Ferdinand 1860-1939 [6]
$680 - €694 - **£425** - FF4 552
Promenade le long du canal Aquarelle/papier (20x27.5cm 7x10in) Bruxelles 2000

COESSIN DE LA FOSSE Charles Alexandre 1829-c.1910 [18]
$9 388 - €10 976 - **£6 595** - FF72 000
Bénédiction des combattants vendéens Huile/toile (132x210.5cm 51x82in) Paris 2000

$2 800 - €3 293 - **£2 014** - FF21 600
Circus performers Oil/canvas (40x33cm 16x13in) Hatfield PA 2001

COESTER Oskar 1886-1955 [10]
$5 395 - €6 135 - **£3 769** - FF40 246
Dasfahrrad Tempera (28x31cm 11x12in) München 2000

$1 606 - €1 687 - **£1 013** - FF11 067
Blühender Baum im Garten Mixed media/paper (40x30cm 15x11in) Stuttgart 2000

COESTER Otto 1902-1990 [14]
$104 - €123 - **£73** - FF804
Berglandschaft Radierung (11.1x18.8cm 4x7in) Düsseldorf 2000

COETZEE Christo 1929 [38]
🖌 $390 - €366 - £241 - FF2 403
Profiles Mixed media (63x49cm 24x19in)
Johannesburg 1999

COETZER Willem Hermanus 1900-1983 [161]
🖌 $10 659 - €9 994 - £6 586 - FF65 557
Nagmaal, Middelburg Oil/canvas/board (121x242cm 47x95in) Johannesburg 1999
🖌 $1 079 - €1 119 - £684 - FF7 342
Bandolies Koppies (near Pietersburg, Eastern Transvaal) Oil/canvas/board (39x59cm 15x23in) Johannesburg 2000
🖌 $736 - €636 - £444 - FF4 172
Drakensberg under Snow Oil/canvas (30x40cm 11x15in) Johannesburg 1998
🖌 $619 - €693 - £430 - FF4 548
Oribi Gorge, Natal Gouache/paper (39.5x49.5cm 15x19in) Johannesburg 2001

COEYLAS Henri c.1845-? [3]
🖌 $4 000 - €3 932 - £2 570 - FF25 791
Les heureuses mères Oil/canvas (63.5x48.5cm 25x19in) New-York 1999

COFFERMANS Marcellus 1520/30-c.1578 [15]
🖌 $32 900 - €36 336 - £22 800 - FF238 350
Maria mit dem Kind, der heiligen Katharina und Agnes Oil/panel (105x72cm 41x28in) Wien 2001

COFFEY Alfred J. 1869-1950 [55]
🖌 $414 - €488 - £291 - FF3 202
Kechimale Mosque, Colombo Oil/canvas/board (28.5x38cm 11x14in) Sydney 2000
🖌 $159 - €139 - £96 - FF914
Landscape Watercolour/paper (24x32.5cm 9x12in) Melbourne 1998

COFFIN Elizabeth Rebecca c.1851-1930 [3]
🖌 $4 500 - €3 851 - £2 709 - FF25 259
Arab Boy Oil/board (33x27cm 13x11in) New-York 1998

COFFIN William Anderson 1855-1925 [19]
🖌 $1 200 - €1 209 - £748 - FF7 932
Crescent Moon over the Lake Oil/canvas (36x50cm 14x20in) Delray-Beach FL 2000

COFFIN William Haskell 1878-1941 [22]
🖌 $3 250 - €3 378 - £2 048 - FF22 161
Portrait of a Lady Oil/canvas (71x55cm 28x22in) Bethesda MD 2000
🖌 $2 310 - €1 971 - £1 393 - FF12 926
Magazine cover: pretty woman in grey fur, pink background Pastel/paper (66x45cm 26x18in) New-York 1998

COFFRE Benoît Bénédict 1671-1722 [7]
🖌 $1 510 - €1 453 - £944 - FF9 534
Der Apostel Petrus Öl/Leinwand (82x63cm 32x24in) Wien 1999

COGELS Joseph 1786-1831 [17]
🖌 $1 032 - €1 227 - £715 - FF8 049
Ruine Schloss Wilhelmstein bei Aachen Watercolour (26.7x44cm 10x17in) Köln 2000

COGEN Félix 1838-1907 [6]
🖌 $5 776 - €6 509 - £4 000 - FF42 694
The returning Fishermen Oil/canvas (46.5x82.5cm 18x32in) London 2000

COGGHE Rémy 1854-1935 [22]
🖌 $7 866 - €8 690 - £5 454 - FF57 000
La douane Huile/toile (122x157cm 48x61in) Lille 2001

COGHLAN Edgardo 1928-1995 [4]
🖌 $2 395 - €2 237 - £1 478 - FF14 671
«Plan de Barrancas, Jal.» Acuarela/papel (50x39cm 19x15in) México 1999

COGHUF Ernst Stocker 1905-1976 [56]
🖌 $1 986 - €2 179 - £1 349 - FF14 292
Jura-Landschaft im Winter Öl/Leinwand (40x44cm 15x17in) Basel 2000
🖌 $281 - €328 - £194 - FF2 150
Printemps/Été/Automne/Hiver Ink/paper (22x14.5cm 8x5in) Bern 2000
🖌 $148 - €159 - £99 - FF1 044
Frau mit Oellampe Lithographie (28x44cm 11x17in) Zofingen 2000

COGIOLA Jean-Ange, G. Angelo 1768-1831 [1]
🖌 $17 646 - €17 782 - £11 000 - FF116 639
Venus standing, holding drapery and a nest of chicks in her left hand Marble (H146cm H57in) London 2000

COGNE François Victor 1876-1932 [4]
🖌 $3 148 - €3 049 - £1 980 - FF20 000
Clemenceau Bronze (68x41.5x24cm 26x16x9in) Paris 2000

COGNÉE Philippe 1957 [33]
🖌 $3 070 - €3 049 - £1 912 - FF20 000
Trois chevaux Huile/toile (160x131cm 62x51in) Paris 1999

COGNIET Léon 1794-1880 [18]
🖌 $655 - €732 - £419 - FF4 800
Femme pansant un homme blessé Crayon (16.5x22.5cm 6x8in) Paris 2000

COGORNO Santiago 1915 [4]
🖌 $1 700 - €1 975 - £1 194 - FF12 956
Figura de día Técnica mixta/papel (70x50cm 27x19in) Buenos-Aires 2001

COHELEACH Guy Joseph 1933 [12]
🖌 $12 000 - €10 253 - £7 203 - FF67 252
A Tiger Crouching in he Grass Oil/canvas (38x76cm 14x29in) New-York 1998
🖌 $4 500 - €4 091 - £2 710 - FF26 833
Tiger Watercolour/paper (33x23cm 13x9in) Hayden ID 1998

COHEN Arthur Morris 1928 [3]
🖌 $350 - €414 - £248 - FF2 716
Broklyn Bridge, Plate 8 Etching, aquatint (22x37.5cm 8x14in) Boston MA 2000

COHEN Carol 1939 [2]
🖌 $9 000 - €8 591 - £5 624 - FF56 353
Fish I Sculpture, glass (37x40.5x30.5cm 14x15x12in) New-York 1999

COHEN Ellen Gertrude 1846-? [1]
🖌 $1 985 - €2 305 - £1 400 - FF15 119
Moments of Inquietude Watercolour (39x28cm 15x11in) London 2001

COHEN Isaac Michael 1884-1951 [8]
🖌 $25 000 - €23 416 - £15 370 - FF153 602
Portrait of a Lady with a Dog Oil/canvas (204.5x148.5cm 80x58in) New-York 1999

COHEN Katherine M. 1859-1914 [3]
🖌 $700 - €665 - £430 - FF4 494
Bust Portrait of a Young Woman Bronze (H20.3cm H7in) Washington 1999

COHEN Minnie Agnes 1864-? **[5]**
🖐 **$58 273** - €54 693 - **£36 000** - FF358 761
  At the Capstan Bars Oil/canvas (113x176cm 44x69in) Billingshurst, West-Sussex 1999

COHEN-GAN Pinjas 1942 **[19]**
🖐 **$1 486** - €1 677 - **£1 045** - FF11 000
  «The Foundation of the State of Israel» Technique mixte (70x50cm 27x19in) Paris 2001
🖐 **$900** - €1 067 - **€655** - FF6 998
  Walking Man Collage (68.5x47cm 26x18in) Tel Aviv 2001

COHILL Charles c.1812-c.1860 **[1]**
🖐 **$5 750** - €4 824 - **£3 373** - FF31 645
  Portrait of Lieut. Col./Mrs William Massey Huddy Oil/canvas (67x54cm 26x21in) New-Orleans LA 1998

COHN Max Arthur 1903-1998 **[19]**
🖐 **$1 700** - €1 933 - **£1 178** - FF12 682
  Flemington Train Station Gouache/paper (34x54cm 13x21in) Chicago IL 2000

COIGNARD James 1925-1997 **[806]**
🖐 **$5 880** - €5 709 - **£3 630** - FF37 450
  Le bleu Oil/canvas (130x161cm 51x63in) Stockholm 1999
🖐 **$1 211** - €1 380 - **£845** - FF9 055
  «Abs» Mischtechnik (65x50cm 25x19in) Hamburg 2001
🖐 **$544** - €557 - **£336** - FF3 656
  Komposition Mixed media (40x31cm 15x12in) Stockholm 2000
🖐 **$733** - €686 - **£449** - FF4 500
  Mannequins Technique mixte/papier (33x15.5cm 12x6in) Paris 1998
🖐 **$306** - €313 - **£189** - FF2 056
  Komposition Etching in colors (57x44cm 22x17in) Stockholm 2000

COIGNARD Louis 1812-1883 **[28]**
🖐 **$2 668** - €2 287 - **£1 605** - FF15 000
  Personnage à la campagne le soir Huile/panneau (31.7x52cm 12x20in) Saint-Germain-en-Laye 1998

COIGNET Jules Louis Philippe 1798-1860 **[98]**
🖐 **$3 184** - €3 049 - **£1 962** - FF20 000
  Peintre en forêt Huile/toile (65x48cm 25x18in) Calais 1999
🖐 **$2 556** - €2 744 - **£1 710** - FF18 000
  Études d'arbres dans des paysages montagneux Huile/toile (35.5x27.5cm 13x10in) Paris 2000
🖐 **$373** - €368 - **£240** - FF2 415
  House by a Pond Watercolour (19x25cm 7x9in) London 1999

COIGNET Marie XIX-XX **[7]**
🖐 **$3 788** - €3 201 - **£2 253** - FF21 000
  Azalées Huile/toile (31x46cm 12x18in) Aubagne 1998

COINCHON Jacques Antoine Th. 1814-1881 **[13]**
🖐 **$1 473** - €1 753 - **£1 020** - FF11 500
  Le joueur de flûte Bronze (H64cm H25in) Sceaux 2000

COINDRE Gaston XIX **[7]**
🖐 **$687** - €762 - **£477** - FF5 000
  Le boulevard Haussmann Technique mixte/papier (31.5x23cm 12x9in) Besançon 2001

COINER Charles 1898-1989 **[4]**
🖐 **$800** - €744 - **£493** - FF4 879
  «Give It Your Best!» Poster (71x50cm 28x20in) New-York 1999

COIZET Louis 1816-1876 **[3]**
🖐 **$1 525** - €1 646 - **£1 054** - FF10 800
  Portrait d'homme/Portrait de femme Pastel/papier (107x76.5cm 42x30in) Lyon 2001

COKE Diana ?-1895 **[1]**
🖐 **$4 489** - €5 339 - **£3 200** - FF35 024
  Captain Edward Thomas Coke of the 45th Regiment Watercolour (44x31cm 17x12in) London 2000

COKE Edward Thomas 1807-1888 **[1]**
🖐 **$4 489** - €5 339 - **£3 200** - FF35 024
  Captain Edward Thomas Coke of the 45th Regiment Watercolour (44x31cm 17x12in) London 2000

COKE-SMYTH Frederick XIX **[3]**
🖐 **$4 812** - €4 849 - **£3 000** - FF31 810
  Sketches of british Costume from William I to William IV Watercolour (23.5x18cm 9x7in) London 2000

COKER Peter Godfrey 1926 **[25]**
🖐 **$7 030** - €6 069 - **£4 200** - FF39 810
  Agave Oil/canvas (152.5x132cm 60x51in) London 1998
🖐 **$1 186** - €1 281 - **£820** - FF8 404
  Reclining Male Pencil (26x36cm 10x14in) London 2001

COL Jan David 1822-1900 **[57]**
🖐 **$29 322** - €27 441 - **£18 162** - FF180 000
  Scène de genre Huile/toile (95x131cm 37x51in) Paris 1999
🖐 **$17 000** - €15 808 - **£10 494** - FF103 693
  Playing in the Barn Oil/canvas (53x79cm 21x31in) Portland ME 1999
🖐 **$2 794** - €2 727 - **£1 716** - FF17 886
  Le panier de volaille Huile/bois (26x20cm 10x7in) Antwerpen 2001

COLACICCHI Giovanni 1900-1993 **[31]**
🖐 **$4 000** - €4 147 - **£2 400** - FF27 200
  Nudo sull'erba Olio/tela (51x71cm 20x27in) Roma 1999
🖐 **$1 560** - €1 348 - **£1 040** - FF8 840
  Ritratto femminile con collana di corallo Olio/cartone/tela (30x40cm 11x15in) Firenze 1998

COLACICCO Salvatore 1935 **[98]**
🖐 **$1 942** - €1 828 - **£1 200** - FF11 993
  America's Cup Yacht Columbia racing in the Mediterranean Oil/panel (86.5x122cm 34x48in) London 1999

COLAO Domenico 1881-1943 **[7]**
🖐 **$3 500** - €3 628 - **£2 100** - FF23 800
  Natura morta Olio/tavola (50x64cm 19x25in) Roma 2001

COLATRELLA Marie-Odile 1967 **[4]**
🖐 **$451** - €503 - **£304** - FF3 300
  Petit trop d'entraînement Huile/toile (16x22cm 6x8in) Deauville 2000

COLAVINI Arturo Marion 1862-1938 **[5]**
🖐 **$4 025** - €4 173 - **£2 415** - FF27 370
  Gentildonna a cavallo Olio/tela (70.5x36.5cm 27x14in) Roma 1999
🖐 **$1 449** - €1 586 - **£1 000** - FF10 406
  Lady reclining in an opulent Interior Watercolour/paper (32x48cm 12x18in) London 2001

COLAY Mary XX **[7]**
🖐 **$1 200** - €1 053 - **£728** - FF6 904
  «Poppies» Poster (97x39cm 38x15in) New-York 1999

C

COLBURN Elanor 1866-1939 [9]
$7 000 - €6 410 - £4 266 - FF42 048
In Her Hogan Oil/canvas (101x81cm 40x32in)
Bloomfield-Hills MI 1999

COLBY George Ernest 1859-? [11]
$2 400 - €2 661 - £1 666 - FF17 453
Loisiana Swamp Scene Oil/canvas (45x30cm
18x12in) New-Orleans LA 2001

COLE Alfred Benjamin XIX [4]
$6 283 - €5 935 - £3 800 - FF38 928
In Arundel Park Oil/canvas (54.5x39cm 21x15in)
Billingshurst, West-Sussex 1999

COLE Alphaeus Philemon 1876-1988 [29]
$600 - €692 - £422 - FF4 541
Venetian Market Oil/canvas (30x40cm 12x16in)
Norwalk CT 2000

COLE George 1810-1883 [104]
$15 000 - €14 396 - £9 403 - FF94 432
The Watering Place Oil/canvas (90x135cm 35x53in)
New-York 1999
$5 776 - €6 295 - £4 000 - FF41 291
View of Arundel Park, Sussex Oil/canvas
(51x76cm 20x29in) London 2001
$1 068 - €1 241 - £750 - FF8 140
The Valley Farm, Surrey Oil/board (11.5x16cm
4x6in) London 2001

COLE George Vicat 1833-1893 [118]
$3 227 - €3 099 - £2 000 - FF20 329
In St.Bride's Bay, Pembrokenshire Oil/canvas
(114x182cm 44x71in) London 1999
$7 316 - €6 755 - £4 500 - FF44 308
The Mill Pond at Albury, Guildford Oil/canvas
(52x64cm 20x25in) London 1999
$1 346 - €1 305 - £840 - FF8 558
Sunset, Henley on Thames Oil/board (19x54cm
7x21in) Henley-on-Thames, Oxon 1999
$2 319 - €2 538 - £1 600 - FF16 650
Cader Idris, near Dolgellau, North Wales
Watercolour/paper (35.5x68.5cm 13x26in) London 2001
$809 - €792 - £500 - FF5 193
Pastoral Landscape with Haymakers Lithograph
(67x102cm 26x40in) Berwick-upon-Tweed 1999

COLE James act.1856-1885 [8]
$1 171 - €1 250 - £800 - FF8 202
«Winchelsea, Sussex» Oil/canvas (44x59.5cm
17x23in) Billingshurst, West-Sussex 2001
$3 244 - €3 593 - £2 200 - FF23 566
Play Time Oil/canvas (34x44cm 13x17in)
Billingshurst, West-Sussex 2001

COLE James William act.1849-1889 [19]
$4 350 - €4 146 - £2 757 - FF27 194
The Riding Lesson Oil/board (45x58cm 18x23in)
Cleveland OH 1999
$5 250 - €4 648 - £3 210 - FF30 488
**Friends, a Black and Tan and a Blenheim
Spaniel** Oil/canvas (31x37cm 12x14in) New-York
1999

COLE John Vicat 1903-1975 [22]
$1 270 - €1 364 - £850 - FF8 945
Apothecary's Shop at Rye Oil/board (30.5x40.5cm
12x15in) London 2000

COLE Joseph Foxcroft 1837-1892 [20]
$2 200 - €2 150 - £1 395 - FF14 104
Landscape with Cattle by a Stream Oil/canvas
(60x86cm 24x34in) Bolton MA 1999

$1 000 - €1 181 - £708 - FF7 750
Haycock Oil/canvas (30.5x46cm 12x18in) Boston MA
2000
$50 - €54 - £34 - FF351
Shepherd with Flock, thatched Cottage on Left
Etching (22x27cm 9x11in) Thomaston ME 2001

COLE Joseph Greenleaf 1806-1858 [5]
$400 - €367 - £245 - FF2 410
Portrait of a Minister Oil/canvas (91x73cm 36x29in)
Portsmouth NH 1999

COLE Philip Tennyson c.1860-1930 [5]
$9 960 - €11 572 - £7 000 - FF75 909
**Portrait of the sixth Marquess of Donegal and
his Mother** Oil/canvas (155x119.5cm 61x47in)
London 2001
$1 914 - €1 989 - £1 200 - FF13 046
**Young Blue-Eyed Girl in a Fur-Lined Coat and
Hood** Watercolour/paper (48x32.5cm 18x12in)
Loughton, Essex 2000

COLE Rex Vicat 1870-1940 [29]
$1 958 - €2 206 - £1 350 - FF14 470
Woodland Springtime Oil/panel (41.5x51.5cm
16x20in) London 2000
$1 314 - €1 249 - £800 - FF8 195
Southwark Cathedral Oil/board (37x24cm 14x9in)
London 1999

COLE Robert Ambrose 1959-1994 [3]
$5 432 - €5 831 - £3 635 - FF38 250
Untitled Mixed media (69.5x50cm 27x19in) Sydney
2000
$971 - €1 089 - £679 - FF7 143
Three Spirits Screenprint (56.5x76cm 22x29in)
Melbourne 2001

COLE Roderick M. XIX [3]
$500 - €7 970 - £5 252 - FF52 283
Portrait of Abraham Lincoln Salt print (18x13cm
7x5in) New-York 1999

COLE Thomas 1801-1848 [20]
$7 500 - €7 774 - £4 755 - FF50 995
**Tree by a Stream in the Afternoon (landscape
Sketch)** Oil/board (11.5x9cm 4x3in) New-York 2000

COLEBROOKE Robert Hyde 1762-1808 [8]
$5 634 - €6 617 - £4 400 - FF43 404
**View of Garden Reach and the Hooghly From
the Governor-General's House** Watercolour
(35x57cm 13x22in) London 2000

COLEMAN Arthur P. 1852-1939 [1]
$2 800 - €2 577 - £1 680 - FF16 904
Walking Between Malvern & Wooster Oil/canvas
(30x50cm 12x20in) Chicago IL 1999

COLEMAN Carlo 1807-1874 [4]
$39 000 - €33 691 - £26 000 - FF221 000
Vita contadina nella campagna Olio/tela
(62x112cm 24x44in) Roma 1998

COLEMAN Charles Caryl 1840-1928 [30]
$18 000 - €16 994 - £11 190 - FF111 475
Lime Kiln Capri Oil/canvas (106x226cm 42x89in)
Milford CT 1999
$150 000 - €164 122 - £99 645 - FF1 079 520
**Still Life with Plum Blossoms in an Oriental
Vase** Oil/canvas (150x29.5cm 59x11in) New-York
2000
$5 000 - €5 367 - £3 346 - FF35 205
Reading Under a Tree Oil/canvas (30x25cm
12x10in) Portland ME 2000

$1 200 - €1 418 - £850 - FF9 301
Untitled Pastel/paper (17x35cm 7x14in) Crossville TN 2000

COLEMAN Enrico 1846-1911 **[62]**
$13 000 - €13 476 - £7 800 - FF88 400
Lago di Albano Olio/tela (45x110cm 17x43in) Prato 2000

$7 200 - €6 220 - £4 800 - FF40 800
Cavalli e buttero nella Campagna Olio/tela (31x40cm 12x15in) Roma 1998

$2 078 - €2 060 - £1 300 - FF13 512
Cattle in a Landscape Watercolour/paper (27x53cm 10x20in) London 1999

COLEMAN Francesco 1851-1918 **[32]**
$1 817 - €2 147 - £1 288 - FF14 086
Römische Villa Oil/panel (12x18cm 4x7in) Ahlden 2000

$1 578 - €1 490 - £980 - FF9 775
Alms for the Poor/An old Man standing by a Ruins Watercolour (37.5x25.5cm 14x10in) Billingshurst, West-Sussex 1998

COLEMAN Glen O. 1897-1932 **[14]**
$3 250 - €3 450 - £2 199 - FF22 629
Sky View Oil/canvas (86x46cm 34x18in) Delray-Beach FL 2001

$1 900 - €1 780 - £1 168 - FF11 673
The Mirror Lithograph (38.5x31cm 15x12in) New-York 1999

COLEMAN Michael 1946 **[42]**
$56 100 - €52 392 - £34 624 - FF343 668
Last glow Blankfeet Encampment Oil/canvas (101x152cm 40x60in) Dallas TX 1999

$2 750 - €2 568 - £1 697 - FF16 846
Spring Trapper Oil/board (54x45cm 21x18in) Dallas TX 1999

$900 - €1 057 - £635 - FF6 931
Squaw Man Oil/board (26.5x20.5cm 10x8in) New-York 2000

$4 750 - €5 099 - £3 179 - FF33 447
A Winter Encampment Gouache/board (34x25.5cm 13x10in) San-Francisco CA 2000

COLEMAN Scott XX **[2]**
$1 000 - €932 - £604 - FF6 113
Showing Her Bottom Watercolour/paper (46x37cm 18x14in) New-Orleans LA 1999

COLEMAN Simon 1916-1999 **[19]**
$685 - €635 - £424 - FF4 164
In the Phoenix Park Oil/paper/board (60x50cm 24x20in) Dublin 1999

$454 - €508 - £308 - FF3 331
Feeding the Chickens Oil/canvas (15x20cm 5x7in) Dublin 2000

COLEMAN William Stephen 1829-1904 **[97]**
$12 000 - €14 103 - £8 319 - FF92 512
On the Terrace Oil/canvas (65.5x42cm 25x16in) New-York 2000

$465 - €513 - £309 - FF3 365
The Couple Oil/board (38x19.5cm 14x7in) Woollahra, Sydney 2000

$1 474 - €1 358 - £900 - FF8 910
Children at a Cottage Stile - Isle of Wight Watercolour, gouache/paper (17x24.5cm 6x9in) London 1998

COLEMAN William, Bill 1922-1992 **[163]**
$1 150 - €1 066 - £708 - FF7 257
The Washerwoman Oil/canvas/board (45x60.5cm 17x23in) Melbourne 1999

$390 - €456 - £271 - FF2 989
The Footbath Oil/board (29.5x19cm 11x7in) Melbourne 2000

$219 - €190 - £133 - FF1 248
Shopping Watercolour/paper (17.5x20cm 6x7in) Sydney 1998

COLERIDGE Francis George ?-1914 **[22]**
$613 - €632 - £380 - FF4 147
Windsor Castle Watercolour/paper (34x60cm 13x23in) London 2000

COLIN Alexandre Marie 1798-1873 **[27]**
$8 921 - €10 367 - £6 269 - FF68 000
Le retour de l'exilé Huile/toile (147.5x177.5cm 58x69in) Pau 2001

$43 988 - €42 686 - £27 384 - FF280 000
Telasco et la princesse Amazili/Jeune fille inca offerte en mariage Huile/toile (39x54.5cm 15x21in) Paris 1999

COLIN André XIX-XX **[6]**
$1 363 - €1 514 - £950 - FF9 929
Country Doctor's lecture/Hard Day's Work Watercolour (12.5x36cm 4x14in) London 2001

COLIN Charles François 1795-1858 **[2]**
$6 288 - €6 098 - £3 956 - FF40 000
Nature morte aux perdreau gris et vanneau sur un entablement de marbre Huile/toile (57.5x42.5cm 22x16in) Paris 1999

COLIN François 1798-1864 **[5]**
$900 - €1 009 - £611 - FF6 619
Pastoral Scenes Gouache/paper (27x34cm 11x13in) Cleveland OH 1999

COLIN Georges 1876-1917 **[27]**
$4 054 - €4 607 - £2 800 - FF30 222
Le rameur Bronze (H84cm H33in) London 2000

$943 - €1 125 - £672 - FF7 378
Ägyptische Seherin Bronze (H48cm H18in) Bonn 2000

COLIN Gérard Philippe XVIII **[1]**
$10 041 - €8 509 - £6 000 - FF55 813
The Town Gate of Malines, with Horsemen and Other Figures Oil/panel (50x64cm 19x25in) London 1998

COLIN Gustave 1828-1910/19 **[168]**
$2 017 - €1 906 - £1 220 - FF12 500
Élégante à la fleur rose Huile/toile (65x54cm 25x21in) Paris 1999

$2 100 - €2 102 - £1 295 - FF13 790
Puerto francés Oleo/lienzo (32x41cm 12x16in) Madrid 2000

COLIN Jean 1912-1982 **[48]**
$422 - €457 - £292 - FF3 000
«Supershell avec ICA, le plus puissant des carburants» Gouache/papier (119x158cm 46x62in) Paris 2001

$273 - €305 - £184 - FF2 000
«Cirage Kiwi, exclusivité PPZ pour tous» Affiche (115x155cm 45x61in) Orléans 2000

COLIN Jean 1881-1961 **[66]**
$444 - €496 - £310 - FF3 252
Portrait de garçonnet à cinq ans Huile/toile (70x50cm 27x19in) Bruxelles 2001

$189 - €183 - £119 - FF1 200
Portrait de garçonnet Huile/toile (35.5x29cm 13x11in) Paris 1999

COLIN Paul 1892-1985 [640]

$1 482 - €1 372 - **£918** - FF9 000
11e Jeux Universitaires de 1947 Huile/panneau
(101x69cm 39x27in) Paris 1999
$1 361 - €1 448 - **£900** - FF9 500
La Revue Nègre Crayons couleurs/papier (33x25cm
12x9in) Paris 2000
$800 - €769 - **£493** - FF5 046
«Silence» Poster (60x38cm 23x14in) New-York 1999

COLIN Paul Alfred 1838-1916 [10]

$1 614 - €1 789 - **£1 120** - FF11 738
Landschaft mit einem Jungen in der Wiese
Öl/Leinwand (40.5x54cm 15x21in) Köln 2001
$3 376 - €3 201 - **£2 053** - FF21 000
Scènes de parc Huile/panneau (31.5x40.5cm
12x15in) Paris 1999

COLIN Paul Émile 1867-1949 [111]

$2 420 - €2 439 - **£1 508** - FF16 000
Paysages de Tahiti Pastel/papier (70x100cm
27x39in) Reims 2000

COLIN-LIBOUR Uranie Alphonsine 1833-? [4]

$7 500 - €6 502 - **£4 583** - FF42 651
Second Helpings Oil/panel (37.5x46.5cm 14x18in)
New-York 1999

COLINET Claire Jeanne Robert ?-1940 [130]

$3 000 - €2 570 - **£1 803** - FF16 859
Egyptian Dancer Bronze (H42.5cm H16in) New-
York 1998

COLIZZI Mauro XX [5]

$273 - €283 - **£163** - FF1 856
«Piccolo Cesare» Affiche couleur (200x140cm
78x55in) Torino 2000

COLKETT Samuel David 1806-1863 [50]

$1 363 - €1 144 - **£800** - FF7 504
**Study From Nature, Queens College Grove,
Cambridge** Oil/canvas (58x43cm 23x17in) Aylsham,
Norfolk 1998
$2 166 - €2 441 - **£1 500** - FF16 010
River Scene at Thorpe near Norwich Oil/panel
(20x30.5cm 7x12in) Ipswich 2000

COLL Joseph Clement 1881-1921 [6]

$3 750 - €4 200 - **£2 605** - FF27 552
**Soaring Warrior Woman, Soldiers going into
Battle** Ink (36x25cm 14x10in) New-York 2001

COLLAERT Adriaen c.1560-1618 [43]

$400 - €464 - **£284** - FF3 043
**Landscapes with Religious Scenes, after Hans
Bol** Engraving (13x20cm 5x8in) Chicago IL 2000

COLLAERT Hans 1566-1628 [9]

$471 - €562 - **£336** - FF3 689
Die Taufe Christi, nach Hendrik Goltzius
Radierung (21.1x15.8cm 8x6in) Berlin 2000

COLLAMARINI René 1904-1983 [4]

$1 960 - €2 287 - **£1 377** - FF15 000
Tête de Mona Doll Pierre (31x21x21cm 12x8x8in)
Pontoise 2000

COLLARD Auguste Hippolyte XIX [8]

$3 879 - €4 573 - **£2 727** - FF30 000
**Album du chemin de fer du Bourbonnais, Moret
- Nevers - Vichy** Tirage albuminé (18.5x47cm 7x18in)
Paris 2000

COLLART Marie 1842-1911 [8]

$2 365 - €2 727 - **£1 650** - FF17 886
Vaches s'abreuvant à la rivière Huile/toile
(62x73cm 24x28in) Bruxelles 2001

COLLAS Louis Antoine 1775-1856 [9]

$18 000 - €16 777 - **£10 879** - FF110 050
Madame Furcy Verret Oil/canvas (66x53cm 26x21in)
New-Orleans LA 1999

COLLE Auguste Michel 1872-1949 [40]

$833 - €915 - **£536** - FF6 000
Coucher de soleil aux roches à Malzéville
Huile/toile (52x77cm 20x30in) Saint-Dié 2000

COLLET John c.1725-1780 [15]

$5 250 - €4 341 - **£3 081** - FF28 473
Landscape with Ruined Abbey Oil/canvas
(46x63cm 18x25in) New-York 1998

COLLETT William R. XIX [1]

$7 745 - €7 438 - **£4 800** - FF48 790
Views at Bahia, Brazil Watercolour (33x25cm
12x9in) London 1999

COLLETTE Aubrey 1920-1992 [1]

$13 448 - €14 436 - **£9 000** - FF94 694
Prime Ministers Ink (28.5x22cm 11x8in) London
2000

COLLIANDER Ina 1905-1985 [37]

$200 - €168 - **£117** - FF1 102
Stilleben Woodcut (36.5x42.5cm 14x16in) Helsinki
1998

COLLIER Alan Caswell 1911-1990 [82]

$1 703 - €1 637 - **£1 049** - FF10 735
All Silent here - BC Oil/board (40.5x91.5cm 15x36in)
Vancouver, BC. 1999
$647 - €756 - **£450** - FF4 956
«Autumn Hills» Oil/board (30.5x40.5cm 12x15in)
Toronto 2000
$518 - €604 - **£360** - FF3 965
«North Saskatchewan River #1» Watercolour/paper
(30.5x40.5cm 12x15in) Toronto 2000

COLLIER Evert / Edwaert c.1640-c.1706 [62]

$284 682 - €242 372 - **£170 000** - FF1 589 857
**Vanitas Still Life with a Candlestick, Musical
Instruments** Oil/canvas (98x129.5cm 38x50in)
London 1998
$58 006 - €56 967 - **£36 000** - FF373 676
**Vanitas Still Life of a Casket of Jewels, a Silver
Candlestick** Oil/canvas (88.5x125cm 34x49in)
London 1999
$20 428 - €23 520 - **£13 942** - FF154 279
**Vanitasstilleben mit einem Globus, einer Laute
und einem Buch** Öl/Leinwand (39.5x32cm 15x12in)
München 2000

COLLIER John 1850-1934 [32]

$8 454 - €7 806 - **£5 200** - FF51 201
**Portrait of Diana Atkinson, as The young Diana,
in a Landscape** Oil/canvas (142.5x112cm 56x44in)
London 1999
$3 316 - €2 871 - **£2 000** - FF18 832
**Mrs J.Marillier, quarter-length, in a White fur
Coat** Oil/canvas (61x51cm 24x20in) London 1998

COLLIER Thomas 1840-1891 [80]

$682 - €573 - **£400** - FF3 759
Surrey Common Watercolour/paper (59x89cm
23x35in) Billingshurst, West-Sussex 1998

COLLIER Thomas Frederick act.1848-1888 [16]

$1 488 - €1 585 - **£980** - FF10 398
Still Life of Pansies Watercolour (19.5x27.5cm
7x10in) Billingshurst, West-Sussex 2000

COLLIGNON Ennemond, Edmond 1822-1890 [2]
  $18 260 - €15 245 - **£10 710** - FF100 000
  Auguste Vinchon dans son atelier Huile/toile
  (35.5x27cm 13x10in) Tours 1998

COLLIGNON François c.1609-1657 [5]
  $215 - €204 - **£133** - FF1 341
  Ein Zwerg mit Trommel Radierung (10.6x10.8cm
  4x4in) Berlin 1999

COLLIGNON Georges 1923 [243]
  $3 757 - €4 214 - **£2 618** - FF27 642
  Peinture Huile/toile (97x130cm 38x51in) Bruxelles
  2001
  $1 456 - €1 611 - **£1 014** - FF10 569
  Lady Farenheit Technique mixte/panneau (90x45cm
  35x17in) Liège 2001
  $462 - €496 - **£310** - FF3 252
  Composition abstraite Technique mixte (18x26.5cm
  7x10in) Liège 2000
  $677 - €694 - **£428** - FF4 552
  Composition bleue Aquarelle/papier (25x31.5cm
  9x12in) Bruxelles 2000
  $233 - €235 - **£145** - FF1 544
  Composition Monotype (40x49cm 15x19in) Bruxelles
  2000

COLLIN Albéric 1886-1962 [64]
  $7 462 - €6 449 - **£4 498** - FF42 302
  Lynx couché Bronze (25x25x37cm 9x9x14in)
  Bruxelles 1998

COLLIN DE VERMONT Hyacinthe 1693-1761 [5]
  $35 000 - €39 203 - **£24 318** - FF257 152
  Allegory of the Four Seasons Oil/canvas
  (87.5x106.5cm 34x41in) New-York 2001

COLLIN Édouard XX [9]
  $400 - €351 - **£242** - FF2 301
  Liberté Poster (98x60cm 38x24in) New-York 1999

COLLIN Marcus 1882-1966 [167]
  $2 514 - €2 859 - **£1 744** - FF18 754
  Landskap Oil/canvas/panel (29x58cm 11x22in)
  Helsinki 2000
  $1 359 - €1 261 - **£816** - FF8 274
  Landskap från Karelen Oil/canvas (33x46cm
  12x18in) Helsinki 1999
  $711 - €774 - **£468** - FF5 074
  I tåget Pastel/paper (45x48cm 17x18in) Helsinki 2000

COLLIN Nicolas Pierre 1820-? [3]
  $1 910 - €1 850 - **£1 200** - FF12 135
  Young Girl knitting Oil/board (23.5x18cm 9x7in)
  London 1999

COLLIN Paul-Louis 1834-? [8]
  $7 475 - €6 397 - **£4 500** - FF41 962
  The Well Dancers Oil/canvas (96x71cm 37x27in)
  London 1998

COLLIN Raphaël 1850-1916 [17]
  $1 000 - €1 037 - **£634** - FF6 805
  Gentlemen in Long Coats and Wearing Wigs
  Oil/canvas (60x50cm 24x20in) Pittsburgh PA 2000

COLLINGS Albert Henry ?-1947 [15]
  $282 - €327 - **£200** - FF2 147
  Portrait of a Lady Holding a Parasole Watercolour
  (32.5x20.5cm 12x8in) London 2000

COLLINGWOOD William 1819-1903 [24]
  $799 - €820 - **£500** - FF5 381
  Figures on a Mountain Track, Burda Watercolour
  (31.5x44.5cm 12x17in) London 2000

COLLINGWOOD William Harding 1848-1922 [1]
  $4 009 - €3 966 - **£2 500** - FF26 018
  **Kensington High Street on Queen Victoria's
  Diamond Jubilee** Watercolour (17.5x22.5cm 6x8in)
  London 1999

COLLINGWOOD-SMITH William 1815-1887 [69]
  $453 - €529 - **£320** - FF3 470
  Beach at Weston Super Mare Watercolour/paper
  (23x30cm 9x11in) Channel-Islands 2000

COLLINI Paolo 1950 [3]
  $1 040 - €1 348 - **£780** - FF8 840
  «L'età riflessa» Olio/tela (30x50cm 11x19in) Milano
  2001

COLLINS Cecil 1908-1989 [53]
  $2 885 - €3 237 - **£2 000** - FF21 235
  Pastoral Oil/paper (25.5x37cm 10x14in) London 2000
  $3 318 - €3 723 - **£2 300** - FF24 420
  Visionary Landscape Ink (25x37.5cm 9x14in)
  London 2000
  $1 082 - €1 231 - **£750** - FF8 074
  Harlequin Etching (39x28.5cm 15x11in) London 2000

COLLINS Charles c.1818-1899 [3]
  $3 116 - €3 650 - **£2 200** - FF23 940
  **Summertome, Cattle resting on a Riverbank
  with a passing Hay Barge** Oil/canvas (50x76cm
  20x30in) Leicester 2001

COLLINS Charles c.1680-1744 [15]
  $22 684 - €21 815 - **£14 000** - FF143 099
  **Still Life of dead Game, a Mallard, an english
  Partridge, other Birds** Oil/canvas (97x112.5cm
  38x44in) London 1999

COLLINS Charles II 1851-1921 [43]
  $2 120 - €1 779 - **£1 250** - FF11 671
  **Village Scene with Cows and Calf with Three
  Figures and a Church** Oil/canvas (49x74cm
  19x29in) Bransford, Worcester 1998
  $449 - €534 - **£320** - FF3 502
  **Cattle in a Meadow, Wooded Landscape
  Beyond** Watercolour (18x28cm 7x11in) Bath 2000

COLLINS Hannah 1956 [2]
  $7 217 - €7 809 - **£5 000** - FF51 222
  Arrows III Gelatin silver print (200x250cm 78x98in)
  London 2001

COLLINS Henry 1782-1824 [2]
  $25 390 - €29 633 - **£18 000** - FF194 382
  The brig Concord in two positions off the coast
  Oil/canvas (58x90cm 22x35in) London 2001

COLLINS Hugh ?-1896 [19]
  $3 522 - €3 483 - **£2 200** - FF22 846
  The Toy Soldier Oil/canvas (91x76.5cm 35x30in)
  Glasgow 1999

COLLINS James 1939 [9]
  $800 - €829 - **£480** - FF5 440
  «Vatching Joyce» Photo couleurs (152x100.5cm
  59x39in) Prato 2001

COLLINS Patrick 1911-1994 [33]
  $91 920 - €101 580 - **£63 744** - FF666 320
  Liffey Quaysides Oil/board (107x129.5cm 42x50in)
  Dublin 2001
  $18 330 - €17 776 - **£11 536** - FF116 606
  Blue Landscape Oil/board (39.5x49.5cm 15x19in)
  Dublin 1999
  $20 112 - €19 046 - **£12 228** - FF124 935
  The Pink Cyclamen Oil/board (30x40cm 12x16in)
  Dublin 1999

$938 - €889 - **£570** - FF5 830
Man with Dog Mixed media/paper (16x25cm 6x10in)
Dublin 1999

COLLINS William 1788-1847 **[59]**
$6 158 - €6 637 - **£4 200** - FF43 539
Figures Conversing by a Fisherman's Hut
Oil/board (42x54.5cm 16x21in) London 2001
$2 400 - €2 291 - **£1 500** - FF15 030
Picking Flowers Oil/panel (23x19cm 9x7in) London 1999

COLLINS William Wiehe 1862-1951 **[40]**
$549 - €516 - **£340** - FF3 386
The Castello d'Ischia Watercolour/paper (18x33cm 7x12in) London 1999

COLLINSON James 1825-1881 **[19]**
$1 565 - €1 781 - **£1 100** - FF11 685
The Embroiderer Oil/canvas (35.5x30.5cm 13x12in) London 2001

COLLIS Peter 1929 **[67]**
$11 350 - €11 047 - **£6 973** - FF72 462
Ballinafunshoge Oil/canvas (121x147cm 48x58in) Dublin 1999
$4 558 - €4 317 - **£2 771** - FF28 318
Still Life with jug Oil/canvas (76x86cm 30x34in) Dublin 1999
$930 - €1 054 - **£650** - FF6 916
Two Figures in a dark Landscape Oil/board (13x16.5cm 5x6in) London 2001
$389 - €406 - **£246** - FF2 665
Country Road Pastel/paper (29x25.5cm 11x10in) Dublin 2000

COLLISHAW Mat 1966 **[10]**
$6 016 - €5 807 - **£3 800** - FF38 090
Infectious Flowers II - Zoster of Supravicular Dermatomes Sculpture (50x50x11cm 19x19x4in) London 1999
$7 324 - €7 129 - **£4 500** - FF46 762
John Luca & Paco Photograph in colors (61x55x9cm 24x21x3in) London 1999

COLLISTER Alfred James 1895-1939 **[20]**
$561 - €599 - **£380** - FF3 927
Peel Harbour, Isle of Man Watercolour/paper (22x30cm 9x12in) Lewes, Sussex 2001

COLLOMB Fernand 1902-1981 **[42]**
$392 - €457 - **£274** - FF3 000
La pause devant les huttes Huile/toile (50x65cm 19x25in) Paris 2000

COLLOMB Paul 1921 **[62]**
$498 - €579 - **£350** - FF3 800
Neige dans le Jura Huile/toile (65x54cm 25x21in) Paris 2001
$459 - €534 - **£322** - FF3 500
Neige sur le Crêt d'eau Huile/toile (27x35.5cm 10x13in) Paris 2001

COLLS Bernard XX **[6]**
$1 053 - €1 252 - **£750** - FF8 215
Diamond, a Jack Russell Terrier/Snuff, a Fox Terrier/Darkie, a Fox Watercolour (39.5x28cm 15x11in) London 2000

COLLS Ebenezer 1812-1897 **[19]**
$2 183 - €2 610 - **£1 500** - FF17 119
Men-O-War Off the Coast of Dover Oil/canvas (39x66cm 15x26in) Billingshurst, West-Sussex 2000
$2 125 - €2 520 - **£1 500** - FF16 527
Figures before a Harbour Scene at Low Tide/Shipping in a stiff Breeze Oil/canvas (30.5x50.5cm 12x19in) West-Midlands 2000

COLLVER Ethel Blanchard 1875-1955 **[3]**
$4 500 - €3 854 - **£2 656** - FF25 281
In Front of the Birdcage Oil/canvas (81.5x86cm 32x33in) New-York 1998

COLLYER Joseph 1748-1827 **[4]**
$1 369 - €1 437 - **£907** - FF9 429
Portrait de Luiza z Hohenzollernow Radziwillowa, d'après Bardou Gravure cuivre (28.5x21.5cm 11x8in) Warszawa 2000

COLLYER Margaret H. XIX-XX **[12]**
$5 132 - €5 077 - **£3 200** - FF33 303
Barn Yard Friends Oil/canvas (66x89cm 25x35in) London 1999
$12 000 - €13 069 - **£8 264** - FF85 730
Companions Oil/canvas (32x40.5cm 12x15in) New-York 2001

COLMAN Roi Clarkson 1884-1945 **[19]**
$700 - €756 - **£483** - FF4 958
«The Surge» Oil/canvas (56x76cm 22x29in) Bethesda MD 2001
$1 200 - €1 071 - **£734** - FF7 027
«The Amber Sea-Laguna, Calif» Oil/canvas (30x40cm 12x16in) Altadena CA 1999

COLMAN Samuel, Sam 1832-1920 **[53]**
$25 254 - €30 034 - **£18 000** - FF197 013
Tintern Abbey with Elegant Figures Oil/canvas (87x117cm 34x46in) London 2000
$3 800 - €3 599 - **£2 310** - FF23 606
Near Cordova, Spain Oil/canvas (23x38cm 9x14in) New-York 2000
$1 500 - €1 420 - **£931** - FF9 314
Western Scene, Three Covered Wagons, Horses and High Mountains Watercolour/paper (8x15cm 3x6in) Wallkill NY 1999

COLMEIRO GUIMARAS Manuel 1901-1999 **[61]**
$7 920 - €7 208 - **£4 800** - FF47 280
Paisaje con niños Oleo/tabla (38x46cm 14x18in) Madrid 1999
$1 122 - €1 321 - **£770** - FF8 668
Pescadoras Lápiz/papel (30x42cm 11x16in) Madrid 2000

COLMENAREZ Asdrúbal 1936 **[11]**
$1 200 - €1 212 - **£825** - FF7 950
Correspondencia IV Técnica mixta/lienzo (74.5x102cm 29x40in) Caracas 1999

COLMO Giovanni 1867-1947 **[73]**
$3 600 - €3 110 - **£1 800** - FF20 400
Pecetto di Macugnaga Olio/cartone (50x70cm 19x27in) Vercelli 1999
$1 020 - €881 - **£510** - FF5 780
Collina torinese Olio/cartone (27x38cm 10x14in) Torino 1999

COLMORE Nina 1889-1973 **[16]**
$844 - €812 - **£520** - FF5 324
Up-Rooter: Study of a Horse in a Landscape Oil/canvas (62x80cm 24x31in) Billingshurst, West-Sussex 1999
$844 - €812 - **£520** - FF5 324
Sheila & Jane: Head Studies of Horses Oil/canvas (30x40cm 11x15in) Billingshurst, West-Sussex 1999

CÖLN von David 1689-1763 **[2]**
$15 221 - €17 866 - **£10 741** - FF117 195
Fjälluggla Oil/canvas (81x64cm 31x25in) Stockholm 2000

COLNOT Arnout 1887-1983 **[93]**
- **$3 152** - €3 403 - **£2 155** - FF22 324
  A Winterlandscape with a House along a Waterway Oil/canvas (40x60cm 15x23in) Amsterdam 2001
- **$2 254** - €2 223 - **£1 388** - FF14 585
  Still Life with Fruit Oil/canvas (30x40.5cm 11x15in) Amsterdam 1999
- **$211** - €227 - **£141** - FF1 488
  Dorpsstraat Chalks (32x50cm 12x19in) Dordrecht 2001

COLNOT Karel 1921 **[18]**
- **$1 761** - €2 042 - **£1 247** - FF13 394
  Still Life with Porcelain Figures, a Teapot and Flowers on a Book Oil/canvas (107x100cm 42x39in) Amsterdam 2000

COLOM Y AUGUSTI Juan 1879-1969 **[20]**
- **$2 170** - €2 102 - **£1 330** - FF13 790
  Jardín con figuras Oleo/lienzo (50x61cm 19x24in) Barcelona 1999
- **$384** - €361 - **£240** - FF2 370
  Molinos de Mallorca Acuarela (33x42cm 12x16in) Madrid 1998

COLOMB Denise 1902 **[53]**
- **$584** - €579 - **£354** - FF3 800
  Portrait de Max Ernst sur les toits Tirage argentique (28x22cm 11x8in) Paris 2000

COLOMBEL Nicolas 1644-1717 **[3]**
- **$216 945** - €215 187 - **£135 000** - FF1 411 533
  Portrait of a Lady returning from the Hunt Oil/copper (65.5x81cm 25x31in) London 1999

COLOMBI Plinio 1873-1951 **[101]**
- **$712** - €685 - **£439** - FF4 492
  Winterlandschaft im Berner Oberland Öl/Leinwand/Karton (73.5x72.5cm 28x28in) Bern 1999
- **$251** - €287 - **£176** - FF1 883
  Die Jungfrau in der Wintersonne Watercolour (47x56cm 18x22in) Bern 2001
- **$1 300** - €1 417 - **£900** - FF9 292
  «Lotschberg» Poster (101x64cm 40x25in) New-York 2001

COLOMBO Ambrogio 1821-1890 **[4]**
- **$2 400** - €2 784 - **£1 707** - FF18 263
  Figural Group Bronze (H73cm H29in) Chicago IL 2000

COLOMBO Gianni 1937-1993 **[9]**
- **$15 433** - €18 354 - **£11 000** - FF120 397
  Spazio elastico, 16 quadrati Acrylic (120x120cm 47x47in) London 2000
- **$8 400** - €10 885 - **£6 300** - FF71 400
  Spazio elastico Acrilico/tavola (50.5x50.5x7cm 19x19x2in) Milano 2001
- **$28 848** - €33 905 - **£20 000** - FF222 400
  Strutturazione Pulsante Assemblage (120x120x22cm 47x47x8in) London 2000
- **$13 671** - €15 882 - **£9 607** - FF104 181
  «Supercie Pulsante» Sculpture, wood (27x24x7cm 10x9x2in) Amsterdam 2001

COLOMBO Giovanni Battista 1717-1793 **[12]**
- **$116 000** - €150 315 - **£87 000** - FF986 000
  Rovine archittoniche con figure Olio/tela (104x146cm 40x57in) Napoli 2000
- **$12 850** - €12 507 - **£7 896** - FF82 042
  Landschaft mit Mühle /raubenlese Öl/Leinwand (85.5x99.5cm 33x39in) Zürich 1999

COLOMBO Joe 1930-1971 **[2]**
- **$9 821** - €11 680 - **£7 000** - FF76 616
  Tube Chair Sculpture (61x50cm 24x19in) London 2000

COLOMBO Renzo 1856-1885 **[10]**
- **$4 200** - €4 480 - **£2 797** - FF29 384
  Boheme orientale (bust) Gilded bronze (H38cm H14in) New-York 2001

COLOMBO Virgilio XIX **[12]**
- **$728** - €807 - **£494** - FF5 293
  Interior Family Scene Watercolour/paper (18.5x26.5cm 7x10in) Toronto 2000

COLOMBOTTO ROSSO Enrico 1925-1998 **[85]**
- **$800** - €1 037 - **£600** - FF6 800
  Testina in verde Olio/tela (50x40cm 19x15in) Vercelli 2001
- **$600** - €622 - **£360** - FF4 080
  Bimbo Olio/tela (40x30cm 15x11in) Torino 2000
- **$160** - €207 - **£120** - FF1 360
  Figura Acquarello/carta (55x55cm 21x21in) Vercelli 2000

COLONELLI-SCIARRA Salvatore c.1700-c.1740 **[2]**
- **$51 000** - €44 058 - **£34 000** - FF289 000
  Il Campidoglio/Piazza del Quirinale Olio/tela (49.5x65cm 19x25in) Milano 1998

COLONIA Adam 1634-1685 **[13]**
- **$5 782** - €6 734 - **£4 000** - FF44 173
  Ladscape with Troopers and Soldiers Beneath a Rocky Arch Oil/canvas (66.5x57cm 26x22in) London 2000
- **$3 505** - €3 270 - **£2 115** - FF21 451
  Die Verkündigung an die Hirten Oil/panel (25.5x28cm 10x11in) Wien 2000

COLONIA Adam Louisz. 1574-c.1651 **[2]**
- **$5 880** - €5 004 - **£3 500** - FF32 826
  A Fire in a Village at Night Oil/panel (39x32cm 15x12in) London 1998

COLOT Robert 1927-1993 **[23]**
- **$414** - €496 - **£284** - FF3 252
  Visser (pêcheur) Huile/panneau (50x40cm 19x15in) Antwerpen 2000

COLOTTE Aristide 1885-1959 **[10]**
- **$4 674** - €3 964 - **£2 774** - FF26 000
  Vase à décor de festons et de zigzags Sculpture verre (H17cm H6in) Paris 1998

COLQUHOUN Alexander 1862-1941 **[6]**
- **$592** - €550 - **£365** - FF3 611
  Spring Cottage Oil/canvas/board (24.5x34.5cm 9x13in) Melbourne 1999

COLQUHOUN Ithell 1906-1988 **[42]**
- **$402** - €387 - **£265** - FF2 541
  Hibiscus Plant Watercolour (34.5x18cm 13x7in) London 1999

COLQUHOUN Robert 1914-1962 **[79]**
- **$21 193** - €23 630 - **£14 500** - FF155 000
  The Performer Oil/canvas (76x61cm 29x24in) Perthshire 2000
- **$6 922** - €7 649 - **£4 800** - FF50 174
  Pig Oil/canvas (30.5x40.5cm 12x15in) London 2001
- **$586** - €632 - **£400** - FF4 146
  Figure on Horseback Ballpoint pen (24.5x19.5cm 9x7in) London 2001

C

$606 - €523 - **£360** - FF3 428
Head of Absolum Lithograph (57.5x45cm 22x17in)
Glasgow 1998

COLSON Charles J.-Baptiste 1810-? **[2]**
$3 800 - €3 897 - **£2 375** - FF25 563
Portrait of a young Gentleman Oil/canvas
(91x73cm 36x29in) New-Orleans LA 2000

COLSON Jean-François Gilles 1733-1803 **[8]**
$38 000 - €42 084 - **£25 771** - FF276 051
La petite rêveuse Oil/canvas (61x50.5cm 24x19in)
New-York 2000
$7 000 - €7 257 - **£4 200** - FF47 600
Ritratto di fanciulla Olio/tavola (39.5x32.5cm
15x12in) Venezia 2000

COLSOULLE Gustaaf 1843-1895 **[13]**
$458 - €499 - **£315** - FF3 274
A Horse in a Stable Oil/canvas (42.5x52cm 16x20in)
Amsterdam 2001

COLTHURST Francis Edward 1874-? **[12]**
$3 979 - €3 690 - **£2 400** - FF24 203
The Bread Sellers Oil/canvas (39.5x56cm 15x22in)
London 1999

COLUCCI Gio 1892-1974 **[268]**
$1 070 - €915 - **£648** - FF6 000
Scène aux environs du Caire Huile/carton
(50x65cm 19x25in) Paris 1998
$276 - €305 - **£191** - FF2 000
Portrait Feutre (40.5x32cm 15x12in) Paris 2001

COLUCCI Vincenzo 1898-1968 **[30]**
$2 070 - €1 788 - **£1 380** - FF11 730
Parigi Olio/tela (60x50cm 23x19in) Milano 1998
$267 - €256 - **£162** - FF1 676
Mediterrane Landschaft Oil/panel (32x41.8cm
12x16in) Bielefeld 1999

COLUNGA Alejandro 1948 **[39]**
$15 000 - €14 595 - **£9 232** - FF95 734
Concierto 4.40 Oil/canvas (165x124.5cm 64x49in)
New-York 1999
$8 500 - €8 250 - **£5 292** - FF54 116
El Mago de la Lluvia Oil/canvas (101.5x80cm
39x31in) New-York 1999
$16 995 - €18 171 - **£11 583** - FF119 196
Los magos que esperan IV Bronze (198x88x215cm
77x34x84in) México 2001
$1 595 - €1 507 - **£995** - FF9 885
Sin título Litografía (90x67cm 35x26in) Monterrey NL
2001

COLVILLE Alexander 1920 **[44]**
$2 929 - €2 507 - **£1 763** - FF16 443
The Landrover Gouache/papier (22x27.5cm 8x10in)
Toronto 1999
$1 564 - €1 496 - **£980** - FF9 812
New Moon Silkscreen (38x45.5cm 14x17in)
Vancouver, BC. 1999

COLVILLE George Garden 1887-1970 **[25]**
$459 - €507 - **£311** - FF3 324
The Settlers Camp Oil/board (27.5x38.5cm 10x15in)
Woollahra, Sydney 2000

COLWELL Elizabeth 1881-? **[3]**
$1 155 - €1 151 - **£701** - FF7 551
Winter Birds Woodcut (8x12cm 3x5in) Pittsfield MA
2000

COLYN David 1582-c.1668 **[6]**
$35 553 - €33 756 - **£21 789** - FF221 427
Die Arche Noah Öl/Leinwand (108x160cm 42x62in)
Zürich 1999

$53 013 - €59 441 - **£36 000** - FF389 905
A Village Kermesse Oil/panel (74x138cm 29x54in)
London 2000

COMAN Charlotte Buell 1833-1924 **[8]**
$3 500 - €4 090 - **£2 498** - FF26 831
Chicken s in farm scene Oil/canvas (30x46cm
12x18in) Altadena CA 2001

COMBA Pierre 1860-1934 **[94]**
$419 - €473 - **£292** - FF3 100
Halte de Chasseurs Alpins devant Antibes
Aquarelle/papier (16.5x34cm 6x13in) Nice 2001
$501 - €428 - **£300** - FF2 809
«Aix les Bains» Poster (112x77cm 44x30in) London
1998

COMBAS Robert 1957 **[1330]**
$9 967 - €11 434 - **£6 817** - FF75 000
Ne pleure pas Acrylique/toile (162x130cm 63x51in)
Paris 2000
$3 978 - €3 432 - **£2 400** - FF22 514
Le Révolutionnaire Acrylic/board (80x39.5cm
31x15in) London 1998
$776 - €838 - **£536** - FF5 500
Femme Acrylique (16x11.5cm 6x4in) Paris 2001
$2 356 - €2 269 - **£1 473** - FF14 883
The Scarecrow Plaster (H82cm H32in) Amsterdam
1999
$1 327 - €1 220 - **£815** - FF8 000
Sculpture vase Céramique (H25cm H9in) Paris 1999
$561 - €640 - **£389** - FF4 200
Personnage au casque Feutre/papier (31.5x22cm
12x8in) Paris 2000
$275 - €290 - **£181** - FF1 900
May All Being Be Happy Sérigraphie couleurs
(56x76cm 22x29in) Paris 2000

COMBAZ Gisbert 1869-1941 **[30]**
$841 - €818 - **£521** - FF5 365
L'avocat Affiche (74.5x42.5cm 29x16in) Bruxelles
1999

COMBER Mélanie 1970 **[3]**
$4 980 - €5 865 - **£3 500** - FF38 469
Pylon Mixed media (175x150.5cm 68x59in) London
2000

COMBET-DESCOMBES Pierre 1885-1966 **[82]**
$759 - €732 - **£471** - FF4 800
Bouquet de fleurs Aquarelle/papier (38.5x29cm
15x11in) Lyon 1999
$381 - €412 - **£263** - FF2 700
Nus Monotype (30.5x24.5cm 12x9in) Lyon 2001

COMBETTE Joseph 1770-c.1840 **[5]**
$156 - €183 - **£192** - FF23 500
Portrait d'une femme en robe prune Huile/toile
(55x46cm 21x18in) Dijon 2001

COMENSOLI Mario 1922-1993 **[63]**
$13 062 - €12 577 - **£8 168** - FF82 498
Alternativ II Technique mixte/toile (170x170cm
66x66in) Zürich 1999
$1 479 - €1 608 - **£974** - FF10 551
**Bergige Landschaft mit Haus in der
Dämmerung** Öl/Karton (39x49cm 15x19in) Bern
1999
$1 277 - €1 251 - **£786** - FF8 203
I maggio, Diritto al lavoro Mischtechnik/Papier
(72.5x50.5cm 28x19in) Zürich 1999

COMERINER Erich XX **[5]**
$2 397 - €2 045 - **£1 446** - FF13 414
Beine Vintage gelatin silver print (24x18.3cm 9x7in)
Köln 1998

COMERRE Léon François 1850-1916 **[82]**
- $44 336 - €51 833 - **£31 144** - FF340 000
  Câlinerie Huile/toile (137x98cm 53x38in) Paris 2000
- $5 574 - €5 793 - **£3 511** - FF38 000
  Chauffeuse au volant de sa voiture sous la neige Huile/toile (70x75cm 27x29in) Paris 2000
- $2 412 - €2 820 - **£1 694** - FF18 500
  Dernier regard avant la nuit Huile/toile (46x34.5cm 18x13in) Paris 2000

COMERRE-PATON Jacqueline 1859-? **[7]**
- $5 301 - €4 940 - **£3 300** - FF32 406
  A young Beauty Oil/canvas (71x58.5cm 27x23in) London 1999

COMFORT Charles Fraser 1900-1994 **[36]**
- $5 462 - €5 286 - **£3 368** - FF34 671
  Midsummer Calm Oil/canvas (61x82cm 24x32in) Toronto 1999
- $1 704 - €1 610 - **£1 058** - FF10 559
  «Igneous Rock Formations, Georgian Bay» Oil/panel (30.5x41cm 12x16in) Nepean, Ont. 1999
- $356 - €416 - **£247** - FF2 726
  Sitting Nude Pencil/paper (48.5x31.5cm 19x12in) Toronto 2000
- $194 - €227 - **£135** - FF1 487
  Skiing Serigraph (8x9.5cm 3x3in) Toronto 2000

COMHAIRE Georges 1909-2000 **[113]**
- $511 - €595 - **£352** - FF3 902
  Nature morte à l'essuie Huile/toile (51x66cm 20x25in) Liège 2000
- $362 - €421 - **£249** - FF2 764
  Batardeau, la Meuse Huile/panneau (24x33cm 9x12in) Liège 2000
- $248 - €273 - **£160** - FF1 788
  Prairie et arbres Feutre/papier (52x73cm 20x28in) Liège 2000
- $90 - €99 - **£58** - FF650
  St Paul, Liège Eau-forte (46x32cm 18x12in) Liège 2000

COMINS Eben Farrington 1875-1949 **[4]**
- $750 - €733 - **£475** - FF4 887
  The Jade Necklace, Portrait of a Woman Oil/canvas (91x66cm 36x26in) Bolton MA 1999

COMIOTTO Hans 1906-1972 **[1]**
- $3 080 - €3 600 - **£2 199** - FF23 615
  Portrait von Augusto Giacometti Pastell/Papier (28x22cm 11x8in) Zürich 2001

COMMARMOND Pierre 1897-1983 **[92]**
- $400 - €362 - **£244** - FF2 376
  «Le Maelar» Poster (104x74cm 41x29in) New-York 1998

COMMERE Jean Yves 1920-1986 **[245]**
- $3 319 - €2 744 - **£1 947** - FF18 000
  Scène de port Huile/toile (88x116cm 34x45in) Paris 1998
- $646 - €762 - **£454** - FF5 000
  L'église derrière les branchages Huile/toile (22x27cm 8x10in) Fontainebleau 2000
- $297 - €305 - **£187** - FF2 000
  Sans titre Encre/papier (26x33cm 10x12in) Versailles 2000

COMMON Violet M. XIX-XX **[7]**
- $662 - €613 - **£400** - FF4 023
  Garden Path Watercolour/paper (28x36cm 11x14in) Little-Lane, Ilkley 1999

COMMUNAL Jean Joseph Ernest 1911 **[33]**
- $826 - €915 - **£560** - FF6 000
  Fleurs de printemps Huile/panneau (50x62cm 19x24in) Paris 2000

COMMUNAL Joseph Victor 1876-1962 **[68]**
- $2 041 - €1 982 - **£1 261** - FF13 000
  Matinée au lac du Bourget, mars Huile/panneau (44.5x63.5cm 17x25in) Grenoble 1999
- $542 - €610 - **£373** - FF4 000
  Chalet dans la Thauvière, Val d'Isère Huile/panneau (32x40cm 12x15in) Lons-Le-Saunier 2000

COMOLERA de Mélanie c.1800-c.1860 **[9]**
- $4 035 - €4 878 - **£2 819** - FF32 000
  Nature morte au vase de fleurs sur un entablement Huile/panneau (47x38cm 18x14in) Paris 2000

COMOLÉRA Paul 1818-c.1897 **[45]**
- $1 526 - €1 524 - **£954** - FF10 000
  Le faisan Bronze (H52.5cm H20in) Soissons 1999

COMOLLI Luigi, Gigi 1893-1976 **[30]**
- $1 432 - €1 495 - **£906** - FF9 805
  Lavandières Huile/panneau (65x55cm 25x21in) Genève 2000
- $750 - €777 - **£450** - FF5 100
  Paesaggio montano Olio/tavola (30x40cm 11x15in) Vercelli 2000

COMPAGNO Scipione 1624-c.1680 **[13]**
- $17 688 - €18 294 - **£11 136** - FF120 000
  Caprice architectural, l'embarquement de la Reine de Saba Huile/toile (72.5x91.5cm 28x36in) Paris 2000

COMPARD Émile 1900-1977 **[107]**
- $956 - €991 - **£606** - FF6 500
  Rue de village Huile/toile (50x61cm 19x24in) Paris 2000
- $200 - €236 - **£141** - FF1 550
  Bateau à quai Aquarelle/papier (21x24cm 8x9in) Brest 2000

COMPIGNÉ XVIII **[13]**
- $4 639 - €5 412 - **£3 226** - FF35 500
  Château fortifié au bord d'un fleuve animé de bateaux Gouache (10.5x14.5cm 4x5in) Nice 2000

COMPRIS Maurice 1885-1939 **[11]**
- $750 - €831 - **£503** - FF5 453
  Flower Piece Oil/canvas (60x50cm 24x20in) Dedham MA 2000

COMPTE-CALIX François Claudius 1813-1880 **[28]**
- $9 000 - €9 893 - **£5 767** - FF64 893
  Sunday in the Park Oil/canvas (61.5x46cm 24x18in) New-York 2000
- $1 800 - €2 134 - **£1 311** - FF13 997
  The old Friend Oil/panel (40x33cm 16x13in) Chicago IL 2001

COMPTON Charles 1828-1884 **[6]**
- $2 027 - €2 353 - **£1 400** - FF15 433
  A Young Boy with a recorder Oil/canvas (62x52cm 24x20in) London 2000

COMPTON Edward Harrison 1881-1960 **[383]**
- $2 228 - €2 556 - **£1 524** - FF16 769
  Sommertag am Watzmann Öl/Leinwand (139x87cm 54x34in) Heidelberg 2000
- $2 075 - €2 301 - **£1 440** - FF15 092
  Taubertal Öl/Leinwand (40.5x59.5cm 15x23in) Heidelberg 2001
- $470 - €435 - **£288** - FF2 856
  Hügelige Landschaft mit kleiner Hütte Öl/Leinwand (29x37.5cm 11x14in) Bern 1999

C

$1 019 - €883 - £618 - FF5 789
Wacholderdrossel vor Waldhintergrund
Watercolour (36x28cm 14x11in) München 1998

COMPTON Edward Theodor 1849-1921 [255]
$31 505 - €27 274 - **£19 000** - FF178 907
Saleinaz Glacier Oil/canvas (114.5x185.5cm 45x73in)
London 1998
$13 255 - €12 271 - **£8 114** - FF80 493
Belebter Fischereihafen vor Gebirgshintergrund
Öl/Leinwand (54.5x90.5cm 21x35in) Hamburg 1999
$3 209 - €3 579 - **£2 158** - FF23 477
Im Hochgebirge Öl/Leinwand (31x48.5cm 12x19in)
Köln 2000
$1 532 - €1 431 - **£926** - FF9 390
In der Ramsau, Bursch und Kuhhirtin auf dem Weg Aquarell/Papier (27x42.5cm 10x16in) Berlin 1999

COMTE Jacques Louis c.1781-? [8]
$1 584 - €1 800 - **£1 104** - FF11 808
Mére et ses trois enfants Technique mixte/papier
(31x24.7cm 12x9in) Budapest 2001

COMTE Meiffren 1630-c.1705 [21]
$28 233 - €27 567 - **£18 000** - FF180 828
Still Life of two Silver late Renaissance Ewers, silver Plate, a Book Oil/canvas (102x123.5cm 40x48in) London 1999
$24 655 - €23 375 - **£15 000** - FF153 333
Ornemental Silver Ewer, Silver-gilt Cup and Cover, Stone, gold Jug Oil/canvas (90.5x122cm 35x48in) London 1999

COMTE Pierre Charles 1823-1895 [14]
$1 670 - €1 982 - **£1 215** - FF13 000
Jeune fille lisant Huile/toile (38x46cm 14x18in) Lyon 2001
$1 514 - €1 448 - **£922** - FF9 500
Soldats de la Renaissance près d'un camp
Huile/panneau (35x26cm 13x10in) Troyes 1999

CONANT Lucy Scarborough 1867-1921 [6]
$350 - €384 - **£225** - FF2 518
Landscape scene with high Mts Watercolour/paper
(39x23cm 15x9in) Wallkill NY 2000

CONCA Giacomo 1787-1852 [2]
$4 000 - €5 183 - **£3 000** - FF34 000
Papa Gregorio XVI Altieri benedice e consacra Ludovico Altieri nella Basilica Olio/tela
(202x270cm 79x106in) Roma 2001

CONCA Sebastiano 1680-1764 [53]
$28 800 - €24 880 - **£19 200** - FF163 200
La Trinità con i Santi in Gloria Olio/tela (67x249cm 26x98in) Roma 1998
$14 224 - €12 054 - **£8 500** - FF79 069
Clio Acknowledged by Fame Oil/canvas
(74x108.5cm 29x42in) London 1998
$3 275 - €3 043 - **£2 000** - FF19 960
An Allegory of Fortitude Ink (21x16.5cm 8x6in)
London 1998

CONCONI Luigi 1852-1917 [35]
$25 000 - €25 916 - **£15 000** - FF170 000
Nudo femminile sul mare Olio/tela (78.5x129cm 30x50in) Milano 2000
$3 500 - €3 628 - **£2 100** - FF23 800
Volto di ragazzo Olio/tela/tavola (36x38cm 14x14in)
Milano 2000
$2 280 - €1 970 - **£1 520** - FF12 920
Le tre sorelle Acquarello/carta (17x14cm 6x5in) Prato 1998

CONCONI Mauro 1815-1860 [4]
$2 284 - €1 974 - **£1 142** - FF12 947
Ritratto maschile Olio/tela (65x51cm 25x20in)
Milano 1999

CONDAMY de Charles Fernand c.1855-? [190]
$6 500 - €7 731 - **£4 632** - FF50 709
Greys with Hounds in Stables Oil/board (49x37cm 19x14in) New-York 2000
$1 130 - €1 329 - **£810** - FF8 720
Ohne Titel Aquarell/Papier (43x87cm 16x34in)
München 2001

CONDÉ John ?-1794 [4]
$763 - €795 - **£480** - FF5 217
Mrs Fitzherbert, after Richard Cosway Engraving
(42.5x34cm 16x13in) London 2000

CONDE Miguel 1939 [21]
$560 - €601 - **£370** - FF3 940
Personaje Acuarela/papel (37.5x27cm 14x10in)
Madrid 2000
$76 - €90 - **£55** - FF591
Figuras Grabado (71x50cm 27x19in) Madrid 2001

CONDEIXA Ernesto Ferreira 1858-1933 [2]
$16 340 - €18 943 - **£11 400** - FF124 260
Milheiral Oleo/tabla (21x27.5cm 8x10in) Lisboa 2001

CONDER Charles Edward 1868-1909 [131]
$8 766 - €9 635 - **£5 617** - FF63 204
Portrait of a Lady Oil/canvas (92x71.5cm 36x28in)
Melbourne 2000
$8 005 - €8 593 - **£5 357** - FF56 366
«Après le bal» Oil/canvas (44x36cm 17x14in)
Melbourne 2000
$2 613 - €2 457 - **£1 618** - FF16 119
Ladies on a Terrace Watercolour (34.5x24cm 13x9in) Melbourne 1999
$473 - €441 - **£293** - FF2 895
The Dance Lithograph (30x45cm 11x17in) Sydney 1999

CONDER Josiah 1852-1920 [2]
$29 886 - €32 080 - **£20 000** - FF210 432
Jittoku Reisho Zu Ink (164.5x161cm 64x63in)
London 2000

CONDO George 1957 [166]
$20 000 - €19 220 - **£12 320** - FF126 078
Blue Study Oil/canvas (216x124cm 85x48in) New-York 1999
$5 044 - €6 098 - **£3 524** - FF40 000
«The Eye of the Brain» Huile/toile (116x89cm 45x35in) Paris 2000
$1 200 - €1 392 - **£828** - FF9 133
Untitled Oil/canvas (30.5x38cm 12x14in) New-York 2000
$2 000 - €2 321 - **£1 380** - FF15 222
Shot Sheriff (Secret Agent) Ink (40x30.5cm 15x12in) New-York 2000
$1 100 - €1 188 - **£760** - FF7 795
Landscape Etching (51x34cm 20x13in) New-York 2001

CONDOY Honorio Garcia 1900-1953 [20]
$5 601 - €5 972 - **£3 800** - FF39 174
Seated Female Figure Bronze (H48cm H18in)
London 2001

CONDY Nicholas 1793-1857 [44]
$5 768 - €6 374 - **£4 000** - FF41 812
Shepherds on a Hillside with their Flock
Oil/board (40x43.5cm 15x17in) London 2001

$6 164 - €5 920 - **£3 800** - FF38 831
View of the Exe, near Topsham, Devon Oil/copper
(15x21.5cm 5x8in) London 1999

$1 464 - €1 572 - **£980** - FF10 311
**The Russian Corvette, Prince of Warsawa, at
Plymouth; The Grand Duke** Watercolour (15x22cm
5x8in) London 2000

CONDY Nicholas Matthew, Jr 1816-1851 **[49]**

$32 372 - €34 073 - **£20 000** - FF199 890
**The Falcon running up the China Coast
towards Hong Kong with Ships** Oil/canvas
(53.5x76.5cm 21x30in) London 1999

$7 519 - €8 341 - **£5 000** - FF54 712
**Paddle Steamer in Plymouth Sound off
Mt.Edgcumbe/Paddle Steamer** Oil/board (18x23cm
7x9in) London 2000

$1 643 - €1 764 - **£1 100** - FF11 573
The Noon Gun Watercolour (10.5x8.5cm 4x3in)
London 2000

CONE Martin D. 1891-1965 **[9]**

$27 500 - €32 096 - **£19 412** - FF210 537
Still Life with Fruit and Flowers Oil/canvas
(40x45cm 16x18in) Cedar-Falls IA 2000

CONEJO Andrés 1913-1994 **[14]**

$1 120 - €1 201 - **£740** - FF7 880
**Retrato de la pintora Esperanza Ruiz Vázquez-
Villamil** Oleo/lienzo (81x61cm 31x24in) Madrid 2000

CONELY William Brewster 1830-1911 **[9]**

$300 - €343 - **£208** - FF2 251
**William Dana Off the Coast of Pointe du Chene
on St.Claire River** Oil/canvas (45x30cm 18x12in)
New-Orleans LA 2000

CONGDON Anne Ramsdell 1873-1958 **[14]**

$7 500 - €6 975 - **£4 644** - FF45 574
Nantucket Street Scene Oil/canvas (55x45cm
22x18in) East-Dennis MA 1999

$4 200 - €3 906 - **£2 600** - FF25 622
Street Scene in Nantucket Oil/board (22x17cm
9x7in) East-Dennis MA 1999

$5 800 - €5 394 - **£3 591** - FF35 383
Nantucket Dune Scene Watercolour/paper
(30x50cm 12x20in) East-Dennis MA 1999

CONGNET Michiel XVII **[4]**

$5 045 - €5 338 - **£3 200** - FF35 013
Dido and Aeneas Oil/panel (54x75cm 21x29in)
London 2000

CONINCK de David Romelaer c.1636-c.1705 **[34]**

$39 000 - €39 042 - **£24 050** - FF256 100
Bodegón de caza Oleo/lienzo (130x179cm 51x70in)
Madrid 2000

$8 202 - €9 471 - **£5 737** - FF62 126
**Bergslandskap med katt vaktande på duvor i en
korg** Oil/canvas (64x76cm 25x29in) Stockholm 2001

$15 862 - €15 988 - **£9 900** - FF104 874
**Erlegtes Federwild von einem Jagdhund
bewacht** Öl/Leinwand (47x34cm 18x13in) Wien 2000

CONINCK de Pierre Louis Joseph 1828-1910 **[12]**

$33 310 - €30 914 - **£20 000** - FF202 784
Girls at the Fountain Oil/canvas (153.5x105cm
60x41in) London 1999

$2 702 - €3 176 - **£1 873** - FF20 836
The Fortune Teller Oil/canvas (77.5x54cm 30x21in)
Amsterdam 2000

CONINXLOO van Gillis III 1544-1607 **[17]**

$10 950 - €12 706 - **£7 560** - FF83 344
**Wooded Landscape with a Biblical Scene of
kings Near a Cornfield** Oil/panel (59.5x122.5cm
23x48in) Amsterdam 2000

$140 000 - €149 513 - **£95 396** - FF980 742
**Woodcutters working beside a Forest path near
a River** Oil/copper (30.5x42cm 12x16in) New-York
2001

CONNARD Philip 1875-1958 **[92]**

$1 406 - €1 352 - **£866** - FF8 869
The Thames Oil/canvas (60x70cm 23x27in)
Melbourne 1999

$2 479 - €2 720 - **£1 600** - FF17 842
Richmond Park Oil/board (32.5x40.5cm 12x15in)
London 2000

$299 - €349 - **£210** - FF2 291
Whitstable Watercolour (20x28.5cm 7x11in)
Crewkerne, Somerset 2000

CONNAWAY Jay Hall 1893-1970 **[39]**

$3 100 - €3 348 - **£2 142** - FF21 960
«A Big Sea» Oil/canvas/board (40.5x51cm 15x20in)
Bethesda MD 2001

$850 - €760 - **£520** - FF4 983
«Fall in the Hollow» Oil/canvas (30x40cm 12x16in)
Boston MA 2000

CONNER Angela XX **[4]**

$9 685 - €9 479 - **£6 200** - FF62 177
Bust of Sir Alec Douglas-Home Bronze (H43cm
H16in) London 1999

$624 - €611 - **£400** - FF4 027
Portrait of General Charles de Gaulle Gouache
(28.5x40.5cm 11x15in) London 1999

CONNER Bruce 1933 **[10]**

$8 000 - €6 716 - **£4 692** - FF44 052
Untitled Drawing Ink/paper (51x51cm 20x20in)
Beverly-Hills CA 1998

CONNER Charles 1857-1905 **[2]**

$1 430 - €1 354 - **£888** - FF8 879
Farm at the edge of woods Oil/canvas (20x30cm
8x12in) North-Berwick ME 1999

CONNER John Anthony 1892-1971 **[32]**

$850 - €770 - **£523** - FF5 053
Desert near Indio, CA Oil/canvas (63x76cm
25x30in) Mystic CT 1999

$715 - €729 - **£448** - FF4 781
Eucalyptus Oil/canvas/board (30x22cm 12x9in)
Altadena CA 2000

CONNER John Ramsey 1869-1952 **[13]**

$1 900 - €2 138 - **£1 308** - FF14 027
The Cup of Water Oil/canvas (76x64cm 29x25in)
Philadelphia PA 2000

CONNER Paul 1881-1968 **[12]**

$1 200 - €1 104 - **£720** - FF7 244
California Landscape Oil/canvas (60x76cm 24x30in)
Pasadena CA 1999

CONNOLLY Howard XX **[2]**

$3 000 - €3 497 - **£2 077** - FF22 939
Woman Riding Horse in Autumnal Landscape
Oil/canvas (86x71cm 34x28in) New-York 2000

CONNOR Arthur Bentley XX **[2]**

$10 264 - €11 062 - **£7 000** - FF72 565
**Portrait of Arthur Strutt, Full-Length, in a White
Coat and Shorts** Oil/canvas (155x96.5cm 61x37in)
London 2001

C

CONNOR Kevin Leslie 1932 [57]
- **$16 010** - €17 186 - **£10 715** - FF112 733
  Woman on Balcony (Victoria Street) Oil/board (182.5x136cm 71x53in) Melbourne 2000
- **$1 822** - €2 033 - **£1 267** - FF13 336
  Pyrmont Roadway Oil/canvas (92x92cm 36x36in) Sydney 2001
- **$562** - €477 - **£339** - FF3 131
  Sydney Harbour Oil/board (29x39cm 11x15in) Sydney 1998

CONNOR Linda S. 1944 [9]
- **$550** - €491 - **£339** - FF3 218
  Seven Sacred Pools, Maui, Hawaii Silver print (23x18cm 9x7in) New-York 1999

CONOLLY Ellen XIX [2]
- **$18 000** - €16 684 - **£11 192** - FF109 441
  The Bookworm Oil/canvas (91.5x71cm 36x27in) New-York 1999

CONOLLY Thurloe XX [7]
- **$1 727** - €1 934 - **£1 200** - FF12 688
  Painting No.XLIII Oil/board (40.5x61cm 15x24in) London 2001

CONOR William 1884-1968 [126]
- **$33 334** - €35 553 - **£22 204** - FF233 212
  Rousing Chorus Oil/canvas (76x63cm 30x25in) Dublin 2000
- **$9 876** - €9 142 - **£6 117** - FF59 968
  The Bog Road Oil/canvas (39x31cm 15x12in) Dublin 1999
- **$9 785** - €10 735 - **£6 500** - FF70 419
  The Mill Girls Pastel/paper (38x27.5cm 14x10in) London 2000

CONRAD Charles 1912 [5]
- **$2 320** - €2 592 - **£1 572** - FF17 000
  Chat observant une tortue Bronze (13x20.5x13cm 5x8x5in) Pontoise 2000

CONRAD-KICKERT Conrad Jean Théodore 1882-1965 [45]
- **$426** - €457 - **£285** - FF3 000
  Cruche, bassine et livre Huile/toile (68x46cm 26x18in) Paris 2000
- **$666** - €619 - **£406** - FF4 059
  Chêne Liège Oil/canvas/panel (27.5x35cm 10x13in) Amsterdam 1998
- **$877** - €998 - **£608** - FF6 548
  Paysages de Bretagne Etching (17.5x23.5cm 6x9in) Haarlem 2000

CONRADE Alfred Charles 1863-1955 [34]
- **$777** - €901 - **£550** - FF5 911
  Figures before a Statue of Minerva in a Classical Temple Watercolour (46.5x57cm 18x22in) London 2001

CONROY Stephen 1964 [10]
- **$1 834** - €2 043 - **£1 200** - FF13 403
  Young Man with Glasses Mixed media/paper (63x46cm 24x18in) Edinburgh 2000
- **$644** - €779 - **£450** - FF5 110
  Man at Window Etching (29x14.5cm 11x5in) Edinburgh 2000

CONSADORI Silvio 1909-1994 [30]
- **$1 800** - €1 866 - **£1 080** - FF12 240
  Pittrice Olio/tela (60.5x45.5cm 23x17in) Milano 2000
- **$660** - €570 - **£330** - FF3 740
  Paesaggio Olio/tavola (18x27cm 7x10in) Prato 1999

CONSAGRA Pietro 1920 [106]
- **$22 400** - €29 026 - **£16 800** - FF190 400
  Colloquio mitico Bronzo (87x71x18cm 34x27x7in) Milano 2001
- **$2 800** - €3 628 - **£2 100** - FF23 800
  Trasparenti N.3 Bronzo (40x26x6.5cm 15x10x2in) Milano 2000
- **$165** - €171 - **£99** - FF1 122
  Nudo China/carta (30x19.5cm 11x7in) Prato 2000

CONSEMÜLLERS Erich 1902-1957 [5]
- **$3 000** - €2 505 - **£1 782** - FF16 429
  Abstraction Gelatin silver print (11x8cm 4x3in) New-York 1998

CONSETTI Antonio 1686-1766 [5]
- **$1 320** - €1 140 - **£660** - FF7 480
  Santo inginocchiato con angeli Matita (31x21.5cm 12x8in) Milano 1999

CONSORTI Paolo 1964 [1]
- **$2 880** - €3 732 - **£2 160** - FF24 480
  Idolo Tecnica mista/tela (100x100cm 39x39in) Milano 2001

CONSTABLE John 1776-1837 [180]
- **$311 600** - €290 690 - **£188 000** - FF1 906 800
  The Lambert Children Öl/Leinwand (61x51cm 24x20in) Wien 2000
- **$106 437** - €97 340 - **£65 000** - FF638 508
  Williamstown Strand/Study of Hollyhocks Oil/board (17x26.5cm 6x10in) London 1998
- **$25 083** - €24 500 - **£16 000** - FF160 708
  A Girl and a Dog in a Landscape Watercolour (32x19.5cm 12x7in) London 1999

CONSTABLE Lionel Bicknell 1828-1887 [15]
- **$6 416** - €6 466 - **£4 000** - FF42 414
  Landscape with a Distant Spire Oil/canvas (24.5x35cm 9x13in) London 2000

CONSTANS Charles Louis ?-c.1840 [1]
- **$36 596** - €42 686 - **£25 452** - FF280 000
  Bouquet de fleurs peint sur une plaque de porcelaine, d'après Van Daël Huile/toile (39.5x31.5cm 15x12in) Nice 2000

CONSTANT (C. Nieuwenhuys) 1920 [169]
- **$17 329** - €17 464 - **£10 803** - FF114 556
  Komposition Oil/canvas (60x70cm 23x27in) Köbenhavn 2000
- **$24 148** - €22 860 - **£15 000** - FF149 953
  Composition Oil/canvas (24x30cm 9x11in) London 1999
- **$16 027** - €19 059 - **£11 424** - FF125 017
  Eivormige constructie Sculpture (60x50x50cm 23x19x19in) Amsterdam 2000
- **$8 593** - €9 983 - **£6 039** - FF65 485
  Mother and Baby Monkey Watercolour/paper (50x34cm 19x13in) Amsterdam 2001
- **$507** - €544 - **£339** - FF3 571
  Het uitzicht van de duif Woodcut in colors (34x26.5cm 13x10in) Amsterdam 2000

CONSTANT Benjamin 1845-1902 [115]
- **$23 800** - €21 023 - **£14 700** - FF137 900
  Zoco árabe Oleo/lienzo (255x164cm 100x64in) Madrid 1999
- **$2 844** - €2 744 - **£1 785** - FF18 000
  Prisonniers Marocains Huile/toile (30x58cm 11x22in) Bourges 1999
- **$5 196** - €4 573 - **£3 165** - FF30 000
  Danseuse orientale Huile/toile (33x24cm 12x9in) Paris 1999

✐ **$4 253** – €3 887 – **£2 603** – FF25 500
Femmes au harem Fusain (36x58cm 14x22in)
Enghien 1999

CONSTANT Eugène XIX **[17]**
✐ **$4 551** – €5 229 – **£3 151** – FF34 300
Baptisteriet i Markuskirken i Venedig Oil/canvas
(104x88cm 40x34in) København 2000
📷 **$952** – €1 022 – **£637** – FF6 707
Forum Romanum Salt print (17.8x23.4cm 7x9in)
München 2000

CONSTANT George Z. 1892-1978 **[23]**
✐ **$650** – €737 – **£454** – FF4 834
Still Life with Flowers Watercolour/paper
(74x53.5cm 29x21in) New-York 2001

CONSTANT Joseph 1892-1969 **[70]**
🦅 **$1 600** – €1 698 – **£1 082** – FF11 140
Two Gazelles Bronze (H27cm H10in) Tel Aviv 2001
✐ **$280** – €273 – **£177** – FF1 792
Seated Boy Watercolour/paper (27.5x18cm 10x7in)
Tel Aviv 1999

CONSTANT-DUVAL 1877-? **[105]**
📜 **$177** – €179 – **£108** – FF1 503
«Paris-Orléans Railway, Villandry» Affiche
(100x65cm 39x25in) Chartres 2000

CONSTANTIN XX **[8]**
📜 **$240** – €243 – **£150** – FF1 591
«Skiing in France» Poster (61x41cm 24x16in)
London 2000

CONSTANTIN Auguste Fernand 1824-1895 **[22]**
☞ **$21 000** – €20 796 – **£13 074** – FF136 411
Rustic Still Life Oil/canvas (131x98.5cm 51x38in)
New-York 1999

CONSTANTIN D'AIX Jean Antoine 1756-1844 **[54]**
☞ **$4 875** – €4 573 – **£3 012** – FF30 000
Barque sur le fleuve Huile/toile (41x52cm 16x20in)
Nîmes 1999
☞ **$3 442** – €3 887 – **£2 399** – FF25 500
Ermite en prière dans une grotte Huile/panneau
(20.5x15.5cm 8x6in) Bayeux 2001
✐ **$1 267** – €1 372 – **£804** – FF9 000
Le château fort de la Barbin Aquarelle (25.5x33cm 10x12in) Paris 2000

CONSTANTIN Demetre XIX **[2]**
📷 **$2 534** – €2 211 – **£1 532** – FF14 500
Fouilles à Eleusis Tirage papier salé (27.2x37.4cm 10x14in) Paris 1998

CONSTANTIN Guy 1802-1892 **[11]**
✐ **$1 929** – €1 873 – **£1 191** – FF12 284
Zuaven und Mädchen beim Kartenspiel Encre
(20x25.5cm 7x10in) Zürich 1999

CONSTANTINE George Hamilton 1878-1967 **[119]**
☞ **$735** – €676 – **£454** – FF4 435
Plough, Horses and Farm in Derbyshire
Oil/board (25x35cm 10x14in) Manchester 1999
✐ **$1 264** – €1 224 – **£780** – FF8 027
Fisherfolk Emptying the Catch Watercolour/paper
(21.5x33cm 8x12in) West-Yorshire 1999

CONSTANTINEAU Fleurimond 1905-1981 **[92]**
☞ **$336** – €309 – **£201** – FF2 030
Les Sucres, Ste-Julienne, P.Q. Huile/toile
(50x81cm 19x31in) Montréal 1999
✐ **$193** – €167 – **£116** – FF1 094
Sugar Bush Oil/board (23x32.5cm 9x12in) Nepean, Ont. 1998

CONSTANTINI Giuseppe XIX-XX **[7]**
☞ **$13 627** – €15 128 – **£9 500** – FF99 231
Artisan's Family in an Interior Oil/panel
(24.5x42cm 9x16in) London 2001

CONTE Dante 1885-1919 **[6]**
☞ **$10 710** – €11 103 – **£6 426** – FF72 828
Porto Olio/cartone (36x51cm 14x20in) Milano 1999

CONTE del Jacopino 1510-1598 **[2]**
☞ **$17 226** – €16 769 – **£10 582** – FF110 000
La Sainte Famille Huile/panneau (129x101.5cm 50x39in) Paris 1999

CONTE Domenico 1813-1885 **[1]**
☞ **$6 622** – €7 006 – **£4 200** – FF45 955
Classical Landscape with Egeria Mourning over Numa Oil/canvas (52.5x66cm 20x25in) London 2000

CONTENCIN Charles Henry XX **[34]**
☞ **$827** – €732 – **£504** – FF4 800
Le lac d'Eychauda Huile/toile (60x81cm 23x31in)
Chambéry 1999

CONTESTABILE Niccolo 1759-1824 **[3]**
☞ **$7 750** – €8 034 – **£4 650** – FF52 700
Paesaggio fluviale con ponte e figure
Olio/carta/tela (50x63cm 19x24in) Prato 2000

CONTI Carlo 1740-1795 **[1]**
📜 **$2 310** – €2 761 – **£1 588** – FF18 114
Ansicht der Salzfahrt auf dem Gmundner-see in Oberösterreich Farbradierung (30x41cm 11x16in)
Salzburg 2000

CONTI Francesco XVII **[1]**
☞ **$16 075** – €18 168 – **£10 850** – FF119 175
Madonna mit Kind mit den Heiligen Josef und Franziskus Öl/Leinwand (185.5x157.5cm 73x62in)
Wien 2000

CONTI Primo 1900-1988 **[80]**
☞ **$18 400** – €23 843 – **£13 800** – FF156 400
Ritratto di giovane esploratore, Eros Chini
Olio/tela (150x120cm 59x47in) Prato 2001
☞ **$2 400** – €3 110 – **£1 800** – FF20 400
Natura morta Olio/tela (64x51cm 25x20in) Prato 2000
☞ **$1 000** – €1 296 – **£750** – FF8 500
Fiori Tempera (40x30cm 15x11in) Torino 2000
📜 **$140** – €145 – **£84** – FF952
Figure Acquaforte (32x24.5cm 12x9in) Prato 1999

CONTI Regina 1890-1960 **[11]**
☞ **$1 292** – €1 506 – **£894** – FF9 881
Tessiner Dorfkirche in der Nachmittagssonne
Öl/Leinwand (50.5x61cm 19x24in) Bern 2000

CONTI Tito 1842-1924 **[66]**
☞ **$13 000** – €12 352 – **£7 909** – FF81 027
The Flower Arranger Oil/canvas (72.5x57cm 28x22in) New-York 1999
☞ **$1 982** – €1 815 – **£1 208** – FF11 906
Friedrich Franz III, Grand Duke of Mecklenburg-Schwerin (1851-1897) Oil/panel (42.5x24cm 16x9in)
Amsterdam 1999
✐ **$1 533** – €1 505 – **£960** – FF9 887
Study of an Arab Watercolour (36x20.5cm 14x8in)
London 1999

CONTINI Massimiliano, Max 1850-? **[1]**
🦅 **$16 299** – €15 583 – **£10 000** – FF102 221
Boy wearing breeches and kneeling drinking from a bucket Bronze (28x100cm 11x42in)
Billingshurst, West-Sussex 1999

CONTINSOUZAS Dany XX **[12]**
$1 658 - €1 829 - £1 096 - FF12 000
Grand cerf au brame Bronze (25.5x21x7cm
10x8x2in) Paris 2000

CONTRERAS Y MUÑOZ José Marcelo 1827-
1890/92 **[6]**
$7 950 - €9 010 - £5 400 - FF59 100
El pintor y la modelo Oleo/lienzo (65x54cm
25x21in) Madrid 2000

CONTWAY Jay XX **[16]**
$1 297 - €1 499 - £908 - FF9 831
Wild horse Race Bronze (H36cm H14in) Calgary,
Alberta 2001

CONVERT Robert Alexandre 1889-1977 **[1]**
$1 000 - €962 - £617 - FF6 308
«Vier Jahreszeiten» Poster (109.5x75.5cm 43x29in)
New-York 1999

CONWAY Frederick E. 1900-1972 **[55]**
$450 - €525 - £321 - FF3 443
The Flamingo Acrylic/board (40x50cm 16x20in) St.
Louis MO 2000
$325 - €379 - £232 - FF2 486
Bass Rocks Watercolour/paper (36x56cm 14x22in)
St. Louis MO 2000

CONWAY J.A. XIX-XX **[2]**
$1 961 - €1 792 - £1 200 - FF11 758
Two Springer Spaniels Watercolour/paper (13x8cm
5x3in) Rotherham 1999

CONZ Gustav 1832-1914 **[8]**
$3 805 - €3 835 - £2 372 - FF25 154
Spaziergang am Nachmittag Öl/Leinwand
(71x64cm 27x25in) Düsseldorf 2000

CONZ Walter 1872-1947 **[64]**
$378 - €434 - £267 - FF2 850
Halbportrait einer jungen Frau Öl/Leinwand
(67x56cm 26x22in) Radolfzell 2001

COOK Beryl 1926 **[90]**
$9 961 - €11 729 - £7 000 - FF76 939
The Dykes' Party Oil/board (59.5x93cm 23x36in)
London 2000
$384 - €381 - £240 - FF2 501
The Joggers Color lithograph (43x36cm 16x14in)
London 1999

COOK Charles J. XIX-XX **[3]**
$800 - €864 - £553 - FF5 668
«Fluent» Photograph (20x15cm 8x6in) Cincinnati OH
2001

COOK Ebenezer Wake 1843-1926 **[100]**
$1 574 - €1 358 - £950 - FF8 911
Bathers in a Classical Roman Palace Garden
Watercolour (38x55cm 14x21in) London 1998

COOK George S. XIX **[5]**
$600 - €563 - £370 - FF3 690
Portrait of Munford Thomas Taylor in Uniform
Albumen print (11x7cm 4x3in) New-York 1999

COOK Gordon 1927-1985 **[17]**
$2 400 - €2 729 - £1 676 - FF17 904
Sculpture, Hat Form and Cap on Circus Stand
Watercolour (25.5x27cm 10x10in) Beverly-Hills CA
2000

COOK Herbert Moxon 1844-1928 **[63]**
$485 - €456 - £300 - FF2 988
Alpine Landscape in Winter Watercolour (34x53cm
13x20in) Leyburn, North Yorkshire 1999

COOK Howard Norton 1901-1980 **[106]**
$6 000 - €5 062 - £3 519 - FF33 204
Complex City Oil/canvas (81.5x111.5cm 32x43in)
New-York 1998
$3 200 - €3 029 - £1 990 - FF19 868
Harbor Skyline, preparatory study Indian ink
(30x40cm 11x15in) New-York 1999
$1 600 - €1 817 - £1 095 - FF11 917
Portrait of B/Studio Bed Print (18x28cm 7x11in)
New-York 2000

COOK John A. 1870-1936 **[21]**
$350 - €339 - £216 - FF2 225
Harbour Scene Watercolour/paper (18x23cm 7x9in)
Mystic CT 1999

COOK Juan 1948 **[35]**
$1 569 - €1 829 - £1 087 - FF12 000
Porteuse d'eau au chat Huile/toile (73x60cm
28x23in) Strasbourg 2000

COOK Nelson 1817-1892 **[1]**
$4 000 - €3 882 - £2 520 - FF25 464
Father and Child Oil/canvas (110x93cm 43x37in)
New-York 1999

COOK OF PLYMOUTH Samuel 1806-1859 **[17]**
$580 - €537 - £350 - FF3 525
**Vessels Off St Michaels Mount in Stormy
Waters** Watercolour/paper (34.5x48.5cm 13x19in)
Billingshurst, West-Sussex 1999

COOK OF PLYMOUTH William c.1830-c.1890 **[44]**
$520 - €473 - £318 - FF3 102
North Cornish Coast near Trebarwith
Watercolour/paper (30x51cm 12x20in) Norwalk CT
1998

COOK Otis Pierce 1900-1980 **[20]**
$2 500 - €2 625 - £1 690 - FF17 216
Gloucester Fog Oil/canvas (49x59cm 19x23in)
Fairfield ME 2001
$1 000 - €1 081 - £665 - FF7 093
Fishing Boats at a Dock Oil/board (28x39cm
11x15in) Plainville CT 2000

COOK Theodore XIX **[1]**
$4 835 - €5 641 - £3 455 - FF37 000
Paysage animé à la calèche Huile/toile (89x116cm
35x45in) Montastruc 2000

COOK William Delafield Jr 1936 **[16]**
$32 637 - €36 911 - £22 968 - FF242 118
Monument, Broken Hill Oil/canvas (89.5x305cm
35x120in) Malvern, Victoria 2001
$5 718 - €6 138 - £3 827 - FF40 262
The Kimono Charcoal/paper (133x105cm 52x41in)
Melbourne 2000

COOKE Arthur Claude 1867-? **[6]**
$7 500 - €7 413 - £4 590 - FF48 623
Country Cousins Oil/canvas (87x129cm 34x51in)
Detroit MI 2000

COOKE Barrie 1931 **[15]**
$5 176 - €6 095 - £3 637 - FF39 979
Woman Under Slieve Na Gluisadh Oil/canvas
(129.5x170.5cm 50x67in) Dublin 2000
$2 922 - €3 365 - £1 994 - FF22 071
After Rembrandt, Danae Oil/canvas (76x91cm
30x36in) Blackrock, Co.Dublin 2000
$3 127 - €3 682 - £2 197 - FF24 154
Coast of Mullaghmore I Oil/board (33x38cm
12x14in) Dublin 2000
$1 301 - €1 397 - £807 - FF9 161
Ginger Plants Watercolour/paper (26.5x24cm 10x9in)
Dublin 2000

COOKE Edward William 1811-1880 **[147]**

$172 494 - €172 118 - **£105 000** - FF1 129 023
On the Dutch Coast at Camperdown: a Squally Day, Tide out Oil/canvas (90x138cm 35x54in) London 2000

$30 000 - €30 231 - **£18 702** - FF198 300
Evening on the Cornice, Gulf of Genoa Oil/canvas (47x75cm 18x29in) New-York 2000

$10 439 - €11 096 - **£7 000** - FF72 782
Dutch Harbour Scene Oil/board (14.5x34.5cm 5x13in) Lymington 2001

$1 505 - €1 285 - **£900** - FF8 427
San Giorgio Maggiore, Venice Pencil/paper (17x19cm 6x7in) London 1998

COOKE Isaac 1846-1922 **[44]**

$455 - €420 - **£280** - FF2 757
A faggot Gatherer on a wooded Path Oil/panel (25x35.5cm 9x13in) London 1999

$641 - €647 - **£400** - FF4 241
Old Flats Moored near Winnington Looking down the River Weaver Watercolour/paper (32x51cm 12x20in) Newbury, Berkshire 2000

COOKE-COLLIS Sylvia 1899-1973 **[5]**

$1 703 - €1 592 - **£1 050** - FF10 446
Standing Stone near Baltimore Watercolour, gouache/paper (23x32cm 9x12in) Co. Kilkenny 1999

COOKESLEY Margaret Murray c.1850-1927 **[22]**

$955 - €929 - **£588** - FF6 097
Arabisk bygata med folkliv Oil/canvas (25x31cm 9x12in) Stockholm 1999

COOL de Gabriel 1854-? **[7]**

$13 000 - €12 352 - **£7 909** - FF81 027
In the Boudoir Pastel/canvas (183x104cm 72x40in) New-York 1999

COOL Jan Daemen 1589-1660 **[5]**

$14 234 - €12 118 - **£8 500** - FF79 492
Portrait of a Gentleman, half Length Oil/panel (67x51cm 26x20in) London 1998

COOLE Brian XIX-XX **[19]**

$1 500 - €1 688 - **£1 033** - FF11 074
British Sailboats Oil/canvas (49x74cm 19x29in) Chicago IL 2000

$1 980 - €1 968 - **£1 198** - FF12 912
Mt. Desert, Me. Oil/panel (27x43cm 11x17in) Hampden MA 2000

COOLIDGE Cassius Marcellus 1844-1934 **[15]**

$26 000 - €30 308 - **£18 002** - FF198 809
Dog Family Gathered Around the Piano Oil/board (58x42cm 23x16in) New-York 2000

COOMANS Auguste 1855-? **[19]**

$2 220 - €2 479 - **£1 550** - FF16 260
Jeune femme à l'écriture Huile/panneau (55.5x43.5cm 21x17in) Bruxelles 2001

$950 - €831 - **£575** - FF5 454
Interior Scene of Barn with Sheep, Chickens and Rooster Oil/panel (23x31cm 9x12in) Saugerties NY 1998

COOMANS Heva XIX-XX **[10]**

$30 000 - €31 819 - **£19 896** - FF208 719
Portrait of Young Woman with Mandolin Oil/canvas (78x101cm 31x40in) South-Deerfield MA 2000

$9 000 - €9 719 - **£6 219** - FF63 755
An Offering to the Goddess Oil/canvas (44x34.5cm 17x13in) New-York 2001

COOMANS Joseph 1816-1889 **[61]**

$159 600 - €135 831 - **£95 000** - FF890 995
The Last Hour of Pompeii, The House of the Poet Oil/canvas (101x158cm 39x62in) London 1998

$14 000 - €12 977 - **£8 705** - FF85 121
Interior scene with classical figures, children and dogs dancing Oil/board (58x84cm 23x33in) Asheville NC 1999

COOMBS Delbert Dana 1850-1938 **[24]**

$2 200 - €1 993 - **£1 346** - FF13 072
Yosemite Valley Oil/canvas (66x101cm 26x40in) Portland ME 1998

$1 100 - €1 012 - **£660** - FF6 641
River Landscape, Train on Tressel Oil/canvas (27x55cm 11x22in) Pasadena CA 1999

COOP Hubert 1872-1953 **[59]**

$3 617 - €3 906 - **£2 500** - FF25 624
Norfolk Landscape with Windmill and River Oil/canvas (63x76cm 25x30in) Bristol, Avon 2001

$1 466 - €1 334 - **£900** - FF8 748
River Estuary with moored Barge named St Ives Transport Watercolour/paper (44x74cm 17x29in) West-Midlands 1999

COOPER Abraham 1787-1868 **[49]**

$31 855 - €26 919 - **£19 000** - FF176 580
Master Fitzgibbon on his Pony, Lion Oil/canvas (100.5x126cm 39x49in) Bath 1998

$3 133 - €2 940 - **£1 936** - FF19 284
Kurier zu Pferde vor einem Burgherrn Öl/Leinwand (63x74cm 24x29in) Ahlden 1999

$6 424 - €6 236 - **£4 000** - FF40 903
A Gamekeeper with his Pony and Pointers Oil/panel (23.5x28.5cm 9x11in) London 1999

COOPER Alexander Davis c.1820-c.1890 **[11]**

$523 - €590 - **£362** - FF3 867
Making Friends Oil/canvas (51x61cm 20x24in) Toronto 2000

COOPER Alfred Egerton 1883-1974 **[67]**

$2 022 - €1 714 - **£1 200** - FF11 245
Hiding Oil/canvas (151x71.5cm 59x28in) Billingshurst, West-Sussex 1998

$505 - €429 - **£300** - FF2 811
A country Village Oil/canvas/board (29.5x44.5cm 11x17in) Billingshurst, West-Sussex 1998

$215 - €239 - **£150** - FF1 566
Tree-Lined rural Lane Watercolour/paper (34x42cm 13x16in) Bristol, Avon 2001

COOPER Alfred Heaton 1863-1929 **[87]**

$1 528 - €1 443 - **£950** - FF9 464
Autumnal Woodland Scene with Snow Capped Mountains in the background Watercolour/paper (58x41cm 23x16in) Scarborough, North-Yorshire 1999

COOPER Alice XIX **[1]**

$1 843 - €2 140 - **£1 300** - FF14 039
Late Watercolour/paper (34.5x25cm 13x9in) London 2001

COOPER Astley David M. 1856-1924 **[30]**

$13 500 - €16 061 - **£9 340** - FF105 352
Portrait of the Scandalous Hochie-Koochie Dancer Oil/canvas (256x303cm 101x119in) New-Orleans LA 2000

$1 600 - €1 785 - **£1 047** - FF11 709
Sunset in the Wood/Sunrise in the Wood Oil/canvas (127x60cm 50x24in) St. Louis MO 2000

$3 400 - €3 645 - **£2 249** - FF23 912
Red Cloud's Summer Camp Oil/board (21x53cm 8x21in) New-Orleans LA 2000

C

C

COOPER Austin 1890-1964 **[24]**
📺 **$717** - €686 - **£449** - FF4 497
«London's Leisure Hours, Tramways» Poster
(102x64cm 40x25in) London 1999

COOPER Colin Campbell 1856-1937 **[130]**
🎨 **$6 000** - €5 034 - **£3 536** - FF33 021
Hollyhocks Oil/canvas (40x60cm 16x24in) Greenwich
CT 1998
🖌 **$1 100** - €1 188 - **£760** - FF7 792
Mountain Shadows Oil/board (11x17cm 4x6in)
Altadena CA 2001
🖌 **$1 200** - €1 402 - **£856** - FF9 199
Fountain at Spanish villa Watercolour/paper
(36x27cm 14x11in) Altadena CA 2001

COOPER Edwin, of Beccles 1785-1833 **[50]**
🎨 **$7 471** - €8 020 - **£5 000** - FF52 608
A Side-Saddled Bay Hunter with a Groom in a
Landscape Oil/canvas (48.5x61cm 19x24in) London
2000
🖌 **$2 215** - €2 291 - **£1 400** - FF15 031
Studies of three spaniels Watercolour (20x27cm
7x10in) London 2000

COOPER Eileen 1953 **[9]**
🎨 **$4 559** - €3 933 - **£2 750** - FF25 801
«Leaving Home» Oil/canvas (122x91.5cm 48x36in)
London 1998

COOPER Emma Lambert 1860-1920 **[17]**
🎨 **$2 000** - €2 345 - **£1 438** - FF15 382
Market Scene Oil/canvas/board (38x45.5cm 14x17in)
New-York 2001
🎨 **$650** - €758 - **£452** - FF4 974
«In a Swiss Town» Oil/canvas/board (26x20cm
10x8in) Altadena CA 2000

COOPER Gerald 1898-1975 **[40]**
🎨 **$6 276** - €6 737 - **£4 200** - FF44 790
End of Summer Oil/canvas (76x63.5cm 29x25in)
London 2000

COOPER Henry M. act.1842-1872 **[54]**
🎨 **$544** - €658 - **£380** - FF4 315
Study of Sheep in a wooded Landscape with
Pond in foreground Oil/canvas (41x61.5cm 16x24in)
Cirencester, Gloucestershire 2000

COOPER Mary XX **[9]**
🖌 **$666** - €581 - **£403** - FF3 812
Noddy and Mrs Monkey Driving/Noddy and the
Girl Doll Watercolour (11x12.5cm 4x4in) London 1998

COOPER Michael XX **[1]**
📷 **$6 586** - €6 189 - **£4 000** - FF40 598
The Rolling Stones Photograph (28x28cm 11x11in)
London 1999

COOPER Richard T. XX **[1]**
📺 **$1 693** - €1 964 - **£1 200** - FF12 882
«The Boat Race Centenary, Saturday March
23rd, 1929» Poster (29x47cm 11x18in) London 2000

COOPER Thomas George 1836-1901 **[22]**
🎨 **$2 750** - €2 381 - **£1 658** - FF15 618
Cattle and Sheep on a River Bank with a Village
beyond Oil/canvas (51.5x76cm 20x29in) San-
Francisco CA 1998
🖌 **$1 895** - €2 155 - **£1 300** - FF14 134
The King of the Jungle Watercolour/paper
(80x58.5cm 31x23in) London 2000

COOPER Thomas Sydney 1803-1902 **[412]**
🎨 **$59 772** - €64 160 - **£40 000** - FF420 864
On a Dairy Farm Oil/canvas (122x183cm 48x72in)
London 2000

🎨 **$22 492** - €21 659 - **£14 000** - FF142 072
Canterbury Meadows Oil/panel (50x61cm 19x24in)
London 1999
🎨 **$4 692** - €5 057 - **£3 200** - FF33 172
Cattle watering Oil/paper/panel (23x28cm 9x11in)
London 2001
🖌 **$1 216** - €1 360 - **£820** - FF8 922
Cattle and Sheep on Hilltop Watercolour/paper
(20x33cm 8x13in) Leominster, Herefordshire 2000

COOPER W. Savage XIX-XX **[23]**
🎨 **$7 698** - €7 615 - **£4 800** - FF49 954
Man Smoking a Pipe Overlooking the Thames
with the Monument Oil/canvas (127x76.5cm
50x30in) London 1999
🎨 **$497** - €533 - **£340** - FF3 498
Still Life with Letter Stand Oil/board (21.5x30cm
8x11in) London 2001

COOPER William F. XX **[4]**
🖌 **$473** - €508 - **£316** - FF3 331
The Lough on the Bog Watercolour/paper (22x38cm
8x14in) Dublin 2001

COOPER William Heaton 1903-1995 **[76]**
🖌 **$1 710** - €1 688 - **£1 040** - FF11 074
Lakeland Landscape with Sunlight on the Fells
Watercolour/paper (36x55cm 14x21in) Kirkby-
Lonsdale, Cumbria 2000

COOPER William Sidney 1854-1927 **[138]**
🎨 **$13 820** - €12 759 - **£8 500** - FF83 694
Summer on the Thames Oil/canvas (102x152.5cm
40x60in) London 1999
🎨 **$3 733** - €4 185 - **£2 600** - FF27 449
Sheep in a Landscape, with a View of a Distant
Town Oil/canvas (51x92cm 20x36in) Leyburn, North
Yorkshire 2001
🎨 **$1 265** - €1 221 - **£800** - FF8 010
Cattle watering near a Lock Oil/canvas/board
(25.5x35.5cm 10x13in) London 1999
🖌 **$1 089** - €1 147 - **£720** - FF7 527
Cows and Chickens before a thatched barn
Watercolour/paper (24x34.5cm 9x13in) London 2000

COORNHERT Dirk Volkertsz. 1522-1590 **[5]**
📺 **$527** - €613 - **£370** - FF4 024
Patientiae Triumphus, nach Marten Heemskerck
Kupferstich (18x25.5cm 7x10in) Hamburg 2001

COORTE Adriaen XVII-XVIII **[6]**
🎨 **$48 000** - €54 504 - **£32 850** - FF357 525
Stilleben mit Waldbeeren und Blüten in einem
Tongefäss Öl/Leinwand (32.5x24cm 12x9in) Wien
2000

COOSEMANS Alexander 1627-1689 **[19]**
🎨 **$34 952** - €39 761 - **£24 412** - FF260 814
Stilleben med druvor, persikor och majs Oil/can-
vas (59x80cm 23x31in) Stockholm 2000

COOSEMANS Joseph Théodore 1828-1904 **[35]**
🎨 **$4 716** - €4 462 - **£2 934** - FF29 268
Soir en Campine Huile/toile (49x77cm 19x30in)
Bruxelles 1999
🎨 **$349** - €297 - **£210** - FF1 951
Paysage fluvial Huile/toile (28.5x33.5cm 11x13in)
Bruxelles 1998

COPE Charles West 1811-1890 **[42]**
🎨 **$5 050** - €6 007 - **£3 600** - FF39 402
Garden Party Oil/panel (62x76cm 24x29in) Bath
2000
🖌 **$258** - €260 - **£160** - FF1 705
Young Woman with a Parasol Pencil (13x16cm
5x6in) London 2000

COPE Elizabeth 1952 **[16]**
- **$1 213** - €1 397 - **£827** - FF9 161
  Still Life with Pears and Brushes Oil/board
  (37x47cm 14x18in) Dublin 2000

COPE George 1855-1929 **[21]**
- **$15 000** - €17 428 - **£10 542** - FF114 318
  Quail (Short Bill)/Snipe (Long Bill) Oil/canvas
  (57x38cm 22x14in) New-York 2001
- **$3 300** - €3 212 - **£2 027** - FF21 068
  Fisherman in River Oil/canvas (10x12cm 4x5in)
  Hatfield PA 1999

COPE Leslie 1913 **[15]**
- **$900** - €1 008 - **£625** - FF6 612
  Horses and a barn Oil/board (38x30cm 15x12in)
  Newark OH 2001

COPELAND Charles G. 1858-1945 **[11]**
- **$750** - €875 - **£526** - FF5 741
  Rocky Coast Gouache/board (45.5x71cm 17x27in)
  Boston MA 2000

COPER Hans 1920-1981 **[15]**
- **$8 882** - €8 353 - **£5 500** - FF54 792
  Stoneware spade form vase Ceramic (H16.5cm
  H6in) London 1999

COPIEUX Albert XIX-XX **[37]**
- **$158** - €152 - **£97** - FF1 000
  Paysage aux ormes Aquarelle/papier (34x50cm
  13x19in) Le Havre 1999

COPLANS John Rivers 1920 **[19]**
- **$3 500** - €4 030 - **£2 388** - FF26 435
  Self-Portrait (Clenched Fist) Gelatin silver print
  (92.5x116.5cm 36x45in) New-York 2000

COPLEY John Singleton 1738-1815 **[20]**
- **$260 000** - €309 206 - **£185 302** - FF2 028 260
  Mrs.Elizabeth Coffin Amory Oil/canvas (77x63.5cm
  30x25in) New-York 2000
- **$115 000** - €134 128 - **£80 948** - FF879 819
  Portrait of Mrs. Joseph Barrell Pastel/paper
  (56x43cm 22x17in) South-Deerfield MA 2001

COPLEY William Nelson 1919-1996 **[118]**
- **$9 880** - €11 760 - **£7 061** - FF77 139
  Ladida Oil/canvas (122x183cm 48x72in) Berlin 2000
- **$6 294** - €7 158 - **£4 365** - FF46 954
  Ohne Titel Acryl/Leinwand (61x92.5cm 24x36in)
  Hamburg 2000
- **$6 588** - €6 124 - **£4 000** - FF40 172
  Untitled Oil/canvas (27x35cm 10x13in) London 1998
- **$1 535** - €1 534 - **£960** - FF10 061
  Liegender weiblicher Akt Charcoal/paper
  (45.8x59.5cm 18x23in) Hamburg 1999

COPPEDGE Fern Isabell 1883-1951 **[55]**
- **$31 000** - €31 238 - **£19 325** - FF204 910
  **Summer Sea, Cove Scene with Shore Line,
  Houses and five Boats** Oil/canvas (63x76cm
  25x30in) Hatfield PA 2000
- **$8 000** - €9 255 - **£5 662** - FF60 710
  Winter Landscape with Stone House Oil/board
  (30x40cm 12x16in) Hatfield PA 2000

COPPENOLLE van XIX **[13]**
- **$2 046** - €1 951 - **£1 245** - FF12 800
  Vase de fleurs Huile/toile (65x54cm 25x21in) Paris
  1999

COPPENOLLE van Edmond 1846-1914 **[93]**
- **$4 000** - €4 715 - **£2 810** - FF30 926
  Still Life with Roses and Fluted Brass Vase
  Oil/canvas (53x64cm 21x25in) New-Orleans LA 2000

- **$1 805** - €1 753 - **£1 115** - FF11 500
  Jeté de roses et lilas Huile/toile (60x25cm 23x9in)
  Melun 1999

COPPENOLLE van Jacques 1878-1915 **[52]**
- **$1 224** - €1 372 - **£858** - FF9 000
  La basse cour Huile/panneau (55.5x37cm 21x14in)
  Paris 2001
- **$610** - €641 - **£404** - FF4 203
  Stilleben mit einem umgekippten Korb Oil/panel
  (15.5x22cm 6x8in) Zürich 2000

COPPENS Omer 1864-1926 **[57]**
- **$941** - €1 091 - **£651** - FF7 154
  Les ponts de Bruges Huile/toile (65x80.5cm
  25x31in) Bruxelles 2000
- **$650** - €726 - **£434** - FF4 762
  Bruges, Bridge Over a Canal Oil/panel
  (24.5x32.5cm 9x12in) Amsterdam 2000

COPPI DEL MELGLIO Jacopo 1523-1591 **[1]**
- **$26 000** - €26 302 - **£15 875** - FF172 533
  The Madonna and Child with Saint Anne
  Oil/panel (71.5x53.5cm 28x21in) New-York 2000

COPPIN John Stephens 1904-1986 **[18]**
- **$900** - €926 - **£570** - FF6 071
  Easter Greetings Oil/canvas (93x73cm 37x29in)
  Detroit MI 2000

COPPOLA Andrew 1941-1992 **[1]**
- **$9 000** - €10 236 - **£6 241** - FF67 141
  Black Odyssey Bronze (55x50cm 22x20in)
  Cincinnati OH 2000

COPPOLA Antonio 1839-? **[39]**
- **$4 500** - €4 212 - **£2 788** - FF27 630
  Scene near Naples Oil/canvas (50x63cm 20x25in)
  Detroit MI 1999
- **$1 360** - €1 762 - **£1 020** - FF11 560
  Pescatori sulla spiaggia Olio/cartone (23.5x31.5cm
  9x12in) Roma 2001
- **$1 080** - €933 - **£720** - FF6 120
  Eruzione del Vesuvio Gouache/carta (41.5x64cm
  16x25in) Napoli 1998

COPPOLA Carlo ?-c.1672 **[7]**
- **$18 000** - €15 789 - **£10 929** - FF103 568
  The Martyrdom of Saint Januarius Oil/canvas
  (117x157cm 46x61in) New-York 1999
- **$28 730** - €28 203 - **£17 815** - FF185 000
  Attaque d'une ville fortifiée Huile/toile
  (63.5x103cm 25x40in) Bordeaux 1999

COQUELIN Gabriel Eugène 1907-1996 **[57]**
- **$1 280** - €1 082 - **£761** - FF7 100
  Baigneuse Bronze (30x8x12cm 11x3x5in) Senlis
  1998

COQUES Gonzales 1618-1684 **[26]**
- **$44 829** - €48 120 - **£30 000** - FF315 648
  A Family Portrait Oil/panel (70x83cm 27x32in)
  London 2000
- **$6 276** - €6 737 - **£4 200** - FF44 190
  Self Portrait of the Artist Oil/panel (12.5x9.5cm
  4x3in) London 2000

COQUILLAY Jacques 1935 **[17]**
- **$1 574** - €1 829 - **£1 106** - FF12 000
  Fillette Bronze (41.5x11.5cm 16x4in) Paris 2001

CORA Sebastiano 1857-1930 **[3]**
- **$7 512** - €8 721 - **£5 280** - FF57 204
  **Blick über den Canal Grande auf die Kirche
  Santa Maria della Salute** Öl/Leinwand (50x73.5cm
  19x28in) Wien 2001

C

CORAZZO Alexander 1908-1971 **[9]**
$2 300 - €2 616 - £1 595 - FF17 158
Untitled Oil/masonite (60x50cm 24x20in) Chicago IL 2000
$1 000 - €955 - £615 - FF6 264
Abstract Gouache/paper (15x17cm 6x7in) Cincinnati OH 1999

CORBAUX Fanny Doetger 1812-1883 **[12]**
$729 - €818 - £508 - FF5 365
Jeune fille blonde lisant Aquarelle (38x32.5cm 14x12in) Bruxelles 2001

CORBAZ Aloise XX **[2]**
$9 017 - €10 477 - £6 337 - FF68 724
«Luxembourg, Noël» Coloured chalks (70x50cm 27x19in) Lausanne 2001

CORBELLI Edgardo 1918-1989 **[51]**
$1 250 - €1 296 - £750 - FF8 500
Giuliana seduta Olio/tavola (70x50cm 27x19in) Vercelli 2001
$900 - €777 - £450 - FF5 100
Paesaggio montano Olio/cartone (27x37cm 10x14in) Torino 1999
$80 - €104 - £60 - FF680
Studio per nudo seduto Inchiostro (23x33cm 9x12in) Vercelli 2000

CORBELLINI Luigi 1901-1968 **[180]**
$850 - €777 - £532 - FF5 097
L'église des Abesses, Montmartre Oil/canvas (45x60cm 18x24in) New-York 1999
$772 - €762 - £476 - FF5 100
Baigneuse dans un paysage Huile/toile (35x27cm 13x10in) Paris 1999

CORBELLINI Quintilio XIX **[1]**
$15 485 - €14 483 - £9 376 - FF95 000
Fillette se penchant Marbre (H97cm H38in) Senlis 1999

CORBERO OLIVELLA Xavier 1935 **[20]**
$560 - €571 - £351 - FF3 743
La cena Bronze (28x48cm 11x18in) Barcelona 2000

CORBET Edith Ellenborough c.1850-1920 **[6]**
$934 - €1 048 - £650 - FF6 877
Arabs resting in a shaded Interior Oil/panel (24.5x38cm 9x14in) London 2001

CORBETT Julian S. XIX **[1]**
$4 423 - €4 899 - £3 000 - FF32 136
Garden, Pwlty-Pant Oil/canvas (38.5x28cm 15x11in) Billingshurst, West-Sussex 2000

CORBIJN Anton 1955 **[6]**
$1 618 - €1 815 - £1 121 - FF11 906
«Stones Stripped» Photograph (45x45cm 17x17in) Amsterdam 2000

CORBINEAU Charles 1835-1901 **[6]**
$2 000 - €2 073 - £1 200 - FF13 600
Il ventaglio rosso Olio/tela (55x46.5cm 21x18in) Venezia 2000

CORBINO Jon 1905-1964 **[42]**
$1 000 - €1 144 - £695 - FF7 503
Dancers Oil/canvas/board (50x40cm 20x16in) Cincinnati OH 2000
$2 200 - €2 310 - £1 387 - FF15 153
The Polo Match Oil/canvas (33x40.5cm 12x15in) Washington 2000

CORBOULD Alfred ?-c.1875 **[6]**
$35 000 - €40 665 - £24 598 - FF266 742
Elford, the Favourite Hunter of Hugo F.Meynell Ingram Oil/canvas (107x157.5cm 42x62in) New-York 2000
$5 612 - €6 674 - £4 000 - FF43 780
The Artist's Children Oil/canvas (77x84cm 30x33in) London 2000

CORBOULD Aster R.C. XIX **[9]**
$2 764 - €2 967 - £1 850 - FF19 465
Pheasant Shooting Oil/board (15x20cm 5x7in) Bath 2000

CORBOULD Edward Henry 1815-1905 **[33]**
$28 998 - €24 357 - £17 000 - FF159 774
«Hai! Here comes the conquering Hero»/The Procession Oil/canvas (122x152.5cm 48x60in) London 1998
$21 656 - €21 823 - £13 500 - FF143 148
The Elopement Oil/canvas (112x86.5cm 44x34in) London 2000
$295 - €334 - £200 - FF2 194
Young Woman in elaborate Golden Armour Watercolour/paper (15.5x11cm 6x4in) London 2000

CORBOULD Richard 1757-1831 **[6]**
$813 - €920 - £550 - FF6 035
Hercules talking to two young Women/Seated Man in a Turban Watercolour/paper (10x7.5cm 3x2in) London 2000

CORCHON Y DIAQUE Federico 1853-? **[15]**
$4 240 - €4 040 - £2 500 - FF26 500
Visite au Prado Huile/panneau (23.5x33cm 9x12in) Paris 1999

CORCOS Lucille 1908-1973 **[8]**
$2 000 - €2 275 - £1 387 - FF14 920
Fire Island Tempera/board (20x25cm 8x10in) Chicago IL 2000

CORCOS Vittorio Matteo 1859-1933 **[92]**
$95 000 - €81 962 - £57 313 - FF537 633
An Afternoon on the Porch Oil/canvas (150x150cm 59x59in) New-York 1998
$9 993 - €9 274 - £6 000 - FF60 835
Portrait of a Lady Oil/canvas (85.5x74cm 33x29in) London 1999
$10 000 - €12 958 - £7 500 - FF85 000
Ritratto di Kitty Olio/tela (47x34cm 18x13in) Milano 2001
$750 - €777 - £450 - FF5 100
Ritratto di ragazza China/carta (14.5x19.5cm 5x7in) Milano 1999

CORCUERA Francisco 1944 **[19]**
$15 000 - €16 101 - £10 038 - FF105 615
Untitled Oil/canvas (219.5x189cm 86x74in) New-York 2000

CORDERO Francisco XIX-XX **[28]**
$1 982 - €1 952 - £1 235 - FF12 805
Paisaje con finca Oleo/lienzo (24.5x39.5cm 9x15in) Madrid 1999

CORDES Johann Wilhelm 1824-1869 **[7]**
$9 126 - €10 226 - £6 290 - FF67 078
Ostseestrand Öl/Leinwand (56x90cm 22x35in) Hamburg 2000

CORDEY Frédéric Samuel 1854-1911 **[38]**
$2 185 - €2 134 - £1 393 - FF14 000
Jeune femme lisant dans un paysage Huile/isorel (45x54cm 17x21in) Paris 1999

C

$879 - €854 - **£547** - FF5 600
Chemin près des arbres Huile/toile (33x41cm 12x16in) La Varenne-Saint-Hilaire 1999

CORDIER Charles Henri Joseph 1827-1905 **[65]**
$150 000 - €168 093 - **£104 550** - FF1 102 620
Jeune femme fellah en costume de harem Gilded bronze (H82.5cm H32in) New-York 2001
$24 000 - €22 480 - **£14 755** - FF147 458
Buste de juive d'Alger Bronze (H39.5cm H15in) New-York 1999

CORDIVIOLA Luis Adolfo 1892-1967 **[4]**
$4 800 - €5 323 - **£3 193** - FF34 918
Paisaje montañoso con cabras Oleo/cartón (60x80cm 23x31in) Buenos-Aires 2000

CORDREY John c.1765-1825 **[14]**
$8 775 - €8 389 - **£5 500** - FF55 027
A Curricle and Grooms on a Road in an extensive Landscape Oil/canvas (51x81.5cm 20x32in) London 1999
$7 000 - €8 133 - **£4 919** - FF53 348
The Brighton to London Royal Mail Oil/board (31.5x47.5cm 12x18in) New-York 2001

CORDSEN Paul XX **[1]**
$14 299 - €13 868 - **£9 000** - FF90 968
A Whippet,a Terrier and a Parrot/A Cockatoo and Hounds after J.B.Oudry Oil/canvas (71x91.5cm 27x36in) London 1999

CORELLI Augusto 1853-1910 **[32]**
$921 - €1 017 - **£638** - FF6 673
Neapel Gouache/paper (18x26cm 7x10in) Wien 2001

CORELLI Giuseppe 1858-1921 **[6]**
$3 249 - €3 161 - **£2 000** - FF20 737
Scenes of Naples Gouache/paper (16.5x23cm 6x9in) London 1999

CORELLI Rosa XIX **[9]**
$600 - €605 - **£374** - FF3 966
Seascape of Capri from the Shore Depicting Fishermen, Boats Watercolour, gouache/paper (33x42cm 13x16in) St. Petersburg FL 2000

CORENZIO Belisario 1558/60-1640/43 **[10]**
$1 500 - €1 555 - **£900** - FF10 200
Conversione di Saulo Inchiostro (25x21cm 9x8in) Milano 2001

COREY Bernard XX **[17]**
$425 - €422 - **£260** - FF2 767
Boy Fishing Oil/board (25x35cm 10x14in) Mystic CT 2000

CORINTH Lovis 1858-1925 **[1839]**
$149 112 - €139 041 - **£90 000** - FF912 051
Rider in Mecklenburg Oil/canvas (109x133cm 42x52in) London 1999
$61 351 - €69 887 - **£42 388** - FF458 430
Weiblicher Akt, Kniestück Öl/Leinwand (85x46cm 33x18in) Zürich 2000
$33 868 - €28 624 - **£20 266** - FF187 762
Anemonen Öl/Karton (20.5x23.5cm 8x9in) Berlin 1998
$2 191 - €1 891 - **£1 317** - FF12 403
Engel und Maler (Malerbuch) Indian ink/paper (31.5x25cm 12x9in) München 1998
$432 - €516 - **£308** - FF3 383
Aus gullivers Reise ins Land der Riesen Lithographie (22.5x17cm 8x6in) Hamburg 2000

CORIOLANO Bartolommeo 1599-1676 **[20]**
$718 - €838 - **£507** - FF5 500
Une sibylle, d'après Guido Reni Estampe (28x19.5cm 11x7in) Paris 2000

CORLEY Philip A. 1944 **[70]**
$750 - €756 - **£467** - FF4 957
Picnic by the Lake Oil/board (40x50cm 16x20in) Delray-Beach FL 2000
$650 - €765 - **£449** - FF5 021
Rue Madelaine Oil/canvas (30x40cm 12x16in) Delray-Beach FL 2000

CORM Daoud 1842-1930 **[1]**
$12 174 - €13 693 - **£8 500** - FF89 819
Melons Oil/canvas (58x71cm 22x27in) London 2001

CORMIER Joseph Em. Descomps 1869-1950 **[77]**
$1 150 - €1 239 - **£795** - FF8 130
Bachanale avec faune et muses Sculpture (H49cm H19in) Bruxelles 2001

CORMIERE Gaston XX **[40]**
$248 - €274 - **£172** - FF1 800
Scène de régates Aquarelle/papier (30x63cm 11x24in) Paris 2001

CORMON Fernand 1845-1924 **[81]**
$8 606 - €9 554 - **£6 000** - FF62 669
Moret-sur-Loing Oil/canvas (38x56cm 14x22in) London 2001
$2 388 - €2 668 - **£1 597** - FF17 500
Jeune femme orientaliste assise Huile/toile (45x35cm 17x13in) Paris 2000

CORNEILLE (C. van Beverloo) 1922 **[2039]**
$7 590 - €6 557 - **£5 043** 010
Senza titolo Serigrafia/tela (150x280cm 59x110in) Milano 1998
$8 740 - €8 622 - **£5 382** - FF56 555
La Belle Mina Acrylic/paper/canvas (64.5x50cm 25x19in) Amsterdam 1999
$2 346 - €2 592 - **£1 626** - FF17 000
Soleil bleu Technique mixte (46x33cm 18x12in) Paris 2001
$4 477 - €4 311 - **£2 799** - FF28 277
Sculpture sur bois I Sculpture, wood (117x111cm 46x43in) Amsterdam 1999
$1 526 - €1 815 - **£1 088** - FF11 906
Animal complice Sculpture, wood (H69cm H27in) Amsterdam 2000
$3 591 - €3 109 - **£2 179** - FF20 393
Les boxeuses Gouache (38x34cm 14x13in) Amsterdam 1998
$335 - €335 - **£209** - FF2 200
Femme et chat Lithographie couleurs (111.6x81cm 43x31in) Paris 1999

CORNEILLE DE LYON Claude 1510-c.1574 **[10]**
$159 280 - €181 004 - **£110 000** - FF1 187 307
Charles de la Rochefoucauld, bust-Length, in a Slashed Doublet Oil/panel (16x14cm 6x5in) London 2000

CORNEILLE Jean-Baptiste 1649-1695 **[4]**
$4 585 - €4 878 - **£3 040** - FF32 630
Apparition du Christ Réssuscité à Ste.Thérèse d'Avila & St.Jean Huile/toile (98x66.5cm 38x26in) Paris 2000

CORNEILLE Michel I 1602-1664 **[14]**
$120 000 - €131 657 - **£79 716** - FF863 616
The Marriage of the Virgin Oil/canvas (256.5x176.5cm 100x69in) New-York 2000

$14 762 - €16 769 - **£10 329** - FF110 000
Enée et les Troyens reçus par Didon Huile/toile
(52.5x65.5cm 20x25in) Paris 2001

$2 183 - €2 137 - **£1 400** - FF14 017
Diana and Endymion Ink (23.5x37.5cm 9x14in)
London 1999

CORNEILLE Michel II 1642-1708 [52]

$22 000 - €24 137 - **£14 614** - FF158 329
**The Meeting of Jacob and Rachel at Haran's
Well** Oil/canvas (132.5x203.5cm 52x80in) New-York
2000

$10 000 - €8 317 - **£5 870** - FF54 555
The Triumph of Galatea Oil/canvas (89.5x119.5cm
35x47in) New-York 1998

$1 043 - €1 037 - **£650** - FF6 802
The Death of Cleopatra Ink (14x24cm 5x9in)
London 1999

CORNELIUS (Cornelius Müller) XIX [6]

$2 521 - €2 723 - **£1 724** - FF17 859
A Coach by a Chalet/The Hayharvest Oil/panel
(10.5x20.5cm 4x8in) Amsterdam 2001

CORNELIUS Jean Georges 1880-1963 [34]

$1 633 - €1 753 - **£1 092** - FF11 500
L'envol Huile/toile (73x100cm 28x39in) Quimper 2000

CORNELL Joseph 1903-1972 [108]

$37 500 - €43 511 - **£25 890** - FF285 412
Mathematics in Nature (Circe and her Lovers)
Collage/board (33x42.5cm 12x16in) New-York 2000

$70 000 - €65 373 - **£43 204** - FF428 820
Cassiopeia #2 Construction (25.5x41x9.5cm
10x16x3in) New-York 1999

$22 000 - €20 710 - **£13 591** - FF135 847
«The Puzzle of the Reward 1670» Collage
(30.5x23cm 12x9in) New-York 1999

$1 700 - €1 638 - **£1 050** - FF10 742
Hôtel du Nord Screenprint (53x41cm 21x16in)
Chicago IL 1999

$42 000 - €48 354 - **£28 660** - FF317 184
Bébé Marie Gelatin silver print (24x21cm 9x8in) New-
York 2000

CORNER Thomas 1865-1938 [7]

$2 700 - €2 990 - **£1 831** - FF19 614
Still Life with Peaches and Grapes Oil/canvas
(27x43cm 11x17in) New-York 2000

CORNILLIET Jean Baptiste Alfred 1807-1895 [2]

$519 - €583 - **£360** - FF3 822
Mozart in Vienne, after Haman Engraving
(70x94cm 27x37in) London 2000

CORNISH Hubert 1757-1832 [15]

$4 225 - €4 963 - **£3 000** - FF32 553
**Palanquin Bearers and Holy Men Restig
Beneath a Banyan...,** Bengal Watercolour
(37.5x54cm 14x21in) London 2000

CORNISH Norman 1919 [12]

$7 274 - €8 624 - **£5 300** - FF56 573
Pit Road in the Wet Oil/canvas (58.5x94.5cm
23x37in) Newcastle-upon-Tyne 2001

$2 550 - €2 722 - **£1 700** - FF17 853
Pigeon Crees Ink (19x29cm 7x11in) Leyburn, North
Yorkshire 2000

CORNOYER Paul 1864-1923 [61]

$8 500 - €7 938 - **£5 246** - FF52 071
December, Gloucester Mixed media/canvas
(56.5x68.5cm 22x26in) Boston MA 1999

$5 500 - €6 415 - **£3 928** - FF42 081
Verdant Spring Landscape Oil/canvas (25x17cm
10x7in) St. Louis MO 2000

CORNU Jean-Jean 1819-1876 [12]

$3 480 - €3 756 - **£2 335** - FF24 637
**En hyrde ser ud over landskabet ved egnen
omkring Beauvais** Oil/canvas (42x60cm 16x23in)
Köbenhavn 2000

CORNU Pierre 1895-1996 [888]

$892 - €1 037 - **£627** - FF6 800
«D 300 Le modèle au canapé» Huile/toile
(46x51cm 18x20in) Paris 2001

$500 - €534 - **£317** - FF3 500
Le sommeil Huile/toile (27x46cm 10x18in) Paris 2000

$276 - €229 - **£162** - FF1 500
Femme allongée/Femme pensive Aquarelle/papier
(48x63cm 18x24in) Paris 1998

CORNU Vital 1851-1927 [7]

$1 025 - €1 143 - **£715** - FF7 500
Victoire triomphante Bronze (H74cm H29in)
Entzheim 2001

CORNWALL W.H. XIX [2]

$13 448 - €14 436 - **£9 000** - FF94 694
Waterloo Bridge with St.Paul's in the Distance
Oil/canvas (99.5x168cm 39x66in) London 2000

CORNWELL Dean 1892-1960 [67]

$10 000 - €11 657 - **£6 924** - FF76 465
Man Standing Outside of House At Night
Oil/canvas (74x54cm 29x21in) New-York 2000

$2 500 - €2 914 - **£1 731** - FF19 116
**John Smith and Crew preparing to Sail, Waving
Crowds** Mixed media (25x34cm 10x13in) New-York
2000

$2 530 - €2 158 - **£1 526** - FF14 157
**Preliminary for calendar: Lewis and Clark with
others on buff** Pencil (87x112cm 34x44in) New-York
1998

COROMALDI Umberto 1870-1948 [30]

$1 140 - €985 - **£760** - FF6 460
Gregge nella campagna romana Olio/tavola
(18x36cm 7x14in) Milano 1998

CORONA Vittorio 1901-1966 [3]

$4 800 - €6 220 - **£3 600** - FF40 800
«Dinamismo aria vento» Tempera/carta (50x70cm
19x27in) Milano 2000

CORONEL Pedro 1923-1985 [44]

$50 000 - €58 092 - **£35 140** - FF381 060
Los Tlacuilos II Oil/canvas (120x120cm 47x47in)
New-York 2001

$2 358 - €2 615 - **£1 568** - FF17 155
El León y el Buho Serigrafia (100x74cm 39x29in)
México 2000

CORONEL Rafael 1932 [104]

$35 000 - €37 569 - **£23 422** - FF246 435
Sueños antiguos V Oil/canvas (120x100cm 47x39in)
New-York 2000

$7 500 - €6 338 - **£4 473** - FF41 574
El vagabundo Oil/canvas (120.5x99.5cm 47x39in)
San-Francisco CA 1998

$2 985 - €3 514 - **£1 800** - FF16 950
Nuturaleza muerta Técnica mixta/papel
(48.5x31.5cm 19x12in) México 1998

$550 - €520 - **£342** - FF3 410
Man Silkscreen in colors (70.5x81cm 27x31in) San-
Francisco CA 1999

CORONELLI Vincenzo Maria XVII [6]

$700 - €813 - **£491** - FF5 332
**Part-gore showing Carpentaria and Van
Diemen's Land** Copper engraving (43x29.5cm
16x11in) Sydney 2000

C

COROT Camille Jean-Bapt. 1796-1875 **[731]**
- **$1 450 000** - €1 359 685 - **£895 955** - FF8 918 950
  La Solitude, souvenir de Vigen, Limousin
  Oil/canvas (95x130cm 37x51in) New-York 1999
- **$170 000** - €190 291 - **£118 558** - FF1 248 225
  Environs de Mantes, le gué sur la Seine Oil/canvas (38.5x45.5cm 15x17in) New-York 2001
- **$73 700** - €78 580 - **£50 000** - FF515 450
  Fontainebleau, route du Bas-Bréau Oil/paper/canvas (40.5x36cm 15x14in) London 2001
- **$8 000** - €6 828 - **£4 784** - FF44 792
  Jeune baigneuse couchée sur l'herbe
  Pencil/paper (20x28cm 7x11in) New-York 1998
- **$950** - €1 054 - **£632** - FF6 915
  Souvenir de Toscane Etching (13.5x18.5cm 5x7in)
  New-York 2000

CORPATAUX Jean-Pierre 1950 **[33]**
- **$730** - €851 - **£505** - FF5 585
  Auf der Pferderennbahn Mischtechnik/Papier (39x59cm 15x23in) Bern 2000

CORPET Armand-Etienne 1877-1954 **[2]**
- **$4 179** - €4 067 - **£2 572** - FF26 677
  Nature morte Oil/canvas (33x41cm 12x16in)
  Stockholm 1999

CORPORA Antonio 1909 **[346]**
- **$9 000** - €9 330 - **£5 400** - FF61 200
  Memoria della prateria Olio/tela (132x162cm 51x63in) Prato 2001
- **$3 500** - €3 628 - **£2 100** - FF23 800
  Composizione astratta Olio/carta/tela (84.5x59cm 33x23in) Vercelli 2001
- **$900** - €933 - **£540** - FF6 120
  Mediterraneo Olio/carta (40x30cm 15x11in) Vercelli 2001
- **$800** - €1 037 - **£600** - FF6 800
  «Il sogno e il mistero» Acquarello/carta (51x36cm 20x14in) Milano 2000
- **$179** - €204 - **£125** - FF1 341
  Verde Mare Farbserigraphie (60x48cm 23x18in)
  München 2000

CORPRON Carlotta M. 1901-1988 **[26]**
- **$1 400** - €1 175 - **£821** - FF7 705
  Chambered Nautilus Gelatin silver print (5.5x6.5cm 2x2in) New-York 1998

CORRADI Alfonso 1889-1972 **[25]**
- **$800** - €1 037 - **£600** - FF6 800
  Paesaggio con canale e barche Olio/tela (50x70cm 19x27in) Vercelli 2000
- **$800** - €829 - **£480** - FF5 440
  San Lorenzo a Milano Olio/tavoletta (22.5x30.5cm 8x12in) Milano 1999

CORRADI Konrad 1813-1878 **[17]**
- **$2 019** - €2 285 - **£1 412** - FF14 988
  Trogen Gouache/paper (32x46cm 12x18in) St. Gallen 2001

CORREDOYRA DE CASTRO Jesús Rodríguez 1889-1939 **[10]**
- **$5 225** - €5 706 - **£3 325** - FF37 430
  Retrato de Julián Blanco Oleo/lienzo (100x80cm 39x31in) Madrid 2000
- **$3 850** - €4 205 - **£2 450** - FF27 580
  El tonto del pueblo Oleo/lienzo (41x33cm 16x12in) Madrid 2000

CORREGGIO Antonio Allegri c.1489-1534 **[10]**
- **$157 080** - €135 698 - **£78 540** - FF890 120
  La Maddonna col Bambino e i santi Giovanni, Giuseppe e Antonio Olio/tela (160x120cm 62x47in) Venezia 1999

- **$15 601** - €17 074 - **£10 785** - FF112 000
  «Noli me tangere» Huile/toile (115x84cm 45x33in)
  Aubagne 2001
- **$5 332** - €5 374 - **£3 324** - FF35 248
  Maria Magdalene Oil/canvas (24x17cm 9x6in)
  København 2000

CORREGGIO Josef 1810-1891 **[24]**
- **$2 095** - €2 045 - **£1 326** - FF13 415
  Jagdstilleben Öl/Leinwand (120x71cm 47x27in)
  Bremen 1999
- **$1 972** - €2 301 - **£1 385** - FF15 092
  Früchtestilleben Öl/Leinwand (23x29cm 9x11in)
  Kempten 2000

CORREGGIO Josef Kaspar 1870-1962 **[8]**
- **$1 201** - €1 176 - **£739** - FF7 714
  Ländliche Idylle Öl/Leinwand (30x24cm 11x9in)
  Stuttgart 1999

CORREGGIO Ludwig 1846-1920 **[45]**
- **$635** - €716 - **£439** - FF4 695
  Küstenlandschaft Oil/canvas/panel (8.5x26cm 3x10in) München 2000

CORREIA Joaquim 1920 **[1]**
- **$22 800** - €19 879 - **£13 600** - FF130 400
  Sim titulo Sculpture (H68cm H26in) Lisboa 1998

CORRELL Richard V. XX **[2]**
- **$600** - €576 - **£369** - FF3 779
  Air Raid Wardens Woodcut (25x38.5cm 9x15in)
  New-York 1999

CORRENS Erich 1821-1877 **[6]**
- **$2 287** - €2 550 - **£1 565** - FF16 727
  Paysage alpin Huile/toile (68x86cm 26x33in)
  Warszawa 2000

CORRENS Jozef Cornelius 1814-1907 **[14]**
- **$2 688** - €2 975 - **£1 884** - FF19 512
  Scène d'intérieur Huile/panneau (70x91cm 27x35in)
  Bruxelles 2001

CORRODI Herman David Salomon 1844-1905 **[178]**
- **$66 250** - €61 971 - **£40 250** - FF406 500
  Gezicht op de tiber en de engelenburcht te Rome Oil/canvas (86.5x165cm 34x64in) Lokeren 1999
- **$17 284** - €18 151 - **£10 936** - FF119 064
  Arabs Camping, the Pyramids in the Distance
  Oil/canvas/panel (36.5x72cm 14x28in) Amsterdam 2000
- **$4 073** - €3 707 - **£2 500** - FF24 317
  Rome and the Tiber from the Roman Campagna
  Oil/canvas (26x42cm 10x16in) London 1999
- **$1 758** - €1 943 - **£1 219** - FF12 744
  Ansicht von Rom Aquarell/Papier (17.5x10cm 6x3in)
  München 2001

CORRODI Salomon 1810-1892 **[60]**
- **$2 962** - €2 813 - **£1 815** - FF18 452
  Blick auf Venedig Aquarell/Papier (24x35cm 9x13in)
  Zürich 1999

CORSELLIS Jane 1940 **[12]**
- **$4 869** - €4 682 - **£3 000** - FF30 715
  Laid up for the Winter, Port Washington Oil/canvas (81x63.5cm 31x25in) London 1999
- **$811** - €780 - **£500** - FF5 119
  Winter Sunshine, Trafalgar Square
  Watercolour/paper (42x25.5cm 16x10in) London 1999

CORSETTI Carlos XIX-XX **[3]**
- **$3 100** - €2 672 - **£1 841** - FF17 525
  Vista de Montevideo Oleo/cartón (21x62cm 8x24in)
  Montevideo 1998

CORSI Carlo 1879-1966 [12]

$1 050 - €1 088 - **£630** - FF7 140
Studio di capitello Carboncino/carta (83x12cm 32x4in) Firenze 2000

CORSI de Nicola 1886-1956 [89]

$3 350 - €3 473 - **£2 010** - FF22 780
Marina napoletana Olio/tela (70x90cm 27x35in) Milano 1999

$1 600 - €1 659 - **£960** - FF10 880
Paesaggio Olio/cartone (27x40cm 10x15in) Napoli 1999

CORSI DI BOGNASCO Giacinto 1829-1909 [22]

$1 320 - €1 140 - **£880** - FF7 480
Mareggiata sulla costa ligure Olio/tela (80x120cm 31x47in) Roma 1998

$600 - €518 - **£400** - FF3 400
Alberi nel paesaggio Olio/tavola (18.5x33cm 7x12in) Roma 1998

CORSI Santi XIX-XX [2]

$16 000 - €15 844 - **£9 961** - FF103 932
The Saturn Room, Palazzo Pitti, Florence Oil/canvas (104x129.5cm 40x50in) New-York 1999

CORT Cornelis 1533-1578 [53]

$377 - €363 - **£234** - FF2 381
Large castle with dome and a round and a square tower Engraving (14.5x20cm 5x7in) Haarlem 1999

CORT de Hendrik Frans 1742-1810 [16]

$22 458 - €22 631 - **£14 000** - FF148 450
Launceston Castle, Cornwall Oil/panel (86.5x118cm 34x46in) London 2000

$9 412 - €10 696 - **£6 500** - FF70 159
View of a Town with Figures by a Canal Oil/panel (28x35cm 11x13in) London 2000

CORTAZAR Roberto 1962 [9]

$10 000 - €10 734 - **£6 692** - FF70 410
Cuatro figuras en una habitación Mixed media/panel (99.5x90cm 39x35in) New-York 2000

$300 - €252 - **£177** - FF1 653
Sin Título Lápiz/papel (69x45cm 27x17in) México 1998

CORTAZZO Oreste 1836-? [27]

$9 500 - €9 770 - **£6 025** - FF64 085
The Artist and His Model Oil/panel (48x35cm 19x14in) Columbia SC 2000

$2 840 - €3 049 - **£1 900** - FF20 450
Scène de magie Huile/panneau (13x18cm 5x7in) Paris 2000

$2 250 - €2 332 - **£1 350** - FF15 300
Processione Tecnica mista/carta (85x145cm 33x57in) Trieste 2001

CORTBEMDE van Balthazar 1612-1663 [2]

$6 544 - €6 098 - **£4 036** - FF40 000
Nativité Huile/panneau (106x73cm 41x28in) Lille 1999

CORTE de la Gabriel 1648-1694 [10]

$42 400 - €48 052 - **£28 800** - FF315 200
Guirnalda de flores Oleo/lienzo (61x80cm 24x31in) Madrid 2000

CORTE de la Juan c.1597-c.1660 [10]

$34 200 - €29 545 - **£22 800** - FF193 800
Interno di cattedrale con l'incoronazione di Carlo V Olio/tela (116x156cm 45x61in) Roma 1998

CORTELLINI Y HERNANDEZ Angel María 1820-1882 [5]

$3 360 - €3 604 - **£2 280** - FF23 640
Retrato femenino Oleo/lienzo (58.5x49cm 23x19in) Madrid 2001

CORTES Antonio Cordero 1827-1908 [34]

$648 - €721 - **£444** - FF4 728
Cabras Oleo/lienzo (33x61.5cm 12x24in) Madrid 2001

$2 025 - €2 363 - **£1 422** - FF15 500
Berger et son troupeau Huile/panneau (32.5x24cm 12x9in) Pontoise 2000

CORTES Édouard 1882-1969 [836]

$26 000 - €29 934 - **£17 742** - FF196 352
Porte Saint Denis Oil/canvas (51x66cm 20x25in) New-York 2000

$22 458 - €22 631 - **£14 000** - FF148 450
La marché aux fleurs, Place de la République, Paris Oil/canvas (33.5x46cm 13x18in) London 2000

$12 458 - €13 264 - **£8 200** - FF87 007
The Saint Martin Gates, Paris, Evening Gouache/paper (26x43cm 10x16in) Billingshurst, West-Sussex 2000

$965 - €811 - **£567** - FF5 317
Paris Street Scene Lithograph (45x53cm 18x21in) Calgary, Alberta 1999

CORTES PEREZ Daniel 1873-1919 [3]

$3 332 - €3 811 - **£2 350** - FF25 000
Orientale aux bijoux Huile/toile (73x48.5cm 28x19in) Paris 2001

CORTES Y AGUILAR Andrés 1810-1879 [90]

$17 820 - €19 821 - **£11 880** - FF130 020
El descanso del pastor Oleo/lienzo (158x210cm 62x82in) Madrid 2000

$3 085 - €2 592 - **£1 813** - FF17 000
Troupeau de vaches et moutons sur le chemin Huile/toile (65x54cm 25x21in) Lille 1998

$1 343 - €1 410 - **£889** - FF9 247
Fischer mit Pferdefuhrwerk am Strand Oil/panel (21x41cm 8x16in) Zürich 2000

CORTESE Federico 1829-1913 [20]

$12 818 - €14 377 - **£8 932** - FF94 308
Vue de la campagne romaine Huile/toile (76x150cm 29x59in) Bruxelles 2001

$1 400 - €1 814 - **£1 050** - FF11 900
Nello stagno Olio/tela (32x39cm 12x15in) Prato 2001

CORTESE IL BORGOGNONE Guglielmo 1628-1679 [23]

$21 000 - €18 141 - **£14 000** - FF119 000
Scena dall'Eneide Olio/tela (69x77cm 27x30in) Milano 1998

$16 000 - €17 087 - **£10 902** - FF112 084
Portrait of a Gentlemen, small bust-length, wearing a Black Tunic Oil/canvas (41.5x31.5cm 16x12in) New-York 2001

$3 000 - €2 592 - **£1 500** - FF17 000
Mosè fa scaturire le acque Inchiostro (26x20cm 10x7in) Milano 1999

CORTEZO Victor Maria 1908-1978 [44]

$255 - €300 - **£180** - FF1 970
Boceto para decorado de la obra Suite Goyescas Acuarela/papel (19x27cm 7x10in) Madrid 2000

CORTI Giovanni Battista 1907-1946 [3]

$1 991 - €1 920 - **£1 227** - FF12 595
Der Gekreuzigte Öl/Karton (41.5x28cm 16x11in) Bern 1999

CORTIELLO Mario 1907-1982 **[35]**
- $800 – €829 – £480 – FF5 440
  Riviera di Posillipo Olio/tela (60x70cm 23x27in)
  Napoli 1999
- $300 – €389 – £225 – FF2 550
  Costiera amalfitana Olio/tela (25x35cm 9x13in)
  Vercelli 2000

CORTIER Amédée 1921-1976 **[22]**
- $1 242 – €1 487 – £852 – FF9 756
  Composition Huile/toile (70x50cm 27x19in)
  Antwerpen 2000

CORTIJO MERIDA Francisco 1936 **[13]**
- $1 056 – €961 – £656 – FF6 304
  Mujer sentada Oleo/tablex (123x75cm 48x29in)
  Madrid 1999

CORTOT Jean 1925 **[24]**
- $413 – €457 – £280 – FF3 000
  Sans titre (texte de l'auteur) Gouache (27.5x20cm
  10x7in) Paris 2000

CORVER(S) J.C. XIX-XX **[15]**
- $2 862 – €3 659 – £1 747 – FF17 440
  **Winter Landscape with Figures on a frozen
  Waterway** Oil/canvas (43.5x65cm 17x25in)
  Amsterdam 1998
- $788 – €817 – £500 – FF5 361
  **Fields outside a Church in Winter Landscape
  with Skaters** Oil/panel (17.5x23cm 6x9in) West-
  Yorkshire 2000

CORVI Domenico 1721-1803 **[11]**
- $28 886 – €33 671 – £20 000 – FF220 870
  **Allegories of the Arts: Modelli for Ceiling
  Decorations** Oil/canvas (73x70cm 28x27in) London
  2000
- $1 419 – €1 524 – £950 – FF9 995
  A Seated Male Academy Black chalk (56.5x43cm
  22x16in) London 2000

CORVINA Magdalena XVII **[1]**
- $3 929 – €3 644 – £2 400 – FF23 904
  **Portrait of a Young Gentleman Holding Gloves
  and Leaning on a Table** Gouache/vellum (14x12cm
  5x4in) London 1998

CORWIN Charles Abel 1857-1938 **[17]**
- $500 – €500 – £3 821 – FF40 409
  «Waterlillies» Oil/canvas (50x101cm 20x40in)
  Cincinnati OH 2001

CORYN Celest E. XX **[1]**
- $18 000 – €20 082 – £11 782 – FF131 727
  Indiana War Memorial Oil/canvas (81x66cm
  32x26in) Chicago IL 2000

CORZA Jean XX **[1]**
- $807 – €779 – £500 – FF5 109
  **«Un homme invisible vous voit...et vous ne le
  voyez pas!»** Poster (28x23cm 11x9in) London 1999

CORZAS Francisco 1936-1983 **[54]**
- $3 249 – €2 901 – £1 990 – FF19 030
  Horse and Figures Watercolour/paper (32x42.5cm
  12x16in) New-York 1999

COSCHELL Moritz Max Kocheles 1873-? **[8]**
- $4 638 – €4 294 – £2 800 – FF28 164
  A good Read Oil/canvas (53.5x48.5cm 21x19in)
  London 1999

COSENZA Giuseppe 1846/7-1922 **[18]**
- $4 249 – €3 681 – £2 606 – FF24 143
  Fishing Boats, Bay of Naples Oil/panel
  (28x17.5cm 11x6in) New-York 1999

COSEY (Bernard Cosendai) 1950 **[3]**
- $1 830 – €2 058 – £1 285 – FF13 500
  Jonathan, pl.42 de «Kate» Encre Chine/papier
  (32x26cm 12x10in) Paris 2001

COSEYN Pieter XVII **[1]**
- $7 731 – €8 622 – £5 044 – FF56 555
  **Italianate wooded Landscape with Travellers
  and Horsemen** Oil/canvas (65.5x92.5cm 25x36in)
  Amsterdam 2000

COSGROVE Stanley Morel 1911 **[378]**
- $2 694 – €3 143 – £1 924 – FF20 618
  Forêt Huile/toile (51x61cm 20x24in) Montréal 2000
- $1 089 – €1 033 – £661 – FF6 777
  Two Pines Oil/canvas (30x25cm 11x9in) Calgary,
  Alberta 1999
- $550 – €591 – £378 – FF3 877
  Nue Charcoal/paper (40.5x30.5cm 15x12in) Toronto
  2001
- $163 – €191 – £116 – FF1 250
  Study of a Nude Lithographie (51x40.5cm 20x15in)
  Montréal 2001

COSIJNS Gies 1920-1997 **[26]**
- $1 051 – €1 091 – £668 – FF7 154
  Sneeuwlandschap Oil/canvas (40x50cm 15x19in)
  Lokeren 2000

COSOLA Demetrio 1851-1895 **[29]**
- $3 000 – €2 592 – £1 500 – FF17 000
  Estate Olio/cartone (22.5x16.5cm 8x6in) Vercelli 1999
- $160 – €207 – £120 – FF1 360
  Maternità Carboncino/carta (29.5x19.5cm 11x7in)
  Milano 2000

COSOMATI Ettore 1871-1960 **[19]**
- $792 – €919 – £547 – FF6 030
  Engadiner Landschaft Öl/Leinwand (48.5x64cm
  19x25in) Luzern 2000

COSSAAR Johannis W. Cornelis 1874-1966 **[77]**
- $969 – €908 – £603 – FF5 953
  Church Interior Oil/panel (94.5x74.5cm 37x29in)
  Amsterdam 1998
- $821 – €908 – £569 – FF5 953
  Buiten met haar pop (Outside with her doll)
  Oil/board (34x26cm 13x10in) Amsterdam 2001
- $394 – €340 – £238 – FF2 232
  St Bartholomeus Watercolour (24.5x35.5cm 9x13in)
  Amsterdam 1999

COSSARD Adolphe 1880-1952 **[21]**
- $334 – €285 – £200 – FF1 872
  «Nice Coni, Nouvelle Ligne» Poster (100x62cm
  39x24in) London 1998

COSSIAU van Jan Joost c.1660-1732 **[5]**
- $7 000 – €6 085 – £4 236 – FF39 918
  **Italianate River Landscape, with Herdsmen and
  Animals** Red chalk (45.5x60cm 17x23in) New-York
  1999

COSSIERS Jan 1600-1671 **[25]**
- $34 450 – €32 225 – £21 320 – FF211 380
  La diseuse d'aventure Huile/toile (129.5x178.4cm
  50x70in) Antwerpen 1999
- $9 506 – €8 842 – £5 887 – FF58 000
  Madeleine repentante Huile/toile (64x49cm
  25x19in) Biarritz 2000

COSSIO Pancho Fr. Gutiérrez 1894-1970 **[40]**
- $15 750 – €15 016 – £9 500 – FF98 500
  Marina Oleo/lienzo (54x73cm 21x28in) Madrid 1999
- $2 160 – €2 403 – £1 440 – FF15 760
  Bodegón: brevas, pera y dominó Acuarela,
  gouache/papel (22x29.5cm 8x11in) Madrid 2000

COSSMANN

COSSMANN Alfred 1870-1951 **[16]**
- $155 - €179 - £109 - FF1 173
  Portrait Hans Meid Radierung (18x12.8cm 7x5in)
  Hamburg 2001

COSSMANN Hermann Maurice 1821-1890 **[15]**
- $3 124 - €3 354 - £2 090 - FF22 000
  Le joueur de mandoline Huile/toile (62.5x46.5cm
  24x18in) Bordeaux 1999

COSSON Marcel Jean Louis 1878-1956 **[688]**
- $3 886 - €4 421 - £2 697 - FF29 000
  Danseuses et hommes en habit au foyer
  Huile/toile (60x73cm 23x28in) Paris 2000
- $2 878 - €2 470 - £1 739 - FF16 200
  Les coulisses du Cirque d'hiver Huile/toile
  (33x47cm 12x18in) Paris 1998
- $813 - €945 - £571 - FF6 200
  Soirée à l'Opéra Aquarelle, gouache/papier (30x23cm
  11x9in) Paris 2001

COSTA Angelo Maria c.1670-1721 **[3]**
- $38 000 - €33 445 - £23 134 - FF219 385
  Mediterranean Port Scenes with Classical
  Ruins/Naval Engagements Oil/canvas (38x76cm
  14x29in) New-York 1999

COSTA Antonio 1804-1875 **[2]**
- $2 100 - €1 814 - £1 050 - FF11 900
  Angelo che suona la lira Inchiostro (36x27cm
  14x10in) Milano 1999

COSTA da Adriano Artur Eugen. 1884/90-1949 **[3]**
- $18 480 - €20 937 - £12 600 - FF137 340
  Brincando na praia Oleo/lienzo (44.5x80cm
  17x31in) Lisboa 2000
- $1 980 - €2 243 - £1 395 - FF14 715
  Paisagem com casas e árvores Oleo/cartón
  (19x27cm 7x10in) Lisboa 2001

COSTA da Catherine c.1668-1756 **[1]**
- $4 000 - €3 669 - £2 464 - FF24 066
  Double Portrait of Two Children Gouache
  (13x11cm 5x4in) New-York 1999

COSTA da John 1867-1931 **[7]**
- $3 623 - €3 803 - £2 400 - FF24 944
  Portrait of Marjorie Armstrong Oil/canvas
  (36x27cm 14x11in) Par, Cornwall 2000

COSTA Emanuele 1875-? **[17]**
- $3 000 - €3 427 - £2 112 - FF22 479
  Afternoon on the Terrazzo Oil/canvas (45x88cm
  18x35in) Chicago IL 2001

COSTA Emmanuel 1833-1921 **[52]**
- $561 - €655 - £389 - FF4 296
  Reisigsammler am Waldrand Öl/Leinwand
  (81x64.5cm 31x25in) Bern 2000
- $2 620 - €2 454 - £1 610 - FF16 098
  Wäscherinnen am Ufer Öl/Leinwand (29x42.5cm
  11x16in) Lindau 1999
- $1 084 - €1 265 - £754 - FF8 300
  Ste Marguerite Aquarelle/papier (22.5x34.5cm
  8x13in) Nice 2000

COSTA Giovanni 1833-1893 **[2]**
- $18 272 - €20 966 - £12 500 - FF137 525
  Portrait of a Young Lady Wearing a Bonnet
  Oil/canvas (129x68cm 51x27in) Heathfield, E. Sussex
  2000

COSTA Giovanni 1826-1903 **[72]**
- $10 200 - €13 217 - £7 650 - FF86 700
  Castel dell'Ovo dalla Riviera di Chiaia Olio/tela
  (40.5x62cm 15x24in) Roma 2001

- $5 500 - €5 702 - £3 300 - FF37 400
  Barca sulla spiaggia Olio/tavola (12x37cm 4x14in)
  Milano 1999

COSTA Olga 1913-1993 **[25]**
- $27 000 - €28 982 - £18 068 - FF190 107
  Muchacha del collar Oil/paper (69x59cm 27x23in)
  New-York 2000

COSTA Oreste 1851-1901 **[34]**
- $7 670 - €6 437 - £4 498 - FF42 224
  Nature morte au lièvre et au faisan Huile/toile
  (112x82cm 44x32in) Liège 1998

COSTA VILA Josep 1953 **[14]**
- $432 - €481 - £288 - FF3 152
  La Habana, Cuba Oleo/lienzo (46x55cm 18x21in)
  Barcelona 2000

COSTAIN Harold Haliday 1895-1994 **[29]**
- $1 800 - €1 998 - £1 254 - FF13 106
  Lindbergh seaplane on the East River, New York
  Gelatin silver print (38x49.5cm 14x19in) New-York
  2001

COSTANTINI Giuseppe 1843-1893 **[27]**
- $22 000 - €22 806 - £13 200 - FF149 600
  Mosca cieca Olio/tela (43x61.5cm 16x24in) Milano
  1999
- $4 500 - €4 665 - £2 700 - FF30 600
  Piccoli contadini con chitarra Olio/tela (27x41cm
  10x16in) Milano 2000

COSTANTINI Virgilio 1882-1940 **[11]**
- $2 852 - €3 049 - £1 942 - FF20 000
  Le Mont Cervin Huile/toile (72.5x92.5cm 28x36in)
  Lyon 2001

COSTANZI Placido 1690-1759 **[15]**
- $60 000 - €52 808 - £36 528 - FF346 398
  Narcissus and Echo Oil/canvas (136x99cm 53x38in)
  New-York 1999
- $18 775 - €21 886 - £13 000 - FF143 565
  The Virgin and Child with Saint Anne Oil/canvas
  (65x48cm 25x18in) London 2000

COSTE Jean-Baptiste XVIII-XIX **[4]**
- $1 727 - €1 601 - £1 074 - FF10 500
  Paysage animé avec une montagne et un
  temple Encre (23x31cm 9x12in) Paris 1999

COSTE Victor 1844-1923 **[16]**
- $2 014 - €2 287 - £1 399 - FF15 000
  Paysage fluvial Huile/toile (33x45cm 12x17in)
  Marseille 2001

COSTER Gordon H. 1906-1991 **[59]**
- $1 200 - €1 120 - £726 - FF7 349
  Cyclists Racing Gelatin silver print (16x23.5cm
  6x9in) New-York 1999

COSTER Hendrick 1638-1659 **[3]**
- $8 218 - €7 792 - £5 000 - FF51 111
  Personification of Poetry by Candlelight, sharpening a Quill at Table Oil/canvas (66x47.5cm
  25x18in) London 1999

COSTER Howard 1885-1959 **[6]**
- $573 - €532 - £350 - FF3 491
  T.E. Lawrence Silver print (24x16.5cm 9x6in) London
  1999

COSTETTI Giovanni 1878-1949 **[30]**
- $14 400 - €12 440 - £7 200 - FF81 600
  Il Maestro Vittorio Gui Olio/tela (123x92.5cm
  48x36in) Prato 1999

$6 900 - €5 961 - £3 450 - FF39 100
La vecchia Olio/tavola (26.5x18.5cm 10x7in) Firenze 1999

$570 - €492 - £285 - FF3 230
Vecchio contadino Acquarello/carta (20.5x15cm 8x5in) Prato 1999

COSTETTI Romeo 1871-1957 [10]
$1 320 - €140 - £660 - FF7 480
Maschere Acquaforte, acquatinta (38x51cm 14x20in) Firenze 1999

COSTI Rochelle 1961 [1]
$5 000 - €5 801 - £3 452 - FF38 055
Quartos-Sao Paulo Cibachrome print (183x230cm 72x90in) New-York 2000

COSTIGAN John Edward 1888-1972 [114]
$15 000 - €17 933 - £10 378 - FF117 630
Mother and Children #2 Oil/canvas (127x152cm 50x60in) Milford CT 2000

$11 000 - €9 820 - £6 736 - FF64 418
«Woman with Goats-Winter» Oil/canvas (63x76cm 25x30in) Altadena CA 1999

$1 000 - €969 - £619 - FF6 359
Winter Snow Scene Oil/board (20x25cm 8x10in) Mystic CT 1999

$1 400 - €1 586 - £978 - FF10 406
Mother and Child in the Autumn Woods Watercolour, gouache (61x46.5cm 24x18in) New-York 2001

$160 - €148 - £99 - FF973
The Bathers Etching (22x29cm 8x11in) York PA 1999

COSWAY Richard 1742-1821 [139]
$49 617 - €43 264 - £30 000 - FF283 794
The Boyle Children: Group Portrait of the Children of Edmund Boyle Oil/canvas (235x145cm 92x57in) London 1998

$2 380 - €2 310 - £1 500 - FF15 153
Portrait of George fifth Duke of Marlborough wearing classical Robes Miniature (7x5.5cm 2x2in) Newbury, Berkshire 1999

$2 845 - €3 306 - £2 000 - FF21 688
Portrait of Sir Peter Paul Rubens, bust-length Ink (21x13.5cm 8x5in) London 2001

COSYN Pieter 1630-c.1667 [7]
$5 177 - €4 799 - £3 000 - FF31 481
Wooded Landscape with Travellers resting on a track before a Ruin Oil/panel (40x47cm 15x18in) London 1999

COT Pierre-Auguste 1837-1883 [17]
$68 318 - €66 258 - £43 000 - FF434 626
Young Street Musicians Oil/canvas (146.5x107cm 57x42in) London 1999

$32 500 - €38 538 - £22 360 - FF252 794
Ophelia Oil/canvas (125.5x78cm 49x30in) New-York 2000

$23 000 - €25 686 - £14 729 - FF168 486
Little Lord Fauntleroy Oil/canvas (38x32.5cm 14x12in) New-York 2000

COTARD-DUPRÉ Thérèse 1877-? [5]
$12 000 - €13 401 - £7 684 - FF87 906
Feeding the Chickens Oil/canvas (66x81cm 25x31in) New-York 2000

COTE Adelard 1899-1974 [17]
$500 - €534 - £339 - FF3 504
Horse with Mane and Tail Sculpture, wood (25x27cm 10x11in) Portsmouth NH 2001

COTÉ Bruno 1940 [58]
$689 - €652 - £428 - FF4 280
«Près de la rivière St Jean» Oil/masonite (51x61cm 20x24in) Calgary, Alberta 1999

COTELLE Adrien XIX [1]
$10 934 - €11 739 - £7 315 - FF77 000
Cour de ferme animée Huile/toile (32x42cm 12x16in) Grenoble 2000

COTELLE Jean II 1642-1708 [4]
$18 284 - €22 105 - £12 774 - FF145 000
La toilette de Vénus devant la façade d'un palais imaginaire Huile/toile (145x112cm 57x44in) Paris 2000

COTES Francis 1726-1770 [51]
$10 643 - €9 734 - £6 500 - FF63 850
Portrait of Mrs Francis Vernon, later Countess Shipbrook Oil/canvas (76x63.5cm 29x25in) London 1998

$6 724 - €7 218 - £4 500 - FF47 347
Portrait of a Gentleman, in Military Dress Pastel/paper (59.5x44.5cm 23x17in) London 2000

COTHARIN Kate Leah 1866-? [2]
$2 400 - €2 836 - £1 700 - FF18 601
Figures on the Beach/As it was Clearing/In the Parching August Wind Pastel/paper (11x26cm 4x10in) Boston MA 2000

COTMAN Frederick George 1850-1920 [68]
$1 630 - €1 444 - £1 000 - FF9 475
Extensive River Landscape with Sailing Boats by the Moonlight Oil/canvas (58x73cm 23x29in) Aylsham, Norfolk 1999

$1 445 - €1 234 - £850 - FF8 095
Firework Display at the Crystal Palace Oil/canvas (24x40.5cm 9x15in) Godalming, Surrey 1998

$890 - €835 - £550 - FF5 477
The Market Square Ripon Watercolour/paper (35x25cm 14x10in) Aylsham, Norfolk 1999

COTMAN John Joseph 1814-1878 [75]
$1 452 - €1 345 - £900 - FF8 821
View near Postwick Grove, Norfolk Watercolour (26x86cm 10x33in) London 1999

COTMAN John Sell 1782-1842 [149]
$3 765 - €4 369 - £2 600 - FF28 662
The mounth of The Yare Oil/canvas (53.5x80cm 21x31in) London 2000

$33 672 - €40 046 - £24 000 - FF262 684
Wooded Landscape at Whitlingham near Norwich Oil/panel (25.5x40.5cm 10x15in) London 2000

$4 797 - €4 620 - £3 000 - FF30 303
Millbank on the Thames Pencil/paper (16x24cm 6x9in) London 1999

$135 - €116 - £80 - FF761
Castle of Lillebonne Etching (22x33.5cm 8x13in) Ipswich 1998

COTMAN Miles Edmund 1810-1858 [33]
$901 - €831 - £550 - FF5 449
The Font at Twyford Church, Norfolk Pencil (20x14.5cm 7x5in) London 1998

COTTAAR Piet Johannes 1878-1950 [29]
$274 - €295 - £183 - FF1 934
Rhododendrons in glazen vaas Oil/canvas (60x82cm 23x32in) Dordrecht 2000

COTTAVOZ André 1922 [523]
$2 031 - €2 287 - £1 426 - FF15 000
«Sable rouge» Huile/toile (41x83.5cm 16x32in) Paris 2001

C

$1 154 - €1 143 - £699 - FF7 500
Nature morte noire Huile/toile (19x27cm 7x10in)
Paris 2000

$461 - €457 - £279 - FF3 000
Harem Pastel/papier (25x33cm 9x12in) Paris 2000

COTTAVOZ Félix 1810-1886 [3]
$5 680 - €6 098 - £3 800 - FF40 000
**Scène de chasse à la bécasse en automne en
Dauphiné** Huile/toile (72x58cm 28x22in) Grenoble
2000

COTTET Charles 1863-1925 [196]
$2 911 - €2 820 - £1 829 - FF18 500
Sunrise Huile/carton (40x60cm 15x23in) Nantes 1999
$1 328 - €1 296 - £817 - FF8 500
Paysanne bretonne Huile/toile (40x27cm 15x10in)
Argenteuil 1999

$928 - €884 - £588 - FF5 800
Le dîner à la ferme Fusain/papier (34x42cm 13x16in)
Douarnenez 1999

$206 - €229 - £140 - FF1 500
**Bretonnes sur le quai/Douleur au pays de la
mer/Paysage marin** Lithographie (14.5x19cm 5x7in)
Paris 2000

COTTINGHAM Robert 1935 [47]
$12 500 - €10 493 - £7 331 - FF68 832
Shell Truck Oil/canvas (124.5x197cm 49x77in)
Beverly-Hills CA 1998
$4 980 - €4 573 - £3 087 - FF30 000
G & S Auto Stores Aquarelle/papier (54x54cm
21x21in) Paris 1999

$375 - €434 - £265 - FF2 850
Radio City Deli Lithograph (36x36cm 14x14in) New-
York 2000

COTTO Pedro Onofre 1669-1713 [2]
$13 500 - €16 218 - £9 450 - FF106 380
Ruinas arquitectónicas Oleo/lienzo (70.5x97cm
27x38in) Madrid 2000
$31 020 - €28 231 - £18 800 - FF185 180
San Jerónimo en paisaje Pintura (35x44cm
13x17in) Madrid 1999

COTTON Alan 1936 [7]
$999 - €920 - £600 - FF6 034
Cottages near Gordes, Provence Oil/canvas
(51x66cm 20x26in) London 1999
$838 - €708 - £500 - FF4 646
«Provence», Summer Fields Oil/canvas (23x28cm
9x11in) Penzance, Cornwall 1998

COTTON John Wesley 1868-1931 [21]
$11 000 - €11 807 - £7 361 - FF77 451
On a Bruges Canal Oil/canvas (76x101cm 30x40in)
Altadena CA 2000
$600 - €644 - £401 - FF4 224
River landscape with bridge and moon Aquatint
(36x45cm 14x18in) Altadena CA 2000

COTTON Shane 1964 [9]
$12 093 - €13 555 - £8 457 - FF88 914
Hopa Oil/canvas (185.5x155cm 73x61in) Auckland
2001
$3 385 - €3 794 - £2 360 - FF24 886
Te Paku o te Rangi Oil/canvas (65x83cm 25x32in)
Wellington 2001
$1 946 - €2 181 - £1 357 - FF14 309
«Np» Oil/canvas (20x20cm 7x7in) Wellington 2001

COTTON William H. 1880-1958 [10]
$5 500 - €4 640 - £3 226 - FF30 437
Sonny Oil/canvas (76x63.5cm 29x25in) New-York
1998

COTUGNO Teodoro 1943 [4]
$750 - €777 - £450 - FF5 100
La torre Acquaforte (30x21cm 11x8in) Torino 1999

COUBINE Othon 1883-1969 [148]
$6 647 - €6 287 - £4 140 - FF41 239
Paysage de Provence Huile/toile (53x54cm
20x21in) Praha 2000
$2 239 - €2 515 - £1 559 - FF16 500
Le berger Huile/panneau (24x17cm 9x6in) Honfleur
2001
$158 - €150 - £99 - FF986
Petite chapelle à Simiane IV Eau-forte (20x24.5cm
7x9in) Praha 2000

COUCHAUX Marcel 1877-1939 [60]
$6 485 - €7 622 - £4 700 - FF50 000
Voiliers dans le port de Dieppe Huile/toile
(60x81cm 23x31in) Rouen 2001

COUCHÉ Jacques 1759-? [7]
$949 - €920 - £601 - FF6 037
La fuite à dessein, nach J.-H. Fragonard
Farbradierung (35.7x25.7cm 14x10in) München 1999

COUDER Alexandre Jean 1808-1879 [25]
$2 217 - €2 053 - £1 357 - FF13 467
Stilleben mit Fruchtkorb und Trauben
Öl/Leinwand (46x55cm 18x21in) Bern 1999
$1 835 - €1 540 - £1 076 - FF10 100
Le repas des petits rongeurs Huile/panneau
(16x21.5cm 6x8in) Troyes 1998

COUDER Gustave Émile 1845-1903 [13]
$18 000 - €17 076 - £10 935 - FF112 012
Peonies and Plums Oil/canvas (55.5x79.5cm
21x31in) New-York 1998

COUDER L. Charles Auguste 1790-1873 [15]
$5 814 - €4 878 - £3 427 - FF32 000
**Achille près d'être englouti par la Xanthe et le
Simoïs** Huile/toile (38.5x59.5cm 15x23in) Paris 1998

COUDON Roland XX [16]
$641 - €732 - £445 - FF4 800
«La maison du travail CGT» Affiche (120x99cm
47x38in) Paris 2000

COUDRAIN Brigitte 1934 [37]
$179 - €204 - £125 - FF1 341
Enlèvements Etching, aquatint in colors (43.5x31.5cm
17x12in) München 2000

COUDRAY Georges Charles ?-1903 [40]
$1 462 - €1 351 - £877 - FF8 865
Busto de Napoleon Terracotta (72x43x27cm
28x16x10in) Barcelona 1999

COUGHTRY John Graham 1931 [8]
$11 262 - €12 472 - £7 638 - FF81 812
Orientale Oil/canvas (213.5x183cm 84x72in) Toronto
2000

COULANGE-LAUTREC Emmanuel 1824-1898 [22]
$392 - €427 - £269 - FF2 800
Paysage animé à la cascade Huile/toile (76x50cm
29x19in) Nîmes 2001

COULAUD Martin ?-1906 [13]
$2 069 - €2 363 - £1 455 - FF15 500
Troupeau en marche Huile/toile (49x65cm 19x25in)
Fontainebleau 2001

COULDERY Horatio Henry 1832-c.1893 [70]
$16 000 - €14 164 - £9 782 - FF92 910
Cornered Oil/canvas (30.5x61cm 12x24in) New-York
1999

C

$6 040 - €5 877 - **£3 717** - FF38 549
Thick as Thieves Oil/board (30.5x40.5cm 12x15in)
Malvern, Victoria 1999

COULIOU Jean-Yves 1916-1994 **[12]**
$1 742 - €1 829 - **£1 098** - FF12 000
Retour au port à Concarneau Huile/toile (60x92cm
23x36in) Besançon 2000

COULON de Éric 1888-1956 **[36]**
$1 193 - €1 007 - **£700** - FF6 603
«Alpes & Jura» Poster (99x60cm 38x23in) London
1998

COULON George David 1823-1904 **[25]**
$2 100 - €1 957 - **£1 269** - FF12 839
Spring Oil/canvas (23x31cm 9x12in) New-Orleans LA
1999
$12 000 - €11 185 - **£7 252** - FF73 366
Nature Morte of a Wood Duck Watercolour/paper
(53x38cm 21x15in) New-Orleans LA 1999

COULON George J.A. 1854-1922 **[3]**
$5 000 - €5 627 - **£3 444** - FF36 913
Nature morte Pastel/paper (49x49cm
19x15in) New-Orleans LA 2000

COULON Louis 1819-1855 **[5]**
$7 494 - €6 956 - **£4 500** - FF45 626
The Prick of the Needle Oil/canvas (66x54.5cm
25x21in) London 1999

COULTER William Alexander 1849-1936 **[48]**
$9 000 - €9 661 - **£6 022** - FF63 369
Full Moon Along the Coast Oil/canvas (90x136cm
35x53in) San-Francisco CA 2000
$6 000 - €7 052 - **£4 159** - FF46 256
Moonlight at Sea Oil/canvas (61x46cm 24x18in)
Beverly-Hills CA 2000

COULY-RAYMOND F. XX **[2]**
$6 662 - €6 183 - **£4 000** - FF40 556
Rue de Paris Oil/canvas (27x41cm 10x16in) London
1999

COUMONT Charles 1822-1889 **[18]**
$2 397 - €2 723 - **£1 681** - FF17 859
**A Shepherd and his Flock in an Italian
Landscape** Oil/canvas (56x74cm 22x29in) Amsterdam
2001
$693 - €665 - **£436** - FF4 360
Kuh und Stier in antiker Landschaft Oil/panel
(22x29cm 8x11in) Konstanz 1999

COUNHAYE Charles 1884-1971 **[104]**
$571 - €595 - **£362** - FF3 902
Femme dans un intérieur Huile/toile (60x50cm
23x19in) Bruxelles 2000
$162 - €149 - **£100** - FF975
L'ombre Lavis/papier (34.5x25.5cm 13x10in) Bruxelles
1999

COUNIHAN Noel Jack 1913-1986 **[85]**
$34 308 - €36 827 - **£22 962** - FF241 572
Woman and Child, mural Study, IV Oil/board
(228.5x122cm 89x48in) Melbourne 2000
$6 529 - €6 125 - **£4 097** - FF40 777
**Woman with Candle, a Childhood Memory (No
2)** Oil/canvas (91.5x121.5cm 36x47in) Melbourne 1999
$2 292 - €2 674 - **£1 595** - FF17 541
**Cleaning and Reclaiming Bricks from the Ruins
of Warsaw** Oil/board (12.5x20cm 4x7in) Melbourne
2000
$605 - €630 - **£382** - FF4 131
Falling Figures/The Drive Ink/paper (30x45cm
11x17in) Melbourne 2000

$291 - €322 - **£194** - FF2 109
Image 10 Lithograph (36x49cm 14x19in) Melbourne

COUPER William A. 1853-1942 **[13]**
$3 500 - €2 953 - **£2 053** - FF19 369
A Labour of Love Bronze (48x32cm 18x12in) New-
York 1998

COURAGEUX Claude 1938 **[2]**
$5 640 - €5 183 - **£3 464** - FF34 000
Composition Huile/toile (92x73cm 36x28in) Paris
1999

COURANT Maurice 1847-1926 **[100]**
$1 505 - €1 524 - **£936** - FF10 000
Coucher de soleil sur la grève Huile/toile
(47x65cm 18x25in) Soissons 2000
$1 361 - €1 265 - **£834** - FF8 300
Honfleur, la sortie des barques de pêche
Huile/panneau (27x35cm 10x13in) Honfleur 1998
$623 - €579 - **£381** - FF3 800
Vieux port Aquarelle/papier (23x40cm 9x15in)
Honfleur 1998

COURBET Gustave 1819-1877 **[270]**
$441 868 - €427 553 - **£280 000** - FF2 804 564
Femme à la guirlande Oil/canvas (125x133cm
49x52in) London 1999
$52 000 - €58 272 - **£36 244** - FF382 241
Paysage Guyère Oil/canvas (46.5x55cm 18x21in)
New-York 2001
$20 750 - €18 885 - **£12 736** - FF123 876
Petite falaise en bord de lac Huile/toile/panneau
(19x24cm 7x9in) Zürich 1999
$19 768 - €17 074 - **£11 939** - FF112 000
La prairie ensoleillée Graphite (24.5x31cm 9x12in)
Barbizon 1998

COURCHINOUX Edouard 1891-1968 **[2]**
$1 345 - €1 444 - **£900** - FF9 473
«Le Touquet» Poster (100x62cm 39x24in) London
2000

COURDOUAN Vincent 1810-1893 **[81]**
$10 662 - €11 891 - **£7 168** - FF78 000
Lavandières dans la vallée de l'Argens
Huile/toile (40x69cm 15x27in) Saint-Martin-de-Crau
2000
$4 102 - €4 878 - **£2 924** - FF32 000
Sous-bois de pins Huile/toile (29x45cm 11x17in)
Toulon 2000
$1 468 - €1 372 - **£906** - FF9 000
Château en bord de mer Aquarelle/papier (15x23cm
5x9in) Le Touquet 1999

COURMES Alfred 1898-1993 **[133]**
$52 190 - €51 833 - **£32 640** - FF340 000
Le marin au bar Huile/toile (136x106cm 53x41in)
Paris 1999
$13 248 - €12 196 - **£7 952** - FF80 000
Paysage du Lavandou Huile/toile (73x92cm
28x36in) Paris 1999
$4 539 - €4 573 - **£2 829** - FF30 000
Nature morte Huile/toile (36x26cm 14x10in) Paris
2000
$1 159 - €1 067 - **£695** - FF7 000
Le fermier et son cheval Crayon/papier (24.5x21cm
9x8in) Paris 1999
$726 - €732 - **£452** - FF4 800
Le radeau de la Méduse Eau-forte (40x50cm
15x19in) Paris 2000

COURNAULT Étienne 1891-1948 **[36]**

$8 998 - €8 385 - **£5 439** - FF55 000
Maingus descernetite, Fond d'oeil Peinture (40x70cm 15x27in) Nancy 1999

COURT Emily 1880-1957 **[22]**

$1 326 - €1 144 - **£800** - FF7 504
A Walk in the Afternoon Oil/board (13x15cm 5x5in) London 1998

COURT Joseph Désiré 1797-1865 **[24]**

$8 200 - €7 775 - **£5 125** - FF51 000
Jeunes femmes en comédiennes Huile/toile (130x98cm 51x38in) Vichy 1999

$3 778 - €3 506 - **£2 267** - FF23 000
Portrait de l'architecte Guillaume Abel Blouet Huile/toile (65.5x54.5cm 25x21in) Paris 1999

COURT Sidney A. XX **[2]**

$1 443 - €1 455 - **£900** - FF9 543
Coastal Landscape Watercolour/paper (27.5x37.5cm 10x14in) London 2000

COURTAT Louis c.1850-1909 **[7]**

$47 500 - €45 134 - **£28 899** - FF296 062
After the Bath Oil/canvas (123x94cm 48x37in) New-York 1999

COURTEILLE de Nicolas c.1768-c.1835 **[2]**

$30 000 - €26 081 - **£18 156** - FF171 078
«The Constancy of Eleazar» Oil/canvas (112x145cm 44x57in) New-York 1999

COURTEN von Angelo 1848-1925 **[16]**

$12 160 - €11 412 - **£7 410** - FF74 860
Es una ganga Oleo/lienzo (131x86cm 51x33in) Madrid 1999

COURTENS Alfred 1889-1967 **[22]**

$1 177 - €1 339 - **£826** - FF8 780
La reine Astrid Terracotta (H40cm H15in) Bruxelles 2001

COURTENS Frans 1854-1943 **[131]**

$9 614 - €9 420 - **£5 888** - FF61 788
Le bois sous la neige Oil/canvas (176x146cm 69x57in) Lokeren 1999

$5 236 - €5 453 - **£3 454** - FF35 772
Barque amarrée au coucher du soleil Huile/toile (100x62cm 39x24in) Bruxelles 2000

$1 651 - €1 611 - **£1 014** - FF10 569
Lever de lune Huile/toile/panneau (30.5x49.5cm 12x19in) Bruxelles 1999

COURTENS Herman 1884-1956 **[62]**

$1 848 - €1 735 - **£1 141** - FF11 382
Nature morte aux fleurs et aux fruits Huile/toile (60x80cm 23x31in) Antwerpen 1999

$924 - €793 - **£560** - FF5 203
Nature morte aux pommes, raisins et citrons Huile/panneau (30x40cm 11x15in) Bruxelles 1998

COURTET Augustin 1821-1891 **[3]**

$5 812 - €5 641 - **£3 618** - FF37 000
Centauresse et faune Bronze (46x41cm 18x16in) Paris 1999

COURTIN F. XIX **[5]**

$371 - €420 - **£252** - FF2 758
Vista de Sevilla Litografía (40x50cm 15x19in) Madrid 1999

COURTIN Pierre Louis 1921 **[44]**

$110 - €91 - **£64** - FF600
Sans titre Lithographie couleurs (46x64cm 18x25in) Paris 1998

COURTOIS DE BONNENCONTRE Ernest 1859-1955 **[8]**

$12 000 - €11 135 - **£7 332** - FF73 044
The Harvest Oil/canvas (192.5x104cm 75x40in) New-York 1999

COURTOIS LE BOURGUIGNON Jacques 1621-1676 **[57]**

$15 000 - €16 130 - **£10 222** - FF105 804
Cavalry Skirmish between Ottomans and Turks Oil/canvas (162.5x250cm 63x98in) Beverly-Hills CA 2001

$17 677 - €17 534 - **£11 000** - FF115 013
Cavalry Battle Oil/canvas (37x59cm 14x23in) London 1999

$4 550 - €3 904 - **£2 795** - FF25 610
Batalla Oleo/lienzo (31x41cm 12x16in) Madrid 1998

$1 350 - €1 534 - **£938** - FF10 061
Reitergefecht Ink (14.5x26.5cm 5x10in) Köln 2001

COURTOIS Raphael XIX-XX **[2]**

$1 800 - €1 731 - **£1 111** - FF11 354
«As de Trèfle» Poster (119x156.5cm 46x61in) New-York 1999

COURTRIGHT Robert 1926 **[10]**

$2 600 - €2 713 - **£1 639** - FF17 797
Untitled CLXXIX Gouache (49x52cm 19x20in) New-York 2000

COURVOISIER XVIII-XIX **[4]**

$217 - €183 - **£127** - FF1 200
Vue de Paris, Quai Bonaparte Gravure (50x40cm 19x15in) Bernay 1998

COURVOISIER Jules 1884-1936 **[9]**

$722 - €787 - **£500** - FF5 165
«Exposition d'affiches» Poster (99x66cm 38x25in) London 2001

COUSE Eanger Irving 1866-1936 **[129]**

$90 000 - €84 983 - **£55 890** - FF557 451
Ute Waterbottle Oil/canvas (61x73.5cm 24x28in) Beverly-Hills CA 1999

$14 000 - €16 454 - **£9 706** - FF107 931
Serenade Oil/masonite (20.5x25.5cm 8x10in) Beverly-Hills CA 2000

$2 600 - €3 056 - **£1 802** - FF20 044
Indian Portrait Watercolour/paper (25.5x18cm 10x7in) Beverly-Hills CA 2000

COUSIN Charles act.c.1904-c.1955 **[99]**

$1 459 - €1 616 - **£990** - FF10 600
Canal à Venise Huile/carton (54x45cm 21x17in) Lyon 2000

$700 - €751 - **£468** - FF4 928
Country Landscape Oil/board (19x27cm 7x11in) St. Petersburg FL 2000

COUSIN Charles Louis Aug. 1807-1887 **[2]**

$2 535 - €2 994 - **£1 800** - FF19 638
Gondolas and other Boats on a Venetian Lagoon/Gondola on a Canal Oil/panel (16x22cm 6x8in) London 2001

COUSIN Jean I c.1490-c.1560 **[2]**

$2 052 - €2 287 - **£1 396** - FF15 000
Minerve Encre/papier (8x14cm 3x5in) Nice 2000

COUSINS Harold B. 1916 **[13]**

$427 - €471 - **£279** - FF3 089
Structure «Star Lights» Fer (47x22x23cm 18x8x9in) Bruxelles 2000

COUSINS Samuel 1801-1887 **[35]**

$151 - €156 - **£95** - FF1 024
Law: The Honorable Sir John Patterson, after Margaret Carpenter Engraving (50x35cm 19x13in) London 1999

COUSSENS Armand 1881-1935 **[51]**

$252 - €274 - **£173** - FF1 800
Le Maquignon Vernis mou couleurs (21x37cm 8x14in) Nîmes 2001

COUSTOU Guillaume I 1677-1746 **[25]**

$1 416 - €1 239 - **£857** - FF8 129
Palefrenier et cheval de Marly Bronze (H60cm H23in) Genève 1998

COUSTURIER Lucie 1870-1925 **[44]**

$9 365 - €8 690 - **£5 722** - FF57 000
Paysage du Midi fauve Huile/toile (73x92cm 28x36in) Paris 1999

$1 170 - €1 311 - **£820** - FF8 600
Étude de nu Huile/carton/toile (28x22cm 11x8in) Paris 2001

$654 - €762 - **£458** - FF5 000
Kissidougou Aquarelle/papier (21x27cm 8x10in) Paris 2000

COUTAN Jules Félix 1848-1939 **[13]**

$60 000 - €57 222 - **£36 522** - FF375 354
Music Bronze (H266.5cm H104in) New-York 1999

COUTAUD Lucien 1904-1977 **[460]**

$2 435 - €2 897 - **£1 736** - FF19 000
Tête et poissons Huile/toile (70x60cm 27x23in) Dreux 2000

$801 - €945 - **£563** - FF6 200
L'automate Huile/toile (22x27cm 8x10in) Fontainebleau 2000

$1 000 - €862 - **£603** - FF5 600
Dames des algues le Dimanche Gouache/papier (34.5x44cm 13x17in) Saint-Germain-en-Laye 1998

$129 - €152 - **£90** - FF1 000
Jeune personne des environs de Joucas Eau-forte (56x38cm 22x14in) Nîmes 2000

COUTTS Alice 1880-1973 **[10]**

$1 300 - €1 248 - **£815** - FF8 184
American Indian seated Child in Bed of Flowers, In Wonderland Oil/board (22x17cm 9x7in) Altadena CA 1999

COUTTS Gordon 1868-1937 **[60]**

$2 500 - €2 136 - **£1 512** - FF14 011
Afternoon Showers Oil/canvas (61x71cm 24x27in) San-Francisco CA 1998

$1 469 - €1 725 - **£1 037** - FF11 313
Head of a Turbanned Man Oil/canvas/board (39x30.5cm 15x12in) Melbourne 2000

COUTTS Hubert ?-1921 **[5]**

$2 923 - €3 259 - **£2 000** - FF21 379
Highland Croft Watercolour (56x99cm 22x38in) Perthshire 2000

COUTURE Thomas 1815-1879 **[65]**

$20 944 - €24 322 - **£14 718** - FF159 544
Herde Oil/canvas (221x189cm 87x74in) Stockholm 2001

$3 404 - €2 897 - **£2 031** - FF19 000
Tête de femme voilée Huile/toile (49x33cm 19x12in) Bordeaux 1998

$6 500 - €7 644 - **£4 660** - FF50 140
Young Beauty Oil/canvas (40.5x32.5cm 15x12in) New-York 2001

$1 213 - €1 361 - **£840** - FF8 929
Portret van een man met snor en ontbloot bovenlichaam Aquarelle/papier (29x23.3cm 11x9in) The Hague 2000

COUTURIER Jean Claude Nicolas 1796-1875 **[1]**

$2 496 - €2 439 - **£1 582** - FF16 000
Jeune Zouave devant le Fort des Dardanelles Aquarelle/papier (73x49cm 28x19in) Paris 1999

COUTURIER Philibert Léon 1823-1901 **[59]**

$22 955 - €23 630 - **£14 461** - FF155 000
Basse-cour effrayée par un épervier Huile/toile (224x307cm 88x120in) Paris 2000

$3 491 - €3 354 - **£2 123** - FF22 000
La basse-cour Huile/toile (45x36cm 17x14in) Paris 1999

$1 760 - €1 829 - **£1 108** - FF12 000
La basse-cour, poules et dindons Huile/toile (30x41cm 11x16in) Tours 2000

COUTURIER Robert 1905 **[44]**

$3 241 - €3 020 - **£2 000** - FF19 813
Nu allongé Bronze (20.5x39.5cm 8x15in) London 1999

COUTY Jean 1907-1991 **[107]**

$1 712 - €1 753 - **£1 075** - FF11 500
Le presbytère, L'Ile Barbe Huile/toile (60x73cm 23x28in) Lyon 2000

$328 - €381 - **£233** - FF2 500
Maternité Fusain/papier (61x46cm 24x18in) Coutances 2001

COUTY Jean-Frédéric 1829-1904 **[12]**

$2 776 - €2 973 - **£1 889** - FF19 500
Nature morte aux poissons Huile/toile (51.5x73.5cm 20x28in) Rennes 2001

COUVERCHEL Alfred 1834-1867 **[5]**

$3 750 - €3 887 - **£2 250** - FF25 500
Cavallo con fantino Olio/tela (59x73cm 23x28in) Milano 2000

COUWENBERG Abraham Johannes 1806-1844 **[5]**

$4 813 - €4 538 - **£2 983** - FF29 766
The Ferry Oil/panel (33.5x43cm 13x16in) Amsterdam 1999

COUWENBERGH van Christian Gillisz. 1604-1667 **[9]**

$16 204 - €18 151 - **£11 260** - FF119 064
The Finding of Moses Oil/panel (122x117cm 48x46in) Amsterdam 2001

$14 943 - €16 040 - **£10 000** - FF105 216
Lady Playing a Lute Oil/panel (74x59cm 29x23in) London 2000

COVARRUBIAS Luis 1918-1987 **[2]**

$8 712 - €8 133 - **£5 376** - FF53 352
Paisaje de México Técnica mixta/lienzo (60x90cm 23x35in) México 1999

COVARRUBIAS Miguel 1904-1957 **[165]**

$35 442 - €33 032 - **£21 420** - FF216 678
Balinesa Oil/canvas (51x36cm 20x14in) Singapore 1999

$4 645 - €4 329 - **£2 866** - FF28 398
Balinese beauties bathing Pencil (26x21cm 10x8in) Singapore 1999

$1 400 - €1 344 - **£863** - FF8 819
Rumba Lithograph (23.5x34cm 9x13in) New-York 1999

COVENTRY Frederick Halford 1905 [3]

$900 - €865 - £550 - FF5 672
«Make the most of the Autumn Leaves, Southern Railway» Poster (102x64cm 40x25in) London 1999

COVENTRY Gertrude Mary 1886-1964 [11]

$3 122 - €2 985 - £1 965 - FF19 580
Hamnbild med segelbåt Oil/panel (29x34cm 11x13in) Stockholm 1999

COVENTRY Keith 1958 [29]

$14 048 - €12 002 - £8 500 - FF78 731
White abstract (Two Boys in Henry's holy Shade) Mixed media (171.5x160x7.6cm 67x62x2in) London 1998

$7 471 - €8 020 - £5 000 - FF52 608
White Abstract (White's) Mixed media (80x65x5cm 31x25x1in) London 2000

$11 553 - €12 590 - £8 000 - FF82 582
White Abstract (Horseguard) Sculpture (178x127x10cm 70x50x3in) London 2001

COVENTRY Robert McGown 1855-1914 [45]

$150 - €1 286 - £780 - FF8 433
West Coast Scene Oil/canvas (50x75cm 19x29in) Edinburgh 2000

$1 155 - €1 158 - £700 - FF7 597
Breezy Day, Carradale Oil/canvas (30x50cm 11x19in) Edinburgh 2000

$1 585 - €1 647 - £1 000 - FF10 801
Hôtel de Ville Watercolour (19.5x24.5cm 7x9in) London 2000

COWAN Jack XX [2]

$9 250 - €9 165 - £5 612 - FF60 120
Winter Scene of Hunters and Geese Watercolour/paper (48.5x61cm 19x24in) New-York 2000

COWARD Noël 1899-1973 [39]

$20 160 - €17 158 - £12 000 - FF112 546
On the Promenade Mixed media/canvas (61x76cm 24x29in) London 1998

$2 604 - €2 967 - £1 800 - FF19 465
Figures on a Coastal Promenade Oil/canvas (39.5x29cm 15x11in) London 2000

$4 781 - €5 133 - £3 200 - FF33 669
Man Among the Leaves Gouache/paper (34.5x28.5cm 13x11in) London 2000

COWELL William Wilson 1856-? [4]

$2 250 - €2 479 - £1 501 - FF16 261
Sailing in Narragnsett Bay Watercolour/paper (15x49cm 6x19in) Portsmouth NH 2000

COWEN Lionel J. XIX-XX [9]

$1 300 - €1 400 - £895 - FF9 184
Feeding the Birds Oil/canvas (66x45cm 26x18in) New-York 2001

COWEN William 1797-1861 [19]

$374 - €313 - £220 - FF2 056
«Aosta», with figures on the road Watercolour/paper (23x35cm 9x14in) London 1998

COWIE James 1886-1956 [28]

$3 573 - €3 413 - £2 200 - FF22 389
Alice Pencil/paper (32x26cm 12x10in) Edinburgh 1999

COWIESON Agnes M. XIX-XX [18]

$113 - €132 - £80 - FF864
Fallen thrush amongst Leaves Oil/board (22x29cm 8x11in) Cambridge 2001

COWIN Jack Lee 1947 [27]

$244 - €287 - £172 - FF1 884
«Shot Gun Shells» Etching (9.5x9cm 3x3in) Calgary, Alberta 2000

COWLES Russell 1887-1979 [10]

$3 250 - €2 777 - £1 966 - FF18 216
Still Life in the Artist's Studio with Plants, Fruit, Books and Dice Oil/canvas (104x71cm 40x27in) San-Francisco CA 1998

COWPER Frank Cadogan 1877-1958 [23]

$126 270 - €150 173 - £90 000 - FF985 068
The Cathedral Scene from Faust: Margaret tormented by the Evil Spirit Oil/canvas (190.5x144.5cm 75x56in) London 2000

$278 000 - €325 945 - £200 000 - FF2 138 060
Titania Sleeps: a Midsummer Night's Dream Oil/canvas (90x114cm 35x44in) London 2001

$55 600 - €65 189 - £40 000 - FF427 612
Mariana in the South Watercolour (50x33cm 19x12in) London 2001

COX Albert J. 1876-1955 [4]

$1 241 - €1 160 - £750 - FF7 607
Orient Line to Australia, Captain Cook Poster (100x62cm 39x24in) London 1999

COX David I 1783-1859 [423]

$4 170 - €4 203 - £2 600 - FF27 569
Returning from Market Oil/canvas (29x57.5cm 11x22in) London 2000

$5 240 - €4 792 - £3 200 - FF31 434
An Angler on the River Llugwy, Bettws-y-Coed Oil/canvas (38.5x26.5cm 15x10in) London 1998

$2 725 - €3 025 - £1 900 - FF19 845
Figures returning from Harvest Watercolour (42.5x57.5cm 16x22in) London 2001

COX David I or II XIX [5]

$472 - €454 - £293 - FF2 977
Breezy Day Aquarelle/papier (19x28cm 7x11in) Montréal 1999

COX David II 1809-1885 [176]

$582 - €681 - £415 - FF4 464
Cottage with Haycart/Cottage with Shepherd and Folk Watercolour/paper (38x56cm 14x22in) Amsterdam 2001

COX Garstin 1892-1933 [85]

$609 - €658 - £420 - FF4 313
The Lake from Bulmershe/View of Bulmershe Oil/canvas (45x90.5cm 17x35in) Billingshurst, West-Sussex 2001

$613 - €644 - £387 - FF4 227
Paysage montagneux Pastel/carton (60x100cm 23x39in) Bruxelles 2001

COX Graham 1941 [14]

$1 923 - €2 146 - £1 337 - FF14 077
Ethereal Quamby Oil/canvas/board (60x75.5cm 23x29in) Sydney 2001

COX Jack XX [115]

$418 - €388 - £250 - FF2 546
Morston Cut Oil/canvas (48x58cm 19x23in) Aylsham, Norfolk 2000

$225 - €228 - £140 - FF1 495
Beached Boat at Sunset Oil/canvas (20x25cm 8x10in) Aylsham, Norfolk 2000

$174 - €167 - £110 - FF1 094
Fishing Boats at the East Quay Wells-next-the-Sea Watercolour/paper (20x25cm 8x10in) Aylsham, Norfolk 1999

COX Jan 1919-1980 **[66]**
$13 200 - €12 394 - **£8 150** - FF81 300
La descente de croix Huile/toile (148x133cm 58x52in) Antwerpen 1999
$8 602 - €8 428 - **£5 304** - FF55 284
Studie for the Maenades Oil/canvas (114.5x74cm 45x29in) Lokeren 1999

COX John Rogers 1915 **[6]**
$600 - €576 - **£371** - FF3 779
Wheat Shocks Lithograph (22.5x30cm 8x11in) New-York 1999

COX Kenyon 1856-1919 **[7]**
$2 800 - €2 399 - **£1 683** - FF15 735
Serenity Oil/canvas (45x60cm 18x24in) Cincinnati OH 1998

COX Marjorie XX **[77]**
$172 - €193 - **£120** - FF1 268
Jan Pastel/paper (44x30.5cm 17x12in) London 2001

COX Mary Constance ?-c.1935 **[2]**
$935 - €1 067 - **£652** FF7 002
Highland Croft with Figures and a Cow and her Calf Watercolour/paper (38x53cm 15x21in) Berwick-upon-Tweed 2000

COX Neil 1955 **[7]**
$938 - €1 015 - **£650** - FF6 658
Woodcock in Natural Habitat, Winter Watercolour/paper (33x40cm 13x16in) Aylsham, Norfolk 2001

COX Palmer 1840-1924 **[6]**
$1 800 - €2 098 - **£1 246** - FF13 763
Brownies Hiding in Hollow Tree And Behind Boulder Ink (29x23cm 11x9in) New-York 2000

COX Tim 1957 **[1]**
$6 000 - €6 813 - **£4 168** - FF44 688
Listening for the Bell Mare Oil/board (30x40cm 12x16in) Dallas TX 2001

COX Walter I. 1866-1930 **[23]**
$1 600 - €1 485 - **£960** - FF9 740
Farming by the Sea Oil/canvas (66x86cm 26x34in) Milford CT 1999
$1 500 - €1 281 - **£907** - FF8 406
By the Sea Oil/board (30.5x38cm 12x14in) San-Francisco CA 1998

COX William, Will XX **[13]**
$740 - €864 - **£520** - FF5 666
Falling Asleep Oil/canvas (74x107cm 29x42in) Par, Cornwall 2000

COXIE de Goris XVII **[1]**
$39 330 - €43 448 - **£27 274** - FF285 000
Paysage panoramique avec Diane et Actéon Huile/toile (123x247cm 48x97in) Lille 2001

COXIE Michiel II c.1560-1616 **[1]**
$90 100 - €84 280 - **£55 760** - FF552 840
Le Mariage Mystique de la Vierge Huile/panneau (177x155cm 69x61in) Antwerpen 1999

COXON Raymond James 1896-1997 **[53]**
$489 - €440 - **£340** - FF3 595
«Pastoral» Oil/canvas (127x75cm 50x29in) London 2001
$690 - €774 - **£480** - FF5 075
«Kismet» Ink (50x36.5cm 19x14in) London 2001

COYNE Petah 1953 **[1]**
$2 400 - €2 576 - **£1 630** - FF16 897
«Untitled #735 Monks II» Gelatin silver print (50.5x76cm 19x29in) Beverly-Hills CA 2001

COYPEL Antoine 1661-1722 **[40]**
$60 000 - €64 181 - **£40 908** - FF421 002
The Triumph of Galatea Oil/canvas (111x144cm 43x56in) New-York 2001
$21 015 - €22 867 - **£14 445** - FF150 000
Vierge à l'Enfant Huile/toile (49x56.5cm 19x22in) Versailles 2001
$13 253 - €14 860 - **£9 000** - FF97 476
Judith and Holofernes Oil/canvas (23x18cm 9x7in) London 2000
$12 332 - €14 330 - **£8 666** - FF94 000
La conception de la Vierge Trois crayons/papier (45.5x55.5cm 17x21in) Paris 2001

COYPEL Charles-Antoine 1694-1752 **[56]**
$160 000 - €175 543 - **£106 288** - FF1 151 488
Andromache and Pyrrhus Oil/canvas (130.5x163cm 51x64in) New-York 2000
$50 000 - €49 977 - **£30 545** - FF327 825
The Fortune Teller Oil/canvas (89x68.5cm 35x26in) New-York 2000
$3 203 - €3 439 - **£2 143** - FF22 559
Minerva führt den jungen König Louis XV Pencil (38.2x27.6cm 15x10in) Bern 2000
$145 - €156 - **£96** - FF1 024
Quijote Grabado (30x32cm 11x12in) Madrid 2000

COYPEL Noël Nicolas 1690-1734 **[13]**
$68 506 - €64 073 - **£42 000** - FF420 294
Pan and Syrinx Oil/canvas (93x130cm 36x51in) London 1998
$47 052 - €54 882 - **£32 724** - FF360 000
Le reniement de Saint Pierre Huile/toile (123x96cm 48x37in) Bordeaux 2001

COYSEVOX Antoine 1640-1720 **[11]**
$14 699 - €16 121 - **£9 485** - FF105 750
La Vierge à l'Enfant Plâtre (54x20.5x17.5cm 21x8x6in) Monte-Carlo 2000

COZAR VIEDMA José 1944 **[39]**
$162 - €180 - **£108** - FF1 182
Portal de Valdigna, Valencia Oleo/tabla (26.5x19cm 10x7in) Madrid 2000

COZENS Alexander 1717-1786 **[28]**
$602 - €620 - **£380** - FF4 070
Study of a Tree Wash (20x26cm 7x10in) Cambridge 2000

COZENS John Robert 1752-1799 **[20]**
$35 863 - €38 496 - **£24 000** - FF252 518
View near Interlaken on the Banks of Lake Thun, Switzerland Pencil (24x36cm 9x14in) London 2000

COZZARELLI Guidoccio di Giovan. 1450-c.1516/17 **[2]**
$75 000 - €74 965 - **£45 817** - FF491 737
The Flight into Egypt Tempera/panel (28.5x57cm 11x22in) New-York 2000

COZZENS Frederick Schiller 1846-1928 **[100]**
$4 500 - €4 830 - **£3 011** - FF31 684
European Coastal Shipping Oil/board (30x44cm 12x17in) East-Dennis MA 2000
$1 200 - €1 119 - **£744** - FF7 339
Fishermen along the Shore Watercolour/paper (34.5x60cm 13x23in) New-York 1999
$175 - €188 - **£117** - FF1 236
Under Minot's Light Ledge Lithograph (35x50cm 14x20in) East-Dennis MA 2000

CRABEELS Florent Nicolas 1829-1896 **[50]**
- $5 405 - €6 353 - £3 747 - FF41 672
  At the Market Oil/canvas (39x54cm 15x21in)
  Amsterdam 2000
- $540 - €644 - £387 - FF4 227
  Grazende koeien (vaches au pâturage)
  Huile/panneau (20x31cm 7x12in) Antwerpen 2000

CRABETH Wouter Pietersz. II 1593-1644 **[5]**
- $9 250 - €9 589 - £5 550 - FF62 900
  Uomo morso da un granchio Olio/tela (87x107cm
  34x42in) Milano 2000
- $4 860 - €4 462 - £2 988 - FF29 268
  Scène de cabaret Huile/panneau (34x38cm 13x14in)
  Bruxelles 1999

CRADDOCK James XIX **[2]**
- $1 200 - €1 120 - £726 - FF7 349
  Ganges River Study Albumen print (24x58.5cm
  9x23in) New-York 1999

CRADOCK Marmaduke c.1660-1717 **[48]**
- $12 012 - €13 416 - £8 140 - FF88 000
  Scène de basse-cour Huile/toile (72x92cm 28x36in)
  Paris 2000
- $9 923 - €8 653 - £6 000 - FF56 758
  **Peacock, a Turkey, a Hen, Doves, Chicks and a
  Pheasant by a Lake** Oil/panel (32x39.5cm 12x15in)
  London 1998

CRAEN Laurens c.1620-1665/71 **[7]**
- $65 000 - €57 209 - £39 572 - FF375 264
  Peaches, Plums and Grapes in a Wicker Basket
  Oil/panel (56x67.5cm 22x26in) New-York 1999

CRAENHALS François 1926 **[16]**
- $219 - €213 - £136 - FF1 400
  **Pom et Teddy; reprise d'une case de la pl.36 de
  Zone Interdite** Encres couleurs/papier (35x27cm
  13x10in) Paris 1999

CRAESBEECK van Joos c.1605-1660 **[29]**
- $8 088 - €6 857 - £4 800 - FF44 980
  **Military Encampment with an Officer Reading a
  Letter** Oil/canvas/panel (70x82.5cm 27x32in) London
  1998
- $2 475 - €2 874 - £1 739 - FF18 855
  I vårdshusträdgården Oil/panel (26x23cm 10x9in)
  Stockholm 2001

CRAFFONARA Aurelio 1875-1945 **[25]**
- $4 350 - €4 509 - £2 610 - FF29 580
  Al mercato Olio/tela (32x41cm 12x16in) Genova 2000
- $1 000 - €1 037 - £600 - FF6 800
  Paesaggio Tecnica mista/carta (16x48cm 6x18in)
  Firenze 2000

CRAFT Percy Robert 1856-1934 **[30]**
- $1 027 - €945 - £616 - FF6 197
  Auf einem Bazar in Damaskus Öl/Leinwand
  (51x66cm 20x25in) Wien 1999
- $1 553 - €1 801 - £1 100 - FF11 813
  A Village Grain Market, Syria Oil/board
  (41.5x25.5cm 16x10in) London 2000

CRAFTY Victor Geruzez, dit 1840-1906 **[25]**
- $511 - €427 - £299 - FF2 800
  La rencontre des cavaliers dans la campagne
  Aquarelle/papier (27x44cm 10x17in) Provins 1998

CRAGG Tony 1949 **[113]**
- $16 710 - €14 123 - £10 000 - FF92 640
  «Paysage Suisse» Mixed media/panel (21x32cm
  8x12in) London 1998
- $26 043 - €25 347 - £16 000 - FF166 265
  Grey Moon Installation (394x222.5cm 155x87in)
  London 1999

- $4 734 - €4 581 - £3 000 - FF30 048
  Five standing Bottles Installation (30.5x100.5cm
  12x39in) London 1999
- $203 - €194 - £123 - FF1 274
  Ohne Titel Radierung (34x39.5cm 13x15in) Bielefeld
  1999

CRAHAY Albert 1881-1914 **[20]**
- $1 384 - €1 361 - £889 - FF8 929
  Three Fishermen overlooking the Sea Oil/panel
  (40x49cm 15x19in) Amsterdam 1999

CRAIG Charles 1846-1931 **[22]**
- $18 000 - €19 754 - £11 590 - FF129 578
  Meeting on the Mesa Oil/canvas (76x127.5cm
  29x50in) Beverly-Hills CA 2000
- $3 200 - €3 524 - £2 167 - FF23 149
  Colorado Landscape Oil/canvas (19x28cm 7x11in)
  New-York 2000

CRAIG Edward Henry Gordon 1872-1966 **[20]**
- $3 442 - €3 821 - £2 400 - FF25 067
  «Hunger» Ink (23.5x16.5cm 9x6in) London 2001
- $573 - €637 - £400 - FF4 178
  Figure near a Town Woodcut (24x17.5cm 9x6in)
  London 2001

CRAIG Henry Robertson 1916-1984 **[32]**
- $2 367 - €2 539 - £1 614 - FF16 658
  Promenade, South of France Oil/board (43x56cm
  16x22in) Dublin 2001
- $4 250 - €4 571 - £2 896 - FF29 984
  Boys playing at the River Oil/board (23x36cm
  9x14in) Dublin 2001

CRAIG James Humbert 1878-1944 **[193]**
- $12 004 - €11 380 - £7 500 - FF74 647
  Children playing by the River Oil/canvas
  (51.5x41.5cm 20x16in) London 1999
- $5 810 - €5 455 - £3 600 - FF35 784
  Cattle returning Oil/panel (29x38cm 11x14in)
  London 1999
- $1 147 - €1 333 - £806 - FF8 745
  Seascape/Hauling in the Boats Watercolour/paper
  (11x14cm 4x5in) Dublin 2001

CRAIG James Stephenson act.1854-? **[13]**
- $5 548 - €5 268 - £3 400 - FF34 555
  The Proud Mother Oil/canvas (66.5x79cm 26x31in)
  London 1999
- $4 279 - €4 446 - £2 700 - FF29 164
  Highland Courtship Oil/canvas (35.5x31cm 13x12in)
  London 2000

CRAIG Johnny XX **[2]**
- $6 000 - €6 440 - £4 015 - FF42 246
  The Vault Keeper Specialty Painting
  Oil/canvas/board (35.5x45.5cm 13x17in) New-York
  2000
- $1 500 - €1 610 - £1 003 - FF10 561
  **Ad Page from Three Dimensional EC Classics
  No.1** Ink (45.5x33cm 17x12in) New-York 2000

CRAIG Sybil 1901-1989 **[49]**
- $198 - €219 - £132 - FF1 436
  Near Black Rock Acrylic (35x45cm 13x17in)
  Melbourne 2000
- $279 - €260 - £172 - FF1 707
  Nude Study Pencil (12x9cm 4x3in) Melbourne 1999

CRAIG Thomas Bigelow 1849-1924 **[61]**
- $2 600 - €2 219 - £1 554 - FF14 557
  The Close of a Showery Day Oil/canvas (60x86cm
  24x34in) New-York 1998

$1 500 - €1 489 - £920 - FF9 767
Cows at the River Oil/canvas (25x35cm 10x14in)
Mystic CT 2000

CRAIG William 1829-1875 [12]
$800 - €859 - £535 - FF5 632
Indian Brook Falls near Cold Spring Watercolour, gouache (33x23cm 13x9in) Bolton MA 2000

CRAIG William Marshall 1765-1834 [15]
$1 326 - €1 144 - £800 - FF7 504
«Little Blue Boy» Wash/paper (7.5x8cm 2x3in)
London 1998

CRAIG-MARTIN Michael 1941 [7]
$14 790 - €13 613 - £8 877 - FF89 298
Untitled Acrylic/canvas (199x152.5cm 78x60in)
Amsterdam 1999
$3 500 - €3 757 - £2 342 - FF24 646
Small Table Painting (87.5x86.5cm 34x34in) Beverly-Hills CA 2000

CRAIG-WALLACE Robert 1886-1969 [41]
$6 315 - €7 103 - £4 400 - FF46 593
In the Bitanic Gardens, Glasgow Oil/canvas
(48x58cm 18x22in) Edinburgh 2001
$1 992 - €2 314 - £1 400 - FF15 181
Rustic Interlude/Farmyard near Lanark, Scotland Oil/canvas/board (30.5x38cm 12x14in)
London 2001
$397 - €370 - £240 - FF2 429
«Yacht Racing, Hunters Quay, Firth of Clyde»
Watercolour (35.5x45.5cm 13x17in) Glasgow 1998

CRALI Tullio 1910 [47]
$6 600 - €5 702 - £3 300 - FF37 400
«Assalto di motori» Olio/tela (60x80cm 23x31in)
Milano 1999
$3 000 - €3 110 - £1 800 - FF20 400
Elementi essenziali di aeropaesaggio Olio/carto-ne (34.5x43.5cm 13x17in) Vercelli 1999
$1 500 - €1 555 - £900 - FF10 200
Eliche Gouache/carta (24x33cm 9x12in) Milano 1999

CRAMB John XIX [1]
$14 915 - €14 483 - £9 215 - FF95 000
Palestine Tirage albuminé (16.5x22cm 6x8in) Paris
1999

CRAMER Konrad 1888-1963 [30]
$35 000 - €39 743 - £23 954 - FF260 694
Improvisation Oil/board (41x48cm 16x18in) New-York 2000
$2 250 - €2 098 - £1 395 - FF13 764
Richfield Ink/paper (32x48.5cm 12x19in) New-York
1999

CRAMER Peter 1726-1782 [15]
$1 977 - €1 744 - £1 190 - FF11 443
Sydtysk landskab/Wilhelm Tells Kapel Oil/canvas
(14x20cm 5x7in) København 1998

CRAMER Rie 1887-1977 [27]
$749 - €726 - £467 - FF4 762
View of Montastruc Pastel/paper (15x11.5cm 5x4in)
Amsterdam 1999
$144 - €159 - £97 - FF1 041
Vrouw zich buigend over een put Etching
(19.9x17.2cm 7x6in) Haarlem 2000

CRANACH Lucas I 1472-1553 [161]
$418 404 - €449 122 - £280 000 - FF2 946 048
Hercules at the Court of Omphale Oil/panel
(83.5x120.5cm 32x47in) London 2000
$34 222 - €38 859 - £23 780 - FF254 896
Lucretia Oil/panel (21.5x16.5cm 8x6in) Köln 2001

$1 152 - €1 140 - £720 - FF7 477
Marcus Curtius Plunging into the Chasm
Woodcut (33x23.5cm 12x9in) London 1999

CRANACH Lucas II 1515-1586 [22]
$139 897 - €156 857 - £95 000 - FF1 028 916
The Lamentation Oil/panel (49x74.5cm 19x29in)
London 2000
$65 000 - €60 154 - £40 560 - FF401 141
Saint Paul Oil/panel (20.5x15cm 8x5in) New-York
1999
$240 - €245 - £150 - FF1 609
Luther Martin, Ganzfigurig Woodcut (16x11.5cm
6x4in) Köln 2000

CRANCH Christopher P. 1813-1892 [11]
$4 250 - €4 520 - £2 686 - FF29 651
A View of Laurel Hills, New Jersey Oil/canvas
(35x53cm 14x21in) New-York 2000

CRANDALL Reed XX [1]
$5 000 - €5 367 - £3 346 - FF35 205
Genesis: Six page story from Weird Science Fantasy No.29 Ink (45x33.5cm 17x13in) New-York
2000

CRANDELL John Bradshaw 1896-1966 [15]
$6 500 - €7 280 - £4 516 - FF47 756
Seated Woman in blue Dress holding Fan
Pastel/paper (104x76cm 41x30in) New-York 2001

CRANE Alan Horton 1901-1969 [18]
$150 - €154 - £94 - FF1 012
Amecameca Pilgrims/Clouds and Spires/Haunted Garden Lithograph (34x24cm
13x9in) Bolton MA 2000

CRANE Bruce 1857-1937 [121]
$6 000 - €6 566 - £4 138 - FF43 072
Spring in the Valley Oil/canvas (35.5x51cm 13x20in)
New-York 2001
$2 400 - €2 498 - £1 506 - FF16 384
Evening Color Oil/canvas (30x40cm 12x16in)
Chicago IL 2000

CRANE Walter 1845-1915 [79]
$39 240 - €36 813 - £24 242 - FF241 480
Allegorie der drei Erdteile Afrika, Asien und Europa Oil/panel (145x125cm 57x49in) Ahlden 1999
$4 869 - €4 682 - £3 000 - FF30 715
Maiden and youth at a Fountain Oil/board
(53x36cm 20x14in) London 1999
$1 043 - €977 - £649 - FF6 407
View of Holland Street, London, from the artists window Watercolour (49x35.5cm 19x13in) London
1999
$749 - €649 - £452 - FF4 256
La Danseuse aux Cymbales Lithograph
(43.5x31cm 17x12in) New-York 1998

CRANE William H. XIX-XX [2]
$5 977 - €6 416 - £4 000 - FF42 086
Syracuse Theatre, Sicily Watercolour (25x34cm
9x13in) London 2000

CRANS Johan Michael S. 1830-1908 [5]
$3 654 - €4 346 - £2 604 - FF28 508
An der Wiege Öl/Leinwand (102x81cm 40x31in)
Köln 2000

CRANSTOUN James Hall 1821-1907 [14]
$1 761 - €1 741 - £1 100 - FF11 423
Loch Lomond Oil/canvas (41x61.5cm 16x24in)
Glasgow 1999

CRAPELET Louis Amable 1822-1867 **[104]**
- $26 188 - €29 728 - **£18 193** - FF195 000
  Vue d'Egypte sur les bords du Nil Tempera (187x382cm 73x150in) Grasse 2001
- $45 745 - €53 357 - **£31 815** - FF350 000
  Nubie, Haute Egypte Huile/toile (66x96cm 25x37in) Paris 2000
- $3 198 - €2 729 - **£1 926** - FF17 900
  Caravane devant les trois pyramides Huile/carton (24x30cm 9x11in) Provins 1999
- $1 045 - €1 220 - **£727** - FF8 000
  Le vieux quartier du Caire Aquarelle/papier (28.5x21.5cm 11x8in) Paris 2000

CRAS Monique 1910 **[150]**
- $23 395 - €22 689 - **£14 725** - FF148 830
  Nemadis Women, Oualata Oil/canvas (194x252cm 76x99in) Amsterdam 1999
- $2 049 - €2 439 - **£1 419** - FF16 000
  Les deux guerriers assis Huile/toile (92x65cm 36x25in) Paris 2000
- $476 - €534 - **£332** - FF3 500
  Remparts de ville Aquarelle/papier (18x42cm 7x16in) Paris 2001

CRAVEN William, 2nd Earl 1809-1866 **[55]**
- $3 974 - €4 427 - **£2 600** - FF29 040
  Thatched Cottage with Two Figures Albumen print (23x28.5cm 9x11in) Devon 2000

CRAVO Jorge XX **[1]**
- $1 600 - €1 596 - **£998** - FF10 469
  Flowers Tapestry (140x125cm 55x49in) Cincinnati OH 2000

CRAVO NETO Mario 1947 **[16]**
- $3 000 - €3 068 - **£1 890** - FF20 126
  Man carrying fish Silver print (44x44cm 17x17in) New-York 2000

CRAWFORD Edmund Thornton 1806-1885 **[38]**
- $3 011 - €3 129 - **£1 900** - FF20 522
  Dundas Castle Oil/board (40.5x56cm 15x22in) London 2000
- $1 578 - €1 637 - **£1 000** - FF10 739
  Shipping in a Dutch Estuary Oil/board (16.5x24cm 6x9in) Penzance, Cornwall 2000

CRAWFORD James W. 1832 **[2]**
- $7 000 - €5 997 - **£4 208** - FF39 337
  Brooke Trout White Mountains, NH Oil/canvas (30x50cm 12x20in) Cleveland OH 1998

CRAWFORD Ralston 1906-1978 **[67]**
- $26 000 - €21 935 - **£15 251** - FF143 884
  «Construction #6» Oil/canvas (71x102cm 27x40in) New-York 1998
- $600 - €568 - **£372** - FF3 725
  Box Car, Red Yellow and Black Color lithograph (42.5x26cm 16x10in) New-York 1999
- $5 000 - €4 701 - **£3 096** - FF30 838
  Girders Silver print (16x24cm 6x9in) New-York 1999

CRAWFORD Robert Cree 1842-1924 **[33]**
- $1 105 - €1 290 - **£780** - FF8 463
  «Farm in Sark» Oil/canvas (33x49.5cm 12x19in) Toronto 2000

CRAWFORD Will 1869-1944 **[7]**
- $1 760 - €1 501 - **£1 061** - FF9 849
  «Don't blame the motorist» Ink/paper (44x72cm 17x28in) New-York 1998

CRAWFORD William Caldwell 1879-1960 **[13]**
- $12 352 - €11 749 - **£7 500** - FF77 067
  Picnic in Lothian, with the Artist's Wife Janet,Children Joan & Robert Oil/canvas (102x127cm 40x50in) Edinburgh 1999
- $3 294 - €3 133 - **£2 000** - FF20 551
  North Uist, Outer Hebrides Oil/canvas (61x91.5cm 24x36in) Edinburgh 1999

CRAWHALL Joseph II 1861-1913 **[37]**
- $1 827 - €1 564 - **£1 100** - FF10 257
  Sketch of a Black Cat Watercolour (15x11cm 5x4in) Banbury, Oxfordshire 1998

CRAXTON John 1922 **[65]**
- $10 827 - €9 251 - **£6 500** - FF60 682
  Boy on a Wall Oil/board (122x56.5cm 48x22in) London 1998
- $13 267 - €14 661 - **£9 200** - FF96 167
  «Two Greek Sailors Dancing» Oil/canvas (30.5x40.5cm 12x15in) London 2001
- $4 200 - €4 885 - **£3 000** - FF32 045
  Black Landscape Watercolour, gouache (45x51.5cm 17x20in) London 2001

CRAYER de Gaspard 1584-1669 **[22]**
- $65 000 - €57 209 - **£39 572** - FF375 264
  The Deposition with Saints Francis of Assisi and Elizabeth of Hungary Oil/canvas (216x163cm 85x64in) New-York 1999
- $37 588 - €43 772 - **£26 000** - FF287 125
  Portrait of Frederick de Marteelaer (1584-1670) Oil/canvas (104x79cm 40x31in) London 2000

CREDIDO di Robert XX **[4]**
- $1 939 - €2 287 - **£1 363** - FF15 000
  Jazz Huile/toile (92x73cm 36x28in) Garches 2000

CREGAN Martin 1788-1870 **[14]**
- $1 892 - €2 032 - **£1 266** - FF13 326
  Edward Henry Hoare Oil/canvas (74x61cm 29x24in) Dublin 2000

CREHAY Gérard Antoine 1844-1936 **[23]**
- $487 - €446 - **£297** - FF2 926
  Zondagswandeling in het park Huile/panneau (12x17cm 4x6in) Antwerpen 1999

CREHEN Charles G. 1829-c.1891 **[1]**
- $662 - €734 - **£449** - FF4 812
  Modern Street view of Point Levi, and Quebec in The Distance Lithograph (26.5x36.5cm 10x14in) Toronto 2000

CREIXAMS PICO Pere / Pedro 1893-1965 **[327]**
- $3 840 - €3 604 - **£2 400** - FF23 640
  Dos gitanas Oleo/lienzo (115x110cm 45x43in) Madrid 1999
- $2 085 - €2 062 - **£1 300** - FF13 529
  Harlequin Oil/canvas (73x60cm 28x23in) Leyburn, North Yorkshire 1999
- $594 - €661 - **£407** - FF4 334
  Desnudo femenino Oleo/lienzo (22x33cm 8x12in) Barcelona 2001
- $205 - €244 - **£141** - FF1 600
  Corrida Aquarelle, gouache/papier (42x21cm 16x8in) Saint-Dié 2000

CRELINGER Marie XIX **[3]**
- $1 752 - €2 035 - **£1 232** - FF13 347
  Vogelnest im Schnee Öl/Leinwand (35x43cm 13x16in) Wien 2001

CREMA Giovan Battista 1883-1964 **[23]**
- $8 000 - €8 293 - **£4 800** - FF54 400
  Tra i vasi di fiori Olio/legno (101x61cm 39x24in) Roma 2000

$2 100 - €2 177 - **£1 260** - FF14 280
Nudo di donna Olio/tela (27.5x30cm 10x11in)
Milano 1999

CREMER Fritz 1906-1993 **[49]**
$3 299 - €3 988 - **£2 303** - FF26 160
Arbeitermutter Bronze (52x22.5x27cm 20x8x10in)
Berlin 2000
$73 - €82 - **£52** - FF536
Frauen und Mädchen Lithographie (27.5x41cm
10x16in) Berlin 2001

CREMER Jan 1940 **[81]**
$13 804 - €12 706 - **£8 285** - FF83 344
Tulips in Blue Mixed media/canvas (120x150cm
47x59in) Amsterdam 1999
$1 268 - €1 361 - **£848** - FF8 929
Untitled Oil/panel (90x73cm 35x28in) Amsterdam
2000
$1 359 - €1 588 - **£970** - FF10 418
Ibiza Wax crayon (64x49cm 25x19in) Amsterdam 2001
$360 - €363 - **£224** - FF2 381
Tulpen III Serigraph (73.5x54.5cm 28x21in)
Amsterdam 2000

CRÉMIERE Léon 1831-1913 **[12]**
$931 - €1 022 - **£600** - FF6 707
**Chef Touareg venu à Paris pour engager des
relations commerciales** Albumen print (24x18cm
9x7in) London 2000

CREMIEUX Édouard 1856-1944 **[19]**
$2 335 - €2 134 - **£1 429** - FF14 000
Saint-Cyr Les Lecques Huile/toile (46x55cm
18x21in) Arles 1999

CREMONA Italo 1905-1979 **[31]**
$3 120 - €2 695 - **£1 560** - FF17 680
Nuda in piedi Olio/tavola (75.5x23.5cm 29x9in)
Torino 1999
$1 200 - €1 244 - **£720** - FF8 160
Figura femminile in un interno Olio/cartone
(34.5x23.5cm 13x9in) Torino 2000

CREMONA Tranquillo 1837-1878 **[14]**
$13 452 - €11 621 - **£6 726** - FF76 228
Ritratto di Amalia Sirtori Olio/tela (54x45cm
21x17in) Milano 1999
$2 359 - €2 000 - **£1 400** - FF13 119
Study of a Pageboy Watercolour (16.5x11cm 6x4in)
Billingshurst, West-Sussex 1998

CREMONINI Leonardo 1925 **[84]**
$39 910 - €39 637 - **£24 856** - FF260 000
Les silences fragiles Huile/toile (73x192.5cm
28x75in) Paris 1999
$14 356 - €12 958 - **£8 848** - FF85 000
Sans titre Huile/toile (50x65cm 19x25in) Paris 1999
$2 600 - €3 369 - **£1 950** - FF22 100
«Il Reno a Basilea» Olio/tela/cartone (22.5x29cm
8x11in) Milano 2000
$200 - €207 - **£120** - FF1 360
Tra le diagonali del sonno Acquaforte, acquatinta a
colori (43x25.5cm 16x10in) Prato 1999

CRENIER Camille Henri 1880-1914/18 **[1]**
$3 513 - €3 354 - **£2 195** - FF22 000
Devant le crépuscule Marbre (67x52x63cm
26x20x24in) Orléans 1999

CREPAX Guido 1933 **[19]**
$375 - €389 - **£225** - FF2 550
«Peppercorns» Inchiostro/carta (39x32cm 15x13in)
Torino 2001

CRÉPIN Fleury Joseph 1875-1948 **[21]**
$7 780 - €8 690 - **£5 204** - FF57 000
Temple No.13 Huile/toile (47.5x29.5cm 18x11in)
Paris 2000

CRÉPIN Louis-Philippe 1772-1851 **[51]**
$19 669 - €19 818 - **£12 259** - FF130 000
Paysage de rivière à la lavandière et au pêcheur
Huile/toile (147x116cm 57x45in) Nantes 2000
$492 - €570 - **£347** - FF3 739
Canal animé Huile/toile (30x55cm 11x21in) Bruxelles
2000
$2 586 - €3 049 - **£1 818** - FF20 000
**Paysage de sous-bois à la cascade animée de
personnages** Huile/panneau (26.5x19.5cm 10x7in)
Paris 2000
$6 301 - €6 250 - **£3 919** - FF41 000
La bataille de Navarin Encre (31x53cm 12x20in)
Paris 1999

CREPS Olivier 1954 **[2]**
$2 284 - €2 134 - **£1 409** - FF14 000
Cinq demi-Lunes Construction (14x21.5cm 5x8in)
Bourg-en-Bresse 1999

CRESCIMBENI Angelo 1734-1781 **[2]**
$1 800 - €1 555 - **£900** - FF10 200
Ritratto di gentildonna Pastelli/carta (59x44.5cm
23x17in) Roma 1999

CRESPELLE Émile 1831-? **[3]**
$11 551 - €11 891 - **£7 277** - FF78 000
Scène bachique d'après Thomas Couture
Huile/toile (130x205cm 51x80in) Paris 2000

CRESPI Antonio c.1704-1781 **[4]**
$15 200 - €19 696 - **£11 400** - FF129 200
**Pesche, uva, albicocche, pere e vaso di
fiori/Uva, melograni, funghi** Olio/tela (92.5x127cm
36x50in) Milano 2000

CRESPI Daniele 1598-1630 **[22]**
$4 500 - €3 887 - **£2 250** - FF25 500
Studio di demone Matita/carta (27.5x25cm 10x9in)
Milano 1999

CRESPI Enrico 1854-1929 **[6]**
$4 651 - €3 980 - **£2 800** - FF26 110
Vigilia del Natale Oil/panel (39.5x29cm 15x11in)
London 1998

CRESPI IL CERANO Giovanni Battista 1575-1633
[9]
$20 390 - €19 910 - **£13 000** - FF130 598
**Eight Studies of Hands/Study of Saint Francis
adoring the Cross** Red chalk (21x28cm 8x11in)
London 1999

CRESPI LO SPAGNOLO Giuseppe Maria 1665-
1747 **[37]**
$135 000 - €139 948 - **£81 000** - FF918 000
**Le ninfe di Diana disarmano gli amorini addor-
mentati** Olio/tela (151x178cm 59x70in) Milano 2000
$38 000 - €40 582 - **£25 893** - FF266 201
The Flight into Egypt Oil/canvas (56.5x41.5cm
22x16in) New-York 2001
$4 165 - €4 318 - **£2 499** - FF28 322
S. Francesco di Paola Olio/tela (31.5x25cm 12x9in)
Venezia 2000
$3 100 - €3 214 - **£1 860** - FF21 080
Studio di putti Matita (13.5x17cm 5x6in) Milano
2001

CRESPIN Adolphe 1851-1944 **[24]**
$4 224 - €3 966 - **£2 608** - FF26 016
Vue de plage Aquarelle/papier (27x37cm 10x14in)
Antwerpen 1999

CRESPIN Louis Charles 1892-1953 **[16]**
$2 322 - €2 231 - £1 431 - FF14 634
Vue du Marly Huile/toile (22.5x37.5cm 8x14in)
Bruxelles 1999

CRESPY LE PRINCE de Charles Édouard 1784-? **[5]**
$37 500 - €34 715 - £22 638 - FF227 718
Julie and Saint-Preux on Lake Geneva Oil/canvas
(97.5x129.5cm 38x50in) New-York 1999

CRESS Frederick 1938 **[63]**
$1 486 - €1 596 - £995 - FF10 468
Eaters 3 Acrylic (50x66cm 19x25in) Melbourne 2000
$368 - €416 - £259 - FF2 726
Seated Figure Watercolour (54.5x37cm 21x14in)
Malvern, Victoria 2001
$74 - €78 - £47 - FF512
Apple & Pear Color lithograph (76x56cm 29x22in)
Sydney 2000

CRESSWELL William Nichol 1822-1888 **[31]**
$475 - €451 - £297 - FF2 957
Boaters on a Beach/Coastal Storm
Watercolour/paper (19.5x29cm 7x11in) Washington
1999

CRESTI IL PASSIGNANO Domenico 1558-1638 **[10]**
$4 500 - €4 490 - £2 739 - FF29 452
The Finding of the True Cross Ink (20.5x22cm
8x8in) New-York 2000

CRESTON René-Yves 1898-1964 **[38]**
$463 - €488 - £305 - FF3 200
Pichet «Jistr» à décor de bretons en goguette
Céramique (H21cm H8in) Douarnenez 2000
$509 - €427 - £299 - FF2 800
Paysages de la région de Guérande, (étude de cheval de dos) Gouache/papier (42x53cm 16x20in)
Rennes 1998
$364 - €305 - £214 - FF2 000
Le port de Saint-Nazaire, le Normandie en construction Gravure bois (27.5x78cm 10x30in)
Rennes 1998

CRESTY Marguerite 1841-? **[2]**
$7 500 - €7 558 - £4 675 - FF49 575
Three-Paneled Screen Decorated with Flowers
Oil/canvas (150.5x45cm 59x17in) New-York 2000

CRESWELL Alexander XX **[8]**
$521 - €593 - £360 - FF3 893
Carrick Castle, Argyll Watercolour/paper (49x41cm
19x16in) London 2000

CRESWICK Thomas 1811-1869 **[141]**
$20 854 - €21 014 - £13 000 - FF137 846
View of Windsor Castle Oil/canvas (96.5x147.5cm
37x58in) London 2000
$6 492 - €6 243 - £4 000 - FF40 953
The old Mill Oil/board (48.5x61cm 19x24in) London
1999
$1 238 - €1 448 - £870 - FF9 500
Aux abords de la chaumière Huile/toile (35x35cm
13x13in) Paris 2000
$865 - €1 017 - £600 - FF6 672
A Herder with Cattle and a Dog on a Wooded Track Watercolour (54x39.5cm 21x15in) London 2000

CRETEN Georges 1887-1966 **[149]**
$832 - €793 - £505 - FF5 203
Femme au poisson Huile/panneau (67x52cm
26x20in) Bruxelles 1999
$405 - €372 - £250 - FF2 439
Femme assise Fusain/papier (105x70cm 41x27in)
Bruxelles 1999

CRETEN Victor 1878-1966 **[58]**
$85 - €99 - £58 - FF650
Architectures et paysages Aquarelle/papier
(33x24cm 12x9in) Liège 2000

CRETI IL DONATINO Donato 1671-1749 **[60]**
$2 640 - €2 281 - £1 320 - FF14 960
Studio per l'Adorazione dei Magi Inchiostro
(23x17cm 9x6in) Milano 1999

CRETOT-DUVAL Raymond 1895-1986 **[12]**
$1 932 - €2 134 - £1 339 - FF14 000
Porte de ville au Maroc Huile/panneau (33x41cm
12x16in) Paris 2001

CREVEL René 1900-1935 **[14]**
$1 690 - €1 829 - £1 158 - FF12 000
Automne Aquarelle/papier (65x50cm 25x19in) Paris
2001

CREWDSON Gregory 1962 **[13]**
$1 900 - €1 838 - £1 171 - FF12 059
Untitled Print in colors (51x61cm 20x24in) New-York
1999
$3 942 - €4 654 - £2 800 - FF30 529
Untitled Type C color print (101.5x127cm 39x50in)
London 2001

CRIDLAND Helen XIX-XX **[2]**
$17 000 - €20 217 - £12 115 - FF132 617
Dandie Dinmont and Puppy Oil/canvas (51x77cm
20x30in) New-York 1999

CRILEY Theodore Morrow 1880-1930 **[27]**
$6 000 - €6 440 - £4 015 - FF42 246
Orchard in Bloom Oil/canvas (53x66cm 20x25in)
San-Francisco CA 2000

CRIMINI Gino XIX **[1]**
$8 000 - €7 662 - £5 034 - FF50 262
Frigates in stormy seas Oil/canvas (58x73cm
23x29in) Portland ME 1999

CRIPPA Roberto 1921-1972 **[529]**
$7 500 - €7 775 - £4 500 - FF51 000
Geometrie Olio/tavola (80x150cm 31x59in) Vercelli
2000
$3 150 - €3 265 - £1 890 - FF21 420
Oiseau Tecnica mista (73x92cm 28x36in) Prato 2000
$1 600 - €2 073 - £1 200 - FF13 600
Oiseau Tecnica mista (40x33cm 15x12in) Milano 2001
$3 000 - €3 110 - £1 800 - FF20 400
Composizione Bronzo (H41.5cm H16in) Milano
$2 070 - €1 788 - £1 380 - FF11 730
La luna nel canneto China/carta (98x147cm
38x57in) Milano 1998
$480 - €622 - £360 - FF4 080
Composizione con testa e natura morta
Monotype (30x39.5cm 11x15in) Milano 2001

CRIPPS Peter 1948 **[2]**
$6 749 - €6 997 - £4 049 - FF45 898
«Spirali» Olio/tela (70x78cm 27x30in) Milano 1999

CRISCONIO Luigi 1893-1946 **[18]**
$640 - €829 - £480 - FF5 440
Napoli Olio/tavola (17x23cm 6x9in) Napoli 2000

CRISENOY de Pierre Émile XIX **[3]**
$4 910 - €4 537 - £3 061 - FF31 862
Französische Kriegsschiffe und Segelboote im Hafen von Cherbourg Öl/Leinwand (40x65cm
15x25in) Ahlden 1999

CRISP James Alexandre 1879-1962 **[3]**
- **$938** - €1 004 - **£618** - FF6 586
  Kookaburras on a Branch Watercolour/paper (54.5x24cm 21x9in) Woollahra, Sydney 2000

CRISS Francis 1901-1973 **[19]**
- **$2 500** - €2 954 - **£1 771** - FF19 377
  Nembutal Broadside Oil/masonite (58.5x89cm 23x35in) Boston MA 2000
- **$3 250** - €3 640 - **£2 258** - FF23 878
  «El Station» Oil/canvas (40x25cm 16x10in) Cincinnati OH 2001
- **$4 000** - €4 542 - **£2 737** - FF29 793
  Study for Third Avenue El Gouache (19x21.5cm 7x8in) New-York 2000

CRISTALL Joshua c.1767-1847 **[50]**
- **$484** - €445 - **£300** - FF2 916
  A Fisherman on a Lake with a Town beyond Watercolour (15x22.5cm 5x8in) London 1999

CRISTELLYS Vincente XIX-XX **[8]**
- **$132** - €152 - **£93** - FF1 000
  «La corrida de la peur» Affiche (120x160cm 47x62in) Paris 2001

CRISTIANO Renato 1926 **[4]**
- **$2 337** - €2 447 - **£1 468** - FF16 051
  Balinese Icon Mixed media/board (40x30cm 15x11in) Singapore 2000

CRISTOFORO DI BENEDETTO XV **[1]**
- **$60 000** - €51 833 - **£30 000** - FF340 000
  Tre predelle, Storie della vita della Vergine Tempera/tavola (29.5x45cm 11x17in) Milano 1999

CRITCHER Catharine Carter 1879-1964 **[2]**
- **$96 739** - €91 703 - **£60 432** - FF601 533
  Light Lightning Oil/canvas (76x63.5cm 29x25in) Washington 1999

CRITE Allan Rohan 1910 **[31]**
- **$900** - €861 - **£548** - FF5 645
  Nativity Mixed media (51x38cm 20x14in) Boston MA 1999
- **$3 500** - €3 921 - **£2 437** - FF25 723
  «David and bathsheba»/«Eve» Relief (10x5cm 4x2in) Watertown MA 2001
- **$2 400** - €2 071 - **£1 442** - FF13 582
  The Woman in Red Watercolour/paper (37x35.5cm 14x10in) Boston MA 1998
- **$3 000** - €3 406 - **£2 053** - FF22 345
  I Love a Parade Lithograph (20.5x25.5cm 8x10in) New-York 2000

CRIVELLI Carlo 1430/35-1494/95 **[3]**
- **$60 000** - €64 181 - **£40 908** - FF421 002
  Saint Lawrence Tempera/panneau (57x38cm 22x14in) New-York 2001
- **$150 000** - €160 193 - **£102 210** - FF1 050 795
  A Male Saint holding a Book Tempera/panel (27x20.5cm 10x8in) New-York 2001

CRIVELLI Giovanni Crivellino ?-1760 **[22]**
- **$18 917** - €17 532 - **£11 293** - FF115 000
  Nature morte aux oiseaux Huile/toile (111x166cm 43x65in) Paris 1999
- **$4 679** - €4 579 - **£3 000** - FF30 036
  Hawk Flushing Ducks Oil/canvas (58.5x72.5cm 23x28in) London 1999

CRIVELLI IL CRIVELLONE Angelo Maria ?-1730/60? **[30]**
- **$22 089** - €24 767 - **£15 000** - FF162 460
  A Peacock, Jay and Pigeons in a Landscape/Herons and their Young Oil/canvas (110x160cm 43x62in) London 2000

- **$8 500** - €8 812 - **£5 100** - FF57 800
  Natura morta Olio/tela (75x100cm 29x39in) Milano 1999

CROATTO Bruno 1875-1948 **[51]**
- **$4 800** - €4 147 - **£3 200** - FF27 200
  Signora in rosso Olio/tela (91x44cm 35x17in) Roma 1998
- **$1 011** - €1 049 - **£606** - FF6 878
  Figure nel parco Olio/cartone (19.5x22cm 7x8in) Milano 1999

CROCETTI Venanzio 1913 **[5]**
- **$11 500** - €11 922 - **£6 900** - FF78 200
  La fanciulla del frutteto Bronzo (H133cm H52in) Roma 2000

CROCICCHI Luca 1958 **[2]**
- **$2 000** - €2 592 - **£1 500** - FF17 000
  Le ali della libertà Olio/tavola (45x50cm 17x19in) Vercelli 2000

CROCKART James Bisset 1885-1974 **[2]**
- **$1 088** - €1 253 - **£750** - FF8 221
  «Canadian Pacific, Banff in the Canadian Rockies» Poster (102x64cm 40x25in) London 2000

CROCKER Charles Matthew 1877-1950 **[4]**
- **$1 500** - €1 673 - **£1 008** - FF10 971
  Landscape with Cypress Trees and Lake Pastel/paper (50x60cm 20x24in) Portsmouth NH 2000

CROCKER John Denison 1823-1879 **[6]**
- **$6 750** - €7 439 - **£4 498** - FF48 798
  Riverscape with Westerners on Shore Trading with Indians Oil/canvas (71x99cm 28x39in) Portsmouth NH 2000

CROCKFORD Duncan MacKinnon 1920-1991 **[72]**
- **$1 105** - €1 290 - **£780** - FF8 463
  «Summer Along the Ghost River, Alberta» Oil/canvas (40.5x51cm 15x20in) Calgary, Alberta 2000
- **$720** - €857 - **£496** - FF5 619
  Seashore Scene Oil/canvas (30x36cm 7x14in) Calgary, Alberta 2000

CRODEL Charles, Carl 1894-1973 **[80]**
- **$198** - €220 - **£137** - FF1 442
  Mädchen mit Ziegen Farblithographie (35x26cm 13x10in) Heidelberg 2001

CRODEL Paul Eduard 1862-1928 **[27]**
- **$360** - €409 - **£246** - FF2 683
  Vor dem Wirtshaus Öl/Leinwand (50x55cm 19x21in) München 2000

CROEGAERT Georges 1848-1923 **[102]**
- **$29 170** - €27 185 - **£18 000** - FF178 322
  A Pinch od Snuff Oil/panel (46x37.5cm 18x14in) London 2000
- **$8 349** - €8 181 - **£5 148** - FF53 658
  Dans le boudoir Oil/panel (32.5x24.5cm 12x9in) Lokeren 1999
- **$1 751** - €1 696 - **£1 100** - FF11 123
  Just a little Juice Watercolour/paper (27x23cm 10x9in) London 1999

CROFOOT Russel XX **[2]**
- **$4 000** - €3 831 - **£2 471** - FF25 127
  The Scorpion Wearing Green Mask, Book Jacket Cover Illustration Gouache/paper (59x40cm 23x16in) New-York 1999

CROFT Arthur 1828-? **[21]**
- **$1 001** - €941 - **£620** - FF6 175
  The Glacier Watercolour/paper (37x47.5cm 14x18in) London 1999

C

CROFT Marianne Dalton XIX [1]
$3 465 - €3 631 - **£2 300** - FF23 818
Travellers in a Classical Wooded Landscape/Goatherders in Landscape Oil/panel
(30.5x39.5cm 12x15in) London 2000

CROFTS Ernest 1847-1911 [64]
$29 196 - €28 146 - **£18 000** - FF184 627
The Battle of Waterloo Oil/canvas (157.5x124.5cm 62x49in) London 1999
$11 528 - €11 240 - **£7 000** - FF73 731
George II at the Battle of Dettingen Oil/canvas (67x126cm 26x49in) London 2000
$3 565 - €2 940 - **£2 100** - FF19 283
The Guide at Marston Oil/canvas (33x28cm 12x11in) Newbury, Berkshire 1998

CROÏN Jos 1894-1949 [28]
$1 209 - €1 361 - **£833** - FF8 929
Bridges over the Seine in Paris Oil/canvas (76x62cm 29x24in) Maastricht 2000

CROISSANT Auguste 1870-1941 [22]
$922 - €1 022 - **£640** - FF6 707
«Maxburg, Hambacher Schloss» Öl/Leinwand (30x39.5cm 11x15in) Heidelberg 2001

CROISSANT Eugen 1898-1957 [30]
$690 - €792 - **£472** - FF5 198
Segelboot am Ufer des Chiemsees Watercolour (47.5x62.5cm 18x24in) Heidelberg 2000

CROISSANT Michael 1928 [23]
$6 294 - €7 158 - **£4 365** - FF46 954
Kopf Metal (50x18x12.5cm 19x7x4in) München 2000
$1 316 - €1 208 - **£813** - FF8 384
Studien zu einer Figur Indian ink (51.3x15.5cm 20x6in) München 1999

CROISY Aristide 1840-1899 [19]
$726 - €732 - **£452** - FF4 800
Ernest Bradfer Bronze (H63.5cm H25in) Senlis 2000

CROLA Georg Heinrich Croll 1804-1879 [16]
$2 601 - €2 958 - **£1 784** - FF19 400
Wernigerode bei Nacht Öl/Leinwand (22.5x24cm 8x9in) Zürich 2001

CROLA Hugo 1841-1910 [1]
$4 840 - €4 649 - **£3 000** - FF30 494
Portrait of a Lady in a white Dress and Hat Oil/canvas (120x85cm 47x33in) London 1999

CROMBIE Charles XX [4]
$143 - €137 - **£90** - FF901
Scared by a Dog Watercolour (38x28cm 14x11in) Billingshurst, West-Sussex 1999

CROME John 1768-1821 [37]
$3 100 - €2 862 - **£1 930** - FF18 774
Landscape with Old Mill Oil/canvas (70x89cm 27x35in) Washington 1999
$1 621 - €1 389 - **£950** - FF9 108
Summer Landscape with a Figure on a Track Oil/panel (28x36cm 11x14in) Devon 1998
$95 - €91 - **£60** - FF597
Near Colney Soft ground (15x22cm 6x9in) Aylsham, Norfolk 1999

CROME John Berney 1794-1842 [33]
$40 617 - €39 750 - **£26 000** - FF260 746
A View of Rouen looking from the Base of Mount St. Catherine Oil/canvas (109x183cm 42x72in) London 1999
$2 100 - €2 443 - **£1 500** - FF16 022
Norfolk Wood Oil/canvas (51x41cm 20x16in) Norfolk 2001

$2 345 - €2 174 - **£1 400** - FF14 258
Moonlight River Scene Oil/canvas (25x43cm 10x17in) Aylsham, Norfolk 1999

CROME William Henry 1806-1873 [26]
$5 825 - €5 463 - **£3 600** - FF35 835
Landscape with a View of a Village Church Oil/canvas (53.5x74cm 21x29in) London 1999
$1 409 - €1 380 - **£908** - FF9 055
Personen und Schafe an einem Weiher vor einem englischen Kastell Öl/Leinwand (23x30cm 9x11in) Kempten 1999

CROMEK Thomas Hartley 1809-1873 [34]
$2 323 - €2 050 - **£1 400** - FF13 448
Giotto's Tower, Florence Watercolour (58.5x35.5cm 23x13in) London 1998

CROMER Carlo Max. 1889-1964 [9]
$519 - €499 - **£321** - FF3 270
Maskenball im Hotel Belvedere in Davos Aquarell/Papier (32x44cm 12x17in) Zürich 1999

CROMIERES Huguette 1920 [5]
$562 - €566 - **£350** - FF3 715
«Saint Gervais» Poster (100x64cm 39x25in) London 2000

CROMMELYNCK Aldo XX [3]
$3 950 - €3 835 - **£2 439** - FF25 154
Atelier à Cannes (Intérieur rouge), after Picasso Etching, aquatint in colors (65.5x50cm 25x19in) München 1999

CROMMELYNCK Robert 1895-1968 [42]
$374 - €446 - **£268** - FF2 926
Paysage vallonné Huile/toile (69x100cm 27x39in) Liège 2000

CROMPTON Henrietta Matilda 1793-1881 [4]
$2 123 - €2 413 - **£1 466** - FF15 825
Clew Bay, Co Mayo Watercolour/paper (38x109cm 15x43in) Dublin 2000

CROMPTON James Shaw 1853-1916 [18]
$613 - €663 - **£420** - FF4 350
Something passing Pencil (36.5x26cm 14x10in) Lenton-Lane, Nottingham 2001

CROMWELL Joane 1884-1969 [31]
$2 200 - €2 465 - **£1 533** - FF16 171
Lonely Grandeur Oil/canvas (51x61cm 20x24in) Beverly-Hills CA 2001
$600 - €700 - **£417** - FF4 591
San Jacinto River Oil/canvas/board (27x35cm 11x14in) Altadena CA 2000

CRONE Robert c.1718-1779 [3]
$13 059 - €14 706 - **£9 000** - FF96 464
Figures Resting Before a Lake in an Italianate Landscape Oil/canvas (29x45cm 11x17in) London 2000

CRONEBORG Betty 1799-1866 [2]
$7 401 - €8 420 - **£5 169** - FF55 231
Stilleben med blommor, frukter och fågelbo Oil/canvas (61x49cm 24x19in) Stockholm 2000

CRONQVIST Lena 1938 [120]
$10 747 - €12 040 - **£7 491** - FF78 980
Målaren II Oil/canvas (150x135cm 59x53in) Stockholm 2001
$3 727 - €3 626 - **£2 250** - FF23 786
Strandvegetation, Koster Oil/canvas (46x55cm 18x21in) Stockholm 2001
$2 208 - €2 422 - **£1 466** - FF15 886
Sydkoster Oil/canvas (34x36cm 13x14in) Stockholm 2000

$1 870 - €2 170 - **£1 291** - FF14 235
Stående flicka med händerna i sidan Bronze
(H17cm H6in) Stockholm 2000

$1 150 - €1 340 - **£803** - FF8 787
**August Strindberg, ett drömspel med valda tex-
ter ur ett drömspel** Color lithograph (73x52.5cm
28x20in) Stockholm 2000

CROOK P.J. 1945 [1]
$8 823 - €8 891 - **£5 500** - FF58 319
Harry's Bar Acrylic/canvas (87.5x118cm 34x46in)
London 2000

CROOKE Ray Austin 1922 [602]
$12 080 - €11 754 - **£7 434** - FF77 098
Cape York Settlement Oil/canvas/board (96.5x155cm
37x61in) Melbourne 1999
$6 475 - €6 105 - **£4 013** - FF40 044
Kimberley Landscape Oil/canvas (75x121cm
29x47in) Melbourne 1999
$1 753 - €1 927 - **£1 123** - FF12 640
Landscape Oil/canvas/board (24.5x28cm 9x11in)
Melbourne 2000
$840 - €793 - **£523** - FF5 204
Islander on the Beach Gouache/paper (11.5x16.5cm
4x6in) Sydney 1999
$247 - €289 - **£172** - FF1 893
«Woman with Flowers» Serigraph (37.5x48.5cm
14x19in) Melbourne 2000

CROOKS Ron 1925 [2]
$2 250 - €2 646 - **£1 618** - FF17 357
Many Pony Tracks Oil/canvas (60x91cm 24x36in)
Hatfield PA 2001

CROOS van der Anthony Jansz. 1606-1662 [44]
$8 052 - €9 147 - **£5 634** - FF60 000
Le passage du gué Huile/panneau (38x51.5cm
14x20in) Paris 2001
$10 231 - €8 837 - **£6 167** - FF57 967
**A Village by a River with Peasants on a Track in
the Foreground** Oil/canvas (9.2x19.8cm 3x7in)
Amsterdam 1998

CROOS van der Jacob c.1635-c.1700 [18]
$5 124 - €5 368 - **£3 389** - FF35 215
Schloss Rijswijk Oil/panel (34x60cm 13x23in)
München 2000

CROOS van der Pieter 1609-1701 [9]
$5 264 - €5 814 - **£3 648** - FF38 136
Fischerboote auf bewegter See Oil/panel
(44x41cm 17x16in) Wien 2001

CROPSEY Jasper Francis 1823-1900 [152]
$2 255 540 - €2 243 391 - **£1 400 000** -
FF14 715 680
Richmond Hill in the Summer Oil/canvas
(137x244cm 53x96in) London 1999
$60 000 - €62 194 - **£38 046** - FF407 964
Wyoming Valley, Pennsylvania Oil/canvas
(41.5x76cm 16x29in) New-York 2000
$42 500 - €46 512 - **£29 316** - FF305 099
Sketches Oil/canvas (4.5x7.5cm 1x2in) New-York
2001
$11 000 - €11 402 - **£6 975** - FF74 793
Richmond Hill Watercolour/paper (40.5x66cm
15x25in) New-York 2001

CROS Charles 1842-1888 [1]
$5 942 - €6 555 - **£4 024** - FF43 000
Autoportrait au carnet de croquis Crayon/papier
(18x10.5cm 7x4in) Paris 2000

CROS Henri 1840-1911 [150]
$6 014 - €6 250 - **£3 788** - FF41 000
Thésée et Ariane Huile/carton (70x48cm 27x18in)
Tours 2000
$9 384 - €10 367 - **£6 507** - FF68 000
Femme pensive Bas-relief (16x11cm 6x4in) Paris
2001
$269 - €229 - **£160** - FF1 500
Femme nu assise Fusain/papier (65x45cm 25x17in)
Paris 1998

CROSATO Giovanni Battista 1686-1758 [10]
$190 000 - €202 911 - **£129 466** - FF1 331 007
Moses striking the Rock Oil/canvas (64x90cm
25x35in) New-York 2001

CROSBIE William 1915-1999 [65]
$4 736 - €5 327 - **£3 300** - FF34 945
Wild Piece Oil/board (75x49.5cm 29x19in) Edinburgh
2001
$2 850 - €2 436 - **£1 725** - FF15 977
Nude Oil/board (44.5x20.5cm 17x8in) Edinburgh 1998
$921 - €1 053 - **£650** - FF6 905
Chinese bottle with flowers Watercolour/paper
(53x35.5cm 20x13in) Glasgow 2001

CROSBY William 1830-1910 [9]
$4 129 - €4 602 - **£2 886** - FF30 185
Moving Melody Öl/Leinwand (71x91cm 27x35in)
München 2001
$2 214 - €2 028 - **£1 350** - FF13 305
Feeding the Baby Oil/panel (30.5x23cm 12x9in)
Ipswich 1999

CROSIO Luigi 1835-1915 [23]
$10 000 - €10 367 - **£6 000** - FF68 000
L'Italena Olio/tela (54.5x73.5cm 21x28in) Torino 1999
$10 800 - €9 330 - **£5 400** - FF61 200
Ritorno dal pascolo d'inverno Olio/tela
(42.5x32cm 16x12in) Vercelli 1999

CROSLAND Enoch 1860-1945 [6]
$997 - €1 073 - **£680** - FF7 038
**The Placid River Derwent near Ambergate,
Derbyshire** Oil/canvas (18.5x26cm 7x10in) West-
Yorkshire 2001

CROSS Henri Edmond 1856-1910 [349]
$356 960 - €350 633 - **£221 490** - FF2 300 000
Paysage (dit de Cabasson) Huile/toile (60x81cm
23x31in) Paris 1999
$20 068 - €18 525 - **£12 000** - FF121 514
Homme à la barque Oil/panel (13x27cm 5x10in)
London 1999
$1 139 - €1 296 - **£790** - FF8 500
Mer agitée Mine plomb (15x22.5cm 5x8in) Paris 2000
$1 200 - €1 403 - **£843** - FF9 202
Les Champs-Élysées Color lithograph (20.5x26.5cm
8x10in) New-York 2000

CROSS Henri H. 1837-1918 [19]
$2 000 - €2 147 - **£1 338** - FF14 082
Chief Quick Eye, Apache Oil/board (24x19cm
9x7in) Portland ME 2000

CROSS van der Anthony Jansz. c.1606-c.1665 [3]
$22 019 - €20 595 - **£13 500** - FF135 094
**Voorhout, the Church Spire seen Rising above
the Trees** Oil/panel (14.5x18.5cm 5x7in) London 1998

CROSSLAND James Henry 1852-1904 [33]
$1 933 - €1 923 - **£1 200** - FF12 613
Faggot Gatherers on a Woodland Path Oil/can-
vas/board (48.5x63.5cm 19x25in) Billingshurst, West-
Sussex 1999

C

$579 - €541 - £350 - FF3 552
Rocky River Landscape Oil/canvas (25.5x38cm 10x14in) London 1999

CROTCH William 1775-1847 [26]
$134 - €144 - £90 - FF946
High Peak, Sidmouth Watercolour (12x17cm 4x6in) Bath 2000

CROTTI Jean 1878-1958 [125]
$3 007 - €3 354 - £2 098 - FF22 000
«Les oiseaux des grands espaces» Huile/toile (91x73cm 35x28in) Evreux 2001
$2 982 - €3 201 - £1 995 - FF21 000
Tête terre de Sienne Technique mixte/carton (33x25cm 12x9in) Paris 2000
$1 228 - €1 372 - £821 - FF9 000
Portrait de femme Crayons couleurs/papier (65x50cm 25x19in) Paris 2000

CROUCH William c.1800-c.1850 [26]
$1 062 - €1 240 - £750 - FF8 134
Continental Town Watercolour/paper (9x14cm 3x5in) London 2000

CROWE Eyre 1824-1910 [19]
$2 968 - €2 690 - £1 800 - FF17 647
«How Happy I Could be with Either» Oil/panel (39x69cm 15x27in) Billingshurst, West-Sussex 1998

CROWE Victoria 1945 [8]
$2 751 - €3 065 - £1 800 - FF20 105
The Watcher from Pompeii Oil/board (29.5x45cm 11x17in) Edinburgh 2000
$516 - €581 - £360 - FF3 812
Back Garden, Summer Watercolour, gouache/paper (36x51cm 14x20in) Edinburgh 2001

CROWELL Anthony Elmer 1862-1851 [9]
$700 - €679 - £435 - FF4 456
Miniature Common Golden Eye Drake Sculpture (6x10cm 2x4in) Bolton MA 1999

CROWELL Tom XX [10]
$1 298 - €1 534 - £920 - FF10 061
Grosses Blumenstilleben Oil/panel (91x71cm 35x27in) Ahlden 2000

CROWLEY Donald, Don 1926 [6]
$4 200 - €4 769 - £2 918 - FF31 282
Security Blanket Pencil/paper (35x27cm 14x11in) Dallas TX 2001

CROWQUILL Alfred H. Forrester 1804-1872 [10]
$434 - €469 - £300 - FF3 075
The Fairy's Mirror Ink (26x17.5cm 10x6in) Billingshurst, West-Sussex 2001

CROWTHER Henry XIX-XX [37]
$613 - €515 - £360 - FF3 375
Flint of Ardagh, a Pointer in a Landscape Oil/canvas (28x36cm 11x14in) Ilkley, West-Yorkshire 1998

CROWTHER John XIX-XX [10]
$449 - €421 - £280 - FF2 762
View of a Garden with Horse-chestnut Trees and a Sundial Watercolour (26x42cm 10x16in) London 1999

CROXFORD William Edwards XIX-XX [81]
$313 - €365 - £220 - FF2 397
At a Quay-Side Watercolour/paper (38x54.5cm 14x21in) Godalming, Surrey 2001

CROZATIER Charles 1795-1855 [4]
$1 018 - €840 - £600 - FF5 509
Allegorical Group, Gentleman Standing Beside a Naked Young Woman Bronze (H51cm H20in) London 1998

CROZET Vincent XIX-XX [4]
$639 - €726 - £444 - FF4 762
«Dunlop Nagel-band» Poster (109.5x158.5cm 43x62in) Hoorn 2001

CROZIER William 1930 [72]
$5 918 - €6 349 - £4 035 - FF41 645
Cromwell Series Oil/canvas (152.5x122cm 60x48in) Dublin 2001
$1 706 - €1 651 - £1 052 - FF10 827
Abstract Oil/canvas/board (122x91.5cm 48x36in) Dublin 1999
$1 311 - €1 524 - £921 - FF9 994
Abstract on a Sheet of Newspaper, the Nursing Mirror Acrylic (30x41cm 11x16in) Dublin 2001
$1 240 - €1 397 - £864 - FF9 182
Landscape Pencil (76x56cm 29x22in) Dublin 2001

CRUAÑAS Josep 1942 [76]
$672 - €721 - £456 - FF4 728
Vista de Amsterdam Oleo/lienzo (73x92cm 28x36in) Madrid 2001
$224 - €240 - £148 - FF1 576
Puerto Acuarela/papel (35.5x50.5cm 13x19in) Barcelona 2000

CRUICKSHANK Frederick 1800-1868 [14]
$2 924 - €2 833 - £1 840 - FF18 585
Young Gentleman and Lady Miniature (13x10cm 5x3in) London 1999

CRUICKSHANK William 1848-1922 [182]
$553 - €473 - £334 - FF3 101
Still Life of Flowers and Bird's Nest with Blue Eggs Huile/carton (10x12.5cm 3x4in) Montréal 1998
$601 - €588 - £370 - FF3 860
Apple Blossom and Eggs on a Bank Watercolour/paper (15x22cm 6x9in) Aylsham, Norfolk 1999

CRUIKSHANK George 1792-1878 [105]
$370 - €430 - £260 - FF2 819
Mann entering a Room in which a young Woman in her petticoat Watercolour (12x20cm 4x7in) London 2001
$209 - €225 - £140 - FF1 473
Game of Chess Engraving (35.5x25.5cm 13x10in) Suffolk 2000

CRUIKSHANK Isaac c.1756-1811/16 [18]
$317 - €351 - £220 - FF2 304
Purchasing a servant Watercolour (14.5x23cm 5x9in) London 2001

CRUIKSHANK Robert Isaac 1789-1856 [18]
$709 - €823 - £500 - FF5 400
Study for Guy Fawkes Drawing (21.5x16cm 8x6in) London 2001

CRUISE Boyd 1909-1988 [5]
$3 400 - €3 151 - £2 114 - FF20 672
Still Life of Flowers on a Silk Shawl Watercolour/paper (30x25cm 12x10in) New-Orleans LA 1999

CRUMB Robert 1943 [6]
$18 000 - €17 365 - £11 376 - FF113 904
«The Adventures of Fuzzy the Bunny» Ink (31x21cm 12x8in) New-York 1999

CRUMBO Woodrow Wilson 1912-1989 **[18]**
🏛 **$250** - €237 - **£155** - FF1 552
Indian praying Lithograph (22x27cm 9x11in) St.
Ignatius MT 1999

CRUPI Giovanni 1859-1925 **[3]**
📷 **$2 327** - €2 744 - **£1 636** - FF18 000
Taormine, Sicile Tirage albuminé (16x22.5cm 6x8in)
Paris 2000

CRUSSENS Anthonie, Anton XVII **[3]**
✏ **$4 200** - €4 499 - **£2 868** - FF29 511
**Winter Landscape with Figures on a Road
Carrying Kindling** Ink (13x13cm 5x5in) New-York
2001

CRUYL Lieven 1640-1720 **[10]**
✏ **$9 000** - €9 641 - **£6 146** - FF63 239
**View of Rome, Looking Along the Tiber, over
the Castel Sant'Angelo** Ink (15.5x21.5cm 6x8in)
New-York 2001

CRUZ CANO de la Juan XVIII **[2]**
🏛 **$476** - €457 - **£295** - FF3 000
Le fameux Pedro Romero Gravure cuivre
(24x17.5cm 9x6in) Paris 1999

CRUZ DIEZ Carlos 1923 **[91]**
☞ **$25 000** - €24 265 - **£15 565** - FF159 165
Physichromie 119 Acrylic (122x109cm 48x42in)
New-York 1999
☞ **$4 611** - €4 287 - **£2 800** - FF28 121
«Physiochromie No.519» Mixed media/board
(72x72cm 28x28in) London 1998
☞ **$980** - €1 143 - **£688** - FF7 500
«Physichromie» Technique mixte (12x19cm 4x7in)
Paris 2000
✏ **$529** - €555 - **£350** - FF3 641
Sin título Acuarela/papel (12.5x11cm 4x4in) Caracas
($) 2000
🏛 **$179** - €204 - **£125** - FF1 341
Transchromies Farbserigraphie (19x19cm 7x7in)
Hamburg 2001

CRUZ HERRERA José 1890-1972 **[79]**
☞ **$90 650** - €106 714 - **£63 700** - FF700 000
Le prince Huile/toile (130x102cm 51x40in) Paris 2000
☞ **$3 885** - €4 573 - **£2 730** - FF30 000
Enfant au coq Huile/toile (55x46cm 21x18in) Paris
2000
☞ **$1 878** - €2 134 - **£1 296** - FF14 000
Portrait d'enfant marocain Huile/panneau
(36.5x28.5cm 14x11in) Paris 2000

CRUZEIRO-SEIXAS Artur 1920 **[9]**
☞ **$1 475** - €1 246 - **£875** - FF8 175
Abstracto Técnica mixta (20x24cm 7x9in) Lisboa
1998
✏ **$2 200** - €2 493 - **£1 550** - FF16 350
Kitandeira Tinta/papel (21x15cm 8x5in) Lisboa 2001

CSABA Vilmos Perllott 1880-1955 **[1]**
☞ **$5 200** - €5 431 - **£3 098** - FF29 066
Village under the Snow Oil/canvas (93x75cm
36x29in) New-York 1998

CSAKY Joseph 1888-1971 **[351]**
🗝 **$14 290** - €16 000 - **£9 943** - FF105 000
«L'oiseau snob» Bronze (96x50x21cm 37x19x8in)
Versailles 2001
🗝 **$4 431** - €5 206 - **£3 129** - FF34 146
Coq assis Marbre (H50cm H19in) Antwerpen 2000
✏ **$758** - €884 - **£532** - FF5 800
Femme et sa fille Encre Chine/papier (23.5x15.5cm
9x6in) Pontoise 2001

CSOK István 1865-1961 **[31]**
☞ **$3 522** - €3 811 - **£2 412** - FF25 000
Repas champêtre Huile/toile (70x60cm 27x23in)
Troyes 2001

CSUZY Karoly XIX **[1]**
☞ **$12 291** - €13 613 - **£8 337** - FF89 298
Portrait of a Man seated Oil/canvas (130x105cm
51x41in) Amsterdam 2000

CUADRAS Joaquim ?-1877 **[1]**
☞ **$7 068** - €8 042 - **£4 968** - FF52 752
**Portraet af ung sydamerikansk kvinde med
orange törklaede** Oil/canvas (53x38cm 20x14in)
Vejle 2001

CUBLEY Henry Hadfield c.1850-c.1930 **[100]**
☞ **$797** - €763 - **£500** - FF5 002
Near Tynault Oban Oil/canvas (51x77cm 20x30in)
Lichfield, Staffordshire 1999
☞ **$471** - €406 - **£280** - FF2 664
**Highland Cattle Watering in a Mountainous
Landscape** Oil/canvas (38x30.5cm 14x12in) London
1998

CUCCHI Enzo 1950 **[163]**
☞ **$37 500** - €38 874 - **£22 500** - FF255 000
Piogge sante Olio/tela (270x426cm 106x167in) Prato
1999
☞ **$13 639** - €11 387 - **£8 000** - FF74 696
Untitled Tempera (76x111x3.5cm 29x43x1in) London
1998
☞ **$4 500** - €4 860 - **£3 110** - FF31 880
«5 elefanti per Vedere» Mixed media (14.5x99.5cm
5x39in) New-York 2001
☞ **$7 140** - €7 402 - **£4 284** - FF48 552
Senza titolo Fer (30x85x298cm 11x33x117in) Venezia
1999
✏ **$2 250** - €2 332 - **£1 350** - FF15 300
Senza titolo Inchiostro/carta (14x19cm 5x7in) Prato
2000
🏛 **$831** - €762 - **£512** - FF5 000
Sans titre Gravure (96x138cm 37x54in) Paris 1999

CUCCIONI Tomaso XIX **[9]**
📷 **$319** - €363 - **£220** - FF2 383
Rom, Forum Romanum Albumen print
(22.2x30.6cm 8x12in) Wien 2000

CUCUEL Edward 1879-1951 **[158]**
☞ **$75 000** - €71 697 - **£47 010** - FF470 302
Tea in the Park Oil/canvas (146x115cm 57x45in)
New-York 1999
☞ **$25 000** - €29 177 - **£17 722** - FF191 390
«In the Herbstland (in the Forest)» Oil/canvas
(79.5x65cm 31x25in) New-York 2001
☞ **$3 728** - €4 346 - **£2 612** - FF28 508
Dorf Bichl bei Kochel Oil/panel (25x34cm 9x13in)
München 2000
☞ **$6 000** - €6 932 - **£4 201** - FF45 468
Musing Watercolour/paper (33x25cm 12x9in) New-
York 2001

CUDENNEC Patrice 1952 **[90]**
☞ **$800** - €762 - **£500** - FF5 000
Pêcheur à la Madone Huile/toile (65x54cm 25x21in)
Douarnenez 1999
☞ **$614** - €610 - **£382** - FF4 000
Trois pêcheurs Huile/toile (33x24cm 12x9in) Brest
1999

CUDWORTH Jack 1930 **[30]**
☞ **$883** - €915 - **£560** - FF6 005
Evening Snow Acrylic/board (61x77cm 24x30in)
West-Yorkshire 2000

C

$580 - €660 - £405 - FF4 331
Riverside Hut and Anglers Oil/board (35x39cm
13x15in) Dublin 2000

CUECO Henri Aguilella, dit 1929 [89]
$554 - €549 - £335 - FF3 600
Chaussure Huile/toile (24x19cm 9x7in) Paris 2000
$690 - €762 - £478 - FF5 000
Moutons Mine plomb (53x76cm 20x29in) Paris 2001

CUENI August 1883-1966 [22]
$1 784 - €2 098 - £1 292 - FF13 765
«Weisse Rosen» Öl/Leinwand (57x48cm 22x18in)
Zofingen 2001

CUEVAS José Luis 1934 [165]
$850 - €827 - £523 - FF5 427
Retrato del natural en el manicomio Ink/paper
(63x48cm 24x18in) New-York 1999
$300 - €283 - £186 - FF1 858
Los Papeles de Salazar Lithograph (61.5x86.5cm
24x34in) San-Francisco CA 1999

CUEVAS Raymond, Ray 1932 [6]
$1 400 - €1 288 - £840 - FF8 452
Cityscape, Civic Center from Elysian Park
Oil/canvas (55x71cm 22x28in) Pasadena CA 1999

CUEVAS Telesforo 1849-1934 [18]
$249 - €288 - £172 - FF1 891
Paisaje de campo Carboncillo (41x27cm 16x10in)
Madrid 2000

CUGAT Delia 1930 [14]
$10 000 - €8 697 - £6 029 - FF57 050
Sin título Oil/canvas (96.5x146.5cm 37x57in) New-
York 1998

CUGAT Xavier 1898-1990 [71]
$192 - €192 - £118 - FF1 260
La espiritual Lilian Tinta/papel (25x16cm 9x6in)
Madrid 2000
$624 - €721 - £432 - FF4 728
Caricaturas Litografía (27x38.5cm 10x15in)
Barcelona 2001

CUGUEN Victor Louis 1882-1969 [12]
$653 - €640 - £402 - FF4 280
Marché du Cours Lafayette à Toulon Huile/carton
(33x42cm 12x16in) Toulon 1999

CUI ZIFAN 1915 [9]
$1 600 - €1 717 - £1 070 - FF11 265
Fish in Lotus Pond Ink (137x70cm 53x27in) San-
Francisco CA 2000

CUIRBLANC Berthe XIX [1]
$4 247 - €4 203 - £2 600 - FF27 571
**Chrysnathemums in a Vase with Books on a
Draped table** Oil/canvas (91.5x71cm 36x27in)
London 2000

CUISINIER Pierre XX [2]
$3 427 - €2 897 - £2 038 - FF19 000
Le passage de l'obstacle Huile/toile (73x92cm
28x36in) Paris 1998

CUITT George I 1743-1818 [26]
$35 075 - €41 715 - £25 000 - FF273 630
View of Shrewsbury Oil/canvas (66x102cm 25x40in)
London 2000
$1 402 - €1 672 - £1 000 - FF10 968
View of a Country House in North Yorkshire
Oil/canvas (21x24cm 8x9in) Leyburn, North Yorkshire
2000

$172 704 - €193 441 - £120 000 - FF1 268 892
**View from Marsh Edge/Easby Ruins/The Round
Howe/Easby Abbey/Richmond** Watercolour
(43x56cm 16x22in) London 2001

CUIXART Modesto 1925 [105]
$25 925 - €25 528 - £15 725 - FF167 450
Serpentaria Oleo/lienzo (164x131cm 64x51in)
Barcelona 2000
$4 970 - €5 336 - £3 325 - FF35 000
Composition #4 Technique mixte/toile (80x30cm
31x11in) Paris 2000
$2 287 - €2 252 - £1 462 - FF14 775
Pic de Benfato Técnica mixta/lienzo (33x24cm
12x9in) Barcelona 1999
$855 - €901 - £570 - FF5 910
Sin título Técnica mixta/papel (32x24cm 12x9in)
Madrid 2000
$140 - €150 - £92 - FF985
Figura femenina Litografía a color (72x52cm
28x20in) Madrid 2000

CUKIER Aniela 1900-1944 [1]
$1 029 - €1 105 - £689 - FF7 249
Vieille ville, Varsovie Gravure bois couleurs
(30x24cm 11x9in) Warszawa 2000

CULIN Alice 1875-1950 [3]
$3 012 - €2 813 - £1 859 - FF18 454
«The New York World's Fair» Poster (71x101cm
27x39in) Oostwoud 1999

CULL Alma Claude Burlton 1880-1931 [22]
$2 242 - €2 407 - £1 500 - FF15 786
A Battleship Entering an Estuary Watercolour
(26x45.5cm 10x17in) London 2000

CULLBERG Erland 1931 [132]
$1 120 - €1 290 - £772 - FF8 461
Figurer i grönt Oil/canvas (150x150cm 59x59in)
Stockholm 2000
$606 - €658 - £383 - FF4 318
Ansikte Oil/canvas (73x65cm 28x25in) Stockholm
2000

CULLEN Isaac J. act.1881-1947 [32]
$42 148 - €46 241 - £28 000 - FF303 324
The Finish Oil/canvas (91.5x155cm 36x61in) London
2000
$4 584 - €3 780 - £2 700 - FF24 793
Training/Before the Race Oil/canvas (33x43cm
12x16in) Newbury, Berkshire 1998

CULLEN Maurice Galbraith 1866-1934 [57]
$13 296 - €12 915 - £8 310 - FF84 716
The Cache River Oil/panel (37.5x46cm 14x18in)
Toronto 1999
$4 060 - €4 005 - £2 500 - FF26 272
Printemps à Terrebonne Huile/panneau (26x35cm
10x13in) Montréal 1999
$3 276 - €2 823 - £1 946 - FF18 518
«Northmount, Montreal» Pastel/paper (38x45.5cm
14x17in) Toronto 1998

CULLEN Tom XX [9]
$519 - €485 - £320 - FF3 183
Merchants Arch, Dublin Oil/board (43x30cm
16x11in) Co. Kilkenny 1999

CULTRERA Armand 1901 [87]
$1 956 - €2 287 - £1 396 - FF15 000
**Marabout de Sidé-Abder-Rahman à
Casablanca** Huile/panneau (50x65cm 19x25in) Paris
2001

CULVER Charles 1908-1967 [73]
$1 000 - €941 - £617 - FF6 174
Reclining Raccoon Watercolour (30x44cm 12x17in) Bloomfield-Hills MI 1999

CULVERHOUSE Johann Mongels 1820-1891 [51]
$4 500 - €4 260 - £2 801 - FF27 944
Woman and Children in a Candlelit Interior setting Oil/canvas (45x60cm 18x24in) Detroit MI 1999
$1 500 - €1 296 - £906 - FF8 498
Moonlight Rowing Party Oil/canvas (35x30cm 14x12in) Watertown MA 1998

CUMBERWORTH Charles 1811-1852 [28]
$16 963 - €14 635 - £10 195 - FF96 000
Porteuse d'eau Bronze (H113cm H44in) Clairefontaine 1998
$1 624 - €1 707 - £1 071 - FF11 200
Enfants se couvrant Bronze (38x26x20cm 14x10x7in) Paris 2000

CUMBO Ettore 1833-1899 [47]
$7 600 - €9 848 - £5 700 - FF64 600
Veduta di paese con fiume Olio/tela (98x160cm 38x62in) Firenze 2000
$2 160 - €1 866 - £1 440 - FF12 240
Rose variegate Olio/tela (60x48cm 23x18in) Firenze 1998
$480 - €622 - £360 - FF4 080
Veduta di Roma al tramonto Olio/cartone (20x28cm 7x11in) Firenze 2000

CUMBRAE-STEWART Janet Agnes 1885-1960 [56]
$5 259 - €5 781 - £3 370 - FF37 922
Nude Pastel/paper (49x34cm 19x13in) Melbourne 2000

CUMING Fred 1930 [79]
$2 540 - €2 727 - £1 700 - FF17 891
Winchelsea Beach Oil/board (50.5x61cm 19x24in) London 2000
$1 119 - €1 078 - £700 - FF7 070
Arcachon Oil/board (25.5x24.5cm 10x9in) London 1999

CUMING Frederick G. Rees 1865-1949 [12]
$1 050 - €1 228 - £750 - FF8 054
Black Pansies Oil/board (19.5x15cm 7x5in) London 2001

CUMMING Constance Fredericka 1837-1924 [38]
$992 - €928 - £600 - FF6 088
Study of Indian Rubber Trees at Peradehia Watercolour (51.5x67.5cm 20x26in) London 1999

CUMMING James 1922-1991 [11]
$1 884 - €2 171 - £1 300 - FF14 238
Ewer, Flask and Lantern Oil/canvas (100x74cm 39x29in) Newbury, Berkshire 2000

CUMMING R.H. Neville XIX-XX [6]
$174 - €199 - £120 - FF1 304
Sailboats on a River Watercolour (22.5x31cm 8x13in) London 2000

CUMMINGS Edward Estlin / e.e. 1894-1962 [10]
$800 - €933 - £561 - FF6 120
Sunset with Nude Oil/canvas (36x49cm 14x19in) Dedham MA 2000
$1 500 - €1 749 - £1 053 - FF11 475
Portrait of Marion Moore Oil/board (39x28cm 15x11in) Dedham MA 2000

CUMMINGS Melvin Earl 1876-1936 [1]
$7 000 - €6 527 - £4 342 - FF42 815
Seated Male Nude on Globe Bronze (H38cm H14in) New-York 1999

CUMMINGS Michael 1919-1997 [30]
$781 - €764 - £500 - FF5 014
Churchill Shocking the Establishment Ink (37x27cm 14x11in) London 1999

CUNAEUS Conradijn 1828-1895 [41]
$10 448 - €8 835 - £6 248 - FF57 952
Setters with a Patridge Oil/canvas (55.5x75cm 21x29in) Amsterdam 1998
$4 347 - €4 084 - £2 620 - FF26 789
Gun Dogs in a 17th Century Interior Oil/panel (25x27.5cm 9x10in) Amsterdam 1999
$903 - €998 - £600 - FF6 548
A Gundog retrieving a Bird Watercolour/paper (23x32.5cm 9x12in) Amsterdam 2001

CUNDALL Charles Ernest 1890-1971 [107]
$2 849 - €3 312 - £2 000 - FF21 728
Watney's Stag Brewery Oil/canvas (53.5x43cm 21x16in) Billingshurst, West-Sussex 2001
$1 005 - €1 124 - £700 - FF7 374
V.E.Day Celebrations, Westminster Oil/canvas/board (28x38cm 11x14in) Penzance, Cornwall 2001
$294 - €330 - £200 - FF2 166
Part of the Medici Fountain Watercolour/paper (19.5x25cm 7x9in) Sudbury, Suffolk 2000

CUNDALL Joseph 1818-1895 [2]
$4 250 - €3 963 - £2 565 - FF25 997
Photographic Tour among the Abbeys of Yorkshire Albumen print (29x24cm 11x9in) New-York 1999

CUNDARI M. XX [6]
$324 - €381 - £232 - FF2 500
Le pavot Aquarelle/papier (61x51cm 24x20in) Nice 2001

CUNEGO Domenico 1727-1794 [9]
$270 - €300 - £175 - FF1 970
Clemens Decimustertius Pontifex Maximus Venetus Aguafuerte (57x42cm 22x16in) Madrid 2000

CUNEO Cyrus 1879-1916 [16]
$26 000 - €28 534 - £16 741 - FF187 168
The Japanese Bridge Oil/canvas (77.5x63.5cm 30x25in) Beverly-Hills CA 2000
$250 - €266 - £170 - FF1 747
Elegant Lady in an Interior Grisaille (45x35.5cm 17x13in) Billingshurst, West-Sussex 2001

CUNEO José 1887-1977 [62]
$19 000 - €16 374 - £11 288 - FF107 408
Luna sobre la Estancia Oleo/lienzo (71x50cm 27x19in) Montevideo 1998
$300 - €291 - £185 - FF1 906
Perro durmiendo Lápiz/papel (29.5x20cm 11x7in) Montevideo 1999

CUNEO Rinaldo 1877-1939 [31]
$12 000 - €12 881 - £8 030 - FF84 492
San Anselmo Oil/canvas (51x61cm 20x24in) San-Francisco CA 2000
$1 700 - €1 987 - £1 213 - FF13 032
Figures near house in wooded landscape Oil/canvas (28x30cm 11x12in) Altadena CA 2001

CUNEO Terence Tenison 1907-1996 [145]
$38 851 - €41 704 - £26 000 - FF273 561
Night Freight (Condor) Oil/canvas (244x309cm 96x122in) London 2000
$9 661 - €8 943 - £6 000 - FF58 659
Winter Express - German State Railways Oil/canvas (40.5x61cm 15x24in) London 1999

C

$3 892 - €4 563 - £2 800 - FF29 932
Venetian Gondolas Oil/canvas (30.5x45.5cm
12x17in) London 2001
$1 129 - €1 309 - £800 - FF8 588
«Track Laying by Night, British Railways» Poster
(102x127cm 40x50in) London 2000

CUNNINGHAM Earl 1893-1977 [8]
$2 750 - €3 208 - £1 964 - FF21 040
Sailing Gunship on the Water Oil/wood (28x50cm
11x20in) Detroit MI 2000

CUNNINGHAM Imogen 1883-1976 [168]
$3 000 - €3 454 - £2 047 - FF22 656
The Unmade Bed Gelatin silver print (26.5x34cm
10x13in) New-York 2000

CUNNINGHAM John 1926-1998 [25]
$4 377 - €3 775 - £2 640 - FF24 761
«Glasgow townscape» Oil/canvas (82x127cm
32x50in) Glasgow 1998
$1 434 - €1 592 - £1 000 - FF10 444
Gardens, Toledo Gouache/paper (34x49cm 13x19in)
London 2001

CUNZ Martha 1876-1961 [96]
$2 184 - €2 126 - £1 342 - FF13 947
Piz neir bei Bivio Öl/Leinwand (58x50cm 22x19in)
Zürich 1999
$1 542 - €1 501 - £947 - FF9 845
Risch am Zugersee Öl/Leinwand/Karton
(31.5x40cm 12x15in) Zürich 1999
$881 - €993 - £610 - FF6 511
Alp Frutt (Obwalden) Pastell/Papier (33x50cm
12x19in) Zürich 2000
$963 - €938 - £592 - FF6 153
Niesen Woodcut (30.5x34.9cm 12x13in) Zürich 1999

CUPRIEN Frank William 1871-1948 [40]
$9 500 - €10 646 - £6 621 - FF69 835
The Arch, Arch Beach Oil/canvas (40.5x56cm
15x22in) Beverly-Hills CA 2001
$1 400 - €1 503 - £936 - FF9 857
Texas Twin Oaks with Twins Oil/masonite
(25x40cm 10x16in) Altadena CA 2000

CUPSA Victor 1932 [8]
$1 958 - €1 937 - £1 221 - FF12 707
Fourrures Huile/toile (73x91cm 28x35in) Genève
1999

CURIE Parvine 1936 [14]
$5 054 - €5 946 - £3 623 - FF39 000
La morada Bronze (44x36x32cm 17x14x12in) Paris
2001

CURIO Sabine 1950 [2]
$1 993 - €1 637 - £1 157 - FF10 738
Baum am Haff Etching, aquatint (33x25cm 12x9in)
Berlin 1998

CURLEY Donald 1940 [7]
$485 - €567 - £338 - FF3 717
«Holly» Oil/canvas (76x61cm 29x24in) Toronto 2000

CURLING Peter 1955 [35]
$8 456 - €8 888 - £5 305 - FF58 303
Last Furlong Oil/canvas (61x91.5cm 24x36in) Dublin
2000
$2 142 - €2 286 - £1 427 - FF14 992
Lester Piggot Oil/canvas (18x18cm 7x7in) Dublin
2000
$2 513 - €2 920 - £1 766 - FF19 156
The Huntsman Watercolour/paper (48x66cm 18x25in)
Dublin 2001

CÜRLIS Peter 1924-1997 [18]
$730 - €635 - £440 - FF4 163
Berlin: Kriegstrümmer Vintage gelatin silver print
(29.7x23.2cm 11x9in) Berlin 1998

CURNOCK James 1812-1870 [9]
$1 379 - €1 553 - £950 - FF10 189
The Gypsy Girl Oil/board (42x35cm 16x13in)
London 2000

CURNOCK James Jackson 1839-1892 [44]
$884 - €820 - £550 - FF5 377
Loch Coruisk Watercolour/paper (32x61cm 12x24in)
London 1999

CUROS Jordi 1930 [316]
$384 - €361 - £240 - FF2 370
Jardín Oleo/lienzo (60x73cm 23x28in) Madrid 1998
$100 - €108 - £68 - FF709
Autorretrato Lápiz/papel (52x37.5cm 20x14in)
Barcelona 2001

CURR Tom XX [8]
$1 000 - €1 166 - £702 - FF7 650
«Summer Holidays by Cunard» Poster (31x50cm
12x19in) New-York 2000

CURRADI Francesco 1570-1661 [33]
$19 500 - €20 215 - £11 700 - FF132 600
Mosè salvato dalle acque Olio/tela (178x218cm
70x85in) Firenze 2000
$6 808 - €6 860 - £4 243 - FF45 000
Sainte Marie Madeleine Huile/toile (66.5x53.5cm
26x21in) Paris 2000
$1 965 - €1 826 - £1 200 - FF11 976
Study of a Man Standing in Supplication Black
chalk (37.5x20cm 14x7in) London 1998

CURRAN Allen XX [2]
$4 008 - €3 883 - £2 500 - FF25 470
Imagine, Statue of John Lennon Bronze (H30.5cm
H12in) London 1999

CURRAN Charles Courtney 1861-1942 [115]
$27 500 - €30 096 - £18 969 - FF197 417
The Boulder Oil/canvas (76x63.5cm 29x25in) New-
York 2001
$6 500 - €7 706 - £4 735 - FF50 547
Nude Oil/canvas (17x11cm 7x4in) Chicago IL 2001
$32 000 - €35 291 - £21 670 - FF231 491
Summer Walk Pastel/canvas (30.5x23cm 12x9in)
New-York 2000

CURREY Fanny W. 1848-1917 [1]
$2 149 - €2 453 - £1 493 - FF16 088
A Family of Swans on a River Akvarell/papper
(35x52cm 13x20in) Stockholm 2001

CURRIE Sidney act.1892-1930 [20]
$505 - €490 - £320 - FF3 213
**Figures in a Lane with a half-timbered House
beyond** Watercolour/paper (24.5x36cm 9x14in) London 1999

CURRIER & IVES (Publisher) act.1857-1907 [723]
$400 - €457 - £281 - FF2 997
Untitled Print (27x38cm 11x15in) Chicago IL 2001

CURRIER Joseph Frank 1843-1909 [12]
$2 500 - €2 360 - £1 554 - FF15 482
Landscape Sketch Oil/board (22x27cm 9x11in)
Milford CT 1999
$1 900 - €1 971 - £1 205 - FF12 932
Landscape Number 12 Pastel/paper (21x43cm
8x16in) Boston MA 2000

CURRIER Nathaniel 1813-1888 [151]
- $650 - €758 - £457 - FF4 972
  The Rubber Lithograph (58x45cm 23x18in) Delaware OH 2001

CURRIER Walter Barron 1879-1934 [9]
- $1 500 - €1 753 - £1 070 - FF11 499
  Coastal landscape Oil/canvas/board (40x30cm 16x12in) Altadena CA 2001

CURRIN John 1962 [19]
- $117 194 - €114 062 - £72 000 - FF748 195
  The Magnificent Bosom Oil/canvas (91.5x71cm 36x27in) London 1999
- $17 000 - €19 725 - £11 736 - FF129 387
  Untitled Watercolour/paper (43x28cm 16x11in) New-York 2000

CURRY Adolf 1879-1939 [18]
- $863 - €1 017 - £607 - FF6 673
  Actaion trifft auf Artemis Öl/Leinwand (15x21.1cm 5x8in) Wien 2001

CURRY John Stuart 1897-1946 [148]
- $2 200 - €2 335 - £1 488 - FF15 318
  The Sermon Watercolour (40x31cm 16x12in) Delray-Beach FL 2001
- $1 300 - €1 218 - £799 - FF7 987
  «Storm Over Stone City» Lithograph (27x43cm 10x16in) New-York 1998

CURRY Robert Franz 1872-1945 [90]
- $1 080 - €1 125 - £684 - FF7 378
  Abendsonne über verschneiter Bergwelt Öl/Leinwand (63x74.5cm 24x29in) München 2000

CURSITER Stanley 1887-1976 [61]
- $10 743 - €9 871 - £6 600 - FF64 751
  The Ming Bowl Oil/canvas (39x45cm 15x17in) Oxfordshire 1999
- $14 755 - €16 482 - £10 000 - FF108 117
  The Embroiderer, possibly Jessie Cursiter Oil/canvas (24x16.5cm 9x6in) Edinburgh 2000
- $2 336 - €2 090 - £1 400 - FF13 712
  Orkney/Summer Landscape Watercolour (33.5x48.5cm 13x19in) Perthshire 1998
- $721 - €727 - £450 - FF4 771
  Nude Lithograph (21.5x15.5cm 8x6in) London 2000

CURTI Francesco 1603-1670 [6]
- $298 - €256 - £179 - FF1 676
  Schlafender Amor Radierung (17.5x12.7cm 6x5in) Berlin 1998

CURTIS Edward Sherrif 1868-1954 [759]
- $5 000 - €5 367 - £3 396 - FF35 202
  Winter-Apsaroke Gelatin silver print (13x19cm 5x7in) Beverly-Hills CA 2001

CURTIS George 1826-1881 [6]
- $4 500 - €5 114 - £3 108 - FF33 546
  The broken Mast Oil/canvas (76x63.5cm 29x25in) New-York 2000
- $5 000 - €4 529 - £3 060 - FF29 709
  Off Three Sisters, Eastham, Cape Cod Oil/canvas (30x50cm 12x20in) Portland ME 1998

CURTIS George Vaughan 1859-1943 [2]
- $47 500 - €40 583 - £28 514 - FF266 209
  Portrait of a Lady on the Champs Elysées Oil/canvas (92x73cm 36x28in) New-York 1998

CURTIS James Waltham c.1839-1901 [30]
- $1 598 - €1 537 - £984 - FF10 079
  The Swagman's Track Watercolour/paper (40.5x62cm 15x24in) Melbourne 1999

CURTIS Leland 1897-? [15]
- $2 750 - €2 350 - £1 664 - FF15 414
  Grand Teton and Mt. Owen Oil/canvas (61x81.5cm 24x32in) San-Francisco CA 1998

CURTIS Ralph Wormsley 1854-1922 [12]
- $5 500 - €4 648 - £3 270 - FF30 489
  View of Santa Maria della Salute, Venice Oil/board (30.5x40.5cm 12x15in) Washington 1998
- $2 200 - €2 616 - £1 567 - FF17 162
  Washerwomen in Venice Watercolour (28.5x43cm 11x16in) New-York 2000

CURTIS Robert Emerson 1899-1996 [31]
- $227 - €214 - £137 - FF1 407
  Building the Underpass of the Gladesville Bridge Coloured inks (44x66cm 17x25in) Sydney 1999

CURTS K. XX [1]
- $4 532 - €4 266 - £2 800 - FF27 984
  «Belle Récolte» Bronze (H16cm H6in) London 1999

CURTY Joseph Emmanuel 1750-1813 [2]
- $5 074 - €5 920 - £3 531 - FF38 835
  Pont de la Zintre près Charmey païs de la Gruyère Canton de Fribourg Gouache (25.7x37.7cm 10x14in) Bern 2000

CURZON de Alfred P. 1820-1895 [21]
- $4 974 - €4 612 - £3 000 - FF30 254
  Ilot et montagne de la presqu'île de Methana, Golfe d'Athènes Oil/canvas (34.5x61.5cm 13x24in) London 1999
- $2 112 - €1 952 - £1 300 - FF12 805
  Campesina rezando a la Virgen Oleo/tabla (21x27cm 8x10in) Madrid 1999

CUSACHS Y CUSACHS Josep 1851-1908 [80]
- $80 692 - €86 616 - £54 000 - FF568 166
  Una Pausa en la Batalla (a Pause in the Battle) Oil/canvas (231x133cm 90x52in) London 2000
- $25 920 - €28 831 - £17 760 - FF189 120
  Paisaje con burro Oleo/lienzo (60x120cm 23x47in) Madrid 2001
- $4 900 - €4 205 - £2 940 - FF27 580
  El descanso de la infanteria Oleo/tabla (48x28cm 18x11in) Madrid 1998
- $1 595 - €1 652 - £1 017 - FF10 835
  Nubes de tormenta en el pinar Aquarelle/papier (34x66cm 13x25in) Barcelona 2000

CUSACK Ralph 1912-1965 [5]
- $529 - €609 - £361 - FF3 997
  Winter Woodland Oil/canvas (66x56cm 25x22in) Dublin 2000

CUSATI Gaetano ?-1720 [8]
- $20 095 - €17 109 - £12 000 - FF112 225
  A Still Life of various Flowers in a Gilt Vase Oil/canvas (101x127.5cm 39x50in) London 1998
- $15 580 - €14 534 - £9 400 - FF95 340
  Natura morta con meloni e uva Öl/Leinwand (75.5x62cm 29x24in) Wien 1999

CUSDEN Leonard XX [2]
- $706 - €819 - £500 - FF5 372
  «Droitwich Spa, Gwr & Lms, Greatest Natural Brine Baths» Poster (102x64cm 40x25in) London 2000

CUSHING Howard Gardiner 1869-1916 [1]
- $15 000 - €17 485 - £10 386 - FF114 697
  Portrait of a Lady Oil/canvas (76x63cm 30x25in) South-Natick MA 2000

CUSSETTI Carlo 1866-1949 **[12]**
📖 **$245** - €229 - **£151** - FF1 500
Plm. Service direct pour l'Italie par le Mont-Cenis Affiche (107x72cm 42x28in) Paris 1999

CUSTER Edward L. 1837-1886 **[11]**
🖼 **$1 300** - €1 241 - **£812** - FF8 140
Fetching the Water Oil/board (21x16cm 8x6in) Dedham MA 1999

CUSTIS Eleanor Parke 1897-1983 **[47]**
✏ **$600** - €582 - **£371** - FF3 815
Woman reading Watercolour/paper (36x34cm 14x13in) Mystic CT 1999
📷 **$1 400** - €1 468 - **£877** - FF9 628
Setting Sun, Gloucester Mass. Photograph (33x25cm 13x10in) New-York 2000

CUSTOS Dominicus c.1550-1612 **[6]**
📖 **$958** - €1 006 - **£635** - FF6 600
Reges Poloniae potentiss Gravure cuivre couleurs (54x40cm 21x15in) Warszawa 2000

CUTANDA Y TORAYA Vicente 1850-1925 **[7]**
$1 836 - €2 042 - **£1 292** - FF13 396
La despedida Grisaille (52x38cm 20x14in) Madrid 2001

CUTLER Carl Gordon 1873-1945 **[3]**
🖼 **$3 000** - €3 499 - **£2 106** - FF22 951
Peasant Woman in a Garden Oil/canvas (72x68cm 28x26in) Boston MA 2000

CUTLER Cecil E.L. act.1866-1934 **[11]**
✏ **$528** - €565 - **£360** - FF3 704
«The Marquis of Salisbury K.G.», Portrait of a Gentleman Watercolour/paper (32x24.5cm 12x9in) Loughton, Essex 2001

CUTRONE Ronnie 1948 **[31]**
✏ **$425** - €428 - **£265** - FF2 810
Patriotic Smurf Watercolour (104x74cm 41x29in) Chicago IL 2000

CUTTOLI Marie XX **[6]**
📖 **$4 800** - €5 353 - **£3 132** - FF35 111
Blanc, after Fernand Léger Tapestry (265x140cm 104x55in) New-York 2000

CUTTS Gertrude Spurr 1858-1941 **[29]**
✏ **$500** - €453 - **£307** - FF2 972
The Grand River-Ontario/Waiting for the Tide/English Scene Oil/board (25x35cm 10x14in) Mystic CT 1999

CUVELIER Eugène 1837-1900 **[33]**
📷 **$1 900** - €1 772 - **£1 146** - FF11 621
Dormoir aux vaches Salt print (20x26cm 7x10in) New-York 1999

CUVELIER Paul 1923-1978 **[15]**
$2 128 - €2 355 - **£1 444** - FF15 447
Brigitte et son chien Huile/toile (32x42cm 12x16in) Bruxelles 2000
✏ **$861** - €793 - **£516** - FF5 200
Corentin Encre Chine (18x12cm 7x4in) Paris 1999

CUVILLON de Louis Robert 1848-? **[6]**
✏ **$550** - €628 - **£388** - FF4 122
Portrait of a Maiden Watercolour, gouache (32x24cm 12x9in) Boston MA 2001

CUYLENBORCH van Abraham c.1610-1658 **[29]**
🖼 **$7 200** - €6 220 - **£4 800** - FF40 800
Diana e le sue ancelle in un antro con rovine antiche Olio/tavola (50x74cm 19x29in) Roma 1998

🖼 **$2 269** - €2 287 - **£1 414** - FF15 000
Le bain de Diane et de ses Nymphes dans un décor de grotte Huile/panneau (29.5x23cm 11x9in) Paris 2000

CUYLENBURG van Cornelis 1758-1827 **[11]**
🖼 **$3 020** - €2 659 - **£1 839** - FF17 440
Geflügelverkäuferin Öl/Leinwand (35x48cm 13x18in) Köln 1999
🖼 **$2 880** - €3 270 - **£1 971** - FF21 451
Holländische Flusslandschaft mit einem Dorf, Booten und Windmühle Oil/panel (30x41.5cm 11x16in) Wien 2000
✏ **$1 698** - €1 633 - **£1 046** - FF10 715
Portrait of Cornelis Ascanius Van Sypesteyn Pastel/paper (38x26.5cm 14x10in) Amsterdam 1999

CUYP Aelbert 1620-1691 **[28]**
🖼 **$27 336** - €23 586 - **£16 494** - FF154 715
River Landscape with Cows and Sheep Oil/canvas (106x147cm 41x57in) Amsterdam 1998
🖼 **$60 000** - €52 808 - **£36 528** - FF346 398
River Landscape with Peasants Unloading a Barge, Dordrecht beyond Oil/panel (69x90cm 27x35in) New-York 1999
✏ **$2 600 000** - €2 776 673 - **£1 771 640** - FF18 213 780
Dordrecht from the End of the Papendrechtse Bank of the River Noord Black chalk (16x50.5cm 6x19in) New-York 2001

CUYP Benjamin Gerritsz 1612-1652 **[38]**
🖼 **$14 472** - €15 882 - **£9 317** - FF104 181
The Adoration of the Shepherds Oil/panel (50.5x70cm 19x27in) Amsterdam 2000
🖼 **$10 168** - €11 798 - **£7 020** - FF71 451
The Sense of Smell, a Boy Mocking an Old Man Oil/panel (34x25.5cm 13x10in) Amsterdam 2000

CUYP Jacob Gerritsz. 1594-1651/52 **[18]**
🖼 **$6 184** - €6 935 - **£4 200** - FF45 488
Portrait of a Gentleman, wearing black/Portrait of a Lady Oil/panel (110x76cm 43x29in) London 2000
🖼 **$4 000** - €3 792 - **£2 433** - FF24 875
Boors in a Tavern Oil/panel (37x33cm 14x12in) New-York 1999

CUYPER de Alfons 1887-1950 **[10]**
🖼 **$9 055** - €7 532 - **£5 316** - FF49 405
A Fair in Ghent Oil/canvas (122x143cm 48x56in) Amsterdam 1998
🖼 **$621** - €744 - **£426** - FF4 878
Stilleven met koffiekan (nature morte à la cafetière) Huile/toile (44x50cm 17x19in) Antwerpen 2000

CUYPERS Franciscus R.H. 1820-1866 **[2]**
🖼 **$12 000** - €13 816 - **£8 188** - FF90 624
Portrait of an Upholsterer Oil/canvas (104x91.5cm 40x36in) New-York 2000

CYBIS Jan 1897-1972 **[38]**
🖼 **$6 967** - €5 760 - **£4 087** - FF37 783
Still Life with Hat Oil/canvas (60x73cm 23x28in) Warszawa 1998
🖼 **$4 288** - €5 112 - **£3 057** - FF33 530
Pont sur Seine Huile/toile (32x41cm 12x16in) Warszawa 2000
✏ **$1 102** - €1 297 - **£793** - FF8 507
Paysage de Kuznica Crayons couleurs/papier (16x23.5cm 6x9in) Warszawa 2000

CYRÉN Gunnar 1931 **[8]**
🗿 **$305** - €352 - **£210** - FF2 307
Fasetterad skål dekorerad i klarglas från Orrefors Sculpture, glass (15x30cm 5x11in) Stockholm 2000

CZACHORSKI Wladyslaw 1850-1911 **[18]**
- **$70 000** – €60 393 – **£42 231** – FF396 151
  The Actors before Hamlet Oil/canvas (112x218.5cm 44x86in) New-York 1998
- **$32 032** – €34 383 – **£21 434** – FF225 540
  Fille à l'éventail Huile/toile (57x43cm 22x16in) Warszawa 2000
- **$9 202** – €10 815 – **£6 381** – FF70 941
  Portrait de Helena Romerowna Huile/panneau (36x23.5cm 14x9in) Warszawa 2000

CZAJKOWSKI Józef 1872-1947 **[7]**
- **$2 745** – €2 947 – **£1 837** – FF19 332
  Paysage avec feu de camps Huile/panneau (14.4x23cm 5x9in) Warszawa 2000

CZAJKOWSKI Stanislaw 1878-1954 **[35]**
- **$2 339** – €2 153 – **£1 404** – FF14 124
  Route traversant le village Oil/board (45x66.5cm 17x26in) Warszawa 1999
- **$952** – €924 – **£588** – FF6 064
  Route de Pulawy à Kazimierz Oil/board (21.5x26.5cm 8x10in) Warszawa 1999

CZAPSKI Joseph 1896-1993 **[25]**
- **$3 670** – €3 699 – **£2 289** – FF24 267
  Nature morte aux poires Oil/canvas (38.6x46.5cm 15x18in) Warszawa 2000
- **$1 647** – €1 768 – **£1 102** – FF11 599
  Procida Aquarelle, gouache (32.5x43cm 12x16in) Kraków 2000

CZECH Emil 1862-1929 **[23]**
- **$1 600** – €1 865 – **£1 121** – FF12 235
  Male Nude Oil/canvas (53x43cm 21x17in) Cleveland OH 2000
- **$3 413** – €2 867 – **£2 006** – FF18 806
  «Weihnachtsabend» Watercolour (77x56.5cm 30x22in) Bern 1998

CZEGKA Bertha XIX-XX **[4]**
- **$2 308** – €2 555 – **£1 600** – FF16 760
  «St.Anton, Arlberg» Poster (69x47cm 27x18in) London 2001

CZENCZ János 1885-1960 **[15]**
- **$893** – €933 – **£613** – FF6 117
  Tea for Two Oil/board (80x59cm 31x23in) Sydney 2000

CZERNOTZKY Ernst 1869-1939 **[22]**
- **$3 840** – €3 813 – **£2 400** – FF25 009
  Table Set for a Feast Oil/canvas (70.5x100.5cm 27x39in) London 1999
- **$2 000** – €2 417 – **£1 396** – FF15 857
  Tabletop Still Life of Tankard, Compote Dish and Book Oil/panel (27x21cm 10x8in) Bethesda MD 2000

CZERNY Alfred 1934 **[19]**
- **$505** – €435 – **£300** – FF2 856
  Pferdeköpfe/Pferderennen Indian ink (12.5x20cm 4x7in) Wien 1998

CZERNY Ludwig 1821-1889 **[7]**
- **$1 645** – €1 817 – **£1 140** – FF11 917
  Schloss Stixenstein in Niederösterreich Aquarell/Papier (23x32cm 9x12in) Wien 2001

CZESCHKA Carl Otto 1878-1960 **[35]**
- **$510** – €581 – **£352** – FF3 813
  August Pencil (40.5x22.6cm 15x8in) Wien 2000
- **$366** – €409 – **£246** – FF2 683
  Buntpapiere Color lithograph (52x70cm 20x27in) München 2000

CZIGANY Dezsö 1883-1937 **[10]**
- **$9 240** – €8 888 – **£5 726** – FF58 300
  Girl in a White Dress Oil/canvas (95x46.5cm 37x18in) Budapest 1999

CZOBEL Bela Adalbert 1883-1976 **[109]**
- **$7 891** – €7 318 – **£4 761** – FF48 000
  Paysage Huile/toile (60x73cm 23x28in) Paris 1999
- **$1 480** – €1 278 – **£894** – FF8 386
  Früchtestilleben Öl/Karton (24.2x39cm 9x15in) Köln 1998
- **$406** – €396 – **£257** – FF2 600
  Nu debout Encre Chine/papier (32x23cm 12x9in) Paris 1999
- **$169** – €204 – **£118** – FF1 341
  Lesendes Mädchen Drypoint (24.3x17.2cm 9x6in) Berlin 2000

CZOERNIG-GOBANZ Herta 1886-1970 **[13]**
- **$558** – €562 – **£347** – FF3 689
  Wiener Strassenszene Pastel (27x25.5cm 10x10in) Düsseldorf 2000

CZOK Maria 1947 **[4]**
- **$2 100** – €1 814 – **£1 400** – FF11 900
  «Rocking Horse Garden» Olio/tela (50x40cm 19x15in) Roma 1998

CZYZEWSKI Tytus 1880-1945 **[8]**
- **$14 513** – €16 596 – **£9 966** – FF108 860
  Portrait de garçon en chapeau Huile/toile (80.5x60cm 31x23in) Warszawa 2000

D

D'ACCARDI Gian Rodolfo 1906-1993 **[48]**
- **$375** – €389 – **£225** – FF2 550
  Cavallini nel bosco Olio/tela (50x60cm 19x23in) Vercelli 2001
- **$300** – €311 – **£180** – FF2 040
  Autunno Olio/cartone/tela (40x30cm 15x11in) Vercelli 2000

D'AMBROSIO Louis 1879-1946 **[1]**
- **$27 000** – €25 773 – **£16 872** – FF169 060
  Jeune fille et la colombe Marble (H175cm H68in) New-York 1999

D'ANCONA Edward XX **[1]**
- **$6 500** – €7 577 – **£4 500** – FF49 702
  Shapely Woman Catching a Fish Oil/canvas (76x60cm 30x24in) New-York 2000

D'ANNA Alessandro 1743-1810 **[14]**
- **$22 766** – €27 136 – **£16 233** – FF178 000
  «Veduta di Salerno presa dalla Strada di Vietri» Gouache/papier (44x64.5cm 17x25in) Châtellerault 2000

D'ARCANGELO Allan 1930 **[56]**
- **$192** – €191 – **£120** – FF1 250
  Landscape 1 Screenprint in colors (60.5x50cm 23x19in) Amsterdam 1999

D'ARIENZO Miguel A. 1950 **[7]**
- **$15 000** – €17 428 – **£10 542** – FF114 318
  El asado u orfeo en el infierno Tempera (166x270cm 65x106in) New-York 2001
- **$19 000** – €20 394 – **£12 714** – FF133 779
  Coming to America Mixed media (119.5x43.5cm 47x17in) New-York 2000
- **$19 000** – €22 075 – **£13 353** – FF144 802
  Tristes noches de Xochimilco Collage (95x190cm 37x74in) New-York 2001

D'ASCENZO Nicola 1871-? [21]

$450 - €408 - £277 - FF2 675
Cloudy Landscape Oil/canvas (35x43cm 14x17in)
Mystic CT 1999

$150 - €161 - £100 - FF1 056
Garden Landscape with Stone House
Watercolour/paper (45x38cm 18x15in) Hatfield PA 2000

D'EZY XX [3]

$414 - €397 - £260 - FF2 601
«**Thé de Chine**» Poster (133x97cm 52x38in) London
1999

D'LEINDRE Zélie 1795-1858 [1]

$13 353 - €12 958 - £8 313 - FF85 000
Bouquet de fleurs, tulipes, pivoines, myosotis, marguerites Aquarelle, gouache/papier (58.5x38.5cm 23x15in) Cheverny 1999

D'ORA Madame (Dora Kalmus) 1881-1960 [129]

$602 - €610 - £374 - FF4 000
Chapeaux Photo (21x16cm 8x6in) Paris 2000

D'OYLEY Charles, Bt. 1781-1845 [51]

$28 116 - €26 299 - £17 000 - FF172 509
Travellers on Elephants passing through a wooded mountainous Landscape Oil/canvas
(43x56.5cm 16x22in) London 1999

$737 - €743 - £460 - FF4 877
An Indian Figure with His Buffalo Watercolour
(15.5x27.5cm 6x10in) London 2000

D'OYLY Charles Walters, Maj 1822-1900 [38]

$738 - €814 - £500 - FF5 340
An Indian Figure with his Buffalo Watercolour
(15.5x27.5cm 6x10in) London 2000

D'YLEN Jean 1886-1938 [64]

$3 830 - €4 269 - £2 576 - FF28 000
«**Cap Corse Quinquina L.N.Mattéi**» Gouache
(141x91cm 55x35in) Orléans 2000

$1 300 - €1 250 - £802 - FF8 200
«**Fiorino**» Poster (160x116cm 62x45in) New-York
1999

DA CHONGGUANG 1623-1692 [6]

$25 740 - €24 410 - £15 660 - FF160 120
Jiangnan in Autumn Ink (20x256.5cm 7x100in)
Hong-Kong 1999

DA CUNHA Héctor 1915-1996 [21]

$308 - €330 - £209 - FF2 167
Composición Oleo/papel (31x21cm 12x8in) Madrid
2001

$649 - €661 - £407 - FF4 334
Constructivo Gouache/papier (30x21cm 11x8in)
Madrid 2000

DA RIMINI Lattanzio XV-XVI [1]

$8 383 - €7 084 - £5 000 - FF46 468
Head of Christ Oil/panel (30x27.5cm 11x10in)
London 1998

DA RIOS Luigi 1844-1892 [14]

$9 750 - €10 107 - £5 850 - FF66 300
Ragazza lombarda Olio/tela (54x42cm 21x16in)
Venezia 2000

DA Tony 1940 [12]

$18 000 - €17 842 - £11 259 - FF117 034
Ceramic Bear Ceramic (12x19cm 4x7in) New-York
1999

$3 500 - €3 740 - £2 382 - FF24 533
Bird Watercolour/paper (26x36cm 10x14in) Cloudcroft
NM 2001

DAALHOFF van Henri 1867-1953 [176]

$420 - €454 - £287 - FF2 976
A Punter on a Canal Oil/canvas (32x51.5cm
12x20in) Amsterdam 2001

$445 - €386 - £270 - FF2 530
Farmhouses Oil/board (30x41cm 11x16in)
Amsterdam 1999

$1 026 - €906 - £618 - FF5 943
«**Lentemorgen**»/**Untitled** Pastel/paper (14.5x19cm
5x7in) Amsterdam 1998

DABADIE Henri 1867-1949 [30]

$14 520 - €15 245 - £9 150 - FF100 000
Baie d'Along Huile/toile (100x224cm 39x88in) Laval
2000

$576 - €637 - £400 - FF4 181
Bouzghala, Algeria Oil/canvas (54x64.5cm 21x25in)
London 2001

$936 - €915 - £593 - FF6 000
Ruines de Carthage Huile/toile (24x35cm 9x13in)
Paris 1999

DABAT Alfred 1869-1935 [3]

$4 986 - €4 573 - £3 099 - FF30 000
Danseuse en rouge Huile/toile (100x91cm 39x35in)
Paris 1999

DABERT Louis XX [8]

$726 - €610 - £426 - FF4 000
Composition fruitière Huile/toile (46x55cm 18x21in)
Maubeuge 1998

DABHOLKAR R.P. XX [2]

$2 390 - €2 566 - £1 600 - FF16 834
Radha's Dream Watercolour (46x66cm 18x25in)
London 2000

DABIT Eugène 1878-1936 [5]

$706 - €686 - £436 - FF4 500
Hôtel du Nord, scène du café Encre/papier
(17x22cm 6x8in) Paris 1999

DABO Leon 1868-1960 [61]

$3 500 - €3 975 - £2 395 - FF26 072
Bognor, England Oil/canvas/board (50x40cm
19x15in) New-York 2000

$4 300 - €4 515 - £2 711 - FF29 617
Nocturne in Green Oil/canvas (25x33cm 10x13in)
Cleveland OH 2000

$368 - €305 - £216 - FF2 000
«**La Syrie et le Liban**» Affiche (105x75cm 41x29in)
Paris 1998

DACHAUER Wilhelm 1881-1951 [19]

$195 - €182 - £121 - FF1 191
«**Kriegsbilder-Ausstellung**» Poster (63x95cm
24x37in) Wien 2001

DACHINGER Hugo 1908-? [6]

$765 - €872 - £529 - FF5 720
Weiblicher Akt, liegend Pastel (39.4x58.4cm
15x22in) Wien 2000

DACOSTA António 1914 [4]

$4 446 - €3 876 - £2 652 - FF25 428
Retrato de señora Técnica mixta/cartón (29x22cm
11x8in) Lisboa 1998

$3 060 - €3 390 - £2 040 - FF22 236
Fonte de Sintra Gouache/papier (26x34cm 10x13in)
Lisboa 2000

DADAMAINO 1935 [26]

$5 077 - €5 899 - £3 568 - FF38 695
Untitled Mixed media (64x63cm 25x24in) Amsterdam
2001

$3 800 - €4 924 - £2 850 - FF32 300
«Volume a moduli sfasati» Sculpture bois
(60x40cm 23x15in) Prato 2000

$1 500 - €1 555 - £900 - FF10 200
Il movimento delle cose China/carta (112x83cm
44x32in) Roma 1999

DADD Frank 1851-1929 **[28]**

$1 112 - €1 060 - £675 - FF6 956
Something to Keep out the Cold
Watercolour/paper (36x26cm 14x10in) Stratford-upon-
Avon, Warwickshire 1999

DADD Richard 1817-1886 **[13]**

$6 488 - €6 255 - £4 000 - FF41 028
The Diadonus Oil/board (20x53.5cm 7x21in) London
1999

$66 720 - €78 227 - £48 000 - FF513 134
The Rabbit Hutch Watercolour (19x13cm 7x5in)
London 2001

DADDI Bernardo c.1310-c.1348/55 **[4]**

$32 000 - €30 106 - £19 968 - FF197 484
Madonna and Child enthroned with attending
Angels and Saints Tempera (53x32cm 20x12in)
New-York 1999

$146 799 - €137 300 - £90 000 - FF900 630
The Crucifixion/The Dead Christ on the Cross
Tempera/panel (31.5x23.5cm 12x9in) London 1998

DADDI Bernardo c.1512-1570 **[6]**

$460 - €525 - £320 - FF3 447
Frieze with the Triumph of Love, After Raphael
Engraving (11x41.5cm 4x16in) London 2000

DADE Ernest 1868-1936 **[53]**

$388 - €428 - £270 - FF2 806
Seascape Oil/panel (18x28cm 7x11in) Cambridge
2001

$1 171 - €1 378 - £840 - FF9 037
Coastal Scene with Figures, Horses and Carts
on a Beach Watercolour (34x51.5cm 13x20in) West-
Yorkshire 2001

DADO Miodrag Djuric, dit 1933 **[443]**

$6 500 - €6 056 - £4 011 - FF39 728
Composition Oil/canvas (161.5x129.5cm 63x50in)
New-York 1999

$3 015 - €2 897 - £1 869 - FF19 000
Deux personnages Huile/toile (60x60cm 23x23in)
Paris 1999

$954 - €884 - £593 - FF5 800
Quatre collages anatomiques Technique mixte
(26x19cm 10x7in) Versailles 1999

$823 - €884 - £551 - FF5 800
Les arachnides Encre (65x50cm 25x19in) Douai
2000

$146 - €137 - £90 - FF900
Sans titre Lithographie (50x39cm 19x15in) Paris 1999

DADSWELL Lyndon Raymond 1908-1986 **[17]**

$461 - €513 - £309 - FF3 363
Design for Theatre Watercolour, gouache/paper
(75x101cm 29x39in) Nedlands 2000

DAEL van Jan Frans 1764-1840 **[33]**

$330 000 - €365 464 - £223 806 - FF2 397 285
Roses, Tulips, Morning Glories and Other
Flowers in a Basket Oil/panel (64.5x54.5cm
25x21in) New-York 2000

$208 640 - €243 918 - £146 560 - FF1 600 000
Vase de fleur Huile/toile (40.5x32.5cm 15x12in) Paris
2000

$27 180 - €30 490 - £19 020 - FF200 000
Nature morte aux raisins, prunes, pêches et
ananas avec un papillon Aquarelle, gouache/papier
(35x44.5cm 13x17in) Paris 2001

DAELE van den Casimir 1818-1880 **[14]**

$1 434 - €1 487 - £912 - FF9 756
Jonge vrouw in mijmering Oil/panel (56.5x50cm
22x19in) Lokeren 2000

DAELE van den Charles XIX **[3]**

$6 473 - €6 070 - £4 000 - FF39 817
The loving Parents Oil/panel (70x91cm 27x35in)
London 1999

DAELLIKER Johann Rudolf 1694-1769 **[7]**

$1 927 - €1 858 - £1 188 - FF12 188
Halbfigurporträt einer Dame Öl/Leinwand
(83.5x64.5cm 32x25in) Bern 1999

DAENS Antoine 1871-1946 **[28]**

$348 - €397 - £240 - FF2 601
Village au bord de l'eau Huile/toile (50x70cm
19x27in) Bruxelles 2000

DAEPP Hans Arnold 1886-1949 **[31]**

$421 - €491 - £291 - FF3 222
Motiv in Oppligen Öl/Leinwand (46x55.5cm
18x21in) Bern 2000

DAEYE Hippolyte 1873-1952 **[20]**

$9 450 - €10 411 - £6 174 - FF68 292
Petit nu, Suzanne Huile/toile (55x38cm 21x14in)
Bruxelles 2000

$599 - €694 - £414 - FF4 552
Tête de paysan Huile/panneau (24.5x16cm 9x6in)
Bruxelles 2000

$3 587 - €3 099 - £2 162 - FF20 325
Portrait de jeune fille Technique mixte/papier
(37x29cm 14x11in) Bruxelles 1999

DAFFINGER Moritz Michael 1790-1849 **[52]**

$4 494 - €4 360 - £2 772 - FF28 602
Bildnis eines ungarischen Edelmanns in
Uniformjacke Miniature (8.5x7cm 3x2in) Wien 1999

$6 289 - €6 904 - £4 180 - FF45 286
Junge Dame Watercolour (9.3x7.3cm 3x2in) Wien
2000

DAGNAC-RIVIERE Charles Henri Gaston 1864-
1945 **[57]**

$1 333 - €1 113 - £781 - FF7 300
Arabes devant une ville en bord de mer
Huile/panneau (50x61cm 19x24in) Provins 1998

$827 - €773 - £500 - FF5 068
Boats moored at a Quay Oil/panel (24x18.5cm
9x7in) London 1999

DAGNAN Isidore 1794-1873 **[15]**

$2 777 - €2 748 - £1 700 - FF18 027
Travellers on a Wooded Track with Cattle resting
beyond Oil/canvas (38x51cm 14x20in) London 2000

$3 834 - €4 116 - £2 565 - FF27 000
La remontée des filets Huile/toile (32.5x44.5cm
12x17in) Paris 2000

DAGNAN-BOUVERET Pascal Adolphe Jean 1852-
1929 **[46]**

$2 149 - €1 829 - £1 279 - FF12 000
La prière Huile/toile (65x54cm 25x21in) Brest 1998

$4 016 - €4 458 - £2 800 - FF29 245
Paysage aux peupliers Oil/panel (24x18.5cm 9x7in)
London 2001

$1 741 - €1 829 - £1 150 - FF12 000
La jeune copiste au Louvre Encre Chine/papier
(36x27cm 14x10in) Paris 2000

D

DAGNAUX Albert Marie A. 1861-1933 **[24]**
- $15 000 - €16 488 - £9 612 - FF108 156
  The Promenade Along the Seine Oil/canvas (105.5x146cm 41x57in) New-York 2000
- $4 966 - €5 793 - £3 488 - FF38 000
  Jeune fille dans l'atelier du peintre Huile/toile (34x55cm 13x21in) Versailles 2000

DAGNEAU Henry XIX **[6]**
- $6 300 - €7 229 - £4 310 - FF47 422
  Still Life of Late Summer Flowers and Fruit Oil/canvas (53x45cm 21x18in) Cleveland OH 2000

DAGONET Ernest 1856-1926 **[4]**
- $1 918 - €2 287 - £1 368 - FF15 000
  Combat de cerfs Bronze (27x58x27cm 10x22x10in) Strasbourg 2000

DAGUERRE Louis J. Mandé 1787-1851 **[5]**
- $2 770 - €2 744 - £1 679 - FF18 000
  Torrent - Cascade Photo (25x30cm 9x11in) Paris 2000

DAHL Carl 1812-1865 **[13]**
- $104 650 - €87 379 - £62 205 - FF573 170
  Udsigt fra Larsens Plads til Toldboden Oil/canvas (79x111cm 31x43in) København 1998
- $3 211 - €3 551 - £2 228 - FF23 290
  Fregatten Freya Oil/canvas (23x21.5cm 9x8in) Vejle 2001

DAHL Carl 1810-1887 **[4]**
- $6 180 - €5 109 - £3 626 - FF33 512
  Das Heidelberger Schloss von Osten mit Blick auf die Stadt Öl/Leinwand (37.5x47cm 14x18in) Heidelberg 1998

DAHL Hans 1849-1937 **[204]**
- $21 820 - €25 212 - £15 280 - FF165 380
  Til kirke på Strynsvand i Nordfjord Oil/canvas (93x145cm 36x57in) Oslo 2001
- $9 820 - €11 527 - £6 930 - FF75 610
  Bergslandskap med ung vallflicka Oil/canvas (119x79cm 46x31in) Stockholm 2000
- $905 - €998 - £591 - FF6 548
  Noorse fjord Oil/panel (24x34cm 9x13in) Den Haag 2000

DAHL Hans Andreas 1881-1919 **[30]**
- $15 000 - €17 310 - £10 561 - FF113 545
  Mountain Girl with Goat seated at the Edge of a Fjord Oil/canvas (154x96cm 61x38in) Norwalk CT 2000
- $3 294 - €3 728 - £2 304 - FF24 456
  Fra Vestlandet Oil/canvas (41x51cm 16x20in) Oslo 2001

DAHL J. XX **[1]**
- $12 535 - €11 739 - £7 077 - FF77 000
  Sujet d'après Rubens Huile/toile (137x167cm 53x65in) Paris 1999

DAHL Johan 1818-1885 **[4]**
- $4 084 - €4 693 - £2 828 - FF30 782
  Marine med Fregatten Jylland i Sundet ud for Kronborg Oil/canvas (63x98cm 24x38in) København 2000

DAHL Johan Christian C. 1788-1857 **[63]**
- $77 360 - €79 251 - £47 740 - FF519 854
  Gebirgslandschaft mit Wildbach bei Hemsedal Öl/Leinwand (154x127cm 60x50in) Düsseldorf 2000
- $54 600 - €64 925 - £38 896 - FF425 880
  Kveldslandskap med gutt som fisker Oil/canvas (52x69cm 20x27in) Oslo 2000

DAHL
- $9 519 - €11 248 - £6 747 - FF73 785
  Weite Sommerlandschaft, die mit dem Horizont zu verschmelzen scheint Öl/Leinwand (25x34.5cm 9x13in) Stuttgart 2000
- $945 - €904 - £595 - FF5 928
  Husmannstue Etching (16x22cm 6x8in) Oslo 1999

DAHL Jørgen 1825-1890 **[13]**
- $1 399 - €1 542 - £933 - FF10 115
  Sejlskibe på havet Oil/canvas (58x84cm 22x33in) Vejle 2000
- $408 - €469 - £282 - FF3 078
  Barkskibet «Faders Minde» af Nyborg Gouache (43.5x70cm 17x27in) København 2000

DAHL Michael 1656/59-1743 **[42]**
- $14 059 - €13 760 - £9 000 - FF90 258
  Portrait of Sir Charles Shuckburgh, standing, wearing a green Coat Oil/canvas (124x99cm 48x38in) London 1999
- $5 047 - €5 577 - £3 500 - FF36 585
  Portrait of a Lady Oil/canvas (74.5x62cm 29x24in) London 2001

DAHL Ole Gabriel 1926 **[2]**
- $8 568 - €7 417 - £5 200 - FF48 651
  Young Girl in a Fjord Landscape Oil/canvas (43.5x61.5cm 17x24in) London 1998

DAHL Peter 1934 **[357]**
- $26 910 - €25 304 - £16 672 - FF165 982
  Gin och tonic Oil/canvas (150x200cm 59x78in) Stockholm 1999
- $3 946 - €3 711 - £2 445 - FF24 344
  Självporträtt i väst och vit kimono Oil/canvas (66x54cm 25x21in) Stockholm 1999
- $960 - €895 - £592 - FF5 874
  Älskande par Akvarell/papper (32x46cm 12x18in) Stockholm 1999
- $277 - €302 - £181 - FF1 982
  Älskande par Color lithograph (43x29cm 16x11in) Uppsala 2000

DAHL Siegwald Johannes 1827-1902 **[22]**
- $2 373 - €2 352 - £1 440 - FF15 426
  Snelandskab med hjort Oil/canvas (68x90cm 26x35in) Vejle 2000

DAHL-WOLFE Louise 1895-1989 **[65]**
- $2 000 - €1 893 - £1 243 - FF12 417
  Jean Patchett, Grenada, Harper's Bazaar Gelatin silver print (40x50cm 16x20in) New-York 1999

DAHLAGER Jules 1884-1952 **[13]**
- $2 500 - €2 273 - £1 505 - FF14 907
  Snow on the Ridge Oil/board (10x12cm 4x5in) Hayden ID 1998

DAHLBERG Erik Jönsson 1625-1703 **[9]**
- $93 - €112 - £65 - FF732
  Vue de Poznan Eau-forte (25x31.5cm 9x12in) Lódz 2000

DAHLGREEN Charles William 1864-1955 **[21]**
- $3 750 - €4 407 - £2 599 - FF28 910
  Brown County Landscape Oil/canvas (55x66cm 22x26in) Cincinnati OH 2000
- $800 - €895 - £557 - FF5 874
  Note in Pattern Etching, aquatint (25x30cm 9x11in) New-York 2001

DAHLGREN Carl Christian 1841-1920 **[22]**
- $1 700 - €1 781 - £1 076 - FF11 685
  Artist's Still Life Oil/canvas/board (69x79cm 27x31in) Austinburg OH 2000

DAHLMAN Helge 1924-1979 **[75]**

$1 045 - €1 177 - **£720** - FF7 722
Strandlandskap Oil/canvas (54x66cm 21x25in)
Helsinki 2000

$1 611 - €1 377 - **£946** - FF9 033
Helsingfors hamn Oil/panel (21x26cm 8x10in)
Helsinki 1998

DAHLSKOG Ewald Albin Filip 1894-1950 **[60]**

$1 420 - €1 239 - **£859** - FF8 125
Italienskt landskap Mixed media (46.5x55.5cm 18x21in) Stockholm 1998

DAHLWEIN Andreas XVIII **[1]**

$3 244 - €3 270 - **£2 025** - FF21 451
Gastmahl des Laban und Jacob Öl/Leinwand (27.5x38cm 10x14in) Wien 2000

DAHM H.P.C. 1787-1844 **[2]**

$4 221 - €4 040 - **£2 622** - FF26 502
Den danske fregat «Diana» commanderet af Capt. N.C. Meyer... Gouache/paper (51x68cm 20x26in) København 1999

DAHM Helen 1878-1968 **[132]**

$1 486 - €1 429 - **£915** - FF9 375
Komposition Huile/panneau (73x49cm 28x19in) St. Gallen 1999

$1 103 - €1 060 - **£683** - FF6 950
Selbstporträt Technique mixte/toile (48.5x32cm 19x12in) Zürich 1999

$887 - €965 - **£584** - FF6 330
Ohne Titel Mischtechnik/Papier (56x61.5cm 22x24in) Bern 2000

$284 - €281 - **£177** - FF1 844
Drei tanzende Frauenfiguren vor Stadt Lithographie (40x31cm 15x12in) St. Gallen 1999

DAHMEN Karl Fred 1917-1981 **[454]**

$23 973 - €22 344 - **£14 486** - FF146 565
Die Stunde Azur Oil/canvas (135x115cm 53x45in) München 1999

$4 052 - €4 602 - **£2 816** - FF30 185
«Lebende Steine» Mixed media (80x56cm 31x22in) München 2001

$3 253 - €2 863 - **£1 980** - FF18 781
Ohne Titel Mixed media (42x37.5cm 16x14in) Stuttgart 1999

$1 762 - €2 096 - **£1 256** - FF13 751
Teleobjekt Sculpture (59x34x6.8cm 23x13x2in) München 2000

$2 639 - €2 940 - **£1 726** - FF19 284
Ohne Titel Mixed media/paper (94.4x77cm 37x30in) München 2000

$202 - €204 - **£123** - FF1 341
Ohne Titel Farbradierung (65x60cm 25x23in) Stuttgart 1999

DAHMS Lise 1966 **[4]**

$150 - €146 - **£91** - FF959
Three Lemons Monotype (27.5x25cm 10x9in) Tel Aviv 2000

DAHN Walter 1954 **[158]**

$3 810 - €4 090 - **£2 550** - FF26 831
Die Nacht Öl/Leinwand (200x150cm 78x59in) Köln 2000

$523 - €562 - **£350** - FF3 689
Porträt Paul Maenz Charcoal/paper (41.8x29.5cm 16x11in) Köln 2000

$714 - €767 - **£478** - FF5 030
Ohne Titel Pochoir (38.3x24.3cm 15x9in) Köln 2000

DAHN-FRIES Sophie 1835-1898 **[2]**

$7 348 - €7 669 - **£4 650** - FF50 308
Blumenstrauss auf Steinbank, im Hintergrund Starnberger See Öl/Leinwand (102x73cm 40x28in) München 2000

DAI BENXIAO 1621-c.1691 **[2]**

$32 100 - €35 052 - **£20 650** - FF229 925
Misty, Rainy Landscape Ink/paper (85x37.5cm 33x14in) Hong-Kong 2000

DAI CANG XVII **[1]**

$41 024 - €48 218 - **£28 448** - FF316 288
Holding a Qin and Having the Wutong Tree Washed - Porträt of Wang Ink (31.5x126cm 12x49in) Hong-Kong 2000

DAI JIN 1388-1462 **[1]**

$51 480 - €48 820 - **£31 320** - FF320 240
Pines by Waterfall Ink/paper (31x485cm 12x190in) Hong-Kong 1999

DAI XI 1801-1860 **[10]**

$19 230 - €21 845 - **£13 500** - FF143 295
Retreat at Yunting Ink/paper (30x98cm 11x38in) Hong-Kong 2001

DAILEY Dan 1947 **[10]**

$6 000 - €5 727 - **£3 749** - FF37 569
Vessel from the Science Fiction Series Sculpture, glass (30x21.5x15.5cm 11x8x6in) New-York 1999

DAINGERFIELD Elliott 1859-1932 **[20]**

$6 000 - €6 387 - **£4 087** - FF41 898
Madonna and Child Oil/canvas/panel (101.5x81cm 39x31in) New-York 2001

$6 250 - €6 856 - **£4 245** - FF44 971
Homage to Albert Pinkham Ryder Oil/canvas (30x40cm 12x16in) New-Orleans LA 2000

DAINI Augusto 1860-1920 **[18]**

$994 - €1 002 - **£620** - FF6 574
The Recital Watercolour/paper (46x64cm 18x25in) Billingshurst, West-Sussex 2000

DAINTREY Adrian Maurice 1902-1988 **[59]**

$812 - €801 - **£500** - FF5 254
East River, New York Huile/toile (51x76cm 20x29in) Montréal 1999

DAIWAILLE Alexander Joseph 1818-1888 **[29]**

$4 690 - €5 336 - **£3 307** - FF35 000
Paysage Huile/toile (43.5x61.5cm 17x24in) Paris 2001

$5 764 - €5 445 - **£3 596** - FF35 719
Wooded River Landscape Oil/canvas (33x44cm 12x17in) Amsterdam 1999

DAKE Carel Lodewijk, Jr. 1886-1946 **[56]**

$1 489 - €1 651 - **£1 032** - FF10 830
Dimhöjt berg i indonesiskt landskap Oil/panel (46x60cm 18x23in) Malmö 2001

DAKIN Joseph act.1859-1914 **[8]**

$926 - €1 077 - **£650** - FF7 066
Rest by the Wayside Watercolour/paper (25x35cm 9x13in) Billingshurst, West-Sussex 2001

DAKIN Sidney Tilden 1876-1935 **[12]**

$800 - €935 - **£566** - FF6 134
Landscape at Sunset Oil/canvas (63x76cm 25x30in) Cedar-Falls IA 2001

DAKON Stefan 1904-1992 **[21]**

$1 194 - €1 017 - **£719** - FF6 672
Hockender Frauenakt Ceramic (H57cm H22in) Wien 1998

DALBERT Yolande XIX-XX **[1]**
$2 123 - €2 102 - **£1 300** - FF13 785
Souvenir de l'Oued-el-Hakum Oil/board (48x23cm 18x9in) London 2000

DALBONO Edoardo 1841-1915 **[94]**
$12 000 - €15 550 - **£9 000** - FF102 000
Fuochi e mare alla Festa del Carmine Olio/tela (90x150cm 35x59in) Roma 2000
$8 800 - €11 403 - **£6 600** - FF74 800
Pescatori a riva Olio/tela (63x128cm 24x50in) Roma 2001
$1 869 - €2 104 - **£1 287** - FF13 800
Les cavaliers Huile/carton (17.5x21.5cm 6x8in) Paris 2000
$1 300 - €1 348 - **£780** - FF8 840
Al traghetto Acquarello/cartone (25x33cm 9x12in) Roma 2000

DALBY OF YORK David 1794-c.1850 **[57]**
$8 000 - €6 835 - **£4 802** - FF44 835
Mr. Poole's Tawny with Jockey Up Oil/canvas (65x83cm 25x32in) New-York 1998

DALBY OF YORK John 1841-?? **[40]**
$26 325 - €25 167 - **£16 500** - FF165 082
The Kill Oil/canvas (45.5x64cm 17x25in) London 1999
$9 721 - €9 349 - **£6 000** - FF61 328
Over the Hedge Oil/canvas (23.5x44cm 9x17in) London 1999

DALEE Justus c.1800-c.1850 **[4]**
$2 600 - €2 777 - **£1 771** - FF18 213
William Palmer/Susan Richardson Palmer Miniature (7x12cm 3x5in) New-York 2001
$22 000 - €21 797 - **£13 347** - FF142 982
Miniature Portrait of a Child in Pink Seated in a Fancy Chair Watercolour/paper (7.5x5.5cm 2x2in) New-York 2000

DALEN van Jan 1611-1677 **[3]**
$23 196 - €21 474 - **£14 002** - FF140 863
Vanitas Stilleben Oil/panel (66.5x95cm 26x37in) Heidelberg 1999

DALENS Dirk I 1600-1676 **[15]**
$6 552 - €7 318 - **£4 440** - FF48 000
La grappe de la Terre Promise Huile/panneau (39x52cm 15x20in) Paris 2000

DALENS Dirk II 1658/59-1688 **[12]**
$35 863 - €38 496 - **£24 000** - FF252 518
Hawking Party in a wooded parkland Landscape, Water Fountain, Villa Oil/canvas (91x176.5cm 35x69in) London 2000
$30 880 - €35 656 - **£21 600** - FF233 888
Landskap med figurer/Byggnader Oil/canvas (80x115cm 31x45in) Stockholm 2001
$6 308 - €5 443 - **£3 806** - FF35 703
Wooded river landscape with peasant woman on a path Wash (24.9x30.2cm 9x11in) Amsterdam 1998

DALENS Dirk III 1688-1753 **[9]**
$7 019 - €6 868 - **£4 500** - FF45 054
River Landscape with Shepherds resting by a Torrent Oil/canvas (43x71cm 16x27in) London 1999

DALEY William P. 1925 **[3]**
$12 000 - €12 431 - **£7 638** - FF81 543
The Wall Sculpture (198x274x36cm 77x107x14in) New-York 2000
$4 000 - €4 144 - **£2 546** - FF27 181
Axial In Ceramic (32.5x53.5x56cm 12x21x22in) New-York 2000

DALGAS Carlos 1820-1851 **[13]**
$4 724 - €5 372 - **£3 300** - FF35 236
Får på en høj ved Skarritsøen Oil/canvas (69x101cm 27x39in) København 2000
$5 620 - €6 032 - **£3 762** - FF39 568
Lille vogterdreng med hat siddende i landskab omgivet af får Oil/canvas (35x42cm 13x16in) København 2000

DALGLISH William 1860-1909 **[13]**
$328 - €312 - **£200** - FF2 044
Figures in a Wooded Glen Watercolour/paper (34x48cm 13x18in) Sighthill 1999

DALI Louis 1905 **[28]**
$450 - €515 - **£312** - FF3 376
Paris Street Oil/canvas (20x25cm 8x10in) Cincinnati OH 2000

DALI Salvador 1904-1989 **[4289]**
$150 304 - €170 743 - **£105 504** - FF1 120 000
Oeil fleuri Tempera (240x190cm 94x74in) Vernou en Sologne 2001
$252 496 - €244 316 - **£160 000** - FF1 602 608
Personnage aux tiroirs Oil/canvas (179x50cm 70x19in) London 1999
$260 000 - €288 622 - **£172 900** - FF1 891 916
Hypnagogic Monument Oil/panel (39.5x31cm 15x12in) New-York 2000
$56 745 - €68 602 - **£39 645** - FF450 000
Vénus de Milo aux Tiroirs Bronze (114x34x10cm 44x13x3in) Paris 2000
$1 559 - €1 848 - **£1 100** - FF12 119
Hommage to Newton Bronze (H36cm H14in) London 2000
$13 490 - €14 483 - **£9 025** - FF95 000
Monde fantastique Aquarelle (16x26.5cm 6x10in) Paris 2000
$531 - €599 - **£368** - FF3 930
Les tiroirs, from Secret Poems by Apollinaire Etching (31.5x23.5cm 12x9in) Toronto 2000

DALL Hans Mathias 1862-1920 **[56]**
$429 - €404 - **£267** - FF2 648
Kystparti med personer og både på stranden Oil/canvas (37x52cm 14x20in) Vejle 1999

DALL'OCCA BIANCA Angelo 1858-1942 **[57]**
$12 000 - €15 550 - **£9 000** - FF102 000
Laghetto Olio/tela (136x140cm 53x55in) Roma 2000
$9 300 - €8 034 - **£6 200** - FF52 700
Canale a Venezia Olio/tela (80x90cm 31x35in) Milano 1998
$7 200 - €9 330 - **£5 400** - FF61 200
Figura femminile sulla neve Olio/tavoletta (34x22cm 13x8in) Genova 2001
$1 120 - €1 451 - **£840** - FF9 520
Volto femminile Pastelli/carta (48x34cm 18x13in) Roma 2001

DALL'OGLIO Egidio 1705-1748 **[4]**
$42 000 - €36 283 - **£28 000** - FF238 000
L'inverno Olio/tela (109x237cm 42x93in) Prato 1998

DALLA NOCE G. XIX **[2]**
$54 000 - €51 311 - **£32 853** - FF336 576
Reclining Nude Oil/canvas (137x145cm 53x57in) New-York 1999

DALLACQUA Daniel 1910-1982 **[13]**
$600 - €653 - **£412** - FF4 450
Woman with her Hands resting on her Feet, «Intermission» Marble (25x32cm 10x12in) Downington PA 2001

DALLAIRE Jean-Guy 1943 **[61]**
- $408 - €381 - £251 - FF2 500
  Famille avec jumeaux Bronze (14x13x8.5cm
  5x5x3in) Paris 1999

DALLAIRE Jean-Philippe 1916-1965 **[85]**
- $13 656 - €13 214 - £8 422 - FF86 678
  Chicken à la King Oil/board (51x61cm 20x24in)
  Toronto 1999
- $3 562 - €4 156 - £2 479 - FF27 262
  Two Birds Gouache/paper (26x33.5cm 10x13in)
  Toronto 2000

DALLEVES Raphy 1878-1940 **[12]**
- $1 672 - €1 967 - £1 212 - FF12 904
  Evolénarde Aquarelle (34x17.5cm 13x6in) Sion 2001
- $1 509 - €1 717 - £1 046 - FF11 261
  «Walliser Herbstfest Sitten..» Affiche couleur
  (101x63cm 39x24in) Sion 2000

DALLIN Cyrus Edwin 1861-1944 **[53]**
- $4 500 - €4 091 - £2 710 - FF26 833
  Appeal to the Great Spirit Bronze (H99cm H39in)
  Hayden ID 1998
- $7 500 - €6 993 - £4 652 - FF45 873
  On the Warpath Bronze (H22cm H8in) New-York
  1999

DALLINGER VON DALLING Alexander Johann
1783-1844 **[23]**
- $1 099 - €1 090 - £688 - FF7 150
  Pferde am Wegrand Oil/panel (23.3x30.5cm 9x12in)
  Wien 1999

DALOU Aimé Jules 1838-1902 **[517]**
- $1 633 - €1 753 - £1 092 - FF11 500
  Paysan relevant ses manches Bronze (H44cm
  H17in) Marseille 2000

DALPAYRAT Adrien Pierre 1844-1910 **[5]**
- $2 112 - €2 439 - £1 478 - FF16 000
  Masque souriant Grès (H19.5cm H7in) Paris 2001

DALSGAARD Christen 1824-1907 **[76]**
- $1 866 - €1 615 - £1 132 - FF10 596
  Landskab med stenet vej Oil/canvas (36x50cm
  14x19in) København 1998
- $587 - €565 - £364 - FF3 709
  **Kystparti fra Lundeborg med stråtaekt gård og
  skov i baggrunden** Oil/canvas (33.5x44cm 13x17in)
  København 1999

DALSGAARD Sven 1914-1999 **[330]**
- $7 884 - €7 538 - £4 944 - FF49 448
  Notat fra Dagbogen Mixed media (170x90cm
  66x35in) København 1998
- $1 441 - €1 346 - £890 - FF8 829
  Fire minutter Oil/canvas (43x50cm 16x19in)
  København 1999
- $352 - €349 - £214 - FF2 291
  Måne Oil/canvas (11x8.5cm 4x3in) Vejle 2000
- $866 - €808 - £522 - FF5 298
  Signeret Iron (H31cm H12in) København 1999
- $355 - €336 - £216 - FF2 207
  Et spil Gouache/paper (27x22cm 10x8in) København
  1999
- $291 - €269 - £181 - FF1 765
  Komposition Color lithograph (46x36cm 18x14in)
  Viby J, Århus 1999

DALVIT Oskar 1911-1975 **[63]**
- $281 - €327 - £194 - FF2 148
  Komposition in Rosa und Schwarz Öl/Leinwand
  (33x40cm 12x15in) Bern 2000

DALWOOD Dexter 1960 **[1]**
- $19 525 - €22 962 - £14 000 - FF150 620
  «Studio 54» Oil/canvas (152.5x183cm 60x72in)
  London 2001

DALY Kathleen Frances 1898-1994 **[51]**
- $804 - €887 - £531 - FF5 818
  Basque Fisherman Oil/panel (45.5x38cm 17x14in)
  Vancouver, BC. 2000
- $2 362 - €2 004 - £1 424 - FF13 143
  Canmore Reflection Oil/canvas/board (33x41cm
  12x16in) Calgary, Alberta 1998
- $546 - €529 - £336 - FF3 467
  **Alicee Quingalik, Heroine of Nanook of the
  North/Inuit Woman tanning** Pencil/paper (37x29cm
  14x11in) Toronto 1999

DALZIEL Owen 1860-1942 **[8]**
- $17 000 - €15 646 - £10 203 - FF102 634
  Watching the Regatta Oil/canvas (40x55cm
  16x22in) Chicago IL 1999

DAM VAN ISSELT van Lucie 1871-1949 **[15]**
- $2 522 - €2 496 - £1 543 - FF16 371
  Still Life with Chestnuts Oil/board (40x50cm
  15x19in) Amsterdam 2000

DAMANE-DEMARTRAIS Michel Fr. 1763-1827 **[4]**
- $2 464 - €2 698 - £1 700 - FF17 695
  **«Vue de Kremlin/Vue de Palais moderne, à
  Moscou/Vue de l'Académie»** Aquatint in colors
  (33x52.5cm 12x20in) London 2001

DAMARÉ L. ?-1927 **[17]**
- $1 100 - €1 283 - £772 - FF8 415
  **«Nouveau cirque, fête de nuit des artistes
  lyriques»** Poster (89x123cm 35x48in) New-York 2000

DAMAS Eugène 1848-1917 **[10]**
- $1 512 - €1 454 - £936 - FF9 540
  Riverbank in Summer Oil/canvas (47x59cm
  18x23in) Budapest 1999

DAMERON Émile Charles 1848-1908 **[65]**
- $2 625 - €2 220 - £1 570 - FF14 561
  The Chicken Run Oil/canvas (38x56cm 14x22in)
  Amsterdam 1998
- $1 168 - €1 296 - £811 - FF8 500
  La Plage de la Salice et les remparts d'Antibes
  Huile/toile (33x46cm 12x18in) Poitiers 2001

DAMIANI Jorge 1931 **[15]**
- $550 - €648 - £379 - FF4 253
  Amanecer en el campo Técnica mixta (50x60cm
  19x23in) Montevideo 2000

DAMIANO Bernard 1926 **[81]**
- $664 - €762 - £454 - FF5 000
  Sans titre Huile/toile (73x50cm 28x19in) Paris 2000
- $265 - €305 - £181 - FF2 000
  Sans titre Gouache/papier (50x65cm 19x25in) Paris
  2000

DAMIANOS Constantin 1869-1953 **[19]**
- $1 054 - €1 022 - £653 - FF6 707
  Liegende Akte Pencil/paper (23.5x34cm 9x13in) Graz
  1999

DAMIEN François Joseph 1879-1973 **[17]**
- $3 016 - €3 222 - £2 054 - FF21 138
  De danseressen Huile/toile (50x40cm 19x15in)
  Lokeren 2001

DAMIN Georges XX **[13]**
- $827 - €793 - £510 - FF5 200
  La chapelle Sainte-Anne Huile/toile (54x73cm
  21x28in) Lyon 1999

DAMIN Victor Louis XX [3]
💰 $5 572 – €5 396 – **£3 500** – FF35 393
Bowl of Strawberries with Bottles/Decanter with a Glass and Lemons Oil/canvas (54.5x65cm 21x25in) London 1999

DAMINI Pietro 1592-1631 [5]
💰 $10 000 – €11 618 – **£7 028** – FF76 212
Fantasy Portrait of Ugo Alberti IV, seated, half-length, with a Sword Oil/canvas (150x115.5cm 59x45in) New-York 2001

DAMIOLI Aldo 1952 [4]
💰 $1 880 – €2 436 – **£1 410** – FF15 980
«**Venezia New York**» Acrilico/tela (70x90cm 27x35in) Milano 2001

DAMISCH Günter 1958 [132]
✏️ $377 – €436 – **£264** – FF2 860
«**Köpflerwelten**» Aquarell/Papier (15x21cm 5x8in) Linz 2001
🎨 $256 – €291 – **£179** – FF1 906
Ohne Titel Radierung (17x70cm 46x27in) Wien 2001

DAMM C. c.1860-1935 [6]
🖌 $1 420 – €1 346 – **£864** – FF8 829
Sejlskib til ankers ved en kyst Oil/canvas (116x74cm 45x29in) København 1999

DAMM Johan Frederik 1820-1894 [4]
🖌 $7 676 – €8 729 – **£5 362** – FF57 258
Opstilling med melon, ananas, jordbaer samt glas med rodvin på en karm Oil/canvas (55x68cm 21x26in) København 2000

DAMMANN Hans 1867-? [4]
💰 $212 – €230 – **£145** – FF1 509
Sich anschleichender Tiger Bronze (H28cm H11in) Berlin 2001

DAMME van Frans 1858-1925 [71]
🖌 $872 – €817 – **£543** – FF5 357
Bleach Field by a Waterside Oil/canvas (65x99cm 25x38in) Amsterdam 1999
🖌 $493 – €460 – **£304** – FF3 018
Binnenschiffer in der Scheldemündung im Licht der untergehenden Sonne Ol/Leinwand (29x46cm 11x18in) Köln 1999

DAMME van Suzanne 1901-1987 [121]
🖌 $660 – €620 – **£407** – FF4 065
Marine Huile/toile (130x81cm 51x31in) Bruxelles 1999

DAMME-SYLVA van Émile 1853-1935 [44]
🖌 $1 404 – €1 637 – **£972** – FF10 740
Kühe am Seeufer Ol/Leinwand (77x127.5cm 30x50in) Bern 2000
🖌 $559 – €595 – **£381** – FF3 902
Vaches au bord de l'étang Huile/panneau (24x38cm 9x14in) Bruxelles 2001

DAMMEIER Rudolf 1851-1936 [10]
🖌 $299 – €277 – **£180** – FF1 819
Still Life of Dead Game and Vegetable Oil/board (45x58.5cm 17x23in) Billingshurst, West-Sussex 1999

DAMOISELET Florentin 1644-c.1690 [1]
🖌 $33 000 – €38 867 – **£22 822** – FF254 954
Putto Holding a Garland of Flowers and Seated on a Drum, with a Helmet Oil/canvas (138x80.5cm 54x31in) New-York 2000

DAMON René Louis XIX-XX [3]
🖌 $9 381 – €7 880 – **£5 500** – FF51 691
Portrait of Ada Rogerson, née Burr Oil/canvas (86.5x67.5cm 34x26in) London 1998

DAMOUR Charles 1813-? [9]
✏️ $1 794 – €1 982 – **£1 244** – FF13 000
Paysage animé Pastel/papier (67.5x92cm 26x36in) Paris 2001

DAMOYE Pierre Emmanuel Eug. 1847-1916 [235]
🖌 $4 205 – €4 802 – **£2 957** – FF31 500
Paysage de Sologne Huile/toile (47x87cm 18x34in) Fontainebleau 2001
🖌 $1 742 – €1 524 – **£1 055** – FF10 000
Bord de Seine par matinée brumeuse Huile/panneau (18x33cm 7x12in) Paris 1998

DAMRONG WONG-UPARAJ 1936 [4]
🖌 $3 825 – €4 114 – **£2 565** – FF26 985
Fishing Village Tempera (35x45cm 13x17in) Bangkok 2000
🎨 $1 402 – €1 508 – **£940** – FF9 894
Abstract Woodcut (63x44cm 24x17in) Bangkok 2000

DAMSCHROEDER Jan Jac Matthys 1825-1905 [49]
🖌 $1 122 – €1 017 – **£700** – FF6 670
Washing Day Oil/canvas (38x47.5cm 14x18in) London 1999

DANBY Francis 1793-1861 [37]
🖌 $1 613 – €1 854 – **£1 117** – FF12 162
The Rock Pool Oil/canvas (36x48cm 14x19in) Hamilton, Lanarkshire 2000
🖌 $3 397 – €4 039 – **£2 354** – FF26 495
Sonnenaufgang am Meer Ol/Leinwand (31x40.5cm 12x15in) Bremen 2000
✏️ $2 665 – €2 603 – **£1 700** – FF17 075
Mountain Landscape with a Wolf and Birds, Norway Watercolour (18x24cm 7x9in) London 1999

DANBY James Francis 1816-1875 [25]
🖌 $9 463 – €10 158 – **£6 332** – FF66 632
Boats on Lake at Sunset Oil/canvas (58x89cm 22x35in) Dublin 2000
🖌 $3 140 – €3 301 – **£1 970** – FF21 655
Sunset at Low Tide Oil/canvas (10.5x17.5cm 4x6in) Dublin 2000

DANBY Kenneth Edison, Ken 1940 [65]
🖌 $4 882 – €4 178 – **£2 939** – FF27 405
«**The Bread Wagon**» Tempera/board (61x81.5cm 24x32in) Toronto 1994
✏️ $1 619 – €1 889 – **£1 127** – FF12 392
Kentvale Watercolour (51x71cm 20x27in) Toronto 2000
🎨 $195 – €228 – **£137** – FF1 497
Trail Serigraph in colors (43x86.5cm 16x34in) Calgary, Alberta 2001

DANBY Thomas 1818-1886 [30]
🖌 $1 608 – €1 778 – **£1 115** – FF11 660
Woman walking in a River Landscape Oil/canvas (29x38cm 11x14in) Dublin 2001
✏️ $408 – €349 – **£240** – FF2 189
A Cottage in Herfordshire Watercolour/paper (17x25cm 7x10in) Bristol, Avon 1998

DANCE Nathaniel 1734-1811 [32]
🖌 $57 927 – €55 158 – **£36 000** – FF361 548
Charlott, Countess of Abingdon, in coronation Robes, holding a Coronet Oil/canvas (217x143.5cm 85x56in) London 1999
🖌 $2 595 – €2 824 – **£1 800** – FF18 815
Portrait of Charles Manners 4th Duke of Rutland (1754-1787) Oil/canvas (74x61.5cm 29x24in) London 2001
✏️ $426 – €496 – **£300** – FF3 253
Two Men on a Cliff Top, one suspended over the edge hanging Watercolour/paper (19.5x31.5cm 7x12in) London 2001

DANCHIN Léon 1887-1939 **[187]**
$196 - €229 - £138 - FF1 500
Tête de cheval Lithographie couleurs (44x34cm 17x13in) Blois 2001

DANCIGER Alice 1914-1991 **[18]**
$657 - €634 - £415 - FF4 162
Harbour Morning Oil/canvas (49x61cm 19x24in) Sydney 1999

DANDINI Cesare c.1595-1658 **[33]**
$672 435 - €721 803 - £450 000 - FF4 734 720
Tobias and the Angel Oil/canvas (220x168cm 86x66in) London 2000
$34 370 - €35 791 - £21 777 - FF234 773
Die Madonna mit dem Christuskind und dem Johannesknaben Öl/Leinwand (83x70cm 32x27in) München 2000
$6 489 - €6 541 - £4 050 - FF42 903
Bildnis eines jungen Dame Öl/Leinwand (37.5x33.5cm 14x13in) Wien 2000

DANDINI Pietro 1646-1712 **[43]**
$30 000 - €25 916 - £15 000 - FF170 000
Adorazione dei Magi Olio/tela (130x100cm 51x39in) Firenze 1999
$5 934 - €6 555 - £4 115 - FF43 000
Héliodore chassant les marchands du temple Huile/toile (44x69cm 17x27in) Paris 2001
$1 089 - €927 - £650 - FF6 079
Figure of a Draped Man, Standing Ink (41x24cm 16x9in) London 1998

DANDINI Vincenzo 1607-1675 **[10]**
$11 400 - €12 949 - £8 000 - FF84 940
A Stemma celebrating the Marriage of Antonio di Francesco Michelozzi Oil/canvas/panel (228x194cm 89x76in) London 2001
$263 - €282 - £180 - FF1 852
Study of St Paul, for Altarpiece at Ognissanti, Florence Black chalk/paper (41.5x28cm 16x11in) London 2001

DANDOY Albert 1885-1977 **[21]**
$707 - €793 - £492 - FF5 203
La porte de Sambre et Meuse Huile/panneau (39x29cm 15x11in) Antwerpen 2001

DANDOY Armand 1834-1898 **[3]**
$8 008 - €7 669 - £4 947 - FF50 308
La Province de Namur monumentale et pittoresque Albumen print (22x29.5cm 8x11in) Köln 1999

DANDOY Giuliam XVII **[3]**
$41 097 - €41 423 - £25 650 - FF271 719
Stilleben mit Früchten, einem Weinglas und einer Pastete Öl/Leinwand (55x70cm 21x27in) Wien 2000

DANDOY Jan Baptist XVII **[4]**
$14 640 - €15 339 - £9 684 - FF100 617
Stilleben mit Austern, Zitronen, Trauben, Teller mit Krebsen Öl/Leinwand (51x65cm 20x25in) München 2000

DANDRÉ-BARDON Michel-François 1700-1778 **[22]**
$7 069 - €6 860 - £4 401 - FF45 000
Étude de mains tenant une bouteille Sanguine/papier (28x34.5cm 11x13in) Montfort L'Amaury 1999

DANDRIDGE Bartholomew 1691-c.1755 **[12]**
$5 000 - €4 197 - £2 932 - FF27 533
Portrait of a Child, full length, in a white dress, holding a garland Oil/canvas (118x80.5cm 46x31in) New-York 1998

$3 686 - €3 483 - £2 300 - FF22 846
Double Portrait of the Countess of Castlemaine and Child Watercolour/paper (127x101cm 50x40in) Fernhurst, Haslemere, Surrey 1999

DANEDI IL MONTALTO Giovanni Stefano 1608-1689 **[11]**
$21 376 - €24 279 - £15 000 - FF159 262
The Decollation of Saint John the Baptist Oil/canvas (176x237cm 69x93in) London 2001

DANEDI IL MONTALTO Giuseppe 1618-1688 **[4]**
$20 000 - €20 733 - £12 000 - FF136 000
Amor Sacro e Amor Profano Olio/tela (118.5x87.5cm 46x34in) Milano 1999

DANGEL van Miguel 1946 **[16]**
$1 050 - €1 078 - £700 - FF7 070
Crucificíon Técnica mixta/lienzo (104x61cm 40x24in) Caracas 2000

DANGELO Sergio 1932 **[86]**
$570 - €492 - £285 - FF3 230
«Mistero di O» Tecnica mista/tela (80x40cm 31x15in) Prato 1999
$201 - €237 - £140 - FF1 556
Absract Composition Ink (46x34cm 18x13in) London 2000

DANGER Henri Camille 1857-1937 **[18]**
$10 000 - €11 753 - £6 933 - FF77 094
Allegory of Industry and Labor Oil/canvas (168x135cm 66x53in) New-York 2001

DANGUY Jean Célestin 1863-1926 **[12]**
$289 - €244 - £171 - FF1 600
Jeune femme dénudée Fusain/papier (36x25cm 14x9in) Paris 1998

DANHAUSER Josef 1805-1845 **[44]**
$10 995 - €10 901 - £6 885 - FF71 505
Frau des Fischers am Meeresufer Oil/panel (39.5x48.5cm 15x19in) Wien 1999
$1 893 - €2 180 - £1 293 - FF14 301
Portraitkopf Oil/panel (35.5x26cm 13x10in) Wien 2000
$700 - €716 - £438 - FF4 695
Zwei sitzende junge MÄdchen mit Kopftüchern Pencil (11.5x22.5cm 4x8in) Köln 2000

DANIELI Giuseppe 1865-1931 **[25]**
$3 250 - €3 369 - £1 950 - FF22 100
Nevicata Olio/tavola (38.5x61cm 15x24in) Vercelli 1999
$1 500 - €1 296 - £750 - FF8 500
Natura morta di frutta Olio/tavola (27.5x40.5cm 10x15in) Vercelli 1999

DANIELL Samuel 1775-1811 **[22]**
$290 - €342 - £200 - FF2 241
Studies of Dancing Natives Pencil/paper (17x14cm 6x5in) Cape Town 2000
$992 - €1 107 - £647 - FF7 261
The Koodoo/The Pallah/Boosh Wannah's/Kaffers on a March Aquatint in colors (32.5x45.5cm 12x17in) Johannesburg 2000

DANIELL Thomas 1749-1840 **[101]**
$63 968 - €61 597 - £40 000 - FF404 052
Landscape in India Oil/canvas (98x137cm 38x53in) London 1999
$84 510 - €99 253 - £60 000 - FF651 060
View of Ryacotta, South India Oil/canvas (88.5x128.5cm 34x50in) London 2000
$2 988 - €3 208 - £2 000 - FF21 043
View of the Palace at Rhotas Ghur, Bihar Pencil (30.5x49cm 12x19in) London 2000

D

▥▥ **$1 599** - €1 540 - **£1 000** - FF10 101
Dusasumade Gaut at Bernares on the Ganges
Aquatint (59x45.5cm 23x17in) London 1999

DANIELL Thomas & William 1749/69-1840/37 **[117]**

✏ **$2 535** - €2 977 - **£1 800** - FF19 531
Studies of Indian Fishing Vessels Pencil/paper
(15x12cm 5x4in) London 2000

▥▥ **$1 077** - €1 156 - **£720** - FF7 584
**Mausoleum of Nawaub Assoph Khan,
Rajemahel** Aquatint (48x63.5cm 18x25in) London
2000

DANIELL William 1769-1837 **[153]**

◒ **$77 165** - €91 772 - **£55 000** - FF601 986
Kemaes Head, Cardiganshire Oil/canvas
(77.5x104cm 30x40in) London 2000

◒ **$5 214** - €6 050 - **£3 600** - FF39 686
On the Thames near Hampton Court Oil/board
(30.5x46cm 12x18in) London 2000

◒ **$4 033** - €3 958 - **£2 500** - FF25 966
**Hindu Temple on the Island of Rameswaram
near Cape Comorin** Watercolour (40x63cm 15x24in)
London 1999

▥▥ **$850** - €787 - **£520** - FF5 164
East India Company Docks Aquatint in colors
(45x78cm 18x31in) Chicago IL 1999

DANIELS Alfred 1926 **[33]**

◒ **$781** - €764 - **£500** - FF5 014
Portrait of Bobbie Marmor Oil/canvas (76x51cm
29x20in) London 1999

◒ **$624** - €595 - **£380** - FF3 905
**Magdalen College from the botanical Gardens,
Oxford** Oil/board (30.5x37cm 12x14in) London 1999

DANIELS Andries 1580-? **[26]**

◒ **$16 000** - €14 082 - **£9 740** - FF92 372
**The Virgin and Child with Scenes from the Life
of Christ** Oil/canvas (126.5x95cm 49x37in) New-York
1999

◒ **$31 716** - €26 157 - **£18 684** - FF171 576
Blumenkorb auf einem Tisch Oil/panel (51x64cm
20x25in) Wien 1998

◒ **$2 873** - €3 212 - **£2 000** - FF21 071
**The Virgin and Child surrounded by a Garland
of Flowers** Oil/copper (30.5x23cm 12x9in) London
2001

DANIELS George Fisher 1821-1879 **[1]**

◒ **$30 000** - €34 989 - **£21 063** - FF229 512
Pastoral Landscape with Distant Shore Oil/can-
vas (59.5x120.5cm 23x47in) Boston MA 2000

DANIëLS René 1950 **[17]**

◒ **$40 000** - €44 803 - **£27 792** - FF293 888
«In de wolken, de geniale zônes» Oil/canvas
(190.5x240cm 75x94in) New-York 2001

◒ **$27 000** - €27 227 - **£16 998** - FF178 596
La muse venale Oil/canvas (40x40cm 15x15in)
Amsterdam 1999

◒ **$2 224** - €2 496 - **£1 541** - FF16 371
Untitled Watercolour/paper (26x20.5cm 10x8in)
Amsterdam 2000

▥▥ **$1 901** - €1 815 - **£1 188** - FF11 906
Elba - St. Helena Etching (65x51cm 25x20in)
Amsterdam 1999

DANIELS William 1813-1880 **[11]**

◒ **$5 230** - €5 614 - **£3 500** - FF36 825
Homeless Oil/canvas (49x33cm 19x12in) London
2000

DANIELSEN Jacob 1888-1938 **[3]**

✏ **$423** - €483 - **£294** - FF3 169
Kajakmaend jager hvalros, Diskobugt juni
Watercolour/paper (10x15cm 3x5in) Köbenhavn 2000

DANIELSON-GAMBOGI Elin 1861-1919 **[46]**

◒ **$27 036** - €30 273 - **£18 774** - FF198 576
Sommardag i en italiensk by Oil/canvas (51x36cm
20x14in) Helsinki 2001

◒ **$15 460** - €16 818 - **£10 190** - FF110 320
Onningeby Oil/canvas (20x37cm 7x14in) Helsinki
2000

✏ **$410** - €437 - **£278** - FF2 868
Blicken Chalks/paper (31x24cm 12x9in) Helsinki 2001

DANIELSSON Emil 1882-1967 **[14]**

◒ **$1 308** - €1 514 - **£926** - FF9 928
Örhänge Oil/canvas (41x44cm 16x17in) Helsinki 2000

DANIELSZ. H. (Hendrick Dzn.?) XVI-XVII **[3]**

◒ **$12 070** - €12 958 - **£8 075** - FF85 000
Le destin de Salomon et de la Reine de Saba
Huile/panneau (84x98.5cm 33x38in) Paris 2000

DANIFER Sigurd 1894-1958 **[9]**

◒ **$592** - €566 - **£373** - FF3 714
Badende gutter Oil/panel (50x61cm 19x24in) Oslo
1999

DANIOTH Heinrich 1896-1953 **[62]**

◒ **$4 354** - €4 952 - **£3 019** - FF32 486
Bauernfamilie Tempera/panel (50x55.5cm 19x21in)
Zofingen 2000

◒ **$1 916** - €1 876 - **£1 179** - FF12 304
Blumenstilleben Tempera (30x38.5cm 11x15in)
Zürich 1999

✏ **$315** - €312 - **£196** - FF2 049
Allegorische Frauenfigur auf Kugel stehend
Aquarelle (35x15cm 13x5in) St. Gallen 1999

DANKMEYER Charles B. 1861-1923 **[61]**

◒ **$1 153** - €998 - **£700** - FF6 548
**A nocturnal View of Amsterdam with barges
along a quay** Oil/canvas (59.5x86cm 23x33in)
Amsterdam 1999

◒ **$826** - €794 - **£515** - FF5 209
View of the «Vispoort» Harderwijk Oil/canvas
(33x41cm 12x16in) Amsterdam 1999

DANLER Herbert 1928 **[7]**

◒ **$1 851** - €2 180 - **£1 302** - FF14 301
Gerstbichl bei Telfes Oil/panel (24x44.5cm 9x17in)
Wien 2000

✏ **$1 550** - €1 453 - **£958** - FF9 534
Blick von Neustift auf den Stubaier Gletscher
Aquarell, Gouache/Papier (48.5x65cm 19x25in) Wien
1999

DANLOUX Henri Pierre 1753-1809 **[58]**

◒ **$10 000** - €11 075 - **£6 782** - FF72 645
Portrait of Etiennette Roussée Oil/canvas
(90.5x71cm 35x27in) New-York 2000

◒ **$8 000** - €9 295 - **£5 622** - FF60 969
**Portrait of a Gentleman, said to be the Poet
Roger Delile** Oil/canvas (37.5x32cm 14x12in) New-
York 2001

✏ **$5 678** - €6 095 - **£3 800** - FF39 982
**Portrait of the Dancer Jean-Etienne Despreaux,
in Profile** Black chalk/paper (17.5x14.5cm 6x5in)
London 2000

DANNAT William Turner 1853-1929 **[12]**

◒ **$3 153** - €2 782 - **£1 900** - FF18 251
Harem Scene Oil/panel (40.5x30.5cm 15x12in)
London 1998

DANNENBERG Alice 1861-? **[14]**
- $2 760 - €3 049 - **£1 914** - FF20 000
Bébé Huile/toile (38x44cm 14x17in) Le Mans 2001

DANNER Sara Kolb 1894-1969 **[25]**
- $1 300 - €1 239 - **£824** - FF8 126
View of Montmartre Oil/board (50x40cm 20x16in)
New-Orleans LA 1999

DANS María Antonia 1932-1988 **[52]**
- $4 800 - €4 505 - **£2 925** - FF29 550
Campesinos con la vaca Oleo/tablex (50x70cm
19x27in) Madrid 1999
- $1 080 - €1 201 - **£740** - FF7 880
Pueblo Técnica mixta (29x50cm 11x19in) Madrid
2000
- $1 540 - €1 652 - **£1 017** - FF10 835
Jarra con flores Pastel/papier (50x70cm 19x27in)
Madrid 2000

DANSAERT Léon Marie Constant 1830-1909 **[32]**
- $5 276 - €5 899 - **£3 672** - FF38 695
Le petit dessinateur Oil/panel (38x46cm 14x18in)
Amsterdam 2001
- $1 951 - €1 785 - **£1 195** - FF11 707
Richelieu recevant des notables Huile/panneau
(31x40cm 12x15in) Bruxelles 1999

DANSLER Robert 1900-1972 **[7]**
- $1 800 - €1 731 - **£1 111** - FF11 354
«Cycles Roold» Poster (156x117cm 61x46in) New-
York 1999

DANTAN Antoine L. 1798-1878 **[10]**
- $3 289 - €3 115 - **£2 000** - FF20 434
Jeune fille Napolitaine jouant au tambourin
Bronze (H40cm H15in) London 1999

DANTAN Edouard J. 1848-1897 **[10]**
- $46 997 - €43 798 - **£29 000** - FF287 297
Fastening the Nets Oil/canvas (156x243cm 61x95in)
London 1999
- $9 182 - €9 452 - **£5 784** - FF62 000
Le jeu du disque Huile/toile (51x99cm 20x38in)
Paris 2000
- $1 697 - €2 033 - **£1 164** - FF13 333
**De jonge matrozen aan de waterkant (les
jeunes matelots surle rivage)** Huile/panneau
(18x39cm 7x15in) Antwerpen 2000

DANTAN Jean-Pierre le Jeune 1800-1869 **[15]**
- $366 - €381 - **£242** - FF2 550
Portrait charge de Louis Jansenne (b.1809)
Plâtre (H22.5cm H8in) Paris 2000

DANTI Gino 1881-1968 **[9]**
- $550 - €570 - **£330** - FF3 740
Carro con buoi bardati a festa Olio/tavoletta
(13.5x22.5cm 5x8in) Firenze 2001

DANTI Ignazio 1537-1586 **[1]**
- $163 080 - €182 939 - **£113 040** - FF1 200 000
**Vue topographique de la Terre Sainte aux
armoiries papales de Pie V** Huile/toile (82x146cm
32x57in) Paris 2000

DANTU Georges 1867-? **[23]**
- $1 150 - €1 235 - **£769** - FF8 100
Érables et chrysanthèmes au Japon Huile/toile
(65x81.5cm 25x32in) Paris 2000

DANVERS Verney L. XIX-XX **[9]**
- $1 200 - €1 199 - **£733** - FF7 867
«Bournemouth» Poster (101x125cm 40x49in) New-
York 2000

DANVIN Victor 1802-1842 **[3]**
- $11 205 - €9 699 - **£6 800** - FF63 621
**Extensive River Landscape with a View of the
Château d'Ambroise** Oil/canvas (61.5x89.5cm
24x35in) London 1998

DANY (Daniel Henrotin) 1943 **[20]**
- $422 - €389 - **£253** - FF2 550
Histoire sans héros, pl.7 Encre Chine/papier
(42.5x32.5cm 16x12in) Paris 1999

DANZEL Jacques Claude 1737-1809 **[1]**
- $1 071 - €925 - **£535** - FF6 069
**Vulcain présentant à Venus des armes d'après
F.Boucher** Gravure (55x66cm 21x25in) Venezia 1999

DANZINGER Itzhak 1916-1979 **[35]**
- $42 000 - €49 792 - **£30 597** - FF326 617
Sheep of the Negev Bronze (H19cm H7in) Tel Aviv
2001
- $2 200 - €2 457 - **£1 408** - FF16 116
Indian Dancer Pencil/paper (28x13cm 11x5in) Tel
Aviv 2000

DAPELS van Philippe c.1620-c.1670 **[4]**
- $9 288 - €8 924 - **£5 724** - FF58 536
Paysage boisé avec voyageurs Huile/toile
(78x113cm 30x44in) Bruxelles 1999

DAPENA PARILLA Juan XX **[2]**
- $4 200 - €4 039 - **£2 592** - FF26 494
«Sevilla» Poster (160x108.5cm 62x42in) New-York
1999

DAPLYN Alfred James 1844-1926 **[4]**
- $5 454 - €6 043 - **£3 700** - FF39 642
Clifton Gardens Oil/canvas (54.5x74.5cm 21x29in)
Sydney 2000

DAQUINO Francisco XX **[65]**
- $384 - €360 - **£228** - FF2 364
Paisaje de Sallent de Gállego Oleo/tabla (46x55cm
18x21in) Madrid 1999
- $352 - €330 - **£220** - FF2 167
Uvas Oleo/lienzo/tabla (35x27cm 13x10in) Madrid
1999

DARANYAGALA Justin Pieris 1903-1967 **[2]**
- $4 482 - €4 812 - **£3 000** - FF31 564
Landscape with Train and Farm Labourers
Oil/canvas (85x91cm 33x35in) London 2000
- $3 287 - €3 529 - **£2 200** - FF23 147
Lady Seated by Chair Ink (61x46cm 24x18in)
London 2000

DARASSE Georges XIX-XX **[4]**
- $3 288 - €3 049 - **£1 984** - FF20 000
Le port de Beaulieu Huile/toile (24.5x50cm 9x19in)
Paris 1999

DARBES Joseph Friedrich A. 1747-1810 **[7]**
- $6 139 - €5 303 - **£3 701** - FF34 783
**Portrait of Anna Charlotte Dorothea,
Rechsgräfin von Biron** Oil/canvas (70.4x57.1cm
27x22in) Amsterdam 1998

DARBOUR Marguerite Mary XIX-XX **[12]**
- $871 - €1 037 - **£604** - FF6 800
**La place de la Concorde, vue du jardin des
Tuileries** Huile/toile (50x65cm 19x25in) Paris 2000

DARBOVEN Hanne 1941 **[38]**
- $3 938 - €3 374 - **£2 367** - FF22 131
Ohne Titel Graphit (63.5x87.2cm 25x34in) Hamburg
1998
- $163 - €184 - **£114** - FF1 207
Ohne Titel Farbserigraphie (33.5x95cm 13x37in)
Stuttgart 2001

DARCHE Joseph 1846-1906 **[5]**
$716 - €686 - £441 - FF4 500
Jeune femme étendant son linge Huile/toile
(65x43cm 25x16in) La Varenne-Saint-Hilaire 1999

DARCIS Jean-Louis ?-1801 **[12]**
$384 - €325 - £230 - FF2 130
Le départ/Le retour, after J.B. Isabey Engraving
(42x33.5cm 16x13in) London 1998

DARDEL von Fritz 1817-1901 **[46]**
$393 - €397 - £245 - FF2 602
Vue d'Ulriksdal Mixed media/paper (26x38cm
10x14in) Stockholm 2000

DARDEL von Ingrid 1922-1962 **[3]**
$246 - €285 - £175 - FF1 872
Mor och dotter Akvarell/papper (41x32cm 16x12in)
Stockholm 2000

DARDEL von Nils 1888-1943 **[102]**
$10 023 - €8 476 - £5 990 - FF55 598
«Den Trevliga Sommaröndagen» Mixed media
(36x48cm 14x18in) Stockholm 1998
$1 920 - €1 864 - £1 185 - FF12 228
Figurkomposition Mixed media (21x13.5cm 8x5in)
Stockholm 1999
$2 392 - €2 249 - £1 482 - FF14 754
Italienska Pencil/paper (66x48cm 25x18in) Stockholm
1999

DARDENNE Léon 1865-1912 **[14]**
$655 - €635 - £412 - FF4 167
Arrival of the Ferry Watercolour (19x29cm 7x11in)
Amsterdam 1999

DARDOIZE Louis Émile 1826-1901 **[16]**
$21 000 - €18 590 - £12 839 - FF121 944
The Harvest Oil/canvas (92x142.5cm 36x56in) New-
York 1999

DAREL Georges 1892-1943 **[61]**
$473 - €515 - £311 - FF3 376
**Stilleben mit antikem Torso und Cézanne-
Bildnis** Öl/Leinwand (81.5x100.5cm 32x39in) Bern
2000

DARET Ernesto, Monsu XVII **[1]**
$9 723 - €8 400 - £4 861 - FF55 100
Paesaggio con cacciatori Olio/tela (90x128cm
35x50in) Roma 1999

DAREY Louis XIX **[12]**
$823 - €915 - £574 - FF6 000
Le chien Fox Huile/toile (90x66cm 35x25in)
Versailles 2001

DARGAUD Victor P.J. c.1850-? **[7]**
$42 500 - €39 808 - £26 129 - FF261 124
The Hôtel de Ville, Paris Oil/canvas (60x81.5cm
23x32in) New-York 1999
$4 603 - €5 183 - £3 233 - FF34 000
Rue animée dans une ville méditerranéenne
Huile/toile (39.5x25.5cm 15x10in) Tarbes 2001

DARGELAS André Henri 1828-1906 **[34]**
$61 582 - €57 391 - £38 000 - FF376 458
The Doctor's Visit Oil/panel (50.5x40.5cm 19x15in)
London 1999
$15 822 - €14 684 - £9 500 - FF96 322
Playing Marbles Oil/panel (35x26.5cm 13x10in)
London 1999

DARGEN Ernst 1866-1929 **[8]**
$461 - €511 - £319 - FF3 353
«Florenz, Ponte Veccio» Aquarell/Papier (40x53cm
15x20in) Kempten 2001

DARGER Henry J. 1892-1973 **[5]**
$27 000 - €23 294 - £16 348 - FF152 801
**«A Battle near McHollester Run»/At Wichey
Sansinia meet Gertrude** Pencil (48x121cm 18x47in)
New-York 1999

DARGIE William Alexander 1912 **[31]**
$787 - €819 - £497 - FF5 371
Mountain Road Autumn Oil/canvas/board
(19.5x25cm 7x9in) Melbourne 2000

DARGOUGE Georges Edmond 1897-1990 **[15]**
$3 247 - €2 744 - £1 931 - FF18 000
Bretagne - Bénédiction de la mer Huile/toile
(48x68cm 18x26in) Calais 1998

DARIEN Henri Gaston 1864-1926 **[42]**
$103 261 - €95 834 - £62 000 - FF628 630
A bustling Street Scene, Paris Oil/canvas
(123.5x203cm 48x79in) London 1999
$2 824 - €3 049 - £1 952 - FF22 000
Nature morte au bocal, aux cerises et fromage
Huile/toile (46x71cm 18x27in) La Varenne-Saint-Hilaire
2001
$725 - €854 - £509 - FF5 603
Girl on the Donkey Oil/canvas (44x36cm 17x14in)
Sydney 2000
$3 495 - €3 390 - £2 200 - FF22 236
The Young Fisherboy Pastel/paper (55x46cm
21x18in) London 1999

DARJOU Alfred H. 1832-1874 **[17]**
$5 318 - €4 878 - £3 305 - FF32 000
Le marchand ambulant de fruits et légumes
Huile/toile (65x46.5cm 25x18in) Paris 1999

DARLEY Felix Octavius Carr 1822-1888 **[29]**
$900 - €850 - £559 - FF5 573
Praying at a Wayside Chapel Watercolour/paper
(23x33cm 9x13in) Milford CT 1999

DARLING Wilder M. 1856-1933 **[8]**
$7 500 - €8 050 - £5 019 - FF52 807
The Haymaker Oil/canvas (60x48cm 24x19in) Cedar-
Falls IA 2000

DARLING William S. 1882-1963 **[26]**
$1 500 - €1 620 - £1 036 - FF10 625
«Box Canyon» Oil/masonite (50x76cm 20x30in)
Altadena CA 2001

DARNAUD Maxime 1931 **[18]**
$500 - €558 - £327 - FF3 659
Industrial Landscape Oil/canvas (45x60cm 18x24in)
Chicago IL 2000

DARNAUT Hugo 1851-1937 **[118]**
$12 750 - €10 899 - £7 650 - FF71 490
Weidelandschaft mit Schafen Oil/Karton (45x61cm
17x24in) Wien 1998
$5 805 - €5 450 - £3 600 - FF35 752
**Motiv aus Wieselburg (Blick auf die
Wieselburger Brauerei)** Öl/Karton (31.5x44cm
12x17in) Wien 1999
$2 979 - €3 237 - £1 917 - FF21 451
Blick auf Wien vom Kahlenberg aus
Aquarell/Papier (25x37cm 9x14in) Wien 2000

DARPY Lucien Gilbert 1875-? **[5]**
$3 955 - €4 116 - £2 668 - FF27 000
Roses Technique mixte (64x64cm 25x25in) Paris 2000

DARRAH Ann Sophia Towne 1819-1881 **[2]**
$4 000 - €4 407 - £2 668 - FF28 909
Smith's Farm, Glass Head, Manchester Oil/board
(25x46cm 10x18in) Portsmouth NH 2000

DARRO Thomas P. 1946 **[2]**
$4 200 - €4 787 - **£2 930** - FF31 403
Girl at Sunset Oil/canvas (36x54cm 14x21in) Dallas TX 2001

DARROW Whitney 1909 **[9]**
$996 - €1 157 - **£700** - FF7 590
Elderly Couple, Wife sitting on her Husband's Knee Ink (25x17.5cm 9x6in) London 2001

DARRU Louise c.1840-? **[9]**
$2 500 - €2 167 - **£1 527** - FF14 217
Still Life with Flowers in an Urn Oil/canvas (106.5x78.5cm 41x30in) New-York 1999

DAS Arup 1927 **[14]**
$2 713 - €2 998 - **£1 881** - FF19 663
Three Women Oil/canvas (57x80cm 22x31in) Singapore 2001

DASBURG Andrew Michael 1887-1979 **[29]**
$10 500 - €9 850 - **£6 488** - FF64 615
Landscape with White House Oil/canvas/panel (35x50cm 14x20in) Cleveland OH 1999
$12 000 - €14 103 - **£8 319** - FF92 512
Landscape with Pueblos Watercolour (37x52cm 14x20in) Beverly-Hills CA 2000

DASHWOOD Geoffrey 1947 **[10]**
$2 597 - €2 496 - **£1 600** - FF16 373
Squirrel Bronze (H26cm H10in) London 1999

DASSELBORNE Lucien 1873-1962 **[7]**
$2 540 - €2 961 - **£1 780** - FF19 423
Village Scene Oil/canvas (44x59cm 17x23in) Cleveland OH 2000

DASSON Henry 1825-1896 **[13]**
$5 000 - €5 892 - **£3 446** - FF38 652
Figural Group Bronze (H61cm H24in) New-York 2000

DASSONVILLE Jacques 1619-c.1670 **[8]**
$219 - €188 - **£132** - FF1 234
La Pipe allumée/La Mère nourrice à l'estaminet Radierung (9.5x9cm 3x3in) München 1998

DASSONVILLE William E. 1879-1957 **[23]**
$3 250 - €2 774 - **£1 943** - FF18 199
Untitled Gelatin silver print (22x18cm 8x7in) San-Francisco CA 1998

DASTUGUE Maxime 1851-1909 **[9]**
$6 000 - €6 236 - **£3 781** - FF40 908
An Elegante Ride in the Park Oil/panel (31.5x41cm 12x16in) New-York 2000

DATER Judy R. Lichtenfeld 1941 **[43]**
$2 200 - €2 118 - **£1 375** - FF13 895
Imogen and Twinka, Yosemite Gelatin silver print (25.5x20.5cm 10x8in) New-York 1999

DATHAN Johann Georg 1703-1748 **[2]**
$12 096 - €10 223 - **£7 238** - FF67 058
Hl. Familie mit dem Johannesknaben Oil/panel (62x46cm 24x18in) Berlin 1998

DATSENKO Lidya 1948 **[45]**
$561 - €555 - **£350** - FF3 642
Composition with Three Apricots Oil/canvas (40x50cm 15x19in) Fernhurst, Haslemere, Surrey 1999
$363 - €351 - **£228** - FF2 300
Abricots et fleurs des champs Huile/toile (41x30cm 16x11in) L'Isle-Adam 1999

DAUBER Miriam 1946 **[1]**
$4 500 - €5 065 - **£3 100** - FF33 222
The Ball Oil/board (60x90cm 23x35in) Herzelia-Pituah 2000

DAUBIGNY Charles François 1817-1878 **[401]**
$48 000 - €52 678 - **£30 907** - FF345 542
Les bords de l'Oise Oil/canvas (84x157.5cm 33x62in) New-York 2000
$18 146 - €21 328 - **£12 581** - FF139 900
Pont de Paris Oil/panel (34x54cm 13x21in) Amsterdam 2000
$6 141 - €7 013 - **£4 319** - FF46 000
Paysage du Valmondois Huile/panneau (23.5x41cm 9x16in) Fontainebleau 2001
$1 167 - €1 296 - **£813** - FF8 500
Étude de sous-bois Pierre noire/papier (29.5x48cm 11x18in) Versailles 2001
$224 - €256 - **£155** - FF1 676
Les ruines du Château de Crémieux Radierung (9.2x7.3cm 3x2in) Berlin 2000

DAUBIGNY Karl 1846-1886 **[203]**
$15 217 - €12 781 - **£8 945** - FF83 837
Alte Eichen am Wasser im Wald von Barbizon, Abendstimmung Öl/Leinwand (110x163cm 43x64in) Köln 1998
$3 692 - €3 964 - **£2 470** - FF26 000
Silhouettes aux abords d'un torrent Huile/toile (46x98cm 18x38in) Paris 2000
$3 204 - €3 201 - **£2 003** - FF21 000
La ramassage de coquillages - la Cancalaise Huile/toile (46.5x33.5cm 18x13in) Pontoise 1999
$4 690 - €4 726 - **£2 923** - FF31 000
Le port de Honfleur Sanguine/papier (27.5x42.5cm 10x16in) Paris 2000

DAUCHEZ André 1870-1948 **[255]**
$1 278 - €1 372 - **£855** - FF9 000
Paysage aux quatre arbres Huile/toile (46x55cm 18x21in) Douarnenez 2000
$427 - €408 - **£267** - FF2 676
Paysage aux grands arbres et deux personnes Oil/panel (28x41cm 11x16in) Zofingen 1999
$96 - €110 - **£67** - FF720
La jetée de Trouville Aquarelle/papier (27x19cm 10x7in) Quimper 2001
$125 - €137 - **£87** - FF900
Quai de Launac Eau-forte (25x39cm 9x15in) Brest 2001

DAUCHOT Gabriel 1927 **[279]**
$760 - €732 - **£469** - FF4 800
Fête au bois Huile/toile (40x80cm 15x31in) Le Havre 1999
$331 - €305 - **£198** - FF2 000
Sur la plage/Le Sulky Huile/toile (12x22cm 4x8in) Soissons 1999

DAUDÉ André 1897-1979 **[11]**
$2 000 - €2 324 - **£1 405** - FF15 242
Pianos Daude Color lithograph (159.5x119.5cm 62x47in) New-York 2000

DAUGHERTY James Henry 1889-1974 **[25]**
$3 500 - €3 980 - **£2 427** - FF26 110
Rural Life, Mural Study Oil/canvas (104x76cm 41x30in) Chicago IL 2000
$2 400 - €2 725 - **£1 642** - FF17 876
Homage a Galileo Pastel (23x23cm 9x9in) New-York 2000

DAULLÉ Jean 1703-1763 **[15]**
$204 - €240 - **£144** - FF1 576
Que de trésors répandus sur la terre!, según François Boucher Grabado (32x26.5cm 12x10in) Madrid 2000

DAUMAL René 1908-1944 **[13]**
* $428 - €457 - £291 - FF3 000
  Un enduri Dessin (15x21cm 5x8in) Paris 2001

DAUMIER Honoré 1808-1879 **[935]**
* $20 716 - €19 922 - **£12 784** - FF130 678
  La lecture Öl/Leinwand (44x62cm 17x24in) Bern 1999
* $13 947 - €16 401 - **£10 000** - FF107 586
  La soupe Oil/paper/canvas (15x32cm 5x12in) London 2001
* $12 000 - €11 360 - **£7 453** - FF74 514
  Lameth Bronze (H14.5cm H5in) New-York 1999
* $4 441 - €4 116 - **£2 762** - FF27 000
  Deux hommes nus Crayon (20.5x28cm 8x11in) Paris 1999
* $248 - €282 - **£170** - FF1 850
  Croquis d'expressions Lithograph (26x40cm 10x15in) Edinburgh 2000

DAUMILLER Adolf Gustav 1876-? **[13]**
* $927 - €766 - **£543** - FF5 026
  «Die Stehende» Porcelain (H38.5cm H15in) München 1998

DAUPHIN Eugène Baptiste E. 1857-1930 **[9]**
* $6 000 - €6 753 - **£4 133** - FF44 296
  Morning at Creux St.Georges, near Toulon on the Mediteranenan Oil/canvas (115x89cm 45x35in) New-Orleans LA 2000

DAUR Hermann 1870-1925 **[19]**
* $5 296 - €6 230 - **£3 838** - FF40 865
  «Sommerlandschaft im Schwarzwald mit Sicht auf den Blauen» Öl/Leinwand (61x83cm 24x32in) Zofingen 2001

DAUREA Giovanni 1955 **[32]**
* $140 - €181 - **£105** - FF1 190
  Primavera Olio/tela (40x30cm 15x11in) Vercelli 2000

DAUSCH Constantin 1841-1908 **[1]**
* $11 229 - €11 316 - **£7 000** - FF74 225
  Vestal Marble (H120.5cm H47in) London 2000

DAUSSY Raymond 1918 **[3]**
* $2 900 - €3 049 - **£1 914** - FF20 000
  Autoportrait à la faux Huile/toile (46.5x33.5cm 18x13in) Paris 2000

DAUX Charles Edmond/Émile 1855-? **[23]**
* $2 791 - €2 556 - **£1 701** - FF16 769
  Junge Orientalin, mit einem Wellensittich auf ihren Schultern Öl/Leinwand (56x38.5cm 22x15in) München 1999
* $514 - €553 - **£350** - FF3 627
  Study of a Girl Watercolour/paper (52x35.5cm 20x13in) Billingshurst, West-Sussex 2001

DAUZATS Adrien 1804-1868 **[52]**
* $50 208 - €48 784 - **£31 392** - FF320 000
  Les environs de Damas Huile/toile/panneau (101x140.5cm 39x55in) Paris 1999
* $1 480 - €1 372 - **£920** - FF9 000
  Paysage de Sicile Aquarelle (24x19.5cm 9x7in) Paris 1999

DAVAGIAN Bryan XX **[4]**
* $1 200 - €1 147 - **£730** - FF7 526
  Midsummers Still Life Acrylic/canvas (61x45.5cm 24x17in) Boston MA 1999

DAVELOOZE Jean-Baptiste 1807-1886 **[9]**
* $6 126 - €5 095 - **£3 597** - FF33 424
  A Panoramic Wooded Landscape with a Herdsman and his Flock Oil/canvas (63.5x84.5cm 25x33in) Amsterdam 1998

DAVENPORT Henry 1882-? **[9]**
* $1 700 - €1 785 - **£1 149** - FF11 707
  Portrait of a young Woman Oil/canvas (44x36cm 17x14in) Fairfield ME 2001

DAVENPORT Ian 1966 **[9]**
* $11 660 - €9 963 - **£7 000** - FF65 350
  Poured Painting: Black, White, Black Mixed media (183x183cm 72x72in) London 1998
* $4 332 - €4 721 - **£3 000** - FF30 968
  «Poured Painting: Lime Green, Pale Yellow, Lime Green» Mixed media (61.5x61.5cm 24x24in) London 2001

DAVENPORT Leslie 1905-1973 **[41]**
* $245 - €225 - **£150** - FF1 479
  Restoration to a Norwich Church with Cathedral Watercolour/paper (73x43cm 29x17in) Aylsham, Norfolk 1998

DAVENT Léon act.1540-1556 **[20]**
* $1 200 - €1 129 - **£741** - FF7 409
  Diana Resting after Primaticcio Etching (15x28cm 5x11in) New-York 1999

DAVERNY G. XX **[1]**
* $2 934 - €3 049 - **£1 840** - FF20 000
  Diane aux bouquetins Bronze (H56cm H22in) Paris 2000

DAVEY Randall 1887-1964 **[48]**
* $1 800 - €2 044 - **£1 263** - FF13 410
  Trophy of the Hunt Oil/canvas (61x46.5cm 24x18in) New-York 2001

DAVID D'ANGERS Pierre Jean 1788-1856 **[215]**
* $629 - €732 - **£442** - FF4 800
  Allégorie de la Liberté Bronze (H23cm H9in) Paris 2001

DAVID DE MARSEILLE Joseph Antoine 1725-1789 **[6]**
* $1 094 - €1 220 - **£744** - FF8 000
  Paysage animé avec une cascade Sanguine/papier (41x52cm 16x20in) Nice 2000

DAVID Ferdinand 1860-? **[42]**
* $239 - €229 - **£145** - FF1 500
  A l'orée du bois Huile/carton (22x28cm 8x11in) Toulouse 1999

DAVID Fernand 1872-1927 **[5]**
* $1 571 - €1 524 - **£978** - FF10 000
  Jeune fille assise sur un tabouret Bronze (H43cm H16in) Montfort L'Amaury 1999

DAVID Giovanni 1743-1790 **[11]**
* $13 000 - €13 476 - **£7 800** - FF88 400
  Scena di stregoneria Inchiostro (24x31cm 9x12in) Milano 2001
* $1 165 - €1 278 - **£791** - FF8 384
  Il sacrificio di Polissena Radierung (22.5x30.7cm 8x12in) Berlin 2000

DAVID Gustave 1824-1891 **[22]**
* $2 113 - €2 515 - **£1 463** - FF16 500
  Jeune femme taquinant le chat Huile/panneau (24x19cm 9x7in) Saint-Dié 2000
* $688 - €775 - **£480** - FF5 081
  A tête-à-tête/The Philanderer Watercolour (30x23.5cm 11x9in) London 2001

DAVID Hermine 1886-1971 **[182]**
* $1 286 - €1 448 - **£903** - FF9 500
  Paysage du Tarn Huile/panneau (65.5x54cm 25x21in) Paris 2001

$422 - €457 - **£289** - FF3 000
Thonon-le-Bains Aquarelle/papier (31x41cm 12x16in) Troyes 2001

DAVID Jacques Louis 1748-1825 **[66]**
$14 805 - €13 720 - **£9 207** - FF90 000
Vue de l'entrée du Capitole Encre (15.5x19.5cm 6x7in) Paris 1999

DAVID José Maria 1944 **[147]**
$5 254 - €5 641 - **£3 515** - FF37 000
Lionne couchée Bronze (30x67x40cm 11x26x15in) Nice 2000

DAVID Jules 1808-1892 **[47]**
$14 458 - €12 144 - **£8 500** - FF79 662
«A la Comete» Oil/canvas (84x129.5cm 33x50in) London 1998
$426 - €457 - **£285** - FF3 000
La mode illustrée Aquarelle (28x22cm 11x8in) Paris 2000

DAVID Louis 1792-1868 **[12]**
$1 708 - €1 657 - **£1 082** - FF10 868
Scène dans un parc Watercolour, gouache/paper (26x22cm 10x8in) Warszawa 1999

DAVID Michael 1954 **[17]**
$1 300 - €1 515 - **£900** - FF9 940
The Archer's Plum Print in colors (26x51cm 10x20in) New-York 2000

DAVIDOVA Marina 1951 **[22]**
$371 - €347 - **£225** - FF2 275
Geese Oil/canvas/board (27x35cm 10x13in) Fernhurst, Haslemere, Surrey 1999

DAVIDSON Alexander ?-1887 **[6]**
$6 091 - €5 754 - **£3 800** - FF37 746
Granny's Servants Oil/canvas (34x29cm 13x11in) Perthshire 1999

DAVIDSON Allan Douglas 1873-1932 **[40]**
$1 428 - €1 347 - **£900** - FF8 838
A Warrior/An Angel Oil/board (38x24cm 14x9in) Godalming, Surrey 1999

DAVIDSON Bessie 1879-1965 **[57]**
$23 355 - €22 867 - **£14 370** - FF150 000
Le faisan Huile/panneau (138x106cm 54x41in) Paris 1999
$17 127 - €16 769 - **£10 538** - FF110 000
Jeune fille au miroir Huile/toile (73x60cm 28x23in) Paris 1999
$2 491 - €2 439 - **£1 532** - FF16 000
Rivière d'Ecosse Huile/panneau (32.5x41cm 12x16in) Paris 1999
$2 024 - €1 982 - **£1 245** - FF13 000
Guéthary, bord de mer Gouache/papier (18x23cm 7x9in) Paris 1999

DAVIDSON Bruce 1933 **[51]**
$3 000 - €2 802 - **£1 813** - FF18 381
Teenage Couple by Cigarette Machine Vintage gelatin silver print (16x25cm 6x10in) New-York 1999

DAVIDSON Clara 1874-1962 **[65]**
$800 - €685 - **£485** - FF4 495
Lady with a Black Hat Oil/canvas (50x40cm 20x16in) New-York 1999
$850 - €729 - **£515** - FF4 778
Garden scenes Oil/board (30x38cm 12x15in) New-York 1999
$800 - €685 - **£485** - FF4 495
European Landscapes Watercolour/paper (29x38cm 11x15in) New-York 1999

DAVIDSON George XIX-XX **[10]**
$3 688 - €4 121 - **£2 500** - FF27 029
Spring Idyll Oil/canvas (62x75cm 24x29in) Edinburgh 2000

DAVIDSON Janet Sutherland XIX-XX **[2]**
$1 731 - €1 665 - **£1 080** - FF10 920
Dutch women working in a Field Oil/canvas (30.5x38cm 12x14in) Stansted Mountfitchet, Essex 1999

DAVIDSON Joseph, Jo 1883-1952 **[32]**
$850 - €913 - **£569** - FF5 987
Bust of Abraham Lincoln Terracotta (H25cm H10in) Bolton MA 2000

DAVIDSON Lilian Lucy 1893-1954 **[15]**
$8 380 - €9 523 - **£5 787** - FF62 467
Sheep in a Mountain Pasture Oil/canvas (60x50cm 24x20in) Dublin 2000
$8 380 - €9 523 - **£5 787** - FF62 467
Village Below Croagh Patrick Oil/canvas (35x40cm 14x16in) Dublin 2000

DAVIDSON Robert Charles 1946 **[8]**
$12 710 - €14 749 - **£8 775** - FF96 745
Mood Metal (4.5x6.5x5cm 1x2x1in) Vancouver, BC. 2000
$926 - €994 - **£629** - FF6 521
Every Year the Salmon Come Silkscreen in colors (29.5x41.5cm 11x16in) Calgary, Alberta 2001

DAVIDSON Thomas XIX-XX **[14]**
$8 816 - €8 329 - **£5 500** - FF54 633
Tam O'Shanter Oil/canvas (71x102.5cm 27x40in) Perthshire 1999
$2 589 - €2 438 - **£1 600** - FF15 991
Study of a Naval Officer Oil/board (19.5x14.5cm 7x5in) London 1999

DAVIDSON Willy 1890-1933 **[4]**
$4 630 - €5 266 - **£3 211** - FF34 545
«Vatikan» Öl/Leinwand (95x65cm 37x25in) Hamburg 2000

DAVIE Alan 1920 **[265]**
$12 997 - €14 163 - **£9 000** - FF92 905
"For a Gay Tom-Cat" Oil/canvas (152.5x121.5cm 60x47in) London 2001
$3 751 - €4 209 - **£2 600** - FF27 606
It's a fine Day, let's follow the Birds Oil/paper/canvas (47x58cm 18x22in) London 2000
$1 713 - €1 636 - **£1 070** - FF10 732
Trick Box Gouache/paper (56x77cm 22x30in) Köln 1999
$151 - €172 - **£104** - FF1 126
Windows Farblithographie (63x82cm 24x32in) Zofingen 2000

DAVIE Karen 1965 **[10]**
$4 250 - €4 931 - **£2 934** - FF32 346
Liar I Mixed media (124.5x96.5cm 49x37in) New-York 2000
$8 500 - €9 862 - **£5 868** - FF64 693
Lazy Susan #5/Lazy Susan #6 Oil/canvas (51x101.5cm 20x39in) New-York 2000

DAVIES Albert Webster 1889-1967 **[12]**
$2 500 - €2 940 - **£1 792** - FF19 284
Summer's Day Oil/masonite (46.5x60.5cm 18x23in) Philadelphia PA 2001
$3 500 - €3 975 - **£2 455** - FF26 076
The Webster Auction, Salem depot, New Hampshire Oil/canvas/board (29x40cm 11x16in) New-York 2001

DAVIES Arthur Bowen 1862-1928 **[187]**
- $55 000 - €52 341 - £34 402 - FF343 332
  The Sphynx Oil/canvas (167.5x91.5cm 65x36in) New-York 1999
- $3 400 - €4 110 - £2 373 - FF26 957
  Dawn Light Oil/canvas (56x43cm 22x16in) Bethesda MD 2000
- $1 600 - €1 913 - £1 099 - FF12 547
  Cows in a Wood Pasture Oil/board (23x28cm 9x11in) Chicago IL 2000
- $1 300 - €1 344 - £821 - FF8 819
  Standing Female Nude Pastel (42.5x30.5cm 16x12in) New-York 2000
- $250 - €303 - £174 - FF1 985
  Greek Athletes Lithograph (26x20.5cm 10x8in) Bethesda MD 2000

DAVIES Arthur Edward 1893-1989 **[239]**
- $567 - €609 - £380 - FF3 998
  Springtime Flowers Oil/canvas (61x51cm 24x20in) Reepham, Norwich 2000
- $353 - €358 - £220 - FF2 350
  Still Life Study of Flowers in a Grey and Bleu Vase on a Table Oil/canvas (27x20cm 11x8in) Aylsham, Norfolk 2000
- $482 - €489 - £300 - FF3 205
  Devil's Tower, Riverside, Norwich Watercolour/paper (27x40cm 11x16in) Aylsham, Norfolk 2000

DAVIES David 1864-1939 **[34]**
- $95 370 - €92 791 - £58 695 - FF608 670
  A Normandy Village Oil/canvas (100.5x73cm 39x28in) Melbourne 1999
- $6 999 - €6 617 - £4 343 - FF43 403
  Country Farmhouse at Dusk Oil/canvas (30.5x43.5cm 12x17in) Malvern, Victoria 1999
- $2 012 - €2 248 - £1 288 - FF14 745
  Quiet River Watercolour/paper (31.5x37.5cm 12x14in) Malvern, Victoria 2000

DAVIES Edgar W. XIX-XX **[1]**
- $2 918 - €2 824 - £1 800 - FF18 526
  Allegory of Love Watercolour/paper (62x48cm 24x18in) London 1999

DAVIES Edward 1841-1920 **[15]**
- $328 - €300 - £200 - FF1 971
  Scottish Landscape with Cattle, mist and Stream Watercolour/paper (20x38cm 7x14in) Leamington-Spa, Warwickshire 1999

DAVIES James Hey 1844-? **[7]**
- $3 040 - €2 902 - £1 900 - FF19 038
  Returning Home with the Flock Oil/canvas (71x107cm 27x42in) London 1999

DAVIES John 1946 **[23]**
- $4 614 - €5 099 - £3 200 - FF33 449
  Head Sculpture, glass (H30.5cm H12in) London 2001
- $606 - €670 - £420 - FF4 394
  Figure Coloured pencils (42x66cm 16x25in) London 2001

DAVIES Llewellyn 1950 **[4]**
- $7 133 - €8 316 - £5 000 - FF54 551
  Elephant Bronze (H77cm H30in) London 2000

DAVIES Peter 1970 **[1]**
- $30 683 - €36 083 - £22 000 - FF236 689
  «Text Painting» Acrylic/canvas (254x203.5cm 100x80in) London 2001

DAVIES William 1826-1910 **[22]**
- $6 892 - €6 512 - £4 300 - FF42 713
  Glen Lean, Argyllshire/Near Ardentinny, Argyllshire Oil/canvas (54x44cm 21x17in) Perthshire 1999
- $3 287 - €3 001 - £2 000 - FF19 685
  Cattle in a Highland Landscape Oil/board (28x20.5cm 11x8in) London 1998

DAVILA José Antonio 1935 **[23]**
- $1 920 - €1 829 - £1 200 - FF12 000
  Sin título Oleo/tabla (33.5x51cm 13x20in) Caracas 1999

DAVILA Juan Domingo 1946 **[12]**
- $473 - €534 - £333 - FF3 505
  «The Field» Color lithograph (98x67cm 38x26in) Malvern, Victoria 2001

DAVIS Arthur Alfred act.1877-? **[29]**
- $20 052 - €16 947 - £12 000 - FF111 168
  Drawing a Covert/On the Scent/The Chase/Gone to Ground Oil/panel (175.5x205.5cm 69x80in) London 1998
- $28 000 - €32 532 - £19 678 - FF213 393
  The Hunt Oil/canvas (142x61cm 55x24in) New-York 2001
- $2 279 - €2 650 - £1 600 - FF17 383
  Hounds in a Kennel Oil/canvas (25.5x30.5cm 10x12in) London 2001
- $668 - €565 - £400 - FF3 705
  A Huntsman with his Hounds in an extensive Landscape Watercolour/paper (33x45cm 12x17in) London 1998

DAVIS Arthur H. act.1871-1893 **[14]**
- $616 - €658 - £420 - FF4 315
  Pheasant in a Cornfield Oil/canvas (24.5x37cm 9x14in) Billingshurst, West-Sussex 2001

DAVIS Catherine XIX **[2]**
- $16 000 - €13 858 - £9 812 - FF90 904
  View of the State House Oil/panel (51x61cm 20x24in) New-York 1999

DAVIS Cecil Clark 1877-1955 **[2]**
- $4 250 - €4 562 - £2 844 - FF29 927
  Joan D'Avigdor with a Falcon Oil/canvas (81x66cm 31x25in) San-Francisco CA 2000

DAVIS Charles Harold 1856-1933 **[43]**
- $80 000 - €93 367 - £56 712 - FF612 448
  Summer Clouds Oil/canvas (131x196cm 51x77in) New-York 2001
- $22 000 - €24 242 - £14 632 - FF159 016
  View of Newburyport Harbour Oil/canvas (66x81cm 26x32in) Haverhill MA 2000
- $4 000 - €3 948 - £2 432 - FF25 900
  Autumn Landscape Oil/canvas (33.5x40.5cm 13x15in) New-York 2000
- $1 600 - €1 842 - £1 091 - FF12 083
  Sailboat Watercolour/paper (38x54.5cm 14x21in) New-York 2000

DAVIS Edward 1813-1878 **[1]**
- $23 027 - €25 792 - £16 000 - FF169 185
  Two Lovers Marble (H94cm H37in) London 2001

DAVIS Edward Thompson 1833-1867 **[18]**
- $74 667 - €71 798 - £46 000 - FF470 966
  Market Scene, with a Performance of Punch Oil/canvas (71x92cm 27x36in) London 1999

DAVIS Frédéric 1919-1996 **[5]**
- $4 339 - €3 750 - £2 575 - FF24 600
  France Gouache/papier (43x43cm 16x16in) Bourges 1998

DAVIS Frederick Williams 1862-1919 **[7]**
$4 180 - €4 282 - **£2 600** - FF28 090
A Game of Dice Oil/canvas (64.5x115.5cm 25x45in)
Billingshurst, West-Sussex 2000

DAVIS Gene 1920-1985 **[48]**
$2 900 - €3 014 - **£1 827** - FF19 772
Untitled Acrylic/canvas (174x120.5cm 68x47in)
Washington 2000
$800 - €854 - **£545** - FF5 604
Composition Mixed media (76x111cm 30x44in)
Philadelphia PA 2001
$275 - €314 - **£193** - FF2 060
Untitled Lithograph (63x78cm 25x31in) Chicago IL
2001

DAVIS Gladys Rockmore 1901-1967 **[39]**
$1 400 - €1 199 - **£841** - FF7 867
Portrait of a Young Girl holding a Toy Reindeer
Oil/canvas (55x48cm 22x19in) Cleveland OH 1998
$850 - €795 - **£524** - FF5 212
Portrait of a Woman Oil/canvas (38x33cm 15x13in)
New-Orleans LA 1999

DAVIS Harry XX **[2]**
$1 591 - €1 719 - **£1 100** - FF11 274
«**Worcester Cathedral**» Ink (15x11.5cm 5x4in)
London 2001

DAVIS Henry William Banks 1833-1914 **[55]**
$74 592 - €64 355 - **£45 000** - FF422 140
Gathering the Flock, Loch Maree Oil/canvas
(122x214.5cm 48x84in) London 1998
$6 000 - €5 758 - **£3 761** - FF37 773
The Way to the Sanctuary Oil/canvas (92x82cm
36x32in) New-York 1999
$2 887 - €2 910 - **£1 800** - FF19 086
Summertime Oil/canvas (33x48cm 12x18in) London
2000

DAVIS J.A. ?-1854 **[1]**
$2 600 - €2 243 - **£1 574** - FF14 714
Young Man Watercolour (18x14cm 7x5in) New-York
1999

DAVIS Jack 1926 **[38]**
$1 600 - €1 543 - **£1 011** - FF10 124
«**The Grand Old Party**» Watercolour (43x40.5cm
16x15in) New-York 1999

DAVIS John Phillip «Pope» 1784-1862 **[2]**
$4 622 - €5 009 - **£3 200** - FF32 855
**Portrait of Bertel Thorvaldsen, the sculptor
(1770-1844)** Oil/canvas (99x74.5cm 38x29in)
Billingshurst, West-Sussex 2001

DAVIS John Scarlett 1804-1845 **[18]**
$10 532 - €10 124 - **£6 500** - FF66 439
**View of a Venetian Canal with a religious
Procession on a Bridge** Oil/canvas (61x40cm
24x15in) London 1999
$1 145 - €1 289 - **£800** - FF8 453
Rue Saint Martin, Paris Watercolour (15x11cm
5x4in) London 2001

DAVIS Joseph Hilliard 1811-1865 **[13]**
$27 000 - €25 330 - **£16 683** - FF166 155
**Young Boy holding an opened Book and a Cap,
posed with his Pet Dog** Watercolour (23x17cm
9x6in) New-York 1999

DAVIS Lucien 1860-1941 **[18]**
$208 - €210 - **£130** - FF1 378
Lady painting at a Table Watercolour (42.5x33cm
16x12in) London 2000

DAVIS Lynn 1944 **[16]**
$4 000 - €4 543 - **£2 806** - FF29 801
Evening Northumberland III Gelatin silver print
(71x71cm 27x27in) New-York 2001

DAVIS Phil 1906-1964 **[2]**
$1 600 - €1 717 - **£1 070** - FF11 265
Mandrake Sunday Page Ink (56x44.5cm 22x17in)
New-York 2000

DAVIS Richard Barrett 1782-1854 **[33]**
$74 028 - €72 042 - **£45 570** - FF472 564
Jaktscen med John Musters Esq.of Colwick
Oil/canvas (96x126cm 37x49in) Stockholm 1999
$11 224 - €13 349 - **£8 000** - FF87 561
**Two Hunters by a Stable with a Landscape
Beyond** Oil/canvas (63x76cm 24x29in) London 2000
$3 600 - €4 281 - **£2 565** - FF28 083
Study of Group of Foxhounds Oil/panel
(13.5x17cm 5x6in) New-York 2000

DAVIS Richard Thomas 1947 **[4]**
$562 - €604 - **£382** - FF3 961
Outcrop Silkscreen (23x31cm 9x12in) Calgary, Alberta
1999

DAVIS Ronald Wendel 1937 **[33]**
$8 000 - €7 556 - **£4 838** - FF49 565
Bridge Acrylic/canvas (289.5x312.5cm 113x123in)
New-York 1999

DAVIS Samuel 1757-1819 **[11]**
$13 231 - €12 376 - **£8 000** - FF81 180
**The Esplanade, Calcutta from the Chowringhee
Road, with the Hooghly** Watercolour (48.5x70cm
19x27in) London 1999

DAVIS Stan 1942 **[13]**
$14 000 - €15 896 - **£9 727** - FF104 273
Silent, Solitary, and Resolute Oil/canvas (91x76cm
36x30in) Dallas TX 2001

DAVIS Stark 1885-? **[12]**
$7 000 - €6 039 - **£4 207** - FF39 615
Monkeys, a Decorative Composition Oil/canvas
(107.5x107.5cm 42x42in) Boston MA 1998

DAVIS Stuart 1894-1964 **[77]**
$300 000 - €350 127 - **£212 670** - FF2 296 680
Smith's Cove Oil/canvas (25.5x35.5cm 10x13in)
New-York 2001
$50 000 - €59 463 - **£35 635** - FF390 050
The Vaudeville Show Watercolour/paper (38x28cm
14x11in) New-York 2000
$14 000 - €16 454 - **£9 706** - FF107 931
Theatre on the Beach Lithograph (28x38cm
11x14in) New-York 2000

DAVIS Tyddesley R. c.1800-c.1870 **[2]**
$6 382 - €6 101 - **£4 000** - FF40 020
**Philip Payne, Huntsman to the Duke of
Beaufort,on his favourite Hunter** Oil/canvas
(61x79cm 24x31in) London 1999

DAVIS W.H. ?-1865 **[6]**
$2 073 - €2 155 - **£1 300** - FF14 133
River Landscape with Harvest Scene Oil/canvas
(61x107cm 24x42in) Suffolk 2000

DAVIS Warren B. 1865-1928 **[44]**
$11 000 - €10 390 - **£6 652** - FF68 152
Lady with St Bernard Oil/canvas (76x63cm 29x24in)
New-York 1999
$1 100 - €1 092 - **£687** - FF7 163
The Angler Oil/canvas/board (29.5x24.5cm 11x9in)
New-York 1999

⟅⟅⟅ **$200** - €199 - **£124** - FF1 308
Reclining Nude Etching (15x20cm 6x8in) St. Louis
MO 1999

DAVIS William 1812-1873 [11]
⌒ **$12 263** - €13 759 - **£8 500** - FF90 251
Landscape at Bidston Oil/canvas (23x31.5cm
9x12in) London 2000

DAVIS William Henry c.1795-1885 [22]
⌒ **$20 000** - €17 088 - **£12 006** - FF112 088
**King David with Jockey Up and held by a
Trainer at Newcastle** Oil/canvas (263.5x76cm
103x29in) New-York 1998
⌒ **$2 245** - €2 263 - **£1 400** - FF14 845
Longhorned Bull in a Landscape Oil/canvas
(44.5x61cm 17x24in) London 2000

DAVIS William Moore 1829-1920 [17]
⌒ **$12 000** - €12 563 - **£7 539** - FF82 406
Gathering Berries by the Shore Oil/canvas
(35x45cm 14x18in) East-Moriches NY 2000
⌒ **$3 400** - €4 017 - **£2 409** - FF26 352
Small Marine Depicting Three Sailboats Oil/can-
vas (18x23cm 7x9in) East-Moriches NY 2000
⟋ **$11 000** - €11 516 - **£6 911** - FF75 539
Methodist Church, Mount Sinai, L.I., N.Y Charcoal
(29x45cm 11x18in) East-Moriches NY 2000

DAVIS Willis E. 1855-1910 [1]
⌒ **$10 000** - €11 667 - **£6 960** - FF76 532
**Coastal Landscape, Sausalito from Marin
Headlands** Oil/canvas (50x66cm 20x26in) Altadena
CA 2000

DAVIS Wynne XX [1]
⟅⟅⟅ **$1 936** - €1 869 - **£1 200** - FF12 261
«Champagne» Poster (91.5x35.5cm 36x13in) London
1999

DAVISON Nora XIX-XX [37]
⟋ **$725** - €817 - **£500** - FF5 359
The Field, Eton Watercolour/paper (26x40cm
10x15in) London 2000

DAVISON Thomas Raffles 1853-1937 [12]
⟋ **$1 063** - €1 235 - **£750** - FF8 099
«Evening light, Hey Tor, Devon» Coloured
chalks/paper (19x30.5cm 7x12in) London 2001

DAVISSON Homer G. 1866-1957 [7]
⌒ **$3 500** - €4 004 - **£2 433** - FF26 262
Pastoral Landscape Oil/board (45x55cm 18x22in)
Cincinnati OH 2000

DAVOL Joseph B. 1864-1923 [5]
⌒ **$1 200** - €1 305 - **£791** - FF8 561
Sunset on a rocky Coast Oil/canvas (20.5x36cm
8x14in) Boston MA 2000

DAVRINGHAUSEN Heinrich Maria 1894-1970 [93]
⌒ **$5 030** - €4 345 - **£3 038** - FF28 501
Ohne Titel Öl/Leinwand (97x131cm 38x51in) Luzern
1998
⌒ **$1 288** - €1 247 - **£794** - FF8 179
Ohne Titel Öl/Leinwand (50x61cm 19x24in) Zürich
1999
⟋ **$877** - €1 022 - **£614** - FF6 707
Komposition III Pencil (61x50cm 24x19in) München
2000
⟅⟅⟅ **$230** - €256 - **£160** - FF1 676
Der tanz des Irren Lithographie (61.5x62.5cm
24x24in) Heidelberg 2001

DAWE George 1781-1829 [11]
⌒ **$18 746** - €18 346 - **£12 000** - FF120 344
**Portrait of Princess Charlotte Augusta, wearing
a blue and gold Dress** Oil/canvas (139.5x109.5cm
54x43in) London 1999

DAWID (Björn Dawidson) 1949 [18]
◉⁻ **$465** - €430 - **£286** - FF2 818
«2873» Gelatin silver print (24x19cm 9x7in)
Stockholm 1999

DAWS Frederick Thomas 1878-? [20]
⌒ **$1 600** - €1 631 - **£1 002** - FF10 698
Fives Scotties Oil/board (20.5x34.5cm 8x13in) New-
York 2000

DAWS Lawrence 1927 [112]
⌒ **$8 045** - €7 565 - **£5 058** - FF49 623
Edge of the Forest Mixed media/board (115x130cm
45x51in) Sydney 1999
⌒ **$2 588** - €2 457 - **£1 614** - FF16 118
Lovers Mixed media/canvas (61x61cm 24x24in)
Sydney 1999
⌒ **$781** - €930 - **£557** - FF6 098
The Hanging Man Acrylic (45x32.5cm 17x12in)
Melbourne 2000
⟋ **$699** - €680 - **£430** - FF4 463
Sydney Harbour Bridge Watercolour, gouache
(29.5x27cm 11x10in) Melbourne 1999

DAWSON Alfred XIX [21]
⌒ **$875** - €731 - **£520** - FF4 792
Holy Trinity Church, Stratford-on-Avon Oil/board
(22.5x30cm 8x11in) Salisbury, Wiltshire 1998

DAWSON Henry 1811-1878 [51]
⌒ **$262 126** - €307 631 - **£185 000** - FF2 017 924
The New Houses of Parliament, Westminster
Oil/canvas (180x272cm 70x107in) London 2000
⌒ **$15 622** - €15 289 - **£10 000** - FF100 287
**Landscape with a Fisherman at the Foot of a
deep Gorge** Oil/canvas (121x98cm 47x38in) London
1999
⌒ **$800** - €920 - **£551** - FF6 038
Figure in the Woods of a Country Estate Oil/can-
vas (23x30cm 9x12in) Boston MA 2000

DAWSON Henry Thomas, Jnr. act.1860-1896 [6]
⌒ **$13 233** - €14 680 - **£8 800** - FF96 294
On the Medway at Dusk Oil/canvas (71x106.5cm
27x41in) London 2000

DAWSON Lucy 1958 [40]
⟋ **$1 000** - €1 089 - **£688** - FF7 144
Tutsy, a Cat Pastel/paper (23x29cm 9x11in) New-York
2001
⟅⟅⟅ **$800** - €871 - **£551** - FF5 715
Sleeping Sealyham Copper engraving (20.5x25.5cm
8x10in) New-York 2001

DAWSON Mabel 1887-1965 [9]
⟋ **$450** - €384 - **£270** - FF2 518
Child standing in arched cathedral doorway
Gouache/paper (48x38cm 19x15in) Norwalk CT 1999

DAWSON Manierre 1887-1969 [6]
⌒ **$20 000** - €21 468 - **£13 384** - FF140 820
Fourteen Oil/canvas (66x55.5cm 25x21in) New-York
1999

DAWSON Montague 1895-1973 [456]
⌒ **$37 500** - €36 716 - **£23 958** - FF240 843
British Extreme Clipper Spray of the Ocean
Oil/canvas (60x91cm 24x36in) Detroit MI 1999

$2 094 - €2 338 - **£1 400** - FF15 339
The Lone Sentiel, original illustration for Naval Magazine Oil/board (34x44cm 13x17in) Kirkby-Lonsdale, Cumbria 2000

$5 889 - €6 321 - **£4 000** - FF41 465
Preparatory Sketch of a Naval Engagement Watercolour (45x72cm 17x28in) London 2001

$160 - €162 - **£100** - FF1 060
Night Mists Color lithograph (61x77cm 24x30in) London 2000

DAWSON Neil 1948 [3]
$3 049 - €3 204 - **£2 007** - FF21 016
Interior 8 Metal (33x15.5x15cm 12x6x5in) Auckland 2000

DAWSON Nelson Ethelred 1859-1941 [23]
$314 - €353 - **£220** - FF2 313
Deserted Beach with Sailing Boats on the Horizon Watercolour/paper (35x47.5cm 13x18in) London 2001

DAWSON-WATSON Dawson 1864-1939 [28]
$8 000 - €6 712 - **£4 693** - FF44 028
Picking Cotton in Texas Oil/canvas (101x76cm 40x30in) New-Orleans LA 1998

$4 500 - €4 825 - **£2 977** - FF31 649
Western Landscape Oil/canvas (35x43cm 14x17in) New-Orleans LA 2000

DAXHELET Paul 1905-1993 [200]
$2 422 - €2 355 - **£1 482** - FF15 447
Panorama de la ville de Liège Huile/toile (130x200cm 51x78in) Liège 1999

$602 - €694 - **£414** - FF4 552
Scène de marché Huile/toile (50x100.5cm 19x39in) Liège 2000

$310 - €347 - **£215** - FF2 276
Femmes Huile/carton (37x25cm 14x9in) Antwerpen 2001

$307 - €297 - **£194** - FF1 951
Maternité Pastel/papier (57.5x31cm 22x12in) Liège 1999

$114 - €124 - **£75** - FF813
La Fontaine de la Tradition Eau-forte couleurs (60x40cm 23x15in) Liège 2000

DAY Forshaw 1837-1903 [7]
$2 732 - €2 622 - **£1 713** - FF17 201
Indian Encampment Overlooking the River Oil/canvas (46x76cm 18x29in) Montréal 1999

DAY Francis James 1863-1942 [14]
$17 000 - €18 748 - **£11 512** - FF122 979
Woman with a Harp Oil/canvas (51.5x41.5cm 20x16in) New-York 2000

$4 000 - €4 411 - **£2 708** - FF28 936
Quiet Moment Watercolour/paper (52x68.5cm 20x26in) New-York 2000

DAY Fred Holland 1864-1933 [14]
$1 100 - €1 026 - **£664** - FF6 728
Clarence White Platinum print (24x19cm 9x7in) New-York 1999

DAY G.F. XIX [3]
$3 638 - €4 350 - **£2 500** - FF28 532
Study of a Young Boy and a Dog in a Landscape Oil/canvas (70x90cm 27x35in) Billingshurst, West-Sussex 2001

DAY Marian XIX [1]
$1 500 - €1 602 - **£1 022** - FF10 510
Landscape with Gothic House and Bridge Watercolour (44x54cm 17x21in) New-York 2001

DAY William Cave 1862-1924 [32]
$334 - €324 - **£210** - FF2 123
Gorse and a Cornish Cottage Oil/board (25x38cm 10x15in) Par, Cornwall 1999

DAYAL Lala Deen 1844-1910 [9]
$2 582 - €2 894 - **£1 800** - FF18 982
Indian scenes Albumen print (17x13.5cm 6x5in) London 2001

DAYES Edward 1763-1804 [57]
$1 578 - €1 531 - **£1 000** - FF10 040
Vale Crucis Abbey Watercolour (43.5x58.5cm 17x23in) London 1999

DAYEZ Georges 1907-1991 [136]
$1 500 - €1 456 - **£926** - FF9 553
Femme se coiffant Oil/board (51x66cm 20x25in) Stockholm 1999

DAYNES-GRASSOT Suzanne 1884-1976 [199]
$4 924 - €5 793 - **£3 530** - FF38 000
Les rubans Huile/toile (130x100cm 51x39in) Senlis 2001

$453 - €534 - **£325** - FF3 500
Vase de dahlias Huile/toile (72x54cm 28x21in) Senlis 2001

$220 - €259 - **£157** - FF1 700
Fruits Huile/toile/carton (33x40.5cm 12x15in) Senlis 2001

$129 - €152 - **£92** - FF1 000
Etude de nature morte au panier de fruits/Femme au collier Mine plomb (63x81cm 24x31in) Senlis 2001

DAYNGANGGAN 1892-? [2]
$4 772 - €5 090 - **£3 184** - FF33 385
Birrkulda Ceremony Mixed media (147x50cm 57x19in) Melbourne 2000

DE Biren 1926 [11]
$3 250 - €3 696 - **£2 270** - FF24 245
The Net Acrylic/canvas (67.5x106cm 26x41in) New-York 2000

DE FERRANTE Mario 1898-1992 [7]
$2 500 - €2 789 - **£1 636** - FF18 295
Abstraction Oil/canvas (76x60cm 30x24in) Chicago IL 2000

DE FRANÇA Manuel Joachim 1808-1865 [5]
$10 000 - €11 601 - **£7 118** - FF76 099
Portrait of Actuary, Joseph Roberts, Jr., with Telescope Oil/canvas (81x91cm 32x36in) Downington PA 2001

DE LA RUE P. XVII [2]
$425 - €390 - **£260** - FF2 558
Sourie - Terre Sainte moderne Engraving (38.5x53.5cm 15x21in) London 1999

DE LACY Charles John 1860-1936 [86]
$2 558 - €2 149 - **£1 500** - FF14 097
Untitled Oil/canvas (81x45.5cm 31x17in) Billingshurst, West-Sussex 1998

$483 - €566 - **£340** - FF3 710
Fishing Boats in Coastal Waters Oil/canvas (20x30.5cm 7x12in) Oxfordshire 2000

$513 - €591 - **£350** - FF3 878
Sailing into Harbour Watercolour (52.5x36.5cm 20x14in) Billingshurst, West-Sussex 2000

DE LALL Oscar Daniel 1903-1971 [47]
$580 - €562 - **£388** - FF3 685
River Landscape in Winter Oil/canvas (61x81.5cm 24x32in) Toronto 1999

DE MARIA Nicola 1954 **[170]**
- $44 829 - €48 120 - **£30 000** - FF315 648
  Regno dei Piori Acrylic/canvas (110x150.5cm
  43x59in) London 2000
- $15 690 - €16 843 - **£10 500** - FF110 481
  Festa della Poesia Acrylic (50x40cm 19x15in)
  London 2000
- $13 368 - €11 298 - **£8 000** - FF74 112
  «Testa Donna» Acrylic/canvas (40x30cm 15x11in)
  London 1998
- $1 840 - €1 815 - **£1 133** - FF11 906
  Untitled Wax crayon (23x22.5cm 9x8in) Amsterdam
  1999

DE MEJO Oscar 1911 **[7]**
- $1 300 - €1 492 - **£889** - FF9 784
  The Birth of Virginia Dare Acrylic/canvas
  (89x125cm 35x49in) Charlottesville VA 2000

DE NITTIS Giuseppe 1846-1884 **[120]**
- $112 007 - €111 204 - **£70 000** - FF729 449
  Signora Napolitana Oil/canvas (95x75cm 37x29in)
  London 1999
- $15 000 - €15 550.- **£9 000** - FF102 000
  Paesaggio meridionale Olio/tela (10x16cm 3x6in)
  Milano 2000
- $3 400 - €4 406 - **£2 550** - FF28 900
  Arabo stanco Acquarello/carta (37x26cm 14x10in)
  Milano 2000
- $1 040 - €1 348 - **£780** - FF8 840
  Donna assisa Acquaforte (21x27cm 8x10in) Milano
  2000

DE ROCCHI Francesco 1902-1978 **[43]**
- $7 200 - €6 220 - **£4 800** - FF40 800
  Venezia Olio/tela (90x72cm 35x28in) Roma 1998
- $5 750 - €5 961 - **£3 450** - FF39 100
  Venezia, San Giorgio Olio/tavola (35x45cm 13x17in)
  Milano 1999

DE SENLIS Séraphine-Louise 1864-1942 **[5]**
- $5 124 - €6 098 - **£3 548** - FF40 000
  Les marguerites Huile/panneau (60x49cm 23x19in)
  Paris 2000

DE SOTO Raphael 1904-1987 **[6]**
- $5 000 - €5 569 - **£3 270** - FF36 532
  **Pulp magazine cover: woman surprised by
  bloody knife** Oil/canvas (48x35cm 19x14in) New-
  York 2000

DE VILLE Vickers 1856-1925 **[23]**
- $1 327 - €1 154 - **£800** - FF7 570
  Windy Day Oil/canvas (42x50.5cm 16x19in)
  Godalming, Surrey 1998
- $651 - €634 - **£400** - FF4 156
  The Close of Day Oil/board (11x20cm 4x8in) Little-
  Lane, Ilkley 1999

DE WITT Antonio Antony 1876-1967 **[3]**
- $8 100 - €6 997 - **£4 050** - FF45 900
  Nevicata Olio/tela (72x58cm 28x22in) Prato 1999

DE YONGHE John 1856-1917 **[2]**
- $900 - €852 - **£559** - FF5 588
  «The New York Times» Poster (74x48cm 29x18in)
  New-York 1999

DE'PREY Juan 1906-1962 **[3]**
- $7 000 - €6 104 - **£4 232** - FF40 037
  Motherhood Oil/canvas (61.5x73cm 24x28in) New-
  York 1998

DEABATE Teonesto 1898-1981 **[22]**
- $750 - €777 - **£450** - FF5 100
  Figura in un interno Olio/tavola (55x42cm 21x16in)
  Torino 2001

DEACON Richard 1949 **[16]**
- $32 000 - €35 109 - **£21 257** - FF230 297
  Art for Other People #14 Metal (170x50x50cm
  66x19x19in) New-York 2000

DEAK-HENCZNE Adrienne Hermine 1895-1956
[49]
- $1 592 - €1 658 - **£1 000** - FF10 874
  **Still Life of White and Pink Carnations in a
  Glass Vase** Oil/canvas (79.5x59.5cm 31x23in) London
  2000

DEAKIN Andrew XIX **[1]**
- $2 113 - €1 951 - **£1 300** - FF12 800
  «Children in a wooded Landscape»/«Cottage in
  the Vale of Llangollen» Oil/canvas (25.5x35.5cm
  10x13in) London 1999

DEAKIN Edwin, Edward 1838-1923 **[44]**
- $18 000 - €16 618 - **£11 070** - FF109 006
  Notre-Dame, Paris Oil/canvas (140x167.5cm
  55x65in) New-York 1999
- $4 000 - €4 675 - **£2 855** - FF30 664
  San Xavier Mission in atmospheric landscape
  Oil/board (41x60cm 16x24in) Altadena CA 2001
- $5 250 - €5 015 - **£3 305** - FF32 896
  Still Life of Grapes Oil/canvas (29x19cm 11x7in)
  York PA 1999

DEALY Jane M. Lewis XIX-XX **[10]**
- $32 464 - €31 217 - **£20 000** - FF204 768
  And she went to Market all on a Market Day
  Oil/canvas (102x127cm 40x50in) London 1999
- $505 - €640 - **£360** - FF3 940
  «Sad Little Pickle» Watercolour (46x35cm 18x13in)
  Bath 2000

DEAN Frank 1865-1947 **[30]**
- $448 - €481 - **£300** - FF3 156
  Untitled Watercolour/paper (22x33cm 9x13in)
  Aylsham, Norfolk 2000

DEAN Hugh Primrose c.1740/50-c.1784 **[2]**
- $2 947 - €2 695 - **£1 800** - FF17 681
  **An Italianate wooded Landscape with the rest
  on the Flight** Oil/copper (29x29cm 11x11in) London
  1998

DEAN John c.1750-1798 **[9]**
- $357 - €316 - **£220** - FF2 072
  Augustus and Cleopatra Engraving (57x48cm
  22x18in) Godalming, Surrey 1999

DEAN Judith XX **[1]**
- $4 505 - €5 319 - **£3 200** - FF34 890
  Tableaux Construction (76.5x162x50cm 30x63x19in)
  London 2001

DEAN Tacita 1965 **[2]**
- $36 105 - €39 343 - **£25 000** - FF258 070
  Disappearance at sea I-IV Chalks (240x240cm
  94x94in) London 2001

DEAN Walter Lofthouse 1854-1912 **[14]**
- $1 100 - €996 - **£673** - FF6 536
  A Study on the Shore, Concarneau Oil/board
  (20x33cm 8x13in) Portland ME 1998

DEARDEN Harold 1888-1969 **[24]**
- $476 - €457 - **£300** - FF2 995
  Milking Time Oil/canvas (53x73cm 21x29in) Aylsham,
  Norfolk 1999

DEARE John 1760-1798 **[2]**
- $310 000 - €347 223 - **£215 388** - FF2 277 632
  The young Bacchus feeding the Panther Relief
  (33x52.5cm 12x20in) New-York 2001

DEARLE John H. act.1852-? **[4]**
- **$6 503** - €6 004 - **£4 000** - FF39 385
  Sunday Morning Oil/canvas (76.5x63.5cm 30x25in) London 1999

DEARLE John Henry 1860-1932 **[7]**
- **$3 679** - €3 140 - **£2 200** - FF20 599
  St. George and the Dragon Watercolour/paper (12.5x18cm 4x7in) London 1998

DEARMAN John ?-c.1857 **[21]**
- **$2 750** - €3 039 - **£1 926** - FF19 937
  Horses Drinking along the River Oil/canvas (47x60cm 18x24in) Chicago IL 2001
- **$3 707** - €3 143 - **£2 200** - FF20 616
  Cattle, Sheep and Figures in a Coastal Landscape Oil/panel (24.5x35cm 9x13in) Billingshurst, West-Sussex 1998

DEARMER Mabel 1872-1915 **[5]**
- **$2 200** - €2 467 - **£1 527** - FF16 185
  «Ibsen's Brand» Poster (77x50cm 30x20in) New-York 2001

DEARN Raymond XIX-XX **[9]**
- **$1 572** - €1 358 - **£950** - FF8 911
  Corn Mill, Ballaugh Glen, Isle of Man Oil/canvas (55x76cm 22x30in) Isle-of-Man 1998

DEARTH Henry Golden 1864-1918 **[14]**
- **$7 000** - €8 232 - **£5 019** - FF53 997
  River in a Landscape Oil/canvas (84x129.5cm 33x50in) Philadelphia PA 2001

DEAS Charles 1818-1867 **[6]**
- **$22 000** - €18 796 - **£13 206** - FF123 296
  Friends Watercolour/paper (19x25cm 7x9in) New-York 1998

DEBAT Roger-Marius XIX **[3]**
- **$1 749** - €1 951 - **£1 176** - FF12 800
  La leçon Huile/toile (33x46cm 12x18in) Narbonne 2000

DEBAT-PONSAN Édouard 1847-1913 **[45]**
- **$2 982** - €3 201 - **£1 995** - FF21 000
  Jeune fermière Huile/toile (65x50cm 25x19in) Avignon 2000

DeBECK William Morgan 1890-1942 **[10]**
- **$900** - €966 - **£602** - FF6 336
  Barney Google Daily Strips Ink (11.5x44.5cm 4x17in) New-York 2000

DEBELLE Alexandre 1805-1897 **[57]**
- **$96** - €107 - **£64** - FF700
  Intérieur du Grand Salon à Uriage Gravure (34x46cm 13x18in) Grenoble 2000

DeBELLE Charles Ernest 1873-1939 **[53]**
- **$409** - €393 - **£257** - FF2 580
  Coucher de soleil/Winter Evening Pastel/paper (35.5x45.5cm 13x17in) Montréal 1999

DEBERDT Françoise 1934 **[23]**
- **$98** - €114 - **£67** - FF750
  Le corral Color lithograph (49x61cm 19x24in) Calgary, Alberta 2000

DEBERITZ Peder 1880-1945 **[22]**
- **$2 940** - €3 496 - **£2 094** - FF22 932
  Hostfarger Oil/canvas (68x59cm 26x23in) Oslo 2000

DEBON Fr.-Hipolyte 1807-1872 **[4]**
- **$6 006** - €6 708 - **£4 070** - FF44 000
  Henri III, roi de France, reçu par le Doge à Venise Huile/toile (83x133cm 32x52in) Paris 2000

DEBRÉ Olivier 1920-1999 **[509]**
- **$10 627** - €12 501 - **£7 617** - FF82 000
  «Rouge d'été» Huile/toile (138x148cm 54x58in) Versailles 2001
- **$6 463** - €6 403 - **£3 918** - FF42 000
  Fjord sombre et clair Huile/toile (60x81cm 23x31in) Paris 2000
- **$2 278** - €2 592 - **£1 581** - FF17 000
  «Tolède, rose ocre taches vertes» Huile/toile (24x33cm 9x12in) Douai 2000
- **$2 251** - €2 134 - **£1 369** - FF14 000
  Signe Encre Chine/papier (120x80.5cm 47x31in) Paris 1999
- **$258** - €213 - **£151** - FF1 400
  Composition Eau-forte couleurs (120x80cm 47x31in) Paris 1999

DEBRET Jean-Baptiste 1768-1848 **[14]**
- **$4 840** - €4 649 - **£3 000** - FF30 494
  Nègres en commission par un temps de pluie Watercolour/paper (15x21cm 5x8in) London 1999

DEBRUS Alexandre 1843-1905 **[19]**
- **$7 777** - €8 168 - **£4 921** - FF53 578
  Swags of Roses by a Garden-Wall Oil/canvas (92x125cm 36x49in) Amsterdam 2000
- **$893** - €869 - **£550** - FF5 702
  Studies of Roses Oil/panel (18x15cm 7x6in) Fernhurst, Haslemere, Surrey 1999

DEBUCOURT Philibert Louis 1755-1832 **[190]**
- **$5 098** - €5 031 - **£3 168** - FF33 000
  Le montreur de marionettes Huile/panneau (16x22cm 6x8in) Paris 1999
- **$2 591** - €2 211 - **£1 563** - FF14 500
  L'heureux accident Lavis (19x28cm 7x11in) La Flèche 1998
- **$387** - €457 - **£272** - FF3 000
  Le menuet de la mariée/La noce au château Gravure (37x26.5cm 14x10in) Paris 2000

DEBUS-DIGNEFF Maria 1876-1956 **[12]**
- **$779** - €818 - **£526** - FF5 366
  Frühlingsblumen in Vase Öl/Karton (47.5x47.5cm 18x18in) Kempten 2001

DEBUT Jean Didier 1824-1893 **[63]**
- **$1 518** - €1 296 - **£907** - FF8 500
  Le petit marchand de fruits Bronze (H29cm H11in) Paris 1998

DÉBUT Marcel 1865-1933 **[70]**
- **$1 157** - €1 073 - **£720** - FF7 040
  Porteur d'eau tunisien Bronze (H63cm H24in) London 1999

DECABOOTER Lieven 1961 **[2]**
- **$952** - €992 - **£600** - FF6 504
  Let's go fishing in the River of Life Technique mixte/papier (114x121cm 44x47in) Antwerpen 2000

DeCAMP Joseph Rodefer 1858-1923 **[15]**
- **$15 000** - €16 416 - **£10 347** - FF107 682
  Summer in the Country Oil/canvas (40.5x51cm 15x20in) New-York 2001
- **$34 000** - €37 496 - **£23 024** - FF245 959
  Theodore Lambert DeCamp as an Infant Oil/canvas (35.5x40.5cm 13x15in) New-York 2000

DeCAMP Ralph Earl 1858-1936 **[5]**
- **$3 500** - €3 816 - **£2 445** - FF26 110
  Buffalo Overlooking Indian Encampment Oil/canvas (35x50cm 14x20in) Mystic CT 2000

D

DECAMPS Alexandre Gabriel 1803-1860 **[181]**
- **$3 573** - €3 659 - **£2 244** - FF24 000
  Signe au miroir Huile/toile (38x46.5cm 14x18in)
  Lyon 2000
- **$2 880** - €2 439 - **£1 731** - FF16 000
  Le rat retiré du monde Huile/panneau (20x25.5cm
  7x10in) Paris 1998
- **$1 372** - €1 524 - **£919** - FF10 000
  Le chevrier des Abruzzes Aquarelle/papier
  (32x39cm 12x15in) Toulouse 2000

DECAMPS Maurice 1892-1953 **[36]**
- **$770** - €917 - **£550** - FF6 014
  Mixed Flowers in a Latticed Vase on a Ledge
  Oil/canvas (65.5x54cm 25x21in) London 2000

DECAN Eugène 1829-1894 **[7]**
- **$1 258** - €1 159 - **£755** - FF7 600
  Promeneuse au bord de l'étang Huile/panneau
  (38x25.5cm 14x10in) Soissons 1999

DECANIS Théophile 1847-1917 **[8]**
- **$2 820** - €3 201 - **£1 959** - FF21 000
  Paysage provençal Huile/toile (40x65.5cm 15x25in)
  Marseille 2001

DECARAVA Roy 1919 **[17]**
- **$4 000** - €4 440 - **£2 788** - FF29 126
  Roy DeCarava Photogravure (30.5x20.5cm 12x8in)
  New-York 2001

DECARIS Albert 1901-1988 **[123]**
- **$5 176** - €6 098 - **£3 580** - FF40 000
  Panneaux à décor incisé d'animaux Huile/pan-
  neau (187x57cm 73x22in) Paris 2000
- **$1 736** - €1 982 - **£1 207** - FF13 000
  **Baigneuses et éléphant sur fond de palais néo-
  classiques** Lavis (51x62cm 20x24in) Paris 2001
- **$174** - €168 - **£108** - FF1 100
  Un corral Gravure bois (51x36cm 20x14in) Paris 1999

DECARLI Albert Joseph 1907-1996 **[12]**
- **$226** - €263 - **£158** - FF1 723
  Repos sur un banc Huile/toile (31x25cm 12x9in)
  Genève 2000

DECHENAUD Adolphe 1868-1929 **[4]**
- **$13 000** - €12 122 - **£8 063** - FF79 514
  Portrait of a seated Gentleman Oil/canvas
  (109x121cm 42x47in) New-York 2001

DECK Leo 1908-1997 **[169]**
- **$403** - €373 - **£246** - FF2 448
  **Gartenpartie mit Schubkarre vor blühenden
  Sonnenblumen** Huile/panneau (58x77cm 22x30in)
  Bern 1999
- **$326** - €274 - **£191** - FF1 798
  «Am Wohlensee» Oil/panel (29x35.5cm 11x13in)
  Bern 1998
- **$167** - €161 - **£103** - FF1 054
  **Hügelige Sommerlandschaft mit Strasse und
  Feldern** Craies couleurs/papier (22.5x28cm 8x11in)
  Bern 1999

DECK Théodore 1823-1891 **[20]**
- **$904** - €838 - **£552** - FF5 500
  **Pot couvert à décor dans le goût chinois imi-
  tant le cloisonné** Céramique (H17cm H6in) Paris
  1999

DECKER Albert 1817-1871 **[13]**
- **$855** - €945 - **£592** - FF6 197
  Zwei Knaben, auf einem Sofa sitzend
  Aquarell/Papier (21x25cm 8x9in) Wien 2001

DECKER Coenraet 1651-c.1709 **[3]**
- **$436** - €427 - **£276** - FF2 800
  Allégorie du Temps Eau-forte (32.5x24.5cm 12x9in)
  Paris 1999

DECKER Cornelis Gerritsz c.1625-1678 **[34]**
- **$32 000** - €28 069 - **£19 430** - FF184 121
  Landscape with a Watermill Oil/canvas
  (113.5x159cm 44x62in) New-York 1999
- **$6 246** - €5 922 - **£3 800** - FF38 844
  Cottage interior with a Washerwoman Oil/panel
  (35x49.5cm 13x19in) London 1999
- **$6 239** - €6 105 - **£4 000** - FF40 048
  Weaver's Workshop Oil/panel (33.5x47cm 13x18in)
  London 1999

DECKER de Jos 1912-2000 **[39]**
- **$9 586** - €7 974 - **£5 629** - FF52 305
  Girl Bronze (H163cm H64in) Amsterdam 1998
- **$1 740** - €1 639 - **£1 185** - FF12 195
  Dansers Bronze (23.5x31.5cm 9x12in) Lokeren 2001

DECKER Frans 1684-1751 **[2]**
- **$26 198** - €24 295 - **£16 000** - FF159 363
  **An Interior with an Amorous Couple, a
  Procuress in the Doorway** Oil/panel (35x27.5cm
  13x10in) London 1998

DECKER Joseph 1853-1924 **[12]**
- **$8 000** - €9 242 - **£5 601** - FF60 624
  Abandoned Oil/canvas (20.5x22cm 8x8in) New-York
  2001

DECKER Robert Melvin 1847-1912 **[9]**
- **$2 800** - €2 652 - **£1 702** - FF17 393
  Fall landscape Oil/canvas (51x76.5cm 20x30in) New-
  York 1999
- **$800** - €874 - **£515** - FF5 730
  Apple Blossoms Oil/board (7x15cm 3x6in) Mystic
  CT 2000

DECKERS Émile 1885-1968 **[72]**
- **$9 612** - €8 860 - **£5 758** - FF58 119
  Tutsi dancers Oil/canvas (79x54cm 31x21in)
  Amsterdam 1998
- **$5 444** - €6 098 - **£3 784** - FF40 000
  Portrait de jeune algérienne Huile/panneau
  (30x28cm 11x11in) Paris 2001
- **$3 885** - €4 573 - **£2 730** - FF30 000
  Vases de roses Pastel/papier (65x91.5cm 25x36in)
  Paris 2000

DECOENE Henri 1798-1866 **[12]**
- **$3 774** - €4 214 - **£2 635** - FF27 642
  Scène de réjouissance devant une maison
  Huile/panneau (50x57cm 19x22in) Bruxelles 2001

DECOEUR Émile 1876-1953 **[14]**
- **$839** - €991 - **£596** - FF6 500
  Hiver/Printemps Bas-relief (25.5x20.5cm 10x8in)
  Neuilly-sur-Seine 2001

DECOMBE Claude XIX **[2]**
- **$5 830** - €6 630 - **£4 000** - FF43 492
  **Lilies, Roses and other Flowers decorating a
  Tomb** Oil/canvas (98.5x73cm 38x28in) Oxfordshire
  2000

DECORCHEMONT François Émile 1880-1971 **[37]**
- **$1 731** - €1 677 - **£1 087** - FF11 000
  Grenouille Sculpture verre (5.5x13.5cm 2x5in) Paris
  1999

DeCREEFT José 1884-1982 **[27]**
- **$1 600** - €1 817 - **£1 095** - FF11 917
  Heads Stone (24x24.5x17.5cm 9x9x6in) New-York
  2000

DECRIND Paul Jean 1916-1995 **[31]**
$1 012 - €991 - **£622** - FF6 500
Paysage de neige Huile/toile (45x60cm 17x23in)
Belfort 1999
$391 - €366 - **£242** - FF2 400
Lecture sous les parasols Aquarelle/papier
(24x30cm 9x11in) Besançon 1999

DeDIEGO Julio 1900-1979 **[16]**
$600 - €644 - **£401** - FF4 224
Menu Design for Hotel Nacional de Cuba
Gouache (35.5x25.5cm 13x10in) New-York 2000

DEDREUX-DORCY Pierre-Joseph 1789-1874 **[6]**
$1 303 - €1 481 - **£900** - FF9 714
Portrait of a Young Lady Pastel/paper (47.5x41cm
18x16in) London 2000

DEEM George C. 1932 **[2]**
$1 000 - €1 071 - **£680** - FF7 026
Eight Woman Oil/canvas (121x91cm 48x36in)
Chicago IL 2001

DEENY Gillian XX [3]
$2 604 - €2 793 - **£1 775** - FF18 323
Soft Rain on the Burren Oil/canvas (70x79cm
27x31in) Dublin 2001

DEFAUX Alexandre 1826-1900 **[260]**
$5 338 - €5 183 - **£3 298** - FF34 000
Berger et son troupeau sous les arbres
Huile/toile (111x131cm 43x51in) Melun 1999
$4 508 - €4 375 - **£2 806** - FF28 700
Vue de Sorques en Seine-et-Marne Huile/toile
(40x68cm 15x26in) Fontainebleau 1999
$3 337 - €3 583 - **£2 232** - FF23 500
Basse-cour Huile/toile (27x41cm 10x16in) Versailles
2000
$557 - €610 - **£385** - FF4 000
Paysanne en forêt Fusain/papier (29x20cm 11x7in)
Fontainebleau 2001

DEFERNEX Jean-Baptiste 1729-1783 **[6]**
$3 092 - €3 049 - **£1 988** - FF20 000
Buste de jeune femme Terracotta (H34cm H13in)
Paris 1999

DEFESCHE Pieter 1921-1998 **[53]**
$1 242 - €1 452 - **£887** - FF9 525
«Straatweg bij Toledo» (Street near Toledo)
Oil/canvas (90x80cm 35x31in) Amsterdam 2001
$942 - €908 - **£589** - FF5 953
Compositie met Moeder en Kind Gouache
(24x31cm 9x12in) Amsterdam 1999

DeFOREST Roy Dean 1930 **[27]**
$12 000 - €13 647 - **£8 384** - FF89 521
«Brothers Beneath the Skin» Oil/canvas
(172x172cm 67x67in) Beverly-Hills CA 2000
$1 700 - €1 635 - **£1 049** - FF10 723
Portrait of a Dog/Warrior Oil/canvas (56x43cm
22x16in) Washington 1999
$2 600 - €2 586 - **£1 613** - FF16 963
Untitled Coloured crayons (71x101.5cm 27x39in)
Beverly-Hills CA 1999

DEFOSSEZ Alfred, Freddy 1932 **[78]**
$2 029 - €1 982 - **£1 293** - FF13 000
Arcachon Huile/toile (55x81cm 21x31in) Paris 1999
$1 611 - €1 829 - **£1 102** - FF12 000
Le champ vert Huile/toile (27x35cm 10x13in) Paris
2000

DEFRANCE Léonard 1735-1805 **[13]**
$9 667 - €9 494 - **£6 000** - FF62 279
**Tavern Interiors with Figures eating, drinking
and playing Cards** Oil/panel (34.5x48cm 13x18in)
London 1999

DEFREGGER von Franz 1835-1921 **[244]**
$17 308 - €20 452 - **£12 268** - FF134 156
Porträt eines Mannes im Dreiviertelprofil
Öl/Leinwand (63x50cm 24x19in) Stuttgart 2000
$10 562 - €12 271 - **£7 423** - FF80 493
Mädchen mit Hut Oil/panel (37x29cm 14x11in)
Hamburg 2001
$1 331 - €1 227 - **£797** - FF8 048
Dirndl, Brustbild/Rücks, Alm mit Sennerin
Gouache (30.5x24.5cm 12x9in) Dresden 1998

DEGAND Eugène 1829-? **[2]**
$4 107 - €3 506 - **£2 456** - FF23 000
Halte de cavaliers Huile/panneau (23x37cm 9x14in)
Paris 1998

DEGAS Edgar 1834-1917 **[949]**
$320 000 - €262 686 - **£190 688** - FF1 788 704
Après le bain Oil/canvas (46.5x65.5cm 18x25in)
New-York 1999
$39 760 - €42 686 - **£26 600** - FF280 000
Dante et Béatrice Huile/papier/toile (22x32cm
8x12in) Paris 2000
$10 460 100 - €11 228 053 - **£7 000 000** -
FF73 651 200
Petite danseuse de quatorze ans Bronze (H98cm
H38in) London 2001
$181 311 - €213 218 - **£130 000** - FF1 398 618
Grande arabesque, premier temps Bronze
(H49cm H19in) London 2001
$107 800 - €115 144 - **£66 000** - FF689 700
Three Women Drawing (47.5x39cm 18x15in) Tokyo
2001
$1 734 - €1 945 - **£1 204** - FF12 757
«Au Louvre, la peinture, Mary Cassatt» Etching,
aquatint (31.5x15.5cm 12x5in) Luzern 2001
$18 000 - €15 028 - **£10 695** - FF98 577
Ludovic Halévy Gelatin silver print (9x9cm 3x3in)
New-York 1998

DEGENHARDT Gertrude 1940 **[66]**
$562 - €670 - **£401** - FF4 398
Ted Fury spielt uns was vor Watercolour
(50x33.7cm 19x13in) Hamburg 2000
$126 - €153 - **£88** - FF1 006
Dem Tod ein Schnippchen schlagen Offset
(34.4x47.5cm 13x18in) Berlin 2000

DEGLUME Henri 1865-1940 **[53]**
$881 - €942 - **£660** - FF6 178
Étang en hiver Huile/toile (50x70cm 19x27in)
Lokeren 2001

DEGNER Arthur 1887-1972 **[28]**
$434 - €511 - **£311** - FF3 353
Am Fluss Aquarell/Papier (26.5x34.5cm 10x13in)
Düsseldorf 2001

DEGODE Wilhelm 1862-1931 **[19]**
$2 299 - €1 943 - **£1 371** - FF12 743
Bad Zwischenahner Heide Oil/canvas/panel
(41x52cm 16x20in) Düsseldorf 1998

DEGOTTEX Jean 1918-1988 **[242]**
$11 409 - €10 891 - **£7 130** - FF71 438
«Sabi (l)» Oil/canvas (195x97cm 76x38in) Amsterdam
1999
$3 530 - €4 269 - **£2 466** - FF28 000
Rose écrite Huile/papier/toile (75x105cm 29x41in)
Paris 2000

$2 284 - €2 134 - **£1 409** - FF14 000
Sans titre Huile/bois (31x31x3cm 12x12x1in) Nantes
1999

$2 404 - €2 744 - **£1 672** - FF18 000
Composition Aquarelle/papier (49x64cm 19x25in)
Paris 2001

$481 -€442 - **£295** - FF2 900
Composition Sérigraphie (73x73cm 28x28in) Paris
1999

DEGOUVE DE NUNCQUES William 1867-1935
[110]

$5 596 - €4 834 - **£3 373** - FF31 707
La neige au verger Huile/toile (48x59cm 18x23in)
Bruxelles 1999

$2 130 - €2 479 - **£1 520** - FF16 260
Meules à Verrewinkel Huile/carton (35x45cm
13x17in) Bruxelles 2001

$651 -€545 - **£382** - FF3 577
Vue des Ardennes Pastel/papier (27x36.5cm
10x14in) Bruxelles 1998

DEGRAVE Jules A.Patrouillard XIX-XX **[5]**

$11 000 - €10 881 - **£6 858** - FF71 377
Le banc des nouveaux Vénus Oleo/tabla
(35x26.5cm 13x10in) Buenos-Aires 1999

DEGREEF Amédée 1878-1969 **[64]**

$590 -€595 - **£367** - FF3 902
Paysage en Campine Huile/toile (46x70.5cm
18x27in) Bruxelles 2000

DEHN Adolf Arthur 1895-1968 **[198]**

$7 000 - €7 661 - **£4 828** - FF50 251
«Summer Night» Oil/masonite (61x91.5cm 24x36in)
New-York 2001

$1 300 - €1 190 - **£792** - FF7 809
Rural Landscape with barn and Farmhouse
Watercolour/paper (48x69cm 19x27in) Bloomfield-Hills
MI 1999

$250 -€296 - **£172** - FF1 944
Street scene Lithograph (24x33cm 9x12in) New-York
2000

DEHN Georg 1843-1904 **[3]**

$366 - €383 - **£230** - FF2 515
Chioggia Madonna Öl/Leinwand/Karton (26x18cm
10x7in) Bremen 2000

DEHNER Dorothy 1901-1994 **[27]**

$1 100 - €1 227 - **£720** - FF8 050
Abstract Form Bronze (27x40cm 11x16in) Chicago
IL 2000

$1 500 - €1 440 - **£924** - FF9 449
New York Landscape Etching (22.5x30.5cm 8x12in)
New-York 1999

DEHODENCQ Alfred 1822-1882 **[121]**

$39 275 - €38 112 - **£24 450** - FF250 000
Les fils du Pacha Huile/toile (144.5x96cm 56x37in)
Cheverny 1999

$3 294 - €3 049 - **£2 040** - FF20 000
Le joueur de guitare Huile/toile (34x26cm 13x10in)
Paris 1999

$544 -€610 - **£369** - FF4 000
**Croquis de personnages en costumes
Renaissance** Crayon/papier (18.5x27.5cm 7x10in)
Paris 2000

DEHOY Charles 1872-1940 **[55]**

$884 -€992 - **£600** - FF6 504
Fillette et chèvres Huile/toile (40.5x50.5cm 15x19in)
Bruxelles 2000

$200 -€173 - **£121** - FF1 137
Dame au chapeau Dessin (49x39cm 19x15in)
Antwerpen 1998

DEIKER Carl 1879-1952 **[24]**

$565 -€665 - **£398** - FF4 359
Fuchs in verschneiter Landschaft Öl/Leinwand
(100x80.5cm 39x31in) Köln 2001

DEIKER Carl Friedrich 1836-1892 **[70]**

$9 526 - €10 226 - **£6 376** - FF67 078
Zwölfender auf einer Anhöhe im Morgenlicht
Öl/Leinwand (118x103cm 46x40in) Köln 2000

$1 708 - €1 789 - **£1 129** - FF11 738
Brunfthirsch im Herbstwald Öl/Leinwand
(86x97cm 33x38in) München 2000

$921 -€920 - **£576** - FF6 037
**Ein Jagdhund einen Keiler im Winterwald ver-
bellend** Öl/Leinwand (34x37cm 13x14in) Köln 1999

DEIKER Johannes Christian 1822-1895 **[24]**

$1 629 - €1 943 - **£1 162** - FF12 744
«Reinecke auf der Suche» Öl/Leinwand
(58.5x48cm 23x18in) Ahlden 2000

$855 -€818 - **£521** - FF5 366
Zwei Jagdhunde stellen einen Hirsch Grisaille
(40x55cm 15x21in) Staufen 1999

DEINEKA Alexander Alexandrov 1889-1969 **[6]**

$19 654 - €21 684 - **£13 000** - FF142 239
The Highway Oil/canvas (55x47cm 21x18in) London
2000

DEITERS Heinrich 1840-1916 **[20]**

$2 086 - €2 454 - **£1 472** - FF16 098
Mühle in sommerlicher Landschaft Öl/Leinwand
(66x99cm 25x38in) Köln 2001

DEJEAN Louis 1872-1953 **[17]**

$8 064 - €9 147 - **£5 682** - FF60 000
Corps de femme Marbre (104x30.5x29cm
40x12x11in) Paris 2001

$1 857 - €2 113 - **£1 288** - FF13 860
Parisienne au manteau Bronze (36x19cm 14x7in)
Sion 2000

DEJONGHE Gerben 1886-1967 **[2]**

$2 221 - €2 592 - **£1 587** - FF17 000
Jeune femme à l'éventail Huile/panneau (33x23cm
12x9in) Lyon 2000

DEJOUX Daniel 1935 **[62]**

$786 - €838 - **£498** - FF5 500
Port de pêche Huile/toile (46x38cm 18x14in) Muret
2000

$479 -€545 - **£330** - FF3 577
Le petit pont Huile/toile (22x27cm 8x10in) De Panne
2000

DEJUINNE François Louis 1786-1844 **[3]**

$15 886 - €16 007 - **£9 901** - FF105 000
Portrait présumé de Conélie Falcon Huile/toile
(82x65cm 32x25in) Paris 2000

DEKEN de Albert 1915 **[129]**

$1 677 - €1 611 - **£1 046** - FF10 569
Jeune femme enfilant ses bas Huile/toile
(100x80cm 39x31in) Bruxelles 1999

$112 -€124 - **£78** - FF813
Liggend naakt (Nu allongé) Sanguine/papier
(29x40cm 11x15in) Antwerpen 2001

DEKKER Henricus Nicol.,Henk 1897-1974 **[72]**

$1 117 - €1 140 - **£699** - FF7 479
Marine Huile/toile (60x80cm 23x31in) Bruxelles 2000

$500 -€481 - **£308** - FF3 154
Sunset on the Harbor Oil/canvas (29.5x50cm
11x19in) Boston MA 1999

DEKKERS Ed 1938-1974 **[28]**

💷 **$11 960** - €11 798 - **£7 365** - FF77 391
Plusteken in dubbenvierkant Oil/wood (60x120cm 23x47in) Amsterdam 1999

💷 **$2 827** - €2 723 - **£1 768** - FF59 753
Verschoven Kwadraten Mixed media (37x37x3cm 14x14x1in) Amsterdam 1999

✒ **$11 427** - €11 344 - **£7 140** - FF74 415
Verschoven achthoeken no I Relief (160x160cm 62x62in) Amsterdam 1999

✒ **$7 820** - €7 714 - **£4 816** - FF50 602
Eerst fase van cirkel naar omgeschreven vierkant Sculpture, wood (H40cm H15in) Amsterdam 1999

📖 **$845** - €908 - **£565** - FF5 953
Lines Screenprint (30x60cm 11x23in) Amsterdam 2000

DEKKERS Ger 1929 **[8]**

📷 **$915** - €1 089 - **£652** - FF7 143
Nine Breakwater of Basalt with Cloudbanks near Westhoek, Friesland Cibachrome print (100x70cm 39x27in) Amsterdam 2000

DEKKERT Eugene 1865-1956 **[66]**

🎨 **$928** - €998 - **£632** - FF6 548
Boats in a Harbour Oil/canvas (70x101cm 27x39in) Amsterdam 2001

🎨 **$368** - €358 - **£229** - FF2 347
Gebirgsdorf mit Figuren, im Hintergrund Bergmassiv/Studie ohne Titel Öl/Karton (33x40cm 12x15in) Bad-Vilbel 1999

DEL BON Angelo 1898-1952 **[96]**

🎨 **$2 750** - €2 851 - **£1 650** - FF18 700
Natura morta Olio/tela (54x65cm 21x25in) Milano 2000

✒ **$480** - €622 - **£360** - FF4 080
Nudo inginocchiato Pastelli (43.5x38.5cm 17x15in) Vercelli 2001

DEL BRINA Francesco c.1540-1585/86 **[7]**

🎨 **$14 190** - €15 012 - **£9 000** - FF98 475
The Madonna and Child with the Infant Saint John The Baptist Oil/panel (58x42cm 22x16in) London 2000

DEL DEVEZ Jean 1910-1982 **[125]**

✒ **$36** - €43 - **£25** - FF280
La petite bête Gouache/papier (18x14cm 7x5in) Paris 2000

DEL MARLE Félix Aimé 1889-1952 **[20]**

🎨 **$9 200** - €9 076 - **£5 666** - FF59 532
Composition Oil/canvas (30x38cm 11x14in) Amsterdam 1999

✒ **$2 010** - €2 287 - **£1 395** - FF15 000
Fugue Crayon gras/papier (33x16cm 12x6in) Paris 2000

DEL MARTINO Don act.1874-1879 **[3]**

✒ **$2 620** - €2 907 - **£1 824** - FF19 068
Innenansicht des Petersdomes Aquarell/Papier (52x74cm 20x29in) Salzburg 2001

DEL PACCHIA Girolamo 1477-c.1533 **[1]**

🎨 **$43 447** - €42 556 - **£28 000** - FF279 148
The Madonna and Child Oil/panel (51x43cm 20x16in) London 1999

DEL PEZZO Lucio 1933 **[229]**

🎨 **$1 200** - €1 555 - **£900** - FF10 200
Essenziale Acrilico (60x75cm 23x29in) Vercelli 2001

🎨 **$600** - €518 - **£400** - FF3 400
Cromatico fondo oro Tecnica mista/tavola (30x25cm 11x9in) Prato 1998

✎ **$2 400** - €2 073 - **£1 600** - FF13 600
Composizione Sculpture bois (57x44x20cm 22x17x7in) Milano 1998

✒ **$375** - €389 - **£225** - FF2 550
Geometrie Acquarello (23.5x21.5cm 9x8in) Vercelli 2000

📖 **$100** - €104 - **£60** - FF680
Geometrie Serigrafia (105x74cm 41x29in) Vercelli 2001

DEL TORRE Giulio 1856-1932 **[37]**

🎨 **$3 180** - €3 579 - **£2 191** - FF23 477
Die Waschenden Kinder Oil/panel (27x21cm 10x8in) München 2000

DELABRIERRE Édouard Paul 1829-1912 **[186]**

✎ **$1 148** - €1 287 - **£800** - FF8 445
Tethered Hound Bronze (21.5x31cm 8x12in) London 2001

DELACHAUX Léon 1850-1919 **[15]**

🎨 **$4 531** - €3 909 - **£2 722** - FF25 641
«Sur les bords du Loing (femme au bateau)» Oil/panel (55x44cm 21x17in) Bern 1998

DELACHAUX Théodore 1879-1949 **[25]**

🎨 **$954** - €877 - **£586** - FF5 751
Chemin de campagne Öl/Leinwand (74x56cm 29x22in) Zürich 1999

DELACOU Yvonne XX **[41]**

✎ **$2 151** - €2 134 - **£1 338** - FF14 000
Elisa Bronze (H45cm H17in) Brest 1999

DELACOUR Clovis XIX-XX **[4]**

✎ **$3 475** - €3 811 - **£2 360** - FF25 000
La source Sculpture (H27cm H10in) Lille 2000

DELACOUR Hyppolite XIX **[8]**

🎨 **$2 507** - €2 134 - **£1 492** - FF14 000
Bateaux à quai Huile/panneau (32x60cm 12x23in) Montpellier 1998

DELACROIX Auguste 1809-1868 **[36]**

✒ **$348** - €396 - **£241** - FF2 600
Laveuses sur la Seine Mine plomb (13x21cm 5x8in) Fontainebleau 2000

DELACROIX Eugène 1798-1863 **[640]**

🎨 **$400 000** - €345 102 - **£241 320** - FF2 263 720
Study of a Reclining Nude Oil/canvas (33x49.5cm 12x19in) New-York 1998

🎨 **$51 203** - €50 836 - **£32 000** - FF333 462
Le corps de Saint-Étienne relevé par les disciples Oil/paper/canvas (43.5x35.5cm 17x13in) London 1999

🎨 **$5 500** - €5 874 - **£3 748** - FF38 532
Studies of Putti and a Female Nude Drawing (26x40.5cm 10x15in) New-York 2001

📖 **$492** - €579 - **£353** - FF3 800
Arabes d'Oran Eau-forte (28.5x33cm 11x12in) Paris 2001

DELACROIX Henry-Eugène 1845-1930 **[10]**

🎨 **$1 141** - €1 067 - **£690** - FF7 000
Paysage à la rivière Huile/toile (24x33cm 9x12in) Lille 1999

DELACROIX Michel 1933 **[31]**

📖 **$260** - €302 - **£180** - FF1 984
Paris Street Scene Color lithograph (48x59cm 19x23in) Calgary, Alberta 2000

DELACROIX Victor 1842-? **[6]**

🎨 **$4 692** - €4 421 - **£2 842** - FF29 000
Victor Delacroix déjeunant avec son modèle Huile/toile (68x61cm 26x24in) Paris 1999

DELAFONTAINE Pierre-Maximilien 1774-1860 **[4]**
$28 494 - €27 441 - £17 694 - FF180 000
Portrait d'Alexandre-Marie Lenoir (1762-1839), sa femme et sa fille Huile/toile (125.5x105.5cm 49x41in) Paris 1999

DELAFONTAINE Rosalie XIX **[1]**
$6 014 - €6 250 - £3 788 - FF41 000
Portrait de petite fille et son panier Huile/toile (65x55cm 25x21in) Melun 2000

DELAFOSSE Jean-Charles 1734-1789 **[26]**
$1 740 - €1 829 - £1 092 - FF12 000
Vierge à l'Enfant avec des Saints Crayon (19.5x19.5cm 7x7in) Paris 2000

DELAHAUT Jo 1911-1992 **[103]**
$11 287 - €9 771 - £6 849 - FF64 095
Reol Oil/canvas (96.5x162cm 37x63in) Amsterdam 1998
$1 112 - €1 289 - £769 - FF8 455
Juxtaposition Nº1 Huile/panneau (41x61cm 16x24in) Bruxelles 2000
$817 - €942 - £562 - FF6 178
Composition polygonale Gouache/paper (49.5x34.6cm 19x13in) Lokeren 2000
$146 - €124 - £87 - FF812
Abstraction Lithographie (73x57cm 28x22in) Liège 1998

DELAHOGUE Alexis-Auguste 1867-1950 **[98]**
$4 313 - €5 031 - £2 999 - FF33 000
El-Kantara Huile/toile (37x54cm 14x21in) Paris 2000
$1 633 - €1 829 - £1 135 - FF12 000
Kérouan Huile/toile (33x46cm 12x18in) Paris 2001

DELAHOGUE Eugène Jules 1867-c.1935 **[51]**
$1 359 - €1 509 - £947 - FF9 990
Pèlerins devant la mosquée Sadi ben Ziad à Tunis Huile/panneau (34x18.5cm 13x7in) Paris 2001
$568 - €610 - £380 - FF4 000
Marché oriental Gouache/papier (23x18cm 9x7in) Quimper 2000

DELAISSEMENT Émile 1873-1955 **[4]**
$1 036 - €991 - £650 - FF6 500
Pêcheur l'après-midi au bord de la Sarthe Huile/toile (47x56cm 18x22in) Angers 1999

DELAISTRE François Nicolas 1746-1832 **[3]**
$5 766 - €6 403 - £4 019 - FF42 000
Buste de Louis Lazare Hoche, général en chef Plâtre (H66cm H25in) Paris 2001

DELAMAIN Paul 1821-1882 **[5]**
$19 680 - €22 867 - £14 025 - FF150 000
Fantasia Huile/toile (47x77.5cm 18x30in) Paris 2001

DELAMARRE Jacques Barthélemy XVIII **[5]**
$6 643 - €6 555 - £4 093 - FF42 000
Portrait d'un chien blanc sur un coussin rouge Huile/toile (50x60.5cm 19x23in) Neuilly-sur-Seine 1999
$6 551 - €6 411 - £4 200 - FF42 051
Still Life of a Bichon, a Quill, an Encrier, a Letter upon a Table Top Oil/canvas (25x33.5cm 9x13in) London 1999

DELAMARRE Raymond 1890 **[14]**
$7 100 - €7 622 - £4 825 - FF50 000
Mogli Bronze (53x80x20cm 20x31x7in) Paris 2001

DELAMARRE Théodore Didier 1824-1883 **[2]**
$4 451 - €4 960 - £3 111 - FF32 537
Interiör med spisende kineser Oil/wood (21x16cm 8x6in) Köbenhavn 2001

DELAMOTTE Philip Henry 1820-1889 **[11]**
$4 250 - €3 963 - £2 565 - FF25 997
Photographic Tour Among the Abbeys of Yorkshire Albumen print (29x24cm 11x9in) New-York 1999

DELAMOTTE William Alfred 1775-1863 **[41]**
$4 482 - €4 812 - £3 000 - FF31 564
Pope's Villa, Twickenham Oil/panel (24.5x44cm 9x17in) London 2000
$490 - €438 - £300 - FF2 873
Goar Tower, Rhine Watercolour/paper (35x26cm 14x10in) Par, Cornwall 1999
$1 286 - €1 461 - £900 - FF9 585
Original Views of Oxford, Its Colleges, Chapels and Gardens Lithograph (25x35.5cm 9x13in) London 2001

DELANCE-FEURGARD Julie 1859-1892 **[21]**
$4 370 - €3 811 - £2 642 - FF25 000
Jeune fille au jardin Huile/toile (92x65cm 36x25in) Paris 1998

DELANEY Arthur 1927-1987 **[16]**
$5 771 - €5 231 - £3 500 - FF34 313
St Ann's Square, Manchester, in the Rain Oil/board (35x48cm 14x19in) Manchester 1998
$4 570 - €5 280 - £3 200 - FF34 633
Girl in red hat Oil/board (33x23cm 13x9in) Manchester 2001

DELANEY Beauford 1901-1979 **[23]**
$20 736 - €24 392 - £14 864 - FF160 000
Composition jaune Huile/toile (194.5x130cm 76x51in) Paris 2001
$12 249 - €13 720 - £8 514 - FF90 000
Sans titre Huile/toile (107x96cm 42x37in) Paris 2001
$3 698 - €3 049 - £2 178 - FF20 000
Sans titre Huile/toile (41x33cm 16x12in) Paris 1998
$647 - €534 - £381 - FF3 500
Silhouette noire Encre Chine/papier (33.5x22cm 13x8in) Paris 1998

DELANGLADE Frédéric Marcou 1907-1970 **[19]**
$130 - €122 - £80 - FF800
Arlequin à la mandoline/Don Quichotte et Sancho Pança/Composition/Dali Crayon (12x22cm 4x8in) Tours 1999

DELANO Gerard Curtis 1890-1972 **[24]**
$92 500 - €84 087 - £55 712 - FF551 577
Evening Cloud Oil/canvas (101x121cm 40x48in) Hayden ID 1998
$22 500 - €20 454 - £13 551 - FF134 167
In Canyon del Muerto Oil/board (71x83cm 28x33in) Hayden ID 1998
$8 500 - €7 727 - £5 119 - FF50 685
Riders in Monument Valley Oil/board (35x43cm 14x17in) Hayden ID 1998
$7 500 - €6 818 - £4 517 - FF44 722
Canyon Del Muerto Watercolour/paper (55x50cm 22x20in) Hayden ID 1998

DELANO Jack 1914-1997 **[22]**
$900 - €841 - £544 - FF5 514
Ex-Slave, Greene County, Ga. Vintage gelatin silver print (34x25cm 13x10in) New-York 1999

DELANOY Hippolyte 1849-1899 **[5]**
$7 226 - €7 013 - £4 498 - FF46 000
Nature morte aux fleurs et à l'ombrelle Huile/toile (65x81cm 25x31in) Pontoise 1999

DELANOY Jacques 1820-1890 **[4]**

🖱 **$4 608** - €4 376 - **£2 824** - FF28 703
Küchenstilleben mit Hummer Öl/Leinwand
(60x73cm 23x28in) Zürich 1999

DELAPCHIER Louis XX **[4]**

🖱 **$1 304** - €1 524 - **£931** - FF10 000
Jeune fille dansant Bronze (H61.5cm H24in) Paris 2001

DELAPIERRE Roger 1935 **[22]**

🖱 **$754** - €858 - **£523** - FF5 631
L'Abbatiale de Payerne Huile/toile (55x46cm 21x18in) Sion 2000

DELAPLANCHE Eugène 1836-1891 **[28]**

🖱 **$6 179** - €5 641 - **£3 759** - FF37 000
Sans titre Bronze (H97cm H38in) Clermont-Ferrand 1998

🖱 **$1 428** - €1 601 - **£969** - FF10 500
Allégorie du sommeil Porcelain (44x35x31cm 17x13x12in) Paris 2000

DELAPORTE Maurice Eugène 1878-1964 **[5]**

🖱 **$1 500** - €1 453 - **£935** - FF9 531
Versailles, la Chambre de Louis XIV Pastel/paper (63.5x50cm 25x19in) Beverly-Hills CA 1999

DELAPUENTE Fernando 1909-1976 **[38]**

🖱 **$1 440** - €1 351 - **£900** - FF8 865
Bodegón con botella de vino Oleo/tablex (53x40cm 20x15in) Madrid 1999

🖱 **$994** - €841 - **£588** - FF5 516
El puerto de San Sebastián Oleo/tablex (27x41cm 10x16in) Madrid 1998

🖱 **$196** - €210 - **£129** - FF1 379
Niños con pájaros Tinta/papel (20x15cm 7x5in) Madrid 2000

DELAROCHE Paul 1797-1856 **[54]**

🖱 **$35 347** - €34 301 - **£22 275** - FF225 000
Cécile de Poilly, Comtesse de Fitz-James Huile/toile (72x56cm 28x22in) Paris 1999

🖱 **$4 303** - €4 777 - **£3 000** - FF31 334
Head Studies of Monks Oil/canvas (24.5x32.5cm 9x12in) London 2001

🖱 **$800** - €758 - **£486** - FF4 975
Saint Cecilia and her husband Valerius crowned by an Angel Black chalk (22.5x35.5cm 8x13in) New-York 1999

DELARUE Lucien 1925 **[12]**

🖱 **$11 000** - €11 412 - **£6 979** - FF74 860
Port de Nice Oil/canvas (94x129cm 37x51in) Pittsburgh PA 2000

🖱 **$700** - €705 - **£436** - FF4 627
View to the Sea Oil/canvas (46x55cm 18x22in) Chicago IL 2000

DELARUE-NOUVELLIERE Pierre Charles XX **[7]**

🖱 **$725** - €835 - **£500** - FF5 480
«Dunlop, tout ce qui roule est équipe par Dunlop» Poster (158x117cm 62x46in) London 2000

DELATRE Eugène 1864-1938 **[105]**

🖱 **$256** - €274 - **£171** - FF1 800
La Seine à Genevilliers Eau-forte, aquatinte couleurs (32.5x59.5cm 12x23in) Paris 2000

DELATTRE Henri 1801-1876 **[4]**

🖱 **$2 540** - €2 439 - **£1 593** - FF16 000
Chevaux à l'écurie Huile/toile (55x80.5cm 21x31in) Angers 1999

DELATTRE Joseph 1858-1912 **[72]**

🖱 **$6 715** - €7 622 - **£4 665** - FF50 000
Les trois-mâts à Croisset Huile/toile (48.5x73cm 19x28in) Rouen 2001

🖱 **$1 668** - €1 829 - **£1 132** - FF12 000
La Seine près de Rouen Huile/panneau (25x44cm 9x17in) Calais 2000

🖱 **$837** - €762 - **£512** - FF5 000
Brume du matin Aquarelle/papier (13x36cm 5x14in) Cherbourg 1998

DELATTRE Mathilde 1871-? **[4]**

🖱 **$3 266** - €3 049 - **£1 978** - FF20 000
Les rhododendrons Aquarelle/papier (116x154cm 45x60in) Avignon 1999

DELAUNAY Jules, dit Duval c.1845-1906 **[22]**

🖱 **$1 240** - €1 250 - **£773** - FF8 200
Nature morte aux gibiers et attributs du chasseur Huile/toile (80x56cm 31x22in) Argenteuil 2000

🖱 **$834** - €915 - **£566** - FF6 000
Cheval d'officier, sellé Huile/panneau (32x41cm 12x16in) Paris 2000

DELAUNAY Jules-Élie 1828-1891 **[29]**

🖱 **$28 842** - €31 871 - **£20 000** - FF209 060
Reclining nude Oil/canvas (103.5x116cm 40x45in) London 2001

🖱 **$2 765** - €2 592 - **£1 662** - FF17 000
Femme au miroir Huile/toile (46x32.5cm 18x12in) Paris 1999

DELAUNAY Maurice **[10]**

🖱 **$770** - €841 - **£518** - FF5 516
Vista de París Oleo/cartón (26x35cm 10x13in) Madrid 2000

DELAUNAY Robert 1885-1941 **[128]**

🖱 **$110 550** - €117 870 - **£75 000** - FF773 175
Portrait de Madame Heim Oil/board (107.5x72.5cm 42x28in) London 2001

🖱 **$216 934** - €240 869 - **£151 206** - FF1 580 000
Esquisse pour l'Hommage à Blériot Huile/papier (27x26.5cm 10x10in) Paris 2001

🖱 **$26 532** - €28 289 - **£18 000** - FF185 562
Tour Eiffel Ink (29x17cm 11x6in) London 2001

🖱 **$2 498** - €2 940 - **£1 764** - FF19 284
«Place de l'étoile (arc de triomphe)» Lithographie (21x21cm 8x8in) Berlin 2001

DELAUNAY-TERK Sonia 1885-1979 **[1063]**

🖱 **$95 000** - €110 227 - **£65 588** - FF723 045
Rythme couleur, No.876 Oil/canvas (116x86cm 45x33in) New-York 2001

🖱 **$9 690** - €8 428 - **£5 780** - FF55 284
Composition Huile/panneau (40x30cm 15x11in) Bruxelles 1998

🖱 **$4 500** - €4 665 - **£2 700** - FF30 600
Composition aux carrés Tempera/carta (32x25cm 12x9in) Milano 2000

🖱 **$879** - €872 - **£550** - FF5 721
Thunderbird Color lithograph (52.5x42cm 20x16in) London 1999

DELAUNE Étienne 1518/19-1595 **[40]**

🖱 **$32 757** - €32 053 - **£21 000** - FF210 256
Design for a Frieze Ink (9x26.5cm 3x10in) London 1999

🖱 **$427** - €420 - **£266** - FF2 758
Geometría/Aritmética Grabado (8x6.5cm 3x2in) Madrid 1999

DELAVALLÉE Henri 1862-1943 **[170]**

🖱 **$4 764** - €4 726 - **£3 000** - FF31 000
Sur les bords de l'Aven Huile/toile (53x73cm 20x28in) Brest 1999

D

D

$2 824 - €3 049 - £1 952 - FF20 000
Neige en Bretagne Huile/toile (33x47cm 12x18in)
Quimper 2001

$2 706 - €2 287 - £1 609 - FF15 000
Bouquet de fleurs Pastel/papier (54x42cm 21x16in)
Quimper 1998

$183 - €198 - £126 - FF1 300
La route de Landemeur, pointe de la Hague
Vernis mou (18.5x26cm 7x10in) Quimper 2001

DELAVILLA Friedrich Karl 1884-1967 [7]
$632 - €613 - £390 - FF4 024
Ein trauriges Stuecklein Woodcut in colors
(14x39.5cm 5x15in) München 1999

DELAVILLE Louis c.1770-1841 [6]
$11 968 - €12 958 - £7 599 - FF85 000
Buste représentant le Christ Terracotta (30x14cm
11x5in) Paris 2000

DELAWARR Valentine, Val act.1880-1900 [47]
$377 - €425 - £260 - FF2 786
Coastal Views Oil/canvas (20x25cm 7x9in) London
2000

DELAYE Alice 1884-1963 [3]
$16 500 - €14 607 - £10 088 - FF95 813
Faithful Friends Oil/canvas (142x185cm 55x72in)
New-York 1999

DELAYE Théophile Jean 1896-1973 [15]
$3 297 - €3 201 - £2 037 - FF21 000
Marrakech, souk de Derb Dabbaghi
Gouache/papier (24x33.5cm 9x13in) Paris 1999

DELCAMBRE Élysée 1930 [59]
$696 - €717 - £441 - FF4 700
Bord du Loing Huile/toile (46x55cm 18x21in) Bernay
2000

DELCOURT Maurice 1877-1917 [20]
$1 377 - €1 524 - £918 500
Place Saint-Georges Gravure bois couleurs
(32x19.5cm 12x7in) Paris 2000

DELCROIX Eugene 1892-1967 [50]
$175 - €198 - £121 - FF1 296
«Old Slave Quarters» Gelatin silver print (11x16cm
4x6in) New-Orleans LA 2000

DELCROIX Giacomo 1894-1972 [11]
$1 500 - €1 296 - £1 000 - FF8 500
Paesaggio Olio/tavoletta (50x80cm 19x31in) Firenze
1998

DELDERENNE Léon 1864-1921 [33]
$720 - €793 - £486 - FF5 203
Bosgezicht in de herfst (Sous-bois en automne)
Huile/toile (77x90cm 30x35in) Antwerpen 2000

DELECLUZE Eugène 1882-? [27]
$539 - €503 - £333 - FF3 300
Douarnenez Huile/carton (25x33cm 9x12in) Le Havre
1999

DELEIDI IL NEBBIA Luigi 1774-1853 [2]
$11 700 - €13 720 - £8 415 - FF90 000
Paysage de neige Huile/toile (48x60.5cm 18x23in)
Paris 2001

DELEN van Dirk 1605-1671 [26]
$319 020 - €297 276 - £196 755 - FF1 950 000
**Arcade de palais avec des personnes élé-
gants** Huile/panneau (111x164cm 43x64in) Lille 1999
$48 612 - €54 454 - £33 780 - FF357 192
**Architectural Capriccio of a Portico, with an
Italianate Landscape** Oil/panel (62.5x88.5cm
24x34in) Amsterdam 2001

DELERIVE Nicolas Louis Albert 1755-1818 [15]
$19 065 - €18 491 - £12 000 - FF121 291
Portrait of a Gentleman and a Lady, Full-Length
Oil/canvas (119.5x94cm 47x37in) London 1999
$1 158 - €1 316 - £800 - FF8 635
Man seated by a Toked Horse in a Landscape
Oil/panel (15.5x11.5cm 6x4in) London 2000

DELÉTANG Robert-Adrien 1874-1951 [24]
$16 309 - €18 751 - £11 512 - FF123 000
Le Fandango Huile/panneau (71x113cm 27x44in)
Menton 2001

DELEURAN Thorvald 1877-1968 [8]
$4 800 - €4 766 - £3 000 - FF31 262
The Seamstress Oil/canvas (68x56.5cm 26x22in)
London 1999

DELFF Cornelis Jacobsz. 1571-1643 [10]
$29 332 - €34 033 - £20 250 - FF223 245
**Kitchen Still Life with a Man Holding a Cockerel
and a Girl Showing** Oil/panel (97x146.5cm 38x57in)
Amsterdam 2000
$15 134 - €14 025 - £9 034 - FF92 000
Nature morte aux huîtres et au verre de vin
Huile/panneau (74x105cm 29x41in) Paris 1999

DELFF Willem Jacobsz 1580-1638 [2]
$1 124 - €1 305 - £800 - FF8 557
**Portrait of Frederik V of Bohemia/Elizabeth
Queen of Bohemia** Engraving (43x30cm 16x11in)
London 2000

DELFGAAUW Gerardus Johannes 1882-1947 [143]
$1 910 - €1 815 - £1 162 - FF11 906
Dordts stadsgezicht Oil/canvas (38.5x58cm
15x22in) Den Haag 1999
$581 - €544 - £362 - FF3 571
View of the Rotterdam Harbour Oil/canvas
(18x24cm 7x9in) Amsterdam 1999

DELFO XX [4]
$357 - €305 - £215 - FF2 000
«La Beauté du Diable» Affiche couleur (160x120cm
62x47in) Paris 1998

DELFOSSE Georges Marie Joseph 1869-1939 [92]
$1 010 - €1 179 - £721 - FF7 732
Vieille maison St.Vincent de Paul Huile/toile
(20.5x37cm 8x14in) Montréal 2000
$188 - €220 - £134 - FF1 443
Vase Fusain/papier (51x36cm 20x14in) Montréal 2000

DELGADO RAMOS Alvaro 1922 [145]
$2 700 - €3 003 - £1 900 - FF19 700
Retrato Oleo/lienzo (65x54cm 25x21in) Madrid 2001
$1 980 - €2 162 - £1 260 - FF14 184
Retrato de mujer con sombrero Oleo/tablex
(34x26cm 13x10in) Madrid 2000
$1 280 - €1 201 - £780 - FF7 880
Campesino vallecano Acuarela/papel (72x50cm
28x19in) Madrid 1999
$315 - €271 - £184 - FF1 777
Lazarillo de Tormes Serigrafia (52x36.5cm 20x14in)
Madrid 1998

DELHAYE José 1921-1991 [25]
$694 - €646 - £431 - FF4 227
Valentin Huile/panneau (90x60cm 35x23in) Liège
1999
$453 - €421 - £282 - FF2 764
Eté Technique mixte/papier (86x59.5cm 33x23in) Liège
1999

DELHOMMEAU Charles 1883-1970 **[9]**
🐾 **$2 730** - €3 049 - **£1 850** - FF20 000
   Un lémurien assis Terracotta (23.5x13.5x21.5cm
   9x5x8in) Pontoise 2000

DELI Antal 1886-1960 **[4]**
✏ **$323** - €365 - **£228** - FF2 394
   «Coritono 926» Aquarelle/papier (43x32cm 16x12in)
   Budapest 2001

DELIGNY Théodore 1798-1863 **[3]**
🖌 **$7 565** - €7 622 - **£4 715** - FF50 000
   Vues de la côte Amalfitaine Huile/toile (23x34cm
   9x13in) Paris 2000

DELIN C. c.1760-c.1810 **[3]**
🖌 **$6 000** - €5 580 - **£3 715** - FF36 603
   Portrait of Captain Baxter of Nantucket Oil/can-
   vas (49x40cm 19x16in) Nantucket MA 1999
🖌 **$13 000** - €12 090 - **£8 049** - FF79 307
   Portrait of Captain James Russell of Nantucket
   Oil/canvas (42x33cm 16x13in) Nantucket MA 1999

DELIN Johannes 1776-1811 **[1]**
🖌 **$4 867** - €5 793 - **£3 370** - FF38 000
   Enfant au chien Huile/toile (56x68cm 22x26in)
   Rodez 2000

DELIN Jozef 1821-1892 **[7]**
🖌 **$1 413** - €1 363 - **£885** - FF8 943
   **Portrait d'André le Candele, époux de Mme. de
   Gilman** Huile/toile (100x87cm 39x34in) Bruxelles
   1999

DELIOTTI Walter 1925 **[62]**
🖌 **$1 300** - €1 396 - **£870** - FF9 158
   Montevideo Oleo/cartón (50x61cm 19x24in)
   Montevideo 2000
🖌 **$448** - €481 - **£304** - FF3 152
   Calle Oleo/cartón (20x25cm 7x9in) Madrid 2001

DELIUS Charles XIX-XX **[16]**
📷 **$450** - €434 - **£283** - FF2 850
   Blick vom neuen R.C.A. Building Photograph
   (18x13cm 7x5in) München 1999

DELL Christian 1893-1974 **[1]**
🐾 **$3 296** - €3 068 - **£2 027** - FF20 123
   Maske Sculpture (24.3x13.4cm 9x5in) München 1999

DELL John Henry c.1836-1888 **[18]**
🖌 **$1 115** - €1 312 - **£800** - FF6 606
   The Last Load/Untitled Oil/panel (17x15cm 7x6in)
   Little-Lane, Ilkley 2001

DELLA BELLA Stefano 1610-1667 **[396]**
✏ **$2 823** - €2 757 - **£1 800** - FF18 082
   Flying eagle holding an arrow in its beak Black
   chalk (5x18cm 1x7in) London 1999
▥ **$347** - €409 - **£250** - FF2 683
   Trois enfants avec une Soucoupe, nach G.Reni
   Radierung (15.5x13cm 6x5in) Hamburg 2001

DELLA ROCCA Giovanni 1788-1858 **[5]**
🖌 **$3 887** - €3 354 - **£2 336** - FF22 000
   Scène de taverne Huile/toile (40x65cm 15x25in)
   Aubagne 1998

**DELLA ROVERE, IL FIAMMENGHINO Giovanni
Battista** I c.1561-c.1630 **[21]**
✏ **$2 160** - €1 866 - **£1 080** - FF12 240
   Studio di pala con cornice Acquarello (26x16.5cm
   10x6in) Milano 1999

DELLA TORRE Enrico 1931 **[28]**
🖌 **$520** - €674 - **£390** - FF4 420
   «Concentramento» Tecnica mista (20.5x50.5cm
   8x19in) Torino 2000

▱ **$432** - €373 - **£216** - FF2 448
   Notte africana Pastelli/carta (22.5x31cm 8x12in)
   Torino 1999

DELLA VALLE Angel 1855-1903 **[1]**
🖌 **$5 600** - €5 473 - **£3 551** - FF35 901
   Toros en un paisaje Oleo/tabla (23x36cm 9x14in)
   Buenos-Aires 1999

DELLAVEDOVA Mario 1958 **[6]**
🖌 **$550** - €570 - **£330** - FF3 740
   Monogramma Acrilico (18x24cm 7x9in) Milano 2000

DELLE VEDOVE Antonio 1865-? **[3]**
🖌 **$13 200** - €11 403 - **£6 600** - FF74 800
   L'atelier Olio/tela (143x105cm 56x41in) Genova 1999
🖌 **$4 750** - €4 438 - **£2 959** - FF29 111
   Grapes and Flowers Oil/canvas (81x116cm 32x46in)
   Mystic CT 1999

DELLEANI Lorenzo 1840-1908 **[147]**
🖌 **$105 300** - €90 966 - **£52 650** - FF596 700
   Luci crepuscolari Olio/tela (104.5x134.5cm
   41x52in) Milano 1999
🖌 **$5 000** - €4 479 - **£3 750** - FF42 500
   Posa di schiena Olio/tela (38x46cm 14x18in) Torino
   2000
🖌 **$12 000** - €11 334 - **£7 257** - FF74 348
   A Walk in the Countryside Oil/panel (31x44.5cm
   12x17in) New-York 1999
▱ **$720** - €622 - **£360** - FF4 080
   **Figura d'uomo con parrucca in abito settecen-
   tesco** Matita/carta (33x17.5cm 12x6in) Milano 1999

DELLEPIANE David 1866-1925 **[49]**
🖌 **$44 829** - €48 120 - **£30 000** - FF315 648
   Les rives de Bosphore Oil/canvas (101x180.5cm
   39x71in) London 1999
🖌 **$9 452** - €9 376 - **£5 879** - FF61 500
   Barque sous voiles sur fond d'olivier Huile/toile
   (73x54cm 28x21in) Brest 1999
🖌 **$1 360** - €1 601 - **£975** - FF10 500
   Paysanne et son âne Huile/carton (27x35cm
   10x13in) Paris 2001
▥ **$1 321** - €1 369 - **£792** - FF8 982
   «Chemin de fer Chamonix-Montenvers» Affiche
   couleur (108x78cm 42x30in) Torino 2000

DELLEPIANE IL MULINARETTO Giovanni Maria
1660-1745 **[4]**
🖌 **$29 500** - €30 581 - **£17 700** - FF200 600
   Ritratto di giovane patrizio con cavallo Olio/tela
   (111x87cm 43x34in) Milano 1999

DELMAET & DURANDELLE Hyacinthe & L.Émile
1828/39-1862/1917 **[5]**
📷 **$5 291** - €4 998 - **£3 200** - FF32 782
   Le Pont d'Arcole Albumen print (28x38.5cm
   11x15in) London 1999

DELMOTTE Marcel 1901-1984 **[308]**
🖌 **$3 468** - €2 975 - **£2 100** - FF19 512
   Le secret est pour l'éternité Huile/panneau
   (183x122cm 72x48in) Bruxelles 1998
🖌 **$2 055** - €1 859 - **£1 260** - FF12 195
   Cambrinus Huile/panneau (124x92cm 48x36in)
   Bruxelles 1999
🖌 **$494** - €471 - **£300** - FF3 089
   Composition fantastique Huile/panneau
   (36x24.5cm 14x9in) Bruxelles 1999
✏ **$221** - €248 - **£150** - FF1 626
   Tête d'homme Encre/papier (50x38cm 19x14in)
   Bruxelles 2000

DELOBBE Alfred 1835-1920 **[27]**
$30 000 - €33 224 - **£20 346** - FF217 935
  The Hay Gatherers at Rest in a Field Oil/canvas
  (96.5x131cm 37x51in) New-York 2000
$1 429 - €1 448 - **£897** - FF9 500
  Fillette assise Huile/toile (25x19cm 9x7in) Saint-Dié
  2000

DELOBEL Christian 1934 **[132]**
$199 - €213 - **£131** - FF1 400
  Village franc-comtois sous la neige Huile/pan-
  neau (18x24cm 7x9in) Lons-Le-Saunier 2000

DELOBRE Alfred François 1835-1920 **[4]**
$3 600 - €3 978 - **£2 496** - FF26 095
  Little Girl in Repose Oil/canvas (26x34cm 10x13in)
  New-Orleans LA 2001

DELOBRE Émile Augustin V. 1873-1956 **[21]**
$3 600 - €4 208 - **£2 548** - FF27 603
  After the Swim Oil/board (43x30cm 17x12in)
  Columbia SC 2001

DELORAS Henriette 1901-1941 **[181]**
$896 - €762 - **£534** - FF5 000
  Portrait de Mme. B. Pastel/papier (28x22cm 11x8in)
  Grenoble 1998

DELORME Anthonie c.1610-1673 **[14]**
$435 726 - €407 871 - **£270 000** - FF2 675 457
  **The Interior of the Grote Kerk, Rotterdam, with
  Figures and Dog** Oil/canvas (112.5x111cm 44x43in)
  London 1999
$18 620 - €18 238 - **£12 000** - FF119 635
  **Interior of a Palace at Night with an Elegant
  couple** Oil/canvas (62.5x47.5cm 24x18in) London
  1999

DELORME H.E. XIX **[1]**
$7 000 - €7 054 - **£4 363** - FF46 270
  Basket of Strawberries and Liserons Oil/canvas
  (61x77cm 24x30in) New-York 2000

DELORME Marguerite 1876-1946 **[11]**
$1 891 - €1 829 - **£1 166** - FF12 000
  Le petit marchand de fleurs Huile/panneau
  (60.5x42.5cm 23x16in) Paris 1999

DELORME Raphaël 1886-1962 **[52]**
$90 000 - €77 105 - **£54 108** - FF505 773
  «Amazones» Oil/canvas (184x174cm 72x68in) New-
  York 1998
$7 135 - €7 622 - **£4 865** - FF50 000
  Modèle dans l'atelier Huile/panneau (48x36cm
  18x14in) Limoges 2001
$2 981 - €3 354 - **£2 081** - FF22 000
  Femmes au voile et colombes Crayons couleurs
  (60.5x44cm 23x17in) Paris 2001
$1 600 - €1 365 - **£965** - FF8 953
  «Royan» Poster (73.5x104.5cm 28x41in) New-York
  1998

DELORT Charles Edouard 1841-1895 **[32]**
$25 000 - €21 569 - **£15 082** - FF141 482
  **Romeo and Juliet (Act II, Scene II: Capulet's
  Garden)** Oil/panel (54.5x34.5cm 21x13in) New-York
  1998
$1 800 - €1 769 - **£1 156** - FF11 606
  Cordial Greetings Oil/panel (32x42cm 12x16in)
  New-York 1999
$540 - €640 - **£381** - FF4 200
  Cavalier saluant Encre (29x20.5cm 11x8in) Paris
  2000

DELPECH François 1778-1825 **[9]**
$173 - €194 - **£120** - FF1 274
  **Cheval de Cavalerie Francaise, after Carle
  Vernet** Lithograph (30x52cm 11x20in) London 2000

DELPECH Hermann 1865-1918 **[15]**
$1 956 - €1 829 - **£1 184** - FF12 000
  Composition florale sur une table Huile/toile
  (60x92cm 23x36in) Pau 1999

DELPERÉE Émile 1850-1896 **[19]**
$819 - €793 - **£518** - FF5 203
  Portrait d'un garçonnet Huile/toile/panneau
  (25x20cm 9x7in) Liège 1999

DELPY Henri Jacques 1877-1957 **[233]**
$1 614 - €1 524 - **£976** - FF10 000
  Lavandières au soleil couchant Huile/panneau
  (41.5x71cm 16x27in) Paris 1999
$1 028 - €960 - **£634** - FF6 300
  Pêcheur en barque Huile/toile (24.5x50cm 9x19in)
  Melun 1999

DELPY Hippolyte-Camille 1842-1910 **[361]**
$8 389 - €7 775 - **£5 217** - FF51 000
  Paysage à l'église Huile/toile (45x69cm 17x27in)
  Rouen 1999
$2 412 - €2 744 - **£1 674** - FF18 000
  Bord de rivière Huile/panneau (16.5x26cm 6x10in)
  Fontainebleau 2000

DELPY Lucien Victor F. 1898-1967 **[148]**
$2 207 - €2 561 - **£1 524** - FF16 800
  Der Hafen von Algier Öl/Leinwand (50x61cm
  19x24in) Luzern 2000
$859 - €732 - **£511** - FF4 800
  Thoniers sous voiles près de la Ville Close
  Huile/panneau (20x27cm 7x10in) Brest 1998
$814 - €808 - **£506** - FF5 300
  Chalutier en route pour la marée Gouache/papier
  (48x62cm 18x24in) Brest 1999

DELSAUX Willem Charles L. 1862-1945 **[64]**
$624 - €595 - **£379** - FF3 902
  Paysage de dunes Huile/toile (73x94cm 28x37in)
  Bruxelles 1999

DELTIL Jean Julien 1791-1863 **[8]**
$1 563 - €1 448 - **£951** - FF9 500
  Les trois lavandières Huile/toile (47x39cm 18x15in)
  Paris 1999

DELTOMBE Paul 1878-1971 **[34]**
$1 913 - €2 134 - **£1 335** - FF14 000
  Paysage Huile/panneau (36x65cm 14x25in) Lons-Le-
  Saunier 2001

DELUC Gabriel 1850-1916 **[9]**
$3 537 - €3 429 - **£2 190** - FF22 492
  Rue de village Huile/toile (46x51cm 18x20in) Genève
  1999

DeLUCE Percival 1847-1914 **[12]**
$54 050 - €49 698 - **£33 381** - FF325 997
  «Gone for a Row» Oil/canvas (45x60cm 18x24in)
  Portsmouth NH 1998

DeLUE Donald 1897-1988 **[6]**
$4 500 - €3 845 - **£2 643** - FF25 224
  Jason Bronze (H47.5cm H18in) Boston MA 1998

DELVAUX Laurent 1696-1778 **[6]**
$6 384 - €5 949 - **£3 936** - FF39 024
  Charles de Lorraine Plâtre (59x51cm 23x20in)
  Bruxelles 1999

DELVAUX Paul 1897-1994 **[1008]**

🖼 $533 140 - €634 062 - £380 000 - FF4 159 176
La grande allée Oil/canvas (140x211cm 55x83in)
London 2000

🖼 $235 840 - €251 456 - £160 000 - FF1 649 440
La table Oil/canvas (89.5x76cm 35x29in) London
2001

🖼 $47 292 - €54 454 - £32 280 - FF357 192
Les Trois Grâces Oil/board (40x30cm 15x11in)
Amsterdam 2000

✒ $2 900 - €2 479 - £1 760 - FF16 260
Dame à l'enfant Crayon/papier (22x14cm 8x5in)
Antwerpen 1998

▥ $3 027 - €2 558 - £1 800 - FF16 781
Hat 1900 Color lithograph (59.5x39.5cm 23x15in)
London 1998

DELVILLE Jean 1867-1953 **[37]**

🖼 $10 652 - €8 860 - £6 254 - FF58 119
Le crime/Nudes Oil/canvas (65x54cm 25x21in)
Amsterdam 1998

✒ $5 400 - €4 958 - £3 320 - FF32 520
La mort Pastel/carton (62x52cm 24x20in) Bruxelles
1999

DELVOYE Wim 1965 **[20]**

🖼 $17 586 - €19 703 - £12 258 - FF129 240
Bétonnière Sculpture (129x151cm 50x59in)
Stockholm 2001

▥ $576 - €637 - £400 - FF4 181
Untitled Print in colors (68x49.5cm 26x19in) London
2001

DELYEN Jean-François 1684-1761 **[3]**

🖼 $41 158 - €39 637 - £25 558 - FF260 000
Buveur sur une treille Huile/toile (127.5x97cm
50x38in) Paris 1999

DEMACHY Pierre-Antoine 1723-1807 **[62]**

🖼 $60 154 - €57 931 - £37 354 - FF380 000
**Rotonde imaginaire avec la statue de Louis XIV
par Desjardins** Huile/panneau (51.5x38.5cm 20x15in)
Paris 1999

🖼 $8 579 - €8 395 - £5 500 - FF55 067
Paris, The Theatre de l'Odéon Oil/panel
(27x32.5cm 10x12in) London 1999

✒ $1 538 - €1 296 - £908 - FF8 500
Fantaisie architecturale Encre (16.7x23.2cm 6x9in)
Paris 1998

▥ $845 - €838 - £525 - FF5 500
Vue de Paris Gravure (39x60.5cm 15x23in) Paris
1999

DEMACHY Robert 1859-1936 **[39]**

📷 $2 255 - €1 906 - £1 341 - FF12 500
**Nu féminin assis au voile vert/Nu féminin allon-
gé** Autochrome (9.8x6.7cm 3x2in) Chartres 1998

DEMAN Albert 1927 **[56]**

🖼 $1 974 - €1 829 - £1 178 - FF12 000
Le faisan Huile/toile (141x66cm 55x25in) La Roche-
sur-Yon 1999

✒ $335 - €381 - £229 - FF2 500
Le sémaphore Fusain/papier (63x47cm 24x18in) La
Roche-sur-Yon 2000

DEMAND Carlo XX **[1]**

✒ $1 833 - €1 906 - £1 155 - FF12 500
Mercédès et Alfa-Roméo en course Fusain/papier
(64x67cm 25x26in) Paris 2000

DEMAND Thomas 1964 **[6]**

📷 $42 000 - €47 043 - £29 181 - FF308 582
Zimmer Type C color print (172x232cm 67x91in)
New-York 2001

DEMANET Victor 1895-1964 **[74]**

🖼 $1 185 - €998 - £700 - FF6 547
An Iron Worker Bronze (H55cm H21in) Amsterdam
1998

DEMAREST Suzanne 1900-1985 **[17]**

🖼 $1 207 - €1 119 - £751 - FF7 341
Kvinnor och barn i park Oil/canvas (25x33cm
9x12in) Malmö 1999

DEMARIA Bernabé 1824-1910 **[2]**

🖼 $4 250 - €3 884 - £2 600 - FF25 480
The Goucho Oil/canvas (39.5x32.5cm 15x12in)
Boston MA 1999

DeMARIA Walter 1935 **[26]**

🖼 $155 000 - €134 183 - £93 480 - FF880 183
Circle, Rectangle 7 Metal (13x132x176.5cm
5x51x69in) New-York 1998

✒ $7 040 - €8 311 - £5 600 - FF54 516
Rome Eats Shit Pencil/paper (100x152cm 39x59in)
London 2001

DEMARNE Jean-Louis 1752-1829 **[94]**

🖼 $11 044 - €11 129 - £6 883 - FF73 000
La collation le long de la route Huile/panneau
(43x53cm 16x20in) Paris 2000

🖼 $4 476 - €4 878 - £2 934 - FF32 000
L'abreuvoir Huile/panneau (29x38.5cm 11x15in)
Louviers 2000

DEMARQUAY Barthélémy Eugène 1818-? **[1]**

✒ $1 286 - €1 453 - £868 - FF9 534
Bildnis eines Mädchens mit Blume im Haar
Pastell/Papier (44x35cm 17x13in) Wien 2000

DEMARTEAU Gilles I 1722-1776 **[66]**

▥ $303 - €281 - £183 - FF1 844
La jardinière, nach Huet Engraving (31.5x24cm
12x9in) Heidelberg 1999

DEMARTEAU Gilles II / le Jeune 1750-1802 **[43]**

▥ $172 - €153 - £105 - FF1 006
Nymphe de Diane, nach Taillasson Kupferstich
(47.5x40.5cm 18x15in) Pforzheim 1999

DeMARTELLY John Stockton 1903-1979 **[89]**

🖼 $11 000 - €12 490 - £7 528 - FF81 932
Michigan Kids Oil/canvas (77x101cm 30x39in) New-
York 2000

▥ $475 - €547 - £327 - FF3 590
Chore Boy Lithograph (22x30cm 9x12in) Cleveland
OH 2000

DeMARTINI Joseph 1896-1984 **[23]**

🖼 $2 750 - €2 952 - £1 840 - FF19 362
The Wreck of the St.Christopher Oil/canvas
(76x101.5cm 29x39in) New-York 2000

🖼 $750 - €642 - £450 - FF4 214
Artist's Studio Oil/masonite (33x30cm 13x12in)
Cincinnati OH 1998

DEMAY Jean-François 1798-1850 **[31]**

🖼 $9 480 - €9 147 - £5 994 - FF60 000
**Scène de bal dans un village/Scène de kermes-
se** Huile/toile/panneau (38x46cm 14x18in) Paris 1999

🖼 $3 244 - €3 201 - £1 999 - FF21 000
La visite à la nourrice Huile/toile (19.5x24.5cm
7x9in) Dijon 1999

DEMEL Franz 1878-1947 **[28]**

✒ $329 - €363 - £228 - FF2 383
Das Fasszieherhaus in Wien Aquarell/Papier
(32x23cm 12x9in) Wien 2001

D

DEMETROPOULOS Charles 1912-1976 **[19]**
  $325 - €333 - **£203** - FF2 187
    Backyards in Winter Watercolour/paper (50x64cm 20x25in) Bolton MA 2000

DEMETZ Karl 1909-1986 **[49]**
  $829 - €920 - **£578** - FF6 037
    «Schafherde auf Waldweg» Öl/Leinwand (51x60cm 20x23in) Stuttgart 2001

DEMEURISSE René 1895-1961 **[44]**
  $361 - €351 - **£229** - FF2 300
    Village dans la campagne Huile/toile (65x101cm 25x39in) Paris 1999

DeMEYER Adolf, Baron 1868-1946 **[80]**
  $1 300 - €1 087 - **£769** - FF7 127
    Fashion Study Silver print (23x17cm 9x7in) New-York 1998

DEMING Edwin Willard 1860-1942 **[69]**
  $3 500 - €3 263 - **£2 171** - FF21 407
    Helping Hand Oil/canvas (36x61.5cm 14x24in) New-York 1999
  $1 900 - €1 886 - **£1 165** - FF12 372
    Indians in a Canoe Oil/panel (15x22cm 6x9in) Mystic CT 2000
  $1 000 - €1 135 - **£694** - FF7 448
    Defiance, Alert Gouache/paper (17x22cm 7x9in) Detroit MI 2001

DEMME Paul 1866-1953 **[6]**
  $991 - €867 - **£600** - FF5 690
    «Ausblick vom Birchi auf die Stadt Solothurn» Aquarell/Papier (53x70cm 20x27in) Zofingen 1998

DEMMIN Erich 1911-1997 **[56]**
  $404 - €434 - **£271** - FF2 850
    Ansicht von Amsterdam, Grachtenszene Oil/panel (10x12cm 3x4in) Berlin 2000

DEMONGIN Victor 1873-? **[5]**
  $2 983 - €3 506 - **£2 067** - FF23 000
    Les chatons Huile/panneau (44x31cm 17x12in) Brest 2000

DEMONT Adrien 1851-1918 **[10]**
  $5 000 - €4 915 - **£3 212** - FF32 239
    Children by a River Oil/panel (35x56cm 13x22in) New-York 1999

DEMONT-BRETON Virginie 1859-1935 **[15]**
  $85 000 - €97 860 - **£58 004** - FF641 920
    L'homme est en mer Oil/canvas (161x134.5cm 63x52in) New-York 2000
  $3 052 - €3 049 - **£1 908** - FF20 000
    Jeune fille aux fleurs Huile/toile (34x26cm 13x10in) Pontoise 1999

DEMOTT John 1954 **[10]**
  $12 000 - €10 909 - **£7 227** - FF71 556
    Lakota Sisters Oil/canvas (121x91cm 48x36in) Hayden ID 1998

DEMUTH Charles 1883-1935 **[71]**
  $55 000 - €54 516 - **£34 402** - FF357 604
    Landscape No.4 Oil/board (30.5x40cm 12x15in) New-York 1999
  $35 000 - €36 280 - **£22 193** - FF237 979
    Waiters at the Brevoort Watercolour (16x23cm 6x9in) New-York 2000

DENATO Olivier 1968 **[78]**
  $357 - €347 - **£222** - FF2 276
    La plage Huile/toile (14x18cm 5x7in) St.Idesbald 1999

DENÉCHEAU Séraphin 1831-1912 **[6]**
  $24 072 - €26 983 - **£16 337** - FF177 000
    Diane couchée sur croissant de lune Marbre (H102cm H40in) Paris 2000

DÉNEUX Gabriel Charles 1856-? **[30]**
  $24 964 - €25 154 - **£15 559** - FF165 000
    Les vendanges Huile/toile (116x164cm 45x64in) Senlis 2000
  $1 300 - €1 290 - **£797** - FF8 465
    Quai Voltaire, Paris Oil/panel (23x32cm 9x12in) Mystic CT 2000
  $270 - €274 - **£168** - FF1 800
    Le pont Royal Aquarelle/papier (24x33cm 9x12in) Paris 2000

DENG FEN 1894-1964 **[33]**
  $4 494 - €4 932 - **£2 894** - FF32 350
    Birthday Wishes from Ma Gu Ink (109.5x48cm 43x18in) Hong-Kong 2000

DENG SANMU 1898-1963 **[1]**
  $2 709 - €2 555 - **£1 680** - FF16 758
    Calligraphy Couplet in Li Shu Ink/paper (136x32.5cm 53x12in) Hong-Kong 1999

DENIES Isaac 1647-1690 **[11]**
  $16 049 - €14 910 - **£9 800** - FF97 804
    Foxgloves, Roses, a Poppy and a Marigold in a Glass Vase Oil/canvas (52x43cm 20x16in) London 1998

DENIS Jean-Claude 1951 **[12]**
  $726 - €732 - **£452** - FF4 800
    Black Betty Pastel/papier (29.5x23.5cm 11x9in) Paris 2000

DENIS Maurice 1870-1943 **[592]**
  $37 825 - €38 112 - **£23 575** - FF250 000
    Jésus chez Marthe et Marie Huile/toile (100x156cm 39x61in) Paris 2000
  $19 891 - €16 959 - **£12 000** - FF111 244
    Delphes, Fontaine Castalie Oil/cardboard (42x62cm 16x24in) London 1998
  $8 736 - €9 757 - **£5 920** - FF64 000
    Le Sphinx et les pyramides Huile/carton (28x33.5cm 11x13in) Paris 2000
  $2 549 - €2 897 - **£1 789** - FF19 000
    Annonciation Gouache/papier (15x22.5cm 5x8in) Paris 2001
  $800 - €757 - **£496** - FF4 967
    Allégorie Color lithograph (27x41cm 10x16in) New-York 1999

DENIS Simon 1755-1813 **[47]**
  $40 466 - €39 778 - **£26 000** - FF260 925
    Bay of Naples with Drovers, animals/Landscape with a Bull, a Dog Oil/canvas (170x240cm 66x94in) London 1999
  $24 000 - €25 631 - **£16 353** - FF168 127
    View of the Bay of Naples and Mount Vesuvius erupting Oil/canvas (54x72cm 21x28in) New-York 2001
  $8 418 - €9 299 - **£5 837** - FF61 000
    Vache romaine Huile/papier (19x29cm 7x11in) Tarbes 2001

DENIS-VALVÉRANE Louis 1870-? **[22]**
  $1 125 - €1 220 - **£762** - FF8 000
    Rue des Petits Marquis à Graoux? Huile/toile (55x46cm 21x18in) Paris 2000
  $675 - €732 - **£457** - FF4 800
    Maisons dans un jardin Huile/toile (46x33cm 18x12in) Paris 2000

$2 251 - €2 439 - £1 524 - FF16 000
L'entrée du port à Barfleur Aquarelle/papier
(45x54cm 17x21in) Paris 2000

DENISOFF Victor, Deni 1893-1946 [9]
$816 - €915 - £553 - FF6 000
«Mettons le terrible vampire fasciste au tribunal...» Affiche couleur (49.5x41.5cm 19x16in) Paris
2000

DENNER Balthasar 1685-1749 [43]
$2 446 - €2 744 - £1 695 - FF18 000
Portrait d'une vieille femme en buste Huile/toile
(43.5x35.5cm 17x13in) Paris 2000

DENNERY Gustave L. 1863-? [6]
$1 420 - €1 524 - £950 - FF10 000
Marché sur la place de l'Église Pastel/papier
(34x43cm 13x16in) Douarnenez 2000

DENNEULIN Jules 1835-1904 [13]
$14 000 - €12 393 - £8 559 - FF81 296
A Tough Catch Oil/canvas (81x105cm 31x41in) New-
York 1999

DENNIS Morgan 1892-1960 [39]
$265 - €245 - £160 - FF1 609
The Campbells are Coming Etching (23x23cm
9x9in) Little-Lane, Ilkley 1999

DENNY Gideon Jacques 1830-1886 [12]
$4 250 - €3 631 - £2 571 - FF23 821
Storm Off Point Bonita Oil/canvas (51x91.5cm
20x36in) San-Francisco CA 1998

DENNY Robyn 1930 [50]
$1 229 - €1 328 - £850 - FF8 712
«Sweet Nature, 27» Gouache (60.5x80cm 23x31in)
London 2001
$218 - €257 - £150 - FF1 689
Square in Blue, Pink and Grey Screenprint in
colors (76x50cm 29x19in) London 2000

DENON Dominique Vivant 1747-1825 [41]
$1 486 - €1 753 - £1 045 - FF11 500
Paysanne de la Bourgogne Pierre noire
(24.5x16cm 9x6in) Paris 2000

DENONNE Alexandre 1879-1953 [82]
$624 - €744 - £447 - FF4 878
Tram rue du Bailly Huile/toile (70x60cm 27x23in)
Bruxelles 2000

DENOYEZ XIX [7]
$823 - €884 - £551 - FF5 800
Rose dans un verre sur un entablement
Huile/carton (32x23cm 12x9in) Paris 2000

DENSLOW William Wallace 1856-1915 [4]
$2 420 - €2 064 - £1 459 - FF13 542
Denslow's Mary had a little Lamb Ink/paper
(35x27cm 14x11in) New-York 1998

DENT Aileen Rose 1890-1979 [25]
$980 - €921 - £606 - FF6 044
Lillies Oil/canvas (59.5x69.5cm 23x27in) Melbourne
1999
$260 - €304 - £181 - FF1 993
Winters Morning Oil/canvas/board (33.5x39cm
13x15in) Melbourne 2000

DENT Rupert Arthur XIX-XX [4]
$3 400 - €3 703 - £2 341 - FF24 290
A Maltese on a blue Chair Oil/canvas (33x43cm
12x16in) New-York 2001

DENTE DA RAVENNA Marco ?-1527 [18]
$476 - €400 - £280 - FF2 624
The Massacre of the Innocents Engraving
(40.5x56.5cm 15x22in) London 1998

DENTON Kenneth 1932 [10]
$328 - €302 - £200 - FF1 978
Autumn Morning, Hyde Park Oil/canvas/board
(61x91.5cm 24x36in) London 1998

DEPERO Fortunato 1892-1960 [240]
$13 200 - €17 105 - £9 900 - FF112 200
Pesce futurista Olio/tela (65x80cm 25x31in) Milano
2001
$10 500 - €10 885 - £6 300 - FF71 400
Gallo nucleare Bronzo (93x94cm 36x37in) Prato
2000
$17 600 - €22 806 - £13 200 - FF149 600
Guizzo dei pesci Bronzo (55x93x18cm 21x36x7in)
Prato 2000
$3 060 - €2 643 - £2 040 - FF17 340
Due collage, figure Tecnica mista/carta (26x34cm
10x13in) Prato 2000
$2 400 - €2 073 - £1 600 - FF13 600
Il pavone Tapisserie (66x57cm 25x22in) Milano 1998

DEPERTHES Jacques 1936 [25]
$2 133 - €1 860 - £1 290 - FF12 204
Paris, la Place du Tertre Huile/toile (46x38cm
18x14in) Genève 1998
$2 489 - €2 151 - £1 505 - FF14 238
Vue de Peissy Huile/toile (35x27cm 13x10in) Genève
1998

DEPOLETTI Francesco 1779-1854 [2]
$135 000 - €150 479 - £94 648 - FF987 079
The Shield of Achilles Mixed media (26x20.5cm
10x8in) New-York 1999

DEPPE Gustav 1913-1999 [46]
$1 184 - €1 023 - £715 - FF6 709
Turmkopf Tempera (54x40cm 21x15in) Köln 1998
$159 - €153 - £98 - FF1 006
Kleine Ruhrlandschaft Lithographie (19.5x30cm
7x11in) Köln 1999

DEPUY Hal XX [1]
$798 - €919 - £550 - FF6 030
«It may be right, it may be wrong» Poster
(112x91cm 44x35in) London 2000

DEQUENE Albert Charles 1897-1973 [10]
$7 486 - €7 260 - £4 712 - FF47 625
African Still Life Oil/canvas (100x81cm 39x31in)
Amsterdam 1999

DEQUENE Jean-Pierre 1905-1954 [11]
$5 216 - €6 098 - £3 724 - FF40 000
L'odalisque endormie Pastel (87x134cm 34x52in)
Paris 2001

DEQUEVAUVILLER François 1745-c.1807 [15]
$281 - €290 - £177 - FF1 900
L'Assemblée au salon/L'Assemblée au concert
Eau-forte (46x55.5cm 18x21in) Orléans 2000

DERAIN André 1880-1954 [1040]
$180 000 - €172 872 - £110 970 - FF1 133 964
Nature morte Oil/canvas (75x203cm 29x79in) New-
York 1999
$24 000 - €23 078 - £14 786 - FF151 384
Fleurs dans un vase bleu Oil/canvas (53x47cm
20x18in) New-York 1999
$7 960 - €7 681 - £5 000 - FF50 381
Portrait d'Anne Oil/canvas (41x33cm 16x12in)
London 1999

$12 408 - €12 196 - **£7 968** - FF80 000
Figure aux boules Bronze (20.5x12.5x90.5cm
8x4x35in) Paris 1999

$1 410 - €1 296 - **£866** - FF8 500
Bouquet de fleurs Mine plomb (20x24cm 7x9in)
Paris 1999

$381 - €381 - **£238** - FF2 500
Paysage du midi Lithographie couleurs (39.5x57cm
15x22in) Paris 1999

DERBRÉ Louis 1925 [34]

$834 - €762 - **£513** - FF5 000
Femme nue debout Bronze (28.5x12x6.5cm
11x4x2in) Paris 1999

DERBY William 1786-1847 [10]

$1 658 - €1 442 - **£1 000** - FF9 462
Pisserache Waterfall, the Simplon pass
Watercolour (28x42cm 11x16in) London 1998

DERCHEU Jules Derchieu 1864-1912 [8]

$4 800 - €5 120 - **£3 197** - FF33 582
La vague Bronze (H28.5cm H11in) New-York 2000

DEREHUS Mikhail Gordeyevich 1904 [6]

$1 300 - €1 449 - **£874** - FF9 508
Taras Bul'ba Oil/cardboard (20x33cm 7x12in) Kiev
2000

DERGES Susan 1931 [1]

$7 943 - €8 655 - **£5 500** - FF56 775
The Observer and the Observed #12 Gelatin silver print (84x67.5cm 33x26in) London 2001

DERIANS A. XIX [6]

$1 500 - €1 389 - **£918** - FF9 109
Homeward Oil/canvas (50x64cm 20x25in) Chicago IL
1999

DERIB (Cl.de Ribeaupierre) 1944 [7]

$396 - €381 - **£246** - FF2 500
Attila/Spécial 33 ans Encre Chine/papier (51x37cm
20x14in) Paris 1999

DERING JOHNSTON Henrietta c.1674-1729 [1]

$240 000 - €285 286 - **£166 296** - FF1 871 352
**Members of the Southwell and Percival
Families** Pastel/paper (35.5x25.5cm 13x10in) New-
York 2000

DERKERT Siri 1888-1973 [74]

$1 028 - €1 104 - **£688** - FF7 243
Blomsterstilleben Oil/canvas (48x37cm 18x14in)
Stockholm 2000

$4 094 - €4 090 - **£2 560** - FF26 831
Mutter und Kind Bronze (21.5x7x4cm 8x2x1in)
Hamburg 1999

$286 - €336 - **£198** - FF2 206
Landskap Pastel/paper (27x22cm 10x8in) Helsinki
2000

DERKZEN VAN ANGEREN Anthonius Philippus
1878-1961 [40]

$90 - €100 - **£61** - FF654
Delfshaven Etching (19.7x21cm 7x8in) Haarlem 2000

DeROME Albert Thomas 1885-1959 [37]

$1 600 - €1 473 - **£960** - FF9 659
Afternoon Haze, July Days Oil/canvas (16x21cm
6x8in) Pasadena CA 1999

$950 - €912 - **£595** - FF5 980
Merrick Butte - Monument Valley, Arizona
Watercolour/paper (14x19cm 5x7in) Altadena CA 1999

DEROUET & GRILLERES Edgard & Georges XX
[2]

$800 - €769 - **£493** - FF5 046
«Loterie Nationale» Poster (149x98cm 58x38in)
New-York 1999

DEROUET & LESACQ Georges & Charles XX [8]

$4 000 - €4 480 - **£2 779** - FF29 388
«Streamlined Car speeding past stylized Trees»
Poster (39x28cm 15x11in) New-York 2001

$108 - €127 - **£74** - FF833
«Loterie Nationale Sports d'Hiver» Poster
(60x40cm 23x15in) Hoorn 2000

DEROUET Edgard 1910 [37]

$207 - €198 - **£129** - FF1 300
«Orléans, Fêtes de Jeanne d'Arc» Affiche couleur
(120x80cm 47x31in) Orléans 1999

DEROY Isidore Laurent 1797-1886 [38]

$155 - €175 - **£109** - FF1 149
«Vue de Lausanne prise de la route de Berne»
Lithographie (15.5x23cm 6x9in) Bern 2001

DERUET Claude 1588-1662 [4]

$470 283 - €534 147 - **£330 000** - FF3 503 775
Equestrian Portrait of a Nobleman Oil/canvas
(251.5x267cm 99x105in) London 2001

$22 423 - €25 154 - **£15 543** - FF165 000
La bataille des amazones Huile/toile (90x116cm
35x45in) Paris 2000

DES CLAYES Berthe 1877-1968 [80]

$2 046 - €1 991 - **£1 259** - FF13 057
Autumn Ploughing Oil/canvas (38x48cm 15x19in)
Nepean, Ont. 1999

$908 - €1 028 - **£639** - FF6 741
**«On the South Terrace, Holland house, London,
Gardens»** Oil/board (26.5x34cm 10x13in) Vancouver,
BC. 2001

$827 - €783 - **£514** - FF5 136
Old Farm in Picardy, France Pastel/paper (24x24cm
9x9in) Calgary, Alberta 1999

DES FONTAINES André 1869-? [34]

$376 - €396 - **£248** - FF2 600
Chemin vers le toit rouge Pastel/papier
(21.5x17.5cm 8x6in) Neuilly-sur-Seine 2000

DES GACHONS Jean XX [19]

$997 - €1 037 - **£628** - FF6 800
Virage de Thillois, Étancelin, Fangio et Farina
Aquarelle, gouache/papier (22x31cm 8x12in) Paris 2000

DESAN Charles XIX [12]

$1 345 - €1 239 - **£833** - FF8 130
Vaches et moutons paissant Huile/panneau
(30x40.5cm 11x15in) Bruxelles 1999

DESBOIS Jules 1851-1935 [28]

$3 637 - €3 201 - **£2 215** - FF21 009
L'hiver Bronze (H52cm H20in) Villeneuve-les-Avignon
1999

DESBOUTIN Marcellin 1823-1902 [47]

$2 159 - €1 982 - **£1 327** - FF13 000
Portrait d'Erik Satie Huile/toile (32x23cm 12x9in)
Paris 1999

DESBROSSES Jean 1835-1906 [30]

$1 099 - €1 067 - **£684** - FF7 000
Effet du matin, prairie Huile/toile (33x54cm
12x21in) Fontainebleau 1999

DESCATOIRE Alexandre 1874-1949 [21]

$1 327 - €1 494 - **£914** - FF9 800
Les adieux du soldat Bronze (26x19cm 10x7in)
Dijon 2000

DESCHAMPS Gabriel 1919 [63]
- **$1 908** - €2 032 - **£1 300** - FF13 326
  View of a French Villa Oil/canvas (52x64cm 20x25in) Billingshurst, West-Sussex 2001

DESCHAMPS Gérard 1937 [69]
- **$409** - €488 - **£291** - FF3 200
  «9» Technique mixte (60x60cm 23x23in) Paris 2000
- **$11 790** - €11 434 - **£7 470** - FF75 000
  Filles-Lastex Accumulation (120x100cm 47x39in) Paris 1999
- **$1 104** - €1 220 - **£765** - FF18 500
  «The fun starts here» Construction (40x40cm 15x15in) Paris 2001

DESCHAMPS Henri 1898-1990 [14]
- **$484** - €511 - **£323** - FF3 349
  Cinquante années de lithographie aux ateliers Mourlot, d'après Picasso Litografía (75x50cm 29x19in) Madrid 2000

DESCHAMPS Louis 1846-1902 [25]
- **$1 400** - €1 196 - **£822** - FF7 847
  Interior Scene with Figures Oil/canvas/board (104x54cm 41x21in) Columbia SC 1998
- **$1 525** - €1 502 - **£950** - FF9 850
  Rostro de Cristo portando la cruz Oleo/lienzo (33x22cm 12x8in) Madrid 1999

DESCHWANDEN von Melchior Paul 1811-1881 [20]
- **$1 380** - €1 318 - **£862** - FF8 646
  Der Schutzengel und das Mädchen, der richtige Weg Öl/Leinwand (96x63cm 37x24in) Zofingen 1999

DESCOURS Michel Hubert 1707-1775 [7]
- **$7 810** - €8 385 - **£5 225** - FF55 000
  Portrait de Monsieur du Saunay Huile/toile (81x65cm 31x25in) Paris 2000
- **$9 786** - €9 153 - **£6 000** - FF60 042
  François-Alexandre Pierre Garsault (1673-1778) Oil/canvas (23x16.5cm 9x6in) London 1998

DESCOURTIS Charles Melchior 1753-1820 [65]
- **$1 477** - €1 636 - **£1 001** - FF10 732
  Untitled, in Paul et Virginie, after F.Schall Coloured pencils (32x40.5cm 12x15in) Hamburg 2000
- **$832** - €781 - **£507** - FF5 122
  Soldado raptando a una mujer Grabado (46x37cm 18x14in) Madrid 1999

DESETA Enrico 1908 [4]
- **$182** - €189 - **£109** - FF1 241
  «Filumena Marturano» Affiche couleur (195x140cm 76x55in) Torino 2000

DESFRICHES Aignan Thomas 1715-1800 [54]
- **$1 766** - €1 982 - **£1 236** - FF13 000
  Bateaux pris dans la tempête Encre Chine (16.5x24.5cm 6x9in) Paris 2001

DESGOFFE Alexandre 1805-1882 [8]
- **$3 155** - €2 744 - **£1 902** - FF18 000
  Forêt de Fontainebleau Huile/papier (28.2x23.1cm 11x9in) Paris 1998

DESGOFFE Blaise Alexandre 1830-1901 [29]
- **$6 423** - €5 946 - **£3 978** - FF39 000
  L'orée du bois Huile/toile (40x54cm 15x21in) Paris 1999
- **$811** - €686 - **£482** - FF4 500
  Nature morte au vase et à la parure de bijoux Huile/panneau (23x18cm 9x7in) Calais 1998

DESGRANGES B. XIX [1]
- **$4 722** - €4 573 - **£2 970** - FF30 000
  Vue d'un lac italien Huile/toile (90x112cm 35x44in) Paris 1999

DESHAYES Charles 1831-1895 [52]
- **$1 121** - €1 220 - **£739** - FF8 000
  Le petit pêcheur Huile/toile (56x38cm 22x14in) Paris 2000
- **$955** - €908 - **£581** - FF5 953
  Landweg in heuvellandschap Oil/panel (14.5x20cm 5x7in) Den Haag 1999

DESHAYES DE COLLEVILLE Jean-Baptiste 1729-1765 [39]
- **$13 930** - €13 416 - **£8 650** - FF88 000
  Saint-Pierre délivré de prison Huile/toile (57x42cm 22x16in) Paris 1999
- **$14 000** - €12 280 - **£8 500** - FF80 553
  Caravan of Peasants and Animals Oil/paper/board (29x29cm 11x11in) New-York 1999
- **$3 500** - €3 070 - **£2 125** - FF20 138
  The Education of the Virgin Wash (33x24.5cm 12x9in) New-York 1999

DESHAYES Eugène 1828-1890 [181]
- **$1 602** - €1 829 - **£1 126** - FF12 000
  Paysage de rivière Huile/toile (51x74cm 20x29in) Fontainebleau 2001
- **$813** - €915 - **£559** - FF6 000
  Chantier naval Huile/panneau (13x25.5cm 5x10in) Paris 2000
- **$146** - €168 - **£103** - FF1 100
  Les grands arbres Mine plomb (14.5x22.5cm 5x8in) Fontainebleau 2001

DESHAYES Eugène François A. 1868-1939 [103]
- **$2 186** - €2 134 - **£1 384** - FF14 000
  Rivage d'Orient Huile/toile (60x80cm 23x31in) Calais 1999
- **$2 283** - €2 211 - **£1 447** - FF14 500
  Campement de nomades Huile/panneau (23x55cm 9x21in) Paris 1999

DÉSI HUBER Istvan 1895-1944 [3]
- **$12 540** - €14 251 - **£8 740** - FF93 480
  Baie Huile/toile (54x43cm 21x16in) Budapest 2001

DESIDERIO DA SETTIGNANO 1428-1464 [1]
- **$40 000** - €41 466 - **£24 000** - FF272 000
  Cherubino tra cornucopie Relief (35x48.5cm 13x19in) Firenze 2001

DESIRÉ-LUCAS Louis Marie 1869-1949 [168]
- **$3 044** - €2 592 - **£1 812** - FF17 000
  La baie de Menton vue de Roquebrune Huile/toile (54x65cm 21x25in) Brest 1998
- **$1 162** - €1 220 - **£770** - FF8 000
  Femme en prière dans l'église Huile/toile (41x33cm 16x12in) Quimper 2000
- **$1 032** - €945 - **£626** - FF6 000
  Port au pays basque Gouache/papier (37x45cm 14x17in) Douarnenez 1998

DESJARDINS Louis Léon 1823-1914 [59]
- **$267** - €290 - **£185** - FF1 900
  Sous-bois Huile/carton (19.5x16cm 7x6in) Paris 2001

DESJOBERT Louis Rémy Eugène 1817-1863 [8]
- **$11 000** - €9 738 - **£6 725** - FF63 875
  Peasants on a Wooded path Oil/canvas (77.5x117cm 30x46in) New-York 1999

DESLIENS Marie 1856-1938 [1]
- **$4 709** - €4 421 - **£2 908** - FF29 000
  Intérieur de cuisine Huile/toile (54x75cm 21x29in) Paris 1999

DESMARAIS Jean-Baptiste Fr. 1756-1813 [5]
- **$7 293** - €8 180 - **£5 082** - FF53 658
  Marc Antoine montrant au peuple romain César assassiné Encre (26.5x48cm 10x18in) Bruxelles 2001

DESMARÉES Georg 1697-1776 **[19]**
- $6 588 - €6 902 - £4 357 - FF45 277
  Bildnis einer jungen, adligen Dame im Karnevalskostüm Öl/Leinwand (81x65cm 31x25in) München 2000

DESMAZIERES Erik XX **[40]**
- $286 - €335 - £205 - FF2 200
  «**La danse du diable**» Eau-forte, aquatinte (34.5x27cm 13x10in) Paris 2001

DESMEURES Victor Jean 1895-? **[11]**
- $671 - €762 - £466 - FF5 000
  «**Exposition coloniale**» Affiche (160x120cm 62x47in) Paris 2001

DESMOND Nerine 1908-1993 **[25]**
- $346 - €386 - £225 - FF2 532
  Xhosa Women Tending their Goats Oil/canvas/board (48x73.5cm 18x28in) Johannesburg 2000

DESMOULINS Augustin François B. 1788-1856 **[4]**
- $3 858 - €4 573 - £2 811 - FF30 000
  Saint Louis emprisonné Huile/toile (41x32cm 16x12in) Neuilly-sur-Seine 2001
- $1 383 - €1 372 - £860 - FF9 000
  Égyptien tirant le tarot à une dame, espionnée par un homme Aquarelle (24.5x19.5cm 9x7in) Paris 1999

DESNOS Ferdinand 1901-1958 **[115]**
- $862 - €1 006 - £600 - FF6 597
  The Harvesters Oil/canvas (50x73.5cm 19x28in) London 2000
- $552 - €625 - £386 - FF4 100
  Les canards Huile/toile (27x35cm 10x13in) Paris 2001

DESNOYER François 1894-1972 **[208]**
- $2 648 - €3 049 - £1 808 - FF20 000
  Femme blonde au hamac Huile/toile (45x53cm 17x20in) Lyon 2000
- $1 787 - €1 524 - £1 078 - FF10 000
  Rivage de Bretagne Huile/panneau (17x34cm 6x13in) Calais 1998
- $499 - €457 - £304 - FF3 000
  Le village Gouache/papier (23x32cm 9x12in) Paris 1999

DESNOYERS Auguste Gaspard L. 1779-1857 **[6]**
- $2 080 - €1 952 - £1 300 - FF12 805
  Recueil d'après des peintures antiques italiennes Grabado (59x43cm 23x16in) Madrid 1999

DESOUTTER Roger Charles 1923 **[4]**
- $1 561 - €1 744 - £1 000 - FF11 438
  Estuary Low Tide/Venice Oil/canvas (50x76cm 19x29in) London 2000

DESPIAU Charles 1874-1946 **[158]**
- $37 758 - €32 014 - £22 407 - FF210 000
  Athlète Bronze (H116cm H45in) Paris 1998
- $4 800 - €5 569 - £3 313 - FF36 532
  Reclining Nude Bronze (16.5x28x12.5cm 6x11x4in) New-York 2000
- $903 - €991 - £600 - FF6 500
  Nu féminin Sanguine/papier (29x19.5cm 11x7in) Paris 2000

DESPIERRE Jacques Ceria, dit 1912-1995 **[127]**
- $529 - €534 - £330 - FF3 500
  Nature morte aux fruits Huile/papier (11x18.5cm 4x7in) Paris 2000
- $247 - €229 - £153 - FF1 500
  Port jaune, mer Égée Aquarelle/papier (12x19cm 4x7in) Paris 1999

DESPORTES Alexandre François 1661-1743 **[33]**
- $92 646 - €99 448 - £62 000 - FF652 339
  Portrait of a Huntsman, three-quarter length, holding a rifle Oil/canvas (147x113.5cm 57x44in) London 2000
- $49 007 - €56 996 - £35 000 - FF373 866
  Portrait of a Gentleman, three-quarter length, standing Oil/canvas (116x93cm 45x36in) London 2001

DESPORTES DE LA FOSSE Emma Andrée Félicité 1810-1869 **[11]**
- $21 000 - €18 590 - £12 839 - FF121 944
  Still Life of Peonies Oil/canvas (63x51cm 24x20in) New-York 1999
- $11 000 - €9 738 - £6 725 - FF63 875
  Roses in a Round Vase Oil/paper (47.5x31.5cm 18x12in) New-York 1999
- $8 109 - €8 171 - £5 054 - FF53 600
  Corbeille de fruits avec des feuillages et un perroquet Aquarelle, gouache/papier (23x34cm 9x13in) Bergerac 2000

DESPORTES Francisque 1849-1899 **[13]**
- $2 228 - €2 134 - £1 373 - FF14 000
  Femme à l'éventail Huile/panneau (65x53cm 25x20in) Calais 1999

DESPREST Jean-Baptiste 1778-1821 **[1]**
- $18 000 - €15 530 - £10 859 - FF101 867
  Still Life with Flowers, Peaches and Grapes Oil/panel (60x44.5cm 23x17in) New-York 1998

DESPRET Georges 1862-1952 **[18]**
- $1 306 - €1 524 - £922 - FF10 000
  Tête de faune Sculpture verre (H20cm H7in) Neuilly-sur-Seine 2000

DESPREZ Louis Jean 1743-1804 **[40]**
- $12 537 - €12 201 - £7 717 - FF80 031
  Påskmässan i Peterskyrkan med illumination av fastlagskorset Indian ink (49x32cm 19x12in) Stockholm 1999
- $2 865 - €2 789 - £1 764 - FF18 292
  Promotion médicale/Indulgences Plenières Etching (55.5x87cm 21x34in) Stockholm 1999

DESPUJOLS Jean 1886-1965 **[16]**
- $3 972 - €3 964 - £2 418 - FF26 000
  Pique-nique bouleversé par un vol Huile/toile (200x260cm 78x102in) Paris 2000
- $3 000 - €2 678 - £1 837 - FF17 568
  Young Girl in Black Oil/canvas (45.5x38cm 17x14in) New-York 1999

DESRAIS Claude Louis 1746-1816 **[33]**
- $896 - €762 - £534 - FF5 000
  La lanterne magique Encre (27x21.5cm 10x8in) Paris 1999

DESRUELLES Félix 1865-1943 **[5]**
- $2 144 - €1 829 - £1 293 - FF12 000
  Le faucheur au repos Bronze (H62.5cm H24in) La Flèche 1998

DESSAR Louis Paul 1867-1952 **[19]**
- $3 000 - €2 859 - £1 901 - FF18 752
  The Restful Hour, The Wood Cart Oil/canvas (44x89cm 17x35in) Cleveland OH 1999

DESSERPRIT Roger 1923-1985 **[76]**
- $865 - €793 - £527 - FF5 200
  Composition abstraite Huile/papier/panneau (36x51cm 14x20in) Paris 1999
- $588 - €701 - £419 - FF4 600
  Composition Huile/panneau (33x46cm 12x18in) Paris 2000

$4 536 - €5 336 - **£3 251** - FF35 000
Le voyageur Bronze (H113cm H44in) Paris 2001
$3 976 - €4 269 - **£2 660** - FF28 000
Dos à dos Bronze (H53cm H20in) Paris 2000

DESSI Gianni 1955 [37]
$1 200 - €1 244 - **£720** - FF8 160
«Appeso» Olio/tavola (49x42cm 19x16in) Prato 1999
$350 - €363 - **£210** - FF2 380
Senza titolo Tempera/carta (32x22cm 12x8in) Milano 1999

DESSOUSLAVY Thomas XIX [6]
$12 456 - €14 341 - **£8 500** - FF94 073
An Italian Landscape, a Capriccio Oil/canvas
(81.5x120cm 32x47in) London 2000

DESTOUCHES Paul Émile 1794-1874 [10]
$1 932 - €2 134 - **£1 339** - FF14 000
Couple enlacé Encre (20.5x13cm 8x5in) Paris 2001

DESTOUCHES von Johanna 1869-1956 [49]
$1 792 - €1 553 - **£1 078** - FF10 059
Herbststrauss in einem Zinnkrug Öl/Leinwand
(82x55cm 32x21in) München 1998

DESTRÉE Johannes Josephus 1827-1888 [39]
$4 880 - €4 805 - **£3 040** - FF31 520
Paisaje Oleo/lienzo (70x95cm 27x37in) Madrid 1999
$1 479 - €1 588 - **£990** - FF10 418
Vue d'Ebenstein avec le château Oil/panel
(33x42cm 12x16in) Amsterdam 2000

DESURMONT XIX-XX [1]
$3 237 - €3 811 - **£2 275** - FF25 000
Buste d'Antar/Buste d'Abla Terracotta (45x47cm
17x18in) Paris 2000

DESVALLIERES Georges 1861-1950 [74]
$2 868 - €3 354 - **£2 015** - FF22 000
Élegante au manteau Huile/papier (36.5x17cm
14x6in) Paris 2000
$255 - €259 - **£158** - FF1 700
Personnage dans un portique Crayon/papier
(25x17cm 9x6in) Paris 2000

DESVARREUX Raymond 1876-1961 [56]
$2 185 - €2 439 - **£1 430** - FF16 000
Moutons s'abreuvant à Fontainebleau Huile/toile
(64.5x82cm 25x32in) Fontainebleau 2000
$782 - €908 - **£554** - FF5 953
French Soldiers on a Horse-Back in a Village
Oil/board (24x32.5cm 9x12in) Amsterdam 2000

DESVARREUX-LARPENTEUR James 1847-1937 [33]
$2 200 - €2 516 - **£1 529** - FF16 507
Shepherd and his flock Oil/canvas (73x92cm
29x36in) Philadelphia PA 2000

DESVERNOIS Joseph Eug. 1790-1872 [2]
$834 - €869 - **£528** - FF5 701
Blick auf Montreux mit Schloss Chillon am
Genfersee Ink/paper (40.3x57.8cm 15x22in) München 2000

DESVIGNES Emily XIX [5]
$1 126 - €1 294 - **£780** - FF8 491
Landscape with Sheep on the Grassey Banks
of a River, Sailing Boat Oil/canvas (28x38cm
11x14in) Harrogate, North Yorkshire 2000

DESVIGNES Herbert Clayton XIX [3]
$2 635 - €2 450 - **£1 600** - FF16 069
Cattle and Sheep Oil/canvas (35x45cm 13x17in)
Doncaster, South-Yorkshire 1998

DETAILLE Charles Jean-Bapt. XIX [17]
$2 056 - €1 906 - **£1 227** - FF12 500
Projet de programme de courses Encre
(52x38.5cm 20x15in) Paris 1999

DETAILLE Édouard 1848-1912 [207]
$28 000 - €26 606 - **£17 035** - FF174 521
After the Skirmish Oil/canvas (162.5x221cm
63x87in) New-York 1999
$18 000 - €15 530 - **£10 859** - FF101 867
Pointing the way Oil/canvas (85x59cm 33x23in)
New-York 1998
$325 - €349 - **£217** - FF2 291
Military Figure on Horse Oil/paper/panel (20x15cm
8x6in) Hatfield PA 2000
$765 - €656 - **£460** - FF4 300
La revue Crayon (53x43cm 20x16in) Melun 1998
$574 - €640 - **£387** - FF4 200
La charge des cuirassiers à Reichhauffen
Lithographie (52x62.5cm 20x24in) Deauville 2000

DETHOMAS Maxime 1867-1929 [19]
$1 324 - €1 372 - **£839** - FF9 000
Jeune femme à la chaise Crayon gras (74x50cm
29x19in) Paris 2000

DETMOLD Charles Maurice 1883-1908 [22]
$1 804 - €2 002 - **£1 200** - FF13 131
Old Man Amidst Vines Watercolour (37x20.5cm
14x8in) London 2000

DETMOLD Edward Julian 1883-1957 [78]
$788 - €887 - **£550** - FF5 818
Humming Bird beside a Flower Watercolour
(12.5x15.5cm 4x6in) London 2001
$320 - €303 - **£200** - FF1 986
Four Deer Etching (20x36cm 8x14in) Fernhurst,
Haslemere, Surrey 1999

DETOUCHE Henry-Julien 1854-1913 [24]
$247 - €229 - **£153** - FF1 500
Bord de rivière Aquarelle/papier (31x48cm 12x18in)
Paris 1999
$1 200 - €1 339 - **£785** - FF8 731
«22e Exposition des Cent de juillet à fin septembre» Poster (62.5x41cm 24x16in) New-York 2000

DETOUCHE Laurent Didier 1815-1882 [2]
$5 000 - €4 751 - **£3 042** - FF31 164
At the Pawn Broker's Oil/canvas (40.5x30.5cm
15x12in) New-York 1999

DÉTRIER Pierre Louis 1822-1897 [27]
$2 111 - €2 211 - **£1 326** - FF14 500
La maternité Bronze (55x30cm 21x11in) Villefranche-
sur-Saône 2000

DETROY Léon 1857-1955 [156]
$1 100 - €1 209 - **£761** - FF8 000
Coupe poire Huile/panneau (62x48cm 24x18in)
Clermont-Ferrand 2001
$522 - €457 - **£316** - FF3 000
Bord de mer et arbres Aquarelle, gouache/papier
(47x62cm 18x24in) Paris 1998

DETTHOW Eric 1888-1952 [88]
$1 618 - €1 381 - **£967** - FF9 059
Le chemin à St Cloud Oil/canvas (65x50cm
25x19in) Stockholm 1998
$371 - €337 - **£230** - FF2 212
Utan titel Oil/panel (35x27cm 13x10in) Stockholm 1999

DETTI Cesare Auguste 1847-1914 [92]
$150 000 - €172 694 - **£102 360** - FF1 132 800
A musical Interlude Oil/canvas (98x152.5cm
38x60in) New-York 2000

DETTMANN

$7 000 – €8 167 – £4 872 – FF53 572
Il Cavaliere Oil/canvas (54x45cm 21x18in) Delray-Beach FL 2000

$7 000 – €6 651 – £4 258 – FF43 630
Summer Day by the Pond Oil/panel (27x21.5cm 10x8in) New-York 1999

$1 115 – €1 296 – £794 – FF8 500
Arabe tenant un fusil Aquarelle/papier (29x16.5cm 11x6in) Paris 2001

DETTMANN Ludwig 1865-1944 [17]

$2 693 – €2 321 – £1 600 – FF15 223
Emin Pasha Bodycolour (36x28cm 14x11in) London 1998

DETTMANN Walter 1914-1984 [9]

$596 – €665 – £400 – FF4 360
Meeresbrandung Öl/Leinwand (70x100cm 27x39in) Satow 2000

DETWILLER Frederick K. 1882-1953 [9]

$60 – €68 – £42 – FF447
Artist painting Watercolour/paper (20x19cm 8x7in) Philadelphia PA 2001

$1 300 – €1 248 – £805 – FF8 189
The Williamsburg Bridge, July Fourth Etching, aquatint (44x27.5cm 17x10in) New-York 1999

DEUCHERT Heinrich 1840-1923 [15]

$2 186 – €2 556 – £1 536 – FF16 769
Bauern bei der Kornernte in Vorgebirgslandschaft Oil/panel (10x18cm 3x7in) München 2000

DEULLY Eugène 1860-1933 [53]

$967 – €902 – £600 – FF5 915
Gentleman at his Desk Oil/canvas (46x61cm 18x24in) London 1999

$2 100 – €2 239 – £1 424 – FF14 690
Kvinna med katt Oil/panel (27x21.5cm 10x8in) Stockholm 2001

DEURER Ludwig 1806-1847 [4]

$41 397 – €40 083 – £26 000 – FF262 925
The Turkish Rider Oil/canvas (73x60cm 28x23in) London 1999

DEUSKAR Gopal Damodar XX [1]

$5 028 – €5 867 – £3 500 – FF38 486
Milkmaid Oil/board (82.5x47cm 32x18in) London 2000

DEUTMANN Frans 1867-1915 [18]

$1 260 – €1 180 – £784 – FF7 739
The First Knitting Lesson Watercolour/paper (68x52cm 26x20in) Amsterdam 1999

DEUTSCH Hans Emil 1927 [15]

$451 – €436 – £278 – FF2 862
Südliche Landschaft Öl/Leinwand (35x50cm 13x19in) Zürich 1999

DEUTSCH Ludwig 1855-1935 [99]

$2 900 000 – €2 751 157 – £1 761 750 – FF18 046 410
The Palace Guard Oil/canvas (132.5x94cm 52x37in) New-York 1999

$40 032 – €36 588 – £24 504 – FF240 000
El Azhar, université arabe au Caire Huile/toile (73.5x99.5cm 28x39in) Paris 1999

$4 003 – €3 659 – £2 450 – FF24 000
Femme et enfant vus de dos Huile/panneau (36.5x27cm 14x10in) Paris 1999

DEUX Fred 1924 [109]

$885 – €732 – £519 – FF4 800
Personnages fantastiques Encre/papier (45.5x24.5cm 17x9in) Paris 1998

DEVADE Marc 1943-1983 [27]

$3 216 – €3 659 – £2 232 – FF24 000
Composition géométrique blanche et bleue Acrylique/toile (200x150cm 78x59in) Paris 2000

$403 – €488 – £281 – FF3 200
Sans titre Pastel/papier (50x50cm 19x19in) Paris 2000

DEVAL Pierre 1897-1993 [295]

$2 032 – €2 287 – £1 399 – FF15 000
Pont à Paris Huile/isorel (38x46cm 14x18in) Albi 2000

$3 226 – €2 912 – £1 988 – FF19 100
La robe mauve Huile/toile (33x41cm 12x16in) Arles 1999

$1 003 – €930 – £624 – FF6 100
Jeune fille pensive dans un intérieur Aquarelle/papier (30x24cm 11x9in) Arles 1999

DEVAMBEZ André 1867-1943 [123]

$34 554 – €39 637 – £23 634 – FF260 000
Une première au théâtre Montmartre Huile/toile (127x150cm 50x59in) Paris 2000

$13 441 – €13 263 – £8 282 – FF87 000
L'assaut Huile/toile (71.5x79cm 28x31in) Paris 1999

$1 336 – €1 524 – £928 – FF10 000
Le voeu Huile/panneau (13.5x10cm 5x3in) Paris 2000

$719 – €838 – £504 – FF5 500
Guitariste et chanteur au cabaret Aquarelle (17.5x28.5cm 6x11in) Neuilly-sur-Seine 2000

DEVAS Anthony 1911-1958 [48]

$1 494 – €1 604 – £1 000 – FF10 521
Standing Female Nude Oil/canvas (76x50.5cm 29x19in) London 2000

$2 789 – €3 060 – £1 800 – FF20 072
Feeding the Gulls Oil/canvas (20x25.5cm 7x10in) London 2000

$1 345 – €1 444 – £900 – FF9 473
Standing Female Nude Watercolour (31.5x21.5cm 12x8in) London 2000

DEVAUX Jules Ernest 1837-? [6]

$3 644 – €3 374 – £2 200 – FF22 129
La gouteuse de soupe Oil/panel (24.5x19cm 9x7in) London 1999

DEVÉ Eugène 1826-1887 [7]

$5 396 – €5 793 – £3 610 – FF38 000
Le ramassage du bois Huile/toile (60x73.5cm 23x28in) Bayeux 2000

DEVEDEUX Louis 1820-1874 [55]

$2 624 – €3 049 – £1 870 – FF20 000
Dans les jardins du sérail Huile/toile (38x55cm 14x21in) Paris 2001

$2 059 – €2 287 – £1 435 – FF15 000
Courtisanes dans le jardin du harem Huile/panneau (16.5x12cm 6x4in) Paris 2001

DEVENTER van Jan Frederik 1822-1886 [8]

$8 089 – €7 669 – £4 921 – FF50 308
Sommertag auf dem Lande, ein Weg, Wiesen und Bauernhöfe unter Bäumen Öl/Leinwand (81x131cm 31x51in) Köln 1999

DEVENTER van Willem Antonie 1824-1893 [33]

$49 530 – €43 353 – £30 000 – FF284 376
Boats by a Quayside Oil/canvas (62.5x82cm 24x32in) London 1998

D

$803 - €709 - **£484** - FF4 651
A Two-master at Anchor in a Harbour Oil/board
(40x25cm 15x9in) Amsterdam 1998

DEVENYNS Steve 1953 **[1]**
$6 000 - €6 839 - **£4 186** - FF44 861
Start of a long Day Oil/board (40x30cm 16x12in)
Dallas TX 2001

DEVER Alfred XIX **[4]**
$4 326 - €4 781 - **£3 000** - FF31 359
The Tea Party Oil/canvas (45.5x61cm 17x24in)
London 2001

DEVÉRIA Achille 1800-1857 **[106]**
$409 - €457 - **£262** - FF3 000
Femme prenant le thé Lavis/papier (23.5x18cm
9x7in) Paris 2000
$193 - €223 - **£133** - FF1 462
Robo de Eloisa Grabado (40x47cm 15x18in)
Barcelona 2000

DEVERIA Eugène 1808-1865 **[112]**
$3 000 - €3 452 - **£2 067** - FF22 644
Portrait of a French Military Officer Oil/canvas
(55x45cm 22x18in) New-Orleans LA 2000
$1 996 - €2 258 - **£1 350** - FF14 813
Going to Market Oil/canvas (42.5x35.5cm 16x13in)
London 2000
$546 - €610 - **£370** - FF4 000
Porteuse d'eau au Béarn Encre (29.5x42cm
11x16in) Paris 2000

DEVERIA Théodule 1831-1871 **[44]**
$643 - €686 - **£428** - FF4 500
Étude de statue égyptienne, buste Tirage papier
salé (27x21cm 10x8in) Paris 2000

DEVETTA Edoardo 1912-1993 **[20]**
$2 000 - €2 073 - **£1 200** - FF13 600
Fiori Olio/tela (80x60cm 31x23in) Trieste 1999
$425 - €441 - **£255** - FF2 890
Marina Olio/tela (30x40cm 11x15in) Trieste 2000

DEVILLARIO René Marie Léon 1874-1942 **[12]**
$3 800 - €3 647 - **£2 382** - FF23 922
Quietude Oil/board (46x55cm 18x21in) New-York
1999

DEVILLE Henry Wilfrid 1871-c.1932 **[8]**
$900 - €1 052 - **£632** - FF6 901
Brooklyn Bridge Etching (46x75.5cm 18x29in) New-
York 2000

DEVILLE Maurice 1860-? **[6]**
$826 - €961 - **£580** - FF6 306
«La tourbe médicale» Poster (126x98cm 49x38in)
London 2001

DEVILLE-CHABROLLE Marie-Paule 1952 **[205]**
$11 594 - €10 824 - **£7 021** - FF71 000
Belle comme un miroir Bronze (H97cm H38in)
Bourges 1999
$4 227 - €5 031 - **£2 927** - FF33 000
Margaux Bronze (H29cm H11in) Château-Thierry
2000
$804 - €762 - **£502** - FF5 000
Femme nue Sanguine (55x44cm 21x17in) L'Isle-
Adam 2000

DEVIS Anthony 1729-1816 **[88]**
$478 - €513 - **£320** - FF3 366
Woodland Scene with Figures by a Bridge Ink
(13x19.5cm 5x7in) Bath 2000

DEVIS Arthur 1708-1787 **[30]**
$32 000 - €30 106 - **£19 968** - FF197 484
Anne (née Lee) and George Venables Vernon
standing in a Landscape Oil/canvas (61x41.5cm
24x16in) New-York 1999

DEVIS Arthur William 1763-1822 **[21]**
$12 804 - €12 223 - **£8 000** - FF80 180
A Gentleman out shooting with a Spaniel
Oil/canvas (83.5x67.5cm 32x26in) London 1999
$21 500 - €18 748 - **£13 000** - FF122 977
Portrait of Horatio, Viscount Nelson, K.B. in
Vice-Admiral's uniform Oil/canvas (35.5x30.5cm
13x12in) London 1998

DEVOISINS Jean XX **[3]**
$2 921 - €3 125 - **£1 924** - FF20 500
Collioure Huile/toile (46x55cm 18x21in) Albi 2000

DeVOLL Frederick Usher 1873-1941 **[18]**
$7 500 - €8 050 - **£5 019** - FF52 807
Coming Up the Harbor, New York City Oil/canvas
(81x91cm 32x36in) Portland ME 2000
$1 500 - €1 749 - **£1 053** - FF11 475
Old Colonial Village of Poquctanick, Conn
Oil/board (28x39cm 11x15in) Cambridge MA 2000

DEVORE Richard 1933 **[9]**
$5 000 - €5 180 - **£3 182** - FF33 976
Deep Bowl Ceramic (21.5x35.5cm 8x13in) New-York
2000

DeVORSS Billy 1908-1985 **[1]**
$3 000 - €3 360 - **£2 084** - FF22 041
Fresh-faced Woman just out of the Shower,
Calendar Illustration Pastel/paper (59x41cm
23x16in) New-York 2001

DEVOS Léon 1897-1974 **[121]**
$1 530 - €1 487 - **£948** - FF9 756
Enfant aux immortelles Huile/toile (70x73cm
27x28in) Bruxelles 1999

DEVOSGE François 1732-1811 **[3]**
$961 - €1 067 - **£665** - FF7 000
Allégorie Encre (27.5x10.5cm 10x4in) Paris 2001

DEVOTO John c.1730-c.1790 **[2]**
$10 460 - €11 228 - **£7 000** - FF73 651
Capriccio with a Castello and Figures by the
Farnese Hercules Oil/canvas (70.5x91cm 27x35in)
London 2000

DEVREESE Godefroid 1861-1941 **[30]**
$6 390 - €7 436 - **£4 560** - FF48 780
Baigneuse Marbre Carrare (H87cm H34in) Bruxelles
2001
$1 039 - €1 115 - **£697** - FF7 317
Vieille femme assise sur son âne Bronze
(54x52x17cm 21x20x6in) Bruxelles 2000

DEWASNE Jean 1921-1999 **[109]**
$5 642 - €6 445 - **£3 978** - FF42 276
Le roi de carreau Huile/panneau (96x130cm
37x51in) Antwerpen 2001
$4 536 - €5 336 - **£3 251** - FF35 000
L'amour, l'amour Peinture (49x65cm 19x25in) Paris
2001
$2 502 - €2 744 - **£1 699** - FF18 000
Composition Gouache/papier (49x65cm 19x25in)
L'Isle-Adam 2000

DEWEY Charles Melville 1849-1937 **[11]**
$5 500 - €5 724 - **£3 452** - FF37 547
Sunset after Rain Oil/canvas (45x60cm 18x24in)
Chicago IL 2000

D

$550 - €609 - £382 - FF3 994
Landscape Oil/board (16x23cm 6x9in) New-Orleans
LA 2001

DEWEY David XX [2]
$1 600 - €1 492 - £992 - FF9 786
Late Jetstream, Harbour Head Light
Watercolour/paper (59x105cm 23x41in) New-York 1999

DEWHURST Wynford 1864-1941 [71]
$2 561 - €2 976 - £1 800 - FF19 519
Glen Falloch, Scotland Oil/canvas (53.5x73.5cm
21x28in) London 2001
$290 - €273 - £180 - FF1 793
Houses by the Creuse Pastel/paper (31.5x22cm
12x8in) London 1999

DEWING Maria Oakey 1845-1928 [3]
$1 000 000 - €1 167 089 - £708 900 - FF7 655 600
Poppies and Italian Mignonette Oil/canvas
(58.5x43cm 23x16in) New-York 2001

DEWING Thomas Wilmer 1851-1938 [22]
$140 000 - €134 635 - £86 408 - FF883 148
The Duet - Interlude Oil/canvas (51x76cm 20x29in)
Boston MA 1999
$280 000 - €307 201 - £186 004 - FF2 015 104
Woman in Black - Portrait of Maria Oakey
Dewing Oil/panel (48x31.5cm 18x12in) New-York
2000
$7 000 - €6 626 - £4 347 - FF43 466
Reclining Nude Pastel/board (16x25cm 6x10in)
Wallkill NY 1999

DEWS John Steven 1949 [43]
$90 000 - €93 547 - £56 718 - FF613 629
Endeavour II Jumps the Gun, Race IV, 1937
America's Cup Rhode Island Oil/canvas
(101.5x152.5cm 39x60in) New-York 2000
$38 000 - €35 222 - £23 628 - FF231 043
Sopwith's Luff Oil/canvas (76x101.5cm 29x39in)
New-York 1999

DEXEL Walter 1890-1973 [201]
$7 373 - €7 158 - £4 554 - FF46 954
Der Pastor Tempera/Karton (65x50.2cm 25x19in)
München 1999
$4 496 - €5 113 - £3 118 - FF33 539
Ohne Titel (Scheibe im Quadrat) Tempera
(40x31.5cm 15x12in) Hamburg 2000
$2 035 - €1 943 - £1 271 - FF12 744
Ruinenberg bei Sanssouci Watercolour (20x24cm
7x9in) Köln 1999
$275 - €234 - £194 - FF2 123
«Weisses Zeichen» Farbserigraphie (51.5x42.5cm
20x16in) Berlin 2001

DEXTER Walter 1876-1958 [21]
$2 100 - €2 443 - £1 500 - FF16 022
Still Life of Strawberries Redcurrants Peaches
and a Stoneware Jug Oil/canvas (18x25.5cm
7x10in) Norfolk 2001

DEY Manishi XX [9]
$1 785 - €1 716 - £1 100 - FF11 256
Seated Woman Tempera/paper (59.5x29.5cm
23x11in) London 1999

DEY Mukul 1895-1989 [7]
$3 000 - €3 545 - £2 126 - FF23 252
Odalisque After Ingres Watercolour (18.5x38.5cm
7x15in) London 2001

DEYKIN Henry Cotterill 1905 [4]
$6 633 - €7 330 - £4 600 - FF48 083
Aston Villa v Sunderland Oil/canvas (59.5x182.5cm
23x71in) London 2001

DEYNUM van Guilliam XVII [8]
$44 870 - €53 357 - £31 990 - FF350 000
Nature morte aux raisins et aux huîtres
Huile/panneau (36.5x45cm 14x19in) Neuilly-sur-Seine
2000
$68 202 - €71 615 - £43 000 - FF469 762
Oysters and a Prawn on a Pewter Plate, a Partly
Peeled Lemon Oil/canvas (33.5x45cm 13x17in)
London 2000

DeYONG Joseph, Joe F. 1894-1975 [12]
$13 000 - €13 939 - £8 600 - FF91 431
Men of the Open Range Oil/canvas (35x50cm
14x20in) Hayden ID 2000
$900 - €1 058 - £624 - FF6 941
Pastoral Scene with Cattle and Riders Ink
(15x40.5cm 5x15in) Beverly-Hills CA 2000
$500 - €443 - £306 - FF2 906
Western Scenes Etching (5x3cm 2x1in) Cincinnati
OH 1999

DEYROLLE Jean 1911-1967 [182]
$4 175 - €3 923 - £2 516 - FF25 734
Opus 12 Oil/canvas (60x120cm 23x47in) Stockholm
1999
$1 808 - €1 677 - £1 091 - FF11 000
Pol Tempera/toile (41x33cm 16x12in) Paris 1999
$1 207 - €1 296 - £807 - FF8 500
Sans titre Gouache/papier (36x26cm 14x10in) Paris
2000
$407 - €381 - £252 - FF2 500
Composition Lithographie couleurs (69x49cm
27x19in) Quimper 1999

DEYROLLE Théophile Louis 1844-1923 [111]
$8 606 - €9 554 - £6 000 - FF62 669
Playing with Snowballs Oil/canvas (106x196cm
41x77in) London 2001
$4 281 - €3 887 - £2 674 - FF25 500
Paysage Huile/toile (50x125cm 19x49in) Rennes 1999
$979 - €915 - £604 - FF6 000
Jeune femme et son enfant en costume de par-
don Huile/panneau (34x21cm 13x8in) Brest 1999

DEYSTER de Louis, Lodewyck c.1656-1711 [11]
$9 282 - €10 411 - £6 468 - FF68 292
Saint Pierre et le centurion Huile/toile (143x212cm
56x83in) Antwerpen 2001
$900 - €850 - £558 - FF5 574
Hagar comforted by an Angel Etching (16.5x13cm
6x5in) New-York 1999

DEZAUNAY Émile Alfred 1854-1938 [138]
$3 020 - €3 364 - £1 976 - FF22 064
Byn vid kusten Oil/canvas (50x61.5cm 19x24in)
Helsinki 2000
$1 619 - €1 509 - £998 - FF9 900
Bord de rivière à Saint-Sébastien, Loire
Huile/toile (34x27cm 13x10in) Nantes 1999
$1 311 - €1 448 - £909 - FF9 500
Au café à Camaret Aquarelle/papier (23x31cm
9x12in) Nantes 2001
$706 - €610 - £424 - FF4 000
Jeunes bretonnes en coiffe Eau-forte (30x39cm
11x15in) Brest 1998

DEZENTJÉ Ernest 1885-1972 [66]
$801 - €680 - £483 - FF4 460
Flamboyant in Djakarta Oil/board (46x46cm
18x18in) Den Haag 1998

DEZEUZE Daniel 1942 [21]
$426 - €457 - £285 - FF3 000
Sans titre Crayon/papier (36.5x48cm 14x18in) Paris
2000

DHAMARRANDJI Gunguyuma c.1916-1970 [1]
$6 561 - €6 998 - **£4 379** - FF45 905
Marrana Mixed media (114x61cm 44x24in)
Melbourne 2000

DHURANDHAR Mahadev Vishvanath 1867-1944 [24]
$6 209 - €6 012 - **£3 900** - FF39 438
Pooja Festival Oil/canvas (46x61cm 18x24in) London 1999

$2 706 - €2 621 - **£1 700** - FF17 191
Village Scene Watercolour/paper (17.5x29.5cm 6x11in) London 1999

DI CARLO Vittorio Maria 1939 [91]
$350 - €363 - **£210** - FF2 380
Le amiche Olio/tela (50x50cm 19x19in) Vercelli 2001

$180 - €233 - **£135** - FF1 530
Ragazza di Manila Olio/tela (40x30cm 15x11in) Vercelli 2001

DI CREDI Lorenzo 1459-1537 [4]
$300 000 - €263 148 - **£182 160** - FF1 726 140
Drapery Study: the Christ Child Standing on the Madonna's Left Knee Ink (27x20cm 10x7in) New-York 1999

DI MACCIO Gérard 1948 [12]
$42 563 - €47 259 - **£29 605** - FF310 000
Femme Acrylique/papier/panneau (97x130cm 38x51in) Paris 2001

$1 361 - €1 524 - **£946** - FF10 000
Personnage fantastique Huile/toile (54x65cm 21x25in) Vernou en Sologne 2001

DI MARINO Francesco 1892-1954 [34]
$550 - €570 - **£330** - FF3 740
Barche di pescatori Olio/tavola (25x35cm 9x13in) Torino 2000

DI ROSA Hervé 1959 [301]
$4 607 - €5 183 - **£3 172** - FF34 000
Paravent Huile/toile (210x270cm 82x106in) Paris 2000

$1 597 - €1 494 - **£967** - FF9 800
Le festin Acrylique/toile (46x55cm 18x21in) Paris 1999

$255 - €290 - **£174** - FF1 900
Le pistolet Acrylique/toile (16x14cm 6x5in) Paris 2000

$575 - €686 - **£418** - FF4 500
Tête Gouache (45x30cm 17x11in) Paris 2000

$204 - €244 - **£145** - FF1 600
La découverte Sérigraphie couleurs (101x103cm 39x40in) Paris 2000

DI ROSA Richard, «Buddy» 1963 [52]
$303 - €335 - **£210** - FF2 200
Chandelier Métal (H65cm H25in) Paris 2001

$3 029 - €3 354 - **£2 054** - FF22 000
Sans titre (texte de Juliette Benzoni) Aquarelle, gouache/papier (30x21cm 11x8in) Paris 2000

$1 539 - €1 753 - **£1 086** - FF11 500
Pinochio Aquatinte (93x40x40cm 36x15x15in) Versailles 2001

DI SUVERO Mark 1933 [82]
$65 000 - €62 466 - **£40 040** - FF409 753
Lickflap Metal (132x99x106.5cm 51x38x41in) New-York 1999

$14 000 - €15 364 - **£9 014** - FF100 783
Untitled Metal (25x54.5x27cm 9x21x10in) New-York 2000

$4 000 - €4 320 - **£2 764** - FF28 335
Fire Jump/Rilke/Marianne Moore/Tendresse/Lady Day/Magnetic Borealis Color lithograph (78.5x121.5cm 30x47in) New-York 2001

DIAGO Roberto 1920-1957 [10]
$80 000 - €92 823 - **£55 232** - FF608 880
Extasis Oil/canvas (99x129.5cm 38x50in) New-York 2000

$18 000 - €15 542 - **£10 980** - FF101 948
Danze Oil/canvas (77.5x63.5cm 30x25in) Miami FL 1999

DIAMANT David S. 1849-1912 [1]
$2 500 - €2 136 - **£1 512** - FF14 011
Evening along the Shoreline Oil/canvas (32x20.5cm 12x8in) San-Francisco CA 1998

DIAMANTINI Giuseppe 1621-1705 [8]
$588 - €511 - **£354** - FF3 352
Saturn und Rhea Radierung (25.9x19.7cm 10x7in) Berlin 1998

DIAMANTINO Riera 1912-1961 [278]
$159 - €152 - **£97** - FF1 000
Nature morte au pot vert Huile/toile (65x92cm 25x36in) Paris 1999

$95 - €91 - **£58** - FF600
Barques Huile/papier (27x35cm 10x13in) Paris 1999

DIAMOND Hugh Welch 1809-1886 [2]
$4 538 - €5 182 - **£3 200** - FF33 994
Still life with hare Albumen print (18.5x9cm 7x3in) London 2001

DIANA Benedetto c.1460-1525 [1]
$11 490 - €11 248 - **£7 070** - FF73 785
Sacra conversazione, Madonna mit Kind zwischen zwei Assistenzfiguren Oil/panel (59x82cm 23x32in) Stuttgart 1999

DIANÉ Aboubacar XX [8]
$700 - €815 - **£500** - FF5 347
«Arts antiques»/«Les français de nos ancêtres les gaulois» Acrylic (31x44cm 12x17in) London 2000

DIANO Giacinto 1731-1804 [18]
$41 715 - €41 161 - **£25 704** - FF270 000
L'Apothéose des héros de l'Antiquité, projet de plafond Huile/toile (95.5x147.5cm 37x58in) Paris 1999

$14 000 - €14 513 - **£8 400** - FF95 200
S. Caterina d'Alessandria Olio/tela (64x50cm 25x19in) Napoli 1999

DIAO David, Diao Deqian 1943 [9]
$23 772 - €22 293 - **£14 779** - FF146 234
Barnett Newman : Paintings in Scale Acrylic/canvas (152x229cm 59x90in) Taipei 1999

$3 660 - €3 073 - **£2 148** - FF20 160
Little Suprematist Prison #23 Acrylic/canvas (41x82cm 16x32in) Taipei 1998

DIAQUÉ Ricardo C. XIX [12]
$15 181 - €17 244 - **£10 651** - FF113 110
An elegant Company on the Beach Oil/panel (35.5x51cm 13x20in) Amsterdam 2001

DIAS Antonio 1944 [3]
$35 000 - €37 569 - **£23 422** - FF246 435
The Illustration of Light Acrylic/canvas (120x120cm 47x47in) New-York 2000

$30 000 - €34 809 - **£20 712** - FF228 330
The poet and the pornographer Object (120x420cm 47x94in) New-York 2000

D

DIAS Cicerio 1907 **[5]**

🌂 **$80 000** - €92 948 - **£56 224** - FF609 696
La pensée rêveuse Oil/canvas (63x52,5cm 24x20in)
New-York 2001

✏ **$40 000** - €47 097 - **£28 108** - FF308 936
Aurora mulher Watercolour (31x21cm 12x8in) New-York 2000

DIAZ CANEJA Juan Manuel 1905-1988 **[10]**

🌂 **$10 400** - €12 013 - **£7 200** - FF78 800
Paisaje Oleo/lienzo (55x46cm 21x18in) Seville 2000

DIAZ Carlos 1968 **[5]**

🌂 **$784** - €841 - **£518** - FF5 516
Casa de Ciutat Vella Oleo/lienzo (65x54cm 25x21in)
Barcelona 2000

DIAZ CASTILLA Luciano 1940 **[54]**

🌂 **$1 485** - €1 622 - **£945** - FF10 658
Paisaje con luna Oleo/lienzo (60x73cm 23x28in)
Madrid 2000

DIAZ DE LA PEÑA Narcisse Virgile 1807-1876 **[508]**

🌂 **$19 878** - €18 402 - **£12 000** - FF120 706
The Forest of Fontainebleau Oil/canvas
(98x129.5cm 38x50in) London 1999

🌂 **$13 000** - €14 765 - **£9 122** - FF96 855
Paysage avec vaches Oil/canvas (60x93cm
23x36in) New-York 2001

🌂 **$4 125** - €4 116 - **£2 575** - FF27 000
Boisière dans la clairière Huile/toile/carton
(19x33cm 7x12in) Fontainebleau 1999

✏ **$611** - €686 - **£428** - FF4 500
**Les quatre saisons, d'après Pierre Paul
Prud'hon** Crayon (24x12cm 9x4in) Paris 2001

DIAZ FERRER Jesús 1922 **[36]**

🌂 **$728** - €841 - **£504** - FF5 516
París Oleo/tablex (121x60cm 47x23in) Madrid 2000

✏ **$228** - €228 - **£140** - FF1 497
Marina Acuarela/papel (19x24.5cm 7x9in) Madrid
2000

DIAZ Gérard 1938 **[31]**

✏ **$1 587** - €1 524 - **£984** - FF10 000
Exotique Pastel/papier (160x110cm 62x43in) Paris
1999

DIAZ José 1930-1990 **[28]**

🌂 **$840** - €901 - **£570** - FF5 910
Tauromaquia y menina Oleo/lienzo (73x73cm
28x28in) Madrid 2000

DIAZ SANTOS Santiago 1940 **[43]**

🌂 **$204** - €240 - **£148** - FF1 576
Palacio de Oriente, Madrid Oleo/lienzo (46x55cm
18x21in) Madrid 2001

DIBBETS Jan 1941 **[35]**

✏ **$24 551** - €26 753 - **£17 000** - FF175 487
Four Courts, Dublin Study I Pencil (72.5x101.5cm
28x39in) London 2001

▦ **$1 010** - €1 116 - **£700** - FF7 321
Untitled Print in colors (75.5x10cm 29x3in) London
2001

📷 **$2 689** - €2 887 - **£1 800** - FF18 938
Untitled/Untitled II/Untitled III Photograph (73x73cm
38x38in) London 2001

DIBDIN Thomas R. Colman 1810-1893 **[107]**

✏ **$821** - €882 - **£550** - FF5 786
Greenwich-Observatory/A Mediaeval Village
Watercolour/paper (25x35.5cm 9x13in) London 2000

DICEY Frank ?-1888 **[1]**

🌂 **$4 861** - €4 531 - **£3 000** - FF29 720
Springtime Beauty Oil/canvas (121x71cm 48x28in)
Bury St. Edmunds, Suffolk 1999

DICHTL Erich 1890-1955 **[22]**

🌂 **$1 860** - €1 534 - **£1 095** - FF10 060
Uhu auf Kiefernast, in den Klauen erlegter Hase
Öl/Leinwand (108x74cm 42x29in) Lindau 1998

DICK Karl Theophil 1884-1967 **[52]**

🌂 **$877** - €876 - **£548** - FF5 746
Pferdespänner auf Feldweg Öl/Leinwand
(46x61cm 18x24in) Zofingen 1999

🌂 **$367** - €427 - **£254** - FF2 800
Stilleben mit Skulptur Öl/Leinwand (44x30cm
17x11in) Luzern 2000

DICK William Reid 1879-1961 **[25]**

▨ **$4 051** - €4 375 - **£2 800** - FF28 699
The Boy with a Sling Bronze (H48.5cm H19in)
London 2001

DICKERHOF Urs 1941 **[55]**

▥ **$103** - €117 - **£72** - FF766
«Blues for Mr.Hubbuch» Drypoint (25x44.5cm
9x17in) Bern 2001

DICKERSON Robert Henry, Bob 1924 **[598]**

🌂 **$26 050** - €31 619 - **£17 500** - FF203 215
The Figure in the Wilderness Oil/board
(182x122cm 71x48in) Melbourne 2000

🌂 **$12 080** - €11 754 - **£7 434** - FF77 098
Girl with ginger Cat Oil/canvas (60x50cm 23x19in)
Melbourne 1999

🌂 **$5 259** - €5 781 - **£3 370** - FF37 922
Lone figure Oil/canvas/board (29.5x24.5cm 11x9in)
Melbourne 2000

✏ **$3 087** - €3 314 - **£2 066** - FF21 741
Tranquility Charcoal/paper (55x37cm 21x14in) Sydney
2000

▥ **$501** - €553 - **£336** - FF3 625
Out of the Barrier Color lithograph (51x69cm
20x27in) Malvern, Victoria 2000

DICKEY Robert L. 1861-1944 **[2]**

✏ **$3 000** - €3 291 - **£1 935** - FF21 587
The Trotter Cresceus Watercolour/paper (46x69cm
18x27in) York PA 2000

DICKINSON Anson 1779-1852 **[8]**

🌂 **$5 250** - €6 123 - **£3 686** - FF40 164
Gentleman with White Stock and Blue Coat
Miniature (6x5cm 2x2in) Portsmouth NH 2000

DICKINSON Edwin Walter 1891-1978 **[26]**

🌂 **$24 000** - €28 140 - **£17 265** - FF184 586
Elisabeth Miller Oil/board (45.5x35.5cm 17x13in)
New-York 2001

🌂 **$10 000** - €9 367 - **£6 148** - FF61 441
View of Wellfleet from Fraziers Oil/canvas
(25.5x30.5cm 10x12in) New-York 1999

✏ **$1 100** - €1 026 - **£682** - FF6 728
Portrait of an old Man with a Beard
Charcoal/paper (50.5x37cm 19x14in) New-York 1999

DICKINSON Preston 1891-1930 **[20]**

✏ **$9 000** - €8 467 - **£5 616** - FF55 542
Watertower at high Bridge Ink (54.5x37.5cm
21x14in) New-York 1999

DICKMAN Charles John 1863-1943 **[6]**

🌂 **$5 000** - €4 272 - **£3 025** - FF28 022
Evening Oil/canvas (78.5x122cm 30x48in) San-
Francisco CA 1998

DICKSEE Francis B., Frank 1853-1928 **[36]**
- $8 000 - €7 493 - **£4 918** - FF49 152
  Romeo and Juliet Oil/wood (19.5x14.5cm 7x5in)
  New-York 1999
- $258 - €237 - **£160** - FF1 555
  After the Battle Watercolour/paper (11x15cm 4x5in)
  Devon 1999

DICKSEE Herbert Thomas 1862-1942 **[194]**
- $25 084 - €21 411 - **£15 000** - FF140 449
  «Suspense» Oil/canvas (33.5x49cm 13x19in) Leeds
  1998
- $1 700 - €1 505 - **£1 039** - FF9 871
  Border Collie Black & white chalks (37.5x28.5cm
  14x11in) New-York 1999
- $523 - €505 - **£330** - FF24 199
  Cindarella Etching (60.5x40.5cm 23x15in) London
  1999

DICKSEE Thomas Francis 1819-1895 **[20]**
- $17 931 - €19 248 - **£12 000** - FF126 259
  Patricia Oil/canvas (51x40.5cm 20x15in) London 2000
- $42 203 - €40 582 - **£26 000** - FF266 198
  Ophelia Oil/panel (22x20cm 8x7in) London 1999

DICKSON Charles Edward 1872-1934 **[3]**
- $3 436 - €3 689 - **£2 300** - FF24 199
  **Steamship at Harbour with Tugs and Distant
  Masted Vessels** Watercolour (37x54cm 14x21in)
  Edinburgh 2000

DICKSON Frank 1862-1936 **[5]**
- $14 792 - €14 056 - **£9 000** - FF92 199
  **Portrait of Margaret, Daughter of J.C.Imthurn
  Esq.** Oil/canvas (71x51cm 27x20in) London 1999

DICKSON William XIX-XX **[3]**
- $2 761 - €2 637 - **£1 700** - FF17 300
  Good Day's Sport on the Tay Oil/canvas (50x88cm
  19x34in) Edinburgh 1999

DIDAY François 1802-1877 **[98]**
- $5 140 - €5 003 - **£3 158** - FF32 816
  **Engelhörner et glacier de Rosenlaui, coucher
  de soleil** Oil/paper/canvas (47x45cm 18x17in) Zürich
  1999
- $1 976 - €1 816 - **£1 214** - FF11 912
  Landschaft mit Anglern am Seeufer/Segelboot
  Öl/Karton (4x5.5cm 1x2in) Zürich 1999
- $394 - €374 - **£246** - FF2 455
  Segler am Steg bei Sturm Aquarell/Papier
  (14x25.5cm 5x10in) Luzern 1999

DIDDAERT Henri 1819-1893 **[3]**
- $266 - €248 - **£165** - FF1 626
  La paysanne au repos Huile/toile (42x27cm
  16x10in) Antwerpen 1999

DIDERON Louis Jules 1901-? **[12]**
- $4 566 - €4 878 - **£3 104** - FF32 000
  Nu assis se coiffant Marbre (28.5x13.5x18.5cm
  11x5x7in) Pontoise 2001
- $541 - €610 - **£377** - FF4 000
  Nu lové Fusain/papier (40x49cm 15x19in) Paris 2001

DIDIER Clovis François-Aug. 1858-? **[14]**
- $18 000 - €20 102 - **£11 527** - FF131 859
  The Laundress Oil/canvas (130x184cm 51x72in)
  New-York 2000
- $1 650 - €1 829 - **£1 142** - FF12 000
  Chasseresse et son chien Huile/toile (55x33cm
  21x12in) Troyes 2001
- $4 318 - €4 421 - **£2 711** - FF29 000
  L'attente Huile/toile (41x33cm 16x12in) Lille 2000

DIDIER Jules 1831-1892 **[46]**
- $7 800 - €6 738 - **£3 900** - FF44 200
  Campagna romana con guado fluviale Olio/tela
  (96x144cm 37x56in) Prato 1999
- $2 286 - €2 565 - **£1 600** - FF16 825
  Arriving at the Village Oil/canvas (80x64cm
  31x25in) London 2001
- $2 286 - €2 454 - **£1 530** - FF16 098
  **Weidelandschaft mit Vieh und Hirten an einem
  Bach** Öl/Leinwand (33.5x47cm 13x18in) Köln 2000
- $781 - €838 - **£522** - FF5 500
  Troupeau près du campement Lavis (10.5x16.5cm
  4x6in) Paris 2000

DIDIER Luc 1954 **[166]**
- $1 412 - €1 524 - **£976** - FF10 000
  Le marais à Bourges Huile/toile (45x60cm 17x23in)
  La Varenne-Saint-Hilaire 2001
- $1 016 - €1 143 - **£699** - FF7 500
  Marée haute à Saint Cado, Morbihan Huile/toile
  (27x41cm 10x16in) La Varenne-Saint-Hilaire 2000

DIDIER Pierre 1929 **[33]**
- $1 988 - €2 134 - **£1 330** - FF14 000
  Nature morte à la mappemonde Huile/toile
  (33x41cm 12x16in) Saint-Dié 2000

DIDIER-POUGET William 1864-1959 **[77]**
- $12 585 - €14 635 - **£8 851** - FF96 000
  Château de Montfort Huile/toile (178x272cm
  70x107in) Tours 2001
- $2 700 - €2 363 - **£1 635** - FF15 500
  «Fenêtre fleurie de ma maison normande»
  Huile/toile (56x46cm 22x18in) Paris 1998
- $1 380 - €1 296 - **£855** - FF8 500
  Bord de mer Huile/panneau (23.5x58.5cm 9x23in)
  Deauville 1999

DIEBENKORN Richard 1922-1993 **[318]**
- $1 150 000 - €1 262 067 - **£740 485** - FF8 278 620
  Round Table Oil/canvas (177.5x161.5cm 69x63in)
  New-York 2000
- $380 000 - €425 628 - **£264 024** - FF2 791 936
  «Girl in Profile» Oil/canvas (51x45.5cm 20x17in)
  New-York 2001
- $55 000 - €46 478 - **£32 807** - FF304 876
  Valentine Day Oil/canvas (33x42cm 12x16in) San-
  Francisco CA 1998
- $40 000 - €41 741 - **£25 228** - FF273 800
  Ocean Park Gouache (63x45cm 24x17in) New-York
  2000
- $5 200 - €4 881 - **£3 212** - FF32 014
  Untitled #1 #2 #4 #5 Etching (101x66cm 39x25in)
  New-York 1999

DIEBOLDT ?-1821/22 **[3]**
- $6 489 - €6 541 - **£4 050** - FF42 903
  **Hafenlandschaft mit ankernden Schiffen und
  vielen Figuren** Öl/Leinwand (28.5x40cm 11x15in)
  Wien 2000

DIEBOLDT Jean-Michel 1779-c.1825 **[4]**
- $4 982 - €4 092 - **£2 893** - FF26 845
  **Südliche Meeresbucht mit ankernden
  Grosseglern** Öl/Leinwand (33x46cm 12x18in)
  Berlin 1998

DIEDEREN Jef 1920 **[41]**
- $422 - €454 - **£282** - FF2 976
  A table still life Oil/canvas (40x50cm 15x19in)
  Amsterdam 2000
- $310 - €363 - **£221** - FF2 381
  «N.N» Watercolour (50x60cm 19x23in) Amsterdam
  2001

〔▢〕 **$95** - €113 - **£68** - FF744
Composition Linocut in colors (57.5x71.5cm
22x28in) Amsterdam 2000

DIEDERICH William Hunt 1884-1953 **[17]**
🐾 **$7 500** - €6 327 - **£4 399** - FF41 505
Group of Two Playing Cats Bronze (H20.5cm H8in)
New-York 1998

DIEFFENBACH Anton 1831-1914 **[24]**
👁 **$14 493** - €13 613 - **£8 736** - FF89 298
The Arrival of Grandfather and Grandmother
Oil/canvas (109x132cm 42x51in) Amsterdam 1999
👁 **$3 000** - €2 531 - **£1 759** - FF16 602
Hide and Seek Oil/panel (40x33cm 16x13in) Mystic
CT 1998

DIEFFENBACH Carl Wilhelm 1851-1913 **[14]**
👁 **$10 582** - €12 015 - **£7 353** - FF78 816
In der blauen Grotte auf Capri Öl/Leinwand
(142x96cm 55x37in) Köln 2001
👁 **$2 302** - €2 556 - **£1 601** - FF16 769
Du sollst nicht töten Oil/panel (49.5x34.5cm
19x13in) Heidelberg 2001
✏ **$1 854** - €2 161 - **£1 283** - FF14 177
Porträt von Richard Wagner Watercolour
(54x44.5cm 21x17in) Bern 2000

DIEFFENBACH P. XIX **[2]**
👁 **$2 245** - €2 034 - **£1 400** - FF13 341
Apples Oil/canvas/panel (23x31cm 9x12in) London
1999

DIEFFENBACHER August Wilhelm 1858-1940 **[26]**
✏ **$889** - €869 - **£564** - FF5 701
**Blick auf die Blaue Gumpe im Reintal bei
Garmisch** Pastell/Papier (98x147cm 38x57in)
München 1999

DIEFFENBRUNNER Johann Georg 1718-1786 **[1]**
👁 **$9 612** - €8 178 - **£5 736** - FF53 646
Memento Mori Öl/Leinwand (31x25cm 12x9in)
München 1998

DIEGHEM van Jacob ?-1873 **[32]**
👁 **$2 325** - €2 496 - **£1 555** - FF16 371
Lamb laying with its mother in a meadow
Oil/panel (16.5x24cm 6x9in) Amsterdam 2000

DIEHL Arthur Vidal 1870-1929 **[122]**
👁 **$1 200** - €1 288 - **£803** - FF8 449
Rolling Surf with Sand Dunes and Seagulls
Oil/canvas (48x71cm 19x28in) East-Dennis MA 2000
👁 **$650** - €667 - **£406** - FF4 375
Still Life with Fruit Oil/canvas (30x45cm 12x18in)
Bolton MA 2000

DIEHL Gösta 1899-1964 **[39]**
👁 **$1 565** - €1 766 - **£1 100** - FF11 583
De hemlösa Oil/canvas (80x100cm 31x39in) Helsinki
2001
👁 **$547** - €605 - **£379** - FF3 971
Arbetare Oil/canvas (33x46cm 12x18in) Helsinki 2001
✏ **$507** - €471 - **£304** - FF3 089
Strandlandskap Akvarell/papper (46x62cm 18x24in)
Helsinki 1999

DIEHL Hanns 1877-1946 **[17]**
👁 **$672** - €581 - **£405** - FF3 813
Weissenkirchen in der Wachau Öl/Leinwand
(54x45cm 21x17in) Wien 1999

DIEHL von Hugo 1821-1883 **[1]**
👁 **$3 351** - €3 835 - **£2 304** - FF25 154
Szene aus den Napoleonischen Kriegen
Öl/Leinwand (39x57.5cm 15x22in) München 2000

DIELMAN Frederick 1847-1935 **[10]**
👁 **$5 500** - €5 209 - **£3 344** - FF34 166
Boy Peeling an Orange Oil/canvas (43x31cm
16x12in) New-York 1999
✏ **$7 000** - €7 993 - **£4 935** - FF52 429
The Artist's Studio Watercolour/paper (53x34cm
20x13in) Boston MA 2001

DIELMAN Marguerite c.1880-? **[12]**
👁 **$1 083** - €1 041 - **£680** - FF6 829
Les fleurs blanches Huile/toile (75x55cm 29x21in)
Bruxelles 1999

DIELMANN Jakob Fürchtegott 1809-1885 **[34]**
👁 **$6 554** - €6 135 - **£4 062** - FF40 246
Ländliches Idyll Oil/panel (17.5x22.3cm 6x8in)
Heidelberg 1999
✏ **$2 488** - €2 147 - **£1 481** - FF14 084
Schäfers Klagelied Aquarell/Papier (9x10.5cm
3x4in) München 1998

DIELS Jef 1952 **[5]**
👁 **$2 300** - €2 479 - **£1 590** - FF16 260
«Yin Yang» Huile/panneau (32x32cm 12x12in)
Antwerpen 2001

DIEMER Bruno 1924-1962 **[3]**
👁 **$3 342** - €3 835 - **£2 286** - FF25 154
Lesende Öl/Leinwand (80x60cm 31x23in) Dettelbach-
Effeldorf 2000

DIEMER Michael Zeno 1867-1939 **[107]**
👁 **$5 401** - €5 624 - **£3 422** - FF36 892
Dreimaster auf bewegter See Öl/Leinwand
(100x143cm 39x56in) München 2000
👁 **$6 383** - €6 647 - **£4 044** - FF43 600
Dreimaster auf bewegter See Öl/Leinwand
(85x111cm 33x43in) München 2000
✏ **$489** - €486 - **£305** - FF3 186
Gebirgslandschaft im Abendlicht Watercolour
(31.2x20.3cm 12x7in) München 1999

DIENER-DENES Rudolf 1889-1956 **[8]**
👁 **$714** - €687 - **£442** - FF4 500
Resting Woman Oil/canvas (63x90cm 24x35in)
Budapest 1999

DIENES de André 1913-1985 **[35]**
📷 **$943** - €1 125 - **£672** - FF7 378
Unter Wasser, Modell Virginia De Lee Photograph
(30.4x26.1cm 11x10in) München 2000

DIEPENBEECK van Abraham Jansz. 1596-1675
[48]
👁 **$17 111** - €19 429 - **£11 890** - FF127 448
Die Anbetung der Könige Öl/Kupfer (59x44cm
23x17in) Köln 2001
👁 **$1 750** - €2 019 - **£1 232** - FF13 247
**Portrait of a Seated Young Woman in a
Landscape playing a Mandolin** Oil/canvas
(38x30cm 15x12in) Norwalk CT 2000
✏ **$1 321** - €1 271 - **£814** - FF8 334
The Vision of St Bernard of Clairvaux Black chalk
(44x30.5cm 17x12in) Amsterdam 1999

DIEPRAAM Abraham 1622-1670 **[6]**
👁 **$5 548** - €5 183 - **£3 423** - FF34 000
Homme dans une taverne Huile/panneau
(20x16.5cm 7x6in) Vannes 1999

DIEPRAAM Willem 1944 **[10]**
📷 **$781** - €908 - **£549** - FF5 953
«Jerry Hall, Parijs» Silver print (48x59cm 18x23in)
Amsterdam 2001

DIER Erhard Amadeus 1893-1969 [47]
$281 - €329 - £197 - FF2 155
Bauerngesellschaft Aquarell/Papier (19.5x18cm
7x7in) Luzern 2000

DIERA G.L. XX [2]
$1 962 - €2 134 - £1 293 - FF14 000
Place animée à Marrakech Huile/panneau
(35x27cm 13x10in) Paris 2000

DIERCKX Pierre Jacques 1855-1947 [20]
$2 640 - €2 479 - £1 630 - FF16 260
La cuisson du pain Huile/toile (72x55cm 28x21in)
Antwerpen 2000

DIERICKX Joseph 1865-1959 [9]
$369 - €372 - £229 - FF2 439
Vue animée de Blankenberge Huile/toile
(91x116cm 35x45in) Bruxelles 2000

DIES Albert Christophe 1755-1822 [36]
$2 723 - €2 325 - £1 628 - FF15 251
Bewaldetes Felsstück Ink (34x46cm 13x18in) Wien
1998
$151 - €169 - £105 - FF1 106
«Tivoli» Radierung (28.5x37.5cm 11x14in) Heidelberg
2001

DIESNER Gerhild 1915-1995 [28]
$6 830 - €7 267 - £4 320 - FF47 670
Stilleben mit Geschirr und Blumen Öl/Leinwand
(40x50cm 15x19in) Salzburg 2000
$4 229 - €3 997 - £2 634 - FF26 218
Felsen von Capri Öl/Leinwand (32x27.5cm 12x10in)
Wien 1999
$3 910 - €3 268 - £2 317 - FF21 438
Blaue Blumen Charcoal (61x46.5cm 24x18in) Wien
1998

DIEST van Adriaen 1655/56-1704 [34]
$11 279 - €11 077 - £7 000 - FF72 659
Mountainous Coastal Landscape with Figures
Loading a Ship Oil/canvas (87x136.5cm 34x53in)
London 1999
$2 233 - €2 045 - £1 361 - FF13 415
Südliche Hafenstadt vor mächtigem Felsmassiv
Oil/panel (25x31cm 9x12in) Berlin 1999

DIEST van Hieronymus 1631-1673 [7]
$26 000 - €22 883 - £15 828 - FF150 105
Fishermen Unloading their Catch in Calm
Waters Oil/panel (39.5x53cm 15x20in) New-York
1999

DIEST van Johann 1695-1757 [1]
$8 682 - €9 631 - £6 000 - FF63 178
Portrait of Field-Marshall George Wade (1673-
1748) Oil/canvas (124.5x99cm 49x38in) London 2001

DIEST van Willem Hermansz. c.1600-1673 [18]
$43 310 - €46 491 - £28 981 - FF304 964
Marine Oil/panel (60x71cm 23x27in) Zürich 2000
$11 736 - €13 720 - £8 379 - FF90 000
Embarcations sur une mer légèrement agitée
Huile/panneau (19.5x25.5cm 7x10in) Paris 2001

DIETER Hans 1881-1978 [30]
$1 383 - €1 605 - £984 - FF10 530
Familie Koblick badet Oil/canvas (59x73cm
23x28in) Stockholm 2000

DIETERLE Marie, née Marcke 1856-1935 [41]
$5 216 - €5 107 - £3 209 - FF33 500
Troupeau au bord du ruisseau Huile/toile
(93x108cm 36x42in) Angers 1999

DIETLER Johann Friedrich 1804-1874 [48]
$667 - €787 - £469 - FF5 160
Herrenbildnis Öl/Leinwand (89x72cm 35x28in) Bern
2000
$8 899 - €10 490 - £6 254 - FF68 811
Brienzersee-Schifferinnen Öl/Leinwand
(32x40.5cm 12x15in) Bern 2000
$1 291 - €1 208 - £800 - FF7 927
Mathilde Gaulthier de Rigny, Marquise de
Banneville (1824-1877) Black chalk (44.5x31cm
17x12in) London 1999

DIETMAN Erik 1937 [161]
$402 - €470 - £276 - FF3 084
Utan titel Mixed media (58.5x73.5cm 23x28in)
Stockholm 2000
$612 - €565 - £376 - FF3 708
«43,2 cm of Taylors Zinc Oxide Plaster B P C»
Mixed media (19x11.5cm 7x4in) Stockholm 1999
$586 - €657 - £408 - FF4 308
A Short Story by Erik Dietman Objet (15x10cm
5x3in) Stockholm 2001
$353 - €427 - £246 - FF2 800
Sans titre Aquarelle (44x54cm 17x21in) Paris 2000
$397 - €336 - £237 - FF2 204
«Proposition pour une sculpture à Amsterdam»
Engraving (75x53cm 29x20in) København 1998

DIETRICH Adelheid 1827-? [43]
$42 188 - €40 399 - £26 553 - FF265 000
Nature morte aux raisins, prunes,pêches et
fleurs sur des entablements Huile/toile
(96.5x71cm 37x27in) Paris 1999
$35 000 - €34 692 - £21 892 - FF227 566
Floral Still Life Oil/canvas (35.5x30.5cm 13x12in)
New-York 2000

DIETRICH Adolf 1877-1957 [150]
$58 730 - €66 180 - £40 670 - FF434 110
Sonnenblumen vor Seelandschaft Öl/Karton
(89x71cm 35x27in) Zürich 2000
$19 998 - €23 783 - £14 252 - FF156 006
Landschaft mit Zaunkönig Oil/panel (25x19cm
9x7in) Zürich 2000
$1 986 - €1 876 - £1 236 - FF12 307
Alt Berlingen, Blick über das Dorf und den See
Pencil/paper (14x17cm 5x6in) St. Gallen 1999
$57 - €56 - £35 - FF369
Park Scherbenhof Weinfelden Lithographie
(16x14cm 6x5in) St. Gallen 1999

DIETRICHSON Mathilde 1837-1921 [15]
$5 270 - €5 965 - £3 686 - FF39 129
Kvinne med folkedrakt ved fontenen Oil/canvas
(130x90cm 51x35in) Oslo 2001
$1 638 - €1 814 - £1 111 - FF11 902
Guttehode, studie Oil/canvas (41x34cm 16x13in)
Oslo 2000

DIETRICY Christian Wilhelm E. 1712-1774 [302]
$30 133 - €25 816 - £18 114 - FF169 341
Das überraschte Liebespaar Öl/Leinwand
(109x138cm 42x54in) Köln 1998
$12 832 - €12 271 - £7 814 - FF80 493
Arkadische Landschaft mit jungen Frauen
Öl/Leinwand (58x82cm 22x32in) Stuttgart 1999
$3 260 - €3 049 - £1 974 - FF20 000
Portrait de jeune femme parée de fleurs
Huile/panneau (45x33cm 17x12in) Lille 1999
$536 - €639 - £382 - FF4 192
Bauern mit Pferden am Wegesrand rastend Ink
(18.8x33cm 7x12in) Berlin 2000

D

▭ **$123** - €133 - £84 - FF872
Drei Köpfe Kupferstich (3.5x9.5cm 1x3in) Rudolstadt-Thüringen 2001

DIETZ Herman R. 1860-1923 [1]
🖼 **$5 500** - €4 891 - £3 363 - FF32 083
The Ella Roliffs Steaming off San Francisco Oil/canvas (71x101.5cm 27x39in) New-York 1999

DIETZSCH Barbara Regina 1706-1783 [24]
🖼 **$1 505** - €1 285 - **£900** - FF8 427
Still Life of a Rose and Butterflies Bodycolour (35x26cm 13x10in) London 1998

DIETZSCH Johann Christoph 1710-1769 [48]
🖼 **$400** - €428 - £272 - FF2 806
Landscape with two Men on a Path near a Tree Ink (12x12cm 4x4in) New-York 2001
▭ **$62** - €51 - £36 - FF335
Landschaft mit Wanderern auf Weg und rastender Familie am Wegesrand Radierung (14x18cm 5x7in) Lindau 1998

DIETZSCH Margaretha Barbara 1716-1795 [4]
🖼 **$3 800** - €4 191 - **£2 573** - FF27 489
Clematis with a Bee Bodycolour (28x20cm 11x7in) New-York 2000

DIEU Antoine 1662-1727 [5]
🖼 **$2 823** - €2 757 - £1 800 - FF18 082
Saint Benedict casting out the devil from a possessed Monk Red chalk (10x27.5cm 3x10in) London 1999

DIEUDONNÉ de Emmanuel XIX-XX [17]
🖼 **$107 589** - €115 489 - **£72 000** - FF757 555
A Beauty at Her Bath Oil/canvas (183x128cm 72x50in) London 2000
🖼 **$4 000** - €3 918 - **£2 577** - FF25 699
Preparing for the Walk Oil/panel (80.5x63.5cm 31x25in) New-York 1999
🖼 **$2 201** - €2 363 - **£1 472** - FF15 500
L'Egyptienne au bord du Nil Huile/toile (46x33cm 18x12in) Paris 2000

DIEVENBACH Hendricus Anthonius 1872-1946 [39]
🖼 **$1 352** - €1 611 - **£968** - FF10 569
Appels schillen, interieur met moeder en kinderen Oil/canvas (40x50cm 15x19in) Lokeren 2000

DIEY Yves 1892-1984 [79]
🖼 **$765** - €732 - **£480** - FF4 800
Modèle nu assis Huile/toile (55.5x46.5cm 21x18in) Paris 1999

DIEZ Julius 1870-1957 [38]
🖼 **$2 126** - €2 301 - **£1 457** - FF15 092
Bei der Toilette Gouache/Karton (42x69cm 16x27in) Stuttgart 2001
▭ **$35** - €41 - **£25** - FF268
Schneckenfrau mit Putto Radierung (17.9x27cm 7x10in) Leipzig 2000

DIEZ Samuel 1803-1873 [3]
🖼 **$2 381** - €2 556 - **£1 594** - FF16 769
Kleines Mädchen in weissem Spitzenkleid mit roten Schleifen Öl/Leinwand (39x32cm 15x12in) Stuttgart 2000

DIEZ von Wilhelm 1839-1907 [41]
🖼 **$1 073** - €1 125 - **£679** - FF7 378
Der Heilige Martin Oil/panel (54x39.5cm 21x15in) Köln 2000
🖼 **$2 075** - €1 943 - **£1 286** - FF12 744
Kleinkind mit Hund in Wiesenlandschaft Oil/panel (19.1x15.1cm 7x5in) Heidelberg 1999

DIEZLER Jakob 1789-1855 [9]
🖼 **$7 890** - €9 203 - **£5 539** - FF60 365
Das alte Kloster am Apollinarisberg bei Remagen Oil/panel (32x56cm 12x22in) Luzern 2000
🖼 **$3 911** - €4 602 - **£2 761** - FF30 184
Ideale Flusslandschaft Öl/Karton (32x45cm 12x17in) Köln 2001

DIGBY R. David 1936 [15]
🖼 **$566** - €532 - **£350** - FF3 491
Partridge Watercolour, gouache/paper (30.5x22.5cm 12x8in) London 1998

DIGGELMANN Alex Walter 1902-1987 [56]
▭ **$1 764** - €1 598 - **£1 100** - FF10 482
«St.Moritz» Poster (102x64cm 40x25in) London 1999

DIGHTON Denis 1792-1827 [7]
🖼 **$1 403** - €1 469 - **£912** - FF10 945
Prussian Army Officers, Dragoons of the Guard Watercolour (37x26.5cm 14x10in) London 2000

DIGHTON Joshua 1831-1908 [16]
🖼 **$1 200** - €1 104 - **£720** - FF7 244
Horse and Jockey Oil/canvas (55x66cm 22x26in) Chicago IL 1999
🖼 **$1 077** - €929 - **£650** - FF6 097
«Sir Tatton Sykes in his 91st Year, sat for at Doncaster Watercolour (19.5x14cm 7x5in) London 2000

DIGHTON Richard 1795-1880 [52]
🖼 **$364** - €392 - **£250** - FF2 570
Portrait of Henry Edmund Gurney Watercolour (26.5x20cm 10x7in) London 2001
▭ **$224** - €226 - **£140** - FF1 484
Trying on new Boots Etching (24x28cm 9x11in) London 2000

DIGHTON Robert 1752-1814 [36]
🖼 **$2 241** - €2 406 - **£1 500** - FF15 782
John Gilpin's return from Ware Ink (30x25cm 11x9in) London 2000
▭ **$656** - €746 - **£450** - FF4 895
Draw Caricature Map of England and Wales Engraving (21.5x18cm 8x7in) Oxfordshire 2000

DIGNAM Mary Ella Williams 1860-1938 [24]
🖼 **$518** - €604 - **£360** - FF3 965
Floral Still Life Oil/canvas (54.5x91.5cm 21x36in) Toronto 2000

DIGNIMONT André 1891-1965 [1035]
🖼 **$1 467** - €1 448 - **£912** - FF9 500
La rue chaude Huile/toile (28.5x33.5cm 11x13in) Nice 1999
🖼 **$442** - €374 - **£262** - FF2 450
Livres et bouquet Gouache/papier (62x48cm 24x18in) Senlis 1998
▭ **$117** - €136 - **£80** - FF894
Femme nue couchée Lithographie couleurs (32x51cm 12x20in) Liège 2000

DIJKSTRA Johan 1896-1978 [143]
🖼 **$15 624** - €18 151 - **£10 980** - FF119 064
Kerkje te dorkwerd Oil/canvas (60x100cm 23x39in) Amsterdam 2001
🖼 **$2 014** - €2 269 - **£1 388** - FF14 883
The Fun-Fair Watercolour (31x22.5cm 12x8in) Amsterdam 2000
▭ **$329** - €363 - **£223** - FF2 381
Kalkovens Groningen Etching, aquatint (29.8x42.4cm 11x16in) Haarlem 2000

DIJKSTRA Rineke 1959 [37]

◫ **$46 000** - €53 373 - **£31 758** - FF350 106
Jalta, Ukraine, July 29 Print in colors (153x129cm 60x50in) New-York 2000

◉ **$9 500** - €10 423 - **£6 311** - FF68 372
Tamale, Ghana, Africa March Photograph in colors (44.5x30.5cm 17x12in) New-York 2000

DIJSSELHOF Gerrit Willem 1866-1924 [49]

⌓ **$2 898** - €2 723 - **£1 747** - FF17 859
Poonen Oil/canvas (44x38cm 17x14in) Amsterdam 1999

⌓ **$1 231** - €1 361 - **£854** - FF8 929
Kameleon vissen Oil/canvas (24.5x35cm 9x13in) Amsterdam 2001

✎ **$675** - €681 - **£421** - FF4 464
Ray/Eelpout/Sole Watercolour/paper (12x16cm 4x6in) Amsterdam 2001

DIKE Philip Latimer, Phil 1906-1990 [12]

⌓ **$5 000** - €5 876 - **£3 446** - FF38 547
Gulls Oil/canvas (51x61cm 20x24in) Beverly-Hills CA 2000

DIKENMANN Rudolf 1832-1888 [70]

◫ **$80** - €91 - **£56** - FF596
«Berne»/Christoffelturm und Münster Aquatinta (7.5x11cm 2x4in) Bern 2001

DIL S.M.Louis Malaveille 1907-? [3]

◫ **$1 100** - €1 227 - **£717** - FF8 046
«L'école des Beaux-Arts Bal» Poster (117x74cm 46x29in) New-York 2000

DILICH Wilhelm 1572-1650 [4]

◫ **$263** - €256 - **£164** - FF1 676
Bremen: Delineatio Fori Tab: XVII, Ansicht des Marktplatzes Kupferstich (13.5x20.5cm 5x8in) Bremen 1999

DILL Laddie John 1943 [27]

◫ **$420** - €459 - **£285** - FF3 009
Ashland Series #1, #2, #3, #4 Etching, aquatint in colors (56x75.5cm 22x29in) New-York 2000

DILL Ludwig 1848-1940 [198]

⌓ **$3 456** - €3 323 - **£2 132** - FF21 800
Gruppe von Silberpappeln an einem Fluss Öl/Leinwand (63.2x48cm 24x18in) Köln 1999

⌓ **$1 877** - €1 738 - **£1 164** - FF11 403
Krabbenfischer Öl/Karton (12x23cm 4x9in) Stuttgart 1999

✎ **$879** - €1 022 - **£617** - FF6 707
Pfefferminz im Sumpf Aquarell/Papier (33.5x19.5cm 13x7in) Hamburg 2001

DILL Otto 1884-1957 [431]

⌓ **$40 432** - €40 904 - **£24 688** - FF268 312
Geführte Hengste Öl/Leinwand (100x120cm 39x47in) Stuttgart 2000

⌓ **$5 072** - €5 624 - **£3 513** - FF36 892
«Zwei Pferde auf der Koppel» Öl/Karton (36x50.5cm 14x19in) Kempten 2001

⌓ **$3 287** - €3 783 - **£2 266** - FF24 818
Auf dem Rennplatz (in Führring) Öl/Leinwand (30x37cm 11x14in) Saarbrücken 2000

✎ **$773** - €716 - **£479** - FF4 695
Winterliche Alpenlandschaft Gouache/paper (15x20cm 5x7in) Stuttgart 1999

◫ **$94** - €94 - **£58** - FF615
Pferderennen Lithographie (22x28.5cm 8x11in) Zofingen 1999

DILLENS Adolf Alexander 1821-1877 [44]

⌓ **$3 584** - €3 966 - **£2 400** - FF26 016
Paysage montagneux animé d'un couple de bergers Huile/panneau (60x48cm 23x18in) Antwerpen 2000

⌓ **$928** - €1 091 - **£651** - FF7 154
Paysage animé de pêcheurs au bord de mer Huile/toile (34x22cm 9x12in) Liège 2000

DILLENS Albert 1844-? [21]

⌓ **$4 103** - €4 724 - **£2 800** - FF30 987
A Family in a Kitchen interior Oil/panel (58.5x75.5cm 23x29in) London 2000

DILLENS Henri Jozef 1812-1872 [24]

⌓ **$12 737** - €14 316 - **£8 943** - FF93 903
Meisterliche Darstellung eines Tanzenden Paares vor einem Hauseingang Oil/panel (81x89.5cm 31x35in) Eltville-Erbach 2001

⌓ **$5 629** - €5 624 - **£3 520** - FF36 892
Kinder pflanzen den Freiheitsbaum Oil/panel (42.5x37cm 16x14in) Köln 1999

DILLENS Juliaan 1849-1904 [13]

◿ **$9 570** - €8 170 - **£5 610** - FF53 592
Allégro Bronze (H85cm H33in) Bruxelles 1998

◿ **$457** - €545 - **£327** - FF3 577
Tête de femme Bronze (H30cm H11in) Antwerpen 2000

DILLER Burgoyne 1906-1965 [26]

✎ **$4 200** - €4 769 - **£2 874** - FF31 283
Third Theme Coloured pencils (15x15cm 5x5in) New-York 2000

◫ **$4 600** - €4 757 - **£2 906** - FF31 206
Still Life Lithograph (29x24cm 11x9in) New-York 2000

DILLER Fritz XX [9]

◿ **$270** - €307 - **£187** - FF2 012
Aufwartender Dackel Porcelain (H15cm H5in) München 2001

DILLEY Ramon 1933 [156]

⌓ **$853** - €884 - **£541** - FF5 800
El vaporetto de Saint-Tropez Huile/toile (50x50cm 19x19in) Paris 2000

⌓ **$678** - €762 - **£472** - FF5 000
«La toilette» Huile/toile (33x41cm 12x16in) Honfleur 2001

◫ **$105** - €107 - **£66** - FF700
L'aéroport de Deauville Lithographie couleurs (55x44cm 21x17in) Quimper 2000

DILLINGHAM Rick 1952-1996 [2]

◿ **$22 000** - €22 791 - **£14 003** - FF149 496
Patch Pot closed top Ceramic (43x48.5cm 16x19in) New-York 2000

DILLIS Cantius 1779-1856 [19]

⌓ **$8 988** - €8 181 - **£5 616** - FF53 662
Nach Sonnenuntergang, Fischer am See Öl/Leinwand (53x66cm 20x25in) München 1999

⌓ **$567** - €562 - **£355** - FF3 689
Am Dum See bey Reichenhall Pencil (21.5x27.5cm 8x10in) München 1999

DILLIS von Johann Georg 1759-1841 [176]

⌓ **$13 312** - €12 270 - **£7 972** - FF80 484
Wasserfall im Gebirge Öl/Leinwand (86x68.5cm 33x26in) Dresden 1998

⌓ **$5 337** - €4 857 - **£3 334** - FF31 862
Josef Kirchmaier (1797-1887) Oil/panel (19.3x16cm 7x6in) München 1999

$720 - €818 - £500 - FF5 366
Landschaft mit einem Torbogen Ink (10.5x15.5cm
4x6in) Berlin 2001

DILLON Cyril 1890-1970 [28]
$98 - €92 - £60 - FF601
«The Swimming Pool Coombe Cottage» Etching
(24x25.5cm 9x10in) Melbourne 1999

DILLON Frank 1823-1909 [24]
$6 750 - €7 246 - £4 599 - FF47 533
«A Corner in a Japanese Curio Shop» Oil/canvas
(61x51cm 24x20in) Boston MA 2001
$976 - €897 - £600 - FF5 886
Nubian Slaves, Asouan Watercolour (24.5x40cm
9x15in) Oxfordshire 1999

DILLON Gerard 1916-1971 [171]
$13 123 - €12 697 - £8 092 - FF83 290
Under the Moon Oil/canvas (61x76cm 24x29in)
Dublin 1999
$6 254 - €5 336 - £3 727 - FF34 999
Study of a young Man in Blue Oil/board
(49.5x21.5cm 19x8in) Dublin 1998
$4 022 - €3 809 - £2 445 - FF24 987
Near Moyard Watercolour/paper (20x33cm 8x13in)
Dublin 1999
$815 - €851 - £515 - FF5 580
Fisherman and the Lobster Pots Woodcut in
colors (15.5x20.5cm 6x8in) Dublin 2000

DIMEO Laura 1965 [4]
$2 500 - €2 157 - £1 513 - FF14 151
Elementry Images, Tablet XX Mixed media
(40x36x6cm 15x14x2in) Tel Aviv 1999

DIMITRIADIS Christina 1967 [1]
$4 320 - €4 805 - £2 880 - FF31 520
Julia, Hallensee, Berlin Type C color print
(120x120cm 47x47in) Athens 2000

DIMITRIJEVIC Braco 1948 [18]
$281 - €305 - £193 - FF2 000
Triptychos post historicus Aquarelle/papier
(49x37cm 19x14in) Paris 2001

DINE Jim 1935 [1041]
$60 000 - €56 034 - £37 032 - FF367 560
Car Crash Mixed media (152.5x162.5cm 60x63in)
New-York 1999
$31 500 - €32 655 - £18 900 - FF214 200
Composizione Tecnica mista (120.5x91cm 47x35in)
Prato 1999
$17 000 - €16 347 - £10 473 - FF107 230
Flowers Synthetic polymer silkscreened/canvas
(20.5x20.5cm 8x8in) New-York 1999
$65 000 - €62 466 - £40 040 - FF409 753
Bouquet Bronze (135x61x61cm 54x24x24in) New-
York 1999
$20 000 - €16 790 - £11 730 - FF110 132
Two Venuses Bronze (60x38x33cm 23x14x12in)
Beverly-Hills CA 1999
$9 000 - €7 555 - £5 278 - FF49 559
Untitled Watercolour, gouache (76x57cm 29x22in)
Beverly-Hills CA 1998
$2 200 - €2 107 - £1 359 - FF13 820
Black and white Bathrobe Lithograph (91.5x61cm
36x24in) New-York 1999

DINET Étienne, Nasreddine 1861-1929 [315]
$40 620 - €45 735 - £28 290 - FF300 000
Les trois vieillards Huile/toile (76x100cm 29x39in)
Paris 2001
$6 958 - €7 470 - £4 655 - FF49 000
Les porteurs d'eau à l'oasis Huile/toile
(33.5x25.5cm 13x10in) Versailles 2000

$2 353 - €2 287 - £1 471 - FF15 000
Tête de femme Aquarelle, gouache/papier (17x11cm
6x4in) Paris 1999
$1 380 - €1 524 - £957 - FF10 000
Abdel Ghourem et Nour el Aïn Eau-forte (72x55cm
28x21in) Paris 2001

DING ERZHONG 1868-1935 [1]
$1 926 - €2 103 - £1 239 - FF13 795
Calligraphy Couplet in Jinwen Ink/paper
(145x38cm 57x14in) Hong-Kong 2000

DING FUZHI 1879-1949 [10]
$3 595 - €3 926 - £2 312 - FF25 751
Lychee Ink (23.5x38cm 9x14in) Hong-Kong 2000

DING XIONGQUAN 1929 [14]
$11 628 - €13 202 - £8 170 - FF86 602
Lady with Parrots Acrylic/paper/canvas (96x178cm
37x70in) Taipei 2001
$10 144 - €11 840 - £6 944 - FF77 664
L'ombrelle Acrylic/paper/canvas (100x73cm 39x28in)
Taipei 2000
$20 976 - €19 439 - £13 041 - FF127 512
Romance, four fold screen Ink (175.5x48cm
69x18in) Taipei 1999

DING YANYONG 1902-1978 [190]
$18 360 - €20 846 - £12 900 - FF136 740
Cat Oil/canvas (45x60.5cm 17x23in) Taipei 2001
$11 340 - €10 433 - £6 804 - FF68 436
Summer frogs Oil/board (45x30.5cm 17x12in) Taipei
1999
$5 128 - €5 779 - £3 584 - FF37 908
Mandarin Ducks Ink/paper (137x68.5cm 53x26in)
Hong-Kong 2001

DING YUNPENG 1547-c.1628 [4]
$12 000 - €10 448 - £7 154 - FF68 532
Sweeping the Elephant Ink (91.5x30.5cm 36x12in)
New-York 1998

DINGEMANS Jan 1921 [53]
$186 - €208 - £121 - FF1 366
Figures Talking near Houses Oil/canvas/board
(41x34cm 16x13in) Johannesburg 2000

DINGEMANS Waalko Jans I 1873-1925 [31]
$954 - €886 - £582 - FF5 813
**Horse-Drawn Carts on a Quay along the Maas,
Rotterdam** Oil/canvas (38x57cm 14x22in) Amsterdam
1998
$1 049 - €975 - £640 - FF6 393
**Horse Market with the Townhall beyond
Middelburg** Oil/canvas (38x29cm 14x11in)
Amsterdam 1998
$64 - €73 - £43 - FF476
Sluis te Gorinchem Etching (25x39cm 9x15in)
Dordrecht 2000

DINGEMANS Waalko Jans II 1912-1991 [7]
$1 310 - €1 271 - £824 - FF8 334
Zulu Warriors Oil/canvas (76x61cm 29x24in)
Amsterdam 1999

DINGLE Adrian, John Darley 1911-1974 [34]
$461 - €541 - £331 - FF3 547
The Wet Pier Oil/board (71x55cm 28x22in)
Vancouver, BC. 2001

DINGLE Kim 1951 [3]
$17 000 - €19 725 - £11 736 - FF129 387
Big Babies mashing Puppies Oil/canvas
(183x152.5cm 72x60in) New-York 2000

DINGLE Thomas, Jnr. XIX-XX [15]
$1 159 - €1 280 - £800 - FF8 396
Fort William Trebarwith Strand, North Cornwall
Watercolour (72.5x36cm 28x14in) Hockley,
Birmingham 2001

DINGLI Edward Caranua 1876-1950 [7]
$8 021 - €8 083 - £5 000 - FF53 018
The Grand Harbour, Valletta, Malta
Watercolour/paper (26x37.5cm 10x14in) London 2000

DINKEL Ernest Michael 1894-1983 [4]
$1 200 - €1 154 - £740 - FF7 569
«Visit The Empire» Poster (101x62.5cm 39x24in)
New-York 1999

DINNERSTEIN Harvey 1928 [12]
$200 - €215 - £133 - FF1 408
Row Home City Landscape Pastel/paper (25x33cm
10x13in) Hatfield PA 2000

DINSDALE John Bentham 1927 [27]
$2 800 - €3 182 - £1 933 - FF20 871
**The Engagement between the Boxer and the
Enterprise, 5th Sept.1813** Oil/canvas (63.5x76cm
25x29in) New-York 2000
$2 200 - €2 500 - £1 519 - FF16 399
Action between the Frolic and the Wasp
Oil/masonite (20.5x25.5cm 8x10in) New-York 2000

DIOR Christian 1905-1957 [11]
$945 - €884 - £579 - FF5 800
«Le 2 janvier 1940» Aquarelle (21x12cm 8x4in) Paris
1998

DIOTTI Giuseppe 1779-1846 [4]
$4 000 - €5 183 - £3 000 - FF34 000
Quattro teste per il giuramento di Pontida
Olio/tela (46.5x76cm 18x29in) Milano 2001
$1 440 - €1 866 - £1 080 - FF12 240
Il conte Ugolino Matita/carta (34x33cm 13x12in)
Milano 2001

DIRANIAN Sarkis 1854-1918 [23]
$3 750 - €3 168 - £2 252 - FF20 778
Summer Landscape Oil/canvas (54x77cm 21x30in)
New-York 1999
$2 726 - €2 254 - £1 600 - FF14 787
Bord de rivière Oil/canvas (33x46cm 12x18in)
London 1998
$7 158 - €5 917 - £4 200 - FF38 816
Lady at the Bath Pastel/paper (55x38cm 21x14in)
London 1998

DIRCKINCK-HOLMFELD Helmuth 1835-1912 [13]
$1 961 - €2 280 - £1 378 - FF14 956
Italiensk folkelivsscene Oil/canvas (65.5x113cm
25x44in) København 2001

DIRCKX Antonius Bernardus 1878-1927 [44]
$607 - €681 - £422 - FF4 464
Molenlandschap met vergezicht op Overschie
Oil/canvas (50x64cm 19x25in) Rotterdam 2001
$459 - €446 - £280 - FF2 926
Vue du Lac Majeur Huile/panneau (20x31cm 7x12in)
Bruxelles 1999
$451 - €499 - £313 - FF3 274
A panoramic summer Landscape Watercolour
(33x48cm 12x18in) Amsterdam 2001

DIRIKS Karl Edvard 1855-1930 [55]
$18 335 - €21 171 - £12 825 - FF138 871
Vinterdag i Paris, gatuliv ved Seine Oil/canvas
(99x150cm 38x59in) Stockholm 2001
$1 314 - €1 453 - £915 - FF9 664
Vinterparti Oil/canvas (46x56cm 18x22in) Viby J,
Århus 2001

$835 - €926 - £567 - FF6 072
Stille vann Oil/canvas (33x43cm 12x16in) Oslo 2000

DIRKS Andreas 1866-1922 [36]
$1 571 - €1 687 - £1 052 - FF11 067
**Fischerboote auf stürmischer See vor der
Küste** Oil/Leinwand (61.5x81cm 24x31in) Köln 2000
$2 051 - €2 147 - £1 289 - FF14 086
Segelboote in schneller Fahrt bei frischer Brise
Oil/panel (30x45cm 11x17in) Hamburg 2000

DIRKSEN Reyn 1924-1999 [77]
$224 - €227 - £139 - FF1 488
«Hellebrekers, Genever en Likeuren» Poster
(115x82.5cm 45x32in) Haarlem 2000

DIRR Johann Georg 1723-1779 [1]
$6 379 - €7 158 - £4 422 - FF46 954
Engelskopf Marble (H17cm 6in) München 2000

DISBROW Jay XX [1]
$1 700 - €1 825 - £1 137 - FF11 969
Julian Apollo Sunday Page Ink (71x49.5cm
27x19in) New-York 2000

DISCART Jean Baptiste XIX-XX [14]
$224 145 - €240 601 - £150 000 - FF1 578 240
The Curiosity Dealer Oil/panel (65x47.5cm 25x18in)
London 2000
$11 157 - €13 121 - £8 000 - FF86 068
The Head of a Berber in a red Fez Oil/board
(40x33cm 15x12in) London 2001

DISCHER Fritz 1880-1983 [1]
$1 364 - €1 375 - £850 - FF9 017
A Female Nude Sitting on a Bed Oil/canvas
(60.5x80cm 23x31in) London 2000

DISCHLER Hermann 1866-1935 [77]
$4 141 - €4 504 - £2 729 - FF29 543
Grundhof Rohrbach bei Furtwangen Öl/Leinwand
(65x88.5cm 25x34in) Bern 2000
$1 804 - €1 789 - £1 122 - FF11 738
Winteransicht von hinterzarten mit der Kirche
Öl/Leinwand (30x50cm 11x19in) Merzhausen 1999
$1 978 - €1 892 - £1 204 - FF12 409
Verschneite Tannen am Feldberg Aquarell/Papier
(10x14cm 3x5in) Staufen 1999

DISCOVOLO Antonio 1874-1956 [10]
$8 000 - €8 293 - £4 800 - FF54 400
Marina Olio/cartone (47x58cm 18x22in) Roma 2000

DISDERI André Adolphe Eugène 1819-1890 [36]
$577 - €488 - £343 - FF3 200
Palais de Versailles, Salon de l'oeil de Boeuf
Tirage albuminé (36.5x27.7cm 14x10in) Chartres 1998

DISEN Andreas Edvard 1845-1923 [16]
$1 372 - €1 156 - £810 - FF7 581
Berglandskap i snö Oil/canvas (24x32cm 9x12in)
Stockholm 1998

DISERTORI Benvenuto 1887-1969 [15]
$350 - €363 - £210 - FF2 380
Borgo s.Antonio a Perugia Acquaforte (29.5x24cm
11x9in) Milano 2001

DISFARMER Michael Meyer, Mike 1884-1959 [5]
$850 - €912 - £577 - FF5 985
Portraits Gelatin silver print (8x14cm 3x5in) Beverly-
Hills CA 2001

DISLER Martin 1949-1996 [233]
$6 856 - €6 283 - £4 189 - FF41 212
Ohne Titel Acryl/Leinwand (180x180cm 70x70in)
Zürich 1999

$1 905 - €2 045 - £1 275 - FF13 415
Ohne Titel Acrylic (109.7x79.8cm 43x31in) Hamburg
2000

$662 - €789 - £473 - FF5 174
Ohne Titel Charcoal/paper (59x42cm 23x16in) Zürich
2000

$322 - €299 - £196 - FF1 961
Figur Lithographie (85x63.5cm 33x25in) Bern 1999

DISMORR Jessica 1885-1939 **[11]**
$1 314 - €1 249 - £800 - FF8 195
Street in a Coastal Town Watercolour (38x27cm
14x10in) London 1999

DISNEY Walt 1901-1966 **[25]**
$59 - €71 - £41 - FF469
Pluto Offset (30x22cm 11x8in) Bad-Vilbel 2000

DISNEY Walt (Studio) XX **[1420]**
$3 500 - €3 757 - £2 342 - FF24 643
Conceptual Study of the Sorcerer's Lair
Oil/paper (24x29cm 9x11in) New-York 2000

$95 000 - €101 972 - £63 574 - FF668 895
Steiff Plush Mohair Noah's Arc Sculpture
Assemblage (305x457x457cm 120x179x179in) New-
York 2000

$7 500 - €8 050 - £5 019 - FF52 807
Young Tarzan Sculpture (H28cm H11in) New-York
2000

$2 200 - €2 063 - £1 359 - FF13 535
Snow White and the Seven Dwarfs, Doc Gouache
(25x30cm 10x12in) New-York 1999

$3 618 - €4 122 - £2 500 - FF27 039
Donald Duck Photograph in colors (38x40.5cm
14x15in) London 2000

DISSARD Michel ?-1837 **[3]**
$32 - €36 - £22 - FF234
Pariser Geschichte Kupferstich (24x29.5cm 9x11in)
Staufen 2001

DISTLER Rudolph 1948 **[35]**
$173 - €199 - £118 - FF1 308
**Bärensee I, Blick über den See, im Hintergrund
eine Bergsilhouette** Etching, aquatint in colors
(31.5x25.7cm 12x10in) Heidelberg 2000

DITKO Steve 1927 **[3]**
$2 250 - €2 171 - £1 422 - FF14 240
Strange Tales No.131 Ink (47x32cm 18x12in) New-
York 1999

DITSCHEINER Adolf Gustav 1846-1904 **[14]**
$5 331 - €6 135 - £3 681 - FF40 246
Klostergarten bei Salzburg Öl/Leinwand
(74x144cm 29x56in) München 2001

$2 185 - €2 165 - £1 325 - FF14 200
Landscape with River Oil/panel (15x31cm 6x12in)
New-Orleans LA 2000

DITTEN von Johannes 1848-1924 **[14]**
$654 - €764 - £466 - FF5 013
Vestlandsfjord med isbre Oil/canvas (67x100cm
26x39in) Oslo 2001

DITTRICH Simon 1940 **[69]**
$350 - €409 - £246 - FF2 683
Spalierobstzüchter Coloured pencils (41x34.5cm
16x13in) Königstein 2001

$76 - €71 - £47 - FF469
Blumenstrauss Farbserigraphie (58x47cm 22x18in)
Stuttgart 1999

DITZ Walter 1888-1925 **[6]**
$77 - €91 - £53 - FF595
«Vaterland-Familie-Zukunft, 8.Kriegsanleihe»
Poster (67x53cm 26x20in) Hoorn 2000

DIULGHEROFF Nicolas 1901-1982 **[43]**
$3 280 - €4 250 - £2 460 - FF27 880
Composizione Tempera/cartone (50x35cm 19x13in)
Milano 2001

$1 200 - €1 037 - £800 - FF6 800
Composizione Pastelli/cartone (16.5x16cm 6x6in)
Prato 1998

$848 - €879 - £508 - FF5 766
«Amaro Cora» Affiche couleur (198x139cm 77x54in)
Torino 2000

DIVEKY von Joseph 1887-1951 **[14]**
$172 - €160 - £106 - FF1 048
«Kriegsausstellung Wien - Kaisergarten» Poster
(63x92cm 24x36in) Wien 1999

DIVIS Alen 1900-1956 **[6]**
$2 196 - €2 077 - £1 368 - FF13 626
Cactus Huile/toile (54.5x69.5cm 21x27in) Praha 2000

$1 300 - €1 230 - £810 - FF8 068
Ester a Nardocheus Fusain (57.5x45.5cm 22x17in)
Praha 2000

DIVOLA John 1949 **[3]**
$2 600 - €2 791 - £1 765 - FF18 305
Zuma #7, #8, #19, #21 Photograph in colors
(37x45.5cm 14x17in) Beverly-Hills CA 2001

DIX Otto 1891-1969 **[1173]**
$89 600 - €76 225 - £53 450 - FF500 000
Portrait eines Kriegsgefangenen Tempera
(64x48cm 25x18in) Paris 1998

$12 275 - €14 316 - £8 618 - FF93 909
Vase mit Glockenblumen Öl/Karton (48.3x31.5cm
19x12in) Köln 2000

$8 576 - €9 408 - £5 825 - FF61 711
Amazonenschlacht Ink (34.2x44.2cm 13x17in)
Berlin 2000

$1 615 - €1 841 - £1 126 - FF12 074
Nelly II Radierung (19.5x14cm 7x5in) Hamburg 2001

DIXEY Frederick Charles act.1881-1914 **[25]**
$289 - €268 - £180 - FF1 759
South Country River Landscape with Boats
Watercolour/paper (19x25cm 7x9in) Cheshire 1999

DIXIE Ethel May 1876-1973 **[9]**
$423 - €439 - £268 - FF2 879
**Erica Blenna/Disa Uniflora/Gladiolus
Spathaceus** Watercolour (26x18cm 10x7in)
Johannesburg 2000

DIXON Alec R. XX **[1]**
$7 731 - €9 243 - £5 333 - FF60 632
«Quiet Moment» Oil/canvas (76x101.5cm 29x39in)
Penzance, Cornwall 2000

DIXON Alfred XIX **[5]**
$7 471 - €8 020 - £5 000 - FF52 608
Waiting Oil/canvas (91.5x71cm 36x27in) London 2000

DIXON Anna 1873-1959 **[33]**
$291 - €339 - £205 - FF2 222
«Breton Market» Watercolour/paper (28x40cm
11x15in) Calgary, Alberta 2001

DIXON Annie c.1817-1901 **[10]**
$2 486 - €2 505 - £1 550 - FF16 435
**Portrait of Liana Susan Penelope Norman,
Dressed as a Sibyl** Watercolour/paper (50x42cm
19x16in) Newbury, Berkshire 2000

DIXON Arthur A. XX **[5]**
$2 025 - €2 187 - £1 400 - FF14 349
**An Animated Discussion by the Fireside/A
Quiet Moment/The Embrace** Oil/board
(21.5x14.5cm 8x5in) London 2001

DIXON Arthur Percy XIX-XX **[15]**

$2 964 - €2 820 - £1 800 - FF18 496
The red Fan Oil/canvas (40.5x33cm 15x12in)
Edinburgh 1999

DIXON Charles Edward 1872-1934 **[278]**

$6 246 - €6 975 - £4 000 - FF45 755
The Battle of Jutland Oil/canvas (51x91.5cm
20x36in) London 2000

$4 522 - €4 252 - £2 800 - FF27 894
Shipping in the Pool of London Watercolour
(37.5x54cm 14x21in) London 1999

$1 000 - €962 - £617 - FF6 308
White Star Line Poster (78x102cm 30x40in) New-York 1999

DIXON Harry 1861-1942 **[9]**

$8 591 - €8 385 - £5 439 - FF55 000
La chasse au tigre Bronze (37x45cm 14x17in)
Calais 1999

DIXON Henry, Lt Col. 1824-1883 **[5]**

$1 147 - €1 278 - £750 - FF8 384
Old London Carbon print (21x17cm 8x7in) London
2000

DIXON James 1887-1970 **[67]**

$4 317 - €4 836 - £3 000 - FF31 722
«The Rice Brothers» Oil/paper (38x56cm 14x22in)
London 2001

$2 159 - €2 419 - £1 500 - FF15 865
The Greenland Owl Oil/paper (39.5x24cm 15x9in)
London 2001

DIXON John 1895-1970 **[3]**

$3 166 - €3 546 - £2 200 - FF23 263
West End Village, Tory Island Oil/board
(51.5x75.5cm 20x29in) London 2001

$4 317 - €4 836 - £3 000 - FF31 722
Imaginary view of Shipping on the Thames
Watercolour/paper (27.5x48.5cm 10x19in) London 2001

DIXON John 1720-1804 **[7]**

$1 443 - €1 322 - £880 - FF8 672
A Tigress, after George Stubbs Mezzotint
(48x58cm 19x23in) Cheltenham, Gloucestershire 1999

DIXON Karl XX **[1]**

$6 157 - €5 750 - £3 800 - FF37 717
**Two Carved Limestone Seats in the Form of the
Giants, Gog and Magog** Sculpture (H50cm H19in)
Billingshurst, West-Sussex 1999

DIXON Leng 1916-1968 **[12]**

$475 - €530 - £310 - FF3 477
Cape Malay Quarter Watercolour (10x22cm 3x8in)
Johannesburg 2000

DIXON Maynard 1875-1946 **[137]**

$1 200 000 - €1 410 349 - £831 960 - FF9 251 280
The Pony Boy Oil/canvas (91.5x183cm 36x72in)
Beverly-Hills CA 2000

$55 000 - €64 170 - £38 280 - FF420 926
«Caliente Hills #2» Oil/masonite (40x50cm 16x20in)
Altadena CA 2000

$40 000 - €46 748 - £28 556 - FF306 644
The Snow Patch» Oil/canvas (45x30cm 18x12in)
Altadena CA 2000

$3 600 - €4 231 - £2 495 - FF27 753
Navajo Charcoal/paper (19.5x12.5cm 7x4in) Beverly-Hills CA 2000

$1 200 - €1 410 - £832 - FF9 251
Indian Drummer Etching (14.5x9.5cm 5x3in)
Beverly-Hills CA 2000

DIXON Nellie Gertrude XIX-XX **[7]**

$6 724 - €7 218 - £4 500 - FF47 347
Girls Gathering Firewood Oil/canvas (46.5x40.5cm
18x15in) London 2000

DIXON Paul 1956 **[13]**

$1 448 - €1 205 - £850 - FF7 903
Zecras - Stormy Skies Pastel/paper (74x109cm
29x42in) London 1998

DIXON Percy 1862-1924 **[22]**

$439 - €422 - £280 - FF2 770
Coastal Scene Watercolour/paper (44x70cm 17x27in)
London 1999

DIXON Samuel XVIII **[3]**

$4 602 - €4 363 - £2 800 - FF28 622
**Red Leddged Barbery Partridge and Two
Pheasants** Mixed media (24x20cm 9x7in) Sighthill
1999

DIXON William 1774-c.1827 **[1]**

$2 400 - €2 644 - £1 601 - FF17 345
**Harbor Celebration with Central View of a
British Man-of-War** Watercolour/paper (11x76cm
4x30in) Portsmouth NH 2000

DIZIANI Antonio, Lo Zoppo 1737-1797 **[23]**

$35 000 - €36 283 - £21 000 - FF238 000
Allegoria dell'amore filiale Olio/tela (83x213cm
32x83in) Imbersago (Lecco) 2001

$17 979 - €16 431 - £11 000 - FF107 781
**River Landscape with a Shepherdess and a
Figure, Mountains beyond** Oil/canvas (36.5x50cm
14x19in) London 1999

$1 858 - €1 527 - £1 079 - FF10 014
Mythologische Szene Ink (14x15.5cm 5x6in) Wien
1998

DIZIANI Gaspare 1689-1767 **[99]**

$32 000 - €28 164 - £19 481 - FF184 745
The Satyr and the Peasant Oil/canvas (97x134.5cm
38x52in) New-York 1999

$18 760 - €21 343 - £13 230 - FF140 000
Le Triomphe de Neptune Huile/toile (98x80cm
38x31in) Paris 2001

$9 005 - €8 351 - £5 500 - FF54 781
Esau Selling his Burthright to Jacob Oil/canvas
(42.5x37cm 16x14in) London 1998

$2 651 - €2 595 - £1 700 - FF17 020
The Ascension/St Andrew and another Saint Ink
(30.5x22cm 12x8in) London 1999

DJAMIN Nasjah 1924-1997 **[7]**

$3 956 - €4 372 - £2 743 - FF28 676
View of the Sea Oil/canvas (135x135cm 53x53in)
Singapore 2001

$2 582 - €2 933 - £1 767 - FF19 237
Flowers Oil/canvas (60x80cm 23x31in) Singapore
2000

DJAMSHID [2]

$2 915 - €2 515 - £1 752 - FF16 500
Une princesse persane à aigrette Gouache
(114x45cm 44x17in) Nice 1998

DJANBARDI Ronnie 1925 **[5]**

$986 - €954 - £625 - FF6 260
Namerrodo Mixed media (99.5x44.5cm 39x17in)
Malvern, Victoria 1999

DJAWA 1905-1980 **[10]**

$4 656 - €5 130 - £3 091 - FF33 650
Djalamu Mortuary Ceremony Mixed media
(139x60cm 54x23in) Woollahra, Sydney 2000

DJIRNA I Made 1957 [8]
$2 835 - €2 643 - £1 713 - FF17 334
Women Oil/canvas (70x90cm 27x35in) Singapore 1999

DJURIC Casimir 1941 [1]
$1 383 - €1 448 - £869 - FF9 500
Sans titre Crayon (22x15.5cm 8x6in) Versailles 2000

DLOUHY Bedrich 1932 [9]
$6 647 - €6 287 - £4 140 - FF41 239
Étude Encre (57x82cm 22x32in) Praha 2001

DLUGACH Mikhail O. 1893-1989 [15]
$400 - €351 - £242 - FF2 301
V Sem Chasov Vechera Poster (72x100cm 28x39in)
New-York 1999

DMITRIENKO Pierre 1925-1974 [181]
$4 917 - €5 946 - £3 435 - FF39 000
Carrière Huile/toile (146x114cm 57x44in) Paris 2004
$1 833 - €1 906 - £1 150 - FF12 500
Composition Huile/toile (58x65cm 22x25in) Paris 2000
$1 491 - €1 448 - £921 - FF9 500
Composition Huile/panneau (44x31cm 17x12in) Paris 1999
$659 - €640 - £407 - FF4 200
Les pluies Lavis/papier (45.5x54cm 17x21in) Paris 1999

DMITRIJEW Wladimir Wladimirow. 1900-1948 [6]
$41 979 - €49 957 - £30 000 - FF327 696
Madonna with Moscow in Background Oil/canvas (192x268cm 75x105in) London 2000
$8 115 - €9 658 - £5 800 - FF63 354
Stage Design for Zori, Dawn Watercolour (38x48.5cm 14x19in) London 2000

DNOBIK Alexander 1890-1968 [1]
$6 320 - €5 814 - £3 912 - FF38 136
Gehöft im Schnee Oil/panel (75x104cm 29x40in) Wien 1999

DO AMARAL Tarsila 1886-1973 [4]
$65 000 - €56 532 - £39 188 - FF370 825
Paisagem Oil/panel (71.5x58.5cm 28x23in) New-York 1998

DO QUAN EM 1942 [3]
$5 086 - €5 621 - £3 527 - FF36 869
Woman Oil/canvas (80x64cm 31x25in) Singapore 2001

DOBBENBURGH van Aart 1899-1988 [26]
$49 - €54 - £33 - FF357
Kerkje in St Pancras Lithograph (33.7x46.3cm 13x18in) Haarlem 2000

DOBBERMANN Jakob 1682-1745 [1]
$30 166 - €25 666 - £18 000 - FF168 361
Figure of a nobleman, possibly William the Silent of Orange (1533-84) Sculpture (H23cm H9in) London 1998

DOBBIN John 1815-1888 [17]
$1 475 - €1 418 - £920 - FF9 302
View of Harlech Castle behind Fishing Boats and Cottages Watercolour/paper (44.5x64cm 17x25in) Stansted Mountfitchet, Essex 1999

DOBBIN Kate 1886-1948 [11]
$1 370 - €1 169 - £816 - FF7 666
Roses Watercolour/paper (31x40cm 12x16in) Dublin 1998

DÖBELI Othmar 1874-1922 [88]
$1 345 - €1 177 - £814 - FF7 723
Bauernhaus in Wikon mit Blick auf das Schloss Öl/Leinwand (60x75cm 23x29in) Zofingen 1998

DOBELL William 1899-1970 [172]
$27 940 - €32 952 - £19 706 - FF216 150
«Conversation Piece» Oil/wood (42.5x52cm 16x20in) Woollahra, Sydney 2001
$11 007 - €10 378 - £6 822 - FF68 074
Street in Royal Oak, London Oil/wood (31.5x39.5cm 12x15in) Melbourne 1999
$1 253 - €1 157 - £764 - FF7 588
Road through Hills, New Guinea Watercolour, gouache/paper (14x24cm 5x9in) Melbourne 1998

DOBIASCHOFSKY Franz Joseph 1818-1867 [6]
$5 944 - €5 733 - £3 706 - FF38 569
Kind am Spiegel Öl/Leinwand (63x79cm 24x31in) Ahlden 1999

DOBIE James 1849-c.1923 [12]
$150 - €170 - £102 - FF1 118
Dinner Scene, After Walter Sadler Etching (54x39cm 21x15in) St. Petersburg FL 2000

DOBLAS PINTO Manuel 1957 [107]
$182 - €210 - £126 - FF1 379
El espejo Oleo/lienzo (65x54cm 25x21in) Barcelona 2001

DOBRINSKY Isaac 1891-1973 [129]
$657 - €762 - £467 - FF5 000
Portrait de Paulette Huile/toile (38x55cm 14x21in) Paris 2001

DOBROWOLSKI Odo 1883-1917 [16]
$675 - €666 - £416 - FF4 370
Portrait d'une femme avec foulard de montagnarde Pastel/board (40x34.6cm 15x13in) Warszawa 1999

DOBROWSKY Josef 1889-1964 [350]
$10 188 - €8 724 - £5 964 - FF57 228
An der Donau Öl/Leinwand (60.2x69.2cm 23x27in) Wien 1998
$2 472 - €2 907 - £1 716 - FF19 068
Spannende Lektüre Tempera (30.5x26cm 12x10in) Wien 2000
$1 832 - €1 817 - £1 147 - FF11 917
Dorf auf der Anhöhe Charcoal/paper (43x31.7cm 16x12in) Wien 1999

DOBSON Cowan 1894-1980 [32]
$425 - €499 - £300 - FF3 272
The Farmer Oil/canvas (51x61cm 20x24in) London 2000

DOBSON Frank 1888-1963 [109]
$1 972 - €1 874 - £1 200 - FF12 293
Standing Female Nude Ink (51x36cm 20x14in) London 1999

DOBSON Henry John 1858-1928 [69]
$1 800 - €1 966 - £1 158 - FF12 894
The Workshop Oil/canvas (45x35cm 18x14in) Mystic CT 2000
$1 037 - €1 156 - £700 - FF7 585
Warm Hearth Oil/canvas (28.5x40cm 11x15in) Edinburgh 2000
$1 298 - €1 450 - £880 - FF9 514
Knit One Purl One Watercolour/paper (18x26cm 7x10in) Edinburgh 2000

DOBSON Henry Raeburn 1901-? [9]
🔄 $1 333 - €1 343 - £831 - FF8 812
   Interiör med mor og far, der betragter deres spaedbarn i vuggen Oil/canvas (70x91cm 27x35in) Köbenhavn 2000
🖊 $1 169 - €1 342 - £800 - FF8 801
   Cottage Interior with Figures Watercolour/paper (25x35cm 10x14in) Little-Lane, Ilkley 2000

DOBSON Robert XIX-XX [22]
🖊 $643 - €605 - £400 - FF3 971
   Horse and Cart in Country Lane with Figures in Conversation Watercolour/paper (41x59cm 16x23in) Leominster, Herefordshire 1999

DOBSON William 1611-1646 [4]
🔄 $9 806 - €10 836 - £6 800 - FF71 080
   Portrait of an Officer Oil/canvas (60.5x49.5cm 23x19in) London 2001

DOBSON William Charles Th. 1817-1898 [24]
🔄 $2 400 - €2 782 - £1 700 - FF18 252
   The Favorite Oil/board (47x54.5cm 18x21in) New-York 2000
🔄 $2 900 - €2 884 - £1 800 - FF18 920
   Little Fern Gatherer Oil/panel (30.5x25.5cm 12x10in) London 1999
🖊 $3 105 - €3 601 - £2 200 - FF23 618
   Gathering Flowers Watercolour (53.5x42cm 21x16in) London 2000

DOBUZHINSKII Mstislaw Valerianov. 1875-1957 [141]
🖊 $850 - €792 - £524 - FF5 196
   Costume Designs «Salome» Persian Dancers Watercolour/paper (29x21cm 11x8in) Chester NY 1999

DOCHARTY Alexander Brownlie 1862-c.1940 [50]
🔄 $1 933 - €1 816 - £1 200 - FF11 914
   A Highland Croft Oil/canvas (35.5x51cm 13x20in) London 1999
🔄 $1 155 - €1 115 - £730 - FF7 317
   Spate on the Docharty Oil/canvas (33x43cm 13x17in) Carlisle, Cumbria 1999

DOCKING Shay 1928-1998 [26]
🖊 $224 - €234 - £141 - FF1 535
   Hills Near Gundagai Pastel (37.5x46cm 14x18in) Sydney 2000

DODD Arthur Charles XIX-XX [21]
🔄 $2 020 - €2 186 - £1 400 - FF14 342
   Huntsman with hounds by Kennels Oil/canvas (53x38cm 21x15in) Aylsham, Norfolk 2001

DODD Daniel act.1752-1780 [7]
🔄 $16 582 - €14 355 - £10 000 - FF94 162
   The Ashby Family of Isleworth and Bromley Oil/canvas (97x116cm 38x45in) London 1998

DODD Francis H. 1874-1949 [79]
🖊 $418 - €393 - £260 - FF2 581
   Battersea Rise Watercolour/paper (23.5x30.5cm 9x12in) London 1999
📷 $142 - €152 - £95 - FF999
   Porta Della Carta, Palazzo Ducale, Venice Etching, aquatint (40x22cm 15x8in) Swindon, Wiltshire 2000

DODD Howell 1910 [3]
🔄 $2 100 - €2 339 - £1 373 - FF15 343
   Magazine cover: blonde and man with two policemen Oil/board (44x38cm 17x15in) New-York 2000
🔄 $2 800 - €2 681 - £1 729 - FF17 589
   Teenagers Warily smoking Marijuana Gouache/paper (44x34cm 17x13in) New-York 1999

DODD Hugh 1948 [6]
🖊 $2 057 - €2 128 - £1 300 - FF13 958
   Racing Caricatures Watercolour, gouache (33x25cm 12x9in) London 2000

DODD Lamar William 1909-1996 [1]
🔄 $8 500 - €9 000 - £5 626 - FF59 037
   Sand, Sea and Sky Tempera/canvas (51x71cm 20x27in) New-York 2000

DODD Louis 1943 [72]
🔄 $4 037 - €3 797 - £2 500 - FF24 905
   The U.S.S. «Columbus» and the Sloop of War «Vincennes», 1845-1848 Oil/panel (40x60cm 15x23in) London 1999
🔄 $3 068 - €2 886 - £1 900 - FF18 928
   San Giorgio Maggiori, Venice Oil/panel (32x41cm 12x16in) London 1999

DODD Robert 1748-1816 [40]
🔄 $39 037 - €43 596 - £25 000 - FF285 972
   The «Cirencester» in Full Sail off St.Helena Oil/canvas (84x144cm 33x56in) London 2000
🔄 $19 423 - €18 284 - £12 000 - FF119 934
   The Morning after the Battle of the Nile Oil/canvas (62x90cm 24x35in) London 1999
📷 $1 198 - €1 279 - £800 - FF8 387
   Victory of Trafalgar Aquatint (44.5x70.5cm 17x27in) London 2000

DODDS Peggy 1900-1987 [11]
🔄 $700 - €590 - £410 - FF3 873
   Ballerinas Oil/canvas (63x76cm 25x30in) Mystic CT 1998

DODEIGNE Eugène 1923 [125]
🖊 $2 325 - €2 496 - £1 555 - FF16 371
   Figure Bronze (H24cm H9in) Amsterdam 2000
🖊 $728 - €762 - £457 - FF5 000
   Nu Fusain/papier (50x73cm 19x28in) Lille 2000

DÖDERHULTAREN Axel Petersson 1868-1952 [173]
🖊 $1 656 - €1 880 - £1 132 - FF12 334
   Fingerkrok Sculpture, wood (27x42cm 10x16in) Uppsala 2000

DODGE John Wood 1807-1893 [9]
🔄 $2 600 - €2 243 - £1 574 - FF14 714
   Daniel Dodge, age 66, Facing Right in Black Jacket Miniature (5x4cm 2x1in) New-York 1999

DODGE William De Leftwich 1867-1935 [22]
🔄 $12 000 - €11 914 - £7 500 - FF78 151
   Woman by the Sea Oil/canvas (119.5x81cm 47x31in) New-York 1999

DODIYA Atul 1959 [8]
🔄 $6 000 - €6 956 - £4 250 - FF45 630
   Man Walking Mixed media/canvas (183x122cm 72x48in) New-York 2000
🔄 $4 750 - €5 402 - £3 318 - FF35 435
   Paper Tree Mixed media/paper (183.5x122cm 72x48in) New-York 2000

DODSON Tom [3]
🔄 $1 920 - €1 833 - £1 200 - FF12 024
   In a Manchester Pub Oil/board (31x23cm 12x9in) Cheshire 1999

DODWELL Edward 1767-1832 [10]
📷 $20 854 - €21 014 - £13 000 - FF137 846
   Views in Greece Aquatint (51x35.5cm 20x13in) London 2000

DOELEMAN Johan Hendrik 1848-1913 **[33]**
- $319 - €363 - £220 - FF2 381
  Keuterboerderij Oil/board (32x45cm 12x17in)
  Dordrecht 2000

DOEPLER Karl Emil I 1824-1905 **[4]**
- $13 526 - €12 706 - £8 153 - FF83 344
  Italian Renaissance Garden Party Oil/canvas
  (115.5x84cm 45x33in) Amsterdam 1999

DOEPLER Karl Emil II 1855-1922 **[6]**
- $6 756 - €6 353 - £4 183 - FF41 672
  La soirée Oil/panel (67x54cm 26x21in) Amsterdam
  1999

DOERR Carl 1777-1842 **[11]**
- $1 380 - €1 278 - £845 - FF8 384
  Der Wartberg bey Heilbronn Aquatinta (26x37.5cm
  10x14in) Heilbronn 1999

DOES van der Jacob 1623-1673 **[9]**
- $5 842 - €5 450 - £3 525 - FF35 752
  Ziegen und Schafe in der römischen Campagna
  Oil/panel (26x28.5cm 10x11in) Wien 1999

DOES van der Simon 1653-c.1717 **[24]**
- $6 306 - €6 672 - £4 000 - FF43 766
  The Flight into Egypt Oil/canvas/panel (41.5x52cm
  16x20in) London 2000
- $772 - €920 - £550 - FF6 037
  **Hirten mit Ziegen und Schafen auf einer
  Landstrasse** Ink (18.3x16cm 7x6in) Köln 2000

DOES van der Willem 1889-1966 **[43]**
- $462 - €499 - £316 - FF3 274
  **An Indonesian Landscape with a Vulcano in the
  Distance** Oil/board (40x60cm 15x23in) Amsterdam
  2001

DOESER Jacobus Johannes 1884-1970 **[95]**
- $336 - €363 - £229 - FF2 381
  Sunset near Toulson Oil/canvas (71x117cm
  27x46in) Amsterdam 2001

DOETECHUM van Joannes I XVI-XVII **[1]**
- $2 897 - €2 812 - £1 804 - FF18 446
  **Landschaft mit der Taufe Christi, after Lucas
  Gassel** Etching (24.4x23.7cm 9x9in) Berlin 1999

DOETECHUM van Lucas A. XVI **[1]**
- $2 897 - €2 812 - £1 804 - FF18 446
  **Landschaft mit der Taufe Christi, after Lucas
  Gassel** Etching (24.4x23.7cm 9x9in) Berlin 1999

DOEVE Eppo 1907-1982 **[31]**
- $179 - €204 - £125 - FF1 339
  «Tentoonstelling motoren Bromfield Rijwielen»
  Poster (79x113cm 31x44in) Hoorn 2001

DOGARTH Erich Josef 1927 **[37]**
- $1 833 - €2 180 - £1 308 - FF14 301
  Blumenstück mit Schmetterling Oil/panel
  (52x34cm 20x13in) Wien 2000
- $1 830 - €1 817 - £1 142 - FF11 917
  Blumenstück Oil/panel (34.5x27cm 13x10in) Wien
  1999

DOGARTH Oskar Robert 1898-1961 **[21]**
- $2 029 - €2 250 - £1 408 - FF14 757
  Blumenstilleben mit Rosen, Tulpen Oil/panel
  (60x50cm 23x19in) Köln 2001
- $835 - €767 - £513 - FF5 030
  Blumenstilleben Öl/Leinwand (41x31cm 16x12in)
  Stuttgart 1999

DOGGETT Ruth 1881-1974 **[8]**
- $1 400 - €1 637 - £1 000 - FF10 738
  Wiltshire Downs Oil/canvas (39.5x62.5cm 15x24in)
  London 2001

DOHANOS Stevan 1907-1994 **[70]**
- $3 000 - €3 497 - £2 077 - FF22 939
  **Doctor and boy Examine Glow-in-the-Dark
  Skeleton Model** Oil/canvas (76x71cm 30x28in) New-
  York 2000
- $1 400 - €1 666 - £968 - FF10 925
  Grey Clapboard Buildings Watercolour/paper
  (52x95cm 20x37in) Plainville CT 2000
- $425 - €489 - £293 - FF3 209
  «Venice Gondolas, along the Grand Canal»
  Linocut (25x20cm 10x8in) Cleveland OH 2000

DOHLMANN Augusta 1847-1914 **[51]**
- $786 - €671 - £470 - FF4 403
  En potte med vintergaekker Oil/canvas (32x26cm
  12x10in) Viby J, Århus 1998

DOHMEN Léo 1929-1999 **[28]**
- $1 420 - €1 524 - £950 - FF10 000
  La passion de Copernic Photo (45x34cm 17x13in)
  Paris 2000

DOIG Peter 1959 **[17]**
- $154 631 - €150 498 - £95 000 - FF987 202
  Lunker Oil/canvas (200x266cm 78x104in) London
  1999
- $25 983 - €28 112 - £18 000 - FF184 401
  «Pinto» Oil/canvas (49.5x69cm 19x27in) London 2001
- $3 500 - €3 939 - £2 459 - FF26 128
  «Bean Farmer» Gouache/paper (30x21cm 11x8in)
  New-York 2001

DOIG Stephen 1964 **[17]**
- $70 000 - €78 405 - £48 636 - FF514 304
  «Pink Briey» Oil/canvas (183x213cm 72x83in) New-
  York 2001

DOIGNEAU Édouard 1865-1954 **[122]**
- $6 811 - €6 418 - £4 125 - FF42 400
  Chasse à courre Huile/toile (162x110cm 63x43in)
  Brest 1999
- $1 368 - €1 189 - £827 - FF7 800
  Deux éléphants et leur cornac Huile/toile
  (49x65cm 19x25in) Paris 1999
- $2 103 - €2 287 - £1 386 - FF15 000
  A la fontaine Huile/panneau (41x33cm 16x12in) Paris
  2000
- $805 - €915 - £555 - FF6 000
  Notre Dame d'Afrique à Alger Gouache (32x43cm
  12x16in) Paris 2000

DOISNEAU Robert 1912-1994 **[383]**
- $1 454 - €1 411 - £905 - FF9 256
  Concert Mayol Vintage gelatin silver print
  (24.5x18.1cm 9x7in) Berlin 1999

DOKOUPIL Jiri Georg 1954 **[149]**
- $7 620 - €8 181 - £5 100 - FF53 662
  Ohne Titel Acryl/Leinwand (220x160cm 86x62in)
  Köln 2000
- $1 890 - €2 102 - £1 260 - FF13 790
  Sin título Acrílico/lienzo (50x50cm 19x19in) Madrid
  2000
- $1 047 - €1 125 - £701 - FF7 378
  U.H.U Sculpture (H20cm H1in) Köln 2000
- $953 - €1 125 - £672 - FF7 378
  Ohne Titel Oil chalks/paper (66x51cm 25x20in) Köln
  2001
- $765 - €900 - £530 - FF5 902
  Ohne Titel Farbserigraphie (69.5x69.5cm 27x27in)
  Stuttgart 2000

DOLA Georges 1872-1950 **[44]**
- $252 - €290 - £172 - FF1 900
  «**Dans l'engrenage**» Gouache/papier (70x52cm 27x20in) Paris 2000
- $194 - €227 - £133 - FF1 488
  «**La Comtesse Maritza, Opérette en 3 actes**» Poster (120x80cm 47x31in) Hoorn 2000

DOLAN Patrick 1926-1980 **[8]**
- $873 - €940 - £595 - FF6 163
  Ex Machina Acrylic (91x81cm 35x31in) Dublin 2001

DOLARD Camille 1810-1884 **[7]**
- $8 125 - €7 622 - £5 020 - FF50 000
  Le chat dans l'office Huile/toile (82x92.5cm 32x36in) Soissons 1999

DOLCI Carlo 1616-1686 **[2]**
- $2 422 - €2 076 - £1 421 - FF13 619
  Árkeängeln Gabriel Oil/canvas (73x58cm 28x22in) Stockholm 1998
- $2 581 - €2 866 - £1 800 - FF18 800
  Rescuing a Mother and her Child Oil/canvas (23.5x29cm 9x11in) London 2001

DOLE William 1917-1983 **[17]**
- $8 000 - €9 098 - £5 589 - FF59 680
  Grievance Machinery Mixed media (47.5x63cm 18x24in) Beverly-Hills CA 2000
- $3 000 - €3 412 - £2 096 - FF22 380
  Signatory Mixed media (30.5x45.5cm 12x17in) Beverly-Hills CA 2000
- $2 000 - €1 678 - £1 173 - FF11 007
  Ultima Thule Collage/paper (36x51cm 14x20in) New-York 1998

DOLENDO Bartholomeus Willemz c.1571-? **[2]**
- $2 522 - €2 132 - £1 500 - FF13 985
  A Man with a Flute Engraving (18.5x14cm 7x5in) London 1998

DOLENDO Zacharias ?-c.1604 **[8]**
- $295 - €281 - £183 - FF1 844
  Das letzte Abendmahl/Die Gefangennahmr Christi Kupferstich (15.2x10.5cm 5x4in) Berlin 1999

DOLEZEL Jenny 1964 **[2]**
- $2 122 - €2 418 - £1 466 - FF15 858
  «**Picture of Mr Punch Trying to Woo Miss Judy**» Pastel/paper (56.5x75cm 22x29in) Auckland 1998

DOLICE Leon Louis 1892-1960 **[68]**
- $550 - €594 - £380 - FF3 897
  New York Skyline Pastel/paper (28x46cm 11x18in) Cincinnati OH 2001
- $270 - €252 - £166 - FF1 653
  From the Corner of Madison and 20th Street NYC Etching (44x30cm 17x12in) Cleveland OH 1999

DOLL Anton 1826-1887 **[187]**
- $7 753 - €7 669 - £4 834 - FF50 308
  Winterfreuden Öl/Leinwand (75.5x112cm 29x44in) Ahlden 1999
- $6 502 - €5 629 - £3 921 - FF36 924
  Flusslandschaft Oil/panel (28x40cm 11x15in) München 1998
- $1 287 - €1 278 - £804 - FF8 384
  Dorfkirche am Fluss Watercolour (15.5x20cm 6x7in) München 1999

DOLLA Noël 1945 **[19]**
- $2 556 - €2 744 - £1 710 - FF18 000
  Croix Technique mixte (191x193cm 75x75in) Paris 2000
- $1 408 - €1 524 - £964 - FF10 000
  Sans titre Huile/panneau (70x50cm 27x19in) Paris 2001

DOLLIAN Guy 1887-? **[10]**
- $294 - €335 - £205 - FF2 200
  «**Moulin de la Galette, Montmartre, bal de la Sainte Catherine**» Affiche (59.5x39cm 23x15in) Paris 2001

DOLLMAN John Charles 1851-1934 **[40]**
- $31 343 - €36 438 - £22 000 - FF239 016
  Mowgli, Made Leader of the Bandar-log Oil/canvas (137x183cm 53x72in) London 2001
- $17 958 - €21 358 - £12 800 - FF140 098
  The London to York Coach Outside the Black Swan Oil/canvas (71x101.5cm 27x39in) London 2000
- $1 424 - €1 656 - £1 000 - FF10 864
  Tigers Watercolour/paper (25.5x44.5cm 10x17in) Billingshurst, West-Sussex 2001

DOLLOND William Anstey 1858-1929 **[43]**
- $6 468 - €6 085 - £4 000 - FF39 914
  Waiting/At the Fountain Watercolour/paper (45x45cm 18x18in) Little-Lane, Ilkley 1999

DOLPH John Henry 1835-1903 **[46]**
- $5 500 - €4 640 - £3 226 - FF30 437
  Feeding the Puppies and Kittens Oil/canvas (35.5x51.5cm 13x20in) New-York 1998
- $2 500 - €2 485 - £1 512 - FF16 303
  Study of a Setter Oil/canvas (25x20cm 10x8in) New-York 2000

DOLPHIJN Victor, Vic 1909-1993 **[74]**
- $399 - €446 - £261 - FF2 926
  Nature morte aux légumes et à la cruche de vin Huile/toile (52x74cm 20x29in) Antwerpen 2000
- $399 - €446 - £261 - FF2 926
  Fermes dans un paysage Huile/carton (29x35cm 11x13in) Antwerpen 2000

DOLS Jean 1909-1994 **[85]**
- $175 - €173 - £109 - FF1 138
  L'arbre de la science du bien et du mal Eau-forte (50x40cm 19x15in) Liège 1999

DOM Paul 1885-1978 **[28]**
- $4 541 - €3 853 - £2 739 - FF25 274
  Bruggetje over stadsgracht Oil/canvas (59x59cm 23x23in) Den Haag 1998
- $1 050 - €1 134 - £718 - FF7 441
  «**Rue de Mirbel, Paris**» Black chalk (46x60.5cm 18x23in) Amsterdam 2001

DOM ROBERT 1907-1997 **[9]**
- $10 582 - €11 281 - £6 711 - FF74 000
  Le chat noir Tapisserie (245x128cm 96x50in) Paris 2000

DOMBROWSKI von Carl Ritter 1872-1951 **[54]**
- $2 900 - €2 812 - £1 837 - FF18 446
  Hirsch mit Rudel auf einer Waldlichtung Öl/Leinwand (142x160cm 55x62in) München 1999
- $745 - €869 - £523 - FF5 701
  Rehbock im Unterholz Öl/Karton (51x70cm 20x27in) Kempten 2000

DOMELA César 1900-1992 **[114]**
- $5 980 - €5 899 - £3 682 - FF38 695
  Untitled Oil/board (46x65cm 18x25in) Amsterdam 1999

$140 030 - €149 302 - **£95 000** - FF979 355
De Stijl, Composition Oil/canvas (36.5x30.5cm
14x12in) London 2001

$13 437 - €12 348 - **£8 253** - FF81 000
Untitled, #48 Relief (86x110cm 33x43in) Paris 1999

$2 210 - €2 187 - **£1 378** - FF14 347
Sans titre Sculpture (H53cm H20in) Luzern 1999

$3 906 - €4 538 - **£2 745** - FF29 766
Untitled Gouache (77.5x62cm 30x24in) Amsterdam
2001

$271 - €291 - **£185** - FF1 906
Konstruktive Studien Serigraph (36x27cm 14x10in)
Wien 2001

DOMENCHIN DE CHAVANNES Pierre Salomon
1673-1744 [9]

$10 679 - €9 909 - **£6 409** - FF65 000
**Repos de bergers dans un paysage de rivière
et de ruines romaines** Huile/toile (51x65cm
20x25in) Paris 1999

DOMENGE Y ANTIGA Melchor 1871-1939 [7]

$549 - €541 - **£351** - FF3 546
La Siega Oleo/lienzo (23x44cm 9x17in) Madrid 1999

DOMENICI Carlo 1898-1981 [222]

$1 400 - €1 814 - **£1 050** - FF11 900
Paesaggio Olio/faesite (45x75cm 17x29in) Prato 2001

$1 200 - €1 244 - **£720** - FF8 160
Zingari Olio/faesite (24.5x28.5cm 9x11in) Prato 2000

DOMENJOZ Raoul 1896-1978 [61]

$604 - €560 - **£370** - FF3 673
**Hafenarbeiter beim Überholen eines
Segelschiffes** Öl/Leinwand (38x46cm 14x18in) Bern
1999

$250 - €297 - **£178** - FF1 950
Plage de Safi n.10 à Mogador Maroc Huile/carton
(17x46cm 6x18in) Genève 2000

DOMERGUE Jean-Gabriel 1889-1962 [1607]

$25 404 - €23 630 - **£15 732** - FF155 000
French Cancan Huile/toile (140x140cm 55x55in)
Biarritz 2001

$5 382 - €5 946 - **£3 732** - FF39 000
La petite Lili Huile/isorel (55x46cm 21x18in) Lille
2001

$4 199 - €3 537 - **£2 480** - FF23 200
Le regard bleu Huile/toile (46x30cm 18x11in) Lille
1998

$1 353 - €1 143 - **£804** - FF7 500
Tenue de soirée dans l'escalier Aquarelle
(43x62cm 16x24in) Senlis 1998

$442 - €488 - **£299** - FF3 200
«Bagheera» Affiche couleur (80x120cm 31x47in)
Nice 2000

DOMICENT Martin 1823-1898 [7]

$2 454 - €2 287 - **£1 513** - FF15 000
Chasseur et ses chiens Huile/panneau
(32.5x24.5cm 12x9in) Lille 1999

DOMINGO (D. Alvarez Gómez) 1942 [40]

$224 - €192 - **£134** - FF1 260
Figura femenina de espaldas Pastel (61x50cm
24x19in) Barcelona 1999

DOMINGO FALLOLA Roberto 1883-1956 [228]

$2 850 - €2 853 - **£1 757** - FF18 715
Sin brillo de caireles Oleo/lienzo (50x65cm
19x25in) Madrid 2000

$728 - €841 - **£504** - FF5 516
Entrando al ruedo Gouache/papier (20x25cm 7x9in)
Madrid 2000

DOMINGO Y MARQUES Francisco 1842-1920 [159]

$197 600 - €228 247 - **£136 800** - FF1 497 200
Paisaje Oleo/lienzo (300x232cm 118x91in) Madrid
2000

$14 000 - €15 427 - **£9 311** - FF101 192
Paisaje con ovejas y personajes Oleo/tabla
(45x55cm 17x21in) Buenos-Aires 2000

$3 850 - €4 205 - **£2 450** - FF27 580
Reunión de caballeros Oleo/tabla (9.5x10cm 3x3in)
Madrid 2000

$432 - €481 - **£288** - FF3 152
Personajes Acuarela, gouache (13x24cm 5x9in)
Madrid 2000

DOMINGOS ALVAREZ José 1906-1942 [1]

$4 218 - €3 678 - **£2 516** - FF24 124
Paisagem com montanhas Oleo (14.5x18.5cm
5x7in) Lisboa 1998

DOMINGUE Maurice 1918 [97]

$275 - €277 - **£172** - FF1 819
St.Antoine, Richelieu Watercolour/paper (37.5x56cm
14x22in) Toronto 2000

DOMINGUEZ BÉCQUER Joaquín 1817-1879 [8]

$18 200 - €19 521 - **£12 025** - FF128 050
Maja y torero Oleo/lienzo (62x41.5cm 24x16in)
Madrid 2000

DOMINGUEZ BÉCQUER Valeriano 1834-1870 [13]

$8 750 - €7 527 - **£5 125** - FF49 375
La heroína o Alegoría de la Libertad Oleo/lienzo
(101x75cm 39x29in) Madrid 1998

$780 - €721 - **£480** - FF4 728
Escena popular, Mujeres junto a un pozo
Acuarela/papel (30x27.5cm 11x10in) Madrid 1999

DOMINGUEZ Nelson 1947 [5]

$8 000 - €6 907 - **£4 880** - FF45 310
La Lluvia Blanca Oil/canvas (100x100cm 39x39in)
Miami FL 1999

DOMINGUEZ Oscar 1906-1957 [531]

$61 320 - €60 980 - **£38 040** - FF400 000
Crucifixion Huile/panneau (120x220cm 47x86in) Paris
1999

$24 358 - €28 965 - **£17 366** - FF190 000
Nature morte Huile/toile (45x54cm 17x21in) Calais
2000

$18 023 - €15 550 - **£10 832** - FF102 000
«Le Grisou I» Technique mixte (20x21cm 7x8in) Paris
1998

$17 910 - €15 245 - **£10 660** - FF100 000
Personnage au coq Fer (H190cm H74in) L'Isle-
Adam 1998

$10 464 - €12 196 - **£7 336** - FF80 000
Violon Bronze (H54cm H21in) Neuilly-sur-Seine 2000

$4 192 - €3 583 - **£2 516** - FF23 500
Composition surréaliste Encre (38x46cm 14x18in)
Paris 1998

$544 - €481 - **£336** - FF3 152
Bodegón surrealista Grabado (20.5x17cm 8x6in)
Madrid 1999

DOMINGUEZ Y SANCHEZ Manuel 1839-1906 [9]

$2 520 - €2 403 - **£1 520** - FF15 760
Romería Oleo/lienzo (38x52cm 14x20in) Madrid 1999

DOMINICIS de Achille 1851-1917 [18]

$610 - €694 - **£425** - FF4 552
Repos dans un jardin à Rome Aquarelle/papier
(50x32cm 19x12in) Antwerpen 2000

DOMINICIS de Gino 1947-1998 [33]

- **$99 930** - €92 743 - **£60 000** - FF608 352
  L'Astronave Mixed media/board (176.5x280.5cm 69x110in) London 1999
- **$22 500** - €23 325 - **£13 500** - FF153 000
  Senza titolo Tecnica mista (50x42cm 19x16in) Prato 1999
- **$10 000** - €10 367 - **£6 000** - FF68 000
  Senza titolo Idropittura (27x22cm 10x8in) Prato 2000
- **$3 250** - €3 369 - **£1 950** - FF22 100
  Senza titolo Pastelli/cartone (48x48cm 18x18in) Roma 1999

DOMINIK Tadeusz 1928 [19]

- **$1 498** - €1 658 - **£1 041** - FF10 873
  Arbres II Huile/toile (73.5x92cm 28x36in) Warszawa 2001

DOMINIQUE John August 1893-1994 [22]

- **$2 800** - €3 291 - **£1 941** - FF21 586
  A Bright Day Oil/canvas (51x61cm 20x24in) Beverly-Hills CA 2000

DOMINIQUE S. XX [4]

- **$900** - €1 044 - **£640** - FF6 848
  Street Scene with a View of Sacre Coeur, Paris Oil/canvas (33x46cm 12x18in) Washington 2000

DOMMERSEN William Raymond 1850-1927 [239]

- **$3 270** - €2 908 - **£2 000** - FF19 074
  «Iriza, Gulf of Taranto, Italy» Oil/canvas (51.5x76cm 20x29in) London 1999
- **$2 196** - €2 345 - **£1 500** - FF15 379
  Zerckzee on the Scheldt, Holland Oil/canvas (29x39cm 11x15in) Billingshurst, West-Sussex 2001

DOMMERSHUIJZEN Cornelis Christaan 1842-1928 [96]

- **$7 966** - €9 244 - **£5 500** - FF60 637
  Blustery Day on the Amstel Oil/canvas (51x76.5cm 20x30in) London 2000
- **$4 559** - €5 300 - **£3 200** - FF34 766
  Dutch Town Scene Oil/canvas (28x21.5cm 11x8in) London 2001
- **$949** - €822 - **£582** - FF5 395
  Views of a Canal in Holland Watercolour/paper (53.5x76cm 21x29in) New-York 1999

DOMMERSHUIJZEN Pieter Cornelis 1834-1908 [198]

- **$28 000** - €24 900 - **£17 124** - FF163 332
  St Michael's Mount Oil/canvas (105.5x151cm 41x59in) New-York 1999
- **$6 481** - €6 807 - **£4 101** - FF44 649
  A Summer Landscape with Shipping on a River Oil/canvas (50x80cm 19x31in) Amsterdam 2000
- **$8 103** - €7 551 - **£5 000** - FF49 534
  On the Spaarne, Haarlem Oil/panel (30.5x40.5cm 12x15in) London 1999

DOMOTO Insho 1891-1975 [8]

- **$6 860** - €6 691 - **£4 200** - FF43 890
  Silent Morning Drawing (125x30cm 49x11in) Tokyo 1999

DOMSAITIS Pranas 1880-1965 [37]

- **$1 970** - €1 857 - **£1 193** - FF12 180
  Karoo at Dawn Oil/board (52.5x62.5cm 20x24in) Cape Town 1999
- **$705** - €786 - **£460** - FF5 159
  Figures Outside a Hut Oil/board (40.5x40.5cm 15x15in) Johannesburg 2000

DON Jean 1900-1985 [18]

- **$294** - €335 - **£205** - FF2 200
  «Contrexeville source Pavillon, pour le régime» Affiche (100x64cm 39x25in) Paris 2001

DONADONI Stefano 1844-1911 [32]

- **$3 280** - €4 250 - **£2 460** - FF27 880
  L'Arco di Tito Olio/tela (76x62cm 29x24in) Roma 2001
- **$1 600** - €2 073 - **£1 200** - FF13 600
  Al pozzo Olio/tela (30.5x23.5cm 12x9in) Milano 2001
- **$1 255** - €1.177 - **£775** - FF7 722
  Vy från Rom, Forum Romanum Akvarell/papper (50x35cm 19x13in) Helsinki 1999

DONALD Tom 1856-1883 [2]

- **$4 160** - €3 972 - **£2 600** - FF26 053
  The Riverside Path Oil/canvas (61x92cm 24x36in) London 1999

DONALDSON Andrew Benjamin 1840-1919 [18]

- **$293** - €267 - **£180** - FF1 751
  Fisherwomen Hauling in a Boat Watercolour (34.5x75cm 13x29in) Billingshurst, West-Sussex 1998

DONALDSON David Abercrombie 1916-1996 [20]

- **$15 021** - €13 438 - **£9 000** - FF88 148
  «Marysia at her Dressing Table» Oil/canvas (116x106.5cm 45x41in) Perthshire 1998
- **$3 588** - €4 036 - **£2 500** - FF26 473
  «Exodus I» Oil/canvas (44x44cm 17x17in) Edinburgh 2001
- **$6 412** - €6 057 - **£4 000** - FF39 733
  Pots and Lamp Oil/canvas (71x19.5cm 27x7in) Perthshire 1998
- **$1 299** - €1 447 - **£850** - FF9 494
  The Ark Watercolour (34x31cm 13x12in) Edinburgh 2000

DONALDSON Kim 1952 [28]

- **$489** - €546 - **£319** - FF3 583
  Kudus at the Watering Hole Pastel/paper (73x54cm 28x21in) Johannesburg 2000

DONAS Marthe Tour-Donas 1885-1967 [35]

- **$3 564** - €2 975 - **£2 088** - FF19 512
  Doubles (cycliste) Oil/canvas (50x40cm 19x15in) Lokeren 1998

DONAT Frederick Reginald 1830-1907 [24]

- **$730** - €869 - **£520** - FF5 701
  Eine indiskrete Frage, am Hafen sitzender Fischer Oil/panel (53x42cm 20x16in) Hildrizhausen 2000
- **$2 250** - €2 204 - **£1 450** - FF14 458
  A Fisherman and his Wife Oil/panel (47x25cm 18x9in) New-York 1999

DONAT M. XIX [12]

- **$571** - €595 - **£360** - FF3 902
  Moulin Saint-Pierre à Woluwé Saint Pierre Huile/toile (45x30cm 17x11in) Antwerpen 2000

DONATI Enrico 1909 [42]

- **$16 000** - €15 413 - **£9 886** - FF101 105
  Metamorphosis Oil/canvas (101x127cm 40x50in) Chicago IL 1999
- **$6 600** - €6 555 - **£4 128** - FF43 000
  Composition abstraite Acrylique/papier (64x76.5cm 25x30in) Paris 1999
- **$2 500** - €2 098 - **£1 466** - FF13 759
  Surrealist Composition Mixed media/board (35.5x28cm 13x11in) New-York 1998

D

D

DONCK Gerrit c.1610-c.1640 **[7]**
$19 494 - €31 323 - **£19 000** - FF205 464
Lady, Wearing a Red Satin Dress, Embroidered Bodice and White Ruff Oil/panel (47.5x35.5cm 18x13in) London 2000
$5 142 - €4 442 - **£3 100** - FF29 135
A Poultry seller on a Quay Oil/panel (43.3x32.3cm 17x12in) Amsterdam 1998

DONCKER Herman Mijnerts c.1620-c.1656 **[9]**
$5 640 - €5 299 - **£3 400** - FF34 759
Portrait of a West Frisian Couple with their two Children Oil/panel (67x56.5cm 26x22in) London 1998

DONCRE Guillaume Dominique 1743-1820 **[11]**
$3 500 - €3 920 - **£2 431** - FF25 715
«Messire Albert de Trazgnies, vicomte Darmuiden 1695» Oil/canvas (80x65cm 31x25in) New-York 2001
$4 539 - €4 573 - **£2 829** - FF30 000
Nature morte au vase de fleurs, dessin et montre gousset Huile/toile (39.5x31cm 15x12in) Paris 2000

DONDUCCI IL MASTELLETTA Giovanni Andrea 1575-1655 **[13]**
$68 737 - €73 784 - **£46 000** - FF483 993
The Baptism of Christ Oil/canvas (32.5x39cm 12x15in) London 1998
$2 820 - €2 436 - **£1 410** - FF15 980
La predica di San Giovanni Battista Matita (34x22.5cm 13x8in) Milano 1999

DONE Ken 1940 **[30]**
$148 - €128 - **£88** - FF841
Beach Silkscreen (60x62cm 23x24in) Sydney 1998

DONEAUD Jean Eugène 1834-? **[2]**
$9 214 - €10 748 - **£6 584** - FF70 000
Dans l'atelier du peintre Huile/toile (70x94cm 27x37in) Versailles 2000

DONELSON Earl Tomlinson 1908 **[3]**
$5 500 - €6 255 - **£3 814** - FF41 031
Through the Trees Oil/canvas (76x81cm 30x32in) Chicago IL 2000

DONEUX Alexandre XIX **[2]**
$12 253 - €11 891 - **£7 628** - FF78 000
Vues de Spa, groupe d'enfants et scène de rue Huile/panneau (34x44cm 13x17in) Montfort L'Amaury 1999

DONG BANGDA 1699-1769 **[9]**
$51 360 - €56 083 - **£33 040** - FF367 880
Miniatre Landscapes after Yan and Ming Masters Ink/paper (10.5x14cm 4x5in) Hong-Kong 1999

DONG GAO 1740-1818 **[1]**
$115 560 - €126 187 - **£74 340** - FF827 730
«Places of Scenic Beauty in Jiangdong, East of the Yangzi River» Ink (28x39.5cm 11x15in) Hong-Kong 2000

DONG JI XIV **[2]**
$37 087 - €34 976 - **£23 000** - FF229 425
Poetry in Cao Shu Ink (28x53.5cm 11x21in) Hong-Kong 2000

DONG QICHANG 1555-1636 **[45]**
$7 051 - €8 010 - **£4 950** - FF52 541
Imperial Edict in standard Script Calligraphy Ink/paper (25.5x274cm 10x107in) Hong-Kong 2001

DONG SHOUPING 1904 **[4]**
$1 000 - €1 073 - **£669** - FF7 041
Bamboo Ink/paper (137x70cm 53x27in) San-Francisco CA 2000

DONGEN van Dyonis 1748-1819 **[7]**
$5 861 - €4 990 - **£3 500** - FF32 732
Pastoral Landscape with Shepherdesses Bathing Oil/panel (21.5x30cm 8x11in) London 1998
$4 026 - €4 573 - **£2 826** - FF30 000
Berger ramenant son troupeau/Le chemin menant à la ferme Gouache (57.5x76cm 22x29in) Paris 2001

DONGEN van Kees 1877-1968 **[1062]**
$1 474 000 - €1 571 597 - **£1 000 000** - FF10 309 000
Femme aux bas noirs Oil/canvas (129.5x195.5cm 50x76in) London 2001
$180 000 - €208 852 - **£124 272** - FF1 369 980
Portrait de femme Oil/canvas (61x47cm 24x18in) New-York 2000
$47 500 - €40 545 - **£28 405** - FF265 957
Tulips Oil/canvas (40.5x32.5cm 15x12in) New-York 1998
$20 000 - €21 599 - **£13 822** - FF141 678
Nu Bronze (H25cm H9in) New-York 2001
$10 664 - €9 766 - **£6 500** - FF64 061
Nu couché Charcoal (27.5x45.5cm 10x17in) London 1999
$534 - €453 - **£322** - FF2 973
Dame met ring Lithograph (25x18cm 9x7in) Den Haag 1998

DONGHI Antonio 1897-1963 **[45]**
$20 000 - €20 733 - **£12 000** - FF136 000
Gianicolo visto dal Lungotevere dei Fiorentini Olio/tela (45x45cm 17x17in) Roma 2000
$2 400 - €2 073 - **£1 200** - FF13 600
Ritratto del pittore Dario Galeazzi Sanguina (26.5x18.5cm 10x7in) Prato 1999

DONIZETTI Mario 1932 **[3]**
$1 360 - €1 762 - **£1 020** - FF11 560
Personaggio Tempera (25x18cm 9x7in) Milano 2001

DONLEAVY James Patrick 1926 **[17]**
$551 - €635 - **£376** - FF4 164
Woman in Hat Watercolour (24x29cm 9x11in) Dublin 2000

DONNAY Auguste 1862-1921 **[94]**
$4 590 - €4 462 - **£2 808** - FF29 268
Les bouleaux Huile/carton (48x73cm 18x28in) Liège 1999
$1 465 - €1 239 - **£875** - FF8 125
Paysage enneigé Huile/panneau (23x37.5cm 9x14in) Liège 1998
$858 - €942 - **£554** - FF6 178
Salon des Beaux-Arts de Liège: projet d'affiche Aquarelle/papier (28.5x20.5cm 11x8in) Liège 2000
$112 - €124 - **£78** - FF813
Promenade équestre Eau-forte (27x19cm 10x7in) Liège 2001

DONNAY Jean 1897-1992 **[108]**
$639 - €744 - **£450** - FF4 878
L'enterrement Huile/panneau (64.5x80cm 25x31in) Liège 2001
$266 - €248 - **£164** - FF1 626
Nu III Fusain (42x62cm 16x24in) Bruxelles 1999
$82 - €89 - **£54** - FF585
Usines et Terril Eau-forte (49x39.5cm 19x15in) Liège 2000

DONNER Carl XX **[35]**
🖌 **$279 - €314 - £190** - FF2 057
Woodcock in a Winter Landscape
Watercolour/paper (35x22cm 14x9in) Aylsham, Norfolk
2000

DONNER Iwar 1884-1964 **[4]**
📼 **$1 000** - €962 - **£617** - FF6 308
«Polisens Villebrad» Poster (100x70cm 39x27in)
New-York 1994

DONNINI Emilio 1809-1886 **[5]**
👝 **$2 250** - €2 332 - **£1 350** - FF15 300
Paesaggio costiero con barche e pescatori
Olio/tela (32x48cm 12x18in) Roma 1999

DONNINI Girolamo 1681-1743 **[2]**
👝 **$38 500** - €39 911 - **£23 100** - FF261 800
Achille affidato a Chirone Olio/tela (186x360cm
73x141in) Milano 2001

DONNY Désiré 1798-1861 **[22]**
👝 **$1 383** - €1 534 - **£960** - FF10 061
**Trocken aufliegende Schiffe an der belgischen
Küste** Öl/Leinwand (24.5x34cm 9x13in) Köln 2001

DONO Heri 1960 **[2]**
👝 **$5 739** - €6 517 - **£3 928** - FF42 746
Barong Gunda Oil/canvas (100x100cm 39x39in)
Singapore 2000

DONOHO Gaines Ruger 1857-1916 **[4]**
👝 **$16 000** - €16 409 - **£10 001** - FF107 633
Bords de forêt Oil/canvas (68x53cm 27x21in) New-
Orleans LA 2000

DONZEL Charles 1824-1889 **[31]**
👝 **$20 000** - €22 716 - **£14 034** - FF149 008
Gentleman and a Lady on Horseback Oil/canvas
(73x58.5cm 28x23in) New-York 2001
$496 - €579 - **£348** - FF3 800
Paysage au château Huile/panneau (34x17cm
13x6in) Paris 2000

DONZELLI Bruno 1941 **[95]**
👝 **$550** - €570 - **£330** - FF3 740
Atelier de Chirico Acrilico/tela (70x70cm 27x27in)
Prato 2000

DOOLITTLE Amos 1754-1832 **[4]**
📼 **$2 000** - €2 332 - **£1 404** - FF15 300
**The Prodigal Son in Misery/The Prodigal Son
Returned to his Father** Engraving (34x25cm
13x10in) Portsmouth NH 2000

DOOLITTLE James N. 1886-1954 **[7]**
📷 **$4 000** - €3 343 - **£2 368** - FF21 930
Marlene Dietrich Silver print (40x32cm 16x12in)
New-York 1998

DOOMER Lambert c.1623-1700 **[19]**
👝 **$13 020** - €14 521 - **£8 496** - FF95 251
**Travellers in a Horse-Drawn Cart on a Path, a
Village beyond** Oil/panel (47x63.5cm 18x25in)
Amsterdam 2000
🖌 **$10 764** - €11 891 - **£7 464** - FF78 000
**Le Burg Katz et Saint Goarhausen sur la rive
droite du Rhin** Aquarelle (20x36cm 7x14in) Paris
2001

DOOMS Vic 1912-1994 **[23]**
👝 **$2 496** - €2 975 - **£1 788** - FF19 512
Vue sur l'église de Deurle Huile/toile (41x49cm
16x19in) Antwerpen 2000
👝 **$1 306** - €1 091 - **£765** - FF7 154
Landschap Oil/panel (15x20cm 5x7in) Lokeren 1998

DOOREN van Edmond 1895-1965 **[79]**
👝 **$644** - €694 - **£431** - FF4 552
Paysage Huile/toile (50x60cm 19x23in) Antwerpen
2000
🖌 **$177** - €198 - **£123** - FF1 300
Mendiants Fusain/papier (48x64cm 18x25in)
Antwerpen 2000

DOOREN van Emile 1865-1949 **[2]**
👝 **$3 270** - €3 842 - **£2 294** - FF25 203
Hiver en Campine au clair de lune Huile/toile
(70x100cm 27x39in) Bruxelles 2000

DOORN van Adrianus 1825-1903 **[4]**
👝 **$1 047** - €1 125 - **£701** - FF7 378
Im Kinderzimmer Oil/panel (26.8x41.5cm 10x16in)
Königstein 2000

DOOYEWAARD Jaap Jacob 1876-1969 **[81]**
👝 **$1 300** - €1 149 - **£794** - FF7 537
Still Life Oil/canvas (56x61cm 22x24in) New-York
1999
👝 **$1 200** - €1 037 - **£712** - FF6 802
Peasant woman cooking Oil/board (33x25cm
13x10in) Chicago IL 1998
🖌 **$169** - €181 - **£113** - FF1 190
Young girl sitting on a chair Pencil/paper
(16x10.5cm 6x4in) Amsterdam 2000

DOOYEWAARD Willem 1892-1980 **[85]**
👝 **$4 983** - €4 214 - **£2 980** - FF27 640
Ballerina en repos Oil/canvas (100.5x50cm 39x19in)
Amsterdam 1998
👝 **$2 190** - €2 496 - **£1 514** - FF16 371
Market Scene Oil/canvas (30x40cm 11x15in)
Amsterdam 2000
🖌 **$1 733** - €2 042 - **£1 199** - FF13 394
Girl near a Fountain Black chalk (78.5x62cm
30x24in) Amsterdam 2000

DORAZIO Piero 1927 **[628]**
👝 **$25 000** - €25 916 - **£15 000** - FF170 000
Fine e chiaro Acrilico/tela (110x110cm 43x43in)
Prato 1999
👝 **$5 066** - €4 917 - **£3 154** - FF32 254
«Ah lala» Öl/Leinwand (65x45cm 25x17in) Luzern
1999
👝 **$2 820** - €2 436 - **£1 880** - FF15 980
«Rubra I» Olio/tela (34x42cm 13x16in) Prato 1998
🖌 **$1 120** - €1 451 - **£840** - FF9 520
Senza titolo Tempera/carta (43.5x54cm 17x21in)
Prato 2000
📼 **$150** - €179 - **£107** - FF1 175
Ohne Titel Radierung (19x21.2cm 7x8in) Berlin 2000

DORCHIN Yaacov 1946 **[22]**
🪨 **$3 600** - €3 864 - **£2 409** - FF25 347
Angel Iron (100x58cm 39x22in) Tel Aviv 2000
🪨 **$3 000** - €3 387 - **£2 089** - FF22 215
Untitled Iron (32.5x46cm 12x18in) Tel Aviv 2001

DORDA RODRIGUEZ Enrique 1869-1944 **[4]**
🖌 **$1 982** - €1 952 - **£1 267** - FF12 805
Retrato de la Marquesa de Aldama Pastel/papier
(111x164cm 43x64in) Madrid 1999

DORDIO GOMES Simão César 1890-? **[4]**
👝 **$79 200** - €89 731 - **£54 000** - FF588 600
Alentejo, terra de Promissão Oleo/lienzo
(75x96.5cm 29x37in) Lisboa 2000

DORÉ Armand 1824-c.1882 **[6]**
👝 **$5 000** - €5 038 - **£3 117** - FF33 050
After the Ball Oil/canvas (65x112cm 25x44in) New-
York 2000

DORÉ Gustave 1832-1883 [317]

$40 579 - €48 292 - **£29 000** - FF316 772
La famille du saltimbanque: l'enfant blessé
Oil/canvas (195.5x130.5cm 76x51in) London 2000

$12 000 - €10 135 - **£7 207** - FF66 482
Cinderella at the Ball Oil/canvas (72.5x114.5cm 28x45in) New-York 1998

$4 074 - €4 269 - **£2 578** - FF28 000
Pantagruel Huile/toile (33x41cm 12x16in) Paris 2000

$22 000 - €26 087 - **£15 136** - FF171 122
La Danse Bronze (106.5x15cm 41x5in) New-York 2000

$14 592 - €14 940 - **£9 163** - FF98 000
Madone Bronze (71x24x22cm 27x9x8in) Lille 2000

$1 580 - €1 601 - **£992** - FF10 500
Le déluge Pastel (60x75cm 23x29in) Saint-Dié 2000

$400 - €427 - **£267** - FF2 798
Illustration for Tennyson's Elaine Lithograph (43x31cm 17x12in) Baltimore MD 2000

DORÉ Jacques XX [11]

$20 605 - €22 805 - **£14 352** - FF149 592
In het estaminet (A l'estaminet) Huile/toile (45x60cm 17x23in) Antwerpen 2001

DOREN van Emile 1865-1949 [22]

$631 - €595 - **£391** - FF3 902
Moulin à vent dans un paysage Huile/toile (59x69cm 23x27in) Antwerpen 1999

DOREN van Raymond 1906-1991 [12]

$884 - €843 - **£537** - FF5 528
Portrait de femme en buste Pastel/papier (73x54.5cm 28x21in) Bruxelles 1999

DORFI (Albert Dorfinant) 1881-1976 [17]

$1 100 - €938 - **£663** - FF6 155
«San Juan - Exposicion de Blanco» Poster (32x40cm 12x15in) New-York 1998

DORIGNAC Georges 1879-1925 [17]

$811 - €793 - **£517** - FF5 200
Petites filles jouant dans la rue Aquarelle/papier (24x31.5cm 9x12in) Paris 1999

DORIGNY Michel 1617-1685 [13]

$254 184 - €256 114 - **£158 424** - FF1 680 000
Le Christ en croix Huile/toile (148.5x88cm 58x34in) Paris 2000

$38 000 - €40 582 - **£25 893** - FF266 201
Bacchanal Black chalk (28.5x21cm 11x8in) New-York 2001

DORIGNY Nicolas 1657-1746 [16]

$1 574 - €1 848 - **£1 111** - FF12 121
Untitled, after Raphael Pencil/paper (45x34cm 17x13in) Melbourne 2000

$613 - €716 - **£432** - FF4 695
Die Geschichte von Amor und Psyche, nach Raphael Kupferstich (38x65cm 14x25in) Berlin 2001

DÖRING Adam Lude, Rudolf 1925 [77]

$909 - €920 - **£555** - FF6 037
Profil II Mischtechnik/Karton (25x25cm 9x9in) Stuttgart 2000

$189 - €204 - **£129** - FF1 341
Frau mit blonden Haaren Mischtechnik/Papier (20x11.5cm 7x4in) Stuttgart 2001

$108 - €118 - **£74** - FF771
Dialog Farbserigraphie (41x41cm 16x16in) Stuttgart 2001

DORIVAL Georges, Géo 1879-1968 [135]

$473 - €473 - **£295** - FF3 100
«La Côte» Affiche (86x60cm 33x23in) Orléans 1999

DORMAN Dave XX [1]

$2 250 - €2 171 - **£1 422** - FF14 240
Batman Watercolour, gouache/paper (48x33cm 18x12in) New-York 1999

DORMOY H. XIX-XX [10]

$320 - €320 - **£200** - FF2 100
«Antar-Gel» Affiche (79.5x58.5cm 31x23in) Orléans 1999

DORN Carl 1831-1919 [1]

$5 109 - €4 224 - **£2 997** - FF27 707
Woman with a Swan Bronze (H54cm H21in) Warszawa 1998

DORN-FLADERER Johanna 1913-1988 [3]

$1 570 - €1 453 - **£972** - FF9 534
Kartenspieler Oil/panel (78x91cm 30x35in) Wien 1999

DORNBACH Hans 1900-1992 [1]

$1 227 - €1 431 - **£861** - FF9 390
Küste Watercolour (39.5x57.2cm 15x22in) Köln 2000

DÖRNBERGER Karl Johannes 1864-1940 [30]

$3 880 - €3 355 - **£2 307** - FF22 007
Smeltende sne Oil/canvas (80x101cm 31x39in) København 1998

DORNE van Martin 1736-1808 [4]

$19 366 - €19 513 - **£12 070** - FF128 000
Vase en pierre sculpté, fleurs et fruits posés sur un entablement Huile/toile (97x74cm 38x29in) Paris 2000

DORNER Johann Jakob II 1775-1852 [44]

$10 980 - €11 248 - **£6 776** - FF73 785
Salzburger Hütte (Eisenhammer) Öl/Leinwand/Karton (46x54cm 18x21in) Düsseldorf 2000

$4 847 - €5 368 - **£3 287** - FF35 215
Sägewerk im Gebirge Öl/Leinwand (27x36.5cm 10x14in) Hamburg 2000

$1 030 - €882 - **£620** - FF5 784
«Partie an d.Isar bei München» Pencil/paper (22.5x32cm 8x12in) München 1998

DORNY Bertrand 1931 [60]

$98 - €114 - **£67** - FF750
«393» Etching in colors (15x14cm 6x5in) Calgary, Alberta 2000

DORO Theo 1896-1973 [13]

$1 100 - €1 041 - **£683** - FF6 830
«Chemins de Fer de l'Est» Poster (100x62cm 39x24in) New-York 1999

DORPH Anton Lauritz Johan. 1831-1914 [66]

$1 508 - €1 690 - **£1 004** - FF10 555
Parti i en gård, med arbejdende mand i sit vaerksted Oil/canvas (48x65cm 18x25in) København 2000

$578 - €539 - **£349** - FF3 533
Kystparti med optrukne joller Oil/canvas (32x48cm 12x18in) København 1999

DORPH Bertha Green 1875-1960 [32]

$1 015 - €942 - **£609** - FF6 180
Tulipaner i vase Oil/canvas (103x90cm 40x35in) København 1999

$466 - €429 - **£288** - FF2 811
Zenia Oil/canvas (27x42cm 10x16in) Vejle 1998

DÖRR Ferdinand 1880-1968 [89]

$58 - €56 - **£35** - FF368
Titisee mit Feldberg im Hintergrund Radierung (23x27cm 9x10in) Staufen 1999

DÖRRIES Bernhard 1898-1978 **[6]**

$1 715 - €2 045 - £1 223 - FF13 415
Sommertag, gedeckter Tisch mit Blick auf einen See und Ruderer Watercolour (62x50cm 24x19in) Königstein 2000

DORSCH Ferdinand 1875-1938 **[33]**

$29 781 - €27 818 - £18 000 - FF182 471
Sommerabend Oil/canvas (112x136cm 44x53in) London 1999

$4 138 - €3 550 - £2 501 - FF23 284
Blaue Stühle Oil/panel (69x52.5cm 27x20in) München 1998

DORSCHFELDT G.A. 1898-1979 **[30]**

$536 - €511 - £327 - FF3 353
Blumenstilleben in Porzellanvase Öl/Leinwand (63x50cm 24x19in) Stuttgart 1999

DORSEY William 1942 **[72]**

$1 650 - €1 682 - £1 033 - FF11 033
Landscape, Eucalyptus Flower Field Oil/masonite (55x73cm 22x29in) Altadena CA 2000

$1 000 - €1 013 - £627 - FF6 645
California Scene with Lake and Mountains behind Eucalyptus Trees Oil/canvas (23x18cm 9x7in) Cincinnati OH 2000

DORT van Willem Jr 1905-1986 **[81]**

$162 - €181 - £112 - FF1 190
Gevarieerd stilleven van plant Oil/canvas (48x68cm 18x26in) Rotterdam 2001

$89 - €100 - £61 - FF654
Deboot Nijmegen Drawing (30x46cm 11x18in) Rotterdam 2001

DORVILLE Noël XIX-XX **[12]**

$725 - €835 - £500 - FF5 480
«Société la Française, marque Diamant, Paris» Poster (153x110cm 60x43in) London 2000

DOSAMANTES Francisco 1911-1986 **[15]**

$400 - €334 - £234 - FF2 190
«Women of Oaxaca» Lithograph (33x21cm 13x8in) Shaker-Heights OH 1998

DOSSENA Alceo 1878-1937 **[4]**

$8 500 - €8 812 - £5 100 - FF57 800
Madonna col Bambino Marbre (68x47cm 26x18in) Roma 2001

DOSSO DOSSI Giovanni Luteri 1489-1541 **[5]**

$1 400 760 - €1 376 926 - £900 000 - FF9 032 040
Venus awakened by Cupid Oil/canvas (120.5x157cm 47x61in) London 1999

DOTREMONT Christian 1922-1979 **[133]**

$8 340 - €8 072 - £5 142 - FF52 950
Dansante evidence blanche Acrylic/canvas (54x65cm 21x25in) Köbenhavn 1999

$1 449 - €1 373 - £881 - FF9 005
Komposition Gouache/paper (28x38cm 11x14in) Köbenhavn 1999

$179 - €211 - £130 - FF1 382
Un match, et avant, et après Lithographie couleurs (43x56cm 16x22in) Bruxelles 2001

$3 620 - €3 811 - £2 390 - FF25 000
Mon coeur à ses idées Photo (18x27cm 7x10in) Paris 2000

DOTTORI Gerardo 1884-1977 **[71]**

$19 000 - €19 696 - £11 400 - FF129 200
Lago umbro-alba Olio/tavola (124x151.5cm 48x59in) Prato 1999

$28 000 - €29 026 - £16 800 - FF190 400
Bombardamento aereo Tempera/tavola (50x35cm 19x13in) Milano 2000

$3 500 - €3 628 - £2 100 - FF23 800
Paesaggo umbro Olio/tavola (32.5x23.5cm 12x9in) Roma 1999

$1 440 - €1 244 - £720 - FF8 160
Il golfo di La Spezia Matite colorate/carta (25x35cm 9x13in) Prato 1999

DOU Gerrit 1613-1675 **[12]**

$68 499 - €69 025 - £42 700 - FF452 776
Die Fischverkäuferin Öl/Leinwand (47x35cm 18x13in) Stuttgart 2000

$340 000 - €343 956 - £207 604 - FF2 256 206
An Old Hermit Oil/panel (18x13cm 7x5in) New-York 2000

DOUAIHY Saliba 1912-1994 **[1]**

$9 739 - €10 954 - £6 800 - FF71 855
Sulaymania Mosque Watercolour (49x39cm 19x15in) London 2001

DOUBLET Georges XX **[20]**

$424 - €366 - £252 - FF2 400
Vaches dans un pré Huile/toile (46x55cm 18x21in) Vernon 1998

DOUBRERE **[3]**

$541 - €457 - £321 - FF3 000
Bouquet de roses blanches Aquarelle/papier (33.5x58cm 13x22in) Tarbes 1998

DOUCET Henri Lucien 1856-1895 **[10]**

$42 000 - €47 066 - £29 274 - FF308 733
The Eager Suitor Oil/canvas (98x124cm 38x48in) New-York 2001

$1 728 - €1 677 - £1 075 - FF11 000
Jeune femme au coin du poêle dans son intérieur Huile/toile (33x46cm 12x18in) Pontoise 1999

DOUCET Jacques 1924-1994 **[286]**

$15 288 - €16 007 - £9 607 - FF105 000
Remuements souterrains Huile/toile (162x130cm 63x51in) Versailles 2000

$4 788 - €4 037 - £2 841 - FF26 478
Ansigtskomposition Acrylic (65x50cm 25x19in) Köbenhavn 1998

$1 922 - €2 134 - £1 339 - FF14 000
Sans titre Technique mixte (17.5x22cm 6x8in) Douai 2001

$1 768 - €1 983 - £1 232 - FF13 008
Composition Gouache/papier (65x40cm 25x15in) Bruxelles 2001

$157 - €159 - £98 - FF1 041
Eté à Sint-Christol A Serigraph (105x75cm 41x29in) Amsterdam 2000

DOUDELET Charles 1861-1938 **[17]**

$436 - €520 - £312 - FF3 414
L'aveugle Watercolour (33x26.5cm 12x10in) Lokeren 2000

DOUFFET Gérard 1594-c.1665 **[4]**

$137 423 - €116 925 - £82 000 - FF766 978
Ecce Homo Oil/canvas (124.5x116cm 49x45in) London 1998

DOUGHERTY Parke Custis 1867-? **[7]**

$4 200 - €4 707 - £2 927 - FF30 873
Spring Landscape Oil/canvas (35.5x51cm 13x20in) Beverly-Hills CA 2001

DOUGHERTY Paul 1877-1947 **[44]**

$5 500 - €5 000 - £3 312 - FF32 796
California Coast Oil/canvas (66x91cm 26x36in) Bethesda MD 1998

$3 500 - €3 923 - £2 439 - FF25 730
Surf on Clodgy Oil/board (32.5x40.5cm 12x15in) Beverly-Hills CA 2001

D

$4 000 - €4 390 - **£2 575** - FF28 795
Coast Below Monterey Watercolour, gouache/paper (36x51cm 14x20in) Beverly-Hills CA 2000

DOUGHTY Thomas 1793-1856 **[34]**
$15 000 - €12 992 - **£9 199** - FF85 222
Ben Lomond Oil/canvas (66x91.5cm 25x36in) New-York 1999

DOUGLAS Andrew 1870-1935 **[13]**
$1 439 - €1 438 - **£900** - FF9 434
Cattle Watering, Loch Achray Oil/board (29x41cm 11x16in) Edinburgh 1999
$5 610 - €5 300 - **£3 500** - FF34 766
Edinburgh Castle from Calton Hill/Princes Street from Calton Hill Watercolour (55x77cm 21x30in) Perthshire 1999

DOUGLAS Edward Algernon S. c.1850-c.1920 **[38]**
$4 781 - €5 133 - **£3 200** - FF33 669
Going to Weigh/The Stone Wall Oil/board (70.5x28cm 27x11in) London 2000
$8 123 - €7 904 - **£5 000** - FF51 844
Departing for the Hunt Oil/panel (18x25.5cm 7x10in) London 1999
$1 196 - €1 285 - **£820** - FF8 432
The Hunt Watercolour/paper (18.5x33cm 7x12in) London 2001

DOUGLAS Edwin 1848-1914 **[37]**
$35 075 - €41 715 - **£25 000** - FF273 630
Ferretting Oil/canvas (127x96.5cm 50x37in) London 2000
$7 383 - €6 984 - **£4 600** - FF45 814
The Gypsy Freebooter Oil/canvas (90x70cm 35x27in) London 1999
$1 800 - €1 960 - **£1 239** - FF12 859
Pride of Place Oil/board (20.5x30.5cm 8x12in) New-York 2001

DOUGLAS James 1858-1911 **[21]**
$1 106 - €945 - **£650** - FF6 202
The Fish Seller Watercolour (47x29.5cm 18x11in) Glasgow 1998

DOUGLAS Jessie Ogsten XIX-XX **[2]**
$4 481 - €4 248 - **£2 800** - FF27 868
Seated Girl with Rabbits in an Orchads Watercolour, gouache/paper (48x65.5cm 18x25in) London 1999

DOUGLAS Stan 1960 **[5]**
$3 000 - €3 291 - **£1 992** - FF21 590
View of Kleeptee Settlement from Clearcut from Nootka Sound Series Photograph in colour (46x56cm 18x22in) New-York 2000

DOUGLAS Walter 1868-1948 **[12]**
$800 - €855 - **£544** - FF5 607
Chickens in Barnyard Oil/board (20x25cm 8x10in) New-Orleans LA 2001

DOUGLAS William 1780-1832 **[7]**
$6 314 - €7 509 - **£4 500** - FF49 258
Huntsmen with their Dogs Resting in a Wooded Landscape Oil/canvas (64x77cm 25x30in) London 2000

DOUGLAS William Fettes 1822-1891 **[22]**
$3 686 - €3 483 - **£2 300** - FF22 846
Refluctant Lovers Oil/panel (34x51cm 13x20in) Perthshire 1999

DOUMET Zacharie Félix 1761-1818 **[14]**
$10 000 - €10 116 - **£6 106** - FF66 359
The Roofs of a Villa/Figures in a Kitchen Garden Bodycolour (41.5x54.5cm 16x21in) New-York 2000

DOURDIL Luis 1914 **[4]**
$840 - €997 - **£600** - FF6 540
Mulheres Lápiz/papel (46x32.5cm 18x12in) Lisboa 2001

DOUTHWAITE Patricia, Pat 1939 **[6]**
$574 - €646 - **£400** - FF4 235
Woman in green Coloured chalks/paper (69.5x47cm 27x18in) Edinburgh 2001

DOUTRELEAU Pierre 1938 **[71]**
$978 - €838 - **£588** - FF5 500
Le jockey Huile/toile (80x80cm 31x31in) Fontainebleau 1998
$540 - €488 - **£333** - FF3 200
New York Huile/toile (41x34cm 16x13in) Arles 1999

DOUVEN Jacques 1908 **[12]**
$1 018 - €942 - **£634** - FF6 178
Zilverberken aan de rand van het bos Oil/canvas (60x70cm 23x27in) Lokeren 1999

DOUW van Simon Johannes c.1630-c.1680 **[30]**
$7 039 - €8 168 - **£4 860** - FF53 578
A Cavalry Battle Between Turks and Christians Oil/canvas (63.5x87.5cm 25x34in) Amsterdam 2000
$4 074 - €3 857 - **£2 533** - FF25 301
Horsemen in a Mountainous Landscape Oil/panel (26x33.5cm 10x13in) Amsterdam 1999

DOUZETTE Fritz 1878-1955 **[13]**
$2 699 - €2 232 - **£1 583** - FF14 641
Petite fille et chien Oil/panel (22.5x19cm 8x7in) Warszawa 1998

DOUZETTE Louis, Carl Ludwig 1834-1924 **[90]**
$2 364 - €2 812 - **£1 685** - FF18 446
Mondschein über der Gracht einer holländischen Stadt Öl/Leinwand (83.5x122cm 32x48in) Köln 2000
$1 167 - €1 130 - **£720** - FF7 410
Coastal Scene by Moonlight with a Figure Standing on a Quayside Oil/panel (13x18cm 5x7in) West-Yorshire 1999
$596 - €613 - **£375** - FF4 024
Knorrige Weide in Wiesen- und Knicklandschaft Aquarell/Papier (20x16cm 7x6in) Berlin 2000

DOVA Gianni 1925-1991 **[326]**
$9 000 - €9 330 - **£5 400** - FF61 200
Scultura Olio/tela (129x99cm 50x38in) Prato 1999
$5 000 - €5 183 - **£3 000** - FF34 000
Attesa Olio/tela (60x50cm 23x19in) Vercelli 2001
$2 000 - €2 073 - **£1 200** - FF13 600
Composizione Olio/tela (35x45cm 13x17in) Venezia 1999
$1 440 - €1 244 - **£720** - FF8 160
Composizione Tecnica mista, disegno (48.5x35cm 19x13in) Prato 1999
$120 - €155 - **£90** - FF1 020
Senza titolo Litografia a colori (93x68.5cm 36x26in) Milano 2001

DOVASTON Margaret 1884-? **[34]**
$14 990 - €14 714 - **£9 292** - FF96 516
The Empire Builders Oil/canvas (45.5x61cm 17x24in) Toronto 1999
$4 811 - €4 760 - **£3 000** - FF31 221
The Connoisseur Oil/panel (23.5x29cm 9x11in) Leyburn, North Yorkshire 1999

DOVE Arthur Garfield 1880-1946 **[42]**

- **$500 000** - €495 604 - **£312 750** - FF3 250 950
  Running River Oil/metal (51x38cm 20x14in) New-York 1999
- **$80 000** - €95 140 - **£57 016** - FF624 080
  Wood Pile Oil/canvas (26x36cm 10x14in) New-York 2000
- **$19 550** - €18 532 - **£12 212** - FF121 563
  Willow Watercolour/paper (12x17cm 5x7in) Bethesda MD 1999

DOVERA Achille 1838-1895 **[21]**

- **$7 696** - €9 172 - **£5 513** - FF60 162
  Milano Huile/toile (56x83cm 22x32in) Antwerpen 2000
- **$3 400** - €3 525 - **£2 040** - FF23 120
  Pescatori Olio/tavoletta (26.5x46cm 10x18in) Genova 2000
- **$1 750** - €1 814 - **£1 050** - FF11 900
  Portico del Palazzo Ducale di Venezia Acquarello/cartone (49.5x39.5cm 19x15in) Milano 2000

DOVIANE Auguste 1825-1887 **[12]**

- **$2 814** - €3 049 - **£1 948** - FF20 000
  «La revanche» Huile/toile (101x70cm 39x27in) Paris 2001

DOVIZIELLI Pietro XIX **[3]**

- **$2 138** - €1 982 - **£1 320** - FF13 000
  Panorama du Colisée, Rome Tirage albuminé (61x144cm 24x56in) Paris 1999

DOW Arthur Wesley 1857-1922 **[53]**

- **$8 000** - €8 588 - **£5 450** - FF56 332
  Autumn/A Landscape Sketch Oil/canvas (35.5x51cm 13x20in) Boston MA 2001
- **$30 000** - €35 002 - **£20 880** - FF229 596
  The Pond on the Hilltop Oil/board (21x26cm 8x10in) Bloomfield-Hills MI 2000
- **$1 600** - €1 785 - **£1 047** - FF11 709
  Willows in Bloom Woodcut in colors (13x8cm 5x3in) Chicago IL 2000

DOWD James Henry 1883-1956 **[6]**

- **$265** - €312 - **£190** - FF2 044
  Child and Cat Etching (10x15cm 3x5in) London 2001

DOWD Robert 1936-1995 **[17]**

- **$6 000** - €5 451 - **£3 719** - FF35 758
  Color certificate 0690 Acrylic/canvas (76x152.5cm 29x60in) New-York 1999

DOWELL Charles Rennie ?-1935 **[7]**

- **$1 738** - €2 017 - **£1 200** - FF13 228
  The Campsie Hills, Scotland Oil/canvas (71x91.5cm 27x36in) London 2000

DOWLING Robert Hawke 1827-1886 **[7]**

- **$18 688** - €20 591 - **£12 406** - FF135 065
  Mrs Margaret McArthur of Meningoort Oil/canvas (98.5x74cm 38x29in) Woollahra, Sydney 2000
- **$38 148** - €37 116 - **£23 478** - FF243 468
  The Artist's Father/The Artist's Step-Mother Oil/board (30.5x25.5cm 12x10in) Malvern, Victoria 1999

DOWNARD Ebenezer Newman act.1849-1889 **[8]**

- **$6 750** - €7 664 - **£4 689** - FF50 274
  Cat and Mouse Oil/canvas (60x50cm 24x20in) Portsmouth NH 2001
- **$59 761** - €69 434 - **£42 000** - FF455 456
  Gulliver diverting the Emperor of Lilliput Oil/canvas (36x30cm 14x11in) London 2001

DOWNES Bernard XVIII **[1]**

- **$2 100** - €2 095 - **£1 311** - FF13 740
  Lady Diana Stockton Pastel/paper (135x100cm 53x39in) St. Louis MO 1999

DOWNES Rackstraw 1939 **[13]**

- **$31 000** - €27 568 - **£18 959** - FF180 832
  Union, Clary Hill, Round Pond, Seven trees Pond Oil/canvas (82.5x222.5cm 32x87in) New-York 1999
- **$1 800** - €2 079 - **£1 260** - FF13 640
  «Washington County Drizzle, October» Oil/canvas (52x76cm 20x30in) New-York 2001
- **$2 000** - €1 678 - **£1 173** - FF11 007
  The I.R.T. Elevated Station at Broadway and 125th Street Graphite (47.5x89cm 18x35in) New-York 1998

DOWNIE John Patrick 1871-1945 **[25]**

- **$2 444** - €2 726 - **£1 650** - FF17 881
  Swans and Cygnets Oil/board (24x35cm 9x13in) Edinburgh 2000
- **$448** - €482 - **£300** - FF3 161
  Shipping in Choppy Seas Watercolour (26.5x35cm 10x13in) London 2000

DOWNIE Patrick 1854-1945 **[58]**

- **$12 423** - €13 852 - **£8 500** - FF90 862
  Ducks Oil/canvas (51x61cm 20x24in) Perthshire 2000
- **$1 074** - €1 190 - **£729** - FF7 807
  Kustsamhälle Oil/panel (26x34cm 10x13in) Stockholm 2000
- **$503** - €425 - **£300** - FF2 788
  Fishing Trawler Off the Ayrshire Coast Watercolour (26.5x37cm 10x14in) Glasgow 1998

DOWNING Delapoer XIX-XX **[17]**

- **$2 346** - €2 529 - **£1 600** - FF16 586
  Feeding Time Oil/canvas (86.5x64.5cm 34x25in) London 2001

DOWNING Joe 1925 **[18]**

- **$1 326** - €1 289 - **£811** - FF8 455
  Abstraction Huile/toile (46x55cm 18x21in) Liège 1999

DOWNMAN John 1750-1824 **[137]**

- **$75 249** - €85 725 - **£52 000** - FF562 322
  John Mortlock, in a Landscape/Elizabeth Mortlock, Wearing Brown Dress Oil/canvas (127x101.5cm 50x39in) London 2000
- **$68 737** - €73 784 - **£46 000** - FF483 993
  Rev. Thomas Eyre, his Sister Frances and her Husband Major R.Sherwood Oil/canvas (98x122cm 38x48in) London 2000
- **$2 430** - €2 337 - **£1 500** - FF15 332
  Frederick William Hallet Hodges, in a green Coat, with a black Spaniel Oil/canvas (30.5x24cm 12x9in) London 1999
- **$1 492** - €1 298 - **£900** - FF8 516
  Portrait of Queen Charlotte Watercolour (19x15cm 7x5in) London 1998

DOWNS David Jarinyanu c.1925-1995 **[18]**

- **$8 551** - €8 249 - **£5 404** - FF54 111
  Whale Fish vomiting Jonah Acrylic (112x137cm 44x53in) Melbourne 1999
- **$2 287** - €2 455 - **£1 530** - FF16 104
  Untitled Mixed media/paper (70x92.5cm 27x36in) Melbourne 2000

DOWS Olin 1904-1981 **[2]**

- **$4 200** - €4 536 - **£2 902** - FF29 752
  Val Kill Cottage, the country Retreat of Eleanor Roosevelt Watercolour/paper (34.5x47cm 13x18in) New-York 2001

D

DOWSON Russell XIX-XX **[4]**
🖌 **$557** - €656 - **£400** - FF4 303
Pilchard Boats fishing off Penzance
Watercolour/paper (38x58cm 15x23in) Church-Stretton, Shropshire 2001

DOYEN Gabriel François 1726-1806 **[12]**
🖎 **$80 000** - €87 772 - **£53 144** - FF575 744
La lecture: young Woman reading with a Dog on her Knees Oil/canvas (73x58cm 28x22in) New-York 2000
🖎 **$2 269** - €2 556 - **£1 596** - FF16 769
Heilige Familie mit Engeln Öl/Leinwand (33x24cm 12x9in) Stuttgart 2001

DOYLE Charles Altamont 1832-1893 **[24]**
🖌 **$843** - €1 003 - **£600** - FF6 576
In the Shade Watercolour (18x26cm 7x10in) London 2000

DOYLE D'Arcy W. 1932 **[60]**
🖎 **$7 038** - €7 531 - **£4 636** - FF49 398
Brumby's Dash Oil/masonite (45x90cm 17x35in) Sydney 2000
🖎 **$1 158** - €1 314 - **£816** - FF8 620
Landscape in Blue Oil/board (24x29cm 9x11in) Sydney 2001

DOYLE Richard 1824-1883 **[45]**
🖌 **$2 200** - €2 564 - **£1 523** - FF16 822
Man at the Ledge of the Pits of Hell Watercolour, gouache (33x23cm 13x9in) New-York 2000

DOYLE William Massey S. 1769-1828 **[4]**
🖌 **$22 000** - €20 366 - **£13 281** - FF133 595
Portrait of Abby Ann Duchesne Seated in a Bamboo Chair Pastel/paper (68.5x55.5cm 26x21in) New-York 1999

DOYLY-JOHN C.R. 1906-1993 **[40]**
🖎 **$353** - €334 - **£220** - FF2 191
Fishing Boat in the Harbour Oil/canvas/board (49x67cm 19x26in) London 1999

DOZE Jean-Marie Melchior 1827-1913 **[7]**
🖎 **$2 500** - €2 918 - **£1 764** - FF19 139
The New Born Christ Oil/canvas (40x33cm 16x13in) Cedar-Falls IA 2000

DOZIER Otis 1904-1987 **[2]**
🖎 **$5 500** - €5 824 - **£3 640** - FF38 200
Fisherman Oil/masonite (70x91.5cm 27x36in) New-York 2000

DRACHKOVITCH-THOMAS Albert 1928 **[29]**
🖎 **$2 597** - €2 897 - **£1 812** - FF19 000
Paysage d'hiver, mare au saule cassé Huile/panneau (55x52cm 21x20in) Entzheim 2001

DRACHMANN Holger 1846-1908 **[126]**
🖎 **$2 975** - €3 350 - **£2 050** - FF21 977
Sejlskibe på havet, solen bryder gennem skydaekket Oil/canvas (43x64cm 16x25in) København 2000
🖎 **$2 040** - €1 953 - **£1 287** - FF12 809
Marine med fyrskib og damer Oil/canvas (24x32cm 9x12in) København 1999

DRAHONET Alexandre J. Dubois 1791-1834 **[11]**
🖎 **$12 146** - €13 627 - **£8 500** - FF89 387
Portrait of a Lady in a Black Evening Gown Oil/canvas (128x98cm 50x38in) London 2001
🖌 **$6 099** - €6 059 - **£3 800** - FF39 742
Capriccio of Roman Ruins Bodycolour (48.5x78cm 19x30in) London 1999

DRAINS Georges A. XIX-XX **[8]**
🖌 **$76** - €89 - **£54** - FF585
Canard, étude Gouache/papier (23.5x30.5cm 9x12in) Bruxelles 2001

DRAKE Frank 1868-1922 **[2]**
🖎 **$800** - €757 - **£496** - FF4 967
Living Room Area Showing Fireplace Watercolour/paper (38x53cm 15x21in) Wallkill NY 1999

DRAKE Heinrich 1903-1994 **[2]**
🖎 **$4 240** - €4 116 - **£2 640** - FF26 998
Sitzendes Mädchen Bronze (60x25x65cm 23x9x25in) Berlin 1999

DRAMARD de Georges 1839-1900 **[9]**
🖎 **$910** - €851 - **£550** - FF5 579
Tulips in a Basket Oil/canvas (46x56cm 18x22in) London 1999

DRANSY Jules Isnard 1883-c.1945 **[27]**
🎞 **$641** - €746 - **£450** - FF4 891
«Pippermint Get» Poster (140x100cm 55x39in) London 2001

DRAPER Charles F. 1870-1910 **[3]**
🖎 **$18 370** - €20 248 - **£12 000** - FF132 819
View of Benacre Hall Oil/canvas (70x111cm 27x43in) London 2000

DRAPER Herbert James 1864-1920 **[13]**
🖎 **$1 122 400** - €1 334 868 - **£800 000** - FF8 756 160
The Mountain Mists Oil/canvas (126x119cm 49x46in) London 2000
🖎 **$39 841** - €46 289 - **£28 000** - FF303 637
Pot pourri Oil/canvas (51x68.5cm 20x26in) London 2001

DRAPPIER Edmond XIX-XX **[12]**
🖎 **$1 499** - €1 677 - **£1 010** - FF11 000
Homme faisant reculer un cheval Bronze (34x50x24cm 13x19x9in) Orléans 2000

DRATHMANN Christoffer 1856-1932 **[24]**
🖎 **$357** - €409 - **£248** - FF2 683
Waldstück mit Fuchs Öl/Leinwand (79x66cm 31x25in) Rudolstadt-Thüringen 2000

DRAVER Orrin 1895-1964 **[6]**
🖎 **$800** - €933 - **£556** - FF6 122
Vista from the Orchard Oil/canvas (71x91cm 28x36in) Delray-Beach FL 2000

DRAYTON Grace Gebbie 1877-1936 **[10]**
🖌 **$1 800** - €2 016 - **£1 250** - FF13 225
Little Girl banished to the Corner Charcoal (44x25cm 17x10in) New-York 2001

DREBER Heinrich 1822-1875 **[30]**
🖎 **$4 991** - €5 113 - **£3 080** - FF33 539
Dionysische Szene Öl/Leinwand (130x105cm 51x41in) Düsseldorf 2000
🖎 **$2 745** - €2 812 - **£1 694** - FF18 446
Malerin im Atelier, möglicherweise Elisabeth Seeburg Oil/panel (56.5x39.5cm 22x15in) Düsseldorf 2000
🖌 **$625** - €639 - **£391** - FF4 192
Grasbewachsene Felsbrocken unter Bäumen und in Landschaft Ink (14x27cm 5x10in) Köln 2000

DRECHSLER Johann Baptist 1756-1811 **[23]**
🖎 **$18 424** - €20 348 - **£12 768** - FF133 476
Blumenstrauss in einer ornamental verzierten Vase und Weintrauben Öl/Leinwand (72x54.5cm 28x21in) Wien 2001

D

⌐◦ **$10 046** - €10 124 - **£6 262** - FF66 407
Früchte in einem Korb, Insekten, Nüsse und ein Vogel Oil/panel (31x45cm 12x17in) Stuttgart 2000
⌐◦ **$10 528** - €11 628 - **£7 296** - FF76 272
Stilleben von Weintrauben, Äpfeln Gouache/paper (26.5x35.2cm 10x13in) Wien 2001

DRECHT van Johannes 1737-1807 **[5]**
⌐◦ **$6 524** - €6 102 - **£4 000** - FF40 028
Landscape with Travellers on a Path near Trees Oil/canvas (43x49cm 16x19in) London 1998

DREESEN Walter XX **[2]**
⌐◦ **$11 478** - €13 033 - **£7 856** - FF85 492
The hermit Oil/panel (32x22cm 12x8in) Singapore 2000

DREGER von Tom Richard 1868-1949 **[21]**
⌐◦ **$2 494** - €2 137 - **£1 500** - FF14 020
Pablo Casals Oil/canvas (10.3x8.6cm 4x3in) London 1998

DREHER Peter 1932 **[3]**
⌐◦ **$2 406** - €2 301 - **£1 465** - FF15 092
Drei Sonnenuntergänge Öl/Karton (26.5x35.5cm 10x13in) Staufen 1999

DREI Ercole 1886-1973 **[22]**
🖎 **$960** - €1 244 - **£720** - FF8 160
Estasi d'amore Céramique (H38cm H14in) Roma 2001

DREIBHOLTZ Christiaan 1799-1874 **[16]**
⌐◦ **$7 291** - €8 168 - **£5 067** - FF53 578
Riviergezicht met platbodems bij een stad Oil/canvas (47x63cm 18x24in) Rotterdam 2001

DREIER Katherine Sophie 1877-1952 **[5]**
▥ **$2 173** - €2 556 - **£1 575** - FF16 769
1 to 40 Variations Lithograph (37.5x29cm 14x11in) Hamburg 2001

DRENKHAHN Reinhard 1926-1959 **[10]**
⌐◦ **$951** - €1 135 - **£678** - FF7 442
«Krebs im Sand» Oil/board (27x67.5cm 10x26in) Hamburg 2000

DRENTHE van Albertus Jacobus Sap 1835-c.1883 **[11]**
⌐◦ **$1 015** - €861 - **£612** - FF5 649
Molens en figuren aan poldervaart Oil/panel (25x36cm 9x14in) Den Haag 1998

DRESSLER Adolf 1833-1881 **[15]**
⌐◦ **$10 076** - €9 623 - **£6 204** - FF63 123
Le chemin dans la montagne Oil/canvas (113x80cm 44x31in) Warszawa 1999
⌐◦ **$1 680** - €1 815 - **£1 161** - FF11 906
Wooded landscape with a Bridge Oil/cardboard (25x36cm 9x14in) Amsterdam 2001

DRESSLER August Wilhelm 1886-1970 **[96]**
✐ **$326** - €358 - **£221** - FF2 347
Das schwarze Haar Indian ink (44x33.1cm 17x13in) Berlin 2000
▥ **$182** - €174 - **£113** - FF1 140
Sitzender weiblicher Akt Radierung (27.6x17.3cm 10x6in) Berlin 1999

DREUX de Alfred 1810-1860 **[121]**
⌐◦ **$310 000** - €360 172 - **£217 868** - FF2 362 572
«Lady Alice and Lady Blanche Egerton» Oil/canvas (116x146cm 45x57in) New-York 2001
⌐◦ **$90 000** - €96 605 - **£60 228** - FF633 690
Out Hunting Oil/canvas (85.5x122cm 33x48in) New-York 2000

⌐◦ **$23 076** - €27 441 - **£16 452** - FF180 000
Sonneur à cheval Huile/toile (32.5x40.5cm 12x15in) Neuilly-sur-Seine 2000
⌐◦ **$12 500** - €11 586 - **£7 772** - FF76 001
Gentleman and his Mount Watercolour/paper (21.5x34.5cm 8x13in) New-York 1999
✐ **$317** - €320 - **£198** - FF2 100
Mille tonnères/Chevaux en liberté Lithographie (63x76cm 24x29in) Paris 2000

DREVET Joannès, Joanny 1854-1940 **[68]**
⌐◦ **$7 250** - €8 012 - **£5 028** - FF52 556
Grand Canal, Venice Oil/canvas (45x64cm 18x25in) New-Orleans LA 2001
✐ **$302** - €305 - **£188** - FF2 000
La rue Saint-Georges Aquarelle/papier (23x14.5cm 9x5in) Lyon 2000

DREVET Pierre 1663-1738 **[19]**
▥ **$331** - €288 - **£206** - FF1 891
«Retrato de André Hercules, cardenal de Fleury» Grabado (52x39.5cm 20x15in) Madrid 1999

DREVET Pierre Imbert 1697-1739 **[5]**
▥ **$490** - €427 - **£296** - FF2 800
Jacques-Benigne Bossuet, d'après H. Rigaud Burin (50x34cm 19x13in) Paris 1998

DREVILLE André Georges 1872-? **[6]**
▥ **$903** - €991 - **£613** - FF6 500
«Terrot & Cie Dijon, rouler sur une bicyclette Terrot» Affiche couleur (156x116cm 61x45in) Paris 2000

DRÉVILLE Jean 1906 **[8]**
[◉] **$2 601** - €2 592 - **£1 579** - FF17 000
Jazz Photo (29x38cm 11x14in) Argenteuil 2000

DREW Clement 1806-1889 **[44]**
⌐◦ **$4 750** - €5 540 - **£3 335** - FF36 342
Entrance to Gloucester Harbor Gale Coming on Oil/canvas (45x76cm 17x29in) Boston MA 2000
⌐◦ **$2 400** - €2 644 - **£1 601** - FF17 345
Ship Laying to Off Cape Horn Oil/board (16x22cm 6x9in) Portsmouth NH 2000

DREW Dudley Joseph 1924 **[25]**
⌐◦ **$647** - €607 - **£400** - FF3 980
Delphiniums Oil/canvas (81x60cm 31x23in) Melbourne 1999

DREW George W. 1875-1968 **[76]**
⌐◦ **$1 600** - €1 567 - **£1 022** - FF10 276
The Shores of Lake Lugano Oil/canvas (60x91cm 24x36in) Norwalk CT 1999
⌐◦ **$500** - €504 - **£311** - FF3 305
Summer House by the Pond Oil/canvas (30x22cm 12x9in) New-York 2000

DREWES Werner 1899-1985 **[136]**
⌐◦ **$4 000** - €4 549 - **£2 774** - FF29 840
«Composition Contrasts» Oil/canvas (81x106cm 32x42in) Cincinnati OH 2000
⌐◦ **$2 380** - €2 812 - **£1 681** - FF18 446
Broken Rainbow Öl/Leinwand (19.5x24cm 7x9in) Köln 2001
▥ **$550** - €569 - **£347** - FF3 734
Pennsylvania Farm Woodcut (24.5x36.5cm 9x14in) New-York 2000

DREWS Kai 1884-1964 **[175]**
⌐◦ **$325** - €302 - **£202** - FF1 982
Solbelyst interiör Oil/canvas (47x37cm 18x14in) Malmö 1999
⌐◦ **$249** - €242 - **£154** - FF1 588
Interiör Oil/canvas (40x31cm 15x12in) Vejle 1999

DREWS Svend 1919 [34]

⮑ $592 - €511 - £358 - FF3 353
Fossende elv Oil/canvas (65x55cm 25x21in) Vejle 1999

DREYER Carl 1889-1968 [1]

📷 $19 842 - €18 741 - £12 000 - FF122 932
L'étrange aventure de David Gray Silver print (16.5x22cm 6x8in) London 1999

DREYER Dankvart 1816-1852 [30]

⮑ $1 888 - €2 144 - £1 292 - FF14 062
Dronning Dagmar og Valdemar Sejr Oil/canvas (65x46cm 25x18in) Vejle 2000

⮑ $3 808 - €4 289 - £2 624 - FF28 131
Vildtvoksende orkidéer Oil/canvas (18x25cm 7x9in) København 2000

DREYFUS-LEMAITRE Henri 1859-1946 [36]

⮑ $972 - €1 143 - £696 - FF7 519
La lessive Huile/toile (46x55cm 18x21in) Paris 2001

⮑ $181 - €213 - £130 - FF1 400
Deux baigneuses Huile/panneau (28x32.5cm 11x12in) Paris 2001

DRIAN Étienne Adrien 1885-1961 [71]

⮑ $10 000 - €9 687 - £6 237 - FF63 542
Map to Versailles, Villa Trianon Oil/canvas (185.5x211cm 73x83in) Beverly-Hills CA 1999

⮑ $2 199 - €2 592 - £1 521 - FF17 000
Nu de dos Huile/panneau (20x28cm 7x11in) Paris 2000

⮑ $988 - €1 146 - £700 - FF7 519
The Puppet Show Watercolour (73x51cm 28x20in) London 2000

📰 $449 - €435 - £280 - FF2 852
Sisters Drypoint (31.5x47cm 12x18in) London 1999

DRIBEN Peter 1902-1968 [14]

⮑ $10 000 - €9 258 - £6 121 - FF60 728
Bikini clad redhead reaching back to adjust her shoe, cover for Wink Oil/board (73x54cm 29x21in) New-York 1999

DRIELENBURGH van Willem 1635-1677 [2]

⮑ $7 613 - €7 994 - £4 800 - FF52 438
Wooded Landscape with Herdsmen and Cattle at a Fountain, a Lake Oil/panel (59x84cm 23x33in) London 2000

DRIELST van Egbert 1746-1818 [18]

⮑ $5 662 - €5 445 - £3 488 - FF35 719
Wooded Landscape with Animals Drinking in a Stream and Peasants Watercolour (30.5x46.5cm 12x18in) Amsterdam 1999

DRIESSCHE van den Jan 1954 [17]

📰 $523 - €545 - £330 - FF3 577
Le décès de mon père Technique mixte/papier (73x54cm 28x21in) Antwerpen 2000

DRIESSCHE van den Lucien 1926-1991 [55]

📰 $300 - €248 - £176 - FF1 624
Le temple Technique mixte/papier (40x60cm 15x23in) Antwerpen 1998

DRIESTEN van Arend Jan 1878-1969 [69]

📰 $917 - €1 044 - £644 - FF6 846
«Aan de Linge» Oil/canvas/panel (33x52cm 12x20in) Amsterdam 2001

⮑ $1 008 - €998 - £617 - FF6 548
Ruïne of Slot Teyring Oil/canvas (47.5x31cm 18x12in) Amsterdam 2000

📰 $1 020 - €998 - £654 - FF6 548
A Farmhouse Watercolour/paper (29x43cm 11x16in) Amsterdam 1999

DRING William Dennis 1904-1990 [43]

⮑ $1 150 - €1 093 - £700 - FF7 171
Self-Portrait of the Artist Oil/canvas (61x91cm 24x35in) London 1999

DRINKWATER Milton XIX-XX [30]

📰 $555 - €577 - £350 - FF3 786
Lakeland Landscape with Figures on the Shore Line/Figures in a Boat Watercolour (28.5x43.5cm 11x17in) Leyburn, North Yorkshire 2000

DRISCOLE M.A. or H.A. XIX-XX [3]

⮑ $5 000 - €4 853 - £3 113 - FF31 833
Clamming, Jamaica Bay, New York Oil/canvas (35x50cm 14x20in) Bolton MA 1999

DRIVER Thomas 1791-1852 [4]

📰 $8 193 - €7 547 - £5 000 - FF49 505
View of St George's Harbour, Bermuda Watercolour (33x49.5cm 12x19in) London 1998

DRIVIER Léon Ernest 1878-1951 [31]

🔨 $13 457 - €12 404 - £8 061 - FF81 365
Young African woman Sculpture (H88.5cm H34in) Amsterdam 1998

📰 $744 - €838 - £518 - FF5 500
Nu de profil marchant Encre (31x23cm 12x9in) Paris 2001

DROESE Felix 1952 [220]

📰 $344 - €391 - £241 - FF2 563
«Hemdchen» Ink (33.5x24cm 13x9in) Zürich 2001

📰 $124 - €133 - £84 - FF872
Die Kommission - Notenbankversuchsabteilungsberungsstelle Radierung (44x37cm 17x14in) Bamberg 2001

DROHAN Walter 1933 [7]

⮑ $1 918 - €2 059 - £1 303 - FF13 508
De Havilland Tigermoth (U.K.) S.Africa Oil/canvas (28x36cm 11x14in) Calgary, Alberta 2001

DROIT Jean 1884-1961 [32]

📰 $517 - €610 - £363 - FF4 600
La Paume Estampe couleurs (50x45cm 19x17in) Paris 2000

DROLLING Martin 1752-1817 [49]

⮑ $151 240 - €144 827 - £95 190 - FF950 000
Portrait de Joseph Merceron, avocat au parlement de Paris Huile/toile (210x140cm 82x55in) Paris 1999

⮑ $19 000 - €15 950 - £11 143 - FF104 625
«Say your Mea Culpa» Oil/canvas (73.5x59cm 28x23in) New-York 1998

⮑ $4 539 - €4 573 - £2 829 - FF30 000
La jeune paysanne sortant de la ferme/L'accaparneur de blé Huile/panneau (30.5x23cm 12x9in) Paris 2000

📰 $2 247 - €2 232 - £1 400 - FF14 642
Portrait of a Mother and her three Children Standingat a Window Black chalk (21x15cm 8x5in) London 1999

DROLLING Michel-Martin 1786-1851 [26]

⮑ $62 068 - €60 794 - £40 000 - FF398 784
Portrait of the Artist, in a brown jacket with a black collar Oil/canvas (60.5x50cm 23x19in) London 1999

📰 $1 229 - €1 220 - £764 - FF8 000
Homme nu coiffé d'un chapeau portant ses habits sur l'épaule Fusain (25.5x15.5cm 10x6in) Paris 1999

DROMIK (Dominique Richard) 1953 **[106]**
- $506 - €564 - £340 - FF3 700
  Femme aux géraniums Huile/toile (46x38cm 18x14in) Toulouse 2000

DROOGSLOOT Cornelis 1630-1673 **[31]**
- $13 664 - €14 316 - £9 038 - FF93 909
  Vor dem Wirtshaus sitzen Bauern beim Mahl am Tisch Oil/panel (43x58.2cm 16x22in) München 2000
- $9 212 - €10 174 - £6 384 - FF66 738
  Rastende Bauern in einer Landschaft Oil/panel (30x40cm 11x15in) Wien 2001

DROOGSLOOT Josst Cornelisz. 1586-1666 **[136]**
- $32 277 - €32 014 - £20 076 - FF210 000
  Villageois vaquant à leurs occupations Huile/toile (101x150cm 39x59in) Lille 1999
- $24 918 - €26 749 - £16 674 - FF175 459
  Belebte Dorfstrasse Oil/panel (48x74cm 18x29in) Zürich 2000
- $10 293 - €12 271 - £7 339 - FF80 493
  Fröhliche Gesellschaft Oil/panel (35x41.5cm 13x16in) Köln 2000

DROUAIS François Hubert 1727-1775 **[23]**
- $52 536 - €50 308 - £33 066 - FF330 000
  Portrait de jeune femme au collier de perles Huile/toile (62x51cm 24x20in) Paris 1999
- $19 716 - €18 294 - £11 832 - FF210 000
  Portrait de la Marquise de Pompadour Huile/toile (42.5x35cm 16x13in) Paris 1999

DROUAIS Jean Germain 1763-1788 **[5]**
- $24 309 - €28 203 - £17 297 - FF185 000
  Académie d'homme assis Huile/toile (57x52cm 22x20in) Paris 2001

DROUET Jean Guillaume 1764-1836 **[1]**
- $41 158 - €39 637 - £25 558 - FF260 000
  Trompe-l'oeil aux crustacés, coquillages, poissons et oiseaux Huile/toile (65x75cm 25x29in) Paris 1999

DROUET-AZAM Suzanne 1908 **[1]**
- $6 168 - €7 013 - £4 232 - FF46 000
  La ferme Huile/panneau (32.5x41cm 12x16in) Toulouse 2000

DROUET-REVEILLAUD Suzanne 1885-1973 **[7]**
- $4 206 - €4 573 - £2 772 - FF30 000
  Une porte de la Mosquée des Andalous, Fès Huile/panneau (46.5x38cm 18x14in) Paris 2000

DROUILLET Gérard XX **[8]**
- $2 245 - €2 515 - £1 560 - FF16 500
  Sans titre Huile/papier (200x120cm 78x47in) Paris 2001
- $1 633 - €1 829 - £1 135 - FF12 000
  Sans titre Gouache/papier (83x122cm 32x48in) Paris 2001

DROUIN J. XIX **[2]**
- $3 909 - €4 337 - £2 600 - FF28 450
  Running in and Out of Le Havre Oil/canvas (48.5x72.5cm 19x28in) London 2000

DROUOT Édouard 1859-1945 **[278]**
- $3 000 - €2 601 - £1 833 - FF17 060
  «Inspiration» Bronze (H81cm H31in) New-York 1999
- $1 100 - €1 175 - £731 - FF7 708
  Runner at the Finish Bronze (H45cm H18in) Cleveland OH 2000

DRTIKOL Frantisek 1883-1961 **[427]**
- $809 - €765 - £504 - FF5 020
  Akte in Landschaft Oil/panel (39x46cm 15x18in) Praha 2000
- $578 - €547 - £360 - FF3 586
  Baeume Öl/Karton (30x49cm 11x19in) Praha 2001
- $520 - €492 - £324 - FF3 227
  Rochers au bord de lac Pastel/papier (46.5x62cm 18x24in) Praha 2001
- $375 - €355 - £234 - FF2 330
  Nue avec crâne Lithographie (27.5x23.5cm 10x9in) Praha 2000
- $701 - €818 - £485 - FF5 366
  Akt Vintage gelatin silver print (12.4x9.3cm 4x3in) Köln 2000

DRUBI Hafiz 1914-1991 **[1]**
- $9 739 - €10 954 - £6 800 - FF71 855
  The Family Oil/canvas (89x69cm 35x27in) London 2001

DRÜCK Hermann 1856-1931 **[37]**
- $695 - €665 - £423 - FF4 360
  Abendstimmung Öl/Karton (37x57.5cm 14x22in) Stuttgart 1999

DRUCKER Mort XX **[37]**
- $4 500 - €4 341 - £2 844 - FF28 476
  «Mad» No.234 Watercolour (43x47cm 16x18in) New-York 1999

DRUET Bernard XX **[8]**
- $556 - €640 - £393 - FF4 200
  Nu Sanguine/papier (65x50cm 25x19in) Barbizon 2001

DRUET Eugène 1868-1917 **[20]**
- $4 400 - €4 839 - £3 051 - FF31 741
  Study of Rodin's Salome Silver print (22x16cm 9x6in) New-York 2001

DRUILLET Philippe 1944 **[34]**
- $907 - €1 067 - £650 - FF7 000
  «Portrait narcissique et provisoire de l'auteur» Technique mixte (48x65cm 18x25in) Versailles 2001
- $2 847 - €3 201 - £1 999 - FF21 000
  Lone Sloane, pl.8 des 6 voyages de Lone Sloane Encre Chine/papier (85x65cm 33x25in) Paris 2001

DRUKS Michael 1940 **[52]**
- $2 000 - €2 147 - £1 338 - FF14 082
  Figure Oil/wood (40.5x59.5cm 15x23in) Tel Aviv 2000
- $8 200 - €9 721 - £5 973 - FF63 768
  Untitled Assemblage (36.5x58.5cm 14x23in) Tel Aviv 2001
- $650 - €771 - £473 - FF5 058
  Head of a Woman Gouache (31.5x30cm 12x11in) Tel Aviv 2001

DRUMAUX Angelina 1881-1959 **[53]**
- $16 575 - €16 112 - £10 205 - FF105 690
  Grand vase de chrysanthèmes dans un intérieur Huile/toile (130x178cm 51x70in) Bruxelles 1999
- $1 642 - €1 834 - £1 147 - FF12 032
  Vase fleuri d'anémones Huile/toile (65x50cm 25x19in) Bruxelles 2001

DRUMMOND Arthur 1871-1951 **[13]**
- $2 113 - €1 951 - £1 300 - FF12 800
  Reflections Oil/panel (30x20cm 11x7in) London 1999

DRUMMOND James 1816-1877 **[29]**
- $653 - €732 - £450 - FF4 799
  Fisher boy/Fisher Girl Watercolour/paper (17x12cm 7x5in) Birmingham 2000

D

DRUMMOND Julian E. XIX [9]
- $1 292 - €1 448 - £900 - FF9 501
  View of St.Mary's Church, Whitby from the Harbour Watercolour (41x29cm 16x11in) Leyburn, North Yorkshire 2001

DRUMMOND Malcolm 1880-1945 [23]
- $17 786 - €20 666 - £12 500 - FF135 557
  Interior, a Sculptor's studio Oil/canvas (54x57cm 21x22in) London 2001
- $2 097 - €1 926 - £1 300 - FF12 637
  Landscape, Donegal Oil/panel (25x35cm 9x13in) London 1999

DRUMMOND-DAVIES Nora 1862-1949 [5]
- $3 007 - €2 542 - £1 800 - FF16 675
  A Partridge Shoot Watercolour (51x75cm 20x29in) London 1998

DRUMMOND-FISH George, Captain XIX-XX [37]
- $450 - €417 - £280 - FF2 737
  O'Connel Bridge, Dublin Watercolour/paper (32x23.5cm 12x9in) London 1999

DRURY Alfred Ed. Briscoe 1859-1944 [22]
- $1 718 - €1 855 - £1 188 - FF12 170
  Bust of a Young Girl Bronze (H37cm H14in) Johannesburg 2001

DRURY Chris 1948 [2]
- $3 402 - €3 178 - £2 100 - FF20 844
  Falcon II Bronze (H63.5cm H25in) Billinghurst, West-Sussex 1999

DRURY Paul Dalou 1903-1988 [21]
- $432 - €367 - £260 - FF2 406
  March Morning Etching (13.5x16.5cm 5x6in) London 1998

DRYDEN Ernst Deutsch 1883-1938 [20]
- $3 207 - €2 905 - £2 000 - FF19 058
  Ski Fashion, Sketches Watercolour (46x29cm 18x11in) London 1999
- $1 064 - €944 - £650 - FF6 193
  «Kupferberg Riesling» Affiche couleur (58x88cm 22x34in) London 1999

DRYDEN Helen 1887-1981 [3]
- $2 300 - €2 681 - £1 592 - FF17 586
  Fashionable Women Pausing Outside Hat Shop Watercolour (46x34cm 18x13in) New-York 2000

DRYSDALE Alexander John 1870-1934 [280]
- $2 500 - €2 497 - £1 562 - FF16 381
  Bayou Landscape with the Live Oak and Waterlilies Oil/board (50x76cm 20x30in) New-Orleans LA 1999
- $2 000 - €1 818 - £1 204 - FF11 926
  Oak at Bayou's Edge Mixed media/board (30x45cm 12x18in) New-Orleans LA 1998
- $1 250 - €1 197 - £770 - FF7 851
  Louisiana Bayou Pastel/paper (50x74cm 20x29in) Portsmouth NH 1999

DRYSDALE George Russell, Sir 1912-1981 [208]
- $547 600 - €611 584 - £350 667 - FF4 011 725
  Mother and Child, North Queensland Oil/canvas (102x127.5cm 40x50in) Malvern, Victoria 2000
- $83 552 - €94 492 - £58 800 - FF619 824
  Mrs Fardakas of the Acropolis Cafe Oil/canvas (76x61cm 29x24in) Malvern, Victoria 2001
- $15 567 - €17 436 - £10 815 - FF114 375
  «Head of a Boy» Oil/board (20x14.5cm 7x5in) Melbourne 2001
- $2 971 - €2 732 - £1 837 - FF17 921
  Girl Carrying a Child Ink (32x25cm 12x9in) Melbourne 1998

$1 158 - €1 001 - £699 - FF6 564
  Black's Camp Lithograph (79x57cm 31x22in) Malvern, Victoria 1998

DU BOIS Guy Pène 1884-1958 [86]
- $28 000 - €30 055 - £18 737 - FF197 148
  Dancer Resting Oil/canvas (50.5x40.5cm 19x15in) New-York 2000
- $15 000 - €16 416 - £10 347 - FF107 682
  Washington Square Oil/canvas (30.5x40.5cm 12x15in) New-York 2001
- $1 400 - €1 592 - £978 - FF10 444
  Nude Study Pencil/paper (33x21cm 13x8in) New-York 2000

DU CAMP Maxime 1822-1894 [70]
- $4 086 - €4 573 - £2 844 - FF30 000
  Seconde Cataracte, 24 mars Tirage papier salé (16x22.5cm 6x8in) Paris 2001

DU PASSAGE Edouard Guy, comte 1872-1925 [7]
- $5 337 - €4 573 - £3 210 - FF30 000
  «Miss chienne de chasse» Bronze (H37cm H14in) Valence 1998

DU TOIT Paul 1922-1986 [19]
- $1 582 - €1 864 - £1 094 - FF12 228
  The Forest clearing Oil/board (55x75.5cm 21x29in) Cape Town 2000

DUARTE DE ALMEIDA Maria do Carmo XX [5]
- $1 056 - €1 196 - £744 - FF7 848
  Barco encalhado no areal do Tejo Oleo/lienzo (33x24cm 12x9in) Lisboa 2001

DUASSUT Curtius XIX-XX [28]
- $736 - €668 - £460 - FF4 385
  Thatched Cottage by a Pond Watercolour/paper (18x25cm 7x9in) London 1999

DUATMIKA Made 1970 [3]
- $1 285 - €1 346 - £807 - FF8 828
  Kampong Life Acrylic/canvas (94x81cm 37x31in) Singapore 2000

DUBACH Margaretha 1938 [7]
- $2 599 - €2 619 - £1 617 - FF17 178
  Das verstummte Lied Mischtechnik (52x21x14cm 20x8x5in) Zürich 2000

DUBAN Félix 1797-1870 [4]
- $3 045 - €3 583 - £2 183 - FF23 500
  Frontispice de l'album de mariage, duc de Montpensier & M.L.F Bourbon Aquarelle, gouache (43.5x62cm 17x24in) Paris 2001

DUBASTY Adolphe Henri 1814-1884 [10]
- $5 130 - €4 462 - £3 060 - FF29 268
  Maternité Huile/panneau (46x37cm 18x14in) Bruxelles 1998
- $1 393 - €1 604 - £950 - FF10 520
  A Break for Lunch Oil/panel (33x25.5cm 12x10in) London 2000

DUBASTY Joseph XIX [8]
- $2 040 - €2 287 - £1 384 - FF15 000
  Homme en habit bleu et lunettes Miniature (6.5x5cm 2x1in) Paris 2000

DUBAUT Pierre Olivier 1886-1968 [209]
- $237 - €229 - £146 - FF1 590
  Jokey à l'entrainement Aquarelle (23.5x32cm 9x12in) Paris 1999

DUBBELS Hendrick Jacobsz. 1620/21-1676 **[20]**
🖌 **$29 473** - €27 332 - **£18 000** - FF179 283
    An Evening Landscape with Dutch Men o'War and other Vessels Oil/panel (70.5x93cm 27x36in) London 1998

DUBE Mattie 1861-? **[2]**
🖌 **$5 000** - €4 328 - **£3 015** - FF28 393
    Reclining Nude in a Forest Oil/canvas (82.5x125cm 32x49in) San-Francisco CA 1998

DUBIEZ Claudius XIX-XX **[3]**
🖌 **$30 000** - €28 100 - **£18 444** - FF184 323
    Still Life with Roses, Grapes and Peaches Oil/canvas (100x81.5cm 39x32in) New-York 1999

DÜBLIN Jacques 1901-1978 **[25]**
🖌 **$652** - €701 - **£436** - FF44 595
    Bauer mit Pferd vor dem Stall Öl/Karton (43x60cm 16x23in) Zofingen 2000

DUBOC Ferdinand 1810-? **[4]**
🖌 **$6 062** - €5 336 - **£3 692** - FF35 000
    Cavaliers au soleil couchant Huile/toile (59.5x97cm 23x38in) Paris 1999

DUBOIS Charles Edouard 1847-1885 **[19]**
🖌 **$4 025** - €3 445 - **£2 423** - FF22 598
    Sumpfwiese im Sommer Huile/toile (42x25cm 16x9in) Zürich 1998

DUBOIS Edward Du Bois 1619-1696 **[2]**
✏ **$5 023** - €4 277 - **£3 000** - FF28 056
    Studies of four Putti Black, red & white chalks (9.5x11cm 3x4in) London 1998

DUBOIS Ernest Henri 1863-1931 **[10]**
🖌 **$5 770** - €6 555 - **£4 050** - FF43 000
    Fauconnier arabe sur son pur-sang cabré Bronze (H70cm H27in) Paris 2001

DUBOIS François 1790-1871 **[3]**
🖌 **$2 798** - €3 049 - **£1 834** - FF20 000
    Distribution des drapeaux aux gardes par le roi Louis-Philippe, 9 août Huile/toile (25x42.5cm 9x16in) Louviers 2000

DUBOIS Guillam 1610-1680 **[26]**
🖌 **$5 731** - €6 391 - **£3 853** - FF41 923
    Dünenlandschaft in der Umgebung von Haarlem Oil/panel (34.5x51.2cm 13x20in) Köln 2000
🖌 **$1 944** - €2 178 - **£1 351** - FF14 287
    Hilly Landscape with Horseman and other Figures on a Path Oil/panel (27x36cm 10x14in) Amsterdam 2001
✏ **$452** - €486 - **£302** - FF3 186
    Hügelige Landschaft Black chalk/paper (13.2x18.7cm 5x7in) Berlin 2000

DUBOIS Hippolyte Henri P. 1837-1909 **[10]**
🖌 **$20 000** - €18 559 - **£12 220** - FF121 740
    After the Bath Oil/canvas (169x130cm 66x51in) New-York 1999
🖌 **$4 172** - €4 878 - **£2 931** - FF32 000
    La discrète Huile/toile (41x32.5cm 16x12in) Paris 2000

DUBOIS Jean 1789-1849 **[17]**
🖌 **$296** - €249 - **£174** - FF1 635
    Ansicht von Saint-Gingolph Aquatinta (14.4x20.7cm 5x8in) Bern 1998

DUBOIS Jean 1923-1990 **[24]**
🖌 **$379** - €372 - **£235** - FF2 439
    Composition Huile/toile (100x80cm 39x31in) Bruxelles 1999

DUBOIS Louis 1830-1880 **[28]**
🖌 **$4 784** - €5 488 - **£3 272** - FF36 000
    Jeune fille sur un sofa Huile/toile (65.5x44cm 25x17in) Pau 2000
🖌 **$653** - €686 - **£429** - FF4 500
    La plage Huile/toile (25x50cm 9x19in) Lyon 2000

DUBOIS Maurice P. XIX-XX **[9]**
🖌 **$2 998** - €3 201 - **£2 047** - FF21 000
    Cantinière Révolutionnaire Huile/toile (104x73cm 40x28in) Paris 2001

DUBOIS Paul 1859-1938 **[23]**
🖌 **$1 758** - €1 486 - **£1 050** - FF9 750
    David Bronze (H56cm H22in) Antwerpen 1998

DUBOIS Paul 1829-1905 **[141]**
🖌 **$5 691** - €5 202 - **£3 482** - FF34 122
    Young Shepherd Bronze (H96cm H37in) Warszawa 1999
🖌 **$1 982** - €1 876 - **£1 232** - FF12 305
    Gladiateur Bronze (H38cm H14in) Montréal 1999

DUBOIS Paul Elie 1886-1949 **[69]**
🖌 **$7 880** - €7 622 - **£4 860** - FF50 000
    Touaregs dans le Hoggar Huile/carton (50x60cm 19x23in) Paris 1999
🖌 **$908** - €1 082 - **£647** - FF7 100
    Femmes Arabes Huile/papier (22x30cm 8x11in) Belfort 2000
🖌 **$1 962** - €1 906 - **£1 212** - FF12 500
    Targui Aquarelle, gouache (57x38cm 22x14in) Paris 1999

DUBOIS Raphaël 1888-? **[84]**
🖌 **$914** - €892 - **£561** - FF5 853
    Le passage du train à vapeur Huile/toile (56x70cm 22x27in) Bruxelles 1999
🖌 **$485** - €520 - **£329** - FF3 414
    Jeux d'enfants Huile/carton (25x19cm 9x7in) Bruxelles 2001

DUBOIS Simon 1632-1708 **[7]**
🖌 **$2 712** - €2 989 - **£1 821** - FF19 607
    Frances Somers, Daughter of Richard Somers Huile/toile (76x63.5cm 29x25in) Montréal 2000

DUBOIS-PILLET Albert 1845-1890 **[28]**
🖌 **$133 576** - €123 117 - **£80 000** - FF807 592
    Le Puy : La place ensoleillée Oil/canvas (82.5x61cm 32x24in) London 1998
🖌 **$9 499** - €10 671 - **£6 615** - FF70 000
    Bord de rivière Huile/toile (27x41cm 10x16in) Honfleur 2001

DUBOIS-TESSELIN Frederic François 1832-? **[1]**
🖌 **$5 500** - €5 098 - **£3 419** - FF33 440
    Brig. Gen. P.G.T Beauregard at Charleston after L.M.D Guillaume Engraving (13x52cm 5x20in) New-Orleans LA 1999

DUBORD Jean-Pierre 1949 **[197]**
🖌 **$1 376** - €1 189 - **£831** - FF7 800
    Neige au pré des loups Huile/toile (50x65cm 19x25in) Rouen 1998
🖌 **$579** - €488 - **£342** - FF3 200
    Rouen, rue du Mont Gargan Huile/toile (22x27cm 8x10in) Grenoble 1998

DUBOS Yves XX **[20]**
🖌 **$390** - €473 - **£273** - FF3 100
    L'atelier du peintre Acrylique (81x60cm 31x23in) Lavaur 2000

DUBOSCQ-SOLEIL Louis Jules 1817-1886 **[8]**
$7 073 - €6 555 - **£4 368** - FF43 000
  Nature morte aux instruments d'optique
  Daguerreotype (8.5x17.5cm 3x6in) Paris 1999

DUBOST Antoine 1769-1825 **[3]**
$210 000 - €233 112 - **£146 391** - FF1 529 115
  Le retour d'Hélène Oil/canvas (131x192cm 51x75in)
  New-York 2001

DUBOURCQ Pierre Louis 1815-1873 **[12]**
$5 593 - €6 353 - **£3 924** - FF41 672
  The Ferry Oil/canvas (64x80cm 25x31in) Amsterdam
  2001
$2 050 - €1 771 - **£1 236** - FF11 618
  **View of a Road along the River Teppia approa-
  ching Cori** Pencil/paper (28.5x44cm 11x17in)
  Amsterdam 1998

DUBOURG Louis Alexandre 1825-1891 **[61]**
$9 152 - €9 757 - **£5 804** - FF64 000
  Les cueilleurs d'herbe Huile/toile (33x55cm
  12x21in) Honfleur 2000
$1 930 - €2 058 - **£1 224** - FF13 500
  Honfleur, la lieutenance Huile/toile (26.5x23cm
  10x9in) Deauville 2000
$3 452 - €3 735 - **£2 364** - FF24 500
  Femmes de pêcheur à Honfleur Pastel/papier
  (14x20cm 5x7in) Granville 2001

DUBOURG Matthew XVIII-XIX **[19]**
$250 - €229 - **£156** - FF1 501
  Forum of Nerva/Grotto of Egeria Aquatint
  (21x29cm 8x11in) New-York 1999

DUBOUT Albert 1906-1976 **[172]**
$723 - €762 - **£477** - FF5 000
  Le policier Sculpture (H39cm H15in) Paris 2000
$816 - €796 - **£568** - FF6 000
  Scène érotique Encres couleurs/papier (31x27cm
  12x10in) Paris 2001
$533 - €457 - **£322** - FF3 000
  «Le Duralumin» Affiche (80x58cm 31x22in) Paris
  1998

DUBOVSKOIJ Nikolaj Nikanorovich 1859-1918 **[23]**
$11 954 - €12 832 - **£8 000** - FF84 172
  Summer - View over the Gulf of Finland Oil/can-
  vas (101.5x132cm 39x51in) London 2000
$13 840 - €14 534 - **£8 720** - FF95 340
  Wolga, Flusslandschaft mit Booten Öl/Leinwand
  (84x105cm 33x41in) Wien 2000
$1 126 - €1 308 - **£777** - FF8 580
  Winteransicht einer Stadt Öl/Leinwand (26x33.5cm
  10x13in) Wien 2000

DUBOY Paul 1830-c.1887 **[12]**
$1 423 - €1 220 - **£856** - FF8 000
  Buste de Béatrix Bronze (H42cm H16in) Royan
  1998

DUBRAY Vital Gabriel 1813-1892 **[3]**
$5 537 - €5 890 - **£3 500** - FF38 633
  The Empress Joséphine Bronze (H57cm H22in)
  London 2000

DUBREUIL André 1951 **[1]**
$28 000 - €30 055 - **£18 737** - FF197 148
  Prototype «Spine» Chair Iron (H87.5cm H34in)
  New-York 2000

DUBREUIL Chéri 1828-c.1880 **[53]**
$5 608 - €6 098 - **£3 696** - FF40 000
  **Flotte française dans un port, grands vaisseaux
  amarrés, chaloupe** Huile/toile (80x150cm 31x59in)
  Paris 2000

$7 000 - €7 954 - **£4 834** - FF52 178
  **The Egyptus in stormy Seas off the Coast of
  Constantinople** Oil/canvas (88x120cm 34x47in)
  New-York 2000
$1 690 - €1 973 - **£1 193** - FF12 944
  Zanzibar ile prise/Etree de la rade Oil/canvas
  (24x35cm 9x13in) Toronto 2000

DUBREUIL Pierre 1872-1944 **[57]**
$24 000 - €22 412 - **£14 493** - FF147 014
  Antithèse Photograph (25x20cm 9x7in) New-York
  1999

DUBREUIL Toussaint c.1651-1602 **[1]**
$28 233 - €27 567 - **£18 000** - FF180 828
  **Lot's wife looking back towards the destruction
  of Sodom and Gomorrah** Black chalk (21.5x27cm
  8x10in) London 1999

DUBREUIL Victor act.1880-1910 **[8]**
$130 000 - €111 070 - **£78 039** - FF728 572
  Barrels of Money Oil/canvas (63.5x76cm 25x29in)
  New-York 1998
$6 000 - €6 566 - **£4 138** - FF43 072
  100 Franc note Oil/canvas (22x26.5cm 8x10in) New-
  York 2001

DUBUC Jean-Louis 1946 **[32]**
$2 740 - €2 942 - **£1 833** - FF19 300
  Les musiciens Huile/toile (61x50cm 24x19in)
  Provins 2000

DUBUC Roland 1924-1998 **[636]**
$850 - €884 - **£535** - FF5 800
  Vue de Montmartre sous la neige Huile/toile
  (46x55cm 18x21in) Le Havre 2000
$355 - €381 - **£235** - FF2 500
  Les musiciens Aquarelle/papier (50x65cm 19x25in)
  Provins 2000

DUBUCAND Alfred 1828-1894 **[262]**
$1 704 - €1 829 - **£1 140** - FF12 000
  Grand cerf, douze cors Bronze (30x37cm 11x14in)
  Paris 2000

DUBUFE Claude-Marie 1790-1864 **[29]**
$8 804 - €9 452 - **£5 890** - FF62 000
  Portrait de la fille du Général Philippe Vigogne
  Huile/toile (64x53cm 25x20in) Nîmes 2000

DUBUFE Édouard Louis 1820-1883 **[38]**
$7 275 - €7 622 - **£4 605** - FF50 000
  Méditation Huile/toile (60x50cm 23x19in) Paris 2000
$3 500 - €3 210 - **£2 156** - FF21 058
  **Mme Rachel, The French Jewish Tragic Actress,
  in the Role of Phedre** Oil/canvas (28x24cm 11x9in)
  New-York 1999
$3 473 - €3 249 - **£2 100** - FF21 310
  **Jean Frederic Andre Poulbert, Baron de
  Neuflize/His Brother M.Poubert** Watercolour/paper
  (48x39.5cm 18x15in) London 1999

DUBUFE Édouard M. Guillaume 1853-1909 **[43]**
$33 087 - €31 252 - **£20 602** - FF205 000
  La cigale/La fourmi Huile/toile (218x105cm 85x41in)
  Paris 1999
$4 604 - €5 196 - **£3 239** - FF34 082
  Mutter mit Kind auf dem Rücken Öl/Leinwand
  (91x78cm 35x30in) Bern 2001
$579 - €534 - **£347** - FF3 500
  Étude pour Erato Crayon (43x30cm 16x11in)
  Soissons 1999

DUBUFFET Jean 1901-1985 **[1534]**
$252 735 - €275 398 - **£175 000** - FF1 806 490
  «Raisons et lieux» Oil/canvas (97x130cm 38x51in)
  London 2001

$133 471 - €129 903 - **£82 000** - FF852 111
Paysage aux oiseaux Mixed media/canvas
(73.5x92cm 28x36in) London 1999

$11 515 - €10 671 - **£7 161** - FF70 000
Assemblage d'empreintes Technique mixte
(15x10cm 5x3in) Versailles 1999

$90 000 - €101 812 - **£62 964** - FF667 845
Pantalon aux chausses Metal (113x63.5x47cm
44x25x18in) New-York 2001

$120 000 - €131 694 - **£77 268** - FF863 856
Buste faunesque Sculpture (71x31.5x23cm
27x12x9in) New-York 2000

$22 331 - €23 203 - **£14 000** - FF152 203
Le cadastre Felt pen (46x68cm 18x26in) London
2000

$2 671 - €2 462 - **£1 600** - FF16 151
Delegation Silkscreen in colors (78x55cm 30x21in)
London 1998

DUBUIS Fernand 1908-1991 [171]

$746 - €732 - **£481** - FF4 800
Fête en Valais Huile/toile (82x50cm 32x19in)
Divonne-les-Bains 1999

$171 - €168 - **£110** - FF1 100
La pochade Huile/carton (35x24cm 13x9in) Divonne-
les-Bains 1999

DUBUISSON Alexandre 1805-1870 [25]

$3 631 - €4 269 - **£2 632** - FF28 000
Equipage de halage sur le Rhône Huile/toile
(71x110cm 27x43in) Lyon 2001

DUC Antoine 1932 [25]

$877 - €884 - **£546** - FF5 800
L'écuyère aux seins nus Huile/toile (54x73cm
21x28in) Paris 2000

DUC Franck 1940 [11]

$575 - €671 - **£398** - FF4 400
Paysage provençal Huile/toile (73x60cm 28x23in)
Strasbourg 2000

DUCAROIR Claudine 1946 [6]

$313 - €335 - **£213** - FF2 200
Sans titre Aquarelle (50x68cm 19x26in) Paris 2001

DUCE Alberto 1916 [43]

$260 - €240 - **£164** - FF1 576
Merienda campestre con sandias Tinta (70x50cm
27x19in) Madrid 1999

DUCHAMP Marcel 1887-1968 [212]

$450 000 - €426 622 - **£273 780** - FF2 798 460
Chessboard Mixed media (70x70cm 27x27in) New-
York 1999

$30 000 - €32 923 - **£19 317** - FF215 964
Some French Moderns Says McBride Mixed
media (30x23.5cm 11x9in) New-York 2000

$67 344 - €80 092 - **£48 000** - FF525 369
**De ou par Marcel Duchamp ou Rrose Selavy
(La boîte en valise)** Object (40x37.5x9cm
15x14x3in) London 2000

$779 472 - €760 411 - **£480 000** - FF4 987 968
**Study for Chess Players (Étude pour les
joueurs d'échecs)** Charcoal/paper (49.5x50.5cm
19x19in) London 1999

$3 295 - €3 506 - **£2 083** - FF23 000
Tiré à quatre épingles Eau-forte (64x46cm 25x18in)
Paris 2000

DUCHAMP Suzanne 1889-1963 [55]

$588 - €686 - **£413** - FF4 500
Le rocher dans la crique Huile/toile (66x81cm
25x31in) Versailles 2000

$654 - €610 - **£403** - FF4 000
Nature-morte à la carafe Gouache/papier
(41.5x51cm 16x20in) Orléans 1999

$923 - €991 - **£617** - FF6 500
Portrait de Marcel Duchamp Gravure (23.5x17.5cm
9x6in) Paris 2000

DUCHAMP-VILLON Raymond 1876-1918 [19]

$11 842 - €10 228 - **£7 152** - FF67 092
Cheval Bronze (36.2x37x12cm 14x14x4in) Köln 1998

DUCHENNE DE BOULOGNE Guillaume Benjamin 1806-1875 [10]

$946 - €991 - **£594** - FF6 500
Expériences électro-physiques Tirage albuminé
(13.5x11cm 5x4in) Paris 2000

DUCHOISELLE XIX [19]

$3 500 - €4 184 - **£2 414** - FF27 447
Indian Brave in a Canoe Bronze (34x55cm 13x22in)
Milford CT 2000

DUCIS Louis 1775-1847 [8]

$4 305 - €3 721 - **£2 595** - FF24 405
Paysage italien animé avec ruines et Vésuve
Huile/toile (90.5x106.5cm 35x41in) Bruxelles 1998

DUCK Jacob 1600-1660 [35]

$26 877 - €29 496 - **£17 303** - FF193 479
**Officer and a Courtesane playing Cards in a
Brothel** Oil/panel (48.5x38.5cm 19x15in) Amsterdam
2000

$47 170 - €40 741 - **£28 435** - FF267 245
**A Kortegaardje: A Woman flirting with an
Ensign in an Inn** Oil/panel (34x26.9cm 13x10in)
Amsterdam 1998

DÜCKER Eugen Gustav 1841-1916 [30]

$3 238 - €3 579 - **£2 246** - FF23 477
**Küstenlandschaft mit Ansiedlung und
Personen** Öl/Leinwand (57.5x96cm 22x37in) Berlin
2001

$1 398 - €1 534 - **£949** - FF10 061
Am Meer Öl/Karton (30x47cm 11x18in) Düsseldorf
2000

DUCKER John M. XIX-XX [30]

$286 - €298 - **£180** - FF1 957
Highland Scene at Dusk Oil/canvas (51x76cm
20x29in) London 2000

DUCKETT Mathilde 1844-? [6]

$437 - €488 - **£304** - FF3 200
La jeune aquarelliste Huile/toile (21x16cm 8x6in)
Paris 2001

DUCKWORTH Ruth 1919 [18]

$10 000 - €10 359 - **£6 365** - FF67 953
Large Vessel Split #R81 Ceramic
(45.5x58.5x53.5cm 17x23x21in) New-York 2000

DUCLERE Teodoro 1816-1867 [19]

$12 500 - €12 958 - **£7 500** - FF85 000
Taormina Olio/tela (35.5x55cm 13x21in) Venezia 2000

$11 052 - €11 582 - **£7 000** - FF75 970
Strada Di Posilipo Oil/canvas (30x44cm 11x17in)
London 2000

$960 - €1 244 - **£720** - FF8 160
Paesaggio sorrentino Matita (23x29cm 9x11in)
Napoli 2000

DUCLOS Antoine Jean 1742-1795 [9]

$751 - €838 - **£522** - FF5 500
**Le concert/Le bal paré, d'après Saint-Aubin
Auguste** Gravure (34x45cm 13x17in) Paris 2001

DUCLOU Pierre XX **[7]**
📖 **$570 – €610 – £388 –** FF4 000
«Contine» Technique mixte/papier (37x90cm 14x35in)
Paris 2001

DUCMELIC Zdravko 1923-1989 **[3]**
💺 **$2 500 – €2 905 – £1 757 –** FF19 053
«Mujer joven del pasado» Oleo/cartón (25x19cm
9x7in) Buenos-Aires 2001

DUCOMMUN Jean 1920-1958 **[21]**
💺 **$3 999 – €4 420 – £2 773 –** FF28 993
Après l'orage Huile/toile (46x55cm 18x21in) Genève
2001
💺 **$2 965 – €3 477 – £2 115 –** FF22 809
Café à Paris Huile/toile (30x41cm 11x16in) Genève
2000

DUCOS DE LA HAILLE Pierre-Henri 1889-1972 **[8]**
💺 **$518 – €610 – £371 –** FF4 000
Paturage en bord de mer Huile/toile (72x53cm
28x20in) Nantes 2001

DUCQ Joseph François 1762-1829 **[8]**
💺 **$22 000 – €18 297 – £12 914 –** FF120 021
«The Heroism of a Scythian» Oil/canvas
(276.5x399cm 108x157in) New-York 1998
💺 **$4 236 – €4 269 – £2 640 –** FF28 000
La Jeunesse et L'Amour Huile/toile (49x35.5cm
19x13in) Paris 2000

DUCREL D. XIX **[2]**
💺 **$11 000 – €11 403 – £6 600 –** FF74 800
La cruche cassée (La brocca rotta) Olio/tela
(110x84cm 43x33in) Prato 2000

DUCRET Maurice 1953 **[16]**
📖 **$274 – €264 – £170 –** FF1 731
Composition Mischtechnik/Papier (43x30.5cm
16x12in) Zürich 1999

DUCREUX Joseph 1735-1802 **[13]**
📖 **$3 220 – €3 659 – £2 260 –** FF24 000
Portrait de Monsieur Jean Dusaulx Pastel/papier
(68x54cm 26x21in) Paris 2001

DUCROS Abraham Louis R. 1748-1810 **[46]**
💺 **$6 695 – €6 555 – £4 119 –** FF43 000
Personnages sur un pont contemplant un torrent Huile/papier/toile (103x66.5cm 40x26in) Paris
1999
📖 **$6 486 – €6 276 – £4 000 –** FF41 168
River Anio above the Cascade at Tivoli near the
Temple of the Sybil Watercolour/paper
(81.5x124.5cm 32x49in) London 1999
🎨 **$4 878 – €5 488 – £3 358 –** FF36 000
Les jardins de la villa Doria-Pamphili Eau-forte
(51x73.5cm 20x28in) Paris 2000

DUCROS Édouard 1856-1936 **[12]**
💺 **$1 923 – €2 287 – £1 333 –** FF15 000
Martigues Huile/toile (73x55cm 28x21in) Aix-en-
Provence 2000

DUDA Gary 1951 **[3]**
💺 **$2 300 – €2 467 – £1 538 –** FF16 182
Kinetic Impressions of Acadia #9 Oil/canvas
(40x50cm 16x20in) Bolton MA 2000

DUDA-GRACZ Jerzy 1941 **[32]**
💺 **$3 758 – €4 123 – £2 553 –** FF27 045
Débauche au crépuscule Huile/toile (81x70cm
31x27in) Warszawa 2000

DUDAN Gabriel-Dominique XIX **[2]**
💺 **$7 766 – €8 385 – £5 368 –** FF55 000
Nature morte aux fruits Huile/toile (59x49.5cm
23x19in) Paris 2001

DUDANT Roger 1929-1991 **[85]**
💺 **$537 – €595 – £376 –** FF3 902
Composition Huile/toile (97x62cm 38x24in)
Bruxelles 2001

DUDLEY Arthur act.c.1890-c.1907 **[58]**
📖 **$624 – €549 – £380 –** FF3 603
Still Life, Cherries and Lemons Watercolour/paper
(25.5x74cm 10x29in) London 1999

DUDLEY Charles XIX-XX **[25]**
💺 **$773 – €716 – £480 –** FF4 698
Setters Retrieving Black Grouse in the Scottish
Highlands Oil/canvas (45x73cm 18x29in) Carlisle,
Cumbria 1999
💺 **$683 – €782 – £470 –** FF5 129
The Unwelcome Visitor Oil/canvas (30.5x23cm
12x9in) Lymington 2000

DUDLEY Frank Virgil 1868-1957 **[27]**
💺 **$26 450 – €22 824 – £15 981 –** FF149 717
Sandland in winter (Sandland's evening song)
Oil/canvas (96x127cm 38x50in) Bethesda MD 1999
💺 **$10 000 – €10 803 – £6 924 –** FF70 861
Day to remember Oil/canvas (68x76cm 27x30in)
Cincinnati OH 2001
💺 **$2 200 – €2 502 – £1 525 –** FF16 412
Summer Afternoon Oil/board (30x40cm 12x16in)
Cincinnati OH 2001

DUDLEY Thomas, Tom 1857-1935 **[27]**
📖 **$362 – €426 – £260 –** FF2 797
«Pike How, Langdale» Watercolour (24.5x35cm
9x13in) West-Yorshire 2001

DUDOVICH Marcello 1878-1962 **[149]**
💺 **$950 – €985 – £570 –** FF6 460
L'amico fedele Tempera/carta (42x28cm 16x11in)
Trieste 2001
🎨 **$1 695 – €1 757 – £1 017 –** FF11 526
«Brigg's Waterproofs» Affiche couleur (100x70cm
39x27in) Torino 2000

DUDREVILLE Leonardo 1885-1976 **[40]**
💺 **$9 000 – €9 330 – £5 400 –** FF61 200
Marina con figure Olio/cartone (40x55cm 15x21in)
Milano 1999
💺 **$2 820 – €2 436 – £1 880 –** FF15 980
L'ansa di Feriolo Olio/tavola (27x37cm 10x14in)
Trieste 1998

DUEREN van Jan XVII **[1]**
💺 **$4 460 – €4 958 – £2 980 –** FF32 520
Nature morte aux grimoires Huile/panneau
(32x42cm 12x16in) Bruxelles 2000

DUESSEL Henry A. XIX-XX **[14]**
💺 **$1 800 – €2 055 – £1 269 –** FF13 481
Gentleman Fishing in an Autumn Landscape
Oil/canvas (76.5x127.5cm 30x50in) Boston MA 2001

DUEZ Ernest Ange 1843-1896 **[35]**
💺 **$82 880 – €70 663 – £50 000 –** FF463 520
Mère et fille sur la plage Oil/canvas (46.5x56cm
18x22in) London 1998
💺 **$10 256 – €12 196 – £7 312 –** FF80 000
Élégante sur la plage de Villerville Huile/panneau
(40x31cm 15x12in) Neuilly-sur-Seine 2000

DUFAU Clémentine Hélène 1869-1937 **[20]**
💺 **$1 506 – €1 537 – £942 –** FF10 081
La baigneuse Huile/toile (80x53cm 31x20in)
Bruxelles 2000
🎨 **$15 000 – €16 735 – £9 819 –** FF109 773
«Pelote basque dans le parc du cercle de
St.James» Poster (145.5x105.5cm 57x41in) New-York
2000

D

DUFAUX Frédéric 1852-1943 **[71]**
- 🏛 **$2 786** - €3 170 - **£1 932** - FF20 791
  Venise Huile/toile (48x68cm 18x26in) Sion 2000
- 🏛 **$1 301** - €1 415 - **£857** - FF9 285
  Frau auf einem Feldweg Öl/Karton (15x23cm 5x9in) Bern 2000

DUFAUX Henri Rochefort 1879-1981 **[14]**
- 🏛 **$11 471** - €12 706 - **£7 781** - FF83 344
  Sénégal-Mauritanie: puits aux abords d'un village Oil/canvas (114x114cm 44x44in) Amsterdam 2000

DUFEU Édouard Jacques 1840-1900 **[104]**
- 🏛 **$1 505** - €1 524 - **£944** - FF10 000
  Vue de port Huile/toile (35x59cm 13x23in) Aix-en-Provence 2000
- 🏛 **$418** - €488 - **£290** - FF3 200
  Mon chien, Lion, couché Huile/toile (16.5x30.5cm 6x12in) Nice 2000
- 🖋 **$137** - €152 - **£95** - FF1 000
  Chameau Mine plomb (15.5x19.5cm 6x7in) Paris 2001

DUFF John Robert Keitley 1862-1938 **[18]**
- 🖋 **$283** - €263 - **£170** - FF1 728
  Sheep grazing beneath blossoming Trees Pastel/paper (28x35cm 11x13in) London 1999

DUFFAUT Préfète 1923 **[64]**
- 🏛 **$706** - €610 - **£424** - FF4 000
  Ile dans le port Huile/toile (40x50cm 15x19in) Paris 1998
- 🏛 **$325** - €313 - **£200** - FF2 051
  Ville Imaginaire Oil/canvas (40.5x30.5cm 15x12in) Washington 1999

DUFFIELD Mary Elizabeth 1819-1914 **[54]**
- 🖋 **$1 315** - €1 493 - **£900** - FF9 794
  Still Life with Roses, Hollyhocks and Lily in a Vase with Fruit Below Watercolour/paper (41x33cm 16x12in) Bury St. Edmunds, Suffolk 2000

DUFFIELD William D. 1816-1863 **[17]**
- 🏛 **$6 342** - €5 674 - **£3 800** - FF37 218
  A Scottish Still Life Oil/canvas (71x91.5cm 27x36in) Perthshire 1998
- 🏛 **$2 819** - €2 452 - **£1 700** - FF16 086
  Grapes, Plums, a Peach, a Groud and a Chine Vase Oil/canvas (25.5x35.5cm 10x13in) London 1998

DUFFY Patrick Vincent 1836-1909 **[7]**
- 🏛 **$1 968** - €1 905 - **£1 213** - FF12 493
  Sunset Oil/board (23x30.5cm 9x12in) Dublin 1999

DUFLOS Claude Augustin 1700-1786 **[6]**
- 🏛 **$242** - €244 - **£150** - FF1 600
  Les premiers pas de l'enfance/La mère qui intercède, d'après Schenau Eau-forte (49x36cm 19x14in) Paris 2000

DUFLOS Robert 1898-? **[64]**
- 🖋 **$314** - €305 - **£194** - FF2 000
  Nu de dos Fusain (34x26cm 13x10in) Entzheim 1999

DUFNER Edward 1871/72-1957 **[27]**
- 🏛 **$8 000** - €6 852 - **£4 723** - FF44 944
  Bedroom Still Life Oil/canvas (40.5x50.5cm 15x19in) New-York 1998

DUFOUR Bernard 1922 **[141]**
- 🏛 **$925** - €1 098 - **£653** - FF7 200
  Sans titre Huile/toile (100x81cm 39x31in) Paris 2000

DUFRAIS Simon XX **[1]**
- 🏛 **$10 930** - €12 207 - **£7 000** - FF80 072
  Well Under Way Oil/canvas (75x100cm 29x39in) London 2000

DUFRENE François 1930-1982 **[30]**
- 🏛 **$2 458** - €2 592 - **£1 623** - FF17 000
  Sans titre Affiche lacérée, arrachage (45x88cm 17x34in) Paris 2000
- 🏛 **$2 315** - €2 592 - **£1 570** - FF17 000
  Personnages et animaux Huile/toile (26x48cm 10x18in) Paris 2000
- 🏛 **$1 437** - €1 448 - **£895** - FF9 500
  Sans titre Affiche (24.5x25cm 9x9in) Paris 2000

DUFRENE Maurice 1876-1955 **[14]**
- 🏛 **$1 200** - €1 336 - **£745** - FF7 451
  «Rayon des Soieries» Poster (120x78.5cm 47x30in) New-York 1999

DUFRENOY Georges Léon 1870-1942 **[32]**
- 🏛 **$1 730** - €1 753 - **£1 086** - FF11 500
  Nature morte aux poires Huile/panneau (88x68cm 34x26in) Saint-Dié 2000

DUFRESNE Charles 1876-1938 **[365]**
- 🏛 **$5 282** - €5 793 - **£3 507** - FF38 000
  La chasse au lion Huile/toile (79x98cm 31x38in) Paris 2000
- 🏛 **$927** - €991 - **£618** - FF6 500
  Les centaures Huile/toile (18x20.5cm 7x8in) Paris 2000
- 🖋 **$882** - €915 - **£559** - FF6 000
  Personnages Encre Chine (26x38cm 10x14in) Paris 2000
- 🏛 **$344** - €381 - **£233** - FF2 500
  Le repos dans l'oasis II Eau-forte (12x20cm 4x7in) Paris 2000

DUFRESNOY Charles Alphonse 1611-1668 **[3]**
- 🏛 **$26 000** - €21 838 - **£15 285** - FF143 249
  Paris and Oenone Oil/canvas (129x97cm 50x38in) New-York 1998
- 🏛 **$16 514** - €14 000 - **£9 800** - FF91 835
  Allegory of Painting Oil/canvas (63x77.5cm 24x30in) London 1998

DUFTAS Robert XX **[5]**
- 🏛 **$1 740** - €2 045 - **£1 206** - FF13 415
  Weiblicher Rückenakt Oil/panel (23x36cm 9x14in) Stuttgart 2000

DUFY Jean 1888-1964 **[1390]**
- 🏛 **$35 000** - €39 203 - **£24 318** - FF257 152
  Le cirque Oil/canvas (96.5x129.5cm 37x50in) New-York 2001
- 🏛 **$17 000** - €17 329 - **£10 652** - FF113 673
  Nature morte au bouquet de fleurs Oil/canvas (61x50cm 24x19in) New-York 2000
- 🏛 **$8 362** - €7 719 - **£5 000** - FF50 631
  Le bouquet Oil/canvas (41x33cm 16x12in) London 1999
- 🖋 **$3 319** - €2 744 - **£1 947** - FF18 000
  Paysage cubiste Aquarelle/papier (63x48cm 24x18in) Paris 1998
- 🏛 **$352** - €396 - **£247** - FF2 600
  Les clowns Lithographie (46x63cm 18x24in) Pont-Audemer 2000

DUFY Raoul 1877-1953 **[2562]**
- 🏛 **$500 000** - €480 801 - **£308 050** - FF3 153 850
  La place d'Hyères: l'obélisque et le kiosque à musique Oil/canvas (129.5x161.5cm 50x63in) New-York 1999
- 🏛 **$111 930** - €118 910 - **£75 036** - FF780 000
  L'atelier de la rue Séguier Huile/toile (81x65cm 31x25in) Cannes 2000
- 🏛 **$38 080** - €42 686 - **£25 844** - FF280 000
  Nu allongé Huile/masonite (16x30.5cm 6x12in) Paris 2000

D

$70 000 - €78 405 - **£48 636** - FF514 304
Vase aux baigneuses Glazed ceramic (H47cm H18in) New-York 2001

$6 039 - €6 860 - **£4 239** - FF45 000
Vence Mine plomb (46x61cm 18x24in) Paris 2001

$391 - €366 - **£236** - FF2 400
Baigneuse à Saint Adresse Eau-forte (40x54cm 15x21in) Paris 1999

DUGDALE John 1961 **[11]**

$2 500 - €2 775 - **£1 738** - FF18 206
«**The Gloaming, Ulster County, N.Y.**» Photograph (24x19cm 9x7in) New-York 2001

DUGDALE Thomas Cantrell 1880-1952 **[11]**

$1 053 - €1 252 - **£750** - FF8 215
From Tel El Ful Watercolour (24.5x33.5cm 9x13in) London 2000

DUGHET Gaspard 1615-1675 **[66]**

$31 000 - €26 491 - **£18 209** - FF173 767
View from Tivoli Oil/canvas (144x194cm 57x76in) New-Orleans LA 1998

$19 740 - €21 802 - **£13 680** - FF143 010
Römische Landschaft mit einem Wasserfall Öl/Leinwand (59x75cm 23x29in) Wien 2001

$26 000 - €30 032 - **£18 000** - FF197 000
Paisaje con arquitecturas Oleo/lienzo (29x45cm 11x17in) Madrid 2000

$26 000 - €22 603 - **£15 735** - FF148 267
Classical Landscape, Thought to be a View of Tivoli Red chalk/paper (34x51.5cm 13x20in) New-York 1999

DUGMORE Arthur Radclyffe 1870-1955 **[3]**

$6 000 - €6 998 - **£4 212** - FF45 902
Elephants at the Watering Hole Oil/canvas (55x100cm 22x39in) Boston MA 2000

DUGMORE OF SWAFFHAM John 1793-1871 **[1]**

$1 925 - €1 940 - **£1 200** - FF12 724
View of the Castle of Carisbrooke on the Isle of Wight, Kenmore Ink (45x30cm 17x11in) London 2000

DUGOURC Jean Démosthène 1749-1825 **[27]**

$7 500 - €8 157 - **£4 944** - FF53 508
Interior with Mother and Child Oil/canvas (46x33cm 18x12in) New-York 2000

$2 172 - €1 829 - **£1 282** - FF12 000
Élévation de la fabrique gothique de la vige de Marolles Encre (49x71.9cm 19x28in) Paris 1998

DUGOURD Pascal 1958 **[24]**

$1 120 - €1 037 - **£685** - FF6 800
L'élégante Huile/toile (65x81cm 25x31in) Rambouillet 1999

DUGUAY Rodolphe 1891-1973 **[57]**

$546 - €524 - **£342** - FF3 440
L'Enfant Jésus Oil/board (28x35.5cm 11x13in) Montréal 1999

DUGUID Henry XIX **[7]**

$12 508 - €11 331 - **£7 800** - FF74 328
A Prospect of Edinburgh looking north towards Arthur Seat Oil/canvas (29.5x45cm 11x17in) Glasgow 1999

DUHEM Henri Aimé 1860-1941 **[53]**

$307 - €366 - **£213** - FF2 400
Paysage de neige Huile/panneau (24x33cm 9x12in) Paris 2000

DUHEM Marie Geneviève 1871-1918 **[8]**

$869 - €1 022 - **£623** - FF6 707
Geschwister in Landschaft Öl/Leinwand (45x59cm 17x23in) München 2001

DUINEN van Jacob Hendrik 1840-1885 **[5]**

$2 258 - €2 496 - **£1 566** - FF16 371
Choppy Seas Oil/canvas (43.5x64.5cm 17x25in) Amsterdam 2001

DUJARDIN Karel 1621/22-1678 **[82]**

$11 722 - €9 980 - **£7 000** - FF65 464
A Pastoral Scene with Cattle, Sheep and a Donkey resting Oil/canvas (53.5x42cm 21x16in) London 1998

$1 316 - €1 431 - **£867** - FF9 390
Tiere am Wasser Oil/panel (25x22.8cm 9x8in) Heidelberg 2000

$1 226 - €1 180 - **£755** - FF7 739
Italianate Landscape with Ruins Black chalk (12.5x15.5cm 4x6in) Amsterdam 1999

$194 - €193 - **£121** - FF1 265
The Village on the Hill Etching (12.2x15.5cm 4x6in) Haarlem 1999

DUKE Alfred ?-c.1905 **[47]**

$3 501 - €4 072 - **£2 500** - FF26 709
On the Scent Oil/canvas (91.5x71cm 36x27in) London 2001

$6 724 - €7 218 - **£4 500** - FF47 347
A Rough Coated Terrier Outside a Kennel Another Terrier Within Oil/canvas (40x30cm 15x11in) Bath 2000

$2 729 - €2 577 - **£1 650** - FF16 907
The faithful Guardian Watercolour/paper (25.5x35.5cm 10x13in) Billingshurst, West-Sussex 1999

DUKES Charles XIX **[5]**

$5 070 - €5 883 - **£3 500** - FF38 589
Lavinia Oil/canvas (61x46cm 24x18in) London 2000

DULAC Charles Marie 1865-1898 **[10]**

$1 482 - €1 601 - **£1 000** - FF10 500
Bord de canal Fusain (47.5x30.5cm 18x12in) Paris 2001

$517 - €610 - **£363** - FF4 000
Paysage Lithographie (66x50cm 25x19in) Paris 2000

DULAC Edmond/Edmund 1882-1953 **[53]**

$7 825 - €7 662 - **£5 000** - FF50 258
Prince Ahmed finds the Enchantress Watercolour (28x25cm 11x9in) London 1999

DULIN James Harvey 1883-? **[2]**

$1 002 - €1 143 - **£696** - FF7 500
«**Jeux interalliés**» Affiche (120x80cm 47x31in) Paris 2000

DULIN Pierre 1669-1748 **[2]**

$4 781 - €5 133 - **£3 200** - FF33 669
The Coronation of King Louis XV at Rheims on 25 October Red chalk/paper (34.5x52cm 13x20in) London 2000

DULL John 1862-1949 **[13]**

$400 - €470 - **£287** - FF3 085
City street corner with cathedral Watercolour/paper (25x20cm 10x8in) Hatfield PA 2001

DULLAH 1919-1996 **[47]**

$23 752 - €19 928 - **£13 936** - FF130 720
Barong Dance in Bali Oil/canvas (110x200cm 43x78in) Singapore 1998

$3 516 - €3 543 - **£2 191** - FF23 239
Portrait of an Old Lady Oil/canvas (94x63cm 37x24in) Singapore 2000

$3 650 - €3 401 - **£2 252** - FF22 312
Jambu Oil/canvas (36x31cm 14x12in) Singapore 1999

DULMEN KRUMPELMAN van Erasmus Bernard
1897-1987 **[68]**
$3 473 - €3 857 - **£2 416** - FF25 301
Zuidlaarder markt Oil/canvas/panel (48.5x68.5cm 19x26in) Groningen 2001
$562 - €544 - **£350** - FF3 571
View of a Canal in Amsterdam Watercolour/paper (35x47cm 13x18in) Amsterdam 1999

DULONG Jean-Louis 1800-1868 **[2]**
$8 900 - €9 543 - **£5 888** - FF62 595
Aristocrat in the Artist's Studio with Still Life of Fowl and Fruit Oil/canvas (91x73cm 36x29in) New-Orleans LA 2000

DULUARD Hippolyte F. Léon 1871-? **[18]**
$1 018 - €1 011 - **£636** - FF6 633
The Standard Bearer Oil/canvas (81.5x63.5cm 32x25in) Toronto 1999
$1 727 - €1 958 - **£1 206** - FF12 844
El abanderado Oleo/tabla (42x34cm 16x13in) Barcelona 2000

DUMA William, Bill 1936 **[47]**
$375 - €317 - **£225** - FF2 081
Near Bragg Creek Acrylic/canvas/board (30x41cm 11x16in) Calgary, Alberta 1998

DUMAIGE Henry Étienne 1830-1888 **[88]**
$7 529 - €8 557 - **£5 200** - FF56 127
Et in Arcadia Ego Bronze (H81.5cm H32in) London 2000
$1 900 - €1 638 - **£1 128** - FF10 746
Classical Maiden Bronze (39x17cm 15x7in) Bethesda MD 1998

DUMAS Aimée act.1861-1876 **[1]**
$1 632 - €1 860 - **£1 128** - FF12 200
Allégorie du printemps Pastel/papier (76.5x51cm 30x20in) Angers 2000

DUMAS Alice Dick 1878-? **[6]**
$795 - €743 - **£480** - FF4 874
«Allons tous à la consultation» Poster (89x126cm 35x49in) London 1999

DUMAS Antoine 1932 **[47]**
$6 725 - €6 190 - **£4 037** - FF40 601
Chez Simmons Huile/toile (91.5x101.5cm 36x39in) Montréal 1999

DUMAS Jean-Joseph 1838-? **[1]**
$676 - €789 - **£470** - FF5 178
Romont Lithograph (24x32.5cm 9x12in) Bern 2000

DUMAS Marlene 1953 **[46]**
$4 000 - €3 870 - **£2 466** - FF25 387
(Mis)using your Wounds Ink/paper (29x42cm 11x16in) New-York 1999
$288 - €292 - **£192** - FF2 029
«Barbie with Pearl Neck Lace» Farblithographie (49.9x38.2cm 19x15in) Hamburg 2000

DUMAS Tancrede R. ?-1905 **[9]**
$1 151 - €1 067 - **£711** - FF7 000
Vues de Beyrouth Tirage albuminé (29x39.5cm 11x15in) Paris 1999

DUMAX Ernest Joachim 1811-? **[7]**
$961 - €1 143 - **£685** - FF7 500
Bord de côte Huile/toile (20x40cm 7x15in) Nantes 2000

DUMAY Victor 1901-1981 **[3]**
$296 - €290 - **£183** - FF1 900
«Terrot Cycles Dijon» Affiche (160x120cm 62x47in) Paris 1999

DUME Edmé 1792-1861 **[2]**
$3 810 - €4 269 - **£2 648** - FF28 000
Les Moulins au bord de l'estuaire Huile/toile (41x69cm 16x27in) Vernou en Sologne 2001

DUMESNIL Pierre Louis II 1698-1781 **[4]**
$12 780 - €13 720 - **£8 550** - FF90 000
Le Prêtre du catéchisme Huile/toile (33x41cm 12x16in) Paris 2000

DUMINIL Frank 1933 **[142]**
$742 - €640 - **£448** - FF4 200
Composition Huile/toile (80x80cm 31x31in) Paris 1999
$311 - €305 - **£191** - FF2 000
Sans titre Technique mixte/papier (20x20cm 7x7in) Paris 1999

DUMITRESCO Natalia 1915-1997 **[149]**
$3 356 - €3 278 - **£2 139** - FF21 500
Composition Huile/toile (120x120cm 47x47in) Paris 1999
$1 594 - €1 829 - **£1 090** - FF12 000
Sans titre Huile/toile (60x92cm 23x36in) Paris 2000
$401 - €412 - **£250** - FF2 700
Composition abstraite Technique mixte/papier (28x43cm 11x16in) Paris 2000

DuMOND Frank Vincent 1865-1951 **[26]**
$6 000 - €5 595 - **£3 721** - FF36 699
The Grove Oil/canvas (71x76cm 27x29in) New-York 1999
$809 - €920 - **£561** - FF6 037
Kavalier in historischem Gewand Öl/Leinwand (27x46cm 10x18in) Hamburg 2000

DUMOND-ROUGET A. XIX **[1]**
$4 515 - €5 335 - **£3 200** - FF34 997
Vase de fleurs aux papillons Oil/canvas (81x65cm 31x25in) London 2000

DUMONSTIER Daniel 1574-1646 **[3]**
$16 000 - €16 186 - **£9 769** - FF106 174
Portrait of a Bearded Man, bust-length Black, red & white chalks/paper (34.5x28.5cm 13x11in) New-York 2000

DUMONSTIER Geoffroy 1510-1560/73 **[2]**
$1 715 - €2 045 - **£1 223** - FF13 415
Die Anbetung der Hirten Radierung (24.2x19.7cm 9x7in) Berlin 2000

DUMONT Alfred 1828-1894 **[13]**
$4 256 - €4 595 - **£2 855** - FF30 142
Venise Huile/toile (36x54cm 14x21in) Genève 2000

DUMONT Charles XIX-XX **[3]**
$3 692 - €3 964 - **£2 470** - FF26 000
Le relais de chasse Huile/toile (92x65cm 36x25in) Louviers 2000

DUMONT Claude 1938 **[125]**
$142 - €168 - **£103** - FF1 100
Le clown musicien, aubade à l'accordéon Huile/toile (33x41cm 12x16in) Provins 2001

DUMONT François / Frans c.1850-? **[12]**
$436 - €496 - **£304** - FF3 252
L'appréciation dans l'atelier Huile/panneau (68x41cm 26x16in) Antwerpen 2000

D

DUMONT François I 1751-1831 **[46]**
- $28 784 – €32 240 – **£20 000** – FF211 482
  Jean-Pierre Pagin, holding an Alto in his left Hand Miniature (18x12.5cm 7x4in) London 2001
- $2 514 – €2 820 – **£1 759** – FF18 500
  Portrait de jeune homme en buste Trois crayons (31.5x25.5cm 12x10in) Paris 2001

DUMONT Henri Julien 1856-1921 **[18]**
- $548 – €564 – **£348** – FF3 702
  Blomstrende rosengren Oil/canvas (75x56cm 29x22in) Vejle 2000

DUMONT Jean-Claude 1805-1874 **[1]**
- $3 945 – €4 601 – **£2 769** – FF30 182
  Stilleben mit Rosen Öl/Leinwand (73.5x60.5cm 28x23in) Luzern 2000

DUMONT LE ROMAIN Jean, ou Jacques 1701-1781 **[19]**
- $828 – €915 – **£574** – FF6 000
  Scène de sacrifice Encre (10.5x18.5cm 4x7in) Paris 2001

DUMONT Pierre 1884-1936 **[273]**
- $11 144 – €10 671 – **£7 014** – FF70 000
  Nature morte aux objets et tissus orientaux Huile/toile (107x157cm 42x61in) Saumur 1999
- $1 896 – €2 211 – **£1 329** – FF14 500
  Déchargement de marchandises dans le port Huile/toile (36.5x44.5cm 14x17in) Paris 2000
- $2 500 – €2 432 – **£1 538** – FF15 955
  Port de St Nazare Oleo/lienzo (33x46cm 12x18in) Buenos-Aires 1999

DUMONT Pierre 1920-1987 **[33]**
- $3 588 – €4 040 – **£2 520** – FF26 500
  Notre-Dame de Paris Huile/toile (60x73cm 23x28in) Pont-Audemer 2001

DUMONT-SMITH Robert 1908 **[19]**
- $438 – €489 – **£300** – FF3 206
  Still Life, a Porcelain Vase with Summer Flowers Oil/canvas (66x55cm 26x22in) Oxford 2000

DUMOUCHEL Albert 1916-1971 **[68]**
- $198 – €179 – **£119** – FF1 121
  La Cigale de Nuit Eau-forte (25x20cm 9x7in) Montréal 2000

DUMOULIN Émile 1850-? **[2]**
- $30 286 – €28 755 – **£18 561** – FF188 623
  Liegender weiblicher Akt Öl/Leinwand (98x210cm 38x82in) Zürich 1999

DUMOULIN Louis 1860-1924 **[23]**
- $1 285 – €1 524 – **£935** – FF10 000
  Fantasia Huile/toile (32x115cm 12x45in) Lyon 2001

DUMOULIN Romeo 1883-1943 **[150]**
- $3 201 – €2 727 – **£1 925** – FF17 886
  Les baigneurs Huile/carton (40x50cm 15x19in) Bruxelles 1998
- $559 – €644 – **£384** – FF4 227
  Un p'tit verre dans l'nez Watercolour (20.5x15cm 8x5in) Lokeren 2000
- $1 007 – €1 091 – **£699** – FF7 154
  Le jeu de balle Eau-forte, aquatinte (65x71cm 25x27in) Maisieres-Mons 2001

DUNAND Bernard 1908-1998 **[6]**
- $7 000 – €7 514 – **£4 684** – FF49 287
  Figure Amongst Stylized Palm Leaves Oil/wood (131x31x1cm 51x12xin) Chicago IL 2000

DUNAND Jean 1877-1942 **[145]**
- $37 680 – €36 588 – **£23 280** – FF240 000
  Grand paravent, motifs géométriques, deux carrés en décrochement Huile/panneau (300x325cm 118x127in) Paris 1999
- $15 504 – €14 483 – **£9 566** – FF95 000
  Couple de panthères Technique mixte (67x87cm 26x34in) Paris 1999
- $2 633 – €2 949 – **£1 829** – FF19 347
  Marabou standing in the Water Painting (42x23cm 16x9in) Amsterdam 2001
- $22 704 – €25 154 – **£15 229** – FF165 000
  Coloquinte Bronze (H17cm H6in) Paris 2000
- $2 305 – €2 287 – **£1 434** – FF15 000
  Hérons devant la cascade (projet pour décor mural) Gouache (15.5x17cm 6x6in) Paris 1999

DUNAND Pierre XX **[2]**
- $24 000 – €22 835 – **£14 916** – FF149 791
  Prancing Horses Oil/panel (180x254cm 70x100in) New-York 1999

DUNBAR George Bauer 1927 **[16]**
- $2 295 – €2 139 – **£1 416** – FF14 033
  Untitled Mixed media/board (25x67cm 10x26in) New-Orleans LA 1999
- $1 700 – €1 584 – **£1 027** – FF10 393
  Gold and Silver Composition Mixed media (25x30cm 10x12in) New-Orleans LA 1999

DUNBAR Harold C. 1882-1953 **[49]**
- $600 – €644 – **£401** – FF4 224
  Barnstable Dunes Oil/board (38x55cm 15x22in) East-Dennis MA 2000
- $550 – €591 – **£368** – FF3 875
  View of the Mill Pond from My Studio Oil/board (25x30cm 10x12in) East-Dennis MA 2000

DUNCAN Edward 1803-1882 **[218]**
- $6 039 – €6 705 – **£4 042** – FF43 983
  Shipwreck on the Calf of Man, kustlandskap med skeppsbrott Oil/canvas (64x107cm 25x42in) Stockholm 2000
- $1 835 – €1 954 – **£1 250** – FF12 818
  Landscape with Windmill Oil/canvas (24.5x47cm 9x18in) Billingshurst, West-Sussex 2001
- $1 984 – €1 730 – **£1 200** – FF11 351
  Furness Abbey, the Harvesters returning at Evening, Cumbria Watercolour (23.5x47cm 9x18in) London 1998
- $389 – €415 – **£260** – FF2 725
  Little Wonder Aquatint (41x53cm 16x20in) London 2000

DUNCAN James 1806-1881 **[10]**
- $4 306 – €4 769 – **£2 920** – FF31 281
  Opposite Beauport below Point Levi, Quebec Watercolour/paper (23x31.5cm 9x12in) Toronto 2000

DUNCAN John McKirdy 1866-1945 **[22]**
- $1 537 – €1 443 – **£949** – FF9 463
  A tranquil Sea Oil/canvas (30.5x40cm 12x15in) London 1999
- $1 051 – €987 – **£649** – FF6 473
  A bearded Man Charcoal/paper (75.5x54cm 29x21in) London 1999

DUNCAN Mary 1885-c.1967 **[9]**
- $4 852 – €5 714 – **£3 410** – FF37 480
  The Ferry Crossing Oil/canvas (48.5x71cm 19x27in) Dublin 2000
- $2 757 – €2 579 – **£1 700** – FF16 914
  Breton Woman Peeling Vegetables Oil/board (32x24cm 12x9in) Co. Kilkenny 1999

D

DUNCAN Robert 1952 **[3]**
- $10 000 - €11 355 - £6 948 - FF74 481
  Trail of the Fur Brigade Oil/board (50x101cm
  20x40in) Dallas TX 2001

DUNCAN Walter, A.R.W.S. 1848/51-1932 **[61]**
- $594 - €591 - £360 - FF3 879
  The Harvesters Watercolour/paper (14x22.5cm 5x8in)
  London 2001

DUNCANSON Robert Scott 1821-1872 **[13]**
- $110 000 - €130 756 - £76 219 - FF857 703
  View of Ashville North Ca Oil/board (33x47cm
  13x18in) Detroit MI 2000
- $20 000 - €23 105 - £14 004 - FF151 562
  Watermelons and Peaches Pastel/paper
  (35.5x56cm 13x22in) New-York 2001

DUNDAS Douglas Robert 1900-1981 **[51]**
- $1 275 - €1 229 - £788 - FF8 059
  The Way Home Oil/canvas (59.5x74.5cm 23x29in)
  Sydney 1999
- $414 - €488 - £291 - FF3 202
  Autumn Morning, Cascade Street, Paddington
  Oil/board (28x34cm 11x13in) Sydney 2000

DUNDAS G. XIX **[2]**
- $2 800 - €3 005 - £1 873 - FF19 714
  Portrait of Mrs Bui C.Coffin, formely Lucy Wass
  Watercolour/paper (16x11cm 6x4in) Portland ME 2000

DUNET Alfred 1889-1939 **[51]**
- $3 755 - €3 506 - £2 274 - FF23 000
  Rue de l'épicerie Pastel/papier (57x46cm 22x18in)
  Évreux 1999

DUNHAM Carroll 1949 **[95]**
- $45 000 - €50 403 - £31 266 - FF330 624
  Demon Tower Mixed media (274x216cm 107x85in)
  New-York 2001
- $15 000 - €16 772 - £10 111 - FF110 016
  Character Study #1 Mixed media (83.5x61cm
  32x24in) New-York 2000
- $7 000 - €8 122 - £4 832 - FF53 277
  Untitled Acrylic (34x26cm 13x10in) New-York 2000
- $14 000 - €13 454 - £8 624 - FF88 254
  Untitled Gouache (103x61cm 40x24in) New-York
  1999
- $1 000 - €886 - £613 - FF5 812
  Full Spectrum Lithograph (106x71cm 41x27in) New-York 1999

DUNKARTON Robert John 1744-1811 **[8]**
- $4 252 - €4 583 - £2 900 - FF30 062
  The Night blowing Cereus Mezzotint (56x42cm
  22x16in) Bury St. Edmunds, Suffolk 2001

DUNKEL Joachim 1925 **[15]**
- $1 415 - €1 687 - £1 009 - FF11 067
  Kreuzigungsgruppe Bronze (35x35x7cm
  13x13x2in) Berlin 2000

DUNKER Balthasar Anton 1746-1807 **[53]**
- $1 253 - €1 251 - £783 - FF8 209
  Selbstportrait des Künstlers Watercolour
  (28.5x21cm 11x8in) Zofingen 1999
- $311 - €361 - £214 - FF2 369
  Vüe de Lausanne, nach Johann Ludwig Aberli
  Radierung (20.7x35.1cm 8x13in) Zürich 2000

DUNKERLEY Joseph XVIII **[4]**
- $7 500 - €6 471 - £4 541 - FF42 444
  **Elegant Young Lady facing Right in White Lace
  Dress** Miniature (3x2cm 1x1in) New-York 1999

DUNLOP Brian James 1938 **[92]**
- $14 736 - €17 198 - £10 402 - FF112 814
  Pomegranates Oil/canvas (106x120cm 41x47in)
  Malvern, Victoria 1998
- $4 699 - €5 315 - £3 307 - FF34 865
  The trumpeter Oil/canvas (90x64cm 35x25in)
  Malvern, Victoria 2001
- $1 010 - €929 - £624 - FF6 093
  «Musician, Peter Thin» Gouache/paper (57x36cm
  22x14in) Melbourne 1998
- $251 - €281 - £175 - FF1 846
  Rising, Sleep Series Color lithograph (55x75cm
  21x29in) Sydney 2001

DUNLOP Elizabeth Maria 1820-1883 **[3]**
- $3 239 - €3 632 - £2 200 - FF23 827
  North America Oil/paper (9x12.5cm 3x4in) London
  2000

DUNLOP Ronald Ossory 1894-1973 **[425]**
- $2 551 - €2 178 - £1 500 - FF14 285
  Shepperton-on-Thames Oil/canvas (35.5x45.5cm
  13x17in) London 1998
- $821 - €783 - £500 - FF5 138
  Portrait of A Man With Cravat Oil/canvas
  (40.5x30.5cm 15x12in) London 1999
- $305 - €308 - £190 - FF2 019
  Reclining Female Nude Watercolour (37x48cm
  14x18in) London 2000

DUNN Arthur XIX-XX **[3]**
- $2 581 - €2 866 - £1 800 - FF18 800
  News of the Day - Trompe l'oeil composition Ink
  (67.5x100cm 26x39in) London 2001

DUNN Harvey T. 1884-1952 **[26]**
- $19 000 - €22 148 - £13 155 - FF145 283
  **Elegantly Clad Mask-Wearing Man Holding Two
  Men in Office** Oil/canvas (101x76cm 40x30in) New-York 2000

DUNN-GARDNER Violet XIX-XX **[4]**
- $3 454 - €3 869 - £2 400 - FF25 377
  **Summer in the Garden, Celia, later Countess of
  Scarbrough as a Child** Oil/canvas (68x89cm
  26x35in) London 2001

DUNNING Jeanne 1960 **[17]**
- $4 500 - €4 225 - £2 788 - FF27 715
  Detail 7 Cibachrome print (54.5x43cm 21x16in) New-York 1999

DUNNING Robert Spear 1829-1905 **[22]**
- $50 000 - €46 402 - £30 020 - FF304 380
  Still Life with fruit, Flowers and Honeycomb
  Oil/canvas (41x54cm 16x21in) Milford CT 1999
- $5 000 - €5 343 - £3 403 - FF35 048
  Still Life of cherries Oil/board (13x25cm 5x10in)
  New-Orleans LA 2001

DUNNINGTON Albert 1860-1928 **[58]**
- $924 - €891 - £570 - FF5 846
  Interior Barn Scene Oil/canvas (50x76cm 20x30in)
  Birmingham 1999
- $983 - €1 145 - £680 - FF7 509
  Deganwy, near Conway, North Wales Oil/canvas
  (31x46cm 12x18in) Cheshire 2000
- $253 - €296 - £180 - FF1 943
  Thatched Cottage Watercolour/paper (35x24cm
  14x9in) Whitby, Yorks 2001

DUNOUY Alexandre 1757-1841 **[28]**
- $35 000 - €34 984 - £21 381 - FF229 477
  **Arcadian Landscape with Maidens Gathering
  Flowers by a River Bank** Oil/canvas
  (208.5x232.5cm 82x91in) New-York 2000

$20 000 - €22 149 - **£13 564** - FF145 290
View of Tivoli Oil/panel (37.5x54cm 14x21in) New-York 2000

$6 259 - €7 318 - **£4 468** - FF48 000
Paysage classique de la campagne romaine avec une rivière Huile/toile (32x46cm 12x18in) Paris 2001

$2 486 - €2 120 - **£1 500** - FF13 905
Landscapes with Animals Etching (44x30cm 17x11in) London 1998

DUNOYER DE SEGONZAC André 1884-1974 **[940]**
$5 163 - €4 269 - **£3 029** - FF28 000
Église de Villiers-sur-Morin Huile/toile (55x81cm 21x31in) Paris 1998

$1 612 - €1 857 - **£1 100** - FF12 178
Provence Ink (34.5x48cm 13x18in) London 2000

$179 - €198 - **£121** - FF1 300
Versailles, le grand Trianon vu du canal Eau-forte (17.5x13cm 6x5in) Paris 2000

DUNSTAN Bernard 1920 **[192]**
$6 096 - €6 143 - **£3 800** - FF40 293
Reclining Nude with Leg bent Oil/canvas (46x55cm 18x21in) London 2000

$2 551 - €3 023 - **£1 800** - FF19 832
The Mirror, Venice Oil/board (28x20cm 11x7in) London 2000

$1 302 - €1 407 - **£900** - FF9 229
Woman Washing her Hair Pastel/paper (41.5x24.5cm 16x9in) London 2001

DUNTON William Herbert 1878-1936 **[31]**
$110 000 - €105 156 - **£68 948** - FF689 777
Hostile Tribes Oil/canvas (99x63.5cm 38x25in) New-York 1999

$15 000 - €16 462 - **£9 658** - FF107 982
The Overlook Oil/canvas/board (31x48.5cm 12x19in) Beverly-Hills CA 2000

$2 000 - €1 818 - **£1 204** - FF11 926
Elk Lithograph (29x25cm 11x10in) Hayden ID 1998

DUNTZE Johannes Bertholomus 1823-1895 **[70]**
$32 396 - €34 857 - **£22 048** - FF228 644
En vintertag på en kanal med smådrenge Oil/canvas (98x130cm 38x51in) København 2001

$7 581 - €6 900 - **£4 653** - FF45 262
Fischerboot in einem Fjord Öl/Leinwand (68x101cm 26x39in) Zürich 1999

$3 216 - €3 835 - **£2 293** - FF25 154
Hochgebirgslandschaft mit Wildwasser und angeInden Kindern Oil/panel (25.5x39cm 10x15in) Berlin 2000

DUNZENDORFER Albrecht 1907-1980 **[8]**
$2 943 - €3 270 - **£1 971** - FF21 451
Mühlviertler Landschaft mit Bauernhof Oil/panel (70x100cm 27x39in) Linz 2000

DUPAGNE Adrien 1889-1980 **[115]**
$649 - €545 - **£380** - FF3 572
Nature morte aux fleurs Huile/toile (65x80cm 25x31in) Liège 1998

DUPAGNE Arthur 1895-1961 **[64]**
$2 023 - €2 355 - **£1 425** - FF15 447
Lanceur de javelot africain Bronze (H42cm H16in) Antwerpen 2001

DUPAIN Edmond Louis 1847-? **[22]**
$2 326 - €2 287 - **£1 494** - FF15 000
Gondole dans le canal à Venise Huile/toile (92.5x73cm 36x28in) Paris 1999

DUPAIN Maxwell Spencer, Max 1911-1992 **[164]**
$1 672 - €1 739 - **£1 105** - FF11 410
Sunbaker, Culburra, NSW Gelatin silver print (36x44.5cm 14x17in) Sydney 2000

DUPAIN Rex 1954 **[30]**
$421 - €396 - **£260** - FF2 598
Man Walking Gelatin silver print (48x47cm 18x18in) Melbourne 1999

DUPAS Jean 1882-1964 **[97]**
$200 000 - €237 851 - **£142 540** - FF1 560 200
Untitled Oil/canvas (199x223cm 78x87in) New-York 2000

$18 000 - €20 913 - **£12 650** - FF137 181
Untitled Oil/canvas (56x52cm 22x20in) New-York 2001

$4 396 - €4 269 - **£2 716** - FF28 000
Portrait d'un gentilhomme Huile/papier (20x17cm 7x6in) Paris 1999

$5 500 - €6 391 - **£3 865** - FF41 919
Les heures à la pendule Charcoal (33x28cm 12x11in) New-York 2001

$3 766 - €4 260 - **£2 546** - FF27 945
Les Amoureux Etching (59x76.5cm 23x30in) Zürich 2001

DUPÉRAC Étienne 1525-1601/04 **[6]**
$950 - €1 111 - **£667** - FF7 288
Parte del Monte Palatino verso il Foro Romano Etching (21.5x38.5cm 8x15in) New-York 2000

DUPIN Léon XX **[27]**
$335 - €381 - **£233** - FF2 500
«André Ledun Fécamp» Affiche (150x100cm 59x39in) Paris 2001

DUPLAIN Albert 1890-1978 **[12]**
$502 - €547 - **£331** - FF3 587
Sommerlandschaft mit Blumenwiese am Genfersee Öl/Leinwand (55x80.5cm 21x31in) Bern 2000

DUPLESSI-BERTAUX Jean 1747-1819 **[35]**
$5 049 - €5 934 - **£3 500** - FF38 924
«L'Innocence» Oil/panel (24.5x20cm 9x7in) London 2000

$896 - €962 - **£600** - FF6 313
A Carthusian Monk Rejecting the Uniform of a Soldier Red chalk/paper (35x23cm 13x9in) London 2000

$777 - €915 - **£557** - FF6 000
Vue intérieure de Paris Eau-forte (41x66cm 16x25in) Paris 2001

DUPLESSIS Joseph-Siffrède 1725-1802 **[13]**
$5 000 - €4 773 - **£3 124** - FF31 308
Louis XIV Wearing the Orders of Saint Esprit and the Golden Fleece Oil/canvas (67.5x53cm 26x20in) New-York 1999

DUPON Josué 1864-1935 **[12]**
$7 704 - €8 924 - **£5 328** - FF58 536
Deux groupes de deux marabouts Bronze (29.5x17x15.5cm 11x6x6in) Bruxelles 2000

$1 421 - €1 584 - **£956** - FF10 390
Fleurs dans un vase en verre Pastel/papier (51x37cm 20x14in) Warszawa 2000

DUPONT Gainsborough c.1754-1797 **[32]**
$48 000 - €57 057 - **£33 259** - FF374 270
George Drummond, standing Three-quarter Length in a Landscape Oil/canvas (125.5x100cm 49x39in) New-York 2000

$2 923 - €3 259 - **£2 000** - FF21 379
Portrait of a Brother of Trinity House Oil/canvas
(121x96cm 48x38in) Oxford 2000
$4 614 - €5 099 - **£3 200** - FF33 449
**A Woman, Standing, full-length, her Right arm
Resting on a Ledge** Chalks (32x18cm 12x7in)
London 2001

DUPONT Jacques XX **[20]**
$165 - €183 - **£114** - FF1 200
**Les revenants: beaux modèles de costumes de
robes** Aquarelle/papier (24x32cm 9x12in) Paris 2001

DUPONT Louis R. 1734-1765 **[4]**
$51 319 - €56 406 - **£32 634** - FF370 000
Portrait d'un homme en armure Huile/toile
(91x73cm 35x28in) Paris 2000

DUPONT Pieter 1870-1911 **[89]**
$3 572 - €3 857 - **£2 442** - FF25 301
A City View with Figures at a Canal Oil/canvas
(37.5x30cm 14x11in) Amsterdam 2001
$133 - €147 - **£90** - FF967
Wilg Etching (25.5x15.5cm 10x6in) Haarlem 2000

DUPONT Richard John Munro 1920-1977 **[8]**
$882 - €873 - **£550** - FF5 728
Out Hunting Oil/canvas (51x61cm 20x24in) London
1999

DUPRA Giuseppe 1703-1784 **[1]**
$12 500 - €12 958 - **£7 500** - FF85 000
**Ritratto di Benedetto Maria Maurizio, duca di
Chiablese** Olio/tela (104x72cm 40x28in) Venezia 1999

DUPRAT Albert Ferdinand 1882-? **[53]**
$2 144 - €2 439 - **£1 488** - FF16 000
Vue de Venise Huile/toile (38x55cm 14x21in)
Versailles 2000

DUPRAT Sophie c.1810-? **[4]**
$3 272 - €3 049 - **£2 018** - FF20 000
Sainte Cécile Huile/panneau (17.5x13cm 6x5in) Paris
1999

DUPRAY Henry Louis 1841-1909 **[55]**
$2 097 - €2 014 - **£1 300** - FF13 214
**Royal Marines landing on a Mediterranean
Coast** Oil/canvas (65x91.5cm 25x36in) London 1999
$2 128 - €1 799 - **£1 266** - FF11 800
Officiers en tournée d'inspection Huile/toile
(32x41cm 12x16in) Calais 1998

DUPRÉ Daniël 1752-1817 **[15]**
$588 - €511 - **£354** - FF3 352
Die Piazza Rotonda mit dem Pantheon in Rom
Watercolour (11.8x14.6cm 4x5in) Berlin 1998
$6 293 - €6 713 - **£4 200** - FF44 032
Vue du Panthéon à Rome Etching (51x73cm
20x28in) London 2000

DUPRE E. XIX **[1]**
$4 050 - €3 809 - **£2 507** - FF24 985
Peasant Children with a Pram Oil/canvas
(61x70cm 24x27in) Melbourne 1999

DUPRÉ Jules 1811-1889 **[413]**
$8 414 - €7 318 - **£5 073** - FF48 000
La fermette Huile/toile (61x50cm 24x19in) Paris 1998
$3 770 - €3 659 - **£2 347** - FF24 629
Paysage à la mare Huile/panneau (24x33.5cm
9x13in) Pontoise 1999
$756 - €884 - **£531** - FF5 800
Pêcheur Aquarelle/papier (10.5x12.5cm 4x4in) Paris
2000

DUPRÉ Julien 1851-1910 **[175]**
$19 590 - €23 313 - **£14 000** - FF152 924
Laitière gardant ses vaches Oil/canvas
(44.5x60.5cm 17x23in) London 2000
$526 - €534 - **£330** - FF3 500
Les foins Aquarelle (50x70cm 19x27in) Saint-Dié
2000

DUPRÉ Louis 1789-1837 **[19]**
$7 498 - €6 199 - **£4 400** - FF40 665
«Un suliste à Corfou» Watercolour (36.5x25cm
14x9in) London 1998
$1 200 - €1 156 - **£750** - FF7 580
**Greek Official of Levadia/Greek Priest and a
Turk** Lithograph (45.5x35.5cm 17x13in) London 1999

DUPRÉ Victor 1816-1879 **[292]**
$6 416 - €6 466 - **£4 000** - FF42 414
Cattle and Farmhands in a Pasture Oil/canvas
(51x79.5cm 20x31in) London 2000
$3 759 - €3 755 - **£2 349** - FF24 629
Bauernhaus am Fluss Öl/Leinwand (27x41cm
10x16in) Zofingen 1999
$3 265 - €2 820 - **£1 972** - FF18 500
Vacher et son troupeau près du grand arbre
Aquarelle/papier (17.5x30.5cm 6x12in) Barbizon 1998

DUPRÉ-LAFON Paul 1900-1971 **[5]**
$21 980 - €21 343 - **£13 580** - FF140 000
Paravent articulé bleu Huile/toile (170x371cm
66x146in) Paris 1999

DUPUIS Émile 1877-1956 **[5]**
$671 - €762 - **£466** - FF5 000
«Fabrique nationale...automobiles, cycles»
Affiche (93x69cm 36x27in) Paris 2001

DUPUIS Maurice 1882-1959 **[40]**
$991 - €1 164 - **£700** - FF7 635
Fish and Shrimps Oil/panel (19.5x29cm 7x11in)
London 2000

DUPUIS Pierre 1610-1682 **[7]**
$322 740 - €335 388 - **£202 400** - FF2 200 000
**Nature morte aux choux, artichauds et abricots
sur un entablement** Huile/toile (109x85cm 42x33in)
Paris 2000

DUPUIS Toon 1877-1937 **[4]**
$11 296 - €10 891 - **£6 964** - FF71 438
Staand vrouwlijk naakt Bronze (H106cm H41in)
Rotterdam 1999

DUPUY Paul Michel 1869-1949 **[89]**
$9 940 - €10 671 - **£6 650** - FF70 000
Campement de nomades Huile/toile (113x162cm
44x63in) Villefranche-sur-Saône 2000
$4 351 - €4 223 - **£2 709** - FF27 700
Le village de Jussy au bord du lac Léman
Huile/panneau (43x57cm 16x22in) Pontoise 1999

DUQUESNOY, Fattore di Putti François 1594-1643
[5]
$2 111 - €1 913 - **£1 300** - FF12 551
Putto Standing Naked with Left Arm Raised
Bronze (H33cm H12in) London 1999

DUQUETTE Tony 1914-1999 **[5]**
$1 900 - €2 043 - **£1 295** - FF13 404
Tulips in Vases Watercolour/paper (63.5x51cm
25x20in) Beverly-Hills CA 2001

DUQUIN DE SAINT-PREUX Louise, née Toscan XIX
[2]
$16 000 - €15 259 - **£9 739** - FF100 094
Still Life with Butterflies Oil/canvas (39.5x49cm
15x19in) New-York 1999

DURA Alberto 1888-1971 **[22]**
- $700 - €728 - £442 - FF4 774
  Paisaje desde el Cerro Arequita Oleo/lienzo (44x47cm 17x18in) Montevideo 2000

DURA Gaetano XIX **[6]**
- $1 000 - €1 109 - £665 - FF7 274
  Life in and around Naples Lithograph (18x22cm 7x9in) San-Francisco CA 2000

DURA Otto XX **[2]**
- $430 - €400 - £266 - FF2 621
  «Rolandbühne» Poster (60x96cm 23x37in) Wien 1999

DURACK Elizabeth 1915-2000 **[30]**
- $1 557 - €1 730 - £1 043 - FF11 350
  Kimberley Rythms Oil/canvas/board (67.5x77.5cm 26x30in) Nedlands 2000
- $1 837 - €2 156 - £1 296 - FF14 141
  Leading from the Rim Mixed media (29x53cm 11x20in) Nedlands 2000
- $1 315 - €1 223 - £812 - FF8 024
  Aboriginal Group Watercolour/paper (44.5x57cm 17x22in) Melbourne 1999

DURAN BENET Rafael 1931 **[63]**
- $792 - €721 - £492 - FF4 728
  Moll del Rellotge Oleo/tablex (54x65cm 21x25in) Barcelona 1999
- $230 - €216 - £144 - FF1 418
  Paisaje del Alto Apurdán Gouache (45x54cm 17x21in) Barcelona 1999

DURAN Jori **[5]**
- $1 390 - €1 372 - £864 - FF9 000
  Les Parapluies de l'Été Huile/toile (100x81cm 39x31in) Nice 1999

DURANCAMPS Rafael 1891-1979 **[123]**
- $13 725 - €13 515 - £8 550 - FF88 650
  Toreando una vaca Oleo/tablex (38x46cm 14x18in) Barcelona 1999
- $6 534 - €6 860 - £4 320 - FF45 000
  Venise Huile/panneau (21x27cm 8x10in) Paris 2000
- $810 - €901 - £570 - FF5 910
  Tauromaquia Lápiz (14.5x21.5cm 5x8in) Madrid 2001

DURAND Alex XIX-XX **[2]**
- $5 000 - €5 809 - £3 514 - FF38 106
  The Andora at Sea Oil/panel (86.5x122cm 34x48in) New-York 2001

DURAND Asher Brown 1796-1886 **[26]**
- $150 000 - €148 681 - £93 825 - FF975 285
  View in the Catskills Oil/canvas (97x137.5cm 38x54in) New-York 1999
- $10 000 - €11 355 - £6 844 - FF74 484
  A Study from Nature Oil/canvas (37.5x47cm 14x18in) New-York 2000
- $1 241 - €1 438 - £875 - FF9 430
  Les présentations Huile/panneau (28x21cm 11x8in) Bruxelles 2000

DURAND Gabriel 1812-? **[5]**
- $1 555 - €1 601 - £988 - FF10 500
  Autoportrait Pastel/papier (90x71.5cm 35x28in) Toulouse 2000

DURAND Gustave XIX-XX **[2]**
- $5 514 - €6 403 - £3 927 - FF42 000
  Nu Huile/toile (136x85cm 53x33in) Limoges 2001

DURAND Jean 1894-1977 **[10]**
- $24 498 - €27 441 - £17 028 - FF180 000
  Le cortège de la mariée Huile/panneau (107x147cm 42x57in) Paris 2001
- $648 - €762 - £464 - FF5 000
  Eléphant Pastel gras/papier (62x46cm 24x18in) Paris 2001

DURAND Jean 1914 **[1]**
- $3 929 - €3 354 - £2 349 - FF22 000
  Touareg au repos Gouache (73.5x60cm 28x23in) Paris 1998

DURAND Simon 1838-1886 **[34]**
- $3 870 - €3 271 - £2 316 - FF21 458
  Blumenstilleben mit Katzen Öl/Leinwand (118x76cm 46x29in) Berlin 1998
- $2 135 - €2 293 - £1 429 - FF15 039
  Wenn die Mutter aus dem Hause... Oil/panel (35x32cm 13x12in) Zofingen 2000

DURAND-BRAGER Jean-Baptiste Henri 1814-1879 **[92]**
- $6 087 - €5 793 - £3 784 - FF38 000
  Bateaux au mouillage près d'une côte orientale Huile/toile (40x65cm 15x25in) Evreux 1999
- $1 599 - €1 611 - £994 - FF10 569
  Le départ du Scheldeboot Huile/panneau (29.5x50cm 11x19in) Bruxelles 2000
- $528 - €579 - £350 - FF3 800
  Combat naval Encre (16x22cm 6x8in) Paris 2000

DURANDELLE Louis Émile Édouard 1839-1917 **[22]**
- $596 - €686 - £410 - FF4 500
  Le château de Bercy Tirage albuminé (16x22cm 6x8in) Paris 2000

DURANTE Domenico Maria 1879-1944 **[2]**
- $3 000 - €2 592 - £1 500 - FF17 000
  Paesaggio montano, frazione con chiesetta Olio/tavola (30.5x39.5cm 12x15in) Vercelli 1999

DURANTE Giorgio 1685-1755 **[5]**
- $7 210 - €7 267 - £4 500 - FF47 670
  Wildenten an einem Teich Öl/Leinwand (67x84cm 26x33in) Wien 2000
- $2 838 - €3 002 - £1 800 - FF19 695
  Still Life of a Turkey, a Bantam, a Barn Owl and a Grey Partridge Oil/canvas (31x41cm 12x16in) London 2000

DURBAN Arne 1912-1993 **[17]**
- $668 - €741 - £453 - FF4 858
  Stående pike Bronze (H16cm H6in) Oslo 2000

DURDEN James 1878-1964 **[33]**
- $2 566 - €2 586 - £1 600 - FF16 965
  Apple Blossom, Millbeck Oil/canvas (63.5x76cm 25x29in) London 2000
- $437 - €365 - £260 - FF2 396
  Dale's Road Oil/canvas/board (40x30cm 15x11in) London 1998
- $370 - €309 - £220 - FF2 027
  Darlydale Church and Cows Watercolour/paper (91x45cm 35x17in) London 1998

DUREAU George 1930 **[101]**
- $3 600 - €3 106 - £2 175 - FF20 377
  Four Standing Nudes Oil/canvas (195x243cm 77x96in) New-Orleans LA 1999
- $650 - €631 - £404 - FF4 138
  Street Study Charcoal (101x81cm 40x32in) New-Orleans LA 1999

📷 **$475** - €553 - **£334** - FF3 625
«**Troy Brown**» Gelatin silver print (35x35cm 14x14in)
New-Orleans LA 2001

DUREL Gaston Jules L. 1879-1954 [50]
🖝 **$952** - €1 067 - **£662** - FF7 000
Foule animée descendant la colline Huile/toile
(38x46cm 14x18in) Paris 2001
🖝 **$1 339** - €1 143 - **£801** - FF7 500
Femmes à la fontaine Huile/panneau (46x33cm
18x12in) Paris 1998

DURENNE Eugène Antoine 1860-1944 [133]
🖝 **$4 065** - €4 573 - **£2 838** - FF30 000
Sur le pont d'Endoume, près de Marseille
Huile/toile (50x65cm 19x25in) Paris 2001
🖝 **$792** - €656 - **£465** - FF4 300
Portrait de jeune garçon Huile/toile (35x28cm
13x11in) Romans-sur-Isère 1998
🖊 **$230** - €229 - **£143** - FF1 500
Sur la route Aquarelle (35.5x21cm 13x8in) Paris 1999

DÜRER Albrecht 1471-1528 [2003]
🖊 **$430 000** - €373 823 - **£260 236** - FF2 452 118
**The Goddess Isis Kneeling with her Hands
Folded** Ink (6.5x4cm 2x1in) New-York 1999
▭ **$1 900** - €2 085 - **£1 226** - FF13 675
**St.Peter and St.John Healing the Cripple, from
the Engraved Passion** Engraving (12x70.5cm
4x27in) New-York 2000

DÜRER Hans 1478/90-c.1538 [2]
🖝 **$150 000** - €141 124 - **£93 600** - FF925 710
**Altarpiece: St. Christopher & St. George/St.
Catherine & St. Barbara** Oil/panel (102x40cm
40x15in) New-York 1999

DURET Francisque Joseph 1804-1865 [59]
🖾 **$43 074** - €48 284 - **£30 000** - FF316 719
**Vendangeur improvisant sur un sujet comique,
souvenir de Naples** Bronze (183x13cm 72x5in)
London 2001
🖾 **$1 420** - €1 524 - **£950** - FF10 000
La loi (esquisse) Terracotta (22.5x10x7.5cm 8x3x2in)
Paris 2000

DURET Pierre Jacques 1729-? [5]
▭ **$362** - €315 - **£218** - FF2 066
Vue des environs de Naples Kupferstich (54x75cm
21x29in) Zofingen 1998

DURET-DUJARRIC Isabelle 1949 [93]
🖝 **$10 696** - €9 968 - **£6 600** - FF65 384
Escalier intérieur Oil/paper (24x32cm 9x12in)
London 1999
🖊 **$1 989** - €1 716 - **£1 200** - FF11 257
Les cerises Ink (61x46cm 24x18in) London 1998

DUREY René 1890-1959 [92]
🖝 **$686** - €762 - **£478** - FF5 000
Les usines Huile/toile (81x100cm 31x39in) Paris
2001

DURHEIM Carl 1810-1890 [5]
▭ **$1 424** - €1 238 - **£858** - FF8 123
Boltigen im Simmental Lithographie (17.7x26.5cm
6x10in) Bern 2000

DURHEIM Johann Ludwig Rudolf 1811-1895 [6]
🖝 **$6 000** - €6 932 - **£4 201** - FF45 468
**Conversation in the Interior Courtyard of a
Mosque, Istambul** Oil/canvas (48x63cm 19x25in)
New-York 2001

DURIEUX Caroline Wagon 1896-1989 [36]
▭ **$350** - €403 - **£239** - FF2 646
Young Sarai Lithograph (61x49cm 24x19in) New-
Orleans LA 2000

DURIEZ Irénée 1950 [2]
🖾 **$2 690** - €2 479 - **£1 620** - FF16 260
Nu Bronze (H70cm H27in) Antwerpen 1999

DÜRIG Rolf 1926-1985 [61]
🖝 **$672** - €622 - **£411** - FF4 081
Fische zwischen Wasserpflanzen Öl/Leinwand
(46x38cm 18x14in) Bern 1999

DURINGER Henri 1892-1980 [534]
🖝 **$198** - €213 - **£133** - FF1 400
Chevaux dans la roulotte Huile/carton (40x50cm
15x19in) Brest 2000
🖝 **$99** - €107 - **£66** - FF700
Nature morte aux oeufs Huile/carton (41x33cm
16x12in) Brest 2000
🖊 **$75** - €88 - **£52** - FF580
Fresque animalière Aquarelle/papier (21x28cm
8x11in) Brest 2000

DURMAN Alan XX [4]
▭ **$452** - €525 - **£320** - FF3 444
«**Broadstairs, British Railways, Southern
Region**» Poster (102x64cm 40x25in) London 2001

DÜRR Louis 1896-1975 [54]
🖝 **$863** - €745 - **£518** - FF4 884
«**Am Silvaplanersee (Oberengadin)**» Öl/Leinwand
(45.5x56cm 17x22in) Bern 1998

DURRANT Roy Turner 1925-1998 [77]
🖝 **$440** - €458 - **£280** - FF3 002
Sunset in September Hills Oil/canvas/board
(19.5x36.5cm 7x14in) London 2000

DÜRRENMATT Friedrich, Fritz 1921-1991 [12]
▭ **$208** - €201 - **£129** - FF1 319
Ohne Titel Lithographie (29.7x49.5cm 11x19in) Zürich
1999

DURRIE George Henry Harvey 1820-1863 [35]
🖝 **$15 000** - €15 396 - **£9 415** - FF100 989
**Two Boys and Their Dog in a Landscape, One
Holding a Book** Oil/canvas (134x104cm 53x41in)
Bolton MA 2000
🖝 **$65 000** - €60 009 - **£39 975** - FF393 633
A Sleigh Ride in the Snow Oil/canvas (56x76cm
22x29in) New-York 1999
🖝 **$16 000** - €15 226 - **£10 008** - FF99 878
Storm clearing, Winter Oil/panel (25x33cm 10x13in)
New-York 1999

DURRIE John 1818-1898 [9]
🖝 **$7 150** - €6 059 - **£4 272** - FF39 744
Still life of two pears, one red and one yellow
Oil/panel (10x15cm 4x6in) Thomaston ME 1998

DURRIO Paco F. Durrieu de M 1876-1940 [1]
🖾 **$192** - €6 098 - **£4 268** - FF40 000
«**Tête fantastique**» Céramique (H17cm H6in) Paris
1998

DURST André XX [2]
📷 **$3 392** - €3 810 - **£2 200** - FF24 992
Lyla Zelensky modelling Rose Descat Silver print
(24x18cm 9x7in) London 2000

DURST Auguste 1842-1930 [17]
🖝 **$1 747** - €1 617 - **£1 069** - FF10 610
Gehöft mit Puten und Hühnern am Teich
Öl/Leinwand (60x92.5cm 23x36in) Bern 1999

DURU Jean-Baptiste XVII-XVIII **[3]**
- $34 826 - €33 539 - **£21 626** - FF220 000
  Le Milord Anglois Huile/toile (49.5x58cm 19x22in) Paris 1999

DURY Antoine,Tony 1819-? **[9]**
- $3 222 - €2 820 - **£1 951** - FF18 500
  Portrait d'homme devant le Théâtre des Variétés Huile/toile (73x60cm 28x23in) Paris 1998

DUSART Cornelis 1660-1704 **[104]**
- $7 125 - €8 093 - **£5 000** - FF53 087
  Tavern Interior with a Man drinking and another reading a Letter Oil/panel (23.5x21cm 9x8in) London 2001
- $3 519 - €4 084 - **£2 430** - FF26 789
  Four Peasants Looking at a Basket Inscription Ink (12.5x12cm 4x4in) Amsterdam 2000
- $407 - €486 - **£290** - FF3 186
  Das grosse Dorffest Radierung (26x33.8cm 10x13in) Berlin 2000

DUSAUTOY Jacques-Léon 1817-1894 **[4]**
- $10 878 - €12 806 - **£7 644** - FF84 000
  Mascarade improvisée par les artistes, le jour de mardi gras Huile/toile (98x130cm 38x51in) Toulouse 2000

DUSEN van Peter XX **[1]**
- $7 500 - €6 399 - **£4 515** - FF41 976
  Seated Elderly Flower Vendor Oil/canvas (58x89cm 23x35in) Norwalk CT 1999

DUSS Carlos 1932-1990 **[38]**
- $320 - €294 - **£196** - FF1 930
  Felder Aquarell/Papier (34x30cm 13x11in) Zürich 1999

DUSSEK Eduard Adrian 1871-1930 **[10]**
- $6 886 - €5 657 - **£4 000** - FF37 105
  Young Boy, a small dog at his feet/Young Girl holding a Cat Oil/canvas (136.5x70.5cm 53x27in) London 1998

DUTCHER H.F. XX **[6]**
- $455 - €442 - **£283** - FF2 900
  New York, Church and Cortland, 19 mars Tirage argentique (16.8x11.7cm 6x4in) Paris 1999

DUTEURTRE Pierre 1911-1989 **[42]**
- $839 - €762 - **£524** - FF5 000
  Jeune fille blonde au bouquet Huile/toile (55x46cm 21x18in) Rennes 1999

DUTILLEUX Constant 1807-1865 **[18]**
- $7 342 - €8 385 - **£5 164** - FF55 000
  Ville du Nord au bord de la rivière Huile/toile (64x80cm 25x31in) Fontainebleau 2001
- $1 574 - €1 524 - **£990** - FF10 000
  Vers la rue de Cambions près du Bourg de Fleurboix, Pas-de-Calais Huile/toile/panneau (35x26cm 13x10in) Paris 1999

DUTTA ROY Shyamal 1934 **[15]**
- $862 - €1 006 - **£600** - FF6 597
  Old Memories Watercolour/paper (48x64cm 18x25in) London 2000

DUTTON Thomas Goldsworth c.1820-1891 **[42]**
- $1 398 - €1 501 - **£950** - FF9 848
  «The Yacht Lacerta under Full Sail» Watercolour/paper (21x31cm 8x12in) London 2001
- $787 - €894 - **£550** - FF5 862
  Captain Hans Busk's Schooner Yacht Lady Busk Lithograph (36x48cm 14x18in) London 2001

DUTZSCHOLD Henri 1841-1891 **[2]**
- $1 881 - €2 031 - **£1 300** - FF13 324
  Les laveuses Oil/canvas (46x33cm 18x12in) Newbury, Berkshire 2001

DUVAL Béatrice 1880-1973 **[7]**
- $1 939 - €2 287 - **£1 363** - FF15 000
  Pommiers bretons Huile/papier/toile (24x31.5cm 9x12in) Paris 2000

DUVAL Étienne 1824-1914 **[18]**
- $3 237 - €3 811 - **£2 275** - FF25 000
  Au bord du Nil Huile/panneau (36x50.5cm 14x19in) Paris 2000

DUVAL Eugène S.G. 1845-? **[3]**
- $13 448 - €14 436 - **£9 000** - FF94 694
  The Piper at Rest Oil/canvas (104x190cm 40x74in) London 2000

DUVAL Eustache François XVIII-XIX **[5]**
- $5 977 - €6 555 - **£4 059** - FF43 000
  L'arrivée de la diligence Huile/panneau (24x32.5cm 9x12in) Lille 2000

DUVAL Pierre XX **[1]**
- $4 281 - €4 581 - **£2 820** - FF30 050
  The Entrapment Oil/canvas (118x87cm 46x34in) Sydney 2000

DUVAL Rémy 1907-1984 **[27]**
- $408 - €457 - **£277** - FF3 000
  Assia Tirage argentique (39x28.5cm 15x11in) Paris 2000

DUVAL Victor act.1833-? **[6]**
- $6 058 - €6 445 - **£4 134** - FF42 276
  Une galerie du Louvre Huile/toile (66x82cm 25x32in) Bruxelles 2001

DUVAL-GOZLAN Léon 1853-1941 **[58]**
- $1 760 - €1 829 - **£1 108** - FF12 000
  Bords du lot à Albas Huile/toile (51x77.5cm 20x30in) Paris 2000

DUVAL-LECAMUS Pierre 1790-1854 **[15]**
- $66 740 - €71 651 - **£44 650** - FF470 000
  La partie de piquet de deux invalides Huile/toile (46.5x35.5cm 18x13in) Paris 2000
- $732 - €686 - **£440** - FF4 500
  Joueur de vielle Huile/toile (22x16.5cm 8x6in) Paris 1999

DUVALL Fanny Eliza 1861-1934 **[6]**
- $3 750 - €3 204 - **£2 269** - FF21 018
  Roses in Sunlight Oil/canvas (36x61cm 14x24in) San-Francisco CA 1998

DUVALL John 1816-1892 **[33]**
- $1 534 - €1 742 - **£1 050** - FF11 427
  Waiting the Return of the Boats Oil/canvas (60x46cm 23x18in) Bury St. Edmunds, Suffolk 2000
- $638 - €663 - **£400** - FF4 348
  Suffolk Punch Oil/canvas (32x40.5cm 12x15in) Suffolk 2000

DUVENECK Frank 1848-1919 **[40]**
- $18 000 - €18 709 - **£11 343** - FF122 725
  Portrait of a girl with hat Oil/canvas (147x91cm 58x36in) Asheville NC 2000
- $18 000 - €21 155 - **£12 479** - FF138 769
  Portrait of a Young Boy Oil/canvas (129.5x76cm 50x29in) Beverly-Hills CA 2000
- $1 600 - €1 863 - **£1 106** - FF12 221
  Venetian Bridge Etching (26.5x40cm 10x15in) New-York 2000

DUVERGER Théophile Emmanuel 1821-1886 **[54]**
- 😏 **$26 000** - €29 531 - **£18 244** - FF193 710
  Blowing Bubbles Oil/panel (55.5x44cm 21x17in)
  New-York 2001
- 😏 **$13 182** - €11 411 - **£8 000** - FF74 848
  The Young Fortune Teller Oil/panel (27x21cm
  10x8in) London 1998

DUVET Jean 1485-c.1561 **[9]**
- ⬚ **$5 000** - €5 597 - **£3 487** - FF36 712
  **The Beast with seven Heads and ten Horns,
  from the Apocalypse** Engraving (30x22cm 11x8in)
  New-York 2001

DUVIEUX Henri 1855-? **[151]**
- 😏 **$3 312** - €3 811 - **£2 282** - FF25 000
  Venise, le Grand Canal Huile/toile (40x65cm
  15x25in) Poitiers 2000
- 😏 **$2 014** - €2 287 - **£1 399** - FF15 000
  Les chasseurs en plaine Huile/panneau (26x37cm
  10x14in) Barbizon 2001
- ✍ **$2 849** - €3 354 - **£2 002** - FF22 000
  Vue de Venise Aquarelle/papier (13.6x20cm 5x7in)
  Argenteuil 2000

DUVILLIER René 1919 **[160]**
- 😏 **$962** - €884 - **£596** - FF5 800
  Averse de feu Peinture (130x96cm 51x37in) Paris
  1999
- 😏 **$540** - €488 - **£333** - FF3 200
  Composition Huile/toile (54x65cm 21x25in) Paris
  1999

DUVIVIER Guillaume 1687-1761 **[3]**
- ⬚ **$1 000** - €1 109 - **£665** - FF7 276
  The temptation of St.Anthony Etching (31.5x25cm
  12x9in) New-York 2000

DUVIVIER Ignaz 1758-1832 **[3]**
- ✍ **$1 974** - €2 180 - **£1 368** - FF14 301
  **Blick auf den Palazzo Donn'Anna am Fusse des
  Posilippo** Ink (26.1x41.5cm 10x16in) Wien 2001

DUVIVIER Thomas Germain 1735-1814 **[4]**
- 😏 **$17 000** - €18 827 - **£11 529** - FF123 496
  **Marble Statue of Bacchus, a Violin, a Flute,
  Sheet Music, a Book** Oil/canvas (72x57.5cm
  28x22in) New-York 2000

DUVOCELLE Julien Adolphe 1873-1961 **[3]**
- 😏 **$4 500** - €4 250 - **£2 721** - FF27 880
  Man with red Cap Oil/canvas (65x54cm 25x21in)
  New-York 1999
- 😏 **$2 440** - €2 423 - **£1 524** - FF15 894
  Sovende ung kvinde Oil/canvas (33.5x28cm
  13x11in) Köbenhavn 1999

DUWE Harald 1926-1984 **[16]**
- 😏 **$1 371** - €1 534 - **£924** - FF10 061
  Landschaft mit Häusern Oil/panel (35x47.5cm
  13x18in) München 2000

DUWEE Henri-Joseph 1810-1884 **[4]**
- 😏 **$16 000** - €14 987 - **£9 836** - FF98 305
  Paris and Helen Oil/canvas (147x118cm 57x46in)
  New-York 1999

DUXA Carl 1871-1937 **[71]**
- 😏 **$1 426** - €1 453 - **£892** - FF9 534
  Holländisches Mädchen auf der Blumenwiese
  Öl/Leinwand (55.5x69cm 21x27in) Wien 2000
- 😏 **$635** - €613 - **£401** - FF4 024
  Holländerin in der Stube Öl/Leinwand (43x31cm
  16x12in) München 1999

DUYET XX **[5]**
- ✍ **$603** - €549 - **£370** - FF3 600
  **Portrait d'homme de type Moï/Portrait de
  femme de Caobang** Pastel/papier (29x21cm 11x8in)
  Paris 1999

DUYFHUYSEN Pieter Jacobsz. 1608-1677 **[4]**
- 😏 **$23 970** - €22 689 - **£14 905** - FF148 830
  **A Man drinking Beer and a Woman spinning
  Wool in a Kitchen Interior** Oil/panel (21x27.5cm
  8x10in) Amsterdam 1999

DUYNEN van Isaac c.1630-1677/81 **[16]**
- 😏 **$8 995** - €10 437 - **£6 210** - FF68 461
  **Still Life with a Cod, a salomon, a Turbot, a Ray
  and other Fish** Oil/canvas (91x155.5cm 35x61in)
  Amsterdam 2000
- 😏 **$7 276** - €8 428 - **£5 032** - FF55 284
  Nature morte aux poissons et crabe Huile/pan-
  neau (77x106cm 30x41in) Bruxelles 2000

DUYTS den Gustave 1850-1897 **[21]**
- 😏 **$672** - €744 - **£468** - FF4 878
  Femme lisant Huile/panneau (36x26.5cm 14x10in)
  Bruxelles 2001
- ✍ **$1 827** - €2 107 - **£1 258** - FF13 821
  Landschap met beek Watercolour/paper (24x44cm
  9x17in) Lokeren 2000

DUYTS van Jan 1629-1676 **[1]**
- 😏 **$15 729** - €15 850 - **£9 805** - FF103 970
  Kinderbacchanal Öl/Leinwand (82.5x116.5cm
  32x45in) Heidelberg 2001

DUYVEN van Steven XVII **[4]**
- 😏 **$7 500** - €8 023 - **£5 113** - FF52 625
  Woman in Kitchen Oil/canvas (95x107.5cm 37x42in)
  New-York 2001

DVORAK Bohuslav 1867-1951 **[15]**
- 😏 **$1 271** - €1 203 - **£792** - FF7 889
  Journée ensoleillée dans les champs Huile/toile
  (55x75cm 21x29in) Praha 2001

DVORAK Franz / Frantisek 1862-1927 **[49]**
- 😏 **$1 907** - €1 804 - **£1 188** - FF11 833
  Portrait de fille Huile/toile (48.5x39cm 19x15in)
  Praha 2000
- ✍ **$491** - €465 - **£306** - FF3 048
  Portrait of a Girl Pencil (31x26.5cm 12x10in) Praha
  2000

DVORSKY Bohumír 1902-1976 **[34]**
- 😏 **$1 213** - €1 148 - **£756** - FF7 530
  Jaro na sv. Kopecku Huile/toile (38x90cm 14x35in)
  Praha 2000

DWIGHT Mabel 1876-1955 **[68]**
- ⬚ **$750** - €699 - **£463** - FF4 587
  Merchanic Marvel of the Age Lithograph (31x23cm
  12x9in) Cleveland OH 1999

DWURNIK Edward 1943 **[16]**
- 😏 **$327** - €382 - **£229** - FF2 506
  Trente et un policier Huile/toile (67.5x59cm
  26x23in) Torun 2000

DYBRIS Freddie 1922-1993 **[34]**
- 😏 **$654** - €565 - **£395** - FF3 706
  «Traeerne er begyndt at skygge» Oil/canvas
  (46x61cm 18x24in) Vejle 1998

DYCK Paul 1917 **[2]**
- 😏 **$5 000** - €4 545 - **£3 011** - FF29 815
  Crow Camp Mixed media (76x101cm 30x40in)
  Hayden ID 1998

DYCK van Abraham 1635/36-1672 **[11]**

🖼 $23 275 - €22 798 - **£15 000** - FF149 544
Hunting Still Life with a Dead bittern and implements of the Chase Oil/canvas (121x105cm 47x41in) London 1999

🖼 $20 000 - €19 991 - **£12 218** - FF131 130
Young Woman, Small Half-Length, in a Brown Dress with a Red Mantle Oil/canvas (60.5x51.5cm 23x20in) New-York 2000

🖼 $55 000 - €60 343 - **£36 536** - FF395 824
A Bearded Old Man Oil/canvas (42x36.5cm 16x14in) New-York 2000

✏ $2 628 - €2 268 - **£1 586** - FF14 876
Standing man in a hat, leaning on a ballustrade Ink (11.9x8cm 4x3in) Amsterdam 1998

DYCK van Albert 1902-1951 **[135]**

🖼 $2 783 - €2 727 - **£1 716** - FF17 886
Lezeresjes Oil/panel (38.5x44.5cm 15x17in) Lokeren 1999

🖼 $529 - €446 - **£313** - FF2 926
Paysage à Schilde Huile/toile (30x40cm 11x15in) Antwerpen 1998

🖼 $293 - €248 - **£175** - FF1 626
Enfant près de la table Crayon/papier (21x33cm 8x13in) Antwerpen 1998

DYCK van Anthonius 1599-1641 **[127]**

🖼 $315 000 - €300 325 - **£200 000** - FF1 970 000
Retorno de la huida a Egipto Oleo/lienzo (155x143cm 61x56in) Madrid 1999

🖼 $220 000 - €192 975 - **£133 000** - FF1 265 836
Eerryk de Putte (Erycius Puteanus) 1574-1646 Oil/canvas (71x67cm 27x26in) New-York 1999

🖼 $212 134 - €197 197 - **£130 000** - FF1 293 526
Saint Augustine in Ecstasy Oil/panel (44x28.5cm 17x11in) London 1998

✏ $1 000 - €1 179 - **£705** - FF7 736
Figure study of three men Drawing (18x28cm 7x11in) New-Orleans LA 2001

📖 $500 - €518 - **£300** - FF3 400
Ritratto di Franciscus Frank Acquaforte (24.5x16cm 9x6in) Roma 1999

DYCK van Floris 1575-1651 **[6]**

🖼 $110 445 - €123 835 - **£75 000** - FF812 302
An Uitgestal Still Life of Pears, Apples and Grapes on Porcelain Bowls Oil/panel (49.5x77cm 19x30in) London 2000

DYCK van Victor 1862-? **[2]**

🖼 $3 689 - €3 842 - **£2 433** - FF25 203
Le gardien Huile/toile (85x64cm 33x25in) Bruxelles 2000

DYCKMANS Josephus Laurentius 1811-1888 **[13]**

🖼 $63 289 - €58 737 - **£38 585** 289
A peaceful Interlude Oil/panel (49.5x38.5cm 19x15in) London 1999

🖼 $3 995 - €4 538 - **£2 803** - FF29 766
Girl doing Needlework Oil/panel (20x18cm 7x7in) Amsterdam 2001

DYE Charlie 1906-1972 **[20]**

🖼 $42 500 - €45 619 - **£28 441** - FF299 242
Cheyenne Sundown Oil/masonite (76x122cm 29x48in) San-Francisco CA 2000

🖼 $27 500 - €29 486 - **£18 194** - FF193 413
Pay Day Mixed media (18x27cm 7x11in) Hayden ID 2000

DYE Clarkson 1869-1955 **[7]**

🖼 $1 500 - €1 706 - **£1 048** - FF11 190
Museum of Natural History Balboa Park, San Diego, Ca Oil/board (43x51cm 17x20in) Mystic CT 2000

DYER Charles Gifford 1851-1912 **[3]**

🖼 $4 184 - €4 491 - **£2 800** - FF29 460
Fishermen in the Bay of Naples with Vesuvius/The Waterfront at Naples Oil/canvas (44.5x66cm 17x25in) London 2000

DYER Hezekiah Anthony 1872-1943 **[52]**

✏ $425 - €367 - **£256** - FF2 407
Pershore Bridge and Abbey Watercolour/paper (26x36cm 10x14in) Watertown MA 1998

DYER Lowell 1856-1915 **[1]**

🖼 $4 820 - €5 051 - **£3 200** - FF33 133
Lady in a Florentine Cloister Oil/canvas (63.5x48.5cm 25x19in) London 2000

DYER William Henry XIX-XX **[51]**

✏ $148 - €126 - **£88** - FF824
«On the East Dart» Watercolour/paper (26x36cm 10x14in) Devon 1998

DYF Marcel Dreyfus, dit 1899-1985 **[524]**

🖼 $30 738 - €35 826 - **£21 291** - FF235 000
Paris, la Seine, vue du pont Alexandre III Huile/toile (130x162cm 51x63in) Calais 2000

🖼 $8 552 - €8 099 - **£5 200** - FF53 129
Le plus beau choix Oil/canvas (56x45.5cm 22x17in) London 1999

🖼 $3 336 - €3 049 - **£2 042** - FF20 000
La roulotte des Gitans Huile/toile (24x33cm 9x12in) Calais 1999

DYK van Philip le Petit 1680-1753 **[17]**

🖼 $13 826 - €13 127 - **£8 473** - FF86 110
Familienportrait in einem Interieur Huile/panneau (59x75cm 23x29in) Zürich 1999

DYKE Samuel P. XIX **[4]**

🖼 $3 000 - €3 624 - **£2 094** - FF23 785
Cows and Sheep in a River Landscape Oil/canvas (56.5x89cm 22x35in) Bethesda MD 2000

DYKEN van Derk 1945 **[5]**

🖼 $1 062 - €1 180 - **£739** - FF7 739
Stilleven met klokhuis Oil/masonite (18x24cm 7x9in) Groningen 2001

DYSON William Henry, Will 1880-1938 **[17]**

📖 $223 - €215 - **£137** - FF1 411
Henry Lawson Etching (32x24.5cm 12x9in) Melbourne 1999

DYXHOORN Pieter Aarnout 1810-1889 **[3]**

🖼 $4 600 - €4 958 - **£3 080** - FF32 520
Marine Huile/panneau (38x54cm 14x21in) Antwerpen 2000

DZHOGIN Pavel Pavlovich 1834-1885 **[3]**

🖼 $19 550 - €19 341 - **£12 190** - FF126 868
Alandskap Oil/canvas (120x168cm 47x66in) Helsinki 1999

DZIGURSKI Alexander 1911-1995 **[70]**

🖼 $1 600 - €1 866 - **£1 142** - FF12 241
Rocky Coastal Scene Oil/canvas (60x76cm 24x30in) St. Louis MO 2000

DZUBAS Friedel 1915-1994 **[78]**

🖼 $5 921 - €6 886 - **£4 228** - FF45 168
«Heath» Acrylic/canvas (183x183cm 72x72in) Toronto 2001

$5 000 - €5 600 - **£3 474** - FF36 736
«**Current**» Acrylic/canvas (101.5x101.5cm 39x39in)
New-York 2001

$225 - €236 - **£150** - FF1 548
«**Nightstar**»/«**Ihgne**» Screenprint in colors
(62x48.5cm 24x19in) New-York 2001

E

EADIE Robert 1877-1954 [44]

$449 - €453 - **£280** - FF2 969
Feeding Chickens Watercolour/paper (29x37cm
11x14in) Newbury, Berkshire 2000

$1 195 - €1 143 - **£749** - FF7 499
«**Ayr**» Poster (102x127cm 40x50in) London 1999

EADIE William XIX-XX [14]

$2 578 - €2 532 - **£1 600** - FF16 607
Country Gentleman in an Interior Oil/canvas
(28x44cm 11x17in) Penzance, Cornwall 1999

EAKINS Susan H. MacDowell 1851-1938 [5]

$2 500 - €2 512 - **£1 727** - FF17 709
Portrait of Jozef Anton Kowalewski
Oil/canvas/board (56x45.5cm 22x17in) Bethesda MD
2001

EAKINS Thomas Cowperthwait 1844-1916 [27]

$60 000 - €51 263 - **£36 018** - FF336 264
Portrait of Lucy Langdon Williams Wilson
Oil/canvas (51x40.5cm 20x15in) New-York 1998

$48 000 - €51 263 - **£32 121** - FF337 968
**Group of Sketches: Eakins father/Table with
Oranges** Oil/paper/board (25.5x34.5cm 10x13in) New-
York 2000

$5 500 - €6 575 - **£3 793** - FF43 131
Nymph with Bittern Bronze (H23cm H9in) Milford
CT 2000

$4 200 - €3 922 - **£2 543** - FF25 724
Mrs. William H. Mac Dowell Platinum print
(14.5x12cm 5x4in) New-York 1999

EAMES Catherine R. XX [1]

$2 400 - €2 654 - **£1 605** - FF17 408
Easy Street Boat Basin, Nantucket Oil/board
(20x25cm 8x10in) Nantucket MA 2000

EARDLEY Joan Kathleen H. 1921-1963 [86]

$17 780 - €19 825 - **£12 000** - FF130 044
Landscape, Catterline Oil/board (122x122cm
48x48in) Edinburgh 2000

$13 335 - €14 869 - **£9 000** - FF97 533
Tenement Doorway, Glasgow Oil/canvas/board
(60x30cm 23x11in) Edinburgh 2000

$10 096 - €11 867 - **£7 000** - FF77 840
Sunset, Catterline Oil/board (21.5x57cm 8x22in)
Edinburgh 2000

$5 072 - €5 269 - **£3 200** - FF34 564
Girl in a striped Jumper Coloured chalks/paper
(15x11cm 5x4in) London 2000

EARL George 1824-1917 [53]

$11 000 - €12 780 - **£7 730** - FF83 833
Feeding the goats Oil/canvas (101.5x127cm
39x50in) New-York 2001

$9 000 - €9 661 - **£6 131** - FF63 373
Portrait of a Terrier Oil/canvas (53.5x68.5cm
21x26in) Boston MA 2001

$3 711 - €3 564 - **£2 300** - FF23 378
Head of a Maltese Terrier Oil/board (25.5x21cm
10x8in) London 1999

EARL Jack 1908-1994 [1]

$6 734 - €6 685 - **£4 130** - FF43 850
Ketch Kathleen Gillett Oil/canvas (91x56cm
35x22in) Auckland 2000

EARL Maud 1864-1943 [77]

$19 425 - €20 852 - **£13 000** - FF136 780
Three Pekingese with a Macaw Oil/canvas
(180.5x183cm 71x72in) London 2000

$7 468 - €6 453 - **£4 500** - FF42 327
The Terrier's Tea Oil/canvas (44x59.5cm 17x23in)
Billingshurst, West-Sussex 1998

$10 000 - €11 816 - **£7 087** - FF77 508
Parrots Mixed media/canvas (15x25cm 5x9in) Boston
MA 2000

$3 537 - €3 624 - **£2 200** - FF23 769
**Catching the Ball/Rolling Over: Studies of Black
Spaniels** Watercolour (30x50.5cm 11x19in)
Billingshurst, West-Sussex 2000

EARL Percy 1874-1947 [28]

$8 803 - €8 403 - **£5 500** - FF55 123
Insurance Oil/canvas (63.5x76cm 25x29in) London
1999

$2 400 - €2 447 - **£1 503** - FF16 048
Binks, a Favourite Pup Oil/canvas (35.5x25.5cm
13x10in) New-York 2000

EARL Ralph 1751-1801 [8]

$17 000 - €19 303 - **£11 634** - FF126 622
Portrait of a Man Oil/canvas (89x69cm 35x27in)
New-York 2000

EARL Thomas William c.1815-c.1885 [14]

$6 000 - €6 116 - **£3 759** - FF40 120
Waiting for Dinner Oil/canvas (45.5x30.5cm 17x12in)
New-York 2000

EARLE Charles 1832-1893 [23]

$786 - €749 - **£480** - FF4 915
Evening on the Common Watercolour (23x49cm
9x19in) Bury St. Edmunds, Suffolk 1999

EARLE Eyvind 1916-2000 [20]

$850 - €958 - **£594** - FF6 282
Silent Thunder Serigraph in colors (60x79cm
24x31in) Portland OR 2001

EARLE Kathleen Irene, Kate XIX-XX [2]

$3 246 - €3 122 - **£2 000** - FF20 476
The Children's Hour Oil/panel (15x27cm 5x10in)
London 1999

EARLE Lawrence Carmichael 1845-1921 [18]

$800 - €768 - **£495** - FF5 039
**Waist-length portrait of a Woman in Profile dra-
ped in fabric** Oil/canvas (30x22cm 12x9in) St. Louis
MO 1999

$1 200 - €1 066 - **£734** - FF6 993
After the Hunt Watercolour/paper (52x41cm 20x16in)
New-Orleans LA 1999

EARLE Thomas ?-c.1831 [1]

$9 685 - €8 966 - **£6 000** - FF58 811
Boarding the Ferry/Unloading the Catch
Oil/panel (27x37cm 10x14in) London 1999

EARLOM Richard 1743-1822 [130]

$576 - €546 - **£360** - FF3 583
Going to Market after Wheatley Engraving
(49x61cm 19x24in) Crewkerne, Somerset 1999

EARLY Miles J. 1886-? [23]

$650 - €739 - **£450** - FF4 849
Landscape with a Lake Oil/board (40x50cm
16x20in) Cincinnati OH 2000

EARP Edwin XIX-XX **[115]**
🖉 **$265** - €282 - **£180** - FF1 847
    Lake Landscape Scenes with Cattle and Boats
    Watercolour/paper (42x65cm 16x25in) Crewkerne,
    Somerset 2001

EARP Henry I 1831-1914 **[99]**
🖉 **$1 020** - €1 209 - **£720** - FF7 933
    Drover and Cattle resting by a Pond Oil/canvas
    (23x35.5cm 9x13in) West-Midlands 2001
🖉 **$661** - €711 - **£450** - FF4 662
    Cattle and Drover on a country Lane Watercolour
    (24x53.5cm 9x21in) Billingshurst, West-Sussex 2001

EARP William Henry XIX **[66]**
🖉 **$217** - €234 - **£150** - FF1 537
    **Coastal Scenes with Distant Hills and Small
    Boats** Watercolour/paper (25x53cm 10x21in) Henley-
    on-Thames, Oxon 2001

EAST Alfred 1849-1913 **[193]**
☞ **$9 250** - €10 903 - **£6 500** - FF71 521
    Autumn Riverscape with Shorebird Oil/canvas
    (96x152cm 38x60in) New-Orleans LA 2000
☞ **$2 360** - €2 503 - **£1 608** - FF16 419
    A Grey Morning at Aberfoyle Oil/board (40.5x61cm
    15x24in) London 2001
🖉 **$2 104** - €1 975 - **£1 300** - FF12 955
    Mountain Sunset Oil/panel (23x15.5cm 9x6in)
    Billingshurst, West-Sussex 1999
🖉 **$826** - €939 - **£580** - FF6 158
    Chateau Gouillard Watercolour (53x68cm 20x26in)
    West-Midlands 2001
🖾 **$151** - €146 - **£95** - FF958
    Country Road Etching (15.5x20cm 6x7in) London
    1999

EASTLAKE Charles Lock 1793-1865 **[11]**
☞ **$3 200** - €4 147 - **£2 400** - FF27 200
    Agar ed Ismaele Olio/tela (75x96cm 29x37in) Milano
    2001
🖉 **$7 009** - €7 450 - **£4 700** - FF48 868
    **Young Shepherdess Surrounded by Eight Putti
    and an Angel by her Side** Pencil (80x102cm
    31x40in) West-Midlands 2001

EASTLAKE Mary Alexandra Bell 1864-1951 **[14]**
☞ **$1 895** - €1 820 - **£1 174** - FF11 938
    Fishermen preparing Nets on a Wharf Oil/canvas
    (40.5x51cm 15x20in) Toronto 1999

EASTMAN Emily 1804-? **[1]**
🖉 **$14 000** - €12 079 - **£8 477** - FF79 230
    Woman with Veil over Her Face Watercolour
    (36x26cm 14x10in) New-York 1999

EASTMAN Seth 1808-1875 **[5]**
🖉 **$120 000** - €138 633 - **£84 024** - FF909 372
    Worship of the Sun Dakota Dancers
    Watercolour/paper (15x29cm 5x11in) New-York 2001

EASTON Reginald 1807-1893 **[13]**
☞ **$564** - €655 - **£400** - FF4 294
    Anne Maria Horton/Rear Admiral Horton
    Miniature (11x9cm 4x3in) Tunbridge-Wells, Kent 2000

EASTWOOD Walter 1867-1943 **[11]**
🖉 **$325** - €317 - **£200** - FF2 078
    By the Tarn Side, Urswick Watercolour/paper
    (25x35cm 9x13in) Penrith, Cumbria 1999

EATON Charles Harry 1850-1901 **[15]**
☞ **$4 000** - €4 730 - **£2 424** - FF24 466
    Still Life with Watermelons Oil/canvas (56x68.5cm
    22x26in) New-York 1999

EATON Charles Warren 1857-1937 **[63]**
☞ **$7 000** - €5 997 - **£4 208** - FF39 337
    «Forest in Winter» Oil/canvas (55x40cm 22x16in)
    Cleveland OH 1998
☞ **$1 500** - €1 654 - **£1 015** - FF10 851
    Standing Pines Oil/canvas (40.5x30.5cm 15x12in)
    New-York 2000
☞ **$2 600** - €2 486 - **£1 583** - FF16 308
    Nocturne, Village Overlooking a Lake Pastel/can-
    vas (71x56cm 27x22in) Boston MA 1999

EATON Dorothy 1893-1968 **[9]**
☞ **$1 200** - €1 061 - **£733** - FF6 957
    June Flowers Oil/canvas (76x63.5cm 29x25in) New-
    York 1999

EATON Marjorie 1901-1986 **[1]**
☞ **$6 250** - €5 392 - **£3 756** - FF35 370
    Taos Man Seated Oil/canvas (55x45cm 21x18in)
    Santa-Fe NM 1998

EATON Wyatt 1849-1896 **[1]**
☞ **$9 000** - €9 661 - **£6 131** - FF63 373
    An Open Field at Dusk Oil/canvas (50.5x60.5cm
    19x23in) Boston MA 2001

EBATARINJA Cordula 1919-1973 **[27]**
🖉 **$321** - €354 - **£213** - FF2 322
    The Winding Valley Watercolour/paper (27x36cm
    10x14in) Melbourne 2000

EBATARINJA Walter 1915-1969 **[35]**
🖉 **$172** - €190 - **£116** - FF1 246
    The Purple Hills of Arunta Watercolour/paper
    (35x51.5cm 13x20in) Sydney 2000

EBEL Fritz 1835-1895 **[26]**
☞ **$5 072** - €4 345 - **£3 048** - FF28 503
    Waldinneres mit Kindern am Bach Öl/Leinwand
    (94x70cm 37x27in) Köln 1998
☞ **$937** - €971 - **£593** - FF6 132
    Frau beim Wasserholen Öl/Leinwand/Karton
    (23.5x28.5cm 9x11in) Rudolstadt-Thüringen 2000

EBENSPERGER Hans 1929-1971 **[2]**
🖉 **$1 184** - €1 022 - **£712** - FF6 704
    Expressive Alpenlandschaft Gouache/paper
    (43x57cm 16x22in) München 1998

EBERHARD Heinrich 1884-1973 **[37]**
☞ **$980** - €1 022 - **£617** - FF6 707
    Schwäbische Ortschaft mit Schloss Öl/Leinwand
    (40x50cm 15x19in) Stuttgart 2000

EBERL François Zdenek 1887-1962 **[64]**
🖉 **$765** - €854 - **£532** - FF5 600
    Jeune fille au sein nu Huile/toile (60x49cm
    23x19in) Paris 2001
☞ **$655** - €732 - **£456** - FF4 800
    Jeune fille aux cheveux roux Huile/toile (30x25cm
    11x9in) Paris 2001

EBERL Josef 1792-1880 **[1]**
🖉 **$1 945** - €2 325 - **£1 337** - FF15 254
    Stift Lambach Gouache/paper (20x27cm 7x10in)
    Salzburg 2000

EBERLE Abastenia St. Leger 1878-1942 **[15]**
🖎 **$3 200** - €3 435 - **£2 141** - FF22 531
    Omar Khayyam Bookends Bronze (H15.5cm H6in)
    New-York 2000

EBERLE Adolf 1843-1914 **[41]**
☞ **$8 936** - €10 226 - **£6 146** - FF67 078
    Musik in der Bauernstube Oil/panel (58x68cm
    22x26in) München 2000

$2 887 - €2 910 - **£1 800** - FF19 086
A Portrait of a Young Lady, Half-Length, Wearing a Hat Oil/panel (26x19cm 10x7in) London 2000

EBERLE Robert 1815-1860 **[10]**
$5 665 - €5 624 - **£3 539** - FF36 892
Hirtenknabe, auf dem Wiesenhang lagernd Öl/Karton (30x24cm 11x9in) München 1999

EBERLEIN Gustav Heinrich 1847-1926 **[8]**
$1 511 - €1 467 - **£941** - FF9 625
Junge Frau mit Handspiegel Bronze (H41cm H16in) Zürich 1999

EBERLEIN Otto 1827-1896 **[1]**
$5 502 - €6 135 - **£3 699** - FF40 246
Mittägliche Rast Öl/Leinwand (49.5x61cm 19x24in) Ahlden 2000

EBERS Hermann 1881-1955 **[24]**
$456 - €511 - **£309** - FF33 353
Bachlandschaft Öl/Leinwand (60x65cm 23x25in) München 2000

EBERSBACH Hartwig 1940 **[15]**
$3 650 - €4 090 - **£2 542** - FF26 831
Gelber Kaspar Oil/panel (133x81cm 52x31in) Berlin 2001
$972 - €1 176 - **£679** - FF7 714
Kaspar seitwärts Gouache/Karton (102x73.2cm 40x28in) Berlin 2000

EBERSBACH Johan Daniël 1822-1900 **[1]**
$4 091 - €3 857 - **£2 535** - FF25 301
Figures Strolling Along a Canal Oil/panel (21.5x16cm 8x6in) Amsterdam 1999

EBERSBERG von Carl Martin 1818-1880 **[7]**
$3 275 - €3 068 - **£2 013** - FF20 123
Der elegante Leutnant hoch zu Ross vor Landschaftshintergrund Öl/Leinwand (37.5x46.5cm 14x18in) Lindau 1999

EBERSBERGER Max 1852-? **[7]**
$4 644 - €4 360 - **£2 880** - FF28 602
Früchtestilleben Öl/Leinwand (71x118cm 27x46in) Wien 1999

EBERT Albert 1906-1976 **[8]**
$2 961 - €3 579 - **£2 067** - FF23 477
Aschermittwoch Oil/panel (12.5x14.1cm 4x5in) Berlin 2000

EBERT Anton 1845-1896 **[67]**
$2 957 - €2 545 - **£1 753** - FF16 691
Mädchen am Fenster Öl/Leinwand (117x86cm 46x33in) Wien 1998
$2 496 - €2 422 - **£1 584** - FF15 890
Portraetter af en brevskrivende og en brevlaesende ung kvinde Oil/panel (21x17cm 8x6in) Viby J, Århus 1999

EBERT Carl 1821-1885 **[52]**
$4 328 - €4 896 - **£3 027** - FF32 118
Laubwald mit vom Sturm geknickten Bäumen Öl/Leinwand (37x57cm 14x22in) St. Gallen 2001
$2 435 - €2 454 - **£1 518** - FF16 098
Sonnenbeschienene Waldlichtung Oil/paper/canvas (34.7x43cm 13x16in) Stuttgart 2000

EBERT Charles H. 1873-1959 **[18]**
$35 000 - €38 761 - **£23 737** - FF254 257
Monhegan Island, Maine Oil/canvas (63.5x76.5cm 25x30in) New-York 1999
$7 500 - €8 517 - **£5 133** - FF55 866
Fishing Boats/Fishing Boarts Entering Safe Harbour Oil/panel (20x25.5cm 7x10in) New-York 2000

EBERZ Josef 1880-1942 **[128]**
$11 247 - €10 737 - **£7 026** - FF70 431
Strasse Öl/Leinwand (70x58cm 27x22in) Köln 1999
$2 646 - €2 965 - **£1 843** - FF19 452
Kanalansicht mit Brücke und Architekturstaffage Öl/Karton (42.5x33cm 16x12in) Leipzig 2001
$909 - €869 - **£553** - FF5 701
Giardino Falconieri Indian ink (30x42cm 11x16in) Bielefeld 1999
$247 - €230 - **£152** - FF1 549
Zwei Mädchen Woodcut (21x15.7cm 8x6in) Hamburg 1999

EBLE Theo 1899-1974 **[27]**
$6 425 - €6 194 - **£3 961** - FF40 629
Mädchen im Fasnachtskostüm Öl/Leinwand (111x80.5cm 43x31in) Bern 1999
$1 663 - €1 974 - **£1 211** - FF12 949
Portrait de Femme/Studie Öl/Leinwand (43x33cm 16x12in) Zürich 2001

EBNER Lajos Deàk 1850-1934 **[18]**
$900 - €1 040 - **£630** - FF6 820
Village Scene with Figures by a Pathway Oil/canvas/board (38x33.5cm 14x13in) Bethesda MD 2001

EBNETH von Lajos 1902-1982 **[1]**
$21 672 - €20 348 - **£13 384** - FF133 476
Ohne Titel Öl/Leinwand (57x46cm 22x18in) Wien 1999

EBSTER Manfred 1941 **[8]**
$1 243 - €1 163 - **£752** - FF7 627
Flora und Fauna Oil/panel (40x30cm 15x11in) Wien 1999

EBY Kerr 1889-1946 **[97]**
$350 - €358 - **£219** - FF2 350
Scout Planes at Dawn Etching (32x22cm 12x8in) Cleveland OH 1999

ECCARDT John Giles c.1720-1779 **[3]**
$36 478 - €43 383 - **£26 000** - FF284 575
Portrait of Horace Walpole, Half-Length, Wearing van Dyck Dress Oil/canvas (43x34.5cm 16x13in) London 2000

ECEVIT Nazli 1908 **[2]**
$1 575 000 - €1 787 465 - **£1 050 000** - FF11 725 000
Nature morte aux fleurs Aquarelle (55x38.5cm 21x15in) Istanbul 2001

ECHAVE ORIO de Balthasar I XVII **[2]**
$28 192 - €23 250 - **£16 608** - FF152 512
Christus und die Samariterin am Brunnen Öl/Kupfer (44.5x59cm 17x23in) Wien 1998

ECHENA José 1845-1912 **[13]**
$20 920 - €22 456 - **£14 000** - FF147 302
A Musical Interlude Oil/panel (37x23cm 14x9in) London 2000
$315 - €300 - **£195** - FF1 970
Bosque Pastel/papier (30x20cm 11x7in) Madrid 1999

ECHEVARRIA de Federico 1911 **[24]**
$3 705 - €3 904 - **£2 470** - FF25 610
Paseo de España anocheciendo (Málaga) Oleo/lienzo (91x73cm 35x28in) Madrid 2000

ECHEVARRIA José Luis 1922 **[36]**
$448 - €481 - **£296** - FF3 152
Playa de San Sebastián Oleo/cartón (24x42cm 9x16in) Madrid 2000

ECHEVARRIA Y ZURICALDAY de Juan 1875-1931 [8]

$33 150 - €39 042 - **£24 050** - FF256 100
Jardín del Palacio de Picavea Oleo/lienzo
(80x105cm 31x41in) Madrid 2001

ECHTLER Adolf 1843-1914 [21]

$2 214 - €2 198 - **£1 383** - FF14 421
Italienerin mit Schleiertuch und Fächer Oil/canvas/panel (74x47cm 29x18in) München 1999

$4 250 - €4 082 - **£2 620** - FF26 774
Children in yard feeding doves and fowl
Oil/panel (31x16cm 12x6in) Cambridge MA 1999

ECKARDT Christian 1832-1914 [96]

$6 390 - €6 057 - **£3 888** - FF39 730
Redningsbåden kommer de nödstedte til hjaelp
Oil/canvas (120x190cm 47x74in) Köbenhavn 1999

$1 221 - €1 278 - **£767** - FF8 384
**Dänische Seelandschaft mit Wandererin und
Kind** Öl/Leinwand (35x56cm 13x22in) Bremen 2000

$1 000 - €1 073 - **£681** - FF7 036
Marine fra kysten ud for Korsor, daggry Oil/canvas (28x50cm 11x19in) Köbenhavn 2001

ECKART Christian 1959 [9]

$2 051 - €2 201 - **£1 393** - FF14 440
Untitled Mixed media/paper (59x22cm 23x8in)
Calgary, Alberta 2001

ECKELBOOM Hendrick Daniël 1806-1847 [4]

$2 283 - €2 301 - **£1 423** - FF15 092
**Weite schneebedeckte Winterlandschaft mit
Figurenstaffage** Öl/Leinwand (21x27cm 8x10in)
Stuttgart 2000

ECKENBRECHER von Themistokles Karl P. 1842-1921 [119]

$2 281 - €2 556 - **£1 572** - FF16 769
Die Magdalenen Bay auf Spitzbergen
Öl/Leinwand (50x74cm 19x29in) Hamburg 2000

$1 896 - €1 636 - **£1 129** - FF10 731
Bootsanlegestelle Öl/Leinwand (24.5x34cm 9x13in)
München 1998

$126 - €143 - **£88** - FF939
Ein Handelsdampfer wird beladen Aquarell,
Gouache/Papier (8.5x12.5cm 3x4in) München 2001

$900 - €1 022 - **£616** - FF6 707
«N.D.L. - Kaiser Wilhelm der Grosse» Poster
(102x69cm 40x27in) Hannover 2000

ECKENER Alexander 1870-1944 [65]

$126 - €112 - **£77** - FF737
Erdenlos Radierung (48.5x72.5cm 19x28in) Pforzheim
1999

ECKENFELDER Friedrich 1861-1938 [64]

$2 379 - €2 812 - **£1 686** - FF18 446
Zwei pflügende Braune bei Dachau Öl/Leinwand
(55x70cm 21x27in) Stuttgart 2000

$2 924 - €2 863 - **£1 799** - FF18 781
Schimmelgespann auf einer sonnenbeschienenen Waldlichtung Oil/canvas/panel (24x30cm 9x11in)
Stuttgart 1999

ECKERSBERG Christoffer Wilhelm 1783-1853 [244]

$102 667 - €90 586 - **£61 830** - FF594 202
Lyngbyvejen ved Lundehuset, i forgrunden hestekøretöj og personer Oil/canvas (37.5x44cm
14x17in) Köbenhavn 1998

$46 650 - €40 384 - **£28 320** - FF264 900
Klostergården i San Lorenzo Fuori Oil/canvas
(33x45cm 12x17in) Köbenhavn 1998

$3 277 - €3 097 - **£2 042** - FF20 313
Nadveren Pencil (23x16cm 9x6in) Köbenhavn 1999

ECKERSBERG Erling 1808-1889 [4]

$6 115 - €6 980 - **£4 248** - FF45 786
**Udsigt gennem tre af de nordvestlige buer i
amphiteatrets** Watercolour/paper (34x50cm 13x19in)
Köbenhavn 2000

ECKERSBERG Johan Frederick 1822-1870 [26]

$22 287 - €23 248 - **£14 060** - FF152 494
Söndagsutflukt Oil/panel (36x49cm 14x19in) Oslo
2000

$21 080 - €25 078 - **£14 580** - FF164 500
Fra Romsdalen Oil/panel (22x38cm 8x14in) Oslo
2000

ECKERSLEY Tom 1914-? [12]

$618 - €567 - **£380** - FF3 722
Whisky Galore! Poster (152.5x51cm 60x20in)
London 1999

ECKERT Henri Ambrose 1807-1840 [9]

$7 268 - €8 181 - **£5 008** - FF53 662
Vor der Hufschmiede Oil/panel (32x43cm 12x16in)
Stuttgart 2000

ECKL Vilna 1892-1982 [19]

$2 432 - €2 761 - **£1 706** - FF18 114
Tanz Oil chalks/paper (44x57.5cm 17x22in) Wien 2001

ECKMANN Otto 1865-1902 [26]

$300 - €307 - **£188** - FF2 012
Wenn der Frühling kommt Lithograph
(25.5x11.2cm 10x4in) Hamburg 2000

ECONOMOU Ioannis 1860-1931 [4]

$12 960 - €14 416 - **£8 640** - FF94 560
Summer Fruits Oil/canvas (58x70cm 22x27in) Athens
2000

$2 070 - €1 753 - **£1 207** - FF11 500
Taling a Break Watercolour/paper (24x16.5cm 9x6in)
Athens 1999

ECONOMOU Michalis 1888-1933 [11]

$32 400 - €36 039 - **£21 600** - FF236 400
Bridge Oil/canvas (46x61cm 18x24in) Athens 2000

$1 620 - €1 513 - **£1 000** - FF9 925
A Greek Coastal View Watercolour/paper (30x44cm
12x17in) Fernhurst, Haslemere, Surrey 1999

ED Carl Frank Ludwig 1890-1959 [4]

$450 - €483 - **£301** - FF3 168
Harold teen Daily Strips Ink (12.5x42cm 4x16in)
New-York 2000

EDDIS Eden Upton 1812-1901 [7]

$2 704 - €2 576 - **£1 650** - FF16 896
The little Fortune Teller Oil/panel (30x24.5cm
11x9in) Bury St. Edmunds, Suffolk 1999

EDDY Don 1944 [30]

$181 - €216 - **£129** - FF1 420
Williams Barbequed Chicken Farblithographie
(59x45cm 23x17in) Hamburg 2000

EDE Basil 1931 [90]

$12 000 - €10 253 - **£7 203** - FF67 252
Pintails Rising Oil/canvas (71x91.5cm 27x36in) New-York 1998

$893 - €859 - **£550** - FF5 632
Long Tailed Tits Watercolour (18.5x23cm 7x9in)
London 1999

EDE Frederick Ch. Vipont 1865-1943 [31]

$1 335 - €1 524 - **£939** - FF10 000
Les maisons au pont de pierre Huile/toile
(50x62cm 19x24in) Fontainebleau 2001

EDELFELT Albert 1854-1905 **[214]**
- $151 759 - €132 827 - £91 956 - FF871 291
  Första snön Oil/canvas (69.5x60cm 27x23in) Helsinki 1998
- $16 328 - €14 291 - £9 894 - FF93 746
  Skiss för målningen Kristus och Magdalena Oil/panel (32x24cm 12x9in) Helsinki 1998
- $1 533 - €1 682 - £987 - FF11 032
  En natt i Augsburg Indian ink (25x27cm 9x10in) Helsinki 2000
- $576 - €538 - £355 - FF3 530
  Man på visthustrappan Etching (17x19.5cm 6x7in) Helsinki 1999

EDELINCK Gerard I 1640-1707 **[12]**
- $268 - €256 - £163 - FF1 676
  Porträt des flämischen Malers Philippe de Champagne Copper engraving (39.5x32.7cm 15x12in) Köln 1999

EDELMANN Albert 1886-1963 **[13]**
- $1 427 - €1 377 - £896 - FF9 035
  Blumenstrauss in vase/Blumenstrauss Öl/Karton (63x48cm 24x18in) St. Gallen 1999

EDELMANN Heinz 1934 **[2]**
- $1 010 - €1 116 - £700 - FF7 321
  «The yellow Submarine» Poster (104x68.5cm 40x26in) London 2001

EDELMANN Yrjö 1941 **[65]**
- $5 548 - €6 120 - £3 758 - FF40 142
  Komposition med papper Oil/canvas (155x148cm 61x58in) Stockholm 2000
- $3 480 - €3 379 - £2 148 - FF22 164
  Skrynkliga papper Oil/canvas (60x60cm 23x23in) Stockholm 2000
- $966 - €1 071 - £656 - FF7 026
  Ett barn försvinner (A Child Disappears) Gouache/paper (50x38cm 19x14in) Stockholm 2000
- $213 - €235 - £147 - FF1 544
  Ljusröd och Ljusblå Serigraph (74x53.5cm 29x21in) Helsinki 2001

EDEMA van Gerard 1652-1700 **[13]**
- $32 500 - €30 087 - £19 620 - FF197 356
  Extensive Mountainous Landscape with Figures in the Foreground Oil/canvas (113x175cm 44x68in) New-York 1999
- $11 324 - €10 498 - £7 000 - FF68 864
  Winter Landscape with Skaters on a Frozen River Oil/canvas/board (62x75cm 24x29in) London 1999

EDEN Emily 1797-1869 **[4]**
- $4 930 - €5 790 - £3 500 - FF37 983
  Portraits of the Princes/People of India Lithograph (51x35.5cm 20x13in) London 2000

EDEN William 1844-1913 **[13]**
- $231 - €259 - £160 - FF1 700
  Study of a Village with three Church Spires Watercolour (24x34cm 9x13in) London 2001

EDER Gyula 1875-1945 **[12]**
- $1 116 - €1 068 - £700 - FF7 003
  Under Cupid's Spell Oil/canvas (62x101.5cm 24x39in) London 1999

EDER Otto 1924-1982 **[16]**
- $878 - €872 - £548 - FF5 720
  Kopf Woodcut in colors (42x60cm 16x23in) Wien 1999

EDERER Carl 1875-1950 **[13]**
- $1 383 - €1 534 - £960 - FF10 061
  Liegende Kühe Öl/Leinwand (29x40.5cm 11x15in) Köln 2001

EDGAR Norman XX **[8]**
- $3 098 - €3 461 - £2 100 - FF22 704
  Towards Strone Oil/canvas (105x100cm 41x39in) Edinburgh 2000

EDGE John William XIX **[6]**
- $1 665 - €1 753 - £1 100 - FF11 500
  Seascape with Shipping and Men-O'-War off the Coast Watercolour (14x22cm 5x8in) London 2000

EDGERTON Harold Eugene 1903-1990 **[120]**
- $1 500 - €1 401 - £906 - FF9 190
  Splash of a Milk Drop/Tennis Forehand Drive, Jenny Tuckey Silver print (30x23cm 12x9in) New-York 1999

EDHOLM Ann 1953 **[5]**
- $1 255 - €1 181 - £778 - FF7 745
  Utan titel Mixed media/paper (30.5x30.5cm 12x12in) Stockholm 1999

EDLINGER Josef/Johann Georg 1741-1819 **[14]**
- $4 494 - €4 090 - £2 808 - FF26 831
  Herrenporträt Öl/Leinwand (54x50cm 21x19in) München 1999

EDMONDSON Edward, Jr. 1830-1883 **[1]**
- $10 000 - €11 553 - £7 002 - FF75 781
  Still Life with Peaches Oil/canvas (43x53cm 16x20in) New-York 2001

EDMONDSON William 1882-1951 **[2]**
- $210 000 - €241 772 - £143 304 - FF1 585 920
  Birthbath Stone (98x77.5x37cm 38x30x14in) New-York 2000

EDMONDSON William John 1868-1966 **[15]**
- $550 - €516 - £339 - FF3 384
  Autumn Landscape Oil/board (22x29cm 9x11in) Cleveland OH 1999

EDOUART Augustin Amant C.F. 1789-1861 **[71]**
- $900 - €768 - £541 - FF5 037
  Gentleman in full cot and hat Silhouette (26x16cm 10x6in) Asheville NC 1999

EDRIDGE Henry 1769-1821 **[87]**
- $1 775 - €1 644 - £1 100 - FF10 782
  In Cassiobury Park, Hertfordshire Watercolour (29.5x39.5cm 11x15in) London 1999

EDSBERG Knud 1911 **[58]**
- $293 - €322 - £187 - FF2 113
  Gårdexteriör med höns Oil/canvas (50x60cm 19x23in) København 1999

EDSON Aaron Allan 1846-1888 **[29]**
- $2 437 - €2 378 - £1 501 - FF15 598
  Preparing the Campsite at Sunset Oil/canvas (42x72.5cm 16x28in) Montréal 1999

EDVI-ILLÉS Aladar 1870-1958 **[28]**
- $623 - €721 - £441 - FF4 732
  Zwei Ochsen an einem Weiher Öl/Karton (39.5x55.5cm 15x21in) Zürich 2000
- $420 - €404 - £260 - FF2 650
  Landscape Oil/cardboard (44x30.5cm 17x12in) Budapest 1999

EDWARDS Alfred Sanderson 1852-1915 **[7]**
- $252 - €270 - £168 - FF1 774
  Crashing Surf Oil/panel (25.5x35.5cm 10x13in) Toronto 2000

EDWARDS Emmet 1906-1981 **[24]**
- $225 - €220 - £138 - FF1 446
  Untitled Watercolour/paper (35.5x50.5cm 13x19in) Washington 1999

EDWARDS George 1694-1773 **[29]**
$179 - €192 - £119 - FF1 260
Black Parrot Engraving (23x19cm 9x7in) Cleveland OH 2000

EDWARDS Harry C. 1868-1922 **[1]**
$5 000 - €4 272 - £3 025 - FF28 022
Gossip/Cowboy Sketching Oil/canvas/board (20.5x25.5cm 8x10in) San-Francisco CA 1998

EDWARDS J.W. XX **[2]**
$2 789 - €3 060 - £1 800 - FF20 072
Portrait of Dylan Thomas Oil/canvas/board (35x26.5cm 13x10in) London 2000

EDWARDS John XVIII-XIX **[1]**
$2 600 - €2 899 - £1 748 - FF19 017
Polyanthus/Medea Watercolour/paper (38x27cm 15x11in) Portsmouth NH 2000

EDWARDS Les 1949 **[4]**
$1 800 - €1 533 - £1 085 - FF10 055
Off to draw the pytchley Acuarela/papel (23.8x36.7cm 9x14in) Buenos-Aires 1998

EDWARDS Lionel Dalhousie R. 1878-1966 **[348]**
$16 221 - €15 578 - £10 000 - FF102 188
Newmarket, The Lime Kilns Oil/canvas (76x101.5cm 29x39in) London 1999
$3 000 - €3 381 - £2 077 - FF22 176
«2nd Whip-Going Home» Watercolour/paper (32x26cm 12x10in) Hatfield PA 2000
$269 - €306 - £190 - FF2 010
The Holderness (the Lambwath Drain) Print in colors (31x29cm 12x19in) Aylsham, Norfolk 2001

EDWARDS Mary A. 1897-1988 **[20]**
$42 735 - €40 291 - £26 485 - FF264 290
Heritage Oil/canvas (151x136cm 59x53in) Melbourne 1999

EDWARDS Nowell M. XX **[1]**
$777 - €901 - £550 - FF5 911
«Southern, For Free Booklet Camping Sites in Southern England» Poster (102x64cm 40x25in) London 2000

EDWARDS Sydenham Teast c.1768-1819 **[32]**
$800 - €864 - £552 - FF5 667
Botanical Subjects Engraving (21.5x25.5cm 8x10in) Miami FL 2001

EDWELL Bernice 1880-1962 **[3]**
$2 233 - €2 046 - £1 364 - FF13 423
Girl in a Red Shawl/Girl in Persian Costume Miniature (14x10cm 5x3in) Melbourne 1999

EDWIN David 1776-1841 **[1]**
$1 000 - €1 061 - £678 - FF6 957
Thomas Jefferson Esqr. President of the United States Engraving (29x23cm 11x9in) New-York 2001

EDY John William XVIII-XIX **[13]**
$1 037 - €880 - £626 - FF5 775
View of the St Ann's or Grand River, after Lt. G. Bulteel Fisher Aquatint (48.5x66cm 19x25in) London 1998

EDY-LEGRAND (Édouard Legrand) 1892-1970 **[68]**
$33 934 - €28 965 - £20 292 - FF190 000
Rassemblement des caïds avant la fantasia Huile/toile (130x163cm 51x64in) Paris 1998
$8 668 - €8 385 - £5 346 - FF55 000
Les femmes du Caïd d'Anemiter Huile/isorel (46x55cm 18x21in) Paris 1999
$1 361 - €1 524 - £946 - FF10 000
Femmes du Haut Atlas Huile/panneau (16x22.5cm 6x8in) Paris 2001

$455 - €534 - £327 - FF3 500
L'enfer de Dante Lavis (23x18cm 9x7in) Paris 2001

EDZARD Dietz 1893-1963 **[283]**
$4 500 - €4 535 - £2 805 - FF29 745
Lady and Child by the Lake Oil/canvas (65x49cm 25x19in) Delray-Beach FL 2000
$1 200 - €1 007 - £704 - FF6 604
Ballerina Oil/canvas (40x33cm 16x13in) New-York 1998

EDZARD Kurt 1890-1972 **[16]**
$908 - €1 022 - £626 - FF6 707
Kleiner Boxer Bronze (H42cm H16in) Bremen 2000

EECKHOUDT van den Jean 1875-1946 **[37]**
$4 288 - €3 966 - £2 672 - FF26 016
Jonge vrouw met hoed Oil/canvas (49x41.5cm 19x16in) Lokeren 1999
$1 722 - €1 488 - £1 038 - FF9 762
Col de Castillon Huile/papier (33x41cm 12x16in) Bruxelles 1998
$1 856 - €1 983 - £1 264 - FF13 008
Portret van Elmisabeth vanden Eeckhoudt Pastel/papier (65x43.5cm 25x17in) Lokeren 2001

EECKHOUT Jacobus Josephus 1793-1861 **[30]**
$8 474 - €9 420 - £5 928 - FF61 788
Petit pêcheur rencontrant une élégante et sa fille Huile/panneau (101x79.5cm 39x31in) Bruxelles 2001

EECKHOUT van den Gerbrandt 1621-1674 **[32]**
$32 748 - €30 368 - £20 000 - FF199 204
A scene from a Pastoral Novel, possibly Daphnis and Chloe Oil/canvas (75x87.5cm 29x34in) London 1998
$17 142 - €19 966 - £11 976 - FF130 970
Potphar's Wife Falsely Accuses Joseph Red chalk (23x20cm 9x7in) Amsterdam 2000

EECKHOUT Victor 1821-1879 **[17]**
$1 182 - €1 125 - £750 - FF7 382
Bazaar in Tangiers Oil/panel (20x30cm 7x11in) Billingshurst, West-Sussex 1999

EEGHEN van Johanna 1822-1868 **[5]**
$4 568 - €3 852 - £2 711 - FF25 267
A Still Life with Cherries, Peonies and Violets Oil/panel (27.5x22cm 10x8in) Amsterdam 1998

EEKMAN Nicolas Mathieu 1889-1973 **[150]**
$1 596 - €1 487 - £984 - FF9 756
La petite fenêtre Huile/panneau (55x38cm 21x14in) Bruxelles 1999
$1 263 - €1 289 - £790 - FF8 455
Trois têtes à caractère Huile/panneau (35x27cm 13x10in) Bruxelles 2000
$590 - €495 - £346 - FF3 248
La bossue aux trois corbeaux Encre (32.5x23cm 12x9in) Bruxelles 1998
$61 - €68 - £41 - FF446
Lezende vrouw Woodcut (12.8x10.4cm 5x4in) Haarlem 2000

EEL Knud P. 1914-1967 **[31]**
$547 - €604 - £370 - FF3 960
Kystparti med huse, Vildsund Oil/canvas (61x101cm 24x39in) Vejle 2000

EELKEMA Eelke Jelles 1788-1839 **[5]**
$6 400 - €6 250 - £4 079 - FF41 000
Nature morte aux pêches et raisins mêlés de fleurs Aquarelle/papier (40.5x32.5cm 15x12in) Paris 1999

E

EEMANS Marc 1907-1998 **[60]**
- **$8 670** - €9 983 - **£5 918** - FF65 485
  L'attitude des apparences Oil/canvas (130x98cm 51x38in) Amsterdam 2000
- **$473** - €545 - **£325** - FF3 577
  Le vainqueur Oil/paper/panel (35x26cm 13x10in) Lokeren 2000
- **$1 792** - €1 859 - **£1 140** - FF12 195
  Compositie Watercolour (47.5x63cm 18x24in) Lokeren 2000

EEMONT van Adriaen c.1627-1662 **[3]**
- **$2 900** - €2 848 - **£1 800** - FF18 683
  Travellers on Horseback resting beside a Well Oil/canvas (23x27.5cm 9x10in) London 1999

EERELMAN Otto 1839-1926 **[107]**
- **$8 789** - €9 983 - **£6 166** - FF65 485
  A Collie Oil/canvas (50x65cm 19x25in) Amsterdam 2001
- **$3 021** - €3 403 - **£2 082** - FF22 324
  Still life with Pink Roses and Wild Flowers Oil/panel (24x15cm 9x5in) Amsterdam 2000
- **$4 300** - €3 625 - **£2 552** - FF23 781
  The Visting-Card Watercolour/paper (30.5x23cm 12x9in) Amsterdam 1998

EERTVELT van Andries 1590-1652 **[22]**
- **$11 116** - €10 174 - **£6 776** - FF66 738
  Ein Dreimaster und andere Schiffe vor einer südlichen Küste Öl/Leinwand (101.5x157.5cm 39x62in) Wien 1999
- **$9 456** - €8 690 - **£5 808** - FF57 000
  Vaisseaux turcs en rade Huile/panneau (72x103cm 28x40in) Paris 1999

EFIAIMBELO c.1925 **[2]**
- **$6 016** - €5 807 - **£3 800** - FF38 090
  Aloalo Pangalatra Omby (Stealing Zebus) Sculpture, wood (199x100x33cm 78x39x12in) London 1999

EFRAT Benni 1936 **[14]**
- **$5 200** - €5 807 - **£3 330** - FF38 092
  Target Metal (H52cm H20in) Tel Aviv 2000

EGAN Felim 1952-? **[14]**
- **$6 778** - €6 364 - **£4 200** - FF41 748
  Hercules/Antaeus Acrylic/canvas (140x160cm 55x62in) London 1999
- **$2 249** - €2 413 - **£1 533** - FF15 825
  Abstract Studies Acrylic/paper (56x45.5cm 22x17in) Dublin 2001

EGEA LOPEZ Alberto XX **[12]**
- **$1 600** - €1 494 - **£1 000** - FF9 800
  Paisaje Oleo/lienzo (49x57cm 19x22in) Caracas 1999

EGEDIUS Alfdan 1877-1899 **[6]**
- **$2 182** - €2 521 - **£1 528** - FF16 538
  Markarbeidere Eika Pencil/paper (11x18cm 4x7in) Oslo 2001

EGELL Augustin 1731-1785 **[2]**
- **$3 743** - €4 295 - **£2 560** - FF28 172
  Bauernkate unter Bäumen, im Vordergrund ein Hirte mit Kuh am Wasser Watercolour (40.4x52.5cm 15x20in) Heidelberg 2000

EGELL Paul 1691-1752 **[1]**
- **$22 332** - €20 452 - **£13 612** - FF134 156
  Hl. Familie Sculpture, wood (H41.4cm H16in) Berlin 1999

EGENBERGER Johannes Henderikus 1822-1897 **[1]**
- **$4 305** - €3 721 - **£2 595** - FF24 405
  Le prince et le peintre Huile/toile (73.5x63cm 28x24in) Bruxelles 1998

EGERSDÖRFER Andreas 1866-1932 **[10]**
- **$1 330** - €1 329 - **£832** - FF8 720
  Bauer mit Kuh und Kalb schaut erstaunt auf die Münzen Öl/Leinwand (32x42cm 12x16in) Lindau 1999

EGERSDÖRFER Konrad 1868-? **[16]**
- **$781** - €716 - **£476** - FF4 695
  Advokat und Bauer beim Verlesen eines Schriftstücks Oil/panel (24x32cm 9x12in) Berlin 1999
- **$3 390** - €3 735 - **£2 261** - FF24 500
  Après-midi d'été Lavis (58x33cm 22x12in) Deauville 2000

EGERTON Daniel Thomas 1800-1842 **[13]**
- **$218 816** - €188 566 - **£130 000** - FF1 236 911
  The Ravine of the Desert Oil/canvas (104x152.5cm 40x60in) London 1998
- **$6 382** - €7 288 - **£4 500** - FF47 804
  Views of Mexico: Guanaxuato Lithograph (42.5x60cm 16x23in) London 2001

EGGELER Stefan 1894-1969 **[19]**
- **$201** - €218 - **£139** - FF1 430
  Wachau, Innenhof mit einem Brunnen und Sonnenblumen Farblithographie (52x50cm 20x19in) Wien 2001

EGGENHOFER Nick 1897-1985 **[68]**
- **$16 000** - €18 673 - **£11 342** - FF122 489
  The Watchers, Dakota Indians Oil/board (37.5x50cm 14x19in) New-York 2001
- **$2 600** - €2 853 - **£1 674** - FF18 716
  Rough Lock (The Army Wagon) Tempera (29x45cm 11x17in) Beverly-Hills CA 2000
- **$2 640** - €2 465 - **£1 629** - FF16 172
  Moving Camp, Indian Buffalo Hunt Ink (30x45cm 12x18in) Dallas TX 1999

EGGENSCHWILER Franz 1930-2000 **[167]**
- **$1 293** - €1 117 - **£781** - FF7 329
  Torso Iron (52x20x20cm 20x7x7in) Luzern 1998
- **$73** - €85 - **£50** - FF559
  Bomba-Eckquartier/Baumfrau Woodcut in colors (44.5x31.5cm 17x12in) Bern 2000

EGGENSCHWILER Urs 1849-1923 **[22]**
- **$4 869** - €4 680 - **£3 000** - FF30 699
  Lion looking over a Valley from a Mountain Oil/canvas (72x100.5cm 28x39in) London 1999

EGGER Jean, Hans 1897-1934 **[6]**
- **$22 440** - €25 154 - **£15 229** - FF165 000
  Tête de femme Huile/toile (46x38cm 18x14in) Paris 2000

EGGER-LIENZ Albin 1868-1926 **[76]**
- **$75 210** - €83 573 - **£50 370** - FF548 205
  Der Bauer und der Tod Öl/Leinwand (63.7x79.8cm 25x31in) Wien 2000
- **$26 000** - €26 953 - **£15 600** - FF176 800
  Montanaro atesino Olio/cartone (43x35cm 16x13in) Roma 1999
- **$3 310** - €3 634 - **£2 200** - FF23 835
  Die Quelle Black chalk (51x79cm 20x31in) Wien 2000

EGGERICKS L.J.J. (?) XIX **[2]**
- **$2 224** - €2 439 - **£1 500** - FF16 000
  Nature morte aux fruits et fleurs Huile/panneau (22x30cm 8x11in) Lille 2000

EGGERT Sigmund 1839-1896 **[10]**
- $4 130 - €4 006 - **£2 600** - FF26 279
  The Reading Lesson Oil/canvas (61.5x49cm 24x19in) London 2001

EGGIMANN Hans 1872-1929 **[67]**
- $68 - €78 - **£48** - FF510
  «Der Bürokrat» Radierung (23.5x12cm 9x4in) Bern 2001

EGGINTON Frank J. 1908-1990 **[209]**
- $2 354 - €2 653 - **£1 630** - FF17 401
  «Muckish, Co.Donegal» Oil/board (45.5x61cm 17x24in) Toronto 2000
- $2 302 - €2 381 - **£1 450** - FF15 617
  Bertraghboy Bay, Connemara Watercolour/paper (37x53cm 14x20in) Bath 2000

EGGINTON Wycliffe 1875-1951 **[149]**
- $3 913 - €3 809 - **£2 404** - FF24 987
  The Cloud swept Moor Oil/canvas (39x54cm 15x21in) Dublin 1999
- $1 120 - €1 203 - **£750** - FF7 891
  Grazing Cattle Watercolour/paper (30x43cm 11x16in) London 2000

EGGLER Josef 1916 **[37]**
- $621 - €532 - **£373** - FF3 491
  Spätwinterlandschaft im Rheintal Öl/Karton (84x58cm 33x22in) St. Gallen 1998

EGGLESTON Benjamin 1867-1937 **[27]**
- $2 250 - €2 462 - **£1 556** - FF16 147
  Still Life with Pewter and Brass Objects and small Elephant Oil/canvas (83x99cm 33x39in) Morris-Plains NJ 2001
- $750 - €769 - **£469** - FF5 048
  The Auburn Locks Oil/canvas (40x30cm 16x12in) Bolton MA 2000

EGGLESTON Edward S. XX **[2]**
- $4 200 - €4 898 - **£2 948** - FF32 131
  «Pennsylvania Railroad, Washington» Poster (63x101cm 24x39in) New-York 2000

EGGLESTON William 1939 **[60]**
- $3 982 - €4 410 - **£2 700** - FF28 927
  Ohne Titel Dye-transfer print (49.5x39.2cm 19x15in) Berlin 2000

EGGLI Jakob 1812-1880 **[2]**
- $2 135 - €2 293 - **£1 429** - FF15 039
  Volksfest bei Bülach Lithographie (39.2x45.8cm 15x18in) Zürich 2000

EGLAU Otto Wilhelm 1917-1988 **[140]**
- $112 - €128 - **£77** - FF838
  «Kyoto I» Farbradierung (49x64.5cm 19x25in) Berlin 2000

EGLEY William 1798-1870 **[24]**
- $1 320 - €1 449 - **£850** - FF9 505
  Frances Sarah Jenkinson, nearly full face in white dress Miniature (6x5cm 2x1in) London 2000

EGLEY William Maw 1826-1916 **[25]**
- $1 367 - €1 456 - **£900** - FF9 549
  The Fishergirl Watercolour/paper (24x15.5cm 9x6in) Billingshurst, West-Sussex 2000

EGMOND Jaap 1913 **[7]**
- $2 538 - €2 949 - **£1 784** - FF19 347
  «Gaufrier Grande» Mixed media (100x100cm 39x39in) Amsterdam 2001

EGMONT van Justus 1601-1674 **[13]**
- $15 862 - €15 988 - **£9 900** - FF104 874
  Bildnis einer jungen Dame als Diana Öl/Leinwand (135x91cm 53x35in) Wien 2000
- $30 770 - €25 916 - **£18 173** - FF170 000
  Portrait présumé de Hortense Mancini Huile/toile (116x92cm 45x36in) Paris 1998
- $18 000 - €19 749 - **£11 957** - FF129 542
  Archduke Loepold Wilhem of Austria (1614-1662), with White Lace Collar Oil/canvas (43x34cm 16x13in) New-York 2000

EGNER Marie 1850-1940 **[139]**
- $29 750 - €25 430 - **£17 850** - FF166 810
  Birken in einer Wiese, in sommerlicher Stimmung Öl/Leinwand (69x54cm 27x21in) Wien 1998
- $10 464 - €11 628 - **£7 008** - FF76 272
  Peuerbach zur Tagesneige Öl/Leinwand (24x30cm 9x11in) Wien 2000
- $2 105 - €2 398 - **£1 455** - FF15 731
  Kahn bei Fiume Aquarell/Papier (19.7x29.6cm 7x11in) Wien 2000

EGORNOV Alexandr Semenovich 1858-1902 **[6]**
- $7 729 - €7 299 - **£4 800** - FF47 877
  Spring Landscape Oil/canvas (51.5x82cm 20x32in) London 1999

EGORNOV Sergei Semenivich 1860-1920 **[3]**
- $11 658 - €10 820 - **£7 000** - FF70 974
  Reclining Nude on a draped Sofa Oil/canvas (125.5x182cm 49x71in) London 1999
- $15 421 - €14 820 - **£9 500** - FF97 216
  Young Woman at Rest Oil/canvas (69x88cm 27x34in) London 1999

EGOROV Andrei Afanas'evich 1878-1954 **[42]**
- $900 - €861 - **£548** - FF5 645
  Horse Drawn Sled in Winter Gouache/paper (23x34cm 9x13in) Cleveland OH 1999

EGRY Jozsef 1883-1951 **[10]**
- $5 180 - €5 442 - **£3 220** - FF35 700
  Ramasseurs de foin Huile/carton (38x52cm 14x20in) Budapest 2000
- $1 110 - €1 166 - **£690** - FF7 650
  Bûcherons au repos Craies/papier (34.5x45cm 13x17in) Budapest 2000

EGUSQUIZA Y BARRENA Rogelio 1845-1915 **[18]**
- $174 - €166 - **£110** - FF1 089
  Vegetables and a Jug Oil/canvas/board (63.5x53.5cm 25x21in) London 1999
- $5 021 - €5 574 - **£3 500** - FF36 561
  The Serenade Oil/canvas (37.5x24.5cm 14x9in) London 2001

EGVILLE d' James T. Herve c.1806-1880 **[15]**
- $742 - €673 - **£450** - FF4 416
  Mazorbo and Burano, Venice Watercolour (35x68cm 13x26in) Billingshurst, West-Sussex 1998

EHLINGER Maurice 1896-1981 **[201]**
- $410 - €381 - **£251** - FF2 500
  Vase de tulipes Huile/toile (73x60cm 28x23in) Paris 1999
- $595 - €564 - **£356** - FF3 600
  Suzy Huile/panneau (31x39cm 12x15in) Paris 1998

EHM Josef 1909-1989 **[16]**
- $635 - €613 - **£399** - FF4 024
  Prager Schaufenster Photograph (14x11cm 5x4in) München 1999

EHMCKE Fritz-Helmut 1878-1965 [1]
📁 **$1 193** - €1 007 - **£700** - FF6 603
«**Pianoforte Fabrik Thein**» Poster (83x109cm 32x42in) London 1998

EHMSEN Heinrich, Heinz 1886-1964 [109]
🖌 **$393** - €409 - **£248** - FF2 683
In der Bar Öl/Papier (20x14.4cm 7x5in) Berlin 2000
🖌 **$772** - €920 - **£550** - FF6 037
Auf der Mole von Cassis sur Mer Watercolour (39.2x49.2cm 15x19in) Berlin 2000
📁 **$219** - €245 - **£152** - FF1 609
«**Heiliger Reigen**» Linocut (28.5x23.2cm 11x9in) Berlin 2001

EHRENBERG Paul 1876-1949 [15]
🖌 **$1 507** - €1 406 - **£910** - FF9 223
Morgenspaziergang (Sommertag am Chiemsee), junger Bauer auf dem Weg Öl/Leinwand (119x90cm 46x35in) Lindau 1999

EHRENBERG Wilhelm Schubert 1630-1676 [5]
🖌 **$9 940** - €10 611 - **£6 650** - FF70 000
La Vierge à l'Enfant avec Saint Jean-Baptiste entourés d'anges Huile/panneau (65.5x143.5cm 25x56in) Paris 2000

EHRENBERGER Ludwig Lutz XIX-XX [7]
📁 **$997** - €1 160 - **£700** - FF7 609
«**Münchener Fashing**» Poster (122x86cm 48x33in) London 2001

EHRENSTRAHL von David Klöcker 1629-1698 [16]
🖌 **$23 400** - €22 276 - **£14 640** - FF146 120
Vanis labor Oil/canvas (131x111cm 51x43in) Stockholm 1999
🖌 **$4 026** - €4 745 - **£2 829** - FF31 123
Carl XI Oil/canvas (93x74cm 36x29in) Malmö 2000

EHRENSVÄRD Carl August 1745-1800 [17]
🖌 **$2 470** - €2 154 - **£1 494** - FF14 132
Mucius Scaevola Wash (22.5x18.9cm 8x7in) Stockholm 1998

EHRET Georg Dyonisius 1710-1770 [61]
🖌 **$6 829** - €7 935 - **£4 800** - FF52 052
Periwinkle, Vinca Major Watercolour (44.5x32cm 17x12in) London 2001

EHRHARDT Alfred 1901-1984 [47]
📷 **$714** - €767 - **£478** - FF5 030
Schlick Photograph (18.1x23.9cm 7x9in) München 2000

EHRHARDT Curt 1895-1972 [42]
🖌 **$5 466** - €5 113 - **£3 311** - FF33 539
Der Dampfer Öl/Karton (64x62cm 25x24in) Stuttgart 1999
🖌 **$2 791** - €3 170 - **£1 910** - FF20 794
Liegende mit Katze Öl/Karton (30x40.3cm 11x15in) Hamburg 2000
🖌 **$737** - €767 - **£465** - FF5 030
Der Selbstmord Charcoal (30.3x26.5cm 11x10in) Berlin 2000

EHRIG William 1892-1962 [5]
🖌 **$500** - €496 - **£311** - FF3 253
Waves crashing on the rocks Oil/canvas (71x96cm 28x38in) Cambridge MA 1999

EHRLICH Franz 1907-1983 [11]
📁 **$1 208** - €1 125 - **£743** - FF7 378
Einladung zum Bauhausfasching Print in colors (29.8x14.8cm 11x5in) München 1999

EHRLICH Georg 1897-1966 [110]
🖌 **$4 219** - €4 090 - **£2 612** - FF26 831
Stilleben mit Blumen, Schale und Vase Öl/Leinwand (51x41cm 20x16in) Graz 1999
🗿 **$756** - €654 - **£456** - FF4 287
Kinderbüste Bronze (H27.5cm H10in) Wien 1998
🖌 **$295** - €281 - **£180** - FF1 844
Study of Three Figures Ink (47x31.5cm 18x12in) London 1999
📁 **$143** - €123 - **£86** - FF804
Porträt der jungen Elisabeth Bergner Lithographie (50x24cm 19x9in) Berlin 1998

EIBISCH Eugeniusz 1896-1987 [41]
🖌 **$6 184** - €5 711 - **£3 852** - FF37 461
Path Oil/canvas (67x83cm 26x32in) Warszawa 1999
🖌 **$5 033** - €5 739 - **£3 476** - FF37 521
Femme tricotant Huile/toile (47x32cm 18x12in) Warszawa 2000

EIBNER Friedrich 1825-1877 [24]
🖌 **$27 450** - €28 121 - **£16 940** - FF184 464
Dom und Severikirche in Erfurt Öl/Leinwand (71x83cm 27x32in) Düsseldorf 2000
🖌 **$7 303** - €6 647 - **£4 563** - FF43 600
Straubing, Blick auf den Theresienplatz mit der Dreifaltigkeitssäule Öl/Papier (32.4x27.5cm 12x10in) München 1999
🖌 **$862** - €971 - **£597** - FF6 372
Florenz, Ponte San Trinità Aquarell/Papier (19x27cm 7x10in) Berlin 2000

EICHENBERG Fritz 1901-1990 [70]
📁 **$450** - €420 - **£278** - FF2 753
«**The Steps**» Woodcut (15x11cm 6x4in) Cleveland OH 1999

EICHHOLTZ Jacob 1776-1842 [10]
🖌 **$8 500** - €9 654 - **£5 964** - FF63 328
Portrait of Robert J.Arundel Oil/canvas (46x63.5cm 18x25in) Philadelphia PA 2001

EICHHORN Albert 1811-1851 [3]
🖌 **$9 282** - €9 353 - **£5 785** - FF61 351
Ansicht der Akropolis Öl/Leinwand (34.7x55.9cm 13x22in) Zürich 2000

EICHHORN Alfred 1909-1972 [172]
🖌 **$679** - €767 - **£478** - FF5 030
Ohne Titel Tempera (60x43cm 23x16in) Stuttgart 2001
🖌 **$391** - €460 - **£271** - FF3 018
Formenrhythmus Öl/Karton (20x32cm 7x12in) Stuttgart 2000
🖌 **$330** - €358 - **£226** - FF2 347
Ohne Titel Indian ink (48x68cm 18x26in) Stuttgart 2001

EICHHORN Peter 1877-1960 [24]
🖌 **$497** - €433 - **£300** - FF2 838
Harvest Time Oil/panel (14x18cm 5x7in) London 1998

EICHHORST Franz 1885-1948 [8]
🖌 **$2 683** - €2 812 - **£1 699** - FF18 446
Erntezeit, Bäuerinnen auf einem Garbenfeld Öl/Leinwand (52x65cm 20x25in) Köln 2000

EICHINGER Erwin 1892-1950 [55]
🖌 **$1 592** - €1 542 - **£1 000** - FF10 112
Cardinal holding his Glasses Oil/board (26x20cm 10x7in) London 1999

EICHINGER Otto 1922 [48]
🖌 **$7 193** - €7 130 - **£4 500** - FF46 773
Card Players Wearing Traditional Costume from the Sarntal, South-Tyrol Oil/canvas (60x78.5cm 23x30in) London 1999

E

$2 749 - €2 514 - £1 679 - FF16 494
Rabbi Oil/board (26x19cm 10x7in) New-York 1998

EICHLER Johann Conrad 1688-1748 [5]
$46 740 - €43 603 - £28 200 - FF286 020
Stilleben von Pfirsichen, Weintrauben, Granatäpfeln Öl/Leinwand (67.5x80cm 26x31in) Wien 1999

EICHLER Joseph 1724-c.1783 [3]
$8 052 - €9 452 - £5 682 - FF62 000
Landskap med tupp, höns och marsvin Oil/canvas (72.5x89cm 28x35in) Stockholm 2000

EICHLER Matthias Gottfried 1748-1818 [7]
$254 - €295 - £175 - FF1 938
Regensberg im Canton Zürich Radierung (11.8x18cm 4x7in) Zürich 2000

EICHLER Reinhold Max 1872-1947 [20]
$1 433 - €1 431 - £896 - FF9 390
Ein Mäusespäher Indian ink (52.8x44.8cm 20x17in) München 1999

EICHLER Theodor 1868-? [16]
$2 209 - €2 045 - £1 352 - FF13 415
Schleiertänzerin Ceramic (H26.5cm H10in) Heilbronn 1999

EICKELBERG Willem Hendrik 1845-1920 [46]
$2 626 - €2 496 - £1 598 - FF16 371
Winters boerendorp Oil/canvas (44x64cm 17x25in) Den Haag 1999
$696 - €792 - £483 - FF5 191
Holländische Kanallandschaft Oil/panel (10.5x12.5cm 4x4in) Zofingen 2000

EICKEMEYER Rudolf, Jr. 1862-1932 [24]
$1 400 - €1 468 - £877 - FF9 628
November on the dunes Silver print (24x17cm 9x7in) New-York 2000

EICKEN von Elisabeth 1862-1940 [25]
$845 - €986 - £593 - FF6 467
Moorlandschaft mit Birken Öl/Leinwand (68x100cm 26x39in) Luzern 2000
$2 566 - €2 505 - £1 625 - FF16 434
Junge Birken am Bodden Öl/Leinwand (38.5x29cm 15x11in) Bremen 1999
$1 753 - €1 994 - £1 216 - FF13 080
Norddeutsche Bauernkate Aquarell, Gouache/Papier (30x40cm 11x15in) Rudolstadt-Thüringen 2000

EICKHOFF Gottfred 1902-1982 [19]
$1 569 - €1 742 - £1 092 - FF11 430
Kvindefigur Stone (H60cm H23in) Köbenhavn 2001

EIDENBERGER Josef 1899-1991 [22]
$104 - €116 - £70 - FF762
Linz-Landhaus Farbradierung (29x22cm 11x8in) Linz 2000

EIDRIGEVICIUS Stasys 1949 [29]
$1 099 - €1 194 - £781 - FF8 597
Miroir Pastel/papier (42.5x29.5cm 16x11in) Warszawa 2000

EIDSON XX [1]
$1 500 - €1 748 - £1 038 - FF11 469
R-100 Dirigible Arriving in Canada, Attached to mooring Post Gouache/paper (30x51cm 12x20in) New-York 2000

EIGENBERGER Gary 1960 [9]
$2 853 - €3 326 - £2 000 - FF21 820
Long Billed Curlew Sculpture, wood (H51cm H20in) London 2000

EIJSEN van B. (Barend ?) XVII [1]
$112 490 - €111 578 - £70 000 - FF731 906
Still Life of Books and Scrolls, an Etching depicting King Charles II Oil/canvas (97x117.5cm 38x46in) London 1999

EIKAAS Ludvig 1920 [45]
$912 - €1 064 - £635 - FF6 977
Komposisjon Oil/canvas (83x45cm 32x17in) Oslo 2000
$361 - €390 - £249 - FF2 561
Komposisjon Color lithograph (61x50cm 24x19in) Oslo 2001

EILERS Conrad 1845-1914 [15]
$1 238 - €1 380 - £860 - FF9 055
Kloster Seeon Öl/Karton (22x42cm 8x16in) München 2001

EILSHEMIUS Louis Michel 1864-1941 [107]
$1 000 - €1 073 - £669 - FF7 041
Outside the Walls of Biskra Oil/canvas (35x50cm 14x20in) Bolton MA 2000
$400 - €446 - £269 - FF2 924
Diana at the Pool Oil/board (19x14cm 7x5in) East-Moriches NY 2000
$850 - €733 - £505 - FF4 807
Bathers at the Sea Watercolour (35x51cm 13x20in) New-York 1998

EINBECK Georges 1871-1951 [30]
$1 330 - €1 249 - £824 - FF8 194
Das Paar Tempera/Karton (65x50cm 25x19in) Luzern 1999
$1 014 - €1 179 - £713 - FF7 731
Nue Tempera/paper (64.5x49.5cm 25x19in) Luzern 2001

EINBERGER Andreas 1878-1953 [6]
$3 281 - €2 812 - £1 972 - FF18 443
Häuser im Schnee Öl/Leinwand (60x100cm 23x39in) Hamburg 1998

EINHART Karl 1884-1967 [30]
$957 - €1 022 - £636 - FF6 707
Hochsommerliche Seelandschaft Öl/Leinwand (45x60cm 17x23in) Konstanz 2000

EINSLE Anton 1801-1871 [19]
$3 694 - €3 270 - £2 259 - FF21 451
Madonna mit Kind Öl/Leinwand (70x56cm 27x22in) Wien 1999

EISEL Fritz, Prof. 1929 [21]
$2 872 - €3 068 - £1 957 - FF20 123
Waldrand am See Öl/Leinwand (48x59cm 18x23in) Satow 2001

EISEN Charles Dom. Joseph 1720-1778 [42]
$43 310 - €46 497 - £28 975 - FF305 000
Allégorie des quatre saisons Huile/toile (65x82cm 25x32in) Neuilly-sur-Seine 2000
$1 194 - €1 361 - £825 - FF8 829
Amusing Children Oil/paper/canvas (38.5x26.5cm 15x10in) Amsterdam 2000
$336 - €383 - £234 - FF2 515
Frankreich in Gestalt der Athena beschützt den Orienthandel Ink (7.5x11cm 2x4in) Berlin 2001

EISEN François c.1695-c.1780 [11]
$3 152 - €3 811 - £2 202 - FF25 000
Allégorie de l'hiver Huile/toile (38.5x26.5cm 15x10in) Paris 2000

EISEN Ikeda, Keisai 1790-1848 **[97]**
▥ **$1 100** - €951 - **£652** - FF6 235
   An Unsigned Frontispiece for a Shunga Album
   Woodcut (26x38cm 10x14in) New-York 1998

EISENBERGER L. XIX-XX **[7]**
◈ **$964** - €1 101 - **£680** - FF7 223
   Figure (cast from a model) Bronze (H28cm H11in)
   London 2001

EISENDIECK Suzanne 1908-1998 **[162]**
◉ **$2 559** - €2 557 - **£1 600** - FF16 771
   Le Cancan Oil/canvas (68.5x45.5cm 26x17in) London
   1999
◉ **$1 331** - €1 278 - **£820** - FF8 384
   Ballettmädchen Öl/Leinwand (27x16cm 10x6in)
   München 1999

EISENHUT Ferencz, Franz 1857-1903 **[25]**
◉ **$2 100** - €1 780 - **£1 255** - FF11 673
   **Portrait of black man with white turban and
   shirt** Oil/canvas (46x39cm 18x15in) Asheville NC 1998
◉ **$13 629** - €15 339 - **£9 390** - FF100 617
   Haremsszene Oil/panel (21.5x27cm 8x10in) Stuttgart
   2000

EISENLOHR Friedrich 1805-1854 **[19]**
✐ **$757** - €869 - **£518** - FF5 701
   Orvieto Pencil/paper (24.8x37.6cm 9x14in) Heidelberg
   2000

EISENMAN Nicole 1963 **[10]**
✐ **$1 800** - €2 007 - **£1 210** - FF13 165
   Untitled Watercolour (70.5x61cm 27x24in) New-York
   2000

EISENSCHITZ Willy 1889-1974 **[205]**
◉ **$23 824** - €24 392 - **£14 960** - FF160 000
   Le pègue Huile/toile (100x180cm 39x70in) Versailles
   2000
◉ **$9 058** - €7 927 - **£5 486** - FF52 000
   Intérieur Huile/toile (68x78cm 26x30in) Paris 1998
◉ **$1 325** - €1 524 - **£913** - FF10 000
   Paysage de Provence Huile/toile (33x41cm
   12x16in) Toulon 2000
✐ **$1 126** - €1 296 - **£776** - FF8 500
   Paysage de Provence Aquarelle/papier (37x51cm
   14x20in) Toulon 2000

EISENSHER Yaacov 1896-1980 **[98]**
◉ **$3 600** - €3 558 - **£2 203** - FF23 339
   Figures in a City Square Oil/canvas (61x46cm
   24x18in) Tel Aviv 2000
✐ **$350** - €372 - **£237** - FF2 440
   The violin Maker Watercolour/paper (15x22cm 5x8in)
   Tel Aviv 2000

EISENSTAEDT Alfred 1898-1995 **[100]**
◉ **$2 400** - €2 604 - **£1 673** - FF17 475
   Prostitute on the rue St.Denis, Paris Gelatin silver
   print (34x26.5cm 13x10in) New-York 2001

EISERMANN Richard 1853-1927 **[5]**
◉ **$6 110** - €7 267 - **£4 360** - FF47 670
   Beim Pfandleiher Öl/Leinwand (75x78cm 29x30in)
   Wien 2000

EISHI Hosoda Jibukyo Toki. 1756-1829 **[47]**
▥ **$3 200** - €3 753 - **£2 283** - FF24 615
   Itsutomi, from the Series Seiro geisha erami
   Print in colors (36.5x25cm 14x9in) New-York 2000

EISHO Chokosai XVIII-XIX **[13]**
▥ **$5 500** - €5 542 - **£3 428** - FF36 355
   **Full-length Portrait of the Courtesan Hanaogi of
   the Ogiva as Fugen** Print (38x24.5cm 14x9in) New-
   York 2000

EISLER Georg 1928-1998 **[84]**
◉ **$1 645** - €1 789 - **£1 084** - FF11 738
   Liegender Frauenakt Öl/Leinwand (81x49cm
   31x47in) Hamburg 2000
◉ **$1 114** - €1 308 - **£790** - FF8 580
   Aktsaal Oil/panel (23.5x32cm 9x12in) Wien 2000
✐ **$463** - €399 - **£275** - FF2 618
   Liegender weiblicher Akt Chalks/paper (28x39.5cm
   11x15in) Wien 1998
▥ **$133** - €153 - **£91** - FF1 006
   **Sitzender weiblicher Akt, sich den Pullover aus-
   ziehend** Drypoint (38x29cm 14x11in) Heidelberg 2000

EISMAN-SEMENOWSKY Emile ?-1911 **[107]**
◉ **$50 000** - €49 514 - **£31 130** - FF320 790
   A Harvest Festival Oil/canvas (85x194.5cm 33x76in)
   New-York 1999
◉ **$11 145** - €10 791 - **£7 000** - FF70 787
   An Oriental Flower Girl Oil/canvas (72x40cm
   28x15in) London 1999
◉ **$3 153** - €2 782 - **£1 900** - FF18 251
   Dark haired Beauty in Gypsy Dress Oil/panel
   (31x23.5cm 12x9in) London 1998

EISMANN Johann Anton 1604-1698 **[12]**
◉ **$52 195** - €48 818 - **£32 000** - FF320 224
   **An Extensive Harbour Scene with English Men
   O'War Anchored Off Shore** Oil/canvas
   (148x212.5cm 58x83in) London 1998
◉ **$16 000** - €20 733 - **£12 000** - FF136 000
   **Paesaggio fluviale con viandanti/Paesaggio flu-
   viale con un gentiluomo** Olio/tela (31.5x44.5cm
   12x17in) Milano 2001

EISMOND Jozef XIX **[1]**
◉ **$3 729** - €3 835 - **£2 364** - FF25 154
   Ernteeinfuhr in Polen Oil/canvas/panel (53x100cm
   20x39in) Stuttgart 2000

EITEL Jacques 1926 **[20]**
◉ **$600** - €644 - **£401** - FF4 224
   Le château d'eau, Normandie Oil/canvas
   (81x100cm 32x39in) New-York 2000

EITNER Ernst Wilhelm H. 1867-1955 **[52]**
◉ **$4 782** - €5 624 - **£3 428** - FF36 892
   **Strandallee mit trocknenden Netzen, vielen
   Personen** Mixed media (41x53cm 16x20in) Hamburg
   2001
◉ **$2 762** - €2 965 - **£1 882** - FF19 452
   Landarbeiter im Felde Öl/Leinwand (41x28cm
   16x11in) Rudolstadt-Thüringen 2001
✐ **$556** - €613 - **£371** - FF4 024
   Landschaft mit Mühle bei Finkenwerder Coloured
   pencils/paper (26x41cm 10x16in) Satow 2000

EIZAN Kikugawa Toshinobu 1787-1867 **[102]**
▥ **$382** - €419 - **£253** - FF2 750
   Dame mit Lampion Print (71.5x23cm 28x9in)
   Stuttgart 2000

EJSMOND Franciszek, Franz 1859-1931 **[13]**
◉ **$22 518** - €19 427 - **£13 585** - FF127 433
   «Babunia» Oil/canvas (106x87cm 41x34in) München
   1998
◉ **$11 886** - €13 791 - **£8 206** - FF90 463
   Nach dem Hagelschlag Oil/panel (32x42cm
   12x16in) Luzern 2000

EJSMOND Stanislaw 1894-1939 **[7]**
✐ **$3 117** - €3 639 - **£2 200** - FF23 871
   Roses blanches Tempera/papier (35.5x25.5cm
   13x10in) Warszawa 2000

EKEDAHL Ivan 1908-1998 **[2]**
∞ **$4 903** - €4 611 - **£3 038** - FF30 245
   Stadsbild vid Johannes Kyrka Oil/panel (50x46cm 19x18in) Stockholm 1999

EKELAND Arne 1908-1994 **[38]**
∞ **$13 080** - €15 202 - **£9 192** - FF99 720
   Fabrikken Oil/paper (165x207cm 64x81in) Oslo 2001
∞ **$6 758** - €7 854 - **£4 749** - FF51 522
   Flyktninger Oil/panel (50x60cm 19x23in) Oslo 2001

EKELS Jan Ekels I 1724-1781 **[11]**
∞ **$12 616** - €10 886 - **£7 612** - FF71 407
   Beverwijk, View from the Peperstraat on the Koningsstraat Oil/panel (42x37cm 16x14in) Amsterdam 1998

EKELS Jan Ekels II 1759-1793 **[4]**
∞ **$44 178** - €49 534 - **£30 000** - FF324 921
   Amsterdam, a View of the Munt Tower and the Doelenshuis on the Singel Oil/panel (40x51.5cm 15x20in) London 2000

EKELUND Poul 1920-1976 **[199]**
∞ **$805** - €781 - **£506** - FF5 122
   Kvinde set bagfra Oil/canvas (66x56cm 25x22in) København 1999
∞ **$261** - €282 - **£180** - FF1 847
   Landskab Oil/board (22x27cm 8x10in) København 2001

EKELUND Ragnar 1892-1960 **[61]**
∞ **$2 147** - €2 102 - **£1 321** - FF13 790
   Tallinnasta Oil/canvas (66x55cm 25x21in) Helsinki 1999
✎ **$249** - €269 - **£172** - FF1 765
   Hus Charcoal/paper (25x31cm 9x12in) Helsinki 2001

EKENAES Jahn 1847-1920 **[28]**
∞ **$2 580** - €2 692 - **£1 628** - FF17 657
   På utflukt Oil/canvas (35x53cm 13x20in) Oslo 2000
∞ **$4 026** - €3 429 - **£2 405** - FF22 490
   To gutter Oil/canvas (41x27cm 16x10in) Oslo 1998

EKIERT Jean 1907-1993 **[36]**
∞ **$241** - €274 - **£170** - FF1 800
   Composition multicolore Huile/carton (16x22cm 6x8in) Paris 2001

EKLUND Claes 1944 **[22]**
✎ **$805** - €940 - **£552** - FF6 168
   Utan titel Tempera/paper (103x67cm 40x26in) Stockholm 2000

EKMAN DE GEER-BERGENSTRÅHLE Marie-Louise 1944 **[90]**
∞ **$2 570** - €2 173 - **£1 536** - FF14 256
   «Good, Bra, Bien» Oil/canvas (50x59cm 19x23in) Stockholm 1998
∞ **$1 790** - €1 965 - **£1 153** - FF12 889
   Homa at an Ape I Collage/canvas (28.5x23cm 11x9in) Stockholm 2000
 $704 - €823 - **£483** - FF5 397
   Utan titel Object (6x10.5x3.5cm 2x4x1in) Stockholm 2000
✎ **$1 670** - €1 413 - **£998** - FF9 266
   «En dam som speglar sig» Collage (15x14.5cm 5x5in) Stockholm 1998
📺 **$428** - €396 - **£263** - FF2 595
   Skulptur mot Baertling Serigraph in colors Stockholm 1999

EKMAN Emil 1880-1951 **[85]**
∞ **$666** - €725 - **£436** - FF4 757
   Marint motiv med fiskebåtar i månljus Oil/canvas (80x131cm 31x51in) Uppsala 2000

EKMAN Robert Wilhelm 1808-1873 **[28]**
∞ **$15 522** - €15 106 - **£9 555** - FF99 086
   Utvandrarna Oil/canvas (74x92cm 29x36in) Stockholm 1999
∞ **$3 060** - €3 027 - **£1 908** - FF19 857
   Flicka i skogen Oil/canvas (41x33cm 16x12in) Helsinki 1999
✎ **$1 314** - €1 430 - **£866** - FF9 377
   Det blåsiga Medelhavet Pastel/paper (32x46cm 12x18in) Helsinki 2000

EKSTAM Alfred 1878-1935 **[4]**
∞ **$4 059** - €3 951 - **£2 499** - FF25 914
   Motiv från Tobyn Oil/panel (33x44cm 12x17in)
✎ **$1 281** - €1 507 - **£928** - FF9 884
   Motiv från Manskog Pastel/paper (45x60cm 17x23in) Stockholm 2001

EKSTRÖM Per 1844-1935 **[441]**
∞ **$9 552** - €9 296 - **£5 880** - FF60 976
   Solglitter i vatten Oil/canvas (99x150cm 38x59in)
∞ **$4 523** - €5 145 - **£3 159** - FF33 752
   Vattendränkt landskap i soldis Oil/canvas (61x46cm 24x18in) Stockholm 2000
∞ **$2 455** - €2 882 - **£1 732** - FF18 902
   Vy över Segerstad Oil/panel (36x44cm 14x17in) Stockholm 2000

EKWALL Emma 1838-1925 **[41]**
∞ **$5 353** - €4 568 - **£3 199** - FF29 966
   En saga Oil/canvas (50x65cm 19x25in) Stockholm 1998
∞ **$1 170** - €1 114 - **£732** - FF7 306
   Stilleben med rosa rosor Oil/canvas/panel (31x23cm 12x9in) Stockholm 1999
∞ **$1 475** - €1 714 - **£1 036** - FF11 240
   Barnporträtt Akvarell/papper (20x15.5cm 7x6in) Stockholm 2001

EKWALL Knut 1843-1912 **[43]**
∞ **$2 415** - €2 575 - **£1 637** - FF16 893
   Vinterlandskap med vanderska Oil/canvas (95x134cm 37x52in) Stockholm 2001
∞ **$2 760** - €2 976 - **£1 852** - FF19 522
   Skidåkare i vintersol Oil/panel (57x82cm 22x32in) Stockholm 2000

EL BAILARIN Antonio XX **[48]**
✎ **$204** - €240 - **£144** - FF1 576
   Figura fantástica Acuarela/papel (33x23cm 12x9in) Madrid 2000

EL GLAOUI Hassan 1924 **[20]**
∞ **$1 334** - €1 220 - **£816** - FF8 000
   La fantasia Huile/isorel (75x107cm 29x42in) Paris 1999
∞ **$5 216** - €6 098 - **£3 724** - FF40 000
   Cavaliers marocains Aquarelle, gouache/papier (50x65cm 19x25in) Paris 2001

ELAM L. Vasser XX **[1]**
📺 **$750** - €813 - **£500** - FF5 334
   «Centenary Pageant» Poster (104x68cm 41x27in) New-York 2000

ELAND Leonardus Jos., Leo 1884-1952 **[129]**
∞ **$805** - €908 - **£555** - FF5 953
   A Floating Market, Indonesia Oil/canvas (61x81cm 24x31in) Amsterdam 2000

ELANDER Kristina A. 1952 **[19]**
✎ **$222** - €258 - **£153** - FF1 692
   Flicka med blomma Indian ink (18x11cm 7x4in) Stockholm 2000

ELBO José 1804-1846 **[2]**
- $44 350 - €37 253 - **£26 000** - FF244 361
  Caballeros/Caballero in the Field Oil/canvas (66x86cm 25x33in) London 1998

ELDERSHAW John Roy 1892-1973 **[35]**
- $337 - €391 - **£236** - FF2 567
  Bush Pub Watercolour/paper (37x51cm 14x20in) Sydney 2000

ELDH Carl 1873-1955 **[87]**
- $1 432 - €1 394 - **£882** - FF9 146
  Le printemps Metal (H13.5cm H5in) Stockholm 1999

ELDRED Lemuel D. 1848-1921 **[44]**
- $4 300 - €4 912 - **£3 027** - FF32 220
  Untitled Oil/canvas (50x76cm 20x30in) Cambridge MA 2001
- $1 200 - €1 154 - **£740** - FF7 569
  Sailboats, Venice Oil/board (31x23.5cm 12x9in) Boston MA 1999
- $750 - €704 - **£464** - FF4 618
  Old Whaler at a Pier Etching (34x56cm 13x22in) Portsmouth NH 1999

ELESZKIEWICZ Stanislas 1900-1963 **[49]**
- $4 313 - €5 031 - **£3 026** - FF33 000
  Rue de village Huile/panneau (65x80cm 25x31in) Paris 2001
- $577 - €495 - **£347** - FF3 247
  Zlozenie do grobu Oil/panel (19.2x24.5cm 7x9in) Warszawa 1998

ELFFERS Dick 1910-1991 **[31]**
- $1 611 - €1 815 - **£1 110** - FF11 906
  Surrealistic Landscape With Houses Gouache (51x73cm 20x28in) Amsterdam 2000
- $134 - €136 - **£83** - FF893
  «Holland Festival» Poster (116x83.5cm 45x32in) Haarlem 2000

ELGOOD George Samuel 1851-1943 **[91]**
- $1 151 - €1 201 - **£725** - FF7 878
  Parkland with Duck in the Foreground Watercolour/paper (23x34cm 9x13in) Little-Lane, Ilkley 2000

ELGORT Arthur 1946 **[3]**
- $2 028 - €1 763 - **£1 222** - FF11 564
  Esmé for Vogue Gelatin silver print (49.8x40cm 19x15in) Berlin 1998

ELIAERTS Jan Frans 1761-1848 **[10]**
- $14 000 - €15 631 - **£9 357** - FF102 530
  Floral Still Life Oil/canvas (75.5x63cm 29x24in) New-York 2000

ELIAS (Etienne Michiels) 1936 **[70]**
- $2 017 - €1 859 - **£1 215** - FF12 195
  Achter een gordijntje Huile/toile (120x100cm 47x39in) Antwerpen 1999
- $1 048 - €908 - **£636** - FF5 953
  Muzikant Oil/canvas (60x60cm 23x23in) Amsterdam 1999

ELIAS Bohumil 1937 **[5]**
- $3 200 - €3 054 - **£1 999** - FF20 036
  Untitled Sculpture, glass (H19.5cm H7in) New-York 1999

ELIAS Nicolaes Pickenoy c.1590-1653/56 **[10]**
- $89 658 - €96 240 - **£60 000** - FF631 296
  Portrait of Pieter van Son, Three-Quarter-length in a Black Doublet Oil/panel (105.5x78.5cm 41x30in) London 2000

ELIASBERG Paul 1907-1984 **[136]**
- $476 - €511 - **£318** - FF3 353
  St.Germain l'Auxerrois Watercolour (47.8x37.7cm 18x14in) Köln 2000
- $95 - €112 - **£69** - FF737
  Hafen (Hamburg) Etching (27.3x40.7cm 10x16in) Hamburg 2001

ELIE Madame XIX **[1]**
- $7 568 - €8 007 - **£4 800** - FF52 520
  Fruit in a Bowl, upon a Stone Ledge/Fruit in a Wicker Basket Watercolour/paper (39x48.5cm 15x19in) London 2000

ELIM Franck XX **[35]**
- $1 349 - €1 448 - **£902** - FF9 500
  Élégante sur cheval Huile/toile (50x60cm 19x23in) Cannes 2000
- $956 - €1 067 - **£646** - FF7 000
  Minoutcher, né en 1948 par Nuageux et Mouchtalette Huile/panneau (26.5x35cm 10x13in) Deauville 2000

ELIOTT Harry 1882-1959 **[185]**
- $2 010 - €2 287 - **£1 395** - FF15 000
  Dîner de chasse Gouache/papier (35x52cm 13x20in) Paris 2000
- $200 - €221 - **£132** - FF1 450
  Le retour de chasse Pochoir (57x24cm 22x9in) Paris 2000

ELK van Gerard 1941 **[20]**
- $8 874 - €8 168 - **£5 326** - FF53 578
  Der Abschied Gouache (82x102cm 32x40in) Amsterdam 1999
- $390 - €454 - **£274** - FF2 976
  The Tree Pets Silkscreen in colors (49x31cm 19x12in) Amsterdam 2001
- $2 958 - €2 723 - **£1 775** - FF17 859
  The Co-founder of the Word O.K Photograph in colors (48x39.5cm 18x15in) Amsterdam 1999

ELLE Edouard 1859-1911 **[19]**
- $327 - €372 - **£228** - FF2 439
  Ostende Aquarelle/papier (30x39cm 11x15in) Maisieres-Mons 2001

ELLE Ferdinand Helle c.1580-c.1640 **[2]**
- $5 460 - €6 403 - **£3 927** - FF42 000
  Portrait présumé de Madame de Sévigné Huile/toile (74x56cm 29x22in) Paris 2001

ELLE Louis, Ferdinand I 1612-1689 **[6]**
- $36 142 - €42 088 - **£25 000** - FF276 082
  Philippe D'Orléans, duc de Chartres (1674-1723), Seated Three-Quarter Oil/canvas (131x98.5cm 51x38in) London 2000
- $15 130 - €16 245 - **£9 430** - FF100 000
  Portrait présumé du chevalier d'Harcourt Huile/toile (118x88.5cm 46x34in) Paris 2000

ELLE Louis, Ferdinand II 1648-1717 **[3]**
- $16 766 - €14 168 - **£10 000** - FF92 937
  Portrait of a Young Girl, Wearing a Lace-Trimmed Dress, holding a Fan Oil/canvas (48.5x37.5cm 19x14in) London 1998

ELLENRIEDER Maria 1791-1863 **[36]**
- $4 494 - €4 090 - **£2 808** - FF26 831
  Die Heilige Rosa von Lima (1586-1617) Oil/panel (50x38.5cm 19x15in) München 1999
- $228 - €256 - **£158** - FF1 676
  Die krönung Marias Pencil/paper (24x17.8cm 9x7in) Berlin 2001

◫◫◫ **$102** - €107 - **£64** - FF704
Die Auferstehung Christi Radierung (19.5x13cm
7x5in) Heidelberg 2000

ELLERBY Thomas XIX **[1]**
🖼 **$10 138** - €11 764 - **£7 000** - FF77 168
**Joseph Gee of Cottingham Hall, in County of
York/Elizabeth Jane Gee** Oil/canvas (127x102cm
50x40in) London 2000

ELLIGER Ottomar I le Vieux 1633-1679 **[13]**
🖼 **$31 012** - €34 033 - **£19 965** - FF223 245
**Swag of Grapes, Prunes, Peaches,
Pomegranates with Butterflies** Oil/panel
(61x44.5cm 24x17in) Amsterdam 2000

ELLIGER Ottomar II le Jeune 1666-1735 **[25]**
🖼 **$11 166** - €9 655 - **£6 638** - FF63 335
**Kaiser Augustus vor dem Totenbett der
Kleopatra** Öl/Leinwand (67.5x55cm 26x21in) Zürich
1998

ELLINGER David Y. 1940 **[69]**
🖼 **$2 100** - €1 939 - **£1 291** - FF12 717
Spring Planting Time Oil/canvas (35x50cm 14x20in)
Hatfield PA 1999
🖼 **$950** - €907 - **£593** - FF5 948
**Potted Tulips and Bird on Heart decorated
Planter** Oil/panel (35x36cm 14x14in) Hatfield PA 1999
✏ **$900** - €979 - **£618** - FF6 425
Theorem of a Basket of Fruit and Bird
Watercolour/paper (14x18cm 5x7in) Downington PA
2001

ELLIOT Ric 1933-1995 **[55]**
🖼 **$1 030** - €999 - **£638** - FF6 552
The Corner Terrace Oil/board (40x55cm 15x21in)
Sydney 1999
🖼 **$447** - €505 - **£314** - FF3 310
Street Scene Oil/board (35.5x38cm 13x14in)
Malvern, Victoria 2001

ELLIOT Thomas XVIII-XIX **[5]**
🖼 **$16 024** - €15 235 - **£10 000** - FF99 934
Men-o'-War in Portsmouth Harbour Oil/canvas
(61x91.5cm 24x36in) London 1999

ELLIOTT Frederick James 1864-1949 **[74]**
✏ **$426** - €412 - **£264** - FF2 703
Through the Heads Watercolour/paper (29x49cm
11x19in) Sydney 1999

ELLIS Arthur 1856-1918 **[13]**
🖼 **$2 525** - €3 003 - **£1 800** - FF19 701
Binny a Yorkshire Terrier Oil/canvas (33x30.5cm
12x12in) London 2000

ELLIS C. Wynn XIX-XX **[9]**
✏ **$571** - €539 - **£360** - FF3 535
The Whip Watercolour/paper (51x45.5cm 20x17in)
Godalming, Surrey 1999

ELLIS Clifford 1907-1985 **[4]**
◫◫◫ **$191** - €199 - **£120** - FF1 305
Composition in grey, Black and Pale Green
Lithograph (37x56cm 14x22in) London 2000

ELLIS Clifford & Rosemary 1907/10-1985/? **[4]**
◫◫◫ **$883** - €969 - **£600** - FF6 356
«**Third Test Match The Oval**» Poster (26x32cm
10x12in) London 2000

ELLIS Edwin John 1841-1895 **[78]**
🖼 **$870** - €960 - **£589** - FF6 296
Mussel gatherers Oil/canvas (44x80cm 17x31in)
Stockholm 2000

🖼 **$662** - €711 - **£450** - FF4 664
«**Fisher Folk off Flamborough Head**» Oil/panel
(10.5x19cm 4x7in) London 2001

ELLIS Fremont F. 1897-1985 **[43]**
🖼 **$17 000** - €19 050 - **£11 849** - FF124 963
Autumn Landscape Oil/canvas (76x61cm 29x24in)
Beverly-Hills CA 2001
🖼 **$4 000** - €4 542 - **£2 779** - FF29 792
San Juan, New Mexico Oil/canvas (20x25cm
8x10in) Dallas TX 2001
✏ **$4 750** - €4 241 - **£2 908** - FF27 816
Atmospheric Landscape Gouache/board (25x33cm
10x13in) Altadena CA 1999

ELLIS Gordon 1921-1979 **[14]**
🖼 **$2 253** - €2 647 - **£1 600** - FF17 361
Off the Needles Oil/board (39x58cm 15x22in)
Burton-on-Trent, Staffs 2000

ELLIS Joseph F. 1783-1848 **[9]**
🖼 **$8 965** - €9 624 - **£6 000** - FF63 129
Amsterdam, Holland Oil/canvas (71x91.5cm
27x36in) London 2000
✏ **$1 807** - €1 803 - **£1 100** - FF11 827
**British Man O'war and other Shipping in a fresh
Breeze** Watercolour (49x61.5cm 19x24in) London
2000

ELLIS Paul H. 1882-1908 **[37]**
🖼 **$865** - €984 - **£600** - FF6 454
The Keepers Cottage, Springfield Oil/canvas
(55x45cm 22x18in) Birmingham 2000
✏ **$656** - €601 - **£400** - FF3 942
The Tower of the Princesses Alhambra Granada
Watercolour/paper (38x31cm 14x12in) Leamington-Spa,
Warwickshire 1999

ELLIS Robert 1930 **[10]**
✏ **$665** - €742 - **£449** - FF4 865
Mt. Eden Watercolour (25x57cm 9x22in) Auckland
2000

ELLIS Tristram James 1844-1922 **[110]**
✏ **$1 128** - €1 052 - **£700** - FF6 902
Cintra, Portugal Watercolour/paper (37.5x27cm
14x10in) London 1999

ELLIS William 1794-1872 **[5]**
📷 **$4 651** - €3 980 - **£2 800** - FF26 110
**Princess Ralefoka/Princess Rabodo, later
Queen Rasoherina** Albumen print (22x17cm 9x7in)
London 1998

ELLMINGER Ignaz 1843-1894 **[39]**
🖼 **$4 669** - €3 999 - **£2 733** - FF26 229
Rast an der Quelle Öl/Leinwand (53x67cm 20x26in)
Wien 1998

ELLSWORTH James Sanford 1802-1874 **[8]**
🖼 **$10 000** - €10 884 - **£6 873** - FF71 393
Girl in Blue Miniature (6x8cm 2x3in) Bolton MA
2001
🖼 **$3 500** - €3 757 - **£2 342** - FF24 643
**Tryphena Pomeroy (1792-1880)/Brother Justrus
Pomeroy (1820-1860)** Watercolour/paper (6x6cm
2x2in) Bolton MA 2000

ELMER Stephen c.1714-1796 **[37]**
🖼 **$8 652** - €9 561 - **£6 000** - FF62 718
Still Life of Fish with a Rod and Basket Oil/can-
vas (109.5x136cm 43x53in) London 2001
🖼 **$5 768** - €6 374 - **£4 000** - FF41 812
Covey of Partridges Oil/canvas (69x89.5cm
27x35in) London 2001

ELMES Willard Frederic XX **[23]**
🏺 **$650** - €589 - **£398** - FF3 864
　　«One Iron in The Fire» Poster (110x91cm 43x36in)
　　New-York 1998

ELMORE Alfred W. 1815-1881 **[35]**
🖎 **$4 074** - €4 045 - **£2 545** - FF26 532
　　Colombus at Porto Santo Oil/canvas (44.5x59.5cm
　　17x23in) Toronto 1999
🖎 **$1 846** - €1 729 - **£1 110** - FF11 344
　　Sittande kvinna Oil/panel (38x26cm 14x10in)
　　Stockholm 1999
✐ **$520** - €613 - **£365** - FF4 023
　　Kvinnor med barn i landskap Akvarell/papper
　　(37x29cm 14x11in) Malmö 2000

ELMORE Richard 1852-1885 **[16]**
🖎 **$821** - €750 - **£500** - FF4 021
　　London from Sydenham Hill Oil/panel
　　(15.5x22.5cm 6x8in) London 1998

ELNATAN Moshe 1904-1969 **[2]**
🖎 **$4 000** - €4 516 - **£2 786** - FF29 620
　　The Way to Jerusalem Oil/canvas (73x90cm
　　28x35in) Tel Aviv 2001

ELOUT Franchoys 1597-1661 **[4]**
🖎 **$64 452** - €63 296 - **£40 000** - FF415 196
　　Box of Draughts, a Clay Brazier of Burning
　　Coals, an Earthenware Jug Oil/canvas (63x80cm
　　24x31in) London 1999

ELOY Mario 1900-1951 **[5]**
✐ **$4 400** - €4 985 - **£3 000** - FF32 700
　　Cabeça de menina Crayon/papier (27x20cm 10x7in)
　　Lisboa 2000

ELRON Baruch 1934 **[7]**
🖎 **$3 820** - €3 272 - **£2 236** - FF21 460
　　«The Sun» Oil/panel (79.5x59.5cm 31x23in) Wien
　　1998

ELSEN Alfred 1850-1914 **[10]**
🖎 **$616** - €644 - **£408** - FF4 207
　　Portrait de jeune fille Huile/toile (50x40cm 19x15in)
　　Bruxelles 2000

ELSENER Jeanne XX **[1]**
✐ **$2 820** - €3 201 - **£1 929** - FF21 000
　　Nature morte aux huîtres et aux oranges
　　Pastel/papier (100x118cm 39x46in) La Roche-sur-Yon
　　2000

ELSHEIMER Adam 1574/78-1610/20 **[8]**
🖎 **$3 705** - €3 904 - **£2 470** - FF25 610
　　San Juan Bautista Oleo/cobre (28.5x22cm 11x8in)
　　Madrid 2000
✐ **$10 519** - €12 252 - **£7 349** - FF80 368
　　Temple Courtyard, the Pool of Bethesda Ink
　　(20.5x16.5cm 8x6in) Amsterdam 2000

ELSHOLTZ Ludwig 1805-1850 **[12]**
🖎 **$7 653** - €8 692 - **£5 353** - FF57 016
　　Bivac aus dem Feldzug Öl/Leinwand (47x61cm
　　18x24in) Berlin 2001
✐ **$1 838** - €1 789 - **£1 129** - FF11 738
　　Neugierige Manöverzuschauer Aquarell,
　　Gouache/Papier (19x27.5cm 7x10in) Berlin 1999

ELSKEN van der Ed 1925-1990 **[16]**
📷 **$1 294** - €1 452 - **£897** - FF9 525
　　Chet Baker Silver print (23.5x17.5cm 9x6in)
　　Amsterdam 2000

ELSLEY Arthur John 1861-1952 **[80]**
🖎 **$373 575** - €401 002 - **£250 000** - FF2 630 400
　　Spring Song, also know as, Baby's Birthday
　　Oil/canvas (100.5x132cm 39x51in) London 2000

$189 405 - €225 259 - **£135 000** - FF1 477 602
　　Home Again Oil/canvas (91.5x71cm 36x27in) London
　　2000
🖎 **$5 976** - €6 943 - **£4 200** - FF45 545
　　Head Study of a young Girl Oil/canvas (26x21.5cm
　　10x8in) London 2001
🏺 **$201** - €204 - **£125** - FF1 339
　　«Pears The Invaders» Poster (39.5x49cm 15x19in)
　　Haarlem 2000

ELSNER Franz 1898-1977 **[19]**
🖎 **$6 170** - €7 267 - **£4 340** - FF47 670
　　Auf dem Weg ins Dorf Öl/Leinwand (76.5x107.5cm
　　30x42in) Wien 2000

ELSNER Otto 1893-1956 **[11]**
✐ **$589** - €613 - **£373** - FF4 024
　　Partie in Rothenburg ob der Tauber Gouache
　　(56.5x44cm 22x17in) München 2000

ELTEN van Hendrik D. Kruseman 1829-1904 **[70]**
🖎 **$22 000** - €24 424 - **£15 301** - FF160 212
　　«Well in the Heath» Oil/canvas (99x149cm 39x59in)
　　Milford CT 2001
🖎 **$1 934** - €2 301 - **£1 378** - FF15 092
　　Flusslandschaft mit Angler Öl/Leinwand (36x56cm
　　14x22in) Köln 2000
🖎 **$1 416** - €1 361 - **£883** - FF8 929
　　Watering Cows Oil/panel (35.5x44cm 13x17in)
　　Amsterdam 1999
✐ **$625** - €726 - **£432** - FF4 762
　　Alpine Landscape with Travellers Overlooking a
　　Lake Wash (9.5x15.5cm 3x6in) Amsterdam 2000

ELTYSHEV Nickolay Ivanovich 1922 **[40]**
🖎 **$485** - €459 - **£300** - FF3 010
　　Village by the River Oil/board (44x53cm 17x20in)
　　London 1999

ELUARD Paul 1895-1952 **[6]**
✐ **$1 049** - €1 220 - **£737** - FF8 000
　　L'oiseau Crayons couleurs/papier (22x16.5cm 8x6in)
　　Paris 2001
📷 **$4 794** - €3 964 - **£2 813** - FF26 000
　　Portrait de Dora Maar Tirage argentique
　　(23.7x16.7cm 9x6in) Paris 1998

ELVGREN Gilette 1914-1980 **[9]**
🖎 **$36 000** - €40 323 - **£25 012** - FF264 499
　　Seated Nude embracing new Fur Oil/canvas
　　(76x60cm 30x24in) New-York 2001

ELWELL D. Jerome 1847-1912 **[9]**
🖎 **$2 500** - €2 854 - **£1 762** - FF18 724
　　Cattle and Figures fording a River Oil/canvas
　　(61x114.5cm 24x45in) Boston MA 2001

ELWELL Frederick William 1870-1958 **[30]**
🖎 **$6 479** - €6 057 - **£4 000** - FF39 730
　　Self Portrait a Cheeky Glint in his Eye Oil/canvas
　　(49x61cm 19x24in) Driffield, East Yorkshire 1999
🖎 **$1 450** - €1 483 - **£909** - FF9 726
　　Italian Lake Scene Oil/board (30x39cm 12x15in)
　　Driffield, East Yorkshire 2000

ELWELL Robert Farrington 1874-1962 **[15]**
🖎 **$4 000** - €3 636 - **£2 409** - FF23 852
　　Custer's Last Stand Oil/canvas (55x40cm 22x16in)
　　Hayden ID 1998
✐ **$450** - €3 863 - **£325** - FF25 342
　　Stage at the Station Ink (36x72cm 14x28in) Hayden
　　ID 1998

ELWYN John 1916-1997 **[19]**
🖎 **$2 343** - €2 293 - **£1 500** - FF15 043
　　Cattle on the Path Oil/canvas (51x61cm 20x24in)
　　London 1999

E

E

ELYARD Samuel 1817-1910 [7]
$379 - €424 - £264 - FF2 778
View of the Shoalhaven Watercolour, gouache/paper
(49x59cm 19x23in) Sydney 2001

ELZINGRE Edouard 1880-1966 [47]
$323 - €357 - £224 - FF2 345
Les militaires Aquarelle/papier (21x28cm 8x11in)
Genève 2001
$1 603 - €1 453 - £1 000 - FF9 529
«Winter Sports» Poster (104x76cm 40x29in) London
1999

EMANUEL Anund 1859-1941 [14]
$1 599 - €1 380 - £962 - FF9 053
Marin med segelbåtar Oil/canvas (110x80cm
43x31in) Malmö 1998

EMANUEL Frank Lewis 1866-1948 [51]
$288 - €319 - £200 - FF2 090
St Ives/St Valery Oil/panel (25.5x34cm 10x13in)
Crewkerne, Somerset 2001

EMBDE von der August 1780-1862 [4]
$11 320 - €13 134 - £7 816 - FF86 156
**Zwei Mädchen unter einem blühenden
Apfelbaum** Öl/Leinwand (65.5x49.1cm 25x19in)
Luzern 2000

EME André 1931 [5]
$1 087 - €1 296 - £775 - FF8 500
«Tau 4» Acrylique/panneau (60x81cm 23x31in) Paris
2000

EMERSON Edith 1888-1965 [5]
$3 500 - €3 920 - £2 431 - FF25 715
**Woman sewing as soldiers look on, Poster
design** Charcoal (67x38cm 26x15in) New-York 2001

EMERSON Peter Henry 1856-1936 [105]
$2 800 - €2 633 - £1 733 - FF17 269
Gunner Working Up to Fowl Platinum print
(18x28cm 7x11in) New-York 1999

EMERSON William C. 1865-? [22]
$2 100 - €1 811 - £1 247 - FF11 877
Landscape with Nymphs Oil/board (71x91cm
28x36in) Cincinnati OH 1998

EMES John ?-c.1805 [1]
$8 269 - €7 211 - £5 000 - FF47 299
**View in the park Hawkstone, the seat of Sir
Richard Hill, Bt.** Watercolour (42x60.5cm 16x23in)
London 1998

EMETT Rowland 1906-1990 [41]
$1 192 - €1 419 - £850 - FF9 305
Happy Christmas Watercolour (29.5x32cm 11x12in)
London 2000

EMIN Tracey 1963 [28]
$4 037 - €4 462 - £2 800 - FF29 268
Self-portrait Acrylic/board (71x45.5cm 27x17in)
London 2001
$1 195 - €1 283 - £800 - FF8 417
Turkish Woman Watercolour (17x13cm 6x5in)
London 2000
$1 494 - €1 604 - £1 000 - FF10 521
Mad Frenzy-Fast Print (41x59cm 16x23in) London
2000
$15 886 - €17 311 - £11 000 - FF113 550
Naked Photos, Life Model Goes Mad Photograph
in colors (53x52cm 20x20in) London 2001

EMIOT Pierre-Paul 1858-? [22]
$921 - €1 037 - £634 - FF6 800
Saint Tropez Huile/toile (46x61cm 18x24in) Corbeil-
Essonnes 2000

EMMENEGGER Hans 1866-1940 [17]
$5 549 - €6 088 - £3 769 - FF39 935
Blumenstilleben Öl/Leinwand (65x46cm 25x18in)
Luzern 2000
$1 728 - €1 944 - £1 206 - FF12 754
Sonnenuntergang am Waldrand Öl/Leinwand
(24x33cm 9x12in) Luzern 2001

EMMERIK van Govert 1808-1882 [51]
$2 800 - €3 218 - £1 939 - FF21 108
**Sejlskibe ud for et havneindlöb, i forgrunden
strandet tremaster** Oil/canvas (66x95cm 25x37in)
Köbenhavn 2000
$1 044 - €1 022 - £642 - FF6 707
Vollschiff und Fischerboot in stürmischer See
Öl/Leinwand (31x48cm 12x18in) Bremen 1999

EMMERSON Henry Hetherington 1831-1895 [18]
$7 471 - €8 020 - £5 000 - FF52 608
**The Parley of an Emissary and Napoleon/The
Requisition of a Farmhouse** Oil/canvas (61x91.5cm
24x36in) London 2000

EMMET Lydia Field 1886-1952 [13]
$26 000 - €24 623 - £15 808 - FF161 514
Portrait of Nora Iselin Oil/canvas (165x108.5cm
64x42in) New-York 1999
$1 200 - €1 142 - £855 - FF9 361
The Red Dress Oil/canvas (101x69cm 39x27in) New-
York 2000

EMMONS Dorothy Stanley 1891-1961 [6]
$1 000 - €1 142 - £705 - FF7 489
Snow Shadows, Newton Mass Oil/canvas/board
(26x20cm 10x7in) Boston MA 2001

EMMS John 1843-1912 [266]
$57 500 - €53 297 - £35 753 - FF349 605
The Huntsman Returns Oil/canvas (128.5x100.5cm
50x39in) New-York 1999
$19 000 - €16 820 - £11 616 - FF110 331
A Group of Clumber Spaniels Oil/canvas
(53.5x43cm 21x16in) New-York 1999
$5 250 - €5 718 - £3 615 - FF37 507
Fox Terriers Oil/canvas (25.5x33.5cm 10x13in) New-
York 2001
$256 - €299 - £180 - FF1 961
**Seated Man Smoking a Pipe, his Dog at his
feet/Elderly Woman Fire** Watercolour/paper
(24x33cm 9x12in) Par, Cornwall 2000

EMOND XIX [1]
$10 251 - €9 683 - £6 200 - FF63 515
L'Hôtel Lesdiguières Albumen print (28x30.5cm
11x12in) London 1999

EMOND Martin 1895-1965 [41]
$958 - €1 004 - £606 - FF6 586
Olivberg Oil/panel (30x41cm 11x16in) Malmö 2000

EMPHINGER Franz 1865-? [5]
$823 - €799 - £508 - FF5 243
Steirisches Motiv Indian ink (15x29cm 5x11in) Wien
2001

EMPI Maurice 1932 [172]
$780 - €930 - £556 - FF6 100
Aux courses Huile/toile (46.5x61.5cm 18x24in)
Soissons 2000
$365 - €412 - £251 - FF2 700
Le 14 juillet sur les Champs Élysées
Gouache/papier (45x89cm 17x35in) La Varenne-Saint-
Hilaire 2000

EMSHWILLER Ed XX [1]
✏ **$2 250** - €2 178 - **£1 426** - FF14 284
«Rat in the Skull» Gouache/board (30.5x28cm
12x11in) New-York 1999

EMSLEY Walter XIX-XX [10]
✏ **$837** - €787 - **£520** - FF5 163
Old Buildings, Whitby Watercolour/paper (35x52cm
13x20in) Salisbury, Wiltshire 1999

EMSLIE Alfred Edward 1848-1918 [23]
👁 **$10 863** - €12 605 - **£7 500** - FF82 685
Young Boy, in a Red Velvet Suit with lace Trim,
Holding a Book Oil/canvas (92x71cm 36x27in)
London 2000
👁 **$1 438** - €1 466 - **£900** - FF9 615
Pilgrims at the River Jordan Watercolour
(24x38.5cm 9x15in) London 2000

ENAS Dato Mohd. Hossein 1924-1995 [7]
👁 **$5 309** - €4 948 - **£3 276** - FF32 454
Portrait of a Nude Oil/canvas (67x57cm 26x22in)
Singapore 1999

ENCKELL Carolus 1945 [4]
✏ **$460** - €471 - **£289** - FF3 089
Utan titel Akvarell/papper (70x50cm 27x19in) Helsinki
2000

ENCKELL Magnus 1870-1925 [31]
👁 **$2 553** - €2 859 - **£1 773** - FF18 754
Höstdag Oil/canvas (32x25cm 12x9in) Helsinki 2001
✏ **$808** - €740 - **£492** - FF4 854
Seglare Akvarell/papper (28x45cm 11x17in) Helsinki
1999

ENDE am Hans 1864-1918 [154]
👁 **$48 392** - €40 898 - **£28 776** - FF268 272
«Letzte Abendsonne» Öl/Leinwand (125x100cm
49x39in) Bremen 1998
👁 **$6 122** - €5 880 - **£3 795** - FF38 569
Abendliche Landschaft mit Torfkahn Öl/Karton
(36x53cm 14x20in) Ahlden 1999
👁 **$5 372** - €5 624 - **£3 375** - FF36 892
Mädchenkopf mit rotem Stirnband
Oil/canvas/panel (32x33cm 12x12in) Bremen 2000
🖌 **$6 049** - €5 112 - **£3 597** - FF33 534
«Worpsweder Kind» Plaster (H30.5cm H12in)
Bremen 1998
✏ **$733** - €716 - **£464** - FF4 695
Magda am Ende, Brustportrait im Profil Ink/paper
(24x17.5cm 9x6in) Bremen 1999
▭▭▭ **$355** - €409 - **£251** - FF2 683
«Die Mühle» Etching, aquatint (42x75.5cm 16x29in)
Bremen 2001

ENDE Edgar 1901-1965 [64]
👁 **$6 540** - €6 135 - **£4 040** - FF40 246
The Mark Oil/panel (71x91cm 27x35in) Stuttgart 1999
✏ **$1 060** - €1 176 - **£736** - FF7 714
Die Mittagsstunde Pencil (64.5x50cm 25x19in)
Heidelberg 2001
▭▭▭ **$119** - €133 - **£83** - FF872
Die Welt der Schirme Lithographie (28x54cm
11x21in) Heidelberg 2001

ENDE von Felix Frhr. 1856-? [5]
👁 **$36 531** - €40 840 - **£25 425** - FF267 894
Autumn elegance Oil/canvas (97x56cm 38x22in)
Amsterdam 2001
👁 **$2 059** - €2 210 - **£1 377** - FF14 499
Lecture intéressante Huile/panneau (33x44cm
12x17in) Warszawa 2000

ENDER Axel 1853-1920 [49]
👁 **$9 486** - €11 285 - **£6 561** - FF74 025
Ved kaien Oil/canvas (97x150cm 38x59in) Oslo 2000
👁 **$13 504** - €13 098 - **£8 500** - FF85 914
Cross Country Skiing Oil/canvas (52.5x40.5cm
20x15in) London 1999
👁 **$3 377** - €2 876 - **£2 017** - FF18 863
Kvinne og mann i interiör Oil/canvas (29x22cm
11x8in) Oslo 1999

ENDER Eduard 1822-1883 [17]
👁 **$1 620** - €1 906 - **£1 161** - FF12 500
Dans la taverne Huile/panneau (31x38cm 12x14in)
Paris 2001

ENDER Johann Nepomuk 1793-1854 [28]
👁 **$25 953** - €26 587 - **£16 016** - FF174 402
Eitelkeit und Bescheidenheit Öl/Leinwand
(123x95.5cm 48x37in) Düsseldorf 2000
👁 **$35 611** - €34 574 - **£22 000** - FF226 791
Young Lady, facing Right in Yellow Dress with
Lace Underdress Miniature (10.5x8.5cm 4x3in)
London 1999
✏ **$346** - €318 - **£211** - FF2 083
Elegant Couple Ink (13.5x10.5cm 5x4in) Amsterdam
1999

ENDER Thomas 1793-1875 [170]
👁 **$20 962** - €21 474 - **£12 936** - FF140 863
Schloss Vöthau des Grafen Daun in Mähren
Öl/Leinwand (52.5x63cm 20x24in) Düsseldorf 2000
👁 **$7 944** - €8 721 - **£5 280** - FF57 204
Burg Kromberg bei Brixlegg Oil/panel (17x24cm
6x9in) Wien 2000
✏ **$4 277** - €4 090 - **£2 604** - FF26 831
Gebirgsdorf, im Hintergrund die Berge
Watercolour (14.5x21.7cm 5x8in) Stuttgart 1999

ENDICOTT & Co. XIX [1]
▭▭▭ **$900** - €966 - **£602** - FF6 336
Portrait of the Side-Wheeler «C.Vanderbilt»
Color lithograph (46x87cm 18x34in) Bolton MA 2000

ENDICOTT George 1802-1848 [1]
▭▭▭ **$2 000** - €1 982 - **£1 213** - FF12 998
Andrew Jackson President of the United States,
After R.E.W Earl Lithograph (53.5x41cm 21x16in)
New-York 2000

ENDRES Louis John 1896-1989 [218]
👁 **$5 217** - €5 793 - **£3 636** - FF38 000
Le souk des dinandiers Huile/toile (104x104cm
40x40in) Paris 2001
👁 **$961** - €1 067 - **£669** - FF7 000
«Paysage, Grand Atlas Maroc» Huile/toile/carton
(28.5x39cm 11x15in) Paris 2001
✏ **$755** - €838 - **£526** - FF5 500
«Mokhazni», vieil homme au fez Pastel/papier
(29x23cm 11x9in) Paris 2001

ENDRIS Irene XX [1]
👁 **$3 500** - €3 920 - **£2 431** - FF25 715
Woman in yellow Grabbed by Gun-Wielding
Thug, she with Telephone Oil/canvas (52x36cm
20x14in) New-York 2001

ENFIELD Henry 1849-1908 [27]
👁 **$890** - €869 - **£563** - FF5 701
Norwegischer Fjord, Morgenstimmung
Öl/Leinwand (72x117cm 28x46in) Bremen 1999

ENG TAY 1947 [2]
👁 **$9 756** - €11 078 - **£6 677** - FF72 668
Gathering Oil/canvas (82.5x101cm 32x39in)
Singapore 2000

ENGALIERE Marius 1824-1857 **[17]**
📐 **$1 358** - €1 189 - **£822** - FF7 800
　　Paysage d'Italie/Paysage de Normandie
　　Gouache/papier (8x13.5cm 3x5in) Paris 1998

ENGBERG Gabriel 1872-1953 **[39]**
☞ **$1 020** - €1 009 - **£636** - FF6 619
　　Landskap Oil/canvas (40x58cm 15x22in) Helsinki
　　1999

ENGEL Hazel Livingston 1906-1999 **[9]**
📐 **$350** - €340 - **£216** - FF2 229
　　Well Kept Farm Watercolour/paper (36x49cm
　　14x19in) Cedar-Falls IA 1999

ENGEL Johann Friedrich 1844-1921 **[18]**
☞ **$2 180** - €2 543 - **£1 540** - FF16 684
　　Satyrknabe als enttäuschter Fischer Oil/panel
　　(23.5x16.5cm 9x6in) Salzburg 2000

ENGEL Morris 1918 **[9]**
📷 **$2 000** - €2 015 - **£1 246** - FF13 220
　　Rebecca Silver print (26x34cm 10x13in) Yonkers NY
　　2000

ENGEL Nissan 1931 **[30]**
🏛 **$230** - €274 - **£164** - FF1 800
　　Agitato Eau-forte, aquatinte couleurs (84x64.5cm
　　33x25in) Paris 2000

ENGEL Otto Heinrich 1866-1949 **[50]**
☞ **$6 878** - €8 181 - **£4 902** - FF53 662
　　Dorfstrasse unter Bäumen im Sommer
　　Öl/Leinwand (62x83cm 24x32in) Köln 2000
☞ **$10 567** - €9 454 - **£6 332** - FF62 017
　　Frischer Wind, Ekensund Öl/Leinwand (33x41cm
　　12x16in) Hamburg 1998
📐 **$645** - €767 - **£447** - FF5 030
　　Knüppelweiden am Ufer der Flensburger Förde
　　Oil chalks/paper (31x48cm 12x18in) Bremen 2000
🏛 **$176** - €204 - **£123** - FF1 341
　　Schiffe auf dem Rhein bei Köln Drypoint
　　(24.5x31.5cm 9x12in) Berlin 2001

ENGEL VON DER RABENAU Carl 1817-1870 **[8]**
☞ **$43 164** - €47 964 - **£28 908** - FF314 622
　　Lachende Mädchen (Die schöne Münchnerin)
　　Öl/Leinwand (82.5x66.5cm 32x26in) Wien 2000
☞ **$2 278** - €2 556 - **£1 579** - FF16 769
　　Porträt des Malers Heubel Öl/Leinwand (42x33cm
　　16x12in) Stuttgart 2000

ENGELBACH Florence Neumengen 1872-1951 **[25]**
☞ **$1 070** - €1 006 - **£650** - FF6 601
　　Still Life with Morning Glory Oil/canvas (56x46cm
　　22x18in) London 1999

ENGELBERTSZ Cornelis I c.1468-1533 **[3]**
☞ **$24 000** - €19 960 - **£14 088** - FF130 932
　　**Crucifixion with Saints Peter, Gregory,
　　Lawrence, Francis of Assisi..** Oil/panel
　　(20.5x28.5cm 8x11in) New-York 1998

ENGELBRECHT Martin 1684-1756 **[18]**
🏛 **$131** - €153 - **£92** - FF1 006
　　Die alte Procuratorie in Venedig Kupferstich
　　(19.5x29.5cm 7x11in) Berlin 2001

ENGELEN Peter 1962 **[2]**
🗎 **$1 479** - €1 588 - **£990** - FF10 418
　　Lion Bronze (H29cm H11in) Amsterdam 2000

ENGELEN van Louis 1856-1940 **[38]**
☞ **$738** - €868 - **£518** - FF5 691
　　Bord de fleuve Huile/toile (50x70cm 19x27in)
　　Bruxelles 2000

☞ **$578** - €595 - **£364** - FF3 902
　　Tricotant près du poêle de Louvain Huile/panneau
　　(26x36cm 10x14in) Antwerpen 2000

ENGELEN van Piet 1863-1924 **[29]**
☞ **$1 841** - €1 735 - **£1 113** - FF11 382
　　Vase fleuri et raisins Huile/toile (113x89cm
　　44x35in) Antwerpen 1999
☞ **$897** - €843 - **£554** - FF5 528
　　Le nid Huile/panneau (26x31cm 10x12in) Bruxelles
　　1999

ENGELHARD Anton 1872-1936 **[162]**
☞ **$236** - €205 - **£140** - FF1 343
　　Rappe Öl/Leinwand (74.5x54cm 29x21in) Heidelberg
　　1998
☞ **$236** - €205 - **£140** - FF1 343
　　Kirchzarten Öl/Leinwand (26x34cm 10x13in)
　　Heidelberg 1998
📐 **$94** - €82 - **£56** - FF537
　　Weiherhäuschen Aquarell/Papier (10x19.5cm 3x7in)
　　Heidelberg 1998

ENGELHARD Julius Ussy 1883-1964 **[24]**
🏛 **$1 159** - €1 336 - **£800** - FF8 761
　　«Adolf Rothschild, für pelze, kleider» Poster
　　(90x61cm 35x24in) London 2000

ENGELHARDT Edna Palmer XX **[10]**
☞ **$950** - €803 - **£548** - FF5 266
　　Snowy Road by Farmhouse Watercolour/paper
　　(26x34cm 10x13in) Hatfield PA 1998

ENGELHARDT Georg 1823-1883 **[36]**
☞ **$2 583** - €2 236 - **£1 568** - FF14 670
　　Berglandschaft mit Hirt auf einem Weg
　　Öl/Leinwand (68x97cm 26x38in) Zürich 1998

ENGELHART Johann Andreas 1801-1858 **[1]**
☞ **$16 854** - €15 339 - **£10 530** - FF100 617
　　Sein, Werden, Vergehen Oil/panel (40.5x46.5cm
　　15x18in) München 1999

ENGELHART Josef 1864-1941 **[82]**
☞ **$9 084** - €8 721 - **£5 700** - FF57 204
　　Die Seilerstätte Oil/panel (46x37.5cm 18x14in) Wien
　　1999
📐 **$432** - €509 - **£310** - FF3 336
　　Bei der Toilette Pencil/paper (34.1x14.1cm 13x5in)
　　Wien 2001

ENGELMÜLLER Ferdinand 1867-1924 **[25]**
☞ **$606** - €574 - **£378** - FF3 765
　　Trees on the Bank of the Lake Oil/cardboard
　　(44x32cm 17x12in) Praha 1999

ENGELS Léo 1882-1952 **[43]**
☞ **$703** - €843 - **£482** - FF5 528
　　De twee oudjes (les deux petits vieux) Huile/toile
　　(78x102cm 30x40in) Antwerpen 2000

ENGELS Lisl 1916-? **[10]**
☞ **$762** - €727 - **£464** - FF4 767
　　Tulpen in graugrünem Krug Tempera/paper
　　(58.5x43.5cm 23x17in) Wien 1999

ENGELSBERG Leon 1908-1999 **[36]**
☞ **$8 260** - €7 603 - **£4 958** - FF49 873
　　Landscape Oil/canvas (70x100cm 27x39in) Tel Aviv
　　1999
📐 **$1 100** - €1 074 - **£696** - FF7 043
　　Landscape Watercolour/paper (43x28.5cm 16x11in)
　　Tel Aviv 1999

ENGELSTED Malthe O. 1852-1930 **[54]**
☞ **$911** - €793 - **£549** - FF5 200
　　At the Well Oil/canvas (44.5x57cm 17x22in) London
　　1998

$258 - €269 - **£163** - FF1 762
Dreng der syr på en paraply Oil/canvas (25x32cm 9x12in) Lyngby 2000

ENGELUND Svend Arne 1908-? [163]
$1 758 - €1 616 - **£1 080** - FF10 598
Interiör med person i forgrunden Oil/canvas (65x81cm 25x31in) Köbenhavn 1999
$611 - €739 - **£426** - FF4 849
Landskab Oil/paper (25x32cm 9x12in) Viby J, Århus 2000
$274 - €308 - **£191** - FF2 020
Landskaber Drawing (22x31cm 8x12in) Viby J, Århus 2001
$94 - €80 - **£55** - FF528
Landskab Color lithograph (37x61cm 14x24in) Viby J, Århus 1998

ENGER Erling 1899-1990 [61]
$5 046 - €4 264 - **£3 030** - FF27 968
Landskap fra Enebakk Oil/canvas (51x61cm 20x24in) Oslo 1998
$2 728 - €2 305 - **£1 638** - FF15 118
Vinterlandskap fra Enebakk Oil/panel (33x41cm 12x16in) Oslo 1998
$165 - €186 - **£115** - FF1 217
Kuer i skog Watercolour/paper (8x12cm 3x4in) Oslo 2001
$442 - €495 - **£307** - FF3 247
Landskap Color lithograph (38x47cm 14x18in) Oslo 2001

ENGL Hugo 1852-1926 [14]
$3 096 - €2 907 - **£1 920** - FF19 068
Die liebste Ressi Oil/panel (32x24cm 12x9in) Wien 1999

ENGLAND E.S. XIX [14]
$565 - €600 - **£380** - FF3 939
Cockerels and Hens Oil/canvas (25.5x35.5cm 10x13in) London 2001

ENGLÄNDER Richard 1859-1919 [3]
$2 127 - €1 816 - **£1 250** - FF11 915
Peter Altenburg und Evelyne Horner Photograph (28.1x32.2cm 11x12in) Wien 1998

ENGLEHEART George 1752-1829 [144]
$2 215 - €1 859 - **£1 300** - FF12 195
William Hayley (1745-1820) in Profile to the Right in Blue Coat Miniature (8.5x7.5cm 3x2in) London 1998

ENGLEHEART John Cox Dillman 1782/84-1862 [38]
$3 727 - €4 090 - **£2 400** - FF26 831
Gentleman, Quarter-Length in Scholars Robes/Lady, Quarter-Length Miniature (9x6.5cm 3x2in) London 2000

ENGLER Friedrich Georg 1877-1905 [1]
$4 000 - €3 839 - **£2 507** - FF25 182
Beauty with rhododendrons Oil/canvas (65x114cm 25x44in) New-York 1999

ENGLISH Frank F. 1854-1922 [67]
$2 100 - €2 017 - **£1 301** - FF13 228
Haywagon with Figures on a Beach, Sailboats Ashore Watercolour/paper (41x64cm 16x25in) St. Louis MO 1999

ENGLISH James 1946 [5]
$831 - €787 - **£505** - FF5 164
Towards Deranmore, Co. Donegal Oil/board (39x28cm 15x11in) Dublin 1999

ENGLISH Mark 1933 [3]
$3 500 - €3 920 - **£2 431** - FF25 715
Cowboy thrown from Horse Oil/masonite (62x99cm 24x39in) New-York 2001

ENGLISH Michael 1941 [5]
$1 231 - €1 428 - **£850** - FF9 370
«Ufo Club, January 13 & 20 1967» Poster (72x99cm 28x38in) London 2000

ENGLISH Simon 1959 [5]
$3 609 - €3 905 - **£2 500** - FF25 615
«Box 1» Oil/canvas (200x400cm 78x157in) London 2001
$6 498 - €7 082 - **£4 500** - FF46 452
«Chairs» Oil/canvas (63x63cm 24x24in) London 2001

ENGLUND Lars 1933 [43]
$1 042 - €1 050 - **£649** - FF6 888
Utan titel Metal (H35.5cm H13in) Stockholm 2000
$1 403 - €1 524 - **£887** - FF9 996
Comunication Monotype (40x21cm 15x8in) Stockholm 2000

ENGMAN Kjell XX [8]
$1 844 - €1 730 - **£1 140** - FF11 347
Bruce Springsteen Sculpture, glass (H52cm H20in) Stockholm 1999

ENGMANN Harald 1903-1968 [84]
$636 - €538 - **£380** - FF3 530
Portraet af en maler Oil/canvas (88x65cm 34x25in) Köbenhavn 1998
$613 - €618 - **£382** - FF4 053
Nyboder Oil/masonite (30x39cm 11x15in) Köbenhavn 2000
$673 - €619 - **£414** - FF4 062
Portvin/Hjemlig hygge Indian ink (50x67cm 19x26in) Köbenhavn 1999

ENGONOPOULOS Nikos 1910-1985 [7]
$17 388 - €14 727 - **£10 143** - FF96 600
The Synagogue in Halkis; main facade on the Street Oil/canvas (56x46.5cm 22x18in) Athens 1998

ENGSTRÖM Albert 1869-1940 [59]
$3 153 - €2 988 - **£1 963** - FF19 559
Kustlandskap Oil/canvas (77x101cm 30x39in) Stockholm 1999
$364 - €346 - **£221** - FF2 268
Gumma med svart katt Ink/paper (19x12cm 7x4in) Stockholm 1999

ENGSTRÖM Leander 1886-1927 [100]
$11 720 - €11 021 - **£7 261** - FF72 294
Kvinna mot röd fond Oil/canvas (73x60cm 28x23in) Stockholm 1999
$1 917 - €1 667 - **£1 156** - FF10 936
Landskap i solnedgång Oil/panel (20x47cm 7x18in) Stockholm 1998
$1 819 - €2 112 - **£1 256** - FF13 851
Ballerinor Akvarell/papper (49x47cm 19x18in) Stockholm 2000

ENHUBER von Karl 1811-1867 [13]
$2 869 - €3 374 - **£2 057** - FF22 135
«Der Liebesbrief» Oil/panel (30.5x23.5cm 12x9in) Hamburg 2001

ENJOLRAS Delphin 1857-1945 [292]
$17 000 - €18 789 - **£11 908** - FF123 248
The Letter Oil/canvas (72x53cm 28x21in) Chicago IL 2001
$5 282 - €5 793 - **£3 587** - FF38 000
Nu au miroir Huile/toile (33x46cm 12x18in) Calais 2000

E

💰 **$6 794** - €6 555 - **£4 265** - FF43 000
La lecture près de la lampe Pastel/papier (54x36cm 21x14in) Paris 1999

📇 **$700** - €781 - **£458** - FF5 122
«Biscuits Lefèvre-Utile» Poster (63.5x44cm 25x17in) New-York 2000

ENKAOUA Daniel 1962 [12]

🖼 **$10 000** - €9 883 - **£6 120** - FF64 831
Landscape Oil/canvas (48x61cm 18x24in) Tel Aviv 2000

🖼 **$7 000** - €6 833 - **£4 433** - FF44 822
Landscape Oil/canvas (36x38cm 14x14in) Tel Aviv 1999

ENKELMANN Siegfried 1905-1978 [29]

📷 **$245** - €256 - **£155** - FF1 676
Die Tänzerin Iene Skorik Vintage gelatin silver print (30.2x23.9cm 11x9in) Berlin 2000

ENNEKING John Joseph 1841-1916 [178]

🖼 **$65 000** - €77 302 - **£46 325** - FF507 065
Coaster's Retreat Oil/canvas (108.5x161.5cm 42x63in) New-York 2000

🖼 **$10 000** - €11 028 - **£6 772** - FF72 341
Spring Flowers Oil/canvas (46x61cm 18x24in) New-York 2000

🖼 **$3 100** - €3 328 - **£2 112** - FF21 828
Near Evening, A Woodland Scene Oil/board (25.5x35cm 10x13in) Boston MA 2001

✎ **$2 000** - €2 147 - **£1 338** - FF14 082
A Stream in the Fall Watercolour/paper (25.5x37cm 10x14in) San-Francisco CA 2000

ENNEKING Joseph Eliot 1881-1942 [35]

🖼 **$2 500** - €2 512 - **£1 502** - FF14 148
«Apple Blossoms» Oil/canvas (41.5x51cm 16x20in) Boston MA 2001

🖼 **$1 200** - €1 418 - **£850** - FF9 301
The Sea Beyond Oil/canvas/board (30.5x40.5cm 12x15in) Boston MA 2000

ENNESS Augustus William 1876-1948 [68]

🖼 **$536** - €576 - **£359** - FF3 779
Nasturtiums Oil/canvas (40.5x50.5cm 15x19in) Toronto 2000

🖼 **$349** - €465 - **£301** - FF3 049
Tree in a Landscape Oil/board (28.5x39.5cm 11x15in) Billingshurst, West-Sussex 2000

ENNION Eric Arnold Roberts 1900-1981 [24]

✎ **$446** - €491 - **£310** - FF3 222
Woodpipers Ink (24x30cm 9x11in) Cambridge 2001

ENNIS George Pearse 1884-1936 [25]

🖼 **$4 750** - €4 568 - **£2 932** - FF29 966
Sailboats, Monhegan Oil/canvas (41x51cm 16x20in) Boston MA 1999

✎ **$475** - €465 - **£301** - FF3 049
Northern Landmark/Fishing Village Watercolour/paper (48x58cm 19x23in) Bolton MA 1999

ENOCK Arthur Henry XIX-XX [66]

✎ **$428** - €487 - **£300** - FF3 195
The Road to Bovey Tracey, a Team of Horses Pulling a Log Wagon Watercolour/paper (36x24cm 14x9in) Devon 2001

ENOTRIO 1920-1989 [54]

🖼 **$1 200** - €1 244 - **£720** - FF8 160
Vicolo in paese Olio/tavola (80x60cm 31x23in) Roma 2000

🖼 **$500** - €518 - **£300** - FF3 400
Piccola natura morta Olio/tela (19x14.5cm 7x5in) Roma 2001

ENRIGHT Maginel Wright 1881-1966 [4]

✎ **$1 700** - €1 574 - **£1 040** - FF10 323
Story ill.: young girl with flowers on blustery day, bird's nest, bird Ink (18x17cm 7x7in) New-York 1999

📇 **$700** - €651 - **£432** - FF4 269
«War Gardens over the Top» Poster (74x56cm 29x22in) New-York 1999

ENRIQUEZ Carlos 1901-1957 [50]

🖼 **$20 000** - €21 332 - **£13 322** - FF139 928
Caballo Oil/canvas (51x40.5cm 20x15in) New-York 2000

🖼 **$12 000** - €11 555 - **£7 468** - FF75 795
Desnudo de Mujer Oil/panel (45.5x32cm 17x12in) New-York 1999

✎ **$7 000** - €6 044 - **£4 270** - FF39 646
Desde el Huron Gouache/paper (43x33cm 16x12in) Miami FL 1999

ENRIQUEZ Nicolás XVIII [9]

🖼 **$14 850** - €16 518 - **£9 900** - FF108 350
Virgen de Guadalupe Oleo/lienzo (103x77.5cm 40x30in) Madrid 2000

🖼 **$2 160** - €2 403 - **£1 440** - FF15 760
Virgen de Guadalupe Oleo/cobre (21x16cm 8x6in) Madrid 2000

ENSINCK Charles Victor 1846-1914 [6]

🖼 **$3 704** - €3 857 - **£2 346** - FF25 301
Bel blazende kinderen Oil/canvas (112x100cm 44x39in) Maastricht 2000

ENSOR James 1860-1949 [992]

🖼 **$96 540** - €90 756 - **£58 440** - FF595 320
Diables turlupant un religieux - Devils teasing a Monk Oil/canvas/board (38x45cm 14x17in) Amsterdam 1999

🖼 **$15 446** - €14 521 - **£9 350** - FF95 251
View of Mariakerke Oil/panel (16.5x27cm 6x10in) Amsterdam 1999

✎ **$6 249** - €7 260 - **£4 392** - FF47 625
Portrait of Captain Borkman Charcoal/paper (56x41cm 22x16in) Amsterdam 2001

📇 **$1 711** - €1 437 - **£1 003** - FF9 425
Affiche de La Plume Lithographie couleurs (53x37cm 20x14in) Liège 1998

ENSOR Mary XIX [15]

🖼 **$828** - €767 - **£513** - FF5 030
Paar Früchtestilleben am Waldboden Öl/Karton (23x28cm 9x11in) Stuttgart 1999

ENTRAYGUES d' Charles Bertrand 1851-? [23]

🖼 **$6 800** - €6 852 - **£4 239** - FF44 948
Off to School Oil/canvas/board (42x54cm 16x21in) New-York 2000

🖼 **$10 559** - €10 275 - **£6 500** - FF67 397
La nichée Oil/canvas (34.5x42cm 13x16in) London 1999

ENWONWU Ben 1921-1994 [12]

✎ **$490** - €571 - **£350** - FF3 743
Africa Dances Watercolour/paper (74x25cm 29x10in) London 2000

ENWRIGHT J.J. 1905-? [25]

🖼 **$850** - €735 - **£504** - FF4 821
York Harbor, Maine Oil/canvas (71x96.5cm 27x37in) Washington 1998

ENZINGER Anton c.1683-1768 [1]

🖼 **$7 246** - €6 893 - **£4 400** - FF45 213
Pheasants with their Young Oil/panel (18x24.5cm 7x9in) London 1999

ENZINGER Hans 1889-1972 **[54]**
- **$852** - €799 - **£526** - FF5 243
  Pferdeschlittenfahrt Oil/panel (9.8x15.1cm 3x5in)
  Wien 1999
- **$2 097** - €2 035 - **£1 293** - FF13 347
  Der Platz am Hof mit dem Radetzkydenkmal
  Aquarell/Papier (29x40cm 11x15in) Wien 1999

EPINAT Fleury 1764-1830 **[14]**
- **$1 100** - €1 294 - **£788** - FF8 485
  «Landscape with Ruins of Aqueduct» Ink
  (46.5x35cm 18x13in) New-York 2001

ÉPINAY d' Marie XIX-XX **[2]**
- **$11 000** - €10 893 - **£6 848** - FF71 453
  Portrait of a young Beauty Oil/canvas (55x46cm
  21x18in) New-York 1999

ÉPINAY d' Prosper 1836-c.1915 **[35]**
- **$11 610** - €10 098 - **£7 000** - FF66 240
  Athenais Marie Grymes, a Bust Marble (H192cm
  H75in) London 1998
- **$2 871** - €3 219 - **£2 000** - FF21 114
  Jeanne d'Arc avant l'attaque Bronze (44x29.5cm
  17x11in) London 2001

EPISCOPIUS Johannes de Bisschop c.1628-1671/86 **[48]**
- **$4 482** - €4 812 - **£3 000** - FF31 564
  Figures by a Ruined Roman Building Black chalk
  (10x16.5cm 3x6in) London 2000

EPISCOPO d' Giovanni XVIII **[1]**
- **$7 600** - €9 843 - **£5 700** - FF64 600
  **La Madonna del Carmine con i Santi Michele e
  Raffaele** Olio/tela (259x200cm 101x78in) Roma 2000

EPP Rudolf 1834-1910 **[98]**
- **$11 268** - €13 081 - **£7 920** - FF85 806
  Ein Kühler Schluck Öl/Leinwand (166x88cm
  65x34in) Wien 2000
- **$4 244** - €4 857 - **£2 919** - FF31 862
  **Tiroler Mädchen in Tracht und mit Almrausch
  am Hut** Öl/Leinwand (76x59.5cm 29x23in) München
  2000
- **$2 294** - €2 556 - **£1 603** - FF16 769
  **Schwarzwälder Bauernmädchen in Gutachter
  Tracht** Öl/Papier (49x28.5cm 19x11in) München 2001

EPPER Ignaz 1892-1969 **[146]**
- **$1 305** - €1 401 - **£873** - FF9 190
  Brücke mit Passanten in der Nacht Indian ink
  (32.5x27.2cm 12x10in) Bern 2000
- **$224** - €222 - **£139** - FF1 455
  Die Eltern, Elternbildnis I Gravure bois (47x63cm
  18x24in) St. Gallen 1999

EPPLE Emil 1877-? **[5]**
- **$2 244** - €2 352 - **£1 484** - FF15 427
  Orpheus Bronze (H69cm H27in) München 2000

EPSTEIN Elisabeth 1879-1956 **[10]**
- **$4 446** - €4 116 - **£2 721** - FF26 998
  Waldinneres mit Ausblick Öl/Karton (48x37.6cm
  18x14in) München 1999

EPSTEIN Henri 1892-1944 **[409]**
- **$7 839** - €6 860 - **£4 747** - FF45 000
  Bouquet et grenades Huile/toile (50x65cm 19x25in)
  Paris 1998
- **$3 005** - €3 354 - **£2 090** - FF22 000
  Les baigneuses Huile/toile (33x41cm 12x16in) Paris
  2001
- **$426** - €396 - **£259** - FF2 600
  Deux femmes Mine plomb (31x23.5cm 12x9in) Paris
  1998

EPSTEIN Jacob 1880-1959 **[507]**
- **$7 227** - €7 015 - **£4 500** - FF46 016
  Third Portrait of Kathleen Bronze (H53.5cm H21in)
  London 1999
- **$2 278** - €2 370 - **£1 450** - FF15 548
  Sunita Pencil/paper (46x55cm 18x21in) London 2000

EPSTEIN Jehudo 1870-1945 **[27]**
- **$12 650** - €11 787 - **£7 873** - FF77 319
  Les buveurs Oil/canvas (99x122cm 38x48in) Tel Aviv
  1999
- **$4 572** - €4 360 - **£2 784** - FF28 602
  Liegende Öl/Leinwand (40x88cm 15x34in) Wien 1999
- **$1 878** - €2 180 - **£1 320** - FF14 301
  Nach der Kirche Öl/Leinwand/Karton (31x41cm
  12x16in) Wien 2001

EQUIPO CRONICA R. Solbes & M.Valdès 1940/42-1981 **[83]**
- **$49 350** - €45 735 - **£30 690** - FF300 000
  Le mas des délices Huile/toile (140x140cm
  55x55in) Paris 1999
- **$15 930** - €17 719 - **£11 210** - FF116 230
  La paleta espejo del alma Acrylique/carton
  (80x110cm 31x43in) Madrid 2001
- **$4 720** - €4 805 - **£2 960** - FF31 520
  Homenaje a Joan Miró Ceramic (32x35x35cm
  12x13x13in) Madrid 2000
- **$10 050** - €9 010 - **£6 150** - FF59 100
  Rembrandt Gouache (112x77cm 44x30in) Madrid
  1999
- **$828** - €721 - **£516** - FF4 728
  Sin título Litografía (70x56cm 27x22in) Madrid 1999

EQUIPO REALIDAD Ballester & Gardells XX **[16]**
- **$124** - €144 - **£86** - FF945
  Composición Litografía (70x68.5cm 27x26in)
  Barcelona 2001

ERB Erno 1878-1943 **[72]**
- **$2 015** - €2 200 - **£1 367** - FF14 429
  Marchandes Huile/carton (49x70cm 19x27in) Torun
  2000
- **$1 096** - €1 225 - **£765** - FF8 033
  Marchandes Huile/carton (26x35cm 10x13in)
  Warszawa 2001
- **$1 248** - €1 333 - **£850** - FF8 744
  Chrysanthèmes dans un vase Gouache/papier
  (49.5x35cm 19x13in) Warszawa 2001

ERBA Carlo 1884-1917 **[34]**
- **$12 000** - €15 550 - **£9 000** - FF102 000
  Pioppeto Olio/tela (40x44cm 15x17in) Milano 2001
- **$8 400** - €7 257 - **£4 200** - FF47 000
  Albero con specchio d'acqua Olio/tela (35x27.5cm
  13x10in) Milano 1999
- **$1 380** - €1 192 - **£920** - FF7 820
  Donna che legge il giornale Matita/carta
  (29.5x19cm 11x7in) Milano 1999

ERBACH Alois 1888-1972 **[13]**
- **$328** - €307 - £199 - FF2 012
  Früchtlinge/Gestürzter Ritter Aquarell/Papier
  (23x30.5cm 9x12in) Berlin 1999

ERBE Paul 1894-1972 **[23]**
- **$568** - €665 - **£399** - FF4 360
  Moorlandschaft Öl/Leinwand (39x48cm 15x18in)
  München 2000
- **$2 278** - €2 556 - **£1 579** - FF16 769
  Früchtestilleben Oil/panel (31x41cm 12x16in)
  München 2000

ERBE Robert 1844-1903 **[29]**
- $323 - €332 - £204 - FF2 180
  Federvieh mit Katze Aquarell/Papier (28x22.5cm 11x8in) Eltville-Erbach 2000

ERBE-VOGEL Hermann 1907-1976 **[29]**
- $571 - €613 - £382 - FF4 024
  Blick auf Erbe-Vogel-Haus von der Flanitz aus Pastell/Papier (33x50cm 12x19in) Zwiesel 2000
- $62 - €61 - £38 - FF402
  Die alte Lampe Linocut (19x9cm 7x3in) Zwiesel 1999

ERBEN Ulrich 1940 **[57]**
- $569 - €665 - £400 - FF4 360
  Ohne Titel Öl/Papier (86x61cm 33x24in) Köln 2000

ERBSLAND Angelika XX **[2]**
- $4 135 - €4 343 - £2 616 - FF28 490
  Portrait of Bradman Oil/canvas (84x68cm 33x26in) Melbourne 2000

ERBSLÖH Adolf 1881-1947 **[29]**
- $162 982 - €194 294 - £116 204 - FF1 274 482
  Gebirge Brannenburg Öl/Leinwand (93x133cm 36x52in) Berlin 2000
- $42 890 - €51 130 - £30 580 - FF335 390
  Schlafende Frau, Akt Öl/Leinwand (68x91.5cm 26x36in) Berlin 2000
- $442 - €383 - £268 - FF2 510
  Weite Landschaft mit Blick auf Warburg in Westfalen Lithographie (30x42.5cm 11x16in) München 1998

ERDELY de Francis 1904-1959 **[56]**
- $2 750 - €2 639 - £1 724 - FF17 312
  Figures, Skiff setting out to Sea Oil/canvas (55x86cm 22x34in) Altadena CA 1999
- $300 - €276 - £180 - FF1 811
  Figure Study, Man with Ball and Chain Charcoal/paper (60x46cm 24x18in) Pasadena CA 1999

ERDMANN Otto 1834-1905 **[24]**
- $13 000 - €11 254 - £7 840 - FF73 821
  «He Loves Me, He Loves Me Not» Oil/canvas (87.5x64cm 34x25in) San-Francisco CA 1998
- $2 065 - €2 102 - £1 295 - FF13 790
  Le peticion Oleo/lienzo (38x27cm 14x10in) Barcelona 2000

ERDMANN-MENZEL Adolf Friedrich 1815-1905 **[2]**
- $180 778 - €148 489 - £105 000 - FF974 022
  Inneres der Klosterkirche zu Ettal Watercolour, gouache/paper (40x26cm 15x10in) London 1999

ERDT Hans Rudi 1883-1918 **[22]**
- $1 900 - €1 621 - £1 146 - FF10 632
  «Elegante Welt» Poster (97x69.5cm 38x27in) New-York 1998

ERDTELT Alois 1851-1911 **[11]**
- $382 - €434 - £267 - FF2 850
  Frauenporträt Öl/Leinwand (56x47cm 22x18in) München 2001
- $3 651 - €3 323 - £2 281 - FF21 800
  Stilleben mit Hummer, Muscheln, Pastetendose, Römerweinglas Oil/board (31x30cm 12x11in) München 1999

ERDTMAN Elias 1863-1945 **[34]**
- $1 291 - €1 115 - £777 - FF7 312
  Utsikt över kust, i förgrunden blommande nyponbuskar Oil/canvas (65x95cm 25x37in) Malmö 1998
- $371 - €384 - £233 - FF2 517
  Landskap i månsken Oil/canvas (46x27cm 18x10in) Stockholm 2000

EREMEYEVICH Boris 1878-1950 **[1]**
- $2 000 - €1 727 - £1 205 - FF11 331
  Hanukah Celebration Gouache/paper (24.5x33.5cm 9x13in) Tel Aviv 1998

ERENTXUN Eloy 1904 **[10]**
- $1 550 - €1 502 - £905 - FF9 850
  Caserío entre montañas Oleo/lienzo (46x55cm 18x21in) Madrid 1999

ERFURTH Hugo 1874-1948 **[69]**
- $1 454 - €1 411 - £905 - FF9 256
  Richard Müller mit Modell im Atelier Vintage gelatin silver print (22.5x17cm 8x6in) Berlin 1999

ERGANIAN Sarkis 1870-1950 **[11]**
- $375 - €374 - £234 - FF2 453
  Mountainous River Scene Oil/masonite (30x39cm 12x15in) St. Louis MO 1999

ERGO Englebert c.1620-c.1667 **[2]**
- $17 000 - €16 498 - £10 711 - FF108 222
  Orpheus charming the Animals Oil/copper (39.5x50cm 15x19in) New-York 1999
- $10 877 - €9 218 - £6 500 - FF60 464
  Aeneas Rescuing his Father From the Sack of Troy Oil/copper (21x27cm 8x10in) London 1998

ERHARD Johann Christoph 1795-1822 **[86]**
- $161 - €179 - £112 - FF1 173
  «Auf der hohen Feste in Salzburg» Radierung (12.5x17.5cm 4x6in) Heidelberg 2001

ERHARDT Georg Friedrich 1825-1881 **[10]**
- $2 483 - €2 556 - £1 565 - FF16 769
  Manöverszene aus der Zeit von 1840 Öl/Leinwand (21x30cm 8x11in) Berlin 2000

ERICHSEN Thorvald 1868-1939 **[28]**
- $25 070 - €29 138 - £17 618 - FF191 130
  Graaveir, Skaane Oil/canvas (65x73cm 25x28in) Oslo 2001
- $10 900 - €12 669 - £7 660 - FF83 100
  Lennart i skogen Oil/panel (37x31cm 14x12in) Oslo 2001

ERICKSON Carl Oscar August 1891-1958 **[11]**
- $950 - €891 - £587 - FF5 846
  Interior Staircase Scene with a formally attired Couple conversing Wash/paper (71x59cm 28x23in) New-York 1999

ERICKSON Oscar B. 1883-1968 **[6]**
- $650 - €725 - £425 - FF4 756
  Indiana Landscape Oil/canvas (35x40cm 14x16in) Chicago IL 2000

ERICSON Johan Erik 1849-1925 **[100]**
- $3 495 - €3 976 - £2 441 - FF26 081
  Västkustmotiv Oil/canvas (68x107cm 26x42in) Stockholm 2000
- $567 - €639 - £391 - FF4 191
  Månsken över sjö Oil/canvas (21x32cm 8x12in) Uppsala 2000

ERIKSEN Edvard 1876-1959 **[10]**
- $30 659 - €30 898 - £19 113 - FF202 676
  Den lille Havfrue Bronze (H100cm H39in) Købenavn 2000
- $912 - €870 - £555 - FF5 710
  Kleine Meerjungfrau Bronze (H24cm H9in) Bern 1999

ERIKSEN Hans 1912-1982 **[24]**
- $476 - €509 - £324 - FF3 340
  Aprilsvejr med drivende skyer, Gothersgade og Kongens Have Oil/canvas (61x61cm 24x24in) Vejle 2001

ERIKSEN Sigurd 1884-1976 **[32]**
$872 - €1 019 - £622 - FF6 684
Skjaergård Oil/canvas (67x73cm 26x28in) Oslo 2001

ERIKSEN Vigilius 1722-1782 **[6]**
$750 - €804 - £511 - FF5 277
Portraet af en dame i rosa kjole Oil/canvas
(65x52cm 25x20in) København 2001

ERIKSSON Christian 1858-1935 **[43]**
$1 028 - €1 104 - £688 - FF7 243
Porträttbyst av Hjalmar Lundbohm Bronze
(H54cm H21in) Stockholm 2000

ERIKSSON Liss 1919-2000 **[24]**
$882 - €989 - £613 - FF6 487
Asmund Arle, sittande figur Bronze (H27cm
H10in) Stockholm 2001

ERIXSON Sven 1899-1970 **[565]**
$43 965 - €49 256 - £30 545 - FF323 100
Målarens hus Oil/panel (250x360cm 98x141in)
Stockholm 2001
$2 735 - €3 065 - £1 906 - FF20 104
Solnedgång, Svolver Oil/panel (61x72cm 24x28in)
Stockholm 2001
$952 - €976 - £588 - FF6 399
Komposition Mixed media (26x40cm 10x15in)
Stockholm 2000
$526 - €601 - £371 - FF3 945
Teckningar från akvariet i Monaco Akvarell/papper
(13x20cm 5x7in) Stockholm 2001
$196 - €170 - £118 - FF1 114
«Drafin» Color lithograph (27.5x35.5cm 10x13in)
Malmö 1998

ERKELENS Frans Willem 1937 **[17]**
$127 - €127 - £77 - FF833
Zeepaardje Oil/panel (45x35.5cm 17x13in)
Amsterdam 2000

ERKER Walter XX **[2]**
$2 880 - €3 270 - £2 020 - FF21 451
«St Christof am Arlberg» Öl/Leinwand (65x100cm
25x39in) Wien 2001

ERLAND Simon 1961 **[3]**
$5 500 - €6 390 - £3 865 - FF41 916
Racehorse with Jockey up Bronze (H30.5cm
H12in) New-York 2001

ERLER Fritz 1868-1940 **[46]**
$3 370 - €3 068 - £2 106 - FF20 123
Stephaniereiter Öl/Leinwand (71x60.5cm 27x23in)
München 1999

ERLER-SAMADEN Erich 1870-1946 **[60]**
$2 415 - €2 198 - £1 509 - FF14 421
Stehender weiblicher Akt in Landschaft
Öl/Leinwand (100x100cm 39x39in) München 1999
$1 010 - €1 119 - £700 - FF7 337
«Winter in Bayern» Poster (72x97cm 28x38in)
London 2001

ERMIEL Naps XIX **[1]**
$3 290 - €3 049 - £2 032 - FF20 000
Boyard donnant à boire à son cheval Bronze
(25x30cm 9x11in) Paris 1999

ERNESTO XX **[5]**
$6 358 - €5 564 - £3 850 - FF36 500
L'Amour à emportée Acrylique/toile (116x89cm
45x35in) Paris 1998

ERNI Hans 1909 **[701]**
$6 783 - €6 174 - £4 163 - FF40 498
Mann mit zwei Zitronen Öl/Leinwand (63x100cm
24x39in) Zürich 1999

$2 305 - €2 593 - £1 609 - FF17 006
«Abstraktion & Realität» Tempera/Karton
(26.5x40cm 10x15in) Luzern 2001
$718 - €692 - £449 - FF4 537
Pan mit Flöte Tempera/papier (35x27cm 13x10in)
Zürich 1999
$228 - €220 - £141 - FF1 443
Zwei Pferde sich begegnend Farblithographie
(74.5x65cm 29x25in) Zürich 1999

ERNST Alfred 1904-1992 **[5]**
$710 - €802 - £500 - FF5 261
«Study of Ships at Night» Silver print (30x36cm
11x14in) London 2001

ERNST Elizabeth 1909-1997 **[3]**
$2 099 - €2 464 - £1 481 - FF16 162
Costa Del Sol, Spain Oil/board (58.5x109cm
23x42in) Melbourne 2001

ERNST Emil von Düsseldorf XIX **[5]**
$3 965 - €3 997 - £2 475 - FF26 218
Staubbachfall im Lauterbrunnertal Öl/Leinwand
(66x81cm 25x31in) Wien 2000

ERNST Helge 1916-1991 **[181]**
$744 - €832 - £497 - FF5 455
Ariel II Oil/canvas (73x100cm 28x39in) København
2000
$481 - €536 - £329 - FF3 519
Komposition Gouache/paper (41x53cm 16x20in)
København 2000

ERNST Jimmy 1920-1984 **[48]**
$4 500 - €4 017 - £2 755 - FF26 352
Untitled Oil/canvas (109x81cm 42x31in) New-York
1999
$600 - €583 - £375 - FF3 823
Untitled Watercolour, gouache/paper (18.5x13cm
7x5in) New-York 1999
$4 000 - €3 741 - £2 418 - FF24 542
Photogram Gelatin silver print (26x19.5cm 10x7in)
New-York 1999

ERNST Max 1891-1976 **[1811]**
$10 000 - €8 214 - £5 808 - FF53 879
Le Grand Ignorant : Screen Mixed media
(186x166cm 73x65in) Tel Aviv 1998
$196 420 - €233 602 - £140 000 - FF1 532 328
La colombe Oil/canvas (46x38cm 18x14in) London
2000
$57 213 - €66 469 - £40 209 - FF436 007
Paysage Oil/panel (14x18cm 5x7in) Köln 2001
$27 523 - €31 324 - £19 339 - FF205 473
Sirènes ailées Bronze (94x48x75cm 37x18x29in)
Zürich 2001
$17 025 - €19 056 - £11 550 - FF125 000
Femmes, Huismes Métal (18x25.2cm 7x9in) Paris
2001
$16 645 - €15 623 - £10 282 - FF102 477
Illustrations de «Je sublime» de B.Peret Dessin
(20.5x21.5cm 8x8in) Genève 1999
$775 - €922 - £552 - FF6 047
Utan titel, from Oiseau en Peril, side no.3 Etching
in colors (30.5x25.5cm 12x10in) Stockholm 2000
$12 573 - €13 720 - £8 532 - FF90 000
Et les papillons se mettent à chanter Tirage
argentique (97x87.5cm 38x34in) Paris 2000

ERNST Otto 1884-1967 **[61]**
$852 - €719 - £500 - FF4 717
«Vallée de Joux» Poster (100x70cm 39x27in)
London 1998

ERNST Rita 1956 [2]
- $2 098 - €2 501 - **£1 495** - FF16 405
  Ohne Titel Acryl/Leinwand (40x40cm 15x15in)
  Luzern 2000

ERNST Rudolph 1854-1932 [180]
- $110 000 - €103 033 - **£67 628** - FF675 851
  The Palace Guard Oil/panel (61x35.5cm 24x13in)
  New-York 1999
- $11 941 - €11 562 - **£7 500** - FF75 843
  The old Man and the Merchant Oil/panel (35x23cm 13x9in) London 1999
- $7 770 - €9 147 - **£5 460** - FF60 000
  La fileuse Aquarelle/papier (33x25cm 12x9in) Paris 2000

ERNST von Alfred 1799-1850 [3]
- $4 740 - €4 090 - **£2 871** - FF26 831
  Schweizer Gebirgslandschaft mit See Burganlagen und Personen Oil/canvas/panel (95x126cm 37x49in) Kempten 1999

ERNSTING Daniel Albert 1749-1820 [10]
- $394 - €383 - **£246** - FF2 515
  Bremen: Arbargen und die umliegende Gegend Kupferstich (23x30cm 9x11in) Bremen 1999

EROLI Erulo 1854-1916 [9]
- $2 200 - €2 376 - **£1 520** - FF15 584
  The Tea Party Watercolour/paper (54.5x81.5cm 21x32in) Bethesda MD 2001

ERP van Theodoor 1874-1959 [2]
- $2 400 - €2 272 - **£1 490** - FF14 902
  «D:16» Poster (99x65cm 38x25in) New-York 1999

ERPIKUM Léon Vuilleminot c.1835-? [9]
- $1 148 - €1 067 - **£697** - FF7 000
  Femmes orientales dans un parc Huile/panneau (29.5x34cm 11x13in) Aubagne 1998

ERRARD Charles II 1606-1689 [3]
- $115 840 - €131 639 - **£80 000** - FF863 496
  Tancred and Erminia Oil/canvas (240.5x241.5cm 94x95in) London 2000
- $12 145 - €14 178 - **£8 574** - FF93 000
  La mort de Saphire Huile/toile (45x62cm 17x24in) Lyon 2000

ERRO Gudmundur 1932 [811]
- $7 128 - €8 385 - **£5 109** - FF55 000
  Gymnasium Acrylique/toile (131x195cm 51x76in) Paris 2001
- $4 544 - €4 421 - **£2 795** - FF29 000
  Sans titre Acrylique/toile (101x73cm 39x28in) Paris 1999
- $1 399 - €1 410 - **£872** - FF9 252
  Kunstner ved staffeli Acrylic/canvas (47x34cm 18x13in) Köbenhavn 2000
- $3 628 - €4 269 - **£2 601** - FF28 000
  «Décor pour Mécamorrons» Assemblage (62x64cm 24x25in) Paris 2001
- $755 - €838 - **£526** - FF5 500
  Sans titre Gouache/papier (31x40cm 12x15in) Douai 2001
- $107 - €122 - **£73** - FF800
  Mao Sérigraphie couleurs (79x59cm 31x23in) Paris 2000

ERTÉ (Romain de Tirtoff) 1892-1990 [921]
- $2 000 - €2 285 - **£1 408** - FF14 986
  Female Nude: Costume Design for the Folies-Bergères Mixed media (28x21cm 11x8in) Pittsfield MA 2001

- $2 500 - €2 297 - **£1 535** - FF15 067
  Heat, a partially draped woman reclining amongst grape vines Bronze (H49cm H19in) St. Petersburg FL 1999
- $1 372 - €1 318 - **£850** - FF8 644
  Costume Design Gouache (35x23cm 13x9in) London 1999
- $500 - €463 - **£301** - FF3 036
  Reflections Color lithograph (50x38cm 20x15in) St. Louis MO 1999

ERTL Marie 1837-c.1890 [6]
- $12 750 - €10 899 - **£7 650** - FF71 490
  «Motiv nächst Alt Ausee, Aussicht vom Fuchsbauer auf den See...» Ol/Leinwand (66x98cm 25x38in) Wien 1998

ERTZ Bruno 1873-1956 [7]
- $375 - €358 - **£236** - FF2 351
  Passenger Pigeons - Extinct Watercolour/paper (68x41cm 27x16in) Milwaukee WI 1999

ERTZ Gordon 1891 [1]
- $1 600 - €1 792 - **£1 111** - FF11 755
  Butterfly fairies picking Flowers in fantastic Landscape Watercolour, gouache (32x51cm 12x20in) New-York 2001

ERWITT Elliot 1928 [104]
- $1 278 - €1 431 - **£888** - FF9 390
  Las Vegas, Nevada Vintage gelatin silver print (16x24cm 6x9in) Köln 2001

ES van Jacob Foppens c.1596-1666 [19]
- $90 403 - €85 710 - **£55 000** - FF562 221
  Fish on a Terracotta platter, Asparagus, Artichokes, Cherries, Crabs Oil/canvas (82x138cm 32x54in) London 1999
- $52 663 - €58 991 - **£36 595** - FF386 958
  Hazelnuts in a Wan-li Bowl with a Bunch of Grapes, an Orange, Oil/panel (27x34.5cm 10x13in) Amsterdam 2001

ESAM Arthur 1850-c.1910 [24]
- $590 - €650 - **£396** - FF4 264
  Journey through the Bush Watercolour/paper (24.5x38cm 9x14in) Malvern, Victoria 2000

ESBENS Emile Etienne 1821-? [5]
- $1 968 - €2 287 - **£1 402** - FF15 000
  Le garde du palais Huile/panneau (18x13cm 7x5in) Paris 2001

ESCADA José 1939-1980 [2]
- $8 100 - €8 973 - **£5 220** - FF58 860
  Abstracto Oleo/lienzo (64x49cm 25x19in) Lisboa 2000
- $1 980 - €2 243 - **£1 395** - FF14 715
  Sem titulo Gouache (19.5x13cm 7x5in) Lisboa 2001

ESCH Mathilde 1820-? [1]
- $2 250 - €2 204 - **£1 450** - FF14 458
  View of a distant Town Oil/panel (29.5x36cm 11x14in) New-York 1999

ESCH von Johann Petrus 1666-1740 [3]
- $8 688 - €7 318 - **£5 131** - FF48 000
  L'Évanouissement d'Esther Huile/papier (58x72cm 22x28in) Paris 1998

ESCHARD Charles 1748-1810 [16]
- $224 940 - €210 380 - **£136 206** - FF1 380 000
  Vue de Marseille - Joute et fête sur l'eau Huile/toile (82.5x120.5cm 32x47in) Lille 1999

$1 602 - €1 601 - £1 001 - FF10 500
Vieux mendiant assis près de son chien dans des ruines romaines Encre (52x41.5cm 20x16in) Paris 1999

ESCHBACH Paul 1881-1961 **[130]**
$900 - €1 067 - £655 - FF7 000
Scène de marché dans la Mayenne Huile/toile (54x65.5cm 21x25in) Paris 2001
$385 - €457 - £281 - FF3 000
Maison sous la neige Huile/toile (33x41cm 12x16in) Paris 2001

ESCHEN Fritz 1900-1964 **[9]**
$714 - €767 - £478 - FF5 030
Georg Kolbe im Atelier Photograph (23.5x17.5cm 9x6in) München 2000

ESCHENBURG von Marianne 1856-1937 **[5]**
$3 641 - €3 997 - £2 420 - FF26 218
Jagdstilleben Öl/Leinwand (79x63cm 31x24in) Wien 2000

ESCHER Johann Heinrich XVIII **[1]**
$1 774 - €1 913 - £1 190 - FF12 547
Horgen am Zürichsee Crayon (27x42cm 10x16in) Zürich 2000

ESCHER Maurits Cornelius 1898-1972 **[346]**
$11 287 - €9 771 - £6 849 - FF64 095
Column Sculpture (H59cm H23in) Amsterdam 1998
$6 000 - €5 070 - £3 579 - FF33 259
Birds Pencil/paper (18x18.5cm 7x7in) San-Francisco CA 1998
$5 500 - €6 405 - £3 804 - FF42 012
Whirlpools Woodcut in colors (54.5x31.5cm 21x12in) New-York 2000

ESCHER Rolf 1936 **[16]**
$96 - €92 - £58 - FF603
Das verlorene Gesicht Lithographie (61x35cm 24x13in) Bielefeld 1999

ESCHKE Herman 1823-1900 **[20]**
$907 - €1 022 - £628 - FF6 707
«Gesundbrunnen bei Berlin» Öl/Leinwand/Karton (35x39cm 13x15in) Berlin 2000

ESCHKE Hermann Richard 1859-1944 **[37]**
$1 180 - €1 329 - £829 - FF8 720
Hafeneinfahrt in Ostende bei Mondschein Öl/Leinwand (62x89cm 24x35in) Stuttgart 2001

ESCOBAR Vicente 1757-1834 **[2]**
$6 000 - €5 823 - £3 575 - FF38 199
D. Augustín de Las Heras y Carazo Oil/canvas (90x68cm 35x26in) New-York 1999

ESCOBEDO PLA XIX-XX **[1]**
$12 160 - €11 412 - £7 410 - FF74 860
Patio Valenciano Oleo/lienzo (103x83cm 40x32in) Madrid 1999

ESCOFET Miriam XX **[1]**
$2 449 - €2 700 - £1 600 - FF17 709
Edge white Ensign and Self Neat and Tidy Auricula in Terracotta Pots Watercolour (43x46cm 16x18in) London 2000

ESCOT Charles 1834-1902 **[3]**
$887 - €991 - £617 - FF6 500
Portrait de jeune femme Pastel/toile (63x51.5cm 24x20in) Paris 2001

ESCTAL Christian 1955 **[60]**
$471 - €457 - £291 - FF3 000
P'tits coqs Sculpture (H72cm H28in) Paris 1999

$441 - €381 - £266 - FF2 500
Fin de siécle Gouache/papier (44x33cm 17x12in) Paris 1998

ESCUDIER Charles Jean Auguste 1848-? **[13]**
$2 964 - €3 292 - £1 984 - FF21 591
Ung kvinna med slända Oil/canvas (74x61cm 29x24in) Stockholm 2000

ESKILSON Peter 1820-1872 **[33]**
$2 287 - €2 691 - £1 657 - FF17 650
Det muntra dryckeslaget Oil/canvas (37x47cm 14x18in) Stockholm 2001

ESKOLA Kalle 1912 **[27]**
$349 - €404 - £247 - FF2 647
Hundloka Oil/canvas (70x60cm 27x23in) Helsinki 2000

ESLER John Kenneth 1933 **[37]**
$67 - €75 - £43 - FF490
Strange Sunset Print (41x37cm 16x14in) Calgary, Alberta 2000

ESMONDE-WHITE Eleanor Frances 1914 **[6]**
$9 676 - €10 030 - £6 129 - FF65 790
Wash Day Oil/canvas (80x111cm 31x43in) Johannesburg 2000

ESPAGNAT d' Georges 1870-1950 **[521]**
$20 300 - €21 343 - £12 740 - FF140 000
La cueillette des pommes Huile/toile (97x130cm 38x51in) Paris 2000
$11 871 - €11 586 - £7 516 - FF76 000
Jeune bohémienne Huile/toile (56x46cm 22x18in) Calais 1999
$2 906 - €3 201 - £1 938 - FF21 000
Nature morte aux fruits Huile/panneau (16x22cm 6x8in) Deauville 2000
$750 - €875 - £526 - FF5 741
Boy Drawing with a Birdcage/Female Bathers Watercolour (26.5x17.5cm 10x6in) Boston MA 2000

ESPALIU Pepe 1955-1993 **[3]**
$8 250 - €9 010 - £5 700 - FF59 100
Sin título Técnica mixta/papel (98x153cm 38x60in) Madrid 2001

ESPALTER Y RULL Joaquín 1809-1880 **[4]**
$2 083 - €2 045 - £1 291 - FF13 415
Madonna mit Kind und dem Johannesknaben vor weiter Landschaft Öl/Leinwand (40x30cm 15x11in) München 2000

ESPARBES d' Jean 1898-1968 **[106]**
$557 - €534 - £343 - FF3 500
La partie d'échec Huile/toile (61x50cm 24x19in) Lyon 1999
$241 - €274 - £167 - FF1 800
L'homme à la poupée Huile/toile (35x27cm 13x10in) Orléans 2001

ESPERLIN Joseph 1707-1775 **[9]**
$3 650 - €4 090 - £2 516 - FF26 831
Auferweckung des Lazarus Öl/Leinwand (83x67cm 32x26in) Frankfurt 2000

ESPIGA PINTO José Manuel 1940 **[1]**
$1 760 - €1 994 - £1 240 - FF13 080
Charrua Tinta/papel (41x27.5cm 16x10in) Lisboa 2001

ESPINA Y CAPO Juan 1848-1933 **[50]**
$504 - €481 - £312 - FF3 152
Paisaje Oleo/tabla (19x32cm 7x12in) Madrid 1999
$190 - €216 - £133 - FF1 418
Paisaje Carboncillo (21x26.5cm 8x10in) Madrid 2001
$97 - €108 - £66 - FF709
Bosque Aguafuerte (18x13cm 7x5in) Madrid 2001

ESPINASSE Raymond 1897-1985 **[130]**
✎ **$318** - €305 - **£194** - FF2 000
Trois personnages Crayons couleurs/papier
(40x30cm 15x11in) Pau 1999

ESPINOS Benito 1748-1818 **[6]**
⌾ **$9 120** - €9 610 - **£5 760** - FF63 040
Ramo de flores Oleo/lienzo (48.5x35.5cm 19x13in)
Madrid 2000
⌾ **$5 518** - €5 838 - **£3 500** - FF38 295
**Bust of a Lady Surrounded by a Garland of
Flowers** Oil/panel (32x25cm 12x9in) London 2000

ESPINOSA de Jerónimo Jacinto 1600-1680 **[6]**
⌾ **$18 460** - €19 818 - **£12 350** - FF130 000
La Vierge du Rosaire Huile/toile (153x115cm
60x45in) Pau 2000

ESPINOZA Manuel 1937 **[13]**
⌾ **$1 436** - €1 692 - **£1 009** - FF11 102
Flores para un velerio Oleo/lienzo (99x64.5cm
38x25in) Caracas ($) 2000

ESPLANDIU Juan 1901-1978 **[56]**
✎ **$639** - €541 - **£378** - FF3 546
Café Gijón Acuarela/papel (43x56cm 16x22in) Madrid
1998

ESPOSITO d' XIX-XX **[19]**
✎ **$999** - €932 - **£620** - FF6 113
«H.M.S.Venus at Sea» Gouache/paper (29x42cm
11x16in) London 1999

ESPOSITO d' Gaetano 1858-1911 **[92]**
⌾ **$2 713** - €2 496 - **£1 677** - FF16 371
A rocky coastal Landscape Oil/canvas (57x75.5cm
22x29in) Amsterdam 1999
⌾ **$1 200** - €1 403 - **£849** - FF9 201
Neapolitan Beauty Oil/canvas (39x30cm 15x12in)
Cedar-Falls IA 2001
✎ **$638** - €741 - **£450** - FF4 860
Harbour Scene Gouache/paper (11x23cm 4x9in)
Cambridge 2001

ESPOSITO d'Vincenzo 1886-1946 **[90]**
✎ **$570** - €487 - **£340** - FF3 192
**British Man O'War off Malta with fishermen
trawling in foreground** Gouache/paper (22x53.5cm
8x21in) Plymouth 1998

ESPOY Angel 1879-1963 **[87]**
⌾ **$4 400** - €3 909 - **£2 694** - FF25 641
Beach Scene with Figures, Horse and Sailboats
Oil/canvas (60x76cm 24x30in) New-Orleans LA 1999
⌾ **$1 300** - €1 248 - **£815** - FF8 184
Flowering atmospheric Landscape Oil/canvas
(22x30cm 9x12in) Altadena CA 1999

ESPRIT Anne-Marie ?-1926 **[2]**
⌾ **$2 521** - €2 973 - **£1 772** - FF19 500
Pardon breton Huile/toile (65x81cm 25x31in) Lyon
2001

ESQUIVEL RIVAS Carlos María 1830-1867 **[3]**
⌾ **$22 780** - €20 422 - **£13 940** - FF133 960
Retrato de D.Mariano Roca de Togores Oleo/lien-
zo (102x82cm 40x32in) Madrid 1999

ESQUIVEL Y SUAREZ DE URBINA Antonio María
1806-1857 **[55]**
⌾ **$24 400** - €24 026 - **£15 200** - FF157 600
Maja desnuda Oleo/lienzo (105x163cm 41x64in)
Madrid 1999
⌾ **$5 100** - €5 106 - **£3 145** - FF33 490
**Retrato de dama de casi medio cuerpo con
vestido marrón y joyas** Oleo/lienzo (70x54.5cm
27x21in) Madrid 2000

$2 760 - €2 409 - **£1 680** - FF15 800
Escena de celos Oleo/lienzo (34.5x25.5cm 13x10in)
Madrid 1998

ESSAIAN Sergei Aramisovich 1939-? **[2]**
🎨 **$9 675** - €11 242 - **£6 800** - FF73 740
«Will you buy me a Wedding Ring ?» Bronze
(56x38.5x43cm 22x15x16in) London 2001

ESSCHE van Maurice 1906-1977 **[72]**
⌾ **$4 289** - €4 041 - **£2 597** - FF26 509
Blue Lamp Oil/board (89x59cm 35x23in) Cape Town
1999
⌾ **$1 635** - €1 575 - **£1 010** - FF10 334
Fisherfolk Oil/canvas/board (35x45.5cm 13x17in)
Johannesburg 1999
✎ **$433** - €485 - **£301** - FF3 183
Harlequin with a white Hat Gouache/paper
(46x25cm 18x9in) Johannesburg 2001

ESSELENS Jacob 1626-1687 **[12]**
⌾ **$30 000** - €26 315 - **£18 216** - FF172 614
Ships in a Calm Sea Oil/canvas (106.5x98cm
41x38in) New-York 1999
⌾ **$13 613** - €13 718 - **£8 485** - FF89 982
Bildnisse eines Amsterdamer Bürgerpaares
Huile/panneau (28.5x23cm 11x9in) Zürich 2000

ESSEN van Cornelis c.1700-c.1770 **[21]**
⌾ **$4 988** - €5 666 - **£3 500** - FF37 165
A highway Robbery by a Cottage Oil/canvas
(47.5x41cm 18x16in) London 2001
⌾ **$406** - €408 - **£267** - FF30 081
**Chevaliers au repos près d'un village hollan-
dais** Huile/panneau (29.2x37cm 11x14in) Antwerpen
1999

ESSEN van Jan 1854-1936 **[39]**
⌾ **$1 749** - €1 906 - **£1 205** - FF12 501
Hunting Still Life Oil/canvas (101x75cm 39x29in)
Amsterdam 2001
⌾ **$810** - €908 - **£563** - FF5 953
Eenden aan de waterkant Oil/canvas (51x31cm
20x12in) Rotterdam 2001

ESSEN van Jan XVII **[1]**
⌾ **$121 975** - €126 446 - **£73 185** - FF829 430
**Veduta di Napoli dal mar, con manifestazione
navale nella rada** Olio/tela (176x276cm 69x108in)
Venezia 2000

ESSEN von Didrik 1856-1922 **[1]**
⌾ **$3 827** - €4 373 - **£2 693** - FF28 683
Cows on the Beach Oil/canvas (67x97.5cm 26x38in)
Helsinki 2001

ESSENHIGH Inka 1969 **[2]**
⌾ **$45 000** - €51 293 - **£31 396** - FF336 460
«Beauty Contest» Oil/canvas (196x216cm 77x85in)
New-York 2001

ESSENTHIER Walter 1892-? **[3]**
🖼 **$1 586** - €1 599 - **£990** - FF10 487
«Cabaret Bonboniere» Poster (86x56cm 33x22in)
Wien 2000

ESSER Max 1885-1943 **[22]**
🐚 **$511** - €436 - **£308** - FF2 859
Möwe auf Welle Porcelain (H42.7cm H16in) Wien
1998

ESSIG George Emerick 1838-1926 **[29]**
⌾ **$1 600** - €1 552 - **£971** - FF10 180
Moonlight, New York Harbor #1 Oil/board
(34x49cm 13x19in) West-Chester PA 2000

E

$475 - €549 - **£332** - FF3 599
Close of Day Watercolour/paper (28x60.5cm 11x23in)
Bethesda MD 2001

ESTALELLA Ramón 1893-1986 **[15]**
$715 - €781 - **£455** - FF5 122
Palacio de La Granja Oleo/cartón (46x37cm
18x14in) Madrid 2000

ESTELA-ANTON Enrique XX **[1]**
$2 400 - €2 799 - **£1 685** - FF18 361
«Sevilla, fiestas de Primavera» Poster
(108.5x157cm 42x61in) New-York 2000

ESTERL Martin 1947 **[3]**
$2 172 - €1 816 - **£1 287** - FF11 910
April, April...,«Thema Fisch» Mischtechnik/Papier
(49x70cm 19x27in) Wien 1998

ESTERLE von Max 1870-1947 **[5]**
$4 784 - €4 678 - **£2 954** - FF30 687
Gebirgswinterlandschaft Gouache/Karton
(34x48cm 13x18in) Zürich 1998

ESTES Richard 1932 **[133]**
$320 000 - €300 342 - **£197 696** - FF1 970 112
Broadway and 64th, Spring '84 Oil/canvas
(100x180cm 39x70in) New-York 1999
$220 000 - €190 453 - **£132 682** - FF1 249 292
Hot Foods Oil/canvas (122x76cm 48x29in) New-York
1998
$1 400 - €1 586 - **£978** - FF10 406
At the Playground Watercolour, gouache (9.8x14cm
3x5in) New-York 2001
$3 400 - €2 930 - **£2 019** - FF19 219
Venezia Murano/Escalator Screenprint in colors
(51x37cm 20x14in) New-York 1998

ESTEVAN Y VICENTE Enrique 1849-1927 **[12]**
$1 116 - €1 081 - **£684** - FF7 092
Salmantinos Oleo/lienzo (39x30cm 15x11in) Madrid
1999

ESTEVE Antonio 1855-1925 **[7]**
$1 025 - €1 184 - **£709** - FF7 769
Camino junto al pinar Oleo/lienzo (52x84cm
20x33in) Barcelona 2000

ESTEVE Maurice 1904-2001 **[575]**
$57 960 - €54 011 - **£35 000** - FF354 287
Charoute Oil/canvas (65x54cm 25x21in) London 1998
$16 592 - €15 321 - **£10 331** - FF100 500
Corbeille de fruits Huile/toile (22x35cm 8x13in)
Douai 1999
$13 048 - €10 754 - **£7 680** - FF70 544
Komposition Akvarell/papper (53x43cm 20x16in)
Köbenhavn 1998
$736 - €696 - **£445** - FF4 563
Lunaire administratif Color lithograph (62x46.5cm
24x18in) Stockholm 1999

ESTEVE Miguel XVI **[2]**
$13 629 - €14 334 - **£9 000** - FF94 025
Noli Me Tangere and The Resurrection Oil/panel
(56.5x50cm 22x19in) London 2000

ESTEVE Y BOTEY Francisco 1884-1955 **[23]**
$2 106 - €2 343 - **£1 443** - FF15 366
El claustro del monasterio de Samos en flor
Acuarela/papel (51x39cm 20x15in) Madrid 2001
$350 - €300 - **£215** - FF1 970
Retrato de Palafox Aguafuerte (33x23cm 12x9in)
Madrid 1998

ESTEVE Y MARQUES Agustín 1753-1809/20 **[10]**
$33 492 - €28 514 - **£20 000** - FF187 042
Portrait of a Lady, Three Quarter length seated
Oil/canvas (112x77.5cm 44x30in) London 1998

ESTIENNE d' Henry 1872-1949 **[387]**
$10 000 - €8 637 - **£6 028** - FF56 657
Young Lady at her Toilet Oil/canvas (148x132cm
58x51in) New-York 1998
$1 424 - €1 677 - **£1 001** - FF11 000
Le bain maure Huile/panneau (40x52cm 15x20in)
Paris 2000
$1 043 - €1 220 - **£744** - FF8 000
Mauresque au jardin Huile/panneau (27x35cm
10x13in) Paris 2001
$1 306 - €1 403 - **£874** - FF9 200
Jeune bretonne attablée Fusain (43x46cm 16x18in)
Nantes 2000

ESTRADA Adolfo 1927 **[20]**
$2 430 - €2 703 - **£1 620** - FF17 730
Mujer sentada Oleo/lienzo (73x92cm 28x36in)
Madrid 2000
$911 - €838 - **£563** - FF5 500
Village d'Espagne Huile/toile (26x33.5cm 10x13in)
Paris 1999

ESTRANY Y ROS Rafael 1884-1958 **[12]**
$2 117 - €1 742 - **£1 247** - FF11 426
Catedral de Burgos Oleo/lienzo (100x81cm
39x31in) Madrid 1998

ESTRUGA Oscar 1933 **[41]**
$308 - €330 - **£209** - FF2 167
Muchachas Gouache/papier (50x65cm 19x25in)
Madrid 2001

ÉTAIX Pierre 1928 **[8]**
$430 - €396 - **£258** - FF2 600
«Mon Oncle» Affiche (120x160cm 47x62in) Paris
1999

ETCHART Severo Rodriguez 1864-? **[2]**
$34 063 - €35 063 - **£21 459** - FF230 000
Femme au harem Huile/toile (132x161cm 51x63in)
Paris 2000

ETCHELLS Frederick 1886-1973 **[6]**
$2 584 - €2 430 - **£1 600** - FF15 939
Portrait of the Artist's Wife Pencil (46x30.5cm
18x12in) London 1999

ETCHEVERRY Denis 1867-1950 **[23]**
$766 - €732 - **£479** - FF4 800
«L'Andalousie au temps des Maures» Affiche
(260x94cm 102x37in) Orléans 1999

ETHOFER Theodor Josef 1849-1915 **[7]**
$5 634 - €6 541 - **£3 960** - FF42 903
Banco del'Lotto in der Via S.Eustachio Oil/panel
(54.5x34.5cm 21x13in) Wien 2001
$2 354 - €2 653 - **£1 630** - FF17 410
Washing Day Oil/panel (29x44.5cm 11x17in) Toronto
2000

ETIDLUI Kingmeata 1915-1989 **[2]**
$430 - €462 - **£292** - FF3 029
Bird Sentinel Print in colors (15.5x22cm 6x8in)
Calgary, Alberta 2001

ÉTIENNE 1952 **[13]**
$22 720 - €24 392 - **£15 200** - FF160 000
Le baiser Bronze (126x78x40cm 49x30x15in) Paris
2000
$4 315 - €4 421 - **£2 685** - FF29 000
La lecture Bronze (34x32cm 13x12in) Paris 2000

ETIENNE Patrick 1953 **[18]**
- $201 - €229 - **£141** - FF1 500
  Charette et moissonneurs Huile/toile (24x33cm 9x12in) Paris 2001

ÉTIENNE-MARTIN 1913-1995 **[43]**
- $104 775 - €114 337 - **£71 100** - FF750 000
  Le dragon Sculpture bois (100x200x80cm 39x78x31in) Paris 2000
- $2 382 - €2 287 - **£1 494** - FF15 000
  Le Sphinx (étude) Sculpture bois (30x27cm 11x10in) Vannes 1999
- $6 500 - €5 608 - **£3 921** - FF36 785
  La Knoud Bronze (53.5x61cm 21x24in) New-York 1998
- $2 212 - €1 829 - **£1 298** - FF12 000
  Maquette pour la nuit d'Oppède Aquarelle (32x31cm 12x12in) Paris 1998

ETNIER Stephen Morgan 1903-1984 **[42]**
- $15 000 - €13 948 - **£9 259** - FF91 494
  Bath Iron Works Oil/canvas (101x127cm 40x50in) Portland ME 1999
- $7 500 - €6 974 - **£4 629** - FF45 747
  Ash Cove, South Harpswell Oil/canvas (40x91cm 16x36in) Portland ME 1999
- $1 800 - €2 026 - **£1 240** - FF13 288
  Study for «The Big Race» Oil/canvas (20x25cm 8x10in) New-Orleans LA 2000

ETROG Sorel 1933 **[76]**
- $12 954 - €15 113 - **£9 016** - FF99 136
  Mythological Figure Bronze (H179cm H70in) Toronto 2000
- $1 460 - €1 653 - **£1 022** - FF10 840
  Pieton Bronze (H21.5cm H8in) Toronto 2001

ETTING Emlen 1905-1992 **[72]**
- $775 - €650 - **£454** - FF4 265
  «Woman with a Shell» Oil/canvas (54x40cm 21x16in) Philadelphia PA 1998

ETTINGER Churchill 1903-1985 **[30]**
- $110 - €118 - **£73** - FF777
  Thunder and Lightning Etching (22x16cm 9x6in) Cleveland OH 2000

ETTY William 1787-1849 **[139]**
- $20 984 - €19 426 - **£13 000** - FF127 424
  Master Hardcastle Oil/canvas (135x110cm 53x43in) London 1999
- $5 743 - €6 438 - **£4 000** - FF42 229
  Seated Nude Oil/board (40x50cm 15x19in) London 2001
- $4 037 - €4 462 - **£2 800** - FF29 268
  Study of a Female Nude Oil/board (18x24cm 7x9in) London 2001
- $400 - €411 - **£250** - FF2 695
  Reclining Male Nude Charcoal (36.5x29.5cm 14x11in) London 2000

EUBANKS Tony 1939 **[2]**
- $15 000 - €17 098 - **£10 465** - FF112 153
  Toas Winter Morning Oil/canvas (81x121cm 32x48in) Dallas TX 2001

EUDES DE GUIMARD Louise 1827-? **[4]**
- $6 965 - €5 946 - **£4 165** - FF39 000
  Orientale aux bracelets Huile/toile (74x61cm 29x24in) Paris 1998

EUGEN OF SWEDEN Prince 1865-1947 **[97]**
- $5 712 - €6 633 - **£4 014** - FF43 512
  Finnboda från Biskopsudden Oil/panel (50x74cm 19x29in) Stockholm 2001

- $5 937 - €5 163 - **£3 580** - FF33 868
  «Studie, djurgården III» Oil/panel (32x35cm 12x13in) Stockholm 1998
- $1 444 - €1 626 - **£995** - FF10 669
  Utsikt från Waldemarsudde Akvarell/papper (22x30cm 8x11in) Stockholm 2000

EUGENE Frank 1865-1936 **[20]**
- $278 - €332 - **£198** - FF2 180
  Willi Geiger Photogravure (17.8x12.8cm 7x5in) München 2000

EULER Pierre Nicolas 1846-1915 **[14]**
- $1 157 - €1 250 - **£800** - FF8 500
  Bouquet de roses Huile/toile (38x53cm 14x20in) Lyon 2001

EULERT Albert 1890-1946 **[6]**
- $45 - €51 - **£31** - FF335
  Rostock: Kröpeliner Tor Radierung (26x18cm 10x7in) Satow 2000

EURICH Richard Ernest 1903-1992 **[116]**
- $7 604 - €8 209 - **£5 200** - FF53 848
  Fawley Beach Oil/canvas (62x75cm 24x29in) Bristol, Avon 2001
- $5 047 - €5 577 - **£3 500** - FF36 585
  Portrait of a Gentleman Oil/canvas (25.5x18cm 10x7in) London 2000

EUSEBIO DA SAN GIORGIO 1465/70-c.1540 **[2]**
- $26 400 - €34 210 - **£19 800** - FF224 400
  Madonna col Bambino Olio/tavola (40x32cm 15x12in) Prato 2000

EUSTACE Alfred William 1820-1907 **[13]**
- $4 168 - €4 957 - **£2 970** - FF32 514
  Man by the Edge of the River Oil/board (34.5x46.5cm 13x18in) Melbourne 2000
- $1 151 - €1 079 - **£712** - FF7 075
  The Stream Oil/canvas (21x29cm 8x11in) Melbourne 1999

EVANS A.E. XIX **[5]**
- $5 000 - €4 634 - **£3 109** - FF30 490
  Courtown, a bay hunter in a stable Oil/canvas (63x76cm 24x29in) New-York 1999

EVANS Bernard Walter 1843-1922 **[53]**
- $1 232 - €1 348 - **£850** - FF8 845
  La Napoule, South of France Watercolour/paper (37x52cm 14x20in) London 2001

EVANS Cerith Wyn 1958 **[3]**
- $4 482 - €4 812 - **£3 000** - FF31 564
  Tix3 Sculpture (14x34x2cm 5x13xin) London 2000

EVANS David 1929-1988 **[8]**
- $350 - €407 - **£250** - FF2 670
  The Haunted Garden Watercolour/paper (73x47.5cm 28x18in) Norfolk 2001

EVANS De Scott 1847-1898 **[29]**
- $60 500 - €57 747 - **£37 655** - FF374 991
  Portrait of Two girls in wide brim hats seated in an orchard bench Oil/canvas (40x50cm 16x20in) Plainfield NH 1999
- $16 000 - €17 763 - **£11 128** - FF116 518
  The Irish Question Oil/canvas (29x24cm 11x9in) Milford CT 2001

EVANS Frederick Henry 1853-1943 **[79]**
- $10 000 - €10 077 - **£6 234** - FF66 100
  The Strength of the Normans Platinum print (18.5x23cm 7x9in) New-York 2000

EVANS Frederick McNamara act.1886-1930 [61]
🖋 **$1 925** - €1 940 - **£1 200** - FF12 724
The Lantern-Newlyn Fisherman's
Watercolour/paper (30x23cm 12x9in) Fernhurst,
Haslemere, Surrey 2000

EVANS James Guy c.1810-1860 [3]
🖼 **$30 000** - €29 724 - **£18 201** - FF194 976
**The second United States Customs House,
New Orleans** Oil/canvas (96.5x78cm 37x30in) New-
York 2000

EVANS Jane 1946 [10]
🖋 **$1 993** - €2 095 - **£1 312** - FF13 741
Wheat Harvest Festival, Provence Gouache/paper
(60x40cm 23x15in) Auckland 2000

EVANS Marjorie c.1850-1907 [2]
🖼 **$2 556** - €2 610 - **£1 600** - FF17 094
Still Life of Roses and a Vase Oil/canvas
(36x132cm 14x51in) London 2000

EVANS Merlyn Oliver 1910-1973 [31]
🖼 **$5 259** - €4 998 - **£3 200** - FF32 782
Composition Oil/board (76.5x152.5cm 30x60in)
London 1999
🗐 **$350** - €323 - **£210** - FF2 116
City at Night Etching (79x56cm 31x22in) Glamorgan
1999

EVANS Minnie Jones 1892-1987 [17]
🖼 **$11 000** - €9 490 - **£6 660** - FF62 252
«At Airlie Garden» Mixed media/canvas (51x61.5cm
20x24in) New-York 1999
🖼 **$3 749** - €3 235 - **£2 270** - FF21 219
«Airlie Oak» Mixed media (33x43cm 12x16in) New-
York 1999
🖼 **$2 000** - €1 726 - **£1 207** - FF11 322
Face in Flowers/Abstract Faces Crayon (44x34cm
17x13in) New-York 1999

EVANS OF BRISTOL William 1809-1858 [11]
🖋 **$1 147** - €1 056 - **£700** - FF6 930
Near Frant, East Sussex Watercolour (25.5x35.5cm
10x13in) London 1998

EVANS OF ETON Samuel T.G. 1829-1904 [8]
🖋 **$5 977** - €6 416 - **£4 000** - FF42 086
**Market Boats on a Lake Traun in the
Salzkammergut, Austria** Watercolour (65x121cm
25x47in) London 2000

EVANS OF ETON William 1798-1877 [21]
🖋 **$2 565** - €2 466 - **£1 600** - FF16 170
**Eton College from the River with Eel Traps to
the Right** Watercolour/paper (26.5x37.5cm 10x14in)
Billingshurst, West-Sussex 1999

EVANS Ray 1920 [3]
🖋 **$515** - €578 - **£360** - FF3 790
«Coal Mine, Hafod» Watercolour (33.5x49cm
13x19in) Billingshurst, West-Sussex 2001

EVANS Rudulph 1878-1960 [1]
🗿 **$13 000** - €15 104 - **£9 136** - FF99 075
George Washington Marble (H152cm H59in) New-
York 2001

EVANS Walker 1903-1975 [451]
📷 **$6 000** - €5 665 - **£3 726** - FF37 163
New York Gelatin silver print (20.5x25.5cm 8x10in)
New-York 1999

EVANS Will 1888-1957 [7]
🖼 **$4 331** - €3 987 - **£2 600** - FF26 151
Swansea Bay and Mumbles from Townhill
Oil/canvas (51x68cm 20x26in) Glamorgan 1999

EVANS 🖋 **$837** - €791 - **£520** - FF5 186
Cattle grazing on Linton Common
Watercolour/paper (33x41cm 13x16in) Little-Lane,
Ilkley 1999

EVAUL William 1949 [2]
🗐 **$700** - €754 - **£477** - FF4 948
New York Skyline Woodcut in colors (28x43cm
11x16in) New-York 2001

EVE Jean 1900-1968 [71]
🖼 **$4 000** - €3 356 - **£2 346** - FF22 014
Printemps : St. Pierre de Bailleul Oil/canvas
(53.5x65.5cm 21x25in) New-York 1998
🖼 **$952** - €1 067 - **£662** - FF7 000
Venise, San Gorgio de Eléna Huile/toile (27x19cm
10x7in) Le Touquet 2001

EVEN André 1918-1996 [123]
🖼 **$448** - €534 - **£319** - FF3 500
Paysage aux fermes et aux champs jaunes
Huile/toile (54x73cm 21x28in) Brest 2000
🖼 **$236** - €259 - **£164** - FF1 700
Pont-Aven Huile/toile (30x40cm 11x15in) Brest 2001

EVEN Jean 1910-1986 [55]
🖋 **$531** - €579 - **£348** - FF3 800
Voilier près des barques Aquarelle/papier (47x63cm
18x24in) Brest 2000
🗐 **$259** - €295 - **£180** - FF1 934
«Air France, Amerique du Nord» Poster
(62x100cm 24x39in) Hoorn 2001

EVENEPOEL Henri Jacques 1872-1899 [86]
🖼 **$4 663** - €4 346 - **£2 877** - FF28 508
Weiblicher Akt Öl/Leinwand (80x50cm 31x19in)
Köln 2001
🖼 **$11 050** - €12 394 - **£7 700** - FF81 300
Le narghile Huile/toile (35.5x27.5cm 13x10in)
Bruxelles 2001
🖋 **$834** - €818 - **£514** - FF5 365
Portret van Hugues Imbert Pencil/paper (29x21cm
11x8in) Lokeren 1999
🗐 **$351** - €409 - **£242** - FF2 682
Femme sur une plage Lithographie (31x25cm
12x9in) Liège 2000

EVENO Edouard 1884-1980 [13]
🖼 **$2 184** - €2 439 - **£1 480** - FF16 000
La panthère noire Huile/toile (60x92cm 23x36in)
Pontoise 2000
🖋 **$1 092** - €1 220 - **£740** - FF8 000
La lionne blessée Crayon (58x78cm 22x30in)
Pontoise 2000

EVERARD Bertha, née King 1873-1965 [3]
🖼 **$2 799** - €2 901 - **£1 773** - FF19 032
Green Trees Oil/board (24x32cm 9x12in)
Johannesburg 2000

EVERARD-HADEN Ruth 1902-1992 [3]
🖼 **$75 009** - €77 749 - **£47 511** - FF509 999
Flat on the Boulevard Edgar Quinet Oil/canvas
(90.5x72cm 35x28in) Johannesburg 2000

EVERARD-STEENKAMP Rosamund King 1907-
1946 [2]
🖼 **$6 640** - €7 705 - **£4 585** - FF50 540
The Blue Furrow Oil/canvas/board (54.5x45.5cm
21x17in) Johannesburg 2000

EVERBAG Frans 1877-1947 [16]
🗐 **$164** - €181 - **£111** - FF1 190
Lijnbaansgracht met links de Lauriergracht
Etching in colors (28.6x23.1cm 11x9in) Haarlem 2000

EVERBROECK van Franz 1638-c.1672 **[5]**
- $18 500 - €17 660 - **£11 558** - FF115 839
  Lady Amongst Chatelaine Oil/canvas (105x84cm 41x33in) Dedham MA 1999

EVERDINGEN van Adrianus 1832-1912 **[43]**
- $1 941 - €2 269 - **£1 386** - FF10 534
  Extensive River Landscape Oil/canvas (75x123cm 29x48in) Amsterdam 2001
- $1 916 - €2 178 - **£1 323** - FF14 287
  Zomerlandschap Oil/panel (27x35cm 10x13in) Dordrecht 2000
- $441 - €458 - **£280** - FF3 003
  Pastoral Landscape at Sunset, with Cattle and Boy on a Lane Watercolour/paper (29x47cm 11x18in) Cheshire 2000

EVERDINGEN van Allart 1621-1675 **[125]**
- $106 027 - €118 881 - **£72 000** - FF779 810
  Extensive Wooded Landscape with a Covered Wagon Approaching a Cottage Oil/canvas (74.5x86.5cm 29x34in) London 2000
- $107 - €102 - **£65** - FF670
  Drei Männer auf dem Felsen, in Gebirgslandschaft Acrylique/masonite (9.1x13.3cm 3x5in) Köln 1999
- $1 592 - €1 355 - **£950** - FF8 885
  Two Men Crossing a Bridge in a Landscape Ink (11x15cm 4x5in) London 1998
- $171 - €184 - **£114** - FF1 207
  Die Landschaft mit der hölzernen Brücke Radierung (16.4x19.2cm 6x7in) Berlin 2000

EVERDINGEN van Caesar Boëtius 1617/21-1678 **[5]**
- $93 384 - €91 795 - **£60 000** - FF602 136
  Artemisia Oil/canvas (79x67cm 31x26in) London 1999

EVEREN van Jay 1875-1947 **[5]**
- $6 500 - €7 381 - **£4 448** - FF48 417
  Abstraction Oil/panel (25x38cm 9x14in) New-York 2000
- $2 000 - €2 345 - **£1 438** - FF15 382
  Abstraction Watercolour/paper (19.5x19.5cm 7x7in) New-York 2001

EVERGOOD Philip Howard 1901-1973 **[91]**
- $6 000 - €6 824 - **£4 192** - FF44 760
  «Shrimp Girl» Oil/canvas (50x40cm 20x16in) New-York 2000
- $1 700 - €1 994 - **£1 223** - FF13 078
  Self Portrait Oil/masonite (35.5x29cm 13x11in) New-York 2001
- $550 - €517 - **£343** - FF3 394
  Let us harvest the Earth together Ink (62x48cm 24x18in) New-York 1999

EVERSDYCK Cornelis Willemsz. c.1590-c.1644 **[2]**
- $13 539 - €13 779 - **£9 500** - FF100 870
  A Still Life of Vegetables and Fruit Oil/canvas (61x73.5cm 24x28in) London 2001

EVERSEN Adrianus 1818-1897 **[155]**
- $45 030 - €51 130 - **£31 290** - FF335 390
  Stadtansicht Öl/Leinwand (41x58cm 16x22in) Köln 2001
- $15 929 - €16 578 - **£10 000** - FF108 746
  Figures in a Dutch Street Oil/panel (27x21.5cm 10x8in) London 2000
- $1 193 - €1 156 - **£797** - FF7 580
  Figures in a Town Square Watercolour (24.5x34.5cm 9x13in) London 1999

EVERSEN Johannes Hendrik 1906-1995 **[33]**
- $13 451 - €12 706 - **£8 391** - FF83 344
  Still Life with Pottery and Eggs on a Pewter Plate Oil/canvas (51x71cm 20x27in) Amsterdam 1999
- $9 158 - €10 891 - **£6 528** - FF71 438
  Still Life of a Pewter Jug, Pears and Walnuts Oil/panel (39x32cm 15x12in) Amsterdam 2000

EVES Reginald Grenville 1876-1941 **[24]**
- $960 - €917 - **£600** - FF6 012
  Lady, quarter-length, in a Blue Dress Oil/canvas (61x51cm 24x20in) London 1999

EVOLA Julius / Giulio 1898-1974 **[10]**
- $38 000 - €39 393 - **£22 800** - FF258 400
  Paesaggio interiore ore 3 A.M Olio/tela (112x65cm 44x25in) Milano 2000
- $15 000 - €15 550 - **£9 000** - FF102 000
  Senza titolo Tempera/carta (90x49cm 35x19in) Milano 2000

EVRARD Paula 1876-1927 **[21]**
- $540 - €496 - **£332** - FF3 252
  Jeune fille au bouquet Pastel/papier (72x55.5cm 28x21in) Bruxelles 1999

EWALD Reinhold 1890-1974 **[14]**
- $943 - €1 125 - **£672** - FF7 378
  Akt mit Mantel Öl/Leinwand (102x81cm 40x31in) Frankfurt 2000

EWART Peter 1918 **[43]**
- $251 - €270 - **£168** - FF1 771
  Whyte & 82nd Ave. Edmonton Oil/canvas/board (25.5x30.5cm 10x12in) Vancouver, BC. 2000

EWBANK John Wilson 1779-1847 **[32]**
- $1 657 - €1 868 - **£1 159** - FF12 251
  Segelfartyg i storm Oil/canvas (111x142cm 43x55in) Stockholm 2001
- $2 584 - €2 897 - **£1 800** - FF19 003
  Mouth of the River Tyne, north and South Shields from the Middens Oil/canvas (63x102cm 24x40in) Leyburn, North Yorkshire 2001

EWBANK Thomas John ?-c.1862 **[2]**
- $8 823 - €8 891 - **£5 500** - FF58 319
  Rosina with Jockey Up on Lincoln Racehorse Oil/canvas (58x73cm 22x28in) London 2000

EWELL James Cady XX **[1]**
- $30 000 - €32 832 - **£20 694** - FF215 364
  The Spirit of Transportation Oil/canvas (132x92cm 51x36in) New-York 2001

EWEN William Patterson 1925 **[10]**
- $4 738 - €4 550 - **£2 936** - FF29 846
  Abstract Acrylic/canvas (30.5x30.5cm 12x12in) Toronto 1999
- $198 - €231 - **£135** - FF1 517
  Abstration au triangle Lithographie (62x46cm 24x18in) Montréal 2000

EWERS Heinrich 1817-1885 **[6]**
- $5 705 - €5 336 - **£3 496** - FF35 000
  Le montreur de singes Huile/toile (112x84cm 44x33in) Paris 1998

EWING G. XIX-XX **[2]**
- $4 482 - €4 812 - **£3 000** - FF31 564
  Village F te Watercolour/paper (76x102cm 29x40in) London 2000

EWING Leckie **[3]**
- $2 292 - €2 126 - **£1 400** - FF13 944
  The First Hole, Maxwell Bank Lade Braes, St Andrews Watercolour/paper (15x24cm 5x9in) Glasgow 1998

EXEL Ria 1915-1985 **[20]**
📖 **$53** - €59 - **£36** - FF387
    Carnaval Lithograph (35.5x45.5cm 13x17in) Haarlem 2000

EXNER Julius 1825-1910 **[129]**
🖎 **$24 860** - €26 828 - **£16 680** - FF175 980
    Almueinteriør med ung pige, der laeser op for sine bedsteforaeldre Oil/canvas (142x173cm 55x68in) København 2000
🖎 **$22 540** - €18 820 - **£13 398** - FF123 452
    «De små naboer» Oil/canvas (70x66cm 27x25in) København 1998
🖎 **$1 777** - €1 614 - **£1 101** - FF10 588
    Portraet af en lille pige og på bagsiden køkkeninteriör Oil/canvas (32x25cm 12x9in) København 1999
✎ **$217** - €215 - **£135** - FF1 411
    En kone, der fejer Pencil/paper (21x17.5cm 8x6in) København 1999

EXPORT Valie 1940 **[16]**
📷 **$2 408** - €2 035 - **£1 430** - FF13 350
    Genitalpanik, Unikat Gelatin silver print (40.6x30.2cm 15x11in) Wien 1998

EXTER Alexandra Alexandrov 1884-1949 **[98]**
🖎 **$26 240** - €30 490 - **£18 440** - FF200 000
    Femme à la corbeille de fruits Huile/toile (93x73cm 36x28in) Paris 2001
🖎 **$22 110** - €23 574 - **£15 000** - FF154 635
    Two Costumed Figures for a Shakespearian Play (Romeo and Juliet) Mixed media (16.5x30x14cm 6x11x5in) London 2001
✎ **$9 840** - €11 434 - **£6 915** - FF75 000
    Projet de costume féminin Gouache/papier (52.5x35cm 20x13in) Paris 2001

EXTER Julius 1863-1939 **[3]**
🖎 **$8 310** - €9 203 - **£5 635** - FF60 370
    Flusslandschaft Öl/Leinwand (65x62cm 25x24in) Hamburg 2000
🖎 **$10 526** - €12 271 - **£7 377** - FF80 493
    Chiemsee Öl/Karton (36x44cm 14x17in) München 2000

EYBL Franz 1806-1880 **[38]**
🖎 **$1 264** - €1 163 - **£758** - FF7 627
    Portrait eines Herrn Öl/Leinwand (53.5x42.5cm 21x16in) Wien 1999
🖎 **$837** - €976 - **£587** - FF6 404
    Portrait de femme Miniature (13.5x9cm 5x3in) Warszawa 2000
✎ **$1 540** - €1 453 - **£956** - FF9 534
    Bildnis des Josef Hrabe Jelacic in Uniform Aquarell/Papier (30x22cm 11x8in) Wien 1999

EYCK Charles 1897-1983 **[73]**
🖎 **$2 592** - €2 496 - **£1 620** - FF16 371
    «Waar Eens de Halles van Parijs Stonden» Oil/canvas (50x60cm 19x23in) Amsterdam 1999
⚒ **$1 225** - €1 180 - **£766** - FF7 739
    Mother with Child Sculpture, wood (H31cm H12in) Amsterdam 1999
✎ **$305** - €352 - **£211** - FF2 306
    Arabier (Arab) Ink (20x16cm 7x6in) Maastricht 2000

EYCK van Gaspar 1613-1673 **[4]**
🖎 **$9 500** - €8 794 - **£5 735** - FF57 688
    Ships in a Calm Sea Oil/panel (36.5x71cm 14x27in) New-York 1999

EYCKEN van den Charles 1809-1891 **[20]**
🖎 **$8 521** - €7 088 - **£5 003** - FF46 492
    An Extensive Mountainous Landscape with a Peasant on a Sandy Track Oil/panel (86x110cm 33x43in) Amsterdam 1998
🖎 **$1 046** - €1 123 - **£700** - FF7 369
    Figures on a Path with the Coast Beyond Oil/canvas (33.5x46cm 13x18in) London 2000

EYCKEN van den Charles, Jnr. 1859-1923 **[59]**
🖎 **$10 656** - €11 898 - **£7 440** - FF78 048
    The Cat Oil/canvas (97x147cm 38x57in) Bruxelles 2001
🖎 **$6 192** - €5 949 - **£3 816** - FF39 024
    Gentille et Manon Huile/toile (52.5x64cm 20x25in) Bruxelles 1999
🖎 **$2 982** - €3 470 - **£2 128** - FF22 764
    Chaton et papillon Huile/panneau (24x18cm 9x7in) Antwerpen 2001

EYCKEN van den Felix XIX **[17]**
🖎 **$1 201** - €1 134 - **£749** - FF7 441
    Domestic Family Scene Oil/panel (27x36cm 10x14in) Amsterdam 1999

EYCKEN van den Marie XIX-XX **[6]**
🖎 **$782** - €838 - **£533** - FF5 500
    Moutons et poules Huile/panneau (18x24cm 7x9in) Calais 2001

EYCKEN van Jean Baptiste 1809-1853 **[4]**
🖎 **$7 616** - €8 428 - **£5 168** - FF55 284
    La belle Vénitienne Huile/toile (122x101cm 48x39in) Antwerpen 2000

EYCKERMANS Arnold XX **[2]**
📖 **$703** - €640 - **£431** - FF4 200
    «Brasserie D.A·V Gosselies» Affiche (65x46.5cm 25x18in) Saint-Cloud 1999

EYDEN William Arnold 1893-1982 **[23]**
🖎 **$450** - €486 - **£311** - FF3 188
    Coastal Scene Oil/canvas (60x76cm 24x30in) Cincinnati OH 2001

EYDZIATOWICZOWA Helena 1840-? **[2]**
🖎 **$1 639** - €1 751 - **£1 117** - FF11 487
    Portrait de fillette Huile/toile (44x33cm 17x12in) Warszawa 2001

EYER Johann Adam 1755-1837 **[6]**
✎ **$9 500** - €9 794 - **£5 735** - FF57 688
    Winged Seraph above crownded Flower: Fraktur Reward of Merit Watercolour (13.5x8cm 5x3in) New-York 1999

EYMER Arnoldus Johannes 1803-1863 **[21]**
🖎 **$5 382** - €4 659 - **£3 267** - FF30 563
    Sommerlandschaft mit Figuren und Schafen Oil/panel (34x56cm 13x22in) Zürich 1998
🖎 **$556** - €544 - **£356** - FF3 571
    Driving in the Cattle before the Storm Bursts Oil/board (25.5x31cm 10x12in) Amsterdam 1999

EYMONNET Jean 1815-? **[3]**
🖎 **$12 307** - €14 635 - **£8 774** - FF96 000
    La toilette Huile/toile (158x107cm 62x42in) Lyon 2000

EYRE Gladstone 1863-1933 **[44]**
✎ **$168** - €174 - **£106** - FF1 142
    Athol Garden Watercolour/paper (25x52cm 9x20in) Sydney 2000

EYRE John 1771-? **[2]**
📖 **$855** - €795 - **£527** - FF5 215
    New South Wales, Views of Sydney Lithograph (33.5x49cm 13x19in) Melbourne 1999

EYRE John c.1850-1927 **[10]**

$2 756 - €2 667 - **£1 700** - FF17 496
Dynchurch on the Romney Marshes - The English Holland Watercolour/paper (30.5x91.5cm 12x36in) London 1999

EYRES Emily c.1850-c.1910 **[5]**

$865 - €956 - **£600** - FF6 271
Portrait of a Young girl with White Bonnet Tied a Pink Ribbon Pastel/paper (40x41cm 15x16in) Oxfordshire 2001

EYSEN Louis 1843-1899 **[5]**

$11 236 - €10 226 - **£7 020** - FF67 078
Früchtestilleben Öl/Leinwand (50.5x70.5cm 19x27in) München 1999

$11 797 - €10 737 - **£7 371** - FF70 431
Motiv aus Bad Kissingen Öl/Leinwand/Karton (27.5x20.3cm 10x7in) München 1999

EYSKENS Félix 1882-1968 **[74]**

$332 - €397 - **£238** - FF2 601
Stilleven met vissen (nature morte aux poissons) Huile/toile (40x60cm 15x23in) Antwerpen 2000

EYTON Anthony 1923 **[44]**

$6 416 - €6 466 - **£4 000** - FF42 414
Seated Female Nude Oil/canvas (127x102cm 50x40in) London 2000

$2 381 - €2 033 - **£1 400** - FF13 333
«Chrys» Oil/canvas (73x81cm 28x31in) London 1998

$1 306 - €1 471 - **£900** - FF9 651
Atlantic Beach I Watercolour/paper (48x63.5cm 18x25in) London 2000

EYÜBOGLU Bedri Rahmi 1913-1975 **[4]**

$4 500 000 - €5 107 042 - **£3 000 000** - FF33 500 000
Jardin Huile/papier (23x33cm 9x12in) Istanbul 2001

$1 800 000 - €2 042 817 - **£1 200 000** - FF13 400 000
Troubadour Gouache/papier (32x24cm 12x9in) Istanbul 2001

EYÜBOGLU Eren 1912-1988 **[2]**

$3 465 000 - €3 932 422 - **£2 310 000** - FF25 795 000
Jeune femme debout Huile/panneau (181x75cm 71x29in) Istanbul 2001

EYVEAU Pietro 1855-? **[2]**

$5 600 - €7 257 - **£4 200** - FF47 600
Donna allo specchio Olio/tela (103x74cm 40x29in) Milano 2001

EZDORF Johann Christian M. 1801-1851 **[22]**

$19 810 - €22 985 - **£13 678** - FF150 773
Seenlandschaft bei abziehendem Gewitter Öl/Leinwand (101.1x138.2cm 39x54in) Luzern 2000

$2 002 - €2 279 - **£1 407** - FF14 946
Landskabsmotiv Oil/canvas (52x43cm 20x16in) Vejle 2001

EZEKIEL Moses Jacob 1844-1917 **[5]**

$4 000 - €3 730 - **£2 481** - FF24 466
Christopher Columbus Bronze (H64cm H25in) New-York 1999

EZEQUIEL (Garcia Lopez) 1940 **[8]**

$1 150 - €1 192 - **£690** - FF7 820
Il ballo Olio/tela (50x50cm 19x19in) Vercelli 2000

$650 - €674 - **£390** - FF4 420
La duetta Olio/masonite (40x30cm 15x11in) Vercelli 2000

EZQUERRA Jerónimo Antonio 1660-1733 **[4]**

$7 410 - €7 808 - **£4 680** - FF51 220
Sagrada Familia Oleo/lienzo (52x41cm 20x16in) Madrid 2000

F

FA RUOZHEN 1613-1696 **[4]**

$51 480 - €48 820 - **£31 320** - FF320 240
Snowly Landscape Ink (229x48.5cm 90x19in) Hong-Kong 1999

FABBI Alberto 1858-? **[3]**

$4 359 - €4 040 - **£2 710** - FF26 500
Danseuse orientale Huile/toile (105x70cm 41x27in) Vitry-Le-François 1999

FABBI Fabio 1861-1946 **[138]**

$42 000 - €36 236 - **£25 338** - FF237 690
A festive Street, Cairo Oil/canvas (102x136cm 40x53in) New-York 1998

$25 216 - €24 392 - **£15 552** - FF160 000
Délassement dans le jardin du palais Huile/toile (46x46cm 18x18in) Paris 1999

$2 429 - €2 607 - **£1 625** - FF17 104
Verkauf einer Sklavin Oil/panel (14x10cm 5x3in) Bremen 2000

$2 400 - €2 073 - **£1 200** - FF13 600
Le tre schiave arabe Tempera/carta (39x29cm 15x11in) Vercelli 1999

FABBIANI Juan Vicente 1910-1989 **[30]**

$1 105 - €1 001 - **£715** - FF6 565
Jarrón con flores y manzanas Oleo/lienzo (41.5x51cm 16x20in) Caracas 1999

FABBRI Agenore 1911-1998 **[75]**

$1 050 - €1 088 - **£630** - FF7 140
Composizione Tecnica mista/cartone (48x63cm 18x24in) Vercelli 2000

$1 800 - €2 332 - **£1 350** - FF15 300
Donna seduta Terracotta (H51cm H20in) Roma 2000

$350 - €363 - **£210** - FF2 380
Cavallo Gouache/carta (63.5x44cm 25x17in) Milano 1999

FABELO Roberto 1951 **[16]**

$21 000 - €22 541 - **£14 053** - FF147 861
Playa Santa María Oil/canvas (150x200cm 59x78in) New-York 2000

$21 000 - €20 432 - **£12 925** - FF134 028
Gran león rojo en el pequeño teatro Oil/canvas (81.5x100.5cm 32x39in) New-York 1999

$10 000 - €11 603 - **£6 904** - FF76 110
Pequeñas historias de amor Watercolour (76x56.5cm 29x22in) New-York 2000

FABER DU FAUR von Hans 1863-1949 **[50]**

$4 552 - €4 346 - **£2 844** - FF28 508
Drei Reiter Öl/Karton (56.7x74.5cm 22x29in) Köln 2000

$596 - €511 - **£358** - FF3 353
Tanzende Watercolour, gouache (16x7.6cm 6x2in) Hamburg 1998

FABER DU FAUR von Otto 1828-1901 **[56]**

$2 857 - €3 068 - **£1 912** - FF20 123
Ophelia Öl/Leinwand (78x113cm 30x44in) München 2000

FABER Herman 1832-1913 **[2]**
📇 $1 300 - €1 362 - **£856** - FF8 937
    Two Civil War Scouts on Horseback with Slaves
    Watercolour/paper (18x24cm 7x9in) Thomaston ME
    2000

FABER Johan 1754-? **[1]**
🖼 $3 736 - €3 732 - **£2 336** - FF24 483
    Puttenbacchanal Öl/Leinwand (134x77.5cm
    52x30in) Heidelberg 1999

FABER Johann XVIII **[4]**
🖼 $1 828 - €1 789 - **£1 124** - FF11 738
    Herakles und Omphale Öl/Leinwand (62x46cm
    24x18in) Stuttgart 1999

FABER Will 1901-1987 **[46]**
🖼 $1 359 - €1 177 - **£825** - FF7 718
    Pintura Tempera/Karton (47x88.3cm 18x34in)
    München 1998

FABI-ALTINI Francesco 1830-1906 **[4]**
🖼 $82 350 - €78 326 - **£50 000** - FF513 785
    Figure of Galatea Marble (H165cm H64in) London
    1999

FABIAN Gottfried 1905-1984 **[13]**
🖼 $5 856 - €5 814 - **£3 656** - FF38 136
    «2-67» Oil/panel (56.5x41cm 22x16in) Wien 1999
🖼 $2 928 - €2 907 - **£1 828** - FF19 068
    Plakatentwurf Indian ink (84x59cm 33x23in) Wien
    1999

FABIAN Max 1873-1926 **[6]**
🖼 $734 - €767 - **£465** - FF5 030
    Blühender Flieder vor einem Haus Öl/Leinwand
    (55x45cm 21x17in) München 2000

FABIANO Fabien 1883-1962 **[31]**
🖼 $812 - €899 - **£550** - FF5 898
    «Michelin Enveloppe Vélo» Poster (117x76cm
    46x29in) London 2000

FABIGAN Hans 1901-1975 **[7]**
🖼 $800 - €933 - **£561** - FF6 120
    «Rainerdiele» Poster (84x119cm 33x46in) New-York
    2000

FABIJANSKI PORAJ Stanislaw Ignacy 1865-1947
[21]
🖼 $771 - €904 - **£550** - FF5 931
    Intérieur de l'église Mariacki à Cracovie
    Huile/carton (38x33.5cm 14x13in) Warszawa 2000
🖼 $1 346 - €1 146 - **£803** - FF7 515
    Marsh Charcoal (32x43cm 12x16in) Warszawa 1998

FABIUS Jan 1820-1889 **[8]**
🖼 $892 - €1 050 - **£646** - FF6 887
    Rue de village Huile/toile (30.5x51cm 12x20in) Sion
    2001

FABRE François-Xavier 1766-1837 **[15]**
🖼 $62 000 - €58 331 - **£38 688** - FF382 626
    Young Man dressed as an Arcadian Shepherd
    Oil/canvas (70x52cm 27x20in) New-York 1999
🖼 $34 911 - €41 161 - **£24 543** - FF270 000
    Philoctète à qui Ulysse demande les flèches
    d'Hercule, île de Lemnos Huile/toile (28x44cm
    11x17in) Paris 2000

FABRE H. XIX **[10]**
🖼 $564 - €655 - **£400** - FF4 294
    Fishermen in the Harbour Oil/canvas (20x53cm
    7x20in) London 2000

FABRE Jan 1958 **[24]**
🖼 $3 676 - €3 107 - **£2 200** - FF20 380
    Spider Sculptures Installation (10x10x10cm
    3x3x3in) London 1998
🖼 $5 000 - €5 690 - **£3 513** - FF37 326
    Untitled Watercolour (231.5x152cm 91x59in) New-
    York 2001
📷 $1 173 - €1 264 - **£810** - FF8 292
    Sans titre Cibachrome print (80x60cm 31x23in)
    Antwerpen 2001

FABRES Y COSTA Antonio María 1854-1936 **[48]**
🖼 $112 332 - €125 268 - **£75 533** - FF821 705
    Sultan und Haremsdame Öl/Leinwand
    (101.5x170.5cm 39x67in) Ahlden 2000
🖼 $945 - €1 051 - **£630** - FF6 895
    Paisaje Oleo/lienzo (75x40cm 29x15in) Madrid 2000
🖼 $2 100 - €2 102 - **£1 295** - FF13 790
    Zingara Oleo/tabla (26x20cm 10x7in) Madrid 2000
🖼 $1 120 - €1 201 - **£760** - FF7 880
    Magistrado Acuarela/papel (26x18.5cm 10x7in)
    Madrid 2001

FABRI Pompeo 1874-1959 **[2]**
🖼 $1 400 - €1 451 - **£840** - FF9 520
    Roma, S. Maria in Aracoeli Acquarello/cartone
    (75x50cm 29x19in) Roma 1999

FABRI Ralph 1894-1975 **[5]**
🖼 $325 - €374 - **£224** - FF2 454
    «Americana (Library of Congress 2)» Etching
    (19x22cm 7x9in) Cleveland OH 2000

FABRIS Pietro act.1754-1804 **[28]**
🖼 $388 518 - €417 042 - **£260 000** - FF2 735 616
    A Mediterranean port scene with Fishermen
    drawing their Catch Oil/canvas (103x157cm
    40x61in) London 2000
🖼 $18 000 - €15 842 - **£10 958** - FF103 919
    Woman Spinning Wool, a Man Mending Shoes,
    and a Young Girl Oil/canvas (50x40.5cm 19x15in)
    New-York 1999
🖼 $7 929 - €9 452 - **£5 654** - FF62 000
    Sans titre Aquarelle/papier (21x39cm 8x15in) Saint-
    Martin-de-Crau 2000

FABRITIUS Barent c.1620-c.1675 **[4]**
🖼 $46 692 - €45 898 - **£30 000** - FF301 068
    Self-Portrait as Saint John the Evangelist
    Oil/canvas (99x83cm 38x32in) London 1999

FABRITIUS Reinhold 1850-1919 **[1]**
🖼 $2 061 - €2 018 - **£1 268** - FF13 238
    Mehiläishaukka Oil/canvas (31x35cm 12x13in)
    Helsinki 1999

FABRO Luciano 1936 **[5]**
🖼 $28 000 - €32 725 - **£19 990** - FF214 665
    Caspar David Friedrich Construction (157x70cm
    61x27in) Zürich 2001
🖼 $6 490 - €7 172 - **£4 500** - FF47 042
    Ogni ordine è contemporaneo d'ogni altro ordi-
    ne Screenprint (91x70cm 35x27in) London 2001

FABRY Ana 1963 **[2]**
🖼 $18 000 - €19 321 - **£12 045** - FF126 738
    Cabecillas y cabezones Mixed media
    (180.5x189.5cm 71x74in) New-York 2000
🖼 $14 000 - €13 622 - **£8 617** - FF89 352
    Demasiado cacique Oil/canvas (146.5x139cm
    57x54in) New-York 1999

FABRY Élysée 1882-1949 **[57]**
🖼 $662 - €793 - **£454** - FF5 203
    Paysage Huile/carton (46x56cm 18x22in) Bruxelles
    2000

F

FABRY Emile 1865-1966 **[22]**
- **$15 500** - €14 521 - **£9 318** - FF95 251
  Cercle de la vie Oil/canvas (135x173cm 53x68in)
  Amsterdam 1999
- **$4 990** - €4 227 - **£3 000** - FF27 726
  Two Young Women Oil/canvas (45x55cm 17x21in)
  London 1998

FABRY Jaro 1912-1953 **[1]**
- **$5 500** - €6 160 - **£3 821** - FF40 409
  Katarine Hepburn in Starry Cape loooking downward, Magazine Cover Gouache/paper
  (43x34cm 17x13in) New-York 2001

FACCHINETTI Nicolau Antonio 1824-1900 **[3]**
- **$14 274** - €14 989 - **£9 000** - FF98 322
  Casa e Chacara do Señor Dr.A.C.Valdectaro, Gavea, Dous Irmão Oil/paper/panel (12x29cm
  4x11in) London 2000

FACCINCANI Athos 1951 **[73]**
- **$1 500** - €1 555 - **£900** - FF10 200
  Cortina Olio/tela (90x100cm 35x39in) Vercelli 1999
- **$950** - €985 - **£570** - FF6 460
  Paesaggio Olio/tela (30x50cm 11x19in) Prato 1999

FACCINI Pietro c.1562-1602 **[21]**
- **$18 775** - €21 886 - **£13 000** - FF143 565
  The Entombment Oil/panel (29x20.5cm 11x8in)
  London 2000
- **$2 400** - €2 488 - **£1 440** - FF16 320
  Ritratto di prelato Sanguina/carta (23.5x20cm 9x7in)
  Milano 2001

FACCIOLI Girolamo ?-1573 **[2]**
- **$897** - €1 022 - **£626** - FF6 707
  Der verwundete Paris, nach Francesco Primaticcio Kupferstich (24x38cm 9x14in) Berlin
  2001

FACCIOLI Raffaele 1846-1916 **[3]**
- **$3 500** - €3 628 - **£2 100** - FF23 800
  Paesaggi invernali Olio/tela (47x32cm 18x12in)
  Roma 2000

FACHNLEIN Louis ?-1930 **[3]**
- **$9 900** - €10 812 - **£6 300** - FF70 920
  Descansado en el rincón del taller Oleo/lienzo
  (184x240cm 72x94in) Madrid 2000

FACKERE van de Jef 1879-1946 **[15]**
- **$621** - €744 - **£426** - FF4 878
  Aronskelken Huile/toile (74x83cm 29x32in)
  Antwerpen 2000
- **$1 973** - €1 815 - **£1 220** - FF11 906
  Portrait of a schoolgirl wearing a white baret
  Pastel/board (74x59cm 29x23in) Amsterdam 1999

FADEN William XVIII-XIX **[21]**
- **$494** - €471 - **£300** - FF3 091
  North America Engraving (53x64cm 20x25in)
  London 1999

FADER Fernando 1882-1935 **[8]**
- **$70 000** - €77 133 - **£46 557** - FF505 960
  Cerrazon Oleo/lienzo (80x100cm 31x39in) Buenos-Aires 2000

FAED James, Jnr. 1857-1920 **[17]**
- **$3 355** - €3 601 - **£2 245** - FF23 621
  Sunshine and Showers, Balenluig Oil/canvas
  (50.5x73.5cm 19x28in) Toronto 2000
- **$2 391** - €2 640 - **£1 500** - FF17 318
  The River Dee at Forrester Hill Oil/board
  (17x25.5cm 6x10in) Crewkerne, Somerset 2001

FAED John 1820-1902 **[27]**
- **$15 145** - €17 801 - **£10 500** - FF116 764
  Portrait of Lucy ashton Oil/board (47x35cm
  18x13in) Edinburgh 2000
- **$3 750** - €4 408 - **£2 600** - FF28 912
  Gatehouse of Flett, Kirkcudbrightshire, Old Girthon Manse, Lightning Watercolour (32x43.5cm
  12x17in) Edinburgh 2000

FAED Thomas 1826-1900 **[83]**
- **$98 210** - €116 801 - **£70 000** - FF766 164
  Farmyard Scene with Milkmaid and a Farm Labourer Oil/canvas (123.5x184cm 48x72in) London
  2000
- **$9 510** - €9 880 - **£6 000** - FF64 809
  Flirtation Oil/canvas (51x42cm 20x16in) London 2000
- **$7 916** - €7 641 - **£5 000** - FF50 119
  Sophia and Olivia Oil/panel (29x23cm 11x9in)
  Ipswich 1999
- **$484** - €510 - **£320** - FF3 345
  Study for «The Disturbed Banquet» Ink (18x23cm
  7x9in) London 2000

FAES Pieter 1750-1814 **[8]**
- **$51 541** - €57 789 - **£35 000** - FF379 074
  Mixed Flowers including Roses, Poppies and Narcissi in a Stone Vase Oil/panel (56.5x41.5cm
  22x16in) London 2000

FAFARD Joseph, Joe 1942 **[25]**
- **$1 134** - €1 223 - **£760** - FF8 023
  Bess Bronze (H17cm H6in) Calgary, Alberta 2000

FAGAN Robert 1761-1816 **[4]**
- **$71 960** - €80 601 - **£50 000** - FF528 705
  Portrait of a Lady Oil/canvas (92x73cm 36x28in)
  London 2001

FAGARD Virginie 1829-? **[2]**
- **$1 159** - €1 067 - **£695** - FF7 000
  Jeune fille aux cerises Pastel/papier (58x47cm
  22x18in) Grenoble 1999

FAGERLIN Ferdinand 1825-1907 **[23]**
- **$16 560** - €17 857 - **£11 115** - FF117 135
  Moderslycka Oil/canvas (73x89cm 28x35in)
  Stockholm 2000

FÄGERPLAN Axel Johan 1798-1865 **[4]**
- **$636** - €642 - **£397** - FF4 209
  Landskap med hästekipage Oil/canvas (33x43cm
  12x16in) Stockholm 2000

FAGES Arthur 1902 **[10]**
- **$969** - €945 - **£596** - FF6 200
  La ville aux toits rouges Huile/toile (46x55.5cm
  18x21in) Rennes 1999

FAGET-GERMAIN Pierre 1903-1961 **[15]**
- **$743** - €884 - **£514** - FF5 800
  Côte rocheuse en Algérie Huile/toile (38x46cm
  14x18in) Tarbes 2000

FAHLCRANTZ Axel 1851-1925 **[41]**
- **$504** - €482 - **£317** - FF3 163
  Kustlandskap med orosmoln Oil/canvas
  (84x130cm 33x51in) Stockholm 1999

FAHLCRANTZ Carl Johan 1774-1861 **[34]**
- **$2 196** - €2 438 - **£1 470** - FF15 994
  Utsikt över Stjernsund och Edö Oil/canvas
  (44.5x60cm 17x23in) Stockholm 2000
- **$714** - €829 - **£501** - FF5 439
  Landskap med vattenfall Oil/canvas (44x35cm
  17x13in) Stockholm 2001

FAHLGREN Carl August 1819-1905 **[28]**
- $496 - €490 - **£305** - FF3 212
  Kustlandskap med fiskeläge i månsken Oil/canvas (48x65cm 18x25in) Stockholm 1999

FAHLSTRÖM Öyvind 1928-1976 **[81]**
- $16 225 - €17 808 - **£10 454** - FF116 812
  Askledarna Oil/canvas (43x60cm 16x23in) Stockholm 2000
- $1 468 - €1 637 - **£1 020** - FF10 740
  La harpe des pauvres Mixed media (16x11.5cm 6x4in) Stockholm 2001
- $4 816 - €4 201 - **£2 913** - FF27 557
  Hundar som har vett att stå stilla Coloured chalks (29.5x39cm 11x15in) Stockholm 1998
- $381 - €409 - **£255** - FF2 683
  Column no.2 Farbserigraphie (76x56cm 29x22in) Köln 2000

FÄHNLE Hans 1903-1968 **[18]**
- $761 - €869 - **£536** - FF5 701
  Bodenseelandschaft Öl/Leinwand (49x70cm 19x27in) Stuttgart 2001

FAHRBACH Carl Ludwig 1835-1902 **[31]**
- $3 483 - €3 270 - **£2 160** - FF21 451
  Rehwild in der Abenddämmerung vor den Toren eines deutschen Schlosses Öl/Leinwand (79x132cm 31x51in) Wien 1999
- $938 - €1 074 - **£645** - FF7 043
  Reh am Waldbach bei Dämmerung Oil/panel (25.5x22.5cm 10x8in) München 2000

FÄHRIG Gustav XIX **[1]**
- $1 775 - €1 647 - **£1 100** - FF10 803
  The Penitent Magdalen, after Pompeo Batoni Pastel/paper (116x86cm 46x34in) London 1999

FAHRINGER Carl 1874-1952 **[119]**
- $6 168 - €5 949 - **£3 864** - FF39 024
  Marché en Autriche Huile/panneau (46x38cm 18x14in) Luxembourg 1999
- $1 740 - €1 738 - **£1 088** - FF11 403
  Ber der Feldarbeit Öl/Karton (33x40cm 12x15in) Köln 1999
- $1 974 - €2 180 - **£1 368** - FF14 301
  Landschaft in den Bergen Watercolour (26x35cm 10x13in) Wien 2001

FAHRNER Kurt 1932-1977 **[19]**
- $4 022 - €4 053 - **£2 507** - FF26 585
  Zwei sich zugeneigte weibliche Figuren Öl/Leinwand (49x120cm 19x47in) Zürich 2000

FAIJA Guglielmo 1803-c.1861 **[2]**
- $12 233 - €13 703 - **£8 500** - FF89 884
  Young Artist, holding artist's palette and paint Brushes Miniature (12.5x10cm 4x3in) London 2001

FAILLA Fabio 1917 **[6]**
- $2 000 - €2 073 - **£1 200** - FF13 600
  Marina Olio/tela (25x40cm 9x15in) Prato 2000

FAINI Fortunato Giulio 1869-1952 **[4]**
- $500 - €518 - **£300** - FF3 400
  Vele in Porto Olio/tavoletta (21x57.5cm 8x22in) Firenze 2001

FAIRCLOUGH Wilfred R.E. 1907-1996 **[22]**
- $1 089 - €1 226 - **£750** - FF8 045
  Sunflowers Oil/board (37.5x38cm 14x14in) London 2000
- $430 - €478 - **£300** - FF3 133
  The Engelberg, Switzerland/Engelberg, The Hahnen Watercolour/paper (26.5x40.5cm 10x15in) Godalming, Surrey 2001

FAIRHURST Angus 1966 **[13]**
- $5 686 - €5 567 - **£3 500** - FF36 517
  When I Woke Up in the Morning, The Feeling was Still There Mixed media (50.5x40cm 19x15in) London 1999
- $2 884 - €3 390 - **£2 000** - FF22 240
  Untitled Acrylic/paper (29.5x21cm 11x8in) London 2000
- $9 762 - €11 481 - **£7 000** - FF75 310
  Man abandoned by Colour Photograph (40.5x51cm 15x20in) London 2001

FAIRHURST Miles XX **[16]**
- $536 - €497 - **£320** - FF3 259
  English Country Landscape Oil/canvas (43x58cm 17x23in) Aylsham, Norfolk 1999
- $484 - €465 - **£300** - FF3 049
  Figure with a Dog on a Beach Oil/board (20x25cm 7x9in) London 1999

FAIRLAND Thomas 1804-1852 **[6]**
- $576 - €637 - **£400** - FF4 181
  Bachelor's Hall Lithograph (34x48cm 13x18in) London 2001

FAIRLEY Barker 1887-1986 **[15]**
- $1 369 - €1 330 - **£855** - FF8 722
  Yellow Day Oil/board (29x35.5cm 11x13in) Toronto 1999

FAIRMAN Frances C. 1836-1923 **[19]**
- $2 049 - €2 188 - **£1 400** - FF14 354
  At the Spinning Wheel Watercolour/paper (51x34.5cm 20x13in) Billingshurst, West-Sussex 2001

FAIRMAN James 1826-1904 **[33]**
- $8 000 - €9 429 - **£5 621** - FF61 853
  Shore View near Venice Oil/canvas (86x116cm 34x46in) East-Dennis MA 2000

FAIRNINGTON Mark 1957 **[2]**
- $2 241 - €2 406 - **£1 500** - FF15 782
  «The Greek Madonna» Oil/panel (83x68cm 32x26in) London 2000

FAIRWEATHER Ian 1891-1974 **[51]**
- $131 514 - €141 172 - **£88 021** - FF926 026
  Chi-Tien Goes Begging Oil/cardboard (89x150cm 35x59in) Melbourne 2000
- $38 850 - €36 628 - **£24 078** - FF240 264
  Family Group with Turtle Mixed media (96.5x69cm 37x27in) Melbourne 1999
- $10 489 - €9 535 - **£6 317** - FF62 546
  Indonesian Household Gouache (32x46cm 12x18in) Woollahra, Sydney 1998

FAISTAUER Anton 1887-1930 **[87]**
- $73 808 - €71 582 - **£46 452** - FF469 546
  Stilleben mit Blumenstrauss und Obstschale Öl/Leinwand (49.5x60cm 19x23in) München 1999
- $27 320 - €29 069 - **£17 280** - FF190 680
  Landschaft mit Gebirgskulisse Öl/Leinwand/Karton (26x48cm 10x18in) Salzburg 2000
- $2 492 - €2 907 - **£1 760** - FF19 068
  Ferleiten an der Grossglockner Hochalpenstrasse Aquarell/Papier (23x30cm 9x11in) Salzburg 2000

FAISTENBERGER Anton 1663-1708 **[9]**
- $6 886 - €7 994 - **£4 840** - FF52 437
  Weite, gebirgige Landschaft mit einem Sturzbach und Reisenden Öl/Leinwand (107x138cm 42x54in) Wien 2001

$5 886 - €6 541 - **£3 942** - FF42 903
Gebirgige Flusslandschaft mit Kirche und lagernden Zigeunern Öl/Leinwand (68x95.5cm 26x37in) Wien 2000

FAIVRE Abel Jules 1867-1945 **[106]**
$2 163 - €2 134 - **£1 332** - FF14 000
Portrait d'élégante Huile/toile (24x18cm 9x7in) Calais 1999

$236 - €229 - **£149** - FF1 500
«Papa sait-il qu'on est vainqueur?» Aquarelle, gouache/papier (21.5x29cm 8x11in) Paris 1999

$300 - €333 - **£209** - FF2 184
Le Cake Walk Official Lithograph (46x89cm 18x35in) Chicago IL 2001

FAIVRE Antoine J.E., Tony 1830-1905 **[12]**
$9 611 - €10 671 - **£6 699** - FF70 000
Servante au chauffe-lit Huile/toile (45x32cm 17x12in) Paris 2001

FAIVRE Georges XX **[1]**
$2 400 - €2 308 - **£1 481** - FF15 139
«Cycles Météor» Poster (158x118.5cm 62x46in) New-York 1999

FAIVRE Léon Maxime 1856-1914 **[9]**
$11 000 - €10 303 - **£6 762** - FF67 585
A Courtier of Henri III Oil/panel (65x49cm 25x19in) New-York 1999

$6 203 - €6 250 - **£3 866** - FF41 000
Portrait d'un homme à la pipe Huile/toile (42x33cm 16x12in) Libourne 2000

FAIVRE-DUFFER Louis Stanislas 1818-1897 **[9]**
$1 577 - €1 372 - **£951** - FF9 000
Portrait présumé d'une petite fille, Mademoiselle Marguerite de Russet Aquarelle, gouache (25.8x21cm 10x8in) Paris 1998

FAIZAL M. 1965 **[6]**
$1 772 - €1 651 - **£1 071** - FF10 833
Man and Horse Oil/canvas (100x80cm 39x31in) Singapore 1999

FAKEYE Lamidi XX **[1]**
$4 205 - €4 891 - **£3 000** - FF32 083
Yoruba Priest with Cockerel Sculpture, wood (H71cm H28in) London 2000

FALARDEAU Antoine Sébastien 1822-1889 **[11]**
$4 788 - €642 - **£2 964** - FF30 447
Marsias écorché par Apollon Huile/toile (120.5x92.5cm 47x36in) Montréal 1999

FALAT Julian 1853-1929 **[127]**
$22 968 - €21 583 - **£14 259** - FF141 577
Chien, épisode de la chasse Oil/canvas (110x170cm 43x66in) Warszawa 1999

$10 133 - €11 884 - **£7 231** - FF77 951
Gazon devant la maison Huile/toile (46x95cm 18x37in) Warszawa 2000

$3 282 - €3 903 - **£2 340** - FF25 605
Vistule charrie Aquarelle, gouache/carton (43x69cm 16x27in) Warszawa 2000

$4 282 - €4 316 - **£2 670** - FF28 311
Fonte des neiges au printemps et chevreuils Etching (49x139cm 19x54in) Lódz 2000

FALCHETTI Alberto 1878-1951 **[29]**
$1 600 - €1 659 - **£960** - FF10 880
Lago del Nioslet Olio/cartone (35x46cm 13x18in) Vercelli 2001

$2 302 - €2 556 - **£1 619** - FF17 041
Trauben an einer Holzwand Öl/Karton (48x33cm 18x12in) Bern 2001

FALCHETTI Giuseppe 1843-1918 **[38]**
$7 200 - €6 220 - **£4 800** - FF40 800
Natura morta con frutta Olio/tela (60x45cm 23x17in) Roma 1998

$2 880 - €2 488 - **£1 920** - FF16 320
Paesaggio alto canavese Olio/cartone (40x27.5cm 15x10in) Milano 1998

FALCINELLI Marcel 1900-1980 **[15]**
$2 558 - €3 049 - **£1 824** - FF20 000
Les moutons Huile/toile (60x80cm 23x31in) Joigny 1998

FALCONE DELLE BATTAGLIE Aniello 1607-1656 **[24]**
$58 000 - €75 157 - **£43 500** - FF493 000
Assedio di Gerusalemme Olio/tela (104x130cm 40x51in) Roma 2001

$44 178 - €49 534 - **£30 000** - FF324 921
Cavalry Engagement Between Turks and Christians Oil/canvas (74.5x112cm 29x44in) London 2000

$1 637 - €1 603 - **£1 050** - FF10 512
Study of a Male Nude with Left Arm Outstreched, Facing Left Red chalk/paper (25x19cm 9x7in) London 1999

FALCONET Étienne Maurice 1716-1791 **[38]**
$6 841 - €6 485 - **£4 274** - FF42 541
Figure of Diana Bronze (H82.5cm H32in) Woollahra, Sydney 1999

$2 303 - €1 973 - **£1 350** - FF12 943
Venus Marble (H51cm H20in) London 1998

FALCONET Louis c.1710-c.1775 **[2]**
$4 690 - €4 726 - **£2 923** - FF31 000
Amour tenant un arc Marbre (H68cm H26in) Riom 2000

FALCONET Pierre Étienne 1741-1791 **[9]**
$6 360 - €5 491 - **£3 800** - FF36 019
Elizabetha Bridgetta Stepney, Mrs Joseph Gulston Oil/canvas (28x23cm 11x9in) Llandeilo, Carmarthenshire 1998

FALCONI Bernardo XVII **[1]**
$87 956 - €84 696 - **£55 000** - FF555 571
Bust of Mercury looking to Dexter, his Head surmounted by a Pegasus Marble (H79cm H31in) London 1999

FALCONNIER Léon 1811-1876 **[1]**
$3 200 - €3 413 - **£2 131** - FF22 388
Group of Abraham Lincoln's Emancipation of the Slaves Bronze (H54.5cm H21in) New-York 2000

FALCUCCI Robert 1900-1989 **[123]**
$486 - €534 - **£314** - FF3 500
Les meules Huile/toile (46x55cm 18x21in) Coutances 2000

$569 - €662 - **£400** - FF4 345
«Veuve Amiot» Poster (155x115cm 61x45in) London 2001

FALDA Giovan Battista 1648-1678 **[14]**
$801 - €777 - **£500** - FF5 094
Bird's eye view of St Peter's with Forecourt and Colonnades Etching (79x55cm 31x21in) London 1999

FALDI Arturo 1856-1911 **[12]**
$16 500 - €17 105 - **£9 900** - FF112 200
Il figlio nella culla Olio/tela (51x70cm 20x27in) Prato 2000

FALENS von Carel 1683-1733 **[44]**
- $17 367 - €19 059 - **£11 180** - FF125 017
  Peasant Woman meeting a Shepherd on a River in a Summer Landscape Oil/canvas (54x64.5cm 21x25in) Amsterdam 2000
- $6 400 - €7 267 - **£4 380** - FF47 670
  Ausritt zur Falkenjagd Öl/Kupfer (23.5x30cm 9x11in) Wien 2000

FALERO Luis Ricardo 1851-1896 **[30]**
- $19 000 - €16 392 - **£11 462** - FF107 526
  Muse of the Night Oil/canvas (74x40.5cm 29x15in) New-York 1998
- $5 687 - €5 336 - **£3 514** - FF35 000
  Jeune fille nue assise devant une architecture mauresque Huile/panneau (40x25cm 15x9in) La Rochelle 1999

FALGUIERE Jean Alexandre 1831-1900 **[154]**
- $5 000 - €4 272 - **£3 001** - FF28 022
  Diana, Goddess of the Hunt Bronze (H5905cm H2324in) New-York 1998
- $2 195 - €2 439 - **£1 470** - FF16 000
  L'enfant vainqueur au combat de coq Bronze (H79.5cm H31in) Toulouse 2000

FALIZE Pierre 1876-1953 **[9]**
- $2 000 - €1 893 - **£1 242** - FF12 419
  «Prunier, Livre Vite et Bien» Poster (213.5x132.5cm 84x52in) New-York 1999

FALK Denise 1960 **[1]**
- $18 000 - €19 091 - **£12 204** - FF125 229
  Pinkie Acrylic (207x166.5x10cm 81x65x3in) Tel Aviv 2001

FALK Hans 1918 **[163]**
- $747 - €847 - **£522** - FF5 554
  Komposition Mixed media (70x50cm 27x19in) Zürich 2001
- $1 076 - €932 - **£653** - FF6 112
  Zwei Elefanten vor Zirkuszelt Indian ink (27x20cm 10x7in) Zürich 1998
- $219 - €212 - **£135** - FF1 390
  Frauenakt Lithographie (37x25.5cm 14x10in) Zürich 2000

FALK Hjalmar 1856-1938 **[30]**
- $850 - €871 - **£525** - FF5 713
  Bränningar Akvarell/papper (25x55cm 9x21in) Stockholm 2000

FALK Jeremias 1619-1677 **[11]**
- $14 251 - €16 186 - **£10 000** - FF106 175
  Still Life of variegated Tulips, Morning Glory, Narcissi, Lilies Oil/panel (44.5x35.5cm 17x13in) London 2001
- $233 - €256 - **£158** - FF1 676
  Susanna und die beiden Alten Kupferstich (32.4x38.5cm 12x15in) Berlin 2000

FALK Lars Erik 1922 **[57]**
- $906 - €1 058 - **£621** - FF6 939
  Målning Oil/panel (27x81cm 10x31in) Stockholm 2000
- $906 - €1 058 - **£621** - FF6 939
  Relief i vitt Oil/panel (24.5x50.5cm 9x19in) Stockholm 2000
- $956 - €900 - **£592** - FF5 901
  Modulskulptur Metal (41x65cm 16x25in) Stockholm 1999

FALK Robert Rafaelovich 1886-1958 **[40]**
- $5 797 - €5 474 - **£3 600** - FF35 908
  Still Life with Red Onions and Fruit Oil/canvas (54x64cm 21x25in) London 1999

- $2 038 - €1 765 - **£1 237** - FF11 578
  Heilige Stadt Samarkand Oil/panel (38x38cm 14x14in) München 1998

FALKEISEN Johann Jakob 1804-1883 **[4]**
- $21 927 - €25 159 - **£15 000** - FF165 030
  The arrival of Goudal at the Market Place of Kadikoÿ Oil/board (27.5x39cm 10x15in) London 2000

FALKENBERG Georg Richard 1850-c.1915 **[6]**
- $4 708 - €5 533 - **£3 264** - FF36 295
  Pêcheur amoureux Huile/toile (87x135cm 34x53in) Warszawa 2000

FALKENSTEIN Claire 1908-1997 **[12]**
- $1 152 - €1 311 - **£812** - FF8 600
  Sans titre Métal (H98cm H38in) Paris 2001

FALKMAN Severin 1831-1889 **[4]**
- $4 638 - €5 045 - **£3 057** - FF33 096
  Brud Oil/canvas (50x42cm 19x16in) Helsinki 2000

FALL George c.1848-1925 **[103]**
- $768 - €767 - **£480** - FF5 031
  York Minster Viewed from over the River Watercolour/paper (30x20cm 12x8in) Rotherham 1999

FALLER Louis-Clément 1819-1901 **[36]**
- $370 - €442 - **£264** - FF2 900
  Paysage Huile/panneau (17x34cm 6x13in) Paris 2000

FALTER John Philip 1910-1982 **[24]**
- $22 000 - €20 835 - **£13 376** - FF136 666
  Memory of an Old Parade Oil/canvas (76x102cm 29x40in) New-York 1999
- $13 000 - €14 761 - **£8 897** - FF96 829
  Huckleberry Finn Oil/masonite (22x23cm 8x9in) New-York 2000

FALZONI Giulio 1900-1978 **[21]**
- $600 - €518 - **£300** - FF3 400
  Vecchia Milano Acquarello/carta (26.5x38.5cm 10x15in) Milano 1999

FAMARS TESTAS de Willem 1834-1896 **[49]**
- $1 482 - €1 633 - **£968** - FF10 715
  Arabieren bij Noord-Afrikaanse stad Oil/canvas (34x52.5cm 13x20in) Den Haag 2000
- $5 100 - €4 991 - **£3 270** - FF32 742
  Arab Merchants resting Oil/panel (27x50cm 10x19in) Amsterdam 1999
- $854 - €998 - **£609** - FF6 548
  The Artist's Son, Henri Baudouin, playing on a Rug Watercolour/paper (15x25cm 5x9in) Amsterdam 2001

FAMEY L. XIX **[1]**
- $3 550 - €3 811 - **£2 375** - FF25 000
  Paolo et Francesca Huile/toile (128x90cm 50x35in) Ourville-en-Caux 2000

FAMIN Constant 1827-1888 **[44]**
- $710 - €762 - **£475** - FF5 000
  Arbres en forêt Tirage albuminé (31x23.5cm 12x9in) Bièvres 2000

FAN RUI XIX **[1]**
- $1 595 - €1 534 - **£984** - FF10 061
  Der Unterbliche Li Tieguai Indian ink/paper (168.5x104.5cm 66x41in) Stuttgart 1999

FAN ZENG 1938 **[3]**
- $4 879 - €5 328 - **£3 138** - FF34 948
  Monkey and a Gentleman Ink (135.5x68.5cm 53x26in) Hong-Kong 2000

F

FANART Alphonse Cl. Antonin 1831-1903 **[39]**
$3 782 - €3 811 - £2 357 - FF25 000
Pêcheur au bord du lac Huile/toile (38x61cm
14x24in) Calais 2000

FANCELLI Pietro 1764-1850 **[10]**
$3 074 - €3 049 - £1 912 - FF20 000
Le Christ devant Ponce Pilate Fusain (26.5x18.5cm
10x7in) Paris 1999

FANCHER Louis 1884-1944 **[2]**
$950 - €1 036 - £658 - FF6 793
«Over there, in the Air Service» Poster (102x76cm
40x30in) New-York 2001

FANELLI Francesco 1863-1924 **[15]**
$2 000 - €2 592 - £1 500 - FF17 000
Ritratto di gentiluomo Olio/tela (120x78cm
47x30in) Prato 2000
$3 870 - €3 232 - £2 300 - FF21 198
Nessus and Deianeira Bronze (H22cm H8in)
London 1998

FANELLI-SEMAH Louis Joseph 1804-1875 **[6]**
$6 072 - €5 183 - £3 631 - FF34 000
Le repentir Huile/toile (46x39cm 18x15in) Paris 1998

FANET A. XIX **[2]**
$2 513 - €2 439 - £1 584 - FF16 000
Bouquet de roses dans un vase à la grecque,
sur un entablement Aquarelle/papier (45x37cm
17x14in) Paris 1999

FANFANI Enrico XIX **[25]**
$2 000 - €1 864 - £1 208 - FF12 227
Contemplation Before the Altar Flame Oil/canvas
(66x45cm 26x18in) Boston MA 1999

FANFANI Paolo, Paul 1823-? **[2]**
$18 937 - €21 654 - £13 000 - FF142 041
A Siren Marble (H166cm H65in) London 2000

FANG SHISHU 1692-1751 **[4]**
$46 224 - €50 475 - £29 736 - FF331 092
Landscape Ink/paper (48x32.5cm 18x12in) Hong-
Kong 2000

FANG WANYI 1732-1779 **[1]**
$5 920 - €5 618 - £3 597 - FF36 850
Flowers and Insects Ink (21x15.5cm 8x6in) Hong-
Kong 1999

FANG ZHAOLIN 1914 **[16]**
$4 487 - €5 274 - £3 111 - FF34 594
Poem in Running Script Calligraphy Ink/paper
(170x93.5cm 66x36in) Hong-Kong 2000

FANNEN J. XIX-XX **[4]**
$1 297 - €1 246 - £800 - FF8 175
The Topsail Schooner Heinrich in the Channel
Oil/canvas (40.5x62.5cm 15x24in) London 1999

FANNER Alice Maud 1865-1930 **[24]**
$1 000 - €1 162 - £702 - FF7 621
Crossing the Channel Oil/canvas (25x40cm
10x16in) Cincinnati OH 2001

FANNING Ralph 1889-? **[5]**
$700 - €813 - £492 - FF5 334
St.Theresa Watercolour/paper (22x30cm 9x12in)
Newark OH 2001

FANSHAW Elizabeth Christiana 1778-1856 **[1]**
$4 533 - €5 291 - £3 200 - FF34 707
North Eastern Italian Coast:
Pisa/Lucca/Massa/Carrara/Sarzana/Spezia Ink
(21.5x30.5cm 8x12in) London 2000

FANTACCHIOTTI Cesare 1844-1922 **[5]**
$29 604 - €28 037 - £18 000 - FF183 909
Romeo and Juliet Marble (H202cm H79in) London

FANTIN-LATOUR Henri-Théodore 1836-1904 **[609]**
$100 000 - €96 160 - £61 610 - FF630 770
Nature morte aux fruits Oil/canvas (46x52.5cm
18x20in) New-York 1999
$31 518 - €30.584 - £20 000 - FF200 616
Nature morte, pêche et raisin Oil/canvas (22x28cm
8x11in) London 1999
$442 - €495 - £307 - FF3 247
Stående kvinneakt Pencil/paper (13.5x7cm 5x2in)
Oslo 2001
$325 - €320 - £202 - FF2 100
Le gloire Estampe (40.5x31cm 15x12in) Paris 1999

FANTIN-LATOUR Théodore 1805-1872 **[17]**
$7 700 - €7 759 - £4 800 - FF50 897
Marine, effet du matin Oil/canvas (16.5x23cm 6x9in)
London 2000
$1 824 - €1 587 - £1 100 - FF10 409
Portrait of a Young Lady Wearing a Red Lace
Trimmed Dress Pastel/paper (68.5x56cm 26x22in)
Godalming, Surrey 1998

FANTIN-LATOUR Victoria 1840-1926 **[24]**
$17 601 - €17 475 - £11 000 - FF114 627
Red, pink, white and yellow Chrysanthemums
Oil/canvas (35x46cm 13x18in) London 1999
$30 485 - €26 679 - £18 462 - FF175 000
Vase de roses Huile/toile (41x29cm 16x11in) Paris
1998

FANTONI Marcello XX **[14]**
$600 - €574 - £369 - FF3 768
Musicians Glazed ceramic (H37cm H14in) Chicago
IL 1999

FANTUZZI Eliano 1909-1987 **[128]**
$560 - €726 - £420 - FF4 760
Ragazza con fiori in mano Olio/tela (70x50cm
27x19in) Prato 2001
$400 - €415 - £240 - FF2 720
Venezia Olio/cartone/tela (20x30cm 7x11in) Roma
2000

FAR-SI Georges 1866-? **[2]**
$19 587 - €19 056 - £12 050 - FF125 000
Femme nue allongée Huile/toile (97x196cm
38x77in) Paris 1999

FARAGO Géza 1877-1928 **[9]**
$2 600 - €2 901 - £1 702 - FF19 027
«Tungsram Wolframlámpa» Poster (124.5x92.5cm
49x36in) New-York 2000

FARAONI Enzo 1920 **[68]**
$550 - €570 - £330 - FF3 740
Natura morta Olio/tela (40x50cm 15x19in) Prato
1999
$375 - €389 - £225 - FF2 550
Fiori Olio/tavola (28x28cm 11x11in) Firenze 2000

FARASYN Luc 1822-1899 **[4]**
$5 133 - €5 173 - £3 200 - FF33 931
Impressive Still Life Oil/canvas (83x115cm 32x45in)
London 2000

FARAZYN Edgard 1858-1938 **[142]**
$7 875 - €8 676 - £5 320 - FF56 910
De kruisafneming (La descente de croix)
Huile/toile (145x110cm 57x43in) Antwerpen 2000
$920 - €992 - £616 - FF6 504
Port Huile/toile (50x70cm 19x27in) Antwerpen 2000

F

$464 - €496 - **£316** - FF3 252
Vue de plage Huile/panneau (14x23cm 5x9in)
Antwerpen 2001

$236 - €223 - **£143** - FF1 463
Marine Aquarelle/papier (34x49cm 13x19in)
Antwerpen 1999

FARCY Andry 1882-1950 **[17]**
$633 - €610 - **£391** - FF4 000
Cycles & motos magnat-Debon, Grenoble, Médaille d'or du TCF Affiche (120x157.5cm 47x62in) Paris 1999

FARE Arthur Cecil 1876-1958 **[30]**
$445 - €404 - **£270** - FF2 647
«V.W.H Pack in Cirencester» Watercolour (37x52cm 14x20in) Bristol, Avon 1998

FAREL Pierre 1957 **[6]**
$1 657 - €1 906 - **£1 170** - FF12 500
Violons pour la mer Huile/toile (80x80cm 31x31in) Barbizon 2001

FAREY Cyril Arthur 1888-1954 **[16]**
$2 127 - €2 288 - **£1 450** - FF15 008
A View of Houses of Parliment with London Bridge Foreground Watercolour (36.5x56cm 14x22in) West-Yorshire 2001

FARGE Pierre 1878-1947 **[27]**
$4 579 - €5 445 - **£3 264** - FF35 719
Soieries Oil/canvas (41x100cm 31x39in) Amsterdam 2000

FARGEOT Ferdinand 1880-1957 **[11]**
$9 940 - €10 671 - **£6 650** - FF70 000
Le café concert Huile/toile (60x72cm 23x28in) Paris 2000

FARHAT Ammar 1911-1986 **[9]**
$9 420 - €10 147 - **£5 820** - FF60 000
Tourbet el Bey, Tunis Huile/carton (37.5x46cm 14x18in) Paris 1999

FARIA de Candido Aragonez 1849-1911 **[48]**
$2 010 - €2 287 - **£1 395** - FF15 000
«Circuit de Dieppe» Affiche (117x77cm 46x30in) Paris 2000

$773 - €663 - **£467** - FF4 350
«Ilka De Mynn» Affiche (127x92.5cm 50x36in) Paris 1998

FARIA Estrela 1910 **[13]**
$860 - €997 - **£600** - FF6 540
Rapariga com cáo Acuarela/papel (25.5x22cm 10x8in) Lisboa 2001

$351 - €335 - **£218** - FF2 200
«Les Meteor's créateur des Statues lumineuses» Affiche (90x125cm 35x49in) Paris 1999

FARIA Jacques 1898-1956 **[30]**
$669 - €640 - **£415** - FF4 400
«Attentat sur la voie ferrée» Affiche (160x120cm 62x47in) La Varenne-Saint-Hilaire 1999

FARINATI Orazio 1559-c.1620 **[16]**
$10 688 - €12 140 - **£7 500** - FF79 631
The Entombment Oil/panel (49x38.5cm 19x15in) London 2001

$659 - €665 - **£411** - FF4 360
Sechs Engel mit den Marterinstrumenten des Heilandes Radierung (17.2x28.6cm 6x11in) Stuttgart 2000

FARINATI Paolo 1524-1606 **[34]**
$74 707 - €73 436 - **£48 000** - FF481 708
The Entombment Oil/panel (50.5x38cm 19x14in) London 1999

$11 463 - €10 650 - **£7 000** - FF69 860
The Madonna and Child with St Catherine, St John the Baptist Oil/paper/panel (46.5x34cm 18x13in) London 1998

$2 400 - €2 073 - **£1 200** - FF13 600
Tre putti che sorreggono Cupido Inchiostro (24x19cm 9x7in) Milano 1999

$850 - €994 - **£597** - FF6 521
The Penitent Magdalen Etching (20.5x14.5cm 8x5in) New-York 2000

FARINGTON Joseph 1747-1821 **[34]**
$14 840 - €14 524 - **£9 500** - FF95 272
An extensive View of Loch Lomond Oil/canvas (53.5x102cm 21x40in) London 1999

$261 - €299 - **£180** - FF1 964
The Cobbler's Shop Watercolour (19x24cm 7x9in) West-Midlands 2000

FARKAS Etienne Istvan 1887-1944 **[5]**
$12 250 - €13 553 - **£8 050** - FF88 900
Man reading Oil/cardboard (64x80cm 25x31in) Budapest 2000

FARKASHAZY Miklos 1895-1964 **[22]**
$4 810 - €5 054 - **£2 990** - FF33 150
Petite allée avec un pont au second plan Huile/toile (59x72cm 23x28in) Budapest 2000

$272 - €307 - **£192** - FF2 016
Au bord de l'eau Aquarelle/papier (43x31cm 16x12in) Budapest 2001

FARLEIGH John 1900-1965 **[6]**
$647 - €546 - **£380** - FF3 584
«Swinburne» Poster (100x64cm 39x25in) London 1998

FARLEY Richard Blossom 1875-1954 **[7]**
$7 000 - €6 527 - **£4 342** - FF42 815
Low Tide Oil/canvas (63.5x101.5cm 25x39in) New-York 1999

FARLOW Harry 1882-1956 **[5]**
$825 - €933 - **£557** - FF6 120
Woman at Table Oil/canvas (54x44cm 21x17in) Plainville CT 2000

FARMER Josephus 1894-1989 **[2]**
$10 000 - €8 628 - **£6 055** - FF56 593
Daniel in the Lion's Den Sculpture, wood (36x84.5cm 14x33in) New-York 1999

FARNDON Walter 1876-1964 **[74]**
$4 500 - €3 796 - **£2 639** - FF24 903
Boats in an Inlet Oil/masonite (35.5x46cm 13x18in) New-York 1998

$5 750 - €4 958 - **£3 414** - FF32 522
Mid-day at the Beach Oil/board (20x25cm 8x10in) Cambridge MA 1998

$1 600 - €1 385 - **£971** - FF9 084
Overlooking the Harbour Gouache/paper (45x55cm 18x22in) Mystic CT 1998

FARNETI Stefano 1855-1926 **[3]**
$5 881 - €6 360 - **£4 090** - FF45 000
Jeune orientale aux oranges Huile/toile (68.5x59cm 26x23in) Paris 2000

FARNHAM Ammi Merchant 1846-1922 **[4]**
$3 000 - €3 265 - **£2 061** - FF21 417
Coastal Landscape with Boats in the Distance Oil/canvas/board (50x91cm 20x36in) St. Petersburg FL 2001

FARNSWORTH Alfred Villiers 1858-1908 **[13]**
✏ **$2 750** – €2 350 – **£1 664** – FF15 414
The Champs Élysée Watercolour/paper (37.5x55cm 21x21in) San-Francisco CA 1998

FARNSWORTH Jerry 1895-1983 **[30]**
🞕 **$1 500** – €1 373 – **£909** – FF9 009
A seated Girl in a green Hat Oil/canvas (86x63cm 34x25in) East-Dennis MA 1998
🞕 **$850** – €717 – **£498** – FF4 703
Adele Oil/canvas (40x35cm 16x14in) Mystic CT 1998

FARNY Henry Francis 1847-1916 **[60]**
🞕 **$675 000** – €756 050 – **£468 990** – FF4 959 360
Morning of a New Day Oil/canvas (47.5x72.5cm 18x28in) New-York 2001
✏ **$155 000** – €146 359 – **£96 255** – FF960 054
The Ford Watercolour, gouache/paper (24x16.5cm 9x6in) Beverly-Hills CA 1999
▥ **$850** – €999 – **£589** – FF6 553
Indian Woman with Papoose Lithograph (20x15cm 8x6in) Cincinnati OH 2000

FARQUHARSON David 1840-1907 **[118]**
🞕 **$7 248** – €6 811 – **£4 500** – FF44 680
Loch Awe Oil/canvas (40.5x61cm 15x24in) London 1999
🞕 **$2 735** – €3 254 – **£1 950** – FF21 343
Sennen Cove, Figures on the Beach, Evening Oil/canvas (30.5x51cm 12x20in) Bath 2000
🞕 **$261** – €295 – **£181** – FF1 933
Herding Sheep to Pasture Watercolour/paper (30.5x40.5cm 12x15in) Toronto 2000

FARQUHARSON John 1865-1931 **[27]**
✏ **$354** – €338 – **£220** – FF2 214
Loch Duich, Ross-Shire Watercolour/paper (39x56.5cm 15x22in) Toronto 1999

FARQUHARSON Joseph 1846-1935 **[140]**
🞕 **$124 402** – €108 196 – **£75 000** – FF709 717
The Silence of the Snow -Bucket Mill, on the Feugh, Finzean Oil/canvas (152.5x106.5cm 60x41in) Glasgow 1998
🞕 **$19 210** – €18 998 – **£12 000** – FF124 618
Tending the Sheep Oil/canvas (51x76cm 20x29in) Glasgow 1999
🞕 **$6 078** – €6 072 – **£3 800** – FF39 832
Morar Oil/canvas (27x50.5cm 10x19in) Edinburgh 1999

FARR Ellen Frances 1840-1907 **[7]**
🞕 **$3 750** – €4 382 – **£2 677** – FF28 747
Pepper tree Oil/canvas (60x40cm 24x16in) Altadena CA 2001
🞕 **$3 500** – €4 090 – **£2 498** – FF26 831
California poppies in Indian basket Oil/canvas (30x40cm 12x16in) Altadena CA 2001

FARR Helen 1911 **[7]**
🞕 **$2 000** – €2 144 – **£1 323** – FF14 066
Windy Sky Oil/board (29x39cm 11x15in) New-Orleans LA 2000

FARRE Henri 1871-1934 **[10]**
🞕 **$1 479** – €1 448 – **£910** – FF9 500
Gabriel Fauré à son piano Huile/toile (38x46cm 14x18in) Paris 1999

FARRELL Frederick Arthur 1882-1935 **[21]**
▥ **$204** – €220 – **£137** – FF1 442
The Meuse at Giver Drypoint (26x49cm 10x19in) Berlin 2000

FARRELL Michael 1940-2000 **[23]**
🞕 **$1 601** – €1 778 – **£1 116** – FF11 660
A Series Red, Yellow, Blue Oil/canvas (54x183cm 21x72in) Dublin 2001
✏ **$1 312** – €1 270 – **£809** – FF8 329
Storm in a Tea Cup Watercolour/paper (56x76cm 22x29in) Dublin 1999
▥ **$341** – €330 – **£201** – FF2 165
Snake in a Bottle Lithograph (76x56cm 29x22in) Dublin 1999

FARREN Robert 1832-? **[9]**
🞕 **$1 008** – €998 – **£617** – FF6 548
Sheep in Woodland Oil/canvas (72x92cm 28x36in) Amsterdam 2000

FARRER Henry 1843-1903 **[36]**
✏ **$3 500** – €3 248 – **£2 101** – FF21 306
Summer Sunset Watercolour/paper (27x43cm 11x17in) Milford CT 1999

FARRERAS RICART Francisco 1927 **[43]**
🞕 **$1 770** – €1 802 – **£1 110** – FF11 820
Pintura No.55 Técnica mixta/tabla (116x90cm 45x35in) Madrid 2000
✏ **$193** – €214 – **£128** – FF1 403
Número 3 Collage/papier (48x60cm 18x23in) México 2000

FARROUKH Mustapha 1901-1957 **[3]**
🞕 **$17 187** – €19 331 – **£12 000** – FF126 804
Aïn Al Mraiseh (Beirut) Oil/canvas (69x99cm 27x38in) London 2001
✏ **$5 013** – €5 638 – **£3 500** – FF36 984
View of Damascus Watercolour (25x34cm 9x13in) London 2001

FARSKY Otto XIX-XX **[10]**
🞕 **$700** – €817 – **£487** – FF5 357
Landscapes Oil/board (22x27cm 9x11in) Altadena CA 2000

FARUFFINI Federico 1831-1869 **[13]**
🞕 **$11 500** – €11 922 – **£6 900** – FF78 200
Convegno galante in gondola Olio/tela (100x155cm 39x61in) Roma 1999
🞕 **$13 000** – €13 476 – **£7 800** – FF88 400
Venezia, rivali in amore Olio/tela (38x30cm 14x11in) Roma 2000
🞕 **$3 000** – €3 887 – **£2 250** – FF25 500
Ciociara con brocca/Ciociara in piedi/Ciociara seduta Acquarello/carta (32x22.5cm 12x8in) Milano 2001

FASANELLA Ralph 1914-1997 **[6]**
🞕 **$15 000** – €14 524 – **£9 421** – FF95 271
Schoolyard Line up Oil/canvas (80.5x116cm 31x45in) New-York 1999

FASANOTTI Gaetano 1831-1882 **[18]**
🞕 **$3 495** – €3 623 – **£2 097** – FF23 766
Paesaggio con contadini Olio/tela (29.5x42cm 11x16in) Milano 1999
✏ **$960** – €1 244 – **£720** – FF8 160
Paesaggio invernale Acquarello/carta (10x15.5cm 3x6in) Milano 2000

FASCE Gianfranco 1927 **[7]**
🞕 **$1 800** – €1 866 – **£1 080** – FF12 240
Composizione Olio/tela (60x46cm 23x18in) Vercelli 1999

FASCH Johann Ludwig c.1738-c.1778 **[2]**
✏ **$2 980** – €2 592 – **£1 796** – FF17 400
«Clytemnestre et Electre»/«Ninias et Azema» Lavis (10x11cm 3x4in) Paris 1998

FASCIOTTI Titta 1927-1993 **[17]**
  $389 - €403 - **£253** - FF2 847
  Pool, Eastern Cape Oil/canvas/board (29.5x40cm
  11x15in) Johannesburg 2000

FASSBENDER Adolf 1884-1980 **[13]**
  $1 800 - €1 681 - **£1 087** - FF11 029
  Venetian Byways Carbon print (46x34cm 18x13in)
  New-York 1999

FASSBENDER Joseph 1903-1974 **[53]**
  $2 080 - €2 454 - **£1 467** - FF16 098
  Ohne Titel Oil/paper/panel (61x92cm 24x36in) Köln
  2001
  $1 333 - €1 431 - **£892** - FF9 390
  Ohne Titel Indian ink (41.5x48.5cm 16x19in) Köln
  2000
  $269 - €307 - **£187** - FF2 012
  Abstrakte Kompositionen Lithographie (62x81cm
  24x31in) Hamburg 2001

FASSIANOS Alexandre, Alecos 1935 **[350]**
  $41 031 - €47 240 - **£28 000** - FF309 873
  Red Bather Mixed media (166.5x119.5cm 65x47in)
  London 2000
  $5 051 - €4 269 - **£3 004** - FF28 000
  Deux oiseaux rouges Huile/toile (74x80cm 29x31in)
  Versailles 1998
  $2 758 - €2 639 - **£1 713** - FF17 313
  Dimanche matin Technique mixte/panneau
  (40x36.5cm 15x14in) Zürich 1999
  $704 - €762 - **£482** - FF5 000
  Nu à la plume Mine plomb (14x20cm 5x7in) Paris
  2001
  $144 - €152 - **£95** - FF1 000
  Sans titre Lithographie couleurs (60x44cm 23x17in)
  Paris 2000

FASSIN de Nicolas Henri J. 1728-1811 **[12]**
  $7 100 - €7 622 - **£4 750** - FF50 000
  **Bergers gardant leur bétail dans les ruines du
  Colisée** Huile/toile (69x60cm 27x23in) Paris 2000

FATTAH Ismail 1934 **[2]**
  $5 729 - €6 444 - **£4 000** - FF42 268
  Man & Woman Gouache (157x118cm 61x46in)
  London 2001

FATTORI Giovanni 1825-1908 **[240]**
  $225 000 - €233 247 - **£135 000** - FF1 530 000
  L'Arno alle Cascine Olio/tela (70.5x135.5cm
  27x53in) Prato 1999
  $27 000 - €23 325 - **£13 500** - FF153 000
  Cavalleggero Olio/tavola (10.5x9cm 4x3in) Prato
  1999
  $13 250 - €13 736 - **£7 950** - FF90 100
  Soldato a cavallo Acquarello/carta (27.5x10.5cm
  10x4in) Milano 2001
  $550 - €570 - **£330** - FF3 740
  Sentiero nel bosco Acquaforte (25x14cm 9x5in)
  Prato 2000

FAU Fernand 1858-1917 **[6]**
  $621 - €686 - **£421** - FF4 500
  «Salon des Cent» Affiche couleur (40x60cm
  15x23in) Nice 2000

FAUBERT Jean 1946 **[243]**
  $432 - €396 - **£252** - FF2 600
  Musicien Huile/panneau (27x18cm 10x7in) Paris 1999
  $325 - €351 - **£218** - FF2 300
  Deux personnages Aquarelle, gouache/papier
  (20x30cm 7x11in) Grenoble 2000

FAUCON Bernard 1950 **[37]**
  $755 - €838 - **£526** - FF5 500
  Les pastèques Tirage Fresson (31.5x30.5cm
  12x12in) Paris 2001

FAUCONNET Guy Pierre 1882-1920 **[6]**
  $1 500 - €1 610 - **£1 003** - FF10 561
  Le clown Watercolour (30x23cm 11x9in) New-York
  2000

FAUERHOLDT Viggo 1832-1883 **[38]**
  $2 486 - €2 683 - **£1 668** - FF17 598
  Sommerdag ved en klippekyst Oil/canvas
  (42x63cm 16x24in) Köbenhavn 2000
  $1 615 - €1 744 - **£1 084** - FF11 438
  Caledonia udfor Sölyst Oil/canvas (25x35cm
  9x13in) Köbenhavn 2000

FAUGERON Adolphe 1866-1944 **[10]**
  $1 189 - €1 416 - **£850** - FF9 287
  **A Gondola on a Sunlit Venetian Canal/A
  Gondola Under a Bridge** Oil/canvas (26.5x40.5cm
  10x15in) London 2000

FAULKNER Barry 1892-1966 **[1]**
  $3 500 - €4 043 - **£2 450** - FF26 523
  **The Declaration of Independence/Constitution
  of the United State** Watercolour/paper (10x23cm
  4x9in) New-York 2001

FAULKNER Charles XIX **[6]**
  $1 417 - €1 350 - **£900** - FF8 853
  **Study of a Chestnut Hunter in a Stable/Study of
  Dark Bay Hunter** Oil/canvas (42x52cm 16x20in)
  Billingshurst, West-Sussex 1999
  $2 100 - €2 155 - **£1 316** - FF14 136
  Fox Hunting Scenes Oil/board (15x29cm 6x11in)
  Downington PA 2000

FAULKNER John 1835-1894 **[156]**
  $4 761 - €4 060 - **£2 872** - FF26 631
  Figures on a Country Riad Oil/canvas/board
  (76x101cm 30x40in) Dublin 1998
  $2 162 - €1 852 - **£1 300** - FF12 151
  Among the Hills of Donegal Watercolour/paper
  (45x75cm 17x29in) Edinburgh 1998

FAULKNER Richard 1917 **[2]**
  $959 - €984 - **£600** - FF6 457
  «Northern Ireland» Poster (102x64cm 40x25in)
  London 2000

FAURE Amandus 1874-1931 **[69]**
  $827 - €869 - **£521** - FF5 701
  Markt in Marokko Öl/Karton (34.5x53cm 13x20in)
  Stuttgart 2000
  $1 666 - €1 738 - **£1 049** - FF11 403
  **Nächtliche Versammung auf dem Stuttgarter
  Schlossplatz** Öl/Karton (27x36cm 10x14in) Stuttgart
  2000

FAURE DE BROUSSÉ Vincent Désiré 1908 **[8]**
  $2 996 - €3 470 - **£2 072** - FF22 764
  Improvisatrice Bronze (H72cm H28in) Bruxelles
  2000

FAURE Elisabeth 1906-1964 **[41]**
  $440 - €488 - **£304** - FF3 200
  Case sous les cocotiers, Nassi Bé, Madagascar
  Huile/panneau (41x56.5cm 16x22in) Paris 2001
  $247 - €274 - **£171** - FF1 800
  Buvette au Zouma, Tamanari, Madagascar
  Aquarelle/papier (29.5x50.5cm 11x19in) Paris 2001

FAURE Jean Victor Louis 1786-1879 **[6]**

- $2 175 - €2 470 - **£1 488** - FF16 200
  Vue de Saint Maurice dans le Valais Huile/toile
  (32x40cm 12x15in) Troyes 2000

FAURE Paul David XX **[2]**

- $3 182 - €3 659 - **£2 246** - FF24 000
  L'orchestre de chambre Huile/panneau (60x90cm
  23x35in) Lavaur 2001

FAURE-DUJARRIC Louis Lucien 1872-? **[14]**

- $700 - €781 - **£458** - FF5 122
  «Claudine à l'école et à Paris par Willy» Poster
  (140x100cm 55x39in) New-York 2000

FAURER Louis 1916-2001 **[37]**

- $1 600 - €1 612 - **£997** - FF10 576
  «Freudian Hand Clasp»/«New York» Gelatin silver
  print (29x19cm 11x7in) New-York 2000

FAURET Léon J.J. 1863-1955 **[18]**

- $1 694 - €1 829 - **£1 171** - FF12 000
  Les bateaux-lavoirs au Pont-Marie Huile/toile
  (38x61cm 14x24in) Soissons 2001
- $653 - €686 - **£433** - FF4 500
  Maisons en bord de mer en bretagne Huile/pan-
  neau (27x35cm 10x13in) Quimper 2000

FAUSTINO Modesto 1839-1891 **[4]**

- $28 000 - €28 215 - **£17 455** - FF185 080
  The Suitor Oil/canvas (51x102cm 20x40in) New-York
  2000
- $2 265 - €1 957 - **£1 132** - FF12 838
  Idillio pompeano Olio/cartone (21.5x18cm 8x7in)
  Milano 1999

FAUTRIER Jean 1898-1964 **[735]**

- $478 176 - €513 282 - **£320 000** - FF3 366 912
  All Alone Mixed media (89x146cm 35x57in) London
  2000
- $90 000 - €93 299 - **£54 000** - FF612 000
  Tourbes Olio/carta/tela (50x60cm 19x23in) Milano
  1999
- $38 851 - €41 704 - **£26 000** - FF273 561
  Petit nu noir Oil/canvas (34.5x27cm 13x10in) London
  2000
- $7 077 - €8 212 - **£4 886** - FF53 865
  Petit masque Bronze (H16cm H6in) Stockholm 2000
- $3 626 - €4 264 - **£2 600** - FF27 972
  Untitled Gouache (32.5x24.5cm 12x9in) London 2001
- $531 - €625 - **£380** - FF4 100
  Sans titre Eau-forte couleurs (79.5x56.5cm 31x22in)
  Paris 2001

FAUVEL Georges Henri 1890-? **[24]**

- $29 000 - €26 880 - **£18 032** - FF176 322
  A Brace of Hounds Oil/canvas (121x150cm 47x59in)
  New-York 1999
- $1 707 - €1 829 - **£1 162** - FF12 000
  Les deux petits chiots Huile/toile (43x56cm
  16x22in) Calais 2001
- $1 050 - €1 220 - **£748** - FF8 000
  Bassets griffons au terrier Huile/panneau
  (36.5x40.5cm 14x15in) Senlis 2001

FAUVELET Jean-Baptiste 1819-1883 **[14]**

- $4 000 - €3 818 - **£2 499** - FF25 046
  Ladies at the Table Oil/canvas (38x46cm 15x18in)
  Dedham MA 1999
- $1 250 - €1 056 - **£743** - FF6 929
  Girl Reading Huile/panneau (15x12cm 6x4in)
  Philadelphia PA 1998

FAUX-FROIDURE Eugénie 1886-? **[43]**

- $960 - €908 - **£599** - FF5 953
  Pink Roses in a Jar Watercolour/paper (51x37.5cm
  20x14in) Amsterdam 1999

FAVAI Gennaro 1882-1958 **[34]**

- $2 749 - €2 514 - **£1 679** - FF16 494
  Venice Oil/canvas (52x72cm 20x28in) New-York 1998
- $1 200 - €1 037 - **£800** - FF6 800
  Veduta di Venezia con barche Olio/tavola
  (32.5x24.5cm 12x9in) Firenze 1998

FAVANNE de Henri Antoine 1668-1752 **[27]**

- $5 382 - €5 946 - **£3 732** - FF39 000
  La naissance d'Adonis Huile/toile (57.5x57cm
  22x22in) Lille 2001

FAVELLE R. XIX **[9]**

- $2 359 - €2 613 - **£1 600** - FF17 139
  Children Lighting a Campfire Oil/panel (17x26cm
  6x10in) Billingshurst, West-Sussex 2000

FAVÉN Antti 1882-1948 **[63]**

- $12 127 - €13 791 - **£8 413** - FF90 462
  Midsommardans Oil/canvas (120x120cm 47x47in)
  Helsinki 2000
- $2 253 - €2 523 - **£1 564** - FF16 548
  Sommarkväll Oil/canvas/board (71x103cm 27x40in)
  Helsinki 2001
- $1 721 - €1 598 - **£1 033** - FF10 480
  Landskap Oil/canvas (25x20cm 9x7in) Helsinki 1999

FAVIER Philippe 1957 **[77]**

- $4 241 - €3 506 - **£2 488** - FF23 000
  Nénuphars Peinture (15x19.5cm 5x7in) Paris 1998
- $1 375 - €1 448 - **£908** - FF9 500
  «Il arrive que Betty» Gouache/papier (19x10cm
  7x3in) Paris 2000

FAVORIN Ellen 1853-1919 **[44]**

- $3 697 - €4 205 - **£2 565** - FF27 580
  Sommarlandskap Oil/canvas (48x76cm 18x29in)
  Helsinki 2000
- $2 401 - €2 102 - **£1 455** - FF13 786
  Vy frân Lojoåsen Oil/panel (20x26.5cm 7x10in)
  Helsinki 1998

FAVORY André 1888-1937 **[198]**

- $1 549 - €1 677 - **£1 061** - FF11 000
  Nu couché sur l'herbe Huile/toile (50x73cm
  19x28in) Paris 2001

FAVRAY de Antoine 1706-1798 **[17]**

- $7 000 - €8 133 - **£4 919** - FF53 348
  **Asclepius, the God of Healing and Medicine,
  seated half-length** Oil/canvas (79x64cm 31x25in)
  New-York 2001
- $3 350 - €3 049 - **£2 094** - FF20 000
  Roses et myosotis Huile/toile (21.5x16cm 8x6in)
  Saint-Dié 1999

FAVRE DE THIERRENS Jacques 1895-1973 **[16]**

- $341 - €381 - **£231** - FF2 500
  Les Roses Huile/bois (22x32cm 8x12in) Nîmes 2000

FAVRE Georges XX **[12]**

- $915 - €915 - **£572** - FF6 000
  «Cycles Griffon» Affiche (117x77cm 46x30in)
  Orléans 1999

FAVRETTO Giacomo 1849-1887 **[46]**

- $13 500 - €13 995 - **£8 100** - FF91 800
  Signora con libro Olio/tela (57x30cm 22x11in)
  Torino 2000
- $3 600 - €4 665 - **£2 700** - FF30 600
  Giovane di profilo Olio/tela (40x28cm 15x11in)
  Roma 2001

$2 000 - €2 073 - **£1 200** - FF13 600
Ritratto del padre del pittore Acquarello/carta
(22x18cm 8x7in) Milano 1999

FAWCETT Robert 1903-1967 **[11]**
$3 000 - €3 497 - **£2 077** - FF22 939
Pitched Battle at the Alamo Watercolour, gouache
(38x88cm 15x35in) New-York 2000

FAWKES Lionel Grimston 1849-1931 **[5]**
$3 865 - €4 634 - **£2 400** - FF23 938
**Queen's House, Barbados/Queen's House
Windmill/View from Drawing-Room**
Watercolour/paper (14.5x23cm 5x9in) London 1999

FAXON Richard XIX **[5]**
$4 208 - €3 961 - **£2 600** - FF25 985
A Two-Master heading into Royan, France
Oil/canvas (54.5x81.5cm 21x32in) London 1999

FAY Clark 1894-1956 **[2]**
$38 000 - €42 584 - **£26 486** - FF279 330
Legend of Woksis Oil/canvas (96.5x86.5cm 37x34in)
Beverly-Hills CA 2001

FAY Georges ?-1916 **[4]**
$1 108 - €1 067 - **£684** - FF7 000
**«Le quartier, Cabaret-Salon artistique et littérai-
re, Rue Cujas»** Affiche (121.5x80.5cm 47x31in) Paris
1999

FAY Hanns 1888-1957 **[30]**
$3 645 - €3 374 - **£2 200** - FF22 135
Weinlese in der Pfalz Öl/Leinwand (90x101cm
35x39in) Heidelberg 1999
$284 - €266 - **£176** - FF1 744
Der Holzmarkt in Speyer Watercolour (47x36cm
18x14in) Heidelberg 1999

FAYDHERBE Jean Lukas 1654-1704 **[1]**
$5 362 - €4 563 - **£3 200** - FF29 930
Venus Sculpture (H26cm H10in) London 1998

FAYE Harold 1910-1980 **[2]**
$3 600 - €3 880 - **£2 455** - FF25 450
«Bid Dip» Lithograph (39x30cm 15x11in) New-York
2001

FAYRAL XX **[6]**
$544 - €610 - **£378** - FF4 000
Femme au cerveau Sculpture (H46cm H18in) Blois
2001

FAZZINI Pericle 1913-1987 **[90]**
$1 200 - €1 244 - **£720** - FF8 160
Pifferaio Bas-relief (31x31cm 12x12in) Trieste 2000
$475 - €492 - **£285** - FF3 230
Paesaggio Pastelli/carta (50.5x39cm 19x15in) Prato
2001

FAZZINO Charles XX **[2]**
$5 539 - €6 250 - **£3 895** - FF41 000
«Money doesn't grow on the Trees» Sérigraphie
(98x78cm 38x30in) Paris 2001

FEARNLEY Thomas 1802-1842 **[31]**
$47 367 - €49 635 - **£30 000** - FF325 587
En plein air, Sorrento Oil/paper/canvas (38x45.5cm
14x17in) London 2000
$7 741 - €8 075 - **£4 884** - FF52 971
Djevelen frister Kristus all verdens herlighet
Oil/canvas (27x32cm 10x13in) Oslo 2000
$11 040 - €10 091 - **£6 915** - FF66 195
Parti med fossende elv i Alperne, Schweiz
Pastel/paper (124x83cm 48x32in) København 1999

FEARON Hilda 1878-1917 **[7]**
$30 618 - €25 718 - **£18 000** - FF168 697
Afternoon Sunshine Oil/canvas (70x90cm 27x35in)
Devon 1998

FEBVRE Édouard XIX-XX **[142]**
$1 059 - €991 - **£641** - FF6 500
Jour de marché Huile/toile (65x53.5cm 25x21in)
Lille 1999
$434 - €381 - **£263** - FF2 500
14 juillet à l'Arc de Triomphe Huile/panneau
(27x34cm 10x13in) Paris 1999
$204 - €229 - **£138** - FF1 500
La roulotte Fusain (24x31cm 9x12in) Paris 2000

FECHENBACH Hermann 1897-1986 **[29]**
$282 - €294 - **£180** - FF1 930
Portrait of Theodor Herzl Oil/canvas (61x51cm
24x20in) London 1999

FECHIN Nicolai Ivanovich 1881-1955 **[27]**
$80 000 - €95 140 - **£57 016** - FF624 080
Young Girl Oil/canvas (51.5x44.5cm 20x17in) New-
York 2000
$70 000 - €82 270 - **£48 531** - FF539 658
The Little Burro Oil/board (26.5x35.5cm 10x13in)
Beverly-Hills CA 2000

FECTEAU Marcel 1927 **[38]**
$492 - €561 - **£340** - FF3 677
Approaching Storm Clouds Oil/canvas (40.5x51cm
15x20in) Montréal 2000

FEDDEN A. Romilly 1875-1939 **[25]**
$306 - €259 - **£180** - FF1 698
Canal at Malines Watercolour/paper (36.5x44.5cm
14x17in) Oxford 1998

FEDDEN Mary 1915 **[456]**
$28 414 - €27 553 - **£18 000** - FF180 736
The Harlequin Coffee Pot Oil/canvas (98x131cm
38x51in) London 1999
$9 549 - €8 974 - **£5 800** - FF58 867
Still Life with Fruit Oil/canvas (30.5x61cm 12x24in)
London 1999
$4 184 - €4 491 - **£2 800** - FF29 460
Red Flowers Oil/board (39.5x29.5cm 15x11in)
London 2000
$2 689 - €2 887 - **£1 800** - FF18 938
The Farm Watercolour/paper (22.5x17.5cm 8x6in)
London 2000
$256 - €254 - **£160** - FF1 667
Still Life Color lithograph (76x57cm 29x22in) London
1999

FEDDER Otto 1873-1919 **[51]**
$1 787 - €2 045 - **£1 229** - FF13 415
**Fischer im Kahn und Kühe bei der Tränke am
Flussufer** Oil/canvas/panel (73x106cm 28x41in)
München 2001
$1 009 - €1 125 - **£705** - FF7 378
Heuernte auf einer Wiese am Seeufer Oil/panel
(11x18cm 4x7in) München 2001
$276 - €307 - **£191** - FF2 012
«Seeufer» Pencil/paper (25x19cm 9x7in) Kempten
2001

FEDDERS Julius, Yuli Ivanov. 1838-1909 **[3]**
$24 156 - €22 809 - **£15 000** - FF149 617
Heading for Shore Oil/canvas (108.5x149.5cm
42x58in) London 1999

FEDDERSEN Hans Peter II 1848-1941 **[13]**
$6 600 - €6 503 - **£3 955** - FF38 733
Landskab med vandlob hvori store sten Oil/can-
vas (39x54cm 15x21in) København 1998

FEDDES Pieter 1586-1634 **[2]**
- $1 165 - €1 278 - **£791** - FF8 384
  Die Dornenkrönung Christi Radierung (16x12.6cm 6x4in) Berlin 2000

FEDDON Mary 1915 **[2]**
- $12 000 - €11 915 - **£7 500** - FF78 155
  Portugal Oil/board (51x76cm 20x29in) London 1999

FEDELER Carl 1837-1897 **[7]**
- $8 000 - €8 062 - **£4 987** - FF52 880
  Bringing in the Catch Oil/canvas (67.5x110cm 26x43in) New-York 2000

FEDELI IL MAGGIOTTO Domenico 1713-1794 **[21]**
- $11 554 - €13 469 - **£8 000** - FF88 348
  Joseph Interpreting the Dreams of Pharaoh's Butler and Baker Oil/canvas (110x130cm 43x51in) London 2000
- $26 963 - €28 313 - **£17 000** - FF185 719
  Shepherds with a Gourd and a Peasant Boy Playing Pipes Oil/canvas (59.5x79cm 23x31in) London 2000
- $8 646 - €8 385 - **£5 478** - FF55 000
  Jeune garçon tenant une écuelle Huile/toile (43.5x36cm 17x14in) Paris 1999

FEDER Adolphe 1886-c.1943 **[115]**
- $1 307 - €1 524 - **£907** - FF10 000
  L'orientale Huile/toile (65x54cm 25x21in) Paris 2001
- $177 - €198 - **£120** - FF1 300
  Église vue à travers les arbres Encre (31x27.5cm 12x10in) Paris 2000

FEDERAU Bernt 1945 **[10]**
- $594 - €588 - **£370** - FF3 857
  Paris, Fenster mit Katze Vintage gelatin silver print (38.9x29.8cm 15x11in) Berlin 1999

FEDERICO Michele 1884-1966 **[78]**
- $872 - €936 - **£583** - FF6 141
  Isle of Capri Oil/canvas (68.5x89cm 26x35in) Montréal 2000

FEDERLE Helmut 1944 **[38]**
- $32 078 - €37 723 - **£23 000** - FF247 447
  «Tree of Inside and Outside» Oil/canvas (271x176cm 106x69in) London 2001
- $13 000 - €11 561 - **£7 950** - FF75 832
  Nach Unten Abnehmende Form Oil/canvas (40x60cm 15x23in) New-York 1999

FEDI Antonio 1771-1843 **[1]**
- $9 000 - €7 775 - **£4 500** - FF51 000
  Ritratto di signora seduta in un giardino Olio/tela (19x13.5cm 7x5in) Firenze 1999

FEDI Giuseppe ?-c.1819 **[1]**
- $7 000 - €7 713 - **£4 669** - FF50 591
  Melantho of Whitby, George Parry, Master Watercolour/paper (46x65cm 18x25in) Portsmouth NH 2000

FÉDIER Franz 1922 **[62]**
- $449 - €434 - **£277** - FF2 844
  Morgen Huile/toile (66.5x49.5cm 26x19in) Bern 1999
- $261 - €297 - **£181** - FF1 949
  Venezia Aquarell/Papier (36.5x53cm 14x20in) Zofingen

FEDKOWICZ Jerzy 1891-1959 **[17]**
- $5 032 - €4 803 - **£3 144** - FF31 506
  Peasants in the Fields, a Village behind Oil/canvas (85x100cm 33x39in) Warszawa 1999

FEDOROVA Maria 1859-1934 **[23]**
- $1 267 - €1 244 - **£786** - FF8 163
  Aftonpromenad Oil/canvas (40x30cm 15x11in) Helsinki 1999

FEDOTOV Pawel Andreievich 1815-1852 **[4]**
- $10 460 - €11 228 - **£7 000** - FF73 651
  Sleeping Beauty by a Candle Oil/panel (40x32cm 15x12in) London 2000

FEER LADER van der Elisabeth, Else 1897-1984 **[5]**
- $2 026 - €2 042 - **£1 263** - FF13 394
  Vijver, a Pond Oil/board (22.5x27cm 8x10in) Amsterdam

FEGUIDE Marcel 1888-1974 **[19]**
- $549 - €488 - **£336** - FF3 200
  Conversation Pastel/papier (50x65cm 19x25in) Avignon 1999

FEHDMER Richard Henri 1860-1945 **[28]**
- $1 686 - €1 892 - **£1 168** - FF12 409
  Motiv aus Antwerpen, Abendstimmung Oil/panel (32x23.4cm 12x9in) München 2000
- $1 597 - €1 789 - **£1 100** - FF11 738
  Niederländische Landschaft mit Segelbooten Watercolour (38.3x57.2cm 15x22in) Hamburg 2000

FEHER Emeric 1904-1966 **[19]**
- $406 - €457 - **£283** - FF3 000
  Nu de femme assise Tirage argentique (18.5x12cm 7x4in) Paris 2001

FEHÉR Laszlo 1953 **[7]**
- $1 400 - €1 549 - **£920** - FF10 160
  In the Water Pastel/paper (63.5x48.5cm 25x19in) Budapest 2000

FEHR Friedrich 1862-1927 **[16]**
- $783 - €767 - **£482** - FF5 030
  Polling bei Weilheim, Stilleben mit Rosen, Rittersporn Öl/Leinwand (67.5x65cm 26x25in) Bremen 1999

FEHR Henri 1890-1964 **[46]**
- $1 193 - €1 246 - **£755** - FF8 171
  Bouquet de fleurs Huile/toile (54x65cm 21x25in) Genève 2000
- $732 - €626 - **£443** - FF4 106
  Jeune femme nue avec drap rose Pastel/papier (51x42cm 20x16in) Genève 1998

FEHRLE Jacob Wilhelm 1884-1974 **[55]**
- $1 308 - €1 227 - **£808** - FF8 049
  Verkündigung Bronze relief (31x35cm 12x13in) Stuttgart 1999

FEIBUSCH Hans 1898-1998 **[17]**
- $269 - €289 - **£180** - FF1 893
  Diana Black & white chalks/paper (51x36cm 20x14in) London 2000

FEID Josef 1806-1870 **[30]**
- $2 317 - €2 543 - **£1 540** - FF16 684
  Am Heimweg Oil/panel (46x64cm 18x25in) Wien 2000
- $4 746 - €4 602 - **£2 939** - FF30 185
  Waldbach Oil/panel (22x28.5cm 8x11in) Graz 1999

FEIFFER Jules 1929 **[3]**
- $2 400 - €2 673 - **£1 569** - FF17 553
  Sequential drawing; woman assesses who to blame Ink (18x34cm 7x13in) New-York 2000

FEIGIN Dov 1907-? **[33]**
- $300 - €318 - **£203** - FF2 088
  Figure Ink/paper (33x21cm 12x8in) Tel Aviv 2001

FEIGL Bedrich, Friedrich 1884-1965 **[65]**
- $2 164 - €2 556 - £1 528 - FF16 769
  Gebirgsfluss mit Kühen Öl/Leinwand (49.5x62cm 19x24in) Köln 2001
- $295 - €307 - £186 - FF2 012
  Am Ufer des Gardasee bei Abendstimmung Indian ink (36x48cm 14x18in) Berlin 2000

FEILER Paul 1918 **[69]**
- $19 639 - €23 411 - £14 000 - FF153 563
  Enclosed Verticals Oil/canvas (167.5x184cm 65x72in) London 2000
- $7 136 - €6 880 - £4 400 - FF45 131
  Floating Form, white Oil/canvas (56x46cm 22x18in) London 1999
- $2 351 - €2 267 - £1 450 - FF14 872
  Orbis L Oil/canvas (15x18cm 5x7in) London 1999
- $1 181 - €1 386 - £850 - FF9 089
  Abstract Charcoal (30.5x30.5cm 12x12in) London 2001

FEILHAMMER Franz Anton 1817-1888 **[7]**
- $813 - €945 - £572 - FF6 197
  Blühende Pflanzenbouquets Öl/Karton (30x27cm 11x10in) Wien 2001

FEIN Martha XX **[1]**
- $5 482 - €5 450 - £3 405 - FF35 752
  Egon Schiele am Totenbett Vintage gelatin silver print (12.5x18.5cm 4x7in) Wien 1999

FEIN Nat 1914-2000 **[14]**
- $2 000 - €2 147 - £1 358 - FF14 081
  Babe Ruth Bows Out/Jackie Robinson Slides Home Gelatin silver print (25.5x33cm 10x12in) Beverly-Hills CA 2001

FEININGER Andreas 1906-1999 **[148]**
- $2 200 - €2 442 - £1 533 - FF16 019
  «Orchard Street, Jewish Barber Shop» Gelatin silver print (24x19cm 9x7in) New-York 2001

FEININGER Lyonel 1871-1956 **[1230]**
- $478 176 - €513 282 - £320 000 - FF3 366 912
  Mädchen mit grünen Strümpfen Oil/canvas (90x80cm 35x31in) London 2000
- $9 496 - €11 171 - £6 703 - FF73 280
  Dorfstrasse in Neppermin Coloured chalks/paper (22x28cm 8x11in) Berlin 2001
- $1 375 - €1 175 - £807 - FF7 707
  Dorfkirche Woodcut (14x12cm 5x4in) Staufen 1998

FEININGER Theodore Lux 1910 **[24]**
- $3 230 - €3 374 - £2 119 - FF22 135
  Cherbourg: La Place de Napoléon et l'église de la Trinité Öl/Karton (35x45.5cm 13x17in) München 2000
- $1 394 - €1 646 - £989 - FF10 799
  Lyonel Feininger mit Modellyacht auf dem Balkon in Weimar Vintage gelatin silver print (12x9cm 4x3in) Berlin 2001

FEINSTEIN David XX **[1]**
- $1 700 - €1 758 - £1 074 - FF11 533
  Reference Room, New York Public Library Lithograph (35x42cm 13x16in) New-York 2000

FEINT Adrian George 1894-1971 **[126]**
- $6 151 - €5 799 - £3 812 - FF38 041
  Still Life Oil/wood (44.5x39.5cm 17x15in) Melbourne 1999
- $726 - €756 - £456 - FF4 958
  Still Life - Hydrangeas and Apples Oil/board (27.5x23cm 10x9in) Melbourne 2000

- $201 - €225 - £140 - FF1 476
  Long Reef Pencil/paper (24.5x30cm 9x11in) Sydney 2001
- $80 - €76 - £50 - FF499
  Barbara Lane Mullins' Bookplate Woodcut in colors (6x5.5cm 2x2in) Sydney 1999

FEITELSON Lorser 1898-1978 **[8]**
- $19 000 - €21 608 - £13 275 - FF141 741
  Cobalt with Red Acrylic/canvas (152.5x152.5cm 60x60in) Beverly-Hills CA 2000

FEITH Gustav 1875-1951 **[37]**
- $1 974 - €2 180 - £1 368 - FF14 301
  Herbstblumen in einem Glas Aquarell/Papier (41x30cm 16x11in) Wien 2001

FEITO LOPEZ Luis 1929 **[316]**
- $8 166 - €7 882 - £5 059 - FF51 700
  1351-Q Huile/toile (200x300cm 78x118in) Montréal 1999
- $3 692 - €3 964 - £2 470 - FF26 000
  Composition Huile/toile (90x50cm 35x19in) Paris 2000
- $864 - €961 - £576 - FF6 304
  Sin título Gouache/papier (11x17.5cm 4x6in) Madrid 2000
- $162 - €180 - £108 - FF1 182
  Círculos Litografía (76x56cm 29x22in) Madrid 2000

FEJES Emerik 1904-1969 **[4]**
- $561 - €655 - £389 - FF4 296
  Ansicht von Novisad Aquarell, Gouache/Papier (40.5x58.5cm 15x23in) Bern 2000

FEKETE Esteban 1924 **[147]**
- $110 - €102 - £66 - FF670
  Das alte Pferd Woodcut (55x40cm 21x15in) Heidelberg 1999

FELBER Carl Friedrich 1880-1932 **[63]**
- $637 - €665 - £401 - FF4 360
  Augustmorgen, Bernina Öl/Karton (49.5x70cm 19x27in) München 2000

FELBRA Walter Feller-Brand 1917 **[19]**
- $333 - €393 - £234 - FF2 580
  Vater mit Tochter auf dem Sonntagsspaziergang Oil/panel (10x10.5cm 3x4in) Bern 2000

FELDAIN Bernard 1950 **[1]**
- $7 274 - €6 403 - £4 431 - FF42 000
  Énergie bleue Technique mixte (100x81cm 39x31in) Marseille 1999

FELDBAUER Max 1869-1948 **[41]**
- $2 033 - €1 789 - £1 237 - FF11 738
  Bergbauer Öl/Karton (71x56cm 27x22in) Stuttgart 1999
- $1 018 - €873 - £615 - FF5 727
  Partie beim Krummbad Öl/Leinwand (28x24cm 11x9in) München 1998
- $249 - €230 - £155 - FF1 509
  Pferdegespann mit Heuwagen/Kuhstudie Pastell/Papier (26x36.5cm 10x14in) Zwiesel 1999
- $108 - €102 - £66 - FF670
  Reiterin Radierung (38x47.5cm 14x18in) München 1999

FELDHUSEN Anna 1867-1951 **[35]**
- $72 - €82 - £50 - FF536
  Feldweg mit alter Eiche Radierung (33.5x44.5cm 13x17in) Bremen 2000

F

FELDHÜTTER Ferdinand 1842-1898 **[60]**
- **$3 775** - €3 579 - **£2 296** - FF23 477
  Sommertag an einem Alpensee Öl/Leinwand
  (75x114cm 29x44in) Köln 1999
- **$1 802** - €1 789 - **£1 126** - FF11 738
  Gebirgssee mit Bauernhäusern Öl/Karton
  (29x40cm 11x15in) München 1999

FELDMANN Peter 1790-1871 **[3]**
- **$1 348** - €1 534 - **£935** - FF10 061
  Blick auf das antike Syrakus mit Amphitheater
  Aquarell/Papier (52x72.5cm 20x28in) Lindau 2000

FELDMANN Wilhelm 1859-1932 **[38]**
- **$829** - €869 - **£546** - FF5 701
  Am kleinen Wannsee Öl/Leinwand (74.3x39.5cm
  29x15in) Leipzig 2000

FELDSTEIN Al XX **[2]**
- **$7 500** - €8 050 - **£5 019** - FF52 807
  Death Must Come!: Eight page story Ink
  (45.5x33cm 17x12in) New-York 2000

FELDTMANN Hugo XX **[4]**
- **$224** - €197 - **£136** - FF1 290
  George Washington Poster (83x59cm 33x23in)
  New-York 1999

FELEZ Mariano 1883-1942 **[12]**
- **$1 998** - €2 222 - **£1 332** - FF14 578
  Albarracín Oleo/lienzo (55x45cm 21x17in) Madrid
  2000

FELGENTREFF Paul 1854-1933 **[27]**
- **$1 586** - €1 841 - **£1 128** - FF12 074
  Wenn dich die bösen Buben locken Öl/Leinwand
  (69x55cm 27x21in) Erlangén 2000

FELGUÉREZ Manuel 1928 **[27]**
- **$20 000** - €17 439 - **£12 092** - FF114 394
  Tierra Insólita Oil/canvas (115x135cm 45x53in) New-
  York 1998
- **$494** - €529 - **£337** - FF3 467
  Formas Serigrafia (56.5x47cm 22x18in) México 2001

FELIX Karl Eugen 1837-1906 **[28]**
- **$1 086** - €1 079 - **£678** - FF7 075
  Venice Oil/canvas (40x59.5cm 15x23in) Toronto 1999

FELIX Nelson Félix 1954 **[1]**
- **$16 000** - €18 565 - **£11 046** - FF121 776
  Untitled Sculpture (H96.5cm H37in) New-York 2000

FELIXMÜLLER Conrad 1897-1977 **[658]**
- **$46 326** - €43 272 - **£28 000** - FF283 844
  Bildnis Frau Sofie Isakowitz Oil/canvas (58x67.5cm
  22x26in) London 1999
- **$3 043** - €2 556 - **£1 789** - FF16 767
  «Bildnis eines Mannes» Öl/Leinwand (38.5x29.5cm
  15x11in) Stuttgart 1998
- **$873** - €9 203 - **£5 738** - FF60 370
  Küstenlandschaft bei Le Lavandou Watercolour,
  gouache (34.5x50cm 13x19in) Köln 2000
- **$657** - €767 - **£462** - FF5 030
  Das Mädchen von Prachatitz Woodcut (50.5x40cm
  19x15in) Königstein 2001

FELL Sheila 1931-1979 **[27]**
- **$8 385** - €9 765 - **£5 800** - FF64 051
  Hillside with Farms Oil/board (167.5x101.5cm
  65x39in) London 2000
- **$6 256** - €5 880 - **£3 800** - FF38 568
  Fields in Winter Oil/canvas (51x61cm 20x24in)
  London 1999

FELLER Bob XX **[1]**
- **$3 500** - €3 362 - **£2 128** - FF22 055
  **Feller's Life-size hand holding a Ball in legen-
  dary fastball grip** Plaster (H26.5cm H10in) New-
  York 1999

FELLER Frank 1848-1908 **[14]**
- **$288** - €275 - **£180** - FF1 803
  Eagle with prey, above the Alps Watercolour
  (46x56cm 18x22in) Cheshire 1999

FELLINI Federico 1920-1993 **[5]**
- **$2 161** - €2 463 - **£1 493** - FF16 154
  Eine antike Villa, umgewandelt in ein Bordell
  Felt pen (31x22.5cm 12x8in) Zürich 2000

FELLOWS Charles 1799-1860 **[2]**
- **$20 000** - €18 559 - **£12 220** - FF121 740
  The Acropolis, Athens Oil/canvas (40.5x60cm
  15x23in) New-York 1999

FELLOWS Fred 1934 **[15]**
- **$4 400** - €4 109 - **£2 715** - FF26 954
  Hopes and Dreams Oil/board (22x30cm 9x12in)
  Dallas TX 1999
- **$4 100** - €4 655 - **£2 848** - FF30 537
  Down from the High Country Bronze (H48cm
  H19in) Dallas TX 2001

FÉLON Joseph 1818-1896 **[24]**
- **$984** - €838 - **£586** - FF5 500
  Au salon Mine plomb (44.5x37cm 17x14in) Paris
  1998
- **$252** - €283 - **£175** - FF1 858
  Le Soire Lithograph (31x22.5cm 12x8in) London 2000

FELSER Anton XIX **[1]**
- **$3 209** - €3 579 - **£2 158** - FF23 477
  Blick durchs Schlüsselloch Oil/panel (37x21cm
  14x8in) Ahlden 2000

FELY-MOUTTET 1893-1953 **[13]**
- **$4 863** - €4 726 - **£3 041** - FF31 000
  Composition polychrome Huile/carton (126x92cm
  49x36in) Lyon 1999

FEMENIA Gabriel XVIII **[3]**
- **$13 056** - €12 253 - **£8 160** - FF80 376
  David y Abigail Oleo/lienzo (116.5x100.5cm 45x39in)
  Palma de Mallorca 1999

FÉNASSE Paul 1899-1976 **[17]**
- **$36 596** - €42 686 - **£25 452** - FF280 000
  La baie d'Alger Huile/toile (74x164cm 29x64in) Paris
  2000
- **$2 957** - €2 744 - **£1 832** - FF18 600
  Jardin d'Alger Huile/toile (60x78cm 23x30in)
  Toulouse 1999
- **$2 614** - €3 049 - **£1 818** - FF20 000
  Villa mauresque sur la hauteurs d'Alger
  Huile/toile (33x41cm 12x16in) Paris 2000

FENDI Peter 1796-1842 **[40]**
- **$2 658** - €2 454 - **£1 655** - FF16 098
  **Betende Nonne in ihrer Zelle vor einem
  Schreibtisch** Oil/panel (23x19cm 9x7in)
  Hildrizhausen 1999
- **$1 316** - €1 453 - **£912** - FF9 534
  Auf der Flucht nach Ägypten Pencil/paper
  (42x53.5cm 16x21in) Wien 2001
- **$540** - €613 - **£375** - FF4 024
  **«Peter Fendi und seine Mutter am Wege vom
  Heumarkt in die Stadt»** Radierung (17.5x24cm
  6x9in) Berlin 2001

FENECK Vincenzo XIX [4]
- $1 604 - €1 616 - £1 000 - FF10 603
  Venditore di latte Maltese Watercolour/paper (19x11.5cm 7x4in) London 2000

FENEON Félix 1861-1944 [13]
- $2 518 - €2 744 - £1 744 - FF18 000
  Autoportrait Crayon (27x21cm 10x8in) Paris 2001

FENETY Frederick M. 1854-1915 [6]
- $2 500 - €2 730 - £1 609 - FF17 909
  Roses and Compote Oil/canvas (55x46cm 22x18in) Mystic CT 2000
- $8 000 - €8 823 - £5 417 - FF57 872
  Still Life of Roses Oil/panel (35.5x25cm 13x9in) New-York 2000

FENEUILLE Louis Auguste 1733-1799 [1]
- $2 097 - €1 964 - £1 300 - FF12 881
  Design for a Domed Palace Ink (26x39.5cm 10x15in) London 1999

FENG CHAORAN 1882-1945 [17]
- $5 791 - €5 492 - £3 523 - FF36 027
  Travelling in Autumn Mountain Ink (31x446cm 12x175in) Hong-Kong 1999

FENG DAZHONG 1948 [1]
- $45 045 - €42 718 - £27 405 - FF280 210
  Tiger Ink (132.5x105cm 52x41in) Hong-Kong 1999

FENG FANG 1492-1563 [2]
- $8 385 - €7 869 - £5 180 - FF51 616
  Cursive Script Calligraphy Ink/paper (110.5x38.5cm 43x15in) Hong-Kong 1999

FENG LINZHANG 1943 [5]
- $14 060 - €13 342 - £8 543 - FF87 520
  Autumn Daisies Ink (95x145cm 37x57in) Hong-Kong 1999

FENG MINGQIU 1951 [2]
- $3 846 - €4 574 - £2 649 - FF30 003
  Calligraphy Ink/paper (234.5x35cm 92x13in) Hong-Kong 2000

FENG ZIKAI 1898-1975 [34]
- $4 871 - €5 534 - £3 420 - FF36 301
  Drunk under a Pine Tree Ink (97x39.5cm 38x15in) Hong-Kong 2001

FENN Harry 1838-1911 [23]
- $2 100 - €2 353 - £1 462 - FF15 434
  Still Life with Fruit Oil/canvas (23.5x18.5cm 9x7in) Washington 2001
- $475 - €450 - £295 - FF2 949
  Hudson River Scene Pencil/paper (17x23cm 7x9in) Wallkill NY 1999

FENN Otto 1913-1993 [5]
- $1 188 - €1 176 - £741 - FF7 714
  Stilleben Vintage gelatin silver print (42x34.5cm 16x13in) Berlin 1999

FENNEKER Josef 1895-1956 [12]
- $5 500 - €6 136 - £3 600 - FF40 250
  «Der Fürst von Pappenheim» Poster (143.5x95.5cm 56x37in) New-York 2000

FENNER-BEHMER Hermann 1866-1913 [4]
- $42 380 - €39 637 - £25 662 - FF260 000
  De quoi écrire? Huile/toile (93x73cm 36x28in) Chartres 1999

FENOSA Apelles 1899-1988 [91]
- $2 247 - €2 515 - £1 524 - FF16 500
  Danseuse Bronze (H18cm H7in) Paris 2000

FENOUIL Hervé XX [3]
- $2 564 - €3 049 - £1 828 - FF20 000
  Le phare de Cassis Huile/toile (38x55cm 14x21in) Toulon 2001

FENOUIL Jean César XVIII [5]
- $3 188 - €3 049 - £1 942 - FF20 000
  Portrait d'un magistrat tenant un livre aux armes Huile/toile (95x80cm 37x31in) Troyes 1999

FENOYL de Pierre 1945-1987 [14]
- $816 - €793 - £508 - FF5 200
  Paris Tirage argentique (47.7x32cm 18x12in) Paris 1999

FENSON Robert, Robin XIX-XX [23]
- $1 157 - €1 250 - £800 - FF8 199
  Harvest Time Oil/canvas/board (57x95.5cm 22x37in) London 2001

FENTON Beatrice 1887-1983 [6]
- $13 500 - €15 194 - £9 300 - FF99 666
  Shell Fountain Bronze (H78.5cm H30in) Philadelphia PA 2000

FENTON Roger 1819-1869 [151]
- $5 181 - €5 803 - £3 600 - FF38 066
  «Door, Lindisfarne» Albumen print (29.5x25cm 11x9in) London 2001

FENWICK Thomas ?-c.1850 [7]
- $2 219 - €2 305 - £1 400 - FF15 122
  Highland Loch Oil/canvas (46.5x61.5cm 18x24in) London 2000

FÉNYES Adolphe 1867-1945 [17]
- $8 000 - €7 866 - £5 000 - FF51 600
  Sunlit farm-yard Oil/canvas (65.5x81cm 25x31in) Budapest 1999
- $2 310 - €2 625 - £1 610 - FF17 220
  Abords de village Huile/bois (12x17cm 4x6in) Budapest 2001

FENZONI Ferraù 1562-1645 [12]
- $40 000 - €42 718 - £27 256 - FF280 212
  The Entombment Oil/copper (21.5x24cm 8x9in) New-York 2001
- $30 039 - €28 965 - £18 525 - FF190 000
  Moïse et les serpents Crayon (39x27cm 15x10in) Paris 1999

FEODOROVA Maria Alekseevna 1859-1934 [17]
- $747 - €841 - £514 - FF5 516
  Huts on the Beach Oil/canvas (20x31cm 7x12in) Helsinki 2000

FEOLI Vincenzo 1646-1720 [4]
- $1 080 - €1 399 - £810 - FF9 180
  La Sala degli animali del Museo Pio-Clementino Gravure (61x73cm 24x28in) Venezia 2000

FER de Nicolas 1646-1720 [8]
- $251 - €282 - £174 - FF1 850
  Noveau canal d'Orléans et celui de Briare Eau-forte (47.5x71.5cm 18x28in) Orléans 2001

FER Edouard 1887-1959 [32]
- $756 - €915 - £528 - FF6 000
  Paysage Huile/panneau (10.5x23cm 4x9in) Paris 2000

FÉRAT Serge, Sergej 1881-1958 [64]
- $4 118 - €4 421 - £2 755 - FF29 000
  La maison rose Huile/toile (81x60cm 31x23in) Paris 2000
- $6 112 - €7 308 - £4 200 - FF47 935
  L'homme à la guitare et au chien Oil/paper (27.5x18.5cm 10x7in) London 2000

F

$615 - €577 - **£380** - FF3 786
Nature morte Ink (18x26cm 7x10in) London 1999

FÉRAUD Albert 1921 **[163]**
$1 092 - €1 220 - **£740** - FF8 000
Sans titre Métal (112x42x26cm 44x16x10in)
Versailles 2000
$909 - €945 - **£570** - FF6 200
Sans titre Métal (47x44x34cm 18x17x13in) Paris
2000

FERBER Herbert 1906-1991 **[10]**
$13 500 - €11 647 - **£8 144** - FF76 400
Calligraph in cage with cluster no.I.II Bronze
(104x66x58.5cm 40x25x23in) New-York 1998

FERENCZI Noémi 1890-1957 **[7]**
$510 - €576 - **£360** - FF3 780
La semeuse Aquarelle/papier (42x19cm 16x7in)
Budapest 2001

FERENCZY Jozef 1866-1925 **[3]**
$9 100 - €10 068 - **£5 980** - FF66 040
Love Oil/canvas (115x85cm 45x33in) Budapest 2000

FERENCZY Karoly 1862-1917 **[9]**
$20 350 - €21 381 - **£12 650** - FF140 250
Monsieur Cézar et son épouse Huile/toile
(96x91cm 37x35in) Budapest 2000

FEREY Prosper XIX **[10]**
$2 392 - €2 287 - **£1 500** - FF15 000
Marine au clair de lune Huile/panneau (48x65cm
18x25in) Angers 1999

FERG Franz de Paula 1689-1740 **[85]**
$26 877 - €29 496 - **£17 303** - FF193 479
**Mediterranean coastal Landscapes with
Peasants and Travellers** Oil/copper (40x53cm
15x20in) Amsterdam 2000
$7 500 - €8 714 - **£5 271** - FF57 162
Suffer the little Children to come unto me
Oil/copper (23x29cm 9x11in) New-York 2001

FERGOLA Francesco XIX **[6]**
$842 - €982 - **£583** - FF6 444
**Süditalienische Küste mit Booten und
Figurenstaffage** Gouache/paper (10.5x13.5cm 4x5in)
Bern 2000

FERGOLA Luigi XVIII-XIX **[2]**
$8 000 - €8 293 - **£4 800** - FF54 400
Mergellina Olio/tela (33x52cm 12x20in) Milano 2000
$8 519 - €9 543 - **£5 928** - FF62 600
Vue de la baie de Naples Gouache/papier (59x90cm
23x35in) Valence 2001

FERGOLA Salvatore 1799-1874/77 **[23]**
$14 500 - €15 031 - **£8 700** - FF98 600
Veduta del Golfo di Napoli dai Camaldoli
Olio/tela (59x90cm 23x35in) Milano 2000
$9 000 - €9 330 - **£5 400** - FF61 200
Napoli da Capodimonte con figure Olio/tela
(30x42cm 11x16in) Roma 1999
$1 488 - €1 448 - **£915** - FF9 500
Port méditerranéen Gouache/papier (17.5x25cm
6x9in) Paris 1999

FERGUSON Edward XX **[3]**
$200 - €230 - **£137** - FF1 509
«The Wheatfield» Lithograph (29x40cm 11x16in)
Cleveland OH 2000

FERGUSON Henry Augustus 1842-1911 **[13]**
$10 000 - €11 102 - **£6 955** - FF72 824
«White Birches, Plymouth, Mass» Oil/canvas
(55x76cm 22x30in) Milford CT 2001

$3 800 - €3 255 - **£2 284** - FF21 354
Island of San Lazaro, Venice Oil/canvas/board
(17x35cm 7x14in) Cleveland OH 1998

FERGUSON James ?-c.1857 **[2]**
$6 081 - €5 805 - **£3 800** - FF38 077
Wayside Conversation Oil/canvas (61x81cm
24x31in) London 1999

FERGUSON Kenneth 1938 **[4]**
$4 000 - €4 144 - **£2 546** - FF27 181
Hare Handle Teapot Glazed ceramic (H68cm H26in)
New-York 2000

FERGUSON Mary XX **[1]**
$1 784 - €1 668 - **£1 100** - FF10 944
**The Drawing Room at 27 Upper Pembroke
Street** Watercolour/paper (40x36cm 15x14in) Co.
Kilkenny 1999

FERGUSON Max 1959 **[5]**
$5 000 - €4 857 - **£3 125** - FF31 859
Up on the Roof Oil/panel (58.5x40.5cm 23x15in)
New-York 1999
$3 000 - €3 131 - **£1 892** - FF20 535
Self-Portrait at Julian's Watercolour/paper
(73.5x51.5cm 28x20in) New-York 2000

FERGUSON Nancy Maybin 1872-1967 **[17]**
$2 500 - €2 773 - **£1 662** - FF18 191
Two Fishing Boats Oil/masonite (40x49cm 16x19in)
Milford CT 2000
$750 - €648 - **£445** - FF4 251
Figures in a Street Oil/board (30x40cm 12x16in)
Provincetown MA 1998

FERGUSON William Gowe 1632-1695 **[29]**
$3 607 - €3 522 - **£2 300** - FF23 105
Still Life of a Finch, a Partridge, Kingfisher
Oil/canvas (64x53cm 25x20in) London 1999

FERGUSON William J. ?-c.1886 **[21]**
$478 - €513 - **£320** - FF3 366
Old Sandpit Near Witley Watercolour/paper
(20x42.5cm 7x16in) London 2000

FERGUSSON John Duncan 1874-1961 **[432]**
$59 020 - €65 929 - **£40 000** - FF432 468
Through the Trees, South of France Oil/canvas
(55.5x61cm 21x24in) Edinburgh 2000
$19 898 - €17 226 - **£12 000** - FF112 994
Towards Juan from Cap d'Antibes Oil/panel
(19x24cm 7x9in) Glasgow 1998
$2 964 - €2 820 - **£1 800** - FF18 496
Eve, Woman and Apples Pencil (31x23cm 12x9in)
Edinburgh 1999

FERIER J. XIX **[1]**
$4 632 - €4 327 - **£2 800** - FF28 384
**Lady, a white Dress and red Wrap, holding rose
Buds in her right Hand** Oil/canvas (99x73.5cm
38x28in) London 1999

FERLINGHETTI Lawrence 1919 **[6]**
$500 - €467 - **£302** - FF3 063
Under the Bodhi Tree - Elephants Fucking!
Ink/paper (30.5x23cm 12x9in) New-York 1999

FERLOV MANCOBA Sonja 1911-1984 **[28]**
$4 503 - €5 093 - **£3 043** - FF33 405
Mand Bronze (H37cm H14in) København 2000
$1 320 - €1 278 - **£814** - FF8 383
Figur Indian ink (19x18.5cm 7x7in) København 1999

FERMARIELLO Sergio 1961 **[5]**
$3 400 - €4 406 - **£2 550** - FF28 900
Senza titolo Acrilico (100x100cm 39x39in) Prato
2000

FERNAND-DUBOIS Émile 1869-? **[5]**
$4 480 - €4 421 - **£2 760** - FF29 000
Devant l'Amour Marbre (40x34x44cm 15x13x17in)
Paris 1999

FERNANDES Constantino 1878-1920 **[4]**
$1 890 - €2 094 - **£1 218** - FF13 734
Paisagem Huile/bois (14.5x19.5cm 5x7in) Lisboa
2000
$3 096 - €3 589 - **£2 160** - FF23 544
Estudo de nú femenino Carbón/papel (48x35cm
18x13in) Lisboa 2001

FERNANDEZ Agustín 1928 **[39]**
$3 200 - €3 077 - **£1 975** - FF20 186
Ariadne Oil/canvas (123x124.5cm 48x49in)
Washington 1999
$400 - €429 - **£272** - FF2 816
Modern drawings Graphite (64x48.5cm 25x19in)
Boston MA 2001
$400 - €420 - **£252** - FF2 755
Le Mille Pattes Yvon Taillander Drypoint
(29x23.5cm 11x9in) Washington 2000

FERNANDEZ ALVARADO José 1875-1935 **[3]**
$2 677 - €2 553 - **£1 615** - FF16 745
Violonista y doncella Oleo/lienzo (40x28cm
15x11in) Madrid 1999

FERNANDEZ Arístides 1904-1934 **[6]**
$14 000 - €13 622 - **£8 617** - FF89 352
Sin Título Watercolour (23x32.5cm 9x12in) New-York
1999

FERNANDEZ CARPIO Manuel 1853-? **[5]**
$8 290 - €7 687 - **£5 000** - FF50 423
The Slave Market Oil/canvas (45.5x66cm 17x25in)
London 1999

FERNANDEZ Eduardo Pelayo 1850-? **[2]**
$4 184 - €4 491 - **£2 800** - FF29 460
Greting the Friar Oil/panel (32x48cm 12x18in)
London 2000

FERNANDEZ Francisco 1897-? **[21]**
$1 632 - €1 648 - **£1 122** - FF10 812
Pozo de Valle Arriba Oleo/lienzo (38.5x46cm
15x18in) Caracas 2001

FERNANDEZ LOPEZ Luis 1900-1973 **[17]**
$21 385 - €19 818 - **£13 299** - FF130 000
Tauromachie Huile/toile (61x38cm 24x14in) Paris
1999
$16 450 - €15 245 - **£10 230** - FF100 000
Le chat Huile/toile (46x33cm 18x12in) Paris 1999

FERNANDEZ MARTIN Trinidad 1937 **[18]**
$3 080 - €3 304 - **£2 090** - FF21 670
«Paisaje asturiano» Oleo/lienzo (50x73cm 19x28in)
Madrid 2001

FERNANDEZ NOSERET Luis XVIII **[4]**
$190 - €183 - **£118** - FF1 200
**Série Colleccion de las principales suertes de
una corrida, pl.IX, XI** Eau-forte (17x24cm 6x9in)
Paris 1999

FERNANDEZ Y GONZALEZ Domingo 1862-? **[12]**
$1 297 - €1 524 - **£940** - FF10 000
Village près de la rivière Huile/panneau (18x32cm
7x12in) Calais 2001

FERNANDI IMPERIALI Francesco 1679-1740 **[9]**
$108 849 - €92 672 - **£65 000** - FF607 886
An Allegorical Monument to King George I
Oil/canvas (182.5x241cm 71x94in) London 1998

$6 500 - €6 738 - **£3 900** - FF44 200
Santa Cecilia Olio/tela (121x97.5cm 47x38in) Milano
2000

FERNE Hortense 1885-1976 **[4]**
$4 750 - €5 270 - **£3 159** - FF34 567
Bathing at the Beach, Gloucester Oil/canvas
(63x76cm 25x30in) Milford CT 2000

FERNEL Fernand 1872-1934 **[27]**
$111 - €107 - **£69** - FF700
«Automobiles et bicyclettes» Affiche (104x21cm
40x8in) Paris 1999

FERNELEY Claude Lorraine 1822-1891 **[27]**
$8 666 - €9 303 - **£5 800** - FF61 025
**A Chestnut Racehorse with Jockey up, with
Horses Exercising Beyond** Oil/canvas (36x47cm
14x18in) London 2000
$6 301 - €7 329 - **£4 500** - FF48 073
«Duncan's Horses, a Scene from Macbeth»
Oil/board (33.5x44.5cm 13x17in) London 2001

FERNELEY John, Jnr. 1815-1862 **[60]**
$9 603 - €9 168 - **£6 000** - FF60 135
Huntsmen and Hounds at a Crossroads Oil/can-
vas (37x53.5cm 14x21in) London 1999
$4 781 - €5 133 - **£3 200** - FF33 669
**The Colt, 1st Charger of Captain Lister-Kaye,
10th Hussars** Oil/board (22x30cm 8x11in) London
2000

FERNELEY John, Snr. 1782-1860 **[146]**
$150 530 - €165 148 - **£100 000** - FF1 083 300
**Thomas Goosey, the Belvoir Hounds leaving
the Kennels, Belvoir Castle** Oil/canvas
(102.5x127.5cm 40x50in) London 2000
$28 810 - €27 503 - **£18 000** - FF180 405
**Mr Ferguson's Chestnut colt Karkaway in an
Landscape** Oil/canvas (71x85cm 27x33in) London
1999
$15 237 - €15 072 - **£9 500** - FF98 868
**Dappled Grey Horse held by a Gentleman on
the Marylebone Road** Oil/canvas (19x23.5cm 7x9in)
London 1999

FERNEZ Louis 1900-1983 **[11]**
$2 310 - €2 592 - **£1 601** - FF17 000
Paysage animé Huile/toile (81x100cm 31x39in) Paris
2000
$642 - €732 - **£441** - FF4 800
**«Chemins de fer algériens de l'Etat, le Sud
Algérien, Touggourt»** Affiche (104x72cm 40x28in)
Paris 2000

FERNHOUT Edgar 1921-1976 **[19]**
$19 966 - €19 059 - **£12 478** - FF125 017
«Stilleven met verflap» Oil/canvas (54x38cm
21x14in) Amsterdam 1999

FERNIER Robert 1895-1977 **[53]**
$9 166 - €9 604 - **£5 802** - FF63 000
Le hameau des Arces Huile/toile (65x210cm
25x82in) Besançon 2000
$2 089 - €2 287 - **£1 444** - FF15 000
Vue de Goux-lès-Usiers Huile/toile (56x44cm
22x17in) Besançon 2001
$715 - €793 - **£496** - FF5 200
Le lac gelé Huile/panneau (12.5x15cm 4x5in)
Besançon 2001
$116 - €130 - **£81** - FF850
**Soeur Abel/Homme debout, le chapeau à la
main** Crayon/papier (42x21cm 16x8in) Besançon 2001

FERNKORN von Anton, Ritter 1813-1878 **[6]**

🔨 **$2 466** - €2 761 - **£1 713** - FF18 114
St.Georg den Drachen tötend Bronze (H59.5cm H23in) Wien 2001

FEROGIO François Fortuné A. 1805-1888 **[20]**

✏️ **$462** - €534 - **£323** - FF3 500
Bateleur Aquarelle/papier (41x26cm 16x10in) Paris 2001

FERON Eloi Firmin 1802-1876 **[3]**

🖼️ **$1 443** - €1 677 - **£1 028** - FF11 000
Retour du marché Huile/toile (24.5x33cm 9x12in) Paris 2001

FERON William 1858-1894 **[17]**

🖼️ **$5 500** - €4 764 - **£3 373** - FF31 248
On the Beach Oil/canvas (59.5x81cm 23x31in) New-York 1999

FERRACCI René 1927-1982 **[52]**

📰 **$243** - €290 - **£168** - FF1 900
«Le Samouraï, Jean-Pierre Melville avec Alain Delon» Affiche (60x80cm 23x31in) Paris 2000

FERRAGUTI Arnaldo 1862-1925 **[17]**

🖼️ **$2 000** - €2 073 - **£1 200** - FF13 600
Bambino fra i ventagli Olio/tela (27x17cm 10x6in) Milano 1999

✏️ **$580** - €654 - **£408** - FF4 288
Der Künstler bei der Arbeit Aquarell/Papier (23x15cm 9x5in) Zürich 2001

FERRANDIZ Y BADENESE Bernardo 1835-c.1885/90 **[10]**

🖼️ **$29 700** - €33 036 - **£19 800** - FF216 700
El trasquilón Oleo/tabla (33x52cm 12x20in) Madrid 2000

🖼️ **$2 565** - €2 703 - **£1 620** - FF17 730
Caballero en su estudio Oleo/tabla (22x16cm 8x6in) Madrid 2000

FERRANT Angel 1891-1961 **[12]**

🔨 **$5 940** - €6 607 - **£3 960** - FF43 340
Pase de muleta Bronze (33x52cm 12x20in) Madrid 2000

FERRANT Y FISCHERMANS Alejandro 1843-1917 **[28]**

🖼️ **$260** - €240 - **£156** - FF1 576
Casas romanas Lápiz/papel (24x18cm 9x7in) Madrid 1999

FERRANT Y LLAUSAS Luis 1806-1868 **[6]**

📰 **$341** - €330 - **£214** - FF2 167
Escenas taurinas Litografía (36.5x51cm 14x20in) Madrid 1999

FERRANTI Carlo XIX **[20]**

✏️ **$1 027** - €1 104 - **£700** - FF7 245
An Italian Couple Walking along a Path Watercolour (55x37cm 21x14in) West-Yorshire 2001

FERRARI Agostino 1938 **[52]**

🖼️ **$250** - €292 - **£150** - FF1 700
Composizione Tecnica mista/cartone (65x50cm 25x19in) Vercelli 2000

FERRARI Antoine 1910-1994 **[122]**

🖼️ **$1 161** - €1 220 - **£732** - FF8 000
Bouquet de fleurs Huile/panneau (86x50cm 33x19in) Nîmes 2000

FERRARI Arturo 1861-1932 **[25]**

🖼️ **$16 800** - €14 513 - **£11 200** - FF95 200
Il Verziere, Milano Olio/tela (64x86cm 25x33in) Milano 1998

🖼️ **$1 298** - €1 435 - **£900** - FF9 412
Choir Boys in a Church Interior/Mother and Child in a church Interior Oil/canvas (44x31cm 17x12in) London 2001

FERRARI Berto 1887-1965 **[35]**

🖼️ **$739** - €684 - **£452** - FF4 489
Felsenküste bei Nervi Öl/Karton (29x39cm 11x15in) Bern 1999

FERRARI Carlo il Ferrarin 1813-1871 **[4]**

🖼️ **$77 100** - €91 469 - **£56 100** - FF600 000
Place du marché à Vérone Huile/toile (136x112cm 53x44in) Lyon 2001

🖼️ **$84 180** - €100 115 - **£60 000** - FF656 712
Market Town, and possibly the Fair of St.Allessandro in Bergamo Oil/canvas (51x71.5cm 20x28in) London 2000

FERRARI DA REGGIO Luca 1605-1654 **[4]**

🖼️ **$27 398** - €27 616 - **£17 100** - FF181 146
König David nach einer siegreichen Schlacht von einem Engel gekrönt Öl/Leinwand (116x88cm 45x34in) Wien 2000

FERRARI de Lorenzo 1680-1744 **[8]**

✏️ **$7 000** - €6 984 - **£4 260** - FF45 815
Flying Figure and a Putto/Sketches of a Kneeling Figure Red chalk (27x41.5cm 10x16in) New-York 1999

FERRARI de Orazio 1605-1657 **[10]**

🖼️ **$25 790** - €23 877 - **£16 000** - FF156 624
The holy Family with a Donor Oil/canvas (111x130cm 43x51in) London 1999

FERRARI Defendente c.1480-c.1540 **[4]**

🖼️ **$78 540** - €67 849 - **£52 360** - FF445 060
S.Giovanni Battista e S.Francesco d'Assisi Olio/tavola (132x76.5cm 51x30in) Venezia 1999

FERRARI dei Gregorio Deferrari 1644/47-1726 **[12]**

🖼️ **$106 870** - €110 787 - **£64 122** - FF726 716
Narciso Olio/tela (115x166cm 45x65in) Roma 1999

🖼️ **$194 259** - €208 521 - **£130 000** - FF1 367 808
The Rest on the Flight Into Egypt Oil/canvas (98.5x74cm 38x29in) London 2000

🖼️ **$6 000** - €7 067 - **£4 149** - FF46 355
Head of a Bearded Man Oil/paper/canvas (43x36.5cm 16x14in) New-York 2000

✏️ **$3 743** - €3 663 - **£2 400** - FF24 029
A Bishop Saint with three Putti Ink (29x21cm 11x8in) London 1999

FERRARI Gaudenzio c.1480-1546 **[6]**

✏️ **$5 500** - €5 892 - **£3 755** - FF38 646
The Holy Family Ink (12x11.5cm 4x4in) New-York 2001

FERRARI Giorgio **[1]**

🔨 **$3 691** - €3 583 - **£2 298** - FF23 500
Le jockey à cheval Bronze (36.5x41.5cm 14x16in) Pontoise 1999

FERRARI Giovanni Andrea 1598-1669 **[11]**

🖼️ **$42 880** - €48 691 - **£29 346** - FF319 389
Johannes der Täufer Öl/Leinwand (120x98cm 47x38in) Wien 2000

FERRARI Giovanni Battista 1829-1906 **[12]**

🖼️ **$12 300** - €10 626 - **£8 200** - FF69 700
Pascolo sul Lago Maggiore con sullo sfondo l'Isola dei Pescatori Olio/tela (46x59cm 18x23in) Milano 1998

🖼️ **$2 400** - €2 782 - **£1 700** - FF18 252
Summer Day Oil/board (21x36cm 8x14in) New-York 2000

FERRARI Luigi 1810-1894 **[3]**
- $8 626 - €8 423 - £5 500 - FF55 253
  Bust of a Woman Marble (H71.5cm H28in) London 1999

FERRARINI E. XIX **[2]**
- $2 000 - €1 941 - £1 235 - FF12 735
  Diana Marble (H49cm H19in) Potomac MD 1999

FERRARINI Giuseppe 1846-? **[3]**
- $5 310 - €4 587 - £2 655 - FF30 090
  Paesaggio lacustre Olio/tela (64.5x110cm 25x43in) Milano 1999

FERRARIS Arthur 1856-c.1930 **[9]**
- $16 000 - €17 279 - £11 057 - FF113 342
  The recital Oil/canvas (181x127cm 71x50in) Bethesda MD 2001
- $160 390 - €188 616 - £115 000 - FF1 237 239
  Negotiations in the Market Place Oil/canvas (85x127cm 33x50in) London 2001

FERRAZZI Benvenuto 1892-1969 **[21]**
- $3 250 - €3 369 - £1 950 - FF22 100
  Il Tevere a Roma Olio/tela (49x62.5cm 19x24in) Torino 2000

FERRAZZI Ferruccio 1891-1978 **[33]**
- $9 000 - €7 775 - £6 000 - FF51 000
  Testa femminile Olio/tela (61.5x47.5cm 24x18in) Prato 1998
- $1 800 - €1 866 - £1 080 - FF12 240
  Mucca Olio/tavola (18x24cm 7x9in) Prato 2001

FERREIRA CHAVES José 1838-1899 **[1]**
- $1 848 - €2 094 - £1 260 - FF13 734
  Marinha Huile/bois (23x34cm 9x13in) Lisboa 2000

FERREIRA Manuel 1927 **[9]**
- $330 - €374 - £225 - FF2 452
  Paisagem com rio Oleo/tablex (17x23cm 6x9in) Lisboa 2000

FERREN John Millard 1905-1970 **[43]**
- $2 556 - €2 744 - £1 710 - FF18 000
  Mouvements Huile/toile (33.5x41cm 13x16in) Paris 2000

FERRER Joachim 1929 **[20]**
- $23 000 - €20 055 - £13 905 - FF131 553
  Carnac - Visite Privée Oil/canvas (150x150cm 59x59in) New-York 1998

FERRER PALLOJA José XIX-XX **[12]**
- $1 100 - €1 201 - £740 - FF7 880
  En la playa Oleo/lienzo (33x41cm 12x16in) Madrid 2000

FERRER Y CABRERA Emilio XIX-XX **[5]**
- $2 475 - €2 252 - £1 500 - FF14 775
  Campesina Oleo/lienzo (68x78cm 26x30in) Madrid 1999

FERRERO Alberto 1888-1963 **[19]**
- $1 750 - €1 814 - £1 050 - FF11 900
  Paesaggio langarolo, il tutore (sostegno) Olio/cartone (25x30cm 9x11in) Vercelli 1999

FERRETTI Giovanni Domenico 1692-1766/69 **[13]**
- $6 000 - €6 220 - £3 600 - FF40 800
  Il transito di San Giuseppe Olio/tela (63x51cm 24x20in) Milano 1999
- $550 - €564 - £344 - FF3 702
  Study for a River God Black & white chalks/paper (21x26.5cm 8x10in) New-York 2000

FERRETTINI ROSSOTTI Emilia 1866-1951 **[30]**
- $1 000 - €1 296 - £750 - FF8 500
  Verso il cascinale Olio/tavola (55x41cm 21x16in) Vercelli 2000
- $750 - €777 - £450 - FF5 100
  Paesaggio lacustre Olio/tavola (34.5x44.5cm 13x17in) Vercelli 2001

FERREZ Marc 1843-1923 **[13]**
- $2 600 - €2 859 - £1 803 - FF18 756
  Sugarloaf/View of central Rio/Corcovado/Flamengo Silver print (9x32cm 3x12in) New-York 2001

FERRI Augusto 1829-1895 **[7]**
- $6 300 - €5 442 - £4 200 - FF35 700
  Veduta di porto Olio/tela (79x123cm 31x48in) Milano 1998
- $1 650 - €1 802 - £1 140 - FF11 820
  Señalando el horizonte/Echando las redes Acuarela/papel (24x37.5cm 9x14in) Madrid 2001

FERRI Ciro 1634-1689 **[22]**
- $120 000 - €121 396 - £73 272 - FF796 308
  Triumph of Bacchus Oil/canvas (141x206cm 55x81in) New-York 2000
- $13 000 - €12 971 - £7 913 - FF85 086
  Stormy Landscape with Fishermen trying to Land their boats in an Inlet Ink (27x42cm 10x16in) New-York 2000

FERRIÉ F. XX **[4]**
- $601 - €623 - £360 - FF4 086
  «Saison d'été, Menton» Affiche couleur (100x62cm 39x24in) Torino 2000

FERRIER Gabriel 1847-1914 **[60]**
- $19 320 - €18 294 - £12 000 - FF120 000
  Le Duc de Guise et la future Duchesse de Magenta Huile/toile (146x115cm 57x45in) Paris 1999
- $8 000 - €9 086 - £5 613 - FF59 603
  The Fairest Oil/canvas (65x54cm 25x21in) New-York 2001
- $1 629 - €1 524 - £1 009 - FF10 000
  Femme à la mandoline Huile/panneau (41x31cm 16x12in) La Grand'Combe 1999
- $1 464 - €1 203 - £850 - FF7 889
  La femme avec l'horloge Watercolour (61x53.5cm 24x21in) London 1998

FERRIERE François 1752-1839 **[9]**
- $6 134 - €5 636 - £3 768 - FF36 971
  L'Illiade d'Homero (trompe l'oeil) Aquarelle/papier (43x55cm 16x21in) Zürich 1999
- $3 134 - €3 018 - £1 960 - FF19 799
  Vue de Morges sur le lac de Genève prise de Launay Radierung (31x46cm 12x18in) Zürich 1999

FERRIERES de Georges, comte 1837-1907 **[8]**
- $3 528 - €4 116 - £2 478 - FF27 000
  Deux chiens se disputant un faisan Bronze (32.5x36x17cm 12x14x6in) Pontoise 2000

FERRIGNO Antonio 1863-? **[5]**
- $3 500 - €3 800 - £2 423 - FF24 327
  Summer Garden with Lady in White Dress Oil/canvas (75x49cm 29x19in) Portland OR 2001

FERRIS Carlisle Keith 1929 **[1]**
- $6 050 - €5 161 - £3 649 - FF33 855
  B-26 in flight Oil/masonite (50x76cm 20x30in) New-York 1998

FERRIS Stephen James 1835-1915 **[2]**
- $700 - €754 - £477 - FF4 948
  Little Girl with Dolls, After Weldon Etching (51x72.5cm 20x28in) New-York 2001

F

FERRO Cesare 1880-1934 **[10]**
- $1 000 - €1 037 - **£600** - FF6 800
  Case di Mangone Olio/tavola (26.5x35cm 10x13in)
  Vercelli 2001

FERRO Gregorio 1742-1812 **[4]**
- $3 600 - €3 604 - **£2 220** - FF23 640
  **Encuentro de Jesús con la cruz a cuesta y
  María** Lápiz (49.5x27cm 19x10in) Madrid 2000

FERRO LA GRÉE Georges 1941 **[118]**
- $653 - €686 - **£411** - FF4 500
  Venise Huile/toile (38x55cm 14x21in) Nîmes 2000

FERRON Jean-Paul 1941 **[15]**
- $1 227 - €1 067 - **£739** - FF7 000
  Sologne Huile/toile (65x92cm 25x36in) Paris 1998

FERRON Marcelle 1924 **[57]**
- $1 372 - €1 509 - **£950** - FF9 897
  Deux figures Huile/toile (14x22.5cm 5x8in) Montréal
  2001

FERRONI Egisto 1835-1912 **[20]**
- $3 750 - €3 887 - **£2 250** - FF25 500
  Fanciulla con fiori Olio/tela (112x70cm 44x27in)
  Roma 2000
- $13 200 - €17 105 - **£9 900** - FF112 200
  Lieto ritorno dalla fonte Olio/tela (47.5x25.5cm
  18x10in) Milano 2000

FERRONI Gianfranco 1927-2001 **[98]**
- $10 000 - €12 958 - **£7 500** - FF85 000
  «Oggetti» Olio/tela (96.5x127cm 37x50in) Prato 2000
- $3 900 - €3 369 - **£1 950** - FF22 100
  La stanza Liberty Tecnica mista (55x40.5cm
  21x15in) Prato 1999
- $6 800 - €8 812 - **£5 100** - FF57 800
  Lo straccio rosa Tecnica mista/cartone (33.5x28cm
  13x11in) Milano 2000
- $5 000 - €6 479 - **£3 750** - FF42 500
  Interno Matita/carta (41.5x38.5cm 16x15in) Milano
  2000
- $500 - €518 - **£300** - FF3 400
  Altarino laico Acquaforte (16.5x22cm 6x8in) Firenze
  2000

FERRUZZI S. XX **[1]**
- $4 206 - €3 993 - **£2 624** - FF26 193
  Beatrice Cenci, after Guido Reni Oil/board
  (64.5x50cm 25x19in) Sydney 1999

FERRY Isabelle H. 1865-1937 **[28]**
- $175 - €160 - **£107** - FF1 049
  Still Life Watercolour/paper (35x27cm 14x11in)
  Cambridge MA 1999

FERTBAUER Leopold 1802-1875 **[4]**
- $7 282 - €7 994 - **£4 840** - FF52 437
  Ein Liebespaar in Alpenlandschaft Oil/panel
  (43.5x36.5cm 17x14in) Wien 2000

FERVILLE-SUAN Charles Georges XIX-XX **[12]**
- $499 - €562 - **£344** - FF3 689
  **Doppelhalsvase als Harfe, die von einer jungen
  Frau gespielt wird** Bronze (H21cm H8in) Stuttgart
  2000

FERY John 1859-1934 **[28]**
- $2 300 - €2 703 - **£1 594** - FF17 731
  Elk in a Landscape Oil/canvas (45x76cm 18x30in)
  Cincinnati OH 2000
- $3 200 - €3 059 - **£2 014** - FF20 069
  Moose in a Snow-covered field Oil/board
  (20x33cm 8x13in) Milwaukee WI 1999

FESER Albert 1901-1993 **[17]**
- $1 318 - €1 380 - **£828** - FF9 055
  **Yachthafen und Restaurant in Teufelsbrück an
  der Elbe** Oil/panel (50x60cm 19x23in) Hamburg 2000
- $1 123 - €1 176 - **£705** - FF7 714
  Hafen von Bornholm Öl/Leinwand/Karton (24x29cm
  9x11in) Hamburg 2000

FESSARD Étienne 1714-1777 **[5]**
- $328 - €373 - **£227** - FF2 448
  Vue d'un Caveau, nach Fragonard Radierung
  (18.4x24.3cm 7x9in) Berlin 2000

FESTA Tano 1938-1988 **[528]**
- $4 000 - €5 183 - **£3 000** - FF34 000
  Senza titolo Olio/tela (120x100cm 47x39in) Vercelli
  2001
- $1 920 - €2 488 - **£1 440** - FF16 320
  Angelo Acrilico/tela (70x100cm 27x39in) Roma 2000
- $1 071 - €925 - **£535** - FF6 069
  Senza titolo Feutre/papier (68x97cm 26x38in) Venezia
  1999

FESZTY Árpád 1856-1914 **[3]**
- $4 160 - €4 724 - **£2 918** - FF30 985
  Kronprinz Eudoph auf dem Totenbett
  Charcoal/paper (62.5x43cm 24x16in) Wien 2001

FETTERS William W. XIX-XX **[3]**
- $1 300 - €1 487 - **£904** - FF9 754
  Mexican Landscape Watercolour/paper (58x76cm
  23x30in) Cincinnati OH 2000

FETTING Rainer 1949 **[194]**
- $17 568 - €17 052 - **£10 938** - FF111 852
  Tulpen Öl/Leinwand (189.5x144.5cm 74x56in) Berlin
  1999
- $11 146 - €9 403 - **£6 537** - FF61 682
  «Selbstportrait mit Palette IV» Oil/canvas
  (100x80cm 39x31in) Berlin 1998
- $1 243 - €1 073 - **£750** - FF7 039
  «Jamaica» Watercolour/paper (38x51cm 14x20in)
  London 1998
- $403 - €460 - **£281** - FF3 018
  Sonnenblumen Farblithographie (122x86cm
  48x33in) Hamburg 2001

FEUCHERE Jean-Jacques 1807-1852 **[39]**
- $2 622 - €2 998 - **£1 800** - FF19 667
  Devil Urns Bronze (H34.5cm H13in) London 2001

FEUCHT Theodor 1867-1944 **[32]**
- $413 - €434 - **£273** - FF2 850
  Abendstimmung am Seeufer Öl/Karton (36x42cm
  14x16in) München 2000

FEUCHTENBERGER Anke 1963 **[2]**
- $2 400 - €2 272 - **£1 490** - FF14 902
  Untitled Poster (85.5x59.5cm 33x23in) New-York
  1999

FEUERBACH Anselm 1829-1880 **[42]**
- $9 208 - €10 226 - **£6 404** - FF67 078
  Nackter Knabe, Flöte spielend Öl/Leinwand
  (82.5x47.5cm 32x18in) Heidelberg 2001
- $1 544 - €1 841 - **£1 100** - FF12 074
  Blick über eine weite Hochgebirgslandschaft
  Oil/canvas/panel (48x33cm 18x12in) Berlin 2000
- $614 - €613 - **£384** - FF4 024
  Stehende junge Frau in Tunika Charcoal (36x18cm
  14x7in) Lindau 1999

FEUERRING Maximilian 1896-1985 **[57]**
- $386 - €438 - **£272** - FF2 873
  Figure Oil/board (60x45cm 23x17in) Sydney 2001

FEUERSTEIN Martin 1856-1931 [6]
- $809 - €908 - £562 - FF5 953
  Der Schutzengel Watercolour, gouache (90.5x68.5cm 35x26in) Luzern 2001

FEUGEREUX Jean 1923-1992 [49]
- $245 - €274 - £170 - FF1 800
  «**Ouistreham**» Aquarelle/papier (43x56cm 16x22in) Versailles 2001

FEUILLASTRE Albert XX [9]
- $244 - €221 - £146 - FF1 450
  Auteuil, un bon saut/Auteuil, chute à la rivière Lithographie couleurs (26x70.5cm 10x27in) Deauville 1998

FEUILLATTE Raymond 1901-1971 [208]
- $166 - €198 - £115 - FF1 300
  Paysage provençal Huile/carton (50x65cm 19x25in) Paris 2000

FEURE de Georges 1868-1943 [146]
- $6 284 - €6 098 - £3 988 - FF40 000
  Le pêcheur Huile/toile (46.5x81cm 18x31in) Paris 1999
- $2 200 - €2 287 - £1 380 - FF15 000
  Paysage méditerranéen Gouache (27x44cm 10x17in) Paris 2000
- $1 200 - €1 427 - £855 - FF9 361
  Les Montmartroises Color lithograph (28x79cm 11x31in) New-York 2000

FEURER Gottlieb 1875-1912 [3]
- $26 838 - €22 968 - £16 155 - FF150 659
  Sennenstreifen Öl/Karton (13x35cm 5x124in) Zürich 1998

FEVRE Pierre 1899-1975 [1]
- $3 250 - €3 606 - £2 161 - FF23 652
  Untitled Gouache/paper (28x20.5cm 11x8in) New-York 2000

FÉVRET DE SAINT-MÉMIN Charles B. Julien 1770-1852 [2]
- $4 200 - €4 769 - £2 874 - FF31 283
  Portrait of Captain Thompson, Philadelphia Charcoal/paper (66x48cm 26x19in) New-York 2000

FEWELL David 1965 [1]
- $616 - €593 - £380 - FF3 890
  Frog Gouache/paper (7.5x7.5cm 2x2in) London 1999

FEYEN Eugène Jacques 1815-1908 [118]
- $4 539 - €4 573 - £2 829 - FF30 000
  Moisson à Cancale Huile/toile (34x53cm 13x20in) Rennes 2000
- $1 984 - €1 677 - £1 180 - FF11 000
  Plage animée en Bretagne Huile/panneau (30x48cm 11x18in) Pontoise 1998
- $1 594 - €1 707 - £1 085 - FF11 200
  Départ à la pêche Fusain/papier (55x88cm 21x34in) Rennes 2001

FEYEN Léon Arie XX [3]
- $1 891 - €2 250 - £1 348 - FF14 757
  Am Flussufer, Fähre und Fischerboote an der Uferbefestigung Oil/panel (60x70cm 23x27in) Köln 2000
- $2 341 - €2 454 - £1 542 - FF16 098
  Bäuerliche Dorfgesellschaft an einem niederländischen Flusslauf Oil/panel (30x40cm 11x15in) Köln 2000

FEYEN-PERRIN François N. Augustin 1826-1888 [59]
- $1 179 - €991 - £693 - FF6 500
  Le retour des pêcheurs Huile/toile (37x46cm 14x18in) Lille 1998
- $1 173 - €1 220 - £739 - FF8 000
  Bretonnes en bord de mer Huile/carton (24.5x34cm 9x13in) Paris 2000

FEYERABEND Johann Rudolf 1779-1814 [8]
- $3 010 - €3 303 - £2 000 - FF21 666
  Copper Pan and Vegetables on a Ledge/Pan, Asparagus, Eggs on a Ledge Watercolour (15x19.5cm 5x7in) London 2000

FFARINGTON Richard Atherton 1823-1855 [1]
- $13 058 - €12 250 - £8 068 - FF80 354
  Perth, Swan River as Viewed from Melville Waters Watercolour/paper (11.5x21.5cm 4x8in) Melbourne 1999

FHEDOROVETZ R. XIX [1]
- $37 835 - €35 063 - £23 529 - FF230 000
  «**Quelques Types de la Russie Méridionale... Odessa**» Photo (14x10cm 5x3in) Paris 1999

FIALETTI Odoardo 1573-1638 [12]
- $466 - €511 - £316 - FF3 353
  Die Zeichenschule Radierung (11.2x15cm 4x5in) Berlin 1998

FIAMBERTI Tommaso ?-1524 [1]
- $156 000 - €202 147 - £117 000 - FF1 326 000
  La Vergine con il Bambino Gesù Relief (65x41cm 25x16in) Firenze 2000

FIASCHI E. XIX [7]
- $14 480 - €16 455 - £10 000 - FF107 937
  Two Lovers Embracing Alabaster (H189cm H74in) London 2000

FIASCHI P.C.E. XIX-XX [25]
- $11 500 - €12 881 - £7 990 - FF84 492
  Nude woman leans on a balustrade Alabaster (H119cm H47in) Philadelphia PA 2001
- $2 300 - €1 985 - £1 389 - FF13 018
  Young Romance, Boy, Maiden and Grapevine Alabaster (64x45x30cm 25x18x12in) St. Petersburg FL 1999

FIASELLA IL SARZANA Domenico 1589-1669 [11]
- $29 886 - €32 080 - £20 000 - FF210 432
  The Stoning of Saint Stephen Oil/canvas (149x173.5cm 58x68in) London 2000

FICATELLI Giuseppe Maria 1639-1703 [1]
- $3 111 - €2 885 - £1 900 - FF18 924
  An Extensive Landscape with Figures by a River Ink (19.5x26cm 7x10in) London 1998

FICHEFET Georges 1864-1954 [37]
- $320 - €335 - £211 - FF2 195
  Porche de ferme Huile/toile (39x56.5cm 15x22in) Bruxelles 2000

FICHEL Eugène 1826-1895 [93]
- $13 000 - €11 490 - £7 945 - FF75 370
  Elegant Figures in an Interior Oil/panel (42x57cm 16x22in) New-York 1999
- $3 883 - €4 515 - £2 725 - FF29 616
  The Leisure Hour Huile/panneau (41x33cm 16x12in) Montréal 2001

FICHET Pierre 1927 [54]
- $1 009 - €915 - £653 - FF6 000
  Sans titre #22 Huile/toile (130x89cm 51x35in) Paris 1998

FICHOT Jean-Michel 1959 **[3]**

$13 593 - €11 767 - **£8 250** - FF77 188
Afrika Bronze (118x27x24cm 46x10x9in) München 1998

FICHOT Michel Charles 1817-1903 **[10]**

$225 - €221 - **£139** - FF1 450
Entrée du Jardin des Tuileries, les Champs Ély-sée, le Bois de Boulogne Lithographie couleurs (78x102cm 30x40in) Orléans 1999

FIDANI Orazio 1610-c.1660 **[6]**

$22 000 - €28 508 - **£16 500** - FF187 000
Giaele e Sisara Olio/tela (120x180cm 47x70in) Roma 2000

FIDANZA Francesco 1747-1819 **[17]**

$4 499 - €3 887 - **£2 999** - FF25 498
Paesaggio con figure Olio/tela (54.5x82.5cm 21x32in) Milano 1998

FIDANZA Giuseppe c.1750-c.1820 **[3]**

$11 500 - €11 922 - **£6 900** - FF78 200
Veduta del porto di Ancona Inchiostro (44x93cm 17x36in) Milano 2000

FIDLER Harry 1856-1935 **[66]**

$1 610 - €1 514 - **£1 000** - FF9 929
The Poacher Oil/canvas (76x66.5cm 29x26in) Salisbury, Wiltshire 1999

$1 600 - €1 841 - **£1 102** - FF12 077
A Small Holder Oil/canvas (40x35cm 16x14in) Newark OH 2000

FIDUS Hugo Höppener 1868-1947 **[44]**

$345 - €383 - **£240** - FF2 515
Sitzendes kleines Kind, einen Ball in der rechten Hand haltend Pencil (37.5x30cm 14x11in) Heidelberg 2001

FIEBIG Carl 1812-1874 **[11]**

$727 - €700 - **£452** - FF4 593
Portraet af dame med kniplingskyste ifört grå plisseret silkekjole... Oil/canvas (38x29cm 14x11in) Köbenhavn 1999

FIEDLER Arnold 1900-1985 **[66]**

$782 - €920 - **£566** - FF6 037
Zirkus Tempera (47x34.8cm 18x13in) Hamburg 2001

$1 133 - €1 125 - **£708** - FF7 378
Blumenstilleben Acryl/Karton (32.9x46.8cm 12x18in) Hamburg 1999

$954 - €818 - **£573** - FF5 365
Zirkus Collage (32.2x50cm 12x19in) Hamburg 1998

FIEDLER Franz 1885-1956 **[27]**

$762 - €818 - **£510** - FF5 366
Akt Photograph (25.2x19.1cm 9x7in) München 2000

FIEDLER Herbert 1891-1962 **[37]**

$1 874 - €2 178 - **£1 317** - FF14 287
Dorpsgezicht Laren Oil/paper (47.5x63cm 18x24in) Amsterdam 2001

$4 101 - €4 765 - **£2 882** - FF31 254
Landschap blaricum Oil/board (21x26cm 8x10in) Amsterdam 2001

$604 - €681 - **£416** - FF4 464
Circus Caravan Gouache/paper (64x44cm 25x17in) Amsterdam 2000

FIEDLER Johann Christian 1697-1765 **[7]**

$2 415 - €2 744 - **£1 666** - FF18 000
Princesse de Hesse-Darmstadt en robe de soie ivoire, rubans bleus Miniature (7x5.5cm 2x2in) Paris 2000

FIELD Charles XVIII **[1]**

$6 734 - €8 009 - **£4 800** - FF52 537
Vanitas Still Life with a Globe Showing the Americas Oil/canvas (38.5x69cm 15x27in) London 2000

FIELD Erastus Salisbury 1805-1900 **[15]**

$90 000 - €84 434 - **£55 611** - FF553 851
Portrait of a Dark-Haired young Girl wearing a green Dress Oil/canvas (157x105cm 61x41in) New-York 1999

$6 000 - €6 408 - **£4 088** - FF42 031
Portrait of a Boy Oil/canvas (68x60cm 27x24in) New-York 2001

$10 000 - €9 355 - **£6 059** - FF61 362
Portrait of Miss Elizabeth Newton Oil/panel (10x8cm 4x3in) Bolton MA 1999

FIELD John 1772-1848 **[72]**

$788 - €817 - **£500** - FF5 361
Gentleman in Profile to Right in Coat with Large Buttons Silhouette (2x1.5cm xin) London 2000

FIELD Robert Nettleton 1899-1987 **[3]**

$4 507 - €4 683 - **£2 826** - FF30 721
Early Morning, Horseshaw Range, North Otago Oil/board (44x60cm 17x23in) Auckland 2000

$1 803 - €2 055 - **£1 246** - FF13 479
Kumeu Landscape Watercolour/paper (50x60cm 19x23in) Auckland 2000

FIELD Walter 1837-1901 **[15]**

$14 885 - €12 979 - **£9 000** - FF85 138
«Waterlillies» Oil/canvas (61x92cm 24x36in) London 1998

FIELDING Anthony V. Copley 1787-1855 **[283]**

$4 600 - €3 941 - **£2 765** - FF25 850
Shore Scape with Boats, Figure and Port in Distance Oil/board (29x43cm 11x17in) New-Orleans LA 1998

$1 528 - €1 260 - **£900** - FF8 264
«Ullwater» Watercolour/paper (17x25.5cm 6x10in) Tyne & Wear 1998

FIELDING Newton Smith Limbird 1799-1856 **[52]**

$968 - €909 - **£600** - FF5 964
An Interior Scene with a small Dog Watercolour (17x25.5cm 6x10in) London 1999

FIELDING Thales 1793-1837 **[13]**

$12 096 - €11 739 - **£7 530** - FF77 000
Portrait d'Eugène Delacroix Huile/toile/carton (34.5x27.2cm 13x10in) Paris 1999

$491 - €585 - **£350** - FF3 837
Figures Beside Fishing Vessels in a Bay Watercolour (12x19.5cm 4x7in) London 2000

FIENE Ernest 1894-1965 **[178]**

$2 500 - €2 141 - **£1 476** - FF14 045
Entering Machias, Maine Oil/canvas (91.5x76cm 36x29in) New-York 1998

$1 500 - €1 265 - **£879** - FF8 301
Fruit on a Stool Oil/canvas (22x40cm 9x16in) Mystic CT 1998

$350 - €382 - **£225** - FF2 507
Fishing Village Watercolour/paper (38x55cm 15x22in) Mystic CT 2000

$650 - €665 - **£407** - FF4 362
Washington Square No.1 Lithograph (27x39cm 11x15in) Cleveland OH 2000

FIERAVINO IL MALTESE Francesco XVII **[24]**

$73 630 - €82 556 - **£50 000** - FF541 535
Still Life of Gilt and Silver Ewers Oil/canvas (97x130.5cm 38x51in) London 2000

$12 000 - €11 290 - £7 488 - FF74 056
Platter of Sweetmeats, an Incense Burner, Statuette of David Oil/canvas (61x78cm 24x30in) New-York 1999

FIERET Gérard 1924 [8]
📷 $572 - €681 - £408 - FF4 464
Selfportrait Silver print (46.5x59.5cm 18x23in) Amsterdam 2000

FIERROS ALVAREZ Dionisio 1827-1894 [13]
$8 100 - €8 109 - £4 995 - FF53 190
Pecados capitales Oleo/lienzo (48.5x35.5cm 19x13in) Madrid 2000

FIETZ Gerhard 1910-1997 [69]
$3 534 - €3 323 - £2 188 - FF21 800
Ohne Titel Tempera (39x51cm 15x20in) Köln 1999
$1 218 - €1 431 - £844 - FF9 390
Komposition 55-45 Indian ink (29.2x35.2cm 11x13in) Stuttgart 2000
$238 - €206 - £144 - FF1 352
Komposition auf Schwarz Farblithographie (34x47.5cm 13x18in) München 1998

FIÉVET Régis & Gisèle 1951/48 [12]
$498 - €534 - £339 - FF3 500
Océane Sculpture verre (H29cm H11in) Albi 2001

FIEVRE Yolande 1907-1983 [65]
$744 - €732 - £478 - FF4 800
Épouvantail jardin Technique mixte (59.5x49cm 23x19in) Paris 1999
$394 - €335 - £234 - FF2 200
Soie-fiction Technique mixte/carton (22x28cm 8x11in) Paris 1998
$419 - €457 - £284 - FF3 000
Sans titre Assemblage (22x28cm 8x11in) Paris 2000

FIGARI Andrea 1858-1945 [5]
$1 500 - €1 469 - £966 - FF9 637
A Lake at Sunset Watercolour/paper (19.5x46cm 7x18in) New-York 1999

FIGARI Pedro 1861-1938 [183]
$39 710 - €34 061 - £24 000 - FF223 428
Preparando el Candombe Oil/board (60x80cm 23x31in) London 1998
$14 250 - €15 016 - £9 000 - FF98 500
Tango Oleo/cartón (40x33cm 15x12in) Madrid 2000

FIGGE Eddie 1904 [73]
$430 - €363 - £255 - FF2 379
Komposition Mixed media/canvas (62x76cm 24x29in) Stockholm 1998

FIGINO Ambrogio Giovanni 1548-1608 [4]
$1 300 000 - €1 390 596 - £886 340 - FF9 121 710
Giovanni Angelo Dannona, Half Length, Holding Gloves and a Letter Oil/panel (59.5x46.5cm 23x18in) New-York 2001

FIGURA Hans 1898-? [75]
$180 - €150 - £105 - FF985
Winter Landscape Etching in colors (43x34cm 17x13in) Shaker-Heights OH 1998

FILARSKI Dirk H.W. 1885-1964 [170]
$12 944 - €14 521 - £8 969 - FF95 251
Alpenglooien Oil/canvas (115x174cm 45x68in) Amsterdam 2000
$5 258 - €5 899 - £3 643 - FF38 695
«Menton» Oil/canvas (47x55.5cm 18x21in) Amsterdam 2000
$718 - €771 - £475 - FF5 060
Landscape with cedar trees Charcoal (44x63cm 17x24in) Amsterdam 2000

FILCER Luis 1927 [9]
$6 968 - €7 727 - £4 634 - FF50 687
Cerro de la estrella Oleo/lienzo (56x80cm 22x31in) México 2000

FILDES Fanny ?-c.1927 [2]
$3 156 - €2 701 - £1 900 - FF17 717
By the Garden Gate, a portrait of Luke Val Fildes Oil/canvas (24x18.5cm 9x7in) London 1998

FILDES Samuel Luke, Sir 1843-1927 [29]
$959 - €984 - £600 - FF6 457
Italian Girl, Bust-Length Wearing a Green Dress Watercolour (24x17.5cm 9x6in) London 2000

FILIGER Charles 1863-1928 [27]
$4 999 - €5 946 - £3 564 - FF39 000
Portrait d'adolescent Huile/panneau (17x16cm 6x6in) Brest 2000
$74 442 - €86 896 - £52 668 - FF570 000
Paysage breton Gouache/carton (32x48cm 12x18in) Paris 2001

FILIP Demetrio 1921-1993 [1]
$1 700 - €1 975 - £1 194 - FF12 956
«Casco de estancia (Chascomus)» Oleo/cartón (24x48cm 9x18in) Buenos-Aires 2001

FILIPKIEWICZ Stefan 1879-1944 [71]
$3 466 - €2 970 - £2 084 - FF19 482
Paysage en hiver avec torrent Oil/canvas (55x65.5cm 21x25in) Warszawa 1998
$2 084 - €2 329 - £1 413 - FF15 274
Hiver Aquarelle/papier (36x49.5cm 14x19in) Warszawa 2000

FILIPPA Corrado 1893-1972 [7]
$390 - €337 - £195 - FF2 210
Paesaggio primaverile/Paesaggio Olio/tavola (10x8cm 3x3in) Vercelli 1999

FILIPPELLI Cafiero 1889-1973 [119]
$3 400 - €4 406 - £2 550 - FF28 900
Figura con vaso di fiori Olio/tavola (80x60cm 31x23in) Prato 2000
$2 100 - €2 177 - £1 260 - FF14 280
Orto toscano Olio/tavola (32x44cm 12x17in) Roma 1999
$1 100 - €1 140 - £660 - FF7 480
Giochi di bambini Carboncino/carta (34.5x48.5cm 13x19in) Prato 1999

FILIPPI Camillo c.1500-1574 [2]
$8 838 - €8 767 - £5 500 - FF57 506
The Nativity Oil/canvas (51x41.5cm 20x16in) London 1999

FILIPPI de Fernando 1940 [49]
$300 - €311 - £180 - FF2 040
Scena Mitologica Acrilico/tela (50x40cm 19x15in) Vercelli 2001

FILIPPINI Antonio ?-1710 [1]
$2 988 - €3 208 - £2 000 - FF21 043
Monument to Pope Gregory XIII Crowned by Putti Red chalk (30x21cm 11x8in) London 2000

FILIPPINI Francesco 1853-1895 [4]
$35 000 - €36 283 - £21 000 - FF238 000
Giornata di pioggia Olio/tela (100x50cm 39x19in) Milano 2000

FILIPPONI Alessandro 1909-1931 [1]
$5 000 - €5 183 - £3 000 - FF34 000
Paesaggio con alberi Tecnica mista (42x42cm 16x16in) Trieste 2000

FILKUKA Anton 1888-1957 **[104]**
- 🖼 $697 - €727 - **£439** - FF4 767
  Bauernhof am Semmering Öl/Leinwand (60x80cm 23x31in) Wien 2000
- 🖼 $670 - €613 - **£408** - FF4 024
  Holzsteg über einen Waldbach Öl/Leinwand (29x40cm 11x15in) München 1999

FILLA Emil 1882-1953 **[217]**
- 🖼 $91 035 - €86 102 - **£56 700** - FF564 795
  Femme caressant un chien Huile/toile (137x97cm 53x38in) Praha 2000
- 🖼 $26 010 - €24 601 - **£16 200** - FF161 370
  Nature morte à la cruche Huile/toile (54x66cm 21x25in) Praha 2000
- 🖼 $10 982 - €10 387 - **£6 840** - FF68 134
  Still Life with Pears Oil/canvas (29.5x35cm 11x13in) Praha 2000
- 🗿 $1 473 - €1 394 - **£918** - FF9 144
  Tête Bronze (H19.5cm H7in) Praha 2001
- ✏ $1 300 - €1 230 - **£810** - FF8 068
  Du cycle combats et luttes Encre (42x30.5cm 16x12in) Praha 2000
- 🖾 $448 - €424 - **£279** - FF2 779
  Nature morte à mandoline Pointe sèche (23x17cm 9x6in) Praha 2000

FILLACIER Jacques 1913 **[3]**
- 🖾 $650 - €650 - **£397** - FF4 264
  «Chamonix» Poster (96x58cm 38x23in) New-York 2000

FILLIA Luigi 1904-1936 **[20]**
- 🖼 $36 000 - €46 649 - **£27 000** - FF306 000
  Figura nello spazio Olio/tela (125x105cm 49x41in) Milano 2000
- 🖼 $31 200 - €26 953 - **£20 800** - FF176 800
  Figure Olio/masonite (58x40cm 22x15in) Milano 1998
- 🖼 $6 000 - €6 220 - **£3 600** - FF40 800
  Sacra Famiglia Olio/tavola (46x33cm 18x12in) Milano 1999

FILLIARD Ernest 1868-1933 **[75]**
- ✏ $1 297 - €1 448 - **£902** - FF9 500
  Fleurs clochettes Aquarelle/papier (38x54cm 14x21in) Paris 2001

FILLIOU Robert 1926-1987 **[46]**
- 🖼 $202 - €204 - **£123** - FF1 341
  Optimistic Box No.1 Object (11x11x11cm 4x4x4in) Stuttgart 2000
- 🖾 $88 - €104 - **£62** - FF683
  Cucumberland sans voir Etching (31.5x49.5cm 12x19in) Stockholm 2000

FILLON Arthur 1900-1974 **[119]**
- 🖼 $837 - €899 - **£560** - FF5 900
  La Seine Huile/toile (65x80cm 25x31in) Compiègne 2000
- 🖼 $447 - €381 - **£266** - FF2 500
  Pêcheur à la ligne Huile/toile (22x50.5cm 8x19in) Paris 1998
- ✏ $369 - €396 - **£247** - FF2 600
  Le kiosque Pastel/papier (48x30cm 18x11in) Compiègne 2000

FILMUS Tully 1903 **[16]**
- 🖼 $3 000 - €2 797 - **£1 860** - FF18 349
  Wintry Day Oil/canvas (28x35.5cm 11x13in) New-York 1999

FILONOV Pavel Nikolaevitch 1883-1941 **[13]**
- 🖼 $63 068 - €61 638 - **£40 000** - FF404 320
  Abstract Composition with Spheres Oil/paper (72x51cm 28x20in) London 1999

FILOQUE T. XVII **[1]**
- 🖼 $60 476 - €66 721 - **£40 000** - FF437 660
  Three Faces with a Horse Watercolour/paper (34.5x31.5cm 13x12in) London 2000

FILOSA Giovanni Battista 1850-1935 **[50]**
- 🖼 $13 188 - €15 184 - **£9 000** - FF99 602
  Mounted Dromedaries Oil/canvas (112x140cm 44x55in) London 2000
- 🖼 $2 987 - €2 636 - **£1 800** - FF17 291
  La Passaggiata Oil/canvas (80x59cm 31x23in) London 1998
- 🖼 $1 000 - €1 097 - **£645** - FF7 195
  Summer landscape scene Watercolour/paper (43x67cm 17x26in) Wallkill NY 2000

FILOSINI C. XIX **[3]**
- 🖼 $4 500 - €4 535 - **£2 805** - FF29 745
  Elegant Salutations Oil/canvas (61x47.5cm 24x18in) New-York 2000
- 🖼 $5 000 - €5 801 - **£3 557** - FF38 049
  Inside the Harem Watercolour/paper (52x76cm 20x29in) Washington 2000

FILSER Maria Caspar 1878-1968 **[1]**
- 🖼 $3 572 - €3 835 - **£2 391** - FF25 154
  Blick auf eine bewaldete Hügellandschaft Öl/Leinwand (110x80cm 43x31in) Stuttgart 2000

FIMA 1916-1991 **[48]**
- 🖼 $1 950 - €1 657 - **£1 178** - FF10 870
  «Calligraphy» Oil/canvas (65x54cm 25x21in) Tel Aviv 1999
- ✏ $400 - €425 - **£270** - FF2 785
  Untitled Watercolour/paper (43x31cm 16x12in) Tel Aviv 2001

FINALE Moïses 1957 **[20]**
- 🖼 $1 588 - €1 601 - **£990** - FF10 500
  Le cirque Technique mixte/toile (164x165cm 64x64in) Paris 2000

FINART Noël-Dieudonné 1797-1852 **[24]**
- 🖼 $7 123 - €6 860 - **£4 432** - FF45 000
  L'amazone Huile/toile (26.5x35cm 10x13in) Montfort L'Amaury 1999
- ✏ $717 - €793 - **£497** - FF5 200
  Cavaliers turcs Aquarelle/papier (15x22cm 5x8in) Lille 2001

FINCH Alfred William 1854-1930 **[94]**
- 🖼 $7 487 - €8 622 - **£5 111** - FF56 555
  Standing Female Nude Oil/canvas (95.5x61cm 37x24in) Amsterdam 2000
- 🖼 $3 727 - €4 205 - **£2 620** - FF27 580
  Strandvy Oil/canvas (32x41cm 12x16in) Helsinki 2001
- ✏ $308 - €303 - **£191** - FF1 985
  I hamnen Charcoal/paper (20x28cm 7x11in) Helsinki 1998
- 🖾 $128 - €126 - **£79** - FF827
  Untitled Etching (21x30cm 8x11in) Helsinki 1999

FINCH E.E. act.1832-1850 **[4]**
- 🖼 $7 600 - €8 121 - **£5 165** - FF53 273
  Portraits of a Maine Couple Oil/canvas (60x50cm 24x20in) Portsmouth NH 2001

FINCH Francis Oliver 1802-1862 **[20]**
- ✏ $594 - €591 - **£360** - FF3 879
  The Fugitive Watercolour/paper (15x24cm 5x9in) London 2000

FINCH Willy 1854-1930 **[8]**
📖 **$330** - **€272** - **£193** - FF1 786
La Tamise à Londres Eau-forte (15x20cm 5x7in)
Bruxelles 1998

FINCK Hazel 1894-1977 **[11]**
🖌 **$13 000** - €13 954 - **£8 699** - FF91 533
May Oil/canvas (46x76.5cm 25x30in) New-York 2000

FINCKEN James Horsey 1860-c.1943 **[2]**
📖 **$1 907** - €1 873 - **£1 182** - FF12 283
American Colonial Architecture Etching
(23.5x34cm 9x13in) Toronto 1999

FIND Ludvig 1869-1945 **[86]**
🖌 **$435** - €496 - **£306** - FF3 253
Interiör med börn omkring bordet Oil/canvas
(41x57cm 16x22in) Vejle 2001
🖌 **$184** - €201 - **£127** - FF1 319
Interiör Oil/canvas (36x30cm 14x11in) Köbenhavn
2001

FINDLEY Albert H. 1880-1975 **[24]**
🖌 **$241** - €225 - **£150** - FF1 473
The Lord Mayor's Parlour Watercolour/paper
(27x38cm 10x14in) Leicestershire 1999

FINELI Claude 1956 **[121]**
🖌 **$1 268** - €1 289 - **£795** - FF8 455
Bataille navale au clair de lune Huile/toile
(46x38cm 18x14in) Luxembourg 2000
🖌 **$1 060** - €915 - **£637** - FF6 000
Bataille navale Huile/toile (33x46cm 12x18in)
Langres 2001

FINES Eugène François 1826-? **[7]**
🖌 **$3 750** - €3 687 - **£2 409** - FF24 182
The Tambourine Oil/canvas (61.5x38.5cm 24x15in)
New-York 1999

FINETTI von Gino, Ritter 1877-1955 **[20]**
📖 **$74** - €66 - **£45** - FF436
Europa auf dem Stier Lithographie (24x19.4cm
9x7in) Pforzheim 1999

FINGESTEN Michael, Michl 1884-1943 **[96]**
✎ **$451** - €506 - **£314** - FF3 320
Ansicht von Almunecor Pastel (49x48cm 19x18in)
Oersberg-bei Kappeln 2001
📖 **$165** - €179 - **£114** - FF1 173
«Der süsse Bronnen» Radierung (31x24.5cm
12x9in) Hamburg 2001

FINI Leonor 1908-1996 **[1228]**
🖌 **$94 686** - €91 619 - **£60 000** - FF600 978
Rasch, Rasch, Rasch Oil/canvas (114x146cm
44x57in) London 1999
🖌 **$8 004** - €9 570 - **£5 500** - FF62 772
La sirène, l'Omnipode Oil/canvas (65x30cm
25x11in) London 2001
🖌 **$3 976** - €4 269 - **£2 660** - FF28 000
Les yeux bruns Huile/toile (41x33cm 16x12in)
Neuilly-sur-Seine 2000
⚒ **$34 320** - €36 588 - **£21 768** - FF240 000
Sans titre Sculpture (220x140x36cm 86x55x14in)
Paris 2000
✎ **$677** - €762 - **£475** - FF5 000
Les trois amies Encre (50x38cm 19x14in) Paris 2001
📖 **$185** - €173 - **£112** - FF1 138
Poezen Etching in colors (9.8x17.8cm 3x7in) Lokeren
1999

FINK A. XIX **[1]**
🖌 **$28 152** - €25 916 - **£16 898** - FF170 000
**Petits métiers et gourmands sur les quais de
Naples** Huile/toile (73x100cm 28x39in) Lyon 1999

FINK Adolphe D. 1802-? **[1]**
✎ **$1 350** - €1 601 - **£953** - FF10 500
Portrait de jeune femme Aquarelle, gouache
(43.5x32.5cm 17x12in) Paris 2000

FINK Anton, Tone 1944 **[33]**
✎ **$504** - €436 - **£304** - FF2 858
«Über Joseph Beuys Katalogsteite»
Mischtechnik/Papier (26x19cm 10x7in) Wien 1998

FINK August 1846-1916 **[39]**
🖌 **$969** - €908 - **£603** - FF5 953
Birch Forest with a Deer by a Stream Oil/canvas
(90.5x75cm 35x29in) Amsterdam 1999
🖌 **$949** - €869 - **£578** - FF5 701
Uferlandschaft Öl/Leinwand (30.5x40cm 12x15in)
München 1999

FINK Waldemar 1893-1948 **[75]**
🖌 **$385** - €372 - **£237** - FF2 437
Herbst auf dem Gurten Öl/Leinwand (60x90.5cm
23x35in) Bern 1999

FINKE Auguste XIX **[5]**
🖌 **$17 058** - €14 328 - **£10 000** - FF93 985
Oriental Figures in an Eastern Town Oil/canvas
(74.5x100.5cm 29x39in) London 1998

FINKELSTEIN Nat 1933 **[25]**
📷 **$652** - €610 - **£394** - FF4 000
Andy Warhol à la Factory Tirage argentique
(30x40cm 11x15in) Paris 1999

FINKELSTEIN Samuel 1890-1942 **[6]**
🖌 **$5 031** - €5 610 - **£3 443** - FF36 799
Vieilles maisons Huile/toile (59.5x68.5cm 23x26in)
Warszawa 2000

FINLAY Virgil 1914-1971 **[6]**
✎ **$1 100** - €1 064 - **£697** - FF6 981
Self Portrait Ink (19x15cm 7x5in) New-York 1999

FINN Herbert John 1860-? **[53]**
🖌 **$286** - €320 - **£200** - FF2 100
Christchurch Oxford, an Interior Oil/canvas
(56x38cm 22x14in) Bath 2001
✎ **$314** - €302 - **£200** - FF1 978
«Lincoln Cathedral from Brayford Pool»
Watercolour/paper (28x40cm 11x15in) London 1999

FINNBERG Gustaf Wilhelm 1784-1833 **[1]**
🖌 **$103 040** - €117 727 - **£72 520** - FF772 240
Arsenalsgatan Tukholmassa Oil/copper
(41.5x55cm 16x21in) Helsinki 2001

FINNE Ferdinand 1910-1999 **[150]**
🖌 **$599** - €604 - **£374** - FF3 965
Grå Morgen, Dosseringen, Mars, Kjöbenhavn
Oil/canvas (46x38cm 18x14in) Köbenhavn 2000
🖌 **$539** - €578 - **£360** - FF3 793
Piken med linhåret Mixed media (39x28cm 15x11in)
Oslo 2000
⚒ **$561** - €602 - **£375** - FF3 952
Ekko fra Jaeren Marble (15x20cm 5x7in) Oslo 2000
✎ **$842** - €904 - **£563** - FF5 928
Alteret pyntes Taormina Watercolour/paper
(35x23cm 13x9in) Oslo 2000
📖 **$494** - €530 - **£330** - FF3 477
Mötestedet Etching in colors (17x20cm 6x7in) Oslo
2000

FINNE Gunnar XX **[5]**
⚒ **$3 304** - €3 700 - **£2 294** - FF24 270
Musa Bronze (H25cm H9in) Helsinki 2001

FINNEMORE Joseph 1860-1939 **[24]**
- $493 - €459 - £304 - FF3 009
  Song of Sleep Watercolour/paper (44x25cm 17x9in) Melbourne 1999

FINNEY Harry XIX-XX **[3]**
- $63 - €76 - £43 - FF500
  «**Le Figaro**» Affiche (83x59cm 32x23in) Paris 2000

FINNIE John 1829-1907 **[12]**
- $8 823 - €8 891 - £5 500 - FF58 319
  River at Sunset Oil/canvas (68.5x91.5cm 26x36in) London 2000

FINOT Émile XX **[4]**
- $950 - €884 - £586 - FF5 797
  «**Pola Néry**» Poster (115x160cm 45x63in) New-York 1999

FINOT Jules, baron 1826-1906 **[22]**
- $2 381 - €2 668 - £1 657 - FF17 500
  Journée de chasse Huile/carton (16.5x24cm 6x9in) Soissons 2001
- $1 760 - €1 707 - £1 107 - FF11 200
  Chasse à courre Gouache/papier (9x15cm 3x5in) Neuilly-sur-Seine 1999

FINSLER Hans 1891-1972 **[27]**
- $857 - €920 - £573 - FF6 037
  Keramik Photograph (23.6x17.8cm 9x7in) München 2000

FINSON Ludovico, Louis 1580-1617 **[10]**
- $131 241 - €110 907 - £78 060 - FF727 500
  Annonciation Huile/toile (117x147cm 46x57in) Monte-Carlo 1998

FINSTER Howard, Reverend 1916 **[66]**
- $504 - €470 - £304 - FF3 080
  Motorcars Oil/board (40x25cm 16x10in) Mystic CT 1998

FINSTERLIN Hermann 1887-1973 **[23]**
- $7 165 - €7 158 - £4 480 - FF46 954
  Zwei Architekturen Watercolour (50x33.2cm 19x13in) Hamburg 1999

FINZI Ennio 1931 **[18]**
- $700 - €726 - £420 - FF4 760
  Senza titolo Olio/cartone/tela (49.5x69.5cm 19x27in) Prato 2001

FIORE del Jacobello c.1370-1439 **[3]**
- $49 788 - €51 613 - £29 872 - FF338 559
  Madonna col Bambino Tempera/tavola (63x45cm 24x17in) Milano 1999

FIORENZI Franco 1912-1992 **[7]**
- $848 - €879 - £508 - FF5 766
  «**La guerra dei mondi**» Affiche couleur (195x140cm 76x55in) Torino 2000

FIORI de Ernesto 1884-1945 **[16]**
- $2 658 - €2 556 - £1 640 - FF16 769
  Selbstbildnis Bronze (H27cm H10in) Köln 1999

FIORILLO Renato 1923 **[12]**
- $350 - €363 - £210 - FF2 380
  Contadini con cesto di frutta Olio/tavola (70x50cm 27x19in) Vercelli 2000

FIORONI Giosetta 1933 **[21]**
- $6 600 - €5 702 - £4 400 - FF37 400
  «**Le dimensioni di un viso**» Smalto/tela (117x89cm 46x35in) Milano 1998
- $600 - €577 - £450 - FF5 100
  Testa di donna Matita (70x50cm 27x19in) Prato 2000

FIOT Maximilien 1886-1953 **[117]**
- $1 273 - €1 375 - £880 - FF9 019
  Bookends Bronze (H19cm H7in) London 2001

FIRLE Walter 1859-1929 **[36]**
- $11 000 - €10 452 - £6 692 - FF68 561
  The Golden Wedding Oil/canvas (127.5x176.5cm 50x69in) New-York 1999
- $1 854 - €1 601 - £1 107 - FF10 500
  Blumenstilleben mit Mohn Öl/Karton (98x72cm 38x28in) Zürich 1998

FIRMENICH Joseph 1821-1891 **[11]**
- $6 953 - €7 158 - £4 383 - FF46 954
  Südliche Ideallandschaft im Abendlicht Öl/Leinwand (93x124cm 36x48in) Berlin 2000

FIRMIN-GIRARD Marie François 1838-1921 **[96]**
- $20 000 - €17 275 - £12 056 - FF113 314
  In the Garden Oil/canvas (46x56cm 18x22in) New-York 1998
- $8 344 - €9 299 - £5 831 - FF61 000
  La jeune fermière Huile/toile (46.5x32.5cm 18x12in) Paris 2001

FIRMIN-GOY Claude 1864-1944 **[47]**
- $2 765 - €2 363 - £1 624 - FF15 500
  La fermière et ses dindons Huile/toile (50x60cm 19x23in) Avignon 1998
- $1 011 - €991 - £652 - FF6 500
  Cour de ferme Huile/toile (40x32cm 15x12in) Avignon 1999

FISAREK Alois 1906-1980 **[25]**
- $693 - €656 - £432 - FF4 303
  Fleurs dans un jardin Huile/toile (40x51cm 15x20in) Praha 1999
- $6 358 - €6 014 - £3 960 - FF39 446
  Südböhmischer Fasching Tapestry (290x235cm 114x92in) Praha 1999

FISCHBACH Johann Heinrich 1797-1871 **[54]**
- $3 641 - €3 997 - £2 420 - FF26 218
  Landschaft mit Wasserfall und Hirsch Oil/panel (78x64cm 30x25in) Wien 2000
- $4 494 - €4 090 - £2 808 - FF26 831
  Dachstein und Hinterer Gosausee Öl/Leinwand (37x26.5cm 14x10in) München 1999
- $349 - €409 - £245 - FF2 683
  Auf dem Rücken liegender, schlafender Bauernbursche Watercolour (14.5x19.5cm 5x7in) München 2000

FISCHBECK Ludwig 1866-1954 **[16]**
- $172 - €169 - £109 - FF1 106
  Birkenweg im Frühling Radierung (42x23.5cm 16x9in) Bremen 1999

FISCHER Adam 1888-1968 **[7]**
- $666 - €672 - £415 - FF4 406
  Cellisten Bronze (H15cm H5in) København 2000

FISCHER Anton Otto 1882-1962 **[80]**
- $3 500 - €4 043 - £2 450 - FF26 523
  A Homecoming Oil/canvas (66x61cm 25x24in) Bethesda MD 2001
- $3 500 - €3 240 - £2 142 - FF21 254
  Two men in small boat approaching by war canoes, Ill. for Moby Dick Oil/canvas (71x50cm 28x20in) New-York 1999

FISCHER Arno 1927 **[15]**
- $684 - €767 - £475 - FF5 030
  «**New York**» Gelatin silver print (28x41cm 11x16in) Köln 2001

FISCHER August 1854-1921 **[196]**
- $1 210 - €1 163 - £750 - FF7 627
  Canal Scene, hamburg Oil/canvas (54x39cm 21x15in) London 1999
- $891 - €808 - £556 - FF5 299
  Parti fra Nürnberg Oil/canvas (33x24cm 12x9in) Köbenhavn 1999

FISCHER Carl 1887-1962 **[114]**
- $449 - €497 - £297 - FF3 257
  Opstilling med en potteplante Oil/canvas (47x38cm 18x14in) Viby J, Arhus 2000
- $499 - €471 - £310 - FF3 090
  Portraet af ung kvinde Oil/paper/canvas (41x30cm 16x11in) Köbenhavn 1999
- $176 - €201 - £124 - FF1 318
  Avislaende mand Collage (50x34.5cm 19x13in) Vejle 2001

FISCHER Carl H. 1885-1955 **[84]**
- $452 - €426 - £280 - FF2 794
  A Bowl of Grapes, a Bottle of Wine and a Wine Glass on a Table Oil/canvas (54.5x65cm 21x25in) London 1999
- $486 - €537 - £329 - FF3 520
  Blomster i vase Oil/canvas (24x30cm 9x11in) Vejle 2000

FISCHER Egon 1935 **[42]**
- $402 - €470 - £283 - FF3 080
  Untitled Iron (H35cm H13in) Köbenhavn 2000

FISCHER Hans 1909-1958 **[150]**
- $1 562 - €1 838 - £1 120 - FF12 054
  Im Krankenbett Indian ink (21.5x63cm 8x24in) Zürich 2001
- $84 - €82 - £52 - FF536
  Katze frisst Vogel Radierung (35x25cm 13x9in) Zürich 1999

FISCHER Hans Christian 1849-1886 **[27]**
- $1 627 - €1 613 - £1 017 - FF10 582
  Udsigt over Golfen ved Castel ouvo Oil/canvas (40x62cm 15x24in) Köbenhavn 1999

FISCHER Heinrich 1820-1886 **[16]**
- $4 000 - €3 971 - £2 500 - FF26 051
  Watermill in an Alpine River Landscape Oil/canvas (84x108cm 33x42in) London 1999
- $201 - €227 - £141 - FF1 491
  «Lucerne Hôtel & Pension du lac» Lithographie (20.5x32.5cm 8x12in) Bern 2001

FISCHER Johann 1919 **[10]**
- $580 - €545 - £358 - FF3 575
  Elephant und Giraffe Pencil (40x30cm 15x11in) Wien 1999

FISCHER Johann George Paul 1786-1875 **[18]**
- $1 964 - €2 336 - £1 400 - FF15 323
  Types of the British Army Watercolour (20.5x29cm 8x11in) London 2000

FISCHER Johann Thomas 1603-1685 **[2]**
- $15 584 - €18 151 - £10 888 - FF119 064
  Studies of Tulips Gouache (30x20.5cm 11x8in) Amsterdam 2000

FISCHER Johannes 1888-1955 **[44]**
- $981 - €1 090 - £657 - FF7 150
  Sturm in der Landschaft Öl/Leinwand (80x70cm 31x27in) Wien 2000
- $18 427 - €18 428 - £11 490 - FF119 566
  Egon Schiele mit seinem Spiegelbild Vintage gelatin silver print (24x18.1cm 9x7in) Berlin 1999

FISCHER Joseph 1769-1822 **[6]**
- $5 202 - €4 920 - £3 240 - FF32 274
  Flowers in Vase Gouache/paper (51x37cm 20x14in) Praha 2000
- $729 - €869 - £519 - FF5 701
  Bootspartie in einer Höhle Etching, aquatint (51.3x68.4cm 20x26in) Berlin 2000

FISCHER Joseph 1761-1843 **[3]**
- $64 928 - €62 433 - £40 000 - FF409 536
  Bouquet of Garden Flowers and Leaves Oil/canvas (22x28cm 8x11in) London 1999

FISCHER Leopold 1814-1864 **[23]**
- $908 - €872 - £570 - FF5 720
  Bildnis einer Dame/Bildnis eines Herrn Aquarell/Papier (31.5x23cm 12x9in) Wien 1999

FISCHER Lothar 1933 **[153]**
- $2 920 - €2 556 - £1 768 - FF16 765
  Verschnürte Hülle Terracotta (109.5x21x18.5cm 43x8x7in) Berlin 1998
- $2 848 - €2 710 - £1 769 - FF17 775
  Kleines Aktbrett Bronze (44.5x11x3cm 17x4x1in) Hamburg 1999
- $309 - €255 - £181 - FF1 675
  Zwei Sitzfigurationen Pencil (28x28.3cm 11x11in) Heidelberg 1998

FISCHER Ludwig Hans 1848-1915 **[40]**
- $1 684 - €1 588 - £1 044 - FF10 418
  Figures in an Arab Streetmarket Oil/panel (31x39cm 12x15in) Amsterdam 1999
- $676 - €726 - £452 - FF4 762
  Busy day in the streets of Vienna Watercolour (23x15.5cm 9x6in) Amsterdam 2000

FISCHER Paul Gustav 1860-1934 **[503]**
- $203 400 - €201 667 - £127 200 - FF1 322 850
  På Höjbro Plads Oil/canvas (171x220cm 67x86in) Köbenhavn 1999
- $22 482 - €24 129 - £15 048 - FF158 274
  På terrassen Oil/canvas (34.5x47cm 13x18in) Köbenhavn 2000
- $6 283 - €7 297 - £4 415 - FF47 863
  Motiv från Kongens Nytorv och den kongelige teater, Köpenhamn Oil/panel (21x22cm 8x8in) Stockholm 2001
- $1 356 - €1 344 - £848 - FF8 819
  Det nye år danses ind Watercolour/paper (22x25cm 8x9in) Köbenhavn 1999

FISCHER Pit XX **[14]**
- $1 074 - €920 - £645 - FF6 035
  Komposition Watercolour (46.2x103.7cm 18x40in) Hamburg 1998

FISCHER Vilhelm Theodor 1857-1928 **[47]**
- $638 - €610 - £400 - FF4 002
  Chickens and Ducks in a Farmyard Oil/canvas (48x63.5cm 18x25in) London 1999

FISCHER Vinzenz 1729-1810 **[5]**
- $8 550 - €9 712 - £6 000 - FF63 705
  The Sacrifice of Iphigenia Oil/panel (36x45cm 14x17in) London 1999

FISCHER-CÖRLIN Ernst Albert 1853-1932 **[27]**
- $899 - €1 022 - £623 - FF6 707
  Bauernhof in Brandenburg Öl/Karton (72x51cm 28x20in) Hamburg 2000
- $4 626 - €5 262 - £3 231 - FF34 519
  Neckerei Gouache/paper (77x106cm 30x41in) Stockholm 2000

FISCHER-HANSEN Else 1905 **[84]**
- $374 - €402 - **£257** - FF2 638
  Komposition Oil/canvas (52x96cm 20x37in)
  København 2001

FISCHER-KÖYSTRAND Carl 1861-1918 **[25]**
- $4 152 - €4 573 - **£2 769** - FF30 000
  Jeune garçon, chien et hérisson Huile/toile
  (64x78cm 25x30in) Deauville 2000
- $235 - €230 - **£144** - FF1 509
  **Die Ahnen, illustre Gesellschaft in einer
  Ahnengalerie** Aquarell/Papier (28.7x29cm 11x11in)
  Stuttgart 1999

FISCHER-TRACHAU Otto 1878-1958 **[16]**
- $453 - €511 - **£318** - FF3 353
  Studie einer Sitzenden Charcoal (32x24cm 12x9in)
  Stuttgart 2001

FISCHES Isaak I 1630/38-1706 **[5]**
- $5 500 - €5 406 - **£3 533** - FF35 462
  Minerva protecting the Arts Oil/canvas (73x52.5cm
  28x20in) New-York 1999

FISCHETTI Fedele 1732-1792 **[22]**
- $80 000 - €82 932 - **£48 000** - FF544 000
  La Primavera/L'Estate/L'Autunno/L'Inverno
  Olio/tela (72.5x59cm 28x23in) Napoli 2000

FISCHHOF Georg 1859-1914 **[94]**
- $1 009 - €1 090 - **£697** - FF7 150
  Fischerhafen Öl/Leinwand (74x100cm 29x39in) Wien
  2001
- $585 - €581 - **£365** - FF3 813
  Kühe in Aulandschaft Oil/panel (46x30cm 18x11in)
  Salzburg 1999

FISCHL Eric 1948 **[199]**
- $200 000 - €227 457 - **£139 740** - FF1 492 020
  Duck, Ode to Julian Schnabel Oil/canvas
  (178x152.5cm 70x60in) Beverly-Hills CA 2000
- $32 500 - €36 339 - **£21 908** - FF238 368
  Untitled Oil/paper (99.5x69.5cm 39x27in) New-York
  2000
- $17 000 - €14 271 - **£9 970** - FF93 612
  Untitled Acrylic/paper (33x41cm 12x16in) Beverly-
  Hills CA 1998
- $120 000 - €134 409 - **£83 376** - FF881 664
  Woman Bending Bronze (141x98x61cm 55x38x24in)
  New-York 2001
- $8 500 - €9 863 - **£5 868** - FF64 696
  Untitled Gouache/paper (45x36cm 17x14in) New-York
  2000
- $3 000 - €2 824 - **£1 853** - FF18 524
  Untitled Etching, aquatint in colors (90x138cm
  35x54in) New-York 1999

FISCHL Franz X. 1891-1962 **[28]**
- $73 - €77 - **£46** - FF503
  Frau Fischl mit Mädchen auf dem Arm Radierung
  (23x33cm 9x12in) Zwiesel 2001

FISCHLI & WEISS Peter & David 1952/46 **[22]**
- $51 991 - €56 653 - **£36 000** - FF371 620
  Car Plaster (52x86.5x138.5cm 20x34x54in) London
  2001
- $6 552 - €7 318 - **£4 440** - FF48 000
  Wurstserie - Moonracher Photo couleurs
  (50x70cm 19x27in) Paris 2000

FISCHLI Hans 1909-1989 **[19]**
- $23 240 - €25 632 - **£15 740** - FF168 132
  **Fünfeckfläche im Raum mit vollem
  Kreisumfang** Metal (26x20x12.5cm 10x7x4in) Zürich
  2000

FISCHLI Peter 1952 **[3]**
- $8 286 - €9 861 - **£5 922** - FF64 686
  Ohne Titel Gelatin silver print (23.5x30.5cm 9x12in)
  Zürich 2000

FISH Anne Harriet 1890-1964 **[7]**
- $1 100 - €1 282 - **£761** - FF8 411
  Couples Dancing, Cupids Attending Ink
  (34x26cm 13x10in) New-York 2000

FISH Janet 1938 **[39]**
- $30 000 - €28 168 - **£18 588** - FF184 773
  Vinegar Bottles Oil/canvas (127x152.5cm 50x60in)
  New-York 1999

FISHER Alexander 1864-? **[1]**
- $28 432 - €24 041 - **£17 000** - FF157 698
  Urania Bronze (H92cm H36in) London 1998

FISHER Alvan 1792-1863 **[12]**
- $10 000 - €11 151 - **£6 724** - FF73 144
  Landscape with Cattle Oil/canvas (76x114cm
  30x45in) Delaware OH 2000
- $2 400 - €2 295 - **£1 461** - FF15 053
  **Mountain Landscape, spaniel Dog in
  Foreground** Oil/board (30x24.5cm 11x9in) Boston
  MA 1999

FISHER Anna S. 1873-1942 **[24]**
- $1 950 - €2 228 - **£1 373** - FF14 615
  Sunlit Barnyard, Fisher Farm Oil/canvas (50x40cm
  20x16in) Pittsfield MA 2001
- $800 - €914 - **£563** - FF5 994
  Back Porch, Fisher Farm Oil/canvas (30x22cm
  12x9in) Pittsfield MA 2001
- $950 - €1 086 - **£669** - FF7 121
  Woman in a Sun dappled Interior Watercolour
  (39x51cm 15x20in) Pittsfield MA 2001

FISHER D.A. 1867-1940 **[15]**
- $302 - €283 - **£187** - FF1 854
  Pikes Peak Oil/canvas (30x22cm 12x9in) Williston
  VT 1999

FISHER Ellen Bowdich Thayer 1847-1911 **[5]**
- $1 600 - €1 866 - **£1 123** - FF12 240
  Sparrow Perches Among Clover and Daisies
  Watercolour, gouache/paper (30x23cm 11x9in) Boston
  MA 2000

FISHER George Bulteel 1764-1834 **[7]**
- $2 595 - €2 868 - **£1 800** - FF18 815
  **The Minto Hills from Teviot Valley,
  Scotland/Rubers Law from the Wells** Watercolour
  (28x40cm 11x15in) London 2001

FISHER Harrison C. 1875-1934 **[35]**
- $520 - €602 - **£368** - FF3 946
  Profile of a Beautiful Lady Pencil/paper (60x48cm
  24x19in) Cleveland OH 2000

FISHER Horace 1861-1928 **[11]**
- $11 750 - €11 155 - **£7 200** - FF73 175
  The Toy Seller Oil/canvas (117x71cm 46x27in)
  London 1999

FISHER Hugo Anton 1854-1916 **[40]**
- $650 - €650 - **£386** - FF3 674
  **Sheep Herder, Dog and Herd, Windmill in dis-
  tance** Watercolour/paper (43x74cm 17x29in) Hatfield
  PA 1998

FISHER Hugo Melville 1876-1946 **[22]**
- $650 - €681 - **£412** - FF4 470
  Impressionistic Country Landscape Oil/canvas
  (66x73cm 26x29in) New-Orleans LA 2000

FISHER Joshua 1859-? **[18]**
📷 **$1 666** - €1 533 - **£1 000** - FF10 058
A Welsh Lake Watercolour/paper (60x90cm 23x35in)
Glamorgan 1999

FISHER Kitty XX **[1]**
🛏 **$1 386** - €1 260 - **£850** - FF8 267
Wool runner, a carpet with coloured horizontal hand-hooked bands Tapestry (58.7x92cm 23x36in)
London 1999

FISHER Larry XX **[3]**
🛋 **$3 500** - €3 856 - **£2 334** - FF25 295
Depicting a Locomotive Crossing a Trestle in a Snow Storm Acrylic (68x53cm 27x21in) Detroit MI 2000

FISHER Leonard Everett 1924 **[7]**
🛋 **$9 500** - €11 139 - **£6 834** - FF73 068
The Fight Oil/canvas (64x89cm 25x35in) New-York 2001

FISHER Mark 1841-1923 **[89]**
🛋 **$2 383** - €2 487 - **£1 503** - FF16 313
Cattle by Canal Oil/canvas (46x66.5cm 18x26in)
Sydney 2000
🛋 **$2 645** - €2 499 - **£1 600** - FF16 391
Landscape with Cattle Oil/canvas (17x26cm 6x10in)
Billingshurst, West-Sussex 1999
📷 **$241** - €281 - **£170** - FF1 843
Cattle in a Meadow Watercolour/paper (33x48cm 13x19in) Lewes, Sussex 2001

FISHER Orville Norman 1911 **[5]**
🛏 **$885** - €851 - **£545** - FF5 582
Memorial to Robbie Burns - Stanley Park, BC Linocut (27.5x32cm 10x12in) Vancouver, BC. 1999

FISHER Paul 1864-1932 **[78]**
🛋 **$9 795** - €11 657 - **£7 000** - FF76 462
On the Beach, Skåne Oil/canvas (47.5x57.5cm 18x22in) London 2000
🛋 **$5 492** - €5 345 - **£3 381** - FF35 061
Köksinteriör Oil/panel (28x25cm 11x9in) Stockholm 1999
🛋 **$1 188** - €1 144 - **£737** - FF7 506
Parti fra Østergade i København ud for Svane Apoteket Indian ink/paper (34x25.5cm 13x10in)
København 1999

FISHER Percy Harland 1867-1944 **[34]**
🛋 **$2 988** - €3 208 - **£2 000** - FF21 043
Young Girl, Seated Three-Quarter-Length in a White Dress and a Cat Oil/board (76x63.5cm 29x25in) London 2000
🛋 **$449** - €453 - **£280** - FF2 969
Portrait of Lila Marchmont Pastel/paper (53.5x43cm 21x16in) London 2000

FISHER Randi 1920 **[9]**
🛋 **$977** - €1 095 - **£681** - FF7 180
Båt under bro Oil/panel (49x75cm 19x29in)
Stockholm 2000

FISHER Rowland 1885-1969 **[116]**
🛋 **$544** - €617 - **£380** - FF4 044
Early Morning, Mevagissey Oil/board (37.5x44.5cm 14x17in) Billingshurst, West-Sussex 2001
🛋 **$426** - €391 - **£260** - FF2 562
Boats on the Shingle, Summer Oil/board (30x40.5cm 11x15in) Ipswich 1999
📷 **$170** - €193 - **£120** - FF1 269
Still life study of cut Wallflowers in a Bowl Watercolour/paper (17x20cm 7x8in) Aylsham, Norfolk 2001

FISHER William 1890-? **[17]**
🛋 **$1 000** - €866 - **£606** - FF5 678
Landscape Oil/canvas (60x50cm 24x20in) Mystic CT 1998

FISHER-CLAY Elizabeth Campbell 1871-1959 **[7]**
🛋 **$5 194** - €5 827 - **£3 600** - FF38 224
Spanish Bullfight Oil/board (14x19.5cm 5x7in)
London 2000

FISHMAN Louise 1939 **[5]**
🛋 **$8 500** - €9 616 - **£5 946** - FF63 074
«Elegy for Tony K» Oil/canvas (127x165cm 50x64in)
New-York 2001

FISHWICK Clifford 1923-1997 **[73]**
🛋 **$492** - €470 - **£300** - FF3 083
Two Hills Oil/board (20x68.5cm 7x26in) London 1999
📷 **$269** - €289 - **£180** - FF1 898
A Bouquet of Memories Ink (33x28cm 12x11in)
London 2000

FISKE Gertrude 1878-1961 **[21]**
🛋 **$10 000** - €8 567 - **£6 012** - FF56 197
A Barn in Algonquin, Maine Oil/canvas (50x68cm 20x27in) Cleveland OH 1998
🛋 **$1 100** - €940 - **£646** - FF6 165
House in Winter Oil/board (30x40cm 11x15in)
Boston MA 1998

FISKE Joseph Winn 1832-? **[5]**
⚖ **$17 000** - €18 166 - **£11 553** - FF119 163
Cow Metal (86x124cm 34x49in) Portsmouth NH 2001

FISQUET Théodore 1813-1890 **[3]**
🛋 **$6 130** - €5 641 - **£3 792** - FF37 000
Scène orientaliste Huile/toile (70x98cm 27x38in)
Libourne 1999

FISSETTE Leopold 1814-1889 **[6]**
🛋 **$6 256** - €5 899 - **£3 877** - FF38 695
In the Tavern Oil/panel (47x54cm 18x21in)
Amsterdam 1999
🛋 **$1 768** - €1 983 - **£1 230** - FF13 008
Intérieur de taverne Huile/panneau (29.5x34.5cm 11x13in) Bruxelles 2000

FISSORE Daniele 1947 **[82]**
🛋 **$750** - €777 - **£450** - FF5 100
Mare e green Olio/cartone (28.5x59.5cm 11x23in)
Vercelli 1999
🛋 **$550** - €570 - **£330** - FF3 740
Mare e green Olio/tela (25x25cm 9x9in) Vercelli 2001

FITCH Walter Hood 1817-1892 **[5]**
🛏 **$2 067** - €2 154 - **£1 300** - FF14 131
Orchids Color lithograph (45.5x33.5cm 17x13in)
London 2000

FITGER Arthur Heinrich 1840-1909 **[4]**
🛋 **$11 470** - €9 720 - **£6 853** - FF63 758
Joseph und Potiphars Weib Öl/Leinwand (158x165cm 62x64in) Bremen 1998

FITLER William Crothers 1857-1915 **[27]**
🛋 **$4 250** - €4 741 - **£2 782** - FF31 102
After the Shower Oil/canvas (53x73cm 21x29in)
Chicago IL 2000
🛋 **$1 900** - €2 228 - **£1 355** - FF14 615
Haystacks in Rural Landscape Oil/canvas (20x25cm 8x10in) Delray-Beach FL 2000
📷 **$300** - €331 - **£200** - FF2 168
Stream with Willows Watercolour/paper (35x50cm 14x20in) Portsmouth NH 2000

FITTKE Arturo 1873-1910 **[6]**
🛋 **$1 000** - €1 037 - **£640** - FF6 800
Paesaggio Olio/cartone (14x23cm 5x9in) Trieste 1999

FITTLER James 1758-1835 **[11]**
📖 $258 - €257 - **£160** - FF1 683
Victory Over the French Fleet, after Paton
Engraving (51x68.5cm 20x26in) Newbury, Berkshire
2000

FITTON E. Hedley 1859-1929 **[47]**
📖 $161 - €149 - **£100** - FF978
Winchester Cross Etching (50x28cm 20x11in)
Leominster, Herefordshire 1999

FITTON James 1899-1982 **[27]**
🖎 $10 427 - €10 507 - **£6 500** - FF68 923
London Landscape Oil/paper (51x61cm 20x24in)
London 2000
📖 $1 136 - €1 311 - **£800** - FF8 600
«Kind Hearts and Coronets» Poster (56x71cm
22x27in) London 2000

FITZ W. Grancel 1894-1963 **[36]**
📷 $3 000 - €2 505 - **£1 782** - FF16 429
Nude Montage Gelatin silver print (25.5x20.5cm
10x8in) New-York 1998

FITZGERALD Florence ?-1927 **[10]**
🖎 $1 424 - €1 656 - **£1 000** - FF10 864
Sunshine and Shade Oil/canvas (40x60cm 15x23in)
Billingshurst, West-Sussex 2001
🖎 $2 064 - €2 286 - **£1 400** - FF14 996
Mending the Nets Watercolour (35.5x52.5cm
13x20in) Billingshurst, West-Sussex 2000

FITZGERALD Frederick R. XIX-XX **[53]**
✏ $378 - €366 - **£240** - FF2 403
Mountain Lake Watercolour/paper (23x29cm 9x11in)
Stansted Mountfitchet, Essex 1999

FITZGERALD Gerald 1873-1935 **[17]**
🖎 $16 220 - €15 420 - **£10 122** - FF101 150
Leura, Blue Mountains Oil/canvas (59x90cm
23x35in) Melbourne 1999
🖎 $350 - €386 - **£232** - FF2 531
Palm Trees Watercolour/paper (55x24.5cm 21x9in)
Melbourne 2000

FITZGERALD James 1899-1971 **[8]**
🖎 $15 000 - €16 101 - **£10 038** - FF105 615
Seiners, Monhegan Oil/board (40x50cm 16x20in)
Portland ME 2000
🖎 $8 500 - €9 124 - **£5 688** - FF59 848
Working Boats Watercolour/paper (45x58cm
18x23in) Portland ME 2000

FITZGERALD John Austen 1832-1906 **[33]**
🖎 $17 931 - €19 248 - **£12 000** - FF126 259
The Flower Girl Oil/canvas (60.5x45.5cm 23x17in)
London 2000
🖎 $238 510 - €283 659 - **£170 000** - FF1 860 684
Death of the Fairy Queen Oil/canvas (20x25.5cm
7x10in) London 2000
🖎 $98 014 - €113 991 - **£70 000** - FF747 733
The Enchanted Forest Watercolour (47x70cm
18x27in) London 2001

FITZGERALD Lionel Lemoine 1890-1956 **[53]**
🖎 $6 098 - €5 970 - **£3 753** - FF39 159
The Red House Oil/canvas (51x42cm 20x16in)
Toronto 1999
✏ $1 054 - €893 - **£633** - FF5 858
Abstract Composition Coloured pencils/paper
(14x21.5cm 5x8in) Vancouver, BC. 1998

FITZGERALD Lloyd 1941 **[11]**
🖎 $2 428 - €2 834 - **£1 690** - FF18 588
Midday - December Acrylic/canvas (54x86.5cm
21x34in) Toronto 2000

FITZGERALD Mary XX **[2]**
✏ $1 302 - €1 397 - **£887** - FF9 161
«Sign Series 17» Mixed media/paper (56x76cm
22x29in) Dublin 2001

FITZGERALD Peggy XX **[1]**
🖎 $3 482 - €3 921 - **£2 400** - FF25 723
Sea Thoughts Oil/canvas (91.5x71cm 36x27in)
London 2000

FITZI Johann Ulrich 1798-1855 **[10]**
🖎 $8 656 - €9 793 - **£6 055** - FF64 236
«Speicher» Oil/panel (30x49cm 11x19in) St. Gallen
2001
🖎 $7 108 - €6 836 - **£4 379** - FF44 839
Speicher, Ansicht von Südosten Aquarelle
(19x28cm 7x11in) St. Gallen 1999
📖 $1 387 - €1 556 - **£963** - FF10 206
Heiden Lithographie (35x53cm 13x20in) Luzern 2001

FIUME Salvatore 1915-1997 **[244]**
🖎 $20 000 - €20 733 - **£12 000** - FF136 000
Gallo Olio/tavola (245x340cm 96x133in) Venezia 1999
🖎 $7 854 - €6 785 - **£5 236** - FF44 568
Isole di Pietra, omaggio a Raffaele Carrieri
Olio/faesite (65x38.5cm 25x15in) Milano 1998
🖎 $5 000 - €5 183 - **£3 000** - FF34 000
Messicani Olio/tavola (27x35.5cm 10x13in) Milano
2000
✏ $2 000 - €2 073 - **£1 200** - FF13 600
Nudi di pietra Pastelli (50x70cm 19x27in) Vercelli
1999
📖 $300 - €311 - **£180** - FF2 040
Somale al vento Serigrafia (70x50cm 27x19in)
Vercelli 1999

FIX-MASSEAU Pierre 1905-1994 **[89]**
✏ $734 - €838 - **£511** - FF5 500
«Dans toutes les mains, la pointe bic» Gouache
(46x55cm 18x21in) Paris 2001
📖 $399 - €381 - **£249** - FF2 540
«Gazoconfort Mirus» Affiche couleur (159.5x120cm
62x47in) Orléans 1999

FIX-MASSEAU Pierre Félix Masseau 1869-1937
[44]
🖎 $10 582 - €12 504 - **£7 500** - FF82 024
La table fleurie Oil/canvas (64x78cm 25x30in)
London 2000
🖎 $8 500 - €8 355 - **£5 461** - FF54 806
Pink Flowers in a blue and white Vase Oil/canvas
(23x33cm 9x12in) New-York 1999
🗝 $2 746 - €2 744 - **£1 717** - FF18 000
Le secret Bronze (H29cm H11in) Paris 1999
📖 $170 - €198 - **£120** - FF1 301
Exactitude, Etat Color lithograph (97x60cm 38x23in)
London 2001

FIZEAU Hippolyte Louis Ar. 1819-1896 **[24]**
📖 $3 637 - €3 436 - **£2 200** - FF22 537
**Notre-Dame, Paris, South Portal and Restes de
l'ancienne Sacristie** Engraving (21.5x16cm 8x6in)
London 1999

FIZELLE Reg. C. Graham, Rah 1891-1964 **[37]**
✏ $304 - €361 - **£215** - FF2 369
Back of the Insitute, Paris Pencil (44x36cm
17x14in) Sydney 2000

FJAESTAD Gustaf 1868-1948 **[107]**
🖎 $16 919 - €14 758 - **£10 233** - FF96 804
Vinterlandskap Oil/canvas (118x146cm 46x57in)
Stockholm 1998
🖎 $7 402 - €7 204 - **£4 557** - FF47 256
Blidväder, vinterlandskap med vattendrag
Oil/panel (61x87cm 24x34in) Stockholm 1999

$963 - €840 - £582 - FF5 511
Snötyngda grenar Oil/panel (30x50cm 11x19in)
Stockholm 1998
$5 962 - €6 783 - £4 164 - FF44 491
Vårlandskap Akvarell/papper (57x70cm 22x27in)
Stockholm 2000

FJAESTAD Maja 1873-1961 **[30]**
$301 - €279 - £184 - FF1 831
Rosor och blåklockor Woodcut in colors (25x32cm 9x12in) Uppsala 1999

FJELL Kai 1907-1989 **[106]**
$88 603 - €85 478 - £56 000 - FF560 700
The Party Oil/canvas (118.5x138.5cm 46x54in)
London 1999
$10 730 - €12 515 - £7 470 - FF82 090
Medaljongen Oil/canvas (51x63cm 20x24in) Oslo 2000
$3 152 - €3 012 - £1 985 - FF19 760
Ventende kvinne Oil/panel (33x24cm 12x9in) Oslo 1999
$960 - €1 037 - £663 - FF6 803
Allsang ved ulykkesstedet Pastel (20x28cm 7x11in) Oslo 2001
$1 412 - €1 525 - £976 - FF10 005
Vårkveld Color lithograph (27x38cm 10x14in) Oslo 2001

FLACHERON Frédéric, Comte 1813-1883 **[15]**
$1 533 - €1 296 - £912 - FF8 500
Base de la colonne Trajane/Arco detto di Giano/Portrait d'homme barbu Tirage papier salé (33.8x25.1cm 13x9in) Chartres 1998

FLACK Audrey 1931 **[12]**
$15 000 - €17 404 - £10 356 - FF114 165
«Self Portrait I» Acrylic (203x162.5cm 79x63in)
New-York 2000

FLADERER Herbert 1913-1981 **[10]**
$358 - €400 - £242 - FF2 621
Bauernkriegzyklus Woodcut (34x25.5cm 13x10in)
Wien 2000

FLAGG Hiram Peabody 1859-1937 **[14]**
$550 - €525 - £342 - FF3 445
Sunset Oil/board (15x20cm 6x8in) Cambridge MA 1999

FLAGG James Montgomery 1877-1960 **[110]**
$8 000 - €9 098 - £5 589 - FF59 680
Alice in Wonderland Oil/canvas (152x45cm 60x18in)
New-York 2000
$1 500 - €1 680 - £1 042 - FF11 020
Beautiful Woman wearing Veil Watercolour/paper (38x27cm 15x11in) New-York 2001
$2 000 - €1 860 - £1 234 - FF12 199
«I Want You for U.S Army» Poster (102x76cm 40x30in) New-York 2000

FLAHERTY Robert Joseph 1884-1951 **[4]**
$2 281 - €2 647 - £1 575 - FF17 364
Nanook of the North: Tookto/Allegoo/The Hunter/Summer/Nyla and Child Photogravure (21x16cm 8x6in) Vancouver, BC. 2000

FLAIG Waldemar 1892-1932 **[14]**
$1 550 - €1 278 - £913 - FF8 383
Segelschiffe auf dem Bodensee, im Vordergrund Weiden Öl/Leinwand (62x66cm 24x25in) Lindau 1998

FLAMAND Georges XIX-XX **[21]**
$2 218 - €2 058 - £1 355 - FF13 500
Femme sortant des branchages Bronze (H21cm H8in) Paris 1999

FLAMEN Albert c.1620-c.1669 **[16]**
$10 000 - €10 712 - £6 829 - FF70 266
Farmhouses and their Surroundings Ink (21.5x16cm 8x6in) New-York 2001
$3 216 - €3 835 - £2 293 - FF25 154
Seconde partie de poissons d'eau douce Kupferstich (10.5x17.5cm 4x6in) Berlin 2000

FLAMEN Anselme I 1647-1717 **[2]**
$60 000 - €52 318 - £36 276 - FF343 182
Diana Bronze (H71cm H27in) New-York 1998

FLAMENG François 1856-1923 **[66]**
$11 270 - €10 671 - £7 000 - FF70 000
La marquise de Yturbe Huile/toile (145x115cm 57x45in) Paris 1999
$28 000 - €30 729 - £18 029 - FF201 566
Pique-nique Oil/panel (38x58.5cm 14x23in) New-York 2000
$5 231 - €5 895 - £3 623 - FF38 669
The Letter Oil/panel (33x19.5cm 12x7in) Toronto 2000
$878 - €838 - £548 - FF5 500
«Aux Merveilles de Paris & de l'Exposition» Affiche couleur (134x83cm 52x32in) Orléans 1999

FLAMENG Léopold 1831-1911 **[17]**
$503 - €562 - £340 - FF3 684
The Defence of Rorke's Drift, after Alphonse de Neuville Engraving (53x86cm 21x34in) Aylsham, Norfolk 2000

FLAMENG Marie-Auguste 1843-1893 **[23]**
$2 305 - €2 134 - £1 428 - FF14 000
Marine Huile/panneau (35x56cm 13x22in) Toulouse 1999

FLAMM Albert 1823-1906 **[34]**
$6 500 - €6 238 - £4 074 - FF40 920
The Resting Place Oil/canvas/board (34x114cm 13x44in) New-York 1999

FLANAGAN Barry 1941 **[59]**
$85 000 - €95 040 - £57 298 - FF623 424
Uni Hare on Cresent and Bell Bronze (134x95.5x57.5cm 52x37x22in) New-York 2000
$6 137 - €5 124 - £3 600 - FF33 613
Untitled Stone (30.5x66x44.5cm 12x25x17in) London 1998

FLANAGAN Francis J. act.1897-1927 **[4]**
$3 800 - €4 191 - £2 573 - FF27 489
Winter Landscape Oil/board (48.5x66cm 19x25in)
New-York 2000

FLANAGAN Terence P. 1929 **[16]**
$4 001 - €3 793 - £2 500 - FF24 882
Winter Orchards Oil/panel (71.5x91cm 28x35in)
London 1999
$1 617 - €1 905 - £1 136 - FF12 493
Fermanagh Landscape Oil/canvas (35.5x44.5cm 13x17in) Dublin 2000
$754 - €889 - £530 - FF5 830
Vegetation Watercolour/paper (76x56cm 29x22in)
Dublin 2000

FLANDIN Eugène Napoléon 1809-1889 **[41]**
$21 165 - €25 009 - £15 000 - FF164 049
Le Palais des Doges, Venise Oil/canvas (51.5x82cm 20x32in) London 2000
$4 065 - €4 573 - £2 799 - FF30 000
Vue de Venise Huile/toile (27x46cm 10x18in) Beaune 2000
$5 637 - €6 250 - £3 903 - FF41 000
Venise, devant le palais de Doges Dessin (18x29cm 7x11in) La Flèche 2001

F

FLANDRIN Hippolyte 1809-1864 **[66]**
$10 200 - €11 434 - **£7 140** - FF75 000
Etude pour la tête de Saint Jean dans la Vocation de Saint Jean Huile/papier (24x18cm 9x7in) Paris 2001
$226 - €248 - **£146** - FF1 626
Composition Mine plomb (46.5x40cm 18x15in) Liège 2000

FLANDRIN Jules 1871-1947 **[312]**
$11 765 - €9 909 - **£6 948** - FF65 000
Le troupeau et les Mas Dauphinois dans la plaine de Moirans Huile/toile (97x196cm 38x77in) Grenoble 1998
$1 857 - €1 753 - **£1 154** - FF11 500
Sous les arcades, la porte du cabaret, Bayonne Huile/carton (61x50cm 24x19in) Neuilly-sur-Seine 1999
$212 - €229 - **£142** - FF1 500
La fontaine de l'Aqua-Acetosa Crayons couleurs/papier (9.5x12.5cm 3x4in) Grenoble 2000

FLANDRIN Paul Jean 1811-1902 **[38]**
$4 995 - €4 573 - **£3 045** - FF30 000
Chemin dans un sous-bois avec un jeune promeneur au repos Huile/toile (61x43.8cm 24x17in) Paris 1999
$3 625 - €3 811 - **£2 275** - FF25 000
Paysage, la Gassaude Huile/papier (26.5x36cm 10x14in) Paris 2000
$639 - €762 - **£456** - FF5 000
Gardeuse de vaches Fusain (27.5x21.5cm 10x8in) Paris 2000

FLANNAGAN John Bernard 1895-1942 **[18]**
$22 000 - €26 164 - **£15 679** - FF171 622
Girl and Horse Stone (H41cm H16in) New-York 2000

FLANNERY Vaughn 1898-1955 **[11]**
$12 000 - €11 258 - **£7 414** - FF73 846
Schooling Yearlings, Greentree Training Track, Saratoga Oil/panel (61x91cm 24x35in) New-York 1999

FLASHAR Bruno Max 1855-1915 **[36]**
$193 - €179 - **£120** - FF1 173
Heimkehr des Invaliden Aquarell/Papier (57x45cm 22x17in) Zwiesel 1999

FLASSCHOEN Gustave 1868-1940 **[145]**
$1 497 - €1 785 - **£1 072** - FF11 707
Déchargement de la péniche Huile/toile/panneau (36x46cm 14x18in) Bruxelles 2000
$777 - €793 - **£486** - FF5 203
Les pêcheurs Huile/carton (27.5x35.5cm 10x13in) Bruxelles 2000

FLATHER Donald M. 1903-1990 **[16]**
$3 084 - €3 489 - **£2 157** - FF22 885
«Step Lakes, Lake Louise, Looking Southeasterly» Oil/canvas (91.5x70cm 36x27in) Toronto 2001

FLATTER Joseph Otto 1894-? **[17]**
$615 - €579 - **£380** - FF3 797
Still Life Study with Bowl of Fruit, Vase of Carnations Oil/board (52x44.5cm 20x17in) West-Sussex 1999

FLAUBERT Paul 1928-1994 **[221]**
$500 - €534 - **£317** - FF3 500
Vue de Rouen sous la neige Huile/panneau (33x55cm 12x21in) Deauville 2000
$422 - €381 - **£260** - FF2 500
Jeune femme et enfants Huile/toile (33x46cm 12x18in) Laudun 1999

FLAVIN Dan 1933-1996 **[130]**
$52 300 - €56 140 - **£35 000** - FF368 256
Untitled (to Charlotte) Sculpture (244x16x9.5cm 96x6x3in) London 2000
$42 000 - €40 638 - **£25 901** - FF266 569
Untitled (to Virginia Dwan) Sculpture (10x244x20cm 3x96x7in) New-York 1999
$4 500 - €4 860 - **£3 110** - FF31 880
«1971 in Daylight and Cool White Fluorescent Light 2 Wide 8 High» Pencil (43x56cm 16x22in) New-York 2001
$1 800 - €2 005 - **£1 177** - FF13 151
«For one Walled Circular Flourescent Light» Lithograph (56x76cm 22x29in) New-York 2000

FLAVITSKY Konstantin Dmitriev. 1830-1866 **[1]**
$88 572 - €83 633 - **£55 000** - FF548 597
Anthony and Cleopatra Oil/canvas (158x165cm 62x64in) London 1999

FLAXMAN John 1755-1826 **[37]**
$1 146 - €1 048 - **£700** - FF6 876
A laplander Ink (23x16cm 9x6in) London 1998

FLECK Karl Anton 1928-1983 **[59]**
$1 009 - €1 017 - **£630** - FF6 673
Vase mit Blumen Pencil/paper (26x20cm 10x7in) Wien 2000
$201 - €218 - **£139** - FF1 430
«Am Neumarkter Mais» Farbradierung (30x39cm 11x15in) Wien 2001

FLEETWOOD-WALKER Bernard 1893-1965 **[49]**
$575 - €645 - **£400** - FF4 229
Portrait of a Girl Oil/canvas (43x31cm 16x12in) London 2001
$515 - €616 - **£355** - FF4 042
«Joan» Watercolour (26.5x20.5cm 10x8in) Penzance, Cornwall 2000

FLEGEL Georg 1563-1638 **[18]**
$268 974 - €288 721 - **£180 000** - FF1 893 888
Allegory of Autumn: Fruit and Vegetable Stall Above the Weinmarket Oil/canvas (169.5x236.5cm 66x93in) London 2000

FLEISCHMANN Adolph Richard 1892-1969 **[137]**
$17 833 - €17 149 - **£10 988** - FF112 492
Ohne Titel Oil/panel (62.5x47.5cm 24x18in) München 1999
$4 945 - €5 624 - **£3 429** - FF36 892
Komposition Gouache/paper (31.5x23.5cm 12x9in) Hamburg 2000
$316 - €332 - **£199** - FF2 180
Komposition Farblithographie (73x59cm 28x23in) Stuttgart 2000

FLEISCHMANN Arthur John 1896-1990 **[9]**
$4 304 - €4 888 - **£2 946** - FF32 061
Lelong dancer Bronze (H36cm H14in) Singapore 2000

FLEISCHMANN August XIX **[7]**
$2 368 - €2 046 - **£1 430** - FF13 418
«Portrait Franz Josef I» Pastell/Papier (54x40cm 21x15in) Konstanz 1998

FLEISCHMANN Carl 1853-? **[2]**
$4 854 - €4 553 - **£3 000** - FF29 863
Reading by Lamplight Oil/canvas (66x76cm 25x29in) London 1999

FLEISCHMANN Charles Louis XIX-XX **[1]**
$6 000 - €6 908 - **£4 094** - FF45 312
Mountain Home Watercolour/paper (38x56cm 14x22in) New-York 2000

FLEISCHMANN Trude 1895-1990 **[75]**
📷 **$523** - €562 - **£350** - FF3 689
Porträt mit Hut Photograph (22.5x17.1cm 8x6in)
München 2000

FLEMING Ian 1906 **[23]**
✎ **$461** - €525 - **£320** - FF3 442
Drystone Dyke, Autumn Watercolour/paper
(48x69cm 18x27in) Edinburgh 2000
▥ **$218** - €189 - **£130** - FF1 238
The Botanic Gardens, Glasgow Etching
(17.5x25cm 6x9in) Glasgow 1998

FLEMING John B. 1792-1845 **[8]**
🖐 **$4 384** - €4 889 - **£3 000** - FF32 069
The Clyde from Greenock Toward Dumbarton
Oil/panel (52.5x76cm 20x29in) Perthshire 2000
🖐 **$5 279** - €4 997 - **£3 300** - FF32 779
Whiteforeland from below Gleenock Oil/panel
(25.5x38.5cm 10x15in) Perthshire 1999

FLEMWELL George XIX-XX **[7]**
▥ **$1 424** - €1 656 - **£1 000** - FF10 864
«Lausanne, Ouchy Plage» Poster (128x91cm
50x35in) London 2001

FLERS Camille 1802-1868 **[89]**
🖐 **$3 197** - €3 506 - **£2 122** - FF23 000
Scène de la vie champêtre Huile/toile (37.5x57cm
14x22in) Melun 2000
🖐 **$4 947** - €4 726 - **£3 084** - FF31 000
Le Bac Huile/toile (32x44.5cm 12x17in) Paris 1999
✐ **$938** - €1 067 - **£651** - FF7 000
Scène champêtre Pastel/papier (15x24.5cm 5x9in)
Fontainebleau 2001

FLETCHER Aaron Dean 1817-1902 **[7]**
🖐 **$6 500** - €6 942 - **£4 429** - FF45 537
Man in Fancy Painted Chair Oil/canvas (66x66cm
26x26in) New-York 2001
🖐 **$2 475** - €2 757 - **£1 618** - FF18 083
**View of Esopus, Catskill Mountains in the
Distance** Oil/canvas (39x31cm 15x12in) Williston VT
2000

FLETCHER Blandford 1858-1936 **[29]**
🖐 **$2 835** - €3 389 - **£1 955** - FF22 231
Feeding the Chikens, Girl before a Cottage
Oil/canvas (49.5x35.5cm 19x13in) Penzance, Cornwall
2000
🖐 **$1 417** - €1 680 - **£1 000** - FF11 018
The Harbour, Porlock Oil/board (16.5x25.5cm
6x10in) London 2000

FLETCHER Blythe 1890-1949 **[10]**
✎ **$190** - €214 - **£132** - FF1 403
Mediterranean Market Watercolour/paper (18x25cm
7x9in) Wellington 2001

FLETCHER Edwin / Edward 1857-1945 **[82]**
🖐 **$1 671** - €1 624 - **£1 020** - FF10 652
Pool of London Oil/canvas (50x76cm 20x30in)
Birmingham 2000
🖐 **$725** - €817 - **£450** - FF5 359
Boats in Calm Seas Oil/canvas (31x40cm 12x15in)
London 2000

FLETCHER Frank Morley 1866-1949 **[2]**
▥ **$1 800** - €2 100 - **£1 252** - FF13 775
«Brotherswater» Print in colors (35x17cm 14x7in)
Altadena CA 2000

FLETCHER Margaret 1862-1943 **[3]**
🖐 **$5 407** - €6 282 - **£3 800** - FF41 208
**Portrait of a Girl, small full-length, in a yellow
Dress** Oil/canvas (68.5x50.5cm 26x19in) London 2001

FLEUR Willy 1888-1967 **[27]**
🖐 **$391** - €431 - **£255** - FF2 827
Gele tulpen Oil/canvas (43.5x34.5cm 17x13in) Den
Haag 2000

FLEURY de James Vivien XIX **[34]**
🖐 **$2 518** - €2 821 - **£1 750** - FF18 504
**Figures and Houses in an italianate Mountain
and Lake Landscape** Oil/canvas (51x81.5cm
20x32in) Bury St. Edmunds, Suffolk 2001

FLEURY Fanny Laurent 1848-? **[19]**
🖐 **$2 367** - €2 211 - **£1 434** - FF14 500
Portrait de femme aux noeuds roses Huile/toile
(25x19cm 9x7in) Paris 1999

FLEURY Jules Amédée 1845-? **[17]**
🖐 **$1 875** - €2 072 - **£1 300** - FF13 593
A Normandy harbour Oil/panel (14.5x24cm 5x9in)
London 2001

FLEURY Léon 1804-1858 **[22]**
🖐 **$10 352** - €12 196 - **£7 160** - FF80 000
Paysage de rivière, bord de la Meuse à Dinan
Huile/toile (53.5x75.5cm 21x29in) Paris 2000
🖐 **$3 681** - €3 201 - **£2 219** - FF21 000
Paysage ombragé dans la forêt de Fontainebleau
Huile/toile (34.4x36.2cm 13x14in) Paris 1998

FLEURY Madeleine XIX-XX **[3]**
🖐 **$9 000** - €7 802 - **£5 499** - FF51 181
Feeding Time Oil/canvas (94.5x100cm 37x39in) New-
York 1999

FLEURY Sylvie 1961 **[35]**
⬚ **$37 549** - €40 916 - **£26 000** - FF268 392
«Skin Crime 3, Givenchy 318» Compression
(90x150x390cm 35x59x153in) London 2001
⬚ **$35 000** - €39 832 - **£24 594** - FF261 282
Louis Vitton Bronze (45.5x78.5x20.5cm 17x30x8in)
New-York 2001
📷 **$4 482** - €4 812 - **£3 000** - FF31 564
«New Woman's Free Diet 2000» Cibachrome print
(160x120cm 62x47in) London 2000

FLEXOR Samson 1907-1971 **[11]**
🖐 **$22 566** - €19 209 - **£13 431** - FF126 000
Va et vient Huile/toile (120x120cm 47x47in) Paris
1998
🖐 **$4 649** - €5 031 - **£3 184** - FF33 000
Composition Huile/toile (54x65cm 21x25in) Paris
2001

FLICK Auguste Emile XIX-XX **[5]**
🖐 **$10 774** - €9 186 - **£6 500** - FF60 257
Ancien Palais du Trocadero, Paris Oil/panel
(32x46cm 12x18in) London 1998

FLICK Carl 1904-1976 **[6]**
🖐 **$1 100** - €1 162 - **£727** - FF7 621
«Highway Through the Village» Oil/board
(33x38cm 13x15in) Cedar-Falls IA 2000

FLICKEL Paul Franz 1852-1903 **[14]**
🖐 **$3 441** - €3 835 - **£2 405** - FF25 154
Strasse in Bordighera Öl/Papier (47x39.5cm
18x15in) München 2001

FLIEHER Karl 1881-1958 **[107]**
🖐 **$991** - €867 - **£600** - FF5 690
Häuser am Dorfbach Tempera/Karton (48x61cm
18x24in) Zofingen 1998
🖐 **$934** - €1 022 - **£646** - FF6 707
**Wiener Blumenfrauen (Wiener Typen), im
Hintergrund die Karlskirche** Öl/Karton (27x21cm
10x8in) Hildrizhausen 2001

$987 - €936 - **£616** - FF6 137
Aus Weissenkirchen Aquarell, Gouache/Papier (23.5x16cm 9x6in) Luzern 1999

FLIESS Max XX [1]
$12 199 - €11 427 - **£7 500** - FF74 956
«**Spione**» Poster (212x96cm 83x37in) London 1999

FLIGHT Claude, Captain 1881-1955 [45]
$4 973 - €4 243 - **£3 000** - FF27 829
The Shore Oil/board (33x41cm 12x16in) London 1998

$311 - €285 - **£190** - FF1 872
River with sloping Willow Watercolour/paper (34x49.5cm 13x19in) Ipswich 1999

$3 174 - €3 080 - **£2 000** - FF20 205
The Conjuror Linocut in colors (33.5x28cm 13x11in) London 1999

FLIGHT Graham XX [3]
$1 100 - €1 170 - **£695** - FF7 674
The Riverboat Delaware Oil/canvas (63x75cm 25x29in) New-York 2000

FLINCK Govaert 1615-1660 [27]
$14 443 - €16 836 - **£10 000** - FF110 435
David with Saul's Arms and Armour: Fragmaent, Made up into a Rectangle Oil/canvas (53x45cm 20x17in) London 2000

$4 511 - €4 487 - **£2 800** - FF29 431
The Head of a Bearded old Man Oil/panel (41.5x31cm 16x12in) London 1999

$29 741 - €25 688 - **£17 928** - FF168 499
Study of two Female seated Nudes Wash (21x26.5cm 8x10in) Amsterdam 1998

FLINDT Albertine XIX [1]
$2 673 - €2 559 - **£1 660** - FF16 784
Krokus, tulipan og liljekonval Oil/panel (24x19cm 9x7in) Köbenhavn 1999

FLINDT Paul ?-c.1618 [2]
$1 159 - €1 125 - **£721** - FF7 378
Deckelpokal mit Amor Radierung (30.3x13.8cm 11x5in) Berlin 1999

FLINT Andreas c.1768-1824 [5]
$772 - €766 - **£483** - FF5 026
Forestilling af Branden... efter C.F.Stanley Copper engraving in colors (22.5x40cm 8x15in) Köbenhavn

FLINT Francis Russell 1915 [68]
$434 - €469 - **£300** - FF3 079
Evening Fishing Watercolour/paper (22.5x16.5cm 8x6in) London 2001

FLINT Leroy Walter 1909-1991 [24]
$801 - €842 - **£505** - FF5 522
Night Desert Oil/board (76x60cm 30x24in) Cleveland OH 2000

$160 - €184 - **£110** - FF1 207
«**Sleepers**» Etching (14x11cm 5x4in) Cleveland OH 2000

FLINT William Russell 1880-1969 [1784]
$74 715 - €80 200 - **£50 000** - FF526 080
The Choice Oil/canvas (87x138cm 34x54in) London 2000

$21 274 - €24 696 - **£15 000** - FF161 998
A conversation in Aragon Oil/canvas (47x66cm 18x25in) London 2001

$7 966 - €6 883 - **£4 800** - FF45 148
The Ski Party's Return Watercolour/paper (33x49.5cm 12x19in) Billingshurst, West-Sussex 1999

$432 - €509 - **£300** - FF3 336
Zoronga Print in colors (40x53.5cm 15x21in) London 2000

FLINTOE Johannes 1786-1870 [10]
$18 023 - €19 450 - **£12 093** - FF127 585
Parti fra Fortundal i Norge Gouache/paper (40x50cm 15x19in) Köbenhavn 2000

FLIPART Charles Jos,Giuseppe 1721-1797 [11]
$18 073 - €16 769 - **£10 846** - FF110 000
La toilette de la courtisane Huile/toile (70.5x58cm 27x22in) Paris 1999

FLIS Giorgio 1941 [22]
$200 - €207 - **£120** - FF1 360
Paesaggio Smalto (30x70cm 11x27in) Vercelli 2001

FLOC'H Jean-Claude 1953 [9]
$277 - €274 - **£169** - FF1 800
Objectif Pub Gouache/papier (29x43.5cm 11x17in) Neuilly-sur-Seine 2000

FLOCH Charles XIX-XX [1]
$1 777 - €1 829 - **£1 119** - FF12 000
Le torpilleur numéro 129 en rade de Brest Fusain (70x99cm 27x38in) Paris 2000

FLOCH Joseph 1895-1977 [147]
$8 294 - €9 447 - **£5 733** - FF61 971
Zwei Frauen auf der Dachterrasse Oil/panel (56.5x50cm 22x19in) Wien 2000

$16 068 - €18 895 - **£11 518** - FF123 942
Mimi Oil/Leinwand (38x25.3cm 14x9in) Wien 2001

$741 - €872 - **£531** - FF5 720
Sitzende Chalks (43.6x32.4cm 17x12in) Wien 2001

$187 - €182 - **£119** - FF1 191
Beim Ringelspiel Lithographie (30x42cm 11x16in) Wien 1999

FLOCH Lionel 1895-1972 [91]
$896 - €823 - **£551** - FF5 400
Bateaux de pêche Huile/panneau (38x46cm 14x18in) Cherbourg 1999

$552 - €579 - **£365** - FF3 800
Bord de mer Huile/panneau (22x27cm 8x10in) Quimper 2000

$159 - €168 - **£105** - FF1 100
Vieille femme de l'île de Sein Eau-forte (24x18cm 9x7in) Quimper 2000

FLOCKENHAUS Heinz 1856-1919 [48]
$888 - €836 - **£549** - FF5 483
A tranquil Sketch of the River Oil/panel (24x15.5cm 9x6in) London 1999

FLOCKTON Frederick XIX [11]
$1 780 - €1 671 - **£1 100** - FF10 962
A Priest Fantasy Watercolour/paper (26.5x20.5cm 10x8in) London 1999

FLÖDIN Ferdinand XIX [3]
$1 075 - €1 016 - **£650** - FF6 663
Nu voilé Carbro-color print (29x22.5cm 11x8in) London 1999

FLODIN Hilda 1877-1958 [10]
$3 246 - €3 532 - **£2 139** - FF23 167
Tidningsutdelarna Mixed media (72x52cm 28x20in) Helsinki 2000

FLODMAN Carl 1863-1888 [10]
$2 318 - €2 500 - **£1 556** - FF16 398
Danvikstull, Stockholm Oil/canvas/panel (23x27cm 9x10in) Stockholm 2000

FLOGNY de Eugène Victor 1825-? **[6]**
- **$4 074** - €4 857 - **£2 905** - FF31 862
  Früchtestilleben Öl/Leinwand (29x38cm 11x14in)
  Ahlden 2000

FLOOD Rex Grattan 1928 **[24]**
- **$375** - €315 - **£220** - FF2 063
  Ducks Alighting in Reeds Watercolour/paper
  (33x48cm 13x19in) Aylsham, Norfolk 1998

FLORA Paul 1922 **[323]**
- **$1 126** - €1 308 - **£792** - FF8 580
  «Theater VII» Indian ink (17x22cm 6x8in) Wien 2001
- **$200** - €203 - **£125** - FF1 334
  Drei Helden Radierung (20x23cm 7x9in) Wien 2000

FLOREANI Roberto 1956 **[2]**
- **$2 200** - €2 851 - **£1 650** - FF18 700
  «Naturale sconosciuto» Smalto/tela (120x70cm
  47x27in) Prato 2000

FLORES Francisco, Poncho 1919-1984 **[9]**
- **$2 208** - €2 597 - **£1 584** - FF17 034
  Quite del Calesero Oleo/lienzo (60x46cm 23x18in)
  México 2001
- **$242** - €286 - **£174** - FF1 873
  Alegoría de Paco Camino Tinta/papel (45x60cm
  17x23in) México 2001

FLORES KAPEROTXIPI Mauricio 1901 **[21]**
- **$2 970** - €3 304 - **£1 980** - FF21 670
  Casero con pipa Oleo/lienzo (46.5x54cm 18x21in)
  Madrid 2000

FLORES Pedro 1897-1967 **[136]**
- **$2 240** - €2 403 - **£1 520** - FF15 760
  Plaza de pueblo con carromatos al amanecer
  Oleo/lienzo (38x46cm 14x18in) Madrid 2001
- **$1 350** - €1 351 - **£832** - FF8 865
  Don Quijote da consejos Oleo/tabla (26x18cm
  10x7in) Madrid 2000
- **$616** - €661 - **£418** - FF4 334
  «Burla de Don Pedro» Gouache/papier (38x32.5cm
  14x12in) Madrid 2001

FLOREZ GONZALEZ Alfredo XIX **[6]**
- **$420** - €450 - **£277** - FF2 955
  Cabeza de moro Oleo/tabla (20x14.5cm 7x5in)
  Madrid 2000

FLORIAN Maximilian 1901-1982 **[34]**
- **$2 289** - €2 543 - **£1 533** - FF16 684
  Die Dirne Öl/Karton (39.6x30.5cm 15x12in) Wien
  2000
- **$914** - €872 - **£556** - FF5 720
  Finale, erotische Darstellung Indian ink
  (43x30.5cm 16x12in) Wien 1999

FLORIDO BERNILS Enrique 1873-1929 **[11]**
- **$3 850** - €3 304 - **£2 310** - FF21 670
  Puerto de Málaga Oleo/tabla (26x44cm 10x17in)
  Madrid 1999

FLORIS Cornelis II 1514-1575 **[6]**
- **$839** - €920 - **£569** - FF6 037
  Entwurf für ein Groteskenornament Kupferstich
  (30.5x20.7cm 12x8in) Berlin 2000

FLORIS Frans I de Vrient 1516/20-1570 **[40]**
- **$12 452** - €14 448 - **£8 597** - FF94 771
  Kreutztragung Christi Oil/panel (125x124cm
  49x48in) Luzern 2000
- **$28 926** - €28 692 - **£18 000** - FF188 204
  Moses being nursed by his Mother Oil/panel
  (97x90cm 38x35in) London 1999

$1 290 - €1 534 - **£894** - FF10 061
  Kampf des Herkules mit Antäus, vor weiter
  Flusslandschaft Ink (23x29cm 9x11in) Köln 2000
- **$386** - €434 - **£271** - FF2 850
  «Sylvanus Deus Nemorum» Kupferstich
  (29.2x22.1cm 11x8in) Köln 2001

FLORIS Frans II 1551-1615 **[1]**
- **$2 698** - €2 601 - **£1 663** - FF17 064
  Firgurenpaar mit Kind in nächtlicher
  Landschaft Huile/toile/panneau (20x27.5cm 7x10in)
  Bern 1999

FLORIT Henri XIX-XX **[17]**
- **$957** - €1 067 - **£644** - FF7 000
  «Lydia Fedowa» Affiche (159x118cm 62x46in)
  Orléans 2000

FLORIT RODERO Josep Lluis 1909 **[61]**
- **$1 716** - €1 562 - **£1 040** - FF10 244
  Paisaje con caballistas Oleo/lienzo (50x61cm
  19x24in) Barcelona 1999.
- **$435** - €457 - **£288** - FF3 000
  Vue de Venise Huile/toile (33x24cm 12x9in) Paris
  2000
- **$364** - €390 - **£240** - FF2 561
  Niñas ochocentistas Acuarela/papel (48.5x34.5cm
  19x13in) Barcelona 2000

FLORSCHUETZ Thomas 1957 **[11]**
- **$1 560** - €1 738 - **£1 021** - FF11 403
  Ohne Titel Gelatin silver print (50x50cm 19x19in)
  Köln 2000

FLORSHEIM Richard Aberle 1916-1979 **[53]**
- **$100** - €84 - **£58** - FF550
  City Landscape/Airport Landscape Lithograph
  (34x24cm 13x9in) Bloomfield-Hills MI 1998

FLÖTER Hubs 1910-1974 **[30]**
- **$900** - €1 074 - **£642** - FF7 043
  Christa Vogel, Kleid von Detlef Albers Photograph
  (29.8x24cm 11x9in) München 2000

FLOUQUET Pierre-Louis 1900-1967 **[33]**
- **$5 300** - €4 958 - **£3 220** - FF32 520
  Silhouettes anthropomorphes Oil/canvas
  (80x70cm 31x27in) Lokeren 1999
- **$488** - €545 - **£338** - FF3 577
  Tête d'homme au chapeau Sanguine/papier
  (34x25cm 13x9in) Antwerpen 2001

FLOUR Jules A. 1864-1921 **[9]**
- **$1 191** - €1 372 - **£813** - FF9 000
  Le baiser Huile/toile (41x32cm 16x12in) Avignon
  2000

FLOUTIER Louis XX **[60]**
- **$2 307** - €2 744 - **£1 589** - FF18 000
  Ferme basque Huile/panneau (39.5x49cm 15x19in)
  Biarritz 2000
- **$1 294** - €1 540 - **£923** - FF10 100
  Maison et mur de pelote au Pays Basque
  Huile/panneau (16x25cm 6x9in) Calais 2000
- **$702** - €781 - **£468** - FF5 122
  La quille Gouache/papier (24.5x61.5cm 9x24in)
  Madrid 2000
- **$480** - €450 - **£292** - FF2 955
  Bolos Pochoir (24x60cm 9x23in) Madrid 1999

FLOWERS Alfred XIX-XX **[8]**
- **$1 168** - €1 327 - **£800** - FF8 706
  Shipping at Anchor, Possibly Falmouth
  Watercolour/paper (23x42.5cm 9x16in) Bury St.
  Edmunds, Suffolk 2000

F

FLOYD Donald H. 1892-1965 **[90]**

🖼 **$597** - €573 - **£380** - FF3 759
Estuary Scene Oil/canvas (36x46cm 14x18in)
London 1999

✏ **$130** - €151 - **£90** - FF992
Summer Garden and Cottages Gouache/paper
(36.5x53cm 14x20in) Bristol, Avon 2000

FLÜCK Johann Peter 1902-1954 **[13]**

🖼 **$1 011** - €1 179 - **£700** - FF7 733
Selbstbildnis am Fenster Oil/panel (60x72.5cm
23x28in) Bern 2000

FLUMIANI Ugo 1876-1938 **[50]**

🖼 **$3 250** - €3 369 - **£1 950** - FF22 100
L'autunno nel parco Olio/tela (80x100cm 31x39in)
Trieste 1999

🖼 **$1 600** - €1 659 - **£960** - FF10 880
San Giusto Olio/tavola (41x29cm 16x11in) Trieste
1999

FLURER Ignaz Franz Josef 1688-1742 **[7]**

🖼 **$7 011** - €6 541 - **£4 230** - FF42 903
**Südlicher Hafen mit antiken Ruinen, einem
Dreimaster und Figuren** Öl/Leinwand (87x115cm
34x45in) Wien 1999

🖼 **$6 489** - €6 541 - **£4 050** - FF42 903
Pilze Öl/Leinwand (24.5x33.5cm 9x13in) Wien 2000

FOÄCHE XX **[3]**

🖼 **$3 400** - €3 965 - **£2 387** - FF26 011
«La Garonne» Poster (51x68.5cm 20x26in) New-York
2000

FOÄCHZ Arthur XX **[3]**

🖼 **$9 971** - €11 586 - **£7 007** - FF76 000
Marché en Afrique Huile/toile (201x150cm 79x59in)
Paris 2001

FOCARDI Alberto XX **[3]**

🖼 **$600** - €777 - **£450** - FF5 100
Solitudine sul mare Olio/tavola (23.5x33.5cm
9x13in) Prato 2001

FOCARDI IL PITTORE DEL GARDA Piero 1889-
1945 **[22]**

🖼 **$29 000** - €30 063 - **£17 400** - FF197 200
Veduta del lago di Garda Olio/tela (145x189cm
57x74in) Milano 2000

🖼 **$3 643** - €3 354 - **£2 186** - FF22 000
Printemps à Pegamas Huile/toile (46x55cm
18x21in) Soissons 1999

🖼 **$1 600** - €1 659 - **£960** - FF10 880
Paesaggio urbano Olio/cartone (19.5x30cm 7x11in)
Torino 2000

FOCARDI Ruggero 1864-1934 **[25]**

🖼 **$13 000** - €14 188 - **£8 820** - FF93 065
In the Field Oil/canvas (150x300cm 59x118in) New-
York 2000

🖼 **$8 000** - €8 293 - **£4 800** - FF54 400
Paesaggio Olio/tela (37x54cm 14x21in) Prato 2000

🖼 **$850** - €881 - **£510** - FF5 780
Paesaggio campestre con casolare Olio/tavoletta
(7x16.5cm 2x6in) Firenze 2000

FOCHT Frédéric C., Fred 1879-? **[8]**

🖼 **$4 500** - €5 228 - **£3 162** - FF34 295
The Spirit of Flight Bronze (66.5x77.5cm 26x30in)
New-York 2001

FOELLER Peter 1945 **[8]**

🖼 **$202** - €204 - **£123** - FF1 341
Zeitwende Farbserigraphie (69.5x54.5cm 27x21in)
Stuttgart 2000

FOGARTY Thomas 1873-1938 **[10]**

✏ **$1 300** - €1 231 - **£807** - FF8 072
Golf Match, Golfers and Spectators Ink (33x22cm
13x9in) Wallkill NY 1999

FOGEL Seymour 1911-1984 **[9]**

🖼 **$5 000** - €5 401 - **£3 462** - FF35 430
Abstract Composition Oil/canvas (76x91cm
30x36in) Cincinnati OH 2001

🖼 **$1 000** - €960 - **£619** - FF6 299
Negro Lithograph (28.5x21.5cm 11x8in) New-York
1999

FOGG Howard 1917-1996 **[6]**

🖼 **$5 500** - €5 282 - **£3 408** - FF34 646
Train Oil/canvas (43x58cm 17x23in) Detroit MI 1999

🖼 **$11 000** - €12 120 - **£7 338** - FF79 500
New York Central Watercolour/paper (43x60cm
17x24in) Detroit MI 2000

FOGGIE David 1878-1948 **[8]**

🖼 **$3 234** - €2 764 - **£1 900** - FF18 129
Resting Pastel/paper (37x47cm 14x18in) Glasgow
1998

FOGGINI Vincenzo c.1700-c.1760 **[4]**

🖼 **$1 936** - €1 813 - **£1 200** - FF11 890
Design for a Statue of Saint Jude Black
chalk/paper (40.5x26.5cm 15x10in) London 1999

FOGGO George 1793-1869 **[1]**

🖼 **$5 047** - €5 577 - **£3 500** - FF36 585
The Conversion of St.Paul Oil/canvas (70x88cm
27x34in) London 2001

FOGGO James 1790-1860 **[1]**

🖼 **$5 047** - €5 577 - **£3 500** - FF36 585
The Conversion of St.Paul Oil/canvas (70x88cm
27x34in) London 2001

FOGTT Andrzej 1950 **[6]**

✏ **$1 107** - €1 285 - **£764** - FF8 429
Possession Tempera/papier (109.5x35cm 43x13in)
Warszawa 2000

FOHN Emanuel 1881-1966 **[36]**

✏ **$538** - €562 - **£353** - FF3 689
Sonne über der Lagune, Venedig Aquarell/Papier
(20x24cm 7x9in) München 2000

FOHR Carl Philipp 1795-1818 **[5]**

✏ **$15 286** - €17 384 - **£10 679** - FF114 032
Vier angeheiterte Studenten auf dem Heimweg
Watercolour, gouache (11.5x16cm 4x6in) München
2000

FOISIL Edith XX **[3]**

🖼 **$2 201** - €2 363 - **£1 472** - FF15 500
Régate de dragons vue de la plage Huile/toile
(64x92cm 25x36in) Douarnenez 2000

FOKKE Jan 1745-1812 **[1]**

✏ **$1 491** - €1 601 - **£997** - FF10 500
**Elèves amenant à un professeur de médecine
des plantes** Encre (15.5x10cm 6x3in) Paris 2000

FOLCHI Ferdinand 1822-1883 **[9]**

✏ **$583** - €663 - **£400** - FF4 349
Retiring to the Music Room Watercolour/paper
(46x34.5cm 18x13in) London 2000

FOLCHI Paolo XIX-XX **[6]**

✏ **$13 234** - €13 336 - **£8 250** - FF87 479
Arab Street Scenes Watercolour/paper (50x33cm
20x13in) Bourton-on-the-Water, Glos. 2000

FÖLDES Imre 1881-1948 **[4]**
📖 **$126** - €131 - **£79** - FF858
  «**Die verkannte Frau**» Poster (126x95cm 49x37in)
  Wien 2000

FOLEY Henry John 1818-1874 **[41]**
🎨 **$896** - €815 - **£550** - FF5 349
  Continental Town Scenes Oil/canvas (26.5x30.5cm
  10x12in) London 1999
🗿 **$1 696** - €1 748 - **£1 050** - FF11 464
  Caracticus Bronze (H76cm H29in) Billingshurst,
  West-Sussex 2000

FOLINSBEE John Fulton 1892-1972 **[36]**
🎨 **$4 250** - €4 045 - **£2 658** - FF26 532
  Floral still Life in a green Vase Oil/canvas
  (45x35cm 18x14in) New-York 1999
🎨 **$4 000** - €3 712 - **£2 401** - FF24 350
  Spring landscape and Houses Oil/board (25x35cm
  10x14in) Milford CT 1999

FOLKARD Charles James 1878-1963 **[21]**
🖌 **$2 867** - €3 240 - **£2 000** - FF21 256
  Bearded Gnome holding a Lantern Watercolour,
  gouache (57x17cm 9x6in) Swindon, Wiltshire 2001

FOLKERTS Poppe 1875-1949 **[19]**
🎨 **$3 663** - €3 835 - **£2 301** - FF25 154
  Auf Norderney Öl/Leinwand (38.5x73cm 15x28in)
  Hamburg 2000
📖 **$381** - €409 - **£259** - FF2 683
  Ausfahrt des Rettungsbootes Radierung (33x44cm
  12x17in) Rudolstadt-Thüringen 2001

FOLKESTAD Bernhard 1879-1933 **[12]**
🎨 **$19 314** - €22 526 - **£13 446** - FF147 762
  Ballerina Oil/canvas (95x90cm 37x35in) Oslo 2000

FOLLENWEIDER Rudolf 1774-1847 **[8]**
🖌 **$1 168** - €1 282 - **£793** - FF8 407
  **Talebene mit Gebäuden, Vieh und Wanderer im
  Berneroberland** Watercolour (37x50cm 14x19in)
  Basel 2000

FOLLET René 1931 **[9]**
🖌 **$215** - €198 - **£129** - FF1 300
  Bracelet Tabou Encre Chine/papier (26.5x23cm
  10x9in) Paris 1999

FOLLINI Carlo 1848-1938 **[93]**
🎨 **$16 500** - €17 105 - **£9 900** - FF112 200
  Campagna con contadino e covoni Olio/tela
  (90x140cm 35x55in) Vercelli 2000
🎨 **$7 200** - €9 330 - **£5 400** - FF61 200
  Fine ottobre nella campagna piemontese
  Olio/tela (65x85cm 26x33in) Vercelli 2000
🎨 **$5 000** - €5 183 - **£3 000** - FF34 000
  Campagna piemontese Olio/tavola (26.5x44cm
  10x17in) Vercelli 2001
🖌 **$800** - €1 037 - **£600** - FF6 800
  Gentildonna/Popolana Acquarello/carta (15x10cm
  5x3in) Vercelli 2001

FOLO Jean 1764-1836 **[2]**
📖 **$44** - €51 - **£31** - FF335
  Bethlem, Kindermord, nach Nicolaus Poussin
  Kupferstich (51.8x61cm 20x24in) Leipzig 2000

FOLON Jean-Michel 1934 **[227]**
🖌 **$1 391** - €1 611 - **£962** - FF10 569
  Le messager de l'automne Aquarelle/papier
  (64x49cm 25x19in) Bruxelles 2000
📖 **$208** - €248 - **£149** - FF1 626
  Compositie Color lithograph (72.5x55cm 28x21in)
  Lokeren 2000

FOLTYN Frantisek 1891-1976 **[60]**
🎨 **$10 496** - €12 196 - **£7 376** - FF80 000
  Composition Huile/toile (80x65cm 31x25in) Paris
  2001
🎨 **$2 312** - €2 187 - **£1 440** - FF14 344
  Landschaft mit Hütten Öl/Leinwand (30x43cm
  11x16in) Praha 1999
🎨 **$1 445** - €1 367 - **£900** - FF8 965
  Composition abstraite Aquarelle/carton (44x34cm
  17x13in) Praha 2001

FOLTZ von Philip 1805-1877 **[7]**
🎨 **$2 903** - €3 302 - **£2 013** - FF21 657
  Des Sängers Fluch, nach L.Uhland Oil/panel
  (38x44cm 14x17in) Zofingen 2000
🖌 **$1 501** - €1 789 - **£1 070** - FF11 738
  **Ein Ritter zu Pferde mit Gefolge, in den Händen
  einen Kelch haltend** Ink (27.3x45cm 10x17in) Berlin
  2000

FOMINE Vladimir 1948 **[19]**
🎨 **$463** - €427 - **£282** - FF2 800
  Promenade sur les Champs-Élysées Huile/toile
  (40x60cm 15x23in) Morlaix 1998

FOMISON Tony 1939-1990 **[9]**
🎨 **$33 104** - €38 881 - **£23 504** - FF255 040
  Hil Top Watcher Oil/canvas (49x84cm 19x33in)
  Auckland 2000
🎨 **$20 690** - €24 300 - **£14 690** - FF159 400
  **Detail from Piero Della Francesca's «The
  Resurrection»** Oil/canvas (44.5x35cm 17x13in)
  Auckland 2000
📖 **$848** - €967 - **£586** - FF6 343
  Maori in a Sunhat Print (78.5x57cm 30x22in)
  Auckland 2000

FON WOO Jade 1911-1983 **[24]**
🖌 **$1 500** - €1 339 - **£918** - FF8 784
  «**East Bay Hills**» Watercolour/paper (55x76cm
  22x30in) Altadena CA 1999

FONDO Nicola XIX **[2]**
🖌 **$1 539** - €1 789 - **£1 080** - FF11 738
  Dreimastbark Leibnitz im Golf von Neapel
  Gouache/Karton (52x76cm 20x29in) Hamburg 2001

FONECHE André XIX-XX **[20]**
🎨 **$877** - €960 - **£609** - FF6 300
  Départ pour la pêche Huile/toile (61x100cm
  24x39in) Brest 2001
🎨 **$544** - €610 - **£381** - FF4 000
  Sur la plage Huile/panneau (20.5x34.5cm 8x13in)
  Paris 2001

FONSECA da Antonio Manuel 1796-1890 **[3]**
🎨 **$48 873** - €56 243 - **£33 748** - FF368 929
  Auf dem Sklavenmarkt Öl/Leinwand (168x188cm
  66x74in) München 2000

FONSECA Gonzalo 1922-1997 **[46]**
🎨 **$11 780** - €11 412 - **£7 220** - FF74 860
  Constructivo con objetos Oleo/tabla (55x54.5cm
  21x21in) Madrid 1999
🎨 **$2 137** - €2 252 - **£1 350** - FF14 775
  Puerto Oleo/lienzo (33x45cm 12x17in) Madrid 2000
🗿 **$42 000** - €48 797 - **£29 517** - FF320 090
  Estela con Baetylos Marble (59.5x30.5x20cm
  23x12x7in) Beverly-Hills CA 2001

FONSSAGRIVES Fernand 1910 **[2]**
📷 **$2 600** - €2 504 - **£1 625** - FF16 422
  Sitting Pretty Peek-a-Boo Chair Gelatin silver print
  (33x26cm 12x10in) New-York 1999

F

FONT Constantin 1890-1954 [52]
🖼 $465 - €534 - **£318** - FF3 500
　　Paysage de Provence Huile/toile (65x54cm
　　25x21in) Soissons 2000

FONTAINE Gabriel 1945 [34]
✏ $4 626 - €4 462 - **£2 862** - FF29 268
　　Fleurs et insectes sur un entablement
　　Aquarelle/papier (58x71cm 22x27in) Bruxelles 1999

FONTAINE Gabrielle XIX [3]
✏ $4 170 - €4 573 - **£2 691** - FF30 000
　　Bouquets de fleurs et fruits, sur un entablement
　　Aquarelle/papier (58x70cm 22x27in) Paris 2000

FONTAINE Pierre François L. 1762-1853 [70]
✏ $6 115 - €6 860 - **£4 279** - FF45 000
　　Cérémonie de magie dans des ruines Aquarelle,
　　gouache/papier (52x73.5cm 20x28in) Paris 2001

FONTAINE Victor 1837-1884 [12]
🖐 $8 000 - €8 970 - **£5 432** - FF58 838
　　A sunny Day of Leisure Oil/panel (62x43cm
　　24x16in) New-York 2000

FONTAN Léo 1884-1965 [40]
🖐 $550 - €510 - **£331** - FF3 345
　　Paris Street Scene Oil/canvas (24x26cm 9x10in)
　　Delray-Beach FL 1999
✏ $1 380 - €1 524 - **£957** - FF10 000
　　Femme au buste nu Crayon (37.5x23.5cm 14x9in)
　　Paris 2001
🖼 $1 700 - €1 972 - **£1 192** - FF12 938
　　«French Line, Ile de France» Poster (101x63cm
　　40x25in) New-York 2000

FONTANA Annibale 1540-1587 [1]
🔨 $1 520 400 - €1 727 763 - **£1 050 000** -
　　FF11 333 390
　　Dragon Bronze (H73.5cm H28in) London 2000

FONTANA Aristide XIX [2]
🔨 $5 355 - €5 551 - **£3 213** - FF36 414
　　Figura femminile con veste di foggia classica
　　Marbre (H72cm H28in) Venezia 1999

FONTANA Ernesto 1837-1918 [17]
✏ $2 856 - €2 467 - **£1 428** - FF16 184
　　Il ventaglio Acquarello/carta (20.5x17cm 8x6in)
　　Milano 1999

FONTANA Franco 1933 [38]
📷 $392 - €381 - **£244** - FF2 500
　　Nus aux tissus bleu et vert Photo couleur
　　(22.4x34cm 8x13in) Paris 1999

FONTANA Giovanni Battista c.1524-1587 [9]
🖐 $3 596 - €3 836 - **£2 400** - FF25 161
　　**Thje Bearing of the Cross, After Domenico
　　Campagnola** Etching (41x65.5cm 16x25in) London
　　2000

FONTANA Lavinia 1552-1614 [17]
🖐 $60 000 - €52 808 - **£36 528** - FF346 398
　　**Anna, Viscountess of Panigarola Standing Full
　　Length Beside a Pillar** Oil/canvas (171.5x89cm
　　67x35in) New-York 1999

FONTANA Louis 1924 [1]
🖐 $6 400 - €8 293 - **£4 800** - FF54 400
　　Concetto spaziale-teatrini Tecnica mista
　　(49.5x49cm 19x19in) Milano 2000

FONTANA Lucio 1899-1968 [1284]
🖐 $449 685 - €417 342 - **£270 000** - FF2 737 584
　　Concetto spaziale, Attese Waterpaint/canvas
　　(120x165cm 47x64in) London 1999

🖐 $149 895 - €139 114 - **£90 000** - FF912 528
　　Concetto spaziale, Attese Waterpaint/canvas
　　(100x80cm 39x31in) London 1999
🖐 $28 711 - €27 610 - **£17 717** - FF181 110
　　Concetto spaziale Mixed media (17.8x19.5cm 7x7in)
　　Köln 1999
🔨 $81 385 - €79 209 - **£50 000** - FF519 580
　　Concetto spaziale Metal (117x57cm 46x22in)
　　London 1999
🔨 $13 684 - €12 954 - **£8 500** - FF84 973
　　Concetto Spaziale Polished bronze (H26cm H10in)
　　London 1999
✏ $4 200 - €3 628 - **£2 800** - FF23 800
　　Concetto spaziale Tempera/carta (15x21.5cm 5x8in)
　　Milano 1998
🖼 $1 222 - €1 143 - **£740** - FF7 500
　　Conception spatiale Lithographie couleurs
　　(49x34.5cm 19x13in) Paris 1999

FONTANA Luigi 1827-1908 [1]
🔨 $4 307 - €4 828 - **£3 000** - FF31 671
　　Bust of the Venus Italica Marble (H52cm H20in)
　　London 2001

FONTANA Prospero 1512-1597 [10]
✏ $1 340 - €1 418 - **£850** - FF9 302
　　**Seated Figure Playing The Bagpipes with an
　　Army in the Background** Black chalk (12x9cm
　　4x3in) London 2000

FONTANA Roberto 1844-1907 [17]
🖐 $3 750 - €3 887 - **£2 250** - FF25 500
　　Bambino in costume bianco Olio/tela (22x17cm
　　8x6in) Milano 2000

FONTANAROSA Lucien Joseph 1912-1975 [225]
🖐 $13 386 - €14 940 - **£8 761** - FF98 000
　　Après-midi musical avec les enfants Huile/toile
　　(145x175cm 57x68in) Besançon 2000
🖐 $2 629 - €2 897 - **£1 753** - FF19 000
　　Scène de plage Huile/toile (38x61cm 14x24in)
　　Deauville 2000
🖐 $1 045 - €1 220 - **£727** - FF8 000
　　Jeune marocaine aux yeux de biche Huile/papier
　　(30x25cm 11x9in) Paris 2000
🖐 $516 - €427 - **£303** - FF2 800
　　**Couple de personnages assis sur une terrasse
　　au bord de la rivière** Gouache/papier (17x26.5cm
　　6x10in) Reims 1998

FONTANESI Antonio 1818-1882 [36]
🖐 $34 400 - €44 576 - **£25 800** - FF292 400
　　Solitudine Olio/tavola (52x70cm 20x27in) Roma 2000
🖐 $14 000 - €18 141 - **£10 500** - FF119 000
　　Impressione a Torrazza Olio/cartone (28x19cm
　　11x7in) Vercelli 2000
✏ $5 000 - €5 183 - **£3 400** - FF34 000
　　Presso Reigner, alta Savoia Carboncino (31x23cm
　　12x9in) Vercelli 1999

FONTANET Noël 1898-1982 [13]
🖼 $2 100 - €2 275 - **£1 399** - FF14 926
　　**«Restaurant Besson, dîners à prix fixe, Route
　　de Rhône.78»** Poster (64x82cm 25x32in) New-York
　　2000

FONTEBASSO Francesco Salvatore 1709-1769
[59]
🖐 $78 380 - €89 024 - **£55 000** - FF583 962
　　**Alexander addressing his Soldiers/The Family
　　of Darius** Oil/canvas (127x127cm 50x50in) London
　　2001

$32 777 - €37 228 - **£23 000** - FF244 202
Portrait of a Young Boy, Half Length, Holding a Medallion Oil/canvas (66.5x49.5cm 26x19in) London 2001

$17 931 - €19 248 - **£12 000** - FF126 259
Diana and Endymion: a Bozzetto Oil/canvas (22.5x16cm 8x6in) London 2000

$5 164 - €5 793 - **£3 613** - FF38 000
Deux académies d'homme Encre (15x31.5cm 5x12in) Paris 2001

$3 787 - €3 665 - **£2 400** - FF24 039
Pope Gregory I praying for the Deliverance of Souls, after Seb.Ricci Etching (46.5x32cm 18x12in) London 1999

FONTENAY de Alexis 1815-? [4]
$732 - €625 - **£442** - FF4 100
Paysage à la chaumière près d'une mare Huile/toile (28x50cm 11x19in) Besançon 1998

FONTIROSSI Roberto 1940 [20]
$660 - €570 - **£440** - FF3 740
Senza titolo Olio/cartone/tela (30x20cm 11x7in) Prato 1998

$510 - €441 - **£255** - FF2 890
Suonatore di trombone Acquarello (30x20cm 11x7in) Prato 1999

FONVILLE Horace Antoine 1832-1914 [36]
$2 757 - €2 363 - **£1 658** - FF15 500
Lavandières sur le chemin Huile/toile (64x110cm 25x43in) Valence 1998

$484 - €488 - **£301** - FF3 200
Le bûcheron Huile/carton (17.5x27cm 6x10in) Lyon 2000

FONVILLE Nicolas Victor 1805-1856 [20]
$2 448 - €2 287 - **£1 526** - FF15 000
Paysage animé de personnages Huile/toile (38.5x57.5cm 15x22in) Grenoble 1999

$539 - €579 - **£361** - FF3 800
Baigneuses Huile/papier (9.5x15cm 3x5in) Grenoble 2000

FOOKS Ursula Mary XX [6]
$1 015 - €986 - **£640** - FF6 465
Pedestrians Linocut in colors (25x16.5cm 9x6in) London 1999

FOOTE Will Howe 1878-1965 [23]
$2 200 - €2 587 - **£1 577** - FF16 970
The Train Bridge Oil/canvas (26x15cm 10x6in) New-York 2001

FOPPIANI Gustavo 1925-1986 [30]
$2 200 - €2 366 - **£1 499** - FF15 517
Citta Antica Oil/panel (45.5x61cm 17x24in) Beverly-Hills CA 2001

$1 000 - €1 075 - **£681** - FF7 053
Lmartitio rel Fiume Oil/panel (40.5x30.5cm 15x12in) Beverly-Hills CA 2001

FORABOSCO Girolamo 1604/05-1679 [6]
$22 500 - €23 325 - **£13 500** - FF153 000
Adam ed Eva Olio/tela (154x127cm 60x50in) Milano 2000

FORAIN Jean-Louis 1852-1931 [776]
$11 794 - €14 025 - **£8 408** - FF92 000
Dame en noir à l'éventail Huile/panneau (35x46cm 13x18in) Neuilly-sur-Seine 2000

$14 000 - €13 218 - **£8 703** - FF86 703
Still Life with white Roses Oil/canvas (35.5x27.5cm 13x10in) New-York 1999

$410 - €457 - **£286** - FF3 000
Quelle affaire! Encre Chine (18.5x24cm 7x9in) Paris 2001

$352 - €348 - **£220** - FF2 284
Fille - mère Etching (39x48cm 15x18in) London 1999

FORBES Alexander ?-1839 [6]
$8 965 - €9 624 - **£6 000** - FF63 129
A Dark Brown Hunter by a Stable Door Oil/canvas (61x76cm 24x29in) London 2000

FORBES Elizabeth A.Stanhope 1859-1912 [55]
$8 921 - €8 568 - **£5 500** - FF56 203
Picking Bluebells Oil/panel (25.5x34cm 10x13in) London 1999

$9 584 - €9 529 - **£6 000** - FF62 503
Pastoral Landscape with Shepherdess and Sheep under Trees in Blossom Watercolour (39x56cm 15x22in) Leicestershire 2000

$239 - €257 - **£160** - FF1 683
Portrait of Lamorna Birch, a Painter Sportsman Print (12x20cm 5x8in) Par, Cornwall 2001

FORBES James 1749-1819 [6]
$4 000 - €4 147 - **£2 400** - FF27 200
Scene in the Ilex Grove, on the Palatine Hill, at Rome Inchiostro (45.5x34.5cm 17x13in) Milano 2000

FORBES John Colin 1846-1925 [21]
$1 700 - €1 510 - **£1 041** - FF9 906
Elegant Lady Oil/canvas (69x92cm 27x36in) New-Orleans LA 1999

FORBES Kenneth Keith 1892-1980 [19]
$8 000 - €7 415 - **£4 974** - FF48 640
Mr. and Mrs. John A.MacDougald with their Mares, Toronto, Canada Oil/canvas (74x109cm 29x42in) New-York 1999

FORBES Leyton XIX-XX [62]
$514 - €447 - **£310** - FF2 933
Cornish Cottage Watercolour (22x14.5cm 8x5in) Solihull, West-Midlands 1998

FORBES Stanhope Alexander 1857-1947 [156]
$1 643 730 - €1 764 408 - **£1 100 000** - FF11 573 760
The Seine Boat Oil/canvas (114.5x157.5cm 45x62in) London 2000

$27 300 - €25 205 - **£17 000** - FF165 335
The blue River Oil/canvas (61x76cm 24x29in) London 1999

$9 811 - €11 007 - **£6 800** - FF72 201
Fishermen Oil/canvas (27x35.5cm 10x13in) London 2000

$269 - €289 - **£180** - FF1 893
Beneath the Viaduct Print in colors (48x58cm 19x23in) Par, Cornwall 2000

FORBES Vivian 1891-1937 [10]
$1 379 - €1 553 - **£950** - FF10 189
Third Round, New York Oil/canvas (30.5x38cm 12x14in) London 2000

$3 951 - €3 714 - **£2 400** - FF24 359
Greek Boy with Rabbit Watercolour (43x26.5cm 16x10in) London 1999

FORCELLA Nicolo XIX-XX [25]
$2 425 - €2 592 - **£1 654** - FF17 000
Baigneuses Huile/toile (36x53cm 14x20in) Arles 2001

$3 925 - €4 116 - **£2 459** - FF27 000
Felouques sur le Nil Huile/panneau (27x50cm 10x19in) Paris 2000

FORCELLA Paolo 1868-? **[1]**
$4 396 - €4 269 - £2 716 - FF28 000
Entrant dans la mosquée Huile/toile (33x46.5cm
12x18in) Paris 1999

FÖRCH Robert 1931 **[26]**
$106 - €102 - £65 - FF670
Lavendelfeld in Senanque Linocut in colors
(53.5x76.5cm 21x30in) Bielefeld 1999

FORCHONDT Willem c.1600-1678 **[3]**
$16 728 - €19 701 - £12 136 - FF129 232
**Moisés recibiendo las tablas de la ley y el festín
de los hebreos** Oleo/cobre (80x114cm 31x44in)
Madrid 2001

FORD Edward Onslow 1852-1901 **[19]**
$15 570 - €18 055 - £11 000 - FF118 435
Bust of James Lever, senior (1809-1897) Bronze
(H70cm H27in) London 2001

FORD Henry Chapman 1828-1894 **[12]**
$1 700 - €1 998 - £1 178 - FF13 109
San Gabriel Mission Engraving (17.5x33cm 6x12in)
Beverly-Hills CA 2000

FORD Henry Justice 1860-1941 **[20]**
$1 658 - €1 435 - £1 000 - FF9 416
**Dunstan - The Friend of Kings, the Sensible
Woman Gets Dunstan...** Watercolour (28.5x18cm
11x7in) London 1998

FORD Herbert XIX **[1]**
$2 405 - €2 380 - £1 500 - FF15 610
Condor House Next to St.Paul's Watercolour
(63x96cm 24x37in) London 1999

FORD Wolfram Onslow XIX-XX **[5]**
$5 389 - €6 256 - £3 800 - FF41 039
Mr. and Mrs. Crompton Hulme Oil/canvas
(102x76cm 40x29in) London 2001

FOREAU Henri Louis 1866-1938 **[104]**
$1 089 - €1 134 - £684 - FF7 438
Winter Streetscape Oil/canvas/board (49.5x60cm
19x23in) Melbourne 2000
$1 236 - €1 082 - £749 - FF7 100
Lavandières et bateau dans la brume Huile/toile
(29x41cm 11x16in) Paris 1998
$580 - €610 - £382 - FF4 816
Le passage du pont Crayon (37x27cm 14x10in)
Paris 2000

FOREST Jean 1636-1712 **[1]**
$5 696 - €6 353 - £3 717 - FF41 672
**Mountainous Wooded Landscape with
Travellers and their Herd** Oil/canvas (59x57.5cm
23x22in) Amsterdam 2000

FOREST Jean-Claude 1930 **[18]**
$405 - €473 - £284 - FF3 100
Barbarella Encre Chine/papier (80x62cm 31x24in)
Versailles 2000

FOREST Pierre 1881-1971 **[43]**
$340 - €320 - £210 - FF2 100
L'allée fleurie Huile/isorel (46x55cm 18x21in) Cannes
1999

FORESTIER Antonin Clair 1865-1912 **[2]**
$4 008 - €4 573 - £2 784 - FF30 000
La ronde des enfants Bronze (18x66x27cm
7x25x10in) Paris 2000

FORESTIER Henri Claudius 1875-1922 **[27]**
$724 - €852 - £525 - FF5 592
Nature morte aux fleurs Huile/toile (46x38cm
18x14in) Sion 2001

$1 154 - €1 278 - £800 - FF8 380
«Ice Skating» Poster (61x50cm 24x19in) London
2001

FORETAY Alfred Jean 1861-1944 **[24]**
$536 - €610 - £376 - FF4 000
Jardinière Nymphe et amour Métal (H28cm H11in)
Paris 2001

FÖRG Günther 1952 **[366]**
$14 202 - €13 743 - £9 000 - FF90 146
Cansons Acrylic (260x148cm 102x58in) London 1999
$7 144 - €7 669 - £4 782 - FF50 308
Ohne Titel Acrylic/panel (60x50cm 23x19in) Köln
2000
$169 - €194 - £119 - FF1 274
Ohne Titel Mischtechnik (29.5x21cm 11x8in) Bremen
2001
$2 857 - €3 068 - £1 912 - FF20 123
Ohne Titel Bronze (H21.2cm H8in) Köln 2000
$4 017 - €3 835 - £2 509 - FF25 154
Ohne Titel Indian ink/paper (22.5x16cm 8x6in) Köln
1999
$324 - €368 - £221 - FF2 414
Linienkompositionen Linocut in colors (29.5x21cm
11x8in) Hamburg 2000
$1 015 - €1 180 - £713 - FF7 739
Untitled Gelatin silver print (59x42cm 23x16in)
Amsterdam 2001

FORGIOLI Attilio 1933 **[41]**
$1 500 - €1 555 - £900 - FF10 200
Parco Sempione Tecnica mista/tela (75x67cm
29x26in) Milano 1999

FORMIS BEFANI Achille 1832-1905 **[38]**
$7 000 - €7 257 - £4 200 - FF47 600
Veduta di Napoli Olio/tela (57x95cm 22x37in)
Milano 1999
$3 500 - €3 030 - £2 110 - FF19 875
«Idle Afternoon on the Venetian Lagoon»
Oil/canvas (40.5x33cm 15x12in) San-Francisco CA
1998

FORNARA Carlo 1871-1968 **[25]**
$37 500 - €38 874 - £22 500 - FF255 000
Una giornata di sole Olio/tela/tavola (40x45cm
15x17in) Milano 1999
$15 000 - €15 550 - £9 000 - FF102 000
Natura morta di frutta Olio/tavola (30x40cm
11x15in) Milano 1999
$8 400 - €10 885 - £6 300 - FF71 400
Paesaggio alpino Pastelli/cartone (75x75cm 29x29in)
Roma 2000

FORNARO D'ATERNO 1936 **[6]**
$9 296 - €10 253 - £6 296 - FF67 252
Sonnenblumen Mixed media (70x100cm 27x39in)
Zürich 2000

FORNASETTI Piero 1913-1988 **[43]**
$5 422 - €5 637 - £3 579 - FF36 975
E.Libri Oil/panel (50x200cm 19x78in) Melbourne 2000

FORNENBURGH van Jan Baptist I c.1590-c.1656
[13]
$100 000 - €101 164 - £61 060 - FF663 590
**Flowers in a Glass Vase on a Ledge with a Frog
and a Lizard** Oil/panel (34x26cm 13x10in) New-York
2000

FORNEROD Rodolphe 1877-1953 **[28]**
$900 - €1 067 - £635 - FF7 000
Paysage Huile/toile (40x65cm 15x25in) Paris 2000

FORNES ISERN Pablo 1932 **[5]**
🖝 **$2 160** - €2 403 - **£1 520** - FF15 760
Dama entre flores Oleo/lienzo (95x69cm 37x27in)
Madrid 2001

FORNS Y ROMANS Rafael 1868-1939 **[11]**
🖝 **$2 790** - €2 703 - **£1 710** - FF17 730
Big Ben, Londres Oleo/lienzo (99x76cm 38x29in)
Madrid 1999

FORREST Archie XX **[5]**
✎ **$673** - €581 - **£400** - FF3 809
An Italian Harbour Gouache/papier (43x67cm
16x26in) Glasgow 1998

FORREST James Haughton Capt. 1826-1925 **[82]**
🖝 **$11 103** - €12 205 - **£7 115** - FF80 058
Narcissus River, MT Ida in the Distance Oil/board
(61x46cm 24x18in) Melbourne 2000
🖝 **$3 590** - €3 369 - **£2 218** - FF22 097
**Wreck of Sir Robert Peel, Eliza and Pandora,
Tynmouth** Oil/board (30.5x46.5cm 12x18in)
Melbourne 1999

FORRESTALL Thomas DeVany, Tom 1936 **[22]**
🖝 **$2 766** - €2 367 - **£1 665** - FF15 529
**«The Odd Fellow's Hall, Annapolis Royal, Nova
Scotia»** Tempera/board (71x112cm 27x44in) Toronto
1998

FORRESTER James 1729-1775 **[4]**
🖝 **$8 392** - €7 880 - **£5 200** - FF51 689
**An Italianate Wooded River Landscape, with
Figures in the Foreground** Oil/canvas (68.5x111cm
26x43in) London 1999

FORRESTER Patricia Tobacco 1940 **[6]**
✎ **$1 500** - €1 258 - **£880** - FF8 255
Gothic Watercolour/paper (100.5x150cm 39x59in)
New-York 1998

FORSBERG Carl Johan 1868-1938 **[37]**
✎ **$336** - €375 - **£235** - FF2 462
**Skitsebog med diverse studier fra København
og Skagen** Pencil/paper (20x25.5cm 7x10in)
København 2001

FORSBERG Howard 1918 **[2]**
✎ **$2 600** - €2 490 - **£1 606** - FF16 332
**Boy and Dog Looking out Window on
Christmas Morning, Magazine Cover**
Gouache/paper (50x40cm 20x16in) New-York 1999

FORSBERG Nils I 1842-1934 **[34]**
🖝 **$955** - €1 067 - **£647** - FF7 000
Portrait d'homme Huile/toile (61x50.5cm 24x19in)
Pontoise 2000
🖝 **$577** - €556 - **£356** - FF3 645
Persikor och plommon Oil/panel (25x33cm 9x12in)
Malmö 1999

FORSETH Einar 1892-1988 **[70]**
🖝 **$412** - €486 - **£289** - FF3 188
Grå stämning över bergen Oil/panel (40x52cm
15x20in) Malmö 2000

FORSLUND Jonas 1754-1809 **[8]**
✎ **$2 261** - €2 573 - **£1 579** - FF16 876
Porträtt av Eva Ulrica Mörner af Morlanda
Pastel/paper (58x45.5cm 22x17in) Stockholm 2000

FORSMAN Erik 1916-1976 **[15]**
✎ **$329** - €387 - **£238** - FF2 541
Tomtar i stallet Akvarell/papper (12x21.5cm 4x8in)
Stockholm 2001

FORSSELL Victor 1846-1931 **[37]**
🖝 **$719** - €818 - **£502** - FF5 369
Arbete på Åkern Oil/panel (15x22cm 5x8in)
Stockholm 2000

FORSTÉN Lennart 1817-1886 **[11]**
🖝 **$1 976** - €1 682 - **£1 180** - FF11 034
Landskap Oil/canvas (37x55cm 14x21in) Helsinki
1998

FÖRSTER Berthold Paul 1851-1925 **[16]**
🖝 **$320** - €332 - **£203** - FF2 180
Sonniges Tal in Thüringen Öl/Leinwand/Karton
(34x42cm 13x16in) Rudolstadt-Thüringen 2000

FORSTER George E. 1817-1896 **[26]**
🖝 **$10 000** - €11 028 - **£6 772** - FF72 341
Still Life of Fish Oil/canvas (51x76.5cm 20x30in)
New-York 2000
🖝 **$10 000** - €11 893 - **£7 127** - FF78 010
Still Life with Strawberries Oil/panel (25x19.5cm
9x7in) New-York 2000

FORSTER Neil 1940 **[9]**
✎ **$2 272** - €2 185 - **£1 400** - FF14 333
Nude with Towel Pastel/paper (21x15cm 8x5in)
London 1999

FORSTER Thomas XIX **[1]**
✎ **$1 268** - €1 489 - **£900** - FF9 770
A Digest of the Different Castes of India
Watercolour (18x10cm 7x3in) London 2000

FORSTER Thomas c.1677-1712 **[19]**
✎ **$2 323** - €2 050 - **£1 400** - FF13 448
Portrait of a Gentleman Mine plomb (11.5x9cm
4x3in) London 1998

FORSTER William James XX **[21]**
✎ **$2 331** - €2 314 - **£1 429** - FF15 179
**Charles Edward Paddlewheel Steamer of the
Anchor Steam Shipping** Watercolour/paper
(28x48cm 11x18in) Auckland 2000

FORSTMANN A. XIX **[12]**
🖝 **$701** - €818 - **£485** - FF5 366
**Süddeutsche Gebirgslandschaft mit einer
Kappelle unter hohen Bäumen** Öl/Leinwand
(47x69cm 18x27in) Buxtehude 2000

FORSYTH Gordon Mitchell 1879-1952 **[4]**
📜 **$981** - €871 - **£600** - FF5 713
«Harrogate» Affiche couleur (102x127cm 40x50in)
London 1999

FORSYTH James Nesfield 1864-c.1927 **[1]**
🗿 **$5 662** - €6 566 - **£4 000** - FF43 067
**Bust of Hon. William Hulme Lever later 2nd
Viscount Leverhulme** Marble (H51cm H20in)
London 2001

FORSYTH William 1854-1935 **[6]**
🖝 **$3 500** - €4 004 - **£2 433** - FF26 262
Spring Landscape Oil/board (40x50cm 16x20in)
Cincinnati OH 2000

FORSYTHE Victor Clyde 1885-1962 **[27]**
🖝 **$2 750** - €2 455 - **£1 684** - FF16 104
«Time to Make Camp» Oil/canvas (60x76cm
24x30in) Altadena CA 1999
🖝 **$1 500** - €1 763 - **£1 040** - FF11 567
Desert Landscape Oil/canvas/board (13.5x14.5cm
5x5in) Beverly-Hills CA 2000
🖝 **$500** - €570 - **£340** - FF3 065
California Mission, vacaqueros on horseback
Gouache/board (35x71cm 14x28in) Pasadena CA 1999

FORT Siméon 1793-1861 **[19]**
- $3 345 - €3 125 - £2 064 - FF20 500
  Personnages sur le chemin, soleil couchant
  Huile/toile (25x35.5cm 9x13in) Melun 1999

FORT Théodore c.1810-? **[71]**
- $605 - €610 - £377 - FF4 000
  Chasseur au poste Huile/toile (12x22cm 4x8in)
  Lyon 2000
- $484 - €488 - £301 - FF3 200
  Le billet de logement Aquarelle/papier (16x24.5cm 6x9in) Paris 2000

FORTE Gaetano 1790-1871 **[3]**
- $9 200 - €11 922 - £6 900 - FF78 200
  Giovane ussaro dell'esercito Olio/tela (92x77cm 36x30in) Napoli 1999

FORTE Vicente 1912-1980 **[12]**
- $2 200 - €2 556 - £1 546 - FF16 766
  «La barca naranja» Oleo/lienzo (50x85cm 19x33in)
  Buenos-Aires 2001

FORTESCUE Henrietta Anne c.1765-1841 **[6]**
- $362 - €397 - £250 - FF2 601
  The Sybil's Temple at Tivoli/St.Peter's and the Vatican Ink (25.5x34.5cm 10x13in) London 2001

FORTESCUE William Banks c.1855-1924 **[43]**
- $4 840 - €4 649 - £3 400 - FF30 494
  Interesting Read Oil/canvas (69x51cm 27x20in)
  London 1999
- $3 750 - €4 291 - £2 579 - FF28 150
  Lost in Thought Oil/canvas (30x22cm 12x9in) New-York 2000

FORTEZA FORTEZA Miguel 1881-? **[11]**
- $1 872 - €1 566 - £1 118 - FF10 270
  «Laya y peñon de Artì» Oleo/lienzo (60x50cm 23x19in) Madrid 1998

FORTEZA Nicolas 1918 **[16]**
- $2 160 - €2 403 - £1 480 - FF15 760
  Cala Mallorquina Oleo/lienzo (53x63cm 20x24in)
  Barcelona 2001

FORTI E. XIX **[3]**
- $40 000 - €44 402 - £27 884 - FF291 260
  Performance on the Balcony Oil/canvas (61.5x98.5cm 24x38in) New-York 2001

FORTI Ettore XIX-XX **[40]**
- $90 440 - €93 755 - £54 264 - FF614 992
  Celebrazione della primavera Olio/tela (93x142cm 36x55in) Venezia 1999
- $50 000 - €55 838 - £32 020 - FF366 275
  The Rug Seller Oil/canvas (59.5x100cm 23x39in)
  New-York 2000
- $8 000 - €8 970 - £5 432 - FF58 838
  Classical Figures by the Sea Oil/panel (27x51cm 10x20in) New-York 2000

FORTIER Fr. Alphonse 1825-1882 **[12]**
- $609 - €701 - £420 - FF4 600
  Eglise de la Madeleine, Pl.8 de Les Monuments de Paris Tirage papier salé (27x37.5cm 10x14in) Paris 2000

FORTIN Marc Aurèle DeFoy 1888-1970 **[228]**
- $10 416 - €8 913 - £6 270 - FF58 465
  «Le port de Montréal» Oil/board (51x66.5cm 20x26in) Toronto 1999
- $2 759 - €3 122 - £1 930 - FF20 476
  Farmstead Oil/canvas (19.5x24cm 7x9in) Toronto 2001
- $1 516 - €1 541 - £948 - FF10 109
  Paysage Aquarelle (19x29.5cm 7x11in) Montréal 2000

FORTUIN Anton 1890-? **[1]**
- $5 106 - €5 899 - £3 575 - FF38 695
  Figure of a Nude Woman Sculpture, wood (H53cm H20in) Amsterdam 2001

FORTUNATO Franco 1946 **[12]**
- $1 100 - €1 140 - £660 - FF7 480
  «L'albero della memoria» Olio/tela (60x50cm 23x19in) Vercelli 2001

FORTUNEY (Andrieux, dit) 1878-1950 **[297]**
- $4 941 - €4 573 - £3 051 - FF30 000
  Embarcations sur la rivière Huile/toile (54x65cm 21x25in) Monte-Carlo 1999
- $435 - €457 - £287 - FF3 000
  Vieux marin Pastel/papier (31x24cm 12x9in) Paris 2000

FORTUNY Marià 1838-1874 **[111]**
- $40 000 - €44 774 - £27 896 - FF293 700
  Summer Day, Morocco Oil/canvas (25.5x66cm 10x25in) New-York 2001
- $4 250 - €5 106 - £2 975 - FF33 490
  El pavo Oleo/lienzo (18x9cm 7x3in) Madrid 2000
- $4 260 - €3 604 - £2 580 - FF23 640
  Colombine Tinta/papel (22.5x17.5cm 8x6in) Madrid 1998
- $324 - €360 - £216 - FF2 364
  Caballero con casaca Grabado (16x11cm 6x4in)
  Madrid 2000

FORTUNY Y MADRAZO Mariano 1871-1949 **[20]**
- $5 244 - €4 573 - £3 171 - FF30 000
  Elégantes sur la place du gouvernement à Alger Huile/toile (55x38cm 21x14in) Toulouse 1998
- $18 343 - €21 674 - £13 000 - FF142 175
  Scene from the Spanish Civil War Oil/canvas (23x28cm 9x11in) London 2000
- $384 - €360 - £240 - FF2 364
  Tarde de verano Aguafuerte (11.5x14.5cm 4x5in)
  Madrid 1999

FORTY Frank 1902-1996 **[15]**
- $156 - €182 - £110 - FF1 192
  Barley, Alderham Bodycolour (27x37cm 10x14in)
  Stansted Mountfitchet, Essex 2001

FORUP Carl Christian 1883-1939 **[39]**
- $421 - €405 - £260 - FF2 657
  Apelsinförsäljning i italiensk landskap Oil/canvas (46x51cm 18x20in) Malmö 1999

FOSCHI Francesco ?-1805 **[25]**
- $27 319 - €27 098 - £17 000 - FF177 748
  Mountainous Winter Landscape with Peasants on a Barge Oil/canvas (98.5x135cm 38x53in) London 1999
- $29 452 - €33 023 - £20 000 - FF216 614
  Winter Landscape with Travellers crossing a Bridge Oil/canvas (47x61cm 18x24in) London 2000

FOSS Harald 1843-1922 **[86]**
- $608 - €670 - £406 - FF4 398
  Landskab med Gudenåen Oil/canvas (49x75cm 19x29in) Vejle 2000
- $503 - €457 - £314 - FF3 001
  Parti fra en fjord med skib, i baggrunden bakket landskab Oil/canvas (23x31cm 9x12in) København 1999

FOSS Olivier 1920 **[60]**
- $450 - €457 - £297 - FF3 138
  Night Scene in Paris Oil/canvas (45x53cm 18x21in)
  Cleveland OH 2000

FOSSATI Andrea 1844-1919 **[5]**

$24 247 - €27 027 - **£17 000** - FF177 286
Castello di Lerici Oil/canvas (43x80cm 16x31in)
London 2001

$15 689 - €17 488 - **£11 000** - FF114 714
Golfo di La Spezia Oil/panel (16.5x50cm 6x19in)
London 2001

FOSSI C. XIX **[3]**

$37 500 - €41 976 - **£26 152** - FF275 343
Hades and Persephone Marble (H122cm H48in)
New-York 2001

$31 252 - €26 221 - **£18 335** - FF172 000
Pauline Borghese alanguie sur un lit de repos une pomme à la main Marbre Carrare
(62x108x38.5cm 24x42x15in) Paris 1998

FOSSOUX Claude 1946 **[84]**

$1 174 - €1 082 - **£703** - FF7 100
Les petits Rats de Paris Huile/toile (38x46cm 14x18in) Paris 1998

FOSTER Benjamin, Ben 1852-1926 **[57]**

$3 750 - €3 480 - **£2 251** - FF22 828
Spring in the Valley Oil/canvas (45x55cm 18x22in)
Milford CT 1999

$2 100 - €2 314 - **£1 397** - FF15 181
Woodland Road Oil/canvas (30x40cm 12x16in)
Portsmouth NH 2000

FOSTER Bernard **[7]**

$917 - €1 064 - **£650** - FF6 980
Feeding Time Watercolour (30x45cm 11x17in)
London 2000

FOSTER Deryck 1924 **[15]**

$1 362 - €1 295 - **£850** - FF8 494
Dragon in the Solent Oil/board (40.5x61cm 15x24in) London 1999

$1 325 - €1 422 - **£900** - FF9 329
West Country Redwings Rounding the Mark/Hornets Racing Gouache/paper (12.5x25cm 4x9in) London 2001

FOSTER Hal, Harold Rudolf 1892-1982 **[24]**

$2 400 - €2 576 - **£1 606** - FF16 898
Partial Prince Valiant Sunday Page Ink
(86.5x58.5cm 34x23in) New-York 2000

FOSTER John B. XIX-XX **[7]**

$475 - €453 - **£301** - FF2 973
Sailing Vessel at Sea/Ship Beside the Pier
Watercolour/paper (48x34cm 19x13in) Boston MA 1999

FOSTER Myles Birket 1825-1899 **[516]**

$3 968 - €3 748 - **£2 400** - FF24 586
Peat Gatherers Watercolour (15x23.5cm 5x9in)
Billingshurst, West-Sussex 1999

FOSTER William Frederick 1883-1953 **[16]**

$1 600 - €1 532 - **£988** - FF10 051
Couple Meeting in the Woods, Story Illustration
Oil/canvas (75x43cm 29x17in) New-York 1999

FOSTER William Gilbert 1855-1924 **[27]**

$2 276 - €2 102 - **£1 400** - FF13 785
Children resting by a Bridge in a wooded Landscape Oil/canvas (56x91.5cm 22x36in) London 1999

$3 010 - €2 569 - **£1 800** - FF16 853
A Mother and Child in a Cottage Garden Stroking the Calves Watercolour (27x37cm 10x14in) Leeds 1998

FOTINSKI Serge 1887-1971 **[19]**

$1 253 - €1 372 - **£864** - FF9 000
Quai au marbre à Marseille Huile/toile (92x73cm 36x28in) Paris 2001

$7 098 - €7 927 - **£4 810** - FF52 000
Orientale Huile/toile (140x38cm 18x12in) Paris 2000

$805 - €899 - **£545** - FF5 900
Sans titre Tapisserie (140x30cm 55x31in) Paris 2000

FOUACE Guillaume R. 1827-1895 **[56]**

$5 633 - €6 250 - **£3 895** - FF41 000
Nature morte au faisan Huile/toile (46.5x65cm 18x25in) Cherbourg 2001

$6 959 - €7 013 - **£4 337** - FF46 000
Vase de Fleurs Huile/toile (35x24cm 13x9in) Calais 2000

FOUBERT Émile Louis 1848-1911 **[33]**

$7 508 - €8 461 - **£5 200** - FF55 503
Grand île sur la Seine à Vetheuil Oil/canvas (65.5x81cm 25x31in) London 2000

$820 - €1 081 - **£1 929** - FF21 000
Paysage verdoyant avec élégante au bord d'une rivière Huile/panneau (32x41cm 12x16in) Orléans 2000

FOUCHÉ Nicolas 1653-1733 **[5]**

$29 927 - €33 991 - **£21 000** - FF222 967
Portrait of a Lady as Flora, accompanied by Zephir Oil/canvas (87.5x68cm 34x26in) London 2001

FOUCHET Bernard 1932 **[2]**

$3 197 - €3 811 - **£2 280** - FF25 000
«Simplicité de la nature» Huile/toile (80x80cm 31x31in) Paris 2000

FOUGASSE (Cyril K. Bird) 1887-1965 **[20]**

$538 - €455 - **£320** - FF2 983
«Hallporter, you Know Everything» Ink (38x27cm 14x10in) London 1998

$670 - €641 - **£420** - FF4 202
«Careless Talk Costs Lives» Poster (32x20cm 12x7in) London 1999

FOUGERON André 1913-1998 **[44]**

$1 738 - €1 677 - **£1 098** - FF11 000
Femme à sa toilette Huile/toile (81x60cm 31x23in)
Paris 1999

FOUGSTEDT Arvid 1888-1949 **[63]**

$2 002 - €2 244 - **£1 396** - FF14 719
Interiör med mor och dotter Oil/canvas (73x60cm 28x23in) Stockholm 2000

$1 473 - €1 385 - **£888** - FF9 082
Den musikaliska familjen Mixed media (33x44cm 12x17in) Stockholm 1999

$907 - €929 - **£560** - FF6 094
Ingres i sin ateljé Akvarell/papper (41x25cm 16x9in)
Stockholm 2000

FOUILHOUZE Félix ?-1885 **[1]**

$12 568 - €12 196 - **£7 976** - FF80 000
Le port de Naples Huile/papier/toile (38x61cm 14x24in) Paris 1999

FOUILLÉ Georges 1909-1994 **[52]**

$738 - €686 - **£452** - FF4 500
Le trois-mâts barque Aquarelle/papier (32x45cm 12x17in) Coutances 1998

$142 - €152 - **£95** - FF1 000
Côtres en mer Sérigraphie (47x33cm 18x12in) Paris 2000

FOUJITA Léonard, Tsuguharu 1886-1968 **[1540]**

$950 000 - €912 378 - **£585 675** - FF5 984 810
Mon portrait Oil/canvas (130x96.5cm 51x37in) New-York 1999

F

$42 000 – €40 387 - **£25 876** - FF264 923
Le nid Oil/canvas (45.5x38cm 17x14in) New-York 1999

$36 262 – €42 643 - **£26 000** - FF279 723
Kiki de Montparnasse Oil/canvas (41.5x33.5cm 16x13in) London 2001

$13 202 – €12 501 - **£8 224** - FF82 000
Petite fille au capuchon sous la neige Encre Chine (35x27cm 13x10in) Cannes 1999

$1 005 – €1 143 - **£697** - FF7 500
«4ème Bal de l'Amicale aux Artistes» Affiche (121x79cm 47x31in) Orléans 2000

FOULCHÉ Thierry XX [2]
$7 800 – €6 588 - **£4 684** - FF43 213
Sleeping Cat, from Les Chats Etching, aquatint (31x37.5cm 12x14in) New-York 1998

FOULLON Lucille 1775-1865 [7]
$9 919 – €9 909 - **£6 201** - FF65 000
Enfant jouant avec un fruit Huile/toile (92x73cm 36x28in) Valence 1999

FOULLONGNE Alfred Charles 1821-1897 [3]
$4 812 – €4 849 - **£3 000** - FF31 810
The Sleeping Beaty Oil/canvas (46.5x65.5cm 18x25in) London 2001

FOUQUERAY Charles Dominique 1869/72-1956 [153]
$1 775 – €1 677 - **£1 105** - FF11 000
La procession Huile/toile (55x81cm 21x31in) Paris 1999

$580 – €610 - **£382** - FF4 000
Napoléonb pensif Aquarelle/papier (25x34.5cm 9x13in) Paris 2000

$101 – €93 - **£62** - FF610
Une fumée au loin Lithographie (17x20cm 6x7in) Douarnenez 1998

FOUQUIERES Jacques c.1580-1659 [16]
$27 398 – €27 616 - **£17 100** - FF181 146
Ein Dorf im Winter Oil/panel (35x48cm 13x18in) Wien 2000

FOURASTIÉ XX [16]
$212 – €244 - **£149** - FF1 600
«Le bossu» Affiche (120x160cm 47x62in) Paris 2001

FOURDRINIER Pierre XVIII [3]
$937 – €795 - **£565** - FF5 214
View of Bellem by Lisbon as before the Late Earthquake Engraving (40.5x78.5cm 15x30in) London 1998

FOURIÉ Albert-Auguste 1854-1896 [15]
$14 000 – €13 864 - **£8 716** - FF90 941
Haymaking in Criquebeuf, Normandie Oil/canvas (145.5x225cm 57x88in) New-York 1999

$6 500 – €7 383 - **£4 561** - FF48 430
Aurora Oil/canvas (92x73cm 36x28in) New-York 2001

FOURMOIS Théodore 1814-1871 [81]
$2 640 – €2 479 - **£1 630** - FF16 260
La Hulpe au mois d'Août Huile/toile (50x64cm 19x25in) Bruxelles 1999

$975 – €842 - **£588** - FF5 525
Abords d'étang Huile/panneau (18x34.5cm 7x13in) Bruxelles 1998

FOURNERY Félix 1865-1938 [9]
$1 063 – €991 - **£657** - FF6 500
«Trouville, Casino municipal, Juin/Septembre» Affiche couleur (104x71cm 40x27in) Paris 1999

FOURNIER Alain A. 1931-1983 [157]
$1 192 – €1 037 - **£718** - FF6 800
Entrée du port Huile/toile (81x100cm 31x39in) Paris 1998

FOURNIER Alexis Jean 1865-1948 [50]
$4 000 – €4 462 - **£2 618** - FF29 272
Autumn Woodland Oil/masonite (50x60cm 20x24in) Chicago IL 2000

$4 000 – €4 701 - **£2 773** - FF30 837
Blue Hills Oil/canvas (26x33cm 10x13in) Cincinnati OH 2000

FOURNIER Gabriel 1893-1963 [61]
$1 317 – €1 220 - **£816** - FF8 000
Nature morte au vase de fleurs Huile/toile (65x54cm 25x21in) Paris 1999

FOURNIER Jean Simon XVIII-XIX [4]
$95 000 – €104 258 - **£61 170** - FF683 886
L'heure du rendez-vous Oil/canvas (51x61cm 20x24in) New-York 2000

$35 000 – €34 984 - **£21 381** - FF229 477
Interior Scenes with a Young Woman Being Offered Flowers by a Suitor Oil/canvas (41x33cm 16x12in) New-York 2000

FOURNIER Jean-Baptiste 1959 [6]
$545 – €620 - **£375** - FF4 065
Provence Huile/toile (22x27cm 8x10in) De Panne 2000

FOURNIER Jean-Claude 1943 [6]
$900 – €892 - **£547** - FF5 853
Couverture journal Spirou Encre Chine (20x20cm 7x7in) Bruxelles 2000

FOURNIER Louis Edouard 1857-? [11]
$4 476 – €3 677 - **£2 600** - FF24 118
The Actor Jean Mounet-Sully in his Dressing Room Oil/board (15x25cm 5x9in) London 1998

FOURNIER-SARLOVEZE de Raymond Joseph 1836-? [12]
$5 515 – €5 322 - **£3 464** - FF34 909
Portrait de la princesse Marie de Bonaparte Huile/toile (55x38cm 21x14in) Genève 1999

$475 – €534 - **£332** - FF3 500
Le Duc Amédée de Broglie distribue les bougeoirs à Chaumont sur Loire Aquarelle (28x19.5cm 11x7in) Paris 2001

FOURRIER-RICOUX Marguerite XX [6]
$1 304 – €1 524 - **£931** - FF10 000
La jeune marocaine au bouquet de fleurs Pastel/carton (63x50cm 24x19in) Paris 2001

FOURY Germaine 1902-1981 [5]
$1 449 – €1 601 - **£1 004** - FF10 500
Jeunes femmes antillaises Pastel/papier (63.5x48.5cm 25x19in) Paris 2001

FOUS Jean 1901-1971 [133]
$509 – €488 - **£320** - FF3 200
Le paradis terrestre Huile/toile (46x55cm 18x21in) Paris 1999

$329 – €305 - **£204** - FF2 000
«Le marché aux puces» Huile/toile (27x35cm 10x13in) Paris 1999

FOUSEK Frank 1913-1979 [10]
$140 – €130 - **£86** - FF855
«Milkweed» Aquatint in colors (41x24cm 16x9in) Cleveland OH 1999

FOWERAKER A. Moulton 1873-1942 **[124]**
- $592 - €699 - £420 - FF4 587
  The Sierras, near Segovia, Spain Oil/canvas
  (45.5x61cm 17x24in) London 2001
- $1 933 - €1 816 - £1 200 - FF11 914
  Moonlight - Figures before an Inn
  Watercolour/paper (22.5x28cm 8x11in) London 1999

FOWLER Robert 1853-1926 **[94]**
- $823 - €797 - £500 - FF5 226
  View of Liverpool Oil/canvas (41x56cm 16x22in)
  London 2000
- $876 - €912 - £550 - FF5 985
  Moonlight Over the Estuary Watercolour/paper
  (41x56cm 16x22in) Billingshurst, West-Sussex 2000

FOWLES Arthur Wellington c.1815-1883 **[39]**
- $27 519 - €31 932 - £19 000 - FF209 457
  **The Indian Troopship Serapis Arriving at
  Portsmouth, with H.R.H.** Oil/canvas (86.5x149cm
  34x58in) London 2000
- $5 500 - €6 250 - £3 798 - FF41 000
  **The H.M.S.Agamemnon laying the Telegraph
  Cable** Oil/canvas (61x106.5cm 24x41in) New-York
  2000
- $3 120 - €3 069 - £2 000 - FF20 133
  **Figures in a Boat setting Sail into the Sun,
  Coastguard on Shore** Oil/canvas (20x30cm 7x11in)
  Bath 1999

FOWLES Joseph 1810-1878 **[5]**
- $10 942 - €9 452 - £6 609 - FF61 999
  Lauristina Oil/canvas (33x44cm 12x17in) Malvern,
  Victoria 1998

FOX Andrew 1960 **[3]**
- $1 176 - €992 - £700 - FF6 508
  Riki's Bar Craies/papier (152x102cm 59x40in)
  Antwerpen 1998

FOX Charles James 1860-c.1937 **[29]**
- $755 - €652 - £450 - FF4 277
  **Evening Landscape with Pond in the
  Foreground** Oil/canvas (70x90cm 27x35in)
  Glamorgan 1998

FOX Edwin M. c.1830-1870 **[17]**
- $2 226 - €2 489 - £1 550 - FF16 330
  **Portrait of a Bay Hunter in a Landscape with
  three arched Bridge** Oil/canvas (63x76cm 25x30in)
  Canterbury, Kent 2001

FOX Emanuel Phillips 1865-1915 **[86]**
- $25 904 - €24 356 - £16 040 - FF159 768
  Breton Fishing Village Oil/canvas (37x45cm
  14x17in) Melbourne 1999
- $12 950 - €12 209 - £8 026 - FF80 088
  Harbourside, Provence Oil/board (34x44cm
  13x17in) Melbourne 1999

FOX Ernest R. XIX-XX **[7]**
- $439 - €470 - £300 - FF3 086
  Mountains of Mourne Watercolour/paper
  (35x60.5cm 13x23in) London 2001

FOX George c.1816-1910 **[30]**
- $706 - €819 - £500 - FF5 372
  An Amusing Passage Oil/panel (33x28cm 12x11in)
  London 2000

FOX Henry Charles 1860-1929 **[315]**
- $989 - €848 - £580 - FF5 600
  Country Lane with a Drover and Cattle
  Watercolour (35.5x52.5cm 13x20in) London 1998

FOX Kathleen 1880-1963 **[10]**
- $2 432 - €2 539 - £1 539 - FF16 658
  Oriental Lillies in a Landscape Oil/canvas
  (67.5x51cm 26x20in) Dublin 2000
- $1 239 - €1 206 - £761 - FF7 912
  Cottages Oil/panel (12x21cm 5x8in) Dublin 1999

FOX Robert Atkinson 1860-1935 **[32]**
- $2 000 - €1 921 - £1 239 - FF12 598
  Cows watering in a Field Oil/canvas (45x64cm
  18x25in) St. Louis MO 1999

FOY Frances 1890-1963 **[1]**
- $5 000 - €5 862 - £3 597 - FF38 455
  Still Life with Liles in a Vase before a Window
  Oil/masonite (71x53.5cm 27x21in) New-York 2001

FOYOT-D'ALVAR Madeleine XIX-XX **[4]**
- $10 000 - €9 903 - £6 226 - FF64 958
  An Elegant Breakfast Oil/canvas (81x100cm
  31x39in) New-York 1999

FRAASS Erich 1893-1974 **[7]**
- $246 - €230 - £149 - FF1 509
  Schafe Woodcut (45.5x55.2cm 17x21in) Berlin 1999

FRACANZANO Francesco 1612-c.1656 **[8]**
- $14 251 - €16 186 - £10 000 - FF106 175
  **Saint John the Baptist preaching to the
  Multitude** Oil/canvas (72.5x61cm 28x24in) London
  2001

FRACCAROLI Innocenzo 1805-1882 **[4]**
- $12 031 - €13 952 - £8 500 - FF91 518
  La Madonna Immacolata Marble (H76cm H29in)
  London 2001

FRACCHIA Luis 1959 **[3]**
- $23 000 - €22 323 - £14 319 - FF146 431
  Cruz de Palma Oil/canvas (92x160cm 36x62in) New-
  York 1999

FRACÉ Charles 1926 **[12]**
- $11 038 - €10 608 - £6 800 - FF69 586
  First Light - Leopard Oil/canvas (58.5x79cm
  23x31in) London 1999
- $250 - €294 - £173 - FF1 529
  Antelope Color lithograph (59.5x47cm 23x18in)
  Beverly-Hills CA 2000

FRADELLE Henri Joseph Fradel 1778-1865 **[7]**
- $2 653 - €2 297 - £1 600 - FF15 065
  **Lady, Small Three quarter length, in a Blue
  Dress** Oil/panel (28x22cm 11x8in) London 1998

FRAGIACOMO Pietro 1856-1922 **[77]**
- $16 000 - €20 733 - £12 000 - FF136 000
  Paesaggio con figure Olio/tela (97x155cm 38x61in)
  Milano 2001
- $6 015 - €5 617 - £3 712 - FF36 848
  Segelboote auf offener See Mixed media
  (39x66cm 15x25in) Luzern 1999
- $3 400 - €4 406 - £2 550 - FF28 900
  Isola dell'estuario Olio/cartone (18x24.5cm 7x9in)
  Milano 2000
- $1 400 - €1 451 - £840 - FF9 520
  L'albero Pastelli/carta (67x48cm 26x18in) Trieste 1999

FRAGONARD Alexandre Évariste 1780-1850 **[55]**
- $8 308 - €9 452 - £5 766 - FF62 000
  La visite du médecin Huile/toile (39x48cm 15x18in)
  Versailles 2000
- $2 200 - €2 086 - £1 330 - FF13 681
  Dismassal of a Suitor, a sketch Oil/canvas
  (40.5x33cm 15x12in) New-York 1999

🖊 **$1 600** – €1 517 - **£973** - FF9 950
Episode from the French Revolution: A Toast
Black chalk (18x24cm 7x9in) New-York 1999

FRAGONARD Jean-Honoré 1732-1806 **[196]**
🖊 **$280 000** – €283 258 - **£170 968** - FF1 858 052
La coquette fixée Oil/canvas (55x45cm 21x17in)
New-York 2000
🖊 **$356 891** – €349 567 - **£230 000** - FF2 293 008
**Interior of a Barn with a Woman and a Child,
Washerwomen nearby** Oil/canvas (30x38cm
11x14in) London 1999
🖊 **$10 000** – €10 116 - **£6 106** - FF66 359
Triumphal Procession, after Salomon de Bray
Ink (30.5x20cm 12x7in) New-York 2000
🖊 **$823** – €715 - **£496** - FF4 692
La Famille du Satyre Radierung (14.5x21.3cm
5x8in) Berlin 1998

FRAGONARD Théophile Evariste 1806-1876 **[15]**
🖊 **$572** – €640 - **£388** - FF4 200
Jeune page frappant à une porte Aquarelle/papier
(19.5x14cm 7x5in) Paris 2000

FRAGUIER de Armand Gabriel 1803-1873 **[12]**
🖊 **$6 225** – €7 318 - **£4 315** - FF48 000
Italienne à la fontaine Huile/toile (138x97cm
54x38in) Paris 2000
🖊 **$1 629** – €1 707 - **£1 031** - FF11 200
Jeune femme à la cape rouge Huile/toile
(81x65cm 31x25in) Besançon 2000
🖊 **$1 942** – €2 287 - **£1 365** - FF15 000
Soldat grec Huile/panneau (31x20cm 12x7in) Paris
2000

FRAHM Hans 1864-? **[12]**
🖊 **$447** – €383 - **£264** - FF2 511
«Dorfstrasse bei Garmisch» Öl/Leinwand
(70.5x90.5cm 27x35in) München 1998
🖊 **$784** – €818 - **£493** - FF5 366
Frühlingsstrasse in Garmisch Oil/panel
(21.5x33cm 8x12in) München 2000

FRAI Felicita Lustig 1914 **[20]**
🖊 **$600** – €518 - **£400** - FF3 400
Pensando a Caravaggio Olio/tela (30x40cm
11x15in) Prato 1998

FRAICHOT Claude Joseph 1732-1803 **[12]**
🖊 **$19 335** – €18 989 - **£12 000** - FF124 558
**Still Life of Cheeses and Pastries, Wine Bottle,
Decanter and Glass** Oil/canvas (105.5x116cm
41x45in) London 1999
🖊 **$6 200** – €7 138 - **£4 230** - FF46 822
**Artichokes and Crayfish on a Porcelaine Dish
with Wine Glasses** Oil/canvas (56x106cm 22x41in)
New-York 2000

FRAIKIN Charles Auguste 1817-1893 **[10]**
🖊 **$765** – €869 - **£523** - FF5 700
Jeune femme nue à la colombe Bronze (H30cm
H11in) Senlis 2000

FRAIKIN Maxime XIX-XX **[7]**
🖊 **$671** – €671 - **£419** - FF4 400
«Pneus vélo Michelin» Affiche (76.5x58cm
30x22in) Orléans 1999

FRAILE ALCALDE Alfonso 1930-1988 **[40]**
🖊 **$10 260** – €11 412 - **£6 840** - FF74 860
«25» Técnica mixta/lienzo (200x155cm 78x61in)
Madrid 2000
🖊 **$2 890** – €2 553 - **£1 785** - FF16 745
Personaje Técnica mixta/cartón (65x50cm 25x19in)
Madrid 1999

🖊 **$1 344** – €1 442 - **£888** - FF9 456
Pintura Oleo/lienzo (21.5x25.5cm 8x10in) Madrid
2000
🖊 **$8 540** – €8 409 - **£5 320** - FF55 160
Dos perros Técnica mixta/papel (110x130cm
43x51in) Madrid 1999

FRAIPONT Gustave 1849-1923 **[43]**
🖊 **$462** – €396 - **£279** - FF2 600
«Exposition Universelle» Affiche (105x73cm
41x28in) Paris 1998

FRAJNDLICH Abe 1946 **[19]**
📷 **$644** – €767 - **£460** - FF5 030
«Alfred Eisenstaedt with two Photographs»
Gelatin silver print (38x38cm 14x14in) Berlin 2000

FRAMPTON Edward 1846-1929 **[3]**
🖊 **$116 032** – €100 108 - **£70 000** - FF656 663
St Catherine Oil/canvas (68.5x122cm 26x48in)
London 1998

FRAMPTON George 1860-1928 **[22]**
🖊 **$13 448** – €14 436 - **£9 000** - FF94 694
Bust of Enid the Fair Bronze (H52cm H20in)
London 2000

FRAMPTON Reginald Edward 1870/72-1923 **[15]**
🖊 **$54 799** – €60 555 - **£38 000** - FF397 214
**Stone Walls do not a Prison Make, nor Iron Bars
a Cage** Oil/canvas (90.5x55cm 35x21in) London 2001

FRAN-BARO (Francisco Baro) 1926-2000 **[135]**
🖊 **$1 852** – €1 952 - **£1 235** - FF12 805
Bateaux de plaisance à Dolean (Bretaña)
Oleo/lienzo (46x56cm 18x22in) Madrid 2000
🖊 **$729** – €747 - **£449** - FF4 900
Le Palais des Doges Huile/toile (22x27cm 8x10in)
Provins 2000

FRANC-LAMY Pierre 1855-1919 **[28]**
🖊 **$2 141** – €1 982 - **£1 292** - FF13 000
Le troupeau au bord de la rivière Huile/panneau
(23x39cm 9x15in) Paris 1999
🖊 **$456** – €503 - **£303** - FF3 300
Terrasse à Versailles Aquarelle/papier (30x47cm
11x18in) Morlaix 2000

FRANÇAIS Anne 1909-1995 **[57]**
🖊 **$1 198** – €991 - **£703** - FF6 500
Quimper, la Cathédrale Huile/toile (92x73cm
36x28in) Reims 1998

FRANÇAIS François Louis 1814-1897 **[136]**
🖊 **$4 025** – €3 811 - **£2 500** - FF25 000
Les lavandières dans le sous-bois Huile/toile
(37x48cm 14x18in) Saint-Dié 1999
🖊 **$2 803** – €3 201 - **£1 971** - FF21 000
Le village au pont de pierre Huile/panneau
(26.5x35cm 10x13in) Fontainebleau 2001
🖊 **$504** – €503 - **£314** - FF3 300
Le temple Lavis (19x27.5cm 7x10in) Fontainebleau
1999
🖊 **$86** – €84 - **£53** - FF550
Sur le chemin Lithographie (23x17cm 9x6in)
Fontainebleau 1999

FRANCALANCIA Riccardo 1886-1965 **[20]**
🖊 **$5 000** – €5 183 - **£3 000** - FF34 000
La Maddalena Olio/tela (38x45cm 14x17in) Vercelli
2001

FRANCANZANO Francesco 1612-1656 **[2]**
🖊 **$15 000** – €14 112 - **£9 360** - FF92 571
A Male Saint holding a Staff Oil/canvas
(77.5x62.5cm 30x24in) New-York 1999

FRANCE Charles XIX [8]
- $3 250 - €2 945 - £2 001 - FF19 320
  Autumn Landscape Oil/canvas (53x78cm 21x31in)
  Mystic CT 1999

FRANCES Y PASCUAL Plácido 1834-1902 [9]
- $18 525 - €19 521 - £12 350 - FF128 050
  Ofrenda a Venus Oleo/lienzo (169.5x123cm 66x48in)
  Madrid 2000

FRANCESCHI de Mariano 1849-1896 [27]
- $1 422 - €1 484 - £900 - FF9 737
  The Coquettes Oil/panel (44x33cm 17x12in) London
  2000
- $1 700 - €1 971 - £1 204 - FF12 931
  Carnevale Watercolour/paper (34.5x53cm 13x20in)
  New-York 2000

FRANCESCHI dei Paolo Fiammingo c.1540-1596 [20]
- $32 000 - €36 336 - £21 900 - FF238 350
  Hirschjagd Öl/Leinwand (118x152cm 46x59in) Wien 2000
- $11 000 - €9 234 - £6 451 - FF60 572
  Pan and Syrinx Oil/canvas (44x75cm 17x29in) New-York 1998

FRANCESCHI Louis Julien, Jules 1825-1893 [8]
- $3 744 - €4 462 - £2 682 - FF29 268
  Chasseresses Bronze (53x32cm 20x12in) Lokeren 2000

FRANCESCHI Edoardo 1928 [56]
- $320 - €415 - £240 - FF2 720
  «Apparizione II» Olio/tela (81x100cm 31x39in)
  Milano 2000

FRANCESCHINI IL VOLTERRANO Baldassare 1611-1689 [68]
- $12 500 - €12 958 - £7 500 - FF85 000
  Elia sul carro Olio/tela (36x56cm 14x22in) Prato 2000
- $3 119 - €3 053 - £2 000 - FF20 024
  Studies of the Forequarters of a Rearing Horse/Sketch of a Woman Black & white chalks/paper (25.5x40.5cm 10x15in) London 1999

FRANCESCHINI Marcantonio 1648-1729 [38]
- $112 072 - €120 301 - £75 000 - FF789 120
  Armida Discovers the Sleeping Rinaldo/Erminia and the Shepherds Oil/canvas (95x129cm 37x50in)
  London 2000
- $120 000 - €134 409 - £83 376 - FF881 664
  The Triumph of Venus Oil/canvas (90.5x117.5cm 35x46in) New-York 2001
- $20 000 - €21 359 - £13 628 - FF140 106
  The Ecstasy of Mary Magdalen with Angels Playing Music Ink (16.5x25.5cm 6x10in) New-York 2001

FRANCESCO DI GIORGIO MARTINI 1439-1501 [1]
- $104 601 - €112 281 - £70 000 - FF736 512
  Archery Tournament with Maiders Drawn in Chariots, with Griffins Oil/panel (34.5x127.5cm 13x50in) London 2000

FRANCESE Franco 1920-1996 [63]
- $2 250 - €2 332 - £1 350 - FF15 300
  Bestario 2, guarda dalla soglia Olio/tela (57x45cm 22x17in) Milano 2001
- $1 100 - €1 140 - £660 - FF7 480
  «Notte d'amore» Inchiostro (47.5x50.5cm 18x19in)
  Milano 2000

FRANCHERE Joseph Charles 1866-1921 [50]
- $2 344 - €2 125 - £1 443 - FF13 937
  Portrait de Firmin Hudon/Portrait d'Azélie d'Orsonnance Huile/toile (68.5x54cm 26x21in)
  Montréal 1999
- $2 425 - €2 829 - £1 732 - FF18 556
  Country Girl Huile/panneau (42.5x23cm 16x9in)
  Montréal 2000

FRANCHI Alessandro 1838-1914 [2]
- $4 000 - €4 225 - £2 644 - FF27 715
  The Birth of Venus Oil/canvas (106x60cm 42x24in)
  Cedar-Falls IA 2000

FRANCHI Cesare c.1580-1615 [4]
- $29 886 - €32 080 - £20 000 - FF210 432
  The Martyrdom of St.Lawrence Gouache
  (16x11.5cm 6x4in) London 2000

FRANCHI Rossello di Jacopo c.1377-1456 [5]
- $72 000 - €62 199 - £48 000 - FF408 000
  Madonna col Bambino in trono tra San Giacomo e San Giovanni Battista Tempera/tavola
  (88.5x50.5cm 34x19in) Milano 1998

FRANCHINA Nino 1912-1988 [14]
- $2 500 - €2 592 - £1 500 - FF17 000
  Piccola astra Fer (66x44cm 25x17in) Milano 2000

FRANCHOYS Lucas II 1616-1681 [4]
- $8 500 - €8 057 - £5 310 - FF52 853
  Portrait of a man in armour Oil/canvas (86x71cm 34x28in) East-Moriches NY 1999
- $2 417 - €2 238 - £1 500 - FF14 683
  Saint Catherine Oil/panel (44.5x34cm 17x13in)
  London 1999

FRANCIA Alexandre Thomas 1813/20-1884 [45]
- $3 661 - €3 506 - £2 256 - FF23 000
  Plage animée à marée basse Huile/toile (40x60cm 15x23in) Calais 1999
- $1 600 - €1 363 - £962 - FF8 943
  Paysage lacustre Aquarelle/papier (41x69cm 16x27in) Bruxelles 1998

FRANCIA Claudio 1952 [3]
- $1 400 - €1 451 - £800 - FF9 520
  «Ready Made in Italy» Collage (60x80cm 23x31in)
  Prato 1999

FRANCIA Francesco Raibolini 1450-1517 [3]
- $120 000 - €105 259 - £72 864 - FF690 456
  Madonna with the Christ Child Holding a Bird Oil/panel (37x29cm 14x11in) New-York 1999

FRANCIA François Thom. Louis 1772-1839 [38]
- $1 167 - €1 254 - £800 - FF8 226
  Prison Galleon off the Shore Watercolour
  (18.5x26cm 7x10in) London 2001

FRANCIA Giacomo Raibolini c.1486-1557 [16]
- $44 625 - €46 261 - £26 775 - FF303 450
  La Madonna col Bambino e S.Giovannino tra i santi Stefano e Lorenzo Olio/tavola (179x147cm 70x57in) Venezia 2000
- $38 851 - €41 704 - £26 000 - FF273 561
  A Sacra Conversazione: The Madonna and Child Oil/canvas (72.5x72.5cm 28x28in) London 2000
- $2 400 - €2 686 - £1 673 - FF17 622
  Cupid adn Psyche, after Raphael Engraving
  (19x27.5cm 7x10in) New-York 2000

FRANCIS Dorothea 1903-1973 [15]
- $1 683 - €1 583 - £1 042 - FF10 384
  Abstract, The Tunnel Oil/canvas (42.5x53cm 16x20in) Melbourne 1999

FRANCIS Ivor Pengelly 1906-1993 **[14]**
$7 566 - €8 336 - **£5 023** - FF54 681
Medical Examination Oil/canvas (34x44cm 13x17in) Woollahra, Sydney 1999

FRANCIS John F. 1808-1886 **[30]**
$5 000 - €4 765 - **£3 169** - FF31 254
Portrait of Juliet Campbell Oil/canvas (76x60cm 30x24in) Cleveland OH 1999
$20 000 - €22 204 - **£13 910** - FF145 648
Strawberries and Cream Oil/canvas (38x31cm 15x12in) Milford CT 2001

FRANCIS Mark 1962 **[32]**
$13 448 - €14 436 - **£9 000** - FF94 694
Colonise Oil/canvas (305x274.5cm 120x108in) London 2000
$5 500 - €6 382 - **£3 797** - FF41 860
Untitled Oil/canvas (61.5x44.5cm 24x17in) New-York 2000

FRANCIS Sam (Samuel Lewis) 1923-1994 **[1379]**
$170 000 - €161 168 - **£103 428** - FF1 057 196
When White Oil/canvas (250x193cm 98x75in) New-York 1999
$20 920 - €22 456 - **£14 000** - FF147 302
Untitled Acrylic/paper (56x76cm 22x29in) London 2000
$7 172 - €7 961 - **£5 000** - FF52 224
Untitled Acrylic/paper (32.5x26cm 12x10in) London 2001
$19 557 - €23 008 - **£14 157** - FF150 925
White Line Gouache/paper (51.5x35.4cm 20x13in) Hamburg 2001
$2 610 - €2 514 - **£1 620** - FF16 493
Serpent on the Stone Farblithographie (63x90cm 24x35in) Zürich 1999

FRANCIS Thomas Edward XIX-XX **[29]**
$225 - €254 - **£156** - FF1 664
«**The Cathedral, Antwerp**» Watercolour/paper (39.5x29cm 15x11in) Toronto 2000

FRANCISCI de Anthony 1887-1964 **[6]**
$5 000 - €4 691 - **£3 089** - FF30 769
Bayade, Harem Dancer Bronze (H48cm H19in) Cleveland OH 1999

FRANCISCO Carlos 1913-1968 **[3]**
$8 608 - €9 775 - **£5 892** - FF64 119
The stick Dance Watercolour (32x50cm 12x19in) Singapore 2000

FRANCISCO de Pietro 1873-1969 **[20]**
$2 300 - €2 384 - **£1 380** - FF15 640
Venezia, Rialto Olio/tela (45x69cm 17x27in) Roma 1999
$1 018 - €1 011 - **£636** - FF6 633
Dancing on the Beach in St-Tropez Oil/canvas (30.5x40.5cm 12x15in) Toronto 1999

FRANCISCO John Bond 1863-1931 **[23]**
$3 000 - €2 563 - **£1 815** - FF16 813
Southern California Landscape Oil/canvas (40.5x51cm 15x20in) San-Francisco CA 1998

FRANCK Albert Jacques 1899-1973 **[31]**
$1 490 - €1 459 - **£917** - FF9 572
Spring Activity Oil/board (40.5x51cm 15x20in) Toronto 1999
$812 - €780 - **£503** - FF5 116
«**Little Italy**» Oil/canvas/board (30.5x40.5cm 12x15in) Toronto 1999

FRANCK Martine 1938 **[18]**
$1 072 - €1 183 - **£709** - FF7 757
Tulku Khentral with Tutor, Nepal Gelatin silver print (40.5x51cm 15x20in) Vancouver, BC. 2000

FRANCK Myriam 1948 **[7]**
$3 580 - €4 040 - **£2 517** - FF26 500
Force de vie Bronze (47x22x12cm 18x8x4in) Paris 2001

FRANCK Philipp 1860-1944 **[78]**
$8 996 - €10 583 - **£6 350** - FF69 423
Kanal unter Bäumen Öl/Leinwand (75x85cm 29x33in) Berlin 2001
$3 826 - €4 346 - **£2 676** - FF28 508
Bootssteg und Ruderkahn an märkischem Seeufer Oil/canvas/panel (32.5x43cm 12x16in) Berlin 2001
$1 667 - €1 789 - **£1 115** - FF11 738
Luganer See Aquarell/Papier (60x46cm 23x18in) Berlin 2000
$107 - €102 - **£66** - FF670
Badende Knaben Radierung (20x27.2cm 7x10in) Berlin 1999

FRANCKEN Ambrosius I 1544-1618 **[14]**
$14 245 - €12 120 - **£8 500** - FF79 503
The Parable of the Rich Man's Feast Oil/panel (95.5x141.5cm 37x55in) London 1998
$12 334 - €10 172 - **£7 266** - FF66 724
Die Verkündigung an Maria Oil/panel (63.5x49cm 25x19in) Wien 1998

FRANCKEN Ambrosius II ?-1632 **[13]**
$24 902 - €24 479 - **£16 000** - FF160 569
Achilles discovered amongst the Daughters of Lycomedes Oil/panel (55x68cm 21x26in) London 1999

FRANCKEN Frans I 1542-1616 **[10]**
$45 220 - €46 877 - **£27 132** - FF307 496
L'Ultima Cena Olio/tavoletta (26.5x20.5cm 10x8in) Venezia 2000

FRANCKEN Frans II 1581-1642 **[211]**
$16 000 - €14 082 - **£9 740** - FF92 372
The Virgin and Child with Scenes from the Life of Christ Oil/canvas (126.5x95cm 49x37in) New-York 1999
$43 260 - €43 603 - **£27 000** - FF286 020
Christus fällt unter dem Kreuz Öl/Leinwand (61x97.5cm 24x38in) Wien 2000
$8 149 - €7 714 - **£5 067** - FF50 602
The Madonna and Child with the Infant Saint John Mixed media/panel (23.5x18.5cm 9x7in) Amsterdam 1999

FRANCKEN Frans III 1607-1667 **[24]**
$32 622 - €30 511 - **£20 000** - FF200 140
The Interior of a Cathedral Oil/panel (41.5x59cm 16x23in) London 1998
$4 093 - €3 796 - **£2 500** - FF24 900
Angels Adoring the Christ Child in a Crib while the Virgin Sews Oil/copper (33x27cm 12x10in) London 1998

FRANCKEN Hiëronymus I 1540-1610 **[6]**
$11 360 - €12 196 - **£7 600** - FF80 000
Lazare et le mauvais riche Huile/panneau (49x74.5cm 19x29in) Paris 2000

FRANCKEN Hiëronymus II 1578-1623 **[11]**
$24 976 - €24 392 - **£15 920** - FF160 000
Scène de collation Huile/panneau (50x65.5cm 19x25in) Paris 1999

$7 471 - €8 020 - **£5 000** - FF52 608
An Elegant Young Man and Woman Looking in a Mirror Oil/panel (19x16cm 7x6in) London 2000

FRANCKEN Hiëronymus III 1611-? **[3]**
$10 260 - €11 412 - **£6 840** - FF74 860
Las obras de misericordia Oleo/cobre (70x89cm 27x35in) Madrid 2000

FRANCKEN Ruth 1924 **[20]**
$469 - €534 - **£325** - FF3 500
Partition V, Paris, Le Soleil noir, série le Livre Objet Métal (32x32x10.5cm 12x12x4in) Paris 2000

FRANCKEN Thomas 1574-c.1626 **[1]**
$5 878 - €5 923 - **£3 664** - FF38 855
Flusslandschaft mit der heilige Magdalena und schwebenden Engeln Öl/Kupfer (51x59.5cm 20x23in) Zürich 2000

FRANCKY BOY F. Boy Sevehon, dit 1954 **[61]**
$440 - €473 - **£294** - FF3 100
No comment Acrylique/toile (54x65cm 21x25in) Paris 2000

FRANCO CORDERO José XIX-XX **[30]**
$3 135 - €3 304 - **£1 980** - FF21 670
Vista de Torrelodones Oleo/lienzo (40x75cm 15x29in) Madrid 2000
$687 - €751 - **£437** - FF4 925
Paisaje al atardecer Oleo/lienzo (22x30cm 8x11in) Madrid 2000

FRANCO IL SEMOLEI Giovanni Battista 1498/1510-1561/80 **[44]**
$12 000 - €10 526 - **£7 286** - FF69 045
Mucius Scaevola Ink (28x35cm 11x13in) New-York 1999
$632 - €613 - **£393** - FF4 024
Der lesende hl. Hieronymus Etching (16.1x13.2cm 6x5in) Berlin 1999

FRANCO Jaime 1963 **[9]**
$8 500 - €7 393 - **£5 124** - FF48 492
«Fuego» Oil/canvas (152.5x114.5cm 60x45in) New-York 1998

FRANCO Siron, Gessiron 1947 **[16]**
$12 000 - €13 923 - **£8 284** - FF91 332
Flagrante Oil/canvas (199x159.5cm 78x62in) New-York 2000

FRANCO Y SALINAS Luis 1850-1897 **[3]**
$10 260 - €11 412 - **£6 840** - FF74 860
El violonista Oleo/tabla (36x25.5cm 14x10in) Madrid 2000

FRANÇOIS André 1915 **[13]**
$900 - €920 - **£564** - FF6 037
Sitzender Affe Indian ink (47.5x48.5cm 18x19in) Hamburg 2000

FRANÇOIS Célestin 1787-1846 **[9]**
$3 536 - €3 966 - **£2 400** - FF26 016
Temple de la Sibylle à Tivoli Huile/toile (77x62cm 30x24in) Bruxelles 2000
$2 953 - €2 704 - **£1 800** - FF17 740
A Lover's Gift Oil/panel (34x25cm 13x9in) Ipswich 1999

FRANÇOIS Georges, Géo 1880-1968 **[32]**
$160 - €181 - **£108** - FF1 190
Stadhuis Middelburg Aquatint in colors (49.5x59.5cm 19x23in) Dordrecht 2000

FRANÇOIS Joseph Charles 1851-1940 **[95]**
$2 688 - €2 975 - **£1 872** - FF19 512
Het groot moeras te genk (Le grand marais à Genk) Huile/toile (159x250cm 62x98in) Antwerpen 2001
$1 177 - €1 363 - **£814** - FF8 943
Lisière de bois ensoleillée Huile/toile (55x75cm 21x29in) Bruxelles 2000

FRANÇOIS Marie Catherine c.1712-1773 **[2]**
$20 500 - €21 251 - **£12 300** - FF139 400
Libraio torinese Giacomo Reycend/Signora Reycend Olio/tela (80x64.5cm 31x25in) Venezia 1999

FRANÇOIS Michel 1956 **[3]**
$7 217 - €7 809 - **£5 000** - FF51 222
Untitled Photograph (39x26cm 15x10in) London 2001

FRANÇOIS Pierre Joseph 1759-1851 **[30]**
$1 185 - €1 239 - **£785** - FF8 130
Rivière en forêt Huile/toile (75x93cm 29x36in) Bruxelles 2000

FRANCQ Philippe 1961 **[8]**
$163 - €137 - **£96** - FF900
«Le Baiser» Sérigraphie couleurs (64x43.5cm 25x17in) Paris 1998

FRANCUCCI Innocenzo da Imola c.1490-c.1545 **[13]**
$24 000 - €24 880 - **£14 400** - FF163 200
Madonna con il Bambino, S. Anna, S. Gerolamo e S. Francesco Olio/tavola (90x71cm 35x27in) Milano 2000
$7 886 - €7 301 - **£4 761** - FF47 891
The Circumcision, a predella Panel Oil/panel (12x31cm 4x12in) Dublin 1999

FRANDSEN Erik August 1956 **[47]**
$897 - €1 006 - **£627** - FF6 596
Our new flag Oil/canvas (77x72cm 30x28in) København 2001
$1 245 - €1 144 - **£765** - FF7 507
Figurkomposition Gouache (110x87cm 43x34in) København 1999
$386 - €416 - **£266** - FF2 726
Komposition Color lithograph (138x99cm 54x38in) København 2001

FRANDZEN Eugene M. 1893-1972 **[7]**
$5 000 - €5 367 - **£3 346** - FF35 205
Eastern Winter Oil/canvas (60x76cm 24x30in) Altadena CA 2000
$450 - €486 - **£311** - FF3 187
Seascape Gouache/board (22x30cm 9x12in) Altadena CA 2001

FRANGI Giovanni 1959 **[10]**
$1 500 - €1 555 - **£900** - FF10 200
Volte femminile Olio/tela (50x40cm 19x15in) Prato 2001

FRANGIAMORE Salvatore 1853-1915 **[22]**
$4 000 - €3 658 - **£2 442** - FF23 995
The Chess Players Oil/canvas (48x61cm 19x24in) New-York 1998

FRANGIPANE Niccolo 1555-1600 **[7]**
$21 280 - €22 825 - **£14 060** - FF149 720
Ecce Homo Oleo/lienzo (40.5x40.5cm 15x15in) Madrid 2000

FRANK (Frank Pé) 1956 **[4]**
$587 - €564 - **£364** - FF3 700
«Comme un animal en cage» Gouache/papier (25x18cm 9x7in) Paris 1999

FRANK Edvard 1909-1972 **[110]**
- $4 220 – €4 857 – **£2 909** – FF31 862
  Komposition Öl/Karton (52x70cm 20x27in)
  Saarbrücken 2000
- $245 – €281 – **£167** – FF1 844
  Sankt Martin zerteilt seinen Mantel Aquarell
  (35x52cm 13x20in) Heidelberg 2000

FRANK Ellen A. 1889-1912 **[5]**
- $2 178 – €2 166 – **£1 350** – FF14 206
  Study of two Gaily coloured Parrots on Branch
  Oil/canvas (24x28cm 9x11in) Lewes, Sussex 2000

FRANK Erna XIX-XX **[21]**
- $89 – €102 – **£62** – FF669
  Pont d'artistes près de Notre-Dame Lithographie
  (18x23cm 7x9in) Lódz 2000

FRANK Eugene C. 1845-1914 **[3]**
- $8 500 – €9 124 – **£5 688** – FF59 848
  Buffalo grazing at sunset Oil/canvas (61x90cm
  24x35in) Philadelphia PA 2000

FRANK Franz 1897-1986 **[26]**
- $1 739 – €2 045 – **£1 246** – FF13 415
  Stilleben am winterlichem Fenster Öl/Karton
  (80x61.5cm 31x24in) Düsseldorf 2001

FRANK Friedrich 1871-1945 **[103]**
- $1 607 – €1 817 – **£1 085** – FF11 917
  Naglergasse in Wien Aquarell/Papier (28x21cm
  11x8in) Wien 2000

FRANK Frigyes 1890-1976 **[17]**
- $1 875 – €2 011 – **£1 278** – FF13 194
  **Tre sommerklaedte piger i lob over en blom-
  strende eng** Oil/canvas (70x100cm 27x39in)
  Köbenhavn 2001
- $440 – €433 – **£275** – FF2 838
  Still Life Mixed media/paper (59x42cm 23x16in)
  Budapest 2000

FRANK Hans 1884-1948 **[97]**
- $1 528 – €1 431 – **£939** – FF9 390
  **Blick von der Höhe über hügelige Landschaft
  mit Burgruine** Öl/Karton (72x90.5cm 28x35in)
  Lindau 1999
- $960 – €1 090 – **£673** – FF7 150
  Sitzender weiblicher Akt Mischtechnik/Papier
  (49x35.5cm 19x13in) Wien 2001
- $201 – €218 – **£139** – FF1 430
  Traunsee Woodcut in colors (22.3x31.5cm 8x12in)
  Wien 2001

FRANK Jean-Michel 1893-1941 **[13]**
- $182 310 – €179 890 – **£112 336** – FF1 180 000
  **Lampadaire à volumes géométriques, coupelle
  dans sa partie médiane** Bronze (H153.5cm H60in)
  Paris 1999
- $39 669 – €43 535 – **£25 543** – FF285 571
  Diabolo Stool Sculpture (42x60x41cm 16x23x16in)
  London 2000
- $2 800 – €2 712 – **£1 746** – FF17 791
  Salon carré de la Villa Trianon Charcoal
  (44.5x50cm 17x19in) Beverly-Hills CA 1999

FRANK Josef 1885-1967 **[14]**
- $952 – €893 – **£588** – FF5 856
  Stilleben med blommor och frukter Akvarell/pap-
  per (52x36cm 20x14in) Stockholm 1999

FRANK Leo 1884-1959 **[46]**
- $156 – €182 – **£111** – FF1 191
  Am Mondsee (Drachenwand) Woodcut in colors
  (32x24cm 12x9in) Wien 2000

FRANK Lucien 1857-1920 **[254]**
- $8 680 – €9 915 – **£6 040** – FF65 040
  Pêcheur au lever du soleil Huile/toile (114x112cm
  44x44in) Bruxelles 2001
- $4 704 – €5 206 – **£3 276** – FF34 146
  Coucher de soleil Huile/toile (60x83.5cm 23x32in)
  Bruxelles 2001
- $2 252 – €2 107 – **£1 394** – FF13 821
  Boulevard Huile/carton (20.5x25.5cm 8x10in)
  Lokeren 1999
- $1 865 – €1 610 – **£1 124** – FF10 562
  Retour à la ferme le soir Technique mixte/papier
  (26.5x21cm 10x8in) Bruxelles 1998

FRANK Mary 1933 **[23]**
- $1 000 – €1 110 – **£697** – FF7 281
  Emerging Woman Terracotta (41.5x25.5x19cm
  16x10x7in) New-York 2001

FRANK Robert 1924 **[340]**
- $6 500 – €7 148 – **£4 507** – FF46 891
  «San Francisco Convention» Silver print
  (32x43cm 12x17in) New-York 2001

FRANK Siegfried 1909 **[4]**
- $3 592 – €3 171 – **£2 165** – FF20 802
  Beachscene in Katwijk Oil/canvas/panel (18x40cm
  7x15in) Amsterdam 1998

FRANK-BOGGS 1855-1926 **[570]**
- $6 865 – €7 622 – **£4 785** – FF50 000
  La Seine à Paris Huile/toile (54.5x65cm 21x25in)
  Paris 2001
- $3 250 – €3 031 – **£2 016** – FF19 881
  Portrait Sketch of a Woman Oil/panel (27.5x21cm
  10x8in) New-York 1999
- $923 – €991 – **£617** – FF6 500
  Trouville, barque de pêche à marée basse
  Aquarelle/papier (26x39cm 10x15in) Cannes 2000

FRANK-KRAUSS Robert 1893-1950 **[65]**
- $772 – €767 – **£482** – FF5 030
  Dachauer Bäuerin Oil/panel (21x16cm 8x6in)
  München 1999

FRANK-WILL 1900-1950 **[864]**
- $2 457 – €2 744 – **£1 665** – FF18 000
  Les grands boulevards,la Porte St Denis
  Huile/toile (66x81cm 25x31in) Nîmes 2000
- $3 290 – €2 897 – **£2 004** – FF19 000
  Voilier Huile/toile (33x41cm 12x16in) Vernon 1999
- $1 602 – €1 906 – **£1 142** – FF12 500
  St Germain de Près Aquarelle/papier (24x33cm
  9x12in) Cherbourg 2000

FRANKE Albert Julius 1860-1924 **[31]**
- $857 – €1 022 – **£611** – FF6 707
  Der Kunstkenner Oil/panel (15.7x21cm 6x8in) Köln
  2000

FRANKE Hanny, Joh. Emil 1890-1973 **[45]**
- $867 – €971 – **£597** – FF6 372
  Alter Weg Seckbach Oil/panel (44x55cm 17x21in)
  Frankfurt 2000
- $912 – €1 022 – **£629** – FF6 707
  Milseburg in der Rhön Öl/Leinwand (19x24.5cm
  7x9in) Frankfurt 2000
- $695 – €665 – **£423** – FF4 360
  Blick über den Main auf den Frankfurter Dom
  Aquarell/Papier (16x21cm 6x8in) Stuttgart 1999

FRANKE Johann Heinrich Chr. 1738-1792 **[2]**
- $21 043 – €24 542 – **£14 812** – FF160 987
  **Friedrich II, Kniestück mit Dreispitz und umhän-
  gendem Stock** Öl/Leinwand (86x70cm 33x27in)
  Königstein 2001

FRÄNKEL Clemens 1872-1944 **[53]**
$456 - €511 - **£317** - FF3 353
«Abend bei Farchant mit Dreitorspitze»
Öl/Leinwand (60x80cm 23x31in) Oersberg-bei Kappeln
2001

FRANKEN Franz 1856-1913 **[1]**
$7 105 - €7 445 - **£4 500** - FF48 838
Oriental Travellers Oil/canvas (107x90cm 42x35in)
London 2000

FRANKEN Paul 1921 **[5]**
$13 140 - €12 271 - **£8 109** - FF80 493
Kaukasische Kandschaft (Kasabek) Öl/Leinwand
(106x190cm 41x74in) Köln 1999

FRANKEN von Paul 1818-1884 **[10]**
$21 028 - €20 348 - **£12 964** - FF133 476
Kaukasische Landschaft Öl/Leinwand (106x190cm
41x74in) Wien 1999

FRANKENTHALER Helen 1928 **[326]**
$60 000 - €68 237 - **£41 922** - FF447 606
Skybanner Acrylic/canvas (178x73.5cm 70x28in)
Beverly-Hills CA 2000
$31 000 - €35 969 - **£21 402** - FF235 941
Ice Flow Oil/canvas (51x96.5cm 20x37in) New-York
2000
$10 500 - €9 540 - **£6 509** - FF62 576
Untitled Acrylic/canvas (16.5x51.5cm 6x20in) New-
York 1999
$4 038 - €4 747 - **£2 800** - FF31 136
Untitled Gouache (21x28cm 8x11in) London 2000
$3 500 - €3 988 - **£2 418** - FF26 157
Orange Downpour Pochoir (75.5x55cm 29x21in)
Beverly-Hills CA 2000

FRANKFORT Eduard 1864-1920 **[19]**
$4 696 - €5 445 - **£3 327** - FF35 719
De Haundwassing Oil/canvas (46x37cm 18x14in)
Amsterdam 2000
$8 000 - €9 077 - **£5 599** - FF59 541
Interior of the Portugese Synagogue,
Amsterdam Watercolour/paper (34x48cm 13x18in)
Tel Aviv 2001

FRANKL Franz 1881-1940 **[49]**
$389 - €460 - **£276** - FF3 018
Sommernachmittag an der Amper Öl/Leinwand
(64x75cm 25x29in) Konstanz 2000

FRANKL Gerhard 1901-1965 **[32]**
$19 297 - €16 708 - **£11 707** - FF109 595
Stilleben Öl/Leinwand (53.5x65.5cm 21x25in) Wien
1998
$3 055 - €3 634 - **£2 180** - FF23 835
Blumenstrauss Watercolour, gouache (45x33.3cm
17x13in) Wien 2000

FRANKLIN George 1898-? **[1]**
$3 500 - €3 980 - **£2 427** - FF26 110
Untitled Oil/canvas (50x30cm 20x12in) Chicago IL
2000

FRANQUELIN Jean Augustin 1798-1839 **[20]**
$13 000 - €14 290 - **£8 330** - FF93 735
Mother and Child Oil/canvas (55.5x46cm 21x18in)
New-York 2000
$6 274 - €6 126 - **£4 000** - FF40 184
Sleeping Child Black & white chalks (11x19.5cm
4x7in) London 1999

FRANQUIN André 1924-1997 **[91]**
$1 597 - €1 859 - **£1 125** - FF12 195
Idées noires, Bonzai, ébauche préparatoire
Dessin (20x30cm 7x11in) Bruxelles 2001

$368 - €335 - **£230** - FF2 200
Babel Oued Sérigraphie (75x55cm 29x21in) Paris
1999

FRANQUINET Eugene 1875-1940 **[9]**
$750 - €875 - **£522** - FF5 739
«Crags Black Rock-looking North from Cliff
Creek Canyon» Oil/masonite (30x40cm 12x16in)
Altadena CA 2000

FRANS Paul 1958 **[22]**
$1 156 - €1 296 - **£804** - FF8 500
Promenade sur la plage Huile/toile (40x40cm
15x15in) Le Touquet 2001

FRANSE Kees 1924-1982 **[6]**
$858 - €797 - **£523** - FF5 228
Stilleven met groene fles Oil/canvas (82x87cm
32x34in) Amsterdam 1998

FRANSELLA Graham 1950 **[6]**
$4 409 - €4 945 - **£3 061** - FF32 434
«Self Portrait» Acrylic (213x153.5cm 83x60in)
Melbourne 2001
$3 430 - €3 683 - **£2 296** - FF24 157
Figure in a Desert Oil/canvas (122x91.5cm 48x36in)
Melbourne 2000

FRANSIOLI Thomas Adrian 1906-1997 **[5]**
$6 500 - €7 283 - **£4 526** - FF47 772
View of Castine, Maine Mixed media/paper
(49x59cm 19x23in) Watertown MA 2001

FRANSSON Bengt 1935 **[9]**
$750 - €846 - **£525** - FF5 549
Tidig vintermorgon (Stockholmsmotiv) Oil/can-
vas (60x73cm 23x28in) Stockholm 2001

FRANTA Hans 1893-1982 **[15]**
$672 - €654 - **£414** - FF4 392
Wassersteg Linz Pastell/Papier (37x28cm 14x11in)
Linz 1999

FRANTZ F. XIX **[8]**
$1 537 - €1 524 - **£956** - FF10 000
Venise Aquarelle/papier (13x20cm 5x7in) Paris 1999

FRANZ (Franz Drappier) 1948 **[18]**
$136 - €152 - **£94** - FF1 000
Le roi des singes, pl.45, de Poupée d'ivoire,
tome 5 Encre Chine/papier (48x38cm 18x14in) Paris
2001

FRANZ Ettore Roesler 1845-1907 **[99]**
$4 250 - €4 739 - **£2 857** - FF31 086
Villa Tivoli Watercolour/paper (76x38cm 30x15in) San
Rafael CA 2000

FRANZEN John Erik 1942 **[82]**
$1 535 - €1 442 - **£925** - FF9 461
Utan titel Oil/canvas (100x84cm 39x33in) Stockholm
1999
$415 - €393 - **£258** - FF2 579
Trä och duk Akvarell/papper (56x69cm 22x27in)
Stockholm 1999
$246 - €264 - **£164** - FF1 732
Low Rider Color lithograph (55x55cm 21x21in)
Stockholm 2000

FRAPPA José 1854-1904 **[42]**
$6 416 - €6 466 - **£4 000** - FF42 414
On the Way to the Ball Oil/canvas (117.5x82cm
46x32in) London 2000
$2 330 - €2 556 - **£1 583** - FF16 769
Ein unerwarteter Mitleser Oil/panel (40.5x28.5cm
15x11in) Düsseldorf 2000

FRASCHETTI Giuseppe 1879-1956 **[7]**
- **$1 320** - €1 710 - **£990** - FF11 220
  La battitura del grano Olio/tavola (38x51.5cm 14x20in) Prato 2000

FRASCONI Antonio 1919 **[34]**
- **$600** - €694 - **£424** - FF4 553
  Brooklyn Bridge II Woodcut in colors (32.5x23.5cm 12x9in) New-York 2000

FRASER Alexander XIX-XX **[13]**
- **$1 980** - €2 219 - **£1 376** - FF14 555
  Boating on a River Oil/panel (28x43cm 11x16in) Johannesburg 2001

FRASER Alexander, Jnr. 1828-1899 **[71]**
- **$2 639** - €2 845 - **£1 800** - FF18 659
  On Loch Falloch Oil/canvas (40.5x61.5cm 15x24in) London 2001
- **$1 364** - €1 146 - **£800** - FF7 518
  Hauling in the Boat Oil/canvas (28x48.5cm 11x19in) Billingshurst, West-Sussex 1998
- **$285** - €269 - **£180** - FF1 767
  A Landscape with Ducks and a Farmhouse beyond Watercolour/paper (35.5x53.5cm 13x21in) Godalming, Surrey 1999

FRASER Alexander, Snr. 1786-1865 **[22]**
- **$7 500** - €6 348 - **£4 489** - FF41 643
  The Poultry Buyer Oil/canvas (63.5x76cm 25x29in) New-York 1998

FRASER Arthur Anderson 1861-1904 **[47]**
- **$724** - €703 - **£460** - FF4 614
  The River Ouse at Newton Blossomville, near Olney, Bucks Watercolour/paper (38x28cm 14x11in) London 1999

FRASER Charles 1782-1860 **[7]**
- **$3 000** - €3 407 - **£2 105** - FF22 351
  Two Young Girls in Antebellum southern Dress Miniature (8x10cm 3x4in) Philadelphia PA 2001

FRASER Charles Gordon XIX **[6]**
- **$3 623** - €3 803 - **£2 400** - FF24 944
  Maidenhood Oil/canvas (73x50cm 29x20in) Par, Cornwall 2000

FRASER Claude Lovat 1890-1921 **[37]**
- **$837** - €722 - **£500** - FF4 739
  At the Theatre Watercolour/paper (31.5x20.5cm 12x8in) London 1998

FRASER Donald Hamilton 1929 **[141]**
- **$4 956** - €4 309 - **£3 000** - FF28 267
  Landscape II Rond Point Oil/canvas (76x76cm 29x29in) London 1999
- **$318** - €307 - **£197** - FF2 014
  Beach Landscape Oil/board (17.5x26.5cm 6x10in) Sydney 1999
- **$1 062** - €978 - **£650** - FF6 414
  Toy Pig with Musician Watercolour (28x21.5cm 11x8in) London 1998
- **$156** - €182 - **£110** - FF1 192
  Toy Hussar Screenprint (43x56cm 16x22in) London 2001

FRASER Frederick Gordon XIX-XX **[62]**
- **$188** - €203 - **£130** - FF1 332
  Norfolk Broads Watercolour/paper (23x51cm 9x20in) Edinburgh 2001

FRASER Garden William 1856-1921 **[83]**
- **$4 154** - €4 235 - **£2 600** - FF27 778
  Hemingford Grey Mill Hunts Watercolour/paper (26.5x38cm 10x14in) London 2000

FRASER George Gordon 1854-1895 **[20]**
- **$9 972** - €11 594 - **£7 000** - FF76 050
  Maidenhood Oil/canvas (76x56cm 29x22in) London 2001
- **$484** - €455 - **£300** - FF2 982
  Beached Fishing Vessels at Low Tide Watercolour (17x24cm 6x9in) London 1999

FRASER James Earle 1876-1953 **[29]**
- **$250 000** - €213 634 - **£146 850** - FF1 401 350
  «End of the Trail» Bronze (H113cm H44in) Boston MA 1998
- **$1 300** - €1 333 - **£812** - FF8 745
  The Roosevelt Bas-relief Bronze (32x25cm 12x10in) Bolton MA 2000

FRASER John 1858-1927 **[39]**
- **$12 073** - €12 959 - **£8 200** - FF85 004
  Ocean Surf Oil/canvas (97x168cm 38x66in) London 1998
- **$1 682** - €1 431 - **£1 003** - FF9 388
  Meereswogen Öl/Leinwand (62x90cm 24x35in) München 1998
- **$1 306** - €1 471 - **£900** - FF9 651
  Santa Cruz harbour, Tenerife Oil/board (25x35cm 9x13in) London 2000
- **$2 827** - €2 658 - **£1 750** - FF17 438
  The Frigate Amphion off Spithead Watercolour (39x63cm 15x24in) London 1999

FRASER John Arthur 1838-1898 **[21]**
- **$584** - €661 - **£411** - FF4 333
  Boating on the River Gouache/paper (19x32cm 7x12in) Vancouver, BC. 2001

FRASER John Simpson c.1840-c.1900 **[8]**
- **$1 635** - €1 605 - **£1 013** - FF10 529
  The Evening Paper Watercolour/paper (45x30.5cm 17x12in) Toronto 1999

FRASER Robert J. Winchester 1872-1930 **[83]**
- **$663** - €693 - **£420** - FF4 544
  Figures in the Watermeadows Watercolour (38x55cm 14x21in) London 2000

FRASER Robert Winchester 1848-1906 **[97]**
- **$664** - €763 - **£460** - FF5 007
  The River Thames at Cookham Watercolour/paper (23x43cm 9x17in) Bristol, Avon 2000

FRASER Thomas Douglass 1883-1955 **[4]**
- **$5 000** - €5 367 - **£3 346** - FF35 205
  Carmel Oil/canvas (45.5x66cm 17x25in) San-Francisco CA 2000

FRASSEK Klaus XX **[2]**
- **$17 217** - €14 142 - **£10 000** - FF92 764
  The Empress Oil/board (148.5x148.5cm 58x58in) London 1998

FRATER William Jock 1890-1974 **[100]**
- **$978** - €920 - **£590** - FF6 032
  View of the Hills Oil/canvas/board (52x62cm 20x24in) Sydney 1999
- **$2 900** - €3 240 - **£1 857** - FF21 251
  Landscape with Gum Trees Oil/canvas (30.5x41cm 12x16in) Malvern, Victoria 2000

FRATIN Christophe 1800-1864 **[322]**
- **$1 855** - €1 982 - **£1 261** - FF13 000
  Singe portant une botte Bronze (18x8.5x14.5cm 7x3x5in) Pontoise 2001

FRATINI Renato XX **[7]**
- **$2 272** - €2 622 - **£1 600** - FF17 201
  «From Russia with Love» Poster (76x101.5cm 29x39in) London 2000

FRATTA Domenico Maria 1696-1763 **[13]**
$1 615 - €1 841 - £1 126 - FF12 074
  Die Zauberin Kirke (La Maga Circe), nach Donato Creti Radierung (28.5x22cm 11x8in) Berlin 2001

FRAU José 1898-1976 **[55]**
$4 160 - €4 805 - £2 880 - FF31 520
  Brisa de oro Oleo/lienzo (73x91.5cm 28x36in) Madrid 2000
$1 950 - €1 952 - £1 202 - FF12 805
  El arbol Oleo/tabla (25x26cm 9x10in) Madrid 2000
$672 - €721 - £456 - FF4 728
  Paisaje Acuarela/papel (32x46cm 12x18in) Madrid 2000

FRAUENDORFER-MÜHLTHALER von Helene XIX-XX **[6]**
$2 069 - €2 045 - £1 266 - FF13 415
  Portrait eines jungen adligen Dame Pastell/Papier (133x66cm 52x25in) Kempten 2000

FRAUENFELDER Hendrik 1885-1922 **[12]**
$1 724 - €1 906 - £1 196 - FF12 501
  Fishermen at Work Oil/canvas (60x73.5cm 23x28in) Amsterdam 2001

FRAYE André 1887-1963 **[41]**
$690 - €640 - £429 - FF4 200
  Port de Noirmoutier Huile/toile (60x73cm 23x28in) Paris 1999

FRAZER William Miller 1864-1961 **[177]**
$3 111 - €3 469 - £2 140 - FF22 757
  At Full Sail, Machrahanish Bay Oil/canvas (49.5x59.5cm 19x23in) Edinburgh 2000
$2 835 - €2 699 - £1 800 - FF17 707
  Fishing Smack off the Coast Oil/canvas/board (24x34.5cm 9x13in) Billingshurst, West-Sussex 1999

FRAZETTA Frank 1928 **[25]**
$11 000 - €10 612 - £6 952 - FF69 608
  «The Silver Warriors» Mixed media/paper (23x16cm 9x6in) New-York 1999

FRAZIER Luke XX **[7]**
$8 000 - €7 272 - £4 818 - FF47 704
  End of a Lagacy Oil/board (60x121cm 24x48in) Hayden ID 1999

FRECHKOP Leonid 1897-1982 **[131]**
$486 - €471 - £300 - FF3 089
  Frère et soeur Huile/toile (64x54cm 25x21in) Bruxelles 1999

FRÉCHON Charles 1856-1929 **[51]**
$12 468 - €13 339 - £8 216 - FF87 500
  Pommiers en fleur Huile/toile (38x55cm 14x21in) Rouen 2000
$2 822 - €3 049 - £1 954 - FF20 000
  Jeune femme près d'une charette Huile/toile (17x26cm 6x10in) Rouen 2001

FRÉCHON Émile 1848-1921 **[10]**
$435 - €488 - £295 - FF3 300
  Appel du Muezzin et musulmans en prière Photo (20x28cm 7x11in) Paris 2000

FRECKLETON Harold, Harry 1890-1979 **[9]**
$1 100 - €1 278 - £773 - FF8 383
  «Summer Days» Oil/canvas (60x91cm 24x36in) New-York 1999

FRED (F. Othon Aristidès) 1931 **[4]**
$591 - €534 - £364 - FF3 500
  L'Ane en Atoll, couverture Encre Chine/papier (33x25cm 12x9in) Neuilly-sur-Seine 1999

FREDDIE Vilhelm 1909-1995 **[330]**
$22 834 - €18 820 - £13 440 - FF123 452
  Mânene forlovede Oil/masonite (114x114cm 44x44in) København 1998
$5 198 - €5 239 - £3 240 - FF34 366
  Kvinde komposition på blå bund Oil/canvas (73.5x60cm 28x23in) København 2000
$4 742 - €5 095 - £3 260 - FF33 424
  Stemmen fra horisonterne Oil/wood (35x45cm 13x17in) København 2001
$504 - €563 - £337 - FF3 695
  Figurkomposition Pencil/paper (16x10cm 6x3in) København 2000
$204 - €175 - £120 - FF1 145
  Min syster Lithograph (17x20cm 6x7in) Viby J, Århus 1998

FREDENTHAL David 1914-1958 **[9]**
$2 300 - €2 616 - £1 595 - FF17 158
  Woman in Kitchen Pencil (41x31cm 16x12in) Chicago IL 2000

FREDERIC Georges 1900-1981 **[36]**
$258 - €297 - £177 - FF1 951
  La vie du moulin Oil/board (30x39cm 11x15in) Lokeren 2000
$1 326 - €1 487 - £900 - FF9 756
  Dimanche, avant la Grand-Messier Fusain/papier (96x112cm 37x44in) Bruxelles 2000

FREDERIC Léon 1856-1940 **[98]**
$1 001 - €1 067 - £634 - FF7 000
  Paysage vallonné Huile/toile/panneau (30x54cm 11x21in) Paris 2000
$800 - €767 - £503 - FF5 030
  Sommerwiese Oil/panel (27.5x43.5cm 10x17in) Köln 1999
$331 - €372 - £232 - FF2 439
  Paysage d'Ardennes Pastel/papier (12x35cm 4x13in) Maisieres-Mons 2001

FREDERICKS Charles de Forest 1823-1894 **[1]**
$3 800 - €4 179 - £2 635 - FF27 413
  Cuba Albumen print (16x20cm 6x8in) New-York 2001

FREDERICKS Ernest 1877-1927 **[58]**
$700 - €675 - £439 - FF4 430
  Fall's First Snow Oil/canvas (60x73cm 24x29in) Chicago IL 1999

FREDERICKS Marshall Maynard 1908-1998 **[44]**
$35 000 - €33 342 - £21 357 - FF218 708
  Eagle Bronze (160x111cm 63x44in) Bloomfield-Hills MI 1999
$9 500 - €9 050 - £5 796 - FF59 363
  Neck Shot Bronze (25x39cm 10x15in) Bloomfield-Hills MI 1999

FREDERICO Cavalier Michèle 1884-1966 **[16]**
$1 301 - €1 197 - £800 - FF7 850
  Waves breaking along the Coast, Capri Oil/canvas (68.5x89cm 26x35in) London 1998

FRÉDOU Jean Martial 1711-1795 **[17]**
$2 414 - €2 592 - £1 615 - FF17 000
  Portrait présumé de Monsieur et Madame de Foresta Pastel/papier (30x24.5cm 11x9in) Paris 2000

FREDRIKS Jan Hendrik 1751-1817 **[7]**
$136 455 - €149 747 - £87 846 - FF982 278
  Melons, Grapes, Lemon Peaches, Plums, Cherries, White Currants Oil/panel (76x59cm 29x23in) Amsterdam 2000

FREDSBERG Olof 1725-1795 **[2]**
$22 195 - €25 628 - **£15 525** - FF168 107
En väldig pumpa Oil/canvas (89x104cm 35x40in)
Stockholm 2001

FREEBAIRN Robert 1765-1808 **[14]**
$6 416 - €6 466 - **£4 000** - FF42 414
Italianate Landscape with a View of a Lake
Oil/canvas (85.5x126.5cm 33x49in) London 2000

FREED Leonard 1929 **[22]**
$1 486 - €1 470 - **£926** - FF9 642
Martin Luther King Vintage gelatin silver print
(25.8x36.7cm 10x14in) Berlin 1999

FREEDMAN Barnett 1901-1958 **[17]**
$652 - €752 - **£450** - FF4 930
**«Everywhere you Go you Can be Sure of Shell,
Swaledale, Yorkshire»** Poster (76x114cm 29x44in)
London 2000

FREEMAN Don 1908-1978 **[69]**
$3 000 - €2 569 - **£1 771** - FF16 854
Relief Line Oil/canvas (48.5x61.5cm 19x24in) New-
York 1998
$300 - €280 - **£185** - FF1 834
Deep in Hollywood Lithograph (23x30cm 9x12in)
Cleveland OH 1999

FREEMAN Mark 1909 **[40]**
$950 - €1 064 - **£662** - FF6 978
«Second Avenue El» Lithograph (26x36.5cm
10x14in) New-York 2001

FREEMAN Richard A. 1932-1991 **[36]**
$1 238 - €1 437 - **£855** - FF9 426
Easy Does It Oil/canvas (76x122cm 29x48in)
Vancouver, BC. 2000

FREEMAN Will. Philip Barnes 1813-1897 **[26]**
$317 - €303 - **£200** - FF1 990
Wooded River Landscape Oil/canvas (33x43cm
13x17in) Aylsham, Norfolk 1999

FREER Henry Branston XIX-XX **[18]**
$453 - €532 - **£320** - FF3 490
Looking up the Cat Water, Plymouth
Watercolour/paper (17.5x34cm 6x13in) London 2000

FREGEVIZE Frédéric 1770-1849 **[11]**
$11 526 - €12 963 - **£8 046** - FF85 030
**Fest auf dem Lande bei Genf mit Blick auf den
Montblanc** Öl/Leinwand (41x52cm 16x20in) Luzern
2001
$11 392 - €9 908 - **£6 867** - FF64 990
«Ansicht des Mont-blanc und der Stadt Genf»
Radierung (36x53cm 14x20in) Bern 1998

FREIESLEBEN Ernst ?-1883 **[1]**
$4 187 - €3 835 - **£2 552** - FF25 154
**Zwei Kinder am Fenster des alten
Bauernhauses** Öl/Leinwand (81x64cm 31x25in)
München 1999

FREILICHER Jane 1924 **[7]**
$14 000 - €12 450 - **£8 562** - FF81 666
Studio Interior Oil/canvas (127x152.5cm 50x60in)
New-York 1999

FREIMAN Lillian 1908-1986 **[28]**
$319 - €375 - **£227** - FF2 463
Breton girl Coloured chalks/paper (31x25cm 12x9in)
Toronto 2000

FREIRE Carlos 1945 **[5]**
$1 084 - €1 220 - **£756** - FF8 000
«Andy Warhol, Paris» Tirage argentique (45x30cm
17x11in) Paris 2001

FREIST Greta 1904-1993 **[83]**
$751 - €872 - **£528** - FF5 720
«Chez soi» Öl/Leinwand (100x100cm 39x39in)
Salzburg 2001
$9 295 - €9 909 - **£5 889** - FF65 000
Autoportrait au chapeau Huile/toile (41x27cm
16x10in) Bayeux 2000
$327 - €363 - **£228** - FF2 383
Die Auferstehung Pencil (41x30cm 16x11in)
Salzburg 2001

FREIXAS ARANGUREN Emilio 1899-1976 **[32]**
$161 - €156 - **£101** - FF1 024
Joven con antifaz Gouache/papier (31x23cm 12x9in)
Madrid 1999

FREIXAS VIVO Amadeo 1912 **[12]**
$1 372 - €1 351 - **£855** - FF8 865
Animación en la medina Oleo/lienzo (60x73cm
23x28in) Madrid 1999

FRÉLAUT Jean 1879-1954 **[264]**
$261 - €244 - **£161** - FF1 600
Le port de Molène Crayon (24x16cm 9x6in) Brest
1999
$130 - €122 - **£80** - FF800
Chaumière dans les arbres, carte de voeux Eau-
forte (9x13cm 3x5in) Brest 1999

FRELINGHUYSEN Suzy 1912-1988 **[1]**
$32 000 - €37 335 - **£22 272** - FF244 902
Untitled Oil/canvas/board (30.5x30.5cm 12x12in)
New-York 2000

FRÉMIET Emmanuel 1824-1910 **[601]**
$24 225 - €27 136 - **£16 856** - FF178 000
Le porte-falot Bronze (184x107cm 72x42in) Soissons
2001
$2 137 - €2 428 - **£1 500** - FF15 926
**Credo, a Knight Holding an Open Scroll Across
his Chest** Bronze (H41cm H16in) Billingshurst, West-
Sussex 2001
$613 - €3 506 - **£2 277** - FF23 000
**Portrait d'E.Fauré à 3 ans, à demi monté sur un
cheval tirant un canon** Crayon (26.5x36.5cm
10x14in) Paris 1999

FREMINET Martin 1567-1619 **[4]**
$78 425 - €76 575 - **£50 000** - FF502 300
**Annunciation, with God the Father flanked by
four allegorical Figures** Black chalk (19.5x29cm
7x11in) London 1999

FREMOND André 1884-1965 **[98]**
$182 - €168 - **£109** - FF1 100
Aspects de ciels Huile/panneau (14x18cm 5x7in) Le
Havre 1999
$149 - €137 - **£89** - FF900
«Exposition A.Fremond» Fusain/papier (65x48cm
25x18in) Le Havre 1999

FREMUND Richard 1928-1969 **[9]**
$1 387 - €1 312 - **£864** - FF8 606
Vue sur Troju Huile/carton (70x86cm 27x33in) Praha
2000

FRÉMY Jacques Noël M. 1782-1867 **[5]**
$9 000 - €7 921 - **£5 479** - FF51 959
**Napoleon Crowning Josephine, after Jacques-
Louis David** Oil/canvas (25x35cm 9x13in) New-York
1999

FRÉMY Zoé XIX **[1]**
$7 000 - €6 527 - **£4 342** - FF42 815
Portrait of a Lady Oil/canvas (52.7x35.6cm 20x14in)
New-York 1999

FRENCH Annie 1872-1965 [98]

$2 175 - €2 044 - **£1 350** - FF13 408
Two Girls reading/Tending the Flowers Mixed media (10x12.5cm 3x4in) London 1999

$1 085 - €971 - **£650** - FF6 370
«Is any Wife so Sweet as You?» Watercolour (21.5x13.5cm 8x5in) Perthshire 1998

FRENCH Daniel Chester 1850-1931 [10]

$6 500 - €6 061 - **£4 031** - FF39 757
Seated Female Figure Bronze (H25.5cm H10in) New-York 1999

FRENCH Leonard William 1928 [82]

$11 675 - €13 077 - **£8 111** - FF85 782
«Rainbow Dragonfly» Enamel (136.5x121cm 53x47in) Melbourne 2001

$8 923 - €10 471 - **£6 296** - FF68 688
Scroll of the Turtle Enamel (90x74.5cm 35x29in) Melbourne 2000

$833 - €972 - **£580** - FF6 378
«Corpse Street 1, 1968» Enamel (35.5x29.5cm 13x11in) Melbourne 2000

$4 132 - €4 021 - **£2 543** - FF26 375
Screaming Head 3 (Study) Watercolour (35x31cm 13x12in) Melbourne 1999

$175 - €193 - **£116** - FF1 265
Boris Gudonov Serigraph in colors (67x50.5cm 26x19in) Melbourne 2000

FRENCH Percy 1854-1920 [161]

$4 313 - €5 079 - **£3 031** - FF33 316
Out Fishing at Kylemore Abbey Watercolour/paper (16.5x21.5cm 6x8in) Dublin 2000

FRENCH, 2nd Earl of Ypres Richard XX [3]

$1 813 - €2 132 - **£1 300** - FF13 986
H.M. The King's Guard, Whitehall Watercolour/paper (26.5x36.5cm 10x14in) London 2001

FRENET Jean-Baptiste, Jean 1814-1889 [76]

$3 231 - €3 277 - **£1 959** - FF21 000
Portraits et scènes diverses Photo (24x18cm 9x7in) Paris 2000

FRENKEL Yitzhak 1899-1981 [95]

$1 500 - €1 555 - **£988** - FF10 201
Zafed the Town of the Kabballa Oil/canvas (46x55cm 18x21in) Herzelia-Pituah 2000

$550 - €584 - **£372** - FF3 832
Woman on a Red Couch Oil/canvas (23x18cm 9x7in) Tel Aviv 2001

$500 - €488 - **£316** - FF3 201
In the Synagogue Gouache/paper (20x13cm 7x5in) Tel Aviv 1999

FRENNET Lucien 1888-? [27]

$506 - €545 - **£349** - FF3 577
Bateaux de pêche près du quai Huile/toile (60x75cm 23x29in) Antwerpen 2001

FRENZEL Oskar 1855-1915 [13]

$983 - €1 125 - **£683** - FF7 378
Landschaft mit Kühen und Bauer Öl/Leinwand (75x99cm 29x38in) Rudolstadt-Thüringen 2000

FRENZENY Paul 1840-1902 [2]

$6 500 - €6 251 - **£4 011** - FF41 003
«The Scout Buffalo Bill» Poster (107x74cm 42x29in) Bern 1999

FREQUENEZ Paul Léon 1876-1943 [14]

$12 000 - €14 112 - **£8 604** - FF92 566
Parc de St.Cloud in the Snow Oil/canvas (154.5x200.5cm 60x78in) New-York 2001

FRERE Ch. Théodore, Bey 1814-1888 [252]

$24 911 - €28 681 - **£17 000** - FF188 137
Ruines de Palmyre Oil/canvas (98x169cm 38x66in) London 2000

$28 479 - €27 475 - **£18 000** - FF180 225
A Game of Chequers Oil/canvas (91.5x73.5cm 36x28in) London 1999

$7 144 - €6 098 - **£4 272** - FF40 000
Marchands de chameaux en Haute-Égypte Huile/panneau (17.5x35cm 6x13in) Paris 1998

$1 822 - €1 982 - **£1 201** - FF13 000
Barques sur le Nil Aquarelle/papier (34.5x24.5cm 13x9in) Paris 2000

FRERE Charles Édouard 1837-1894 [35]

$1 350 - €1 143 - **£811** - FF7 500
La forge Huile/panneau (33x46cm 12x18in) Paris 1998

FRERE Pierre Édouard 1819-1886 [57]

$16 206 - €15 103 - **£10 000** - FF99 068
Worn through Oil/panel (46x37.5cm 18x14in) London 1999

$11 000 - €10 035 - **£6 760** - FF65 828
Interior Scene with Child Warming a Stove Side Oil/board (28x23cm 11x9in) Bloomfield-Hills MI 1998

FRERICHS Wilhelm Charles Ant. 1829-1905 [27]

$5 250 - €6 123 - **£3 686** - FF40 164
Winter Landscape with Bear Oil/canvas/board (35x55cm 14x22in) Portsmouth NH 2000

FRESQUET ALMURIN Pasqual 1930 [67]

$168 - €144 - **£100** - FF945
«Cadaqués» Oleo/lienzo (54x65cm 21x25in) Barcelona 1999

FRESQUET Guillem 1914-1991 [32]

$238 - €204 - **£142** - FF1 339
Masía en Olot, Gerona Acuarela/papel (25x36cm 9x14in) Madrid 1998

FREUD Lucian 1922 [139]

$2 200 000 - €2 128 673 - **£1 356 740** - FF13 963 180
Evening in the Studio Oil/canvas (200x168.5cm 78x66in) New-York 1999

$600 000 - €517 653 - **£360 600** - FF3 395 580
Naked Man on a Bed Oil/canvas (81x71cm 31x27in) New-York 1998

$358 632 - €384 962 - **£240 000** - FF2 525 184
Filly Oil/canvas (19x26.5cm 7x10in) London 2000

$22 113 - €18 574 - **£13 000** - FF121 837
«Ib» Pastel (23x33.5cm 9x13in) London 1998

$6 562 - €6 010 - **£4 000** - FF39 422
Head of Bruce Bernard Etching (29.5x29.5cm 11x11in) London 1999

FREUDENBERG Jacobus 1818-1873 [5]

$3 326 - €3 323 - **£2 080** - FF21 800
Winterliches Eisvergnügen mit Windmühle, Kirche, malerischen Häusern Oil/panel (31.5x41cm 12x16in) Lindau 1999

FREUDENBERGER Sigismond 1745-1801 [85]

$2 390 - €2 566 - **£1 600** - FF16 834
Musical Diversion Ink (15x10.5cm 5x4in) London 2000

$556 - €656 - **£383** - FF4 302
Le retour des champs/La balanceuse Aquatinta (19x14.5cm 7x5in) Bern 2000

FREUDENTHAL Peter 1938 [59]

$794 - €881 - **£550** - FF5 776
Square and Rectangle for PRIAB Oil/canvas (130x90cm 51x35in) Stockholm 2001

F

📖 $264 - €305 - £182 - FF1 999
Komposition Color lithograph (77.5x47.5cm 30x18in)
Stockholm 2000

FREUDWEILER Heinrich 1755-1795 **[6]**
💰 $15 133 - €17 881 - £10 724 - FF117 290
Das Blindekuhspiel Öl/Leinwand (47x57cm
18x22in) Zürich 2000
🖼 $3 962 - €4 597 - £2 735 - FF30 154
**Erinnerungsbild auf die im Kindbett gestorbene
Katharina Wüest-Hirzel** Oil/panel (36x26.5cm
14x10in) Luzern 2000

FREUND Fritz 1859-1942 **[9]**
🖼 $4 654 - €4 857 - £2 945 - FF31 862
Vier Skifahrer im Hochgebirge Öl/Leinwand
(53x44cm 20x17in) München 2000

FREUND Gisèle 1912-2000 **[126]**
📷 $925 - €1 036 - £642 - FF6 797
**André Gide sous le masque de Léopardi chez
lui, rue Vaneau, Paris** Tirage argentique (16x11cm
6x4in) Genève 2001

FREUNDLICH Otto 1878-1943 **[43]**
🖼 $9 780 - €9 147 - £5 994 - FF60 000
Forme et couleur Technique mixte (35x25.5cm
13x10in) Paris 1998
🖼 $10 460 - €12 302 - £7 500 - FF80 694
Composition Gouache/paper (22.5x19cm 8x7in)
London 2001
📖 $696 - €665 - £435 - FF4 360
Komposition Linocut (20.5x12.6cm 8x4in) Köln 1999

FREY Alice 1895-1981 **[97]**
🖼 $1 332 - €1 487 - £924 - FF9 756
Danseurs Huile/toile (70x80cm 27x31in) Antwerpen
2001
🖼 $408 - €397 - £249 - FF2 601
Danseurs Huile/panneau (18x14cm 7x5in) Bruxelles
1999
🖼 $484 - €446 - £291 - FF2 926
Couple dansant Technique mixte/papier (30x25cm
11x9in) Antwerpen 1999

FREY Eleonore 1927-1975 **[4]**
🖼 $1 545 - €1 277 - £906 - FF8 378
«Negerin» Öl/Karton (100x85cm 39x33in) Radolfzell
1998

FREY Johann Jakob 1813-1865 **[39]**
🖼 $5 155 - €5 368 - £3 266 - FF35 215
**Die Bucht von Pozzuoli mit Blick auf das
Städtchen und Insel Nisida** Öl/Leinwand (36x54cm
14x21in) München 2000
🖼 $1 957 - €2 102 - £1 310 - FF13 786
Sonnenbeschienene Gewitterwolken
Öl/Leinwand (29x44cm 11x17in) Zürich 2000

FREY Johann Wilhelm 1830-1909 **[26]**
🖼 $1 316 - €1 450 - £912 - FF9 534
Der Ratzenstadl in Wien Aquarell/Papier
(20.5x28cm 8x11in) Wien 2001

FREY Joseph 1892-1977 **[16]**
🖼 $1 600 - €1 428 - £979 - FF9 369
High Desert and Mountains Oil/canvas (63x76cm
25x30in) Altadena CA 1999

FREY Ludwig 1953 **[87]**
🖼 $285 - €307 - £191 - FF2 012
Landschaft bei Kempten mit Grünten Oil/panel
(14.5x29.5cm 5x11in) Kempten 2000

FREY Max 1902-1955 **[4]**
🖼 $2 097 - €2 020 - £1 305 - FF13 249
Stimmen des Frühlingd, forårets stemmer
Oil/canvas (71x71cm 27x27in) Köbenhavn 1999

FREY Oskar 1883-1966 **[48]**
🖼 $417 - €358 - £251 - FF2 347
Papageien auf der Kletterstange Öl/Karton
(51x40cm 20x15in) Stuttgart 1998

FREY Viola 1933 **[12]**
🖼 $12 000 - €13 942 - £8 433 - FF91 454
The Feeding and Petting of a Poodle Poopy
Glazed ceramic (147x48x48cm 57x18x18in) New-York
2001
🖼 $20 000 - €20 719 - £12 730 - FF135 906
Circular Bench II: the Decline and Fall Glazed
ceramic (45.5x175.5x225cm 17x69x88in) New-York
2000

FREY Wilhelm 1826-1911 **[26]**
🖼 $2 782 - €2 556 - £1 709 - FF16 769
Weidende Kuhherde an einem Flussufer
Öl/Leinwand (50x73cm 19x28in) Stuttgart 1999
🖼 $2 002 - €2 287 - £1 408 - FF15 000
Rue de Vienne animée Aquarelle, gouache/papier
(35.5x45cm 13x17in) Versailles 2001

FREY-MOOCK Adolf 1881-1954 **[115]**
🖼 $1 302 - €1 278 - £807 - FF8 384
Kampf der Centauren Öl/Leinwand (50x70cm
19x27in) München 1999
🖼 $913 - €767 - £536 - FF5 030
«Erdgeist», Mythologische Szene Öl/Karton
(27x17cm 10x6in) Köln 1998

FREY-SURBEK Jeanne Marguerite 1886-1980 **[93]**
🖼 $771 - €743 - £475 - FF4 875
Ansicht von Manhattan mit Brooklyn Bridge
Öl/Leinwand (51x76cm 20x29in) Bern 1999
🖼 $436 - €404 - £267 - FF2 652
Weg zwischen Feldern in einem Alpental
Öl/Leinwand (28.5x34.5cm 11x13in) Bern 1999

FREYBERG Conrad 1842-1915 **[7]**
🖼 $6 349 - €6 647 - £3 989 - FF43 600
**Prinz Friedrich Karl in der Schlacht von
Vionville** Öl/Leinwand (63.5x102cm 25x40in) Bremen
2000

FREYRE Rafael 1917 **[38]**
🖼 $97 - €98 - £60 - FF642
El Cordobés Acuarela/papel (23x29cm 9x11in)
México 2000

FREZZA Giovanni Girolamo 1659-1741 **[4]**
📖 $266 - €312 - £190 - FF2 048
The Adoration of the Magi, after Rubens
Engraving (44.5x36cm 19x14in) London 2000

FRIANT Émile 1863-1932 **[41]**
🖼 $1 698 - €1 448 - £1 025 - FF9 500
Jeune militaire assis et son chien Huile/panneau
(63.5x46.5cm 25x18in) Paris 1998
🖼 $510 - €488 - £318 - FF3 281
Les lutteurs Encre/papier (44.5x33cm 17x12in) Paris
1999

FRIAS Y ESCALANTE de Juan Antonio 1630-1670
[3]
🖼 $19 950 - €21 023 - £12 600 - FF137 900
San Juan Bautista Oleo/lienzo (136x93cm 53x36in)
Madrid 2000
🖼 $7 000 - €5 876 - £4 105 - FF38 546
**Saint Peter Nolasco carried to the Altar by
Angels** Oil/canvas (110.5x82.5cm 43x32in) New-York
1998

FRIBERG Roj 1934 **[66]**

🖉 **$758** - €880 - **£523** - FF5 771
　　Lövverk Pencil/paper (89x94cm 35x37in) Stockholm 2000

FRIBOULET Jef E. 1919 **[230]**

😊 **$1 183** - €1 098 - **£738** - FF7 200
　　Femme de la terre Huile/toile (73x60cm 28x23in) Honfleur 1999

😊 **$322** - €274 - **£191** - FF1 800
　　Jeune fille au panier Technique mixte (40x30cm 15x11in) Paris 1998

😊 **$582** - €503 - **£351** - FF3 300
　　Les buveurs Aquarelle/papier (30x38cm 11x14in) Le Havre 1998

FRICH Joachim 1810-1858 **[15]**

😊 **$10 963** - €9 536 - **£6 609** - FF62 549
　　Hardanger Oil/canvas (28x43cm 11x16in) Oslo 1998

FRICK de Paul 1864-1935 **[40]**

😊 **$525** - €579 - **£355** - FF3 300
　　Autoportrait à la palette Huile/toile (91x45cm 35x17in) Paris 2000

FRID Ludvig 1855-1909 **[3]**

😊 **$3 998** - €4 643 - **£2 809** - FF30 458
　　Midsommardans i Dalarna Oil/canvas (66x110cm 25x43in) Stockholm 2001

FRIDELL Axel 1894-1935 **[259]**

😊 **$2 051** - €2 299 - **£1 430** - FF15 078
　　Två glas rött vin Oil/canvas (79x66cm 31x25in) Stockholm 2001

😊 **$1 887** - €2 055 - **£1 235** - FF13 479
　　Porträtt av konstnärens syster Elvira Oil/canvas (35x32cm 13x12in) Uppsala 2000

🖉 **$1 360** - €1 183 - **£820** - FF7 761
　　«Glädjeflickor» Indian ink/paper (20x26cm 7x10in) Stockholm 1998

📜 **$305** - €257 - **£180** - FF1 688
　　Maureen (An English Girl) Etching (28.8x15.6cm 11x6in) Stockholm 1998

FRIE Peter 1947 **[16]**

😊 **$2 839** - €3 165 - **£1 972** - FF20 764
　　Utan titel Oil/canvas (130x200cm 51x78in) Stockholm 2001

😊 **$4 330** - €5 054 - **£2 967** - FF33 153
　　Landskap Oil/canvas/panel (99x98cm 38x38in) Stockholm 2000

😊 **$926** - €1 081 - **£634** - FF7 093
　　Landskap Oil/paper (18x24cm 7x9in) Stockholm 2000

🖉 **$1 314** - €1 525 - **£907** - FF10 003
　　Landskap Mixed media/paper (10.5x15cm 4x5in) Stockholm 2000

FRIEBEL XIX **[2]**

😊 **$13 349** - €13 873 - **£8 372** - FF91 000
　　Paysage montagneux Huile/toile (101x137cm 39x53in) Boulogne-sur-Seine 2000

FRIED Pal 1893-1976 **[302]**

😊 **$1 575** - €1 499 - **£979** - FF9 833
　　Black Gloves Oil/canvas (76x61cm 29x24in) Toronto 1999

🖉 **$1 089** - €1 022 - **£674** - FF6 707
　　Can can Gouache (74.5x66cm 29x25in) München 1999

FRIEDBERGER Philippe 1938 **[2]**

😊 **$1 256** - €1 220 - **£776** - FF8 000
　　Passage Huile/toile (100x81cm 39x31in) Paris 1999

FRIEDENSON Arthur 1872-1955 **[37]**

😊 **$3 344** - €2 855 - **£2 000** - FF18 726
　　An Extensive Yorkshire Landscape with a Man Oil/canvas (61.5x91cm 24x35in) Leeds 1998

😊 **$933** - €1 090 - **£650** - FF7 147
　　Figure and Cart on a Hillside Lane Oil/panel (26.5x20.5cm 10x8in) West-Yorshire 2000

FRIEDENTHAL David 1914-1958 **[11]**

🖉 **$225** - €228 - **£139** - FF1 495
　　Reclining Young Boy Reading Charcoal (28x36cm 11x14in) Bloomfield-Hills MI 2000

FRIEDERICI Walter 1874-1943 **[9]**

😊 **$824** - €971 - **£579** - FF6 372
　　Pavillion im Zwinger, Dresden Öl/Leinwand (50x68cm 19x26in) Frankfurt 2000

FRIEDLAENDER Alfred von Malheim 1860-1927 **[59]**

😊 **$2 174** - €2 556 - **£1 558** - FF16 769
　　Der überfall Öl/Leinwand (39x47cm 15x18in) München 2001

😊 **$1 076** - €1 163 - **£744** - FF7 627
　　Schlachtengetümmel Öl/Leinwand (36.5x28cm 14x11in) Wien 2001

FRIEDLAENDER Camilla von Malheim 1856-1926 **[23]**

😊 **$1 549** - €1 616 - **£977** - FF10 603
　　Still Life Wildflowers Oil/panel (9.5x12.5cm 3x4in) Sydney 2000

FRIEDLAENDER Friedrich v. Malheim 1825-1901 **[53]**

😊 **$3 300** - €3 997 - **£2 398** - FF26 218
　　Vor dem Rapport Oil/panel (46x36cm 18x14in) Wien 2000

😊 **$2 251** - €2 556 - **£1 541** - FF16 769
　　Mann mit Regenschirm bei der Weinprobe Oil/panel (15x12.5cm 5x4in) München 2000

FRIEDLAENDER Hedwig von Malheim 1863-1916 **[8]**

😊 **$7 944** - €8 721 - **£5 280** - FF57 204
　　Strick Unterricht Oil/panel (36.8x26.8cm 14x10in) Wien 2000

FRIEDLAENDER Johnny 1912-1992 **[846]**

🖉 **$3 058** - €2 648 - **£1 856** - FF17 367
　　Mohn Pencil (34x30cm 13x11in) München 1998

📜 **$354** - €343 - **£218** - FF2 249
　　Trois rouges Aquatinte couleurs (52.5x41cm 20x16in) Zürich 1999

FRIEDLAENDER Julius 1810-1861 **[58]**

😊 **$1 220** - €1 210 - **£763** - FF7 937
　　Parti fra en italiensk kystby Oil/canvas (32x28cm 12x11in) Köbenhavn 1999

FRIEDLANDER Isac 1890-1968 **[62]**

📜 **$800** - €908 - **£547** - FF5 958
　　Backstage Woodcut (34.5x28cm 13x11in) New-York 2000

FRIEDLANDER Lee 1934 **[86]**

📷 **$3 200** - €3 327 - **£2 020** - FF21 826
　　San Diego, California Gelatin silver print (19x28cm 7x11in) New-York 2000

FRIEDLINGER Jeno 1890-? **[9]**

😊 **$872** - €936 - **£583** - FF6 141
　　Parlour Interior Oil/canvas (59.5x81cm 23x31in) Toronto 2000

FRIEDMAN Arnold Aaron 1879-1946 **[20]**

🐟 **$20 000** – €23 342 – **£14 178** – FF153 112
Parkway Oil/canvas (77x92cm 30x36in) New-York 2001

🐟 **$15 000** – €16 612 – **£10 173** – FF108 967
Fresh Mounts Oil/canvas/board (23.5x34.5cm 9x13in) New-York 2000

FRIEDMAN Tom 1965 **[12]**

🐟 **$22 000** – €24 137 – **£14 614** – FF158 329
Two by four Acrylic/wood (122x9.5x4.5cm 48x3x1in) New-York 2001

🐟 **$26 499** – €31 163 – **£19 000** – FF204 413
Curse Sculpture (133x28x28cm 52x11x11in) London 2001

🐟 **$28 000** – €31 362 – **£19 454** – FF205 721
Spider Construction (12.5x10x2.5cm 4x3xin) New-York 2001

📷 **$46 323** – €49 724 – **£31 000** – FF326 169
Untitled Photograph (89x63.5cm 35x25in) London 2000

FRIEDRICH Alexander 1895-1968 **[24]**

📜 **$131** – €123 – **£79** – FF804
Zeche Prospero II Radierung (20x34.8cm 7x13in) Berlin 1999

FRIEDRICH August J.H. 1789-1843 **[4]**

🐟 **$25 144** – €21 252 – **£15 000** – FF139 405
A Farmyard Scene, Pheasant, a Golden Eagle, after M. d'Honechoeter Oil/canvas (109.5x140.5cm 43x55in) London 1998

FRIEDRICH Carolina Friederica 1749-1815 **[5]**

🐟 **$77 658** – €71 573 – **£46 508** – FF469 490
Blumenstilleben, Auf einer Tischplatte steht ein bauchiger Glaskrug Öl/Metall (63.5x44cm 25x17in) Dresden 1999

FRIEDRICH Caspar David 1774-1840 **[22]**

🐟 **$1 158 150** – €1 081 795 – **£700 000** – FF7 096 110
Zwei Männer in Betrachtung des Mondes Oil/canvas (35x44cm 13x17in) London 1999

✏️ **$47 301** – €46 229 – **£30 000** – FF303 240
Fichtenbaum/Wäldchen Pencil/paper (27x21cm 10x8in) London 1999

FRIEDRICH WILHELM IV König von Preussen 1795-1861 **[3]**

✏️ **$1 790** – €1 533 – **£1 076** – FF10 059
Ein Schloss am Meer Ink (28.8x22cm 11x8in) Köln 1998

FRIEND Donald Stuart Leslie 1915-1989 **[595]**

🐟 **$14 247** – €13 396 – **£8 822** – FF87 872
The Kite Tempera (48x63cm 18x24in) Melbourne 1999

🐟 **$3 831** – €3 340 – **£2 316** – FF21 912
Mt Macedon Gothic Oil/board (45x35cm 17x13in) Melbourne 1998

✏️ **$2 429** – €2 336 – **£1 496** – FF15 320
Oh Doktor Mann Watercolour, gouache (63x48cm 24x18in) Melbourne 1999

📜 **$146** – €161 – **£97** – FF1 056
«...In their courtyard bird cages hang from the eaves...» Lithograph (61x48cm 24x18in) Melbourne 2000

FRIEND Washington F. c.1820-1886 **[28]**

✏️ **$1 327** – €1 171 – **£800** – FF7 684
The River Hudson from Fort Putnam Watercolour (24x32.5cm 9x12in) London 1998

FRIER Harry c.1849-1919 **[14]**

🐟 **$2 920** – €2 859 – **£1 796** – FF18 754
Kotimatkalla Oil/canvas (36x46cm 14x18in) Helsinki 1999

FRIER Walter act.1715-1743 **[4]**

🐟 **$182 026** – €211 698 – **£130 000** – FF1 388 647
Portrait of the Princess of Zanzibar with an African Attendant Oil/canvas (65x122cm 25x48in) London 2001

FRIES Bernhard 1820-1879 **[26]**

🐟 **$6 405** – €6 135 – **£4 030** – FF40 246
Blick von erhöhter Warte auf Burg Runkelstein bei Bozen im Etschtal Öl/Leinwand (97.5x130cm 38x51in) Stuttgart 1999

🐟 **$4 549** – €5 113 – **£3 194** – FF33 539
Die Rast Öl/Leinwand (70.5x93.5cm 27x36in) Düsseldorf 2001

🐟 **$1 170** – €1 329 – **£801** – FF8 720
Flusslandschaft Öl/Karton (22x30.5cm 8x12in) München 2000

FRIES Charles Arthur 1854-1940 **[37]**

🐟 **$4 000** – €4 052 – **£2 510** – FF26 582
County Park in Spring Valley Oil/canvas (50x60cm 20x24in) Cincinnati OH 2000

🐟 **$1 600** – €1 803 – **£1 108** – FF11 827
«Wind and Sea» Oil/canvas (27x38cm 11x15in) Hatfield PA 2000

FRIES Ernst 1801-1833 **[22]**

🐟 **$967** – €818 – **£579** – FF5 364
Schloss Sprechenstein bei Sterzing Aquarell/Papier (25x16cm 9x6in) Berlin 1998

📜 **$857** – €1 022 – **£611** – FF6 707
Der gesprengte und der Bibliothek Thurm vom Heidelberger Schlosse Lithographie (26.4x34.3cm 10x13in) Berlin 2000

FRIES Leonhard F. Willy 1881-? **[7]**

📜 **$1 300** – €1 458 – **£902** – FF9 564
«Biswanger Mews» Poster (71x94cm 28x37in) New-York 2001

FRIES Pia 1955 **[1]**

🐟 **$2 163** – €2 391 – **£1 500** – FF15 683
Untitled Oil/board (30x37cm 11x14in) London 2001

FRIESE Richard Bernhard L. 1854-1918 **[26]**

🐟 **$5 852** – €6 647 – **£4 093** – FF43 600
Winterlandschaft mit untergehender Sonne und Elchrudel Öl/Leinwand (92x74cm 36x29in) Berlin 2001

✏️ **$486** – €501 – **£306** – FF3 286
Mähnenlöwe in Senke Indian ink (13.2x19cm 5x7in) Berlin 2000

FRIESEKE Frederick Carl 1874-1939 **[85]**

🐟 **$170 000** – €161 780 – **£106 335** – FF1 061 208
Venus au Soleil Oil/canvas (41.5x51cm 16x20in) New-York 1999

🐟 **$42 000** – €39 659 – **£26 082** – FF260 143
Nude in Dappled Sunlight Oil/board (35x27cm 13x10in) Beverly-Hills CA 1999

🐟 **$7 500** – €7 025 – **£4 611** – FF46 080
Lady Sitting Watercolour/paper (24x31cm 9x12in) New-York 1999

FRIESENDAHL Carl 1886-1948 **[8]**

🐟 **$1 917** – €1 667 – **£1 156** – FF10 936
Vildsvin Bronze (H22cm H8in) Stockholm 1998

FRIESZ Émile-Othon 1879-1949 **[1166]**

🐟 **$29 942** – €33 539 – **£20 834** – FF220 000
Le port de Toulon Huile/toile (90x148cm 35x58in) Clamecy 2001

$8 000 - €7 518 - £4 859 - FF49 316
Chapelle-sous-Roche Oil/canvas (63.5x80cm 25x31in) New-York 1999

$3 399 - €3 354 - £2 094 - FF22 000
Le modèle assis Huile/toile (46.5x26.5cm 18x10in) Paris 1999

$823 - €694 - £490 - FF4 555
Nu Crayon/papier (41x28cm 16x11in) Antwerpen 1998

$173 - €198 - £121 - FF1 300
«Aide Amicale aux Artistes, mai» Affiche (120x80cm 47x31in) Paris 2001

FRIETAG Conrad 1845-1894 **[2]**

$17 000 - €16 403 - £10 677 - FF107 594
Pilot Boat #13 Caldwell H.Colt Oil/canvas (66x91cm 26x36in) Cambridge MA 1999

FRIGERIO R. XIX-XX **[8]**

$3 100 - €3 214 - £1 860 - FF21 080
Interno di osteria con frate e sonatore di chitarra Olio/tela (80x100cm 31x39in) Napoli 2000

FRIGERIO Raffaele XIX-XX **[41]**

$359 - €403 - £250 - FF2 646
Study of an old Man Oil/canvas (32.5x22.5cm 12x8in) London 2001

FRIIS Hans 1839-1892 **[50]**

$1 300 - €1 209 - £802 - FF7 929
Winter Thaw Oil/canvas (31x52cm 12x20in) Portland ME 1999

$429 - €404 - £265 - FF2 649
Aftenstemming Oil/canvas (24x43cm 9x16in) Viby J, Århus 1999

FRILLI Antonio XIX-XX **[44]**

$36 000 - €31 869 - £22 010 - FF209 048
Dancing Girl Marble (H80cm H31in) New-York 1999

$3 322 - €3 534 - £2 100 - FF23 179
Bust of a Woman in a Lace Hat Alabaster (H59cm H23in) London 2000

FRIND August 1852-1924 **[13]**

$986 - €1 165 - £700 - FF7 642
Bavarian Courtship Oil/panel (40x26.5cm 15x10in) London 2001

FRINK Elizabeth 1930-1993 **[495]**

$54 704 - €46 668 - £33 000 - FF306 121
Wild Boar Bronze (H102cm H40in) London 1998

$14 229 - €16 532 - £10 000 - FF108 442
Falling Man Bronze (H68.5cm H26in) London 2000

$5 123 - €6 032 - £3 600 - FF39 569
Horse Lying Down Pencil/paper (56x76cm 22x29in) London 2000

$794 - €903 - £550 - FF5 923
Birds of Prey, Golden Eagle Aquatint in colors (54x46.5cm 21x18in) London 2000

FRIPP Alfred Downing 1822-1895 **[22]**

$1 576 - €1 773 - £1 100 - FF11 628
The Bather Watercolour (68.5x53.5cm 26x21in) London 2001

FRIPP George Arthur 1813-1896 **[127]**

$1 445 - €1 703 - £1 000 - FF11 171
Mill Beside a Weir Oil/canvas (39.5x59cm 15x23in) Devon 2000

$1 345 - €1 571 - £950 - FF10 303
The Borromean Islands, Lago Maggiore Watercolour/paper (23x34.5cm 9x13in) London 2001

FRIPP Thomas William 1864-1931 **[32]**

$613 - €584 - £383 - FF3 829
Preparing to go Fishing Watercolour/paper (23.5x35cm 9x13in) Vancouver, BC. 1999

FRISCH F., Augsburg XIX **[1]**

$1 237 - €1 247 - £771 - FF8 180
Vue de la chute du Rhin à Lauffen, peint par G.F.Gmelin Farbradierung (39.2x56.5cm 15x22in) Zürich 2000

FRISCH Johann Christoph 1738-1815 **[10]**

$3 000 - €3 240 - £2 073 - FF21 251
Cairo, Egypt Oil/canvas (30.5x46.5cm 12x18in) New-York 2001

FRISCHE Heinrich Ludwig 1831-1901 **[15]**

$4 763 - €5 113 - £3 188 - FF33 539
Reisigsammler in gebirgiger Landschaft Öl/Leinwand (104x141cm 40x55in) Köln 2000

FRISCHMANN Marcel 1900-1951 **[26]**

$158 - €184 - £110 - FF1.207
Kanal Lithograph (20.2x27.7cm 7x10in) Berlin 2000

FRISENDAHL Carl 1886-1948 **[10]**

$329 - €366 - £220 - FF2 399
Stående bisonoxe Bronze (H12cm H4in) Stockholm 2000

FRISHMUTH Harriet Whitney 1880-1980 **[158]**

$140 000 - €120 786 - £84 770 - FF792 302
Playdays Bronze (H133cm H52in) New-York 1999

$13 000 - €12 002 - £7 995 - FF78 726
Extase Bronze (H51cm H20in) New-York 1999

FRISIA Donato 1883-1953 **[21]**

$3 500 - €3 628 - £2 100 - FF23 800
Scorcio di cascina con ulivi Olio/tela (104x75cm 40x29in) Milano 1999

$2 380 - €2 467 - £1 428 - FF16 184
Venezia Olio/tavola (27x50cm 10x19in) Milano 2000

FRISIUS Simon Wynouts c.1580-1629 **[17]**

$600 - €672 - £418 - FF4 405
St.Anthonis Poorte in Amsterdam/Overtoom Sluice in Amsterdam Etching (17x21cm 6x8in) New-York 2001

FRISON Barthélémy 1816-1877 **[3]**

$510 - €545 - £347 - FF3 577
Buste van een man Bronze (35x20.5cm 13x8in) Lokeren 2001

FRISON Jehan 1882-1961 **[201]**

$1 170 - €1 239 - £792 - FF8 130
Nature morte au homard et aux citrons Huile/toile (50x60cm 19x23in) Bruxelles 2001

$516 - €496 - £318 - FF3 252
Portrait de l'artiste Huile/panneau (26.5x16.5cm 10x6in) Bruxelles 1999

FRISTROM Carl Magnus Oscar 1856-1918 **[2]**

$2 298 - €2 534 - £1 556 - FF16 623
Kingston Estate, South Coast Line Watercolour/paper (47.5x66cm 18x25in) Woollahra, Sydney 2000

FRISTRUP Niels, Niklaus 1837-1909 **[18]**

$4 296 - €4 170 - £2 653 - FF27 351
Udsigt gennem pergola til by, hav og bjerge, Italien Oil/canvas (121x94cm 47x37in) Vejle 1999

$206 - €228 - £136 - FF1 496
Parti fra Kastellet Oil/canvas (34x45cm 13x17in) Viby J, Århus 2000

FRITH Francis 1822-1898 **[80]**

$2 484 - €2 727 - £1 600 - FF17 887
Sinai & Palestine, London, Glasgow & Edinburgh: Will.MacKenzie Albumen print (44x33cm 17x13in) London 2000

FRITH Frederick XIX **[3]**
- 🖌 **$3 218** - €3 026 - **£2 023** - FF19 849
  Portrait of a Gentleman Watercolour/paper
  (43.5x31.5cm 17x12in) Sydney 1999

FRITH William Powell 1819-1909 **[99]**
- 👝 **$25 254** - €30 034 - **£18 000** - FF197 013
  Lord Foppington Relates his Adventures
  Oil/canvas (98x137cm 38x53in) London 2000
- 👝 **$8 486** - €8 057 - **£5 200** - FF52 849
  The Flower Seller Oil/canvas (76.5x63.5cm 30x25in)
  London 1999
- 👝 **$5 783** - €4 858 - **£3 400** - FF31 865
  Norah Creina Oil/canvas (33x26cm 12x10in) Devon
  1998
- 🖌 **$1 135** - €1 195 - **£750** - FF7 841
  **A young Lady carrying her Daughter through
  the Snow to Safety** Pastel/paper (65x44cm 25x17in)
  London 2000

FRITSCH Elizabeth XX **[3]**
- 🖾 **$10 982** - €10 327 - **£6 800** - FF67 743
  Spiral Vase Ceramic (H39.5cm H15in) London 1999

FRITSCH Ernst 1892-1965 **[39]**
- 👝 **$4 106** - €4 602 - **£2 860** - FF30 185
  Dame mit Cape Öl/Leinwand (75.5x61cm 29x24in)
  Berlin 2001
- 👝 **$3 216** - €3 528 - **£2 184** - FF23 141
  Mädchen auf der Bank Watercolour (47.6x33.7cm
  18x13in) Berlin 2000

FRITSCH Melchior 1826-1889 **[20]**
- 👝 **$2 817** - €3 270 - **£1 980** - FF21 451
  «Felsenpartie aus dem Pinzgau» Öl/Leinwand
  (100x81cm 39x31in) Wien 2001
- 👝 **$1 637** - €1 817 - **£1 140** - FF11 917
  Blick vom Mönchsberg auf Leopoldskron
  Öl/Karton (29x35.5cm 11x13in) Salzburg 2001

FRITZ Andreas 1828-1906 **[40]**
- 👝 **$825** - €738 - **£492** - FF4 841
  Parti fra Århusbugten Oil/canvas (98x72cm
  38x28in) København 1998

FRITZ Charles XX **[7]**
- 👝 **$14 000** - €12 727 - **£8 432** - FF83 482
  Sunlight over Granite Peak Oil/canvas (101x152cm
  40x60in) Hayden ID 1998

FRITZ Max 1849-? **[23]**
- 👝 **$1 290** - €1 431 - **£894** - FF9 386
  Spiegelnde häuser von Olching u der Amper
  Oil/canvas (68x109cm 26x42in) Malmö 2001
- 🖌 **$887** - €953 - **£594** - FF6 250
  Small boats in a river, a village on the horizon
  Watercolour (39x59cm 15x23in) Amsterdam 2000

FRITZEL Wilhelm 1870-1943 **[30]**
- 👝 **$1 481** - €1 278 - **£897** - FF8 384
  **«Niederrhein, Landschaft mit Holzsteg über
  einen Bach»** Öl/Leinwand (33.5x48cm 13x18in)
  Kempten 1999

FRITZSCH Claudius Ditlev 1763-1841 **[8]**
- 👝 **$34 658** - €34 928 - **£21 606** - FF229 112
  **Opstilling med meloner, ferskner, druer og kir-
  sebaer** Oil/canvas (130x100cm 51x39in) København
  2000
- 👝 **$6 849** - €7 789 - **£4 785** - FF51 092
  **Opstilling med tulipaner, roser, guldregn og
  syrener** Oil/canvas (71x60cm 27x23in) København
  2000

FRITZVOLD Reidar 1920-1998 **[21]**
- 👝 **$8 400** - €9 988 - **£5 984** - FF65 520
  Vinterlandskap Oil/canvas (124x186cm 48x73in)
  Oslo 2000
- 👝 **$724** - €802 - **£491** - FF5 263
  Höstsol, Telemark Oil/panel (46x55cm 18x21in) Oslo
  2000
- 🖾 **$239** - €280 - **£171** - FF1 838
  Et skogstjern seinhöstes Color lithograph
  (46x62cm 18x24in) Oslo 2001

FRIZE Bernard 1954 **[16]**
- 👝 **$1 450** - €1 753 - **£1 013** - FF11 500
  Le devin (I/IV) Aquarelle (55x75cm 21x29in) Paris
  2000

FRODMAN-CLUZEL Boris M. XIX-XX **[40]**
- 🖾 **$3 398** - €3 964 - **£2 386** - FF26 000
  Danseuse orientale Bronze (H14.5cm H5in) Paris
  2000

FROEHLICH Bernhard 1823-1885 **[8]**
- 👝 **$2 750** - €2 492 - **£1 693** - FF16 348
  Children Playing with their Boats Oil/canvas
  (30x50cm 12x20in) Mystic CT 1999

FROHAWK Frederick William 1861-1946 **[6]**
- 🖌 **$2 005** - €1 695 - **£1 200** - FF11 116
  Woodcock Watercolour/paper (27x38cm 10x14in)
  London 1998

FRÖHLICH Fritz 1910 **[31]**
- 👝 **$8 964** - €8 721 - **£5 520** - FF57 204
  Was wollen diese Leute? Acryl/Leinwand
  (64x90cm 25x35in) Linz 1999
- 👝 **$588** - €654 - **£394** - FF4 290
  Wackeliges Gebäude Mischtechnik (17x22cm
  6x8in) Linz 1999
- 🖌 **$629** - €727 - **£440** - FF4 767
  Ohne Titel Aquarell/Papier (25x20cm 9x7in) Linz
  2001

FROHNER Adolf 1934 **[218]**
- 👝 **$10 016** - €11 628 - **£7 040** - FF76 272
  «Die Herausforderung» Öl/Leinwand (130x90cm
  51x35in) Wien 2001
- 👝 **$794** - €872 - **£528** - FF5 720
  Ohne Titel Indian ink (38x27cm 14x10in) Wien 2000
- 🖾 **$153** - €182 - **£111** - FF1 191
  «Frauen-Leiden» Radierung (46.5x36.5cm 18x14in)
  Salzburg 2001

FRØLICH Lorenz 1820-1908 **[61]**
- 👝 **$2 363** - €2 547 - **£1 611** - FF16 710
  Thor og Hymer Oil/canvas (36x54cm 14x21in)
  København 2001
- 👝 **$655** - €603 - **£405** - FF3 954
  Landskab med ko Oil/canvas (27x32cm 10x12in)
  Vejle 1998
- 🖌 **$405** - €390 - **£252** - FF2 561
  Kong Skjold frembaeres for folket Pencil/paper
  (20.5x35.5cm 8x13in) København 1999

FRÖLICHER Otto 1840-1890 **[59]**
- 👝 **$3 687** - €3 888 - **£2 435** - FF25 502
  Landschaft mit Figur Öl/Leinwand (76x110cm
  29x43in) Zürich 2000
- 👝 **$1 005** - €1 094 - **£662** - FF7 174
  Naturstudie Öl/Leinwand/Karton (21x39cm 8x15in)
  Bern 2000

FROMANGER Gérard 1939 **[195]**
- 👝 **$12 042** - €13 720 - **£8 271** - FF90 000
  **«Comment dites-vous?» Serie: Annoncer la
  couleur** Huile/toile (200x150cm 78x59in) Paris 2000

🖼 **$7 465** - €6 860 - **£4 585** - FF45 000
L'autre, série: Boulevard des italiens
Acrylique/toile (100x100cm 39x39in) Paris 1999

🖼 **$214** - €183 - **£129** - FF1 200
Chimère 83 Acrylique/toile (18x12.5cm 7x4in) Paris 1998

✏ **$645** - €534 - **£378** - FF3 500
Il Campo Pastel/papier (101x71cm 39x27in) Paris 1998

▥ **$130** - €137 - **£86** - FF900
La vie est une marchandise Lithographie couleurs (56x90cm 22x35in) Paris 2000

FROMENT Jeanne XIX-XX **[5]**
🖼 **$2 356** - €2 287 - **£1 467** - FF15 000
Troupeau dans la plaine Huile/toile (65x81cm 25x31in) Fontainebleau 1999

FROMENT Yvette 1937 **[4]**
🖼 **$2 921** - €3 305 - **£2 043** - FF21 680
«Hôtel de ville» Acrylic/canvas (137x76cm 53x29in) Toronto 2001

FROMENT-MEURICE Jacques 1864-1948 **[11]**
🗿 **$1 582** - €1 637 - **£1 000** - FF10 736
A Family of Sheep Bronze (24x28cm 9x11in) London 2000

FROMENTIN Eugène 1820-1876 **[184]**
🖼 **$41 841** - €49 204 - **£30 000** - FF322 758
The River crossing Oil/canvas (103.5x141.5cm 40x55in) London 2001

🖼 **$10 742** - €10 824 - **£6 695** - FF71 000
Chevaux arabes rentrant à l'écurie Huile/panneau (33x56cm 12x22in) Neuilly-sur-Seine 2000

🖼 **$3 584** - €3 067 - **£2 157** - FF20 119
Strasse in Algerien mit zahlreichen Händlern und Passanten Öl/Leinwand (41x33cm 16x12in) München 1998

✏ **$777** - €915 - **£546** - FF6 000
Enfant arabe assis en tailleur, de profil Crayon (21x13.5cm 8x5in) Paris 2000

FROMILLER Joseph Ferdinand 1693-1760 **[6]**
🖼 **$51 912** - €52 324 - **£32 400** - FF343 224
Die Vertreibung aus dem Paradies Öl/Leinwand (98x127.5cm 38x50in) Wien 2000

✏ **$686** - €818 - **£489** - FF5 366
Mariä Verkündigung Red chalk (27.3x17cm 10x6in) Köln 2000

FROMMEL Carl Ludwig 1789-1863 **[33]**
🖼 **$2 269** - €2 556 - **£1 596** - FF16 769
Blick auf eine bewaldete Anhöhe mit einem Schloss Öl/Karton (35x46cm 13x18in) Stuttgart 2001

🖼 **$1 612** - €1 493 - **£987** - FF9 794
Landschaft mit Schafherde und aufziehendem Gewitter Öl/Leinwand (27x36cm 10x14in) Bern 1999

✏ **$111** - €128 - **£76** - FF838
Blick auf die Kirche St.Wolfgang in Wehr Pencil (17.5x26.5cm 6x10in) Heidelberg 2000

▥ **$42** - €46 - **£28** - FF301
Waldlandschaft mit kleinem Flusslauf Radierung (32.5x27.5cm 12x10in) Köln 2000

FROMUTH Charles Henry 1861-1937 **[39]**
✏ **$2 798** - €3 049 - **£1 834** - FF20 000
The First Blue net Apperence, Concarneau, July 4th Pastel/papier (59x44cm 23x17in) Dijon 2000

FRONIUS Hans 1903-1988 **[330]**
🖼 **$6 886** - €7 994 - **£4 752** - FF52 437
Etretat, Französische Steilküste Oil/panel (60x83cm 23x32in) Graz 2000

✏ **$531** - €436 - **£308** - FF2 861
Landschaftsstudie Charcoal/paper (40x53.5cm 15x21in) Wien 1998

▥ **$162** - €182 - **£110** - FF1 191
Unterwelt Radierung (15.5x32.1cm 6x12in) Wien 2000

FRÖSCHL Carl 1848-1934 **[12]**
✏ **$4 497** - €4 336 - **£2 772** - FF28 440
Mädchen in rotem Kleid vor einem Paravent Pastell/Papier (118x79cm 46x31in) Bern 1999

FROST Arthur Burdett, Sr. 1851-1928 **[82]**
🖼 **$2 000** - €2 332 - **£1 404** - FF15 300
The Bear Hunt Watercolour, gouache (30.5x44.5cm 12x17in) Boston MA 2000

▥ **$1 500** - €1 749 - **£1 053** - FF11 475
Rabbit Shooting/Pheasant Shooting/Hunting Lithograph (54x72cm 21x28in) Portsmouth NH 2000

FROST Francis Shedd 1825-1902 **[5]**
🖼 **$17 000** - €20 217 - **£12 115** - FF132 617
Moat Mountain, New Hampshire Oil/canvas (45.5x76cm 17x29in) New-York 2000

FROST George 1754-1821 **[15]**
✏ **$448** - €481 - **£300** - FF3 156
The Drayman Pencil/paper (12x10cm 4x3in) Reepham, Norwich 2000

FROST George Albert 1843-1907 **[19]**
🖼 **$4 000** - €4 543 - **£2 806** - FF29 801
Mountain Landscape Oil/canvas (66x102cm 25x40in) Miami FL 2001

🖼 **$1 200** - €1 138 - **£730** - FF7 462
Little Harbor Watercolour/paper (35x55cm 14x22in) South-Natick MA 1999

FROST Gill 1965 **[1]**
🖼 **$6 610** - €5 648 - **£4 000** - FF37 050
Remembrance 2 Oil/canvas (75x100cm 29x39in) London 1998

FROST James XVIII **[1]**
🖼 **$4 210** - €4 671 - **£2 800** - FF30 639
The Glorious First of June, 1754: Lord Howe, After Mather Brown Oil/canvas (43x55cm 16x21in) London 2000

FROST John 1890-1937 **[21]**
🖼 **$47 500** - €55 419 - **£33 060** - FF363 527
Indian Shack Oil/canvas (68x81cm 27x32in) Altadena CA 2000

🖼 **$9 250** - €10 788 - **£6 494** - FF70 766
Southwestern Mesa Oil/canvas (33x40cm 13x16in) Portsmouth NH 2000

✏ **$4 250** - €4 023 - **£2 639** - FF26 390
Three People in Rowboat, Fishing Watercolour/paper (36x56cm 14x22in) Wallkill NY 1999

FROST John Orne Johnson 1852-1928 **[2]**
🖼 **$75 000** - €72 620 - **£47 107** - FF476 355
Marblehead Harbor Oil/board (76x157.5cm 29x62in) New-York 2000

FROST Joseph Ambrose, Mraz 1953 **[53]**
🖼 **$953** - €995 - **£601** - FF6 525
Grange Beach, Adelaide Oil/canvas (37x19cm 14x7in) Sydney 2000

✏ **$855** - €825 - **£540** - FF5 411
Harbour from Cremorne Gouache/paper (13x18cm 5x7in) Sydney 1999

FROST Terry 1915 **[308]**
🖼 **$9 819** - €11 705 - **£7 000** - FF76 781
Red, Yellow and Blue Oil/canvas (72.5x178.5cm 28x70in) London 2000

F

$4 170 - €4 203 - **£2 600** - FF27 569
Abstract Oil/canvas (91.5x91.5cm 36x36in) London 2000

$1 299 - €1 281 - **£800** - FF8 405
Construction, hanging Form Mixed media (53x17.5cm 20x6in) London 1999

$1 136 - €1 121 - **£700** - FF7 355
Blue, yellow and red Watercolour (30.5x28.5cm 12x11in) London 1999

$597 - €642 - **£400** - FF4 208
Summers Day Silkscreen in colors (87x70cm 34x27in) London 2000

FROST William Edward 1810-1877 **[75]**
$1 714 - €1 924 - **£1 200** - FF12 619
Fête Champêtre Oil/canvas (57x77cm 22x30in) London 2001

$841 - €1 001 - **£600** - FF6 567
The Birth of Venus Oil/canvas (21x26cm 8x10in) London 2000

$156 - €181 - **£110** - FF1 187
Femal Nude/Lady, Seated Full Length, Wearing a Pink Dress Watercolour (18.5x11.5cm 7x4in) London 2000

FROSTERUS-SÅLTIN Alexandra 1837-1916 **[6]**
$1 774 - €2 018 - **£1 231** - FF13 238
Gamling och barn Oil/canvas (31x38cm 12x14in) Helsinki 2000

FROSTERUS-SEGERSTRÅLE Hanna 1867-1946 **[11]**
$1 366 - €1 211 - **£838** - FF7 943
Systrarna Pastel/paper (48x56cm 18x22in) Helsinki 1999

FROUD Brian 1947 **[4]**
$1 576 - €1 364 - **£950** - FF8 949
Pixie Girl Coloured pencils (27x18cm 10x7in) London 1998

FRUGE Nestor 1914 **[18]**
$125 - €138 - **£87** - FF908
The Pontalba and Cabildo/Pirate's Alley Watercolour/paper (36x26cm 14x10in) New-Orleans LA 2001

FRUHMANN Johann 1928-1985 **[12]**
$5 418 - €5 087 - **£3 346** - FF33 369
Ohne Titel Tempera/canvas (97.5x114cm 38x44in) Wien 1999

FRÜHTRUNK Günter 1923-1983 **[156]**
$17 146 - €18 407 - **£11 476** - FF120 740
Centre d'Energie Acryl/Leinwand (118x113cm 46x44in) Hamburg 2001

$9 906 - €11 248 - **£6 883** - FF73 785
Offenes Grün II Acrylic (80x70cm 31x27in) München 2001

$5 105 - €4 857 - **£3 172** - FF31 862
Ikone Oil/panel (37.2x35.7cm 14x14in) Hamburg 1999

$243 - €204 - **£143** - FF1 341
Vertikale Strahlung Farbserigraphie (69x69cm 27x27in) Stuttgart 1998

FRUWIRTH Carl 1810-1878 **[1]**
$1 965 - €2 180 - **£1 368** - FF14 301
Mittagsrast italienischer Hirten Oil/panel (45x35cm 17x13in) Wien 2001

FRY John Hemming 1861-1946 **[2]**
$2 900 - €3 383 - **£2 071** - FF22 188
Haystacks Oil/panel (21x30cm 8x12in) St. Louis MO 2000

FRY Roger Elliot 1866-1934 **[51]**
$5 621 - €5 456 - **£3 500** - FF35 790
The Barn at Charleston Oil/canvas (45.5x61cm 17x24in) London 1999

$5 480 - €6 055 - **£3 800** - FF39 721
Venice Oil/board (25.5x33.5cm 10x13in) London 2001

FRYDLENDER Barry 1954 **[3]**
$3 377 - €3 811 - **£2 375** - FF25 000
Premiers chaussons Photo (75.5x100cm 29x39in) Paris 2001

FRYE Thomas 1710-1762 **[27]**
$35 980 - €40 300 - **£25 000** - FF264 352
Two young Children, the Elder Girl building House of Cards on a Table Oil/canvas (156x121cm 61x47in) London 2001

$3 486 - €4 100 - **£2 500** - FF26 896
Half length portrait of a gentleman with white stock Oil/canvas (73x60cm 29x24in) Oxford 2001

$1 300 - €1 218 - **£799** - FF7 987
Self Portrait Mezzotint (47x35cm 18x13in) New-York 1999

FRYER Wilfred Moody 1891-? **[20]**
$363 - €318 - **£220** - FF2 085
Boys on a Rowboat Watercolour/paper (36x48cm 14x18in) London 1998

FRYMIRE Jacob 1765/74-1822 **[1]**
$35 000 - €31 851 - **£21 868** - FF208 932
Daniel Clarke, Seated by a Desk, View to a Country Home Oil/canvas (72x60cm 28x24in) Bolton MA 1999

FU BAOSHI 1904-1965 **[107]**
$36 036 - €34 174 - **£21 924** - FF224 168
Madam Xiang Ink (52x61cm 20x24in) Hong-Kong 1999

FU SHAN 1605-1690 **[8]**
$19 000 - €16 402 - **£11 350** - FF107 587
Running-Cursive Script Calligraphy Ink (191.5x47.5cm 75x18in) New-York 1998

FUA HARIPITAK 1910-1993 **[14]**
$4 590 - €4 937 - **£3 078** - FF32 382
Backyards of Rome Ink/paper (50x34cm 19x13in) Bangkok 2000

FUCHS Bernie 1932 **[23]**
$5 000 - €5 569 - **£3 270** - FF36 532
Dustjacket illustration and book cover: Flower seller Oil/canvas (51x79cm 20x31in) New-York 2000

FUCHS Ernst 1930 **[999]**
$5 341 - €5 087 - **£3 262** - FF33 369
Cherub, himmlischer Fürst Tempera/panel (92x73cm 36x28in) Wien 1999

$1 153 - €1 163 - **£720** - FF7 627
Daphne Bronze (H39.5cm H15in) Wien 2000

$1 565 - €1 817 - **£1 100** - FF11 917
Eva Christina Black chalk (62x46cm 24x18in) Wien 2001

$243 - €270 - **£161** - FF1 770
Allegorie Aquatint in colors (39x29cm 15x11in) Bern 2000

FUCHS Michael XX **[6]**
$156 - €172 - **£108** - FF1 191
Landschaft Radierung (54x40cm 21x15in) Wien 2000

FUCHS Rudolf 1868-1918 **[8]**
$4 000 - €4 591 - **£2 445** - FF23 227
A Ball to Remember Oil/canvas (75x109cm 29x42in) New-York 1999

FUCHS Therese 1849-? **[28]**
- $809 - €869 - £542 - FF5 701
  Norwegische Fjordlandschaft Öl/Leinwand (62x104.5cm 24x41in) Bremen 2000

FUECHSEL Hermann 1833-1915 **[10]**
- $7 500 - €8 326 - £5 216 - FF54 618
  «**Sunset Glow**» Oil/board (16x30cm 6x12in) Milford CT 2001

FUENTETAJA Jose Luis 1951 **[18]**
- $561 - €511 - £348 - FF3 349
  Grupo infantil Pastel (43.5x36cm 17x14in) Barcelona 1999
- $112 - €102 - £68 - FF669
  Cuatro aguafuertes sobre Nepal Aguafuerte (61x52cm 24x20in) Madrid 1999

FUERTES Louis Agassiz 1874-1927 **[50]**
- $3 750 - €4 079 - £2 472 - FF26 757
  Black-capped Chickadee Gouache (19x12cm 7x4in) Boston MA 2000

FÜGER Friedrich Heinrich 1751-1818 **[71]**
- $16 800 - €14 298 - £10 000 - FF93 789
  Poseidon Enthroned Oil/canvas (143.5x110.5cm 56x43in) London 1998
- $6 400 - €7 267 - £4 380 - FF47 670
  Augusta Gräfin Khevenhüller/Exzellenz Gemahl Öl/Papier (55x45cm 21x17in) Wien 2000
- $3 200 - €3 634 - £2 190 - FF23 835
  Die büssende Magdalena Öl/Leinwand (39.5x32cm 15x12in) Wien 2000
- $874 - €1 022 - £614 - FF6 707
  Zweigesichtige Herme auf einem Sockel Ink (38.7x28.9cm 15x11in) München 2000

FUGERE Henry 1872-1944 **[39]**
- $919 - €942 - £581 - FF6 178
  Jeune femme charmant un cabri Bronze (30x43cm 11x16in) Bruxelles 2000

FUHR Franz Xaver 1898-1973 **[145]**
- $21 910 - €23 008 - £13 815 - FF150 925
  Pfarrkirche St.Kilian in Heilbronn Öl/Leinwand (141.5x107.5cm 55x42in) Stuttgart 2000
- $10 075 - €11 504 - £7 103 - FF75 462
  «**Französische Küste**» Oil/panel (60x80cm 23x31in) Stuttgart 2001
- $3 542 - €3 323 - £2 188 - FF21 800
  Alpenvorland Öl/Karton (20.5x30cm 8x11in) Stuttgart 1999
- $2 014 - €1 764 - £1 220 - FF11 568
  Frachtschiff Gouache (36x61cm 14x24in) Berlin 1998

FÜHRICH von Josef 1800-1876 **[32]**
- $6 987 - €7 158 - £4 312 - FF46 954
  Heiliger Christopherus Öl/Leinwand (103.5x75cm 40x29in) Düsseldorf 2000
- $1 607 - €1 817 - £1 085 - FF11 917
  Engel in rotem Mantel, die Gesetzestafeln haltend Aquarell/Papier (58x37cm 22x14in) Wien 2000

FUHRMANN Arend 1918-1984 **[8]**
- $1 490 - €1 777 - £1 062 - FF11 656
  Ohne Titel Öl/Leinwand (54x81cm 21x31in) Luzern 2000

FUHRMANN Ernest 1886-1956 **[11]**
- $857 - €920 - £573 - FF6 037
  Kirschen Photograph (23.9x17.9cm 9x7in) München 2000

FUHRMANN Max 1860-1908 **[11]**
- $1 694 - €1 585 - £1 026 - FF10 397
  Planmagenkarawane bei Wetterwechsel in den Alpen Öl/Leinwand (70x90cm 27x35in) Bremen 1999

- $3 605 - €3 323 - £2 159 - FF21 797
  Gefahr im Anzug Öl/Leinwand (35x25cm 13x9in) Dresden 1998

FÜHRMANN Rudolf 1909-1977 **[6]**
- $3 810 - €4 386 - £2 600 - FF28 773
  Carnival Charcoal (50x32cm 19x12in) London 2000

FUJISHIMA Takeji 1867-1943 **[3]**
- $30 000 - €33 098 - £19 842 - FF217 107
  Casa dei Vetti (House of the Vettii, Pompeii) Oil/canvas (34.5x26cm 13x10in) New-York 2000

FUJITA Kyohei 1921 **[2]**
- $3 000 - €3 108 - £1 909 - FF20 385
  «**Flower Vase**» Sculpture, glass (16.5x21.5cm 6x8in) New-York 2000

FUKUDA HEIHACHIRO 1892-1974 **[8]**
- $14 000 - €14 108 - £8 727 - FF92 540
  Take (Bamboo) Mixed media (27x24cm 10x9in) New-York 2000
- $28 000 - €28 215 - £17 455 - FF185 080
  Shuntei (early Spring) Mixed media drawing (54x36cm 21x14in) New-York 2000

FUKUI Ryonosuke 1924-1986 **[10]**
- $13 720 - €13 382 - £8 400 - FF87 780
  Winter Oil/canvas (53x33.5cm 20x13in) Tokyo 1999
- $15 680 - €15 294 - £9 600 - FF100 320
  Woman in Kimono Oil/canvas (33.5x24.5cm 13x9in) Tokyo 1999
- $3 200 - €3 449 - £2 182 - FF22 622
  Blue Tower with two Leaves/Blue Flower with three Leaves Bodycolour (36.5x26cm 14x10in) New-York 2001

FULDE Edward B. XIX-XX **[4]**
- $5 574 - €5 793 - £3 496 - FF38 000
  Le quai Saint Pierre à Cannes Huile/toile (53x77cm 20x30in) Paris 2000

FULIGNOT Guido XX **[1]**
- $6 500 - €7 484 - £4 435 - FF49 091
  Portrait of Jacqueline Kennedy Pastel/paper (58.5x42cm 23x18in) New-York 2000

FULLBROOK Samuel Sydney 1922 **[62]**
- $5 827 - €5 494 - £3 611 - FF36 039
  Flowers Oil/canvas (50.5x46cm 19x18in) Melbourne 1999
- $4 039 - €3 712 - £2 461 - FF24 348
  Nocturne Oil/canvas (37x39.5cm 14x15in) Melbourne 1998
- $693 - €631 - £420 - FF4 136
  Pool on Callandoon Creek Pastel/papier (29x39cm 11x15in) Sydney 1998

FULLER Arthur Davenport 1889-1966 **[21]**
- $600 - €561 - £373 - FF3 677
  Ducks in Flight Watercolour/paper (35x50cm 14x20in) Mystic CT 2000

FULLER Buckminster 1895-1983 **[2]**
- $6 000 - €6 531 - £3 706 - FF36 939
  Inventions: Twelve Around One Screenprint (75.5x100cm 29x39in) New-York 1999

FULLER Edmund G. XIX-XX **[28]**
- $2 650 - €2 845 - £1 800 - FF18 659
  Coastal Reflections Oil/canvas (40x56cm 15x22in) London 2001
- $132 - €147 - £90 - FF961
  Cornish Coastline at Sunset Watercolour/paper (39x53cm 15x20in) London 2000

FULLER Florence Ada 1867-1946 **[6]**
- $17 265 - €16 180 - **£10 681** - FF106 135
  Whilst Yet the Days are Wintry Oil/canvas
  (125.5x101.5cm 49x39in) Melbourne 1999
- $1 458 - €1 735 - **£1 039** - FF11 380
  Country Path Oil/board (38.5x22cm 15x8in)
  Melbourne 2000

FULLER George 1822-1884 **[13]**
- $6 000 - €6 813 - **£4 106** - FF44 690
  Study for The Quadroon Oil/canvas (76.5x64cm
  30x25in) New-York 2000
- $1 600 - €1 598 - **£1 000** - FF10 484
  Steamboat Race on the Mississipi Lithograph
  (50x68cm 20x27in) New-Orleans LA 1999

FULLER Isaac 1606-1672 **[3]**
- $7 000 - €6 140 - **£4 250** - FF40 276
  Woman, Bust Length Ink (14.5x12.5cm 5x4in) New-
  York 1999

FULLER Richard Henry 1822-1871 **[12]**
- $2 750 - €2 320 - **£1 613** - FF15 218
  Figure by the River Oil/canvas (50x76cm 20x30in)
  Mystic CT 1998

FULLER Robert E. 1972 **[3]**
- $4 181 - €4 756 - **£2 900** - FF31 196
  Hares on the Run Oil/board (44x121cm 17x48in)
  Driffield, East Yorkshire 2000

FULLEYLOVE John 1847-1908 **[79]**
- $3 938 - €3 749 - **£2 500** - FF24 593
  Tenby Oil/panel (24x34cm 9x13in) Billingshurst, West-
  Sussex 1999
- $789 - €918 - **£563** - FF6 022
  Holborn Viaduct Watercolour/paper (17x12.5cm
  6x4in) Toronto 2001

FULLJAMES Penelope 1942 **[10]**
- $3 138 - €3 659 - **£2 200** - FF24 002
  Tiger in the Garden Oil/canvas (57x70cm 22x27in)
  London 2000

FULLWOOD Albert Henry 1864-1930 **[116]**
- $10 656 - €11 901 - **£6 823** - FF78 066
  European Valley Oil/canvas/board (102.5x129cm
  40x50in) Malvern, Victoria 2000
- $33 472 - €28 911 - **£20 217** - FF189 644
  Sad News Oil/canvas (76x101.5cm 29x39in) Malvern,
  Victoria 1998
- $1 907 - €1 856 - **£1 173** - FF12 173
  Harbour Entrance Oil/canvas/board (19.5x15cm
  7x5in) Malvern, Victoria 1999
- $526 - €489 - **£324** - FF3 209
  Sydney Beach Scene Watercolour, gouache/paper
  (11.5x23.5cm 4x9in) Melbourne 1999

FULLWOOD John 1854-1931 **[59]**
- $1 125 - €1 153 - **£700** - FF7 562
  Amberley Oil/canvas (40x59.5cm 15x23in)
  Billingshurst, West-Sussex 2000
- $374 - €414 - **£260** - FF2 717
  Country Lane Watercolour/paper (16x23cm 6x9in)
  London 2001
- $71 - €86 - **£50** - FF567
  Buttermere/Crummock Water and Red Pike
  Drypoint (20x15cm 8x6in) Aylsham, Norfolk 2000

FULOP Karoly 1898-1963 **[14]**
- $16 000 - €17 559 - **£10 302** - FF115 180
  The Ceremony Oil/panel (69x56cm 27x22in)
  Beverly-Hills CA 2000

FULTON David 1848-1930 **[72]**
- $2 590 - €2 904 - **£1 800** - FF19 050
  Children on a Rocky Shore Oil/canvas (41x52cm
  16x20in) Little-Lane, Ilkley 2001
- $1 247 - €1 069 - **£750** - FF7 010
  Faggot Gatherers Oil/canvas (34.5x29.5cm 13x11in)
  Edinburgh 1998

FULTON Fitch Burt 1879-1955 **[18]**
- $3 250 - €2 991 - **£1 950** - FF19 621
  The Narrow Path Oil/canvas (66x76cm 26x30in)
  Pasadena CA 1999

FULTON Hamish 1946 **[62]**
- $5 600 - €5 230 - **£3 456** - FF34 305
  Sierra Nevada Photograph (83.5x110cm 32x43in)
  New-York 1999

FULTON Samuel 1855-1941 **[25]**
- $4 121 - €4 281 - **£2 600** - FF28 083
  Cairn Terrier Oil/canvas (46x36cm 18x14in) London
  2000
- $1 964 - €2 336 - **£1 400** - FF15 323
  A Scottie Oil/canvas (36x26cm 14x10in) London 2000

FULWIDER Edwin L. 1913 **[8]**
- $12 000 - €13 648 - **£8 322** - FF89 522
  Receiving News of Pearl Harbor Oil/masonite
  (55x76cm 22x30in) Chicago IL 2000

FUMAKOSHI XX [1]
- $4 000 - €3 818 - **£2 499** - FF25 046
  Box with Lacquer Cover Sculpture, glass
  (78x23x20cm 7x9x7in) New-York 1999

FUMERON René 1921 **[16]**
- $3 008 - €3 506 - **£2 083** - FF23 000
  Nocturne Tapisserie (150x238cm 59x93in) Calais
  2000

FUMIANI Giovanni Antonio 1643-1710 **[6]**
- $18 526 - €21 042 - **£13 000** - FF138 027
  Abraham and the Three Angels Oil/canvas
  (129x183cm 50x72in) London 2001

FUNCKEN Fred 1921 **[12]**
- $215 - €198 - **£129** - FF1 300
  Doc Silver Encre Chine/papier (38x28cm 14x11in)
  Paris 1999

FUNI Achille 1890-1972 **[103]**
- $5 750 - €5 961 - **£3 450** - FF39 100
  Natura morta con carciofo e statua Tempera/car-
  tone (40x55cm 15x21in) Milano 2001
- $1 680 - €2 177 - **£1 260** - FF14 280
  Studio Acquarello/carta (55x41cm 21x16in) Milano
  2001

FUNK Emil XIX **[2]**
- $8 526 - €8 934 - **£5 400** - FF58 605
  The Family Gathering Oil/canvas (78x90cm
  30x35in) London 2000

FUNKE Helene 1869-1957 **[45]**
- $2 342 - €2 325 - **£1 462** - FF15 254
  Seine Canal, Paris Oil/Leinwand (53x65cm 20x25in)
  Wien 1999
- $1 905 - €1 817 - **£1 160** - FF11 917
  Segelboote/Südliche Landschaft Pencil
  (28.5x32.5cm 11x12in) Wien 1999

FUNKE Jaromír 1896-1945 **[64]**
- $7 500 - €6 293 - **£4 400** - FF41 277
  Light Abstraction Gelatin silver print (23.5x29cm
  9x11in) New-York 1998

FUNNO Michele c.1830-c.1880 **[4]**
✏ **$14 000** - €14 509 - **£8 870** - FF95 174
    Ship Joshua Mauran, Capt. Barton entering the port of Naples Gouache/paper (51x76cm 20x30in) Portsmouth NH 2000

FURCY DE LAVAULT Albert Tibule 1847-1915 **[56]**
✏ **$4 500** - €4 115 - **£2 748** - FF26 994
    Basket of flowers Oil/canvas (43x56cm 17x22in) New-York 1998
  $1 876 - €1 753 - **£1 168** - FF11 500
    Le panier de pensées Huile/panneau (33x41cm 12x16in) Cherbourg 1999

FURET François 1842-1919 **[58]**
  $10 000 - €10 077 - **£6 234** - FF66 100
    Weasel on Watch Oil/canvas (150.5x100.5cm 59x39in) New-York 2000
  $533 - €622 - **£369** - FF4 081
    Walddickicht Öl/Leinwand (65x54.5cm 25x21in) Bern 2000
  $616 - €595 - **£387** - FF3 901
    Landschaft Öl/Leinwand (14.5x22.5cm 5x8in) Zürich 1999

FURINI Francesco 1603/4-1646 **[19]**
  $91 392 - €78 952 - **£60 928** - FF517 888
    Ghismonda riceve il cuore dell'amato Olio/tela (247x177cm 97x69in) Venezia 1998
  $35 000 - €29 382 - **£20 527** - FF192 731
    Saint Ursula Oil/canvas (91.5x75.5cm 36x29in) New-York 1998

FURLETTI Severino 1886-1970 **[22]**
✏ **$200** - €207 - **£120** - FF1 360
    Al Valentino Acquarello/carta (37x28.5cm 14x11in) Torino 2000

FURLONGER Joe, Joseph Maxwell 1952 **[24]**
✏ **$465** - €513 - **£309** - FF3 365
    Still Life Watercolour/paper (23x27.5cm 9x10in) Woollahra, Sydney 2000

FURNEAUX Charles 1835-1913 **[2]**
  $13 000 - €14 337 - **£9 012** - FF100 222
    Kilauea Oil/wood (34.5x50cm 13x19in) Beverly-Hills CA 2000

FURNISH T. XIX **[1]**
✏ **$4 490** - €4 442 - **£2 800** - FF29 140
    Haymaking in Wensleydale Watercolour (41x60cm 16x23in) Leyburn, North Yorkshire 1999

FURNISS Harry 1854-1925 **[12]**
✏ **$428** - €485 - **£300** - FF3 182
    «The great liberal Party» Ink (32x50cm 12x19in) Swindon, Wiltshire 2001

FURSE Charles Wellington 1868-1904 **[17]**
  $298 571 - €288 185 - **£185 000** - FF1 890 367
    Cubbing with the York and Ainsty - The Children of Mrs Green Oil/canvas (209x288cm 82x113in) London 1999
  $2 420 - €2 337 - **£1 500** - FF15 327
    «Withers Mare'- a sketch by Furse Cubbing York and Ainsty» Oil/canvas (53x35.5cm 20x13in) London 1999
  $3 550 - €3 427 - **£2 200** - FF22 480
    Cubbing with the York and Ainsty' - The Children of Mrs E.L Green Oil/panel (18x25.5cm 7x10in) London 1999

FÜRST Albert 1920 **[2]**
✏ **$2 552** - €2 454 - **£1 572** - FF16 098
    Komposition in Blautönen mit Weiss Aquarell, Gouache/Papier (51x70cm 20x27in) Köln 1999

FUSARO Jean 1925 **[137]**
  $3 142 - €2 897 - **£1 882** - FF19 000
    «Lyon rouge» Huile/toile (73x92cm 28x36in) Paris 1998
  $2 168 - €2 104 - **£1 349** - FF13 800
    Ciel de suie sur Lyon Huile/toile (22x33cm 8x12in) Paris 1999
✏ **$821** - €762 - **£511** - FF5 000
    Les régates Pastel/papier (24x32cm 9x12in) Paris 1999

FUSI Walter 1924 **[24]**
  $390 - €337 - **£195** - FF2 210
    Senza titolo Olio/cartone (50x70cm 19x27in) Prato 1999

FUSS Adam 1961 **[47]**
📷 **$8 500** - €7 333 - **£5 108** - FF48 104
    Nasturtium Cibachrome print (101.5x76cm 39x29in) New-York 1998

FUSS Albert 1889-1969 **[15]**
▥ **$534** - €499 - **£329** - FF3 274
    «Hamburg-Amerika Linie, nach New-York» Poster (60x83.5cm 23x32in) Oostwoud 1999

FUSSELL Charles Lewis 1840-1909 **[11]**
  $9 500 - €8 771 - **£5 842** - FF57 531
    The Backyard Watercolour, gouache/paper (60.5x50cm 23x19in) New-York 1999

FÜSSLI Hans Caspar 1743-1786 **[1]**
  $9 618 - €9 076 - **£5 934** - FF59 532
    Flowers and Fruit in Baskets with Peaches and Roses on Ledges Oil/panel (37x27cm 14x10in) Amsterdam 1999

FÜSSLI Johann Heinrich 1741-1825 **[123]**
  $130 000 - €142 629 - **£86 359** - FF935 584
    The Vision of the Deluge Oil/canvas (247x206cm 97x81in) New-York 2000
  $56 000 - €65 451 - **£39 980** - FF429 330
    Euphrosyne, den Tanz der Landleute besuchend Öl/Leinwand (91x70.5cm 35x27in) Zürich 2001
✏ **$18 000** - €19 322 - **£12 263** - FF126 747
    Salome with the head John the Baptist Ink (31x22cm 12x8in) Boston MA 2001

FÜSSLI Johann Melchior 1677-1736 **[15]**
  $724 - €823 - **£500** - FF5 396
    The Lord Shall Make the Pestilence Cleave into you Wash (29x20.5cm 11x8in) London 2000

FUSSMANN Klaus 1938 **[437]**
  $17 664 - €16 464 - **£10 674** - FF107 995
    Frühjahr, Barbara F.R. und G.P. im Garten in Gelting Oil/canvas (170x160cm 66x62in) München 1999
  $4 824 - €5 292 - **£3 276** - FF34 712
    Rose, Margeriten und Gladiolen Öl/Papier (43x53.4cm 16x21in) Berlin 2000
  $3 048 - €3 272 - **£2 040** - FF21 465
    Pfingstrosen Öl/Karton (24x30.8cm 9x12in) Hamburg 2000
✏ **$2 578** - €2 403 - **£1 590** - FF15 763
    Gelbe Blüten in einer Vase Aquarell/Papier (35.7x48cm 14x18in) Hamburg 1999
▥ **$208** - €245 - **£151** - FF1 609
    Selbst im Spiegel Aquatint (42.2x45cm 16x17in) Hamburg 2001

FUSTER VALIENTE José Antonio 1892-1964 **[2]**
  $2 080 - €1 952 - **£1 300** - FF12 805
    Vista de Mallorca Oleo/cartón (29x38cm 11x14in) Madrid 1999

FUSTIER Geo, Georges 1891-1982 **[12]**
- $6 460 - €7 280 - **£4 473** - FF47 752
  Dans un coin de l'atelier Öl/Leinwand (65x54cm 25x21in) Zürich 2000
- $482 - €469 - **£296** - FF3 076
  «Quinzaine de Genève» Affiche couleur (89x64cm 35x25in) Bern 1999

FUTTERER Josef 1871-1930 **[24]**
- $433 - €486 - **£301** - FF3 186
  «Auf der Pilzpirsch» Öl/Leinwand (26.5x37.5cm 10x14in) Oersberg-bei Kappeln 2001

FYFE S.H. XIX-XX **[3]**
- $3 100 - €3 456 - **£2 092** - FF22 673
  Schooner Yacht Crusader Leaving the Mediterranean Oil/panel (18x27cm 7x11in) York PA 2000

FYFE William B. Collier 1836-1882 **[11]**
- $5 798 - €6 449 - **£3 600** - FF35 744
  The Young Housewife Oil/canvas (49.5x64cm 19x25in) London 1999
- $5 007 - €4 479 - **£3 000** - FF29 382
  The Little Housewife Oil/canvas (40.5x28cm 15x11in) Perchtolsdorf 1998

FYT Jan 1611-1661 **[53]**
- $17 942 - €16 781 - **£11 000** - FF110 077
  Still Life of Fowl in a Landscape Oil/canvas (44x67.5cm 17x26in) London 1998
- $2 400 - €2 763 - **£1 637** - FF18 124
  Hunting Dog Retriever a Mallard Oil/canvas (19x25.5cm 7x10in) New-York 2000
- $8 500 - €9 105 - **£5 804** - FF59 726
  Study of a Mastiff with a Leather Collar Black chalk/paper (19x24cm 7x9in) New-York 2001
- $118 - €138 - **£83** - FF905
  Zwei Hunde bei einem Brunnen Radierung (16.5x22cm 6x8in) Hamburg 2001

G

GAAL Ferenc 1891-1956 **[8]**
- $605 - €665 - **£411** - FF4 360
  Ungarische Zigeunerfamilie vor einem strohge-deckten Haus Öl/Leinwand (59x78cm 23x30in) Saarbrücken 2000

GABAIN Ethel 1883-1950 **[61]**
- $438 - €498 - **£300** - FF3 264
  Flowers and Stripes Oil/board (51x41cm 20x16in) Bury St. Edmunds, Suffolk 2000
- $160 - €151 - **£101** - FF992
  Woman by the Mirror Lithograph (36x21cm 14x8in) Sydney 1999

GABANI Giuseppe 1846-1899 **[29]**
- $96 169 - €89 169 - **£58 000** - FF584 912
  The Lion Hunt Oil/canvas (153x287cm 60x112in) London 1999
- $3 654 - €3 127 - **£2 200** - FF20 515
  Horsemen guarding an Encampment Watercolour (61.5x98cm 24x38in) London 1998

GABARD Ernest 1879-1957 **[4]**
- $1 622 - €1 797 - **£1 100** - FF11 787
  «Pau-Aviation» Poster (79x119cm 31x46in) London 2000

GABBIANI Antonio Domenico 1652-1726 **[25]**
- $18 000 - €21 200 - **£12 448** - FF139 066
  Musicians Playing a Viola Da Gamba, Two Violins and a Clavichord Oil/canvas (110.5x136.5cm 43x53in) New-York 2000
- $10 815 - €10 901 - **£6 750** - FF71 505
  Bildnis eines jungen Mediceer Prinzen Öl/Leinwand (48x33cm 18x12in) Wien 2000
- $687 - €639 - **£420** - FF4 191
  Study of a Heavily Robed Seated Male Figure Red chalk/paper (39.5x28cm 15x11in) London 1998

GABE Nicolas Edward 1814-1865 **[25]**
- $3 391 - €3 293 - **£2 095** - FF21 500
  Marines animées Huile/toile (45x61cm 17x24in) Pau 1999
- $3 402 - €3 811 - **£2 365** - FF25 000
  Femme surprise par quatre orientaux Huile/toile (24x33.5cm 9x13in) Paris 2001

GABINO Amadeo 1922 **[39]**
- $112 - €120 - **£76** - FF788
  Sin título Serigrafía (65x50cm 25x19in) Madrid 2000

GABINO Santiago 1928 **[5]**
- $1 953 - €1 862 - **£1 240** - FF12 214
  El port Oleo/lienzo (54x81cm 21x31in) Barcelona 1999

GABL Alois 1845-1893 **[3]**
- $12 867 - €15 339 - **£9 174** - FF100 617
  Der Kasperl-Verkäufer Oil/panel (65.5x54cm 25x21in) Ahlden 2000

GABO Naum 1890-1977 **[37]**
- $458 838 - €442 655 - **£290 000** - FF2 903 625
  Vertical Construction No.1 Sculpture (H203cm H79in) London 1999
- $36 850 - €39 290 - **£25 000** - FF257 725
  Monument for an Airport Construction (9.5x27x14cm 3x10x5in) London 2001
- $10 758 - €11 943 - **£7 500** - FF78 341
  Study with red Pencil (26x33.5cm 10x13in) London 2001
- $637 - €613 - **£398** - FF4 024
  Composition Farblithographie (17.5x19cm 6x7in) München 1999

GABOR Jenö 1893-1971 **[7]**
- $4 620 - €4 444 - **£2 860** - FF29 150
  Nudes Oil/canvas (85x75cm 33x29in) Budapest 1999
- $2 310 - €2 222 - **£1 430** - FF14 575
  A Parisian Boulevard at Night Mixed media/paper (20x24.5cm 7x9in) Budapest 1999

GABORJANI Szabó Kálmán 1897-1955 **[1]**
- $5 920 - €6 220 - **£3 680** - FF40 800
  Senteur de lilas Tempera (122x55cm 48x21in) Budapest 2000

GABRIEL François 1893-1993 **[76]**
- $2 338 - €2 134 - **£1 422** - FF14 000
  Nature morte aux fruits Huile/panneau (77x62cm 30x24in) Saint-Dié 1998

GABRIEL Isabelle 1902-1990 **[17]**
- $2 000 - €2 371 - **£1 457** - FF15 553
  Floral Still Life Oil/panel (91x71cm 36x28in) Chicago IL 2001

GABRIëL Paul Joseph Const. 1828-1903 **[133]**
- $125 606 - €117 983 - **£75 712** - FF773 916
  Zomer (polder bij Kortenoef) Oil/canvas (91x150cm 35x59in) Amsterdam 1999
- $14 580 - €14 873 - **£9 120** - FF97 560
  Un matin à Veenendaal, Gueldre Huile/toile (40x62cm 15x24in) Bruxelles 2000

$7 206 - €6 807 - **£4 359** - FF44 649
Ruine Van Brederode Oil/panel (22.5x28.5cm 8x11in) Amsterdam 1999

$1 999 - €2 178 - **£1 377** - FF14 287
River Landscape with a Mill Watercolour/paper (7.5x16.5cm 2x6in) Amsterdam 2001

GABRINI Alfonso XX [3]
$1 250 - €1 296 - **£750** - FF8 500
Villa Borghese Olio/tela (44x70cm 17x27in) Roma 1999

GABRINI Pietro 1856-1926 [103]
$6 111 - €6 067 - **£3 818** - FF39 798
The Festival of Spring Oil/canvas (136.5x100.5cm 53x39in) Toronto 1999

$4 200 - €4 232 - **£2 618** - FF27 762
The Fisherman's Serenade Oil/canvas (51x76.5cm 20x30in) New-York 2000

$2 380 - €2 461 - **£1 428** - FF16 184
Giovane ciociara Olio/tela (32x22cm 12x8in) Milano 1999

$1 500 - €1 454 - **£928** - FF9 539
Woman at the Shore Watercolour/paper (38x51cm 15x20in) Mystic CT 1999

GABRITSCHEVSKY Eugène 1893-1979 [31]
$524 - €610 - **£368** - FF4 000
Composition Aquarelle/papier (21x25cm 8x9in) Paris 2001

GABRON Guilliam 1619-1678 [6]
$54 468 - €54 882 - **£33 948** - FF360 000
Sept faucons pèlerins perchés sur des rochers avec des gants Huile/toile (115x143cm 45x56in) Paris 2000

$144 630 - €143 458 - **£90 000** - FF941 022
Silver salt-cellar and upturned Tazza, a Pewter Flagon, a Roemer Oil/panel (84.5x97cm 33x38in) London 1999

GACHET Mario 1879-1983 [49]
$880 - €1 140 - **£669** - FF7 480
«Castiglione, riva del Po» Olio/tela (50x63cm 19x24in) Vercelli 2001

$450 - €466 - **£270** - FF3 060
Contadina in costume Olio/cartone (45x35cm 17x13in) Torino 2000

GACHET Niclaus 1736-1817 [3]
$6 678 - €5 609 - **£3 925** - FF36 794
«Vue du Chateau de Chatelare près de Vevey canton de Berne» Aquarell/Papier (34.6x59cm 13x23in) Bern 1999

GADAN Antoine 1854-1934 [45]
$5 516 - €5 336 - **£3 402** - FF35 000
Bergères et troupeau sur un chemin côtier Huile/toile (57x100cm 22x39in) Paris 1999

GADANYI Jenö 1896-1960 [7]
$2 220 - €2 332 - **£1 380** - FF15 300
Nature morte avec des fleurs Huile/toile (51x42cm 20x16in) Budapest 2000

$1 330 - €1 471 - **£874** - FF9 652
Nude with Violin Mixed media/paper (80x60cm 31x23in) Budapest 2000

GADBOIS Louis 1770-1826 [11]
$55 000 - €48 244 - **£33 396** - FF316 459
Extensive Italian Landscapes with Peasants Oil/canvas (94x132.5cm 37x52in) New-York 1999

$3 334 - €3 201 - **£2 072** - FF21 000
Groupe de personnages avec chasseurs dans un paysage Gouache/papier (64.3x101.5cm 25x39in) Paris 1999

GADDI Agnolo c.1350-1396 [5]
$49 700 - €53 357 - **£33 250** - FF350 000
Madone en trône allaitant l'Enfant, deux anges volants et les Saints Tempera (100x58cm 39x22in) Paris 2000

$342 408 - €336 582 - **£220 000** - FF2 207 832
The Martyrdom of Saint Andrew Tempera/panel (27x37cm 10x14in) London 1999

GADDI Taddeo c.1300-1366 [4]
$130 000 - €138 834 - **£88 582** - FF910 689
Saint John the Evangelist Tempera/panel (55.5x35cm 21x13in) New-York 2001

GADE Hari Ambadas 1917 [6]
$1 000 - €863 - **£597** - FF5 662
Untitled Gouache/paper (55x36cm 21x14in) New-York 1998

GADEGAARD Paul 1920 [72]
$1 444 - €1 346 - **£871** - FF8 830
Konstruktivistisk komposition Oil/canvas (130x97cm 51x38in) København 1999

$2 474 - €2 681 - **£1 714** - FF17 588
Komposition Oil/canvas (73x92cm 28x36in) København 2001

$1 563 - €1 744 - **£1 069** - FF11 438
Komposition Oil/canvas (30x37cm 11x14in) København 2000

$530 - €538 - **£329** - FF3 526
Komposition Gouache/paper (59x72cm 23x28in) København 2000

GADENNE Charles 1926 [4]
$2 948 - €3 354 - **£2 046** - FF22 000
La muleta Bronze (58x29x20cm 22x11x7in) Douai 2000

GADOUD L. XIX-XX [10]
$1 094 - €1 220 - **£736** - FF8 000
«Vins camp romain, rouge, rosé, blanc» Affiche (159x118cm 62x46in) Orléans 2000

GAEL Barend c.1630-c.1690 [66]
$13 989 - €15 686 - **£9 500** - FF102 891
Figures and Sportsmen gathered outside an Inn Playing Oil/canvas (50x66cm 19x25in) London 2000

$10 607 - €10 379 - **£6 800** - FF68 083
Landscape with Horsemen resting by a Fountain Oil/copper (13x19cm 5x7in) London 1999

$779 - €908 - **£544** - FF5 953
Washerwoman by a well, with Ruins to the Right Black chalk (24.5x21.5cm 9x8in) Amsterdam 2000

GAELEN van Alexander 1670-1728 [5]
$2 848 - €3 176 - **£1 858** - FF20 836
A Battle Scene with two Horsemen/A Battle Scene with three Horsemen Oil/canvas (41x52cm 16x20in) Amsterdam 2000

GAENSLY Guilherme William XIX-XX [1]
$5 200 - €5 719 - **£3 606** - FF37 512
Coemrcio Street/Teatro Sao Joao/Porto da Barra/Praca Riachuelo Albumen print (18x23cm 7x9in) New-York 2001

GAERTNER Carl Frederick 1898-1952 [54]
$850 - €911 - **£580** - FF5 975
«Monday» Oil/masonite (38x53cm 15x21in) Cleveland OH 2001

$700 - €760 - **£484** - FF4 985
Old Mill Oil/canvas (22x30cm 9x12in) Cleveland OH 2001

G

$650 - €697 - £444 - FF4 570
The Moors Gouache/board (43x73cm 17x29in)
Cleveland OH 2001

GAERTNER Eduard 1801-1877 [12]
$22 880 - €27 267 - £16 390 - FF178 860
Visser voor het dorp (pêcheur devant le village)
Huile/toile (34x52cm 13x20in) Antwerpen 2000
$4 392 - €4 602 - £2 905 - FF30 185
Berliner Salon Watercolour (20.9x27.9cm 8x10in)
München 2000

GAETA Enrico 1840-1887 [8]
$3 400 - €4 406 - £2 550 - FF28 900
Interno di chiesa Olio/tela (105x82cm 41x32in)
Roma 2000

GÄFGEN Wolfgang 1936 [25]
$1 115 - €1 296 - £783 - FF8 500
Sans titre Crayon/papier (57x45cm 22x17in) Paris
2001

GAG Wanda 1893-1946 [27]
$950 - €1 024 - £648 - FF6 719
Tumble Timbers Linocut (10.5x16cm 4x6in) New-
York 2001

GAGARIN Prince Grigori Grigorievich 1810-1893
[16]
$4 384 - €4 837 - £2 900 - FF31 730
Young Greek Warrior Watercolour, gouache
(43x28.5cm 16x11in) London 2000

GAGEN Robert Ford 1847-1926 [23]
$268 - €316 - £190 - FF2 071
Frenchman's Bay Watercolour/paper (17x28cm
6x11in) Toronto 2000

GAGEY André XX [4]
$7 132 - €7 410 - £4 500 - FF48 606
**Working in the Garden/House with the red
Roof/French Village** Oil/canvas (60x73.5cm 23x28in)
London 2000

GAGGINI Antonello 1478-1536 [1]
$16 884 - €19 831 - £11 988 - FF130 086
Die Auferstehung Christi Relief (82x77cm 32x30in)
Zürich 2000

GAGLIARDINI Julien Gustave 1846/48-1927 [81]
$2 851 - €3 354 - £2 043 - FF22 000
Martigues Huile/panneau (38x55.5cm 14x21in) Paris
2001
$2 088 - €2 231 - £1 422 - FF14 634
Village ensoleillé Huile/panneau (26.5x41cm
10x16in) Lokeren 2001

GAGNEAU Paul Léon ?-1910 [6]
$11 120 - €12 196 - £7 552 - FF80 000
Retour à la ferme Huile/toile (148x225cm 58x88in)
Pontoise 2000

GAGNEREAUX Bénigne 1756-1795 [15]
$147 260 - €165 113 - £100 000 - FF1 083 070
The Education of Achilles Oil/canvas
(97.5x125.5cm 38x49in) London 2000
$18 435 - €17 503 - £11 298 - FF114 814
Lesender Knabe Öl/Leinwand (46x38cm 18x14in)
Zürich 1999
$1 656 - €1 829 - £1 148 - FF12 000
Venus transporté dans l'Olympe par Iris Encre
(32.5x47.5cm 12x18in) Paris 2001

GAGNEUX Paul ?-1892 [5]
$11 000 - €12 965 - £7 729 - FF85 048
Une écluse sur le Sichon/Canal at Sichon
Oil/canvas (100x149cm 39x59in) New-Orleans LA
2000

GAGNON Clarence Alphonse 1881-1942 [119]
$4 422 - €4 228 - £2 771 - FF27 731
L'Église de Goteig, Suisse Oil/panel (11.5x18cm
4x7in) Vancouver, BC. 1999
$991 - €1 157 - £679 - FF7 589
Village Co.Charlevoix Mine plomb (20x33cm
7x12in) Montréal 2000
$260 - €304 - £183 - FF1 997
«Rouen» Etching (16.5x10cm 6x3in) Calgary, Alberta
2001

GAI Qi 1774-1829 [11]
$800 - €818 - £501 - FF5 365
**Ladies in a Courtyard of a Pavilion with
Soldiers Outside** Ink (129.5x52cm 50x20in)
Washington 2000

GAIDAN Louis 1847-1925 [42]
$40 000 - €44 372 - £26 600 - FF291 064
Sous les pins à Carqueiranne Oil/canvas
(110.5x151cm 43x59in) New-York 2000
$9 355 - €7 858 - £5 500 - FF51 546
La route de Sommieres Oil/canvas (54x73cm
21x28in) London 1998

GAIGG Lois XX [5]
$816 - €953 - £559 - FF6 250
«Blaupunkt» Poster (118.5x84.5cm 46x33in) Hoorn
2000

GAIGNERON de Jean 1890-1976 [14]
$966 - €1 098 - £666 - FF7 200
Marocains dans la palmeraie Huile/carton
(27x35cm 10x13in) Paris 2000

GAIL Wilhelm 1804-1890 [33]
$2 752 - €3 068 - £1 924 - FF20 123
Italienischer Burghof Öl/Leinwand (44x54.5cm
17x21in) München 2001
$1 473 - €1 534 - £933 - FF10 061
**Santa Anna in Barcelona, Blick in einen goti-
schen Kreuzgang** Öl/Metall (32.5x27.5cm 12x10in)
München 2000

GAILLARD René 1719-1790 [9]
$1 400 - €1 399 - £855 - FF9 179
«Cocaine» Poster (160x117cm 63x46in) New-York
2000

GAILLARDOT Pierre 1910 [181]
$880 - €915 - £554 - FF6 000
Jockeys et chevaux, avant le départ Huile/toile
(38x46cm 14x18in) Le Havre 2000
$401 - €442 - £266 - FF2 900
Le port de Trouville Aquarelle/papier (21x26cm
8x10in) Deauville 2000

GAILLIARD Franz, François 1861-1932 [76]
$58 258 - €54 631 - £36 000 - FF358 358
Leda and the Swan Oil/canvas/board
(181.5x121.5cm 71x47in) London 1999
$2 079 - €1 735 - £1 218 - FF11 382
Canal de Willebroeck Huile/toile (32x56cm 12x22in)
Bruxelles 1998

GAILLIARD Jean-Jacques 1890-1976 [150]
$3 536 - €4 214 - £2 533 - FF27 642
Le Wellington d'Ostende Oil/canvas (45x55cm
17x21in) Lokeren 2000
$540 - €644 - £387 - FF4 227
Le navire école (Ostende) Huile/panneau (29x39cm
11x15in) Bruxelles 2000
$400 - €471 - £288 - FF3 089
San Leo au château Encre Chine (26.5x35.5cm
10x13in) Bruxelles 2001

GAINSBOROUGH Thomas 1727-1788 **[211]**
- $248 651 - €250 559 - **£155 000** - FF1 643 558
  Portrait of Admiral Vernon (1684-1757) Three-Quarter Length Oil/canvas (124x99.5cm 48x39in) London 2000
- $56 120 - €66 743 - **£40 000** - FF437 808
  Claudius Amyand (1718-1774), half length, wearing a Blue Coat Oil/canvas (74x62cm 29x24in) London 2000
- $20 308 - €19 875 - **£13 000** - FF130 373
  Landscape with Rustics on a Path Oil/paper/board (20x23cm 7x9in) London 1999
- $22 551 - €21 191 - **£14 000** - FF139 007
  Study of a mounted Horseman, possibly George, Prince of Wales Black chalk (17x13.5cm 6x5in) London 1999
- $182 - €170 - **£113** - FF1 114
  The Gipsies Etching (50x45cm 19x17in) London 1999

GAISSER Jakob Emanuel 1825-1899 **[63]**
- $2 963 - €2 556 - **£1 764** - FF16 767
  Zechkumpane Öl/Leinwand (80x61cm 31x24in) München 1998
- $2 138 - €2 543 - **£1 526** - FF16 684
  Höfische Gesellschaft Öl/Leinwand (40x31cm 15x12in) Wien 2000

GAISSER Max 1857-1922 **[56]**
- $4 198 - €4 326 - **£2 600** - FF28 376
  The Lovers Oil/panel (49x34cm 19x13in) London 2000
- $1 718 - €1 789 - **£1 088** - FF11 738
  Skatbrüder: Mönch, Feldherr und Landsknecht im Kellergewölbe Oil/panel (32x24.5cm 12x9in) München 2000

GAITIS Yannis 1923-1984 **[50]**
- $3 309 - €2 838 - **£2 000** - FF18 619
  Dragonfly Oil/canvas (65x100cm 25x39in) London 1998

GAITONDE Vasudeo. S. 1924 **[12]**
- $26 000 - €30 144 - **£18 418** - FF197 732
  Untitled Oil/canvas (127x101.5cm 50x39in) New-York 2000
- $11 577 - €10 829 - **£7 000** - FF71 033
  Abstract Oil/canvas (75.5x125.5cm 29x49in) London 1999

GAJARDO José Vicente XX **[1]**
- $5 500 - €6 382 - **£3 797** - FF41 863
  Sin título Marble (32x41.5x29cm 12x16x11in) New-York 2000

GAKUTEI Yashima XVIII-XIX **[15]**
- $449 - €511 - **£311** - FF3 353
  Reiskuchen auf Lackschale und Pflaumenblüten Woodcut in colors (13.6x18.3cm 5x7in) Köln 2000

GAL Jean-Claude 1942-1994 **[3]**
- $949 - €1 067 - **£666** - FF7 000
  Arn, pl.11 de la Vengeance d'Arn Encre Chine/papier (53x41cm 20x16in) Paris 2001

GAL Menchu 1919 **[30]**
- $3 825 - €4 505 - **£2 700** - FF29 550
  Paisaje Oleo/tabla (40x45cm 15x17in) Madrid 2001
- $5 175 - €5 043 - **£3 225** - FF29 550
  Robles de Estívaliz Oleo/tabla (30.5x21.5cm 12x8in) Madrid 1999
- $1 620 - €1 802 - **£1 110** - FF11 820
  Jinetes en el bosque Acuarela (31.5x21.5cm 12x8in) Madrid 2001

$346 - €330 - **£209** - FF2 167
  Marina Aguafuerte (38x58cm 14x22in) Madrid 1999

GALAN Julio 1959 **[26]**
- $21 000 - €24 399 - **£14 758** - FF160 045
  Aladino y la reina Victoria Acrylic (229.5x149.5cm 90x58in) New-York 2001
- $10 000 - €8 697 - **£6 029** - FF57 050
  Luna, bola de cristal y pelota Mixed media/canvas (59.5x120cm 23x47in) New-York 1998
- $2 873 - €3 354 - **£2 032** - FF22 000
  Untitled Pastel/papier (60x48cm 23x18in) Paris 2001

GALAND Léon 1872-1960 **[57]**
- $554 - €648 - **£395** - FF4 252
  French Soldier on the Beach with his Horse Huile/toile (38x46cm 14x18in) Montréal 2001
- $907 - €915 - **£565** - FF6 000
  Nature morte à la brioche Huile/toile (27x35cm 10x13in) Paris 2000

GALANDA Mikulas 1895-1938 **[5]**
- $4 913 - €4 647 - **£3 060** - FF30 481
  Nature morte aux fruits Huile/panneau (25x30cm 9x11in) Praha 2000

GALANIS Demetrius 1882-1966 **[63]**
- $249 - €244 - **£158** - FF1 600
  Corbeille de fruits Eau-forte (32x34.5cm 12x13in) Paris 1999

GALANTE Francesco 1884-1972 **[21]**
- $2 200 - €2 851 - **£1 650** - FF18 700
  Interno borghese Olio/tavola (45x55cm 17x21in) Napoli 2000
- $760 - €985 - **£570** - FF6 460
  Fanciulla addormentata Olio/tavola (18x24cm 7x9in) Napoli 2000

GALANTE Nicola 1883-1969 **[12]**
- $7 200 - €9 330 - **£5 400** - FF61 200
  Paesaggio a Vasto Olio/tela (40x55cm 15x21in) Torino 2000
- $4 250 - €4 406 - **£2 550** - FF28 900
  Spiaggia Olio/tela (25x33.5cm 9x13in) Torino 1999
- $400 - €415 - **£240** - FF2 720
  «Terzetto al caffe» Stampa (13.5x18.5cm 5x7in) Milano 2001

GALARD de Gustave 1779-1841 **[7]**
- $12 725 - €12 348 - **£8 019** - FF81 000
  Fillette et papillons Huile/toile (141x106cm 55x41in) Paris 1999

GALAREYA Jimmy c.1937 **[3]**
- $3 946 - €3 807 - **£2 494** - FF24 974
  Yingarna Mixed media (154x61.5cm 60x24in) Melbourne 1999

GALBALLY Cecil ?-1995 **[3]**
- $1 936 - €1 651 - **£1 153** - FF10 833
  Summer Afternoon, Kilmurvey Oil/board (33x44cm 13x17in) Dublin 1998

GALBUSERA Gioachimo 1871-1942 **[32]**
- $3 933 - €4 585 - **£2 723** - FF30 074
  Blumenstrauss mit Rosen Öl/Leinwand (84x59cm 33x23in) Bern 2000
- $1 656 - €1 801 - **£1 091** - FF11 817
  Zwei Hütten in bergiger Landschaft Huile/panneau (16.5x28.5cm 6x11in) Bern 2000

GALDI Vincenzo XIX-XX **[16]**
- $713 - €706 - **£444** - FF4 628
  Junger Mann mit Schal Albumen print (22.3x16.2cm 8x6in) Berlin 1999

GALE Dennis 1828-1903 **[8]**
✐ **$970** - €1 083 - **£675** - FF7 104
    Crossing to Levis in Canoes Aquarelle/papier
    (15x22cm 5x8in) Montréal 2001

GALE Martin 1949 **[10]**
  $6 624 - €7 111 - **£4 433** - FF46 642
    Watching the River Oil/canvas (120.5x138.5cm
    47x54in) Dublin 2000
  $2 840 - €3 047 - **£1 937** - FF19 989
    Wicklow Landscape Oil/canvas/board (30.5x76.5cm
    12x30in) Dublin 2001
✐ **$1 348** - €1 587 - **£947** - FF10 411
    Greenhouse at Canyon Pyon Watercolour/paper
    (15x70.5cm 5x27in) Dublin 2000

GALE William 1823-1909 **[31]**
  $26 078 - €23 711 - **£16 000** - FF155 534
    The captured Runaway Oil/canvas (126x96cm
    49x37in) London 1999
  $6 578 - €7 548 - **£4 500** - FF49 509
    Middle Eastern Woman with a Water Jug
    Oil/panel (19.5x14.5cm 7x5in) London 2000
✐ **$13 329** - €15 852 - **£9 500** - FF103 984
    **The Croquet Game/The Wedding Reception/The
    Christening/The Goodnight** Watercolour
    (21.5x28cm 8x11in) London 2000

GALEA Luigi Maria 1847-1917 **[109]**
  $6 151 - €5 773 - **£3 800** - FF37 869
    An extensive View of Valetta Harbour Oil/board
    (26x80cm 10x31in) Billingshurst, West-Sussex 1999
  $2 850 - €3 042 - **£1 900** - FF19 954
    The Grand Harbour, Valetta at Sunset Oil/board
    (22x56cm 8x22in) Leyburn, North Yorkshire 2000

GALEK Stanislaw 1876-1961 **[19]**
  $1 028 - €1 140 - **£684** - FF7 479
    Étang dans les Tatras Huile/toile/carton
    (27.5x39.5cm 10x15in) Warszawa 2000

GALEMA Arjen 1886-1974 **[5]**
  $1 039 - €1 180 - **£722** - FF7 739
    «De Vliegende Hollander» Poster (65.5x99.5cm
    25x39in) Hoorn 2001

GALEOTA Leopoldo 1868-1938 **[17]**
  $1 916 - €2 235 - **£1 345** - FF14 660
    Landstrasse mit Bauernvolk Öl/Leinwand
    (35x51cm 13x20in) Luzern 2000
  $1 200 - €1 244 - **£728** - FF7 683
    Marina Olio/tela (29.5x43.5cm 11x17in) Torino 2000

GALEOTTI Sebastiano c.1676-1746 **[7]**
✐ **$2 138** - €1 982 - **£1 329** - FF13 000
    Projet de décoration Encre (41x32cm 16x12in) Paris
    1999

GALESTRUZZI Giovanni Battista 1618-1661 **[7]**
  $175 - €204 - **£123** - FF1 341
    Seeungeheuer Radierung (8.5x12.5cm 3x4in) Berlin
    2001

GALEY Gaston Pierre 1880-1959 **[13]**
✐ **$1 232** - €1 171 - **£750** - FF7 683
    Flowers in a Basket Beside a Window
    Gouache/paper (12.5x16.5cm 4x6in) London 1999

GALHARDO Joao Carlos XIX-XX **[1]**
  $20 520 - €17 891 - **£12 240** - FF117 360
    Paisagem saloia Oleo/lienzo (100x125cm 39x49in)
    Lisboa 1998

GALI-FABRA Francisco 1880-1965 **[3]**
  $1 500 - €1 673 - **£981** - FF10 977
    **«Tous les attraits du tourisme en un seul pays:
    l'Espagne»** Poster (96.5x63.5cm 37x25in) New-York
    2000

GALIBERT Pierre XIX **[2]**
  $3 000 - €3 110 - **£1 800** - FF20 400
    **Natura morta di frutta/Natura morta con brocca
    di rame** Olio/tela (28.5x36.5cm 11x14in) Napoli 2000
  $4 017 - €3 964 - **£2 496** - FF26 000
    Gaston et Jules, chiens dans l'atelier du peintre
    Aquarelle/papier (35x43cm 13x16in) Paris 1999

GALICE Louis 1864-1935 **[49]**
  $384 - €328 - **£230** - FF2 153
    «Résurrection» Poster (177x122.5cm 69x48in)
    London 1998

GALICIA César 1957 **[4]**
  $6 380 - €6 607 - **£4 180** - FF43 340
    Calavera sobre alfeira Oleo/tabla (65x54cm
    25x21in) Madrid 2000
  $260 - €300 - **£185** - FF1 970
    Paisaje de Nueva York Grabado (49x49cm 19x19in)
    Madrid 2001

GALIEN-LALOUE Eugène 1854-1941 **[1120]**
  $4 371 - €4 878 - **£2 860** - FF32 000
    Village au bord de l'eau Huile/toile (49x65cm
    19x25in) Fontainebleau 2000
  $2 765 - €2 592 - **£1 662** - FF17 000
    Bateaux à quai Huile/panneau (17.5x36cm 6x14in)
    Paris 1999
✐ **$13 000** - €14.967 - **£8 871** - FF98 176
    Les quais de Paris Watercolour, gouache (19x31cm
    7x12in) New-York 2000

GALIMSKI Wladyslaw Mihailov. 1860-1940 **[10]**
  $5 154 - €4 759 - **£3 210** - FF31 218
    **Farmers on a Road, Windmills in the back-
    ground** Oil/canvas (62x101cm 24x39in) Warszawa
    1999

GALINDO Florencio 1947 **[5]**
  $1 960 - €2 102 - **£1 295** - FF13 790
    Ventana al jardín Oleo/tabla (100x81cm 39x31in)
    Madrid 2000

GALIZIA Fede 1578-c.1630 **[6]**
  $94 737 - €86 221 - **£58 150** - FF565 575
    Flechtkorb mit Quitten Huile/panneau (41x54cm
    16x21in) Zürich 1999
  $60 000 - €52 630 - **£36 432** - FF345 228
    Dish of Fruit Resting on a Table Oil/panel
    (28.5x39cm 11x15in) New-York 1999

GALJAARD Johannes Philippus 1812-1867 **[4]**
  $3 593 - €3 857 - **£2 404** - FF25 301
    Figures on a Country Road near Loosduinen
    Oil/panel (50x66cm 19x25in) Amsterdam 2000

GALL François, Ferenç 1912-1987 **[643]**
  $4 005 - €4 488 - **£2 792** - FF29 438
    Tvätterskor Oil/canvas (50x62cm 19x24in) Stockholm
    2001
  $2 123 - €2 463 - **£1 465** - FF16 159
    Gatuserveringen Oil/canvas (27x34cm 10x13in)
    Stockholm 2000
  $1 087 - €1 278 - **£754** - FF8 384
    Jeune fille à la terrasse du café Charcoal
    (56x45cm 22x17in) Stuttgart 2000

GALLACCIO Anya 1963 **[1]**
  $5 066 - €4 890 - **£3 200** - FF32 076
    Monika Mixed media (100x100x3cm 39x39x1in)
    London 1999

GALLAGHER Ellen 1967 **[2]**
- **$100 000** - €112 007 - **£69 480** - FF734 720
  Soma Oil/canvas (244x213.5cm 96x84in) New-York 2001

GALLAGHER Sears 1869-1955 **[35]**
- **$7 500** - €7 558 - **£4 675** - FF49 575
  Sand Dunes Oil/canvas (50x58cm 20x23in) Wilton NH 2000
- **$1 400** - €1 650 - **£983** - FF10 824
  Nothern New England Winter Scene Watercolour/paper (22x27cm 9x11in) East-Dennis MA 2000

GALLAIT Louis 1810-1887 **[45]**
- **$1 863** - €1 596 - **£1 100** - FF10 466
  The Forbidden Book Oil/panel (51x40.5cm 20x15in) Ipswich 1998
- **$1 300** - €1 440 - **£881** - FF9 443
  The Scholar Oil/panel (23x18cm 9x7in) New-York 2000
- **$459** - €446 - **£280** - FF2 926
  Le Cardinal Granvelle Crayon (21x13.5cm 8x5in) Bruxelles 1999

GALLAND André 1886-1965 **[51]**
- **$324** - €305 - **£201** - FF2 040
  Longchamp, partie de campagne Aquarelle/papier (26x40cm 10x15in) Deauville 1999
- **$205** - €229 - **£143** - FF1 500
  «L'Angleterre avec ses 15 millions d'ouvriers sur 22 millions...» Affiche (115x79cm 45x31in) Chartres 2001

GALLAND Gilbert 1870-1956 **[56]**
- **$6 535** - €7 622 - **£4 545** - FF50 000
  Lavandières à la Roche d'or de Bou saâda Huile/toile (65x100cm 25x39in) Paris 2000
- **$10 380** - €11 434 - **£6 892** - FF75 000
  La traversée de l'oued Huile/panneau (73x155cm 28x61in) Deauville 2000
- **$900** - €901 - **£555** - FF5 910
  La Mezquita de Ortakeil Oleo/tabla (24x33cm 9x12in) Madrid 2000
- **$952** - €838 - **£580** - FF5 500
  Bateaux à quai à Marseille Aquarelle/papier (26.5x37cm 10x14in) Lyon 1999

GALLAND Pierre Victor 1822-1892 **[16]**
- **$34 247** - €35 063 - **£21 505** - FF230 000
  Paravent à décor floral Huile/toile (230x300cm 90x118in) Lille 2000

GALLARD de Michel 1921 **[98]**
- **$1 320** - €1 448 - **£896** - FF9 500
  Le pot de fleurs Huile/toile (60x50cm 23x19in) Orléans 2000

GALLARD-LÉPINAY Paul Ch. Emmanuel 1842-1885 **[41]**
- **$2 911** - €3 125 - **£1 947** - FF20 500
  Marine Huile/toile (36x61cm 14x24in) Paris 2000
- **$1 876** - €2 058 - **£1 274** - FF13 500
  Clair de lune sur un port du Nord Huile/panneau (24x18.5cm 9x7in) Lille 2000

GALLARDO RUIZ Gustavo 1891-1971 **[6]**
- **$3 705** - €3 904 - **£2 340** - FF25 610
  Venta de San Fernando Oleo/lienzo (31x50cm 12x19in) Madrid 2000

GALLATIN Albert Eugene 1882-1952 **[9]**
- **$6 000** - €5 595 - **£3 721** - FF36 699
  «No.20» Oil/canvas (25.5x35.5cm 10x13in) New-York 1999

GALLE Cornelius I 1576-1650 **[17]**
- **$442** - €486 - **£300** - FF3 186
  Pictura, after Rubens Etching (29.3x20cm 11x7in) Berlin 2000

GALLÉ Émile 1846-1904 **[53]**
- **$1 388** - €1 296 - **£840** - FF8 500
  Pichet, gravé en camée à l'acide de baies rouges Sculpture verre (H19cm H7in) La Varenne-Saint-Hilaire 1999

GALLÉ Hieronymus I 1626-c.1680 **[8]**
- **$42 500** - €44 058 - **£25 500** - FF289 000
  Vari uccelli, anatra in un cesto/Cacciagione, vari uccelli Olio/tela (152x187.5cm 59x73in) Milano 1999

GALLE Philip 1537-1612 **[54]**
- **$643** - €767 - **£458** - FF5 030
  Die Geschichte des Königs Josua, nach Marten van Heemskerck Kupferstich (21.5x25.5cm 8x10in) Berlin 2000

GALLE Theodore 1571-1633 **[10]**
- **$386** - €460 - **£275** - FF3 018
  Staphae, vive Stapedes, der Hufschmied, nach Johannes Stradanus Kupferstich (19.9x27cm 7x10in) Berlin 2000

GALLEGO Fernando c.1468-c.1507 **[3]**
- **$226 950** - €228 674 - **£141 450** - FF1 500 000
  Vierge à l'enfant couronnée par deux anges Huile/panneau (150x75cm 59x29in) Paris 2000

GALLEGOS Y ARNOSA José 1859-1917 **[66]**
- **$54 542** - €54 961 - **£34 000** - FF360 522
  Ladies in a Sun-dapped Courtyard Oil/panel (40x52cm 15x20in) London 2000
- **$23 881** - €20 059 - **£14 000** - FF131 579
  El rosario Oil/panel (18x28cm 7x11in) London 1998
- **$2 660** - €2 853 - **£1 805** - FF18 715
  «Vista de Venecia» Acuarela/papel (56x35cm 22x13in) Madrid 2001

GALLELLI Massimo 1863-1956 **[4]**
- **$12 000** - €14 103 - **£8 319** - FF92 512
  The Lyrist's Serenade Oil/canvas (62x102cm 24x40in) New-York 2001

GALLEN-KALLELA Akseli 1865-1931 **[166]**
- **$326 570** - €285 831 - **£197 880** - FF1 874 930
  Den stora gäddan Oil/canvas (138x123cm 54x48in) Helsinki 1998
- **$50 204** - €47 091 - **£31 024** - FF308 896
  Kölddag Oil/canvas (60x48cm 23x18in) Helsinki 1999
- **$12 631** - €13 236 - **£8 000** - FF86 823
  Year Old Snow Oil/board (21x26cm 8x10in) London 2000
- **$2 319** - €2 270 - **£14 103** - FF14 893
  Kesäaamun sarastaessa Akvarell/papper (30x23cm 11x9in) Helsinki 1999
- **$599** - €639 - **£406** - FF4 192
  Gamla furor Etching (13.5x7.5cm 5x2in) Helsinki 2001

GALLI Edoardo 1854-? **[4]**
- **$11 270** - €10 671 - **£7 000** - FF70 000
  La loge Huile/panneau (74x31cm 29x12in) Paris 1999

GALLI Federica 1932 **[10]**
- **$350** - €363 - **£210** - FF2 380
  Albero Acquaforte (69x29cm 27x11in) Milano 1999

GALLI Giuseppe 1868-1953 **[11]**
- **$400** - €415 - **£240** - FF2 720
  Paesaggio montano Olio/tavola (23.5x34cm 9x13in) Milano 2000

G

GALLI Leopoldo XIX [2]

$8 042 - €8 163 - £5 000 - FF53 545
**The Madonna del Cardellino, after Raffaello
Sanzio** Oil/canvas (107x75cm 42x29in) London 2000

GALLI Riccardo 1869-1944 [23]

$2 160 - €1 866 - £1 080 - FF12 240
Cascinali a Macugnaga Olio/tavola (50x60cm
19x23in) Milano 1999

$1 400 - €1 451 - £840 - FF9 520
Nervi, mattina di burrasca Olio/tavola (24.5x35cm
9x13in) Milano 1999

GALLI Stefano 1950 [34]

$425 - €441 - £255 - FF2 890
«Solo all'attacco» Acrilico/tela (80x80cm 31x31in)
Vercelli 2001

GALLIAC Louis 1849-1934 [7]

$1 683 - €1 982 - £1 183 - FF13 000
Portrait de femme africaine Huile/toile (54x40cm
21x15in) Paris 2000

GALLIAN Octave Georges V.L. 1855-? [9]

$1 307 - €1 555 - £932 - FF10 200
Village de Provence Huile/toile (50x100cm 19x39in)
Toulon 2000

GALLIANI Omar 1954 [83]

$3 750 - €3 887 - £2 250 - FF25 500
Tra la voce e il silenzio 2 Olio/tela (150x100cm
59x39in) Prato 2000

$2 250 - €2 332 - £1 350 - FF15 300
Ombre Olio/tela (80x80cm 31x31in) Prato 2000

$2 000 - €2 073 - £1 200 - FF13 600
Modern Monnalisa Tecnica mista/cartone (30x30cm
11x11in) Roma 1999

$720 - €622 - £360 - FF4 080
Senza titolo Matita/carta (36.5x31.5cm 14x12in) Prato
1999

GALLIARI Bernardino 1707-1794 [9]

$16 000 - €20 733 - £12 000 - FF136 000
L'Olimpo Olio/tela (120x144cm 47x56in) Milano 2000

$11 685 - €10 901 - £7 050 - FF71 505
Die Musik Öl/Leinwand (97x107.5cm 38x42in) Wien
1999

$3 352 - €3 323 - £2 097 - FF21 800
Bühnenprospekt (Innenansicht eines Kerkers)
Ink (20.5x28cm 8x11in) München 1999

GALLIEN Pierre Antoine 1896-1963 [6]

$26 130 - €22 867 - £15 825 - FF150 000
Composition abstraite Huile/toile (73x116cm
28x45in) Paris 1998

GALLIS Pieter 1633-1697 [7]

$15 000 - €17 428 - £10 542 - FF114 318
**Roses, Carnations, Poppies and other Flowers
by a Tree Trunk** Oil/canvas (106x83cm 41x32in) New-
York 2001

GALLISON Henry Hammond 1850-1910 [10]

$9 000 - €10 281 - £6 336 - FF67 438
Extensive Summer Landscape Oil/canvas
(101x137cm 40x54in) Pittsfield MA 2001

GALLO Beppe 1942 [43]

$550 - €570 - £330 - FF3 740
Frutti d'autunno Olio/tela (60x70cm 23x27in)
Vercelli 2000

$250 - €259 - £150 - FF1 700
Langa Olio/tavola (18x24cm 7x9in) Vercelli 2000

GALLO Frank 1933 [26]

$1 300 - €1 478 - £908 - FF9 698
Erotic Lovers Sculpture (26x43x25cm 10x17x10in)
Chicago IL 2000

GALLO Giuseppe 1954 [19]

$3 600 - €4 665 - £2 700 - FF30 600
Alzai gli occhi Tecnica mista (47x111.5cm 18x43in)
Prato 2000

$480 - €622 - £360 - FF4 080
Senza titolo Carboncino (46.5x37cm 18x14in) Milano
2000

GALLOCHE Louis 1670-1761 [7]

$20 000 - €19 956 - £12 174 - FF130 902
Seated Woman, her left arm raised Black, red &
white chalks/paper (40.5x51.5cm 15x20in) New-York
2000

GALLON Richard [2]

$7 893 - €7 654 - £5 000 - FF50 204
Highland Cattle Oil/canvas (44x34cm 17x13in) Little-
Lane, Ilkley 1999

GALLON Robert 1845-1925 [117]

$8 505 - €9 166 - £5 800 - FF60 125
Guildford Castle, Surrey Oil/canvas (86.5x157.5cm
34x62in) London 2001

$6 000 - €6 440 - £4 015 - FF42 246
Mountainous Landscape with Figures Oil/canvas
(60x101cm 24x40in) Bloomfield-Hills MI 2000

$750 - €805 - £501 - FF5 280
Leigh-on-Sea, Essex Oil/board (20x30cm 8x12in)
Hendersonville NC 2000

$392 - €467 - £280 - FF3 064
Kenilworth Castle Watercolour/paper (24x35cm
9x13in) Bath 2000

GALLOP Herbert Reginald 1890-1958 [46]

$1 012 - €1 129 - £704 - FF7 409
Garie Beach Oil/board (37.5x45.5cm 14x17in)
Sydney 2001

$595 - €622 - £375 - FF4 078
The Homestead Oil/board (29x44cm 11x17in)
Sydney 2000

GALLOTTI Alessandro 1879-1961 [10]

$1 600 - €2 073 - £1 200 - FF13 600
Bosco con figure Olio/tela (60.5x40.5cm 23x15in)
Milano 2001

GALLOWAY William 1878-? [3]

$798 - €908 - £553 - FF5 953
**Young Women in national Costume on the
Beach** Etching in colors (17.8x26cm 7x10in) Haarlem
2000

GALOFRE Y GIMÉNEZ Baldomero 1849-1902 [101]

$38 250 - €45 049 - £26 250 - FF295 500
Marina Oleo/lienzo (90x145.5cm 35x57in) Madrid
2000

$20 000 - €19 074 - £12 174 - FF125 118
Rainy Day on the Pontine Marches Oil/canvas
(77.5x132cm 30x51in) New-York 1999

$15 000 - €14 854 - £9 339 - FF97 437
The Country Fair Oil/panel (21x35cm 8x13in) New-
York 1999

$2 430 - €2 703 - £1 620 - FF17 730
Pescadores en la playa Acuarela/papel (21.5x45cm
8x17in) Madrid 2000

GALOYER François 1944 [16]

$1 712 - €1 829 - £1 164 - FF12 000
Sitelle de Torchepot Bronze (16.5x21.5cm 6x8in)
Pontoise 2001

GALT Cameron 1964 [4]
- $6 630 - €5 720 - **£4 000** - FF37 523
  Vanity Oil/canvas (119.5x58.5cm 47x23in) London 1998
- $6 746 - €6 547 - **£4 200** - FF42 948
  Study for The Old Haunt Charcoal (122x153cm 48x60in) London 1999

GALTER Pietro act.1881-1887 [9]
- $6 780 - €7 927 - **£4 841** - FF52 000
  Felouques sur le Nil Huile/toile (45x74cm 17x29in) Paris 2001
- $5 450 - €6 051 - **£3 800** - FF39 690
  Venetian Fishermen returning Home Oil/canvas (26x41cm 10x16in) London 2001

GALVANO Albino 1907-1991 [46]
- $850 - €881 - **£510** - FF5 780
  Fiori Olio/tavola (50x40cm 19x15in) Torino 2000
- $500 - €518 - **£300** - FF3 400
  Composizione Olio/cartone/tela (35x45cm 13x17in) Vercelli 2000
- $200 - €207 - **£120** - FF1 360
  «Eva» Acquarello/carta (31x21cm 12x8in) Vercelli 2000

GALWEY Y DE GARCIA Enrique 1864-1931 [36]
- $1 890 - €2 102 - **£1 330** - FF13 790
  Paisaje Oleo/lienzo (35x46cm 13x18in) Barcelona 2001
- $693 - €661 - **£418** - FF4 334
  Paisaje con montaña Oleo/lienzo (22.5x29.5cm 8x11in) Barcelona 1999

GAMAGE Parker XX [12]
- $1 150 - €1 234 - **£769** - FF8 097
  Monhegan Island from Shore, Rocks and Pine Trees in Foreground Oil/canvas (91x73cm 36x29in) Thomaston ME 2000
- $400 - €433 - **£274** - FF2 838
  New harbor, Main in Autumn Oil/board (30x40cm 12x16in) Thomaston ME 2001

GAMAIN Louis 1803-1871 [20]
- $2 863 - €2 668 - **£1 765** - FF17 500
  Voiliers à l'entrée du port du Havre Huile/toile (43x59cm 16x23in) Le Havre 1999

GAMARRA José 1934 [30]
- $35 000 - €34 054 - **£21 542** - FF223 380
  La Incógnita Oil/canvas (150x150cm 59x59in) New-York 1999
- $2 094 - €2 439 - **£1 462** - FF16 000
  Composition Huile/toile (80x94cm 31x37in) Paris 2000

GAMBA DE PREYDOUR Jules-Alexandre 1846-? [8]
- $7 283 - €6 022 - **£4 273** - FF39 500
  Panier de roses sur un banc de pierre dans un jardin Huile/toile (136x72cm 53x28in) Tarbes 1998
- $3 950 - €4 668 - **£2 800** - FF30 622
  Roses/Marguerites Oil/canvas (22x16cm 8x6in) London 2000

GAMBA Enrico 1831-1883 [55]
- $8 800 - €11 403 - **£6 600** - FF74 800
  Sul Tago a Belem Olio/tela (35.5x62cm 13x24in) Roma 2001
- $2 000 - €2 073 - **£1 200** - FF13 600
  Giovane popolana Olio/tavola (29.5x21cm 11x8in) Vercelli 1999
- $120 - €155 - **£90** - FF1 020
  Gentiluomo Matita/carta (31.5x14.5cm 12x5in) Milano 2001

- $1 211 - €1 255 - **£726** - FF8 234
  «Esposizione Generale Italiana, Torino» Affiche couleur (99x72cm 38x28in) Torino 2000

GAMBA Francesco 1818-1887 [3]
- $26 000 - €26 980 - **£16 494** - FF176 974
  Village Marketplace Oil/canvas (88x132.5cm 34x52in) Boston MA 2000

GAMBACCIANI A. XIX-XX [1]
- $7 000 - €6 676 - **£4 260** - FF43 791
  Bust of a Young Woman on Pedestal Marble (H74.5cm H29in) New-York 1999

GAMBARD Henri Augustin 1819-? [3]
- $3 500 - €3 939 - **£2 411** - FF25 839
  Portrait of a Lady in Black, Possibly a Member of the Gaudet Family Oil/canvas (101x81cm 40x32in) New-Orleans LA 2000

GAMBARINI Giuseppe 1680-1725 [12]
- $10 665 - €10 414 - **£6 800** - FF68 312
  Meanad beating a Tambourine with an Infant, a Goat in a Formal Garden Oil/canvas (74.5x62cm 29x24in) London 1999
- $8 516 - €7 911 - **£5 200** - FF51 896
  A Sheet of Figure Studies Wash (32x39.5cm 12x15in) London 1998

GAMBARTES Leonidas 1909-1963 [15]
- $3 400 - €3 950 - **£2 389** - FF25 912
  Conjuro Técnica mixta/cartón (22x33cm 8x12in) Buenos-Aires 2001
- $1 600 - €1 859 - **£1 124** - FF12 193
  Dos figuras Acuarela/cartulina (23x30cm 9x11in) Buenos-Aires 2001

GAMBIER-PARRY Ernest, Major c.1854-1936 [3]
- $3 270 - €2 908 - **£2 000** - FF19 074
  Spring Days Oil/canvas (110.5x85.5cm 43x33in) London 1999

GAMBLE John Marshall 1863-1957 [56]
- $47 500 - €48 101 - **£29 801** - FF315 523
  California Landscape Oil/canvas (49x74cm 19x29in) Morris-Plains NJ 2000
- $17 000 - €16 169 - **£10 322** - FF106 063
  October, Wild Buckwheat Oil/canvas (30.5x40.5cm 12x15in) Beverly-Hills CA 1999
- $3 500 - €4 090 - **£2 498** - FF26 831
  «Field of Yellow» Watercolour/paper (15x25cm 6x10in) Altadena CA 2001

GAMBOGI Émile XIX [10]
- $1 175 - €1 296 - **£782** - FF8 500
  La porteuse d'eau Huile/toile (70x44cm 27x17in) Biarritz 2000

GAMBOGI G. XIX-XX [13]
- $9 045 - €8 567 - **£5 500** - FF56 194
  Pearl Nymph Marble (H109cm H42in) London 1999
- $1 976 - €1 880 - **£1 200** - FF12 330
  Figure of a young Girl Alabaster (H55cm H21in) London 1999

GAMBOGI Raffaello 1874-1943 [16]
- $520 - €2 177 - **£1 680** - FF14 280
  Parco di Villa Fabricotti Olio/tela (58x69cm 22x27in) Prato 1998
- $2 000 - €2 592 - **£1 500** - FF17 000
  Marian ad Antignano Olio/cartone (29.5x37cm 11x14in) Prato 2000

GAMELIN Jacques 1738-1803 [42]
- $12 378 - €11 891 - **£7 675** - FF78 000
  Portrait d'un général révolutionnaire Huile/toile (194x107cm 76x42in) Montastruc 1999

G

$952 - €1 067 - **£666** - FF7 000
Sainte Cécile Huile/toile (26x21cm 10x8in) Paris
2001

$1 654 - €1 448 - **£1 002** - FF9 500
Choc de cavalerie Encre (30x43.5cm 11x17in)
Toulouse 1998

$256 - €281 - **£174** - FF1 844
Der Tod auf dem Schlachtfeld Radierung
(14.5x29cm 5x11in) Berlin 2000

GAMES Abram 1914-1996 **[28]**

$375 - €407 - **£250** - FF2 670
«Visit Israel, Land of the Bible» Poster (74x49cm
29x19in) New-York 2000

GAMLEY Andrew Archer 1869-1949 **[24]**

$330 - €308 - **£200** - FF2 023
Unloading the Catch Watercolour/paper (34x42.5cm
13x16in) Edinburgh 1999

GAMMELL Robert Hale Ives 1893-1981 **[30]**

$5 000 - €5 908 - **£3 543** - FF38 754
Wellfleet Bay Oil/canvas (56x81.5cm 22x32in) Boston
MA 2000

$475 - €532 - **£330** - FF3 491
Ischia Oil/panel (17x28cm 7x11in) Watertown MA
2001

$500 - €475 - **£306** - FF3 113
Portrait of Ariel Hall Pastel/paper (62x48cm 24x19in)
Boston MA 2000

GAMMON Reginald William 1894-1997 **[41]**

$817 - €850 - **£520** - FF5 576
Washer Women Oil/board (45.5x56cm 17x22in)
London 2000

$152 - €176 - **£105** - FF1 157
Cattle in the Water Meadow Watercolour
(28x38.5cm 11x15in) Bristol, Avon 2000

GAMP von Botho Freiherr 1894-1977 **[62]**

$1 677 - €1 841 - **£1 080** - FF12 074
Blick auf südliche Kirche mit Figurenstaffage
Öl/Leinwand (51x60cm 20x23in) Lindau 2000

GAMPENRIEDER Karl 1860-1930 **[8]**

$2 975 - €2 543 - **£1 785** - FF16 681
**Bildnis einer jungen bayrischen Prinzessin im
Reitkostüm** Öl/Leinwand (78x38cm 30x14in) Wien
1998

GAMY (Marguerite Montaut) XIX-XX **[81]**

$389 - €379 - **£240** - FF2 488
**Juvisy, Paris, de Lambert sur son Biplan
Wright-Aeriel** Color lithograph (45x90cm 17x35in)
London 1999

GANASSINI Marzio di Colantonio XVII **[1]**

$18 000 - €17 182 - **£11 246** - FF112 708
Venus and Mars Surrounded by Putti Oil/copper
(36.5x49cm 14x19in) New-York 1999

GANDIA Vicente 1935 **[13]**

$12 864 - €14 266 - **£8 556** - FF93 576
Naturaleza muerta Oleo/lienzo (100x120cm 39x47in)
México 2000

$14 000 - €13 622 - **£8 617** - FF89 352
La mesa recobrada Acrylic/canvas (80x90cm
31x35in) New-York 1999

$828 - €885 - **£566** - FF5 804
Las bañistas Aguafuerte (23x19.5cm 9x7in) México
2001

GANDINI DEL GRANO Giorgio 1489-1538 **[6]**

$21 000 - €24 814 - **£14 882** - FF162 766
Saint George and the Dragon Oil/canvas (76x63cm
29x24in) Boston MA 2000

$22 500 - €22 450 - **£13 695** - FF147 264
Study of Two Saints Kneeling Red chalk/paper
(10.5x17cm 4x6in) New-York 2000

GANDOLFI Gaetano 1734-1802 **[98]**

$24 477 - €22 753 - **£15 000** - FF149 253
Saint Peter in Penitence Oil/canvas (45x37.5cm
17x14in) London 1998

$88 385 - €87 669 - **£55 000** - FF575 069
**Allegory of Prudence/Allegory of temperance
(studies for Pendentives)** Oil/canvas (34.5x43.5cm
13x17in) London 1999

$5 500 - €4 824 - **£3 339** - FF31 645
Three Heads of Young Women Ink (15x19.5cm
5x7in) New-York 1999

$643 - €767 - **£458** - FF5 030
Die Schlägerei im Wirtshaus Radierung
(12.1x15.8cm 4x6in) Berlin 2000

GANDOLFI Mauro 1764-1834 **[21]**

$29 359 - €27 460 - **£18 000** - FF180 126
The Education of the Virgin Oil/canvas (75x53cm
29x20in) London 1998

$4 161 - €5 031 - **£2 907** - FF33 000
Sainte Anne, saint Joachim et l'Enfant Jésus
Huile/toile (30.5x23cm 12x9in) Paris 2000

$6 500 - €6 738 - **£3 900** - FF44 200
Ritratto di giovane donna Acquarello (11x13.5cm
4x5in) Milano 2001

$156 - €168 - **£104** - FF1 100
**Se in Opre di Pennel, divino Ingeno...A Allegri
detto Il Corregion** Eau-forte (69x45.5cm 27x17in)
Paris 2000

GANDOLFI Ubaldo 1728-1781 **[57]**

$100 000 - €94 082 - **£62 400** - FF617 140
The Holy Family in the Carpenter's Shop Oil/can-
vas (43x33cm 16x12in) New-York 1999

$2 989 - €3 354 - **£2 092** - FF22 000
**Etude de personnages pour sainte Hélène
retrouvant la vraie Croix** Encre (30.5x21.5cm
12x8in) Paris 2001

GANDON Adolphe 1828-1889 **[10]**

$3 400 - €4 007 - **£2 389** - FF26 287
Camp de Boulogne, 1805 Oil/canvas (53x64cm
21x25in) New-Orleans LA 2000

GANDY Joseph Michael 1771-1843 **[6]**

$4 196 - €3 885 - **£2 600** - FF25 484
Jason Before a Temple to Amphitrite Watercolour
(45x63cm 17x24in) London 1999

GANDY William c.1655-1729 **[1]**

$4 910 - €5 840 - **£3 500** - FF38 308
**Portrait of Sir Richard Pyne, Lord Chief Justice
of the Common Pleas** Oil/canvas (74x62cm
29x24in) London 2000

GANGOLF Paul 1879-c.1945 **[38]**

$878 - €869 - **£547** - FF5 701
Tiermarkt Radierung (11.9x15.7cm 4x6in) Berlin 1999

GANGOOLY Jamini Prokash 1876-1953 **[8]**

$2 856 - €2 772 - **£1 800** - FF18 184
A Bengali Beauty Oil/canvas (33x26cm 12x10in)
London 1999

GANLY Rose Brigid 1909 **[14]**

$1 725 - €2 032 - **£1 212** - FF13 326
Daffodils in a Vase Oil/canvas/board (61x49.5cm
24x19in) Dublin 2000

$1 748 - €2 032 - **£1 229** - FF13 326
Connemara Lake Landscape Oil/board (25x35cm
9x13in) Dublin 2001

GANNAM John 1907-1965 **[11]**
$1 500 - €1 389 - £918 - FF9 109
Outdoor circus scene with elephants; ill. for American Magazine Watercolour/paper (33x45cm 13x18in) New-York 1999

GANRYO 1798-1852 **[4]**
$1 521 - €1 789 - £1 102 - FF11 738
Brüllender Tiger an einem Felsen im Regen Indian ink (100.5x37cm 39x14in) Köln 2001

GANSO Emil 1895-1941 **[150]**
$850 - €964 - £594 - FF6 321
Reclining Female Nude Oil/board (42x56.5cm 16x22in) New-York 2001
$1 500 - €1 512 - £935 - FF9 915
Seated Nude Oil/masonite (31x23cm 12x9in) Delray-Beach FL 2000
$550 - €569 - £347 - FF3 734
Woman in a Chemise Seen from Behind Watercolour (29x19.5cm 11x7in) New-York 2000
$325 - €303 - £200 - FF1 988
Bather, Model Standing Etching (24x17cm 9x6in) Cleveland OH 1999

GANTNER Bernard 1928 **[383]**
$1 250 - €1 372 - £804 - FF9 000
Ferme dans la forêt Huile/toile (66x54cm 25x21in) Saint-Dié 2000
$505 - €427 - £300 - FF2 800
Coin de forêt Gouache (22.5x31cm 8x12in) Saint-Dié 1998
$101 - €107 - £66 - FF700
Paysage Lithographie (46x61cm 18x24in) Saint-Dié 2000

GANTZ John 1772-1853 **[5]**
$5 352 - €6 286 - £3 800 - FF41 233
Arjuna's penance, Mahabalipuram Watercolour (33.5x44.5cm 13x17in) London 2000

GANTZ Justinian Walter 1802-1862 **[17]**
$3 586 - €3 849 - £2 400 - FF25 251
View from the Governor's Camp near Kistnagherry Watercolour (31x36cm 12x14in) London 2000

GANZ Edwin 1871-1957 **[33]**
$346 - €372 - £232 - FF2 439
Paysage montagneux Huile/toile (46x38cm 18x14in) Liège 2000

GANZ Valerie 1936 **[5]**
$3 143 - €3 523 - £2 200 - FF23 108
British Steel, Port Talbot Watercolour (48x73cm 18x28in) Billingshurst, West-Sussex 2001

GANZER Jim XX **[3]**
$4 000 - €4 455 - £2 616 - FF29 225
Sea of Desire Etching, aquatint in colors (25x50cm 9x19in) New-York 2000

GAO CEN c.1643-1682 **[1]**
$33 384 - €36 454 - £21 476 - FF239 122
Landscapes Ink/paper (22x14.5cm 8x5in) Hong-Kong 2000

GAO FENGHAN 1683-1748 **[4]**
$7 704 - €8 412 - £4 956 - FF55 182
Calligraphy in Li Shu of «Yan Ming» (Inscription on inkstone) Ink/paper (35.5x217cm 13x85in) Hong-Kong 2000

GAO JIAN 1634-1707 **[4]**
$9 009 - €8 544 - £5 481 - FF56 042
Landscape Ink (122x50.5cm 48x19in) Hong-Kong 1999

GAO JIANFU 1879-1951 **[49]**
$4 902 - €4 623 - £3 040 - FF30 324
Calligraphy Couplet in Cao Shu Ink/paper (133x31.5cm 52x12in) Hong-Kong 1999

GAO QIFENG 1889-1933 **[13]**
$66 924 - €63 466 - £40 716 - FF416 312
Growling Tiger Ink (108.5x54.5cm 42x21in) Hong-Kong 1999

GAO XIANG 1688-1754 **[5]**
$4 200 - €3 626 - £2 509 - FF23 782
Snapping Fingers Pavilion Ink (73x35.5cm 28x13in) New-York 1998

GARA Emmerich 1903-1964 **[5]**
$1 500 - €1 574 - £993 - FF10 325
Leonard Bernstein Silver print (33x25cm 13x10in) New-York 2000

GARACCIONI Oreste 1881-? **[3]**
$16 104 - €16 332 - £10 000 - FF107 132
Reclining Semi-draped Nude Holding a Cigarette Oil/canvas (68x118cm 26x46in) London 2000

GARAT Francis c.1870-? **[106]**
$2 854 - €3 049 - £1 902 - FF20 000
Le marché aux fleurs Huile/panneau (29x23cm 11x9in) Paris 2000
$725 - €701 - £447 - FF4 600
L'Hôtel de Ville Gouache/papier (20x26cm 7x10in) Bordeaux 1999

GARATE Cecilia 1933 **[4]**
$3 900 - €3 904 - £2 405 - FF25 610
Descanso Oleo/lienzo (65x54cm 25x21in) Madrid 2000

GARATE Y CLAVERO Juan José 1870-1939 **[41]**
$4 326 - €4 269 - £2 665 - FF28 000
Vue de Brousse en Turquie représentant l'entrée de l'armée ottomane Huile/toile (58x79cm 22x31in) Saint-Dié 1999
$1 624 - €1 742 - £1 102 - FF11 426
Los Apeninos Oleo/cartón (21x29.5cm 8x11in) Madrid 2001
$1 080 - €1 201 - £720 - FF7 880
Panticosa Acuarela/papel (26x37cm 10x14in) Madrid 2000

GARAUD Gustave Césaire 1847-1914 **[18]**
$1 897 - €2 134 - £1 306 - FF14 000
La mare aux fées, Fontainebleau Huile/toile (46.5x61cm 18x24in) Barbizon 2000

GARAVILLA Angel 1906-1961 **[4]**
$6 100 - €6 006 - £3 800 - FF39 400
Familia Vasca Oleo/lienzo (54x81cm 21x31in) Madrid 1999

GARAY de Marie XIX-XX **[11]**
$8 000 - €9 509 - £5 543 - FF62 378
Innocent Pastime, Blowing Bubbles in the Garden Oil/wood (10x14cm 4x5in) New-Orleans LA 2000

GARAY Y ARÉVALO Manuel XIX **[11]**
$4 575 - €4 505 - £2 850 - FF29 550
Devanando la madeja Oleo/tabla (43x52.5cm 16x20in) Madrid 1999
$2 600 - €3 003 - £1 800 - FF19 700
Proposición Oleo/tabla (35x27cm 13x10in) Madrid 2001

GARBE Herbert 1888-1945 **[6]**
$3 518 - €3 388 - £2 200 - FF22 222
Elephant Bronze (H45.5cm H17in) London 1999

G

GARBE Richard 1876-1957 **[8]**
$886 - €899 - £550 - FF5 896
Fate Porcelain (H26.5cm H10in) London 2000

GARBELL Alexandre, Sacha 1903-1970 **[426]**
$1 315 - €1 220 - £803 - FF8 000
La halle aux viandes Huile/toile (131x146cm 51x57in) Paris 1998
$573 - €640 - £383 - FF4 200
Paysage Huile/toile (65x91cm 25x35in) Paris 2000
$312 - €320 - £196 - FF2 100
Sans titre Huile/toile (27x35cm 10x13in) Versailles 2000
$180 - €168 - £110 - FF1 100
Le phare Aquarelle/papier (14x14cm 5x5in) Paris 1998

GARBER Daniel 1880-1958 **[37]**
$250 000 - €238 991 - £156 700 - FF1 567 675
Corn Oil/canvas (106.5x128cm 41x50in) New-York 1999
$2 000 - €2 015 - £1 246 - FF13 220
Tohickon, Landscape with Hillside Village Etching (16x18cm 6x7in) Hatfield PA 2000

GARBER Johann 1947 **[8]**
$132 - €145 - £85 - FF953
Frau Felt pen/paper (21x14.6cm 8x5in) Wien 2000

GARBIERI IL NEPOTE Lorenzo 1580-1654 **[5]**
$14 420 - €14 534 - £9 000 - FF95 340
Die Beweinung Christi, Flügel eines Renaissance-Altars Oil/panel (146x129cm 57x50in) Wien 2000
$500 - €518 - £300 - FF3 400
San Carlo Borromeo che benedice un gruppo di credenti Inchiostro (29.5x21cm 11x8in) Milano 2001

GARBO del Raffaello de'Carli c.1479-c.1524 **[3]**
$72 215 - €84 179 - £50 000 - FF552 175
Portrait of a Young Lady, with a Pearl Headdress, a Landscape Beyond Oil/panel (36x28cm 14x11in) London 2000

GARBUZ Yair 1945 **[46]**
$5 000 - €5 644 - £3 482 - FF37 025
Untitled Mixed media (130x130cm 51x51in) Tel Aviv 2001
$1 700 - €1 825 - £1 137 - FF11 969
Objects in Landscape Mixed media (40x59.5cm 15x23in) Tel Aviv 2000
$500 - €488 - £316 - FF3 201
Figures Mixed media/paper (34x49cm 13x19in) Tel Aviv 1999

GARCEMENT Alfred XIX-XX **[12]**
$907 - €1 067 - £650 - FF7 000
Village de Morvan Huile/toile (43x55cm 16x21in) Besançon 2001

GARCIA BARRENA Carmelo 1926 **[50]**
$2 970 - €3 304 - £1 980 - FF21 670
Puerto Oleo/lienzo (73x93cm 28x36in) Madrid 2000
$132 - €132 - £81 - FF866
Payaso Acuarela/papel (24x16cm 9x6in) Madrid 2000

GARCIA CARRILERO Enrique 1900-? **[6]**
$3 640 - €3 904 - £2 430 - FF25 610
Retrato de la Reina Victoria Eugenia Oleo/lienzo (87x62cm 34x24in) Madrid 2001

GARCIA Daniel 1959 **[7]**
$7 500 - €6 523 - £4 521 - FF42 787
«Blind Head» Acrylic/canvas (144x142cm 56x55in) New-York 1998

GARCIA DE BENABARRE Pedro c.1425-1496 **[2]**
$162 000 - €180 195 - £108 000 - FF1 182 000
La última cena Oleo/tabla (163x98cm 64x38in) Madrid 2000

GARCIA DE PAREDES Vicente c.1845-1903 **[20]**
$5 940 - €6 607 - £4 180 - FF43 340
Velada andaluza Oleo/lienzo (64x81cm 25x31in) Madrid 2001
$804 - €721 - £492 - FF4 728
«Richelieu y Corneille con M.de Medicis» Acuarela/papel (18x24cm 7x9in) Madrid 1999

GARCIA Diego XIX **[3]**
$4 050 - €4 505 - £2 625 - FF29 550
Flamenqueo Oleo/lienzo (53x66cm 20x25in) Madrid 2000

GARCIA ERGÜIN Ignacio 1934 **[30]**
$2 520 - €2 108 - £1 505 - FF13 825
Costa brumosa Oleo/lienzo (46x65cm 18x25in) Madrid 1998

GARCIA Hector XX **[3]**
$750 - €874 - £519 - FF5 734
David alfaro Siqueiros, Lecumberri, Mexico Gelatin silver print (35x27.5cm 13x10in) Caracas ($) 2000

GARCIA HISPALETO Manuel 1838-1898 **[16]**
$434 - €420 - £266 - FF2 758
Joven con traje gris Aguada/papel (35x25cm 13x9in) Madrid 1999

GARCIA HISPALETO Rafael 1833-1854 **[2]**
$5 400 - €6 006 - £3 800 - FF39 400
Jugando a las cartas Oleo/lienzo (46x58.5cm 18x23in) Madrid 2001

GARCIA LORCA Federico XX **[5]**
$3 445 - €3 904 - £2 340 - FF25 610
Dama en el balcón Tinta/papel (32x25cm 12x9in) Madrid 2000

GARCIA MENCIA Antonio 1853-1915 **[39]**
$7 000 - €6 548 - £4 232 - FF42 949
The Introduction Oil/canvas (27x35cm 10x13in) New-York 1999
$180 - €216 - £126 - FF1 418
Tipo toledano Acuarela/papel (18x12cm 7x4in) Madrid 2000

GARCIA NUÑEZ Armando 1883-1965 **[37]**
$630 - €677 - £421 - FF4 440
Iglesia Huile/masonite (30x20cm 11x7in) México 2000
$294 - €316 - £196 - FF2 127
Decorado teatral, boceto Acuarela/papel (13x32cm 5x12in) México 2000

GARCIA OCHOA Luis 1920 **[81]**
$4 060 - €4 205 - £2 590 - FF27 580
Mujeres peinándose Oleo/lienzo (65x80cm 25x31in) Madrid 2000
$710 - €601 - £420 - FF3 940
Bodegón Tinta/papel (35x50cm 13x19in) Madrid 1998
$70 - €60 - £42 - FF394
Domine Cabra Litografía (49x37cm 19x14in) Madrid 1999

GARCIA RAMON Leopoldo 1876-1958 **[2]**
$10 494 - €12 489 - £7 500 - FF81 924
Cosiendo la vela Oil/canvas (56.5x75cm 22x29in) London 2000

GARCIA RIVERA Oscar 1915-1971 **[4]**
$12 000 - €11 647 - £7 471 - FF76 399
Guateque Oil/canvas (76x107cm 29x42in) New-York 1999

GARCIA RODRIGUEZ Francisco XIX-XX **[4]**
⌒ **$9 100** - €7 808 - **£5 460** - FF51 220
   Primavera en Sevilla Oleo/lienzo (109x69cm
   42x27in) Madrid 1998

GARCIA ROMERO Manuel, «Hispaletto» 1921 **[25]**
⌒ **$457** - €450 - **£285** - FF2 955
   Campesino Oleo/lienzo (114x88cm 44x34in) Madrid
   1999

GARCIA SEVILLA Ferrán 1949 **[40]**
⌒ **$10 640** - €11 412 - **£7 030** - FF74 860
   Pintura Oleo/lienzo (150x150cm 59x59in) Madrid
   2000
⌒ **$2 380** - €2 553 - **£1 572** - FF16 745
   El paso de un cometa Oleo/papel (70x52cm
   27x20in) Madrid 2000
✎ **$4 270** - €4 205 - **£2 730** - FF27 580
   Composición Técnica mixta/papel (116x80cm
   45x31in) Madrid 1999
▥ **$162** - €150 - **£97** - FF985
   Composición sobre fondo negro Litografía
   (76x56cm 29x22in) Barcelona 1999

GARCIA Y PARAMO Ventura ?-1881 **[4]**
⌒ **$2 136** - €2 439 - **£1 502** - FF16 000
   Le marchand d'armes Huile/panneau (30x24cm
   11x9in) Versailles 2001

GARCIA Y RAMOS José 1852-1912 **[53]**
⌒ **$22 750** - €21 023 - **£14 000** - FF137 900
   El ventilador Oleo/lienzo (54x35cm 21x13in) Madrid
   1999
⌒ **$16 437** - €17 644 - **£11 000** - FF115 737
   Fiesta en el jardin (The Garden Party) Oil/canvas
   (32x16cm 12x6in) London 2000
⌒ **$576** - €542 - **£360** - FF3 555
   Anciana italiana Aguada/papel (34x17cm 13x6in)
   Madrid 1998

GARCIA Y RODRIGUEZ Manuel 1863-1925 **[138]**
⌒ **$15 555** - €15 317 - **£9 945** - FF100 470
   Junto al pozo Oleo/lienzo (105.5x133cm 41x52in)
   Madrid 1999
⌒ **$15 750** - €13 515 - **£9 675** - FF88 650
   Paisaje con río y figura Oleo/lienzo (72x128cm
   28x50in) Madrid 1998
⌒ **$6 080** - €5 706 - **£3 800** - FF37 430
   Niños en la playa de la Jara, Sanlúcar Oleo/tabla
   (16x25cm 6x9in) Madrid 1999
⌒ **$1 300** - €1 478 - **£908** - FF9 698
   Vistas sevillanas Acuarela/papel (16x29cm 6x11in)
   Buenos-Aires 2000

GARCIN Gilles 1647-1702 **[1]**
⌒ **$10 783** - €9 909 - **£6 623** - FF65 000
   Narcisse dans un paysage Huile/toile (63x76.5cm
   24x30in) Paris 1999

GARDELL-ERICSON Anna 1853-1939 **[255]**
✎ **$1 238** - €1 394 - **£853** - FF9 145
   Motiv från Marstrand Akvarell/papper (25x33cm
   9x12in) Stockholm 2000

GARDET Georges 1863-1939 **[139]**
⌁ **$1 490** - €1 389 - **£900** - FF9 110
   A Setter Flushing Bronze (H29cm H11in) London
   1998

GARDIER du Raoul 1871-1952 **[15]**
✎ **$5 218** - €5 946 - **£3 584** - FF39 000
   Vers l'embarcadère Huile/toile (81x59.5cm 31x23in)
   Paris 2000

GARDINER Alfred Clive 1891-1960 **[12]**
▥ **$396** - €460 - **£280** - FF3 015
   «At London's Service» Poster (102x64cm 40x25in)
   London 2000

GARDINER Eliza Draper 1871-1955 **[58]**
▥ **$425** - €403 - **£265** - FF2 642
   Woman at a Table Lithograph (23x15cm 9x6in)
   Cincinnati OH 1999

GARDINER Gerald 1902-1959 **[18]**
⌒ **$1 104** - €1 144 - **£707** - FF7 506
   Studio Interior Oil/canvas (76x61cm 29x24in) West-
   Yorkshire 2000
✎ **$283** - €294 - **£180** - FF1 930
   **St. John's College, Oxford/The Canterbury
   Quadrangle** Black chalk/paper (61x42cm 24x16in)
   West-Yorkshire 2000

GARDINER Stanley Horace 1887-1952 **[22]**
✎ **$1 050** - €895 - **£626** - FF5 873
   **Mounts Bay from above Madron/Spring in our
   Valley** Oil/board (37x44.5cm 14x17in) Bath 1998

GARDNER Alexander 1821-1882 **[80]**
▣ **$4 000** - €3 751 - **£2 471** - FF24 604
   The Hanging of the Lincoln Conspirators
   Albumen print (16x21cm 6x8in) New-York 1999

GARDNER Daniel 1750-1805 **[65]**
⌒ **$40 615** - €39 518 - **£25 000** - FF259 220
   **Angelica Kauffman, wearing a red Dress, and
   Dark blue Headdress** Oil/canvas (63x48cm 24x18in)
   London 1999
✎ **$5 892** - €7 008 - **£4 200** - FF45 969
   **Lady Charlotte Hill, Countess Talbot, Bust-
   Lenght, in a White Dress** Pastel (25x20cm 9x7in)
   London 2000

GARDNER Derek George M. 1914 **[16]**
⌒ **$6 474** - €6 095 - **£4 000** - FF39 978
   **Northern Waters: Loch Vennachar/The Waimate
   bound out New Zealand** Oil/canvas (35.5x46cm
   13x18in) London 1999
✎ **$1 278** - €1 418 - **£850** - FF9 303
   Greenwich Hospital from the Thames
   Watercolour/paper (26x38cm 10x14in) London 2000

GARDNER James XX **[2]**
▥ **$639** - €656 - **£400** - FF4 304
   «Imperial Airways» Poster (62x97cm 24x38in)
   London 2000

GARDNER William Biscombe 1847-1919 **[26]**
✎ **$930** - €938 - **£580** - FF6 150
   Tonbridge Castle, Kent Watercolour/paper
   (20x13.5cm 7x5in) Newbury, Berkshire 2000

GARDUÑO Flor 1957 **[19]**
▣ **$850** - €794 - **£515** - FF5 208
   La Mujer, Juchitan, Mexico Gelatin silver print
   (23.5x31.5cm 9x12in) New-York 1999

GARDY Claude 1994 **[55]**
⌒ **$800** - €838 - **£503** - FF5 500
   Marine Huile/toile (41x33cm 16x12in) Cap d'Ail 2000

GARDY Eugène Benoît 1856-? **[1]**
✎ **$1 920** - €1 829 - **£1 164** - FF12 000
   Scènes de cirque/Roulottes/Décors
   Aquarelle/papier (31x50cm 12x19in) Paris 1999

GAREIS Antonín 1837-1922 **[3]**
⌒ **$1 156** - €1 093 - **£720** - FF7 172
   Card Players, Study Oil/canvas (26x30cm 10x11in)
   Praha 1999

GAREL Philippe 1945 **[39]**

$3 134 - €3 049 - **£1 928** - FF20 000
Portrait d'homme Pastel/papier (118x79cm 46x31in)
Paris 1999

GARELLA Antonio 1864-1919 **[10]**

$65 000 - €77 077 - **£44 720** - FF505 589
Apollo and Daphné Marble (152,5x85cm 60x33in)
New-York 2000

$1 951 - €2 045 - **£1 236** - FF13 415
Büste eines jungen Mädchens Poésie Marble
(H30cm H11in) Köln 2000

GAREMYN Jan Anton 1712-1799 **[16]**

$1 415 - €1 361 - **£872** - FF8 929
Sheet of Figure Studies Red chalk (45x27cm
17x10in) Amsterdam 1999

GARF Salomon 1879-1943 **[36]**

$1 180 - €1 134 - **£736** - FF7 441
Farmer's Camp Oil/canvas (60x80cm 23x31in)
Amsterdam 1999

$2 618 - €2 949 - **£1 805** - FF19 347
A Summers Day at the Beach of Zandvoort
Watercolour (12x14cm 4x5in) Amsterdam 2000

GARGALEIRO Manuel 1927 **[1]**

$6 794 - €6 555 - **£4 265** - FF43 000
Composition Huile/toile (55x46cm 21x18in) Senlis
1999

GARGALLO Pablo 1881-1934 **[46]**

$24 840 - €23 147 - **£15 000** - FF151 837
Torse de jeune gitan Bronze (H92cm H36in)
London 1998

$68 160 - €73 176 - **£45 600** - FF480 000
Maternité Bronze (32.5x18x18cm 12x7x7in) Paris
2000

$2 028 - €2 343 - **£1 404** - FF15 366
Arlequín con guitarra Tinta/papel (21x17.5cm 8x6in)
Madrid 2000

GARGIULO Domenico 1612-1679 **[36]**

$164 160 - €154 067 - **£102 600** - FF1 010 610
**La Adoración de los Reyes Magos/Cristo expul-
sando a los mercaderes** Oleo/lienzo (103x130cm
40x51in) Palma de Mallorca 1999

$11 000 - €11 403 - **£6 600** - FF74 800
**San Bruno dona la Regola certosina ai suoi
confratelli da Stanzione M.** Olio/tela (101x74.5cm
39x29in) Roma 2001

$2 179 - €2 263 - **£1 511** - FF17 000
Feuille d'étude avec un guerrier casqué Encre
(14x20cm 5x7in) Paris 2000

GARGIULO Sergio XX **[5]**

$1 057 - €970 - **£649** - FF6 363
My Darling Clementine Poster (104x68.5cm
40x26in) London 1999

GARIAZZO Pier Antonio 1879-1963 **[49]**

$400 - €415 - **£240** - FF2 720
L'albero Olio/cartone (54x69cm 21x27in) Torino 1999

GARIBALDI Joseph 1863-1941 **[48]**

$3 878 - €4 345 - **£2 698** - FF28 500
Entrée de port Huile/toile (31x61cm 12x24in)
Montpellier 2001

$1 942 - €1 753 - **£1 197** - FF11 500
Village en bord de mer Huile/panneau (33x41cm
12x16in) Arles 1999

GARIN Louis 1888-1959 **[38]**

$1 538 - €1 829 - **£1 096** - FF12 000
Le port du Bono en rivière d'Auray Huile/toile
(73x92cm 28x36in) Brest 2000

$510 - €495 - **£323** - FF3 244
Landscape of Provence Oil/board (22x27cm
8x10in) Warszawa 1999

$3 069 - €2 820 - **£1 885** - FF18 500
Jour de régate à Paimpol Pastel/papier (46x60cm
18x23in) Soissons 1999

GARIN Paul 1898-1963 **[253]**

$261 - €229 - **£158** - FF1 500
Le port d'Antibes Huile/toile (46x61cm 18x24in)
Paris 1998

$174 - €152 - **£105** - FF1 000
Vue du village aux cyprès Huile/toile (41x33cm
16x12in) Paris 1998

GARINEI Michele 1871-1960 **[14]**

$1 000 - €1 137 - **£698** - FF7 460
Chef Oil/canvas (26x16cm 10x6in) Mystic CT 2000

GARINO Angelo 1860-1945 **[28]**

$4 781 - €5 624 - **£3 465** - FF36 892
«Dörfer in den Alpen» Öl/Leinwand (73x92cm
28x36in) Frankfurt 2001

GARINO Piero 1922 **[29]**

$450 - €466 - **£270** - FF3 060
Paese Tecnica mista/tela (50x70cm 19x27in) Torino
2000

$200 - €207 - **£120** - FF1 360
Diano Marina Tecnica mista/carta (24x35cm 9x13in)
Torino 2000

GARIOT Paul Césaire 1811-1880 **[7]**

$4 508 - €4 878 - **£3 088** - FF32 000
La marchande de coco Huile/carton (32x21cm
12x8in) Chartres 2001

GARLAND Charles Trevor 1855-1906 **[6]**

$18 763 - €15 761 - **£11 000** - FF103 383
The naughty Boy Oil/canvas (65.5x92cm 25x36in)
London 1998

GARLAND Henry act.1854-1890 **[62]**

$18 273 - €15 638 - **£11 000** - FF102 576
Village Gossips Oil/canvas (102x170cm 40x66in)
London 1998

$2 000 - €2 015 - **£1 246** - FF13 220
Highland Cattle on the Move Oil/canvas
(75.5x122cm 29x48in) New-York 2000

$720 - €768 - **£480** - FF5 041
**Lady Seated Sewing at a Window, Probably the
Artist's Sister** Oil/canvas (36x39cm 14x15in)
Leyburn, North Yorkshire 2000

GARLAND Valentine Thomas ?-1914 **[27]**

$3 500 - €3 812 - **£2 410** - FF25 004
Maternity Oil/canvas (35.5x47cm 13x18in) New-York
2001

$5 807 - €5 775 - **£3 600** - FF37 883
Terriers and Dachshunds on Cottage Steps
Oil/panel (31x22cm 12x9in) Lewes, Sussex 2000

GARLICK Harry 1877-1910 **[3]**

$2 050 - €2 392 - **£1 439** - FF15 688
Study of Dogs Heads and Figures Ink (27x20cm
10x7in) Sydney 2000

GARLIEB Louise XIX **[2]**

$26 000 - €22 432 - **£15 685** - FF147 141
**Still Life with Streptocarpusm Oleander calla
Lily, Cactus Flowers** Oil/canvas (121x94cm 47x37in)
New-York 1998

GARLING Frederick 1806-1873 **[17]**

$1 340 - €1 399 - **£845** - FF9 177
The Essex Watercolour/paper (25x38cm 9x14in)
Sydney 2000

GARMAN Ed 1914 **[2]**
📷 **$13 000** - €14 761 - **£8 897** - FF96 829
Untitled Oil/masonite (76x76cm 29x29in) New-York 2000

GARNELL Jean-Louis XX **[3]**
📷 **$2 143** - €2 592 - **£1 497** - FF17 000
Mer II Photo couleur (96x120cm 37x47in) Paris 2000

GARNELO Y ALDA José 1866-1945 **[12]**
😊 **$3 840** - €3 604 - **£2 400** - FF23 640
Mujer en el Templo de Paestum Oleo/lienzo (107x84cm 42x33in) Madrid 1999
😊 **$3 780** - €3 604 - **£2 280** - FF23 640
Reunión en un salón Oleo/lienzo (29x46cm 11x18in) Madrid 1999

GARNER Charles S.,Jr. 1890-1933 **[5]**
😊 **$2 000** - €2 147 - **£1 338** - FF14 082
Back Yards Oil/canvas (76x91cm 30x36in) Hatfield PA 2000

GARNERAY Hippolyte 1787-1858 **[21]**
😊 **$2 188** - €2 439 - **£1 489** - FF16 000
Le Vieux Rouen Huile/toile (24x18cm 9x7in) Nice 2000

GARNERAY Louis Ambroise 1783-1857 **[42]**
😊 **$6 871** - €6 403 - **£4 237** - FF42 000
Navire entrant dans un port anglais sous la tempête Huile/toile (38x47cm 14x18in) Lille 1999
😊 **$7 924** - €8 521 - **£5 400** - FF55 894
Naval Engagement Oil/canvas (30.5x38.5cm 12x15in) Billingshurst, West-Sussex 2001
✏ **$2 617** - €2 439 - **£1 614** - FF16 000
Vue du port de Gênes Aquarelle/papier (18x28cm 7x11in) Lille 1999
🖼 **$378** - €323 - **£225** - FF2 116
Parti fra Köbenhavn med skibe og folkeliv ved börsen Aquatint (32x44cm 12x17in) Vejle 1998

GARNETT William A. 1916 **[20]**
📷 **$950** - €892 - **£587** - FF5 851
Desert Sagebrush, near Kelso, California Gelatin silver print (50x40cm 19x15in) New-York 1999

GARNIER Étienne Barthélémy 1759-1849 **[6]**
😊 **$13 164** - €11 281 - **£7 918** - FF74 000
Consternation de Priam et de sa famille après le combat d'Achille Huile/toile (74x100cm 29x39in) Besançon 1998

GARNIER Geoffrey Sneyd 1889-c.1971 **[50]**
🖼 **$123** - €112 - **£75** - FF732
The Sand Cart Aquatint (21x22cm 8x9in) Penzance, Cornwall 1998

GARNIER Hippolyte 1802-1855 **[4]**
🖼 **$485** - €460 - **£295** - FF3 018
Lola Montez, Darstellung der Tänzerin und Kurtisane in Reitkleid Lithographie (38x53cm 14x20in) München 1999

GARNIER Jean 1853-1910 **[10]**
🗿 **$1 491** - €1 601 - **£997** - FF10 500
Le jeune violoniste Bronze (H41.5cm H16in) Soissons 1999

GARNIER Michel 1753-1819 **[8]**
😊 **$560 000** - €599 026 - **£381 808** - FF3 929 352
Fashionably Dressed Young Woman in the Arcade of the Palais Royal Oil/canvas (45x37cm 17x14in) New-York 2001

GARNIER Pierre 1847-? **[22]**
😊 **$2 883** - €2 744 - **£1 792** - FF18 000
Bouquet de roses sur un entablement Huile/toile (65x54cm 25x21in) Mâcon 1999

GARMAN

😊 **$539** - €534 - **£336** - FF3 500
Roses près de l'étang Huile/toile (24x33cm 9x12in) Lyon 1999

GARNIER Simon XX **[2]**
🖼 **$1 603** - €1 453 - **£1 000** - FF9 529
«Ecole de ski de la Côte d'Azur» Poster (100x62cm 39x24in) London 1999

GARNIER Tony 1869-1948 **[2]**
🖼 **$2 800** - €3 122 - **£1 827** - FF20 481
«Exposition Internationale, La Cité Moderne» Poster (115x156cm 45x61in) New-York 2000

GARNSEY Julian E. 1887-? **[2]**
✏ **$1 100** - €1 092 - **£674** - FF7 162
Diamond Head Watercolour, gouache/paper (34x40cm 13x16in) Mystic CT 2001

GAROFALO Benvenuto Tisi da 1481-1559 **[19]**
😊 **$59 772** - €64 160 - **£40 000** - FF420 864
The Holy Family with Saint-Catherine Oil/canvas (40x31.5cm 15x12in) London 2000

GAROLA Pietro Francesco 1638-1716 **[11]**
😊 **$7 500** - €7 775 - **£4 500** - FF51 000
Presentazione al tempio Olio/tela (98.5x71.5cm 38x28in) Milano 1999

GAROUSTE Gérard 1946 **[72]**
😊 **$21 636** - €25 428 - **£15 000** - FF166 800
Untitled Oil/canvas (161.5x129.5cm 63x50in) London 2000
😊 **$6 500** - €6 738 - **£3 900** - FF44 200
Senza titolo Olio/tela (64.5x50cm 25x19in) Prato 2000
✏ **$3 886** - €4 421 - **£2 697** - FF29 000
Sans titre Gouache/papier (65x50cm 25x19in) Douai 2000
🖼 **$227** - €221 - **£141** - FF1 450
Sans titre Gravure (30x23cm 11x9in) Paris 1999

GARRALDA Elías 1920 **[7]**
😊 **$4 355** - €3 904 - **£2 665** - FF25 610
«Trilal de Hostalets de Bas» Oleo/lienzo (80.5x100cm 31x39in) Madrid 1999

GARRAUD Léon 1877-1961 **[55]**
😊 **$835** - €991 - **£607** - FF6 500
Bouquet de roses Huile/toile/panneau (55.5x45cm 21x17in) Lyon 2001
😊 **$1 032** - €991 - **£647** - FF6 500
Nature morte aux raisins noirs Huile/panneau (23x33cm 9x12in) Lyon 1999
✏ **$732** - €671 - **£447** - FF4 400
Bord du Rhône Aquarelle/papier (20x25cm 7x9in) Lyon 1999

GARREAU Georges 1885-? **[8]**
🗿 **$2 840** - €3 049 - **£1 900** - FF20 000
Le Méhariste Bronze (H60.5cm H23in) Epinal 2000

GARRETT Edmund Henry 1853-1929 **[19]**
😊 **$3 405** - €3 735 - **£2 312** - FF24 500
Portrait de Jean-Paul Laurens Huile/toile (65x55cm 25x21in) Lille 2000
✏ **$350** - €392 - **£243** - FF2 572
Wooded Landscape Watercolour/paper (34x23cm 13x9in) Watertown MA 2001

GARRETT Thomas Balfour 1879-1952 **[210]**
😊 **$937** - €1 094 - **£652** - FF7 175
Chikens Feeding at the Old Barn Oil/board (31.5x54.5cm 12x21in) Melbourne 2000
😊 **$1 007** - €944 - **£623** - FF6 191
Curl Curl Watercolour/paper (21x29cm 8x11in) Melbourne 1999

$1 331 - €1 386 - **£836** - FF9 091
The Shaded Pool Monotype (24.5x31.5cm 9x12in)
Melbourne 2000

GARRETTO Paolo Federico 1903-1991 **[22]**
$152 - €157 - **£91** - FF1 033
«Pitagora scopri la tavola pitagorica...» Affiche
(100x70cm 39x27in) Torino 2000

GARRI Giorgio c.1670-c.1731 **[1]**
$5 600 - €7 257 - **£4 200** - FF47 600
**Natura morta di frutta e fiori con frammenti
archeologici** Olio/tela (86x115cm 33x45in) Napoli
2000

GARRIDO Eduardo Léon 1856-1949 **[140]**
$44 917 - €45 262 - **£28 000** - FF296 900
The finishing Touches Oil/canvas (130x97cm
51x38in) London 2000
$14 850 - €16 518 - **£10 175** - FF108 350
Ensoñación Oleo/tabla (62x44cm 24x17in) Madrid
2001
$4 900 - €4 205 - **£3 010** - FF27 580
Soldado Oleo/tabla (33x24cm 12x9in) Madrid 1998

GARRIDO Louis Édouard 1893-1982 **[68]**
$1 400 - €1 372 - **£902** - FF9 000
Fenaison Huile/panneau (38x54cm 14x21in)
Coutances 1999
$948 - €960 - **£594** - FF6 300
Le port Saint-Vaast la Hougue Huile/carton
(24x35cm 9x13in) Coutances 2000

GARROS Catherine 1954 **[82]**
$691 - €777 - **£475** - FF5 100
Saint Jean de Luz Huile/toile (55x46cm 21x18in)
Albi 2000
$2 403 - €2 744 - **£1 690** - FF18 000
Sanary Huile/toile (21x28cm 8x11in) Valence 2001

GARROW Simon 1946 **[43]**
$723 - €842 - **£500** - FF5 526
The Audience Oil/canvas (43x56cm 16x22in) London
2000
$597 - €642 - **£400** - FF4 208
Audience Oil/canvas (40.5x30.5cm 15x12in) London
2000
$1 092 - €1 270 - **£768** - FF8 329
Never Ending Story Watercolour/paper (41x51cm
16x20in) Dublin 2001

GARRY Charley 1891-1973 **[25]**
$705 - €794 - **£486** - FF5 210
**Vornehme Dame in gelbem Kleid einen sitzen-
den Papagei fütternd** Öl/Leinwand (99x72cm
38x28in) Basel 2000

GARSIDE Oswald 1879-1942 **[35]**
$749 - €635 - **£450** - FF4 163
Unloading the Catch Watercolour/paper (40.5x62cm
15x24in) London 1998

GARSIDE Thomas Hilton 1906-1980 **[122]**
$748 - €640 - **£453** - FF4 196
Birches in the Spring Huile/toile (40.5x51cm
15x20in) Montréal 1998
$383 - €414 - **£257** - FF2 716
Winter River and Mountain Oil/board (19x23.5cm
7x9in) Calgary, Alberta 2000

GARSON Etta Corbett 1898-1968 **[1]**
$3 400 - €3 490 - **£2 134** - FF22 890
New England Port Scenes Oil/board (33x40cm
13x16in) St. Louis MO 2000

GARSTIN Alethea 1894-1978 **[45]**
$8 732 - €10 439 - **£6 000** - FF68 478
Portrait of Dod Proctor Oil/board (75.5x51cm
29x20in) Billingshurst, West-Sussex 2000
$1 811 - €1 702 - **£1 100** - FF11 164
Big Hat, little Girl Oil/board (35.5x25.5cm 13x10in)
London 1999
$948 - €990 - **£622** - FF6 496
Study of a Child Watercolour/paper (34x21cm
13x8in) Dublin 2000

GARSTIN Norman 1847-1926 **[68]**
$712 - €828 - **£500** - FF5 432
Figures outside a Church, Brittany Oil/canvas
(59x72.5cm 23x28in) Billingshurst, West-Sussex 2001
$1 211 - €1 408 - **£850** - FF9 239
Interior Oil/panel (29.5x23.5cm 11x9in) Billingshurst,
West-Sussex 2001
$1 183 - €1 270 - **£807** - FF8 329
The White Horse Watercolour/paper (24x30cm
9x11in) Dublin 2001

GARTEGEN Robert Pajer 1886-1944 **[2]**
$6 837 - €7 158 - **£4 296** - FF46 954
Ein Sonntagnachmittag im Prater Öl/Leinwand
(66x82cm 25x32in) Hamburg 2000

GARTHWAITE William 1821-1899 **[6]**
$3 735 - €4.010 - **£2 500** - FF26 304
**Paddlesteamer Britannia of Leith - Off Holy
Island - Currie Line Flag** Oil/canvas (66x87cm
25x34in) Edinburgh 2000

GARTMEIER Hans 1910-1985 **[147]**
$1 067 - €1 244 - **£739** - FF8 163
In der Schmiedewerkstatt Oil/panel (49.5x59.5cm
19x23in) Bern 2000
$533 - €622 - **£369** - FF4 081
Bauernfamilie vor dem Haus Oil/panel (24x32cm
9x12in) Bern 2000

GÄRTNER Fritz 1882-1958 **[88]**
$816 - €767 - **£506** - FF5 030
Wiesenräumen Öl/Leinwand (79x89cm 31x35in)
München 1999

GÄRTNER Johann 1697-1750 **[2]**
$2 840 - €2 403 - **£1 720** - FF15 760
Marina Oleo/lienzo (30x50cm 11x19in) Madrid 1998

GARTNER L. XIX-XX **[7]**
$1 226 - €1 088 - **£749** - FF7 137
Waiting for the Catch Oil/canvas (81.5x51cm
32x20in) London 1999

GARZI Luigi 1638-1721 **[14]**
$39 902 - €45 322 - **£28 000** - FF297 290
Diana and Callisto Oil/canvas (100x151.5cm
39x59in) London 2000
$10 572 - €8 719 - **£6 228** - FF57 192
**Lapidazione di Santo Stefano, Steinigung des
heiligen Stephan** Öl/Leinwand (84x99cm 33x38in)
Wien 1998
$15 068 - €15 823 - **£9 500** - FF103 789
The Finding of Moses Oil/canvas (28x24.5cm
11x9in) London 2000

GARZOLINI Ciro 1883-1972 **[21]**
$1 100 - €1 140 - **£660** - FF7 480
Paese di alta montagna Olio/faesite (60x80cm
23x31in) Trieste 2001

GASCARD Henri 1635-1701 **[14]**
$14 697 - €13 531 - **£9 000** - FF88 757
**Portrait of Louise de Kerouaille, Duchesse of
Portsmouth** Oil/canvas (124x99cm 48x38in) London
1998

$18 000 - €20 161 - **£12 506** - FF132 249
Portrait of a Lady Oil/canvas (117x91.5cm 46x36in)
New-York 2001

GASCOIGNE Rosalie Norah King 1917-1999 [36]
$21 375 - €23 958 - **£14 946** - FF157 154
«**Shoreline**» Mixed media (53.5x107.5cm 21x42in)
Melbourne 2000
$44 400 - €49 588 - **£28 432** - FF325 275
Promised Land Assemblage (110.5x250cm 43x98in)
Malvern, Victoria 2000
$9 339 - €10 291 - **£6 211** - FF67 504
Private Beach Assemblage (58x39cm 22x15in)
Melbourne 2000
$1 879 - €2 126 - **£1 323** - FF13 946
Close Owly Color lithograph (76x49.5cm 29x19in)
Malvern, Victoria 2001

GASIOROWSKI Gérard 1930-1986 [51]
$1 264 - €1 220 - **£799** - FF8 000
Soldat Acrylique/papier (40x47cm 15x18in) Paris 1999
$584 - €564 - **£369** - FF3 700
Abstraction Acrylique/papier (42x32cm 16x12in)
Paris 1999
$363 - €351 - **£229** - FF2 300
Compositions Technique mixte/papier (50x65cm
19x25in) Paris 1999

GASKELL Anna XX [1]
$16 000 - €17 554 - **£10 628** - FF115 148
Untitled #21 (Override) Cibachrome print
(144x174.5cm 56x68in) New-York 2000

GASKELL George Arthur XIX-XX [6]
$1 884 - €2 062 - **£1 300** - FF13 528
Time for Tea Watercolour/paper (73.5x54.5cm
28x21in) London 2001

GASPAR Jean-Marie 1861-1931 [7]
$2 220 - €2 479 - **£1 550** - FF16 260
Lionne couchée Bronze (25x42.5cm 9x16in)
Bruxelles 2001

GASPARD Leon Schulman 1882-1964 [86]
$160 000 - €188 046 - **£110 928** - FF1 233 504
Flowers Oil/canvas/board (60x61cm 23x24in) Beverly-
Hills CA 2000
$12 000 - €13 447 - **£8 364** - FF88 209
Portrait of a Mongolian Oil/canvas/board (38x22cm
14x8in) Beverly-Hills CA 2001
$1 500 - €1 294 - **£901** - FF8 489
Mongolian Horseman Sketch Graphite (13x18cm
5x7in) Santa-Fe NM 1998

GASPARI Luciano 1913 [11]
$1 100 - €1 140 - **£660** - FF7 480
Figura Olio/tela (62x46cm 24x18in) Venezia 2000
$1 100 - €1 140 - **£660** - FF7 480
Dormiente Olio/tela (39.5x31cm 15x12in) Venezia
2000

GASPARINI Bruna 1917-1998 [4]
$1 250 - €1 296 - **£750** - FF8 500
Composizione Tempera/cartone (60x31cm 23x12in)
Vercelli 2000

GASPARINI Luigi 1865-? [1]
$6 000 - €5 701 - **£3 650** - FF37 397
Arrival of the Suiter Oil/canvas (70x95.5cm 27x37in)
New-York 1999

GASQ Paul J.-Baptiste 1860-1944 [21]
$2 047 - €2 210 - **£1 400** - FF14 497
Diana the Huntress Bronze (H76cm H29in)
Billingshurst, West-Sussex 2001

GASSE Albert XIX-XX [1]
$2 000 - €1 923 - **£1 234** - FF12 616
«**Modes Parisiennes**» Poster (127.5x98cm 50x38in)
New-York 1999

GASSEL van Lucas, dit Helmont c.1500-c.1570 [13]
$78 220 - €90 756 - **£54 000** - FF595 320
Abraham and the Angels Oil/panel (71x91cm
27x35in) Amsterdam 2000
$26 505 - €22 867 - **£15 990** - FF150 000
Couple d'élégants dans un parc Huile/panneau
(32x45cm 12x17in) Paris 1998
$42 471 - €40 840 - **£26 163** - FF267 894
**Panoramic Mountainous Estuary Landscape
with Christ and the Woman** Ink (27x38.5cm
10x15in) Amsterdam 1999

GASSELIN Noël XVII-XVIII [3]
$14 507 - €13 431 - **£9 000** - FF88 101
**Architectural Capriccio with Travellers Beneath
and Arcade, Landscape** Oil/canvas/board
(110x119cm 43x46in) London 1999

GASSER Henry Martin 1909-1981 [131]
$800 - €758 - **£499** - FF4 974
Man in a Skiff Watercolour/paper (35x51cm 14x20in)
Mystic CT 1999

GASSIES Jean-Bapt. Georges 1829-1919 [29]
$1 068 - €1 220 - **£751** - FF8 000
Chevreuils en forêt Huile/panneau (26.5x35cm
10x13in) Fontainebleau 2001
$459 - €534 - **£322** - FF3 500
Cerf et biches en forêt Aquarelle/papier (51x36cm
20x14in) Blois 2001

GASTALDI Andrea 1826-1889 [3]
$33 600 - €29 026 - **£22 440** - FF190 400
**Damaianti dormiente in una selva abbandonata
da suo marito Nalo** Olio/tela (134x225cm 52x88in)
Milano 1998

GASTALDI Michel XX [3]
$3 550 - €3 811 - **£2 375** - FF25 000
Cannes, la Croisette Huile/toile (60x73cm 23x28in)
Romorantin-Lanthenay 2000

GASTÉ Constant Georges 1869-1910 [31]
$8 775 - €9 681 - **£5 943** - FF63 500
Laveuses bédouines en Algérie dans l'oued
Huile/toile (100x81cm 39x31in) Angers 2000
$1 839 - €2 134 - **£1 309** - FF14 000
Femme au foulard vert Huile/toile (41.5x33cm
16x12in) Compiègne 2000

GASTEIGER Anna Sophie 1878-1954 [30]
$2 850 - €3 323 - **£1 998** - FF21 800
Sommerblumenstrauss Öl/Karton (50.5x70cm
19x27in) München 2001

GASTEMANS Emiel 1883-1956 [156]
$720 - €594 - **£422** - FF3 897
Le nettoyage du poisson Huile/toile (73x84cm
28x33in) Antwerpen 1998
$900 - €743 - **£528** - FF4 872
Les nettoyeuses de peaux Huile/carton (17x37cm
6x14in) Antwerpen 1998
$238 - €248 - **£150** - FF1 626
Dames de cour Pastel/papier (43x48cm 16x18in)
Antwerpen 2000

GASTINEAU Henry 1791-1876 [43]
$937 - €868 - **£580** - FF5 693
Cattle by the Trent, Nottingham Castle beyond
Watercolour (17x25cm 6x9in) London 1999

G

GASTINI Marco 1938 **[18]**
💰 **$849** - €881 - **£509** - FF5 778
   Senza titolo Tecnica mista/carta (70x100cm 27x39in)
   Milano 1999

GASTO VILANOVA Pere 1908/09-1997 **[72]**
🖼 **$1 690** - €1 952 - **£1 170** - FF12 805
   Actor Oleo/lienzo (46.5x38cm 18x14in) Madrid 2000
💰 **$313** - €330 - **£203** - FF2 167
   Pareja de actores Técnica mixta/papel (32x45cm
   12x17in) Madrid 2000

GASTYNE de Marc 1889-? **[8]**
🖼 **$3 174** - €3 513 - **£2 200** - FF23 045
   «Davos» Poster (57x37cm 22x14in) London 2001

GAT Eliahu 1919-1987 **[28]**
🖼 **$2 600** - €2 791 - **£1 739** - FF18 306
   Landscape Oil/canvas (48.5x68.5cm 19x26in) Tel
   Aviv 2000
💰 **$500** - €531 - **£338** - FF3 481
   Mountain Landscape Ink/paper (32.5x46.5cm
   12x18in) Tel Aviv 2001

GATE JONSSON Simon 1883-1945 **[8]**
🖼 **$4 263** - €5 070 - **£3 040** - FF33 259
   Flickan vid bäcken Oil/canvas (60x40cm 23x15in)
   Stockholm 2000

GATEHOUSE Charles E. 1866-1952 **[10]**
🖼 **$1 263** - €1 502 - **£900** - FF9 855
   **Basket, a Dapple Grey Hunter on a Wooded
   track** Oil/canvas (41x51.5cm 16x20in) London 2000
🖼 **$2 380** - €2 769 - **£1 700** - FF18 163
   Wire haired Jack Russell Terrier Oil/canvas
   (30.5x38cm 12x14in) London 2001

GATIER Pierre 1878-1944 **[22]**
🖼 **$222** - €259 - **£159** - FF1 700
   Chalutiers/Goëlette au sec Burin (20x25cm 7x9in)
   Paris 2001

GATTA della Anacleto, Nino 1868 **[5]**
🖼 **$375** - €389 - **£225** - FF2 550
   Paesaggio con casolare/Paesaggio con Stagno
   Olio/tavoletta (8.5x7cm 3x2in) Firenze 2001

GATTA della Saverio, Xavier act.1777-1827 **[105]**
🖼 **$2 942** - €3 066 - **£1 850** - FF20 110
   Classical Roman View Watercolour/paper (27x39cm
   10x15in) Stratford-upon-Avon, Warwickshire 2000

GATTI Oliviero 1579-? **[1]**
🖼 **$5 489** - €5 360 - **£3 500** - FF35 161
   **The Arms of a Borghese Cardinal, in a car-
   touche flanked by Putti** Black chalk (20.5x29cm
   8x11in) London 1999

GATTO Victor Joseph 1893-1965 **[10]**
🖼 **$24 000** - €25 631 - **£16 353** - FF168 127
   Night Club Scene Oil/canvas (81x71cm 31x27in)
   New-York 2001

GATTORNO Antonio 1904-1980 **[8]**
🖼 **$8 500** - €10 008 - **£5 973** - FF65 648
   Naturaleza muerta Oil/canvas (56x45cm 22x17in)
   New-York 2000

GAUBAULT Alfred Émile ?-1895 **[15]**
🖼 **$850** - €802 - **£528** - FF5 264
   **French Officer at Ease/French Officer smoking
   Pipe** Oil/panel (30x21cm 12x8in) Cleveland OH 1999

GAUCHER Yves 1934 **[16]**
🖼 **$265** - €288 - **£182** - FF1 887
   Cardinal Raga Sérigraphie (56x56cm 22x22in)
   Montréal 2001

GAUCI A.M. XIX **[5]**
🖼 **$4 460** - €4 193 - **£2 700** - FF27 504
   Hereford Cow in a Landscape Oil/canvas
   (51x66cm 20x25in) London 1999

GAUCI Paul c.1800-c.1855 **[3]**
🖼 **$682** - €664 - **£420** - FF4 354
   View in the Neighbourhood of Sevenoaks Color
   lithograph (34x40cm 13x15in) London 1999

GAUD Léon 1844-1908 **[26]**
🖼 **$1 239** - €1 446 - **£870** - FF9 486
   Liegender weiblicher Halbakt Öl/Leinwand
   (38.5x46cm 15x18in) Luzern 2000

GAUDEFROY Alphonse 1845-1936 **[10]**
🖼 **$6 000** - €6 236 - **£3 781** - FF40 908
   Gathering by the Hearth After the Hunt Oil/can-
   vas (64.5x78.5cm 25x30in) New-York 2000

GAUDENZI Pietro 1880-1955 **[16]**
🖼 **$2 100** - €2 177 - **£1 260** - FF14 280
   Maternità Olio/tavola (60x47.5cm 23x18in) Roma
   2001
💰 **$1 500** - €1 555 - **£900** - FF10 200
   Purezza Pastelli/tavola (68.5x41cm 26x16in) Torino
   2000

GAUDET Etienne 1891-1963 **[12]**
🖼 **$141** - €152 - **£96** - FF1 000
   Rue du vieux Blois Aquarelle/papier (27x17.5cm
   10x6in) Blois 2001

GAUDEZ Adrien Étienne 1845-1902 **[158]**
🖼 **$2 500** - €2 533 - **£1 569** - FF16 614
   Étole du matin Bronze (H89cm H35in) Detroit MI
   2000
🖼 **$1 632** - €1 371 - **£959** - FF8 994
   An einem Baumstumpf lehnendes Mädchen
   Bronze (H55cm H21in) Bern 1998

GAUDFROY Fernand 1885-1964 **[8]**
🖼 **$2 563** - €2 727 - **£1 749** - FF17 886
   Le Rétameur Huile/toile (91x71cm 35x27in)
   Bruxelles 2001

GAUDIER-BRZESKA Henri 1891-1915 **[168]**
🖼 **$1 800** - €2 044 - **£1 231** - FF13 407
   Study of a Seated Woman Writing Ink (38.5x26cm
   15x10in) New-York 2000

GAUDISSARD Émile 1872-1956 **[16]**
🖼 **$2 493** - €2 287 - **£1 549** - FF15 000
   Scènes de hammam Huile/toile (60x73cm 23x28in)
   Paris 1999

GAUDRY ALLARD Julie XIX-XX **[5]**
🖼 **$2 952** - €3 354 - **£2 065** - FF22 000
   Le fumeur de cigare Huile/toile (35x27cm 13x10in)
   Paris 2001

GAUDY E. XIX-XX **[1]**
🖼 **$1 231** - €1 372 - **£828** - FF9 000
   **«Circuit international, critérium de régularité
   touriste»** Affiche (59x89cm 23x35in) Orléans 2000

GAUDY Georges 1872-? **[25]**
🖼 **$700** - €651 - **£432** - FF4 269
   «Circuit International» Poster (59x89cm 23x35in)
   New-York 1999

GAUERMANN Carl 1804-1829 **[2]**
💰 **$1 498** - €1 453 - **£924** - FF9 534
   Gebirgslandschaft mit einem Angler am Fluss
   Aquarell/Papier (20x28cm 7x11in) Wien 1999

GAUERMANN Friedrich 1807-1862 **[118]**
- 🐟 **$135 831** - €154 253 - **£95 000** - FF1 011 835
  Wasserjagd am Chiemsee (hunt on the shores of the Chiemsee) Oil/panel (84x73.5cm 33x28in) London 2001
- 🐟 **$5 106** - €4 359 - **£3 054** - FF28 596
  Junge Bäuerin von hinten auf einem Hauhaufen sitzend/Junger Bauer Öl/Papier (24x15cm 9x5in) Wien 1998
- **$1 466** - €1 453 - **£918** - FF9 534
  Tanzunterhaltung in einem Wirtshaus Pencil/paper (21.5x31.7cm 8x12in) Wien 1999
- 🎨 **$449** - €436 - **£277** - FF2 860
  Der schützende Baum Radierung (16.6x22cm 6x8in) Wien 1999

GAUERMANN Jacob 1773-1843 **[13]**
- 📝 **$987** - €1 090 - **£684** - FF7 150
  Gebirgslandschaft mit figürlicher Staffage Ink (49x69cm 19x27in) Wien 2001
- 🎨 **$316** - €307 - **£196** - FF2 400
  Die Walfahrt der drey heil Etching (33.7x42.1cm 13x16in) Berlin 1999

GAUFFIER Louis 1762-1801 **[11]**
- 🐟 **$20 000** - €21 394 - **£13 636** - FF140 334
  Abraham Accepting Hagar Oil/canvas (54x65cm 21x25in) New-York 2001
- 🐟 **$28 000** - €30 720 - **£18 600** - FF201 510
  Portrait of a young Man, with Mount Vesuvius beyond Oil/canvas (9.5x7.5cm 3x21in) New-York 2000

GAUFFRIAUX Emile 1877-1957 **[62]**
- 📝 **$388** - €457 - **£273** - FF3 000
  Bord de rivière Huile/toile (46x55cm 18x21in) Paris 2000
- 🐟 **$340** - €366 - **£228** - FF2 400
  Marine - mer agitée et voiles rouges Huile/panneau (33x41cm 12x16in) Douarnenez 2000

GAUGAIN Thomas 1748-1810 **[17]**
- 🎨 **$268** - €288 - **£182** - FF1 891
  Perros bailando Grabado (40.5x54.5cm 15x21in) Madrid 2000

GAUGUIN Jean René 1881-1961 **[77]**
- 🦎 **$645** - €738 - **£442** - FF4 839
  Tyrekalv Terracotta (H32cm H12in) Köbenhavn 2000

GAUGUIN Paul 1848-1903 **[528]**
- 🐟 **$791 100** - €763 198 - **£500 000** - FF5 006 250
  Course de chiens dans la prairie Oil/canvas (92x72.5cm 36x28in) London 2001
- 🐟 **$145 652** - €140 313 - **£89 998** - FF920 390
  Nature morte Oil/canvas (33x40.5cm 12x15in) New-York 1999
- 🦎 **$16 000** - €17 921 - **£11 116** - FF117 555
  «La Hina» Bronze (35x12.5x5.5cm 13x4x2in) New-York 2001
- 📝 **$61 236** - €51 436 - **£36 000** - FF337 395
  Projet de décoration pour une bibliothèque Watercolour/paper (47x64cm 18x25in) London 1998
- 🎨 **$12 922** - €12 782 - **£8 057** - FF83 847
  Manao Tupapao Lithographie (18.1x27.3cm 7x10in) Berlin 1999

GAUGUIN Paul René 1911-1976 **[33]**
- 🎨 **$226** - €244 - **£156** - FF1 600
  Komposisjon Serigraph (34x34cm 13x13in) Oslo 2001

GAUGUIN Pola 1883-1961 **[14]**
- 🐟 **$683** - €738 - **£471** - FF4 838
  En lille legende dreng Oil/canvas (46x46cm 18x18in) Köbenhavn 2001

GAUL Arrah Lee 1888-1980 **[25]**
- 🐟 **$2 500** - €2 772 - **£1 732** - FF18 184
  Valley Panorama through the Cherry Blossoms Oil/canvas (63x76cm 25x30in) St. Petersburg FL 2001

GAUL August 1869-1921 **[197]**
- 🦎 **$2 164** - €2 556 - **£1 528** - FF16 769
  Grasender Esel Bronze (H9.5cm H3in) Köln 2001
- 📝 **$632** - €613 - **£393** - FF4 024
  Panther, Löwe und Gänsegruppe Pencil (22.6x15.4cm 8x6in) Berlin 1999
- 🎨 **$104** - €112 - **£70** - FF737
  Kamele und Soldaten Lithographie (32.5x24.7cm 12x9in) München 2000

GAUL Gilbert William 1855-1919 **[46]**
- 🐟 **$16 000** - €18 805 - **£11 092** - FF123 350
  Indian Scout Oil/canvas/board (77x51cm 30x20in) Beverly-Hills CA 2001
- 🐟 **$3 500** - €3 975 - **£2 395** - FF26 072
  Going Fishing Oil/canvas/board (40x30cm 15x11in) New-York 2000

GAUL Gustav 1836-1888 **[15]**
- 🐟 **$2 400** - €2 563 - **£1 635** - FF16 812
  Portrait of a Young Actress of the Burgtheater Oil/canvas (68x55cm 27x22in) New-Orleans LA 2001

GAUL Winfred 1928 **[87]**
- 🐟 **$9 864** - €11 760 - **£7 033** - FF77 139
  Ohne Titel Öl/Leinwand (140x100cm 55x39in) Berlin 2000
- 📝 **$1 093** - €1 022 - **£662** - FF6 707
  Komposition Gouache (49.6x64.6cm 19x25in) Stuttgart 1999
- 🎨 **$83** - €97 - **£58** - FF637
  Rotes Dreieck auf blauem Grund/Oranges Dreieck auf lila Grund Farbserigraphie (25x25cm 9x9in) Berlin 2000

GAULD David 1865-1936 **[53]**
- 🐟 **$5 610** - €5 300 - **£3 500** - FF34 766
  The old Watermill Oil/canvas (61x76cm 24x29in) Perthshire 1999
- 🐟 **$2 164** - €2 045 - **£1 350** - FF13 414
  La ville basse Oil/canvas (30x51cm 11x20in) Perthshire 1999

GAULIS Fernand 1860-1924 **[10]**
- 📝 **$390** - €459 - **£282** - FF3 011
  Bateau au port Aquarelle/papier (28.5x19cm 11x7in) Sion 2001

GAULLI BACICCIA Giovan Battista 1639-1709 **[39]**
- 🐟 **$97 202** - €82 703 - **£58 000** - FF542 497
  Saint Francis receiving the Stigmata Oil/canvas (99.5x75cm 39x29in) London 1998
- 📝 **$3 200** - €3 718 - **£2 249** - FF24 387
  Bearded Nude seated on a Rock in Profile to the Right Red chalk (41.5x55cm 16x21in) New-York 2001

GAULT de Jacques Joseph 1738-? **[7]**
- 🐟 **$16 000** - €17 554 - **£10 628** - FF115 148
  Cadmus and Hermione Oil/panel (10x7.5cm 3x2in) New-York 2000

GAULT George 1916 **[17]**
- 🐟 **$765** - €889 - **£537** - FF5 830
  Village, County Wicklow Oil/panel (36x47cm 14x18in) Dublin 2000
- 🐟 **$260** - €226 - **£160** - FF1 482
  Ashprington, Near Totnes Devon Oil/board (25x32.5cm 9x12in) Bayswater, London 1999

GAULTIER Léonard 1561-1630/41 **[5]**
📖 **$469** - €522 - **£326** - FF3 421
    Das jüngste Gericht Kupferstich (31.5x23.5cm
    12x9in) Heidelberg 2001

GAUNT William Norman 1900-1980 **[66]**
✏️ **$496** - €463 - **£300** - FF3 036
    «Point to Point in the Paddock» Gouache
    (35.5x47cm 13x18in) London 1998

GAUPP Gustav Adolf 1844-1918 **[8]**
👉 **$986** - €1 111 - **£693** - FF7 289
    Stehende Dame mit Früchteschale Öl/Leinwand
    (109x77cm 42x30in) Zürich 2001

GAUQUIÉ Henri Désiré 1858-1927 **[28]**
🔨 **$1 355** - €1 239 - **£825** - FF8 130
    Le semeur Bronze (H63cm H24in) Antwerpen 1999

GAUSACHS Josep 1891-1959 **[46]**
👉 **$306** - €360 - **£210** - FF2 364
    Pueblo nevado Oleo/lienzo (46x61cm 18x24in)
    Barcelona 2000

GAUSE Wilhelm 1853-1916 **[22]**
✏️ **$2 103** - €2 120 - **£1 311** - FF13 906
    Auf dem Naschmarkt Fusain (31.5x41.5cm 12x16in)
    Zürich 2000

GAUSSEN Adolphe 1871-1954 **[42]**
👉 **$46 168** - €44 210 - **£29 058** - FF290 000
    Le port de Marseille Huile/toile (122x202cm
    48x79in) Marseille 1999
👉 **$2 853** - €3 354 - **£2 068** - FF22 000
    Nature morte aux fruits et faïence Huile/toile
    (38x55cm 14x21in) Lyon 2001
👉 **$3 040** - €2 744 - **£1 873** - FF18 000
    La corniche et les îles Huile/toile (33x41cm
    12x16in) Arles 1999

GAUSSON Léo 1860-1944 **[77]**
👉 **$2 149** - €2 058 - **£1 352** - FF13 500
    Paysage Huile/toile (49x73cm 19x28in) Arcachon
    1999
👉 **$2 014** - €2 287 - **£1 399** - FF15 000
    Travaux des champs Huile/toile (26.5x40.5cm
    10x15in) Pontoise 2001

GAUTHERIN Jean 1840-1890 **[23]**
🔨 **$1 000** - €960 - **£619** - FF6 299
    Clotide de Surville Bronze (H34cm H13in) Chicago
    IL 1999

GAUTHEY Emiland Marie 1732-1806 **[1]**
✏️ **$1 300** - €1 524 - **£935** - FF10 000
    **Plans, profils et élévation d'une entrée principa-
le** Encre Chine (46.5x59cm 18x23in) Paris 2001

GAUTHIER Alain 1939 **[2]**
📖 **$800** - €892 - **£523** - FF5 854
    «Clairette de Die, de la gaieté...naturellement...»
    Poster (114.5x154.5cm 45x60in) New-York 2000

GAUTHIER Joachim George 1897-1988 **[34]**
👉 **$682** - €661 - **£421** - FF4 333
    St.Fabien, Que Oil/canvas/board (25.5x30.5cm
    10x12in) Toronto 1999

GAUTHIER L. XX **[2]**
📖 **$534** - €610 - **£371** - FF4 000
    «La Baule» Affiche (109x75cm 42x29in) Paris 2000

GAUTHIER Marie XIX-XX **[2]**
👉 **$8 000** - €7 922 - **£4 980** - FF51 966
    Wild Flowers Oil/canvas (130x75.5cm 51x29in) New-
    York 1999

GAUTHIER Oscar 1921 **[137]**
👉 **$1 760** - €1 906 - **£1 205** - FF12 500
    Terrain Huile/toile (73x60cm 28x23in) Paris 2001
✏️ **$958** - €915 - **£598** - FF6 000
    Composition Gouache (32x48cm 12x18in) Douai
    1999

GAUTIER D'AGOTY Jacques Fabien 1710-1781 **[5]**
📖 **$20 000** - €19 258 - **£12 506** - FF126 326
    **Exposition anatomique des organes des sens,
First Edition** Mezzotint (40.5x27cm 15x10in) New-
    York 1999

GAUTIER Gérard 1723-1795 **[1]**
🔨 **$47 490** - €45 735 - **£29 490** - FF300 000
    **Bas-relief commémorant le sacre de Louis XVI
et son mariage** Bas-relief (59x41.5cm 23x16in) Paris
    1999

GAUTIER Jean Rodolphe 1764-c.1820 **[3]**
✏️ **$3 662** - €3 811 - **£2 315** - FF25 000
    Vue du port de Marseille Aquarelle/papier
    (35x54.5cm 13x21in) Paris 2000

GAUTIER Louis François 1855-1947 **[15]**
👉 **$2 826** - €2 744 - **£1 746** - FF18 000
    Paysage méditerranéen Huile/toile (45.5x59.5cm
    17x23in) Paris 1999

GAUTIER Lucien 1850-1925 **[24]**
📖 **$127** - €137 - **£85** - FF900
    Bergère et ses moutons en sous-bois
    Lithographie (55.5x66cm 21x25in) Paris 2000

GAUTIER Philippe 1928 **[14]**
👉 **$1 396** - €1 372 - **£866** - FF9 000
    La mèche de cheveux Huile/toile (50x50cm
    19x19in) Lyon 1999

GAUTIER Pierre J. 1811-1872 **[1]**
👉 **$14 522** - €12 272 - **£8 637** - FF80 500
    Portrait d'une dame en nymphe Huile/toile
    (100x82cm 39x32in) Monte-Carlo 1998

GAUVREAU Pierre 1922 **[12]**
👉 **$5 947** - €6 942 - **£4 076** - FF45 534
    Composition Huile/panneau (42x33cm 16x12in)
    Montréal 2000

GAUZY Jeanne L. 1886-? **[20]**
👉 **$674** - €571 - **£408** - FF3 743
    Bodegón Oleo/lienzo (38x46cm 14x18in) Madrid
    1998

GAVAGNIN Natale 1851-? **[15]**
👉 **$2 000** - €2 073 - **£1 200** - FF13 600
    Veduta della laguna Olio/tela (20.5x50.5cm 8x19in)
    Venezia 1999

GAVARNI Paul 1804-1866 **[262]**
👉 **$2 683** - €2 287 - **£1 599** - FF15 000
    Le collectionneur de tableaux Huile/panneau
    (17x14.5cm 6x5in) Paris 1998
✏️ **$436** - €412 - **£264** - FF2 700
    Deux jeunes femmes, l'une de dos assise
    Aquarelle/papier (19x15cm 7x5in) Paris 1999
📖 **$234** - €271 - **£168** - FF1 811
    Les Artistes Lithograph (20x15.5cm 7x6in) Hamburg
    2001

GAVARRONE Domenico c.1820-c.1880 **[3]**
✏️ **$3 750** - €3 508 - **£2 272** - FF23 013
    **Ship Brandywine Brunswik P.C Merryman
Commander** Watercolour/paper (46x67cm 18x26in)
    Bolton MA 1999

G

GAVIN Robert 1827-1883 **[12]**
- $4 611 - €4 386 - **£2 800** - FF28 772
  Spanish Girl with a Fan Oil/canvas (60x44.5cm 23x17in) Edinburgh 1999
- $1 268 - €1 317 - **£800** - FF8 641
  The Truant Oil/canvas/panel (33x28.5cm 12x11in) London 2000

GAW William A. 1891-1973 **[9]**
- $1 400 - €1 512 - **£967** - FF9 917
  Rock Quarry Oil/canvas (38x45cm 15x18in) Altadena CA 2001
- $3 500 - €3 780 - **£2 418** - FF24 793
  Begonia in red Clay Pot Oil/canvas (35x27cm 14x11in) Altadena CA 2001

GAWELL Oskar 1888-1955 **[44]**
- $809 - €920 - **£561** - FF6 037
  Nordafrikanische Dorfansicht mit Palmen Aquarell/Papier (47x61cm 18x24in) Staufen 2000

GAWRIS Iwan Trophimowitsch XX **[1]**
- $10 752 - €9 954 - **£6 582** - FF65 297
  Stilleben mit Violine, Fruchtkorb und Büchern Öl/Papier (79x63cm 31x24in) Bern 1999

GAWTHORN Henry George 1879-1941 **[12]**
- $4 000 - €4 641 - **£2 806** - FF30 442
  «**Cruden Bay**» Poster (101x63cm 40x25in) New-York 2000

GAY Abel 1877-1961 **[25]**
- $519 - €518 - **£324** - FF3 400
  Coin de verger au printemps Huile/panneau (51x67cm 20x26in) Lyon 1999

GAY Arthur Wilson 1901-1948 **[10]**
- $190 - €218 - **£130** - FF1 430
  A Pony on the Isles of Scilly Watercolour/paper (8x10cm 3x4in) Par, Cornwall 2000

GAY Edward B. 1837-1928 **[95]**
- $5 500 - €4 661 - **£3 286** - FF30 572
  River scene Oil/canvas (45x60cm 18x24in) Thomaston ME 1998
- $1 300 - €1 227 - **£808** - FF8 351
  The Night Train Oil/panel (24x40cm 9x16in) Milford CT 1999
- $1 100 - €1 114 - **£690** - FF7 310
  Golden Waves Watercolour/paper (48x33cm 19x13in) Cincinnati OH 2000

GAY George Howell 1858-1931 **[145]**
- $1 100 - €1 051 - **£677** - FF6 891
  Path through the Woods Oil/paper (76x40cm 30x16in) Cincinnati OH 1999
- $600 - €558 - **£370** - FF3 659
  Coastal View, New England Watercolour/paper (23x49cm 9x19in) Portland ME 1999

GAY Jean Joseph Pascal 1775-1832 **[1]**
- $2 947 - €2 733 - **£1 808** - FF17 928
  Two Ghosts Appearing From a Tomb in the Crypt of a Romanesque Church Watercolour (37x33cm 14x12in) London 1998

GAY Walter 1856-1937 **[72]**
- $20 000 - €23 252 - **£14 038** - FF152 520
  The Gallery Oil/board (59x45cm 23x17in) New-York 2001
- $894 - €838 - **£537** - FF5 500
  Jeune femme Huile/panneau (18x14.5cm 7x5in) Paris 1999
- $1 740 - €1 829 - **£1 092** - FF12 000
  Chambre à coucher Aquarelle, gouache (27x36cm 10x14in) Paris 2000

GAY Winckworth Allan 1821-1910 **[29]**
- $9 000 - €10 634 - **£6 378** - FF69 757
  A Bay Near Hong Kong Oil/canvas (43x58.5cm 16x23in) Boston MA 2000
- $2 100 - €2 284 - **£1 384** - FF14 982
  Trip Hammer Road, Hingham Oil/board (20.5x30.5cm 8x12in) Boston MA 2000

GAYA Ramón 1910 **[52]**
- $10 370 - €10 211 - **£6 460** - FF66 980
  Homenaje a Tiépolo Oleo/lienzo (45.5x35.5cm 17x13in) Madrid 1999
- $1 080 - €1 081 - **£666** - FF7 092
  Pintores junto al Sena Lápiz/papel (20x27cm 7x10in) Madrid 2000
- $2 400 - €2 252 - **£1 500** - FF14 775
  Agua para una infanta/La gente/El principe Baltasar Carlos Litografía (50x65cm 19x25in) Madrid 1999

GAYFORD Stephen 1954 **[17]**
- $4 769 - €3 967 - **£2 800** - FF26 022
  Snow Leopard Acrylic/board (45x61cm 17x24in) London 1998

GAYRARD Paul 1807-1855 **[31]**
- $1 898 - €2 019 - **£1 200** - FF13 245
  Recumbent Chihuahua Bronze (10.5x16cm 4x6in) London 2000

GAZZERA Romano 1906-1985 **[25]**
- $3 000 - €3 110 - **£1 800** - FF20 400
  Le grandi dalie Olio/tela/tavola (70x90cm 27x35in) Vercelli 2000
- $1 250 - €1 296 - **£750** - FF8 500
  Les Roches Rouges Olio/carta (24x28.5cm 9x11in) Torino 2000

GAZZERI Ernesto 1866-? **[6]**
- $23 000 - €25 745 - **£16 040** - FF168 877
  Apollo and Daphne Marble (H127cm H50in) New-York 2001
- $6 223 - €6 137 - **£4 000** - FF40 258
  Figure of a Classical Maiden with a Lyre Marble (H77cm H30in) London 2001

GDANIETZ Wilhelm 1893-1962 **[34]**
- $839 - €716 - **£506** - FF4 694
  «**Pfeife rauchender Bauer mit Wanderstab**» Öl/Leinwand (61x71cm 24x27in) Kempten 1998

GE Nikolai Nikolaevich. 1831-1894 **[2]**
- $8 219 - €8 823 - **£5 500** - FF57 873
  Portrait of a Woman in a black Veil Oil/canvas (55.5x47.5cm 21x18in) London 2000

GEACH Portia Stranston 1873-1959 **[20]**
- $3 430 - €3 683 - **£2 296** - FF24 157
  The Beach, Beaumaris Oil/board (22.5x33.5cm 8x13in) Melbourne 2000
- $2 105 - €2 457 - **£1 486** - FF16 116
  «**Procession of the Hours**» Watercolour (25.5x80cm 10x31in) Malvern, Victoria 2000

GEAR Mabel 1900-1997 **[103]**
- $1 819 - €1 702 - **£1 100** - FF11 162
  Feeding the Chickens Oil/canvas (41x41cm 16x16in) London 1999
- $2 500 - €2 213 - **£1 528** - FF14 517
  Tug o'War Oil/panel (28.5x42cm 11x16in) New-York 1999
- $533 - €634 - **£380** - FF4 517
  Kitten with Foxgloves and a Bee Watercolour (32x21.5cm 12x8in) Bath 2000

G

GEAR William 1915-1997 **[171]**
- **$4 461** – €3 878 – **£2 700** – FF25 440
  September landscape Oil/canvas (84x68.5cm 33x26in) London 1999
- **$1 311** – €1 492 – **£900** – FF9 785
  Tapis Rouge Acrylic/paper (29x39cm 11x15in) London 2000
- **$2 092** – €2 246 – **£1 400** – FF14 730
  Nude Studies Drawing (41.5x29cm 16x11in) London 2000

GEARHART Frances Hammel 1869-1958 **[39]**
- **$1 800** – €2 007 – **£1 250** – FF13 162
  «**Fall**» Woodcut in colors (28x23cm 11x9in) New-York 2001

GEBAUER Christian David 1777-1831 **[28]**
- **$557** – €470 – **£334** – FF3 086
  Kronhjort med sine hinder på en höj, morgenbelysning Oil/wood (25x36cm 9x14in) Köbenhavn 1998
- **$1 011** – €857 – **£600** – FF5 622
  Arab Horses Lithograph (34x42cm 13x16in) London 1998

GEBHARD Albert 1869-1937 **[30]**
- **$2 330** – €2 186 – **£1 440** – FF14 341
  Roddare Oil/canvas (56x82cm 22x32in) Helsinki 1999
- **$582** – €572 – **£361** – FF3 750
  Insjölandskap Oil/canvas (31x44cm 12x17in) Helsinki 1999
- **$319** – €370 – **£226** – FF2 427
  Hemstrand Watercolour/paper (24x38cm 9x14in) Helsinki 2000

GEBHARD Johannes 1894-1976 **[54]**
- **$498** – €538 – **£344** – FF3 530
  Spirea Oil/canvas (51x35cm 20x13in) Helsinki 2001
- **$137** – €151 – **£94** – FF992
  Lador i Norrmark Watercolour/paper (28x42cm 11x16in) Helsinki 2001

GEBHARDT Ludwig 1830-1908 **[27]**
- **$2 492** – €2 301 – **£1 532** – FF15 092
  Mond über dem See Öl/Leinwand (43x57cm 16x22in) München 1999
- **$1 000** – €1 125 – **£698** – FF7 378
  Herbstliche Landschaft Oil/panel (19.5x28cm 7x11in) Lindau 2001

GEBHARDT von Eduard 1838-1925 **[78]**
- **$1 165** – €1 278 – **£791** – FF8 384
  Die Verurteilung Christi Öl/Leinwand (105x86cm 41x33in) Düsseldorf 2000
- **$600** – €716 – **£428** – FF4 695
  Bildnis einer alten Frau mit gestreiftem Umhang Oil/panel (26.5x17.5cm 10x6in) Königstein 2000

GEBLER Friedrich Otto 1838-1917 **[55]**
- **$10 388** – €11 654 – **£7 200** – FF76 448
  Stable Interior Oil/panel (50x68cm 19x26in) London 2000
- **$4 557** – €5 113 – **£3 159** – FF33 539
  Heimkehrende Schafe und Hund vor dem Stall Oil/panel (21.5x28.5cm 8x11in) München 2000

GEBRAN Gébran Khalil 1883-1931 **[2]**
- **$27 258** – €30 678 – **£18 780** – FF201 234
  Der Verschneite Weg nach München Öl/Leinwand (78x102cm 30x40in) München 2000

GECELLI Johannes 1925 **[20]**
- **$4 763** – €5 113 – **£3 188** – FF33 539
  Warmkreis Acryl/Leinwand (100x89.5cm 39x35in) Köln 2000

GEHR... – €1 636 – **£1 024** – FF10 732
  Greenwalk Aquarell, Gouache (67.5x51cm 26x20in) Heidelberg 2001

GECHTER Jean-Fr. Théodore 1796-1844 **[87]**
- **$1 666** – €1 982 – **£1 188** – FF13 000
  Cheval romantique Bronze (19x25cm 7x9in) Paris 2001

GECHTOFF Leonid XX **[23]**
- **$200** – €202 – **£124** – FF1 322
  Arabian Street Scene Pastel/paper (43x51cm 17x20in) Hatfield PA 2000

GEDDA Hans 1942 **[2]**
- **$1 076** – €1 201 – **£748** – FF7 876
  Olof Palme Gelatin silver print (38x29.5cm 14x11in) Stockholm 2001

GEDDES Andrew 1783-1844 **[12]**
- **$11 157** – €13 121 – **£8 000** – FF86 068
  Double Portrait of Wilkie Collins and Charles Alston Collins Oil/canvas (95x120cm 37x47in) Tunbridge-Wells, Kent 2001

GEDDES Ewan 1866-1935 **[12]**
- **$417** – €385 – **£260** – FF2 528
  Redhouse, East Lothian Watercolour/paper (19.5x13cm 7x5in) Edinburgh 1999

GEDDES William 1841-1884 **[17]**
- **$4 246** – €3 909 – **£2 600** – FF25 640
  A Hamlet on the Banks of a River/Extensive Landscape with Figures Oil/canvas (46x61cm 18x24in) Newbury, Berkshire 1998

GEDLEK Ludwig 1847-1904 **[55]**
- **$7 641** – €8 866 – **£5 275** – FF58 155
  Ungarische Rieterturppe bei Sonnenuntergang Oil/panel (37x56cm 14x22in) Luzern 2000
- **$2 947** – €3 270 – **£2 052** – FF21 451
  An der Überfuhre Oil/panel (18x23cm 7x9in) Wien 2001

GEDO Ilka 1921-1985 **[4]**
- **$3 850** – €4 259 – **£2 530** – FF27 940
  Spring Oil/paper/canvas (44.5x59cm 17x23in) Budapest 2000

GEDOVIUS Germán 1867-1937 **[5]**
- **$6 500** – €6 215 – **£3 958** – FF40 769
  Portrait of Ana Julie Grillo Peoh Oil/canvas (150x66cm 59x26in) Columbia SC 1999

GEE David 1793-1871 **[1]**
- **$12 469** – €11 419 – **£7 600** – FF74 902
  Horse and Foal in stable Steeing Oil/canvas (69x89cm 27x35in) Leamington-Spa, Warwickshire 1999

GEEL van Jean-Louis 1787-1852 **[1]**
- **$3 322** – €3 534 – **£2 100** – FF23 179
  Bust of a Woman Plaster (H64cm H25in) London 2000

GEEL van Joost 1631-1698 **[3]**
- **$14 420** – €14 534 – **£9 000** – FF95 340
  Bewaldete Flusslandschaft mit einer Hütte und Bauern Oil/canvas (26x35cm 10x13in) Wien 2000

GEER de Carl Johan 1940 **[8]**
- **$1 125** – €1 255 – **£782** – FF8 234
  U.S.A., Mördare Print in colors (52x45cm 20x17in) Stockholm 2001

GEERARDS Jasper c.1620-c.1654 **[5]**
- $25 116 - €28 134 - **£17 453** - FF184 549
  Still Life with a silver Ewer, a Lobster on a Porcelain Plate Oil/panel (59.5x51cm 23x20in) Amsterdam 2001

GEERLINGS Gerald Kenneth 1897-1998 **[33]**
- $1 300 - €1 125 - **£784** - FF7 382
  Electrical Building at Night (Grand Canal America) Etching (30x22.5cm 11x8in) New-York 1998

GEERTSEN Hendrik 1892-1969 **[25]**
- $44 - €50 - **£31** - FF325
  Dorpsgezicht (Vue de village) Aquarelle/papier (32x36cm 12x14in) Antwerpen 2001

GEERTSEN Ib 1919 **[42]**
- $962 - €1 073 - **£658** - FF7 039
  Blaa rum II Oil/canvas (92x73cm 36x28in) København 2000
- $1 182 - €1 341 - **£833** - FF8 796
  «Rum II» Oil/canvas (41x33cm 16x12in) København 2001

GEEST de Wybrand Simonsz. 1592-1660 **[6]**
- $32 000 - €34 174 - **£21 804** - FF224 169
  Family Portrait of two Brothers, two Sisters Oil/panel (79.5x115cm 31x45in) New-York 2001

GEETERE de Frans 1895-1968 **[12]**
- $845 - €908 - **£565** - FF5 953
  Tulips in a vase Watercolour, gouache/paper (71x58.5cm 27x23in) Amsterdam 2000

GEETS Willem 1838-1919 **[28]**
- $4 500 - €3 776 - **£2 652** - FF24 766
  Young Lady Embroidering in an Interior Oil/panel (49x38cm 19x15in) Greenwich CT 1998

GEFFCKEN Walter 1872-1950 **[43]**
- $966 - €920 - **£589** - FF6 037
  Gesellschaft im Park Öl/Karton (38x47cm 14x18in) Stuttgart 1999
- $650 - €674 - **£390** - FF4 420
  Scena d'interno in abiti settecenteschi Olio/tavoletta (33x46cm 12x18in) Milano 2001

GEFFELS de Frans c.1615-1659/71 **[3]**
- $17 724 - €17 406 - **£11 000** - FF114 178
  Figures Playing Music and Dancing in a Garden Oil/canvas (89x115cm 35x45in) London 1999

GEGERFELT von Wilhelm 1844-1920 **[342]**
- $2 094 - €2 432 - **£1 471** - FF15 954
  Sydländsk stadsbild Oil/canvas (60x40cm 23x15in) Stockholm 2001
- $1 207 - €1 341 - **£808** - FF8 796
  Hus och figur i vinterlandskap Oil/canvas (27x41cm 10x16in) Stockholm 2000
- $381 - €360 - **£236** - FF2 360
  Båtar på strand Akvarell/papper (17x23cm 6x9in) Stockholm 2001

GEGO Gertrudis Goldschmit 1912-1994 **[14]**
- $50 000 - €43 598 - **£30 230** - FF285 985
  Sin título Metal (100x70cm 39x27in) New-York 1998
- $11 000 - €10 703 - **£6 770** - FF70 205
  Sin título Ink/paper (55x50cm 21x19in) New-York 1999

GEHLIN Hugo 1889-1953 **[8]**
- $775 - €922 - **£552** - FF6 047
  Gammal maltug - motiv från St.Clemens gata i Helsingborg Oil/panel (25x17cm 9x6in) Stockholm 2000

GEHR Ferdinand 1896-1996 **[186]**
- $2 830 - €3 284 - **£1 954** - FF21 539
  Christus, das Kreuz tragend Painting (54x54cm 21x21in) St. Gallen 2000
- $3 231 - €3 107 - **£1 790** - FF20 381
  Verklärter Christus Peinture (37x32cm 14x12in) St. Gallen 1999
- $5 040 - €4 847 - **£3 105** - FF31 795
  Zinnie Aquarell/Papier (24x32cm 9x12in) St. Gallen 1999
- $326 - €350 - **£218** - FF2 297
  Komposition Woodcut in colors (35x34.5cm 13x13in) Zofingen 2000

GEHRTS Carl 1853-1898 **[19]**
- $181 - €204 - **£125** - FF1 341
  Bildergeschichte zu Märchen-Illustrationen mit König und Gnomen Indian ink/paper (14x35cm 5x13in) Zwiesel 2000

GEHRY Frank 1929 **[6]**
- $10 000 - €9 576 - **£6 163** - FF62 814
  Bubbles Chaise lounge Construction (86x208x71cm 34x82x28in) Chicago IL 1999
- $11 000 - €10 500 - **£6 873** - FF68 876
  Easy Edge Dining Table and Six Side Chairs Sculpture (73.5x206x91cm 28x81x35in) New-York 1999

GEIBEL Margarete 1876-1955 **[19]**
- $225 - €245 - **£148** - FF1 609
  Treppe zum Büstenzimmer/Treppe im Goethehaus Woodcut (28x40cm 11x15in) Hamburg 2000

GEIGENBERGER Otto 1881-1946 **[23]**
- $893 - €1 050 - **£640** - FF6 888
  Wasserburg am Inn Öl/Leinwand (53x68cm 20x26in) Bern 2001
- $657 - €767 - **£461** - FF5 030
  Sulzfeld am Main Aquarell/Papier (55x79cm 21x31in) München 2000

GEIGER Conrad 1751-1808 **[8]**
- $4 170 - €4 573 - **£2 832** - FF30 000
  Allégorie de l'Espérance Huile/toile (88x69cm 34x27in) Lille 2000

GEIGER Ernst Samuel 1876-1965 **[58]**
- $5 588 - €5 335 - **£3 491** - FF34 996
  Über der Bucht von Auvernier Öl/Leinwand (56x65cm 22x25in) Zofingen 1999
- $321 - €310 - **£198** - FF2 031
  Stadt an einem Fluss Aquarell/Papier (20x30cm 7x11in) Bern 1999

GEIGER Peter Johann Nepomuk 1805-1880 **[12]**
- $4 128 - €4 857 - **£2 914** - FF31 861
  Der Maler Van Dyck unter seinen Freunden im Salon Öl/Karton (36.5x45cm 14x17in) Köln 2001

GEIGER Raimund 1889-1968 **[6]**
- $1 300 - €1 450 - **£851** - FF9 513
  «Cirkus Reinhardt» Poster (94.5x68.5cm 37x26in) New-York 2000

GEIGER Richard 1870-1945 **[113]**
- $982 - €1 070 - **£680** - FF7 019
  The Tambourine Girl Oil/canvas (79x59cm 31x23in) London 2001

GEIGER Rupprecht 1908 **[219]**
- $43 716 - €42 438 - **£26 999** - FF278 373
  Komposition Öl/Leinwand (151.5x146.5cm 59x57in) München 1999

G

G

$16 352 - €14 313 - **£9 903** - FF93 886
Ohne Titel Öl/Leinwand (101x76cm 39x29in) Berlin 1998

$33 772 - €38 347 - **£23 115** - FF251 542
Objektziffer O (Metapher Zahl 0) Sculpture, wood (110x120x21cm 43x47x8in) Berlin 2000

$1 749 - €1 994 - **£1 220** - FF13 080
Komposition Pencil (51x70cm 20x27in) Hamburg 2001

$241 - €225 - **£145** - FF1 475
Blau-Schwarz Farblithographie (51x47cm 20x18in) Hamburg 1999

GEIGER Willi 1878-1971 [201]

$1 093 - €1 022 - **£662** - FF6 707
Bunter Blumenstrauss in einer Vase Oil/panel (54.5x70cm 21x27in) Stuttgart 1999

$263 - €256 - **£162** - FF1 767
Felsenhäuser in Spanien Aquarell, Gouache/Papier (33.8x50.5cm 13x19in) München 1999

$184 - €184 - **£115** - FF1 207
Stierkampf Etching, aquatint in colors (50x84cm 19x33in) München 1999

GEIKIE Walter 1795-1837 [3]

$2 964 - €2 820 - **£1 800** - FF18 496
The itinerant bagpiper Oil/canvas (30.5x25.5cm 12x10in) Edinburgh 1999

GEISEL Theodor S. Dr. Seuss 1904-1991 [18]

$15 000 - €14 365 - **£9 267** - FF94 228
Goat Eating Machine Parts, Billboard Advertisement Mixed media (30x68cm 12x27in) New-York 1999

$13 000 - €14 561 - **£9 032** - FF95 513
Magazine Cartoon, Man spanking Cat as others wait their Turns Ink (21x19cm 8x7in) New-York 2001

GEISER Karl 1898-1957 [69]

$4 480 - €5 236 - **£3 198** - FF34 346
David Bronze (H77.5cm H30in) Zürich 2001

$532 - €574 - **£357** - FF3 764
Weibliche Akte Encre Chine/papier (14x22cm 5x8in) Zürich 2000

$242 - €274 - **£169** - FF1 798
Sitzende Radierung (33.5x23.5cm 13x9in) Zürich 2001

GEISLER E. XX [1]

$5 118 - €5 113 - **£3 200** - FF33 539
Im Englischen Garten Oil/panel (108.5x87.5cm 42x34in) Hamburg 1999

GEISSER Johann Joseph 1824-1894 [43]

$691 - €778 - **£482** - FF5 101
Genferseelandschaft Öl/Leinwand (37x55.5cm 14x21in) Luzern 2001

$936 - €892 - **£586** - FF5 853
Bergère dans un paysage montagneux Huile/toile (35x25cm 13x9in) Antwerpen 1999

GEISSLER Christian Gottlieb 1729-1814 [6]

$1 972 - €2 301 - **£1 384** - FF15 091
«Vue de Genève prise depuis Cologny» Aquarelle (26.5x42.5cm 10x16in) Genève 2000

$1 972 - €2 301 - **£1 384** - FF15 091
Vue des ponts du Rhône, de la Place Bel Air et de l'Isle Eau-forte (32.5x54cm 13x21in) Genève 2000

GEISSLER Claude 1955 [4]

$434 - €427 - **£269** - FF2 800
Neige en Savoie Aquarelle/papier (50x60cm 19x23in) Lyon 1999

GEISSLER Paul 1881-1965 [31]

$100 - €107 - **£66** - FF704
Rothenburg Engraving (18x27cm 7x11in) Hendersonville NC 2000

GEISSLER Robert 1819-1893 [4]

$1 684 - €1 636 - **£1 052** - FF10 732
Bremen: Rathhaus/Domshof/Börse/Grosse Weserbrücke/Hillmann's Hotel/... Lithographie (8x12cm 3x4in) Bremen 1999

GEIST August Christian 1835-1868 [8]

$9 550 - €8 692 - **£5 967** - FF57 016
Idyllische Landschaft mit einem Schafhirten und seiner Herde am Wasser Oil/panel (42.5x53cm 16x20in) München 1999

GEITLINGER Ernst 1895-1972 [34]

$425 - €491 - **£297** - FF3 220
Untitled Watercolour, gouache/paper (51x40cm 20x15in) Bethesda MD 2001

GELATI Lorenzo 1824-1893 [13]

$17 000 - €17 623 - **£10 200** - FF115 600
Veduta di Firenze Olio/carta/tela (37x86.5cm 14x34in) Milano 2000

$2 200 - €2 851 - **£1 650** - FF18 700
Paesaggio Olio/cartone (24x32.5cm 9x12in) Prato 2001

GELATI Lorenzo 1880-1955 [2]

$11 500 - €11 922 - **£6 900** - FF78 200
Paesaggio lacustre Olio/tela (40x58.5cm 15x23in) Prato 2000

$5 100 - €4 406 - **£3 400** - FF28 900
Staggia Olio/tela/cartone (13x40cm 5x15in) Prato 1998

GELDER de Aert 1645-1727 [7]

$72 000 - €63 370 - **£43 833** - FF415 677
The Archangel Raphael Oil/canvas (53x43cm 20x16in) New-York 1999

$24 486 - €22 497 - **£15 043** - FF147 571
Der pissende Soldat vor dem Bordell Oil/panel (31.5x25.9cm 12x10in) München 1999

GELDER F.V. XVII [1]

$10 477 - €9 700 - **£6 500** - FF63 628
Still Life of Peaches, Plums, Pears, Grapes and Butterfly upon a Stone Oil/panel (40.5x52cm 15x20in) London 1999

GELDER van Dirk 1907-1990 [7]

$219 - €250 - **£152** - FF1 637
«Veere» Woodcut (12.6x22.9cm 4x9in) Haarlem 2000

GELDER van Eugène J. Adolphe 1856-? [10]

$588 - €508 - **£354** - FF3 331
Mahieux au cabaret Huile/panneau (29.5x22.5cm 11x8in) Bruxelles 1998

GELDEREN van Simon 1905-1986 [36]

$1 142 - €1 190 - **£753** - FF7 804
Le jour des cuivres Huile/toile (74x60cm 29x23in) Bruxelles 2000

GELDHOF Herbert 1929 [12]

$1 287 - €1 438 - **£899** - FF9 430
Ours polaire Bronze (H27cm H10in) Bruxelles 2001

GELDORP Gortzius 1553-1618 [27]

$13 687 - €12 782 - **£8 447** - FF83 847
Anna Selbdritt Oil/panel (129.5x123.5cm 50x48in) Köln 2001

$6 877 - €7 669 - **£4 624** - FF50 308
Allegorie der Liebe Oil/panel (67x50.5cm 26x19in) Köln 2000

GELENG Otto Friedrich XIX **[15]**
- $13 000 - €13 100 - **£8 104** - FF85 930
  The Ruins of Pompeii Oil/canvas (106.5x167.5cm 41x65in) New-York 1999
- $1 030 - €1 022 - **£643** - FF6 707
  Bucht bei Amalfi Oil/canvas/panel (40x64.5cm 15x25in) München 1999

GELENG Rinaldo XX **[3]**
- $969 - €1 004 - **£581** - FF6 589
  «Passione di Zingara» Affiche couleur (140x100cm 55x39in) Torino 2000

GELFAND Sydney XX **[1]**
- $2 500 - €2 426 - **£1 556** - FF15 916
  National Theater Pencil/paper (15x22cm 6x9in) New-Orleans LA 1999

GELHAAR Emil 1862-1934 **[5]**
- $2 200 - €2 153 - **£1 353** - FF14 126
  Evening in New England Town Oil/canvas (22x26cm 8x10in) Washington 1999

GELHAY Édouard 1856-? **[17]**
- $1 279 - €1 079 - **£750** - FF7 079
  «Clou de l'Exposition» Poster (193x138cm 75x54in) London 1998

GÉLIBERT Gaston 1850-1931 **[27]**
- $694 - €777 - **£471** - FF5 100
  Chasse aux lapins et au faisan Aquarelle, gouache/paper (45x31.5cm 17x12in) Libourne 2000

GÉLIBERT Jules Bertrand 1834-1916 **[68]**
- $4 402 - €4 726 - **£2 945** - FF31 000
  Le repos des chasseurs Huile/toile (60x73cm 23x28in) Paris 2001
- $1 005 - €945 - **£622** - FF6 200
  Les petits braconniers Huile/panneau (30x23cm 11x9in) Toulouse 1999
- $4 500 - €5 045 - **£3 055** - FF33 096
  Druid, the Bloodhound of Imperial Prince Napoleon Bronze (H34cm H13in) Cleveland OH 2000
- $694 - €777 - **£471** - FF5 100
  Chasse aux lapins et au faisan Aquarelle, gouache/paper (45x31.5cm 17x12in) Libourne 2000

GELISSEN Maximilien Lambert 1786-1867 **[9]**
- $2 278 - €2 677 - **£1 598** - FF17 563
  Chemin creux animé Huile/toile (38x51cm 14x20in) Bruxelles 2000

GELLER Johann Nepomuk 1860-1954 **[45]**
- $2 317 - €2 543 - **£1 540** - FF16 684
  Motiv aus Stein an der Donau Öl/Karton (32x20.5cm 12x8in) Wien 2000
- $1 248 - €1 163 - **£769** - FF7 627
  Beflaggte Dorfstrasse Aquarell/Papier (23x21cm 9x8in) Linz 1999

GELLER Judith 1975 **[1]**
- $3 748 - €4 104 - **£2 655** - FF28 508
  Knabenporträt Daguerreotype (28.4x37.2cm 11x14in) Lindau 2001

GELLERSTEDT Albert Theodor 1836-1914 **[15]**
- $375 - €412 - **£249** - FF2 700
  Solnedgång Gouache/paper (11x18cm 4x7in) Stockholm 2000

GELLERT Hugo 1892-? **[21]**
- $550 - €513 - **£339** - FF3 364
  Century of the Common Man Silkscreen in colors (38x32cm 15x12in) Cleveland OH 1999

GELLI Edoardo 1852-1933 **[6]**
- $48 003 - €47 659 - **£30 000** - FF312 621
  Festa nella taverna Oil/canvas (95.5x200cm 37x78in) London 1999

GELPKE André 1947 **[17]**
- $676 - €588 - **£407** - FF3 854
  Yvonne Gelatin silver print (32.7x22cm 12x8in) Berlin 1998

GEMAYEL César 1898-1958 **[1]**
- $8 307 - €9 343 - **£5 800** - FF61 288
  Am Irzal (the tree house) Oil/canvas (36x44.5cm 14x17in) London 2001

GEMIGNANI Valmore 1879-1958 **[10]**
- $800 - €829 - **£480** - FF5 440
  Levriero Bronze (20x26cm 7x10in) Milano 1999

GEMITO Vincenzo 1852-1929 **[172]**
- $5 000 - €5 183 - **£3 000** - FF34 000
  Studio di giovane Tecnica mista/cartone (54x45cm 21x17in) Roma 2000
- $1 120 - €1 451 - **£840** - FF7 923
  Pescatorello con canna Bronzo (H19cm H7in) Roma 2001
- $1 600 - €2 073 - **£1 200** - FF13 600
  Giovane donna di profilo Matita/carta (41x45cm 16x17in) Roma 2001

GEMMELL William XIX-XX **[1]**
- $18 091 - €17 134 - **£11 000** - FF112 389
  Mrs Ernest Guinness, half-length, in striped décolleté dress Pastel/paper (74x56.5cm 29x22in) London 2001

GEMPT te Bernhard 1826-1879 **[29]**
- $39 649 - €47 259 - **£28 272** - FF310 000
  Chien couché près de la sellerie/L'étalon et le lévrier Huile/toile (112x141cm 44x55in) Lyon 2000
- $5 500 - €6 391 - **£3 865** - FF41 919
  Toy Spaniel Oil/panel (47x61.5cm 18x24in) New-York 2001
- $1 400 - €1 367 - **£886** - FF8 964
  Dogs at Play Oleo/tabla (22.5x31cm 8x12in) Buenos-Aires 1999

GEN PAUL Eugène Paul, dit 1895-1975 **[2280]**
- $6 358 - €6 174 - **£3 928** - FF40 500
  Le clown jongleur Huile/panneau (55x33cm 21x12in) Paris 1999
- $2 734 - €3 049 - **£1 908** - FF20 000
  Violoniste et pianiste Huile/panneau (41x27cm 16x10in) Versailles 2001
- $1 099 - €1 296 - **£772** - FF8 500
  Le théâtre de l'atelier Crayons couleurs/papier (28.5x37cm 11x14in) Paris 2000
- $175 - €160 - **£106** - FF1 050
  Sanary Lithographie couleurs (52x67cm 20x26in) Versailles 1998

GEN Yamaguchi 1903-1976 **[4]**
- $1 400 - €1 356 - **£873** - FF8 895
  Abstract Woodcut (65.5x47cm 25x18in) New-York 1999

GENBERG Anton 1862-1939 **[204]**
- $7 916 - €6 884 - **£4 774** - FF45 158
  Skymning över åre Oil/canvas (106x170cm 41x66in) Stockholm 1998
- $1 302 - €1 504 - **£911** - FF9 867
  Vinterlandskap med vattendrag, skymning Oil/panel (45x62cm 17x24in) Stockholm 2001
- $1 113 - €968 - **£671** - FF6 350
  Fjällgård Oil/canvas (27x51cm 10x20in) Stockholm 1998

G

G

GENCE Robert XVII-XVIII [4]
👁 $5 368 – €6 098 – **£3 756** – FF40 000
Portrait de jeune femme en flore Huile/toile
(120x96cm 47x37in) Paris 2001

GENDALL John 1790-1865 [16]
✎ $1 730 – €1 912 – **£1 200** – FF12 543
View on the Exe towards Topsham, Devon
Watercolour (25.5x37cm 10x14in) London 2001

GENEAU Alain 1935 [13]
👁 $1 400 – €1 508 – **£963** – FF9 890
«**Chaconne**» Oil/canvas (45x54cm 18x21in) New-
York 2001

GENEGEN van Joseph 1857-1936 [72]
👁 $408 – €397 – **£249** – FF2 601
Vue de village Huile/toile (45x65cm 17x25in)
Bruxelles 1999
👁 $336 – €372 – **£234** – FF2 439
Paysage de neige animé de personnages
Huile/toile (30x39.5cm 11x15in) Bruxelles 2001

GENELLI Bonaventura 1798-1868 [3]
✎ $745 – €818 – **£506** – FF5 366
**Gewandstudie zu einer sitzenden Frau mit
Ölkrug/Figurenstudie** Pencil/paper (25.2x15.2cm
9x5in) Berlin 2000

GENESEN van Franz 1887-1945 [49]
👁 $387 – €372 – **£243** – FF2 439
Rivière à Deurne Huile/toile (70x80cm 27x31in)
Bruxelles 1999

GENET Alexandre 1799-? [4]
👁 $3 169 – €2 897 – **£1 939** – FF19 000
**Route du Dey, Place Bab-el-Oued et le Fort des
24 heures, Alder** Aquarelle/papier (28x37cm
11x14in) Paris 1999

GENEVIEVE (Geneviève Pezet) 1918 [3]
🤚 $3 683 – €4 040 – **£2 445** – FF26 500
Orphée Bronze (36x21x20cm 14x8x7in) Paris 2000

GÉNICOT Robert 1890-1981 [31]
👁 $2 140 – €1 829 – **£1 296** – FF12 000
Village au Sud Marocain Huile/toile (74x93cm
29x36in) Paris 1998
👁 $1 023 – €991 – **£648** – FF6 500
Anemiter, Vallée d'Ounila, Grand Atlas Huile/iso-
rel (23.5x18.5cm 9x7in) Paris 1999

GENILLION Jean-Baptiste Franç. c.1750-1829 [6]
👁 $25 000 – €29 445 – **£17 290** – FF193 147
**River Landscape with a Roman Temple/River
Landscape with Aqueducts** Oil/canvas
(34.5x48.5cm 13x19in) New-York 2001
✎ $2 325 – €2 592 – **£1 582** – FF17 000
Vue de Béziers Gouache/papier (38x54cm 14x21in)
Nice 2000

GENIN Antoine act.c.1750-? [2]
✎ $4 697 – €5 336 – **£3 286** – FF35 000
**Personnages à l'Antique dans des paysages
architecturés** Aquarelle/papier (43x61cm 16x24in)
Paris 2001

GENIN John 1830-1895 [6]
👁 $5 000 – €4 995 – **£3 125** – FF32 762
Portrait of Miss MacLeod Oil/canvas (58x48cm
23x19in) New-Orleans LA 1999

GENIN Lucien 1894-1953 [719]
👁 $4 941 – €4 573 – **£2 982** – FF30 000
Port animé Huile/toile (60x73cm 23x28in) Paris 1999
👁 $576 – €549 – **£358** – FF3 500
Montmartre: la place du Tertre Huile/isorel
(27x35cm 10x13in) Besançon 1999

✎ $844 – €915 – **£571** – FF6 000
Paris, la place Pigalle Gouache/papier (32x40cm
12x15in) Provins 2000

GENIN Robert 1884-1943 [50]
👁 $1 286 – €1 534 – **£917** – FF10 061
**Männlicher Rückenakt vor dramatischer
Landschaft** Öl/Leinwand (92x83cm 36x32in) Berlin
2000
✎ $516 – €511 – **£322** – FF3 353
**Caritas (drei weibliche Gestalten umsorgen
einen Knaben)** Pastell/Papier (26x22cm 10x8in)
Berlin 2000

GENIS René 1922 [108]
👁 $1 755 – €1 677 – **£1 094** – FF11 000
Petit bouquet bleu fatigué Huile/toile (55x46cm
21x18in) Paris 1999

GÉNISSON Jules Victor 1805-1860 [38]
👁 $16 001 – €15 886 – **£10 000** – FF104 207
A Church Interior Oil/canvas (144x116cm 56x45in)
London 1999
👁 $4 752 – €4 622 – **£2 985** – FF30 185
**Laurentiuskirche in Nürnberg, Blick in den
Chorraum, auf Altar** Öl/Leinwand (82x65.5cm
32x25in) Berlin 1999
👁 $1 200 – €1 188 – **£747** – FF7 795
Interior de iglesia Oleo/tabla (19x14cm 7x5in)
Buenos-Aires 1999

GENKINGER Fritz 1934 [48]
👁 $1 701 – €1 841 – **£1 165** – FF12 074
«**Helle Rückenfigur und Ball**» Acrylic/panel
(90x65cm 35x25in) Stuttgart 2001
▥ $109 – €102 – **£66** – FF670
Fussballer Farblithographie (56x76cm 22x29in)
Stuttgart 1999

GENN Robert 1936 [123]
👁 $651 – €730 – **£452** – FF4 786
Green Islet Light Oil/canvas (49x60cm 19x24in)
Calgary, Alberta 2001
👁 $403 – €344 – **£240** – FF2 257
Afternoon, Wells Lake Oil/canvas (20.5x25.5cm
8x10in) Vancouver, BC. 1998

GENNADIOS Cleonice XIX [1]
👁 $20 343 – €24 194 – **£14 500** – FF158 705
Greek Girl in Regional Costume Oil/canvas
(123.5x85cm 48x33in) London 2000

GENNAI Guido XX [4]
✎ $1 200 – €1 555 – **£900** – FF10 200
Perugia, Porta etrusca Acquarello/carta (49x40cm
19x15in) Prato 2000

GENNARELLI Amadeo XIX-XX [70]
🤚 $4 140 – €4 573 – **£2 871** – FF30 000
Le messager Bronze (H143cm H56in) Paris 2001
🤚 $2 216 – €2 058 – **£1 389** – FF13 500
Femme nue assise Bronze (H23.5cm H9in) Paris
1999

GENNARI Bartolomeo 1594-1661 [4]
👁 $3 200 – €4 147 – **£2 400** – FF27 200
Santo vescovo Olio/tela (92x65cm 36x25in) Prato
2000

GENNARI Benedetto il Giovane 1633-1715 [31]
👁 $64 000 – €60 065 – **£40 000** – FF394 000
María de Modena y el Prícipe James Oleo/lienzo
(189x125cm 74x49in) Madrid 1999
👁 $90 000 – €96 116 – **£61 326** – FF630 477
David with the Head of Goliath Oil/canvas
(115.5x92.5cm 45x36in) New-York 2001

G

◢ **$2 500** – €2 592 – **£1 500** – FF17 000
Madonna con il bambino Inchiostro (20x13cm 7x5in) Milano 2001

GENNARI Cesare 1637-1688 **[9]**
🖾 **$19 573** – €18 307 – **£12 000** – FF120 084
The Madonna and Child Oil/canvas (135x108.5cm 53x42in) London 1998
🖾 **$18 600** – €16 068 – **£9 300** – FF105 400
David Olio/tela (80x65.5cm 31x25in) Firenze 1999

GENOD Michel Philibert 1795-1862 **[8]**
🖾 **$4 865** – €5 336 – **£3 304** – FF35 000
La confession/La confidence Huile/toile (60x48cm 23x18in) Lille 2000

GENOELS Abraham II 1640-1723 **[28]**
🖾 **$9 940** – €10 671 – **£6 650** – FF70 000
Vénus et Adonis dans un paysage italien Huile/toile (54x87cm 21x34in) Paris 2000
▥ **$175** – €204 – **£122** – FF1 341
Arkadische Landschaften Radierung (19.5x15cm 7x5in) Berlin 2000

GENOVES Juan 1930 **[53]**
🖾 **$9 150** – €9 010 – **£5 700** – FF59 100
La Huída Acrílico/lienzo (180x250cm 70x98in) Madrid 1999
🖾 **$5 950** – €5 106 – **£3 570** – FF33 490
Figuras Oleo/lienzo (90x130cm 35x51in) Madrid 1998
🖾 **$1 350** – €1 351 – **£832** – FF8 865
Mujer sentada Oleo/tablex (39x25cm 15x9in) Madrid 2000
◢ **$1 020** – €1 021 – **£629** – FF6 698
Dos figuras Gouache/papier (20x14cm 7x5in) Madrid 2000
▥ **$184** – €168 – **£114** – FF1 103
A la resistencia antifascista chilena Grabado (40x50cm 15x19in) Madrid 1999

GENSO Okuda 1912 **[4]**
🖾 **$47 040** – €45 881 – **£28 800** – FF300 960
Under the Moon Light Painting (52x61cm 20x24in) Tokyo 1999

GENT van Joannes Bapt. Nic. 1891-1974 **[17]**
🖾 **$453** – €431 – **£274** – FF2 827
Gevarieerd stilleven Oil/canvas (39x59cm 15x23in) Rotterdam 1999

GENTH Lillian M. 1876-1953 **[40]**
🖾 **$3 520** – €3 008 – **£2 067** – FF19 731
Portrait of Young Woman with Hat Oil/canvas (48x40cm 19x16in) Chester NY 1998

GENTHE Arnold 1869-1942 **[84]**
📷 **$2 287** – €2 117 – **£1 400** – FF13 889
Greta Garbo Gelatin silver print (30x23cm 12x9in) London 1999

GENTILESCHI Artemisia c.1593-1652/53 **[10]**
🖾 **$217 896** – €214 188 – **£140 000** – FF1 404 984
Portrait of a Lady, dressed in a Gold-Embroidered Elaborate Costume Oil/canvas (128.5x96cm 50x37in) London 1999
🖾 **$619 818** – €579 712 – **£380 000** – FF3 802 660
Woman Playing the Lute, Possibly a Self Portrait of the Artist Oil/canvas (80.5x68.5cm 31x26in) London 1998

GENTILESCHI Orazio 1563-1639 **[6]**
🖾 **$3 287 460** – €3 528 817 – **£2 200 000** – FF23 147 520
The Holy Family with the Infant Saint-John the Baptist in a Landscape Oil/copper (56.5x42.5cm 22x16in) London 2000

GENTILINI Franco 1909-1981 **[237]**
🖾 **$80 400** – €69 456 – **£40 200** – FF455 600
Cattedrale di San Zeno Olio/tela (95x130cm 37x51in) Milano 1999
🖾 **$30 248** – €29 186 – **£19 000** – FF191 447
Ragazza con tulipano Oil/canvas (66x51cm 25x20in) London 1999
🖾 **$9 600** – €12 440 – **£7 200** – FF81 600
«Bagnanta n.2» Olio/cartone (32x41cm 12x16in) Milano 2001
◢ **$3 750** – €3 887 – **£2 250** – FF25 500
Ragazzo con pera Bronzo (67.5x77.5x24cm 26x30x9in) Milano 1999
◢ **$2 160** – €1 866 – **£1 080** – FF12 240
Paesaggio Carboncino/carta (34x25cm 13x9in) Prato 1999
▥ **$240** – €249 – **£144** – FF1 632
Figura femminile Litografia (47x35cm 18x13in) Torino 1999

GENTILS Vic 1919-1997 **[129]**
◢ **$2 868** – €2 975 – **£1 824** – FF19 512
Zonder titel Relief (99x42.5cm 38x16in) Lokeren 2000
◢ **$1 872** – €2 231 – **£1 341** – FF14 634
Zonder titel Metal (H5cm H1in) Lokeren 2000
◢ **$396** – €372 – **£244** – FF2 439
Bateau devant la rade d'Anvers Technique mixte/papier (71x100cm 27x39in) Antwerpen 1999

GENTLEMAN David XX **[18]**
▥ **$119** – €132 – **£80** – FF866
Lord's Print in colors (48x43cm 19x17in) Norwich 2000

GENTRY Herbert 1919 **[10]**
🖾 **$388** – €403 – **£246** – FF2 641
Komposition Oil/canvas (70x60cm 27x23in) Viby J, Århus 2000

GENTZ Ismaël 1862-1914 **[12]**
🖾 **$1 658** – €1 738 – **£1 050** – FF11 403
Strasse in Jerusalem Öl/Karton (37.5x21.5cm 14x8in) Köln 2000
◢ **$448** – €481 – **£300** – FF3 156
Market Place in Tunis Watercolour/paper (36.5x26cm 14x10in) London 2000

GENTZ Wilhelm Karl 1822-1890 **[18]**
🖾 **$17 036** – €16 361 – **£10 500** – FF107 324
Gebetsruf der Muezzins bei Sonnenaufgang Öl/Leinwand (136x105cm 53x41in) Ahlden 1999
🖾 **$13 000** – €13 954 – **£8 699** – FF91 533
At the Watering Hole Oil/canvas (43x60cm 17x24in) Bloomfield-Hills MI 2000

GENZKEN Isa 1948 **[31]**
🖾 **$1 446** – €1 329 – **£888** – FF8 720
Basic Research Öl/Leinwand (45x60cm 17x23in) Bielefeld 1999
◢ **$9 766** – €9 505 – **£6 000** – FF62 349
Beton Fenster Metal (291x293cm 114x115in) London 1999
◢ **$2 884** – €3 187 – **£2 000** – FF20 906
«Galway» Sculpture (20.5x35.5x7cm 8x13x2in) London 2001

GENZMER Berthold 1858-1927 **[12]**
🖾 **$1 177** – €1 176 – **£736** – FF7 714
Fischerboote an der Küste Öl/Leinwand (80x100cm 31x39in) Köln 1999

GÉO HAM (Georges Hamel) 1900-1972 **[270]**
🖾 **$3 837** – €4 573 – **£2 736** – FF30 000
Bugatti Huile/carton (23.5x32cm 9x12in) Paris 2000

G

$981 - €1 067 - **£646** - FF7 000
  Paquebot en cale sèche Gouache/papier (42x62cm 16x24in) Paris 2000
$557 - €579 - **£351** - FF3 800
  Bugatti au Cap d'Antibes Lithographie (38x55cm 14x21in) Paris 2000

GÉO-FOURRIER Georges 1898-1966 **[64]**
$110 - €122 - **£77** - FF800
  Coutances Dessin (17.5x11.5cm 6x4in) Quimper 2001
$141 - €152 - **£94** - FF1 000
  Portrait de Bretonne Pochoir (23x15cm 9x5in) Rennes 2000

GEOFFROY Henry J. Jean 1853-1924 **[83]**
$8 472 - €8 537 - **£5 280** - FF56 000
  Jeune fille lisant, 16 mai Huile/toile (54x40.5cm 21x15in) Paris 2000
$2 097 - €2 014 - **£1 300** - FF13 214
  The Connoisseurs Oil/canvas (35x27cm 13x10in) London 1999
$2 008 - €2 363 - **£1 439** - FF15 500
  La cantine Aquarelle/papier (19.5x29.5cm 7x11in) Paris 2001

GEOFFROY Jean-Baptiste 1769-1845 **[3]**
$2 083 - €1 943 - **£1 257** - FF12 744
  Abendliche Sommerlandschaft mit Teich, malerischem Gehöft Öl/Leinwand (55.5x74cm 21x29in) Lindau 1999

GEOFFROY Rose XIX **[14]**
$744 - €625 - **£437** - FF4 100
  Jeune femme et sa fille d'après Vigée Le Brun Pastel/papier (86x66cm 33x25in) Tarbes 1998

GÉOLUC (Louis C. Anglés) 1894-? **[5]**
$407 - €381 - **£252** - FF2 500
  Champ de courses Huile/panneau (40x50cm 15x19in) Paris 1999

GEORGE Ernest 1839-1922 **[119]**
$504 - €523 - **£320** - FF3 432
  Avignon Watercolour/paper (34x24cm 13x9in) Cheshire 2000

GEORGE Herbert XIX-XX **[15]**
$385 - €359 - **£240** - FF2 356
  A Shepherd seated beneath Olive Trees Tivoli Watercolour (35x48.5cm 13x19in) London 1999

GEORGE James, Lt. Colonel 1782-1828 **[4]**
$15 863 - €17 529 - **£11 000** - FF114 983
  View at Chittagong/View of Rungunneah on the Chittagong Watercolour/paper (36x52cm 14x20in) London 2001

GEORGE T. XIX **[1]**
$1 999 - €1 840 - **£1 200** - FF12 069
  Portrait of a Woman, wearing a black Dress and a purple Shawl Watercolour (17.5x14cm 6x5in) Glamorgan 1999

GEORGE-JUILLARD Jean Philippe 1818-1888 **[72]**
$1 538 - €1 673 - **£1 013** - FF10 973
  Alpenlandschaft mit Gehöft und weidendem Vieh Öl/Leinwand (44x60.5cm 17x23in) Bern 2000
$685 - €782 - **£483** - FF5 131
  Flusslandschaft mit Bauernhaus unter wolkigem Himmel Öl/Karton (23.5x34.5cm 9x13in) Bern 2001

GEORGES Alain XX **[8]**
$517 - €610 - **£363** - FF4 000
  Satisfaction Huile/toile (80x65cm 31x25in) Paris 2000

GEORGES Claude 1929-1988 **[82]**
$812 - €762 - **£503** - FF5 000
  Composition Huile/toile (92x73cm 36x28in) Paris 1999

GEORGES Jean-Louis ?-1893/94 **[7]**
$8 267 - €9 400 - **£5 775** - FF61 663
  Opstilling med brod, fad med ost og nodder samt skraellet aeble Oil/canvas (48x59cm 18x23in) Köbenhavn 2000

GEORGET Elisa Antoinette ?-1914 **[2]**
$5 509 - €5 641 - **£3 459** - FF37 000
  Fleurs et fruits Huile/toile (88x68cm 34x26in) Lille 2000

GEORGET Guy 1911-1992 **[28]**
$184 - €157 - **£110** - FF1 030
  «Air Afrique» Poster (95.5x150cm 37x59in) London 1998

GEORGET Jean-Charles 1833-1895 **[12]**
$433 - €488 - **£298** - FF3 200
  La mare en sous-bois Huile/toile (40.5x62cm 15x24in) Barbizon 2000

GEORGI Edwin 1896-1964 **[15]**
$990 - €845 - **£597** - FF5 540
  Woman holding up her long blonde hair Gouache (39x33cm 15x13in) New-York 1998

GEORGI Friedrich Otto 1819-1874 **[26]**
$3 184 - €3 323 - **£2 015** - FF21 800
  Weite Landschaft, rechts auf einem Hügel Burganlage Öl/Leinwand (50x43cm 19x16in) München 2000
$3 644 - €3 374 - **£2 261** - FF22 135
  Italienische Landschaft mit einer Klosteranlage Oil/canvas/panel (27x38cm 10x14in) Stuttgart 1999

GEORGI Walter 1871-1924 **[15]**
$2 801 - €2 403 - **£1 692** - FF15 760
  Unwetter Öl/Leinwand (68.3x89.5cm 26x35in) München 1998

GEPPERT Eugeniusz 1890-1979 **[33]**
$3 344 - €3 322 - **£2 083** - FF21 793
  Chevaux Oil/canvas (59x79cm 23x31in) Warszawa 1999
$1 494 - €1 666 - **£1 038** - FF10 926
  Officier à cheval Huile/carton (32x46cm 12x18in) Warszawa 2001

GERALE N., Gérard Alexandre 1914-? **[11]**
$722 - €728 - **£452** - FF4 776
  «Plaisir de neige, SNCF» Poster (100x62cm 39x24in) London 2000

GERALIS Apostolos 1886-1983 **[26]**
$8 039 - €9 225 - **£5 500** - FF60 511
  Wooded Landscape Oil/board (35x50cm 13x19in) London 2000

GERALIS Loucas 1875-1958 **[8]**
$5 847 - €6 709 - **£4 000** - FF44 008
  Lady with her Dog Oil/canvas (99x80.5cm 38x31in) London 2000

GERANZANI Cornelio 1880-1955 **[8]**
$11 500 - €11 922 - **£6 900** - FF78 200
  Contadine Olio/tela (50x47cm 19x18in) Roma 2000
$2 500 - €2 592 - **£1 500** - FF17 000
  Prospettiva interna di antico edificio romano Olio/tela (52x25cm 20x9in) Milano 2000

GÉRARD Calixte M. XIX [2]
$4 730 - €4 726 - **£2 957** - FF31 000
Pur sang Bronze (55x67.5x31.5cm 21x26x12in)
Pontoise 1999

GERARD Charles XIX [1]
$3 175 - €2 965 - **£1 959** - FF19 452
Kleines Mädchen auf einem Stuhl sitzend
Oil/panel (32.5x28.5cm 12x11in) Köln 1999

GÉRARD François 1770-1837 [61]
$182 505 - €175 316 - **£112 585** - FF1 150 000
Corinne au Cap-Misène Huile/toile (211x171cm
83x67in) Bayeux 1999
$48 546 - €47 259 - **£29 822** - FF310 000
Portrait de Jean-François Ducis (1733-1816)
Huile/toile (65x54.5cm 25x21in) Paris 1999
$3 743 - €3 663 - **£2 400** - FF24 029
Study of a Boy, half-Length Black chalk/paper
(9x6cm 3x2in) London 1999

GÉRARD Gaston 1859-? [21]
$271 - €263 - **£171** - FF1 727
Portrait einer jungen Frau mit Haube Aquarelle
(41.5x29cm 16x11in) Zürich 1999

GERARD Henry 1860-1925 [25]
$3 346 - €3 506 - **£2 118** - FF23 000
Caïque sur le Bosphore Huile/toile (50x64cm
19x25in) Paris 2000

GERARD Lucien 1852-1935 [24]
$3 010 - €3 346 - **£2 011** - FF21 951
**Jeune femme assise nourrissant son
chien/Jeune homme dans une auberge**
Huile/toile (48x37cm 18x14in) Bruxelles 2000
$911 - €768 - **£539** - FF5 040
Fumeur de pipe Huile/toile (30x23cm 11x9in)
Antwerpen 1998

GÉRARD Marguerite 1761-1837 [39]
$100 000 - €87 716 - **£60 720** - FF575 380
Lady with her Daughter, in a Parkland Setting
Oil/canvas (48x40cm 18x15in) New-York 1999
$26 000 - €21 838 - **£15 285** - FF143 249
**Doctor François Thiery, Seated Half Length in
an Interior** Oil/panel (21.5x16cm 8x6in) New-York
1998
$2 359 - €2 744 - **£1 684** - FF18 000
L'enfant et le chat Eau-forte (23.5x17.5cm 9x6in)
Paris 2001

GÉRARD Michel XX [1]
$798 - €762 - **£499** - FF5 000
«Bambi» Affiche couleur (160x120cm 62x47in) Paris
1999

GÉRARD Pascal 1941 [38]
$544 - €610 - **£378** - FF4 000
La terrasse Huile/toile (55x65cm 21x25in) Paris 2001

GÉRARD Théodore 1829-1895 [125]
$17 212 - €19 108 - **£12 000** - FF125 338
Cafe Conversation Oil/canvas (119.5x139.5cm
47x54in) London 2001
$8 064 - €8 924 - **£5 652** - FF58 536
L'assistance publique Huile/toile (80x115cm
31x45in) Bruxelles 2001
$1 245 - €1 064 - **£753** - FF6 981
Scène d'auberge Huile/toile (40.5x31cm 15x12in)
Genève 1998

GERARDIN Roland Marie 1907-1935 [11]
$11 780 - €11 281 - **£7 274** - FF74 000
Les vendanges Huile/toile (217x216cm 85x85in)
Besançon 1999

$706 - €823 - **£489** - FF5 400
Jeune femme mélancolique Huile/toile (81x65cm
31x25in) Besançon 2000

GERARDS Marcus II 1561/62-1635 [8]
$244 965 - €225 516 - **£150 000** - FF1 479 285
Portrait of a Lady Oil/canvas (220.5x136cm 86x53in)
London 1998
$125 907 - €116 555 - **£78 000** - FF764 548
Frances Knyvett, Countess of Rutland Oil/panel
(90x70cm 35x27in) London 1999

GERASCH August 1822-1908 [26]
$1 308 - €1 453 - **£876** - FF9 534
Bärenfamilie am Gebirgsbach Öl/Leinwand
(34.2x42cm 13x16in) Wien 2000

GERASCH Franz 1826-1893 [19]
$524 - €509 - **£323** - FF3 336
Die Kapelle bei der Hundsturmlinie
Aquarell/Papier (16x20cm 6x7in) Wien 1999

GERBAUD Abel 1888-1954 [24]
$552 - €579 - **£350** - FF3 800
Honfleur Huile/toile (46x55cm 18x21in) Paris 2000

GERBAULT Henry 1863-1930 [30]
$227 - €213 - **£136** - FF1 400
Portrait de femme Aquarelle/papier (20x15cm 7x5in)
Paris 1999
$1 373 - €1 372 - **£858** - FF9 000
«Chocolat Carpentier» Affiche (130x93cm 51x36in)
Orléans 1999

GERBIG Alexander 1878-1948 [15]
$484 - €562 - **£340** - FF3 689
Selbstporträt Öl/Leinwand (46x37cm 18x14in)
Rudolstadt-Thüringen 2001

GERBINO Rosario Urbino 1900-1972 [3]
$1 400 - €1 592 - **£960** - FF10 442
Bacchusa Oil/canvas (15x13cm 5x5in) Hampden MA
2000

GERCHMAN Rubens 1942 [4]
$35 000 - €40 665 - **£24 598** - FF266 742
«Dream Team, a seleçao dos seleçoes» Acrylic
(160x223cm 62x87in) New-York 2001
$35 000 - €37 569 - **£23 422** - FF246 435
Virgem dos labios de mel Oil/canvas (120x90cm
47x35in) New-York 2000
$12 000 - €13 942 - **£8 433** - FF91 454
«Burnt Perfume» Construction (6x24.5x31.5cm
2x9x12in) New-York 2001

GERDAGO Gerda Iro 1906-? [14]
$6 100 - €5 661 - **£3 800** - FF37 132
Exotic Dancer in a Floral Costume Ivory, bronze
(H32cm H12in) London 1999

GERE Charles March 1860-1959 [22]
$3 786 - €3 559 - **£2 300** - FF23 344
Classical Landscape with Oxen and Cart
Oil/canvas/board (39x40cm 15x15in) London 1999
$850 - €726 - **£500** - FF4 761
Portrait of a Young Lady Watercolour/paper
(20x18cm 7x7in) Godalming, Surrey 1998

GERELL Greta 1898-1982 [80]
$561 - €609 - **£355** - FF3 998
Landskap med kor vid insjö Oil/canvas (56x63cm
22x24in) Stockholm 2000
$496 - €550 - **£344** - FF3 610
Sittande flicka Oil/paper (26x23cm 10x9in) Malmö
2001

G

GERGELY Imre 1868-1914 **[40]**
$1 150 – €945 – **£668** – FF6 199
Blick auf Dubrovnik Öl/Leinwand (53x75cm
20x29in) Wien 1998

GERHARD Johan Friedrich 1695-1748 **[3]**
$5 339 – €5 732 – **£3 573** – FF37 598
Bildnis eines jungen Herrn mit Mütze Öl/Kupfer
(25.5x23cm 10x9in) Zürich 2000

GERHARDI Ida 1867-1927 **[3]**
$3 098 – €3 645 – **£2 187** – FF23 912
Pfingstrosen in Türkisfarbener Vase Öl/Leinwand
(55.5x80cm 21x31in) Berlin 2001

GERHARDINGER Constantin 1888-1970 **[41]**
$2 722 – €2 556 – **£1 687** – FF16 769
Kallmünz Öl/Leinwand (47x55.5cm 18x21in)
München 1999
$571 – €613 – **£391** – FF4 024
Herrenporträt Öl/Karton (31x30cm 12x11in)
München 2001

GERHARDT Eduard 1813-1888 **[5]**
$1 756 – €1 994 – **£1 220** – FF13 080
Italienischer Klosterhof im Abendlicht
Watercolour (20.5x26.5cm 8x10in) Berlin 2001

GÉRICAULT Théodore 1791-1824 **[248]**
$743 715 – €635 427 – **£450 000** – FF4 168 125
Turc monté sur un cheval alezan brûlé Oil/canvas
(38x46cm 14x18in) London 1998
$82 635 – €70 603 – **£50 000** – FF463 125
Deux chevaux dans une écurie Oil/canvas
(40.5x32cm 15x12in) London 1998
$25 640 – €30 490 – **£17 780** – FF200 000
Étude d'homme Encre (18x21cm 7x8in) Paris 2000
$1 460 – €1 278 – **£884** – FF8 382
**Ein Mameluck verteidigt einen verletzten
Trompeter** Lithographie (34.4x27.9cm 13x10in) Berlin
1998

GERINI Niccolo di Pietro c.1368-1415 **[6]**
$239 088 – €256 641 – **£160 000** – FF1 683 456
The Annunciation Oil/panel (23.5x39cm 9x15in)
London 2000

GERITZ Franz 1895-1945 **[11]**
$550 – €529 – **£341** – FF3 467
Mt. Shasta Woodcut in colors (23x30.5cm 9x12in)
New-York 1999

GERKE Johann Philipp 1811 **[1]**
$5 000 – €4 331 – **£3 066** – FF28 407
The Three Kings Oil/canvas (40.5x53cm 15x20in)
New-York 1999

GERLACH Georg 1874-1962 **[16]**
$1 373 – €1 308 – **£838** – FF8 580
Café de Paris M. Carlo Öl/Leinwand (42.5x52cm
16x20in) Wien 1999
$553 – €509 – **£342** – FF3 336
In Schönbrunn Gouache/paper (37.5x51cm 14x20in)
Wien 1999

GERLIC XX **[1]**
$4 288 – €3 659 – **£2 587** – FF24 000
«L'Atalante» Affiche couleur (160x240cm 62x94in)
Paris 1998

GERLOVIN Valeriy 1945 **[3]**
$7 000 – €7 771 – **£4 868** – FF50 976
«Vintage» Photograph (101.5x117cm 39x46in) New-
York 2001

GERLOVINA Rimma 1951 **[3]**
$7 000 – €7 771 – **£4 868** – FF50 976
Untitled Photograph (101.5x117cm 39x46in) New-
York 2001

GERLWH Gerardus Ladage 1878-1932 **[10]**
$1 765 – €1 906 – **£1 207** – FF12 501
Sunlit Mountain Watercolour/paper (33x17cm
12x6in) Amsterdam 2001

GERMA H. XIX-XX **[4]**
$425 – €396 – **£263** – FF2 600
Po & Midi. Chemin de fer & Hôtels de montagne
Affiche couleur (107x77cm 42x30in) Paris 1999

GERMAIN Jacques 1915 **[299]**
$1 815 – €2 077 – **£1 247** – FF13 624
Banlieue Oil/canvas (80x100cm 31x39in) Köbenhavn
2000
$648 – €762 – **£464** – FF5 000
Composition Huile/papier (24x19cm 9x7in) Versailles
2001
$356 – €335 – **£215** – FF2 200
Composition Aquarelle/papier (31.5x47cm 12x18in)
Paris 1999

GERMAIN Jean-Baptiste 1841-1910 **[31]**
$829 – €762 – **£509** – FF5 000
La jeune fille au bouquet Bronze (H50cm H19in)
Soissons 1999

GERMAIN-THILL Alphonse 1873-1925 **[15]**
$560 – €610 – **£369** – FF4 000
Porte d'une ville marocaine Huile/panneau
(21.5x15cm 8x5in) Paris 2000

GERMAN Christopher S. XIX **[3]**
$45 000 – €42 197 – **£27 805** – FF276 795
Portrait of Abraham Lincoln Daguerreotype
(11x8cm 4x3in) New-York 1999

GERMAN LLORENTE Bernardo c.1680-1759 **[10]**
$15 600 – €18 019 – **£10 800** – FF118 200
Divina Pastora Oleo/lienzo (196x124cm 77x48in)
Madrid 2000
$5 400 – €4 516 – **£3 225** – FF29 625
Divina pastora Oleo/lienzo (106.5x79cm 41x31in)
Madrid 1998

GERMANA Mimmo 1944-1992 **[96]**
$2 000 – €2 592 – **£1 500** – FF17 000
Senza titolo Olio/tela (80x60cm 31x23in) Vercelli
2001
$750 – €777 – **£450** – FF5 100
Bagnante Tecnica mista/carta (73x102cm 28x40in)
Vercelli 1999

GERMELA Raimund 1868-1945 **[23]**
$832 – €945 – **£583** – FF6 197
«Carnevall in Venedig» Öl/Leinwand (64x82.5cm
25x32in) Wien 2001

GERNAY Pierre Noël 1801-1858 **[2]**
$5 237 – €5 899 – **£3 610** – FF38 695
Floral Opulence/Butterflies Amidst Blossoming
Oil/canvas (63x82cm 24x32in) Amsterdam 2000

GERNES Poul 1925 **[13]**
$1 333 – €1 343 – **£831** – FF8 812
Geometrisk komposition Oil/masonite (91x91cm
35x35in) Köbenhavn 2000

GERNEZ Paul-Élie 1888-1948 **[493]**
$9 091 – €10 214 – **£6 331** – FF67 000
Nu couché au tapis d'Orient Huile/toile
(114x146cm 44x57in) Honfleur 2001

$4 924 - €5 793 - £3 530 - FF38 000
«Place du marché Sainte Catherine à Honfleur»
Huile/carton (46x55cm 18x21in) Paris 2001

$3 240 - €3 049 - £2 004 - FF20 000
La Touque à Trouville Huile/toile (33x46cm 12x18in)
Deauville 1999

$2 793 - €2 592 - £1 742 - FF17 000
Trouville Aquarelle/papier (30x47cm 11x18in)
Deauville 1999

GEROLD (Gerold Hunziker) 1914-1980 [5]

$1 000 - €877 - £607 - FF5 753
Bugatti Poster (56x39cm 22x15in) New-York 1999

GEROME François 1895-? [48]

$787 - €749 - £489 - FF4 916
Les Parisiennes Oil/canvas (51x61cm 20x24in)
Toronto 1999

GÉROME Jean-Léon 1824-1904 [428]

$210 000 - €181 178 - £126 693 - FF1 188 453
«O Pti Cien» Oil/canvas (87x66cm 34x25in) New-
York 1998

$42 000 - €46 622 - £29 278 - FF305 823
On the Watch Oil/canvas (25x33cm 9x12in) New-
York 2001

$105 000 - €117 532 - £73 227 - FF770 962
La joueuse de boules Marble (H91cm H35in) New-
York 2001

$8 000 - €7 982 - £4 869 - FF52 360
Horse Bronze (H31cm H12in) New-York 2000

$1 476 - €1 677 - £1 032 - FF11 000
Étude d'homme en toge Crayon/papier (36x23.5cm
14x9in) Paris 2001

GERRITS Geo, Ger 1893-1965 [31]

$4 228 - €4 538 - £2 829 - FF29 766
Composition Oil/canvas (80x100cm 31x39in)
Amsterdam 2000

$6 300 - €5 454 - £3 823 - FF35 774
Untitled Gouache/paper (58.5x49cm 23x19in)
Amsterdam 1998

$1 249 - €1 452 - £878 - FF9 525
«Variate III op comp.39» Woodcut (14x18cm 5x7in)
Amsterdam 2001

GERRITZ Harrie 1940 [11]

$202 - €204 - £126 - FF1 339
Zonder titel Serigraph (73x55cm 28x21in) Amsterdam
2000

GERRY Samuel Lancaster 1813-1891 [53]

$7 000 - €6 341 - £4 284 - FF41 592
Sketching Moat Mountain from the Artist's
Camp Oil/canvas (35x60cm 14x24in) Portland ME
1998

$1 600 - €1 660 - £1 015 - FF10 890
Still Life with Orange and Glass of Wine
Oil/board (23.5x18.5cm 9x7in) Boston MA 2000

GERSH Stephen XX [11]

$750 - €706 - £464 - FF4 628
Dali Atomicus Silver print (26x33cm 10x13in) New-
York 1999

GERSHOV Solomon Moiseevich 1906-1989 [23]

$509 - €486 - £318 - FF3 187
Tallinn, Estonia Gouache/board (58x81cm 23x32in)
Cedar-Falls IA 1999

GERSHUNI Moshe 1936 [22]

$3 000 - €3 291 - £1 935 - FF21 587
Composition Oil/cardboard (63x100cm 24x39in) Tel
Aviv 2000

$1 400 - €1 190 - £845 - FF7 803
«The Majesty, the Power, the Triumph and the
Glory» Mixed media/paper (57x44cm 22x17in) Tel
Aviv 1999

GERSON Wojciech 1831-1901 [17]

$9 196 - €10 088 - £6 108 - FF66 176
Tête de femme Oil/board (31.8x25.8cm 12x10in)
Warszawa 1999

$4 404 - €4 439 - £2 746 - FF29 120
Conversation Watercolour, gouache/paper
(16.7x20.3cm 6x7in) Warszawa 2000

GERSTEIN David 1944 [2]

$14 782 - €13 606 - £8 872 - FF89 247
Spring in Jerusalem Oil/canvas (110x213cm
43x83in) Tel Aviv 1999

GERSTENBRAND Alfred 1891-1977 [15]

$4 695 - €5 450 - £3 300 - FF35 752
«Die Ankunft mit der Postkutsche in St.Gilgen»
Öl/Karton (38x47cm 14x18in) Salzburg 2001

GERSTENHAUER Johann Georg 1858-1931 [3]

$517 - €544 - £341 - FF3 571
Woodgatherers Oil/panel (22.5x32cm 8x12in)
Amsterdam 2000

GERSTNER Karl 1930 [30]

$115 - €111 - £71 - FF731
Color Dome, CS 46-2K/I Acryl/Papier (21.5x8cm
8x3in) Bern 1999

$1 214 - €1 448 - £865 - FF9 497
Carro 64. (Serie 1 Gelb-Grau-Blau Tongleich)
Sculpture (37.5x37.5x4cm 14x14x1in) Luzern 2000

GERTLER Mark 1892-1939 [70]

$40 002 - €39 716 - £25 000 - FF260 517
The Sari Oil/board (91.5x56cm 36x22in) London 1999

$27 413 - €30 755 - £19 000 - FF201 738
Portrait of the Artist's Sister, Sophie Oil/canvas
(41x30.5cm 16x12in) London 2000

$1 971 - €1 880 - £1 200 - FF12 333
Man In A Hat Pencil/paper (19.5x19cm 7x7in) London
1999

GERTNER Christoph c.1574-c.1623 [4]

$4 000 - €3 932 - £2 570 - FF25 791
Diana and a Satyr Wash (20.5x35cm 8x13in) New-
York 1999

GERTNER Johan Vilhelm 1818-1871 [25]

$472 - €509 - £326 - FF3 342
Barfodet ung pige baerer trug ud fra en staldby-
gning Oil/canvas (18.5x24cm 7x9in) Købenavn 2001

GERTSCH Franz 1930 [59]

$17 472 - €16 176 - £10 696 - FF106 108
Liegendes Paar Tempera (71.5x103.5cm 28x40in)
Bern 1999

$4 852 - €5 541 - £3 421 - FF36 344
Liebespaar Collage/paper (64x124cm 25x48in) Bern
2001

$1 190 - €1 354 - £825 - FF8 879
Late Breakfast Lithographie (59x86cm 23x33in)
Zofingen 2000

GERVAIS Lise 1933-1998 [124]

$1 021 - €969 - £620 - FF6 354
Untitled, Abstract Oil/canvas (77x76cm 30x29in)
Calgary, Alberta 1999

$162 - €188 - £113 - FF1 233
Ombres de nuages Encre/papier (28x22cm 11x8in)
Montréal 2000

G

GERVEX Henri 1852-1929 **[104]**
- $96 110 - €106 714 - **£66 990** - FF700 000
  Dans les bois Huile/toile (209x95cm 82x37in) Paris 2001
- $6 000 - €6 611 - **£3 990** - FF43 368
  Jeune fille assise avec chien Oleo/lienzo (81x65cm 31x25in) Buenos-Aires 2000
- $17 040 - €18 294 - **£11 400** - FF120 000
  La loge Huile/toile (33x24.5cm 12x9in) Paris 2000
- $3 066 - €3 049 - **£1 902** - FF20 000
  Conversation galante Gouache (26.5x56cm 10x22in) Neuilly-sur-Seine 1999

GERZSO Gunther 1915-2000 **[97]**
- $32 000 - €37 179 - **£22 489** - FF243 878
  «Amarillo, verde, azul» Oil/masonite (65x54cm 25x21in) New-York 2001
- $29 000 - €31 128 - **£19 406** - FF204 189
  Paisaje Oil/canvas/board (35x29cm 15x11in) New-York 2000
- $26 000 - €25 235 - **£16 187** - FF165 531
  Semblantes Bronze (58.5x78x6cm 23x30x2in) New-York 1999
- $848 - €996 - **£602** - FF6 532
  Muro naranja y azul Grabado (39x34cm 15x13in) México 2000

GESELSCHAP Eduard 1814-1878 **[9]**
- $5 000 - €6 501 - **£3 452** - FF38 055
  Family Bath Oil/canvas (118x96cm 46x37in) New-York 2000

GESMAR Charles, Carl 1900-1928 **[99]**
- $273 - €305 - **£186** - FF2 000
  Danseuse orientale, projet de costume pour le Music-Hall Aquarelle, gouache (46x30.5cm 18x12in) Paris 2000
- $2 600 - €2 280 - **£1 578** - FF14 959
  Mistinguett Poster (313x112cm 123x44in) New-York 1999

GESNE de Jean Victor Albert 1834-1903 **[16]**
- $1 465 - €1 702 - **£1 029** - FF11 167
  Jagdszene mit Hirsch und Hundemeute Öl/Leinwand (50.5x60cm 19x23in) Luzern 2001
- $2 656 - €3 082 - **£1 834** - FF20 216
  Huntsman with his Dogs Oil/canvas (39.5x31.5cm 15x12in) Johannesburg 2000

GESSA Y ARIAS Sebastián 1840-1920 **[35]**
- $4 491 - €4 526 - **£2 800** - FF29 690
  An Upturned Basket of Grapes and Figs Oil/canvas (46.5x56.5cm 18x22in) London 2000
- $784 - €841 - **£518** - FF5 516
  Pensamientos Oleo/lienzo (27x18cm 10x7in) Madrid 2000
- $156 - €180 - **£108** - FF1 182
  Flores Acuarela, gouache/papel (25x18cm 9x7in) Madrid 2000

GESSEN Tanke 1721-1809 **[5]**
- $523 - €562 - **£350** - FF3 689
  Ein Betrunkener in Beamtenkleidung Indian ink (128.8x28.8cm 50x11in) Köln 2000

GESSI Giovanni Francesco 1588-1649 **[12]**
- $21 685 - €25 253 - **£15 000** - FF165 649
  Saint Ursula Oil/canvas (114x84cm 44x33in) London 2000

GESSNER Johann Conrad 1764-1826 **[32]**
- $7 425 - €7 482 - **£4 628** - FF49 081
  Reiterschlacht zur offenem Feld/Reiterschlacht vor einer Stadt Öl/Leinwand (75x90cm 29x35in) Zürich 2000

- $10 449 - €10 061 - **£6 534** - FF65 998
  Schimmel und Brauner im Stall Öl/Leinwand (28.5x41.5cm 11x16in) Zürich 1999

GESSNER Richard 1894-1989 **[35]**
- $726 - €613 - **£433** - FF4 024
  Am Rhein bei Kaiserwerth Öl/Karton (34x45cm 13x17in) Düsseldorf 1998

GESSNER Robert S. 1908-1982 **[17]**
- $509 - €591 - **£351** - FF3 877
  Accordion Watercolour (38x50cm 14x19in) Zürich 2000

GESSNER Salomon 1730-1788 **[53]**
- $900 - €963 - **£613** - FF6 315
  Grove in Arcadia with a Woman and two Men Watercolour (20.5x28.5cm 8x11in) New-York 2001
- $97 - €102 - **£61** - FF670
  Ein Satyr, von zwei anderen begleitet Radierung (11.7x14.4cm 4x5in) Heidelberg 2000

GESSNITZER T.C. XIX **[5]**
- $8 936 - €10 226 - **£6 146** - FF67 078
  Alte Hafenstadt (Antwerpen) mit zahlreichen Segelbooten und Kähnen Öl/Leinwand (160x251cm 62x98in) München 2000

GESTEL Leo 1881-1941 **[414]**
- $41 013 - €47 647 - **£28 822** - FF312 543
  «Stilleven» Oil/canvas (51.5x51.5cm 20x20in) Amsterdam 2001
- $8 593 - €9 983 - **£6 039** - FF65 485
  Lezend naakt Oil/canvas (22x48cm 8x18in) Amsterdam 2001
- $1 908 - €2 269 - **£1 360** - FF14 883
  Portrait of an Gestel, the wife of the Artist Charcoal/paper (59x45.5cm 23x17in) Amsterdam 2000

GETZ Arthur 1913-1996 **[4]**
- $5 500 - €6 160 - **£3 821** - FF40 409
  Magazine Cover, Park Avenue looking south from about 96th Street Tempera/paper (60x45cm 24x18in) New-York 2001

GEUDENS Albert 1869-1949 **[84]**
- $666 - €744 - **£465** - FF4 878
  La salle d'attente Huile/toile (50x60cm 19x23in) Bruxelles 2001
- $1 047 - €1 091 - **£664** - FF7 154
  Le repas Pastel/papier (60x80cm 23x31in) Bruxelles 2000

GEURTS Joris XX **[2]**
- $1 415 - €1 588 - **£981** - FF10 418
  Composition Gouache/paper (102.5x122.5cm 40x48in) Amsterdam 2000

GEVA Tsibi 1951 **[6]**
- $9 000 - €9 990 - **£6 273** - FF65 533
  «Thorn» Acrylic (175.5x225.5cm 69x88in) Tel Aviv 2001
- $4 347 - €4 002 - **£2 609** - FF26 249
  Kaffiya Mixed media/canvas (100x80cm 39x31in) Tel Aviv 1999

GEX E. XIX-XX **[11]**
- $499 - €427 - **£299** - FF2 800
  «Suprême Pernot» Affiche (86x123cm 33x48in) Paris 1998

GEYER Alexius 1816-1883 **[15]**
- $474 - €460 - **£295** - FF3 018
  Blick auf Damaskus vom Palmyra Tor aus Chalks/paper (23.2x30cm 9x11in) Berlin 1999

GEYER Fritz 1875-1947 **[38]**
$646 - €662 - **£399** - FF4 342
Stadsbild med fontän Oil/panel (59x49cm 23x19in)
Stockholm 2000

GEYER Georg 1823-1912 **[52]**
$1 802 - €1 817 - **£1 125** - FF11 917
Blick auf Heiligen Blut mit Grossglockner
Öl/Leinwand (58x46cm 22x18in) Wien 2000
$1 565 - €1 817 - **£1 100** - FF11 917
«Partie beim Waldbach Strubb, Hallstatt»
Öl/Papier (23x32.5cm 9x12in) Wien 2001
$794 - €872 - **£511** - FF5 720
Blick von einer Terrasse auf Kairo Watercolour
(22x34.5cm 8x13in) Wien 2001

GEYER Johann 1807-1875 **[7]**
$13 093 - €12 697 - **£8 240** - FF83 290
Engagement to Marry Oil/canvas (111.5x141cm
43x55in) Dublin 1999

GEYGER Ernst Moritz 1861-1941 **[21]**
$1 312 - €1 490 - **£920** - FF9 777
An Archer Bronze (H39cm H15in) Billingshurst, West-
Sussex 2001

GEYLING Karl Michael 1814-1880 **[4]**
$5 856 - €5 814 - **£3 656** - FF38 136
Hohen Salzburg vom Fusse des Kreuzberges
Öl/Karton (41x49cm 16x19in) Wien 1999

GEYP Adrianus Marinus 1855-1926 **[73]**
$1 180 - €1 134 - **£736** - FF7 441
Shepherd with his Flock Oil/canvas (50x70cm
19x27in) Amsterdam 1999
$2 202 - €1 906 - **£1 337** - FF12 501
View of a farm with moored sailing vessels
Oil/panel (22.5x33cm 8x12in) Amsterdam 1999

GFELLER Werner 1895-1985 **[9]**
$628 - €717 - **£442** - FF4 703
Stilleben mit Äpfeln Öl/Leinwand/Karton (25x49cm
9x19in) Bern 2001
$1 122 - €1 017 - **£700** - FF6 670
«Hiver à Zweisimmen» Poster (100x70cm 39x27in)
London 1999

GHEDUZZI Augusto 1883-1969 **[3]**
$3 200 - €4 147 - **£2 400** - FF27 200
Tramonto sul porto Olio/cartone (38x59cm 14x23in)
Torino 2000

GHEDUZZI Cesare 1894-1944 **[79]**
$3 900 - €3 369 - **£1 950** - FF22 100
«Baite di pecetto» Olio/tavola (65x50cm 25x19in)
Milano 1999
$1 800 - €1 866 - **£1 080** - FF12 240
Paesaggio alpino (Valle d'Aosta) Olio/tavola
(30x40cm 11x15in) Torino 2000

GHEDUZZI Giuseppe 1889-1957 **[65]**
$4 400 - €4 702 - **£3 300** - FF37 400
Estate a Valtournanche Olio/tela (60x80cm
23x31in) Vercelli 2001
$2 460 - €2 125 - **£1 230** - FF13 940
Ormeggio a Pallanza Olio/tavola (20x27.5cm
7x10in) Vercelli 1999

GHEDUZZI Mario 1891-1970 **[14]**
$1 850 - €1 918 - **£1 110** - FF12 580
«Campagna Vercellese» Olio/tavola (40x50cm
15x19in) Vercelli 2001
$900 - €933 - **£540** - FF6 120
Valtourenza, sfondo Tournalin Olio/tavola
(24x30cm 9x11in) Vercelli 2000

GHEDUZZI Ugo 1853-1925 **[13]**
$10 000 - €10 367 - **£6 000** - FF68 000
**Marina di Montecarlo vista dai giardini Hanbury,
Ventimiglia** Olio/tela (100x155cm 39x61in) Milano
1999
$1 600 - €2 073 - **£1 200** - FF13 600
«Pre S. Didier» Olio/tavola (38x58.5cm 14x23in)
Vercelli 2001

GHEE Robert Edgar Taylor 1872-1951 **[55]**
$3 026 - €3 150 - **£1 900** - FF20 662
The Dandenongs from Kalorama Oil/canvas
(65x50cm 25x19in) Melbourne 2000
$719 - €674 - **£445** - FF4 422
Making Hay Oil/board (27x39cm 10x15in) Melbourne
1999

GHELLI Giuliano 1944 **[63]**
$400 - €518 - **£300** - FF3 400
«L'albero dei vaggi» Olio/tela (50x40cm 19x15in)
Vercelli 2000
$350 - €363 - **£210** - FF2 380
La serenità della luna Olio/tela (20x40cm 7x15in)
Vercelli 2000

GHENT Peter 1856-1911 **[33]**
$2 727 - €2 748 - **£1 700** - FF18 026
Tranquil River with a Church beyond Oil/canvas
(76x127cm 29x50in) London 2000
$405 - €448 - **£280** - FF2 938
Snowy Village Scene with Figures
Watercolour/paper (37x24cm 14x9in) Hockley,
Birmingham 1999

GHERARDI Antonio 1644-1702 **[2]**
$19 500 - €20 215 - **£11 700** - FF132 600
Santa Caterina Olio/tela (90x67cm 35x26in) Milano
1999
$8 200 - €10 626 - **£6 150** - FF69 700
**Santa Cecilia, bozzetto per la pala nella cappel-
la in S.Carlo** Olio/tavola (42x25cm 16x9in) Roma
2000

GHERARDI Giuseppe, Joseph XIX **[7]**
$900 - €777 - **£600** - FF5 100
Veduta di Casa Torrigiani Acquarello/carta
(23x33cm 9x12in) Firenze 1998

GHERARDINI Alessandro 1655-1723 **[11]**
$50 000 - €43 858 - **£30 360** - FF287 690
The Annunciation to the Immaculate Virgin
Oil/canvas (90x155cm 35x61in) New-York 1999

GHERARDINI IL CERANINO Melchiorre 1607-1675
[9]
$839 - €920 - **£569** - FF6 037
**Ansichten italienischer Plätze in Mailand,
Palermo, Piacenza, Turin** Radierung (5.5x7.5cm
2x3in) Berlin 2000

GHERARDINI Stéphane 1696-1756 **[3]**
$7 066 - €7 927 - **£4 898** - FF52 000
Jeune paysanne devant un panier d'oeufs
Huile/toile (52x43cm 20x16in) Paris 2000

GHERING Anton Gunther ?-1667 **[4]**
$11 000 - €9 649 - **£6 679** - FF63 291
Interior of a Church Oil/canvas (77.5x98.5cm
30x38in) New-York 1999

GHERRI-MORO Bruno 1899-1967 **[84]**
$1 075 - €995 - **£658** - FF6 529
Tschiertschen Öl/Leinwand (59.5x80cm 23x31in)
Bern 1999
$1 647 - €1 575 - **£1 004** - FF9 897
Capucines in einer weissen Vase Öl/Leinwand
(41x33cm 16x12in) Zürich 1999

✐ **$964** - €810 - **£567** - FF5 314
Segelboot in der Lagune von Venedig
Watercolour (31.5x24cm 12x9in) Bern 1998

GHERWEN van Reynier XVII [1]
🖙 **$13 870** - €12 894 - **£8 500** - FF84 576
Mercenary Love Oil/canvas (81x99cm 31x38in)
London 1998

GHESIO-VOLPENGO Amedeo 1847-1889 [1]
🖙 **$10 000** - €10 367 - **£6 000** - FF68 000
Paesaggio al tramonto Olio/cartone (27.5x38cm
10x14in) Milano 2000

GHESQUIERE Christophe 1968 [7]
🖙 **$901** - €843 - **£547** - FF5 528
La digue Huile/toile (22x27cm 8x10in) Arlon 1999

GHESQUIERE Napoléon François 1812-1862 [10]
🖙 **$9 373** - €10 358 - **£6 500** - FF67 944
Admiring the Baby Oil/panel (61x77cm 24x30in)
London 2001
🖙 **$1 800** - €1 983 - **£1 176** - FF13 008
Tricoteuse à la fenêtre Huile/panneau (43x33cm
16x12in) Bruxelles 2000

GHEYN de Jacob I, II, or III XVI-XVII [2]
▥ **$935** - €991 - **£623** - FF6 500
**La diseuse de bonne aventure et une jeune
femme** Gravure (30.5x20.5cm 12x8in) Paris 2000

GHEYN de Jacob II 1565-1629 [50]
✐ **$30 000** - €32 136 - **£20 487** - FF210 798
**Soldier Transferring his Hand to the Lower end
of the Ramrod** Ink (26.5x18.5cm 10x7in) New-York
2001
▥ **$314** - €358 - **£218** - FF2 347
**Die zwölf Söhne Jakobs, nach Karel van
Mander** Radierung (15.9x11.3cm 6x4in) Berlin 2000

GHEZZI Pier Leone 1674-1755 [72]
✐ **$3 500** - €3 749 - **£2 390** - FF24 593
Père Pierre de Charlevois, S.J. Black chalk
(29.5x21.5cm 11x8in) New-York 2001

GHIBERTI Lorenzo 1378-1443 [1]
🔨 **$228 000** - €295 446 - **£171 000** - FF1 938 000
Madonna con Bambino Relief (96x74cm 37x29in)
Firenze 2000

GHIDONI Matteo dei Pitocchi c.1626-1689 [10]
🖙 **$13 500** - €13 930 - **£8 100** - FF91 800
Cavalieri e pitocchi Olio/tela (41x58cm 16x22in)
Milano 2001

GHIGLIA Oscar 1876-1945 [50]
🖙 **$27 000** - €27 990 - **£16 200** - FF183 600
Ritratto della Marchesa de'Fornari Olio/tela
(99x77cm 38x30in) Prato 2000
🖙 **$8 368** - €9 841 - **£6 000** - FF64 551
L'enfant endormi Oil/board (33.5x47cm 13x18in)
London 2001

GHIGLIA Paulo 1905-1979 [71]
🖙 **$5 576** - €5 781 - **£3 345** - FF37 920
Ritratto di artista Olio/tavoletta (158x103cm
62x40in) Roma 2000
🖙 **$1 440** - €1 244 - **£720** - FF8 160
Alla finestra Olio/tela (60x40cm 23x15in) Prato 1999
🖙 **$1 300** - €1 348 - **£780** - FF8 840
Signora con cappello Olio/cartone (35x30cm
13x11in) Roma 2000

GHIGLIA Valentino 1903-1960 [77]
🖙 **$1 100** - €1 140 - **£660** - FF7 480
Natura morta con pesci Olio/cartone (45x59cm
17x23in) Prato 2000

🖙 **$650** - €674 - **£390** - FF4 420
Bagnante Olio/cartone (44.5x23cm 17x9in) Prato
2000

GHIGLION-GREEN Maurice 1913 [62]
🖙 **$756** - €762 - **£471** - FF5 000
**Les bords de la petite Creuse, souvenir de
Boussac** Huile/toile (54.5x73cm 21x28in) Paris 2000
🖙 **$1 434** - €1 592 - **£1 000** - FF10 444
La rue Norvins, Montmartre Oil/board (42x33.5cm
16x13in) London 2001

GHIJSBRECHT-VANDERBORGHT Simone 1888-
1969 [1]
🔨 **$7 486** - €7 260 - **£4 712** - FF47 625
Sleeping Woman Bronze (H43cm H16in) Amsterdam
1999

GHIKA Nikos Hadjikyriakos 1906-1994 [57]
🖙 **$2 618** - €2 455 - **£1 619** - FF16 106
Komposition i rött Mixed media (49x69cm 19x27in)
Stockholm 1999
🖙 **$8 059** - €9 279 - **£5 500** - FF60 867
Cabins on the Beach Oil/board (16.5x35.5cm
6x13in) London 2000
🖙 **$4 677** - €5 367 - **£3 200** - FF35 206
Bridge in an English Garden Watercolour
(30x22cm 11x8in) London 2000
▥ **$874** - €847 - **£550** - FF5 555
Aypika for the Greek poems by A.Iolas Color
lithograph (49x34.5cm 19x13in) London 1999

GHIRLANDAIO Davide Bigordi 1452-1525 [5]
🖙 **$380 000** - €406 482 - **£259 084** - FF2 666 346
**The Dead Christ supported by The Virgin, St
John The Evangelist** Tempera/panel (88x81cm
34x31in) New-York 2001

GHISI Diana Mantuana c.1536-c.1587 [7]
▥ **$6 433** - €7 669 - **£4 587** - FF50 308
**Das Martyrium des Heilige Katharina von
Alexandria, nach Giulio Romano** Kupferstich
(56x43cm 22x16in) Berlin 2000

GHISI Giorgio Mantovano 1520/24-1582 [88]
▥ **$494** - €562 - **£343** - FF3 689
Allegorie der Jagd, nach Luca Penni Kupferstich
(36x25.5cm 14x10in) Berlin 2000

GHISI Giovanni Battista 1498-1563/75 [5]
▥ **$1 398** - €1 534 - **£949** - FF10 061
**Die Trojaner drängen die Griechen, nach Giulio
Romano** Kupferstich (40.7x58cm 16x22in) Berlin
2000

GHISLANDI Vittore Fra'Galgario 1655-1743 [18]
🖙 **$55 000** - €57 016 - **£33 000** - FF374 000
Ritratto di giovanetto Olio/tela (63x47.5cm 24x18in)
Milano 2001

GHISOLFI Enrico 1837-1897 [1]
🖙 **$6 000** - €6 183 - **£3 540** - FF34 000
Di ritorno al Presbiterio Olio/tela (46x66cm
18x25in) Torino 1999

GHISOLFI Giovanni 1623/32-1683 [31]
🖙 **$104 601** - €112 281 - **£70 000** - FF736 512
**Capriccio of a Mediterranean Port with
Bandits/Capriccio of a Port** Oil/canvas
(120.5x195cm 47x76in) London 2000
🖙 **$12 212** - €13 111 - **£8 170** - FF86 000
**Paysage de ruines antiques animé de person-
nages** Huile/toile (96x74cm 37x29in) Paris 2000

GHITTI Pompeo 1631-1703 **[9]**
$484 - €453 - **£300** - FF2 972
The Visitation Black & white chalks (24x36cm 9x14in) London 1999

GHITTONI Francesco 1855-1928 **[1]**
$5 500 - €5 702 - **£3 300** - FF37 400
Madonna Olio/tavola (45x22cm 17x8in) Milano 2000

GHIVARELLO Benedetto 1882-1955 **[36]**
$380 - €492 - **£285** - FF3 230
Poesia dell'ora Olio/cartone (20x23cm 7x9in) Torino 2000

GHOSE Gopal 1913-1980 **[10]**
$2 000 - €2 319 - **£1 416** - FF15 210
Fish Watercolour/paper (18x28cm 7x11in) New-York 2000

GHOSH Kali Charan XIX-XX **[4]**
$2 597 - €2 496 - **£1 600** - FF16 373
Cat and Parrot Watercolour/paper (45.5x26.5cm 17x10in) London 1999

GIACOMELLI Mario 1925-2000 **[74]**
$1 268 - €1 361 - **£848** - FF8 929
Scanno Gelatin silver print (29x39cm 11x15in) Amsterdam 2000

GIACOMETTI Alberto 1901-1966 **[1163]**
$120 000 - €139 235 - **£82 848** - FF913 320
Diego dans son atelier Oil/canvas (46x38cm 18x14in) New-York 2000
$400 000 - €464 116 - **£276 160** - FF3 044 400
Tête noire Oil/canvas (41x33cm 16x12in) New-York 2000
$210 000 - €235 215 - **£145 908** - FF1 542 912
Lampadaire à noeud Bronze (H148.5cm H58in) New-York 2001
$120 000 - €102 429 - **£71 760** - FF671 892
Buste de Diego Bronze (H20.5cm H8in) New-York 1998
$13 052 - €14 011 - **£8 734** - FF91 907
Portrait d'Olivier Larronde assis Pencil/paper (28.2x22.6cm 11x8in) Bern 2000
$3 000 - €3 358 - **£2 088** - FF22 030
The Artist's mother seated I Lithograph (51.5x38cm 20x14in) New-York 2001

GIACOMETTI Alberto & Diego 1901/02-1966/85 **[41]**
$82 360 - €88 420 - **£55 100** - FF580 000
Lampadaire, tête de femme Bronze (H155cm H61in) Paris 2000
$42 320 - €41 494 - **£26 000** - FF270 181
Lampe tête de femme Bronze (H50.5cm H19in) London 1999

GIACOMETTI Augusto 1877-1947 **[130]**
$192 753 - €184 616 - **£121 304** - FF1 211 004
Orangenverkäufer I Öl/Leinwand (140.5x101.5cm 55x39in) Bern 1999
$139 525 - €164 085 - **£100 050** - FF1 076 325
Katze Öl/Leinwand (36.5x48cm 14x18in) Bern 2001
$42 370 - €49 839 - **£30 704** - FF326 921
«Rosen in Glasvase» Öl/Leinwand (28x35cm 11x13in) Zofingen 2001
$10 517 - €11 981 - **£7 266** - FF78 588
Le vieux port à Marseille Pastell/Papier (25x36.3cm 9x14in) Zürich 2000
$1 279 - €1 079 - **£750** - FF7 079
«Les Grisons Suisse le Pays du Soleil» Poster (102x65cm 40x25in) London 1998

GIACOMETTI Diego 1902-1985 **[508]**
$100 000 - €116 029 - **£69 040** - FF761 100
Fauteuil à têtes de lionnes: 2eme version, pieds antérieurs en griffes Bronze (H95.5cm H37in) New-York 2000
$55 000 - €63 816 - **£37 972** - FF418 605
Tabouret en X, troisième version Bronze (H49cm H19in) New-York 2000
$3 000 - €3 240 - **£2 073** - FF21 251
«La Licorne» Watercolour (26x24cm 10x9in) New-York 2000
$12 552 - €14 761 - **£9 000** - FF96 827
La promenade des amis Tapestry (174x239cm 68x94in) London 2001

GIACOMETTI Giovanni 1868-1933 **[245]**
$130 526 - €140 112 - **£87 340** - FF919 072
Il Mattino, Morgenritt Öl/Leinwand (111x120cm 43x47in) Bern 2000
$130 620 - €125 767 - **£81 680** - FF824 980
Fiori e frutta (Blumen und Früchte) Öl/Leinwand (60.5x51cm 23x20in) Zürich 2001
$72 215 - €85 883 - **£51 467** - FF563 355
Stampa im Winter Öl/Leinwand (24x34.5cm 9x13in) Zürich 2001
$5 197 - €5 016 - **£3 282** - FF32 904
Camargue Aquarelle/papier (22.7x29cm 8x11in) Bern 1999
$1 413 - €1 376 - **£868** - FF9 024
Otto Vautier aud dem Totenbett Woodcut (24.5x30cm 9x11in) Zürich 1999

GIACOMI de Eugenio 1852-1917 **[1]**
$19 000 - €19 696 - **£11 400** - FF129 200
Corteggiamento Olio/tela (78x114cm 30x44in) Milano 2000

GIALLINA Angelos 1857-1939 **[177]**
$4 184 - €4 491 - **£2 800** - FF29 460
The Coast of Corfu Watercolour/paper (28x54.5cm 11x21in) London 2000

GIAMBOLOGNA Jean de Boulogne c.1529-1608 **[76]**
$1 701 - €1 429 - **£1 000** - FF9 372
Mercury Bronze (H84cm H33in) London 1998
$4 480 - €3 811 - **£2 672** - FF25 000
Vénus au bain Sculpture (H1.32cm Hin) Paris 1998

GIAMPICCOLI Giuliano 1698-1759 **[9]**
$270 - €233 - **£135** - FF1 530
Clemente VII riceve Carlo V a Bologna Maria de Medici Acquaforte (61.5x35cm 24x13in) Firenze 1999

GIAMPICCOLI Marco Sebastiano ?-1782 **[14]**
$316 - €271 - **£190** - FF1 777
«Pastorale Landschaft mit Hirten an einem Fluss» nach Marco Ricci Radierung (25.1x36.2cm 9x14in) Berlin 1998

GIAMPIETRI Settimio 1842-1924 **[6]**
$917 - €1 064 - **£650** - FF6 980
A Figure Standing before a Roman Arch Watercolour (49.5x32.5cm 19x12in) London 2000

GIANI Felice 1758-1823 **[39]**
$1 700 - €1 762 - **£1 020** - FF11 560
Annunciazione/Putti in volo Matita/carta (17.5x12cm 6x4in) Roma 2000

GIANI Giovanni 1866-1937 **[18]**
$1 920 - €2 488 - **£1 440** - FF16 320
Barche di pescatori nel Golfo di Napoli Olio/legno (25x30cm 9x11in) Roma 2000

G

GIANLISI Antonio c.1677-1727 **[21]**
- $24 840 - €22 867 - **£14 910** - FF150 000
  Vanité aux instruments de musique et à l'horloge Huile/toile (92x145.5cm 36x57in) Paris 1999
- $48 455 - €39 961 - **£28 545** - FF262 130
  Natura morta di tappeti e frutti Öl/Leinwand (81.5x110.5cm 32x43in) Wien 1998

GIANNETTI Raffaele 1832-1916 **[8]**
- $8 500 - €9 435 - **£5 925** - FF61 892
  Ladt at Rest within a Neoclassical Interior Oil/panel (40.5x51cm 15x20in) New-York 2001
- $3 980 - €3 462 - **£2 400** - FF22 711
  Memories Oil/panel (29.5x21.5cm 11x8in) Glasgow 1998

GIANNI XIX **[2]**
- $17 541 - €20 127 - **£12 000** - FF132 024
  Jerusalem, from the Mount of Olives Oil/canvas (53x107cm 20x42in) London 2000
- $1 905 - €2 194 - **£1 300** - FF14 391
  Figures on a track above the bay of Naples Oil/canvas (26x39.5cm 10x15in) London 2000

GIANNI C.A. XIX **[1]**
- $15 410 - €14 799 - **£9 500** - FF97 078
  British Squadron of the Red Saluting it's Arrival off Piraeus, Greece Watercolour (76x137.5cm 29x54in) London 1999

GIANNI Ettore XIX-XX **[10]**
- $400 - €388 - **£251** - FF2 542
  Venetian Canal Gouache/paper (18x41cm 7x16in) Norwalk CT 1999

GIANNI Giacinto 1837 **[3]**
- $16 356 - €13 435 - **£9 500** - FF88 125
  A View from St. Paul Bay, from San Paul Ta-Targa, Malta Oil/canvas (31x64cm 12x25in) London 1998

GIANNI Gian XIX-XX **[68]**
- $15 781 - €13 505 - **£9 500** - FF88 588
  Sliema and Manoel Island from Marsamuscetto Oil/canvas (36x103.5cm 14x40in) London 1998
- $6 414 - €6 166 - **£4 000** - FF40 446
  View of the Harbour, Valletta, Malta Oil/board (21x54cm 8x21in) London 1999
- $8 491 - €9 066 - **£5 800** - FF59 468
  Street Scenes, Valetta Gouache/paper (21.5x15.5cm 8x6in) Billingshurst, West-Sussex 2001

GIANNI Girolamo 1837-1895 **[54]**
- $12 090 - €11 274 - **£7 500** - FF73 950
  The Three Cities from Valletta, Malta Oil/canvas (37x103cm 14x40in) London 1999
- $4 513 - €4 209 - **£2 800** - FF27 608
  The Entrace to the Grand Harbour, Valletta by Night Oil/canvas (21x66cm 8x25in) London 1999

GIANNI Giuseppe 1829-1885 **[3]**
- $4 087 - €3 635 - **£2 500** - FF23 843
  Valletta Harbour Oil/board (18x36cm 7x14in) London 1999

GIANNI M. XIX-XX **[81]**
- $337 - €340 - **£210** - FF2 231
  Gondoliers, Venice Watercolour, gouache/paper (31x47cm 12x18in) Billingshurst, West-Sussex 2000

GIANNI Maria XIX-XX **[54]**
- $484 - €456 - **£300** - FF2 988
  The Flower Vendor Watercolour (48x30cm 18x11in) London 1999

GIANNI V. XIX-XX **[3]**
- $1 900 - €1 970 - **£1 140** - FF12 920
  Vicolo Tempera/carta (48x30cm 18x11in) Napoli 1999

GIANNI Y. XIX-XX **[31]**
- $400 - €416 - **£251** - FF2 730
  Napoli da Via Casso Watercolour/paper (29x48cm 11x19in) Chicago IL 2000

GIANNICOLA DI PAOLO XV-XVI **[1]**
- $190 000 - €166 661 - **£115 368** - FF1 093 222
  Madonna and Child Enthroned before a Landscape Mixed media/panel (172.5x167.5cm 67x65in) New-York 1998

GIANNINI Giovanni 1930 **[28]**
- $541 - €473 - **£327** - FF3 100
  Femme au calice Pastel/papier (120x80cm 47x31in) Paris 1998

GIANNUZZI XIX **[1]**
- $2 586 - €3 049 - **£1 818** - FF20 000
  Vue de Meshed, Iran Tirage papier salé (19x23.5cm 7x9in) Paris 2000

GIANOLI Louis 1868-1957 **[40]**
- $571 - €652 - **£402** - FF4 280
  Sonniger Wintertag in den Walliser Alpen Öl/Leinwand (27x35cm 10x13in) Bern 2001

GIANQUINTO Alberto 1929 **[44]**
- $2 080 - €2 695 - **£1 560** - FF17 680
  «Jesolo» Olio/tela (100x73cm 39x28in) Torino 2000

GIAQUINTO Corrado 1703-1766 **[50]**
- $19 740 - €21 802 - **£13 680** - FF143 010
  Die heilige Familie mit Heiligen Öl/Leinwand (130x99cm 51x38in) Wien 2001
- $25 500 - €26 435 - **£15 300** - FF173 400
  Cristo deposto Olio/tela (62x50cm 24x19in) Prato 1999
- $6 222 - €5 770 - **£3 800** - FF37 848
  A Seated Nude Holding a Cross Red chalk (40x27cm 15x10in) London 1998

GIARDIELLO Carmine 1871-? **[9]**
- $6 312 - €5 402 - **£3 800** - FF35 435
  Una festa a Napoli Oil/canvas (49.5x103.5cm 19x40in) London 1998

GIARDIELLO G. XIX-XX **[10]**
- $2 019 - €2 180 - **£1 395** - FF14 301
  Junge Italienerin, aus Meer hinausblickend Öl/Leinwand (40x25.5cm 15x10in) Wien 2001

GIARDIELLO Giovanni XIX-XX **[12]**
- $876 - €971 - **£608** - FF6 372
  Alter Fischer von Capri Oil/panel (23.5x17.5cm 9x6in) Köln 2001

GIARDIELLO Giuseppe XIX-XX **[40]**
- $2 382 - €2 573 - **£1 646** - FF16 875
  Fiskare vid stranden Oil/canvas (46x68cm 18x26in) Stockholm 2001
- $1 200 - €1 555 - **£900** - FF10 200
  Sorrento Olio/tavola (31x43cm 12x16in) Napoli 2000

GIAUQUE Ferdinand 1895-1973 **[20]**
- $537 - €498 - **£329** - FF3 264
  Ohne Titel Gouache/papier (49x32cm 19x12in) Bern 1999

GIBAULT Eugène XIX **[4]**
- $6 669 - €6 403 - **£4 183** - FF42 000
  Jeté de fleurs Huile/toile (64x92cm 25x36in) Lyon 1999

GIBB Harry Phelan 1870-1948 **[37]**
  $420 - €351 - **£250** - FF2 304
    Passing Through the Town Oil/canvas (63.5x76cm 25x29in) London 1998

GIBB John 1831-1909 **[5]**
  $3 395 - €3 868 - **£2 346** - FF25 372
    Horse and Cart on a Winding Road in the Otira Gorge Oil/canvas (60x43.5cm 23x17in) Auckland 2000

GIBB Robert II 1845-1932 **[15]**
  $13 631 - €15 199 - **£9 200** - FF99 700
    Full, Composition Cartoon for The Thin Red Line Chalks (58x116cm 22x45in) Edinburgh 2000

GIBB Thomas Henry XIX **[20]**
  $400 - €385 - **£250** - FF2 527
    Ullswater Oil/canvas (21x36cm 8x14in) West-Yorkshire 1999

GIBBONS Gladys 1903-1977 **[3]**
  $448 - €468 - **£282** - FF3 068
    The Lovers Linocut (23x18cm 9x7in) Sydney 2000

GIBBONS William XIX **[16]**
  $2 339 - €2 149 - **£1 450** - FF14 095
    Low Tide, Lynmouth Oil/canvas (45x75.5cm 17x29in) Devon 1999
  $3 120 - €3 069 - **£2 000** - FF20 133
    Figures on the Beach, above the Artillery Tower Oil/canvas (43x22cm 17x9in) Tavistock, Devon 1999

GIBBS George 1870-1942 **[6]**
  $3 400 - €3 650 - **£2 316** - FF23 941
    Marigolds Pastel/paper (83.5x55cm 32x21in) Boston MA 2001

GIBBS Harry ?-c.1907 **[1]**
  $5 912 - €6 280 - **£3 900** - FF41 196
    Cliff Top Adventure Oil/canvas (75x134.5cm 29x52in) Penzance, Cornwall 2000

GIBBS Jane 1884-? **[2]**
  $4 800 - €4 936 - **£3 044** - FF32 379
    Jazz Club Scene Oil/masonite (66x67cm 26x26in) New-Orleans LA 2000

GIBBS Leonard, Len 1929 **[43]**
  $488 - €548 - **£339** - FF3 592
    Travel Home Etching (26x19cm 10x7in) Calgary, Alberta 2001

GIBELE Johann Nepomuk ?-c.1836 **[3]**
  $737 - €768 - **£471** - FF5 040
    Vue perspective de la Place Royale, d'après C.Janssens Lithographie couleurs (60x84cm 23x33in) Bruxelles 2000

GIBERT Lucien 1904-1988 **[350]**
  $2 349 - €2 592 - **£1 553** - FF17 000
    Paysanne Plâtre (H124cm H48in) Paris 2000
  $691 - €762 - **£457** - FF5 000
    Visage de femme II Pierre (H39cm H15in) Paris 2000
  $334 - €381 - **£236** - FF2 500
    Le modèle Dessin (30.5x49cm 12x19in) Rennes 2001

GIBINSKI Stanislaw 1882-1971 **[7]**
  $4 187 - €3 853 - **£2 512** - FF25 275
    Le traîneau sur le chemin de la forêt Oil/canvas (60x90cm 23x35in) Warszawa 1999

GIBSON Bessie 1868-1961 **[11]**
  $1 839 - €1 775 - **£1 139** - FF11 644
    Seated Nude Watercolour/paper (23x19cm 9x7in) Sydney 1999

GIBSON Charles Dana 1867-1944 **[58]**
  $3 800 - €4 170 - **£2 446** - FF27 355
    Girl in Tangerine Oil/canvas (117x92.5cm 46x36in) Beverly-Hills CA 2000
  $400 - €439 - **£258** - FF2 878
    Lady and man Golfers sitting on fairway Ink (22x34cm 9x13in) Wallkill NY 2000

GIBSON Colin 1948 **[11]**
  $341 - €381 - **£231** - FF2 498
    «**Balligan Church**» Oil/board (29x39cm 11x15in) Dublin 2000

GIBSON George 1904 **[7]**
  $1 400 - €1 344 - **£877** - FF8 813
    Monday and Santa Prisca, Taxco, Mexico Watercolour/paper (55x76cm 22x30in) Altadena CA 1999

GIBSON John 1790-1866 **[7]**
  $14 802 - €14 018 - **£9 000** - FF91 954
    Hylas and the Naiades Plaster (164x121x73cm 64x47x28in) London 1999
  $28 000 - €25 921 - **£16 903** - FF170 030
    Bust of Cupid Marble (H57.5cm H22in) New-York 1999

GIBSON Ralph 1939 **[105]**
  $970 - €1 067 - **£622** - FF7 000
    The Somnambulist Tirage argentique (18.5x12.5cm 7x4in) Paris 2000

GIBSON Richard 1615-1690 **[7]**
  $14 568 - €14 144 - **£9 000** - FF92 778
    Young Girl in the Guise of Diana the Huntress, Full Length Miniature (17.5x11cm 6x4in) London 1999

GIBSON Thomas c.1680-1751 **[6]**
  $15 000 - €16 457 - **£9 964** - FF107 952
    Mawdistly Best (d.1795) of Chilston Park, Kent Wearing a Red Dress Oil/canvas (125x99cm 49x38in) New-York 2000

GIBSON William Alfred 1866-1931 **[63]**
  $2 884 - €3 390 - **£2 000** - FF22 240
    Barges on a Dutch Canal Oil/canvas (40.5x51cm 15x20in) Edinburgh 2000
  $1 912 - €1 639 - **£1 150** - FF10 749
    Drying the Sails Oil/canvas (30.5x40.5cm 12x15in) Edinburgh 1998

GID Raymond 1905-2000 **[28]**
  $550 - €600 - **£381** - FF3 934
    «**Exposition ethnographique**» Poster (59x39cm 23x15in) New-York 2001

GIDAL Tim 1909-1996 **[31]**
  $657 - €654 - **£408** - FF4 290
    An der Klagemauer, Jerusalem Gelatin silver print (21.8x30.6cm 8x12in) Wien 1999

GIDE François Théophile 1822-1890 **[32]**
  $4 092 - €4 878 - **£2 918** - FF32 000
    Au couvent Huile/toile (66x82cm 25x32in) Nice 2000
  $15 000 - €14 050 - **£9 222** - FF92 161
    Man smoking a Pipe, View of Constantinople beyond Oil/canvas (40.5x32cm 15x12in) New-York 1999
  $908 - €838 - **£565** - FF5 500
    Relais de chiens Aquarelle, gouache/papier (76x54cm 29x21in) Paris 1999

GIEBEL Heinrich 1865-1951 **[11]**
  $1 529 - €1 431 - **£947** - FF9 390
    Weite oberhessische Landschaft Öl/Leinwand (38x63cm 14x24in) Heidelberg 1999

G

$1 656 - €1 534 - £1 000 - FF10 061
Grüngraue Landschaft mit Feldweg Öl/Leinwand
(22x34.5cm 8x13in) Heidelberg 1999

GIEBERICH Oscar H. 1886-? [18]
$850 - €918 - £588 - FF6 023
Still Life Oil/canvas (73x91cm 29x36in) Cincinnati OH 2001
$425 - €476 - £295 - FF3 122
«Laundry and Sunflowers» Monotype (41x31cm 16x12in) Cincinnati OH 2001

GIEL van Frans 1892-1975 [37]
$852 - €992 - £608 - FF6 504
Boer en boerin bij de haard (couple de paysans près de l'âtre) Huile/toile (48x68cm 18x26in) Antwerpen 2000

GIELNIAK József 1932-1972 [11]
$915 - €982 - £612 - FF6 444
Arbre Linogravure (35.5x27.5cm 13x10in) Warszawa 2000

GIEROWSKI Stefan 1925 [3]
$1 498 - €1 658 - £1 041 - FF10 873
Sans titre Aquarelle/papier (72.5x50.5cm 28x19in) Warszawa 2001

GIERSING Harald 1881-1927 [128]
$2 914 - €2 827 - £1 835 - FF18 545
Skovtykning Oil/canvas (61x51cm 24x20in) Köbenhavn 1999
$933 - €1 006 - £642 - FF6 597
Havebillede Oil/canvas (21x20cm 8x7in) Köbenhavn 2001
$217 - €241 - £151 - FF1 582
Nögen kvindemodel Charcoal/paper (31.5x24cm 12x9in) Köbenhavn 2001

GIERYMSKI Aleksander 1850-1901 [17]
$56 914 - €52 019 - £34 826 - FF341 220
Portret Brata Alberta-Adama Chmielowskiego Oil/canvas/board (50x38cm 19x14in) Warszawa 1999
$13 077 - €15 359 - £9 285 - FF100 751
Paysage au bord de l'eau Huile/carton (31x42cm 12x16in) Warszawa 2000
$23 507 - €27 438 - £16 104 - FF179 982
Étude de garçon Gouache/carton (61x41.5cm 24x16in) Warszawa 2000

GIERYMSKI Maksymilian 1846-1874 [15]
$38 295 - €35 938 - £23 655 - FF235 740
Landscape with Cottage and Carriage Oil/canvas (38x53cm 14x20in) Warszawa 1999
$53 781 - €49 248 - £32 781 - FF323 043
Recognition of the Austrian Hussars Oil/canvas (31x43cm 12x16in) Warszawa 1999
$16 038 - €15 006 - £9 721 - FF98 432
Small Village in Winter Watercolour/paper (26x48.3cm 10x19in) Warszawa 1999

GIES Joseph W., Joe 1860-1935 [18]
$2 800 - €3 328 - £1 940 - FF21 832
Lady Wearing a Straw Bonnet with a Basket for Flowers by the Ocean Oil/board (25x20cm 10x8in) Detroit MI 2000

GIES Ludwig 1887-1966 [26]
$296 - €256 - £178 - FF1 676
Harlekin mit Augenmaske und Fächer Porcelain (H19.2cm H7in) Köln 1998

GIESE Wilhelm 1883-? [9]
$179 - €204 - £124 - FF1 341
Hochbahn am Alexanderplatz Radierung (25.3x23.1cm 9x9in) Berlin 2000

GIESSEL Franz 1902-1982 [9]
$1 550 - €1 453 - £958 - FF9 534
Mittagsrast Öl/Leinwand (120x90cm 47x35in) Wien 1999

GIETL von Josua 1847-1922 [34]
$1 218 - €1 125 - £749 - FF7 378
Moorsee Öl/Karton (40x31cm 15x12in) München 1999
$664 - €613 - £408 - FF4 024
Kirche in Marzoll Aquarell/Papier (20x18cm 7x7in) München 1999

GIFFARD Léon XIX-XX [6]
$2 800 - €2 399 - £1 683 - FF15 735
Venice at Sunset Oil/board (17x27cm 7x11in) Cleveland OH 1998

GIFFORD Charles Henry 1839-1904 [55]
$60 000 - €64 311 - £40 842 - FF421 854
Three masted Sailing Ship with several Sailing Yachts Oil/canvas (76x109cm 30x43in) Thomaston ME 2001
$3 900 - €3 619 - £2 432 - FF23 739
Moonlit Harbor Scene Oil/canvas (35x22cm 14x9in) East-Dennis MA 1999
$1 900 - €2 216 - £1 334 - FF14 535
Sunset with sailboat Watercolour/paper (10x20cm 4x8in) Cambridge MA 2000

GIFFORD John XIX [41]
$6 096 - €6 143 - £3 800 - FF40 293
The Day's Bag Oil/canvas (101.5x127cm 39x50in) London 2000
$3 500 - €4 066 - £2 459 - FF26 674
Two Setters and Game Oil/canvas (61x91.5cm 24x36in) New-York 2001

GIFFORD Robert Swain 1840-1905 [46]
$4 400 - €4 245 - £2 763 - FF27 848
Haying Time Oil/canvas (38x63cm 15x25in) Columbia SC 1999
$600 - €644 - £401 - FF4 224
Moonlit Shore Scene with Skiff Oil/canvas (30x45cm 12x18in) East-Dennis MA 2000
$870 - €751 - £468 - FF4 928
Arab Sheik Watercolour/paper (20x25cm 8x10in) East-Dennis MA 2000

GIFFORD Sanford Robinson 1823-1880 [81]
$50 000 - €53 670 - £33 460 - FF352 050
Scene in the Catskills Oil/canvas (60x51cm 23x20in) Philadelphia PA 2000
$39 000 - €42 117 - £26 952 - FF276 272
Genoa Oil/canvas (19x26cm 7x10in) San Rafael CA 2001

GIGANTE Achille 1823-1846 [4]
$4 500 - €4 665 - £2 700 - FF30 600
Strada di Posillipo Olio/tela (16x25.5cm 6x10in) Milano 2000

GIGANTE Ercole 1815-1860 [35]
$11 932 - €14 025 - £8 480 - FF92 000
Moines en prière devant la côte amalfitaine Huile/toile (48x57cm 14x22in) Bernay 2001
$3 162 - €3 278 - £1 897 - FF21 505
Scorcio del Golfo di Napoli Olio/tela (12.5x15cm 4x5in) Roma 1999
$3 422 - €3 278 - £2 154 - FF21 500
La Baie de Naples, vue de la terrasse d'une auberge du Pausilippe Aquarelle, gouache/papier (19x28cm 7x11in) Paris 1999

GIGANTE Giacinto 1806-1876 [73]

- $22 000 - €28 508 - £16 500 - FF187 000
  Penisola sorrentinal al tramonto Olio/tela (46x62cm 18x24in) Milano 2001
- $21 000 - €21 770 - £12 600 - FF142 800
  Marinella Olio/tela (24.5x35cm 9x13in) Milano 2000
- $2 291 - €2 577 - £1 600 - FF16 907
  Figures and a Dog before the Temples at Paestum Watercolour (20x29cm 7x11in) London 2001

GIGER Hansruedi, H. Rudolf 1940 [68]

- $38 962 - €45 873 - £27 377 - FF300 909
  Lilith, Todesengel Acrylic/paper (200x140cm 78x55in) Zürich 2000
- $7 792 - €9 175 - £5 475 - FF60 181
  Kim I Painting (127.4x89.8cm 50x35in) Zürich 2000
- $2 293 - €2 610 - £1 611 - FF17 122
  Biomechanische Landschaft Acryl/Papier (41.5x28cm 16x11in) Zürich 2001
- $622 - €722 - £429 - FF4 788
  Am Swimmingpool Ink/paper (20x29.8cm 7x11in) Zürich 2000
- $276 - €329 - £197 - FF2 156
  Ohne Titel Serigraph (110x80cm 43x31in) Zürich 2000

GIGLI [4]

- $3 435 - €3 201 - £2 137 - FF21 000
  Le Colysée Aquarelle/papier (33x48cm 12x18in) Toulouse 1999

GIGLI Ormond 1925 [9]

- $3 200 - €3 552 - £2 230 - FF23 300
  Rio de Janeiro Gelatin silver print (24.5x43.5cm 9x17in) New-York 2001

GIGLI Roberto 1846-1922 [13]

- $900 - €907 - £561 - FF5 949
  St.Peter's Cathedral Watercolour, gouache/paper (25.5x36.5cm 10x14in) New-York 2000

GIGNOUS Eugenio 1850-1906 [50]

- $15 240 - €15 357 - £9 500 - FF100 738
  A Tranquil River Landscape/Leaving Port Oil/canvas (35x66.5cm 13x26in) London 2000
- $10 000 - €12 958 - £7 500 - FF85 000
  Bambini nell'Aia Olio/tela (25x36cm 9x14in) Milano 2001

GIGNOUS Lorenzo 1862-1958 [45]

- $3 300 - €2 851 - £1 650 - FF18 700
  Lago Maggiore Olio/tela (45x65cm 17x25in) Vercelli 1999
- $800 - €829 - £480 - FF5 440
  Scorcio di paese con figure Olio/legno (21x15cm 8x5in) Roma 1999

GIGNOUX Regis François 1816-1882 [21]

- $6 000 - €6 661 - £4 173 - FF43 694
  Peaceful Harbor Oil/canvas (35x50cm 14x20in) Milford CT 2001
- $4 000 - €4 549 - £2 794 - FF29 840
  Country Road Oil/canvas (30x40cm 12x16in) New-York 2000

GIGOLA Giovanni Battista 1769-1841 [6]

- $2 880 - €2 488 - £1 920 - FF16 320
  Ritratto di bambina Miniature (3.5x3cm 1x1in) Milano 1998
- $4 000 - €4 147 - £2 400 - FF27 200
  Gita in barca sul lago Inchiostro (29.5x28.5cm 11x11in) Milano 2000

GIGOTTI Lorenzo 1908-1994 [3]

- $2 000 - €2 073 - £1 200 - FF13 600
  Nudo femminile in un interno Olio/tela (40x35cm 15x13in) Roma 2000

GIGOUX DE GRANDPRÉ Pierre Emile 1826-? [7]

- $8 670 - €7 436 - £5 250 - FF48 780
  Paysage oriental avec felouques Huile/panneau (35x55cm 13x21in) Bruxelles 1998

GIHON Clarence Montfort 1871-1929 [36]

- $18 000 - €19 983 - £12 519 - FF131 083
  Breezy Day Oil/canvas (81x100cm 32x39in) Milford CT 2001
- $929 - €884 - £577 - FF5 800
  Sur les quais à Paris Huile/carton (22x27cm 8x10in) Lille 1999

GIJSELS Philips XVII [2]

- $20 239 - €23 570 - £14 000 - FF154 606
  Still Life of a Lemon, Hazelnuts and a Crab on a Pewter Dish Oil/panel (74x63cm 29x24in) London 2000

GIL GARCIA Juan 1879-c.1930 [46]

- $4 000 - €3 454 - £2 440 - FF22 655
  Paisaje con Palmeras Oil/canvas (66x91.5cm 25x36in) Miami FL 1999

GIL Ignacio 1913 [26]

- $6 145 - €6 480 - £4 059 - FF42 504
  Plaza de Cataluña, Barcelona Öl/Leinwand (73x100cm 28x39in) Zürich 2000

GILADI Aharon 1907-1993 [81]

- $1 400 - €1 451 - £922 - FF9 521
  Refectory in Affikim Oil/canvas (50x65cm 19x25in) Herzelia-Pituah 2000
- $450 - €483 - £301 - FF3 171
  Figures by the Sea of Galilée Oil/canvas/board (15.5x29cm 6x11in) Tel Aviv 2000
- $300 - €356 - £218 - FF2 333
  Figures in the Village Pathway Watercolour/paper (24x31.5cm 9x12in) Tel Aviv 2001

GILARDI Irene 1879-1951 [1]

- $5 000 - €5 183 - £3 000 - FF34 000
  Bambina sul prato Pastelli/carta (64x106.5cm 25x41in) Milano 2000

GILARDI Pier Celestino 1837-1905 [15]

- $18 250 - €18 919 - £10 950 - FF124 100
  Machiavelli nello studio Olio/tela (167x108cm 65x42in) Prato 2000
- $2 800 - €3 628 - £2 100 - FF23 800
  Tirata d'orecchi Olio/cartone (50x35cm 19x13in) Milano 2001
- $7 464 - €6.492 - £4 500 - FF42 583
  News from Afar Oil/panel (23x17cm 9x6in) London 1998

GILARDI Piero 1942 [73]

- $8 000 - €8 293 - £4 800 - FF54 400
  Giardino d'autunno Tecnica mista (200x204x25cm 78x80x9in) Milano 2000
- $2 400 - €2 073 - £1 600 - FF13 600
  «Prato» Tecnica mista (101x99cm 39x38in) Prato 1998
- $880 - €1 140 - £660 - FF7 480
  «Sottobosco» Tecnica mista (15x30.5x30.5cm 5x12x12in) Milano 2001
- $1 300 - €1 348 - £780 - FF8 840
  Campo di papaveri Scultura (50x50cm 19x19in) Vercelli 2001

GILBAULT Joseph Eugène XIX [4]
- $11 000 – €11 085 – **£6 857** – FF72 710
  Still Life with Roses, Peaches, Plums and Figs Oil/canvas (64x92cm 25x36in) New-York 2000

GILBERT & GEORGE 1943/1942 [145]
- $19 200 – €16 586 – **£12 800** – FF108 800
  «Cloud Head Work» Collage/cartone (240x175cm 94x68in) Prato 1998
- $10 560 – €12 467 – **£7 500** – FF81 779
  Cross of St.Bartholomew Mixed media (140x82cm 55x32in) London 2001
- $12 000 – €11 532 – **£7 392** – FF75 646
  City Lion World Collage (247.5x181.5cm 97x71in) New-York 1999
- $207 – €244 – **£148** – FF1 600
  «City Drop» Affiche (49x92cm 19x36in) Paris 2001
- $110 000 – €103 242 – **£67 958** – FF677 226
  Bead Boards No.13 Photograph (185x154cm 72x60in) New-York 1999

GILBERT Albert ?-1927 [6]
- $3 795 – €3 718 – **£2 355** – FF24 390
  Soubrette Huile/panneau (51x39cm 20x15in) Bruxelles 1999

GILBERT Alfred 1854-1934 [40]
- $6 747 – €7 828 – **£4 734** – FF51 348
  Awakening of the Pierrot Ivory, bronze (H58cm H22in) Melbourne 2000

GILBERT Arthur 1819-1895 [70]
- $4 065 – €4 269 – **£2 688** – FF28 000
  Troupeau près d'une rivière Huile/toile (52x90cm 20x35in) Paris 2000
- $1 715 – €1 664 – **£1 080** – FF10 916
  River Scene in Kent Oil/canvas (18x25.5cm 7x10in) London 1999

GILBERT Arthur Hill 1894-1970 [41]
- $4 000 – €4 675 – **£2 855** – FF30 664
  Canyon de Chelley Oil/canvas (60x76cm 24x30in) Altadena CA 2001
- $1 500 – €1 295 – **£915** – FF8 495
  Landscape Oil/board (19x24cm 7x9in) Oakland CA 1999

GILBERT Ferdinand ?-1877 [2]
- $1 719 – €2 045 – **£1 225** – FF13 415
  Orientalische Hafenstadt mit Moschee Öl/Leinwand (53x41.5cm 20x16in) Köln 2000

GILBERT Horace Walter 1855-? [12]
- $4 055 – €3 895 – **£2 500** – FF25 547
  Early Autumn, May Hill Gloucester Oil/canvas (45.5x61cm 17x24in) London 1999

GILBERT John, Sir 1817-1897 [69]
- $8 015 – €7 572 – **£5 000** – FF49 666
  Cardinal Wolsey and the Duke of Buckingham Oil/canvas (107x183cm 42x72in) Perthshire 1999
- $302 – €274 – **£183** – FF1 800
  Scene from the Merchant of Venice Watercolour/paper (27.5x33.5cm 10x13in) Sydney 1998

GILBERT Joseph Francis 1792-1855 [12]
- $4 500 – €4 250 – **£2 721** – FF27 880
  Village on the Edge of a Vale Oil/canvas (61x106.5cm 24x41in) New-York 1999
- $3 575 – €4 063 – **£2 469** – FF26 652
  Glengarriffe, Co.Cork Oil/board (30x40cm 12x16in) Dublin 2000

GILBERT Kate Elizabeth 1843-? [6]
- $231 – €250 – **£160** – FF1 640
  Untitled Oil/panel (17x25cm 7x10in) Bristol, Avon 2001

GILBERT Pierre Julien 1783-1860 [13]
- $10 824 – €9 147 – **£6 438** – FF60 000
  Le combat naval entre le «Québec» et la «Surveillante» Huile/toile (73x110cm 28x43in) Paris 1998

GILBERT Stephen 1910 [96]
- $2 247 – €2 518 – **£1 566** – FF16 514
  Utan titel Oil/panel (46x55cm 18x21in) Stockholm 2001
- $269 – €289 – **£180** – FF1 893
  Abstract in black and red Mixed media (26.5x21cm 10x8in) London 2000
- $194 – €209 – **£130** – FF1 370
  Streched Man Ink (19.5x24cm 7x9in) London 2000

GILBERT Victor 1847-1933 [222]
- $16 000 – €14 987 – **£9 836** – FF98 305
  Her new Friend Oil/canvas (46x38cm 18x14in) New-York 1999
- $2 887 – €2 910 – **£1 800** – FF19 086
  Playtime in the Summerhouse Oil/canvas (25.5x35cm 10x8in) London 2000
- $4 508 – €4 269 – **£2 808** – FF28 000
  Les marchandes de fruits et les enfants sur les quais Aquarelle, gouache/papier (23x30cm 9x11in) Cannes 1999

GILBERT W.J. XIX [6]
- $7 471 – €8 020 – **£5 000** – FF52 608
  Gentleman Dribing a Gig Pulled by a Trotting Grey Oil/canvas (53x41.5cm 20x25in) Suffolk 2000

GILCHRIST William Wallace Jr. 1879-1926 [14]
- $40 000 – €37 195 – **£24 692** – FF243 984
  After Breakfast Oil/canvas (66x83cm 26x33in) Portland ME 1999
- $8 500 – €10 162 – **£5 863** – FF66 657
  Silk and Satin Oil/canvas (22x30cm 9x12in) Milford CT 2000

GILDEMEISTER Gustav 1876-1951 [6]
- $25 000 – €27 733 – **£16 625** – FF181 915
  The Harvesters Oil/canvas (86x99cm 33x38in) New-York 2000

GILDEMEISTER Karl 1820-1869 [1]
- $1 473 – €1 431 – **£921** – FF9 390
  Das Rathaus in Bremen Lithographie (68x72cm 26x28in) Bremen 1999

GILDOR Jacob 1948 [51]
- $3 000 – €3 350 – **£1 921** – FF21 976
  Landscape Oil/paper/canvas (70.5x100.5cm 27x39in) Tel Aviv 2000
- $1 900 – €1 970 – **£1 252** – FF12 921
  On the Beach Oil/wood (16x30cm 6x11in) Herzelia-Pituah 2000
- $1 300 – €1 463 – **£895** – FF9 597
  Nude in the Window Mixed media/paper (46x47cm 18x18in) Herzelia-Pituah 2000
- $662 – €613 – **£400** – FF4 024
  Schlafender weiblicher Akt mit angewinkelten Beinen Etching, aquatint (88.5x118cm 34x46in) Heidelberg 1999

GILE Selden Connor 1877-1947 [55]
- $32 000 – €35 118 – **£20 604** – FF230 361
  Bathers at Corinthian Island, Belvédère Oil/canvas (46.5x38.5cm 18x15in) Beverly-Hills CA 2000
- $7 500 – €6 408 – **£4 538** – FF42 033
  Beach Road at Cove Road Oil/board (20.5x25.5cm 8x10in) San-Francisco CA 1998

GILES Carl Ronald 1916-1995 **[19]**
  $1 471 - €1 470 - £920 - FF9 643
  **Scotland Yard? About Your Prize Winners, 8-11
  Year Old Group** Ink/paper (33x49.5cm 12x19in)
  London 1999

GILES Godfrey Douglas 1857-1941 **[23]**
  $3 808 - €4 422 - £2 676 - FF29 008
  «The Prospect» Oil/canvas (61x50.5cm 24x19in)
  Stockholm 2001
  $916 - €850 - £550 - FF5 576
  Black Horse in a Stable Oil/canvas (28x34cm
  11x13in) Carlisle, Cumbria 1999

GILES Howard Everett 1876-1955 **[5]**
  $2 000 - €2 275 - £1 387 - FF14 920
  «Northern Shores» Oil/canvas (76x91cm 30x36in)
  Cincinnati OH 2000

GILES James William 1801-1870 **[35]**
  $10 424 - €9 443 - £6 500 - FF61 940
  Trees at Castle Fraser, Aberdeenshire Oil/card-
  board (35.5x53.5cm 13x21in) Glasgow 1999
  $1 426 - €1 482 - £900 - FF9 721
  Fishing on the Dee Oil/panel (25.5x35.5cm 10x13in)
  London 2000

GILES John 1885-? **[3]**
  $4 560 - €4 324 - £2 849 - FF28 361
  Circular Quay Oil/board (27.5x44cm 10x17in)
  Woollahra, Sydney 1999

GILES John West XIX **[5]**
  $304 - €302 - £190 - FF1 979
  The Coxeter Coat Lithograph (48x73cm 18x28in)
  London 1999

GILES Tony 1925-1994 **[36]**
  $269 - €289 - £180 - FF1 893
  Limmifet Mine Oil/board (50x76cm 20x30in) Par,
  Cornwall 2000

GILETTA Jean XIX-XX **[5]**
  $1 089 - €1 220 - £758 - FF8 000
  Italie, Riviera Tirage albuminé (21x27cm 8x10in) Paris
  2001

GILFILLAN Tom XX **[11]**
  $621 - €597 - £380 - FF3 916
  «Caledonian Canal, LMS» Poster (100x62cm
  39x24in) London 1999

GILHOOLEY David James 1943 **[61]**
  $1 300 - €1 099 - £775 - FF7 206
  **Large Baked Potato with Sour Cream and
  Frogs** Glazed ceramic (H23cm H9in) San-Francisco
  CA 1998

GILI Y ROIG Baldomero 1837-1926 **[19]**
  $3 000 - €3 003 - £1 850 - FF19 700
  Pueblo de Cataluña Oleo/lienzo (80x56cm 31x22in)
  Madrid 2001
  $594 - €661 - £407 - FF4 334
  Lavandera en el río Oleo/lienzo (22x28cm 8x11in)
  Madrid 2001
  $255 - €300 - £185 - FF1 970
  El camino Acuarela/papel (13x24cm 5x9in) Madrid
  2001

GILIOLI Émile 1911-1977 **[190]**
  $2 948 - €3 354 - £2 079 - FF22 000
  Babet Bronze (H49cm H19in) Paris 2001
  $690 - €686 - £432 - FF4 500
  Composition Pastel (64.5x50.5cm 25x19in) Paris
  1999

$82 - €77 - £49 - FF503
  White Sun Farbserigraphie (57.5x48cm 22x18in)
  Stuttgart 1999

GILL André Gosset de Gui. 1840-1885 **[11]**
  $32 430 - €35 826 - £22 489 - FF235 000
  Portraits Huile/panneau (55x36cm 21x14in) Enghien
  2001

GILL DeLancey Walker 1859-1940 **[3]**
  $4 250 - €5 138 - £2 967 - FF33 700
  Landscape at Twilight Oil/board (47x67cm 18x26in)
  Bethesda MD 2000

GILL Edmund Ward 1820-1894 **[55]**
  $3 946 - €3 381 - £2 372 - FF22 180
  Landschaft mit Wasserfall und Ziegen
  Öl/Leinwand (38x58.5cm 14x23in) Zürich 1998
  $2 005 - €2 021 - £1 250 - FF13 254
  On the Conway, North Wales, The River Stealing
  Oil/panel (39x29cm 15x11in) London 2000
  $1 295 - €1 451 - £900 - FF9 516
  Irish Abbeys and Castles Pencil (31.5x44cm
  12x17in) London 2001

GILL Edward act.1842-1872 **[1]**
  $4 290 - €4 809 - £3 000 - FF31 544
  **Rocky Scene with Waterfall/Waterfall, Scottish
  Scene** Oil/canvas (40x61cm 15x24in) London 2001

GILL Eric 1882-1940 **[149]**
  $5 268 - €4 951 - £3 200 - FF32 478
  Madonna and Child, suckling Plaster (H16cm
  H6in) London 1999
  $1 012 - €1 179 - £700 - FF7 735
  Crouched Nude Pencil/paper (24x30cm 9x11in)
  London 2000
  $193 - €218 - £135 - FF1 432
  Skaters Copper engraving (12x12cm 4x4in) Swindon,
  Wiltshire 2001

GILL F.H. XIX **[1]**
  $6 912 - €6 708 - £4 303 - FF44 000
  La promenade à cheval Huile/toile (52x67cm
  20x26in) Montfort L'Amaury 1999

GILL Mariquita 1915 **[5]**
  $11 363 - €9 401 - £6 664 - FF62 233
  «A bit of my garden, Giverny» Oil/canvas
  (32x40cm 12x16in) Marshfield MA 1998

GILL Samuel Thomas 1818-1880 **[73]**
  $3 048 - €3 595 - £2 149 - FF23 580
  Night Corroboree Watercolour, gouache/paper
  (30x42cm 11x16in) Woollahra, Sydney 2001
  $114 - €132 - £80 - FF869
  Ophir at the Junction Lithograph (32x25cm 12x9in)
  Sydney 2000

GILL William Ward 1823-1894 **[18]**
  $600 - €650 - £400 - FF4 265
  View of a Waterfall Oil/board (26.5x20cm 10x7in)
  Billingshurst, West-Sussex 2000

GILLAR Rob XIX-XX **[3]**
  $7 500 - €7 025 - £4 611 - FF46 080
  Arrival of the Caravan Oil/canvas (80x127cm
  31x50in) New-York 1999

GILLARD William XIX **[13]**
  $4 969 - €4 694 - £3 100 - FF30 793
  The Day's Bag Oil/canvas (60x90cm 23x35in)
  Perthshire 1999

GILLBERG Jacob 1724-1793 **[6]**
  $6 210 - €5 406 - £3 870 - FF35 460
  Puerto con faro y pescadores Oleo/lienzo
  (68x85cm 26x33in) Madrid 1999

GILLBERG Jakob Axel 1769-1845 **[17]**
- $375 - €422 - £260 - FF2 765
  Porträtt av Gustaf Erik Ruuth Miniature (7.5x6cm 2x2in) Stockholm 2000

GILLCHREST Joan 1918 **[33]**
- $1 243 - €1 320 - £820 - FF8 661
  Sancred - The Church and Memorial Oil/board (56x48cm 22x18in) Penzance, Cornwall 2000
- $261 - €243 - £160 - FF1 594
  The Well Wisher's figures before a house Oil/cardboard (17x12cm 7x5in) Penzance, Cornwall 1999

GILLE Christian Friedrich 1805-1899 **[20]**
- $2 896 - €3 323 - £1 981 - FF21 800
  Jäger mit angelegtem Gewehr und schnuppern- dem Jagdhund vor Gebüsch Öl/Leinwand (21.5x25.5cm 8x10in) Berlin 2000

GILLEMANS Jan Pauwel I 1618-c.1680 **[46]**
- $13 018 - €15 104 - £8 988 - FF99 079
  Stilleben mit Früchten, Schinken, Austern und Gläsern Öl/Leinwand (58x84cm 22x33in) Luzern 2000
- $21 068 - €20 004 - £12 912 - FF131 216
  Blumen in einer Glasvase Huile/panneau (39.5x28cm 15x11in) Zürich 1999

GILLEMANS Jan Pauwel II 1651-1704 **[36]**
- $10 467 - €11 891 - £7 324 - FF78 000
  Nature morte à la guirlande de fruits ornant une fontaine Huile/toile (52x37cm 20x14in) Paris 2001
- $6 770 - €6 268 - £4 280 - FF41 113
  Grapes, Apples, Figs, Melons, Cherries, Raspberries in a Bowl Oil/canvas (29.5x37.5cm 11x14in) London 1999

GILLER William c.1805-c.1870 **[8]**
- $391 - €383 - £250 - FF2 511
  John Myton, Esquire of Halson Salop, riding to Hounds in Landscape Engraving (53x61cm 21x24in) Leominster, Herefordshire 1999

GILLES Barthel 1891-1977 **[43]**
- $2 077 - €2 454 - £1 467 - FF16 098
  Waldlichtung Öl/Leinwand (65x55.5cm 25x21in) Köln 2001
- $4 020 - €4 410 - £2 730 - FF28 927
  Hyazinthe Oil/panel (41x32cm 16x12in) Berlin 2000
- $952 - €1 022 - £637 - FF6 707
  Schwertlilien und Klatschmohn Aquarell/Papier (40.7x54.3cm 16x21in) Köln 2000

GILLES Werner 1894-1961 **[211]**
- $3 061 - €3 410 - £2 003 - FF22 370
  Stilleben Oil/panel (49x60cm 19x23in) München 2000
- $5 853 - €6 647 - £4 067 - FF43 600
  Der Priesterschüler Öl/Karton (43x29.5cm 16x11in) München 2001
- $1 499 - €1 764 - £1 058 - FF11 570
  Fischer mit Booten am Strand Aquarell, Gouache (46x60.5cm 18x23in) Berlin 2001
- $337 - €384 - £235 - FF2 516
  «Der Junge Tobias» Farblithographie (37.5x51cm 14x20in) München 2000

GILLES-MURIQUE Jeannine 1924 **[53]**
- $1 778 - €1 829 - £1 128 - FF12 000
  Archias Huile/toile (81x100cm 31x39in) Paris 2000

GILLESPIE George K. 1924-1996 **[62]**
- $4 246 - €4 825 - £2 932 - FF31 650
  Bundorragh River, Delphi, Connemara Oil/canvas (50x76cm 20x30in) Dublin 2000

- $1 748 - €2 032 - £1 229 - FF13 326
  Donegal Landscape Oil/canvas/board (20x23cm 7x9in) Dublin 2001

GILLESPIE Gregory 1936-2000 **[3]**
- $45 000 - €50 403 - £31 266 - FF330 624
  Portrait of a Painter Oil/board (58.5x50.5cm 23x19in) New-York 2001

GILLESPIE Jessie 1888-1972 **[4]**
- $4 500 - €5 012 - £2 943 - FF32 878
  Magazine cover: Young woman at writing desk with floral lamp Gouache/paper (40x29cm 16x11in) New-York 2000

GILLET Frédéric 1814-1884 **[2]**
- $5 500 - €6 382 - £3 797 - FF41 860
  Place de la République/Place Bastille Oil/canvas (33x45cm 13x18in) New-York 2000

GILLET Roger-Edgard 1924 **[196]**
- $8 049 - €7 620 - £5 000 - FF49 984
  Réunion de parents d'élèves Oil/canvas (97x130cm 38x51in) London 1999
- $2 385 - €2 211 - £1 483 - FF14 500
  Personnage accoudé Huile/toile (92x65cm 36x25in) Arles 1999
- $399 - €403 - £249 - FF2 643
  Komposition Oil/canvas (40x33cm 15x12in) Köbenhavn 2000
- $279 - €250 - £171 - FF1 700
  Sans titre Encre/papier (45x37cm 17x14in) Paris 1999

GILLHAUSEN Rolf 1922 **[12]**
- $814 - €971 - £581 - FF6 372
  John F.Kennedy, Reise in die Nacht Photograph (28.3x41.3cm 11x16in) München 2000

GILLI Alberto Maso 1840-1894 **[2]**
- $45 000 - €50 254 - £28 818 - FF329 647
  Soldiers Combing their Hair Oil/canvas (100x175.5cm 39x69in) New-York 2000

GILLI Claude 1938 **[61]**
- $2 148 - €2 439 - £1 470 - FF16 000
  La prairie Huile/panneau (57x76cm 22x29in) Paris 2000
- $3 530 - €4 269 - £2 466 - FF28 000
  Ex-Voto Technique mixte (30.5x20.5cm 12x8in) Paris 2000
- $4 413 - €5 336 - £3 083 - FF35 000
  Coulée de cinq pots Sculpture bois (250x195x60cm 98x76x23in) Paris 2000

GILLIAM Sam 1933 **[34]**
- $5 500 - €6 354 - £3 851 - FF41 679
  «Clear Around» Oil/canvas (132x122cm 51x48in) Bethesda MD 2001
- $400 - €462 - £280 - FF3 031
  Untitled Watercolour/paper (91.5x61cm 36x24in) Bethesda MD 2001
- $500 - €580 - £355 - FF3 804
  «Coffee Thyme II» Screenprint in colors (76x103cm 29x40in) Washington 2000

GILLIES William George 1898-1973 **[142]**
- $10 759 - €11 549 - £7 200 - FF75 755
  Autumn Landscape Oil/canvas (56x71cm 22x27in) Edinburgh 2000
- $3 999 - €3 995 - £2 500 - FF26 205
  Still Life of Melon and Jug Oil/canvas (25.5x52cm 10x20in) Edinburgh 1999
- $2 881 - €2 850 - £1 800 - FF18 692
  The Croft, Kirkord Watercolour/paper (38x56cm 14x22in) Glasgow 1999

GILLIG Jacob 1636-1701 **[14]**
- $5 927 - €5 800 - **£3 800** - FF38 046
  Pike, Carp, Roach and other fish in a Landscape with Baskets Oil/canvas (74.5x101cm 29x39in) London 1999

GILLIS Nicolaes 1580-1632 **[2]**
- $82 186 - €88 220 - **£55 000** - FF578 688
  Still Life of Fraises-de-Bois in a Wan-Li Porcelain Bowl, Redcurrants Oil/panel (19x21cm 7x8in) London 2000

GILLOT Claude 1673-1722 **[19]**
- $43 334 - €46 516 - **£29 000** - FF305 126
  La Passion de la Guerre Red chalk/paper (18x35.5cm 7x13in) London 2000
- $390 - €381 - **£247** - FF2 500
  Les Sabbats: Est-ce un enchantement/Errant pendant la nuit Eau-forte (24.5x33.5cm 9x13in) Paris 1999

GILLOT Eugène Louis 1867-1925 **[70]**
- $2 269 - €2 287 - **£1 414** - FF15 000
  Londres Huile/toile (49.5x59cm 19x23in) Paris 2000
- $367 - €396 - **£253** - FF2 600
  Bord de Seine Aquarelle/papier (13x19cm 5x7in) Quimper 2001

GILLRAY James 1756/57-1815 **[294]**
- $3 538 - €4 103 - **£2 500** - FF26 917
  Seated Prisoner, reading a Book, three Head Studies Ink (17.5x11.5cm 6x4in) London 2001
- $1 119 - €1 078 - **£700** - FF7 070
  Tiddy-Doll, the great French Gingerbread Baker Etching (38x26cm 14x10in) London 1999

GILMAN Harold 1876-1919 **[26]**
- $11 924 - €14 214 - **£8 500** - FF93 239
  Landscape, Somerset Oil/canvas (51x77cm 20x30in) London 2000
- $7 226 - €6 672 - **£4 500** - FF43 765
  Romney Marsh Oil/canvas (25.5x35.5cm 10x13in) London 1999

GILMET Roberto 1947 **[4]**
- $540 - €601 - **£370** - FF3 940
  Escultura de hombre Oleo/cartón (33.5x10cm 13x3in) Madrid 2001

GILMOUR Leon 1907-1989 **[5]**
- $500 - €593 - **£344** - FF3 889
  Cement Finishers Woodcut (26x21cm 10x8in) New-York 2000

GILOT Françoise 1921 **[59]**
- $7 580 - €7 499 - **£4 726** - FF49 190
  Le tribut de Minos Öl/Leinwand (100x81cm 39x31in) Luzern 1999
- $5 770 - €6 555 - **£4 050** - FF43 000
  Seule Huile/toile (41x33cm 16x12in) Paris 2001
- $846 - €838 - **£513** - FF5 500
  La chouette au clair de lune Aquarelle/papier (33x25cm 12x9in) Paris 2000

GILPIN Laura 1891-1979 **[64]**
- $4 500 - €3 757 - **£2 673** - FF24 644
  Young Trees Gelatin silver print (25x35cm 9x13in) New-York 1998

GILPIN Sawrey 1733-1807 **[54]**
- $30 106 - €33 030 - **£20 000** - FF216 660
  Groom offering a feeding Sieve to a Bay Pony, in a wooded Landscape Oil/canvas (96.5x131cm 37x51in) London 2000

- $15 806 - €17 341 - **£10 500** - FF113 751
  Mare and Stallion in a wooded Landscape, beside a Lake Oil/canvas (63.5x72.5cm 25x28in) London 2000
- $4 800 - €5 708 - **£3 421** - FF37 444
  A Chestnut Horse Oil/panel (11x16cm 4x6in) New-York 2000
- $1 424 - €1 473 - **£900** - FF9 663
  Horses and a Donkey by a Rocky Outcrop Watercolour (45.5x66cm 17x25in) London 2000

GILPIN William, Rev. 1724-1804 **[22]**
- $285 - €252 - **£170** - FF1 654
  Lake and Mountainous Landscape Wash (16.5x25.5cm 6x10in) London 1998

GILQUIN François c.1695-1750 **[1]**
- $1 563 - €1 751 - **£1 089** - FF11 488
  Författarinna Marianne Greenwood Pencil/paper (27x21cm 10x8in) Stockholm 2001

GILROY John Thomas Young 1898-1985 **[79]**
- $527 - €490 - **£320** - FF3 213
  Portrait of Lord Mountbatten of Burma Bodycolour (36x25cm 14x9in) London 1998
- $833 - €854 - **£520** - FF5 605
  «A Sane Lunch Party - Guinness Time» Poster (79x53cm 31x20in) London 2000

GILSOUL Victor 1867-1939 **[192]**
- $8 730 - €7 436 - **£5 250** - FF48 780
  Canal à Bruges Huile/toile (105.5x200.5cm 41x78in) Bruxelles 1998
- $1 774 - €1 611 - **£1 098** - FF10 569
  L'abbaye du Rouge Cloître Huile/toile (80x100cm 31x39in) Bruxelles 1999
- $559 - €644 - **£390** - FF4 227
  Vues de rues de Rouen Huile/panneau (39x31cm 15x12in) Bruxelles 2001

GILSOUL-HOPPE Ketty 1868-1939 **[32]**
- $559 - €595 - **£381** - FF3 902
  Le vestibule Aquarelle/papier (36x26cm 14x10in) Bruxelles 2001

GILST van Arnout 1898-1981 **[31]**
- $582 - €681 - **£415** - FF4 464
  Horses ploughing Oil/canvas (50x70cm 19x27in) Amsterdam 2001

GIMENEZ y MARTIN Juan 1855-1901 **[15]**
- $1 402 - €1 652 - **£990** - FF10 835
  La volverá! Oleo/lienzo (73x50cm 28x19in) Madrid 2000
- $201 - €216 - **£133** - FF1 418
  Casas rurales Acuarela/papel (30x23.5cm 11x9in) Madrid 2000

GIMENO Andrés 1879-? **[11]**
- $2 400 - €2 252 - **£1 500** - FF14 775
  Paisaje Oleo/cartón (23.5x30.5cm 9x12in) Madrid 1999

GIMENO ARASA Francesc 1858-1927 **[58]**
- $48 450 - €51 055 - **£32 300** - FF334 900
  Paisaje Oleo/lienzo (136x100cm 53x39in) Madrid 2000
- $20 800 - €19 521 - **£13 000** - FF128 050
  Paisaje fluvial Oleo/lienzo (76.5x115.5cm 30x45in) Madrid 1999
- $5 120 - €4 805 - **£3 200** - FF3 124
  Paisaje Oleo/lienzo (25x22cm 9x8in) Madrid 1999
- $540 - €601 - **£380** - FF3 940
  Paisaje Carbón/papel (31.5x21cm 12x8in) Barcelona 2001

G

GIMIGNANI Giacinto 1611-1681 **[29]**
- $50 000 - €64 791 - **£37 500** - FF425 000
  Allegoria della Modestia che respinge l'Ambizione in favore della Vita Olio/tela (140x157cm 55x61in) Roma 2000
- $8 000 - €8 960 - **£5 558** - FF58 777
  Truth being revealed by Time, a fragment Oil/canvas/board (86.5x99.5cm 34x39in) New-York 2001
- $913 - €920 - **£569** - FF6 037
  Einnahme von Tournay/Schlacht von Covenstein Radierung (29x41cm 11x16in) Stuttgart 2000

GIMIGNANI Ludovico 1648-1697 **[5]**
- $550 - €564 - **£344** - FF3 702
  Mythological Scene Black chalk (18x28cm 7x11in) New-York 2000

GIMMI Wilhelm 1886-1965 **[364]**
- $5 936 - €4 986 - **£3 489** - FF32 706
  «Paysanne espagnole» Öl/Leinwand (72x58.5cm 28x23in) Bern 1998
- $2 313 - €2 230 - **£1 426** - FF14 626
  Am Tisch sitzendes Paar Oil/panel (33x41cm 12x16in) Bern 1999
- $462 - €519 - **£321** - FF3 402
  Selbstbildnis auf Stuhl sitzend Charcoal/paper (32x24cm 12x9in) Luzern 2001

GIMOND Marcel 1894-1961 **[34]**
- $2 760 - €3 049 - **£1 914** - FF20 000
  Buste de Marguerite Marie Bronze (34x17cm 13x6in) Paris 2001

GINDERTAEL van Roger 1899-1982 **[103]**
- $6 831 - €6 693 - **£4 212** - FF43 902
  De stier Oil/canvas (38.5x50cm 15x19in) Lokeren 1999
- $3 376 - €3 966 - **£2 400** - FF26 016
  La palmeraie Huile/toile (32.5x43cm 12x16in) Bruxelles 2000
- $344 - €397 - **£236** - FF2 601
  Zittend naakt Charcoal/paper (74x50cm 29x19in) Lokeren 2000

GINDRA Jozef XIX **[3]**
- $1 260 - €1 271 - **£786** - FF8 334
  Playing Kittens Oil/canvas (31.5x42.5cm 12x16in) Amsterdam 2000

GINE Alexander Vasiliev. 1830-1880 **[5]**
- $18 775 - €18 168 - **£11 575** - FF119 175
  Blick auf Svjatogorsky Kloster an dem Fluss Donetz in der Ostukraine Öl/Leinwand (60x79cm 23x31in) Wien 1999

GINER BUENO Luis 1935 **[9]**
- $870 - €901 - **£555** - FF5 910
  Begonias y granadas Oleo/lienzo (65x46cm 25x18in) Barcelona 2000

GINER Vicente c.1640-c.1680 **[6]**
- $52 700 - €51 055 - **£32 300** - FF334 900
  Capricho arquitectónico con figuras Oleo/lienzo (120x195cm 47x76in) Madrid 1999
- $21 000 - €18 019 - **£12 900** - FF118 200
  Capricho arquitectónico Oleo/lienzo (73.5x97cm 28x38in) Madrid 1998

GINESI Edna 1902 **[4]**
- $4 751 - €4 941 - **£3 000** - FF32 409
  The Auction Oil/canvas (64x81.5cm 25x32in) London 2000

GINGELEN van Jacques 1801-1864 **[17]**
- $3 744 - €4 462 - **£2 682** - FF29 268
  Petit baigneur et pêcheur près d'un village portuaire Huile/toile (68x106cm 26x41in) Bruxelles 2000
- $1 030 - €942 - **£645** - FF6 178
  Landskab med hyrdedreng og kvaeg Oil/panel (31x40cm 12x15in) København 1999

GINKEL Johan Godfried 1827-1863 **[1]**
- $2 980 - €2 949 - **£1 824** - FF19 347
  Catharijne Poort, Utrecht Oil/panel (25x33.5cm 9x13in) Amsterdam 2000

GINNER Charles 1878-1952 **[54]**
- $11 924 - €14 214 - **£8 500** - FF93 239
  The Building of HMS The Prince of Wales Oil/canvas (51x38cm 20x14in) London 2000
- $2 059 - €2 211 - **£1 377** - FF14 500
  Le chemin aux peupliers Huile/toile (46x33cm 18x12in) Paris 2000
- $5 543 - €5 764 - **£3 500** - FF37 811
  Batheaston Watercolour (40x28cm 15x11in) London 2000

GINOVSZKY Josef 1800-1857 **[3]**
- $3 971 - €4 724 - **£2 834** - FF30 985
  Winterliche Jagdgesellschaft Öl/Karton (33x42cm 12x16in) Wien 2000

GINSBERG Allen 1926-1997 **[31]**
- $800 - €747 - **£483** - FF4 901
  Tyger Felt pen/paper (61x45.5cm 24x17in) New-York 1999
- $800 - €747 - **£483** - FF4 901
  Jack Kerouac at Staten Island Ferry Dock Print (61x94cm 24x37in) New-York 1999
- $3 250 - €3 036 - **£1 964** - FF19 916
  Neal Cassady Young & Handsome Age 29 Gelatin silver print (47x31cm 18x12in) New-York 1999

GIOJA Belisario 1829-1906 **[45]**
- $10 000 - €9 903 - **£6 226** - FF64 958
  The Lute Player Oil/canvas (124x70cm 48x27in) New-York 1999
- $1 787 - €1 739 - **£1 100** - FF11 405
  Caught! Watercolour/paper (35x50cm 13x19in) London 1999

GIOJA Camillo XIX **[5]**
- $802 - €808 - **£500** - FF5 301
  The Young Waters Carriers Watercolour/paper (46x31cm 18x12in) Newbury, Berkshire 2000

GIOLFI Antonio, abbé c.1722-1796 **[3]**
- $2 749 - €2 850 - **£1 649** - FF18 698
  Veduta del Palazzo del Sig. Marcello Durazzo Burin (45x68cm 17x26in) Genova 2000

GIOLFINO Nicolo II Ursino V. 1476-1555 **[4]**
- $5 927 - €5 800 - **£3 800** - FF38 046
  A Female allegorical Figure Ink (12x11cm 4x4in) London 1999

GIOLI Francesco 1846-1922 **[24]**
- $7 712 - €8 279 - **£5 161** - FF54 308
  Südliche Landschaft mit Beerensammlerinnen Öl/Leinwand (35.5x55cm 13x21in) Zürich 2000
- $6 900 - €5 961 - **£3 450** - FF39 100
  «Sull'Arno fuori di Porta alle Piagge, Pisa» Olio/cartone (20x27cm 7x10in) Prato 1999

GIOLI Luigi 1854-1947 **[79]**
- $9 200 - €11 922 - **£6 900** - FF78 200
  Buttero a cavallo Olio/tavola (61x39cm 24x15in) Milano 2000

$3 600 - €3 110 - **£2 400** - FF20 400
Caccia al cinghiale Olio/tavola (32.5x14cm 12x5in)
Prato 1998

$1 320 - €1 140 - **£880** - FF7 480
Il Guado Disegno (28x42cm 11x16in) Firenze 1998

GIONIMA Antonio 1697-1732 **[12]**

$95 000 - €98 482 - **£57 000** - FF646 000
Muzio scevola dinnanzi a re porsenna Olio/tela
(151x198cm 59x77in) Milano 2000

GIORDANO Felice 1880-1964 **[154]**

$2 400 - €2 488 - **£1 440** - FF16 320
Mercatino in città Olio/tavola (35x50cm 13x19in)
Milano 2000

$1 100 - €942 - **£667** - FF6 181
Busy Day at Market Oil/board (22x27cm 9x11in)
New-York 1999

GIORDANO Luca Fa Presto 1632-1705 **[170]**

$55 000 - €61 604 - **£38 214** - FF404 096
**Saint Gregory interceding with the Madonna for
Souls in Purgatory** Oil/canvas (153x194cm 60x76in)
New-York 1999

$30 142 - €25 663 - **£18 000** - FF168 337
Saint John the Evangelist Oil/canvas (85x110.5cm
33x43in) London 1998

$3 000 - €2 592 - **£1 880** - FF17 000
Fuga in Egitto Sanguina (44x31cm 17x12in) Milano
1999

$269 - €307 - **£187** - FF2 012
Christus, Maria und St.Anna Radierung
(32.8x25.3cm 12x9in) Hamburg 2000

GIORGETTI Angelo 1899-1960 **[26]**

$783 - €891 - **£543** - FF5 847
Liegender Frauenakt Öl/Leinwand (54x65cm
21x25in) Zofingen 2000

GIOVANNELLI Roberto 1947 **[2]**

$700 - €726 - **£420** - FF4 760
Come un flusso Tecnica mista/carta (73.5x98.5cm
28x38in) Prato 1999

GIOVANNI di Luigi 1856-1938 **[10]**

$720 - €933 - **£540** - FF6 120
Giovane modella Acquarello/carta (26x18cm 10x7in)
Milano 2000

GIOVANNI DI PIAMONTE XV **[1]**

$75 000 - €65 787 - **£45 540** - FF431 535
Saint Stephen and Saint Lawrence, a Diptych
Oil/panel (164x45cm 64x17in) New-York 1999

GIOVANNINI Vincenzo 1816/17-c.1885 **[17]**

$10 619 - €10 508 - **£6 500** - FF68 928
Noblemans' Carriage Oil/canvas (46x92.5cm
18x36in) London 2000

$3 000 - €2 879 - **£1 880** - FF18 886
Roman Aqueduct Oil/canvas (25.5x54.5cm 10x21in)
New-York 1999

GIOVANNINO DI PIETRO DA VENEZIA XV **[5]**

$57 852 - €57 383 - **£36 000** - FF376 408
The Madonna and child Oil/panel (57x46cm
22x18in) London 1999

GIOVANNOZZI Ottavio XIX **[1]**

$4 749 - €4 573 - **£2 955** - FF30 000
**Buste de Léopold II, grand duc de Toscane et
archiduc d'Autriche** Marbre (H57cm H22in)
Montfort L'Amaury 1999

GIOVENONE Girolamo 1486/87-1555 **[4]**

$39 146 - €36 613 - **£24 000** - FF240 168
Madonna and Child Oil/panel (56x38cm 22x14in)
London 1998

GIPKENS Julius E.F. 1883-1960 **[12]**

$737 - €654 - **£450** - FF4 289
«Kupferberg Gold» Affiche couleur (70x95cm
27x37in) London 1999

GIR Charles F. Girard 1883-1941 **[147]**

$235 - €198 - **£139** - FF1 300
Caruso, de l'Opéra Encre Chine/papier (11x14cm
4x5in) Paris 1998

$345 - €381 - **£234** - FF2 500
«Arlequin avant la lettre» Affiche couleur
(80x120cm 31x47in) Nice 2000

GIRALDEZ Y PEÑALVER Adolfo c.1840-c.1920 **[17]**

$3 190 - €3 304 - **£2 035** - FF21 670
Puerto de Barcelona Oleo/lienzo (60x100cm
23x39in) Madrid 2000

GIRALT Agustin **[2]**

$3 920 - €4 205 - **£2 590** - FF27 580
La adivina Oleo/lienzo (50x68cm 19x26in) Madrid
2000

GIRAN Émile G. 1870-1902 **[4]**

$5 467 - €5 336 - **£3 461** - FF35 000
Petit bain de soleil en bord de rivière Huile/toile
(54x65cm 21x25in) Calais 1999

$1 602 - €1 906 - **£1 142** - FF12 500
«Ouverture de la patisserie Lisboa» Affiche
(134x100cm 52x39in) Orléans 2000

GIRAN-MAX Léon 1867-1927 **[97]**

$1 296 - €1 524 - **£929** - FF10 000
Nature morte Huile/panneau (47.5x82.5cm 18x32in)
Paris 2001

$641 - €762 - **£457** - FF5 000
La ramasseuse de fagot Huile/toile (33x28cm
12x11in) Brest 2001

GIRAO José de Sousa Moura 1840-1916 **[5]**

$7 310 - €8 475 - **£5 100** - FF55 590
Rebanho ao pôr-do-dol Oleo/lienzo (16x26.5cm
6x10in) Lisboa 2001

GIRARD Albert 1839-1920 **[24]**

$3 726 - €4 116 - **£2 583** - FF27 000
La campagne romaine Huile/toile (55x80cm
21x31in) Lille 2001

$2 462 - €2 744 - **£1 656** - FF18 000
Vieille maison à Alger Huile/toile (36x40cm
14x15in) Mayenne 2000

GIRARD Alexander XX **[8]**

$270 - €302 - **£187** - FF1 983
«Snake» Silkscreen in colors (64x208cm 25x82in)
Cincinnati OH 2001

GIRARD Alexis-François 1789-1870 **[1]**

$991 - €986 - **£600** - FF6 465
La cueille des figures, After O.Guet Color lithograph (66x77cm 26x30in) London 2000

GIRARD André 1901-1968 **[94]**

$639 - €656 - **£400** - FF4 304
«Tout est plus beau...avec une Peugeot» Poster
(112x76cm 44x29in) London 2000

GIRARD Eugène Léonard 1842-1917 **[50]**

$5 181 - €5 031 - **£3 201** - FF33 000
Danseuse au Tambourin, Le Printemps Sculpture
(96x50x36cm 37x19x14in) Paris 1999

$785 - €762 - **£485** - FF5 000
Buste de femme Terracotta (44x25x18cm 17x9x7in)
Paris 1999

G

GIRARD Johann Peter 1769-1851 [6]
- $3 213 - €3 126 - **£1 978** - FF20 507
  Vue de Nidau Gouache/papier (35x43cm 13x16in)
  Bern 1999
- $978 - €933 - £595 - FF6 118
  1re Vue de Bienne Lithographie (28.8x42.4cm
  11x16in) Bern 1999

GIRARD Karine XX [62]
- $864 - €961 - £576 - FF6 304
  Niños en la playa Oleo/tabla (49x64.5cm 19x25in)
  Madrid 2000
- $538 - €640 - £383 - FF4 200
  Place de l'Opéra sous la neige Huile/panneau
  (27x22cm 10x8in) Lyon 2000

GIRARD Pierre 1806-1872 [2]
- $10 368 - €12 196 - **£7 432** - FF80 000
  **Vue de la ville de Taormina depuis l'amphithéâtre
  avec l'Etna** Huile/toile (158x219cm 62x86in) Paris
  2001

GIRARDET Edouard Henri 1819-1880 [20]
- $12 552 - €14 761 - **£9 000** - FF96 827
  Resting at Sunset Oil/canvas (72x90cm 28x35in)
  London 2001

GIRARDET Eugène 1853-1907 [129]
- $15 000 - €16 488 - **£9 612** - FF108 156
  A Game of Boules Oil/canvas (63.5x99.5cm
  25x39in) New-York 2000
- $5 500 - €4 655 - **£3 292** - FF30 538
  M.Linzeler at his Easel Oil/panel (26x41cm
  10x16in) New-York 1998
- $471 - €407 - **£280** - FF2 671
  Dogs Attacking a Bedouin Watercolour/paper
  (21.5x26cm 8x10in) London 1998

GIRARDET Jean 1709-1788 [1]
- $4 004 - €3 887 - **£2 494** - FF25 499
  Portrait of Josephe Jacob Oil/canvas (63x46cm
  24x18in) Warszawa 1999

GIRARDET Jules 1856-1946 [55]
- $4 290 - €4 573 - **£2 718** - FF30 000
  Les petites gardiennes d'oies Huile/toile
  (61x51cm 24x20in) Bayeux 2000
- $1 760 - €2 068 - **£1 250** - FF13 563
  Feeding the Chickens Watercolour/paper (53x45cm
  21x18in) Leominster, Herefordshire 2000

GIRARDET Karl 1813-1871 [92]
- $5 004 - €4 573 - **£3 063** - FF30 000
  Cérémonie sous les cèdres du Liban Huile/toile
  (43x36cm 16x22in) Paris 1999
- $2 955 - €2 849 - **£1 822** - FF18 689
  Sommerlandschaft mit Bauernhof
  Öl/Leinwand/Karton (23.5x40cm 9x15in) Bern 1999
- $214 - €244 - **£149** - FF1 602
  Kuhwitz auf dem Seelisberg Pencil/paper
  (12.5x19cm 4x7in) Zofingen 2000

GIRARDET Léon 1857-1895 [18]
- $14 000 - €13 113 - **£8 607** - FF86 017
  The Departure of the Queen Oil/canvas
  (171.5x183cm 67x72in) New-York 1999
- $750 - €728 - **£472** - FF4 777
  New Tricks Watercolour (35x59cm 14x23in) New-
  York 1999

GIRARDET Paul 1821-1893 [4]
- $4 400 - €4 933 - **£2 988** - FF32 361
  **New York, Winter Scene in Broadway, After
  Sebron** Aquatint (71x98cm 27x38in) New-York 2000

GIRARDIN de Louis Alexandre Fr. 1777-1848 [3]
- $37 052 - €42 084 - **£26 000** - FF276 055
  **View of La Brasserie at Ermenonville, with
  Sportsmen Shooting Duck** Oil/canvas (58x71.5cm
  22x28in) London 2001

GIRARDIN Julien 1824-1896 [3]
- $21 000 - €19 670 - **£12 910** - FF129 026
  Wild Flowers Oil/canvas (143x110.5cm 56x43in)
  New-York 1999

GIRARDIN Pauline, née Joannis 1818-? [7]
- $11 000 - €9 649 - **£6 679** - FF63 291
  Branch of Lilac Bodycolour (56.5x43cm 22x16in)
  New-York 1999

GIRARDON François 1628-1715 [8]
- $48 000 - €45 886 - **£30 086** - FF300 993
  Equestrian Statue of Louis XIV Bronze
  (203x86x66.5cm 79x33x26in) New-York 1998

GIRARDOT Ernest Gustave act.1860-1893 [31]
- $2 321 - €2 615 - **£1 600** - FF17 150
  The Favourite Jewel Oil/canvas (53.5x43cm
  21x16in) London 2000
- $4 353 - €4 902 - **£3 000** - FF32 154
  The Love Token Oil/canvas (38x30cm 14x11in)
  London 2000

GIRARDOT Louis-Auguste 1856-1933 [67]
- $9 810 - €8 724 - **£6 000** - FF57 223
  La sieste Oil/canvas (40x54cm 15x21in) London 1999
- $1 900 - €2 100 - **£1 317** - FF13 772
  Country House Laundry Day Oil/canvas (30x45cm
  12x18in) New-Orleans LA 2001

GIRARDOT Philippe XX [13]
- $1 269 - €1 220 - **£783** - FF8 000
  Vieux gréement dans la tempête Pastel/papier
  (60x41cm 23x16in) Bayeux 1999

GIRAUD Eugène Pierre Fr. 1806-1881 [44]
- $37 212 - €42 686 - **£25 452** - FF280 000
  La Czarda Huile/toile (105x196cm 41x77in) Paris
  2000
- $7 785 - €7 402 - **£4 858** - FF48 552
  Spanish Dancers Oil/canvas (82x65cm 32x25in)
  Melbourne 1999
- $459 - €534 - **£317** - FF3 500
  Caricature de Fernand de Preaulx Lavis (24x21cm
  9x8in) Paris 2000

GIRAUD Jean 1938 [59]
- $1 179 - €991 - **£693** - FF6 500
  Portrait de Blueberry de trois quarts Aquarelle
  (29x22cm 11x8in) Paris 1998
- $181 - €152 - **£106** - FF1 000
  Starwatcher I Sérigraphie couleurs (76x56cm
  29x22in) Paris 1998

GIRAUD Jules XIX [2]
- $14 000 - €13 864 - **£8 716** - FF90 941
  **Still life of Cherries and Peaches/Still Life of the
  Lobster** Oil/canvas (110x175cm 43x68in) New-York
  1999

GIRAUD Sébastien Charles 1819-1892 [17]
- $13 822 - €14 483 - **£8 749** - FF95 000
  Trophée Huile/toile (175x140cm 68x55in) Paris 2000
- $3 387 - €3 811 - **£2 332** - FF25 000
  Le badinage Huile/panneau (47x37cm 18x14in)
  Barbizon 2000
- $1 760 - €1 829 - **£1 108** - FF12 000
  Le couple au Rouet Huile/panneau (32.5x23.5cm
  12x9in) Paris 2000

GIRAUDON A. XIX [4]

📷 **$13 620** - €15 245 - **£9 480** - FF100 000
Ateliers d'artistes Tirage albuminé (21.5x26.5cm 8x10in) Paris 2001

GIRAUDON Charles XX [102]

🖼 **$153** - €183 - **£109** - FF1 200
Église à Manosque Huile/panneau (57x35cm 22x13in) Toulon 2000

🖼 **$127** - €152 - **£91** - FF1 000
Maison à la tour Huile/carton (33x24cm 12x9in) Toulon 2000

✏ **$127** - €152 - **£91** - FF1 000
Vieille rue Aquarelle/papier (33x24cm 12x9in) Toulon 2000

GIRAULT DE PRANGEY Joseph Philibert 1804-1892 [14]

📷 **$8 542** - €9 375 - **£5 500** - FF61 493
Central Pavilion of the Tuileries Palace, Paris Daguerreotype (11x9cm 4x3in) London 2000

GIRBAL Gaston 1888-c.1978 [28]

🖼 **$165** - €183 - **£112** - FF1 200
«Jo Privat accordéon Fratelli Crosio» Affiche couleur (80x120cm 31x47in) Nice 2000

GIRIEUD Pierre 1876-1948 [37]

🖼 **$1 232** - €1 143 - **£767** - FF7 500
Le château des Templiers à Greoux-les-Bains Huile/panneau (38x46cm 14x18in) Paris 1999

🖼 **$2 617** - €2 439 - **£1 582** - FF16 000
Paysage d'Italie Huile/carton (30x37cm 11x14in) Aix-en-Provence 1999

GIRIN David 1848-1917 [95]

🖼 **$10 179** - €9 009 - **£6 253** - FF65 000
L'embarcadère/L'arrivée à quai Huile/toile/panneau (100x225cm 39x88in) Paris 1999

🖼 **$3 637** - €3 201 - **£2 215** - FF21 000
Nature morte aux fleurs et fruits Huile/toile (107x93cm 42x36in) Saint-Dié 1999

🖼 **$448** - €534 - **£319** - FF3 500
Femme à son ouvrage Huile/carton (26.5x24cm 10x9in) Lyon 2000

GIRKE Raimund 1930 [142]

🖼 **$9 648** - €10 584 - **£6 553** - FF69 425
Caput Mortuum Öl/Leinwand (120.5x100.3cm 47x39in) Berlin 2000

🖼 **$4 144** - €3 580 - **£2 503** - FF23 482
Geschiebe Mischtechnik (64x88cm 25x34in) Köln 1998

🖼 **$2 192** - €2 556 - **£1 539** - FF16 769
Ohne Titel Tempera (34x29cm 13x11in) Köln 2000

✏ **$1 169** - €1 125 - **£721** - FF7 378
Ohne Titel Gouache/Karton (29.9x54.8cm 11x21in) Köln 1999

🖼 **$145** - €138 - **£90** - FF905
Komposition Print (70x51.7cm 27x20in) Hamburg 1999

GIROD DE L'AIN Hélène 1926 [12]

🖼 **$238** - €244 - **£149** - FF1 600
Rêveuse Rose Huile/toile (65x92cm 25x36in) Versailles 2000

GIROD-LAMBERT Claude François XVIII-XIX [1]

✏ **$1 637** - €1 518 - **£1 000** - FF9 960
The Rape of the Sabine Women, after Poussin Ink (58x72cm 22x28in) London 1998

GIRODET DE ROUCY TRIOSON Anne-Louis 1767-1824 [47]

🖼 **$112 072** - €120 301 - **£75 000** - FF789 120
Portrait of a Young Man, Half-Length, Seated in a White Shirt Oil/canvas (79x65cm 31x25in) London 2000

🖼 **$40 000** - €40 465 - **£24 424** - FF265 436
Head of a young Woman Oil/canvas (40x32cm 15x12in) New-York 2000

✏ **$8 187** - €7 592 - **£5 000** - FF49 801
Anacreon Receiving a Silver Vase From Two Standing Figures Black chalk/paper (22.5x18cm 8x7in) London 1998

GIRON Léon 1839-1914 [1]

🖼 **$2 164** - €2 428 - **£1 500** - FF15 926
The Love Letter Oil/panel (26.5x21.5cm 10x8in) London 2000

GIRONCOLI Bruno 1936 [83]

✏ **$4 392** - €4 360 - **£2 742** - FF28 602
Ohne Titel Indian ink (57x80cm 22x31in) Wien 1999

🖼 **$195** - €218 - **£132** - FF1 430
Hundederby-Objektentwurf/Objekt Scharnierkette und zwei Hanflieger Serigraph (41x58.5cm 16x23in) Wien 2000

GIRONELLA Alberto 1929-1999 [23]

🖼 **$8 500** - €10 008 - **£5 973** - FF65 648
Del greco Oil/canvas (100.5x80cm 39x31in) New-York 2000

🖼 **$585** - €548 - **£361** - FF3 592
Picador Serigrafia (65x84cm 25x33in) México 1999

GIROSI Franco 1896-1987 [7]

🖼 **$1 680** - €2 177 - **£1 260** - FF14 280
Paesaggio Olio/cartone (48x70cm 18x27in) Napoli 2000

GIROUX Achille 1820-1894 [15]

🖼 **$3 770** - €3 964 - **£2 366** - FF26 000
King Charles sur une chaise damassée Huile/toile (47x61cm 18x24in) Paris 2000

🖼 **$2 599** - €2 363 - **£1 565** - FF15 500
Repos après la chasse Huile/toile (40.5x32.5cm 15x12in) Aubagne 1998

GIROUX André 1895-1965 [11]

🖼 **$234** - €200 - **£140** - FF1 310
«Gorges du Tarn, Circuit au départ de Millau et Rocamadour» Poster (99.5x61.5cm 39x24in) London 1998

GIROUX André 1801-1879 [19]

🖼 **$490** - €427 - **£296** - FF2 800
Marine Huile/toile (25.5x37.5cm 10x14in) Paris 1998

📷 **$52 316** - €44 210 - **£31 117** - FF290 000
Maison près d'une rivière Tirage papier salé (27x36cm 10x14in) Paris 1998

GIROUX Antoine XX [20]

🖼 **$295** - €347 - **£211** - FF2 276
Paysage méditerranéen Huile/panneau (50x60cm 19x23in) Bruxelles 2000

GIROUX Charles c.1828-c.1890 [3]

🖼 **$67 500** - €56 634 - **£39 602** - FF371 493
Bayou Tech Landscape with River Settlement and Steamboat Oil/canvas (35x55cm 14x22in) New-Orleans LA 1998

🖼 **$13 000** - €14 366 - **£9 015** - FF94 233
On the Bayou, Rural Louisiana Landscape with Steamboat Oil/board (16x20cm 6x8in) New-Orleans LA 2001

G

GIROUX Ernest 1851-? [4]
$11 000 - €10 564 - **£6 816** - FF69 293
The boating Party Oil/canvas (15x18.3cm 5x7in)
Bethesda MD 1999

GIRSIK Jozsef 1804-1857 [2]
$14 946 - €14 316 - **£9 405** - FF93 909
**Bildnis einer jungen Dame der guten
Gesellschaft** Öl/Leinwand (88x108cm 34x42in)
Stuttgart 1999

GIRTIN Thomas 1775-1802 [60]
$8 795 - €8 470 - **£5 500** - FF55 557
**Okehampton Castle, Devon, with Cattle and a
Herdsman in the foreground** Watercolour
(10x13.5cm 3x5in) London 1999

GISBERT Antonio 1835-1901 [13]
$9 591 - €9 507 - **£6 000** - FF62 364
The Arrival of the Pilgrim Fathers Oil/canvas
(58x80.5cm 22x31in) London 1999
$560 - €601 - **£378** - FF3 940
Apunte de escena valenciana Oleo/tabla (38x30cm
14x11in) Madrid 2000

GISBERT Roca XX [1]
$1 710 - €1 802 - **£1 140** - FF11 820
Hiladora ibicenca Carboncillo (64x49cm 25x19in)
Madrid 2000

GISCHIA Léon 1903-1991 [132]
$2 000 - €2 073 - **£1 200** - FF13 600
Composizione viola, verde e blue Idropittura/tela
(65x92cm 25x36in) Vercelli 1999
$749 - €777 - **£449** - FF5 098
Senza titolo Olio/tela (30x20cm 11x7in) Milano 1999
$356 - €305 - **£214** - FF2 000
Tauréador Encre/papier (16x10cm 6x3in) Paris 1998

GISELA Josef 1851-1899 [13]
$11 712 - €12 504 - **£8 000** - FF82 024
The Chessplayers Oil/panel (43x35cm 16x13in)
Billingshurst, West-Sussex 2001

GISLANDER William 1890-1937 [123]
$639 - €606 - **£397** - FF3 972
Marker ved hösttid med flyvende aender Oil/can-
vas (69x80cm 27x31in) København 1999

GISSING Roland 1895-1967 [181]
$1 072 - €1 183 - **£709** - FF7 757
Saddle Mountain Oil/canvas (56x76cm 22x29in)
Vancouver, BC. 2000
$648 - €749 - **£454** - FF4 915
Bow Lake Oil/canvas (30x40cm 12x16in) Calgary,
Alberta 2001

GISSON André 1928 [305]
$2 800 - €2 554 - **£1 721** - FF16 755
Floral Still Lifes Oil/canvas (40x50cm 16x20in) New-
York 1999
$1 600 - €1 723 - **£1 101** - FF11 303
Les jeunes filles dans le musée Oil/canvas
(22x30cm 9x12in) New-York 2001

GITTARD Alexandre 1832-1904 [23]
$11 000 - €12 936 - **£7 887** - FF84 852
The Old Bridge, Touraine Oil/canvas (54.5x110.5cm
21x43in) New-York 2001
$922 - €1 037 - **£643** - FF6 802
Landschaft bei Gewitterstimmung Oil/panel
(15x26.5cm 5x10in) Luzern 2001

GIUDICI del Luigi XVIII-XIX [4]
$8 143 - €7 927 - **£5 002** - FF52 000
Scène de danse villageoise/La fileuse
Aquarelle/papier (37.5x27.5cm 14x10in) Paris 1999

GIULIANI Giovanni 1663-1744 [3]
$20 000 - €19 956 - **£12 174** - FF130 902
Austrian Figures, Pieta and two Angels Terracotta
(H21cm H8in) New-York 2000

GIULIANO Bartolomeo 1825-1909 [25]
$36 400 - €34 464 - **£22 750** - FF226 070
Galante Szene Öl/Leinwand (113x155cm 44x61in)
Praha 1999
$4 500 - €5 218 - **£3 188** - FF34 226
The Daydreamer Oil/canvas (41.5x50cm 16x19in)
New-York 2000
$1 200 - €1 555 - **£900** - FF10 200
Marina Olio/tela (24.5x32.5cm 9x12in) Vercelli 2000

GIULIANO DI SIMONE act.c.1389 [1]
$50 000 - €53 484 - **£34 090** - FF350 835
The Crucifixion: a fragment Tempera/panel
(30.5x37cm 12x14in) New-York 2001

GIUNTA Joseph 1911 [132]
$634 - €600 - **£394** - FF3 937
Fleurs Huile/carton/toile (61x51cm 24x20in) Montréal
1999
$336 - €309 - **£201** - FF2 030
Autumn, Ste-Adèle, Qué Huile/panneau
(20.5x25.5cm 8x10in) Montréal 1999

GIUNTOTARDI Filippo 1768-1831 [9]
$1 943 - €2 086 - **£1 300** - FF13 682
The Dancing Bear Watercolour/paper (21x32cm
8x12in) London 2000

GIUSTI Guglielmo 1824-c.1916 [48]
$2 531 - €2 659 - **£1 596** - FF17 440
**Oberitalienische Landschaft mit figürlicher
Staffage auf einer Brücke** Öl/Leinwand (29x38cm
11x14in) Heidelberg 2000
$1 476 - €1 433 - **£935** - FF9 390
Südliche Küstenlandschaft Gouache/board
(27.5x40cm 10x15in) München 1999

GIUSTO Fausto XIX-XX [22]
$5 702 - €5 190 - **£3 500** - FF34 044
Fishermen unloading their Catch Oil/canvas
(84x112cm 33x44in) London 1999
$2 873 - €3 222 - **£1 950** - FF21 138
Promenade sur la digue d'Ostende Huile/toile
(29.5x50cm 11x19in) Bruxelles 2000
$2 539 - €3 001 - **£1 800** - FF19 685
View of Notre-Dame, Paris Watercolour, gouache
(18x32cm 7x12in) London 2000

GIVANIAN Mo ?-1900 [8]
$3 287 - €3 529 - **£2 200** - FF23 147
Embassy Garden in Constantinople Oil/canvas
(52x71cm 20x27in) London 2000

GJEDSTED Rolf 1947 [60]
$954 - €807 - **£570** - FF5 295
«Regnbuedrömme» Oil/canvas (100x130cm
39x51in) København 1998
$559 - €538 - **£344** - FF3 528
Blå konkurbine Acrylic/canvas (100x100cm 39x39in)
København 1999

GJERDEVIK Niels Erik 1962 [63]
$837 - €938 - **£585** - FF6 156
Figurkomposition med mandsfigur i forgrunden
Mixed media (175x210cm 68x82in) København 2001

GLACKENS William James 1870-1938 [129]
$250 000 - €297 314 - **£178 175** - FF1 950 250
Two in a Garden Oil/canvas (45.5x61cm 17x24in)
New-York 2000

$19 000 – €18 332 – **£11 933** – FF120 252
Children, strollers and sailboats in a park
Oil/panel (16x21cm 6x8in) Downington PA 1999
$7 000 – €6 527 – **£4 342** – FF42 815
New York City Park Pastel/paper (22x30cm 8x11in)
New-York 1999

GLAIN Léon act.c.1748-c.1778 [3]
$5 256 – €6 250 – **£3 620** – FF41 000
**Portrait d'homme de qualité/Portrait de femme
de qualité** Pastel/papier (60x48cm 23x18in) Biarritz
2000

GLAIZE Auguste Barthélémy 1807-1893 [15]
$3 402 – €3 811 – **£2 367** – FF25 000
Portrait de jeune fille aux roses Huile/toile
(100x81cm 39x31in) Pau 2001

GLAIZE Léon P. 1842-1932 [24]
$1 800 – €2 134 – **£1 311** – FF13 997
The Secret Oil/canvas (50x60cm 20x24in) Chicago IL
2001
$1 400 – €1 317 – **£870** – FF8 642
Head of a Young Girl Oil/canvas (32x25cm 12x10in)
East-Dennis MA 1999

GLANCY Michael 1950 [9]
$55 000 – €59 037 – **£36 806** – FF387 255
Nucleic Genesis Sculpture (162.5x127x127cm
63x50x50in) New-York 2000
$12 000 – €11 455 – **£7 498** – FF75 138
Ruby Plume Sculpture, glass (24x15cm 9x5in) New-
York 1999

GLANSDORFF Hubert 1877-1964 [108]
$1 597 – €1 328 – **£937** – FF8 713
Stil Life with Flowers Oil/canvas (78x59cm 30x23in)
Amsterdam 1998

GLARNER Fritz 1899-1972 [45]
$6 000 – €6 962 – **£4 142** – FF45 666
Tondo with Echo Pencil/paper (52x33.5cm 20x13in)
New-York 2000
$1 665 – €1 973 – **£1 174** – FF12 945
Tondo Farblithographie (61x46cm 24x18in) Zürich
2000

GLASCO Joseph 1925-1996 [7]
$4 000 – €3 853 – **£2 471** – FF25 276
Reclining Figure Metal (10x31x7cm 4x12x3in)
Chicago IL 1999

GLASER Milton 1929 [17]
$1 760 – €1 501 – **£1 061** – FF9 849
Portrait of Shakespeare Watercolour (20x18cm
8x7in) New-York 1998
$93 – €109 – **£63** – FF741
«Woodstock» Poster (61x92cm 24x36in) Hoorn 2000

GLASER Otto 1915 [5]
$511 – €431 – **£300** – FF2 830
«Bioro» Poster (127x90cm 50x35in) London 1998

GLASS John Hamilton act.1890-1925 [46]
$521 – €492 – **£325** – FF3 228
Corn Stooks by a Loch/Untitled Watercolour/paper
(27x36cm 11x14in) Fernhurst, Haslemere, Surrey 1999

GLASS John Hamilton 1820-1885 [49]
$648 – €606 – **£400** – FF3 973
Lower Largo, Fife Watercolour/paper (22x35cm
8x13in) Sighthill 1999

GLASS Margaret XX [21]
$454 – €445 – **£280** – FF2 921
Early Spring Day Pastel/paper (38x48cm 15x19in)
Aylsham, Norfolk 1999

GLASS William Mervyn 1885-1965 [29]
$5 635 – €4 862 – **£3 400** – FF31 895
The Dutchman's Cap seen from Iona Oil/board
(37x45cm 14x17in) London 1998
$6 276 – €6 737 – **£4 200** – FF44 190
The Sound of Iona Oil/board (35x45cm 13x17in)
London 2000

GLATTACKER Adolf 1878-1971 [33]
$149 – €128 – **£87** – FF837
Kleopatra Pencil (23x19cm 9x7in) Staufen 1998

GLATTFELDER Hans-Jörg 1939 [22]
$4 085 – €4 870 – **£2 912** – FF31 947
«Ungleichraum III» Oil/canvas (75x136cm 29x53in)
Luzern 2000

GLATZ Oscar 1872-1958 [22]
$3 009 – €3 343 – **£2 125** – FF21 930
Resting in the Afternoon Oil/canvas (55x70cm
21x27in) Budapest 1999

GLAUBER Johannes Polidoro 1646-1726/28 [34]
$11 801 – €11 891 – **£7 355** – FF78 000
**Paysage de rivière dans la campagne romaine,
animé de personnages** Huile/toile (49x63cm
19x24in) Paris 2000
$17 336 – €16 769 – **£10 692** – FF110 000
Paysages animés Huile/toile (31.5x37.5cm 12x14in)
Paris 1999

GLAUS Alfred 1890-1971 [28]
$570 – €652 – **£402** – FF4 275
«Bergbild» Öl/Leinwand (62x55cm 24x21in) Bern
2001
$130 – €141 – **£85** – FF928
Mattenberg Watercolour (35.5x32cm 13x12in) Bern
2000

GLAX Stefanie XIX-XX [2]
$1 400 – €1 562 – **£916** – FF10 245
«Wintercurort Und Seebad Abbazia» Poster
(81.5x110cm 32x43in) New-York 1999

GLAZUNOV Ilja 1930 [3]
$5 190 – €5 450 – **£3 270** – FF35 752
Ester Schnee Öl/Karton (49x79cm 19x31in) Wien
2000

GLEASON Joe Duncan 1881-1959 [17]
$7 700 – €7 849 – **£4 824** – FF51 487
Polynesian Oil/canvas (50x40cm 20x16in) Altadena
CA 2000
$1 200 – €1 146 – **£738** – FF7 517
Afternoon Walk Oil/board (25x17cm 10x7in)
Cincinnati OH 1999

GLEESON James Timothy 1915 [207]
$16 948 – €17 639 – **£10 640** – FF115 707
The Gifts of the Techno-Magi Oil/canvas
(181x272.5cm 71x107in) Melbourne 2000
$20 345 – €19 795 – **£12 521** – FF129 849
Captives in a threatening Landscape I Oil/canvas
(61.5x49.5cm 24x19in) Melbourne 1999
$2 550 – €2 457 – **£1 576** – FF16 119
The Sentry Oil/board (14.5x12cm 5x4in) Sydney 1999
$1 052 – €1 187 – **£740** – FF7 788
Man in Psychoscape Ink (19.5x14.5cm 7x5in)
Malvern, Victoria 2001
$425 – €478 – **£276** – FF3 136
The Judgement of Paris III Color lithograph
(56.5x76.5cm 22x30in) Malvern, Victoria 2000

GLEESON Joseph Michael 1861-? [2]
$6 000 – €6 720 – **£4 083** – FF44 083
Mowgli and his Animal Friends Watercolour,
gouache/paper (69x36cm 27x14in) New-York 2001

G

GLEGHORN Thomas 1925 [66]
- **$1 098 – €1 038 – £684 –** FF6 806
  Souvenir No.4 Oil/canvas (175x132cm 68x51in)
  Sydney 1999
- **$478 – €499 – £301 –** FF3 270
  Park Dream Acrylic/canvas (60x60cm 23x23in)
  Sydney 2000
- **$224 – €234 – £141 –** FF1 535
  Landscape Oil/board (30x29cm 11x11in) Sydney
  2000
- **$220 – €229 – £140 –** FF1 501
  Study Gouache/paper (48x32cm 18x12in) London
  2000

GLEHN de Jane Erin Emmet 1873-1961 [8]
- **$5 669 – €6 719 – £4 000 –** FF44 072
  The White Villa Oil/board (46x61cm 18x24in) London
  2001

GLEHN de Wilfred Gabriel 1870-1951 [146]
- **$9 961 – €11 729 – £7 000 –** FF76 939
  The Artist's House at Stratford Tony, Wiltshire
  Oil/canvas (53x69cm 20x27in) London 2000
- **$2 800 – €3 179 – £1 916 –** FF20 855
  Brooklyn Bridge Oil/canvas (30.5x30.5cm 12x12in)
  New-York 2000
- **$1 290 – €1 207 – £780 –** FF7 915
  Coastal View Watercolour (31x46.5cm 12x18in)
  London 1999

GLEICH John 1879-? [32]
- **$2 184 – €2 343 – £1 482 –** FF15 366
  Bailarina árabe Oleo/tablex (61x52cm 24x20in)
  Madrid 2001
- **$1 794 – €1 533 – £1 077 –** FF10 059
  Frachtdampfer im Hamburger Niederhafen
  Öl/Leinwand (31x41cm 12x16in) Hamburg 1998

GLEICHEN Helena 1873-1947 [9]
- **$2 380 – €2 769 – £1 700 –** FF18 163
  **«Ptarmigan» a grey Hunter with Blanche
  Buxton up** Oil/board (43x53.5cm 16x21in) London
  2001

GLEICHEN-RUSSWURM von Heinrich Ludwig
1836-1901 [32]
- **$1 091 – €1 227 – £761 –** FF8 049
  Blick vonder Höhe über Hag Öl/Leinwand
  (71.5x51cm 28x20in) Lindau 2001
- **$609 – €562 – £379 –** FF3 689
  Haus am Dorfrand Gouache/paper (22.5x30.5cm
  8x12in) Rudolstadt-Thüringen 1999
- **$102 – €118 – £71 –** FF771
  Am Waldrand Radierung (17x28cm 6x11in)
  Rudolstadt-Thüringen 2000

GLEICHMANN Otto 1887-1963 [60]
- **$1 606 – €1 534 – £1 003 –** FF10 061
  Frauenbildnis Aquarell/Karton (62.4x39.1cm
  24x15in) Köln 1999
- **$215 – €204 – £133 –** FF1 341
  Die Tafelrunde Lithographie (27x21.5cm 10x8in)
  Berlin 1999

GLEIM Eduard 1812-1899 [9]
- **$2 185 – €2 165 – £1 325 –** FF14 200
  Landscape with Stream Oil/canvas (26x36cm
  10x14in) New-Orleans LA 2000

GLEITSMAN Raphael 1910-? [9]
- **$3 700 – €3 885 – £2 332 –** FF25 484
  Early American Church Oil/masonite (64x84cm
  25x33in) Cleveland OH 2000

GLEIZE Claude P. Emile ?-1892 [3]
- **$1 967 – €2 211 – £1 370 –** FF14 500
  **Elégante devant les bouquinistes sur les quais
  de Seine** Huile/panneau (40x32cm 15x12in) Cannes
  2001

GLEIZES Albert 1881-1953 [606]
- **$97 662 – €95 051 – £60 000 –** FF623 496
  Pour l'esprit, les verts ou composition Oil/canvas
  (183x148cm 72x58in) London 1999
- **$30 360 – €33 539 – £21 054 –** FF220 000
  Composition Huile/panneau (46x38cm 18x14in) Paris
  2001
- **$6 750 – €7 493 – £4 705 –** FF49 150
  «Analogue» Oil/board (18x14cm 7x5in) New-York
  2001
- **$4 823 – €5 336 – £3 349 –** FF35 000
  Femme à sa toilette Crayon (29x22cm 11x8in)
  Villeneuve-les-Avignon 2001
- **$879 – €818 – £540 –** FF5 366
  Centre Noir Lithographie (35.8x26.5cm 14x10in)
  Hamburg 1999

GLENAVY Beatrice, née Elvery 1883-1970 [18]
- **$6 007 – €5 968 – £3 743 –** FF39 146
  Owl Oil/canvas (45x36cm 18x14in) Dublin 1999
- **$5 965 – €5 005 – £3 500 –** FF32 833
  White Hand Oil/canvas (40x30cm 16x12in) Co.
  Kilkenny 1998
- **$15 053 – €16 515 – £10 000 –** FF108 330
  Muses Relief (50x25cm 19x9in) London 2000

GLENDINING Alfred Augustus, Jr. 1861-1907 [163]
- **$12 369 – €10 610 – £7 476 –** FF69 600
  **Shepherd and Flock in Tranquil Summer
  Landscape** Oil/canvas (49.5x75cm 19x29in) Toronto
  1998
- **$2 932 – €3 161 – £2 000 –** FF20 733
  On the Thames, Laleham Oil/canvas (30.5x51cm
  12x20in) London 2001
- **$4 605 – €3 868 – £2 700 –** FF25 375
  Glower Sellers on the Banks of the Seine
  Watercolour/paper (48.5x74cm 19x29in) Billinghurst,
  West-Sussex 1998

GLENDENING Alfred Augustus, Sr. act.1861-
1903/10 [52]
- **$12 401 – €11 713 – £7 500 –** FF76 833
  Alfriston, Sussex Oil/canvas (39x64.5cm 15x25in)
  Billinghurst, West-Sussex 1999
- **$12 469 – €12 359 – £7 800 –** FF81 073
  Ripley, Surrey/The Thames at Maple Durham
  Oil/canvas (31x51cm 12x20in) London 1999
- **$2 506 – €2 776 – £1 700 –** FF18 210
  The Love Letter Watercolour (19x13.5cm 7x5in)
  Billinghurst, West-Sussex 2000

GLENDENING Alfred, Jnr. or Snr. XIX-XX [87]
- **$10 922 – €10 742 – £7 000 –** FF70 466
  A Highland River with Cattle watering Oil/canvas
  (30x56cm 11x22in) Bath 1999
- **$7 846 – €8 843 – £5 434 –** FF58 004
  **On the Thames near Hampton, Surrey/River
  Scene with Man Punting** Oil/canvas (21x38cm
  8x14in) Toronto 2000

GLENNIE Arthur 1803-1890 [7]
- **$320 – €323 – £200 –** FF2 120
  **Cattle and Goats in a Mountainous Landscape
  Beside a Ruin** Watercolour (44.5x63cm 17x24in)
  London 2000

GLENNIE

GLENNIE E. Maud, Miss XIX-XX [4]
$269 - €281 - **£170** - FF1 841
Doves in the Courtyard of a Country House
Watercolour (34x21.5cm 13x8in) London 2000

GLENNIE George F. XIX [24]
$445 - €498 - **£300** - FF3 268
View in Cawdry Park, Midhurst Watercolour
(30x47.5cm 11x18in) London 2000

GLIBERT Albert 1832-1917 [2]
$15 470 - €17 352 - **£10 780** - FF113 820
Entre deux feux Huile/panneau (55.5x75cm 21x29in)
Bruxelles 2001

GLIKSBERG Chaim 1904-1970 [32]
$9 500 - €10 197 - **£6 357** - FF66 889
House Among Trees Oil/canvas (47x55cm 18x21in)
Tel Aviv 2000
$2 500 - €2 053 - **£1 452** - FF13 469
Synagogue in Safed Watercolour (36x40cm
14x15in) Tel Aviv 1998

GLINDONI Henri Gillard 1852-1913 [64]
$8 706 - €9 804 - **£6 000** - FF64 309
A Fortune in a Tea Cup Oil/panel (43x56cm
16x22in) London 2000
$1 503 - €1 450 - **£950** - FF9 511
The latest News Oil/panel (15x20.5cm 5x8in)
London 1999
$553 - €478 - **£333** - FF3 133
**Dansande kvinna med tamburin/Dansande man
med klarinett** Watercolour/paper (36x25cm 14x9in)
Malmö 1998

GLINN Burt 1925 [9]
$4 800 - €5 452 - **£3 368** - FF35 761
**Elizabeth Taylor during the filming of Suddenly
Last Summer** Gelatin silver print (24x35.5cm 9x13in)
New-York 2001

GLINTENKAMP Hendrik 1887-1946 [12]
$9 500 - €10 852 - **£6 688** - FF71 185
«The Black Barn» Oil/canvas (60x76cm 24x30in)
Pittsfield MA 2001
$1 900 - €2 153 - **£1 327** - FF14 122
Window Shopper Watercolour/paper (38x28.5cm
14x11in) New-York 2001
$160 - €184 - **£110** - FF1 207
Farm in the Valley Woodcut (10x15cm 4x6in)
Cleveland OH 2000

GLINZ Theo 1890-1962 [73]
$890 - €955 - **£595** - FF6 266
Pfingstrosen und Akelei Oil/panel (80x60cm
31x23in) Zofingen 2000
$511 - €438 - **£307** - FF2 875
«Tessiner Dorf» Oil/panel (23x26cm 9x10in) St.
Gallen 1998

GLOAG Isabel Lilian 1865-1917 [7]
$8 288 - €7 150 - **£5 000** - FF46 904
A Legend of Provence Oil/canvas (183x138cm
72x54in) London 2000

GLOCKENDON Albrecht I c.1432-? [3]
$576 - €570 - **£360** - FF3 738
The Crowning with Thorns Engraving (14x10cm
5x3in) London 1999

GLOCKENDON Georg II 1492-1553 [1]
$8 000 - €6 955 - **£4 841** - FF45 620
Coat-of-Arms Gouache (12.5x9.5cm 4x3in) New-York
1999

GLOCKENDON Nikolaus I c.1490-1533/34 [1]
$22 414 - €24 060 - **£15 000** - FF157 824
Ecce Homo/The Flagellation Oil/panel (69x32cm
27x12in) London 2000

GLÖCKNER Hermann 1889-1987 [67]
$7 144 - €7 669 - **£4 782** - FF50 308
Profil mit Lichtstrahl 26.1 Painting (29.3x23.7cm
11x9in) Köln 2001
$4 010 - €4 602 - **£2 743** - FF30 185
Zwei gleiche Dreiecke einander durchdringend
Metal (42x50x30cm 16x19x11in) Dettelbach-Effeldorf
2000
$1 692 - €2 045 - **£1 181** - FF13 415
Ohne Titel (abstrakte Komposition) Tempera/paper
(30.7x45cm 12x17in) Berlin 2000
$234 - €220 - **£145** - FF1 442
Konstruktion Farbserigraphie (36.3x25.6cm 14x10in)
Heidelberg 1999

GLOECKNER Michiel 1915-1989 [62]
$225 - €268 - **£156** - FF1 759
The Sea Oil/canvas (76x76cm 30x30in) Plainville CT
2000
$150 - €154 - **£95** - FF1 013
Abstract Mixed media (38x27cm 15x11in) Plainville
CT 2000

GLOEDEN von Wilhelm, Freiherr 1856-1931 [200]
$886 - €767 - **£538** - FF5 034
Porträt eines Jungen Photograph (21.3x16.5cm
8x6in) München 1998

GLOSSOP Allerley 1870-1955 [33]
$257 - €242 - **£160** - FF1 588
South African Mountain Range Oil/board
(26x36.5cm 10x14in) Salisbury, Wiltshire 1999

GLOVER Ablade 1934 [5]
$1 401 - €1 630 - **£1 000** - FF10 694
Market Lane I Oil/canvas (101x101cm 40x40in)
London 2000

GLOVER Henry XIX [1]
$1 917 - €1 844 - **£1 181** - FF12 095
Grand Inter-Colonial Cricket Match Lithograph
(44.5x64cm 17x25in) Melbourne 1999

GLOVER John 1767-1849 [144]
$14 373 - €13 090 - **£8 800** - FF85 867
The Port of Westminster Oil/canvas (53x76cm
20x29in) Malvern, Victoria 1998
$2 089 - €1 960 - **£1 290** - FF12 856
View of a Lake - Estuary through a Clearing
Watercolour/paper (18x26.5cm 7x10in) Melbourne 1999

GLOVER John Jnr. 1790-1868 [4]
$3 647 - €4 337 - **£2 599** - FF28 450
Mountainous Lake Landscape Oil/canvas
(80x120cm 31x47in) Woollahra, Sydney 2000
$9 349 - €10 641 - **£6 570** - FF69 798
**Sketch Book of Properties in the Longford
Region of Tasmania** Wash (14x24cm 5x9in)
Woollahra, Sydney 2001

GLOVER Sybil Mullen XX [31]
$158 - €172 - **£110** - FF1 126
On the Deben-Woodbridge Watercolour/paper
(17x33cm 7x13in) Aylsham, Norfolk 2001

GLOWACKI Jan Nepomuk 1802-1847 [2]
$2 739 - €3 054 - **£1 903** - FF20 031
Paysage de montagne Huile/toile (44x34cm
17x13in) Warszawa 2001

GLOWCZEWSKI W. XX **[3]**
🛏 **$273** - €280 - **£170** - FF1 838
«Femme et quatre tulipes» Affiche (70x50cm
27x19in) Kraków 2000

GLUCK Eugène 1820-1898 **[10]**
🖼 **$7 300** - €7 927 - **£5 054** - FF52 000
Le cabaret du pot d'étain Huile/toile (73x94cm
28x37in) Tours 2001

GLUCK Hannah Gluckstein 1895-1978 **[8]**
🖼 **$82 186** - €88 220 - **£55 000** - FF578 688
Flowering Cactus Oil/canvas (68.5x43cm 26x16in)
London 2000

GLÜCKLICH Simon 1863-1943 **[7]**
🖼 **$5 000** - €4 331 - **£3 066** - FF28 407
The Flower-Gatherers Oil/canvas (66x52.5cm
25x20in) New-York 1999
🖼 **$5 304** - €5 010 - **£3 207** - FF32 863
Visage de fillette Oil/canvas (27x21cm 10x8in)
Warszawa 1999

GLUCKMANN Grigory 1898-1973 **[64]**
🖼 **$3 243** - €3 583 - **£2 248** - FF23 500
Réunion de personnages Huile/toile (50x40cm
19x15in) Paris 2001
✏ **$4 000** - €4 412 - **£2 384** - FF22 384
The swells Watercolour (38x32.5cm 14x12in) New-
York 1998

GLUSHENKO Nicolas 1902-1977 **[10]**
🖼 **$4 000** - €4 274 - **£2 718** - FF28 038
Parisian Night Oil/canvas (100x80cm 39x31in) Kiev
2001

GLÜSING Martin Franz 1885-1956 **[28]**
🖼 **$545** - €613 - **£383** - FF4 432
Im Abendlicht heimkehrende Finkenwärder
Fischerboote Öl/Karton (53x80cm 20x31in) Hamburg
2001

GLYDE Henry Georges 1906-1998 **[107]**
🖼 **$1 497** - €1 481 - **£935** - FF9 712
Boat Houses, Sidney, BC Oil/canvas (40.5x51cm
15x20in) Calgary, Alberta 1999
🖼 **$910** - €1 063 - **£642** - FF6 970
Oak Bay, Victoria, BC Oil/board (25.5x30.5cm
10x12in) Calgary, Alberta 2000
✏ **$388** - €452 - **£273** - FF2 963
Studies for Christmas Cards Watercolour
(12x6.5cm 4x2in) Calgary, Alberta 2001

GMELIN Johann Georg 1810-1854 **[12]**
🖼 **$14 289** - €15 339 - **£9 564** - FF100 617
Fischerszene im Golf von Sorrent
Oil/canvas/panel (136.3x92.3cm 53x36in) Hamburg
2000
🖼 **$12 860** - €13 805 - **£8 607** - FF90 555
Blick auf den Monte Pelegrino bei Palermo
Oil/canvas/panel (70.4x96.2cm 27x37in) Hamburg 2000

GMELIN Wilhelm Friedrich 1760-1820 **[41]**
🛏 **$225** - €263 - **£158** - FF1 724
La Cascata del Velino à Terni/La Grotta di
Nettuno à Tivoli Eau-forte (51.5x36.5cm 20x14in)
Genève 2000

GNACCARINI Filipo 1804-1875 **[3]**
🖼 **$90 000** - €84 300 - **£55 332** - FF552 969
The Dancers Marble (H180.5cm H71in) New-York
1999

GNOLI Domenico 1933-1970 **[98]**
🖼 **$126 100** - €152 449 - **£88 100** - FF1 000 000
«La pelisse» Huile/toile (160x100cm 62x39in) Paris
2000

🖼 **$72 000** - €62 199 - **£48 000** - FF408 000
Pressed Shirt Tecnica mista/tela (92x127cm 36x50in)
Prato 1998
🖼 **$11 600** - €15 031 - **£8 700** - FF98 600
«A man and his wife» Tecnica mista/cartone
(27x19cm 10x7in) Milano 2001
✏ **$2 100** - €2 177 - **£1 260** - FF14 280
Confessional Acquarello (42x35.5cm 16x13in) Roma
2000
🛏 **$400** - €415 - **£240** - FF2 720
Le false confidenze Acquaforte (25x17cm 9x6in)
Prato 2000

GOBAUT Gaspard 1814-1882 **[47]**
✏ **$863** - €991 - **£590** - FF6 500
Bordeaux, voiliers près des quais Aquarelle/papier
(12x20cm 4x7in) Arcachon 2000

GOBBAIRTS Emile [1]
🖼 **$8 745** - €8 224 - **£5 500** - FF53 946
Extensive Street Scene with Numerous Figures
with Children Oil/canvas (76x122cm 29x48in) Co.
Kilkenny 1999

GOBBIS de Giuseppe act.1772-1783 **[5]**
🖼 **$40 000** - €35 205 - **£24 352** - FF230 932
The Nun's Parlor Oil/canvas (82x114cm 32x44in)
New-York 1999

GÖBELL Gerrit Hendrik 1786-1833 **[7]**
🖼 **$11 186** - €12 706 - **£7 848** - FF83 344
Winter Landscape with a Woodgatherer crossing a Bridge and a peasant Oil/panel (51x73cm
20x28in) Amsterdam 2001
🖼 **$13 911** - €13 613 - **£8 919** - FF89 298
A Summer Landscape with Peasants by a
Farm/Winter Landscape Oil/canvas (33.5x41cm
13x16in) Amsterdam 1999

GOBER Robert 1954 **[84]**
🖼 **$3 800** - €4 409 - **£2 623** - FF28 921
Untitled Technique mixte (56.5x35.5cm 22x13in) New-
York 2000
🖼 **$35 000** - €38 400 - **£23 250** - FF251 888
Rat Bait Mixed media (23x15x5cm 9x5x1in) New-
York 2000
🗿 **$290 000** - €272 185 - **£179 162** - FF1 785 414
Crib Sculpture, wood (114x133x84cm 44x52x33in)
New-York 1999
🗿 **$74 000** - €82 885 - **£51 415** - FF543 692
Untitled Sculpture (8x19.5x7.5cm 3x7x2in) New-York
2001
✏ **$48 000** - €55 694 - **£33 139** - FF365 328
Sink Pencil/paper (28x35.5cm 11x13in) New-York
2000
🛏 **$3 500** - €3 387 - **£2 158** - FF22 214
Untitled Offset (57x30.5cm 22x12in) New-York 1999
📷 **$50 000** - €56 903 - **£35 135** - FF373 260
«Untitled», Self Portrait Gelatin silver print
(51x40.5cm 20x15in) New-York 2001

GOBERT Julie XIX **[6]**
🖼 **$4 139** - €3 964 - **£2 605** - FF26 000
Nature morte au gibier Huile/toile (103x103cm
40x40in) La Rochelle 1999

GOBERT Pierre 1662-1744 **[26]**
🖼 **$27 979** - €31 371 - **£19 000** - FF205 783
Portrait of the young Louis XV of France, full
Length Oil/canvas (144x110.5cm 56x43in) London
2000
🖼 **$19 575** - €19 056 - **£12 025** - FF125 000
Portrait de Louise-Diane d'Orléans, princesse
de Conti en Iris Huile/toile (108x88cm 42x34in) Paris
1999

G

$3 782 - €3 811 - **£2 357** - FF25 000
Portrait de jeune femme à la robe bleue
Huile/toile (42.5x33cm 16x12in) Paris 2000

GOBILLARD Paule 1869-1946 **[18]**
$26 862 - €28 203 - **£16 927** - FF185 000
Enfants de Julie Manet dans le parc du Mesnil
Huile/toile (81x60cm 31x23in) Paris 2000

GÖBL-WAHL Camilla 1871-1965 **[50]**
$828 - €909 - **£550** - FF5 965
Peonies in a Vase with a Bowl of Forget-Me-Nots and a Beaker Oil/canvas (61x80cm 24x31in)
London 2000

GOBLE Warwick 1862-1943 **[29]**
$320 - €328 - **£200** - FF2 152
A River Landscape Watercolour (34x22.5cm 13x8in)
London 2000
$706 - €819 - **£500** - FF5 372
«Bristol, An Ideal Centre for the West Country,Express Trains by LMS» Poster
(102x64cm 40x25in) London 2000

GOBO Georges Gobeau 1876-1958 **[284]**
$401 - €457 - **£277** - FF3 000
Marine Huile/toile (16x22cm 6x8in) Angers 2000
$115 - €114 - **£71** - FF750
Sur un marché en Italie Encre (12x10cm 4x3in)
Brest 1999
$83 - €76 - **£50** - FF500
Place animée en Provence Lithographie (17x15cm 6x5in) Douarnenez 1998

GODARD Armand XIX-XX **[10]**
$10 260 - €11 412 - **£7 030** - FF74 860
Danseuse à la bulle Bronze (H91cm H35in) Madrid 2000
$3 075 - €2 895 - **£1 900** - FF18 989
St Marks's Square Ivory, bronze (H39.5cm H15in)
London 1999

GODCHAUX XIX-XX **[203]**
$1 627 - €1 524 - **£978** - FF10 000
Barque sur la grève Huile/toile (40.5x65cm 15x25in)
Paris 1999
$657 - €762 - **£453** - FF5 000
Paysage de montagne Huile/toile (32x46cm 12x18in) Toulouse 2000

GODCHAUX Alfred 1835-1895 **[65]**
$1 807 - €1 982 - **£1 199** - FF13 000
Barques de pêcheurs sur la grève, la tempête
Huile/toile (62x85cm 24x33in) Melun 2000
$2 937 - €2 744 - **£1 812** - FF18 000
Balade sur le lac près de la villa/Village au bord du lac Huile/panneau (17.5x36cm 6x14in) Melun 1999

GODCHAUX Émile 1860-1938 **[96]**
$2 119 - €2 058 - **£1 309** - FF13 500
Rivage normand Huile/toile (68x83.5cm 26x32in)
Grenoble 1999
$1 210 - €1 220 - **£754** - FF8 000
Bateau à vapeur entrant au port Huile/toile
(26.5x45.5cm 10x17in) Lyon 2000

GODCHAUX Roger 1878-1958 **[84]**
$5 044 - €4 991 - **£3 087** - FF32 742
Still Life with Dahlia's in a Vase Oil/canvas
(65x92cm 25x36in) Amsterdam 2000
$3 750 - €4 291 - **£2 579** - FF28 150
Figures of Lions Bronze (H21cm H8in) New-York 2000

GODDARD George Bouverie 1832-1886 **[8]**
$6 500 - €7 383 - **£4 561** - FF48 430
Bay Hunter by a Gate Oil/canvas (25.5x76.5cm 10x30in) New-York 2001
$2 650 - €2 454 - **£1 600** - FF16 094
Losing the Scent Watercolour/paper (102.5x154cm 40x60in) Billingshurst, West-Sussex 1999

GODDERIS Jack 1916-1971 **[103]**
$374 - €363 - **£233** - FF2 381
Still Life of Flowers Oil/canvas (80x60cm 31x23in)
Amsterdam 1999
$124 - €149 - **£89** - FF975
Heuvelachtig landschap (paysage accidenté)
Huile/carton (25x35cm 9x13in) Antwerpen 2000

GODEFROID Marie Eléonore 1778-1849 **[2]**
$18 000 - €19 749 - **£11 957** - FF129 542
Portrait de Madame Campan (1752-1822), in a Black Dress Oil/canvas (188x129.5cm 74x50in) New-York 2000
$4 830 - €5 336 - **£3 349** - FF35 000
Un jeune garçon nourrissant des petits chiots
Huile/toile (24.5x32.5cm 9x12in) Paris 2001

GODEFROY Adrien Pierre F. 1777-1865 **[2]**
$581 - €686 - **£409** - FF4 500
Le thé parisien, d'après un dessin de Harriet F.J. Eau-forte (36.5x45cm 14x17in) Paris 2000

GODEFROY Jean 1771-1839 **[7]**
$377 - €390 - **£247** - FF2 561
Batalla de Austerlitz, según F.Gerard Grabado
(55x100cm 21x39in) Madrid 2001

GODET Henri 1863-1937 **[34]**
$3 297 - €3 884 - **£2 280** - FF25 475
A Scantily-Clad Maiden seated on a Rock and Watching two Love Birds Bronze (H77cm H30in)
Cape Town 2000

GODFREY Adelaide Anne 1827-1915 **[1]**
$5 230 - €5 614 - **£3 500** - FF33 825
Floral Studies Watercolour (38x28cm 14x11in)
London 2000

GODFREY William Frederick G. 1884-1971 **[31]**
$163 - €148 - **£101** - FF969
In the Park Linocut in colors (18x25.5cm 7x10in)
Toronto 2000

GODFRINON Ernst Jean Joseph 1878-1927 **[34]**
$1 530 - €1 487 - **£936** - FF9 756
Le bouquet de dahlias Huile/toile (64x74cm 25x29in) Bruxelles 1999
$1 351 - €1 537 - **£948** - FF10 081
Les joueurs de carte Huile/panneau (27.5x36cm 10x14in) Bruxelles 2001

GODIE Lee 1908-1994 **[7]**
$1 300 - €1 478 - **£908** - FF9 698
«Prince of a City» Oil/canvas (84x130cm 33x51in)
Chicago IL 2000

GODINAU Jacobus Ludovicus 1811-1873 **[5]**
$9 495 - €11 155 - **£6 840** - FF73 170
Les musiciens ambulants Huile/panneau (82x64cm 32x25in) Bruxelles 2001
$2 925 - €3 222 - **£1 911** - FF21 138
La souricière Huile/panneau (36x28.5cm 14x11in)
Bruxelles 2000

GODLEVSKY Ivan Ivanovitch 1908-1988 **[232]**
$1 111 - €1 048 - **£700** - FF6 874
Figures by a Monastery Oil/canvas (68.5x51cm 26x20in) Godalming, Surrey 1999

GODOY CASTRO Federico 1869-1939 **[7]**
- $6 000 - €7 115 - **£4 128** - FF46 669
  Picking Grapes Oil/canvas (65.5x85cm 25x33in) New-York 2000

GODWARD John William 1861-1922 **[117]**
- $160 000 - €179 300 - **£111 520** - FF1 176 128
  At the Garden Shrine, Pompeii Oil/canvas (64x26cm 25x10in) New-York 2001
- $49 728 - €42 398 - **£30 000** - FF278 112
  Head of a Girl, the Priestess Oil/canvas (34x29cm 13x11in) London 1998
- $24 864 - €21 452 - **£15 000** - FF140 713
  A Choice Blossom Watercolour/paper (25.5x15cm 10x5in) London 1998

GODWIN Frank 1889-1959 **[8]**
- $9 400 - €10 726 - **£6 533** - FF70 356
  Untitled Oil/canvas (114x76cm 45x30in) Del Co PA 2001
- $1 600 - €1 532 - **£988** - FF10 051
  Cockfighting Scene, Story Illustration Watercolour/paper (33x66cm 13x26in) New-York 1999

GODWIN Mary 1887-1960 **[15]**
- $1 203 - €1 212 - **£750** - FF7 952
  View at 69 Fellows Road, London Oil/canvas (61x51cm 24x20in) London 2000

GODWIN Ted 1933 **[39]**
- $717 - €842 - **£506** - FF5 520
  Beaver Dam Oil/panel (45.5x61cm 17x24in) Calgary, Alberta 2000
- $647 - €753 - **£455** - FF4 938
  «Lost Creek» Oil/panel (30.5x37.5cm 12x14in) Calgary, Alberta 2001
- $910 - €1 063 - **£642** - FF6 970
  Beaver Pond Kananaskis Watercolour/paper (73.5x54.5cm 28x21in) Calgary, Alberta 2000

GOEBEL Gottfried 1906-1975 **[26]**
- $250 - €291 - **£176** - FF1 906
  «Schweine und Kartoffelkorb» Pencil/paper (30x48cm 11x18in) Salzburg 2001

GOEBEL Hermann 1885-1945 **[18]**
- $1 891 - €1 841 - **£1 161** - FF12 074
  Regennasse Strasse mit eiligen Passanten Öl/Leinwand (68x64cm 26x25in) Berlin 1999

GOEBEL Karl 1824-1899 **[81]**
- $774 - €669 - **£466** - FF4 387
  Vid lägerelden Oil/canvas (21.5x27cm 8x10in) Malmö 1998
- $749 - €727 - **£462** - FF4 767
  Dalmatiner in Tracht, aid einem Stein sitzend Aquarell/Papier (47x35cm 18x13in) Wien 1999

GOEBEL Karl Peter 1791-1823 **[7]**
- $26 410 - €28 965 - **£17 936** - FF190 000
  Portrait d'une femme en robe blanche Huile/toile (187x108cm 73x42in) Lille 2000
- $15 480 - €14 534 - **£9 600** - FF95 340
  Portrait zweier Schwestern Öl/Leinwand (95x84cm 37x33in) Wien 1999

GOEBEL Rod 1946-1993 **[8]**
- $8 000 - €9 084 - **£5 558** - FF59 584
  Quiet Springs of Jenny Oil/canvas (76x101cm 30x40in) Dallas TX 2001

GOEDVRIEND Theodor Franciskus 1879-1969 **[74]**
- $385 - €454 - **£266** - FF2 976
  De Kalkput Bij Het Inbouw Zijnde huis Rhederenk Oil/board (60.5x46cm 23x18in) Amsterdam 2000

GOEJE de Pieter 1789-1859 **[8]**
- $5 809 - €5 438 - **£3 600** - FF35 672
  Peasants and Cattle by a Cottage in a River Landscape Oil/canvas (49.5x60cm 19x23in) London 1999

GOENEUTTE Norbert 1854-1894 **[197]**
- $11 000 - €9 501 - **£6 630** - FF62 322
  Self-Portrait Oil/panel (65x67.5cm 25x26in) New-York 1998
- $5 804 - €6 403 - **£3 931** - FF42 000
  Autoportraits aux livres Huile/panneau (35x26.5cm 13x10in) Paris 2000
- $2 952 - €2 744 - **£1 792** - FF18 000
  Rêverie Pastel/papier (55x38cm 21x14in) Paris 1998
- $250 - €274 - **£169** - FF1 800
  «Bords de la Meuse à Rotterdam» Pointe sèche (20x32cm 7x12in) Pontoise 2000

GOEREE Jan 1670-1731 **[31]**
- $174 - €181 - **£109** - FF1 190
  Discuserende geleerden Ink/paper (21x16cm 8x6in) Dordrecht 2000

GOERG Édouard 1893-1969 **[531]**
- $3 958 - €4 421 - **£2 682** - FF29 000
  Le voyeur Huile/toile (64.5x54cm 25x21in) Paris 2000
- $2 356 - €2 287 - **£1 467** - FF15 000
  Figure sur fond gris Huile/toile (41x33cm 16x12in) Paris 1999
- $355 - €381 - **£237** - FF2 500
  Jeune fille au chapeau Fusain/papier (32x25cm 12x9in) Paris 2000
- $192 - €213 - **£130** - FF1 400
  Le feu d'artifice à l'exposition Eau-forte (44.5x29.5cm 17x11in) Paris 2000

GOERING C. Anton 1836-1905 **[14]**
- $1 069 - €1 227 - **£731** - FF8 049
  Salvador de Bahia, Dampfer und ankernde Segelboot Charcoal (26x36cm 10x14in) Berlin 2000

GOERITZ Mathías 1915-1990 **[22]**
- $3 604 - €4 233 - **£2 560** - FF27 764
  Salvador de Auschwitz Bronze (44x30cm 17x11in) México 2000
- $2 178 - €2 033 - **£1 344** - FF13 338
  El duende Gouache (56x41cm 22x16in) México 1999

GOETHE Franz XIX **[1]**
- $11 658 - €10 820 - **£7 000** - FF70 974
  Venus Oil/canvas (172.5x109cm 67x42in) London 1999

GOETHE von Johann Wolfgang 1749-1832 **[5]**
- $135 - €153 - **£92** - FF1 006
  Landschaften, nach A.Thiele Radierung (17.5x14.5cm 6x5in) München 2000

GOETHEM van Edward 1857-1924 **[9]**
- $787 - €750 - **£500** - FF4 918
  Boys Playing near a Village Watercolour (36x26cm 14x10in) Billingshurst, West-Sussex 1999

GOETSCH Gustave F. 1877-1969 **[27]**
- $675 - €583 - **£403** - FF3 822
  Still Life with Green Glass Bottle, Porcelain Teapot, Vase Oil/canvas/board (34x43cm 13x17in) St. Louis MO 1998
- $500 - €520 - **£313** - FF3 413
  Corona Watercolour/paper (36x46cm 14x18in) Chicago IL 2000

GOETZ Gottfried Bernhard 1708-1774 **[29]**
- $1 633 - €1 585 - **£1 016** - FF10 397
  Die hl. Rachel/Der hl. Ignatius Indian ink (11.7x9cm 4x3in) Berlin 1999

🎨 **$1 615** - €1 841 - **£1 126** - FF12 074
Die vier Erdteile Radierung (18.5x11.5cm 7x4in)
Berlin 2001

GOETZ Henri 1909-1989 [867]

😊 **$4 013** - €3 887 - **£2 524** - FF25 500
Sans titre Huile/toile (114x146cm 44x57in) Paris 1999

😊 **$1 722** - €1 829 - **£1 154** - FF12 000
Anjou Huile/toile (53x54cm 20x21in) Cannes 2000

😊 **$1 554** - €1 326 - **£937** - FF8 700
L'animal des profondeurs Huile/papier (23x25cm 9x9in) Saint-Germain-en-Laye 1998

✏️ **$1 084** - €1 220 - **£746** - FF8 000
«Jour de pluie» Pastel/toile (78x98cm 30x38in) Paris 2000

🎨 **$167** - €143 - **£100** - FF938
Nature morte Etching, aquatint (33.9x43.5cm 13x17in) Hamburg 1998

GOETZE Otto 1868-1931 [13]

🎨 **$179** - €153 - **£107** - FF1 006
Erotische Darstellung/Stehendes Mädchen in kurzem Hemdchen, Strümpfen Etching (21.5x23.7cm 8x9in) Berlin 1998

GOETZE Rolf XX [4]

🎨 **$307** - €297 - **£190** - FF1 945
«Bei Anruf Mord!» Poster (82.5x60cm 32x23in) London 1999

GOFF Frederick E.J. 1855-1931 [113]

✏️ **$1 674** - €1 740 - **£1 050** - FF11 415
Yacht, Steam Yacht and Other Vessels on the Thames Watercolour (63.5x34cm 25x13in) Suffolk 2000

GOFF Lloyd Lózes 1917-1983 [13]

😊 **$1 200** - €1 414 - **£843** - FF9 278
Monument Valley Huile/papier (30x43cm 12x17in) New-Orleans LA 2000

✏️ **$3 000** - €3 291 - **£2 037** - FF21 585
Storm Damage Tempera/paper (38x50cm 15x20in) New-Orleans LA 2000

GOFF Robert Charles, Col. 1837-1922 [37]

✏️ **$791** - €724 - **£480** - FF4 752
On The Ponte Vecchio, Florence Pencil (26x18cm 10x7in) London 1998

GOFFINON Aristide 1881-1952 [15]

😊 **$1 226** - €1 363 - **£819** - FF8 943
Vase garni de roses Huile/toile (40x55cm 15x21in) Bruxelles 2000

GOGARTEN Heinrich 1850-1911 [47]

😊 **$1 465** - €1 534 - **£929** - FF10 061
Winterabend vor dem Dorf Öl/Leinwand (35x53cm 13x20in) Bremen 2000

😊 **$961** - €1 143 - **£666** - FF7 500
Vue de Paris animée Huile/toile (35x27cm 13x10in) Paris 2000

GOGARTY Brenda St. John XX [1]

🔨 **$4 515** - €4 954 - **£3 000** - FF32 499
Head of Jack Butler Yeats, R.H.A Bronze (H42.5cm H16in) London 2000

GOGH van Vincent 1853-1890 [148]

😊 **$1 600 000** - €1 755 920 - **£1 030 240** - FF11 518 080
L'entrée du parc de Voyer-d'Argenson à Asnières Oil/canvas (54.5x66.5cm 21x26in) New-York 2000

😊 **$4 000 000** - €3 412 419 - **£2 412 800** - FF22 384 000
Les chaumières à Auvers Oil/canvas (34x41.5cm 13x16in) New-York 1998

🖊️ **$408 494** - €482 356 - **£290 000** - FF3 164 045
The Beach at Scheveningen Watercolour, gouache (28x46cm 11x18in) London 2001

🎨 **$381** - €421 - **£258** - FF2 761
Old Vineyard with Peasant Woman Lithograph (22x25cm 9x10in) Calgary, Alberta 2000

GOGIN Charles 1844-1931 [9]

😊 **$9 739** - €9 365 - **£6 000** - FF61 430
After Waterloo Oil/canvas (76x142cm 29x55in) London 1999

GOGOIS Pierre 1935 [150]

😊 **$388** - €335 - **£235** - FF2 200
Le parc du chateau Huile/toile (46x61cm 18x24in) Doullens 1999

🖊️ **$702** - €793 - **£494** - FF5 200
Le Pont des Arts Pastel (24x33cm 9x12in) Paris 2001

GOGOS Basil XX [1]

🖊️ **$3 000** - €3 360 - **£2 084** - FF22 041
Portraits of Basil Rathbone and Peter Lorre Gouache/paper (20x36cm 8x14in) New-York 2001

GÖHLER Hermann 1874-1959 [44]

😊 **$1 558** - €1 636 - **£982** - FF10 732
Sommer am Starnberger See Öl/Leinwand (70x80cm 27x31in) Heidelberg 2000

GOHLKE Frank W. 1942 [4]

📷 **$1 200** - €1 121 - **£725** - FF7 352
House and Cypress Trees/Aerial View Silver print (35x43cm 14x17in) New-York 1999

GOINGS Ralph 1928 [20]

😊 **$45 000** - €50 315 - **£30 334** - FF330 048
Interior with trash Cans Oil/canvas (96.5x132cm 37x51in) New-York 2000

GOIS Étienne P. 1731-1823 [3]

🏛️ **$23 355** - €22 867 - **£14 370** - FF150 000
Buste de jeune fille les cheveux tombant sur les épaules Terracotta (H49cm H19in) Paris 1999

GOLA Emilio 1851-1923 [33]

😊 **$31 200** - €26 953 - **£20 800** - FF176 800
Lavandaia a Mondonico Olio/tavola (75x48.5cm 29x19in) Milano 1998

😊 **$2 100** - €2 177 - **£1 260** - FF14 280
Paesaggio lombardo Olio/tavoletta (34x24cm 13x9in) Trieste 2000

✏️ **$2 856** - €2 961 - **£1 713** - FF19 420
Figura femminile Acquarello/carta (35x24.5cm 13x9in) Milano 2000

GOLAY Mary 1869-1944 [21]

🎨 **$1 343** - €1 524 - **£933** - FF10 000
«Le pavot»/«La giroflée»/«Le parfum»/«La rose» Affiche (38x31cm 14x12in) Paris 2001

GOLDBECK Eugene Omar XX [15]

📷 **$550** - €588 - **£362** - FF3 860
Freaks and Novelties Gelatin silver print (25x111cm 10x44in) New-Orleans LA 2000

GOLDBERG Eric 1890-1969 [30]

😊 **$779** - €881 - **£545** - FF5 781
Circus Couple Oil/canvas/board (51x40.5cm 20x15in) Toronto 2001

😊 **$614** - €661 - **£422** - FF4 333
Cleaning Codfish Oil/panel (24x33cm 9x12in) Toronto 2001

GOLDBERG Michael 1924 [28]

😊 **$23 000** - €22 157 - **£14 211** - FF145 339
House Oil/canvas (208x195cm 82x77in) Chicago IL 1999

G

$3 250 - €3 407 - **£2 036** - FF22 351
Oregon Territory Oil/canvas (76x88cm 30x35in)
Norwalk CT 2000

GOLDBERG Rube 1883-1970 **[17]**
$750 - €694 - **£459** - FF4 554
Baseball players distracted by woman Ink
(20x38cm 8x15in) New-York 1999

GOLDEN Rolland 1931 **[28]**
$500 - €532 - **£340** - FF3 491
Up Close Watercolour/paper (72.5x54cm 28x21in)
Miami FL 2001

GOLDENSKY Elias XIX-XX **[2]**
$3 000 - €2 821 - **£1 857** - FF18 503
Female Nude Studies Platinum print (22x17cm
9x7in) New-York 1999

GOLDIE Charles Frederick 1870-1947 **[14]**
$95 174 - €111 782 - **£67 574** - FF733 240
**Portrait of Anahe te Rahui famed Maori Carved
from Rotorua** Oil/canvas (76x63.5cm 29x25in)
Auckland 2000
$21 109 - €22 181 - **£13 896** - FF145 498
Anxious Moment «The Last Match»
Oil/canvas/board (37x42cm 14x16in) Auckland 2000
$3 126 - €2 652 - **£1 886** - FF17 397
Pipi Hacre aka Kia Ora Pencil/paper (32x25cm
12x9in) Sydney 1998

GOLDIN Nan 1953 **[382]**
$3 200 - €3 684 - **£2 183** - FF24 166
Cookie in her Casket, N.Y.C. Cibachrome print
(33x50cm 12x19in) New-York 2000

GOLDING Tomás 1909-1985 **[89]**
$1 875 - €1 963 - **£1 125** - FF12 875
Flores Oleo/lienzo (50x40cm 19x15in) Caracas 2000

GOLDSCHEIDER (Manufacture) XIX-XX **[120]**
$1 991 - €1 906 - **£1 237** - FF12 500
La laitière Terracotta (H82cm H32in) Rennes 1999
$896 - €1 067 - **£620** - FF7 000
Jeune fille à la robe à volants Chryséléphantine
(H34.5cm H13in) Paris 2000

GOLDSCHMIDT Hilde 1897-1980 **[29]**
$5 337 - €6 135 - **£3 769** - FF40 246
Stilleben mit Milchkanne Öl/Karton (85.5x40cm
33x15in) Bremen 2001

GOLDSMITH Walter H. c.1860-c.1930 **[32]**
$17 305 - €19 123 - **£12 000** - FF125 436
«Boulter's Weir, Old Windsor» Oil/canvas
(101.5x153cm 39x60in) London 2001
$1 176 - €1 306 - **£820** - FF8 564
Children by a Cottage Oil/canvas (36x67cm
14x26in) Birmingham 2001
$324 - €303 - **£200** - FF1 985
**A Farm in a Valley with Cann Hill and Melbury
Hill beyond** Watercolour/paper (33x47cm 12x18in)
London 1999

GOLDSTEEN Arthur 1908-1985 **[9]**
$303 - €354 - **£207** - FF2 321
«Parijs per Pullman» Poster (100x65cm 39x25in)
Hoorn 2000

GOLDSTEIN Jack 1945 **[23]**
$3 000 - €2 817 - **£1 858** - FF18 477
Untitled (#26) Acrylic/canvas (244x152.5cm 96x60in)
New-York 1999

GOLDSWORTHY Andy 1956 **[20]**
$5 480 - €6 055 - **£3 800** - FF39 721
Dandelions collected on the Way to Bretton
Cibachrome print (50x50cm 19x19in) London 2001

GOLDTHWAITE Harold XIX-XX **[40]**
$547 - €517 - **£340** - FF3 391
Evening in the Downs, Parham Oil/panel
(23x34cm 9x13in) Billingshurst, West-Sussex 1999

GOLDYNE Joseph XX **[6]**
$1 000 - €944 - **£621** - FF6 193
«What did You say?» Monotype (80.5x121cm
31x47in) San-Francisco CA 1999

GOLE Jacob 1660-1737 **[12]**
$428 - €511 - **£305** - FF3 353
**Violinspieler mit zwei zechenden jungen
Männern** Pochoir (24.9x19.1cm 9x7in) Berlin 2000

GOLICKE Wilhelm Alexandrow. ?-1848 **[3]**
$330 - €3 477 - **£2 072** - FF22 806
**Grinsender Bauernbursch, die Arme auf
Holztisch gestützt** Öl/Leinwand (36x28cm 14x11in)
Berlin 2000

GOLINKEN Joseph XX **[1]**
$1 100 - €1 185 - **£750** - FF7 776
Art Lovers Lithograph (36.5x44.5cm 14x17in) New-
York 2001

GOLINKIN Joseph Webster 1896-1977 **[36]**
$3 000 - €2 993 - **£1 826** - FF19 635
**Flagman, US Goal, 1930 International/Argentine
Grooms and Pony** Watercolour/paper (28x25.5cm
11x10in) New-York 2000
$450 - €420 - **£278** - FF2 753
First Round Knockout Lithograph (40x50cm
16x19in) Cleveland OH 1999

GOLLER Bruno 1901-1998 **[38]**
$9 152 - €9 909 - **£6 266** - FF65 000
Composition KRR Huile/carton (100x75cm 39x29in)
Paris 2001
$2 960 - €2 557 - **£1 788** - FF16 773
Pendeluhr Pencil (64.7x50cm 25x19in) Köln 1998

GOLLINGS William Elling 1878-1932 **[16]**
$60 000 - €64 332 - **£39 696** - FF421 992
Range Riders Oil/board (35x50cm 14x20in) Hayden
ID 2000
$38 000 - €42 768 - **£26 178** - FF280 542
Tall in the Saddle Oil/canvas (25.5x35.5cm 10x13in)
Philadelphia PA 2000
$7 644 - €8 725 - **£5 310** - FF57 232
En spejdende indianer på hesteryg Watercolour,
gouache/paper (34x28cm 13x11in) København 2000

GOLLON Chris XX **[1]**
$6 630 - €5 720 - **£4 000** - FF37 523
Mother and Daughter Mixed media/panel
(122x61cm 48x24in) London 1998

GOLOVIN Alexander Yakovlev. 1864-1930 **[19]**
$19 479 - €18 721 - **£12 000** - FF122 799
**Set Design for Scene 8, the Ballroom, in
Masquerade** Gouache (71x96.5cm 27x37in) London
1999

GOLOWKOW Gerassim S. 1863-1909 **[2]**
- $2 245 - €2 035 - **£1 383** - FF13 347
  Fischerboote im Hafen Öl/Karton (24.5x34.5cm 9x13in) Wien 1999

GOLTZIUS Hendrik 1558-1617 **[370]**
- $124 136 - €121 588 - **£80 000** - FF797 568
  Virgin and Child music-making Angels and the Annunciation Oil/canvas (134x100cm 52x39in) London 1999
- $29 014 - €26 862 - **£18 000** - FF176 202
  Portrait of a bearded man holding a Scroll of Paper Oil/panel (48.5x38cm 19x14in) London 1999
- $58 987 - €56 722 - **£36 337** - FF372 075
  Allegoric Female Figure Ink (21.5x13cm 8x5in) Amsterdam 1999
- $813 - €915 - **£593** - FF6 000
  L'Adoration des bergers, planche de la vie de la Vierge Burin (48x35.5cm 18x13in) Paris 2000

GOLTZIUS Hubert 1526-1583 **[5]**
- $1 427 - €1 470 - **£900** - FF9 641
  Icones Imperatorum Romanorum Woodcut (37x23.5cm 14x9in) London 2000

GOLTZSCHE Dieter 1934 **[34]**
- $98 - €92 - **£59** - FF603
  Kahlkopf W. Etching (14.6x9.8cm 5x3in) Berlin 1999

GOLUB Leon 1922 **[48]**
- $41 030 - €39 701 - **£26 000** - FF260 423
  The Go-Ahead Acrylic/canvas (305x487.5cm 120x191in) London 1999
- $12 000 - €13 923 - **£8 284** - FF91 332
  Pope Paul Acrylic (76x66cm 29x25in) New-York 2000
- $3 500 - €3 285 - **£2 162** - FF21 548
  Sphinx Crayon (70.5x73.5cm 27x28in) New-York 1999
- $73 - €87 - **£51** - FF570
  Selbstbildnis Farbserigraphie (20x17.9cm 7x7in) Braunschweig 2000

GOMANSKY Edmund 1854-? **[13]**
- $1 266 - €1 074 - **£751** - FF7 044
  Goldfasan Bronze (23x10cm 9x3in) München 1998

GOMBAR Andras 1946 **[23]**
- $489 - €457 - **£302** - FF3 000
  Composition aux cerises Huile/panneau (30x40cm 11x15in) Brides-les-Bains 1999

GOMES Karel 1930 **[46]**
- $923 - €908 - **£593** - FF5 953
  An elegant Lady standing Bronze (H50cm H19in) Amsterdam 1999

GOMEZ GIL Guillermo 1862-1942 **[59]**
- $3 087 - €2 853 - **£1 852** - FF18 715
  Vista de una bahia con niños jugando Oleo/lienzo (36x60cm 14x23in) Barcelona 1999
- $1 306 - €1 171 - **£799** - FF7 683
  Marina al amanecer Oleo/lienzo (37x24.5cm 14x9in) Madrid 1999

GOMEZ MARTIN Enrique XIX-XX **[16]**
- $2 002 - €2 312 - **£1 386** - FF15 169
  Maniobras militares Oleo/lienzo (41x75.5cm 16x29in) Seville 2000

GOMEZ MAYORGA Guillermo 1887-1962 **[14]**
- $14 157 - €13 217 - **£8 736** - FF86 697
  El Popocatépetl Oleo/lienzo (80x100cm 31x39in) México 1999

GOMEZ MIR Eugenio 1877-1938 **[21]**
- $930 - €931 - **£573** - FF6 107
  La torre del castillo Oleo/cartón (40.5x31.5cm 15x12in) Madrid 2000

GOMEZ MORENO Y GONZALEZ Manuel 1834-1918 **[1]**
- $15 073 - €15 668 - **£9 500** - FF102 774
  Christopher Columbus in His Study Oil/canvas (70x100cm 27x39in) Leyburn, North Yorkshire 2000

GOMEZ NEDERLEYTNER German XIX **[3]**
- $1 650 - €1 802 - **£1 140** - FF11 820
  La Dueña Oleo/tabla (33x24.5cm 12x9in) Madrid 2001

GOMIDES Antonio Gonçalves 1895-1967 **[4]**
- $5 000 - €4 814 - **£3 112** - FF31 581
  Figuras Danzantes Oil/canvas (50x60cm 19x23in) New-York 1999

GOMIEN Paul 1799-1846 **[5]**
- $1 656 - €1 817 - **£1 100** - FF11 920
  Young Lady, Full Face White Dress with Puffed Sleeves Miniature (9.5x7.5cm 3x2in) London 2000

GOMIER-PRÉVOT Marie-Eugénie XIX **[1]**
- $4 400 - €4 525 - **£2 790** - FF29 681
  Portrait of a Viennese Aristocrat Oil/canvas (68x54cm 27x21in) New-Orleans LA 2000

GOMMAERTS Fernand 1894-1975 **[8]**
- $3 108 - €3 470 - **£2 170** - FF22 764
  «Hommage à Gauguin» Huile/panneau (85.5x113cm 33x44in) Bruxelles 2001

GÖMÖRY Imre 1902-1969 **[1]**
- $4 200 - €4 628 - **£2 760** - FF30 360
  Passage Oil/canvas (70x100cm 27x39in) Budapest 2000

GONÇALVES Fausto 1893-? **[1]**
- $4 620 - €5 234 - **£3 150** - FF34 335
  Paisagem com casas e rio com lavadeiras Oleo/lienzo (61.5x66cm 24x25in) Lisboa 2000

GONCHAROVA Nataliia Sergeevna 1881-1962 **[363]**
- $60 000 - €55 548 - **£36 726** - FF364 368
  Spring Oil/canvas (242x79cm 95x31in) Chicago IL 1999
- $16 320 - €18 294 - **£11 076** - FF120 000
  Magnolias, raisins et pommes Huile/toile (46x55cm 18x21in) Paris 2000
- $2 986 - €2 744 - **£1 834** - FF18 000
  Bouquet de fleurs de cerisier Huile/carton (41.5x33cm 16x12in) Paris 1999
- $2 676 - €2 287 - **£1 606** - FF15 000
  La foire de Sorochensky Gouache/papier (41x56cm 16x22in) Paris 1998
- $1 274 - €1 368 - **£852** - FF8 972
  Judas Iscariot Pochoir (67x49.5cm 26x19in) London 2000

GONCOURT de Jules Alfred Huot 1830-1870 **[4]**
- $2 311 - €2 287 - **£1 441** - FF15 000
  Portrait de Blanche Passy à son chevalet Crayon/papier (23.5x15.5cm 9x6in) Paris 1999

GONDOUIN Emmanuel 1883-1934 **[73]**
- $1 561 - €1 524 - **£995** - FF10 000
  Bouquet de fleurs Huile/panneau (51x41cm 20x16in) Paris 1999

GONG XIAN 1599-1689 **[18]**
- $11 000 - €9 496 - **£6 571** - FF62 287
  Plum Blossom Poems in Running-Cursive Script Ink (98.5x49.5cm 38x19in) New-York 1998

GONGORO Jean & Lucien XX **[3]**
🎨 **$611** - €616 - **£380** - FF4 038
«Valais, Switzerland» Poster (102x64cm 40x25in)
London 2000

GOÑI SUAREZ Lorenzo 1911-1992 **[27]**
✏️ **$214** - €252 - **£155** - FF1 654
Cabeza de mujer gatuna Tinta/papel (39x29cm
15x11in) Madrid 2001

GONIN Francesco 1808-1889 **[135]**
🖼️ **$51 289** - €59 050 - **£35 000** - FF387 341
At the Slave Market Oil/canvas (100x126cm
39x49in) London 2000
🖼️ **$1 452** - €1 645 - **£990** - FF10 791
Retrato de Sua Magestade Carlo Alberto, Rei da
Sardenha Huile/papier (54x44.5cm 21x17in) Lisboa
2000
🖼️ **$1 223** - €1 189 - **£765** - FF7 800
Portraits présumés d'Angela Gonin, épouse de
l'artiste Huile/toile (17x40cm 6x15in) Paris 1999
✏️ **$455** - €518 - **£318** - FF3 400
Tableau de chasse Aquarelle/papier (50x32cm
19x12in) Rennes 2000

GONSCHIOR Kuno 1935 **[18]**
🖼️ **$3 945** - €4 602 - **£2 770** - FF30 185
«R/K Orange/BL» Acryl (35x35cm 13x13in) Köln
2000

GONTIER Clément 1876-1918 **[36]**
🖼️ **$2 277** - €2 515 - **£1 579** - FF16 500
Fête au bord de l'eau à Trentemoult près de
Nantes Huile/toile (35x65cm 13x25in) La Roche-sur-
Yon 2001

GONTIER Pierre Camille 1840-? **[21]**
🖼️ **$6 500** - €6 944 - **£3 969** - FF38 992
Flowers in an ornate jardinière Oil/canvas
(93x107cm 37x42in) New-York 1998

GONZAGA Giovanfrancesco 1921 **[93]**
🖼️ **$1 800** - €1 866 - **£1 080** - FF12 240
«Il corsiero nero» Olio/tela (50x40cm 19x15in)
Vercelli 2000
🖼️ **$1 050** - €1 088 - **£630** - FF7 140
Cavaliere berbero fra le acque Olio/tela (40x30cm
15x11in) Vercelli 2000
🖼️ **$500** - €518 - **£300** - FF3 400
Cavaliere di Savoia al galoppo Tecnica mista/carta
(48x34cm 18x13in) Vercelli 1999
🎨 **$125** - €130 - **£75** - FF850
Corsiero bianco Litografia (64x88cm 25x34in)
Vercelli 2001

GONZAGA Pietro di Gottardo 1751-1831 **[12]**
✏️ **$968** - €906 - **£600** - FF5 945
The Courtyard of a Gothic Palace Ink (24.5x20cm
9x7in) London 1999

GONZALES Eva 1849-1883 **[22]**
🖼️ **$5 172** - €6 098 - **£3 648** - FF40 000
Ane Huile/carton (56x48cm 22x18in) Bourges 2001
🖼️ **$32 000** - €37 129 - **£22 092** - FF243 552
La demoiselle Oil/canvas/board (40.5x28cm 15x11in)
New-York 2000
✏️ **$20 224** - €19 513 - **£12 697** - FF128 000
Citron et verre/Poire et radis Aquarelle/papier
(22.5x18.5cm 8x7in) Paris 1999

GONZALES Marcel XX **[15]**
🖼️ **$261** - €305 - **£183** - FF2 000
L'église et les toits Huile/carton/toile (37.5x54.5cm
14x21in) Paris 2000

GONZALEZ ALACREU Juan 1937 **[2]**
🖼️ **$3 835** - €3 904 - **£2 405** - FF25 610
Salto Gouache/papier (40x50cm 15x19in) Madrid 2000

GONZALEZ BRAVO Justo 1944 **[7]**
🖼️ **$2 200** - €2 493 - **£1 550** - FF16 350
Duas figuras Oleo/lienzo (116x81cm 45x31in) Lisboa
2001

GONZALEZ CAMACHO Fernando 1925 **[7]**
🖼️ **$1 560** - €1 802 - **£1 080** - FF11 820
Los limones Oleo/lienzo (86x66cm 33x25in) Madrid
2001

GONZALEZ CAMERANA Jorge 1908-1981 **[9]**
🖼️ **$6 500** - €7 552 - **£4 568** - FF49 541
«Mutación femenina No.1» Oil/canvas (50x70cm
19x27in) New-York 2001
✏️ **$4 183** - €4 907 - **£3 009** - FF32 186
Las bañistas Lápiz/papel (32x41cm 12x16in) México
2001

GONZALEZ Carmelo 1920 **[5]**
🖼️ **$4 500** - €3 885 - **£2 745** - FF25 487
Mesa con Frutas Oil/canvas (51.5x89cm 20x35in)
Miami FL 1999
🖼️ **$5 500** - €5 338 - **£3 424** - FF35 016
Sin Título Oil/canvas (35.5x40.5cm 13x15in) New-
York 1999

GONZALEZ GONZALEZ Pedro 1927 **[17]**
🖼️ **$3 100** - €3 003 - **£1 950** - FF19 700
Composición Oleo/lienzo (95x80cm 37x31in) Madrid
1999

GONZALEZ Juan XVII **[1]**
🖼️ **$60 000** - €57 775 - **£37 344** - FF378 978
Allegories of the ten Commandments Oil/panel
(44x59cm 17x23in) New-York 1999

GONZALEZ Juan Antonio 1842-1914 **[26]**
🖼️ **$9 600** - €9 010 - **£5 850** - FF59 100
Recibiendo las noticias Oleo/lienzo (50.5x72.5cm
19x28in) Madrid 1999
🖼️ **$2 204** - €2 592 - **£1 598** - FF17 000
La tentation des moines Huile/panneau (27x22cm
10x8in) Calais 2001

GONZALEZ Julio 1876-1942 **[313]**
🖼️ **$31 518** - €30 584 - **£20 000** - FF200 616
Deux bouteilles Enamel (15x11cm 5x4in) London
1999
🔨 **$630 360** - €611 674 - **£400 000** - FF4 012 320
Forme sévère Iron (H90cm H35in) London 1999
🔨 **$173 349** - €168 210 - **£110 000** - FF1 103 388
Masque Montserrat criant Bronze (H47.5cm H18in)
London 1999
✏️ **$14 183** - €13 763 - **£9 000** - FF90 277
Tête de femme criant Ink (15.5x20cm 6x7in)
London 1999
🎨 **$2 048** - €1 988 - **£1 300** - FF13 040
Deux paysannes au bord du village Etching
(21x32cm 8x12in) London 1999

GONZALEZ MARCOS Angel 1900-1977 **[67]**
🖼️ **$486** - €541 - **£342** - FF3 546
Escena taurina Oleo/lienzo (54x65cm 21x25in)
Madrid 2001
✏️ **$264** - €252 - **£159** - FF1 654
Picador y torero Gouache/papier (38x50cm 14x19in)
Madrid 1999

GONZALEZ Modesto XIX **[1]**
🖼️ **$5 200** - €5 767 - **£3 460** - FF37 827
Soldados de la guerra del Paraguay Oleo/lienzo
(64.5x41cm 25x16in) Buenos-Aires 2000

GONZALEZ PALMA Luis 1957 [9]
📷 **$3 800** - €3 951 - **£2 399** - FF25 919
La Rosa Gelatin silver print (44.5x44.5cm 17x17in)
New-York 2000

GONZALEZ Pedro Angel 1901-1981 [20]
🐝 **$7 608** - €8 967 - **£5 346** - FF58 822
Arrabal caraqueño Oleo/cartón (53x64cm 20x25in)
Caracas ($) 2000

GONZALEZ PELLICER Juan 1868-1908 [2]
✎ **$901** - €1 021 - **£612** - FF6 698
Elegante Pastel (36x25cm 14x9in) Madrid 2000

GONZALEZ Rafael Ramón 1894-1975 [21]
🐝 **$2 040** - €1 848 - **£1 320** - FF12 120
Casa de Hacienda Oleo/lienzo (61x70cm 24x27in)
Caracas 2000

GONZALEZ SANTOS Manuel 1875-1949 [8]
✎ **$2 240** - €2 108 - **£1 400** - FF13 825
El otoño Pastel/papier (66x74cm 25x29in) Madrid
1998

GONZALEZ SUAREZ Antonio 1915-1975 [1]
✎ **$1 425** - €1 502 - **£950** - FF9 850
Paisaje de Canarias Acuarela/papel (48x62cm
18x24in) Madrid 2000

GONZALEZ VELASQUEZ Antonio 1723-1794 [6]
🐝 **$52 000** - €48 052 - **£31 200** - FF315 200
San Lorenzo Oleo/lienzo (146.5x105cm 57x41in)
Madrid 1999
🐝 **$13 500** - €15 016 - **£9 250** - FF98 500
El ángel anuncia a San José la huida a Egipto
Oleo/lienzo (101x76cm 39x29in) Madrid 2001

GONZALEZ VELAZQUEZ Isidoro 1765-1829 [10]
✎ **$52 562** - €62 504 - **£37 474** - FF410 000
**Vue du lac du jardin Borghese/Vue de l'entrée
du jardin Borghese** Aquarelle (32x58.5cm 12x23in)
Monte-Carlo 2000
▥ **$578** - €511 - **£357** - FF3 349
**«Vista del Prado de Madrid tomada desde la
fuente La Cibéles»** Grabado (39.5x63cm 15x24in)
Madrid 1999

GONZALEZ VELAZQUEZ Zacarías 1763-1834 [22]
🐝 **$10 080** - €9 610 - **£6 480** - FF63 040
Immaculada Oleo/lienzo (166x100cm 65x39in)
Madrid 1999
▥ **$16 800** - €18 019 - **£11 400** - FF118 200
**Boceto para el techo del cuarto del Rey en el
Palacio de Aranjuez** Oleo/lienzo (64.5x51.5cm
25x20in) Madrid 2000
🐝 **$12 825** - €14 568 - **£9 000** - FF95 557
Saint Joseph and the Christ Child in Glory
Oil/canvas (42x29.5cm 16x11in) London 2001

GONZALEZ Xavier 1898-1993 [25]
🐝 **$4 000** - €3 990 - **£2 497** - FF26 173
Abstraction Oil/canvas (91x60cm 36x24in) Cincinnati
OH 1999

GONZALEZ Zacarías 1923 [35]
🐝 **$1 760** - €1 652 - **£1 100** - FF10 835
Alacena Oleo/cartón (53.5x43.5cm 21x17in) Madrid
1999
✎ **$313** - €330 - **£198** - FF2 167
Estrella errante Gouache/papier (26x32cm 10x12in)
Madrid 2000

GONZALEZ-TORRES Felix 1957-1996 [50]
🐝 **$280 000** - €313 621 - **£194 544** - FF2 057 216
Bloodworks Acrylic (35.5x66cm 13x25in) New-York
2001

🐝 **$14 623** - €14 315 - **£9 000** - FF93 901
Untitled Mixed media (19x24cm 7x9in) London 1999
🐝 **$40 250** - €45 083 - **£27 965** - FF295 724
Legal Size White Installation (165x24x28cm
64x9x11in) New-York 2001
🐝 **$50 000** - €58 014 - **£34 520** - FF380 550
Untitled Metal (42x84cm 16x33in) New-York 2000
🐝 **$36 000** - €40 725 - **£25 185** - FF267 138
«Untitled, T-Cell Count» Graphite (48.5x38cm
19x14in) New-York 2001
▥ **$4 500** - €5 121 - **£3 162** - FF33 593
Parkett 39 Screenprint (317x691.5cm 124x272in)
New-York 2001
📷 **$16 000** - €17 921 - **£11 116** - FF117 555
Lover's Letter Type C color print (19x24cm 7x9in)
New-York 2001

GONZALVO Pablo 1827-1896 [6]
🐝 **$8 100** - €9 010 - **£5 700** - FF59 100
Puerta de la Universidad de Salamanca
Oleo/lienzo (75x58cm 29x22in) Madrid 2001

GONZATO Guido 1896-1955 [3]
🐝 **$4 273** - €4 080 - **£2 670** - FF26 761
Rustico metaphisica Öl/Karton (54x40cm 21x15in)
Zofingen 1999

GOOBALATHELDIN Dick Roughsey 1924-1985 [22]
🐝 **$2 396** - €2 850 - **£1 708** - FF18 695
**Returning From Fish Hunting, Mornington
Island** Acrylic (30.5x51cm 12x20in) Woollahra,
Sydney 2000

GOOCH Georgina Anne, Miss ?-1858 [6]
🐝 **$2 755** - €3 037 - **£1 800** - FF19 922
Knight of Malta, after Titian Oil/canvas (79x62cm
31x24in) London 2000
✎ **$1 224** - €1 350 - **£800** - FF8 854
Portrait of Emperor Charles V, after Titian
Watercolour/paper (11.5x9cm 4x3in) London 2000

GOOD Bernard Stafford 1887-1969 [1]
🐝 **$8 500** - €8 140 - **£5 251** - FF53 396
**Trapper Defending Himself Against Wolf, Pulp
Magazine Cover** Oil/canvas (91x63cm 36x25in) New-
York 1999

GOOD Minnetta 1895-1946 [2]
▥ **$1 200** - €1 241 - **£758** - FF8 140
**Dry Sand Molding of Dredge Bucket Lip, Taylor
Wharton Iron** Lithograph (26.5x30.5cm 10x12in)
New-York 2000

GOODACRE Glenna 1939 [7]
🐝 **$2 900** - €3 293 - **£2 014** - FF21 599
Fantasy Bronze (H28cm H11in) Dallas TX 2001

GOODALL Agnes M. XIX-XX [7]
✎ **$1 825** - €1 577 - **£1 100** - FF10 346
**Treckers Resting Round a Campfire in South
African Landscape** Watercolour (24x39cm 9x15in)
Billingshurst, West-Sussex 1999

GOODALL Edward Angelo 1819-1908 [133]
✎ **$1 322** - €1 314 - **£800** - FF8 507
The Silk Market Watercolour (35.5x53.5cm 13x21in)
London 2000

GOODALL Frederick 1822-1904 [227]
🐝 **$5 116** - €5 870 - **£3 500** - FF38 507
On the Banks of the Nile Oil/canvas (53.5x39.5cm
21x15in) London 2000
🐝 **$1 711** - €1 943 - **£1 171** - FF12 744
Portraet af arabisk fiskerdreng Oil/canvas
(31x23cm 12x9in) Vejle 2000

G

$544 - €613 - **£380** - FF4 020
Camels in the Desert with the Pyramids beyond
Watercolour (17x32.5cm 6x12in) London 2001

GOODALL George XIX-XX **[18]**
$421 - €501 - **£300** - FF3 288
Italian Lake Landscape with Figures on a Path
Watercolour/paper (30x42.5cm 11x16in) London 2000

GOODALL Howard 1850-1874 **[2]**
$4 465 - €3 811 - **£2 670** - FF25 000
Scène animée au bord du Nil Huile/toile
(62x127cm 24x50in) Paris 1998

GOODALL John Edward XIX-XX **[16]**
$700 - €690 - **£450** - FF4 529
Scene in the Langham Sketch Club Watercolour
(16x24.5cm 6x9in) London 1999

GOODALL John Strickland 1908-1996 **[83]**
$892 - €858 - **£550** - FF5 631
Lucy, Dot and Amy Watercolour/paper (14x11.5cm
5x4in) London 1999

GOODALL Walter 1830-1889 **[28]**
$1 113 - €1 047 - **£700** - FF6 865
Watching the hens feed Watercolour/paper
(30x45cm 11x17in) Bristol, Avon 1999

GOODAN Till P. 1896-1958 **[3]**
$4 500 - €5 282 - **£3 176** - FF34 645
Chuckwagon at Dusk Oil/canvas (76x101.5cm
29x39in) New-York 2000

GOODE Joe 1937 **[26]**
$4 000 - €4 549 - **£2 794** - FF29 840
Oak Rock Acrylic/canvas (132x244cm 51x96in)
Beverly-Hills CA 2000
$500 - €574 - **£342** - FF3 763
Untitled, from the Tissue Tear Series
Collage/board (50x65.5cm 19x25in) New-York 2000
$2 600 - €3 021 - **£1 827** - FF19 815
Bed Pencil/paper (50x65cm 19x25in) Beverly-Hills CA
2001
$700 - €814 - **£492** - FF5 338
Untitled, from Tissue Tear Series Color lithograph
(50x65.5cm 19x25in) Beverly-Hills CA 2001

GOODELL Ira Chaffee 1800-c.1875 **[2]**
$5 500 - €5 115 - **£3 405** - FF33 553
Lady in Fancy White Headpiece and Lace Collar
Oil/panel (76x60cm 30x24in) Portsmouth NH 1999

GOODES Edward A. 1832-1910 **[1]**
$5 500 - €6 019 - **£3 793** - FF39 483
Still Life with Fruit Oil/canvas (74.5x91.5cm 29x36in)
New-York 2001

GOODIN Walter 1907-1992 **[39]**
$750 - €812 - **£520** - FF5 327
Still Life, spring Flowers in Jug Oil/hardboard
(59x49cm 23x19in) Driffield, East Yorkshire 2001

GOODING Maria Simmonds XX **[6]**
$1 147 - €1 232 - **£767** - FF8 079
Road Down by the Sea Oil/paper (56x73.5cm
22x28in) Dublin 2001

GOODMAN Arthur Jule ?-1926 **[2]**
$2 800 - €2 650 - **£1 739** - FF17 386
«Buffalo Bill's Wild West» Poster (76.5x51.5cm
30x20in) New-York 2000

GOODMAN Bertram 1904-1988 **[10]**
$1 200 - €1 118 - **£740** - FF7 335
«Burlesk» Lithograph (37x28cm 14x11in) Cleveland
OH 1999

GOODMAN Brenda 1943 **[16]**
$1 300 - €1 529 - **£932** - FF10 028
Abstarct portrait Oil/masonite (35x25cm 14x10in)
Detroit MI 2001
$1 100 - €1 048 - **£671** - FF6 873
Black Cloud Pencil/paper (104x51cm 41x20in)
Bloomfield-Hills MI 1999

GOODMAN John Reginald 1878-? **[48]**
$414 - €391 - **£250** - FF2 565
Near Yapton/Rustington Watercolour (24.5x34.5cm
9x13in) Billingshurst, West-Sussex 1999

GOODMAN Maude Scanes 1860-1938 **[8]**
$25 000 - €27 919 - **£16 010** - FF183 137
A Wonderful Story Oil/canvas (51.5x76cm 20x29in)
New-York 2000
$3 287 - €3 529 - **£2 200** - FF23 147
My Dear! Oil/canvas (46x33cm 18x12in) London 2000

GOODMAN Robert Gwelo 1871-1939 **[54]**
$4 974 - €4 664 - **£3 073** - FF30 593
Victoria Falls Oil/canvas (50x45cm 19x17in)
Johannesburg 1999
$425 - €409 - **£262** - FF2 686
Two Rondavels and a Wagon Pastel/paper
(53x45.5cm 20x17in) Johannesburg 1999

GOODMAN Walter 1838-? **[1]**
$375 000 - €320 394 - **£225 112** - FF2 101 650
The Printseller's Window Oil/canvas (133x114cm
52x44in) New-York 1998

GOODNOUGH Robert Arthur 1917 **[80]**
$3 000 - €3 240 - **£2 073** - FF21 251
«Grey, White, Blue» Acrylic (123x174cm 48x68in)
New-York 2001
$1 216 - €1 355 - **£850** - FF8 889
Horses racing Acrylic/canvas (91.5x101.5cm
36x39in) Near Ely 2001

GOODRICH William Ralph E. 1887-1956 **[36]**
$337 - €391 - **£240** - FF2 567
The Old Cornmill, Hallam Yorkshire
Watercolour/paper (22x31cm 9x12in) Woodford,
Cheshire 2000

GOODWIN Albert 1845-1932 **[515]**
$8 644 - €9 832 - **£6 094** - FF64 491
Luzern mir Rigi Öl/Leinwand (106.5x142cm 41x55in)
Zürich 2001
$315 045 - €366 400 - **£225 000** - FF2 403 427
**«The Afterglow, San Giorgio Maggiore and the
Dogana, Venice»** Oil/board (61x92cm 24x36in)
London 2001
$3 081 - €2 981 - **£1 900** - FF19 555
Windsor Castle Mixed media (27.5x38cm 10x14in)
London 1999
$2 317 - €2 689 - **£1 600** - FF17 638
Christchurch, hants Watercolour/paper (24.5x36cm
9x14in) London 2000

GOODWIN Arthur Clifton 1864-1929 **[147]**
$9 000 - €9 329 - **£5 706** - FF61 194
Harbor in Winter Oil/canvas (74.5x84.5cm 29x33in)
New-York 2000
$350 - €299 - **£205** - FF1 961
View of the Dome Oil/board (12x12cm 5x5in)
Portsmouth NH 1998
$3 000 - €3 545 - **£2 126** - FF23 252
View of the Boston public Garden Pastel/paper
(24x32cm 9x12in) Boston MA 2000

GOODWIN Betty Roodish 1923 [16]
- $2 030 - €1 950 - £1 258 - FF12 791
  «Still Life 15» Oil/masonite (40.5x84cm 15x33in)
  Toronto 1999
- $1 466 - €1 702 - £1 012 - FF11 165
  Night Etching (23x27.5cm 9x10in) Vancouver, BC.
  2000

GOODWIN Harry c.1840-1925 [66]
- $597 - €548 - £370 - FF33 596
  Sunday Evening, Hastings Watercolour/paper
  (23.5x16.5cm 9x6in) Devon 1999

GOODWIN Philip Russell 1882-1935 [22]
- $80 000 - €85 776 - £52 928 - FF562 656
  Crossing the Flathead Oil/canvas (60x91cm
  24x36in) Hayden ID 2000
- $1 700 - €1 555 - £1 038 - FF10 198
  Tamarack and Spruce Oil/canvas/board (19x27cm
  7x11in) Boston MA 2001

GOODWIN Richard LaBarre 1840-1910 [39]
- $3 200 - €3 159 - £1 945 - FF20 720
  Hanging Duck Oil/canvas (71x49cm 27x19in) New-
  York 2000
- $3 200 - €3 435 - £2 141 - FF22 531
  The Day's Catch Oil/canvas (30x40cm 12x16in)
  Portland ME 2000

GOODWIN Sidney Paul 1867-1944 [80]
- $962 - €925 - £600 - FF6 067
  Northfleet, Kent Watercolour (28.5x47.5cm 11x18in)
  West-Yorshire 1999

GOOKINS James F. 1840-1904 [4]
- $7 806 - €7 121 - £4 800 - FF46 712
  Psycheland, colourful Flowers, Psyche and
  Butterflies Oil/canvas (92.5x57cm 36x22in) Co.
  Kilkenny 1999

GOOL van Jan 1685-c.1764 [37]
- $6 580 - €7 267 - £4 560 - FF47 670
  Felsentor in einer Landschaft mit Hirten und
  Herde Oil/panel (43.5x63cm 17x24in) Wien 2001
- $4 000 - €4 389 - £2 657 - FF28 787
  The Interior of a Barn with Sheep and Ducks
  Resting Oil/panel (31.5x37.5cm 12x14in) New-York
  2000

GOOL van Studio XX [200]
- $321 - €274 - £194 - FF1 800
  Pinocchio, illustration originale, double-page
  66/67 Gouache (32.5x50cm 12x19in) Paris 1998

GOOS Pieter 1615/16-1675 [4]
- $476 - €420 - £287 - FF2 757
  Cust Van Hollant Tusschen de Maes ende Texel
  Engraving (42.5x53cm 16x20in) Amsterdam 1998

GOOSE William Henry XIX [74]
- $396 - €468 - £280 - FF3 072
  The New Arrival Watercolour/paper (40x27cm
  16x11in) Aylsham, Norfolk 2001

GOOSEN Frits J. 1943 [9]
- $700 - €833 - £484 - FF5 462
  Dutch River Scene Oil/canvas (22x40cm 9x16in)
  Norwalk CT 2000

GOOSEY George Turland XIX-XX [15]
- $1 867 - €2 088 - £1 300 - FF13 696
  Fishing Fleet in St.Ives Harbour Oil/panel
  (29x38.5cm 11x15in) Penzance, Cornwall 2001

GOOSSENS Josse 1876-1929 [10]
- $2 899 - €2 812 - £1 824 - FF18 446
  Früchtestilleben mit Weinflasche Öl/Leinwand
  (65x65cm 25x25in) München 1999

GOPAS Rudolf 1913-1983 [9]
- $1 172 - €1 232 - £772 - FF8 083
  Landscape Watercolour/paper (19x24cm 7x9in)
  Auckland 2000

GÖRANSSON Åke 1902-1942 [83]
- $28 244 - €26 539 - £17 020 - FF174 087
  Gula pappersrosor Oil/canvas/panel (52x40cm
  20x15in) Stockholm 1999
- $4 903 - €4 611 - £3 038 - FF30 245
  Sköterskan, Lillhagen Oil/canvas (29x22cm 11x8in)
  Stockholm 1999
- $155 - €166 - £105 - FF1 087
  Modellstudie Pencil/paper (31x24cm 12x9in)
  Stockholm 2001

GORBATOV Konstantin Ivanovich 1876-1945 [93]
- $162 330 - €156 006 - £100 000 - FF1 023 330
  Portrait of the Artist's Wife relaxing on the
  Verandah Oil/canvas (134x187.5cm 52x73in) London
  1999
- $11 157 - €13 121 - £8 000 - FF86 068
  «Herbstgold» Oil/canvas/board (59.5x73.5cm
  23x28in) London 2001
- $4 417 - €4 953 - £3 000 - FF32 492
  Fishing-boats Off Amalfi Oil/board (21.5x29cm
  8x11in) London 2001
- $3 000 - €3 489 - £2 140 - FF22 888
  On the Grand Canal Watercolour (33x41cm 13x16in)
  New-York 2000

GÖRBITZ Johan 1782-1853 [7]
- $6 148 - €6 959 - £4 300 - FF45 651
  «Ved inngangen til landsbyen Favergetti»
  Oil/canvas (64x80cm 25x31in) Oslo 2001
- $1 365 - €1 623 - £972 - FF10 647
  Hyrdescene Oil/canvas (32x40cm 12x15in) Oslo 2000

GORDE Gaston 1908-1995 [41]
- $496 - €464 - £300 - FF3 041
  Bières Edelweiss Poster (100x64cm 39x25in)
  London 1999

GORDER van Luther Emerson 1861-1931 [16]
- $2 500 - €2 775 - £1 738 - FF18 206
  «Sherburne Lake and Mountains, Glacier
  National Park» Oil/canvas (45x60cm 18x24in)
  Milford CT 2001
- $4 500 - €4 996 - £3 129 - FF32 770
  Young Girl with Paper Lantern Oil/canvas
  (50x30cm 20x12in) Milford CT 2001

GORDIGIANI Edoardo 1867-1961 [62]
- $1 500 - €1 555 - £900 - FF10 200
  Natura morta in giardino Olio/tela (62x72cm
  24x28in) Prato 2000
- $900 - €777 - £450 - FF5 100
  Marina Olio/tavola (17.5x25cm 6x9in) Firenze 1999

GORDIGIANI Michele 1830-1909 [34]
- $19 000 - €19 146 - £11 844 - FF125 590
  Nude with Putto Oil/canvas (160x109cm 62x42in)
  New-York 2000
- $2 750 - €2 851 - £1 650 - FF18 700
  Ritratto di giovane donna Olio/tela (55x39cm
  21x15in) Prato 1999
- $1 650 - €1 710 - £990 - FF11 220
  Fanciulla con Fiori Olio/tela (29x22cm 11x8in)
  Firenze 2001

GORDIJN Araun 1947 [4]
- $2 827 - €2 723 - £1 768 - FF17 859
  «Buick 1947, San Francisco» Oil/canvas
  (100x100cm 39x39in) Amsterdam 2000

G

GORDILLO Luis Rodríguez 1934 **[100]**
- $36 400 - €42 045 - **£25 200** - FF275 800
  Serie mosaico No.6 Acrílico/tabla (156x107cm 61x42in) Seville 2000
- $7 280 - €7 808 - **£4 940** - FF51 220
  «Supra I» Acrílico (120x80cm 47x31in) Madrid 2001
- $930 - €901 - **£570** - FF5 910
  Personaje Técnica mixta (25x16.5cm 9x6in) Madrid 1999
- $810 - €901 - **£555** - FF5 910
  Oasis Crayon gras (24x17cm 9x6in) Madrid 2001
- $238 - €270 - **£162** - FF1 773
  Alma Nok Serigrafía (54x40cm 21x15in) Madrid 2000

GORDINE Dora 1906-1991 **[5]**
- $2 433 - €2 345 - **£1 500** - FF15 385
  Sea rose Bronze (H41cm H16in) London 1999

GORDON Arthur 1883-1944 **[24]**
- $2 500 - €2 682 - **£1 704** - FF17 592
  Putney Bridge, Fulham Oil/canvas (51x77cm 20x30in) Köbenhavn 2001
- $1 032 - €1 146 - **£720** - FF7 520
  Evening Glow Windsor Watercolour/paper (53x74cm 21x29in) Birmingham 2001

GORDON John Watson 1788-1864 **[26]**
- $3 507 - €4 171 - **£2 500** - FF27 363
  Portrait of William Gilpin, Full Length, Seated in a Study Oil/canvas (190x149cm 74x58in) London 2000
- $4 611 - €4 386 - **£2 800** - FF28 772
  Contemplation Oil/canvas (76x63.5cm 29x25in) Edinburgh 1999

GORDON Julia Isabella, Lady 1772-1867 **[1]**
- $1 599 - €1 540 - **£1 000** - FF10 101
  Parliament Street, Westminster Watercolour (19.5x30.5cm 7x12in) London 1999

GORDON Michail act.c.1945 **[7]**
- $436 - €467 - **£303** - FF3 336
  Unser Ziel Poster (29.5x19.5cm 11x7in) Wien 2000

GORDON Thomas Edward 1832-1914 **[1]**
- $1 613 - €1 549 - **£1 000** - FF10 164
  The Roof of the World Lithograph (26x18cm 10x7in) London 1999

GORDON William J. XX **[1]**
- $1 300 - €1 487 - **£904** - FF9 754
  Acrobats Gouache/board (60x40cm 24x16in) Cincinnati OH 2000

GORDON Witold XX **[3]**
- $4 400 - €3 859 - **£2 671** - FF25 316
  III Olympic Winter Games Poster (100x62cm 39x24in) New-York 1999

GORDY Robert 1933-1986 **[52]**
- $2 000 - €2 194 - **£1 358** - FF14 390
  Female Nude Mixed media/paper (60x50cm 24x20in) New-Orleans LA 2000
- $500 - €467 - **£308** - FF3 065
  W.W.II Serigraph (73x85cm 29x33in) New-Orleans LA 1999

GORE Charles 1729-1807 **[9]**
- $700 - €846 - **£488** - FF5 550
  The fleet in Heavy Seas Ink (22x33cm 9x13in) Philadelphia PA 2000

GORE Frederick 1913 **[99]**
- $5 830 - €6 630 - **£4 000** - FF43 492
  Les Baux de Provence Oil/canvas (51x61cm 20x24in) London 2000

$375 - €315 - **£220** - FF2 063
  Sunflowers Offset (63x81cm 25x32in) London 1998

GORE Millicent XIX-XX **[1]**
- $2 540 - €2 176 - **£1 500** - FF14 272
  Minding the Baby Watercolour, gouache/paper (38x26.5cm 14x10in) Ipswich 1998

GORE Spencer Frederick 1878-1914 **[30]**
- $22 482 - €20 757 - **£14 000** - FF136 158
  A Garden Square in Camden Town Oil/canvas (51x61cm 20x24in) London 1999
- $11 056 - €9 437 - **£6 500** - FF61 904
  Window in Granby Street Oil/canvas (40.5x30.5cm 15x12in) London 1998

GORE William Crampton 1871-1946 **[21]**
- $4 153 - €4 645 - **£2 800** - FF30 466
  Cottages at Dooagh, Achill Oil/panel (37.5x46cm 14x18in) London 2000
- $1 530 - €1 778 - **£1 075** - FF11 660
  On the Beach, Brittany Oil/canvas/board (30.5x40cm 12x15in) Dublin 2001

GORE William Henry XIX-XX **[21]**
- $49 640 - €57 625 - **£35 000** - FF377 996
  In Disgrace Oil/canvas (76x51cm 29x20in) London 2001

GOREN STRAUSS Yael 1971 **[4]**
- $900 - €777 - **£544** - FF5 094
  Elephants 1 Charcoal (65x93.5cm 25x36in) Tel Aviv 1999

GOREY Edward 1929-2000 **[10]**
- $3 500 - €3 977 - **£2 417** - FF26 089
  The Ghost in the Mirror Watercolour/paper (23x33cm 9x12in) New-York 2000

GÖRG Jürgen 1951 **[16]**
- $170 - €198 - **£120** - FF1 301
  Classical Composition Study Color lithograph (52.5x38cm 20x14in) London 2000

GORGE Paul 1856-1941 **[23]**
- $1 305 - €1 289 - **£795** - FF8 455
  Deux amis Huile/toile (100.5x72cm 39x28in) Bruxelles 2000

GORGUET Auguste-François 1862-1927 **[29]**
- $500 - €537 - **£334** - FF3 520
  La répétiton Ink (26.5x38cm 10x14in) New-York 2000

GORI Alessandro XVII **[8]**
- $8 412 - €7 799 - **£5 200** - FF51 156
  French partridge with a thrush, a robin/Sparrowhawk, blue tits Oil/canvas (38x48cm 14x18in) London 1999

GORI Georges XX **[20]**
- $593 - €640 - **£397** - FF4 200
  La femme aux dogues Métal (52x80cm 20x31in) Rennes 2000

GORI Gino Paolo 1911-1991 **[30]**
- $360 - €311 - **£180** - FF2 040
  «A Firenze» Olio/tela (30.5x40.5cm 12x15in) Prato 1999

GORIN Jean 1899-1981 **[69]**
- $7 014 - €8 181 - **£4 924** - FF53 662
  Composition-Spazio-Temporelle No.82 Relief (50x50cm 19x19in) Köln 2000
- $199 - €168 - **£117** - FF1 102
  Geometrisk komposition Lithograph (60x60cm 23x23in) Stockholm 1998

GORKY Arshile 1904-1948 **[84]**
- **$2 000 000** – €2 320 579 – **£1 380 800** – FF15 222 000
  Khorkom Oil/canvas (101.5x132cm 39x51in) New-York 2000
- **$35 000** – €38 411 – **£22 536** – FF251 958
  The City Oil/canvas (66x51.5cm 25x20in) New-York 2000
- **$42 000** – €36 236 – **£25 338** – FF237 690
  Untitled Oil/canvas (16x21cm 6x8in) New-York 1998
- **$17 000** – €18 359 – **£11 748** – FF120 426
  Untitled Indian ink (43x28cm 16x11in) New-York 2001

GÖRLICH Ulrich 1952 **[1]**
- **$3 332** – €3 234 – **£2 074** – FF21 213
  Brandenburger Tor Photograph (100x100cm 39x39in) Berlin 1999

GORMAN Greg 1949 **[13]**
- **$826** – €920 – **£540** – FF6 037
  Ohne Titel Gelatin silver print (56.3x46.5cm 22x18in) Köln 2000

GORMAN Rudolph Carl 1932 **[70]**
- **$500** – €466 – **£308** – FF3 057
  Hand Graphics Impression I «Expectations» Print (55x76cm 22x30in) Bloomfield-Hills MI 1999

GORMLEY Antony 1950 **[50]**
- **$2 689** – €2 887 – **£1 809** – FF18 938
  Untitled Acrylic (32x38cm 12x14in) London 2000
- **$52 300** – €56 140 – **£35 000** – FF368 256
  Body Bronze (202x86x65cm 79x33x25in) London 2000
- **$15 647** – €14 545 – **£9 500** – FF95 410
  Man Rock Stone (54x46x44cm 21x18x17in) London 1998
- **$2 731** – €2 528 – **£1 671** – FF16 585
  Comfort in Distance I-III Indian ink (19x14cm 7x5in) München 1999

GÖRMS Wilhelm 1864-c.1903 **[2]**
- **$2 936** – €2 959 – **£1 831** – FF19 413
  Commérages Gouache/board (92x71.5cm 36x28in) Warszawa 2000

GORNIK April 1953 **[24]**
- **$11 000** – €12 266 – **£7 396** – FF80 458
  «Desert Lake» Oil/canvas (172x213.5cm 67x84in) New-York 2000

GORNIK Friedrich 1877-1943 **[27]**
- **$652** – €727 – **£427** – FF4 767
  Pflügende Bäuerin Bronze (26x62cm 10x24in) Wien 2000

GORNY Hein 1904-1967 **[10]**
- **$591** – €512 – **£358** – FF3 356
  Berliner Planken Photograph (23.1x17.4cm 9x6in) München 1998

GORODINE Alexis 1944 **[14]**
- **$150** – €175 – **£103** – FF1 147
  Stones Serigrafia (40.5x40cm 15x15in) Caracas ($) 2000

GORP van Henri Nicolas 1756-1819 **[37]**
- **$10 000** – €10 971 – **£6 643** – FF71 968
  Gentleman, Small Seated Full-Length, Holding La Gazette Nationale Oil/panel (46.5x38cm 18x14in) New-York 2000
- **$2 800** – €3 224 – **£1 910** – FF21 145
  Portrait of Amity Thayer, Age 12, Small Half-Length/Harriet Thayer Oil/panel (22x17cm 8x6in) New-York 2000

GORSKI Konstanty 1868-1934 **[5]**
- **$1 101** – €1 110 – **£686** – FF7 280
  Un moment de frayeur Oil/board (34x22.5cm 13x8in) Warszawa 2000

GORSKI Stanislaw 1887-1955 **[16]**
- **$1 372** – €1 474 – **£918** – FF9 666
  Portrait d'une montagnarde Pastel/carton (50x35cm 19x13in) Torun 2000

GORSLINE Douglas Warner 1913-1985 **[18]**
- **$400** – €454 – **£273** – FF2 979
  Express Stop Etching (16x15cm 6x5in) New-York 2000

GORSON Aaron Henry 1872-1933 **[32]**
- **$6 500** – €6 977 – **£4 350** – FF45 769
  At the Riverhead Oil/canvas (40.5x50.5cm 15x19in) New-York 2000
- **$3 169** – €3 244 – **£2 244** – FF20 790
  Industrial Pittsburgh Scene Oil/panel (25x35cm 10x14in) Hatfield PA 1998

GORTER Arnold Marc 1866-1933 **[165]**
- **$15 444** – €18 151 – **£10 708** – FF119 064
  A Peasantwoman and a Child on a Path Amidst Birchtrees Oil/canvas (100x135.5cm 39x53in) Amsterdam 2000
- **$4 227** – €4 933 – **£2 983** – FF32 360
  River Landscape with Cattle and Woman Herding Oil/canvas (51x38cm 20x14in) Toronto 2000
- **$3 636** – €3 403 – **£2 262** – FF22 324
  Ducks in a Meadow, in Spring Oil/canvas (32.5x42cm 12x16in) Amsterdam 1999
- **$608** – €666 – **£420** – FF4 370
  Dutch Lane Watercolour/paper (32.5x45.5cm 12x17in) London 2001

GORUS Pieter 1881-1941 **[53]**
- **$860** – €992 – **£604** – FF6 504
  Enfant jouant sous le pommier en fleurs Huile/toile (45x55cm 17x21in) Bruxelles 2000
- **$928** – €1 041 – **£646** – FF6 829
  Pâturage au bord de l'eau Huile/panneau (19x23.5cm 7x9in) Bruxelles 2001

GORY Affortunato 1895-1925 **[89]**
- **$7 179** – €8 047 – **£5 000** – FF52 786
  Bust of a Woman Gilded bronze (H177cm H69in) London 2001
- **$3 500** – €3 034 – **£2 138** – FF19 903
  Seated Allegorical Female Nude Marble (H53cm H20in) New-York 1999

GOS Albert H. 1852-1942 **[92]**
- **$1 193** – €1 246 – **£755** – FF8 171
  Le printemps au bord du lac Huile/toile (55x65cm 21x25in) Genève 2000
- **$669** – €787 – **£484** – FF5 161
  Yvoire Huile/toile (29x47cm 11x18in) Sion 2001

GOS François Marc Eug. 1880-1975 **[81]**
- **$1 112** – €1 311 – **£781** – FF8 601
  Pinien am Strand Öl/Leinwand (130x80cm 51x31in) Bern 2000
- **$557** – €656 – **£404** – FF4 301
  Le Gd Combin, de la Dt de Morcles Huile/carton (32.5x40cm 12x15in) Sion 2001
- **$508** – €585 – **£350** – FF3 840
  «Chocolats Peter & Kohler» Poster (38x99cm 14x38in) London 2000

GÖSCHEL Eberhard 1943 **[10]**
- **$109** – €123 – **£76** – FF804
  Abstrakte Komposition Farbradierung (49.5x32cm 19x12in) Berlin 2001

G

GOSE ROVIRA Francisco Javier 1876-1915 **[16]**
🖌 **$363** - €330 - **£220** - FF2 167
Retrato Acuarela/papel (27x20cm 10x7in) Madrid 1999

GOSHUN Matsumura 1752-1811 **[2]**
🖋 **$180 000** - €198 910 - **£124 830** - FF1 304 766
Fishermen Ink (153.5x348cm 60x137in) New-York 1999

GOSLING William 1824-1883 **[24]**
🖌 **$583** - €542 - **£350** - FF3 553
A punt moored by the Edge of a River
Watercolour (19x34cm 7x13in) London 1999

GOSSAERT Jan Mabuse 1478/88-c.1536 **[5]**
🖋 **$180 000** - €192 816 - **£122 922** - FF1 264 788
The Holy Family Ink (15.5x12.5cm 6x4in) New-York 2001

GOSSE Nicolas Louis 1787-1878 **[20]**
🖻 **$80 000** - €67 195 - **£47 032** - FF440 768
Monks Fleeing before a Marshall Oil/canvas (96x151cm 37x59in) New-York 1998
🖻 **$10 288** - €12 196 - **£7 496** - FF80 000
«Charles-Eustache-Gabriel comte d'Osmond, menin de M. le dauphin..» Huile/toile (97.5x77.5cm 38x30in) Paris 2001

GOSSE Sylvia Laura 1881-1968 **[45]**
🖻 **$2 891** - €2 785 - **£1 800** - FF18 266
Continental Street Vendor Oil/canvas (61x61cm 24x24in) London 1999
🖻 **$512** - €583 - **£360** - FF3 824
Trees in Sunlight, near Hastings Oil/board (35x27cm 13x10in) London 2001

GOSSELIN Albert 1862-1931 **[10]**
🖻 **$1 316** - €1 227 - **£812** - FF8 049
An der Loire Oil/panel (63.5x83cm 25x32in) Bremen 1999

GOSSELIN family XIX **[3]**
🖌 **$2 595** - €2 502 - **£1 600** - FF16 411
La moinerie, Serk Ink (18.5x22.5cm 7x8in) London 1999

GOSSELIN Gérard 1769-1859 **[2]**
🖌 **$1 622** - €1 564 - **£1 000** - FF10 257
View near Beddington, Surrey Ink (27x37.5cm 10x14in) London 1999

GOSSELIN Joshua 1739-1813 **[56]**
🖌 **$2 189** - €2 111 - **£1 350** - FF13 847
View near the Grand Mieles, Guernsey Ink (12.5x24cm 4x9in) London 1999

GOSSELIN Joshua, Jnr. 1763-1789 **[5]**
🖌 **$486** - €469 - **£300** - FF3 077
Village of Appleshaw Watercolour/paper (23.5x37cm 9x14in) London 1999

GOSSIN Louis XIX-XX **[15]**
🗿 **$1 944** - €2 287 - **£1 393** - FF15 000
David et Goliath Bronze (H82cm H32in) Paris 2001
🗿 **$1 686** - €1 982 - **£1 168** - FF13 000
Orphée Bronze (H69cm H27in) Brest 2000

GOTCH Bernard Cecil 1876-? **[23]**
🖌 **$407** - €374 - **£250** - FF2 452
Evening Light, Battersea Watercolour (24.5x35.5cm 9x13in) Oxfordshire 1999

GOTCH Thomas Cooper 1854-1931 **[98]**
🖻 **$7 114** - €8 266 - **£5 000** - FF54 221
Seated Girl Oil/canvas (61x51cm 24x20in) London 2001

🖻 **$8 262** - €8 776 - **£5 450** - FF57 570
Penzance from Newlyn - View Across Mounts Bay Oil/canvas (30.5x51cm 12x20in) Penzance, Cornwall 2000
🖌 **$1 449** - €1 341 - **£900** - FF8 798
Two Studies of Angels Pencil/paper (20x9.5cm 7x3in) London 1999

GÖTH Moricz 1873-1939 **[26]**
🖻 **$3 236** - €3 630 - **£2 242** - FF23 812
Amsterdam canal Gouache/paper (50x60cm 19x23in) Amsterdam 2000

GOTHEIN Werner 1890-1968 **[62]**
🖻 **$17 799** - €19 106 - **£11 910** - FF125 328
Baum am Wege Öl/Karton (64.5x54cm 25x21in) Bern 2000
🪵 **$153** - €143 - **£94** - FF939
Raucher Woodcut (24.7x13.5cm 9x5in) Hamburg 1999

GOTLIB Marcel Gotlieb, dit 1934 **[8]**
🖌 **$245** - €274 - **£170** - FF1 800
Gai Luron Encre Chine/papier (44x33cm 17x12in) Paris 2001

GOTSCH Friedrich Karl 1900-1984 **[252]**
🖻 **$14 993** - €17 639 - **£10 584** - FF115 706
«Stilleben» Öl/Leinwand (43.5x57.5cm 17x22in) Berlin 2001
🖻 **$2 143** - €2 301 - **£1 434** - FF15 092
Monserrato, Elba II Gouache/Karton (71x48cm 27x18in) Köln 2001
🪵 **$262** - €281 - **£175** - FF1 844
Selbstbildnis mit Sommerhut Woodcut in colors (23x15.5cm 9x6in) Hamburg 2000

GÖTSCH Joseph 1728-1793 **[1]**
🏺 **$7 168** - €6 134 - **£4 315** - FF40 239
Der hl. Joseph verehrt das Jesuskind Relief (H23cm H9in) München 1998

GOTT Joseph 1785-1860 **[12]**
🏺 **$10 322** - €11 431 - **£7 000** - FF74 984
King Charles Spaniel, a kitten and an upturned basket of fruit Marble (31.5x68.5x33cm 12x26x12in) London 2000

GOTTFREDSON Floyd 1905-1987 **[11]**
🖌 **$1 673** - €1 753 - **£1 059** - FF11 500
Mickey Mouse, 3 strips Encre Chine/papier (42x65cm 16x25in) Paris 2000

GOTTLIEB Adolph 1903-1974 **[183]**
🖻 **$90 000** - €100 807 - **£62 532** - FF661 248
«Low Land» Oil/canvas (122x228.5cm 48x89in) New-York 2001
🖻 **$12 500** - €11 116 - **£7 645** - FF72 916
Untitled No.75 Acrylic (38x51cm 14x20in) New-York 1999
🖻 **$13 000** - €12 523 - **£8 032** - FF82 148
Untitled Acrylic/paper (22x30cm 9x12in) Chicago IL 1999
🖻 **$8 500** - €9 180 - **£5 874** - FF60 216
Abstract Composition Pastel (25x30cm 9x11in) New-York 2001
🪵 **$800** - €751 - **£494** - FF4 925
Pink Ground Screenprint in colors (94x69.5cm 37x27in) New-York 1999

GOTTLIEB Harry 1895-1992 **[47]**
🖻 **$1 200** - €1 066 - **£734** - FF6 993
Mexican mine Workers with picks Oil/canvas (61x102cm 24x40in) Saugerties NY 1999
🖻 **$500** - €513 - **£312** - FF3 363
Dock Workers Watercolour/paper (34x39cm 13x15in) Bolton MA 2000

G

⊞ $375 - €403 - **£251** - FF2 645
Home Sweet Home Lithograph (23x34cm 9x13in)
Cleveland OH 2000

GOTTLIEB Henry 1892-1966 **[64]**
⌐ **$1 733** - €1 485 - **£1 042** - FF9 741
Nature morte aux fruits Oil/canvas (46x61cm
18x24in) Warszawa 1998
✎ $417 - €420 - **£260** - FF2 756
Man with an Ox Watercolour/paper (25.5x35.5cm
10x13in) London 2000

GOTTLIEB Leopold 1883-1933 **[38]**
⌐ $14 748 - €16 750 - **£10 314** - FF109 872
Portrait de Helena Rubinstein Huile/toile
(116.5x89cm 45x35in) Warszawa 2001
✎ **$2 750** - €2 380 - **£1 669** - FF15 614
Roof Tops Gouache/paper (63x48cm 25x19in) Mystic
CT 1998

GOTTLIEB Moritz, Maurycy 1856-1879 **[13]**
⌐ **$183 465** - €171 659 - **£111 211** - FF1 126 007
Powitanie Natana przez Reche Oil/canvas
(110x80cm 43x31in) Warszawa 1999
⌐ **$14 000** - €16 650 - **£9 977** - FF109 214
Portrait of a Jewish Man Oil/canvas/board
(25.5x14cm 10x5in) New-York 2000

GOTTLOB Fernand Louis 1873-1935 **[22]**
⊞ **$1 600** - €1 539 - **£987** - FF10 093
«Salon des Cent» Poster (57.5x38cm 22x14in) New-
York 1999

GOTTLOB Maurice, Mau XIX-XX **[4]**
✥ $558 - €640 - **£381** - FF4 200
Max Linder Plâtre (H40cm H15in) Paris 2000

GOTTMAN Lorens, Lars 1708-1779 **[1]**
⌐ **$19 257** - €16 396 - **£11 500** - FF107 549
**Italianate landscape with travellers resting and
drinking from a river** Oil/canvas (55.9x66.5cm
22x26in) London 1998

GOTTSCHALK Albert 1866-1906 **[70]**
⌐ **$1 327** - €1 542 - **£932** - FF10 117
Landskab med traeer Oil/canvas (37x53cm 14x20in)
Köbenhavn 2001
⌐ $796 - €858 - **£548** - FF5 629
Portraet af mand med röd fez Oil/board (24x17cm
9x6in) Köbenhavn 2001

GOTTWALD Frederick C. 1860-1941 **[14]**
⌐ **$1 401** - €1 622 - **£992** - FF10 637
Interior Scene: The Lesson Oil/canvas (45x55cm
18x22in) Cleveland OH 2000

GÖTZ Hermann 1848-1901 **[4]**
⌐ **$15 140** - €16 617 - **£9 744** - FF109 000
Chasse à courre Huile/toile (135x332cm 53x130in)
Nancy 2000

GÖTZ Karl Otto 1914 **[288]**
⌐ **$26 065** - €22 486 - **£15 664** - FF147 501
«Trefang» Mixed media/canvas (120x150cm 47x59in)
Köln 1998
⌐ **$12 069** - €11 248 - **£7 447** - FF73 785
Figuren und Symbole IV Acrylic (36x48cm
14x18in) Hamburg 1999
✎ **$2 167** - €2 556 - **£1 529** - FF16 769
Spanisches Gouache/paper (30.8x40.3cm 12x15in)
Köln 2001
⊞ $210 - €245 - **£146** - FF1 609
Kallo Farblithographie (59.5x69.8cm 23x27in) Köln
1999

GÖTZ-RÄCKNITZ Paul 1873-1952 **[74]**
⌐ $260 - €230 - **£159** - FF1 509
«Mann mit Tonpfeife» Öl/Karton (50x40cm 19x15in)
München 1999

GÖTZE Karl Alexander 1887-? **[3]**
✎ **$2 224** - €2 496 - **£1 541** - FF16 371
Untitled Watercolour (68x53cm 26x20in) Amsterdam
2000

GÖTZINGER Hans 1867-1941 **[44]**
✎ $680 - €581 - **£407** - FF3 812
Biedermeierinterieur mit Gitarre Watercolour/paper
(26x34cm 10x13in) Wien 1998

GÖTZLOFF Karl Wilhelm 1799-1866 **[36]**
⌐ **$17 468** - €17 895 - **£10 780** - FF117 386
Blick auf den Golf von Neapel Öl/Leinwand
(57.5x83cm 22x32in) Düsseldorf 2000
⌐ **$16 001** - €15 886 - **£10 000** - FF104 207
Vue prise de l'hôtel/Salerno/Atrani près d'amalfi
Oil/canvas (20x25cm 7x9in) London 1999
✎ **$2 566** - €2 914 - **£1 783** - FF19 117
Blick auf Palermo und den Monte Pellegrino
Watercolour (23.5x33cm 9x12in) Berlin 2001

GOUBAU Antoon 1616-1698 **[13]**
⌐ **$63 765** - €71 425 - **£44 330** - FF468 520
**A Southern Landscape with a Market near clas-
sical Ruins** Oil/canvas (136x175cm 53x68in) Uppsala
2001
⌐ **$16 896** - €15 857 - **£10 560** - FF104 016
La Crucificación Oleo/lienzo (66.5x49cm 26x19in)
Palma de Mallorca 2001

GOUBAU Laureys XVII **[3]**
⌐ **$6 420** - €6 378 - **£4 000** - FF41 834
Peasant Family seated by a Barm Oil/panel
(34.5x45.5cm 13x17in) London 1999

GOUBERT Lucien 1887-1964 **[137]**
⌐ $958 - €838 - **£580** - FF5 503
Effet de vague dans la Hague Huile/toile (46x61cm
18x24in) Cherbourg 1998
⌐ $412 - €457 - **£285** - FF3 000
Effet de vague Huile/carton (27x35cm 10x13in)
Cherbourg 2001
✎ $252 - €221 - **£153** - FF1 450
Pêcheur à pied Dessin (18.8x26.4cm 7x10in)
Cherbourg 1998

GOUBIE Jean Richard 1842-1899 **[25]**
⌐ **$8 264** - €6 788 - **£4 800** - FF44 526
An Afternoon Ride Oil/canvas (46.5x55.5cm
18x21in) London 1998
⌐ **$8 494** - €9 715 - **£5 833** - FF63 724
Reiterin und Reiter auf rassigen Pferden
Öl/Leinwand (35.5x43cm 13x16in) Lindau 2000

GOUD Laxma 1940 **[23]**
⌐ **$2 250** - €2 559 - **£1 572** - FF16 785
Untitled Pencil (44.5x72.5cm 17x28in) New-York
2000

GOUDIACHVILI Lado 1896-1980 **[10]**
⌐ **$6 775** - €7 622 - **£4 665** - FF50 000
Vue sur le lac et les montagnes Huile/toile
(72.5x59cm 28x23in) La Varenne-Saint-Hilaire 2000
✎ **$2 898** - €3 201 - **£2 009** - FF21 000
Parisienne à la terrasse d'un café Crayon gras
(41x26cm 16x10in) Paris 2001

GOUDIE Alexander 1933 **[41]**
⌐ **$8 649** - €8 080 - **£5 337** - FF53 000
Le ramassage des pommes de terre Huile/toile
(115x100cm 45x39in) Brest 1999

G

$512 - €610 - £365 - FF4 000
Composition au pichet fleuri Aquarelle/papier
(38x28cm 14x11in) Brest 2000

GOUDT Hendrick 1582/88-1630/48 [63]
$3 896 - €4 538 - £2 722 - FF29 766
Group of Three Men Talking Together, Drawn
Over a Faint Study Ink (10.5x8.5cm 4x3in)
Amsterdam 2000

$650 - €728 - £453 - FF4 775
Landscape at Dawn: Aurora, after Elsheimer
Engraving (16x18cm 6x7in) New-York 2001

GOUDY William Frederic 1865-1947 [1]
$6 000 - €7 052 - £4 159 - FF46 256
Figure in Kimono Oil/canvas (71x71cm 27x27in)
Beverly-Hills CA 2000

GOUGH J. XIX [1]
$5 000 - €5 038 - £3 117 - FF33 050
The M.M. Jones Oil/canvas (35.5x61cm 13x24in)
New-York 2000

GOULD & HART John H. & William M. 1804/30-1881/1908 [15]
$250 - €268 - £165 - FF1 761
Hylonympha Macrocerca Hummingbirds
Lithograph (50x34cm 20x13in) New-Orleans LA 2000

GOULD & RICHTER John H. & H. Const. 1804/21-1881/1902 [133]
$325 - €358 - £217 - FF2 350
Gennaeus Nycthemerus Color lithograph (38x55cm 15x22in) East-Dennis MA 2000

GOULD Alexander Carruthers 1870-1948 [51]
$514 - €477 - £328 - FF3 129
The Road through Porlock Oil/board (28x36cm 11x14in) London 1999

GOULD Chester 1900-1987 [8]
$800 - €859 - £535 - FF5 632
Five Dick Tracy Daily Strips Ink (13x42cm 5x16in)
New-York 2000

GOULD David XIX-XX [11]
$8 965 - €9 624 - £6 000 - FF63 129
Calves Resting in a Barn Oil/canvas (51x76.5cm 20x30in) London 2000

GOULD Elisabeth 1804-1841 [17]
$1 010 - €1 133 - £700 - FF7 432
Otus Bengalensis Lithograph (44.5x33cm 17x12in)
London 2000

GOULD John H. 1804-1881 [627]
$182 - €213 - £126 - FF1 395
Prioniturus Flavicans Lithograph (55.5x37.5cm 21x14in) Melbourne 2000

GOULD John H. & Elizabeth 1804-1881/41 [5]
$233 - €257 - £155 - FF1 684
Estrelda Bichenovii Color lithograph (50x33.5cm 19x13in) Sydney 2000

GOULD Joseph J., Jr. 1880-1935 [17]
$1 500 - €1 700 - £1 048 - FF11 149
Winner and Still Champion Black chalk (24x37cm 9x14in) New-York 2001

$549 - €599 - £380 - FF3 927
«Lippincott's February» Poster (48x28cm 18x11in)
London 2001

GOULD Walter 1829-1893 [1]
$9 000 - €10 413 - £6 370 - FF68 305
Henry Clay Oil/canvas (86x68cm 34x27in) Cleveland OH 2000

GOULD William Buelow 1803-1853 [9]
$7 791 - €8 867 - £5 475 - FF58 165
Still Life, Fruit and Flowers Oil/canvas (62.5x75cm 24x29in) Woollahra, Sydney 2001

GOULDEN Jean 1878-1947 [3]
$28 875 - €32 014 - £19 992 - FF210 000
Le vol des mouettes Email (53x40cm 20x15in) Paris 2001

GOULT de Alfred XIX [2]
$23 472 - €27 441 - £16 758 - FF180 000
Le marché aux esclaves/La danse orientale
Huile/toile (135x73cm 53x28in) Paris 2001

GOUNAROPOULOS Giorgios 1889-1977 [34]
$6 578 - €7 548 - £4 500 - FF49 509
Oil/canvas (55.5x46cm 21x18in) London 2000

GOUNOD François Louis 1758-1823 [4]
$3 964 - €4 726 - £2 827 - FF31 000
Portrait du maréchal de Castellane Huile/toile (86x53cm 33x20in) Lyon 2000

GOUPIL Ernest ?-1841 [8]
$9 662 - €9 124 - £6 000 - FF59 847
The Astrolabe and Zelée off Elephant Island
Pencil (24x41cm 9x16in) London 1999

GOUPIL Jules Adolphe 1839-1883 [23]
$5 084 - €4 931 - £3 200 - FF32 344
Portrait of a Young Girl Wearing a Feathered Hat
Oil/canvas (81x65.5cm 31x25in) London 1999

GOUPIL Léon Lucien 1834-1890 [12]
$2 409 - €2 727 - £1 628 - FF17 886
Les politiques Huile/panneau (27x37cm 10x14in)
Bruxelles 2000

GOUPY Joseph 1689-1763 [9]
$2 539 - €2 359 - £1 550 - FF15 473
Tobias and the Angel in a Rocky Landscape
Gouache/paper (26.5x41cm 10x16in) London 1998

GOURDAULT Pierre 1880-1915 [15]
$557 - €534 - £350 - FF3 500
Pont et rivière Huile/toile (38x55cm 14x21in)
Neuilly-sur-Seine 1999

GOURDON Michel 1925 [13]
$331 - €305 - £198 - FF2 000
Meurtre dans les Alpilles Gouache/papier (34x31.5cm 13x12in) Paris 1999

GOURDON René 1855-? [14]
$960 - €901 - £585 - FF5 910
Campesina en el bosque Oleo/lienzo (50.5x73cm 19x28in) Madrid 1999

GOUREAU P.E. XX [3]
$810 - €908 - £550 - FF5 953
Jockey Max Dearly Bronze (H32cm H12in)
Amsterdam 2000

GOURGUE Jacques Enguerrand 1930-1996 [52]
$1 400 - €1 453 - £888 - FF9 529
Maison inachevée Oil/masonite (65.5x81cm 25x31in) Boston MA 2000

GOURY Juliette 1878-? [2]
$1 007 - €1 134 - £694 - FF7 441
Bouquet de roses Watercolour (37x73cm 14x28in)
Amsterdam 2000

GOUSSÉ Henri XIX-XX [4]
$3 721 - €3 664 - £2 379 - FF24 034
Trabajandoen el muelle Oleo/lienzo (81x100cm 31x39in) Barcelona 1999

GOUSSEV Vladimir 1957 **[57]**
- $702 - €781 - £481 - FF5 122
  Invierno en el pueblo Oleo/lienzo (60x80cm 23x31in) Madrid 2000
- $316 - €305 - £198 - FF2 000
  En cueillant des coquelicots Huile/toile/carton (27x41cm 10x16in) L'Isle-Adam 1999

GOUVERNEUR Arthur 1852-? **[10]**
- $488 - €457 - £302 - FF3 000
  E.Veil Picard Aquarelle/papier (47x30cm 18x11in) Senlis 1999

GOUVRANT Gérard 1946 **[196]**
- $1 389 - €1 524 - £894 - FF10 000
  Retour au port Huile/toile (46x55cm 18x21in) Thonon-les-Bains 2000
- $462 - €503 - £317 - FF3 300
  Les petits fiances Huile/toile (22x27cm 8x10in) Reze 2001

GOUWE Adriaan Herman 1875-1965 **[87]**
- $3 268 - €3 403 - £2 070 - FF22 324
  Boer met ploegende ossen Oil/canvas (46x95cm 18x37in) Maastricht 2000
- $467 - €511 - £323 - FF3 353
  Hirtenjunge mit äesenden Schafen in einer Waldlichtung Öl/Leinwand (33x44cm 12x17in) Heidelberg 2001
- $325 - €363 - £217 - FF2 381
  Beach with Seagulls and a Boat Watercolour/paper (26.5x37cm 10x14in) Amsterdam 2000

GOUWELOOS Jean 1868-1943 **[87]**
- $2 838 - €2 727 - £1 749 - FF17 886
  Nu debout de côté Huile/toile (63x35cm 24x13in) Bruxelles 1999
- $1 559 - €1 376 - £940 - FF9 029
  «A l'ami J.Dupont» Oil/panel (24x31cm 9x12in) Bristol, Avon 1999

GOUWEN van der Willem / Gillem act.1669/70-1720 **[4]**
- $652 - €767 - £469 - FF5 030
  Der gestrandete Walfisch zwischen Scheveningen und Katwijk Kupferstich (27.5x34cm 10x13in) Hamburg 2001

GOVAERTS Abraham 1589-1626 **[25]**
- $55 580 - €50 871 - £33 880 - FF333 690
  Rastende Bauern an einer Waldstrasse nahe einem Fluss Öl/Kupfer (44x65cm 17x25in) Wien 1999

GOVAERTS Hendrik 1669-1720 **[14]**
- $6 539 - €6 403 - £4 023 - FF42 000
  Réunion de musiciens/Danse dans un intérieur Huile/toile (48x56cm 18x22in) Paris 1999
- $7 600 - €9 848 - £5 700 - FF64 600
  Compagnia allegra Olio/tavola (30x39cm 11x15in) Milano 2000

GOVAN Mary Maitland XIX-XX **[2]**
- $5 697 - €5 545 - £3 500 - FF36 370
  Young Mother and Child Oil/board (36x26cm 14x10in) Penrith, Cumbria 1999

GOW James ?-1886 **[1]**
- $3 363 - €3 973 - £2 383 - FF26 064
  Junge Familie Öl/Leinwand (81.7x59.2cm 32x23in) Zürich 2000

GOW Marie Louise 1851-1929 **[12]**
- $3 503 - €4 108 - £2 626 - FF26 949
  His Lordship, the Baby Watercolour/paper (35.5x18.5cm 13x7in) Manchester 2000

GOWER Ronald Sutherland 1845-1915 **[4]**
- $14 000 - €15 681 - £9 727 - FF102 860
  Marie Antoinette heading for Execution by Guillotine Bronze (H116cm H46in) St. Louis MO 2001

GOWIN Emmet 1941 **[44]**
- $2 000 - €2 303 - £1 364 - FF15 104
  Edith, Danville, Virginia Gelatin silver print (13x17cm 5x6in) New-York 2000

GOWING Lawrence 1918 **[7]**
- $7 471 - €8 020 - £5 000 - FF52 608
  Boy Reading Oil/canvas (40.5x50.5cm 15x19in) London 2000

GOYA Y LUCIENTES Francisco 1746-1828 **[1012]**
- $420 000 - €360 389 - £252 000 - FF2 364 000
  La muerte de San Francisco Javier Oleo/lienzo (106x78cm 41x30in) Madrid 1998
- $450 000 - €455 236 - £274 770 - FF2 986 155
  Hannibal the Conqueror, viewing Italy from the Alps for the First Time Oil/canvas (31x40.5cm 12x15in) New-York 2000
- $140 000 - €149 513 - £95 396 - FF980 742
  Portrait of Cesar Arbasia, Bust-Length Red chalk/paper (17.5x10.5cm 6x4in) New-York 2001
- $550 - €578 - £372 - FF3 790
  Correccion Etching (18x13cm 7x5in) Boston MA 2001

GOYEN van A. XVIII **[2]**
- $3 506 - €4 084 - £2 449 - FF26 789
  View of a Village Black chalk/paper (11.5x22.5cm 4x8in) Amsterdam 2000

GOYEN van Jan Jozefsz. 1596-1656 **[309]**
- $380 000 - €334 451 - £231 344 - FF2 193 854
  River Landscape with Passengers and Cows on a Ferry near a Cottage Oil/canvas (112.5x152cm 44x59in) New-York 1999
- $149 770 - €123 517 - £88 230 - FF810 220
  Holländische Flusslandschaft mit einem bewohnten Turm, Segelbooten Öl/Leinwand (77x65cm 30x25in) Wien 1998
- $46 932 - €54 454 - £32 400 - FF357 192
  Figures Standing on a Hill, with a Farm beyond Oil/panel (32x43cm 12x16in) Amsterdam 2000
- $18 460 - €15 944 - £11 128 - FF104 586
  A Village Harbour along a River Wash (17x29cm 6x11in) Amsterdam 1998

GOYO Hachiguchi c.1880-1921 **[34]**
- $13 000 - €13 100 - £8 104 - FF85 930
  Woman in Indian Dress and Cranes Ink (145x39.5cm 57x15in) New-York 2000
- $3 500 - €3 868 - £2 427 - FF25 373
  Kyoto Sanjo Ohashi (Great Bridge at Sanjo, Kyoto) Woodcut (29.5x48.5cm 11x19in) New-York 2001

GOZZARD James Walter 1888-1950 **[27]**
- $627 - €611 - £380 - FF4 011
  The Young Anglers Oil/canvas (30.5x40.5cm 12x15in) London 2000
- $641 - €647 - £400 - FF4 241
  Figures on a Path approaching cottages at dusk Watercolour (25x36cm 10x14in) Dorchester, Dorset 2000

GRAADT VAN ROGGEN Johannes 1867-1959 **[30]**
- $273 - €318 - £189 - FF2 083
  Portret van Engelsman met baret/ Oil/canvas (46x32cm 18x12in) Groningen 2000

G

G

▭▭▭ **$70** - €82 - **£48** - FF535
Voor anker liggende bomschuiten Etching
(42.5x69cm 16x27in) Groningen 2000

GRAAF de Josua 1640/45-c.1712 **[19]**
🖌 **$4 500** - €4 806 - **£3 066** - FF31 526
View near Maastricht/Sketch of a Village Ink
(13x20.5cm 5x8in) New-York 2001

GRAAFLAND Rob 1875-1940 **[12]**
🖌 **$4 188** - €4 175 - **£2 543** - FF27 384
Zigeunermeisje in een duinpan Oil/canvas
(60x40cm 23x15in) Amsterdam 2000
🖌 **$3 528** - €3 971 - **£2 430** - FF26 045
Young Lady Oil/canvas (36x21cm 14x8in) Maastricht
2000
🖌 **$928** - €998 - **£632** - FF6 548
Vrouw leunend tegen een deur Pencil/paper
(45x21cm 17x8in) Maastricht 2001

GRAAT Barend 1628-1709 **[15]**
🖌 **$10 086** - €9 879 - **£6 500** - FF64 802
**Reclining youth holding Fruit and Flowers with
a Brother and Sister** Oil/canvas (78x141.5cm
30x55in) London 1999
🖌 **$3 000** - €3 291 - **£1 992** - FF21 590
Diana the Huntress in a Landscape
Oil/canvas/panel (33.5x44.5cm 13x17in) New-York
2000

GRAB von Bertha 1846-c.1921 **[10]**
🖌 **$2 400** - €2 383 - **£1 500** - FF15 631
Sailing Boats off the Coast Oil/canvas
(48.5x60.5cm 19x23in) London 1999

GRAB Walter 1927-1989 **[26]**
🖌 **$612** - €592 - **£377** - FF3 885
Auf meinem Balkon Huile/panneau (73x60cm
28x23in) Zürich 1999

GRABACH John R. 1886-1981 **[45]**
🖌 **$17 000** - €19 303 - **£11 634** - FF126 622
Connecticut River in Winter, Deerfield Oil/canvas
(107x122cm 42x48in) New-York 2000
🖌 **$1 900** - €1 603 - **£1 114** - FF10 514
Nude with Fan Oil/canvas/panel (45.5x35.5cm
17x13in) New-York 1998
🖌 **$749** - €867 - **£530** - FF5 688
Grand Central Coachman Oil/wood (39x30cm
15x11in) Cleveland OH 2001

GRABAR Igor Emanuilovich 1871-1960 **[12]**
🖌 **$9 071** - €10 008 - **£6 000** - FF65 649
Stalin Giving Advice Oil/canvas (119x139cm
46x54in) London 2000
🖌 **$10 467** - €9 884 - **£6 500** - FF64 834
Still Life Oil/canvas (44x57.5cm 17x22in) London
1999
🖌 **$2 003** - €2 325 - **£1 382** - FF15 254
Kleine Winterlandschaft Öl/Karton (20x31cm
7x12in) Wien 2000

GRÄBHEIN Wilhelm 1859-? **[18]**
🖌 **$515** - €499 - **£321** - FF3 274
Ein Fuchs schlägt eine Wildente Öl/Papier
(31.5x47cm 12x18in) Zürich 1999

GRABILL John C.H. XIX-XX **[7]**
📷 **$325** - €387 - **£224** - FF2 536
«Fort Meade, Dak» Albumen print (16x21cm 6x8in)
Baltimore MD 2000

GRABINSKI Henryk 1842-1903 **[3]**
🖌 **$3 766** - €3 524 - **£2 283** - FF23 116
Polish Landscape Oil/canvas (30x45.5cm 11x17in)
Warszawa 1999

GRABMAYER Franz 1927 **[18]**
🖌 **$6 110** - €7 267 - **£4 360** - FF47 670
Waldviertler Landschaft Öl/Leinwand (130x147cm
51x57in) Wien 2000
🖌 **$1 280** - €1 431 - **£863** - FF9 390
Materialbild Mixed media (120x93cm 47x36in)
München 2000

GRABNER Pepo 1897-1991 **[9]**
🖌 **$826** - €799 - **£509** - FF5 243
Der Kreuzberglteich Aquarell/Papier (66x55cm
25x21in) Klagenfurt 1999

GRABOWSKI Andrzej 1833-1866 **[3]**
🖌 **$4 229** - €4 913 - **£2 971** - FF32 228
Règlement de compte avec Arendarz
Huile/toile/panneau (29x29cm 11x11in) Warszawa 2001

GRACE A.L. XIX **[19]**
🖌 **$805** - €864 - **£538** - FF5 669
Contemplation Oil/canvas (50.5x40.5cm 19x15in)
Toronto 2000

GRACE Alfred Fitzwalter 1884-1903 **[7]**
🖌 **$645** - €767 - **£460** - FF5 034
On the South Downs Watercolour (24x35.5cm
9x13in) Bath 2000

GRACE James Edward 1851-1908 **[29]**
🖌 **$1 000** - €1 050 - **£676** - FF6 886
Fall Landscape Oil/canvas (51x33cm 20x13in)
Fairfield ME 2001
🖌 **$457** - €516 - **£317** - FF3 383
«Inlet of a Pond» Oil/board (34.5x25cm 13x9in)
Toronto 2000
🖌 **$542** - €632 - **£380** - FF4 145
**Figures Fishing by a Mountain Lake/Thirlmere,
Cumberland** Watercolour (24x35cm 9x13in)
Crewkerne, Somerset 2000

GRACEY Theodore J. 1895-1959 **[16]**
🖌 **$275** - €310 - **£190** - FF2 036
Near Gweedore, Co. Donegal Watercolour/paper
(18x25cm 7x9in) London 2000

GRACH Pierre 1898-1987 **[7]**
▭▭▭ **$1 000** - €1 083 - **£666** - FF7 107
«Le Parisen, tous lisent Le Parisien» Poster
(160x116cm 63x46in) New-York 2000

GRADA de Raffaele 1885-1957 **[103]**
🖌 **$9 500** - €9 848 - **£5 700** - FF64 600
La raccolta delle olive Olio/tela (95x140cm
37x55in) Milano 1999
🖌 **$4 000** - €4 147 - **£2 400** - FF27 200
Campagna toscana Olio/tela (60x70.5cm 23x27in)
Milano 1999
🖌 **$1 680** - €2 177 - **£1 260** - FF14 280
Paesaggio svizzero Olio/tavola (28x39cm 11x15in)
Milano 2000
🖌 **$240** - €311 - **£180** - FF2 040
Paesaggio Inchiostro/carta (27x34cm 10x13in) Milano
2000

GRADL Hermann 1883-1964 **[51]**
🖌 **$1 476** - €1 431 - **£935** - FF9 390
Moorlandschaft bei Abendstimmung
Öl/Leinwand (38x75cm 14x29in) München 1999
🖌 **$1 176** - €1 125 - **£737** - FF7 378
Bei Nesselwangen Öl/Karton (24x31cm 9x12in)
Hamburg 1999
▭▭▭ **$140** - €138 - **£90** - FF905
Baumallee mit Kirchdorf im Hintergrund
Radierung (19x14.5cm 7x5in) Hildrizhausen 1999

GRADY Napoleone Luigi 1860-1949 **[13]**
- **$3 237** - €3 113 - **£1 997** - FF20 418
  Bildnis einer jungen Frau Öl/Leinwand (55x39.5cm 21x15in) Bern 1999

GRAEB Carl Georg Anton 1816-1884 **[14]**
- **$16 723** - €19 429 - **£11 753** - FF127 448
  Ansicht von Spoleto Öl/Leinwand (63x90cm 24x35in) Hamburg 2001
- **$5 989** - €6 135 - **£3 696** - FF40 246
  Kircheninterieur Oil/panel (27x20.6cm 10x8in) Düsseldorf 2000
- **$913** - €920 - **£569** - FF6 037
  Blick auf Burg Stolzenfels und den Rhein Ink (32x41cm 12x16in) Heidelberg 2000

GRAECEN Edmund 1877-1949 **[6]**
- **$2 000** - €2 141 - **£1 361** - FF14 045
  Study in Pink Oil/board (40x30cm 16x12in) Portsmouth NH 2001

GRAEF de Timotheus c.1650/70-? **[3]**
- **$8 671** - €9 174 - **£5 500** - FF60 179
  Evening Landscape with Travellers and Fisherman on a Track Oil/canvas (90.5x74cm 35x29in) London 2000

GRAEF Robert A. c.1878-1951 **[2]**
- **$22 000** - €24 642 - **£15 285** - FF161 638
  Man battling alien Monster Gouache/paper (47x41cm 18x16in) New-York 2001

GRAEFF Werner 1901-1978 **[20]**
- **$5 848** - €5 624 - **£3 609** - FF36 892
  Stijl 20 L. Tempera/canvas (75x75cm 29x29in) Köln 1999
- **$215** - €204 - **£133** - FF1 341
  Ligriklo Woodcut in colors (50.5x65cm 19x25in) Hamburg 1999

GRAEME Colin 1858-1910 **[117]**
- **$2 000** - €2 178 - **£1 377** - FF14 288
  A Winter Morning Oil/canvas (40.5x51cm 15x20in) New-York 2001
- **$2 152** - €2 466 - **£1 300** - FF13 159
  Pointers in a Highland Landscape Oil/canvas (25.5x35.5cm 10x13in) London 1998

GRAESER Camille 1882-1980 **[71]**
- **$1 752** - €1 923 - **£1 190** - FF12 611
  Komplementäres Spannungsfeld Acrylic/board (46x46cm 18x18in) Luzern 2000
- **$1 752** - €1 923 - **£1 190** - FF12 611
  Translokation C Acrylic/board (32x32cm 12x12in) Luzern 2000
- **$1 731** - €1 959 - **£1 211** - FF12 847
  «2 volumen 1:1» Sculpture (48x48x5cm 18x18x1in) Zürich 2001
- **$3 290** - €3 016 - **£2 010** - FF19 781
  Stufenrhythmus Crayons couleurs/papier (14x14cm 5x5in) Zürich 1999
- **$199** - €237 - **£141** - FF1 553
  «Blau, rot 3:1» Farbserigraphie (60x60cm 23x23in) Zürich 2000

GRAF Carl C. 1890-1947 **[10]**
- **$4 500** - €4 467 - **£2 760** - FF29 302
  Brown Country Scene Oil/board (63x91cm 25x36in) Mystic CT 2000

GRAF Emil 1901-1980 **[12]**
- **$2 669** - €2 866 - **£1 786** - FF18 799
  Appenzeller Bauernhof, im Vordergrund Sennen beim Schellenschötte Huile/panneau (32x42cm 12x16in) St. Gallen 2000

$1 796 - €1 550 - **£1 083** - FF10 166
  Grosser Dorfplatz mit Passanten und Pferdefuhrwagen Pencil (50x61cm 19x24in) St. Gallen 1998

GRAF Ernst 1909-1988 **[42]**
- **$106** - €115 - **£71** - FF752
  Drachen am Strand Linocut in colors (31x52cm 12x20in) St. Gallen 2000

GRAF Gerhard 1883-1960 **[52]**
- **$952** - €1 022 - **£637** - FF6 707
  Rathaus von Posen in der Wintersonne Öl/Karton (60x50cm 23x19in) Bremen 2000

GRAF Gottfried 1881-1938 **[36]**
- **$194** - €204 - **£122** - FF1 341
  Baldur-Motiv Farbradierung (61.5x38cm 24x14in) Stuttgart 2000

GRAF Karl 1902-1986 **[18]**
- **$359** - €332 - **£216** - FF2 180
  Wanderer auf der Strasse vor Gleiswiler Watercolour (59x64.7cm 19x25in) Heidelberg 1999

GRAF Ludwig Ferdinand 1868-1932 **[14]**
- **$34 785** - €32 703 - **£21 060** - FF214 515
  In Erwartung Öl/Leinwand (142x158cm 55x62in) Wien 1999
- **$11 595** - €10 901 - **£7 020** - FF71 505
  Rosenstrauss in Vase Öl/Karton (71x55.5cm 27x21in) Wien 1999
- **$13 080** - €14 534 - **£8 760** - FF95 340
  Urteil des Paris Oil/panel (40x39cm 15x15in) Wien 2000

GRAF Oskar 1873-1957 **[52]**
- **$625** - €716 - **£430** - FF4 695
  Festliche Gesellschaft im Park bei einer Fontaine Oil/board (59x54cm 23x21in) München 2000
- **$90** - €77 - **£53** - FF502
  Stadtansicht Radierung (14x13cm 5x5in) München 1998

GRAF Paul Edmund 1856/66-1903 **[20]**
- **$3 750** - €3 430 - **£2 290** - FF22 498
  A Game of Cards Oil/canvas (45.5x61cm 17x24in) New-York 1998

GRAF Philip 1874-1947 **[40]**
- **$1 388** - €1 534 - **£962** - FF10 061
  Chiemsee mit Fraueninsel und Kloster Öl/Leinwand (70x95cm 27x37in) München 2001
- **$250** - €281 - **£170** - FF1 844
  Winterlandschaft Aquarell/Papier (35x45cm 13x17in) München 2000

GRAF Urs c.1485-1527 **[19]**
- **$215** - €250 - **£148** - FF1 637
  Ein Papst empfängt eine Abordnung Rechtsgelehrter und Mönche Woodcut (23.5x19.5cm 9x7in) Zürich 2000

GRAFF Anton 1736-1813 **[74]**
- **$5 516** - €5 298 - **£3 418** - FF34 751
  Bildnis des Christian Fürchtegott Gellert Öl/Leinwand (60x43cm 23x16in) Zürich 1999
- **$5 768** - €5 814 - **£3 600** - FF38 136
  Selbstbildnis eines Künstlers Oil/paper/panel (19.5x15.5cm 7x6in) Wien 2000
- **$895** - €869 - **£557** - FF5 701
  Brustbild einer Dame im Profil nach links Pencil (9.2x7cm 3x2in) Berlin 1999
- **$343** - €409 - **£244** - FF2 683
  Basse, Kaufmann aus Frankfurt am Main Radierung (18.4x11.8cm 7x4in) Berlin 2000

GRAFFENRIED von Karl Adolf 1801-1859 [4]

- **$2 466** - €2 368 - **£1 528** - FF15 535
  Italienische Stadtvedute Öl/Leinwand (27x42cm 10x16in) Zürich 1999

GRAFTON Robert Wadsworth 1876-1936 [14]

- **$6 000** - €6 694 - **£3 927** - FF43 909
  Young woman sewing Oil/canvas (60x50cm 24x20in) Chicago IL 2000
- **$4 000** - €4 715 - **£2 810** - FF30 926
  Fishing Boats Oil/panel (38x27cm 15x11in) New-Orleans LA 2000

GRAGNOLI Ovidio XX [17]

- **$560** - €726 - **£420** - FF4 760
  Stalla toscana Olio/tavola (50x70cm 19x27in) Prato 2001
- **$700** - €726 - **£420** - FF4 760
  Sensali alla fiera del bestiame Olio/tavola (27x39cm 10x15in) Prato 2000

GRAHAM Anne Marie 1925 [22]

- **$1 284** - €1 415 - **£854** - FF9 281
  Covent Gardens Oil/canvas (60x90cm 23x35in) Melbourne 2000

GRAHAM Ben XX [9]

- **$173** - €203 - **£120** - FF1 334
  Bit of Dartmoor Watercolour/paper (17x48cm 7x19in) Lewes, Sussex 2000

GRAHAM Colin D. 1915 [30]

- **$325** - €365 - **£226** - FF2 393
  Alberta Landscape Watercolour/paper (53x73cm 21x29in) Calgary, Alberta 2001

GRAHAM Dan 1942 [33]

- **$11 000** - €12 299 - **£7 415** - FF80 678
  Pavillion Sculpture for Park Setting Construction (23.5x44.5x44.5cm 9x17x17in) New-York 2000
- **$6 478** - €5 409 - **£3 800** - FF35 481
  Court Steps, New York City/Side Facade of Suburban House Photograph (89x63.5cm 35x25in) London 1998

GRAHAM David 1926 [17]

- **$937** - €917 - **£600** - FF6 017
  Edith, Ferry across the Thames Oil/canvas (61x51cm 24x20in) London 1999

GRAHAM George II 1881-1949 [89]

- **$1 053** - €983 - **£650** - FF6 451
  Bolton Castle Oil/canvas (71x91.5cm 27x36in) London 1999
- **$849** - €803 - **£525** - FF5 267
  Parish Church Whitby Oil/canvas (28x44cm 11x17in) Whitby, Yorks 1999
- **$225** - €242 - **£150** - FF1 585
  Saint Aubins, Jersey Watercolour (25.5x38cm 10x14in) London 2000

GRAHAM James 1806-1869 [4]

- **$2 796** - €2 592 - **£1 727** - FF17 000
  Pozzuoli, la via Appia Tirage albuminé (29x22cm 11x8in) Paris 1999

GRAHAM James Lillie 1873-1965 [20]

- **$582** - €680 - **£405** - FF4 461
  «Cloudy Day near la Malbaie» Oil/panel (18x25.5cm 7x10in) Toronto 2000
- **$637** - €684 - **£426** - FF4 488
  Grazing Cattle Pastel/paper (27x37cm 10x14in) Montréal 2000

GRAHAM John 1754-1817 [6]

- **$34 368** - €33 635 - **£22 000** - FF220 631
  The Reception of Princess Caroline Amelia/The Marriage of George Oil/canvas (54.5x64cm 21x25in) London 1999

GRAHAM John D. 1881/87/90-1961 [24]

- **$200 000** - €188 271 - **£123 560** - FF1 234 980
  Woman with Dodecahedron Mixed media/board (152.5x101.5cm 60x39in) New-York 1999
- **$40 000** - €38 441 - **£24 640** - FF252 156
  Poniatowsky Oil/canvas (76x61cm 29x24in) New-York 1999
- **$35 000** - €38 400 - **£23 250** - FF251 888
  Still Life Oil/canvas (35.5x43.5cm 13x17in) New-York 2000
- **$47 000** - €44 244 - **£29 036** - FF290 220
  Portrait of a Woman with the Third Eye of Perception Pencil (56.5x43cm 22x16in) New-York 1999

GRAHAM Laura Margaret 1912 [12]

- **$6 000** - €7 136 - **£4 276** - FF46 806
  Summer Afternoon Oil/canvas/board (51x60.5cm 20x23in) New-York 2000

GRAHAM Patrick XX [8]

- **$3 871** - €3 303 - **£2 307** - FF21 666
  Study of Joe Coloured chalks (38x56cm 14x22in) Dublin 1998

GRAHAM Peter 1836-1921 [69]

- **$10 848** - €9 705 - **£6 500** - FF63 662
  Sea-Girt Crags Oil/canvas (101.5x152.5cm 39x60in) Perthshire 1998
- **$2 065** - €1 796 - **£1 245** - FF11 783
  «Misty Morn» Oil/canvas (86.5x112cm 34x44in) Toronto 1998
- **$882** - €889 - **£550** - FF5 832
  Wooded Landscape «Evening» Oil/canvas (18x26cm 7x10in) Oxford 2000

GRAHAM Robert 1938 [43]

- **$28 000** - €27 850 - **£17 379** - FF182 683
  Elizabeth Bronze (149x48.5x48.5cm 58x19x19in) Beverly-Hills CA 1999
- **$3 800** - €3 659 - **£2 376** - FF24 001
  Untitled Sculpture (24x21.5x1.5cm 9x8xin) Beverly-Hills CA 1999
- **$1 300** - €1 293 - **£806** - FF8 481
  Untitled No.35 Print (53.5x46cm 21x18in) Beverly-Hills CA 1999

GRAHAM Robert Alexander 1873-1946 [6]

- **$4 500** - €4 830 - **£3 011** - FF31 684
  A Summer Stream Oil/canvas (76x91.5cm 29x36in) San-Francisco CA 2000

GRAHAM Robert MacDonald XIX-XX [2]

- **$4 250** - €4 768 - **£2 952** - FF31 225
  «Coal Miners» Oil/masonite (66x121cm 26x48in) Cincinnati OH 2001

GRAHAM Rodney 1948 [5]

- **$6 000** - €6 709 - **£4 044** - FF44 000
  Bookshelves for Freud's First Editions - The Future of an Illusion Pencil (65.5x85cm 25x33in) New-York 2000
- **$10 000** - €11 381 - **£7 027** - FF74 652
  Tree on Site of Former Camera Obscura Type C color print (114.5x96.5cm 45x37in) New-York 2001

GRAHAM Thomas Alexander 1840-1906 [5]

- **$3 798** - €4 044 - **£2 500** - FF26 526
  Lovers on Westminster Bridge Oil/canvas (67.5x49.5cm 26x19in) Billingshurst, West-Sussex 2000

GRAHAM William 1841-1910 **[9]**
- $700 - €810 - £495 - FF5 312
  Venetian Doorway Scene Oil/canvas (40x50cm 16x20in) Hatfield PA 2000

GRAILLON César A. 1831-? **[1]**
- $6 950 - €7 622 - £4 720 - FF50 000
  La baignade Huile/toile (52x77cm 20x30in) Enghien 2000

GRAILLY de Victor 1804-1889 **[56]**
- $5 514 - €6 403 - £3 927 - FF42 000
  Paysage animé avec cavalières en amazone Huile/toile (54x73cm 21x28in) Senlis 2001
- $2 536 - €2 744 - £1 737 - FF18 000
  Vue de Vaugirard Huile/toile (26x19cm 10x7in) Provins 2001

GRAM Gyda 1851-1906 **[1]**
- $6 552 - €7 258 - £4 446 - FF47 610
  Liten pike med paerer Oil/canvas (34x29cm 13x11in) Oslo 2000

GRAM KLEEN Andrea 1853-1927 **[2]**
- $4 254 - €4 916 - £2 979 - FF32 249
  Kunstnerens söster Margrethe Oil/canvas (36.5x36.5cm 14x14in) Oslo 2001

GRAMART R. XX **[2]**
- $2 840 - €3 049 - £1 900 - FF20 000
  Scène portuaire Aquarelle (15x23cm 5x9in) Paris 2000

GRAMATTÉ Walter 1897-1929 **[129]**
- $4 901 - €5 624 - £3 352 - FF36 892
  Fortgehen, weibliche Gestalt in langem Gewand Aquarell (39.4x29cm 15x11in) Heidelberg 2000
- $476 - €511 - £318 - FF3 353
  Bildnis Siddi Heckel Woodcut (58x44.5cm 22x17in) Hamburg 2000

GRAMATYKA Antoni 1841-1922 **[7]**
- $4 850 - €5 450 - £3 404 - FF35 752
  Paysage de campagne Huile/toile (46x95cm 18x37in) Katowice 2001
- $2 139 - €2 291 - £1 456 - FF15 026
  Procession Huile/carton (33.5x47cm 13x18in) Lódz 2001

GRAMATZKI Eve 1935 **[9]**
- $848 - €991 - £600 - FF6 500
  Sans titre Crayon (129x193cm 50x75in) Paris 2001

GRAMMATICA Antiveduto 1571-1626 **[12]**
- $41 865 - €35 643 - £25 000 - FF233 802
  Madonna and Child with a Still Life of Flowers in a Vase Oil/canvas (96.5x76cm 37x29in) London 1998
- $7 200 - €9 330 - £4 800 - FF61 200
  Quattro donne Olio/tela (35x45cm 13x17in) Roma 2000

GRAN Daniel 1694-1757 **[17]**
- $16 000 - €18 168 - £10 950 - FF119 175
  Das Martyrium des Heiligen Stephan Öl/Leinwand (77.5x41cm 30x16in) Wien 2000
- $1 165 - €1 278 - £791 - FF8 384
  Die Apotheose Maria Theresias, Kaiserin von Österreich Ink (28.9x41.4cm 11x16in) Berlin 2000

GRAN Enrique 1928 **[11]**
- $5 200 - €6 006 - £3 600 - FF39 400
  Sin título Oleo/tabla (67.5x122cm 26x48in) Seville 2000

GRANATA Louis XIX-XX **[12]**
- $1 088 - €1 220 - £756 - FF8 000
  «Rencontre à Bou Saada» Huile/panneau (81.5x61.5cm 32x24in) Paris 2001

GRANCHI-TAYLOR Achille 1857-1921 **[75]**
- $529 - €457 - £319 - FF3 000
  Pêcheur de Concarneau Huile/bois (24x16cm 9x6in) Provins 1998
- $541 - €457 - £321 - FF3 000
  Fouesnantaise en costume du Dimanche Fusain (56x40cm 22x15in) Quimper 1998

GRAND-CARTERET Jean-Albert 1903 **[17]**
- $1 900 - €2 039 - £1 294 - FF13 378
  An Elegant Profile, Portrait of a Woman Pastel/paper (59.5x44.5cm 23x17in) Boston MA 2001

GRANDE Severin 1869-1934 **[17]**
- $1 417 - €1 647 - £995 - FF10 803
  Röde tulipaner Oil/canvas (61x67cm 24x26in) Oslo 2001
- $1 090 - €1 267 - £766 - FF8 310
  Oppstilling med blomster i krukke og epler Oil/canvas/panel (40x39cm 15x15in) Oslo 2001

GRANDEE Joe Ruiz, John 1929 **[9]**
- $1 000 - €1 135 - £694 - FF7 448
  Low Dog Watercolour/paper (38x34cm 15x13in) Dallas TX 2001

GRANDGÉRARD Lucien 1880-1970 **[60]**
- $565 - €549 - £358 - FF3 600
  La sieste Huile/panneau (50x64.5cm 19x25in) Paris 1999

GRANDHOMME Paul XIX **[2]**
- $9 498 - €9 147 - £5 940 - FF60 000
  Andromède Email/panneau (9x6cm 3x2in) Lyon 1999

GRANDI Francesco 1831-1891 **[6]**
- $4 700 - €4 872 - £2 820 - FF31 960
  Rabbino della Sinagoga di Roma Olio/cartone (38x24cm 14x9in) Roma 2000

GRANDI Giuseppe Domenico 1848-1894 **[6]**
- $1 400 - €1 451 - £840 - FF9 520
  Donna che piange Bronzo (H32cm H12in) Milano 2000

GRANDIN Eugène 1833-1919 **[26]**
- $3 043 - €2 897 - £1 903 - FF19 000
  Trois-mâts par gros temps Huile/toile (66x81cm 25x31in) Paris 1999
- $1 553 - €1 342 - £938 - FF8 800
  Le trois-mâts barque Quevilly Aquarelle/papier (24x37cm 9x14in) Le Havre 1998

GRANDIO Constantino, Tino 1926-1977 **[76]**
- $4 200 - €4 505 - £2 775 - FF29 550
  Bailando el tango Oleo/lienzo (65x50cm 25x19in) Madrid 2000
- $1 458 - €1 622 - £1 026 - FF10 638
  Pueblo de Lugo Oleo/lienzo (35x26.5cm 13x10in) Madrid 2001
- $3 080 - €3 304 - £2 090 - FF21 670
  Máscaras de carnaval en Galicia Craies/papier (72x50cm 28x19in) Madrid 2001

GRANDJEAN Edmond Georges 1844-1908 **[7]**
- $20 469 - €17 194 - £12 000 - FF112 782
  Femme nue allongée Oil/canvas (89x146cm 35x57in) London 1998
- $10 000 - €10 394 - £6 302 - FF68 181
  A Family Outing Oil/panel (32.5x23.5cm 12x9in) New-York 2000

G

GRANDMAISON de Nicholas 1892-1978 [66]

- $4 909 - €4 789 - **£3 023** - FF31 412
  Boy Chief Mixed media (52x42cm 20x16in) Montréal 1999
- $1 958 - €1 654 - **£1 176** - FF10 849
  «Naposis» Oil/canvas (33x28cm 12x11in) Calgary, Alberta 1998
- $2 347 - €2 618 - **£1 531** - FF17 170
  Indian Child, File Hills, Saskatchewan
  Pastel/paper (22x15cm 8x5in) Calgary, Alberta 2000

GRANDMAISON de Oreste, Rick 1932-1985 [67]

- $1 035 - €1 204 - **£728** - FF7 901
  «Season's End & New Moon» Oil/board (46x61cm 18x24in) Calgary, Alberta 2001
- $339 - €324 - **£211** - FF2 125
  Mountain Morning, Whiskey Creek, Banff National Park, Alberta, Canada Oil/board (25.5x30.5cm 10x12in) Calgary, Alberta 1999
- $179 - €210 - **£126** - FF1 375
  Skyline of Calgary Pastel/paper (14.5x18cm 5x7in) Calgary, Alberta 2001

GRANDVILLE (Jean Ignace Gérard) 1803-1847 [57]

- $2 662 - €3 011 - **£1 800** - FF19 751
  Tortoise, Snail, Swallow, Crane and other Birds and Animals Watercolour (6.5x7.5cm 2x2in) London 2000
- $372 - €409 - **£253** - FF2 683
  Karikatur auf die Bedrohung der Pressefreiheit Lithographie (21.4x31.1cm 8x12in) Berlin 2000

GRANELL Eugenio Fernandez 1912 [48]

- $13 200 - €12 013 - **£8 200** - FF78 800
  Figuras Oleo/lienzo (55x110cm 21x43in) Madrid 1999
- $2 279 - €2 583 - **£1 548** - FF16 942
  Horizonte lunar Oleo/lienzo/tabla (23x13.5cm 9x5in) Madrid 2000
- $1 120 - €1 201 - **£740** - FF7 880
  Figuras Tinta (20.5x30cm 8x11in) Madrid 2000

GRANER Ernst 1865-1943 [119]

- $3 270 - €3 634 - **£2 190** - FF23 835
  Ausfahrt Kaiser Franz Josef vor dem Schweizertor Aquarell/Papier (36x46.6cm 14x18in) Wien 2000

GRANER Y ARRUFI Luis 1863-1929 [127]

- $38 400 - €36 039 - **£23 400** - FF236 400
  Cena de pescadores, puerto Oleo/lienzo (101x121cm 39x47in) Barcelona 1999
- $7 680 - €7 208 - **£4 800** - FF47 280
  Joven en un interior Oleo/lienzo (116x80cm 45x31in) Madrid 1999
- $1 830 - €1 802 - **£1 170** - FF11 820
  Interior con escritorio Oleo/lienzo (28x36cm 11x14in) Madrid 1999
- $572 - €661 - **£396** - FF4 334
  «Puerto de Buenos Aires» Acuarela (27x35cm 10x13in) Madrid 2001

GRANERI Giovanni Michele 1736-c.1778 [2]

- $43 511 - €36 871 - **£26 000** - FF241 859
  A Cheese Seller/A Travelling Conjurer Oil/canvas (87x69.5cm 34x27in) London 1998

GRANET François-Marius 1775-1849 [89]

- $4 970 - €5 336 - **£3 325** - FF35 000
  La messe à l'intérieur du choeur de l'église des Capucins à Rome Huile/panneau (46x37.5cm 18x14in) Paris 2000
- $4 784 - €5 336 - **£3 216** - FF35 000
  La Bénédiction des fruits de la terre chez Madame de Forbin Huile/toile (30x40cm 11x15in) Saint-Martin-de-Crau 2000

GRANDMAISON de

- $2 327 - €2 744 - **£1 636** - FF18 000
  Ruelle dans une ville italienne Aquarelle (14x10cm 5x3in) Paris 2000

GRANFELT Erik 1919-1990 [41]

- $751 - €841 - **£521** - FF5 516
  Stilleben Oil/canvas (56x68cm 22x26in) Helsinki 2001
- $82 - €84 - **£51** - FF531
  Stadsmuren Lithograph (35x42cm 13x16in) Helsinki 2000

GRANFELT Sigrid 1868-1942 [4]

- $6 803 - €7 736 - **£4 719** - FF50 747
  Storby Oil/canvas (75x100cm 29x39in) Helsinki 2000

GRANINGER Leopold 1852-1941 [15]

- $4 476 - €3 677 - **£2 600** - FF24 118
  A River Torrent in an Autumnal Mountain Landscape Oil/canvas (75.5x142cm 29x55in) London 1998
- $1 252 - €1 453 - **£880** - FF9 534
  Schafe auf der Weide im Frühling Gouache/Karton (42x55cm 16x21in) Wien 2001

GRANT Alistair 1925-1997 [18]

- $1 350 - €1 438 - **£920** - FF9 431
  Girls at a Window Oil/canvas (60x73cm 23x28in) Billingshurst, West-Sussex 2001

GRANT Allan XX [3]

- $2 680 - €2 957 - **£1 772** - FF19 394
  Grace Kelly and Audrey Hepburn Backstage at the Academy Awards Gelatin silver print (51x40.5cm 20x15in) Vancouver, BC. 2000

GRANT Carleton c.1860-c.1899 [29]

- $806 - €904 - **£563** - FF5 927
  English Village Scene with Cartman and Maid in Conversation Watercolour/paper (39x59.5cm 15x23in) Auckland 2001

GRANT Clement Rollins 1849-1893 [14]

- $1 800 - €2 127 - **£1 275** - FF13 951
  Winding Yarn Oil/canvas (63.5x76cm 25x29in) Boston MA 2000
- $2 000 - €2 345 - **£1 438** - FF15 382
  Gathering Flowers Watercolour/paper (26x40cm 10x15in) New-York 2001

GRANT Donald 1930 [60]

- $2 745 - €3 047 - **£1 913** - FF19 989
  Elephant browsing Oil/canvas (51x76cm 20x29in) Dublin 2001
- $1 055 - €1 015 - **£650** - FF6 656
  Wild Dog Charcoal/paper (32x46.5cm 12x18in) London 1999

GRANT Duncan J. Corrow 1885-1978 [410]

- $7 299 - €7 036 - **£4 500** - FF46 156
  Baffle Board II Oil/panel (96.5x105.5cm 37x41in) London 1999
- $2 242 - €2 407 - **£1 500** - FF15 786
  Portrait of a Girl Oil/canvas/board (45x31.5cm 17x12in) London 2000
- $1 604 - €1 616 - **£1 000** - FF10 603
  The Ancient Mariner Charcoal (51x28cm 20x11in) London 2000
- $266 - €301 - **£180** - FF1 975
  Washing Day Color lithograph (77x57.5cm 30x22in) London 2000

GRANT Francis 1803-1878 [38]

- $215 450 - €252 607 - **£155 000** - FF1 656 996
  Daisy Grant, the artist's daughter, full length, wearing a black Dress Oil/canvas (223.5x132.5cm 87x52in) London 2001

$12 404 - €11 602 - **£7 500** - FF76 107
  Viscount Hardinge, Governor-General of India accompagnied, Col. Wood Oil/canvas (52x70cm 20x27in) London 2001

GRANT Frederic Milton 1886-1959 **[30]**
$6 500 - €6 484 - **£4 057** - FF42 531
  Venice Oil/canvas (167x220cm 66x87in) Cincinnati OH 1999
$5 500 - €6 255 - **£3 814** - FF41 031
  Autumn Landscape with Figures Oil/canvas (78x83cm 31x33in) Cincinnati OH 2000

GRANT Gordon Hope 1875-1962 **[228]**
$5 250 - €6 123 - **£3 686** - FF40 164
  China Trade Clipper Ship Oil/canvas (66x91cm 26x36in) Portsmouth NH 2000
$1 800 - €1 706 - **£1 128** - FF11 192
  Harbour Traffic Oil/board (30x40cm 12x16in) Mystic CT 1999
$1 000 - €951 - **£621** - FF6 241
  Caribbean Fisherman in Boats Watercolour/paper (35x48cm 14x19in) San Rafael CA 1999
$180 - €207 - **£124** - FF1 358
  Men at Dock Lithograph (23x30cm 9x12in) Cleveland OH 2000

GRANT Henry ?-c.1893 **[2]**
$4 037 - €4 462 - **£2 800** - FF29 268
  A wayside Conversation Oil/canvas (76x101.5cm 29x39in) London 2001

GRANT J. Jeffrey 1883-1960 **[11]**
$1 200 - €1 435 - **£824** - FF9 410
  Horse Drawn Cart in the Village Oil/canvas (39x34cm 15x13in) Chicago IL 2000
$850 - €1 016 - **£584** - FF6 665
  The Mail Delivery Watercolour/paper (43x55cm 17x22in) Chicago IL 2000

GRANT Keith 1930 **[50]**
$2 301 - €2 186 - **£1 400** - FF14 342
  Storm over the Hebrides Oil/canvas (126x101.5cm 49x39in) London 1999
$173 - €191 - **£120** - FF1 254
  «Aurora Borealis» Watercolour/paper (25.5x34cm 10x13in) London 2001

GRANT William James 1829-1866 **[5]**
$5 804 - €6 536 - **£4 000** - FF42 873
  A Visit to the Old Sodier Oil/canvas (82x134cm 32x52in) London 2000

GRANZOW Wladimir, Wladyslaw 1872-? **[3]**
$2 408 - €2 439 - **£1 512** - FF16 000
  L'espagnole à la mantille Huile/panneau (42x28cm 16x11in) Saint-Dié 2000

GRARD George 1901-1984 **[36]**
$23 100 - €24 788 - **£15 500** - FF162 600
  Plénitude Bronze (H111cm H43in) Antwerpen 2000
$444 - €496 - **£310** - FF3 252
  Nu s'étirant Bronze (H21cm H8in) Bruxelles 2001

GRAS Jean-Pierre 1879-1964 **[33]**
$532 - €473 - **£325** - FF3 100
  Ecce Homo Huile/toile (100x81cm 39x31in) Avignon 1999
$2 904 - €3 049 - **£1 830** - FF20 000
  Nus allongés Bronze (21x58cm 8x22in) Avignon 2000

GRASHOF Otto 1812-1876 **[9]**
$80 000 - €77 033 - **£49 792** - FF505 304
  Parada en el Campo Oil/canvas (80.5x105.5cm 31x41in) New-York 1999

$8 451 - €9 925 - **£6 000** - FF65 106
  La Sambacueca, Chile Watercolour (29x20.5cm 11x8in) London 2000

GRASS Günter 1927 **[60]**
$727 - €844 - **£501** - FF5 533
  Pilze Charcoal (48x64cm 18x25in) Köln 2000
$182 - €204 - **£126** - FF1 341
  «Der Butt» Radierung (28x37cm 11x14in) Kempten 2001

GRASS-MICK Auguste 1873-1963 **[66]**
$1 425 - €1 677 - **£1 021** - FF11 000
  Baigneuses et danseuses Huile/toile (81x116cm 31x45in) Paris 2001
$1 011 - €991 - **£652** - FF6 500
  Intérieur Huile/carton (24x32.5cm 9x12in) Versailles 1999

GRÄSSEL Franz 1861-1948 **[21]**
$4 392 - €4 602 - **£2 905** - FF30 185
  Enten am Weiher unter Bäumen im Sommer Öl/Leinwand (51x61cm 20x24in) München 2000
$4 324 - €4 194 - **£2 721** - FF27 513
  Enten am Bach Aquarell/Papier (63x40cm 24x15in) München 1999

GRASSET Adèle XIX **[3]**
$8 520 - €9 147 - **£5 700** - FF60 000
  Portrait de Madame François, fille du Baron Fain Huile/toile (73x59cm 28x23in) Paris 2000

GRASSET Eugène 1841-1917 **[179]**
$1 862 - €1 982 - **£1 235** - FF13 000
  La Justice (projet d'affiche) Gouache/papier (60x45cm 23x17in) Paris 2000
$1 400 - €1 562 - **£916** - FF10 245
  «1e Exposition d'Art Décoratif» Poster (128x80cm 50x31in) New-York 2000

GRASSI Josef c.1758-1838 **[15]**
$9 397 - €10 943 - **£6 500** - FF71 781
  Portrait of Pauline Herzogin Von Würtemberg, Princess Metternich Oil/canvas (84.5x66cm 33x25in) London 2000

GRASSI Niccola 1682-1750 **[16]**
$50 027 - €46 830 - **£31 000** - FF307 182
  Venus Presenting Arms to Aeneas Oil/canvas (166.5x113.5cm 65x44in) London 1999
$13 566 - €11 719 - **£6 783** - FF76 874
  Giobbe deriso Olio/tela (56x86cm 22x33in) Milano 1999
$2 306 - €2 556 - **£1 601** - FF16 769
  Die Anbetung der Heiligen Drei Könige Öl/Kupfer (17x22cm 6x8in) Köln 2001
$7 471 - €8 020 - **£5 000** - FF52 608
  Allegory with Hercules Pointing to a Monument Decorated Red chalk/paper (20.5x14.5cm 8x5in) London 2000

GRASSIS Giuseppe 1870-1949 **[11]**
$3 000 - €3 110 - **£1 800** - FF20 400
  Rododendri sotto il Monte Bianco Olio/tela (45x60cm 17x23in) Vercelli 2001
$792 - €888 - **£550** - FF5 822
  Count Filippo Giordano delle Lanze Miniature (21.5x12cm 8x4in) London 2001

GRATALOUP Guy-Rachel 1935 **[4]**
$1 456 - €1 524 - **£915** - FF10 000
  Sans titre Technique mixte/papier (81x65cm 31x25in) Versailles 2000

GRATCHEV Alexei Petrovitch c.1780-? **[24]**
- $3 000 - €3 485 - **£2 108** - FF22 863
  Soldier on horseback kissing a maiden Bronze (H26.5cm H10in) New-York 2001

GRATCHEV Georgi Ivanovich 1860-1893 **[3]**
- $3 393 - €3 594 - **£2 291** - FF23 577
  Le baiser de séparation Bronze (H22.5cm H8in) Bruxelles 2001

GRATCHEV Vassily Yacovlevitch 1831-1905 **[37]**
- $2 000 - €2 133 - **£1 332** - FF13 992
  Cossack saying Goodbye Bronze (H24.5cm H9in) New-York 2000

GRATE Erik 1896-1983 **[94]**
- $1 255 - €1 181 - **£778** - FF7 745
  Knäböjande kvinna Bronze (H19cm H7in) Stockholm 1999
- $1 701 - €1 742 - **£1 050** - FF11 427
  Komposition med borg och figurer Chalks/paper (37x27cm 14x10in) Stockholm 2000

GRATH Anton 1881-? **[11]**
- $453 - €511 - **£319** - FF3 353
  Amazone Porcelain (H38cm H14in) Stuttgart 2001

GRATHWOL Ray 1900-1992 **[23]**
- $600 - €668 - **£421** - FF4 383
  Farm Landscape, Summit County Oil/canvas (53x76cm 21x30in) Cleveland OH 2001

GRATON Jean 1923 **[11]**
- $335 - €305 - **£209** - FF2 000
  Le motard Ch. Bourgeois sur sa Yamaha Encre Chine/papier (30x47cm 11x18in) Paris 1999
- $136 - €152 - **£94** - FF1 000
  Le pilote sans visage Sérigraphie (80x60cm 31x23in) Paris 2001

GRATTAN George 1787-1819 **[1]**
- $12 403 - €13 967 - **£8 640** - FF91 619
  Blind Piper Oil/canvas (64x43cm 25x16in) Dublin 2001

GRÄTZ Theodor 1859-1947 **[54]**
- $4 824 - €5 488 - **£3 348** - FF36 000
  La malle poste devant l'auberge Huile/toile (70.5x100cm 27x39in) Fontainebleau 2000
- $177 - €184 - **£112** - FF1 207
  Untertänigste Begrüssung Indian ink (57x49.5cm 22x19in) Zwiesel 2000

GRAU Enrique 1920 **[23]**
- $28 000 - €27 243 - **£17 234** - FF178 704
  Desnudo de mujer Oil/canvas (90x121cm 35x47in) New-York 1999

GRAU SANTOS Julián 1937 **[83]**
- $2 632 - €2 823 - **£1 786** - FF18 518
  «Mercado de Villafranca» Oleo/lienzo (55x46cm 21x18in) Madrid 2001
- $1 485 - €1 652 - **£1 017** - FF10 835
  Jardín Oleo/lienzo (46x33cm 18x12in) Madrid 2000
- $252 - €270 - **£171** - FF1 773
  Tipos Dibujo (26x34cm 10x13in) Madrid 2001
- $156 - €132 - **£92** - FF866
  Casa Litografía (30x21cm 11x8in) Madrid 1998

GRAU Xavier 1951 **[16]**
- $3 640 - €3 904 - **£2 470** - FF25 610
  Los Oficios XVII Oleo/lienzo (100x81cm 39x31in) Madrid 2001

GRAU-GARRIGA Joseph 1929 **[12]**
- $154 - €168 - **£100** - FF1 103
  Pobre i bo Tapisserie (110x65cm 43x25in) Barcelona 2000

GRAU-SALA Emilio 1911-1975 **[1068]**
- $15 900 - €18 019 - **£10 800** - FF118 200
  Niña con jaula Oleo/lienzo (137x104cm 53x40in) Madrid 2000
- $22 000 - €19 988 - **£13 637** - FF131 113
  Paddock Oil/canvas (48.5x59.5cm 19x23in) New-York 1999
- $6 737 - €6 789 - **£4 200** - FF44 535
  Le chat noir Oil/board (41x33cm 16x12in) London 2000
- $2 824 - €3 049 - **£1 952** - FF20 000
  Le hameau au printemps Gouache/papier (32x40cm 12x15in) Paris 2001
- $190 - €204 - **£129** - FF1 339
  El quiqué rojo Litografía (23x16cm 9x6in) Madrid 2001

GRAUBNER Gotthard 1930 **[181]**
- $31 944 - €30 678 - **£19 692** - FF201 234
  Mondlicht III Mixed media (125x130cm 49x51in) München 1999
- $2 857 - €3 068 - **£1 912** - FF20 123
  Ohne Titel (Fliessblatt) Öl/Leinwand (61.5x40.5cm 24x15in) Köln 2000
- $909 - €920 - **£555** - FF6 037
  Ohne Titel Öl/Papier (24x21.5cm 9x8in) Stuttgart 2000
- $1 782 - €1 633 - **£1 089** - FF10 715
  Farbraum Aquarell/Papier (41x31cm 16x12in) Zürich 1999
- $150 - €179 - **£107** - FF1 175
  Ohne Titel Radierung (20.8x14.8cm 8x5in) Berlin 2000

GRAVELOT Hubert Fr. d'Anville 1699-1773 **[34]**
- $1 200 - €1 285 - **£819** - FF8 431
  Scenes from the Life of Christ Ink (21.5x14cm 8x5in) New-York 2001

GRÄVENITZ von Fritz 1892-1952 **[7]**
- $3 552 - €3 323 - **£2 152** - FF21 800
  Reh Bronze (H18cm H7in) Stuttgart 1999

GRAVEROL Jane 1907/10-1984 **[24]**
- $1 022 - €1 190 - **£720** - FF7 804
  «La vie de bohème» Huile/toile (117x73cm 46x28in) Liège 2001
- $712 - €838 - **£516** - FF5 500
  La Statue de la Liberté Crayon (35.5x15.5cm 13x6in) Paris 2001

GRAVES Abbott Fuller 1859-1936 **[83]**
- $78 695 - €87 298 - **£52 332** - FF572 636
  Peonies and Chinese Jar Oil/canvas (101x127cm 40x50in) Milford CT 2000
- $23 000 - €21 293 - **£14 078** - FF139 674
  «Roses» Oil/canvas (74x49cm 29x19in) South-Deerfield MA 1999
- $3 250 - €2 781 - **£1 956** - FF18 245
  Pont Alexandre, 3RD - Over the Seine Oil/board (23x15cm 9x6in) New-York 1998
- $3 800 - €3 442 - **£2 325** - FF22 578
  The Flower Vendor Pastel/paper (34x23cm 13x9in) Portland ME 1998

GRAVES Betsy 1888-1964 **[3]**
- $4 500 - €4 184 - **£2 777** - FF27 448
  Portrait of Edward Lee Oil/canvas (60x48cm 24x19in) Portland ME 1999

GRAVES Henry Richard, Hon. c.1820-c.1885 **[11]**
- $4 268 - €4 639 - **£3 000** - FF32 532
  Portrait of Alice Charlotte Arobin Oil/canvas (107x91.5cm 42x36in) London 2001

GRAVES Morris 1910-2001 **[61]**
- $13 000 - €12 122 - **£8 063** - FF79 514
  Study of the Kass, sleeping Dog Pencil/paper (60.5x46cm 23x18in) New-York 1999

GRAVES Nancy Stevenson 1940-1995 **[54]**
- $7 500 - €7 558 - **£4 675** - FF49 575
  Schatten Oil/canvas (175x175x20cm 68x68x7in) New-York 2000
- $8 000 - €8 348 - **£5 045** - FF54 760
  Fracture 2 Oil/canvas (86.5x66cm 34x25in) New-York 2000
- $20 000 - €22 401 - **£13 896** - FF146 944
  «Evergrowing Mobility» Iron (148x129.5x35.5cm 58x50x13in) New-York 2001
- $6 000 - €6 440 - **£4 015** - FF42 246
  Gulu Watercolour/paper (63.5x101.5cm 25x39in) Beverly-Hills CA 2000
- $650 - €758 - **£450** - FF4 970
  Saille Etching, aquatint in colors (50.5x60cm 19x23in) New-York 2000

GRAVINA Antonio 1934 **[40]**
- $959 - €1 143 - **£684** - FF7 500
  Paris, les bouquinistes sur les quais Huile/toile (50x60cm 19x23in) Paris 2000

GRAY Alfred XX **[2]**
- $1 150 - €1 270 - **£761** - FF8 329
  Herder and Castle at Dusk Oil/canvas (45x60cm 17x23in) Dublin 2000

GRAY Alice XIX-XX **[1]**
- $2 432 - €2 354 - **£1 500** - FF15 438
  Thistledown Watercolour/paper (23.5x39.5cm 9x15in) London 1999

GRAY Cedric XIX-XX **[7]**
- $483 - €481 - **£300** - FF3 153
  Mountainous lakeland scene with sheep grazing Oil/canvas (48x73cm 19x29in) Manchester 1999

GRAY Cleve 1918 **[8]**
- $5 000 - €4 963 - **£3 067** - FF32 558
  Abstract City Scene Oil/canvas (121x76cm 48x30in) Mystic CT 2000

GRAY Douglas Stannus 1890-1959 **[8]**
- $1 604 - €1 616 - **£1 000** - FF10 603
  Still Life with Oranges Roses Oil/canvas (25.5x30.5cm 10x12in) London 2000

GRAY Eilen 1879-1976 **[4]**
- $154 090 - €148 550 - **£95 000** - FF974 424
  Untitled Painting (140x160cm 55x62in) London 1999
- $12 165 - €11 728 - **£7 500** - FF76 928
  Rug Design'Centimetre' for E-1027 Gouache/paper (15.5x18cm 6x7in) London 1999

GRAY Harold 1894-1968 **[6]**
- $1 700 - €1 982 - **£1 177** - FF12 999
  Annie Approaches Daddy Warbucks About the Tramp's Secret Ink (13x49cm 5x19in) New-York 2000

GRAY Henri 1858-c.1924 **[106]**
- $1 357 - €1 296 - **£848** - FF8 500
  «Automobiles & Cycles Georges Richard» Affiche (184x120cm 72x47in) Orléans 1999

GRAY Henri Peters 1819-1877 **[3]**
- $1 700 - €1 972 - **£1 209** - FF12 936
  Portrait of a Young Woman in a Landscape Oil/canvas (35.5x30.5cm 13x12in) Washington 2000

GRAY Jack Lorimer 1927-1981 **[34]**
- $7 500 - €6 993 - **£4 652** - FF45 873
  Ambrose Light Ship Oil/canvas (66x91.5cm 25x36in) New-York 1999
- $1 700 - €2 009 - **£1 204** - FF13 176
  Lobsterman Laying His Traps Watercolour/paper (18x28.5cm 7x11in) Boston MA 2000

GRAY James ?-1947 **[14]**
- $1 425 - €1 204 - **£850** - FF7 899
  «Country Bouquet» Watercolour (52.5x35cm 20x13in) Glasgow 1998

GRAY Kate, Kathryn ?-1931 **[5]**
- $1 300 - €1 519 - **£920** - FF9 967
  Portrait of a young Girl with Basket of Flowers in a Landscape Oil/canvas (60x50cm 24x20in) Columbia SC 2001

GRAY Kate, née Newenham act.1864-1875 **[14]**
- $2 161 - €2 542 - **£1 550** - FF16 675
  «Feeding the Nestlings» Oil/canvas (46x36cm 18x14in) Cheshire 2001

GRAY Monica XIX-XX **[3]**
- $1 300 - €1 325 - **£814** - FF8 692
  Ch.Hildewell Ba-Tang/Hildewell Xane Oil/panel (22x19.5cm 8x7in) New-York 2000

GRAY Norah Neilson 1882-1931 **[3]**
- $4 615 - €5 425 - **£3 200** - FF35 584
  Sleeping Watercolour (39x18cm 15x7in) Edinburgh 2000

GRAY Percy 1869-1952 **[141]**
- $27 500 - €23 496 - **£16 640** - FF154 121
  «Mount Tamalpais» Oil/canvas (66x81.5cm 25x32in) San-Francisco CA 1998
- $4 500 - €3 845 - **£2 722** - FF25 219
  Purple Haze, Lands End, San Francisco Oil/canvas/board (25.5x35.5cm 10x13in) San-Francisco CA 1998
- $8 500 - €9 124 - **£5 688** - FF59 848
  Monterey Dunes Watercolour/paper (28x39.5cm 11x15in) San-Francisco CA 2000
- $9 155 - €10 753 - **£6 500** - FF70 536
  «Coming Home Dinner to Sir Ernest Shackleton April 9, Bohemian's Club» Poster (89x48.5cm 35x19in) London 2000

GRAYBACH John R. 1880-1981 **[1]**
- $4 500 - €4 470 - **£2 790** - FF29 318
  Swimming on the Hudson Oil/canvas (63x76cm 25x30in) Norwalk CT 2000

GRAZI L. XIX **[1]**
- $6 638 - €7 318 - **£4 416** - FF48 000
  La répétition/Le Baptème Huile/toile (55.5x72cm 21x28in) Biarritz 2000

GRAZIANI CICCIO NAPOLETANO Francesco XVII **[24]**
- $7 500 - €6 479 - **£3 750** - FF42 500
  Dopo la battaglia Olio/tela (35x71.5cm 13x28in) Firenze 1999
- $7 716 - €8 721 - **£5 208** - FF57 204
  Reitergefecht Öl/Leinwand (23.5x37.5cm 9x14in) Wien 2000

GRAZIANI Ercole I 1651-1726 **[3]**
- $77 703 - €83 408 - **£52 000** - FF547 123
  The Liberation of Saint Peter Oil/canvas (146x192cm 57x75in) London 2000
- $2 456 - €2 282 - **£1 500** - FF14 970
  Rebecca and Eliezer at the Well Ink (26x19cm 10x7in) London 1998

G

GRAZIANI Pietro XVII-XVIII [8]

$16 113 - €15 824 - **£10 000** - FF103 799
Cavalry Skirmishes Oil/canvas (49.5x65cm 19x25in)
London 1999

$2 680 - €2 836 - **£1 700** - FF18 600
Cavalry Skirmish Oil/canvas (21x29cm 8x11in)
London 2000

GRAZZINI Renzo 1912-1989 [35]

$475 - €492 - **£285** - FF3 254
Paesaggio Olio/tavola (50x70cm 19x27in) Prato 2000

$350 - €363 - **£210** - FF2 380
La raccolta delle olive Pastelli/carta (31x47cm 12x18in) Firenze 2001

GREACEN Edmund William 1877-1949 [23]

$2 000 - €2 015 - **£1 246** - FF13 220
Floral Arrangement on Table Oil/canvas (38x43cm 15x17in) Delray-Beach FL 2000

$1 700 - €1 585 - **£1 054** - FF10 398
The Silver Mirror Oil/canvas/board (40.5x30.5cm 15x12in) New-York 1999

GREACEN Nan 1909 [13]

$700 - €824 - **£484** - FF5 408
Roses on a Table Oil/canvas (50x40cm 20x16in) Delray-Beach FL 2000

$2 100 - €2 008 - **£1 278** - FF13 171
Pink and white petunias Oil/canvas/board (40.5x33cm 15x12in) Boston MA 1999

GREASON William 1884-? [13]

$1 200 - €1 063 - **£736** - FF6 975
The Canal at Morning Light Oil/canvas (60x91cm 24x36in) Cincinnati OH 1999

GREAVES Christopher XX [2]

$706 - €819 - **£500** - FF5 372
«The Boat Race, Go By Tramways» Poster (76x51cm 29x20in) London 2000

GREAVES Derrick 1927 [33]

$3 287 - €3 123 - **£2 000** - FF20 488
Studies from the Japanese, First Series Oil/canvas (95x74cm 37x29in) London 1999

$79 - €75 - **£50** - FF491
Red Petal Etching in colors (30x30cm 11x11in) London 1999

GREAVES Harry E. 1854-1919 [5]

$4 250 - €3 969 - **£2 623** - FF26 038
The Tempest from David Copperfield Sérigraphie/toile (64x129.5cm 25x50in) Boston MA 1999

GREAVES Henry & Walter 1850/46-1900/30 [11]

$9 623 - €9 519 - **£6 000** - FF62 443
The Old Swan, Chelsea Watercolour (51x63.5cm 20x25in) London 1999

GREAVES Walter 1846-1930 [86]

$1 700 - €1 856 - **£1 153** - FF12 173
Boating near a Tranquil Shore Oil/canvas (56x45cm 22x17in) New-York 2000

$352 - €320 - **£220** - FF2 097
Hungerford Bridge Crayon (17x28cm 6x11in) London 1999

GREAVES William 1852-1938 [28]

$713 - €832 - **£500** - FF5 455
Sherwood Forest, Nottinghamshire/Bolton Woods, Yorkshire Oil/board (14x22.5cm 5x8in) Crewkerne, Somerset 2000

GREBBER de Pieter Fransz. c.1600-1653 [18]

$11 342 - €12 706 - **£7 882** - FF83 344
Susannah and the Elders Oil/canvas (102.5x78cm 40x30in) Amsterdam 2001

GREBE Fritz 1850-1925 [21]

$975 - €1 022 - **£618** - FF6 707
Laerdal am Sognefjord Öl/Leinwand (54x81cm 21x31in) Köln 2000

GREBER Henri 1855-1941 [11]

$6 627 - €6 180 - **£4 000** - FF40 535
Joan of Arc, standing in armour with arms outstreched Gilded bronze (H188cm H74in) London 1999

$3 250 - €3 195 - **£2 038** - FF20 958
Athlete lifting a Rock Bronze (H59.5cm H23in) New-York 1999

GRECO Alberto 1931-1965 [27]

$14 260 - €13 815 - **£8 740** - FF90 620
Sin título Oleo/lienzo (150x100cm 59x39in) Madrid 1999

$3 422 - €3 544 - **£2 183** - FF23 246
Personajes Técnica mixta (49x64cm 19x25in) Madrid 2000

$1 836 - €2 042 - **£1 224** - FF13 396
Personajes Técnica mixta/papel (38x27cm 14x10in) Madrid 2000

GRECO el Dom. Theotocopoulos c.1541-1614 [19]

$1 400 000 - €1 399 345 - **£855 260** - FF9 179 100
Saint Paul Oil/canvas (104x81cm 40x31in) New-York 2000

$1 737 600 - €1 974 587 - **£1 200 000** - FF12 952 440
The Flight into Egypt Oil/panel (16x21.5cm 6x8in) London 2000

GRECO Emilio 1913-1995 [231]

$1 254 - €1 330 - **£850** - FF8 724
Mixed Flowers in a Glass vase on a Marble Plinth Oil/canvas (61x51cm 24x20in) London 2001

$65 000 - €60 704 - **£40 118** - FF398 190
Grande Figura seduta Bronze (132x34.5x60cm 51x13x23in) New-York 1999

$12 500 - €12 958 - **£7 500** - FF85 000
Ritratto di Maria Baldassarre Bronzo (H63cm H24in) Roma 2001

$1 700 - €1 762 - **£1 020** - FF11 560
Modella China/carta (70x50cm 27x19in) Roma 1999

$390 - €337 - **£260** - FF2 210
Euriclea Acquaforte (17.5x38.5cm 6x15in) Prato 1998

GRECO Gennaro Mascacotta 1663-1714 [39]

$10 260 - €11 967 - **£7 331** - FF78 500
Artistes dans des ruines romaines Huile/toile (111x77cm 43x30in) Versailles 2000

$13 000 - €12 994 - **£7 941** - FF85 234
Architectural Capriccio with Classical Ruins and Figures Oil/copper (25x21cm 9x8in) New-York 2000

GREE de Pieter J. Balthasar 1751-1789 [2]

$6 338 - €7 365 - **£4 455** - FF48 308
Cupids playing with a Gazehound Oil/canvas (125x205cm 49x80in) Dublin 2001

GREEF de Jean-Baptiste 1852-1894 [62]

$1 422 - €1 487 - **£942** - FF9 756
Printemps Huile/panneau (52x80.5cm 20x31in) Bruxelles 2000

$448 - €496 - **£314** - FF3 252
Chasseur à l'affût Huile/panneau (23x35cm 9x13in) Bruxelles 2001

GREEN Alfred H. XIX [33]

$1 169 - €1 342 - **£800** - FF8 801
A Highland Pass Oil/canvas (50x76cm 20x30in) Par, Cornwall 2000

$3 173 - €3 266 - **£2 000** - FF21 426
The Show Off, study of a young boy balancing a stick on his chin Oil/board (24x19cm 9x7in) Lichfield, Staffordshire 2000

GREEN Allan 1932 [24]

$952 - €1 022 - **£637** - FF6 707
No 155 Mischtechnik (72x96cm 28x37in) Köln 2000

GREEN Anthony Eric Sandall 1939 [29]

$1 886 - €2 125 - **£1 300** - FF13 938
The Proposal Oil/board (91.5x99cm 36x38in) London 2000

GREEN Benjamin c.1736-c.1800 [4]

$1 600 - €1 537 - **£986** - FF10 079
The Horse and Lioness, after Stubbs Mezzotint (45.5x57cm 17x22in) New-York 1999

GREEN Charles 1840-1898 [47]

$1 600 - €1 737 - **£1 108** - FF11 395
The Caricature Watercolour/paper (30x22cm 12x9in) Cleveland OH 2001

GREEN Charles Edwin Lewis 1844-1915 [18]

$3 400 - €3 678 - **£2 329** - FF24 127
Fall Landscape Oil/canvas (20x30cm 8x12in) Thomaston ME 2001

GREEN David Gould 1854-1918 [11]

$664 - €624 - **£410** - FF4 090
Unloading the Boats, North Berwick Watercolour (26x50.5cm 10x19in) Billingshurst, West-Sussex 1999

GREEN Dennis 1942 [19]

$886 - €805 - **£549** - FF5 283
Winter Bullfinch/Robin and Jasmine Watercolour (19.5x26.5cm 7x10in) Billingshurst, West-Sussex 1999

GREEN E.F. XIX [1]

$8 021 - €8 083 - **£5 000** - FF53 018
Old Man, half-length, holding his stick and cap Oil/canvas (76x63.5cm 29x25in) London 2000

GREEN Elizabeth Shippen 1871-1954 [4]

$15 000 - €17 485 - **£10 386** - FF114 697
Young Woman Holding Medal of Honor Watercolour (27x26cm 11x10in) New-York 2000

GREEN Frank Russell 1856-1949 [17]

$1 600 - €1 488 - **£987** - FF9 759
Preparing for Market Oil/canvas (64x79cm 25x31in) Portland ME 1999

$720 - €756 - **£454** - FF4 959
The Angelus, Normandy Oil/canvas (30x40cm 12x16in) Cleveland OH 2000

GREEN Henry Towneley 1836-1899 [10]

$778 - €835 - **£520** - FF5 480
Young lady and her pet dog Watercolour (13.5x10cm 5x3in) Billingshurst, West-Sussex 2000

GREEN John Kenneth 1828-1875 [10]

$1 700 - €1 605 - **£1 056** - FF10 528
The Fisherman Oil/canvas (50x76cm 20x30in) Milford CT 1999

$3 177 - €3 082 - **£2 000** - FF20 215
Children in a Clearing Oil/canvas (30.5x46cm 12x18in) London 1999

GREEN Madeleine XIX-XX [9]

$241 - €243 - **£150** - FF1 545
Study of a Horse with Jockey Up Watercolour (20.5x16.5cm 8x6in) Billingshurst, West-Sussex 2000

GREEN Nathaniel Everett c.1833-1899 [29]

$263 - €282 - **£180** - FF1 852
The Alps Thuru Watercolour/paper (20.5x28cm 8x11in) London 2001

GREEN OF AMBLESIDE William 1761-1823 [10]

$740 - €701 - **£450** - FF4 597
Romantic Lake View Watercolour/paper (32x42.5cm 12x16in) Penrith, Cumbria 1999

GREEN Roland 1896-1972 [246]

$601 - €581 - **£380** - FF3 809
Song Thrush Amidst Violets Watercolour (13x20cm 5x7in) Ipswich 1999

GREEN Tony 1954 [1]

$1 000 - €1 842 - **£1 091** - FF12 083
Fallen Lovers Watercolour/paper (51x71cm 20x28in) New-Orleans LA 2000

GREEN Valentine 1739-1813 [51]

$150 - €161 - **£102** - FF1 055
General Washington Mezzotint (63x40cm 25x16in) New-Orleans LA 2001

GREENAWAY Kate 1846-1901 [60]

$2 514 - €2 844 - **£1 700** - FF18 654
Girl in a blue Sash carrying a Wreath of Ivy Watercolour/paper (8.5x6.5cm 3x2in) London 2000

GREENBAUM Joseph 1864-1940 [14]

$3 000 - €3 220 - **£2 007** - FF21 123
A Rocky Landscape Oil/canvas (63.5x89cm 25x35in) San-Francisco CA 2000

$800 - €935 - **£571** - FF6 132
Atmospheric landscape Oil/canvas/board (21x28cm 8x11in) Altadena CA 2001

GREENE Albert van Nesse 1887-? [26]

$600 - €605 - **£374** - FF3 966
Spring Meadow Landscape Oil/board (30x40cm 12x16in) Hatfield PA 2000

$250 - €294 - **£179** - FF1 928
Chester County, PA, farmhouse with cypress trees Pastel (22x27cm 9x11in) Hatfield PA 2001

GREENE Bruce R. 1954 [2]

$8 250 - €8 855 - **£5 520** - FF58 088
Seven Miles Since Sunup Oil/canvas (76x81cm 30x32in) Houston TX 2000

GREENE John Beasley 1832-1856 [44]

$6 476 - €7 254 - **£4 500** - FF47 583
Egypt, Architectural Study Salt print (22.5x29.5cm 8x11in) London 2001

GREENE Milton H. 1922-1985 [111]

$1 360 - €1 140 - **£800** - FF7 476
Marilyn Monroe Lying Down Full Stretch Photograph (85x101.5cm 33x39in) London 1998

GREENE Stephen 1917-1999 [5]

$4 500 - €4 860 - **£3 110** - FF31 880
«Pleasure Dome #12» Oil/canvas (81x56cm 31x22in) New-York 2001

GREENE Walter L. XIX-XX [11]

$2 100 - €1 983 - **£1 305** - FF13 005
The Flower Garden Oil/board (45x60cm 18x24in) Milford CT 1999

$7 000 - €8 122 - **£4 911** - FF53 274
«Adirondack Mountains, Lake Placid» Poster (102x67cm 40x26in) New-York 2000

GREENHALGH Thomas XIX [39]

$589 - €634 - **£400** - FF4 146
Oxford viewed from the River Watercolour (48.5x69cm 19x27in) London 2001

GREENHAM Peter 1909-1992 **[37]**

- **$2 657** - €2 931 - **£1 800** - FF19 226
  Frightened Child Oil/canvas (76x63.5cm 29x25in)
  London 2000

- **$1 479** - €1 406 - **£900** - FF9 220
  Mundesley Beach Oil/board (21.5x33cm 8x12in)
  London 1999

GREENHAM Robert Duckworth 1906-1975 **[87]**

- **$1 297** - €1 434 - **£900** - FF9 407
  «Frills and Stripes: Miss Ann Todd as Madeleine Smith» Oil/canvas (48x36cm 18x14in)
  London 2001

- **$2 110** - €2 082 - **£1 300** - FF13 659
  Portrait of Anna Stern Oil/canvas (20.5x15cm 8x5in)
  London 1999

GREENHILL Harold 1914-1995 **[27]**

- **$1 469** - €1 725 - **£1 037** - FF11 313
  Vedettes du pont Neuf Oil/board (56x71.5cm 22x28in) Nedlands 2000

- **$901** - €778 - **£544** - FF5 105
  Brighton Pier, Manly Oil/board (31.5x43cm 12x16in)
  Malvern, Victoria 1998

GREENLAW Alexander John 1818-1870 **[8]**

- **$3 546** - €4 049 - **£2 500** - FF26 562
  Gateway East of Hampi Photograph (30x38cm 11x14in) London 2001

GREENLEAF Jacob I. 1887-1968 **[33]**

- **$1 800** - €1 890 - **£1 217** - FF12 396
  Foggy Day Oil/canvas (39x48cm 15x19in) Fairfield ME 2000

GREENOUGH Horatio 1805-1852 **[5]**

- **$159 280** - €181 004 - **£110 000** - FF1 187 307
  Bust of President John Adams (1735-1826) Plaster (H60cm H23in) London 2000

GREENWOOD Christopher & John XIX **[17]**

- **$134** - €155 - **£95** - FF1 019
  County Map of Durham Engraving (61x70cm 24x27in) Stansted Mountfitchet, Essex 2000

GREENWOOD Ethan Allen 1779-1856 **[8]**

- **$2 100** - €2 497 - **£1 446** - FF16 382
  Portrait of a Gentleman Oil/canvas (63x49cm 25x19in) Bolton MA 2000

GREENWOOD George Parker XIX-XX **[5]**

- **$1 375** - €1 334 - **£835** - FF8 748
  The Arno Oil/canvas (45x66cm 18x26in) Gray ME 2000

GREENWOOD Joseph H. 1857-1927 **[23]**

- **$1 900** - €2 169 - **£1 339** - FF14 230
  «Spring Meadow» Oil/canvas (51x63.5cm 20x25in) Boston MA 2001

- **$750** - €641 - **£440** - FF4 206
  The Autumn Wood Oil/canvas/board (30.5x40.5cm 12x15in) Boston MA 1998

GREENWOOD Marion 1909-1970 **[46]**

- **$6 750** - €6 701 - **£4 140** - FF43 953
  Rendez-vous Oil/canvas (76x63cm 30x25in) Mystic CT 2000

- **$80** - €82 - **£50** - FF536
  Waif Lithograph (33x20cm 13x8in) Cleveland OH 2000

GREENWOOD Orlando 1892-1989 **[190]**

- **$544** - €598 - **£350** - FF3 920
  Venus and the Looking Glass Oil/canvas (76x63.5cm 29x25in) London 2000

- **$836** - €984 - **£600** - FF6 455
  Gypsy encampment at Whitby Abbey Watercolour/paper (51x61cm 20x24in) Whitby, Yorks 2001

GREENWOOD Parker 1850-1904 **[8]**

- **$14 943** - €16 040 - **£10 000** - FF105 216
  The White Star Liner Majestic at Sea Oil/canvas (76x127cm 29x50in) London 2000

GREER Aubrey Dale 1904-1998 **[19]**

- **$2 000** - €1 876 - **£1 235** - FF12 307
  Still Life with mixed Roses Oil/canvas (81x101cm 32x40in) Houston TX 1999

GREER Blanche 1833-? **[2]**

- **$2 000** - €2 331 - **£1 384** - FF15 293
  Group of Louging Young People Charcoal (33x43cm 13x17in) New-York 2000

GREG Michel Régnier, dit 1932-1999 **[17]**

- **$339** - €381 - **£238** - FF2 500
  Achille Talon, le sapin de Noël, pl.56 Encre Chine/papier (45x30cm 17x11in) Paris 2001

GREGER Gregor 1802/08-1835 **[2]**

- **$6 400** - €6 354 - **£4 000** - FF41 682
  Summer Flowers in an elaborate Vase with Peaches, Apples, Pears Oil/canvas (105.5x83cm 41x32in) London 1999

GREGERSEN Emil 1921-1993 **[31]**

- **$408** - €377 - **£244** - FF2 472
  Interieur med figur Oil/canvas (75x58cm 29x22in) Köbenhavn 1999

- **$423** - €456 - **£291** - FF2 990
  Opstilling med to appelsiner Oil/masonite (15x21cm 5x8in) Köbenhavn 2001

GREGOIR Henri 1818-1853 **[7]**

- **$3 036** - €2 975 - **£1 872** - FF19 512
  Jonge vrouw met bloemenguirlande Oil/panel (54.5x43cm 21x16in) Lokeren 1999

GRÉGOIRE Jean Louis 1840-1890 **[75]**

- **$11 000** - €9 501 - **£6 630** - FF62 322
  Perseus and Andromeda Bronze (H89cm H35in) New-York 1998

- **$1 608** - €1 677 - **£1 070** - FF11 000
  Femme au tambourin Bronze (H63cm H24in) Bordeaux 2000

GREGOOR Gillis Smak 1770-1843 **[16]**

- **$3 900** - €4 095 - **£2 458** - FF26 862
  Cows and Horse in Pasture Oil/wood (40x50cm 16x20in) Cleveland OH 2000

- **$1 955** - €2 269 - **£1 350** - FF14 883
  A Bull and a Cow by a pollarded Willow, Dordrecht Beyond, in Summer Oil/panel (26.5x35cm 10x13in) Amsterdam 2000

GREGOR Harold 1929 **[7]**

- **$15 000** - €15 115 - **£9 351** - FF99 150
  Illinois Corn Crib #20 Acrylic (109x167.5cm 42x65in) New-York 2000

GREGORI Gino 1906-1973 **[182]**

- **$204** - €198 - **£126** - FF1 300
  Crustacés Huile/toile (73x100cm 28x39in) Paris 1999

GREGORIO de Marco 1829-1876 **[8]**

- **$3 000** - €3 110 - **£1 800** - FF20 400
  Paesaggio Olio/tela (22x27cm 8x10in) Milano 2000

GREGOROVIUS Michael Christoph 1786-1850 **[1]**

- **$30 000** - €27 839 - **£18 330** - FF182 610
  A View of Danzig Oil/canvas (100x82.5cm 39x32in) New-York 1999

GREGORY Angela 1903-1990 **[3]**
- **$3 600** - €4 142 - **£2 481** - FF27 173
  Still Life with Vase and Elephant Oil/board (39x41cm 15x16in) New-Orleans LA 2000
- **$4 500** - €5 178 - **£3 101** - FF33 966
  Head of a Black Woman Bronze (25x15x8cm 10x6x3in) New-Orleans LA 2000

GREGORY Arthur Victor 1867-1957 **[36]**
- **$1 210** - €1 260 - **£760** - FF8 264
  Cutty Sark off Cape Horn Watercolour (47.5x62cm 18x24in) Melbourne 2000

GREGORY Charles 1810-1896 **[10]**
- **$4 791** - €5 022 - **£3 200** - FF32 945
  Racing Cutters Neck and Neck Oil/canvas (45.5x61cm 17x24in) London 2001

GREGORY Charles 1849-1920 **[12]**
- **$794** - €828 - **£500** - FF5 366
  Abendidylle, Dorfstrasse mit heimkehrendem Fischer und Kindern Aquarell/Papier (36x53cm 14x20in) Berlin 2000

GREGORY Edward John 1850-1909 **[30]**
- **$41 688** - €40 383 - **£26 000** - FF264 895
  Portrait of Mabel, Daughter of Charles Galloway Oil/canvas (152.5x113cm 60x44in) Billingshurst, West-Sussex 1999
- **$15 000** - €12 941 - **£9 049** - FF84 889
  Midday repose Oil/canvas (29.5x46cm 11x18in) New-York 1998
- **$871** - €991 - **£604** - FF6 500
  Joueuse de luth Aquarelle/papier (20x14cm 7x5in) Paris 2000

GREGORY Eliot 1854-1915 **[4]**
- **$2 000** - €1 906 - **£1 213** - FF12 501
  Portrait of a Boy Oil/canvas (91x73cm 36x29in) New-York 1999

GREGORY George 1849-1938 **[76]**
- **$4 210** - €4 671 - **£2 800** - FF30 639
  Beached Vessels and Hulks in the Upper Reaches of Portsmouth Harbour Oil/canvas (45.5x80cm 17x31in) London 2000
- **$1 942** - €2 085 - **£1 300** - FF13 678
  Hulks in Portsmouth Harbour Oil/canvas (20.5x30.5cm 8x12in) London 2000
- **$1 399** - €1 365 - **£850** - FF8 953
  Shipping in a Swell/Pulling in the Nets/Coastal Scenes Watercolour/paper (9x12.5cm 3x4in) London 2000

GREGORY John W. 1903 **[8]**
- **$850** - €1 004 - **£602** - FF6 588
  Provincetown Street Scene Lithograph (28x21cm 11x8in) Provincetown MA 2000

GREGORY Robert 1881-1918 **[2]**
- **$12 967** - €14 602 - **£9 033** - FF95 783
  Burren Oil/canvas (61x91.5cm 24x36in) Dublin 2001

GREIF XX **[1]**
- **$919** - €785 - **£550** - FF5 149
  «Partez P.L.M, Les Alpes et le Jura» Poster (100x61cm 39x24in) London 1998

GREIFFENHAGEN Maurice William 1862-1931 **[35]**
- **$303** - €261 - **£180** - FF1 714
  «Outsailed», from «Many Cargoes» Gouache (40.5x27cm 15x10in) Glasgow 1998
- **$6 831** - €6 399 - **£4 200** - FF41 975
  «London by LMS» Poster (115.5x103cm 45x40in) London 1999

GREIG Donald 1916 **[23]**
- **$565** - €588 - **£360** - FF3 860
  Construction Works alongside the Thames Oil/board (36.5x78.5cm 14x30in) London 2000

GREIL Alois 1842-1902 **[26]**
- **$771** - €872 - **£520** - FF5 720
  Alter Bauer mit Pfeife und seinem Hund Aquarell/Papier (22x17cm 8x6in) Wien 2000

GREINER (K.P.M., Berlin) XIX **[1]**
- **$24 705** - €23 498 - **£15 000** - FF154 135
  L'épanouissement Porcelaine (58x49.5cm 22x19in) London 1999

GREINER Otto 1869-1916 **[131]**
- **$704** - €818 - **£494** - FF5 366
  Sitzender männlicher Rückenakt Coloured chalks (40.5x25.5cm 15x10in) Hamburg 2001
- **$350** - €307 - **£212** - FF2 011
  Bildnis von Max Klinger in Leipzig Lithographie (21x17.8cm 8x7in) Berlin 1998

GREIS Otto 1913 **[17]**
- **$2 392** - €2 301 - **£1 476** - FF15 092
  Var No.5 Tempera/canvas (34.8x27cm 13x10in) Köln 1999
- **$1 428** - €1 534 - **£956** - FF10 061
  Komposition Aquarell (46.5x46.8cm 18x18in) Hamburg 2000

GREISALMER Alphonse [2]
- **$2 276** - €2 211 - **£1 406** - FF14 500
  Les attributs du culte et de la Thora Huile/panneau (12x15cm 4x5in) Paris 1999

GREIVE Johan Conrad, Jnr. XIX-XX **[8]**
- **$31 447** - €29 496 - **£19 435** - FF193 479
  The Royal Barge Receiving a Salute by the Royal Yacht Oil/panel (37.5x53.5cm 14x21in) Amsterdam 1999

GREIVE Johan Conrad, Snr. 1837-1891 **[24]**
- **$17 977** - €20 420 - **£12 613** - FF133 947
  A View of the Damrak, Amsterdam, with the Palace on Dam Square beyond Oil/canvas (40x67cm 15x26in) Amsterdam 2001
- **$7 345** - €7 714 - **£4 647** - FF50 602
  A View of the Oudezijds Voorburgwal, Amsterdam Oil/panel (36x23.5cm 14x9in) Amsterdam 2000
- **$660** - €635 - **£412** - FF4 167
  Vie of the IJ from Amsterdam looking North with a Boomhuisje Black chalk (35.5x47cm 13x18in) Amsterdam 1999

GREKOFF Elie 1914 **[2]**
- **$2 126** - €1 982 - **£1 315** - FF13 000
  Le jardin d'Eden Tapisserie (164x221cm 64x87in) Paris 1999

GRELLE Martin 1954 **[6]**
- **$16 500** - €17 711 - **£11 041** - FF116 176
  Piegan Winter Oil/canvas (101x76cm 40x30in) Houston TX 2000

GRELLET Georges XIX-XX **[24]**
- **$295** - €335 - **£207** - FF2 200
  Elégante au miroir Eau-forte (39x29cm 15x11in) Avignon 2001

GREMLICH Adolf 1915-1971 **[4]**
- **$20 764** - €20 035 - **£13 043** - FF131 424
  Die vier Jahreszeiten: Frühling/Sommer/Herbst/Winter Öl/Karton (128x98cm 50x38in) St. Gallen 1999

G

GRENET DE JOIGNY
- $2 979 - €2 814 - £1 855 - FF18 460
Le Pianiste Jean Verd Öl/Karton (63x48cm 24x18in)
St. Gallen 1999

GRENET DE JOIGNY Dominique Adolphe 1821-1885 **[9]**
- $2 637 - €3 037 - £1 800 - FF19 920
A River Town with a Castle Beyond Oil/canvas (36x54.5cm 14x21in) London 2000

GRENIER DE SAINT MARTIN François, Francisque 1793-1867 **[14]**
- $2 335 - €2 287 - £1 437 - FF15 000
Sainte-Geneviève Huile/toile (33x24.5cm 12x9in) Paris 1999

GRENIER Henry, Henri XX **[25]**
- $912 - €961 - £576 - FF6 304
Calles de París Acuarela/cartulina (34x49cm 13x19in) Madrid 2000

GRENNESS Johannes 1875-1963 **[23]**
- $472 - €537 - £330 - FF3 523
Uvejrsskyer over en fyrreskov Oil/canvas (65x105cm 25x41in) København 2000

GRESLAND Camille 1872-? **[1]**
- $10 425 - €11 434 - £6 922 - FF75 000
Le désir Marbre (76x86cm 29x33in) Melun 2000

GRESLEY Frank 1855-1936 **[51]**
- $721 - €848 - £500 - FF5 564
Figures Seated on a River Bank before a Village Watercolour (30x49.5cm 11x19in) London 2000

GRESLEY Harold 1892-1967 **[35]**
- $662 - €743 - £450 - FF4 873
Trent Swarkestone Bridge, Derbyshire Watercolour/paper (23x34cm 9x13in) Aylsham, Norfolk 2000

GRESLEY James Stephen 1829-1908 **[28]**
- $646 - €754 - £450 - FF4 948
Bolton Abbey on the River Wharfe Watercolour (27x38cm 10x14in) West-Yorshire 2000

GRESLY Gaspard, Gabriel 1712-1756 **[19]**
- $23 275 - €22 798 - £15 000 - FF149 544
Peasant Boy, holding a Hat full of Fruit/Peasant Girl, with a Bowl Oil/canvas (68x52cm 26x20in) London 1999

GRESY Prosper 1810-1974 **[8]**
- $4 359 - €4 269 - £2 682 - FF28 000
Le passage du col de montagne Huile/toile (65x101cm 25x39in) Aix-en-Provence 1999

GRETER Robert 1885-? **[2]**
- $4 307 - €4 828 - £3 000 - FF31 671
Walking Camel Bronze (40x53cm 15x20in) London 2001

GRETZNER Harold 1902-1977 **[28]**
- $1 000 - €1 073 - £669 - FF7 041
China Town Watercolour/paper (51x69cm 20x27in) Altadena CA 2000

GREUTHER Matthäus c.1566-1638 **[6]**
- $1 423 - €1 518 - £950 - FF9 959
The Birth of the Virgin, After Bartholomaes Spranger Engraving (48.5x32cm 19x12in) London 2000

GREUZE Jean-Baptiste 1725-1805 **[133]**
- $160 000 - €152 732 - £99 968 - FF1 001 856
Cimon and Pero «Roman Charity» Oil/canvas (63x79.5cm 24x31in) New-York 1999

- $32 000 - €35 109 - £21 257 - FF230 297
Interior with a Man playing a Harp and a Woman reading beside Him Oil/canvas (25.5x18.5cm 10x7in) New-York 2000
- $23 154 - €25 916 - £15 708 - FF170 000
Une jeune fille implorant une statue de l'Amour Encre (34.5x29.5cm 13x11in) Paris 2000

GREUZE Louis 1863-1950 **[3]**
- $150 000 - €141 124 - £93 600 - FF925 710
Girl with a blue Ribbon in her Hair Oil/canvas (41.5x34cm 16x13in) New-York 1999

GREVEDON Pierre Louis, Henri 1776-1860 **[19]**
- $342 - €381 - £239 - FF2 500
Portrait de femme Pierre noire (30x23cm 11x9in) Paris 2001
- $650 - €606 - £392 - FF3 974
S.A.R Madame La Duchesse de Nemours, after F.X Wiinterhalter Lithograph (65x44cm 25x17in) New-Orleans LA 1999

GREVENBROECK Alessandro XVII-XVIII **[11]**
- $42 000 - €45 049 - £27 750 - FF295 500
Paisaje italianizante con puerto y galeón Oleo/lienzo (95.5x130cm 37x51in) Madrid 2000
- $42 000 - €45 049 - £27 750 - FF295 500
Marina con barcos y puerto Oleo/lienzo (90x130cm 35x51in) Madrid 2000

GREVENBROECK Charles Laurent XVIII **[1]**
- $66 576 - €73 176 - £42 336 - FF480 000
Vues de l'entrée du port Huile/toile (95x130cm 37x51in) Paris 2000

GREVENBROECK Orazio c.1670-1743 **[43]**
- $8 862 - €8 703 - £5 500 - FF57 089
Capriccio of a Mediterranean Harbour at Sunset Oil/canvas (66.5x92cm 26x36in) London 1999
- $9 713 - €10 426 - £6 500 - FF68 390
Winter landscape with figures crossing a bridge Oil/panel (21x38cm 8x14in) London 2000

GRÉVIN Alfred 1827-1892 **[106]**
- $1 784 - €1 983 - £1 248 - FF13 008
Madame Coq/Mademoiselle Poule Bronze (H33cm H12in) Bruxelles 2001
- $86 - €76 - £52 - FF500
Conversation galante Crayon/papier (32.5x22cm 12x8in) Vendôme 1999

GREWENIG Leo 1898-1991 **[12]**
- $3 398 - €2 942 - £2 062 - FF19 297
Blume im Flug Oil/panel (100x80cm 39x31in) München 1998

GREY Alfred 1845-1926 **[17]**
- $922 - €1 082 - £663 - FF7 095
Cows and Sheep in Landscape Oil/canvas (40x51cm 16x20in) Vancouver, BC. 2001
- $655 - €762 - £460 - FF4 997
Cattle feeding Watercolour/paper (24.5x34.5cm 9x13in) Dublin 2001

GREY Charles 1808-1892 **[2]**
- $565 - €5 233 - £3 500 - FF34 329
Study of a Chestnut Horse in a Landscape with the Sugar Loaf beyond Oil/canvas (48x66cm 18x25in) Co. Kilkenny 1999

GREY Gregor ?-c.1911 **[10]**
- $3 934 - €4 571 - £2 765 - FF29 984
Farmyard Recital Oil/canvas (51x61cm 20x24in) Dublin 2001

GREY-SMITH Guy Edward 1916-1981 **[53]**

$18 235 - €21 686 - **£12 995** - FF142 250
Woman washing-Ceylon Oil/board (121.5x181cm
47x71in) Melbourne 2000

$6 315 - €7 371 - **£4 458** - FF48 349
«Evening Performance» Oil/board (76x69.5cm
29x27in) Malvern, Victoria 2000

$721 - €801 - **£483** - FF5 254
Landscape with Palm Trees Watercolour (28x22cm
11x8in) Nedlands 2000

$157 - €147 - **£97** - FF962
Rigged and Unrigged Yachts Silkscreen in colors
(30x44cm 11x17in) Melbourne 1999

GRIBBLE Bernard Finegan 1873-1962 **[62]**

$912 - €774 - **£550** - FF5 077
Vessels Off the Coast Oil/panel (36.5x51.5cm
14x20in) Billingshurst, West-Sussex 1998

$262 - €298 - **£180** - FF1 957
Clipper at Sea Watercolour/paper (30x44cm 11x17in)
London 2000

GRIBKOV Sergei Ivanovich 1820-1893 **[5]**

$9 572 - €10 733 - **£6 500** - FF70 404
Preparation for the Meal Oil/canvas (65.5x47cm
25x18in) London 2000

GRIDEL Émile 1839-1901 **[6]**

$3 420 - €3 604 - **£2 160** - FF23 640
Pescadores en un puerto de la Costa Azul
Oleo/lienzo (55x75cm 21x29in) Madrid 2000

GRIEBEL Otto 1895-1972 **[6]**

$67 408 - €77 608 - **£46 000** - FF509 077
The naked Whore Watercolour (31.5x23cm 12x9in)
London 2000

GRIEKEN van Jef 1950 **[40]**

$2 496 - €2 975 - **£1 788** - FF19 512
«Minas-Gerais III» Oil/canvas (90x130cm 35x51in)
Lokeren 2000

$1 113 - €1 190 - **£758** - FF7 804
Recife I Pastel/papier (52x74cm 20x29in) Lokeren
2001

GRIENT de Cornelis 1691-1783 **[8]**

$2 099 - €2 355 - **£1 463** - FF15 447
**Bateaux voguant sur des flots légèrement tour-
mentés** Lavis (21x30cm 8x11in) Bruxelles 2001

GRIER Louis Monro c.1864-1920 **[19]**

$2 745 - €2 582 - **£1 700** - FF16 935
Moonlit Coastal Scene Oil/canvas (76x153cm
30x60in) London 1999

$498 - €505 - **£310** - FF3 311
The Fishing Fleet Oil/panel (25x34cm 10x13in) Par,
Cornwall 2000

GRIERA CALDERON Rafael 1934 **[99]**

$513 - €571 - **£351** - FF3 543
Canal urbano Oleo/lienzo (46x61cm 18x24in)
Barcelona 2001

$176 - €192 - **£115** - FF1 260
Barcas en un puerto Oleo/cartón (30x38.5cm
11x15in) Barcelona 2000

$95 - €108 - **£64** - FF709
Embarcaciones en un río Acuarela/papel (30x45cm
11x17in) Barcelona 2000

GRIERSON Charles Mac Iver 1864-1939 **[41]**

$5 080 - €5 454 - **£3 400** - FF35 773
Full House Oil/canvas (47x58.5cm 18x23in) London
2000

$758 - €862 - **£520** - FF5 654
**Photographer on the Thames at Kew/River
Landscape** Watercolour/paper (16x24.5cm 6x9in)
London 2000

GRIESHABER Helmut A.P., Hap 1909-1981 **[1429]**

$134 340 - €153 390 - **£94 710** - FF1 006 170
Männerwald Tempera (200x480cm 78x188in)
Stuttgart 2001

$2 610 - €3 068 - **£1 809** - FF20 123
Noways Ambassador Gouache (56x76cm 22x29in)
Stuttgart 2000

$335 - €383 - **£230** - FF2 515
Gefangener ai Woodcut (17.6x10cm 6x3in) Lindau
2000

GRIESS Rudolf 1863-1941 **[6]**

$762 - €716 - **£427** - FF4 695
Für Karl Schmidt-Rottluf Woodcut in colors
(49.5x34cm 19x13in) München 1999

GRIESSLER Franz 1897-c.1950 **[4]**

$235 - €254 - **£162** - FF1 668
«Allgemeine Wäschesammlung» Poster (95x63cm
37x24in) Wien 2001

GRIEVE Robert Henderson 1924 **[36]**

$416 - €496 - **£297** - FF3 251
«Ultramarine Motif» Mixed media (64.5x49.5cm
25x19in) Melbourne 2000

GRIFFIER Jan I c.1645/56-1718 **[49]**

$26 458 - €26 009 - **£17 000** - FF170 605
**Extensive Rhenish Landscape, with moored
Boats, Castle and Mountainous** Oil/canvas
(60.5x71cm 23x27in) London 1999

$83 795 - €71 296 - **£50 000** - FF467 670
**Rhenish Landscape with Peasants and Boats in
the foreground** Oil/panel (34x40.5cm 13x15in)
London 1998

GRIFFIER John, Jan II c.1690-c.1773 **[10]**

$29 452 - €33 023 - **£20 000** - FF216 614
Extensive rhenish Landscape Oil/panel
(34x47.5cm 13x18in) London 2000

$4 773 - €4 090 - **£2 869** - FF26 826
Phantastische Rheinlandschaft Öl/Kupfer
(25x34cm 9x13in) Köln 1998

GRIFFIER Robert 1688-1750 **[26]**

$17 304 - €17 441 - **£10 800** - FF114 408
**Rheinlandschaft mit Korbflechtern auf einem
Boot** Öl/Leinwand (74x110cm 29x43in) Wien 2000

GRIFFIN Rick 1944-1991 **[5]**

$142 - €149 - **£90** - FF978
«The Who - Hollywood Palladium June 13»
Poster (57.5x40cm 22x15in) London 2000

GRIFFIN Thomas Bartholomew 1858-1918 **[43]**

$1 250 - €1 068 - **£734** - FF7 006
Mountain Stream Oil/canvas (40x50cm 16x20in) St.
Petersburg FL 1998

$925 - €1 007 - **£635** - FF6 603
Fall Landscape in gold Tones Oil/canvas (30x40cm
12x16in) St. Louis MO 2001

GRIFFIN Vaughan Murray 1903-1992 **[33]**

$525 - €579 - **£349** - FF3 797
The Journey No.5 Linocut in colors (45.5x35cm
17x13in) Melbourne 2000

GRIFFIN Walter P. S. 1861-1935 **[27]**

$6 000 - €6 604 - **£4 170** - FF44 908
The Orchard at Borgnesville Oil/canvas (68x81cm
27x32in) Dedham MA 2001

G

GRIFFING Robert XX [3]
- $75 000 - €80 415 - **£49 620** - FF527 490
  Welcome to Logstown Oil/canvas (76x127cm 30x50in) Hayden ID 2000

GRIFFITH David 1939 [3]
- $3 572 - €4 003 - **£2 500** - FF26 259
  Portrait of Sir Kyffin Williams Oil/canvas (59.5x49.5cm 23x19in) Billingshurst, West-Sussex 2001

GRIFFITH Ella N. act.1894-1901 [4]
- $7 500 - €8 517 - **£5 133** - FF55 866
  Still Life with Parlor Matches Oil/canvas (30.5x36cm 12x14in) New-York 2000

GRIFFITH Louis Oscar 1875-1956 [17]
- $7 000 - €8 227 - **£4 853** - FF53 965
  Woman in a Garden Oil/canvas (76x86cm 30x34in) Cincinnati OH 2000
- $3 000 - €2 796 - **£1 851** - FF18 339
  River Hands Oil/canvas/board (25x35cm 10x14in) New-Orleans LA 1999
- $425 - €483 - **£294** - FF3 170
  Sailboats Aquatint in colors (33x27cm 13x11in) Cincinnati OH 2000

GRIFFITH Marie Osthaus XX [7]
- $1 900 - €2 052 - **£1 315** - FF13 463
  Roses Oil/canvas (66x45cm 26x18in) Cincinnati OH 2001

GRIFFITH Moses 1747-1819 [23]
- $917 - €844 - **£550** - FF5 536
  Nantwich Church, Cheshire Watercolour (13.5x18cm 5x7in) Glamorgan 1999

GRIFFITH William Alexander 1866-1940 [16]
- $6 500 - €6 225 - **£4 015** - FF40 832
  Quiet Afternoon at the Firehouse, Calendar Illustration Oil/masonite (59x76cm 23x30in) New-York 1999
- $2 200 - €2 243 - **£1 378** - FF14 710
  Canyon Landscape Oil/canvas/board (17x22cm 7x9in) Altadena CA 2000
- $5 000 - €5 876 - **£3 466** - FF38 547
  Flowering Landscape Pastel/board (39x47.5cm 15x18in) Beverly-Hills CA 2000

GRIFFITHS Harley Cameron 1908-1981 [31]
- $1 749 - €1 585 - **£1 060** - FF10 400
  Still Life Oil/canvas/board (68x56cm 26x22in) Sydney 1998
- $514 - €484 - **£323** - FF3 175
  Contemplation Oil/canvas/board (37x27cm 14x10in) Sydney 1999

GRIG Alex 1938 [6]
- $2 161 - €2 439 - **£1 520** - FF16 000
  Jazz I Huile/toile (73x116cm 28x45in) Paris 2001

GRIGGS Frederick Landseer 1876-1938 [74]
- $532 - €497 - **£330** - FF3 258
  Launds Etching (17x25cm 6x9in) London 1999

GRIGGS Samuel W. 1827-1898 [25]
- $2 600 - €2 243 - **£1 562** - FF14 714
  «On the Pemigewasset» Oil/canvas (45.5x76cm 17x29in) Boston MA 1998
- $2 000 - €1 860 - **£1 238** - FF12 201
  Pastoral Landscape Oil/panel (13x21cm 5x8in) Nantucket MA 1999

GRIGIOTTI Francesco XVII [1]
- $2 750 - €2 851 - **£1 650** - FF18 700
  Marte e MInerva, sullo sfondo il Tempio della Pace Gouache (24x21cm 9x8in) Milano 2000

GRIGNION Charles 1754-1804 [7]
- $530 - €623 - **£380** - FF4 088
  View of Ranelagh Garden, after Canalet Engraving (26x40cm 10x15in) London 2001

GRIGNON P.F. [2]
- $1 400 - €1 633 - **£982** - FF10 710
  «Pianos A.Bord, Blondel» Poster (46x64cm 18x25in) New-York 2000

GRIGORESCU Nicolas Jon 1838-1907 [16]
- $4 781 - €5 336 - **£3 129** - FF35 000
  Vue du village de Barbizon Huile/toile (38x55cm 14x21in) Fontainebleau 2000
- $1 309 - €1 200 - **£800** - FF7 871
  Woman before a House in a sunlit Courtyard Oil/board (25x36cm 9x14in) London 1999

GRIGORIEV Boris Dimitrevich 1886-1939 [70]
- $11 383 - €13 225 - **£8 000** - FF86 753
  Still Life with Bread and Onions Oil/canvas (60x72cm 23x28in) London 2001
- $1 620 - €1 817 - **£1 100** - FF11 918
  The Milkmaid and her Admirer Pencil (17x23.5cm 6x9in) London 2000

GRILL Oswald 1878-1964 [34]
- $2 924 - €2 907 - **£1 768** - FF19 068
  Ein verschneiter Pfad Öl/Leinwand (80x95cm 31x37in) Wien 2000

GRILLON Roger 1881-1938 [94]
- $477 - €442 - **£296** - FF2 900
  Nu allongé Huile/toile (65x150cm 25x59in) Paris 1999
- $406 - €457 - **£285** - FF3 000
  Carnaval Huile/carton (32x24cm 12x9in) Garches 2001

GRIM XIX-XX [3]
- $1 200 - €1 339 - **£785** - FF8 781
  «Manufacture d'Herstal-Lez-Liège, cycles, motos, voiturettes» Poster (157x113.5cm 61x44in) New-York 2000

GRIMALDI IL BOLOGNESE Giovan Francesco 1606-1680 [59]
- $4 184 - €4 491 - **£2 800** - FF29 460
  Figures in Landscape Ink (20x29.5cm 7x11in) London 2000
- $505 - €429 - **£300** - FF2 811
  L'homme debout près d'autres assis, after Titan Etching (33.5x46.5cm 13x18in) London 1998

GRIMANI Guido 1871-1933 [14]
- $2 600 - €2 695 - **£1 560** - FF17 680
  Pescatori di telline Olio/cartone (42x30cm 16x11in) Trieste 2001

GRIMBALDSON Walter XVIII [1]
- $19 333 - €19 229 - **£12 000** - FF126 134
  London, View of the Villages of New Riverhead and Bagridge Wells Oil/canvas (60x139.5cm 23x54in) London 1999

GRIMELUND Johannes Martin 1842-1917 [53]
- $5 348 - €4 652 - **£3 224** - FF30 512
  Mennesker i elvelandskap Oil/panel (54x38cm 21x14in) Oslo 1998
- $4 352 - €4 800 - **£2 948** - FF31 484
  Fjällbacka Oil/canvas (33x44cm 12x17in) Stockholm 2000

GRIMM Arthur 1883-1948 [16]
- $4 822 - €5 624 - **£3 385** - FF36 892
  Pariser Landschaft Öl/Leinwand (80x100cm 31x39in) Köln 2000

GRIMM Ludwig Emil 1790-1865 **[74]**
▱ **$895 - €869 - £557** - FF5 701
 Maria und Elisabeth mit Christus,
 Johannesknaben vor Landschaft Indian ink
 (27.6x24.8cm 10x9in) Berlin 1999
▭ **$197 - €235 - £140** - FF1 542
 Bairische Bauern vom Schliersee/Bairische
 Bäuerinnen vom Schliersee Radierung
 (14.5x10.1cm 5x3in) Berlin 2000

GRIMM Paul 1892-1974 **[163]**
⌐ **$3 000 - €2 810 - £1 803** - FF18 435
 San Jacinto & San Gorgonio Oil/canvas (60x76cm
 24x30in) Portland OR 1999
⌐ **$1 600 - €1 870 - £1 142** - FF12 265
 Landscape Oil/board (30x40cm 12x16in) Altadena
 CA 2001

GRIMM Pierre 1898-1979 **[18]**
⌐ **$1 207 - €1 296 - £807** - FF8 500
 Harmonique Huile/toile (88x117cm 34x46in) Paris
 2001

GRIMM Samuel Hieronymus 1733-1794 **[51]**
▱ **$1 795 - €1 753 - £1 144** - FF11 500
 Promeneurs devant un château en ruine
 Aquarelle (18x26cm 7x10in) Paris 1999

GRIMM Walter Otto 1894-1919 **[18]**
▱ **$764 - €869 - £530** - FF5 701
 Sitzendes Mädchen an einem Tisch mit
 Blumenvase Pencil (13.8x9cm 5x3in) Berlin 2000
▭ **$157 - €179 - £109** - FF1 173
 Liegende und stehende weibliche Akte
 Lithographie (35.5x47.5cm 13x18in) Berlin 2000

GRIMM Wilhelm 1904-1986 **[212]**
⌐ **$2 582 - €2 236 - £1 567** - FF14 665
 Blumenstilleben Tempera (28x37cm 11x14in)
 München 1998
⌐ **$355 - €409 - £251** - FF2 683
 Wattlandschaft Ink (31x47.7cm 12x18in) Hamburg
 2001
▭ **$148 - €138 - £89** - FF905
 Sterngucker/Mädchen Lithographie (47.5x28.5cm
 18x11in) Hamburg 1999

GRIMMER Abel c.1560-c.1619 **[34]**
⌐ **$29 886 - €32 080 - £20 000** - FF210 432
 The Interior of a Cathedral with Elegant Figures
 Oil/canvas (66x82cm 25x32in) London 2000
⌐ **$235 616 - €264 181 - £160 000** - FF1 732 912
 Spring, an Extensive Landscape with a View of
 a Country-House Oil/panel (27x36.5cm 10x14in)
 London 2000

GRIMMER Jacob 1525-1592 **[31]**
⌐ **$47 817 - €51 328 - £32 000** - FF336 691
 Landscape with peasants resting under trees
 Oil/panel (52.5x69cm 20x27in) London 2000
⌐ **$82 186 - €88 220 - £55 000** - FF578 688
 Landscape with Villagers Playing Ketspel and
 Picking Apples Oil/panel (27.5x38cm 10x14in)
 London 2000
▱ **$4 247 - €4 084 - £2 616** - FF26 789
 Panoramic Landscape with View across a
 Village to a Distant Shoreline Ink (12x18.5cm
 4x7in) Amsterdam 1999

GRIMOU Alexis 1680-1740 **[33]**
⌐ **$17 000 - €14 912 - £10 322** - FF97 814
 The Young Guardsman Oil/canvas (80.5x66cm
 31x25in) New-York 1999
⌐ **$3 070 - €3 506 - £2 159** - FF23 000
 Portrait de jeune fille en buste Huile/toile
 (25x27cm 9x10in) Versailles 2001

GRIMSHAW Arthur Edmund 1868-1913 **[6]**
⌐ **$8 859 - €9 928 - £6 200** - FF65 123
 «Conwy Castle, Moonrise» Oil/canvas (51x36cm
 20x14in) Billingshurst, West-Sussex 2001
⌐ **$10 671 - €12 399 - £7 500** - FF81 331
 Evening, Whitby Harbour Oil/board (20x30.5cm
 7x12in) London 2001

GRIMSHAW John Atkinson 1836-1893 **[260]**
⌐ **$190 624 - €164 462 - £115 000** - FF1 078 803
 Old Chelsea Oil/canvas (76.5x64cm 30x25in) London
 1998
⌐ **$56 783 - €60 952 - £38 000** - FF399 820
 Whitby from Scotch Head Oil/board (28.5x43cm
 11x16in) London 2000
▱ **$73 220 - €78 596 - £49 000** - FF515 558
 Whitby Sands, Sunset Watercolour (26.5x40.5cm
 10x15in) London 2000

GRIMSHAW Louis H. 1870-1943 **[21]**
⌐ **$61 266 - €65 764 - £41 000** - FF431 385
 The Royal Mile, Edinburgh Oil/canvas (45.5x69cm
 17x27in) London 2000
⌐ **$24 407 - €28 702 - £17 500** - FF188 275
 Shipping in a Moonlit Harbour with Buildings
 beside a Quay Oil/board (18x38cm 7x14in) West-
 Yorkshire 2001
▱ **$502 - €587 - £350** - FF3 848
 Petergate, York Ink (27x21.5cm 10x8in) West-
 Yorkshire 2000

GRIMT Carole 1957 **[69]**
▱ **$177 - €198 - £123** - FF1 300
 Nature morte Aquarelle/papier (32x24cm 12x9in)
 Paris 2001

GRINNELL George Victor 1878-1946 **[6]**
⌐ **$2 800 - €2 577 - £1 680** - FF16 904
 Mystic Connecticut, Old Mystic Vista Oil/canvas
 (76x91cm 30x36in) Chicago IL 1999

GRINSSON Boris 1907-? **[141]**
▭ **$300 - €259 - £181** - FF1 700
 «La mélodie du bonheur», de Stuart Heisler
 Affiche couleur (120x160cm 47x62in) Argenteuil 1999

GRIPENHOLM Ulf 1943 **[26]**
⌐ **$2 685 - €2 947 - £1 730** - FF19 334
 Burkar på soptipp Oil/canvas (54.5x69cm 21x27in)
 Stockholm 2000
⌐ **$1 398 - €1 535 - £901** - FF10 070
 Därute I Oil/canvas (41.5x38cm 16x14in) Stockholm
 2000
▭ **$175 - €211 - £122** - FF1 387
 Badande Color lithograph (44x56cm 17x22in)
 Stockholm 2000

GRIPPO Victor 1936 **[1]**
🖾 **$18 000 - €20 913 - £12 650** - FF137 181
 Pan Plaster (50x33x14cm 19x12x5in) New-York 2001

GRIPS Charles Joseph 1825-1920 **[17]**
⌐ **$26 620 - €22 968 - £16 000** - FF150 659
 The Pet Bird Oil/panel (45x55cm 17x21in) Leyburn,
 North Yorkshire 1998
⌐ **$11 954 - €12 832 - £8 000** - FF84 172
 Minding the Baby Oil/panel (40x31cm 15x12in)
 London 2000

GRIPS Frits 1869-1961 **[2]**
⌐ **$13 982 - €15 882 - £9 810** - FF104 181
 Clearing the Dishes Oil/canvas (62x49cm 24x19in)
 Amsterdam 2001

G

GRIS Juan 1887-1927 **[230]**
- $925 000 - €889 482 - £569 892 - FF5 834 622
  Guitare et papier à musique Oil/canvas (65x80.5cm 25x31in) New-York 1999
- $233 285 - €282 031 - £162 985 - FF1 850 000
  Pipe et paquet de tabac Huile/toile (33x19cm 12x7in) Paris 2000
- $17 849 - €19 818 - £12 441 - FF130 000
  Etude de personnage pour l'Assiette au beurre Encre (39x32cm 15x12in) Paris 2001
- $1 353 - €1 143 - £809 - FF7 500
  Marcelle la brune Lithographie (30x22.5cm 11x8in) Paris 1998

GRISEL Philippe 1930-1998 **[13]**
- $1 804 - €1 524 - £1 073 - FF10 000
  Vision florale Huile/toile (65x80cm 25x31in) Compiègne 1998

GRISET Ernest 1844-1907 **[78]**
- $352 - €356 - €220 - FF2 332
  Taking Notes in the Great Swampy Forest Bodycolour (20x16cm 8x6in) Dorchester, Dorset 2000

GRISON François-Adolphe 1845-1914 **[82]**
- $9 000 - €7 802 - £5 499 - FF51 181
  The Arrival of the Horsemen in the Inn Oil/canvas (45.5x38cm 17x14in) New-York 1999
- $1 680 - €1 555 - £1 028 - FF10 202
  Rastendes Pferd im Stall Öl/Leinwand (24x33cm 9x12in) Bern 1999

GRISOT Pierre 1911-1995 **[281]**
- $1 849 - €1 753 - £1 155 - FF11 500
  Matinée d'automne Huile/toile (54x65cm 21x25in) L'Isle-Adam 1999
- $1 440 - €1 234 - £844 - FF8 093
  Jeune femme Huile/panneau (35x28cm 13x11in) Genève 1998

GRISWOLD Casimir Clayton 1834-1918 **[5]**
- $2 200 - €2 351 - £1 497 - FF15 421
  Green Fields & Trees Oil/canvas (48x25cm 19x10in) Pleasant-Valley NY 2001

GRITCHENKO Alexis Vasilievich 1883-1977 **[25]**
- $1 502 - €1 677 - £1 045 - FF11 000
  Le panier de langoustines Huile/panneau (49x65cm 19x25in) Paris 2001

GRITSENKO Nikolai Nikolaievich 1856-1900 **[3]**
- $4 980 - €5 786 - £3 500 - FF37 954
  The Church of Saint Nicholas in Tolmachi, Moscow Watercolour (45x28cm 17x11in) London 2001

GRITTEN Henry C. 1818-1873 **[27]**
- $11 646 - €12 718 - £7 496 - FF83 424
  View of the Yarra, Knockanda, Alphington Oil/canvas (49.5x77cm 19x30in) Melbourne 2000
- $5 215 - €4 888 - £3 226 - FF32 061
  Still Waters Oil/board (29.5x44cm 11x17in) Melbourne 1999

GRIVAZ Eugène 1852-1915 **[20]**
- $796 - €908 - £550 - FF5 953
  Flower Girl Oil/canvas (41x27.5cm 16x10in) Amsterdam 2000
- $800 - €786 - £514 - FF5 158
  The Picnic Watercolour/board (36x50cm 14x19in) New-York 1999

GRIVEAU Lucien XIX **[1]**
- $2 600 - €2 788 - £1 720 - FF18 286
  Tranquil French Landscape Oil/canvas (46x34cm 18x13in) New-Orleans LA 2000

GRIVOLAS Antoine 1843-1902 **[12]**
- $1 400 - €1 372 - £902 - FF9 000
  Bouquet de fleurs Huile/toile (68x48cm 26x18in) Avignon 1999

GRIVOLAS Pierre 1823-1906 **[34]**
- $1 608 - €1 829 - £1 116 - FF12 000
  Sous la pinède Huile/toile (28x33cm 11x12in) Marseille 2000

GROB Konrad 1828-1904 **[15]**
- $13 000 - €12 502 - £8 023 - FF82 006
  Shepherd with Flutes and Dancing Maiden in a Bucolic Landscape Oil/canvas (110x89cm 43x35in) Boston MA 1999

GROBE German 1857-1938 **[54]**
- $1 956 - €2 301 - £1 402 - FF15 092
  In den Dünen Öl/Leinwand (51x60.5cm 20x23in) Düsseldorf 2001
- $1 074 - €1 074 - £672 - FF7 043
  Hafenszene Oil/panel (45x33cm 17x12in) Köln 1999

GROBON François Frédéric 1815-1901/02 **[18]**
- $5 102 - €4 955 - £3 152 - FF32 500
  Paysage, soleil couchant Huile/toile (98.5x114.5cm 38x45in) Grenoble 1999
- $2 285 - €2 104 - £1 371 - FF13 800
  Moulin de Saint-Servan, près de Saint-Malo Huile/panneau (20.5x42.5cm 8x16in) Mâcon 1999

GROBON Jean Michel 1770-1853 **[14]**
- $11 507 - €13 568 - £8 090 - FF89 000
  Scène animée devant l'abbaye Saint-Martin d'Ainay Huile/panneau (28x25.5cm 11x10in) Lyon 2000

GROEN Hendrik Pieter/ Piet 1886-1964 **[85]**
- $587 - €499 - £354 - FF3 270
  Gevarieerd stilleven Oil/canvas (45x55cm 17x21in) Rotterdam 1998
- $725 - €681 - £448 - FF4 464
  Baggerwerkzaameheden bij Rotterdam Oil/panel (18x25cm 7x9in) Rotterdam 1999

GROENEVELD Cornelis 1882-1952 **[8]**
- $655 - €771 - £453 - FF5 060
  Melktijd Oil/board (48x38cm 18x14in) Amsterdam 2000

GROENEWEGEN Adrianus Johannes 1874-1963 **[121]**
- $3 847 - €3 264 - £2 320 - FF21 409
  Melkbocht Oil/canvas (50x68cm 19x26in) Rotterdam 1998
- $1 193 - €1 109 - £728 - FF7 272
  Milking Time Oil/canvas (31.5x46.5cm 12x18in) Amsterdam 1998
- $1 684 - €1 612 - £1 046 - FF10 572
  Milking Time Watercolour/paper (29x39.5cm 11x15in) Calgary, Alberta 1999

GROENEWEGEN Gerrit 1754-1826 **[16]**
- $4 011 - €3 857 - £2 470 - FF25 301
  Shipping Outside the Harbour of Vlaardingen, Schiedam Beyond Ink (16x25.5cm 6x10in) Amsterdam 1999
- $1 255 - €1 108 - £756 - FF7 268
  Rotterdam van de Maas te zien Etching (18x27.5cm 7x10in) Amsterdam 1998

GROENEWEGEN van Pieter Anthonisz. ?-1658 **[11]**
- $7 051 - €8 385 - £5 027 - FF55 000
  Le forum romain et le Mont Palatin Huile/panneau (51x67cm 20x26in) Monte-Carlo 2000

$51 555 - €51 277 - **£32 000** - FF336 358
Travellers on a Path with Roman Ruins beyond
Oil/panel (27.5x34.5cm 10x13in) London 1999

GROESBECK Daniel Sayre 1878-1950 [2]
$3 750 - €4 084 - **£2 582** - FF26 790
Wedding Procession Oil/board (49x56cm 19x22in)
Altadena CA 2001

GRÖGER Friedrich Carl 1766-1838 [13]
$4 225 - €3 581 - **£2 524** - FF23 489
«Frau de Coninck», Brustportrait in weissem Kleid und roter Stola Öl/Leinwand (71x62.5cm 27x24in) Bremen 1998

GROISEILLIEZ de Marcelin 1837-1880 [8]
$1 611 - €1 818 - **£1 133** - FF11 928
Dorf in der Bretagne Öl/Leinwand (43x64cm 16x25in) Bern 2001

GROLIG Curtius 1805-1863 [13]
$4 485 - €4 269 - **£2 788** - FF28 000
Paysage orientaliste Huile/toile (68x92cm 26x36in) Chambéry 1999
$5 004 - €4 573 - **£3 063** - FF30 000
Alger vue de Lapérouse Huile/toile (27x40.5cm 10x15in) Paris 1999

GROLL Albert Lorey 1866-1952 [33]
$3 750 - €4 164 - **£2 608** - FF27 312
Desert Storm Oil/canvas (71x91cm 28x36in) Milford CT 2001
$1 700 - €1 588 - **£1 059** - FF10 418
Inlet Oil/canvas (30x40cm 12x16in) Mystic CT 1999

GROLL Andreas 1850-1907 [3]
$14 022 - €13 081 - **£8 460** - FF85 806
Was ihr dem Geringsten getan Öl/Leinwand (126.5x182cm 49x71in) Wien 1999

GRÖLL Henriette 1910-1996 [29]
$1 648 - €1 601 - **£1 018** - FF10 500
Jeune femme à la violette Huile/toile (65x54cm 25x21in) Grenoble 1999

GROLL Theodor 1857-1913 [4]
$3 775 - €3 579 - **£2 296** - FF23 477
Klosterruine Himmerod bei Manderscheid in der Eifel Öl/Leinwand (66x86cm 25x33in) Köln 1999
$2 370 - €2 045 - **£1 435** - FF13 415
Segelboot und Gondoliere vor Stadtsilhouette von Venedig Öl/Leinwand/Karton (32.5x22cm 12x8in) Kempten 1999

GROLLERON Paul Louis Narcisse 1848-1901 [42]
$27 000 - €32 016 - **£18 576** - FF210 014
Soldiers Outside a Thatched Cottage Oil/canvas (157x210cm 61x82in) New-York 2000
$4 249 - €3 886 - **£2 595** - FF25 492
Soldier on his mount Oil/canvas (70x51cm 27x20in) New-York 1998

GROLLIER de Marquise de Fuligny 1742-1828 [2]
$6 390 - €6 860 - **£4 275** - FF45 000
Études de roses Huile/toile (33x24cm 12x9in) Paris 2000

GROLMAN Johan Paul C. 1841-1927 [2]
$9 000 - €10 212 - **£6 299** - FF66 984
Interior View of the Ashkenazi Synagogue in Maarssen Watercolour (36.5x26.5cm 14x10in) Tel Aviv 2001

GROM-ROTTMAYER Hermann 1877-1953 [42]
$22 500 - €24 976 - **£15 684** - FF163 833
Diana the Huntress Oil/panel (124.5x99cm 49x38in) New-York 2001

$812 - €872 - **£554** - FF5 720
Sitzende Dame Öl/Leinwand (68.5x55.5cm 26x21in) Wien 2001

GROMAIRE Marcel 1892-1971 [841]
$56 800 - €60 980 - **£38 000** - FF400 000
La moisson Huile/toile (287x168cm 112x66in) Paris 2000
$21 486 - €21 038 - **£13 220** - FF138 000
Personnages à l'orée d'un bois Huile/toile (81x100cm 31x39in) Paris 1999
$6 700 - €7 622 - **£4 650** - FF50 000
«Tête de paysanne» Huile/bois (41x33cm 16x12in) Douai 2000
$1 706 - €1 306 - **£1 156** - FF12 500
Nu debout de dos Encre Chine/papier (32.5x25cm 12x9in) Paris 2000
$281 - €335 - **£195** - FF2 200
La Sorcière Pointe sèche (28x23cm 11x9in) Saint-Dié 2000

GROMME Owen J. 1896-1991 [39]
$9 500 - €8 912 - **£5 870** - FF58 462
Turkeys in the Woods Oil/canvas (39.5x48cm 15x18in) New-York 1999

GRÖNHOLM Paul 1907-1992 [31]
$800 - €672 - **£470** - FF4 411
Hus Oil/canvas (54x65cm 21x25in) Helsinki 1998

GRÖNLAND René 1849-1892 [8]
$2 750 - €2 851 - **£1 650** - FF18 700
Anatra morta Olio/tela (63x48.5cm 24x19in) Venezia 2000

GRØNLAND Theude 1817-1876 [19]
$7 206 - €6 807 - **£4 359** - FF44 649
Fruit still Life Oil/panel (35x45.5cm 13x17in) Amsterdam 1999

GRONOWSKI Tadeusz 1894-1990 [9]
$1 400 - €1 562 - **£916** - FF10 245
«Odparcia Najazdu» Poster (99x68.5cm 38x26in) New-York 2000

GRØNVOLD Bernt Borchgrevink 1859-1923 [4]
$5 018 - €5 799 - **£3 514** - FF38 037
Kvinne og gutt i interiör Oil/canvas (80x64cm 31x25in) Oslo 2001

GRÖNVOLD Henrik 1858-1940 [5]
$731 - €703 - **£450** - FF4 609
Hooded Crow Watercolour (48.5x34.5cm 19x13in) London 1999

GRØNVOLD Marcus 1845-1929 [21]
$3 584 - €3 262 - **£2 200** - FF21 399
Maidens on a Rocky Shore Oil/canvas (57x92cm 22x36in) London 1999

GROOME William Henry Ch. XIX-XX [22]
$263 - €282 - **£180** - FF1 852
Wheedling Watercolour/paper (48x33cm 18x12in) London 2001

GROOMS Red, Charles Roger 1937 [234]
$22 000 - €25 526 - **£15 188** - FF167 442
Lateria Oil/canvas (198x147.5cm 77x58in) New-York 2000
$3 800 - €3 930 - **£2 401** - FF25 779
Nude Reclining in Bed Oil/board (14x19cm 5x7in) New-York 2000
$32 000 - €37 129 - **£22 092** - FF243 552
Eighth Avenue Snow Scene (Wall Relief) Relief (99x130x48.5cm 38x51x19in) New-York 2000

G

$3 500 - €3 980 - **£2 445** - FF26 110
Shoot Out (Wagon Piece) Bronze (31x50x26cm 12x20x10in) Chicago IL 2000

$7 000 - €5 873 - **£4 106** - FF38 525
Study for «The Tycoon» Gouache/paper (100.5x148.5cm 39x58in) New-York 1998

$1 200 - €1 152 - **£739** - FF7 559
Subway Color lithograph (74.5x92cm 29x36in) New-York 1999

GROOT de Joseph 1828-1899 **[12]**

$883 - €1 041 - **£621** - FF6 831
Familij framför sin målerisamling Oil/panel (25x33cm 9x12in) Malmö 2000

GROOTE de A. XX **[20]**

$1 494 - €1 604 - **£1 000** - FF10 521
Figures on a Quay Oil/panel (35.5x51.5cm 13x20in) London 2000

$1 122 - €1 131 - **£700** - FF7 422
Figures on a frozen Lake/Figures by a Canal Oil/panel (19.5x25.5cm 7x10in) London 2000

GROOTH George Christopher 1716-1749 **[4]**

$9 624 - €9 203 - **£5 860** - FF60 370
Porträt des Grafen Johann Franz von Rothenstein Öl/Leinwand (88x69cm 34x27in) Stuttgart 1999

GROOTH Johann Niklaus 1723-1797 **[2]**

$18 157 - €15 717 - **£11 020** - FF103 100
Margarethe Elisabeth Tscharner-von Wattenvyl/Beat Albrecht Tscharner Huile/toile (81.5x66.2cm 32x26in) Zürich 1998

GROOTVELT van Jan Hendrik 1808-1865 **[23]**

$3 505 - €3 994 - **£2 442** - FF26 196
Der blinde Geiger Oil/panel (44.2x57.4cm 17x22in) Zürich 2000

$3 974 - €4 726 - **£2 833** - FF31 000
Le charme du cordonnier Huile/panneau (39x31cm 15x12in) Lyon 2000

GROOVER Jan 1943 **[47]**

$2 000 - €2 200 - **£1 387** - FF14 428
Tulip, large Squash, three Pears Silver print (29x37cm 11x14in) New-York 2001

GROPEANO Nicolae 1865-? **[5]**

$2 593 - €2 820 - **£1 709** - FF18 500
Naydé, beauté de Bou-Saâda Pastel/carton (65x50cm 25x19in) Paris 2000

GROPPER William 1897-1977 **[182]**

$5 500 - €4 711 - **£3 247** - FF30 899
Musicians Oil/canvas (61x51cm 24x20in) New-York 1998

$600 - €629 - **£400** - FF4 125
Workers Unite Ink (25x25cm 9x9in) New-York 2001

$130 - €158 - **£91** - FF1 034
Point of Order/For the Record Etching (14.5x9.5cm 5x3in) Bethesda MD 2000

GROS Baron Antoine Jean 1771-1835 **[23]**

$8 965 - €9 624 - **£6 000** - FF63 129
The Death of Patroclus Oil/paper/canvas (31.5x39.5cm 12x15in) London 2000

$9 411 - €9 189 - **£6 000** - FF60 276
Ulysses killing the suitors of Penelope Black chalk (16x22cm 6x8in) London 1999

GROS Baron Jean-Baptiste 1793-1870 **[15]**

$23 598 - €20 581 - **£14 269** - FF135 000
Vue de l'Acropolis et d'une partie de la ville d'Athènes... Daguerreotype (15x20cm 5x7in) Paris 1998

GROS Lucien Alphonse 1845-1913 **[52]**

$1 224 - €1 372 - **£856** - FF9 000
Couple de promeneurs dans un paysage champêtre Huile/toile (54x65cm 21x25in) Paris 2001

$4 863 - €4 421 - **£2 929** - FF29 000
Les pêcheurs aux Sables d'Olonne Huile/panneau (31.5x41cm 12x16in) Soissons 1998

$4 083 - €3 857 - **£2 470** - FF25 301
Breton Marketscene Watercolour (43x62cm 16x24in) Amsterdam 1999

GROS Mario 1888-1977 **[2]**

$848 - €879 - **£508** - FF5 766
«1a festa nazionale dell'uva» Affiche couleur (100x70cm 39x27in) Torino 2000

GROSBARD Yehoshua 1900-1992 **[3]**

$4 500 - €5 025 - **£2 881** - FF32 964
Haifa Oil/canvas (60x82cm 23x32in) Tel Aviv 2000

GRÖSCHEL Rudolf 1891-1985 **[16]**

$1 959 - €2 045 - **£1 240** - FF13 415
Vor dem Neuschnee Öl/Leinwand (54x90cm 21x35in) München 2000

GROSCLAUDE Louis Aimé 1784/86-1869 **[6]**

$17 725 - €20 581 - **£12 501** - FF135 000
Portrait de Jeanne Seillière à l'âge de cinq ans Huile/toile (95x81cm 37x31in) Paris 2001

GROSE Daniel Charles 1865-1890 **[27]**

$900 - €1 046 - **£632** - FF6 859
Fishing along the River Oil/canvas (38x66cm 15x26in) New-York 2001

$650 - €555 - **£381** - FF3 643
Primitive Landscapes Oil/canvas (20x30cm 8x12in) Timonium MD 1998

GROSE Francis, Captain 1731-1791 **[11]**

$917 - €1 070 - **£650** - FF7 021
Chatham Church and barracks/Upnor Castle on the Medway Pencil (16x39cm 6x15in) London 2001

GROSE Harriet Estella 1863-1914 **[1]**

$4 250 - €4 833 - **£2 969** - FF31 705
Walther's Preislied Oil/canvas (60x91cm 24x36in) Chicago IL 2000

GROSJEAN Henry 1864-1948 **[36]**

$564 - €610 - **£390** - FF4 000
Route montagneuse Huile/toile (66x93cm 25x36in) Lyon 2001

$2 500 - €2 754 - **£1 659** - FF18 068
Paysage Oleo/tabla (25x34.5cm 9x13in) Buenos-Aires 2000

GROSPERRIN Claude 1936-1977 **[75]**

$900 - €803 - **£551** - FF5 725
«Eglise romane, Grand Pressigny»/«Les remparts du Grand Pressigny» Oil/canvas (81x65cm 31x25in) New-York 1999

GROSPIETSCH Florian 1789-1830 **[16]**

$5 147 - €5 011 - **£3 162** - FF32 868
Olevano, Monte Serone und weite Ebene mit fernem Kastell und See Oil/paper/canvas (17.5x32.5cm 6x12in) Berlin 1999

$4 194 - €4 602 - **£2 849** - FF30 185
Panoramaansicht der Stadt Florenz Watercolour (36.5x52cm 14x20in) Berlin 2000

$516 - €613 - **£357** - FF4 024
Golf von Neapel mit qualmendem Vesuv Etching (31.5x45cm 12x17in) Köln 2000

GROSS Anthony 1905-1984 **[112]**

$574 - €635 - £398 - FF4 167
Sunday Afternoon at the Beach Ink (37x50cm 14x19in) Amsterdam 2001

$364 - €340 - £226 - FF2 229
Rustic Pupils Etching (21x18cm 8x7in) London 1999

GROSS Chaim 1904-1991 **[210]**

$14 000 - €15 028 - £9 368 - FF98 574
Homage to Marc Chagall Bronze (H89cm H35in) New-York 2000

$1 500 - €1 399 - £930 - FF9 174
Patron Bronze (H13.5cm H5in) New-York 1999

$600 - €560 - £362 - FF3 676
Portrait with an Angel Ink/paper (29x35.5cm 11x13in) New-York 1999

$150 - €147 - £95 - FF964
Women and Children Lithograph (46x25cm 18x10in) Bolton MA 1999

GROSS F. XIX **[1]**

$3 078 - €3 664 - £2 200 - FF24 031
Crimera Executed in Honour of Emperor Alexander II Nicholaevich Pencil/paper (53x40cm 20x15in) London 2000

GROSS Frantisek 1909-1985 **[57]**

$549 - €519 - £342 - FF3 406
Landscape at Night Oil/cardboard (23.5x33.5cm 9x13in) Praha 1999

GROSS George XX **[6]**

$2 800 - €3 264 - £1 938 - FF21 410
Catcher Fielding Fly Ball Crashes Into Stands Oil/canvas (49x34cm 19x13in) New-York 2000

$4 250 - €4 734 - £2 779 - FF31 052
Paperback book cover: man playing solitaire, woman stretching on couch Watercolour/paper (34x25cm 13x10in) New-York 2000

GROSS Mijael 1920 **[24]**

$20 000 - €22 201 - £13 942 - FF145 630
«Portrait of the Sculptor Bar-Even» Oil/canvas (160x100.5cm 62x39in) Tel Aviv 2001

$6 000 - €6 773 - £4 179 - FF44 430
Portrait Oil/canvas (80x60cm 31x23in) Tel Aviv 2001

GROSS Peter Alfred 1849-1914 **[15]**

$1 354 - €1 296 - £841 - FF8 500
«Cycles Rudge» Affiche (105.5x74.5cm 41x29in) La Varenne-Saint-Hilaire 1999

GROSSBERG Carl 1894-1940 **[9]**

$77 535 - €76 695 - £48 345 - FF503 085
Jacquard-Weberei Oil/panel (50x40cm 19x15in) Berlin 1999

GROSSI de Adelchi 1852-1892 **[17]**

$1 003 - €1 128 - £700 - FF7 401
The Gesture Watercolour (50.5x35cm 19x13in) London 2001

GROSSI Proferio 1923-2000 **[17]**

$425 - €441 - £255 - FF2 890
Natura morta Olio/masonite (50x70cm 19x27in) Vercelli 2000

GROSSLAND James Henry XIX **[2]**

$2 685 - €2 300 - £1 614 - FF15 089
Englische Flusslandschaft im Sommer Öl/Leinwand (61x92cm 24x36in) Stuttgart 1998

GROSSMAN Elias 1898-1947 **[8]**

$107 - €115 - £71 - FF755
Winter on Fifth Avenue/Summer Fun on the River Etching (17x22cm 6x8in) Toronto 2000

GROSSMAN Nancy 1940 **[14]**

$9 500 - €10 260 - £6 565 - FF67 300
Untitled Sculpture (40.5x20x20cm 15x7x7in) New-York 2001

$6 000 - €5 034 - £3 520 - FF33 021
Man Standing Watercolour (122x93cm 48x36in) New-York 1998

GROSSMAN Sid 1915-1955 **[2]**

$2 600 - €2 173 - £1 539 - FF14 254
Child Kicking Up her Heels, Coney Island Silver print (22x19cm 9x7in) New-York 1998

GROSSMANN Rudolf 1882-1941 **[281]**

$5 328 - €4 603 - £3 218 - FF30 191
Beim Parkkonzert Oil/panel (81.5x55.5cm 32x21in) Köln 1998

$1 071 - €1 022 - £669 - FF6 707
Sonnenuntergang über dem Schwarzwald Oil/panel (37x34.8cm 14x13in) Köln 1999

$214 - €256 - £152 - FF1 676
Die Sammlerin Hermine Feist-Wollheim und der Sammler Marcel von Nemecs Charcoal (43x58.5cm 16x23in) Köln 2000

$110 - €128 - £77 - FF838
Hämisches Publikum Lithographie (32x36cm 12x14in) Berlin 2001

GROSSO Giacomo 1860-1938 **[45]**

$11 557 - €10 116 - £7 000 - FF66 354
Portrait of the Actress Virginia Oil/canvas (161x121cm 63x47in) London 1998

$4 000 - €4 147 - £2 400 - FF27 200
Ritratto di gentiluomo Olio/tela (72x55cm 28x21in) Torino 1999

$2 880 - €2 488 - £1 440 - FF16 320
La monaca, bozzetto per il dipinto «Rimpianti» Olio/tavola (32x19.5cm 12x7in) Milano 1999

GROSSO Y SANCHEZ Alfonso 1893-1983 **[23]**

$20 160 - €21 623 - £13 680 - FF141 840
Bodegón con frutas Oleo/lienzo (100x130cm 39x51in) Madrid 2001

$6 720 - €7 208 - £4 200 - FF47 280
Preparándose para la Feria de Abril Oleo/lienzo (81x61cm 31x24in) Madrid 2000

GRØSTAD Terje 1925 **[7]**

$162 - €187 - £114 - FF1 227
Sildefiske Color lithograph (39x59cm 15x23in) Oslo 2000

GROSZ George 1893-1959 **[1243]**

$11 000 - €12 763 - £7 594 - FF83 721
Nude on beach, artist's wife Oil/paper (50x36cm 19x14in) New-York 2000

$6 500 - €6 119 - £4 015 - FF40 136
Bandit, Dummy Charcoal (63.5x48.5cm 25x19in) New-York 1999

$301 - €281 - £181 - FF1 844
Das ungleiche Paar Lithographie (29x21cm 11x8in) Berlin 1999

GROTEMEYER Fritz 1864-? **[4]**

$15 000 - €12 992 - £9 199 - FF85 222
Conversation Over Tea Oil/canvas (117x172.5cm 46x67in) New-York 1998

GROTH Jan 1938 **[16]**

$405 - €408 - £252 - FF2 678
Komposition mot vitt Black chalk/paper (62x88cm 24x34in) Stockholm 2000

GROTH Vilhelm Georg 1842-1899 **[48]**
- $887 - €835 - £553 - FF5 474
  Udsigt over sommerlandskab ved Silkeborg
  Oil/canvas (47x68cm 18x26in) Vejle 1999

GROTT Teodor 1884-1972 **[27]**
- $996 - €932 - £603 - FF6 114
  Flowers in a Vase Watercolour/paper (59.3x48cm
  23x18in) Warszawa 1999

GROTTGER Artur 1837-1867 **[11]**
- $38 035 - €43 259 - £26 815 - FF283 760
  Mädchen mit Früchtekorb Öl/Leinwand
  (94.5x73.3cm 37x28in) Zürich 2001
- $8 361 - €8 306 - £5 208 - FF54 484
  Règlement de comptes entre élèves Oil/paper
  (30.5x39cm 12x15in) Warszawa 1999

GROUX de Charles 1825-1870 **[30]**
- $742 - €793 - £505 - FF5 203
  Procession Pastel/papier (33x46.5cm 12x18in)
  Lokeren 2001

GROUX de Henri 1867-1930 **[120]**
- $819 - €793 - £505 - FF5 203
  La bague rouge Pastel/panneau (102x72cm 40x28in)
  Bruxelles 1999

GROVER Jeannette Elisabeth XIX **[2]**
- $6 961 - €6 716 - £4 400 - FF44 055
  A Visit from the Bishop Oil/canvas (64.5x86.5cm
  25x34in) London 1999

GROVER Oliver Dennett 1861-1927 **[30]**
- $2 400 - €2 222 - £1 469 - FF14 574
  Self Portrait Oil/canvas/board (76x55cm 30x22in)
  Chicago IL 1999
- $400 - €444 - £277 - FF3 083
  Summer in the Valley Oil/board (22x33cm 9x13in)
  Cincinnati OH 2000

GROVES John Michael XX **[4]**
- $1 586 - €1 520 - £1 000 - FF9 969
  Landing the Catch Pastel/paper (49x74cm 19x29in)
  Billingshurst, West-Sussex 1999

GROVES Robert E. ?-c.1944 **[19]**
- $5 798 - €6 932 - £4 000 - FF45 474
  «Off to the Fishing Grounds» Watercolour
  (67.5x101.5cm 26x39in) Penzance, Cornwall 2000

GRUAU René 1909 **[198]**
- $12 790 - €15 245 - £9 120 - FF100 000
  Femme à la rose Huile/toile (161x120cm 63x47in)
  Paris 2000
- $611 - €610 - £381 - FF4 000
  Étude de ballerine Gouache/papier (32.5x25.5cm
  12x10in) La Varenne-Saint-Hilaire 1999
- $256 - €305 - £182 - FF2 000
  «Bal du Moulin Rouge» Affiche (160x120cm
  62x47in) Orléans 2000

GRUBACS Carlo 1810-c.1870 **[68]**
- $45 640 - €53 357 - £32 585 - FF350 000
  **Caprice: vue de Venise avec le pont du Rialto,
  d'après Palladio** Huile/toile (55x79cm 21x31in) Paris
  2001
- $9 900 - €8 552 - £4 950 - FF56 100
  Venezia, piazza San Marco Olio/tela (20x27.5cm
  7x10in) Milano 1999
- $2 774 - €2 592 - £1 711 - FF17 000
  Vue du Palais des Doges à Venise Gouache/papier
  (11x16cm 4x6in) Paris 1999

GRUBACS Giovanni 1829-1919 **[30]**
- $10 710 - €11 103 - £6 426 - FF72 828
  **Notturno con la sagra di Santa Marta/Notturno
  col ponte votivo** Oleo/tabla (32.5x50.5cm 12x19in)
  Venezia 1999
- $12 710 - €12 327 - £8 000 - FF80 860
  **Elegant Figures in Piazza San Marco/Gondolas
  on the Grand Canal** Oil/panel (15x25cm 5x9in)
  London 1999

GRUBACS Marco 1839-1910 **[35]**
- $1 211 - €1 163 - £760 - FF7 627
  Blick auf den Dogenpalast Oil/panel (14x27cm
  5x10in) Wien 1999

GRUBER Francis 1912-1948 **[93]**
- $15 972 - €16 769 - £10 098 - FF110 000
  Portrait de Mlle Nordmann Huile/toile (100x80cm
  39x31in) Paris 2000
- $2 856 - €3 201 - £1 938 - FF21 000
  Paysage au chemin Huile/isorel (33x41cm 12x16in)
  Paris 2000
- $2 561 - €2 622 - £1 608 - FF17 000
  Femme nue debout Mine plomb (59x43cm 23x16in)
  Paris 2000

GRUBER Franz Xaver 1801-1862 **[14]**
- $1 645 - €1 817 - £1 140 - FF11 917
  Stilleben mit Trauben auf einem Felsen
  Aquarell/Papier (53x36cm 20x14in) Wien 2001

GRUBER Jacques 1870-1936 **[50]**
- $13 344 - €12 196 - £8 168 - FF80 000
  **Des oiseaux volent parmi des frondaisons au-
  dessus des eaux** Peinture (202x180cm 79x70in)
  Chartres 1999
- $160 - €152 - £97 - FF1 000
  **Dessin de tissus pour dossier de chaise de
  salon (projet)** Aquarelle (41x28cm 16x11in) Paris
  1999

GRUBER-GLEICHENBERG Franz 1886-1940 **[5]**
- $742 - €847 - £523 - FF5 558
  «Stilleben mit Bronzefigur» Öl/Leinwand
  (77.5x60cm 30x23in) Bern 2001

GRUBHOFER Tony 1854-1935 **[9]**
- $249 - €291 - £176 - FF1 906
  Altstadt Innsbruck mit Helblinghaus Indian ink
  (19x12cm 7x4in) Salzburg 2000

GRUBICY DE DRAGON Vittore 1851-1920 **[10]**
- $7 735 - €8 019 - £4 641 - FF52 598
  La sera Olio/cartone (56x66cm 22x25in) Venezia 2000

GRUBINSKI Jan 1874-1945 **[7]**
- $1 414 - €1 501 - £950 - FF9 849
  Country Road Oil/canvas (74x95.5cm 29x37in)
  London 2001

GRUEBER Albrecht 1847-1888 **[2]**
- $1 730 - €1 912 - £1 200 - FF12 543
  The Proposal Oil/canvas (37x29.5cm 14x11in)
  London 2001

GRUELLE Johnny 1880-1938 **[8]**
- $2 600 - €2 407 - £1 591 - FF15 789
  **Frolicking woodland sprites: endpaper ill. for
  The Friendly Fairies** Watercolour (25x32cm 10x12in)
  New-York 1999

GRUELLE Richard Buckner 1851-1914 **[5]**
- $1 400 - €1 624 - £996 - FF10 653
  Landscape Watercolour/paper (35x50cm 14x20in)
  Carmel IN 2000

GRUEN John, Bob 1946 [18]

📷 **$526** - €495 - **£320** - FF3 247
The Group Led Zepplin standing in front of their jet Photograph (26.5x34cm 10x13in) London 1999

GRÜN Jules-Alexandre 1868-1934 [176]

$1 739 - €1 933 - **£1 216** - FF12 682
L'enfant aux oranges Huile/panneau (50x61cm 19x24in) Bruxelles 2001

$464 - €396 - **£276** - FF2 600
Roses dans un vase Huile/carton (33x24cm 12x9in) Bruxelles 1998

$1 306 - €1 252 - **£822** - FF8 210
«Théâtre du Cinématographique Pathé, 5 Boulevard Montmartre» Affiche (131x90cm 51x35in) Bern 1999

GRÜN Maurice 1869-1947 [38]

$1 805 - €1 753 - **£1 115** - FF11 500
Intérieur de ferme Huile/toile (65x54.5cm 25x21in) Paris 1999

$1 920 - €1 753 - **£1 168** - FF11 500
Retour de pêche à Audierne Huile/panneau (23x32cm 9x12in) Douarnenez 1998

GRÜNBAUM Johann 1760-1827 [4]

$6 000 - €5 826 - **£3 705** - FF38 215
Karl Otto Bonnier vid terrassbordet Oil/panel (65x54cm 25x21in) Stockholm 1999

$2 634 - €3 068 - **£1 840** - FF20 123
Brustbild einer jungen Dame mit brauner Lockenfrisur in weissem Kleid Miniature (11x9cm 4x3in) München 2000

GRÜNBERG Wolfgang XX [11]

$952 - €1 022 - **£637** - FF6 707
Gelbe Rose Oil/canvas/panel (27.5x22.5cm 10x8in) Köln 2000

GRUND Johann 1808-1887 [19]

$1 604 - €1 534 - **£1 005** - FF10 061
Drei Generationen beim Tee Öl/Leinwand (66x54cm 25x21in) Hamburg 1999

$2 528 - €2 301 - **£1 579** - FF15 092
Junges Mädchen im Gebet an einem Tisch, auf dem das Gesangbuch liegt Öl/Leinwand (36.8x36.2cm 14x14in) München 1999

GRÜND Norbert Joseph Carl 1717-1767 [33]

$11 271 - €10 660 - **£7 020** - FF69 927
Lucretia Oil/wood (17.5x13cm 6x5in) Praha 2000

GRUNDIG Hans 1901-1958 [27]

$1 057 - €1 278 - **£738** - FF8 384
Sitzendes Mädchen Charcoal (60x46cm 23x18in) Berlin 2000

$101 - €112 - **£66** - FF737
Frau am Webstuhl Woodcut (31.8x20.9cm 12x8in) Leipzig 2000

GRUNDMANN Basilius 1726-1798 [5]

$2 369 - €2 543 - **£1 585** - FF16 684
Mondbeschienene Flusslandschaft mit steinerner Bogenbrücke, Figuren Oil/panel (17x27cm 6x10in) Wien 2000

GRÜNENWALD Jakob 1822-1896 [29]

$32 452 - €38 347 - **£23 002** - FF251 542
Die Attacke Öl/Leinwand (121x100cm 47x39in) Stuttgart 2001

$2 688 - €2 300 - **£1 618** - FF15 089
Landschaft mit Zigeunerstaffage Oil/paper/canvas (45.5x67.5cm 17x26in) München 1998

$1 430 - €1 636 - **£982** - FF10 732
Prachtvolle alte Weide im sonnigen Gegenlicht an einem Frühlingstag Öl/Leinwand/Karton (42x31cm 16x12in) Lindau 2001

$900 - €1 022 - **£625** - FF6 707
Wintervergnügen Ink (23.5x30cm 9x11in) Berlin 2001

GRUNER Elioth 1882-1939 [108]

$14 527 - €15 119 - **£9 120** - FF99 177
Playing in the Shallows Oil/canvas (26.5x64cm 10x25in) Melbourne 2000

$11 063 - €12 082 - **£7 121** - FF79 252
Stocks in a Vase Oil/canvas/board (43.5x35cm 17x13in) Melbourne 2000

$229 - €246 - **£156** - FF1 616
Out West Etching (17x13cm 6x5in) Sydney 2001

GRÜNEWALD Isaac 1889-1946 [527]

$10 880 - €11 999 - **£7 370** - FF78 710
På stranden II Oil/canvas (250x60cm 98x23in) Stockholm 2001

$10 960 - €10 480 - **£6 871** - FF68 742
Interiör med amaryllis och hätskulptur Oil/panel (75x59cm 29x23in) Stockholm 1999

$4 165 - €3 906 - **£2 576** - FF25 623
Stilleben med frukter Oil/panel (22x27cm 8x10in) Stockholm 1999

$1 567 - €1 818 - **£1 081** - FF11 927
Teaterkostym, eldfågel Akvarell/papper (50x31cm 19x12in) Stockholm 1999

$195 - €223 - **£137** - FF1 461
Gossporträtt Lithograph (28.5x20.5cm 11x8in) Stockholm 2001

GRÜNFELD Thomas 1956 [19]

$29 886 - €32 080 - **£20 000** - FF210 432
Misfit (Nandu) Sculpture (120x70x30cm 47x27x11in) London 2000

$2 816 - €3 324 - **£2 000** - FF21 806
Untitled Installation (65x90x37cm 25x35x14in) London 2001

GRÜNHUT Isidoro 1862-1896 [1]

$7 250 - €7 516 - **£4 590** - FF49 300
Musicisti Olio/tela (77x55cm 30x21in) Trieste 1999

GRUNSWEIGH Nathan 1880-c.1966/77 [24]

$1 180 - €1 375 - **£816** - FF9 022
Pariser Strassenszene Öl/Leinwand (38x55cm 14x21in) Bern 2000

GRÜNWALD Béla Iványi 1867-1940 [51]

$2 400 - €2 360 - **£1 500** - FF15 480
Scene of Village Oil/canvas (70x100cm 27x39in) Budapest 1999

$4 000 - €3 933 - **£2 500** - FF25 800
Picking Flowers Pastel/paper (48x38cm 18x14in) Budapest 1999

GRUNZWEIG Bedrich 1910 [31]

📷 **$1 600** - €1 717 - **£1 086** - FF11 264
«Between Heaven and Earth» Gelatin silver print (40x39.5cm 15x15in) Beverly-Hills CA 2001

GRUPPE Charles Paul 1860-1940 [203]

$4 000 - €3 730 - **£2 481** - FF24 466
Clipper at Sea Oil/canvas (76.5x102cm 30x40in) New-York 1999

$2 970 - €2 680 - **£1 830** - FF17 582
Rainy Street Oil/panel (20x25cm 8x10in) Batavia NY 1999

$700 - €801 - **£486** - FF5 252
Sketch of Two Women Watercolour/paper (15x10cm 6x4in) Cincinnati OH 2000

G

GRUPPE Emile Albert 1896-1978 **[398]**
- $8 000 - €8 587 - **£5 353** - FF56 328
  Banyan Tree Oil/canvas (61x51cm 24x20in) San-Francisco CA 2000
- $3 250 - €2 988 - **£2 007** - FF19 602
  Gloucester Fishing Boats Oil/canvas (35x35cm 14x14in) Hampton-Falls NH 1998
- $500 - €473 - **£310** - FF3 104
  Harbor Scene with Sailboats Pencil/paper (23x34cm 9x13in) Wallkill NY 1999

GRÜTZKE Johannes 1937 **[168]**
- $16 432 - €19 403 - **£11 665** - FF127 276
  «Durchbruch» Öl/Leinwand (130.5x135cm 51x53in) Berlin 2001
- $4 552 - €4 346 - **£2 844** - FF28 508
  Wir Beide Öl/Leinwand (60.5x96cm 23x37in) Köln 1999
- $3 354 - €3 066 - **£2 136** - FF20 113
  Freundschaft Oil/canvas/panel (17.5x21.5cm 6x8in) München 1998
- $857 - €920 - **£573** - FF6 037
  Die Figur des Lichtbringers Pastel (62.6x44.6cm 24x17in) Köln 2000
- $132 - €153 - **£92** - FF1 006
  Köpfe Radierung (34x25cm 13x9in) Berlin 2001

GRÜTZNER von Eduard 1846-1925 **[158]**
- $17 423 - €19 429 - **£11 715** - FF127 448
  Nach der Mahlzeit Öl/Leinwand (48x40cm 18x15in) Ahlden 2000
- $8 484 - €8 692 - **£5 236** - FF57 016
  Falstaff Oil/panel (20.5x15.5cm 8x6in) Düsseldorf 2000
- $412 - €353 - **£248** - FF2 313
  Bildnis eines Geistlichen Red chalk/paper (20x17cm 7x6in) München 1998

GRUYERE Théodore Charles 1814-1885 **[1]**
- $190 000 - €225 958 - **£133 415** - FF1 482 190
  Seated Indian Marble (H119.5cm H47in) New-York 2000

GRUYTER Jacob Willem 1817-1880 **[31]**
- $3 622 - €3 069 - **£2 164** - FF20 134
  Küstensegler auf stürmisch bewegter See Öl/Leinwand (40.5x50.5cm 15x19in) Bremen 1998
- $2 870 - €2 477 - **£1 730** - FF16 250
  Une barque de pêche échouée Huile/panneau (33x26cm 12x10in) Bruxelles 1998

GRYEFF de Adriaen 1670-1715 **[80]**
- $6 400 - €7 267 - **£4 380** - FF47 670
  Jagdstilleben in einem Schlosspark von einem Hund bewacht Öl/Kupfer (47x38cm 18x14in) Wien 2000
- $4 674 - €4 360 - **£2 820** - FF28 602
  Jagdbeute von Hunden bewacht Öl/Leinwand (24x20cm 9x7in) Wien 1999

GRYGLEWSKI Aleksander 1833-1879 **[1]**
- $3 340 - €3 899 - **£2 358** - FF25 576
  Intérieur d'église gothique Huile/toile (36.5x24.5cm 14x9in) Warszawa 2000

GRZIMEK Waldemar 1918-1984 **[49]**
- $1 633 - €1 841 - **£1 131** - FF12 074
  Stehender Akt Bronze (H42cm H16in) Berlin 2000

GSCHOSMANN Ludwig 1894/1901-1988 **[144]**
- $1 033 - €971 - **£639** - FF6 372
  Chiemgaulandschaft Öl/Leinwand (70x80cm 27x31in) München 1998
- $112 - €128 - **£77** - FF838
  Partie am Starnberger See Aquarell/Papier (55x65.5cm 21x25in) München 2000

GSELL Georg 1673-1740 **[2]**
- $4 962 - €5 445 - **£3 194** - FF35 719
  Nobleman wearing a yellow lined Light brown Velvet Cloak Oil/canvas (87x66cm 34x25in) Amsterdam 1999

GSELL Henry Alfred 1859-1920 **[1]**
- $14 421 - €15 935 - **£10 000** - FF104 530
  Nu au divan Oil/canvas (126.5x171.5cm 49x67in) London 2001

GSELL Laurent 1860-1944 **[59]**
- $2 402 - €2 134 - **£1 471** - FF14 000
  Le port de Monaco Huile/toile (53x45cm 20x17in) Limoges 1999

GU LINSHI 1865-1929 **[5]**
- $12 226 - €11 595 - **£7 438** - FF76 057
  Landscapes after Ancient Masters Ink/paper (16x21.5cm 6x8in) Hong-Kong 1999

GU LUO 1763-c.1840 **[2]**
- $14 846 - €12 586 - **£8 878** - FF82 558
  Capturing enemies in Mountain Range Coloured inks/paper (49x183cm 19x72in) Hong-Kong 1998

GU MEI 1934 **[11]**
- $6 410 - €7 534 - **£4 445** - FF49 420
  Landscape in Misty Clouds Ink (136.5x63cm 53x24in) Hong-Kong 2000

GU WENDA 1955 **[3]**
- $14 491 - €12 099 - **£8 500** - FF79 365
  United Nation Series : Hong Kong monument Mixed media (305x244cm 120x96in) London 1998

GU YUN 1835-1896 **[4]**
- $2 564 - €2 913 - **£1 800** - FF19 106
  Landscape after Li Tang Ink (25x25.5cm 9x10in) Hong-Kong 2001

GUACCIMANNI Vittorio 1859-1938 **[12]**
- $3 647 - €3 382 - **£2 200** - FF22 186
  Moorish Guard Oil/panel (28x17cm 11x6in) London 1999

GUALA Antonio 1892-1972 **[4]**
- $750 - €777 - **£450** - FF5 100
  Riflessi Olio/cartone (33x27.5cm 12x10in) Vercelli 2000

GUALA Pier Francesco 1698-1757 **[9]**
- $6 000 - €6 220 - **£3 600** - FF40 800
  Ritratto di frate Olio/tela (80x60.5cm 31x23in) Milano 2001

GUALDI Antonio 1796-1865 **[3]**
- $14 000 - €18 141 - **£10 500** - FF119 000
  Imelda Lambertazzi e Bonifacio de'Geremei Olio/tela (82.5x107.5cm 32x42in) Prato 2000

GUALDI Pietro 1716-? **[1]**
- $1 829 - €1 906 - **£1 150** - FF12 501
  Monumentos de Mejico Lithograph (39x52.5cm 15x20in) London 2000

GUAN LIANG 1900-1986 **[41]**
- $20 605 - €24 050 - **£14 105** - FF157 755
  «Arbor day» Oil/canvas (60.5x35.5cm 23x13in) Taipei 2000
- $6 992 - €6 557 - **£4 347** - FF43 010
  Yu-Wong Temple Oil/paper/board (26x34cm 10x13in) Taipei 1999
- $1 417 - €1 304 - **£850** - FF8 554
  Berth Watercolour/paper (30x36cm 11x14in) Taipei 1999

GUAN SHANYUE 1912-2000 **[22]**
- $11 840 – €11 236 – **£7 194** – FF73 701
  Snow Games Ink (131.5x69cm 51x27in) Hong-Kong 1999

GUANSE Antonio 1926 **[105]**
- $447 – €488 – **£293** – FF3 200
  La fenêtre Huile/toile (46x38cm 18x14in) Douai 2000

GUARANA Jacopo 1720-1808 **[22]**
- $5 100 – €4 406 – **£3 400** – FF28 900
  Allegoria dell'inverno Olio/tela (37x70cm 14x27in) Prato 1998
- $4 000 – €4 147 – **£2 400** – FF27 200
  Testa di donna/Studio di mano destra Matita (29.5x22.5cm 11x8in) Milano 2001

GUARDABASSI Guerrino 1841-? **[40]**
- $475 – €411 – **£282** – FF2 696
  Woman by a roadside Shrine Watercolour/paper (53.5x34.5cm 21x13in) Washington 1998

GUARDASSONI Alessandro 1819-1888 **[2]**
- $10 500 – €10 885 – **£6 300** – FF71 400
  Dario Re di Persia morente Olio/tela (173x246cm 68x96in) Formigine, Mo 2000

GUARDI Francesco 1712-1793 **[166]**
- $121 040 – €121 959 – **£75 440** – FF800 000
  Venise: Vue de l'église san Giovanni e Paolo Huile/toile (95x127.5cm 37x50in) Paris 2000
- $475 794 – €407 039 – **£283 554** – FF2 670 000
  Vue de San Marco animée de personnages Huile/toile (40.5x62cm 15x24in) Cannes 1998
- $77 123 – €65 173 – **£46 000** – FF427 510
  Venice, the Grand Canal and the Rialto Bridge from the South Oil/panel (18x31.5cm 7x12in) London 1998
- $14 943 – €16 040 – **£10 000** – FF105 216
  Figures in a Loggia near a Church Wash (39.5x31.5cm 15x12in) London 2000

GUARDI Giacomo 1764-1835 **[187]**
- $18 000 – €18 660 – **£10 800** – FF122 400
  Veduta della Piazza di S.Marco Olio/tela (68.5x94cm 26x37in) Venezia 2000
- $16 000 – €18 168 – **£10 950** – FF119 175
  Venezianisches Capriccio mit verfallenem Torbogen bei einem Hafen Öl/Leinwand (8.5x11.3cm 3x4in) Wien 2000
- $8 000 – €6 955 – **£4 841** – FF45 620
  The Rialto Bridge, Venice Gouache/paper (13x24cm 5x9in) New-York 1998

GUARDI Giovanni Antonio 1698/99-1760 **[30]**
- $60 000 – €51 833 – **£40 000** – FF340 000
  Immacolata Olio/tela (170x100cm 66x39in) Prato 1998
- $24 000 – €31 100 – **£18 000** – FF204 000
  Il trionfo di un condottiero Olio/tela (46.5x60cm 18x23in) Milano 2001
- $17 931 – €19 248 – **£12 000** – FF126 259
  Study of a Standing Nude/Nude Seated on a Rock Red chalk/paper (41x27.5cm 16x10in) London 2000

GUARIENTI Carlo 1923 **[72]**
- $6 500 – €6 738 – **£3 900** – FF44 200
  Natura morta Tecnica mista/cartone (122x133cm 48x52in) Milano 2000
- $1 800 – €1 866 – **£1 080** – FF12 240
  Chiesa Tempera (53x38.5cm 20x15in) Prato 2001
- $1 200 – €1 244 – **£720** – FF8 160
  Diana cacciatrice Matita/carta (46x33cm 18x12in) Roma 2000

GUARINO Domenico 1683-1750 **[4]**
- $10 041 – €8 509 – **£6 000** – FF55 813
  Susannah and the Elders Oil/canvas (120x94cm 47x37in) London 1998

GUARINO Francesco 1611-1654 **[11]**
- $14 000 – €18 141 – **£10 500** – FF119 000
  San Francesco in preghiera Olio/tela (91.5x70.5cm 36x27in) Milano 2001

GUARLOTTI Giovanni 1869-1954 **[26]**
- $2 120 – €2 747 – **£1 590** – FF18 020
  Verso il pascolo Olio/cartone (36x49,5cm 14x19in) Torino 2000
- $1 000 – €1 296 – **£750** – FF8 500
  Ritratto di donna Olio/cartone (42x31.5cm 16x12in) Vercelli 2001

GUARNIERI Luciano 1930 **[31]**
- $300 – €311 – **£180** – FF2 040
  Ritratto maschile Matita/carta (33x24cm 12x9in) Prato 1999

GUASTALLA Pierre 1891-1968 **[92]**
- $682 – €793 – **£479** – FF5 200
  L'église d'Ascain Huile/toile (47x61.5cm 18x24in) Paris 2001

GUASTALLA Roberto 1855-1912 **[8]**
- $5 000 – €5 183 – **£3 000** – FF34 000
  Mekinez - (Marrueco) El'Magreb Olio/tavola (18x28cm 7x11in) Roma 2000

GUAYASAMIN Oswaldo 1919-1999 **[186]**
- $15 000 – €17 428 – **£10 542** – FF114 318
  El pingullo Oil/paper/board (75.5x56cm 29x22in) New-York 2001
- $1 530 – €1 425 – **£935** – FF9 350
  Guitarrista Tinta china/papel (43x30cm 16x11in) Caracas 1998
- $162 – €180 – **£105** – FF1 182
  La pareja Litografía (63x43cm 24x16in) Madrid 2000

GUBBELS Klaas 1934 **[63]**
- $1 725 – €1 588 – **£1 035** – FF10 418
  Coffee pot Oil/canvas (24x18cm 9x7in) Amsterdam 1999
- $759 – €817 – **£517** – FF5 357
  Coffee pot Sculpture, glass (H33cm H12in) Amsterdam 2001
- $666 – €577 – **£404** – FF3 787
  A teapot Watercolour (17.5x12cm 6x4in) Amsterdam 1998

GUBLER Eduard 1891-1971 **[7]**
- $19 952 – €18 158 – **£12 246** – FF119 111
  Familie beim Lampenlicht Öl/Leinwand (120x130cm 47x51in) Zürich 1999

GUBLER Ernst 1895-1958 **[15]**
- $431 – €488 – **£301** – FF3 204
  Zwei Kinder Charcoal/paper (81.5x53.5cm 32x21in) Zürich 2001

GUBLER Jakob 1891-1963 **[7]**
- $14 704 – €13 732 – **£9 075** – FF90 074
  Nachtlandschaft mit Gaswerk Schlieren Unterengstringen Öl/Leinwand (33x46cm 12x18in) Luzern 1999

GUBLER Max 1898-1973 **[123]**
- $39 726 – €37 524 – **£24 738** – FF246 144
  Landschaft mit Kloster Fahr im Vorfrühling Öl/Leinwand (97x130cm 38x51in) St. Gallen 1999
- $17 748 – €19 129 – **£11 901** – FF125 475
  Nacht Öl/Leinwand (46x55cm 18x21in) Zürich 2000

G

G

$1 151 - €1 299 - £809 - FF8 520
**Illustration zu «The old man and the sea» von
Hemingway** Pastel (47.5x33cm 18x12in) Bern 2001

GUCCIONE Piero 1935 [80]
$17 500 - €18 141 - £10 500 - FF119.000
«Villa Balestra dopo il tramonto» Olio/tela
(94x85cm 37x33in) Roma 2001
$17 200 - €22 288 - £12 900 - FF146 200
«Linee del mare» Olio/tela (18.5x56cm 7x22in)
Roma 2001
$4 000 - €4 147 - £2 400 - FF27 200
Appunto per la siepe Pastelli (34.5x40cm 13x15in)
Roma 2001
$400 - €415 - £240 - FF2 720
Mare Acquaforte, acquatinta (39x30cm 15x11in) Roma
2001

GUCHT van de Rob XX [2]
$11 580 - €12 706 - £7 694 - FF83 344
Deux femmes Oil/canvas (95x91cm 37x35in)
Amsterdam 2000

GUCHT van Jose 1913-1980 [39]
$181 - €211 - £127 - FF1 382
Vue sur Rupelmonde Aquarelle/papier (50x70cm
19x27in) Antwerpen 2001

GUDAPI Moima XX [6]
$6 289 - €6 752 - £4 209 - FF44 288
Rainbow Serpents Come Out of the Water
Acrylic/canvas (102x84cm 40x33in) Melbourne 2000

GUDAPI Willie 1916-1996 [13]
$3 289 - €3 173 - £2 078 - FF20 812
Untitled Acrylic/canvas (148x142cm 58x55in)
Melbourne 1999
$6 289 - €6 752 - £4 209 - FF44 288
Rainbow Serpents Come Out of the Water
Acrylic/canvas (102x84cm 40x33in) Melbourne 2000

GUDE Hans Fredrik 1825-1903 [118]
$180.000 - €155 296 - £108 594 - FF1 018 674
Ships Off a Wooded Coast Oil/canvas (91x139cm
35x54in) New-York 1998
$43 176 - €49 116 - £30 156 - FF322 182
Bergigt landskap, Norge Oil/canvas (48x72cm
18x28in) Stockholm 2000
$7 686 - €8 699 - £5 376 - FF57 064
Seilskute Oil/panel (18x13cm 7x5in) Oslo 2001
$4 172 - €4 722 - £2 918 - FF30 977
Utsyn over sjöen ved Arran Mixed media/paper
(26x43cm 10x16in) Oslo 2001

GUDE Nils 1859-1908 [6]
$1 197 - €1 145 - £754 - FF7 508
Sittende kvinne med rose Oil/panel (31x23cm
12x9in) Oslo 1999

GUDERNA Ladislav 1921 [4]
$5 202 - €4 920 - £3 240 - FF32 274
Femme écrivant une lettre Huile/toile (70x95cm
27x37in) Praha 2000

GUDGEON Ralston 1910-1984 [133]
$432 - €486 - £300 - FF3 185
Cock Pheasant Taking flight Watercolour/paper
(45.5x73.5cm 17x28in) Penrith, Cumbria 2000

GUDIASCHWILI Wladimir Davidovich 1896-1980 [2]
$58 904 - €66 045 - £40 000 - FF433 228
Celebration in Georgia Oil/canvas (170x303cm
66x119in) London 2000
$35 572 - €41 330 - £25 000 - FF271 105
View of Svanetia, Georgia Oil/canvas (73x60cm
28x23in) London 2001

GUDIN Henriette Herminie 1825-? [143]
$3 445 - €3 442 - £2 153 - FF22 576
Marine, les bateaux au clair de lune Oil/panel
(14x21cm 5x8in) Zofingen 1999
$1 270 - €1 372 - £852 - FF9 000
Bateaux et pêcheurs à marée basse
Gouache/papier (6.5x9cm 2x3in) Rennes 2000

GUDIN Théodore, baron 1802-1880 [158]
$50 640 - €59 492 - £35 520 - FF390 240
Le grand canal de Venise animé Huile/toile
(106x152cm 41x59in) Bruxelles 2000
$4 438 - €4 269 - £2 738 - FF28 000
Trois-mâts dans une mer forte Huile/toile
(49x65cm 19x25in) Le Havre 1998
$1 740 - €1 829 - £1 092 - FF12 000
Bord de mer Huile/toile (26.5x42cm 10x16in) Nice
2000
$900 - €1 067 - £635 - FF7 000
Cérmonie au pied de la colonne de juillet Encre
(21.5x37.5cm 8x14in) Paris 2000

GUDIOL COROMINAS Monserrat 1933 [24]
$5 500 - €6 105 - £3 834 - FF40 048
Girl seated by a Tree Oil/canvas (65x81.5cm
25x32in) New-York 2001
$440 - €4 805 - £2 960 - FF31 520
Figura femenina de perfil Oleo/tabla (28x45cm
11x17in) Barcelona 2000
$151 - €168 - £106 - FF1 103
Personajes Litografía (76x56cm 29x22in) Barcelona
2001

GUDNASON Svavar 1909-1988 [63]
$4 255 - €4 827 - £2 998 - FF31 665
Skumringslys Oil/canvas (78x100cm 30x39in)
København 2001
$848 - €860 - £526 - FF5 642
Rosa-Brud Watercolour (52x40cm 20x15in)
København 2000

GUDNI Georg 1961 [11]
$3 740 - €4 340 - £2 582 - FF28 471
Landskap Oil/canvas (170x150cm 66x59in)
Stockholm 2000
$984 - €992 - £613 - FF6 505
Utan titel Oil/canvas (30x30cm 11x11in) Stockholm
2000

GUDUPI Willie 1916-1996 [1]
$10 140 - €10 815 - £6 767 - FF70 944
Dance and Song Cycles Acrylic/canvas
(244x135cm 96x53in) Melbourne 2000

GUEDEN Colette XX [7]
$726 - €732 - £452 - FF4 800
Masque african Céramique (H34cm H13in) Paris
2000

GUÉDY Gaston Édouard 1874-1955 [6]
$82 186 - €88 220 - £55 000 - FF578 688
Harem Dancer Oil/canvas (181.5x148.5cm 71x58in)
London 2000

GUEDY Jules 1805-1876 [2]
$9 102 - €10 824 - £6 489 - FF71 000
Vue de Grenoble, soleil couchant Huile/toile
(60x90cm 23x35in) Grenoble 2000

GUELDRY Ferdinand Joseph 1858-1945 [59]
$6 642 - €5 793 - £4 016 - FF38 000
Course d'aviron Huile/toile (90x123cm 35x48in)
Paris 1998
$4 623 - €5 107 - £3 205 - FF33 500
La Baie de St Tropez Huile/toile (34x42cm 13x16in)
Paris 2001

GUELTZL de Marco 1958-1992 **[20]**
- **$3 983** - €3 887 - **£2 521** - FF25 500
  Petite table d'appoint Fer (50x50x42cm
  19x19x16in) Versailles 1999

GUENIN Joachim 1776-1816 **[2]**
- **$4 531** - €4 358 - **£2 796** - FF28 585
  Herrenportrait Öl/Leinwand (96.5x73cm 37x28in)
  Bern 1999

GUÉNOT Auguste 1882-1966 **[9]**
- **$2 800** - €2 794 - **£1 768** - FF18 326
  Polo Player Bronze (H29cm H11in) New-York 2000

GUERARD Amédée 1824-1908 **[6]**
- **$1 671** - €1 601 - **£1 030** - FF10 500
  Scène familiale Huile/toile (40x33cm 15x12in) Calais
  1999

GUÉRARD Charles-Jean 1790-1830 **[1]**
- **$11 498** - €11 586 - **£7 166** - FF76 000
  Vues de parc avec cannotage Huile/toile
  (63x41cm 24x16in) Paris 2001

GUÉRARD von Eugen Johann Joseph 1811-1901
[39]
- **$120 802** - €117 535 - **£74 347** - FF770 982
  Southern Italian Coastal Scene Oil/canvas
  (71x104cm 27x40in) Melbourne 1999
- **$55 037** - €51 890 - **£34 110** - FF340 374
  Creek at the Foot of Mount Kosciusko Oil/board
  (42x32cm 16x12in) Melbourne 1999
- **$247** - €289 - **£172** - FF1 893
  **Moroka River Falls, Foot of Mount Kent
  Gippsland** Color lithograph (32x52.5cm 12x20in)
  Melbourne 1999

GUERBE Raymond XX **[4]**
- **$14 598** - €14 073 - **£9 000** - FF92 313
  Diana hunting Deer Oil/canvas (94.5x158cm
  37x62in) London 1999
- **$1 100** - €1 077 - **£708** - FF7 067
  Lamp, Woman in the Egyptian Taste Bronze
  (50x34x10cm 20x13x4in) Naples FL 1999

GUERIE Félix Paul 1819-1895 **[5]**
- **$3 892** - €3 811 - **£2 395** - FF25 000
  La marchande de buis Huile/toile (60x47cm
  23x18in) Paris 1999

GUÉRIN Armand Manago 1913-1983 **[106]**
- **$593** - €499 - **£349** - FF3 270
  Der Place du Tertre in Paris Oil/panel (60x73cm
  23x28in) Bern 1998

GUÉRIN Charles François 1875-1939 **[78]**
- **$1 443** - €1 220 - **£858** - FF8 000
  Femme au turban vert Huile/toile (65x54cm
  25x21in) Mâcon 1998
- **$634** - €610 - **£391** - FF4 000
  David jouant à la harpe devant Saül Huile/toile
  (32x21cm 12x8in) Troyes 1999

GUÉRIN Ernest 1887-1952 **[224]**
- **$13 080** - €15 245 - **£9 170** - FF100 000
  Le grand pardon de Sainte-Anne de la Palude
  Huile/toile (65x92cm 25x36in) Paris 2000
- **$1 704** - €1 829 - **£1 140** - FF12 000
  Automne en Bretagne Aquarelle, gouache/papier
  (26x33cm 10x12in) Soissons 2000

GUERIN François c.1740-c.1795 **[8]**
- **$9 720** - €11 586 - **£6 931** - FF76 000
  Danaë Huile/toile (67x147cm 26x57in) Riom 2000

GUÉRIN Gabriel 1869-1916 **[7]**
- **$2 830** - €3 284 - **£1 954** - FF21 539
  La grand mère Öl/Leinwand (81x45cm 31x17in)
  Luzern 2000

GUÉRIN Jean Urbain 1761-1836 **[24]**
- **$839** - €906 - **£580** - FF5 944
  Portrait of a young Lady wearing a wihte Dress
  Miniature (6x5cm 2x2in) Little-Lane, Ilkley 2001

GUERIN Jules 1866-1946 **[19]**
- **$4 750** - €5 320 - **£3 300** - FF34 899
  Shepherd with Flock of Sheep Oil/board (75x49cm
  29x19in) New-York 2001
- **$2 100** - €2 470 - **£1 505** - FF16 199
  Independence Hall Gouache (76x50cm 29x19in)
  Philadelphia PA 2001

GUERIN LE GUAY André 1872-c.1945 **[29]**
- **$765** - €869 - **£531** - FF5 700
  Santa Maria delle Salute Huile/toile (45x80.5cm
  17x31in) Le Raincy 2001

GUÉRIN Paulin Jean-Bapt. 1783-1855 **[5]**
- **$3 679** - €4 269 - **£2 618** - FF28 000
  Sainte Famille Huile/toile (188x156cm 74x61in) Paris
  2001

GUÉRIN Pierre Narcisse 1774-1833 **[19]**
- **$12 352** - €11 749 - **£7 500** - FF77 067
  Sapho Oil/canvas (82x70cm 32x27in) London 1999
- **$8 000** - €8 880 - **£5 576** - FF58 252
  Hector leaving Andromeda Ink (35.5x28.5cm
  13x11in) New-York 2001
- **$156** - €168 - **£104** - FF1 100
  Le vigilant/Le paresseux Lithographie (27x19.5cm
  10x7in) Paris 2000

GUERMACHEV Mikhail M., Michel 1868-1930 **[29]**
- **$828** - €930 - **£580** - FF6 099
  Tree-lined Country Lane in Evening Light
  Oil/canvas (46x55.5cm 18x21in) London 2001
- **$1 351** - €1 308 - **£833** - FF8 580
  Der Ostertisch Öl/Karton (20x24cm 7x9in) Wien
  1999

GUERRA Achille 1832-1903 **[11]**
- **$16 119** - €18 558 - **£11 000** - FF121 735
  Raphael before Pope Julius II Oil/canvas
  (99.5x138cm 39x54in) London 2000
- **$7 500** - €7 172 - **£4 567** - FF47 042
  The Arrival of his Emminence Oil/canvas
  (48.5x95cm 19x37in) Boston MA 1999

GUERRA Giovanni 1544-1618 **[12]**
- **$400** - €428 - **£272** - FF2 806
  Old testament Scene Ink (19.5x21cm 7x8in) New-
  York 2001

GUERRA Giuseppe act.1740-1761 **[1]**
- **$85 000** - €91 956 - **£58 233** - FF603 194
  **Capriccio of a Mediterranean Port with a
  Volcano Erupting** Oil/canvas (63.5x100.5cm
  25x39in) New-York 2001

GUERRA Isabel 1947 **[5]**
- **$6 160** - €6 607 - **£4 180** - FF43 340
  Bodegón Oleo/lienzo (50x75cm 19x29in) Madrid
  2001

GUERRA Noémia 1920 **[5]**
- **$5 500** - €6 391 - **£3 865** - FF41 919
  Roses de juin Oil/canvas (73x50cm 28x19in) New-
  York 2001

G

G

GUERRA Vincent XX [15]

🎨 **$642** - €732 - **£441** - FF4 800
«Air France, West Africa, Equatorial Africa»
Affiche (100x62cm 39x24in) Paris 2000

GUERRA ZAMORA Evaristo 1942 [41]

🖼 **$3 410** - €3 304 - **£2 090** - FF21 670
Montes de Velez, malaga Oleo/lienzo (97x146cm 38x57in) Barcelona 1999

🖼 **$2 025** - €2 252 - **£1 350** - FF14 775
La cosecha Oleo/lienzo (65x81cm 25x31in) Madrid 2000

🖼 **$1 775** - €1 502 - **£1 050** - FF9 850
«Calle de los Arcos» Oleo/lienzo (41x33cm 16x12in) Madrid 1998

GUERRERO GALVAN Jesús 1910-1973 [62]

🖼 **$45 000** - €52 283 - **£31 626** - FF342 954
El nacimiento de Quetzacoatl Oil/canvas (125.5x100.5cm 49x39in) New-York 2001

🖼 **$17 000** - €19 725 - **£11 736** - FF129 387
Niñas con aves Oil/canvas (70x90cm 27x35in) New-York 2000

GUERRERO José 1787-1803 [1]

🖼 **$2 100** - €2 102 - **£1 295** - FF13 790
Sta. Agueda Oleo/cobre (46x34cm 18x13in) Madrid 2000

GUERRERO José 1914-1991 [84]

🖼 **$20 300** - €21 023 - **£12 950** - FF137 900
Negro con bandas rojas Oleo/lienzo (130x97cm 51x38in) Madrid 2000

🖼 **$9 750** - €9 010 - **£5 850** - FF59 100
Comienzo Oleo/lienzo (65x100cm 25x39in) Barcelona 1999

🖼 **$4 845** - €5 706 - **£3 515** - FF37 430
Composición Gouache (61x47cm 24x18in) Madrid 2001

🎨 **$306** - €360 - **£222** - FF2 364
Composición azul, roja y negra Litografía (75x56cm 29x22in) Madrid 2001

GUERRERO MALAGON Mariano Cecilio 1909-1996 [20]

🖼 **$3 200** - €3 003 - **£2 000** - FF19 700
Noviembre Oleo/tablex (85.5x137.5cm 33x54in) Madrid 1999

🖼 **$871** - €781 - **£533** - FF5 122
Rincón de Cuenca Oleo/lienzo (24x15cm 9x5in) Madrid 1999

GUERRESCHI Giuseppe 1929-1985 [38]

🖼 **$1 246** - €1 337 - **£850** - FF8 771
Mother and Child Oil/canvas (98.5x78.5cm 38x30in) London 2001

GUERRICCHIO Luigi 1932 [23]

🖼 **$750** - €777 - **£450** - FF5 100
Panni stesi Olio/tela (70x60cm 27x23in) Roma 2000

GUERRIER Madeleine 1885-1959 [84]

🎨 **$178** - €183 - **£111** - FF1 200
Les Quais animés, vue de l'ancien Trocadero Aquarelle/papier (13x19cm 5x7in) Deauville 2000

GUERRIER Raymond 1920 [125]

🖼 **$933** - €915 - **£601** - FF6 000
Le fruit vert Huile/toile (100x100cm 39x39in) Versailles 1999

GUERRIERI Giovanni Francesco 1589-1665 [3]

🖼 **$31 200** - €26 953 - **£20 800** - FF176 800
Apollo e Pan Olio/tela (132x94cm 51x37in) Roma 1998

GUERRINI Giovanni 1887-1972 [4]

✏ **$2 400** - €2 073 - **£1 200** - FF13 600
Frati distratti Acquarello/carta (20x26cm 7x10in) Genova 1999

GUERRY Louis XIX-XX [4]

🎨 **$1 088** - €991 - **£668** - FF6 500
«Annecy Thônes» Affiche (105.5x75cm 41x29in) Saint-Cloud 1999

GUERSANT Pierre Sébastien 1789-1853 [1]

🏺 **$158 300** - €152 449 - **£98 300** - FF1 000 000
Statue représentant Henri de Bourbon (1820-1883) Duc de Bordeaux Porcelain (H121cm H47in) Paris 1999

GUÉRY Armand 1850-1912 [135]

🖼 **$13 000** - €15 279 - **£9 012** - FF100 222
Soir d'automne (Champagne) - Lever de lune sur la Suippe Oil/canvas (164x243cm 64x95in) New-York 2000

🖼 **$6 004** - €5 564 - **£3 733** - FF36 500
Berger et ses moutons dans un paysage Huile/toile (80x126cm 31x49in) Saint-Germain-en-Laye 1999

🖼 **$2 300** - €2 212 - **£1 419** - FF14 508
Coastal Views Oil/panel (14x23.5cm 5x9in) Boston MA 1999

GUÉRY-COLAS Fernand XX [2]

🖼 **$1 350** - €1 434 - **£890** - FF9 409
Still Life with Pears Oil/masonite (23x33cm 9x13in) Cleveland OH 2000

GUES Alfred François 1833-? [14]

🖼 **$1 467** - €1 724 - **£1 017** - FF11 311
Halberdier Oil/panel (29.5x20cm 11x7in) Amsterdam 2000

GUESDON Alfred 1808-1876 [10]

🎨 **$179** - €192 - **£121** - FF1 260
Vista de Sevilla Litografía (39x55cm 15x21in) Madrid 2000

GUESNET Louis Félix 1843-? [1]

🖼 **$13 521** - €12 256 - **£8 200** - FF80 392
The Farmyard Oil/canvas (82x110cm 32x43in) Billingshurst, West-Sussex 1998

GUET Charlemagne Oscar 1801-1871 [12]

🖼 **$8 506** - €7 775 - **£5 207** - FF51 000
Femme au châle Huile/toile (66x54cm 25x21in) Paris 1999

GUÉTAL Laurent, abbé 1841-1892 [43]

🖼 **$1 538** - €1 829 - **£1 096** - FF12 000
Pré en fleurs et vue sur le Néron Huile/toile (52.5x92.5cm 20x36in) Grenoble 2000

🖼 **$843** - €991 - **£584** - FF6 500
Coucher de soleil sur le Casque du Néron Huile/panneau (28x47cm 11x18in) Grenoble 2000

GUEVARA Alvaro 1894-1951 [8]

🖼 **$9 879** - €9 284 - **£6 060** - FF60 897
Figures in the four Eiffel Restaurant Oil/board (43x51cm 16x20in) London 1999

✏ **$4 610** - €4 332 - **£2 800** - FF28 418
The Graduation Red chalk (52x77cm 20x30in) London 1999

GUEVARA MORENO Luis 1926 [55]

🖼 **$540** - €554 - **£360** - FF3 636
Rostro Oleo/lienzo (44x32cm 17x12in) Caracas 2000

✏ **$432** - €497 - **£294** - FF3 262
Figuras Técnica mixta/papel (32x46cm 12x18in) Caracas ($) 2000

GUEYLON G. XIX **[4]**
$1 826 - €1 534 - £1 073 - FF10 060
Mozart, die Violine spielend Bronze (H66cm H25in) Köln 1998

GUFFENS Godfried Egide 1823-1901 **[6]**
$4 576 - €5 453 - £3 278 - FF35 772
Dromend meisje Oil/canvas (110x86.5cm 43x34in) Lokeren 2000

GUGEL Karl Adolf 1820-1885 **[22]**
$2 247 - €2 045 - £1 404 - FF13 415
Bildnis des Generals von Krazeisen Öl/Leinwand (71x57.5cm 27x22in) München 1998

GUGGENBERGER Theodor Otto Michael 1866-1929 **[20]**
$470 - €562 - £323 - FF3 689
Blick auf ein Dorf in den Bergen Öl/Leinwand (61x90cm 24x35in) München 2000

GUGGENBICHLER Johann Meinrad 1649-1723 **[5]**
$44 800 - €50 871 - £30 660 - FF333 690
Sitzende Engel mit Flügeln Sculpture (H55cm H21in) Wien 2001

GUGLIELMI Gennaro 1804-? **[14]**
$13 636 - €13 741 - £8 500 - FF90 135
Impersonating The Teacher Oil/canvas (48.5x37cm 19x14in) London 2000
$3 750 - €3 887 - £2 250 - FF25 500
Uova fresche! Olio/tela (42x33.5cm 16x13in) Roma 2000

GUGLIELMI Gregorio 1714-1773 **[3]**
$7 500 - €8 034 - £5 121 - FF52 699
King Solomon Receiving the Queen of Sheba Gouache (43x59cm 16x23in) New-York 2001

GUGLIELMI O. Louis 1906-1956 **[20]**
$65 000 - €71 136 - £44 837 - FF466 622
Women of Peterboro Oil/canvas (61x76cm 24x29in) New-York 2001

GUHR Richard 1873-? **[1]**
$4 153 - €3 554 - £2 500 - FF23 312
The Triumphant Return Tempera (43x26cm 16x10in) London 1998

GUHRS Vic 1943 **[12]**
$1 623 - €1 560 - £1 000 - FF10 233
Luangwa Morning - Buffalo Oil/canvas (70x95.5cm 27x37in) London 1999

GUI FU 1736-1805 **[1]**
$2 564 - €3 014 - £1 778 - FF19 768
Calligraphy in Clerical Script (Lishu) Ink/paper (145x79cm 57x31in) New-York 1998

GUIARD Y LARRAURI Adolfo 1860-1916 **[4]**
$5 572 - €5 336 - £3 507 - FF35 000
Le déjeuner au bord de la mer Huile/toile (61x46cm 24x18in) Nice 1999

GUIAUD Jacques 1811-1876 **[12]**
$3 260 - €3 311 - £2 327 - FF25 000
La sortie de la messe en Bretagne Huile/toile (63x42cm 24x16in) Angers 2001
$802 - €685 - £480 - FF4 494
Figures beside the water's edge with a Continental City beyond Watercolour (12.5x22.5cm 4x8in) London 1998

GUIBERT Maurice XIX **[9]**
$4 505 - €5 183 - £3 104 - FF34 000
Toulouse-Lautrec avec Tremolada, devant l'affiche de Chéret Tirage argentique (12x17cm 4x6in) Chartres 2000

GUICHARD Joseph Benoit 1806-1880 **[9]**
$782 - €915 - £549 - FF5 000
Vénus endormie et Cupidon Huile/panneau (31x41cm 12x16in) Paris 2000

GUIDALEVITCH Victor 1892-1962 **[25]**
$1 200 - €1 338 - £841 - FF8 774
Workers Silver print (22x16cm 9x6in) New-York 2001

GUIDI Giuseppe 1881-1931 **[13]**
$5 500 - €6 411 - £3 808 - FF42 055
Harem Woman reclining on a Couch Oil/canvas (34x48cm 13x19in) Delaware OH 2000
$1 408 - €1 654 - £1 000 - FF10 851
Interior Scene, two Figures at a Table in Richly decorated surroundin Watercolour/paper (51x35cm 20x14in) Leominster, Herefordshire 2000

GUIDI Guido XIX **[2]**
$7 299 - €7 010 - £4 500 - FF45 984
J.O.R.Fairlie of Myres, dressed as a mid-Fifteenth Century Troubadour Oil/board (75x36cm 29x14in) London 1999

GUIDI Guido 1901 **[16]**
$250 - €259 - £150 - FF1 700
Ponte e barche Olio/tavola (40x50cm 15x19in) Prato 2000

GUIDI Virgilio 1891-1984 **[437]**
$7 600 - €9 848 - £5 700 - FF64 600
Figure nello spazio Olio/tela (101x127cm 39x50in) Prato 2000
$5 100 - €4 406 - £2 550 - FF28 900
Marine di San Giorgio Olio/tela (50x60cm 19x23in) Prato 1999
$1 750 - €1 814 - £1 050 - FF11 900
Volto Olio/tela (40x30cm 15x11in) Milano 2001
$500 - €518 - £300 - FF3 400
Volto Biro (47x39cm 18x15in) Milano 2000

GUIDOBONO Bartolomeo 1654-1709 **[9]**
$230 000 - €216 389 - £143 520 - FF1 419 422
Cupid and Psyche Oil/canvas (156x120cm 61x47in) New-York 1999
$4 740 - €4 573 - £2 997 - FF30 000
La Vierge en prière Huile/toile (58.5x44.5cm 23x17in) Paris 1999

GUIDOTTI Antonio 1881-1958 **[2]**
$2 500 - €2 592 - £1 500 - FF17 000
Il Canal Grande, Venezia Acquarello/cartone (29.5x49cm 11x19in) Vercelli 2000

GUIDOTTI Salvatore 1836-? **[3]**
$2 273 - €2 556 - £1 587 - FF16 769
Fisher in der Bucht von Neapel mit dem Vesuv in Hintergrund Öl/Leinwand (40x25.5cm 15x10in) Lindau 2001

GUIETTE René 1893-1976 **[296]**
$1 032 - €1 190 - £710 - FF7 804
Compositie Oil/paper/canvas (73.5x45.8cm 28x18in) Lokeren 2000
$600 - €495 - £352 - FF3 248
Personnage Huile/papier (22x15cm 8x5in) Antwerpen 1998
$777 - €868 - £539 - FF5 691
Composition abstraite, noir-blanc Lavis/papier (62x92cm 24x36in) Antwerpen 2001

GUIGNARD Alberto da Veiga 1896-1962 **[3]**
$690 000 - €664 652 - £428 421 - FF4 359 834
Vaso de flores Oil/canvas (89.5x69.5cm 35x27in) New-York 1999

GUIGNARD Alexandre-Gaston 1848-1922 **[36]**
$1 500 - €1 713 - £1 057 - FF11 234
The Day's End - A Sheep Herder Oil/canvas (54.5x81.5cm 21x32in) Boston MA 2001

GUIGNERY Louis Jules 1818-? **[1]**
$4 300 - €5 081 - £3 047 - FF33 328
Foxhunt at Murs, France, a Great Stand of Trees, Bonfire Oil/canvas (64x92cm 25x36in) New-Orleans LA 2000

GUIGON Charles Louis 1807-1882 **[32]**
$935 - €807 - £561 - FF5 291
Waldlichtung am Vierwaldstättersee Öl/Karton (39x47cm 15x18in) Bern 1998

GUIGOU Paul Camille 1834-1871 **[112]**
$36 900 - €34 301 - £22 410 - FF225 000
Chasse dans la plaine de Crau Huile/toile (44x80cm 17x31in) Uzès 1998
$11 866 - €11 448 - £7 500 - FF75 093
River Landscape with Hillside Village Oil/panel (28x46cm 11x18in) London 1999

GUIGUET François Joseph 1860-1937 **[152]**
$4 137 - €4 878 - £2 908 - FF32 000
Portrait de Madame Marie-Louise Perrier Huile/toile (77.5x59cm 30x23in) Lyon 2000
$1 390 - €1 601 - £949 - FF10 500
Fillette Huile/toile/carton (15x19cm 5x7in) Lyon 2000
$351 - €351 - £219 - FF2 300
La lecture Dessin (20x19.5cm 8x7in) Lyon 1999

GUIJARRO Antonio 1923 **[24]**
$1 120 - €1 201 - £740 - FF7 880
El cabracho arlequín Oleo/lienzo (38x46cm 14x18in) Madrid 2000

GUILBERT D'ANELLE Charles Michel 1820-1889 **[2]**
$257 - €248 - £158 - FF1 625
Bildnisse eines jungen Paars in Festtagskleidung Öl/Karton (22.5x17.5cm 8x6in) Bern 1998

GUILBERT Maurice 1876-1938 **[31]**
$711 - €694 - £436 - FF4 552
Après-midi d'été au jardin Huile/panneau (69x101cm 27x39in) Bruxelles 1999

GUILBERT Narcisse 1878-1942 **[143]**
$4 817 - €4 497 - £2 917 - FF29 500
Vallée de la Seine Huile/toile (46x65cm 18x25in) Évreux 1999

GUILBERT Robert 1920-1992 **[241]**
$331 - €305 - £198 - FF2 000
Pommiers en fleurs Huile/toile (50x65cm 19x25in) Le Havre 1999
$276 - €229 - £162 - FF1 500
Nature morte aux poires Huile/toile (33x46cm 12x18in) Le Havre 1998
$265 - €244 - £159 - FF1 600
Péniches à quai Gouache/papier (50x65cm 19x25in) Le Havre 1999

GUILEV Iouri 1951 **[9]**
$6 048 - €5 599 - £3 702 - FF36 729
Klavierkonzert in eleganter Abendgeselschaft Öl/Leinwand (67x100cm 26x39in) Bern 1999

GUILLAIN Marthe 1890-1974 **[40]**
$844 - €793 - £521 - FF5 203
Péniche à quai Huile/toile (54x65cm 21x25in) Bruxelles 1999

GUILLARD Alfred 1810-1880 **[2]**
$14 904 - €17 532 - £10 683 - FF115 000
Jeune grecque secourant un blessé Huile/toile (76x81.5cm 25x32in) Paris 2001

GUILLAUD Charles XX **[24]**
$989 - €1 067 - £663 - FF7 000
Bergère à Volterra Huile/toile (73x92cm 28x36in) Grenoble 2000
$707 - €762 - £474 - FF5 000
La chaude journée Huile/toile (33x41cm 12x16in) Grenoble 2000

GUILLAUME Albert 1873-1942 **[186]**
$8 500 - €7 333 - £5 128 - FF48 104
A Private Box at the Opera Oil/panel (81.5x65cm 32x25in) New-York 1998
$4 970 - €5 336 - £3 325 - FF35 000
Le coucher Huile/panneau (41x33cm 16x12in) Paris 2000
$151 - €152 - £94 - FF1 000
Gros Chagrin Encre/papier (31.5x24cm 12x9in) Paris 2000
$686 - €686 - £429 - FF4 500
«Transformation du Gil Blas» Affiche (195x123cm 76x48in) Orléans 1999

GUILLAUME Eugène 1822-1905 **[4]**
$13 176 - €12 196 - £8 160 - FF80 000
Jeune femme ailée coiffée d'un chignon, symbolisant Psyché Marbre (68x50cm 26x19in) Paris 1999

GUILLAUME Louis 1865-1942 **[3]**
$514 - €499 - £318 - FF3 271
Paysage du Jura Huile/toile (86x116cm 33x45in) Genève 1999

GUILLAUME Paul XX **[6]**
$598 - €686 - £409 - FF4 500
Par fil spécial Encre/papier (31x47.5cm 12x18in) Paris 2000

GUILLAUME R. M. 1876-? **[10]**
$4 515 - €5 335 - £3 200 - FF34 997
Tiens chouchou! Oil/canvas (90x70cm 35x27in) London 2000

GUILLAUMET Gustave 1840-1887 **[120]**
$3 533 - €3 406 - £2 178 - FF22 345
Rastende Beduinenfamilie unter einem Baum Öl/Leinwand (65x54cm 25x21in) Bern 1999
$2 107 - €1 943 - £1 262 - FF12 743
Steilküste und schmaler Strand mit einer Frau und ihrem Kind vorn Öl/Karton (24.5x32.5cm 9x12in) Dresden 1999
$965 - €1 037 - £646 - FF6 800
Jeune femme berbère, cardant la laine Pierre noire (41x29.5cm 16x11in) Paris 2000

GUILLAUMIN Armand 1841-1927 **[733]**
$17 688 - €18 859 - £12 000 - FF123 708
Paysage de la Creuse, la Creuse à Genetin Oil/canvas (254.5x66cm 100x25in) London 2001
$40 000 - €38 416 - £24 660 - FF251 992
Le quai de la Rapée Oil/canvas (40.5x54.5cm 15x21in) New-York 1999
$10 159 - €9 715 - £6 186 - FF63 724
Herbstliche Landstrasse mit Haus Öl/Leinwand (32x42cm 12x16in) Staufen 1999
$8 606 - €9 554 - £6 000 - FF62 669
Vue de Mont St Sauveur Pastel/paper (44.5x58.5cm 17x23in) London 2001
$534 - €573 - £357 - FF3 759
Petit enfant au lit Farblithographie (42.5x42cm 16x16in) Bern 2000

GUILLEMARD Sophie 1780-? **[1]**
$10 094 - €10 174 - **£6 300** - FF66 738
Joseph und die Frau des Potiphar Öl/Leinwand (100x80.5cm 39x31in) Wien 2000

GUILLEMER Ernest 1839-1913 **[26]**
$3 056 - €3 049 - **£1 908** - FF20 000
Bouvier et ses vaches Huile/toile (50x65.5cm 19x25in) Fontainebleau 1999
$2 074 - €1 789 - **£1 234** - FF11 737
Verschilfter Teich Oil/panel (21x35cm 8x13in) München 1998

GUILLEMET Antoine J.-Bapt. 1843-1918 **[172]**
$4 992 - €5 031 - **£3 111** - FF33 000
Chaumières Huile/toile (38x47cm 14x18in) Calais 2000
$2 870 - €3 278 - **£2 018** - FF21 500
Sur le chemin du village en Bretagne Huile/panneau (13.5x23.5cm 5x9in) Fontainebleau 2001

GUILLEMIN Alexandre 1817-1880 **[22]**
$2 596 - €2 949 - **£1 821** - FF19 347
The Miller and his Son on their Way to the Market Oil/canvas (57x76.5cm 22x30in) Amsterdam 2001
$3 899 - €4 346 - **£2 725** - FF28 508
Bewunderung für das Marienbild Oil/panel (35x29cm 13x11in) München 2001

GUILLEMIN Émile Coriolan H. 1841-1907 **[98]**
$12 705 - €10 671 - **£7 469** - FF70 000
«Femme arabe» Bronze (H130cm H51in) Marseille 1998
$1 190 - €1 329 - **£806** - FF8 720
Nordafrikanischer Jäger mit Gewehr und Jagdfalken auf Araberhengt Bronze (H69.5cm H27in) Nürnberg 2000

GUILLEMINET Claude 1821-1860 **[103]**
$1 746 - €1.829 - **£1 105** - FF12 000
Basse-cour Huile/panneau (55x45.5cm 21x17in) Paris 2000
$1 998 - €1 753 - **£1 213** - FF11 500
Basse cour Huile/panneau (40x32cm 15x12in) Paris 1999

GUILLERMOT C.T. XIX **[7]**
$45 000 - €38 824 - **£27 148** - FF254 668
Le Pont Neuf à la Belle Époque Oil/canvas (89x116cm 35x45in) New-York 1998

GUILLERY Theodor 1900-1976 **[28]**
$356 - €383 - **£245** - FF2 515
Waldlandschaft mit Bachlauf Öl/Leinwand (57x75.5cm 22x29in) München 2001

GUILLOBEL Joaquim Cândido 1787-1859 **[2]**
$2 855 - €2 998 - **£1 800** - FF19 664
Figures hauling a Cask, Rio de Janeiro/Two Figures carrying Provisions Watercolour/paper (20x25cm 7x9in) London 2000

GUILLOD Thomas Walker XIX **[5]**
$671 - €720 - **£449** - FF4 724
Leading the Flock to Pasture Oil/canvas (35.5x47cm 13x18in) Vancouver, BC. 2000

GUILLON Adolphe 1829-1896 **[6]**
$23 166 - €27 227 - **£16 062** - FF178 596
Cannes in January Oil/canvas (96x139cm 37x54in) Amsterdam 2000

GUILLONNET Octave 1872-1967 **[295]**
$1 331 - €1 220 - **£812** - FF8 000
Jeunes archers Huile/toile (55x65cm 21x25in) Lyon 1999

$335 - €290 - **£202** - FF1 900
La bénédiction Huile/panneau (35x27cm 13x10in) Paris 1998

GUILLOT Anatole 1865-1911 **[6]**
$1 342 - €1 342 - **£839** - FF8 800
Jeune fille à la cruche Bronze (H46cm H18in) Paris 1999

GUILLOT Gabriel Paul 1850-1914 **[2]**
$4 319 - €3 696 - **£2 600** - FF24 245
An Arab Prince Oil/canvas (56.5x46.5cm 22x18in) London 1998

GUILLOU Alfred 1844-1926 **[65]**
$3 177 - €3 430 - **£2 196** - FF22 500
L'arrière-port de Concarneau Huile/toile (32x56cm 12x22in) Quimper 2001
$3 372 - €3 354 - **£2 092** - FF22 000
Sur le quai Huile/toile (24.5x35cm 9x13in) Neuilly-sur-Seine 1999

GUILLOU Sophie XVIII **[3]**
$1 237 - €1 296 - **£820** - FF8 500
Le Bon Père/La Bonne Mère Aquarelle/papier (42x41cm 16x16in) Toulouse 2000

GUILLOUX Charles Victor 1866-1946 **[75]**
$2 618 - €2 866 - **£1 818** - FF18 800
Les bouquinistes sur les quais de la Seine à Paris Huile/toile (33x55cm 12x21in) Brest 2001
$1 900 - €1 810 - **£1 204** - FF11 876
View of Paris at Evening, from the River Oil/board (32x27.5cm 7x9in) Cleveland OH 1999

GUIMARAES de José 1939 **[29]**
$1 176 - €992 - **£700** - FF6 508
Ballerine Gouache/papier (37x30cm 14x11in) Antwerpen 1998

GUIMARD Hector 1867-1934 **[9]**
$9 591 - €10 519 - **£6 368** - FF69 000
Élément de décoration, feuillages et graines en bouquet jaillissant Fer (97x52cm 38x20in) Paris 2000
$6 321 - €6 597 - **£4 000** - FF43 276
Bench Elements Iron (H73cm H28in) London 2000

GUINAND Emma 1857-1920 **[2]**
$1 003 - €1 180 - **£727** - FF7 742
«Grand Hôtel du Cervin, St Luc, Val d'Anniviers» Affiche couleur (83x59cm 32x23in) Sion 2001

GUINAND René 1892-1983 **[37]**
$735 - €854 - **£508** - FF5 600
Les Quais Huile/toile (38x55cm 14x21in) Genève 2000
$353 - €341 - **£217** - FF2 234
Liegender weiblicher Akt Öl/Karton (14.5x29cm 5x11in) Bern 1999

GUINART Francesc 1888-1974 **[12]**
$980 - €1 051 - **£665** - FF6 895
Playa de Lloret Oleo/lienzo (54x65cm 21x25in) Barcelona 2001

GUINDON Jean 1883-1976 **[27]**
$1 474 - €1 677 - **£1 023** - FF11 000
Scène de marché Huile/toile (54x73cm 21x28in) Marseille 2000
$1 228 - €1 448 - **£863** - FF9 500
Marché provençal Gouache/papier (46x94cm 18x37in) Cabestany 2000

GUINDRAND Antoine 1801-1843 **[13]**

- $456 - €521 - £322 - FF3 420
  Holländische Uferlandschaft mit Hütte bei Sonnenuntergang Öl/Leinwand (61.5x93cm 24x36in) Bern 2001
- $645 - €744 - £444 - FF4 878
  Riviergezicht Oil/panel (20x18cm 7x7in) Lokeren 2000

GUINEA Y UGALDE Anselmo 1855-c.1906 **[11]**

- $3 355 - €3 304 - £2 090 - FF21 670
  Caserío Acuarela/papel (50x66cm 19x25in) Madrid 1999

GUINEGAULT Georges Pierre 1893-? **[43]**

- $379 - €427 - £261 - FF2 800
  Marchands place Djema-el-Fna à Marrakech Gouache/papier (49x33cm 19x12in) Corbeil-Essonnes 2000

GUINIER Henri 1867-1927 **[45]**

- $2 673 - €3 125 - £1 877 - FF20 500
  File de Plougastel Huile/toile (69.5x56.5cm 27x22in) Paris 2000
- $770 - €762 - £480 - FF5 000
  Bigoudène buvant dans un bol Pastel/papier (48x32cm 18x12in) Paris 1999

GUINNESS GUEVARA Meraud 1904-1993 **[2]**

- $4 280 - €4 023 - £2 600 - FF26 389
  Portrait of a seated Woman Oil/paper (44.5x36.5cm 17x14in) London 1999

GUINNESS May 1863-1955 **[28]**

- $4 515 - €4 954 - £3 000 - FF32 499
  Still Life with Apples and a White Cloth Oil/canvas (46x61.5cm 18x24in) London 2000
- $4 438 - €5 079 - £3 052 - FF33 316
  Woman at a Window Oil/panel (30x25cm 12x10in) Dublin 2000
- $1 406 - €1 397 - £876 - FF9 161
  Woman in a Teashop Pastel/paper (28x22cm 11x9in) Dublin 1999

GUINO Michel 1926 **[8]**

- $938 - €1 067 - £661 - FF7 000
  Relief Relief (38.5x48.5x7cm 15x19x2in) Paris 2001

GUINO Richard 1890-1973 **[170]**

- $121 940 - €106 714 - £73 850 - FF700 000
  Grande Vénus debout - Vénus Vitrix Bronze (H180cm H70in) Paris 1998
- $5 112 - €5 488 - £3 420 - FF36 000
  Tête de danseuse Bronze (H17cm H6in) Paris 2000
- $272 - €274 - £169 - FF1 800
  Femme assise se coiffant Sanguine/papier (30.5x19cm 12x7in) Paris 2000

GUINOVART Josep 1927 **[262]**

- $4 480 - €4 805 - £2 960 - FF31 520
  Fang Acrílico (208x205cm 81x80in) Barcelona 2000
- $2 200 - €2 403 - £1 400 - FF15 760
  Abstracción Técnica mixta/tabla (56x40cm 22x15in) Madrid 2000
- $1 088 - €1 021 - £680 - FF6 698
  Composición Técnica mixta/cartón (16x18cm 6x7in) Madrid 1999
- $1 122 - €1 021 - £680 - FF6 698
  Composición Gouache (49x64cm 19x25in) Madrid 1999
- $172 - €192 - £115 - FF1 260
  Composición Litografía (32x23cm 12x9in) Madrid 2000

GUINY Jean-Marie 1954 **[56]**

- $276 - €305 - £184 - FF2 000
  Adeona Gravure (40x58cm 15x22in) Dozulé 2000

GUIRAGOSSIAN Paul 1926 **[2]**

- $12 174 - €13 693 - £8 500 - FF89 819
  Le prisme de la mémoire Oil/canvas (72x59cm 28x23in) London 2001

GUIRAMAND Paul 1926 **[149]**

- $942 - €991 - £591 - FF6 500
  Nature morte aux poissons et au crabe Huile/toile (65x80cm 25x31in) Paris 2000
- $4 631 - €4 497 - £2 861 - FF29 500
  Cavalier et cheval Bronze (29x30.5x25.5cm 11x12x10in) Paris 1999
- $600 - €534 - £367 - FF3 500
  Deux cavaliers sous un arbre Aquarelle/papier (56x76cm 22x29in) Paris 1999
- $80 - €92 - £54 - FF602
  Abstract Composition Color lithograph (89x63cm 35x25in) Cleveland OH 2000

GUIRAND DE SCÉVOLA Lucien Victor 1871-1950 **[145]**

- $6 993 - €8 232 - £4 914 - FF54 000
  Promenade en barque Huile/toile (175x126cm 68x49in) Toulouse 2000
- $1 688 - €1 943 - £1 163 - FF12 744
  Rosen mit Mohn Öl/Leinwand (46x38.5cm 18x15in) Heidelberg 2000
- $786 - €915 - £552 - FF6 000
  Torero Pastel (72.5x59.5cm 28x23in) Paris 2001

GUIRAUD-RIVIERE Maurice 1881-? **[98]**

- $4 529 - €3 964 - £2 743 - FF26 000
  Le joueur de chistera Huile/toile (81x65cm 31x25in) Paris 1998
- $69 537 - €72 571 - £44 000 - FF476 036
  Figure of a Jester on a Globe, her Arms raised above her Head Bronze (H88cm H34in) London 2000
- $1 379 - €1 296 - £831 - FF8 500
  Le guitariste Bronze (H42cm H16in) Toulouse 1999

GUISE Konstantin 1811-1858 **[9]**

- $3 902 - €4 431 - £2 711 - FF29 065
  Spalenschwibbogen Aquarell/Papier (37x30.5cm 14x12in) Basel 2001

GUITET James 1925 **[104]**

- $1 747 - €1 829 - £1 098 - FF12 000
  60.F.9.72 Huile/toile (97x130cm 38x51in) Versailles 2000
- $1 337 - €1 448 - £915 - FF9 500
  40.P. Huile/toile (100x73cm 39x28in) Paris 2001

GUITRY Sacha 1885-1957 **[49]**

- $624 - €579 - £388 - FF3 800
  Portrait de Marguerite Moreno Encre Chine/papier (15x21cm 5x8in) Paris 1999
- $1 900 - €1 621 - £1 146 - FF10 632
  «K.K.O. - L.S.K.» Poster (119.5x63.5cm 47x25in) New-York 1999

GUITTET Georges Henri 1871-1902 **[6]**

- $7 511 - €8 842 - £5 278 - FF58 000
  Le grand porteur d'eau arabe Bronze (H102cm H40in) Paris 2000

GUIZZARO Innocente XVII **[1]**

- $1 791 - €1 738 - £1 115 - FF11 403
  Augusta Praetoria Aosta (Grosse Gesamtansicht von Aosta) Copper engraving (47.2x117cm 18x46in) Berlin 1999

GULACSY Lajos 1882-1932 **[7]**
- **$4 620** - €5 250 - **£3 220** - FF34 440
  Promeneurs dans un parc Huile/carton (18x28.5cm 7x11in) Budapest 2001
- **$2 100** - €2 323 - **£1 380** - FF15 240
  Court of the Monastery Pastel/paper (19x24cm 7x9in) Budapest 2000

GULBRANSSON Olaf 1873-1958 **[98]**
- **$454** - €431 - **£276** - FF82 625
  Skibsportraet af DFDS ruteskibet «Holar» Oil/canvas (28x40cm 11x15in) København 1999
- **$670** - €665 - **£419** - FF4 360
  Mahlzeit, Anderson, Cafehausszene Indian ink (25x23cm 9x9in) München 1999

GULGEE Ismail 1926 **[5]**
- **$5 379** - €5 774 - **£3 600** - FF37 877
  Allah Oil/canvas (152.5x122cm 60x48in) London 2000

GULIK van Franciscus Lodewijk 1841-1899 **[16]**
- **$12 000** - €11 159 - **£7 407** - FF73 195
  In the Square Oil/canvas (69x87cm 27x34in) Portland ME 1999
- **$1 816** - €1 541 - **£1 095** - FF10 109
  Winters bosgezicht Oil/panel (24.5x32cm 9x12in) Den Haag 1998

GULIUNY E. XIX-XX **[2]**
- **$10 500** - €12 246 - **£7 372** - FF80 329
  Autumnal Village Landscape with Ducks Oil/canvas (58x106cm 23x42in) Portsmouth NH 2000

GULLBY Folke 1912-1982 **[44]**
- **$198** - €180 - **£122** - FF1 179
  Roman Etching (9.6x12.3cm 3x4in) Stockholm 1999

GULLEY Catherine B. XIX-XX **[19]**
- **$632** - €694 - **£420** - FF4 554
  The Choice Watercolour (53.5x35.5cm 21x13in) London 2000

GULLICHSEN Alvar 1961 **[13]**
- **$216** - €202 - **£133** - FF1 323
  Griskontakt Color lithograph (66x44cm 25x17in) Helsinki 1999

GULLY John 1819-1888 **[18]**
- **$5 556** - €6 459 - **£3 900** - FF42 371
  Mountainous Landscape, New Zealand Watercolour (36x64cm 14x25in) Billingshurst, West-Sussex 1999

GULSTON Alan Stepney 1844-1919 **[18]**
- **$602** - €520 - **£360** - FF3 412
  Welsh Giants off the Coast of Pembrokeshire Watercolour/paper (49.5x71cm 19x27in) Llandeilo, Carmarthenshire 1998

GUMANA Birriktji 1898-1982 **[2]**
- **$3 084** - €3 399 - **£2 047** - FF22 293
  Banumbirr Morning Star Ceremony Mixed media (133x71.5cm 52x28in) Woollahra, Sydney 2000

GUMERY Adolphe 1861-1943 **[25]**
- **$2 804** - €3 049 - **£1 848** - FF20 000
  Au cimetière des Princesses, Alger Huile/toile (59x81.5cm 23x32in) Paris 2000

GUMLICH-KEMPF Anna 1860-1940 **[13]**
- **$703** - €673 - **£437** - FF4 417
  Opstilling med clivia, bog og kinesisk por-ceansfigur Oil/canvas (70x57cm 27x22in) København 1999

GUMMESON Per 1858-1928 **[51]**
- **$577** - €556 - **£356** - FF3 645
  Gamlegatan 3-5, Falsterbo Oil/canvas (50x61cm 19x24in) Malmö 1999

GUN Karl Fedorovich 1830-1877 **[2]**
- **$8 829** - €7 279 - **£5 200** - FF47 750
  Bazaar in Central Asia Oil/canvas (40.5x32cm 15x12in) London 1998

GUNARSA Nyoman 1944 **[25]**
- **$4 591** - €5 213 - **£3 142** - FF34 196
  Wayang Figures Oil/canvas (146x195cm 57x76in) Singapore 2000
- **$1 417** - €1 321 - **£856** - FF8 667
  Dogs Oil/canvas (66x66cm 25x25in) Singapore 1999
- **$1 870** - €1 958 - **£1 174** - FF12 841
  Legong Dancer Watercolour/paper (76x56cm 29x22in) Singapore 2000

GUNAWAN Hendra 1918-1983 **[80]**
- **$31 564** - €35 841 - **£21 604** - FF235 103
  Mother Carrying Her Child Oil/canvas (140x100cm 55x39in) Singapore 2000
- **$15 438** - €12 953 - **£9 058** - FF84 968
  Wanita Bawa Ikan: Girl carrying Fish Oil/canvas (155x58cm 61x22in) Singapore 1998

GUNDELACH Matthäus 1566-1653 **[4]**
- **$3 116** - €2 907 - **£1 880** - FF19 068
  Kaiser Matthias und seine Gemahlin Kaiserin Anna Öl/Kupfer (16x12.5cm 6x4in) Wien 1999

GUNDERSEN Gunnar S. 1921-1983 **[54]**
- **$17 918** - €21 316 - **£12 393** - FF139 825
  Komposisjon Oil/canvas (120x130cm 47x51in) Oslo 2000
- **$2 975** - €3 302 - **£2 073** - FF21 662
  Komposisjon 3 Oil/canvas (63x71cm 24x27in) Oslo 2001
- **$453** - €507 - **£314** - FF3 328
  Komposisjon, soft-og hard-edge Serigraph in colors (46x62cm 18x24in) Oslo 2001

GUNDERSEN Helene 1858-1934 **[6]**
- **$3 163** - €3 656 - **£2 215** - FF23 980
  Interiör vinter Oil/canvas (65x70cm 25x27in) Oslo 2001

GUNDLACH F.C. 1926 **[93]**
- **$1 087** - €1 278 - **£779** - FF8 384
  Grit Hübscher mit Pudel, Berlin Gelatin silver print (31x35cm 12x13in) Berlin 2001

GUNER Nizam 1941 **[26]**
- **$1 042** - €1 037 - **£646** - FF6 800
  Repli Bronze (H42cm H16in) Grenoble 1999

GUNN Archibald, Archie 1863-1930 **[8]**
- **$2 873** - €2 767 - **£1 797** - FF18 149
  Stilleben mit Früchten Öl/Leinwand (33x45cm 12x17in) Zürich 1999

GUNN Herbert James 1893-1964 **[65]**
- **$8 821** - €8 726 - **£5 500** - FF57 239
  Duke of York's Column Oil/canvas (61x46cm 24x18in) London 1999
- **$8 115** - €9 065 - **£5 500** - FF59 564
  Cornflowers in a Glass Vase Oil/canvas (45x35cm 17x13in) Edinburgh 2000

GUNSAM Karl Josef 1900-1972 **[31]**
- **$3 665** - €3 634 - **£2 295** - FF23 835
  Kahlenbergerdorf Oil/panel (64.4x76.8cm 25x30in) Wien 1999

G

🖋 **$1 148** - €1 308 - **£793** - FF8 580
Landschaft in Niederösterreich Aquarell/Papier
(42.5x52.5cm 16x20in) Wien 2000

GUNST van Pieter Stevens 1659-1724 **[4]**
🗐 **$596** - €669 - **£415** - FF4 390
**Vertu plaît quoique vaincue, d'après Charles le
Brun** Burin (71x162.5cm 27x63in) Bruxelles 2001

GUNSTON Audley J. XIX-XX **[2]**
🖋 **$1 604** - €1 616 - **£1 000** - FF10 603
Joy Watercolour/paper (36x26cm 14x10in) Oxford
2000

GÜNSUR Nedim 1924 **[4]**
🖋 **$9 000 000** - €10 214 084 - **£6 000 000** -
FF67 000 000
Lachée de balons Huile/toile (90x44cm 35x17in)
Istanbul 2001

GÜNTHER Christian Aug. 1759-1824 **[8]**
🗐 **$169** - €164 - **£106** - FF1 073
Hirschjagd Radierung (45x59cm 17x23in) Berlin 1999

GÜNTHER Erwin Carl Wilhelm 1864-1927 **[47]**
🖋 **$1 522** - €1 687 - **£1 056** - FF11 067
Marine Öl/Leinwand (66x100cm 25x39in) Köln 2001

GÜNTHER Herta 1934 **[30]**
🖋 **$1 099** - €1 329 - **£767** - FF8 720
Frau mit Hut am Strand Pastell/Karton
(39.2x53.6cm 15x21in) Berlin 2000
🗐 **$164** - €184 - **£114** - FF1 207
«Variété» Lithographie (42x30.5cm 16x12in) Berlin
2001

GÜNTHER Ignaz 1725-1775 **[5]**
🗿 **$21 700** - €20 348 - **£13 412** - FF133 476
Engel Sculpture, wood (H87cm H34in) Wien 1999
🗿 **$30 732** - €28 639 - **£18 558** - FF187 857
Putto Sculpture (72x45cm 28x17in) Dresden 1998

GÜNTHER Kurt 1893-1955 **[9]**
🖋 **$826** - €920 - **£540** - FF6 037
Ohne Titel Watercolour (34.2x27.8cm 13x10in)
Dettelbach-Effeldorf 2000

GÜNTHER Matthäus 1705-1788 **[11]**
🖋 **$27 259** - €23 517 - **£16 228** - FF154 261
Die Madonna Immaculata auf der Weltkugel...
Öl/Leinwand (157.5x84.5cm 62x33in) München 1998
🖋 **$7 238** - €7 994 - **£5 016** - FF52 437
Aeneas tritt vor den Thron des Fürsten Evander
Öl/Leinwand (20x27cm 7x10in) Wien 2001
🖋 **$385** - €358 - **£235** - FF2 347
Der Hl. Johann Nepomuk Radierung (14.6x23.4cm
5x9in) München 1999

GÜNTHER-NAUMBURG Otto 1856-1941 **[26]**
🖋 **$239** - €230 - **£147** - FF1 509
**Kircheninterieur des Würzburger Domes mit
Betenden** Aquarell/Papier (60x45cm 23x17in) Berlin
1999

GUO WEI 1960 **[7]**
🖋 **$5 706** - €6 660 - **£3 906** - FF43 686
«Memory of the Fairy Car» Mixed media/canvas
(97x130cm 38x51in) Taipei 2000

GUPTA Ajit XX **[3]**
🖋 **$4 443** - €4 312 - **£2 800** - FF28 287
Musicians Gouache/board (27x16.5cm 10x6in)
London 1999

GUPTA Jagdish 1924 **[2]**
🖋 **$3 885** - €4 170 - **£2 600** - FF27 356
Deepshrinkhala Wash/paper (37.5x26.5cm 14x10in)
London 2000

GUPTA Manindra Bhusan XX **[1]**
🖋 **$1 724** - €2 012 - **£1 200** - FF13 195
Pilgrims in the Himalayas Watercolour (54x36cm
21x14in) London 2000

GUR-ARIE Meir 1891-1951 **[39]**
🖋 **$1 200** - €1 186 - **£734** - FF7 779
Jerusalem Watercolour/paper (24x26.5cm 9x10in) Tel
Aviv 2000

GURANOWSKI Józef 1852-1922 **[15]**
🖼 **$8 908** - €10 398 - **£6 288** - FF68 204
Paysage forestier Huile/toile (160.5x120.5cm
63x47in) Warszawa 2000
🖼 **$2 503** - €2 430 - **£1 559** - FF15 937
A tranquil River Landscape Oil/canvas
(80.3x140.5cm 31x55in) Warszawa 1999

GURDON Nora 1881-1974 **[13]**
🖼 **$460** - €428 - **£284** - FF2 808
Mediterranean Harbour Scene Oil/board (23x18cm
9x7in) Melbourne 1999

GURK Eduard 1801-1841 **[4]**
🖋 **$898** - €872 - **£554** - FF5 720
**Österreichische Kalkbauern/Zeiselwagen/Der
Schiffzug, nach J.Höchles** Etching in colors
(32x44cm 12x17in) Wien 1999

GURLITT Ludwig H. Theodor 1812-1897 **[40]**
🖋 **$56 180** - €51 130 - **£35 100** - FF335 390
**Italienische Küstenlandschaft mit einer Bäuerin
und Kindern** Öl/Leinwand (99x138cm 38x54in)
München 1999
🖼 **$16 995** - €16 873 - **£10 678** - FF110 678
Bucht von Baia bei Neapel Öl/Leinwand
(43x59.5cm 16x23in) München 1999
🖋 **$2 305** - €2 286 - **£1 441** - FF14 992
Huse ved fjorden Oil/canvas (14x23cm 5x9in)
København 1999
🖋 **$422** - €469 - **£294** - FF3 077
Ruinlandskab Pencil/paper (40x57cm 15x22in)
København 2001

GURR Lena 1897-? **[12]**
🗐 **$300** - €347 - **£212** - FF2 276
Central Park, New York Screenprint in colors
(26x38cm 10x14in) New-York 2000

GURSCHNER Gustav 1873-1971 **[37]**
🔨 **$705** - €767 - **£464** - FF5 030
Trinkende Bronze (H26cm H10in) Ahlden 2000

GURSCHNER Herbert 1901-1975 **[51]**
🖋 **$5 279** - €5 663 - **£3 600** - FF37 150
Tirol Oil/canvas (59x64cm 23x25in) London 2001
🖋 **$2 691** - €2 325 - **£1 622** - FF15 254
Gasse in Innsbruck Tempera (45.5x29.5cm 17x11in)
Wien 1999
🖋 **$2 031** - €2 180 - **£1 386** - FF14 301
«Bei Volterra Toscana» Aquarell/Papier (21x25.5cm
8x10in) Wien 2001
🗐 **$511** - €581 - **£359** - FF3 813
Bauerntanz Linocut in colors (15x16cm 5x6in) Wien
2001

GURSKY Andreas 1955 **[75]**
📷 **$19 629** - €21 986 - **£13 639** - FF144 217
Niagara Falls Photograph in colors (75x58cm
29x22in) Köln 2001

GURUWIRRI Mithinari 1929-1976 **[2]**
🖋 **$5 260** - €5 090 - **£3 333** - FF33 386
Thunderman Mixed media (95x45.5cm 37x17in)
Malvern, Victoria 1999

GURVICH José 1927-1974 **[58]**

⟲ **$10 200** - €10 606 - **£6 440** - FF69 573
Composición de Montevideo con el Frigorífico Switt Oleo/cartón (42x50cm 16x19in) Montevideo 2000

⟲ **$2 050** - €2 164 - **£1 354** - FF14 192
Bodegón Oleo/cartón (36x21.5cm 14x8in) Caracas ($) 2000

✐ **$3 000** - €3 485 - **£2 108** - FF22 863
Composición urbana de Madrid Acuarela/papel (15x21cm 5x8in) Buenos-Aires 2001

GUSEV Vladimir 1957 **[107]**

⟲ **$1 816** - €1 696 - **£1 100** - FF11 122
By the Lake Oil/canvas (33x55cm 12x21in) Fernhurst, Haslemere, Surrey 1999

⟲ **$502** - €433 - **£300** - FF2 843
The Pink Ribbon Oil/canvas/board (42x33cm 16x12in) St. Helier, Jersey 1998

GUSSINYÉ GIRONELLA Pere 1898-1980 **[20]**

⟲ **$5 100** - €6 006 - **£3 500** - FF39 400
Paisaje con figuras Oleo/lienzo (54x73cm 21x28in) Barcelona 2000

✐ **$540** - €601 - **£380** - FF3 940
Paisaje de Olot Pastel (34x45cm 13x17in) Barcelona 2001

GUSSONI Vittorio 1893-1968 **[37]**

⟲ **$2 700** - €2 332 - **£1 800** - FF15 300
Madrilena Olio/tavola (60x50cm 23x19in) Milano 1998

⟲ **$1 320** - €1 710 - **£994** - FF11 220
Natura morta con crostacei e frutti di mare Olio/cartone (40x31cm 15x12in) Torino 2000

GUSTAFSON Mats 1951 **[5]**

✐ **$1 364** - €1 584 - **£942** - FF10 388
Basker Akvarell/papper (35x44cm 13x17in) Stockholm 1999

GUSTAND Denis XX **[2]**

⟲ **$4 874** - €5 488 - **£3 423** - FF36 000
«Ouverture» Huile/toile (73x92cm 28x36in) Garches 2001

GUSTAVSON Leland R. 1899-1966 **[6]**

⟲ **$2 600** - €2 912 - **£1 806** - FF19 102
Magazine Cover, Group of People at Church Supper Oil/canvas (86x78cm 34x31in) New-York 2001

GUSTON Philip 1913-1980 **[152]**

⟲ **$300 000** - €334 943 - **£200 520** - FF2 197 080
White Painting II Oil/canvas (127x129cm 50x50in) New-York 2000

⟲ **$70 000** - €79 187 - **£48 972** - FF519 435
«Page» Oil/board (76x101.5cm 29x39in) New-York 2001

⟲ **$38 000** - €31 900 - **£22 287** - FF209 250
«Two Heads» Oil/masonite (30.5x40.5cm 12x15in) Beverly-Hills CA 1998

✐ **$21 000** - €23 481 - **£14 156** - FF154 022
Untitled Ink/paper (48.5x64.5cm 19x25in) New-York 2000

▥ **$1 600** - €1 787 - **£1 024** - FF11 720
Studio Forms Lithograph (81x110.5cm 31x43in) New-York 2000

GUTCH John Wheeley Gough 1802-1862 **[5]**

◉ **$5 469** - €6 126 - **£3 800** - FF40 181
«Great Fire of Sugar House» Salt print (20.5x15cm 8x5in) London 2001

GÜTE F.W. XVIII **[2]**

⟲ **$5 764** - €5 483 - **£3 500** - FF35 964
Meyer Criskis, Half-Length, Wearing a Grey Fur-Lined Jacket Oil/canvas (82x64cm 32x25in) London 1999

GUTEKUNST Frederick 1831-1917 **[7]**

◉ **$6 000** - €5 642 - **£3 715** - FF37 006
Selected Studies from «The Mind Unveiled» Salt print (11x8cm 4x3in) New-York 1999

GUTEKUNST Lewis XIX **[1]**

◉ **$3 250** - €3 392 - **£2 056** - FF22 248
Joseph (Parrish) Jr. at his Lesson/Dillwyn Parrish Salt print (19x14cm 7x5in) New-York 2000

GÜTERSLOH Albert Paris 1887-1973 **[88]**

✐ **$2 971** - €2 545 - **£1 739** - FF16 691
«Im Park» Mischtechnik/Papier (15.7x15.6cm 6x6in) Wien 1998

GUTFREUND Otto 1889-1927 **[71]**

⬳ **$2 256** - €2 120 - **£1 392** - FF13 904
Don Quichotte Bronze (H38cm H14in) Praha 1999

✐ **$346** - €328 - **£216** - FF2 151
Im Kaffeehaus Pencil/paper (17x12cm 6x4in) Praha 2001

GUTHRIE James 1859-1930 **[15]**

⟲ **$2 025** - €2 308 - **£1 400** - FF15 139
Portrait of a Lady, Seated Three-Quarter-Length, Wearing a Bonnet Oil/canvas (127.5x101cm 50x39in) London 2000

GUTIERREZ DE LA VEGA José 1791-1865 **[15]**

⟲ **$12 375** - €13 515 - **£8 550** - FF88 650
Retrato de Señora con niño Oleo/lienzo (90x75cm 35x29in) Madrid 2001

GUTIERREZ HERNANDEZ Ernesto 1873-1934 **[30]**

⟲ **$1 296** - €1 442 - **£888** - FF9 456
Cigarral de Toledo Oleo/lienzo (42x53cm 16x20in) Madrid 2001

⟲ **$2 025** - €2 252 - **£1 425** - FF14 775
Rincón toledano Oleo/tabla (30x20cm 11x7in) Madrid 2001

GUTIERREZ Rafael Joachim XVII-XVIII **[1]**

⟲ **$7 016** - €5 939 - **£4 200** - FF38 960
The Visitation/The Annunciation/The Nativity/The Presentation Oil/copper (45x33cm 17x12in) London 1998

GUTKNECHT Carl 1878-1970 **[2]**

✐ **$1 700** - €1 839 - **£1 164** - FF12 063
Woman at their Bath Watercolour/paper (59x115cm 23x45in) Chicago IL 2001

GUTMAN Nachum 1898-1980 **[185]**

⟲ **$74 000** - €62 877 - **£44 696** - FF412 446
Ships at Port Oil/canvas (76.5x102.5cm 30x40in) Tel Aviv 1999

⟲ **$23 000** - €25 531 - **£16 033** - FF167 474
Neve Tsedek Oil/canvas (24.5x35.5cm 9x13in) Tel Aviv 2000

✐ **$7 000** - €7 679 - **£4 517** - FF50 371
Tiberias Watercolour/paper (36.5x55cm 14x21in) Tel Aviv 2000

GUTMAN Nathan 1914 **[54]**

✐ **$189** - €213 - **£133** - FF1 400
La tailleur Gouache/papier (42x32cm 16x12in) Paris 2001

GUTMANN Bernhard 1869-1936 **[8]**

⟲ **$24 000** - €26 331 - **£15 943** - FF172 723
Elms at Sunrise Oil/canvas (71x71cm 27x27in) New-York 2000

G

GUTMANN John 1905-1998 **[33]**
$3 500 - €3 757 - **£2 377** - FF24 644
Images Gelatin silver print (35.5x28cm 13x11in)
Beverly-Hills CA 2001

GUTTENBERG Carl Gottlieb 1743-1792 **[7]**
$375 - €365 - **£230** - FF2 394
The tea-Tax-Templest/The Anglo-American Revolution Engraving (38x44cm 14x17in) London 1999

GUTTENBRUNN Ludwig c.1770-1813 **[5]**
$3 801 - €3 681 - **£2 388** - FF24 148
Amor flieht die ihn anflehende Psyche Oil/panel (52x35cm 20x13in) Berlin 1999

GUTTER Piet 1944 **[4]**
$1 345 - €1 452 - **£919** - FF9 525
Still Life with Bottles and a Box Oil/board (38.5x28.5cm 15x11in) Amsterdam 2001

GUTTUSO Renato 1912-1986 **[813]**
$20 500 - €21 251 - **£12 300** - FF139 400
Ritratto di Titina Maselli Olio/tela (165x115cm 64x45in) Prato 1999
$27 600 - €23 843 - **£18 400** - FF156 400
Fiori Olio/tela (38x46cm 14x18in) Milano 1998
$11 100 - €9 589 - **£7 400** - FF62 900
Piccolo nudo Olio/tela (30x40cm 11x15in) Roma 1998
$2 250 - €2 332 - **£1 350** - FF15 300
Nudo China/carta (51x36.5cm 20x14in) Prato 1999
$425 - €441 - **£255** - FF2 890
Figure Litografia (46x53cm 18x20in) Torino 2001

GUY James 1909-1963 **[6]**
$7 500 - €8 441 - **£5 166** - FF55 370
Reflections Oil/canvas (51x66cm 20x25in) Washington 2000
$2 000 - €1 731 - **£1 213** - FF11 356
The Old Faro Dealer Gouache/paper (38x27cm 15x11in) Mystic CT 1998

GUY Louis Jean-Bapt. 1824-1888 **[45]**
$1 060 - €1 250 - **£745** - FF8 200
Scène orientale Huile/panneau (20x26.5cm 7x10in) Lyon 2000

GUY Seymour Joseph 1824-1910 **[34]**
$47 500 - €52 605 - **£32 214** - FF345 063
Now I'm Ready for Your Portrait, Portrait of an Artist Oil/canvas (61x50.5cm 24x19in) New-York 2000
$24 347 - €26 851 - **£16 488** - FF176 134
Guilty Oil/canvas (34x26.5cm 13x10in) New-York 2000

GUYBET Viviane 1940 **[8]**
$5 456 - €4 955 - **£3 409** - FF32 500
Baigneuse Bronze (H71cm H27in) Rennes 1999

GUYOMARD Gérard 1936 **[114]**
$2 144 - €2 318 - **£1 488** - FF16 000
La plage Acrylique/toile (65x92cm 25x36in) Douai 2000
$275 - €290 - **£181** - FF1 900
Scène érotique Mine plomb (50x65cm 19x25in) Paris 2000

GUYOT Georges Lucien 1885-1973 **[188]**
$457 - €534 - **£318** - FF3 500
Nature morte à la corneille Huile/isorel (72x53.5cm 28x21in) Paris 2000

$4 800 - €5 553 - **£3 397** - FF36 426
Washington Square Oil/board (30.5x40cm 12x15in) New-York 2000

$2 755 - €3 217 - **£1 945** - FF21 100
Ours assis Bronze (H17cm H6in) Neuilly-sur-Seine 2000
$796 - €732 - **£489** - FF4 800
Panthère Fusain (56x64cm 22x25in) Paris 1999
$392 - €457 - **£275** - FF3 000
Panthère Lithographie (41x55cm 16x21in) Pontoise 2000

GUYOT Louise 1869-1927 **[3]**
$2 600 - €2 523 - **£1 618** - FF16 553
Flock of Sheep on the Hillside Oil/panel (41x30cm 16x12in) New-Orleans LA 1999

GUYS Constantin 1802-1892 **[476]**
$1 316 - €1 250 - **£807** - FF8 201
Les Hussards Aquarelle (6.5x13cm 2x5in) Zürich 1999

GUZZARDI Giuseppe 1845-1914 **[16]**
$580 - €654 - **£400** - FF4 290
The Dancing Master Oil/canvas (29.5x22cm 11x8in) Billingshurst, West-Sussex 2000

GUZZI Beppe 1902-1982 **[31]**
$840 - €726 - **£560** - FF4 760
Paesaggio Olio/tela (50x70cm 19x27in) Prato 1998

GUZZONE Sebastiano 1856-1890 **[7]**
$2 400 - €3 110 - **£1 800** - FF23 400
Chierichetti in sagrestia Olio/tela (25x45cm 9x17in) Roma 2001

GWATHMEY Robert 1903-1988 **[75]**
$8 000 - €6 852 - **£4 723** - FF44 944
Picking Cotton Oil/canvas (51x40.5cm 20x15in) New-York 1998
$5 000 - €4 282 - **£2 952** - FF28 090
Seated Musician Oil/canvas (30.5x25.5cm 12x10in) New-York 1998
$2 500 - €2 141 - **£1 476** - FF14 045
«World, Series #1» Watercolour (71x55.5cm 27x21in) New-York 1998
$1 400 - €1 344 - **£863** - FF8 819
Sharecroppers Screenprint in colors (37x30.5cm 14x12in) New-York 1999

GWOZDECKI Gustaw 1880-1935 **[9]**
$4 395 - €4 857 - **£3 049** - FF31 863
Femme dans le pré Huile/carton (23.5x15.5cm 9x6in) Warszawa 2001
$850 - €915 - **£579** - FF6 000
Jeune femme de profil Monotype (36.5x28cm 14x11in) Paris 2001

GWYNNE-JONES Allan 1892-1982 **[33]**
$4 269 - €5 027 - **£3 000** - FF32 974
Spring Lane, near Aldbrough Oil/canvas (61x51cm 24x20in) London 2000

GYARMATHY Tihamér 1915 **[24]**
$3 200 - €3 147 - **£2 000** - FF20 640
Speedily in the Streets Oil/board (60x80cm 23x31in) Budapest 1999
$1 540 - €1 704 - **£1 012** - FF11 176
In Memoriam Martyn Ferenc Oil/canvas (30x20cm 11x7in) Budapest 2000
$798 - €768 - **£494** - FF5 035
Lights Indian ink/paper (70x50cm 27x19in) Budapest 2000

GYBERSON Indiana 1879-c.1928 **[3]**
$1 500 - €1 706 - **£1 040** - FF11 190
Woman in an Interior Oil/board (25x20cm 10x8in) Cincinnati OH 2000

GYENES Gitta 1888-1960 [3]
$6 650 – €7 328 – £4 370 – FF48 070
Hotel Garni Oil/board (100x68cm 39x26in) Budapest 2000

GYLLENSTIERNA Malin 1889-1980 [2]
$11 900 – €11 679 – £7 380 – FF76 610
Ateljé, studie Oil/canvas (65x86cm 25x33in) Stockholm 1999

GYOKU Akasofu XIX [2]
$5 500 – €5 036 – £3 352 – FF33 037
Warrior Bronze (H79.5cm H31in) New-York 1999

GYOKUDO Kawai 1873-1957 [13]
$38 220 – €37 278 – £23 400 – FF244 530
Village in Spring Painting (123x41.5cm 48x16in) Tokyo 1999
$46 060 – €44 925 – £28 200 – FF294 690
Landscape Drawing (49x60cm 19x23in) Tokyo 1999

GYOKUSHO Kawabata 1842-1913 [2]
$3 000 – €3 430 – £2 059 – FF22 502
Egrets Ink (176.5x105cm 69x41in) Beverly-Hills CA 2000

GYSBRECHTS Cornelis Norbertus 1659/60-? [11]
$35 332 – €34 033 – £21 832 – FF223 245
Trompe-l'oeil: Documents, a Quill, a Set of Engravings, an Almanac Oil/canvas (77.5x57.5cm 30x22in) Amsterdam 1999

GYSBRECHTS Franciscus XVII [13]
$9 058 – €8 616 – £5 500 – FF56 516
Still Life of a Candle, a Skull, Ears of Corn, a Drape, Books Oil/canvas (76x58cm 29x22in) London 1999

GYSELINCKX Joseph 1845-? [22]
$2 702 – €3 176 – £1 873 – FF20 836
The Little Cherry-Eaters Oil/panel (59x46cm 23x18in) Amsterdam 2000

GYSELMAN Warner 1827-? [7]
$3 220 – €3 457 – £2 155 – FF22 676
Village Square with Figures Oil/panel (33.5x45.5cm 13x17in) Toronto 2000

GYSELS Peter 1621-1690 [64]
$12 815 – €14 025 – £8 859 – FF92 000
Sans titre Huile/toile (108x165cm 42x64in) Versailles 2001
$79 400 – €72 725 – £48 400 – FF476 700
Vertumnus und Pomona bei einem steinernen Brunnen auf der Terrasse Öl/Leinwand (78x96cm 30x37in) Wien 1999
$62 256 – €61 197 – £40 000 – FF401 424
Village Scene with a Horse-drawn Cart on a Track, Figures Oil/copper (16.5x22.5cm 6x8in) London 1999

GYSIN Brion 1916-1986 [13]
$3 000 – €2 802 – £1 813 – FF18 381
Naked Lunch Watercolour (38x56cm 14x22in) New-York 1999

GYSIS Nicholaos 1842-1901 [45]
$397 800 – €336 912 – £232 050 – FF2 210 000
The Gossips Oil/canvas (61x79cm 24x31in) Athens 1998
$27 000 – €30 032 – £18 000 – FF197 000
Smoking Girl Oil/canvas/panel (26x17cm 10x6in) Athens 2000
$4 776 – €4 625 – £3 000 – FF30 337
Standing male Nude Pencil/paper (41x29cm 16x11in) London 1999

$195 – €230 – £141 – FF1 506
«München, Jahresausstellung» Affiche (109x65cm 42x25in) Sion 2001

H

HAACKE Hans 1936 [4]
$5 769 – €6 781 – £4 000 – FF44 480
Mobil: on the Right Track Screenprint in colors (152.5x109cm 60x42in) London 2000

HAAG Carl 1820-1915 [261]
$3 460 – €4 069 – £2 481 – FF26 692
Kinder bei einer Schneeballschlacht Öl/Leinwand (73.5x60cm 28x23in) Zürich 2001
$1 368 – €1 534 – £929 – FF10 061
Araber, an eine Mauer gelehnt Öl/Leinwand (41x31cm 16x12in) München 2000
$1 718 – €1 844 – £1 150 – FF12 099
Mosi Guelle (The Well of Moses) Watercolour (12x34.5cm 4x13in) Newbury, Berkshire 2000

HAAG Hans Johann 1841-1919 [16]
$2 891 – €2 806 – £1 800 – FF18 406
Masters with their Hounds/Over the Fence Oil/panel (23.5x29cm 9x11in) London 1999

HAAG Jean-Paul c.1850-c.1895 [10]
$22 000 – €19 045 – £13 268 – FF124 929
«The Student's Recital» Oil/canvas (70.5x100cm 27x39in) San-Francisco CA 1998

HAAG Tethart Ph. Christ. 1737-1812 [8]
$1 333 – €1 151 – £803 – FF7 552
Two Dogs resting in a hilly Landscape Wash (20.5x22.5cm 8x8in) Amsterdam 1998

HAAGEN van der Jacobus ?-1686 [1]
$10 764 – €10 247 – £6 734 – FF67 215
Stilleben med frukter och pipkanna Oil/canvas (81x63cm 31x24in) Stockholm 1999

HAAGEN van der Joris Abrahamsz. c.1615-1669 [22]
$28 357 – €31 765 – £19 705 – FF208 362
Extensive wooded River Landscape with Traveller Oil/panel (40x58cm 15x22in) Amsterdam 2001

HAALAND Lars Laurits Larsen 1855-1938 [40]
$9 486 – €11 285 – £6 561 – FF74 025
Möte ved kysten Oil/canvas (98x150cm 38x59in) Oslo 2000
$7 487 – €6 512 – £4 513 – FF42 716
Sköyte i opprört sjö Oil/canvas (38x55cm 14x21in) Oslo 1998
$4 620 – €5 494 – £3 291 – FF36 036
Nordlandsjekte på havet Oil/canvas (33x44cm 12x17in) Oslo 2000

HAAN de Dirk 1832-1886 [3]
$4 500 – €4 830 – £3 011 – FF31 684
Early Morning Sail Oil/canvas (53x74cm 21x29in) New-York 2000

HAAN de Jürgen 1936 [25]
$506 – €544 – £345 – FF3 571
Untitled Pastel/paper (49x64cm 19x25in) Amsterdam 2001

HAAN de Wim 1913-1967 [15]
$3 090 – €2 949 – £1 931 – FF19 347
Blue Composition Mixed media (45x60cm 17x23in) Amsterdam 1999

HAANEN Adriana Johanna 1814-1895 **[34]**
🖘 $25 096 - €29 496 - **£17 400** - FF193 479
A Still Life with Grapes and Apricots Oil/canvas
(44.5x60.5cm 17x23in) Amsterdam 2000
🖘 $10 588 - €9 983 - **£6 562** - FF65 485
Still Life with a Peach, Grapes and Violets
Oil/panel (15x19cm 5x7in) Amsterdam 1999

HAANEN van Cecil 1844-1914 **[20]**
🖘 $5 000 - €5 142 - **£3 171** - FF33 729
**Portrait of a young Jewish Boy rebed in Velvet,
wearing a Yarmulke** Oil/canvas (79x54cm 31x21in)
New-Orleans LA 2000

HAANEN van George Gillis 1807-1876/81 **[42]**
🖘 $4 640 - €3 966 - **£2 816** - FF26 016
Intérieur d'église Huile/toile (70x60cm 27x23in)
Antwerpen 1998

HAANEN van Remigius Adrianus 1812-1894 **[116]**
🖘 $8 764 - €10 174 - **£6 160** - FF66 738
Winterlandschaft im Abendrot Oil/panel
(35.5x56cm 13x22in) Wien 2001
🖘 $5 399 - €5 113 - **£3 283** - FF33 539
**Sommerlandschaft mit einer Bäuerin und ihrem
Maultier** Oil/panel (28.5x38cm 11x14in) München
1999
✏ $693 - €654 - **£430** - FF4 290
Motiv aus Holland mit Windmühlen Watercolour
(22x18cm 8x7in) Wien 1999

HAAPANEN John Nichols 1891-? **[19]**
🖘 $850 - €856 - **£525** - FF5 618
Autumn Oil/board (40x49cm 16x19in) Wilton NH

HAARLEM van Cornelis Cornelisz. 1562-1638 **[27]**
🖘 $319 750 - €381 123 - **£228 000** - FF2 500 000
Pâris et Oenone Huile/toile (180x176cm 70x69in)
Nice 2000
🖘 $40 000 - €39 981 - **£24 436** - FF262 260
The Finding of Moses Oil/panel (49.5x70cm
19x27in) New-York 2000
🖘 $23 083 - €21 781 - **£14 241** - FF142 876
Amor and Psyche Oil/panel (20x25.5cm 7x10in)
Amsterdam 1999

HAARTMAN Axel 1877-1969 **[48]**
🖘 $1 541 - €1 514 - **£956** - FF9 928
Stilleben Oil/canvas (60x47cm 23x18in) Helsinki 1999
🖘 $1 546 - €1 514 - **£951** - FF9 928
Hiekkajaaloja rannassa Oil/panel (32x40cm
12x15in) Helsinki 1999

HAAS de Aad 1920-1972 **[35]**
〰 $253 - €272 - **£172** - FF1 786
Untitled Linocut (37x53cm 14x20in) Amsterdam 2001

HAAS de Jean Hubert Léonard 1832-1908 **[64]**
🖘 $3 024 - €3 176 - **£1 913** - FF20 836
Cows by a Well Oil/canvas (46x70cm 18x27in)
Amsterdam 2000
🖘 $3 648 - €3 966 - **£2 400** - FF26 016
Grazend vee Oil/panel (31.5x47cm 12x18in) Lokeren
2000
✏ $5 403 - €5 445 - **£3 368** - FF35 719
The Little Cowherd Watercolour (78x66cm 30x25in)
Amsterdam 2000

HAAS de Mauritz Frederik H. 1832-1895 **[79]**
🖘 $37 500 - €41 040 - **£25 867** - FF269 205
Ship off a Stormy Coast Oil/canvas (96.5x153cm
37x60in) New-York 2001
🖘 $11 287 - €9 517 - **£6 699** - FF62 426
Three-Master at Sea Oil/canvas (62.5x85cm
24x33in) Amsterdam 1998

🖘 $4 000 - €4 441 - **£2 782** - FF29 129
High Clouds Oil/canvas (31x49cm 12x19in) Milford
CT 2001

HAAS de Willem Frederik 1830-1880 **[13]**
🖘 $6 500 - €5 454 - **£3 831** - FF35 773
Children by the Riverside Oil/canvas (53x91cm
21x36in) Greenwich CT 1998
🖘 $8 500 - €9 413 - **£5 764** - FF61 748
Sunset Landscape with Branchless Tree Oil/can-
vas (20.5x35.5cm 8x13in) New-York 2000

HAAS Ernst 1921-1986 **[55]**
📷 $1 377 - €1 534 - **£900** - FF10 061
Homecoming Prisoners, Vienna Gelatin silver print
(50.4x40.6cm 19x15in) Köln 2000

HAAS HEMKEN de Willem 1831-1911 **[21]**
✏ $718 - €771 - **£480** - FF5 060
Diligence in a street in Enkhuizen Watercolour
(16.5x25cm 6x9in) Amsterdam 2000

HAAS Michel 1934 **[31]**
✏ $2 293 - €2 610 - **£1 611** - FF17 122
La danse Mischtechnik/Papier (229x124cm 90x48in)
Zürich 2001

HAAS Richard 1936 **[23]**
〰 $300 - €289 - **£188** - FF1 898
Flatiron Building Etching (88x32cm 35x12in)
Chicago IL 1999

HAAS van der Hermina 1843-1921 **[13]**
✏ $676 - €726 - **£452** - FF4 762
Still life with grapes, peaches and a melon
Watercolour (37.5x47cm 14x18in) Amsterdam 2000

HAASE Ove 1894-1989 **[10]**
🖘 $5 186 - €5 899 - **£3 656** - FF38 694
Rosen in einer Vase Öl/Leinwand (43.3x35.2cm
17x13in) Zürich 2001

HAASE von Carl Friedrich M.E. 1844-? **[3]**
🖘 $3 351 - €3 835 - **£2 304** - FF25 154
Jägerlatein Öl/Leinwand (62x54cm 24x21in)
München 2000

HAASE-ILSENBURG Hermann 1879-1960 **[12]**
🗿 $2 189 - €2 463 - **£1 528** - FF16 155
Schreitender Akt mit Kessel und Tuch Bronze
(H65.5cm H25in) Luzern 2001

HAAXMAN Peter 1854-1937 **[9]**
🖘 $2 908 - €2 723 - **£1 810** - FF17 859
«Als Voorheen» Oil/panel (46.5x36.5cm 18x14in)
Amsterdam 1999

HAAXMAN Pieter Alardus 1814-1884 **[22]**
🖘 $5 106 - €4 305 - **£3 030** - FF28 240
The Happy Family Oil/canvas (55x70cm 21x27in)
Amsterdam 1998
🖘 $1 634 - €1 815 - **£1 137** - FF11 906
Voornaam echtpaar in landschap Oil/panel
(16.5x24.5cm 6x9in) Groningen 2001
✏ $933 - €920 - **£600** - FF6 038
Young Girl Knitting Watercolour/paper (20x12.5cm
7x4in) London 1999

HABBE Nikolai 1827-1889 **[21]**
🖘 $708 - €806 - **£495** - FF5 285
En so med sine pattegrise Oil/canvas (19x36cm
7x14in) København 2000

HABENSCHADEN Sebastian 1813-1868 **[13]**
🖘 $2 640 - €2 556 - **£1 658** - FF16 769
**Angelfreuden, Waldsee und drei, mit Hund auf
der Lauer liegende Jäger** Öl/Leinwand (48x73cm
18x28in) Berlin 1999

HABERLE John 1856-1933 **[14]**
- $130 000 - €111 070 - **£78 039** - FF728 572
  The palette Oil/canvas (45x62cm 17x24in) New-York 1998
- $900 - €771 - **£541** - FF5 057
  Trompe l'oeil Still Life with Moonlit Scene Watercolour/paper (15x17cm 6x7in) Cleveland OH 1998

HABERMANN von Franz 1788-1866 **[8]**
- $1 792 - €1 631 - **£1 100** - FF10 699
  Palazzo Doria, Genoa Watercolour (22x34cm 8x13in) London 1999

HABERMANN von Franz Xaver 1721-1796 **[5]**
- $205 - €200 - **£126** - FF1 312
  Die Anländung der Englischen Trouppen zu Neu Yorck Copper engraving in colors (24.3x39cm 9x15in) Bern 1999

HABERMANN von Hugo, Freiherr 1849-1929 **[95]**
- $1 236 - €1 125 - **£772** - FF7 378
  Bildnis einer alten Dame Öl/Karton (72x52cm 28x20in) München 1999
- $534 - €613 - **£365** - FF4 024
  Interieur mit Frau und Blumenvase auf dem Tisch Öl/Karton (25.5x32cm 10x12in) Heidelberg 2000
- $546 - €511 - **£331** - FF3 353
  Mädchenbildnis, sitzend Chalks (37.5x31cm 14x12in) Stuttgart 1999

HABERT François XVII **[1]**
- $149 430 - €160 401 - **£100 000** - FF1 052 160
  Stephanois, Primroses, Snowdrops and Other Flowers in a Blue Bowl Oil/panel (27.5x36cm 10x14in) London 2000

HACCOU Johannes Cornelius 1798-1839 **[6]**
- $2 419 - €2 269 - **£1 495** - FF14 883
  Sailing Vessels in a Calm Oil/panel (27x34cm 10x13in) Amsterdam 1999
- $2 532 - €2 949 - **£1 769** - FF19 347
  A Herder and his Cow Crossing A Bridge/Two Men in a Boats Watercolour (15.5x20cm 6x7in) Amsterdam 2000

HACCOU Lodewijk Gillis 1792-c.1830 **[7]**
- $1 296 - €1 452 - **£900** - FF9 525
  Riviergezicht met vele schepen Watercolour/paper (50x71.5cm 19x28in) Rotterdam 2001

HACKAERT Jan 1629-1699 **[26]**
- $4 899 - €4 510 - **£3 000** - FF29 585
  Landscape with Figures and Cattle around a Waterfall Oil/canvas (37x40cm 14x15in) Newbury, Berkshire 1998
- $1 877 - €2 178 - **£1 296** - FF14 287
  A Mountainous Wooded River Landscape with Travellers on a Road Ink (17x26cm 6x10in) Amsterdam 2000
- $153 - €153 - **£96** - FF1 006
  Landschaft mit vier Bäumen Radierung (19.4x21.8cm 7x8in) Hamburg 1999

HACKE Rudolf 1881-1952 **[3]**
- $21 508 - €20 090 - **£13 000** - FF131 784
  Das weisse Tuch Oil/panel (85x58.5cm 33x23in) London 1999

HACKER Arthur 1858-1919 **[46]**
- $24 064 - €20 792 - **£14 500** - FF136 387
  The Wonder Story Oil/canvas (125.5x100cm 49x39in) Billingshurst, West-Sussex 1999
- $6 903 - €6 302 - **£4 200** - FF41 338
  A Skyphos, a Kylix, a Wine Jug and an Egyptian Necklace Oil/canvas (51x61cm 20x24in) London 1998

HACKER Dieter 1942 **[44]**
- $5 317 - €5 113 - **£3 281** - FF33 539
  Der Traum Bronze (H45cm H17in) Köln 1999

HACKER Horst 1842-1906 **[30]**
- $1 317 - €1 380 - **£871** - FF9 055
  Am Lago Maggiore, Blick auf Felsen, Zypressen Öl/Leinwand (65x94cm 25x37in) München 2000

HACKERT Carl Ludwig 1740-1796 **[23]**
- $7 985 - €8 181 - **£4 928** - FF53 662
  Flussbrücke mit Angler Öl/Leinwand (37.5x46cm 14x18in) Düsseldorf 2000
- $1 817 - €1 757 - **£1 136** - FF11 478
  Vue de la source de l'Arveron Radierung (34.5x46cm 13x18in) Zürich 1999

HACKERT Georg Abraham 1755-1805 **[9]**
- $7 471 - €8 020 - **£5 000** - FF52 608
  Villagers in a Hilly Landscape Ink (34.5x45.5cm 13x17in) London 2000
- $415 - €486 - **£291** - FF3 186
  I.ième vue des ruines du Pont d'Auguste, nach J.Ph.Hackert Kupferstich (43x57.5cm 16x22in) München 2000

HACKERT Jacob Philipp 1737-1807 **[151]**
- $119 544 - €128 321 - **£80 000** - FF841 728
  English Frigates in Rough Seas Oil/canvas (146x191.5cm 57x75in) London 2000
- $74 865 - €76 695 - **£46 200** - FF503 085
  Mittelmeerhafen mit stürmischem Meer Öl/Leinwand (74x99cm 29x38in) Düsseldorf 2000
- $146 960 - €167 694 - **£102 080** - FF1 100 000
  Pêcheurs près d'un navire amarré Huile/cuivre (30.5x42.5cm 12x16in) Paris 2000
- $5 384 - €6 403 - **£3 708** - FF42 000
  Moines et personnages dans un paysage montagneux près d'une fontaine Pierre noire (56x81.5cm 22x32in) Paris 2000
- $552 - €613 - **£384** - FF4 024
  «Sophora» Radierung (48.5x37cm 19x14in) Heidelberg 2001

HACKERT Johann Gottlieb 1744-1773 **[6]**
- $8 400 - €7 257 - **£5 600** - FF47 600
  Paesaggio con il Ponte Milvio e viandanti Matita (35x47cm 13x18in) Roma 1998

HACKING Grant 1964 **[7]**
- $1 141 - €1 331 - **£800** - FF8 728
  Watchful, Cheetah Oil/canvas (19x34cm 7x13in) London 2000

HADAD Marie 1890-1973 **[1]**
- $16 471 - €18 526 - **£11 500** - FF121 520
  Lebanese Moutain Landscape Oil/canvas (44.5x54cm 17x21in) London 2001

HADAMARD Auguste 1823-1886 **[4]**
- $5 806 - €5 336 - **£3 566** - FF35 000
  Le valet de chambre courtisant la soubrette Huile/toile (54x59cm 21x23in) Paris 1999

HADDON Arthur Trevor 1864-1941 **[140]**
- $3 197 - €2 998 - **£1 976** - FF19 667
  Conversation at the Marketplace in Venice Oil/canvas (75x62.5cm 29x24in) Johannesburg 1999
- $525 - €481 - **£320** - FF3 153
  Girl with Pitchers Watercolour/paper (50x35cm 20x14in) Whitby, Yorks 1999

HADDON David W. XIX-XX **[112]**

- $798 - €814 - £500 - FF5 342
  Portrait of a Girl on a Pathway in Front of a Cottage Oil/board (42.5x54cm 16x21in) London 2000
- $849 - €786 - £520 - FF5 158
  Young Girl trying bonnet on before a toilet Mirror/Young Girl looking Oil/board (40x25cm 16x10in) Birmingham 1999
- $418 - €387 - £260 - FF2 541
  Old Salt/Cornish Fishwoman Watercolour/paper (30x22cm 11x8in) Cheshire 1999

HADENGUE Louis Michel act.1875-1893 **[9]**

- $14 513 - €14 940 - £9 143 - FF98 000
  Le cirque Huile/toile (108x136cm 42x53in) Paris 2000
- $13 636 - €13 741 - £8 500 - FF90 135
  Summer Flowers in a Chinese Ceramic Vase/A Tureen and a Magpie Eating Oil/canvas (93x65.5cm 36x25in) London 2000

HADER Ernst 1866-1910 **[8]**

- $4 025 - €4 015 - £2 512 - FF26 339
  Pifferari Oil/canvas (48.8x37cm 19x14in) Warszawa 1999

HAECHT van Willem II 1593-1637 **[1]**

- $379 920 - €365 878 - £236 400 - FF2 400 000
  L'atelier d'Apelle Huile/panneau (76x114cm 29x44in) Montfort L'Amaury 1999

HAECKEN Antoine 1709-1749 **[1]**

- $20 000 - €17 543 - £12 144 - FF115 076
  Parkland Setting with Elegant Company Seated to Lunch Oil/copper (46.5x61.5cm 18x24in) New-York 1999

HAEN de Abraham 1707-1748 **[6]**

- $868 - €987 - £600 - FF6 476
  Ruin of the Ameyde Castle Wash (19.5x28.5cm 7x11in) London 2000

HAENSBERGEN van Jan 1642-1705 **[28]**

- $3 079 - €3 319 - £2 100 - FF21 769
  Classical Landscape with Nymphs discovering an Infant Oil/copper (18.5x25.5cm 7x10in) Bury St. Edmunds, Suffolk 2001

HAER de Adolf 1892-1944 **[11]**

- $45 000 - €49 919 - £29 925 - FF327 447
  Mädchen mit Blumen Oil/canvas (100x68cm 39x26in) New-York 2000
- $503 - €575 - £350 - FF3 770
  «Der Geile Tod» Woodcut (30.5x42cm 12x16in) London 2000

HAERNING August 1874-1961 **[28]**

- $1 120 - €940 - £657 - FF6 167
  Mand og to kvinder i robåd Oil/canvas (56x85cm 22x33in) Vejle 1998

HAES Y FORTUNY de Carlos 1826-1898 **[64]**

- $207 000 - €180 652 - £126 000 - FF1 185 000
  Bosque con leñadores Oleo/lienzo (236x172cm 92x67in) Madrid 1998
- $28 000 - €30 032 - £18 500 - FF197 000
  La ribera Oleo/lienzo (50x79cm 19x31in) Madrid 2000
- $3 900 - €3 904 - £2 405 - FF25 610
  Paisaje Oleo/tabla (18x29cm 7x11in) Madrid 2000
- $2 517 - €2 853 - £1 757 - FF18 715
  Tormenta en al acantilado Acuarela/papel (24x41.5cm 9x16in) Madrid 2001
- $130 - €153 - £91 - FF1 005
  Paisaje Aguafuerte (8.5x10.5cm 3x4in) Madrid 2000

HAESE Gunter 1924 **[7]**

- $6 137 - €7 158 - £4 309 - FF46 954
  Astron Metal (29.5x27x25.5cm 11x10x10in) Köln 2000

HAESEKER Alexandra Sandy 1945 **[6]**

- $1 257 - €1 349 - £853 - FF8 850
  Untitled (Bull's eye) Watercolour/paper (20.5x28cm 8x11in) Calgary, Alberta 2001
- $397 - €426 - £269 - FF2 794
  Last summer Color lithograph (22x27.5cm 8x10in) Calgary, Alberta 2001

HAFFENRICHTER Hans 1897-1981 **[39]**

- $361 - €358 - £225 - FF2 347
  Das Blühen für Frau Maass Watercolour (26.5x21cm 10x8in) München 1999

HAFFNER Léon 1881-1972 **[280]**

- $570 - €610 - £389 - FF4 000
  Yawl remontant au vent Gouache (44.5x32.5cm 17x12in) Paris 2001
- $367 - €335 - £223 - FF2 200
  Vaisseau royal sous voiles Lithographie (78x40cm 30x15in) Douarnenez 1998

HAFFNER Louis XIX-XX **[2]**

- $2 345 - €1 982 - £1 394 - FF13 000
  Voiliers Gouache/papier (39x78.5cm 15x30in) Châtellerault 1998

HAFFNER von Johan Heinrich W. 1746-1808 **[5]**

- $644 - €606 - £401 - FF3 973
  Portraet af Georg Wilhelm Greve af Sponeck/Hylleborg von Eppengen Pastel/paper (25x22cm 9x8in) Vejle 1999

HAFFTEN von Karl, Freiherr 1831-1884 **[7]**

- $1 251 - €1 431 - £870 - FF9 390
  Grosses Seestück mit untergehendem Kriegsschiff Öl/Leinwand (80x146cm 31x57in) Rudolstadt-Thüringen 2000

HAFFTER Martha 1873-1951 **[7]**

- $2 648 - €2 502 - £1 649 - FF16 409
  Schafherde mit schwarzem Schaf Öl/Leinwand (13x34cm 5x13in) St. Gallen 1999

HÄFLIGER Leopold 1929-1988 **[158]**

- $1 285 - €1 410 - £873 - FF9 248
  Bewölkte Feldlandschaft Öl/Leinwand (46x60cm 18x23in) Luzern 2000
- $526 - €502 - £328 - FF3 293
  Der Clown Öl/Papier (48x31cm 18x12in) Zofingen 1999
- $286 - €314 - £194 - FF2 323
  Hummer Oil chalks/paper (48x60cm 18x23in) Luzern 2000

HAFNER Rudolf 1893-1951 **[12]**

- $7 332 - €8 721 - £5 232 - FF57 204
  Winterliches Salzburg Oil/panel (89x104cm 35x40in) Wien 2000

HAFSTRÖM Axel Gillis 1841-1909 **[18]**

- $2 029 - €1 975 - £1 249 - FF12 957
  På promenad Oil/canvas (42x30cm 16x11in) Stockholm 1999

HÅFSTRÖM Jan 1937 **[72]**

- $3 126 - €3 150 - £1 949 - FF20 665
  Pompeji Oil/canvas (125x290cm 49x114in) Stockholm 2000
- $837 - €787 - £518 - FF5 163
  Den undre världen Mixed media (51.5x46.5cm 20x18in) Stockholm 1999

$195 - €219 - **£136** - FF1 436
Skogsaltare Mixed media (32x25x9cm 12x9x3in)
Stockholm 2001
$195 - €223 - **£137** - FF1 461
Robinson Mixed media/paper (28x35cm 11x13in)
Stockholm 2001

HAGARTY James XVIII **[2]**
$5 839 - €5 608 - **£3 600** - FF36 787
View at Hammersmith Oil/canvas (49.5x68.5cm 19x26in) London 1999

HAGARTY Mary S. act.1882-1938 **[34]**
$602 - €669 - **£420** - FF4 386
Local Festivities on Bastille Day Watercolour (28.5x17.5cm 11x6in) London 2001

HAGARTY Parker 1859-1934 **[36]**
$348 - €303 - **£210** - FF1 986
In the Vale of Glamorgan Watercolour/paper (27.5x37.5cm 10x14in) Glamorgan 1998

HAGBERG Rune 1924 **[40]**
$735 - €678 - **£451** - FF4 450
Ikonoklassi Tempera/canvas (84x46.5cm 33x18in) Stockholm 1999
$303 - €303 - **£189** - FF1 987
Abstrakt motiv i rött och grått Indian ink (76x101cm 29x39in) Uppsala 1999

HAGBORG August Wilhelm N. 1852-1921 **[186]**
$6 874 - €8 069 - **£4 851** - FF52 927
Skärgårdslandskap, motiv från Dalarö Oil/canvas (130x195cm 51x76in) Stockholm 2000
$4 416 - €4 762 - **£2 964** - FF31 236
Vy över blasieholmen och skeppsholmen Oil/panel (81x64cm 31x25in) Stockholm 2000
$1 459 - €1 333 - **£913** - FF8 745
Young Girl Wearing a White Bonnet Oil/panel (36x23cm 14x9in) Dublin 1999

HAGEDORN Edward XX **[6]**
$375 - €426 - **£260** - FF2 797
Destruction Etching (54x39cm 21x15in) Chicago IL 2000

HAGEDORN Friedrich c.1814-c.1889 **[11]**
$15 000 - €17 661 - **£10 540** - FF115 851
View of Rio de Janeiro Gouache/paper (38.5x75cm 15x29in) New-York 2000

HAGEDORN Karl 1889-1969 **[109]**
$985 - €940 - **£600** - FF6 166
The back Garden Oil/canvas (56x46cm 22x18in) London 1999
$829 - €706 - **£500** - FF4 633
Shire Oaks Farm, Chapel en le Frith, Derbyshire Watercolour (35.5x51cm 13x20in) London 1998

HAGEDORN-OLSEN Thorvald 1902-1996 **[151]**
$512 - €471 - **£315** - FF3 091
Vinterlandskab Oil/canvas (66x91cm 25x35in) Vejle 1999
$246 - €268 - **£170** - FF1 759
Fiskere på havnen Oil/canvas (27x33cm 10x12in) Köbenhavn 2001

HAGELGANS Michel Christoph Em. 1725-1766 **[5]**
$15 650 - €18 168 - **£11 000** - FF119 175
Bildnis des Erzherzogs Josef/Bildnis seiner Schwester Pastel (36x27cm 14x10in) Wien 2001

HAGELSTEIN Paul 1825-1868 **[25]**
$427 - €488 - **£297** - FF3 200
Portrait de Napolitaine Huile/toile (99.5x77.5cm 39x30in) Paris 2000

HAGEMANN de Godefroy c.1820-1877 **[19]**
$1 300 - €1 223 - **£808** - FF8 025
Stream, Cattle, Farmyard and Boatman all beneath spring foliage Oil/canvas (46x38cm 18x15in) East-Dennis MA 1999
$3 554 - €3 964 - **£2 389** - FF26 000
Scène animée à l'entrée de la ville Huile/toile (41.5x35cm 16x13in) Narbonne 2000

HAGEMANN Oskar H. 1888-1985 **[53]**
$399 - €434 - **£263** - FF2 850
Welkender Blumenstrauss Öl/Leinwand (56x65.5cm 22x25in) Heidelberg 2000

HAGEMANS Maurice 1852-1917 **[287]**
$14 760 - €14 873 - **£9 180** - FF97 560
Berger et son troupeau Huile/toile (200x127cm 78x50in) Bruxelles 2000
$3 461 - €3 879 - **£2 032** - FF18 884
Portrait, Modèle Oil/canvas (59x49cm 23x19in) Amsterdam 1998
$854 - €818 - **£537** - FF5 366
Flusslandschaft mit Schäfer und Herde, Herbststimmung Oil/panel (27x44cm 10x17in) Köln 1999
$1 439 - €1 476 - **£900** - FF9 685
A Figure Beside the Edge of a Lake Watercolour (52x91cm 20x35in) London 2000

HAGEMANS Paul 1884-1959 **[156]**
$1 506 - €1 487 - **£918** - FF9 756
Chalutiers au port de Zeebrugge Huile/panneau (80x99cm 31x38in) Bruxelles 2000.
$1 085 - €1 140 - **£685** - FF7 479
Les moutons Huile/panneau (30x31cm 11x12in) Bruxelles 2000
$896 - €793 - **£547** - FF5 203
«La lettre anonyme» Aquarelle, gouache/papier (34x21cm 13x8in) Antwerpen 1999

HAGEMEISTER Karl 1848-1933 **[81]**
$18 992 - €22 343 - **£13 407** - FF146 561
Elster im Birkenwald Öl/Leinwand (198.5x118cm 78x46in) Berlin 2001
$4 495 - €5 055 - **£3 137** - FF33 161
In Sommerfeld stehendes Bauernmädchen Öl/Leinwand (107x74cm 42x29in) Luzern 2001
$1 440 - €1 620 - **£1 005** - FF10 628
Winterlandschaft mit Bäumen am See Pastel/canvas (102x71cm 40x27in) Luzern 2001

HAGEMEYER Johan 1884-1962 **[29]**
$3 500 - €3 653 - **£2 214** - FF23 959
David Alberto (Arms Crossed) Photograph (16x12cm 6x4in) New-York 2000

HAGEN Michael 1809-1873 **[1]**
$10 055 - €8 555 - **£6 000** - FF56 120
Saint Sebastian Relief (H40.5cm H15in) London 1998

HAGEN Theodor Joseph 1842-1919 **[46]**
$1 201 - €1 380 - **£848** - FF9 055
Hohlweg im Wald Öl/Leinwand/Karton (35.5x53cm 13x20in) Bremen 2001
$1 439 - €1 329 - **£896** - FF8 720
Dorfkirche im Sonnenlicht Öl/Karton (29x38cm 11x14in) Rudolstadt-Thüringen 1999

HAGEN Thomas [1]
$4 500 - €4 288 - **£2 729** - FF28 129
Sailing Vessels Oil/canvas (60x91cm 24x36in) New-York 1999

HAGEN van der J.C. / Johann 1675-c.1745 **[3]**
🖇 **$21 996** - €23 705 - **£15 000** - FF155 497
Double Portrait of a Young Boy and Girl Oil/canvas (128x101.5cm 50x39in) London 2001
🖇 **$14 274** - €14 989 - **£9 000** - FF98 322
Rhenish Harbour with a Man-O-War Firing a Salute Oil/canvas (63x123cm 24x48in) London 2000

HAGEN van der William ?-c.1745 **[5]**
🖇 **$115 463** - €120 626 - **£75 772** - FF791 255
Capriccio Southern Landscape with Anglers Oil/canvas (191x206cm 75x81in) Dublin 2000
🖇 **$22 086** - €23 705 - **£15 000** - FF155 496
Admiral of the Blue Squadron arriving at Gibraltar Oil/canvas (85x124cm 33x48in) London 2001

HAGEN von Eduard 1834-1909 **[6]**
🖇 **$692** - €619 - **£414** - FF4 062
A Musketeer Smoking a Pipe Oil/panel (21x16cm 8x6in) Amsterdam 1998

HAGENAUER (Manufacture) XX **[34]**
🖇 **$1 456** - €1 371 - **£900** - FF8 995
Sailor Playing an Accordian and Singing Metal (H19cm 7in) London 1999

HAGENAUER Franz 1906-1986 **[155]**
🖇 **$1 010** - €945 - **£622** - FF6 197
Liegender Hirsch Sculpture, wood (31x39.5cm 12x15in) Wien 1999

HAGENAUER Karl 1898-1956 **[110]**
🖇 **$958** - €1 090 - **£664** - FF7 150
Eingeborenenjunge mit Lanze und Schild Metal (H26cm H10in) Wien 2000

HAGER Albert 1857-1940 **[10]**
🖇 **$3 496** - €3 998 - **£2 400** - FF26 223
A pair af sparring Elephants Bronze (15.5x23cm 6x9in) London 2000

HAGER Marie 1872-1947 **[8]**
🖇 **$4 269** - €4 704 - **£2 849** - FF30 855
«Weite norddeutsche Sommerlandschaft mit Kornhocken» Öl/Karton (46x62cm 18x24in) Satow 2000

HAGERBAUMER David 1921 **[11]**
🖇 **$700** - €785 - **£475** - FF5 148
Ducks in Flight Watercolour/paper (20x25cm 8x10in) Cleveland OH 2000

HAGERUP Nels 1864-1922 **[54]**
🖇 **$900** - €995 - **£630** - FF6 524
Seascape Oil/board (35x56cm 14x22in) Chicago IL 2001
🖇 **$650** - €625 - **£403** - FF4 097
Seascape Oil/board (30x50cm 12x20in) Oakland CA 1999

HÄGG Herman 1884-1966 **[20]**
🖇 **$715** - €768 - **£478** - FF5 038
Marin med fullriggare Oil/canvas (47x39cm 18x15in) Stockholm 2000
🖇 **$317** - €351 - **£220** - FF2 300
Vy över Gamla stan Oil/panel (27x22cm 10x8in) Stockholm 2001

HÄGG Jakob 1839-1931 **[36]**
🖇 **$26 352** - €29 259 - **£17 640** - FF191 928
Skeppet Adolph Fredrik utanför Vaxholm Oil/canvas (100x150cm 39x59in) Stockholm 2000
🖇 **$876** - €874 - **£546** - FF5 733
Segelskutor Oil/canvas (22.5x33cm 8x12in) Uppsala 1999

HAGGIN Ben Ali 1882-1951 **[2]**
🖇 **$22 000** - €24 374 - **£14 751** - FF159 880
Yellow Jacket, Portrait of Juliette Day Oil/canvas (233x142cm 92x56in) Dedham MA 2000

HAGHE Charles 1810-1888 **[2]**
🖇 **$10 564** - €12 407 - **£7 500** - FF81 387
Sketches in Scinde from drawings by Lieut.Wm.Edwards, 86th.Regt. Lithograph (55.5x45cm 21x17in) London 2000

HAGHE Louis 1806-1885 **[270]**
🖇 **$1 933** - €1 923 - **£1 200** - FF12 613
Side Aisle of St Gudule, Brussels Watercolour/paper (63x46cm 25x18in) Manchester 1999
🖇 **$937** - €884 - **£581** - FF5 800
Petra (excavations at the End of the Valley), d'après David Roberts Lithographie (24x34cm 9x13in) Paris 1999

HAGIO Kunio 1947 **[1]**
🖇 **$30 000** - €32 202 - **£20 076** - FF211 230
Raging Bull - United Artists Oil/masonite (60x45cm 24x18in) Beverly-Hills CA 2000

HAGIWARA Hideo 1913 **[11]**
🖇 **$639** - €615 - **£393** - FF4 031
Man in Armour No.9 Woodcut in colors (91x60cm 35x23in) Melbourne 1999

HAGN von Ludwig 1819-1898 **[12]**
🖇 **$3 090** - €3 602 - **£2 139** - FF23 629
Der unartige Knabe Öl/Leinwand (46.5x38cm 18x14in) Bern 2000

HAGUE Joshua Anderson 1850-1916 **[61]**
🖇 **$1 138** - €1 322 - **£800** - FF8 675
The Watermill Oil/canvas (76.5x63cm 30x24in) London 2001

HAGUE K. XIX **[1]**
🖇 **$806** - €802 - **£500** - FF5 261
H.M.S.Shannon and the American Frigate Shakespear, after Schetky Lithograph (38x47.5cm 14x18in) Newbury, Berkshire 2000

HAGUE Michael XX **[6]**
🖇 **$3 500** - €3 352 - **£2 162** - FF21 986
Bear Trick-or-Treater in Cornfield, Calendar Illustration Ink (26x24cm 10x9in) New-York 1999

HAGUETTE Georges J.-Marie 1854-1906 **[3]**
🖇 **$2 104** - €2 009 - **£1 314** - FF13 175
Fruits, hommage à l'automne Oil/panel (14.5x23cm 5x9in) Zofingen 1999

HAHN Albert Pieter 1877-1918 **[7]**
🖇 **$558** - €522 - **£344** - FF3 423
«Koloniale Tentoonstelling Semarang» Poster (80x109cm 31x42in) Oostwoud 1999

HAHN Albert, Jnr. 1894-1953 **[10]**
🖇 **$134** - €113 - **£79** - FF744
«Den Nieuwen Dag Tegemoet S.D.A.P. Lijst 17 Vliegen» Poster (74x108cm 29x42in) Haarlem 1998

HAHN Friedemann 1949 **[51]**
🖇 **$4 478** - €5 113 - **£3 157** - FF33 539
Marilyn Monroe Öl/Leinwand (100x90cm 39x35in) Stuttgart 2001
🖇 **$1 303** - €1 534 - **£943** - FF10 061
Portrait einer Filmdiva Chalks (81.2x93.4cm 31x36in) Hamburg 2001

HAHN Josef 1839-1906 **[16]**
🎨 $719 - €665 - £442 - FF4 360
**Winterlandschaft, auf einem verschneiten Weg
Bauern mit Karren** Oil/panel (16x33cm 6x12in)
München 1999

HAHN Karl 1892-1980 **[10]**
✏️ $491 - €511 - £310 - FF3 353
Stehende Frau mit aufgestütztem Arm Aquarell
(61x32.5cm 24x12in) Berlin 2000

HAHN Siegbert B. XX **[16]**
🎨 $2 118 - €2 134 - £1 320 - FF14 000
Animaux fantastiques Huile/toile (40x30cm
15x11in) Paris 2000

HAHN William, Karl Wilh. 1829-1887 **[24]**
🎨 $5 175 - €4 993 - £3 722 753
Barnyard Scene Oil/canvas (73x89cm 29x35in)
Oakland CA 1999
🎨 $3 000 - €3 133 - £1 903 - FF20 420
Filling the Hay Wagon Oil/canvas (30.5x51cm
12x20in) Boston MA 2000

HAHNEL Julius Heinrich 1823-1909 **[5]**
🗿 $5 858 - €5 241 - £3 500 - FF34 381
A Walking Asiatic Lion Cleaning his Paw Bronze
(21x34.5cm 8x13in) Perthshire 1998

HÄHNISCH Anton 1817-1897 **[8]**
✏️ $719 - €665 - £442 - FF4 360
Junges Mädchen im Sessel Aquarell/Papier
(29x21cm 11x8in) München 1999

HAID Johann Elias 1739-1809 **[4]**
🖼️ $157 - €169 - £105 - FF1 106
Portrait Johann Jakob Haid, nach Anton Graff
Pochoir (39.9x26.5cm 15x10in) Berlin 2000

HAID Johann Jakob 1704-1767 **[20]**
🖼️ $241 - €230 - £150 - FF1 509
Kinderszenen Mezzotint (21.2x26.5cm 8x10in) Berlin
1999

HAIDER Hermann 1938 **[6]**
🎨 $3 459 - €3 997 - £2 420 - FF26 218
«Blumen» Öl/Leinwand (94x119cm 37x46in) Linz
2001

HAIDER Karl 1846-1912 **[10]**
🎨 $3 370 - €3 068 - £2 106 - FF20 123
Wiesental mit einem Bachlauf und einer Kirche
Öl/Leinwand (70.5x89cm 27x35in) München 1999
🎨 $5 824 - €5 368 - £3 488 - FF35 211
**Oberbayerisches Bauernmädchen mit weissem
Kopftuch** Öl/Leinwand (38x31.5cm 14x12in) Dresden
1998

HAIER Josef 1816-1891 **[15]**
🎨 $3 295 - €2 853 - £2 000 - FF18 712
The First Knitting Lesson Oil/canvas (63x50cm
24x19in) London 1998

HAIG Axel Herman 1835-1921 **[85]**
🖼️ $63 - €74 - £45 - FF485
The Aisles of Chartres Etching (38x53cm 14x20in)
London 2000

HAIG The Earl George A. 1918 **[12]**
🎨 $854 - €812 - £520 - FF5 327
Study for the Rocky Road Oil/canvas (50.5x50.5cm
19x19in) London 1999
✏️ $260 - €239 - £160 - FF1 569
Study for Pigeons at Frascati Pencil (25x20cm
10x8in) Northumberland 1999

HAIGH Alfred Grenfell 1870-1963 **[32]**
🎨 $3 038 - €3 192 - £2 000 - FF20 941
**Father and Son Mounted on a Chesnut Hunter
& a Bay Pony in a Parkland** Oil/canvas (88x119cm
35x47in) Dorchester, Dorset 2000

HAIGH-WOOD Charles 1856-1927 **[5]**
🎨 $17 000 - €19 309 - £11 928 - FF126 656
The Fortune Teller Oil/canvas (44x56cm 17x22in)
New-York 2001

HAIGHT Charles T. 1904-1980 **[41]**
✏️ $100 - €97 - £62 - FF637
House by the Sea Watercolour/paper (43x58cm
17x23in) Norwalk CT 1999

HAILER Max 1818-1854 **[2]**
🎨 $30 289 - €35 791 - £21 469 - FF234 773
**Ludwig I, König von Bayern im Krönungsornatn
nach J.Stieler** Öl/Leinwand (245x170cm 96x66in)
München 2000

HAIM Franz Anton 1830-1890 **[2]**
🎨 $17 246 - €14 879 - £10 404 - FF97 600
Ankunft auf der Alp Öl/Papier (23x32cm 9x12in) St.
Gallen 1998

HAIMANN Giuseppe 1828-1883 **[4]**
🎨 $1 560 - €1 348 - £1 040 - FF8 840
Contadina e alberi Olio/tela (26x39.5cm 10x15in)
Prato 1998

HAINARD Robert 1906-1999 **[51]**
🗿 $6 967 - €7 924 - £4 831 - FF51 978
Chouette Sculpture bois (52x19cm 20x7in) Sion 2000
🖼️ $469 - €436 - £287 - FF2 860
Spielende Spatzen Farblithographie (27x36cm
10x14in) Bern 1999

HAINDL-LAPOIRIE Elfy 1907-1969 **[1]**
🎨 $560 - €7 267 - £4 450 - FF47 670
Stilleben Öl/Leinwand (60x73cm 23x28in) Wien 2000

HAINES Frederick Stanley 1879-1960 **[96]**
🎨 $1 977 - €1 675 - £1 188 - FF10 985
Pine River near Alliston Oil/canvas/board (51x66cm
20x25in) Vancouver, BC. 1998
🎨 $456 - €529 - £315 - FF3 472
Wanapetei Bay Oil/canvas/board (25x30cm 10x12in)
Calgary, Alberta 2000
🖼️ $194 - €227 - £135 - FF1 487
«On Gull River» Aquatint in colors (25x21cm 9x8in)
Toronto 2000

HAINES William Henry 1812-1884 **[14]**
🎨 $54 665 - €55 375 - £34 000 - FF363 239
**View of Venice at the Entrance to the Grand
Canal** Oil/canvas (62x113.5cm 24x44in) Crewkerne,
Somerset 2000

HAINS Raymond 1926 **[168]**
🎨 $11 500 - €11 922 - £6 900 - FF78 200
Senza titolo Decollage (109x149cm 42x58in) Prato
1999
🎨 $10 082 - €10 824 - £6 745 - FF71 000
J.Dubuffet Coucou Bazar Affiche lacérée, arrachage
(100x100cm 39x39in) Versailles 2000
🎨 $2 964 - €2 756 - £1 800 - FF18 077
Untitled Collage/board (33x41.5cm 12x16in) London
1998
🗿 $4 500 - €4 665 - £2 700 - FF30 600
Saffa Sculpture bois (110x22x11cm 43x8x4in) Milano
2000
✏️ $4 611 - €4 287 - £2 800 - FF28 121
Untitled Collage (48x46cm 18x18in) London 1998

$546 - €610 - £370 - FF4 000
American Express Sérigraphie (58x42cm 22x16in)
Paris 2000

$1 513 - €1 524 - **£943** - FF10 000
Les palissades de Versailles Photo couleur
(60x90cm 23x35in) Paris 2000

HAIR Thomas Henry XIX [6]
$5 000 - €4 677 - **£3 023** - FF30 678
View of Durham Oil/canvas (48.5x69cm 19x27in)
New-York 1999

HAITE Georges Charles 1855-1924 [59]
$6 193 - €5 631 - **£3 800** - FF36 939
A Street in Morocco Oil/canvas (54x95.5cm
21x37in) London 1999
$712 - **€828** - **£500** - FF5 432
Shop in the Market Place, Tangiers Oil/panel
(15x23.5cm 5x9in) Billingshurst, West-Sussex 2001
$399 - €453 - **£280** - F£2 972
Curio Shop, Tangiers Watercolour/paper (35x34cm
14x13in) Leominster, Herefordshire 2001

HAIZMANN Richard 1895-1963 [17]
$7 921 - €9 203 - **£5 567** - FF60 370
Vogelwesen Bronze (37.5x27x34.5cm 14x10x13in)
Hamburg 2001
$1 760 - €2 045 - **£1 237** - FF13 415
Landschaft Aquarell, Gouache/Karton (48x60.5cm
18x23in) Hamburg 2001

HAJDU Étienne 1907-1996 [73]
$4 260 - €4 573 - **£2 800** - FF30 000
Composition Marbre (H34cm H13in) Paris 2000

HAJEK Otto Herbert 1927 [146]
$1 754 - €2 045 - **£1 230** - FF13 415
«Bildobjekt 88/3 K» Oil/panel (70x25x6cm
27x9x2in) Köln 2001
$1 066 - €920 - **£640** - FF6 034
Untitled Relief (17.7x26.5cm 6x10in) München 1998
$1 665 - €1 943 - **£1 169** - FF12 744
Ohne Titel Gouache (62.5x44cm 24x17in) Köln 2000
$144 - €143 - **£90** - FF939
Ohne Titel Lithographie (63.5x50cm 25x19in)
München 1999

HAJEK-HALKE Heinz 1898-1983 [152]
$514 - €613 - **£367** - FF4 024
«Wasserfloh» Heliogravure (39.8x29.9cm 15x11in)
München 2000
$700 - **€780** - **£490** - FF5 118
Nude Montage Silver print (34x24cm 13x9in) New-
York 2001

HAJOS Imre 1905-1977 [3]
$2 310 - €2 625 - **£1 610** - FF17 220
Nu à la guitare Huile/toile (68.5x56.5cm 26x22in)
Budapest 2001

HAKUHO Hirano 1879-1957 [5]
$1 300 - €1 250 - **£810** - FF8 197
Woman before a Mirror Print (40x28cm 15x11in)
New-York 1999

HALAPY János 1893-1960 [5]
$2 252 - €2 359 - **£1 425** - FF15 475
Kvinna vid soligt fönster Oil/canvas (100x75cm
39x29in) Malmö 2000

HALAUSKA Ludwig 1827-1892 [43]
$25 963 - €30 514 - **£18 000** - FF200 160
Abedlandschaft Mit Kirchenruine Oil/canvas
(100x143cm 39x56in) London 2000
$2 504 - €2 907 - **£1 760** - FF19 068
Blick auf den wolkenverhangenen Dachstein
Öl/Leinwand (56x68cm 22x26in) Wien 2001

HALBACH David 1931 [7]
$1 700 - €1 998 - **£1 178** - FF13 109
Windmills of Your Mind Watercolour, gouache/paper
(38x57cm 14x22in) Beverly-Hills CA 2000

HALBART Gustave 1846-1913 [15]
$1 062 - €891 - **£622** - FF5 846
Marine Huile/toile (44x65.5cm 17x25in) Liège 1998

HALBAX Michael c.1661-1711 [2]
$26 010 - €24 601 - **£16 200** - FF161 370
Simeon s Jeziskem Huile/toile (111x90cm 43x35in)
Praha 2000

HALBERG-KRAUSS Fritz 1874-1951 [265]
$2 595 - €2 504 - **£1 630** - FF16 428
Bauern bei der Feldarbeit Öl/Karton (50x68.5cm
19x26in) Zürich 1999
$1 217 - €1 431 - **£872** - FF9 390
Landschaft mit Personenstaffage Öl/Karton
(29x35cm 11x13in) München 2001

HALDANKAR Sawalaram Laxman 1882-1969 [10]
$2 390 - €2 566 - **£1 600** - FF16 834
Ancient Glory, Elephanta Caves Watercolour/paper
(38x56cm 14x22in) London 2000

HALDAR Asit Kumar 1890-1964 [7]
$3 980 - €3 854 - **£2 500** - FF25 281
Buddha Watercolour/paper (59x38.5cm 23x15in)
London 1999

HALDENWANG Christian 1770-1831 [17]
$128 - €153 - **£91** - FF1 006
Die heimkehrende Herde Copper engraving
(54.5x67.3cm 21x26in) Berlin 2000

HALDER Asit 1890-1964 [1]
$3 307 - €3 094 - **£2 000** - FF20 295
Mother and Child Watercolour/paper (28x33.5cm
11x13in) London 1999

HALE Edward Matthew 1852-1924 [13]
$9 453 - €8 595 - **£5 800** - FF56 381
The Sirens Oil/canvas (76x127cm 29x50in) London
1999

HALE Ellen Day 1855-1940 [12]
$1 350 - €1 541 - **£938** - FF10 107
Daisies Oil/canvas (60x45cm 24x18in) Cleveland OH
1999

HALE Kathleen 1898-? [3]
$3 615 - €3 436 - **£2 200** - FF22 537
Bloomsbury Rooftops Oil/board (41x32.5cm
16x12in) London 1999

HALE Lilian Westcott 1881-1963 [19]
$24 000 - €26 579 - **£16 276** - FF174 348
Agnes Dogget as a Bride Oil/canvas (76.5x63.5cm
30x25in) New-York 1999
$11 000 - €13 082 - **£7 839** - FF85 811
Yesterday, Rose Charcoal/paper (38x28cm 14x11in)
New-York 1999

HALE Philip Leslie 1865-1931 [27]
$14 000 - €13 387 - **£8 526** - FF87 812
**Portrait of Jeanette Farren seated and holding a
Fan** Oil/canvas (106.5x90.5cm 41x35in) Boston MA
1999
$2 500 - €2 331 - **£1 550** - FF15 291
Landscape with a Stream Oil/canvas (40.5x30.5cm
15x12in) New-York 1999

HALEMAN Thomas 1665-1706 **[2]**
- $10 067 - €9 529 - **£6 260** - FF62 508
  The Sacrifice of Manoah (Samson's Birth foretold) Oil/canvas (64x83.5cm 25x32in) Amsterdam 1999

HALEVY Aharon 1887-1957 **[1]**
- $4 000 - €4 147 - **£2 636** - FF27 204
  Olive grove Ink/paper (53.5x75cm 21x29in) Herzelia-Pituah 2000

HALEY John Charles 1905 **[1]**
- $1 700 - €1 565 - **£1 020** - FF10 263
  Golden Gate Avenue, Point Richmond
  Gouache/paper (35x48cm 14x19in) Pasadena CA 1999

HALFNIGHT Richard William 1855-1925 **[28]**
- $305 - €283 - **£190** - FF1 857
  Shepherd and Flock on a Country Lane
  Watercolour/paper (25x36cm 9x14in) Cheshire 1999

HALHED Harriet 1851-1933 **[5]**
- $3 302 - €3 894 - **£2 328** - FF25 545
  Portrait of a young Woman with Blossoms
  Oil/canvas (57x32cm 22x12in) Woollahra, Sydney 2001

HALICKA Alice 1895-1975 **[42]**
- $959 - €1 143 - **£684** - FF7 500
  Élégantes au bord de la mer Collage (44x34cm 17x13in) Paris 2000

HALIL PASA 1857-1937 **[7]**
- $29 811 - €28 965 - **£18 639** - FF190 000
  Portrait du Sultan Abdulmedjid Ier (1839-1861)
  Huile/toile (41x27cm 16x10in) Paris 1999

HALKETT François Jos.Clément 1856-1921 **[12]**
- $4 000 - €3 658 - **£2 442** - FF23 995
  The buffalo hunt Oil/canvas (59x99cm 23x39in) New-York 1998

HALL Charles XIX **[1]**
- $4 350 - €3 759 - **£2 581** - FF24 659
  View of the valley Oil/canvas (71x121cm 28x48in) Houston TX 1998

HALL Chenovet, Chenny 1908 **[2]**
- $2 250 - €1 941 - **£1 352** - FF12 733
  Between Tuscon and Nogales Watercolour/paper (36x46cm 14x18in) Santa-Fe NM 1998

HALL Christopher Compton 1930 **[19]**
- $391 - €386 - **£240** - FF2 530
  Rosebush, Dyfed Oil/board (20x39.5cm 7x15in) London 1999

HALL Clifford Eric Martin 1904-1973 **[367]**
- $796 - €688 - **£480** - FF4 514
  Listening to a Broadcast, Paris Oil/board (51x40.5cm 20x15in) Billingshurst, West-Sussex 1999
- $566 - €532 - **£350** - FF3 491
  Brixham, Morning Oil/board (24x16.5cm 9x6in) London 1999
- $250 - €245 - **£160** - FF1 604
  Seated Woman Crayon (35.5x25.5cm 13x10in) London 1999

HALL Frederick 1860-1948 **[103]**
- $8 033 - €7 735 - **£5 000** - FF50 740
  Returning from the Fields Oil/canvas (46x61cm 18x24in) London 1999
- $2 274 - €2 446 - **£1 550** - FF16 043
  Extensive Landscape with Corn stooks in a Field and a Village beyond Oil/board (31x39.5cm 12x15in) West-Yorkshire 2001

HALL Frederick Garrison 1879-1946 **[13]**
- $22 000 - €20 228 - **£13 587** - FF132 690
  «Beatrice», portrait of a lady with a guitar
  Oil/canvas (111x88cm 44x35in) Hampton-Falls NH 1998
- $500 - €558 - **£336** - FF3 657
  Scene in Tours Etching (31x20cm 12x8in) Portsmouth NH 2000

HALL George Henry 1825-1913 **[38]**
- $6 500 - €6 738 - **£4 121** - FF44 196
  Still Life with Holly and Fruit Oil/canvas (39.5x61cm 15x24in) New-York 2000
- $25 000 - €27 360 - **£17 245** - FF179 470
  Peaches and Grapes Oil/canvas (30.5x40.5cm 12x15in) New-York 2001

HALL George Lowthian 1825-1888 **[30]**
- $414 - €366 - **£250** - FF2 401
  The Wild Sea Watercolour/paper (54.5x101.5cm 21x39in) London 1998

HALL Gilbert XIX **[1]**
- $5 503 - €5 165 - **£3 400** - FF33 883
  Waiting for a Bite Oil/canvas (68.5x94cm 26x37in) Billinghurst, West-Sussex 1999

HALL H.R. XIX-XX **[35]**
- $963 - €911 - **£600** - FF5 975
  Highland Cattle, Loch Linnhe Oil/canvas (62x52cm 24x20in) London 1999

HALL Harry 1814-1882 **[102]**
- $35 000 - €40 665 - **£24 598** - FF266 742
  Mr.F.L.Popham's Wild Dayrell with Robert Sherwood up and Mr.Rickaby Oil/canvas (120.5x151cm 47x59in) New-York 2001
- $5 500 - €4 764 - **£3 373** - FF31 248
  Bay Racehorse, the Property of Lord Anglesey, with Tom Cannon Up Oil/canvas (58.5x76cm 23x29in) New-York 1999

HALL Kenneth 1913-1946 **[11]**
- $7 746 - €7 274 - **£4 800** - FF47 713
  Portrait of Lucy Wertheim Oil/canvas (76x51cm 29x20in) London 1999
- $2 129 - €2 286 - **£1 424** - FF14 992
  Irish Island Village Oil/canvas (25x48cm 9x18in) Dublin 2000
- $449 - €483 - **£306** - FF3 165
  Still life Watercolour (24x18cm 9x7in) Dublin 2001

HALL Lida XX **[2]**
- $1 600 - €1 823 - **£1 105** - FF11 956
  Life in the Recreational Hot Spot Silver print (10x7cm 4x3in) New-York 2000

HALL Lindsay Bernard 1859-1935 **[22]**
- $18 880 - €20 802 - **£12 675** - FF136 451
  In the Studio Oil/canvas (105.5x81cm 41x31in) Malvern, Victoria 2000
- $1 563 - €1 859 - **£1 113** - FF12 192
  Flinders Pastoral Oil/board (40x29.5cm 15x11in) Melbourne 2000

HALL Norma Bassett 1889-1957 **[12]**
- $350 - €407 - **£246** - FF2 667
  Drying Chile Print in colors (20x25cm 8x10in) Cincinnati OH 2001

HALL Oliver 1869-1957 **[68]**
- $381 - €410 - **£260** - FF2 691
  Grey Stems, Winter Sunshine Overlooking Easington Fell Oil/board (35x46cm 13x18in) West-Yorkshire 2001

H

$531 - €586 - **£360** - FF3 845
Study of Tree near Egdean/Road to Orton, Westmorland Oil/canvas (33x46cm 12x18in) London 2000

$224 - €241 - **£150** - FF1 578
Middleham Castle & Village, Coverdale Yorks Etching (15x22.5cm 5x8in) London 2000

HALL Patrick 1906-1992 [27]
$437 - €497 - **£300** - FF3 261
Le Crotoy-Somme Watercolour/paper (43.5x76cm 17x29in) London 2000

HALL Peter Adolf 1739-1793 [34]
$11 004 - €10 671 - **£6 923** - FF70 000
Portrait de jeune homme au tricorne Huile/panneau (20x17cm 7x6in) Paris 1999

HALL Thomas P. c.1810-c.1870 [16]
$6 690 - €6 963 - **£4 200** - FF45 673
Young Love Oil/canvas (76.5x63.5cm 30x25in) London 2000

$3 138 - €3 368 - **£2 100** - FF22 095
Tryst Oil/canvas (30x38cm 11x14in) London 2000

HALL-NEALE Maud c.1870-1950 [24]
$4 964 - €5 762 - **£3 500** - FF37 799
Portrait of Mrs Bryce Smith Oil/canvas (117x89cm 46x35in) London 2001

$992 - €1 152 - **£700** - FF7 559
A moorland stream Oil/panel (23.5x32.5cm 9x12in) London 2001

HALLAM Joseph Sydney 1889-1953 [25]
$512 - €495 - **£315** - FF3 250
Penn Rapids (Algonquin Park) Oil/canvas (25.5x30.5cm 10x12in) Toronto 1999

HALLATZ Emil 1837-1888 [8]
$4 982 - €4 877 - **£3 065** - FF31 992
Kaksi hevosta ja ajuri Oil/canvas (95x120cm 37x47in) Helsinki 1999

HALLÉ Charles Edward 1846-1919 [21]
$9 713 - €10 426 - **£6 500** - FF68 390
The Tempter Oil/canvas (152.5x91.5cm 60x36in) London 2000

HALLÉ Claude Guy 1652-1736 [8]
$6 075 - €5 183 - **£3 665** - FF34 000
Descente de croix Huile/toile (46x37.5cm 18x14in) Paris 1998

$4 078 - €3 982 - **£2 600** - FF26 119
Adonis resting with his Dog Black chalk (9x7.5cm 3x2in) London 1999

HALLÉ Noël 1711-1781 [28]
$139 819 - €135 680 - **£88 110** - FF890 000
La Sainte Famille Huile/toile (64x48cm 25x18in) Paris 1999

$3 580 - €3 964 - **£2 428** - FF26 000
La Charité Huile/papier/toile (17x33.5cm 6x13in) Paris 1999

$17 408 - €19 513 - **£12 185** - FF128 000
Portrait d'homme barbu Pastel/papier (43.5x32cm 17x12in) Paris 2001

HALLE Samuel Baruch Ludwig 1824-1889 [12]
$1 138 - €1 051 - **£700** - FF6 892
Doorway Companions Oil/board (28x23cm 11x9in) London 1999

HALLE William 1912 [5]
$1 085 - €1 172 - **£750** - FF7 687
Kennington Street Oil/canvas (63.5x76cm 25x29in) London 2001

HALLENGREN Manne, Aug. Emanuel 1875-? [9]
$7 768 - €8 827 - **£5 456** - FF57 904
De Badande Wännernas paviljong i Visby Oil/canvas (72x91cm 28x35in) Stockholm 2001

HALLENSLEBEN Ruth 1898-1977 [98]
$1 141 - €1 278 - **£793** - FF8 384
«Kokereianlage» Vintage gelatin silver print (21x17cm 8x6in) Köln 2001

HALLER Hermann 1880-1950 [26]
$11 665 - €13 873 - **£8 313** - FF91 003
Jüngling Bronze (H97cm H38in) Zürich 2000

$1 436 - €1 383 - **£898** - FF9 074
Sitzender Akt Terracotta (H36.5cm H14in) Zürich 1999

HALLER VON HALLERSTEIN Christoph 1771-1839 [12]
$242 - €240 - **£151** - FF1 577
Junge Frau in Tracht mit Tuch Watercolour (18.5x12.5cm 7x4in) München 1999

$264 - €230 - **£159** - FF1 508
«Manara» Radierung (27x19.2cm 10x7in) Berlin 1998

HALLET André 1890-1959 [217]
$5 486 - €6 445 - **£3 952** - FF42 276
Fêtes rituelles dans un village africain Huile/toile (100x160cm 39x62in) Bruxelles 2001

$1 917 - €1 609 - **£1 124** - FF10 556
Bord de fleuve en Afrique Huile/toile (70x79cm 27x31in) Liège 1998

$231 - €248 - **£157** - FF1 626
Paysage à Heikant Huile/carton (28x36.5cm 11x14in) Bruxelles 2001

HALLETT Hendricks A. 1847-1921 [31]
$12 000 - €12 452 - **£7 612** - FF81 680
Schooners and Sailing Vessels Along an Animated Coastline Oil/canvas (72.5x101.5cm 28x39in) Boston MA 2000

$575 - €488 - **£343** - FF3 198
Portrait of a Three Masted Schooner in Rough Seas Watercolour/paper (48x73cm 19x29in) South-Natick MA 1998

HALLEY Peter 1953 [62]
$52 500 - €59 390 - **£36 729** - FF389 576
«Yellow Cell with Conduit» Acrylic (153.5x114.5cm 60x45in) New-York 2001

$2 092 - €2 246 - **£1 400** - FF14 730
Untitled Acrylic (43x54.5cm 16x21in) London 2000

$2 000 - €1 706 - **£1 206** - FF11 192
Untitled Mixed media/paper (54.5x43cm 21x16in) New-York 1998

HALLMARK George 1949 [1]
$17 000 - €19 303 - **£11 811** - FF126 617
Ochenta Oil/canvas (91x121cm 36x48in) Dallas TX 2001

HALLOWELL George Hawley 1871-1926 [19]
$4 250 - €4 064 - **£2 588** - FF26 660
Clouds off the Dalmatian Coast Watercolour/paper (31.5x23.5cm 12x9in) Boston MA 1999

HALLSTRÖM Björn 1916-1982 [18]
$775 - €922 - **£552** - FF6 047
Ingefärskruka och kaffekanna - stilleben Oil/canvas (80x65cm 31x25in) Stockholm 2000

HALLSTRÖM Carl 1850-1929 [12]
$4 806 - €5 382 - **£3 337** - FF35 302
Månsken Oil/canvas (84.5x134cm 33x52in) Helsinki 2001

HALLSTRÖM Eric 1893-1946 **[258]**
- **$1 666** - €1 562 - **£1 030** - FF10 249
  Pojke med kärra (Höst) Oil/panel (45.5x55cm 17x21in) Stockholm 1999
- **$622** - €690 - **£422** - FF4 528
  Flicka med rutig klänning Mixed media (31.5x22.5cm 12x8in) Stockholm 2000
- **$1 564** - €1 319 - **£928** - FF8 652
  Kvinna vid byrå Gouache/paper (75x98cm 29x38in) Stockholm 1998

HALLSTRÖM Staffan 1914-1976 **[219]**
- **$3 600** - €3 496 - **£2 223** - FF22 929
  Arkbusering Oil/canvas (104x116cm 40x45in) Stockholm 1999
- **$1 904** - €1 786 - **£1 177** - FF11 713
  Ingens Hundar Mixed media (47x54cm 18x21in) Stockholm 1999
- **$544** - €557 - **£336** - FF3 656
  Badstenen Oil/canvas (28x40cm 11x15in) Stockholm 2000
- **$712** - €674 - **£442** - FF4 422
  Säby-udd Akvarell/papper (26x40cm 10x15in) Stockholm 1999
- **$370** - €402 - **£234** - FF2 639
  Ingens hundar Color lithograph (45x52cm 17x20in) Stockholm 2000

HALM von Peter 1854-1923 **[75]**
- **$73** - €77 - **£46** - FF503
  Von der Reichenau, Blick durch ein geöffnetes Fenster Radierung (25x14.5cm 9x5in) Heidelberg 2000

HALMI Artur Lajos 1866-1939 **[12]**
- **$702** - €654 - **£436** - FF4 290
  Gemeinsame Ministerkonferenz unter dem Vorsitz des Kaisers Pencil/paper (39x28cm 15x11in) Wien 1999

HALONEN Emil 1875-1950 **[19]**
- **$1 731** - €1 685 - **£1 065** - FF11 051
  Två flickor Bronze (H45.5cm H17in) Stockholm 1999

HALONEN Pekka 1865-1933 **[144]**
- **$14 983** - €13 115 - **£9 079** - FF86 026
  Insjölandskap Oil/canvas (80x48cm 31x18in) Helsinki 1998
- **$4 745** - €4 205 - **£2 910** - FF27 580
  Bod Oil/canvas (34x30cm 13x11in) Helsinki 1999

HALPERT Samuel T. 1884-1930 **[12]**
- **$7 000** - €7 948 - **£4 790** - FF52 138
  Still Life with Fruit with View of Street from Window Oil/canvas (45.5x38cm 17x14in) New-York 2000

HALS Dirck 1591-1656 **[45]**
- **$100 860** - €98 791 - **£65 000** - FF648 024
  Elegant company at Table in an interior Oil/panel (33x53cm 12x20in) London 1999
- **$12 978** - €13 081 - **£8 100** - FF85 806
  Elegante Gesellschaft mit einem Musikanten in einem Wirtshaus Oil/panel (24x32cm 9x12in) Wien 2000

HALS Frans I 1582/85-1666 **[10]**
- **$3 112 800** - €3 059 835 - **£2 000 000** - FF20 071 200
  Gentleman, in a black Hat, his Gloves in his left Hand Oil/canvas (108x79.5cm 42x31in) London 1999

HALS Harmen 1611-1669 **[13]**
- **$5 060** - €5 892 - **£3 500** - FF38 651
  Study of an Old Man with a Skull Oil/panel (47.5x35cm 18x13in) London 2000

- **$4 456** - €4 991 - **£3 096** - FF32 742
  The School Master Oil/panel (33.5x27.5cm 13x10in) Amsterdam 2001

HALS Johannes c.1620-? **[4]**
- **$24 105** - €23 910 - **£15 000** - FF156 837
  Young Peasant Woman, in a brown Dress and a white Cap Oil/panel (32.5x26cm 12x10in) London 1999

HALSALL William Formby 1841-1919 **[24]**
- **$3 800** - €3 639 - **£2 341** - FF23 869
  Entering Boston Harbor with Pilot Boat Oil/canvas (50x76cm 20x30in) Portsmouth NH 1999
- **$2 300** - €1 970 - **£1 382** - FF12 925
  Ships at Sea Oil/panel (17x27cm 7x11in) Dedham MA 1998

HALSE George XIX-XX **[4]**
- **$5 062** - €5 385 - **£3 200** - FF35 321
  Young Girl with a Theatrical Mask Marble (H60cm H23in) London 2000

HALSEY William Melton 1915 **[2]**
- **$1 000** - €927 - **£621** - FF6 080
  «Houses and Minaret, Rhodes, Greece» Gouache/paper (49x65cm 19x25in) New-Orleans LA 1999

HALSMAN Philippe 1906-1979 **[341]**
- **$951** - €941 - **£593** - FF6 171
  Walter W.Frese, aus der Serie Jump Pictures Vintage gelatin silver print (25.3x20.2cm 9x7in) Berlin 1999

HALSTEAD Elizabeth XX **[3]**
- **$3 206** - €3 029 - **£2 000** - FF19 866
  On the Moors in Winter/Minding the Herd Oil/board (65x94cm 25x37in) Perthshire 1999

HALSWELLE Keeley 1832-1891 **[74]**
- **$4 010** - €4 041 - **£2 500** - FF26 509
  Near the Gravel Pit, Suffolk Oil/canvas (35.5x61cm 13x24in) London 2000
- **$1 775** - €1 667 - **£1 100** - FF10 934
  Siesta, Grotta Ferrata Watercolour (10.5x18.5cm 4x7in) London 1999

HÄLSZEL Johann Baptist 1710/12-1777 **[7]**
- **$13 078** - €10 743 - **£7 595** - FF70 469
  Bunter Blumenstrauss in gläsernerm godronierter Vase Öl/Kupfer (47x38cm 18x14in) Berlin 1998

HALTER Jean H. XX **[5]**
- **$5 700** - €6 423 - **£3 947** - FF42 134
  Winter Village Scene with Figures and Train in background Oil/canvas (45x60cm 18x24in) Hatfield PA 2000
- **$4 000** - €4 508 - **£2 770** - FF29 568
  «Lamberville» Oil/masonite (30x40cm 12x16in) Hatfield PA 2000

HALTIA Kaarlo 1863-1938 **[1]**
- **$26 892** - €30 273 - **£18 522** - FF198 576
  Aino Bronze (H128cm H50in) Helsinki 2000

HAMADA Shoji 1894-1978 **[42]**
- **$8 000** - €8 932 - **£5 347** - FF58 588
  Untitled Ceramic (H16.5cm H6in) New-York 2000

HAMAGUCHI Yozo 1909-2000 **[232]**
- **$3 831** - €3 232 - **£2 247** - FF21 203
  14 Kirschen Etching, aquatint in colors (52.3x31.2cm 20x12in) Berlin 1998

HÄMÄLÄINEN Väinö 1876-1940 **[92]**

🐦 **$2 306** - €2 186 - **£1 402** - FF14 341
Roddare på sjön Oil/canvas (65.5x50.5cm 25x19in) Helsinki 1999

✏️ **$189** - €202 - **£128** - FF1 323
Oihonna i södra hamnen Pencil/paper (14x24cm 5x9in) Helsinki 2001

HAMANAKA XX **[1]**

🗿 **$22 864** - €24 392 - **£14 480** - FF160 000
Vénus Sculpture bois (H135.5cm H53in) Paris 2000

HAMBACH Johann Michael XVII **[8]**

🐦 **$32 000** - €31 455 - **£20 560** - FF206 329
Still Life of Bread, Cheese and Butter on a Table Oil/canvas (59.5x79.5cm 23x31in) New-York 1999

HAMBLEN Sturtevant J. XIX **[2]**

🐦 **$60 000** - €59 448 - **£36 402** - FF389 952
Portrait of a Child in Blue Posed with a Black and White Dog Oil/canvas (64x54cm 25x21in) New-York 2000

HAMBLETT Theora 1895-1977 **[5]**

🐦 **$5 500** - €5 241 - **£3 486** - FF34 379
Figures among Trees Oil/canvas (40x50cm 16x20in) New-Orleans LA 1999

HAMBLING Maggie 1945 **[36]**

🐦 **$1 120** - €1 310 - **£800** - FF8 591
«Kensal Rises» Oil/canvas (53.5x43cm 21x16in) London 2001

✏️ **$822** - €883 - **£550** - FF5 793
Study for Fife: Max Looking Up Charcoal/paper (50x38.5cm 19x15in) London 2000

HAMBOURG André 1909-1999 **[702]**

🐦 **$8 971** - €8 690 - **£5 643** - FF57 000
Les tentes sur la plage de Trouville Huile/toile (60x73cm 23x28in) Paris 1999

🐦 **$4 219** - €4 726 - **£2 957** - FF31 000
«La corbeille de raisins» Huile/toile (12x22cm 4x8in) Paris 2001

✏️ **$907** - €1 067 - **£650** - FF7 000
Embarcation au large de Deauville Encre Chine (28x26cm 11x10in) Paris 2001

🗂️ **$153** - €183 - **£109** - FF1 200
Les bateaux de pêche Lithographie couleurs (31x49cm 12x19in) Paris 2000

HAMBRESIN Albert 1850-1938 **[12]**

🗿 **$1 112** - €1 289 - **£790** - FF8 455
Buste de jeune femme Bronze (H70cm H27in) Bruxelles 2001

HAMBRIDGE Jay 1867-1924 **[7]**

🐦 **$3 500** - €3 248 - **£2 101** - FF21 306
Afternoon Reading Oil/canvas/board (35x27cm 14x11in) Milford CT 1999

✏️ **$1 800** - €2 098 - **£1 286** - FF13 763
New York Street Children Dancing to the Music of a Barrel Organ Gouache/paper (84x51cm 33x20in) New-York 2000

HAMBÜCHEN Georg 1901-1971 **[26]**

🐦 **$714** - €767 - **£478** - FF5 030
Segelschiffe im Hafen Öl/Leinwand (40x60cm 15x23in) München 2000

HAMBÜCHEN Wilhelm 1869-1939 **[73]**

🐦 **$1 711** - €1 636 - **£1 041** - FF10 732
Strandszene mit anlegenden Schiffen und einem Pferdefuhrwerk Öl/Leinwand (61x81cm 24x31in) Bielefeld 1999

HAMEL Jack 1890-1951 **[20]**

🐦 **$3 171** - €3 403 - **£2 121** - FF22 324
Portrait of Amerigio Martinucci Oil/canvas (81x65cm 31x25in) Amsterdam 2000

HAMEL Otto 1886-1950 **[98]**

🐦 **$1 000** - €853 - **£602** - FF5 596
San Marco Cathedral, Venice Oil/canvas (60x81cm 24x32in) Norwalk CT 1999

🐦 **$285** - €307 - **£191** - FF2 012
Holländischer Hafen mit Fischerbooten Öl/Karton (21.5x27.5cm 8x10in) München 2000

HAMEL Théophile 1817-1870 **[8]**

🐦 **$5 462** - €5 286 - **£3 368** - FF34 671
Portrait of George Edward Aird Oil/canvas (76x63.5cm 29x25in) Toronto 1999

HAMEN Y LEON van der Juan 1596-c.1632 **[17]**

🐦 **$236 600** - €253 774 - **£156 325** - FF1 664 650
San Juan Bautista en oración Oleo/lienzo (184x143.5cm 72x56in) Madrid 2000

🐦 **$120 000** - €124 398 - **£72 000** - FF816 000
Limoni, melagrane e pere in una frutteria di porcellana Olio/tela/tavola (44x61cm 17x24in) Venezia 1999

🐦 **$151 200** - €168 182 - **£100 800** - FF1 103 200
Bodegón con membrillo, granada y frutas confitadas Oleo/lienzo (20x32cm 7x12in) Madrid 2000

HAMILTON Ann 1956 **[5]**

🗿 **$24 000** - €27 847 - **£16 569** - FF182 664
Untitled (Hair Collar) Sculpture (18x51x51cm 7x20x20in) New-York 2000

📷 **$10 000** - €11 603 - **£6 904** - FF76 110
Untitled (The Body Object Series) #4 Gelatin silver print (58x53cm 22x20in) New-York 2000

HAMILTON Charles act.1831-1867 **[5]**

🐦 **$4 184** - €4 491 - **£2 800** - FF29 460
An Arab Horseman Holding a Falcon Oil/board (50x61cm 19x24in) London 2000

HAMILTON de Carl Wilhelm 1668-1754 **[20]**

🐦 **$5 746** - €6 425 - **£4 000** - FF42 142
Birds, a Lizard, a red Snake, a white Butterfly and a Wasp among Oil/canvas (54.5x42.5cm 21x16in) London 2001

🐦 **$7 204** - €6 681 - **£4 400** - FF43 824
A Still Life of a Snake, a Snail, a Toad and a Butterfly Oil/panel (34.5x24cm 13x9in) London 1998

HAMILTON de Franz XVII **[5]**

🐦 **$15 000** - €13 886 - **£9 055** - FF91 087
Trompe l'oeil Still Lifes: Game Birds Oil/canvas (43x35cm 16x13in) New-York 1999

HAMILTON de Johann Georg 1672-1737 **[22]**

🐦 **$67 674** - €66 461 - **£42 000** - FF435 955
Soldier Leading a Grey Stallion by the Reins Oil/canvas (41x58.5cm 16x23in) London 1999

🐦 **$756** - €6 098 - **£4 164** - FF40 000
Le chien surveillant le trophée de chasse Huile/toile (27x34.5cm 10x13in) Paris 1999

HAMILTON de Philipp Ferdinand 1664-1750 **[28]**

🐦 **$26 840** - €30 490 - **£18 780** - FF200 000
Volatiles, singes et chiens dans un paysage Huile/toile (127x166cm 50x65in) Paris 2001

🐦 **$16 680** - €18 294 - **£11 328** - FF120 000
Perroquet, poules, faisans et singe dans un paysage Huile/toile (72x91cm 28x35in) Poitiers 2000

$80 000 - €80 931 - **£48 848** - FF530 872
Two Female Snowy Owls in a Mountainous Landscape Oil/paper/canvas (23x30cm 9x11in) New-York 2000

HAMILTON Eva Henrietta 1876-1960 [23]
$8 159 - €9 123 - **£5 500** - FF59 844
Harvesting in Mayo Oil/board (38x46cm 14x18in) London 2000
$7 417 - €8 294 - **£5 000** - FF54 404
The Flower Pickers Oil/panel (24.5x34cm 9x13in) London 2000

HAMILTON Gavin 1723-1798 [7]
$4 061 - €3 952 - **£2 500** - FF25 922
The Muse of Painting Oil/canvas (72x59.5cm 28x23in) London 1999

HAMILTON Gawen 1697-1737 [6]
$85 921 - €84 088 - **£55 000** - FF551 578
The Norris Family Conversation Piece Oil/canvas (61.5x74.5cm 24x29in) London 1999

HAMILTON George 1812-1883 [21]
$3 212 - €3 539 - **£2 132** - FF23 214
Overlanders Crossing Cattle over the Murray in the Year Pencil (17.5x27cm 6x10in) Woollahra, Sydney 2000

HAMILTON Hamilton 1847-1928 [34]
$6 500 - €7 771 - **£4 483** - FF50 973
Haystacks Oil/canvas (50x60cm 20x24in) Milford CT 2000
$18 000 - €21 007 - **£12 760** - FF137 800
Gust of Wind Oil/canvas (51x30.5cm 20x12in) New-York 2001

HAMILTON Helen 1889-1970 [4]
$4 500 - €5 380 - **£3 104** - FF35 289
Whitecaps on the Coast of Maine Oil/canvas (64x81cm 25x32in) Milford CT 2000

HAMILTON Hugh Douglas 1739-1808 [66]
$23 434 - €20 230 - **£14 000** - FF132 701
Elizabeth Bridgetta Stepney, Mrs Gulston Oil/canvas (147x144.5cm 57x56in) Llandeilo, Carmarthenshire 1998
$3 201 - €3 035 - **£2 000** - FF19 906
Portrait of a Gentleman of the Armstrong Family of Kisharvan Oil/canvas (74.5x61.5cm 29x24in) London 1999
$7 225 - €7 927 - **£4 800** - FF51 998
Portrait Mrs Playford, Bust-length/Portrait of Mr Playford Pastel/paper (23.5x19cm 9x7in) London 2000

HAMILTON James 1819-1878 [35]
$3 100 - €2 964 - **£1 887** - FF19 444
Ship in Rough Seas Oil/canvas (61x91.5cm 24x36in) Boston MA 1999

HAMILTON James Whitelaw 1860-1932 [36]
$2 639 - €2 845 - **£1 800** - FF18 659
Wharfdale Oil/canvas (63.5x77cm 25x30in) London 2001
$947 - €993 - **£600** - FF6 511
Early Spring Oil/board (26x34cm 10x13in) Edinburgh 2000

HAMILTON Letitia Marion 1878-1964 [160]
$11 964 - €11 428 - **£7 456** - FF74 961
Bantry Bay with a Sailing Boat Oil/canvas (50x60cm 19x23in) Dublin 1999
$7 446 - €6 352 - **£4 437** - FF41 666
The Reaper and the Binder Oil/board (32.5x35cm 12x13in) Dublin 1998

$3 990 - €4 698 - **£2 803** - FF30 817
La Charité-sur-Loire Watercolour/paper (42.5x53cm 16x20in) Dublin 2000

HAMILTON Mary Riter 1873-1954 [11]
$2 048 - €1 982 - **£1 263** - FF13 001
Market Scene Oil/paper/board (25x35cm 9x13in) Toronto 1999

HAMILTON Richard 1922 [227]
$149 688 - €125 731 - **£88 000** - FF824 744
Glorious Techniculture (Hers is a Lush Situation III) Mixed media (123x122.5cm 48x48in) London 1998
$2 000 - €1 986 - **£1 240** - FF13 030
Follow the Crowd Mixed media/paper (58x73cm 23x29in) Norwalk CT 2000
$926 - €933 - **£577** - FF6 123
Interiör Etching, aquatint (53x41.5cm 20x16in) Stockholm 2000
$993 - €926 - **£600** - FF6 073
Bathers Dye-transfer print (40x54.5cm 15x21in) London 1998

HAMILTON Vereker Monteith 1856-1931 [1]
$8 004 - €9 570 - **£5 500** - FF62 772
Les Sylphides Oil/canvas (100x150.5cm 39x59in) Billingshurst, West-Sussex 2000

HAMILTON William Osborne 1751-1801 [36]
$12 913 - €11 954 - **£8 000** - FF78 415
Lord Burleigh's Courtship Oil/canvas (30x25cm 11x9in) London 1999
$3 518 - €3 388 - **£2 200** - FF22 222
Winter Amusement/Summer Amusement/Children playing Hoop/Children Watercolour (16x20cm 6x7in) London 1999

HAMLET-GRIFFIT Charles 1848-? [2]
$2 800 - €3 213 - **£1 915** - FF21 073
Shoreline with Fishing Boats Oil/canvas (48x99cm 19x39in) Cleveland OH 2000

HAMM Eugen 1885-1930 [14]
$1 014 - €1 022 - **£632** - FF6 707
Portrait der Elisabeth Hengst, geborene Hentschel Pastell/Papier (32x28cm 12x11in) Frankfurt 2000

HAMM Manfred 1944 [15]
$547 - €647 - **£388** - FF4 242
«Fred Thieler in seinem Atelier in Berlin-Schöneberg» Gelatin silver print (23.5x29.5cm 9x11in) Berlin 2001

HAMMAD Mahmoud 1923-1988 [1]
$3 580 - €4 027 - **£2 500** - FF26 417
Mosque Oil/canvas (43x33cm 16x12in) London 2001

HAMMAN Édouard J. Conrad 1819-1888 [25]
$15 822 - €15 264 - **£10 000** - FF100 125
On the Beach Oil/panel (48x60cm 18x23in) London 1999
$2 406 - €2 304 - **£1 671** - FF17 500
Promeneuses au jardin Huile/panneau (32.5x24cm 12x9in) Soissons 2001
$580 - €610 - **£364** - FF4 000
Portrait en pied d'un homme appuyé sur un cla-vecin Fusain (62.5x34.5cm 24x13in) Paris 2000

HAMMAN Edouard Michel F. XIX-XX [13]
$1 113 - €935 - **£654** - FF6 132
«Le repos sous bois» Öl/Leinwand (61.5x46cm 24x18in) Bern 1998

HAMME van Alexis 1818-1875 **[39]**
- **$16 205** - €13 611 - **£9 500** - FF89 285
  An elegant Compagny Oil/panel (71x57cm 27x22in)
  London 1998

HAMME-VOITUS von Peter 1880-1936 **[6]**
- **$1 398** - €1 308 - **£846** - FF8 580
  Jagdstilleben Öl/Leinwand (70.5x57cm 27x22in)
  Wien 1999

HAMMEE van Antoine 1836-1903 **[3]**
- **$3 349** - €3 857 - **£2 286** - FF25 301
  Une cour de palais dans l'ancienne Rome
  Oil/panel (38x53cm 14x20in) Amsterdam 2000

HAMMER Christian Gottlob 1779-1864 **[23]**
- **$428** - €460 - **£286** - FF3 018
  Teich im Wald Ink (30.4x25.3cm 11x9in) Hamburg
  2000
- **$981** - €1 099 - **£682** - FF7 208
  Vue du Kreml et de ses environs à Moscau
  Etching (43x54cm 16x21in) Uppsala 2001

HAMMER William 1821-1889 **[34]**
- **$60 000** - €57 222 - **£36 522** - FF375 354
  Fruits of the Garden and Field Oil/canvas
  (223x168.5cm 87x66in) New-York 1999
- **$1 875** - €2 011 - **£1 278** - FF13 194
  **Kurv med ananas, druer og blommer på en
  karm** Oil/canvas (23x26cm 9x10in) København 2001

HAMMERSCHMIDT Wilhelm act.c.1855-c.1872 **[17]**
- **$471** - €562 - **£336** - FF3 689
  **Temple de Mouth à Karnak, Statues de la
  Déesse Pacht** Albumen print (23.6x31.3cm 9x12in)
  Berlin 2000

HAMMERSHØI Svend 1873-1948 **[111]**
- **$1 140** - €1 077 - **£708** - FF7 064
  Udstrakt landskab Oil/canvas (64x82cm 25x32in)
  København 1999
- **$474** - €470 - **£282** - FF3 085
  Landskab med ruin antagelig Koldinghus
  Oil/canvas (38x32cm 14x12in) Vejle 2000

HAMMERSHØI Vilhelm 1864-1916 **[93]**
- **$66 640** - €75 050 - **£45 920** - FF492 296
  Landskab Oil/canvas (38x46cm 14x18in) København
  2000
- **$8 691** - €7 515 - **£5 168** - FF49 296
  Selvportraet Oil/canvas (33x28cm 12x11in)
  København 1998
- **$882** - €938 - **£591** - FF6 153
  Portraet af Stine Kramer fra Thisted Pencil/paper
  (31x28cm 12x11in) Viby J, Århus 2001

HAMMICK Jeremy 1956 **[13]**
- **$1 362** - €1 133 - **£800** - FF7 435
  In the Bush Watercolour/paper (38x76cm 14x29in)
  London 1998

HAMMOND Arthur J. 1875-1947 **[26]**
- **$800** - €881 - **£533** - FF5 781
  Church of the Sacred Heart, Paris Oil/board
  (16x23cm 6x9in) Portsmouth NH 2000

HAMMOND Aubrey 1893-? **[2]**
- **$1 200** - €1 339 - **£785** - FF8 781
  «The Daily Mirror, International Fashion Fair»
  Poster (76x50cm 29x19in) New-York 2000

HAMMOND Bill 1947 **[12]**
- **$36 279** - €40 665 - **£25 371** - FF266 742
  The Quik and the Ded Oil/panel (200x160cm
  78x62in) Auckland 2001

- **$5 172** - €6 075 - **£3 672** - FF39 850
  Pack of Five Oil/panel (75x52.5cm 29x20in)
  Auckland 2000
- **$4 256** - €4 423 - **£2 669** - FF29 014
  **«It's a Frame of Mind That You're In, It's a
  Frame,...(Lingr Lewis)»** Enamel (40.5x32cm
  15x12in) Auckland 2000
- **$586** - €616 - **£386** - FF4 041
  The Greeting Indian ink/paper (51x79cm 20x31in)
  Auckland 2000
- **$564** - €633 - **£394** - FF4 149
  Untitled Lithograph (56.5x75cm 22x29in) Auckland
  2001

HAMMOND Gertrude E. Demain 1862-1953 **[16]**
- **$1 337** - €1 142 - **£800** - FF7 490
  Harmony Watercolour (38x42cm 14x16in) London
  1998

HAMMOND Horace XIX-XX **[20]**
- **$678** - €631 - **£420** - FF4 138
  Figure and Cattle outside «The Bell Inn»
  Watercolour/paper (16x23cm 6x9in) Birmingham 1999

HAMMOND Jane 1950 **[8]**
- **$2 000** - €2 194 - **£1 290** - FF14 391
  Untitled Monotype (72.5x81.5cm 28x32in) New-York
  2000

HAMMOND John A. 1843-1939 **[99]**
- **$1 365** - €1 321 - **£842** - FF8 667
  Venice with Fishing Boats Oil/panel (33x48.5cm
  12x19in) Toronto 1999
- **$885** - €851 - **£545** - FF5 582
  Falls in B.C Oil/board (21.5x34cm 8x13in) Vancouver,
  BC. 1999

HAMMOND Robert John ?-1911 **[61]**
- **$4 243** - €4 028 - **£2 600** - FF26 424
  Spring Time Oil/canvas (40.5x61cm 15x24in) London
  1999
- **$1 269** - €1 424 - **£880** - FF9 343
  Watching the Ducks Oil/canvas (18x25.5cm 7x10in)
  London 2000

HAMMONS David 1943 **[9]**
- **$4 000** - €4 320 - **£2 764** - FF28 335
  Rage and Requiem Mixed media (101.5x76cm
  39x29in) New-York 2001
- **$409 500** - €458 670 - **£284 520** - FF3 008 678
  Untitled Installation (137x152.5x40.5cm 53x60x15in)
  New-York 2001
- **$16 000** - €15 481 - **£9 867** - FF101 550
  Untitled (Speakers) Accumulation (57x43x38cm
  22x16x14in) New-York 1999
- **$24 000** - €26 882 - **£16 675** - FF176 332
  «Puzzling Times» Pastel/paper (61x51cm 24x20in)
  New-York 2001

HAMNETT Nina 1890-1956 **[14]**
- **$525** - €501 - **£320** - FF3 288
  Figures By The Bar, Douarnenez Pencil/paper
  (25x28cm 9x11in) London 1999

HAMON-DUPLESSIS Michel act.1791-1799 **[39]**
- **$15 565** - €15 550 - **£9 730** - FF102 000
  Cavaliers et paysans dans la cour de la ferme
  Huile/panneau (44x58cm 17x22in) Paris 1999
- **$3 489** - €3 964 - **£2 441** - FF25 660
  Scène de port animé de cavaliers Huile/panneau
  (24x32cm 9x12in) Paris 2001

HAMONET Louis XX **[20]**
- **$205** - €244 - **£146** - FF1 600
  Abri côtier et bord de mer, Erquy Aquarelle/papier
  (41x23cm 16x9in) Brest 2000

HAMPE Guido 1839-1902 **[80]**
- $1 500 - €1 687 - **£1 047** - FF11 067
  Widelandschaft mit Gehöft Öl/Leinwand
  (68x98.5cm 26x38in) Lindau 2001
- $1 133 - €1 125 - **£708** - FF7 378
  Bauernhaus an Gebirgsbach Oil/panel (26.5x35cm
  10x13in) München 1999

HAMPEL Angela 1956 **[25]**
- $84 - €102 - £59 -FF670
  Ohne Titel (Paar) Lithographie (42.5x56cm 16x22in)
  Berlin 2000

HAMPEL Sigmund Walter 1868-1949 **[56]**
- $1 572 - €1 817 - **£1 100** - FF11 917
  «Tanzszene» Mischtechnik (49x47cm 19x18in) Linz
  2001
- $976 - €1 022 - **£645** - FF6 707
  Frauengruppe am Schlossteich Watercolour,
  gouache (40.5x31.5cm 15x12in) München 2000

HAMPSHIRE Ernest Llewellyn 1882-? **[18]**
- $8 187 - €6 877 - **£4 800** -FF45 112
  Gathering Bluebells in the Woods Oil/canvas
  (76x102cm 29x40in) Billingshurst, West-Sussex 1998

HAMPTON John Wade 1918-2000 **[12]**
- $12 000 - €14 066 - **£7 471** - FF79 145
  The old Chisholm Trail Oil/canvas (81x121cm
  32x48in) Dallas TX 2001
- $500 - €588 - **£358** - FF3 856
  Round-up Oil/canvas (35x30cm 14x12in) New-York
  2001

HAMZA Hans 1879-1945 **[18]**
- $6 500 - €6 550 - **£4 052** - FF42 965
  A Busy marketplace Oil/panel (10x15.5cm 3x6in)
  New-York 2000

HAMZA Johann 1850-1927 **[64]**
- $34 610 - €38 245 - **£24 000** - FF250 872
  A difficult recital Oil/canvas (58x71cm 22x27in)
  London 2001
- $8 000 - €9 408 - **£5 736** - FF61 711
  Coquettish Exchange Oil/panel (25x19cm 9x7in)
  New-York 2001

HANAK Anton 1875-1934 **[38]**
- $1 698 - €1 454 - **£994** - FF9 538
  Brennender Mensch Bronze (H29.5cm H11in) Wien
  1998
- $927 - €1 090 - **£664** - FF7 150
  Studie zu einer Kaokoongruppe Indian ink
  (22.8x14.6cm 8x5in) Wien 2001

HANBRIDGE J.E. XX **[1]**
- $5 500 - €6 101 - **£3 657** - FF40 021
  Solitude Oil/canvas (55x81cm 22x32in) Milford CT
  2000
- $1 800 - €1 966 - **£1 158** - FF12 894
  In the Shoals Loch Lomond Oil/panel (25x34cm
  10x13in) Mystic CT 2000

HANCOCK Charles 1795/1802-1868/77 **[25]**
- $1 964 - €2 336 - **£1 400** - FF15 323
  «Punch», a grey Horse by the Side of a Barn
  Oil/panel (25x35.5cm 9x13in) London 2000

HANCOCK James Carl 1890-1966 **[19]**
- $150 - €147 - **£92** - FF963
  Untitled Etching (23x18cm 9x7in) New-Orleans LA
  1999

HAND Thomas 1771-c.1804 **[13]**
- $3 798 - €3 928 - **£2 400** - FF25 768
  Full Cry Oil/canvas (49.5x64.5cm 19x25in) London
  2000

- $1 504 - €1 565 - **£950** - FF10 263
  Cottagers and Donkeys in Winter Oil/canvas
  (21x26cm 8x10in) Newbury, Berkshire 2000

HANDLEN F. XIX-XX **[6]**
- $11 000 - €12 066 - **£7 471** - FF79 145
  Seascape with crashing Waves Oil/masonite
  (104x134cm 41x53in) Thomaston ME 2000
- $2 000 - €2 194 - **£1 358** - FF14 390
  Seascape Oil/canvas (71x96cm 28x38in) Thomaston
  ME 2000

HÄNDLER Paul 1833-1903 **[2]**
- $17 307 - €15 850 - **£10 549** - FF103 970
  **Die Einwohner Berlins auf dem Schlachtfeld
  von Grossbeeren am Morgen** Öl/Leinwand
  (102x138cm 40x54in) Berlin 1999

HANDLER Richard 1932 **[85]**
- $165 - €1 817 - **£1 100** - FF11 917
  Blumenstilleben Oil/panel (45.5x37.5cm 17x14in)
  Wien 2001

HANDLEY-READ Edward Harry 1870-1935 **[14]**
- $1 767 - €1 647 - **£1 100** - FF10 802
  The Iceskaters Bodycolour (50x74.5cm 19x29in)
  London 1999

HANDMANN Emmanuel Jakob 1718-1781 **[19]**
- $11 005 - €10 583 - **£6 791** - FF69 422
  Rudolf von Erlach im Alter von vierzehn Jahren
  Öl/Leinwand (49x39cm 19x15in) Bern 1999

HANDSCHIN Johannes 1899-1948 **[28]**
- $1 924 - €1 743 - **£1 200** - FF11 435
  «Silvaplana» Poster (100x70cm 39x27in) London
  1999

HANDYSIDE K.M. XIX-XX **[7]**
- $4 611 - €4 386 - **£2 800** - FF28 772
  Young Girl Carrying a Bundle of Sticks Oil/can-
  vas (59x49cm 23x19in) Penzance, Cornwall 1999
- $790 - €752 - **£480** - FF4 932
  Corn Stooks Oil/canvas (43.5x33.5cm 17x13in)
  Penzance, Cornwall 1999

HÄNEL Georg 1879-1945 **[8]**
- $2 928 - €3 068 - **£1 936** - FF20 123
  **Rast des Ziegenhirten mit seinen Ziegen auf
  Gebirgswiese im Sonnenlicht** Öl/Leinwand
  (80x100cm 31x39in) München 2000

HANFSTAENGL Franz 1804-1877 **[27]**
- $42 - €49 - **£30** - FF323
  Hound Engraving (20x21cm 7x8in) London 2000

HANFSTÄNGL Ernst 1840-1897 **[4]**
- $1 604 - €1 789 - **£1 079** - FF11 738
  Villa auf Capri Öl/Leinwand (73x50.5cm 28x19in)
  Ahlden 2000

HÄNGER Max I 1874-1955 **[187]**
- $1 147 - €1 074 - **£695** - FF7 043
  **Elf Hühner und ein Truthahn am Futternapf vor
  einem Bauernhaus** Oil/panel (14x24cm 5x9in)
  Bamberg 1999

HÄNGER Max II 1898-1961 **[20]**
- $731 - €767 - **£482** - FF5 030
  Hühnervolk Oil/panel (9.5x16cm 3x6in) Köln 2000

HANICOTTE Augustin 1870-1957 **[40]**
- $2 840 - €3 049 - **£1 900** - FF20 000
  Canal du Nord Huile/toile (46x65cm 18x25in) Paris
  2000
- $2 208 - €2 439 - **£1 531** - FF16 000
  Deux paysans hollandais Huile/toile (33x41cm
  12x16in) Paris 2001

HANIEL von Gerhart 1888-1955 **[19]**
$2 392 - €2 301 - **£1 474** - FF15 092
Rottach-Egern Öl/Leinwand (65.5x80.5cm 25x31in)
München 1999

HANIN René 1873-1943 **[22]**
$1 254 - €1 098 - **£759** - FF7 200
Le pont des Arts, Paris Huile/panneau (45.5x55cm
17x21in) Paris 1998

HANKE Henry Aloysius 1901-1989 **[54]**
$7 261 - €8 144 - **£5 042** - FF53 421
Gypsy Dancer and card Player Oil/canvas
(138x153cm 54x60in) Melbourne 2001
$592 - €661 - **£379** - FF4 337
St Severin, Paris Oil/canvas (59.5x49cm 23x19in)
Melbourne 2000
$422 - €503 - **£292** - FF3 300
Vegetable Vendors, Venise Canal Oil/board
(13.5x36.5cm 5x14in) Sydney 2000

HANKE Willy XX **[3]**
$874 - €817 - **£539** - FF5 357
**«Norddeutscher Lloyd Bremen, Bremen-New
York»** Poster (59.5x85.5cm 23x33in) Oostwoud 1999

HANKINS Abraham P. 1903-1963 **[15]**
$500 - €588 - **£358** - FF3 856
Street with figure in a doorway Oil/canvas/board
(34x26cm 13x10in) Philadelphia PA 2001

HANLON Jack Paul 1913-1968 **[37]**
$2 657 - €2 793 - **£1 667** - FF18 323
Two Figures by a Woodland Path Oil/board
(37x45cm 14x17in) Dublin 2000
$5 073 - €5 333 - **£3 183** - FF34 981
Still Life with Lemons Oil/canvas (14.5x21.5cm
5x8in) Dublin 2000
$1 555 - €1 719 - **£1 078** - FF11 277
Christ carrying the Cross Watercolour/paper
(51x33cm 20x13in) Dublin 2001

HANLY Pat 1932 **[26]**
$38 294 - €42 924 - **£26 780** - FF281 561
«Girl Asleep 14» Oil/canvas (54.5x70.5cm 21x27in)
Auckland 2001
$677 - €759 - **£472** - FF4 977
«Mt Eden» Watercolour/paper (21x23cm 8x9in)
Wellington 2001
$725 - €813 - **£507** - FF5 334
«Untitled» Screenprint (59x78cm 23x30in) Auckland
2001

HANNA Forman 1882-1950 **[12]**
$1 200 - €1 128 - **£743** - FF7 401
Female Nude Studies Silver print (26x34cm
10x13in) New-York 1999

HANNA-BARBERA Studios XX **[8]**
$289 - €336 - **£200** - FF2 204
**Scooby Doo Sitting Down and Scrappy Doo
Flying in the Air** Gouache (23x29.5cm 9x11in)
London 2000

HANNAFORD Charles A., Jnr. 1887-1972 **[30]**
$171 - €208 - **£120** - FF1 362
Boat by a River Watercolour/paper (20x30cm 8x12in)
Aylsham, Norfolk 2000

HANNAFORD Charles E. 1863-1955 **[88]**
$406 - €398 - **£202** - FF2 608
Figure with Ducks on River Bank
Watercolour/paper (25x35cm 10x14in) Aylsham,
Norfolk 1999

HANNAUX Emmanuel 1855-1934 **[16]**
$18 000 - €20 102 - **£11 527** - FF131 859
Poète and La Sirène Marble (H81cm H31in) New-
York 2000
$6 307 - €6 770 - **£4 220** - FF44 408
Sirien Marble (H75cm H29in) Toronto 2000

HANNEMAN Adriaan c.1601-1671 **[9]**
$78 388 - €72 165 - **£48 000** - FF473 371
Portrait of an officer Oil/canvas (133.5x116.5cm
52x45in) London 1998

HANNEY Clifford 1890-1990 **[100]**
$281 - €243 - **£170** - FF1 594
«Season of Mists and Mellow Fruitfulness»
Oil/board (49x59cm 19x23in) Bristol, Avon 1998

HANNOCK Stephen XX **[1]**
$6 500 - €6 783 - **£4 099** - FF44 492
Squid Boats on the Gulf of Siam Oil/canvas
(76x127cm 29x50in) New-York 2000

HANNON Théodore 1851-1916 **[24]**
$5 051 - €4 421 - **£3 059** - FF29 000
Portrait du Père Frédé Aquarelle/papier (61x89cm
24x35in) Paris 1998

HANNOT Johannes 1633-1685 **[3]**
$161 130 - €158 241 - **£100 000** - FF1 037 990
**Roemer, a Flute, a Jug, Nuts in a Wan-li
Porcelain Bowl** Oil/panel (50x87.5cm 19x34in)
London 1999

HANNOTIAU Alexandre 1863-1901 **[7]**
$1 500 - €1 634 - **£1 038** - FF10 721
«A.J.Kymeulen» Poster (72x42cm 28x16in) New-
York 2001

HANOTEAU Hector Ch. 1823-1890 **[24]**
$7 148 - €6 098 - **£4 312** - FF40 000
Bergère et son troupeau au bord du ruisseau
Huile/toile (81x116cm 31x45in) Pontoise 1998

HANOTEL Auguste XIX-XX **[7]**
$519 - €545 - **£327** - FF3 577
Jour de pêche Huile/panneau (24.5x35.2cm 9x13in)
Bruxelles 2000

HANRIOT Jules Armand 1853-1877 **[10]**
$4 510 - €4 726 - **£2 855** - FF31 000
Jeune femme au bain Huile/toile (73x50cm
28x19in) Paris 2000

HANS Josephus Gerardus 1826-1891 **[34]**
$8 663 - €8 168 - **£5 369** - FF53 578
The Approaching Thunderstrom Oil/panel
(40x55cm 15x21in) Amsterdam 1999
$1 930 - €2 269 - **£1 338** - FF14 883
**A Peasantwoman on a Path in a Wooded
Landscape** Oil/panel (28x26cm 11x10in) Amsterdam
2000

HANSCH Anton 1813-1876 **[43]**
$5 525 - €4 723 - **£3 315** - FF30 979
**Rehwild am Bachufer, im Hintergrund das
Dachsteinmassiv** Oil/panel (57x79cm 22x31in) Wien
1998

HÄNSCH Johannes 1875-1945 **[64]**
$401 - €460 - **£274** - FF3 018
Am Christelsee, Hessen Öl/Leinwand (79x100cm
31x39in) Berlin 2000

HANSEN Al, Alfred Earl 1927-1995 **[56]**
$1 000 - €995 - **£620** - FF6 524
Gimme A Hug! Mixed media (35x25cm 13x9in)
Beverly-Hills CA 1999

📖 $390 · €454 · £274 · FF2 976
«Smavset Baby» Collage (31x30cm 12x11in)
Amsterdam 2001

HANSEN Armin Carl 1886-1957 [72]
📷 $18 000 · €16 997 · £11 178 · FF111 490
Monterey Dock Scene/Ship in Harbor, Monterey
Oil/board (35.5x47cm 13x18in) Beverly-Hills CA 1999
📷 $30 000 · €35 061 · £21 417 · FF229 983
Fishermen on the beach Oil/board (30x48cm
12x19in) Altadena CA 2001
📖 $2 500 · €2 232 · £1 531 · FF14 640
«The Landing Party» Crayon (20x28cm 8x11in)
Altadena CA 1999
🗒 $850 · €879 · £537 · FF5 769
Fisher Harbour Drypoint (7x9cm 2x3in) New-York
2000

HANSEN Arne L. 1921 [84]
📷 $495 · €563 · £339 · FF3 691
Fra den store industri, koldt mod varmt Oil/can-
vas (50x73cm 19x28in) København 2000

HANSEN Asor 1862-1929 [6]
📷 $3 645 · €4 161 · £2 532 · FF27 295
Norsk bondestue, i forgrunden sovende born
Oil/canvas (57x49cm 22x19in) København 2000

HANSEN Constantin 1804-1880 [154]
📷 $1 017 · €1 008 · £636 · FF6 614
Thor på vandring Oil/canvas (47x41cm 18x16in)
København 1999
📷 $811 · €871 · £543 · FF5 715
Mytologisk sceneri, Odysseus og Nauskaa
Oil/canvas (52x20cm 9x7in) København 2000
📖 $256 · €242 · £159 · FF1 589
Studie til musernes frise i universitetes vestibu-
le Pencil/paper (34.5x37cm 13x14in) København 1999

HANSEN Emile 1878-1952 [99]
📷 $188 · €201 · £128 · FF1 943
Strandparti, vinter, i baggrunden Aarhus Oil/can-
vas (40x63cm 15x24in) Vejle 2001
📷 $171 · €148 · £103 · FF970
Vaskekoner Oil/canvas (24x30.5cm 9x12in) Vejle
1999

HANSEN Hans 1769-1828 [7]
📷 $1 801 · €1 748 · £1 112 · FF11 469
Portraet af Susanna Jacoba Fabritius (1741-
1762) Oil/canvas (35x27cm 13x10in) Vejle 1999

HANSEN Hans 1874-1948 [22]
📷 $1 207 · €1 225 · £750 · FF8 036
Blossom in Two vases on a Table Oil/canvas
(59.5x46.5cm 23x18in) London 2000

HANSEN Hans Jacob 1859-1942 [21]
📖 $505 · €529 · £320 · FF3 472
North African Bazaar Watercolour/paper (17x12cm
6x4in) Edinburgh 2000

HANSEN Hans Nicolaj 1853-1923 [78]
📷 $699 · €673 · £435 · FF4 416
Slaedekörsel Oil/canvas (55x74cm 21x29in)
København 1999
📖 $214 · €207 · £130 · FF1 358
The Bull Fight, Seville Watercolour/paper
(17x24.5cm 6x9in) London 2000

HANSEN Harald H. 1890-1967 [42]
📖 $536 · €457 · £319 · FF2 998
Interieur med stol Oil/canvas (94x110cm 37x43in)
Vejle 1998

HANSEN Heinrich 1821-1890 [99]
📷 $6 664 · €6 053 · £4 131 · FF39 708
Kirkeinteriör fra St.Jacques, Antwerpen Oil/can-
vas (76x97cm 29x38in) København 1999
📷 $1 607 · €1 811 · £1 108 · FF11 877
Kirkeinteriör, Baptisteriet i Ravenna Oil/canvas
(32x38cm 12x14in) København 2000

HANSEN Herman Wendelborg 1854-1924 [28]
📷 $60 000 · €56 655 · £37 260 · FF371 634
Attack on the Wagon Train Oil/canvas (91.5x127cm
36x50in) Beverly-Hills CA 1999
📖 $5 000 · €5 946 · £3 563 · FF39 005
Bear Hunt Watercolour (21.5x33cm 8x12in) New-York
2000

HANSEN Jacob XIX-XX [23]
📷 $1 289 · €1 475 · £896 · FF9 673
Frederiksdal Slot set fra Barokhaven Oil/canvas
(42x54cm 16x21in) København 2000
📷 $588 · €671 · £408 · FF4 402
Parti fra Forum Romanum med kig gennem
Castor og Pollux templets Oil/wood (40x32cm
15x12in) København 2000

HANSEN Johannes Christian 1903-1995 [18]
🗒 $10 999 · €11 411 · £6 978 · FF74 851
Stående nögen kvinde Bronze (H166cm H65in)
Viby J, Århus 2000

HANSEN Jop 1899-1960 [7]
📷 $6 648 · €7 714 · £4 590 · FF50 602
Noordenplantsoen Mixed media (51.5x63.5cm
20x25in) Groningen 2000

HANSEN Jørgen 1862-1937 [6]
📷 $15 587 · €16 750 · £10 687 · FF109 875
Badende börn Oil/canvas (108x132cm 42x51in) Vejle
2001

HANSEN Josef Theodor 1848-1912 [155]
📷 $5 800 · €7 516 · £4 350 · FF49 300
Interno di palazzo Olio/tela (40x50cm 15x19in)
Venezia 2000
📷 $2 500 · €2 682 · £1 704 · FF17 592
Timandsrådets sal i Dogepaladset Oil/canvas
(47x32cm 18x12in) København 2001
📖 $352 · €363 · £223 · FF2 380
Havneparti med småbåde og Det
Kgl.Assistenshus Watercolour/paper (33.5x22.5cm
13x8in) Vejle 2000

HANSEN Niels 1880-1946 [28]
📷 $582 · €671 · £402 · FF4 401
Marine Oil/canvas (81x101cm 31x39in) København
2000

HANSEN Niels Christian 1834-1922 [18]
📷 $28 059 · €27 306 · £17 272 · FF179 117
Lekande pojkar i strandbrynet Oil/canvas
(117x146cm 46x57in) Stockholm 1999
📷 $2 162 · €2 549 · £1 520 · FF16 720
Strandparti med dreng og pige i klitterne
Oil/canvas (45x59.5cm 17x23in) Vejle 2000

HANSEN Peter Marius 1868-1928 [121]
📷 $1 154 · €1 342 · £824 · FF8 804
Älefiskere på isen Oil/canvas (55x77cm 21x30in)
Aarhus 2001
📷 $815 · €939 · £562 · FF6 162
Pigeportraet Oil/canvas (37x34cm 14x13in)
København 2000
📖 $389 · €470 · £271 · FF3 085
Parti fra København Watercolour/paper (23x35cm
9x13in) Viby J, Århus 2000

HANSEN Sigvard Marius 1859-1938 **[148]**
🖼 **$1 034** - €1 140 - **£700** - FF7 480
Parti fra Lago de Como, med huse og udsigt til søen Oil/canvas (50x70cm 19x27in) Vejle 2000

HANSEN Sikker Aage 1897-1955 **[9]**
🖼 **$59** - €68 - **£41** - FF446
«F.D.B.Møbler» Poster (64x91.5cm 25x36in) Hoorn 2001

HANSEN Theodore Brooke 1870-1945 **[4]**
🖼 **$2 487** - €2 929 - **£1 748** - FF19 213
Too Late Oil/canvas (96x121cm 37x47in) Sydney 2000

HANSEN von Theophil 1813-1891 **[1]**
🖊 **$2 632** - €2 907 - **£1 824** - FF19 068
«Ansicht des neuen Waffenmuseums im k.k.Artillerie Arsenal» Watercolour (38x57cm 14x22in) Wien 2001

HANSEN-BAHIA Karl Heinz 1915-1978 **[136]**
🖼 **$174** - €164 - **£108** - FF1 073
Stierfänger Woodcut (37.1x56.5cm 14x22in) Heidelberg 1999

HANSEN-REISTRUP Karl Frederik 1863-1929 **[68]**
🖼 **$733** - €739 - **£457** - FF4 846
To dragoner til hest i samtale, vinter Oil/canvas (50x64cm 19x25in) København 2000
🖼 **$412** - €377 - **£258** - FF2 471
Ridende dragon og göende hund Oil/canvas (36x31cm 14x12in) København 1999
🖊 **$351** - €388 - **£243** - FF2 548
Fransk byparti med hestevogn foran vinhandel Watercolour (32.5x48.5cm 12x19in) København 1999

HANSI (Jean-Jacques Waltz) 1873-1951 **[76]**
🖊 **$1 557** - €1 418 - **£973** - FF9 300
L'église de Burnkirch près de Illfurth Aquarelle/papier (16x23cm 6x9in) Belfort 1999
🖼 **$95** - €107 - **£66** - FF700
«2ème emprunt de la Défence Nationale, souscrivez, aidez-nous..» Affiche (37x28cm 14x11in) Chartres 2001

HANSON Albert J. 1866-1914 **[10]**
🖼 **$25 952** - €24 672 - **£16 196** - FF161 840
The Harvest Oil/canvas (83x156cm 32x61in) Melbourne 1999
🖼 **$14 751** - €13 720 - **£9 135** - FF90 000
Vues d'un port animées Huile/toile (58x77cm 22x30in) Biarritz 1999
🖊 **$1 462** - €1 423 - **£900** - FF9 332
Mermaids Watercolour (37.5x62cm 14x24in) Melbourne 1999

HANSON Christian Heinrich 1790-1863 **[2]**
🖼 **$5 215** - €5 368 - **£3 287** - FF35 215
Der Fischer Öl/Leinwand (63x48cm 24x18in) Berlin 2000

HANSON Duane 1925-1996 **[14]**
🖼 **$120 000** - €116 109 - **£74 004** - FF761 628
Policeman Sculpture (183x46x38cm 72x18x14in) New-York 1999
🖼 **$85 000** - €81 687 - **£52 360** - FF535 831
Motorcycle Accident Sculpture (52x185.5x203cm 20x73x79in) New-York 1999

HANSON Leon William 1918 **[55]**
🖼 **$375** - €351 - **£232** - FF2 302
Snowcapped Mountains Oil/panel (48x59cm 19x23in) Philadelphia PA 1999
🖼 **$182** - €213 - **£126** - FF1 395
North Head to Manly Oil/board (14x36.5cm 5x14in) Melbourne 2000

HANSON OF SUSANVILLE XIX **[1]**
📷 **$26 000** - €27 134 - **£16 450** - FF177 988
Two Groups of Miners posing with Water Wheels Albumen print (19.5x24cm 7x9in) New-York 2000

HANSPERS Olle 1923 **[28]**
🖼 **$349** - €294 - **£206** - FF1 929
«California, I love you» Copper engraving (63.5x49.5cm 25x19in) Stockholm 1998

HANSSON Rolf 1953 **[30]**
🖼 **$3 538** - €4 106 - **£2 443** - FF26 932
Uahoe Oil/panel (112x132cm 44x51in) Stockholm 2000
🖼 **$3 315** - €3 115 - **£1 998** - FF20 436
Utan titel Oil/panel (61x60cm 24x23in) Stockholm 1999
🖼 **$448** - €512 - **£316** - FF3 361
Komposition Serigraph in colors (112x94cm 44x37in) Stockholm 2001

HANSTEEN Aasta 1824-1908 **[3]**
🖼 **$36 363** - €37 930 - **£22 940** - FF248 806
En avskjed Oil/canvas (57x73cm 22x28in) Oslo 2000

HANSTEEN Niels 1855-1912 **[65]**
🖼 **$6 825** - €8 116 - **£4 862** - FF53 235
Hest og slede i vinterlandskap Oil/canvas (90x150cm 35x59in) Oslo 2000
🖼 **$2 858** - €3 219 - **£1 970** - FF21 115
Sneklaedt norsk skovlandskab Oil/canvas (81x65.5cm 31x25in) København 2000
🖼 **$519** - €442 - **£310** - FF2 902
Fra Meaelven i Selbu Oil/canvas (19x27cm 7x10in) Oslo 1998

HANTAï Simon 1922 **[104]**
🖼 **$41 472** - €48 784 - **£29 728** - FF320 000
Sans titre Acrylique/toile (150x130cm 59x51in) Paris 2001
🖼 **$23 580** - €22 867 - **£14 940** - FF150 000
«C-2-8-19» Acrylique/papier/toile (79x72.5cm 31x28in) Paris 1999
🖼 **$5 118** - €5 031 - **£3 286** - FF33 000
Sans titre Huile/papier (10x24cm 3x9in) Paris 1999
🖊 **$4 508** - €4 878 - **£3 088** - FF32 000
Personnage Technique mixte/papier (21.5x11cm 8x4in) Paris 2001

HANTMAN Carl 1935 **[10]**
🖼 **$2 800** - €3 120 - **£1 956** - FF20 466
Rails of Change Oil/canvas (50x82cm 20x32in) Delray-Beach FL 2001

HANZEN Aleksei Vasilievich 1876-1937 **[10]**
🖼 **$3 468** - €3 280 - **£2 160** - FF21 516
Sailing Boats by the Seashore Oil/canvas (81x113cm 31x44in) Praha 2000

HAPASKA Siobhan 1963 **[3]**
🖼 **$5 769** - €6 781 - **£4 000** - FF44 480
Heart Construction (146x110x16.5cm 57x43x6in) London 2000

HAPPEL Karl 1819-1914 **[11]**
🖼 **$2 247** - €2 045 - **£1 404** - FF13 415
Damenporträt Öl/Leinwand (39.5x30.5cm 15x12in) München 1999

HAPSHASH AND THE COLOURED COAT XX **[21]**
🖼 **$598** - €657 - **£380** - FF4 311
«Sunday at the Saville» Poster (76x49.5cm 29x19in) London 2000

HAQUETTE Georges Jean Marie 1854-1906 **[50]**
$3 000 - €2 570 - **£1 803** - FF16 859
Fishermen sailing in Choppy Seas Oil/canvas
(44x54cm 17x21in) St. Louis MO 1998
$1 298 - €1 246 - **£804** - FF8 176
Die Rückkehr der Fischer Öl/Leinwand (36x24.5cm
14x9in) Zürich 1999

HARA Jacques 1933 **[83]**
$357 - €366 - **£222** - FF2 400
Fin d'après-midi Huile/toile (22x27cm 8x10in) Paris
2000

HARALD XX **[3]**
$3 400 - €2 900 - **£2 050** - FF19 026
**«Grande Semaine d'Aviation
d'Egypte/Héliopolis»** Poster (117x157cm 46x61in)
New-York 1998

HARARI Hanahiah 1912 **[15]**
$1 100 - €1 026 - **£682** - FF6 728
The Artist's Palette Watercolour, gouache/paper
(25x29.5cm 9x11in) New-York 1999
$950 - €1 099 - **£672** - FF7 212
City Signs Screenprint in colors (46x30.5cm 18x12in)
New-York 2000

HARBURGER Edmund 1846-1906 **[33]**
$3 370 - €3 068 - **£2 106** - FF20 123
**Im Gespräch stehen zwei Bauern und eine alte
Frau in der Stube** Oil/panel (43x64.5cm 16x25in)
München 1999

HARCOURT George 1869-1947 **[5]**
$130 000 - €110 965 - **£77 740** - FF727 883
Borrowed plumes Oil/canvas (126.5x101.5cm
49x39in) New-York 1998

HARDENBERG B.F. XVIII-XIX **[1]**
$6 332 - €6 098 - **£3 932** - FF40 000
**Buste de Francis Seymour-Conway, second
Marquis de Hertford(1743-1822)** Marbre (H69cm
H27in) Paris 1999

HARDER Heinrich 1858-c.1930 **[5]**
$382 - €358 - **£234** - FF2 347
**Herbstwald mit Bachlauf und sonnigem
Lichteinfall** Öl/Leinwand (67x57cm 26x22in) Lindau
1999

HARDIE Charles Martin 1858-1916 **[40]**
$3 929 - €3 644 - **£2 400** - FF23 904
Gorse in Bloom on the Links Oil/canvas
(91.5x71cm 36x27in) Glasgow 1999
$2 923 - €3 259 - **£2 000** - FF21 379
By the Gate - Springtime Oil/canvas (46x30.5cm
18x12in) Perthshire 2000

HARDIE Martin 1875-1952 **[71]**
$384 - €349 - **£240** - FF2 287
Afternoon at Ajaccio, Corsic Watercolour
(26x38cm 10x14in) Glasgow 1999
$74 - €82 - **£50** - FF541
Street at Semur Etching (25x15cm 10x6in) Aylsham,
Norfolk 2000

HARDIME Peter 1677-1758 **[15]**
$11 417 - €10 679 - **£7 000** - FF70 049
**Roses, Peonies, a Variegated Tulip, Carnations,
Daisies and Others** Oil/canvas (86.5x69cm 34x27in)
London 1998

HARDIME Simon 1664-1737 **[5]**
$8 425 - €7 143 - **£5 000** - FF46 855
Roses, Hyacinths, Tulips, and Other Flowers
Oil/canvas (54.5x48.5cm 21x19in) London 1998

HARDIN Helen 1943-1984 **[12]**
$6 500 - €7 586 - **£4 588** - FF49 763
Untitled Oil/panel (58x49cm 22x19in) New-York 2000
$4 500 - €4 261 - **£2 806** - FF27 948
Untitled Oil/canvas (40x30cm 16x12in) St. Ignatius
MT 1999
$1 700 - €1 817 - **£1 157** - FF11 916
Male Pueblo Dancer Watercolour/paper (27x18cm
11x7in) Cloudcroft NM 2001

HARDING B. XX **[6]**
$513 - €508 - **£320** - FF3 330
**Cock and Hen Pheasants in a Woodland
Clearing** Watercolour (37.5x53.5cm 14x21in) London
1999

HARDING Ch. Chester 1792-1866 **[3]**
$2 365 - €2 727 - **£1 617** - FF17 886
Marine à la pleine lune Huile/panneau (31x35cm
12x13in) Bruxelles 2000

HARDING Charles T. XIX **[1]**
$4 489 - €5 339 - **£3 200** - FF35 024
Frigate and a Ship of the Line off the Coast
Oil/panel (31x31cm 12x12in) London 2000

HARDING Charlotte 1873-1951 **[1]**
$4 000 - €4 663 - **£2 769** - FF30 586
Four Women PLaying Cards on Veranda
Charcoal (63x39cm 25x15in) New-York 2000

HARDING Edward J. 1804-1870 **[2]**
$3 913 - €4 294 - **£2 600** - FF28 165
**Family Portrait of Gentleman, his wife and their
child** Watercolour (50.5x37cm 19x14in) London 2000

HARDING George Perfect 1775-1853 **[59]**
$467 - €537 - **£320** - FF3 520
Henry VII, full length Miniature (18x11cm 7x4in)
Little-Lane, Ilkley 2000
$599 - €582 - **£380** - FF3 815
**Portrait of Jeffrey Hudson, holding a walking
Stick and Rose** Watercolour (23.5x14cm 9x5in)
London 1999

HARDING James Duffield 1797-1863 **[127]**
$31 244 - €30 577 - **£20 000** - FF200 574
Verona Oil/canvas (102x150cm 40x59in) London 1999
$5 977 - €6 416 - **£4 000** - FF42 086
**View of a Continental Town on a River with
Barges** Oil/canvas (32x50cm 12x19in) London 2000
$581 - €556 - **£356** - FF3 644
Studies of Peasants Pencil (16.5x25cm 6x9in)
London 1999
$289 - €329 - **£200** - FF2 158
The Park & the Forest Lithograph (55x37cm
21x14in) London 2000

HARDING Samuel A. XIX-XX **[13]**
$593 - €686 - **£420** - FF4 503
Horse, Cart and Dog on a Forest Road
Watercolour/paper (71x54cm 28x21in) Cheadle-Hulme-
Cheshire 2000

HARDING W.H. XIX-XX **[2]**
$6 158 - €6 637 - **£4 200** - FF43 539
**St.Mark's Square, Venice/Santa Maria delle
Salute from the Grand Canal** Oil/canvas
(54.5x67.5cm 21x26in) London 2001

HARDINGE OF PENSHURST Charles, 1st Baron
XIX **[1]**
$11 577 - €10 829 - **£7 000** - FF71 033
Collection of official and unofficial Photographs
Photograph (28x36cm 11x14in) London 1999

HARDMAN John XVIII-XIX **[5]**
- $6 424 - €6 236 - £4 000 - FF40 903
  A dapple grey Gelding in an extensive Landscape Oil/canvas (63.5x76cm 25x29in) London 1999

HARDMEYER Robert 1876-1919 **[6]**
- $4 800 - €4 616 - £2 962 - FF30 279
  «Washanstalt Zürich» Poster (127.5x91cm 50x35in) New-York 1999

HARDOUIN D.T. XIX **[2]**
- $4 104 - €4 573 - £2 877 - FF30 000
  Femmes turques marchandant un collier à Constantinople Huile/toile (77.5x50cm 30x19in) Paris 2001

HARDOUIN Ernest Alfred 1820-1854 **[2]**
- $4 326 - €4 269 - £2 665 - FF28 000
  Scènes de rue en Turquie Huile/toile (78x50.5cm 30x19in) Aubagne 1999

HARDRICK John Wesley 1891-1968 **[30]**
- $2 800 - €3 203 - £1 947 - FF21 009
  Wooded Stream Oil/board (40x50cm 16x20in) Cincinnati OH 2000
- $1 600 - €1 859 - £1 124 - FF12 193
  Autumn Landscape Oil/board (33x40cm 13x16in) Cincinnati OH 2001

HARDS Charles G. XIX **[1]**
- $5 676 - €6 786 - £3 900 - FF44 511
  In a Summer Garden Oil/canvas (90.5x60.5cm 35x23in) Billingshurst, West-Sussex 2000

HARDWICK Alice R. 1876-? **[2]**
- $3 750 - €4 282 - £2 644 - FF28 090
  Country Lane in Spring Oil/canvas (58.5x68.5cm 23x26in) Boston MA 2001

HARDWICK John Jessop 1832-1917 **[25]**
- $970 - €838 - £580 - FF5 497
  Spring Time Watercolour/paper (19x16cm 7x6in) Llandeilo, Carmarthenshire 1998

HARDWICK Melbourne Havelock 1857-1916 **[30]**
- $20 000 - €21 468 - £13 384 - FF140 820
  Summer on the Coast Oil/canvas (58x69cm 23x27in) Portland ME 2000
- $600 - €700 - £421 - FF4 590
  The Letter Watercolour/paper (34x48cm 13x19in) Dedham MA 2000

HARDWICK William Noble 1805-1865 **[11]**
- $1 647 - €1 566 - £1 000 - FF10 275
  The High Street, Edinburgh Watercolour (38x28cm 14x11in) Edinburgh 1999

HARDY André 1887-1986 **[332]**
- $594 - €610 - £372 - FF4 000
  L'auberge Huile/papier (35x50cm 13x19in) Deauville 2000
- $494 - €427 - £298 - FF2 800
  La couture Huile/toile/carton (30x38cm 11x14in) Bayeux 1999
- $684 - €762 - £460 - FF5 000
  «Saint-Aubin/Mer, Calvados, la reine de l'iode» Affiche (100x62cm 39x24in) Orléans 2000

HARDY Anna Elizabeth 1839-1934 **[16]**
- $8 500 - €9 472 - £5 718 - FF62 135
  Still Life of Roses Oil/canvas (27x35cm 11x14in) Portsmouth NH 2000

HARDY Cyril XIX **[48]**
- $716 - €614 - £432 - FF4 029
  In old Tunisia/A Moorish Street Watercolour/paper (28x19cm 11x7in) Toronto 1998

HARDY David c.1835-c.1885 **[19]**
- $2 022 - €1 741 - £1 200 - FF11 417
  Cottage Interior Oil/board (21x30.5cm 8x12in) London 1998
- $1 998 - €1 855 - £1 200 - FF12 167
  A young Girl seated on a grassy bank holding a bunch of wild Flowers Watercolour (24x18cm 9x7in) London 1999

HARDY DeWitt 1940 **[16]**
- $600 - €549 - £365 - FF3 604
  Young Woman in an Interior Scene Watercolour/paper (73x53cm 29x21in) Bloomfield-Hills MI 1999

HARDY Dorofield XIX-XX **[6]**
- $2 098 - €2 498 - £1 500 - FF16 384
  Portrait of the Queen Anne Oil/canvas (125x116cm 49x45in) Billingshurst, West-Sussex 2000

HARDY Dorothy XX **[9]**
- $238 - €229 - £147 - FF1 500
  Twelve miles from Home/A Move towards Covert Pochoir (19x49cm 7x19in) Senlis 1999

HARDY Dudley 1865-1922 **[125]**
- $15 781 - €13 505 - £9 500 - FF88 588
  Idle Moments Oil/board (38x46cm 14x18in) London 1998
- $729 - €684 - £450 - FF4 488
  The Return Watercolour (18.5x24.5cm 7x9in) Billingshurst, West-Sussex 1999
- $767 - €648 - £450 - FF4 249
  «D'Oyly Carte Opera Company» Poster (77x51cm 30x20in) London 1998

HARDY Florence, née Small c.1860-1933 **[2]**
- $7 015 - €8 343 - £5 000 - FF54 726
  Mischief Oil/canvas (127x94cm 50x37in) London 2000

HARDY Frederick Daniel 1826-1911 **[61]**
- $15 651 - €18 185 - £11 000 - FF119 286
  Bed-Time Oil/canvas (56x43.5cm 22x17in) London 2001
- $4 184 - €4 491 - £2 800 - FF29 460
  The Money Lender Oil/canvas (29.5x21.5cm 11x8in) London 2000
- $1 192 - €1 418 - £850 - FF9 303
  The Apprentice Cooper Watercolour (22x18cm 8x7in) Bath 2000

HARDY George 1822-1909 **[11]**
- $4 181 - €3 999 - £2 546 - FF26 229
  Pastoral Scenes of English Countryside Oil/canvas (40x60cm 16x24in) New-Orleans LA 1999

HARDY Heywood 1843-1933 **[219]**
- $110 000 - €93 982 - £66 033 - FF616 484
  The Presentation Oil/canvas (91.5x222cm 36x87in) New-York 1998
- $30 000 - €32 202 - £20 076 - FF211 230
  Hounds at Covert Oil/canvas (122x91.5cm 48x36in) New-York 2000
- $7 500 - €7 446 - £4 687 - FF48 844
  The Postman Oil/panel (20.5x40.5cm 8x15in) New-York 1999
- $1 464 - €1 563 - £1 000 - FF10 253
  Stuck in the Snow Watercolour (49x99cm 19x38in) Billingshurst, West-Sussex 2001

HARDY James, Jnr. 1832-1889 **[141]**
- $16 030 - €15 143 - £10 000 - FF99 333
  Still Life of Dead Game Oil/canvas (95x140cm 37x55in) Perthshire 1999

$28 000 - €23 923 - **£16 808** - FF156 923
Three Setters in a Landscape Oil/canvas
(48.5x65cm 19x25in) New-York 1998

$5 690 - €5 254 - **£3 500** - FF34 462
Children Fishing Oil/panel (14.5x10.5cm 5x4in)
London 1999

$2 646 - €2 307 - **£1 600** - FF15 135
**Children sitting on a Hayrick, watching a
Farmer** Watercolour (26.5x38cm 10x14in) London
1998

HARDY James, Snr. 1801-1879 **[5]**

$4 615 - €5 425 - **£3 200** - FF35 584
Scenes in Stirlingshire Oil/canvas (18x35.5cm
7x13in) Edinburgh 2000

$2 137 - €2 484 - **£1 500** - FF16 296
Pulling the Cart Watercolour (37x51cm 14x20in)
Billingshurst, West-Sussex 2001

HARDY Marc 1957 **[2]**

$983 - €945 - **£610** - FF6 200
La Patrouille des Libellules, pl.24 Encre
Chine/papier (50x33cm 19x12in) Paris 1999

HARDY Nina XIX-XX **[4]**

$7 236 - €7 412 - **£4 500** - FF48 618
The letter Oil/canvas (64.5x54.5cm 25x21in)
Billingshurst, West-Sussex 2000

HARDY Norman H. c.1864-1914 **[3]**

$3 308 - €3 630 - **£2 198** - FF23 812
La pesée du caoutchouc Watercolour (34x50cm
13x19in) Amsterdam 2000

HARDY Thomas Bush 1842-1897 **[625]**

$13 116 - €14 648 - **£8 400** - FF96 086
H.M.S Illustrious, Portsmouth Harbour Oil/canvas
(38x76cm 14x29in) London 2000

$988 - €963 - **£600** - FF6 319
Fisherfolk on a Quay Oil/canvas (35.5x25.5cm
13x10in) London 2000

$2 154 - €1 859 - **£1 300** - FF12 195
French Fishing Boats Watercolour (28x61cm
11x24in) London 1998

HARE Augustus J. Cuthbert 1834-1903 **[24]**

$348 - €370 - **£220** - FF2 428
Study of Corfe Castle Watercolour (25x35cm
9x13in) London 2000

HARE John 1908 **[13]**

$500 - €463 - **£308** - FF3 036
Provincetown Harbor Watercolour/paper (25x30cm
10x12in) East-Dennis MA 1999

HARE John Knowles 1882-1947 **[45]**

$850 - €925 - **£584** - FF6 068
Moonlight in Provincetown Watercolour/paper
(30x25cm 12x10in) St. Petersburg FL 2001

HARE Saint George 1857-1933 **[8]**

$10 460 - €11 228 - **£7 000** - FF73 651
The Salvation Army Oil/canvas (73.5x56cm 28x22in)
London 2000

$6 500 - €6 977 - **£4 428** - FF45 769
«Listen» Oil/canvas (33.5x24cm 13x9in) Boston MA
2001

HARE Samuel 1780-1859 **[7]**

$6 000 - €5 503 - **£3 696** - FF36 099
Daniel Mendoza Oil/canvas (30.5x25cm 12x9in)
New-York 1999

HARE William 1815-1865 **[5]**

$11 550 - €9 870 - **£6 784** - FF64 742
Portrait of the Ann Maria Oil/canvas (55x68cm
22x27in) Timonium MD 1998

HAREUX Ernest 1847-1909 **[77]**

$1 641 - €1 829 - **£1 147** - FF12 000
Chemin de hallage Huile/toile (60x81.5cm 23x32in)
Paris 2001

$1 256 - €1 220 - **£776** - FF8 000
Nuit tombante, retour du troupeau à la ferme
Huile/toile (16x24cm 6x9in) Grenoble 1999

HARFAUX Artür 1906-1995 **[8]**

$2 008 - €2 363 - **£1 455** - FF15 500
**Univers surréaliste composé d'un personnage
aux ongles acérés** Encre/papier (25x19cm 9x7in)
Paris 2001

$1 418 - €1 228 - **£860** - FF8 054
Sitzender Akt Photograph (14x21cm 5x8in) München
1998

HARFORD William Henry XIX-XX **[9]**

$170 - €187 - **£110** - FF1 226
In the Trossacks Watercolour/paper (25x33cm
10x13in) Woodford, Cheshire 2000

HARGENS Charles W. 1893-1997 **[29]**

$1 700 - €1 832 - **£1 159** - FF12 018
**Springtime, Illustration of White Horse and
brown Colt in meadow** Oil/canvas (66x50cm
26x20in) Hatfield PA 2001

$1 000 - €1 157 - **£707** - FF7 588
The Old Scotter Studio Oil/board (30x40cm
12x16in) Hatfield PA 2000

$275 - €296 - **£184** - FF1 939
Prairie Fire Charcoal (25x45cm 10x18in) Hatfield PA
2000

HARGITT Edward 1835-1895 **[63]**

$1 195 - €1 283 - **£800** - FF8 417
Highland Cattle in a Mountainous Landscape
Oil/canvas (24x30.5cm 9x12in) London 2000

$692 - €634 - **£420** - FF4 158
A View of Bass Rock off the Scottish Coast
Watercolour (23x35cm 9x13in) London 1998

HARGREAVES Toni 1965 **[4]**

$3 895 - €3 744 - **£2 400** - FF24 559
Meopard Pair Acrylic/board (42.5x103.5cm 16x40in)
London 1999

HARING Keith 1958-1990 **[925]**

$40 000 - €43 886 - **£26 572** - FF287 872
Sneeze (Via Picasso) Acrylic/canvas
(152.5x152.5cm 60x60in) New-York 2000

$16 000 - €15 376 - **£9 856** - FF100 862
Untitled Acrylic/canvas (61x61cm 24x24in) New-York
1999

$12 000 - €11 267 - **£7 435** - FF73 909
Untitled Acrylic/panel (36x28cm 14x11in) New-York
1999

$37 883 - €35 215 - **£23 000** - FF230 993
Rose Selavy's Dress Holder Sculpture (H160cm
H62in) London 1998

$3 861 - €3 222 - **£2 262** - FF21 138
Vaas Ceramic (33x39cm 12x15in) Lokeren 1998

$7 500 - €7 042 - **£4 647** - FF46 193
Untitled Ink (57x76.5cm 22x30in) New-York 1999

$2 750 - €2 604 - **£1 708** - FF17 078
Pop Shop V Silkscreen in colors (29x37cm 11x14in)
New-York 1999

$3 200 - €3 435 - **£2 173** - FF22 529
King King for a Day Gelatin silver print (37x25cm
14x9in) Beverly-Hills CA 2001

HARITONOFF Nicholas Basil 1880-1944 **[4]**
- $4 000 - €4 715 - **£2 810** - FF30 926
  Before the Wedding, Young Bride with Sisters and Mother Oil/canvas (38x53cm 15x21in) New-Orleans LA 2000

HARKE Evelyn XIX-XX **[22]**
- $1 836 - €1 693 - **£1 100** - FF11 104
  Waiting Oil/canvas (32x51cm 12x20in) London 1998
- $1 669 - €1 539 - **£1 000** - FF10 094
  The Plough Team Oil/canvas (25.5x31cm 10x12in) London 1998

HARLES Victor Joseph 1894-1975 **[18]**
- $450 - €512 - **£312** - FF3 357
  Paris Street in Winter Oil/board (40x50cm 16x20in) Cincinnati OH 2000
- $425 - €459 - **£294** - FF3 011
  California Coast Oil/board (30x20cm 12x8in) Cincinnati OH 2001

HARLFINGER Richard 1873-1948 **[25]**
- $1 712 - €1 955 - **£1 207** - FF12 827
  «Kaufladen» Öl/Leinwand (74.5x100.5cm 29x39in) Bern 2001
- $793 - €799 - **£495** - FF5 243
  «Ausstellung Secession» Poster (63x47cm 24x18in) Wien 2000

HARLOFF Guy 1933-1991 **[34]**
- $349 - €363 - **£209** - FF2 378
  The Wheel of Light Tecnica mista/carta (25x25.5cm 9x10in) Milano 2000

HARLOW George Henry 1787-1819 **[41]**
- $13 778 - €15 186 - **£9 000** - FF99 614
  Portrait of Sir Thomas Gooch, 5th Bt. (1767-1851) wearing a black Coat Oil/canvas (141x111cm 55x43in) London 2001
- $5 080 - €5 454 - **£3 400** - FF35 773
  Portrait of Frances Coke, daughter of D'Ewes Coke Oil/canvas (86x66cm 33x25in) London 2000
- $6 416 - €6 466 - **£4 000** - FF42 414
  The Proposal/the Engagement Oil/canvas (39.5x31.5cm 15x12in) London 2000
- $5 230 - €5 615 - **£3 500** - FF36 830
  Portrait of Mrs.Sarah Siddons (1755-1831), Bust-Length, Holding a Book Pencil (22x18cm 8x7in) London 2000

HARLOW Louis Kinney 1850-1930 **[22]**
- $200 - €219 - **£135** - FF1 439
  Birches by a pond Watercolour/paper (12x15cm 5x6in) Cambridge MA 2000

HARMAN Fred 1902-1982 **[5]**
- $6 600 - €7 084 - **£4 416** - FF46 470
  Rolling Wheels Oil/canvas (60x91cm 24x36in) Houston TX 2000

HARMAN Jean C. 1897-? **[2]**
- $2 400 - €2 701 - **£1 653** - FF17 718
  View of South Lake, Taboe, California Oil/canvas (97x112cm 38x44in) Washington 2000

HARMAR Fairlie 1876-1945 **[13]**
- $1 120 - €1 203 - **£750** - FF7 891
  The New Hat Oil/canvas (68x52.5cm 26x20in) London 2000

HARMER Alexander F. 1856-1925 **[12]**
- $14 000 - €16 454 - **£9 706** - FF107 931
  Santa Barbara Mission Watercolour/paper (25.5x35cm 10x13in) Beverly-Hills CA 2000

HARMS Anton Friedrich 1695-1745 **[3]**
- $4 927 - €5 113 - **£3 126** - FF33 539
  Darstellung eines Schwimmvogels Öl/Leinwand (55x75cm 21x29in) Magdeburg 2000

HARNETT William Michael 1848/51-1892 **[43]**
- $90 000 - €76 895 - **£54 027** - FF504 396
  The Broker's Table Oil/canvas (23.5x31cm 9x12in) New-York 1998
- $200 - €223 - **£139** - FF1 463
  Study of Two Women Pencil (6x7cm 2x3in) Cleveland OH 2001

HARNEY Paul E. 1850-1915 **[17]**
- $2 250 - €1 898 - **£1 319** - FF12 451
  Back Porch Oil/board (55x45cm 22x18in) Mystic CT 1998
- $500 - €499 - **£312** - FF3 271
  Bust-Length Portrait of a Monk Oil/board (40x30cm 16x12in) St. Louis MO 1999

HAROUARD Émile A. XIX **[1]**
- $1 829 - €2 134 - **£1 272** - FF14 000
  Promeneurs au Caire Huile/toile (41x27cm 16x10in) Paris 2000

HAROUTOUNIAN William T. XX **[2]**
- $5 987 - €5 130 - **£3 600** - FF33 649
  Portrait of Aaron Copland with an autograph quotation Photograph (44x38cm 17x14in) London 1998

HAROUTUNIAN Haren 1967 **[4]**
- $3 600 - €3 106 - **£2 178** - FF20 377
  Farewell Mixed media (90x100cm 35x39in) Tel Aviv 1999
- $2 400 - €2 071 - **£1 452** - FF13 585
  A Voyage to the Sky Mixed media (40x30cm 15x11in) Tel Aviv 1999

HARPER Edward Steel, Jnr. 1878-1951 **[11]**
- $1 135 - €1 090 - **£700** - FF7 153
  Portrait of a Gentleman, in a black Suit and white Shirt Oil/canvas/panel (90.5x49cm 35x19in) London 1999

HARPER Henry Andrew 1835-1900 **[54]**
- $852 - €716 - **£500** - FF4 694
  Loch and Broch and Hills in Misty Background Watercolour (42x75cm 16x29in) London 1998

HARPER Thomas XIX **[21]**
- $212 - €195 - **£130** - FF1 282
  Figures by Stream on Mountain Road Watercolour/paper (25x19.5cm 9x7in) St. Helier, Jersey 1998

HARPER William St-John 1851-1910 **[7]**
- $25 000 - €21 360 - **£15 007** - FF140 110
  Wood Pinks Oil/canvas (114x152.5cm 44x60in) New-York 1998
- $9 500 - €11 357 - **£6 553** - FF74 499
  Long Island Dunes Oil/canvas (76x111cm 30x44in) Milford CT 2000

HARPIGNIES Henri Joseph 1819-1916 **[1042]**
- $46 000 - €51 490 - **£32 080** - FF337 755
  Bords de la Royat près de Vintimille Oil/canvas (133x165.5cm 52x65in) New-York 2001
- $8 400 - €7 394 - **£5 116** - FF48 500
  Paysage Huile/toile (38x47cm 14x18in) Fontainebleau 1999
- $3 200 - €3 071 - **£2 006** - FF20 145
  Thick Forest Oil/canvas (35.5x26.5cm 13x10in) New-York 1999

$756 - €899 - **£524** - FF5 900
Paysage au grand arbre Crayon/papier (28x36cm 11x14in) Paris 2000

HARPLEY Sydney 1927-1992 **[12]**
$2 922 - €2 883 - **£1 800** - FF18 913
Girl on a Swing Bronze (H58.5cm H23in) London 1999

HARPSAU C. XIX **[1]**
$2 200 - €2 135 - **£1 369** - FF14 006
Chickens in the Barnyard Oil/canvas (24x34cm 9x13in) New-Orleans LA 1999

HARR Karl Erik 1940 **[18]**
$454 - €387 - **£271** - FF2 539
Isak bryter sten Etching (61x75cm 24x29in) Oslo 1998

HARRACH von Ferdinand Graf 1832-1915 **[7]**
$2 047 - €2 045 - **£1 280** - FF13 415
Die Versuchung Christi Oil/panel (18.5x26.5cm 7x10in) Köln 1999

HARRADEN Richard Bankes 1778-1862 **[28]**
$34 143 - €31 522 - **£21 000** - FF206 774
The Bay of Naples as seen from the Posilippo Oil/canvas (45.5x89.5cm 17x35in) London 1999
$2 993 - €2 807 - **£1 849** - FF18 411
View of a House with a Lady and her Dog walking in the Garden Oil/panel (29.5x46cm 11x18in) London 1999
$1 989 - €1 697 - **£1 200** - FF11 131
View of St. Catharine's College Cambridge Watercolour (30x47cm 11x18in) Suffolk 1998

HARRADINE Leslie XX **[1]**
$4 026 - €4 083 - **£2 500** - FF26 783
Sunshine Girl's H.N.1344 Ceramic (H13cm H5in) London 2000

HARRER Hugo Paul 1836-1876 **[1]**
$2 841 - €3 068 - **£1 963** - FF20 123
Zwiebelschäler an südländischer Küste Öl/Leinwand (37.5x29cm 14x11in) Frankfurt 2001

HARRI Juhani 1939 **[9]**
$689 - €757 - **£444** - FF4 964
Brinnande sten Collage (72x63cm 28x24in) Helsinki 2000

HARRIET Fulchran Jean 1778-1805 **[3]**
$2 827 - €2 744 - **£1 794** - FF18 000
Daphnis d'après un poème de Gessner Lavis (42x34cm 16x13in) Paris 1999

HARRINGTON Charles 1865-1943 **[52]**
$649 - €753 - **£460** - FF4 938
Heathland Landscape with Horsedrawn Cart and Figure by a River Watercolour/paper (25x38cm 10x15in) Tunbridge-Wells, Kent 2000

HARRINGTON George 1832-1911 **[7]**
$1 000 - €1 088 - **£687** - FF7 139
View of the Houghton Family Homestead in Lancaster, Massachusetts Oil/canvas (20x28cm 8x11in) Bolton MA 2001

HARRINGTON Robert 1800-1882 **[9]**
$1 960 - €2 280 - **£1 400** - FF14 954
Saddled Horses ina Castle yard Oil/board (43x54.5cm 16x21in) London 2001

HARRIOTT William Henry act.1811-1839 **[19]**
$175 - €189 - **£120** - FF1 242
The Erschenheimer Gate Frankfurt Pencil (35.5x26cm 13x10in) Lenton-Lane, Nottingham 2001

HARRIS Brent 1956 **[15]**
$4 076 - €4 451 - **£2 623** - FF29 198
On Becoming (Yellow No.2) Oil/canvas (244x130cm 96x51in) Melbourne 2000

HARRIS Charles Gordon 1891-? **[27]**
$1 000 - €1 097 - **£679** - FF7 195
Fall Landscape with Bridge over Stream Oil/canvas (63x76cm 25x30in) Thomaston ME 2000
$700 - €806 - **£491** - FF5 355
Nantucket Moors in October Looking Towards Sanketey Head Light Oil/canvas/board (36x31cm 14x12in) Boston MA 2000

HARRIS Charles X. 1856-? **[6]**
$45 000 - €52 483 - **£31 594** - FF344 268
Coastal Scene with Children at Shore Oil/canvas (30x40cm 12x16in) Portsmouth NH 2000

HARRIS Edwin 1855-1906 **[70]**
$15 420 - €17 542 - **£10 770** - FF115 065
Vid vaggan Oil/canvas (105x125cm 41x49in) Stockholm 2000
$15 758 - €16 141 - **£9 800** - FF105 880
A Quiet Read Oil/canvas (39.5x49.5cm 15x19in) Billingshurst, West-Sussex 2000
$4 781 - €5 133 - **£3 200** - FF33 669
Portrait of an Old Woman Oil/board (20.5x15cm 8x5in) London 2000

HARRIS George F. 1856-1924 **[10]**
$2 499 - €2 300 - **£1 500** - FF15 087
Ripening Muscatts, Grown by the Marquess of Bute Oil/canvas/board (44x27cm 17x10in) Glamorgan 1999

HARRIS George Walter act.1864-1893 **[4]**
$1 877 - €1 676 - **£1 150** - FF10 997
Still Life of Grapes, Apples and Cherries/Still Life of Apples, Pears Oil/canvas (28.5x33.5cm 11x13in) London 1999

HARRIS Henry 1852-1926 **[51]**
$1 028 - €1 193 - **£710** - FF7 827
Boys Fishing in the Frome by the Old Snuffmill, Stapleton Oil/canvas (65.5x110cm 25x43in) Bristol, Avon 2000
$410 - €442 - **£280** - FF2 902
Stapleton Bridge, Bristol with Figures Oil/canvas (12x38cm 5x15in) Bristol, Avon 2001

HARRIS J. XIX **[12]**
$486 - €496 - **£304** - FF3 252
Fox-Hunting, d'après J.F.Herring Lithographie couleurs (72x123cm 28x48in) Bruxelles 2000

HARRIS John 1811-1865 **[3]**
$308 - €298 - **£190** - FF1 955
The 3rd or Scots Fusilier Guards Color lithograph (29x22cm 11x8in) London 1999

HARRIS John c.1686-c.1740 **[3]**
$257 - €247 - **£160** - FF1 623
The East Prospect of Birmingham, after W Wesley Engraving (40x86cm 15x33in) Leicestershire 1999

HARRIS John II c.1791-1873 **[36]**
$348 - €381 - **£240** - FF2 500
Scène de chasse à courre, d'après Herring Gravure (69x125cm 27x49in) Vendôme 2001

HARRIS Lawren Stewart H. 1885-1970 **[111]**
$16 295 - €18 909 - **£11 250** - FF124 032
The Spirit Settling into the Heaven World State Oil/canvas (108x127cm 42x50in) Vancouver, BC. 2000

H

HARRIS
- $10 720 - €11 827 - £7 089 - FF77 577
  Abstract LSH #130 Oil/canvas (101.5x81cm 39x31in)
  Vancouver, BC. 2000
- $47 074 - €53 250 - £32 929 - FF349 297
  Lake Superior Sketch CVIII Oil/board (27.5x35.5cm
  10x13in) Toronto 2001
- $331 - €367 - £224 - FF2 406
  Maligne Lake, Jasper Park Print (13.5x18cm 5x7in)
  Toronto 2000

HARRIS Lyle Ashton 1965 [8]
- $2 750 - €3 075 - £1 853 - FF20 169
  Constructs #10 Photograph (183x122cm 72x48in)
  New-York 2000

HARRIS OF SWANSEA James, Snr. 1810-1887 [17]
- $2 919 - €2 804 - £1 800 - FF18 393
  **Close Run Thing/A Barque running Inshore bet-
  ween an Island** Oil/canvas (30.5x56cm 12x22in)
  London 1999
- $7 144 - €8 006 - £5 000 - FF52 519
  «Between Oystermouth Castle and Swansea»
  Oil/board (14.5x24.5cm 5x9in) Billingshurst, West-
  Sussex 2001

HARRIS Robert 1849-1919 [33]
- $2 484 - €2 751 - £1 684 - FF18 046
  Portrait of William Rein Wadsworth Oil/canvas
  (77.5x64.5cm 30x25in) Toronto 2000
- $1 295 - €1 511 - £901 - FF9 913
  At the Edge of the Forest Prince Edward Island
  Oil/board (43x30.5cm 15x12in) Toronto 2000

HARRIS Robert George 1911 [7]
- $2 600 - €2 490 - £1 606 - FF16 332
  **Elegant Woman and Soldier in Front of Lingerie
  Shop's Window** Oil/canvas (44x33cm 17x13in) New-
  York 2000

HARRIS Sam Hyde 1889-1977 [117]
- $3 000 - €3 506 - £2 141 - FF22 998
  Mountain landcape Oil/canvas/board (40x50cm
  16x20in) Altadena CA 2001
- $2 250 - €2 629 - £1 606 - FF17 248
  Works boats in Newport Harbor Oil/board
  (30x40cm 12x16in) Altadena CA 2001
- $650 - €621 - £440 - FF4 071
  Scene with Large Windblown Tree Woodcut
  (25x20cm 10x8in) Cincinnati OH 1999

HARRIS William B. 1930 [2]
- $629 - €697 - £426 - FF4 571
  Band's Island, Georgian Bay Print (50.5x75.5cm
  19x29in) Toronto 2000

HARRIS William Cornwallis 1807-1848 [13]
- $329 - €342 - £208 - FF2 241
  Hyaena Crocuta/Hyaena Fusca/Hyaena Venatica
  Color lithograph (36x50cm 14x19in) Johannesburg 2000

HARRIS William Edward c.1860-c.1930 [43]
- $2 518 - €2 405 - £1 550 - FF15 774
  Old Homestead at Romney Oil/canvas (43x87cm
  16x34in) Edinburgh 1999

HARRIS-CHING Raymond, Ray 1935 [12]
- $1 141 - €1 331 - £800 - FF8 728
  North Auskland and New Zealand Pigeon
  Pencil/paper (53x36cm 20x14in) London 2000

HARRISON Alexander, Thomas 1853-1930 [30]
- $14 000 - €12 925 - £8 610 - FF84 782
  Curling Breakers, Brittany Oil/canvas (76x152.5cm
  29x60in) New-York 1999

HARRISON Birge Lowell 1854-1929 [19]
- $4 250 - €4 562 - £2 844 - FF29 924
  Moonlight Meadow Oil/board (45x58cm 18x23in)
  Hatfield PA 2000

HARRISON Charles Harmony 1842-1902 [117]
- $597 - €694 - £420 - FF4 554
  Patting Dyke, Norfolk Watercolour/paper (22x33cm
  9x13in) Lewes, Sussex 2001

HARRISON Claude 1922 [28]
- $1 573 - €1 457 - £950 - FF9 556
  Lover Boy Oil/board (48x51cm 18x20in)
  Leicestershire 1999
- $1 192 - €1 104 - £720 - FF7 242
  Love's Barren Shore Oil/panel (36x42cm 14x16in)
  Leicestershire 1999

HARRISON Clifford XX [15]
- $2 645 - €2 499 - £1 600 - FF16 391
  Alcove with 17th Century English Delft Ware
  Oil/board (91x65.5cm 35x25in) Billingshurst, West-
  Sussex 1999

HARRISON John Cyril 1898-1985 [488]
- $1 418 - €1 646 - £1 000 - FF10 799
  Covey of Partridge Watercolour/paper (33x23cm
  12x9in) Cambridge 2001
- $159 - €147 - £95 - FF967
  Woodcock in Flight over a Snow Covered Field
  Print in colors (30x43cm 12x17in) Aylsham, Norfolk
  1999

HARRISON Lowell Birge 1854-1929 [6]
- $7 100 - €6 477 - £4 365 - FF42 486
  St.Lawrence from Québec Oil/canvas (63x76cm
  25x30in) North-Harwich MA 1999
- $2 250 - €2 498 - £1 565 - FF16 388
  Landscape with Houses Oil/canvas/board (20x25cm
  8x10in) Milford CT 2001
- $500 - €5 136 - £3 394 - FF33 693
  Early Morning Low Tide Pastel/paper (59.5x80cm
  23x31in) Boston MA 1999

HARRISON Sarah Cecilia 1863-1941 [4]
- $11 174 - €12 697 - £7 717 - FF83 290
  Study of a Young Woman Reading Oil/canvas
  (60x50cm 24x20in) Dublin 2000
- $11 913 - €10 163 - £7 100 - FF66 666
  Portrait Study of Ernest Oil/panel (27.5x20.5cm
  10x8in) Dublin 1998

HARRISON Ted 1926 [21]
- $1 911 - €1 619 - £1 149 - FF10 618
  Alaskan Fireworks Acrylic/canvas (91.5x61cm
  36x24in) Vancouver, BC. 1998

HARROWING Walter ?-c.1904 [42]
- $2 725 - €2 574 - £1 700 - FF16 886
  A Chestnut Horse in a Landscape Oil/canvas
  (50x59cm 20x23in) Fernhurst, Haslemere, Surrey 1999
- $750 - €630 - £440 - FF4 130
  Scottish Return Home Oil/canvas (23x33cm 9x13in)
  New-York 1998

HART C. XIX [1]
- $8 500 - €7 869 - £5 131 - FF51 616
  **William Powers holding a Top and Esther
  Powers holding Strawberries** Oil/canvas (45x35cm
  18x14in) New-York 1999

HART Ernest H. 1910 [9]
- $110 - €120 - £76 - FF786
  «Aces Three» Lithograph (24x34cm 9x13in)
  Cleveland OH 2001

HART Frederick Elliot 1943-1999 [13]
🖎 **$3 750** - €3 592 - **£2 359** - FF23 560
  Sacred Mysteries - Act of Light (Male) Sculpture
  (78x60cm 31x24in) Houston TX 1999

HART J. Lawrence c.1830-1907 [20]
🖎 **$188** - €203 - **£130** - FF1 332
  The House of the three Gables, Breston-on-Stour Watercolour (14x21cm 5x8in) West-Midlands
  2001

HART James Mac Dougal 1828-1901 [90]
🖎 **$15 000** - €16 416 - **£10 347** - FF107 682
  Afternoon Concert Oil/canvas (99x136cm 38x53in)
  New-York 2001
🖎 **$6 000** - €6 961 - **£4 268** - FF45 658
  Morning in the Pasture Oil/canvas (49x69cm
  19x27in) Chicago IL 2000
🖎 **$4 910** - €5 113 - **£3 111** - FF33 539
  **Bauernmädchen mit Enten und Truthähnen am
  Bachufer unter Bäumen** Öl/Leinwand (43.5x29cm
  17x11in) München 2000

HART Joel Tanner 1810-1877 [4]
🖎 **$17 000** - €15 845 - **£10 274** - FF103 936
  Portrait Bust Marble (H63cm H25in) New-Orleans
  LA 1999

HART Laetitia Bonnet 1867-? [7]
🖎 **$6 500** - €6 044 - **£4 012** - FF39 647
  Puzzle (presumably self-portraits) Oil/canvas
  (50x40cm 20x16in) Portland ME 1999

HART Mary Theresa G. 1829-1921 [4]
🖎 **$6 500** - €6 044 - **£4 012** - FF39 647
  Puzzle (prezumably self-portraits) Oil/canvas
  (50x40cm 20x16in) Portland ME 1999

HART Pop(George Overbury) 1868-1933 [38]
🖎 **$1 800** - €2 141 - **£1 282** - FF14 041
  Picnic at the Beach Watercolour, gouache/paper
  (33.5x54cm 13x21in) New-York 2000
🖎 **$260** - €242 - **£160** - FF1 589
  «Happy Days» Etching (26x21cm 10x8in) Cleveland
  OH 1999

HART Pro (Kevin Charles) 1928 [512]
🖎 **$1 786** - €1 676 - **£1 104** - FF10 991
  Study for Gold Mining Area Oil/canvas
  (116x120.5cm 45x47in) Sydney 1999
🖎 **$1 789** - €1 721 - **£1 102** - FF11 288
  The Gatemaker Oil/board (90.5x60cm 35x23in)
  Melbourne 1999
🖎 **$560** - €602 - **£381** - FF3 952
  Waterbirds Oil/board (24x28cm 9x11in) Sydney 2001
🖎 **$144** - €139 - **£91** - FF915
  Back Street, Broken Hill Etching (15x20cm 5x7in)
  Sydney 1999

HART Solomon Alexander 1806-1881 [9]
🖎 **$70 000** - €64 206 - **£43 120** - FF421 162
  The Temple of the Jews at Shilo Oil/canvas
  (127x165cm 50x64in) New-York 1999
🖎 **$42 763** - €47 358 - **£29 000** - FF310 648
  **Alee Moham'Mad Beg who Accompanied the
  Horses Presented by the Ima'm** Oil/panel
  (46x35.5cm 18x13in) Plymouth 2000

HART Thomas act.c.1776 [1]
🖎 **$6 000** - €6 364 - **£4 068** - FF41 743
  **Major Robert Rogers, Commander in Chief of
  the Indians** Mezzotint (35x24.5cm 13x9in) New-York
  2001

HART Thomas 1830-1916 [58]
🖎 **$576** - €612 - **£380** - FF4 014
  Shrimping on the Lizard Coastline
  Watercolour/paper (18x48cm 7x18in) Penzance,
  Cornwall 2000

HART Thomas ?-1886 [7]
🖎 **$606** - €670 - **£420** - FF4 394
  **Fishermen hauling in the Nets with St Michaels
  Mount in the Distance** Watercolour (42x61cm
  16x24in) London 2001

HART William M. 1823-1894 [106]
🖎 **$7 000** - €6 629 - **£4 256** - FF43 484
  Cattle Watering Oil/canvas/panel (52x34.5cm
  20x13in) New-York 1999
🖎 **$4 500** - €4 489 - **£2 809** - FF29 444
  Autumn Landscape with Cattle Beside a Stream
  Oil/canvas (20x30cm 8x12in) St. Louis MO 1999
🖎 **$1 500** - €1 610 - **£1 003** - FF10 561
  A Winter Landscape Mixed-media/paper
  (11.5x19.5cm 4x7in) San-Francisco CA 2000

HART William Matthew 1830-1908 [26]
🖎 **$4 794** - €5 114 - **£3 200** - FF33 548
  **Monograph of the Trochilidae - Family of
  Humming-Birds, After J.Gould** Lithograph
  (55.5x38.5cm 21x15in) London 2000

HARTA Felix Albrecht 1884-1967 [77]
🖎 **$3 723** - €3 997 - **£2 541** - FF26 218
  Selbstporträt als junger Mann Öl/Karton
  (45.6x35.5cm 17x13in) Wien 2001
🖎 **$4 739** - €5 087 - **£3 234** - FF33 369
  «Salzburg im Schnee» Öl/Karton (32.2x43.5cm
  12x17in) Wien 2001
🖎 **$750** - €636 - **£452** - FF4 175
  View of Puchberg Watercolour/paper (29.5x40cm
  11x15in) Sydney 1998

HARTER Earl XX [1]
🖎 **$2 800** - €2 604 - **£1 728** - FF17 078
  «Grand Central Terminal» Poster (104x68cm
  41x27in) New-York 1999

HARTIG Carl Christoph 1888-? [20]
🖎 **$2 144** - €2 352 - **£1 456** - FF15 427
  Blattpflanze auf Mahagonitisch Öl/Leinwand
  (75x60cm 29x23in) Berlin 2001

HARTIG Hans 1873-1936 [41]
🖎 **$1 155** - €1 125 - **£709** - FF7 378
  Ruine Hoff in Pommern Öl/Leinwand (66x80.5cm
  25x31in) Berlin 1999

HARTIGAN Grace 1922 [23]
🖎 **$12 000** - €13 441 - **£8 337** - FF88 166
  The Gallow Ball Oil/canvas (96.5x128.5cm 37x50in)
  New-York 2001
🖎 **$4 400** - €4 986 - **£3 074** - FF32 704
  Abstract Composition Oil/paper (57.5x72cm
  22x28in) New-York 2001
🖎 **$800** - €709 - **£490** - FF4 650
  The Hero Leaves his Ship IV Lithograph
  (53.5x76cm 21x29in) New-York 1999

HARTING Lloyd 1901-1976 [8]
🖎 **$1 500** - €1 381 - **£900** - FF9 056
  Southern Tavern with Figures Watercolour/paper
  (55x76cm 22x30in) Pasadena CA 1999

HARTINGER Anton 1806-1890 [18]
🖎 **$1 490** - €1 534 - **£939** - FF10 061
  Blumenstilleben Aquarell, Gouache/Papier (31x26cm
  12x10in) München 2000

HARTLAND Albert Henry 1840-1893 **[55]**
- $529 - €609 - £361 - FF3 997
  Haystacks in a Field Watercolour/paper (17x23cm 6x9in) Dublin 2000

HARTLEY Alex 1963 **[6]**
- $11 157 - €13 121 - £8 000 - FF86 068
  Untitled, Ronan Point Installation (200x90x35cm 78x35x13in) London 2001
- $11 238 - €9 602 - £6 800 - FF62 985
  Untitled (Sackler) Sculpture (74x122x23cm 29x48x9in) London 1998
- $8 965 - €9 624 - £6 000 - FF63 129
  Untitled (Model) Photograph in colour (110x170x30cm 43x66x11in) London 2000

HARTLEY Alfred 1855-1933 **[16]**
- $9 000 - €9 967 - £6 103 - FF65 380
  Portrait of Ina Wigan, Aged Eight Oil/canvas (76x63.5cm 29x25in) New-York 2000

HARTLEY Jonathan Scott 1845-1912 **[8]**
- $6 000 - €5 722 - £3 652 - FF37 535
  Figural Group: Joy of Life Bronze (H43cm H16in) New-York 1999

HARTLEY Marsden 1878-1943 **[99]**
- $2 000 000 - €2 378 510 - £1 425 400 - FF15 602 000
  Abstraction Oil/canvas (119.5x100.5cm 47x39in) New-York 2000
- $190 000 - €221 747 - £134 691 - FF1 454 564
  New Mexico Recollections Oil/canvas (54.5x79.5cm 21x31in) New-York 2001
- $80 000 - €95 140 - £57 016 - FF624 080
  White Hibiscus Oil/board (41x30.5cm 16x12in) New-York 2000
- $4 125 - €3 939 - £2 539 - FF25 841
  Woodcutters Pencil/paper (30x22cm 12x9in) Portsmouth NH 1999
- $2 800 - €3 134 - £1 952 - FF20 559
  Flowers in a Goblet #3 Lithograph (41.5x26cm 16x10in) New-York 2001

HARTMAN John 1950 **[3]**
- $3 638 - €3 906 - £2 471 - FF25 620
  The Artist's Home in Winter Mixed media/canvas (41x57.5cm 16x22in) Calgary, Alberta 2001

HARTMAN Mauno 1930 **[10]**
- $1 533 - €1 682 - £987 - FF11 032
  X.CIII Sculpture, wood (40x40cm 15x15in) Helsinki 2000

HARTMANN Erich 1886-1974 **[37]**
- $2 393 - €2 556 - £1 592 - FF16 769
  Schreibende Frau am Fenstertisch Tempera (72.5x86cm 28x33in) Hamburg 2000
- $229 - €273 - £163 - FF1 790
  Selbstbildnis Watercolour (22.7x15cm 8x5in) Hamburg 2000

HARTMANN Hugo Friedrich 1870-1943 **[11]**
- $3 621 - €4 021 - £2 520 - FF26 379
  Hvilende tiger Oil/canvas (62x88cm 24x34in) København 2001

HARTMANN Johann Joseph 1753-1830 **[25]**
- $2 348 - €2 010 - £1 413 - FF13 182
  Die St. Peterinsel Gouache/papier (29x42.5cm 11x16in) Zürich 1998
- $316 - €357 - £222 - FF2 343
  «Biéz d'Etoz au Doubs Frontière de la Franche-Comté»/«Le Précipice» Radierung (14x16.5cm 5x6in) Bern 2001

HARTMANN Johannes Jacob c.1658-1738/45 **[15]**
- $29 423 - €34 768 - £20 855 - FF228 065
  Bewaldete Landschaft mit Reisenden Öl/Leinwand (60.5x81cm 23x31in) Ahlden 2000
- $24 565 - €23 234 - £15 300 - FF152 405
  Flight to Egypt Oil/metal (34x47cm 13x18in) Praha 2000

HARTMANN Ludwig 1835-1902 **[38]**
- $2 165 - €2 182 - £1 349 - FF14 315
  Schwatz mit dem Pferdehändler Huile/panneau (31x61.5cm 12x24in) Zürich 2000
- $1 464 - €1 534 - £968 - FF10 061
  Landhaus in einem Park Öl/Leinwand (24x29cm 9x11in) München 2000

HARTMANN Oluf 1879-1910 **[42]**
- $966 - €1 007 - £608 - FF6 608
  Maske af Beethoven Oil/canvas (35x27cm 13x10in) København 2000
- $556 - €512 - £342 - FF3 356
  Forarbejde til Ixion Indian ink (13x13cm 5x5in) København 1999

HARTMANN Werner 1945-1993 **[20]**
- $821 - €812 - £512 - FF5 329
  Metallplastik Fer (20x4x4cm 7x1x1in) Luzern 1999
- $204 - €243 - £145 - FF1 597
  Ohne Titel Indian ink (18x14cm 7x5in) Luzern 2000

HARTRATH Lucie 1868-1962 **[7]**
- $16 000 - €18 302 - £11 126 - FF120 056
  The Foot Bridge Oil/canvas (58x71cm 23x28in) Cincinnati OH 2000
- $6 500 - €7 284 - £4 530 - FF47 783
  The Cabins Oil/canvas (33x38cm 12x14in) Beverly-Hills CA 2001

HARTUNG Eduard XIX-XX **[84]**
- $125 - €143 - £87 - FF939
  Bach durch schroffe Berglandschaft Öl/Karton (71x42cm 27x16in) Rudolstadt-Thüringen 2000

HARTUNG Hans Heinrich Ernst 1904-1989 **[1468]**
- $77 952 - €73 176 - £48 288 - FF480 000
  T 1965 - H 33 Acrylique/toile (102x130cm 40x51in) Paris 1999
- $15 516 - €18 294 - £10 908 - FF120 000
  Composition Technique mixte/carton (76x107cm 29x42in) Paris 2000
- $7 497 - €7 772 - £4 498 - FF50 979
  T 1986-R4 Acrilico/tela (22x16cm 8x6in) Milano 2000
- $9 500 - €9 848 - £5 700 - FF64 600
  Senza titolo Tecnica mista, disegno (48.5x65cm 19x25in) Milano 1999
- $427 - €420 - £273 - FF2 728
  Composición abstracta Litografía (59.5x86.5cm 23x34in) Barcelona 1999

HARTUNG Heinrich 1851-1919 **[38]**
- $14 156 - €13 139 - £8 500 - FF86 183
  In the Orchard Oil/canvas (91.5x132.5cm 36x52in) London 1999
- $3 210 - €3 430 - £2 139 - FF22 500
  Place du village animée Huile/toile (56x86cm 22x33in) Paris 2000

HARTUNG Johann XIX-XX **[12]**
- $1 465 - €1 534 - £920 - FF10 061
  Vier Dackelwelpen Oil/panel (18.5x26.5cm 7x10in) Bremen 2000

HARTUNG Karl 1908-1967 **[44]**
- $9 644 - €11 248 - £6 771 - FF73 785
  Komposition I Bronze (H30cm H11in) Köln 2000

H

✏ $750 - €767 - £470 - FF5 030
Atelierszene Indian ink (20.5x26.7cm 8x10in)
Hamburg 2000

▥ $215 - €204 - £133 - FF1 341
Komposition Woodcut (43x30.5cm 16x12in)
Hamburg 1999

HARTWELL George Kenneth 1891-1949 [7]
▥ $1 000 - €1 169 - £702 - FF7 668
Subway Lithograph (25.5x20.5cm 10x8in) New-York
2000

HARTWICH Hermann 1853-1926 [22]
☞ $2 379 - €2 812 - £1 686 - FF18 446
**Porträt des Malers Christian Mali in seinem
Atelier** Öl/Leinwand (55x68cm 21x26in) Stuttgart 2000

HARTWICK George Gunther ?-1899 [7]
☞ $7 200 - €8 563 - £5 131 - FF56 167
Girola Path Oil/canvas (76x112cm 29x44in) New-
York 2000

HARTWIG Heinie 1939 [106]
☞ $1 100 - €1 118 - £691 - FF7 333
High Mountain Camp Oil/board (45x60cm 18x24in)
Oakland CA 2000
☞ $500 - €508 - £312 - FF3 332
Rocky Mountain Peaks Oil/masonite (30x45cm
12x18in) Portland OR 2000

HARTWIG Josef 1850-1956 [6]
⚒ $7 481 - €8 692 - £5 258 - FF57 016
Bauhaus-Schachspiel Installation (7.5x13.5x13.5cm
2x5x5in) München 2001

HARTWIG Max 1873-1939 [55]
☞ $547 - €613 - £371 - FF4 024
Dorfansicht Öl/Karton (8x12cm 3x4in) München
2000

HARTZ Lauritz 1903-1987 [61]
☞ $1 269 - €1 475 - £892 - FF9 677
Skovparti med figur Oil/canvas (68x50cm 26x19in)
Köbenhavn 2001

HARTZ Louis 1869-1935 [20]
☞ $907 - €767 - £539 - FF5 030
Früchtestilleben Öl/Leinwand (55x46cm 21x18in)
Bremen 1998

HARTZ Wilhelm XIX-XX [3]
▥ $1 300 - €1 109 - £784 - FF7 274
«Internationale Photographische Ausstellung»
Poster (62.5x97.5cm 24x38in) New-York 1998

HARUNOBU Suzuki 1724-1770 [98]
▥ $7 000 - €7 282 - £4 454 - FF47 770
Eight Views of Omi (Omi Hakke) Woodcut in colors
(15.5x32.5cm 6x12in) New-York 2000

HARVEY G. 1933 [42]
☞ $67 500 - €61 361 - £40 655 - FF402 502
God's Gift to the Cowboy Oil/canvas (127x101cm
50x40in) Hayden ID 1998
☞ $16 000 - €18 167 - £11 116 - FF119 169
Country Place Oil/canvas (76x60cm 30x24in) Dallas
TX 2001
☞ $7 700 - €7 191 - £4 752 - FF47 170
Early out Oil/board (27x17cm 11x7in) Dallas TX 1999
⚒ $4 200 - €4 769 - £2 918 - FF31 282
Taking Stock Bronze (H27cm H11in) Dallas TX 2001

HARVEY George 1806-1876 [21]
☞ $2 600 - €2 365 - £1 591 - FF15 513
Still Life of Apples Oil/canvas (34x44cm 13x17in)
New-Orleans LA 1998

HARVEY George Wainwright 1855-1930 [16]
☞ $3 700 - €4 315 - £2 597 - FF28 306
Frozen Pond and Snow Covered Hills Oil/canvas
(61x91.5cm 24x36in) Boston MA 2000

HARVEY Gerald Jones 1933 [5]
▥ $700 - €822 - £494 - FF5 392
Changing of the Rangeland Print (42x63.5cm
16x25in) New-York 2000

HARVEY Harold C. 1874-1941 [127]
☞ $57 812 - €53 376 - £36 000 - FF350 121
The Road to market Oil/canvas (109x127cm
42x50in) London 1999
☞ $20 876 - €19 274 - £13 000 - FF126 432
Haulers on a Country Road, Newlyn Oil/canvas
(76.5x91.5cm 30x36in) London 1999
☞ $17 617 - €15 030 - £10 500 - FF98 591
Feeding Time Oil/canvas (35.5x30.5cm 13x12in)
London 1998
✏ $1 867 - €2 179 - £1 300 - FF14 294
Gertrude Harvey (Study for the Sunlit Room)
Pencil/paper (37x49cm 14x19in) London 2000

HARVEY Herbert Johnson 1884-1928 [15]
☞ $7 114 - €8 266 - £5 000 - FF54 221
Head and Shoulder Portrait of a young Girl
Oil/canvas (29.5x24cm 11x9in) Leamington-Spa,
Warwickshire 2001

HARVEY Marcus 1963 [2]
☞ $12 891 - €11 014 - £7 800 - FF72 247
Doggy Oil/canvas (213x213cm 83x83in) London 1998

HARVEY Marion Rodger Hamil. 1886-1971 [32]
✏ $1 120 - €1 108 - £700 - FF7 269
Pekinese Coloured chalks/paper (39.5x49.5cm
15x19in) Glasgow 1999

HARVEY Paul 1878-1948 [1]
☞ $6 500 - €6 977 - £4 349 - FF45 766
Santa Barbara, California Oil/canvas (71x76cm
28x30in) Portland ME 2000

HARVEY Seymour Garstin XIX-XX [5]
☞ $8 965 - €9 624 - £6 000 - FF63 129
The Lady of Shalott Oil/panel (67.5x47cm 26x18in)
London 2000

HARWOOD John ?-c.1829 [3]
☞ $33 224 - €35 337 - £21 000 - FF231 798
The Choir of York Minster Looking West Oil/panel
(94.5x75cm 37x29in) London 2000

HARY Gyula 1864-1946 [19]
☞ $680 - €768 - £480 - FF5 040
Viaduc Huile/toile (60x82cm 23x32in) Budapest 2001
☞ $528 - €605 - £368 - FF3 968
Oszi impresszio Oil/wood (19x24cm 7x9in)
Budapest 2000

HARZE Léopold 1831-1893 [14]
⚒ $2 009 - €1 736 - £1 211 - FF11 389
Mendiant, jeune fille et chien Terracotta
(28x28.5x19cm 11x11x7in) Bruxelles 1998

HASBROUCK Du Bois Fenelon 1860-1934 [25]
☞ $3 100 - €2 620 - £1 855 - FF17 186
Evening Oil/board (23x30cm 9x12in) Hatfield PA
1998
✏ $475 - €454 - £292 - FF2 978
Landscape in Winter Watercolour/paper (22x33cm
9x13in) Charlottesville VA 1999

HASCH Carl 1834-1897 [80]
☞ $2 928 - €3 068 - £1 936 - FF20 123
Gebirgssee Öl/Leinwand (73x100cm 28x39in)
München 2000

HASCH
☞ **$3 193** - €3 126 - **£1 965** - FF20 508
An der Schlitza in Kärnten/Bei Lugano, südliche Schweiz Öl/Leinwand (32x47cm 12x18in) Zürich 1999

HASCH Victor 1945 **[11]**
☞ **$1 473** - €1 753 - **£1 020** - FF11 500
Seychelles Huile/toile (130x62cm 51x24in) Nancy 2000

HASEGAWA Kiyoshi 1891-1980 **[340]**
▥ **$1 800** - €1 823 - **£1 119** - FF11 960
Anemones Drypoint (25x21cm 9x8in) New-York 2000

HASEGAWA Soichi 1929 **[117]**
✎ **$1 394** - €1 618 - **£962** - FF10 613
View of the City Watercolour/paper (37x27.5cm 14x10in) Johannesburg 2000
▥ **$158** - €160 - **£99** - FF1 050
Indifférence Gravure (65x50cm 25x19in) Orléans 2000

HASEGAWA Tomisaburô 1910 **[9]**
▥ **$63** - €60 - **£40** - FF394
View of Mount Fuji Woodcut in colors (38x50cm 14x19in) London 1999

HASELEER Frans 1804-1890 **[4]**
☞ **$14 437** - €14 549 - **£9 000** - FF95 432
Rembrandt engraving the Raising of Lazarus Oil/panel (50.5x39cm 19x15in) London 2000

HASELL William XVIII **[1]**
☞ **$3 936** - €4 476 - **£2 700** - FF29 361
Mixed Flowers in a Gilt Urn on a Ledge in a Niche Oil/canvas (124.5x81cm 49x31in) Oxfordshire 2000

HASELTINE Charles Field 1840-1915 **[1]**
☞ **$7 500** - €7 081 - **£4 642** - FF46 448
On the Ganges, Benares, India Oil/canvas (91x114cm 36x45in) Milford CT 1999

HASELTINE Herbert 1877-1962 **[40]**
⚏ **$16 000** - €18 008 - **£11 022** - FF118 123
Sheep Bronze (H12.5cm H4in) Washington 2000

HASELTINE William Stanley 1835-1900 **[39]**
☞ **$10 450** - €8 855 - **£6 244** - FF58 087
Landscape Oil/board (60x50cm 24x20in) MT. Morris NY 1998
☞ **$120 000** - €123 149 - **£75 228** - FF807 804
New England Seascape with figures on a rocky shore Oil/canvas (25x55cm 10x22in) Downington PA 2000

HASEMANN Wilhelm Gustav F. 1850-1913 **[13]**
☞ **$2 402** - €2 269 - **£1 498** - FF14 883
Spinning German Peasant Woman Oil/canvas (61.5x46.5cm 24x18in) Amsterdam 1999

HASENCLEVER Johann Peter 1810-1853 **[11]**
☞ **$17 468** - €17 895 - **£10 780** - FF117 386
Kandidat Jobs im Examen Öl/Leinwand (79x105.5cm 31x41in) Düsseldorf 2000
☞ **$3 500** - €3 818 - **£2 405** - FF24 987
Waist Length Portrait of a Woman wearing a Black Shawl and Floral Oil/canvas (26x22cm 10x9in) St. Louis MO 2001

HASENPFLUG Carl Georg Adolf 1802-1858 **[19]**
☞ **$4 491** - €4 602 - **£2 772** - FF30 185
Klosterhalle im Schnee Öl/Leinwand (43.8x39cm 17x15in) Düsseldorf 2000
☞ **$19 729** - €23 520 - **£14 066** - FF154 279
Blick auf einen winterlichen Friedhof Öl/Leinwand (27.3x31cm 10x12in) Köln 2000

HASKELL Ernest 1876-1925 **[12]**
▥ **$2 400** - €2 615 - **£1 661** - FF17 155
«Truth Xmas» Poster (50x35cm 20x14in) New-York 2001

HASKELL Joseph A. 1808-1894 **[5]**
☞ **$850** - €874 - **£539** - FF5 736
Portrait of a Lady in black Oil/canvas (76x64cm 30x25in) New-Orleans LA 2000

HASLEHURST Ernest William 1866-1949 **[67]**
✎ **$617** - €734 - **£440** - FF4 815
River Estuary, Devon Watercolour/paper (32.5x49.5cm 12x19in) Bath 2000

HASLUND Otto 1842-1917 **[39]**
☞ **$2 131** - €2 018 - **£1 326** - FF13 240
En gammel bondekone ved sin rok Oil/canvas (51x44cm 20x17in) Köbenhavn 1999
☞ **$421** - €469 - **£288** - FF3 079
Interiör med legende börn Oil/paper (37x28cm 14x11in) Viby J, Arhus 2000

HASS Siegfried A. Sofus 1848-1908 **[26]**
☞ **$496** - €471 - **£302** - FF3 089
I parken Oil/canvas (78x66cm 30x25in) Helsinki 1999

HASSALL John 1868-1948 **[62]**
✎ **$385** - €382 - **£240** - FF2 509
Guilty Pencil (29x22cm 11x8in) London 1999
▥ **$500** - €558 - **£327** - FF3 659
«The New Barmaid» Poster (74x51cm 29x20in) New-York 2000

HASSAM Childe F. 1859-1935 **[331]**
☞ **$330 000** - €369 624 - **£229 284** - FF2 424 576
Moonrise at sunset, Cape Ann Oil/canvas (45.5x56cm 17x22in) New-York 2001
☞ **$115 000** - €126 719 - **£76 486** - FF831 220
Cottages on a Country Road Oil/canvas (25x38cm 10x15in) Haverhill MA 2000
☞ **$40 000** - €39 714 - **£25 000** - FF260 504
Gloucester Inner Harbor Pastel (21.5x28cm 8x11in) New-York 1999
▥ **$1 700** - €1 898 - **£1 088** - FF12 453
Old Dominy House Etching (23x30cm 9x11in) New-York 2000

HASSAN Faik 1914-1992 **[1]**
✎ **$6 875** - €7 732 - **£4 800** - FF50 721
Two Women Gouache/board (49x33cm 19x12in) London 2001

HASSEBRAUCK Ernst 1905-1974 **[104]**
☞ **$1 395** - €1 380 - **£870** - FF9 055
Blumenstilleben Mischtechnik/Karton (76.2x55.2cm 29x21in) Berlin 1999
✎ **$351** - €405 - **£240** - FF2 683
Der Chirurg Prof.Dr.Fromme Charcoal (48x35.5cm 18x13in) Berlin 2000
▥ **$101** - €112 - **£66** - FF737
Frau Brief lesend Radierung (49x30cm 19x11in) Leipzig 2000

HASSEBRAUCK-KÖRTLING Johanna XIX-XX **[6]**
☞ **$1 295** - €1 109 - **£758** - FF7 276
The Apostle Thomas, after Nicolaes Maes Oil/canvas (122x91cm 48x35in) Amsterdam 1998

HASSELBACH Wilhelm 1846-? **[7]**
☞ **$8 341** - €9 203 - **£5 517** - FF60 370
Die zerbrochene Butzenscheibe Oil/panel (75x98cm 29x38in) Hamburg 2000

HASSELBERG Per 1850-1894 **[22]**
⚏ **$1 844** - €1 980 - **£1 234** - FF12 990
Farfadern Bronze (H30cm H11in) Stockholm 2000

HASSELBLATT Adolf 1823-1896 **[4]**
> **$2 592** - €2 723 - **£1 640** - FF17 859
Children Playing on the Ice Oil/canvas (22x36cm 8x14in) Amsterdam 2000

HASSELGREN Gustaf Erik 1781-1827 **[4]**
> **$3 655** - €4 348 - **£2 519** - FF28 519
Figurscen Oil/canvas (83x135cm 32x53in) Stockholm 2000

HASSELL Edward XIX **[3]**
> **$1 638** - €1 397 - **£976** - FF9 166
Mansion in Galway Oil/paper (10x10cm 4x4in) Dublin 1998

HASSELT van Willem 1882-1963 **[75]**
> **$1 107** - €1 189 - **£741** - FF7 800
Le port de l'île d'Yeu Huile/toile (54x65cm 21x25in) Nantes 2000
> **$677** - €762 - **£471** - FF5 000
Paysage en Ile de France Huile/carton (22x25cm 8x9in) Paris 2001
> **$2 312** - €1 982 - **£1 391** - FF13 000
«Grand Match de Football Rugby» Affiche (120.5x117cm 47x46in) Orléans 1998

HASSENTEUFEL Hans 1887-1943 **[25]**
> **$2 299** - €1 943 - **£1 371** - FF12 743
Akt in rotem Samtumhang Öl/Leinwand (61x40.5cm 24x15in) Düsseldorf 1998

HÄSSLER Uwe 1938 **[7]**
> **$973** - €818 - **£572** - FF5 365
Liebespaare Pencil (43x60.5cm 16x23in) Stuttgart 1998

HASTAIRE Claude Hilaire 1946 **[30]**
> **$828** - €915 - **£574** - FF6 000
«Sur la genèse» Technique mixte (45x45cm 17x17in) Paris 2001
> **$432** - €457 - **£286** - FF3 000
Grand paysage exotique Lithographie (107x77cm 42x30in) Dozulé 2000

HASTIE Grace H. XIX-XX **[23]**
> **$364** - €424 - **£260** - FF2 780
Fishing Vessels Moored on Beach at Low Tide Watercolour (30x25cm 11x9in) Cambridge 2000

HASTREL d' Adolphe 1805-1874 **[5]**
> **$84 160** - €72 525 - **£50 000** - FF475 735
Praia de D.Manuel Oil/canvas (37.5x60.5cm 14x23in) London 1998
> **$4 000** - €3 407 - **£2 411** - FF22 346
«Portenita» Técnica mixta/papel (39.5x26cm 15x10in) Buenos-Aires 1998

HASUI Kawase Bunjiro 1883-1957 **[241]**
> **$30 000** - €35 181 - **£21 408** - FF230 772
Sailing Boat in an Inlet Mixed media (163x163.5cm 64x64in) New-York 2000
> **$1 800** - €2 115 - **£1 247** - FF13 876
Zundai Yama Watercolour/paper (35.5x45.5cm 13x17in) Beverly-Hills CA 2000
> **$678** - €658 - **£430** - FF4 318
Nagasaki Villa Woodcut (16.5x45.5cm 6x17in) Toronto 1999

HASWELLE Keeley 1832-1891 **[2]**
> **$5 400** - €5 055 - **£3 346** - FF33 157
Sonming Bridge Oil/canvas (35x60cm 14x24in) Norwalk CT 1999

HATHAWAY George M. 1856-1903 **[30]**
> **$1 100** - €1 141 - **£697** - FF7 487
Coastal View Oil/board (15x26cm 5x10in) Boston MA 2000

HATHAWAY James S. act.1839-1847 **[1]**
> **$21 000** - €19 531 - **£13 003** - FF128 112
Portrait of Levi Starbuck Coffin and his Sister Eunice Coffin Oil/canvas (96x73cm 38x29in) Nantucket MA 1999

HATHAWAY Rufus 1770-1822 **[3]**
> **$90 000** - €77 648 - **£54 495** - FF509 337
Joseph Robertson Tolman Oil/canvas (77.5x64cm 30x25in) New-York 1999

HATHERELL William 1855-1928 **[8]**
> **$1 910** - €1 859 - **£1 176** - FF12 195
Läsande kvinna med parasoll i roddbåt Akvarell/papper (21x28.5cm 8x11in) Stockholm 1999

HATLEM John Carsten XX **[2]**
> **$2 140** - €2 117 - **£1 334** - FF13 885
Bow of the Queen Mary Vintage gelatin silver print (23.9x16cm 9x6in) Berlin 1999

HATOUM Mona 1952 **[16]**
> **$86 669** - €93 032 - **£58 000** - FF610 252
Marbles Carpet Installation (600x400cm 236x157in) London 2000
> **$16 000** - €15 481 - **£9 867** - FF101 550
+ And - Sculpture (7.5x30x30cm 2x11x11in) New-York 1999
> **$32 000** - €35 842 - **£22 233** - FF235 110
Performance Still, Roadworks Gelatin silver print (76.5x108cm 30x42in) New-York 2001

HATTERSLEY Frederick William 1860-? **[32]**
> **$721** - €797 - **£500** - FF5 226
Figures & Horses on a Windswept Path Watercolour/paper (14.5x35cm 5x13in) Kirkby-Lonsdale, Cumbria 2001

HATTICH van Petrus XVII **[1]**
> **$31 000** - €32 136 - **£18 600** - FF210 800
Diana e Atteone/Paesaggio con rovine classiche e astanti presso Olio/rame (39x66cm 15x25in) Roma 2001

HATTON Helen Howard ?-c.1894 **[2]**
> **$739** - €836 - **£500** - FF5 486
Young Beauty Pastel/paper (43.5x67cm 17x26in) London 2000

HATZ Felix 1904-1999 **[64]**
> **$514** - €435 - **£307** - FF2 851
Stilleben Oil/canvas (65x82cm 25x32in) Stockholm 1998

HATZIS Vassilios 1870-1915 **[16]**
> **$11 694** - €13 418 - **£8 000** - FF88 016
Fishermen Coming in to Shore Oil/canvas (47.5x34cm 18x13in) London 2000
> **$3 654** - €4 193 - **£2 500** - FF27 505
Boats in a Harbour, Sunset Oil/canvas (24.5x15cm 9x5in) London 2000

HATZOPOULOS Georgio 1858-1935 **[1]**
> **$5 400** - €6 006 - **£3 600** - FF39 400
The Acropolis at Sunset Oil/canvas (53x74.5cm 20x29in) Athens 2000

HAU Tran Luu 1928 **[7]**
> **$2 295** - €2 607 - **£1 571** - FF17 098
Still Life Acrylic/canvas (80x90cm 31x35in) Singapore 2000
> **$1 781** - €1 495 - **£1 045** - FF9 804
Mountain Village Gouache/paper (68x79cm 26x31in) Singapore 1998

H

HAU Woldemar Ivanovich 1816-1895 **[13]**
$1 718 - €1 682 - £1 057 - FF11 032
Konstantine Opotchinine Akvarell/papper
(15x12cm 5x4in) Helsinki 1999

HAUBENSTOCK-RAMATI Roman 1919-1994 **[8]**
$960 - €1 090 - £673 - FF7 150
«Konstellationen» Farbradierung (61x41cm 24x16in)
Wien 2001

HAUBER Josef 1766-1834 **[18]**
$1 685 - €1 534 - £1 053 - FF10 061
**Bildnis einer Münchener Bürgersfrau mit
Riegelhaube** Öl/Leinwand (75x58.5cm 29x23in)
München 1999

HAUBERG Peter Christian 1844-1928 **[1]**
$3 250 - €3 885 - £2 241 - FF25 486
A Scenic Rest Oil/canvas (93x78cm 37x31in) Milford
CT 2000

HÄUBLIN Nicolaus XVII **[1]**
$2 107 - €2 045 - £1 312 - FF13 415
**Bildnis des theosophischen Mystikers Jakob
Böhme in Umarmung** Radierung (44.7x35.2cm
17x13in) Berlin 1999

HAUDEBOURT-LESCOT Hortense Antoinette 1784-
1845 **[32]**
$7 566 - €9 147 - £5 286 - FF60 000
Un médecin pique-assiette Huile/toile
(55.5x46.5cm 21x18in) Paris 2000
$11 000 - €10 349 - £6 864 - FF67 885
A Swiss Guard Oil/canvas (37x28cm 14x11in) New-
York 1999
$1 990 - €2 211 - £1 387 - FF14 500
Théâtre de rue en Italie Aquarelle/papier (17x24cm
6x9in) Paris 2001

HAUEISEN Albert 1872-1954 **[101]**
$3 279 - €3 068 - £1 986 - FF20 123
Schlafendes Bauernmädchen Öl/Leinwand
(81x100cm 31x39in) Stuttgart 1999
$146 - €153 - £92 - FF1 006
Selbstbildnis Indian ink (20.3x20.5cm 7x8in)
Heidelberg 2000
$74 - €71 - £45 - FF469
Flusslandschaft mit zwei Anglern Radierung
(38.5x35.2cm 15x13in) Bielefeld 1999

HAUER Hans 1586-1660 **[1]**
$8 000 - €6 955 - £4 841 - FF45 620
Coat-of-Arms Gouache (10x9cm 3x3in) New-York
1999

HAUER Leopold 1896-1984 **[37]**
$2 817 - €3 270 - £1 980 - FF21 451
Kathedrale Oil/canvas/panel (59x49cm 23x19in) Wien
2001
$2 102 - €1 816 - £1 267 - FF11 910
Blumen Öl/Leinwand (29x25.5cm 11x10in) Wien 1998
$807 - €872 - £558 - FF5 720
Bauernhaus in Frankreich Indian ink (34.3x24.5cm
13x9in) Wien 2001

HAUG Kristian 1862-1953 **[8]**
$2 950 - €3 350 - £2 020 - FF21 972
Efterårslandskab med rådyr Oil/canvas
(80.5x90.5cm 31x35in) Vejle 2000

HAUG von Robert 1857-1922 **[70]**
$777 - €664 - £456 - FF4 356
Rückenfiguren von zwei Soldaten im Felde
Oil/canvas (47x38cm 18x14in) Stuttgart 1998
$1 074 - €1 227 - £757 - FF8 049
Reiter Öl/Karton (23x37cm 9x14in) Stuttgart 2001

HAUGEN SØRENSEN Arne 1932 **[79]**
$10 176 - €8 611 - £6 086 - FF56 486
«Dame uden dyr» Oil/canvas (130x194cm 51x76in)
København 1998
$3 268 - €3 096 - £1 987 - FF20 306
Favn og nymfe Oil/canvas (70x70cm 27x27in)
København 1999
$397 - €377 - £241 - FF2 472
Figur Watercolour/paper (39x28cm 15x11in)
København 1999
$159 - €134 - £95 - FF881
Figurkomposition Woodcut (40x36cm 15x14in)
København 1998

HAUGEN SØRENSEN Jørgen 1934 **[81]**
$691 - €673 - £424 - FF4 412
Untitled Bronze (H25cm H9in) København 1999

HAUGHTON Moses, Jnr. 1772/74-1848 **[1]**
$2 806 - €3 337 - £2 000 - FF21 890
**Dead Grouse, Killed on Lord Powis's Hills by
J.C.Molineaux** Oil/panel (28x42cm 11x16in) London
2000

HAUGHTON Moses, Snr. 1734-1804 **[6]**
$3 605 - €3 984 - £2 500 - FF26 132
Still Life of Fruit and a Melon Oil/panel
(43.5x53.5cm 17x21in) London 2001

HAUGK von Gustav 1804-1861 **[5]**
$6 750 - €6 997 - £4 050 - FF45 900
Venditori sul golfo Olio/tela (45x72cm 17x28in)
Venezia 2000

HAUKELAND Arnold 1920-1983 **[2]**
$12 876 - €15 017 - £8 964 - FF98 508
Mor og unge Bronze (H33cm H12in) Oslo 2000

HAUMONT Émile Richard XIX-XX **[5]**
$3 250 - €3 755 - £2 275 - FF24 628
Sun Drenched Courtyard Oil/canvas (33x45cm
13x18in) New-York 2001

HAUN August C. 1815-1894 **[4]**
$1 894 - €1 841 - £1 184 - FF12 074
**Panorama von Bremen, nach Anton v. Lowtzow
(1842-1854)** Lithographie (34x140cm 13x55in)
Bremen 1999

HAUNOLD Carl 1813-1876 **[43]**
$740 - €872 - £520 - FF5 720
Träumendes Mädchen am Felsvorsprung
Öl/Leinwand (24.6x32cm 9x12in) Wien 2000

HAUNOLD Karl Franz Emanuel 1832-1911 **[37]**
$725 - €613 - £431 - FF4 024
Malerische Burgruine im sonnigen Licht
Oil/panel (31x24cm 12x9in) Lindau 1998

HAUPT Karl Hermann 1904-1983 **[25]**
$24 723 - €23 008 - £15 205 - FF150 925
Abstrakte Komposition Öl/Leinwand (100x125cm
39x49in) München 1999
$18 099 - €19 429 - £12 114 - FF127 448
Aufstrebende Konstruktion Öl/Leinwand
(75x95.2cm 29x37in) Köln 2000
$2 381 - €2 556 - £1 594 - FF16 769
Studien Gouache/Karton (9.4x6.3cm 3x2in) Köln 2000

HAUPT Matti 1912-1999 **[75]**
$221 - €252 - £152 - FF1 654
Naken Mixed media (40x28cm 15x11in) Helsinki 2000
$636 - €538 - £379 - FF3 529
Kvinnohuvud Terracotta (H32cm H12in) Helsinki
1998
$257 - €303 - £178 - FF1 985
Rygg Pastel/paper (26x35cm 10x13in) Helsinki 2000

HAUPTMANN Ivo 1886-1973 **[176]**
- $5 960 - €6 647 - **£4 007** - FF43 600
  Frau mit Geige Öl/Leinwand (65x50cm 25x19in)
  Satow 2000
- $1 042 - €971 - **£643** - FF6 372
  Seinebrücke in Paris Watercolour (32.5x41cm
  12x16in) Hamburg 1999

HAUPTMANN Karl 1880-1947 **[78]**
- $5 604 - €5 368 - **£3 526** - FF35 215
  **Frühling im Schwarzwald, inmitten blühender
  Wiesen** Öl/Leinwand (38x50cm 14x19in) Stuttgart
  1999
- $4 087 - €3 835 - **£2 525** - FF25 154
  **Oberitalienisches Stadttor mit Figurenstaffage
  an einem Sommertag** Öl/Leinwand (45x35cm
  17x13in) Staufen 1999
- $2 180 - €2 045 - **£1 346** - FF13 415
  Falkenstein (Blick auf die Elbe vom Falkenstein)
  Watercolour (38.5x46cm 15x18in) Stuttgart 1999

HAUPTMANN Sven 1911-1984 **[49]**
- $373 - €376 - **£232** - FF2 467
  Komposition Collage (15x20cm 5x7in) København
  2000

HAURI Edi 1911-1988 **[5]**
- $386 - €389 - **£240** - FF2 554
  «Berner Oberland, Schweiz» Poster (102x64cm
  40x25in) London 2000

HAUSCHILD Maximilien Albert 1810-1895 **[3]**
- $2 379 - €2 812 - **£1 686** - FF18 446
  Blick in das Langhaus des Mailänder Domes
  Öl/Leinwand (68x55cm 26x21in) Stuttgart 2000

HAUSER Carry 1895-1985 **[151]**
- $5 499 - €6 541 - **£3 924** - FF42 903
  Das grosse Buschbild Oil/panel (66.5x90cm
  26x35in) Wien 2000
- $1 099 - €1 090 - **£688** - FF7 150
  Frohe Weihnachten Indian ink (19x12.9cm 7x5in)
  Wien 1999
- $156 - €182 - **£111** - FF1 191
  Der Heilige Antonius Linocut (26x17cm 10x6in)
  Wien 2000

HAUSER Erich 1930 **[36]**
- $3 993 - €3 835 - **£2 461** - FF25 154
  Stele Metal (50x13cm 19x4x5in) München 1999
- $617 - €688 - **£403** - FF4 511
  Konstruktion Chalks/paper (100x70cm 39x27in)
  München 2000
- $78 - €87 - **£51** - FF570
  M.Z.3.66 H Drypoint (41.2x41.5cm 16x16in) Köln
  2000

HAUSER Heinrich 1901-1955 **[18]**
- $228 - €256 - **£159** - FF1 676
  «Bojen» Gelatin silver print (17x22.5cm 6x8in) Köln
  2001

HAUSER Johann 1926-1996 **[21]**
- $432 - €509 - **£300** - FF3 336
  Weiblicher Akt Pencil/paper (25x14cm 9x5in) Wien
  2000

HAUSER John 1859-1913 **[14]**
- $7 500 - €8 815 - **£5 200** - FF57 823
  Chief Bald Eagle, Sioux Oil/canvas (30.5x20.5cm
  12x8in) Beverly-Hills CA 2000
- $19 000 - €16 392 - **£11 419** - FF107 526
  On the Snake River Gouache/paper (24x33cm
  9x13in) Santa-Fe NM 1998

HAUSER Renée Yolande 1919 **[69]**
- $282 - €237 - **£165** - FF1 553
  Kleiner Trockenblumenstrauss Oil/panel (27x22cm
  10x8in) Bern 1998

HAUSHOFER Alfred 1872-1943 **[22]**
- $1 274 - €1 448 - **£892** - FF9 500
  Deux élégantes au balcon Aquarelle (54x43cm
  21x16in) Paris 2001

HAUSHOFER Maximilian 1811-1866 **[30]**
- $2 619 - €2 383 - **£1 638** - FF15 633
  Landscape with a classical Temple Oil/canvas
  (46x68cm 18x26in) Praha 1999
- $260 - €246 - **£162** - FF1 613
  Mountain Peak Oil/cardboard (39x27.5cm 15x10in)
  Praha 1999

HÄUSLE Martin 1903-1966 **[2]**
- $34 430 - €39 970 - **£24 200** - FF262 185
  «Flieder mit Tonkrug» Öl/Leinwand (75x96cm
  29x37in) Wien 2001

HAUSLEITNER Rudolf 1840-1918 **[16]**
- $3 055 - €2 543 - **£1 799** - FF16 681
  An der Staffelei Oil/panel (57.5x70.5cm 22x27in)
  Wien 1998

HAUSMAN René 1936 **[16]**
- $761 - €701 - **£457** - FF4 600
  Laïyna Encres couleurs/papier (40x30cm 15x11in)
  Paris 1999

HAUSMANN Ernst 1856-1914 **[7]**
- $2 881 - €3 241 - **£2 011** - FF21 257
  Aufforderung zum Tanz Öl/Leinwand (58x68cm
  22x26in) Luzern 2001

HAUSMANN Raoul 1886-1971 **[109]**
- $5 014 - €5 586 - **£3 280** - FF36 641
  Construction mobile dans une dimension
  Gouache (63.7x50cm 25x19in) München 2000
- $276 - €317 - **£189** - FF2 079
  Fiat Modes Gelatin silver print (17.9x12.8cm 7x5in)
  Heidelberg 2000

HAUSNER Rudolf 1914-1995 **[272]**
- $39 599 - €32 526 - **£23 000** - FF213 357
  Bei Sonnenaufgang Acrylic (103x128cm 40x50in)
  London 1998
- $224 - €256 - **£156** - FF1 676
  Adam Farbserigraphie (51x22.5cm 20x8in) Hamburg
  2001

HAUSNER Xenia 1951 **[2]**
- $17 544 - €20 452 - **£12 296** - FF134 156
  Kissenschlacht Acrylic/panel (130x170cm 51x66in)
  München 2000

HÄUSLER Robert 1924 **[11]**
- $526 - €613 - **£364** - FF4 024
  Industrieaufnahmen Vintage gelatin silver print
  (30x23.3cm 11x9in) Köln 2000

HAUSTRATE Gaston 1878-1949 **[150]**
- $2 308 - €2 355 - **£1 444** - FF15 447
  Vue de Bruxelles Huile/toile (100x121cm 39x47in)
  Bruxelles 2000
- $724 - €843 - **£516** - FF5 528
  Cul de sac à Bruxelles Huile/toile (93x81cm
  36x31in) Bruxelles 2001
- $261 - €297 - **£182** - FF1 951
  Pont Huile/carton (22x27cm 8x10in) Maisieres-Mons
  2001

HAUSWIRTH Hans Johan Jakob 1808-1871 **[11]**
🖊 **$16 564** - €18 016 - **£10 917** - FF118 174
    Blumenbouquet mit springenden Hirschen und Hasen Silhouette (25x33cm 9x12in) Bern 2000

HAUTERIVE d' Henri XIX-XX **[8]**
🖊 **$191** - €213 - **£129** - FF1 400
    Gorges dans les Pyrénées Aquarelle/papier (28x21cm 11x8in) Tarbes 2000

HAVARD James 1937 **[62]**
🖎 **$4 750** - €3 986 - **£2 787** - FF26 144
    «Cree Camp» Acrylic/canvas (152.5x122cm 60x48in) New-York 1999

HAVELKA Roman 1877-1950 **[24]**
🖎 **$635** - €601 - **£396** - FF3 944
    Sous la neige Huile/toile (50x65cm 19x25in) Praha 2000

HAVELL Alfred Charles 1855-1928 **[17]**
🖎 **$2 574** - €2 450 - **£1 610** - FF16 073
    Ekipage i park Oil/canvas (31x57cm 12x22in) Stockholm 1999

HAVELL Daniel XVIII-XIX **[13]**
🍶 **$525** - €568 - **£360** - FF3 728
    Ruine of the Fort at Juanpore on the River Goomtee, after Henry Salt Aquatint (46.5x62.5cm 18x24in) Lenton-Lane, Nottingham 2001

HAVELL Edmund, Jnr. 1819-1894 **[19]**
🖎 **$65 000** - €55 535 - **£39 019** - FF364 286
    Sir John Cope with his Hounds on the Steps of Bramshill House Oil/canvas (93x146cm 36x57in) New-York 1998

HAVELL Robert, Jnr. 1793-1878 **[60]**
🖎 **$5 500** - €6 499 - **£3 897** - FF42 629
    Fauns Leap, N.Y. Oil/canvas (68.5x51cm 26x20in) Boston MA 2000
🍶 **$2 500** - €2 477 - **£1 516** - FF16 248
    Pigeon Hawk (Plate XCII), After J.J Audubon Etching, aquatint in colors (69.5x52cm 27x20in) New-York 2000

HAVELL Robert, Snr. 1769-1832 **[4]**
🍶 **$800** - €744 - **£495** - FF4 880
    Sandwich Tern, No.52 Engraving (67x99cm 26x39in) East-Dennis MA 1999

HAVELL Robert, Snr. or Jnr. XVIII-XIX **[2]**
🍶 **$865** - €956 - **£600** - FF6 271
    Rough-Legged Falcon-Buteo Lagopus, after Audubon Engr (68x61cm 26x24in) London 2001

HAVELL William 1782-1857 **[30]**
🖎 **$8 537** - €9 919 - **£6 000** - FF65 065
    Landscape in the Lake District with the Vale of St.John Oil/canvas (51x61cm 20x24in) London 2001
🖎 **$724** - €840 - **£500** - FF5 512
    Brathag Hall, Windermere Watercolour (24x34cm 9x13in) London 2000

HAVEN de Frank, Franklin 1856-1934 **[65]**
🖎 **$2 300** - €1 965 - **£1 351** - FF12 892
    «Sheep in a Storm» Oil/canvas (61x76cm 24x29in) Boston MA 1998
🖎 **$1 100** - €932 - **£657** - FF6 114
    Landscape with River Bend at Sunset Oil/canvas (45x30cm 18x12in) South-Natick MA 1998

HAVENS James Dexter 1900-1960 **[17]**
🍶 **$140** - €143 - **£87** - FF939
    Fungus Woodcut in colors (26x21cm 10x8in) Cleveland OH 2000

HAVERKAMP Gerhard Christiaan 1872-1926 **[25]**
🖊 **$2 424** - €2 269 - **£1 508** - FF14 883
    Pollard-willows along a stream with brick houses in the distance Pastel (49x65cm 19x25in) Amsterdam 1999

HAVERKAMP Wilhelm 1864-1929 **[3]**
🦅 **$4 000** - €4 090 - **£2 508** - FF26 831
    Bocksprung Bronze (H50cm H19in) Berlin 2000

HAVERMAN Hendrik Johannes 1857-1928 **[52]**
🖎 **$12 077** - €11 344 - **£7 280** - FF74 415
    The Young Apollo Oil/canvas (162.5x82.5cm 63x32in) Amsterdam 1999
🖎 **$816** - €793 - **£508** - FF5 200
    Alger Huile/panneau (49.5x33cm 19x12in) Paris 1999
🖎 **$854** - €998 - **£600** - FF5 548
    Townsquare in Biskra, Algeria Oil/canvas (22x29.5cm 8x11in) Amsterdam 2001

HÄVERÖ Bert-Håge 1932 **[7]**
🖎 **$8 236** - €9 795 - **£5 873** - FF64 251
    Midsommarafton - lövade Waxholmsbåtar Oil/canvas (130x170cm 51x66in) Stockholm 2000
🖎 **$1 020** - €976 - **£642** - FF6 401
    Slaktar Bladlund och Kakelugnsmakaren Oil/canvas (54x63cm 21x24in) Stockholm 1999

HAVERS Alice Mary 1850-1890 **[9]**
🖎 **$20 000** - €21 444 - **£13 232** - FF140 664
    Belle of the Village Oil/canvas/board (82x139cm 32x55in) New-Orleans LA 2000
🖎 **$10 672** - €12 400 - **£7 500** - FF81 336
    Caught Scrumping Oil/canvas (34.5x42cm 13x16in) London 2001

HAVET Henri 1862-1913 **[7]**
🖎 **$3 141** - €3 448 - **£2 027** - FF22 615
    Trädgårdsinteriör med kvinna och barn Oil/canvas (46x54cm 18x21in) Lund 2000

HAVILAND Paul Burty 1880-1950 **[10]**
📷 **$1 500** - €1 728 - **£1 034** - FF11 334
    Lady in Lace Autochrome (16x12cm 6x5in) New-York 2000

HAVINDEN John Oliver 1908-1987 **[16]**
📷 **$700** - €772 - **£488** - FF5 100
    «Tune» Gelatin silver print (19.5x15.5cm 7x6in) New-York 2001

HAVRANEK Bedrich 1821-1899 **[30]**
🖎 **$1 734** - €1 640 - **£1 080** - FF10 758
    Carlstein Castle Oil/cardboard (24.5x34.5cm 9x13in) Praha 2000
🖎 **$260** - €246 - **£162** - FF1 613
    Vallée Aquarelle/papier (30x42cm 11x16in) Praha 2000

HAVSTEEN-MIKKELSEN Sven 1912-1999 **[51]**
🖎 **$1 777** - €2 010 - **£1 201** - FF13 186
    Islandske huse Oil/canvas (43x66cm 16x25in) Köbenhavn 2001
🖎 **$1 327** - €1 474 - **£924** - FF9 672
    Huse ved havet Oil/canvas (33x46cm 12x18in) Köbenhavn 2001

HAWARDEN Clementina 1822-1865 **[3]**
📷 **$2 734** - €3 063 - **£1 900** - FF20 090
    Portrait of Viscount Hawarden in the Drawing Room, 5 Princes Gardens Albumen print (19.5x14.5cm 7x5in) London 2001

HAWES Josiah Johnson 1808-1908 **[5]**
📷 **$12 000** - €11 283 - **£7 430** - FF74 012
    Beacon Street Below Spruce Street/Brattle Square Church Gelatin silver print (33x28cm 12x11in) New-York 1999

HAWKINS Louis Welden 1849-1910 **[78]**
🖼 **$6 528** - €7 318 - **£4 564** - FF48 000
Femme dans un verger Huile/toile (73x60cm 28x23in) Paris 2001
🖼 **$1 360** - €1 524 - **£923** - FF10 000
Paysage, effet d'automne Huile/panneau (14x22cm 5x8in) Paris 2000
🖼 **$1 587** - €1 865 - **£1 100** - FF12 236
A Young Girl in a Wood Watercolour (56.5x45cm 22x17in) London 2000

HAWKINS Weaver 1893-1977 **[116]**
🖼 **$4 151** - €4 650 - **£2 884** - FF30 500
Winter Landscape Oil/board (49x60cm 19x23in) Melbourne 2001
🖼 **$891** - €820 - **£551** - FF5 376
Study for Moth Preparing, Double Bay Ink (26.5x35cm 10x13in) Melbourne 1998
🖼 **$284** - €296 - **£178** - FF1 944
A Nursing Mother Linocut (22.5x30cm 8x11in) Sydney 2000

HAWKINS William L. 1895-1990 **[19]**
🖼 **$29 000** - €24 212 - **£17 008** - FF158 818
Buffalo Hunter Enamel (122x152cm 48x59in) New-York 1998
🖼 **$9 000** - €7 765 - **£5 449** - FF50 933
Untitled Cityscape Enamel/panel (86.5x95cm 34x37in) New-York 1998

HAWKS Rachel M. 1879-? **[2]**
🖼 **$10 000** - €11 787 - **£7 027** - FF77 317
Girl Holding Butterfly Bronze (H91cm H36in) Detroit MI 2000

HAWKSLEY Dorothy Webster 1884-c.1971 **[13]**
🖼 **$1 149** - €1 042 - **£700** - FF6 835
«Two Female Bathers Changing on the Beach» Watercolour/paper (32x17.5cm 12x6in) Solihull, West-Midlands 1998
🖼 **$847** - €982 - **£600** - FF6 441
«Isle of Man, LMS, Travel via LMS» Poster (102x64cm 40x25in) London 2000

HAWLEY Hughson 1850-1936 **[15]**
🖼 **$16 000** - €18 168 - **£10 950** - FF119 174
Woolworth Building, New York Gouache (181x81.5cm 71x32in) New-York 1999

HAWLICEK Vincenz 1864-1914 **[24]**
🖼 **$1 316** - €1 453 - **£912** - FF9 534
Dorf mit Windmühle und Ententeich Watercolour (59x74cm 23x29in) Wien 2001

HAWORTH Bobs Cogill 1900-1988 **[32]**
🖼 **$651** - €557 - **£391** - FF3 654
«Caledon Hill» Gouache/papier (51x63.5cm 20x25in) Toronto 1998

HAWORTH Peter 1889-1986 **[28]**
🖼 **$226** - €243 - **£155** - FF1 597
Boats with Markers Gouache (63.5x51cm 25x20in) Toronto 2001

HAWTHORNE Charles Webster 1872-1930 **[38]**
🖼 **$60 000** - €59 472 - **£37 530** - FF390 114
Motherhood Triumphant Oil/panel (152.5x122cm 60x48in) New-York 1999
🖼 **$10 000** - €11 671 - **£7 089** - FF76 556
The Lovers Tempera/panel (101.5x101.5cm 39x39in) New-York 2000
🖼 **$12 692** - €14 483 - **£8 825** - FF95 000
Pêcheurs en barque Huile/carton (24x35cm 9x13in) Paris 2001

🖼 **$3 000** - €3 328 - **£1 995** - FF21 829
Nude by Firelight Watercolour, gouache/paper (64x46cm 25x18in) Milford CT 2000

HAXTON Elaine Alys 1909-1995 **[89]**
🖼 **$15 567** - €17 436 - **£10 815** - FF114 375
Summer, Pittwater, Summer Bouquet Oil/canvas (110.5x110cm 43x43in) Melbourne 2001
🖼 **$6 993** - €6 805 - **£4 304** - FF44 635
Stage Scene, War Time New Guinea Oil/board (51x61cm 20x24in) Malvern, Victoria 1999
🖼 **$2 328** - €2 565 - **£1 545** - FF16 825
Monkeys Oil/board (39.5x39.5cm 15x15in) Woollahra, Sydney 2000
🖼 **$388** - €366 - **£240** - FF2 402
Centaur Gouache (38x53.5cm 14x21in) Malvern, Victoria 2000
🖼 **$223** - €208 - **£138** - FF1 364
«Dark Nude» Aquatint (35x32.5cm 13x12in) Melbourne 1998

HAY Bernard, Bernardo 1864-? **[65]**
🖼 **$4 103** - €4 724 - **£2 800** - FF30 987
A Coastal Inlet with Figures on a Beach, Capri Oil/canvas (35.5x55.5cm 13x21in) London 2000
🖼 **$1 024** - €975 - **£650** - FF6 398
Water Carriers, Capri Oil/canvas (40x24cm 15x9in) Billingshurst, West-Sussex 1999

HAY George H. 1831-1912 **[14]**
🖼 **$1 949** - €1 862 - **£1 200** - FF12 212
The Billet-Doux Oil/canvas (51x41cm 20x16in) Edinburgh 1999

HAY James Hamilton 1874-1916 **[15]**
🖼 **$2 215** - €1 859 - **£1 300** - FF12 195
Breaking Waves Oil/canvas (42x51.5cm 16x20in) London 1998

HAY Peter Alexander 1866-1952 **[34]**
🖼 **$7 767** - €7 284 - **£4 800** - FF47 781
Portrait of a Lady with a Parasol Oil/canvas (117x84cm 46x33in) London 1999
🖼 **$308** - €298 - **£190** - FF1 955
Flower Girls with a Donkey before a Palace Watercolour (35x51cm 13x20in) London 1999

HAY Thomas Marjoribanks 1862-1921 **[20]**
🖼 **$486** - €469 - **£300** - FF3 077
Castle by the Coast Watercolour/paper (17x24cm 6x9in) Edinburgh 1999

HAY William M. c.1820-c.1900 **[11]**
🖼 **$1 139** - €1 047 - **£700** - FF6 869
A Young Beauty Oil/canvas/board (29x24cm 11x9in) London 1998

HAYAKAWA Miki 1904-1953 **[5]**
🖼 **$12 000** - €12 881 - **£8 030** - FF84 492
Music Oil/canvas (91.5x86.5cm 36x34in) San-Francisco CA 2000

HAYAMI Gyoshū 1894-1935 **[4]**
🖼 **$22 000** - €25 799 - **£15 699** - FF169 232
Ranka nishu (Two orchids) Ink (29x41cm 11x16in) New-York 2000

HAYD Karl 1882-1945 **[38]**
🖼 **$896** - €872 - **£552** - FF5 720
Blühende Kirschenzweige in Vase Oil/panel (80x90cm 31x35in) Linz 1999
🖼 **$488** - €581 - **£348** - FF3 833
Fischer am Traunsee-Traunkirchen Öl/Karton (32x26cm 12x10in) Linz 2000
🖼 **$336** - €327 - **£207** - FF2 145
Ländliche Idylle Aquarell/Papier (28x40cm 11x15in) Linz 1999

HAYDEN Charles H. 1856-1901 **[7]**
- $2 200 - €1 993 - **£1 346** - FF13 072
  Early Autumn Oil/canvas (45x55cm 18x22in) Portland ME 1998
- $2 500 - €2 594 - **£1 586** - FF17 016
  Spring Landscape Oil/canvas (30.5x40.5cm 12x15in) Boston MA 2000

HAYDEN Edward Parker 1858-1922 **[8]**
- $1 600 - €1 477 - **£996** - FF9 690
  New England Summer Landscape Oil/canvas (45.5x61cm 17x24in) Washington 1999

HAYDEN Henri 1883-1970 **[458]**
- $5 094 - €4 915 - **£3 200** - FF32 243
  Vue de Saint-Tropez Oil/canvas (38x46cm 14x18in) London 1999
- $1 951 - €2 028 - **£1 228** - FF13 300
  Paris sous la neige Huile/papier/toile (32.5x46cm 12x18in) Paris 2000
- $1 369 - €1 480 - **£947** - FF9 705
  Baie Le Poulde Aquarelle/papier (19.5x25cm 7x9in) Warszawa 2001
- $113 - €105 - **£69** - FF686
  Landscape View Color lithograph (44.5x48cm 17x18in) London 1998

HAYDEN Palmer Cole 1893-1973 **[3]**
- $36 000 - €42 813 - **£25 657** - FF280 836
  New York City Hall Oil/canvas (61x76cm 24x29in) New-York 2000

HAYDON Benjamin Robert 1786-1846 **[18]**
- $30 866 - €36 709 - **£22 000** - FF240 794
  Heracles and Persephone Oil/canvas (235.5x175.5cm 92x69in) London 2000
- $461 - €542 - **£320** - FF3 558
  A portrait of the Head of a Young Boy Black chalk (33x23cm 12x9in) London 2000

HAYEK von Hans 1869-1940 **[34]**
- $696 - €767 - **£464** - FF5 030
  Militärische Zeremonie Öl/Leinwand (60x80cm 23x31in) Satow 2000

HAYES Claude 1852-1922 **[297]**
- $1 233 - €1 389 - **£850** - FF9 111
  Extensive Country Landscape, with Seagulls Oil/canvas (51x87cm 20x34in) London 2000
- $5 133 - €5 173 - **£3 200** - FF33 931
  Dutch Fishing Boats Oil/panel (20x28cm 7x11in) London 2000
- $670 - €613 - **£420** - FF4 018
  In a Dutch Village Watercolour (35x25cm 13x9in) Suffolk 1999

HAYES Colin 1919 **[24]**
- $1 446 - €1 562 - **£1 000** - FF10 249
  Boats in Harbour, Greece Oil/canvas (50x61cm 19x24in) London 2001

HAYES Edward 1797-1864 **[17]**
- $1 092 - €1 270 - **£768** - FF8 329
  Gentleman in top hat and two ladies Watercolour/paper (53.5x43cm 21x16in) Dublin 2001

HAYES Edwin 1819-1904 **[181]**
- $6 360 - €5 981 - **£4 000** - FF39 233
  Fishing Boats in Rough Waters Oil/board (49x75cm 19x29in) Co. Kilkenny 1999
- $2 841 - €3 301 - **£1 997** - FF21 655
  Sailing Boat at SUnset with Lookout Tower in Distance Oil/panel (18x28cm 7x11in) Dublin 2001
- $1 411 - €1 423 - **£880** - FF9 331
  Ship Wreckers Watercolour/paper (16.5x36cm 6x14in) Newbury, Berkshire 2000

HAYES Ernest 1914-1978 **[7]**
- $5 563 - €5 968 - **£3 793** - FF39 146
  Interior Oil/canvas (68x53cm 26x20in) Dublin 2001
- $5 918 - €6 349 - **£4 035** - FF41 645
  Long Meadow Oil/canvas (44.5x35.5cm 17x13in) Dublin 2001

HAYES Frederick William 1848-1918 **[20]**
- $3 304 - €3 856 - **£2 300** - FF25 291
  Elterwater Oil/canvas (33.5x51.5cm 13x20in) West-Yorkshire 2000
- $521 - €452 - **£320** - FF2 964
  Arundel Castle Oil/canvas/board (33x43cm 12x16in) Billingshurst, West-Sussex 1999

HAYES Gabriel 1909-1978 **[1]**
- $30 106 - €33 030 - **£20 000** - FF216 660
  The Cork Bowler Oil/panel (124.5x94cm 49x37in) London 2001

HAYES John 1786-1866 **[7]**
- $17 000 - €18 515 - **£11 707** - FF121 451
  Mischief Oil/canvas (71x91.5cm 27x36in) New-York 2001

HAYES Michael Angelo 1820-1877 **[8]**
- $1 005 - €940 - **£620** - FF6 168
  Military Charging on Horseback Watercolour/paper (27x41cm 10x16in) Co. Kilkenny 1999

HAYES Sidney ?-c.1923 **[3]**
- $6 519 - €5 928 - **£4 000** - FF38 883
  Discretion in the Better Part of Valour Oil/board (25.5x35.5cm 10x13in) London 2001

HAYES William 1729-1799 **[16]**
- $800 - €881 - **£533** - FF5 781
  Study of Three Shore Birds Gouache/paper (50x35cm 20x14in) Portsmouth NH 2000

HAYET Louis 1864-1940 **[213]**
- $5 807 - €6 632 - **£4 084** - FF43 500
  Paysage près de Pontoise Huile/toile (45x56cm 17x22in) Aubagne 2001
- $2 994 - €3 354 - **£2 081** - FF22 000
  Arbres au printemps Huile/toile/carton (18x12cm 7x4in) Paris 2001
- $2 449 - €2 744 - **£1 702** - FF18 000
  Nocturne Aquarelle (18x22.5cm 7x8in) Paris 2001

HAYEZ Francesco 1791-1882 **[35]**
- $975 000 - €841 186 - **£588 217** - FF5 517 817
  Bathsheba Oil/canvas (150x115.5cm 59x45in) New-York 1998
- $56 000 - €55 065 - **£35 000** - FF361 200
  Lovers, Bice del Balzo and Ottorino Oil/canvas (69.5x89cm 27x35in) Budapest 1999
- $30 000 - €25 916 - **£20 000** - FF170 000
  La famiglia di Loth Olio/tavola (30x38cm 11x14in) Milano 1998
- $3 684 - €3 136 - **£2 200** - FF20 574
  Romeo and Julie Drawing (22x15cm 8x5in) London 1998

HAYGREEN Philip XX **[1]**
- $4 899 - €4 510 - **£3 000** - FF29 585
  Trafalgar Square Oil/panel (25.5x35.5cm 10x13in) London 1998

HAYLLAR Edith 1860-1948 **[8]**
- $75 000 - €71 528 - **£45 652** - FF469 192
  The First of October Oil/canvas (64x91.5cm 25x36in) New-York 1999

H

HAYLLAR James 1829-1920 **[44]**
- **$28 842** - €31 871 - **£20 000** - FF209 060
  The Tame Jackdaw Oil/canvas (152.5x101.5cm 60x39in) London 2001
- **$4 033** - €3 705 - **£2 500** - FF24 303
  All Serene Oil/canvas (49.5x60cm 19x23in) Devon 1999
- **$2 487** - €2 153 - **£1 500** - FF14 124
  «More Bother than its Worth» Oil/canvas (34x30cm 13x11in) London 1998
- **$9 713** - €10 427 - **£6 500** - FF68 394
  Bandaging the Wounded Finger Watercolour (33x23.5cm 12x9in) London 2000

HAYLLAR Jessica 1858-1940 **[14]**
- **$5 500** - €5 387 - **£3 544** - FF35 336
  Goods and Chattels I have selected as those to be the first sacrificed Oil/panel (25x17cm 9x6in) New-York 1999

HAYLS John ?-1679 **[5]**
- **$9 806** - €10 836 - **£6 800** - FF71 080
  Portrait of Lady Mary Bertie Oil/canvas (74x62cm 29x24in) London 2001

HAYMAN Francis c.1708-1776 **[14]**
- **$86 352** - €96 721 - **£60 000** - FF634 446
  Joseph Henry of Straffan, Co.Kildare, seated at a Table writing Oil/canvas (60x50.5cm 23x19in) London 2001
- **$14 059** - €13 760 - **£9 000** - FF90 258
  Sight Oil/panel (30.5x24cm 12x9in) London 1999

HAYMAN Patrick 1915-1988 **[47]**
- **$1 459** - €1 407 - **£900** - FF9 231
  Perseus at the Door of the Underworld Tempera (18.5x24.5cm 7x9in) London 1999
- **$686** - €613 - **£420** - FF4 022
  Still Life with Figures Gouache/paper (25x34cm 10x13in) Par, Cornwall 1999

HAYMANN Ernst 1873-1947 **[46]**
- **$231** - €194 - **£136** - FF1 274
  «Pflügender Bauer» Öl/Karton (16.5x21cm 6x8in) München 1998

HAYNES Frank Jay 1853-1921 **[23]**
- **$800** - €747 - **£484** - FF4 899
  Golden Gate and Pillar Albumen print (41.5x55.5cm 16x21in) New-York 1999

HAYNES Frederick XIX **[7]**
- **$9 056** - €10 114 - **£5 800** - FF66 345
  Fresh Breeze, Shipping off the South Foreland Oil/canvas (76x127cm 29x50in) London 2000

HAYNES John William 1836-1908 **[19]**
- **$3 110** - €3 352 - **£2 120** - FF21 987
  Milady's favourite Oil/canvas (47x37cm 18x14in) Köbenhavn 2001
- **$2 800** - €2 470 - **£1 711** - FF16 259
  Beg Sir Oil/board (23x30.5cm 9x12in) New-York 1999

HAYS George A. 1854-1934 **[71]**
- **$1 400** - €1 327 - **£874** - FF8 705
  Cows Grazing Oil/canvas (66x91cm 26x36in) Mystic CT 1999
- **$800** - €769 - **£493** - FF5 046
  Portrait of a Cow Oil/canvas (30.5x45.5cm 12x17in) Boston MA 1999

HAYTER George 1792-1871 **[51]**
- **$2 932** - €3 161 - **£2 000** - FF20 733
  Portrait of Lady Elisabeth Harcourt, Seated Half-Length, in Red Dress Oil/panel (75x58.5cm 29x23in) London 2001

- **$2 242** - €2 649 - **£1 588** - FF17 376
  Portrait von Lord Byron in Halbfigur Miniature (17.4x13.7cm 6x5in) Zürich 2000
- **$463** - €527 - **£320** - FF3 460
  Portrait of Queen Victoria, Standing Full-Length by a Pillar Watercolour (26.5x18cm 10x7in) London 2000

HAYTER John 1800-1891 **[25]**
- **$64 030** - €74 393 - **£45 000** - FF487 989
  Portraits of the Children of the Rev.Joseph Arkwright of Mark Hall Oil/canvas (87.5x113cm 34x44in) London 2001
- **$231** - €216 - **£140** - FF1 417
  Double Portrait of Jane Dorothea Forbes-Shirreff Pastel/paper (55x43cm 21x16in) Glasgow 1998

HAYTER Stanley William 1901-1988 **[363]**
- **$2 572** - €2 592 - **£1 603** - FF17 000
  Flash Huile/toile (54x65cm 21x25in) Paris 2000
- **$457** - €421 - **£280** - FF2 761
  Abstract Composition Coloured inks/paper (62x67cm 24x26in) London 1998
- **$700** - €624 - **£431** - FF4 092
  Danae Engraving (41x30cm 16x11in) New-York 1999

HAYTLEY Edward c.1700-c.1780 **[4]**
- **$12 000** - €10 870 - **£7 344** - FF71 301
  Portrait of Mlle. Violette (later Mrs. David Garrick) Oil/canvas (34x28cm 13x11in) Portland ME 1998

HAYWARD Alfred Frederick W. 1856-1939 **[37]**
- **$750** - €813 - **£500** - FF5 331
  Still Life of White Roses in a Vase Oil/canvas (39.5x26cm 15x10in) Billingshurst, West-Sussex 2000

HAYWARD Alfred Robert 1875-1971 **[48]**
- **$1 454** - €1 264 - **£880** - FF8 291
  Beer Harbour, Devon Oil/panel (16.5x24cm 6x9in) London 1999

HAYWARD Arthur 1889-1971 **[54]**
- **$2 551** - €2 178 - **£1 500** - FF14 285
  Shrimping, Normandy Coast Oil/canvas/board (35.5x51cm 13x20in) London 1998
- **$2 431** - €2 054 - **£1 450** - FF13 475
  Morning Light, St Ives Oil/board (23x33cm 9x13in) Penzance, Cornwall 1998

HAYWARD Frank Harold 1867-1945 **[19]**
- **$1 000** - €1 102 - **£667** - FF7 227
  Stream Running Through a Forest in the Fall Oil/canvas (17x12cm 7x5in) Detroit MI 2000

HAYWARD-HARRIS Martin 1959 **[6]**
- **$5 706** - €6 653 - **£4 000** - FF43 640
  Sitting Hare Bronze (H30.5cm H12in) London 2000

HAYWOOD Mary Carolyn 1898-? **[1]**
- **$900** - €1 004 - **£589** - FF6 586
  «Postum Cereals, Build Strong Teeth» Poster (66.5x95cm 26x37in) New-York 2000

HAZARD Arthur Merton 1872-1930 **[17]**
- **$9 250** - €10 192 - **£6 141** - FF66 852
  Portrait of Leah Porchard Pollard and her Children Oil/canvas (243x137cm 96x54in) Beverly MA 2000
- **$1 800** - €1 542 - **£1 062** - FF10 112
  Portrait of a Woman in Green and Peach Dress Oil/canvas (101.5x56cm 39x22in) New-York 1998

HAZARD John Bevan ?-1892 **[3]**
$4 500 - €4 209 - **£2 720** - FF27 610
Untitled (Man and his Dog) Salt print (7.5x12.5cm
2x4in) New-York 1999

HAZELL Frank XX **[2]**
$1 600 - €1 856 - **£1 122** - FF12 177
«West Point» Poster (104x68cm 41x27in) New-York
2000

HAZELTON Mary Brewster 1868-1953 **[11]**
$5 000 - €5 978 - **£3 449** - FF39 210
The Blue Shawl Oil/canvas (76x63cm 30x25in)
Milford CT 2000

HAZELZET D.J. 1889-1953 **[9]**
$420 - €454 - **£287** - FF2 976
Figures in a Street in Mechelen Oil/panel
(62x43cm 24x16in) Amsterdam 2001

HAZLEDINE Alfred 1876-1954 **[57]**
$889 - €942 - **£600** - FF6 178
Le jour du marché Huile/toile (61x45cm 24x17in)
Bruxelles 2001

HAZON Barthélémy-Michel 1722-1822 **[2]**
$1 357 - €1 601 - **£954** - FF10 500
Elévation du choeur d'une église Pierre noire
(48x48cm 18x18in) Paris 2001

HAZON DE SAINT-FIRMIN de Jane XIX **[1]**
$4 500 - €5 218 - **£3 188** - FF34 226
Feline Frolic Watercolour/board (41.5x54cm 16x21in)
New-York 2000

HAZOUMÉ Romuald 1962 **[1]**
$4 749 - €4 584 - **£3 000** - FF30 071
Le saxophoniste (The Saxophonist) Metal
(47x29x25cm 18x11x9in) London 1999

HE BAILI Ho Paklee 1945 **[31]**
$12 198 - €13 320 - **£7 847** - FF87 371
Misty Landscapes Ink (45x41.5cm 17x16in) Hong-
Kong 2000

HE SHAOJI 1799-1873 **[13]**
$2 400 - €2 072 - **£1 433** - FF13 590
Running Script Calligraphy Ink/paper (36x93.5cm
14x36in) New-York 1998

HE TIANJIAN 1893-1974 **[12]**
$2 323 - €1 963 - **£1 395** - FF12 875
Yuping Peak of Mount Huang Coloured inks/paper
(65x44cm 25x17in) Hong-Kong 1998

HEAD B.G. XIX-XX **[7]**
$1 438 - €1 466 - **£900** - FF9 615
«Tales of...» Oil/canvas (90x70cm 35x27in) London
2000

HEAD Edith XX **[5]**
$1 600 - €1 514 - **£995** - FF9 934
Sketch of Jacqueline Kennedy Charcoal (44x65cm
17x25in) New-York 1999

HEAD Guy 1753-1800 **[3]**
$13 149 - €14 115 - **£8 800** - FF92 590
Rev.John Disney D.D.F.S.A, in a black Coat, hol-
ding a Jockey whip Oil/canvas (91.5x72cm 36x28in)
London 2000

HEADE Martin Johnson 1819-1904 **[83]**
$280 000 - €326 785 - **£198 492** - FF2 143 568
Cherokee Roses in a Glass Oil/canvas (52x31.5cm
20x12in) New-York 2001
$150 000 - €168 011 - **£104 220** - FF1 102 080
Marshes at Boston Harbor Oil/canvas (25.5x56cm
10x22in) New-York 2001

$3 500 - €3 023 - **£2 114** - FF19 829
Flowers, Bird Nest, Eggs Watercolour/paper
(27x22cm 11x9in) Chester NY 1998

HEALY George Peter Alex. 1813-1894 **[16]**
$1 300 - €1 508 - **£924** - FF9 892
Portrait of Miss Brown of Providence, Rhode
Island Oil/canvas (65.5x54cm 25x21in) Washington
2000

HEALY Henry 1909-1982 **[27]**
$1 433 - €1 651 - **£978** - FF10 827
Summer Day Oil/board (51x61cm 20x24in) Dublin
2000
$1 705 - €1 905 - **£1 155** - FF12 493
Galway Landscape, Cottages in Mauve Oil/board
(36x44cm 14x17in) Dublin 2000

HEALY Michael 1873-1941 **[13]**
$300 - €292 - **£184** - FF1 915
Study of a Horse Watercolour/paper (10x15cm 4x6in)
Dublin 1999

HEALY Robert 1743-1771 **[3]**
$42 179 - €40 632 - **£26 064** - FF266 528
Portrait of the Countess of Clancarty, standing
in a Landcsape Chalks/paper (58x42cm 22x16in)
Dublin 1999

HEAPHY Thomas 1775-1835 **[27]**
$968 - €930 - **£600** - FF6 098
Lady and her Dog by a Stile Watercolour
(50.5x40.5cm 19x15in) London 1999

HEAPS Maud D. XIX-XX **[5]**
$2 500 - €2 600 - **£1 578** - FF17 052
Pekingese Pastel/paper (38x52.5cm 14x20in) New-
York 2000

HEARD Hugh Percy XIX-XX **[17]**
$476 - €400 - **£280** - FF2 624
Sheep in the Field/Sheep on the Moor
Watercolour/paper (25.5x36.5cm 10x14in) Devon 1998

HEARD OF LIVERPOOL Joseph 1799-1859 **[19]**
$8 000 - €7 114 - **£4 892** - FF46 666
The East Indiamen the «Seaking» and the
«Loodiannah» off a Coast Oil/canvas (61x91.5cm
24x36in) New-York 1999

HEARMAN Louise 1963 **[11]**
$2 242 - €2 470 - **£1 505** - FF16 203
Untitled #578 Oil/board (69x53cm 27x20in) Malvern,
Victoria 2000
$2 331 - €2 614 - **£1 630** - FF17 144
Untitled Oil/board (37.5x28.5cm 14x11in) Melbourne
2001

HEARNE Thomas 1744-1817 **[51]**
$1 190 - €1 038 - **£720** - FF6 811
Naworth Castle, Cumberland Wash (18.5x26cm
7x10in) London 1998

HEARTFIELD John, H. Herzfelde 1891-1968 **[17]**
$557 - €533 - **£349** - FF3 497
«Jahrestag Oktoberrevolution» Poster (82x60cm
32x23in) London 1999
$356 - €353 - **£222** - FF2 314
London, Sloane Square Gelatin silver print
(29.9x24cm 11x9in) Berlin 1999

HEASLIT William 1898-1965 **[3]**
$300 - €356 - **£206** - FF2 333
Propeller/The Intruder Etching, aquatint (20x28cm
7x11in) New-York 2000

HEATH Adrian 1920-1992 **[59]**
- $2 757 - €2 658 - **£1 700** - FF17 437
  Vaynor No.I Oil/canvas (76x63.5cm 29x25in) London 1999
- $3 978 - €3 394 - **£2 400** - FF22 263
  Composition with red & blue Oil/canvas (30.5x41cm 12x16in) London 1998
- $437 - €428 - **£280** - FF2 808
  Abstract Watercolour (23x20cm 9x7in) London 1999

HEATH Frank Gascoigne 1873-1936 **[25]**
- $12 900 - €12 066 - **£7 800** - FF79 151
  Preparing the Tea Oil/canvas (61x51cm 24x20in) London 1999
- $1 959 - €2 207 - **£1 350** - FF14 478
  The Witch Oil/panel (25x35.5cm 9x13in) Newbury, Berkshire 2000

HEATH Henry XIX **[1]**
- $1 523 - €1 476 - **£950** - FF9 683
  The Dancing Lesson, Fishing Party, Smoaking, a Shooting Party Etching (16x19cm 6x7in) London 1999

HEATH James 1757-1834 **[14]**
- $30 000 - €25 883 - **£18 165** - FF169 779
  George Washington, after Gilbert Stuart Coloured crayons (49.5x34cm 19x13in) New-York 1999
- $176 - €170 - **£110** - FF1 112
  The Dead Soldier, after J.Wright Engraving (48x61cm 19x24in) London 1999

HEATH William 1795-1840 **[40]**
- $842 - €928 - **£550** - FF6 087
  Life Guard Trumpeter Watercolour/paper (26x21.5cm 10x8in) London 2000
- $425 - €363 - **£255** - FF2 383
  The Battle of Waterloo Aquatint in colors (45.5x59.5cm 17x23in) New-York 1998

HEAZLE William ?-1872 **[1]**
- $7 827 - €7 618 - **£4 809** - FF49 974
  A boy asleep on the steps of the Cork Opera House Oil/canvas (30x40cm 12x16in) Dublin 1999

HEBBAR Kattingeri Krishna 1911-1996 **[44]**
- $34 731 - €32 487 - **£21 000** - FF213 099
  Spring Oil/canvas (114x137cm 44x53in) London 1999
- $8 000 - €9 275 - **£5 667** - FF60 840
  Life and Death Oil/canvas (92x77cm 36x30in) New-York 2000
- $974 - €936 - **£600** - FF6 140
  Bandra Bridge Oil/paper (11x15cm 4x5in) London 1999
- $1 488 - €1 392 - **£900** - FF9 132
  Dancing Couple Ink (56x38cm 22x14in) London 1999

HEBENSTREIT Ferdinand XVI **[1]**
- $2 058 - €2 454 - **£1 467** - FF16 098
  Ein weiblicher Kopf Red chalk (22x15.5cm 8x6in) Köln 2000

HEBERER Charles XX **[2]**
- $13 000 - €14 433 - **£9 041** - FF94 671
  French Farm Girl Oil/canvas (97x129cm 38x51in) Milford CT 2001
- $2 600 - €2 581 - **£1 594** - FF16 930
  Champion Gouvernor Moscow/Champion Prairie Queen Oil/canvas (20x30cm 8x12in) Mystic CT 2000

HÉBERT Adrien 1890-1967 **[46]**
- $1 594 - €1 726 - **£1 091** - FF11 325
  Sans titre Huile/bois (38x50cm 14x19in) Montréal 2001

HÉBERT Émile Pierre Eugène 1828-1893 **[27]**
- $2 372 - €2 302 - **£1 476** - FF15 100
  Méphistophélès Bronze (45x22cm 17x8in) Cléon d'Andran 1999

HÉBERT Ernest Antoine 1817-1908 **[34]**
- $3 822 - €3 278 - **£2 242** - FF21 500
  Sainte Marguerite Huile/toile (66x35cm 25x13in) Paris 1998
- $2 076 - €1 994 - **£1 287** - FF13 082
  Heilige mit Lilie Huile/panneau (42.5x22cm 16x8in) Zürich 1999
- $1 160 - €1 220 - **£728** - FF8 000
  Paysan italien Crayon (27x17.5cm 10x6in) Paris 2000

HEBERT Jules 1812-1897 **[32]**
- $372 - €351 - **£225** - FF2 300
  Les hallebardier Mine plomb (14.5x11cm 5x4in) Paris 1999

HEBERT Louis-Philippe 1850-1917 **[15]**
- $14 821 - €17 288 - **£10 586** - FF113 403
  Fleur des bois Bronze (H53cm H20in) Montréal 2000

HEBUTERNE Jeanne 1898-1920 **[3]**
- $16 205 - €17 684 - **£10 996** - FF116 000
  Portrait de femme Huile/toile (62x47cm 24x18in) Paris 2000
- $2 556 - €2 744 - **£1 710** - FF18 000
  Portrait de Modigliani Crayon/papier (21x24cm 8x9in) Paris 2000

HECHT Joseph 1891-1951 **[69]**
- $653 - €762 - **£458** - FF5 000
  Bouquet de fleurs Huile/toile (59x49cm 23x19in) Paris 2001
- $700 - €800 - **£492** - FF5 245
  Face depicting a young woman Bronze (H19cm H7in) Morris-Plains NJ 2001
- $445 - €464 - **£288** - FF3 043
  Swiss Landscape I Etching (15x25.5cm 5x10in) London 2000

HECHT van der Hendrik 1841-1901 **[24]**
- $1 032 - €1 190 - **£720** - FF7 804
  Travaux de champs sur fond de paysage avec ferme Huile/toile (40x49cm 15x19in) Bruxelles 2001

HECK Georg 1897-1982 **[11]**
- $643 - €767 - **£458** - FF5 030
  Mann mit Zylinder Woodcut (66.5x28cm 26x11in) Königstein 2000

HECK van der Claesz Dircksz 1571-c.1650 **[5]**
- $33 110 - €35 029 - **£21 000** - FF229 775
  Wooded Landscape with Huntsmen in the fore-ground Oil/panel (52x107cm 20x42in) London 2000

HECK van der Nicolaes 1575/81-1652 **[1]**
- $25 637 - €28 134 - **£16 504** - FF184 549
  View of Egmont Abbey Oil/panel (20.5x59.5cm 8x23in) Amsterdam 2000

HECKE van Arthur 1924 **[109]**
- $1 074 - €1 220 - **£746** - FF8 000
  Abstraction Huile/toile (99x78.5cm 38x30in) Saint-Omer 2001

HECKE van den Jan Frans XVII **[1]**
- $9 002 - €10 174 - **£6 076** - FF66 738
  Stilleben mit Weintrauben, Pfirsichen und einem gefüllten Weinglas Oil/panel (58.5x83cm 23x32in) Wien 2000

HECKE van den Jan I 1620-1684 **[24]**
- $17 527 - €16 351 - **£10 575** - FF107 257
  Blumenstilleben Öl/Leinwand (48x68cm 18x26in) Wien 1999

$19 333 - €19 229 - **£12 000** - FF126 134
Still Life of Roses, Tulips and other Flowers in a Glass Vase Oil/panel (33.5x23.5cm 13x9in) London 1999

HECKE van Willem 1893-1976 **[158]**
$995 - €916 - **£611** - FF6 000
Plage Huile/toile (81x65cm 31x25in) Paris 1999
$621 - €595 - **£381** - FF3 902
Figure Huile/papier (37x25cm 14x9in) Bruxelles 1999

HECKEL Erich 1883-1970 **[1400]**
$302 910 - €293 997 - **£188 600** - FF1 928 492
Ziegelei (Gehöft am Niederrhein) Öl/Leinwand (79x94.5cm 31x37in) Berlin 1999
$14 387 - €16 361 - **£9 977** - FF107 324
«Schlafend»/«Küstenlandschaft» Tempera (43.6x36.5cm 17x14in) Hamburg 2000
$12 360 - €10 218 - **£7 252** - FF67 024
«Landschaft in Kärnten mit Karawanken» Aquarell/Papier (55.5x68.5cm 21x26in) Radolfzell 1998
$950 - €1 149 - **£663** - FF7 535
Bildnis E.G. Lithograph (49x38cm 19x14in) Bethesda MD 2000

HECKEL von August 1824-1883 **[15]**
$1 861 - €1 609 - **£1 106** - FF10 555
König Lear verstösst Cordelia Öl/Leinwand (59x71cm 23x27in) Zürich 1998

HECKENDORF Franz 1888-1962/64 **[341]**
$4 503 - €5 113 - **£3 129** - FF33 539
Häuser am Wannsee Öl/Leinwand (36.5x46.5cm 14x18in) Berlin 2001
$1 362 - €1 278 - **£841** - FF8 384
Friedhofskapelle im Walde (vermutlich Timmendorfer Strand) Oil/board (33.2x40.2cm 13x15in) Stuttgart 1999
$711 - €665 - **£430** - FF4 360
Liegender Frauenakt vor rot-blauem Hintergrund Charcoal (24x24cm 9x9in) Berlin 1999
$346 - €286 - **£203** - FF1 876
Zwei Beduinen mit Dromedaren Farblithographie (30.5x41.2cm 12x16in) Bremen 1998

HECKER Franz 1870-1944 **[181]**
$3 876 - €3 835 - **£2 417** - FF25 154
Winterlandschaft mit Kirche Öl/Leinwand (61x82cm 24x32in) Heilbronn 1999
$4 138 - €4 540 - **£2 748** - FF29 779
Ville au bord d'un canal Oil/panel (45x34.7cm 17x13in) Warszawa 2000
$526 - €613 - **£369** - FF4 024
Am Zaub Etching, aquatint (20.5x26.8cm 8x10in) Osnabrück 2000

HECKMAN Albert 1893-1971 **[10]**
$475 - €547 - **£327** - FF3 590
«Oil Yards at Kingston» Lithograph (26x33cm 10x13in) Cleveland OH 2000

HECKROTH Hein 1901-1970 **[23]**
$650 - €758 - **£450** - FF4 971
At the Mouth of the River Oil/canvas (41x51cm 16x20in) London 2000

HECQ Émile 1924 **[67]**
$513 - €549 - **£349** - FF3 600
Composition Huile/toile (95x106cm 37x41in) Abbeville 2001
$208 - €229 - **£134** - FF1 500
Composition abstraite aux allumettes Gouache/papier (43x60cm 16x23in) Bernay 2000

HEDA Gerrit Willemsz. c.1620-c.1702 **[16]**
$64 890 - €65 405 - **£40 500** - FF429 030
Stilleben mit Prunkgefässen, Zinntellern, Austern und Haselnüssen Oil/panel (57x71cm 22x27in) Wien 2000

HEDA Willem Claesz. 1594-1680/82 **[19]**
$400 000 - €427 180 - **£272 560** - FF2 802 120
Hock of Ham, Knife with Slices of Ham, peeled Lemon, Wineglass Oil/panel (59.5x79cm 23x31in) New-York 2001

HEDBERG Hans 1917 **[28]**
$1 547 - €1 451 - **£956** - FF9 517
Äpple Ceramic (H12cm H4in) Stockholm 1999

HEDIN Sven 1865-1952 **[1]**
$14 000 - €15 543 - **£9 737** - FF101 953
Tibet Photograph (12.5x17cm 4x6in) New-York 2001

HEDLEY Ralph 1851-1913 **[65]**
$9 809 - €9 464 - **£6 200** - FF62 077
Draining the Marsh Oil/canvas (139.5x117.5cm 54x46in) London 1999
$6 716 - €7 993 - **£4 800** - FF52 431
A Good Read Oil/canvas (51x40.5cm 20x15in) London 2000
$2 865 - €2 789 - **£1 764** - FF18 292
Interiör med kvinnor Oil/panel (32.5x40cm 12x15in) Stockholm 1999

HEDLUND Bertil Bull 1893-1950 **[7]**
$5 661 - €6 569 - **£3 908** - FF43 092
Under parasollet Oil/canvas (67x67cm 26x26in) Stockholm 2000

HEEL van Jan 1898-1990 **[122]**
$5 704 - €5 445 - **£3 565** - FF35 719
«Winter» Oil/canvas (100x150cm 39x59in) Amsterdam 1999
$2 618 - €2 949 - **£1 805** - FF19 347
Spaans Drop VII Oil/canvas (50x60cm 19x23in) Amsterdam 2000
$1 483 - €1 327 - **£888** - FF8 706
Paris Oil/board (34x23.5cm 13x9in) Amsterdam 1998
$646 - €635 - **£415** - FF4 167
Rotsformatie Spanje Watercolour/paper (45.5x31cm 17x12in) Amsterdam 1999

HEEM de Cornelis 1631-1695 **[53]**
$93 864 - €108 907 - **£64 800** - FF714 384
Peaches, Grapes, Walnuts, Mushrooms and a Thistle, on a River Bank Oil/canvas (49.5x45.5cm 19x17in) Amsterdam 2000
$104 325 - €103 636 - **£65 000** - FF679 809
Still Life of a Peeled Lemon, Grapes, a Fig and Cherries Oil/panel (34x24.5cm 13x9in) London 1999

HEEM de David Cornelisz 1663-1718 **[8]**
$80 000 - €66 535 - **£46 960** - FF436 440
Roses, Poppies, Ears of Corn and other Flowers in a glass Vase Oil/canvas (63.5x52cm 25x20in) New-York 1998

HEEM de Jan Davidsz. 1606-1683/84 **[25]**
$279 800 - €304 898 - **£183 400** - FF2 000 000
Nature morte de fruits et huîtres dans une niche de pierre Huile/toile (63x74cm 24x29in) Dijon 2000
$67 674 - €66 461 - **£42 000** - FF435 955
Peeled Lemon, Oranges, Nuts in a Blue and White Porcelain Bowl Oil/panel (32x39.5cm 12x15in) London 1999

HEEM de Jan II Jansz 1650-c.1695 **[3]**
- $362 000 - €411 372 - **£250 000** - FF2 698 425
  A Silver Tazza and a Basket Laden with Fruit, Silver Platters Oil/canvas (83x108cm 32x42in) London 2000

HEEMSKERCK VAN BEEST van Jacob Eduard 1828-1894 **[19]**
- $7 204 - €7 260 - **£4 491** - FF47 625
  Shipping on a rough Sea Oil/canvas (60x106cm 23x41in) Amsterdam 2000
- $1 925 - €1 815 - **£1 193** - FF11 906
  Dutch Sailing Vessel at Sea Oil/panel (25x34.5cm 9x13in) Amsterdam 1999

HEEMSKERCK VAN BEEST van Jacoba 1876-1923 **[37]**
- $48 465 - €47 039 - **£30 176** - FF308 558
  Hafen, Bild 2 Öl/Leinwand (100.5x119.5cm 39x47in) Berlin 1999
- $43 076 - €40 167 - **£26 000** - FF263 481
  Am Meer (By the Sea) Oil/canvas (98x98cm 38x38in) London 1999
- $5 655 - €5 445 - **£3 536** - FF35 719
  Kleurstudie Oil/canvas (38.5x38.5cm 15x15in) Amsterdam 1999
- $505 - €499 - **£307** - FF3 274
  Composition with Fish Woodcut (22x32cm 8x12in) Amsterdam 2000

HEEMSKERCK van Egbert I 1634/35-1704 **[59]**
- $3 205 - €3 811 - **£2 285** - FF25 000
  Réunion des paysans dans une auberge Huile/panneau (33.5x48cm 13x18in) Neuilly-sur-Seine 2000
- $2 769 - €2 592 - **£1 715** - FF17 000
  Scène de taverne Huile/panneau (34.5x27.5cm 13x10in) Tourcoing 1999
- $1 260 - €1 431 - **£876** - FF9 390
  Trinkende Bauern vor der Dorfschänke Chalks (16.5x20.5cm 6x8in) Köln 2001

HEEMSKERCK van Egbert II ?-1744 **[137]**
- $7 191 - €6 807 - **£4 471** - FF44 649
  A Death-Bed Scene with a Notary tipping a Clerk Oil/panel (39.5x51.5cm 15x20in) Amsterdam 1999
- $4 055 - €3 968 - **£2 600** - FF26 031
  Tavern Scene Oil/panel (32.5x26cm 12x10in) London 1999
- $4 482 - €4 812 - **£3 000** - FF31 564
  Tavern Scene/Sketch of a Nude Black chalk (25.5x30.5cm 10x12in) London 2000

HEEMSKERCK van Maerten Jacobsz. 1498-1574 **[22]**
- $27 380 - €30 490 - **£19 240** - FF200 000
  Le couronnement d'épines Huile/panneau (79x69cm 31x27in) Paris 2001
- $53 842 - €46 504 - **£32 457** - FF305 044
  Jezebel sealing the forget Letters Ink (20x25cm 7x9in) Amsterdam 1998
- $1 058 - €920 - **£637** - FF6 033
  Die Passion Christi Radierung (24.7x19.6cm 9x7in) Berlin 1998

HEER de Gerrit Adriaensz. c.1610-c.1660 **[6]**
- $15 771 - €13 607 - **£9 516** - FF89 259
  Portrait of a man, half-length Ink (14.3x15.4cm 5x6in) Amsterdam 1998

HEER de Margareta c.1600-c.1665 **[4]**
- $2 737 - €2 632 - **£1 686** - FF17 264
  Two Turkeys, a Peacock and Three Chickens in a Panoramic Landscape Gouache (35.5x27cm 13x10in) Amsterdam 1999

HEER de Willem 1637/38-1681 **[4]**
- $4 102 - €3 543 - **£2 472** - FF23 240
  A Still Life with dead Songbirds, a Rose, a Tulip, Butterflies Bodycolour (24.5x33cm 9x12in) Amsterdam 1998

HEERDEN van Piet 1917-1991 **[31]**
- $1 238 - €1 387 - **£860** - FF9 097
  Figures walking on a Bridge Oil/canvas/board (39x49cm 15x19in) Johannesburg 2001
- $872 - €733 - **£511** - FF4 807
  Farmhouse with Chickens Oil/canvas (29x49cm 11x19in) Cape Town 1998

HEEREBAART Georgius 1829-1915 **[11]**
- $5 310 - €4 648 - **£3 216** - FF30 486
  Bauer mit Pferdefuhrwerk vor dem Dorfe Oil/panel (35.5x45cm 13x17in) Zofingen 1998

HEEREMANS Thomas 1641-1697 **[148]**
- $16 311 - €15 256 - **£10 000** - FF100 070
  A Winter Landscape with Skaters and Other Figures Feeding Their Horses Oil/canvas (58x81cm 22x31in) London 1998
- $9 820 - €11 527 - **£6 930** - FF75 610
  Vinterlandskap med byggnader och skriskoåkare Oil/panel (32x38.5cm 12x15in) Stockholm 2000

HEERICH Erwin 1922 **[43]**
- $2 411 - €2 812 - **£1 692** - FF18 446
  Ohne Titel Bronze (60.4x60x40.2cm 23x23x15in) Köln 2000

HEERUP Henry 1907-1993 **[738]**
- $1 239 - €1 407 - **£848** - FF9 228
  Klippekyst Oil/canvas (86x140cm 33x55in) Köbenhavn 2000
- $4 113 - €4 084 - **£2 570** - FF26 789
  Miller's Dream Oil/canvas (37x68cm 14x26in) Amsterdam 1999
- $1 246 - €1 076 - **£752** - FF7 060
  Landskab med korntraver Oil/canvas (32x14in) Vejle 1998
- $14 022 - €12 099 - **£8 460** - FF79 362
  «Faerdselsalter» Assemblage (146x47cm 57x18in) Köbenhavn 1998
- $2 370 - €2 680 - **£1 602** - FF17 582
  Hare Stone (H40cm H15in) Köbenhavn 2000
- $498 - €458 - **£306** - FF3 002
  Drengen og storken Gouache (23x14.5cm 9x5in) Köbenhavn 1999
- $157 - €134 - **£92** - FF881
  Hjerteparret Color lithograph (40x52cm 15x20in) Viby J, Århus 1998

HEFFNER Joseph Julius 1877-1951 **[14]**
- $1 635 - €1 534 - **£1 010** - FF10 061
  Sommerliche Ausblicke auf den Titisee Öl/Karton (69x88cm 27x34in) Staufen 1999
- $1 535 - €1 534 - **£960** - FF10 061
  Rauhreif bei Neuhäuser Öl/Karton (43x32cm 16x12in) Staufen 1999

HEFFNER Karl 1849-1925 **[276]**
- $10 400 - €10 326 - **£6 500** - FF67 734
  Landscape at Sunset Oil/canvas (102x143cm 40x56in) London 1999
- $2 824 - €2 417 - **£1 700** - FF15 852
  A Country Track lined with Poplars Oil/canvas (56x61cm 22x24in) London 1998

H

$645 - €767 - £447 - FF5 030
Kleine Flusslandschaft mit Pappeln Öl/Leinwand
(14x19cm 5x7in) Bremen 2000

HEGE Walter 1893-1955 **[11]**
$1 324 - €1 278 - **£832** - FF8 384
Köpfe in Stein aus dem Naumburger Dom
Photograph (22x17cm 8x6in) München 1999

HEGEMANN-RÄDERSCHEIDT Martha 1894-1970
[2]
$1 227 - €1 431 - **£861** - FF9 390
Fischerdorf mit Booten Aquarell/Papier
(29.8x22.6cm 11x8in) Köln 2000

HEGENBARTH Josef 1884-1962 **[273]**
$4 284 - €4 090 - **£2 676** - FF26 831
Im kaffee (Gartenrestaurant) Tempera
(32.9x50.4cm 12x19in) Köln 1999
$2 628 - €2 300 - £1 591 - FF15 089
**Ein Fuchs/Der Vater jagt seinen Sohn aus dem
Haus** Mixed media/canvas (25.9x31.3cm 10x12in)
Berlin 1998
$817 - €716 - **£495** - FF4 694
**Illustrationen zu Grimmelshausen,
Simplicissimus** Indian ink (20x17cm 7x6in) Berlin
1998
$175 - €204 - **£122** - FF1 341
Obstpflücker Drypoint (12.1x9.8cm 4x3in) Berlin
2000

HEGER Frantz 1766-1831 **[3]**
$2 893 - €3 270 - £1 953 - FF21 451
Andacht in Santa Prassede zu Rom Ink
(33.6x40.1cm 13x15in) Wien 2000

HEGG Maria Teresa 1829-1911 **[10]**
$1 511 - €1 304 - **£899** - FF8 551
Rosenstilleben Gouache/paper (48x33.5cm 18x13in)
München 1998

HEGI Franz 1774-1850 **[64]**
$433 - €486 - **£301** - FF3 189
**Vue prise de Beckenried vers Schwytz, nach
Wetzel** Aquatinta (24x31.5cm 9x12in) Luzern 2001

HEIBERG Astri 1883-1967 **[8]**
$10 013 - €11 912 - **€6 925** - FF78 137
Badende kvinner Oil/canvas (97x83cm 38x32in)
Oslo 2000

HEIBERG Jean Hjalmar Dahl 1884-1976 **[30]**
$53 650 - €62 573 - **£37 350** - FF410 450
Efter badet Oil/canvas (162x130cm 63x51in) Oslo
2000
$8 456 - €7 145 - **£5 077** - FF46 865
Kystlandskap Oil/canvas (74x93cm 29x36in) Oslo
1998

HEICHELE Max XX **[26]**
$540 - €639 - **£383** - FF4 192
Stürmische Voralpenlandschaft mit Wegkreuz
Oil/panel (25x38cm 9x14in) Staufen 2000

HEICKE Josef 1811-1861 **[30]**
$4 490 - €4 442 - **£2 800** - FF29 140
New Tricks Oil/canvas (56.5x43cm 22x16in) London
1999

HEICKELL Arthur 1873-1958 **[152]**
$822 - €704 - **£485** - FF4 621
Landskap Oil/canvas (70x60cm 27x23in) Helsinki
1998
$660 - €555 - **£388** - FF3 639
Strandlandskap Oil/canvas (35x45cm 13x17in)
Helsinki 1998

HEIDECK von Karl Wilhelm 1788-1861 **[18]**
$7 340 - €8 181 - **£5 131** - FF53 662
Rast vor dem Brunnen Oil/panel (20x29cm 7x11in)
München 2001

HEIDEKEN von Pehr Gustaf 1781-1864 **[5]**
$5 946 - €5 686 - **£3 728** - FF37 296
Vy över Riddarholmen Oil/canvas (30x42cm
11x16in) Stockholm 1999

HEIDER Klaus 1936 **[7]**
$997 - €1 125 - **£701** - FF7 378
Ohne Titel Farbserigraphie (65x50cm 25x19in)
Stuttgart 2001

HEIDERSBERGER Heinrich 1906-? **[62]**
$857 - €1 022 - **£611** - FF6 707
Materialstudie mit Akt Photograph (40x28.8cm
15x11in) München 2000

HEIGEL Franz Napoleon 1813-1888 **[10]**
$5 161 - €6 135 - **£3 576** - FF40 246
**«Ankunft König Ludwigs II.in Schloss-
Linderhof»** Gouache/paper (57.5x64.5cm 22x25in)
München 2000

HEIJDEN van der Jacques 1928 **[12]**
$5 643 - €4 886 - **£3 424** - FF32 047
Abstract compositions Oil/canvas (26.5x22cm
10x8in) Amsterdam 1998

HEIJENBROCK Herman 1871-1948 **[44]**
$1 618 - €1 906 - £1 119 - FF12 501
«Metaalgieterij» Oil/canvas (52.5x78cm 20x30in)
Amsterdam 2000
$393 - €340 - **£238** - FF2 232
Staalmeester Engeland Pastel/paper (26x21.5cm
10x8in) Amsterdam 1999

HEIJMANS Jan Hendrik 1806-1888 **[2]**
$4 519 - €5 062 - **£3 140** - FF33 203
Junge Wild, und Geflügelhändlerin Öl/Leinwand
(87x65cm 34x25in) Oersberg-bei Kappeln 2001

HEIKE Joseph 1811-1861 **[7]**
$4 420 - €4 633 - **£2 800** - FF30 388
The Woodcutters Oil/canvas (42x52cm 16x20in)
London 2000

HEIKKA Earle Erik 1910-1941 **[35]**
$1 350 - €1 278 - **£842** - FF8 384
Old Time Prospector Bronze (30x40cm 12x16in) St.
Ignatius MT 1999

HEIL Charles Emile 1870-1953 **[14]**
$2 100 - €2 284 - **£1 384** - FF14 982
Last Glow Oil/canvas (25.5x20.5cm 10x8in) Boston
MA 2000
$950 - €1 123 - **£673** - FF7 366
Bluejay Watercolour (30.5x47cm 12x18in) Boston MA
2000

HEIL van Daniel 1604-1662 **[35]**
$14 251 - €16 186 - **£10 000** - FF106 175
Fire in Brussels at Night Oil/canvas (116x166.5cm
45x65in) London 2001
$8 132 - €9 420 - **£5 624** - FF61 788
Paysage hivernal avec patineurs Huile/toile
(41.5x50.5cm 16x19in) Bruxelles 2000

HEILBORN Emil 1900 **[5]**
$3 000 - €2 536 - £1 795 - FF16 632
At the Dog Races Gelatin silver print (38x30cm
14x11in) Beverly-Hills CA 1998

HEILBUTH Ferdinand 1826-1889 **[57]**
- **$18 000** - €20 444 - **£12 630** - FF134 107
  The Intermission Oil/panel (33.5x56cm 13x22in)
  New-York 2001
- **$457** - €512 - **£312** - FF3 343
  Portraet af en rödhåret kvinde Oil/wood (24x19cm 9x7in) Viby J, Århus 2000
- **$4 528** - €5 254 - **£3 126** - FF34 462
  Zwei junge Damen am Waldrand Aquarell, Gouache/Papier (43x69cm 16x27in) Luzern 2000

HEILEMANN Ernst 1870-? **[8]**
- **$5 943** - €5 087 - **£3 577** - FF33 369
  «**Frau dal'Ongaro**» Oil/panel (104x78cm 40x30in) Wien 1998

HEILIGENSTEIN Auguste 1891-1976 **[13]**
- **$28 752** - €24 392 - **£17 344** - FF160 000
  Vase à décor de poissons scalaires sur fond de végétation aquatique Céramique (54.5x28cm 21x11in) Paris 1998

HEILIGER Bernhard 1915-1995 **[115]**
- **$7 269** - €7 056 - **£4 526** - FF46 283
  Doppeltorso Polished bronze (36x18.5x12.7cm 14x7x5in) Berlin 1999
- **$423** - €511 - **£295** - FF3 353
  Weiblicher Akt, nach links unten gebeugt Graphite (42x27.6cm 16x10in) Berlin 2000
- **$149** - €176 - **£105** - FF1 157
  Bildnis Martin Heidegger Lithographie (33x22cm 12x8in) Berlin 2001

HEILMAN-C Gloria 1961 **[13]**
- **$3 750** - €3 169 - **£2 237** - FF20 789
  Hanging Bronze Sculpture Series Bronze (18x18cm 7x7in) San-Francisco CA 1998
- **$3 500** - €3 898 - **£2 289** - FF25 572
  Enquirer Series Print in colors (27.5x23cm 10x9in) New-York 2000
- **$4 000** - €3 390 - **£2 390** - FF22 234
  Enquirer Series Photograph in colour (28x23cm 11x9in) New-York 1998

HEILMANN Gerhard V.E. 1859-1946 **[25]**
- **$850** - €927 - **£588** - FF6 078
  «**Danmarks Fugleliv**» Poster (87x67cm 34x26in) New-York 2001

HEILMANN Jean-Jacques 1822-1859 **[14]**
- **$457** - €534 - **£321** - FF3 500
  Façade de l'église de Morlaas, prise à 14 heures 30 Tirage papier salé (26.5x20cm 10x7in) Paris 2001

HEILMANN Julius 1881-? **[8]**
- **$1 126** - €1 125 - **£704** - FF7 378
  An einem Winterabend im Schwarzwald Öl/Karton (30x40cm 11x15in) Staufen 1999

HEILMANN Karl XX **[14]**
- **$545** - €511 - **£336** - FF3 353
  Glottertäler Bauernhaus an einem Frühlingsmorgen mit Blick ins Tal Öl/Leinwand (45x55cm 17x21in) Staufen 1999
- **$327** - €307 - **£202** - FF2 012
  Brunnen im Schwarzwald an einem Frühlingstag Öl/Karton (18x14cm 7x5in) Staufen 1999

HEILMANN Mary 1940 **[9]**
- **$18 000** - €20 362 - **£12 592** - FF133 569
  «**Red yellow of the Square Pair**» Acrylic/canvas (122x122cm 48x48in) New-York 2001

- **$21 000** - €19 718 - **£13 011** - FF129 341
  Black Sliding Square Acrylic (65x61cm 25x24in) New-York 1999

HEILMAYER Karl 1829-1908 **[54]**
- **$2 076** - €2 003 - **£1 304** - FF13 142
  Rom - der Tiber mit Blick auf die Engelsburg und St. Peter Öl/Leinwand (42x65cm 16x25in) Zürich 1999
- **$953** - €817 - **£563** - FF5 358
  «**Vor der Steilküste**» Oil/panel (24x36cm 9x14in) München 1998

HEIM François Joseph 1787-1865 **[15]**
- **$33 902** - €33 539 - **£21 142** - FF220 000
  La lutte des Sabins contre les Romains Huile/toile (54x67cm 21x26in) Rouen 1999
- **$5 187** - €5 793 - **£3 515** - FF38 000
  Entrée de Charles VIII à Naples Huile/panneau (13x29.5cm 5x11in) Paris 2000

HEIM Liane 1920 **[8]**
- **$401** - €457 - **£282** - FF2 996
  «**Kleine Lebewesen**» Aquarell (43x54cm 16x21in) Zürich 2001

HEIMERDINGER Friedrich 1817-1882 **[6]**
- **$822** - €883 - **£550** - FF5 793
  Hanging-Bird on the Lid of a Cigar Box, a Trompe-l'oeil Oil/canvas (24x18.5cm 9x7in) London 2000

HEIMERL Josef 1867-? **[32]**
- **$1 193** - €1 109 - **£728** - FF7 272
  Two Kittens Oil/canvas (21.5x27cm 8x10in) Amsterdam 1998

HEIMES Heinrich 1855-1933 **[13]**
- **$779** - €716 - **£478** - FF4 695
  Kirchdorf im Sommer Öl/Leinwand (51x60.5cm 20x23in) Stuttgart 1999

HEIMIG Walter 1881-1955 **[46]**
- **$427** - €486 - **£296** - FF3 186
  Zwei junge Damen beim Lesen Oil/panel (30.2x30cm 11x11in) Berlin 2000

HEIN Eduard, Jr. XIX-XX **[7]**
- **$644** - €767 - **£459** - FF5 030
  Winterwald/Sommerlandschaft Öl/Leinwand (35.5x27cm 13x10in) Köln 2000

HEIN Eduard, Sr. XIX-XX **[19]**
- **$1 045** - €1 220 - **£747** - FF8 000
  Château dans un paysage romantique Huile/toile (65x95cm 25x37in) Lyon 2000
- **$1 201** - €1 125 - **£744** - FF7 378
  Winterlandschaft mit an einem Flüsschen gelegenem Bauernhaus Öl/Leinwand (35x27cm 13x10in) Heidelberg 1999

HEIN Hendrik Jan 1822-1866 **[12]**
- **$8 377** - €9 729 - **£5 887** - FF63 817
  Stilleben med fåglar, frukter och vinglas Oil/canvas (73x65cm 28x25in) Stockholm 2001
- **$7 458** - €6 390 - **£4 483** - FF41 916
  Früchtestilleben Oil/panel (26.5x21.8cm 10x8in) Köln 1998

HEINDORFF Michael XX **[6]**
- **$412** - €389 - **£260** - FF2 553
  Lobster Etching, aquatint (75x105.5cm 29x41in) London 1999

HEINE Johann Adalbert 1850-1900 **[19]**
- $2 537 - €2 556 - £1 581 - FF16 769
  Zwei fesche Dirndl beim Plausch mit einem Jägersmann Öl/Leinwand (46x60cm 18x23in) Staufen 2000
- $1 626 - €1 534 - £1 013 - FF10 061
  Heiterer Mönchsvortrag an reich gedeckter Tafel Oil/panel (21.5x27cm 8x10in) Frankfurt 1999

HEINE Thomas Theodor 1867-1948 **[139]**
- $4 016 - €4 458 - £2 800 - FF29 245
  Mountainous Lake Landscape Oil/canvas (80x55cm 31x21in) London 2001
- $464 - €460 - £290 - FF3 018
  Naturgenuss Ink (19.5x29.6cm 7x11in) München 1999
- $2 000 - €1 754 - £1 214 - FF11 507
  Simplicissimus Poster (84x61cm 33x24in) New-York 1999

HEINECKE Wilhelmus, Wim 1895-1978 **[15]**
- $573 - €544 - £348 - FF3 571
  Rotterdams stadsgezicht Oil/canvas (39x59cm 15x23in) Rotterdam 1999

HEINECKEN Robert F. 1931 **[8]**
- $2 400 - €2 266 - £1 490 - FF14 865
  Vary Cliché, Fetishism/Vary Cliché, Auto Eroticism Lithograph (40.5x40.5cm 15x15in) New-York 1999
- $5 500 - €6 247 - £3 859 - FF40 980
  He:She Photograph (22x33cm 8x12in) New-York 2001

HEINEFETTER Johann Baptist 1815-1902 **[18]**
- $1 384 - €1 636 - £981 - FF10 732
  Der Golf von Neapel Öl/Karton (43.5x57cm 17x22in) München 2000

HEINEL Eduard 1835-1895 **[13]**
- $2 148 - €1 840 - £1 291 - FF12 071
  Mittelgebirgslandschaft mit Wassermühle Öl/Leinwand (51x81cm 20x31in) Köln 1998

HEINISCH Karl Adam 1847-1923 **[64]**
- $2 636 - €2 556 - £1 659 - FF16 769
  Bauern mit Schafen in Moorlandschaft Öl/Leinwand (68.5x100.5cm 26x39in) München 1999
- $3 584 - €3 262 - £2 200 - FF21 399
  The Gipsy Camp Oil/canvas (29x35.5cm 11x13in) London 1999

HEINLEIN Heinrich 1803-1885 **[35]**
- $1 841 - €2 045 - £1 280 - FF13 415
  Weite Landschaft Oil/board/canvas (40x52.5cm 15x20in) Heidelberg 2001
- $1 375 - €1 526 - £957 - FF10 010
  Blick ins «Oetz Thal» Öl/Karton (30.5x37cm 12x14in) Wien 2001

HEINONEN Aare 1906 **[24]**
- $411 - €404 - £255 - FF2 647
  Brunnsparken Oil/canvas (33x55cm 12x21in) Helsinki 1999

HEINRICH Frans 1802-1890 **[18]**
- $1 200 - €1 329 - £814 - FF8 720
  Schlossinterieur Aquarell, Gouache/Papier (27.5x33.7cm 10x13in) Hamburg 2000

HEINRICH-HANSEN Adolf 1859-1925 **[100]**
- $2 674 - €2 282 - £1 599 - FF14 971
  Portraet af en hund med et kuld kvalpe Oil/canvas (51x75cm 20x29in) Viby J, Århus 1998
- $481 - €536 - £336 - FF3 517
  Lövesöjlerne på Marcuspladsen i Venedig Oil/canvas (35.5x24cm 13x9in) Köbenhavn 2001

HEINS Armand 1856-1938 **[20]**
- $1 033 - €892 - £615 - FF5 853
  Place Ste-Pharaïlde à Gand Huile/toile (63x95.5cm 24x37in) Bruxelles 1998

HEINS John Theodore, Snr. 1697-1756 **[20]**
- $7 218 - €7 274 - £4 500 - FF47 716
  Miles Branthwayt (d.1751), three-quarter-length, in a brown Coat Oil/canvas (127x103.5cm 50x40in) London 2000
- $2 177 - €2 452 - £1 500 - FF16 082
  Dorothy Branthwayt (d.1769), in a Turquoise Dress and red Wrap Oil/canvas (76x63.5cm 29x25in) London 2000

HEINSIUS Johann Ernst, Julius 1740-1812 **[26]**
- $2 303 - €2 592 - £1 586 - FF17 000
  Portrait d'homme en habit rouge Huile/toile (65x54cm 25x21in) Tarbes 2000
- $2 212 - €1 829 - £1 298 - FF12 000
  Portrait d'homme Pierre noire (57x45cm 22x17in) Paris 1998

HEINTZ Hans (Johann) c.1580-1635 **[1]**
- $4 415 - €4 602 - £2 899 - FF30 185
  Stehender Maler mit Palette, auf eine Stadt herabblickend Ink (16.5x11.2cm 6x4in) Hamburg 2000

HEINTZ Josef I 1564-1609 **[14]**
- $55 000 - €54 879 - £33 478 - FF359 980
  The Madonna and Child with Mary Magdalen Black chalk (25x18cm 9x7in) New-York 2000

HEINTZ Josef II c.1600-c.1678 **[20]**
- $255 000 - €264 347 - £153 000 - FF1 734 000
  Lo sbarco alla Piazzetta di San Marco di un Capitano da Mar Olio/tela (125x230cm 49x90in) Roma 2000
- $35 000 - €36 283 - £21 000 - FF238 000
  Festa in una piazza Olio/tela (79x121cm 31x47in) Venezia 2000
- $8 000 - €8 569 - £5 463 - FF56 212
  Paradise Watercolour (51x153cm 20x60in) New-York 2001

HEINTZ Richard 1871-1929 **[249]**
- $4 260 - €4 958 - £3 000 - FF32 520
  Vieille forge à Nassogne Huile/panneau (40x50cm 15x19in) Liège 2001
- $1 695 - €1 859 - £1 095 - FF12 195
  Juillet à Sy Huile/toile (28x36cm 11x14in) Liège 2000
- $101 - €111 - £65 - FF731
  Paysage Eau-forte (24x31.5cm 9x12in) Liège 2000

HEINTZELMAN Arthur William 1890-1965 **[42]**
- $150 - €144 - £91 - FF943
  Sergey Kousevitzkey Etching (25.5x20cm 10x7in) Boston MA 1999

HEINZE Adolph 1887-1958 **[17]**
- $950 - €842 - £582 - FF5 522
  The Log Cabin Oil/canvas (76x88cm 30x35in) Cincinnati OH 1999

HEINZMANN Carl Friedrich 1795-1846 **[15]**
- $279 - €256 - £170 - FF1 676
  Ansicht vom Kochelsee Lithographie (40.9x47.7cm 16x18in) München 1999

HEISE Wilhelm 1894-1965 **[23]**
- $418 - €486 - £293 - FF3 186
  «Wilder Türkenbund» Print (35.5x25cm 13x9in) Berlin 2001

HEISIG Bernhard 1925 **[76]**
- $83 296 - €97 147 - **£58 482** - FF637 241
  Der Maler und sein Thema Öl/Leinwand (150x240cm 59x94in) Köln 2000
- $14 473 - €14 316 - **£9 024** - FF93 909
  Alte Häuser in Warnau Öl/Leinwand (60.5x80cm 23x31in) Berlin 1999
- $385 - €368 - **£234** - FF2 414
  Tanzplatz im KZ Westhofen Crayon (14.5x12.5cm 5x4in) Dettelbach-Effeldorf 1999
- $101 - €123 - **£70** - FF804
  Sterbender Bauer Lithographie (43x30.5cm 16x12in) Berlin 2000

HEISIG Johannes 1953 **[6]**
- $1 825 - €2 045 - **£1 271** - FF13 415
  «Akt» Oil/panel (50.5x71cm 19x27in) Berlin 2001

HEISKA Joonas 1873-1937 **[28]**
- $1 360 - €1 345 - **£848** - FF8 825
  Kangas pappersbruk Oil/panel (55x48cm 21x18in) Helsinki 1999
- $616 - €605 - **£382** - FF3 971
  Gård Oil/canvas (27x33cm 10x12in) Helsinki 1999
- $289 - €320 - **£200** - FF2 096
  Gårdsvy Watercolour/paper (27x35cm 10x13in) Helsinki 2001

HEISS Johann 1640-1704 **[27]**
- $67 200 - €57 192 - **£40 000** - FF375 156
  The Death of Jezebel Oil/canvas (117.5x140cm 46x55in) London 1998
- $18 000 - €17 182 - **£11 246** - FF112 708
  The Continence of Scipio Oil/canvas (75.5x85cm 29x33in) New-York 1999

HEISTER von Hans Siebert 1888-1967 **[2]**
- $57 907 - €54 090 - **£35 000** - FF354 805
  Drei Manner Oil/canvas (80x63cm 31x24in) London 1999

HEITINGER Paul 1841-1920 **[29]**
- $3 410 - €2 812 - **£2 008** - FF18 444
  Prinzregent Luitpold auf seiner Zweimastjacht vor der Villa Toscana Oil/panel (38x56cm 14x22in) Lindau 1999
- $470 - €562 - **£323** - FF3 689
  Abendliche Landschaft Oil/canvas/panel (21.5x39.5cm 8x15in) München 2000

HEITMANN Günther 1924 **[2]**
- $2 880 - €2 812 - **£1 824** - FF18 446
  Landschaft mit Dorfkirche bei Jever Öl/Leinwand (60x80cm 23x31in) Bremen 1999

HEIZER Michael 1944 **[41]**
- $15 000 - €16 801 - **£10 422** - FF110 208
  Untitled Construction (188x199.5x61cm 74x78x24in) New-York 2001
- $1 456 - €1 702 - **£1 039** - FF111 162
  Demonics Pencil/paper (76x102cm 29x40in) Zürich 2001
- $1 100 - €1 225 - **£719** - FF8 037
  Levitated Mass/Dragged Mass Lithograph (81.5x118cm 32x46in) New-York 2000

HEJNA Václav 1914-1985 **[42]**
- $1 300 - €1 230 - **£810** - FF8 068
  Trois grâces Huile/toile (65x95cm 25x37in) Praha 2000

HEKKING Joseph Antonio 1830-c.1903 **[19]**
- $6 000 - €5 540 - **£3 736** - FF36 337
  Western Landscape Oil/canvas/board (64x50cm 25x20in) Oakland CA 1999

- $1 750 - €2 000 - **£1 232** - FF13 116
  Water's Edge Oil/canvas (17x22cm 7x9in) Pittsfield MA 2001

HEKKING Willem 1796-1862 **[11]**
- $1 289 - €1 227 - **£801** - FF8 049
  Drei Garnelen Aquarell/Papier (9.3x13.2cm 3x5in) Berlin 1999

HELAND Martin Rudolf 1765-1814 **[17]**
- $2 635 - €2 926 - **£1 764** - FF19 192
  La mère/Le triomphe Akvarell/papper (16x20cm 6x7in) Stockholm 2000
- $246 - €213 - **£148** - FF1 396
  Jernvägen i Stockholm Etching (14.5x13cm 5x5in) Stockholm 1999

HELBERGER Alfred Hermann 1871-1946 **[154]**
- $602 - €562 - **£363** - FF3 689
  Weite Havellandschaft mit fernem Grunewaldturm und Segelbooten Öl/Leinwand (60x60cm 19x23in) Berlin 1999

HELBIG Walter 1878-1965 **[80]**
- $2 809 - €3 275 - **£1 945** - FF21 481
  Bagni di Craveggia Öl/Leinwand (89x101cm 35x39in) Bern 2000
- $258 - €590 - **£3 633** - FF39 294
  Stilleben mit Schale, Früchten und Glas Oil/panel (32.2x44cm 12x17in) Zürich 2000
- $113 - €131 - **£80** - FF860
  Madonna mit Jesuskind Woodcut (30x23cm 11x9in) Zürich 2000

HELBING Ferenc 1870-1958 **[1]**
- $5 550 - €5 831 - **£3 450** - FF38 250
  Le baiser Huile/toile (100x90cm 39x35in) Budapest 2000

HELCK Peter 1893-1988 **[25]**
- $11 000 - €12 252 - **£7 195** - FF80 370
  Race car in autumn rain, train in distance Mixed media (40x40cm 16x16in) New-York 2000
- $500 - €478 - **£304** - FF3 136
  Cracked its Engine Block Graphite (16.5x23cm 6x9in) Boston MA 1999
- $210 - €196 - **£129** - FF1 286
  Joe Tracy's Locomobile Etching (21x30cm 8x12in) Cleveland OH 1999

HELD Al 1928 **[113]**
- $10 000 - €11 603 - **£6 904** - FF76 110
  Tri-Step Acrylic/canvas (122x152.5cm 48x60in) New-York 2000
- $7 500 - €7 826 - **£4 730** - FF51 337
  Untitled I-4 Acrylic/paper (60.5x45cm 23x17in) New-York 2000
- $1 000 - €839 - **£586** - FF5 503
  Untitled Ink/paper (57x89cm 22x35in) New-York 1998
- $2 200 - €1 904 - **£1 326** - FF12 492
  Untitled Etching, aquatint in colors (101x67cm 39x26in) New-York 1998

HELD Alma H. 1889-1989 **[20]**
- $750 - €875 - **£529** - FF5 741
  Still Life with Copper Kettle Oil/board (45x60cm 18x23in) Cedar-Falls IA 2000
- $850 - €994 - **£602** - FF6 520
  Summer Landscape Oil/board (35x25cm 14x10in) Cedar-Falls IA 2001

HELD John, Jnr. 1889-1958 **[29]**
- $9 500 - €11 074 - **£6 577** - FF72 641
  Margie Showing her Stockings Oil/canvas (46x27cm 18x11in) New-York 2000

H

🖉 **$1 600** - €1 792 - **£1 111** - FF11 755
Theatrical Chariot Race, Cartoon Drawing
(23x33cm 9x13in) New-York 2001

📜 **$3 800** - €4 141 - **£2 631** - FF27 162
«Northward, the New Haven R.R.» Poster
(105x71cm 41x28in) New-York 2001

HELDER Johannes 1842-1913 **[14]**
🖎 **$4 345** - €5 042 - **£3 000** - FF33 072
Interior Scene Oil/panel (50x37cm 19x14in) London
2000

HELDNER Colette Pope 1902-1990 **[89]**
🖎 **$1 000** - €1 151 - **£682** - FF7 552
Swamp Idyl Oil/canvas (40x50cm 16x20in) New-
Orleans LA 2000

🖎 **$550** - €634 - **£375** - FF4 156
**Old Courtyard on St.Peter St., French Quarter,
New Orleans** Oil/board (17x11cm 7x4in) New-
Orleans LA 2000

🖉 **$1 800** - €2 071 - **£1 240** - FF13 586
Edge of the Old French Quarter, New Orleans
Watercolour/paper (26x37cm 10x14in) New-Orleans LA
2000

HELDNER Knute 1884-1952 **[94]**
🖎 **$3 500** - €4 030 - **£2 053** - FF19 262
St. Tammany Pines Oil/canvas (40x50cm 16x20in)
New-Orleans LA 1998

🖎 **$2 900** - €3 039 - **£1 836** - FF19 933
Arts and Crafts Courtyard Oil/canvas/board
(33x43cm 13x17in) New-Orleans LA 2000

📜 **$400** - €371 - **£248** - FF2 432
Black Figure Fishing Off the Wharf Etching
(15x13cm 6x5in) New-Orleans LA 1999

HELDT von Werner 1904-1954 **[97]**
🖎 **$12 867** - €15 339 - **£9 174** - FF100 617
Strassenszene Oil/panel (40.2x59.7cm 15x23in)
Berlin 2000

🖎 **$4 905** - €4 602 - **£3 030** - FF30 185
Berlin am Meer Aquarell/Papier (24x16cm 9x6in)
Stuttgart 1999

📜 **$1 168** - €1 125 - **£730** - FF7 378
Hinterhäuser Farblithographie (21.5x33,5cm 8x13in)
München 1999

HELE Ivor Henry Thomas 1912-1993 **[17]**
🖎 **$8 901** - €8 660 - **£5 478** - FF56 809
Jupiter and Antiope Oil/board (90x60cm 35x23in)
Melbourne 1999

🖎 **$4 090** - €4 496 - **£2 621** - FF29 495
The Lovers Oil/board (24.5x14cm 9x5in) Melbourne
2000

🖉 **$1 676** - €1 527 - **£1 026** - FF10 017
Jean Seated Pastel/paper (38x27.5cm 14x10in)
Malvern, Victoria 1998

HELENIUS Ester 1875-1955 **[39]**
🖎 **$1 568** - €1 766 - **£1 080** - FF11 583
Blommor i vas Oil/canvas (65x47cm 25x18in)
Helsinki 2000

🖎 **$582** - €572 - **£361** - FF3 750
Flicka Oil/canvas (22x21cm 8x8in) Helsinki 1999

🖎 **$344** - €320 - **£206** - FF2 096
Flickhuvud Pastel/paper (50x36cm 19x14in) Helsinki
1999

HELENIUS Jorma 1955 **[4]**
🖎 **$4 482** - €5 045 - **£3 087** - FF33 096
Ensam hemma Oil/canvas (73x97cm 28x38in)
Helsinki 2000

HELFFERICH Fransiscus Willem 1871-1941 **[26]**
🖎 **$1 437** - €1 269 - **£866** - FF8 321
Ducks on the Waterfront/Ducks in the Grass
Oil/panel (12x16.5cm 4x6in) Amsterdam 1998

HELFOND Riva 1910 **[11]**
📜 **$400** - €377 - **£247** - FF2 470
«Escort» Lithograph (25x29.5cm 9x11in) New-York
1999

HELGUERO PUYUEL Luis 1942 **[40]**
🖉 **$112** - €120 - **£76** - FF788
Catedral de Astorga y Palacio de Gaudí
Acuarela/papel (30x40cm 11x15in) Madrid 2001

HELIKER John Edward 1909-1999 **[19]**
🖎 **$950** - €822 - **£576** - FF5 394
Abstract City Scene Oil/board (33x60cm 13x24in)
Mystic CT 1998

HELINCK Gustave 1884-1954 **[46]**
🖎 **$242** - €235 - **£152** - FF1 544
Vases de fleurs des champs Huile/toile (80x70cm
31x27in) Bruxelles 1999

HÉLION Jean 1904-1987 **[759]**
🖎 **$15 202** - €16 769 - **£10 296** - FF110 000
Duo luxembourgeois Acrylique/toile (130x96cm
51x37in) Paris 2000

🖎 **$7 128** - €8 385 - **£5 109** - FF55 000
Nature morte Huile/toile (81x65cm 31x25in)
Versailles 2001

🖎 **$2 487** - €2 744 - **£1 684** - FF18 000
Dans le miroir Huile/toile (35x27cm 13x10in) Paris
2000

🖎 **$2 814** - €3 201 - **£1 984** - FF21 000
Planches de suite maraîchère Gouache/papier
(61x46.5cm 24x18in) Paris 2001

📜 **$350** - €290 - **£205** - FF1 900
Homme au chapeau Lithographie couleurs
(65x50cm 25x19in) Paris 1998

HELL Friedrich 1869-1957 **[9]**
🖎 **$458** - €509 - **£319** - FF3 336
**Stilleben mit Weisser und roter Pfingstrose in
Wasserglas** Öl/Karton (33x24cm 12x9in) Salzburg
2001

HELL van Johan 1889-1952 **[25]**
🖎 **$24 804** - €29 496 - **£17 680** - FF193 479
Acrobats on a Terrace Oil/canvas (90.5x67cm
35x26in) Amsterdam 2000

📜 **$438** - €499 - **£304** - FF3 274
Laarzen Lithograph (24.2x18.5cm 9x7in) Haarlem
2000

HELLEMANS Pierre Jean 1787-1845 **[6]**
🖎 **$13 724** - €16 361 - **£9 785** - FF107 324
Bewaldete Landschaft mit Hirtenstaffage
Oil/panel (67.5x78.5cm 26x30in) Köln 2000

🖎 **$5 715** - €6 135 - **£3 825** - FF40 246
Vor dem Gewitter Oil/panel (30.2x29cm 11x11in)
Köln 2000

HELLER Adolf 1874-1914 **[8]**
🖎 **$6 188** - €7 186 - **£4 348** - FF47 138
Ung kvinna som arrangerar blommor Oil/canvas
(100x80cm 39x31in) Stockholm 2001

HELLESEN Johanna, Hanna 1801-1844 **[32]**
🖎 **$20 560** - €23 389 - **£14 360** - FF153 420
Blomsterstilleben med korg Oil/canvas (68x88cm
26x34in) Stockholm 2000

🖎 **$5 289** - €4 565 - **£3 182** - FF29 945
Druvklasar samt blomma i glasvas Oil/panel
(30x39cm 11x15in) Malmö 1998

HELLESEN Thorvald 1888-1937 [19]
- $27 630 - €25 962 - **£16 650** - FF170 302
  Flygmaskinen Oil/panel (22x27cm 8x10in) Stockholm 1999
- $2 786 - €2 668 - **£1 716** - FF17 500
  Composition Gouache/papier (31x22cm 12x8in) Douai 1999

HELLEU Jean Helleu-Guérin 1894-? [22]
- $1 678 - €1 906 - **£1 166** - FF12 500
  Le bateau à vapeur Huile/toile (54x65cm 21x25in) Pontoise 2001
- $1 911 - €2 134 - **£1 295** - FF14 000
  Femme couchée dans l'herbe Huile/bois (26.7x35cm 10x13in) Pontoise 2000

HELLEU Paul César 1859-1927 [847]
- $403 461 - €433 082 - **£270 000** - FF2 840 832
  La gare Saint-Lazare Oil/canvas (103x160cm 40x62in) London 2000
- $29 486 - €35 063 - **£21 022** - FF230 000
  Nu debout Huile/toile (56x46.5cm 22x18in) Neuilly-sur-Seine 2000
- $1 884 - €2 151 - **£1 328** - FF14 110
  Porträt einer Dame mit Blauem Hut Öl/Karton (17x12cm 6x4in) Bern 2001
- $9 775 - €9 554 - **£6 200** - FF62 669
  An Elegant Lady Reclining Black, red & white chalks/paper (47.5x57.5cm 18x22in) London 1999
- $1 500 - €1 703 - **£1 026** - FF11 172
  Ellen au profil (the Artist's Daughter) Drypoint (27x21cm 10x8in) New-York 2000

HELLGREWE Rudolf 1860-1935 [59]
- $939 - €1 022 - **£645** - FF6 702
  Märkischer See Öl/Leinwand (76x120.8cm 29x47in) Leipzig 2001
- $608 - €511 - **£357** - FF3 353
  Ufer eines märkischen Sees im Abendlicht Gouache/papier (36.5x60cm 14x23in) Köln 1998

HELLMEIER Otto 1908-1996 [45]
- $844 - €869 - **£532** - FF5 701
  Altes Backhaus in Raisting Öl/Karton (47x60cm 18x23in) München 2000
- $692 - €818 - **£490** - FF5 366
  Gehöft an Weiher Öl/Karton (23x48cm 9x18in) München 2000

HELLRATH Emil 1838-c.1900 [7]
- $2 435 - €2 556 - **£1 646** - FF16 769
  Schäfer mit Herde am Waldrand Öl/Leinwand (61x92cm 24x36in) Kempten 2001

HELLYER Thomas XVIII-XIX [1]
- $1 270 - €1 363 - **£850** - FF8 943
  Battle of the Nile, After Captain J.Weir Aquatint in colors (42.5x69cm 16x27in) London 2000

HELM van den Hendrik 1811-1889 [3]
- $4 012 - €3 857 - **£2 502** - FF25 301
  Sailing Vessels on a Choppy Sea Oil/canvas (61x77cm 24x30in) Amsterdam 1999

HELMANTEL Henk 1945 [19]
- $18 284 - €18 151 - **£11 424** - FF119 064
  Licht en tegenlicht Oil/board (91x82cm 35x32in) Amsterdam 1999
- $12 253 - €11 798 - **£7 662** - FF77 391
  Stilleven met afrikaanse drunkbeker en schep Oil/masonite (40x35cm 15x13in) Amsterdam 1999

HELMBERGER Adolf 1885-1967 [14]
- $2 378 - €2 761 - **£1 672** - FF18 114
  «Am Weg zum Friedhof in St.Gilgen, im Hintergrund das Zwölferhorn» Öl/Leinwand (50x42cm 19x16in) Salzburg 2001
- $1 001 - €1 163 - **£704** - FF7 627
  «Stilleben mit Maiglöckchen in Vase» Öl/Leinwand/Karton (18x14cm 7x5in) Salzburg 2001

HELMBRECKER Dirck Theodor 1633-1696 [16]
- $16 380 - €18 294 - **£11 100** - FF120 000
  Oeuvres de Charité - Distribution de la soupe à la porte d'un couvent Huile/toile (76x100cm 29x39in) Paris 2000
- $3 303 - €3 176 - **£2 034** - FF20 836
  Self-Portrait Red chalk (23x17.5cm 9x6in) Amsterdam 1999

HELME Helge 1894-1987 [111]
- $559 - €564 - **£349** - FF3 701
  Opstilling med pelargonie og aebler i vinduet Oil/canvas (61x50cm 24x19in) Köbenhavn 2000
- $568 - €538 - **£353** - FF3 533
  Ung pige ved vinduet Oil/canvas (42x30cm 16x11in) Köbenhavn 1999

HELMER Philipp 1846-1912 [5]
- $3 258 - €2 965 - **£2 035** - FF19 452
  Im Dachauer Moos Öl/Leinwand (28.3x46cm 11x18in) München 1999

HELMER Robert 1922-1990 [14]
- $160 - €155 - **£99** - FF1 018
  French Quarter Facade Linocut (48x30cm 19x12in) New-Orleans LA 1999

HELMICK Howard 1845-1907 [16]
- $2 376 - €2 221 - **£1 464** - FF14 572
  Recollections, Kustvy med fiskarfamilj Oil/canvas (51x77cm 20x30in) Stockholm 1999
- $3 228 - €2 994 - **£2 000** - FF19 641
  Dejeune a las Fourchette/His Nightcap Oil/board (28x20cm 11x7in) London 1999

HELMONT van Matthieu 1623-1679 [66]
- $22 104 - €20 499 - **£13 500** - FF134 462
  Interior of a Tavern with a Woman cleaning a Cauldron, Three Boers Oil/canvas (48x37cm 18x14in) London 1998
- $6 059 - €6 647 - **£4 115** - FF43 600
  Zechende Bauern im Wirtshaus Oil/panel (28x23cm 11x9in) Bamberg 2000

HELMSLEY William 1819-1906 [2]
- $3 227 - €3 099 - **£2 000** - FF20 329
  Young Rabbits, a Study Oil/panel (17.5x12cm 6x4in) London 1999

HELNWEIN Gottfried 1948 [52]
- $5 403 - €6 135 - **£3 754** - FF40 246
  Warren Beatty Mischtechnik/Karton (34x28.5cm 13x11in) München 2001
- $1 112 - €1 308 - **£772** - FF8 580
  Aggstein Mischtechnik/Papier (36.8x23cm 14x9in) Wien 2000
- $309 - €299 - **£190** - FF1 963
  The Champion Farbserigraphie (85x62cm 33x24in) Zürich 1999

HELPS Francis William 1890-1972 [29]
- $1 094 - €1 013 - **£680** - FF6 648
  Summer Days Oil/canvas (61x51cm 24x20in) London 1999

HELSBY Alfredo H. 1862-1936 **[15]**
⌐ **$7 500** - €8 714 - **£5 271** - FF57 162
Paisaje con arcoiris Oil/canvas (64.5x85cm 25x33in)
New-York 2001

HELST J.-C. XVIII **[1]**
⌐ **$3 844** - €3 583 - **£2 371** - FF23 500
Bouquet de fleurs sur un entablement Huile/panneau (23x17cm 9x6in) Louviers 1999

HELST van der Bartholomeus 1613-1670 **[18]**
⌐ **$38 400** - €33 173 - **£25 600** - FF217 600
Ritratto di gentildonna Olio/tela (151x114cm 59x44in) Milano 1998
⌐ **$85 000** - €85 989 - **£51 901** - FF564 051
Portrait of a Man holding a Plumed Hat Oil/canvas (71x59cm 27x23in) New-York 2000

HELST van der Lodewyck 1642-c.1685 **[2]**
⌐ **$3 128** - €3 630 - **£2 160** - FF23 812
Gentleman, Seated Small Three Quarter length, Wearing Grey Costume Oil/panel (16x13cm 6x5in) Amsterdam 2000

HELSTED Axel 1847-1907 **[30]**
⌐ **$1 554** - €1 744 - **£1 077** - FF11 443
En deputation Oil/canvas (49x64cm 19x25in) Köbenhavn 2000
⌐ **$5 500** - €5 900 - **£3 748** - FF38 702
Lille abbate med boger under armene Oil/canvas (43x35cm 16x13in) Köbenhavn 2001

HELY-HUTCHINSON Nicholas 1955 **[11]**
✎ **$781** - €764 - **£500** - FF5 014
Nude on a Bed Gouache/paper (51x63.5cm 20x25in) London 1999

HEM Raoul Edward XIX-XX **[7]**
▥ **$1 517** - €1 448 - **£948** - FF9 500
«La Saltarella» Affiche couleur (150x250cm 59x98in) Paris 1999

HEM van der Piet 1885-1961 **[186]**
⌐ **$4 439** - €4 084 - **£2 745** - FF26 789
The Rose Garden Oil/canvas (72x52cm 28x20in) Amsterdam 2000
⌐ **$547** - €635 - **£378** - FF4 167
Dansparen Mixed media (25x17cm 9x6in) Rotterdam 2000
✎ **$535** - €590 - **£349** - FF3 869
Zandloper van de politiek 1929-1930/Avondfeest Drawing (50x35cm 19x13in) Den Haag 2000
▥ **$279** - €318 - **£193** - FF2 083
El Rey Lithograph (30x42cm 11x16in) Haarlem 2000

HEM WECHAKORN 1903-1969 **[5]**
✎ **$1 281** - €1 190 - **£792** - FF7 809
Thai Tradition Watercolour (27.5x22.5cm 10x8in) Bangkok 1999

HEMCHE Abdel-Halim 1906-1979 **[8]**
⌐ **$18 226** - €19 818 - **£12 012** - FF130 000
Rue animée à Tlemcen Huile/panneau (64.5x49.5cm 25x19in) Paris 2000
⌐ **$2 355** - €2 287 - **£1 455** - FF15 000
Djamâa Sidi Abder Rahmane Huile/carton (41x33cm 16x12in) Paris 1999

HEMELMAN Albert 1883-1951 **[11]**
▥ **$318** - €372 - **£218** - FF2 440
«S.s.Nieuw Amsterdam Holland-America Line» Poster (67.5x96cm 26x37in) Hoorn 2000

HEMERET Claude 1929 **[21]**
▥ **$113** - €107 - **£70** - FF700
Les iris Lithographie (70x44cm 27x17in) Avignon 1999

HEMESSEN van Jan Sanders 1504-1566 **[8]**
⌐ **$33 243** - €38 571 - **£22 950** - FF253 011
The Last Supper Oil/panel (60x74cm 23x29in) Amsterdam 2000

HEMESSEN van Katherine 1527/28-1587 **[5]**
⌐ **$34 965** - €32 014 - **£21 315** - FF210 000
Portrait de jeune Femme à la robe ornée de bijoux Huile/panneau (21x15.5cm 8x6in) Paris 1999

HEMING Arthur Henry Howard 1870-1940 **[15]**
⌐ **$3 716** - €3 580 - **£2 307** - FF23 485
The Trappers Oil/canvas (51x61cm 20x24in) Toronto 1999

HEMINGWAY Andrew 1955 **[12]**
⌐ **$317** - €271 - **£190** - FF1 779
Bales of Hay and a Rabbit in the Snow Tempera/canvas (18x19cm 7x7in) Leeds 1998

HEMMING Walter XX **[4]**
▥ **$1 100** - €1 276 - **£771** - FF8 371
«Mitropa, Schlafwagen» Poster (100x63cm 39x25in) New-York 2000

HEMMRICH Georg 1874-1939 **[20]**
⌐ **$636** - €665 - **£403** - FF4 360
Postkutsche vor Gasthaus Oil/panel (14x18cm 5x7in) München 2000

HÉMON Jean-Marie XVIII **[4]**
⌐ **$11 930** - €13 873 - **£8 390** - FF91 000
Paysages en ruine Huile/carton (24.5x33cm 9x12in) Tours 2001

HEMPFING Wilhelm 1886-1948/51 **[84]**
⌐ **$716** - €818 - **£505** - FF5 366
Alblandschaft im Herbst Öl/Leinwand (73x97cm 28x38in) Stuttgart 2001

HEMPLER Orval XX **[26]**
✎ **$200** - €168 - **£117** - FF1 101
Italian Interior No.1 Gouache/board (36x49cm 14x19in) Cleveland OH 1998

HEMSLEY William 1819-c.1895 **[65]**
⌐ **$2 845** - €3 306 - **£2 000** - FF21 688
Gathering Round Oil/canvas (61x78cm 24x30in) London 2001
⌐ **$2 589** - €2 429 - **£1 600** - FF15 935
Breakfast Party Oil/canvas (25x20cm 10x8in) Aylsham, Norfolk 1999

HEMY Bernard Benedict c.1855-1913 **[117]**
⌐ **$1 125** - €1 334 - **£820** - FF8 752
Fishing Cobles in Cullercoats Harbour Oil/canvas (45.5x75cm 17x29in) Newcastle-upon-Tyne 2001
✎ **$306** - €361 - **£220** - FF2 366
Coastal Scene with Shipping, Possibly off Tynemouth Watercolour (34x46.5cm 13x18in) West-Yorkshire 2001

HEMY Charles Napier 1841-1917 **[126]**
⌐ **$13 197** - €14 223 - **£9 000** - FF93 298
Returning to the Barge Oil/canvas (92x173cm 36x68in) London 2001
⌐ **$7 790** - €6 721 - **£4 700** - FF44 090
Fresh from the Sea Oil/canvas (82.5x122.5cm 32x48in) London 1998
⌐ **$847** - €982 - **£600** - FF6 441
Figures Before St. Michael's Mount Oil/board (44.5x31cm 17x12in) London 2000
✎ **$1 504** - €1 695 - **£1 081** - FF11 117
«Mending Nets off Pendennis Castle» Watercolour/paper (24.5x34cm 9x13in) Toronto 2000

🛏 $116 - €107 - **£70** - FF704
Racing yachts Engraving (40x73cm 16x29in) Par,
Cornwall 1999

HEMY Thomas M. Madawaska 1852-1937 **[27]**
✎ $989 - €906 - **£600** - FF5 940
A Fishing Boat returning Home Watercolour/paper
(53x73cm 20x28in) London 1998

HENCHOZ Samuel 1905-1976 **[5]**
🛏 $562 - €566 - **£358** - FF3 715
«Caux-Jaman-Naye» Poster (102x64cm 40x25in)
London 2000

HENDERIKSE Jan 1937 **[16]**
⊙ $976 - €1 134 - **£686** - FF7 441
«Pp13-A» Mixed media (45x65cm 17x25in)
Amsterdam 2001

HENDERSON Charles Cooper 1803-1877 **[67]**
⊙ $5 500 - €6 247 - **£3 859** - FF40 977
The Edinburgh to London Royal Mail Coach
Oil/canvas (43x67.5cm 16x26in) New-York 2001
⊙ $2 564 - €2 981 - **£1 800** - FF19 555
Reposa Oil/board (25x35.5cm 9x13in) London 2001
✎ $769 - €789 - **£480** - FF5 175
**The Royal mail Coach passing Through a Flock
of Sheep** Watercolour (24x34.5cm 9x13in) London
2000

HENDERSON Elsie M. 1880-1967 **[12]**
⊙ $675 - €680 - **£420** - FF4 462
Elegant Figures in a park Oil/board (51x61cm
20x24in) London 2000

HENDERSON Fred XIX **[2]**
⊙ $4 750 - €5 099 - **£3 178** - FF33 444
**A Racehorse with a Jockey Up in the Duke of
Westminster's Colors** Oil/canvas (71x91.5cm
27x36in) New-York 2000

HENDERSON James 1871-1951 **[23]**
⊙ $2 607 - €3 025 - **£1 800** - FF19 845
Untitled - Qu'appelle Winter Oil/hardboard
(40x50cm 16x20in) Calgary, Alberta 2000
⊙ $4 074 - €4 782 - **£2 875** - FF31 367
Horse Team and Wagon Oil/board (28x35.5cm
11x13in) Calgary, Alberta 2000

HENDERSON John 1764-1834 **[6]**
✎ $571 - €534 - **£352** - FF3 500
Temple de Vesta et temple de la Fontaine Virile
Crayon/papier (21x28cm 8x11in) Paris 1999

HENDERSON John 1860-1924 **[33]**
⊙ $2 002 - €1 792 - **£1 200** - FF11 753
A Country Lane Oil/canvas (46x61cm 18x24in)
Perthshire 1998
⊙ $1 912 - €1 639 - **£1 150** - FF10 749
Children on the Riverbank Oil/panel (23x31cm
9x12in) Edinburgh 1998

HENDERSON John Black 1827-1918 **[1]**
✎ $3 559 - €3 379 - **£2 220** - FF22 163
Skull Rock, Wilson's Promontory
Watercolour/paper (21x30cm 8x11in) Sydney 1999

HENDERSON Joseph 1832-1908 **[70]**
⊙ $3 231 - €2 761 - **£1 955** - FF18 108
A View near Dornoch Oil/canvas (61x91.5cm
24x36in) Edinburgh 1998
⊙ $1 786 - €1 897 - **£1 200** - FF12 441
Pensive thoughts Oil/board (28x22.5cm 11x8in)
London 2001

HENDERSON Joseph Morris 1863-1936 **[84]**
⊙ $2 727 - €2 748 - **£1 700** - FF18 026
Autumnal River Landscape Oil/canvas (51x66cm
20x25in) London 2000
⊙ $1 081 - €926 - **£650** - FF6 075
A Stream in Summer Oil/panel (25.5x18cm 10x7in)
Edinburgh 1998

HENDERSON Keith 1883-? **[22]**
🛏 $1 976 - €2 291 - **£1 400** - FF15 030
«Western Highlands, LNER & LMS, It's Quicker
by Rail» Poster (102x127cm 40x50in) London 2000

HENDERSON Louise 1912-1994 **[18]**
⊙ $4 232 - €4 742 - **£2 950** - FF31 108
Still life Oil/panel (52x41cm 20x16in) Wellington 2001
✎ $469 - €493 - **£308** - FF3 233
Abstract Composition Pencil (27x39.5cm 10x15in)
Auckland 2001

HENDERSON William 1844-1904 **[5]**
⊙ $2 426 - €2 294 - **£1 500** - FF15 050
Family/Alone/Mated Oil/board (12x18cm 5x7in)
Whitby, Yorks 1999

HENDERSON William XIX **[9]**
⊙ $1 650 - €1 541 - **£999** - FF10 108
To the Rescue Oil/canvas/board (30.5x40.5cm
12x15in) Philadelphia 2001

HENDERSON William Penhallow 1877-1943 **[23]**
⊙ $40 000 - €34 175 - **£24 204** - FF224 176
Figures and Adobes Oil/board (45.5x61cm 17x24in)
San-Francisco CA 1998
✎ $1 800 - €1 542 - **£1 062** - FF10 112
**Three Views of Boston : Old North Church/Old
City Hall/King's Chapel** Pastel (26x19cm 10x7in)
New-York 1998

HENDLER David 1904-1984 **[55]**
✎ $360 - €326 - **£217** - FF2 006
Aviva Uri Charcoal (48x34.5cm 18x13in) Tel Aviv
1999

HENDORF Richard 1861-1939 **[6]**
⊙ $800 - €742 - **£497** - FF4 864
Spring in the Mountains Oil/masonite (41x56cm
16x22in) New-Orleans LA 1999

HENDRA GUNAWAN 1918-1983 **[2]**
⊙ $42 390 - €46 839 - **£29 392** - FF307 245
Three Women by the Sea Oil/canvas (95x140cm
37x55in) Singapore 2001
⊙ $33 183 - €30 923 - **£20 475** - FF202 842
Street Vendor Oil/canvas (60x99cm 23x38in)
Singapore 1999

HENDRICKS Dirck, Teodoro c.1544-c.1618 **[3]**
⊙ $65 000 - €62 047 - **£40 612** - FF407 004
Last Supper Oil/panel (166.5x294cm 65x115in) New-
York 1999

HENDRICKX Jos 1905-1971 **[192]**
✎ $111 - €124 - **£77** - FF813
Antverpia Fusain/papier (23x49cm 9x19in) Antwerpen
2001

HENDRICKX Michel 1847-1906 **[4]**
⊙ $1 856 - €1 983 - **£1 264** - FF13 008
Fleurs Huile/toile (65x90cm 25x35in) Lokeren 2001

HENDRIKS Frederik Hendrik 1808-1865 **[8]**
⊙ $6 411 - €5 440 - **£3 867** - FF35 682
Rustende herder met vee Oil/panel (33.5x48.5cm
13x19in) Den Haag 1998

HENDRIKS Gerhardus 1804-1859 **[26]**
- 🐦 **$9 127** - €8 622 - **£5 694** - FF56 555
  The Departure of the Fishing Fleet Oil/panel
  (38x56cm 14x22in) Amsterdam 1999
- 🐦 **$1 997** - €2 269 - **£1 401** - FF14 883
  Figures near a Ship on a frozen River Oil/panel
  (29x38.5cm 11x15in) Amsterdam 2001

HENDRIKS Wijbrand 1744-1831 **[19]**
- 🐦 **$19 724** - €18 700 - **£12 000** - FF122 666
  **Sportman after the Chase, smoking in an
  Interior** Oil/panel (55.5x46cm 21x18in) London 1999

HENDRIKS Willem 1828-1891 **[25]**
- 🐦 **$1 906** - €1 849 - **£1 200** - FF12 129
  Cattle Resting Before a Cottage in Spring
  Oil/canvas (61.5x93cm 24x36in) London 1999

HENDRIKS Willem 1888-1966 **[23]**
- 🐦 **$1 575** - €1 499 - **£979** - FF9 833
  Winter Landscape Oil/canvas (51x71cm 20x27in)
  Toronto 1999
- 🐦 **$293** - €343 - **£209** - FF2 251
  Autumn Glade, old Holland Huile/toile (26x31cm
  10x12in) Montréal 2001

HENDRIKSE Jan 1937 **[6]**
- 🗒 **$1 279** - €1 271 - **£799** - FF8 334
  You Tall and Blonde, Me Dark with Glasses
  Screenprint (51.5x42x14cm 20x16x5in) Amsterdam
  1999

HENDRIKSEN Sven XIX-XX **[2]**
- 🗒 **$500** - €465 - **£308** - FF3 049
  «Visit Denmark» Poster (100x62cm 39x24in) New-
  York 1999

HENDRIKZ Willem de Sanderes 1910-1959 **[5]**
- 🗝 **$18 667** - €20 814 - **£12 172** - FF136 534
  Marega Bronze (H115cm H45in) Johannesburg 2000

HENEIN Adam 1929 **[7]**
- 🗝 **$20 052** - €22 553 - **£14 000** - FF147 938
  Brise Bronze (89x23x17cm 35x9x6in) London 2001
- 🖌 **$3 580** - €4 027 - **£2 500** - FF26 417
  Man sawing Tree Gouache (53x65cm 20x25in)
  London 2001

HENEL Edwin H.R. 1883-1953 **[20]**
- 🗒 **$631** - €590 - **£389** - FF3 869
  «Internationale Wintersportwoche» Poster
  (63.5x100.5cm 25x39in) Oostwoud 1999

HENG Euan 1945 **[1]**
- 🖌 **$1 457** - €1 633 - **£1 019** - FF10 715
  Charfall Series Drawing (110x100cm 43x39in)
  Melbourne 2001

HENGELER Adolf 1863-1927 **[95]**
- 🐦 **$1 318** - €1 278 - **£835** - FF8 384
  **Heilige Eremit im Mönchshabit, auf Hügel vor
  kleiner Klosteranlage** Öl/Leinwand/Karton
  (47x47cm 18x18in) Lindau 1999
- 🐦 **$559** - €613 - **£379** - FF4 024
  Landschaft im Allgäu Öl/Karton (25.3x20.3cm
  9x7in) Berlin 2000
- **$177** - €204 - **£125** - FF1 341
  Heimfahrt von der Kirchweih I/II Ink (34x48cm
  13x18in) Zwiesel 2001

HENGGE Joseph 1890-1970 **[37]**
- 🐦 **$569** - €665 - **£400** - FF4 360
  Die Forellenfängerin Öl/Leinwand (60x64cm
  23x25in) Kempten 2000

HENGSBACH Franz 1814-1883 **[11]**
- 🐦 **$13 842** - €13 294 - **£8 580** - FF87 201
  Norditalienische Seelandschaft Öl/Leinwand
  (100x148cm 39x58in) Ahlden 1999

HENKEL Irmin 1921-1977 **[9]**
- 🐦 **$396** - €444 - **£275** - FF2 911
  Nude Study Oil/board (70x49.5cm 27x19in)
  Johannesburg 2001

HENKES Gerke 1844-1927 **[23]**
- 🐦 **$399** - €454 - **£275** - FF2 976
  Oude man med pijp Oil/panel (18x14cm 7x5in)
  Dordrecht 2000

HENLE Fritz 1909-1993 **[64]**
- 📷 **$1 029** - €1 227 - **£733** - FF8 049
  «Beauty from Haiti» Photograph (22.8x22.8cm
  8x8in) München 2000

HENLEY Henry W. XIX **[8]**
- 🐦 **$1 091** - €1 299 - **£780** - FF8 520
  Ludlow Castle from the River Teme, Shropshire
  Oil/canvas (76x127cm 30x50in) Bristol, Avon 2000

HENNEBERG Hugo 1863-1918 **[9]**
- 🗒 **$370** - €436 - **£265** - FF2 860
  Dürnstein Woodcut in colors (44.5x44.5cm 17x17in)
  Wien 2001

HENNELL Thomas Barclay 1903-1945 **[34]**
- 🖌 **$513** - €517 - **£320** - FF3 393
  Winter Dawn, Ridley, Kent Watercolour/paper
  (30.5x46.5cm 12x18in) Billingshurst, West-Sussex 2000

HENNEMAN Jeroen 1942 **[48]**
- 🖌 **$494** - €442 - **£296** - FF2 902
  A Piano-player in an Urban Landscape Crayon
  (41x41cm 16x16in) Amsterdam 1998

HENNEMANN Nicolas XIX **[2]**
- 📷 **$3 200** - €3 022 - **£1 987** - FF19 820
  Lacock Abbey Photograph (16x19.5cm 6x7in) New-
  York 1999

HENNEQUIN Philippe Auguste 1763-1833 **[17]**
- 🐦 **$6 228** - €6 098 - **£3 832** - FF40 000
  Paysage historique (hadés) Huile/toile (65x81cm
  25x31in) Paris 1999

HENNER Jean Jacques 1829-1905 **[474]**
- 🐦 **$7 326** - €6 708 - **£4 466** - FF44 000
  Jeune femme de profil à droite au châle bleu
  Huile/toile (55x40cm 21x15in) Paris 1999
- 🐦 **$3 397** - €2 897 - **£2 050** - FF19 000
  Profil de femme rousse Huile/papier/panneau
  (20x12.5cm 7x4in) Paris 1998
- 🖌 **$259** - €305 - **£182** - FF2 000
  Femme dans un paysage Crayon/papier (10x13cm
  3x5in) Paris 2000

HENNESSEY Frank Charles 1893-1941 **[27]**
- 🖌 **$792** - €750 - **£493** - FF4 922
  March Stream Pastel/papier (36x46cm 14x18in)
  Montréal 1999
- 🗒 **$161** - €189 - **£112** - FF1 239
  Wayside Shrine Serigraph (9.5x12cm 3x4in) Toronto
  2000

HENNESSY Patrick 1915-1980 **[60]**
- 🐦 **$13 408** - €15 237 - **£9 260** - FF99 948
  Summer Strand, Co.Cork Oil/canvas (101x121cm
  40x48in) Dublin 2000
- 🐦 **$6 477** - €6 735 - **£4 500** - FF47 587
  Still Life with Apples and Pears Oil/canvas
  (45.5x51cm 17x20in) London 2001

$4 250 - €4 571 - £2 896 - FF29 984
Madame Laperiére & Josephine Bruce Oil/canvas (20x25cm 7x9in) Dublin 2001

$1 954 - €1 686 - £1 174 - FF11 062
Kinderbildnisse : «Berthold Hempel»/«Liv Hempel» Chalks (46x31.5cm 18x12in) Köln 1998

HENNESSY William John 1839-1917 [14]

$10 000 - €10 992 - £6 408 - FF72 104
The Japanese Parasol Oil/canvas (96.5x62.5cm 37x24in) New-York 2000

$3 800 - €4 215 - £2 527 - FF27 651
The Snowball Fight Oil/canvas (20x25cm 8x10in) Milford CT 2000

HENNIG Albert 1907-1998 [120]

$351 - €409 - £245 - FF2 683
Formenspiel Mischtechnik (18.8x14.8cm 7x5in) Berlin 2000

$611 - €665 - £402 - FF4 360
Häuserfront im Mondlicht Coloured pencils (23.5x15.5cm 9x6in) Hamburg 2000

$456 - €511 - £317 - FF3 353
Komposition Woodcut in colors (10.5x16cm 4x6in) Berlin 2001

HENNIG Gustav Adolf 1797-1869 [7]

$22 332 - €20 452 - £13 612 - FF134 156
Geschwisterpaare Öl/Leinwand (170x120cm 66x47in) Berlin 1999

HENNIGS von Gösta 1866-1941 [22]

$1 960 - €1 833 - £1 207 - FF12 021
Solbelyst gata Oil/canvas (55x38cm 21x14in) Stockholm 1999

$2 701 - €2 538 - £1 628 - FF16 651
Flicka i röd hatt Oil/canvas/panel (44x36cm 17x14in) Stockholm 1999

$803 - €695 - £484 - FF4 557
Spansk dansös Akvarell/papper (28.5x22.5cm 11x8in) Stockholm 1999

HENNIN de Adriaen ?-1710 [2]

$6 534 - €6 109 - £4 026 - FF40 073
Grotta med romerska sarkofager samt figurer vid brunn Oil/canvas (106x84cm 41x33in) Stockholm 1999

HENNIN de Jacob 1629-? [1]

$12 942 - €11 998 - £8 000 - FF78 702
Diana and her Nymphs in a wooded Landscape Oil/canvas (87.5x173.5cm 34x68in) London 1999

HENNING Adolf 1809-1900 [8]

$973 - €1 079 - £674 - FF7 075
Lekande barn Oil/canvas (63x51cm 24x20in) Stockholm 2001

HENNING Gerhard 1880-1967 [150]

$82 680 - €69 903 - £49 452 - FF458 536
Siddende pige Bronze (100x86x75cm 39x33x29in) København 1998

$2 074 - €1 952 - £1 294 - FF12 802
Psyche, stående ung kvinde Bronze (H35cm H13in) Vejle 1999

$517 - €484 - £322 - FF3 177
Figurstudie, kvindelig model Pencil/paper (48x32cm 18x12in) København 1999

HENNING John, Snr. 1771-1851 [8]

$5 116 - €5 870 - £3 500 - FF38 507
The Frieze of the Elgin Marbles Relief (6x24cm 2x9in) London 2000

HENNINGER Manfred 1894-1986 [191]

$4 372 - €4 090 - £2 648 - FF26 831
Vorfrühling Öl/Leinwand (92x98cm 36x38in) Stuttgart 1999

$1 336 - €1 534 - £914 - FF10 061
Obststilleben Äpfel Öl/Karton (26.5x35.8cm 10x14in) Dettelbach-Effeldorf 2000

$661 - €716 - £453 - FF4 695
Männliche Akte am See Watercolour (48x66cm 18x25in) Stuttgart 2001

$126 - €128 - £79 - FF838
Venus and Adonis Radierung (24x32cm 9x12in) Hildrizhausen 2000

HENNINGS Ernest Martin 1886-1956 [66]

$420 000 - €401 504 - £263 256 - FF2 633 694
September Glory Oil/canvas (114x109cm 44x42in) New-York 1999

$70 000 - €76 800 - £46 501 - FF503 776
Across the Foothills Oil/canvas (41.5x51.5cm 16x20in) New-York 1999

$25 000 - €29 382 - £17 332 - FF192 735
Arroyo Seco Near Taos Oil/board (35.5x35.5cm 13x13in) Beverly-Hills CA 2000

HENNINGS Johann Friedrich 1838-1899 [12]

$3 427 - €3 323 - £2 171 - FF21 800
Der Marienplatz in München in einer Winternacht Öl/Leinwand (75x59cm 29x23in) München 1999

HENNINGSEN Erik 1855-1930 [136]

$4 776 - €4 625 - £3 000 - FF30 337
Returning Home Oil/canvas (48x44cm 18x17in) London 1999

$330 - €295 - £197 - FF1 936
Sommerlandskab med siddende kvinde iklaedt blå kjole Oil/canvas (20x26.5cm 7x10in) København 1998

$350 - €296 - £210 - FF1 940
Fra Höjbro Plads ved juletid Indian ink/paper (37x31cm 14x12in) København 1998

HENNINGSEN Frants Peter Didrik 1850-1908 [89]

$1 076 - €1 208 - £746 - FF7 922
En dragon til hest Oil/canvas (72x59cm 28x23in) København 1999

$864 - €1 005 - £616 - FF6 591
Portraet af ung pige Oil/board (31x19cm 12x7in) København 2000

$156 - €148 - £97 - FF971
En löbsk hest Pencil/paper (23x20cm 9x7in) København 1999

HENNO Louis 1907-1990 [39]

$287 - €322 - £195 - FF2 113
Roses Huile/toile (70x60cm 27x23in) Bruxelles 2000

HÉNOCQUE Narcisse 1879-1952 [56]

$2 686 - €2 439 - £1 678 - FF16 000
Paysage impressionniste Huile/toile (48.5x65cm 19x25in) Rennes 1999

$648 - €762 - £470 - FF5 000
Vase de fleurs Huile/toile (41x30cm 16x11in) Calais 2001

HENRARD Henry Joseph XIX [2]

$2 669 - €2 592 - £1 649 - FF17 000
La vie à la campagne Huile/toile (21x32cm 8x12in) Entzheim 1999

HENRI Florence 1893-1982 [76]

$762 - €818 - £510 - FF5 366
Hans Harp Photograph (23.2x17.9cm 9x7in) München 2000

HENRI Paolo XIX-XX **[9]**

🎞️ **$176** - €183 - **£116** - FF1 200
«Cycles Clement» Affiche (37x73cm 14x28in)
Corbeil-Essonnes 2000

HENRI Pierre, Peter c.1760-1822 **[2]**

✏️ **$4 000** - €4 272 - **£2 725** - FF28 021
Portrait of a Boy of the Pell Family Watercolour
(11x10cm 4x4in) New-York 2001

HENRI Robert 1865-1929 **[178]**

🖼️ **$57 500** - €54 968 - **£36 041** - FF360 565
«Portrait of Stella» Oil/canvas (61x51cm 24x20in)
New-York 1999

🖼️ **$9 000** - €9 829 - **£5 794** - FF64 472
Coastal View Oil/board (25x36cm 10x14in) Mystic
CT 2000

✏️ **$750** - €643 - **£443** - FF4 215
Lady Seated Graphite (28x21.5cm 11x8in) New-York
1998

HENRICHSEN Carsten Frederik 1824-1897 **[140]**

🖼️ **$1 019** - €938 - **£630** - FF6 150
Sommerstemning ved Möens Klint Oil/canvas
(42x63cm 16x24in) Vejle 1998

🖼️ **$679** - €699 - **£431** - FF4 584
Vinterlandskab med hus i skovkanten Oil/canvas
(25x35cm 9x13in) Vejle 2000

HENRICI Johann-Josef Karl 1737-1823 **[2]**

🖼️ **$3 385** - €3 634 - **£2 265** - FF23 835
Das letzte Abendmahl Öl/Leinwand (87x107cm
34x42in) Wien 2001

HENRICI John H. 1874-1958 **[7]**

🖼️ **$1 500** - €1 422 - **£937** - FF9 327
The Unbidden Guest, a young girl with her porridge Oil/canvas (60x40cm 24x16in) St. Petersburg FL
1999

HENRIKSEN Sven 1890-1935 **[3]**

🎞️ **$550** - €550 - **£336** - FF3 608
«Rejs Til Sonderjylland» Poster (99x62cm 39x24in)
New-York 2000

HENRIKSEN William 1880-1964 **[89]**

🖼️ **$1 178** - €1 340 - **£828** - FF8 792
Herskabeligt interiör Oil/canvas (50x71cm 19x27in)
Vejle 2001

🖼️ **$837** - €939 - **£580** - FF6 162
Sollys i stuen/Solskin i den rode stue Oil/canvas
(30x25cm 11x9in) Köbenhavn 2000

HENRION Armand 1875-? **[71]**

🖼️ **$1 316** - €1 220 - **£882** - FF8 001
Pierrot au bonnet orange/Pierrot au bonnet
mauve Huile/panneau (18x14cm 7x5in) Paris 1999

HENRION Frederic Henri Kay 1914-1992 **[5]**

🎞️ **$900** - €1 004 - **£587** - FF6 583
«A Psychology Pstudent» Poster (100x63cm
39x25in) New-York 2000

HENRIQUES Marie 1866-1944 **[10]**

🖼️ **$2 800** - €2 702 - **£1 758** - FF17 721
Interior Scene with Young Woman at the Piano
Oil/canvas (40x60cm 16x24in) Chicago IL 1999

HENRY D'ARLES Jean 1734-1784 **[21]**

🖼️ **$4 800** - €5 183 - **£3 219** - FF34 000
Paysage avec des baigneuses Huile/toile
(28x38cm 11x14in) Lyon 2000

HENRY DE GRAY Nicolas I 1822-? **[3]**

🖼️ **$7 482** - €8 443 - **£5 263** - FF55 383
Zwei Sopraporten Öl/Leinwand (72x148cm 28x58in)
Bern 2001

HENRY Edward Lamson 1841-1919 **[84]**

🖼️ **$25 000** - €25 914 - **£15 852** - FF169 985
Stopping to Water his Horses Oil/canvas (31x56cm
12x22in) New-York 2000

🖼️ **$25 000** - €23 905 - **£15 225** - FF156 807
Fishing by the Stream Oil/canvas (27.5x49cm
10x19in) Boston MA 1999

✏️ **$5 000** - €4 331 - **£3 066** - FF28 407
Chickens on a Country Street Watercolour/paper
(23x49cm 9x19in) New-York 1999

HENRY Émile 1842-1920 **[22]**

🖼️ **$1 060** - €1 220 - **£730** - FF8 000
Entrée de l'escadre russe à Toulon en octobre
Aquarelle/papier (33x58.5cm 12x23in) Toulon 2000

HENRY George 1858-1943 **[40]**

🖼️ **$119 851** - €133 630 - **£82 000** - FF876 555
Poinsettia Oil/canvas (125.5x177cm 49x69in)
Perthshire 2000

🖼️ **$22 442** - €21 200 - **£14 000** - FF139 066
Pensive Oil/canvas (62.5x81cm 24x31in) Perthshire
1999

✏️ **$4 328** - €4 089 - **£2 700** - FF26 819
An Afternoon Rest Watercolour/paper (26x35cm
10x13in) Perthshire 1999

HENRY George Morrison R. 1891-1983 **[29]**

🖼️ **$1 284** - €1 498 - **£900** - FF9 823
Montagu's Harrier and studies of Pale Harrier
and Marsh Harrier Watercolour (23.5x23.5cm 9x9in)
London 2001

HENRY Grace 1868-1953 **[52]**

🖼️ **$3 060** - €3 555 - **£2 150** - FF23 321
The Dream Oil/canvas (45.5x35.5cm 17x13in) Dublin
2001

🖼️ **$4 762** - €5 079 - **£3 172** - FF33 316
Chinese Dog of Fo and Flowers Oil/board
(30x35cm 12x14in) Dublin 2000

HENRY Harry Raymond 1882-1974 **[10]**

🖼️ **$5 000** - €4 272 - **£3 025** - FF28 022
Santa Monica Canyon Oil/canvas (63.5x76cm
25x29in) San-Francisco CA 1998

HENRY Maurice 1907-1984 **[59]**

🖼️ **$1 367** - €1 588 - **£960** - FF10 418
Figures Oil/canvas (64.5x92cm 25x36in) Amsterdam
2001

✏️ **$535** - €555 - **£321** - FF3 641
Dix minutes au 200 Gouache/carta (41x30cm
16x11in) Milano 2000

HENRY Olive 1902-1989 **[18]**

✏️ **$409** - €457 - **£277** - FF2 998
Landscape with Buildings Watercolour/paper
(28x38cm 11x14in) Dublin 2000

HENRY Paul & Prospère 1849/48-1901/02 **[12]**

📷 **$14 000** - €13 219 - **£8 694** - FF86 714
Observatoire de Paris Albumen print (23x17cm
9x6in) New-York 1999

HENRY Paul, R.H.A. 1876-1958 **[164]**

🖼️ **$56 021** - €53 106 - **£35 000** - FF348 355
On the Path to the Mountains Oil/canvas (41x61cm
16x24in) London 1999

🖼️ **$26 703** - €29 858 - **£18 000** - FF195 856
Mountain and Lough Oil/canvas/board (34.5x39cm
13x15in) London 2000

✏️ **$5 000** - €5 333 - **£3 330** - FF34 981
Head of an Achill Woman Charcoal/paper (20x15cm
8x6in) Dublin 2000

$1 704 - €1 438 - £1 000 - FF9 434
«Connemara, Ireland this Year» Poster (102x64cm
40x25in) London 1998

HENS Frans 1856-1928 [73]
$392 - €403 - £248 - FF2 644
Havneparti med skibe Oil/canvas (48x34cm
18x13in) Vejle 2000

HENSCHE Ada Reyner 1901 [3]
$8 000 - €8 869 - £5 555 - FF58 178
Still life Oil/board (59x49cm 23x19in) New-Orleans
LA 2001

HENSCHE Henry 1901 [7]
$3 200 - €2 930 - £1 941 - FF19 219
Landscape Oil/board (25x30cm 10x12in) East-Dennis
MA 1998

HENSHALL John Henry 1856-1928 [31]
$3 100 - €2 896 - £1 931 - FF18 999
His only Treasure Oil/canvas (111x73cm 44x29in)
Mystic CT 1999
$1 279 - €1 074 - £750 - FF7 046
The Cottage Home Watercolour (37x25.5cm
14x10in) London 1998

HENSHAW Frederick Henry 1807-1891 [73]
$2 952 - €3 151 - £2 000 - FF20 671
Extensive Landscape Scene with River and
Abbey Ruins, Figures Oil/canvas (49x68cm
19x27in) Birmingham 2001
$919 - €834 - £560 - FF5 468
An Extensive Alpine Landscape with a Cottage,
Goats and Figures Oil/panel (19x15.5cm 7x6in)
Solihull, West-Midlands 1998
$698 - €722 - £440 - FF4 739
Children at Play Beneath Beach Trees
Watercolour (46x74cm 18x29in) Bath 2000

HENSHAW Glenn Cooper 1885-1946 [13]
$650 - €674 - £411 - FF4 418
Cityscape - From a Study made in Indianapolis
Pastel/paper (30x36cm 12x14in) Portsmouth NH 2000

HENSON Bill 1955 [51]
$1 652 - €1 820 - £1 109 - FF11 939
Untitled Type C color print (82.5x62cm 32x24in)
Malvern, Victoria 2000

HENSTENBURGH Herman 1667-1726 [24]
$11 000 - €11 128 - £6 716 - FF72 994
Spray of Flowers, including a tulip, roses, poppies, morning glory Watercolour (35.5x29cm
13x11in) New-York 2000

HENTON George Moore c.1859-1924 [13]
$429 - €371 - £260 - FF2 431
St Margaret's Leicester from Lower Church
Gate Watercolour (38.5x28cm 15x11in) London 1999

HENTSCHEL Konrad 1872-1907 [38]
$1 182 - €1 090 - £742 - FF7 150
Mädchen mit Puppenwagen Porcelain (H13.8cm
H5in) Wien 1999

HENTSCHEL William Ernst 1892-1962 [5]
$13 000 - €12 238 - £8 031 - FF80 273
St Francis in the Rooftops Oil/masonite (137x91cm
54x36in) Bloomfield-Hills MI 1999

HENTZE Gudmund 1875-1948 [28]
$599 - €604 - £374 - FF3 965
Tyrkisk haremskvinde, interieur med liggende
kvinde Pastel/paper (43x55cm 16x21in) Köbenhavn
2000

HENZE-MORRO Ingfried Paul 1925-1972 [18]
$582 - €562 - £368 - FF3 689
Blumenstilleben Öl/Leinwand (80x70cm 31x27in)
München 1999

HENZELL Isaac 1823-1875 [24]
$4 312 - €3 751 - £2 600 - FF24 603
Feeding the Calves Oil/canvas (54x46.5cm 21x18in)
Glasgow 1998

HENZIROSS Eugen 1877-1961 [53]
$147 - €137 - £90 - FF899
Lötschbergbahn Farblithographie (100x62.5cm
39x24in) Bern 1999

HEPPENER Johannes Jacobus 1826-1898 [20]
$1 625 - €1 815 - £1 086 - FF11 906
View on Oudewater Oil/panel (46x56cm 18x22in)
Amsterdam 2000
$557 - €656 - £403 - FF4 304
Bord de rivière Huile/panneau (19x26cm 7x10in)
Sion 2001

HEPPER George c.1840-c.1870 [3]
$4 392 - €4 360 - £2 742 - FF28 602
Drei gute Freunde Öl/Leinwand (43.5x54cm
17x21in) Wien 1999

HEPPLE John Wilson 1853-1937 [29]
$2 325 - €2 235 - £1 450 - FF14 662
Young Girl Standing in a Courtyard Holding a
Plate Oil/canvas (41x30.5cm 16x12in) West-Yorshire
1999
$400 - €446 - £270 - FF2 926
Wooded and river landscapes Watercolour/paper
(17x25cm 7x10in) Aylsham, Norfolk 2000

HEPPLE Norman R. 1908-1994 [33]
$1 199 - €1 155 - £750 - FF7 576
Portrait of Effie, the Artists Daughter Oil/canvas
(88x75cm 34x29in) London 1999

HEPPLE Wilson 1854-1937 [55]
$1 089 - €1 226 - £750 - FF8 045
A Foggy Morning Oil/canvas (49.5x75cm 19x29in)
London 2000
$661 - €630 - £420 - FF4 131
Mare and Foal in a Landscape Oil/canvas
(30x50cm 11x19in) Billingshurst, West-Sussex 1999
$2 017 - €2 165 - £1 350 - FF14 204
Two Kittens beside an Ornate Timepiece
Watercolour (25x36.5cm 9x14in) West-Yorshire 2000

HEPWORTH Barbara 1903-1975 [226]
$16 000 - €14 942 - £9 875 - FF98 016
Square Forms II (Green + ochre) Oil/masonite
(91.5x46.5cm 36x18in) New-York 1998
$27 216 - €22 860 - £16 000 - FF149 953
Two Heads of Lisa (mauve) Mixed media
(34.5x30.5cm 13x12in) London 1998
$267 152 - €246 233 - £160 000 - FF1 615 184
Sunion Sculpture (H197cm H77in) London 1998
$40 000 - €43 898 - £25 756 - FF287 952
Three hemispheres Polished bronze (18x37.5x22cm
7x14x8in) New-York 2000
$12 165 - €11 728 - £7 500 - FF76 928
Form in Movement Watercolour (23.5x29cm 9x11in)
London 1999
$960 - €950 - £600 - FF6 230
Rangatria I Silkscreen in colors (76x57.5cm 29x22in)
London 1999

HEPWORTH Philip Dalton 1888-? [4]
$82 500 - €79 233 - £50 861 - FF519 733
Orpheus Maquette 2 Metal (H63.5cm H25in) New-
York 1999

H

HERAIN de François 1877-1962 **[6]**
🖩 **$679** - €638 - **£420** - FF4 185
The Water Carrier Drypoint (29x25.5cm 11x10in)
London 1999

HERALD James Watterson 1859-1914 **[72]**
🖼 **$15 866** - €18 648 - **£11 000** - FF122 320
Morning, Fishwives, East Coast Oil/canvas
(53.5x66cm 21x25in) Edinburgh 2000
🖼 **$3 492** - €2 992 - **£2 100** - FF19 629
A Masque Watercolour/paper (17x26.5cm 6x10in)
Edinburgh 1998

HERAMB Thore 1916 **[21]**
🖼 **$3 137** - €2 650 - **£1 883** - FF17 385
Komposisjon Oil/panel (50x65cm 19x25in) Oslo
1998

HÉRAUT Henri 1894-1980 **[26]**
🖩 **$4 309** - €4 726 - **£2 861** - FF31 000
**L'Annonciation (la Vierge et angelots la couron-
nant, fleurs, colombes)** Tapisserie (240x300cm
94x118in) Paris 2000

HERBERT Alfred c.1820-1861 **[47]**
🖼 **$1 288** - €1 211 - **£800** - FF7 943
Unloading the Catch Watercolour (41x65cm
16x25in) London 1999

HERBERT Harold Brocklebank 1892-1945 **[128]**
✎ **$755** - €881 - **£525** - FF5 780
Beach Baby Blue Watercolour/paper (24x20cm
9x7in) Melbourne 2000

HERBERT John Rogers 1810-1890 **[33]**
🖼 **$26 118** - €24 412 - **£18 000** - FF192 929
«A Well in Valley of Moses, Sinai Desert» Oil/can-
vas (86x170cm 33x66in) London 2000
🖼 **$8 039** - €9 225 - **£5 500** - FF60 511
Study of an Arab Oil/panel (65.5x39cm 25x15in)
London 2000

HERBERT Sydney 1854-1914 **[30]**
🖼 **$2 327** - €2 261 - **£1 420** - FF14 830
Continental Town scenes Oil/board (44x28cm
17x11in) Birmingham 2000

HERBERT Wilfred Vincent XIX **[4]**
🖼 **$1 683** - €2 002 - **£1 200** - FF13 134
On the Marshes, Connemara, Ireland Huile/toile
(50x89cm 19x35in) London 2000

HERBERTE Edward Benjamin 1857-1893 **[74]**
🖼 **$5 513** - €5 249 - **£3 500** - FF34 430
The Meet Oil/canvas (49x79.5cm 19x31in)
Billingshurst, West-Sussex 1999
🖼 **$3 400** - €3 440 - **£2 076** - FF22 562
Steeple Chase Oil/canvas (23x33cm 9x13in) East-
Moriches NY 2000

HERBIG Otto 1889-1971 **[115]**
🖼 **$7 611** - €7 107 - **£4 610** - FF46 619
Fütterung Öl/Leinwand (67x75.5cm 26x29in) Berlin
1999
✎ **$1 263** - €1 278 - **£771** - FF8 384
Ostereier am Baumstamm Pastell/Papier
(48x66.2cm 18x26in) Stuttgart 2000
🖩 **$165** - €164 - **£103** - FF1 073
Mutter beim Kindbaden Lithographie (22.1x16.4cm
8x6in) Berlin 1999

HERBIN Auguste 1882-1960 **[605]**
🖼 **$42 500** - €45 897 - **£29 371** - FF301 065
«Orphée» Oil/canvas (130x96.5cm 51x37in) New-
York 2001

$31 472 - €35 791 - **£21 826** - FF234 773
Nature morte à la cuvette Oil/canvas (81.5x64.5cm
32x25in) München 2000
🖼 **$24 000** - €21 343 - **£14 678** - FF139 999
Paysage au pont Oil/canvas (27.5x35cm 10x13in)
New-York 1999
✎ **$6 180** - €6 098 - **£3 808** - FF40 000
Hardricourt Aquarelle (63x47.5cm 24x18in) Paris
1999
🖩 **$701** - €818 - **£492** - FF5 366
Midi Farbserigraphie (48.7x34.8cm 19x13in) Köln 2000

HERBO Fernand 1905-1995 **[820]**
🖼 **$2 445** - €2 287 - **£1 477** - FF15 000
Le port de Crotoy Huile/toile (50x65cm 19x25in)
Rennes 1999
🖼 **$900** - €945 - **£569** - FF6 200
Remorqueur à quai Huile/toile (33x46.5cm 12x18in)
Paris 2000
✎ **$719** - €793 - **£477** - FF5 200
Saint-Jean-Croix-de-Vie Aquarelle/papier (52x64cm
20x25in) Deauville 2000

HERBO Léon 1850-1907 **[156]**
🖼 **$3 582** - €3 049 - **£2 132** - FF20 000
L'Elégante aux roses blanches Huile/toile
(67x54cm 26x21in) Toulouse 1998
🖼 **$1 083** - €1 141 - **£684** - FF7 486
La jóven artista Oleo/tabla (36x27cm 14x10in)
Madrid 2000

HERBST Adolf 1909-1983 **[125]**
🖼 **$2 888** - €3 435 - **£2 058** - FF22 534
Blumenstrauss Öl/Leinwand (61x46cm 24x18in)
Zürich 2000
🖼 **$1 361** - €1 372 - **£848** - FF8 998
Stilleben Huile/panneau (27x22cm 10x8in) Zürich
2000
🖼 **$635** - €713 - **£441** - FF4 677
Jungen Frau mit Rosenbouquet in blauer Vase
Mischtechnik/Papier (28.5x22cm 11x8in) Luzern 2001

HERBST Thomas Ludwig 1848-1915 **[61]**
🖼 **$6 925** - €7 669 - **£4 696** - FF50 308
Bauernhaus in Landschaft Öl/Karton (34.2x50.5cm
13x19in) Hamburg 2000
🖼 **$2 856** - €2 555 - **£1 711** - FF16 761
Ruhende, helle Kuh im Sonnenlicht Öl/Papier
(26x26cm 10x10in) Hamburg 1998

HERBSTHOFFER Peter Rudolf Karl 1821-1876 **[15]**
🖼 **$1 179** - €1 308 - **£820** - FF8 580
Der Mönch Oil/panel (34x26cm 13x10in) Wien 2001

HERCK van Jacobus Melchior XVII-XVIII **[10]**
🖼 **$6 828** - €6 555 - **£4 282** - FF43 000
Urne fleurie Huile/toile (93x75cm 36x29in) Lyon
1999

HERCZEGH Zoltan 1880-? **[2]**
📷 **$2 000** - €1 877 - **£1 235** - FF12 313
Latent Fire Gelatin silver print (24x30.5cm 9x12in)
New-York 1999

HERDEG Walter 1908 **[8]**
🖩 **$1 443** - €1 455 - **£900** - FF9 543
«St.Moritz» Poster (43x31cm 16x12in) London 2000

HERDER de Dirk 1914 **[9]**
📷 **$424** - €470 - **£288** - FF3 085
Arthur Rubinstein Gelatin silver print (29.3x22.5cm
11x8in) Berlin 2000

HERDIES Oliver 1906-1994 **[4]**
🖼 **$197** - €235 - **£136** - FF1 541
Komposition Indian ink/paper (43x60cm 16x23in)
Stockholm 2000

HERDMAN Robert Duddingstone 1863-1922 **[6]**
- $2 220 - €2 103 - £1 350 - FF13 793
  Sunny Childhood Oil/canvas/board (23x30.5cm 9x12in) Godalming, Surrey 1999

HERDMAN Robert Inerarity 1829-1888 **[33]**
- $385 - €429 - £260 - FF2 817
  Portrait of Rev.W.B.Robertson of Irvine Oil/canvas (63x48cm 24x18in) Edinburgh 2000
- $733 - €791 - £500 - FF5 187
  A Courtier Oil/canvas (24x18cm 9x7in) London 2001
- $2 596 - €3 051 - £1 800 - FF20 016
  The Brigand Watercolour (28x21.5cm 11x8in) Edinburgh 2000

HERDMAN William Gawin 1805-1882 **[15]**
- $354 - €331 - £220 - FF2 169
  Gallows Mill, Liverpool Watercolour (17x30cm 6x11in) Billingshurst, West-Sussex 1999

HERDMAN-SMITH Robert 1879-? **[30]**
- $439 - €429 - £280 - FF2 812
  Young Boy Fishing from a Bridge Watercolour (26x35.5cm 10x13in) Billingshurst, West-Sussex 1999
- $147 - €165 - £100 - FF1 083
  «**The Little Shrine**» Etching in colors (19x23.5cm 7x9in) Billingshurst, West-Sussex 2000

HEREAU Jules 1839-1879 **[24]**
- $2 982 - €3 201 - £1 995 - FF21 000
  Batterie d'artillerie de marine sur la butte Montmartre Huile/toile (66x100cm 25x39in) Grenoble 2000

HERGÉ Georges Rémi, dit 1907-1983 **[281]**
- $1 375 - €1 363 - £836 - FF8 945
  Tintin et Milou dans la potiche devant une rue de Shanghai Oil/canvas (24x18cm 9x7in) Bruxelles 2000
- $739 - €694 - £456 - FF4 552
  «**On a marché sur la lune**» Sérigraphie (82x62cm 32x24in) Antwerpen 1999

HERGENRÖDER Georg Heinrich 1736-c.1794 **[10]**
- $4 728 - €5 368 - £3 285 - FF35 215
  Grotteninterieur mit Diana und Aktäon Oil/panel (52x65cm 20x25in) Köln 2001
- $6 022 - €5 624 - £3 716 - FF36 892
  Zwei Höhlenbilder Oil/panel (23x30.5cm 9x12in) Köln 1999

HERGET Herbert M. 1885-1950 **[11]**
- $2 100 - €1 991 - £1 311 - FF13 058
  Indian Fishing Oil/board (25x50cm 10x20in) Cincinnati OH 1999

HERING George 1884-1936 **[10]**
- $1 565 - €1 680 - £1 047 - FF11 022
  Tre män Oil/canvas (61x80cm 24x31in) Stockholm 2000

HERING George Edwards 1805-1879 **[32]**
- $8 574 - €8 772 - £5 200 - FF60 980
  «**Isola dei pescatore, Lake Maggiore, Italy**» Oil/canvas (48.5x84cm 19x33in) Billingshurst, West-Sussex 1998
- $2 065 - €2 307 - £1 400 - FF15 136
  Lake Como Oil/panel (29.5x24.5cm 11x9in) Edinburgh 2000

HERIOT George 1766-1844 **[21]**
- $406 - €458 - £280 - FF3 003
  Vallée D'Osseau, Pyrénées Pencil (11.5x18cm 4x7in) Newbury, Berkshire 2000

HERIOT Robertine XIX-XX **[4]**
- $6 736 - €6 664 - £4 200 - FF43 710
  Buckingham Palace Oil/canvas (38x45.7cm 14x17in) London 1999

HERKENRATH Peter 1900-1992 **[147]**
- $3 945 - €4 602 - £2 770 - FF30 185
  Vergänglich Öl/Leinwand (125x100cm 49x39in) Köln 2000
- $3 029 - €3 323 - £2 057 - FF21 800
  Rot im Durchbruch Öl/Leinwand (90x70cm 35x27in) Düsseldorf 2000
- $428 - €460 - £286 - FF3 018
  Ohne Titel Gouache/paper (47.5x65cm 18x25in) Köln 2000

HERKOMER von Hubert 1849-1914 **[97]**
- $12 000 - €11 123 - £7 441 - FF72 961
  Sir John, 2nd Duke of Abercorn Oil/canvas (231x140cm 90x55in) New-York 1999
- $2 065 - €1 892 - £1 259 - FF12 409
  Abschied Öl/Leinwand (50.2x77.5cm 19x30in) München 1999
- $1 605 - €1 490 - £1 000 - FF9 771
  Portrait of a Young Girl with Flowers in her Hair Oil/canvas (43x33cm 17x13in) Bristol, Avon 1999
- $1 756 - €1 605 - £1 100 - FF10 525
  Farm Labourer Reading the Parish Notice Board Watercolour/paper (23x16cm 9x6in) Fernhurst, Haslemere, Surrey 1999
- $107 - €102 - £65 - FF670
  Ohne Titel Radierung (15x10cm 5x3in) Stuttgart 1999

HERLAND Emma 1856-1947 **[26]**
- $11 520 - €10 976 - £7 300 - FF72 000
  La jeune mère et son enfant Huile/toile (96x106cm 37x41in) Douarnenez 1999
- $1 341 - €1 243 - £927 - FF5 400
  Dans la cour de ferme à Locronan Pastel/papier (46x30cm 18x11in) Quimper 2001

HERMAN Josef 1911-2000 **[358]**
- $11 241 - €10 379 - £7 000 - FF68 079
  Harvest Oil/board (48.5x63.5cm 19x25in) London 1999
- $4 796 - €4 486 - £2 900 - FF29 428
  Man and Dog Oil/canvas (25x36cm 9x14in) London 1999
- $850 - €726 - £500 - FF4 761
  Three Figures/Peasant Family Ink (20x25cm 7x9in) London 1998
- $196 - €183 - £121 - FF1 200
  Bird Silkscreen (58x44cm 22x17in) London 1999

HERMAN Lipót 1884-1972 **[12]**
- $720 - €708 - £450 - FF4 644
  View from the Studio Oil/canvas (80x61cm 31x24in) Budapest 1999

HERMAN Sali Yakubowitsch 1898-1993 **[179]**
- $27 975 - €27 219 - £17 217 - FF178 543
  Renaissance Oil/canvas (102x203.5cm 40x80in) Malvern, Victoria 1999
- $5 701 - €6 712 - £4 006 - FF44 030
  Paddington Street Scene Oil/canvas (37x50cm 14x19in) Sydney 2000
- $3 571 - €3 440 - £2 207 - FF22 567
  Children playing in the Street Oil/canvas/board (19x24cm 7x9in) Sydney 1999

HERMANJAT Jacques E. Abraham 1862-1932 **[35]**
- $1 661 - €1 783 - £1 111 - FF11 697
  Stilleben mit Früchten Öl/Leinwand (38x46cm 14x18in) Zürich 1999

H

$2 128 - €2 487 - **£1 519** - FF16 314
Paysage du Léman Öl/Karton (22x27.5cm 8x10in)
Zürich 2001

HERMANN (Hermann Huppen) 1938 [17]

$793 - €762 - **£492** - FF5 000
Tonnerre sur Coronado, de la série Bernard Prince, pl.33 Encre Chine/papier (44x36cm 17x14in)
Paris 1999

HERMANN Hans 1813-1890 [13]

$4 816 - €5 622 - **£3 400** - FF36 876
Autumnal Street Scene Oil/canvas (62x82cm 24x32in) London 2000

HERMANN Léon-Charles 1838-1908 [2]

$8 606 - €10 062 - **£6 144** - FF66 000
Les limiers Huile/toile (80.5x60.5cm 31x23in) Angers 2001

HERMANN Ludwig 1812-1881 [66]

$7 219 - €7 275 - **£4 500** - FF47 720
A Bustling Harbour Town Oil/canvas (47.5x67.5cm 18x26in) London 2000

$5 737 - €6 369 - **£4 000** - FF41 779
Town on a River Oil/canvas (31.5x45cm 12x17in) London 2001

$5 575 - €5 802 - **£3 500** - FF38 061
A Dutch Canal Scene Watercolour/paper (61x83cm 24x32in) Billingshurst, West-Sussex 2000

HERMANN Woldemar 1807-1878 [8]

$990 - €1 125 - **£688** - FF7 378
Blick auf Rom Ink (28.5x43cm 11x16in) Berlin 2001

HERMANN-PAUL René 1864-1940 [60]

$5 636 - €6 708 - **£3 902** - FF44 000
Promenade en famille Huile/panneau (32x40cm 12x15in) Chartres 2000

$2 746 - €3 049 - **£1 914** - FF20 000
Élégante sur la plage Crayons couleurs/papier (47x55cm 18x21in) Paris 2001

$268 - €305 - **£186** - FF2 000
«Dame à la pelisse noire» Affiche (55x28cm 21x11in) Paris 2000

HERMANNS Ernst 1914 [7]

$3 726 - €4 346 - **£2 616** - FF28 508
Drei Flächenbahnen (Winkel) Iron (H50.5cm H19in) Köln 2000

HERMANNS Heinrich 1862-1942 [94]

$4 927 - €5 445 - **£3 417** - FF35 719
Flower Market, Amsterdam Oil/canvas (65x91cm 25x35in) Amsterdam 2001

$1 210 - €1 022 - **£721** - FF6 707
Mainzer Dom und Marktplatz Öl/Karton (34x24.5cm 13x9in) Düsseldorf 1998

$1 034 - €869 - **£608** - FF5 701
Innenansicht des Doms von Palermo Aquarell, Gouache/Papier (47x39cm 18x15in) Köln 1998

HERMANS Charles 1839-1924 [65]

$3 750 - €3 718 - **£2 295** - FF24 390
Jeune femme dénudée Huile/toile (87x120cm 34x47in) Bruxelles 1999

$1 596 - €1 487 - **£984** - FF9 756
Élégante au bord de la mer Aquarelle/papier (48x36cm 18x14in) Bruxelles 1999

HERMANS Johannes c.1630-c.1665 [7]

$2 160 - €2 799 - **£1 620** - FF18 360
Selvaggina Olio/tela (20.5x28cm 8x11in) Milano 2000

HERMANSEN Olaf August 1849-1897 [84]

$14 278 - €13 128 - **£8 820** - FF86 112
To börn i skoven Oil/canvas (127x96.5cm 50x37in) Vejle 1998

$3 477 - €3 755 - **£2 402** - FF24 631
En beaglehund med sine hvalpe betragter en skade i vandská¿len Oil/canvas (89x47cm 35x18in) Köbenhavn 2001

$942 - €1 006 - **£627** - FF6 597
Blåmejser på en blomstrende frugtgren Oil/canvas (34.5x26.5cm 13x10in) Köbenhavn 2000

HERMANUS Paul 1859-1911 [41]

$2 453 - €2 727 - **£1 639** - FF17 886
Quai animé Huile/toile (62x76cm 24x29in) Bruxelles 2000

$1 148 - €991 - **£692** - FF6 500
Vaches s'abreuvant Aquarelle/papier (32x45.5cm 12x17in) Bruxelles 1998

HERMELIN Olof 1827-1913 [261]

$1 910 - €1 859 - **£1 176** - FF12 195
Sjölandskap i soldis, motiv från Långängen Oil/canvas (70x41cm 27x16in) Stockholm 1999

$1 044 - €999 - **£657** - FF6 552
På en ö i Kalmar sund Oil/panel (28x41cm 11x16in) Stockholm 1999

HERMES Erich 1881-1971 [47]

$536 - €610 - **£372** - FF4 000
«L'hiver en Suisse» Affiche (100x61cm 39x24in) Paris 2000

HERMES Gertrude Anna B. 1901-1983 [24]

$336 - €314 - **£208** - FF2 057
Remote Control Woodcut in colors (57x39.5cm 22x15in) London 1999

HERMOSO MARTINEZ Eugenio 1883-1963 [19]

$26 980 - €22 825 - **£15 960** - FF149 720
La niña llamada «la peseta» Oleo/lienzo (107x72cm 42x28in) Madrid 1998

HERN Charles Edward 1848-1894 [8]

$1 337 - €1 142 - **£800** - FF7 490
Dusk over the Church of St. Martin in the Fields, London Watercolour/paper (22.5x14cm 8x5in) London 1998

HERNANDEZ CATALAYUD José 1935 [3]

$207 - €1 021 - **£731** - FF6 698
El barón Técnica mixta/papel (46x35cm 18x13in) Madrid 1998

HERNANDEZ Charles L. XIX [1]

$5 500 - €6 065 - **£3 724** - FF39 787
Noon in the Pasture Oil/canvas (30.5x51cm 12x20in) New-York 2000

HERNANDEZ José 1944 [45]

$16 900 - €15 617 - **£10 400** - FF102 440
Prática neufragos II Oleo/lienzo (162x130cm 63x51in) Madrid 1999

$792 - €721 - **£480** - FF4 728
Alienígena Lápiz (34x25.5cm 13x10in) Madrid 1999

$912 - €961 - **£608** - FF6 304
Atlas de anatomía (Série II) Aguafuerte (34x24cm 13x9in) Madrid 2000

HERNANDEZ Luis Alberto 1947 [9]

$790 - €921 - **£547** - FF6 040
Para navegar los sueños Técnica mixta (100x85cm 39x33in) Caracas ($) 2000

HERNANDEZ M.R. XX [1]
- $3 227 - €3 099 - £2 000 - FF20 329
  The Palace of Chapultecpec, Mexico City
  Oil/paper (18x29.5cm 7x11in) London 1999

HERNANDEZ Mateo 1885-1949 [13]
- $3 543 - €3 330 - £2 200 - FF21 844
  Pelican Bronze (38x16cm 14x6in) London 1999

HERNANDEZ MONJO Francisco 1862-1937 [55]
- $3 000 - €3 003 - £1 850 - FF19 700
  Vista costera con barcos Oleo/lienzo (37x68cm 14x26in) Madrid 2000
- $660 - €721 - £420 - FF4 728
  Barco Oleo/tabla (17x30cm 6x11in) Madrid 2000

HERNANDEZ MORILLO Daniel 1856-1932 [70]
- $11 520 - €10 812 - £7 020 - FF70 920
  Baile de máscaras Oleo/tabla (66x35.5cm 25x13in) Madrid 1999
- $2 750 - €3 003 - £1 900 - FF19 700
  Bella mujer Oleo/lienzo (35x27cm 13x10in) Madrid 2001
- $308 - €330 - £209 - FF2 167
  La siesta Grabado (27x21cm 10x8in) Madrid 2001

HERNANDEZ Pablo Wenceslao XX [1]
- $3 520 - €3 354 - £2 200 - FF22 000
  Niña Oil/wood (24x20cm 9x7in) Caracas 1999

HERNANDEZ PIJUAN Joan 1931 [84]
- $8 872 - €9 909 - £6 012 - FF65 000
  Paisatge negre Huile/toile (114x146cm 44x57in) Paris 2000
- $1 820 - €1 952 - £1 235 - FF12 805
  Sin título Pintura (70x100cm 27x39in) Barcelona 2001
- $1 950 - €1 802 - £1 200 - FF11 820
  Blanc Oleo/lienzo (27x35cm 10x13in) Madrid 1999
- $1 121 - €1 141 - £703 - FF7 486
  Composición Tinta/papel (15x7cm 5x2in) Barcelona 2000
- $180 - €162 - £110 - FF1 063
  Roturat Aguafuerte (38x57cm 14x22in) Madrid 1999

HERNANDEZ SANZ Agustín 1931 [58]
- $1 024 - €961 - £640 - FF6 304
  Desnudo femenino Oleo/lienzo (100x81cm 39x31in) Madrid 1999

HERNANDEZ Sergio 1957 [22]
- $24 222 - €28 407 - £17 424 - FF186 340
  Junglas Técnica mixta/lienzo (80x200cm 31x78in) México 2001
- $9 000 - €9 661 - £6 022 - FF63 369
  Meditación Oil/canvas (80x80cm 31x31in) New-York 2000
- $5 500 - €5 338 - £3 424 - FF35 016
  Sin Título Watercolour (52x78cm 20x30in) New-York 1999
- $990 - €1 162 - £712 - FF7 623
  Calacas Litografía (48x69cm 18x27in) México 2001

HERNANDEZ XOCHITIOTZIN Desiderio 1922 [6]
- $3 963 - €4 648 - £2 851 - FF30 492
  Paisaje con Iztlaccihuatl Oleo/lienzo (31x40cm 12x15in) Madrid 2001

HERNANDEZ-DIEZ José Antonio 1964 [3]
- $20 000 - €19 352 - £12 334 - FF126 938
  San Guinefort Construction (146x200x85cm 57x78x33in) New-York 1999

HERNLUND Ferdinand 1838-1902 [10]
- $900 - €874 - £555 - FF5 732
  Gåsapåg med sina gäss Oil/canvas (25x42cm 9x16in) Stockholm 1999

HEROLD Georg 1947 [47]
- $964 - €920 - £602 - FF6 037
  Ohne Titel Mixed media/canvas (25x20.3cm 9x7in) Köln 1999

HÉROLD Jacques 1910-1987 [126]
- $5 354 - €5 793 - £3 667 - FF38 000
  «Le sommeil et le noir» Huile/toile (146x114cm 57x44in) Paris 2001
- $7 156 - €6 174 - £4 301 - FF40 500
  Femme-oiseau sans ailes Huile/carton (47x63cm 18x24in) Paris 1998
- $4 770 - €4 116 - £2 867 - FF27 000
  L'eau à la bouche Huile/toile (15x21cm 5x8in) Paris 1998
- $1 273 - €1 220 - £784 - FF8 000
  Composition Gouache/papier (63x48cm 24x18in) Douai 1999

HERON Hilary 1923-1976 [4]
- $2 362 - €2 286 - £1 456 - FF14 992
  Red Bird Enamel (20.5x13.5cm 8x5in) Dublin 1999
- $3 235 - €3 809 - £2 273 - FF24 987
  Torso Bronze (H36cm H14in) Dublin 1999

HERON Patrick 1920-1999 [125]
- $46 020 - €43 729 - £28 000 - FF286 843
  Rumbold vertical two: reds withs purple and orange: March Oil/canvas (199x122cm 78x48in) London 1999
- $22 444 - €26 755 - £16 000 - FF175 500
  Violet and Ultramarine Through Prussian: June Oil/canvas (76x122cm 29x48in) London 2000
- $10 673 - €12 567 - £7 500 - FF82 435
  Two Dark Ultras in Acid Blue: July Oil/canvas (25.5x35.5cm 10x13in) London 2000
- $7 791 - €8 741 - £5 400 - FF57 336
  Untitled Gouache/paper (23x75cm 9x29in) London 2000
- $1 294 - €1 437 - £900 - FF9 428
  Untitled Screenprint in colors (42.5x52cm 16x20in) London 2001

HÉROULT Antoine Désiré 1802-1853 [24]
- $966 - €945 - £613 - FF6 200
  Paysage fluvial Aquarelle, gouache/papier (53x74cm 20x29in) Paris 1999

HÉROUX Bruno 1868-1944 [63]
- $77 - €82 - £49 - FF536
  Verzweifelter Mann zu Füssen einer auf einer Weltkugel stehenden Radierung (44x25.7cm 17x10in) Heidelberg 2001

HERP van N. XVII [1]
- $5 935 - €5 310 - £3 555 - FF34 829
  Spaniel watching a dead hare hanging from a nail on a stone wall Oil/canvas (71x58cm 27x22in) Amsterdam 1998

HERP van Willem 1614-1677 [44]
- $12 825 - €14 568 - £9 000 - FF95 557
  Isaac blessing Jacob Oil/canvas (114.5x166cm 45x65in) London 2001
- $20 148 - €18 654 - £12 500 - FF122 362
  Barn interior with an old Man and a Child attending to an old Lady Oil/panel (52.5x75.5cm 20x29in) London 1999

HERPEL Franz Carl 1850-? [6]
- $375 - €409 - £258 - FF2 683
  Segelschiffe vor Mole Öl/Leinwand (55.5x90.7cm 21x35in) Leipzig 2001

HERPFER Karl 1836-1897 **[23]**
- **$140 000** - €153 643 - **£90 146** - FF1 007 832
  Evening's Entertainment Oil/canvas (98x125.5cm 38x49in) New-York 2000
- **$17 000** - €18 490 - **£11 206** - FF121 284
  Mother's Helpers Oil/canvas (96x75cm 38x29in) Wethersfield CT 2000

HERR Claudius 1791-1838 **[1]**
- **$2 325** - €2 180 - **£1 437** - FF14 301
  Amor Oil/panel (23.3x18.8cm 9x7in) Wien 1999

HERRAN Saturnino 1887-1918 **[9]**
- **$200 000** - €192 653 - **£124 180** - FF1 263 720
  Campesino Oil/canvas (100x74cm 39x29in) New-York 1999

HERREGOUTS Jan Baptist c.1640-c.1721 **[4]**
- **$16 426** - €19 059 - **£11 340** - FF125 017
  Allegory of the Fortitude of the Liberal Arts Oil/canvas (112x145.5cm 44x57in) Amsterdam 2000

HERREGOUTS Maximilian XVII **[2]**
- **$5 237** - €5 899 - **£3 610** - FF38 695
  Elizer and Rebecca at the Well Oil/canvas (34x42cm 13x16in) Amsterdam 2000

HERREMANS Lievin 1858-1907 **[39]**
- **$848** - €992 - **£604** - FF6 504
  Sortie des barques de pêche Huile/toile (37x99cm 14x38in) Bruxelles 2001

HERRERA BARNUEVO de Sebastian 1619-1671 **[1]**
- **$23 075** - €19 521 - **£13 650** - FF128 050
  Exaltación de la Eucaristía Aguada (42.5x24cm 16x9in) Madrid 1999

HERRERA Francisco el Mozzo 1612/22-1685 **[5]**
- **$7 000** - €7 476 - **£4 769** - FF49 037
  Bearded Saint Holding a Book and a Cross Ink (21x14.5cm 8x5in) New-York 2001

HERRERA Francisco el Viejo c.1576/90-1656 **[11]**
- **$21 600** - €24 026 - **£14 000** - FF157 600
  La Visitación Oleo/lienzo (86x62cm 33x24in) Madrid 2000
- **$6 500** - €6 942 - **£4 429** - FF45 537
  Apostle Holding a Book Ink (31x20cm 12x7in) New-York 2001

HERRERA TORO Antonio 1857-1914 **[10]**
- **$3 200** - €3 049 - **£2 000** - FF20 000
  Rosas Oleo/tabla (29.5x28.5cm 11x11in) Caracas 1999

HERRERA Velino Shije 1902-1973 **[2]**
- **$2 000** - €2 137 - **£1 361** - FF14 019
  Cheyenne Warrior Watercolour/paper (31x23cm 12x9in) Cloudcroft NM 2001

HERRFELDT Marcel René 1890-1965 **[42]**
- **$2 359** - €1 994 - **£1 407** - FF13 078
  Hockender Akt Öl/Leinwand (100x75cm 39x29in) Düsseldorf 1998

HERRICK Frederich Charles 1887-1970 **[4]**
- **$375** - €407 - **£250** - FF2 670
  «Scotland, Anchor Line, New York and Glasgow» Poster (101x63cm 40x25in) New-York 2000

HERRICK William Salter XIX-XX **[4]**
- **$2 136** - €2 492 - **£1 500** - FF16 344
  A Friend in Need Oil/canvas (84x111cm 33x43in) Par, Cornwall 2000

HERRIES William Robert 1818-1845 **[4]**
- **$962** - €970 - **£600** - FF6 362
  Glare Ice or Sleighing on the River St. John, New Brunswick, Canada Watercolour/paper (21.5x30.5cm 8x12in) London 2000

HERRIMAN George 1880-1944 **[40]**
- **$6 500** - €6 977 - **£4 349** - FF45 766
  Krazy Kat Sunday Page Ink (57x37cm 22x14in) New-York 2000

HERRING Benjamin I 1806-1830 **[6]**
- **$17 000** - €14 524 - **£10 205** - FF95 274
  The Great Subscription Purse at York, August Oil/canvas (35x61cm 13x24in) New-York 1998

HERRING Benjamin II 1830-1871 **[21]**
- **$1 925** - €1 940 - **£1 200** - FF12 724
  The Carriage Oil/canvas (50x40cm 19x15in) London 2000
- **$4 500** - €5 352 - **£3 207** - FF35 107
  The Steeplechase Oil/canvas (26.5x37cm 10x14in) New-York 2000

HERRING E.L. XIX **[12]**
- **$175** - €201 - **£120** - FF1 320
  Lakes with Shipping Watercolour/paper (30x50cm 12x20in) Par, Cornwall 2000

HERRING John Frederick, Jnr. 1815-1907 **[343]**
- **$15 000** - €14 555 - **£9 519** - FF95 476
  Goats, Chickens and Mates in a Stable Oleo/lienzo (41.5x62cm 16x24in) Buenos-Aires 1999
- **$7 014** - €8 361 - **£5 000** - FF54 844
  A Mounted Sportsman with a Gamekeeper/A Mounted Gentleman with a Lad Oil/board (16x21cm 6x8in) Leyburn, North Yorkshire 2000
- **$1 242** - €1 158 - **£750** - FF7 596
  Asking the Way Watercolour/paper (20x30.5cm 7x12in) London 1998

HERRING John Frederick, Snr. 1795-1865 **[350]**
- **$98 210** - €116 801 - **£70 000** - FF766 164
  Farmyard Scene with Milkmaid and a Farm Labourer Oil/canvas (123.5x184cm 48x72in) London 2000
- **$39 137** - €42 938 - **£26 000** - FF281 658
  Matilda, a Bay Racehorse with her Groom in a Loosebox Oil/canvas (56x76cm 22x29in) London 2000
- **$12 962** - €12 466 - **£8 000** - FF81 771
  Hen and Chicks Oil/panel (29x23.5cm 11x9in) London 1999
- **$850** - €970 - **£590** - FF6 363
  Racing Horse in a Landscape Acuarela/papel (17.5x23.5cm 6x9in) Buenos-Aires 2000
- **$584** - €689 - **£402** - FF4 517
  Racing-Plate 4. returning to Weigh, Fores's National Sports Aquatinta (33.5x63.2cm 13x24in) Bern 2000

HERRLEIN Johann Andreas 1720-1796 **[8]**
- **$4 120** - €4 090 - **£2 574** - FF26 831
  Bildnis eines geistlichen Kurfürsten Öl/Kupfer (48.5x34.5cm 19x13in) München 1999

HERRLEIN Leonnard XVIII **[1]**
- **$14 251** - €12 043 - **£8 500** - FF78 996
  Vienna, the Interior of the Stephanskirche with a Procession Oil/panel (36.5x26cm 14x10in) London 1998

HERRLIBERGER David 1697-1777 **[59]**
- **$296** - €249 - **£174** - FF1 635
  «Romont» Copper engraving (15.2x26.2cm 5x10in) Bern 1998

HERRMANN Alexander 1814-1845 [7]
- $1 192 - €1 227 - £751 - FF8 049
  Messe in der Cappella Palatina des königlichen Palastes von Palermo Öl/Papier (35x30cm 13x11in) Berlin 2000

HERRMANN Curt 1854-1929 [16]
- $20 450 - €23 296 - £14 129 - FF152 810
  Malvenstrauss Öl/Karton (51.5x33.5cm 20x13in) Zürich 2000
- $12 922 - €12 782 - £8 057 - FF83 847
  Landschaft Öl/Leinwand/Karton (23.7x32.7cm 9x12in) Berlin 1999

HERRMANN Frank Simon 1866-1942 [11]
- $1 359 - €1 299 - £827 - FF8 524
  View along the Seine Watercolour, gouache/paper (41x60cm 16x24in) New-Orleans LA 1999

HERRMANN Hans 1858-1942 [114]
- $15 443 - €14 521 - £9 662 - FF95 251
  Dutch fishing-village at disk with Figures on a Quay Oil/canvas (107x132cm 42x51in) Amsterdam 1999
- $4 500 - €4 115 - £2 748 - FF26 994
  Waiting for the ferry Oil/canvas (49x68cm 19x27in) New-York 1998
- $1 590 - €1 404 - £959 - FF9 212
  Windmills by a Harbour Oil/canvas (33x44.5cm 12x17in) Amsterdam 1998
- $1 108 - €1 227 - £751 - FF8 049
  Fischhalle Amersfoort Aquarell, Gouache/Papier (49.7x32.7cm 19x12in) Hamburg 2000

HERRMANN Léo 1853-1927 [23]
- $2 166 - €2 441 - £1 500 - FF16 015
  Incroyable en promenade Oil/canvas (26x17cm 10x6in) London 2000

HERRMANN Paul 1864-? [38]
- $112 - €128 - £77 - FF838
  Frauenkopf: Hetty Drypoint (12x9cm 4x3in) Berlin 2000

HERRMANN Theodor 1881-1926 [6]
- $1 841 - €2 045 - £1 233 - FF13 415
  Fleethansicht mit Speicherhäusern und Blick auf den Hamburger Michel Öl/Leinwand (36x24cm 14x9in) Buxtehude 2000

HERRMANN Willy 1895-1963 [83]
- $934 - €767 - £542 - FF5 033
  Lagerhallen und kleines Hafenbecken mit Booten Oil/canvas/panel (83x103cm 32x40in) Berlin 1998
- $317 - €358 - £219 - FF2 347
  Lieper Bucht mit Ruderbooten und Segelbooten Öl/Leinwand (10x15cm 3x5in) Berlin 2000

HERSBERGER Margrit 1943 [7]
- $1 782 - €1 633 - £1 089 - FF10 715
  Polissage Nr.51 Gouache/carton (40x40cm 15x15in) Zürich 1999

HERSCHEL Otto John 1871-1937 [22]
- $1 133 - €1 142 - £706 - FF7 490
  Ung kvinde, der betragter sig selv i et spejl Oil/canvas (63x53cm 24x20in) Köbenhavn 2000

HERSCHEND Oscar 1853-1891 [58]
- $666 - €605 - £413 - FF3 970
  To fiskere i klitterne ved Skagen Fyr Oil/canvas (45x72cm 17x28in) Köbenhavn 1999
- $437 - €469 - £292 - FF3 077
  Parti fra Skagen strand Oil/canvas (19x28cm 7x11in) Köbenhavn 2000

HERSENT Louis 1777-1860 [19]
- $4 989 - €5 793 - £3 553 - FF38 000
  Portrait de femme au turban Huile/toile (65x54cm 25x21in) Enghien 2001
- $2 208 - €2 477 - £1 500 - FF16 246
  Ulysses recognised by his Nurse Oil/canvas (32.5x40.5cm 12x15in) London 2000

HERSHBERG Israel 1948 [6]
- $11 500 - €10 659 - £7 154 - FF69 921
  Jerusalem View Oil/canvas/panel (22x33.5cm 8x13in) Tel Aviv 1999

HERSSEN van Alexander XVII [1]
- $9 060 - €8 721 - £5 664 - FF57 204
  Landschaft mit Figuren vor einem Dorf Oil/panel (27x34cm 10x13in) Wien 1999

HERST Auguste 1825-? [25]
- $6 000 - €6 727 - £4 074 - FF44 128
  The Park in Bloom Oil/panel (34.5x63cm 13x24in) New-York 2000
- $977 - €1 080 - £680 - FF7 200
  Le marché aux fleurs Huile/panneau (8x18cm 3x7in) Cannes 2001

HERTEL Albert 1843-1912 [46]
- $357 - €409 - £248 - FF2 683
  Tiber, Landschaft Öl/Leinwand/Karton (13.5x36cm 5x14in) Zwiesel 2000

HERTEL Georg Leopold XVIII [3]
- $1 211 - €1 329 - £823 - FF8 720
  Mariage à la mode Copper engraving (38.1x47cm 14x18in) Berlin 2000

HERTER Adele 1869-1946 [6]
- $3 000 - €2 569 - £1 771 - FF16 854
  Still Life with Pink Gladiolas Oil/canvas (76x51cm 29x20in) New-York 1998

HERTER Albert 1871-1950 [35]
- $110 000 - €109 033 - £68 805 - FF715 209
  The Bouvier Twins Oil/masonite (101.5x122cm 39x48in) New-York 1999
- $24 000 - €23 828 - £15 000 - FF156 302
  Where Love Abides Oil/canvas (61x91.5cm 24x36in) New-York 1999
- $5 000 - €5 367 - £3 346 - FF35 205
  Japanese Pilgrims Watercolour/paper (36x26cm 14x10in) San-Francisco CA 2000

HERTERICH von Ludwig 1856-1932 [13]
- $781 - €767 - £484 - FF5 030
  Emmanuel von Seidl im Kreis von Freunden Öl/Leinwand (82x110cm 32x43in) München 1999
- $1 652 - €1 943 - £1 184 - FF12 744
  Die Rettung der Verwundeten Öl/Leinwand (30x37cm 11x14in) München 2001
- $1 905 - €1 764 - £1 166 - FF11 571
  Feier zu Bismarcks siebzigstem Geburtstag, Königsplatz, 1. April Indian ink (36x56.3cm 14x22in) München 1999

HERTERVIG Lars 1830-1902 [3]
- $3 780 - €4 495 - £2 692 - FF29 484
  Fra Tysvaer Watercolour (34x50cm 13x19in) Oslo 2000

HERTIG Klaus XX [1]
- $3 179 - €3 068 - £1 997 - FF20 123
  Bauhausgebäude Dessau, Gesamtansicht Photograph (22.5x37.8cm 8x14in) München 1999

HERTZ Mogens 1909-1999 **[140]**
- $923 - €1 073 - **£648** - FF7 038
  Gadebillede Oil/canvas (54x81cm 21x31in)
  Köbenhavn 2001
- $483 - €536 - **£336** - FF3 517
  Bondegård med bindingsvaerk Oil/panel
  (32x38cm 12x14in) Köbenhavn 2001

HERTZBERG Axel Gustaf 1832-1878 **[9]**
- $2 508 - €2 486 - **£1 522** - FF16 307
  Den lille konfirmand Oil/canvas (85x73cm 33x28in)
  Vejle 2000

HERTZBERG Frank XX **[1]**
- $37 500 - €37 459 - **£23 441** - FF245 718
  Cityscape Oil/canvas (142x99cm 55x38in) New-York
  1999

HERTZBERG Halfdan 1857-1890 **[8]**
- $2 240 - €2 211 - **£1 380** - FF14 500
  Gamin sifflant Bronze (H51cm H20in) Biarritz 1999

HERVÉ Jules René 1887-1981 **[744]**
- $3 618 - €4 116 - **£2 517** - FF27 000
  Cavaliers dans les sous-bois Huile/toile (54x65cm
  21x25in) Paris 2000
- $1 962 - €2 287 - **£1 359** - FF15 000
  Les enfants jouant Huile/toile (22x27cm 8x10in)
  Calais 2000
- $279 - €259 - **£173** - FF1 700
  Sangliers dans la neige Gouache/papier (15x10.5cm
  5x4in) Le Raincy 1999

HERVÉ Lucien, Elkan Laszlo 1910 **[19]**
- $1 120 - €1 112 - **£700** - FF7 294
  Paris Street Scene Gelatin silver print (18x16cm
  7x6in) London 1999

HERVÉ Régis 1947 **[116]**
- $378 - €381 - **£235** - FF2 500
  Le repos de la chatte Huile/panneau (30x40cm
  11x15in) La Roche-sur-Yon 2000

HERVÉ-MATHÉ Jules Alfred 1868-1953 **[252]**
- $1 299 - €1 220 - **£804** - FF8 000
  Lavandières à Annecy Huile/toile (38x46cm
  14x18in) Deauville 1999
- $672 - €640 - **£425** - FF4 200
  Le bateau rose Huile/panneau (27x34cm 10x13in)
  Douarnenez 1999
- $726 - €610 - **£426** - FF4 000
  Rue animée en Provence Aquarelle/papier
  (50x30cm 19x11in) Le Mans 1998

HERVIER Louis Adolphe 1818-1879 **[134]**
- $1 366 - €1 524 - **£894** - FF10 000
  Ferme en Normandie Huile/toile (38.5x46cm
  15x18in) Fontainebleau 2000
- $1 907 - €1 982 - **£1 201** - FF13 000
  Les ruines d'un château Huile/toile (35x28cm
  13x11in) Paris 2000
- $502 - €428 - **£300** - FF2 805
  A Fishing-Boat on the Shore Watercolour
  (21x28.5cm 8x11in) London 1998
- $123 - €107 - **£74** - FF700
  Les petits dénicheurs Eau-forte (15x10.5cm 5x4in)
  Barbizon 1998

HERVIEU Louise 1878-1954 **[73]**
- $2 126 - €2 301 - **£1 457** - FF15 092
  Le Maske sur le Point Leger Oil/panel (40x30cm
  15x11in) Stuttgart 2001
- $421 - €366 - **£253** - FF2 400
  Poires Fusain/papier (21x27cm 8x10in) Paris 1998

HERVO Väinö 1894-1974 **[41]**
- $372 - €353 - **£226** - FF2 316
  Blomsterstilleben Oil/canvas (55x46cm 21x18in)
  Helsinki 1999

HERWEGEN-MANINI Veronica Maria 1851-1933 **[6]**
- $71 067 - €79 251 - **£47 786** - FF519 854
  Das Forum Romanum Öl/Leinwand (82x136cm
  32x53in) Köln 2000

HERWERDEN van Jacob Dirck 1806-1870 **[4]**
- $14 845 - €12 455 - **£8 710** - FF81 700
  Landscape Oil/canvas (51x69cm 20x27in) Singapore
  1998
- $4 304 - €4 887 - **£2 946** - FF32 059
  View of Java Pastel/paper (25.5x40cm 10x15in)
  Singapore 2000

HERWIJNEN van Jan 1889-1965 **[43]**
- $2 852 - €2 723 - **£1 782** - FF17 859
  **Still Life with a Plant, Apples and Cherries on a
  Plate** Oil/canvas (60x50cm 23x19in) Amsterdam 1999

HERZ Walter 1909-? **[8]**
- $1 755 - €1 678 - **£1 100** - FF11 005
  «Olympic Games, London» Poster (51x38cm
  20x14in) London 1999

HERZBERG Robert A. 1886-? **[2]**
- $4 000 - €4 549 - **£2 774** - FF29 840
  Motor City Oil/board (96x81cm 38x32in) Cincinnati
  OH 2000

HERZEL Paul 1876-1956 **[6]**
- $7 000 - €6 509 - **£4 321** - FF42 697
  Buffalo Hunters Oil/canvas (58x88cm 23x35in)
  Portland ME 1999

HERZGER Walter 1901-1985 **[19]**
- $2 533 - €2 094 - **£1 486** - FF13 739
  «Blühende Seerose in Schale» Aquarell/Papier
  (40x55cm 15x21in) Radolfzell 1998
- $150 - €179 - **£104** - FF1 173
  Hasenjäger Lithographie (36x29.5cm 14x11in)
  Radolfzell 2000

HERZIG Édouard 1860-1926 **[33]**
- $2 285 - €2 668 - **£1 617** - FF17 500
  Puisant l'eau dans l'oued, Sud-algérien
  Huile/toile (43.5x81cm 17x31in) Paris 2001
- $260 - €290 - **£181** - FF1 900
  **«Chemins de Fer Algériens de l'Etat, l'Algérie
  pittoresque, Arris»** Affiche (103x74cm 40x29in)
  Paris 2001

HERZIG Heinrich 1887-1964 **[96]**
- $2 094 - €2 311 - **£1 385** - FF15 157
  Blick vom Hohen Kasten gegen Illtal Öl/Karton
  (46x59cm 18x23in) St. Gallen 2000
- $950 - €814 - **£571** - FF5 339
  «Kirchturm in Rheineck» Öl/Karton (28x23cm
  11x9in) St. Gallen 1998
- $338 - €397 - **£238** - FF2 603
  Abendstimmung über Berglandschaft Coloured
  chalks/paper (15x21cm 5x8in) St. Gallen 2000

HERZIG Wolfgang 1941 **[42]**
- $10 068 - €8 717 - **£6 108** - FF57 180
  «Wunder der Chirurgie» Öl/Leinwand (115x80cm
  45x31in) Wien 1999
- $342 - €327 - **£208** - FF2 145
  Ohne Titel Gouache/paper (19x19.5cm 7x7in) Wien
  1999

HERZMANOWSKY-ORLANDO von Fritz 1877-1954 **[39]**
 $740 - €799 - **£511** - FF5 243
«Nach des Tages Müh' und Plage» Pencil/paper
(18.5x13.5cm 7x5in) Wien 2001

HERZOG August 1885-1959 **[23]**
 $651 - €562 - **£391** - FF3 687
Pietà Öl/Karton (48.5x70cm 19x27in) München 1998
 $1 732 - €1 943 - **£1 176** - FF12 744
Ansicht Ludwigstrasse in München Öl/Karton
(32x39cm 12x15in) München 2000

HERZOG Hermann 1832-1932 **[187]**
 $35 000 - €38 304 - **£24 143** - FF251 258
The old Water Mill Oil/canvas (104x140.5cm
40x55in) New-York 2001
 $9 500 - €8 129 - **£5 719** - FF53 326
Fishing Boat in the Storm Oil/canvas (50x63cm
20x25in) New-York 1998
 $5 000 - €5 551 - **£3 477** - FF36 412
Women in a Tropical Setting Oil/canvas (26x34cm
10x13in) Milford CT 2001

HERZOG Josef 1939-1998 **[4]**
 $524 - €625 - **£373** - FF4 101
Ohne Titel Aquarell/Papier (42x30cm 16x11in) Luzern
2000

HERZOG Walter 1936 **[12]**
 $109 - €102 - **£66** - FF670
Freies Feld Radierung (14.6x36.2cm 5x14in) Berlin
1999

HESELDIN James 1887-1969 **[212]**
 $144 - €147 - **£90** - FF961
Old Newlyn Watercolour/paper (35x25cm 14x10in)
Par, Cornwall 2000

HESLER Alexander 1829-1895 **[24]**
 $2 200 - €2 307 - **£1 378** - FF15 130
Portrait of Abraham Lincoln Albumen print
(21x16cm 8x6in) New-York 2000

HESS Benedikt Franz 1817-? **[4]**
 $5 870 - €5 024 - **£3 533** - FF32 956
Paysans Vaudois récoltant du raisin Huile/toile
(66x91.5cm 25x36in) Zürich 1998

HESS Bruno 1888-1949 **[20]**
 $2 355 - €2 543 - **£1 627** - FF16 684
Planspitze, Gesäuse, Steiermark Öl/Leinwand
(96x82cm 37x32in) Wien 2001

HESS Carl 1801-1874 **[3]**
 $1 831 - €1 829 - **£1 144** - FF12 000
Le renard musicien/Le lièvre conteur
Gouache/papier (17x19cm 6x7in) Soissons 1999

HESS Florence Adelina 1891-1974 **[8]**
 $3 304 - €3 856 - **£2 300** - FF25 291
«Leeds Wharf» Oil/canvas (51x61cm 20x24in) West-
Yorhsire 2000

HESS Hieronymus 1799-1850 **[7]**
 $4 750 - €4 070 - **£2 856** - FF26 698
Neapel, Padre Rocca predigend Grisaille
(28.3x35.2cm 11x13in) Zürich 1998
 $3 971 - €4 535 - **£2 800** - FF29 745
Neapolitan Genre Scenes Etching (17x22cm 6x8in)
London 2001

HESS Hildi 1911-1998 **[2]**
 $1 803 - €2 103 - **£1 266** - FF13 797
Artistin Bronze (H53cm H20in) Luzern 2000

HESS Julius 1878-1957 **[20]**
 $2 668 - €3 068 - **£1 884** - FF20 123
Sommerblumen in weisser Vase Öl/Leinwand
(79x70cm 31x27in) Bremen 2001

HESS Ludwig 1760-1800 **[13]**
 $4 811 - €5 582 - **£3 321** - FF36 616
Voralpenlandschaft mit Wildbach Oil/panel
(52x75cm 20x29in) Zürich 2000
 $2 285 - €2 201 - **£1 429** - FF14 437
Mühle am Fluss Huile/panneau (26x35cm 10x13in)
Zürich 1999

HESS Marcel 1878-1948 **[52]**
 $867 - €820 - **£540** - FF5 379
Still-Life with a Bunch of Flowers, Mirror, Box
Oil/canvas (63x59cm 24x23in) Praha 1999

HESS von Peter 1792-1871 **[36]**
 $30 899 - €28 313 - **£19 305** - FF184 464
Griechische Landschaft mit Reitern an der
Quelle Öl/Leinwand (61.5x77cm 24x30in) München
1999
 $5 000 - €4 740 - **£3 042** - FF31 094
Winter Landscape with horsedrawn Sled, after
Philips Wouwerman Oil/canvas (32x41cm 12x16in)
New-York 1999
 $430 - €511 - **£298** - FF3 353
Thronender Herrscher im Hermelin vor
Rautenwappen Watercolour (34x50.5cm 13x19in)
Köln 2000
 $1 594 - €1 789 - **£1 105** - FF11 738
Das Pferderennen auf dem Münchner
Oktoberfest Radierung (35.3x49.3cm 13x19in)
München 2000

HESSE Bruno 1905 **[99]**
 $263 - €263 - **£164** - FF1 724
Abendspaziergang im Emmental Öl/Karton
(30x25cm 11x9in) Zofingen 1999
 $194 - €188 - **£122** - FF1 232
Paris, Porte de Châtilon: vue sur le Mont
Valérien Aquarelle (12x15cm 4x5in) St. Gallen 1999

HESSE Eva 1936-1970 **[44]**
 $170 000 - €186 515 - **£112 931** - FF1 223 456
Untitled Mixed media (208x157.5cm 81x62in) New-
York 2000
 $100 000 - €109 715 - **£66 430** - FF719 680
Untitled Oil/canvas (87.5x104cm 34x40in) New-York
2000
 $310 000 - €299 949 - **£191 177** - FF1 967 539
Range Mixed media (30.5x30.5x0.5cm 12x12xin)
New-York 1999
 $340 000 - €328 977 - **£209 678** - FF2 157 946
Untitled (Three Nets) Installation (108x29x15cm
42x11x5in) New-York 1999
 $650 000 - €728 048 - **£451 620** - FF4 775 680
Untitled, Kardon Glass Case Plaster (37x26x26cm
14x10x10in) New-York 2001
 $73 700 - €78 580 - **£50 000** - FF515 450
Untitled Pencil (40x28.5cm 15x11in) London 2001

HESSE Georg H. 1845-1920 **[18]**
 $2 146 - €2 045 - **£1 310** - FF13 415
Konstanz in der Abenddämmerung
Öl/Leinwand/Karton (26x39cm 10x15in) Stuttgart 1999

HESSE Henri Joseph 1781-1849 **[26]**
 $15 620 - €16 769 - **£10 450** - FF110 000
Portrait d'une jeune mère et son enfant
Huile/toile (101.5x82cm 39x32in) Paris 2000

H

HESSE Hermann 1877-1962 **[78]**
$3 726 - €4 346 - £2 616 - FF28 508
Ausblick auf den Luganer See in südwestlicher Richtung Watercolour (18x21.3cm 7x8in) Köln 2000

HESSE Marie 1844-1911 **[1]**
$8 274 - €7 217 - £5 004 - FF47 342
Stilleben med frukter och kopparkanna Oil/canvas (80x106cm 31x41in) Stockholm 1998

HESSE Rudolph 1871-1944 **[46]**
$1 635 - €1 534 - £1 010 - FF10 061
Conventsitzung Oil/panel (55x70cm 21x27in) Stuttgart 1999

HESSELBOM Otto 1848-1913 **[53]**
$3 744 - €3 564 - £2 342 - FF23 379
Norrländsk landskapsvy Oil/canvas (49x134cm 19x52in) Stockholm 1999
$1 791 - €1 743 - £1 102 - FF11 433
Före soluppgången Oil/panel (27.5x34cm 10x13in) Stockholm 1999

HESSEN von Heinrich 1926-1999 **[3]**
$1 530 - €1 789 - £1 075 - FF11 738
Liegender Mops auf dem offenen Buch Mopsaik in herbstlicher Landschaft Gouache/paper (11.5x11.5cm 4x4in) München 2000

HESSEN-KASSEL af Augusta 1797-1889 **[2]**
$4 782 - €4 573 - £2 913 - FF30 000
Jeune fille à la rose Pastel/paper (55x46cm 21x18in) Bourges 1999

HESSEN-KASSEL af Louise Caroline 1789-1867 **[3]**
$3 258 - €2 959 - £2 019 - FF19 412
Lyseröde roser Oil/canvas (18x26cm 7x10in) København 1999

HESSING Gustav 1909-1983 **[195]**
$8 946 - €10 174 - £6 286 - FF66 738
Stilleben mit Flaschen Öl/Leinwand (61.5x86.5cm 24x34in) Wien 2001
$1 018 - €872 - £613 - FF5 720
Blumenstrauss Pencil (52x47.5cm 20x18in) Wien 1999

HESSING Leonard 1931 **[8]**
$5 146 - €5 524 - £3 444 - FF36 235
Narrenschiff Oil/board (36x121cm 14x47in) Melbourne 2000

HESSLER Otto Rudolf 1858-? **[13]**
$1 445 - €1 347 - £873 - FF8 833
Parti fra Venedig med Canal Grande Oil/canvas (44x66cm 17x25in) København 1999

HESSMERT Karl 1869-1928 **[16]**
$2 377 - €2 352 - £1 482 - FF15 427
Im Spätsommer Öl/Leinwand (55.5x72cm 21x28in) Berlin 1999

HESTER Edward Gilbert c.1843-1903 **[19]**
$232 - €266 - £160 - FF1 746
Day with the Fox Hounds, After A.C.Havell Engraving (66x43cm 25x16in) West-Midlands 2000

HESTER Joy St Clair 1920-1960 **[66]**
$5 531 - €6 041 - £3 560 - FF39 626
Portrait of a Young Lady Watercolour (74.5x49cm 29x19in) Melbourne 2000

HESTU WAHYUNI Erica 1971 **[6]**
$1 721 - €1 955 - £1 178 - FF12 823
Cart Oil/canvas (50x100cm 19x39in) Singapore 2000

HETSCH Christian Frederik 1830-1903 **[17]**
$266 - €269 - £166 - FF1 762
Relief med en tyr Pencil/paper (29x36cm 11x14in) København 2000

HETSCH von Philipp Friedrich 1758-1839 **[9]**
$14 851 - €14 965 - £9 256 - FF98 162
Agrippina Öl/Leinwand (62.9x47.4cm 24x18in) Zürich 2000

HETTICH Eugen 1848-1888 **[3]**
$1 782 - €1 817 - £1 115 - FF11 917
Kühe an der Tränke Öl/Karton (21.5x37cm 8x14in) Wien 2000

HETTINGA TROMP van T. Geertruida Maria 1872-1962 **[23]**
$923 - €908 - £593 - FF5 953
A Still Life with Apples in a Cane Basket Oil/canvas (26x35cm 10x13in) Amsterdam 1999

HETZ Carl 1828-1899 **[7]**
$3 574 - €4 090 - £2 458 - FF26 831
Junge Bäuerin mit drei Kindern in der Stube am Tisch bei der Mahlzeit Öl/Leinwand (67x51cm 26x20in) München 2000

HETZEL George 1826-1899/1906 **[17]**
$12 000 - €14 264 - £8 314 - FF93 567
Scalp Level Farm Scene with Mill and Barn Oil/canvas/board (55x91cm 22x36in) Pittsburgh PA 2000

HEUBERGER Felix 1888-1968 **[17]**
$2 547 - €2 180 - £1 533 - FF14 301
Morgen Oil/panel (79x90cm 31x35in) Wien 1998

HEUBNER Hermann Ludwig 1843-1915 **[3]**
$1 423 - €1 483 - £902 - FF9 726
Blick in das Eisacktal mit Schloss Tirol Watercolour (43.8x59.5cm 17x23in) München 2000

HEUDEBERT Raymonde 1905 **[10]**
$7 690 - €7 088 - £4 606 - FF46 495
«Costumes pour la circoncision» Oil/canvas (97x76cm 38x29in) Amsterdam 1998

HEUFF Herman 1875-1945 **[17]**
$3 588 - €4 084 - £2 521 - FF26 789
«De Noordermarkt in Amsterdam» Oil/canvas (46x72cm 18x28in) Amsterdam 2001

HEUSCH de Jacob 1657-1701 **[27]**
$40 000 - €41 466 - £24 000 - FF272 000
Paesaggio laziale Olio/tela (133x173cm 52x68in) Prato 2000
$11 900 - €12 336 - £7 140 - FF80 920
Veduta romana col Tevere e l'Aventino con la chiesa di S.Maria Olio/tela (45x71cm 17x27in) Venezia 1999

HEUSCH de Willem 1638-1692 **[32]**
$4 987 - €5 665 - £3 500 - FF37 161
Southern Landscape with drovers and their Mules on a Path beside Lake Oil/panel (51.5x50.5cm 20x19in) London 2001
$44 469 - €42 296 - £27 000 - FF277 443
Italianate Wooded Landscape with Figures and Goats by a Stream Oil/panel (22x30cm 8x11in) London 1999

HEUSCHER Johann Jakob 1843-1901 **[8]**
$22 220 - €26 426 - £15 836 - FF173 340
Gädmen Gouache/paper (35x46cm 13x18in) Zürich 2000

HEUSDEN van Joop 1920 **[7]**

📇 **$111** - €127 - **£77** - FF833
«**Luftfracht KLM**» Poster (60x100cm 23x39in) Hoorn 2001

HEUSDEN van Wout 1896-1982 **[8]**

📇 **$379** - €431 - **£262** - FF2 827
Paardje Etching, aquatint (39.6x24.9cm 15x9in) Haarlem 2001

HEUSER Carl XIX **[13]**

☞ **$442** - €434 - **£274** - FF2 850
Porträt eines alten Mannes mit Bart Oil/panel (16x12cm 6x4in) München 1999

HEUSER Christian 1862-1942 **[8]**

☞ **$4 861** - €5 176 - **£3 200** - FF33 954
Studies of elderly Peasants Oil/panel (16x12cm 6x4in) Billingshurst, West-Sussex 2000

HEUSER Werner 1880-1964 **[22]**

📇 **$179** - €153 - **£107** - FF1 006
Kranich in Landschaft Woodcut (30.8x15.7cm 12x6in) Berlin 1998

HEUVEL de Theodore Bernhard 1817-1906 **[18]**

☞ **$2 808** - €3 346 - **£2 011** - FF21 951
Cache-cache Oil/panel (40x50cm 15x19in) Lokeren 2000

☞ **$2 064** - €1 983 - **£1 272** - FF13 008
L'atelier du peintre Huile/panneau (32x41cm 12x16in) Bruxelles 1999

HEUVEL van den Karel Jan 1913-1991 **[82]**

☞ **$669** - €719 - **£449** - FF4 715
Nature morte à la coupe de fruits et à la cruche Huile/toile (63x79cm 24x31in) Antwerpen 2000

☞ **$227** - €273 - **£156** - FF1 788
Péricles sur le canal Huile/panneau (17x21cm 6x8in) Antwerpen 2000

HEUVELMANS Lucienne Antoinette 1885-? **[10]**

🖎 **$3 924** - €3 489 - **£2 400** - FF22 889
Cupid and Psyche Bronze (H43cm H16in) London 1999

HEUZÉ Edmond Amédée 1884-1967 **[216]**

☞ **$489** - €457 - **£296** - FF3 000
Vase de fleurs Huile/carton (46x38cm 18x14in) Lons-Le-Saunier 1999

☞ **$650** - €610 - **£391** - FF4 000
Péniches Huile/carton (19x33cm 7x12in) Paris 1999

✏ **$230** - €274 - **£164** - FF1 800
Le clown du cirque Médrano Encre (28x20cm 11x7in) Paris 2000

HEWARD Prudence 1896-1947 **[6]**

☞ **$5 208** - €4 456 - **£3 135** - FF29 232
Portrait of Mabel Lockerby Oil/board (61x47cm 24x18in) Toronto 1998

☞ **$2 847** - €3 142 - **£1 883** - FF20 608
Spring, Knowlton, Que. Oil/canvas (30.5x36cm 12x14in) Vancouver, BC. 2000

HEWES Horace G. XIX-XX **[5]**

☞ **$300** - €343 - **£211** - FF2 247
The River's Edge Oil/board (24x30.5cm 9x12in) Boston MA 2001

HEWINS Philip 1806-1850 **[4]**

☞ **$3 250** - €3 582 - **£2 162** - FF23 495
Portraits of a Couple, each Beside a Red Drapery Swag Oil/canvas (76x63cm 30x25in) Portsmouth NH 2000

HEWLETT James 1768-1836 **[4]**

✏ **$4 839** - €4 750 - **£3 000** - FF31 159
Still Life of Flowers on a Marble Ledge Watercolour (37x28cm 14x11in) London 1999

HEWTON Randolf Stanley 1888-1960 **[22]**

☞ **$226** - €263 - **£159** - FF1 726
«**Air Force Officer**» Huile/toile (61x51cm 24x20in) Montréal 2000

☞ **$1 878** - €1 817 - **£1 158** - FF11 920
Haywagon, Winter Oil/canvas (25.5x30.5cm 10x12in) Toronto 1999

HEY Paul 1867-1952 **[96]**

☞ **$927** - €971 - **£587** - FF6 372
Winterlandschaft mit Bauernhaus und Marterl Tempera (11x16cm 4x6in) Köln 2000

✏ **$901** - €873 - **£562** - FF5 729
Bäuerin mit Kuh am Wegesrand Crayon (14.5x27.5cm 5x10in) Zürich 1999

📇 **$238** - €256 - **£159** - FF1 676
Circus im Städtchen (Rothenburg o.d.Tauber) Farblithographie (36.8x47.5cm 14x18in) Berlin 2000

HEYART Sylvie XX **[18]**

📇 **$204** - €198 - **£127** - FF1 300
Variation sur une attente IV Monotype (29.5x29.5cm 11x11in) Paris 1999

HEYBOER Anton 1924 **[555]**

☞ **$3 515** - €4 084 - **£2 470** - FF26 789
«**Sche and Sche and Other Sche as one**» Acrylic/canvas (130x100cm 51x39in) Amsterdam 2001

☞ **$646** - €546 - **£385** - FF3 579
Le système Huile/toile (51x60cm 20x23in) Antwerpen 1998

✏ **$226** - €250 - **£147** - FF1 637
Strand Pastel/paper (36x39cm 14x15in) Rotterdam 2000

📇 **$634** - €681 - **£424** - FF4 464
Function as Etching (66x100cm 25x39in) Amsterdam 2000

HEYDE op den Herman Henry 1813-1857 **[7]**

☞ **$8 118** - €9 076 - **£5 650** - FF59 532
Shipping on a calm Sea Oil/panel (43x61.5cm 16x24in) Amsterdam 2001

HEYDEN Christian 1854-1939 **[5]**

☞ **$1 990** - €2 312 - **£1 398** - FF15 166
Joueur d'orgue de Barbarie Huile/toile (64.5x67.5cm 25x26in) Warszawa 2001

HEYDEN Otto Johann Heinrich 1820-1897 **[10]**

☞ **$2 936** - €3 221 - **£1 994** - FF21 129
Landschaft am Nil, mit Personnenstaffage, Kamelreiter und Schaferde Öl/Leinwand (38x67cm 14x26in) Saarbrücken 2000

HEYDEN van der J.C.J. 1928 **[13]**

☞ **$34 416** - €40 840 - **£25 056** - FF267 894
Untitled Acrylic/canvas (45x40cm 17x15in) Amsterdam 2001

HEYDEN van der Jacob 1573-1645 **[3]**

📇 **$158** - €150 - **£99** - FF986
Rudolphus II Dei Gratia Rom, Imperator semper Augustus Copper engraving (29.7x18.8cm 11x7in) Praha 1999

HEYDEN van der Jan 1637-1712 **[18]**

☞ **$41 893** - €41 142 - **£26 000** - FF269 877
Brussels, a Capriccio of the Porte du Rivage Oil/panel (30.5x27cm 12x10in) London 1999

H

HEYDEN van der Pieter XVI **[14]**

📷 **$896 - €992 - £624** - FF6 504
   La descente de Jésus aux limbes Burin
   (22.5x30cm 8x11in) Liège 2001

HEYDENDAHL Joseph Fried. Nico. 1844-1906 **[59]**

🖙 **$776 - €767 - £474** - FF5 030
   Wildschwein in verschneiter Waldlichtung
   Öl/Leinwand (40x60cm 15x23in) Kempten 2000

🖙 **$1 494 - €1 277 - £878** - FF8 378
   Winterliche Abendstimmung, Figurenstaffage
   Öl/Leinwand (34x45cm 13x17in) Staufen 1998

HEYER Arthur 1872-1931 **[202]**

🖙 **$1 406 - €1 343 - £885** - FF8 811
   Three Kittens playing Oil/canvas (49x68cm 19x27in)
   Vancouver, BC. 1998

🖙 **$607 - €662 - £420** - FF4 340
   On the Hunt Oil/canvas (33x44cm 12x17in) London
   2001

HEYERDAHL Hans Olaf 1857-1913 **[32]**

🖙 **$78 259 - €90 925 - £55 000** - FF596 431
   Fra Montmartre Oil/canvas (100x162cm 39x63in)
   London 2001

🖙 **$27 060 - €23 356 - £16 280** - FF153 208
   Mor och barn Oil/canvas (92x71cm 36x27in) Malmö
   1998

HEYERMANS Jan Arnold 1837-1892 **[13]**

🖙 **$3 000 - €2 539 - £1 795** - FF16 657
   Minding the Baby Oil/canvas (61x46.5cm 24x18in)
   New-York 1998

HEYLIGERS Anton François 1828-1897 **[11]**

🖙 **$13 328 - €15 851 - £9 500** - FF103 979
   Figures in a Laundryroom Oil/canvas (63x48.5cm
   24x19in) London 2000

🖙 **$13 074 - €11 055 - £7 818** - FF72 514
   Cavalrists Playing Dice in a Tavern Oil/panel
   (27.5x22cm 10x8in) Amsterdam 1998

HEYLIGERS Gustaaf A. 1828-1910 **[1]**

🖙 **$3 120 - €3 718 - £2 235** - FF24 390
   Le repos du musicien et son élève Huile/toile
   (65x52cm 25x20in) Bruxelles 2000

HEYLIGERS Hendrik 1877-1967 **[37]**

🖙 **$4 250 - €3 665 - £2 524** - FF24 038
   Playing Dolls Oil/canvas (60x69cm 24x27in)
   Cincinnati OH 1998

HEYMANN Léon XX **[4]**

📷 **$2 412 - €2 744 - £1 674** - FF18 000
   «Peggy Angelo» Affiche (160x120.5cm 62x47in)
   Orléans 2000

HEYMANS Adriaan Jozef 1839-1921 **[109]**

🖙 **$10 332 - €8 929 - £6 228** - FF58 572
   Le retour au bercail Huile/toile (100.5x148.5cm
   39x58in) Bruxelles 1998

🖙 **$2 601 - €2 230 - £1 539** - FF14 625
   Paysage au chariot Huile/toile (60x70cm 23x27in)
   Antwerpen 1998

🖙 **$1 098 - €1 006 - £669** - FF6 598
   **Spaziergänger bei einem Häuschen in einer
   Winterlandschaft** Huile/panneau (14.5x23.5cm
   5x9in) Zürich 1999

HEYNEN-DUMONT Karl 1883-? **[4]**

🖎 **$854 - £818 - £537** - FF5 366
   Trompetender Elefantenbulle Bronze (48x45cm
   18x17in) Köln 1999

HEYRAULD Louis Robert XIX **[9]**

🖙 **$7 458 - €8 842 - £5 434** - FF58 000
   **Équipage du comte d'Osmond/Scène de chas-
   se** Huile/toile (44x64cm 17x25in) Paris 2001

HEYRMAN Doctor Hugo 1942 **[6]**

🖙 **$5 566 - €5 453 - £3 432** - FF35 772
   Smeltende sneeuw Oil/canvas (200x130cm 78x51in)
   Lokeren 1999

HEYSEN Hans 1877-1968 **[276]**

🖙 **$18 132 - €17 049 - £11 228** - FF111 837
   Still Life Oil/canvas (60x65cm 23x25in) Melbourne
   1999

🖙 **$2 416 - €2 351 - £1 486** - FF15 419
   Florence Oil/board (22x33cm 8x12in) Melbourne
   1999

📁 **$3 235 - €3 072 - £2 018** - FF20 148
   Winson, Cotswolds Watercolour/paper (32x40cm
   12x15in) Sydney 1999

HEYSEN Nora 1911-1973 **[27]**

🖙 **$7 023 - €6 124 - £4 247** - FF40 172
   Old Fashioned Roses Oil/canvas (39.5x50.5cm
   15x19in) Melbourne 1998

📁 **$743 - €702 - £462** - FF4 604
   Seated Nude Pencil (44x34cm 17x13in) Sydney 1999

HEYSER Friedrich W. Theodor 1857-1921 **[1]**

🖙 **$6 433 - €7 669 - £4 587** - FF50 308
   Beim Sonntagsfrühstück Öl/Leinwand (71x101cm
   27x39in) Ahlden 2000

HEYTMANN Willem H. 1950 **[22]**

🖙 **$352 - €366 - £232** - FF2 400
   Personnages sur la plage Huile/toile (22x27cm
   8x10in) Besançon 2000

HIBBARD Aldro Thompson 1886-1972 **[155]**

🖙 **$6 500 - €7 422 - £4 582** - FF48 684
   Spring Thaw Oil/canvas (41x51cm 16x20in) Boston
   MA 2001

🖙 **$4 100 - €4 254 - £2 601** - FF27 907
   Vermont Brook Oil/canvas/board (23.5x30.5cm
   9x12in) Boston MA 2000

HIBEL Edna Plotkin 1917 **[65]**

🖙 **$1 000 - €839 - £589** - FF5 503
   Peasants with Baskets in the Fields Mixed media
   (76x101cm 30x40in) Bloomfield-Hills MI 1998

🖙 **$600 - €579 - £376** - FF3 797
   Elderly Couple in a Horse Drawn Wagon Mixed
   media/panel (27x35cm 11x14in) New-Orleans LA 1999

📁 **$400 - €381 - £253** - FF2 497
   Man in a Turban Drawing (34x23cm 13x9in) Chicago
   IL 1999

📷 **$150 - €161 - £102** - FF1 054
   Girl Holding Vase Etching (50x55cm 20x22in)
   Chicago IL 2001

HICK Jacqueline 1919 **[20]**

🖙 **$13 723 - €14 731 - £9 184** - FF96 628
   Lost Identity Oil/board (90x226cm 35x88in)
   Melbourne 2000

HICKEL Joseph 1736-1807 **[9]**

🖙 **$22 500 - €23 325 - £13 500** - FF153 000
   **Fernandino, arciduca d'Austria, governatore di
   Milano (1754-1806)** Olio/tela (151x111cm 59x43in)
   Venezia 2000

🖙 **$38 910 - €38 248 - £25 000** - FF250 890
   **Emperor Josef II (1741-1790) with the Sash of
   the Order of M.Theresa** Oil/canvas (92.5x74cm
   36x29in) London 1999

HICKEN George Arthur ?-c.1881 **[2]**
🖋 **$1 046** - €1 123 - **£700** - FF7 365
   Ducks and Chickens Foraging Watercolour/paper
   (16x23cm 6x9in) London 2000

HICKEY Dale 1937 **[6]**
😊 **$13 602** - €15 246 - **£9 511** - FF100 007
   Foyer, Bursey Theatre Acrylic/canvas (198x244cm
   77x96in) Melbourne 2001

HICKEY Desmond XX **[4]**
😊 **$2 045** - €2 032 - **£1 274** - FF13 326
   Reader's Chair Oil/board (39x31cm 15x12in) Dublin
   1999

HICKEY Patrick 1927-1998 **[32]**
😊 **$1 833** - €2 159 - **£1 288** - FF14 159
   Late Harvest Field, Co.Wicklow Acrylic
   (51x73.5cm 20x28in) Dublin 2000
🖼 **$472** - €457 - **£291** - FF2 998
   Still Life with Copper pot Lithograph (52x70cm
   20x27in) Dublin 1999

HICKEY Thomas 1741-1824 **[25]**
😊 **$23 337** - €23 015 - **£15 000** - FF150 967
   **Portrait of an Indian Princess, full Length, sea-
   ted cross legged** Oil/canvas (75x62cm 29x24in)
   London 2001
😊 **$8 666** - €9 303 - **£5 800** - FF61 025
   **Young Girl, Half-Length in a White Dress and
   Bonnet/Young Boy** Oil/canvas (30x25cm 11x9in)
   London 2000

HICKIN George Arthur XIX **[12]**
😊 **$2 849** - €3 312 - **£2 000** - FF21 728
   Guinea Fowl Oil/canvas (61x51cm 24x20in) London
   2001
🖋 **$1 891** - €1 835 - **£1 200** - FF12 037
   Mother Hen with her Brood Watercolour
   (23x32.5cm 9x12in) London 1999

HICKS Edward 1780-1849 **[9]**
😊 **$1 300 000** - €1 121 581 - **£787 150** - FF7 357 090
   The Residence of David Twining Oil/canvas
   (66x55cm 26x22in) New-York 1999
😊 **$5 000** - €4 314 - **£3 027** - FF28 296
   Still Life with Win Glass and Fruit Oil/board
   (23x52cm 9x20in) New-York 1999

HICKS George Elgar 1824-1914 **[53]**
😊 **$146 088** - €140 475 - **£90 000** - FF921 456
   On the Seashore Oil/canvas (133x181cm 52x71in)
   London 1999
😊 **$43 097** - €37 183 - **£26 000** - FF243 903
   Waiting for the Boats Oil/canvas (76x51cm 29x20in)
   London 1998
😊 **$11 029** - €10 633 - **£6 800** - FF69 748
   The Wedding Breakfast Oil/panel (30.5x25.5cm
   12x10in) London 1999

HICKS Herbert William 1880-1944 **[9]**
🖋 **$134** - €149 - **£90** - FF979
   Hay Tor, Dartmoor Gouache/paper (17.5x27.5cm
   6x10in) Bristol, Avon 2000

HICKS Nicola 1960 **[21]**
🖋 **$460** - €437 - **£280** - FF2 868
   Three Sheep Pastel (28.5x22.5cm 11x8in) London
   1999

HICKS Thomas 1823-1890 **[15]**
😊 **$4 000** - €4 502 - **£2 755** - FF29 530
   **Portrait of Susan Hicks Carle Daughter of
   Edward Hicks** Oil/canvas (76x63cm 30x25in)
   Charlottesville VA 2000

HIDALGO DE CAVIEDES Hipólito 1901-1996 **[76]**
😊 **$1 220** - €1 201 - **£780** - FF7 880
   Ruinas Oleo/lienzo (65x50cm 25x19in) Madrid 1999
😊 **$870** - €901 - **£540** - FF5 910
   Virgen Oleo/tabla (32x27cm 12x10in) Madrid 2000
🖋 **$520** - €601 - **£360** - FF3 940
   Malabarista Crayon gras/papier (55x34cm 21x13in)
   Madrid 2001

HIDDEMANN Friedrich Peter 1829-1892 **[19]**
😊 **$16 110** - €13 803 - **£9 684** - FF90 539
   **Aschenputtel, Junges Mädchen beim
   Taubenfüttern** Öl/Leinwand (91x71cm 35x27in) Köln
   1998
😊 **$2 063** - €2 301 - **£1 387** - FF15 092
   **Nach der Jagd, Kinder einen erlegten Hirsch
   betrachtend** Öl/Leinwand (41.5x34.5cm 16x13in)
   Köln 2000

HIDER Frank 1861-1933 **[134]**
😊 **$471** - €407 - **£280** - FF2 671
   **«Summer Evening, near Babbacombe,
   Devon»/«Near Land's End»** Oil/canvas (36x46cm
   14x18in) Chester 1998
😊 **$329** - €390 - **£240** - FF2 561
   Fishing Boats landing in a sandy Cove Oil/can-
   vas (29x49.5cm 11x19in) Newcastle-upon-Tyne 2001
🖋 **$307** - €263 - **£180** - FF1 725
   Herding the Sheep Watercolour/paper (33x48.5cm
   12x19in) London 1998

HIDER M.C. XIX-XX **[5]**
😊 **$644** - €608 - **£400** - FF3 989
   Sheep on a Highland Path, Dartmoor Oil/canvas
   (30.5x51cm 12x20in) Billingshurst, West-Sussex 1999

HIEKE Heinrich 1890-1975 **[30]**
🖋 **$60** - €56 - **£37** - FF368
   Landschaft mit Holzbrücke Aquarell/Papier
   (16x22.5cm 6x8in) Zwiesel 1999

HIENL-MERRE Franz 1869-1943 **[47]**
😊 **$419** - €409 - **£265** - FF2 683
   Schwandtner Bauer bei Partenkirchen
   Öl/Leinwand (60x80cm 23x31in) Bremen 1999

HIENONEN Erkki 1933 **[7]**
😊 **$1 201** - €1 345 - **£834** - FF8 825
   Olika tillstånd (Herr Blumfeldt bollar) Oil/canvas
   (90x100cm 35x39in) Helsinki 2001

HIEPES Tomás c.1610-1674 **[18]**
😊 **$520 000** - €457 670 - **£316 576** - FF3 002 116
   **Monkey in a Fenced Garden Surrounded by
   Elaborately Decorated Pots** Oil/canvas (101x140cm
   39x55in) New-York 1999
😊 **$589 040** - €660 452 - **£400 000** - FF4 332 280
   **Apples, Pears, Grapes, Plums and Figs on a
   Parcel-Gilt Platter** Oil/canvas (67.5x89.5cm 26x35in)
   London 2000

HIERL Alfred XX **[3]**
🖼 **$2 000** - €1 923 - **£1 234** - FF12 616
   «Grosser Preis von Deutschland» Poster
   (118.5x84cm 46x33in) New-York 1999

HIERSCHEL de Gioachino XIX **[1]**
😊 **$7 000** - €6 421 - **£4 312** - FF42 116
   Jerusalem: Birket Israel Oil/canvas (21x32cm
   8x12in) New-York 1999

HIGASHIYAMA Kaii 1908-1999 **[6]**
😊 **$63 700** - €62 131 - **£39 000** - FF407 550
   Pine Trees Painting (50x58cm 19x22in) Tokyo 1999
🖋 **$100 000** - €100 769 - **£62 340** - FF661 000
   Sankyo no asa (Morning in a Valley) Mixed media
   drawing (24.5x35.5cm 9x13in) New-York 2000

HIGBY Wayne 1943 [5]

$10 000 - €10 359 - **£6 365** - FF67 953
Bear's Ear Pass Glazed ceramic (29x51x35.5cm 11x20x13in) New-York 2000

HIGGINS Eugene 1874-1958 [49]

$1 000 - €851 - **£596** - FF5 581
Pioneers Resting Oil/board (30x40cm 12x16in) New-York 1998

HIGGINS George F. act.c.1850-1884 [20]

$1 900 - €1 842 - **£1 176** - FF12 082
Haying scene Oil/canvas (50x76cm 20x30in) Mystic CT 1999

$600 - €536 - **£367** - FF3 516
The River in Spring Oil/canvas (45x30cm 18x12in) Boston MA 1999

HIGGINS Reginald Edward 1877-1933 [5]

$706 - €819 - **£500** - FF5 372
«Knaresborough,LNER,Guide Free from Council Office or Any LNER Agency» Poster (102x64cm 40x25in) London 2000

HIGGINS Victor, William 1884-1949 [16]

$2 900 - €2 709 - **£1 806** - FF17 773
Landscape Oil/canvas (40x55cm 16x22in) Mystic CT 1999

$23 000 - €23 298 - **£14 306** - FF152 828
Pool in the Rio Grande Oil/canvas (34x37cm 13x14in) Bloomfield-Hills MI 2000

HIGGS Cecil 1900-1986 [40]

$5 300 - €5 494 - **£3 357** - FF36 035
Still Life with Fruit and Vegetables Oil/canvas (36.5x49cm 14x19in) Johannesburg 2000

$1 028 - €1 212 - **£711** - FF7 948
Still Life with Apples and Oranges Oil/panel (21x29cm 8x11in) Cape Town 2000

$175 - €197 - **£122** - FF1 289
Sea Anemone Watercolour (27x33cm 10x12in) Cape Town 2001

HIGHAM Bernard XX [1]

$1 554 - €1 493 - **£950** - FF9 795
«Come to Ulster for a Happy Holiday!» Poster (102x61cm 40x24in) London 1999

HIGHAM Thomas B. XX [2]

$5 750 - €6 172 - **£3 848** - FF40 488
Salt Water Farm, Martha's Vineyard Oil/board (50x81cm 20x32in) East-Dennis MA 2000

HIGHMORE Joseph 1692-1780 [23]

$53 314 - €63 406 - **£38 000** - FF415 917
Three Girls, Three-Quarter-Length in Blue, Pink & Oyster Satin Dresses Oil/canvas (127x103.5cm 50x40in) London 2000

$4 209 - €5 006 - **£3 000** - FF32 835
Portrait of a Gentleman, Half Length, Wearing a Green Coat Oil/canvas (74.5x62cm 29x24in) London 2000

HIGUERO Enrique Marin 1876-? [21]

$1 900 - €1 952 - **£1 202** - FF12 805
Vista de Granada Acuarela/papel (50x34cm 19x13in) Madrid 2000

HILAIRE Camille 1916 [940]

$11 480 - €10 671 - **£6 972** - FF70 000
Fenêtre ouverte sur le jardin Huile/toile (131x162cm 51x63in) Calais 1998

$5 572 - €5 356 - **£3 433** - FF35 000
Nu au miroir Huile/toile (55x33cm 21x12in) Douai 1999

$2 313 - €2 592 - **£1 608** - FF17 000
Versailles, bassin dans le parc Huile/toile (33x41cm 12x16in) Le Touquet 2001

$1 004 - €1 067 - **£673** - FF7 000
Nu de profil Lavis (68x43cm 26x16in) Cannes 2000

$79 - €88 - **£51** - FF578
Les courses Color lithograph (32.5x48cm 12x18in) Johannesburg 2000

HILAIRE Jean-Baptiste 1753-1822 [45]

$86 680 - €83 847 - **£53 460** - FF550 000
Passages des deux Grandes Caravanes à Palmyre, vallée des Mausolées Huile/toile (80x152cm 31x59in) Paris 1999

$46 980 - €45 735 - **£28 860** - FF300 000
L'embarcadère Huile/toile (81x122cm 31x48in) Paris 1999

$7 884 - €9 147 - **£5 610** - FF60 000
Un dromadaire Huile/panneau (24.5x19cm 9x7in) Paris 2001

$2 495 - €2 442 - **£1 600** - FF16 019
View from a Hill-Top over an Ottoman Town, Figures in the Foreground Black chalk . (20.5x33.5cm 8x13in) London 1999

HILARY Hilary Krzysztofiak 1926-1979 [3]

$3 424 - €3 699 - **£2 367** - FF24 263
Wiwisekcja sowy brazowej III Huile/toile (100x81cm 39x31in) Kraków 2001

HILBERT Georges 1900-1982 [6]

$4 182 - €4 878 - **£2 937** - FF32 000
Le fennec Marbre (H37.5cm H14in) Pontoise 2000

HILDEBRANDT brothers (Gregory & Timothy) 1939 [12]

$4 250 - €4 734 - **£2 779** - FF31 052
Paperback book cover: J.R.R. Tolkien and hobbit relaxing Oil/masonite (57x36cm 22x14in) New-York 2000

$1 300 - €1 395 - **£870** - FF9 153
Card No.130 of Cyber vs. Wolverine Acrylic/masonite (28x37.5cm 11x14in) New-York 2000

$639 - €738 - **£450** - FF4 840
«Star Wars» Poster (76x101.5cm 29x39in) London 2000

HILDEBRANDT Eduard 1817-1869 [76]

$13 689 - €15 339 - **£9 435** - FF100 617
Aufsehen erregende Einfahrt einer russischen Radkorvette in den Hafen Öl/Leinwand (105.5x155cm 41x61in) Hamburg 2000

$4 395 - €4 857 - **£3 048** - FF31 862
Fischer am Ufer Öl/Leinwand (45x67cm 17x26in) München 2001

$988 - €1 175 - **£681** - FF7 708
Familj i vinterlandskap Oil/canvas (30x42cm 11x16in) Stockholm 2000

$880 - €1 037 - **£618** - FF6 800
Paysage méditerranéen Aquarelle, gouache/papier (24x34cm 9x13in) Paris 2000

HILDEBRANDT Ferdinand Theodor 1804-1874 [4]

$3 552 - €3 966 - **£2 464** - FF26 016
La lettre Huile/toile (30x36cm 11x14in) Bruxelles 2001

HILDEBRANDT Friedrich, Fritz 1819-1885 [5]

$8 710 - €7 927 - **£5 444** - FF52 000
Le pêcheur et ses enfants sur la côte Normande Huile/toile (40x59cm 15x23in) Saint-Dié 1999

$2 052 - €2 287 - **£1 380** - FF15 000
Mère et son enfant guettant le retour du voilier Huile/toile (32.5x46cm 12x18in) Saint-Dié 2000

HILDEBRANDT Howard Logan 1872-1958 **[21]**
- $1 000 - €1 181 - £708 - FF7 750
  Portrait of a Gypsy Woman Oil/canvas (78x62cm 30x24in) Boston MA 2000

HILDER Jesse Jewhurst 1881-1916 **[53]**
- $2 540 - €2 996 - £1 791 - FF19 650
  «**St.Mary's Cathedral**» Watercolour, gouache/paper (20x18cm 7x7in) Woollahra, Sydney 2001

HILDER Richard H. 1813-1852 **[55]**
- $5 000 - €4 677 - £3 023 - FF30 678
  Wayside rest/The watering Place Oil/canvas (61x51cm 24x20in) New-York 1999
- $2 080 - €1 986 - £1 300 - FF13 026
  Travellers Resting before a Church Ruin Oil/panel (30x40.5cm 11x15in) London 1999

HILDER Rowland 1905-1993 **[127]**
- $3 804 - €3 558 - £2 300 - FF23 339
  Old Mill, Cambridgeshire Oil/canvas/board (49x59.5cm 19x23in) London 1999
- $1 176 - €1 317 - £817 - FF8 642
  «**Landscape with Oast Houses, Kent**» Watercolour (27.5x37cm 10x14in) Johannesburg 2001
- $327 - €314 - £200 - FF2 061
  «**Country Houses and Gardens in Britain,The British Travel Association**» Poster (102x64cm 40x25in) London 1999

HILDITCH George 1803-1857 **[6]**
- $5 936 - €5 810 - £3 800 - FF38 109
  View of Richmond with the Star and Garter Oil/panel (32x50cm 12x19in) London 1999
- $2 014 - €2 269 - £1 388 - FF14 883
  Pond Twickenham Park Oil/panel (24x34cm 9x13in) Amsterdam 2000

HILES Bartram, Fred. John 1872-1927 **[66]**
- $216 - €240 - £145 - FF1 577
  A Sailing Boat Unloading at a River Landing Stage Watercolour/paper (17x25.5cm 6x10in) Bristol, Avon 2000

HILGERS Carl 1818-1890 **[71]**
- $5 946 - €5 445 - £3 624 - FF35 719
  Peasants and a Horse-drawn Sledge in a Snowstorm Oil/canvas (50x69cm 19x27in) Amsterdam 1999
- $6 389 - €5 624 - £3 890 - FF36 892
  Wintervergnügen mit Eisläufern Öl/Leinwand (28x42cm 11x16in) Köln 1999

HILKEN Philip Burnham 1910 **[2]**
- $12 696 - €12 196 - £7 872 - FF80 000
  Sans titre Mobile (H127cm H50in) Paris 1999

HILKER Georg Christian 1807-1875 **[2]**
- $5 865 - €5 911 - £3 656 - FF38 772
  En italiensk loggia Oil/canvas (32x42cm 12x16in) Köbenhavn 2000

HILL & ADAMSON David O. & Robert 1802/21-1870/98 **[55]**
- $5 389 - €6 154 - £3 800 - FF40 368
  St. Andrews, Fishergate, Women and Children Baiting the Lines Salt print (13.5x19cm 5x7in) London 2001

HILL A.W. 1867-1949 **[3]**
- $1 200 - €1 168 - £737 - FF7 661
  Studies, Landscapes, Seascapes, Portraits Bromoil print (29x21cm 11x8in) New-York 1999

HILL Adrian Keith Graham 1897-1977 **[63]**
- $478 - €513 - £320 - FF3 366
  House on the Riverside Oil/canvas (50x60cm 19x23in) London 2000
- $242 - €228 - £150 - FF1 494
  The Coast Road to Kinvara Co Clare Charcoal/paper (13.5x20cm 5x7in) London 1999

HILL Carl Fredrik 1849-1911 **[199]**
- $99 110 - €94 763 - £62 135 - FF621 605
  Stranden vid Luc-sur-Mer Oil/canvas (59.5x73cm 23x28in) Stockholm 1999
- $7 365 - €8 645 - £5 197 - FF56 707
  Skånskt landskap om aftonen strax efter solens nedgång Oil/canvas (26x32cm 10x12in) Stockholm 2000
- $4 039 - €3 776 - £2 488 - FF24 772
  Palatsinteriör med figurer Indian ink (23.5x31cm 9x12in) Stockholm 1999

HILL Daryl 1930 **[5]**
- $1 715 - €1 841 - £1 148 - FF12 078
  Billabong Watercolour (26.5x74cm 10x29in) Melbourne 2000

HILL David Octavius 1802-1870 **[66]**
- $2 108 - €1 880 - £1 300 - FF12 329
  Sketches of Scenery in Perthshire, Drawn from Nature Lithograph (28x43cm 11x16in) London 1999
- $4 500 - €4 209 - £2 720 - FF27 610
  Portrait, Possibly Sheriff Gay Salt print (20x14cm 7x5in) New-York 1999

HILL Derek 1916-2000 **[85]**
- $2 878 - €3 224 - £2 000 - FF21 148
  Portrait of Everett Fahy Oil/canvas (45.5x40.5cm 17x15in) London 2001
- $4 317 - €4 836 - £3 000 - FF31 722
  Apples at Clandeboye Oil/board (30.5x40.5cm 12x15in) London 2001
- $547 - €613 - £380 - FF4 022
  Portrait of Daniel O'Donell Charcoal/paper (42x29cm 16x11in) London 2001

HILL Edward Rufus 1851-1908 **[11]**
- $2 000 - €1 915 - £1 232 - FF12 562
  Sierra Blanca at Sunset, looking East from Palmilia, New Mexico Oil/canvas (35x55cm 14x22in) Portsmouth NH 1999
- $2 000 - €1 893 - £1 242 - FF12 419
  Lake Scene, Two Men in a Small Boat Oil/canvas (25x40cm 10x16in) Wallkill NY 1999

HILL Ernest F. XIX-XX **[15]**
- $632 - €587 - £380 - FF3 852
  Fishing Harbour Watercolour/paper (38x55cm 15x22in) Carlisle, Cumbria 1999

HILL Howard c.1840-c.1880 **[13]**
- $1 000 - €987 - £608 - FF6 475
  Country Landscape Oil/canvas (20.5x30.5cm 8x12in) New-York 2000

HILL James XIX-XX **[6]**
- $750 - €716 - £461 - FF4 698
  Blue and Yellow Flowers Watercolour/paper (27x38cm 11x15in) Cincinnati OH 1999

HILL James John 1811-1882 **[59]**
- $5 865 - €6 321 - £4 000 - FF41 466
  Stepping stones Oil/canvas (76.5x56cm 30x22in) London 2001
- $1 612 - €1 503 - £1 000 - FF9 860
  The Harvester's Family Oil/panel (23x19cm 9x7in) Billingshurst, West-Sussex 1999

HILL Jean XIX **[26]**
- $624 - €595 - **£379** - FF3 902
  Paysage de neige Huile/toile (45.5x56cm 17x22in)
  Bruxelles 1999

HILL John 1770-1850 **[13]**
- $5 500 - €5 160 - **£3 398** - FF33 846
  New York from Weehawken/New York from Heights near Brooklyn Aquatint (44x64cm 17x25in)
  New-York 1998

HILL John Henry 1839-1922 **[24]**
- $6 500 - €7 680 - **£4 606** - FF50 380
  Wild Duck Shooting Oil/canvas (46x81cm 18x31in)
  Boston MA 2000
- $3 000 - €2 885 - **£1 851** - FF18 924
  View of half Dome Watercolour (30x44.5cm 11x17in)
  Boston MA 1999

HILL John William 1812-1879 **[39]**
- $2 500 - €2 331 - **£1 550** - FF15 291
  Still Life with Peaches and Grapes
  Oil/canvas/board (21x30.5cm 8x12in) New-York 1999
- $3 600 - €4 281 - **£2 565** - FF28 083
  Fishing in the White Mountains Watercolour/paper
  (28x44.5cm 11x17in) New-York 2000

HILL Justus XIX **[4]**
- $4 105 - €4 425 - **£2 800** - FF29 026
  Supper for Two Oil/canvas (30.5x23cm 12x9in)
  London 2001

HILL Rowland 1915-1979 **[30]**
- $2 711 - €2 358 - **£1 634** - FF15 465
  «Fishing Boats, Mulroy Bay, Co. Donegal»
  Oil/canvas (61x91.5cm 24x36in) Toronto 1998
- $619 - €660 - **£412** - FF4 331
  Mulroy Bay, Co.Donegal/White Cliffs, Portrush
  Watercolour/paper (36x51cm 14x20in) Dublin 2000

HILL Rowland Henry 1873-1952 **[72]**
- $1 608 - €1 778 - **£1 115** - FF11 660
  Figures on a Beach, West of Ireland Oil/canvas
  (39x49cm 15x19in) Dublin 2001
- $1 034 - €1 207 - **£720** - FF7 917
  Two Figures Walking Along a Beach
  Watercolour/paper (24.5x34cm 9x13in) West-Yorkshire
  2000

HILL Thomas 1829-1908 **[111]**
- $180 000 - €178 711 - **£112 500** - FF1 172 268
  Fishing on the Merced River Oil/canvas
  (91.5x137cm 36x53in) New-York 1999
- $32 000 - €29 090 - **£19 273** - FF190 816
  Vernal Falls, Yosemite Oil/canvas (91x55cm
  36x22in) Hayden ID 1998
- $10 000 - €11 418 - **£7 050** - FF74 899
  Mount Shasta Oil/canvas (33.5x43.5cm 13x17in)
  Boston MA 2001

HILL Thomas J. XIX **[5]**
- $4 000 - €4 031 - **£2 493** - FF26 440
  Mt.Shasta, McCloud River Oil/canvas (40x60cm
  16x24in) Oakland CA 2000
- $1 100 - €1 121 - **£689** - FF7 355
  Itsy Bitsy Spider Oil/canvas (41.5x33cm 16x12in)
  New-York 2000

HILL Vernon 1887-? **[1]**
- $568 - €610 - **£380** - FF4 002
  The Tree Maiden Etching (24.5x5.5cm 9x2in) London
  2000

HILL William Denley XIX **[2]**
- $47 500 - €55 399 - **£33 349** - FF363 394
  Encampment surrounded by Mountains Oil/canvas (71x73cm 28x29in) Dedham MA 2000

HILLEGAERT van Paulus 1596-1640 **[7]**
- $41 232 - €46 232 - **£28 000** - FF303 259
  The Siege of Grol (Groenlo) Oil/canvas
  (127x215.5cm 50x84in) London 2000
- $2 151 - €2 496 - **£1 485** - FF16 371
  An Italianate river with Fortifications on either Side, Three Men Ink (19.5x27cm 7x10in) Amsterdam
  2000

HILLEMACHER Eugène Ernest 1818-1887 **[10]**
- $10 118 - €9 452 - **£6 243** - FF62 000
  La présentation de Poussin à Louis XIII par Cinq-Mars Huile/toile (92x126cm 36x49in) Granville
  1999

HILLENIUS Jaap 1934 **[17]**
- $2 114 - €2 269 - **£1 414** - FF14 883
  Schemer Oil/canvas (45x45cm 17x17in) Amsterdam
  2000

HILLER Anton 1893-1985 **[9]**
- $5 944 - €5 880 - **£3 706** - FF38 569
  Torso I Bronze (70x20x30cm 27x7x11in) Berlin 1999

HILLER Heinrich act.c.1865-1894 **[39]**
- $1 819 - €2 138 - **£1 261** - FF14 023
  Paysage aux alentours de Ramsau Huile/toile
  (48.5x39cm 19x15in) Warszawa 2000

HILLER Karol 1891-1939 **[5]**
- $2 946 - €2 734 - **£1 800** - FF17 932
  Heliographic Composition Silver print (21.5x21cm
  8x8in) London 1999

HILLERN-FÖLL Maria 1880-1943 **[19]**
- $1 475 - €1 380 - **£894** - FF9 055
  Drei Frauen Öl/Leinwand (69x61cm 27x24in)
  Stuttgart 1999

HILLERS John K., Jack 1843-1925 **[49]**
- $1 500 - €1 280 - **£897** - FF8 398
  Zuni Pueblo, New Mexico Albumen print (25x33cm
  9x12in) San-Francisco CA 1998

HILLERSBERG Lars 1937 **[19]**
- $758 - €880 - **£523** - FF5 771
  Utan titel Indian ink (52x70cm 20x27in) Stockholm
  2000

HILLESTRÖM Carl Peter 1760-1812 **[9]**
- $6 800 - €6 727 - **£4 240** - FF44 128
  Landskapsmålningar Mixed media (50x100cm
  19x39in) Helsinki 1999
- $1 178 - €1 321 - **£800** - FF8 664
  Gnarled and Ancient Oak Black chalk/paper
  (50.5x38cm 19x14in) London 2000

HILLESTRÖM Pehr 1733-1816 **[90]**
- $13 328 - €15 478 - **£9 366** - FF101 528
  Stilleben med fiskfat och pepparrot Oil/canvas
  (44x51cm 17x20in) Stockholm 2001
- $20 410 - €17 749 - **£12 309** - FF116 424
  «Gosse bygger korthus»/«En liten flicka leker med sin docka» Oil/canvas (36x30cm 14x11in)
  Stockholm 1998
- $329 - €366 - **£220** - FF2 399
  Studie av två gummor Indian ink (10.3x16cm 4x6in)
  Stockholm 2000

HILLEVELD Adrianus David 1838-1880 **[9]**
- $3 212 - €3 449 - **£2 150** - FF22 621
  Ship of the Line - Stranded Off the Dutch Coast
  Oil/canvas (47x62cm 18x24in) Edinburgh 2000

HILLFON Curt 1943 **[48]**
- $600 - €629 - **£380** - FF4 126
  Komposition i blått Oil/canvas (83x65cm 32x25in)
  Malmö 2000

HILLGRUND Bengt 1935-1981 **[14]**
- $1 107 - €955 - £666 - FF6 267
  Uppställning på blå duk Oil/canvas (91x82cm 35x32in) Malmö 1998

HILLHOUSE May 1908-1989 **[16]**
- $3 020 - €2 832 - £1 866 - FF18 574
  Winter Night, Mowbray Oil/canvas (68x75cm 26x29in) Johannesburg 1999
- $209 - €176 - £122 - FF1 153
  Two Nudes Print (34.5x27cm 13x10in) Cape Town 1998

HILLIARD John 1945 **[3]**
- $3 652 - €4 090 - £2 537 - FF26 831
  Study from «Distorted Vision» Photograph in colors (40x38.5cm 15x15in) Köln 2001

HILLIARD Laurence act.1876-1887 **[3]**
- $2 100 - €2 443 - £1 500 - FF16 022
  November Dawn Watercolour (16.5x24cm 6x9in) London 2001

HILLIARD William Henry 1836-1905 **[32]**
- $950 - €922 - £587 - FF6 051
  Narni, near Rome Oil/canvas (45x35cm 18x14in) New-Orleans LA 1999
- $950 - €986 - £603 - FF6 469
  Marsh at Twilight Oil/canvas (38x30.5cm 14x12in) Boston MA 2000

HILLIER Tristram 1905-1983 **[68]**
- $8 537 - €9 919 - £6 000 - FF65 065
  Glastonbury Fen Oil/canvas (38.5x49.5cm 15x19in) London 2001
- $5 677 - €5 473 - £3 500 - FF35 899
  Villa Escusa de Haro, La Mancha Oil/board (28x40cm 11x15in) London 1999

HILLINGFORD Robert Alexander 1828-1904 **[153]**
- $50 972 - €53 050 - £32 000 - FF347 987
  Peasant of the Campagna Oil/canvas (102x165cm 40x64in) London 2000
- $4 034 - €4 537 - £2 816 - FF29 760
  Übergabe einer Ehrenkanne an den Dombaumeister von Köln Öl/Leinwand (43x65.5cm 16x25in) Luzern 2001
- $2 150 - €1 875 - £1 300 - FF12 297
  «Summoned to Waterloo, Dawn, 16th June 1815» Oil/canvas (29x46cm 11x18in) London 1998

HILLS Anna Althea 1882-1930 **[41]**
- $12 000 - €11 679 - £7 372 - FF76 612
  Laguna Canyon Road Oil/canvas (35x45cm 14x18in) San-Francisco CA 1999
- $4 500 - €4 830 - £3 011 - FF31 684
  Montezuma's Head Oil/canvas/board (25.5x35.5cm 10x13in) San-Francisco CA 2000
- $750 - €711 - £468 - FF4 663
  California Coast Watercolour/paper (25x38cm 10x15in) Cincinnati OH 1999

HILLS Laura Coombs 1859-1952 **[49]**
- $13 200 - €13 819 - £8 293 - FF90 647
  Mixed Flower #2 Pastel/paper (34x41cm 13x16in) Hampton NH 2000

HILLS Robert 1769-1844 **[100]**
- $2 251 - €2 306 - £1 400 - FF15 125
  A Farmyard Scene Watercolour/paper (31.5x42cm 12x16in) Billingshurst, West-Sussex 2000

HILLYARD J.W. XIX **[3]**
- $2 750 - €2 634 - £1 698 - FF17 275
  Fox hunter tending to his Horse Oil/canvas (20x24cm 8x9in) Portsmouth NH 1999

HILPERT Alfred 1878-1933 **[39]**
- $100 - €114 - £70 - FF750
  Rue des trois frères Merlin, Saint Brieuc Aquarelle/papier (18.5x12cm 7x4in) Rennes 2000

HILSDORF Jacob 1872-1916 **[9]**
- $800 - €767 - £494 - FF5 030
  Porträt Annelie Thyssen Vintage gelatin silver print (37.1x26.3cm 14x10in) Köln 1999

HILSDORF Theodor 1868-1944 **[12]**
- $557 - €665 - £397 - FF4 360
  Stefan George im Profil Vintage gelatin silver print (20.3x16.7cm 7x6in) Berlin 2000

HILSØE Hans XX **[64]**
- $1 131 - €1 065 - £700 - FF6 985
  A Summer Garden in full Bloom Oil/canvas (65.5x85.5cm 25x33in) London 1999

HILTON Bo 1961 **[11]**
- $580 - €654 - £400 - FF4 287
  Brighton pier, Evening Light Oil/canvas/board (20x25.5cm 7x10in) London 2000

HILTON Eric 1937 **[1]**
- $6 500 - €6 205 - £4 061 - FF40 699
  Beginning of the Beginning, from the Steuben Project Sculpture, glass (25.5x23x23cm 10x9x9in) New-York 1999

HILTON Henry XIX **[1]**
- $452 - €425 - £280 - FF2 789
  Corn Stooks Arranged Before a Castle Watercolour (59.5x100cm 23x39in) London 1999

HILTON John William 1904-1983 **[23]**
- $1 300 - €1 404 - £898 - FF9 209
  Landscape Oil/board (40x50cm 16x20in) Altadena CA 2001
- $1 200 - €1 288 - £803 - FF8 449
  Passing Storm Oil/board (30x40cm 12x16in) Altadena CA 2000

HILTON Roger 1911-1975 **[212]**
- $11 505 - €10 932 - £7 000 - FF71 710
  February Oil/canvas (91x76cm 35x29in) London 1999
- $2 176 - €1 878 - £1 300 - FF12 322
  Untitled Oil/board (26x22cm 10x8in) London 1998
- $3 293 - €3 095 - £2 000 - FF20 299
  Where's my Sugar? Gouache/paper (38x56cm 14x22in) London 1999
- $791 - €903 - £550 - FF5 925
  Figurative Composition Lithograph (36x48cm 14x18in) London 2000

HILTON Rose, née Phipps 1931 **[36]**
- $1 874 - €1 835 - £1 200 - FF12 034
  Golden Still Life Oil/canvas (91.5x122cm 36x48in) London 1999
- $636 - €617 - £400 - FF4 045
  Woman walking Oil/canvas (28x25cm 11x10in) Par, Cornwall 1999

HILTON William II 1786-1839 **[7]**
- $2 245 - €2 263 - £1 400 - FF14 845
  Studies for the Ascension, St John the Baptist, The Three Graces Ink (29x38cm 11x15in) London 2000

HILTUNEN Eila 1922 **[6]**
- $498 - €538 - £344 - FF3 530
  Sittande dam Bronze (H17cm H6in) Helsinki 2001

HILVERDINK Eduard Alexander 1846-1891 **[35]**

- **$7 500** - €8 702 - **£5 178** - FF57 082
  Holland Canal Scene with Figures beside a Drawbridge Oil/canvas (45.5x68.5cm 17x26in) New-York 2000
- **$4 633** - €5 445 - **£3 212** - FF35 719
  A Streetscene with Horse-Drawn Carts and Villagers Conversing Oil/canvas (41.5x34cm 16x13in) Amsterdam 2000
- **$2 053** - €2 269 - **£1 424** - FF14 883
  A View in Amsterdam, with the Schreierstoren on the Prins Hendrikkade Pencil (32x50cm 12x19in) Amsterdam 2001

HILVERDINK Johann Jakob Anton 1837-1884 **[15]**

- **$2 895** - €3 403 - **£2 007** - FF22 324
  Sailing Vessels near a Town Oil/canvas (40x55cm 15x21in) Amsterdam 2000
- **$739** - €817 - **£512** - FF5 357
  A River Landscape with a Village in the Distance Oil/panel (26x36cm 10x14in) Amsterdam 2001

HILVERDINK Johannes 1813-1902 **[63]**

- **$3 088** - €3 630 - **£2 141** - FF23 812
  Sailingvessel on a Choppy Sea near a Castel Oil/canvas (102x128cm 40x50in) Amsterdam 2000
- **$3 349** - €3 668 - **£2 041** - FF20 123
  Niederländische Landschaft mit einer alten Windmühle am Ufer Oil/Leinwand (51x71cm 20x27in) München 1999
- **$1 531** - €1 724 - **£1 055** - FF11 311
  Fishermen at Work on a Rocky Coast at Dusk Oil/panel (12.5x23.5cm 4x9in) Amsterdam 2000
- **$353** - €340 - **£218** - FF2 232
  Elegant Lady Reading Black chalk/paper (25x31.5cm 9x12in) Amsterdam 1999

HILZ Sepp 1906-1967 **[12]**

- **$1 530** - €1 789 - **£1 075** - FF11 738
  Josef Holzmaier aus Willing Öl/Karton (80x60cm 31x23in) München 2000

HIMELY Sigismond 1801-1872 **[23]**

- **$180** - €180 - **£111** - FF1 182
  Tableau pittoresque des merveilles de la nature Litografía (48x63cm 18x24in) Madrid 2000

HIMMELSTOSS Karl 1878-1967 **[37]**

- **$168** - €182 - **£116** - FF1 191
  Entenpaar Porcelain (7x13.5cm 2x5in) Wien 2001

HINCKLEY Thomas Hewer 1813-1896 **[19]**

- **$7 500** - €6 854 - **£4 588** - FF44 961
  Cattle and Sheep in a Pasture Oil/canvas (63.5x91cm 25x35in) Boston MA 1999
- **$1 600** - €1 768 - **£1 120** - FF11 599
  Cows Resting in Landscape Oil/canvas (22x30cm 9x12in) Chicago IL 2001

HINCKS William act.1773-1797 **[6]**

- **$2 727** - €2 748 - **£1 700** - FF18 026
  The Irish Linen Industry Engraving (40.5x35cm 15x13in) London 2000

HINCZ Gyula 1904-1986 **[4]**

- **$1 188** - €1 350 - **£828** - FF8 856
  Composition avec une tête de grec Huile/toile (50x60cm 19x23in) Budapest 2001

HINDENLANG Charles, Karl 1894-1960 **[51]**

- **$835** - €813 - **£513** - FF5 332
  Artistin Oil/canvas/panel (22.5x22.5cm 8x8in) Zürich 1999

- **$87** - €99 - **£60** - FF649
  Fasnachtsszene Lithographie (47x62cm 18x24in) Zofingen 2000

HINDER Frank (Francis H.C.) 1906-1992 **[120]**

- **$5 079** - €5 980 - **£3 569** - FF39 227
  Brown Construction Oil/masonite (92x71.5cm 36x28in) Sydney 2000
- **$830** - €930 - **£576** - FF6 100
  Abstract Oil/board (44.5x35.5cm 17x13in) Melbourne 2001
- **$502** - €564 - **£325** - FF3 699
  Donkey Man (S.S City of Rayville» Pencil/paper (21.5x16cm 8x6in) Malvern, Victoria 2000
- **$302** - €338 - **£210** - FF2 215
  Bird Emerging Lithograph (21x17cm 8x6in) Sydney 2001

HINE Harry T. 1845-1941 **[25]**

- **$546** - €468 - **£320** - FF3 068
  St. Albans Abbey Watercolour/paper (35x45cm 13x17in) London 1998

HINE Henry George 1811-1895 **[38]**

- **$1 678** - €1 430 - **£1 000** - FF9 380
  Gravesend from the Old Wharf, Milton Watercolour/paper (24x55cm 9x21in) Bath 1998

HINE Lewis W. 1874-1940 **[142]**

- **$4 000** - €3 761 - **£2 476** - FF24 670
  Construction Worker, Empire State Building Silver print (8x6cm 3x2in) New-York 1999

HINE William Egerton 1851-1926 **[12]**

- **$582** - €535 - **£360** - FF3 512
  Peace, View on the South Downs Watercolour/paper (36x51cm 14x20in) Billingshurst, West-Sussex 1999

HINES Frederick, Fred act.1875-? **[179]**

- **$454** - €437 - **£280** - FF2 866
  Figures Resting Under Trees Overlooking a Valley Watercolour (19.5x29cm 7x11in) London 1999

HINES Theodore act.1876-1889 **[80]**

- **$1 600** - €1 583 - **£1 000** - FF10 384
  In Glen Sannox, Arran, N.B Oil/canvas (76x51cm 29x20in) Glasgow 1999
- **$425** - €485 - **£299** - FF3 184
  «Near Loch Catherine» Oil/canvas (44x34cm 17x13in) Chicago IL 2001
- **$248** - €286 - **£169** - FF1 876
  Figures in a Lake Landscape Watercolour/paper (46.5x36cm 18x14in) Billingshurst, West-Sussex 2000

HINEY Harlan XX **[2]**

- **$3 000** - €2 881 - **£1 859** - FF18 898
  #5600 Oil/board (76x91cm 30x36in) Detroit MI 1999

HINGRE Louis Théophile 1832-1911 **[24]**

- **$1 589** - €1 363 - **£962** - FF8 943
  Cheval de trait Bronze (H23cm H9in) Bruxelles 1998
- **$1 600** - €1 539 - **£987** - FF10 093
  «Olibet» Poster (206.5x72.5cm 81x28in) New-York 1999

HINKLE Clarence Keiser 1880-1960 **[34]**

- **$7 770** - €7 714 - **£4 855** - FF50 602
  Dock at Santa Barbara Oil/panel (61x76cm 24x29in) Amsterdam 1999
- **$2 400** - €2 283 - **£1 457** - FF14 973
  Menton, Italy Oil/board (26.5x35cm 10x13in) Beverly-Hills CA 1999

HINKLEIN XX **[3]**

- **$1 813** - €2 133 - **£1 300** - FF13 990
  «Dunlop» Poster (81x61cm 31x24in) London 2001

HINRICHSEN Kurt 1901-1963 **[57]**
$893 - €762 - £539 - FF5 000
Esther et son pianiste Huile/panneau (61x50cm 24x19in) Saint-Germain-en-Laye 1998

HINSBERGER Alexis 1907-1996 **[97]**
$1 256 - €1 220 - £776 - FF8 000
Le plus vieux métier Huile/toile (92x60cm 36x23in) Paris 1999

HINTERHOLZER Franz 1851-1928 **[6]**
$1 962 - €1 817 - £1 215 - FF11 917
Waldstück mit Pilzen und Vogel Öl/Leinwand (47x73cm 18x28in) Wien 1999

HINTERMEISTER Henry, Hy 1897-1972 **[23]**
$6 000 - €5 746 - £3 706 - FF37 691
Roller-Skating Boy Sprawled as Dog Chases Cat, Calendar of Poster Oil/canvas (76x60cm 30x24in) New-York 1999

HINTERREITER Hans 1902-1989 **[26]**
$750 - €856 - £521 - FF5 613
Still Life, Roses in glass Vase Oil/canvas (60x50cm 24x20in) Plainville CT 2001

HINTZ Alexis 1940 **[15]**
$900 - €901 - £555 - FF5 910
Composición Oleo/tabla (51x37cm 20x14in) Madrid 2000

HINZ Johann Georg c.1630-1688 **[23]**
$19 899 - €20 581 - £12 528 - FF135 000
Nature morte verre Rohmer et au homard Huile/toile (102x78cm 40x30in) Paris 2001

HIOLIN Louis Auguste 1846-1910 **[13]**
$2 558 - €2 434 - £1 600 - FF15 968
«Aguador» Bronze (H70cm H27in) London 1999

HIPP Johanna XX **[1]**
$1 200 - €1 339 - £785 - FF8 781
«Deutschen Theaters» Poster (75.5x108.5cm 29x42in) New-York 2000

HIQUILY Philippe 1925 **[176]**
$11 109 - €10 671 - £6 888 - FF70 000
Sans titre Technique mixte (186x101cm 73x39in) Paris 1999
$9 072 - €10 671 - £6 503 - FF70 000
La croupière Bronze (115x43x15cm 45x16x5in) Versailles 2001
$4 482 - €4 812 - £3 000 - FF31 564
Stabile Metal (H58.5cm H23in) London 2000
$268 - €259 - £168 - FF1 700
Personnage Aquarelle (18x18.5cm 7x7in) Paris 1999

HIRAGA Kamesuké 1889-1971 **[6]**
$4 000 - €4 691 - £2 854 - FF30 769
Vieilles maisons sur le quai Oil/panel (57.5x68.5cm 22x26in) New-York 2000

HIRATSUKA Unichi 1895-1997 **[2]**
$500 - €604 - £349 - FF3 964
Temple Woodcut (45.5x61cm 17x24in) Bethesda MD 2000

HIREMY-HIRSCHL Adolf 1860-1933 **[31]**
$8 784 - €8 721 - £5 484 - FF57 204
Allegorie der Fruchtbarkeit Oil/Leinwand (155x94cm 61x37in) Salzburg 1999
$1 565 - €1 819 - £1 100 - FF11 933
Study of the Head of St Cecilia, possibly for Ahasver Black & white chalks (24x32cm 9x12in) London 2001

HIROAKI Tadahashi 1871-1945 **[14]**
$88 - €102 - £60 - FF670
Bergsee «Tôsei-ko» Woodcut in colors (25.6x38.9cm 10x15in) Stuttgart 2000

HIROSHIGE Andô Utagawa 1797-1858 **[877]**
$2 213 - €2 363 - £1 500 - FF15 500
Filet suspendu séchant au-dessus des flots et barques sous voile Encre (31x52.5cm 12x20in) Paris 2001
$1 500 - €1 296 - £890 - FF8 503
Shiojiri Pass in Shinano Province Woodcut (36.5x24.5cm 14x9in) New-York 1998

HIROSHIGE I, II or III **[113]**
$389 - €458 - £270 - FF3 002
Artisans at Work Woodcut (22x34cm 9x13in) Lewes, Sussex 2000

HIROSHIGE II Suzuki Chimpei 1826-1869 **[81]**
$542 - €610 - £373 - FF4 000
Tateyama, dans la série de Itchu, de la série Shokoku Meisho Hyakkei Estampe couleurs (36x24cm 14x9in) Paris 2000

HIRSCH Alexandre-Auguste 1833-1912 **[9]**
$5 708 - €4 878 - £3 353 - FF32 000
Portrait de jeune fille Huile/toile (65x54cm 25x21in) Avignon 1998

HIRSCH Alphonse 1843-1884 **[2]**
$4 808 - €4 497 - £2 911 - FF29 500
Demoiselle en robe de satin et dentelle, devant un piano Huile/toile (48.5x39.5cm 19x15in) Pau 1999

HIRSCH Hermann 1861-1934 **[3]**
$7 193 - €7 130 - £4 500 - FF46 773
The Artist's Model Oil/canvas/board (41x31cm 16x12in) London 1999

HIRSCH Joseph 1910-1981 **[104]**
$4 500 - €5 292 - £3 226 - FF34 712
Couple in blue Acrylic/canvas (91.5x76cm 36x29in) Philadelphia PA 2001
$250 - €262 - £167 - FF1 721
Lunch Hour Lithograph (27.5x30.5cm 10x12in) New-York 2001

HIRSCH Karl Jakob 1892-1952 **[9]**
$20 515 - €23 620 - £14 000 - FF154 936
Martin Ruber Mouring in a Jewish Cemetery Watercolour (35.5x28.5cm 13x11in) London 2000

HIRSCH Karl-Georg 1938 **[12]**
$105 - €123 - £73 - FF804
Blatt 1 zu drei Wetten von Isaak Babel Radierung (29.7x29cm 11x11in) Berlin 2000

HIRSCH Richard 1944 **[2]**
$3 500 - €3 626 - £2 227 - FF23 783
Ceremonial Vessel #15 Ceramic (42x51x51cm 16x20x20in) New-York 2000

HIRSCH Stefan 1899-1964 **[14]**
$1 100 - €1 286 - £773 - FF8 435
New York Night Lithograph (25.5x35.5cm 10x13in) New-York 2000

HIRSCHBERG Carl 1854-1923 **[7]**
$110 000 - €93 982 - £66 033 - FF616 484
Decoration Day Oil/canvas (112x89cm 44x35in) New-York 1998

HIRSCHELY Caspar 1698-1743 **[6]**
$5 040 - €4 289 - £3 000 - FF28 136
Roses, forget-me-nots, morning glory and other flowers Oil/panel (25x17cm 9x6in) London 1998

HIRSCHFELD Albert, Al 1903 **[63]**

$3 500 - €3 898 - £2 289 - FF25 572
Movie publicity artwork: two couples riding in speeding jeep Ink (39x40cm 15x16in) New-York 2000

$425 - €446 - £284 - FF2 923
Cultural Calendar/Ed Koch & Company Lithograph (41x53cm 16x20in) New-York 2001

HIRSCHFELD Emil Benediktoff 1867-1922 **[46]**

$1 304 - €1 172 - £778 - FF7 687
Segelbåtar i hamn Oil/canvas (52x71cm 20x27in) Stockholm 1998

$501 - €549 - £348 - FF3 600
Marine, soleil couchant Huile/panneau (22x27cm 8x10in) Brest 2001

HIRSCHFELD-MACK Ludwig 1893-1965 **[4]**

$1 758 - €1 636 - £1 081 - FF10 732
Postkarte zur Bauhausausstellung Lithographie (15x10.5cm 5x4in) München 1999

HIRSCHVOGEL Augustin Hirssfogel c.1503-1553 **[15]**

$179 - €204 - £124 - FF1 341
Die Heilung des Kranken im Bad von Bethesda Radierung (11.3x14.7cm 4x5in) Hamburg 2000

HIRSH Alice 1888-1935 **[4]**

$5 500 - €5 092 - £3 366 - FF33 400
Impressionist Scene Cityscape, People in the Rain Oil/canvas (74x84cm 29x33in) Wethersfield CT 1999

HIRSHFIELD Morris 1872-1946 **[3]**

$510 000 - €485 340 - £319 005 - FF3 183 624
Girl with Dog Oil/canvas (117x91.5cm 46x36in) New-York 1999

HIRST Claude Raguet 1855-1942 **[18]**

$9 500 - €8 997 - £5 776 - FF59 014
Roses Oil/canvas (21.5x26.5cm 8x10in) New-York 1999

$13 000 - €12 311 - £7 904 - FF80 757
Don Quixote Watercolour (21x26cm 8x10in) New-York 1999

HIRST Damien 1965 **[133]**

$209 205 - €246 021 - £150 000 - FF1 613 790
N-(9-Acridinyl) Maleimide Painting (172.5x152.5cm 67x60in) London 2001

$65 000 - €75 419 - £44 876 - FF494 715
Alprazolam Mixed media/canvas (44x71cm 17x27in) New-York 2000

$13 558 - €14 088 - £8 500 - FF92 409
6 - Azauracil Mixed media/canvas (30.5x25.5cm 12x10in) London 2000

$250 000 - €241 895 - £154 175 - FF1 586 725
Alone yet Together Construction (91x122x12cm 35x48x4in) New-York 1999

$10 706 - €9 952 - £6 500 - FF65 280
Love will tear us apart Assemblage (35.5x51x22.5cm 13x20x8in) London 1998

$3 200 - €3 713 - £2 209 - FF24 355
Spin Drawing Coloured crayons (21x14.5cm 8x5in) New-York 2000

$33 000 - €37 530 - £23 057 - FF246 183
The Last Supper Screenprint in colors (152.5x101.5cm 60x39in) Beverly-Hills CA 2000

$38 000 - €44 091 - £26 235 - FF289 218
With Dead Head Photograph (57x76cm 22x29in) New-York 2000

HIRT Friedrich Wilhelm 1721-1772 **[11]**

$8 009 - €8 598 - £5 359 - FF56 397
Baumreiche Landschaft mit Hirten und Tieren Öl/Leinwand (40x52cm 15x20in) Zürich 2000

$7 257 - €6 134 - £4 342 - FF40 234
Mainlandschaft Oil/panel (25x32cm 9x12in) Berlin 1998

HIRT Heinrich 1841-1902 **[13]**

$22 243 - €21 572 - £14 000 - FF141 506
A Helping hand Oil/canvas (72x83cm 28x32in) London 1999

$10 246 - €9 715 - £6 233 - FF63 724
Die Pusteblume, Schulmädchen auf dem Heimweg Oil/panel (44.5x30.5cm 17x12in) Köln 1999

HIRTH DU FRENES Rudolf 1846-1916 **[46]**

$1 276 - €1 431 - £884 - FF9 390
Junge Magd am Fenster des Bauernhauses Öl/Leinwand (65x48.5cm 25x19in) München 2000

$1 072 - €1 227 - £745 - FF8 049
Sprechstunde des Tierarztes Oil/canvas/panel (26x34cm 10x13in) Rudolstadt-Thüringen 2000

HIS Andreas 1928 **[4]**

$1 959 - €1 886 - £1 225 - FF12 374
Paris, Rue Muffetard/Rue Edouard-Quenu Öl/Papier (40.5x41.5cm 15x16in) Zürich 1999

HIS René 1877-1960 **[114]**

$26 000 - €29 531 - £18 244 - FF193 710
Waterlilies on a tranquil Pond Oil/canvas (230.5x330cm 90x129in) New-York 2001

$2 118 - €2 134 - £1 320 - FF14 000
Bords de l'Eure Huile/toile (46x61cm 18x24in) La Varenne-Saint-Hilaire 2000

HITCHCOCK David Howard 1861-1943 **[12]**

$6 000 - €5 126 - £3 630 - FF33 626
At the End of the Fishermans Day Oil/canvas (51x40.5cm 20x15in) San-Francisco CA 1998

$4 276 - €3 999 - £2 635 - FF26 229
Landskap med palmer, Hawaii Oil/canvas/panel (40x29.5cm 15x11in) Stockholm 1999

HITCHCOCK George 1850-1913 **[42]**

$10 000 - €10 706 - £6 805 - FF70 226
Dutch landscape with Windmill and Daffodils Oil/canvas (44x55cm 17x22in) Portsmouth NH 2001

$8 500 - €9 820 - £5 951 - FF64 413
Mother and Child in a Courtyard Oil/canvas (36.5x31cm 14x12in) New-York 2001

HITCHCOCK Harold 1914 **[26]**

$1 016 - €1 091 - £680 - FF7 154
The Glade Watercolour/paper (30x33.5cm 11x13in) London 2000

HITCHCOCK Malcolm J. 1929-1998 **[18]**

$516 - €486 - £320 - FF3 187
Celtic Circle Tempera (45.5x61cm 17x24in) London 2000

HITCHENS Ivon 1893-1979 **[199]**

$29 196 - €28 146 - £18 000 - FF184 627
Flowers in a Vase Oil/canvas (61x50.5cm 24x19in) London 1999

$9 378 - €10 521 - £6 500 - FF69 015
Woodland gate Oil/canvas (12.5x38.5cm 4x15in) London 2000

$548 - €624 - £380 - FF4 092
Untitled Print in colors (39x72cm 15x28in) London 2000

HITCHENS

HITCHENS John 1940 [62]
   $722 - €728 - **£450** - FF4 776
    Heavy Heat Oil/canvas (43x149.5cm 16x58in) London 2000

HITZ Dora 1856-1930 [16]
   $1 947 - €2 301 - **£1 380** - FF15 092
    Mutter und Kind Pastell/Karton (50.5x60.5cm 19x23in) Ahlden 2000

HITZLER Franz 1946 [89]
   $614 - €716 - **£430** - FF4 695
    Komposition Oil/board/canvas (88x63cm 34x24in) München 2000
   $1 097 - €1 227 - **£739** - FF8 049
    Ohne Titel Öl/Leinwand (35x32cm 13x12in) München 2000
   $457 - €511 - **£308** - FF3 353
    Komposition Mischtechnik/Papier (36x25.5cm 14x10in) München 2000

HJELM Fanny 1861-1940 [8]
   $3 216 - €2 797 - **£1 939** - FF18 345
    Pojke och flicka Coloured chalks/paper (118x75cm 46x29in) Stockholm 1998

HJERTÉN Sigrid 1885-1948 [174]
   $239 365 - €268 173 - **£166 845** - FF1 759 100
    Kvinna i röd interiör Oil/canvas (159x151cm 62x59in) Stockholm 2001
   $28 244 - €26 539 - **£17 020** - FF174 087
    Liljor Oil/panel (73x60cm 28x23in) Stockholm 1999
   $21 582 - €24 175 - **£15 004** - FF158 576
    Ivan vid bordet Oil/panel (41x35cm 16x13in) Stockholm 2001
   $4 591 - €5 145 - **£3 200** - FF33 746
    Blomsterstilleben Akvarell/papper (38x28cm 14x11in) Stockholm 2001

HJORTH Bror 1894-1968 [153]
   $14 016 - €13 986 - **£8 748** - FF91 740
    Flicka i trädgård Oil/canvas (81x54cm 31x21in) Uppsala 1999
   $1 963 - €1 841 - **£1 214** - FF12 079
    Skogslandskap, från Vaksala kyrka Oil/canvas (41x33cm 16x12in) Stockholm 1999
   $1 071 - €1 004 - **£662** - FF6 588
    Sittande flicka med hund Stone (H26.5cm H10in) Stockholm 1999
   $607 - €608 - **£403** - FF4 368
    Sittande kvinna Pencil/paper (40x32cm 15x12in) Stockholm 2000

HJORTH-NIELSEN Søren 1901-1983 [155]
   $1 142 - €1 050 - **£702** - FF6 889
    Landskab fra Mols Oil/canvas (60x80cm 23x31in) København 1999

HJORTZBERG Olle 1872-1959 [308]
   $4 197 - €4 013 - **£2 631** - FF26 326
    Tulpaner och narcisser Oil/panel (54x63cm 21x24in) Stockholm 1999
   $443 - €443 - **£277** - FF2 905
    Salomons Höga Visa Oil/canvas (23x46cm 9x18in) Uppsala 1999
   $748 - €630 - **£442** - FF4 135
    Träd vid husgavel Watercolour/paper (26x37cm 10x14in) Stockholm 1998
   $4 200 - €4 551 - **£2 799** - FF29 853
    «Olympiska spelen, Stockholm» Poster (105x74cm 41x29in) New-York NY 2000

HLAVACEK Anton / Avlov 1842-1926 [70]
   $4 382 - €5 087 - **£3 080** - FF33 369
    Stuem und Wetterhagel Öl/Leinwand (159x250cm 62x98in) Wien 2001

   $2 794 - €3 197 - **£1 971** - FF20 974
    Madatsch Gletscher, Ortlergruppe (Südtirol) Öl/Karton (49.5x43.5cm 19x17in) Wien 2001
   $405 - €472 - **£286** - FF3 098
    Bauerngehöft bei Puchberg Öl/Karton (19x28cm 7x11in) Salzburg 2000

HLINA Ladislav 1947 [49]
   $765 - €869 - **£535** - FF5 701
    Froschkönig Bronze (H42cm H16in) Berlin 2001

HLITO Alfredo 1923-1993 [9]
   $3 200 - €3 718 - **£2 249** - FF24 387
    Sin título Acrilico (50x37cm 19x14in) Buenos-Aires 2001

HLUNGWANE Jackson 1923 [6]
   $1 238 - €1 387 - **£860** - FF9 097
    Angel Sculpture, wood (H52cm H20in) Johannesburg 2001

HO KAN Huo Gang 1931 [10]
   $1 902 - €2 220 - **£1 302** - FF14 562
    Composition Oil/canvas (40x40cm 15x15in) Taipei 2000

HOARE Mrs. Mary XVIII [2]
   $5 788 - €5 047 - **£3 500** - FF33 109
    Study of an oriental Woman holding a Drum Pencil (23x17cm 9x6in) London 1998

HOARE OF BATH William 1706-1799 [56]
   $16 246 - €15 807 - **£10 000** - FF103 688
    Portrait of the Pitt Family Oil/canvas (140x118cm 55x46in) London 2001
   $5 000 - €4 349 - **£3 014** - FF28 525
    Gentleman, Half Length, in a Brown Coat and White Cravat Oil/canvas (76x63cm 29x24in) New-York 1998
   $1 695 - €1 570 - **£1 050** - FF10 296
    Lady, Head and Shoulders, in Profile, Wearing a White Hat Coloured chalks (21.5x17cm 8x6in) London 1999

HOARE Richard Colt, 2nd Bt 1758-1838 [3]
   $560 - €552 - **£360** - FF3 623
    Arcadian Idyll with Figures on a Riverbank Ink (25.5x36cm 10x14in) London 1998

HOBART Clark 1868-1948 [20]
   $7 000 - €6 658 - **£4 250** - FF43 673
    Beside Still Waters Oil/board/canvas (61x76cm 24x29in) Beverly-Hills CA 1999
   $900 - €776 - **£534** - FF5 087
    Woman with a Parasol on a Terrace Monotype (20x20cm 7x7in) New-York 1998

HOBART John R. XIX [10]
   $6 608 - €6 212 - **£4 000** - FF40 747
    Dapple grey Horse in Landscape/Bay Horse with Dog in Landscape Oil/canvas (46x53.5cm 18x21in) London 1999

HOBBEMA Meindert 1638-1709 [28]
   $300 000 - €303 491 - **£183 180** - FF1 990 770
    View of a Fish pond with Figures, a Man Walking, a Washerwoman Oil/panel (41x61cm 16x24in) New-York 2000
   $34 253 - €32 037 - **£21 000** - FF210 147
    A Wooded River Landscape Oil/panel (34x44cm 13x17in) London 2000

HOBBS Morris Henry 1892-1967 [74]
   $3 600 - €3 991 - **£2 499** - FF26 180
    Bromeliad and Bluebirds Watercolour/paper (50x35cm 20x14in) New-Orleans LA 2001

Calendar & auction results : Internet www.artprice.com 3617 ARTPRICE 721

H

$250 - €250 - **£156** - FF1 638
Judith Etching (34x16cm 13x6in) New-Orleans LA
1999

HOBDELL Roy 1911-1961 **[7]**
$5 413 - €6 294 - **£3 800** - FF41 284
**Trompe-l'oeil: Music
Manuscript/Opera/Compendium of Garden
Delights** Watercolour (24.5x19cm 9x7in) Billingshurst,
West-Sussex 2001

HOBDEN Frank XIX-XX **[10]**
$7 573 - €7 330 - **£4 600** - FF48 083
Reclining Lady in a Classical Bath Oil/canvas
(20.5x30.5cm 8x12in) London 2000

HOBERMAN Nicky 1967 **[7]**
$5 769 - €6 781 - **£4 000** - FF44 480
Party Dress Oil/canvas (180x90cm 70x35in) London
2000

HOBLEY Edward George 1866-1916 **[8]**
$2 267 - €2 687 - **£1 600** - FF17 628
Ready for Work Oil/canvas (50x76cm 19x29in) West-
Midlands 2000

HOBSON Cecil James 1874-1918 **[3]**
$9 864 - €11 760 - **£7 033** - FF77 139
Märchenstunde Öl/Leinwand (72x92cm 28x36in)
Ahlden 2000

HOBSON Henry E. XIX **[23]**
$2 564 - €2 981 - **£1 800** - FF19 555
At the Well Oil/panel (15x20.5cm 5x8in) London 2001
$657 - €623 - **£400** - FF4 086
At a Cottage Door Watercolour/paper (33x43cm
12x16in) Godalming, Surrey 1999

HOCH Franz Xaver 1869-1916 **[36]**
$958 - €938 - **£589** - FF6 152
Aus Evolène Öl/Leinwand (54.5x70cm 21x27in)
Zürich 1999

HÖCH Hannah 1889-1978 **[232]**
$2 411 - €2 812 - **£1 692** - FF18 446
Zynien (Zinnien) Öl/Karton (59.7x49.7cm 23x19in)
Köln 2000
$2 537 - €2 556 - **£1 581** - FF16 769
Collage Collage/Karton (19.5x19.5cm 7x7in)
Düsseldorf 2000
$2 315 - €2 505 - **£1 586** - FF16 434
Tiermenschen-Paar Watercolour (15.5x13cm 6x5in)
Stuttgart 2001
$180 - €204 - **£125** - FF1 341
Strasse und Häuser Woodcut (20.5x17cm 8x6in)
Berlin 2001
$30 000 - €25 171 - **£17 601** - FF165 108
Clown Photograph (12.5x9.5cm 4x3in) New-York 1998

HOCH Johann Jacob 1750-1829 **[17]**
$6 608 - €5 622 - **£3 943** - FF36 881
Interieur einer gotischen Kirche Öl/Kupfer
(43x52cm 16x20in) München 1998
$7 204 - €8 181 - **£5 006** - FF53 662
Trompe-l'oeil, Gemälde nach antiken Basreliefs
Öl/Leinwand (42.5x35cm 16x13in) Köln 2001
$890 - €1 049 - **£613** - FF6 884
Orientalische Szene Ink (46x32cm 18x12in) Bern
2000

HOCHARD Gaston 1863-1913 **[18]**
$3 933 - €3 964 - **£2 451** - FF26 000
Chez les bouquinistes Huile/panneau (65x81cm
25x31in) Lille 2000

HOCHECKER Franz 1730-1782 **[23]**
$8 096 - €7 917 - **£5 000** - FF51 933
**Flusslandschaft mit Mühle/Flusslandschaft mit
Dorf und Fischer** Öl/Leinwand (39.5x52cm 15x20in)
Zürich 1999
$4 812 - €4 602 - **£2 930** - FF30 185
**Rastende Reiter an der Tränke, im Hintergrund
Blick in weite Landschaft** Öl/Leinwand
(26.5x34.5cm 10x13in) Stuttgart 1999

HÖCKELMANN Antonius, Anton 1937-2000 **[128]**
$357 - €332 - **£219** - FF2 180
Bar Eigelstein Pencil/paper (40.5x29.5cm 15x11in)
Hamburg 1999
$104 - €118 - **£73** - FF771
Frau und Pferd Linocut (42x29.5cm 16x11in)
Düsseldorf 2001

HÖCKERT Johan Fredrik 1826-1866 **[9]**
$1 207 - €1 341 - **£808** - FF8 796
Lars Petter Sjulen Bartni Oil/canvas (29x26cm
11x10in) Stockholm 2000

HOCKEY Patrick 1948-1992 **[31]**
$1 375 - €1 167 - **£829** - FF7 654
Holiday by the Sea Oil/board (91x122cm 35x48in)
Sydney 1998
$1 029 - €970 - **£648** - FF6 366
Flowers Monotype (75x58cm 29x22in) Sydney 1999

HÖCKNER Rudolf 1864-1942 **[49]**
$2 238 - €2 403 - **£1 498** - FF15 763
**Verhangene weite Wiesenlandschaft mit
Kanalschleuse** Oil/canvas/panel (48x66cm 18x25in)
Berlin 2000
$1 973 - €2 301 - **£1 366** - FF15 092
Norddeutsche Landschaft mit Bauernhaus
Öl/Karton (19.5x23.5cm 7x9in) Buxtehude 2000

HOCKNEY David 1937 **[1858]**
$380 000 - €425 628 - **£264 024** - FF2 791 936
«The Cruel Elephant» Oil/canvas (122x152.5cm
48x60in) New-York 2001
$179 047 - €174 261 - **£110 000** - FF1 143 076
Steps with Shadow (Paper Pool 2) Mixed media
(128x86cm 50x33in) London 1999
$4 641 - €4 004 - **£2 800** - FF26 266
Mount Street, Bradford Oil/board (32x42cm
12x16in) London 1998
$16 000 - €15 376 - **£9 856** - FF100 862
Man listening to Noise Crayon (32x25.5cm 12x10in)
New-York 1999
$2 500 - €2 487 - **£1 551** - FF16 311
Sunflowers I and II Etching, aquatint in colors
(46x38.5cm 18x15in) Beverly-Hills CA 1999
$4 250 - €3 997 - **£2 631** - FF26 220
Gregory and Shinro, Nara, Japan Photograph
(84x74cm 33x29in) New-York 1999

HÖD Edmund XIX **[18]**
$1 830 - €1 817 - **£1 142** - FF11 917
Blick auf Berchtesgaden Oil/panel (16x31.5cm
6x12in) Wien 1999

HODDER Albert c.1850-c.1895 **[3]**
$1 952 - €2 299 - **£1 350** - FF15 080
Crab Boat at Seaton, Dorset Oil/canvas (24x44cm
9x17in) Devon 2000

HODÉ Pierre 1889-1942 **[113]**
$7 360 - €7 165 - **£4 521** - FF47 000
Les remparts de la ville Huile/toile (54x65.5cm
21x25in) Paris 1999
$2 000 - €2 285 - **£1 408** - FF14 986
Still Life with Flowers Oil/canvas (33x24cm 13x9in)
Chicago IL 2001

HODEL Ernst 1881-1955 **[86]**
- $963 - €929 - £594 - FF6 094
  Sommerlandschaft mit Bauern bei der Heuernte Öl/Leinwand/Karton (43x57cm 16x22in) Bern 1999
- $571 - €529 - £349 - FF3 468
  Alpenlandschaft mit Bergsee bei untergehender Sonne Öl/Leinwand/Karton (34x44cm 13x17in) Bern 1999

HODGE Francis Edwin 1883-1949 **[10]**
- $646 - €607 - £400 - FF3 984
  Mrs Robert de Lasaux, nee Ethel Lambert Taylor Oil/canvas (68x53cm 26x20in) London 1999

HODGE Spencer 1943 **[10]**
- $5 421 - €6 320 - £3 800 - FF41 458
  Cheetah at Ngorogoro Crater Oil/canvas (98x118.5cm 38x46in) London 2000
- $439 - €400 - £300 - FF3 086
  Tiger Cub Watercolour/paper (46.5x64cm 18x25in) London 2001

HODGE Thomas XIX **[3]**
- $2 957 - €2 907 - £1 900 - FF19 067
  The Son of his Father Ink (16x11.5cm 6x4in) London 1999

HODGES C.J. XIX **[1]**
- $4 840 - €4 649 - £3 000 - FF30 494
  Battle of Obligado, November 20, 1845: English and French Squadron Watercolour/paper (61x96.5cm 24x37in) London 1999

HODGES Charles Howard 1764-1837 **[14]**
- $2 153 - €1 860 - £1 298 - FF12 200
  Portrait of a Girl, wearing a White Dress Pastel/paper (43x28.5cm 16x11in) Amsterdam 1998

HODGES Gary 1954 **[10]**
- $8 928 - €8 580 - £5 500 - FF56 283
  Jaguar Pencil/paper (32.5x36cm 12x14in) London 1999

HODGES J. Sydney Willis 1829-1900 **[6]**
- $1 497 - €1 569 - £1 000 - FF10 295
  Lord Hood of Avalon as a Midshipman Bombay Harbour in the Background Watercolour (36.5x26cm 14x10in) London 2001

HODGES J.E., of Portsmouth **[1]**
- $4 376 - €4 269 - £2 693 - FF28 000
  Bouquet de fleurs sur un entablement Aquarelle, gouache (52.5x37cm 20x14in) Argenteuil 1999

HODGES Jim 1957 **[2]**
- $35 000 - €39 134 - £23 593 - FF256 704
  A Line to You Plastic (H536cm H211in) New-York 2000
- $7 000 - €7 827 - £4 718 - FF51 340
  A Diary of Flowers (US) Ink (119.5x94cm 47x37in) New-York 2000

HODGES William 1744-1797 **[16]**
- $11 299 - €10 460 - £7 000 - FF68 613
  View of the Rhine Oil/canvas (44x54cm 17x21in) London 1999
- $962 - €970 - £600 - FF6 362
  Select Views in India: View of the Mosque at Mounheer/View of the Toms Aquatint (68.5x52cm 26x20in) London 2000

HODGINS Robert Griffiths 1920 **[6]**
- $4 006 - €4 494 - £2 803 - FF29 478
  «**Office Downtown**» Oil/canvas (120x90cm 47x35in) Cape Town 2001

- $633 - €746 - £437 - FF4 891
  Student Watercolour (41x27cm 16x10in) Cape Town 2000

HODGKIN Eliot 1905-1987 **[96]**
- $4 626 - €4 022 - £2 800 - FF26 383
  Cotton Pods Tempera/board (50x34.5cm 19x13in) London 1999
- $12 806 - €14 879 - £9 000 - FF97 597
  Nine Spring Turnips Oil/panel (28x23cm 11x9in) London 2001
- $569 - €648 - £400 - FF4 249
  Village Study Pencil (29x39cm 11x15in) London 2001

HODGKIN Howard 1932 **[281]**
- $358 094 - €348 522 - £220 000 - FF2 286 152
  Cafeteria at the Grand Palais Oil/panel (124.5x144.5cm 49x56in) London 1999
- $97 129 - €104 260 - £65 000 - FF683 904
  In the Guest Room Oil/panel (40x53cm 15x20in) London 2000
- $30 000 - €28 831 - £18 480 - FF189 117
  Prinzeman's Perspective Oil/wood (28x37cm 11x14in) New-York 1999
- $1 800 - €1 694 - £1 112 - FF11 114
  One Down Color lithograph (91x122cm 35x48in) New-York 1999

HODGKINS Frances 1870-1947 **[70]**
- $37 306 - €35 965 - £23 000 - FF235 913
  Ibiza Oil/canvas (61x72cm 24x28in) London 1999
- $11 975 - €10 260 - £7 200 - FF67 299
  Farmyard in Kent Watercolour/paper (40x54cm 15x21in) Edinburgh 1998
- $2 460 - €2 320 - £1 550 - FF15 221
  Jugs Color lithograph (45.5x61cm 17x24in) London 1999

HODGKINSON Frank George 1919 **[95]**
- $4 304 - €4 147 - £2 660 - FF27 203
  Shikara Lane Oil/canvas (82x196cm 32x77in) Sydney 1999
- $1 400 - €1 544 - £931 - FF10 125
  Day's End Oil/board (69x60cm 27x23in) Melbourne 2000
- $840 - €793 - £523 - FF5 204
  Koongara, kakadu Gouache/paper (55x64cm 21x25in) Sydney 1999
- $113 - €107 - £70 - FF700
  Rainbow Serpent Lithograph (35x49.5cm 13x19in) Sydney 1999

HODGSON David 1798-1864 **[19]**
- $9 533 - €8 703 - £5 800 - FF57 086
  Lower Bridge Street, Chester Oil/canvas (53.5x76.5cm 21x30in) London 1998

HODGSON Frank XX **[1]**
- $4 013 - €3 724 - £2 500 - FF24 429
  Nudes Watercolour, gouache (53x36cm 20x14in) London 1999

HODGSON George 1847-1921 **[10]**
- $1 303 - €1 512 - £900 - FF9 921
  Bridge over the Dochart River, Perthshire Watercolour/paper (36x53.5cm 14x21in) London 2000

HODGSON John Evan 1831-1895 **[12]**
- $18 000 - €19 786 - £11 534 - FF129 787
  Arab Prisoners Oil/canvas (94x185.5cm 37x73in) New-York 2000
- $466 - €553 - £340 - FF3 629
  Sailor and a group of Arab figures seated by a doorway to a temple Ink (27.5x22cm 10x8in) London 2001

HODGSON Olliver Ussison 1810-1878 **[1]**
- $13 278 - €12 995 - **£8 500** - FF85 244
  The Brig British Queen off the Coast at Whitehaven Oil/canvas (66x91cm 25x35in) London 1999

HODGSON William J. XIX-XX **[3]**
- $481 - €468 - **£300** - FF3 067
  In Full Cry Watercolour (22.5x33cm 8x12in) London 1999

HÖDICKE Karl Horst 1938 **[63]**
- $13 936 - €15 288 - **£9 466** - FF100 281
  Defaka Acryl/Leinwand (179.7x150cm 70x59in) Berlin 2000
- $3 101 - €3 068 - **£1 933** - FF20 123
  Drei Kinderköpfe Acryl (60.5x89.5cm 23x35in) Berlin 1999
- $1 300 - €1 534 - **£917** - FF10 061
  Ohne Titel Gouache/paper (89x60.5cm 35x23in) Köln 2001

HODIENER Hugo Hodina 1886-1955 **[30]**
- $1 143 - €1 090 - **£696** - FF7 150
  Vorfrühling im Gesäuse Eingang Gouache/paper (68.5x60.5cm 26x23in) Wien 1999

HODINA Karl 1935 **[15]**
- $2 136 - €2 035 - **£1 304** - FF13 347
  Die Kirschenesser Indian ink (36x30.5cm 14x12in) Wien 1999

HODLER Ferdinand 1853-1918 **[467]**
- $251 145 - €295 352 - **£180 090** - FF1 937 385
  Giulia Leonardi in ganzer Figur, Bewegte Figur für «Das Blühen» Öl/Leinwand (158x88cm 62x34in) Bern 2001
- $185 640 - €187 060 - **£115 710** - FF1 227 030
  Bach bei Néris Öl/Leinwand (89x68cm 35x26in) Zürich 2000
- $24 640 - €28 798 - **£17 591** - FF188 905
  Studie zur Einmütigkeit Oil/paper/canvas (47x22cm 18x8in) Zürich 2001
- $2 770 - €3 134 - **£1 937** - FF20 555
  Zwei nach links schreitende Frauen Pencil/paper (38x27cm 14x10in) St. Gallen 2001
- $375 - €375 - **£235** - FF2 462
  Jenaer Student Lithographie (62x49cm 24x19in) Zofingen 1999

HODSON John XX **[2]**
- $7 958 - €8 595 - **£5 500** - FF56 378
  «Brummagen» Bronze (H26cm H10in) London 2001

HODSON Samuel John 1836-1908 **[11]**
- $1 062 - €944 - **£649** - FF6 195
  The Hotel de Ville, Brussels Watercolour (75x52.5cm 29x20in) London 1999

HODSON William Stephen 1821-1858 **[1]**
- $2 789 - €2 554 - **£1 700** - FF16 754
  Elephants being released from a kraal, India Watercolour (67.5x101.5cm 26x39in) London 1999

HOEBER Arthur 1854-1915 **[28]**
- $6 500 - €7 198 - **£4 408** - FF47 219
  Connecticut Marsh Oil/canvas (30x76cm 12x30in) New-York 2000
- $1 400 - €1 576 - **£964** - FF10 335
  The Tree in the Meadow Oil/canvas (40.5x30.5cm 15x12in) Philadelphia PA 2001

HOECH Anna 1889-1978 **[2]**
- $3 195 - €2 999 - **£1 974** - FF19 675
  Visage masqué Collage/carton (12x10cm 4x3in) Genève 1999

HOECKE van den Gaspar 1585-c.1648 **[15]**
- $42 400 - €48 052 - **£28 800** - FF315 200
  Bodegón con dos personajes, canasta de frutas y verduras Oleo/lienzo (163x209cm 64x82in) Madrid 2000
- $17 671 - €19 813 - **£12 000** - FF129 968
  The Raising of Lazarus Oil/panel (63x100.5cm 24x39in) London 2000
- $24 208 - €24 392 - **£15 088** - FF160 000
  La Parabole du fils prodigue Huile/panneau (27.5x40cm 10x15in) Paris 2000

HOECKE van der Jan 1611-1651 **[8]**
- $74 753 - €75 325 - **£46 593** - FF494 098
  Allegorie der vier Elemente Öl/Leinwand (237x183cm 93x72in) Zürich 2000
- $15 862 - €15 988 - **£9 900** - FF104 874
  Eine Allegorie: die Zeit und die Warheit siegen über Neid und Lüge Oil/panel (32.5x37.5cm 12x14in) Wien 2000

HOEDT Jan Hendrik Willem 1825-1868 **[5]**
- $4 804 - €4 538 - **£2 906** - FF29 766
  Estuary Scene Oil/canvas (47.5x65.5cm 18x25in) Amsterdam 1999
- $15 827 - €14 159 - **£9 481** - FF92 880
  A Beachscene with Moored Vessels on the Shore/A Summer Landscape Oil/panel (22x30cm 8x11in) Amsterdam 1998

HOEF van der Abraham 1611/12-1666 **[20]**
- $29 529 - €33 234 - **£20 364** - FF218 003
  Rast von der Eberjagd Öl/Leinwand (100x129.5cm 39x50in) Bremen 2000
- $7 125 - €8 093 - **£5 000** - FF53 087
  Cavalry Engagement Oil/panel (51.5x83.5cm 20x32in) London 2001

HOEFFLER Adolf Joh. 1825-1898 **[19]**
- $4 233 - €5 002 - **£3 000** - FF32 809
  A Cottage by a Stream Oil/canvas (61x47.5cm 24x18in) London 2000
- $1 957 - €2 147 - **£1 329** - FF14 086
  Italienischer See Öl/Leinwand (21x34cm 8x13in) Düsseldorf 2000
- $2 138 - €2 045 - **£1 302** - FF13 415
  Der Schwanheimer Eichen Pencil (42x61.5cm 16x24in) Stuttgart 1999

HOEFNAGEL Georgius Hufnagel 1542-1600 **[11]**
- $382 755 - €434 480 - **£265 905** - FF2 850 000
  Allégorie des quatre saisons Aquarelle/papier (12.5x18.5cm 4x7in) Clermont-Ferrand 2001
- $466 - €511 - **£316** - FF3 353
  Stilleben mit Maus, Zitrone, Erdbeere, weiteren Pflanzen und Insekten Kupferstich (15.8x20.9cm 6x8in) Berlin 2000

HOEHME Gerhard 1920-1989 **[229]**
- $12 158 - €13 805 - **£8 448** - FF90 555
  «Gouache obscure» Mixed media (100x65cm 39x25in) München 2001
- $2 149 - €2 556 - **£1 532** - FF16 769
  Im Gelb liegend Öl/Karton (15.5x52.5cm 6x20in) München 2000
- $1 348 - €1 534 - **£935** - FF10 061
  Ohne Titel Aquarell/Papier (28.3x19.5cm 11x7in) Hamburg 2000
- $486 - €511 - **£307** - FF3 353
  Vibrierendes Leben Etching, aquatint in colors (71.7x49.5cm 28x19in) Stuttgart 2000

HOEK van Hans 1947 [17]
- $8 456 - €9 076 - **£5 658** - FF59 532
  Black Water Oil/canvas (203x278cm 79x109in)
  Amsterdam 2000
- $2 289 - €2 723 - **£1 632** - FF17 859
  Zwangere vrouw Watercolour (58.5x76.5cm 23x30in)
  Amsterdam 2000

HOEKSEMA Daan 1879-? [3]
- $1 002 - €1 143 - **£699** - FF7 500
  «Cycloïde Simplex, Amsterdam, Holland» Affiche
  (115x52.5cm 45x20in) Paris 2001

HOEN Pieter Cornelis 1814-1880 [23]
- $2 850 - €3 323 - **£1 974** - FF21 800
  **Holländische Winterlandschaft mit Windmühle
  und Personenstaffage** Öl/Leinwand (50x67cm
  19x26in) Buxtehude 2000

HOENIGER Paul 1865-1924 [13]
- $7 269 - €7 056 - **£4 526** - FF46 283
  Kaiser-Wilhelm-Brücke und Schloss, Berlin
  Öl/Leinwand (73.5x92cm 28x36in) Berlin 1999
- $3 002 - €3 579 - **£2 140** - FF23 477
  Berliner Strassenszene bei Nacht Öl/Leinwand
  (41x33cm 16x12in) Berlin 2000

HOENTSCHEL Georges 1855-1915 [3]
- $1 257 - €1 220 - **£796** - FF8 000
  **Coupe japonisante à panse évasée à décor en
  léger relief** Céramique (H8cm H3in) Paris 1999

HOEPFFNER Marta 1912-2000 [21]
- $1 200 - €1 381 - **£818** - FF9 062
  Fotogramm, Hommage à DeFalla (Balletmusik)
  Gelatin silver print (29.5x21cm 11x8in) New-York 2000

HOERLE Heinrich 1895-1936 [53]
- $10 387 - €12 271 - **£7 336** - FF80 493
  Unvollendetes Selbstbildnis Öl/Leinwand
  (46x34.5cm 18x13in) Köln 2001
- $4 603 - €5 368 - **£3 231** - FF35 215
  Porträt Papa Dierse Pencil/paper (54.8x49cm
  21x19in) Köln 2000

HOERMAN Carl 1885-1955 [11]
- $1 325 - €1 113 - **£779** - FF7 300
  Superstition Mountain Oil/canvas (71x78cm
  28x31in) Hendersonville NC 1998

HOERTZ Fred J. XX [5]
- $1 040 - €1 067 - **£650** - FF7 000
  «Europe - White Star» Poster (104x68cm 40x26in)
  London 2001

HOET Gerard I 1648-1733 [61]
- $7 210 - €7 267 - **£4 500** - FF47 670
  Bildnis eines vornehmen Herrn Öl/Leinwand
  (65x54.5cm 25x21in) Wien 2000
- $4 519 - €4 192 - **£2 800** - FF27 498
  Diana and Actaeon Oil/panel (36x28.5cm 14x11in)
  London 1999
- $743 - €862 - **£513** - FF5 655
  The Finding of Moses Pencil (24x36cm 9x14in)
  Amsterdam 2000

HOETERICKX Emile 1858-1923 [18]
- $3 008 - €3 421 - **£2 111** - FF22 438
  Le marché du Sablon Huile/panneau (18x23.5cm
  7x9in) Bruxelles 2001
- $832 - €992 - **£604** - FF6 504
  In de haven te duinkerken Watercolour/paper
  (26.5x38cm 10x14in) Lokeren 2000

HOETGER Bernhard 1874-1949 [91]
- $11 182 - €13 294 - **£7 748** - FF87 201
  Tänzerin Sent M'Ahesa Bronze (H146cm H57in)
  Bremen 2000
- $3 924 - €3 325 - **£2 344** - FF21 812
  «Bettler - Le Mendiant» Bronze (H26.5cm H10in)
  Bremen 1998
- $1 135 - €1 278 - **£782** - FF8 384
  Kauernder weiblicher Akt Indian ink (39.5x54.5cm
  15x21in) Bremen 2000
- $494 - €460 - **£304** - FF3 018
  Der Einäuige No. 1 Radierung (32.5x24.6cm 12x9in)
  Hamburg 1999

HOEVENAAR William Pieter 1808-1863 [8]
- $6 392 - €7 260 - **£4 484** - FF47 625
  Soldiers playing Backgammon in a Tavern
  Oil/panel (34x46.5cm 13x18in) Amsterdam 2001

HOEY de Nicolas act.c.1590-1611/12 [1]
- $19 648 - €18 221 - **£12 000** - FF119 522
  **Joseph Distributing the Harvest to the
  Egyptians and Benjamin** Oil/panel (74x158cm
  29x62in) London 1998

HOEYDONCK van Paul 1925 [131]
- $839 - €942 - **£570** - FF6 178
  Composition Technique mixte (125x94cm 49x37in)
  Bruxelles 2000
- $729 - €793 - **£480** - FF5 203
  Petit observatoire de l'espace Assemblage
  (20x25cm 7x9in) Lokeren 2000
- $450 - €371 - **£264** - FF2 436
  Planète Zafir Technique mixte/papier (61x61cm
  24x24in) Antwerpen 1998

HOF van den Gijs Jacobs 1889-1965 [2]
- $10 936 - €12 706 - **£7 686** - FF83 344
  Female nude rising from the waves Sculpture,
  wood (H35cm H13in) Amsterdam 2000

HOFBAUER Josef, Snr. 1907-1998 [162]
- $599 - €511 - **£361** - FF3 353
  «Entenfamilie am Weiher mit Blick auf
  Dorfsilhouette» Oil/panel (20.5x25.5cm 8x10in)
  Kempten 1998

HOFBAUER Ludwig 1843-? [11]
- $1 187 - €1 125 - **£722** - FF7 378
  Der Stephansdom in Wien Watercolour (18x14.8cm
  7x5in) München 1999

HÖFER Candida 1944 [51]
- $1 158 - €1 380 - **£825** - FF9 055
  Wartesaal Düsseldorf Cibachrome print (50.6x61cm
  19x24in) München 2000

HOFER Carl 1878-1955 [739]
- $107 692 - €100 419 - **£65 000** - FF658 703
  Self-Portrait with Demons Oil/canvas (140.5x120cm
  55x47in) London 2001
- $49 635 - €46 363 - **£30 000** - FF304 119
  Feldblumen in weissem Henkelkrug Oil/canvas
  (49x55.5cm 19x21in) London 1999
- $23 958 - €23 008 - **£14 789** - FF157 925
  Mädchenkopf im Profil Öl/Karton (43x34.5cm
  16x13in) München 1999
- $2 144 - €2 556 - **£1 529** - FF16 769
  Zwei Männer am Tisch Ink (50.5x35cm 19x13in)
  Berlin 2000
- $342 - €383 - **£237** - FF2 515
  Abend Lithographie (39x32cm 15x12in) Köln 2001

HÖFER Heinrich 1825-1878 **[14]**

$4 763 - €5 113 - **£3 188** - FF33 539
Ziegenhirte vor einer Mühle im Alpental
Öl/Leinwand (42x52cm 16x20in) Köln 2000

$13 404 - €15 339 - **£9 219** - FF100 617
Pferdeschlitten und Spaziergänger auf dem Eis des Flüsschens Oil/panel (32.5x41cm 12x16in) München 2000

HOFER Ignaz 1790-1862 **[2]**

$4 989 - €5 501 - **£3 378** - FF36 084
Prospekt fra de östrigske alper med udsigt til byen Maria Zell Oil/canvas (74x111cm 29x43in) Vejle 2000

HOFER Ueli 1952 **[6]**

$402 - €455 - **£283** - FF2 982
Ohne Titel Silhouette (9x9cm 3x3in) Bern 2001

HOFF Charles 1905-1975 **[10]**

$2 500 - €2 609 - **£1 581** - FF17 114
Rubin (Hurricane) Carter VS. James Carter, Madison Square Garden Photograph (19x24cm 7x9in) New-York 2000

HOFF George Rayner 1894-1937 **[4]**

$4 199 - €4 928 - **£2 963** - FF32 324
Amihion Antiopa Bas-relief (61.5x36cm 24x14in) Melbourne 2000

HOFF Jakob 1838-1892 **[3]**

$183 000 - €181 681 - **£114 250** - FF1 191 750
Unter den Linden, Tanzfest in Schwälmer Trachten Öl/Leinwand (97x160cm 38x62in) Wien 1999

HOFF Karl Heinrich 1838-1890 **[8]**

$9 964 - €8 185 - **£5 787** - FF53 691
Sehnsucht Öl/Leinwand (125x90cm 49x35in) Berlin 1998

HOFF Tor 1925-1976 **[11]**

$4 187 - €4 648 - **£2 918** - FF30 487
Komposisjon Acrylic/panel (83x122cm 32x48in) Oslo 2001

HOFF van't Adrianus Johannes 1893-1939 **[24]**

$145 - €136 - **£90** - FF893
«La Hollande Alkmaar, Marché au fromage» Poster (34x52cm 13x20in) Oostwoud 1999

HOFFBAUER Charles C.J. 1875-1957 **[73]**

$11 000 - €10 664 - **£6 811** - FF69 952
Cityscape Oil/canvas (60x76cm 24x30in) Englewood NJ 1999

$2 600 - €2 791 - **£1 739** - FF18 306
Dance Hall Oil/canvas/board (19.5x24.5cm 7x9in) New-York 2000

HOFFENREICH Ludwig XX **[7]**

$945 - €1 125 - **£675** - FF7 378
Wiener Aktionisten Vintage gelatin silver print (24x30cm 9x11in) Berlin 2000

HOFFMAN Frank B. 1888-1958 **[20]**

$32 500 - €34 885 - **£21 749** - FF228 832
The Jockey's Instructions Before the Point to Point Oil/canvas (61x78.5cm 24x30in) New-York 2000

$6 000 - €7 052 - **£4 159** - FF46 256
Night Herding Oil/masonite (30.5x40.5cm 12x15in) Beverly-Hills CA 2000

HOFFMAN Harry Leslie 1874-1966 **[28]**

$1 600 - €1 552 - **£991** - FF10 180
Docked the Caribean Oil/canvas/board (20x25cm 8x10in) New-York 2000

HOFFMAN Irwin D. 1901-1989 **[35]**

$170 - €174 - **£106** - FF1 143
New York 1930 Etching (9x16cm 3x6in) Cleveland OH 2000

HOFFMAN Malvina Cornell 1887-1966 **[47]**

$3 000 - €2 797 - **£1 860** - FF18 349
Shivering Girl Bronze (H24cm H9in) New-York 1999

HOFFMAN Richard Peter 1911 **[4]**

$125 - €135 - **£84** - FF883
Winding Stream, Spring Landscape Watercolour/paper (63x51cm 25x20in) Hatfield PA 2000

HOFFMANN Anker 1904-1985 **[47]**

$895 - €940 - **£564** - FF6 167
Ung pige, portraetbuste Bronze (H31cm H12in) Köbenhavn 2000

HOFFMANN Anton 1863-1938 **[50]**

$1 125 - €1 097 - **£692** - FF7 199
Outside the Tavern Oil/panel (40x60cm 16x24in) Cleveland OH 1999

$1 535 - €1 534 - **£960** - FF10 061
Rast im Manöver Öl/Leinwand (32x42cm 12x16in) Köln 1999

$289 - €332 - **£204** - FF2 180
Schiessübung Ink (11.5x18cm 4x7in) Zwiesel 2001

HOFFMANN August 1810-1872 **[1]**

$9 500 - €9 118 - **£5 955** - FF59 807
Game of Dice Oil/canvas (71x101.5cm 27x39in) New-York 1999

HOFFMANN Dezo XX **[5]**

$625 - €588 - **£380** - FF3 856
Portrait of Jimi Hendrix Photograph (29x39.5cm 11x15in) London 1999

HOFFMANN Georges Johannes 1833-1873 **[14]**

$4 112 - €3 857 - **£2 541** - FF25 301
Full-Rigged Koff in a Breeze, a Paddle Steamer beyond Oil/canvas (36x50cm 14x19in) Amsterdam 1999

$2 021 - €1 906 - **£1 252** - FF12 501
Ships near the Coast Oil/panel (25.5x18.5cm 10x7in) Amsterdam 1999

HOFFMANN Hans c.1530/50-1591/2 **[5]**

$2 400 000 - €2 567 254 - **£1 636 320** - FF16 840 080
Hare in a Forest Oil/panel (157.5x198cm 62x77in) New-York 2001

$229 236 - €212 579 - **£140 000** - FF1 394 428
The Head of a Bearded Man, Turned to the left Ink (27.5x21.5cm 10x8in) London 1998

HOFFMANN Heinrich 1816-1891 **[1]**

$2 852 - €2 659 - **£1 760** - FF17 440
Marktplatz in Nördlingen Aquarell/Papier (34x31.5cm 13x12in) Hamburg 1999

HOFFMANN Helmut 1928-1998 **[7]**

$3 997 - €4 499 - **£2 754** - FF29 514
Akt mit grünem Strumpf Öl/Leinwand (118x80cm 46x31in) München 1999

HOFFMANN Josef 1831-1904 **[20]**

$3 292 - €3 758 - **£2 287** - FF24 654
Italiensk landskab med kvinder og börn Oil/canvas (76x100cm 29x39in) Köbenhavn 2000

HOFFMANN Josef 1870-1956 **[38]**

$487 - €509 - **£307** - FF3 336
Tulpen Ink/paper (29.5x20.7cm 11x8in) Wien 2000

H

HOFFMANN Oskar Adolfovitch 1851-1913 **[14]**
- $3 938 - €3 374 - **£2 367** - FF22 131
  Dorfstrasse in Estland Öl/Leinwand (67x121cm 26x47in) Köln 1998
- $2 920 - €2 859 - **£1 796** - FF18 754
  Mies ja piippu Oil/canvas (41x27cm 16x10in) Helsinki 1999

HOFFMANN-FALLERSLEBEN Franz 1855-1927 **[41]**
- $1 298 - €1 534 - **£920** - FF10 061
  Heidelandschaft Öl/Leinwand (76x131cm 29x51in) Ahlden 2000
- $1 092 - €1 125 - **£688** - FF7 378
  Vögel in winterlicher Waldlandschaft Oil/panel (23.5x43cm 9x16in) München 2000

HOFFMANN-TEDESCO Julia 1843-? **[2]**
- $2 596 - €3 068 - **£1 840** - FF20 123
  Der Ruf der Sirenen Pastell/Papier (56x96cm 22x37in) Ahlden 2000

HOFFMEISTER C.L. XIX **[4]**
- $32 850 - €30 678 - **£20 274** - FF201 234
  Ansicht von Wien Öl/Metall (53x77cm 20x30in) Köln 1999

HOFFMÜLLER Reinhard 1894-1975 **[12]**
- $1 200 - €1 024 - **£723** - FF6 715
  «Alexander - Buffet» Poster (95.5x74cm 37x29in) New-York 1998

HOFKER Willem Gerard 1902-1981 **[176]**
- $4 323 - €4 084 - **£2 697** - FF26 789
  Clown Oil/canvas (100.5x75cm 39x29in) Amsterdam 1999
- $7 125 - €5 978 - **£4 180** - FF39 216
  Woman with a Basket Charcoal (48x29.5cm 18x11in) Singapore 1998
- $478 - €544 - **£332** - FF3 571
  Sleeping Balinese Beauty Mezzotint (21.9x15.2cm 8x5in) Haarlem 2000

HOFKUNST Alfred 1942 **[73]**
- $1 485 - €1 496 - **£925** - FF9 816
  Käse-Mäuse Objet (26x31x18cm 10x12x7in) Zürich 2000
- $685 - €628 - **£418** - FF4 121
  Marmorblock Crayon (69x50cm 27x19in) Zürich 1999
- $146 - €170 - **£101** - FF1 118
  Huhn und Ei Etching, aquatint (49x63cm 19x24in) Bern 2000

HOFLAND Thomas Christopher 1777-1843 **[10]**
- $23 385 - €26 074 - **£16 000** - FF171 035
  Fisherman Loch Awe Oil/panel (27.5x41cm 10x16in) Perthshire 2000

HOFLEHNER Rudolf 1916-1995 **[42]**
- $143 - €145 - **£89** - FF953
  Figuren im Raum XII Radierung (65x65cm 25x25in) Wien 2000

HOFLER Max 1892-1963 **[65]**
- $721 - €653 - **£449** - FF4 284
  Summer Clouds, Brightwell, Berkshire Oil/canvas (51x61cm 20x24in) London 1999
- $300 - €266 - **£183** - FF1 748
  Landscape Oil/board (38x30cm 15x12in) New-Orleans LA 1999

HÖFLINGER Albert 1855-1936 **[5]**
- $1 884 - €2 151 - **£1 328** - FF14 110
  Interieur mit junger Dame und Papagei Öl/Leinwand (43x35cm 16x13in) Bern 2001

HOFMAN Pieter Adrianus H. 1885-1965 **[4]**
- $1 244 - €1 452 - **£852** - FF9 525
  «Mustermesse Utrecht» Poster (96x61.5cm 37x24in) Hoorn 2000

HOFMAN Vlastislav 1884-1964 **[32]**
- $289 - €273 - **£180** - FF1 793
  Kirilov Pencil/paper (34x21cm 13x8in) Praha 2000

HOFMAN Wlastimil 1881-1970 **[218]**
- $17 129 - €17 264 - **£10 682** - FF113 246
  Madone des orphelins Oil/canvas (179x126cm 70x49in) Warszawa 2000
- $4 499 - €4 488 - **£2 808** - FF29 438
  Deux enfants Oil/panel (49.8x35.5cm 19x13in) Warszawa 1999
- $1 705 - €1 905 - **£1 190** - FF12 497
  Satyr Huile/carton (26x33cm 10x12in) Warszawa 2001

HOFMANN Charles C. 1821-1882 **[4]**
- $230 000 - €223 234 - **£143 198** - FF1 464 318
  My Home Oil/metal (40x60cm 16x24in) Downington PA 1999

HOFMANN Egon 1884-1972 **[32]**
- $244 - €291 - **£174** - FF1 906
  Gschnierkar Coloured pencils/paper (35x24cm 13x9in) Linz 2000
- $85 - €94 - **£56** - FF619
  Winterlandschaft Woodcut (23x13cm 9x5in) Linz 2000

HOFMANN Hans 1880-1966 **[255]**
- $170 000 - €163 472 - **£104 737** - FF1 072 309
  Scotch and Burgundy Oil/canvas/panel (155x103.5cm 61x40in) New-York 1999
- $60 000 - €57 696 - **£36 966** - FF378 462
  Landscape Oil/panel (76x91cm 29x35in) New-York 1999
- $11 000 - €12 299 - **£7 415** - FF80 678
  Untitled Oil/paper/canvas (17.5x27.5cm 6x10in) New-York 2000
- $12 000 - €12 959 - **£8 293** - FF85 006
  Untitled Coloured crayons (72.5x57.5cm 28x22in) New-York 2001
- $15 000 - €17 537 - **£10 540** - FF115 032
  Composition in Blue Screenprint in colors (43.5x36cm 17x14in) New-York 2000

HOFMANN Otto 1907-1994 **[25]**
- $484 - €470 - **£301** - FF3 085
  Ohne Titel Aquarell (44x57.6cm 17x22in) Berlin 1999
- $108 - €112 - **£68** - FF737
  Abstrakte Landschaft Woodcut (25.5x38.9cm 10x15in) Leipzig 2000

HOFMANN Samuel 1592-1648 **[3]**
- $6 122 - €6 013 - **£3 800** - FF39 443
  Portrait of Wilhelm Baudart (1565-1640) Oil/panel (94x71cm 37x27in) London 1999

HOFMANN von Ludwig 1861-1945 **[276]**
- $5 471 - €6 130 - **£3 813** - FF40 208
  Solbadande kvinnor Oil/canvas (74x96cm 29x37in) Stockholm 2001
- $1 028 - €869 - **£611** - FF5 700
  «Warmbad» Pastel (21.5x32cm 8x12in) Bremen 1998
- $166 - €179 - **£111** - FF1 173
  Reiter Woodcut (38.7x49.8cm 15x19in) Köln 2000

HOFMANN Walter 1906-1973 **[26]**
- $237 - €254 - **£161** - FF1 668
  «Österreich» Poster (95x63cm 37x24in) Wien 2001

H

HOFMANN Werner 1935 **[6]**

$1 950 - €1 646 - **£1 144** - FF10 794
Blick aus dem Fenster mit Blumenvase
Aquarell/Papier (54.3x75.8cm 21x29in) Berlin 1998

HOFMEIER Karl 1858-1934 **[2]**

$2 200 - €2 376 - **£1 520** - FF15 584
The Threat of Rain Oil/canvas/board (29x21cm
11x8in) New-York 2001

HOFMEISTER Johannes 1721-1800 **[5]**

$5 180 - €5 845 - **£3 644** - FF38 342
«L'Au = près qu'Isle au bord du Lac de Zuric»
Radierung (16x24cm 6x9in) Bern 2001

HOFMEISTER Johannes 1914-1990 **[139]**

$6 723 - €7 241 - **£4 627** - FF47 498
Figurer i landskab Oil/masonite (103x122cm
40x48in) København 2001

$1 999 - €2 015 - **£1 286** - FF13 218
Personer i bakket landskab Oil/canvas (66x87cm
25x34in) København 2000

$559 - €564 - **£349** - FF3 701
Figurer i landskab Oil/paper (26x31cm 10x12in)
København 2000

HOFNER Johann Baptist 1832-1913 **[6]**

$11 985 - €13 613 - **£8 409** - FF89 298
A Flock of Sheep in an extensive Landscape
Oil/canvas (58x100.5cm 22x39in) Amsterdam 2001

$21 910 - €19 941 - **£13 689** - FF130 802
**Junges Mädchen mit Schafen und Ziegen im
Stall bei der Fütterung** Öl/Leinwand (26x40cm
10x15in) München 2000

HOFSTATTER Osias 1905-1995 **[25]**

$400 - €474 - **£291** - FF3 110
Nude Gouache (33.5x38.5cm 13x15in) Tel Aviv 2001

HOGAI Kano 1828-1888 **[2]**

$45 000 - €46 817 - **£28 638** - FF307 098
Ryojusen Ink (133x88cm 52x34in) New-York 2000

HOGAN John 1800-1858 **[2]**

$15 449 - €14 094 - **£9 500** - FF92 452
**Bust, Head and Shoulders, Rev. Theobald
Matthew (1770-1861)** Marble (H58cm H22in) Co.
Kilkenny 1999

HOGAN Ricardo 1843-1891 **[1]**

$4 300 - €4 985 - **£3 000** - FF32 700
Mulher no jardim Acuarela/papel (28.5x17.5cm
11x6in) Lisboa 2001

HOGARTH Paul 1917 **[21]**

$474 - €558 - **£340** - FF3 657
The Blacksmith Ink (36x27cm 14x11in) Tunbridge-
Wells, Kent 2001

$425 - €504 - **£300** - FF3 305
«The Hermitage» Color lithograph (48x66cm
18x25in) London 2000

HOGARTH William 1697-1764 **[293]**

$115 201 - €133 645 - **£82 000** - FF876 653
**Mary Hogarth, Bust-length in a green & brown
Dress/Anne Hogarth** Oil/canvas/panel (46.5x41.5cm
18x16in) London 2001

$52 300 - €56 140 - **£35 000** - FF368 256
**Portrait of a Gentleman, standing in a
Landscape with a Dog** Oil/canvas (40x33cm
15x12in) London 2000

$279 - €253 - **£170** - FF1 660
**An Election Entertainment/Canvassing for
Voate/The Polling/...** Engraving (43x55cm 16x21in)
Solihull, West-Midlands 1998

HOGENBERGH Franz ?-1592 **[16]**

$353 - €344 - **£217** - FF2 255
Luxembourg Copper engraving in colors
(34.8x41.3cm 13x16in) Bern 1999

HÖGER Josef 1801-1877 **[33]**

$847 - €799 - **£525** - FF5 243
Baumstamm Aquarell/Papier (31.5x21cm 12x8in)
Wien 1999

HÖGER Rudolf Alfred 1877-1930 **[41]**

$1 951 - €2 035 - **£1 229** - FF13 347
Treffen am Brunnen Öl/Leinwand (74x100cm
29x39in) Wien 2000

HÖGFELDT Robert 1894-1986 **[467]**

$697 - €809 - **£495** - FF5 304
Badande kvinnor Oil/canvas (50x74cm 19x29in)
Stockholm 2000

$408 - €350 - **£239** - FF2 225
Tre skrattande troll i trädet Mixed media (28x27cm
11x10in) Stockholm 1998

$490 - €549 - **£341** - FF3 604
De lyckliga tu Akvarell, gouache/papper (42x51cm
16x20in) Uppsala 2001

HOGGARTH Graham 1882-? **[3]**

$917 - €1 064 - **£650** - FF6 980
«Isle of Man, Travel by GWR» Poster (102x127cm
40x50in) London 2000

HOGGATT William 1880-1961 **[81]**

$5 080 - €5 454 - **£3 400** - FF35 773
Boats by a Shoreline Oil/board (42x40cm 16x15in)
West-Yorkshire 2000

$1 394 - €1 530 - **£900** - FF10 036
Sulby Glen above Tholt-E-Will Oil/board (17x23cm
7x9in) Isle-of-Man 2000

$2 014 - €2 210 - **£1 300** - FF14 497
Top of the Glen Watercolour/paper (13x18cm 5x7in)
Isle-of-Man 2000

HOGLEY Stephen E. 1874-? **[18]**

$1 408 - €1 379 - **£900** - FF9 046
**Mountainous Landscape with Figures and
Cattle by a River** Oil/canvas (61x107cm 24x42in)
Leyburn, North Yorkshire 1999

HÖGLUND Erik Sylvester 1932-1998 **[20]**

$447 - €480 - **£299** - FF3 149
Kvinno- och manshuvud Relief (30x42cm 11x16in)
Stockholm 2000

HOGUET Charles 1821-1870 **[76]**

$4 289 - €5 113 - **£3 058** - FF33 539
In der Bauernküche Öl/Leinwand (75x59cm
29x23in) Köln 2000

$1 367 - €1 534 - **£947** - FF10 061
**Rastendes Fischerpaar vor an den Strand gezo-
genen Booten** Öl/Leinwand (27.5x40.5cm 10x15in)
München 2000

HOGUET Louis XIX **[5]**

$805 - €844 - **£532** - FF5 533
Waldlandschaft mit Holzfällern bei der Arbeit
Oil/panel (22x13cm 8x5in) München 2000

HOHAUS Hermann 1920 **[1]**

$4 074 - €4 489 - **£2 704** - FF29 444
Mother and Child Sculpture (H39.5cm H15in)
Woollahra, Sydney 2001

HOHE Friedrich 1802-1870 **[4]**

$2 862 - €3 221 - **£1 971** - FF21 129
Hirsche in Alpenlandschaft Öl/Leinwand (82x69cm
32x27in) München 2000

HOHENBERG Marguerite 1883-? [3]
🖼 **$1 600** - €1 820 - **£1 109** - FF11 936
   Abstract Composition Gouache/paper (50x33cm 20x13in) Chicago IL 2000

HOHENLEITER Y CASTRO Francisco 1889-1968 [13]
🖼 **$3 410** - €3 304 - **£2 090** - FF21 670
   Caballos y galgos Oleo/lienzo (38.5x52cm 15x20in) Madrid 1999
🖼 **$2 000** - €1 923 - **£1 234** - FF12 616
   «Sevilla» Poster (99x66cm 38x25in) New-York 1999

HOHENSTEIN Adolf, Adolpho 1854-1917 [53]
🖼 **$3 200** - €3 077 - **£1 975** - FF20 186
   «Bitter Campari» Poster (198x100cm 77x39in) New-York 1999

HOHLWEIN Ludwig 1874-1949 [260]
🖼 **$1 266** - €1 329 - **£856** - FF8 720
   Jagdhund mit Beute Pencil (11x15cm 4x5in) Kempten 2001
🖼 **$1 100** - €1 234 - **£763** - FF8 092
   «Sichert euch Wohnungen» Poster (119x84cm 47x33in) New-York 2001

HOHNECK Adolf 1812-1879 [7]
🖼 **$1 667** - €1 789 - **£1 115** - FF11 738
   Hügelige Landschaft mit einer Burgruine Gouache (28x39cm 11x15in) Stuttgart 2000

HÖHNEL Wilhelm 1872-1941 [7]
🖼 **$2 367** - €2 761 - **£1 672** - FF18 114
   Zwei aufgezäumte Zugpferde Öl/Leinwand (36x45cm 14x17in) Salzburg 2000
🖼 **$305** - €363 - **£218** - FF2 383
   Weisser Hengst Öl/Karton (20x14cm 7x5in) Linz 2000

HOHNSTEDT Peter Lanz 1872-1957 [15]
🖼 **$1 200** - €1 152 - **£752** - FF7 554
   California Landscape Oil/canvas (40x50cm 16x20in) Altadena CA 1999
🖼 **$500** - €576 - **£341** - FF3 776
   Poppie Field Oil/board (15x22cm 6x9in) New-Orleans LA 2000

HOHR Franz Xaver Ludwig 1766-1848 [1]
🖼 **$6 539** - €6 403 - **£4 179** - FF42 000
   Joseph le charpentier avec l'enfant Jésus Gouache/papier (27x23cm 10x9in) Marseille 1999

HOIN Claude Jean-Bapt. 1750-1817 [27]
🖼 **$3 799** - €3 506 - **£2 272** - FF23 000
   Portrait d'un pastelliste Huile/toile (24.5x20cm 9x7in) Paris 1999
🖼 **$557** - €665 - **£397** - FF4 360
   Parklandschaft mit einem Tempel Ink/paper (24.7x18.4cm 9x7in) Berlin 2000

HOINKIS Ewald 1897-1960 [37]
📷 **$1 601** - €1 534 - **£989** - FF10 061
   Rückenakt (Jenny Hoinkis) Vintage gelatin silver print (21.5x16.1cm 8x6in) Köln 1999

HOIT Albert G. 1809-1856 [2]
🖼 **$7 500** - €8 747 - **£5 265** - FF57 378
   Amanda Fiske, Aged 5 Oil/canvas (91x71cm 36x28in) Portsmouth NH 2000

HOITSU Sakai 1761-1829 [8]
🖼 **$70 000** - €67 289 - **£43 652** - FF441 385
   Tale of Ise Ink (107.5x40cm 42x15in) New-York 1999

HOKE Giselbert 1927 [27]
🖼 **$1 103** - €1 308 - **£779** - FF8 580
   Liebespaar Charcoal (36x23cm 14x9in) Klagenfurt 2001

🖼 **$385** - €436 - **£269** - FF2 860
   Ohne Titel Lithographie (74x58cm 29x22in) Klagenfurt 2001

HOKEAH Jack 1902-1969 [1]
🖼 **$2 600** - €2 577 - **£1 626** - FF16 904
   Untitled Gouache/paper (17x25.5cm 6x10in) New-York 1999

HOKKEI Totoya 1780-1850 [47]
🖼 **$723** - €716 - **£451** - FF4 695
   Eine auf einer Gartenbank sitzenden Frau, einen Pinsel haltend Woodcut in colors (20.2x17cm 7x6in) Köln 2000

HOKUBA Arisaka, Teisai 1771-1844 [15]
🖼 **$1 793** - €1 925 - **£1 200** - FF12 625
   A Beauty in the Wind Ink (124x57cm 48x22in) London 2000

HOKUSAI Katsushika 1760-1849 [348]
🖼 **$530** - €566 - **£353** - FF3 711
   Seated Kabuki Actor Watercolour/paper (6x5cm 2x1in) Cleveland OH 2000
🖼 **$6 000** - €5 185 - **£3 561** - FF34 013
   Eight Views of the Ryukyu Islands Woodcut (25.5x38cm 10x14in) New-York 1998

HOLAN Karel 1893-1953 [24]
🖼 **$780** - €738 - **£486** - FF4 841
   Motif from Prague Oil/canvas (43x59cm 16x23in) Praha 1999
🖼 **$361** - €342 - **£225** - FF2 241
   Paysage d'hiver avec une maison Huile/carton (18x25cm 7x9in) Praha 2000

HOLBAK Niels 1884-1954 [71]
🖼 **$315** - €269 - **£188** - FF1 763
   Opstilling med blomster Oil/canvas (49x60cm 19x23in) Vejle 1998

HOLBECH Niels Peter 1804-1889 [16]
🖼 **$1 988** - €2 146 - **£1 334** - FF14 078
   Portraet af baron Hans Joost Dahlerup/Portraet Ursula Dahlerup Oil/canvas (63x50cm 24x19in) Köbenhavn 2000

HOLBEIN Hans II 1497-1543 [11]
🖼 **$27 258** - €30 678 - **£18 780** - FF201 234
   Portrait König Heinrich III, von England Oil/panel (21.5x17cm 8x6in) München 2000
🖼 **$140 000** - €149 968 - **£95 606** - FF983 724
   St. Thomas Ink (20.5x10.5cm 8x4in) New-York 2001
🖼 **$63** - €71 - **£44** - FF469
   Ohne Titel Woodcut (6.5x5cm 2x1in) Stuttgart 2001

HOLD Abel 1815-1891 [38]
🖼 **$2 336** - €2 090 - **£140** - FF13 712
   Grouse Oil/panel (42x53cm 16x20in) Perthshire 1998
🖼 **$1 122** - €1 131 - **£700** - FF7 422
   Still Life of Bird's Nest Oil/board (19x24cm 7x9in) London 2000

HOLD B.L. XIX-XX [3]
🖼 **$7 227** - €7 015 - **£4 500** - FF46 016
   Partridge in a Highland Landscape Oil/canvas (51x76cm 20x29in) London 1999

HOLD Tom XIX-XX [13]
🖼 **$1 420** - €1 525 - **£950** - FF10 002
   Apple Blossom, Bird's Nests/Eggs on a Mossy Bank Oil/canvas (25.5x30.5cm 10x12in) London 2000

HOLDCROFT John Hambleton XX [2]
🖼 **$1 618** - €1 524 - **£1 000** - FF9 994
   View across the East River from Manhattan/Shipping between Manhattan Watercolour (28x49cm 11x19in) London 1999

HOLDEN Albert William 1848-1932 [11]
$2 726 - €2 697 - **£1 700** - FF17 692
Storey's Gate and Great George Street looking Towards Big Ben Oil/canvas (30.5x45.5cm 12x17in) London 1999

HOLDER Edward Henry 1847-c.1922 [82]
$1 800 - €1 932 - **£1 204** - FF12 673
Flosmoddyn on the Fairy Fleu on the Conway Oil/canvas (59x89cm 23x35in) Chicago IL 2000
$825 - €881 - **£550** - FF5 776
Landscape with Children by a Stream Oil/canvas (30x40cm 11x15in) Leyburn, North Yorkshire 2000

HOLDER van Frans 1881-1919 [17]
$1 330 - €1 239 - **£820** - FF8 130
Entrée de la vieille demeure Huile/panneau (49.5x70cm 19x27in) Bruxelles 1999

HOLDICH W. Whyte XIX [2]
$1 943 - €2 086 - **£1 300** - FF13 682
Cattle Grazing on Bexley Heath Oil/canvas (28x53.5cm 11x21in) London 2000

HOLDING Edgar Thomas 1870-1952 [41]
$239 - €257 - **£160** - FF1 683
Untitled Watercolour/paper (27x38cm 11x15in) Aylsham, Norfolk 2000

HOLDING Henry James 1833-1872 [11]
$497 - €460 - **£300** - FF3 017
The Kiss Watercolour (37x54.5cm 14x21in) Billingshurst, West-Sussex 1999

HOLDREDGE Ransome Gillette 1836-1899 [31]
$4 500 - €4 155 - **£2 802** - FF27 253
Mt. Diabolo Oil/canvas (76x127cm 30x50in) Oakland CA 1999
$3 800 - €4 191 - **£2 573** - FF27 489
Western Settlement Oil/board (21x47cm 8x18in) New-York 1999

HOLDSTOCK Alfred Worsley 1820-1901 [39]
$721 - €822 - **£498** - FF5 393
Gatineau River Pastel/paper (34x56.5cm 13x22in) Montréal 2000

HOLE William Brassey 1846-1917 [20]
$2 566 - €2 586 - **£1 600** - FF16 965
Lesson in Astronomy Oil/canvas (35x44.5cm 13x17in) London 2000

HOLGATE Edwin Headley 1892-1977 [71]
$24 348 - €27 543 - **£17 032** - FF180 671
Portrait of a Woman Oil/canvas (65x53.5cm 25x21in) Toronto 2001
$5 464 - €5 245 - **£3 426** - FF34 403
Over the Top Oil/board (20x25cm 7x9in) Montréal 1999
$1 158 - €1 113 - **£713** - FF7 299
Portrait Study Charcoal/paper (35x28cm 13x11in) Vancouver, BC. 1999
$848 - €841 - **£530** - FF5 515
Untitled Engraving (17x11.5cm 6x4in) Calgary, Alberta 1999

HOLGATE Thomas W. XIX-XX [6]
$759 - €809 - **£500** - FF5 305
Bridge on the Thames Oil/canvas/board (24x34cm 9x13in) Billingshurst, West-Sussex 2000

HOLIDAY Gilbert Joseph 1879-1937 [42]
$2 443 - €2 224 - **£1 500** - FF14 590
The End of the Holidays, The White Cliffs of Old England again Pastel/paper (29.5x24.5cm 11x9in) Channel-Islands 1999

HOLIDAY Henry James 1839-1927 [25]
$495 - €574 - **£350** - FF3 764
An Extensive Wooded Landscape Watercolour/paper (13.5x22cm 5x8in) London 2000

HOLL Francis 1815-1884 [6]
$316 - €361 - **£220** - FF2 370
The Railway Station, after William Powell Frith Engraving (51x111cm 20x43in) London 2000

HOLL Frank 1845-1888 [8]
$3 000 - €2 938 - **£1 933** - FF19 274
Contemplation Oil/canvas (38x26cm 14x10in) New-York 1999

HÖLL Werner 1898-1984 [27]
$217 - €256 - **£150** - FF1 676
Ohne Titel Woodcut in colors (62x88cm 24x34in) Stuttgart 2000

HOLLAENDER Alfonso 1845-1923 [34]
$2 000 - €2 073 - **£1 200** - FF13 600
Strada di paese Olio/tavoletta (24x36cm 9x14in) Milano 1999
$1 500 - €1 555 - **£900** - FF10 200
Frate che suona l'organo Carboncino (59x42cm 23x16in) Prato 2000

HOLLAIN N.F.J. 1761-? [1]
$3 574 - €4 090 - **£2 458** - FF26 831
In der Bauernküche sitzt eine junge Mutter beim Rübenschälen Öl/Leinwand (47.5x54.5cm 18x21in) München 2000

HOLLAMS Florence Mabel 1877-1963 [141]
$2 800 - €3 257 - **£2 000** - FF21 363
«Painter's Joy», a dark brown Hunter in a Paddock Oil/canvas (45.5x61cm 17x24in) London 2001
$2 661 - €3 095 - **£1 900** - FF20 300
«John», a chesnut Hunter Oil/panel (33.5x39.5cm 13x15in) London 2001

HOLLAND James 1799/1800-1870 [177]
$4 038 - €4 747 - **£2 800** - FF31 136
Edinburgh, The Royal Mile Oil/panel (58.5x46.5cm 23x18in) Edinburgh 2000
$1 819 - €1 586 - **£1 100** - FF10 405
The Grand Canal, Venice Oil/board (31.5x32cm 12x12in) London 1998
$2 323 - €2 050 - **£1 400** - FF13 448
Still Life of Roses in a Vase Watercolour (33.5x25cm 13x9in) London 1998

HOLLAND John XIX [14]
$578 - €681 - **£400** - FF4 468
Peel Harbour, Isle of Man Oil/board (25x40cm 10x16in) Grantham, Lincolnshire 2000
$2 000 - €1 731 - **£1 206** - FF11 357
Fishing Smacks Offshore with a Dinghy Black chalk (89x152.5cm 35x60in) San-Francisco CA 1998

HOLLAND John, Snr. act.1831-1879 [29]
$1 400 - €1 576 - **£964** - FF10 335
Gathering Fuel Oil/canvas (61x91.5cm 24x36in) Philadelphia PA 2000
$1 740 - €1 679 - **£1 100** - FF11 013
Figures at an Inn, Evening Oil/canvas (25.5x35.5cm 10x13in) London 1999

HOLLAND Kiff XX [7]
$272 - €259 - **£170** - FF1 701
Brunch Watercolour/paper (23x30.5cm 9x12in) Vancouver, BC. 1999

HOLLAND Sidney XIX **[1]**
$4 195 - €4 029 - **£2 600** - FF26 428
Old Mill on the Thames/Millhouse in a Sunlit
Clearing Oil/canvas (35.5x58cm 13x22in) London
1999

HOLLAND Thomas 1799-1870 **[17]**
$970 - €1 131 - **£680** - FF7 418
Botanical Studies Watercolour (11.5x17.5cm 4x6in)
Crewkerne, Somerset 2000

HOLLANDER Hendrik 1823-1884 **[20]**
$2 928 - €3 068 - **£1 936** - FF20 123
Rembrandt malt die Nachtwache Öl/Leinwand
(102x80cm 40x31in) München 2000

HOLLAR VON PRACHNA Wenceslaus 1607-1677
[258]
$15 433 - €18 354 - **£11 000** - FF120 397
View of the Town and Fort, from the South-
east/View from the Bowling Pencil (19.5x62cm
7x24in) London 2000
$558 - €485 - **£336** - FF3 184
Navis Bellica Hollandica Radierung (14x23.1cm
5x9in) Berlin 1998

HOLLAUS Bartholomäus 1877-? **[4]**
$3 531 - €2 985 - **£2 100** - FF19 578
The Execution of Strafford/The Trial of Strafford
Etching (18x25.5cm 7x10in) London 1998

HOLLENBERG Felix 1868-1945 **[77]**
$1 362 - €1 278 - **£841** - FF8 384
Blick ins Lautertal Öl/Karton (31x41.5cm 12x16in)
Stuttgart 1999
$160 - €138 - **£97** - FF905
Ohne Titel Radierung (15x23cm 5x9in) Stuttgart 1998

HOLLENSTEIN Stephanie 1886-1944 **[3]**
$2 749 - €3 270 - **£1 962** - FF21 451
Dorf an einem See Aquarell/Papier (32x44.5cm
12x17in) Wien 2000

HOLLESCH Carlo 1926-1977 **[13]**
$950 - €985 - **£570** - FF6 460
Caduta di Icaro Olio/tela (60x80cm 23x31in) Venezia
2000

HOLLESTELLE Jacob Huybrecht 1858-1920 **[24]**
$549 - €590 - **£367** - FF3 869
View of a waterway, Zeeland (?) Oil/canvas
(51.5x30cm 20x11in) Amsterdam 2000

HOLLOSY Simon 1857-1918 **[5]**
$5 550 - €5 831 - **£3 450** - FF38 250
Prairie broussailleuse Huile/toile (50x50cm
19x19in) Budapest 2000

HOLLOWAY Charles Edward 1838-1897 **[16]**
$375 - €423 - **£260** - FF2 775
Boats Leaving Lowestoft Watercolour/paper
(26.5x37.5cm 10x14in) Ipswich 2000

HOLLYER Eva XIX-XX **[17]**
$2 368 - €2 754 - **£1 691** - FF18 067
The introduction of Tobacco by Sir Walter
Raleigh Oil/canvas (51x68.5cm 20x26in) Toronto 2001
$3 968 - €3 748 - **£2 400** - FF24 586
Learning a new Tune Watercolour (38x56cm
14x22in) Billingshurst, West-Sussex 1999

HOLLYER Frederick 1837-1933 **[8]**
$1 942 - €2 176 - **£1 350** - FF14 275
William Morris Platinum print (14.5x10cm 5x3in)
London 2001

HOLLYER Maud ?-1910 **[17]**
$553 - €475 - **£334** - FF3 113
Mother and Child in a Cottage Garden
Watercolour/paper (49.5x34.5cm 19x13in) Toronto 1998

HOLLYER William P. 1834-1922 **[36]**
$977 - €1 013 - **£620** - FF6 648
Cattle watering in a Highland Landscape
Oil/canvas (59x91cm 23x35in) West-Yorkshire 2000

HOLM Åke 1900-1980 **[64]**
$814 - €902 - **£564** - FF5 920
Noa med duvan Terracotta (H47cm H18in) Malmö
2001

HOLM Anders 1751-1824 **[9]**
$5 583 - €5 220 - **£3 440** - FF34 244
Sjölandskap med byggnader och figurer
Oil/panel (39x53cm 15x20in) Stockholm 1999
$1 206 - €1 393 - **£843** - FF9 136
Landskap med byggnader samt figurer vid vat-
ten Oil/panel (19x27cm 7x10in) Stockholm 2001

HOLM Christian Frederik 1804-1846 **[10]**
$15 921 - €18 020 - **£11 136** - FF118 204
Landskap med jeger og dyr Oil/canvas (52x63cm
20x24in) Oslo 2001

HOLM Heinrich G.Ferdinand 1803-1861 **[33]**
$1 838 - €2 146 - **£1 297** - FF14 080
Parti fra Kronprinsessegade i Köbenhavn
Watercolour/paper (9.5x11cm 3x4in) Köbenhavn 2000

HOLM Just J.C. 1815-1907 **[10]**
$6 540 - €6 135 - **£4 040** - FF40 246
Männliches Figurenbildnis vor der Silhouette
Münchens Öl/Leinwand (96x73cm 37x28in) Ahlden
1999
$2 862 - €2 692 - **£1 786** - FF17 658
Rygvendt kvinde ved åbentstående vindue
Oil/canvas (33x28cm 12x11in) Vejle 1999

HOLM P. XIX **[1]**
$5 492 - €5 345 - **£3 381** - FF35 061
Barck scandia från wifsta warf, commenderad
Capt.Gustaf Bergenstråhle Oil/canvas (63x91cm
24x35in) Stockholm 1999

HOLM Per Daniel 1835-1903 **[25]**
$1 178 - €1 383 - **£831** - FF9 073
Döda fallet, landskap från Jämtland Oil/canvas
(82x108cm 32x42in) Stockholm 2000
$240 - €231 - **£148** - FF1 518
Sommarlandskap med gärdesgård Oil/board
(29x40cm 11x15in) Malmö 1999

HOLM Peter 1798-1875 **[8]**
$969 - €941 - **£588** - FF6 170
Prospect over Aarhus, set fra dyrehaven
Oil/metal (18x25cm 7x9in) Viby J, Århus 2000

HOLM Peter Cristian 1823-1888 **[4]**
$3 940 - €3 834 - **£2 425** - FF25 152
«Iris», Capt. Frans Molander Wisby Oil/canvas
(47x65cm 18x25in) Stockholm 1999

HOLM Wilhelm Lorens 1810-1877 **[1]**
$2 746 - €2 672 - **£1 690** - FF17 530
Stilleben med vinglas och mat Oil/canvas
(41x32.5cm 16x12in) Stockholm 1999

HOLMAN Edwin Charles Pascoe XIX-XX **[14]**
$247 - €282 - **£170** - FF1 848
Moorland Landscapes Watercolour/paper
(27x36.5cm 10x14in) London 2000

HOLMAN Francis c.1740-c.1790 **[13]**
$20 000 – €17 786 - **£12 232** - FF116 666
Four Views of the «Antonetta» Oil/canvas/panel
(75x120cm 29x47in) New-York 1999

HOLMBERG Werner 1830-1860 **[11]**
$10 822 – €11 773 - **£7 133** - FF77 224
Gubbe stoppande en pipa Oil/canvas (37x30.5cm
14x12in) Helsinki 2000

HOLMBOE Thorolf 1866-1935 **[97]**
$2 625 – €3 121 - **£1 870** - FF20 475
Vårløsning Oil/canvas (64x94cm 25x37in) Oslo 2000
$5 040 – €5 993 - **£3 590** - FF39 312
Aftenstemning Mixed media (43x30cm 16x11in)
Oslo 2000
$652 – €550 - **£387** - FF3 605
Sjöfågel på strandklippa Watercolour (79x68cm
31x26in) Stockholm 1998

HOLMEAD Clifford H. Phillips 1889-1975 **[25]**
$2 186 – €2 045 - **£1 324** - FF13 415
Männerkopf Oil/canvas/panel (51x40cm 20x15in)
Bremen 1999

HOLMENS Gérard 1934 **[12]**
$5 712 – €5 949 - **£3 600** - FF39 024
Composition Marbre (H143cm H56in) Antwerpen
2000

HOLMES Billie Justine 1970 **[4]**
$2 400 – €2 361 - **£1 451** - FF15 488
Series of Congratulatory Regrets Watercolour
(48.5x60.5cm 19x23in) Chicago IL 2000

HOLMES Edward ?-c.1893 **[7]**
$3 000 – €3 217 - **£1 984** - FF21 099
The Young Angler Oil/canvas (53x43cm 21x17in)
New-Orleans LA 2000

HOLMES George Augustus ?-1911 **[21]**
$10 541 – €11 254 - **£7 200** - FF73 822
Pushing Family Oil/canvas (54x67.5cm 21x26in)
Billingshurst, West-Sussex 2001
$2 520 – €2 931 - **£1 800** - FF19 227
Inquisitive Terrier Oil/canvas (26.5x23cm 10x9in)
London 2001

HOLMES John J. XX **[11]**
$2 105 – €2 335 - **£1 400** - FF15 319
**Gloucester Schooners Under Full Sail On the
Grand Banks** Oil/canvas (86.5x106cm 34x41in)
London 2000

HOLMES Ralph 1876-1963 **[55]**
$1 500 – €1 620 - **£1 036** - FF10 625
Monterey Coastal Oil/canvas/board (38x49cm
15x19in) Altadena CA 2001
$750 – €876 - **£535** - FF5 749
Hazy atmospheric landscape Oil/board (22x30cm
9x12in) Altadena CA 2001

HOLMES William Henry 1846-1933 **[30]**
$2 400 – €2 901 - **£1 675** - FF19 028
Autumn Landscape/Wadsworth Oil/canvas
(25.5x20.5cm 10x8in) Bethesda MD 2000
$1 100 – €1 232 - **£765** - FF8 084
The old Mill Watercolour/paper (39.5x46.5cm
15x18in) Washington 2001

HOLMGREN Martin 1921-1969 **[7]**
$960 – €932 - **£592** - FF6 114
Mor och barn Bronze (H20.5cm H8in) Stockholm
1999

HOLMGREN Wilhelm 1863-1943 **[47]**
$468 – €445 - **£292** - FF2 922
Fransk skuta Oil/panel (22x27cm 8x10in) Stockholm
1999

HOLMLUND Josefina 1827-1905 **[76]**
$1 747 – €1 471 - **£1 031** - FF9 648
Brusande fors Oil/canvas (116x75cm 45x29in)
Stockholm 1998
$561 – €481 - **£329** - FF3 153
Insjölandskap i månsken Oil/canvas (28x38cm
11x14in) Stockholm 1998

HOLMSKOV Helge 1912-1982 **[29]**
$4 029 – €3 769 - **£2 436** - FF24 724
Komposition Marble (H64.5cm H25in) København
1999

HOLMSTRAND Cajsa 1951 **[16]**
$1 670 – €1 413 - **£998** - FF9 266
«Relationer» Acrylic/canvas (98x96cm 38x37in)
Stockholm 1998

HOLMSTRÖM Tora Vega 1880-1967 **[46]**
$2 717 – €2 370 - **£1 643** - FF15 545
Gossporträtt Oil/canvas (52x43cm 20x16in)
Stockholm 1998
$448 – €492 - **£289** - FF3 230
Stilleben med fågel Oil/panel (34x35cm 13x13in)
Lund 2000

HOLOFCENER Lawrence 1926 **[5]**
$81 234 – €79 501 - **£52 000** - FF521 492
The Allies Bronze (137x183cm 53x72in) London 1999
$3 905 – €3 822 - **£2 500** - FF25 071
**No Man loses his Freedom Except through his
own Weakness, M.Ghandi** Bronze (H28cm H11in)
London 1999

HOLSØE Carl Vilhelm 1863-1935 **[255]**
$24 672 – €28 066 - **£17 232** - FF184 104
Stilla interiör Oil/canvas (82x70cm 32x27in)
Stockholm 2000
$4 263 – €4 467 - **£2 700** - FF29 302
Santa Maria Novella, Florence Oil/board
(27.5x37.5cm 10x14in) London 2000

HOLSØE Niels 1865-1928 **[38]**
$1 491 – €1 481 - **£931** - FF9 713
Interiör Oil/canvas (72x100cm 28x39in) København
1999

HOLST Agda 1886-1976 **[62]**
$546 – €605 - **£378** - FF3 971
Stadsmotiv med figurer på torg Oil/canvas
(49x63cm 19x24in) Stockholm 2001

HOLST Johannes 1880-1965 **[52]**
$3 522 – €4 084 - **£2 495** - FF26 789
The Helios Under Full Sail Oil/canvas (92x135cm
36x53in) Amsterdam 2000
$3 254 – €3 477 - **£2 165** - FF22 806
Dreimast-Vollschiff Öl/Leinwand (70x100cm
27x39in) Hamburg 2000

HOLST Lauritz B. 1848-1934 **[53]**
$2 250 – €2 334 - **£1 350** - FF15 300
Tramonto al Cairo Olio/tela/cartone (39.5x62cm
15x24in) Venezia 2000

HOLST Richard Nic. Roland 1868-1938 **[39]**
$2 244 – €1 994 - **£1 374** - FF13 080
**Dorf und Windmühle vorn einer weiten
Landschaft im wandernden Licht** Oil/panel
(32.5x38cm 12x14in) Hamburg 1999

〰️ **\$496** - €590 - **£353** - FF3 869
Pareldduiker Lithograph (35x42cm 13x16in)
Amsterdam 2000

HOLST von Johan Gustav 1841-1917 [13]
\$2 865 - €2 789 - **£1 764** - FF18 292
Hundvalpar Oil/canvas (44x34cm 17x13in) Stockholm
1999

HOLSTAYN Josef 1930-? [25]
\$16 550 - €18 168 - **£11 000** - FF119 175
**Grosses Blumenstück mit Fayence
Deckelgefäss und Vogelnest** Öl/Leinwand
(73.5x59.5cm 28x23in) Wien 2000

HOLSTAYN Renate 1940 [3]
\$2 191 - €2 543 - **£1 540** - FF16 684
Katzenkinder Öl/Leinwand (30.5x40cm 12x15in)
Wien 2001

HOLSTEYN Pieter I c.1580-1662 [20]
\$6 951 - €6 580 - **£4 322** - FF43 160
**A Turkey, a Peacock and Chickens in a
Landscape before a House** Bodycolour
(38x38.5cm 11x15in) Amsterdam 1999

HOLSTEYN Pieter II 1614-1673/87 [41]
\$485 - €544 - **£336** - FF3 571
Aapje met vrucht Aquarelle/papier (15.5x18cm
6x7in) The Hague 2000

HOLT Edwin Frederick ?-c.1910 [75]
\$2 750 - €2 549 - **£1 709** - FF16 720
Stable Interior Oil/canvas (40x60cm 16x24in) New-
Orleans LA 2000
\$4 000 - €4 294 - **£2 676** - FF28 164
English Springer Spaniel Oil/canvas (35x45.5cm
13x17in) Philadelphia PA 2000

HOLT Eric 1944 [4]
\$3 475 - €4 075 - **£2 500** - FF26 730
Monetarism Tempera/board (39.5x18cm 15x7in)
London 2001

HOLTE Arthur Brandish XIX-XX [8]
\$900 - €1 024 - **£624** - FF6 714
**Fall Scene with Woman and a Girl Carrying
Wood** Oil/canvas (116x93cm 46x37in) East-Moriches
NY 2000

HOLTER Wilhelm 1842-1916 [2]
\$2 196 - €2 474 - **£1 520** - FF16 228
Handelssted ved kysten Oil/canvas (77x120cm
30x47in) Oslo 2000

HÖLTL Josef XIX [1]
\$4 021 - €4 602 - **£2 765** - FF30 185
Die Mittagssuppe nimmt ein Mann am Tisch ein
Öl/Leinwand (37x53cm 14x20in) München 2000

HOLTRUP Jan 1917-? [20]
\$2 374 - €2 124 - **£1 422** - FF13 931
Herfst, Spanderwoud (Scheiwal) Oil/canvas
(60x80cm 23x31in) Amsterdam 1998
\$1 389 - €1 179 - **£838** - FF7 731
Winters landschap met houtsprokkelaarster
Oil/panel (28x38cm 11x14in) Rotterdam 1998

HOLTY Carl Robert 1900-1973 [91]
\$1 200 - €1 133 - **£746** - FF7 431
Abstractions Oil/canvas (71x45cm 28x18in) Milford
CT 1999
\$3 500 - €2 998 - **£2 066** - FF19 663
Untitled Oil/masonite (45.5x30cm 17x11in) New-York
1998
\$950 - €811 - **£566** - FF5 318
Abstract Figures/Untitled Watercolour/paper
(18x13cm 7x5in) New-York 1998

HOLTZ Karl 1889-1978 [55]
\$359 - €409 - **£249** - FF2 683
Frivoles Trio Gouache (19x13.4cm 7x5in) Berlin 2000
〰️ **\$270** - €307 - **£187** - FF2 012
«Bahnhof» Linocut (22x29.5cm 8x11in) Berlin 2001

HOLTZMANN Carl Friedrich 1740-1811 [3]
\$2 088 - €1 789 - **£1 255** - FF11 736
Porträts eines fürstlichen Paares Aquarell/Papier
(22x16cm 8x6in) Stuttgart 1998

HOLUB Georg 1861-1919 [14]
\$2 172 - €1 816 - **£1 287** - FF11 910
Blick auf Dürnstein Öl/Leinwand/Karton (49x68cm
19x26in) Wien 1998

HOLUB Josef 1870-1957 [23]
\$867 - €820 - **£540** - FF5 379
Sommerlandschaft Öl/Karton (50x66cm 19x25in)
Praha 2000

HOLY Adrien 1898-1979 [109]
\$939 - €1 118 - **£671** - FF7 331
Port de Cassis Öl/Leinwand (53x72cm 20x28in)
Zürich 2000
\$473 - €515 - **£311** - FF3 376
Sitzende junge Frau in roter Hose Öl/Leinwand
(46x33cm 18x12in) Bern 2000

HOLY Miloslav 1897-1974 [46]
\$933 - €867 - **£580** - FF5 685
Still Life with Pears Oil/canvas (41x51cm 16x20in)
Praha 1999
\$433 - €410 - **£270** - FF2 689
Banlieue Huile/carton (34.5x45.5cm 13x17in) Praha
1999

HOLYOAKE Rowland XIX-XX [23]
\$1 707 - €1 984 - **£1 200** - FF13 013
Rading by the Fireside Oil/canvas (30.5x25cm
12x9in) London 2001

HOLYOAKE William 1834-1894 [18]
\$3 186 - €3 697 - **£2 200** - FF24 253
Gathering Mussels Oil/canvas (76.5x51cm 30x20in)
London 2001

HOLZ Johann Daniel 1867-1945 [54]
\$1 922 - €1 636 - **£1 147** - FF10 729
Kühe am Wasser Öl/Leinwand (70x80cm 27x31in)
München 1998
\$1 095 - €920 - **£644** - FF6 036
Weidende Schafe im Baumhof Öl/Karton
(27.5x37.5cm 10x14in) Köln 1998

HOLZ Paul 1883-1938 [18]
\$1 165 - €1 278 - **£791** - FF8 384
Ein Herr steigt aus der Kutsche Ink/paper
(43.5x30.5cm 17x12in) Berlin 2000

HOLZAPFEL Carl 1865-1926 [23]
\$536 - €562 - **£339** - FF3 683
Dorf an der Havel im Abendlicht Öl/Leinwand
(46x63.5cm 18x25in) Köln 2000

HÖLZEL Adolf Richard 1853-1934 [175]
\$17 268 - €19 484 - **£12 147** - FF127 809
Anbetung Öl/Leinwand (73x62cm 28x24in) Bern
2001
\$5 198 - €5 624 - **£3 561** - FF36 892
Komposition Sculpture, glass (46x34cm 18x13in)
Stuttgart 2001
\$501 - €4 857 - **£3 112** - FF31 862
Komposition mit Figuren und Häusern Coloured
pencils (24.5x16cm 9x6in) München 1999

HOLZER Adi 1936 [11]

▥ **$171** - €203 - **£121** - FF1 334
Gloria Radierung (14.5x20.5cm 5x8in) Klagenfurt 2000

HOLZER Jenny 1950 [87]

👄 **$3 500** - €3 840 - **£2 325** - FF25 191
«The Living Series: Many Dogs Run Wild in the City...» Enamel (53.5x59cm 21x23in) New-York 2000

🦌 **$12 000** - €10 353 - **£7 212** - FF67 911
Survival Series: «In a Dream You Saw a Way...» Marble (43x61x43cm 16x24x16in) New-York 1998

▥ **$125** - €145 - **£87** - FF952
Truisms Serigraph (42x33cm 16x12in) Miami FL 2001

HOLZER Johann Evangelist 1709-1740 [15]

✍ **$5 158** - €5 113 - **£3 227** - FF33 539
Dreikönigsanbetung Ink (14.5x10cm 5x3in) München 1999

▥ **$474** - €460 - **£295** - FF3 018
Complexio Cholerica, nach J.G. Bergmüller Radierung (28.8x18cm 11x7in) Berlin 1999

HOLZER Joseph 1824-1876 [38]

👄 **$2 504** - €2 907 - **£1 728** - FF19 068
Reitergruppe am Fusse der Ruine Pantenstein Öl/Leinwand (55x69cm 21x27in) Graz 2000

HOLZER-DEFANTI Constantin 1881-1951 [33]

🦌 **$777** - €727 - **£479** - FF4 767
Tänzerin Porcelain (H30.3cm H11in) Wien 1999

HOLZHALB Rudolf 1835-1885 [4]

👄 **$2 536** - €2 812 - **£1 761** - FF18 446
Klosterruine im Schwarzwald Öl/Leinwand (87x125cm 34x49in) Köln 2001

HOLZHANDLER Dora 1928 [32]

✍ **$449** - €433 - **£280** - FF2 841
Moroccan Dancer Watercolour (25.5x16.5cm 10x6in) London 1999

HOLZINGER Rudolf 1898-1949 [14]

✍ **$457** - €436 - **£278** - FF2 860
Wolfgangsee Aquarell, Gouache/Papier (46x62cm 18x24in) Wien 1999

HÖLZL Johann Felix XVIII [1]

👄 **$4 833** - €4 807 - **£3 000** - FF31 533
Still life of Flowers in a Glass Vase on a Stone Ledge Oil/canvas (43x32.5cm 16x12in) London 1999

HOLZMAN Shimshon 1907-1986 [46]

👄 **$1 300** - €1 395 - **£870** - FF9 153
Landscape Oil/canvas (49.5x64.5cm 19x25in) Tel Aviv 2000

✍ **$350** - €346 - **£214** - FF2 271
Figures in a Room Watercolour/paper (35x50cm 13x19in) Tel Aviv 2000

HOLZMEISTER Clemens 1886-1983 [11]

✍ **$686** - €767 - **£462** - FF5 030
Grossglockner/Fuschertörl Watercolour (30x51cm 11x20in) München 2000

HOLZMÜLLER Juliusz 1876-1932 [9]

✍ **$874** - €999 - **£615** - FF6 552
Scène de genre Aquarelle/papier (33.5x49.5cm 13x19in) Warszawa 2001

HØM Paul 1905-1994 [59]

👄 **$888** - €1 005 - **£600** - FF6 593
Drengeportraet Oil/canvas (84x55cm 33x21in) København 2000

HOMANN Johan Baptist 1663-1724 [90]

▥ **$292** - €291 - **£182** - FF1 906
Charte von Amerika, Landkarte Copper engraving in colors (58x45cm 22x17in) Salzburg 1999

HOMANS Nannie 1861-? [1]

👄 **$5 500** - €5 214 - **£3 435** - FF34 199
Young Girl Darning a Stocking Oil/canvas (76x55cm 30x22in) Mystic CT 1999

HOME Robert 1752-1834 [7]

👄 **$40 000** - €35 205 - **£24 352** - FF230 932
Lady as the Cumaean Sibyl Oil/canvas (76x63.5cm 29x25in) New-York 1999

HOMER Winslow 1836-1910 [156]

👄 **$2 600 000** - €2 879 411 - **£1 763 320** - FF18 887 700
Uncle Ned at Home Oil/canvas (35.5x56cm 13x22in) New-York 2000

👄 **$900 000** - €860 366 - **£564 120** - FF5 643 630
Woodchopper in the Adirondacks Oil/canvas (27x40cm 10x15in) New-York 1999

✍ **$340 000** - €380 825 - **£236 232** - FF2 498 048
Boys Fishing, Gloucester Harbor Watercolour/paper (23.5x35cm 9x13in) New-York 2001

▥ **$5 000** - €4 733 - **£3 109** - FF31 044
Mending the Tears Etching (44.5x58cm 17x22in) New-York 1999

HOMPEL Ludwig Ten 1887-? [9]

▥ **$1 100** - €1 227 - **£728** - FF8 050
«Gartenbau-Ausstellung, Duisberg» Poster (89x65cm 35x25in) New-York 1999

HONDECOETER de Gillis Claesz c.1570-1638 [37]

👄 **$20 475** - €22 867 - **£13 875** - FF150 000
Paysage fluvial animé de pêcheurs Huile/panneau (48x74cm 18x29in) Paris 1999

👄 **$9 000** - €8 996 - **£5 498** - FF59 008
Wooded River Landscape with a Traveller and a Dog on a Path Oil/panel (22x38cm 8x14in) New-York 2000

HONDECOETER de Gysbrecht Gillisz. 1604-1653 [8]

👄 **$145 017** - €142 416 - **£90 000** - FF934 191
Cockerel and Hens Oil/canvas (71x91.5cm 27x36in) London 1999

HONDECOETER de Melchior 1636-1695 [36]

👄 **$269 637** - €283 128 - **£170 000** - FF1 857 199
Peacock, a Peahen, a Pheasant, a Turkey, a Cockerel and Chicks Oil/canvas (126.5x154.5cm 49x60in) London 2000

👄 **$70 000** - €77 523 - **£47 474** - FF508 515
Poultry in a Landscape with Ruins, a River Beyond Oil/canvas (82x78.5cm 32x30in) New-York 2000

HONDIUS Abraham Danielsz 1625-1695 [51]

👄 **$9 996** - €8 635 - **£4 998** - FF56 644
Leda e il cigno in un paesaggio Olio/tela (58x92cm 22x36in) Milano 1999

👄 **$1 822** - €2 045 - **£1 263** - FF13 415
Bärenhatz Öl/Leinwand (32.5x43cm 12x16in) München 2000

HONDIUS Gerrit 1891-1970 [76]

👄 **$750** - €875 - **£526** - FF5 741
Still Life with Begonia Oil/masonite (76x61cm 29x24in) Boston MA 2000

HONDIUS Hendrick I 1573-1650 [20]

▥ **$352** - €408 - **£249** - FF2 678
Map of Flanders Etching (39.5x49.5cm 15x19in) Amsterdam 2000

HONDIUS Hendrik II c.1597-c.1644 **[1]**
📖 **$864** - €998 - **£608** - FF6 546
Poli Arctici Copper engraving (43x49cm 16x19in)
Oslo 2000

HONDIUS Jodocus 1563-1611 **[9]**
📖 **$564** - €655 - **£400** - FF4 294
Europe Engraving (37x49.5cm 14x19in) London 2000

HONDIUS Willem 1610-? **[1]**
📖 **$684** - €719 - **£453** - FF4 714
Ludwika Maria Gonzaga, reine de Pologne, d'après Egmont Gravure cuivre (31x21.5cm 12x8in)
Warszawa 2000

HONDT de Lambert I c.1620-1665 **[31]**
🖼 **$23 722** - €22 105 - **£14 630** - FF145 000
Le choc de la cavalerie Huile/toile (102.5x138.5cm 40x54in) Paris 1999
🖼 **$8 942** - €8 232 - **£5 367** - FF54 000
Scène de bataille Huile/toile (62x86cm 24x33in)
Lyon 1999
🖼 **$3 660** - €3 604 - **£2 280** - FF23 640
Batalla de caballeros Oleo/lienzo (27x39.5cm 10x15in) Madrid 1999

HONDT de Lambert II c.1640-c.1690 **[3]**
🖼 **$6 489** - €6 541 - **£4 050** - FF42 903
Reitergefecht in einer Waldlandschaft Öl/Leinwand (28x33cm 11x12in) Wien 2000

HONE David XX **[4]**
🖼 **$6 249** - €5 329 - **£3 770** - FF34 953
Summer, Sandymount Strand Oil/canvas (50x60cm 20x24in) Dublin 1998
🖼 **$1 420** - €1 524 - **£968** - FF9 994
The Lobster Oil/canvas (14x24cm 5x9in) Dublin 2001

HONE Evie Sydney 1894-1955 **[153]**
🖼 **$6 369** - €7 238 - **£4 398** - FF47 475
Graveyard at Ardmore Oil/board (44x72cm 17x28in)
Dublin 2000
🖼 **$887** - €952 - **£593** - FF6 246
Design for Stained Glass Window (Suffer Little Children) Mixed media (20.5x5cm 8x1in) Dublin 2000
🖼 **$1 476** - €1 587 - **£1 005** - FF10 411
Design for Window for Downe Church Pencil/paper (34x22cm 13x8in) Dublin 2001

HONE Nathaniel 1718-1784 **[80]**
🖼 **$58 926** - €70 081 - **£42 000** - FF459 698
The Whiteford Children Playing in Wood Oil/canvas (103.5x128cm 40x50in) London 2000
🖼 **$14 780** - €14 576 - **£9 500** - FF95 612
Portrait of a Gentleman, half Length, playing a Mandolin Oil/canvas (73.5x61cm 28x24in) London 1999
🖼 **$11 925** - €14 183 - **£8 500** - FF93 034
Portrait of a Boy/His Sister, Half-Length, He Wearing a Buff Coat Oil/canvas (44.5x35cm 17x13in) London 2000
✏ **$929** - €1 079 - **£652** - FF7 079
Head of a Lady Pencil (15x11cm 5x4in) Dublin 2001

HONE Nathaniel II, R.H.A. 1831-1917 **[53]**
🖼 **$18 384** - €20 316 - **£12 748** - FF133 264
Landscape near Malahide, wih Cattle resting Oil/canvas (64x93cm 25x36in) Dublin 2001
🖼 **$3 574** - €3 049 - **£2 130** - FF19 999
Coastal Landscape, Malahide Oil/canvas (33x45cm 13x18in) Dublin 1998
✏ **$2 500** - €2 666 - **£1 665** - FF17 490
Landscape Watercolour/paper (11x18cm 4x7in)
Dublin 2000

HONEDER Walter 1906 **[3]**
🖼 **$13 424** - €11 623 - **£8 144** - FF76 240
Alpenblick Öl/Leinwand (120.5x200cm 47x78in)
Wien 1998

HONEGGER Gottfried 1917 **[85]**
🖼 **$6 856** - €6 283 - **£4 189** - FF41 212
Biseautage Z-121 Huile/panneau (75x75cm 29x29in)
Zürich 1999
✏ **$414** - €493 - **£296** - FF3 234
Komposition Pencil (53.5x42cm 21x16in) Zürich 2000
📖 **$78** - €92 - **£54** - FF603
Ohne Titel Lithographie (77.5x56cm 30x22in) Stuttgart 2000

HONEYSETT Martin 1943 **[5]**
🖼 **$1 565** - €1 455 - **£950** - FF9 545
Illustrations Depicting the Months of the Year Ink (19x28.5cm 7x11in) London 1998

HONG TONG 1920-1987 **[37]**
🖼 **$34 650** - €31 879 - **£20 790** - FF209 110
Memory of Heing Chun Mixed media (67x128cm 26x50in) Taipei 1999
🖼 **$25 336** - €20 941 - **£14 821** - FF137 365
A Hundred Dollar fantasy Oil/masonite (28x38cm 11x14in) Taipei 1998
✏ **$15 408** - €16 825 - **£9 912** - FF110 364
Elegant Women Mixed media/paper (43x114cm 16x44in) Hong-Kong 2000

HONG VIET DUNG 1962 **[3]**
🖼 **$3 506** - €3 671 - **£2 202** - FF24 077
Girl with Lotus Leaf Oil/canvas (100x100cm 39x39in) Singapore 2000

HONG WU c.1750-1795 **[5]**
✏ **$51 280** - €60 272 - **£35 560** - FF395 360
Rural Scene Ink/paper (30.5x368.5cm 12x145in)
Hong-Kong 2000

HONG ZHU AN 1955 **[3]**
🖼 **$5 086** - €5 621 - **£3 527** - FF36 869
The Yellow Earth Indian ink (110x110cm 43x43in)
Singapore 2001

HONGYI 1880-1942 **[8]**
✏ **$8 974** - €10 548 - **£6 223** - FF69 188
Calligraphy in Standard Script Ink/paper (65x18cm 25x7in) Hong-Kong 2000

HONIGBERGER Ernst 1885-1976 **[47]**
🖼 **$1 049** - €1 176 - **£729** - FF7 714
«Blumenstilleben» Öl/Leinwand (43x38cm 16x14in)
Staufen 2001
✏ **$460** - €460 - **£288** - FF3 018
Blick auf das Elternhaus des Künstlers in Wehr Aquarell/Karton (24x20cm 9x7in) Staufen 1999

HÖNIGSMANN Bela 1885-? **[11]**
🖼 **$1 333** - €1 431 - **£892** - FF9 390
Roter Malwenstrauss in einem Keramikkrug Öl/Karton (99x55cm 38x21in) Stuttgart 2000

HONKANEN Juhani XX **[5]**
🖼 **$378** - €437 - **£267** - FF2 868
Sommardag, Saimen Oil/canvas (22x33cm 8x12in)
Helsinki 2000

HONNET Jean-Louis 1957 **[122]**
🖼 **$758** - €732 - **£476** - FF4 800
Le chemin Huile/toile (54x65cm 21x25in) Pérenchies 1999
🖼 **$246** - €244 - **£149** - FF1 600
Paysage Provençal Huile/toile (22x27cm 8x10in)
Toulouse 2000

HONSA Jan 1876-1937 **[21]**
- **$1 069** - €1 011 - **£666** - FF6 634
  Quiet Place in the Garden Oil/canvas (42x65cm 16x25in) Praha 2000
- **$332** - €314 - **£207** - FF2 061
  Proti slunci Huile/carton (20x27.5cm 7x10in) Praha 2000

HONT d' Pieter 1917-1997 **[5]**
- **$1 828** - €1 815 - **£1 142** - FF11 906
  Man and Child Bronze (H47.5cm H18in) Amsterdam 1999

HONTHORST van Gerrit 1590-1656 **[29]**
- **$29 832** - €29 564 - **£18 106** - FF193 930
  Hos vildthandleren, ung kvinde med stråhat stående med en hare Oil/canvas (117x103cm 46x40in) Vejle 2000
- **$65 368** - €64 256 - **£42 000** - FF421 495
  Venus and Cupid Oil/canvas (110x92.5cm 43x36in) London 1999

HOOCH de Carel Cornelisz. c.1590-1638 **[14]**
- **$5 710** - €5 996 - **£3 600** - FF39 328
  Figures among Italianate Ruins Oil/panel (63x77.5cm 24x30in) London 2000
- **$9 244** - €9 452 - **£5 797** - FF62 000
  Paysage aux ruines avec des bergers Huile/panneau (28x43.5cm 11x17in) Paris 1999
- **$900** - €1 007 - **£627** - FF6 608
  Octagonal Landscape with large Tree/Ladnscape with a wooden Bridge Etching (9x11cm 3x4in) New-York 2001

HOOCH de David c.1610-c.1680 **[3]**
- **$7 733** - €7 632 - **£4 800** - FF50 453
  Italianate Landscape with Shepherds crossing a Bridge and Watering Oil/canvas (88.5x121.5cm 34x47in) London 1999

HOOCH de Horatius XVII **[9]**
- **$32 900** - €30 490 - **£19 640** - FF200 000
  Paysans s'arrêtant à l'entrée d'un village Huile/toile (79x69cm 31x27in) Paris 1999
- **$1 973** - €2 250 - **£1 377** - FF14 757
  Die Versuchung des Hl.Antonius, nach Jacques Callot Ink (34x48cm 13x18in) Berlin 2001

HOOCH de Pieter 1629-1684 **[19]**
- **$120 000** - €132 896 - **£81 384** - FF871 740
  A Lady and a Gentleman Making Music with Dancing Dogs Oil/canvas (62x53.5cm 24x21in) New-York 2000

HOOD Ernest Burnett 1932-1988 **[27]**
- **$1 937** - €2 179 - **£1 350** - FF14 295
  The Hunt Oil/canvas (70x151cm 27x59in) Edinburgh 2001
- **$287** - €323 - **£200** - FF2 117
  Railway Siding, Kirklee Pastel/paper (18.5x29.5cm 7x11in) Edinburgh 2001
- **$373** - €420 - **£260** - FF2 753
  Launching Day Monotype (46.5x52.5cm 18x20in) Edinburgh 2001

HOOD George Washington 1869-1949 **[5]**
- **$1 300** - €1 448 - **£850** - FF9 498
  Book illustration: Prince bowing to woman in forest Oil/board (42x30cm 16x12in) New-York 2000

HOOG de Bernard Johann 1866/67-1943 **[189]**
- **$8 740** - €8 228 - **£5 400** - FF53 970
  The Happy Family Oil/canvas (64x49.5cm 25x19in) West-Sussex 1999

- **$2 572** - €2 635 - **£1 600** - FF17 286
  Family Group in a Dutch Interior Oil/canvas (29.5x23.5cm 11x9in) Billingshurst, West-Sussex 2000

HOOGERHEYDEN Engel 1740-1809 **[7]**
- **$7 799** - €7 632 - **£5 000** - FF50 061
  Dutch Men-of-War in Choppy Seas Oil/canvas (65x102cm 25x40in) London 1999

HOOGERS Hendrick 1747-1814 **[7]**
- **$1 435** - €1 240 - **£865** - FF8 132
  An Italianate Landscape with a ruined tower on a Hill Wash (15x23.5cm 5x9in) Amsterdam 1998

HOOGHE de Romeyn 1645-1708 **[29]**
- **$4 719** - €4 538 - **£2 907** - FF29 766
  The Bodies of the Brothers de Witt Hung Up by the Feet Ink (5.5x32cm 8x12in) Amsterdam 1999
- **$235** - €252 - **£157** - FF1 654
  Title page from Atlas Maritime Copper engraving in colors (55x40cm 22x16in) Cleveland OH 2000

HOOGKAMER Hendrik Willem 1790-1864 **[1]**
- **$1 252** - €1 452 - **£887** - FF9 525
  Voorstelling der Door-lizing van eenige Koopvaardij,after G.H.Koekkoek Etching, aquatint (55x69cm 21x27in) Amsterdam 2000

HOOGSTEYNS Jan 1935 **[96]**
- **$477** - €446 - **£289** - FF2 926
  Sneeuwlandschap Oil/panel (49x55cm 19x21in) Lokeren 1999
- **$128** - €109 - **£76** - FF715
  Meisje in blauw Watercolour/paper (47x33cm 18x12in) Lokeren 1998

HOOGSTRATEN van Samuel 1627-1678 **[16]**
- **$20 920** - €22 456 - **£14 000** - FF147 302
  Portrait of Axel Gustafsson, Count Oxenstierna (1583-1654) Oil/canvas (76x68.5cm 29x26in) London 2000
- **$14 000** - €14 997 - **£9 560** - FF98 372
  Studies of Three Standing Figures, and of a Head Ink (11.5x7.5cm 4x2in) New-York 2001

HOOK James Clarke 1819-1907 **[38]**
- **$13 448** - €14 436 - **£9 000** - FF94 694
  Dutch Pedlar Oil/canvas (95.5x156.5cm 37x61in) London 2000
- **$19 642** - €23 360 - **£14 000** - FF153 232
  Rest While Gathering Blackberries Oil/canvas (84.5x123cm 33x48in) London 2000
- **$866** - €930 - **£580** - FF6 102
  Study of children climbing rocks by the sea Oil/canvas (33x40cm 13x16in) Bury St. Edmunds, Suffolk 2000

HOOPER John Horace c.1850-c.1899 **[93]**
- **$2 510** - €2 952 - **£1 800** - FF19 365
  Mother and Child on a Wet Country Lane, a Cottage and Trees nearby Oil/canvas (61x91cm 24x35in) West-Yorshire 2001
- **$1 167** - €1 303 - **£780** - FF8 546
  Pastoral scene with figures, sheep, a pond and a farm Oil/canvas (30x51cm 11x20in) West-Midlands 2000

HOORDE van Louis 1886-1935 **[18]**
- **$468** - €446 - **£291** - FF2 926
  Nature morte au vase de roses blanches Huile/toile (60x45cm 23x17in) Antwerpen 1999
- **$582** - €694 - **£417** - FF4 552
  Dans voor de hoeve (danse devant la ferme) Huile/panneau (24x32cm 9x12in) Antwerpen 2000

HOOSTE van Jozef 1884-1940 **[15]**
  $816 - €843 - **£513** - FF5 528
    Ferme dans un paysage hivernal Huile/toile
    (88x98cm 34x38in) Antwerpen 2000

HOOVER Ellison 1888-1955 **[14]**
  $900 - €1 030 - **£619** - FF6 756
    Sunny Side of Broadway/Little German Band
    Crayon (48x61cm 19x24in) New-York 2000
  $325 - €312 - **£201** - FF2 048
    The Statue of Liberty Lithograph (34x23.5cm
    13x9in) New-York 1999

HOOVER Nan 1931 **[3]**
  $2 888 - €3 147 - **£2 000** - FF20 645
    «Impressions» Photograph (60x90cm 23x35in)
    London 2001

HOPE Gabrielle 1916-1962 **[2]**
  $1 876 - €1 972 - **£1 235** - FF12 933
    View of Mangere Mountain Watercolour/paper
    (65.5x54cm 25x21in) Auckland 2000

HOPE James Archi 1818-1892 **[54]**
  $130 000 - €154 603 - **£92 651** - FF1 014 130
    Rainbow Falls, Watkins Glen, New York Oil/canvas
    (198x152.5cm 77x60in) New-York 2000
  $1 700 - €1 816 - **£1 158** - FF11 909
    Fisherman on the Coast of Haifa Oil/canvas
    (44x68cm 17x27in) Chester NY 2001

HOPE Robert 1869-1936 **[34]**
  $1 599 - €1 598 - **£1 000** - FF10 482
    Children Bathing in a River Oil/canvas
    (65.5x40.5cm 25x15in) Edinburgh 1999
  $689 - €632 - **£420** - FF4 146
    The Road to the Harbour Oil/board (23x34cm
    9x13in) Berwick-upon-Tweed 1998

HOPE Thomas 1832-1926 **[1]**
  $10 000 - €9 232 - **£6 150** - FF60 559
    Music Oil/canvas (51x66cm 20x25in) New-York 1999

HOPE William 1863-1931 **[4]**
  $10 355 - €12 045 - **£7 288** - FF79 012
    **«Stormy Day off St.Andrews, York Beach,
    Maine»** Oil/canvas (98.5x146cm 38x57in) Calgary,
    Alberta 2001

HOPF Eduard 1901-1973 **[15]**
  $846 - €511 - **£307** - FF3 353
    Stilleben mit afrikanischen Figuren
    Aquarell/Papier (49x65cm 19x25in) Stuttgart 2000

HOPFER Daniel c.1470-1536 **[79]**
  $448 - €511 - **£313** - FF3 353
    Maximilian I als Heiliger Georg Radierung
    (22.5x15.5cm 8x6in) Berlin 2001

HOPFER Hieronymus ?-1563 **[37]**
  $631 - €716 - **£441** - FF4 695
    Der heilige Christophorus Radierung (14x8.5cm
    5x3in) München 2001

HOPFER Lambert c.1510-c.1550 **[10]**
  $885 - €971 - **£601** - FF6 372
    Die Bekehrung des Heilige Paulus Radierung
    (13.7x8.6cm 5x3in) Berlin 2000

HÖPFNER Wilhelm 1899-1968 **[14]**
  $126 - €153 - **£88** - FF1 006
    Goldfische (China) Etching, aquatint in colors
    (24.7x20cm 9x7in) Berlin 2000

HÖPKER Thomas 1936 **[46]**
  $891 - €882 - **£556** - FF5 785
    Malaysia Vintage gelatin silver print (26.8x38.8cm
    10x15in) Berlin 1999

HOPKIN Robert B. 1832-1909 **[50]**
  $700 - €672 - **£433** - FF4 409
    Seascape, two masted Schooner in Great Lakes
    Oil/canvas (35x50cm 14x20in) Detroit MI 1999
  $600 - €559 - **£370** - FF3 669
    Two Ships on Stormy Seas Watercolour/paper
    (38x23cm 15x9in) Bloomfield-Hills MI 1999

HOPKINS Arthur 1848-1930 **[58]**
  $1 012 - €1 094 - **£700** - FF7 174
    **Penberth with Man/Maid on a Path by the
    Sream** Watercolour/paper (28x38cm 11x14in) Cheshire
    2001

HOPKINS Francis Powell 1830-1913 **[10]**
  $11 207 - €12 031 - **£7 500** - FF78 916
    The Golf Match Watercolour/paper (20.5x30.5cm
    8x12in) London 2001

HOPKINS Milton William 1789-1844 **[2]**
  $12 000 - €13 225 - **£7 983** - FF86 752
    Folk Portrait of Sarah Reed Oil/panel (71x59cm
    28x23in) Portsmouth NH 2001

HOPKINS Tom XX **[7]**
  $1 124 - €1 207 - **£764** - FF7 918
    Untitled (Sunday) Mixed media/paper (21.5x29cm
    8x11in) Calgary, Alberta 2001

HOPKINS William H. ?-1892 **[24]**
  $9 000 - €10 456 - **£6 325** - FF68 590
    The Artist's Pug with Ball Oil/canvas (49.5x59.5cm
    19x23in) New-York 2001
  $2 327 - €2 744 - **£1 641** - FF18 000
    Scènes de chasse Aquarelle/papier (30.5x45cm
    12x17in) Bourges 2001

HOPKINSON Charles Sydney 1869-1962 **[24]**
  $17 000 - €19 827 - **£11 935** - FF130 056
    Portrait of Harriot Sumner Oil/canvas (51x41cm
    20x16in) Boston MA 2000
  $500 - €583 - **£346** - FF3 826
    Study of a Rocky Coast Watercolour/paper
    (26x36cm 10x14in) South-Natick MA 2000

HOPPÉ Emil Otto 1878-1972 **[65]**
  $1 600 - €1 541 - **£1 000** - FF10 106
    New York Gelatin silver print (10x7.5cm 3x2in) New-
    York 1999

HOPPE Erik 1897-1968 **[127]**
  $3 662 - €3 366 - **£2 250** - FF22 080
    Sommerstemning i Söndermarken Oil/canvas
    (50x60cm 19x23in) Köbenhavn 1999
  $1 904 - €1 750 - **£1 170** - FF11 481
    Figur i Söndermarken Oil/canvas (36x40cm
    14x15in) Köbenhavn 1999
  $874 - €739 - **£523** - FF4 849
    Pige i Söndermarken Watercolour/paper (24x31cm
    9x12in) Köbenhavn 1999

HÖPPE Ferdinand Bernhard 1841-1922 **[20]**
  $805 - €864 - **£538** - FF5 669
    **River Landscape with Windmill and City
    Beyond** Watercolour, gouache/paper (53.5x76cm
    21x29in) Toronto 2000

HOPPEN Gerard 1885-1959 **[2]**
  $3 382 - €3 630 - **£2 263** - FF23 812
    Kneeling Nude Sculpture, wood (H69cm H27in)
    Amsterdam 2000

HOPPENBROUWERS Johannes Franciscus
1791/1819-1866 **[85]**
  $9 033 - €9 983 - **£6 265** - FF65 485
    After the Harvest Oil/panel (38.5x54.5cm 15x21in)
    Amsterdam 2001

H

$4 732 - €4 084 - **£2 855** - FF26 789
Winter sunset Oil/panel (13x17cm 5x6in) Amsterdam 1999

HOPPER Edward 1882-1967 **[104]**
$220 000 - €210 312 - **£137 896** - FF1 379 554
Monhegan Houses, Maine Oil/board (24x32.5cm 9x12in) New-York 1999
$23 000 - €23 841 - **£14 584** - FF156 386
Cats Pencil/paper (23.5x20.5cm 9x8in) New-York 2000
$16 000 - €17 587 - **£10 252** - FF115 366
Night Shadows, from The New Republic Portfolio Etching (17.5x21.5cm 6x8in) New-York 2000

HOPPIN Tracy 1882-1956 **[2]**
$4 000 - €4 567 - **£2 820** - FF29 959
Dinner is served Oil/canvas (63x76cm 24x29in) Boston MA 2001

HOPPNER John 1758-1810 **[70]**
$18 000 - €17 992 - **£10 996** - FF118 017
Portrait of lady Boothby, Three-Quarter Length, in a Grey Dress Oil/canvas (127x101.5cm 50x39in) New-York 2000
$9 332 - €9 112 - **£5 950** - FF59 773
Gentleman, said to be Philippe-Jacques de Louthербourg, dark grey Coat Oil/canvas (63.5x48cm 25x18in) London 1999
$4 837 - €5 621 - **£3 400** - FF36 870
Study of an elegant young Lady, Emma Hamilton Pencil (18x22cm 7x8in) London 2001

HOPS Tom 1906-1976 **[26]**
$1 137 - €1 278 - **£798** - FF8 384
Norsee-Fishereihafen bei Ebbe Öl/Leinwand (48x63cm 18x24in) Hamburg 2001

HOPWOOD Henry Silkstone 1860-1914 **[34]**
$3 375 - €3 629 - **£2 300** - FF23 806
A Street in Biskra Oil/panel (14x18cm 5x7in) West-Yorkshire 2001
$1 160 - €1 199 - **£730** - FF7 866
Sittande flicka med bok Akvarell/papper (75x49cm 29x19in) Stockholm 2000

HORACIO 1912-1972 **[50]**
$3 800 - €3 697 - **£2 338** - FF24 252
El niño Oil/canvas (61x46cm 24x18in) New-York 1999

HORAN Michael XX **[3]**
$884 - €980 - **£600** - FF6 427
«Magic Nights...Merry Days...P&O Cruises» Poster (100x62cm 39x24in) London 2000

HÖRBERG Pehr 1746-1816 **[14]**
$2 991 - €3 454 - **£2 092** - FF22 657
Interiör med grosshandlaren Christian Heitmüller med familj Oil/canvas (97x122cm 38x48in) Stockholm 2001

HOREJC Jaroslaw 1886-1983 **[40]**
$809 - €765 - **£504** - FF5 020
Torse Bronze (H34.5cm H13in) Praha 2001

HOREL Albert 1876-1964 **[24]**
$2 875 - €3 354 - **£1 999** - FF22 000
Vue de Fés Huile/toile/panneau (64x91cm 25x35in) Paris 2000

HOREMANS Jan Jozef I 1682-1759 **[97]**
$6 100 - €5 281 - **£3 702** - FF34 638
Fischmarkt Öl/Leinwand (72x81cm 28x31in) Zürich 1998
$8 959 - €8 385 - **£5 549** - FF55 000
Intérieur de cuisine Huile/toile (40x32cm 15x12in) Paris 1999

$1 173 - €1 361 - **£810** - FF8 929
Study of a Woman Wearing a Bonnet/Man Seated at a Table Red chalk/paper (23.5x18.5cm 9x7in) Amsterdam 2000

HOREMANS Jan Jozef II 1714-1790 **[62]**
$19 033 - €19 985 - **£12 000** - FF131 096
Van Den Bosch Family Dining by a House, a Topiary Garden Beyond Oil/canvas (98x77.5cm 38x30in) London 2000
$7 940 - €7 267 - **£4 840** - FF47 670
Im Atelier des Malers Öl/Leinwand (34.4x27cm 13x10in) Wien 1999
$1 887 - €1 815 - **£1 182** - FF11 906
Man standing on a Ladder Red chalk (22.5x19cm 8x7in) Amsterdam 1999

HOREMANS Peter Jacob 1700-1776 **[20]**
$32 748 - €30 368 - **£20 000** - FF199 204
The Colonnade of a Countryhouse with a Lady seated Beside a Statue Oil/canvas (67x84cm 26x33in) London 1998
$20 920 - €22 456 - **£14 000** - FF147 302
Portrait of the Artist Oil/panel (26.5x21cm 10x8in) London 2000

HORLOR George William act.1849-1891 **[59]**
$99 888 - €99 350 - **£62 000** - FF651 694
Day's Sport in Perthshire: Preparing for the Return Oil/canvas (125x152.5cm 49x60in) London 1999
$7 519 - €6 355 - **£4 500** - FF41 688
The Brothers Oil/canvas (76x63.5cm 29x25in) London 1998
$2 152 - €2 006 - **£1 300** - FF13 159
A Watchful Eye Oil/board (21.5x30.5cm 8x12in) London 1998

HORLOR Joseph 1809-1887 **[126]**
$1 180 - €1 086 - **£730** - FF7 123
East Lynn River Oil/canvas (41.5x62cm 16x24in) Bristol, Avon 1999
$712 - €827 - **£500** - FF5 426
Cattle watering before a Cottage in a Mountainous Landscape Oil/canvas (30.5x51cm 12x20in) London 2001

HÖRMANN von Theodor 1814-1895 **[50]**
$3 666 - €4 360 - **£2 616** - FF28 602
Wasserfall im Kolbach Thale Hohe Tatra Öl/Leinwand (68.5x55.5cm 26x21in) Wien 2000
$3 583 - €3 731 - **£2 270** - FF24 475
Friedliche Seelandschaft mit drei Männern Huile/panneau (18x36cm 7x14in) Zürich 2000
$2 996 - €2 907 - **£1 848** - FF19 068
Winterlandschaft Aquarell/Papier (15x34cm 5x13in) Wien 1999

HORN AF EKEBYHOLM Adam 1725-1796 **[6]**
$4 218 - €4 725 - **£2 932** - FF30 994
Sydländsk hamn med figurer Oil/canvas (42x50cm 16x19in) Uppsala 2001

HORN Harry XX **[5]**
$4 250 - €4 580 - **£2 898** - FF30 045
Spring Landscape with blossom and White House Oil/canvas (40x50cm 16x20in) Hatfield PA 2001

HORN Rebecca 1944 **[71]**
$16 000 - €18 209 - **£11 243** - FF119 443
Climbing up the Magic Mountain Installation (230x30x35.5cm 90x11x13in) New-York 2001
$12 000 - €10 353 - **£7 212** - FF67 911
Piece for Buster Keaton's Bedroom Construction (61x16x51cm 24x6x20in) New-York 1998

🖊 **$1 808** - €1 677 - **£1 091** - FF11 000
Kangourou Encre (27.5x21.5cm 10x8in) Paris 1999

📷 **$951** - €1 135 - **£678** - FF7 442
New York Photograph in colors (42.5x50cm 16x19in) Hamburg 2000

HORN Roni 1955 [20]

🖊 **$7 280** - €8 508 - **£5 197** - FF55 812
Ohne Titel Mixed media (34.5x37cm 13x14in) Zürich 2001

🪶 **$55 000** - €63 856 - **£33 880** - FF346 714
Steven's Bouquet Sculpture (107x127x38cm 42x50x14in) New-York 1999

🖊 **$4 750** - €4 565 - **£2 926** - FF29 946
A Social History of Mush-Rooms Gouache (27x35.5cm 10x13in) New-York 1999

📇 **$103** - €122 - **£74** - FF800
Sans titre Offset (84x64cm 33x25in) Paris 2001

📷 **$13 000** - €14 795 - **£9 135** - FF97 047
«Suite No.1» Photograph in colors (38.5x29cm 15x11in) New-York 2001

HORNBROOK Thomas Lyde 1780-1855 [24]

🖊 **$9 423** - €10 114 - **£6 400** - FF66 345
The Battle of San Domingo Oil/canvas (58x97cm 22x38in) London 2001

🖊 **$1 442** - €1 371 - **£900** - FF8 994
A View of St. Malo Watercolour (19x24.5cm 7x9in) London 1999

HORNEL Edward Atkinson 1864-1933 [151]

🖊 **$44 714** - €52 552 - **£31 000** - FF344 720
The Nest Oil/canvas (103x128cm 40x50in) Edinburgh 2000

🖊 **$18 669** - €20 918 - **£13 000** - FF137 212
Three Japanese Girls Oil/canvas (65x51cm 25x20in) Edinburgh 2001

🖊 **$10 419** - €9 843 - **£6 500** - FF64 566
Summer Blossom Oil/board (36x25cm 14x9in) Perthshire 1999

HORNEMANN Christian 1765-1844 [20]

🖊 **$1 262** - €1 502 - **£900** - FF9 850
Head and Shoulders Portrait of Kammerherre Jacob Frederik Van Deurs Pastel/paper (47x38cm 18x14in) Bath 2000

HORNER Friedrich 1800-1864 [24]

🖊 **$2 542** - €2 425 - **£1 547** - FF15 907
Schäumender Wasserfall in bewaldeter Schlucht Aquarelle (50.5x41.5cm 19x16in) Bern 1999

HORNER George Christopher 1829-1881 [2]

🖊 **$50 473** - €55 774 - **£35 000** - FF365 855
Ellen Chapman, the wild beast Tamer Oil/canvas (62x74.5cm 24x29in) London 2001

HORNICK Erasmus ?-1583 [3]

🖊 **$8 000** - €7 017 - **£4 857** - FF46 030
Design for a Wall Lamp, Allegories of Justice, Eloquence, Temperance Ink (32.5x20.5cm 12x8in) New-York 1999

HORNOR Thomas 1785-1844 [5]

🖊 **$2 332** - €2 147 - **£1 400** - FF14 081
River Neath, near Aberdulais Watercolour (17x32.5cm 6x12in) Glamorgan 1999

HORNUNG Charles Émile 1883-1956 [31]

🖊 **$1 090** - €1 002 - **£669** - FF6 572
Femme de Profil Pastel (44x59cm 17x23in) Zürich 1999

HORNUNG Preben 1919-1989 [271]

$5 056 - €4 167 - **£2 976** - FF27 335
Sergels fugle Oil/canvas (158x128cm 62x50in) Köbenhavn 1998

$1 244 - €1 407 - **£841** - FF9 230
Fra teaterrummet Oil/canvas (56x47cm 22x18in) Köbenhavn 2000

$424 - €404 - **£265** - FF2 648
Grentema Oil/canvas (27x46cm 10x18in) Köbenhavn 1999

🖊 **$279** - €282 - **£174** - FF1 850
Tre kompositioner Oil chalks (11x17cm 4x6in) Köbenhavn 2000

HORNUNG-JENSEN Carl 1882-1960 [147]

$399 - €377 - **£248** - FF2 471
Kystparti i naerheden af Hornbaek Oil/canvas (83x122cm 32x48in) Köbenhavn 1999

$320 - €295 - **£198** - FF1 933
Malerens havestue en sommerdag Oil/canvas (28.5x39cm 11x15in) Vejle 1998

HORNY Conrad 1764-1807 [6]

📇 **$247** - €281 - **£172** - FF1 844
Gebirgslandschaften mit Wanderern Radierung (10.5x15.5cm 4x6in) Berlin 2001

HORNY Franz Theobald 1798-1824 [7]

$27 000 - €30 242 - **£18 759** - FF198 374
Italiante Landscape with Ruins Oil/canvas (83.5x109.5cm 32x43in) New-York 2001

$5 256 - €4 600 - **£3 183** - FF30 177
Brücke über einem Fluss in einem Park Watercolour (16.8x21.6cm 6x8in) Berlin 1998

HORNYANSKY Nicholas 1896-1965 [201]

📇 **$162** - €156 - **£100** - FF1 023
«Victoria College in Spring, Toronto» Etching, aquatint in colors (18.5x16cm 7x6in) Toronto 1999

HOROVITZ Leopold 1838-1917 [14]

$62 400 - €58 138 - **£38 800** - FF381 360
Kaiserin Elisabeth von Österreich Öl/Leinwand (160x110cm 62x43in) Wien 1999

$12 000 - €14 346 - **£8 245** - FF94 104
Portrait of a Jewish Youth Oil/canvas (93x73cm 36x28in) Tel Aviv 2000

HORQUES Miguel XIX [6]

$1 056 - €961 - **£640** - FF6 304
Vistas granadinas Oleo/tabla (27x16cm 10x6in) Madrid 1999

HORRIX Hendrikus Mattheus 1845-1923 [27]

$2 043 - €2 269 - **£1 421** - FF14 883
Aardappelschillende jonge Zeeuwse vrouw in interieur Oil/canvas (57x39.5cm 22x15in) Groningen 2001

$440 - €511 - **£309** - FF3 353
Bauernstube Oil/canvas/panel (25x35cm 9x13in) Rudolstadt-Thüringen 2001

HORSFALL Robert Bruce 1869-1948 [4]

🖊 **$1 900** - €2 039 - **£1 294** - FF13 378
Bird study with Sharp-Shinned Hawks Watercolour, gouache (33x23cm 12x9in) Boston MA 2001

HORSFIELD Craigie 1949 [7]

📷 **$8 219** - €8 823 - **£5 500** - FF57 873
Placa de Braus de la Monumental... Barcelona, October Photograph (99.5x96cm 39x37in) London 2000

HORSLEY Hopkins H. Hobday 1807-1890 [8]

$5 698 - €6 625 - **£4 000** - FF43 457
Busy Beach Scene with Archers/Figures in a Rocky Cove Oil/canvas (19.5x29.5cm 7x11in) Billingshurst, West-Sussex 2001

HORSLEY John Calcott 1817-1903 **[26]**
$1 315 - €1 493 - **£900** - FF9 794
The sweep Boy Oil/canvas (53.5x43cm 21x16in)
Bury St. Edmunds, Suffolk 2000

HORSLEY Walter Charles 1855-? **[7]**
$28 479 - €27 475 - **£18 000** - FF180 225
Striking a Bargain Oil/canvas (92x71cm 36x27in)
London 1999

HORST Gerrit Willemsz 1612-1652 **[3]**
$45 214 - €38 494 - **£27 000** - FF252 506
Tobias and the Angel Oil/panel (115x84.5cm
45x33in) London 1998

HORST Horst Paul 1906-1999 **[336]**
$3 444 - €3 323 - **£2 163** - FF21 800
Mainbocher Corset Photograph (50x40cm 19x15in)
München 1999

HORST van der Gerrit 1581/2-1629 **[1]**
$2 733 - €2 359 - **£1 649** - FF15 471
**View o a broad river valley, with boats moored
to the left** Ink (24x41.8cm 9x16in) Amsterdam 1999

HORSTOK van Johannes Petrus 1745-1825 **[6]**
$8 835 - €9 907 - **£6 000** - FF64 984
Figures in a Courtyard Oil/panel (63x46cm
24x18in) London 2000
$4 247 - €3 842 - **£2 604** - FF25 203
L'enfant au hochet Huile/panneau (16.5x12.5cm
6x4in) Bruxelles 1999

HORTER Earl 1881-1940 **[95]**
$800 - €859 - **£535** - FF5 632
Outhouses Graphite (29x38.5cm 11x15in)
Philadelphia PA 2000
$225 - €208 - **£138** - FF1 313
The Kitchen, New Orleans Aquatint (31x26cm
12x10in) New-Orleans LA 1999

HORTON Etty XIX-XX **[57]**
$800 - €854 - **£545** - FF5 604
Near Colchester Oil/canvas (50x76cm 20x30in) St.
Petersburg FL 2001
$327 - €348 - **£220** - FF2 281
**River Landscape with Figure Fishing in the
Foreground** Oil/canvas (24x34.5cm 9x13in) London
2001

HORTON George Edward 1860-? **[47]**
$411 - €488 - **£300** - FF3 202
Street Scene in North Shields Watercolour/paper
(16x22.5cm 6x8in) Newcastle-upon-Tyne 2001

HORTON John M. 1935 **[5]**
$3 570 - €4 037 - **£2 512** - FF26 482
«Resolution at Nootka» Oil/canvas (61x91cm
24x35in) Vancouver, BC. 2001

HORTON William Samuel 1865-1936 **[121]**
$2 600 - €3 048 - **£1 870** - FF19 996
The Pasture Oil/panel (37.5x45.5cm 14x17in) New-
York 2001
$951 - €915 - **£586** - FF6 000
La halte des chameliers Pastel/papier (48x62cm
18x24in) Granville 1999

HORVAT Frank 1928 **[24]**
$1 500 - €1 420 - **£932** - FF9 313
Harper's Bazaar Gelatin silver print (26x38cm
10x15in) New-York 1999

HORVATH George A. 1933 **[21]**
$716 - €803 - **£498** - FF5 265
Landscape of Bygone Days Oil/canvas (55x76cm
22x30in) Calgary, Alberta 2000

$523 - €623 - **£360** - FF4 086
Near Bragg Creek Oil/canvas (12x16cm 4x6in)
Calgary, Alberta 2000

HORWITZ Emmanuel Henry XIX-XX **[3]**
$1 618 - €1 519 - **£1 000** - FF9 965
**A Profile Portrait of a Young Lady, half Length,
seated** Coloured chalks/paper (90x62cm 35x24in)
Billingshurst, West-Sussex 1999

HORWOOD Charles XX **[11]**
$3 800 - €3 554 - **£2 297** - FF23 315
At the Shore Oil/board (28x40.5cm 11x15in) New-
York 1999

HORY de Elmyr 1911-1979 **[69]**
$3 287 - €3 529 - **£2 200** - FF23 147
Trees in Provence, After Paul Cezanne Oil/canvas
(76x56cm 29x22in) London 2000
$530 - €601 - **£360** - FF3 940
Dama elegante Lápices de color/papel (24.5x19.5cm
9x7in) Madrid 2000
$1 008 - €1 081 - **£666** - FF7 092
Flores Acuarela/papel (45x42cm 17x16in) Madrid
2000

HÖSCH Hans 1855-1902 **[4]**
$2 749 - €2 381 - **£1 686** - FF15 621
Taking Cover Oil/panel (30x20cm 11x7in) New-York
1999

HOSCH Karl 1900-1972 **[34]**
$1 029 - €943 - **£627** - FF6 185
Gebirgige Winterlandschaft Öl/Leinwand (58x68cm
22x26in) Zürich 1999

HOSCHÉDÉ-MONET Blanche 1865-1947 **[33]**
$16 000 - €16 123 - **£9 974** - FF105 760
Bord de Seine Oil/canvas (60x73.5cm 23x28in) New-
York 1999

HÖSEL Erich XIX **[10]**
$552 - €613 - **£384** - FF4 024
Zwei Bären aneinander gelehnt sitzend Porcelain
(H10.5cm H4in) Köln 2001

HOSEMANN Theodor 1807-1875 **[66]**
$5 852 - €6 647 - **£4 093** - FF43 600
Rast am Weg Öl/Leinwand (51x63cm 20x24in) Berlin
2001
$3 262 - €3 579 - **£2 216** - FF23 477
Der Uckermärker und die Importierten Oil/panel
(16.3x23.5cm 6x9in) Berlin 2000
$670 - €613 - **£408** - FF4 024
**«Annchen, lieb Annchen, was hast' in Deinem
Kännchen, Rothen Wein...»** Aquarell/Papier
(14x10cm 5x3in) Berlin 1999

HOSHI Joichi 1913-1979 **[13]**
$450 - €494 - **£305** - FF3 240
Constellation 23 Color lithograph (71x49cm 28x19in)
Bolton MA 2000

HOSIASSON Philippe 1898-1978 **[83]**
$4 500 - €3 882 - **£2 714** - FF25 466
Red and Blue Oil/canvas (97x129.5cm 38x50in) New-
York 1998
$1 697 - €1 448 - **£1 024** - FF9 500
Composition Huile/toile (65x81cm 25x31in) Saint-
Germain-en-Laye 1998
$682 - €762 - **£456** - FF5 000
Sans titre Aquarelle/papier (104.5x71.5cm 41x28in)
Paris 2000

HOSKINS Gayle Porter 1887-1962 **[22]**
$4 000 - €4 430 - £2 773 - FF29 056
Three soldiers fighting with knives Oil/canvas (71x76cm 28x30in) Downington PA 2001

HOSKINS John ?-1664/65 **[15]**
$3 551 - €3 579 - £2 214 - FF23 477
Brustbild des Sir Algenon Percy, Earl of Northumberland Miniature (7.9x6.4cm 3x2in) Stuttgart 2000

HOSMER Harriet Goodhue 1830-1908 **[3]**
$5 500 - €6 487 - £3 879 - FF42 549
Portrait of a Distinguished Gentleman Carrare marble (66x36x26cm 26x14x10in) New-Orleans LA 2001

HOSOE Eikoh 1933 **[20]**
$850 - €954 - £589 - FF6 255
Kamaitachi #8 Gelatin silver print (30x20cm 12x8in) New-York 2000

HOSOTTE Georges 1936 **[36]**
$2 145 - €2 439 - £1 472 - FF16 000
Paysage pastoral Huile/toile (73x60cm 28x23in) Provins 2000

HOSSEIN Mohammed XIX **[2]**
$50 512 - €42 686 - £30 212 - FF280 000
Une princesse qajar Huile/toile (163x80cm 64x31in) Paris 2001

HØST Oluf 1884-1966 **[298]**
$35 991 - €36 271 - £22 437 - FF237 924
Solnedgang over Østerlars Oil/canvas (89x143cm 35x56in) København 2001
$7 968 - €8 582 - £5 484 - FF56 294
Figur på en klippe, Gudhjem Oil/canvas (63x55cm 24x21in) København 2001
$3 661 - €3 095 - £2 185 - FF20 299
Personer foran gård Oil/canvas (27x33cm 10x12in) København 1998
$540 - €457 - £323 - FF2 998
Ildebrand, Bognemark Soft pencil (22x17cm 8x6in) København 1998
$188 - €214 - £129 - FF1 406
Figurer ved rundkirke på Bornholm Color lithograph (56x73cm 22x28in) Vejle 2000

HOSTEIN Édouard 1804-1889 **[25]**
$33 000 - €39 131 - £22 704 - FF256 683
View of the City of Lyon Oil/canvas (98x216cm 38x85in) New-York 2001
$939 - €1 023 - £650 - FF6 712
«Castelnau» Oil/canvas (48.5x57.5cm 19x22in) London 2001
$2 608 - €2 439 - £1 579 - FF16 000
Paysage de campagne Huile/toile (36x44cm 14x17in) Reims 1999

HOTERE Ralph 1931 **[35]**
$40 310 - €45 183 - £28 190 - FF296 380
«Painting'77 Yellow» Enamel (240x120cm 94x47in) Auckland 2001
$8 513 - €8 846 - £5 338 - FF58 029
Ninteen Eighty Four, Polaris Mixed media (77.5x77cm 30x30in) Auckland 2000
$4 031 - €4 518 - £2 819 - FF29 638
«Drawing for Ian Weddes Pathway to the Sea» Watercolour (56x76cm 22x29in) Auckland 2001
$1 061 - €1 209 - £733 - FF7 929
Untitled Serigraph (106x71cm 41x27in) Auckland 2000

HOTTOT Louis 1829-1905 **[33]**
$4 400 - €3 831 - £2 623 - FF25 128
A Servant Holding a Tray with a Dagger in his Sash Sculpture (H109cm H43in) St. Louis MO 1998
$782 - €843 - £540 - FF5 528
Figure d'une femme orientale tenant une poulie de métier à tisser Métal (H52cm H20in) Antwerpen 2001

HÖTZENDORFF von Theodor 1898-1974 **[21]**
$1 890 - €2 045 - £1 295 - FF13 415
Südländische Dorf am Meer Oil/panel (44x62cm 17x24in) Stuttgart 2001

HOU Axel 1860-1948 **[39]**
$909 - €1 005 - £630 - FF6 591
Pavillon, efterår Oil/canvas (74x87cm 29x34in) København 2001

HOUASSE Michel-Ange c.1680-1730 **[6]**
$14 560 - €16 818 - £10 080 - FF110 320
Muchacha criolla Oleo/tabla (39x28cm 15x11in) Madrid 2000
$6 587 - €6 432 - £4 200 - FF42 193
Saint Joseph seated, looking to the right, his hands clasped Black & white chalks (28.5x19cm 11x7in) London 1999

HOUBEN Charles 1871-1931 **[72]**
$340 - €397 - £243 - FF2 601
Un personnage avec rivière et cascade arborées Huile/toile (49x73.5cm 19x28in) Liège 2001
$185 - €173 - £114 - FF1 138
Maison au bord de l'eau Huile/carton (34x40cm 13x15in) Bruxelles 1999

HOUBEN Henri 1858-1931 **[78]**
$13 920 - €14 873 - £9 480 - FF97 560
Riviergezicht met koeienhoedster Huile/toile (100x160.5cm 39x63in) Lokeren 2001
$1 792 - €1 859 - £1 140 - FF12 195
Dreef met koeien Oil/canvas (70x100cm 27x39in) Lokeren 2000

HOUBRAKEN Jacobus 1698-1780 **[22]**
$190 - €204 - £127 - FF1 341
Bildnis des Cornelis Troost, nach Cornelis Troost Kupferstich (37.4x26.8cm 14x10in) Berlin 2000

HOUBRON Frédéric Anatole 1851-1908 **[24]**
$5 131 - €4 348 - £3 065 - FF28 523
Belebte Pariser Strassenszenerie Gouache/paper (25x33cm 9x12in) Bremen 1998

HOUDON Jean-Antoine 1741-1828 **[94]**
$1 238 - €1 181 - £754 - FF7 749
Knabenbüste Plâtre (H30.5cm H12in) Bern 1999

HOUëL Jean Pierre Louis L. 1735-1813 **[32]**
$4 184 - €4 491 - £2 800 - FF29 460
An open landscape with a woman and her horse on a path Oil/panel (16x20cm 6x7in) London 2000
$5 977 - €6 416 - £4 000 - FF42 086
Classical Landscape with a Tomb Gouache/paper (52x62cm 20x24in) London 2000

HOUGAARD Henning 1922-1995 **[38]**
$481 - €463 - £297 - FF3 037
Andpar vid sjökant Oil/canvas (61x82cm 24x32in) Malmö 1999

HOUGH William B. act.1857-1894 **[9]**
$3 287 - €3 001 - £2 000 - FF19 685
Apples and Raspberries on a mossy Bank/Plums and redcurrants Oil/canvas (25.5x40.5cm 10x15in) London 1998

⬦ **$1 014** - €1 110 - **£700** - FF7 284
Plums and Pears on a Mossy Bank
Watercolour/paper (25.5x35.5cm 10x13in) London 2001

HOUGHTON William [1]
⬦ **$2 000** - €1 906 - **£1 267** - FF12 500
Repos en sous-bois Pastel/papier (63x82cm 24x32in) Douarnenez 1999

HOUGHTON William B. XIX-XX **[5]**
⬦ **$1 707** - €1 984 - **£1 200** - FF13 013
Still Life of pink Roses on a marble topped Table Watercolour (20.5x30cm 8x11in) London 2001

HOUGHTON William Robert 1826-1897 **[1]**
⬦ **$2 977** - €2 784 - **£1 800** - FF18 265
Malabar Point, Bombay/Bombay Harbour
Oil/canvas (18x35.5cm 7x13in) London 1999

HOUPIN Louis XX **[5]**
⬦ **$245** - €229 - **£151** - FF1 500
Chemin de fer de l'État. La Côte d'Émeraude. Cap Frehelo Affiche couleur (104x72cm 40x28in)
Paris 1999

HOURREGUE Jean XX **[31]**
⬦ **$217** - €213 - **£140** - FF1 400
Pontacq Aquarelle/papier (31.5x43.5cm 12x17in)
Tarbes 1999

HOURY Charles Borromée A. 1823-1898 **[5]**
⬦ **$15 000** - €12 941 - **£9 049** - FF84 889
Catching the trolley Oil/canvas (141.5x100.5cm 55x39in) New-York 1998

HOUSE Gordon 1932 **[20]**
⬦ **$311** - €370 - **£220** - FF2 424
«Triangle» Screenprint (86x43cm 33x16in) London 2000

HOUSER Allan Houzous 1914-1994 **[11]**
⬦ **$25 000** - €29 178 - **£17 647** - FF191 397
Apache Buffalo Hunt Oil/canvas (157x107cm 61x42in) New-York 1999
⬦ **$12 000** - €11 894 - **£7 506** - FF78 022
Holders of Knowledge Bronze (H51cm H20in)
New-York 1999

HOUSEZ Charles Gustave 1822-c.1880 **[9]**
⬦ **$16 612** - €14 216 - **£10 000** - FF93 251
Intérieur d'une Verrerie Oil/canvas (100.5x81.5cm 39x32in) London 1998

HOUSMAN Laurence 1865-1959 **[5]**
⬦ **$2 410** - €2 391 - **£1 500** - FF15 683
Young Lady watering Plants in a Formal Garden
Ink (18x11.5cm 7x4in) London 1999

HOUSSER Yvonne McKague 1898-1996 **[31]**
⬦ **$2 030** - €1 950 - **£1 258** - FF12 791
Old Mine Shaft, Colbalt Oil/panel (40.5x32cm 15x12in) Toronto 1999

HOUSSIN Edouard 1847-1917 **[6]**
⬦ **$11 229** - €11 316 - **£7 000** - FF74 225
Esmeralda Bronze (H120cm H47in) London 2000

HOUSSOT Louis 1824-1890 **[3]**
⬦ **$3 670** - €4 090 - **£2 565** - FF26 831
Fêtes galantes Öl/Leinwand (13x16.5cm 5x6in)
München 2001

HOUSTON Cody XX **[1]**
⬦ **$15 000** - €13 636 - **£9 034** - FF89 445
Circle Cross Cutback Bronze (H129cm H51in)
Hayden ID 1998

HOUSTON George 1869-1947 **[205]**
⬦ **$6 572** - €6 209 - **£4 100** - FF40 726
Spring on the Caff Water, North Ayrshire Oil/canvas (102x127cm 40x50in) Perthshire 1999
⬦ **$3 155** - €3 503 - **£2 200** - FF22 978
A Sunny Winter's Day Oil/canvas (45.5x61cm 17x24in) London 2001
⬦ **$1 179** - €1 193 - **£720** - FF7 824
Woodland Scene Oil/canvas (31x46cm 12x18in)
Sighthill 2000
⬦ **$691** - €650 - **£420** - FF4 262
Groatholm Farm Watercolour (44x59cm 17x23in)
London 1999

HOUSTON Ian 1934 **[53]**
⬦ **$991** - €1 164 - **£700** - FF7 635
Horse and Cart on a Winters Day Oil/board (51x76cm 20x29in) Manchester 2000
⬦ **$646** - €754 - **£450** - FF4 948
The Harbour, Portofino Oil/board (13.5x23cm 5x9in) London 2000

HOUSTON John 1930 **[37]**
⬦ **$3 129** - €2 976 - **£1 900** - FF19 523
Running bather and Man Oil/canvas (51x61cm 20x24in) Edinburgh 1999
⬦ **$545** - €613 - **£380** - FF4 024
Red Landscape Gouache (27x36.5cm 10x14in)
Edinburgh 2001

HOUSTON John Adam Plimmer 1812-1884 **[27]**
⬦ **$333** - €350 - **£220** - FF2 294
Invercoe Watercolour (25x35.5cm 9x13in)
Billingshurst, West-Sussex 2000

HOUSTON John Rennie McKenzie 1856-1932 **[18]**
⬦ **$971** - €1 043 - **£650** - FF6 841
Peeling Potatoes Oil/canvas (45.5x35.5cm 17x13in)
London 2001
⬦ **$801** - €726 - **£500** - FF4 764
Darning Time Watercolour (43x33,5cm 16x13in)
Glasgow 1999

HOUSTON Richard 1721-1775 **[18]**
⬦ **$207** - €179 - **£125** - FF1 176
Childers, the Fleetest Horse that Ever run at Newmarket after Seymour Mezzotint (29.5x35cm 11x13in) Stockholm 1999

HOUSTON Robert 1891-1940 **[40]**
⬦ **$1 575** - €1 370 - **£950** - FF8 989
The Cobbler from Arrochar Oil/canvas (40.5x51cm 15x20in) Glasgow 1998

HOUT M.D. XVII **[2]**
⬦ **$1 410** - €1 588 - **£972** - FF10 418
Le Roi boit, after Cornelis Saftleven Oil/panel (44x62cm 17x24in) Amsterdam 2000

HOUTEN van den Henricus Leonardus 1801-1879
[10]
⬦ **$217 090** - €189 293 - **£131 274** - FF1 241 680
The Exploring Party Coming upon an Encampment of Natives Oil/canvas (133x219cm 52x86in) Melbourne 1998
⬦ **$8 755** - €9 648 - **£5 823** - FF63 285
The Trout Stream Oil/canvas (44x60cm 17x23in)
Melbourne 2000

HOUTHUESEN Albert 1903-1979 **[50]**
⬦ **$1 067** - €1 257 - **£750** - FF8 243
Marble Dust Acrylic (51x40.5cm 20x15in) Suffolk 2000
⬦ **$996** - €1 173 - **£700** - FF7 694
Yellow Flowers in Glass Oil/board (30.5x25.5cm 12x10in) Suffolk 2000

🖊 $569 - €670 - £400 - FF4 396
Roadside Madonna with Beggar Ink (35.5x25.5cm 13x10in) Suffolk 2000

HOUTMAN Martinus I 1746-1819 [1]
🕊 $32 104 - €36 302 - £22 592 - FF238 128
Portrait of Willem Borski (1765-1814) Oil/canvas (90.5x67.5cm 35x26in) Amsterdam 2001

HOVE van Bartholomäus 1850-1914 [4]
🕊 $9 987 - €11 344 - £7 007 - FF74 415
A Town Scene with Figures on a frozen Canal Oil/panel (45.5x54cm 17x21in) Amsterdam 2001

HOVE van Bartholomeus J. 1790-1880 [75]
🕊 $25 096 - €29 496 - £17 400 - FF193 479
A Cappriccio View of the Hooglandse Kerk, Leiden, in Winter Oil/canvas (57.5x47.5cm 22x18in) Amsterdam 2000
🕊 $12 065 - €11 344 - £7 470 - FF74 415
Capricio View with Figures leaving a Church in Winter Oil/panel (29.5x22cm 11x8in) Amsterdam 1999
🕊 $2 593 - €2 723 - £1 635 - FF17 859
View in Deventer (?) with a moored Barge on a Canal Watercolour (29x37.5cm 11x14in) Amsterdam 2000

HOVE van Francine 1942 [1]
🕊 $86 499 - €96 043 - £60 165 - FF630 000
Le divan Huile/toile (90x115cm 35x45in) Paris 2001

HOVE van Hubertus, Huib 1814-1864 [48]
🕊 $2 687 - €2 266 - £1 595 - FF14 863
The Inundation Oil/panel (57.5x45cm 22x17in) Amsterdam 1998
🕊 $4 837 - €4 079 - £2 871 - FF26 754
A Servant Girl with poultry Oil/panel (26x21cm 10x8in) Amsterdam 1998
🖊 $445 - €499 - £308 - FF3 274
De Haagse visbank Aquarelle/papier (14.5x10cm 5x3in) The Hague 2001

HOVEN Hendrik Lodewijk B. 1822-c.1880 [2]
🕊 $4 902 - €4 710 - £3 021 - FF30 894
Le petit-déjeuner Huile/toile (52x39cm 20x15in) Bruxelles 1999

HOVENDEN Thomas 1840-1895 [17]
🕊 $55 000 - €57 011 - £34 875 - FF373 967
The Story of the Hunt Oil/canvas (63.5x79cm 25x31in) New-York 2000
🕊 $3 000 - €3 517 - £2 158 - FF23 073
Couple in an Interior Oil/canvas (25.5x38cm 10x14in) New-York 2001

HOVENER Jan 1936 [12]
🕊 $1 038 - €1 180 - £717 - FF7 739
Draaimolen op de kermis Oil/panel (63x83cm 24x32in) Dordrecht 2000

HOVEY Charles Mason 1810-? [1]
🖊 $12 000 - €11 258 - £7 414 - FF73 846
The old Hovey Tavern, Cambridgeport, Massachusetts Watercolour (34x47.5cm 13x18in) New-York 1999

HOVI Mikko 1879-1962 [25]
🕊 $379 - €336 - £232 - FF2 206
Mor och barn Bronze (H29cm H11in) Helsinki 1999

HOW Beatrice Julia 1867-1932 [45]
🕊 $2 943 - €2 617 - £1 800 - FF17 167
Maternity Oil/canvas (65x81.5cm 25x32in) London 1999
🖊 $1 148 - €1 052 - £700 - FF6 898
Bébé au joujou bleu Pastel/paper (43x34cm 16x13in) London 1999

HOWARD Bessie Jeannette 1890-1962 [10]
🕊 $900 - €865 - £555 - FF5 677
Swan Boat, Boston Public Garden Oil/canvas/board (51x40.5cm 20x15in) Boston MA 1999

HOWARD Cecil de Blaquière 1888-? [8]
🕊 $3 064 - €3 354 - £2 114 - FF22 000
Baigneuse aux bras levés Bronze (H45cm H17in) Paris 2001

HOWARD Eloise 1899-? [5]
🕮 $1 000 - €960 - £619 - FF6 299
Opening the Road Woodcut (23x29.5cm 9x11in) New-York 1999

HOWARD Frank 1805-1866 [2]
🖊 $3 135 - €3 062 - £2 000 - FF20 088
Scenes from Shakespeare's Plays Pencil/paper (24x17cm 9x6in) London 2001

HOWARD George of Carlisle 1843-1911 [54]
🕊 $18 202 - €21 170 - £13 000 - FF138 864
«The Palatine, Rome» Oil/canvas (61x96.5cm 24x37in) London 2001
🕊 $819 - €781 - £500 - FF5 120
Kroustar, Walsh River, the Boer War Oil/panel (16.5x23.5cm 6x9in) Bury St. Edmunds, Suffolk 1999
🖊 $604 - €640 - £400 - FF4 197
View of Girgenti, Sicily Watercolour (12x45cm 4x17in) Penrith, Cumbria 2000

HOWARD Henry 1769-1847 [6]
🕊 $14 195 - €15 238 - £9 500 - FF99 955
Diana and her Nymphs Oil/canvas (127x103cm 50x40in) London 2000
🕊 $4 860 - €4 675 - £3 000 - FF30 664
Fairies on the Sea Shore Oil/canvas (51x61cm 20x24in) London 1999

HOWARD Ken 1932 [260]
🕊 $7 471 - €8 020 - £5 000 - FF52 608
The Silk Shirt Oil/canvas (122x101.5cm 48x39in) London 2000
🕊 $2 834 - €3 359 - £2 000 - FF22 036
Charlotte Reclining Oil/canvas (40.5x51cm 15x20in) London 2000
🕊 $1 144 - €1 231 - £780 - FF8 073
A Beach Scene with Figures and a Wind Breake nearby Oil/canvas (20.5x25.5cm 8x10in) West-Yorshire 2001
🖊 $651 - €703 - £450 - FF4 612
Seated Female Nude beside a Vase of Flowers Watercolour/paper (24x17.5cm 9x6in) London 2001

HOWARD Lucile 1885-1960 [9]
🕊 $500 - €481 - £308 - FF3 154
Overlooking the Hillside Oil/paper/board (15x20.5cm 5x8in) Boston MA 1999

HOWARD Marion P. 1883-? [7]
🕊 $28 000 - €30 729 - £18 029 - FF201 566
Home of the Eagle Oil/canvas (76x61.5cm 29x24in) Beverly-Hills CA 2000
🕊 $2 000 - €1 709 - £1 210 - FF11 208
A Woman Reading in the Woods Oil/board (28x35.5cm 11x13in) San-Francisco CA 1998

HOWARD Norman 1899-1955 [5]
🕮 $1 000 - €1 090 - £692 - FF7 147
«Egyptian State Railways» Poster (99x59cm 39x23in) New-York 2001

HOWARD Richard E. 1912-1996 [4]
🕮 $500 - €547 - £335 - FF3 589
Of East Dennis Village Print (48x56cm 19x22in) East-Dennis MA 2000

H

HOWARD William XIX [12]
$1 599 - €1 540 - **£1 000** - FF10 101
A Riverside Town View Oil/canvas (78x130cm 30x51in) London 1999

HOWARD-JONES Ray 1903-1996 [24]
$666 - €613 - **£400** - FF4 023
Picton Point Watercolour, gouache (23.5x32.5cm 9x12in) Glamorgan 1999

HOWARTH Albany E. 1872-1936 [47]
$98 - €114 - **£70** - FF748
Rheims Cathedral Etching (72x54cm 28x21in) Cambridge 2000

HOWD van Doug XX [2]
$3 111 - €3 069 - **£2 000** - FF20 129
Water Buffalo with three Birds Bronze (29x42cm 11x16in) London 1999

HOWE John 1957 [2]
$2 487 - €2 153 - **£1 500** - FF14 124
The Cygnet and the Firebird Watercolour (49.6x73.7cm 19x29in) London-1998

HOWE William Henry 1846-1929 [30]
$1 600 - €1 728 - **£1 105** - FF11 334
On the Strand Egmond Holland Oil/canvas (60x81cm 24x32in) Detroit MI 2001
$1 500 - €1 653 - **£1 000** - FF10 841
Sand Dunes with Scrub Pine Oil/panel (31x40cm 12x16in) Portsmouth NH 2000

HOWELL Felicia Waldo 1897-1968 [7]
$101 451 - €95 294 - **£61 152** - FF625 086
Wall Street - The Noon Hour Oil/canvas (102x76cm 40x29in) Amsterdam 1999
$4 000 - €4 726 - **£2 834** - FF31 003
Portrait of the Residence at 1609 sixteenth Street, N.W., Washington Gouache 39.5x30cm 15x11in) Boston MA 2000

HOWELL Peter 1932 [10]
$961 - €1 087 - **£650** - FF7 132
Jockey Up Oil/canvas (49x58cm 19x23in) Northumberland 2000

HOWES Jerome 1955 [46]
$850 - €787 - **£525** - FF5 161
Still Life with Cherries and Basket Oil/board (40x45cm 16x18in) East-Dennis MA 1999

HOWES Samuel P. 1806-1881 [4]
$2 000 - €2 303 - **£1 364** - FF15 104
A Dark-haired Young Woman wearing a Bertha Collar over a Black Dress Oil/canvas (68.5x56cm 26x22in) New-York 2000

HOWET Marie 1897-1984 [135]
$1 377 - €1 189 - **£830** - FF7 800
Soir d'été à Naômé Huile/toile (53x64cm 20x25in) Bruxelles 1998
$379 - €421 - **£253** - FF2 764
Petit bouquet d'automne Huile/toile (38x38cm 14x14in) Bruxelles 2000
$231 - €248 - **£157** - FF1 626
Autour de Mycènes Aquarelle/papier (28.5x35cm 11x13in) Bruxelles 2001

HOWIE James 1780-1836 [4]
$4 207 - €3 946 - **£2 600** - FF25 881
A Bay Hunter Romulus in a Landscape Oil/canvas (75x60cm 29x23in) London 1999

HOWITT John Newton 1885-1958 [21]
$2 500 - €2 785 - **£1 635** - FF18 266
Magazine cover: Soldier and father with gun collection Oil/canvas/board (57x61cm 22x24in) New-York 2000

HOWITT William Samuel 1756-1822 [91]
$1 195 - €1 283 - **£800** - FF8 417
Rustics with a Horse and cart by a Barn Watercolour (15.5x20.5cm 6x8in) London 2000
$198 - €184 - **£121** - FF1 207
Jagdstiche Radierung (15x20cm 5x7in) Ahlden 1999

HOWLAND Alfred Cornelius 1838-1909 [20]
$30 000 - €32 832 - **£20 694** - FF215 364
On the Bridge Oil/canvas (44x59cm 17x23in) New-York 2001
$700 - €751 - **£468** - FF4 928
Cottage beside the River Oil/board (10x18cm 4x7in) Bolton MA 2000

HOWLAND Georges 1865-1928 [2]
$950 - €1 020 - **£635** - FF6 689
The Canal - Montreuil sur mer Pastel/canvas (59x72cm 23x28in) New-York 2000

HOWLETT Robert 1830-1858 [14]
$1 871 - €2 096 - **£1 300** - FF13 746
The Leviathan, group including Isambard Kingdom Brunel Albumen print (26x20cm 10x7in) London 2001

HOWLEY John Richard 1931 [22]
$390 - €456 - **£271** - FF2 989
«The Remote Control Man» Acrylic/paper (46x62cm 18x24in) Melbourne 2000

HOWSON Peter 1958 [91]
$2 923 - €3 259 - **£2 000** - FF21 379
Below the Bridge Oil/canvas (91.5x76cm 36x29in) Perthshire 2000
$2 493 - €2 687 - **£1 700** - FF17 627
Man Kneeling before a Disused Building Oil/canvas (38x30.5cm 14x12in) London 2001
$578 - €673 - **£400** - FF4 417
Study for the Scottish Opera's Production of Don Giovanni Crayon (20.5x25cm 8x9in) London 2000
$305 - €340 - **£200** - FF2 233
Four Scottish Scenes Lithograph (61x46cm 24x18in) Edinburgh 2000

HOYER Edward XIX [20]
$9 063 - €10 399 - **£6 200** - FF68 212
Moonlight over Constantinople Oil/canvas (29x50cm 11x19in) London 2000

HØYER Peter Julius XIX [5]
$1 257 - €1 411 - **£880** - FF9 254
Victorian Warship of the Royal Navy in the Open Sea Oil/canvas (76.5x127cm 30x50in) London 2001

HOYLAND John 1934 [125]
$3 563 - €3 909 - **£2 299** - FF25 643
Untitled Oil/canvas (203x152.5cm 79x60in) London 2000
$2 135 - €2 037 - **£1 300** - FF13 360
Abstract Oil/canvas (76x51cm 29x20in) London 1999
$1 604 - €1 616 - **£1 000** - FF10 603
Untitled Watercolour (47x71cm 18x27in) London 2000
$308 - €288 - **£191** - FF1 886
Wandering Moon Silkscreen in colors (94.5x79.5cm 37x31in) London 1999

HOYLES William R. c.1870-c.1935 **[11]**
🖉 $640 - €581 - **£400** - FF3 813
Bettys-Y-Coed Watercolour (33.5x45.5cm 13x17in)
London 1999

HOYNCK VAN PAPENDRECHT Jan 1858-1933 **[46]**
⌒ $18 152 - €19 059 - **£11 445** - FF125 017
Royal Netherland Infantry of the 17th Battalion Infantry circa 1815 Oil/canvas (90x136cm 35x53in)
Amsterdam 2000
⌒ $3 668 - €3 630 - **£2 245** - FF23 812
The Barouche of Prince Hendrik Oil/canvas
(53.5x36.5cm 21x14in) Amsterdam 2000
⌒ $2 702 - €3 176 - **£1 873** - FF20 836
Hussars in the Dunes Oil/canvas (29x55cm
11x21in) Amsterdam 2000
🖉 $834 - €817 - **£535** - FF5 357
An Infantryman Watercolour (35x26cm 13x10in)
Amsterdam 1999

HOYNINGEN-HUENE George 1900-1968 **[85]**
📷 $3 200 - €3 511 - **£2 125** - FF23 029
Portrait of Elsie de Wolfe as Refugee Gelatin silver
print (35x27.5cm 13x10in) Beverly-Hills CA 2000

HOYOLL Philipp 1816-? **[20]**
⌒ $16 320 - €15 494 - **£10 000** - FF101 633
Put Salt on their Tails, so catch them Oil/canvas
(53.5x43cm 21x16in) London 1999

HOYOS Anna Mercedes 1942 **[55]**
⌒ $35 000 - €33 714 - **£21 731** - FF221 151
Bazurto Oil/canvas (118x118cm 46x46in) New-York
1999
⌒ $13 000 - €11 335 - **£7 859** - FF74 255
Bazurto Oil/canvas (100x100cm 39x39in) New-York
1998
⌒ $5 000 - €5 801 - **£3 452** - FF38 055
Plátanos Oil/canvas (30x30cm 11x11in) New-York
2000

HØYRUP Carl 1893-1961 **[71]**
⌒ $239 - €276 - **£170** - FF1 812
Perro de caza Oleo/lienzo (65x75cm 25x29in) Madrid
2001

HOYT William H. XIX **[2]**
⌒ $11 000 - €10 010 - **£6 872** - FF65 664
Formal Still Life with Fruit and Baskets Arranged on a Marble Slab Oil/canvas (45x60cm
18x24in) Bolton MA 1999

HOYTE John Barr Clarke 1835-1913 **[53]**
🖉 $1 481 - €1 660 - **£1 032** - FF10 887
Lake landscape Watercolour/paper (24x34cm 9x13in)
Wellington 2001

HOYTEMA van Theodoor van Hoytemo 1863-1917
[32]
🖉 $587 - €544 - **£363** - FF3 571
Leguaan op rots Pastel/paper (28.5x47cm 11x18in)
Dordrecht 1999
▥ $292 - €249 - **£175** - FF1 636
Kraai Lithograph (16.3x24.9cm 6x9in) Haarlem 1998

HOYTON Edward Bouverie c.1900-1988 **[40]**
▥ $164 - €176 - **£110** - FF1 157
Tithe Barn, Abbotsbury Etching (20x30cm 8x12in)
Par, Cornwall 2000

HRADIL Béla 1885-? **[38]**
⌒ $399 - €336 - **£235** - FF2 205
Stilleben med frukt Oil/panel (24x30cm 9x11in)
Stockholm 1998

HRADIL Rudolf 1925 **[36]**
▥ $122 - €145 - **£89** - FF953
«Salzburg» Farblithographie (37.5x53cm 14x20in)
Salzburg 2001

HRDLICKA Alfred 1928 **[656]**
⌒ $8 410 - €7 263 - **£5 070** - FF47 640
Portrait Erich Fried Öl/Leinwand (100x70cm
39x27in) Wien 1998
⚒ $31 479 - €29 353 - **£19 000** - FF192 544
Stele with Female Figure Marbre Carrare
(135x20x20cm 53x7x7in) London 1999
⚒ $1 382 - €1 329 - **£853** - FF8 720
Strip tease triste Bronze (37.5x13x9.7cm 14x5x3in)
Köln 1999
🖉 $964 - €920 - **£602** - FF6 037
Ohne Titel Mixed media/paper (47.6x62.5cm 18x24in)
Köln 1999
▥ $145 - €160 - **£93** - FF1 048
200 Jahre Revolution Radierung (17x31.5cm
6x12in) Wien 2000

HRSKA Alexandr Vladimir 1890-1954 **[5]**
▥ $600 - €600 - **£366** - FF3 933
«Clovek V Kleci» Poster (99x69cm 39x27in) New-
York 2000

HRYNKOWSKI Jan 1891-1971 **[20]**
🖉 $1 712 - €1 849 - **£1 183** - FF12 131
Au verger Aquarelle (13.5x12.5cm 5x4in) Kraków
2001

HSIEH MING CHANG 1955 **[1]**
🖉 $3 936 - €4 191 - **£2 496** - FF27 492
Recalling Memories of the old Town
Watercolour/paper (80x60.5cm 31x23in) Taipei 2000

HSU PI-HUA 1957 **[2]**
⌒ $4 544 - €4 262 - **£2 825** - FF27 956
Gallop Mixed media/canvas (45.5x53cm 17x20in)
Taipei 1999

HSUEH Ava 1956 **[2]**
⌒ $6 292 - €5 901 - **£3 912** - FF38 709
Untitled Mixed media (76x102cm 29x40in) Taipei
1999

HU BAIK-RYUN 1891-1977 **[4]**
🖉 $2 400 - €2 652 - **£1 664** - FF17 396
River Landscape Ink (34.5x139.5cm 13x54in) New-
York 2001

HU NIANZU 1927 **[12]**
🖉 $5 136 - €5 636 - **£3 308** - FF36 972
Landscape Ink (55x85cm 21x33in) Hong-Kong 2000

HU YEFO 1908 **[13]**
🖉 $8 717 - €9 824 - **£6 092** - FF64 443
Autumn Breeze Ink (18.5x51cm 7x20in) Hong-Kong
2001

HU YONGKAI 1945 **[10]**
🖉 $4 487 - €5 274 - **£3 111** - FF34 594
Picking Lotus Ink (102x51cm 40x20in) Hong-Kong
2000

HUA GUAN 1740-c.1819 **[1]**
🖉 $10 939 - €10 374 - **£6 655** - FF68 051
Portrait of Yong Rong Ink/paper (31.5x104.5cm
12x41in) Hong-Kong 1999

HUA YAN 1682-1756 **[22]**
🖉 $41 024 - €48 218 - **£28 448** - FF316 288
Lotus Pond Ink (169x128.5cm 66x50in) Hong-Kong
2000

HUANG Anton 1935-1985 **[9]**
- **$8 181** - €8 565 - **£5 139** - FF56 180
  Three Dancers Oil/canvas (84x82cm 33x32in)
  Singapore 2000
- **$3 839** - €3 578 - **£2 320** - FF23 473
  Portrait of a Balinese Dancer Oil/canvas (43x35cm
  16x13in) Singapore 1999

HUANG BINHONG 1864-1955 **[115]**
- **$4 341** - €5 049 - **£3 100** - FF33 118
  **Landscape Scene of a Scholar carrying a Quin
  crossing the Bridge** Drawing (146.5x39cm 57x15in)
  London 2001

HUANG DAOZHOU 1585-1646 **[5]**
- **$20 720** - €19 662 - **£12 590** - FF128 977
  Poem in Running Script Calligraphy Ink
  (163x52.5cm 64x20in) Hong-Kong 1999

HUANG DAZENG XIX-XX **[2]**
- **$6 340** - €7 400 - **£4 340** - FF48 540
  Portrait of a Lady Oil/canvas (42.5x57cm 16x22in)
  Taipei 2000

HUANG FONG 1936 **[11]**
- **$2 337** - €2 447 - **£1 468** - FF16 051
  Fish Market Oil/canvas (80x100cm 31x39in)
  Singapore 2000
- **$1 492** - €1 694 - **£1 021** - FF11 114
  Seated Lady Pastel/paper (45x36cm 17x14in)
  Singapore 2000

HUANG HUANWU 1906-1985 **[7]**
- **$1 801** - €1 709 - **£1 096** - FF11 208
  Fishing Boats by the Shore Ink (29x86.5cm
  11x34in) Hong-Kong 1999

HUANG JINHUI XIX **[2]**
- **$3 846** - €4 520 - **£2 667** - FF29 652
  Mist over the Mountains Ink/paper (57.5x53.53cm
  22x21in) Hong-Kong 2000

HUANG JUN 1775-1850 **[1]**
- **$3 700** - €3 511 - **£2 248** - FF23 031
  White Clouds Encircling Mountain Peaks
  Ink/paper (26x31.5cm 10x12in) Hong-Kong 1999

HUANG JUNBI 1898-1991 **[63]**
- **$5 136** - €5 608 - **£3 304** - FF36 788
  Duet by a Moutain Spring Ink (132x44cm 51x17in)
  Hong-Kong 2000

HUANG MING-CH'ANG 1952 **[8]**
- **$42 840** - €48 640 - **£30 100** - FF319 060
  Satured Green (from the rice field Series)
  Oil/canvas (162x112cm 63x44in) Taipei 2001
- **$25 171** - €23 327 - **£15 649** - FF153 014
  Rice Field with Red Dragonfly Oil/canvas
  (80.5x116.5cm 31x45in) Taipei 1999

HUANG MINGZHE Michell Hwang 1948 **[10]**
- **$9 792** - €11 118 - **£6 880** - FF72 928
  Fighter from the East Oil/canvas (90.5x116cm
  35x45in) Taipei 2001

HUANG PINHUNG 1864-1955 **[2]**
- **$4 750** - €4 890 - **£3 039** - FF32 078
  Landscape Ink (72x34cm 28x13in) New-York 2000

HUANG SHAN 1959 **[1]**
- **$3 846** - €4 574 - **£2 649** - FF30 003
  Spring Flower Ink (132x66cm 51x25in) Hong-Kong
  2000

HUANG SHAOQIANG 1901-1942 **[3]**
- **$1 548** - €1 460 - **£960** - FF9 576
  Bodhidharma Ink/paper (17.5x50.5cm 6x19in) Hong-
  Kong 1999

HUANG SHEN 1687-1772 **[11]**
- **$5 805** - €5 448 - **£3 586** - FF35 734
  Liu Hai playing with the three-legged Toad Ink
  (92x120cm 36x47in) Hong-Kong 1999

HUANG SHULIANG 1958 **[11]**
- **$3 845** - €3 564 - **£2 390** - FF23 377
  Roses with Cage Oil/canvas (57.5x66.5cm 22x26in)
  Taipei 1999

HUANG YONGYU 1924 **[13]**
- **$8 333** - €9 466 - **£5 850** - FF62 094
  Owls Ink (27.5x38cm 10x14in) Hong-Kong 2001

HUANG ZHONG XVII **[1]**
- **$5 920** - €5 618 - **£3 597** - FF36 850
  Running Script Calligraphy Ink/paper (259x58cm
  101x22in) Hong-Kong 1999

HUANG ZHONGFANG 1943 **[3]**
- **$7 051** - €8 385 - **£4 856** - FF55 005
  Landscape Ink (137x68.5cm 53x26in) Hong-Kong
  2000

HUANG ZHOU 1925-1997 **[23]**
- **$4 487** - €5 097 - **£3 150** - FF33 435
  Uighur Girl Ink (105x54cm 41x21in) Hong-Kong 2001

HUBACEK Josef 1899-1931 **[4]**
- **$2 167** - €2 050 - **£1 350** - FF13 447
  «At a Yard» Oil/canvas (55x64cm 21x25in) Praha 2001

HUBACHER Hermann 1881-1976 **[22]**
- **$1 038** - €1 114 - **£694** - FF7 310
  Mädchenkopf einer Aegypterin Bronze (H24cm
  H9in) Zofingen 2000

HUBBARD Eric Hesketh 1892-1957 **[20]**
- **$670** - €641 - **£420** - FF4 202
  «Northern Ireland» Poster (102x125cm 40x49in)
  London 1999

HUBBARD Richard William 1816/17-1888 **[5]**
- **$18 000** - €19 851 - **£12 189** - FF130 213
  Afternoon by the River Oil/board (21x18cm 8x7in)
  New-York 2000

HUBBELL Henry Salem 1870-1949 **[1]**
- **$2 251** - €2 269 - **£1 403** - FF14 883
  Pont-Neuf, Paris Oil/board (19x13cm 7x5in)
  Amsterdam 2000

HUBBUCH Karl 1891-1979 **[396]**
- **$38 106** - €35 533 - **£23 000** - FF233 079
  Myriam with a Cat Oil/masonite (135x79cm 53x31in)
  London 1999
- **$6 719** - €6 647 - **£4 189** - FF43 600
  Marianne Öl/Karton (40.8x29.9cm 16x11in) Berlin
  1999
- **$1 169** - €1 125 - **£720** - FF7 378
  Jazzkapelle Indian ink/paper (28.5x22cm 11x8in)
  München 1999
- **$234** - €245 - **£147** - FF1 609
  Die Suche nach dem Koffer Radierung
  (24.2x26.7cm 9x10in) Bremen 2000

HUBER Carl Rudolf S. 1839-1896 **[14]**
- **$4 991** - €5 113 - **£3 080** - FF33 539
  Fürstin Salm mit Lipizzaner Oil/panel (56x44cm
  22x17in) Düsseldorf 2000
- **$3 096** - €2 907 - **£1 920** - FF19 068
  Der Schäfer mit seiner Herde Öl/Leinwand
  (25.5x50.5cm 10x19in) Wien 1999

HUBER Conrad 1752-1830 **[6]**
- $2 044 – €2 301 – **£1 408** - FF15 092
  **Brustbilder der Apostel Paulus/Des Petrus
  Schlüssel** Öl/Leinwand (32x24cm 12x9in) Stuttgart
  2000

HUBER Emil 1884-1943 **[1]**
- $1 000 – €962 – **£697** - FF6 308
  «S.R.B» Poster (127.5x90cm 50x35in) New-York 1999

HUBER Ernst 1895-1960 **[695]**
- $13 980 – €14 534 – **£8 900** - FF95 340
  Capri Öl/Leinwand (100x130cm 39x51in) Wien 2000
- $6 291 – €6 541 – **£4 005** - FF42 903
  Stilleben mit Gemüse und Brot Öl/Karton
  (45.9x53.5cm 18x21in) Wien 2000
- $2 097 – €2 180 – **£1 335** - FF14 301
  Rastende Bauern vor dem Dorf Oil/panel
  (20.9x28.6cm 8x11in) Wien 2000
- $1 015 – €1 090 – **£693** - FF7 150
  «Marktplatz» Aquarell/Papier (16x23.5cm 6x9in)
  Wien 2001
- $349 – €363 – **£222** - FF2 383
  Kapelle am See Monotype (47x61.5cm 18x24in)
  Wien 2000

HUBER Hermann 1888-1967 **[70]**
- $838 – €718 – **£504** - FF4 708
  Weilblicher Halbakt Huile/toile (100.5x73.5cm
  39x28in) Zürich 1998

HUBER Jakob Wilhelm 1787-1871 **[6]**
- $10 280 – €10 006 – **£6 316** - FF65 633
  Italienische Küstenlandschaft/Ansicht von Rom
  Aquarell/Papier (29.5x44cm 11x17in) Zürich 1999

HUBER Jean Daniel 1754-1845 **[10]**
- $4 610 – €5 185 – **£3 218** - FF34 012
  Milchwirtschaft im Berner Oberland Öl/Leinwand
  (76x105.5cm 29x41in) Luzern 2001

HUBER Johann Rudolf 1668-1748 **[14]**
- $2 242 – €2 649 – **£1 588** - FF17 376
  Ursula von Freudenreich, geboren Fischer
  Öl/Leinwand (83x64cm 32x25in) Zürich 2000

HUBER Léon Charles 1858-1928 **[90]**
- $4 476 – €3 677 – **£2 600** - FF24 118
  **Plums in a Basket, Strawberries on a Plate, a
  Wine Glass** Oil/canvas (51x66cm 20x25in) London
  1998
- $1 610 – €1 418 – **£981** - FF9 300
  Deux chatons jouant avec une fleur Huile/pan-
  neau (24.5x33cm 9x12in) Vernon 1999

HUBER Rudolf 1770-1844 **[6]**
- $1 606 – €1 817 – **£1 130** - FF11 919
  «Burgdorf vom Girisberg aufgenommen»
  Lithographie (34.5x47cm 13x18in) Bern 2001

HUBER Wolfgang ?-c.1943 **[33]**
- $838 – €872 – **£534** - FF5 720
  **Trockau/Bei
  Vossen/Dettendorf/Odelzhausen/Krotoschin**
  Aquarell/Papier (48.2x63.5cm 18x25in) Wien 2000
- $153 – €160 – **£97** - FF1 048
  Bergwiese mit Dorf Linocut in colors (11.5x16.5cm
  4x6in) Wien 2000

HUBER Wolfgang c.1490-1553 **[7]**
- $3 860 – €4 602 – **£2 752** - FF30 185
  Die Anbetung der Könige Woodcut (11.7x9.2cm
  4x3in) Berlin 2000

HUBER-SULZEMOOS Hans 1873-1951 **[21]**
- $1 224 – €1 278 – **£775** - FF8 384
  Madonna mit Kind Öl/Karton (13.5x10cm 5x3in)
  München 2001

HUBERT-GAUTIER Jean 1872-? **[5]**
- $1 831 – €1 677 – **£1 111** - FF11 000
  Marché en Bretagne Huile/panneau (41x33cm
  16x12in) Douarnenez 1998

HUBERT-ROBERT Marius XIX-XX **[44]**
- $915 – €838 – **£558** - FF5 500
  Saint-Paul-de-Vence Huile/toile (45.5x55cm
  17x21in) Paris 1999
- $343 – €381 – **£239** - FF2 500
  Pagode au Siam/Palais dans un jardin au Siam
  Aquarelle/papier (38.5x29cm 15x11in) Neuilly-sur-
  Seine 2001

HUBERTI & BAER XIX-XX **[1]**
- $2 737 – €2 585 – **£1 700** - FF16 956
  A Panorama of Rio de Janeiro Carbon print
  (22x138.5cm 8x54in) London 1999

HUBERTI Antonio Glauberman 1907 **[92]**
- $354 – €347 – **£219** - FF2 276
  Composition à l'instrument de musique
  Aquarelle/papier (23x18.5cm 9x7in) Bruxelles 1999

HUBERTI Edouard Jules Joseph 1818-1880 **[33]**
- $851 – €818 – **£534** - FF5 365
  Paysage enneigé Huile/toile (35.5x56.5cm 13x22in)
  Bruxelles 1999
- $1 033 – €892 – **£622** - FF5 853
  Printemps Huile/toile (24x40cm 9x15in) Bruxelles
  1999

HUBLIN Émile Auguste 1830-c.1891 **[6]**
- $14 000 – €13 905 – **£8 680** - FF91 214
  **Portrait of a Young Expecting Mother in Tattered
  Clothes with Basket** Oil/canvas (93x63cm 37x25in)
  Norwalk CT 2000

HUBMANN Franz 1914 **[9]**
- $809 – €869 – **£542** - FF5 701
  **Jacqueline, Wohnen mit Picasso, Villa «La
  Californie», Cannes** Photograph (30x30cm 11x11in)
  München 2000

HÜBNER Carl Wilhelm 1814-1879 **[46]**
- $2 679 – €2 454 – **£1 633** - FF16 098
  Der Freiersmann Öl/Leinwand/Karton (58x72cm
  22x28in) München 1999
- $1 445 – €1 347 – **£873** - FF8 833
  Akskeden, interiör med to kvinder ved vugge
  Oil/canvas (42x36cm 16x14in) Köbenhavn 1999

HÜBNER Heinrich 1869-1945 **[23]**
- $737 – €818 – **£512** - FF5 366
  Männlicher Akt Öl/Leinwand (61x51cm 24x20in)
  Köln 2001

HÜBNER Julius 1806-1882 **[11]**
- $13 974 – €14 316 – **£8 624** - FF93 909
  Junge mit Weinglas vor Landschaft Oil/panel
  (61.6x48cm 24x18in) Düsseldorf 2000

HÜBNER Ulrich 1872-1932 **[43]**
- $1 905 – €2 045 – **£1 275** - FF13 415
  Travemünde Öl/Karton (38x46cm 14x18in) Berlin
  2000
- $1 742 – €1 817 – **£1 097** - FF11 917
  Fischerboote vor Anker Öl/Karton (30x40cm
  11x15in) Wien 2000
- $2 009 – €1 841 – **£1 225** - FF12 074
  Aus Hamburg Charcoal/paper (48x65cm 18x25in)
  Berlin 1999

HUC Eugène 1891-? **[3]**
- $12 860 – €12 958 – **£8 015** – FF85 000
  Femme jouant du luth Huile/toile (146.5x114cm 57x44in) Paris 2000

HUCHET Urbain 1930 **[190]**
- $910 – €762 – **£535** – FF5 000
  Chalutiers sur l'Aven, Kerdruc Acrylique/toile (65x81cm 25x31in) Rennes 1998
- $83 – €91 – **£55** – FF600
  Les voiliers Lithographie (17x26cm 6x10in) Dozulé 2000

HUCHTENBURG van Jacob c.1640/45-1675 **[9]**
- $9 108 – €8 622 – **£5 663** – FF56 555
  An elegant Company making Merry near Classical Ruins Oil/panel (52.5x53cm 20x20in) Amsterdam 1999

HUCHTENBURG van Jan 1647-1733 **[94]**
- $10 376 – €12 196 – **£7 192** – FF80 000
  Charge de cavalerie Huile/toile (89x135cm 35x53in) Brest 2000
- $14 224 – €12 054 – **£8 500** – FF79 069
  A Cavalry Engagement near a Town Oil/canvas (50.5x58.5cm 19x23in) London 1998
- $7 231 – €7 173 – **£4 500** – FF47 051
  Cavalry Battle between Christians and Turks Oil/canvas (25.5x34cm 10x13in) London 1999
- $585 – €665 – **£406** – FF4 360
  Ein berittener Tatar, eine Pistole abfeuernd Red chalk/paper (20x14cm 7x5in) Köln 2001

HUCHTHAUSEN David R. 1951 **[3]**
- $5 500 – €5 250 – **£3 436** – FF34 438
  Fantasy Vessel Sculpture, glass (H19.5cm H7in) New-York 1999

HUCK Johann Gerhard c.1759-1811 **[4]**
- $66 – €61 – **£41** – FF402
  Grosse Szene mit Militärs Lithographie (55x68cm 21x26in) Rudolstadt-Thüringen 1999

HUCLEUX Jean-Olivier 1923 **[33]**
- $11 664 – €13 720 – **£8 361** – FF90 000
  Portrait de Bernard Lamarche-Vadel Crayon/papier (223x149cm 87x58in) Paris 2001
- $151 – €168 – **£101** – FF1 100
  Portrait de Joseph Beuys Lithographie (75x55cm 29x21in) Paris 2000

HUDDERSFORD George, Rev. 1749-1809 **[1]**
- $4 170 – €4 203 – **£2 600** – FF27 569
  Portrait of the Artist, half-length, in a black coat and white ruff Oil/canvas (76x63.5cm 29x25in) London 2000

HUDECEK Antonín 1872-1941 **[68]**
- $2 312 – €2 187 – **£1 440** – FF14 344
  Cours d'eau Huile/toile (100x133.5cm 39x52in) Praha 1999
- $578 – €547 – **£360** – FF3 586
  «Meadow with Flowers» Oil/paper (44x60cm 17x23in) Praha 2001
- $462 – €437 – **£288** – FF2 868
  Humeur froid Huile/carton (28x37cm 11x14in) Praha 2000

HUDECEK Frantisek 1909-1990 **[62]**
- $4 046 – €3 827 – **£2 520** – FF25 102
  Rue Saint Dominique Huile/carton (32x25.5cm 12x10in) Praha 2001
- $274 – €260 – **£171** – FF1 703
  Homme et l'univers Encre (29.5x24cm 11x9in) Praha 2000

HUDELET Henry Paul 1849-1878 **[2]**
- $4 149 – €4 116 – **£2 581** – FF27 000
  Le joueur de dés Bronze (H60cm H23in) Montpellier 1999

HUDNUT Alexander M. XX **[5]**
- $1 400 – €1 641 – **£1 007** – FF10 767
  Along the Docks Watercolour (45.5x60.5cm 17x23in) New-York 2001

HUDON Normand 1929-1997 **[68]**
- $840 – €903 – **£578** – FF5 926
  «Les skieurs» Mixed media (27x35.5cm 10x13in) Toronto 2001

HUDSON Charles Bradford 1865-1939 **[7]**
- $3 000 – €3 220 – **£2 007** – FF21 123
  October Sea Oil/canvas (35x55cm 14x22in) Altadena CA 2000

HUDSON Grace Carpenter 1865-1937 **[58]**
- $45 000 – €42 491 – **£27 945** – FF278 725
  Hunter, Tick-E-Dy Oil/canvas (56x40.5cm 22x15in) Beverly-Hills CA 1999
- $5 000 – €5 343 – **£3 403** – FF35 048
  Hudson Oil/board (20x15cm 8x6in) New-Orleans LA 2001

HUDSON John XIX **[2]**
- $2 092 – €2 246 – **£1 400** – FF14 730
  The Dare of Portsmouth Oil/canvas (56.5x82.5cm 22x32in) London 2000

HUDSON Robert, Snr. 1826-1885 **[3]**
- $1 056 – €1 136 – **£720** – FF7 452
  A Still Life of Roses, Fushias and Other Flowers Oil/board (23x28cm 9x11in) West-Yorshire 2001

HUDSON Samuel John XIX **[1]**
- $1 438 – €1 677 – **£996** – FF11 000
  Rouen, Rue de Gros-Horloge Aquarelle/papier (42x27cm 16x10in) Le Havre 2000

HUDSON Thomas 1701-1779 **[70]**
- $21 287 – €19 468 – **£13 000** – FF127 701
  Portrait of Philip Yorke, Lord Hardwicke, 1st Earle of Hardwicke Oil/canvas (127x101.5cm 50x39in) London 1998
- $7 961 – €6 924 – **£4 800** – FF45 421
  Anne Sneyd, Three-quarter Length, Wearing a Silver Dress Oil/canvas (108x91.5cm 42x36in) Godalming, Surrey 1998

HUE Alexandre L. XIX **[2]**
- $8 000 – €9 422 – **£5 532** – FF61 807
  Landscape with Mountains Beyond Oil/panel (22x38cm 8x14in) New-York 2000

HUE Charles Désiré 1842-1899 **[16]**
- $20 508 – €18 781 – **£12 500** – FF123 195
  La jeune soubrette Oil/canvas (46.5x38.5cm 18x15in) London 1999
- $650 – €2 470 – **£1 634** – FF16 200
  Courtisane Huile/panneau (32.5x41cm 12x16in) Besançon 1999

HÜE DE BRÉVAL Virginie XVIII-XIX **[4]**
- $1 025 – €1 085 – **£650** – FF7 114
  Portrait of a Gentleman Wearing a Stock Black & white chalks/paper (36x27.5cm 14x10in) London 2000

HUÉ Jean-François 1751-1823 **[30]**
- $17 000 – €18 651 – **£11 293** – FF122 345
  View of the Hôtel de Chassins Curtilly Oil/canvas (130x160cm 51x62in) New-York 2000

$10 000 - €11 201 - **£6 948** - FF73 472
Fishermen and other figures along a Shoreline with a Sailboat Oil/panel (50.5x72.5cm 19x28in) New-York 2001

$5 768 - €5 814 - **£3 600** - FF38 136
Südlicher Hafen mit Fischern «Abend» Oil/panel (23.5x28.5cm 9x11in) Wien 2000

$1 311 - €1 448 - **£909** - FF9 500
Paysans et troupeaux dans un sous-bois Crayon (35x52cm 13x20in) Paris 2001

HUEBER Luc 1888-1974 [14]

$907 - €1 067 - **£650** - FF7 000
Paysage vosgien avec ruines de château Huile/panneau (70x60cm 27x23in) Entzheim 2001

HUEFFER Catherine Madox B. 1850-1927 [2]

$22 414 - €24 060 - **£15 000** - FF157 824
Laura Alma-Tadema Watercolour/paper (78.5x51cm 30x20in) London 2000

HUENS Jean Léon 1921 [3]

$1 600 - €1 532 - **£988** - FF10 051
Knight on Horseback Approaching Lounging Creature: Book Cover Watercolour (28x18cm 11x7in) New-York 1999

HUERTAS Marcos [2]

$5 318 - €5 024 - **£3 317** - FF32 953
Simbiosis Lápiz/papel (102x121cm 40x47in) Monterrey NL 2001

HUET Christophe 1694-1759 [11]

$22 143 - €25 154 - **£15 543** - FF165 000
Nature morte, fruits et perroquet Huile/toile (77.5x106cm 30x41in) Paris 2001

$8 155 - €7 628 - **£5 000** - FF50 035
Architectural Capricci with Still Life in Ornamental Gardens Oil/canvas (41.5x28cm 16x11in) London 1998

HUET François Villiers 1772-1813 [10]

$7 500 - €7 587 - **£4 579** - FF49 769
Extensive River Landscape with the Ruins of an Abbey Bodycolour (40x54.5cm 15x21in) New-York 2000

$874 - €911 - **£550** - FF5 978
Rudiments of Cattle Etching (28x35cm 11x13in) London 2000

HUET Jean-Baptiste 1745-1811 [207]

$40 000 - €47 112 - **£27 664** - FF309 036
Flower-Seller Setting off For Market Oil/canvas (138x125cm 54x49in) New-York 2000

$11 685 - €10 976 - **£7 050** - FF71 505
Schäferszene bei einem Brunnen in einer bewaldeten Flusslandschaft Öl/Leinwand (46.5x81cm 18x31in) Wien 1999

$12 688 - €13 324 - **£8 000** - FF87 397
Portrait of Marie-Joseph Chérier, Small Full-Length Oil/panel (30.5x23.5cm 12x9in) London 2000

$2 590 - €3 049 - **£1 820** - FF20 000
Berger dans une étable avec un boeuf, un âne, un mouton et un chat Pierre noire (22.5x35.5cm 8x13in) Paris 2000

$172 - €192 - **£115** - FF1 260
Cabras Grabado (47x35cm 18x13in) Madrid 2000

HUET Paul 1803-1869 [279]

$25 000 - €27 984 - **£17 435** - FF183 562
Marais salants aux environs de Saint-Valèry en Somme, Picardie Oil/canvas (97x162cm 38x63in) New-York 2001

$4 845 - €5 412 - **£3 283** - FF35 500
Chasse au Mont d'Ussy, Fontainebleau Huile/panneau (34.5x48.5cm 13x19in) Pontoise 2000

$3 060 - €2 592 - **£1 839** - FF17 000
Devant l'orage, rayons sous les nuages Huile/carton (27x35cm 10x13in) Paris 1998

$2 540 - €2 727 - **£1 700** - FF13 161
View of Rocco Bruna, Italy Watercolour (23x29cm 9x11in) London 2000

$216 - €244 - **£149** - FF1 600
Pont en Auvergne Eau-forte (29x37cm 11x14in) Paris 2000

HUF Paul 1924 [12]

$422 - €454 - **£282** - FF2 976
Torremolinos Cibachrome print (16x24.5cm 6x9in) Amsterdam 2000

HUFF Byron 1949 [1]

$1 600 - €1 785 - **£1 047** - FF11 709
«U.S.Open Golf» Poster (56.5x81cm 22x31in) New-York 2000

HUFFINGTON John C. 1864-1929 [4]

$1 400 - €1 561 - **£941** - FF10 240
Autumnal Landscape with Pond Gouache/paper (26x18cm 10x7in) Portsmouth NH 2000

HUFFMAN Layton Alton 1854-1931 [44]

$600 - €626 - **£379** - FF4 107
Untitled Photograph (20x35cm 8x14in) San-Francisco CA 2000

HUFFORD Nick XX [1]

$5 500 - €6 126 - **£3 597** - FF40 185
Calendar illustration: SChool crossing guard attract attention Oil/board (66x54cm 26x21in) New-York 2000

HUG Charles 1899-1979 [34]

$1 437 - €1 240 - **£867** - FF8 133
Garten bei Greifenstein Oil/panel (36x46cm 14x18in) St. Gallen 1998

$563 - €605 - **£377** - FF3 968
Mädchen aus Tourah, Brustbild Öl/Leinwand (25.5x18cm 10x7in) Zofingen 2000

HUG Fritz Rudolf 1921-1989 [366]

$1 023 - €877 - **£615** - FF5 750
Landschaft mit Blick auf den Zürichsee Öl/Leinwand (74x100cm 29x39in) Zürich 1998

$509 - €435 - **£304** - FF2 851
Ziege Öl/Leinwand (24x35cm 9x13in) Zürich 1998

$708 - €594 - **£417** - FF3 898
«Löwin» Charcoal/paper (33x47.5cm 12x18in) Bern 1998

$130 - €112 - **£78** - FF733
Rothirsch Farblithographie (37.5x53cm 14x20in) Zürich 1998

HUG Nicolaus 1771-1852 [5]

$659 - €665 - **£411** - FF4 360
Sommerwirtschaft auf dem Fürstenberg Radierung (8x14cm 3x5in) Radolfzell 2000

HUGARD DE LA TOUR Claude Sébastien 1816-1885 [20]

$7 850 - €7 622 - **£4 850** - FF50 000
Paysage de montagne, Haute-Savoie Huile/toile (55x95cm 21x37in) Grenoble 1999

$1 184 - €1 377 - **£845** - FF9 033
Herder and cows by a Woodland Stream Oil/canvas (38.5x29cm 15x11in) Toronto 2001

HUGENTOBLER Ivan Edwin 1886-1972 [119]

$2 200 - €1 918 - **£1 507** - FF15 974
Kopf eines gezäumten Schimmels Öl/Karton (38x29cm 14x11in) Basel 2000

H

📝 **$467** - €437 - **£288** - FF2 866
Galoppierendes Pferd Aquarelle (36x43.5cm 14x17in) Luzern 1999

🎨 **$168** - €186 - **£111** - FF1 222
Hohe Schule Offset (24x21cm 9x8in) Bern 2000

HUGER Emily H(amilton) 1881-1946 [2]

🖼 **$11 500** - €12 749 - **£7 985** - FF83 631
Paradise Grove, Breaux Bridge, Louisiana Oil/canvas (78x91cm 31x36in) New-Orleans LA 2001

🖼 **$2 750** - €3 049 - **£1 909** - FF20 002
«Sea Gulls, Gloucester, Mass» Oil/board (28x21cm 11x8in) New-Orleans LA 2001

HUGGINS James Miller XIX [3]

🖼 **$9 856** - €9 835 - **£6 000** - FF64 515
Bringing in the Catch, Low tide/Shipping off the Coast in a Breeze Oil/canvas (40.5x51cm 15x20in) London 2000

HUGGINS William 1820-1884 [88]

🖼 **$7 471** - €8 020 - **£5 000** - FF52 608
Bideston Farmhouse with Cattle and Ducks in the foreground Oil/canvas (56x41cm 22x16in) London 2000

🖼 **$2 438** - €2 252 - **£1 500** - FF14 769
Hens and a Cockerel in a wooded Landscape Oil/canvas (30.5x35.5cm 12x13in) London 1999

🖼 **$3 638** - €3 173 - **£2 200** - FF20 811
A Lioness Coloured chalks (17.5x25.5cm 6x10in) London 1998

HUGGINS William John 1781-1845 [44]

🖼 **$35 937** - €37 669 - **£24 000** - FF247 092
An East Indiaman Under Full Sail in Two Positions off Dover Oil/canvas (91x152.5cm 35x60in) London 2001

🖼 **$1 030** - €1 106 - **£700** - FF7 256
The Lord Saumarez, 201 tons, outward bound to Africa, December Oil/canvas (47.5x63cm 18x24in) London 2001

🎨 **$250** - €239 - **£157** - FF1 569
The Ship H.M.S Winchester Engraving (34x51cm 13x20in) Boston MA 1999

HUGGLER Arnold 1894-1988 [17]

🗿 **$1 959** - €1 886 - **£1 225** - FF12 374
Stehender weiblicher Akt Bronze (H45cm H17in) Zürich 1999

HUGGLER Hans 1877-1947 [2]

🗿 **$2 858** - €3 201 - **£1 988** - FF21 000
«Le cerf» Sculpture bois (H79cm H31in) Valence 2001

HUGHES Arthur 1832-1915 [79]

🖼 **$43 001** - €37 495 - **£26 000** - FF245 954
Sir Galahad Oil/canvas (89x135cm 35x53in) London 1998

🖼 **$16 836** - €20 023 - **£12 000** - FF131 342
The Rescue Oil/canvas (110x53cm 43x20in) London 2000

🖼 **$7 015** - €8 343 - **£5 000** - FF54 726
Coastal Scene Oil/board (26x46cm 10x18in) London 2000

🖼 **$1 657** - €1 430 - **£1 000** - FF9 380
Angels O'er the Realms of Glory Pencil/paper (25x28.5cm 9x11in) London 1998

HUGHES Arthur Foord 1856-1934 [18]

📝 **$1 649** - €1 494 - **£1 000** - FF9 803
At the Spinet Watercolour (62x52cm 24x20in) Billingshurst, West-Sussex 1998

HUGHES Edward 1832-1908 [25]

🖼 **$7 916** - €8 867 - **£5 500** - FF58 162
Lucy Celia Ashton, née Dunn-Gardiner, later Countess of Scarbrough Oil/canvas (142x99cm 55x38in) London 2001

🖼 **$28 000** - €25 983 - **£17 108** - FF170 436
An English Artist collecting Costumes in Brittany Oil/canvas (87x122.5cm 34x48in) New-York 1999

HUGHES Edward John 1913 [80]

🖼 **$20 726** - €24 181 - **£14 425** - FF158 617
Looking North over Shawnigan Lake Acrylic/canvas (96.5x129.5cm 37x50in) Toronto 2000

🖼 **$24 348** - €27 543 - **£17 032** - FF180 671
South of Chilliwack» Oil/canvas (81.5x101.5cm 32x39in) Toronto 2000

🖼 **$5 075** - €5 007 - **£3 125** - FF32 841
Promenade en canoé Huile/isorel (25x17cm 9x6in) Montréal 1999

📝 **$3 402** - €3 252 - **£2 132** - FF21 332
River's Inlet, B.C. Pencil/paper (37.5x47cm 14x18in) Vancouver, BC 1999

🎨 **$1 362** - €1 309 - **£839** - FF8 588
Old Empress Figurehead, Stanley Park Linocut (23x30.5cm 9x12in) Vancouver, BC. 1999

HUGHES Edward Robert 1851-1914 [37]

🖼 **$3 461** - €3 824 - **£2 400** - FF25 087
Sketch for a Pastoral Oil/board (19.5x19cm 7x7in) London 2001

📝 **$8 606** - €9 554 - **£6 000** - FF62 669
Returning Home Watercolour (50x70cm 19x27in) London 2001

HUGHES Edwin XIX [20]

🖼 **$1 195** - €1 283 - **£800** - FF8 417
Below Stairs Oil/canvas (34x44cm 13x17in) London 2000

HUGHES George 1907-1990 [12]

🖼 **$8 500** - €9 521 - **£5 905** - FF62 451
Magazine Cover, young Couple goes out on a Date, Family looking on Oil/masonite (72x71cm 28x28in) New-York 2001

HUGHES George Frederick XIX-XX [4]

🖼 **$9 493** - €9 158 - **£6 000** - FF60 075
A Tug O'War Oil/canvas (61x91.5cm 24x36in) London 1999

HUGHES George Hart 1839-1921 [14]

🖼 **$1 691** - €1 669 - **£1 041** - FF10 947
Campement indien Huile/toile (31x38.5cm 12x15in) Montréal 1999

HUGHES John 1849-? [1]

🗿 **$7 120** - €7 962 - **£4 800** - FF52 228
A Kneeling Nude with a Child Holding a Fish Bronze (H28cm H11in) London 2000

HUGHES John 1805-1880 [1]

🖼 **$30 000** - €33 054 - **£20 013** - FF216 819
The American Down Easter Premier Outward Bound Off the South Stack Oil/canvas (60x89cm 24x35in) Portsmouth NH 2000

HUGHES Joseph Johan ?-1909 [32]

🖼 **$868** - €937 - **£600** - FF6 149
Country landscape with Figures on a Road in the Foreground Oil/canvas (39.5x65cm 15x25in) London 2001

HUGHES Nigel 1940 [21]

🖼 **$5 756** - €6 448 - **£4 000** - FF42 296
The Gulf of Nicoya Oil/canvas (68.5x111.5cm 26x43in) London 2001

H

📎 $43 - €47 - **£30** - FF307
Dovecote à La Buissière Convent, Burgundy
Watercolour/paper (32x22.5cm 12x8in) Bristol, Avon
2001

HUGHES Patrick 1939 **[38]**
🖼 $9 819 - €11 705 - **£7 000** - FF76 781
Up Town Construction (101.5x108x36cm 39x42x14in)
London 2000
▥ $224 - €241 - **£150** - FF1 578
Made in Sky Screenprint in colors (54x54cm 21x21in)
London 2000

HUGHES Paul XX **[1]**
🖼 $4 800 - €4 650 - **£2 993** - FF30 500
Intérieur à la commode Oil/canvas (46x38cm
18x14in) Beverly-Hills CA 1999

HUGHES Robert Morson 1873-1953 **[54]**
🖼 $159 - €154 - **£100** - FF1 011
Near Lamorna Oil/board (25x34cm 10x13in) Par,
Cornwall 1999

HUGHES S.G. XIX **[2]**
▥ $518 - €591 - **£360** - FF3 878
**Travelling on the Liverpool/Manchester Railway,
After I Shaw** Aquatint in colors (25.5x66.5cm
10x26in) London 2000

HUGHES Talbot 1869-1942 **[28]**
🖼 $16 566 - €17 688 - **£11 286** - FF116 028
The Island of the Sacred Swans Oil/canvas
(136.5x166cm 53x65in) Vejle 2001
🖼 $7 916 - €8 867 - **£5 500** - FF58 162
Shadows Oil/panel (48.5x65cm 19x25in) London
2001
🖼 $4 625 - €4 806 - **£2 900** - FF31 527
Maid Serving Claret to a Gentleman in a Library
Oil/panel (22.5x30cm 8x11in) Oxfordshire 2000

HUGHES Thomas John XIX-XX **[9]**
🖼 $1 120 - €1 069 - **£700** - FF7 014
Vanity Oil/panel (30.5x23cm 12x9in) London 1999

HUGHES William 1842-1901 **[75]**
🖼 $4 650 - €4 991 - **£3 111** - FF32 742
Branch with plums against a gold background
Oil/canvas (76.5x41cm 30x16in) Amsterdam 2000
🖼 $1 227 - €1 317 - **£821** - FF8 707
**Still Life Study of Pears, Apple and Grapes on a
Bank** Oil/canvas (27x40cm 11x16in) Aylsham, Norfolk
2001

HUGHES-STANTON Blair 1902 **[16]**
▥ $431 - €493 - **£300** - FF3 231
«Estuary» Woodcut in colors (15x71cm 5x27in)
London 2000

HUGHES-STANTON Herbert Ed. Pelham 1870-1937
[35]
📎 $387 - €452 - **£270** - FF2 968
**Figure Beside a Path in an Extensive
Landscape with a Castle Beyond** Watercolour
(34x48.5cm 13x19in) West-Yorshire 2000

HÜGIN Karl Otto 1887-1963 **[42]**
🖼 $1 018 - €982 - **£703** - FF7 754
Auf dem Balkon Mischtechnik/Karton (79x31cm
31x12in) Zürich 2000
🖼 $522 - €503 - **£326** - FF3 299
Im Kaffeehaus Tempera/papier (89x31.5cm 35x12in)
Zürich 1999

HUGNET Georges 1904-1974 **[39]**
🖼 $1 891 - €2 287 - **£1 321** - FF15 000
Personnage Huile/panneau (21.5x8.5cm 8x3in) Paris
2000

📎 $1 997 - €1 875 - **£1 233** - FF12 297
La chevelure Collage/papier (21x16cm 8x6in) Genève
1999
📷 $1 600 - €1 760 - **£1 109** - FF11 542
Huit jours à Trebaumec Photograph (23x16cm
9x6in) New-York 2001

HUGO Charles Victor 1826-1871 **[12]**
📷 $1 373 - €1 524 - **£957** - FF10 000
Le rocher de l'Ermitage Tirage papier salé
(18x22.5cm 7x8in) Paris 2001

HUGO Georges-Victor 1868-1925 **[20]**
🖼 $6 447 - €6 403 - **£4 032** - FF42 000
**Vue de Saint Malo, vu de la plage de l'écluse à
Dinard** Huile/toile (59x74cm 23x29in) Paris 1999
📎 $331 - €335 - **£202** - FF2 200
**Cheminée de la maison de Victor Hugo à
Guernesey** Aquarelle/papier (9.5x12.5cm 3x4in)
Clermont-Ferrand 2000

HUGO Jean 1894-1984 **[209]**
🖼 $475 - €549 - **£332** - FF3 599
Herder with Cow in Village Oil/canvas (77x107.5cm
30x42in) Bethesda MD 2001
🖼 $2 500 - €2 136 - **£1 468** - FF14 013
Village Street Oil/panel (19x27cm 7x10in) New-York
1998
📎 $1 701 - €1 429 - **£1 000** - FF9 372
Village en montagne Ink (33x49cm 12x19in)
London 1998

HUGO Valentine 1887-1968 **[180]**
🖼 $226 980 - €274 408 - **£158 580** - FF1 800 000
Portrait des poètes surréalistes Huile/panneau
(120x100cm 47x39in) Paris 2000
🖼 $23 722 - €22 105 - **£14 326** - FF145 000
Nijinski dans l'après-midi d'un Faune Huile/pan-
neau (54x45cm 21x17in) Paris 1998
🖼 $898 - €991 - **£608** - FF6 500
Autoportrait Crayon (31x24cm 12x9in) Paris 2000
▥ $317 - €274 - **£191** - FF1 800
«Sussex». Boulogne Sur Mer Gravure bois
(34x46cm 13x18in) Paris 1998

HUGO Victor Marie 1802-1885 **[55]**
📎 $8 638 - €7 392 - **£5 200** - FF48 490
A castle in a Landscape Ink (3.5x11cm 1x4in)
London 1998

HUGON Geneviève 1945 **[4]**
▥ $256 - €305 - **£183** - FF2 000
Promesse de l'aube Carborundum in colors
(89x71cm 35x27in) Paris 2000

HUGON Roland 1911 **[37]**
▥ $600 - €526 - **£364** - FF3 452
8 jours de neige blanche Poster (99x61cm 39x24in)
New-York 1999

HUGREL Claude Honoré 1880-1944 **[18]**
🖼 $1 794 - €2 134 - **£1 244** - FF14 000
Labour en mâconnais Huile/carton (93x73cm
36x28in) Paris 2000
📎 $1 046 - €884 - **£622** - FF5 800
Basse-cour sous des pommiers en fleurs Pastel
(45x60cm 17x23in) Senlis 1998

HUGUENIN-VIRCHAUX Henri Edouard 1878-1958
[38]
📎 $473 - €515 - **£311** - FF3 376
Walliser Gebirgslandschaft mit Hütte am Hang
Öl/Leinwand (38x46cm 14x18in) Bern 2000
🖼 $436 - €404 - **£267** - FF2 652
Reideralp im Wallis Huile/panneau (24.5x32cm
9x12in) Bern 1999

HUGUENY Jean 1767-1817 **[2]**
$2 698 - €2 897 - £1 805 - FF19 000
Colin et Colette, pour «le devin du village» de J.J.Rousseau Aquarelle/papier (44.5x33cm 17x12in) Paris 2000

HUGUES Jean-Baptiste 1849-1930 **[2]**
$3 160 - €3 049 - £1 998 - FF20 000
La muse de la source Bronze (54x47cm 21x18in) Paris 1999

HUGUES Paul Jean 1891-c.1950 **[16]**
$2 634 - €2 211 - £1 545 - FF14 500
Le bureau dans le hall Huile/toile (55x65cm 21x25in) Bordeaux 1998
$1 845 - €2 058 - £1 287 - FF13 500
Intérieur avec bureau plat/Intérieur avec cheminée Huile/toile (36x27cm 14x10in) Entzheim 2001

HUGUES Talbot 1869-1942 **[1]**
$1 741 - €1 961 - £1 200 - FF12 862
The Game Larder Oil/panel (30.5x35.5cm 12x13in) London 2001

HUGUES Victor Louis 1827-1879 **[4]**
$1 071 - €1 021 - £646 - FF6 698
Dama jugando con un perro Oleo/tabla (20x16cm 7x6in) Madrid 1999

HUGUET Victor Pierre 1835-1902 **[104]**
$9 639 - €8 842 - £5 991 - FF58 000
Le cortège de la mariée Huile/toile (47x68cm 18x26in) Paris 1999
$3 096 - €2 820 - £1 896 - FF18 500
La rencontre Huile/toile (21.5x27.5cm 8x10in) Cherbourg 1998

HUHN Friedrich Wilhelm 1821-? **[4]**
$3 952 - €4 710 - £2 831 - FF30 894
Personnages dans un paysage Huile/toile (78x100cm 30x39in) Antwerpen 2000

HUHNEN Fritz 1895-1981 **[38]**
$308 - €358 - £212 - FF2 347
Indianer Gouache/paper (62x47.5cm 24x18in) Köln 2000

HUIBERS Jan Derk 1829-1919 **[7]**
$3 709 - €3 319 - £2 222 - FF21 769
Motherly Admonition Oil/panel (64x44cm 25x17in) Amsterdam 1998

HUILLIOT Claude 1632-1702 **[5]**
$14 480 - €12 196 - £8 552 - FF80 000
Nature morte au panier de fleurs, perroquet et chien Huile/toile (38x46cm 14x18in) Paris 1998

HUILLIOT Pierre Nicolas 1674-1751 **[26]**
$7 952 - €8 537 - £5 320 - FF56 000
Vase de fleurs, pastèque et panier de fruits près d'un muret Huile/toile (92.5x81cm 36x31in) Paris 2000

HUISMAN Jopie 1922-2000 **[10]**
$14 720 - €14 521 - £9 065 - FF95 251
Pair of Shoes Oil/canvas (20x25cm 7x9in) Amsterdam 1999
$15 624 - €18 151 - £10 980 - FF119 064
Old Coast and Trousers hanging from a Hatrack Coloured inks (30x31cm 11x12in) Amsterdam 2001

HUITTI Ilmari 1897-1960 **[22]**
$948 - €807 - £566 - FF5 296
Stugan Oil/canvas (38x46cm 14x18in) Helsinki 1998

HULBERT Charles Allen ?-1939 **[4]**
$2 000 - €1 939 - £1 238 - FF12 718
Tea Time Oil/canvas (60x76cm 24x30in) Mystic CT 1999

HULDAH Cherry Jeffe XX **[19]**
$3 250 - €3 226 - £1 993 - FF21 162
Having Fun on the Carrousel Oil/canvas (91x101cm 36x40in) Delray-Beach FL 2000

HULETT J.G. XIX **[2]**
$2 000 - €2 051 - £1 250 - FF13 454
White Rock Dam on Pawtucket River/Shannock Brook, Conn. Oil/canvas (15x20cm 6x8in) Bolton MA 2000

HULEWICZ Jerzy 1886-1941 **[2]**
$10 319 - €10 611 - £6 543 - FF69 602
Faune jouant Oil/canvas (74x60cm 29x23in) Kraków 2000

HULINGS Clark 1922 **[26]**
$42 500 - €38 635 - £25 597 - FF253 427
Posada Sn Antonio Oil/board (66x76cm 26x30in) Hayden ID 1998
$4 250 - €3 863 - £2 559 - FF25 342
Fresh Fruit Oil/canvas (20x25cm 8x10in) Hayden ID 1998
$5 500 - €6 411 - £3 808 - FF42 055
Man Leading Donkey Pulling Cart Watercolour/paper (32x51cm 12x20in) New-York 2000

HULK Abraham I 1813-1897 **[268]**
$12 112 - €11 389 - £7 500 - FF74 705
Shipping in a Calm Oil/canvas (55x84cm 22x33in) Guildford, Surrey 1999
$8 539 - €9 166 - £5 800 - FF60 125
Dutch Boats off a Breakwater with a Beached Fishing Boat Oil/panel (19x26cm 7x10in) London 2001
$555 - €661 - £395 - FF4 333
Küstenlandschaft mit Schiffen Aquarell, Gouache/Papier (28.5x42cm 11x16in) Zürich 2000

HULK Abraham I or II XIX **[31]**
$241 - €274 - £169 - FF1 799
Figure gathering kindling in open Landscape Oil/canvas (20x25cm 8x10in) Aylsham, Norfolk 2001

HULK Abraham II 1851-1922 **[234]**
$1 005 - €1 173 - £700 - FF7 697
Wooded Landscape with Figure, a Cottage Beyond Oil/canvas (75x54cm 29x21in) Billingshurst, West-Sussex 2000
$744 - €843 - £520 - FF5 531
Calm evening Oil/canvas (21.5x31.5cm 8x12in) Billingshurst, West-Sussex 2001
$122 - €109 - £75 - FF715
Cattle in Landscape Watercolour/paper (12x17cm 4x6in) Newbury, Berkshire 1999

HULK Hendrick 1842-1937 **[40]**
$5 764 - €5 445 - £3 596 - FF35 719
Bomschuiten on the beach of Zandvoort, Noord Holland Oil/canvas (56x83.5cm 22x32in) Amsterdam 1999
$1 893 - €2 087 - £1 236 - FF13 692
Zeilschepen aan de waterkant Oil/panel (20x27.5cm 7x10in) Den Haag 2000

HULK John Frederick I 1829-1911 **[57]**
$2 796 - €3 176 - £1 962 - FF20 836
A Canal in a Dutch Town Oil/panel (46x35.5cm 18x13in) Amsterdam 2001

$7 876 - €6 660 - **£4 710** - FF43 688
A View of Meppel with Figures Standing near a Tollhouse Oil/panel (40.5x31.5cm 15x12in) Amsterdam 1998

HULK John Frederick II 1855-1913 [25]

$19 425 - €20 852 - **£13 000** - FF136 780
Unloading Ships at a Dutch Port Oil/canvas (61x92cm 24x36in) London 2000

$1 632 - €1 829 - **£1 136** - FF12 000
Vue de Harlem Huile/panneau (8x27cm 3x10in) Paris 2001

HULK William Frederick 1852-c.1906 [90]

$1 770 - €1 978 - **£1 200** - FF12 974
Cattle in Country Lane Oil/canvas (60x50cm 23x19in) Doncaster, South-Yorkshire 2000

$560 - €533 - **£340** - FF3 843
Woman on a Wooded Country Lane Oil/panel (12.5x10cm 4x3in) Penzance, Cornwall 1999

HULL Edward ?-c.1877 [16]

$626 - €574 - **£380** - FF3 762
Fotheringway Castle on the River Nen/The Remains of Bambletye House Watercolour (14x22.5cm 5x8in) London 1998

HULL Gregory Stewart 1950 [4]

$2 000 - €2 326 - **£1 426** - FF15 259
Reclining Nude Female Figure Oil/canvas (45x76cm 18x30in) Bloomfield-Hills MI 2000

HULL Marie Atkinson 1890-1980 [12]

$3 500 - €4 128 - **£2 468** - FF27 076
European village Oil/board (44x34cm 17x14in) New-Orleans LA 2001

$9 000 - €10 356 - **£6 203** - FF67 932
Sally Watercolour/paper (69x54cm 27x21in) New-Orleans LA 2000

HULL William 1820-1880 [26]

$998 - €943 - **£620** - FF6 184
A Woodland rest Watercolour/paper (52x36.5cm 20x14in) Billingshurst, West-Sussex 1999

HULLGREN Oscar 1869-1948 [54]

$812 - €839 - **£511** - FF5 506
Hamnmotiv med båtar, Lofoten Oil/panel (39x51cm 15x20in) Stockholm 2000

HULLMANDEL Charles Joseph 1789-1850 [9]

$245 - €275 - **£170** - FF1 805
Cossack Horse, after James Ward Lithograph (33x45cm 12x17in) London 2000

HULME Frederick William 1816-1884 [76]

$10 523 - €12 515 - **£7 500** - FF82 093
Snowdon, North Wales Oil/canvas (107x152.5cm 42x60in) London 2000

$9 500 - €8 228 - **£5 826** - FF53 974
The Walker's Rest Oil/canvas (45.5x45.5cm 17x17in) New-York 1999

$1 685 - €1 594 - **£1 050** - FF10 457
Near Dorking Oil/canvas (30.5x46cm 12x18in) London 1999

HULOT Suzanne XIX-XX [10]

$1 000 - €1 166 - **£702** - FF7 650
«Sables d'Or les Pins» Poster (63x99.5cm 24x39in) New-York 2000

HULSDONCK Gillis Jacobsz. 1626-c.1675 [6]

$29 482 - €28 877 - **£19 000** - FF189 422
Partly peeled lemon and an Orange in a blue and white Wanli Kraak Oil/panel (48x38.5cm 18x15in) London 1999

HULSDONCK van Jacob 1582-1647 [18]

$217 200 - €246 823 - **£150 000** - FF1 619 055
Grapes on the Vine and Peaches in a Basket on a Table, with Butterfly Oil/panel (49.5x64cm 19x25in) London 2000

$117 489 - €109 217 - **£72 000** - FF716 414
Plums and Nectarines in a Porcelain Bowl with Cherries Oil/panel (32x41.5cm 12x16in) London 1998

HULSHOFF POL Albertus Gerhard 1883-1957 [22]

$382 - €363 - **£232** - FF2 381
Wilgen in rivierlandschap Oil/canvas (58.5x78.5cm 23x30in) Den Haag 1999

HULSMAN Johann 1600-1660 [4]

$13 259 - €12 974 - **£8 500** - FF85 103
Diana and her Nymphs resting on the Edge of a Forest Oil/canvas (139x138cm 54x54in) London 1999

HULST de Frans 1610-1661 [31]

$18 496 - €21 854 - **£13 107** - FF143 355
Kanallandschaft mit Wehrturm und Booten Oil/panel (39x52cm 15x20in) Zürich 2000

$6 257 - €7 260 - **£4 320** - FF47 625
Fortified Town on a River, with Fishermen in a Rowing Boats Oil/panel (30.5x40.5cm 12x15in) Amsterdam 2000

HULST van der Jean Baptist 1790-1862 [4]

$4 845 - €4 710 - **£2 983** - FF30 894
Portrait d'une dame de qualité Huile/toile (124x95cm 48x37in) Bruxelles 1999

$3 588 - €4 116 - **£2 454** - FF27 000
Melle Emma de Franeau de Gommegnies avec son épagneul Huile/toile (31x25cm 12x9in) Pau 2000

HULST van der Maerten Fransz 1605-1645 [8]

$3 000 - €2 844 - **£1 825** - FF18 656
River Landscape with Fishermen in a Rowboat on a River Oil/panel (23x28.5cm 9x11in) New-York 1999

HULST van der Peter IV 1651-1727 [6]

$37 650 - €37 182 - **£23 250** - FF233 900
Paysage, pèlerins devant un crucifix, moines saluant un cardinal Huile/toile (119x208.3cm 46x82in) Antwerpen 1999

$16 100 - €13 443 - **£9 570** - FF88 180
Prospekt over København set fra skovbund med rugende due omgivet Oil/wood (34x43cm 13x16in) København 1998

HULSTIJN van Cornelis Johannes 1813-c.1887 [14]

$354 - €386 - **£243** - FF2 530
Woman cutting Vegetables Oil/panel (33.5x22.5cm 13x8in) Amsterdam 2001

HULSWIT Jan 1766-1822 [18]

$545 - €635 - **£381** - FF4 167
Village Seen Across Fields, with a Standing Man in the Foreground Ink (24.5x35cm 9x13in) Amsterdam 2000

HULTBERG Charles Evald 1874-1948 [10]

$300 - €348 - **£213** - FF2 282
The Attack Watercolour/paper (33x48cm 13x19in) Chicago IL 2000

HULTÉN Carl Otto 1916 [90]

$2 142 - €2 009 - **£1 324** - FF13 177
Lianvärld Oil/canvas (81x100cm 31x39in) Stockholm 1999

$1 794 - €1 687 - **£1 111** - FF11 065
Utan titel Mixed media (28x22cm 11x8in) Stockholm 1999

$585 - €670 - £402 - FF4 395
Komposition Gouache/paper (21x24cm 8x9in)
Köbenhavn 2000

HULTSTRÖM Karl 1884-1973 [6]
$3 952 - €4 389 - £2 646 - FF28 789
Diana och Orfeus med hindar Bronze relief
(30x97cm 11x38in) Stockholm 2000

HUMBERT ESTEVE Manuel 1890-1975 [13]
$3 250 - €3 754 - £2 250 - FF24 625
La modelo del pintor Oleo/lienzo (81x65cm
31x25in) Madrid 2000

$810 - €901 - £540 - FF5 910
Muchacha en un sillón Técnica mixta/papel
(49x42cm 19x16in) Barcelona 2000

HUMBERT Jean-Charles Ferd. 1813-1881 [45]
$3 759 - €3 755 - £2 349 - FF24 629
**Hirtenmädchen mit Kühen und Ziegen auf dem
Heimweg** Öl/Leinwand (76x115cm 29x45in) Zofingen
1999

$501 - €590 - £363 - FF3 871
Chèvres Huile/carton (25x34cm 9x13in) Sion 2001

HUMBERT-VIGNOT Léonie 1878-1960 [32]
$716 - €671 - £443 - FF4 400
Bretonne tenant un livre Huile/toile (61x50cm
24x19in) Morlaix 1999

HUMBLOT Emmeline 1816-1895 [1]
$4 972 - €4 955 - £3 019 - FF32 500
**Composition florale sur une console en bois
doré** Huile/toile (113x85cm 44x33in) Tarbes 2000

HUMBLOT Robert 1907-1962 [141]
$3 423 - €3 201 - £2 097 - FF21 000
«Le phare d'Eckmul» Huile/toile (73.5x92cm
28x36in) Paris 1998

$2 525 - €2 134 - £1 502 - FF14 000
Rue de village Huile/toile (27x41cm 10x16in) Calais
1998

HUMBORG Adolf 1847-1921 [53]
$12 800 - €12 709 - £8 000 - FF83 365
The Recital Oil/canvas (57x73cm 22x28in) London
1999

$2 982 - €3 323 - £2 084 - FF21 800
Der Geniesser Oil/panel (37x30cm 14x11in)
München 2001

HUME Edith, née Dunn ?-1906 [17]
$6 373 - €7 395 - £4 400 - FF48 506
**The Dutch Fisherman's Family Awaiting the
Return of the Fleet** Oil/canvas (51x66cm 20x25in)
London 2000

$4 274 - €4 969 - £3 000 - FF32 593
Dutch Girls reading a Letter by the Shore
Watercolour (23x30cm 9x11in) Billingshurst, West-
Sussex 2001

HUME Gary 1962 [32]
$83 682 - €98 408 - £60 000 - FF645 516
Like Father Like Son Mixed media (200x162cm
78x63in) London 2001

$86 652 - €94 422 - £60 000 - FF619 368
Untitled, Portrait of Zoe Enamel (104.5x73cm
41x28in) London 2001

$1 000 - €1 160 - £690 - FF7 611
London Plane Leaves Indian ink/paper (20x12.5cm
7x4in) New-York 2000

$976 - €951 - £600 - FF6 235
Untitled Screenprint (82.5x66cm 32x25in) London
1999

$6 628 - €6 413 - £4 200 - FF42 068
Ugly Self-Portraits Cibachrome print (52x42cm
20x16in) London 1999

HUMMEL Berta 1909-1946 [1]
$2 669 - €2 556 - £1 649 - FF16 769
Der neue Stern Charcoal/paper (68x48cm 26x18in)
Kempten 1999

HUMMEL Carl 1769-? [5]
$3 114 - €3 270 - £1 962 - FF21 451
Kaiser Franz I.von Österreich Miniature (13x9.5cm
5x3in) Wien 2000

HUMMEL Carl Maria Nicolaus 1821-1907 [91]
$9 435 - €11 248 - £6 727 - FF73 785
**Dünenlandschaft bei Midsroy (Insel Wollin), im
Hintergrund die Ostsee** Öl/Leinwand (38.5x58cm
15x22in) Berlin 2000

$1 168 - €1 022 - £707 - FF6 706
Felsige Flusslandschaft Öl/Leinwand (28.3x40.5cm
11x15in) Berlin 1998

$579 - €690 - £412 - FF4 527
Sommertag in den Albaner Bergen
Aquarell/Papier (42x56cm 16x22in) Bonn 2000

$175 - €153 - £106 - FF1 005
Das Aquäduktental bei Tivoli Radierung
(15.7x21.6cm 6x8in) Berlin 1998

HUMMEL Eugen 1812-? [3]
$3 163 - €3 068 - £1 990 - FF20 123
Ferdinand I. (1793-1875), Kaiser von Österreich
Öl/Leinwand (65x54.5cm 25x21in) München 1999

HUMMEL Johann Erdmann 1769-1852 [4]
$5 268 - €5 113 - £3 280 - FF33 539
**Das Mausoleum der Königin Luise im
Charlottenburger Schlosspark** Watercolour
(41.2x49.4cm 16x19in) Berlin 1999

HUMMEL Theodor 1864-1939 [26]
$788 - €767 - £484 - FF5 030
Kieswerk bei Dachau Öl/Karton (51x77cm 20x30in)
Stuttgart 1999

HUMPHREY Elizabeth B. c.1845-c.1890 [1]
$2 800 - €2 681 - £1 729 - FF17 589
**Smiling Girl Holding Holly: Greeting Card
Design** Watercolour/paper (25x21cm 10x8in) New-
York 1999

HUMPHREY Jack Weldon 1901-1967 [29]
$3 015 - €3 326 - £1 993 - FF21 818
Driftwood Duck Tempera (71x91.5cm 27x36in)
Vancouver, BC. 2000

$3 674 - €3 512 - £2 302 - FF23 038
Three Riveters Oil/masonite (40.5x30.5cm 15x12in)
Vancouver, BC. 1999

$737 - €813 - £487 - FF5 333
Sailor Pencil/paper (39.5x26.5cm 15x10in) Vancouver,
BC. 2000

HUMPHREY Maud XIX [4]
$7 000 - €6 704 - £4 324 - FF43 973
**Young Girl Holding Cup With Flower, Easter
Greeting Card Design** Watercolour/paper (25x21cm
10x8in) New-York 1999

HUMPHREY Ozias 1742-1810 [39]
$2 558 - €2 479 - £1 610 - FF16 262
**Mrs Crewe as the Fate Clotho, facing right in
white dress** Miniature (7.5x6cm 2x3in) London 1999

$545 - €542 - £340 - FF3 555
Five Male Heads Black chalk (40.5x51cm 15x20in)
London 1999

HUMPHREY Ralph 1932-1990 **[27]**
$13 000 - €14 706 - **£9 094** - FF96 466
«Chinatowns, Tracks» Acrylic (122x122x7.5cm 48x48x2in) New-York 2001

HUMPHREY Tom 1858-1922 **[3]**
$8 741 - €8 241 - **£5 417** - FF54 059
Eltham Oil/canvas (71x138cm 27x54in) Melbourne 1999

HUMPHREY Walter Beach 1892-1966 **[5]**
$4 750 - €4 549 - **£2 934** - FF29 839
Standing Woman wearing Riding Gear, Magazine Cover Oil/canvas (71x53cm 28x21in) New-York 1999

HUMPHREY William 1740-1810 **[1]**
$1 450 - €1 424 - **£900** - FF9 341
The Good Girl, Who Can Find a Virtuous Woman ? Mezzotint (26.5x36cm 10x14in) London 1999

HUMPHREYS Malcolm 1894-? **[5]**
$2 250 - €2 314 - **£1 427** - FF15 178
Female Nude Among Laurel Oil/canvas (102x81cm 40x32in) Detroit MI 2000

HUMPHRISS Charles Harry 1867-1934 **[38]**
$7 500 - €6 408 - **£4 538** - FF42 033
Bucking Bronco Bronze (H48.5cm H19in) San-Francisco CA 1998

HUMPHRYS William 1794-1865 **[2]**
$937 - €1 052 - **£650** - FF6 901
The Meet at Melton, after F.Grant Engraving (54x78cm 21x30in) London 2000

HUNDERTWASSER Friedensreich 1928-2000 **[1191]**
$103 982 - €113 306 - **£72 000** - FF743 241
Rain of Blood Dropping into Japanese Waters in an Austrian Garden Mixed media (130x161cm 51x63in) London 2001
$2 239 - €2 601 - **£1 573** - FF17 062
Chinois dans les tropiques Technique mixte (82.5x66.5cm 32x26in) Warszawa 2001
$45 075 - €53 225 - **£32 000** - FF349 136
«Haus für Bäume und auch für Menschen, Zwei Stockwerke» Mixed media (20x29.5cm 7x11in) London 2001
$932 - €1 022 - **£633** - FF6 707
Kunsthaus Wien Ceramic (H24cm H9in) Berlin 2000
$21 225 - €18 168 - **£12 775** - FF119 175
«Die grünen Haare» Aquarell/Papier (22x16cm 8x6in) Wien 1998
$2 100 - €2 446 - **£1 467** - FF16 046
Eyeballnumber Number five Serigraph in colors (46.5x58cm 18x22in) Stockholm 2000

HUNG Francisco 1937 **[22]**
$937 - €1 079 - **£639** - FF7 076
Sin título Oleo/lienzo (65x86cm 25x33in) Caracas ($) 2000

HUNIN Alouis Pierre Paul 1808-1855 **[5]**
$5 212 - €6 126 - **£3 613** - FF40 184
The Baptism Oil/panel (88.5x107cm 34x42in) Amsterdam 2000

HUNN Thomas Henry, Tom 1857-1928 **[74]**
$945 - €890 - **£590** - FF5 835
King Richards Walk, Chichester Watercolour/paper (38x27cm 14x10in) Stansted Mountfitchet, Essex 1999

HUNT Alan M. 1947 **[51]**
$17 120 - €19 959 - **£12 000** - FF130 922
Tiger Stalking Acrylic/board (50x79cm 19x31in) London 2000
$3 066 - €2 550 - **£1 800** - FF16 728
«Is it Safe? -Young Springbok» Acrylic/board (25x61cm 9x24in) London 1998

HUNT Alfred William 1830-1896 **[82]**
$3 529 - €3 556 - **£2 200** - FF23 327
The Gap of Dunloc, Scotland Oil/canvas (35.5x46cm 13x18in) London 2000
$5 133 - €5 173 - **£3 200** - FF33 931
Sunlit Wooded River Valley Oil/canvas (33x33cm 12x12in) London 2000
$8 823 - €8 891 - **£5 500** - FF58 324
Bamburgh Castle at Twilight Watercolour (28x38.5cm 11x15in) London 2000

HUNT Bryan 1947 **[77]**
$5 000 - €5 218 - **£3 153** - FF34 225
Aug 10 Mixed media (213.5x53.5cm 84x21in) New-York 2000
$15 000 - €16 772 - **£10 111** - FF110 016
Dancers Bronze (148x66x59.5cm 58x25x23in) New-York 2000
$5 000 - €5 801 - **£3 452** - FF38 055
Untitled (Waterfall) Bronze (45.5x32x20cm 17x12x7in) New-York 2000
$5 500 - €6 161 - **£3 821** - FF40 412
Black Falls XV Graphite (211x53.5cm 83x21in) New-York 2001
$800 - €751 - **£494** - FF4 925
«Navigator I» Etching, aquatint in colors (137x91.5cm 53x36in) New-York 1999

HUNT Cecil Arthur 1873-1965 **[89]**
$723 - €781 - **£500** - FF5 125
On the Medway Watercolour/paper (27x36cm 11x14in) Par, Cornwall 2001

HUNT Charles 1803-1877 **[66]**
$12 985 - €12 487 - **£8 000** - FF81 907
Rules for Paupers Oil/canvas (92x61cm 36x24in) London 1999
$2 910 - €3 480 - **£2 000** - FF22 826
Gathering Flowers Oil/canvas (24.5x34.5cm 9x13in) Billingshurst, West-Sussex 2000
$208 - €243 - **£145** - FF1 594
Kensington Grand Steeple Chase Aquatint (49x67cm 19x26in) Melbourne 2000

HUNT Charles D. 1840-1914 **[9]**
$750 - €711 - **£456** - FF4 664
Mountain Landscape Study, Preston Pond Oil/canvas (8x15cm 3x6in) South-Natick MA 1999

HUNT Charles, Jnr. 1829-1900 **[59]**
$8 035 - €9 452 - **£5 759** - FF62 000
Le petit malade Huile/toile (61x100cm 24x39in) Paris 2001
$20 810 - €17 480 - **£12 200** - FF114 661
In the Dock Oil/canvas (31x46cm 12x18in) Billingshurst, West-Sussex 1998
$451 - €449 - **£280** - FF2 946
The Liverpool Grand National Steeple Chase Aquatint in colors (58x90cm 22x35in) Newbury, Berkshire 1999

HUNT Claude R. 1863-1949 **[4]**
$10 608 - €10 071 - **£6 500** - FF66 061
The last Move Oil/canvas (63.5x76.5cm 25x30in) London 1999

HUNT Edgar 1876-1953 **[206]**
- $43 192 - €39 271 - **£26 500** - FF257 603
  Our Rustic Friends Oil/canvas (35.5x53cm 13x20in)
  London 1999
- $26 325 - €25 167 - **£16 500** - FF165 082
  Farmyard Studies Oil/canvas (18x23cm 7x9in)
  Leicester 1999

HUNT Edward Aubrey 1855-1922 **[73]**
- $16 066 - €15 471 - **£10 000** - FF101 480
  The Last Boat from Greenwich Oil/canvas
  (142.5x229cm 56x90in) London 1999
- $2 849 - €3 312 - **£2 000** - FF21 728
  The Goose Girl Oil/canvas (76x127cm 29x50in)
  London 2001
- $1 739 - €1 909 - **£1 122** - FF12 519
  Landskap med vattendrag och människor
  Oil/canvas (30x45cm 11x17in) Lund 2000
- $950 - €929 - **£602** - FF6 093
  Marketplace Morocco Watercolour/paper (23x34cm
  9x13in) Bolton MA 1999

HUNT Esther Anna 1875-1951 **[23]**
- $1 629 - €1 396 - **£979** - FF9 155
  Burning Incense Watercolour/paper (45x66cm
  18x26in) Cedar-Falls IA 1998

HUNT George XIX **[10]**
- $402 - €460 - **£280** - FF3 016
  Tom Cribb, after J.J.Jackson Aquatint (39x30.5cm
  15x12in) London 2000

HUNT Lynn Bogue 1878-1960 **[27]**
- $3 600 - €3 076 - **£2 114** - FF20 179
  Setter with Pheasant in Autumn Oil/canvas
  (76x56cm 29x22in) Boston MA 1998
- $800 - €731 - **£489** - FF4 795
  Wildlife of Bird Graphite (35x25cm 14x10in)
  Columbia SC 1999

HUNT Millson act.1875-1900 **[32]**
- $3 051 - €2 882 - **£1 900** - FF18 905
  **At Rhu Head Skye, stranded Ship on Beach
  with Figures** Oil/canvas (74x125cm 29x49in)
  Channel-Islands 1999
- $1 434 - €1 271 - **£880** - FF8 338
  **Sailing Boats by a Continental Town/Sailing
  Vessels at Anchor** Oil/canvas (25x45cm 9x17in)
  West-Midlands 1999

HUNT Reuben 1879-1962 **[6]**
- $2 208 - €2 477 - **£1 500** - FF16 246
  Good Friends Oil/canvas (30.5x25.5cm 12x10in)
  Billingshurst, West-Sussex 2000

HUNT Richard Howard 1935 **[13]**
- $5 600 - €5 594 - **£3 500** - FF36 694
  Hybrid Form Bronze (H105cm H41in) Chicago IL
  1999
- $3 300 - €3 169 - **£2 045** - FF20 788
  Nature's Palette Bronze (43x20x20cm 16x7x7in)
  Washington 1999

HUNT W. XIX **[1]**
- $2 100 - €2 440 - **£1 475** - FF16 004
  Portrait of a man/Portrait of a woman Miniature
  (10x8cm 4x3in) South-Deerfield MA 2001

HUNT Walter 1861-1941 **[58]**
- $51 911 - €61 738 - **£37 000** - FF404 972
  The Orphan Oil/canvas (101.5x169cm 39x66in)
  London 2000
- $25 777 - €25 639 - **£16 000** - FF168 179
  Beseiged Oil/canvas (76x114cm 29x44in) London
  1999

- $9 120 - €7 895 - **£5 500** - FF51 789
  Calves Watering at a Stream Oil/panel (18x28.5cm
  7x11in) London 1998

HUNT William Henry 1790-1864 **[164]**
- $2 125 - €2 520 - **£1 500** - FF16 527
  Blowing Bubbles Watercolour (41.5x26.5cm
  16x10in) West-Midlands 1999

HUNT William Holman 1827-1910 **[53]**
- $753 - €886 - **£540** - FF5 809
  Portrait of William Pink Oil/canvas (61x46cm
  24x18in) Cheshire 2001
- $3 213 - €3 094 - **£2 000** - FF20 296
  **Portrait of the Artist's daughter, Gladys, aged
  Four** Ink (18x11.5cm 7x4in) London 1999

HUNT William Morris 1824-1879 **[33]**
- $3 100 - €2 809 - **£1 908** - FF18 428
  Young Boy Oil/canvas (45x35cm 18x14in) Mystic CT
  1999
- $35 000 - €38 400 - **£23 250** - FF251 888
  The Flight of Night Bronze (47.5x71.5x24cm
  18x28x9in) New-York 2000
- $600 - €549 - **£366** - FF3 599
  Landscape Study Charcoal/paper (13x25cm 5x10in)
  Boston MA 1998
- $1 100 - €1 097 - **£686** - FF7 197
  The Bathers Engraving (48x33cm 19x13in)
  Watertown MA 1999

HÜNTEN Emil 1827-1902 **[25]**
- $3 897 - €4 346 - **£2 620** - FF28 508
  **Attacke des 2.Rheinischen Husarenregiments
  bei Hébécourt, November** Öl/Leinwand (75x93cm
  29x36in) Ahlden 2000

HÜNTEN Franz Johann Wilhelm 1822-1887 **[18]**
- $1 392 - €1 569 - **£979** - FF10 291
  Seelandschaft mit Segelschiffen bei der Küste
  Öl/Leinwand (44x72cm 17x28in) Zürich 2001
- $4 759 - €5 624 - **£3 373** - FF36 892
  Strand bei Blankenese bei Altona Öl/Leinwand
  (25.5x42.5cm 10x16in) Ahlden 2000

HUNTER Clementine 1887-1988 **[360]**
- $2 600 - €2 227 - **£1 563** - FF14 611
  Cotton Pickin Oil/canvas (45x60cm 18x24in) New-
  Orleans LA 1998
- $1 500 - €1 602 - **£1 022** - FF10 508
  Picking Pecans Oil/canvas/panel (30x40cm 12x16in)
  New-Orleans LA 2001
- $13 000 - €14 375 - **£8 694** - FF94 296
  Basket of Zinnias Watercolour/paper (30x40cm
  12x16in) Portsmouth NH 2000
- $6 000 - €6 630 - **£4 161** - FF43 492
  Melrose Manor, African House Tapestry (106x88cm
  42x35in) New-Orleans LA 2001

HUNTER Colin 1841-1904 **[39]**
- $4 018 - €4 520 - **£2 800** - FF29 650
  Give Way Oil/canvas (90x157cm 35x61in) Edinburgh
  2001
- $2 031 - €2 287 - **£1 400** - FF15 005
  Gathering Wood in an Alpine Landscape Oil/can-
  vas (46x76cm 18x29in) London 2000
- $498 - €567 - **£350** - FF3 716
  Beached fishing Boat, Loch Achray Oil/board
  (24x34cm 9x13in) Whitby, Yorks 2001

HUNTER George Leslie 1877-1931 **[174]**
- $31 700 - €32 934 - **£20 000** - FF216 030
  Robinson Crusoe House at Largo Oil/canvas
  (46.5x41.5cm 18x16in) London 2000
- $13 703 - €16 105 - **£9 500** - FF105 644
  Fife Oil/panel (25x43cm 9x16in) Edinburgh 2000

✏ **$3 259** - €3 635 - **£2 200** - FF23 841
Nude by a Window Ink (35x21.5cm 13x8in)
Edinburgh 2000

HUNTER George Sherwood 1846-1919 **[96]**
🖼 **$2 550** - €2 722 - **£1 700** - FF17 853
Salmon Fishermen Emptying a Jumper,
Aberdeen Coast Oil/canvas (75x101cm 29x39in)
Leyburn, North Yorkshire 2000
🖼 **$855** - €872 - **£535** - FF5 720
Venedig, Blick auf San Vidale mit Palazzo
Franchetti Oil/paper/canvas (17x32.5cm 6x12in) Wien
2000

HUNTER Isabel 1878-1941 **[7]**
🖼 **$5 000** - €4 272 - **£3 025** - FF28 022
Monterey Adobe Oil/canvas (51x56cm 20x22in) San-
Francisco CA 1998
✏ **$1 900** - €2 220 - **£1 356** - FF14 565
Palace of Fine Art, San Francisco Mixed
media/paper (44x44cm 17x17in) Altadena CA 2001

HUNTER James, Lieutenant c.1740-1792 **[7]**
✏ **$2 480** - €2 320 - **£1 500** - FF15 221
The third Delhi Gate, Tipu Sultan Fort,
Bangalore Watercolour (27.5x35cm 10x13in) London
1999

HUNTER John Frederick 1893-1951 **[3]**
🖼 **$4 001** - €3 793 - **£2 500** - FF24 882
Leicester Square Oil/canvas (38x53.5cm 14x21in)
London 1999
🖼 **$2 076** - €2 322 - **£1 400** - FF15 233
Saturday Night Oil/board (28x35cm 11x13in) London
2000

HUNTER John Young 1874-1955 **[36]**
🖼 **$1 500** - €1 680 - **£1 042** - FF11 020
«Duet» Oil/canvas (91x60cm 36x24in) Cincinnati OH
2001

HUNTER Mary Ethel Young 1878-1936 **[17]**
🖼 **$498** - €536 - **£340** - FF3 519
A Portrait of David Vardy, Aged 5 Years Oil/canvas
(41.5x33cm 16x12in) West-Yorkshire 2001

HUNTER Philip 1958 **[5]**
🖼 **$4 090** - €4 496 - **£2 621** - FF29 495
Excursion Oil/canvas (198x168cm 77x66in)
Melbourne 2000

HUNTER Robert c.1752-c.1803 **[4]**
🖼 **$30 106** - €33 030 - **£20 000** - FF216 660
James FitzGerald (1722-1773), 20th Earl of
Kildare Oil/canvas (127x101.5cm 50x39in) London
2000

HUNTER Robert 1947 **[7]**
🖼 **$13 602** - €15 246 - **£9 511** - FF100 007
Untitled #1 Acrylic (123x244cm 48x96in) Melbourne
2001

HUNTER Robert Douglas 1928 **[12]**
🖼 **$4 500** - €4 489 - **£2 809** - FF29 444
Still Life Oil/canvas (48x89cm 19x35in) Watertown
MA 1999

HUNTINGTON Daniel 1816-1906 **[16]**
🖼 **$3 600** - €4 159 - **£2 520** - FF27 281
Mount Mansfield, Sunset Oil/canvas (35.5x63.5cm
13x25in) Bethesda MD 2001

HUNTINGTON Dwight W. 1860-1906 **[4]**
✏ **$3 000** - €2 977 - **£1 860** - FF18 349
Duck Shooting Watercolour/paper (32.5x50.5cm
12x19in) New-York 1999

HUNTLEY Victoria Eb. Hutson 1900-1971 **[21]**
📰 **$325** - €332 - **£203** - FF2 181
Looking to New York Lithograph (19x31cm 7x12in)
Cleveland OH 2000

HUNZIKER Frieda 1908-1966 **[14]**
🖼 **$2 852** - €2 723 - **£1 782** - FF17 859
«Geste 1» Oil/canvas (46x55cm 18x21in) Amsterdam
1999

HUNZINGER Werner 1816-1861 **[4]**
🖼 **$75 000** - €64 079 - **£45 022** - FF420 330
Still Life Oil/canvas (61x81.5cm 24x32in) New-York
1998

HUOT Charles Ed. Masson 1855-1930 **[31]**
🖼 **$3 062** - €2 956 - **£1 897** - FF19 387
Vue d'Italie Huile/toile (37x62.5cm 14x24in) Montréal
1999
🖼 **$744** - €734 - **£458** - FF4 816
Vue du Québec prise de la Baie de Lévis
Huile/toile (22.5x30.5cm 8x12in) Montréal 1999
✏ **$476** - €460 - **£295** - FF3 015
Dieppe Aquarelle (23.5x31cm 9x12in) Montréal 1999

HÜPPI Alfonso 1935 **[30]**
📰 **$151** - €174 - **£106** - FF1 140
Ohne Titel Serigraph in colors (86x63cm 33x24in)
Hamburg 2001

HUQUIER L. XVIII **[1]**
✏ **$2 572** - €2 592 - **£1 603** - FF17 000
Danaé Gouache/vélin (24x19.5cm 9x7in) Paris 2000

HURARD Joseph 1887-1956 **[66]**
🖼 **$1 039** - €915 - **£633** - FF6 000
Le vieux port de Martigues Huile/panneau
(48x90cm 18x35in) Lyon 1999

HURD Peter 1904-1984 **[88]**
🖼 **$5 000** - €5 776 - **£3 501** - FF37 890
Portrait of a Young Jockey Oil/canvas (96x68cm
38x27in) New-York 2001
✏ **$2 500** - €2 839 - **£1 737** - FF18 620
Woman on Horse Watercolour/paper (12x17cm
5x7in) Dallas TX 2001
📰 **$350** - €325 - **£218** - FF2 130
The Sheep Herder Lithograph (27x23cm 10x9in)
York PA 1999

HUREL Clément XX **[12]**
📰 **$441** - €381 - **£261** - FF2 500
«A bout de souffle» Affiche (60x80cm 23x31in)
Paris 1999

HURET Grégoire 1606-1670 **[6]**
✏ **$2 641** - €2 897 - **£1 793** - FF19 000
Allégorie des sciences Pierre noire/papier
(26x34.5cm 10x13in) Troyes 2000

HURLEY Edward Timothy 1869-1950 **[22]**
📰 **$475** - €493 - **£313** - FF3 234
Feeding Chickens Etching (29x18cm 11x7in)
Cleveland OH 2000

HURLEY Frank 1885-1962 **[59]**
📷 **$2 083** - €2 431 - **£1 450** - FF15 946
The Crystal Canoe Gelatin silver print (37x29cm
14x11in) Sydney 2000

HURLEY Robert Newton 1894-1980 **[66]**
✏ **$338** - €325 - **£209** - FF2 131
Winter Prairie with Grain Elevator
Watercolour/paper (24x35cm 9x13in) Toronto 1999

HURLEY Wilson 1924 [12]
- $32 000 - €36 335 - **£22 233** - FF238 339
  Bathed in a Firey Sunset Oil/canvas (91x121cm 36x48in) Dallas TX 2001
- $7 500 - €8 815 - **£5 200** - FF57 823
  Sandias Sunset Oil/board (18.5x36cm 7x14in) Beverly-Hills CA 2000

HÜRLIMANN Johann 1793-1850 [12]
- $467 - €437 - **£288** - FF2 866
  Le Repas champêtre, Costumes de Lucerne, nach Gabriel Lory fils Aquatinta (21.5x28.5cm 8x11in) Luzern 1994

HURMERINTA Olavi 1928 [19]
- $553 - €471 - **£330** - FF3 089
  Fåglar Oil/canvas (45x60cm 17x23in) Helsinki 1998

HURNI Rudolf 1914 [5]
- $1 070 - €1 244 - **£752** - FF8 161
  Bild 63 Oil/panel (50x50cm 19x19in) Luzern 2001

HURRELL George 1904-1992 [111]
- $2 000 - €2 147 - **£1 358** - FF14 081
  Portfolio III Gelatin silver print (48x39.5cm 18x15in) Beverly-Hills CA 2001

HURRY Leslie 1909-1978 [70]
- $464 - €396 - **£280** - FF2 595
  Ruins in a Wooded Glade - Design for Swan Lake Watercolour (30x53cm 11x20in) London 1998
- $7 161 - €6 572 - **£4 400** - FF43 107
  Dead of Night Poster (76x101.5cm 29x39in) London 1999

HURST Earl Oliver 1895-1958 [3]
- $2 800 - €2 681 - **£1 729** - FF17 589
  Woman with Umbrella and First Drops of Rain, Magazine Cover Watercolour/paper (59x38cm 23x15in) New-York 1999

HURT Louis Bosworth 1856-1929 [190]
- $39 808 - €34 623 - **£24 000** - FF227 109
  Loch Lubnaig and Ben Vane, Strathyre Oil/canvas (99x145cm 38x57in) Glasgow 1998
- $38 012 - €32 477 - **£23 000** - FF213 037
  Cattle in the Highlands Oil/canvas (76x127cm 29x50in) Edinburgh 1998
- $2 701 - €3 043 - **£1 900** - FF19 962
  Highland Cattle watering Oil/panel (12x21cm 4x8in) Lichfield, Staffordshire 2001

HURTADO Rodolfo XX [2]
- $2 572 - €2 853 - **£1 711** - FF18 715
  El sheik Estampe (139x109cm 54x42in) México 2000

HURTRELLE Simon 1648-1724 [1]
- $87 956 - €84 696 - **£55 000** - FF555 571
  Saturn devouring one of his Children Marble (64x22x24cm 25x8x9in) London 1999

HURTUBISE Jacques 1939 [24]
- $971 - €1 129 - **£681** - FF7 404
  «Griffon gris 85» Acrylique/toile (61x102cm 24x40in) Montréal 2001
- $172 - €175 - **£107** - FF1 148
  Titane Estampe (39.5x66cm 15x25in) Montréal 2000

HURWITZ Sidney 1932 [5]
- $450 - €467 - **£285** - FF3 066
  Green Line Etching, aquatint in colors (49.5x60cm 19x23in) Boston MA 2000

HUSAIN Maqbool Fida 1915 [172]
- $17 000 - €19 334 - **£11 877** - FF126 821
  Pilgrimace Acrylic/canvas (110.5x133.5cm 43x52in) New-York 2000

$10 460 - €11 228 - **£7 000** - FF73 651
  Eternal Lovers Oil/canvas (119.5x73.5cm 47x28in) London 2000
- $3 749 - €3 550 - **£2 338** - FF23 287
  Untitled Oil/board (42x28.5cm 16x11in) New-York 1999
- $3 246 - €3 120 - **£2 000** - FF20 466
  Abstract Watercolour/paper (56x76cm 22x29in) London 1999
- $14 943 - €16 040 - **£10 000** - FF105 216
  Mother Teresa Series Print (40.5x53.5cm 15x21in) London 2000

HUSE Marion 1896-1967 [8]
- $1 300 - €1 241 - **£812** - FF8 140
  Untitled Oil/canvas (53x66cm 21x26in) Dedham MA 1999

HUSER A.C. XIX [1]
- $5 530 - €5 087 - **£3 318** - FF33 369
  Jäger im Winterwald Öl/Leinwand (84x68cm 33x26in) Wien 1999

HUSKISSON Robert Locking 1919-1861 [3]
- $112 072 - €120 301 - **£75 000** - FF789 120
  Titania's Elves Robbing the Squirrel's Nest - Midsummer Night's Dream Oil/panel (38x50cm 14x19in) London 2000

HUSON Thomas 1844-1920 [22]
- $556 - €534 - **£338** - FF3 504
  Just in Time Oil/panel (37x45cm 14x17in) Stockholm 1999
- $265 - €295 - **£181** - FF1 933
  «The House by the Sea NR. Liverpool» Watercolour/paper (23x33cm 9x12in) Toronto 2000

HUSSEM Willem 1900-1974 [89]
- $3 534 - €3 403 - **£2 210** - FF22 324
  Untitled Oil/canvas (46x55cm 18x21in) Amsterdam 1999
- $1 932 - €1 906 - **£1 189** - FF12 501
  Untitled Oil/paper (32.5x25cm 12x9in) Amsterdam 1999
- $1 618 - €1 815 - **£1 121** - FF11 906
  Untitled Gouache/paper (64.5x49.5cm 25x19in) Amsterdam 2000

HUSSEY Philip 1713-1782 [2]
- $10 074 - €11 284 - **£7 000** - FF74 018
  Portrait of Samuel Madden (1686-1765) Oil/canvas (73x60cm 28x23in) London 2001

HUSSMANN Albert Heinrich 1874-1946 [53]
- $1 916 - €1 841 - **£1 188** - FF12 074
  Trabender Hengst Bronze (47x56cm 18x22in) Ahlden 1999

HUSTON William XIX-XX [6]
- $3 600 - €4 281 - **£2 565** - FF28 083
  Early Morning, Long Island Oil/canvas (25.5x45.5cm 10x17in) New-York 2000

HUSZAR Vilmos 1884-1960 [41]
- $59 537 - €63 912 - **£39 850** - FF419 237
  Komposition Öl/Leinwand (146x110.5cm 57x43in) Köln 2000
- $8 820 - €7 635 - **£5 352** - FF50 084
  Still Life of Flowers Oil/canvas (40x30cm 15x11in) Amsterdam 1998
- $399 - €454 - **£276** - FF2 976
  Vier hoofden Etching (14.6x19cm 5x7in) Haarlem 2000

HUTAF August William 1879-1942 **[2]**
📖 **$1 100** - €1 114 - **£684** - FF7 309
«Treat'em Rough! Join the Thanks, United States Tank Corps» Poster (104x53cm 41x21in) Bethesda MD 2000

HUTCHENS Frank Townsend 1869-1937 **[24]**
🖼 **$6 000** - €6 720 - **£4 168** - FF44 083
«New England Landscape» Oil/canvas (76x91cm 30x36in) Cincinnati OH 2001
🖼 **$600** - €566 - **£373** - FF3 715
Fishing Boat at Katwyk Holland Oil/board (23x15cm 9x6in) Milford CT 1999
✎ **$9 500** - €10 867 - **£6 606** - FF71 283
Woman Reading Watercolour/paper (45x30cm 18x12in) Cincinnati OH 2000

HUTCHINSON Frederick William 1871-1953 **[18]**
🖼 **$800** - €707 - **£489** - FF4 638
Own Street Oil/masonite (20x25.5cm 7x10in) New-York 1999

HUTCHINSON Leonard 1896-1980 **[104]**
📖 **$186** - €175 - **£115** - FF1 172
«Ravine» Woodcut in colors (22x26cm 8x10in) Toronto 1999

HUTCHINSON Peter Arthur 1932 **[22]**
✎ **$562** - €534 - **£342** - FF3 500
Apple Triangle Collage (72x49cm 28x19in) Paris 1999

HUTCHISON Robert Gemmell 1855-1936 **[264]**
🖼 **$5 454** - €6 134 - **£3 800** - FF40 239
Full length Portrait of a Boy in a white Ruff Shirt Oil/canvas (161x92cm 63x36in) Edinburgh 2001
🖼 **$7 411** - €7 049 - **£4 500** - FF46 240
Portrait of Nan, the Artist's Daughter Oil/canvas (92x57cm 36x22in) Edinburgh 1999
🖼 **$14 596** - €15 025 - **£9 200** - FF98 559
Boy digging for worms on a sunlit beach Oil/board (25x20cm 9x7in) Cambridge 2000
✎ **$7 204** - €7 124 - **£4 500** - FF46 732
Picnic by the Sea Watercolour (52x74cm 20x29in) Glasgow 1999

HUTH Franz 1876-1970 **[66]**
✎ **$571** - €613 - **£389** - FF4 024
Schillerhaus Pastell/Papier (43x30cm 16x11in) Rudolstadt-Thüringen 2001

HUTH Julius 1838-1892 **[16]**
🖼 **$2 321** - €2 352 - **£1 443** - FF15 427
Teilansicht von Cuxhaven Öl/Leinwand (45x70.5cm 17x27in) Hamburg 2000
✎ **$878** - €920 - **£581** - FF6 037
Fischerboot und Segelschiffe vor der Nordseeküste Watercolour (26.4x39.2cm 10x15in) München 2000

HUTH Walde 1923 **[37]**
📷 **$514** - €613 - **£337** - FF4 024
Ernst Jünger Photograph (40.2x28.8cm 15x11in) München 2000

HUTH Willy Robert 1890-1977 **[66]**
✎ **$381** - €434 - **£266** - FF2 850
Nordfriesische Landschaften Watercolour, gouache/board (15x10cm 5x3in) Hamburg 2001
📖 **$343** - €409 - **£244** - FF2 683
Artisten Lithographie (52x36cm 20x14in) Berlin 2000

📖 **$275** - €307 - **£191** - FF2 012
Frauenbildnis Mischtechnik (26.5x17.5cm 10x6in) München 2001
✎ **$407** - €460 - **£286** - FF3 018
Blumen vor dem Fenster Aquarell/Papier (34.5x26cm 13x10in) Stuttgart 2001

HUTHSTEINER Rudolf 1855-1935 **[15]**
🖼 **$2 047** - €2 045 - **£1 280** - FF13 415
Das Konzert Öl/Leinwand (79x64cm 31x25in) Köln 1999

HÜTTE Axel 1951 **[39]**
📷 **$921** - €1 074 - **£637** - FF7 043
Maschere, Poggio a Caiano Gelatin silver print (31.5x22.5cm 12x8in) Köln 2000

HUTTER Schang 1934 **[65]**
✎ **$355** - €386 - **£233** - FF2 532
Veitstanz Nr.1 Watercolour, gouache (65x50cm 25x19in) Bern 2000
📖 **$92** - €104 - **£64** - FF681
Figurengruppe im Kreis angeordnet Drypoint (20.5x29cm 8x11in) Bern 2001

HUTTER Wolfgang 1928 **[137]**
🖼 **$8 390** - €7 264 - **£5 090** - FF47 650
«Der grosse Kopfschmuck» Oil/panel (51.5x62cm 20x24in) Wien 1998
🖼 **$5 887** - €5 084 - **£3 549** - FF33 348
Die Muse des Poeten Oil/panel (29.3x19.3cm 11x7in) Wien 1998
✎ **$1 143** - €1 090 - **£696** - FF7 150
Zeichen Aquarell/Papier (23.7x16.5cm 9x6in) Wien 1999
📖 **$201** - €218 - **£139** - FF1 430
Im Blumenland Farbradierung (33.5x29cm 13x11in) Wien 1999

HUTTON Thomas Swift 1865-1935 **[121]**
✎ **$553** - €527 - **£350** - FF3 458
A Fisherman on a River in Spate Watercolour (50.5x76.5cm 19x30in) London 1999

HUTTY Alfred Heber 1877-1954 **[116]**
🖼 **$7 000** - €6 552 - **£4 337** - FF42 981
Autumn Oil/canvas (60x74cm 24x29in) Detroit MI 1999
✎ **$3 600** - €3 880 - **£2 414** - FF25 453
Man Netting for Fish Watercolour/paper (30x38cm 12x15in) Marshfield MA 2000
📖 **$800** - €671 - **£469** - FF4 402
City Gate Etching (18x21cm 7x8in) New-Orleans LA 1998

HUVEY Louis 1868-1954 **[7]**
📖 **$3 000** - €3 109 - **£2 106** - FF22 951
«Audibet et Lavirotte» Poster (151.5x109cm 59x42in) New-York 2000

HUYBERTS Cornelis 1669-c.1712 **[2]**
📖 **$219** - €256 - **£154** - FF1 676
Der Triumphzug des Julius Cäsar, nach Andrea Mantegna Radierung (44x41.5cm 17x16in) Berlin 2001

HUYGENS Constantijn 1628-1697 **[8]**
✎ **$30 388** - €35 395 - **£21 231** - FF232 174
View Towards the Manor at Kleef, Near Haarlem Ink (16.5x26cm 6x10in) Amsterdam 2000

HUYGENS François Joseph 1820-1908 **[42]**
🖼 **$3 068** - €3 222 - **£1 937** - FF21 138
Bouquet de fleurs dans la Serre Huile/toile (111x76cm 43x29in) Bruxelles 2000

$1 262 - €1 502 - **£900** - FF9 850
Roses on a Marble Entabulature Oil/panel
(19.5x14cm 7x5in) London 2000

HUYGENS Frederik Lodewijk 1802-1887 **[15]**
$1 801 - €2 147 - **£1 284** - FF14 086
Ländliche Idylle Öl/Leinwand (90x112cm 35x44in)
Bonn 2000

HUYNH Jean-Baptiste 1966 **[1]**
$2 750 - €2 851 - **£1 650** - FF18 700
Nu Photograph (70x70cm 27x27in) Prato 1999

HUYS Balthasar ?-1652 **[3]**
$11 733 - €13 613 - **£8 100** - FF89 298
Still Life with Gherkins, Fruits, a Cabbage, Hens
and a Duck on Table Oil/panel (58.5x83cm 23x32in)
Amsterdam 2000

HUYS Bernhard 1896-1973 **[49]**
$1 097 - €1 022 - **£677** - FF6 707
Heuernte in den Hammewiesen Oil/panel
(49x70cm 19x27in) Bremen 1999

HUYS Franz 1522-1562 **[4]**
$7 375 - €7 158 - **£4 592** - FF46 954
Der Lautenmacher, nach Cornelis Matsys
Kupferstich (28x42.7cm 11x16in) Berlin 1999

HUYS Modest 1874-1932 **[94]**
$19 530 - €22 689 - **£13 725** - FF148 830
Inondation Oil/canvas (98x140cm 38x55in)
Amsterdam 2001
$19 875 - €18 591 - **£12 075** - FF121 950
Middag in de lente, midi au printemps Oil/canvas
(60.5x75.5cm 23x29in) Lokeren 2000
$6 360 - €5 949 - **£3 936** - FF39 024
De beuk Huile/toile (31x45cm 12x17in) Lokeren 1999

HUYS Pieter 1519-1584 **[8]**
$35 568 - €39 637 - **£24 856** - FF260 000
L'Enfer Huile/panneau (44.5x55cm 17x21in) Paris 2001

HUYSMAN P.J. XVIII **[2]**
$7 525 - €7 622 - **£4 725** - FF50 000
Repos de la bergère près de la rivière/Le
Passage du pont Huile/panneau (38.5x46cm
15x18in) Versailles 2000

HUYSMANS Cornelis 1648-1727 **[24]**
$77 342 - €75 955 - **£48 000** - FF498 235
Hilly Wooded Landscape with Peasants and
Cattle at a Watering-Hole Oil/canvas (117x135.5cm
46x53in) London 1999
$7 175 - €7 021 - **£4 600** - FF46 056
Wooded River Valley Landscape with Drovers
and Cattle Oil/canvas (65x79cm 25x31in) London
1999
$2 880 - €3 270 - **£1 971** - FF21 451
Bewaldete Flusslandschaft mit Hirten und
Angler in einem Boot Öl/Leinwand (34x45cm
13x17in) Wien 2000

HUYSMANS Jacob c.1633-1696 **[21]**
$16 916 - €16 825 - **£10 500** - FF110 367
Young boy wearing a Ostrich Feather
Headdress with a Purple Robe Oil/canvas
(170x108cm 66x42in) London 1999
$5 671 - €5 454 - **£3 500** - FF35 774
Portrait of Lady Cotton, seated, in a green and
white satin Dress Oil/canvas (118x100.5cm 46x39in)
London 1999

HUYSMANS Jan Baptist 1826-1906 **[43]**
$8 424 - €8 924 - **£5 688** - FF58 536
Cavaliers près d'un campement Huile/toile
(42.5x50.5cm 16x19in) Bruxelles 2001

$1 505 - €1 735 - **£1 036** - FF11 382
Oosters tafereel Oil/panel (8.7x9.5cm 3x3in) Lokeren
2000
$508 - €534 - **£318** - FF3 500
Un passetemps de Mauresque Aquarelle/papier
(23.5x11.5cm 9x4in) Paris 2000

HUYSMANS Jan Baptist 1654-1716 **[13]**
$14 022 - €13 081 - **£8 460** - FF85 806
Gebirgige Küstenlandschaft Öl/Leinwand
(120x174cm 47x68in) Wien 1999
$7 794 - €8 692 - **£5 241** - FF57 016
Klassische Landschaft mit Frauen an einem
Bachlauf Öl/Leinwand (60x75cm 23x29in) Köln 2000

HUYSUM van Jan 1682-1749 **[72]**
$22 410 - €19 124 - **£13 392** - FF125 442
Blomsterstilleben Oil/canvas (90x60cm 35x23in)
Stockholm 1998
$496 544 - €486 354 - **£320 000** - FF3 190 272
Roses, Morning Glory, Narcissi, Aster, and other
Flowers, Eggs Oil/panel (26x19.5cm 10x7in) London
1999
$3 933 - €3 964 - **£2 451** - FF26 000
Paysage à la rivière Encre (13x21cm 5x8in) Paris
2000

HUYSUM van Justus 1659-1716 **[8]**
$9 222 - €9 147 - **£5 736** - FF60 060
Panier de roses, lys, pivoines sur un entable-
ment avec un tapis Huile/toile (86x70cm 33x27in)
Lille 1999
$8 934 - €9 147 - **£5 610** - FF60 060
La halte des cavaliers près d'une fontaine
Huile/toile (39x33cm 15x12in) Lille 2000

HUYSUM van Michiel c.1700-c.1765 **[4]**
$4 345 - €5 042 - **£3 000** - FF33 072
Study of Roses (Rosa centifolia) Watercolour
(30.5x20cm 12x7in) London 2000

HUZÉ Guy XX **[6]**
$620 - €681 - **£412** - FF4 464
African Women Gouache/paper (53x41cm 20x16in)
Amsterdam 2000

HYAMS William 1878-? **[11]**
$513 - €517 - **£320** - FF3 393
October Morning, Steyning/Haycart on a
Country Road/March on the South Watercolour
(18x26cm 7x10in) Billingshurst, West-Sussex 2000

HYATT Anna Huntington 1876-1973 **[67]**
$75 000 - €77 742 - **£47 557** - FF509 955
Greyhounds at Play Bronze (H98cm H38in) New-
York 2000
$3 600 - €3 457 - **£2 219** - FF22 679
Stretching cougar Bronze (10x33cm 4x13in)
Cambridge MA 1999

HYBERT Fabrice 1961 **[25]**
$8 676 - €9 147 - **£5 730** - FF60 000
Territoires Technique mixte (167x206cm 65x81in)
Paris 2000
$8 190 - €9 147 - **£5 550** - FF60 000
Garde-fou Technique mixte (111x100cm 43x39in)
Paris 2000
$10 368 - €12 196 - **£7 432** - FF80 000
Élevage de mouches Installation (140x100x13cm
55x39x5in) Paris 2001
$2 047 - €2 287 - **£1 387** - FF15 000
Bouteille-estomac Sculpture verre (H35cm H13in)
Paris 2000
$2 457 - €2 744 - **£1 665** - FF18 000
L'oeil Crayon gras (56x75cm 22x29in) Paris 2000

HYDE Helen 1868-1919 **[106]**
- $550 - €529 - **£339** - FF3 469
  Ah Tim and Miss Plum Blossom
  Watercolour/paper (15x8cm 6x3in) Oakland CA 1999
- $500 - €477 - **£307** - FF3 132
  Two Asian Children Woodcut in colors (11x10cm 4x4in) Cincinnati OH 1999

HYDE-POWNALL George 1876-1932 **[60]**
- $665 - €642 - **£420** - FF4 210
  Westminster from the Thames by Moonlight
  Oil/board (24.5x16.5cm 9x6in) Ipswich 1999

HYDMAN-VALLIEN Ulrica 1938 **[56]**
- $1 320 - €1 282 - **£815** - FF8 407
  Flicka med tulpaner och ormar Oil/panel (38x46cm 14x18in) Stockholm 1999
- $773 - €651 - **£456** - FF4 273
  Blomster Mixed media (33x29cm 12x11in) Stockholm 1998
- $317 - €352 - **£220** - FF2 310
  Blommor Akvarell/papper (41x31cm 16x12in) Malmö 2001
- $128 - €143 - **£87** - FF936
  Bröloppet Color lithograph (41x30cm 16x11in) Stockholm 2000

HYNAïS Vojteck 1854-1925 **[19]**
- $2 456 - €2 323 - **£1 530** - FF15 240
  Portrait of Mr.M.H. Oil/canvas (106x71cm 41x27in) Praha 2000
- $578 - €547 - **£360** - FF3 586
  Portrait d'épouse Huile/toile/carton (27x21cm 10x8in) Praha 2000
- $722 - €683 - **£450** - FF4 482
  Pâturage de moutons Gouache/papier (60x39cm 23x15in) Praha 1999

HYNCKES Raoul 1893-1973 **[105]**
- $9 374 - €10 891 - **£6 588** - FF71 438
  The Oilcan Oil/canvas (70x90cm 27x35in) Amsterdam 2001
- $647 - €726 - **£448** - FF4 762
  Marine Pencil/paper (17x13cm 6x5in) Amsterdam 2000

HYNCKES-ZAHN Marguerite 1897-1978 **[14]**
- $1 593 - €1 588 - **£967** - FF10 418
  Stilleven met sokkel, laurier, touw en klassieke portretbuste Oil/canvas (52x66cm 20x25in) Amsterdam 2000

HYNEMAN Herman 1859-1907 **[9]**
- $2 100 - €2 095 - **£1 311** - FF13 740
  Contemplation Oil/canvas (50x40cm 20x16in) Cincinnati OH 1999

HYNES Gladys 1888-1958 **[9]**
- $9 946 - €8 485 - **£6 000** - FF55 658
  Circus Clowns Oil/panel (65.5x52cm 25x20in) London 1998

HYON Georges 1855-? **[32]**
- $1 957 - €2 058 - **£1 291** - FF13 500
  Napoléon Huile/toile (65.5x54.5cm 25x21in) Paris 2000

HYSING Hans 1678-1753 **[6]**
- $3 980 - €4 387 - **£2 600** - FF28 777
  Portrait of a Gentleman of the Gooch Family Oil/canvas (74x61cm 29x24in) London 2000

I

I GUSTI KETUT SUANDI 1921 **[4]**
- $2 308 - €2 151 - **£1 424** - FF14 110
  Fish Market Oil/canvas (69x90cm 27x35in) Singapore 1999

l'ONS Frederick Timpson 1802-1887 **[22]**
- $2 921 - €3 390 - **£2 017** - FF22 237
  Portrait of a Man Oil/canvas (22.5x18cm 8x7in) Johannesburg 2000
- $9 859 - €11 580 - **£7 000** - FF75 957
  South African Portraits (Fingo Girl/Fingo Boy/Bechuana/Caffer...) Watercolour (21.5x15.5cm 8x6in) London 2000

IACOBY Valéri Ivanovitch 1834/36-1909 **[5]**
- $4 831 - €4 562 - **£3 000** - FF29 923
  African Girl with Fruit Oil/board (35x21.5cm 13x8in) London 1999

IACOVLEFF Alexander Evgenevich 1887-1938 **[205]**
- $10 990 - €10 671 - **£6 790** - FF70 000
  Vue de Grasse Huile/toile (108x192cm 42x75in) Paris 1999
- $4 806 - €4 430 - **£2 879** - FF29 059
  Encampment, Chad Oil/canvas (47.5x69cm 18x27in) Amsterdam 1998
- $1 306 - €1 372 - **£823** - FF9 000
  Vue plongeante sur le quartier arabe Peinture (42x25cm 16x9in) Fontainebleau 2000
- $2 032 - €2 134 - **£1 281** - FF14 000
  Anita Lopez en cheftaine scoute Pastel gras (175x78cm 68x30in) Fontainebleau 2000

IACURTO Francesco, Frank 1908 **[61]**
- $2 041 - €1 970 - **£1 264** - FF12 925
  Scène hivernale Huile/carton/toile (41x51cm 16x20in) Montréal 1999
- $1 173 - €1 027 - **£710** - FF6 737
  «Hiver St-Hylarion» Huile/toile/carton (30.5x35.5cm 12x13in) Montréal 1998

IALENTI Antonio 1937 **[59]**
- $800 - €829 - **£480** - FF5 440
  «Campagna molisana» Olio/tela (50x70cm 19x27in) Vercelli 2001
- $325 - €337 - **£195** - FF2 210
  «Fiume Sesia» Olio/tela (30x40cm 11x15in) Vercelli 2001

IANCHELEVICI Idel 1909-1994 **[11]**
- $1 270 - €1 239 - **£780** - FF8 130
  Jeune fille assise Sculpture (H41cm H16in) Bruxelles 1999

IANELLI Vincent 1885-1962 **[1]**
- $5 000 - €5 946 - **£3 563** - FF39 005
  New Jersey Rooftops Oil/canvas (56x72cm 22x28in) New-York 2000

IANNELLI Alfonso 1888-? **[4]**
- $4 500 - €4 380 - **£2 764** - FF28 729
  Bert Leslie, the King of the Slang Tempera/board (68.5x93.5cm 26x36in) New-York 1999

IBAÑEZ DE ALDECOA Y ARANO Julián 1866-1952 **[48]**
- $1 620 - €1 802 - **£1 140** - FF11 820
  Pescadores de Lequeitio Oleo/cartón (40x50cm 15x19in) Madrid 2000
- $1 188 - €1 081 - **£720** - FF7 092
  Puerto Oleo/cartón (29.5x40cm 11x15in) Madrid 1999

IBANEZ Francisco Ramos XIX [2]
- $2 080 - €1 952 - £1 300 - FF12 805
  Procesión Oleo/tabla (21.5x13.5cm 8x5in) Madrid 1999

IBARRA de José 1688-1756 [7]
- $21 060 - €23 907 - £14 720 - FF156 820
  Crucifixión Oleo/lienzo (202x126cm 79x49in) México 2001

IBARROLA GOICOECHEA Agustín 1930 [5]
- $11 200 - €12 013 - £7 400 - FF78 800
  Trabajadores Oleo/lienzo (144x112cm 56x44in) Madrid 2000

IBBETSON Julius Caesar 1759-1817 [113]
- $5 338 - €6 193 - £3 800 - FF40 625
  Children gathering Firewood, an Ox-drawn Cart standing beside Oil/canvas (51.5x64cm 20x25in) London 2001
- $4 037 - €4 462 - £2 800 - FF29 268
  View of a Lake with a Storm Approaching Oil/canvas (29.5x41.5cm 11x16in) London 2001
- $1 193 - €1 002 - £700 - FF6 572
  The Rich and the Poor Watercolour (21x18cm 8x7in) London 1998

IBELS Henri-Gabriel 1867-1936 [124]
- $2 787 - €2 897 - £1 755 - FF19 000
  Paysage Huile/carton (64.5x100cm 25x39in) Paris 2000
- $518 - €610 - £371 - FF4 000
  Scène galante Huile/toile (28x24cm 11x9in) Paris 2001
- $500 - €457 - £305 - FF2 997
  Pierrefort 12R Bonaparte Lithograph (19x25cm 7x10in) Pittsburgh PA 1999

ICARD Honoré 1845-1917 [6]
- $985 - €1 067 - £674 - FF7 000
  Le gentilhomme Bronze (H42cm H16in) Paris 2001

ICART Louis 1888-1950 [2623]
- $70 380 - €77 749 - £48 807 - FF510 000
  L'après-midi d'un faune Huile/toile (167x359cm 65x141in) Paris 2001
- $6 700 - €7 622 - £4 650 - FF50 000
  Matin à Notre-Dame Huile/toile (46x55cm 18x21in) Paris 2000
- $4 931 - €4 878 - £3 075 - FF32 000
  Au rendez-vous Huile/toile (30x40.5cm 11x15in) Abbeville 1999
- $999 - €854 - £600 - FF5 601
  Girl with Bouquet of Flowers, Sketch Watercolour (45x57cm 17x22in) London 1998
- $1 159 - €1 080 - £760 - FF7 085
  Girl with Blue Butterflies Etching, aquatint in colors (64.5x50.5cm 25x19in) London 1998

ICAZA Ernesto 1866-1935 [40]
- $21 300 - €19 913 - £13 160 - FF130 620
  Manganeando a campo abierto Oleo/lienzo (47.5x70.5cm 18x27in) México 1999
- $12 144 - €14 282 - £8 712 - FF93 687
  Mangana a caballo Oleo/tabla (30.5x47cm 12x18in) México 2001

IERSEL van Rik 1961 [11]
- $112 - €113 - £70 - FF744
  Brainthing Serigraph (40x40cm 15x15in) Amsterdam 2000

IEZUMI Toshio 1954 [2]
- $7 000 - €6 682 - £4 374 - FF43 830
  Untitled Sculpture, glass (68x19x8cm 26x7x3in) New-York 1999

IFFLAND Franz 1862-1935 [87]
- $503 - €435 - £304 - FF2 851
  Bogenschütze Bronze (H71cm H27in) Frankfurt 1998

IGERT Paul 1899-? [6]
- $365 - €341 - £220 - FF2 239
  Goodrich Poster (57x39cm 22x15in) London 1999

IGLER Gustav 1842-? [13]
- $3 756 - €4 360 - £2 640 - FF27 000
  Sommertag Öl/Leinwand (85x112cm 33x44in) Wien 2001

IGLESIAS Cristina 1956 [9]
- $8 965 - €9 624 - £6 000 - FF63 129
  Untitled Sculpture, wood (235x116x59cm 92x45x23in) London 2000
- $9 660 - €8 430 - £5 880 - FF55 300
  Sin título Construction (48x30x180cm 18x11x70in) Madrid 1998

IGLESIAS SANZ Antonio 1935 [30]
- $1 050 - €1 051 - £647 - FF6 895
  Bodegón Oleo/lienzo (80x100cm 31x39in) Madrid 2000

IGNATIEV Alexander 1913-1997 [9]
- $575 - €621 - £397 - FF4 076
  Victorian House on Bunker Hill, Los Angeles Watercolour/paper (51x66cm 20x26in) Altadena CA 1999

IGNATOVITCH Boris Vsevolodovich 1899-1976 [20]
- $1 300 - €1 087 - £769 - FF7 127
  Mother Mare Silver print (28x40cm 11x16in) New-York 1998

IHLE Johann Eberhard 1727-1814 [6]
- $17 343 - €18 348 - £11 000 - FF120 358
  The Chariot of Silenus Oil/canvas (82x95cm 32x37in) London 2000
- $5 056 - €4 602 - £3 159 - FF30 185
  Selbstbildnis des Künstlers Öl/Leinwand (27.5x23cm 10x9in) München 1999

IHLEE Rudolph 1883-1968 [57]
- $1 345 - €1 444 - £900 - FF9 473
  The Waterfall Oil/canvas (38x45.5cm 14x17in) London 2000

IHLY Jean Daniel 1854-1910 [27]
- $1 608 - €1 621 - £1 002 - FF10 634
  Der heimliche Beobachter Öl/Leinwand (112x65.5cm 44x25in) Zürich 2000

IHRAN Manne 1877-1917 [8]
- $433 - €371 - £260 - FF2 434
  Uppsala slott Oil/canvas (15x20cm 5x7in) Uppsala 1998

IKEDA Masuo 1934-1997 [22]
- $2 800 - €3 179 - £1 916 - FF20 855
  Kagami no Naoo (Blue in the Mirror) Etching, aquatint in colors (34.5x36.5cm 13x14in) New-York 2000

IKEMURA Leiko 1951 [38]
- $618 - €624 - £385 - FF4 090
  Figuren Fusain (56x42cm 22x16in) Zürich 2000

IKUO Hirayama 1930 [12]
- $56 840 - €55 440 - £34 800 - FF363 660
  Cranes Drawing (24x33.5cm 9x13in) Tokyo 1999

IL PAPERO ROSSO 1940 [4]
- $750 - €777 - £450 - FF5 100
  Eclissi totale strage ecologica Collage (43x31cm 16x12in) Prato 2000

ILIGAN Ralph W. 1895-1960 [3]
- $2 000 - €2 352 - £1 434 - FF15 427
  Winter in the Woods Oil/canvas (51x61cm 20x24in)
  Philadelphia PA 2001

ILLIERS d' Gaston 1876-1952 [73]
- $1 755 - €1 677 - £1 105 - FF11 000
  Sidney Bronze (21x30x9cm 8x11x3in) Deauville 1999

ILLIES Arthur 1870-1952 [82]
- $3 237 - €3 681 - £2 245 - FF24 148
  «**Hochzeitstag**» Öl/Karton (86.4x68.9cm 34x27in)
  Hamburg 2000
- $117 - €138 - £85 - FF905
  Am Berge Radierung (17.5x22cm 6x8in) Hamburg 2001

ILLINGWORTH Michael 1932-1988 [5]
- $12 520 - €13 010 - £7 850 - FF85 337
  Tawera Landscape with Tree Oil/canvas
  (36x30.5cm 14x12in) Auckland 2000
- $297 - €338 - £205 - FF2 220
  **Tawera, from the Barry Lett Gallery Multiple
  Series** Screenprint (43.5x56cm 17x22in) Auckland 2000

ILMONI Einar 1880-1946 [13]
- $8 068 - €7 062 - £4 888 - FF46 321
  Park Oil/canvas (85x77cm 33x30in) Helsinki 1998
- $3 604 - €4 036 - £2 503 - FF26 476
  Skärgårdslandskap Oil/canvas/board (30x25cm 11x9in) Helsinki 2001

ILOSVAI VARGA István 1895-1978 [4]
- $1 036 - €1 088 - £644 - FF7 140
  Vue de Dunara Huile/toile (70x60cm 27x23in)
  Budapest 2000

ILSTED Peter Vilhelm 1861-1933 [661]
- $8 722 - €9 384 - £5 936 - FF61 558
  **Dansk sommerlandskab fra Falster med traer
  på raekke** Oil/canvas (40x82cm 15x32in) Köbenhavn 2001
- $972 - €1 074 - £644 - FF7 043
  Opstilling med vildt Oil/canvas (34x21cm 13x8in)
  Viby i/ Århus 2000
- $1 040 - €1 009 - £660 - FF6 621
  Interiör med to piger ved et klaver Pencil/paper
  (23x21cm 9x8in) Viby i/ Århus 2000
- $462 - €550 - £329 - FF3 607
  **Opstilling med fad med aebler, frimurerglas og
  kande** Aquatint in colors (20x27.8cm 7x10in)
  Köbenhavn 2000

IMAI Toshimitsu 1928 [49]
- $12 998 - €12 725 - £8 000 - FF83 468
  Untitled Mixed media (180x180cm 70x70in) London 1999
- $2 672 - €2 948 - £1 810 - FF19 335
  Komposition Öl/Karton (51.5x65.5cm 20x25in)
  Zürich 2000
- $1 900 - €1 970 - £1 140 - FF12 920
  Il Sole Tecnica mista (34x42cm 13x16in) Milano 1999

IMAM Ali 1924 [2]
- $3 000 - €3 545 - £2 126 - FF23 252
  Street Scene of Ghora Gali Watercolour/paper
  (40.5x51cm 15x20in) New-York 2001

IMANDT Willem 1882-1967 [30]
- $1 891 - €2 042 - £1 293 - FF13 394
  **A Pagoda in a Mountainous Landscape at
  Sunset** Oil/canvas (90x125cm 35x49in) Amsterdam 2001

IMHOF Joseph A. 1871-1955 [19]
- $4 000 - €4 390 - £2 575 - FF28 795
  Southwestern Ranch Oil/board (54.5x45.5cm 21x17in) Beverly-Hills CA 2000
- $7 000 - €6 039 - £4 207 - FF39 615
  Buffalo Dance, Taos Watercolour/paper (58x46cm 23x18in) Santa-Fe NM 1998

IMKAMP Wilhelm 1906-1990 [59]
- $4 519 - €4 346 - £2 784 - FF28 508
  Tropische Vegetation Öl/Karton (62x44cm 24x17in)
  München 1999
- $1 238 - €1 329 - £828 - FF8 720
  Gral Tempera (33.3x19.6cm 13x7in) Königstein 2000

IMMENDORF Jörg 1945 [244]
- $10 746 - €9 459 - £6 543 - FF62 047
  Ohne Titel Mixed media/canvas (155x200cm 61x78in)
  Stuttgart 1999
- $3 477 - €4 090 - £2 520 - FF26 831
  «**Welche? Jean Paul**» Öl/Leinwand (100x100cm 39x39in) Frankfurt 2001
- $1 535 - €1 534 - £960 - FF10 061
  Für alle Lieben in der Welt Acrylic/paper (76x9cm 29x3in) Hamburg 1999
- $1 286 - €1 534 - £917 - FF10 061
  Ohne Titel, zu The Rake's Progress
  Aquarell/Karton (39.9x29.9cm 15x11in) Berlin 2000
- $314 - €358 - £219 - FF2 347
  Wartebleine Farblithographie (106.5x72.5cm 41x28in)
  Hamburg 2001

IMMENRAET Philip Augustijn 1627-1679 [13]
- $12 815 - €14 025 - £8 859 - FF92 000
  Sans titre Huile/toile (108x165cm 42x64in) Versailles 2001

IMMERZEEL Christiaan 1808-1886 [13]
- $956 - €998 - £603 - FF6 548
  Rowing Boat in a Landscape Oil/panel (29x43cm 11x16in) Amsterdam 2000

IMPENS Josse 1840-1905 [70]
- $649 - €694 - £442 - FF4 552
  Jeune fumeur Huile/toile (53x41.5cm 20x16in)
  Lokeren 2001
- $358 - €397 - £249 - FF2 601
  Welverdiende rust (Repos bien mérité) Huile/toile (32x42cm 12x16in) Antwerpen 2001
- $1 400 - €1 500 - £952 - FF9 837
  Portrait of a Young Woman Lithograph (46x58cm 18x23in) Chicago IL 2001

IMPERIALE Girolamo ?-c.1639 [3]
- $772 - €920 - £550 - FF6 037
  Tobias mit dem Engel Radierung (24.8x19.9cm 9x7in) Berlin 2000

IMSCHOOT van Jules 1821-1884 [14]
- $3 825 - €3 718 - £2 340 - FF24 390
  **Épisode de la Bataille des Dunes gagnée par
  les français** Huile/panneau (27x39.5cm 10x15in)
  Bruxelles 1999
- $3 332 - €3 470 - £2 114 - FF22 764
  Scène de bataille Huile/panneau (27x39.5cm 10x15in) Bruxelles 2000

INCE Joseph Murray 1806-1859 [64]
- $1 367 - €1 456 - £900 - FF9 549
  **View near Crickhowell, Sugar Loaf Mountain in
  the Distance/Brecon** Oil/board (30.5x40.5cm 12x15in) Billingshurst, West-Sussex 2000
- $700 - €752 - £480 - FF4 935
  **Harvesting on a Country Estate at Presteigne,
  Radnor** Watercolour (21x33cm 8x12in) London 2001

INCHBOLD John William 1830-1888 **[8]**
🖊 **$9 101** – €10 585 – **£6 500** – FF69 432
Lake Leman Watercolour (24x34.5cm 9x13in) London 2001

INCHBOLD Stanley 1856-? **[16]**
🖊 **$1 608** – €1 845 – **£1 100** – FF12 102
The Mediterranean Sea from the Mountains of Lebanon Watercolour (24x34cm 9x13in) London 2000

INDEN Ernest 1879-1946 **[8]**
🖊 **$932** – €869 – **£575** – FF5 701
Frühlingstag am Weinfelder Maar Öl/Leinwand (60x80cm 23x31in) Köln 1999

INDENBAUM Léon 1892-c.1980 **[19]**
🖊 **$100 000** – €107 339 – **£66 920** – FF704 100
Musicians and Antelopes Marble (H85.5cm H33in) New-York 2000
🖊 **$2 437** – €2 744 – **£1 711** – FF18 000
Modèle nu se coiffant Terracotta (H38cm H14in) Paris 2001

INDIA Bernardino c.1528-1590 **[9]**
🖊 **$18 000** – €17 960 – **£10 956** – FF117 811
Mary Magdalen washing the feet of Christ Ink (22x31cm 8x12in) New-York 2000

INDIANA Robert Clark 1928 **[290]**
🖊 **$81 664** – €88 420 – **£55 912** – FF580 000
«Love is God» Huile/toile (173x173cm 68x68in) Paris 2001
🖊 **$32 500** – €33 691 – **£19 500** – FF221 000
«Decagon» Acrilico/tela (61x56cm 24x22in) Prato 1999
🖊 **$91 520** – €99 092 – **£62 660** – FF650 000
Love Métal (91.5x91.5cm 36x36in) Paris 2001
🖊 **$57 500** – €64 117 – **£38 663** – FF420 578
Love Metal (46x46x22cm 18x18x9in) New-York 2000
🖊 **$850** – €817 – **£527** – FF5 357
Brooklyn Bridge Screenprint in colors (90x63cm 35x24in) New-York 2000

INDONI Filippo ?-c.1883 **[123]**
🖊 **$3 000** – €3 412 – **£2 096** – FF22 380
Young Boy with Hat Oil/canvas (97x73cm 38x29in) Chicago IL 2000
🖊 **$1 400** – €1 576 – **£964** – FF10 335
Le billet doux Watercolour/paper (44.5x63.5cm 17x25in) Philadelphia PA 2000

INDUNO Domenico 1815-1878 **[30]**
🖊 **$36 000** – €37 320 – **£21 600** – FF244 800
Un episodio della strage degli innocenti Olio/tela (138x102.5cm 54x40in) Milano 1999
🖊 **$60 000** – €77 749 – **£45 000** – FF510 000
I contrabbandieri sul lago di Como Olio/tela (77x95cm 30x37in) Milano 2000
🖊 **$2 250** – €2 332 – **£1 350** – FF15 300
Soldato Matita (28x40cm 11x15in) Roma 2000

INDUNO Gerolamo 1827-1890 **[53]**
🖊 **$25 000** – €25 916 – **£15 000** – FF170 000
I due orfanelli Olio/tela (49x40cm 19x15in) Milano 2000
🖊 **$6 545** – €6 785 – **£3 927** – FF44 506
Innamorata! Olio/tavoletta (10x7cm 3x2in) Milano 1999
🖊 **$7 500** – €7 775 – **£4 500** – FF51 000
Il ritorno del soldato a Milano Acquarello/carta (35x21cm 13x8in) Milano 1999

INGALL John Spence XIX-XX **[15]**
🖊 **$244** – €285 – **£170** – FF1 869
Sky and Landscape Study Watercolour (18x25cm 7x9in) West-Yorshire 2000

INGANNI Angelo 1807-1880 **[15]**
🖊 **$56 580** – €48 878 – **£28 290** – FF320 620
Giovane filatrice lombarda Olio/tela (102x74cm 40x29in) Milano 1999
🖊 **$36 000** – €46 649 – **£27 000** – FF306 000
Il cortile del Broletto a Brescia Olio/tela (33.5x39cm 13x15in) Milano 2000

INGELS Domien 1881-1946 **[8]**
🖊 **$2 604** – €2 975 – **£1 812** – FF39 512
Centaure féminin Bronze (H33cm H12in) Bruxelles 2001

INGELS Graham 1915-1991 **[3]**
🖊 **$17 000** – €16 400 – **£10 744** – FF107 576
The Haunt of Fear Ink (46.5x36cm 18x14in) New-York 1999

INGEMANN Lucie M. Mandix 1792-1868 **[10]**
🖊 **$5 314** – €6 043 – **£3 712** – FF39 640
Lyserode roser og forglemmigej på en karn Oil/canvas (14.5x20cm 5x7in) København 2000

INGEN van Hendrikus Alexander 1846-1920 **[25]**
🖊 **$596** – €590 – **£364** – FF3 869
Sunlit Landscape with a Farm on the Horizon Oil/paper/panel (13x25.5cm 5x10in) Amsterdam 2000

INGERLE Rudolph F. 1879-1950 **[17]**
🖊 **$3 250** – €3 640 – **£2 258** – FF23 878
«Stream in Autumn» Oil/canvas (63x76cm 25x30in) Cincinnati OH 2001
🖊 **$1 250** – €1 195 – **£787** – FF7 839
Moonrise Oil/panel (24x34cm 9x13in) Milwaukee WI 1999

INGHAM Alan 1920 **[4]**
🖊 **$3 201** – €3 527 – **£2 125** – FF23 134
Sergeant Michael Kennedy/Ned Kelly/Ned Kelly Bronze (H54cm H21in) Woollahra, Sydney 2000

INGHAM Bryan 1936 **[13]**
🖊 **$2 551** – €3 023 – **£1 800** – FF19 832
St Ives and Scene of the Fire Mixed media (58.5x61cm 23x24in) London 2000

INGLE John Stuart 1933 **[1]**
🖊 **$8 500** – €7 926 – **£5 272** – FF51 990
Cigar Box Watercolour/paper (40x53.5cm 15x21in) New-York 1999

INGLETON Geoffrey C. 1908-1998 **[10]**
🖊 **$164** – €153 – **£101** – FF1 003
«Dawn and Weigh» Etching (22.5x29cm 8x11in) Melbourne 1999

INGLIS James act.1885-1892 **[1]**
🖊 **$4 105** – €4 425 – **£2 800** – FF29 026
Prince Charlie Leaving Scotland/The Abdication of Queen Mary Oil/canvas (40.5x30.5cm 15x12in) London 2001

INGLIS John J. 1867-1946 **[6]**
🖊 **$4 500** – €4 830 – **£3 011** – FF31 684
Goodnight Kiss - Portrait of a Gentleman (Probably the Father) Oil/canvas (48x58cm 19x23in) Portland ME 2001

INGRAM William Ayerst 1855-1913 **[32]**
🖊 **$568** – €610 – **£380** – FF4 002
A Steamship in Choppy Seas Oil/canvas (42x68.5cm 16x26in) London 2000
🖊 **$497** – €491 – **£320** – FF3 220
Three Master Off Shore Watercolour/paper (36x61.5cm 14x24in) London 1999

INGRES Jean Dominique 1780-1867 **[135]**
- $152 432 - €170 743 - **£106 064** - FF1 120 000
  Étude por la figure de jeune femme dite L'odyssée Huile/toile/panneau (29x21.5cm 11x8in) Valence 2001
- $22 500 - €22 450 - **£13 695** - FF147 264
  Paolo and Francesca Black chalk/paper (19.5x13cm 7x5in) New-York 2000
- $2 000 - €2 239 - **£1 394** - FF14 685
  Odalisque Lithograph (13x21cm 5x8in) New-York 2001

INGUIMBERTY Joseph 1896-1971 **[24]**
- $36 738 - €40 594 - **£25 473** - FF266 279
  Le retour du marché (The Return from the Market) Oil/canvas (204x200cm 80x78in) Singapore 2001
- $3 809 - €3 838 - **£2 374** - FF25 177
  Femmes au repos - Women Resting Oil/paper/panel (63x49cm 24x19in) Singapore 2000

INIS XX **[1]**
- $3 304 - €3 887 - **£2 394** - FF25 500
  Marché de fleurs Huile/toile (73x92cm 28x36in) Chambéry 2001

INJALBERT Jean Antoine 1845-1933 **[28]**
- $1 152 - €1 271 - **£780** - FF8 334
  Buste de jeune fille souriante Bronze (H48cm H18in) Amsterdam 2000

INMAN Henry 1801-1846 **[7]**
- $2 750 - €2 512 - **£1 840** - FF19 365
  A Mother and Child Oil/panel (23x19cm 9x7in) San-Francisco CA 2000

INMAN John O'Brien 1828-1896 **[7]**
- $1 200 - €1 329 - **£804** - FF8 720
  The Lady and Dog Oil/panel (21x16cm 8x6in) Dedham MA 2000
- $1 700 - €1 825 - **£1 137** - FF11 969
  In the Forest Watercolour/paper (32x23.5cm 12x9in) San-Francisco CA 2000

INNERST Mark 1957 **[23]**
- $4 800 - €5 376 - **£3 335** - FF35 266
  Tranformer Oil/masonite (26.5x30cm 10x11in) New-York 2001
- $5 000 - €5 038 - **£3 117** - FF33 050
  Roof Top Gouache (33x28cm 12x11in) New-York 2000

INNES Callum 1962 **[22]**
- $7 471 - €8 020 - **£5 000** - FF52 608
  Exposed Painting in Grey No.4 Oil/canvas (210x190cm 82x74in) London 2000
- $9 889 - €10 276 - **£6 200** - FF67 404
  Formed Painting Oil/canvas (110x100cm 43x39in) London 2000

INNES James Dickson 1887-1914 **[36]**
- $25 952 - €25 019 - **£16 000** - FF164 113
  The Fair at Perpignan Oil/canvas (28x38cm 11x14in) London 1999
- $1 327 - €1 470 - **£900** - FF9 640
  Near Carmarthen Watercolour (24.5x34.5cm 9x13in) Billingshurst, West-Sussex 2000

INNES John 1863-1941 **[25]**
- $751 - €727 - **£463** - FF4 767
  When Days are shorter/Across the trackless Desert Oil/board (23.5x31cm 9x12in) Toronto 1999
- $271 - €259 - **£169** - FF1 700
  Saddle Etching (18.5x28cm 7x11in) Calgary, Alberta 1999

INNESS George 1825-1894 **[117]**
- $80 000 - €95 140 - **£57 016** - FF624 080
  Autumn in Montclair Oil/canvas (66x91cm 25x35in) New-York 2000
- $27 500 - €32 704 - **£19 599** - FF214 527
  Étretat Oil/canvas (23.5x33cm 9x12in) New-York 2000
- $17 000 - €16 546 - **£10 444** - FF108 534
  Italian Landscape Watercolour/paper (22x28cm 9x11in) San-Francisco CA 1999

INNESS George, Jr. 1853-1926 **[23]**
- $1 500 - €1 282 - **£881** - FF8 408
  Spring Oil/board (160x60cm 62x23in) Boston MA 1998
- $2 000 - €1 851 - **£1 224** - FF12 145
  Summer Landscape of open Countryside Oil/board (28x44cm 11x17in) Wethersfield CT 1999

INNOCENT Ferenc 1859-1934 **[15]**
- $2 489 - €2 197 - **£1 500** - FF14 409
  The Games Room Oil/panel (25x37cm 9x14in) London 1998

INNOCENT Franck 1912-1983 **[107]**
- $783 - €854 - **£513** - FF5 600
  Bord de l'Eure aux Damps Huile/toile (54x65cm 21x25in) Évreux 2000

INNOCENTI Bruno 1906-1986 **[9]**
- $2 000 - €2 073 - **£1 200** - FF13 600
  Figura femminile in atto rituale (Omaggio a Gauguin) Sculpture bois (H70cm H27in) Prato 2000

INNOCENTI Camillo 1871-1961 **[147]**
- $30 000 - €31 100 - **£18 000** - FF204 000
  Donna di Scanno Olio/tela (170x123.5cm 66x48in) Roma 1999
- $4 000 - €5 183 - **£3 000** - FF34 000
  Figura femminile in abito da sera Olio/tavola (78.5x26cm 30x10in) Milano 2001
- $1 513 - €1 524 - **£943** - FF10 000
  L'amateur d'estampes Huile/panneau (27x22cm 10x8in) Calais 2000
- $1 000 - €1 037 - **£600** - FF6 800
  Portatrice d'acqua Acquarello/carta (16x23cm 6x9in) Roma 1999

INOKUMA Genichiro 1902-1993 **[18]**
- $18 000 - €17 436 - **£11 226** - FF114 375
  Fujin zazo (Seated Woman) Oil/canvas (80x53cm 31x20in) New-York 1999
- $4 900 - €4 779 - **£3 000** - FF31 350
  Woodpecker Watercolour, gouache/paper (65.5x50cm 25x19in) Tokyo 1999

INSHAW David 1943 **[2]**
- $5 068 - €5 270 - **£3 200** - FF34 570
  Stubble Burning, East kennet Oil/canvas (76.5x102cm 30x40in) London 2000

INSKIP John Henry 1864-1947 **[6]**
- $4 250 - €4 406 - **£2 550** - FF28 900
  The Whoclarigte Yard Olio/tela (89x98cm 35x38in) Prato 2000

INSLEY Albert B. 1842-1937 **[28]**
- $9 000 - €9 992 - **£6 259** - FF65 541
  The River's Edge Oil/canvas (36x56cm 14x22in) Milford CT 2001
- $1 000 - €1 181 - **£708** - FF7 750
  Autumn Insley Oil/canvas (20.5x30.5cm 8x12in) Boston MA 2000

INUKAI Kyohei 1886-1954 **[11]**
- $4 000 - €4 294 - **£2 676** - FF28 164
  Portrait Dorothy Hampton Oil/canvas (91.5x76.5cm 36x30in) New-York 2000

INZA Joaquin XVIII **[3]**
- $3 660 - €3 604 - **£2 280** - FF23 640
  Retrato de caballero Oleo/lienzo (81x70.5cm 31x27in) Madrid 1999

IOKI Bunsai 1863-1906 **[12]**
- $4 000 - €4 420 - **£2 774** - FF28 994
  Nikko (Yomei gate) Watercolour (49x66cm 19x25in) New-York 2001

IONDA Franco 1946 **[3]**
- $4 000 - €4 147 - **£2 400** - FF27 200
  «Mistake 3» Tecnica mista, disegno (60x80cm 23x31in) Milano 1999

IONESCO Eugène 1912-1994 **[60]**
- $754 - €691 - **£460** - FF4 533
  Figur Encre Chine/papier (43x30.5cm 16x12in) Zürich 1999
- $310 - €307 - **£193** - FF2 012
  Les Haut Danseurs Farblithographie (62.3x42.4cm 24x16in) Berlin 1999

IONESCO Irina 1935 **[93]**
- $381 - €427 - **£258** - FF2 800
  «Palais de Mucha à Prague» Tirage argentique (22x15cm 8x5in) Paris 2000

IPCAR Dahlov 1919 **[7]**
- $4 000 - €4 294 - **£2 676** - FF28 164
  Horse Farm Oil/canvas (50x101cm 20x40in) Portland ME 2000

IPEELEE Osuitok 1923 **[6]**
- $4 557 - €3 899 - **£2 743** - FF25 578
  Woman and Child Stone (H66cm H25in) Toronto 1998

IPOUSTEGUY Jean Robert 1920 **[52]**
- $9 080 - €9 909 - **£6 162** - FF65 000
  Les mains Fusain (46.5x61.5cm 18x24in) Paris 2000

IPPO 1798-1871 **[2]**
- $2 000 - €1 831 - **£1 219** - FF12 013
  Two Crows in Flight Ink (120x51cm 47x20in) New-York 1999

IPSEN Ernest Ludwig 1869-1934 **[7]**
- $9 500 - €10 332 - **£6 262** - FF67 776
  Schooner in Dry Dock Oil/canvas (76x50.5cm 29x19in) Boston MA 2000

IPSEN Poul Janus 1936 **[76]**
- $809 - €740 - **£507** - FF4 854
  Fragmental Double Portrait II Oil/canvas (71x51cm 27x20in) Köbenhavn 1999

IRAZU Pedro Maria, Pello 1963 **[4]**
- $3 840 - €3 604 - **£2 400** - FF23 640
  Sin título Fer (57.5x65x38.5cm 22x25x15in) Madrid 1999

IRELAND Thomas Tayler ?-c.1927 **[61]**
- $493 - €574 - **£352** - FF3 764
  «Burnham Beeches» Watercolour/paper (36x52.5cm 14x20in) Toronto 2001

IRIARTE Ignacio 1621-1685 **[1]**
- $4 770 - €5 406 - **£3 330** - FF35 460
  Paisaje con el Buen Pastor y monjes trinitarios Oleo/lienzo (49x120cm 19x47in) Madrid 2001

IRIBE Paul 1883-1935 **[25]**
- $29 830 - €28 965 - **£18 430** - FF190 000
  Eléphants formant serre-livres Sculpture bois (13.5x16.5x7cm 5x6x2in) Paris 1999
- $416 - €488 - **£299** - FF3 200
  Monsieur Foreno Encre Chine (20x20cm 7x7in) Paris 2001

IRMER Carl 1834-1900 **[48]**
- $1 337 - €1 483 - **£928** - FF9 726
  Italienische Küstenlandschaft Öl/Leinwand (73x96cm 28x37in) Köln 2001
- $671 - €588 - **£406** - FF3 856
  Die Getreideernte Öl/Karton (24.6x32.3cm 9x12in) Berlin 1998

IRMINGER Valdemar 1850-1938 **[94]**
- $661 - €738 - **£452** - FF4 839
  Almueinteriör med moder og barn Oil/canvas (51x37cm 20x14in) Viby J, Århus 2000
- $310 - €335 - **£214** - FF2 199
  Faun og Nymphe Oil/canvas (33x28.5cm 12x11in) Köbenhavn 2001

IROLLI Vincenzo 1860-1942 **[228]**
- $11 200 - €14 513 - **£8 400** - FF95 200
  Piazzetta di mercato rionale con tre portici Olio/tela (152x100cm 59x39in) Milano 2001
- $13 000 - €14 576 - **£8 828** - FF95 612
  Young Girl with Chicken Oil/canvas (89x46cm 35x18in) New-York 2000
- $5 500 - €5 702 - **£3 300** - FF37 400
  Giovane donna con scialle bianco Olio/tela (29x18cm 11x7in) Milano 2001
- $2 720 - €3 525 - **£2 040** - FF23 120
  Giovane donna in terrazza Acquarello/carta (40x52cm 15x20in) Napoli 2000

IRONSIDE Adelaide Eliza Scott 1831-1867 **[3]**
- $1 302 - €1 549 - **£928** - FF10 160
  Portrait of a Young Woman Crayon (26x20cm 10x7in) Woollahra, Sydney 2000

IRSAI Istvan 1896-1967 **[7]**
- $1 300 - €1 250 - **£802** - FF8 200
  «Tungsram Radio» Poster (123.5x93cm 48x36in) New-York 1999

IRVIN Albert 1922 **[31]**
- $3 244 - €3 127 - **£2 000** - FF20 514
  Precinct Watercolour, gouache (55x78cm 21x30in) London 2001
- $246 - €234 - **£150** - FF1 536
  Idom 9 Screenprint in colors (45x58.5cm 17x23in) London 1999

IRVIN Fred 1914 **[8]**
- $3 250 - €3 009 - **£1 989** - FF19 736
  Young girl artist abandons the easel, cover for American Weekly Mixed media/board (38x32cm 15x12in) New-York 1999
- $2 800 - €3 136 - **£1 945** - FF20 572
  Magazine Cover, Boy wants a new Tricycle, to the Consternation of hiss Gouache/paper (41x38cm 16x15in) New-York 2001

IRVINE Gregory John, Greg 1947 **[56]**
- $328 - €306 - **£203** - FF2 006
  Exotic Interior Watercolour/paper (100x75cm 39x29in) Melbourne 1999

IRVINE Sadie 1887-1970 **[4]**
- $1 200 - €1 351 - **£826** - FF8 859
  Floral Study Watercolour/board (36x25cm 14x10in) New-Orleans LA 2000
- $1 400 - €1 327 - **£874** - FF8 705
  Sailboat at Night with Stars in Sky Woodcut in colors (17x23cm 7x9in) Cincinnati OH 1999

IRVINE Wilson Henry 1869-1936 **[90]**
- $6 500 - €6 156 - **£3 952** - FF40 378
  Flowering Fields Oil/canvas (46x61cm 18x24in) New-York 1999

$3 000 - €2 567 - **£1 806** - FF16 839
Landscape, Connecticut Oil/canvas (30x40cm 12x16in) New-York 1998

$675 - €624 - **£415** - FF4 090
Landscape with Birch Tres Watercolour/paper (35x43cm 14x17in) Hatfield PA 1999

IRVINE Ysobel Rosalind XX **[3]**
$418 - €394 - **£263** - FF2 586
Football Linocut (24.5x23cm 9x9in) Sydney 1999

IRWIN José XX **[17]**
$142 - €165 - **£98** - FF1 082
Boats in Karachi Harbour Watercolour/paper (34.5x24cm 13x9in) Dublin 2000

ISAAC John Raphael ?-1871 **[2]**
$4 224 - €4 110 - **£2 600** - FF26 958
The Fancy Fair, Princes Park, Liverpool, August Watercolour (30x46cm 11x18in) London 1999

ISAACS John 1968 **[2]**
$11 548 - €12 494 - **£8 000** - FF81 956
In Advance of the Institution Sculpture, wax (185.5x66x82cm 73x25x32in) London 2001

ISAAKSZ. Pieter Fransz. 1569-1625 **[8]**
$23 696 - €21 523 - **£14 688** - FF141 184
Christian IV Oil/canvas (125x108cm 49x42in) København 1999
$11 529 - €10 966 - **£7 000** - FF71 929
Jephthah's Daughter Oil/canvas/panel (44x79cm 17x31in) London 1999
$7 048 - €5 813 - **£4 152** - FF38 128
Das Urteil Salomons Oil/panel (47x33cm 18x12in) Wien 1998

ISABEY Eugène Louis Gabriel 1803-1886 **[347]**
$7 589 - €6 555 - **£4 583** - FF43 000
Le départ des bateaux de pêche Huile/toile (47x61.5cm 18x24in) Barbizon 1998
$4 284 - €3 708 - **£2 600** - FF24 325
Low Tide Oil/canvas (27x40.5cm 10x15in) London 1998
$957 - €1 067 - **£669** - FF7 838
L'escalier Aquarelle/papier (20x16cm 7x6in) Paris 2001

ISABEY Jean Baptiste 1767-1855 **[135]**
$3 731 - €3 220 - **£2 249** - FF21 125
Portrait de Mme. Amélie d'Arlincourt née A. de Bazant Miniature (14x10cm 5x3in) Bruxelles 1998
$1 807 - €2 134 - **£1 283** - FF14 168
Vues du château et de la ferme de Vandeneville en Lorraine Crayon (19x28.5cm 7x11in) Paris 2001

ISAILOFF Alexandre 1869-? **[10]**
$818 - €762 - **£504** - FF5 000
L'étendoir Huile/toile (41x32cm 16x12in) Lille 1999

ISAKSEN Christen Holme 1877-1935 **[9]**
$478 - €536 - **£332** - FF3 514
Parti fra Sandö på Faeröerne Oil/canvas/panel (20x27cm 7x10in) Viby J, Århus 2001

ISAKSON Karl 1878-1922 **[69]**
$17 850 - €16 741 - **£11 040** - FF109 815
Stilleben med frukter, krus och fat Oil/canvas (66x78cm 25x30in) Stockholm 1999
$2 931 - €3 402 - **£2 024** - FF22 315
Skogslandskap Oil/paper (24x27cm 9x10in) Stockholm 2000

ISBAK Poul 1943 **[18]**
$897 - €1 006 - **£627** - FF6 596
Boksehandske Stone (15x20x32cm 5x7x12in) København 2001

ISBARY von Alice 1884-1971 **[10]**
$2 247 - €2 180 - **£1 386** - FF14 301
Heiligenkreuzerhof Aquarell/Papier (29x35cm 11x13in) Wien 1999

ISBERG Fredrik 1846-1904 **[42]**
$336 - €366 - **£213** - FF2 399
Gamla Djurgårdsbron Akvarell/papper (10x15.5cm 3x6in) Stockholm 2000

ISBRAND Victor 1897-1988 **[44]**
$410 - €456 - **£286** - FF2 990
Blomsterbuket og petroleumslampe i vindue Oil/canvas (63x48cm 24x18in) København 2001

ISCAN Ferit 1931-1986 **[20]**
$11 775 - €11 434 - **£7 275** - FF75 000
L'équipe Technique mixte (162x130cm 63x51in) Paris 1999

ISELI Rolf 1934 **[215]**
$6 576 - €7 669 - **£4 617** - FF50 308
Nagelskizze Mixed media (140x90cm 55x35in) Köln 2000
$5 569 - €5 612 - **£3 471** - FF36 810
Es wurde doch eine homme cactusse Technique mixte (68x52cm 26x20in) Zürich 2000
$1 542 - €1 656 - **£1 032** - FF10 861
Komposition in Blau, Rot und Gelb Öl/Leinwand (49x30.5cm 19x12in) Bern 2000
$1 799 - €1 734 - **£1 109** - FF11 376
Relief Stockhorn Sculpture, wood (H50cm H19in) Bern 1999
$3 085 - €3 312 - **£2 064** - FF21 723
Elemente, gris pâle Coloured pencils (27.5x39.5cm 10x15in) Bern 2000
$225 - €262 - **£155** - FF1 720
Horcher Radierung (31.5x24.5cm 12x9in) Bern 2000

ISEN'IN Kano 1775-1828 **[2]**
$1 984 - €2 096 - **£1 312** - FF13 751
Landschaft mit Wasserfall und aufgehender Sonne Print in colors (86.5x29.5cm 34x11in) Köln 2000

ISENBART Marie-Victor Émile 1846-1921 **[134]**
$15 888 - €18 294 - **£10 848** - FF120 000
Le retour du faucheur Huile/toile (103x165cm 40x64in) Besançon 2000
$5 619 - €5 488 - **£3 582** - FF36 000
Femmes aux champs Huile/toile (46x65.5cm 18x25in) Argenteuil 1999
$2 100 - €2 439 - **£1 496** - FF16 000
Soir au Bélieu Huile/papier (29x47cm 11x18in) Besançon 2001

ISENBRANT Adriaen c.1490-1551 **[10]**
$129 600 - €144 156 - **£86 400** - FF945 600
Llanto sobre Cristo muerto Oleo/tabla (54.5x40cm 21x15in) Madrid 2001
$100 000 - €106 969 - **£68 180** - FF701 670
Portrait of a Man Oil/panel (22x15cm 8x5in) New-York 2001

ISENBURGER Eric(h) 1905-1994 **[28]**
$883 - €765 - **£536** - FF5 017
Blick auf Häuser und Gärten Öl/Papier (63x48cm 24x18in) München 1998

ISENRING Johann Baptist 1796-1860 **[56]**
$783 - €681 - **£472** - FF4 468
«Ansicht der Stadt Baden, der Bäder und merkwürdigsten Plätze» Aquatinta (35.5x48.5cm 13x19in) Bern 1998

ISEPP Sebastian 1884-1954 **[4]**
- $31 950 - €36 336 - £22 450 - FF238 350
  Blick vom Nassfeld in Gailtal Öl/Leinwand (58.5x76cm 23x29in) Wien 2001

ISERN Y ALIÉ Pedro 1876-1946 **[28]**
- $1 650 - €1 502 - £1 025 - FF9 850
  Mujer Oleo/lienzo (92.5x54.5cm 36x21in) Madrid 1999
- $457 - €450 - £292 - FF2 955
  La Vedette Gouache/papier (26x23cm 10x9in) Madrid 1999

ISGRO Emilio 1937 **[23]**
- $3 000 - €3 110 - £1 800 - FF20 400
  Libro cancellato Objet (38x55cm 14x21in) Milano 1999
- $1 280 - €1 659 - £960 - FF10 880
  Senza titolo Feutre/papier (47x22.5cm 18x8in) Milano 1999

ISHERWOOD Lawrence James 1917-1988 **[30]**
- $346 - €360 - £220 - FF2 359
  Rome (45x61cm 17x24in) Cheshire 2000

ISHIGURO Munemaro 1893-1968 **[9]**
- $2 500 - €2 791 - £1 671 - FF18 309
  Untitled Ceramic (H17cm H6in) New-York 2000

ISHIKAWA KIN'ICHIRO 1871-1945 **[23]**
- $5 270 - €5 627 - £3 600 - FF36 911
  Figures near an Oriental Railway Watercolour/paper (32.5x50cm 12x19in) Billingshurst, West-Sussex 2001

ISHIKAWA Toraji 1875-1964 **[12]**
- $5 500 - €4 753 - £3 264 - FF31 178
  Teasing Woodcut (27.5x43cm 10x16in) New-York 1998

ISHIMOTO Yasuhiro 1921 **[4]**
- $1 000 - €1 122 - £693 - FF7 359
  Chicago Gelatin silver print (23x23cm 9x9in) New-York 2000

ISHIOKA Eiko XX **[1]**
- $1 000 - €936 - £619 - FF6 140
  Apocalypse Now Poster (104x145cm 40x57in) New-York 1999

ISIDORO Jaime 1924 **[2]**
- $3 068 - €2 592 - £1 820 - FF17 004
  Vista de São Pedro de Muel Oleo (14x18cm 5x7in) Lisboa 1998

ISKANDAR Popo 1927 **[30]**
- $4 383 - €4 588 - £2 753 - FF30 096
  Cat Oil/canvas/board (61x48cm 24x18in) Singapore 2000

ISKOWITZ Gershon 1921-1988 **[12]**
- $585 - €590 - £365 - FF3 869
  Composition Watercolour/paper (32.5x56cm 12x22in) Toronto 2000

ISLAS de Andreas XVIII **[2]**
- $3 060 - €2 703 - £1 890 - FF17 730
  San José con el Niño Oleo (27.5x21.5cm 10x8in) Madrid 1999

ISLE de l' Guillaume 1675-1726 **[27]**
- $240 - €278 - £170 - FF1 825
  Africa Engraving (44.5x57cm 17x22in) London 2000

ISMAEL Juan 1907-1981 **[5]**
- $2 100 - €2 102 - £1 295 - FF13 790
  Escena surrealista Aguada (25x17cm 9x6in) Madrid 2000

ISMAIL Adham 1922-1963 **[1]**
- $4 296 - €4 833 - £3 000 - FF31 701
  Nude resting Oil/canvas (49.5x53cm 19x20in) London 2001

ISNARD Vivien 1946 **[14]**
- $157 - €183 - £110 - FF1 200
  Sans titre Technique mixte/papier (76x56cm 29x22in) Paris 2001

ISOM Graham **[18]**
- $1 193 - €1 001 - £700 - FF6 566
  Diamond Stakes, Ascot Oil/canvas (48x73cm 19x29in) Par, Cornwall 1998

ISONAGA K. XIX **[2]**
- $1 470 - €1 361 - £900 - FF8 928
  Bangkok taken from Wat Chang on the West Side of the River Albumen print (20x108cm 8x42in) London 1999

ISOU Isidore 1925 **[19]**
- $634 - €686 - £434 - FF4 500
  Formule de l'amour prodigieux Sérigraphie couleurs (148x121cm 58x47in) Paris 2001

ISOZAKI Arata XX **[5]**
- $475 - €459 - £298 - FF3 010
  Views of La Museum of Contemporary Art Serigraph (45x97cm 18x38in) Chicago IL 1999

ISRAEL Daniel 1859-1901 **[28]**
- $50 950 - €49 333 - £32 000 - FF323 600
  Spoiled for Choice Oil/panel (44.5x64cm 17x25in) London 1999
- $8 203 - €7 512 - £5 000 - FF49 278
  Painting in the Marketplace Oil/panel (25.5x35cm 10x13in) London 1999

ISRAELS Isaac 1865-1934 **[439]**
- $230 840 - €215 118 - £142 440 - FF1 411 080
  Gamelan Players Oil/canvas (116x140.5cm 45x55in) Singapore 1999
- $72 060 - €68 067 - £43 590 - FF446 490
  In the Dressingroom of the Scala Oil/canvas (45x58cm 17x22in) Amsterdam 1999
- $13 437 - €11 330 - £7 975 - FF74 317
  The Gamelan Orchestra Oil/canvas (27.5x36cm 10x14in) Amsterdam 1998
- $4 586 - €4 538 - £2 807 - FF29 766
  Paris by Night Pastel/paper (34x43.5cm 13x17in) Amsterdam 2000
- $758 - €862 - £525 - FF5 655
  Seated Man playing the Banjo Etching (23.2x13.8cm 9x5in) Haarlem 2001

ISRAELS Joseph 1824-1911 **[361]**
- $115 512 - €108 907 - £71 592 - FF714 384
  Pancake-Day Oil/canvas (160x190cm 62x74in) Amsterdam 1999
- $26 323 - €30 584 - £18 500 - FF200 617
  Mending the Nets Oil/panel (42.5x56cm 16x22in) London 2001
- $10 269 - €10 671 - £6 468 - FF70 000
  Retour de pêche Huile/carton (29x42cm 11x16in) Paris 2000
- $1 905 - €2 045 - £1 275 - FF13 415
  Nähende Frau am Fenster Watercolour (50.8x34.2cm 20x13in) Königstein 2000
- $250 - €303 - £174 - FF1 985
  Old Katwyk Woman Etching (15x10cm 5x3in) Bethesda MD 2000

ISSAIEV Nicolas 1891-1977 **[47]**
- **$1 292** - €1 448 - **£898** - FF9 500
  La sortie du théâtre Mine plomb (31x21cm 12x8in)
  Le Touquet 2001

ISSUPOFF Alessio 1889-1957 **[87]**
- **$31 455** - €32 608 - **£18 873** - FF213 894
  Colazione in terrazza Olio/tela (101x136cm
  39x53in) Milano 1999
- **$4 400** - €5 702 - **£3 300** - FF37 400
  Frutta e porcellana Olio/tavola (50x72cm 19x28in)
  Roma 2001
- **$1 920** - €2 488 - **£1 440** - FF16 320
  Mercato Olio/tavola (13x24cm 5x9in) Roma 2000

ISTLER Josef 1919-2000 **[73]**
- **$867** - €820 - **£540** - FF5 379
  Gelbes Bild Öl/Karton (69x50cm 27x19in) Praha
  2000
- **$751** - €711 - **£468** - FF4 661
  Bird's Phantom Oil/canvas (37.3x28.3cm 14x11in)
  Praha 1999
- **$433** - €410 - **£270** - FF2 689
  Personnages Aquarelle (35x24.5cm 13x9in) Praha
  2000
- **$101** - €96 - **£63** - FF627
  Head Aquatint in colors (14.5x11cm 5x4in) Praha 2000

ISTRATI Alexandre 1915-1991 **[159]**
- **$2 658** - €3 049 - **£1 818** - FF20 074
  Sans titre Huile/toile (250x195cm 98x76in) Paris 2000
- **$1 668** - €1 614 - **£1 028** - FF10 590
  Komposition Oil/canvas (54x65cm 21x25in)
  Köbenhavn 1999
- **$936** - €915 - **£597** - FF6 000
  Petit Paradis Gouache (65x50cm 25x19in) Paris 1999

ISTVANFFY Gabriella Brian 1877-1964 **[102]**
- **$1 179** - €1 308 - **£820** - FF8 580
  Katzenfamilie Öl/Leinwand (51x70.4cm 20x27in)
  Wien 2001
- **$713** - €654 - **£436** - FF4 290
  Die Katze und der Schmetterling Oil/panel
  (29x40cm 11x15in) Wien 1999

ITASSE Adolphe 1830-1893 **[4]**
- **$3 692** - €3 964 - **£2 470** - FF26 000
  L'amour vainqueur Bronze (61x17x17cm 24x6x6in)
  Lyon 2000

ITAYA Foussa 1919 **[49]**
- **$457** - €534 - **£317** - FF3 500
  Ville méditerranéenne Huile/toile (55x38cm
  21x14in) Calais 2000

ITEN Hans, Jean 1874-1930 **[38]**
- **$4 228** - €4 444 - **£2 652** - FF29 151
  Bulach, Switzerland Oil/canvas (51x66cm 20x25in)
  Dublin 2000
- **$2 800** - €2 687 - **£1 755** - FF17 627
  The Farm Oil/canvas/board (35x42cm 13x16in) New-
  York 1999

ITHIPOL THANGCHALOK 1946 **[2]**
- **$1 530** - €1 646 - **£1 026** - FF10 794
  Wall J. Etching (57x71cm 22x27in) Bangkok 2000

ITO Shinsui 1898-1972 **[87]**
- **$50 000** - €50 384 - **£31 170** - FF330 500
  Kobai (Red plum) Mixed media (45x52.5cm 17x20in)
  New-York 2000
- **$36 260** - €35 367 - **£22 200** - FF231 990
  Spring Snow Drawing (45x54cm 17x21in) Tokyo
  1999

$2 500 - €2 601 - **£1 591** - FF17 061
**The First Series of Modern Beauties: Gifu
Lantern** Woodcut in colors (42.5x27.5cm 16x10in)
New-York 2000

ITTEN Johannes 1888-1967 **[115]**
- **$24 829** - €23 781 - **£15 625** - FF155 993
  Baum und Ährenfeld Öl/Karton (40x50cm 15x19in)
  Bern 1999
- **$5 478** - €6 401 - **£3 220** - FF30 181
  «Flecken und Texturen» Tempera (31.4x42.4cm
  12x16in) Stuttgart 1998
- **$2 332** - €2 230 - **£1 462** - FF14 626
  Composition Watercolour/paper (35x25cm 13x9in)
  Stockholm 1999
- **$309** - €361 - **£214** - FF2 365
  Gruss und Heil Farblithographie (35x24.5cm 13x9in)
  Bern 2000

ITTENBACH Franz 1813-1879 **[8]**
- **$55 000** - €65 219 - **£37 840** - FF427 806
  The Holy Family Oil/panel (49x33cm 19x12in) New-
  York 2000

ITTER Diane 1946-1989 **[1]**
- **$7 000** - €6 397 - **£4 282** - FF41 963
  Ancient Walls Tapestry (40x23.5cm 15x9in) New-
  York 1999

ITURBIDE Graciela 1942 **[18]**
- **$1 207** - €1 105 - **£754** - FF7 246
  El viaje Photo (40x50cm 15x19in) Caracas 1999

ITURRIA de Ignacio 1949 **[105]**
- **$30 000** - €34 855 - **£21 084** - FF228 636
  Avión azul en la bañera Oil/canvas (100x130cm
  39x51in) New-York 2001
- **$12 000** - €13 647 - **£8 384** - FF89 521
  Los imigrantes Oil/cardboard (55.5x203cm 21x79in)
  Beverly-Hills CA 2000
- **$3 550** - €3 435 - **£2 189** - FF22 534
  Cadaquès Oleo/lienzo (30x30cm 11x11in)
  Montevideo 1999
- **$1 800** - €1 983 - **£1 200** - FF13 010
  Interior Litografía (68x50cm 26x19in) Montevideo
  2000

ITURRINO GONZALEZ Francisco 1864-1924 **[46]**
- **$6 000** - €6 824 - **£4 192** - FF44 760
  Desnudos en Columpio Oil/canvas (54x33cm
  21x13in) Chicago IL 2000
- **$896** - €841 - **£560** - FF5 516
  Contadora de cuentos Grabado (24.5x34.5cm
  9x13in) Madrid 1999

IUDICE Giovanni 1970 **[2]**
- **$1 650** - €1 710 - **£990** - FF11 220
  Messina Matita/carta (23x60cm 9x23in) Roma 2001

IUON Konstantin Fedorov. 1875-1958 **[24]**
- **$14 363** - €15 846 - **£9 500** - FF103 944
  Autumnal View from the Balcony Oil/canvas
  (72x58cm 28x22in) London 2000
- **$1 943** - €2 086 - **£1 300** - FF13 682
  Landscape with Fir Trees Oil/cardboard (16x22.5cm
  6x8in) London 2000
- **$2 390** - €2 566 - **£1 600** - FF16 834
  Summer Dawn Watercolour (46.5x60.5cm 18x23in)
  London 2000

IVACKOVIC Djoka 1930 **[46]**
- **$531** - €610 - **£363** - FF4 000
  Sans titre Technique mixte/toile (100x100cm 39x39in)
  Paris 2000

IVANNE 1949 [6]
- $880 - €838 - **£557** - FF5 500
  Tendresse Huile/toile (50x61cm 19x24in) Les Sables d'Olonne 1999

IVANOV Sergei Vasilevitch 1864-1910 [3]
- $6 296 - €7 493 - **£4 500** - FF49 154
  Religious Procession to the Danilovski Monastery Oil/canvas (97x110cm 38x43in) London 2000

IVARSON Ivan 1900-1939 [243]
- $27 236 - €23 333 - **£16 368** - FF153 054
  Blomsterstilleben med stockrosor, prästkragar, rosor och tulpaner Oil/canvas (67x56cm 26x22in) Uppsala 1998
- $3 689 - €3 460 - **£2 281** - FF22 695
  Strandlandskap Oil/panel (21x32cm 8x12in) Stockholm 1999
- $599 - €514 - **£351** - FF3 369
  Landskap med häst och vagn Watercolour/paper (18x21cm 7x8in) Stockholm 1998

IVERSEN Helen XIX-XX [2]
- $1 371 - €1 534 - **£924** - FF10 061
  Bauerngarten Öl/Leinwand (47x61cm 18x24in) München 2000

IVERSEN Kraesten 1886-1955 [103]
- $483 - €536 - **£336** - FF3 517
  Sydeuropaeisk kystparti med bjerge i baggrunden Oil/canvas (58x100cm 22x39in) Köbenhavn 2001
- $345 - €336 - **£212** - FF2 206
  Nature morte med svampe Oil/canvas (20.5x30.5cm 8x12in) Köbenhavn 1999

IVES Chauncey Bradley 1810-1894 [14]
- $140 000 - €133 231 - **£87 570** - FF873 936
  Undine receiving her Soul Marble (H150cm H59in) New-York 1999
- $38 000 - €37 666 - **£23 769** - FF247 072
  Jephtah's Daughter Marble (H59.5cm H23in) New-York 1999

IVES Hazel c.1900-c.1980 [20]
- $1 100 - €1 027 - **£678** - FF6 738
  Lighthouse, Nantucket Pastel/paper (21x26cm 8x10in) Boston MA 1999

IWANEC Iwan 1893-1946 [1]
- $2 680 - €2 994 - **£1 870** - FF19 638
  Paysage de campagne Huile/carton (40x24cm 15x9in) Warszawa 2001

IWILL (M.J. Léon Clavel) 1850-1923 [93]
- $4 396 - €4 269 - **£2 716** - FF28 000
  Lavandières au bord du ruisseau, Normandie Huile/toile (99x131cm 38x51in) Melun 1999
- $3 815 - €3 201 - **£2 238** - FF21 000
  Paysage d'Ambleteuse Huile/toile (37x59cm 14x23in) Saint-Dié 1998
- $1 547 - €1 693 - **£1 067** - FF11 106
  Le Havre Oil/canvas (27x40cm 11x16in) Vancouver, BC. 2001
- $1 632 - €1 524 - **£1 016** - FF10 000
  Brumes du soir dans la baie de Morsalines Pastel/papier (22.5x37.5cm 8x14in) Cherbourg 1999

IZAGUIRRE Leandro 1867-1941 [8]
- $9 648 - €10 699 - **£6 417** - FF70 182
  Ruinas de Palenque Oleo/lienzo (35x53cm 13x20in) México 2000

IZANT Herbert XIX [3]
- $2 308 - €2 590 - **£1 600** - FF16 988
  My Musical Friend Oil/board (16.5x23cm 6x9in) London 2000

IZARNY d' François 1952 [19]
- $2 599 - €2 744 - **£1 717** - FF18 000
  L'atelier du peintre Huile/toile (65x54cm 25x21in) Brides-les-Bains 2000

IZIS (Israël Bidermanas) 1911-1980 [55]
- $1 500 - €1 401 - **£906** - FF9 190
  Woman with Lips pressed against Window Vintage gelatin silver print (23x17cm 9x7in) New-York 1999

IZQUIERDO María 1906-1950 [30]
- $170 000 - €165 406 - **£104 635** - FF1 084 991
  Retrato del turista (Retrato de Henri de Chatillon) Oil/canvas (160x190cm 62x74in) New-York 1999
- $80 000 - €94 194 - **£56 216** - FF617 872
  Paisaje de cuautla Oil/panel (60.5x50cm 23x19in) New-York 2000

IZU Kenzo XX [2]
- $1 500 - €1 683 - **£1 039** - FF11 038
  Still Life #559 Platinum, palladium print (33x48cm 13x19in) New-York 2000

IZZARD Daniel J. 1923 [15]
- $443 - €422 - **£277** - FF2 765
  Long Beach, Summer's Sunset Oil/masonite (41x51cm 16x20in) Vancouver, BC. 1999

J

JAAKOLA Alpo 1929-1997 [49]
- $1 351 - €1 514 - **£938** - FF9 928
  Kärleken och transformation Oil/canvas (75x99cm 29x38in) Helsinki 2001
- $672 - €588 - **£407** - FF3 860
  Kritikens blommor Oil/panel (33x24cm 12x9in) Helsinki 1998
- $457 - €538 - **£317** - FF3 530
  Vindens skapare Watercolour/paper (41x55cm 16x21in) Helsinki 2000

JAAR Alfredo 1956 [15]
- $24 000 - €27 847 - **£16 569** - FF182 664
  Geography=War Assemblage (101.5x101.5cm 39x39in) New-York 2000
- $5 000 - €5 690 - **£3 513** - FF37 326
  El cuerpo en la mapa Cibachrome print (178x178cm 70x70in) New-York 2001

JABIOT Charles E. XIX [2]
- $4 821 - €5 031 - **£3 039** - FF33 000
  Rue animée Huile/toile (81x64.5cm 31x25in) Toulouse 2000

JABONNEAU Albert XIX-XX [17]
- $587 - €545 - **£365** - FF3 577
  Bateau à vapeur Huile/panneau (27x17cm 10x6in) Liège 1999

JAC (Jacques Saignier) XX [1]
- $1 200 - €1 154 - **£740** - FF7 569
  «Yvonne Blanc» Poster (120x79cm 47x31in) New-York 1999

JACK John XIX [7]
- $3 511 - €3 769 - **£2 350** - FF24 725
  Cardiff Roads Oil/canvas (51x76cm 20x29in) Edinburgh 2000

JACK Kenneth William D. 1924 [129]
- **$5 187** – €5 817 - **£3 602** - FF38 158
  Melbourne Oil/board (90x150cm 35x59in) Melbourne 2001
- **$1 923** – €2 146 - **£1 337** - FF14 077
  Cuballing, W.A. Acrylic/board (46x61cm 18x24in) Sydney 2001
- **$437** – €371 - **£264** - FF2 435
  Bridge Over Woady Yaloak Creek Watercolour, gouache/paper (37.5x55cm 14x21in) Sydney 1998
- **$77** – €75 - **£47** - FF491
  War Memorial Lithograph (37x60cm 14x23in) Sydney 1999

JACK Richard 1866-1952 [47]
- **$913** – €772 - **£548** - FF5 063
  Still Life with Oriental Objects Oil/masonite (51x61cm 20x24in) Calgary, Alberta 1998
- **$2 118** – €2 456 - **£1 500** - FF16 108
  «British Industries, Steel, LMS» Poster (102x127cm 40x50in) London 2000

JÄCKEL Robert Hugo 1872-1952 [3]
- **$4 998** – €4 905 - **£3 099** - FF32 176
  En skål med jordgubbar Oil/panel (21x27cm 8x10in) Stockholm 1999

JACKLIN Bill 1943 [28]
- **$16 658** – €14 232 - **£10 000** - FF93 358
  The Brothers Oil/canvas (152.5x200cm 60x78in) London 1998
- **$6 118** – €5 664 - **£3 800** - FF37 151
  The Dancers, West 42nd Street Oil/paper (100.5x67.5cm 39x26in) London 1999

JACKS Robert 1943 [45]
- **$8 766** – €9 635 - **£5 617** - FF63 204
  Under a Pear Tree Alone Oil/canvas (121x245cm 47x96in) Melbourne 2000
- **$1 850** – €2 201 - **£1 279** - FF14 438
  Cello Oil/canvas (91x91.4cm 35x35in) Sydney 2000
- **$7 348** – €8 624 - **£5 185** - FF56 567
  Molly I/Moly II /Moly III Oil/canvas (39.5x39.5cm 15x15in) Nedlands 2000
- **$3 540** – €3 900 - **£2 376** - FF25 584
  Guitar Bronze (H32.5cm H12in) Malvern, Victoria 2000
- **$361** – €336 - **£223** - FF2 206
  Untitled Mixed media/paper (55x84cm 21x33in) Melbourne 1999

JACKSON Alexander Young 1882-1974 [282]
- **$25 175** – €27 879 - **£17 073** - FF182 875
  Laurentian Village, Winter Oil/canvas (63.5x83.5cm 25x32in) Toronto 2000
- **$6 477** – €7 557 - **£4 508** - FF49 568
  Quebec Farm House in Winter Oil/panel (21x25.5cm 8x10in) Toronto 2000
- **$1 054** – €893 - **£633** - FF5 858
  Fox River, Gaspe Pencil/paper (23x28.5cm 9x11in) Vancouver, BC. 1998
- **$307** – €359 - **£214** - FF2 354
  Pine Island Copper engraving (17x16.5cm 6x6in) Toronto 2000

JACKSON Ashley 1940 [24]
- **$809** – €888 - **£550** - FF5 826
  Village Landscape near Cullen Watercolour/paper (51x73cm 20x29in) Rotherham 2000

JACKSON Carlyle 1891-1940 [48]
- **$288** – €299 - **£181** - FF1 964
  Serenity Watercolour/paper (32.5x43cm 12x16in) Melbourne 2000

JACKSON Elbert McGran 1896-1962 [17]
- **$4 750** – €5 537 - **£3 288** - FF36 320
  Couple and Shopgirl in Flower Shop at Easter Oil/canvas (76x76cm 30x30in) New-York 2000

JACKSON Frederick Hamilton 1848-1923 [17]
- **$1 362** – €1 434 - **£900** - FF9 409
  The Lamb Inn Watercolour (30x48cm 11x18in) London 2000

JACKSON Frederick William 1859-1918 [65]
- **$4 611** – €3 902 - **£2 757** - FF25 595
  Havneparti Oil/canvas (85x112cm 33x44in) Viby J, Århus 1998
- **$3 081** – €3 314 - **£2 100** - FF21 736
  Cattle Grazing beside a Barn with an Extensive Landscape beyond Oil/canvas (31x43cm 12x16in) West-Yorshire 2001
- **$585** – €689 - **£420** - FF4 518
  Archway, Tangier Watercolour, gouache/paper (19.5x15.5cm 7x6in) West-Yorshire 2001

JACKSON George XIX [18]
- **$5 040** – €5 862 - **£3 600** - FF38 454
  Horses watering at a Stream/Horse in a Paddock Oil/canvas (32x45.5cm 12x17in) London 2001

JACKSON Harry 1924 [116]
- **$18 700** – €20 072 - **£12 514** - FF131 666
  Algonquin Chief and Warrior Bronze (H80cm H31in) Houston TX 2000
- **$6 000** – €6 566 - **£4 138** - FF43 072
  Lack of Slack Bronze (H35.5cm H13in) New-York 2001

JACKSON James Ranalph 1882/86-1975 [165]
- **$3 617** – €3 490 - **£2 286** - FF22 893
  Harbour from Cremorne Oil/board (44x59cm 17x23in) Sydney 1999
- **$1 315** – €1 468 - **£915** - FF9 632
  Evening Sky, Berrys Bay Oil/board (28x38cm 11x14in) Sydney 2001

JACKSON John 1778-1831 [12]
- **$7 464** – €6 492 - **£4 500** - FF42 583
  Portrait of Mrs Hardwicke when a Child Oil/canvas (90x70cm 35x27in) London 1998

JACKSON Kurt 1961 [3]
- **$1 092** – €1 270 - **£780** - FF8 331
  Lamorna Cove Watercolour/paper (27x28cm 11x11in) Par, Cornwall 2001

JACKSON Martin Jacob 1871-1955 [27]
- **$700** – €751 - **£468** - FF4 928
  The Enchanted Doorway Oil/masonite (30x40cm 12x16in) Hatfield PA 2000

JACKSON Michael 1961 [19]
- **$17 035** – €14 168 - **£10 000** - FF92 937
  Ever Watchful -Two Tigers Oil/canvas (105x154cm 41x60in) London 1998
- **$1 935** – €1 593 - **£1 200** - FF11 536
  «Violet Sabre winged Hummingbird» Acrylic/canvas (40x30cm 15x11in) Billingshurst, West-Sussex 1999
- **$4 565** – €5 322 - **£3 200** - FF34 912
  Peacock Bodycolour (88.5x42cm 34x16in) London 2000

JACKSON OF BATERSEA John Baptist 1701-c.1780 [21]
- **$642** – €625 - **£395** - FF4 101
  Kreuzabnahme Christi, nach Rembrandt Woodcut (53.5x37.7cm 21x14in) Bern 1999

JACKSON Ronald Threlkeld 1902-1992 **[22]**
- $646 - €618 - £405 - FF4 053
  Mallards Oil/board (61x51cm 24x20in) Vancouver, BC. 1999

JACKSON Samuel 1794-1869 **[41]**
- $3 355 - €3 566 - £2 250 - FF23 394
  Stoke Cottage, near Bristol Oil/panel (25x38cm 9x14in) West-Midlands 2001
- $1 658 - €1 442 - £1 000 - FF9 462
  Harlech castle, North Wales Watercolour (25x38.5cm 9x15in) London 1998

JACKSON Samuel Phillips 1830-1904 **[114]**
- $524 - €562 - £350 - FF3 689
  Bringing in the Catch, Thurlestone Sands, Devon Oil/board (23x38cm 9x14in) London 2000
- $657 - €706 - £440 - FF4 629
  Stepper Point - Mouth of Camel Estuary Watercolour/paper (30x50cm 12x20in) Wadebridge, Cornwall 2000

JACKSON William XX **[9]**
- $567 - €600 - £380 - FF3 998
  Port Acon, Co Donegal - Extensive Shore Scene with Figures on a Beach Oil/canvas (50x60cm 19x23in) Bath 2000

JACKSON William Franklin 1850-1936 **[13]**
- $30 000 - €35 013 - £21 267 - FF229 668
  California Poppies Oil/canvas (51x127cm 20x50in) New-York 2001
- $3 000 - €3 220 - £2 007 - FF21 123
  Suisan Marshes, California Oil/canvas (23x39cm 9x15in) Altadena CA 2000

JACKSON William Henry 1843-1942 **[104]**
- $1 750 - €1 987 - £1 215 - FF13 034
  Indians near Lake Gouache/paper (16x22cm 6x9in) Detroit MI 2001
- $200 - €214 - £131 - FF1 403
  «French Opera House» Lithograph (21x16cm 8x6in) New-Orleans LA 2000
- $1 064 - €1 216 - £750 - FF7 974
  «Mystic Lake, M.T» Albumen print (23x31.5cm 9x12in) London 2001

JACLIN Josée 1947 **[14]**
- $553 - €610 - £368 - FF4 007
  L'adolescent Bronze (H23cm H9in) Morlaix 2000

JACOB (S') Adrienne Jacqueline 1857-1920 **[4]**
- $2 748 - €2 949 - £1 838 - FF19 347
  Rhododendrons Oil/canvas (82x58cm 32x22in) Amsterdam 2000

JACOB Alexandre 1876-1972 **[87]**
- $1 174 - €1 215 - £742 - FF7 969
  Paysage Oil/canvas (54x40.5cm 21x15in) Warszawa 2000
- $656 - €698 - £415 - FF4 581
  Cottages by a riverbank Oil/board (23x24cm 9x9in) Dublin 2000

JACOB Julius I 1811-1882 **[4]**
- $2 956 - €2 761 - £1 786 - FF18 111
  Kinderkopf mit braunen halblangen Locken Öl/Leinwand (35x26.5cm 13x10in) Berlin 1999

JACOB Julius II 1842-1929 **[36]**
- $2 533 - €2 607 - £1 596 - FF17 104
  Vorortstrasse in Mecklenburg Öl/Leinwand/Karton (50x35cm 19x13in) Berlin 2000
- $1 500 - €1 370 - £897 - FF8 328
  The Old Sarazene Castle in Pozzuoli Oil/canvas/board (43x31cm 16x12in) New-York 1998

JACOB Max 1876-1944 **[163]**
- $2 471 - €2 744 - £1 722 - FF18 000
  La Seine devant Notre-Dame Huile/carton (33x41cm 12x16in) Paris 2001
- $1 640 - €1 524 - £996 - FF10 000
  Vue d'un port Gouache/papier (37x44.5cm 14x17in) Paris 1998

JACOB Ned 1938 **[12]**
- $9 000 - €9 661 - £6 022 - FF63 369
  Night guard, Winter Camp of the Crows Oil/canvas (76x107cm 29x42in) San-Francisco CA 2000
- $1 200 - €1 035 - £721 - FF6 791
  Full Trailer Bonnet Charcoal/paper (57x27cm 22x11in) Santa-Fe NM 1998

JACOB Nicolas Henri 1782-1871 **[5]**
- $4 512 - €5 113 - £3 153 - FF33 539
  Genius des Steindrucks Lithographie (18.7x16cm 7x6in) München 2001

JACOB Walter 1893-1964 **[45]**
- $562 - €639 - £392 - FF4 193
  Selbstbildnis mit Mütze und Pfeife Pencil/paper (51x36cm 20x14in) München 2001
- $1 304 - €1 534 - £945 - FF10 061
  Garten Kirchhoff Woodcut in colors (54.5x45cm 21x17in) Hamburg 2001

JACOBBER Moïse 1786-1863 **[10]**
- $3 928 - €4 090 - £2 488 - FF26 831
  Päonien und andere Blüten in einem Strauss Öl/Leinwand (60x50cm 23x19in) München 2000
- $2 165 - €2 042 - £1 342 - FF13 394
  Still Life with Grapes, Prunes and Peaches Oil/panel (15.5x11.5cm 6x4in) Amsterdam 1999
- $30 807 - €32 014 - £19 320 - FF210 000
  Nature morte aux fleurs et aux fruits (plateau) Porcelain (52.5x43cm 20x16in) Paris 2000

JACOBI Eli 1898-1984 **[5]**
- $750 - €776 - £474 - FF5 091
  The Hangout Lithograph (25x35cm 9x13in) New-York 2000

JACOBI Jacques 1887-1957 **[8]**
- $5 509 - €4 525 - £3 200 - FF29 684
  A Summer's Day Oil/canvas (46x55cm 18x21in) London 1998

JACOBI Lotte Johanna 1896-1987 **[180]**
- $1 090 - €1 058 - £679 - FF6 942
  Portrait einer jungen Frau Vintage gelatin silver print (13.5x8.4cm 5x3in) Berlin 1999

JACOBI M.M. XIX **[13]**
- $525 - €564 - £360 - FF3 702
  On the River Dee, North Wales Oil/canvas (31x51.5cm 12x20in) London 2001

JACOBI Marcus 1891-1969 **[75]**
- $601 - €601 - £375 - FF3 940
  Thunersee-Landschaft Öl/Leinwand (70x60cm 27x23in) Zofingen 1999

JACOBI Otto Reinhold 1812-1901 **[68]**
- $2 976 - €2 454 - £1 753 - FF16 096
  Blick in eine alte Strasse mit zahlreichen Passanten und Häusern Öl/Leinwand (59x48.5cm 23x19in) Lindau 1994
- $336 - €393 - £240 - FF2 577
  Paysage à la mare Aquarelle/papier (18x28cm 7x11in) Montréal 2000

JACOBI Rudolf 1889-1972 **[53]**
- $550 - €498 - **£338** - FF3 269
  Town Scene Oil/canvas (63x77cm 25x30in) Mystic CT 1999
- $1 074 - €920 - **£645** - FF6 035
  Fischer beim Flicken der Netze Aquarell/Papier (39.4x36.7cm 15x14in) Hamburg 1998

JACOBS Edgar Pierre 1904-1987 **[47]**
- $828 - €762 - **£497** - FF5 000
  Dragon Encre (26x20cm 10x7in) Paris 1999
- $586 - €534 - **£366** - FF3 500
  «En la marque jaune, débarassée» Sérigraphie (75x55cm 29x21in) Paris 1999

JACOBS François XIX **[10]**
- $6 843 - €6 228 - **£4 200** - FF40 853
  In the Kitchen Oil/panel (44x56.5cm 17x22in) London 1999

JACOBS Helen 1888-1970 **[14]**
- $596 - €515 - **£360** - FF3 377
  Her Heart Grew Bitter Ink (25.5x38.5cm 10x15in) London 1998

JACOBS Herman 1921-1994 **[10]**
- $2 277 - €2 727 - **£1 573** - FF17 886
  Intérieur bourgeois animé d'une couturière au travail Huile/toile (25x32cm 9x12in) Antwerpen 2000

JACOBS Jacob Albrecht M. 1812-1879 **[84]**
- $4 804 - €4 538 - **£2 906** - FF29 766
  House at the Coast Oil/panel (39.5x52cm 15x20in) Amsterdam 1999
- $2 386 - €1 972 - **£1 400** - FF12 938
  Tophane Mosque on the Bosphorus Oil/canvas (27x37cm 10x14in) London 1998

JACOBS Paul Emil 1802-1866 **[11]**
- $27 268 - €22 543 - **£16 000** - FF147 873
  Surprised with his Lover Oil/canvas (195x218cm 76x85in) London 1998

JACOBSEN Antonio Nicolo G. 1850-1921 **[310]**
- $12 000 - €11 265 - **£7 436** - FF73 891
  Olympia and Nanucket Lightship Oil/canvas/board (55x91cm 22x36in) Portsmouth NH 1999
- $8 500 - €7 926 - **£5 272** - FF51 990
  The ship «Glory of the Seas» Oil/board (18.5x22cm 7x8in) New-York 1999

JACOBSEN David 1821-1871 **[24]**
- $721 - €805 - **£493** - FF5 279
  En rygende orientaler Oil/canvas (26x20cm 10x7in) Viby J, Århus 2000

JACOBSEN Egill 1910-1997 **[415]**
- $21 975 - €20 196 - **£13 500** - FF132 480
  Maskerade Oil/canvas (131x97cm 51x38in) Köbenhavn 1999
- $12 370 - €13 406 - **£8 570** - FF87 940
  Savanne Oil/canvas (100x75cm 39x29in) Köbenhavn 2001
- $4 240 - €4 825 - **£2 980** - FF31 651
  Komposition med maske Oil/canvas (41.5x31.5cm 16x12in) Vejle 2001
- $1 025 - €942 - **£630** - FF6 182
  Maske Gouache/paper (32.5x26cm 12x10in) Köbenhavn 2000
- $310 - €363 - **£221** - FF2 381
  Composition Color lithograph (64x47.5cm 25x18in) Amsterdam 2001

JACOBSEN Ludvig 1890-1975 **[315]**
- $450 - €504 - **£312** - FF3 306
  «The Duck Pond» Oil/canvas (45x55cm 18x22in) Cincinnati OH 2001

- $252 - €268 - **£169** - FF1 758
  Holberg scene Oil/canvas (34x45cm 13x17in) Viby J, Århus 2001

JACOBSEN Roald 1935 **[2]**
- $18 852 - €18 151 - **£11 788** - FF119 064
  Untitled Bronze (H83cm H32in) Amsterdam 1999

JACOBSEN Robert 1912-1993 **[704]**
- $6 382 - €7 241 - **£4 498** - FF47 498
  Komposition, drip painting Acrylic/canvas (120x200cm 47x78in) Köbenhavn 2001
- $1 421 - €1 346 - **£864** - FF8 829
  Komposition Acrylic (91x61cm 35x24in) Köbenhavn 1999
- $2 492 - €2 301 - **£1 532** - FF15 092
  Moderne Komposition Mischtechnik (17x23cm 6x9in) München 1999
- $9 608 - €10 731 - **£6 424** - FF70 392
  Figur, Montfermeil Iron (H215cm H84in) Köbenhavn 2000
- $5 514 - €5 946 - **£3 697** - FF39 000
  Sans titre Assemblage (73x75.5x13.5cm 28x29x5in) Paris 2000
- $639 - €645 - **£398** - FF4 229
  Komposition Watercolour/paper (25x32cm 9x12in) Köbenhavn 2000
- $108 - €114 - **£71** - FF750
  Composition Sérigraphie couleurs (29x24cm 11x9in) Paris 2000

JACOBSEN Sophus 1833-1912 **[27]**
- $6 656 - €6 135 - **£3 980** - FF40 242
  Venedig, Blick auf die Isola di S. Giorgio Maggiore bei Abendsonne Öl/Leinwand (82x121cm 32x47in) Dresden 1999

JACOBSSON Fritz **[5]**
- $8 418 - €8 241 - **£5 179** - FF54 056
  Häät Oil/canvas (59x79cm 23x31in) Helsinki 1999

JACOBSZ Lambert c.1598-1636 **[6]**
- $26 000 - €25 988 - **£15 883** - FF170 469
  Saint Paul Writting at a Desk Oil/canvas (114.5x100cm 45x39in) New-York 1999

JACOBY Max 1919 **[18]**
- $515 - €613 - **£368** - FF4 024
  «Igor Stravinsky» Vintage gelatin silver print (29.8x24cm 11x9in) Berlin 2000

JACOMB-HOOD George Percy 1857-1929 **[25]**
- $4 326 - €4 269 - **£2 665** - FF28 000
  Saint-Simeon Stylite Huile/toile (91.5x71.5cm 36x28in) Paris 1999
- $508 - €572 - **£350** - FF3 753
  Portrait of a Lady Seated in a Chair Oil/panel (36x24cm 14x9in) Newbury, Berkshire 2000

JACOMETTI Tarquinio XVI-XVII **[2]**
- $1 600 - €2 073 - **£1 200** - FF13 600
  Sant'Agnese Martire Tempera (12x15cm 4x5in) Milano 2000

JACOMIN Alfred Louis Vigny 1842-1913 **[16]**
- $6 710 - €7 202 - **£4 490** - FF47 243
  The Forge Oil/panel (66x52cm 25x20in) Toronto 2000

JACOMIN Marie Ferdinand 1843/48-1902 **[10]**
- $674 - €786 - **£466** - FF5 155
  Bauernsiedlung mit weidenden Kühen am Waldrand Öl/Papier (38.5x49.5cm 15x19in) Bern 2000

JACOMO XX **[5]**

📶 **$1 079** - €1 006 - **£667** - FF6 600
Caux s/Montreux. Championnat du monde de bobsleighs Affiche couleur (101x64cm 39x25in) Paris 1999

JACOPO DI SANDRO, dit JACONE 1795-1553 **[4]**
🎨 **$35 863** - €38 496 - **£24 000** - FF252 518
Portrait of a Man, Bust-Length, Wearing a Black Cap and Doublet Oil/panel (58.5x50cm 23x19in) London 2000

JACOULET Paul 1902-1960 **[527]**
📶 **$750** - €721 - **£462** - FF4 727
Calme Woodcut in colors (30x39.5cm 11x15in) New-York 1999

JACOVACCI Francesco 1838-1908 **[12]**
🎨 **$3 821** - €3 700 - **£2 400** - FF24 270
Arriving by Gondola Oil/canvas (46x54cm 18x21in) London 1999
🎨 **$7 600** - €8 860 - **£5 326** - FF58 118
Interior Scene with Mother, Baby and Nurse Oil/wood (35x26cm 14x10in) Cleveland OH 2000

JACQUAND Claude, Claudius 1804-1878 **[20]**
🎨 **$24 012** - €19 971 - **£14 095** - FF131 000
Ofrande de raisins Huile/toile (160x204cm 62x80in) Lyon 1998
🎨 **$1 282** - €1 524 - **£914** - FF10 000
Scène de la Ligue Huile/toile (61.5x50cm 24x19in) Neuilly-sur-Seine 2000
🎨 **$1 551** - €1 829 - **£1 090** - FF12 000
Visite de Marie de Médicis dans l'atelier de Rubens Huile/panneau (11.5x16.5cm 4x6in) Lyon 2000

JACQUE Charles Emile 1813-1894 **[572]**
🎨 **$80 000** - €69 020 - **£48 264** - FF452 744
A farmyard Oil/canvas (96.5x161.5cm 37x63in) New-York 1998
🎨 **$8 000** - €7 864 - **£5 140** - FF51 582
Berger s'abreuvant Oil/canvas (48.5x78.5cm 19x30in) New-York 1999
🎨 **$3 500** - €3 201 - **£2 137** - FF20 995
Shepherdess and sheep in a landscape Oil/canvas (41x33cm 16x13in) New-York 1998
✏️ **$651** - €640 - **£418** - FF4 200
Paysan accoudé sur son bâton Fusain (21.5x13cm 8x5in) Paris 1999
📶 **$106** - €91 - **£64** - FF600
Ferme animée Pointe sèche (8.5x14.5cm 3x5in) Pontoise 1998

JACQUE Émile 1848-1912 **[32]**
🎨 **$3 608** - €3 049 - **£2 146** - FF20 000
La bergerie Huile/toile (101x80cm 39x31in) Auvers sur Oise 1998
🎨 **$1 500** - €1 296 - **£906** - FF8 500
Bergère et ses moutons Huile/toile (21.5x16cm 8x6in) Barbizon 1998

JACQUELIN Jean 1905-1989 **[32]**
📶 **$325** - €352 - **£216** - FF2 311
«Les Gorges de la Loire, avec les trains et les autocars» Poster (99x61cm 39x24in) New-York 2000

JACQUEMART Henri Alfred M. 1824-1896 **[62]**
🗿 **$52 156** - €49 867 - **£32 000** - FF327 107
Bloodhounds Iron (H100cm H39in) Billingshurst, West-Sussex 1999
🗿 **$1 904** - €1 736 - **£1 150** - FF11 386
Chien et tortue Bronze (H17cm H7in) Cranbrook, Kent 1998

JACQUEMIN André 1904-1992 **[149]**
📶 **$175** - €152 - **£105** - FF1 000
Olga/Tête de jeune femme/Adolescent en buste Burin (8.2x5.8cm 3x2in) Paris 1998

JACQUES Émile 1874-1937 **[5]**
🎨 **$713** - €793 - **£499** - FF5 203
Portrait de Louis Mussche/Portrait de Madame Mussche Huile/toile (80x60cm 31x23in) Bruxelles 2001

JACQUET Alain 1939 **[173]**
🎨 **$3 240** - €3 811 - **£2 322** - FF25 000
Le Pape-Otto Acrylique/toile (155x102cm 61x40in) Paris 2001
🎨 **$3 499** - €4 116 - **£2 508** - FF27 000
«Miss America» Acrylique/toile (97x91cm 38x35in) Paris 2001
📶 **$1 592** - €1 470 - **£978** - FF9 642
La Plage Serigraph (96x159cm 37x62in) Stockholm 1999

JACQUET Eugène XX **[31]**
🎨 **$212** - €198 - **£130** - FF1 300
Marine Huile/bois (20x25cm 7x9in) Villeneuve-les-Avignon 1999

JACQUET Gustave Jean 1846-1909 **[133]**
🎨 **$40 387** - €47 467 - **£28 000** - FF311 360
La pavane Oil/canvas (236x141.5cm 92x55in) London 2000
🎨 **$14 000** - €13 113 - **£8 607** - FF86 017
A Coquettish Smile Oil/canvas (53.5x46cm 21x18in) New-York 1999
🎨 **$7 454** - €6 901 - **£4 500** - FF45 265
Portrait of a young Beauty, Head and Shoulders, in a pink Shawl Oil/panel (33x25cm 12x9in) London 1999
✏️ **$338** - €366 - **£234** - FF2 400
Etude de têtes Sanguine/papier (28x42cm 11x16in) Biarritz 2001

JACQUET Jan Jozef 1822-1898 **[12]**
🗿 **$5 616** - €6 693 - **£4 023** - FF43 902
Amor en Venus Bronze (90.5x32cm 35x12in) Lokeren 1998

JACQUETTE Yvonne 1934 **[17]**
✏️ **$2 400** - €2 014 - **£1 408** - FF13 208
Chinatown I, San Francisco Pastel/paper (51x60.5cm 20x23in) New-York 1998
📶 **$1 600** - €1 823 - **£1 105** - FF11 956
Northwest View from the Empire State Building Color lithograph (127x88.5cm 50x34in) Beverly-Hills CA 2000

JACQUIER Henry 1878-1921 **[32]**
🎨 **$4 931** - €4 878 - **£3 075** - FF32 000
Intérieur d'atelier, Portrait de Mr PS Huile/toile (68x80cm 26x31in) Lyon 1999

JACQUIN Nicolas joseph XVIII **[1]**
📶 **$940** - €900 - **£573** - FF5 901
Botanical Illustrations Engraving (45x25cm 18x10in) New-Orleans LA 1999

JACQUIOT Thierry 1962 **[57]**
🎨 **$183** - €183 - **£111** - FF1 200
Basse-cour Huile/toile (14x18cm 5x7in) Coulommiers 2000

JADIN Charles Emmanuel XIX **[3]**
🎨 **$16 756** - €17 989 - **£11 210** - FF118 000
L'arrivée au caravansérail Huile/toile (143x108cm 56x42in) Paris 2000

J

JADIN Louis Godefroy 1805-1882 **[13]**
- $1 340 - €1 524 - **£930** - FF10 000
  Chien de chasse Huile/toile (73x60cm 28x23in)
  Reims 2000

JAECKEL Heinrich act.1842-1876 **[17]**
- $3 637 - €3 099 - **£2 162** - FF20 325
  Ville animée de personnages Huile/toile (62x90cm 24x35in) Antwerpen 1998

JAECKEL Willy 1888-1944 **[179]**
- $3 810 - €4 090 - **£2 550** - FF26 831
  Stilleben mit Orangen Öl/Leinwand (60x70cm 23x27in) Köln 2000
- $1 880 - €2 147 - **£1 325** - FF14 086
  Berglandschaft mit Bergsee Oil/panel (37x42cm 14x16in) Stuttgart 2001
- $881 - €1 022 - **£608** - FF6 707
  Baum vor blauem Himmel Oil chalks/paper (47x37cm 18x14in) Köln 2000
- $106 - €118 - **£73** - FF771
  Weib am Abgrund Radierung (25x21.5cm 9x8in) Heidelberg 2001

JAEGER Ernst Gustav 1880-? **[6]**
- $2 393 - €2 821 - **£1 649** - FF18 502
  Aktfigurenpaar mit Grosskatze Bronze (64x55cm 25x21in) Bern 2000

JAEGER Gotthilf 1871-? **[10]**
- $728 - €681 - **£448** - FF4 464
  Classical Warrior Bronze (H38cm H14in) Amsterdam 1999

JAEGER Tyco Christopher 1819-1889 **[2]**
- $20 258 - €20 832 - **£12 849** - FF136 648
  Bergen set fra Natland Oil/canvas (61x92cm 24x36in) Vejle 2000

JAENISCH Hans 1907-1989 **[170]**
- $1 514 - €1 470 - **£943** - FF9 642
  Ohne Titel Öl/Leinwand (35x49.7cm 13x19in) Berlin 1999
- $471 - €562 - **£336** - FF3 689
  Strand-Fugette Tempera (24x28cm 9x11in) Berlin 2000
- $266 - €266 - **£166** - FF1 744
  Fische Aquarell/Papier (14.8x10.5cm 5x4in) Hamburg 1999
- $392 - €450 - **£268** - FF2 951
  Poel Nord Ost Küste Linocut in colors (10x14cm 3x5in) Heidelberg 2000

JAFFE Shirley 1923 **[9]**
- $4 686 - €5 031 - **£3 135** - FF33 000
  Witch's Brother Acrylique/toile (117x56cm 46x22in) Paris 2000
- $2 272 - €2 439 - **£1 520** - FF16 000
  Pandora'x box Acrylique/toile (41x33cm 16x12in) Paris 2000
- $1 227 - €1 444 - **£880** - FF9 471
  Komposition Gouache (65x49.5cm 25x19in) Bern 2001

JAGGER Charles Sargeant 1885-1934 **[11]**
- $48 127 - €55 808 - **£34 000** - FF366 074
  «**Wipers**» Bronze (H46cm H18in) London 2001

JAGODZINSKI Lucjan 1897-1945 **[3]**
- $2 000 - €2 215 - **£1 356** - FF14 529
  «**Moulin Rouge**» Poster (58x81cm 23x32in) New-York 2000

JAHL Wladyslaw Ad. Alojzy 1886-1953 **[16]**
- $2 073 - €2 439 - **£1 486** - FF16 000
  Don Quichotte Huile/toile (50x65cm 19x25in) Paris 2001

- $3 078 - €3 071 - **£1 921** - FF20 142
  Couple de skieurs Oil/board (46.3x30.5cm 18x12in) Warszawa 1999

JAHN Adolf 1858-1925 **[8]**
- $698 - €835 - **£480** - FF5 478
  Figure of a Prophet Bronze (H63cm H24in) Billingshurst, West-Sussex 2000

JAHN Anton 1810-1841 **[1]**
- $4 902 - €5 113 - **£3 086** - FF33 539
  Die Komödianten in rheinischem Städtchen Öl/Leinwand (80x61cm 31x24in) Stuttgart 2000

JAHN Gustav 1879-1919 **[27]**
- $468 - €472 - **£292** - FF3 098
  «**K.k.österr.Staatsbahnen, Zell am See**» Poster (100x65cm 39x25in) Wien 2000

JAHN Hans Emil A. 1834-1902 **[11]**
- $4 879 - €5 495 - **£3 362** - FF36 043
  Skibe ud for Köbenhavns havn, med Christian IV's mastekran Oil/canvas (41x69cm 16x27in) Köbenhavn 2000

JAHNS Rudolf 1896-1983 **[17]**
- $2 114 - €2 269 - **£1 414** - FF14 883
  Still life with Flowers on a ledge by a pond Oil/canvas (106x88.5cm 41x34in) Amsterdam 2000
- $4 820 - €4 602 - **£3 011** - FF30 185
  Ohne Titel Watercolour (28x21.6cm 11x8in) Köln 1999

JAILLOT Alexis Hubert 1632-1712 **[15]**
- $246 - €226 - **£150** - FF1 480
  Iudaea seu Terra Sancta, after N.Sanson Engraving (46x64.5cm 18x25in) London 1999

JAIMES SANCHEZ Humberto 1930 **[14]**
- $3 680 - €3 717 - **£2 530** - FF24 380
  Oración Oleo/lienzo (45x54cm 17x21in) Caracas 1999
- $2 720 - €2 592 - **£1 700** - FF17 000
  Grupo familiar Oleo/lienzo (30x53cm 11x20in) Caracas 2000

JAIS-NIELSEN Jais 1885-1961 **[212]**
- $11 130 - €9 410 - **£6 657** - FF61 726
  Skakspillerne Oil/canvas (135x100cm 53x39in) Köbenhavn 1998
- $1 199 - €1 209 - **£747** - FF7 930
  Blomstrende röd kastanie Oil/canvas (100x70cm 39x27in) Köbenhavn 2000
- $498 - €458 - **£306** - FF3 002
  Maria med barnet Ceramic (H35cm H13in) Köbenhavn 1999
- $218 - €202 - **£136** - FF1 324
  Stjernehimlen Chalks/paper (77x99cm 30x38in) Viby J, Århus 1999

JAK (Raymond A. Jackson) 1927-1997 **[20]**
- $209 - €208 - **£130** - FF1 363
  Could you put your name and adress on the back of your cheque please? Ink (52x59.5cm 20x23in) London 1999

JAKIMCZUK Aleksander XX **[1]**
- $4 422 - €4 851 - **£3 084** - FF31 818
  Récolte de pommes de terre Huile/toile (52x75cm 39x29in) Warszawa 2000

JAKOBIDES Georgios 1853-1932 **[25]**
- $105 508 - €121 474 - **£72 000** - FF796 816
  Portrait of a Young Beauty Oil/canvas (52x40.5cm 20x15in) London 2000
- $49 320 - €41 771 - **£28 770** - FF274 000
  Smoking the Pipe Oil/canvas (35.5x30.5cm 13x12in) Athens 1998

JAKOBSSON Fritz 1940 [39]
- $6 013 - €5 886 - **£3 699** - FF38 612
  Rakastavaiset Oil/canvas (75x90cm 29x35in) Helsinki 1999
- $3 457 - €3 026 - **£2 095** - FF19 852
  Stilleben med svampar Oil/canvas (20x26cm 7x10in) Helsinki 1998
- $1 619 - €1 682 - **£1 015** - FF11 032
  Orrar Akvarell/papper (50x35cm 19x13in) Helsinki 2000

JAKUCHU Ito 1716-1800 [4]
- $21 000 - €23 206 - **£14 563** - FF152 222
  Tortoise under Pine Tree Ink/paper (108.5x35cm 42x13in) New-York 2001

JALABERT Jean 1815-1900 [2]
- $5 460 - €6 098 - **£3 700** - FF40 000
  Portrait de famille Huile/toile (79x105cm 31x41in) Carcassonne 2000

JAMAR Armand 1870-1946 [553]
- $792 - €744 - **£489** - FF4 878
  Le travail Huile/toile (100x150cm 39x59in) Antwerpen 1999
- $379 - €446 - **£266** - FF2 926
  Nature morte aux fleurs Huile/toile (46x37cm 18x14in) Bruxelles 2000
- $298 - €297 - **£186** - FF1 951
  La chaumière Huile/panneau (30x37cm 11x14in) Bruxelles 1999
- $181 - €211 - **£124** - FF1 382
  Vue de Bruges/Le port de l'âne aveugle Fusain/papier (25x31cm 9x12in) Liège 2000

JAMBOR Josef 1887-1964 [20]
- $1 011 - €957 - **£630** - FF6 275
  Sorbes Huile/carton (36.5x56cm 14x22in) Praha 2001
- $953 - €902 - **£594** - FF5 916
  Paysage de la région Ceskomoravske Huile/toile (25x35cm 9x13in) Praha 2000

JAMBOR Lajos, junius 1884-1955 [35]
- $1 751 - €1 696 - **£1 100** - FF11 123
  The pink Parasol Oil/canvas (79.5x61cm 31x24in) London 1999

JAMBULULA c.1908-c.1972 [4]
- $1 315 - €1 269 - **£831** - FF8 324
  Fishing Story Mixed media (53.5x88cm 21x34in) Melbourne 1999

JAMEAUX L. XIX-XX [1]
- $1 067 - €915 - **£642** - FF6 000
  «**Grand concours de gymnastique, Prairie des Mauves, Nantes**» Affiche (190x128cm 74x50in) Orléans 1998

JAMES Alan Gosset 1875-1950 [1]
- $13 035 - €15 125 - **£9 000** - FF99 216
  A Dovecote in its Windrush Valley Setting Oil/canvas (61x91.5cm 24x36in) London 2000

JAMES David ?-1913 [112]
- $5 977 - €6 416 - **£4 000** - FF42 086
  Breaking Waves Oil/canvas (63.5x127cm 25x50in) London 2001
- $2 706 - €3 147 - **£1 900** - FF20 642
  «**Tide Coming in, Cornish Coast**» Oil/canvas (29x49cm 11x19in) Billingshurst, West-Sussex 2001

JAMES Edward 1820-1877 [1]
- $22 000 - €24 239 - **£14 676** - FF159 000
  Schooner Oliver H.Booth, Capt.Oliver Burger, Running Rebel Batteries Watercolour (46x60cm 18x24in) Portsmouth NH 2000

JAMES Francis ?-c.1845 [1]
- $19 904 - €17 311 - **£12 000** - FF113 554
  View of the Arno Facing upstream with a distant View of St. Miniato Oil/canvas (29x47cm 11x18in) London 1998

JAMES Francis Edward 1849-1920 [22]
- $185 - €172 - **£115** - FF1 129
  Still Lives of Bowls of Flowers Watercolour/paper (24.5x34cm 9x13in) Bristol, Avon 1999

JAMES Frederick 1915-1985 [5]
- $350 - €398 - **£242** - FF2 611
  City Shadows Watercolour/paper (48x60cm 19x24in) Chicago IL 2000

JAMES Louis Robert 1920-1996 [43]
- $6 861 - €7 365 - **£4 592** - FF48 314
  Red Night Oil/canvas (100x125.5cm 39x49in) Melbourne 2000
- $1 141 - €1 279 - **£793** - FF8 387
  «**Red Journey**» Oil/board (63x76cm 24x29in) Melbourne 2001

JAMES Walter John 1869-1932 [16]
- $30 223 - €33 852 - **£21 000** - FF222 056
  Autumn Wood Oil/canvas (61x45.5cm 24x17in) London 2001
- $1 727 - €1 934 - **£1 200** - FF12 688
  Running Water Oil/panel (30.5x40.5cm 12x15in) London 2001
- $404 - €453 - **£280** - FF2 969
  Study of Trees in a Meadow Watercolour (24x34cm 9x13in) London 2001

JAMES Will 1892-1942 [4]
- $6 000 - €7 052 - **£4 159** - FF46 256
  Bucking Bronco Graphite (29x20cm 11x7in) Beverly-Hills CA 2000

JAMES William act.1746-1771 [54]
- $47 817 - €51 328 - **£32 000** - FF336 691
  View of the Grand Canal, Venise, looking North-East from Santa Croce Oil/canvas (61x96,5cm 24x37in) London 2000

JAMES Cecil Stuart act.1910-1937 [4]
- $2 561 - €2 976 - **£1 800** - FF19 519
  Portrait of a Lady, Bust-length, in a black feathered Hat Pencil (56x41.5cm 22x16in) London 2001

JAMESON Frank 1899-1968 [67]
- $497 - €460 - **£300** - FF3 017
  Sunbeams, the Yacht Race Oil/board (38x45cm 15x18in) Par, Cornwall 1999
- $143 - €139 - **£90** - FF910
  Boats on The Fal Watercolour/paper (17x35cm 7x14in) Par, Cornwall 1999

JAMESON Joan 1892-1953 [8]
- $3 913 - €4 294 - **£2 600** - FF28 165
  The Road to Dublin Oil/canvas/board (41.5x51cm 16x20in) London 2000
- $1 553 - €1 778 - **£1 068** - FF11 660
  Village with River Walk and figures Oil/board (30x40cm 12x16in) Dublin 2000

JAMET Pauline, née ADAM XIX [3]
- $665 - €747 - **£461** - FF4 900
  Étude de fleur Huile/papier (28x22cm 11x8in) Paris 2000

JAMIESON Alexander 1873-1937 [96]
- $2 200 - €2 371 - **£1 500** - FF15 554
  The Fountain satturne, versailles Oil/board (61x51cm 24x20in) London 2001

$1 424 - €1 217 - **£862** - FF7 984
Samois Oil/panel (32.5x41cm 12x16in) Edinburgh 1998

JAMIESON Frances E. 1895-1950 **[165]**
$454 - €443 - **£280** - FF2 909
Lakeland Landscape Oil/canvas (40.5x60.5cm 15x23in) London 1999
$316 - €355 - **£215** - FF2 328
Lakeland Landscapes with Boats and Figures Watercolour/paper (30x48cm 12x19in) Aylsham, Norfolk 2000

JAMIESON Gil 1934 **[16]**
$1 262 - €1 425 - **£888** - FF9 346
Three Horses Oil/board (106.5x137cm 41x53in) Malvern, Victoria 2001

JAMIESON Mitchell 1915-1976 **[8]**
$1 000 - €1 181 - **£708** - FF7 750
November Farm Watercolour (40.5x52cm 15x20in) Boston MA 2000

JAMIN Diederik Franciscus 1838-1865 **[6]**
$6 563 - €7 714 - **£4 500** FF50 602
The Letter Oil/canvas (60x76cm 23x29in) Amsterdam 2000

JAMINJI Paddy c.1912-1996 **[3]**
$5 260 - €5 090 - **£3 333** - FF33 386
Mount House Mixed media/board (80x116cm 31x45in) Malvern, Victoria 1999

JAMISON Philip 1929 **[20]**
$500 - €569 - **£352** - FF3 730
Children on a Porch Watercolour (53x71cm 21x28in) Philadelphia PA 2001

JAMITZER Wenzel 1508-1585 **[2]**
$35 000 - €37 492 - **£23 901** - FF245 931
Urania Black chalk/paper (12.5x9cm 4x3in) New-York 2001

JAMMES Louis 1958 **[14]**
$1 387 - €1 677 - **£969** - FF11 000
Sans titre Sérigraphie (88x88cm 34x34in) Paris 2000

JAN Elvire 1904-1996 **[154]**
$6 180 - €6 098 - **£3 808** - FF40 000
Composition Huile/toile (97x128.5cm 38x50in) Versailles 1999
$1 784 - €1 982 - **£1 244** - FF13 000
Composition Huile/toile (38x46cm 14x18in) Douai 2001
$1 671 - €1 829 - **£1 160** - FF12 000
Alba Huile/carton (27x35cm 10x13in) Vannes 2001
$557 - €610 - **£386** - FF4 000
Paysage Gouache/carton (27x35cm 10x13in) Vannes 2001

JANCE Paul Claude 1840-1915 **[12]**
$8 500 - €7 525 - **£5 196** - FF49 333
Still Life of Roses with two Books on a Table Oil/canvas (92x67.5cm 36x26in) New-York 1999

JANCO Marcel 1895-1984 **[415]**
$7 000 - €7 902 - **£4 875** - FF51 835
Composition with Owl Oil/canvas (54x73cm 21x28in) Tel Aviv 2001
$10 500 - €11 271 - **£7 026** - FF73 930
Don Quichotte Oil/board (33x45.5cm 12x17in) Tel Aviv 2000
$2 173 - €2 001 - **£1 304** - FF13 124
Architectural Composition Relief (50x35cm 19x13in) Tel Aviv 1999
$800 - €859 - **£535** - FF5 632
Nude Watercolour (32.5x24.5cm 12x9in) Tel Aviv 2000

$180 - €184 - **£112** - FF1 207
Le balcon Farbserigraphie (42.2x59.4cm 16x23in) Hamburg 2000

JANDANY Hector Chundaloo c.1922/27 **[9]**
$901 - €955 - **£601** - FF6 265
Pompey's Pillar Mixed media (91x121cm 35x47in) Melbourne 2000

JANDI David 1893-1944 **[17]**
$2 035 - €2 138 - **£1 265** - FF14 025
Charrette de foin à l'entrée de Nagybanya Huile/toile (73x100cm 28x39in) Budapest 2000
$1 120 - €1 239 - **£736** - FF8 128
Family Oil/cardboard (35.5x43cm 13x16in) Budapest 2000
$1 056 - €1 200 - **£736** - FF7 872
Palfrenier Pastel/papier (30x44cm 11x17in) Budapest 2001

JANEBÉ Jeanne Baraud-Pellet 1907-2000 **[20]**
$1 816 - €1 753 - **£1 141** - FF11 499
Bildnis einer jungen Frau mit Kopftuch Oil/hardboard (64x59cm 25x23in) Zürich 1999

JANECEK Ota 1919-1996 **[82]**
$1 734 - €1 640 - **£1 080** - FF10 758
Ein Strahlen Öl/Leinwand (84x66cm 33x25in) Praha 2000
$809 - €765 - **£504** - FF5 020
Rackove Huile/toile (17x25cm 6x9in) Praha 2000
$317 - €301 - **£198** - FF1 972
Visage de fille Technique mixte/papier (25x18cm 9x7in) Praha 2001

JANES Alfred 1911-1999 **[3]**
$3 572 - €4 003 - **£2 500** - FF26 259
Man praying Oil/board (72.5x47cm 28x18in) Billingshurst, West-Sussex 2001

JANESCH Albert 1889-1973 **[30]**
$1 630 - €1 789 - **£1 050** - FF11 738
Halbfigürliches Portrait eines sitzenden Mädchens Oil/panel (120x97cm 47x38in) Lindau 2000
$626 - €716 - **£442** - FF4 695
Portrait eines alten Juden mit Pelzmütze Oil/panel (43.5x34.5cm 17x13in) Kassel 2001

JANIER Georges 1946 **[38]**
$841 - €991 - **£591** - FF6 500
Le verre de vin rouge Tempera/toile (55x46cm 21x18in) Paris 2000
$323 - €381 - **£227** - FF2 500
Le coquet Tempera/toile (46x33cm 18x12in) Paris 2000

JANIN Louise XIX-XX **[49]**
$6 555 - €7 622 - **£4 600** - FF50 000
Le songe du Mandarin Gouache/papier (70.5x45.5cm 27x17in) Paris 2001

JANIN Louise, née Delarue 1781-1842 **[8]**
$2 163 - €2 556 - **£1 533** - FF16 769
Biedermeierfamilie Miniature (37x28cm 14x11in) Stuttgart 2001

JANINET Jean-François 1752-1814 **[87]**
$646 - €762 - **£454** - FF5 000
Vénus et l'Amour, d'après Boucher Gravure (28x26cm 11x10in) Paris 2000

JANISS Johann 1808-1851 **[1]**
$3 954 - €3 835 - **£2 488** - FF25 154
Aussee Gouache/paper (21.5x36.5cm 8x14in) München 1999

J

JANK Angelo 1868-1940 **[111]**
$856 - €895 - **£562** - FF5 870
Reiter überspringen einen Wassergraben
Öl/Leinwand (50x65cm 19x25in) München 2000

JANKOWSKI J. Wilhelm c.1825-1870 **[61]**
$2 003 - €2 325 - **£1 408** - FF15 254
Blick auf Melk mit der Promenade Öl/Leinwand
(42x53cm 16x20in) Wien 2001
$1 480 - €1 599 - **£1 023** - FF10 487
Stadtmotiv am Fluss Öl/Leinwand (22.5x29cm
8x11in) Wien 2001

JANMOT Jean-Louis 1814-1892 **[22]**
$32 352 - €36 588 - **£21 864** - FF240 000
Allégorie du sommeil Huile/toile (200x139cm
78x54in) Toulouse 2000
$840 - €991 - **£590** - FF6 500
Étude Mine plomb (28x19cm 11x7in) Lyon 2000

JANNECK Franz Christoph 1703-1761 **[43]**
$38 974 - €40 403 - **£23 384** - FF265 027
Paesaggio di riviera con rovine e personaggi
Olio/tela (101x149cm 39x58in) Milano 2000
$42 515 - €39 970 - **£25 740** - FF262 185
Die Sünderin, Gastmahl des Pharisäers
Öl/Kupfer (36x47.5cm 14x18in) Wien 1999
$12 948 - €12 451 - **£7 990** - FF81 674
Der Liebesbrief Huile/panneau (15x18.8cm 5x7in)
Bern 1999

JANNI Guglielmo 1872-1958 **[17]**
$6 000 - €6 220 - **£3 600** - FF40 800
Autoritratto Olio/tela/tavola (58x47cm 22x18in) Roma
1999
$3 000 - €3 110 - **£1 800** - FF20 400
Atleta Olio/tela/tavola (53x23.5cm 13x9in) Roma 2000

JANNIOT Alfred Auguste 1889-1969 **[108]**
$961 - €915 - **£597** - FF6 000
Baigneuse de dos dans un paysage Huile/toile
(41x33cm 16x12in) Paris 1999
$3 140 - €3 049 - **£1 940** - FF20 000
Nu féminin Plâtre (H89cm H35in) Paris 1999
$4 645 - €4 421 - **£2 888** - FF29 000
Vénus et le cheval marin Plâtre (17.5x12x3cm
6x4x1in) Paris 1999
$2 031 - €2 287 - **£1 414** - FF15 000
Nu accroupi Encre (46x34cm 18x13in) Paris 2001
$10 896 - €12 196 - **£7 392** - FF80 000
Reine des prés, Reine des bois Tapisserie
(226x290cm 88x114in) Paris 2000

JANNY Georg 1864-1946 **[79]**
$753 - €643 - **£450** - FF4 217
Figures walking in an Alpine Landscape
Watercolour (45.5x63.5cm 17x25in) London 1998

JANO (F. Fernandez Zarza) 1922-1992 **[16]**
$180 - €180 - **£111** - FF1 182
Maja y torero Gouache/papier (34x23cm 13x9in)
Madrid 2000

JANOSCH Friedrich Eckart 1931 **[19]**
$65 - €77 - **£46** - FF503
Karikatur, Jäger mit erlegtem Hirsch
Farbradierung (25x25cm 9x9in) Kempten 2000

JANOSEK Cestmír 1935 **[9]**
$2 080 - €1 968 - **£1 296** - FF12 909
Sazovky Technique mixte (40x60cm 15x23in) Praha
2001

JANOUSEK Frantisek 1890-1943 **[12]**
$12 138 - €11 480 - **£7 560** - FF75 306
Image Oil/canvas (74x96cm 29x37in) Praha 2000

$7 225 - €6 834 - **£4 500** - FF44 825
Motionless Pilgrim Tempera/canvas (27x41cm
10x16in) Praha 1999
$10 982 - €10 387 - **£6 840** - FF68 134
Paysage surréaliste Pastel (49x67cm 19x26in) Praha
2000

JANS de Edouard 1855-1919 **[14]**
$4 160 - €4 958 - **£2 980** - FF32 520
**Vrouw en diochter van de schilder (femme et
fille du peintre)** Huile/toile (57x47cm 22x18in)
Antwerpen 2000

JANS Jan 1893-1963 **[25]**
$581 - €544 - **£362** - FF3 571
The Harbour of Willemstad Oil/canvas (30x40.5cm
11x15in) Amsterdam 1999

JANS Knud 1915-1986 **[46]**
$238 - €202 - **£142** - FF1 322
«Medvinds Peter» Mixed media (36x43cm 14x16in)
København 1998

JANSA Vaclav 1859-1913 **[24]**
$1 589 - €1 503 - **£990** - FF9 861
Seaside Landscape with a Villa Oil/canvas
(53x76cm 20x29in) Praha 2000

JANSÉ Félix XIX-XX **[14]**
$4 911 - €5 841 - **£3 500** - FF38 312
Out Hunting Oil/canvas (96.5x71cm 37x27in) London
2000
$3 219 - €3 594 - **£2 247** - FF23 577
Au champ de courses Huile/panneau (32.5x23.5cm
12x9in) Bruxelles 2001

JANSEM Jean, Jean-Léon 1920 **[507]**
$24 645 - €22 867 - **£15 345** - FF150 000
Village d'Italie Huile/toile (114x162cm 44x63in) Paris
1999
$10 151 - €8 690 - **£6 110** - FF57 000
La famille Huile/toile (73x100cm 28x39in) Paris 1998
$4 800 - €5 184 - **£3 317** - FF34 002
Scene de maison Oil/canvas (41x33cm 16x12in)
New-York 2001
$1 793 - €1 906 - **£1 202** - FF12 500
Le danseur Crayon (64x49cm 25x19in) Cannes 2000
$480 - €488 - **£292** - FF3 200
Le coin de l'atelier Lithographie couleurs (76x54cm
29x21in) Paris 2000

JANSEN Dirk 1878-1952 **[17]**
$791 - €708 - **£474** - FF4 643
View of Tanger Oil/canvas (65.5x99.5cm 25x39in)
Amsterdam 1999

JANSEN Franz Maria 1885-1958 **[87]**
$175 - €184 - **£110** - FF1 207
Wählt/Schamlos/Die herrschende Klasse
Woodcut (44.5x32.5cm 17x12in) Stuttgart 2000

JANSEN Fritz 1856-1928 **[5]**
$4 586 - €4 538 - **£2 807** - FF29 766
Playing with the Japanese Doll Watercolour
(28x28cm 11x11in) Amsterdam 2000

JANSEN Han 1931-1994 **[9]**
$176 - €204 - **£121** - FF1 339
Onder de blauwe boom Serigraph (50x50cm
19x19in) Groningen 2000

JANSEN Hendrik Willebrord 1855-1908 **[28]**
$1 131 - €1 082 - **£689** - FF7 100
Cour de ferme avec fillette Huile/toile (62x83cm
24x32in) Troyes 1999

JANSEN Johannes Mauritz 1812-1857 **[14]**
- $2 748 - €2 949 - £1 838 - FF19 347
  Peasants on a sandy Trail in a wooded landscape Oil/panel (48x60.5cm 18x23in) Amsterdam 2000
- $2 103 - €1 815 - £1 269 - FF11 906
  A wooded River Landscape with Cattle Drivers on a Sandy track Oil/panel (23.5x29.5cm 9x11in) Amsterdam 1999

JANSEN Joseph 1829-1905 **[16]**
- $5 891 - €4 857 - £3 469 - FF31 858
  «Der Eibsee mit der Zugspitze», Prachtvoller Sonnentag mit Gehöft Öl/Leinwand (94x130cm 37x51in) Lindau 1998
- $4 750 - €5 260 - £3 221 - FF34 506
  Hiker Approaching an Alpine Mountain House Oil/canvas (26.5x105cm 10x41in) New-York 2000

JANSEN Willem George Fred. 1871-1949 **[220]**
- $9 506 - €9 983 - £6 105 485
  A View of Rotterdam Harbour with Holland-America Line in the Distance Oil/canvas (80x162cm 31x63in) Amsterdam 2000
- $4 274 - €3 626 - £2 578 - FF23 788
  Gezicht op Garderen Oil/canvas (68x98cm 26x38in) Rotterdam 1998
- $2 005 - €1 906 - £1 220 - FF12 501
  Gezicht op een stadsgracht met ophaalbrug Oil/panel (13.5x20.5cm 5x8in) Den Haag 1999
- $1 153 - €998 - £700 - FF6 548
  Harbour of harlingen Watercolour/paper (35x47cm 13x18in) Amsterdam 1999

JANSON Johannes Christian 1763-1823 **[9]**
- $2 606 - €2 962 - £1 800 - FF19 428
  Boy Buying Cherries at a Fruit Stall/Woman Talking to a Man Oil/panel (20.5x18cm 8x7in) London 2000

JANSON Johannes, Jacobus 1729-1784 **[41]**
- $1 955 - €2 269 - £1 350 - FF14 883
  Man and a Woman Cleaning the Interior of a Barn Oil/panel (28.5x37.5cm 11x14in) Amsterdam 2000
- $2 172 - €2 500 - £1 500 - FF16 397
  Cattle, Goat and Drovers on a Country Road/Sheep and Shepherd Watercolour (25x22.5cm 9x8in) Billingshurst, West-Sussex 2000

JANSON Knut 1882-1966 **[24]**
- $316 - €301 - £191 - FF1 976
  Djurgårdsbrunnkanalen Oil/canvas (24x35cm 9x13in) Stockholm 1999

JANSON Marc 1930 **[176]**
- $573 - €549 - £353 - FF3 600
  L'oeil noir de la nuit souveraine Huile/toile (46x38cm 18x14in) Douai 1999
- $484 - €488 - £301 - FF3 200
  Sans titre Huile/isorel (41x27cm 16x10in) Paris 1999
- $334 - €320 - £206 - FF2 100
  Sans titre Gouache/papier (49x63cm 19x24in) Douai 1999

JANSON Pieter 1768-1851 **[5]**
- $4 692 - €3 992 - £2 800 - FF26 189
  Cattle and Sheep in a Watermeadow Oil/panel (36x32cm 14x12in) London 1998

JANSONS Andris 1939 **[9]**
- $1 331 - €1 386 - £836 - FF9 091
  Rocky Shores, Bay of Islands Great Ocean Road Victoria Oil/canvas (36x49cm 14x19in) Melbourne 2000

JANSSAUD Mathurin 1857-1940 **[209]**
- $1 902 - €2 058 - £1 302 - FF13 500
  Port breton animé, au coucher du soleil Pastel/papier (26x33cm 10x12in) Troyes 2001

JANSSEN Gerhard 1636-1725 **[1]**
- $9 212 - €10 174 - £6 384 - FF66 738
  Die Verkündigung an die Hirten Mixed media (36.5x28cm 14x11in) Wien 2001

JANSSEN Gerhard 1863-1931 **[19]**
- $1 740 - €1 738 - £1 088 - FF11 403
  Festliche Gesellschaft Oil/panel (29x31cm 11x12in) Köln 1999

JANSSEN Horst 1929-1995 **[2768]**
- $11 299 - €13 294 - £8 179 - FF87 201
  In der Mahlauklasse Tempera (62x48cm 24x18in) Hamburg 2001
- $8 992 - €10 226 - £6 236 - FF67 078
  So du Knuff Mixed media (43x29.4cm 16x11in) Hamburg 2000
- $2 088 - €1 789 - £1 255 - FF11 736
  Computerhirn Pencil (22.5x15.2cm 8x5in) Hamburg 1998
- $210 - €245 - £147 - FF1 609
  Zeus Radierung (16x34.5cm 6x13in) Köln 2001

JANSSEN Ludovic 1888-1954 **[97]**
- $1 150 - €1 339 - £820 - FF8 780
  Marais de Genck Huile/toile (60x80cm 23x31in) Liège 2001

JANSSEN Luplau 1869-1927 **[36]**
- $1 168 - €1 009 - £705 - FF6 619
  Interiör med to piger ved klaveret Oil/canvas (60x70cm 23x27in) Vejle 1998

JANSSENS Abraham 1575-1632 **[13]**
- $114 800 - €99 214 - £69 200 - FF650 800
  Suite allégorique des Quatre Saisons et Douze Mois de l'Année Huile/panneau (68x48.5cm 26x19in) Bruxelles 1998

JANSSENS DEN DANSER Hieronymus 1624-1693 **[32]**
- $38 313 - €35 010 - £24 000 - FF229 653
  Festive Gathering of Elegant Company Before a Country House Oil/canvas (114x167cm 44x65in) Suffolk 1999
- $11 536 - €11 628 - £7 200 - FF76 272
  Elegante Gesellschaft bei einem Festmahl im Saal eines Schlosses Öl/Leinwand (61x85.5cm 24x33in) Wien 2000

JANSSENS Jacques 1809-c.1888 **[4]**
- $1 881 - €2 231 - £1 368 - FF14 634
  Matinée d'automne Huile/toile (92x125cm 36x49in) Antwerpen 2001

JANSSENS Johan 1809-? **[4]**
- $6 230 - €6 703 - £4 240 - FF43 970
  De hjemvendte fiskerte falbyder dagens fangst Oil/canvas (70x79cm 27x38in) Köbenhavn 2001

JANSSENS V. XIX **[3]**
- $3 836 - €3 803 - £2 400 - FF24 945
  The Pantry Oil/panel (41x35cm 16x13in) London 1999

JANSSENS Victor Emile 1807-1845 **[2]**
- $5 400 - €6 006 - £3 700 - FF39 400
  Damas en el tocador Oleo/tabla (55x42cm 21x16in) Madrid 2001

J

JANSSON Alfred 1863-1931 **[27]**
$1 700 - €1 886 - **£1 130** - FF12 370
River Landscape Oil/canvas (76x63cm 30x25in)
Milford CT 2000

JANSSON Alvar 1922-1990 **[7]**
$1 734 - €1 903 - **£1 117** - FF12 486
Självporträtt Oil/canvas (34x30cm 13x11in)
Stockholm 2000

JANSSON Eugène 1862-1915 **[41]**
$96 757 - €112 417 - **£68 000** - FF737 405
Aftonstämning vid kusten (evening mood)
Oil/canvas (49.5x68cm 19x26in) London 2001
$1 910 - €1 859 - **£1 176** - FF12 195
Tidig vår djurgården Oil/paper/panel (29x22.5cm
11x8in) Stockholm 1999
$1 484 - €1 291 - **£895** - FF8 467
Visby ringmur Pastel/paper (14x22cm 5x8in)
Stockholm 1998

JANSSON Johaniss XVII **[15]**
$318 - €295 - **£190** - FF1 935
The County Palatine of Chester Engraving
(43x50cm 17x20in) Godalming, Surrey 1999

JANSSON Karl Emanuel 1846-1874 **[8]**
$3 227 - €3 027 - **£1 994** - FF19 857
Vid fönstret Oil/canvas/panel (23x19cm 9x7in)
Helsinki 1999
$2 241 - €2 102 - **£1 385** - FF13 790
Landskap Akvarell/papper (8x12cm 3x4in) Helsinki
1999

JANSSON Rune 1918 **[119]**
$802 - €700 - **£485** - FF4 592
Komposition med rektangel Oil/canvas (35x98cm
13x38in) Stockholm 1998
$257 - €286 - **£175** - FF1 873
Kust (Coast) Oil/canvas (27x35cm 10x13in)
Stockholm 2000

JANSSON Tove 1914 **[28]**
$2 977 - €2 606 - **£1 804** - FF17 094
Teaterateljén Oil/panel (38x46cm 14x18in) Helsinki
1998
$2 062 - €2 421 - **£1 455** - FF15 878
Vinterlandskap med byggnader Oil/panel
(33x41cm 12x16in) Stockholm 2000
$385 - €458 - **£265** - FF3 006
Muminfigurer Indian ink/paper (31x22cm 12x8in)
Stockholm 2000

JANSSON Viktor 1886-1958 **[8]**
$2 689 - €2 523 - **£1 662** - FF16 548
Galjonsfigur Bronze (H37cm H14in) Helsinki 1999

JANTHUR Richard 1883-1950 **[36]**
$194 - €204 - **£122** - FF1 341
Leda und der Schwan Lithographie (27x34cm
10x13in) Stuttgart 2000

JANVIER Alex Simeon 1935 **[40]**
$860 - €923 - **£584** - FF6 055
Frontline water Walker Acrylic/canvas (48x36cm
18x14in) Calgary, Alberta 2001
$544 - €517 - **£330** - FF3 389
Untitled, Spring Board Gouache/paper (39x57cm
15x22in) Calgary, Alberta 1999

JAPY Louis Aimé 1840-1916 **[212]**
$21 492 - €20 915 - **£13 230** - FF137 196
Franskt sommarlandskap med herde och får,
solnedgång Oil/canvas (154x115cm 60x45in)
Stockholm 1999

$5 421 - €5 946 - **£3 681** - FF39 000
Berger gardant les moutons Huile/toile (65x81cm
25x31in) Lille 2000
$1 912 - €2 134 - **£1 251** - FF14 000
Pâturage près de la rivière Huile/panneau
(32x41cm 12x16in) Fontainebleau 2000
$1 020 - €991 - **£630** - FF6 500
Le passage du bac Encre/papier (17x22cm 6x8in)
Melun 1999

JAQUES Bertha Evelyn 1863-1941 **[30]**
$305 - €291 - **£190** - FF1 912
Jimson Weed/Woodsfolk Etching (20x23cm 8x9in)
Cedar-Falls IA 1999

JAQUES Jean-Pierre 1913 **[6]**
$2 800 - €3 272 - **£1 999** - FF21 466
Frühlingslandschaft bei Genf (Grand Saconnex)
Öl/Leinwand (60x93cm 23x36in) Zürich 2001

JAQUES Pierre 1913 **[14]**
$2 188 - €2 380 - **£1 442** - FF15 615
Petit village Vaudois au Printemps Öl/Leinwand
(54x102.5cm 21x40in) Bern 2000

JAQUET Jacques 1828-1899 **[2]**
$54 000 - €59 492 - **£35 280** - FF390 240
Jeune femme assise sur un tronc d'arbre Marbre
(H136cm H53in) Bruxelles 2000

JARDIN Nicolas Henri 1720-1799 **[2]**
$14 490 - €12 099 - **£8 613** - FF79 362
Interiör fra Christiansborg Slot udfört i anled-
ning af hofbal Ink (38x46cm 14x18in) København
1998

JARDINES José Maria 1862-? **[55]**
$1 950 - €1 802 - **£1 170** - FF11 820
Casas y lavanderas Oleo/lienzo (68x30.5cm
26x12in) Madrid 1999
$997 - €1 051 - **£630** - FF6 895
Niña con pavos Oleo/lienzo (32x22cm 12x8in)
Madrid 2000

JARMAN Derek 1942-1993 **[14]**
$2 006 - €1 852 - **£1 200** - FF12 151
St John the Baptist (after Caravaggio) Chalks
(78x118cm 30x46in) London 1999

JÄRNEFELT Eero 1863-1937 **[136]**
$11 910 - €10 424 - **£7 216** - FF68 379
Landskap Oil/canvas (37x54cm 14x21in) Helsinki
1998
$6 125 - €6 895 - **£4 218** - FF45 231
Aftonljus Oil/canvas (19x22cm 7x8in) Helsinki 2000
$3 178 - €3 111 - **£1 955** - FF20 409
Mäntyjä Akvarell/papper (46x32cm 18x12in) Helsinki
1999
$628 - €537 - **£369** - FF3 525
Snöig skog Etching in colors (25x21.5cm 9x8in)
Helsinki 1998

JÄRNEFELT Laura 1904-1985 **[33]**
$914 - €874 - **£556** - FF5 736
Grönska Oil/canvas (50x61cm 19x24in) Helsinki 1999
$295 - €303 - **£185** - FF1 985
Kastelholm Gouache/paper (31x48.5cm 12x19in)
Helsinki 2000

JAROCKI von Wladyslav 1879-1965 **[18]**
$4 499 - €4 488 - **£2 808** - FF29 438
Yellow Poncho Oil/canvas (101x92cm 39x36in)
Warszawa 1999

JARONEK Bohumír 1866-1933 [7]
- $173 - €164 - £108 - FF1 075
  Paysanne Gravure bois couleurs (55.5x69.5cm 21x27in) Brno 2000

JAROSZYNSKI Józef 1835-1900 [10]
- $2 447 - €2 466 - £1 526 - FF16 178
  Scène champêtre Oil/canvas (22x34.4cm 8x13in) Warszawa 2000

JARRY Alfred 1873-1907 [6]
- $9 268 - €8 994 - £5 770 - FF59 000
  Ubu sortant du puits Encre (14x9cm 5x3in) Paris 1999
- $2 826 - €2 744 - £1 746 - FF18 000
  Programmes pour la création d'Ubu Roi au Théâtre de l'Oeuvre Lithographie (25x32.5cm 9x12in) Paris 1999

JARVILLE act.c.1922 [3]
- $435 - €502 - £300 - FF3 290
  «Prunelle du Velay» Poster (158x117cm 62x46in) London 2001

JARVIS Arnold Henry 1881-1960 [25]
- $244 - €262 - £161 - FF1 718
  Bush Landscape Watercolour/paper (30x45.5cm 11x17in) Sydney 2000

JARVIS Georgina 1944-1990 [27]
- $1 394 - €1 538 - £944 - FF10 086
  The Sugar House Oil/canvas (40x60cm 16x24in) Calgary, Alberta 2000
- $1 178 - €1 402 - £812 - FF9 194
  Mountain Lake Oil/canvas (20x30cm 7x11in) Calgary, Alberta 2000

JARVIS Henry C. 1867-1955 [9]
- $490 - €436 - £300 - FF2 861
  River Landscape with Sheep Grazing Watercolour/paper (19x26.5cm 7x10in) Newbury, Berkshire 1999

JARVIS John Brent 1946 [1]
- $3 400 - €3 875 - £2 372 - FF25 421
  On the Canyon Rim Gouache/paper (27x61cm 11x24in) Dallas TX 2001

JASCHA Johann 1942 [11]
- $273 - €254 - £168 - FF1 668
  Viererbande Felt pen (33x25cm 12x9in) Linz 1999

JASCHIK Almos 1885-1950 [4]
- $630 - €606 - £390 - FF3 975
  In seven League Boots Mixed media/paper (34x23cm 13x9in) Budapest 1999

JASIENSKY Stefan 1899-1990 [8]
- $600 - €666 - £418 - FF4 368
  «Alpgottesdienst» Photograph (7.5x10.5cm 2x4in) New-York 2001

JASINSKI Emilian 1865-? [1]
- $2 008 - €2 369 - £1 416 - FF15 540
  Paysage fluvial au coucher de soleil Huile/panneau (16x29cm 6x11in) Warszawa 2001

JASINSKI Feliks Stanislaw 1862-1901 [11]
- $205 - €222 - £142 - FF1 458
  Marécage, d'après Jozef Chelmonski Eau-forte (21x28.5cm 8x11in) Bydgoszcz 2001

JASINSKI Zdzislaw 1863-1932 [8]
- $4 860 - €5 406 - £3 240 - FF35 460
  Alegoría de la República Oleo/lienzo (75x110cm 29x43in) Madrid 2000

JASUSCH Anton 1882-1965 [2]
- $5 780 - €5 467 - £3 600 - FF35 860
  Ein Zigeunerlager Öl/Leinwand (75x94cm 29x37in) Praha 2000

JAUDON Valérie 1945 [21]
- $3 200 - €3 435 - £2 141 - FF22 531
  Osyaka Oil/canvas (91x91cm 35x35in) Beverly-Hills CA 2000

JAULMES Gustave Louis 1873-1959 [20]
- $2 073 - €2 363 - £1 424 - FF15 500
  La baignade Huile/toile (36x75cm 14x29in) Paris 2000

JAULMES Marc 1928 [15]
- $680 - €686 - £424 - FF4 500
  2 juin 98 Acrylique/toile (81x100cm 31x39in) Paris 2000

JAUNBERSIN J. XIX-XX [4]
- $3 565 - €3 634 - £2 230 - FF23 835
  Palaisinterieur Öl/Leinwand (71x110cm 27x43in) Wien 2000

JAVIER Maximino 1950 [15]
- $1 101 - €1 291 - £792 - FF8 470
  La vaca mecánica Litografía (76x56cm 29x22in) México 2001

JAVUREK Karel 1815-1909 [10]
- $4 335 - €4 100 - £2 700 - FF26 895
  King Ladislav Pohrobek Oil/canvas (93x106cm 36x41in) Praha 2000

JAWLENSKY Andreas 1902-1984 [26]
- $14 016 - €12 268 - £8 488 - FF80 474
  Flusslandschaft mit Figuren Oil/paper/canvas (49.5x73.4cm 19x28in) Berlin 1998
- $9 380 - €10 290 - £6 371 - FF67 497
  Felsenküste Oil/board (22.7x31cm 8x12in) Berlin 2000
- $2 144 - €2 352 - £1 456 - FF15 427
  Komposition Pastell/Papier (20.8x16.5cm 8x6in) Berlin 2000

JAWLENSKY von Alexej 1864-1941 [389]
- $320 000 - €354 979 - £212 800 - FF2 328 512
  Landschaft Oil/board (53x50cm 20x19in) New-York 2000
- $85 000 - €81 634 - £52 402 - FF535 483
  Grosse Meditation (large Meditation) Oil/paper/board (25x17cm 9x6in) New-York 1999
- $5 989 - €5 624 - £3 711 - FF36 892
  Becher mit Blumen Indian ink (16x14cm 6x5in) München 1999
- $5 668 - €4 856 - £3 407 - FF31 856
  Liegender weiblicher Akt II Lithographie (22.9x41.2cm 9x16in) Hamburg 1998

JAY Cecil 1884-? [5]
- $28 833 - €32 014 - £20 097 - FF210 000
  Les Béguines de la ville de Goes à l'office Huile/toile (150x221.5cm 59x87in) Paris 2001
- $5 680 - €6 098 - £3 800 - FF40 000
  La dentellière Huile/toile (68x54cm 26x21in) Paris 2000

JAY Florence XIX-XX [19]
- $3 952 - €4 583 - £2 800 - FF30 060
  Study of a Springer Spaniel Oil/canvas (53x38cm 21x15in) Carmarthen, Wales 2000
- $564 - €530 - £350 - FF3 477
  Golden by Portrait of Horse Oil/canvas (35x44cm 14x17in) Woking, Surrey 1999

J

JAZET Jean Pierre Marie 1788-1871 **[26]**
▥ **$430** - €511 - **£298** - FF3 353
Napoleon Bonaparte, Adieux de Fontainebleau, nach Horace Vernet Aquatinta (57.5x72.5cm 22x28in) Köln 2000

JAZET Paul Léon 1848-? **[19]**
◡ **$562** - €665 - **£398** - FF4 360
Militärparade in einer französischen Kleinstadt Oil/panel (37.5x54.5cm 14x21in) Ahlden 2000
◢ **$4 184** - €4 491 - **£2 800** - FF29 460
French Cavalry Trumpeter Oil/panel (23x16cm 9x6in) London 2000

JEAN Marcel 1900-1994 **[79]**
◡ **$1 400** - €1 451 - **£840** - FF9 520
La barricade Tecnica mista/tela (38x46.5cm 14x18in) Prato 2000
◢ **$2 000** - €1 705 - **£1 206** - FF11 185
«Flag Girls», Costume Design Gouache (28x38cm 11x14in) New-York 1998

JEAN-HAFFEN Yvonne 1895-1993 **[29]**
◢ **$669** - €762 - **£472** - FF5 000
La pointe de Dinan Fusain (24.5x31.5cm 9x12in) Rennes 2001
▥ **$158** - €145 - **£95** - FF950
Bateaux sur la grève Linocut (29.5x50cm 11x19in) Douarnenez 1998

JEANCLOS Georges Jeankelowich 1933-1997 **[34]**
◣ **$8 875** - €7 318 - **£5 227** - FF48 000
Adam et Eve Terracotta (75x67x25cm 29x26x9in) Paris 1998

JEANMAIRE Édouard 1847-1916 **[68]**
◡ **$10 900** - €12 394 - **£7 600** - FF81 300
«Les pavots» Huile/toile (116x143cm 45x56in) Antwerpen 2000
◡ **$1 612** - €1 493 - **£987** - FF9 794
Herbstliche Juralandschaft mit Bauernpaar beim Lauben Öl/Leinwand (72.5x59cm 28x23in) Bern 1999

JEANNE-CLAUDE J.-Cl. Guillebon 1935 **[1]**
◡ **$10 298** - €9 996 - **£6 412** - FF65 568
Wrapped Reichstag, Platz der Republik, Brandenburger Tor Collage/board (35.5x28cm 13x11in) Berlin 1999

JEANNENEY Victor François 1832-1885 **[3]**
◡ **$3 947** - €4 136 - **£2 500** - FF27 132
La pharmacie de l'Abbey Oil/canvas (80x106cm 31x41in) London 2000

JEANNERET Gustave 1847-1927 **[18]**
◡ **$1 856** - €1 871 - **£1 157** - FF12 270
Stilleben mit Blume, Vasen und Schatulle Öl/Leinwand (55x44cm 21x17in) Zürich 2000

JEANNIN Gaëtan XIX-XX **[3]**
◡ **$6 000** - €5 701 - **£3 650** - FF37 397
Bowl of Apples Oil/canvas (61x73cm 24x28in) New-York 1999

JEANNIN Georges 1841-1925 **[200]**
◡ **$11 141** - €11 550 - **£6 685** - FF75 763
Natura morta con fiori/Natura morta con frutta Olio/tela (130x105cm 51x41in) Milano 1999
◡ **$3 312** - €3 659 - **£2 296** - FF24 000
Bouquet de fleurs Huile/toile (38x46cm 14x18in) Le Havre 2001
◡ **$2 613** - €2 287 - **£1 582** - FF15 000
Bouquet de roses Huile/panneau (32x41cm 12x16in) Paris 1998

JEANNIOT Pierre Georges 1848-1934 **[171]**
◡ **$1 545** - €1 448 - **£929** - FF9 500
Femmes au salon Huile/carton (40x44.5cm 15x17in) Paris 1999
◡ **$853** - €915 - **£581** - FF6 000
Paris, les grands boulevards Huile/toile (32x41cm 12x16in) Calais 2001
◢ **$216** - €198 - **£131** - FF1 300
Paysage/Marine Encre/papier (17.5x49.5cm 6x19in) Paris 1999

JEANNOT Joseph-Clément-M. 1855-? **[29]**
◢ **$302** - €335 - **£209** - FF2 200
Ruisselet en sous-bois Aquarelle/papier (48x60cm 18x23in) Troyes 2001

JEAURAT DE BERTRY Nicolas Henry 1728-c.1800 **[8]**
◡ **$47 490** - €45 735 - **£29 550** - FF300 000
Table de cuisine Huile/toile (92x135cm 36x53in) Montfort L'Amaury 1999
◡ **$46 692** - €45 898 - **£30 600** - FF301 068
Still Life of Pipes, a Globe, Musical Score, Violin , a young Girl Oil/canvas (81x100.5cm 31x39in) London 1999

JEAURAT Étienne 1699-1789 **[41]**
◡ **$14 311** - €13 263 - **£8 900** - FF87 000
Le retour des maraîchers Huile/toile (54x65cm 21x25in) Corbeil-Essonnes 1999
◢ **$6 327** - €5 793 - **£3 857** - FF38 000
Trois homme attablés, étude pour Les citrons de Javottes Pierre noire (38.7x29.3cm 15x11in) Paris 1999

JEBENS Adolf 1819-1888 **[1]**
◡ **$3 478** - €4 090 - **£2 493** - FF26 831
Portrait Kaiser Wilhelm I Öl/Leinwand (37x31cm 14x12in) München 2001

JEFFERSON Joseph 1829-1905 **[5]**
◡ **$4 000** - €4 274 - **£2 722** - FF28 038
Louisiana Landscape with Figure on the Road Oil/canvas (50x76cm 20x30in) New-Orleans LA 2001

JEFFERYS Charles William 1869-1951 **[7]**
▥ **$198** - €220 - **£134** - FF1 443
Departure of the Siberian Battery from Petawawa Camp Lithograph (57.5x48.5cm 22x19in) Toronto 2000

JEFFERYS Marcel 1872-1924 **[80]**
◡ **$2 354** - €2 727 - **£1 628** - FF17 886
Nature morte au vase blanc Huile/toile (50x60cm 19x23in) Bruxelles 2000
◡ **$621** - €694 - **£431** - FF4 552
La gitane Technique mixte (35x40cm 13x15in) Antwerpen 2001
◢ **$262** - €297 - **£177** - FF1 951
Le jardin Aquarelle, gouache/papier (24.5x28.5cm 9x11in) Bruxelles 2000

JEGERLEHNER Hans Gordon 1906-1974 **[50]**
▥ **$104** - €119 - **£72** - FF779
Bergdorf Woodcut in colors (30x25cm 11x9in) Zofingen 2000

JEGHER Christoffel 1586-1653 **[30]**
▥ **$1 304** - €1 534 - **£938** - FF10 061
Der Liebesgarten, mit der sitzenden Frau, nach Peter Paul Rubens Woodcut (45.5x59cm 17x23in) Hamburg 2001

JEIHAN SUKMANTORO 1938 **[16]**
◡ **$4 156** - €3 487 - **£2 438** - FF22 876
Mother and Child Oil/canvas (89.5x130cm 35x51in) Singapore 1998

JEJER Anatoli 1937 **[23]**
$428 - €391 - **£260** - FF2 567
In the Farmyard Oil/canvas/board (45.5x51cm
17x20in) London 1998

JELINEK Frantisek A. 1890-1977 **[22]**
$780 - €738 - **£486** - FF4 841
Seated Girl Oil/cardboard (49x39cm 19x15in) Praha
2000

JELINEK Rudolph 1880-? **[40]**
$1 135 - €1 090 - **£712** - FF7 150
Nähende Mutter mit zwei Kindern in der Stube
Öl/Leinwand (55.5x69cm 21x27in) Wien 1999

JELINGER Han 1895-1961 **[8]**
$1 182 - €1 361 - **£816** - FF8 929
Zicht op Brugge (View of Brugge) Oil/canvas
(40x50cm 15x19in) Maastricht 2000

JELINK Hendrikus Johannes 1808-1846 **[4]**
$1 249 - €1 361 - **£860** - FF8 929
Landscape with Cows and a Sheep Oil/canvas
(30.5x36cm 12x14in) Amsterdam 2001

JELLETT Mainie Harriet 1897-1944 **[49]**
$29 670 - €33 176 - **£20 000** - FF217 618
Abstract Composition Oil/canvas (183x91.5cm
72x36in) London 1999
$22 408 - €21 243 - **£14 000** - FF139 342
Three Elements Oil/canvas (91.5x71cm 36x27in)
London 1999
$5 745 - €6 349 - **£3 984** - FF41 645
Still Life Study of a Vase of Flowers
Oil/canvas/board (30x39cm 11x15in) Dublin 2001
$2 570 - €2 920 - **£1 774** - FF19 156
Flower Forms Gouache/paper (8x13cm 3x5in) Dublin
2000

JELLEY James Valentine c.1870-c.1940 **[30]**
$1 632 - €1 549 - **£1 000** - FF10 163
Dog Roses Oil/board (25x18.5cm 9x7in) London
1999

JEM XX **[1]**
$853 - €732 - **£513** - FF4 800
«**Cie Générale de navigation sur le Lac Léman;
Lake of Geneva...**» Affiche (100x65cm 39x25in)
Orléans 1998

JENDRASSIK Jeno 1860-1919 **[5]**
$4 458 - €4 317 - **£2 800** - FF28 315
Deep in the Thought Oil/panel (73x58.5cm 28x23in)
London 1999

JENÉ Edgar 1904-1984 **[40]**
$2 192 - €2 556 - **£1 543** - FF16 769
Versunkenes, jour indécis Öl/Leinwand (65x80cm
25x31in) Königstein 2001
$542 - €581 - **£370** - FF3 813
Kai Aquarell/Papier (47x32.5cm 18x12in) Wien 2001

JENKINS Blanche act.1872-1915 **[6]**
$16 059 - €15 169 - **£10 000** - FF99 502
**Young Girl sitting on a Tree Branch, holding
Flowers in the Air** Oil/canvas (128.5x90.5cm
50x35in) Channel-Islands 1999
$2 900 - €2 785 - **£1 797** - FF18 268
Young Girl with Daisies Oil/canvas (47x33cm
18x13in) Chicago IL 1999

JENKINS Burris, Jnr. 1897-1966 **[2]**
$3 750 - €3 603 - **£2 280** - FF23 633
«**Trib' Sports Coverage is Excellent**»: **Drawing
for the Poster** Pencil/paper (53x46.5cm 20x18in)
New-York 1999

$4 500 - €4 262 - **£2 736** - FF27 954
Babe Ruth Day Print (29x38cm 11x14in) New-York
1999

JENKINS George Henry 1843-1914 **[101]**
$1 145 - €1 063 - **£700** - FF6 973
Prawle Point, South Devon Oil/canvas (54x89cm
21x35in) Penzance, Cornwall 1999
$481 - €485 - **£300** - FF3 181
**River Landscape with a Blossoming Tree in the
foreground** Oil/board (23x38cm 9x15in) Dorchester,
Dorset 2000
$468 - €460 - **£300** - FF3 020
Cattle grazing near a stream, Dartmoor
Watercolour/paper (50x35cm 20x14in) Tavistock, Devon
1999

JENKINS George J. 1920 **[23]**
$274 - €281 - **£173** - FF1 842
Whistle Stop Oil/board (25x35cm 10x14in) Victoria,
B.C. 2000

JENKINS H. ?-1872 **[3]**
$1 860 - €1 534 - **£1 095** - FF10 060
**Gotisches Portal in einer nordfranzösischen
Stadt mit Figurenstaffage** Aquarell/Papier
(41x29cm 16x11in) Lindau 1998

JENKINS Joseph John 1811-1885 **[20]**
$5 215 - €4 742 - **£3 200** - FF31 106
**The Towing Path, Boys Fishing at a Lock at
Dusk** Watercolour (22x38cm 8x14in) London 1999

JENKINS Michael 1957 **[13]**
$411 - €381 - **£248** - FF2 500
Boulier Métal (172x133.5cm 67x52in) Paris 1999

JENKINS Paul 1923 **[585]**
$7 000 - €6 740 - **£4 377** - FF44 214
Phenomena Planetary Walks (II) Acrylic/canvas
(114.5x152.5cm 45x60in) Beverly-Hills CA 1999
$2 273 - €2 206 - **£1 415** - FF14 473
Phenomena celestial vine with Seraph
Öl/Leinwand (116x81cm 45x31in) Luzern 1999
$934 - €1 025 - **£634** - FF6 725
Phaenomena before I am Öl/Leinwand (41x24cm
16x9in) Luzern 2000
$1 194 - €1 153 - **£750** - FF7 561
Phenomena Big Sur Watercolour/paper
(73.5x62.5cm 28x24in) London 1999
$226 - €210 - **£136** - FF1 375
Komposition mit gelb-grün-blauem Streifen
Farblithographie (87.5x61.5cm 34x24in) Heidelberg
1999

JENKINS Wilfred ?-1936 **[55]**
$1 229 - €1 328 - **£850** - FF8 712
Liverpool Docks and Habour by Gas Light
Oil/canvas (41x61cm 16x24in) Cheshire 2001
$745 - €722 - **£460** - FF4 734
**Figure Walking Down a Moonlight Road with a
House Beyond** Oil/canvas (29x39.5cm 11x15in)
West-Yorshire 1999

JENNENS Luke XIX-XX **[2]**
$1 153 - €1 275 - **£800** - FF8 362
Harse and a Jay on a Woodland Path Watercolour
(18.5x26cm 7x10in) London 2001

JENNER Isaac Walter 1836-1901 **[30]**
$5 270 - €5 138 - **£3 200** - FF33 705
H.M.S Royal Albert Ashore in Zea Bay Oil/canvas
(71x101.5cm 27x39in) London 2000
$1 563 - €1 859 - **£1 113** - FF12 192
Dawn over The Brisbane River Oil/board
(13.5x23cm 5x9in) Melbourne 2000

🖊 **$2 557** - €2 836 - **£1 700** - FF18 606
Fisherfolk on the Shore at Brighton with the Chain Pier Beyond Bodycolour (10x24.5cm 3x9in)
London 2000

JENNER William XIX [8]
👁 **$6 742** - €6 483 - **£4 160** - FF42 526
Heavy Weather in the North Sea, towing in a disabled Ship Oil/canvas (77x127cm 30x50in)
Malmö 1999

JENNEY Neil 1945 [35]
👁 **$70 000** - €81 329 - **£49 196** - FF533 484
«North America» Acrylic/panel (65x287cm 25x112in) Beverly-Hills CA 2001
👁 **$75 000** - €84 844 - **£52 470** - FF556 537
Scent and Pud Acrylic/canvas (81.5x123x6.5cm 32x48x2in) New-York 2001

JENNINGS Howard E. XX [1]
📖 **$1 587** - €1 757 - **£1 100** - FF11 527
«Lake Placid» Poster (66x49cm 25x19in) London 2001

JENNY Arnold 1831-1881 [22]
👁 **$850** - €984 - **£602** - FF6 453
Vierwaldstättersee mit Booten Öl/Leinwand (70x104cm 27x40in) Zürich 2000

JENNY Johann Heinrich 1786-1854 [3]
📖 **$1 708** - €1 486 - **£1 030** - FF9 748
«Enneda im Canton Glarus» Aquatinta (35x48cm 13x18in) Bern 1998

JENNYS William c.1770-c.1810 [8]
👁 **$6 500** - €6 942 - **£4 429** - FF45 534
Young Lady in Gray-green Empire Dress, Portrait of Miss Ashley Oil/canvas (73.5x62cm 28x24in) New-York 2001

JENSEN Alfred 1903-1981 [85]
👁 **$35 000** - €32 687 - **£21 602** - FF214 410
The Integer Rules the Universe: Windows in Heaven Oil/canvas (193x127cm 75x50in) New-York 1999
👁 **$10 000** - €11 201 - **£6 948** - FF73 472
«The Earthly Plate» Mixed media (101.5x76cm 39x29in) New-York 2001
👁 **$3 402** - €3 811 - **£2 365** - FF25 000
Projet de diagramme Huile/toile (31x41cm 12x16in) Le Touquet 2001
🖊 **$13 000** - €12 325 - **£7 909** - FF80 844
The First Count in the Great Platonic Year Felt pen (73.5x58.5cm 28x23in) New-York 1999
📖 **$220** - €244 - **£149** - FF1 599
Composition Farbserigraphie (82x70.5cm 32x27in) Zürich 2000

JENSEN Alfred David 1859-1935 [149]
👁 **$1 238** - €1 329 - **£828** - FF8 720
Auslaufendes Segelschiff vor Stralsund Öl/Leinwand (71x100cm 27x39in) Bremen 2000
👁 **$333** - €282 - **£199** - FF1 853
Marine med sejlskib i höj sö Oil/canvas (25x36cm 9x14in) Viby J, Århus 1998
🖊 **$5 500** - €4 910 - **£3 368** - FF32 209
«Magic in Egypt II» Mixed media/paper (47x41cm 18x16in) New-York 1998

JENSEN Arup c.1906 [15]
👁 **$944** - €807 - **£567** - FF5 293
Parti fra Köbenhavns Havn Oil/canvas (83x117cm 32x46in) Köbenhavn 1998

JENSEN Axel P. 1885-1972 [287]
👁 **$391** - €363 - **£235** - FF2 383
Blomstermark Oil/canvas (52x60cm 20x23in) Köbenhavn 1999

JENSEN Berit 1956 [82]
🖊 **$533** - €537 - **£332** - FF3 524
Komposition Gouache/paper (100x70cm 39x27in) Köbenhavn 2000

JENSEN Bill 1945 [35]
📖 **$700** - €768 - **£452** - FF5 040
Etching for Denial Engraving (62x49.5cm 24x19in) New-York 2000

JENSEN Christian Albrecht 1792-1870 [19]
👁 **$8 050** - €6 721 - **£4 785** - FF44 090
Herreportraet Oil/canvas (65x50.5cm 25x19in) Köbenhavn 1998
👁 **$3 978** - €3 768 - **£2 475** - FF24 715
Dameportraet, Omtrent halv figur, en vace til venstre Oil/canvas (23.5x18.5cm 9x7in) Köbenhavn 1999

JENSEN Edvard Michael 1822-1915 [34]
👁 **$390** - €377 - **£241** - FF2 471
Parti fra Ordrup krat, personer ved et hus Oil/paper/canvas (35x23cm 13x9in) Viby J, Århus 1999

JENSEN George 1878-? [15]
👁 **$1 300** - €1 401 - **£886** - FF9 190
Hill & Stream, Northern Michigan Oil/board (36x45cm 14x18in) Hatfield PA 2001

JENSEN Johan Laurents 1800-1856 [382]
👁 **$17 640** - €20 135 - **£12 255** - FF132 075
Opstilling med vandmelon, blommer og nödder på en karm Oil/canvas (68x56cm 26x22in) Köbenhavn 2000
👁 **$8 855** - €7 394 - **£5 263** - FF48 499
Kamelier Oil/wood (23x30cm 9x11in) Köbenhavn 1998
🖊 **$735** - €817 - **£492** - FF5 358
Ängsblommor Pencil (16x11.5cm 6x4in) Stockholm 2000

JENSEN Karl 1851-1933 [53]
👁 **$4 258** - €3 758 - **£2 539** - FF24 648
Interiör fra Frederiksborgmuseet Oil/canvas (38x45cm 14x17in) Köbenhavn 1998

JENSEN Louis 1858-1908 [24]
👁 **$806** - €938 - **£575** - FF6 152
Parti fra Randers Oil/canvas (52x72cm 20x28in) Köbenhavn 2000

JENSEN Olaf Simony 1864-1923 [80]
👁 **$422** - €363 - **£252** - FF2 380
Krointeriör med munke Oil/canvas (43x50cm 16x19in) Viby J, Århus 1998
👁 **$111** - €94 - **£66** - FF617
Munk med kurv Oil/canvas (41x27cm 16x10in) Viby J, Århus 1998

JENSEN Sören Georg 1917-1982 [12]
🖌 **$1 999** - €2 015 - **£1 246** - FF13 218
Utan titel Bronze (H22cm H8in) Köbenhavn 2000

JENSEN Thomas Martin 1831-1916 [7]
👁 **$7 500** - €6 456 - **£4 451** - FF42 348
Spring/Summer/Fall/Winter Oil/canvas (86.5x61cm 34x24in) Los-Angeles CA 1998

JENSEN Ulf Valde 1945 [8]
📖 **$140** - €162 - **£98** - FF1 063
Figurer i Rom Aquatint in colors (32x24cm 12x9in) Oslo 2000

J

JENSSEN Olav Christopher 1954 [14]
- $1 516 - €1 760 - **£1 047** - FF11 542
  Dedikasjon No.52 Oil/panel (22x24cm 8x9in) Stockholm 2000
- $756 - €873 - **£532** - FF5 728
  En ung mann som antagelig er en violinist er kommet til byen Etching (33x69cm 12x27in) Oslo 2000

JENTSCH Adolph Stephan Fried 1888-1977 [56]
- $26 940 - €23 272 - **£16 245** - FF152 655
  Mountain Landscape on the Edge of the Namib Oil/canvas (100x69cm 39x27in) Johannesburg 1998
- $790 - €683 - **£476** - FF4 477
  A Riverbed, Namibia Oil/canvas (13x28cm 5x11in) Johannesburg 1998
- $637 - €740 - **£440** - FF4 851
  Extensive Landscape, Namibia Watercolour/paper (20.5x32.5cm 8x12in) Johannesburg 2000

JENTZEN Friedrich 1804-1875 [4]
- $1 890 - €2 147 - **£1 322** - FF14 086
  König Friedrich Wilhelm III/Zar Nicolaus I von Russland Lithographie (65x50cm 25x19in) Berlin 2001

JENTZSCH Hans Gabriel 1862-? [15]
- $2 845 - €3 306 - **£2 000** - FF21 688
  Sunday morning Oil/canvas (72x53cm 28x20in) London 2001

JEONG-IM LEE 1971 [5]
- $1 300 - €1 264 - **£793** - FF8 292
  Letter Oil/canvas (19x24cm 7x9in) Tel Aviv 2000

JERACE Francesco 1854-1937 [1]
- $7 464 - €6 492 - **£4 500** - FF42 583
  Bust of a woman Marble (H66cm H25in) London 1998

JERECZEK Chistian 1935 [6]
- $1 566 - €1 687 - **£1 078** - FF11 067
  Kaffeegarten am Starnberger See Öl/Leinwand (60.5x50.5cm 23x19in) München 2001

JERICHAU Harald 1851-1878 [56]
- $2 245 - €2 263 - **£1 400** - FF14 845
  By the Banks of the River Tiber Oil/canvas (33.5x58cm 13x22in) London 2000
- $620 - €537 - **£369** - FF3 521
  Landskabsstudie, Italien Oil/canvas (27.5x40.5cm 10x15in) København 1998

JERICHAU Holger Hvitfeldt 1861-1900 [192]
- $808 - €872 - **£542** - FF5 719
  To gående personer på en vej langs Middelhavskysten Oil/canvas (33x55cm 12x21in) København 2000
- $471 - €555 - **£331** - FF3 643
  Marina grande Capri Oil/panel (22x33cm 8x12in) Malmö 2000

JERICHAU Jens Adolf 1816-1883 [19]
- $2 493 - €2 838 - **£1 752** - FF18 613
  The Bathers Ceramic (H21cm H8in) Woollahra, Sydney 2001

JERICHAU Jens Adolf Emil 1890-1916 [49]
- $54 510 - €61 648 - **£36 846** - FF404 386
  Dante Oil/canvas (155x132cm 61x51in) København 2000
- $379 - €350 - **£226** - FF2 295
  Nature morte med grøntsager Pencil/paper (19x26cm 7x10in) København 1999

JERICHAU-BAUMANN Anna Maria Elisabeth 1819-1881 [85]
- $8 232 - €9 396 - **£5 719** - FF61 635
  En aegypterinde legende med sit lille barn Oil/canvas (98x138cm 38x54in) København 2000
- $2 526 - €2 289 - **£1 575** - FF15 014
  Ung pige i nordsjaellandsk dragt Oil/canvas (51x42cm 20x16in) København 1999
- $912 - €805 - **£544** - FF5 281
  Bedende barn med foldede haender Oil/canvas (33x26cm 12x10in) København 1998
- $2 049 - €2 213 - **£1 415** - FF14 515
  Portraet af den svenske operasangerinde Jenny Lind Pencil (19x21.5cm 7x8in) København 2001

JERKEN Erik 1898-1947 [75]
- $510 - €437 - **£299** - FF2 867
  Landskap med kanal Oil/canvas (72x49cm 28x19in) Stockholm 1998

JERNBERG August 1826-1896 [52]
- $2 106 - €2 005 - **£1 317** - FF13 150
  I ett kök tvenne qvinnor sysslande med rengöring Oil/canvas (51x61cm 20x24in) Stockholm 1999
- $2 380 - €2 764 - **£1 672** - FF18 130
  Stilleben med päron och plommon Oil/panel (35x28cm 13x11in) Stockholm 1999

JERNBERG Olaf August Andreas 1855-1935 [79]
- $1 522 - €1 794 - **£1 069** - FF11 716
  Vinterlandskap med rådjur vid tjärn Oil/canvas (47x61cm 18x24in) Malmö 2000

JERNDORFF August Andreas 1846-1906 [31]
- $718 - €673 - **£447** - FF4 413
  Portraet af Agnete Dyrlund/Portraet af Marie Dyrlund Oil/wood (46x37cm 18x14in) København 1999

JÉROME 1946 [1]
- $6 871 - €6 403 - **£4 237** - FF42 000
  La Naissance Huile/toile (50x40cm 19x15in) Toulon 1999

JERVAS Charles c.1675-1739 [31]
- $9 721 - €9 349 - **£6 000** - FF61 328
  Gentleman, in a red Coat and Waistcoat, with classical Landscape Oil/canvas (127x101.5cm 50x39in) London 1999
- $26 229 - €30 474 - **£18 434** - FF199 896
  Mrs Trevor, seated in a wooded Landscape Oil/canvas (45x38cm 17x14in) Dublin 2001

JERZY Richard XX [90]
- $1 000 - €1 176 - **£717** - FF7 713
  Valentine Oil/masonite (121x121cm 48x48in) Detroit MI 2001
- $1 100 - €1 294 - **£788** - FF8 485
  Still life of sunflowers on blue background Oil/panel (53x81cm 21x32in) Detroit MI 2001
- $800 - €941 - **£573** - FF6 171
  View of East Jordan Oil/board (33x45cm 13x18in) Detroit MI 2001
- $900 - €1 058 - **£645** - FF6 942
  Floral still life with multicolored flowers Watercolour/paper (76x66cm 30x26in) Detroit MI 2001

JESPERS Emile 1862-1918 [11]
- $1 664 - €1 983 - **£1 192** - FF13 008
  Buste Bronze (H46cm H18in) Antwerpen 2000

JESPERS Floris 1889-1965 [1041]
- $5 380 - €4 958 - **£3 240** - FF32 520
  Ferme blanche à Knokke Huile/toile (150x200cm 59x78in) Antwerpen 1999

J

$2 499 - €2 108 - £1 487 - FF13 829
Nature morte aux pommes Huile/toile (65x53cm 25x20in) Antwerpen 1998

$664 - €669 - £413 - FF4 390
Paysage Huile/toile (23.5x34cm 9x13in) Bruxelles 2000

$475 - €446 - £293 - FF2 926
Négresse assise Crayon/papier (65x48cm 25x18in) Antwerpen 1999

$352 - €298 - £210 - FF1 952
Clown musicien Eau-forte (27x20.5cm 10x8in) Antwerpen 1998

JESPERS Oscar 1887-1970 [72]

$11 385 - €13 634 - £7 810 - FF89 430
Stervende soldaat Plâtre (H92cm H36in) Antwerpen 2000

$7 240 - €6 807 - £4 383 - FF44 649
Samenspraak - Dialogue Relief (72.5x72.5cm 28x28in) Amsterdam 1999

JESPERSEN Henrik Gamst 1853-1936 [161]

$711 - €673 - £442 - FF4 414
Motiv fra Det Kongelige Haveselvskab på Frederiksberg Oil/canvas (46x70cm 18x27in) Vejle 1999

JESS Collins 1923 [13]

$12 000 - €12 092 - £7 480 - FF79 320
Cover Design for a Lesbian Estate by Lynn Lonidier Mixed media (42x59.5cm 16x23in) New-York 2000

$25 000 - €25 192 - £15 585 - FF165 250
«Passage of the Black Dove from Thebes to Dodane» Collage (44x52.5cm 17x20in) New-York 2000

JESSEN Carl Ludwig 1833-1917 [18]

$1 640 - €1 877 - £1 141 - FF12 311
Ung syende pige fra Deetzbüll Oil/canvas (35x30cm 13x11in) Köbenhavn 2000

JESSUP Frederick Arthur 1920 [16]

$290 - €305 - £182 - FF2 000
Couple d'oiseaux devant un pont sur la Seine Technique mixte (73x93cm 28x36in) Paris 2000

JETT Wilhelm 1846-1877 [1]

$20 000 - €22 387 - £13 948 - FF146 850
Day of Leisure Oil/canvas (87x137cm 34x53in) New-York 2001

JETTEL Eugen 1845-1901 [54]

$28 000 - €26 873 - £17 553 - FF176 274
Horses Watering in a Country Village Oil/panel (51x79cm 20x31in) New-York 1999

$3 013 - €2 761 - £1 843 - FF18 114
Viehweide in Holland Öl/Leinwand (40x25.5cm 15x10in) Wien 2001

$1 986 - €2 180 - £1 278 - FF14 301
Die Ebene bei Cayeux mit Strohtristen Pastell/Papier (40x59.5cm 15x23in) Wien 2000

JETTMAR Rudolf 1869-1939 [23]

$927 - €1 090 - £664 - FF7 150
Jagdszene Öl/Leinwand (44x66cm 17x25in) Wien 2001

$2 877 - €3 272 - £2 010 - FF21 465
Amoretten in italienischer Landschaft Mischtechnik (32.5x45cm 12x17in) München 2000

JEWELS Mary c.1900-c.1965 [8]

$5 611 - €6 689 - £4 000 - FF43 875
Cornubia Oil/canvas (76x51cm 29x20in) London 2001

JEWETT Maud Sherwood 1873-1953 [11]

$7 000 - €8 207 - £5 035 - FF53 837
Flower Holder Bronze (H26.5cm H10in) New-York 2001

JEX Garnet W. 1895-1979 [37]

$2 200 - €2 376 - £1 520 - FF15 584
Georgetown Freeway Oil/canvas (45.5x76cm 17x29in) Bethesda MD 2001

$2 100 - €2 268 - £1 451 - FF14 876
The canal at Fletcher's Oil/board (35.5x40.5cm 13x15in) Bethesda MD 2001

JIANG BAOLING 1781-1840 [1]

$2 322 - €2 190 - £1 440 - FF14 364
Flower and Rock Ink (131x30.5cm 51x12in) Hong-Kong 1999

JIANG CHANGYI 1943 [14]

$20 656 - €17 447 - £12 400 - FF114 448
Lingering Melody Oil/canvas (105.5x87cm 41x34in) Hong-Kong 1998

JIANG GUOFANG 1951 [5]

$45 150 - €42 371 - £27 895 - FF277 935
Forbidden City in Silence Oil/canvas (180x160cm 70x62in) Hong-Kong 1999

JIANG HANTING 1903-1963 [11]

$6 420 - €7 010 - £4 130 - FF45 985
Insects an Summer Plants Ink (107x51cm 42x20in) Hong-Kong 2000

JIANG JIE XVIII [1]

$5 405 - €5 126 - £3 288 - FF33 625
Flowers Ink (24x31.5cm 9x12in) Hong-Kong 1999

JIANG TINGXI 1669-1732 [7]

$3 205 - €3 641 - £2 250 - FF23 882
Flowers, Bird and Butterfly Ink (19x55cm 7x21in) Hong-Kong 2000

JIANG ZHAOHE 1904 [1]

$3 333 - €3 786 - £2 340 - FF24 837
Homework Ink (53x35cm 20x13in) Hong-Kong 2001

JIAO BINGZHEN 1606-c.1687 [3]

$192 600 - €210 311 - £123 900 - FF1 379 550
Auspicious Celebration of the Dragon Bopat Festival Ink (19x14.5cm 7x5in) Hong-Kong 2000

JIAQING Emperor 1796-1820 [1]

$6 420 - €7 010 - £4 130 - FF45 985
Poem in Kai Shu Ink (131x54cm 51x21in) Hong-Kong 2000

JIDÉE XX [7]

$1 856 - €2 134 - £1 310 - FF14 000
«37.2 C» Bronze (40x22cm 15x8in) Barbizon 2001

JIDÉHEM (Jean De Mesmaeker) 1935 [8]

$681 - €793 - £480 - FF5 203
Starter, dans une Fiat 600 Dessin (15x23cm 5x9in) Bruxelles 2001

JIJÉ (Joseph Gillain) 1914-1980 [40]

$1 036 - €991 - £631 - FF6 500
Le retour de Valhardi, pour la pl. n°28 Encre Chine/papier (40x32cm 15x12in) Paris 1999

JILEK Karel 1896-1983 [11]

$1 184 - €1 121 - £738 - FF7 351
Femmes se reposant Huile/carton (37x50cm 14x19in) Praha 2001

JIMENEZ FERNANDEZ Federico 1841-c.1910 [27]

$9 150 - €9 010 - £5 700 - FF59 100
Conejos Oleo/lienzo (62x88cm 24x34in) Madrid 1999

$2 405 - €2 228 - £1 480 - FF14 615
Gallinero Oleo/tabla (13x22cm 5x8in) Madrid 1998

JIMENEZ Y ARANDA José 1837-1903 [81]
$54 585 - €45 849 - £32 000 - FF300 752
The Go-Between Oil/panel (45x56cm 17x22in) London 1998
$14 000 - €12 013 - £8 600 - FF78 800
Desnudo Oleo/tabla (33x19.5cm 12x7in) Madrid 1998
$1 920 - €1 802 - £1 200 - FF11 820
Escena del Quijote Aguada/papel (17.5x24cm 6x9in) Madrid 1999

JIMENEZ Y ARANDA Luis 1845-1928 [68]
$109 171 - €105 321 - £69 000 - FF690 862
The Violin Audition Oil/canvas (51.5x93cm 20x36in) London 1999
$4 800 - €4 505 - £2 925 - FF29 550
Campesina de los Evelynes (Isle de France) Oleo/tabla (48x28cm 18x11in) Madrid 1999
$1 040 - €1 201 - £720 - FF7 880
Escapando Aguada/papel (33x26cm 12x10in) Madrid 2000

JIMENEZ Y MARTIN Juan 1858-1901 [15]
$952 - €1 021 - £646 - FF6 698
«Avila» Oleo/tabla (15x23.5cm 5x9in) Madrid 2001
$4 000 - €4 701 - £2 773 - FF30 837
The Mandolin Serenade Watercolour (54x39cm 21x15in) New-York 2000

JIMENEZ Y PRIETO Manuel 1848-1904 [13]
$16 001 - €15 886 - £10 000 - FF104 207
An attentive audience Oil/panel (48x34.5cm 18x13in) London 1999
$5 440 - €5 106 - £3 400 - FF33 490
El recital Oleo/tabla (34.5x44cm 13x17in) Madrid 1999

JIN CHENG 1878-1926 [16]
$3 846 - €4 574 - £2 649 - FF30 003
Misty Landscape Ink (33x198cm 12x77in) Hong-Kong 2000

JIN JIAZHEN 1964 [1]
$10 256 - €12 197 - £7 064 - FF80 008
Korean Girl Oil/canvas (120x25cm 47x9in) Hong-Kong 2000

JIN JUNMING 1602-1675 [2]
$16 666 - €18 932 - £11 700 - FF124 189
Snow on Yaotai Ink (131x52cm 51x20in) Hong-Kong 2001

JIN LAN 1841-1909 [1]
$2 322 - €2 190 - £1 440 - FF14 364
Appreciating Painting in a Studio Ink/paper (30x249.5cm 11x98in) Hong-Kong 1999

JIN LIYING 1772-1807 [1]
$3 225 - €3 026 - £1 992 - FF19 852
Butterflies and Chrysanthemum Ink (105.5x37cm 41x14in) Hong-Kong 1999

JIN NONG 1687-1764 [25]
$15 468 - €16 909 - £9 924 - FF110 916
«Horse and Groom» Ink (54x76cm 21x29in) Hong-Kong 2000

JIN RUNZO Chin Jun-tso 1922-1983 [1]
$48 336 - €44 794 - £30 051 - FF293 832
Golden Roses Oil/canvas (45x36.5cm 17x14in) Taipei 1999

JIN TINGBIAO ?-1767 [1]
$109 395 - €105 743 - £66 555 - FF680 510
Crossing Bridge Ink (129.5x64.5cm 50x25in) Hong-Kong 1999

JIRA Josef 1929 [35]
$867 - €820 - £540 - FF5 379
Radobil Huile/toile (50x60cm 19x23in) Praha 2000

JIRANEK Milos 1875-1911 [11]
$7 947 - €7 517 - £4 950 - FF49 307
Fossé de cerf Huile/toile (68x82cm 26x32in) Praha 2000
$895 - €847 - £558 - FF5 558
Grande maison Huile/carton (21x26.5cm 8x10in) Praha 2000

JIRASEK Vaclav 1965 [11]
$511 - €509 - £317 - FF3 336
Christus Photograph (13.5x37.6cm 5x14in) Wien 1999

JIRINCOVA-NOVAKOVA Ludmila 1912-1994 [38]
$895 - €847 - £558 - FF5 558
Korab Tempera/carton (22x30cm 8x11in) Praha 2000
$57 - €55 - £36 - FF358
Visage de femme Lithographie (19x13.5cm 7x5in) Praha 2000

JIRLOW Lennart 1936 [474]
$330 33 - €35 193 - £20 940 - FF230 850
Växthuset i byn Oil/canvas (152x185cm 59x72in) Stockholm 2000
$9 604 - €11 144 - £6 631 - FF73 102
Målaren i ateljén Oil/canvas (50x61cm 19x24in) Stockholm 2000
$3 360 - €3 262 - £2 074 - FF21 400
Interiör med kortspelare Oil/canvas (33x24cm 12x9in) Stockholm 1999
$3 488 - €4 148 - £2 487 - FF27 212
Skulptören Bronze (H59cm H23in) Stockholm 2000
$3 707 - €3 486 - £2 297 - FF22 868
Fruktförsäljare Gouache/paper (32x23cm 12x9in) Stockholm 1999
$540 - €504 - £333 - FF3 304
Trädgårdsmästaren Color lithograph (39x27cm 15x10in) Stockholm 1999

JIROUDEK Frantisek 1915-1991 [40]
$462 - €437 - £288 - FF2 868
Nature morte aux sorbes, alisés Huile/toile (50x70cm 19x27in) Praha 2000

JIRU Vaclav 1910-1980 [10]
$708 - €665 - £437 - FF4 360
Sonnenbad Vintage gelatin silver print (18x13cm 7x5in) Köln 1999

JOACHIM Jean 1905-1990 [11]
$2 483 - €2 897 - £1 744 - FF19 000
Le grand-duc Grès (34x11.5x14cm 13x4x5in) Pontoise 2000

JOANES de Joan c.1510-1579 [3]
$56 000 - €48 052 - £33 600 - FF315 200
San Miguel y el Dragon Oleo/tabla (170x140cm 66x55in) Madrid 1998
$192 000 - €180 195 - £120 000 - FF1 182 000
Adoración de Los Magos Oleo/tabla (91x61cm 35x24in) Madrid 1999

JOANNON-NAVIER Etienne Albert 1857-? [4]
$13 113 - €12 056 - £8 100 - FF79 083
«Le lever» Oil/canvas (116x168cm 45x66in) Vejle 1998
$7 500 - €6 348 - £4 489 - FF41 643
A Rainy Day in Paris Oil/panel (40x32cm 15x12in) New-York 1998

JOANOVITCH Paul 1859-1957 [13]
$175 142 - €169 580 - £110 000 - FF1 112 375
The Snake Charmer Oil/canvas (107.5x83cm 42x32in) London 1999

JOB Charles 1853-1930 **[8]**
[icon] **$1 100** – €1 034 – **£681** – FF6 784
Rustic Interiors, Woodland and Lakeside Vistas in England and Normandy Carbon print (35x24cm 14x9in) New-York 1999

JOB J-M. Onfray de Brév. 1858-1931 **[22]**
$4 500 – €4 115 – **£2 748** – FF26 994
At the entrance to the circus Oil/canvas (145x75cm 57x29in) New-York 1998
$601 – €686 – **£419** – FF4 500
Tambour et officier Aquarelle (30x23cm 11x9in) Paris 2001

JOBBÉ-DUVAL Gaston 1856-? **[4]**
$509 – €579 – **£353** – FF3 800
«Excursions en Normandie et Bretagne» Affiche (106x75cm 41x29in) Paris 2000

JOBBINS William H. XIX **[1]**
$2 103 – €1 973 – **£1 300** – FF12 940
Il Traghetto di S.M. Zobenigo, Venezia Oil/panel (22x15cm 8x5in) London 1999

JOBERT Fernand 1876-1949 **[47]**
$325 – €320 – **£196** – FF2 100
Paysage de Bretagne Aquarelle (16x26cm 6x10in) Paris 2000

JOBERT Paul C.F. 1863-? **[13]**
$4 589 – €5 458 – **£3 272** – FF35 800
Barques de pêche et l'Amirauté d'Alger Huile/toile (63x73cm 23x28in) Neuilly-sur-Seine 2000

JOBLING Robert 1841-1923 **[85]**
$7 640 – €6 299 – **£4 500** – FF41 322
«The Voice of Spring» Oil/canvas (91.5x122cm 36x48in) Tyne & Wear 1998
$3 885 – €4 170 – **£2 600** – FF27 356
Sunset in the Harbour Oil/canvas (30x50cm 11x19in) Bath 2000
$178 – €211 – **£130** – FF1 387
Earsdon Farm, Nr.Beehive» Watercolour/paper (16.5x23.5cm 6x9in) Newcastle-upon-Tyne 2001

JOBSON John 1941 **[13]**
$5 681 – €6 095 – **£3 874** – FF39 979
Evening Shadow, Var Oil/board (122x91.5cm 48x36in) Dublin 2001
$1 180 – €1 270 – **£804** – FF8 329
Whitethorn Oil/board (25x30cm 9x11in) Dublin 2001

JOCHAMS Hyacinth XIX **[4]**
$4 373 – €4 086 – **£2 698** – FF26 800
Cheval Bourbonnais Huile/panneau (80x118cm 31x46in) Riom 1999

JOCHEMS Frans 1880-1949 **[10]**
$780 – €744 – **£474** – FF4 878
Le débardeur Bronze (H70cm H27in) Bruxelles 1999

JOCHIMS Reimer 1934 **[37]**
$2 381 – €2 556 – **£1 594** – FF16 769
Schwarzlicht No.8 Acrylic/panel (35x35cm 13x13in) Köln 2000

JODE de Gerhard 1509-1591 **[16]**
$914 – €1 067 – **£645** – FF7 000
Scènes de l'Ancien Testament Burin (20x24.5cm 7x9in) Paris 2000

JODE de Pieter I c.1570-1634 **[23]**
$333 – €358 – **£223** – FF2 347
Abendliche Gesellschaft beim Musizieren Kupferstich (15.4x19.8cm 6x7in) Berlin 2000

JODE de Pieter II de Jonghe 1606-c.1674 **[12]**
$358 – €409 – **£250** – FF2 683
Rinaldo und Armida, nach Anton van Dyck Kupferstich (61x42cm 24x16in) Berlin 2001

JODELET Charles Emmanuel 1883-1969 **[89]**
$568 – €610 – **£380** – FF4 000
Les marins douarneniste au bistrot Huile/toile (22x27cm 8x10in) Douarnenez 2000
$134 – €145 – **£90** – FF950
Les quais de Douarnenez Fusain/papier (22x30cm 8x11in) Douarnenez 2000

JODLOWSKI Tadeusz 1925 **[2]**
$900 – €768 – **£542** – FF5 036
«Swieto Lotnictwa Polskiego» Poster (99.5x69cm 39x27in) New-York 1998

JOE Oreland C. 1958 **[6]**
$4 000 – €4 542 – **£2 779** – FF29 792
Taunting the Soldiers Alabaster (48x33x22cm 19x13x9in) Dallas TX 2001

JOENSEN-MIKINES Samuel 1906-1979 **[135]**
$6 384 – €6 193 – **£4 020** – FF40 622
Skibe ved en kyst Oil/canvas (100x134cm 39x52in) København 1999
$4 102 – €3 770 – **£2 520** – FF24 729
Skt. Hansbål Oil/canvas (80x100cm 31x39in) København 1999
$933 – €940 – **£581** – FF6 168
Bibelsk scene med Jesus på havet Watercolour (22x26.5cm 8x10in) København 2000

JOëTS Jules 1884-1959 **[44]**
$376 – €427 – **£261** – FF2 800
Chemin du Tourniquet Aquarelle/papier (19x31cm 7x12in) Saint-Omer 2001

JOFFE Chantal 1969 **[2]**
$5 288 – €4 519 – **£3 200** – FF29 640
Children Mixed media/board (29x21.5cm 11x8in) London 1998

JOFFE Mark / Mordechai 1864-1941 **[3]**
$12 000 – €14 346 – **£8 245** – FF94 104
View of a Lithuanian Synagogue on Kol Nidre Watercolour (45x33cm 17x12in) Tel Aviv 2000

JOHANNESSEN Erik Harry 1902-1980 **[55]**
$2 339 – €2 592 – **£1 587** – FF17 003
Søsken Oil/canvas (70x100cm 27x39in) Oslo 2000
$378 – €437 – **£266** – FF2 864
Søsken Gouache/paper (27x40cm 10x15in) Oslo 2000
$216 – €249 – **£152** – FF1 636
Landskap Woodcut in colors (30x40cm 11x15in) Oslo 2000

JOHANNESSEN Jens 1934 **[53]**
$51 504 – €60 070 – **£35 856** – FF394 032
Flora og maleren på parnasset Oil/canvas (140x140cm 55x55in) Oslo 2000
$16 095 – €18 772 – **£11 205** – FF123 135
Röd maskerade Oil/canvas (60x60cm 23x23in) Oslo 2000
$6 281 – €6 972 – **£4 377** – FF45 731
«Mordet på Ovrevoll» Oil/canvas (33x41cm 12x16in) Oslo 2001
$702 – €811 – **£494** – FF5 319
Landskap Gouache/paper (24x17cm 9x6in) Oslo 2000
$287 – €322 – **£199** – FF2 110
Kvinne og mann Linocut (30x19cm 11x7in) Oslo 2001

JOHANNESSON Sture XX [7]
$285 - €332 - £203 - FF2 175
«The underground will take over...» Poster
(85x62cm 33x24in) Stockholm 2001

JOHANNOT Tony 1803-1852 [21]
$240 - €274 - £167 - FF1 800
Jeunes Italiennes remerciant le Général
Bonaparte Crayon/papier (8x12cm 3x4in) Paris 2001

JOHANSEN Albert 1890-1975 [9]
$1 826 - €2 045 - £1 268 - FF13 415
Norddeutsche Hochsommerlandschaft mit
Heufeldern und Gehöft Öl/Karton (50x65cm
19x25in) Oersberg-bei Kappeln 2001

JOHANSEN Axel 1872-1938 [49]
$728 - €670 - £450 - FF4 393
Opstilling med frugter og blomster Oil/canvas
(48x42cm 18x16in) Vejle 1998

JOHANSEN John Christian 1876-1964 [11]
$4 400 - €4 116 - £2 666 - FF26 999
October Sear and Gold Oil/canvas (101x101cm
40x40in) Chicago IL 1999
$1 200 - €1 365 - £832 - FF8 952
Venice Oil/board (25x25cm 10x10in) Cincinnati OH
2000

JOHANSEN Svend 1890-1970 [59]
$1 758 - €1 616 - £1 080 - FF10 598
Opstilling med blomster på bord Oil/canvas
(81x65cm 31x25in) København 1999
$254 - €215 - £152 - FF1 410
Kostumeudkast (Teater) Gouache/paper (55x42cm
21x16in) København 1998

JOHANSEN Viggo 1851-1935 [196]
$1 196 - €1 342 - £829 - FF8 803
Kystparti, Refsnaes Oil/canvas (66x98cm 25x38in)
København 2000
$1 152 - €1 340 - £822 - FF8 789
Portraet af Lise Kruse Oil/canvas (40x35cm
15x13in) København 2000
$1 034 - €1 140 - £690 - FF7 476
Portraet af fire drenge Oil chalks/paper (23x54cm
9x21in) Vejle 2000

JOHANSSON Albert 1926-1998 [169]
$797 - €963 - £556 - FF6 319
Målning, abstrakt komposition Oil/panel
(91x122cm 35x48in) Stockholm 2000

JOHANSSON Arvid 1862-1923 [40]
$564 - €540 - £355 - FF3 539
Segelfartyg på öppet hav Oil/canvas (80x53cm
31x20in) Stockholm 1999

JOHANSSON Carl August 1863-1944 [184]
$1 860 - €1 686 - £1 146 - FF11 061
Landskap med insjö Oil/canvas (54x76cm 21x29in)
Stockholm 1999
$933 - €1 036 - £624 - FF6 797
Sommar, utsikt över Ångermanälven Oil/panel
(32x46cm 12x18in) Stockholm 2000

JOHANSSON Eric 1896-1979 [23]
$442 - €486 - £300 - FF3 186
Paar in Umarmung Charcoal (42.7x33cm 16x12in)
Berlin 2000

JOHANSSON Helge 1886-1926 [12]
$3 614 - €4 050 - £2 519 - FF26 566
Gård med blommande fruktträd Oil/canvas
(50x60cm 19x23in) Stockholm 2001

JOHANSSON Johan 1879-1951 [54]
$663 - €614 - £405 - FF4 028
Träd i strandkant, motiv från Skåne Oil/canvas
(49x63cm 19x24in) Uppsala 1998

JOHANSSON Stefan 1876-1955 [27]
$4 296 - €4 991 - £3 019 - FF32 742
Interior Oil/canvas/board (64x48cm 25x18in)
Amsterdam 2001
$4 968 - €5 357 - £3 334 - FF35 140
Utsikt från ett fönster Oil/canvas (40x30cm 15x11in)
Stockholm 2000
$2 710 - €3 002 - £1 837 - FF19 690
Regndis Watercolour (25x28cm 9x11in) Göteborg
2000

JOHANSSON Sven Erik 1924 [19]
$1 842 - €1 731 - £1 110 - FF11 353
Vertikal karneval Oil/canvas (99x69cm 38x27in)
Stockholm 1999

JOHANSSON VON CÖLN Anders 1663-1716 [2]
$26 901 - €29 869 - £18 007 - FF195 926
Karl XII till häst vid slaget vid Düna Oil/canvas
(175x137cm 68x53in) Stockholm 2000

JOHANSSON-THOR Emil 1889-1958 [71]
$861 - €743 - £518 - FF4 874
«Ödekyrkan, Hven» Oil/canvas (48x62cm 18x24in)
Malmö 1998

JOHFRA 1919-1998 [14]
$6 135 - €6 989 - £4 238 - FF45 843
Die Stadt Oil/panel (41x53cm 16x20in) Zürich 2000

JOHN Augustus Edwin 1878-1961 [565]
$28 056 - €33 444 - £20 000 - FF219 376
In Memorium Amadeo Modigliani Oil/canvas
(127x101.5cm 50x39in) London 2000
$8 219 - €8 823 - £5 500 - FF57 873
The Little Railway, Martigues Oil/canvas
(53.5x73cm 21x28in) London 2000
$9 118 - €10 870 - £6 500 - FF71 301
Portrait of Bapsy, Marchioness of Winchester
Oil/canvas (23.5x43cm 9x16in) London 2000
$2 416 - €2 224 - £1 450 - FF14 588
At the Piano Ink (33.5x23cm 13x9in) Glamorgan
1999
$419 - €447 - £280 - FF2 935
Benjamin Evans Etching (13x10.5cm 5x4in) London
2000

JOHN Gwendolen Mary, Gwen 1876-1939 [76]
$4 871 - €4 805 - £3 000 - FF31 522
House at Twilight Watercolour (23x30.5cm 9x12in)
London 1999

JOHN Paul W. 1887-1966 [40]
$371 - €411 - £252 - FF2 699
Geschirrstilleben auf dem Wochenmarkt Vintage
gelatin silver print (21.7x17.2cm 8x6in) Berlin 2000

JOHN Robert Brown XX [6]
$1 136 - €1 311 - £800 - FF8 600
«Goldfinger» Poster (56x71cm 22x27in) London 2000

JOHN Sara 1946 [4]
$3 831 - €3 527 - £2 300 - FF23 133
Priddbwll Valley Oil/canvas (93x123cm 36x48in)
Glamorgan 2000

JOHN Vivien 1916-1994 [17]
$348 - €392 - £240 - FF2 574
Landscape with Trees Oil/board (49.5x26cm
19x10in) Newbury, Berkshire 2000

JOHN William Goscombe 1860-1952 **[12]**

$14 155 - €16 414 - **£10 000** - FF107 669
Bust of Sir William Hesketh Lever later 1st Viscount Leverhulme Marble (H174cm H68in) London 2001

$1 415 - €1 641 - **£1 000** - FF10 766
Bust of the Elizabeth Ellen Hulme, Lady Lever Sculpture (H53cm H20in) London 2001

JOHNS Jasper 1930 **[903]**

$6 500 000 - €6 118 823 - **£4 015 700** - FF40 136 850
Two Flags Oil/canvas (133x176.5cm 52x69in) New-York 1999

$10 500 - €10 885 - **£6 300** - FF71 400
Bread Tecnica mista (58.5x43cm 23x16in) Prato 2000

$580 000 - €649 643 - **£442 984** - FF4 261 376
Green Target Mixed media (21.5x21.5cm 8x8in) New-York 2001

$17 000 - €18 248 - **£11 376** - FF119 697
Light Bulb, from Lead Reliefs Relief (99x43cm 38x16in) Beverly-Hills CA 2000

$24 000 - €23 110 - **£15 007** - FF151 591
High School Days, from Lead Reliefs Relief (58x43cm 22x16in) Beverly-Hills CA 1999

$600 000 - €696 174 - **£414 240** - FF4 566 600
Green Flag Graphite (20x24.5cm 7x9in) New-York 2000

$6 000 - €6 720 - **£4 168** - FF44 083
Ventriloquist Color lithograph (84.5x56.5cm 33x22in) New-York 2001

JOHNSON Andrew XX **[12]**

$1 696 - €1 879 - **£1 150** - FF12 325
«Orient Cruises» Poster (102x64cm 40x25in) London 2000

JOHNSON Arnrid Banniza 1895-? **[1]**

$3 400 - €3 270 - **£2 098** - FF21 447
Regent Park Poster (101x127cm 39x50in) New-York 1999

JOHNSON Charles Edward 1832-1913 **[26]**

$666 - €737 - **£462** - FF4 834
Skotsk klippekyst med sæler Oil/canvas (35x59cm 13x23in) København 2001

JOHNSON Clarence Raymond 1894-1981 **[7]**

$11 000 - €10 303 - **£6 762** - FF67 585
New hope Oil/canvas (60x71cm 24x28in) Chester Heights PA 1999

JOHNSON David 1827-1908 **[109]**

$20 000 - €21 888 - **£13 796** - FF143 576
Esopus River Landscape, Hurly, New York Oil/canvas (35.5x61cm 13x24in) New-York 2001

$9 000 - €10 634 - **£6 378** - FF69 757
Hudson river Landscape Oil/panel (20x31cm 7x12in) Boston MA 2000

JOHNSON Eastman 1824-1906 **[70]**

$2 750 - €2 500 - **£1 687** - FF16 398
Portrait of a Young Gentleman Oil/canvas (53x43cm 21x17in) Nantucket MA 1998

$45 000 - €48 176 - **£30 622** - FF316 017
Preparing Breakfast Oil/board (31x23cm 12x9in) Portsmouth NH 2001

JOHNSON Edward Killingworth 1825-1896 **[32]**

$4 500 - €5 095 - **£3 200** - FF33 423
Expectations Watercolour (66x42cm 25x16in) London 2001

JOHNSON Francis Hans 1888-1949 **[4]**

$672 - €789 - **£477** - FF5 178
Old Fort Metagami Watercolour/board (13x18cm 5x7in) Toronto 2000

JOHNSON Francis Norton 1878-1931 **[13]**

$3 976 - €4 269 - **£2 660** - FF28 000
Jeune femme à la corbeille de fleurs Huile/toile (50x61cm 19x24in) Paris 2000

JOHNSON Frank Tenney 1874-1939 **[88]**

$310 000 - €296 348 - **£194 308** - FF1 943 917
Twilight Rendezvous Oil/canvas (101.5x127cm 39x50in) New-York 1999

$55 000 - €49 998 - **£33 126** - FF327 965
Runaway Buckboard Oil/board (53x83cm 21x33in) Hayden ID 1998

$15 000 - €16 462 - **£9 658** - FF107 982
Navajo Oil/canvas/board (29x21.5cm 11x8in) Beverly-Hills CA 2000

$55 000 - €58 971 - **£36 388** - FF386 826
The Stillness of Night Watercolour/paper (66x40cm 26x16in) Hayden ID 2000

JOHNSON Harry John 1826-1884 **[61]**

$599 - €512 - **£360** - FF3 360
Palanza Watercolour/paper (28x46cm 11x18in) Little-Lane, Ilkley 1998

JOHNSON Harvey W. 1920 **[14]**

$8 000 - €9 084 - **£5 558** - FF59 584
The War no Buffler, no Meat Oil/board (60x86cm 24x34in) Dallas TX 2001

JOHNSON James 1803-1834 **[4]**

$520 - €7 849 - **£5 200** - FF51 485
Lower Berkley Place from Clifton, Bristol Watercolour (33x30cm 12x11in) London 1998

JOHNSON James E. 1810-1858 **[1]**

$7 000 - €5 997 - **£4 208** - FF39 337
The Clark Children of Spencetown, New York Oil/canvas (40x68cm 16x27in) Cleveland OH 1998

JOHNSON Joshua XVIII-XIX **[2]**

$2 700 - €2 643 - **£1 661** - FF17 337
Portrait of a Black Man Watercolour/paper (12x10cm 5x4in) Columbia SC 1999

JOHNSON Kåre Espolin 1907-1994 **[76]**

$1 653 - €1 835 - **£1 152** - FF12 034
Vikingskip Mixed media (30x44cm 11x17in) Oslo 2001

$7 365 - €6 223 - **£4 422** - FF40 818
Grankonglelek Mixed media/paper (33x41cm 12x16in) Oslo 1998

$1 270 - €1 423 - **£883** - FF9 336
Helgeland Serigraph (28x21cm 11x8in) Oslo 2001

JOHNSON Keith XX **[52]**

$136 - €164 - **£95** - FF1 078
Brooke Mere Watercolour/paper (35x50cm 14x20in) Aylsham, Norfolk 2000

JOHNSON Ken 1950 **[19]**

$7 147 - €8 019 - **£4 953** - FF52 601
Terracotta Acrylic/canvas (148x138cm 58x54in) Sydney 2000

JOHNSON Larry 1956 **[2]**

$1 790 - €1 942 - **£1 100** - FF11 430
Untitled (Fella) Photograph in colour (167.5x122cm 65x48in) London 1999

JOHNSON Lester 1919 **[62]**

$1 000 - €1 110 - **£697** - FF7 281
Head Oil/canvas (49.5x51cm 19x20in) New-York 2001

$2 500 - €2 113 - **£1 491** - FF13 858
At the Bar Oil/board (31x40.5cm 12x15in) San-Francisco CA 1998

JOHNSON Marshall 1850-1921 [33]
$6 000 - €6 611 - **£4 002** - FF43 363
Clipper Ship Marco Polo Entering the Bay of Fundy Oil/canvas (71x121cm 28x48in) Portsmouth NH 2000
$4 250 - €4 598 - **£2 911** - FF30 159
Two Men in a Dory, Sailboats at Sea Oil/canvas (25x35cm 10x14in) Thomaston ME 2001

JOHNSON Michael 1938 [32]
$16 837 - €15 832 - **£10 426** - FF103 849
Dangar Oil/canvas (182.5x152.5cm 71x60in) Melbourne 1999
$1 715 - €1 841 - **£1 148** - FF12 078
Ci Lun Oil/paper (75.5x56.5cm 29x22in) Melbourne 2000

JOHNSON Nevill 1911-1998 [17]
$2 051 - €2 127 - **£1 300** - FF13 949
Figure in Moon Park Oil/board (45x53cm 18x21in) Belfast 2000
$1 837 - €1 778 - **£1 132** - FF11 660
Landscape Oil/board (27.5x47cm 10x18in) Dublin 1999

JOHNSON Neville T. XIX [2]
$3 250 - €3 599 - **£2 204** - FF23 609
On the Androscoggin River - Near Bethel, Me Oil/board (24x44cm 9x17in) New-York 2000

JOHNSON Patty, née Townsend XIX-XX [19]
$1 216 - €1 177 - **£750** - FF7 719
Country Cottage Watercolour/paper (24x31.5cm 9x12in) London 1999

JOHNSON Ray 1927-1994 [15]
$3 000 - €3 497 - **£2 077** - FF22 939
Woman About to Be Slugged by Russian Oil/canvas (83x53cm 33x21in) New-York 2000
$1 820 - €2 042 - **£1 261** - FF13 394
Eyelash Arthur Craven Collage/board (30x12.5cm 11x4in) Amsterdam 2000

JOHNSON Robert 1890-1964 [155]
$2 178 - €2 443 - **£1 512** - FF16 026
Bush Road Oil/canvas (37x44.5cm 14x17in) Melbourne 2000
$1 229 - €1 167 - **£767** - FF7 656
View to the River Oil/board (23x32cm 9x12in) Sydney 1999

JOHNSON Samuel Frost 1835-? [2]
$8 000 - €8 292 - **£5 072** - FF54 395
The Dilemma Oil/panel (27x20cm 10x7in) New-York 2000

JOHNSON Sargent Claude 1888-1967 [2]
$3 000 - €3 466 - **£2 100** - FF22 734
Animal Abstraction, Horse Stone (H14cm H5in) New-York 2001

JOHNSON Sydney Yates XIX-XX [172]
$591 - €669 - **£400** - FF4 389
Country Landscape, with Cottage and Figures in the foreground Oil/canvas (49.5x74.5cm 19x29in) London 2000
$418 - €449 - **£280** - FF2 946
Highland Landscapes Oil/canvas (23x34cm 9x13in) Little-Lane, Ilkley 2000
$87 - €98 - **£60** - FF643
Sheep in a Highland Landscape Watercolour (25x36cm 9x14in) London 2000

JOHNSON Tim 1947 [42]
$1 143 - €1 228 - **£765** - FF8 052
Two Bob Acrylic/canvas (61x91cm 24x35in) Sydney 2000

JOHNSON Willes XIX [1]
$2 540 - €2 727 - **£1 700** - FF17 886
Coastal views Oil/canvas (31x39cm 12x15in) London 2000

JOHNSSON August 1873-1900 [6]
$782 - €752 - **£483** - FF4 936
Flicka vid fönster Oil/canvas (24x28cm 9x11in) Malmö 1999

JOHNSSON Ivar 1885-1970 [15]
$604 - €691 - **£425** - FF4 530
Kvinna vid havet Bronze (H42cm H16in) Stockholm 2001

JOHNSTON Alexander 1815-1891 [12]
$441 - €521 - **£310** - FF3 415
Uniformsklädd man Oil/canvas (49x33cm 19x12in) Malmö 2000
$2 014 - €2 257 - **£1 400** - FF14 803
The trysting place Oil/canvas (45.5x34.5cm 17x13in) London 2001

JOHNSTON Alfred Cheney 1884-1971 [43]
$800 - €770 - **£500** - FF5 053
Old Gold Advertisement Gelatin silver print (18x13.5cm 7x5in) New-York 1999

JOHNSTON David 1946 [20]
$5 962 - €4 959 - **£3 500** - FF32 527
«Buffon's Macaw -Ara, ambigua» Oil/panel (41x76cm 16x29in) London 1998
$664 - €733 - **£450** - FF4 806
Calcutua Leadbeateri Watercolour (48x68.5cm 18x26in) London 2000

JOHNSTON David Claypoole 1799-1865 [6]
$3 500 - €3 975 - **£2 395** - FF26 072
Self Portrait Oil/canvas/board (71.5x51.5cm 28x20in) New-York 2000
$14 000 - €12 925 - **£8 610** - FF84 782
Bee Catching Watercolour/paper (25x34cm 9x13in) New-York 1999

JOHNSTON Frank (Franz) Hans 1888-1949 [153]
$5 192 - €4 390 - **£3 104** - FF28 797
The Poetry of Winter Oil/board (63.5x76cm 25x29in) Toronto 1998
$2 365 - €2 278 - **£1 468** - FF14 945
The Doctor in the North Oil/board (30.5x40.5cm 12x15in) Toronto 1999
$1 298 - €1 468 - **£913** - FF9 630
Georgian Bay, First Snow Watercolour/paper (19.5x14.5cm 7x5in) Vancouver, BC. 2001

JOHNSTON Harry Hamilton c.1866-1927 [4]
$10 594 - €9 632 - **£6 500** - FF63 185
The Garden of the British Consulate, Tunis - La Villa Marsa Oil/canvas (53.5x21cm 21x8in) London 1999

JOHNSTON John 1753-1818 [3]
$7 200 - €6 522 - **£4 406** - FF42 781
Portrait of Mrs. Nathaniel Gardner Oil/canvas (76x63cm 30x25in) Portland ME 1998

JOHNSTON Reuben Le Grand 1850-1914 [18]
$1 100 - €1 249 - **£752** - FF8 193
Sunny Meadow Landscape with Heards of Sheep Oil/canvas (31x50cm 12x19in) Windsor CT 2000

J

J

JOHNSTON Ynez 1920 [18]

✎ **$1 400** - €1 590 - **£958** - FF10 427
Umbrian City Watercolour, gouache (53x37cm 20x14in) New-York 2000

⬚ **$224** - €194 - **£135** - FF1 271
«**Inhabited World**» Etching, aquatint in colors (45.5x29cm 17x11in) New-York 1998

JOHNSTONE George Whitton 1849-1901 [18]

😊 **$1 363** - €1 520 - **£920** - FF9 970
The Stile at Gilnockie Road, Canonbie, at Which Drs.Chalmers Oil/canvas (30x45cm 11x17in) Edinburgh 2000

JOHNSTONE Henry James 1835-1907 [31]

😊 **$55 318** - €60 410 - **£35 606** - FF396 264
Backwater of the River Murray, South Australia Oil/canvas (120.5x182cm 47x71in) Melbourne 2000

😊 **$2 462** - €2 683 - **£1 700** - FF18 745
The Cottage Door, ST.Ives, Cornwall Oil/board (26.5x18cm 10x7in) London 2000

😊 **$7 039** - €7 219 - **£4 400** - FF47 352
Gathering Mussels Watercolour (24.5x17cm 9x6in) London 2000

JOHNSTONE John Young 1887-1930 [32]

😊 **$2 734** - €2 336 - **£1 654** - FF15 324
Horse Grazing Beside the Farmhouse Huile/panneau (12.5x17.5cm 4x6in) Montréal 1998

JOHNSTONE William 1897-1983 [78]

😊 **$5 481** - €6 442 - **£3 800** - FF42 256
Composition Oil/board (53.5x75.5cm 21x29in) Edinburgh 2000

✎ **$331** - €307 - **£200** - FF2 011
Abstract, Ochre and Green Watercolour/paper (18x25.5cm 7x10in) Edinburgh 1999

JOINER Harvey 1852-1932 [7]

😊 **$3 750** - €4 200 - **£2 605** - FF27 552
«**Forest Interior**» Oil/canvas (50x101cm 20x40in) Cincinnati OH 2001

JOINVILLE Antoine Edmond 1801-1849 [18]

😊 **$1 635** - €1 789 - **£1 131** - FF11 738
Sonnenuntergang in italienischer Landschaft Öl/Leinwand (26.5x35cm 10x13in) Heidelberg 2001

✎ **$317** - €351 - **£220** - FF2 300
Vue de Palerme en Italie/Paysage avec un temple antique Crayon/papier (15.5x23.5cm 6x9in) Senlis 2001

JOINVILLE François, prince de 1818-1900 [54]

✎ **$2 307** - €2 744 - **£1 589** - FF18 000
Le Cassard se rapprochant dangereusement de la Belle Poule Aquarelle/papier (35x50.5cm 13x19in) Paris 2000

JOIRE Jean 1862-1950 [29]

🖌 **$2 250** - €2 252 - **£1 387** - FF14 775
Dos perros alsacianos Bronze (49x34x70cm 19x13x27in) Madrid 2000

JOKI Olli 1943 [12]

😊 **$375** - €320 - **£224** - FF2 096
Skärgård Oil/canvas (17x40cm 6x15in) Helsinki 1998

JOLE van Jef 1905-1951 [5]

😊 **$1 087** - €1 271 - **£776** - FF8 334
Washerwoman at Work in a Canal in the Hague Oil/canvas (33x49cm 12x19in) Amsterdam 2001

JOLE van Joseph Gerardus 1877-1919 [19]

😊 **$1 800** - €1 556 - **£1 068** - FF10 204
Artist at Work beside a Chicken Coop Oil/canvas (24x42cm 9x16in) Washington 1998

JOLI DE DIPI Antonio c.1700-1777 [62]

😊 **$250 000** - €220 033 - **£152 200** - FF1 443 325
The Campo Vaccino, Rome, Looking Towards S.Francesca Romana Oil/canvas (94x128cm 37x50in) New-York 1999

😊 **$97 500** - €101 074 - **£58 500** - FF663 000
La piana dei templi di Paestum, vista da Levante Olio/tela (49x76.5cm 19x30in) Milano 2001

⬚ **$2 500** - €2 592 - **£1 500** - FF17 000
Palazzo del Duca d'Oria in Strada Nuova/Palazzo del Prencipe d'Oria Burin (45x68cm 17x26in) Genova 2000

JOLIN Einar 1890-1976 [410]

😊 **$11 121** - €12 904 - **£7 678** - FF84 645
Modell med utslaget hår Oil/canvas (169x108cm 66x42in) Stockholm 2000

😊 **$2 795** - €3 001 - **£1 870** - FF19 682
Stilleben med frukt, korg och skål Oil/canvas (45x54cm 17x21in) Stockholm 2000

😊 **$1 408** - €1 187 - **£835** - FF7 786
Stilleben Oil/canvas (40x34cm 15x13in) Stockholm 1998

✎ **$471** - €547 - **£335** - FF3 588
Häger vid Kivikstrand Akvarell/papper (38x55cm 14x21in) Stockholm 2000

⬚ **$337** - €324 - **£208** - FF2 126
Stilleben med flamingo Color lithograph (55x46cm 21x18in) Malmö 1999

JOLIN Ellen 1854-1939 [17]

😊 **$868** - €1 003 - **£607** - FF6 578
Julia Jolin med dottern Ingrid Oil/canvas (91.5x72.5cm 36x28in) Stockholm 2001

JOLIVARD André 1787-1851 [7]

😊 **$3 223** - €3 659 - **£2 239** - FF24 000
Scène de la vie champêtre, au loin Paris Huile/toile (50.5x61.5cm 19x24in) Barbizon 2001

JOLLAIN Nicolas René 1732-1804 [6]

😊 **$6 228** - €6 098 - **£3 832** - FF40 000
Jeunes femmes au bain Huile/toile (66x142cm 25x55in) Paris 1999

😊 **$6 154** - €5 183 - **£3 634** - FF34 000
Allégories de la Guerre et de la Paix Huile/panneau (29.5x35cm 11x13in) Paris 1998

JOLLAIN Pierre 1720-? [3]

😊 **$4 730** - €5 004 - **£3 000** - FF32 825
Diana and Endymion/The Education of Cupid Oil/cardboard (13x16cm 5x6in) London 2000

JOLLEY Martin Gwilt 1859-? [9]

😊 **$8 732** - €10 439 - **£6 000** - FF68 478
Sunshine and Blossom Oil/canvas (72.5x93cm 28x36in) Billingshurst, West-Sussex 2000

JOLLIVET Pierre Jules 1794-1871 [7]

😊 **$5 797** - €6 250 - **£3 886** - FF41 000
Jeunes femmes et servantes au bain antique Huile/toile (38x46.5cm 14x18in) Paris 2000

JOLLO Domenico XIX-XX [1]

🖌 **$20 755** - €21 495 - **£13 211** - FF141 000
Enfant Bronze (122x80cm 48x31in) Bordeaux 2000

JOLLY André 1883-? [8]

😊 **$12 820** - €15 245 - **£9 140** - FF100 000
Thoniers au mouillage à Kerdruc sur l'Aven/Scène de jardin Huile/toile (100x130cm 39x51in) Brest 2000

😊 **$3 408** - €3 659 - **£2 280** - FF24 000
Neige à Pont-Aven Huile/toile (61x50cm 24x19in) Quimper 2000

JOLLY F.R. Auguste 1782-1840? [1]
🖙 $15 830 - €15 245 - **£9 830** - FF100 000
　　Trompe-l'oeil au bas-relief Huile/toile (41x55cm 16x21in) Paris 1999

JOLY Alexis, Alexandre V. 1798-1874 [9]
▥ $890 - €748 - **£523** - FF4 906
　　«Vallée de Lauterbrunn» Lithographie (39.4x55.5cm 15x21in) Bern 1998

JOLYET Philippe 1832-1908 [7]
🖙 $2 557 - €2 211 - **£1 518** - FF14 500
　　La couture près de la fenêtre Huile/panneau (28.5x22cm 11x8in) Dijon 1998

JOMOUTON Frédéric 1858-? [22]
🖙 $390 - €372 - **£237** - FF2 439
　　Le port d'Ostende Huile/toile (50x65cm 19x25in) Bruxelles 1999

JON-AND John 1889-1941 [58]
🖙 $5 520 - €6 055 - **£3 665** - FF39 715
　　Kvarnen Oil/canvas (66x46cm 25x18in) Stockholm 2000
🖙 $1 373 - €1 538 - **£954** - FF10 091
　　Nature morte Oil/canvas (29x28cm 11x11in) Stockholm 2001
▱ $852 - €923 - **£583** - FF6 057
　　Landskap med hus och träd Oil chalks/paper (36.5x44cm 14x17in) Stockholm 2001

JONAS Henri Charles 1878-1944 [24]
🖙 $788 - €908 - **£544** - FF5 953
　　Christus Oil/panel (50x40cm 19x15in) Maastricht 2000
▱ $211 - €227 - **£143** - FF1 488
　　Maastrichterbrug Pencil/paper (9x15cm 3x5in) Maastricht 2001
▥ $94 - €109 - **£65** - FF714
　　Jonas en de walvis (Jona and the Whale) Woodcut (14x15cm 5x5in) Maastricht 2000

JONAS Lucien 1880-1947 [122]
🖙 $1 854 - €1 829 - **£1 142** - FF12 000
　　Saint Jean Cap Ferrat Huile/toile (65x81cm 25x31in) Paris 1999
▱ $494 - €457 - **£302** - FF3 000
　　Retour du soldat blessé Sanguine/papier (74x52cm 29x20in) Metz 1999
▥ $142 - €137 - **£88** - FF900
　　Fêtes commemoratives de la bataille de Denain, 1712-1912 Affiche (156.5x115.5cm 61x45in) Paris 1999

JONAS Rudolf, Carl R. Hugo 1822-1888 [4]
🖙 $1 964 - €2 045 - **£1 244** - FF13 413
　　Composition nach einem Motiv aus Südbaiern Öl/Leinwand (53x78cm 20x30in) München 2000

JONAS Siegfried 1909-1989 [1]
▲ $3 232 - €3 811 - **£2 272** - FF25 000
　　Composition Bronze (H72.5cm H28in) Paris 2000

JONAVILLE Pierre 1827-? [4]
🖙 $4 564 - €5 336 - **£3 258** - FF35 000
　　Femmes se prélassant au harem Huile/panneau (32x41cm 12x16in) Paris 2001

JONCHERE Evariste 1892-1956 [27]
▲ $11 145 - €11 718 - **£8 075** - FF86 000
　　Torse de jeune femme vietnamienne Bronze (H87cm H34in) Soissons 2001
▲ $5 901 - €5 793 - **£3 659** - FF38 000
　　Femme Maori Bronze (H52cm H20in) Paris 1999

JONCHERIE Gabriel Germain c.1800-c.1850 [14]
🖙 $5 295 - €5 336 - **£3 300** - FF35 000
　　Nature morte aux plats de cuisine, brasero et chat Huile/toile (50x61cm 19x24in) Paris 2000
🖙 $16 621 - €16 007 - **£10 342** - FF105 000
　　Guichet de banque Huile/toile (44x35cm 17x13in) Montfort L'Amaury 1999

JONCHERY Charles 1873-? [8]
▲ $14 084 - €14 788 - **£9 341** - FF97 000
　　Lustre à six branches de lumière, décor de fleurs, corps arborescent Bronze (H98cm H38in) Paris 2000

JONCIERES de Léonce 1871-1947 [46]
🖙 $551 - €579 - **£347** - FF3 800
　　Venise Huile/carton (18x21cm 7x8in) Nîmes 2000

JONCKHEER de Jacobus XVII [2]
🖙 $7 000 - €6 636 - **£4 258** - FF43 531
　　Coastal Landscape with Elegant Figures, Travellers by the Walls City Oil/panel (58.5x73.5cm 23x28in) New-York 1999

JONES Adrian, Captain 1845-1938 [18]
🖙 $1 288 - €1 216 - **£800** - FF7 979
　　Bay Horses in stabled Interiors Oil/canvas (49x59.5cm 19x23in) Billingshurst, West-Sussex 1999
▲ $6 931 - €6 598 - **£4 400** - FF43 283
　　Racehorse Bronze (H38cm H14in) Billingshurst, West-Sussex 1999

JONES Allen 1937 [285]
🖙 $22 747 - €22 268 - **£14 000** - FF146 069
　　Thais Oil/canvas (211x152.5cm 83x60in) London 1999
▲ $1 043 - €1 051 - **£650** - FF6 897
　　Chest Sculpture (36.5x25.5x11.5cm 14x10x4in) London 2000
▱ $1 644 - €1 765 - **£1 100** - FF11 578
　　Costume Designs Watercolour (26x36.5cm 10x14in) London 2001
▥ $515 - €550 - **£350** - FF3 608
　　Seated Woman Color lithograph (80x55cm 31x21in) London 2001

JONES Alonso XIX [1]
🖙 $12 300 - €10 614 - **£7 431** - FF69 622
　　Portrait of Agnes Gardner Campbell, Lexington, Ky, in a party dress Oil/canvas (105x99cm 41x39in) Radford VA 1999

JONES Alun Leach 1937 [37]
▥ $156 - €182 - **£108** - FF1 196
　　Untitled Serigraph in colors (61x49cm 24x19in) Melbourne 2000

JONES Arne 1914-1976 [59]
▲ $864 - €754 - **£522** - FF4 946
　　«Delad kontinuitet» Metal (12x25cm 4x10in) Stockholm 1998

JONES Brian J. XX [13]
🖙 $2 896 - €3 361 - **£2 000** - FF22 048
　　Britannia and Ailsa racing at Cowes, 1895 Oil/canvas (61x91.5cm 24x36in) London 2000

JONES Calvert R., Rev. 1802-1877 [61]
▱ $966 - €889 - **£580** - FF5 833
　　Sailing Vessel & Pilot Boats at Sea Ink (18x25.5cm 7x10in) Glamorgan 1999
📷 $4 254 - €4 858 - **£3 000** - FF31 869
　　Reclining male figure Salt print (8x10cm 3x3in) London 2001

JONES Charles 1866-1959 **[64]**

📷 **$6 000** - €6 908 - **£4 094** - FF45 312
Brussels Sprouts Gelatin silver print (15.5x21cm 6x8in) New-York 2000

JONES Charles Lloyd 1878-1958 **[2]**

$2 736 - €2 594 - **£1 709** - FF17 016
Ferry Wharf, Sydney Harbour Oil/board (22.5x29.5cm 8x11in) Woollahra, Sydney 1999

JONES Charles, Sheep 1836-1892 **[77]**

$5 105 - €5 927 - **£3 600** - FF38 879
Cows watering by a River Oil/canvas (60x90cm 23x35in) Cambridge 2001

$3 055 - €3 633 - **£2 177** - FF23 834
Weidende Schafe in Schottischer Seelandschaft Oil/panel (27.8x38cm 10x14in) Zürich 2000

JONES David 1895-1974 **[68]**

$2 576 - €2 385 - **£1 600** - FF15 642
An Afternoon in the Park Coloured pencils (25.5x34cm 10x13in) London 1999

$892 - €1 018 - **£620** - FF6 679
Wounded Knight Drypoint (20x15.5cm 7x6in) London 1999

JONES Francis Coates 1857-1932 **[28]**

$57 652 - €63 954 - **£38 338** - FF419 511
Girl with Flowers Oil/canvas (76x91cm 30x36in) Milford CT 2000

$2 500 - €2 989 - **£1 724** - FF19 605
Brittany Girl at Play Watercolour, gouache/paper (22x16cm 9x6in) Milford CT 2000

JONES Frank 1900-1969 **[2]**

$44 - €49 - **£30** - FF320
Pierrot Ink/paper (17x13.5cm 6x5in) London 2000

JONES H.F./H.J. XIX **[2]**

$4 811 - €4 760 - **£3 000** - FF31 221
Night Mails at the General Post Office: Arrival/Depature Oil/canvas (40.5x61.5cm 15x24in) London 1999

JONES Hampson T. XIX-XX **[10]**

$484 - €445 - **£300** - FF2 916
A River Landscape Watercolour (34.5x62cm 13x24in) London 1999

JONES Herbert H. St.John act.c.1899-c.1936 **[24]**

$1 540 - €1 792 - **£1 100** - FF11 754
«Hotspur», a saddled liver chesnut Hunter with a Dog in a Stable Oil/canvas (56x68.5cm 22x26in) London 2001

$597 - €581 - **£368** - FF3 813
Goldspring Rosalie Öl/Leinwand (30x41cm 11x16in) Linz 1999

JONES Hugh Bolton 1848-1927 **[93]**

$12 000 - €11 420 - **£7 506** - FF74 908
Autumn River Landscape Oil/canvas (60x102cm 24x40in) New-York 1999

$3 500 - €3 361 - **£2 168** - FF22 047
Landscape Oil/canvas (30x45cm 12x18in) Oakland CA 1999

$1 000 - €1 103 - **£677** - FF7 234
Nimes Pencil (23x16cm 9x6in) New-York 2000

JONES John c.1745-1797 **[11]**

$149 - €165 - **£100** - FF1 083
The Father of the Turf, After Wooton Mezzotint (55x36cm 22x14in) Little-Lane, Ilkley 2000

JONES John Llewellyn 1870-1927 **[18]**

$9 714 - €9 134 - **£6 015** - FF59 913
Harbour Scene Oil/canvas/board (20.5x27.5cm 8x10in) Melbourne 1999

JONES Jonah 1919 **[2]**

$3 498 - €3 220 - **£2 100** - FF21 122
Bust of John Cowper Powys Bronze (H77cm H30in) Glamorgan 1999

JONES Joseph, Joe 1909-1963 **[48]**

$2 000 - €2 282 - **£1 389** - FF14 972
Flowers on a Table in Front of a Screen Oil/canvas (101x76cm 40x30in) St. Louis MO 2000

$326 - €304 - **£201** - FF1 993
Missouri Wheat Farmers Lithograph (24x20cm 9x8in) Cleveland OH 1999

JONES Josiah Clinton 1848-1936 **[29]**

$746 - €633 - **£450** - FF4 155
Autumnal Landscape Oil/canvas (54.5x44cm 21x17in) Billingshurst, West-Sussex 1998

JONES Leon Foster 1871-1940 **[2]**

$6 000 - €6 851 - **£4 230** - FF44 939
Hillside, early Spring Oil/canvas (66x63.5cm 25x25in) Boston MA 2001

JONES Lois Mailou 1905-1998 **[1]**

$4 250 - €5 056 - **£2 940** - FF33 166
African Woman Acrylic/paper (71x55cm 28x22in) Plainville CT 2000

JONES Maud Raphael XIX-XX **[15]**

$1 498 - €1 391 - **£900** - FF9 125
Figures harvesting lettuces/Poultry scratching beneath a crab Watercolour (25.5x36cm 10x14in) London 1999

JONES Paul ?-c.1888 **[50]**

$3 047 - €3 014 - **£1 900** - FF19 773
Spaniels and a Terrier in a Barn Oil/canvas (21x26cm 8x10in) Leyburn, North Yorkshire 1999

JONES Paul Osborne 1921-1998 **[51]**

$394 - €461 - **£278** - FF3 021
Bird of Paradise Oil/board (30.5x51cm 12x20in) Malvern, Victoria 2000

$1 042 - €1 239 - **£742** - FF8 128
Bouquet of Australian Wildflowers Watercolour (24x17cm 9x6in) Woollahra, Sydney 2000

JONES Reginald T. 1857-1920 **[25]**

$346 - €357 - **£220** - FF2 339
New Forest Scene Watercolour/paper (22x28cm 9x11in) Petersfield, Hampshire 2000

JONES Richard 1767-1840 **[6]**

$34 210 - €39 785 - **£24 429** - FF260 972
Portrait of Rowland, Viscount Hill on his grey Hunter Oil/canvas (105x130cm 41x51in) Toronto 2001

$22 684 - €21 815 - **£14 000** - FF143 099
Going out: Gentleman with a Chestnut hunter held by a Groom, Blackburn Oil/canvas (71x91.5cm 27x36in) London 1999

JONES Robert act.1906-? **[1]**

$4 020 - €4 118 - **£2 500** - FF27 010
A Group of Figures on the Beach Oil/canvas (30x60cm 11x23in) Billingshurst, West-Sussex 2000

JONES Robert Edmond 1887-1954 **[5]**

$3 250 - €3 011 - **£1 961** - FF18 179
«A Royal Fandango» Design for the Decor in Act II Gouache (24x40.5cm 9x15in) New-York 1998

JONES Robert Gibson XX [1]
- $14 000 - €13 407 - **£8 649** - FF87 946
  Rocketman Speeding Through Earth's Atmosphere, Pulp Magazine Cover Gouache/paper (46x34cm 18x13in) New-York 1999

JONES Robinson XX [6]
- $4 750 - €5 488 - **£3 325** - FF35 996
  British Clipper Ship on the High Seas Oil/canvas (60x91cm 24x36in) New-York 2001

JONES Samuel John Egbert XIX [32]
- $6 096 - €6 143 - **£3 800** - FF40 293
  Gypsy Encampment Oil/canvas (71x91.5cm 27x36in) London 2000
- $3 579 - €3 003 - **£2 100** - FF19 699
  Shooters with Dogs in Landscape Oil/canvas (20x25cm 8x10in) Aylsham, Norfolk 1998
- $1 331 - €1 437 - **£920** - FF9 429
  Jamaica: a View of East Harbour of Port Antonio as seen from Eazon Watercolour/paper (20x31cm 7x12in) Newbury, Berkshire 1999

JONES Sarah 1959 [4]
- $8 952 - €8 713 - **£5 500** - FF57 153
  The Dining Room, Francis Place Photograph (152.5x152.5cm 60x60in) London 1999

JONES T. Hampson 1846-1916 [5]
- $2 987 - €2 581 - **£1 800** - FF16 930
  Children in a Village Lane Watercolour (45.5x75cm 17x29in) Billingshurst, West-Sussex 1999

JONES Thomas 1743-1803 [15]
- $14 437 - €14 549 - **£9 000** - FF95 432
  Coast Scene with Approaching Storm Oil/canvas (61.5x74.5cm 24x29in) London 2000
- $72 639 - €67 243 - **£45 000** - FF441 085
  Lerici from the Convent of the Galoro Watercolour (27x41cm 10x16in) London 1999

JONES William ?-c.1779 [1]
- $3 984 - €4 629 - **£2 800** - FF30 363
  Basket of Strawberries with a Bluetit and Butterfly, on a rocky Bank Oil/canvas (51x63.5cm 20x25in) London 2001

JONG de Frans ?-1705 [1]
- $11 102 - €11 658 - **£7 000** - FF76 472
  Claudius Civilis with the Commanders of the Roman Army Oil/canvas (73x100cm 28x39in) London 2000

JONG de Germ 1886-1967 [68]
- $2 523 - €2 949 - **£1 801** - FF19 347
  Still Life with a Pring Bouquet in a Chinese Vase Oil/canvas (82x73cm 32x28in) Amsterdam 2001
- $675 - €757 - **£469** - FF4 964
  Annalkande regn Oil/canvas (40x31cm 15x12in) Helsinki 2001
- $350 - €363 - **£222** - FF2 381
  Kerkgang Zondiagmorgen Charcoal/paper (23x29.5cm 9x11in) Amsterdam 2000

JONG de Jacqueline 1939 [26]
- $1 725 - €1 588 - **£1 035** - FF10 418
  Woman in Blue Dress Gouache (106x73.5cm 41x28in) Amsterdam 1999

JONG de Tinus 1885-1942 [8]
- $5 329 - €4 997 - **£3 293** - FF32 778
  Wilderness, George Oil/canvas (72x106.5cm 28x41in) Johannesburg 1999

JONGE de Johan Antonie 1864-1927 [48]
- $5 019 - €5 899 - **£3 480** - FF38 695
  A Girl Knitting Oil/canvas/board (54.5x47.5cm 21x18in) Amsterdam 2000
- $1 066 - €998 - **£663** - FF6 548
  Woman in a Beachchair Watercolour (18x12cm 7x4in) Amsterdam 1999

JONGELINGHS K. XIX-XX [12]
- $831 - €694 - **£487** - FF4 552
  Nature morte aux fruits Huile/panneau (25x160cm 9x62in) Antwerpen 1998

JONGERE de Marinus Johannes 1912-1978 [144]
- $1 978 - €1 815 - **£1 219** - FF11 906
  View of Rotterdam Harbour Oil/canvas (40.5x80cm 15x31in) Amsterdam 1999
- $1 701 - €1 906 - **£1 182** - FF12 501
  «De Waalhaven te Rotterdam» Oil/canvas (29x49cm 11x19in) Rotterdam 2001
- $566 - €635 - **£396** - FF4 167
  Havenpanorama met H.A.L.Rotterdam Watercolour, gouache/paper (16.5x69.8cm 6x27in) Dordrecht 2001

JONGERT Jacob 1883-1942 [15]
- $315 - €295 - **£194** - FF1 934
  «Elfde Jaarbeurs Utrecht» Poster (66.5x99cm 26x38in) Oostwoud 1999

JONGH de Gabriel Cornelis 1913 [89]
- $742 - €832 - **£516** - FF5 458
  View of a Stone Bridge Oil/canvas (59x90cm 23x35in) Johannesburg 2001
- $371 - €431 - **£256** - FF2 830
  Near Caledon, Cape Province Oil/canvas (30x45.5cm 11x17in) Johannesburg 2000

JONGH de Ludolf 1616-1679 [18]
- $24 608 - €21 254 - **£14 834** - FF139 419
  Diana and her Companions resting after the Chase Oil/panel (73.3x106.5cm 28x41in) Amsterdam 1998
- $3 377 - €3 835 - **£2 346** - FF25 154
  Kavalier und Bettlerin vor einem Gasthof Oil/panel (46x30cm 18x11in) Köln 2001

JONGH de Oene Romkes 1812-1896 [53]
- $3 888 - €4 084 - **£2 460** - FF26 789
  Figures on a Frozen Canal in a Wintry Town Oil/canvas (68x53cm 26x20in) Amsterdam 2000
- $2 470 - €2 723 - **£1 613** - FF17 859
  Schaatsenrijders bij een koek en zopie te Woudrichem Oil/panel (13x23cm 5x9in) Den Haag 2000

JONGH de Tinus 1885-1942 [206]
- $3 553 - €3 331 - **£2 195** - FF21 852
  Snow on the Mountains, Cape Oil/canvas (45x64cm 17x25in) Johannesburg 1999
- $1 144 - €1 103 - **£707** - FF7 233
  Landscape with a Cottage Oil/canvas (25x29.5cm 9x11in) Johannesburg 1999
- $557 - €647 - **£385** - FF4 245
  Figure Outside a Cottage Pastel/paper (24x37cm 9x14in) Johannesburg 2000
- $137 - €147 - **£91** - FF963
  Entrance to the Castle of Good Hope Engraving (31x22cm 12x8in) Cape Town 2000

JONGHE de Gustave Leonhard 1829-1893 [59]
- $11 500 - €10 454 - **£6 926** - FF68 574
  «Kind Heart» Oil/canvas (86x64cm 34x25in) St. Petersburg FL 1998

J

$200 - €223 - **£134** - FF1 463
Le peintre dans l'atelier Huile/toile (38x30cm
14x11in) Bruxelles 2000

JONGHE de Jan Baptiste 1785-1844 **[26]**
$1 038 - €998 - **£647** - FF6 548
Farm in a Summer Landscape Oil/canvas
(38x55.5cm 14x21in) Amsterdam 1999
$4 674 - €4 360 - **£2 820** - FF28 602
Flusslandschaft mit Wanderern Oil/panel
(29x39cm 11x15in) Wien 1999

JONGKIND Johan-Barthold 1819-1891 **[590]**
$38 610 - €45 378 - **£26 770** - FF297 660
**Figures on a Jetty in the Moonlit Harbour of
Harfleur** Oil/canvas (43.5x60cm 17x23in) Amsterdam
2000
$26 688 - €24 392 - **£16 336** - FF160 000
Voilier en Hollande au couchant Huile/toile
(33x46cm 12x18in) Calais 1999
$3 053 - €3 278 - **£2 042** - FF21 500
Grenoble, les bords du lac Aquarelle/papier
(18x25cm 7x9in) Grenoble 2000
$548 - €640 - **£387** - FF4 200
Jetée en bois dans le port de Honfleur Eau-forte
(24x31.5cm 9x12in) Paris 2000

JONK Nic 1928-1995 **[44]**
$34 650 - €29 996 - **£21 027** - FF196 759
Aarde en Water, de Wachter Bronze (H104cm
H40in) Amsterdam 1998
$1 979 - €1 906 - **£1 237** - FF12 501
Untitled Bronze (H33cm H12in) Amsterdam 1999

JONNAERT Clémence 1866-1941 **[7]**
$3 712 - €3 966 - **£2 528** - FF26 016
Rhododendrons Huile/toile (78x88cm 30x34in)
Lokeren 2001

JONNEVOLD Carl Henrik 1856-1930 **[35]**
$500 - €2 683 - **£1 673** - FF17 602
Carmel Landscape Oil/canvas (45x72.5cm 17x28in)
San-Francisco CA 2000
$1 100 - €1 012 - **£660** - FF6 641
Cattle in Luminescent Landscape Oil/canvas
(30x40cm 12x16in) Pasadena CA 1999

JONNIAUX Alfred 1882-? **[6]**
$2 994 - €3 354 - **£2 081** - FF22 000
Homme accroupi Huile/toile/carton (72.5x59cm
28x23in) Paris 2001

JONSDOTTIR Kirstin Stefansson 1890-1958 **[10]**
$3 024 - €2 556 - **£1 805** - FF16 769
**«Hagavatn», Islandsk landskab med sö og bjerg
i baggrunden** Oil/canvas (80x87cm 31x34in)
Köbenhavn 1998

JONSON Raymond 1891-1982 **[23]**
$32 000 - €35 118 - **£20 604** - FF230 361
Prismatic Figuration Oil/canvas (51x38cm 20x14in)
Beverly-Hills CA 2000

JONSON Sven 1902-1981 **[239]**
$5 400 - €5 243 - **£3 334** - FF34 393
Vilande nät Oil/canvas (39x89cm 15x35in) Stockholm
1999
$2 238 - €2 456 - **£1 442** - FF16 112
Landskap i månsken Oil/canvas/panel (33x40cm
12x16in) Stockholm 2000
$2 099 - €1 831 - **£1 269** - FF12 012
«Horisontell komposition» Gouache/paper
(15x32cm 5x12in) Stockholm 1998
$255 - €218 - **£149** - FF1 433
Komposition med häst Color lithograph (48x39.5cm
18x15in) Stockholm 1998

JONSON van Ceulen Cornelis I 1593-1661 **[11]**
$10 460 - €11 228 - **£7 000** - FF73 651
**Portrait of Lady Palmer, Half-Length, in a Black
Dress with a Collar** Oil/canvas (75x62.5cm 29x24in)
London 2000

JONSSON Asgrimur 1876-1958 **[12]**
$1 008 - €942 - **£609** - FF6 181
Islandsk landskab med fossende elv
Watercolour/paper (38x49cm 14x19in) Köbenhavn 1999

JONSSON Lars 1952 **[120]**
$2 419 - €2 198 - **£1 500** - FF14 420
Winter Fox Oil/canvas (48x58cm 18x22in)
Billingshurst, West-Sussex 1999
$900 - €865 - **£555** - FF5 677
Blackpole Warbler Watercolour (32x25cm 12x9in)
Boston MA 1999
$370 - €373 - **£231** - FF2 449
Storspovar Color lithograph (36x27cm 14x10in)
Stockholm 1999

JÖNSSON Theodor 1888-1966 **[10]**
$804 - €901 - **£559** - FF5 910
Vinter vid Esarps kvarn Oil/canvas (53x64cm
20x25in) Malmö 2001

JONXIS Jan Lodewyk 1789-1867 **[7]**
$2 276 - €2 269 - **£1 382** - FF14 883
**Portret van Schrassert/Portret van
Pierre Ambroise Bert** Oil/canvas (67x55cm 26x21in)
Amsterdam 2000

JONXIS Pieter Hendrik Lod. 1815-1852 **[4]**
$7 341 - €6 807 - **£4 428** - FF44 649
Wijk bij Duurstede Oil/panel (42x33cm 16x12in)
Maastricht 1999

JOO Seah Kim 1939 **[14]**
$1 327 - €1 237 - **£819** - FF8 113
Two Women and a Child Mixed media (85x34cm
33x13in) Singapore 1999

JOORS Eugeen 1850-1910 **[51]**
$5 100 - €4 359 - **£3 060** - FF28 596
Blumenstilleben mit Hyazinthen und Zyklamen
Öl/Leinwand (63x80cm 24x31in) Wien 1998
$873 - €1 041 - **£625** - FF6 829
Stilleven met appelsienen Oil/canvas (30.5x45.5cm
12x17in) Lokeren 2000

JOOS Hildegard 1909 **[21]**
$278 - €327 - **£193** - FF2 145
Madonna mit Jesuskind, Johannes und Engel
Mischtechnik/Papier (48.5x38.5cm 19x15in) Wien 2000

JOOSTENS Dirk Jan Hendrik 1818-1882 **[3]**
$23 164 - €21 781 - **£14 342** - FF142 876
**Still Life with Roses, forget-me-nots,
Columbines and Cornflowers** Oil/panel (29x22cm
11x8in) Amsterdam 1999

JOOSTENS Paul 1889-1960 **[495]**
$1 680 - €1 735 - **£1 057** - FF11 382
La folle Huile/carton (72x43cm 28x16in) Antwerpen
2000
$713 - €793 - **£499** - FF5 203
Ballerine en train de danser Huile/carton (34x29cm
13x11in) Antwerpen 2001
$4 253 - €4 090 - **£2 624** - FF26 831
Ohne Titel Assemblage (H24cm H9in) Köln 1999
$336 - €347 - **£211** - FF2 276
Dominus Vobiseum Crayon/papier (27x21cm
10x8in) Antwerpen 2000
$3 550 - €3 811 - **£2 375** - FF25 000
Les mollusques Lithographie (31x42cm 12x16in)
Paris 2000

JOPLING Louise 1843-1933 [7]
   $3 567 - €3 452 - **£2 200** - FF22 642
     Modern Cinderella Watercolour (26.5x21cm 10x8in)
     London 1999

JORDAENS Hans I c.1539-1630 [6]
   $3 757 - €4 269 - **£2 629** - FF28 000
     Le portement de croix Huile/panneau (37x37.5cm
     14x14in) Paris 2001

JORDAENS Hans III c.1595-1643/44 [25]
   $24 105 - €23 910 - **£15 000** - FF156 837
     **Apollo enthroned, presented with the Gifts of
     the Continents** Oil/canvas (119x200cm 46x78in)
     London 1999
   $19 200 - €21 802 - **£13 140** - FF143 010
     Die Begegnung von Jakob und Josef Oil/panel
     (90x128cm 35x50in) Wien 2000

JORDAENS Jacob 1593-1678 [82]
   $41 238 - €43 302 - **£26 000** - FF284 042
     The Triumph of Apollo Oil/canvas (113x106.5cm
     44x41in) London 2000
   $46 551 - €45 596 - **£30 000** - FF299 088
     Mercury and Argus Oil/canvas/panel (59x79cm
     23x31in) London 1999
   $283 917 - €304 761 - **£190 000** - FF1 999 104
     Head Studies of Two African Men Oil/canvas
     (32x47cm 12x18in) London 2000
   $8 960 - €10 437 - **£6 260** - FF68 461
     The Widow's Mite Black chalk (23.5x29cm 9x11in)
     Amsterdam 2000

JORDAENS Symon 1590-1640 [1]
   $5 120 - €5 814 - **£3 504** - FF38 136
     **Gebirgige Flusslandschaft mit einer steinernen
     Bogenbrücke** Oil/panel (42x69cm 16x27in) Wien
     2000

JORDAN Carl 1863-? [12]
   $2 248 - €2 556 - **£1 559** - FF16 769
     Kaiser Sigismund in Strassburg Öl/Leinwand
     (83x110.5cm 32x43in) Köln 2000

JORDAN Ernst Pasqual 1858-1924 [6]
   $2 697 - €3 068 - **£1 870** - FF20 123
     Dekorationsentwürfe Aquarell, Gouache/Papier
     (52x62cm 20x24in) Hamburg 2000

JORDAN Rudolf 1810-1887 [19]
   $471 - €562 - **£336** - FF3 689
     Die trauernde Fischersfrau am Strand Oil/can-
     vas/panel (23.6x32cm 9x12in) Köln 2000

JORDE Lars 1865-1939 [22]
   $2 644 - €2 935 - **£1 843** - FF19 255
     Utenfor i haven Oil/canvas (70x80cm 27x31in) Oslo
     2001

JORDENS Barend 1888-1962 [2]
   $4 754 - €4 558 - **£2 971** - FF29 766
     Sleeping Beauty Stone (30x45cm 11x17in)
     Amsterdam 1999

JORDENS Jan Gerrit 1883-1962 [16]
   $2 862 - €3 403 - **£2 040** - FF22 324
     Acrobate Oil/canvas (75.5x50cm 29x19in) Amsterdam
     2000
   $2 942 - €3 176 - **£2 011** - FF20 836
     Portrait in Pink Oil/canvas (42.5x33cm 16x12in)
     Amsterdam 2001
   $582 - €681 - **£415** - FF4 464
     Landscape Watercolour, gouache/paper (56x45cm
     22x17in) Amsterdam 2001

JORDI Jorge Mercadé Farrés 1923-1990 [40]
   $544 - €511 - **£340** - FF3 349
     Barcas Oleo/lienzo (38x55cm 14x21in) Barcelona
     1999

JØRGENSEN Aksel 1883-1957 [123]
   $951 - €821 - **£574** - FF5 383
     Opstilling i atelieret på Charlottenborg Oil/canvas
     (47x66cm 18x25in) Vejle 1999

JØRGENSEN Børge 1926 [68]
   $6 517 - €7 371 - **£4 405** - FF48 350
     Kvinde & mand Metal (H205cm H80in) København
     2000
   $779 - €845 - **£539** - FF5 540
     Untitled Metal (H32cm H12in) København 2001

JØRGENSEN Christian A. 1860-1935 [31]
   $6 500 - €6 977 - **£4 349** - FF45 766
     Carmel Oil/canvas (44x76cm 17x29in) San-Francisco
     CA 2000
   $1 200 - €1 317 - **£772** - FF8 638
     **Vast southwestern Californian landscape with
     Ruins** Watercolour/board (22x35cm 9x14in) St.
     Petersburg FL 2000

JØRGENSEN Erling 1905-1977 [28]
   $298 - €335 - **£208** - FF2 196
     Mand & kvinde Oil/canvas (111x90cm 43x35in) Viby
     J, Århus 2001

JØRGENSEN Knut 1937-1991 [32]
   $8 925 - €10 613 - **£6 358** - FF69 615
     Portal Oil/canvas (75x75cm 29x29in) Oslo 2000
   $3 306 - €3 669 - **£2 304** - FF24 069
     Soppen Watercolour/paper (38x37cm 14x14in) Oslo
     2001
   $678 - €732 - **£468** - FF4 802
     No title Etching (13x13cm 5x5in) Oslo 2001

JØRGENSEN Niels 1860-1943 [3]
   $8 136 - €8 067 - **£5 088** - FF52 914
     **Udsigt over New York set fra St.George
     Kystvagten på Staten Island** Oil/canvas (48x90cm
     18x35in) København 1999
   $3 971 - €4 724 - **£2 834** - FF30 985
     New York with Brooklyn Bridge am Morgen
     Oil/panel (23x28cm 9x11in) Wien 2000

JØRGENSEN Sven 1861-1940 [6]
   $3 753 - €3 915 - **£2 368** - FF25 683
     Gård i vinterlandskap Oil/canvas/panel (28x36cm
     11x14in) Oslo 2000

JØRGENSEN Willer XIX-XX [25]
   $1 039 - €1 125 - **£720** - FF7 378
     Winterwald im Sonnenschein Öl/Leinwand
     (39.5x60cm 15x23in) Hamburg 2001

JORHAN Christian I 1727-1804 [1]
   $12 622 - €11 762 - **£7 622** - FF77 155
     Zwei Engel Sculpture (H80cm H31in) Dresden 1998

JORI Marcello 1951 [22]
   $700 - €726 - **£420** - FF4 760
     Composizione Acrilico/tela/tavola (50x38cm
     19x14in) Vercelli 2001

JORIO Albert XX [3]
   $530 - €610 - **£374** - FF4 000
     «La fille du puisatier» Affiche (120x160cm 47x62in)
     Paris 2001

JORIS Pio 1843-1921 [59]
   $8 058 - €9 093 - **£5 668** - FF59 644
     Fischer beim Fischfang Öl/Leinwand (107x182cm
     42x71in) Bern 2001

J

$9 500 - €10 443 - **£6 087** - FF68 501
The Proposal Oil/canvas (101.5x66cm 39x25in) New-York 2000

$850 - €881 - **£510** - FF5 780
Barche sulla spiaggia di Anzio Olio/tavola (17x9cm 6x3in) Roma 1999

$1 680 - €1 451 - **£1 120** - FF9 520
Donna in un vicolo a Tivoli Acquarello/carta (29x46cm 11x18in) Roma 1998

JORLAND Monique XX [1]
$2 673 - €2 287 - **£1 590** - FF15 000
Éclats de rose Huile/toile (46x33cm 18x12in) Paris 1998

JORN Asger Jorgensen 1914-1973 [1620]
$134 181 - €130 112 - **£85 000** - FF853 476
Skörd (Harvest) Oil/canvas (108x139cm 42x54in) London 1999

$34 500 - €35 765 - **£20 700** - FF234 600
Veteran Oil/tela (51x45cm 20x17in) Prato 1999

$6 259 - €5 818 - **£3 800** - FF38 164
«A Gay Bird to Petusha Cochrane» Oil/canvas (17.8x14.5cm 7x5in) London 1998

$5 500 - €5 702 - **£3 300** - FF37 400
Fuori posto Terracotta (27x19x19cm 10x7x7in) Milano 2001

$3 615 - €3 089 - **£2 122** - FF20 265
Komposition Watercolour (20x27cm 7x10in) Viby J, Århus 1998

$387 - €446 - **£266** - FF2 923
Ohne titel Color lithograph (76x53cm 29x20in) Stockholm 2000

JORON Maurice 1883-1937 [8]
$4 020 - €4 573 - **£2 835** - FF30 000
Jour d'hiver près de la cheminée Huile/toile (60x73cm 23x28in) Paris 2001

JÖRRES Carl 1872-1947 [21]
$1 366 - €1 278 - **£827** - FF8 384
Kornernte bei Lilienthal Öl/Leinwand (71x79cm 27x31in) Bremen 1999

JOSEN Hamada 1875-? [3]
$762 - €818 - **£510** - FF5 366
Halbporträt einer jungen, spazierengehenden Frau Woodcut in colors (38.1x24.9cm 14x9in) Köln 2000

JOSEPH George Francis 1764-1846 [5]
$5 047 - €5 577 - **£3 500** - FF36 585
Portrait of Spencer Perceval (1762-1812) Oil/canvas (60x50cm 23x19in) London 2001

JOSEPH Jasmin 1923 [10]
$1 590 - €1 372 - **£955** - FF9 000
Chats et singes Huile/toile (50x123cm 19x48in) Paris 1998

JOSEPH Julian 1882-1964 [7]
$8 000 - €9 084 - **£5 475** - FF59 587
Rain in Union Square Pastel/paper (58x43.5cm 22x17in) New-York 2000

JOSEPH Lily Delissa 1864-1940 [1]
$13 635 - €13 740 - **£8 500** - FF90 130
City of London Skies and Flowers (Roofs of High Holborn) Oil/canvas (135x146cm 53x57in) London 2000

JOSEPHA de OBIDOS DE AYALLA c.1630-1684 [6]
$585 - €689 - **£420** - FF4 518
Madonna and Child Oil/canvas/board (57x49cm 22x19in) Channel-Islands 2001

JOSEPHI Isaac A. ?-1954 [1]
$8 500 - €9 124 - **£5 688** - FF59 851
View of the Waldorf-Astoria Oil/canvas (47x50.5cm 18x19in) New-York 2000

JOSEPHSON Ernst 1851-1906 [179]
$1 890 - €2 016 - **£1 281** - FF13 221
Interiör med barockskåp och silverpokaler Oil/canvas (54x62cm 21x24in) Stockholm 2001

$3 927 - €3 854 - **£2 435** - FF25 281
Advokaten Oil/canvas (24x19cm 9x7in) Stockholm 1999

$2 507 - €2 440 - **£1 543** - FF16 006
Kung David spelar på sin harpa Indian ink/paper (31x19.5cm 12x7in) Stockholm 1999

JOSEPHSON Ken 1932 [2]
$1 800 - €2 073 - **£1 241** - FF13 600
Season's Greetings Silver print (9x12cm 3x5in) New-York 2000

JOSHUA Nellie XIX-XX [1]
$5 665 - €5 317 - **£3 500** - FF34 879
Heatherley's Art School Oil/canvas (60.5x49.5cm 23x19in) London 1999

JOSSE Jean A. XX [1]
$1 200 - €1 154 - **£740** - FF7 569
«Alcyon, Le Tour de France» Poster (119x78cm 46x30in) New-York 1999

JOSSET Lawrence 1910 [9]
$118 - €132 - **£80** - FF864
The Practice Shot Aquatint (35x47cm 13x18in) London 2000

JOSSOT Henri / Abdul Karim 1866-1951 [36]
$763 - €762 - **£477** - FF5 000
«Guignolet Cointreau» Affiche (127x92cm 50x36in) Orléans 1999

JOST Joseph 1888-? [26]
$1 676 - €1 599 - **£1 020** - FF10 487
Blumenstrauss mit Glockenblumen, Nelken, Rittersporn Öl/Leinwand (63.5x52.5cm 25x20in) Wien 1999

$1 078 - €1 210 - **£750** - FF7 940
Good Vintage/Reading the Leaves Oil/panel (20.5x15cm 8x5in) London 2001

JOTTI Carlo 1826-1905 [14]
$1 300 - €1 348 - **£780** - FF8 840
Brughiere di Castano Olio/cartone (13x40cm 5x15in) Milano 2000

JOU I SENABRE Louis 1882-1968 [23]
$397 - €473 - **£275** - FF3 100
Les Baux Aquarelle (13x19cm 5x7in) Marseille 2000

$141 - €168 - **£97** - FF1 100
Berger Gravure bois (24x20cm 9x7in) Marseille 2000

JOUANA Marie José XX [85]
$239 - €274 - **£166** - FF1 800
Marine Huile/toile (24x14cm 9x5in) Romorantin-Lanthenay 2000

JOUANT Jules XIX-XX [3]
$1 241 - €1 392 - **£842** - FF9 131
Sans titre Bronze (H31.5cm H12in) Warszawa 2000

JOUAS Charles 1866-1942 [39]
$525 - €503 - **£330** - FF3 300
Proue en bois sculpté dans les combles de l'Hôtel des Abbés de Fécamp Fusain (46x61cm 18x24in) Paris 1999

JOUBERT Léon 1876-1920 **[21]**
- **$13 000** - €11 254 - **£7 840** - FF73 821
  Quiet Lake Scene with Figures on the Far Shore Oil/canvas (98x161cm 38x63in) San-Francisco CA 1998
- **$1 305** - €1 220 - **£805** - FF8 000
  Bord de rivière Huile/toile (38x55cm 14x21in) Compiègne 1999
- **$6 447** - €6 274 - **£3 969** - FF41 158
  Franskt landskap Oil/canvas (30x45cm 11x17in) Stockholm 1999

JOUBERT Pierre 1910 **[11]**
- **$529** - €488 - **£318** - FF3 200
  La maison du bord des sables Encre Chine/papier (28x19cm 11x7in) Paris 1999

JOUBERT-DROLING Louise Adéone 1797-1831 **[2]**
- **$14 148** - €13 720 - **£8 901** - FF90 000
  La confession Huile/toile (73x60cm 28x23in) Paris 1999
- **$11 808** - €13 720 - **£8 298** - FF90 000
  La leçon de dessin Huile/toile (33.5x24.5cm 13x9in) Paris 2001

JOUBIN Georges 1888-1983 **[338]**
- **$536** - €610 - **£368** - FF4 000
  Les lavandières en Bretagne Huile/toile (89x84cm 35x33in) Versailles 2000
- **$255** - €305 - **£182** - FF2 000
  La couture Aquarelle, gouache/papier (43x33cm 16x12in) Châtellerault 2000

JOUCLARD Adrienne 1881-1971 **[262]**
- **$1 074** - €1 143 - **£679** - FF7 500
  La cantine à la maternelle Huile/toile/carton (65x92cm 25x36in) Paris 2000
- **$447** - €534 - **£319** - FF3 500
  Les vendanges Huile/toile (24x35cm 9x13in) Nancy 2000
- **$340** - €366 - **£228** - FF2 400
  L'attente Fusain (30x24cm 11x9in) Chaumont 2000

JOUENNE Michel 1933 **[162]**
- **$3 415** - €3 659 - **£2 325** - FF24 000
  Les genets en Provence Huile/toile (54x73cm 21x28in) Calais 2001
- **$537** - €518 - **£331** - FF3 400
  Le lac de Guadalcaccin, Espagne Huile/toile (27x35cm 10x13in) Paris 1999
- **$583** - €534 - **£357** - FF3 500
  Paysage d'été en Provence Aquarelle, gouache/papier (48x64cm 18x25in) Calais 1999
- **$293** - €305 - **£186** - FF2 000
  La Provence Lithographie (45x61cm 17x24in) Thionville 2000

JOUETT Matthew Harris 1788-1827 **[2]**
- **$40 000** - €42 582 - **£27 248** - FF279 320
  Portrait of Thomas Jefferson Oil/panel (73.5x60cm 28x23in) New-York 2001

JOUFFROY Pierre 1912-2000 **[38]**
- **$1 011** - €1 180 - **£700** - FF7 733
  Stilleben mit Geflügel Oil/panel (81x65cm 31x25in) Bern 2000
- **$690** - €823 - **£492** - FF5 400
  Paysage de neige en Franche-Comté Huile/panneau (27x41cm 10x16in) Belfort 2000

JOUHANDEAU Marcel 1888-1979 **[3]**
- **$1 576** - €1 677 - **£996** - FF11 000
  Le bal masqué Lithographie couleurs (53.5x76cm 21x29in) Paris 2000

JOUHAUD Léon 1874-1950 **[110]**
- **$3 436** - €3 354 - **£2 175** - FF22 000
  Eymoutiers Email (17x10cm 6x3in) Bourges 1999
- **$456** - €427 - **£279** - FF2 800
  «Vallons au printemps» Pastel/papier (23x32cm 9x12in) Paris 1998

JOULLAIN François 1697-1778 **[4]**
- **$2 500** - €2 173 - **£1 513** - FF14 256
  Head and Shoulders of a Male Nude, seen from behind Red chalk (46.5x36cm 18x14in) New-York 1999

JOULLIN Amedee 1862-1917 **[15]**
- **$4 000** - €4 327 - **£2 740** - FF28 385
  Still Life of Roses Oil/canvas (89x130cm 35x51in) San Rafael CA 2001

JOURDAIN Francis 1876-1958 **[46]**
- **$3 044** - €3 354 - **£2 021** - FF22 000
  Femme sur fond bleu Pastel (91x72cm 35x28in) Deauville 2000

JOURDAIN Henri 1864-1931 **[40]**
- **$417** - €391 - **£260** - FF2 564
  River Landscape with a Village beyond Watercolour (21x26.5cm 8x10in) London 1999

JOURDAIN Roger 1845-1918 **[13]**
- **$1 569** - €1 753 - **£1 063** - FF11 500
  Portrait de Marie Renard Huile/panneau (24x15.5cm 9x6in) Pontoise 2000
- **$897** - €838 - **£542** - FF5 500
  Elégante au bord du lac Aquarelle/papier (38x53cm 14x20in) Paris 1999

JOURDAN Adolphe 1825-1889 **[21]**
- **$14 432** - €16 769 - **£10 142** - FF110 000
  Nymphes et satyres Huile/toile (130x65cm 51x25in) Paris 2001
- **$2 390** - €2 668 - **£1 564** - FF17 500
  Diane chasseresse Huile/panneau (35x27cm 13x10in) Fontainebleau 2000

JOURDAN Émile 1860-1931 **[23]**
- **$39 193** - €38 874 - **£24 378** - FF255 000
  La chapelle de Lanriot au clair de lune Huile/panneau (81x80cm 31x31in) Brest 1999

JOURDAN Théodore 1833-? **[28]**
- **$13 100** - €14 025 - **£8 914** - FF92 000
  La Transhumance Huile/toile (85x150cm 33x59in) Marseille 2001
- **$3 266** - €3 506 - **£2 185** - FF23 000
  Gardienne de moutons Huile/toile (48x73cm 18x28in) Paris 2000
- **$795** - €854 - **£532** - FF5 600
  Chèvres dans la garrigue Huile/toile (21.5x26cm 8x10in) La Varenne-Saint-Hilaire 2000

JOURDEUIL Louis Marie Adrien 1849-1907 **[13]**
- **$3 025** - €2 556 - **£1 804** - FF16 767
  In der Mittagssonne Öl/Leinwand (70x120cm 27x47in) Düsseldorf 1998
- **$1 105** - €1 235 - **£771** - FF8 100
  Paysanne et poules dans un champ fleuri Huile/panneau (44x30cm 17x11in) Tours 2001

JOURNOD Monique 1935 **[22]**
- **$795** - €795 - **£561** - FF6 000
  Lumière du Var Huile/toile (46x38cm 18x14in) Barbizon 2001

JOUSSET Charles 1857-1907 **[3]**
- **$5 753** - €4 964 - **£3 457** - FF32 560
  «La rentrée des barques» Oil/panel (32x45.5cm 12x17in) Bern 1998

JOUSSET Claude 1935 [43]
- $455 - €427 - **£281** - FF2 800
  Visite à la foire aux antiquités à la Bastille
  Huile/toile (55x46cm 21x18in) La Varenne-Saint-Hilaire 1999
- $1 810 - €2 058 - **£1 242** - FF13 500
  Montmartre, les vignes Huile/toile (33x46cm 12x18in) Versailles 2000

JOUVE A. XX [1]
- $1 521 - €1 448 - **£946** - FF9 500
  Tête de tigre Encre Chine (46x59cm 18x23in) Paris 1999

JOUVE Georges 1910-1964 [36]
- $15 030 - €17 074 - **£10 550** - FF112 000
  Sans titre Céramique (95x30cm 37x11in) Paris 2001
- $2 376 - €2 744 - **£1 663** - FF18 000
  Sirène Céramique (H41cm H16in) Paris 2001

JOUVE Paul 1878-1973 [615]
- $72 120 - €84 762 - **£50 000** - FF556 000
  Two Panthers with a Cub Oil/panel (88x298cm 34x117in) London 2000
- $10 288 - €12 196 - **£7 264** - FF80 000
  Panthère tachetée dévorant sa proie Huile/panneau (42x62cm 16x24in) Paris 2000
- $132 - €152 - **£92** - FF1 000
  Aigle en vol et palmiers Métal (35x55cm 13x21in) Paris 2001
- $3 139 - €3 354 - **£2 134** - FF22 000
  L'Aigle du Mont Atbos Encre Chine (34x26.5cm 13x10in) Pontoise 2001
- $1 175 - €1 143 - **£723** - FF7 500
  Tigre au repos Pointe sèche (45x63cm 17x24in) Paris 1999

JOUVENET François Dagobert 1688/94-1756 [2]
- $1 613 - €1 511 - **£1 000** - FF9 909
  Five Women Making Lace by Candlelight Ink (16x17.5cm 6x6in) London 1999

JOUVENET François le Jeune 1664-1749 [4]
- $4 732 - €5 641 - **£3 374** - FF37 000
  Portrait d'homme Huile/toile (72x59cm 28x23in) Chartres 2000

JOUVENET Jean 1644-1717 [21]
- $37 000 - €43 579 - **£25 589** - FF285 858
  Venus at the Forge of Vulcan Oil/canvas (80.5x65cm 31x25in) New-York 2000
- $5 128 - €6 098 - **£3 556** - FF40 000
  Etude d'un personnage à gauche du tableau «La Résurrection de Lazare» Crayon (25x42cm 9x16in) Paris 2000

JOVINGE Torsten 1898-1936 [25]
- $9 770 - €10 946 - **£6 810** - FF71 800
  Svalgången Oil/canvas (51x62cm 20x24in) Stockholm 2001
- $13 248 - €14 531 - **£8 796** - FF95 316
  Stella Oil/canvas (41.5x33cm 16x12in) Stockholm 2000
- $920 - €1 095 - **£656** - FF7 181
  Damer i kyrkan Indian ink (39x30cm 15x11in) Stockholm 2000

JOWETT Ellen XIX-XX [18]
- $88 - €95 - **£60** - FF621
  Portrait, After Gainsborough Mezzotint (43x34cm 17x13in) Carmarthen, Wales 2001

JOWETT Frank B. c.1890-c.1940 [14]
- $518 - €484 - **£320** - FF3 176
  Sheep grazing in Woodland Watercolour/paper (38x53.5cm 14x21in) London 1999

JOWETT John Marshall XIX-XX [3]
- $1 704 - €1 870 - **£1 100** - FF12 266
  Fleshwick Bay Watercolour/paper (48x71cm 19x28in) Isle-of-Man 2000

JOWETT Percy Hague 1882-1955 [40]
- $605 - €506 - **£360** - FF3 318
  Wiltshire Garden Oil/board (29.5x35cm 11x13in) London 1998
- $334 - €289 - **£200** - FF1 895
  Gardens Under Snow, Putney Watercolour (33x24.5cm 12x9in) London 1998

JOY Arthur 1808/9-1838 [2]
- $3 936 - €3 809 - **£2 427** - FF24 987
  Family Disagreement Watercolour/paper (35.5x48.5cm 13x19in) Dublin 1999

JOY George William 1844-1925 [10]
- $35 345 - €34 035 - **£22 000** - FF223 256
  Truth Oil/canvas (259x97cm 101x38in) London 1999
- $9 119 - €10 846 - **£6 500** - FF71 143
  Pamela's Birthday Oil/canvas (122.5x83cm 48x32in) London 2000

JOY John 1925 [24]
- $273 - €264 - **£168** - FF1 733
  Bathurst St Acrylic/board (25.5x20.5cm 10x8in) Toronto 1999

JOY John Cantiloe 1806-1866 [19]
- $1 960 - €2 280 - **£1 400** - FF14 954
  French Lugger Prize to a British Brig of War Watercolour/paper (20x28cm 7x11in) Norfolk 2001

JOY William & John Can. 1803/06-1867/66 [16]
- $5 681 - €5 463 - **£3 500** - FF35 834
  Pulling in the Catch Watercolour/paper (18x26.5cm 7x10in) London 1999

JOY William Cantiloe 1803-1867 [48]
- $16 539 - €14 421 - **£10 000** - FF94 598
  A Squadron at Anchor Oil/canvas (46x61cm 18x24in) London 1998
- $1 780 - €1 676 - **£1 100** - FF10 994
  Shipping in coastal Waters Watercolour/paper (15x23cm 5x9in) London 1999

JOYANT Jules Romain 1803-1854 [29]
- $31 644 - €30 528 - **£20 000** - FF200 250
  The Doges' Palace Oil/canvas (104.5x165.5cm 41x65in) London 1999
- $47 060 - €39 637 - **£27 794** - FF260 000
  Vue du Palais des Doges/Vue du Pont de Rialto Huile/toile (43x60cm 16x23in) Paris 1998
- $7 809 - €7 318 - **£4 694** - FF48 000
  Place à Venise Huile/toile (36x28cm 14x11in) Paris 1999
- $1 155 - €1 296 - **£808** - FF8 500
  La place San Giovanni e Paolo à Venise Aquarelle, gouache (43x35cm 16x13in) Paris 2001

JOYARD Henriette XVIII [2]
- $5 077 - €5 450 - **£3 397** - FF35 752
  Eine Dienerin serviert ihrer Herrin Kaffee Öl/Leinwand (31.5x25cm 12x9in) Wien 2000

JOYCE Ena Elizabeth 1925 [6]
- $1 072 - €1 119 - **£676** - FF7 340
  The Quiet River Oil/board (74x119cm 29x46in) Sydney 2000

JOYEUX Pierre Samuel Louis 1749-1818 [8]
- $5 194 - €4 363 - **£3 053** - FF28 618
  «Le Château de Chillon en allant de Villeneuve à Vevey» Eau-forte (32.8x49.2cm 12x19in) Bern 1998

JOYNT Dick XX [4]
🔨 **$2 739** - €2 666 - **£1 683** - FF17 490
    Mother and Child Marble (H61cm H24in) Dublin 1999

JOZEFCZYK Zygmunt 1881-1966 [6]
🖼 **$7 776** - €7 275 - **£4 713** - FF47 724
    Na mokradlach Oil/board (70x102cm 27x40in) Warszawa 1999

JU JIE 1527-1586 [1]
✎ **$3 846** - €4 520 - **£2 667** - FF29 652
    Landscape Ink (15.5x49cm 6x19in) Hong-Kong 2000

JU LIAN 1828-1904 [27]
🖼 **$2 820** - €3 204 - **£1 980** - FF21 016
    Insects and Flowers Ink (134.5x38cm 52x14in) Hong-Kong 2001

JU MING 1938 [14]
🔨 **$19 680** - €20 956 - **£12 480** - FF137 460
    Taiji Stone (H26cm H10in) Taipei 2000

JUAN DE FLANDES XV-XVI [1]
🖼 **$13 200** - €12 013 - **£8 200** - FF78 800
    La Lanzada Oleo/tabla (71x49.5cm 27x19in) Madrid 1999

JUBIEN Antoine Fr. Louis 1833-1909 [4]
✎ **$1 463** - €1 448 - **£913** - FF9 500
    Jeune femme à la robe blanche Pastel/papier (99x80cm 38x31in) Lyon 1999

JUBIER C.L. XVIII [7]
▥ **$142** - €168 - **£102** - FF1 100
    Le départ d'une foire, d'après Jean-Baptiste Huet Gravure (21.5x27cm 8x10in) Paris 2001

JÜCHSER Hans 1894-1977 [27]
🖼 **$5 019** - €5 624 - **£3 495** - FF36 892
    Grosses Stilleben mit Petroleumlampe und Jugendstilvase Öl/Leinwand (100x69cm 39x27in) Berlin 2001
🖼 **$593** - €665 - **£412** - FF4 360
    «Stilleben» Aquarell (17.4x23.4cm 6x9in) Berlin 2001
▥ **$165** - €158 - **£100** - FF1 039
    Lesender Akt Woodcut (29.9x16.5cm 11x6in) Dettelbach-Effeldorf 1999

JUDD Donald 1928-1994 [272]
🔨 **$179 047** - €174 261 - **£110 000** - FF1 143 076
    Untitled (89-6) Construction (300x50x25cm 118x19x9in) London 1999
🔨 **$80 000** - €92 823 - **£55 232** - FF608 880
    Untitled Construction (15x68.5x61cm 5x26x24in) New-York 2000
▥ **$3 750** - €4 198 - **£2 615** - FF27 534
    Untitled Etching (55.5x69cm 22x27in) New-York 2001

JUDGE Spencer Percival 1874-1956 [5]
✎ **$2 118** - €2 458 - **£1 462** - FF16 126
    Vancouver from the Mouth of the Capilano River Watercolour/paper (28x47.5cm 11x18in) Vancouver, BC. 2000

JUDIKAëL (Pierre Juhel) 1937 [78]
☞ **$720** - €762 - **£477** - FF5 000
    Le pas de deux Huile/toile (46x55cm 18x21in) Strasbourg 2000

JUDSON Jane Berry XX [7]
▥ **$750** - €724 - **£471** - FF4 749
    Mount Monadnock from Jaffrey, N.H Woodcut (15x20cm 6x8in) Boston MA 1999

JUDSON William Lee 1842-1928 [56]
☞ **$3 000** - €3 506 - **£2 141** - FF22 998
    Eucalyptus sunset landscape Oil/canvas (50x60cm 20x24in) Altadena CA 2001
☞ **$3 250** - €2 991 - **£1 950** - FF19 621
    Edge of the Desert Oil/canvas (25x40cm 10x16in) Pasadena CA 1999
✎ **$800** - €864 - **£552** - FF5 667
    Divers Cove Laguna Beach Watercolour/paper (30x47cm 12x18in) Altadena CA 2001

JUEL Jens 1745-1802 [87]
☞ **$16 065** - €18 092 - **£11 070** - FF118 678
    Portraet af en ung pige med lyst langt hår Oil/canvas (65x51cm 25x20in) Köbenhavn 2000
☞ **$12 168** - €10 736 - **£7 328** - FF70 424
    Landskab fra Schweiz, Creux de Genthod Oil/panel (28.5x39.5cm 11x15in) Köbenhavn 1998
✎ **$12 796** - €12 896 - **£7 977** - FF84 595
    Portraet af en ung kvinde Pastel/paper (32x25cm 12x9in) Köbenhavn 2000

JUENGLING Frederick 1848-1889 [2]
✎ **$3 000** - €3 324 - **£2 011** - FF21 801
    Floral Still Lifes Watercolour/paper (33x25cm 13x10in) Dedham MA 2000

JUGELET Jean Marie Auguste 1805-1875 [14]
☞ **$612** - €671 - **£425** - FF4 400
    Mer démontée, le naufrage Huile/carton (16x28cm 6x11in) Brest 2001

JUGLAR Victor Henri 1826 [2]
☞ **$7 379** - €8 181 - **£5 123** - FF53 662
    Der Page liest einen Brief Öl/Leinwand (65x77cm 25x30in) Köln 2001

JUILLARD André 1948 [24]
✎ **$809** - €777 - **£501** - FF5 100
    Le Vieil Homme et la Mer, pl.4 Encres couleurs/papier (40x30cm 15x11in) Paris 1999
▥ **$123** - €136 - **£83** - FF894
    Plume au vent Sérigraphie (89x50cm 35x19in) Bruxelles 2000

JUILLARD Nicolas-Jacques 1715-1790 [3]
☞ **$20 388** - €19 069 - **£12 500** - FF125 087
    A Rocky River Landscape with Ruins, a Washerwoman and other Figures Oil/panel (26.5x43cm 10x16in) London 1998

JUILLERAT Jacques Henri 1777-1860 [21]
✎ **$514** - €579 - **£358** - FF3 800
    «Assaut donné par les Impériaux à la tête de Pont d'Huningue...» Lavis (32x48cm 12x18in) Angers 2001

JUKES Francis 1747-1812 [35]
▥ **$284** - €314 - **£190** - FF2 058
    Fox Hunting Scenes, After L.Loraine Color lithograph (25x26cm 10x10in) Little-Lane, Ilkley 2000

JULES Mervin 1912 [49]
☞ **$1 400** - €1 633 - **£1 000** - FF10 711
    Musicians and Orchestra Conductor Oil/board (61x40cm 24x16in) Detroit MI 2000
▥ **$100** - €86 - **£59** - FF565
    Boy with Flute Woodcut in colors (50x25cm 20x10in) Cambridge MA 1998

JULIA Y CARRERE Luis ?-1908 [17]
☞ **$505** - €440 - **£305** - FF2 884
    Toro costaño Oleo/lienzo (19x25.5cm 7x10in) México 1998

JULIA Y ENTRAIGUES Rafael XIX [8]
$472 - €481 - £296 - FF3 152
Toro en el campo Oleo/papel (25x35cm 9x13in)
Madrid 2000

JULIANA Y ALBERT José 1844-1890 [15]
$1 156 - €1 241 - £773 - FF8 140
Recreo de frailes Acuarela/papel (33x15cm 12x5in)
México 2000

JULIEN Henri Octave 1852-1908 [18]
$1 109 - €937 - £666 - FF6 148
The Buffalo Hunt Graphite (22x33cm 8x12in)
Calgary, Alberta 1998

JULIEN Jean Pierre 1888-1974 [22]
$287 - €274 - £179 - FF1 800
«Aix en Provence» Affiche (76x105cm 29x41in)
Paris 1999

JULIEN Joseph, Jos XIX [3]
$13 000 - €12 477 - £8 149 - FF81 841
The Haymakers Oil/canvas (30.5x40.5cm 12x15in)
New-York 1999

JULIENNE Eugène c.1800-1874 [2]
$9 000 - €7 824 - £5 446 - FF51 323
**Three Designs for the «Toilette de bouche» of
the Viceroy of Egypt** Watercolour, gouache
(41x57.5cm 16x22in) New-York 1999

JULIN Johan Fredrik 1798-1843 [7]
$1 235 - €1 077 - £747 - FF7 066
Utsikt af Brokind i Östergötland Wash (40x56cm
15x22in) Stockholm 1998

JULIUS Per 1951 [45]
$910 - €898 - £560 - FF5 889
Vårdag, landskap med björkar Akvarell/papper
(20x14cm 7x5in) Stockholm 1999

JULLIAN Philippe 1919-1977 [29]
$505 - €442 - £306 - FF2 900
La brocanteuse Aquarelle (28.5x21cm 11x8in) Paris
1998

JULLIARD Nicolas Jacques 1715-1790 [17]
$9 230 - €9 909 - £6 175 - FF65 000
Port de pêche animé Huile/toile (26x37cm 10x14in)
Paris 2000
$20 598 - €24 025 - £14 500 - FF157 594
Le moulin à l'eau, After François Boucher
Tapestry (284x366cm 111x144in) London 2001

JULLIEN Louis Marie XX [1]
$2 176 - €2 287 - £1 435 - FF15 000
Les colombes messagères du Bonheur
Tapisserie (176x241cm 69x94in) Calais 2000

JUN ICHIRO Sekino Jun'ichiro 1914-1988 [31]
$449 - €511 - £311 - FF3 353
Futakawa Woodcut (42.5x55cm 16x21in) Köln 2000

JUNCK Ferdinand XIX [1]
$4 594 - €5 150 - £3 200 - FF33 783
Young woman reading the scriptures Marble
(33x58.5cm 12x23in) London 2001

JUNCKER Justus 1703-1767 [31]
$34 578 - €39 326 - £24 378 - FF257 964
Stilleben mit Gemüse/Stilleben mit Käse
Öl/Leinwand (34.8x47cm 13x18in) Zürich 2001
$4 500 - €3 912 - £2 723 - FF25 661
Awaiting the Doctor's Reply Oil/panel (33x40cm
13x16in) New-York 1999

JUNCKER Wilhelm Karl 1820-1901 [1]
$10 500 - €11 213 - £7 154 - FF73 555
Portrait of a Maiden with Flowers Oil/canvas
(99x78cm 39x31in) New-Orleans LA 2001

JUNDT Gustave Adolphe 1830-1884 [15]
$10 000 - €11 760 - £7 170 - FF77 139
By the Riverbank Oil/canvas (116x160cm 45x62in)
New-York 2001
$641 - €762 - £457 - FF5 000
La fête de l'Aid Kébir Aquarelle/papier (27x43cm
10x16in) Calais 2000

JUNG Charles Frédéric 1865-1936 [27]
$1 020 - €1 143 - £709 - FF7 500
Nature morte Huile/toile (24x41cm 9x16in) Lyon
2001

JUNG Emil Felix 1886-? [3]
$6 923 - €8 181 - £4 907 - FF53 662
Abendliche Gesellschaft Öl/Leinwand (100x119cm
39x46in) Ahlden 2000

JUNG Otto 1867-1966 [34]
$837 - €715 - £491 - FF4 691
Der Feuerbach im Herbst Öl/Leinwand/Karton
(62x44cm 24x17in) Stuttgart 2000

JUNG Simonetta 1917 [12]
$1 284 - €1 487 - £888 - FF9 756
Abstraction Huile/toile (60x90cm 23x35in) Bruxelles
2000

JUNG Théodore 1803-1865 [16]
$2 302 - €2 287 - £1 440 - FF15 000
Champ de bataille de Valmy Aquarelle,
gouache/papier (26.5x46.5cm 10x18in) Paris 1999

JUNG Tom XX [8]
$400 - €443 - £271 - FF2 905
«Star Wars» Poster (104x205cm 41x81in) New-York
2000

JUNGBLUT Johann 1860-1912 [224]
$3 061 - €3 579 - £2 151 - FF23 477
Winterliche Dorflandschaft Öl/Leinwand
(80x120cm 31x47in) München 2000
$1 117 - €1 329 - £796 - FF8 720
Herbstabend Oil/panel (35x26.5cm 13x10in) Köln
2000

JUNGHANNS Julius Paul 1876-1953/58 [180]
$2 790 - €2 812 - £1 739 - FF18 446
Bauer mit Kälbchen vor hügeliger Landschaft
Öl/Leinwand (61x80cm 24x31in) Düsseldorf 2000
$1 545 - €1 534 - £966 - FF10 061
Bergbauer mit Rossen an der Tränke
Öl/Leinwand (27x48cm 10x18in) München 1999
$1 116 - €1 022 - £680 - FF6 707
Pferde an der Tränke in Gebirgsdorf Gouache
(16.8x24cm 6x9in) München 1999

JUNGHEIM Carl 1803-1886 [30]
$2 891 - €3 323 - £2 041 - FF21 800
**Schweizer Alpenlandschaft mit Sennerhütte
und Kühen** Öl/Leinwand (87x122cm 34x48in)
Bremen 2001

JUNGMANN Marten Joh. Balt. 1877-1965 [38]
$1 173 - €1 361 - £810 - FF8 929
Roos in een vaas Oil/panel (50x38cm 19x14in)
Rotterdam 2000
$254 - €295 - £175 - FF1 934
Dode spreeuw Oil/panel (17x24cm 6x9in) Rotterdam
2000

JUNGMANN Nico Wilhelm 1872-1935 [37]
$926 - €994 - **£620** - FF6 523
Study of Young Lady Seated in Ornate Chair
Watercolour/paper (31x22cm 12x9in) Leominster,
Herefordshire 2000

JUNGNICKEL Ludwig Heinrich 1881-1965 [368]
$2 725 - €3 068 - **£1 878** - FF20 123
Ahrenshoop Höhe Bune 12 Öl/Leinwand (58x67cm
22x26in) Satow 2000
$3 735 - €3 634 - **£2 300** - FF23 835
Zwei Lastenesel Mischtechnik (29x39cm 11x15in)
Linz 1999
$957 - €1 090 - **£661** - FF7 150
Liegender weiblicher Akt Charcoal/paper
(33x47.8cm 12x18in) Wien 2000
$293 - €327 - **£198** - FF2 145
Hirschkühe Farblithographie (34.5x50cm 13x19in)
Wien 2000

JUNGSTEDT Axel 1859-1933 [7]
$9 153 - €7 960 - **£5 520** - FF52 214
Kärleksbrevet Oil/canvas (44x31cm 17x12in)
Stockholm 1998

JUNGSTEDT Kurt 1894-1963 [53]
$3 332 - €3 125 - **£2 060** - FF20 498
Flamenco Oil/canvas (90x141cm 35x55in) Stockholm
1999
$748 - €766 - **£462** - FF5 027
Blått linne Oil/canvas (63x53cm 24x20in) Stockholm
2000

JUNGWIRTH Josef 1869-1950 [56]
$22 000 - €22 806 - **£13 200** - FF149 600
Arianna e Bacco Olio/tela (123x168cm 48x66in)
Prato 1999
$1 211 - €1 163 - **£760** - FF7 627
Blumenstilleben Öl/Karton (41x51cm 16x20in) Wien
1999
$600 - €629 - **£380** - FF4 126
Sommarblommor Oil/panel (24x18cm 9x7in) Malmö
2000
$2 091 - €2 180 - **£1 317** - FF14 301
Wicken Gouache/Karton (41x50cm 16x19in) Wien
2000

JUNGWIRTH Martha 1940 [21]
$1 222 - €1 453 - **£872** - FF9 534
Ohne Titel Aquarell/Papier (69x99cm 27x38in) Wien
2000

JUNIPER Robert Litchfield 1929 [77]
$17 154 - €18 414 - **£11 481** - FF120 786
Landscape Oil/canvas (171x144cm 67x56in)
Melbourne 2000
$1 961 - €2 179 - **£1 313** - FF14 293
The Procession Oil/hardboard (45.5x122cm 17x48in)
Nedlands 2000
$1 297 - €1 246 - **£800** - FF8 175
Burnt Trees Oil/canvas (19.5x75cm 7x29in) London
1999
$3 018 - €3 542 - **£2 129** - FF23 232
Artist in a Landscape Mixed media/paper
(56x75.5cm 22x29in) Nedlands 2000

JUNK Rudolf 1880-1943 [7]
$1 895 - €2 035 - **£1 293** - FF13 347
Blick über Dächer Öl/Leinwand (50.2x50.2cm
19x19in) Wien 2001
$3 085 - €3 634 - **£2 170** - FF23 835
Blüte in der Wachau Öl/Karton (24.4x36.2cm
9x14in) Wien 2000

JUNYENT Oleguer 1876-1958 [14]
$1 820 - €1 952 - **£1 235** - FF12 805
Tendiendo la ropa Oleo/lienzo (50x65cm 19x25in)
Madrid 2001
$1 447 - €1 672 - **£1 002** - FF10 969
Personajes en un barco Acuarela (19x25cm 7x9in)
Barcelona 2000

JURADOWITCH Vincent Edward 1904-1983 [18]
$315 - €350 - **£214** - FF2 295
Fort Denison Oil/board (14x19cm 5x7in) Sydney
2000

JURRES Johannes Hendrikus 1875-1946 [106]
$1 116 - €1 271 - **£784** - FF8 334
Traveller resting Oil/canvas (48x64cm 18x25in)
Amsterdam 2001
$1 086 - €1 079 - **£678** - FF7 075
Jael Oil/panel (17x30cm 6x11in) Toronto 1999
$465 - €499 - **£311** - FF3 274
Young soldier in 17th century costume Coloured
chalks (30x40cm 11x15in) Amsterdam 2000

JURY Anne Primerose 1907-1979 [20]
$5 469 - €6 126 - **£3 800** - FF40 163
**From Horn Head Looking Towards
Sheephavern Co.Donegal** Oil/canvas/board
(35.5x46cm 13x18in) London 2001
$640 - €635 - **£400** - FF4 168
Connemara Donkey Oil/canvas (15x15cm 6x6in)
Belfast 1999

JUSELIUS Erik 1891-1948 [21]
$761 - €841 - **£527** - FF5 516
Bätar vid stranden Oil/panel (46.5x55.5cm 18x21in)
Helsinki 2000
$365 - €404 - **£253** - FF2 647
Strandklippor Oil/panel (30x37.5cm 11x14in)
Helsinki 2001

JUSSEL Eugen 1912-1997 [28]
$15 126 - €16 689 - **£10 004** - FF109 473
Abendgesellschaft Öl/Leinwand (110x161cm
43x63in) St. Gallen 2000
$2 648 - €2 502 - **£1 649** - FF16 409
Schloss Albrechtsberg Öl/Leinwand/Karton
(82x62cm 32x24in) St. Gallen 1999
$1 409 - €1 654 - **£994** - FF10 849
Rankweil Oil/canvas/panel (35x45cm 13x14in) St.
Gallen 2000

JUSTE de Juste XVI [4]
$18 400 - €19 074 - **£11 040** - FF125 120
Piramide di sei ginnasti Acquaforte (25x20.5cm
9x8in) Roma 1999

JUSTITZ Alfred 1879-1934 [44]
$11 560 - €10 934 - **£7 200** - FF71 720
Nature morte à la pipe et aux fruits Huile/toile
(35x50cm 13x19in) Praha 2001
$10 404 - €9 840 - **£6 480** - FF64 548
Charriot sur la route Huile/bois (26x35cm 10x13in)
Praha 2001

JUTSUM Henry 1816-1869 [50]
$5 865 - €6 321 - **£4 000** - FF41 466
**A Herd of Deer in a Wooded River Landscape,
near Kenilworth** Oil/canvas (61x95.5cm 24x37in)
London 2001
$1 086 - €1 173 - **£750** - FF7 694
Sheep Grazing in Heathland Oil/canvas
(21.5x29.5cm 8x11in) London 2001
$926 - €994 - **£620** - FF6 523
A Girl and Boy Crossing a Brook
Watercolour/paper (42.5x30.5cm 16x12in) London 2000

JÜTTNER Bruno 1880-? [48]
- $273 - €256 - **£165** - FF1 676
  Baumfäller am Seeufer, Vorfrühlingsstimmung
  Oil/canvas/panel (50x70cm 19x27in) Bremen 1999

JUTZ Carl 1838-1916 [80]
- $27 920 - €27 099 - **£17 384** - FF177 756
  **Geflügelhof, im Hintergrund eine
  Wiesenlandschaft mit einem Schloss**
  Öl/Leinwand (38.2x48.2cm 15x18in) Berlin 1999
- $4 524 - €4 857 - **£3 028** - FF31 862
  Hühnerhof mit Pfau Oil/panel (15.5x20.5cm 6x8in)
  Bremen 1999

JUTZ Carl 1916-1960 [2]
- $6 821 - €5 624 - **£4 017** - FF36 888
  Enten, Küken, Hühner, Hahn und Pfau im Hof
  Oil/panel (24x31.5cm 9x12in) Lindau 1998

JUTZ Carl, Jnr. 1873-1915 [7]
- $1 682 - €1 817 - **£1 162** - FF11 917
  Wäscherinnen am Waldbach Oil/canvas/panel
  (41.5x32.5cm 16x12in) Wien 2001

JUUEL Andreas Thomas 1817-1868 [38]
- $8 720 - €8 181 - **£5 387** - FF53 662
  **Heller Sommertag in einem oberbayerischen
  Dorf** Öl/Leinwand (55.5x78cm 21x30in) Ahlden 1999
- $1 828 - €1 547 - **£1 093** - FF10 149
  En herregård Oil/wood (21x29cm 8x11in) Viby J,
  Århus 1998
- $2 488 - €2 682 - **£1 696** - FF17 590
  Lumskebugten Pencil (20x29cm 7x11in) København
  2001

JUVA Kari 1939 [18]
- $1 502 - €1 682 - **£1 043** - FF11 032
  Läsestund Bronze (H29cm H11in) Helsinki 2001

K

KAAZ Carl Ludwig 1773-1810 [3]
- $2 890 - €3 286 - **£1 982** - FF21 556
  Hüons Flucht vor Oberon Gouache/paper
  (53.5x76cm 21x29in) Zürich 2000

KABAKOV Ilya 1933 [29]
- $2 411 - €2 812 - **£1 692** - FF18 446
  Ohne Titel Indian ink (21.8x44.7cm 8x17in) Köln
  2000

KABELL Ludvig 1853-1902 [47]
- $1 900 - €1 777 - **£1 171** - FF11 657
  **Sommarlandskap med kvinna och gosse på
  byväg** Oil/canvas (48x74cm 18x29in) Stockholm 1999
- $364 - €403 - **£241** - FF2 641
  Solnedgang over marken Oil/panel (31x45cm
  12x17in) Viby J, Århus 2000

KABREGU Enzo Doméstico XX [13]
- $1 200 - €1 035 - **£713** - FF6 786
  «Mujer Paraguaya» Oleo/cartón (54x30cm 21x11in)
  Montevideo 1998

KACERE John 1920 [48]
- $4 299 - €4 726 - **£2 734** - FF31 000
  Sans titre Huile/panneau (64x120cm 25x47in) Paris
  2000
- $1 790 - €2 134 - **£1 276** - FF14 000
  Dianne II Mine plomb (49x75cm 19x29in) Paris 2000

KADAR Béla 1877-1956 [414]
- $3 090 - €3 602 - **£2 139** - FF23 629
  Menschenansammlung vor einer Kirche
  Oil/Papier (80x59cm 31x23in) Bern 2000
- $1 980 - €2 250 - **£1 380** - FF14 760
  Avant le bain Huile/carton (43x34cm 16x13in)
  Budapest 2001
- $1 951 - €2 035 - **£1 229** - FF13 347
  Frau mit Sonnenblumen Gouache (55x39cm
  21x15in) Wien 2000
- $250 - €286 - **£176** - FF1 873
  Couple embracing Woodcut (18x23cm 7x9in)
  Chicago IL 2001

KADAR Géza 1878-1952 [5]
- $1 840 - €1 809 - **£1 150** - FF11 868
  Nagybánya Oil/canvas (68x76.5cm 26x30in) Budapest
  1999

KADELER Hans 1852-1910 [1]
- $2 233 - €2 045 - **£1 361** - FF13 415
  Die kleine Gratulantin Oil/panel (32x22cm 12x8in)
  München 1999

KADERABEK Josef 1915 [5]
- $920 - €971 - **£603** - FF6 372
  Stilleben, Hefegebäck Oil/panel (18x23cm 7x9in)
  Kempten 2000

KADISH Reuben 1913-1992 [2]
- $1 000 - €1 034 - **£631** - FF6 784
  Abstract Composition Etching, aquatint
  (34.5x24.5cm 13x9in) New-York 2000

KADISHMAN Menashe 1932 [166]
- $14 000 - €15 635 - **£8 965** - FF102 557
  Sheep resting Oil/canvas (71x170cm 27x66in) Tel
  Aviv 2000
- $1 649 - €1 785 - **£1 130** - FF11 706
  Head Acrylic/canvas (60x80cm 23x31in) Tel Aviv 2001
- $2 500 - €2 814 - **£1 722** - FF18 456
  View of our Country Iron (H30cm H11in) Herzelia-
  Pituah 2000

KADLEC Dusan 1942 [8]
- $1 924 - €2 269 - **£1 352** - FF14 882
  Old Irving Gate, Halifax Oil/board (25x43cm
  10x17in) Waverley NS 2000

KADLIK Franz 1786-1840 [4]
- $3 179 - €3 007 - **£1 980** - FF19 723
  Saint Wenceslas, Protector of Youth Oil/panel
  (17.5x23.5cm 6x9in) Praha 1999

KADOW Gerhard 1909 [4]
- $782 - €920 - **£561** - FF6 037
  Abstraktion in Gelb Oil/panel (39x28.5cm 15x11in)
  Düsseldorf 2001

KAELIN Charles Salis 1858-1929 [41]
- $10 800 - €11 340 - **£6 809** - FF74 388
  Woodland Stream in Winter Oil/canvas (50x60cm
  20x24in) Cleveland OH 2000
- $3 000 - €2 814 - **£1 853** - FF18 461
  Harbor Scene with Puffy Clouds Oil/board
  (25x31cm 10x12in) Cleveland OH 1999
- $250 - €3 696 - **£2 253** - FF24 245
  Woodland Stream Pastel/paper (44x39cm 17x15in)
  Cincinnati OH 2000

KAEMMERER Frederick Hendrik 1839-1902 [78]
- $47 762 - €40 118 - **£28 000** - FF263 158
  The Promenade Oil/canvas (86x151cm 33x59in)
  London 1998
- $5 423 - €6 192 - **£3 823** - FF40 620
  Junge Frau bei der Näherin Öl/Leinwand
  (60x35cm 23x13in) Bern 2001

$10 108 - €9 420 - **£6 232** - FF61 788
La leçon de patinage Huile/toile (46x32cm 18x12in)
Bruxelles 1999

$1 724 - €1 815 - **£1 138** - FF11 906
Three Children playing on the Beach Watercolour
(11x15cm 4x5in) Amsterdam 2000

KAEMMERER Johan Hendrik 1894-1970 [53]

$576 - €499 - **£350** - FF3 274
A Peasant Woman feeding chickens by a Farm
Oil/canvas (50x80cm 19x31in) Amsterdam 1999

$202 - €227 - **£140** - FF1 488
Voorstellingen van Kasteel de Binckhorst
Oil/canvas (30x40cm 11x15in) Rotterdam 2001

KAENDLER Johann Joachim 1706-1775 [22]

$1 384 - €1 530 - **£981** - FF10 732
Liebespaar Porcelain (H22cm H8in) Ahlden 2000

KAERCHER Amalie XIX [9]

$28 596 - €32 474 - **£20 000** - FF213 018
Stilleben (still life) Oil/canvas (71x80cm 27x31in)
London 2001

$3 593 - €3 857 - **£2 404** - FF25 301
Still life with roses, primulas and morning glory
Oil/canvas (40x31cm 15x12in) Amsterdam 2000

KAERIUS Petrus 1570/71-c.1630 [2]

$1 653 - €1 892 - **£1 150** - FF12 408
Insulae Philippinae Engraving (8.5x12.5cm 3x4in)
London 2000

KAESBACH Rudolf 1873-1955 [48]

$750 - €694 - **£452** - FF4 554
Mythological Female Nude Bronze (H38cm H15in)
St. Louis MO 1999

KÅGE Wilhelm 1889-1960 [22]

$1 190 - €1 124 - **£739** - FF7 373
Drakmamma Glazed ceramic (24x43cm 9x16in)
Stockholm 1999

$214 - €181 - **£127** - FF1 190
Twisting Roads of Love; Comedy Poster
(65.5x92.5cm 25x36in) Haarlem 1998

KAGER Johann Mathias 1575-1634 [8]

$1 964 - €2 045 - **£1 244** - FF13 415
Madonna mit Kind und Johannesknaben
Öl/Kupfer (15.5x11.5cm 6x4in) München 2000

KAGIE Jan, Jnr. 1907-1991 [47]

$218 - €218 - **£132** - FF1 428
Compositie Oil/canvas (110x80cm 43x31in)
Amsterdam 2000

$120 - €136 - **£81** - FF893
Vrouwenpolder Zeeland Watercolour/paper
(29x53cm 11x20in) Dordrecht 2000

KAGY Sheffield H. 1907-1989 [12]

$210 - €196 - **£129** - FF1 286
Sugar Bush Woodcut (27x38cm 11x15in) Cleveland
OH 1999

KAHAN Louis 1905-1997 [57]

$817 - €900 - **£543** - FF5 906
Beark in Life Class Ink (55x72.5cm 21x28in)
Melbourne 1999

$125 - €109 - **£76** - FF713
Two Seated Nudes Etching (11x9cm 4x3in) Sydney
1998

KAHANA Aharon 1905-1967 [105]

$16 000 - €17 309 - **£10 961** - FF113 542
Figures Oil/canvas (95x130cm 37x51in) Tel Aviv 2001

$4 400 - €4 952 - **£3 031** - FF32 483
Couple Oil/paper/canvas (35x48cm 13x18in) Herzelia-
Pituah 2000

$1 500 - €1 688 - **£1 033** - FF11 074
Landscape with Cypress Trees Oil/canvas
(27x35cm 10x13in) Herzelia-Pituah 2000

$550 - €652 - **£401** - FF4 280
Studies Charcoal/paper (47.5x68cm 18x26in) Tel Aviv
2001

KAHLER Carl 1855-1906 [42]

$4 000 - €3 839 - **£2 507** - FF25 182
Elegant Lady at a Flower Stand Oil/canvas
(130.5x79.5cm 51x31in) New-York 1999

$1 751 - €1 930 - **£1 164** - FF12 657
Portrait of Baroness Marie Vetsera Pastel/paper
(93x84cm 36x33in) Melbourne 2000

KAHLHAMER Brad XX [1]

$2 600 - €2 959 - **£1 827** - FF19 409
Untitled Watercolour, gouache (76x56.5cm 29x22in)
New-York 2001

KAHLO Frida 1907-1954 [26]

$1 500 000 - €1 742 767 - **£1 054 200** -
FF11 431 800
Portrait of Cristina, my sister Oil/panel (79x60cm
31x23in) New-York 2001

$200 000 - €235 485 - **£140 540** - FF1 544 680
Autorretrato Miniature (5x4cm 1x1in) New-York
2000

$47 500 - €55 928 - **£33 378** - FF366 861
Untitled Object (8x12x4cm 3x4x1in) New-York 2000

$40 000 - €34 879 - **£24 184** - FF228 788
Sin Título Ink (28x20cm 11x7in) New-York 1998

KAHN Wolf 1927 [62]

$14 000 - €16 415 - **£10 071** - FF107 675
Afterglow II Oil/canvas (106.5x167.5cm 41x65in)
New-York 2001

$7 000 - €8 122 - **£4 832** - FF53 277
Trees Against an Evening Background Oil/canvas
(61x71cm 24x27in) New-York 2000

$4 000 - €4 235 - **£2 522** - FF27 380
Trees in Andalusia Oil/canvas (29x40cm 11x15in)
New-York 2000

$800 - €746 - **£496** - FF4 893
Declicity Pastel/paper (38x49.5cm 14x19in) New-York
1999

KAHRER Max 1878-1937 [37]

$3 179 - €3 007 - **£1 980** - FF19 723
Dornröschen Öl/Leinwand (98x90cm 38x35in) Praha
2000

$1 059 - €1 163 - **£681** - FF7 627
Teich im Waldviertel Aquarell/Karton (47x61cm
18x24in) Wien 2000

KAINEN Jacob 1909-2001 [9]

$160 - €184 - **£110** - FF1 207
Bright Afternoon Etching, aquatint (39x49cm
15x19in) Cleveland OH 2000

KAIPIAINEN Birger 1915-1988 [25]

$1 839 - €2 018 - **£1 184** - FF13 238
Untitled Relief (H102cm H40in) Helsinki 2000

$824 - €923 - **£572** - FF6 054
Kvinna med sjal och hatt Sandstone (30x40cm
11x15in) Stockholm 2001

KAIRA Alice 1913 [21]

$3 796 - €3 364 - **£2 328** - FF22 064
Adam och Eva Oil/canvas (65x81cm 25x31in)
Helsinki 1999

KAISER Eduard 1820-1895 [7]

$2 640 - €2 281 - **£1 760** - FF14 960
Bambino con cane/Ritratto di gentildonna
Miniature (16x13cm 6x5in) Roma 1998

K

KAISER Friedrich 1815-1889 **[18]**
$2 330 - €2 479 - £1 590 - FF16 260
«La bataille de Naseby en 1645» Huile/toile
(26x34cm 10x13in) Bruxelles 2001

KAISER Raffi 1931 **[11]**
$3 400 - €3 827 - £2 342 - FF25 101
Surrealistic Marine battle Oil/board (60x140cm
23x55in) Herzelia-Pituah 2000

KAISER Richard 1868-1941 **[75]**
$1 792 - €1 533 - £1 078 - FF10 059
Blick auf die Fraueninsel im Chiemsee
Öl/Leinwand (110x75cm 43x29in) München 1998
$2 050 - €1 960 - £1 248 - FF12 858
Landscape with Country Road Oil/canvas
(19x59cm 7x23in) Columbia SC 1999

KAISER-HERBST Carl 1858-1940 **[43]**
$990 - €945 - £603 - FF6 197
Landschaften Öl/Karton (15x23cm 5x9in) Wien 1999

KAISERMANN Franz 1765-1833 **[59]**
$3 440 - €4 090 - £2 384 - FF26 831
Die Villa des Maecenas mit Tivoli Watercolour
(30x42.5cm 11x16in) Köln 2000

KAISIN Luc 1901-1963 **[67]**
$322 - €347 - £222 - FF2 276
Le jour du carnaval Huile/toile (70x60cm 27x23in)
Bruxelles 2001
$288 - €248 - £171 - FF1 627
La Régate Huile/panneau (30x33cm 11x12in)
Bruxelles 1998

KAIVANTO Kimmo 1932 **[17]**
$3 951 - €3 868 - £2 431 - FF25 373
Pohjoisluode Oil/canvas (92x73cm 36x28in) Helsinki
1999
$1 546 - €1 514 - £951 - FF9 928
Lämpöisellä reitillä Gouache/paper (49x70cm
19x27in) Helsinki 1999
$443 - €504 - £304 - FF3 309
Brevet Color lithograph (84x60cm 33x23in) Helsinki
2000

KAKANIAS Konstantin 1961 **[2]**
$4 590 - €5 106 - £3 060 - FF33 490
I Am Vlacha (Ex) Acrylic/canvas (50x40cm 19x15in)
Athens 2000

KÅKS Olle 1941 **[68]**
$1 968 - €1 984 - £1 227 - FF13 011
Komposition Oil/canvas (210x90cm 82x35in)
Stockholm 2000
$1 228 - €1 154 - £740 - FF7 569
Utan titel Oil/canvas (112x90cm 44x35in) Stockholm
1999
$216 - €201 - £133 - FF1 321
Guillaume Apollinaire, Dikter till Lou Serigraph in
colors (43x29cm 16x11in) Stockholm 1999

KALAY Necdet 1932-1984 **[2]**
$4 049 999 - €4 596 338 - £2 699 999 -
FF30 150 000
Boeufs tirant la charrue Huile/panneau (70x70cm
27x27in) Istanbul 2001

KÄLBERER Paul 1896-1974 **[16]**
$132 - €148 - £92 - FF972
Vorfrühling Print (28x22cm 11x8in) Dornhan 2001

KALCHER Raimund 1889-1959 **[11]**
$328 - €363 - £222 - FF2 383
Gebirgslandschaft mit Bergsee Aquarell/Papier
(35x27.5cm 13x10in) Klagenfurt 2000

KALCHSCHMIDT Emilio 1902 **[17]**
$200 - €207 - £120 - FF1 360
Cangelasio Acquarello/cartone (35x50cm 13x19in)
Vercelli 2000

KALCKAR Isidor 1850-1884 **[7]**
$956 - €1 074 - £663 - FF7 042
Bondestuinterior med ung pige, der pynter sig
Oil/canvas (23x27cm 9x10in) Köbenhavn 2000

KALCKREUTH von Jo 1912-1984 **[25]**
$5 841 - €5 624 - £3 652 - FF36 892
Der Berg II Öl/Leinwand (73x92cm 28x36in)
München 1999

KALCKREUTH von Leopold Karl Walter 1855-1928
[57]
$3 721 - €3 681 - £2 320 - FF24 148
Blick über Harmsdorf Öl/Leinwand (80x95cm
31x37in) Berlin 1999
$219 - €204 - £132 - FF1 341
Duckdalben im Hamburger Hafen Etching
(21.4x23cm 8x9in) Berlin 1999

KALCKREUTH von Patrick 1898-1970 **[161]**
$1 174 - €1 125 - £739 - FF7 378
Fischerboote in steifer See Öl/Leinwand
(71x100cm 27x39in) Köln 1999

KALDOVA Alois 1875-1934 **[3]**
$2 312 - €2 187 - £1 440 - FF14 344
Sommerlandschaft Öl/Leinwand (45x55cm 17x21in)
Praha 2001

KALF Willem 1619-1693 **[16]**
$108 849 - €92 672 - £65 000 - FF607 886
Still Life with Arms and Armour, Martial
Trumpets Oil/canvas (153x165.5cm 60x65in) London
1998
$471 232 - €528 361 - £320 000 - FF3 465 824
Peeled Lemon, a Roemer, a Wine-glass, a Knife
and a Rug Oil/canvas (51x44cm 20x17in) London
2000
$9 373 - €9 447 - £5 850 - FF61 971
Frau am Brunnen vor dem Haus Oil/panel
(32x25cm 12x9in) Wien 2000

KALINOWSKI Horst Egon 1924 **[81]**
$1 223 - €1 032 - £717 - FF6 771
«Tourrettes s Loop a.M.- «Coeur d'été»
(Mittsommer)» Collage (65x50cm 25x19in) Berlin
1998
$132 - €123 - £80 - FF804
Le nombril d'Adam Lithographie (49x64cm 19x25in)
Heidelberg 1999

KALISCHER Clemens 1921 **[21]**
$877 - €1 022 - £607 - FF6 707
St.Patricks Parade Vintage gelatin silver print
(25.2x20.1cm 9x7in) Köln 2000

KALISH Max 1891-1945 **[27]**
$7 500 - €8 677 - £5 308 - FF56 916
Mother and Child Bronze (H34cm H13in) Cleveland
OH 2000

KALLENBERG Anders 1834-1902 **[30]**
$747 - €714 - £465 - FF4 682
Idylliskt landskap Oil/canvas (36x48.5cm 14x19in)
Stockholm 1999
$1 020 - €966 - £633 - FF6 339
Tvätterskor vid sjö Oil/canvas (38x34cm 14x13in)
Malmö 1999

KALLERT August 1882-1958 **[7]**
- $993 - €971 - £630 - FF6 372
  Dachauer Bäuerin Oil/panel (38x29cm 14x11in)
  München 1999

KALLIN-FISCHER Grit 1897-1973 **[4]**
- $35 000 - €40 295 - £23 884 - FF264 320
  Freddo Gelatin silver print (23.5x15.5cm 9x6in) New-
  York 2000

KALLINA Jean 1956 **[8]**
- $796 - €941 - £565 - FF6 171
  «**Roy Lichtenstein in N.Y.C. Studio**» Gelatin silver
  print (50.5x40.5cm 19x15in) Berlin 2001

KALLIO Kalervo 1909-1969 **[5]**
- $3 436 - €3 868 - £2 366 - FF25 373
  Moderskärlek Marble (H51cm H20in) Helsinki 2000

KALLMORGEN Friedrich 1856-1924 **[131]**
- $4 176 - €4 602 - £2 787 - FF30 185
  Landschaft mit Fluss Öl/Leinwand (58x86cm
  22x33in) Satow 2000
- $3 212 - €2 811 - £1 945 - FF18 442
  **Zwei Schäfer mit blauen Hemdblusen und
  Pfeife im Gespräch** Öl/Leinwand (40x35cm 15x13in)
  Staufen 1998
- $105 - €123 - £74 - FF804
  Holländische Dorfstrasse Farblithographie
  (18x13.5cm 7x5in) Hamburg 2001

KALLOS Paul 1928 **[167]**
- $1 742 - €1 829 - £1 098 - FF12 000
  Composition Huile/toile (73x60cm 28x23in) Paris
  2000
- $272 - €305 - £189 - FF2 000
  Composition Aquarelle/papier (13x18cm 5x7in) Paris
  2001

KALLOUDIS Alexandros 1853-1923 **[1]**
- $9 108 - €7 714 - £5 313 - FF50 600
  Still Life with Pomegranates Oil/canvas
  (27x45.5cm 10x17in) Athens 1998

KALLSTENIUS Gottfrid 1861-1943 **[191]**
- $3 074 - €3 413 - £2 058 - FF22 391
  Glitter Oil/canvas (100x120cm 39x47in) Stockholm
  2000
- $1 134 - €1 104 - £698 - FF7 240
  Skärgårdsklippor i sommarsol Oil/canvas
  (60x74cm 23x29in) Stockholm 1999
- $759 - €778 - £469 - FF5 104
  Insjölandskap i månsken Oil/canvas (27x34cm
  10x13in) Stockholm 2000

KALMAKOFF Nicolaï 1873-1958 **[17]**
- $7 309 - €8 386 - £5 000 - FF55 010
  Le conteur dans le harem Oil/canvas (50x120cm
  19x47in) London 2000
- $4 877 - €4 269 - £2 954 - FF28 000
  Le gladiateur Aquarelle/papier (47x27cm 18x10in)
  Paris 1998

KALMAN Peter 1877-1948 **[17]**
- $2 021 - €2 045 - £1 234 - FF13 415
  Schlafender Akt Öl/Leinwand (96x83cm 37x32in)
  Stuttgart 2000

KALMAN Zsuzanna 1938 **[27]**
- $188 - €213 - £128 - FF1 400
  Le foulard rouge Huile/panneau (18x13cm 7x5in) Le
  Pontet 2000

KALMIKOFF Nicholas 1873-1955 **[2]**
- $2 127 - €2 265 - £1 400 - FF14 855
  Harem Scenes Watercolour, gouache/paper
  (22.5x61cm 8x24in) Billingshurst, West-Sussex 2000

KALMYKOV Nickolai Pavlovich 1924-1994 **[27]**
- $728 - €689 - £450 - FF4 519
  Woman in red, after Bogdanov-Belski Oil/canvas
  (90x69cm 35x27in) London 1999

KALOMA XIX-XX **[5]**
- $662 - €762 - £456 - FF5 000
  **Josephine Earp, de la femme de Wyatt Earp en
  nu** Tirage argentique (22x10.5cm 8x4in) Paris 2000

KALTENBECK Franz XX **[1]**
- $4 644 - €4 360 - £2 868 - FF28 602
  Ohne Titel Chalks (152.7x175.2cm 60x68in) Wien
  1999

KALTENMOSER E. XIX-XX **[16]**
- $108 - €128 - £76 - FF838
  Dachauer Moos Öl/Karton (26x36cm 10x14in)
  München 2000

KALTENMOSER Kaspar 1806-1867 **[11]**
- $4 606 - €5 113 - £3 211 - FF33 539
  «**Familienszene aus Istrien**» Öl/Leinwand
  (55x48cm 21x18in) Stuttgart 2001
- $2 734 - €3 068 - £1 895 - FF20 123
  Tanz in der oberbayerischen Wirtsstube
  Öl/Metall (15x18.5cm 5x7in) München 2000

KALUTA William Michael XX **[2]**
- $1 500 - €1 610 - £1 003 - FF10 561
  Finished pencil and ink specialty work Ink
  (33x43cm 12x16in) New-York 2000

KALVACH Rudolf 1883-1932 **[5]**
- $13 080 - €14 534 - £8 760 - FF95 340
  Träumende Mädchen Oil/panel (71x60cm 27x23in)
  Wien 2000

KALVODA Alois 1875-1934 **[73]**
- $1 618 - €1 531 - £1 008 - FF10 040
  Allée bordée d'arbres Huile/carton (44x67cm
  17x26in) Praha 2000
- $722 - €683 - £450 - FF4 482
  Village in Winter Oil/cardboard (26.5x30.5cm
  10x12in) Praha 1999

KAMA XX **[4]**
- $1 876 - €2 077 - £1 300 - FF13 622
  «**Megève**» Poster (98x67cm 38x26in) London 2001

KAMAL AL-MULK Muhammad XIX-XX **[1]**
- $60 252 - €62 874 - £38 000 - FF412 429
  Portrait of Muzaffar al-Din Shah Qajar Oil/canvas
  (109.5x80cm 43x31in) London 2000

KAMCHORN Soonpongsri 1937 **[4]**
- $7 140 - €7 679 - £4 788 - FF50 372
  Morning Oil/canvas (89x65cm 35x25in) Bangkok 2000

KAMEKE von Otto Werner Henning 1826-1899 **[23]**
- $894 - €1 022 - £621 - FF6 707
  Der Königsee Öl/Leinwand (60x89cm 23x35in)
  Rudolstadt-Thüringen 2000

KAMEKURA Yusaku 1915-? **[6]**
- $962 - €970 - £600 - FF6 362
  «**Xi Olympic Winter Games**» Poster (105x71cm
  41x27in) London 2000

KAMEN Jack XX **[1]**
- $4 000 - €4 294 - £2 676 - FF28 164
  «**Surpise Package**» Ink (44.5x34cm 17x13in) New-
  York 2000

KAMINER Saül 1952 **[4]**
- $13 000 - €12 649 - £8 001 - FF82 969
  La filmación Oil/canvas (130x195cm 51x76in) New-
  York 1999

K

KAMINSKI Max G. 1938 **[18]**
$2 411 - €2 812 - **£1 692** - FF18 446
Die grüne Pflanze Öl/Leinwand (105x96.5cm
41x37in) Köln 2000

KAMINSKI Stan 1952 **[24]**
$1 426 - €1 663 - **£1 000** - FF10 910
Impala Lookout Oil/canvas (60x90cm 23x35in)
London 2000

KAMINSKY Thomas 1945 **[11]**
$744 - €716 - **£459** - FF4 695
Ohne Titel Pencil/paper (54.9x46cm 21x18in) Köln
1999

KAMKE Ivar 1882-1936 **[40]**
$816 - €836 - **£504** - FF5 485
Kvinnlig nakenmodell Oil/panel (54x60cm 21x23in)
Stockholm 2000
$1 227 - €1 441 - **£866** - FF9 451
Strandbild med hus och uppdragna båtar
Pastel/paper (62x47cm 24x18in) Stockholm 2000

KAMM Louis Philippe XX **[12]**
$3 626 - €4 116 - **£2 519** - FF27 000
Petite fille de Hunspach Huile/toile (72x60cm
28x23in) Entzheim 2001
$2 278 - €1 982 - **£1 374** - FF13 000
Paysage Aquarelle/papier (28x38cm 11x14in)
Entzheim 1998

KÄMMERER Robert 1870-1950 **[31]**
$460 - €460 - **£288** - FF3 018
Aus Schwalenberg, Lippe Gouache (30.5x23.9cm
12x9in) Hamburg 1999

KAMOCKI Stanislaw 1875-1944 **[123]**
$12 379 - €12 246 - **£7 717** - FF80 330
Wola Radziszowska Oil/canvas (88x144.5cm
34x56in) Warszawa 1999
$3 705 - €4 140 - **£2 512** - FF27 155
Paysage Huile/toile (64x79cm 25x31in) Warszawa
2000
$2 266 - €2 601 - **£1 550** - FF17 062
Jardin Huile/carton (33x48cm 12x18in) Katowice 2000
$3 660 - €4 160 - **£2 528** - FF77 288
Automne Pastel (50x70cm 19x27in) Warszawa 2000

KAMP Louise Mary 1867-1959 **[33]**
$100 - €118 - **£71** - FF771
**View of porch with rocking settee and wooded
background** Oil/board (22x17cm 9x7in) Hatfield PA
2001

KAMPER Godaert 1614-1679 **[6]**
$8 724 - €9 161 - **£5 500** - FF60 090
**Wooded Landscape with a Herdsman and
Cattle on a Track, Peasants** Oil/panel (46x65.5cm
18x25in) London 2000

KAMPF Arthur 1864-1950 **[80]**
$2 311 - €2 496 - **£1 597** - FF16 371
Boy in a red Beret Oil/canvas (55.5x37cm 21x14in)
Amsterdam 2001
$438 - €409 - **£265** - FF2 683
Gefallene Krieger Gouache (67x53cm 26x20in)
Berlin 1999

KAMPF Eugen 1861-1933 **[77]**
$2 372 - €2 250 - **£1 443** - FF14 757
**Flandrisches Gehöft unter weitem
Wolkenhimmel** Öl/Leinwand (52x61cm 20x24in)
Köln 1999
$1 433 - €1 431 - **£896** - FF9 390
Strasse in einem flandrischen Dorf Oil/panel
(29x32cm 11x12in) Köln 1999

$680 - €581 - **£407** - FF3 812
Weidelandschaft mit tiefem Horizont
Pastell/Papier (34x54cm 13x21in) Wien 1998

KÄMPF Max 1912-1982 **[112]**
$2 968 - €2 493 - **£1 744** - FF16 353
«Sitzender Akt» Öl/Leinwand (69.5x26cm 27x10in)
Bern 1998
$335 - €281 - **£197** - FF1 846
Ansicht einer stehenden Figur mit Hut
Pencil/paper (27x19cm 10x7in) Bern 1998
$128 - €124 - **£79** - FF812
Sitzendes Mädchen Lithographie (47x35cm
18x13in) Bern 1999

KAMPMANN Gustav 1859-1917 **[66]**
$99 - €92 - **£60** - FF603
Frischer Wind Etching (6.5x17cm 2x6in) Heidelberg
1999

KAMPMANN Jack 1914-1989 **[114]**
$694 - €673 - **£437** - FF4 415
Komposition med huse Oil/canvas (54x65cm
21x25in) Köbenhavn 1999
$466 - €429 - **£288** - FF2 811
Huse ved fjorden Oil/canvas (24x33cm 9x12in) Vejle
1998

KAMPPURI Väinö 1891-1972 **[70]**
$2 374 - €2 270 - **£1 445** - FF14 893
Interiör Oil/canvas (51x65cm 20x25in) Helsinki 1999
$1 255 - €1 177 - **£775** - FF7 722
Hus vid forsen Oil/panel (31x39cm 12x15in) Helsinki
1999

KAMSETZER Jan Baptist 1753-1795 **[2]**
$994 - €1 067 - **£665** - FF7 000
Vue du grand aqueduc de Constantinople Encre
(27x44.5cm 10x17in) Paris 2000

KANAGA Consuelo 1894-1978 **[14]**
$2 000 - €1 871 - **£1 209** - FF12 271
Tree after Ice Storm (At the Ice House) Gelatin
silver print (10x7.5cm 3x2in) New-York 1999

KANAYAMA Heizo 1883-1964 **[3]**
$8 000 - €7 749 - **£4 989** - FF50 833
Morning in Seoul Oil/panel (30.5x39.5cm 12x15in)
New-York 1999

KANDEL ROEKA Dewa Kompiang 1916-1975 **[1]**
$5 844 - €6 118 - **£3 671** - FF40 129
Loetoeng Noendjel Oemah Watercolour (48x56cm
18x22in) Singapore 2000

KANDELIN Ole 1920-1947 **[20]**
$5 737 - €5 382 - **£3 545** - FF35 302
Avskedet Oil/panel (70x50cm 27x19in) Helsinki 1999
$7 215 - €7 064 - **£4 439** - FF46 334
Keskustelu Oil/panel (28x28cm 11x11in) Helsinki
1999

KANDINSKY Wassily 1866-1944 **[710]**
$584 850 - €494 301 - **£350 000** - FF3 242 400
Zum Rosa (Toward Pink) Oil/board (71x27cm
27x10in) London 1998
$160 000 - €167 490 - **£106 400** - FF1 164 256
**Kallmunz-Langgasse, Dorfstrasse (Village
Street, Kallmunz)** Oil/canvas/board (26.5x42cm
10x16in) New-York 2000
$85 218 - €71 573 - **£50 092** - FF469 490
«Aus der Tiefe», «De Profundis» Aquarell/Papier
(47.8x34cm 18x13in) Stuttgart 1998
$1 342 - €1 246 - **£820** - FF8 172
Komposition IV Farblithographie (34x52cm 13x20in)
Bern 1999

KANE Art 1925-1995 [8]
📷 **$2 800** - €3 225 - **£1 931** - FF21 156
Louis «Satchmo» Armstrong Dye-transfer print
(71x53cm 28x21in) New-York 2000

KANE Daniel 1954 [16]
📷 **$257** - €307 - **£183** - FF2 012
Canova I, Vatikan/Canova II, Vatikan Gelatin silver
print (15x33.4cm 5x13in) Berlin 2000

KANE John 1860-1934 [6]
🎨 **$21 000** - €17 942 - **£12 606** - FF117 692
Farm Scene with Three Horses Oil/canvas
(45.5x56cm 17x22in) New-York 1998
🎨 **$9 000** - €10 397 - **£6 301** - FF68 202
Dad's Roses Oil/board (43.5x28cm 17x11in) New-
York 2001

KANE Paul 1810-1871 [2]
🎨 **$321 005** - €309 205 - **£199 310** - FF2 028 250
Portrait of Maungwudaus Oil/canvas (63.5x76cm
25x29in) Toronto 1999

KANEDA JU XIX [1]
🗿 **$6 500** - €6 248 - **£4 053** - FF40 985
Elephant on a Globe Bronze (H50cm H19in) New-
York 1999

KANEKO Jun 1942 [7]
🗿 **$21 000** - €21 755 - **£13 366** - FF142 701
Dango with turquoise Stripes Ceramic (H88.5cm
H34in) New-York 2000

KANELBA Rajmund, Raymond 1897-1960 [29]
🎨 **$3 412** - €3 811 - **£2 282** - FF25 000
Nature morte au vase de fleurs Huile/toile
(81x54cm 31x21in) Paris 2000
🎨 **$10 170** - €11 156 - **£6 909** - FF73 181
Portrait d'une petite fille Huile/panneau (34x24cm
13x9in) Warszawa 2000
🎨 **$349** - €398 - **£240** - FF2 609
Portrait of a Lady Gouache/paper (76.5x53.5cm
30x21in) London 2000

KANERVA Aimo 1909-1991 [97]
🎨 **$567** - €538 - **£347** - FF3 530
Landskap Oil/canvas (42x59cm 16x23in) Helsinki
1999
🎨 **$1 195** - €1 345 - **£823** - FF8 825
Blåsig dag Oil/panel (15x25cm 5x9in) Helsinki 2000
$763 - €774 - **£479** - FF5 074
Kuru Akvarell/papper (48x64cm 18x25in) Helsinki
2000

KANERVA Raimo 1941-1999 [16]
📖 **$132** - €118 - **£81** - FF772
Form 1 Color lithograph (28x25cm 11x9in) Helsinki
1999

KANG YOUWEI 1858-1927 [16]
🖌 **$3 870** - €3 650 - **£2 400** - FF23 940
Calligraphy in Xing Shu Ink/paper (56x104.5cm
22x41in) Hong-Kong 1999

KANGXI Emperor 1662-1722 [29]
🗿 **$6 335** - €6 588 - **£4 000** - FF43 212
Famille Verte Rouleau Vase Ceramic (H42cm
H16in) London 2000
🖌 **$15 408** - €16 909 - **£9 924** - FF110 916
Poem in Running Script Calligraphy Ink/paper
(159.5x59cm 62x23in) Hong-Kong 2000

KANJI Maeta 1896-1930 [1]
🎨 **$95 000** - €104 809 - **£62 833** - FF687 505
Portrait of a Boy (Shonen no zo) Oil/canvas
(116.5x80.5cm 45x31in) New-York 2000

KANNEMANS Christiaan Cornelis 1812-1884 [24]
🎨 **$5 593** - €6 353 - **£3 924** - FF41 672
Sailing Vessels on a choppy Seas Oil/canvas
(66x89cm 25x35in) Amsterdam 2001

KANNIK Frans 1949 [54]
🎨 **$1 790** - €1 682 - **£1 087** - FF11 036
Komposition med kvindefigur Chalks (149x88cm
58x34in) Köbenhavn 1999

KANO MUNENOBU 1514-1562 [1]
✏️ **$11 000** - €10 073 - **£6 704** - FF66 075
Chinese Landscape Ink/paper (155x353cm
61x138in) New-York 1999

KANO SADANOBU XVII [1]
✏️ **$3 000** - €2 906 - **£1 871** - FF19 062
Views of Kyoto Coloured inks/paper (28x262.5cm
11x103in) New-York 1999

KANO TANSETSU 1654-1713 [1]
✏️ **$82 788** - €79 563 - **£51 000** - FF521 898
Six-Fold Screen of Flowers Coloured inks/paper
(178.5x61.5cm 70x24in) London 1999

KANO TANSHI 1785-1835 [1]
✏️ **$2 001** - €1 943 - **£1 246** - FF12 744
Landschaft mit einem Gelehrten in einem
Pavillon Indian ink/paper (101.7x47.7cm 40x18in)
Köln 1999

KANO TANYU 1602-1674 [5]
✏️ **$5 288** - €6 135 - **£3 650** - FF40 246
Taube auf Baumstamm Indian ink (90x30cm
35x11in) Stuttgart 2000

KANOLDT Alexander 1881-1939 [143]
🎨 **$23 701** - €23 008 - **£14 638** - FF150 925
Aus Tirol Öl/Karton (52x45.5cm 20x17in) München
1999
📖 **$601** - €690 - **£411** - FF4 527
Kapelle (Klausen in Tirol) Lithographie
(15.8x12.8cm 6x5in) Heidelberg 2000

KANOLDT Edmund Friedrich 1845-1904 [25]
🎨 **$10 128** - €11 248 - **£7 044** - FF73 785
Hero Öl/Leinwand (136.5x106cm 53x41in) Heidelberg
2001
🎨 **$980** - €1 125 - **£670** - FF7 378
Blick auf den Campo d'Annibale bei Cannae
Öl/Leinwand (13.3x41.2cm 5x16in) Heidelberg 2000
✏️ **$469** - €434 - **£283** - FF2 850
Rastender Wanderer im Wald bei Weimar Pencil
(45.5x59.5cm 17x23in) Heidelberg 1999

KANTERS Hans 1947 [16]
🎨 **$3 656** - €3 630 - **£2 284** - FF23 812
De Wachtende Maagden Oil/canvas (104x60cm
40x23in) Amsterdam 1999
🎨 **$1 828** - €1 815 - **£1 142** - FF11 906
Droomwereld Oil/panel (18x40cm 7x15in)
Amsterdam 1999

KANTILLA Kitty c.1928 [4]
🎨 **$20 584** - €22 096 - **£13 777** - FF144 943
Parlini Jilamara (Ancestral Design) Mixed media
(199.5x201cm 78x79in) Melbourne 2000
🎨 **$4 111** - €3 966 - **£2 598** - FF26 016
Parlini Jilmara (Old Designs) Mixed media/canvas
(100x118cm 39x46in) Melbourne 1999

KANTOR Maurice 1896-1974 [13]
🎨 **$5 000** - €4 662 - **£3 101** - FF30 582
Bouquet Oil/canvas (81.5x58.5cm 32x23in) New-York

K

KANTOR Tadeusz 1915-1990 **[47]**
- $3 432 - €3 684 - **£2 296** - FF24 165
  Demoiselles prenant un bain Technique mixte/panneau (39x50cm 15x19in) Kraków 2000
- $1 223 - €1 233 - **£763** - FF8 089
  Composition Indian ink (22x17.2cm 8x6in) Warszawa 2000

KANZAN Shimomura 1873-1930 **[6]**
- $30 000 - €29 061 - **£18 711** - FF190 626
  Shorin asa (Morning in Pine Grove) Coloured inks (145x55.5cm 57x21in) New-York 1999

KAPELL Paul 1876-1943 **[50]**
- $545 - €613 - **£375** - FF4 024
  Mann beim Festmachen eines Flusskahns Öl/Leinwand/Karton (52x55.5cm 20x21in) Bremen 2000

KAPLAN Anatoli Lwowitsch 1902-1980 **[45]**
- $219 - €204 - **£132** - FF1 341
  Anatewka (Dorf in Russland) Lithographie (28.8x40.8cm 11x16in) Berlin 1999

KAPLAN Hubert 1940 **[65]**
- $5 924 - €6 647 - **£4 106** - FF43 600
  Viehmarkt vor einem alten Städtchen Öl/Leinwand (40x51cm 15x20in) München 2000
- $1 739 - €2 045 - **£1 246** - FF13 415
  Sommerviehmarkt in Dachau Oil/canvas/panel (13x18cm 5x7in) Stuttgart 2001

KAPLAN Joseph 1900-1980 **[22]**
- $850 - €817 - **£519** - FF5 357
  Safe Harbor Watercolour, gouache/paper (50x66cm 20x26in) Provincetown MA 1999
- $3 800 - €3 951 - **£2 399** - FF25 919
  Untitled (Street Scene from above with Shadows) Gelatin silver print (24x21.5cm 9x8in) New-York 2000

KAPOOR Anish 1954 **[42]**
- $72 311 - €59 395 - **£42 000** - FF389 608
  Mother as a Ship Sculpture (223.5x108x104cm 87x42x40in) London 1998
- $26 897 - €28 872 - **£18 000** - FF189 388
  Buco Terracotta (39x39x40cm 15x15x15in) London 2000
- $937 - €1 036 - **£650** - FF6 796
  Untitled Etching (29x37cm 11x14in) London 2001

KAPP Gary 1942 **[2]**
- $8 000 - €9 084 - **£5 558** - FF59 584
  Blackfoot Camp Oil/canvas (76x101cm 30x40in) Dallas TX 2001

KAPPEL Philip 1901-1981 **[40]**
- $100 - €107 - **£68** - FF703
  «Boat Builders, Exssex» Etching (24x19cm 9x7in) Thomaston ME 2001

KAPPERS Gerhard A.V. ?-1750 **[1]**
- $115 745 - €109 322 - **£70 000** - FF717 108
  Hound with a Mallard before a Waterfall/A Pointer with a Covey Oil/canvas (136x157.5cm 53x62in) London 1999

KAPPES Alfred 1850-1894 **[2]**
- $75 000 - €86 645 - **£52 515** - FF568 357
  Tattered and Torn Oil/canvas (101.5x81.5cm 39x32in) New-York 2001

KAPPIS Albert 1836-1914 **[93]**
- $36 517 - €33 234 - **£22 815** - FF218 003
  Fischer mit Netzen und Booten am Strand Öl/Leinwand (100x209cm 39x82in) München 1999

KAPRALIK Jacques XX **[1]**
- $7 000 - €8 160 - **£4 846** - FF53 525
  Katharine Hepburn on Horseback Speaking to Robert Taylor Watercolour (28x43cm 11x17in) New-York 2000

KAPROW Alan 1927 **[6]**
- $3 600 - €3 110 - **£2 400** - FF20 400
  «3rd Routine», Trittico Collage/carta (36x27cm 14x10in) Prato 1998

KAPTAN Arif 1906-1982 **[2]**
- $1 800 000 - €2 042 817 - **£1 200 000** - FF13 400 000
  Paysage Huile/toile/panneau (46x36.5cm 18x14in) Istanbul 2001

KAR Ida 1908-1974 **[19]**
- $655 - €539 - **£380** - FF3 533
  William Somerset Maugham Gelatin silver print (58x45cm 23x18in) London 1998

KAR Surendranath 1892-1970 **[2]**
- $8 600 - €8 044 - **£5 200** - FF52 767
  Marble Prison Watercolour (28x20.5cm 11x8in) London 1999

KARAS Michael XX **[4]**
- $1 300 - €1 395 - **£870** - FF9 153
  Deer isle Maine Oil/board (25x17cm 10x7in) Newark OH 2000

KARAVAN Dani 1930 **[13]**
- $18 400 - €17 145 - **£11 452** - FF112 464
  Paralleli Metal (165x67cm 64x26in) Tel Aviv 1999

KARAZIN Nikolai Nikolaevich 1842-1908 **[13]**
- $1 600 - €1 784 - **£1 075** - FF11 703
  Winter Fairytale Watercolour, gouache (18.5x34cm 7x13in) Kiev 2000

KÄRCHER Amalia XIX-XX **[9]**
- $4 323 - €4 193 - **£2 738** - FF27 502
  Früchtestilleben mit Trauben, Pfirsichen und Aprikosen Öl/Leinwand/Karton (55.8x45.8cm 21x18in) München 1999

KARCHER Gustave 1831-1908 **[10]**
- $2 044 - €1 879 - **£1 256** - FF12 323
  Sommerliche Flusslandschaft mit Boot und Figurenstaffage Öl/Leinwand (129x90cm 50x35in) Zürich 1999

KARFIOL Bernard 1886-1952 **[28]**
- $4 500 - €4 489 - **£2 809** - FF29 444
  Still Life Composition Oil/canvas (91x71cm 36x28in) Cincinnati OH 1999

KÄRFVE Fritz 1880-1967 **[67]**
- $782 - €752 - **£483** - FF4 936
  Gårdar på Österlen Oil/canvas (54x69cm 21x27in) Malmö 1999

KARGEL Axel 1896-1971 **[45]**
- $1 852 - €2 116 - **£1 305** - FF13 883
  Hus och träd Oil/canvas/panel (34x49.5cm 13x19in) Stockholm 1999
- $1 860 - €1 806 - **£1 148** - FF11 846
  Sädesfält Oil/canvas (28x40cm 11x15in) Stockholm 1999

KARGER Karl 1848-1913 **[9]**
- $14 000 - €13 113 - **£8 607** - FF86 017
  Distinguished by Kaiser Franz Josef I through the Honor of his Address Oil/canvas (56x77.5cm 22x30in) New-York 1999
- $4 641 - €4 676 - **£2 892** - FF30 675
  Der Sammler Huile/panneau (34.5x28cm 13x11in) Zürich 2000

KARGL Rudolf 1878-1942 **[25]**
- $390 - €409 - **£258** - FF2 683
  Dachstein und Torstein Watercolour (21.4x33.5cm 8x13in) München 2000

KARGOPOULO B. XIX **[2]**
- $10 704 - €12 196 - **£7 352** - FF80 000
  Panorama de Constantinople Tirage albuminé (23x300cm 9x118in) Paris 2000

KARIMO Aarne 1886-1952 **[15]**
- $1 226 - €1 345 - **£789** - FF8 825
  Korsets magiska tecken Oil/canvas (70x49cm 27x19in) Helsinki 2000

KARLINSKY Anton Hans 1872-1945 **[22]**
- $2 708 - €2 907 - **£1 848** - FF19 068
  «Blühender Kastanienbaum» Öl/Leinwand (102.4x125cm 40x49in) Wien 2001
- $342 - €400 - **£244** - FF2 621
  «Künstlerhaus - 1.Jahresausstellung» Poster (121x91cm 47x35in) Wien 2000

KARLOWSKA de Stanislawa 1876-1952 **[18]**
- $3 586 - €3 849 - **£2 400** - FF25 251
  The Wine Shop Oil/board (25.5x33cm 10x12in) London 2000

KARLSSON C. Göran 1944 **[61]**
- $2 316 - €2 334 - **£1 444** - FF15 308
  Bebådelsen Tempera/panel (80x60cm 31x23in) Stockholm 2000
- $579 - €583 - **£361** - FF3 827
  Pyramider Tempera/paper (38x29cm 14x11in) Stockholm 2000

KARLSSON-STIG Ante 1885-1967 **[17]**
- $818 - €742 - **£504** - FF4 866
  Norrlandsmotiv Oil/canvas (39x58cm 15x22in) Stockholm 1999

KARNEC Jean-Étienne 1865-1934 **[59]**
- $974 - €915 - **£601** - FF6 000
  Vue d'Istambul, Le Bosphore Huile/panneau (24x33cm 9x12in) Paris 1999

KÄRNER Theodor 1884-1966 **[92]**
- $431 - €409 - **£262** - FF2 683
  Liegender junger Dackel Porcelain (10x18cm 3x7in) München 1999
- $1 579 - €1 687 - **£1 073** - FF11 067
  Jagdmotive Pastell/Papier (48x64cm 18x25in) Satow 2001

KARNIEIEFF Akim Jegorovitch 1833-1896 **[6]**
- $8 304 - €8 721 - **£5 232** - FF57 204
  Figürliche Szene aus einem italienischen Dorf Watercolour (41.5x31cm 16x12in) Wien 2000
- $493 - €457 - **£306** - FF3 000
  Le jeu de sauter sur la planche/Les patineurs sur la Nerva/Montagne Aquatinte couleurs (25x31cm 9x12in) Paris 1999

KARNIEJ Edward 1890-1942 **[2]**
- $3 315 - €3 307 - **£2 069** - FF21 691
  Jeune femme blonde Oil/panel (40.7x32.5cm 16x12in) Warszawa 1999

KARPELLUS Adolf 1869-1919 **[14]**
- $400 - €400 - **£244** - FF2 622
  «The Wallace Collection» Poster (100x63cm 39x25in) New-York 2000

KARPFF Jean-Jacq., Casimir 1770-1829 **[18]**
- $16 192 - €13 586 - **£9 500** - FF89 118
  The Playwright Collin d'Harleville Facing Left Miniature (9.5x7.5cm 3x2in) London 1998

KARPINSKI Alfons 1875-1961 **[158]**
- $3 605 - €3 155 - **£2 183** - FF20 697
  «Buduar» Oil/panel (56.5x68.7cm 22x27in) Warszawa 1998
- $2 140 - €2 515 - **£1 484** - FF16 498
  Boutons d'or dans un vase blanc Huile/carton (30x50.5cm 11x19in) Warszawa 2000
- $1 378 - €1 621 - **£991** - FF10 633
  Soucis Pastel/carton (31.5x47.5cm 12x18in) Warszawa 2001

KARPINSKI Tony 1965 **[8]**
- $6 132 - €5 100 - **£3 600** - FF33 457
  Elephant -Mother and Calf -Samburu, Kenya» Oil/board (37x75cm 14x29in) London 1998

KARPOFF Ivan 1898-1970 **[65]**
- $720 - €933 - **£540** - FF6 120
  Laguna di Venezia Olio/tela (40x50cm 15x19in) Vercelli 2001

KARPPANEN Matti 1873-1953 **[54]**
- $3 227 - €3 027 - **£1 994** - FF19 857
  Sidensvansar på gren Oil/canvas/panel (62x51cm 24x20in) Helsinki 1999
- $1 235 - €1 430 - **£874** - FF9 377
  Bofinkar Oil/canvas (34x40cm 13x15in) Helsinki 2000

KARS Georges / Jiri 1882-1945 **[219]**
- $5 628 - €6 403 - **£3 969** - FF42 000
  Femme assise Huile/toile (55x46cm 21x18in) Paris 2001
- $247 - €229 - **£153** - FF1 500
  Nu de dos Fusain/papier (33x47.5cm 12x18in) Paris 1999

KARSCH Joachim 1897-1945 **[8]**
- $4 240 - €4 116 - **£2 660** - FF26 998
  Betender Jünger Bronze (28.5x18x21.5cm 11x7x8in) Berlin 1999

KARSEN Eduard 1860-1941 **[24]**
- $8 686 - €8 168 - **£5 378** - FF53 578
  Boersche buurt Oil/canvas (37.5x50.5cm 14x19in) Amsterdam 1999
- $910 - €770 - **£544** - FF5 052
  Aan een slootkant Oil/canvas (33.5x44cm 13x17in) Amsterdam 1998
- $3 653 - €4 084 - **£2 542** - FF26 789
  The Herengracht, Amsterdam Black chalk (34x44.5cm 13x17in) Amsterdam 2001

KARSEN Kasparus 1810-1896 **[52]**
- $10 982 - €9 414 - **£6 498** - FF61 750
  Vue de ville Huile/toile (37.5x45cm 14x17in) Tongeren 1998
- $3 210 - €3 176 - **£1 964** - FF20 836
  Capriccio View in a City Oil/panel (23.5x31.5cm 9x12in) Amsterdam 2000
- $2 123 - €2 496 - **£1 472** - FF16 371
  A Capriccio view of a Town Watercolour (25x34cm 9x13in) Amsterdam 2000

KARSH Yousuf 1908 **[200]**
- $3 231 - €3 083 - **£2 025** - FF20 265
  Winston Churchill Gelatin silver print (51x40.5cm 20x15in) Vancouver, BC. 1999

K

KARSKAYA Ida 1905-1990 **[83]**
$170 - €183 - £114 - FF1 200
Composition Technique mixte/papier (23.5x16.5cm 9x6in) Versailles 2000

KARSTEN Ludwig Peter 1876-1926 **[48]**
$45 066 - €52 561 - £31 374 - FF344 778
Kvinne som steller seg Oil/canvas (55x66cm 21x25in) Oslo 2000
$10 540 - €12 539 - £7 290 - FF82 250
Studie av hest Oil/canvas (37x41cm 14x16in) Oslo 2000

KARTAKOV XX **[6]**
$614 - €581 - £380 - FF3 812
Women collecting Wood by the Shoreline Oil/canvas (15x20cm 5x7in) London 1999

KARVALY Mor 1860-1899 **[9]**
$7 382 - €8 080 - £5 103 - FF53 000
Sans titre Huile/toile (65x41cm 25x16in) Versailles 2001
$2 200 - €2 163 - £1 375 - FF14 190
Man with a Walking Stick Oil/canvas (48.5x32.5cm 19x12in) Budapest 1999

KASAMATSU Shiro 1898-1991 **[22]**
$150 - €153 - £94 - FF1 006
Tree Trunks by Water Woodcut (40x27cm 16x11in) Charlottesville VA 2000

KÄSEBIER Gertrude Stanton 1852-1934 **[49]**
$6 500 - €6 113 - £4 024 - FF40 097
Petty Harbour, St Johns, Newfoundland Gum bichromat print (19x24cm 7x9in) New-York 1999

KASELITZ Albert Friedrich 1821-1884 **[4]**
$3 261 - €3 835 - £2 337 - FF25 154
Küstenlandschaft mit Schiffen, Dorf und Personenstaffage Öl/Leinwand (58x86cm 22x33in) München 2001

KASIMIR Luigi 1881-1962 **[775]**
$325 - €295 - £195 - FF1 938
Schoenbuehel on the Danube Etching, aquatint in colors (23x23cm 9x9in) Bethesda MD 1998

KASIMIR Robert 1914 **[23]**
$133 - €131 - £82 - FF858
Wiener Ansichten Farbradierung (11x10cm 4x3in) Graz 1999

KASIMIR-HOERNES Tanna 1887-1972 **[36]**
$188 - €218 - £133 - FF1 430
Wien, Schottenring mit der Votifkirche Farbradierung (28x37cm 11x14in) Wien 2000

KASKIPURO Pentti 1930 **[20]**
$100 - €84 - £58 - FF551
Nattens väktare Etching (24x39cm 9x15in) Helsinki 1998

KASPAR Paul 1891-1953 **[107]**
$1 619 - €1 534 - £984 - FF10 061
Der Stephansdom in Wien Watercolour (20.2x16.4cm 7x6in) München 1999

KASPARIDES Eduard 1858-1926 **[48]**
$8 652 - €10 174 - £6 006 - FF66 738
Die letzten Sonnenstrahlen Oil/canvas/panel ($150x200cm 59x78in) Wien 2000
$2 900 - €3 113 - £1 940 - FF20 418
The Tryst Oil/canvas (68.5x49cm 26x19in) Philadelphia PA 2000
$1 951 - €2 035 - £1 229 - FF13 347
Stille Landschaft mit goldener Wolke Öl/Karton (29x36.5cm 11x14in) Wien 2000

KASPER Ludwig 1893-1945 **[6]**
$2 143 - €2 301 - £1 434 - FF15 092
Kinderkopf Beate Terracotta (29.3x11.6x10cm 11x4x3in) Köln 2000

KASPROWICZ Jan M. 1920 **[3]**
$3 975 - €3 680 - £2 400 - FF24 141
The Proposal Oil/canvas (62x78cm 24x30in) London 1999

KASPRZYCKI Wincenty 1802-1849 **[2]**
$1 258 - €1 351 - £842 - FF8 860
Wilanow Aquarelle (30x38cm 11x14in) Warszawa 2000

KASSAK Lajos 1887-1967 **[63]**
$8 738 - €10 062 - £5 966 - FF66 000
Kompozicio Huile/toile (62x56cm 24x22in) Lyon 2000
$12 800 - €12 586 - £8 000 - FF82 560
Composition Oil/canvas (28x22.5cm 11x8in) Budapest 1999
$2 572 - €3 049 - £1 816 - FF20 000
Composition constructiviste Collage (31x23cm 12x9in) Bordeaux 2000
$672 - €646 - £416 - FF4 240
Composition Engraving (20x20cm 7x7in) Budapest 1999

KASTEL Roger K. 1931 **[1]**
$1 790 - €1 643 - £1 100 - FF10 776
The Empire Strikes Back Poster (104x68cm 40x26in) London 1999

KASTEN Barbara 1936 **[10]**
$3 400 - €3 649 - £2 275 - FF23 939
Architectural Site #8 Cibachrome print (114x152cm 45x60in) New-York 2000

KASTROPHYLAX George XVIII **[1]**
$8 374 - €7 907 - £5 200 - FF51 867
The Martyrdom of Saint John the Baptist Oil/panel (44x32cm 17x12in) London 1999

KASTRUP E. XIX **[1]**
$3 410 - €3 229 - £2 121 - FF21 184
Roser i en kurv i skovbunden Oil/canvas (24x19cm 9x7in) Köbenhavn 1999

KASYN John 1926 **[91]**
$4 868 - €5 505 - £3 426 - FF36 112
«Off River Street» Oil/board (56x40cm 22x15in) Vancouver, BC. 2001
$1 633 - €1 561 - £1 023 - FF10 239
Back of Richmond St. Oil/board (20.5x35.5cm 8x13in) Vancouver, BC. 1999
$689 - €652 - £428 - FF4 280
Back Yard in Winter, near Shaw Street, Toronto Watercolour/paper (20x15cm 7x5in) Calgary, Alberta 1999

KAT de Anne Pierre 1881-1968 **[107]**
$2 691 - €3 222 - £1 846 - FF21 138
De gitaar (La guitare) Huile/toile (84x134cm 33x52in) Antwerpen 2000
$921 - €843 - £561 - FF5 528
Paysage Huile/panneau (29x32cm 11x12in) Antwerpen 1999
$306 - €347 - £207 - FF2 276
La toilette Aquarelle (16x22cm 6x8in) Bruxelles 2000

KAT de Otto B. 1907-1995 **[74]**
$5 129 - €4 440 - £3 112 - FF29 127
Papavers met testje Oil/canvas (46x61cm 18x24in) Amsterdam 1998

$3 334 - €2 886 - **£2 023** - FF18 933
Les Crêtes, France Oil/canvas (31x46cm 12x18in)
Amsterdam 1998

$604 - €681 - **£416** - FF4 464
The British Museum, London Watercolour,
gouache/paper (27x36.5cm 10x14in) Amsterdam 2000

KATCHADOURIAN Sarkis 1887-1947 **[7]**
$2 500 - €2 877 - **£1 723** - FF18 870
Floral Still Life Oil/canvas (65x49cm 25x19in) New-
Orleans LA 2000

KATCOWER Yuval 1971 **[5]**
$600 - €590 - **£362** - FF3 872
Social Games Print in colors (25x115.5cm 9x45in)
Chicago IL 2000

KÄTHELHÖN Hermann 1884-1940 **[59]**
$175 - €184 - **£110** - FF1 207
Bildnis Professor Karl Budde Radierung
(26.2x32.8cm 10x12in) Heidelberg 2000

KATHELIN Ernest XIX **[2]**
$3 223 - €3 712 - **£2 200** - FF24 347
Sweet Dreams Watercolour (52x38.5cm 20x15in)
London 2000

KATHY Roger 1934-1979 **[48]**
$1 018 - €1 182 - **£703** - FF7 754
Sonnenuntergang in Winterlandschaft
Öl/Leinwand (50x65cm 19x25in) St. Gallen 2000

KATSUGAWA Shuncho act.1777-1821 **[10]**
$1 300 - €1 525 - **£928** - FF10 003
**A Sheet from a Pentaptych Illustrating a Scene
from the Joruri Play** Print in colors (25.5x19cm
10x7in) New-York 2000

KATSUGAWA Shunjo ?-1787 **[1]**
$948 - €1 067 - **£653** - FF7 000
**L'acteur Nakamura Matsue dans un rôle de
femme** Estampe couleurs (30.5x14cm 12x5in) Paris
2000

KATZ Alex 1927 **[328]**
$65 000 - €57 803 - **£39 754** - FF379 164
Vincent and Ada Oil/canvas (183x244cm 72x96in)
New-York 2000

$8 500 - €7 251 - **£5 127** - FF47 566
Study for Times Square Mural Acrylic/board
(42.5x47cm 16x18in) New-York 1998

$7 000 - €7 966 - **£4 918** - FF52 256
Façade Oil/masonite (30.5x23cm 12x9in) New-York
2001

$4 800 - €5 463 - **£3 373** - FF35 833
Crolie Graphite (38x56cm 14x22in) New-York 2001

$934 - €1 038 - **£620** - FF6 808
Portrait of a Woman Screenprint in colors
(65.5x65.5cm 25x25in) London 2001

KATZ Benjamin 1930 **[27]**
$730 - €818 - **£507** - FF5 366
Joseph Beuys Gelatin silver print (49x58cm 19x22in)
Köln 2001

KATZ Hanns Ludwig 1882-1940 **[4]**
$13 772 - €15 988 - **£9 680** - FF104 874
**Selbstbildnis im Handspiegel/Stilleben mit
Aquarium** Oil/panel (100x60cm 39x23in) Wien 2001

$1 195 - €1 387 - **£825** - FF9 097
Magaliesberg Pool, Grootkloof Watercolour/paper
(55x37.5cm 21x14in) Johannesburg 2000

KATZ Hyman 1899-? **[26]**
$170 - €174 - **£106** - FF1 143
Men on Park Bench Etching, aquatint (22x18cm
8x7in) Cleveland OH 2000

KATZEN-FLURY Burkhard 1862-1928 **[23]**
$676 - €789 - **£474** - FF5 174
Katzenbildnis Öl/Leinwand (22x20cm 8x7in) Luzern
2000

$1 351 - €1 425 - **£893** - FF9 350
Drei Katzen Pastell/Papier (25.5x34cm 10x13in)
Zürich 2000

KATZIEFF Julius D. 1892-? **[8]**
$225 - €216 - **£137** - FF1 418
Along the Shore Print (15x21cm 6x8in)
Provincetown MA 1999

KAUBA Carl 1865-1922 **[156]**
$1 620 - €1 815 - **£1 126** - FF11 906
Lady Bronze (H22.5cm H8in) Amsterdam 2001

KAUFFER Edward McKnight 1890-1954 **[88]**
$2 628 - €2 507 - **£1 600** - FF16 444
Ship at Last Light Watercolour (33x25cm 12x9in)
London 1999

$579 - €658 - **£402** - FF4 316
«By the Rushy-fringed Bank...» Poster (63x102cm
24x40in) Hoorn 2001

KAUFFMAN Angelica 1740-1807 **[179]**
$375 300 - €440 026 - **£270 000** - FF2 886 381
**Group Portrait of the Spencer Children, full-
length in a Landscape** Oil/canvas (113.5x145cm
44x57in) London 2001

$123 340 - €101 720 - **£72 660** - FF667 240
Die Trauer Telemache auf der Insel der Calypso
Öl/Leinwand (80x96.5cm 31x37in) Wien 1998

$21 174 - €20 675 - **£13 500** - FF135 621
**Beauty Governed by Reason Rewarded by
Merit** Oil/copper (45.5x30.5cm 17x12in) London 1999

$1 614 - €1 494 - **£1 000** - FF9 801
Study for «Morning Amusement» Black
chalk/paper (30x22cm 11x8in) London 1999

$507 - €562 - **£344** - FF3 689
**Lesende Frau, ein Buch auf einem Kissen hal-
tend** Radierung (9.5x12.2cm 3x4in) Hamburg 2000

KAUFFMANN Hermann 1808-1889 **[61]**
$9 086 - €10 226 - **£6 260** - FF67 078
Pferdfuhrwerk im Schneesturm Öl/Leinwand
(61x84cm 24x33in) München 2000

$3 634 - €4 090 - **£2 504** - FF26 831
Im Galopp zur Feldarbeit Oil/panel (28x35cm
11x13in) München 2000

$716 - €613 - **£430** - FF4 024
Fischerboote am Strand Pencil/paper (13x19.8cm
5x7in) Köln 1998

KAUFFMANN Hermann II 1873-1953 **[10]**
$971 - €920 - **£590** - FF6 037
**Oberbayerischer Jäger, auf sein Gewehr
gestützt, eine Pfeife haltend** Oil/panel
(20.7x16.2cm 8x6in) München 1999

KAUFFMANN Hugo Wilhelm 1844-1915 **[185]**
$18 047 - €16 527 - **£11 000** - FF108 411
The Musician Oil/canvas (46x60.5cm 18x23in)
London 1999

$6 349 - €7 503 - **£4 500** - FF49 214
Portrait of a Man Oil/panel (14.5x11.5cm 5x4in)
London 2000

$504 - €562 - **£352** - FF3 689
Der Bratenrock Ink (18.5x12.6cm 7x4in) München
2001

KAUFFMANN Max 1846-? **[5]**
$11 598 - €10 737 - **£7 100** - FF70 431
Jagdmotive Öl/Leinwand (42x53cm 16x20in)
Hamburg 1999

K

K

$2 189 – €1 865 – **£1 304** – FF12 236
A Clear Brew/A Toast Oil/panel (26x20cm 10x7in)
Bath 1998

KAUFMAN Steve XX [2]

$453 – €537 – **£320** – FF3 525
The Greatest, No.II out of IV Screenprint (78x116cm
30x45in) London 2000

KAUFMANN Adolf 1848-1916 [194]

$2 749 – €3 270 – **£1 962** – FF21 451
Flusslandschaft Öl/Leinwand (60x101cm 23x39in)
Linz 2000

$2 628 – €2 249 – **£1 582** – FF14 754
Schäfer mit seiner Herde in Herbstlandschaft
Öl/Karton (33.5x17.5cm 13x6in) München 1998

KAUFMANN Arthur 1888-1971 [16]

$4 327 – €5 113 – **£3 067** – FF33 539
Auf dem Güterbahnhof Öl/Leinwand (85x105cm
33x41in) Ahlden 2000

KAUFMANN Ferdinand 1864-1942 [24]

$4 000 – €4 320 – **£2 764** – FF28 335
«Morning at Lumbar warf» Oil/canvas (51x61cm
20x24in) Bethesda MD 2001

$3 500 – €4 090 – **£2 498** – FF26 831
«Fishermen's house, Rockport, Mass» Oil/board
(20x25cm 8x10in) Altadena CA 2001

KAUFMANN Isidor 1853-1921 [87]

$95 000 – €90 602 – **£57 826** – FF594 310
Portrait of a Young Yeshiva Boy Oil/panel
(30.5x25cm 12x9in) New-York 1999

$10 000 – €9 733 – **£6 144** – FF63 844
Portrait of a Rabbi Watercolour (25.5x19.5cm
10x7in) Tel Aviv 1999

KAUFMANN Joseph Clemens 1867-1925 [54]

$442 – €437 – **£275** – FF2 869
Stilleben mit Fischen und Zitronen Öl/Leinwand
(37x64cm 14x25in) St. Gallen 1999

$546 – €526 – **£336** – FF3 453
**Kavallerist auf braunem Pferd in bewaldeter
Landschaft** Huile/panneau (41x31.5cm 16x12in) Bern
1999

$169 – €197 – **£117** – FF1 292
Zaun auf Alpweide Pastell/Papier (29.5x43.5cm
11x17in) Luzern 2000

KAUFMANN Karl, Charles 1843-1901 [399]

$7 040 – €6 607 – **£4 290** – FF43 340
En el cuarto de jugar Oleo/lienzo (98x138cm
38x54in) Madrid 1999

$1 947 – €1 870 – **£1 206** – FF12 265
**Venedig, Blick auf Canal Grande und Kirche
Santa Maria della Salute** Öl/Leinwand (37x58cm
14x22in) Zürich 1999

$1 792 – €1 631 – **£1 100** – FF10 699
**The Grand Canal, Venice as seen from the
Piazzetta** Oil/canvas (32x48cm 12x18in) London 1999

KAUFMANN Philipp Friedrich 1888-1969 [33]

$269 – €289 – **£180** – FF1 893
Austrian Landscape Oil/canvas (76x62cm 29x24in)
London 2000

KAUFMANN Wilhelm 1895-1975 [133]

$1 608 – €1 599 – **£972** – FF10 487
Achensee Oil/panel (60x80cm 23x31in) Wien 2000

$957 – €1 000 – **£661** – FF7 150
Steirische Häuser zur Baumblüte
Mischtechnik/Papier (47.3x64.5cm 18x25in) Wien 2000

KAUL J.V. XX [1]

$7 871 – €9 169 – **£5 500** – FF60 144
Wilma Neruda playing the Violin Oil/canvas
(90x70cm 35x27in) Brighton 2000

KAULA Lee Lufkin 1882-1957 [13]

$2 400 – €2 729 – **£1 676** – FF17 904
Table Still Life Oil/canvas (58x45cm 23x18in) Mystic
CT 2000

$1 300 – €1 209 – **£802** – FF7 929
Holding all the Cards Watercolour/paper (34x25cm
13x10in) Portland ME 1999

KAULA William Jurian 1871-1953 [65]

$8 500 – €7 263 – **£4 992** – FF47 645
Late Afternoon, Winter Oil/canvas (61x74cm
24x29in) Boston MA 1998

$2 250 – €1 923 – **£1 361** – FF12 612
**The Little White House, New Ipswich, New
Hampshire** Oil/panel (30.5x38cm 12x14in) San-
Francisco CA 1998

$700 – €625 – **£428** – FF4 099
House in River Landscape Watercolour/paper
(36x30cm 14x12in) Altadena CA 1999

KAULBACH Anton 1864-1930 [56]

$834 – €767 – **£512** – FF5 030
**Zigeunerin, ein Band im Haar und grosses
orientalisches Ohrgehänge** Öl/Karton (52x41cm
20x16in) Konstanz 1999

KAULBACH Friedrich 1822-1903 [12]

$6 021 – €7 158 – **£4 172** – FF46 954
Kaiserin Elisabeth Öl/Leinwand (104x106cm
40x41in) München 2000

KAULBACH Hermann 1846-1909 [69]

$19 820 – €18 151 – **£12 080** – FF119 064
Ruhe auf der Flucht nach Egypt Oil/canvas
(192x152cm 75x59in) Amsterdam 1999

$6 141 – €5 624 – **£3 743** – FF36 892
Stilleben Öl/Leinwand (110x85cm 43x33in) Berlin
1999

$7 211 – €6 646 – **£4 318** – FF43 595
Kleines Mädchen mit rotem Kleid Oil/panel
(17x11cm 6x4in) Dresden 1998

KAULBACH von Friedrich August 1850-1920 [78]

$16 560 – €19 831 – **£11 360** – FF130 080
**Vijf kinderen in pierrotkostuum (Cinq enfants
en costume de pierrot)** Huile/toile (95x135cm
37x53in) Antwerpen 2000

$4 810 – €5 624 – **£3 380** – FF36 892
Mädchenbildnis Öl/Leinwand (62x52cm 24x20in)
München 2000

$2 832 – €2 812 – **£1 769** – FF18 446
Junge Dame in Renaissancegewand Oil/panel
(27.5x22cm 10x8in) München 1999

$619 – €613 – **£387** – FF4 024
**Auf dem Bett sitzende junge Frau mit entblös-
ter Brust** Ink/paper (10x11cm 3x4in) München 1999

KAULBACH von Wilhelm 1804-1874 [32]

$782 – €920 – **£561** – FF6 037
«Anakreon und seine Geliebte»
Öl/Leinwand/Karton (18.5x16.5cm 7x6in) Stuttgart
2001

$360 – €409 – **£250** – FF2 683
**Sich küssendes Liebespaar in mittelalterlicher
Tracht** Ink (37.5x50.5cm 14x19in) Berlin 2001

KAULUM Haakon Jensen 1863-1933 [21]

$982 – €1 153 – **£693** – FF7 561
Fiskare i segelbåt Oil/canvas (60x85cm 23x33in)
Stockholm 2000

KAUS Max 1891-1977 **[238]**
- **$39 984** - €34 750 - **£24 092** - FF227 942
«Badende Frauen und Angler am Rhein»/**Sauerländische Landschaft** Öl/Leinwand (117x142.5cm 46x56in) Berlin 1998
- **$10 316** - €10 226 - **£6 454** - FF67 078
Fischreusen Öl/Leinwand (70x100cm 27x39in) München 1999
- **$2 097** - €2 301 - **£1 424** - FF15 092
Stilleben mit Kanne Gouache (68.7x48.2cm 27x18in) Berlin 2000
- **$549** - €511 - **£337** - FF3 353
Drei Akte Radierung (29.8x24.3cm 11x9in) Hamburg 1999

KAUTZKY Theodore 1896-1953 **[9]**
- **$600** - €557 - **£374** - FF3 652
Dory Beached on Tidal Flats in Rockport, Cape Ann Watercolour/paper (53x73cm 21x29in) East-Dennis MA 1999

KAUZMANN Paul 1874-1951 **[15]**
- **$8 989** - €7 668 - **£5 422** - FF50 302
«Im Kirchturm» Öl/Leinwand (106x76cm 41x29in) Kempten 1998

KAVAN Frantisek 1866-1941 **[72]**
- **$1 329** - €1 257 - **£828** - FF8 247
At Vostrovec (in Vitanov) Oil/paper/canvas (50x67cm 19x26in) Praha 1999
- **$1 011** - €957 - **£630** - FF6 275
Forest Nook seen from Zeleznice Oil/cardboard (24.5x34.5cm 9x13in) Praha 1999

KAVANAGH Joseph Malachy 1856-1918 **[25]**
- **$2 600** - €2 791 - **£1 739** - FF18 306
Tending the Flock Oil/canvas (50x59cm 20x23in) Chicago IL 2000
- **$6 280** - €5 930 - **£3 900** - FF38 900
Winding River Landscape with Cattle Oil/canvas (32.5x22.5cm 12x8in) Billingshurst, West-Sussex 1999

KAVLI Arne 1878-1970 **[81]**
- **$7 855** - €9 076 - **£5 567** - FF59 536
Oppstilling med blomster Oil/canvas (76x64cm 29x25in) Oslo 2001
- **$2 598** - €2 212 - **£1 552** - FF14 510
Fra Rönnes Oil/canvas (26x35cm 10x13in) Oslo 1998

KAWABATA Ryushi 1885-1966 **[32]**
- **$26 000** - €26 200 - **£16 208** - FF171 860
Shumbo Fugaku (Spring view of Mount Fuji) Mixed media (47x57cm 18x22in) New-York 2000
- **$6 000** - €6 046 - **£3 740** - FF39 660
Hakubai (white plum) Mixed media (27x24cm 10x9in) New-York 2000
- **$22 000** - €24 272 - **£14 550** - FF159 211
Kawasemi (Kingfisher) Ink (61x72.5cm 24x28in) New-York 2000

KAWAI Kanjiro 1890-1966 **[7]**
- **$9 000** - €10 048 - **£6 015** - FF65 912
Untitled Ceramic (H19cm H7in) New-York 2000

KAWANO Kaoru 1916-1965 **[42]**
- **$136** - €128 - **£82** - FF838
Geisha Woodcut in colors (38x25.4cm 14x10in) Berlin 1999

KAWARA On 1932 **[37]**
- **$140 000** - €158 375 - **£97 944** - FF1 038 870
«Feb.27,1987» Acrylic (133.5x194.5cm 52x76in) New-York 2001
- **$49 680** - €46 295 - **£30 000** - FF303 675
«Nov. 30, 1985» Acrylic/canvas (46x61cm 18x24in) London 1998

- **$28 000** - €31 362 - **£19 454** - FF205 721
«Sunday, Apr.7,1974, Today Series No.21» Mixed media/canvas (21.5x25.5cm 8x10in) New-York 2001
- **$32 000** - €35 780 - **£21 571** - FF234 700
Tuesday Aug. 12 Assemblage (26x33cm 10x12in) New-York 2000
- **$17 000** - €19 041 - **£11 811** - FF124 902
I Got Up Ink (10.5x14.5cm 4x5in) New-York 2001

KAWASE Shinobu 1950 **[4]**
- **$6 000** - €6 699 - **£4 010** - FF43 941
Untitled Porcelain (H37.5cm H14in) New-York 2000

KAY Archibald 1860-1935 **[84]**
- **$2 416** - €2 270 - **£1 500** - FF14 893
Driving Sheep Oil/canvas (51x40.5cm 20x15in) London 1999
- **$861** - €969 - **£600** - FF6 353
Goodly River Oil/canvas/board (23.5x32cm 9x12in) Edinburgh 2001

KAY James 1858-1942 **[157]**
- **$7 053** - €6 663 - **£4 400** - FF43 706
Parisian Flower Market Oil/canvas (61x51cm 24x20in) Perthshire 1999
- **$1 580** - €1 354 - **£950** - FF8 879
Snow in Perthshire Oil/board (25.5x34.5cm 10x13in) Edinburgh 1998
- **$1 903** - €2 039 - **£1 300** - FF13 375
Scottish Bay on a Summer's Day Watercolour (29.5x44.5cm 11x17in) London 2001

KAY Violet McNeish 1914-1971 **[11]**
- **$789** - €827 - **£500** - FF5 426
Faslane Bay before the War Oil/canvas/board (60x90cm 23x35in) Edinburgh 2000

KAYAMA Matazo 1927 **[32]**
- **$65 000** - €65 500 - **£40 521** - FF429 650
Hana (Flower) Mixed media (39.5x50cm 15x19in) New-York 2000
- **$85 000** - €98 625 - **£58 684** - FF646 935
Kazan (Volcano) Ink (41x60cm 16x23in) New-York 2000
- **$2 462** - €2 744 - **£1 710** - FF18 000
La martin pêcheur Gravure (45x34.5cm 17x13in) Paris 2001

KAYE Otis 1885-1974 **[42]**
- **$80 000** - €88 597 - **£54 256** - FF581 160
Hidden Assets Oil/panel (36x50.5cm 14x19in) New-York 2000
- **$62 000** - €59 002 - **£38 781** - FF387 028
The Key to Success Oil/canvas/panel (20.5x25.5cm 8x10in) New-York 1999
- **$3 500** - €3 263 - **£2 171** - FF21 407
Chicago Street Gouache/paper (19x30cm 7x11in) New-York 1999

KAYYALI Louai 1934-1978 **[2]**
- **$37 239** - €41 884 - **£26 000** - FF274 742
Newspaper Boy Oil/masonite (88x73.5cm 34x28in) London 2001

KAZAN Watanabe 1793-1841 **[3]**
- **$1 360** - €1 310 - **£850** - FF8 590
View of the Mount Fuji with Villages Print (48x77.5cm 18x30in) London 1999

KAZUMASA Nakagawa 1893-1991 **[7]**
- **$58 800** - €57 351 - **£36 000** - FF376 200
Manazuru Oil/canvas (50x65cm 19x25in) Tokyo 1999
- **$20 580** - €20 073 - **£12 600** - FF131 670
Still Life Gouache/paper (34.5x63cm 13x24in) Tokyo 1999

K

KCHAOUDOFF Jeantimir 1941 **[45]**
🖋 **$315** - €290 - **£193** - FF1 900
   La promenade du chien Encre Chine/papier
   (27x47cm 10x18in) Paris 1999

KCHO (A. Leyva Machado) 1970 **[5]**
🖊 **$13 221** - €11 296 - **£8 000** - FF74 100
   Untitled Installation (55x300x122cm 21x118x48in)
   London 1998
🖋 **$4 500** - €4 354 - **£2 775** - FF28 561
   Columna infinita Charcoal/paper (234x152.5cm
   92x60in) New-York 1999

KEARNEY William Henry c.1800-1858 **[6]**
🖋 **$1 077** - €1 257 - **£750** - FF8 247
   **Martin Luther before the Cardinal at the Diet of
   Worns** Watercolour (85x109cm 33x42in) London 2000

KEATING George 1762-1842 **[13]**
🖋 **$107** - €107 - **£65** - FF700
   Setting out for the Fair, after Frances Wheatley
   Mezzotint (31x24cm 12x9in) Leicestershire 2000

KEATING Sean 1889-1977 **[70]**
☞ **$49 681** - €53 329 - **£33 247** - FF349 818
   An Beinnsin Luachra (Two on a Mountain)
   Oil/board (119.5x119.5cm 47x47in) Dublin 2000
☞ **$26 287** - €22 846 - **£15 840** - FF149 857
   **Portrait of a Fireman Seated, Holding a Brass
   Nozzle** Oil/canvas (106x90cm 41x35in) Dublin 1998
🖋 **$2 426** - €2 793 - **£1 655** - FF18 323
   Seated Woman in Shawl Charcoal/paper (25x28cm
   9x11in) Dublin 2000

KEATING Tom 1917-1984 **[135]**
☞ **$1 191** - €1 386 - **£850** - FF9 090
   Exquisite Lady with a Fan, after Velazquez
   Oil/canvas (76x51cm 29x20in) Suffolk 2000
🖋 **$2 806** - €2 457 - **£1 760** - FF16 114
   Crucifixion, in the manner of Rembrandt Oil/can-
   vas (18x25.5cm 7x10in) Suffolk 1998
🖋 **$957** - €838 - **£580** - FF5 497
   Harvesters Resting by a Threshing Circle
   Watercolour (26x37.5cm 10x14in) Suffolk 1998
🖊 **$1 816** - €1 590 - **£1 100** - FF10 427
   After Edgard Degas Estampe (43x32.5cm 16x12in)
   Suffolk 1998

KEATISAK PLITAPORN 1955 **[5]**
🖋 **$1 468** - €1 364 - **£907** - FF8 948
   Rocks by the Rapids Watercolour/paper (53x72cm
   20x28in) Bangkok 1999

KEATS Cecil Jack XIX-XX **[43]**
🖋 **$374** - €412 - **£260** - FF2 703
   Rural Lane Scenes with Cottages and Figures
   Watercolour/paper (18x34cm 7x13in) Burton-on-Trent,
   Staffs 2001

KEATS Charles James XIX-XX **[6]**
🖋 **$372** - €416 - **£260** - FF2 731
   La grosse horloge, Rouen Watercolour (39x28cm
   15x11in) Bath 2001

KEAY Jack 1907 **[15]**
🖋 **$97** - €115 - **£70** - FF753
   **Male and Female Figures in a Moorland
   Landscape with a Cottage nearby**
   Watercolour/paper (46x33cm 18x13in) Send-Woking,
   Surrey 2001

KECK Leo 1906-1987 **[15]**
🖊 **$673** - €610 - **£420** - FF4 002
   «Lenk» Poster (102x64cm 40x25in) London 1999

KECK Otto 1873-1948 **[23]**
☞ **$2 419** - €2 045 - **£1 438** - FF13 413
   Sommertag in den Allgäuer Alpen Öl/Leinwand
   (65x80cm 25x31in) Lindau 1998
🖋 **$1 014** - €971 - **£626** - FF6 372
   Gebirgslandschaft am Reh auf Frühlingswiese
   Aquarell, Gouache/Papier (26x34cm 10x13in) Kempten
   1999

KECK Paul 1904-1973 **[18]**
☞ **$2 023** - €2 301 - **£1 403** - FF15 092
   **Portrait einer jungen hübschen Frau mit schul-
   terfreiem Kleid** Öl/Leinwand (76x55cm 29x21in)
   Lindau 2000

KECK William 1908 **[12]**
📷 **$4 000** - €3 730 - **£2 414** - FF24 466
   Reflections and Mirroring, Variant Photograph
   (33.5x26.5cm 13x10in) New-York 1999

KEDZIERSKI Apoloniusz 1861-1939 **[32]**
☞ **$11 852** - €10 225 - **£7 150** - FF67 070
   Fisherman and Wave Oil/canvas (40x60cm 15x23in)
   München 1998
🖋 **$1 928** - €1 893 - **£1 196** - FF12 417
   Roseaux Watercolour (31.5x25.5cm 12x10in)
   Warszawa 1999

KEELEY John 1849-1930 **[47]**
🖋 **$408** - €392 - **£242** - FF2 572
   Anglers on a Riverbank Watercolour/paper
   (25x35.5cm 9x13in) London 1999

KEELHOFF Frans 1820-1893 **[20]**
☞ **$7 000** - €7 849 - **£4 753** - FF51 483
   At the Farm Oil/canvas (75x99cm 29x38in) New-York
   1999

KEELING David 1951 **[4]**
☞ **$4 129** - €4 629 - **£2 887** - FF30 361
   «Tasmanian Landscape» Oil/canvas (76.5x106.5cm
   30x41in) Melbourne 2001

KEELY Pat (P. Cokayne) ?-1970 **[7]**
🖊 **$233** - €272 - **£159** - FF1 786
   «Meldt u als oorlogsvrijwilliger» Poster (69x40cm
   27x15in) Hoorn 2000

KEENE Charles Samuel 1823-1891 **[33]**
🖋 **$423** - €412 - **£260** - FF2 572
   Desesperate Case/Contented Mind Ink (17x14cm
   6x5in) Newbury, Berkshire 1999

KEENE Elmer XIX-XX **[16]**
🖋 **$883** - €1 027 - **£620** - FF6 735
   Diving Ducks Watercolour, gouache/paper (35x26cm
   13x10in) Billingshurst, West-Sussex 2001

KEENE Paul F., Jr. 1920 **[1]**
☞ **$8 500** - €9 723 - **£5 910** - FF63 779
   Table top still life and chair Mixed media (81x64cm
   32x25in) Philadelphia PA 2000

KEETMAN Peter 1916 **[189]**
📷 **$2 277** - €1 943 - **£1 373** - FF12 743
   Schraubenpumpe Vintage gelatin silver print
   (39.6x30.4cm 15x11in) Köln 1998

KEFER Pierre XX **[26]**
📷 **$1 147** - €991 - **£692** - FF6 500
   **«Blackwell Tunnel» ombres d'une verrière sur
   un grand mur, Londres** Tirage argentique
   (27.4x24cm 10x9in) Paris 1998

KEFER-DORA MAAR (P. Kefer & D. Maar) XX **[2]**
📷 **$1 422** - €1 677 - **£999** - FF11 000
   Mendiante à Barcelone Tirage argentique (24x18cm
   9x7in) Paris 2000

KEGHEL de Désiré 1839-1901 **[10]**
- **$65 000** – €77 077 – **£44 720** – FF505 589
  A Cart of Wild Flowers Oil/canvas (126x176cm 49x69in) New-York 2000
- **$1 664** – €1 983 – **£1 192** – FF13 008
  Orchideeën Oil/canvas (100x81cm 39x31in) Lokeren 2000
- **$2 523** – €2 949 – **£1 801** – FF19 347
  Still Life with yellow Roses Oil/canvas (32x40.5cm 12x15in) Amsterdam 2001

KEHRER Wilhelm 1892-1960 **[9]**
- **$1 502** – €1 431 – **£917** – FF9 390
  Pfronten im Allgäu Öl/Leinwand (50x60cm 19x23in) Stuttgart 1999

KEIGETSU Kikuchi 1879-1955 **[1]**
- **$3 500** – €3 527 – **£2 181** – FF23 135
  Narcissus Ink (40.5x51.5cm 15x20in) New-York 1999

KEIL Alfredo 1851-1907 **[9]**
- **$18 490** – €21 436 – **£12 900** – FF140 610
  Bosque na Alemanha Oleo/lienzo (65.5x50.5cm 25x19in) Lisboa 2001
- **$19 800** – €21 934 – **£12 760** – FF143 880
  Interior de igreja com luz do sol iluminado o altar Oleo/lienzo (37.5x23.5cm 14x9in) Lisboa 2000

KEIL Karl Philipp Franz XIX **[1]**
- **$16 868** – €19 442 – **£11 635** – FF127 448
  Büste von Wilhelm I, König von Preussen Marble (H72cm H28in) München 2000

KEIL Peter 1942 **[188]**
- **$296** – €256 – **£175** – FF1 679
  «Hommage à Pablo Picasso» Öl/Karton (66x50cm 25x19in) Rudolstadt-Thüringen 1998

KEIL Robert 1905-1989 **[10]**
- **$1 576** – €1 789 – **£1 095** – FF11 738
  Stilleben mit Muscheln, Seetieren und rotem Himmel Watercolour, gouache (50.5x65.5cm 19x25in) München 2001

KEILHAU, MONSU BERNARDO Bernhard 1624-1687 **[44]**
- **$22 634** – €22 105 – **£14 427** – FF145 000
  Les buveurs Huile/toile (116x147cm 45x57in) Paris 1999
- **$13 057** – €12 782 – **£8 035** – FF83 847
  Schlafendes Mädchen Öl/Leinwand (58x90cm 22x35in) Bremen 1999

KEIMEL Hermann 1889-1948 **[7]**
- **$551** – €635 – **£380** – FF4 166
  «Pfälzer wein haus münzsr, pikante früstücke auswahlreiche mittag» Poster (126x95cm 49x37in) London 2000

KEINÄNEN Sigfrid August 1841-1914 **[48]**
- **$3 832** – €4 205 – **£2 467** – FF27 580
  Landskap från tavastland Oil/canvas (39x60cm 15x23in) Helsinki 2000
- **$1 839** – €2 018 – **£1 184** – FF13 238
  Fiskaren Oil/canvas (29.5x33.5cm 11x13in) Helsinki 1999

KEINEN Imao 1845-1924 **[3]**
- **$902** – €869 – **£564** – FF5 701
  Keinen Kacho Gafu/Vögel am Wasser mit blühenden Zweigen Woodcut in colors (37x26cm 14x10in) München 1999

KEIRINCX Alexander 1600-1652 **[37]**
- **$42 000** – €44 854 – **£28 618** – FF294 222
  Wooded Landscape wit a Stag Hunt Oil/canvas (100x147cm 39x57in) New-York 2001

$33 120 – €30 490 – **£19 880** – FF200 000
  Cavalier aux abords d'une ville Huile/panneau (57x81cm 22x31in) Lyon 1999
- **$10 086** – €9 879 – **£6 500** – FF64 802
  The Rest on the Flight into egypt Oil/panel (14.5x25.5cm 5x10in) London 1999

KEIRSBLICK van Jules 1833-1896 **[7]**
- **$3 228** – €2 975 – **£1 944** – FF19 512
  Portrait d'une belle italienne Huile/toile (101x81cm 39x31in) Antwerpen 1999
- **$2 201** – €2 439 – **£1 476** – FF16 000
  J'entends le bruit de l'eau: Portrait de femme Huile/panneau (42x35cm 16x13in) Tours 2000

KEISER Ernst 1894-1960 **[2]**
- **$500** – €558 – **£326** – FF3 657
  «I.X.Kantonal Schutzenfest» Poster (128x90cm 50x35in) New-York 2000

KEITA Seydou 1923 **[22]**
- **$4 184** – €4 491 – **£2 800** – FF29 460
  Untitled Photograph (78.5x62.5cm 30x24in) London 2000

KEITEL Simon 1964 **[44]**
- **$1 005** – €915 – **£628** – FF6 000
  Le violon vert Huile/toile (60x73cm 23x28in) Entzheim 1999

KEITH David Barrogill 1891-1979 **[1]**
- **$3 472** – €3 853 – **£2 400** – FF25 271
  J.Taits Shop, Kirkwall/Broad Street Kirkwall Oil/canvas/board (35.5x45.5cm 13x17in) London 2001

KEITH Elizabeth 1887-1956 **[55]**
- **$650** – €625 – **£403** – FF4 097
  Ying LIn Monastery (China) Woodcut in colors (39x27.5cm 15x10in) New-York 1999

KEITH William 1838-1911 **[173]**
- **$82 500** – €74 997 – **£49 689** – FF491 947
  Mt. Hood from Hood River Oil/canvas (101x182cm 40x72in) Hayden ID 1999
- **$6 000** – €5 126 – **£3 630** – FF33 626
  After the Storm Oil/canvas (51x76cm 20x29in) San-Francisco CA 1999
- **$2 000** – €1 942 – **£1 235** – FF12 737
  Forest Interior with Figures Oil/board (16x22cm 6x9in) Cedar-Falls IA 1999
- **$2 500** – €2 683 – **£1 673** – FF17 602
  Sitka, Alaska Pastel/paper (34x47cm 13x18in) San-Francisco CA 2000

KEIZO Koyama 1897-1987 **[4]**
- **$49 000** – €47 793 – **£30 000** – FF313 500
  Roses Oil/canvas (65x53.5cm 25x21in) Tokyo 1999

KELDER Toon 1894-1973 **[189]**
- **$2 668** – €2 356 – **£1 608** – FF15 453
  Landscape Oil/canvas (82.5x99cm 32x38in) Amsterdam 1998
- **$1 479** – €1 588 – **£990** – FF10 418
  Horsemen in landscape Oil/canvas (34x40cm 13x15in) Amsterdam 2000
- **$942** – €908 – **£589** – FF5 953
  Untitled Metal (H71cm H27in) Amsterdam 1999
- **$553** – €544 – **£355** – FF3 571
  A Child next to a Vase of Flowers Watercolour (69.5x54cm 27x21in) Amsterdam 1999

KELER Peter 1898-1982 **[13]**
- **$15 000** – €12 797 – **£9 048** – FF83 940
  «Bauhaus, Weimar» Poster (33x53.5cm 12x21in) New-York 1998

KÉLÉTY

KÉLÉTY Alexandre ?-1940 **[51]**
- **$11 754** – €13 720 – **£8 316** – FF90 000
  Le tournoi Bronze (H93cm H36in) Paris 2001
- **$1 844** – €2 106 – **£1 300** – FF13 814
  Figure (cast from a model) Bronze (H23cm H9in) London 2001

KELL Violet Beatrice XIX-XX **[2]**
- **$1 793** – €1 925 – **£1 200** – FF12 625
  Tennis in the Orchard Watercolour/paper (34.5x25cm 13x9in) London 2000

KELLEN van der David III 1827-1895 **[8]**
- **$13 830** – €14 521 – **£8 720** – FF95 251
  The Fair Oil/panel (45x54cm 17x21in) Amsterdam 2000
- **$4 247** – €4 991 – **£2 944** – FF32 742
  A Lady writing a Letter Oil/panel (33.5x27cm 13x10in) Amsterdam 2000

KELLER Adolphe 1880-1968 **[82]**
- **$592** – €620 – **£392** – FF4 065
  Béguinage à Val Duchesse Huile/toile (65x54cm 25x21in) Bruxelles 2000

KELLER Art XX **[2]**
- **$353** – €427 – **£246** – FF2 800
  Collection Paul Devautour Sérigraphie (65x50cm 25x19in) Paris 2000

KELLER Arthur Ignatius 1866-1924 **[15]**
- **$4 400** – €3 754 – **£2 654** – FF24 622
  «The conspiracy dinner» Oil/canvas/board (42x58cm 16x23in) New-York 1998
- **$2 600** – €2 461 – **£1 614** – FF16 144
  «The Empty Chair» Watercolour/paper (48x33cm 19x13in) Wallkill NY 1999

KELLER Clyde Leon 1872-1962 **[28]**
- **$650** – €758 – **£452** – FF4 974
  Landscape Oil/canvas/board (35x45cm 14x18in) Altadena CA 2000
- **$650** – €732 – **£454** – FF4 804
  Landscape, a Willamette Valley Farm at Dawn Oil/panel (30x40cm 12x16in) Portland OR 2001

KELLER Ferdinand, Prof. 1842-1922 **[47]**
- **$10 317** – €12 271 – **£7 353** – FF80 493
  David spielt Harfe vor Bathseba Öl/Leinwand (86x160cm 33x62in) Köln 2000
- **$7 765** – €7 157 – **£4 650** – FF46 949
  Südliche Insel mit Zypressen und einer Burg Öl/Leinwand (95x120cm 37x47in) Dresden 1998

KELLER Fritz 1915-1994 **[4]**
- **$417** – €486 – **£291** – FF3 186
  Alter Leopard Gouache/paper (63.3x49cm 24x19in) Berlin 2000

KELLER Heinrich 1778-1862 **[27]**
- **$225** – €242 – **£150** – FF1 587
  Aussicht vom Albis gegen Zürich Radierung (16.2x25.4cm 6x10in) Zürich 2000

KELLER Henry George 1869-1949 **[53]**
- **$410** – €468 – **£285** – FF3 072
  Standing Female Nude Pastel/paper (61x36cm 24x14in) Cleveland OH 2001
- **$90** – €95 – **£57** – FF622
  Circus Lithograph (35x48cm 14x19in) Cleveland OH 2000

KELLER Johan Hendrik 1692-1765 **[16]**
- **$6 223** – €5 781 – **£3 800** – FF37 924
  A Band of Travellers Crossing a Bridge Oil/canvas (61x87cm 24x34in) London 1998

- **$2 321** – €2 736 – **£1 600** – FF17 946
  An Allegory of Faith/An Allegory of the Arts Oil/canvas (44.5x34cm 17x13in) London 2000

KELLER von Albert 1844-1920 **[83]**
- **$6 754** – €7 669 – **£4 693** – FF50 308
  Die Hexenverbrennung Öl/Leinwand (99x150.5cm 38x59in) Köln 2001
- **$2 823** – €3 015 – **£1 923** – FF19 777
  Parti fra Venedig Oil/canvas (53x82cm 20x32in) Vejle 2001
- **$917** – €1 022 – **£641** – FF6 707
  Bacchusfamilie vor Bäumen Öl/Leinwand (20x26cm 7x10in) München 2001

KELLER von Friedrich 1840-1914 **[76]**
- **$16 009** – €18 918 – **£11 347** – FF124 094
  Kameltränke bei Bethlehem Öl/Leinwand (123x190cm 48x74in) Stuttgart 2000
- **$3 500** – €3 545 – **£2 177** – FF23 256
  The Stone Breakers Oil/canvas (71x94cm 28x37in) Bloomfield-Hills MI 2000
- **$674** – €767 – **£467** – FF5 030
  Szene am Sterbebett Öl/Karton (24.5x22cm 9x8in) Hamburg 2000

KELLER-HERMANN Marie 1868-1952 **[24]**
- **$810** – €920 – **£554** – FF6 037
  Stilleben Öl/Karton (37x56cm 14x22in) Merzhausen 2000

KELLER-REUTLINGEN Paul Wilhelm 1854-1920 **[84]**
- **$8 521** – €7 157 – **£5 009** – FF46 949
  Schwäbisches Gehöft am Fluss in der sommerlichen Abendsonne Öl/Leinwand (80x120cm 31x47in) Bad-Vilbel 1998
- **$2 010** – €2 301 – **£1 382** – FF15 092
  Kleines Mädchen in Tracht in ein Flusstal mit einer Ortschaft blickend Oil/panel (21x16cm 8x6in) München 2000
- **$770** – €665 – **£458** – FF4 359
  Pompeji Watercolour (29x39.5cm 11x15in) München 1998

KELLEY Mike 1954 **[105]**
- **$31 772** – €34 621 – **£20 000** – FF227 101
  «Center + Peripheries #2» Acrylic (230x236cm 90x92in) London 2001
- **$11 836** – €12 806 – **£8 200** – FF84 004
  Garbage Drawing #59, from Seventy-four Garbage Drawings and One Bush Acrylic/paper (61x112cm 24x44in) London 2001
- **$3 500** – €3 112 – **£2 140** – FF20 416
  Reconstructed History: Bestowing a Blessing on Columbus Mixed media (20.5x25.5cm 8x10in) New-York 1999
- **$50 000** – €48 379 – **£30 835** – FF317 345
  Estral Star #3 Assemblage (80x30.5x16.5cm 31x12x6in) New-York 1999
- **$38 000** – €32 896 – **£22 917** – FF215 786
  Dialogue #5 Installation (41x162x103cm 16x63x40in) New-York 1998
- **$35 000** – €32 850 – **£21 623** – FF215 481
  Cocks and Balls Felt pen/paper (236.5x178cm 93x70in) New-York 1999
- **$1 875** – €2 072 – **£1 300** – FF13 593
  Poetics Country Screenprint in colors (88x91cm 34x35in) London 2001
- **$12 000** – €13 441 – **£8 337** – FF88 166
  The Left Wing and Right Wing of Monkey Island Gelatin silver print (19.5x24cm 7x9in) New-York 2001

KELLIN Nicolas Joseph 1789-1858 **[23]**
- $452 - €381 - **£267** - FF2 500
  Paysage fluvial Crayon (11.3x28.7cm 4x11in) Paris 1998

KELLNER Charles Harry 1890-? **[1]**
- $3 500 - €4 004 - **£2 433** - FF26 262
  Landscape with Houses Oil/canvas (76x91cm 30x36in) Cincinnati OH 2000

KELLY David 1959 **[2]**
- $2 711 - €3 161 - **£1 900** - FF20 734
  Disturbed Crossing, Elephant, Egret and Hippopotamus at the Shire Oil/canvas (60x84.5cm 23x33in) London 2000

KELLY Ellsworth 1923 **[383]**
- $500 000 - €580 145 - **£345 200** - FF3 805 500
  White, Dark Blue Oil/canvas (147.5x84cm 58x33in) New-York 2000
- $88 452 - €74 296 - **£52 000** - FF487 349
  Stèle et Marine (EK 149) Oil/canvas (71x46cm 27x18in) London 1998
- $650 000 - €728 048 - **£451 620** - FF4 775 680
  Blue Curve with white Panel (EK799) Oil/canvas (23x36cm 9x14in) New-York 2001
- $28 000 - €31 307 - **£18 874** - FF205 363
  Mirrored Concorde Sculpture (131.5x76x32.5cm 51x29x12in) New-York 2000
- $20 000 - €22 362 - **£13 482** - FF146 688
  Untitled Collage (78.5x115.5cm 30x45in) New-York 2000
- $2 000 - €2 324 - **£1 405** - FF15 242
  Peach branch Lithograph (120x80cm 47x31in) Beverly-Hills CA 2001

KELLY Felix 1917-1994 **[93]**
- $3 434 - €4 001 - **£2 400** - FF26 245
  St Paul's Oil/board (41x54cm 16x21in) Brighton 2000
- $2 862 - €3 334 - **£2 000** - FF21 870
  Vintage Car, Brighton Oil/board (34x45cm 13x17in) Brighton 2000
- $973 - €935 - **£600** - FF6 131
  The Lovers Gouache/paper (26.5x21cm 10x8in) London 1999

KELLY Francis Robert 1927 **[18]**
- $220 - €237 - **£150** - FF1 552
  Armour Etching, aquatint (37.5x55.5cm 14x21in) London 2001

KELLY Gerald Festus 1879-1972 **[108]**
- $1 982 - €1 724 - **£1 200** - FF11 307
  Mangosteens and a Casket Oil/canvas (63.5x76cm 25x29in) London 1999
- $2 480 - €2 320 - **£1 500** - FF15 221
  Ma seyn Sin, pose II Oil/panel (34x27cm 13x10in) London 1999

KELLY James Edward 1855-1933 **[4]**
- $5 000 - €4 768 - **£3 043** - FF31 279
  Figure of a Gentleman Saddling a Horse Bronze (H53.5cm H21in) New-York 1999

KELLY John 1965 **[3]**
- $5 900 - €6 501 - **£3 961** - FF42 641
  Museum Box II Construction (64x128x56cm 25x50x22in) Malvern, Victoria 1999

KELLY John 1932 **[12]**
- $983 - €1 143 - **£691** - FF7 496
  Christ, Clown of the World Watercolour/paper (37x34cm 14x13in) Dublin 2001

KELLY John Melville 1878-1962 **[14]**
- $800 - €736 - **£480** - FF4 829
  Little Lotus Aquatint (44x34cm 17x13in) Charlottesville VA 1999

KELLY Leon 1901-1982 **[38]**
- $10 000 - €11 725 - **£7 194** - FF76 911
  Insects and Cliffs Oil/canvas (71x112cm 27x44in) New-York 2001
- $4 500 - €5 110 - **£3 080** - FF33 521
  Compote with Fruit Oil/canvas/board (22x30cm 8x11in) New-York 2000
- $800 - €853 - **£507** - FF5 593
  Seated Nude Watercolour/paper (54x41cm 21x16in) Downington PA 2000

KELLY Oisin 1915-1981 **[4]**
- $6 686 - €7 872 - **£4 698** - FF51 639
  Hawk Metal (H16cm H6in) Dublin 2000

KELLY Paul 1968 **[8]**
- $1 420 - €1 651 - **£998** - FF10 827
  Still life with spanish Jug Oil/board (41x52cm 16x20in) Dublin 2001

KELLY Richard B. Talbot 1896-1971 **[50]**
- $609 - €625 - **£380** - FF4 098
  Pink-Footed Geese Watercolour (52x73cm 20x28in) London 2000
- $424 - €492 - **£300** - FF3 225
  «Suffolk, British Railways, Eastern Region, See Britain by Train» Poster (102x64cm 40x25in) London 2000

KELLY Robert George Talbot 1861-1934 **[62]**
- $1 160 - €1 076 - **£700** - FF7 059
  Middle Eastern Dancer Watercolour (37x26.5cm 14x10in) London 1999

KELLY Walt 1913-1973 **[12]**
- $1 800 - €1 666 - **£1 101** - FF10 931
  Longhorn LBJ's New Hampshire campaign hijinks: daily strips Ink (13x50cm 5x20in) New-York 1999

KELM Ursula 1942 **[15]**
- $531 - €588 - **£360** - FF3 857
  Alexander Camaro Gelatin silver print (30.5x40.4cm 12x15in) Berlin 2000

KELPE Paul 1902-1985 **[10]**
- $45 000 - €53 516 - **£32 071** - FF351 045
  Machinist Series Oil/canvas (122x115cm 48x45in) New-York 2000
- $19 000 - €16 447 - **£11 531** - FF107 882
  Industrial Scene Watercolour/paper (46x36cm 18x14in) Mystic CT 1998

KELS Franz 1828-1893 **[6]**
- $3 760 - €3 681 - **£2 314** - FF24 148
  Ein junges Mädchen in bäuerlicher Tracht sitzt am Ufer eines Baches Öl/Leinwand (48x38cm 18x14in) Stuttgart 1999

KELSEY Charles Joshua 1870-1960 **[29]**
- $88 - €82 - **£55** - FF536
  La Cadore near Cannes Pastel/paper (31.5x24cm 12x9in) Bristol, Avon 1999

KELSEY Frank XIX-XX **[18]**
- $720 - €668 - **£440** - FF4 382
  The Inner Harbour at Polperro Watercolour (24x34cm 9x13in) London 1998

KELSY XX **[13]**
- $1 012 - €991 - **£622** - FF6 500
  La vague Bronze (21x43cm 8x16in) Paris 1999

K

KELTERBORN Ludwig Adam 1811-1878 **[4]**
- $3 193 – €3 632 – **£2 214** – FF23 823
  Der Freischütz Oil/panel (33x37cm 12x14in) Zofingen 2000

KEMENEDY Jeno 1860-1925 **[6]**
- $8 283 – €8 621 – **£5 200** – FF56 547
  Talk of the Town Oil/panel (25x33cm 9x12in) London 2000

KEMENY Zoltan 1907-1965 **[31]**
- $8 288 – €7 066 – **£5 000** – FF46 352
  Ailes cassées Mixed media (142.5x60cm 56x23in) London 1998
- $4 539 – €4 573 – **£2 829** – FF30 000
  Conception du temps Relief (63x95cm 24x37in) Reims 2000

KEMEYS Edward 1843-1907 **[11]**
- $3 750 – €3 577 – **£2 282** – FF23 462
  Figure of a Ram Bronze (H37.5cm H14in) New-York 1999

KEMM Robert 1849-1890 **[68]**
- $17 400 – €18 591 – **£11 850** – FF121 950
  Gitans en route vers le marché de Séville Huile/toile (106x152cm 41x59in) Antwerpen 2001
- $5 803 – €5 024 – **£3 500** – FF32 956
  «Andalusian Goatherd» Oil/canvas (71x91.5cm 27x36in) London 1998

KEMMER Hans / Johann c.1495-c.1561 **[1]**
- $119 544 – €128 321 – **£80 000** – FF841 728
  Christ and the Adultress Oil/panel (86.5x96cm 34x37in) London 2000

KEMP Roger 1908-1987 **[26]**
- $2 872 – €3 248 – **£2 021** – FF21 306
  Untitled Oil/paper/canvas (122x152cm 48x59in) Malvern, Victoria 2001
- $2 131 – €2 380 – **£1 364** – FF15 613
  Untitled Oil/paper/canvas (63.5x144.5cm 25x56in) Malvern, Victoria 2000

KEMP-WELCH Lucy Elizabeth 1869-1958 **[110]**
- $10 673 – €12 567 – **£7 500** – FF82 435
  The Starting Post, Goodwood Oil/canvas (127x117cm 50x46in) London 2000
- $7 373 – €8 165 – **£5 000** – FF53 560
  Foam-Horses Oil/canvas/board (34x52cm 13x20in) Billingshurst, West-Sussex 2000
- $1 600 – €1 528 – **£1 000** – FF10 022
  Study of a Horse in a Field Oil/canvas (25.5x35.5cm 10x13in) London 1999
- $879 – €840 – **£549** – FF5 508
  Self-Portrait with Tenpence Pencil/paper (13x18cm 5x7in) London 1999

KEMPE Fritz 1909-1988 **[26]**
- $711 – €792 – **£465** – FF5 198
  Porträt Otto Steinert Vintage gelatin silver print (23.8x18cm 9x7in) Köln 2000

KEMPER Charles Jean 1913-1986 **[47]**
- $72 – €82 – **£50** – FF535
  Ewethheul Ink (37x55cm 14x21in) Rotterdam 2001

KEMPER H.W. XIX **[1]**
- $6 500 – €6 156 – **£3 952** – FF40 378
  Fishing on the River Oil/canvas (51x77cm 20x30in) New-York 1999

KEMPF-HARTENKAMPF Gottlieb Theodor 1871-1964 **[40]**
- $2 325 – €2 180 – **£1 437** – FF14 301
  Das Waldmädchen Öl/Leinwand (43x43cm 16x16in) Wien 1999

- $3 416 – €3 579 – **£2 259** – FF23 477
  Junge Dame am Teich vor dem Bauernhaus Oil/panel (26x32cm 10x12in) München 2000

KENDALL William Sergeant 1869-1938 **[12]**
- $3 750 – €3 246 – **£2 275** – FF21 292
  Brittany Scene Oil/panel (35x25cm 14x10in) Mystic CT 1998
- $6 000 – €6 694 – **£3 927** – FF43 909
  Portrait of a Woman Pastel/paper (50x30cm 20x12in) Chicago IL 2000

KENDERDINE Augustus Fred. L. 1870-1947 **[12]**
- $714 – €807 – **£502** – FF5 296
  The Tumbling Glacier at Berg Lake Oil/canvas (51x76cm 20x29in) Vancouver, BC. 2001

KENDRICK Mel 1949 **[26]**
- $1 900 – €1 684 – **£1 116** – FF11 044
  Woodprints Woodcut (62.5x48cm 24x18in) New-York 1999

KENDRICK Sydney Percy 1874-1955 **[12]**
- $1 247 – €1 277 – **£770** – FF8 379
  Sittande kvinna på klippa Oil/canvas (77x118cm 30x46in) Stockholm 2000

KENNA Michael 1953 **[83]**
- $3 000 – €3 023 – **£1 870** – FF19 830
  «Point of Honor, Versailles»/«Octagonal Basin, Sceaux» Gelatin silver print (19x19cm 7x7in) New-York 2000

KENNEDY Cecil 1905-1997 **[166]**
- $11 954 – €12 832 – **£8 000** – FF84 172
  Californian Poppies Oil/canvas (63.5x76cm 25x29in) London 2000
- $3 293 – €3 095 – **£2 000** – FF20 299
  Still Life with Camellias, Asters and Michaelmas Daisies Oil/canvas (25.5x18cm 10x7in) London 1999

KENNEDY Charles Nappier 1852-1898 **[9]**
- $15 132 – €15 749 – **£9 500** – FF103 308
  Cains First Crime Oil/canvas (166x144cm 65x56in) London 2000
- $4 760 – €5 528 – **£3 345** – FF36 260
  Brevet Oil/canvas (76x46cm 29x18in) Stockholm 2001

KENNEDY William 1860-1918 **[19]**
- $3 111 – €3 469 – **£2 100** – FF22 757
  Military Manoeuvres Oil/canvas (39x60cm 15x23in) Edinburgh 2000
- $4 167 – €3 937 – **£2 600** – FF25 826
  Village Street Oil/panel (28x16cm 11x6in) Perthshire 1999

KENNEDY William W. 1817-c.1870 **[8]**
- $7 000 – €5 844 – **£4 105** – FF38 335
  Portrait of a Dark-Haired, Dark-Eyed Boy Wearing a Blue Costume Oil/canvas (43x31cm 16x12in) New-York 1998

KENNER von Anton Josef 1871-1951 **[4]**
- $5 450 – €5 113 – **£3 367** – FF33 539
  Zyklus von zwölf bildlich dargestellen Sprichwörtern Oil/panel (100x71cm 39x27in) Ahlden 1999

KENNEY John Theodore 1911-1972 **[10]**
- $4 257 – €4 160 – **£2 700** – FF27 291
  The Cottesmore near Burrough on the Hill Oil/canvas (60x91cm 24x36in) Leicester 1999

KENNINGTON Eric Henri 1888-1960 **[38]**
- $2 053 – €2 212 – **£1 400** – FF14 513
  The Canadian Piper Black chalk/paper (75x53cm 29x20in) Bury St. Edmunds, Suffolk 2001

KENNINGTON Thomas Benjamin 1856-1916 **[28]**
- $5 500 - €5 387 - **£3 544** - FF35 336
  Portrait of a seated Lady Oil/canvas (91.5x71cm 36x27in) New-York 1999
- $8 706 - €10 260 - **£6 000** - FF67 299
  Contemplation, Study of a Young Girl, Half Length Oil/canvas (41x30cm 16x11in) Woodbridge, Suffolk 2000

KENNY Michael 1941-2000 **[16]**
- $770 - €900 - **£550** - FF5 906
  «Beyond Truth and Beauty 2» Pencil (68x92.5cm 26x36in) London 2001

KENSETT John Frederick 1816-1872 **[64]**
- $38 000 - €42 187 - **£26 429** - FF276 731
  «White Mountains from Shelburne, N.H.» Oil/canvas (34x55cm 13x22in) Milford CT 2001
- $38 000 - €41 907 - **£25 733** - FF274 895
  View of Lake Champlain Oil/panel (13x21.5cm 5x8in) New-York 2000
- $1 900 - €2 120 - **£1 321** - FF13 907
  Rydall Falls Watercolour (29x18cm 11x7in) Cleveland OH 2001

KENT Leslie 1890-1980 **[26]**
- $662 - €613 - **£400** - FF4 023
  Coastal Chalets Oil/board (33x43cm 13x17in) Par, Cornwall 1999

KENT Rockwell 1882-1971 **[366]**
- $80 000 - €95 140 - **£57 016** - FF624 080
  Calm Oil/canvas (87x112cm 34x44in) New-York 2000
- $16 000 - €17 174 - **£10 707** - FF112 656
  Manana from Monhegan Island Oil/board (12x16cm 5x6in) Portland ME 2000
- $4 000 - €4 052 - **£2 510** - FF26 582
  Starry Night Watercolour/paper (35x43cm 14x17in) Detroit MI 2000
- $800 - €893 - **£512** - FF5 860
  Blue Bird Woodcut (15.5x15.5cm 6x6in) New-York 2000

KENT William 1685-1748 **[9]**
- $12 464 - €14 483 - **£8 759** - FF95 000
  Plan pour le plafond du salon au 44, Berkeley Square, London Aquarelle (33x11cm 12x4in) Paris 2001

KENTRIDGE William 1955 **[28]**
- $2 142 - €2 389 - **£1 397** - FF15 669
  Severed Head Mixed media (31.5x43cm 12x16in) Johannesburg 2000
- $7 888 - €7 260 - **£4 734** - FF47 625
  Cameroon Head Gouache (120x150cm 47x59in) Amsterdam 1999
- $561 - €626 - **£366** - FF4 108
  The Head and the Load Are the Troubles of the Neck Etching (29x37cm 11x14in) Johannesburg 2000

KENWORTHY Jonathan 1943 **[18]**
- $16 612 - €17 669 - **£10 500** - FF115 899
  Charging Cape Buffalo Bronze (33x81cm 12x31in) London 2000

KENYON Henry Rodman 1861-1926 **[12]**
- $850 - €952 - **£591** - FF6 247
  Cows in Landscape Oil/board (22x30cm 9x12in) Watertown MA 2001

KEOGH Tom 1921-1980 **[28]**
- $436 - €457 - **£273** - FF3 000
  Les joueurs de cartes Aquarelle (17x26cm 6x10in) Paris 2000

KEPES György 1906-1989 **[55]**
- $964 - €1 125 - **£668** - FF7 378
  Blick auf die Strasse Gelatin silver print (11.2x7.9cm 4x3in) Köln 2000

KERCKHOVE van den Antoine Joseph 1849-? **[6]**
- $2 552 - €2 727 - **£1 738** - FF17 886
  Jonge vrouw met rozen Bronze (68x42cm 26x16in) Lokeren 2001

KERCKHOVE van den Ernest 1840-1879 **[9]**
- $3 444 - €3 470 - **£2 142** - FF22 764
  La trahison Huile/panneau (73x52.5cm 28x20in) Bruxelles 2000

KERCKHOVEN van de Jacob da Castello c.1637-c.1715 **[18]**
- $59 526 - €56 223 - **£36 000** - FF368 798
  A Boar's Head, a dead Hare, a Mallard, Songbirds with a Cat Oil/canvas (106x143.5cm 41x56in) London 1999
- $18 660 - €16 153 - **£11 328** - FF105 960
  Kalkuner og duer ved et dörslag med kirsebaer, skovjordbaer og agurker Oil/canvas (77x64cm 30x25in) København 1998

KERELS Henri 1896-1956 **[20]**
- $739 - €793 - **£496** - FF5 203
  Nature morte de fleurs et fruits Huile/toile (80x60cm 31x23in) Bruxelles 2000

KERFYSER Georges XX **[10]**
- $212 - €244 - **£149** - FF1 600
  «Bonjour tristesse» Affiche (120x160cm 47x62in) Paris 2001

KERG Théo 1909-1993 **[50]**
- $3 272 - €3 811 - **£2 285** - FF25 000
  La cathédrale Huile/toile (109x80cm 42x31in) Paris 2000
- $690 - €792 - **£472** - FF5 198
  Taktilismus in Grau-Braun Mixed media drawing (50x36cm 19x14in) Heidelberg 2000
- $102 - €118 - **£70** - FF771
  Souvenez-vous de Léopold Sédar Senghor, Komposition mit Schrift Lithographie (51.4x39.7cm 20x15in) Heidelberg 2000

KERGEL Carl Franz-Ludwig 1814-1874 **[12]**
- $8 992 - €10 226 - **£6 236** - FF67 078
  Dresden Öl/Leinwand (34.5x47cm 13x18in) Hamburg 2000

KERINEC Roger XX **[24]**
- $250 - €229 - **£152** - FF1 500
  Brest - l'église St-Louis et les halles Gouache/papier (31x22cm 12x8in) Douarnenez 1998

KERKAM Earl Cavis 1892-1965 **[13]**
- $300 - €252 - **£176** - FF1 652
  But We said Script Miss Marlowe Ink (45x38cm 18x15in) Saugerties NY 1998

KERKHOFF van den Maurits 1830-1909 **[2]**
- $28 986 - €27 227 - **£17 472** - FF178 596
  View in a Kampong near a Volcano Oil/panel (31x44cm 12x17in) Amsterdam 1999

KERKOVIUS Ida 1879-1970 **[403]**
- $10 932 - €10 226 - **£6 622** - FF67 078
  Halbakt Öl/Leinwand (84x66cm 33x25in) Stuttgart 1999
- $4 925 - €5 624 - **£3 472** - FF36 892
  «Punkt-Linie-Fläche» Oil/panel (31x41cm 12x16in) Stuttgart 2001

K

$1 626 - €1 431 - **£990** - FF9 390
Verkündigung Pastell/Papier (9.5x12.5cm 3x4in)
Stuttgart 1999

$236 - €256 - **£161** - FF1 676
Rote Tonalitäten Farbserigraphie (55x47cm 21x18in)
Stuttgart 2001

KERMADEC de Eugène 1899-1976 **[112]**

$3 804 - €4 176 - **£2 451** - FF27 390
Intimité Oil/canvas (46x38cm 18x14in) Stockholm
2000

$2 481 - €2 129 - **£1 500** - FF13 964
Paysage aux formes vivantes Oil/canvas (46x33cm
18x12in) London 1998

$680 - €762 - **£473** - FF5 000
Composition Pastel/papier (31x23cm 12x9in) Paris
2001

KERMARREC Joël 1939 **[167]**

$785 - €762 - **£485** - FF5 000
Sans titre Acrylique/toile (100x81cm 39x31in) Paris
1999

$341 - €381 - **£237** - FF2 500
Scène érotique Mine plomb (23x19cm 9x7in) Paris
2001

KERN Anton 1710-1747 **[10]**

$47 817 - €51 328 - **£32 000** - FF336 691
Bacchus and Ariadne Oil/panel (66.5x114.5cm
26x45in) London 2000

KERN E. XX **[1]**

$833 - €854 - **£514** - FF5 600
Les signes du zodiaque Tapisserie (132x115cm
51x45in) Enghien 2000

KERN Hermann 1839-1912 **[200]**

$4 000 - €4 031 - **£2 493** - FF26 440
Violonist Oil/canvas (47x36cm 18x14in) San Rafael
CA 2000

$5 000 - €4 799 - **£3 134** - FF31 477
In the Wine Cellar Oil/panel (48x32cm 18x12in)
New-York 1999

KERN Leonhard 1588-1662 **[4]**

$14 672 - €16 361 - **£9 865** - FF107 324
Caritas Sculpture (H17cm H6in) Ahlden 2000

KERN Richard 1945 **[9]**

$1 507 - €1 448 - **£934** - FF9 500
Cristina with Guns Photograph (66x100cm 25x39in)
Paris 1999

KERN Richard Hovenden 1821-1853 **[1]**

$24 000 - €26 339 - **£15 453** - FF172 771
View of Upper Colorado River Watercolour,
gouache/paper (18x25cm 7x9in) Beverly-Hills CA 2000

KERNAN Joseph F. 1878-1958 **[24]**

$3 000 - €3 497 - **£2 077** - FF22 939
Happy Children Emerging from Public School
Oil/canvas (52x41cm 20x16in) New-York 2000

KERNBEIS Franz 1935 **[2]**

$2 310 - €2 180 - **£1 434** - FF14 301
Motorrad Pencil (62.5x88cm 24x34in) Wien 1999

KERNN-LARSEN Rita 1914-1998 **[59]**

$799 - €806 - **£498** - FF5 287
Landskab ved St.Jeannet Oil/canvas (65x100cm
25x39in) Köbenhavn 2000

$1 152 - €1 077 - **£696** - FF7 064
Udsigt fra kunstnerens atelier Oil/canvas
(41x33cm 16x12in) Köbenhavn 1999

KERNOFF Harry Aaron 1900-1974 **[146]**

$25 905 - €29 016 - **£18 000** - FF190 333
Dublin Bay from Howth Oil/panel (60x73.5cm
23x28in) London 2001

$5 500 - €6 190 - **£3 788** - FF40 604
Portrait of Sean Keating Oil/board (21x15cm 8x5in)
Philadelphia PA 2000

$4 047 - €4 317 - **£2 696** - FF28 318
Blaskets from Dunquin, Co.Kerry
Watercolour/paper (35x26cm 14x10in) Dublin 2000

$204 - €229 - **£138** - FF1 499
**Bird Never Flew on One Wing or Alcoholics
Anonymous** Color lithograph (39x39cm 15x15in)
Dublin 2000

KERNSTOK Josef Karoly 1873-1940 **[9]**

$1 260 - €1 394 - **£828** - FF9 144
Spring Fields Oil/board (69.5x47.5cm 27x18in)
Budapest 2000

KEROUAC Edie Parker 1922-1993 **[1]**

$2 250 - €2 102 - **£1 360** - FF13 788
Zagg (Portrait of Jack Kerouac) Oil/canvas/board
(40.5x30.5cm 15x12in) New-York 1999

KEROUAC Jack 1922-1969 **[6]**

$15 000 - €14 011 - **£9 066** - FF91 908
Red, White and Blue Abstract Oil/masonite
(40x33cm 15x12in) New-York 1999

$4 500 - €4 203 - **£2 719** - FF27 572
Dr. Sax, The Shroudy Stranger Graphite (28x21cm
11x8in) New-York 1999

KERPEL Leopold 1818-1880 **[11]**

$515 - €613 - **£367** - FF4 024
Häuser an einem See im Salzkammergut
Öl/Leinwand (38.5x54.5cm 15x21in) Köln 2000

KERR David Ord 1951 **[20]**

$4 214 - €4 624 - **£2 800** - FF30 332
Blue Eyed Cockatoo Oil/board (50x75.5cm 19x29in)
London 2000

$767 - €638 - **£450** - FF4 186
Great Grey Owl Watercolour, gouache/paper
(80x56cm 31x22in) London 1998

KERR Frederick B. c.1860-1914 **[39]**

$514 - €479 - **£320** - FF3 142
St. Ives, Cornwall Watercolour/paper (30x26cm
12x10in) Whitby, Yorks 1999

KERR George Cochran XIX-XX **[18]**

$602 - €677 - **£420** - FF4 442
Figures mending Lobster Pots on the Beach
Watercolour (45x75cm 17x29in) London 2001

KERR Henry Wright 1857-1936 **[45]**

$1 021 - €873 - **£600** - FF5 725
**Portrait of James McIntosh Esq. SSC, auditor to
the Court of Session** Watercolour/paper (70x57cm
27x22in) Glasgow 1998

KERR Illingworth Holey 1905-1989 **[192]**

$6 472 - €7 528 - **£4 555** - FF49 383
«Prairie Towers» Acrylic/canvas (103x137cm
40x53in) Calgary, Alberta 2001

$1 303 - €1 513 - **£900** - FF9 922
Foothills Road, Spring Oil/canvas (45x60cm
18x24in) Calgary, Alberta 2000

$804 - €897 - **£525** - FF5 887
Qu'appelle Valley, East of Craven, No.3 Oil/maso-
nite (30x41cm 11x16in) Calgary, Alberta 2000

$325 - €365 - **£226** - FF2 353
Canvas Backs Watercolour/paper (37x54cm 14x21in)
Calgary, Alberta 2001

K

📖 $120 - €114 - **£74** - FF748
Untitled, Wolves Howling Linoblock (23x13cm
9x5in) Calgary, Alberta 1999

KERR Tiko 1953 **[2]**
🖼 $1 694 - €1 966 - **£1 170** - FF12 899
Twilight Success Acrylic/canvas (101.5x76cm
39x29in) Vancouver, BC. 2000

KERR Vernon ?-1982 **[6]**
🖼 $4 500 - €4 860 - **£3 109** - FF31 877
Oaks on flowering Hillside Oil/masonite (40x50cm
16x20in) Altadena CA 2001

KERR-LAWSON James 1865-1939 **[29]**
🖼 $800 - €967 - **£558** - FF6 342
The Harbour Entrance Oil/board (17x22cm 7x9in)
Philadelphia PA 2000

KERRICH Thomas 1748-1828 **[17]**
✏ $5 817 - €6 412 - **£3 800** - FF42 059
**Portrait of John Gooch, D.D., Rector of Ditton,
Cambridge (1729-1804)** Black chalk/paper
(33.5x25.5cm 13x10in) London 2000

KERSCHBAUMER Anton 1885-1931 **[27]**
📖 $279 - €307 - **£190** - FF2 012
Häuser am See II (Gstadt am See)
Farblithographie (30.8x40.3cm 12x15in) Berlin 2000

KERSEBOOM Frederick Causabon 1632-1690 **[1]**
🖼 $21 870 - €21 404 - **£14 000** - FF140 401
**Portrait of Emily and Robert Cecil, in a
Landscape** Oil/canvas (74.5x71cm 29x27in) London
1999

KERSELS Martin 1960 **[7]**
📷 $5 200 - €5 705 - **£3 454** - FF37 423
Tossing a Friend Photograph in colors
(67.5x100.5cm 26x39in) New-York 2000

KERSTING Georg Friedrich 1785-1847 **[9]**
✏ $1 398 - €1 534 - **£949** - FF10 061
**Stehendes Mädchen in Trachtenkleid mit
Sonnenschirm** Pencil/paper (18.3x12.4cm 7x4in)
Berlin 2000

KERTÉSZ André 1894-1985 **[867]**
📷 $3 800 - €3 212 - **£2 274** - FF21 067
Rainy Day, Tokyo Gelatin silver print (25x14cm
9x5in) Beverly-Hills CA 1998

KERTON Sudjana 1922-1994 **[19]**
🖼 $11 876 - €9 964 - **£6 968** - FF65 360
Balloon Seller Oil/canvas/board (98x66.5cm 38x26in)
Singapore 1998

KESSEL van Ferdinand 1648-c.1696 **[19]**
🖼 $7 280 - €7 808 - **£4 810** - FF51 220
Guirnalda de flores enmarcando a San Antonio
Oleo/cobre (73.5x56cm 28x22in) Madrid 2000
🖼 $80 682 - €91 762 - **£56 882** - FF601 916
Schmetterlinge Oil/panel (12x17.5cm 4x6in) Zürich
2001

KESSEL van Hieronymus 1578-1636 **[1]**
🖼 $11 731 - €9 981 - **£7 000** - FF65 473
**Portrait of a Gentleman, aged 52, in a black jer-
kin** Oil/panel (60.5x46cm 23x18in) London 1998

KESSEL van Jan I 1626-1679 **[142]**
🖼 $50 454 - €53 378 - **£32 000** - FF350 134
**Various Flowers and Grapes encircling a
Reliquary** Oil/copper (70x105.5cm 27x41in) London

🖼 $60 000 - €52 808 - **£36 528** - FF346 398
**Cockerel, a Turkey, a Cockatoo, Parrots and
Other Birds in a Landscape** Oil/copper (18.5x24cm
7x9in) New-York 1999

KESSEL van Jan II 1654-1708 **[31]**
🖼 $24 156 - €27 441 - **£16 902** - FF180 000
**Nature morte au bouquet de fleurs sur un enta-
blement** Huile/toile (67x51cm 26x20in) Paris 2001
🖼 $100 000 - €101 164 - **£61 060** - FF663 590
**Waan-Li Kraak Bowl of Fruit, Monkey/Birds,
Cat/Hare Vegetable/Birds...** Oil/copper
(16.5x21.5cm 6x8in) New-York 2000

KESSEL van Jan III 1641/42-1680 **[26]**
🖼 $40 777 - €38 139 - **£25 000** - FF250 175
**Don Luis de la Cerda Fernandez de Cordoba,
9th Duke of Medinaceli** Oil/canvas (52x37.5cm
20x14in) London 1998
🖼 $59 994 - €71 349 - **£42 757** - FF468 018
Das Element Luft Öl/Kupfer (20x26cm 7x10in)
Zürich

KESSEL van Jean Thomas Nicolas 1677-c.1741 **[5]**
🖼 $2 726 - €2 543 - **£1 645** - FF16 684
Fröhliche Gesellschaft im Freien beim Wein
Öl/Leinwand (61x50cm 24x19in) Wien 1999
🖼 $19 512 - €21 953 - **£13 435** - FF144 000
Intérieurs d'auberge Huile/panneau (28.5x41cm
11x16in) Paris 2000

KESSELS Willy 1898-1974 **[113]**
📷 $782 - €920 - **£561** - FF6 037
Akstudie Vintage gelatin silver print (17.3x23.4cm
6x9in) Berlin 2001

KESSLER August 1826-1906 **[19]**
🖼 $2 191 - €2 352 - **£1 466** - FF15 427
Sommernachmittag Jäger Öl/Leinwand
(66.5x90cm 26x35in) Bremen 2000

KESSLER Carl 1876-1968 **[52]**
✏ $285 - €243 - **£172** - FF1 597
Die Hütte am Beatenberg im Winter Pencil
(37.5x52cm 14x20in) Zürich 1998

KESTING Edmund 1892-1970 **[189]**
🖼 $26 105 - €28 022 - **£17 468** - FF183 814
Portrait Herwarth Walden Öl/Karton (48.5x43.5cm
19x17in) Bern 2000
🖼 $1 552 - €1 738 - **£1 078** - FF11 403
Dorf mit weidenden Kühen Watercolour
(15.8x23.8cm 6x9in) Berlin 2001
📖 $165 - €174 - **£104** - FF1 140
Fahrt ins Feld Woodcut (13.5x19.5cm 5x7in)
Heidelberg 2001
📷 $608 - €529 - **£366** - FF3 469
Dresdner Schloss bei Nacht Vintage gelatin silver
print (40x30.3cm 15x11in) Berlin 2000

KET Dick 1902-1940 **[57]**
🖼 $4 854 - €5 445 - **£3 363** - FF35 719
«Schaaps Kooi Bij Ede» Oil/board (40x50cm
15x19in) Amsterdam 2000
🖼 $11 718 - €13 613 - **£8 235** - FF89 298
Stilleven met flessen en een zalfpotje Oil/canvas
(40x29.5cm 15x11in) Amsterdam 2001
✏ $5 073 - €5 445 - **£3 394** - FF35 719
**De Grootmoeder Van De Schilder (Mevrouw
Otten-Van Steenberger)** Black chalk (26x17cm
10x6in) Amsterdam 2001
📖 $388 - €454 - **£277** - FF2 976
Zelfportret Linocut (13x10cm 5x3in) Amsterdam 2001

K

KETEL Cornelis 1548-1616 [4]

➳ **$4 034** – €4 331 – **£2 700** – FF28 408
Bearded Gentleman, wearing a black tunic and white ruff Oil/panel (46x35.5cm 18x13in) London 2000

➳ **$20 619** – €21 651 – **£13 000** – FF142 021
Portrait of an Elderly Man, Bust-Length, in a Jerkin and a Red Cloak Oil/panel (33.5x24.5cm 13x9in) London 2000

KETTEMANN Erwin 1897-1971 [157]

➳ **$676** – €673 – **£420** – FF4 414
Mountain Landscape Oil/canvas (68x98cm 26x38in) London 1999

➳ **$1 054** – €1 176 – **£709** – FF7 714
Fischer auf dem Chiemsee Oil/panel (14x17.5cm 5x6in) Köln 2000

KETTER Clay 1961 [10]

➳ **$9 916** – €8 472 – **£6 000** – FF55 575
Trace Painting Mixed media (120x120cm 47x47in) London 1998

KETTLE Tilly 1735-1786 [35]

➳ **$154 935** – €181 965 – **£110 000** – FF1 193 610
Umdatul-ul-Umara and Amir-ul-Umara, Sons of Nawab Muhammad Ali Khan Oil/canvas (127x96.5cm 50x37in) London 2000

➳ **$8 000** – €9 422 – **£5 532** – FF61 807
Portrait of a Gentleman, Half-Length, Standing and Wearing Blue Coat Oil/canvas (66x71cm 25x27in) New-York 2000

KETTNER Gerhard 1928-1993 [20]

▥ **$91** – €102 – **£63** – FF670
Zwei sitzende Frauen Lithographie (19.5x26cm 7x10in) Berlin 2001

KEUDELL von Maria 1838-1918 [5]

➳ **$2 200** – €2 454 – **£1 479** – FF16 098
Rügen Öl/Leinwand (72x98cm 28x38in) Satow 2000

KEUKEN van der Johan 1938-2001 [11]

◉ **$686** – €817 – **£489** – FF5 357
«Anthropoïds, Sipan, Yugoslavia» Silver print (26.5x37cm 10x14in) Amsterdam 2000

KEULEMANS Johannes Gerardus 1842-1912 [58]

✎ **$581** – €547 – **£360** – FF3 585
Racing Pigeons by a Coop Watercolour (70.5x56cm 27x22in) London 1999

KEULEN van Johannes 1676-1763 [2]

▥ **$1 100** – €1 030 – **£676** – FF6 758
Pas-Kaart van Rio Oronoque Golfo de Paria Met d'Eylanden Engraving (52x60cm 20x23in) New-York 1999

KEULLER Vital 1866-1945 [103]

➳ **$638** – €545 – **£380** – FF3 575
Vue de forêt Huile/panneau (59.5x80cm 23x31in) Bruxelles 1998

✎ **$186** – €223 – **£127** – FF1 463
Bosweg in de herfst (sentier en automne) Gouache/papier (39x29cm 15x11in) Antwerpen 2000

KEUNEN Alexis 1921-1990 [52]

✎ **$121** – €111 – **£72** – FF731
Les migrateurs Lavis/papier (50x65cm 19x25in) Antwerpen 1999

KEUNINCK de Kerstiaen I c.1560-1635 [13]

➳ **$12 800** – €14 534 – **£8 760** – FF95 340
Der Brand von Troya, Aeneas und seine Familie fliehen aus der Stadt Oil/panel (51x85.5cm 20x33in) Wien 2000

KEVER Jacob Simon, Hein 1854-1922 [118]

➳ **$6 805** – €5 754 – **£4 069** – FF37 744
Amusing the Baby Oil/canvas (40.5x50.5cm 15x19in) Amsterdam 1998

➳ **$989** – €908 – **£609** – FF5 953
Portrait of a Baby Oil/canvas (37x37cm 14x14in) Amsterdam 1999

✎ **$3 250** – €3 789 – **£2 250** – FF24 856
Boy in Interior Reading to a Young Girl Watercolour, gouache/paper (49x35cm 19x14in) South-Natick MA 2000

KEVORKIAN Jean 1933 [82]

➳ **$4 127** – €4 400 – **£2 800** – FF28 865
«St. Mammes» Oil/canvas (72x91.5cm 28x36in) London 2001

KEY Adriaen Thomasz II c.1544-c.1590 [9]

➳ **$10 445** – €10 361 – **£6 500** – FF67 962
Portrait of a Lady, in a black Brocade Dress with an organza Ruff Oil/panel (48.5x35.5cm 19x13in) London 1999

KEY John Ross 1832-1920 [26]

➳ **$2 250** – €2 098 – **£1 395** – FF13 764
Chrysanthemums Oil/canvas/board (72.5x48.5cm 28x19in) New-York 1999

➳ **$11 000** – €10 273 – **£6 789** – FF67 386
Watching the Boats, Newport Oil/canvas (30.5x50.5cm 12x19in) Boston MA 1999

KEY Willem c.1515/20-1568 [13]

➳ **$82 186** – €88 220 – **£55 000** – FF578 688
Portrait of a Gentleman Standing Half-Length Before a Green Curtain Oil/panel (58x44cm 22x17in) London 2000

KEYL Friedrich Wilhelm 1823-1871 [22]

➳ **$12 807** – €12 665 – **£8 000** – FF83 079
Sheep in the Highlands Oil/canvas (65x102cm 25x40in) Glasgow 1999

➳ **$4 160** – €3 972 – **£2 600** – FF26 053
Cattle and Sheep Resting in a Mountainous River Landscape Oil/canvas (32.5x46cm 12x18in) London 1999

KEYSER de Albert 1829-1890 [15]

➳ **$487** – €446 – **£297** – FF2 926
Vaches au pâturage Huile/toile (38x58cm 14x22in) Antwerpen 1999

KEYSER de Hendrick 1565-1621 [1]

✎ **$26 000** – €27 812 – **£17 726** – FF182 434
Self-Portrait in a Hat, in Profile to the Left, Bust-Length Ink (11.5x8.5cm 4x3in) New-York 2001

KEYSER de Jean-Baptiste 1857-? [3]

◈ **$1 064** – €992 – **£640** – FF6 504
Lassitude Terracotta (H60cm H23in) Liège 1999

KEYSER de Nicaise 1813-1887 [26]

➳ **$2 154** – €2 414 – **£1 500** – FF15 832
King Lear with Cordelia beside Gothic throne with Landscape Oil/canvas (29x24cm 11x9in) Dorking, Surrey 2001

KEYSER de Thomas 1596/97-1667 [18]

➳ **$29 048** – €27 191 – **£18 000** – FF178 363
Lady full-length Seated, in a Black Dress with White Ruff and Cap Oil/panel (66.5x51cm 26x20in) London 1999

KEYSER Elisabeth 1851-1898 [19]

➳ **$9 473** – €9 927 – **£6 000** – FF65 117
On the Balcony, Paris Oil/canvas (41.5x33cm 16x12in) London 2000

KEYSER Ephraïm 1850-1937 **[6]**
- **$14 000** - €15 446 - **£9 259** - FF101 316
  Figure of Renaissance Lady with a Falcon
  Bronze (H144cm H56in) New-York 2000
- **$6 000** - €5 722 - **£3 652** - FF37 535
  Figural Group: Titania Bronze (H78.5cm H30in)
  New-York 1999

KEYSER Ragnhild 1889-1943 **[11]**
- **$2 865** - €3 180 - **£1 996** - FF20 859
  Stilleben, den rode bog Oil/canvas (46x38cm
  18x14in) Oslo 2001
- **$4 699** - €5 158 - **£3 028** - FF33 835
  Utan titel Gouache/paper (19x9cm 7x3in) Stockholm
  2000

KEYT George 1901-1993 **[36]**
- **$4 545** - €4 368 - **£2 800** - FF28 653
  Musicians Acrylic/canvas (112x79cm 44x31in)
  London 1999
- **$1 800** - €2 087 - **£1 275** - FF13 689
  Untitled Oil/canvas (36.5x29cm 14x11in) New-York
  2000
- **$1 800** - €2 047 - **£1 257** - FF13 428
  Untitled Ink/paper (56x38cm 22x14in) New-York 2000

KHAKHAR Bhupen 1934 **[15]**
- **$12 000** - €13 913 - **£8 500** - FF91 261
  Landscape with Cannon Oil/canvas (107.5x91.5cm
  42x36in) New-York 2000
- **$2 700** - €2 331 - **£1 613** - FF15 288
  She Rejected Five Suiters Watercolour/paper
  (127.5x109cm 50x42in) New-York 1998

KHALDEÏ Evgueni 1917-1997 **[17]**
- **$1 800** - €1 998 - **£1 254** - FF13 106
  **Raising the red Flag over the Reichstag
  Building** Gelatin silver print (26x34cm 10x13in) New-
  York 2001

KHALIP Yakov 1908-1980 **[23]**
- **$1 140** - €1 329 - **£789** - FF8 720
  Torpedoschütze Gelatin silver print (28.3x40.4cm
  11x15in) Köln 2000

KHANAMIRYAN Lidia 1930 **[17]**
- **$619** - €549 - **£380** - FF3 600
  Still Life with Fish and Lemons Oil/canvas
  (60.5x80.5cm 23x31in) London 1999

KHANINE Alexandre 1955 **[166]**
- **$308** - €351 - **£216** - FF2 300
  Danaé Huile/toile (49x49cm 19x19in) Paris 2001

KHANNA Krishen 1925 **[17]**
- **$5 292** - €4 950 - **£3 200** - FF32 472
  The End Oil/canvas (158.5x96.5cm 62x37in) London
  1999
- **$1 298** - €1 248 - **£800** - FF8 186
  Portrait of M.F.Husain Ink (22x17.5cm 8x6in)
  London 1999

KHASTGIR Sudhir Ranjan 1907-1974 **[4]**
- **$1 724** - €2 012 - **£1 200** - FF13 195
  The Dancer Gouache (63.5x47cm 25x18in) London
  2000

KHIEN YIMSIRI 1922-1971 **[1]**
- **$10 688** - €8 968 - **£6 271** - FF58 824
  Courtesy: Embracing Couple Bronze (H60cm
  H23in) Singapore 1998

KHMELUK Vassyl 1903-1986 **[92]**
- **$778** - €884 - **£541** - FF5 097
  Clown au chapeau rouge Huile/toile (55x46cm
  21x18in) Brive-la-Gaillarde 2001

- **$537** - €610 - **£373** - FF4 000
  Bouquet Huile/toile (27x35cm 10x13in) Brive-la-
  Gaillarde 2001

KHNOPFF Fernand 1858-1921 **[150]**
- **$50 640** - €59 492 - **£35 520** - FF390 240
  Le pont de Fosset Huile/toile (43x63cm 16x24in)
  Bruxelles 2000
- **$6 864** - €6 445 - **£4 238** - FF42 276
  Le jardin à Famelettes Huile/toile (22.5x30.2cm
  8x11in) Antwerpen 1999
- **$25 392** - €24 281 - **£16 000** - FF159 270
  Icarus Coloured chalks (15.5x11cm 6x4in) London
  1999
- **$242** - €235 - **£150** - FF1 542
  Ex-Libris pour Isabella Errera Print (14.6x9.9cm
  5x3in) Berlin 1999

KHODOSSIEVITCH-LÉGER Nadia 1904-1982 **[13]**
- **$538** - €613 - **£375** - FF4 024
  Suprématisme I Farblithographie (76x54cm 29x21in)
  Hamburg 2001

KHOKHLOVKINA Elsa 1934 **[17]**
- **$216** - €213 - **£133** - FF1 400
  Muguet Huile/toile (40x35cm 15x13in) L'Isle-Adam
  1999

KIAERSCHOU Frederik Christian 1805-1891 **[209]**
- **$1 246** - €1 076 - **£752** - FF7 060
  Flodlandskab med jolle, i baggrunden huse
  Oil/canvas (53x77cm 20x30in) Vejle 1998
- **$813** - €807 - **£508** - FF5 291
  Parti fra Alperne Oil/panel (24x32cm 9x12in)
  København 1999

KIAKSHUK 1886-1966 **[6]**
- **$226** - €193 - **£134** - FF1 264
  Caribou Hunting Engraving (25.5x30cm 10x11in)
  Vancouver, BC. 1998

KIBEL Wolf 1903-1938 **[48]**
- **$2 656** - €3 082 - **£1 834** - FF20 216
  Antoinette Oil/canvas (33x24cm 12x9in) Johannesburg
  2000
- **$996** - €1 156 - **£687** - FF7 581
  Red Roofed House Pastel/paper (22x24.5cm 8x9in)
  Johannesburg 2000
- **$784** - €756 - **£484** - FF4 960
  Landscape with a House in the Distance
  Monotype (16.5x22cm 6x8in) Johannesburg 1999

KICCO 1969 **[8]**
- **$600** - €622 - **£360** - FF4 080
  «Neuroni Saratoga» Tecnica mista (60x60cm
  23x23in) Vercelli 2001

KICK Cornelis 1635-1681 **[12]**
- **$7 491** - €8 521 - **£5 281** - FF55 892
  **Blumenstilleben in einer Glasvase mit Pflaume
  und Schnecke** Öl/Leinwand (40.5x28cm 15x11in)
  Zürich 2001

KICK Simon 1603-1652 **[5]**
- **$400 000** - €352 054 - **£243 520** - FF2 309 320
  **Company of Soldiers in a Guardroom Preparing
  for Battle** Oil/panel (122x122cm 48x48in) New-York
  1999

KID KOSOLAWAT 1917-1988 **[3]**
- **$2 002** - €1 890 - **£1 237** - FF12 202
  Windswept Rural Scenery Watercolour/paper
  (54x73cm 21x28in) Bangkok 1999

K

KIDD Joseph Bartholomew 1806-1899 **[7]**

📖 **$1 442** - €1 594 - **£1 000** - FF10 453
Clermont Pen, St Mary's Lithograph (25x40cm 9x15in) London 2001

KIDD William 1790-1863 **[20]**

🖼 **$1 613** - €1 739 - **£1 100** - FF11 407
The Pensive Cobbler Oil/panel (30.5x38cm 12x14in) London 2001

KIDDER Harvey W. 1918 **[6]**

🖌 **$700** - €654 - **£432** - FF4 288
Simon Bolivar Presides Watercolour (56x76cm 22x30in) Detroit MI 1999

KIDDER James 1793-1837 **[1]**

🖌 **$5 225** - €4 869 - **£3 224** - FF31 941
Interior of a lottery office Watercolour, gouache/paper (38x27cm 15x11in) Thomaston ME 1999

KIECOL Hubert 1950 **[26]**

🗿 **$10 102** - €9 715 - **£6 233** - FF63 724
Sechs Häuser Sculpture (25.6x8.8x13.4cm 10x3x5in) Köln 1999

📖 **$73** - €82 - **£51** - FF536
Komposition Woodcut (31.5x23cm 12x9in) Heidelberg 2001

KIEFER Anselm 1945 **[150]**

🖼 **$110 000** - €127 632 - **£75 944** - FF837 210
Wurzel Jesse (Tree of Jesse) Mixed media (241x131cm 94x51in) New-York 2000

🖼 **$35 000** - €39 203 - **£24 318** - FF257 152
«Der engel der Geschichte» Mixed media (101.5x109cm 39x42in) New-York 2001

🖼 **$17 000** - €19 725 - **£11 736** - FF129 387
Die Donauquelle (The Source of the Danube) Mixed media (30.5x20x2cm 12x7xin) New-York 2000

🖌 **$28 152** - €26 234 - **£17 000** - FF172 082
«Gilgamesch im Zedernwald» Mixed media/paper (84x58.5cm 33x23in) London 1998

📖 **$652** - €716 - **£443** - FF4 695
Johannis-Nacht Offset (62x67.8cm 24x26in) Berlin 2000

📷 **$2 248** - €2 556 - **£1 559** - FF16 769
Kristalle Photograph (27x39cm 10x15in) Hamburg 2000

KIEFF (Antonio Grediaga) 1936 **[42]**

🗿 **$1 295** - €1 511 - **£901** - FF9 913
Tonadilados No.2 Bronze (H56cm H22in) Toronto 2000

KIELBERG Ole 1911-1985 **[163]**

🖼 **$664** - €737 - **£463** - FF4 836
Sommerdag på Helsingör Strand med Kronborg i baggrunden Oil/canvas (64x97cm 25x38in) Köbenhavn 2001

🖌 **$224** - €241 - **£154** - FF1 583
St.Paul's Watercolour/paper (29x20cm 11x7in) Köbenhavn 2001

KIELDRUP Anton Edvard 1827-1869 **[70]**

🖼 **$1 017** - €1 008 - **£636** - FF6 614
Bjerglandskab med gående personer Oil/canvas (46x61cm 18x24in) Köbenhavn 1999

🖼 **$1 033** - €1 141 - **£684** - FF7 483
Fjordparti med sejlskib Oil/paper (25x35cm 9x13in) Viby J, Århus 2000

KIELLAND Kitty Christine 1843-1914 **[22]**

🖼 **$4 368** - €4 839 - **£2 964** - FF31 740
Landskap Oil/canvas (38x83cm 14x32in) Oslo 2000

🖼 **$87 280** - €100 848 - **£61 120** - FF661 520
Interiör med röd stol Oil/panel (41x32cm 16x12in) Oslo 2001

KIEN Josef 1903-1985 **[43]**

🖼 **$2 515** - €2 812 - **£1 695** - FF18 446
Pittura Öl/Leinwand (111.5x69.5cm 43x27in) München 2000

🖼 **$1 777** - €1 533 - **£1 068** - FF10 056
«Der Maler Weber-Tyrol» Coloured chalks/paper (61x48.5cm 24x19in) München 1998

📖 **$1 303** - €1 124 - **£783** - FF7 375
Visione: zwei Akte Farblithographie (50x70cm 19x27in) München 1998

KIENERK Giorgio 1869-1948 **[17]**

🖼 **$15 000** - €15 550 - **£9 000** - FF102 000
Ombre lunghe Olio/tavola (60x81.5cm 23x32in) Prato 2000

🖼 **$4 500** - €3 887 - **£2 250** - FF25 500
«Motivo toscano» Olio/tavola (45x28cm 17x11in) Prato 1999

KIENHOLZ Edward 1927-1994 **[84]**

🖼 **$1 800** - €2 098 - **£1 246** - FF13 763
The Marriage Icon Mixed media (32.5x133cm 12x52in) New-York 2000

🖼 **$105 000** - €88 145 - **£61 582** - FF578 193
«Boy, Son of John Doe» Assemblage (190.5x51x115.5cm 75x20x45in) Beverly-Hills CA 1998

🗿 **$1 600** - €1 823 - **£1 105** - FF11 956
The Billionaire Deluxe Metal (28x38.5x35.5cm 11x15x13in) Beverly-Hills CA 2000

🖌 **$1 200** - €1 288 - **£803** - FF8 449
For $200.00 Watercolour (31x41.5cm 12x16in) Beverly-Hills CA 2000

📖 **$800** - €933 - **£553** - FF6 117
Documentation Books: 5 Car Stud and Sawdy Offset (29x26.5cm 11x10in) New-York 2000

KIENHOLZ Edward & Nancy 1927/43 **[11]**

🗿 **$15 000** - €17 059 - **£10 480** - FF111 901
The Black Bird Construction (181x59x26cm 71x23x10in) Beverly-Hills CA 2000

KIENMAYER Franz 1886-? **[17]**

🖼 **$476** - €511 - **£318** - FF3 353
Reitergruppe in den Bergen Öl/Leinwand (69x55cm 27x21in) Bremen 2000

🖌 **$675** - €767 - **£472** - FF5 030
Profilporträt eines indonesischen Chalks/paper (70x50cm 27x19in) München 2001

KIERNEK Giorgio 1869-1948 **[3]**

🖼 **$8 750** - €9 071 - **£5 250** - FF59 500
Il pagliaio a Fauglia Olio/cartone (50x66cm 19x25in) Milano 1999

KIERS Petrus 1807-1875 **[16]**

🖼 **$12 784** - €14 521 - **£8 969** - FF95 251
Adieu, au revoir Oil/panel (74.5x60cm 29x23in) Amsterdam 2001

🖼 **$630** - €681 - **£431** - FF4 464
Intérieur effet de chandelle Oil/panel (11x9cm 4x3in) Amsterdam 2001

KIERS-HAANEN van Elisabeth Alida 1809-1845 **[8]**

🖼 **$3 125** - €3 634 - **£2 231** - FF23 838
In the Wine Cellar Oil/canvas (51x38cm 20x14in) Toronto 2001

$13 305 - €11 176 - **£7 800** - FF73 308
Elegant Lady with a Pet Parrot on a Balcony
Oil/panel (43.5x35cm 17x13in) Billingshurst, West-Sussex 1998

KIERSBLICK van Jules 1833-1896 [1]
$2 586 - €3 049 - **£1 818** - FF20 000
Scènes de l'histoire italienne Huile/panneau (45x35cm 17x13in) Paris 2000

KIES Helmut 1933 [33]
$4 669 - €3 999 - **£2 733** - FF26 229
«Die Mauer II» Oil/panel (25x20cm 9x7in) Wien 1998
$378 - €363 - **£233** - FF2 383
Österreich Radierung (55x40cm 21x15in) Wien 1999

KIESEL Conrad 1846-1921 [46]
$3 429 - €2 899 - **£2 050** - FF19 019
After the Ball Oil/canvas (60x78cm 23x30in) Amsterdam 1998
$2 871 - €2 454 - **£1 737** - FF16 094
Edgar, der Sohn des Künstlers Öl/Leinwand (37x29cm 14x11in) München 1998

KIFFER Charles 1902-1992 [64]
$1 087 - €928 - **£650** - FF6 086
«Charles Trenet» Poster (121x81cm 47x31in) London 1998

KIHLE Harald 1905-1997 [106]
$2 534 - €2 813 - **£1 766** - FF18 452
«Oygaards-kuene» Oil/panel (39x45cm 15x17in) Oslo 2001
$1 324 - €1 265 - **£833** - FF8 299
En mann kjører forbi Oil/panel (19x24cm 7x9in) Oslo 1999
$1 356 - €1 464 - **£937** - FF9 604
Telemark Gouache/paper (23x31cm 9x12in) Oslo 2001
$882 - €843 - **£555** - FF5 532
Snöplogen Lithograph (37x50cm 14x19in) Oslo 1999

KIJNO Ladislas 1921 [861]
$1 963 - €2 287 - **£1 371** - FF15 000
«Stele par Pablo Neruda» Technique mixte (215x160cm 84x62in) Paris 2000
$1 108 - €1 037 - **£679** - FF6 800
Composition bleue et mauve Acrylique/papier (97x84cm 38x33in) Paris 1998
$706 - €762 - **£488** - FF5 000
«St John Perse» Acrylique/toile (27x22cm 10x8in) Paris 2001
$912 - €945 - **£578** - FF6 200
Sans titre Technique mixte/papier (38x30cm 14x11in) Paris 2001
$131 - €137 - **£82** - FF900
Composition en rouge, noir et jaune sur fond vert Lithographie (90x63cm 35x24in) Lille 2000

KIKI DE MONTPARNASSE Alice Ernestine Prin 1901-1953 [15]
$3 036 - €3 354 - **£2 105** - FF22 000
Marchande de fleurs Huile/toile (46x55cm 18x21in) Avallon 2001
$2 255 - €1 906 - **£1 341** - FF12 500
Passage des filles du Calvaire Huile/toile (41x33cm 16x12in) Paris 1998
$6 248 - €6 600 - **£4 180** - FF44 000
Portrait de Man Ray Watercolour, gouache (64x48cm 25x18in) Paris 2000

KIKI OF PARIS 1945 [10]
$845 - €915 - **£579** - FF6 000
Ulysse Photo (119.5x83.5cm 47x32in) Paris 2001

KIKOINE Michel 1892-1968 [362]
$6 000 - €5 561 - **£3 730** - FF36 480
Paysage Oil/canvas (54x65cm 21x25in) Tel Aviv 1999
$2 139 - €2 134 - **£1 302** - FF14 000
Autoportrait Huile/toile (24x19cm 9x7in) Paris 2000
$911 - €1 037 - **£632** - FF6 800
Paysage Aquarelle/papier (26x37cm 10x14in) Paris 2000

KILBURNE George Goodwin, Snr. 1839-1924 [310]
$6 644 - €5 686 - **£4 000** - FF37 300
Her First Ball Oil/canvas (91x122cm 35x48in) London 1998
$2 200 - €2 371 - **£1 500** - FF15 554
Setting Off Oil/panel (25.5x18cm 10x7in) London 2001
$4 682 - €3 997 - **£2 800** - FF26 217
Tending the Invalid/A Young girl feeding a Cat Watercolour (26.5x35cm 10x13in) London 1998

KILENYI Julio 1885-1959 [5]
$2 600 - €2 901 - **£1 702** - FF19 027
«Los Angeles Olympics» Poster (99.5x66cm 39x25in) New-York 2000

KILGOUR Andrew Wilkie 1868-1930 [16]
$390 - €334 - **£236** - FF2 189
Early Snow Huile/panneau (26.5x37cm 10x14in) Montréal 1998

KILGOUR Jack Noel 1900-1987 [28]
$1 326 - €1 474 - **£888** - FF9 669
Listening Group Oil/canvas/board (41x51cm 16x20in) Nedlands 2000
$1 307 - €1 260 - **£808** - FF8 263
The Conductor Oil/board (22x14cm 8x5in) Sydney 1999

KILIAN Hannes 1909-1999 [83]
$772 - €920 - **£550** - FF6 037
Der Hund von Ballybunion, Irland Photograph (31x24cm 12x9in) München 2000

KILIAN Lukas 1579-1637 [19]
$1 544 - €1 841 - **£1 100** - FF12 074
Bildnis eines bärtigen Mannes in allegorischer Umrahmung Pencil/paper (18.6x12.7cm 7x5in) Köln 2000
$539 - €613 - **£374** - FF4 024
Pietà, nach Hans von Aachen Kupferstich (46.2x30.4cm 18x11in) Berlin 2000

KILIMNICK Karen 1955 [17]
$6 500 - €7 542 - **£4 487** - FF49 471
Is Pretty Baby finally growing up? Acrylic (87.5x57cm 34x22in) New-York 2000
$7 217 - €7 809 - **£5 000** - FF51 222
«Scene I the Countryside 1600's» Oil/canvas (35x45cm 13x17in) London 2001
$6 500 - €7 353 - **£4 547** - FF48 233
Brief Lives Crayon (89x58.5cm 35x23in) New-York 2001
$4 000 - €4 552 - **£2 810** - FF29 860
Undead Type C color print (43x51cm 16x20in) New-York 2001

KILLI OLSEN Kjell Erik 1952 [4]
$10 469 - €11 619 - **£7 296** - FF76 218
«Fiora des Pesta» Oil/canvas (100x100cm 39x39in) Oslo 2001

KILLINGBECK Benjamin XVIII [9]
$36 000 - €33 368 - **£22 384** - FF218 883
Edward Parr with his Son John and his Horse «Button» Browsholme Hall Oil/canvas (104x133.5cm 40x52in) New-York 1999

$12 000 – €12 473 - **£7 562** – FF81 817
Ancaster Oil/canvas (61x76cm 24x29in) New-York 2000

KILPACK Sarah Louise c.1840-1909 **[163]**
$5 491 – €5 164 - **£3 400** – FF33 871
St Michael's Mount, Cornwall Oil/canvas (56x81.5cm 22x32in) London 1999
$1 135 – €1 090 - **£700** – FF7 153
St.Michael's mount, Cornwall Oil/board (23.5x31cm 9x12in) London 1999

KILPATRICK Aaron Edward 1872-1953 **[25]**
$4 000 – €4 294 - **£2 676** – FF28 164
Oaks in landscape Oil/canvas (60x76cm 24x30in) Altadena CA 2000
$1 200 – €1 296 - **£829** – FF8 500
Landscape Oil/board (31x47cm 12x18in) Altadena CA 2001

KILVINGTON Patrick 1922-1990 **[20]**
$642 – €707 - **£427** – FF4 640
The Royal Mail Series: Departure Oil/canvas (38.5x49cm 15x19in) Melbourne 2000

KIM Tschang-yeul 1929 **[8]**
$35 000 – €39 805 - **£24 454** – FF261 103
Waterdrops No.S 2 Acrylic (181.5x227cm 71x89in) Beverly-Hills CA 2000
$8 000 – €8 840 - **£5 548** – FF57 989
Waterdrop Ink (164x52cm 64x20in) New-York 2001

KIMBEI Kusakabe 1841-1934 **[20]**
$784 – €726 - **£480** – FF4 762
Japanese Landscape, Gardens and Portraits Albumen print (20x25cm 8x10in) London 1999

KIMBEL Richard 1865-1942 **[4]**
$1 500 – €1 404 - **£929** – FF9 210
European Fish Harbor Scene with a small Gothic Cathedral Oil/board (30x39cm 12x15in) Detroit MI 1999

KIMCHI Evi 1945 **[2]**
$1 486 – €1 677 - **£1 045** – FF11 000
Homme debout Métal (52x81x12cm 20x31x4in) Paris 2001

KIMMEL Cornelis 1804-1877 **[19]**
$6 980 – €7 714 - **£4 841** – FF50 602
A rhenish River Landscape with a Herdsman and Cattle Oil/panel (51.5x64.5cm 20x25in) Amsterdam 2001

KIMPE Raymond 1885-1970 **[59]**
$5 246 – €4 873 - **£3 202** – FF31 965
Two cubist Figures Oil/canvas (80x60cm 31x23in) Amsterdam 1998
$2 718 – €3 176 - **£1 940** – FF20 836
Abstract 5 Oil/panel (32x25cm 12x9in) Amsterdam 2001
$874 – €953 - **£602** – FF6 250
«Veere» Black chalk/paper (39x44cm 15x17in) Amsterdam 2001

KIMSOU Kim Heung-Sou 1919 **[12]**
$7 142 – €6 250 - **£4 325** – FF41 000
Profil sur fond rouge Huile/toile (60x37cm 23x14in) Paris 1998

KINCH Hayter 1767-1844 **[5]**
$8 218 – €8 822 - **£5 500** – FF57 868
Mr Whitby's Hunter Cyrus near Newlands Manor Oil/canvas (67.5x89cm 26x35in) London 2000

KINDBORG Johan 1861-1907 **[66]**
$1 111 – €1 120 - **£693** – FF7 347
Metande vid stilla sjö Oil/canvas (45x77cm 17x30in) Stockholm 2000
$496 – €446 - **£296** – FF2 928
Landskap i månsken Oil/canvas (45x35cm 17x13in) Stockholm 1998
$1 932 – €2 083 - **£1 296** – FF13 665
Kvinna i sommarskog Akvarell/papper (31x42cm 12x16in) Stockholm 2000

KINDEL Theodor XX **[8]**
$149 – €160 - **£101** – FF1 048
«Dressing Gown» Poster (46x31cm 18x12in) Wien 2001

KINDER John 1819-1903 **[3]**
$2 122 – €2 418 - **£1 466** – FF15 858
Awatere Valley Watercolour/paper (24.5x65.5cm 9x25in) Auckland 2000

KINDERMANS Jean-Baptiste 1822-1876 **[14]**
$1 326 – €1 487 - **£924** – FF9 756
Paysage animé de personnages Huile/toile (47x55.5cm 18x21in) Bruxelles 2001
$2 721 – €2 286 - **£1 600** – FF14 995
Extensive Landscape with Peasants by a Campfire Oil/panel (31.5x40.5cm 12x15in) London 1998

KINDLER Albert 1833-1876 **[9]**
$2 026 – €2 301 - **£1 408** – FF15 092
Die Lektüre, Interieur mit zwei Frauen am Tisch Oil/panel (16.5x13cm 6x5in) Köln 2001

KINDON Mary Evelina c.1855-c.1925 **[9]**
$160 – €153 - **£100** – FF1 002
G.Engeström, seated three-quarter-length/Agatha Engeström Oil/canvas (66x51.5cm 25x20in) London 1999

KINDT Marie Adelaide 1804-1884 **[5]**
$4 310 – €4 838 - **£3 000** – FF31 733
The patient Mother Oil/canvas (57x47cm 22x18in) London 2001

KING Agnes Gardner XIX-XX **[2]**
$3 065 – €2 944 - **£1 900** – FF19 312
Young Girl with her Pet Lamb Watercolour/paper (53x72cm 20x28in) London 1999

KING Albert F. 1854-1945 **[32]**
$7 000 – €6 341 - **£4 284** – FF41 592
Ammples and basket Oil/canvas (35x50cm 14x20in) Portland ME 1998
$3 000 – €2 885 - **£1 851** – FF18 924
Still Life with Apples from an Overturned Basket Oil/canvas (33x45cm 13x18in) Pittsburgh PA 1999

KING Alexa 1952 **[1]**
$6 500 – €7 552 - **£4 568** – FF49 537
«Thoroughbred Mare and Foal» Bronze (H29cm H11in) New-York 2001

KING Baragwanath John 1864-1939 **[93]**
$369 – €375 - **£230** – FF2 457
Moorland Landscape Watercolour/paper (27x43cm 11x17in) Aylsham, Norfolk 2000

KING Cecil 1921-1986 **[24]**
$1 538 – €1 651 - **£1 049** – FF10 827
Abstract Oil/canvas (46x76cm 18x29in) Dublin 2001
$608 – €635 - **£384** – FF4 164
Red Within Mixed media (35x25.5cm 13x10in) Dublin 2000

$1 183 – €1 270 – £807 – FF8 329
Intrusion orange Gouache/paper (51x73.5cm 20x28in) Dublin 2001

$268 – €305 – £187 – FF1 999
Berlin Suite 2 Lithograph (52.5x39cm 20x15in) Dublin 2000

KING Cecil G. Charles 1881-1942 **[8]**
$3 670 – €4 255 – £2 600 – FF27 912
«Royal Rothesay, LMS & LNER, The Holiday Capital of the Clyde Coast» Poster (102x127cm 40x50in) London 2000

KING Charles Bird 1785-1862 **[20]**
$14 000 – €12 126 – £8 586 – FF79 541
Pomegranate, Grapes and Pineapples Oil/canvas (63.5x76cm 25x29in) New-York 1999
$550 – €501 – £343 – FF3 285
Chon-Ca-Pe Lithograph (40x30cm 16x12in) Bolton MA 1999

KING Edith 1869-1962 **[6]**
$4 021 – €4 168 – £2 547 – FF27 340
Aloes in a Rocky Landscape Watercolour/paper (73x47.5cm 28x18in) Johannesburg 2000

KING Elizabeth XIX-XX **[6]**
$161 – €152 – £100 – FF995
Still Life, Two-handled Bowl Containing White Lilies Watercolour/paper (54x36cm 21x14in) Canterbury, Kent 1999

KING Emma Bird 1858-1933 **[2]**
$4 750 – €4 812 – £2 981 – FF31 566
Still Life Apples and Jugs Oil/canvas (50x60cm 20x24in) Cincinnati OH 2000

KING Eric Meade 1911 **[27]**
$658 – €642 – £400 – FF4 213
The Berkeley Hounds, Oldbury Watercolour (40x55cm 15x21in) London 2000

KING George W. 1836-1922 **[12]**
$2 500 – €2 801 – £1 740 – FF18 374
River Landscape Oil/canvas (45x81cm 18x32in) Watertown MA 2001

KING Gordon 1939 **[15]**
$1 023 – €1 174 – £700 – FF7 701
Flwoer Girl Watercolour/paper (50x40cm 20x16in) Little-Lane, Ilkley 2000

KING Hamilton 1871-1952 **[3]**
$1 800 – €1 713 – £1 125 – FF11 236
Woman in Kimono Pastel/paper (50x20cm 20x8in) New-York 1999

KING Haynes 1831-1904 **[46]**
$3 813 – €3 302 – £2 300 – FF21 657
The Pea Sellers Oil/canvas (63.5x76cm 25x29in) London 1998
$1 900 – €1 627 – £1 345 – FF14 568
«Oranges» Oil/canvas (41x32cm 16x12in) Cedar-Falls IA 2001

KING Henry John Yeend 1855-1924 **[299]**
$59 772 – €64 160 – £40 000 – FF420 864
Haymaking Oil/canvas (153x102cm 60x40in) London 2000
$4 419 – €5 187 – £3 118 – FF34 024
Sommarlandskap med kvinnor vid bro Oil/canvas (51x76cm 20x29in) Stockholm 2000
$948 – €1 115 – £680 – FF7 315
Hill Farm with Turkeys and Hens, by a Stream Oil/canvas (30x40cm 11x15in) Cheshire 2001

$866 – €740 – £520 – FF4 854
Evening Watercolour/paper (24x34cm 9x13in) Little-Lane, Ilkley 1998

KING Jessie Marion 1875-1949 **[45]**
$4 561 – €3 897 – £2 760 – FF25 564
«The Reluctant Dragon» Ink (24x17cm 9x6in) Edinburgh 1998

KING John Gregory 1929 **[9]**
$400 – €451 – £277 – FF2 956
The Lone Fox Watercolour/paper (36x26cm 14x10in) Hatfield PA 2000

KING Paul 1867-1947 **[36]**
$4 250 – €5 081 – £2 920 – FF33 328
Sailing Ships in the Harbor Oil/canvas (61x51cm 24x20in) Chicago IL 2000
$2 750 – €3 288 – £1 896 – FF21 565
Winter in Lansdowne, PA Oil/canvas (20x25cm 8x10in) Milford CT 2000

KING Peter A. XX **[15]**
$459 – €440 – £280 – FF2 883
Razor's Gaelic Prize Watercolour (25x15cm 10x6in) London 2001

KING William Gunning 1859-1940 **[24]**
$2 694 – €3 128 – £1 900 – FF20 519
Feeding time, a Farmer with his Casttle Oil/canvas (43x53cm 16x20in) Cambridge 2001

KINGELEZ Bodys Isek 1948 **[2]**
$11 083 – €10 697 – £7 000 – FF70 166
Kimbembeke Ihunga Construction (51x108x86.5cm 20x42x34in) London 1999

KINGERLEE John 1936 **[17]**
$591 – €635 – £403 – FF4 164
Chip off the Old Block Oil/board (49.5x31.5cm 19x12in) Dublin 2001

KINGMAN Dong 1911-2000 **[87]**
$1 900 – €1 627 – £1 121 – FF10 674
Sailboats on a Canal Watercolour/paper (38x56cm 14x22in) New-York 1999

KINGMAN Eduardo 1911-1997 **[2]**
$12 000 – €13 942 – £8 433 – FF91 454
Payaso Oil/canvas (58.5x53.5cm 23x21in) New-York 2001

KINGMAN RIOFRIO Eduardo 1913-1997 **[36]**
$9 000 – €10 456 – £6 325 – FF68 590
Mujer triste Oil/canvas (79.5x100.5cm 31x39in) New-York 2001
$3 500 – €3 405 – £2 154 – FF22 338
Mujer con canastas Graphite (88.5x63cm 34x24in) New-York 1999

KINGSBURGER Sylvain 1855-1935 **[2]**
$3 970 – €4 141 – £2 500 – FF27 166
Le Preux, standing holding a sword and an axe Ivory, bronze (H60cm H23in) Billingshurst, West-Sussex 2000

KINGSTON Peter 1943 **[14]**
$225 – €212 – £141 – FF1 392
Circular Ski Etching (56x42cm 22x16in) Sydney 1999

KINGSTON Richard XX **[12]**
$4 285 – €4 571 – £2 854 – FF29 984
Ringsend Oil/board (50x76cm 20x30in) Dublin 2000

KINGSTON Steve 1951 **[7]**
$6 420 – €7 485 – £4 500 – FF49 100
African Queen, Lioness Acrylic/board (46.5x84.5cm 18x33in) London 2000

K

$6 168 – €5 928 – **£3 800** – FF38 886
Lion and Lioness Acrylic (14x14cm 5x5in) London 1999

KINGWELL Mabel Amber XIX-XX [12]

$491 – €571 – **£350** – FF3 745
«Toby», a Jack Russell Terrier Watercolour (21.5x18cm 8x7in) London 2001

KINLEY Peter 1926-1988 [68]

$834 – €978 – **£600** – FF6 414
Study for Birds on Water Oil/canvas (40.5x51cm 15x20in) London 2001

$1 397 – €1 332 – **£850** – FF8 740
Studio Interior with Figure Oil/paper (30.5x25.5cm 12x10in) London 1999

KINNAIRD Frederick Gerald c.1840-c.1890 [25]

$1 823 – €2 174 – **£1 300** – FF14 259
Gathers Oil/canvas (76x64cm 29x25in) Leyburn, North Yorkshire 2000

KINNAIRD Henry John act.1880-1920 [219]

$2 988 – €3 208 – **£2 000** – FF21 043
Harvesting by the Thames Oil/canvas (51x76.5cm 20x30in) London 2000

$1 760 – €1 883 – **£1 200** – FF12 349
River with Men loading a Haycart in a Field nearby Watercolour/paper (25x38.5cm 9x15in) Loughton, Essex 2001

KINNAIRD Wiggs (Francis Jos.) 1875-1915 [35]

$527 – €565 – **£360** – FF3 704
Sheep Droving Watercolour/paper (24x34cm 9x13in) London 2001

KINNEAR James 1858-c.1917 [34]

$1 906 – €2 055 – **£1 300** – FF13 480
Shepherd with his Flock on the Scottish Coast Oil/canvas (76.5x117cm 30x46in) London 2001

$1 157 – €1 083 – **£700** – FF7 103
Voe of Papa Stour Oil/board (23.5x38cm 9x14in) London 1999

$539 – €566 – **£340** – FF3 714
The Tweed at Abbotsford Ferry Opposite «Abbotsford» the Home of Scott Watercolour (30.5x45.5cm 12x17in) London 2000

KINOLD Klaus 1939 [15]

$568 – €562 – **£355** – FF3 689
Le Corbusier/Villa Savoye in Poissy Photograph (30.2x24cm 11x9in) München 1999

KINOSHITA Takanori 1894-1973 [3]

$3 332 – €3 250 – **£2 040** – FF21 318
Ballerina Oil/canvas (45.5x38cm 17x14in) Tokyo 1999

KINSBURGER Sylvain 1855-1935 [30]

$890 – €818 – **£547** – FF5 366
La Rêverie, Engel die Geige spielend Bronze (H60cm H23in) Konstanz 1999

KINSELLA James 1857-1923 [3]

$4 000 – €4 757 – **£2 850** – FF31 204
The State House from Park Street, Boston Watercolour (65.5x49.5cm 25x19in) New-York 2000

KINSEY Alberta 1875-1955 [69]

$2 000 – €2 144 – **£1 323** – FF14 066
New Orleans Courtyard Oil/canvas (53x42cm 21x16in) New-Orleans LA 2000

$850 – €849 – **£531** – FF5 569
Arts & Crafts Courtyard, New Orleans Oil/board (24x18cm 9x7in) New-Orleans LA 1999

KINSLEY Albert 1852-1945 [19]

$503 – €425 – **£300** – FF2 788
Country Riverlandscape with Distant Cottage and Field of Sheep Oil/canvas (23x34cm 9x13in) Leamington-Spa, Warwickshire 1998

$434 – €371 – **£242** – FF2 434
«The Edge of Derwentwater» Watercolour (37x52.5cm 14x20in) Leeds 1998

KINSON François-Joseph 1771-1839 [17]

$10 432 – €12 196 – **£7 448** – FF80 000
Portrait de la duchesse d'Angoulême Huile/toile (65x53.5cm 25x21in) Paris 2001

KINUTANI Koji 1943 [11]

$55 000 – €60 679 – **£36 377** – FF398 029
Miki to Moheno no shozo (Portrait of Miki and Moheno) Oil/canvas (117x93.5cm 46x36in) New-York 2000

$5 880 – €5 735 – **£3 600** – FF37 620
Nude Woman Painting (26.5x21cm 10x8in) Tokyo 1999

$4 116 – €4 015 – **£2 520** – FF26 334
Nude Woman Watercolour/paper (37x55.5cm 14x21in) Tokyo 1999

KINZEL Joseph 1852-1925 [40]

$7 740 – €7 267 – **£4 800** – FF47 670
Jäger im Gespräch Oil/panel (50.5x39cm 19x15in) Wien 1999

$3 300 – €3 276 – **£2 024** – FF21 488
Rabbits in Discussion Oil/panel (25x31cm 10x12in) Mystic CT 2000

KINZEL Liesl 1886-1961 [13]

$1 561 – €1 836 – **£1 131** – FF12 044
«Sommerliche Flusslandschaft mit Ausblick auf Dorf» Öl/Karton (40x46cm 15x18in) Zofingen 2001

KIOERBOE Carl Fredrik 1799-1876 [44]

$2 138 – €1 999 – **£1 317** – FF13 114
Sittande räv i vinterlandskap Oil/canvas (60x70cm 23x27in) Stockholm 1999

KIP Jan c.1653-1722 [16]

$262 – €290 – **£174** – FF1 900
St. James's House le Palais Royal de St. James Engraving (35x47.5cm 13x18in) Melbourne 2000

KIPNISS Robert 1931 [26]

$200 – €185 – **£124** – FF1 211
Backyard V Color lithograph (50x45cm 20x18in) Chicago IL 1999

KIPPENBERGER Martin 1953-1997 [106]

$110 000 – €122 194 – **£73 667** – FF801 537
Kasperle V Oil/canvas (180x150cm 70x59in) New-York 2000

$10 460 – €11 228 – **£7 000** – FF73 651
Two Kernteilchen Mit Mutti Oil/canvas (90x75cm 35x29in) London 2000

$2 600 – €3 017 – **£1 795** – FF13 114
Hotel Drawing Oil/paper (29x21cm 11x8in) New-York 2000

$17 931 – €19 248 – **£12 000** – FF126 259
Kippen Noodle Metal (128x40x25cm 50x15x9in) New-York 2000

$8 992 – €10 226 – **£6 236** – FF67 078
Modell Toscana Plaster (57.8x50.3x20cm 22x19x7in) Hamburg 2000

$2 983 – €2 556 – **£1 793** – FF16 766
Ohne Titel Pencil (45.3x64.4cm 17x25in) Hamburg 1998

$11 548 – €12 494 – **£8 000** – FF81 956
2 Mirrors Silkscreen (89x59cm 35x23in) London 2001

KIPRENSKII Orest Adamovich 1782-1836 **[6]**
- **$11 897** - €12 771 - **£7 961** - FF83 772
  Portrait d'un jeune homme Huile/métal (12.5x10cm 4x3in) Warszawa 2000

KIPS Erich 1869-c.1945 **[63]**
- **$1 143** - €1 227 - **£765** - FF8 049
  Hamburger Hafen mit Lotsenbooten und einfahrendem Dampfer Oil/panel (35x50cm 13x19in) Berlin 2000
- **$1 035** - €971 - **£639** - FF6 372
  Hafenprospekt Oil/Karton (22x32cm 8x12in) Stuttgart 1999
- **$809** - €920 - **£561** - FF6 037
  Kolberg Gouache (28.5x43.5cm 11x17in) Hamburg 2000

KIRA Hiromu 1898-1991 **[13]**
- **$3 000** - €2 517 - **£1 760** - FF16 510
  A Pattern Gelatin silver print (34x27cm 13x10in) New-York 1998

KIRALL Emmerich XIX-XX **[7]**
- **$707** - €799 - **£477** - FF5 243
  Magdalenenstrasse Ratzenstadl Aquarell/Papier (21x21cm 8x8in) Wien 2000

KIRBERG Otto Karl 1850-1926 **[22]**
- **$4 185** - €4 716 - **£2 898** - FF30 935
  The Tea Party Oil/canvas (68x81.5cm 26x32in) Toronto 2000

KIRCHBACH Johann Frank 1859-1912 **[12]**
- **$10 093** - €11 248 - **£7 055** - FF73 785
  Ganymed, vom Adler des Zeus emporgetragen zum Olymp Öl/Leinwand (312x200cm 122x78in) München 2001
- **$8 608** - €7 071 - **£5 000** - FF46 382
  Grapes, Apples, Pears, Cauliflower amd Marrows on a table Oil/canvas (71x121cm 27x47in) London 1998

KIRCHER Alexander, Alex 1867-? **[18]**
- **$942** - €920 - **£597** - FF6 037
  Früher Abend im Hafen Öl/Leinwand (79x110cm 31x43in) Bremen 1999

KIRCHHERR Astrid 1938 **[12]**
- **$796** - €882 - **£540** - FF5 785
  Outside the Cavern, Liverpool Gelatin silver print (46.9x59cm 18x23in) Berlin 2000

KIRCHNER Albert Emil 1813-1885 **[44]**
- **$4 813** - €4 602 - **£3 016** - FF30 185
  Castello von Rovereto Oil/panel (71x97cm 27x38in) Hamburg 1999
- **$11 236** - €10 226 - **£7 020** - FF67 078
  Schloss Rendelstein in Süd-Tirol an der Talfer Oil/panel (27.5x23.5cm 10x9in) München 1999
- **$914** - €756 - **£536** - FF4 959
  «Am Lech bei Füssen» Pencil/paper (28.4x23.6cm 11x9in) Heidelberg 2001

KIRCHNER Ernst Ludwig 1880-1938 **[1175]**
- **$130 526** - €140 112 - **£87 340** - FF919 072
  Wald Öl/Leinwand (185x118cm 72x46in) Zürich 2000
- **$718 740** - €688 400 - **£452 320** - FF4 515 610
  Waldweg zwischen jungen Stämmen an der Küste von Fehmarn Öl/Leinwand (120.5x90.5cm 47x35in) Bern 1999
- **$32 500** - €28 902 - **£19 877** - FF189 582
  Weiblicher Akt mit männlicher Figur Oil/canvas (27x19cm 10x7in) New-York 1999
- **$6 139** - €7 121 - **£4 402** - FF47 358
  Zwei sitzende weibliche Akte in ganzer Figur Pencil (27x33cm 10x12in) Bern 2001

$3 320 - €3 170 - **£2 074** - FF20 794
Männerkopf IV Woodcut in colors (26.1x22.3cm 10x8in) Köln 1999

KIRCHNER Eugen 1865-1938 **[59]**
- **$160** - €153 - **£102** - FF1 006
  Die Séance Indian ink (23x31cm 9x12in) Zwiesel 1999
- **$197** - €184 - **£121** - FF1 207
  November Etching, aquatint (31.5x20cm 12x7in) Hamburg 1999

KIRCHNER Otto 1887-1960 **[144]**
- **$825** - €817 - **£505** - FF5 357
  Bavarian Smoking Pipe Oil/panel (60x50cm 23x19in) Amsterdam 2000
- **$647** - €613 - **£393** - FF4 024
  Vesperzeit, Kellermeister bei Brot und Wein an einem Fasstisch Öl/Karton (24x18cm 9x7in) Köln 1999

KIRCHNER Raphael 1876-1917 **[46]**
- **$6 762** - €6 403 - **£4 200** - FF42 000
  Jeune femme, fond vert Huile/toile (119x34cm 46x13in) Paris 1999
- **$733** - €844 - **£500** - FF5 538
  Untitled Ink (41x42.5cm 16x16in) London 2000

KIRCHSBERG von Ernestine 1857-1924 **[19]**
- **$751** - €872 - **£518** - FF5 730
  Partie auf dem Königssee Aquarell/Papier (16.5x23cm 6x9in) Graz 2000

KIRING Alois 1840-1911 **[1]**
- **$2 910** - €2 648 - **£1 820** - FF17 370
  In the Forest Oil/canvas (46x33cm 18x12in) Praha 1999

KIRK Joel 1948 **[22]**
- **$595** - €694 - **£420** - FF4 555
  Swallow in Flight Watercolour/paper (21.5x29cm 8x11in) Channel-Islands 2000

KIRKALL Elisha c.1682-1742 **[5]**
- **$269** - €314 - **£190** - FF2 060
  Architectural Decorations Engraving (19x36.5cm 7x14in) London 2000

KIRKBY Thomas 1824-1900 **[1]**
- **$2 450** - €2 533 - **£1 542** - FF16 617
  Rebecca Oil/panel (17x13.5cm 6x5in) Melbourne 2000

KIRKEBY Per 1938 **[363]**
- **$22 458** - €25 478 - **£15 827** - FF167 124
  Pop-komposition Oil/masonite (122x122cm 48x48in) Köbenhavn 2001
- **$12 663** - €12 762 - **£7 894** - FF83 714
  Don Juan i helvedet Oil/canvas (80x100cm 31x39in) Köbenhavn 2000
- **$1 828** - €1 546 - **£1 093** - FF10 140
  Modifikation Oil/canvas (36x40cm 14x15in) Köbenhavn 1998
- **$2 871** - €2 761 - **£1 771** - FF18 111
  Modell Bronze (20.5x6.3x8cm 8x2x3in) Köln 1999
- **$1 112** - €1 076 - **£685** - FF7 060
  Kompositioner Chalks/paper (30x21cm 11x8in) Köbenhavn 1999
- **$468** - €431 - **£288** - FF2 826
  Blå, lilla komposition Color lithograph (56x75cm 22x29in) Köbenhavn 1999

KIRKPATRICK Joseph 1872-c.1930 **[93]**
- **$693** - €808 - **£480** - FF5 300
  The Tweed at Abbotsford with Lady Waiting for the Ferry Watercolour/paper (17x23cm 6x9in) Cheshire 2000

K

K

KIRKPATRICK [title]
$102 - €86 - £60 - FF562
Shepherd on the South Downs Aquatint (27x38cm 11x15in) Par, Cornwall 1998

KIRKPATRICK Lily XIX-XX [1]
$7 366 - €8 598 - £5 200 - FF56 399
«The Little Fishwife» Oil/canvas (46x41cm 18x16in) London 2000

KIRKUP Simon XX [1]
$2 755 - €3 037 - £1 800 - FF19 922
Portrait of Louisa Catherine Gooch Oil/board (23x20cm 9x7in) London 2000

KIRMSE Marguerite 1885-1954 [81]
$450 - €411 - £274 - FF2 697
The Hound/The Fox Engraving (43x32cm 17x12in) Boston MA 1998

KIRMSE Persis XIX-XX [8]
$850 - €926 - £585 - FF6 072
Fox Terriers Coloured chalks (25.5x17.5cm 10x6in) New-York 2001

KIRNER Johan Baptist 1806-1866 [6]
$5 970 - €5 810 - £3 675 - FF38 110
Min favoritponny idyll med ungt italienskt par som leker med sitt barn Oil/canvas (60x46cm 23x18in) Stockholm 1999

KIRNIG Alois 1840-1911 [17]
$1 734 - €1 640 - £1 080 - FF10 758
Landschaft mit Berg Öl/Leinwand/Karton (47x37cm 18x14in) Praha 2001
$1 062 - €929 - £643 - FF6 097
Ansicht der Contexa - Werke in Schlimmdorf am Schlacker Öl/Leinwand (80x16cm 31x6in) Zofingen 1998

KIROUAC Louise Lecor 1939 [64]
$636 - €687 - £427 - FF4 506
Paysage-Temiscounta, Q.C. Acrylic/canvas (50.5x61cm 19x24in) Calgary, Alberta 2000
$404 - €387 - £251 - FF2 537
Charlevoix, Quebec Acrylic/canvas (28x35.5cm 11x13in) Calgary, Alberta 1999

KIRSCH Hugo Friedrich 1873-1961 [29]
$247 - €281 - £172 - FF1 844
Der Gruss Porcelain (H15cm H5in) München 2001

KIRSCH Johanna 1856-? [5]
$6 272 - €5 368 - £3 775 - FF35 259
Sächsische Spitzenklöpplerin, in der Stube bei der Arbeit Öl/Leinwand (100.2x75cm 39x29in) München 1998

KIRSCHENBAUM Jules 1930 [2]
$3 250 - €3 696 - £2 253 - FF24 245
Time and a Dreamer's World Oil/canvas (76x91cm 30x36in) Chicago IL 2000

KIRSTEIN Adolf 1814-1873 [6]
$7 312 - €6 860 - £4 518 - FF45 000
Village enneigé Huile/toile (49x63cm 19x24in) Epinal 1999

KIRWAN John 1956 [4]
$861 - €762 - £451 - FF4 997
June, Dooega Achill Oil/canvas (50x39cm 19x15in) Dublin 2000

KIRZINGER Marianne 1770-1809 [5]
$5 699 - €6 250 - £3 870 - FF41 000
Turc debout Huile/toile (24.5x15.5cm 9x6in) Lille 2000

KISCHKA Isis 1908-1974 [60]
$1 015 - €1 143 - £713 - FF7 500
Bouquet de pivoines Huile/toile (54x65cm 21x25in) Paris 2001

KISFALUDI STROBL Zsigmond 1884-1975 [1]
$11 200 - €12 342 - £7 360 - FF80 960
Crouching Marble (H38cm H14in) Budapest 2000

KISLING Gabriel 1915 [6]
$660 - €686 - £416 - FF4 500
Vignes au Mas de la Dame Aquarelle/papier (35x47cm 13x18in) Grenoble 2000

KISLING Moïse 1891-1953 [931]
$190 000 - €178 858 - £117 382 - FF1 173 231
Bouquet de fleurs Oil/canvas (127x96cm 50x37in) New-York 1999
$40 000 - €46 412 - £27 616 - FF304 440
Nu allongé Oil/canvas (41x80cm 16x31in) New-York 2000
$35 175 - €32 014 - £21 546 - FF210 000
Vase d'anémones Huile/toile (41x33cm 16x12in) Monte-Carlo 1998
$2 911 - €3 125 - £1 947 - FF20 500
Au café Encre Chine/papier (15x26cm 5x10in) Cannes 1999
$630 - €610 - £388 - FF4 000
Madame D. Le Bec, d'après un tableau de 1927 Lithographie couleurs (68.4x61.5cm 26x24in) Paris 1999

KISLING Philipp Heinrich 1713-? [4]
$2 166 - €2 325 - £1 449 - FF15 254
Lachende Frau mit einem Krug Oil/panel (25x20cm 9x7in) Wien 2000

KISS Joszef 1833-1900 [1]
$5 490 - €5 624 - £3 388 - FF36 892
Franz Liszt Öl/Leinwand (79.5x63.5cm 31x25in) Düsseldorf 2000

KISSELIEV Alexandre Alexandrov 1838-1911 [21]
$2 618 - €2 949 - £1 805 - FF19 347
In the Old Russian Town Oil/canvas (70.5x89cm 27x35in) Amsterdam 2000
$2 689 - €2 523 - £1 662 - FF16 548
Vid floden Oil/canvas (26x45cm 10x17in) Helsinki 1999

KISSELIOFF Alexander Alexeiev. 1855-1927 [1]
$1 812 - €2 018 - £1 185 - FF13 238
Country Road Oil/board (15x23cm 5x9in) Helsinki 2000

KISSLING-PELATI Violette act.1939-? [6]
$644 - €732 - £447 - FF4 800
Deux servales Pastel (20x30cm 7x11in) Pontoise 2001

KISTLER Maria 1884-1963 [10]
$805 - €799 - £502 - FF5 243
Alpenblumen in Tontopf Öl/Karton (35x45cm 13x17in) Salzburg 1999

KITAGAWA TAMIJI 1894-1989 [6]
$12 740 - €12 426 - £7 800 - FF81 510
Cattleya Oil/canvas (38x45.5cm 14x17in) Tokyo 1999

KITAJ Ronald Brooks 1932 [151]
$65 108 - €63 368 - £40 000 - FF415 664
The Drivist Oil/canvas (183x93cm 72x36in) London 1999
$44 829 - €48 120 - £30 000 - FF315 648
The Messianist Oil/canvas (183x61cm 72x24in) London 2000

$13 673 - €11 891 - **£8 244** - FF78 000
Chimera Huile/toile (56x25cm 22x9in) Paris 1998

$29 480 - €31 432 - **£20 000** - FF206 180
New York Madman Charcoal (56x38cm 22x14in) London 2001

$356 - €332 - **£215** - FF2 180
Sitzender Akt Lithographie (51.8x38.8cm 20x15in) Hamburg 1999

KITCHELL Hudson Mindell 1862-1944 [40]

$1 250 - €1 454 - **£892** - FF9 535
Autumn Landscape with Figure in a Clearing Oil/canvas (45.5x61cm 17x24in) Toronto 2001

$550 - €625 - **£384** - FF4 103
Figure in a Landscape Oil/canvas (25x35cm 10x14in) Mystic CT 2000

KITCHIN Thomas XVIII [7]

$139 - €149 - **£95** - FF976
Map of the French Settlements in North America Engraving (16x17cm 6x7in) Aylsham, Norfolk 2001

KITE Joseph Milner 1862-1946 [46]

$2 177 - €2 452 - **£1 500** - FF16 082
Brittany Square Oil/canvas (51x65cm 20x25in) London 2000

$4 122 - €4 425 - **£2 800** - FF29 025
Fishing Vessels at Anchor in a Harbour Oil/panel (25x35cm 9x13in) London 2001

KITO Akira 1925 [36]

$972 - €1 143 - **£696** - FF7 500
Personnages Huile/toile (27x22cm 10x8in) Paris 2001

KITSON Henry Hudson 1865-1947 [3]

$5 250 - €4 866 - **£3 264** - FF31 920
Jefferson Davis Bronze (67x23x20cm 26x9x8in) New-Orleans LA 1999

KITT Ferdinand 1887-1961 [56]

$4 740 - €4 360 - **£2 934** - FF28 602
Törichte Jungfrauen Öl/Leinwand (75x100cm 29x39in) Wien 1999

$955 - €799 - **£566** - FF5 240
Rittersporn Aquarell/Papier (61x47.5cm 24x18in) Wien 1998

KITTELSEN Theodor Severin 1857-1914 [25]

$2 598 - €2 212 - **£1 552** - FF14 510
Höifjeld Mixed media/paper (23x28cm 9x11in) Oslo 1998

KITTENDORFF Johann Adolf 1820-1902 [29]

$182 - €201 - **£121** - FF1 319
Scene fra Tivoli, København med talrige figurer Watercolour (12.5x8.5cm 4x3in) Vejle 2000

KITTENSTEYN van Cornelis c.1600-? [3]

$2 891 - €2 495 - **£1 744** - FF16 364
Bacchus pressing grapes into a dish held by a satyr Ink (11.8x8.7cm 4x3in) Amsterdam 1998

$5 880 - €5 110 - **£3 543** - FF33 521
«Der siegreicht Einzug des Prinzen W.von Oranien» nach W.Buytewech Etching (35.5x27.4cm 13x10in) Berlin 1998

KITZ Marcin 1891-1943 [5]

$4 736 - €4 724 - **£2 956** - FF30 988
Charrettes et chevaux Oil/canvas (50x63cm 19x24in) Warszawa 1999

KITZEL Herbert 1928-1978 [14]

$1 608 - €1 764 - **£1 092** - FF11 571
1. Fassung Mischtechnik/Papier (42x35.6cm 16x14in) Berlin 2000

KITZINGER Maximilian Leonard 1811-1882 [1]

$4 778 - €4 973 - **£3 000** - FF32 623
Cattle in a Meadow with Sailing Boats Beyond Oil/canvas (48x64cm 18x25in) London 2000

KIYOCHIKA Kobayashi 1847-1915 [29]

$800 - €884 - **£554** - FF5 799
Sogo watashiba no zu shinga/Matsuchiyama yuki no tasogare Print (36.5x24.5cm 14x9in) New-York 2001

KIYOHARU Seiya XIX-XX [1]

$3 750 - €3 902 - **£2 386** - FF25 594
Figure of sisters Bronze (H43cm H16in) New-York 2000

KIYOKATA Kaburagi 1878-1973 [5]

$19 600 - €19 117 - **£12 000** - FF125 400
Portrait of a Woman Painting (50.5x42cm 19x16in) Tokyo 1999

$5 603 - €6 548 - **£4 000** - FF42 955
«Tsukushi» Ink (115.5x27cm 45x10in) London 2001

$1 600 - €1 383 - **£949** - FF9 070
Woman of Tsukiji Woodcut (60.5x35cm 23x13in) New-York 1998

KIYOMASU Torii II 1706-1763 [3]

$1 888 - €2 147 - **£1 309** - FF14 086
Stehende Dame in einem Kimono mit grossen Chrysanthemen Woodcut in colors (29.4x15.9cm 11x6in) Köln 2000

KIYOMITSU Torii 1735-1785 [6]

$6 233 - €7 013 - **£4 291** - FF46 000
Pique-nique printanier. Sous une tente improvisée dans la campagne Estampe (42x30.5cm 16x12in) Paris 2000

KIYONAGA Ito 1912 [2]

$21 560 - €21 029 - **£13 200** - FF137 940
Roses Oil/canvas (53x56cm 20x22in) Tokyo 1999

KIYONAGA Torii 1752-1815 [38]

$2 200 - €2 580 - **£1 569** - FF16 923
Nakamura Riko I,Ichikawa Monnosuke II on Stage with Degatari Chanters Print in colors (38x26cm 14x10in) New-York 2000

KIYONOBU Torii c.1664-1729 [2]

$7 000 - €8 209 - **£4 995** - FF53 846
Ukiyo tsurezure (Idleness of the Floating World) Print in colors (22x31cm 8x12in) New-York 2000

KIYOSHI Kobayakawa 1896-1948 [5]

$2 500 - €2 403 - **£1 559** - FF15 763
Modern Day Figures No.5: Black Hair Print (53.5x30.5cm 21x12in) New-York 1999

KIYOSHI Nakajima 1899-1989 [15]

$2 800 - €2 822 - **£1 745** - FF18 508
White Porcelain Woodcut (55x72.5cm 21x28in) New-York 2000

KJAER Anders 1940 [13]

$8 066 - €9 375 - **£5 668** - FF61 494
Uten titel XXXX Oil/canvas (100x135cm 39x53in) Oslo 2001

$216 - €249 - **£152** - FF1 636
Aftenland II Color lithograph (44x64cm 17x25in) Oslo 2000

KJARVAL Johannes S. 1885-1972 [50]

$13 122 - €12 114 - **£7 848** - FF79 461
Fjeldlandskab, Island Oil/canvas (100x135cm 39x53in) Köbenhavn 1999

$3 555 - €4 021 - **£2 403** - FF26 373
Bjerglandskab med bygd, Island Oil/canvas (36x65cm 14x25in) Köbenhavn 2000

K

$2 607 - €2 948 - **£1 762** - FF19 340
Bjerglandskab, Island Oil/canvas (25x37.5cm 9x14in) København 2000

$485 - €471 - **£305** - FF3 090
Figurstudie Pastel (29x45cm 11x17in) København 1999

KJELDGAARD Marinus Jacob XX **[3]**
$2 000 - €2 147 - **£1 339** - FF14 086
Graf Spree Photograph (16x21cm 6x8in) München 2000

KJERNER Esther 1873-1952 **[182]**
$1 833 - €2 117 - **£1 282** - FF13 887
Stilleben med blommor Oil/canvas (46x38cm 18x14in) Stockholm 2001

$2 037 - €1 777 - **£1 232** - FF11 658
«En gammal trädgård, Drottningholm» Oil/canvas (39x35.5cm 15x13in) Stockholm 1998

KLABLENA Eduard 1881-1933 **[29]**
$2 423 - €2 812 - **£1 673** - FF18 446
Schönheit Porcelain (H21.5cm H8in) München 2000

KLAIN Nathaniel M. c.1815-c.1888 **[1]**
$8 000 - €9 210 - **£5 459** - FF60 416
The San Francisco Customs House Albumen print (43x53.5cm 16x21in) New-York 2000

KLAPHECK Konrad 1935 **[86]**
$23 973 - €22 344 - **£14 486** - FF146 565
Das Gelübde Oil/canvas (95.5x90cm 37x35in) München 1999

$204 - €194 - **£126** - FF1 274
Dampfbügeleisen (Die Schwiegermutter) Lithographie (69.6x50cm 27x19in) Hamburg 1999

KLAPISCH Liliane 1933 **[36]**
$5 000 - €5 550 - **£3 485** - FF36 407
Désordre à la croisée Oil/canvas (65x50cm 25x19in) Tel Aviv 2001

$3 200 - €3 601 - **£2 204** - FF23 624
Landscape Oil/canvas (33x45cm 12x17in) Herzelia-Pituah 2000

$350 - €342 - **£222** - FF2 243
Study Mixed media/paper (24x36cm 9x14in) Tel Aviv 1999

KLAPPER Siegfried 1918 **[2]**
$12 722 - €12 348 - **£7 921** - FF80 996
Sonntag Oil/hardboard (52x71.1cm 20x27in) Berlin 1999

KLAR Karel 1866-1919 **[4]**
$4 624 - €4 373 - **£2 880** - FF28 688
Flower-Bed Oil/canvas (70x54cm 27x21in) Praha 2000

KLAR Otto 1908-1994 **[62]**
$1 423 - €1 588 - **£928** - FF10 414
Poinsettias in a Green Vase Oil/board (59.5x44cm 23x17in) Johannesburg 2000

$654 - €630 - **£404** - FF4 133
Extensive Landscape Oil/board (14x49.5cm 5x19in) Johannesburg 1999

$250 - €281 - **£175** - FF1 842
«Namib, S.W.A» Watercolour/paper (10x28cm 3x11in) Cape Town 2001

KLASEN Peter 1935 **[654]**
$4 017 - €4 726 - **£2 879** - FF31 000
«Manette vide charge radioactive S90» Acrylique/toile (132x97.5cm 51x38in) Paris 2001

$3 649 - €3 354 - **£2 241** - FF22 000
Manette, fond bleu 2 flèches Acrylique (73x60cm 28x23in) Paris 1999

$1 027 - €991 - **£649** - FF6 500
Lw-Flèche Acrylique (33x24cm 12x9in) Paris 1999

$999 - €991 - **£625** - FF6 500
Sans titre Aquarelle (30x42cm 11x16in) Paris 1999

$145 - €130 - **£89** - FF850
«CNC.5.» Sérigraphie couleurs (47x35cm 18x13in) Paris 1999

KLASMER Gabi 1950 **[4]**
$5 800 - €6 438 - **£4 043** - FF42 232
Untitled Acrylic (173x343cm 68x135in) Tel Aviv 2001

KLAUBER Catharina XVIII **[2]**
$1 200 - €1 201 - **£740** - FF7 880
Los Cuatro Elementos: Aire, Tierra, Fuego y Agua Grabado (53x71cm 20x27in) Madrid 2000

KLAUBER Johann Baptist 1712-1787 **[8]**
$184 - €179 - **£114** - FF1 173
Die vier Temperamente Radierung (18x23cm 7x9in) Berlin 1999

KLAUKE Jürgen 1943 **[91]**
$2 731 - €2 528 - **£1 671** - FF16 585
Zwei Figuren Aquarell/Papier (41.5x55.6cm 16x21in) München 1999

$3 913 - €4 602 - **£2 805** - FF30 185
Ohne Titel Gelatin silver print (52x61cm 20x24in) Berlin 2001

KLAUS Christian 1843-1893 **[6]**
$1 418 - €1 228 - **£855** - FF8 056
Junger Diskuswerfer und Gelehrter in einer mit Genien Loggia Öl/Leinwand (30x36cm 11x14in) München 1998

KLAUS Karl 1889-? **[5]**
$865 - €1 022 - **£613** - FF6 707
Judith Porcelain (H28.8cm H11in) Ahlden 2000

KLECZYNSKI von Bodhan 1852-1920 **[12]**
$21 996 - €23 705 - **£15 000** - FF155 497
Horse drawn Troikas in a Snow covered Landscape Oil/canvas (60x100cm 23x39in) Bury St. Edmunds, Suffolk 2001

KLEE Paul 1879-1940 **[845]**
$1 400 000 - €1 568 103 - **£972 720** - FF10 286 080
Zwillinge Oil/canvas (60.5x50.5cm 23x19in) New-York 2001

$151 291 - €162 402 - **£101 235** - FF1 065 288
Bedaute Berg-Terrasse Painting (29.4x38.9cm 11x15in) Bern 2000

$63 387 - €74 848 - **£45 000** - FF490 972
«Landschaft mit dem Rad» Watercolour (24x35cm 9x13in) London 2001

$2 381 - €2 556 - **£1 594** - FF16 769
Kopf, bärtiger Mann Lithographie (44.5x31.3cm 17x12in) Köln 2000

KLEEHAAS Theodor 1854-1929 **[47]**
$5 349 - €4 847 - **£3 337** - FF31 701
To små drenge, der leger i gården Oil/canvas (55x70cm 21x27in) København 1999

$2 326 - €2 812 - **£1 624** - FF18 446
Die treuen Spielgefährten (Kleinkind mit Hund und Kaninchen) Oil/panel (17x22cm 6x8in) Düsseldorf 2000

KLEIBER Hans 1887-1967 **[43]**
$425 - €502 - **£301** - FF3 295
Shooting from Duck Blind/Duck hunters/Fishing on Pines/Lone Fisherman Etching (19x14cm 7x5in) Boston MA 2000

KLEIJN Reinhardt Willem 1828-1889 [2]
- $5 617 – €5 899 – £3 554 – FF38 695
  A View of Breda Oil/canvas (57x42cm 22x16in)
  Amsterdam 2000

KLEIJNE David 1754-1805 [7]
- $9 137 – €7 704 – £5 423 – FF50 535
  Sainling Vessels on a Choppy Sea/Ships in a Harbour Oil/panel (27.5x35.5cm 10x13in) Amsterdam 1998

KLEIJNTJENS Jan 1876-1938 [4]
- $4 016 – €4 311 – £2 687 – FF28 277
  Kunstnaaldwerk Oil/canvas (48x41cm 18x16in)
  Amsterdam 2000

KLEIMA Ekke 1899-1958 [4]
- $8 033 – €8 622 – £5 375 – FF56 555
  Kerkje te Breede Oil/canvas (46x61cm 18x24in)
  Amsterdam 2000

KLEIMER Axel 1881-1945 [81]
- $482 – €448 – £300 – FF2 936
  Gård syd Värlinge Oil/canvas (47x72cm 18x28in)
  Malmö 1999
- $590 – €509 – £355 – FF3 342
  Malmöhus Slott Oil/canvas (32x46cm 12x18in)
  Malmö 1998

KLEIN Aart 1909 [12]
- 📷 $585 – €681 – £411 – FF4 464
  «Dukdalven Europoort» Gelatin silver print
  (40x30cm 15x11in) Amsterdam 2001

KLEIN Astrid 1951 [19]
- 📷 $321 – €383 – £229 – FF2 515
  Fotoarbeiten Photograph (40.5x30.4cm 15x11in)
  München 2000

KLEIN Bernhard 1888-1968 [14]
- $1 428 – €1 329 – £878 – FF8 720
  Mediterrane Strassenszene Gouache (36x43.2cm 14x17in) Hamburg 1999

KLEIN Cesar 1876-1954 [70]
- $41 352 – €40 904 – £25 784 – FF268 312
  Madonna Öl/Leinwand (170x150cm 66x59in) Berlin 1999
- $15 000 – €16 102 – £10 219 – FF105 622
  Harbor View Oil/canvas (68x78cm 26x30in) Boston MA 2001
- $1 085 – €1 074 – £676 – FF7 043
  Figürliche Komposition Aquarell/Papier (30x42cm 11x16in) Hildrizhausen 1999

KLEIN Christian Leonhard 1810-1891 [2]
- $3 164 – €3 488 – £2 142 – FF22 882
  Opstilling med georginer på en stenkarm Oil/canvas (24.5x36cm 9x14in) Vejle 2000

KLEIN Frits, Fred 1898-1990 [64]
- $4 367 – €4 311 – £2 655 – FF28 277
  Summerday on the Beach Oil/paper/canvas (38x46cm 14x18in) Amsterdam 2000
- $3 300 – €3 857 – £2 356 – FF25 301
  Beach Oil/canvas (33x46cm 12x18in) Amsterdam 2001
- $698 – €635 – £428 – FF4 167
  «Parc Monceau» Watercolour/paper (12.5x20cm 4x7in) Amsterdam 1999

KLEIN Georges André 1901-1992 [35]
- $4 728 – €4 516 – £2 916 – FF30 000
  Jeune fille en mauve/Marocaine au foulard rose Huile/toile (99x50cm 38x19in) Paris 1999

KLEIN Johan Adam 1792-1875 [253]
- $4 739 – €5 087 – £3 171 – FF33 369
  Der Windhund Öl/Leinwand (70.5x81.3cm 27x32in)
  Wien 2000
- $5 675 – €4 856 – £3 416 – FF31 856
  Braunes Pferd, gesattelt im Stall Oil/paper/board (18x24.6cm 7x9in) München 1998
- $1 147 – €1 278 – £801 – FF8 384
  Pferde an der Tränke Gouache (21.8x27.1cm 8x10in) München 2001
- $160 – €153 – £98 – FF1 006
  Pferde auf einer Weide Radierung (19x25cm 7x9in) Kempten 1999

KLEIN Jozsef 1896-1945 [3]
- $7 700 – €8 485 – £5 060 – FF55 660
  Dream Oil/canvas (49.5x60cm 19x23in) Budapest 2000

KLEIN Medard 1905-? [10]
- $1 800 – €2 059 – £1 251 – FF13 506
  Abstract Composition Oil/board (45x53cm 18x21in)
  Cincinnati OH 2000
- $3 500 – €3 102 – £2 147 – FF20 345
  Arrangement Gouache/paper (38x30cm 15x12in)
  Cincinnati OH 1999

KLEIN Paul Georges 1909-1995 [52]
- $699 – €744 – £477 – FF4 878
  The modern jazz quartet Huile/panneau (37x67cm 14x26in) Bruxelles 2001

KLEIN Philippe 1871-1907 [18]
- $1 368 – €1 534 – £943 – FF10 061
  Dachauer Moos mit Schäfer Öl/Leinwand (95x41cm 37x16in) Frankfurt 2000
- $730 – €818 – £503 – FF5 366
  Vergnügtes Selbstporträt mit Zigarre Öl/Karton (31x25cm 12x9in) Frankfurt 2000

KLEIN VON DIEPOLD Julian 1868-1947 [13]
- $3 838 – €3 835 – £2 400 – FF25 154
  Norddeutsche Bauernhaus Öl/Leinwand (48x60cm 18x23in) Hamburg 1999

KLEIN VON DIEPOLD Leo 1865-1944 [14]
- $831 – €920 – £563 – FF6 037
  Dünenlandschaft Öl/Leinwand (80x100cm 31x39in)
  Hamburg 2000

KLEIN VON DIEPOLD Maximilian 1873-1949 [51]
- $714 – €767 – £478 – FF5 030
  Rotwild auf der Lichtung Öl/Leinwand (61x80cm 24x31in) Köln 2000

KLEIN Wilhelm 1821-1897 [15]
- $1 978 – €2 250 – £1 371 – FF14 757
  Romantische Landschaft Öl/Leinwand (53x75cm 20x29in) Rudolstadt-Thüringen 2000
- $318 – €363 – £220 – FF2 138
  Portrait of a Man Holding Playing Cards Oil/panel (18x14cm 7x5in) Amsterdam 2000

KLEIN William 1928 [130]
- 📷 $2 000 – €1 881 – £1 238 – FF12 337
  Simone & Nina, Spanish Steps, Rome Gelatin silver print (45x32.5cm 17x12in) New-York 1999

KLEIN Yves 1928-1962 [392]
- $1 134 648 – €1 101 014 – £720 000 – FF7 222 176
  I.K.B. 81 Mixed media/canvas (100x200cm 39x78in)
  London 1999
- $254 031 – €272 681 – £170 000 – FF1 788 672
  I.K.B 171 Mixed media (62x50cm 24x19in) London 2000
- $2 833 – €2 744 – £1 780 – FF18 000
  Timbres Bleus Technique mixte (11x2cm 4xin) Paris 1999

K

KLEINEH

$14 399 - €14 132 - **£8 929** - FF92 698
La table d'or Construction (125x100x35cm
49x39x13in) Stockholm 1999

$23 958 - €23 008 - **£14 769** - FF150 925
Venus Bleue Plaster (H68cm H26in) München 1999

$2 298 - €2 515 - **£1 595** - FF16 500
Composition Aquarelle/papier (14x10cm 5x3in)
Vannes 2001

$1 524 - €1 636 - **£1 020** - FF10 732
Blau-Rosa-Gold Farbserigraphie (32x23.4cm 12x9in)
Köln 2000

$3 710 - €4 311 - **£2 607** - FF28 277
Levilation Vintage gelatin silver print (40x50cm
15x19in) Amsterdam 2001

KLEINEH Oscar 1846-1919 **[86]**

$125 510 - €117 727 - **£77 560** - FF772 240
Hamnvy Oil/canvas (84x148cm 33x58in) Helsinki
1999

$22 365 - €25 227 - **£15 720** - FF165 480
Stilla månskensnatt till havs Oil/canvas (75x104cm
29x40in) Helsinki 2001

$8 217 - €9 250 - **£5 659** - FF60 676
Till havs Oil/panel (15.5x20cm 6x7in) Helsinki 2000

KLEINMANN Alain 1953 **[53]**

$1 282 - €1 524 - **£883** - FF10 000
Le musicien Huile/toile (73x60cm 28x23in)
Maubeuge 2000

$3 698 - €3 049 - **£2 178** - FF20 000
La mariée Collage (195x130cm 76x51in) Paris 1998

KLEINSCHMIDT Johann Jakob 1687-1772 **[4]**

$419 - €460 - **£284** - FF3 018
**Bildnis des Erzgiessers Johann Balthasar
Keller, nach Rigaud** Kupferstich (46.3x35.8cm
18x14in) Berlin 2000

KLEINSCHMIDT Paul 1883-1949 **[182]**

$30 000 - €25 198 - **£17 637** - FF165 288
Landscape with Cypress Trees Oil/canvas
(69x89cm 27x35in) Cleveland OH 1998

$2 924 - €2 812 - **£1 801** - FF18 446
Weiblicher Rückenakt Aquarell/Papier (69x50cm
27x19in) München 1999

$173 - €206 - **£123** - FF1 353
Bei der Kartenlegerin Radierung (33x23cm 12x9in)
Hamburg 2000

KLEINT Boris Herbert 1903-1996 **[11]**

$5 263 - €5 089 - **£3 304** - FF38 569
Kreise und Quadrate Öl/Leinwand (46x63cm
18x24in) Saarbrücken 2000

$2 559 - €2 556 - **£1 600** - FF16 769
Komposition Öl/Leinwand (21.9x26.8cm 8x10in)
Hamburg 1999

KLEITSCH Joseph 1886-1931 **[24]**

$10 000 - €11 753 - **£6 933** - FF77 094
Rainy Day, Laguna Oil/masonite (38.5x51cm
15x20in) Beverly-Hills CA 2000

$28 000 - €32 908 - **£19 412** - FF215 863
Diver's Cove, Laguna Oil/canvas/board (22.5x27cm
8x10in) Beverly-Hills CA 2000

KLEIVA Per 1933 **[11]**

$140 - €162 - **£98** - FF1 063
Bölga Serigraph in colors (49x49cm 19x19in) Oslo
2000

KLEMCZYNSKI Pierre 1910 **[44]**

$1 281 - €1 494 - **£887** - FF9 800
Paysage Huile/toile (46x61cm 18x24in) Besançon
2000

KLEMENT Fon 1930 **[42]**

$140 - €146 - **£89** - FF955
Eclore Print (49.5x64.5cm 19x25in) Amsterdam 2000

KLEMENTIEFF Eugène 1901 **[6]**

$8 000 - €9 282 - **£5 523** - FF60 888
Nature morte à la bouteille Oil/canvas (55.5x91cm
21x35in) New-York 2000

KLEMM Barbara 1939 **[24]**

$485 - €522 - **£325** - FF3 421
Madonna, Haute Couture, Paris Photograph
(30.5x40.5cm 12x15in) München 2000

KLEMM Fritz 1902-1990 **[23]**

$2 786 - €2 351 - **£1 634** - FF15 420
Ohne Titel Mixed media/paper (69x50cm 27x19in)
Berlin 1998

KLEMM Walther 1883-1957 **[218]**

$192 - €199 - **£121** - FF1 308
Hirsch in Winterlandschaft Watercolour (35x41cm
13x16in) Rudolstadt-Thüringen 2000

$106 - €123 - **£73** - FF804
**Rettung, Menschen am Strand warten auf ein
ankommendes Boot** Drypoint (29.5x34.9cm
11x13in) Heidelberg 2000

KLEMMER Robert 1938-1971 **[18]**

$1 238 - €1 453 - **£878** - FF9 534
Klemmer breit Mixed media/paper (50x83.5cm
19x32in) Wien 2000

KLENGEL Johann Christian 1751-1824 **[76]**

$453 - €5 087 - **£3 290** - FF33 360
**Die büssende Magdalena in einer bewaldeten
Gebirgslandschaft** Öl/Leinwand (36x47cm 14x18in)
Wien 1999

$810 - €920 - **£563** - FF6 037
Lagerndes Vieh Ink (23x20.5cm 9x8in) Köln 2001

KLEPPER Max Francis 1861-1907 **[5]**

$4 500 - €5 040 - **£3 126** - FF33 062
Young Woman looks on As her Hor is reshod
Oil/canvas (86x60cm 34x24in) New-York 2001

KLERK de Willem 1800-1876 **[48]**

$10 807 - €12 271 - **£7 509** - FF80 493
Rheinlandschaft Oil/panel (34.5x50.5cm 13x19in)
Köln 2001

$1 731 - €1 943 - **£1 200** - FF12 744
Südl.Landschaft mit Wasserfall Öl/Leinwand
(28x36cm 11x14in) Stuttgart 2000

$1 279 - €1 278 - **£800** - FF8 384
Mittelgebirgslandschaft mit einem Fluss
Aquarell/Papier (19.8x27cm 7x10in) Köln 1999

KLESTOVA Irene XIX-XX **[21]**

$1 719 - €1 846 - **£150** - FF12 106
June Everlasting Oil/board (45.5x61cm 17x24in)
London 2000

KLEVER Julian Julianovich 1882-1942 **[13]**

$2 582 - €2 121 - **£1 500** - FF14 429
Daisies and Cherries Oil/canvas (42x60cm 16x23in)
London 1999

$2 434 - €2 340 - **£1 500** - FF15 350
Still Life of Hortensia in a Vase Oil/canvas
(41x29.5cm 16x11in) London 1999

KLEVER Juri 1879-? **[4]**

$354 - €364 - **£217** - FF2 206
Stilleben Oil/canvas (64x50cm 25x19in) Helsinki 1999

KLEVER von Julius Sergius 1850-1924 **[150]**

$10 317 - €12 271 - **£7 353** - FF80 493
**Ländliche Szene mit Windmühle und Kate im
Winter** Öl/Leinwand (125x168cm 49x66in) Köln 2000

K

KLEY Heinrich 1863-1945 **[69]**

🖼 **$5 230** – €5 615 – **£3 500** – FF36 830
Winter - Lakeside Settlement at Sunset Oil/canvas (49.5x72cm 19x28in) London 2000

🖼 **$1 793** – €1 925 – **£1 200** – FF12 625
Winter - Homeward bound at Sunset Oil/board (29.5x41.5cm 11x16in) London 2000

🖼 **$5 158** – €5 113 – **£3 227** – FF33 539
Seeungeheuer Öl/Leinwand (61x47cm 24x18in) München 1999

✏ **$747** – €647 – **£453** – FF4 245
Diskussionsrunde im Caféhaus Ink/paper (29x34cm 11x13in) München 1998

KLEY Louis 1833-1911 **[28]**

🗿 **$572** – €610 – **£362** – FF4 000
Trois angelots Bronze (48x34cm 18x13in) Bayeux 2000

KLEYN Lodewijk Johannes 1817-1897 **[105]**

🖼 **$20 637** – €20 420 – **£12 631** – FF133 947
River Landscape in Autumn with Villagers on a Path along a Water Oil/panel (43.5x59.5cm 17x23in) Amsterdam 2000

🖼 **$8 062** – €6 798 – **£4 785** – FF44 590
Figures in a Winter Landscape Oil/panel (33x44cm 12x17in) Amsterdam 1998

✏ **$559** – €635 – **£386** – FF4 167
Reiziger in sneeuwlandschap Watercolour/paper (22x37cm 8x14in) Dordrecht 2000

KLIEBER Anton XIX-XX **[8]**

🗿 **$1 678** – €1 453 – **£1 018** – FF9 530
Thronende Madonna mit Kind und Engelskonzert Ceramic (H25.3cm H9in) Wien 1998

KLIEBER Eduard 1803-1879 **[9]**

🖼 **$4 758** – €4 724 – **£2 970** – FF30 985
Mädchen mit Weintrauben Öl/Leinwand (82x67cm 32x26in) Wien 1999

KLIEMANN Carl-Heinz 1924 **[93]**

✏ **$603** – €562 – **£364** – FF3 689
Herbstlicher Garten Watercolour (48.5x61.5cm 19x24in) Hamburg 1999

🖼 **$171** – €204 – **£122** – FF1 341
Am Strom Drypoint (59.7x49.7cm 23x19in) Berlin 2000

KLIEN Erika Giovanna 1900-1957 **[8]**

🖼 **$57 907** – €54 090 – **£35 000** – FF354 805
Begegnung Tempera/canvas (77.5x77.5cm 30x30in) London 1999

🖼 **$12 141** – €13 808 – **£8 531** – FF90 573
Schreitende Aquarell/Papier (23.5x10.5cm 9x4in) Wien 2001

KLIER P. act.c.1875-c.1890 **[2]**

📷 **$2 327** – €2 744 – **£1 636** – FF18 000
Birmanie Tirage albuminé (18x25cm 7x9in) Paris 2000

KLIJN Albert 1895-1981 **[10]**

🖼 **$505** – €590 – **£346** – FF3 869
«Regata, reclame-en grafische arbeid tentoonstelling Amsterdam» Poster (110x80cm 43x31in) Hoorn 2000

KLIMEK Ludwig / Ludovic 1912-1992 **[342]**

🖼 **$907** – €1 067 – **£658** – FF7 000
Femmes papillon paysage mauve Huile/carton/toile (50x65cm 19x25in) Lyon 2001

✏ **$621** – €686 – **£430** – FF4 500
Paysage Huile/carton (32x41.5cm 12x16in) Paris 2001

✏ **$320** – €335 – **£202** – FF2 200
Saint Jorgen Aquarelle/papier (25.5x34.5cm 10x13in) Castres 2000

KLIMENKO F. XIX-XX **[5]**

🖼 **$3 893** – €3 739 – **£2 400** – FF24 525
Steam Yachts and other Shipping in a Greek Harbour Oil/canvas (37x57cm 14x22in) London 1999

KLIMSCH Eugen Johann Georg 1839-1896 **[33]**

🖼 **$8 578** – €9 742 – **£6 000** – FF63 905
Die musikstunde (the music lesson) Oil/canvas (57x40cm 22x15in) London 2001

🖼 **$3 950** – €3 835 – **£2 439** – FF25 154
Der Reitertrunk Öl/Karton (24.5x18cm 9x7in) Frankfurt 1999

✏ **$243** – €256 – **£153** – FF1 676
Sitzende Hofdame mit Kammerdiener Pencil (26.3x27.1cm 10x10in) Heidelberg 2000

KLIMSCH Fritz 1870-1960 **[180]**

🗿 **$36 349** – €35 280 – **£22 632** – FF231 419
In Wind und Sonne Bronze (147x42x42cm 57x16x16in) Berlin 1999

🗿 **$2 124** – €2 045 – **£1 328** – FF13 415
Siesta Bronze (25x17x21cm 9x6x8in) München 1999

KLIMSCH Karl 1867-? **[3]**

🖼 **$800** – €892 – **£523** – FF5 854
«Engelhorn's Roman-Bibliothek» Poster (77x52cm 30x20in) New-York 2000

KLIMT Gustav 1862-1918 **[454]**

🖼 **$3 147 920** – €2 935 316 – **£1 900 000** – FF19 254 410
The Tall Poplar Tree I Oil/canvas (80x80cm 31x31in) London 1999

🖼 **$192 015** – €176 980 – **£115 000** – FF1 160 913
Bildnis Emilie Flöges (Portrait of Emilie Flöges) Oil/cardboard (41x24cm 16x9in) London 1998

✏ **$20 000** – €17 072 – **£11 960** – FF111 982
Damenbilnis Pencil (57x37.5cm 22x14in) New-York 1998

🖼 **$263** – €245 – **£162** – FF1 604
Woman Asleep Lithograph (36x54cm 14x21in) Melbourne 1999

KLINCKENBERG Eugen 1858-? **[5]**

🖼 **$8 086** – €8 181 – **£4 937** – FF53 662
In der Sommerfrische Öl/Leinwand (80x106.5cm 31x41in) Stuttgart 2000

KLINE Franz 1910-1962 **[167]**

🖼 **$600 000** – €669 885 – **£401 040** – FF4 394 160
Mycenae Oil/canvas (256x194.5cm 100x76in) New-York 1999

🖼 **$67 500** – €78 319 – **£46 602** – FF513 742
Untitled Oil/board (61x47cm 24x18in) New-York 2000

🖼 **$20 000** – €17 072 – **£11 960** – FF111 982
Untitled Oil/paper (28x21.5cm 11x8in) New-York 1998

✏ **$33 850** – €36 336 – **£22 650** – FF238 350
Ohne Titel Indian ink/paper (37.7x26.7cm 14x10in) Wien 2000

KLING Anton 1881-1963 **[3]**

🖼 **$126** – €143 – **£87** – FF939
Exlibris Magda Mautner von Markhof Lithographie (18x13cm 7x5in) München 2001

KLING Wendell XX **[1]**

✏ **$1 400** – €1 568 – **£972** – FF10 286
Man on Telephone, Woman lounging in Dressing gown Gouache/paper (28x41cm 11x16in) New-York 2001

KLINGELHÖFER Fritz 1832-1903 **[6]**

🖼 **$2 183** – €2 505 – **£1 493** – FF16 434
Romantische Landschaft in Tirol Öl/Leinwand (62x93cm 24x36in) Heidelberg 2000

KLINGER Julius 1876-1950 **[24]**

📱 **$675** – €767 – **£462** – FF5 030
«**Flugzeugrennen Johannisthal**» Poster (68x93cm 26x36in) Hannover 2000

KLINGER Max 1857-1920 **[812]**

🖼 **$54 332** – €61 701 – **£38 000** – FF404 734
Die lautenspielerin (the guitar player) Oil/canvas (130x80.5cm 51x31in) London 2001

🖼 **$5 542** – €6 174 – **£3 626** – FF40 498
Badende, die sich im Wasser spiegelt Bronze (43.5x17.5x17.5cm 17x6x6in) München 2000

$6 434 – €7 307 – **£4 500** – FF47 929
Selbstbildnis (self portrait) Black chalk (49x31cm 19x12in) London 2001

📱 **$493** – €562 – **£344** – FF3 689
Katze mit säugenden Jungen Etching, aquatint (13x11.5cm 5x4in) Hamburg 2001

KLINGSBÖGL Rudolf 1881-1943 **[32]**

🖼 **$217** – €204 – **£134** – FF1 341
Hundebildnis Öl/Leinwand (34x28cm 13x11in) München 1999

KLINGSOR Tristan 1874-1966 **[144]**

🖼 **$406** – €473 – **£285** – FF3 100
Passage sur la Loire Huile/toile (38x46cm 14x18in) Paris 2001

🖼 **$262** – €305 – **£184** – FF2 000
Vase de fleurs Huile/carton (33x24cm 12x9in) Paris 2001

$144 – €168 – **£101** – FF1 100
Château de Cognac Pastel (25x21.5cm 9x8in) Paris 2001

KLINGSTEDT Karl-Gustav 1657-1734 **[21]**

🖼 **$903** – €991 – **£600** – FF6 499
Le Galant Médecin, a Doctor examining the lower half of a young Lady Miniature (5x7cm 1x2in) London 2000

KLINKAN Alfred 1950-1994 **[28]**

✏ **$496** – €545 – **£330** – FF3 575
Frau Ballon Aquarell/Papier (76x57cm 29x22in) Wien 2000

KLINKENBERG Johannes Christiaan 1852-1924 **[119]**

🖼 **$30 888** – €36 302 – **£21 416** – FF238 128
A View along the Amstel in Amsterdam Oil/canvas (70.5x51cm 27x20in) Amsterdam 2000

🖼 **$10 448** – €8 835 – **£6 248** – FF57 952
The Hanging Kitchens of Enkhuizen Oil/canvas (32x44cm 12x17in) Amsterdam 1998

✏ **$5 783** – €4 991 – **£3 490** – FF32 742
A View of a Town with Barges on a Canal Watercolour (34.5x29cm 13x11in) Amsterdam 1999

KLINKERT Walter 1901-1959 **[5]**

📱 **$225** – €256 – **£156** – FF1 676
Berliner Haus II Etching (12x13.5cm 4x5in) Berlin 2001

KLINT af Hilma 1862-1944 **[26]**

🖼 **$514** – €585 – **£359** – FF3 835
Insjölandskap Oil/panel (24.5x37cm 9x14in) Stockholm 2000

🖼 **$503** – €540 – **£336** – FF3 542
Landskap med kanal Akvarell/papper (25x19cm 9x7in) Stockholm 2000

KLIOUNE Ivan 1870-1942 **[51]**

✏ **$20 000** – €17 786 – **£12 232** – FF116 666
Suprematist Composition Watercolour, gouache/paper (24x24cm 9x9in) New-York 1999

KLIPPEL Robert Edward 1920 **[61]**

✏ **$1 545** – €1 421 – **£955** – FF9 318
«**L.S 114**» Mixed media (36.5x49cm 14x19in) Melbourne 1998

🖼 **$23 740** – €21 763 – **£14 688** – FF142 756
Opus 271 Construction (H108cm H42in) Melbourne 1998

🖼 **$2 674** – €2 459 – **£1 653** – FF16 128
«**Opus 206**» Bronze (H40.5cm H15in) Melbourne 1998

✏ **$950** – €874 – **£587** – FF5 734
LS 105 Collage (28.5x39cm 11x15in) Melbourne 1998

KLIPPENBERGER Martin 1953 **[1]**

🖼 **$6 308** – €5 880 – **£3 812** – FF38 569
Ohne Titel Acrylic/canvas/board (101.5x86cm 39x33in) München 1999

KLODT Michail Konstantin. 1832-1902 **[7]**

🖼 **$18 675** – €21 023 – **£12 862** – FF137 900
Calm Day on the Lake Oil/canvas (47x104cm 18x40in) Helsinki 2000

KLODT Nicolaï Alexandrov. 1865-1918 **[3]**

🖼 **$2 689** – €2 887 – **£1 800** – FF18 938
Towards the Forest Oil/board (25x36cm 9x14in) London 2000

KLOEBER von August Karl F. 1793-1864 **[9]**

🖼 **$4 097** – €3 988 – **£2 517** – FF26 160
Königin Luise von Preussen, nach J.G.Schadow Öl/Leinwand (57x46cm 22x18in) Berlin 1999

✏ **$190** – €204 – **£127** – FF1 341
Sich zuprostendes bacchantisches Paar Pencil (17x13.4cm 6x5in) Berlin 2000

KLOMBECK Johann Bernard 1815-1893 **[54]**

🖼 **$12 065** – €11 344 – **£7 470** – FF74 415
Wooded River Valley with Peasants on a Path, Cattle in a meadow beyond Oil/canvas (99.5x126cm 39x49in) Amsterdam 1999

🖼 **$30 000** – €34 809 – **£20 712** – FF228 330
Pastoral Landscape Oil/canvas (94x127cm 37x50in) New-York 2000

🖼 **$4 998** – €5 336 – **£3 412** – FF35 000
Patineurs et villageois dans la forêt Huile/panneau (31.5x40cm 12x15in) Paris 2001

KLOMP Albert Jansz. c.1618-c.1688 **[23]**

🖼 **$6 445** – €6 330 – **£4 000** – FF41 519
Cattle and Sheep in an Open Landscape, with Figures Oil/canvas (89.5x121cm 35x47in) London 1999

🖼 **$4 528** – €4 991 – **£2 957** – FF32 742
Herders met rustend vee aan het water Oil/panel (41.5x33.5cm 16x13in) Den Haag 2000

KLOSE Friedrich Wilhelm 1804-1863 **[4]**

🖼 **$35 000** – €32 479 – **£21 385** – FF213 045
View of Schlossbrücke and Zeughaus Oil/canvas (75.5x98.5cm 29x38in) New-York 1999

🖼 **$3 609** – €4 141 – **£2 468** – FF27 166
Durchblick einer Strasse im Winter Öl/Papier (17.5x13cm 6x5in) Berlin 2000

KLOSE Wilhelm 1830-1914 **[14]**

🖼 **$480** – €450 – **£297** – FF2 951
Südliche Gebirgslandschaft Öl/Karton (28.7x37.6cm 11x14in) Heidelberg 1999

KLOSS Alice, Gene 1903-1996 **[111]**

🖼 **$4 000** – €4 757 – **£2 850** – FF31 204
The Palisades at Blue Mountain Lake Watercolour/paper (51.5x72.5cm 20x28in) New-York 2000

$1 000 - €1 189 - £712 - FF7 801
Far Across the Rio Grande Etching (27.5x35.5cm 10x13in) New-York 2000

KLOSS Robert 1889-1950 [2]
$3 972 - €4 360 - £2 640 - FF28 602
Waldinneres Öl/Leinwand (60x79cm 23x31in) Wien 2000

KLOSSOWSKI Pierre 1905 [21]
$17 250 - €19 056 - £11 962 - FF125 000
«Le jeune Ogier et le frère Chevalier Damiens» Crayons couleurs/papier (116x148cm 45x58in) Paris 2001

$470 - €511 - £309 - FF3 353
Portrait de Roberte Farblithographie (65x50cm 25x19in) Hamburg 2000

KLOTZ Hermann 1850-1932 [6]
$2 560 - €2 907 - £1 796 - FF19 068
Kaiserin Elisabeth von Österreich Porcelain (H46cm H18in) Wien 2001

KLOTZ Konrad 1905-1994 [17]
$333 - €383 - £235 - FF2 515
Winter am Arber Aquarell/Papier (55.5x65cm 21x25in) Zwiesel 2001

KLOTZ Lenz 1925 [53]
$13 026 - €11 937 - £7 959 - FF78 302
Mit halben schrägen Öl/Leinwand (105x125cm 41x49in) Zürich 1999

$1 008 - €1 083 - £674 - FF7 101
Komposition Tempera/paper (34x28.5cm 13x11in) Zofingen 2000

$128 - €124 - £79 - FF812
Abstrakte Komposition Farblithographie (45x65cm 17x25in) Bern 1999

KLUGE Constantin 1912 [123]
$3 192 - €3 295 - £2 000 - FF21 617
Fleurs de la Madeleine Oil/canvas (60x75cm 23x29in) Great Dunwow, Essex 2000

KLUGE Gustav 1947 [69]
$10 837 - €12 782 - £7 645 - FF83 847
«Nymphe Echo» Acryl/Leinwand (194x280cm 76x110in) Köln 2001

$1 124 - €1 278 - £779 - FF8 384
Sitzender Aquarell/Papier (78.3x53cm 30x20in) Hamburg 2000

$296 - €358 - £206 - FF2 347
Kleiner Kopf Woodcut in colors (35x30cm 13x11in) Berlin 2000

KLUGE Harry 1879-1963 [42]
$319 - €295 - £195 - FF1 936
Strandparti Oil/panel (46x61cm 18x24in) Viby J, Århus 1998

KLUMPAR Vladéna 1956 [3]
$6 750 - €6 444 - £4 218 - FF42 267
Untitled #142 Sculpture, glass (24.5x22x22cm 9x8x8in) New-York 1999

KLUMPP Gustav 1902-1980 [6]
$6 000 - €5 176 - £3 633 - FF33 955
The Last Hour Dream of Heaven Oil/canvas (61x75cm 24x29in) New-York 1999

KLUSEMANN Georg 1942-1981 [1]
$3 945 - €4 584 - £2 772 - FF30 067
Stilleben Öl/Karton (39x27cm 15x10in) Zürich 2001

KLUSKA Johann 1904-1973 [32]
$343 - €358 - £216 - FF2 347
Geisselung Christi Öl/Leinwand (115x94cm 45x37in) Stuttgart 2000

KLUTE Jeannette 1918 [1]
$2 750 - €3 166 - £1 876 - FF20 768
Capdinal Flowers Dye-transfer print (47.5x32.5cm 18x12in) New-York 2000

KLUYVER Pieter Lodeviik 1816-1900 [62]
$14 145 - €12 209 - £8 510 - FF80 086
Rissamlande familj, vinter Oil/canvas (78x65cm 30x25in) Malmö 1998

$4 837 - €4 079 - £2 871 - FF26 754
Figures on a Snowy Country Road Oil/panel (23x35.5cm 9x13in) Amsterdam 1998

KLUZIS Gustav Gustavovich 1895-1944 [25]
$7 500 - €8 412 - £5 208 - FF55 176
«Let's send Millions of qualified Worker Cadres...» Poster (142x104cm 56x41in) New-York 2001

$2 800 - €2 633 - £1 733 - FF17 269
The Aim of the Confederation/Heroic Stakhanovites Silver print (10x5cm 4x2in) New-York 1999

KMETTY János 1889-1975 [17]
$9 600 - €9 440 - £6 000 - FF61 920
Painter by the River Bank Oil/canvas (46x59cm 18x23in) Budapest 1999

$1 815 - €2 063 - £1 265 - FF13 530
Nature morte au journal sur une table Aquarelle/papier (29x23cm 11x9in) Budapest 2001

KMIT Michael 1910-1981 [109]
$1 962 - €1 839 - £1 213 - FF12 060
Nude Acrylic/canvas (59x29cm 23x11in) Sydney 1999

$947 - €1 069 - £666 - FF7 009
«Angel» Oil/board (21.5x16.5cm 8x6in) Malvern, Victoria 2001

$376 - €326 - £228 - FF2 139
Prophet Watercolour/paper (44x36.5cm 17x14in) Sydney 1998

KNAB Ferdinand 1834-1902 [19]
$2 047 - €1 770 - £1 217 - FF11 611
Schlosspavillon in Oberbayern Öl/Leinwand (50x40cm 19x15in) Zürich 1998

$1 730 - €2 045 - £1 226 - FF13 415
Architekturszene an Gewässer Öl/Leinwand (45x35cm 17x13in) München 2000

$1 584 - €1 534 - £995 - FF10 061
Byzantinische Schlossanlage im Gebirge über See mit Felsenufern Ink/paper (85x107cm 33x42in) Berlin 1999

KNAP Jan 1949 [5]
$1 284 - €1 529 - £917 - FF10 028
Ohne Titel Aquarell (54x38.5cm 21x15in) Berlin 2000

KNAPP Charles Wilson 1822-1900 [51]
$4 500 - €4 677 - £2 835 - FF30 681
Extensive Landscape with Figures and Cows by a Stream Oil/canvas (66x106cm 26x42in) Bethesda MD 2000

$2 000 - €2 311 - £1 400 - FF15 156
Autumn River Landscape Oil/canvas (25x36cm 10x14in) New-York 2001

KNAPP F. Oskar 1914 [31]
$243 - €256 - £164 - FF1 676
Blumenstrauss mit Vergissmeinnicht in Vase Oil/panel (30x24cm 11x9in) Kempten 2001

KNAPP Stefan 1921 [14]
$827 - €962 - £580 - FF6 310
Figures Oil/canvas (51x61cm 20x24in) Billingshurst, West-Sussex 2001

K

KNARREN Petrus Renier Hub. 1826-1896 **[4]**
- **$21 045** – €25 029 – **£15 000** – FF164 178
  Goodnight Visit Oil/panel (59.5x49.5cm 23x19in)
  London 2000

KNATHS Karl Otto 1891-1971 **[90]**
- **$8 500** – €7 280 – **£5 018** – FF47 753
  Net Mender Oil/canvas (124.5x106.5cm 49x41in)
  New-York 1998
- **$2 750** – €2 596 – **£1 709** – FF17 031
  In Homage to Cezanne Oil/canvas (50x55cm
  20x22in) Milford CT 1999
- **$500** – €480 – **£305** – FF3 151
  Untitled Ink/paper (45x36cm 18x14in) Provincetown
  MA 1999
- **$300** – €259 – **£178** – FF1 700
  Untitled Lithograph (34x46cm 13x18in) Provincetown
  MA 1998

KNAUBER Alma Jordan 1893-? **[7]**
- **$500** – €581 – **£351** – FF3 810
  Southwestern Scene Watercolour/paper (33x25cm
  13x10in) Newark OH 2001

KNAUPP Werner 1936 **[38]**
- **$1 071** – €1 022 – **£669** – FF6 707
  Verbrennung (Indien) Charcoal (75x105cm 29x41in)
  Köln 1999

KNAUS Ludwig 1829-1910 **[120]**
- **$400 000** – €446 706 – **£256 160** – FF2 930 200
  The Golden Wedding Oil/canvas (111.5x167cm
  43x65in) New-York 2000
- **$13 391** – €11 247 – **£7 871** – FF73 777
  Audienz beim Herrn Pfarrer Öl/Leinwand
  (80x100cm 31x39in) Köln 1998
- **$5 135** – €4 980 – **£3 232** – FF32 669
  Die feine Dame Öl/Leinwand (33x44cm 12x17in)
  München 1999
- **$230** – €230 – **£144** – FF1 509
  Figuren und Kopfstudie eines Knaben
  Chalks/paper (44.6x30.5cm 17x12in) Köln 1999

KNAYER Imanuel 1896-1962 **[3]**
- **$3 517** – €4 049 – **£2 400** – FF26 560
  Locomotive Watercolour (13.5x19.5cm 5x7in)
  London 2000

KNEBEL Franz Jnr. 1809-1877 **[37]**
- **$19 964** – €20 452 – **£12 320** – FF134 156
  Wasserfälle bei Tivoli Öl/Leinwand (99x135cm
  38x53in) Düsseldorf 2000
- **$10 545** – €11 760 – **£7 090** – FF77 139
  Campagnalandschaft mit Blick auf Rom
  Öl/Leinwand (59x106cm 23x41in) Köln 2000
- **$2 900** – €2 812 – **£1 796** – FF18 446
  Rast im Gebirge Aquarell/Papier (34.5x49.5cm
  13x19in) Graz 1999

KNEIDL Helga 1939 **[22]**
- **$325** – €281 – **£197** – FF1 845
  Therese Giehse Photograph (14.5x10.5cm 5x4in)
  München 1998

KNELL Adolphus ?-c.1890 **[48]**
- **$5 448** – €5 180 – **£3 400** – FF33 977
  **Three-Deckers, probably Nelson's Victory and
  H.M.S. Duke of Wellington** Oil/canvas (45.5x81.5cm
  17x32in) London 1999
- **$1 714** – €1 924 – **£1 200** – FF12 619
  Ship under tow Amid other Craft Oil/canvas
  (22.5x33cm 8x12in) London 2001

KNELL William Adolphus 1805-1875 **[126]**
- **$10 925** – €10 658 – **£6 727** – FF69 910
  **Scene at the Bank of the Isle of Wright saving
  the Lives** Oil/canvas (81x135cm 32x53in) Chicago IL
  1999
- **$2 143** – €1 943 – **£1 300** – FF12 745
  Shipping in a Channel at Sunset Oil/panel
  (17x24.5cm 6x9in) Billingshurst, West-Sussex 1998
- **$1 537** – €1 647 – **£1 050** – FF10 803
  Becalmed/Evening in the Downs
  Watercolour/paper (30x55.5cm 11x21in) London 2001

KNELL William Callcott c.1830-c.1880 **[121]**
- **$3 204** – €3 047 – **£2 000** – FF19 986
  **Dutch Fishing Boats running before the Wind
  off the North Foreland** Oil/canvas (30.5x61cm
  12x24in) London 1998
- **$1 494** – €1 604 – **£1 000** – FF10 521
  Cutters Rounding the Buoy Oil/canvas
  (22.5x50.5cm 8x19in) London 2000
- **$475** – €498 – **£301** – FF3 269
  Collier Brig. Underway off Gravensend
  Watercolour/paper (19x30cm 7x12in) New-Orleans LA
  2000

KNELLER Godfrey 1646-1723 **[97]**
- **$12 184** – €11 855 – **£7 500** – FF77 766
  **General Charles Churchill (D.1745), standing,
  wearing a green Coat** Oil/canvas (125x100cm
  49x39in) London 1999
- **$4 519** – €4 184 – **£2 800** – FF27 445
  **Young Man Possibly John Vanderbank (1694-
  1739)** Oil/canvas (49x38cm 19x14in) London 1999
- **$5 365** – €4 534 – **£3 200** – FF29 739
  **Lady, said to be Sarah, Duchess of
  Marlborough/Study of a Head** Coloured
  chalks/paper (40x24cm 15x9in) Bath 1998

KNGWARREYE Emily Kame 1910-1996 **[121]**
- **$14 866** – €15 959 – **£9 950** – FF104 681
  My Country Mixed media/canvas (121x213cm
  47x83in) Sydney 2000
- **$4 288** – €4 604 – **£2 870** – FF30 198
  Untitled Mixed media/canvas (61x50cm 24x19in)
  Sydney 2000
- **$17 551** – €18 392 – **£11 117** – FF120 645
  Untitled Acrylic/canvas (18x86cm 7x33in) Sydney
  2000
- **$4 604** – €4 442 – **£2 909** – FF29 136
  A Pair of Carved and Painted Lizards Sculpture,
  wood (H79cm H31in) Melbourne 1999

KNIBBERGEN van François 1597-c.1670 **[8]**
- **$13 701** – €11 255 – **£7 957** – FF73 825
  **Flusslauf zwischen hohen Bergen mit ablegen-
  dem Lastkahn** Oil/wood (45.5x63cm 17x24in) Berlin
  1998
- **$9 204** – €7 800 – **£5 500** – FF51 162
  **A Wooded River Landscape with Cottage, a
  Church Spire beyond** Oil/panel (31.5x47cm
  12x18in) London 1998

KNIE Rolf 1949 **[47]**
- **$2 284** – €2 115 – **£1 398** – FF13 875
  **Abstrakte Komposition mit Pegasus vor einer
  Leiter** Oil/Papier (34x25cm 13x9in) Bern 1999
- **$561** – €655 – **£389** – FF4 296
  Löwe im Käfig Gouache (33x24cm 12x9in) Bern
  2000
- **$347** – €385 – **£235** – FF2 525
  Im Zirkus Farblithographie (76.2x56.2cm 29x22in)
  Zürich 2000

KNIEP Christian Heinrich 1755-1825 **[14]**
$2 024 - €2 352 - £1 422 - FF15 427
Ideale Flusslandschaft mit Schäferin
Chalks/paper (20x26.5cm 7x10in) Hamburg 2001

KNIGHT A. Roland XIX **[110]**
$1 194 - €1 243 - £750 - FF8 156
A Pike on a River bank Oil/canvas (40.5x61cm 15x24in) London 2000
$1 942 - €2 085 - £1 300 - FF13 678
Hooked trout leaping/Hooked trout diving
Oil/canvas (15x20cm 5x7in) Billingshurst, West-Sussex 2000

KNIGHT Charles 1901-1990 **[14]**
$777 - €834 - £520 - FF5 471
Grey Estuary, North Wales Watercolour (31.5x50.5cm 12x19in) Bath 2000

KNIGHT Charles 1743-1826 **[9]**
$648 - €550 - £391 - FF3 609
British Plenty/Indian in Scarcity, after Heny Singleton Engraving (51.5x40.5cm 20x15in) London 1998

KNIGHT Charles Parsons 1829-1897 **[29]**
$1 410 - €1 646 - £1 000 - FF10 799
Fisherfolk on the Jetty Oil/canvas (56x91.5cm 22x36in) London 2001
$331 - €307 - £200 - FF2 011
On the Exe, Tiverton Oil/canvas (19x33cm 7x12in) Billingshurst, West-Sussex 1999
$461 - €423 - £280 - FF2 772
Goatland Watercolour (32.5x50cm 12x19in) London 1998

KNIGHT Charles Robert 1874-1953 **[11]**
$5 500 - €4 699 - £3 301 - FF30 824
Bull/Bear Bronze (H12.5cm H4in) New-York 1998

KNIGHT Clara 1861-? **[10]**
$446 - €464 - £280 - FF3 044
The Country Inn Watercolour (11x17cm 4x6in) Oxfordshire 2000

KNIGHT Daniel Ridgway 1839-1924 **[136]**
$48 000 - €41 412 - £28 958 - FF271 646
The Road to harvest Oil/canvas (98x131cm 38x51in) New-York 1999
$60 000 - €71 355 - £42 762 - FF468 060
Wash Day Oil/canvas (90x130cm 35x51in) New-York 2000
$8 000 - €8 587 - £5 353 - FF56 328
In the Moonlight Oil/canvas (40x33cm 16x13in) Portland ME 2000
$3 961 - €4 594 - £2 799 - FF30 133
La lavandière Aquarelle/papier (27x37cm 10x14in) Montréal 2001

KNIGHT Edward Loxton 1905 **[9]**
$817 - €786 - £500 - FF5 153
«Ely, Cambridgeshire, LNER» Poster (102x64cm 40x25in) London 1999

KNIGHT George XIX **[39]**
$1 014 - €1 177 - £700 - FF7 721
Fishing Boats off a Harbour Oil/canvas (40.5x61cm 15x24in) London 2000
$1 283 - €1 293 - £800 - FF8 482
Leaving Harbour Oil/canvas (40.5x30.5cm 15x12in) London 2000

KNIGHT Harold 1874-1961 **[41]**
$44 829 - €48 120 - £30 000 - FF315 648
Bric-a-Brac Oil/canvas (92x77cm 36x30in) London 2000

$13 326 - €15 886 - £9 500 - FF104 203
Portrait of Laura Knight, Head and Shoulders
Oil/canvas (41x31cm 16x12in) Leyburn, North Yorkshire 2000
$3 010 - €2 569 - £1 800 - FF16 853
A Fisherwoman beside a Cottage sorting out the Catch Watercolour/paper (23x22cm 9x8in) Leeds 1998

KNIGHT Jacob Jaskoviak 1939-1994 **[6]**
$8 000 - €7 650 - £4 872 - FF50 178
Peace on Earth, Christmas Eve on Martha's Vineyard Acrylic/canvas (83.5x62.5cm 32x24in) Boston MA 1999

KNIGHT John William Buxton 1843-1908 **[59]**
$11 229 - €11 316 - £7 000 - FF74 225
Church at Sunset Oil/canvas (152.5x103cm 60x40in) London 2000
$1 104 - €1 238 - £750 - FF8 123
Extensive Landscape Oil/canvas (55x88cm 22x35in) Aylsham, Norfolk 2000
$388 - €417 - £260 - FF2 735
Haymakers Watercolour (27x37.5cm 10x14in) London 2000

KNIGHT Joseph 1837-1909 **[48]**
$725 - €853 - £520 - FF5 594
Landscape with Sheep Grazing beside a Path
Oil/canvas (29.5x39.5cm 11x15in) West-Yorkshire 2001
$609 - €614 - £380 - FF4 529
Woman wearing a white bonnet and a blue checked shawl Watercolour (71x46cm 28x18in) Dorchester, Dorset 2000

KNIGHT Kenneth 1956 **[19]**
$855 - €795 - £527 - FF5 215
Small Cove Oil/board (44.5x64.5cm 17x25in) Melbourne 1999

KNIGHT Laura, née Johnson 1877-1970 **[568]**
$112 273 - €111 060 - £70 000 - FF728 504
Studio Window Oil/canvas (101.5x127cm 39x50in) London 1999
$28 391 - €30 476 - £19 000 - FF199 910
Portrait of an Entertainer Oil/canvas (63.5x76cm 25x29in) London 2001
$14 455 - €14 030 - £9 000 - FF92 033
The Fireside Oil/canvas (40.5x30.5cm 15x12in) London 1999
$1 514 - €1 264 - £900 - FF8 294
Dancing Figure Study Ink (22.5x16cm 8x6in) London 1999
$718 - €654 - £440 - FF4 293
Women Reading Linocut in colors (10x17.5cm 3x6in) Malvern, Victoria 1998

KNIGHT Louis Aston 1873-1948 **[200]**
$30 970 - €28 965 - £18 981 - FF190 000
Vue de Rolleboise, animée de personnages
Huile/toile (108x169cm 42x66in) Paris 1998
$12 000 - €11 240 - £7 377 - FF73 729
Houses Along a Canal Oil/canvas (82x66cm 32x25in) New-York 1999
$1 900 - €1 630 - £1 128 - FF10 746
Cottage Beside a River Oil/panel (30x40cm 12x16in) Cincinnati OH 1998
$1 791 - €1 524 - £1 066 - FF10 000
Le vieux moulin Pastel/papier (54x44cm 21x17in) Paris 1998

KNIGHT Robbert XVII **[1]**
$14 405 - €13 751 - £9 000 - FF90 202
Hawking Accoutrements Oil/canvas (78x66cm 30x25in) London 1999

K

KNIGHT William Henry 1823-1863 **[22]**

⌐ $7 825 - €7 470 - **£4 890** - FF49 000
Jeune mère et ses enfants en bord de mer
Huile/toile (79x109cm 31x42in) Auvers sur Oise 1999

⌐ $4 463 - €5 248 - **£3 200** - FF34 427
Children playing Cricket Oil/panel (9x16cm 3x6in)
London 2001

KNIGHTON-HAMMOND Arthur Henry 1875-1970
[197]

⌐ $739 - €677 - **£450** - FF4 439
Allport Mill Oil/canvas (45.5x61cm 17x24in) London
1999

✍ $831 - €718 - **£500** - FF4 708
Coastal Scene with Figures on a Beach
Watercolour/paper (48x63cm 18x24in) Leyburn, North
Yorkshire 1998

KNIJFF Wouter c.1607-c.1693 **[29]**

⌐ $12 000 - €11 994 - **£7 330** - FF78 678
River Landscape with a Windmill by a Town
Oil/panel (35x51.5cm 13x20in) New-York 2000

⌐ $5 084 - €5 899 - **£3 510** - FF38 695
**Fortified Town on a River, with a Sailing Boat in
the Distance** Oil/panel (25.5x28.5cm 10x11in)
Amsterdam 2000

KNIKKER Aris 1887-1962 **[94]**

⌐ $1 194 - €1 134 - **£726** - FF7 441
Scharrelende kippen bij een huisje Oil/canvas
(43x42cm 16x16in) Den Haag 1999

⌐ $494 - €544 - **£322** - FF3 571
Pluimvee aan de waterkant Oil/panel (22x34cm
8x13in) Rotterdam 2000

KNIKKER Jan II 1911-1990 **[145]**

⌐ $718 - €771 - **£480** - FF5 060
**View of the Prins Hendrikkade with the
Scheierstoren** Oil/canvas (40x60cm 15x23in)
Amsterdam 2000

⌐ $504 - €499 - **£308** - FF3 274
Chicken in a Farmyard Oil/canvas (30x40cm
11x15in) Amsterdam 2000

KNIKKER Jan Simon 1889-1957 **[91]**

⌐ $716 - €681 - **£435** - FF4 464
Buurtschapje Oil/canvas (34x48cm 13x18in)
Rotterdam 1999

⌐ $580 - €544 - **£358** - FF3 571
Bloemstilleven Oil/board (23x29cm 9x11in)
Rotterdam 1999

KNILLE Otto 1832-1898 **[4]**

⌐ $4 982 - €4 877 - **£3 065** - FF31 992
**Gefangene Edelleute im deutschen
Bauernkriege** Oil/canvas (32.5x47.5cm 12x18in)
Helsinki 1999

KNIP August 1819-1861 **[24]**

⌐ $4 153 - €3 835 - **£2 554** - FF25 154
Schäfer mit seiner Herde auf dem Heimweg
Öl/Leinwand (76x105cm 29x41in) München 1999

⌐ $2 547 - €2 407 - **£1 600** - FF16 180
Hunt in progress/A Leaping Stag Oil/canvas
(16x21cm 6x8in) London 1999

KNIP Hendrick Johannes 1819-1897 **[35]**

✍ $1 321 - €1 271 - **£814** - FF8 334
**View of the Pfalzgrafenstein at Kaub on the
River Rhine** Watercolour (43x58.5cm 16x23in)
Amsterdam 1999

KNIP Henriette Geertruida 1783-1842 **[8]**

⌐ $2 990 - €3 222 - **£2 067** - FF21 138
Nature morte au vase de fleurs sur la table
Huile/panneau (34x18cm 13x7in) Antwerpen 2001

KNIP Joseph August 1777-1847 **[70]**

⌐ $2 168 - €2 439 - **£1 492** - FF16 000
Aigles et chevreau Huile/toile (104x75cm 40x29in)
Paris 2000

⌐ $2 052 - €1 812 - **£1 237** - FF11 887
Wild Horses near a Ruin Watercolour/paper
(49x75cm 19x29in) Amsterdam 1998

KNIP Mattheus Derk 1785-1845 **[13]**

✍ $3 845 - €3 322 - **£2 318** - FF21 788
**A Rocky Landscape with Travellers and a
Huntsman with his Dog** Bodycolour (18.5x23.5cm
7x9in) Amsterdam 1998

KNIP Pauline 1781-1851 **[1]**

✍ $16 953 - €20 061 - **£12 000** - FF131 594
Brush Bronze Wing, Phaps Elegant Watercolour
(63x48cm 24x18in) London 2001

KNIP Willem Anton Alex. 1883-1967 **[99]**

⌐ $1 395 - €1 588 - **£980** - FF10 418
Farm in a polder Landscape Oil/panel (40x60cm
23x23in) Amsterdam 2001

⌐ $1 477 - €1 588 - **£1 006** - FF10 418
St.Tropez Oil/panel (29x40cm 11x15in) Amsterdam
2001

KNIPE Emilie Benson 1870-? **[1]**

✍ $2 900 - €2 685 - **£1 775** - FF17 611
**Young girl with black-eyed Susans, fairies loo-
king on: story ill.** Watercolour (13x25cm 5x10in)
New-York 1999

KNIRSCH Otto act.1853-1860 **[1]**

▥ $46 000 - €55 600 - **£32 117** - FF364 715
The Road-winter Lithograph (54x76cm 21x30in)
Bolton MA 2000

KNOBLOCH Josef Rolf 1891-1964 **[109]**

⌐ $450 - €437 - **£281** - FF2 865
Bauer mit Pferdekarren vor dem Haus
Öl/Leinwand (53x61cm 20x24in) Zürich 1999

KNÖCHL Hans 1850-1927 **[9]**

⌐ $2 600 - €2 366 - **£1 624** - FF15 520
Mythological Landscape with Bathers Oil/panel
(23x33cm 9x13in) Chester NY 1999

KNOEBEL Imi 1940 **[120]**

⌐ $21 268 - €20 452 - **£13 124** - FF134 156
Ohne Titel Mixed media/panel (171.5x203cm 67x79in)
Köln 1999

⌐ $3 810 - €4 090 - **£2 550** - FF26 831
Ohne Titel Acrylic (98.3x68.2cm 38x26in) Köln 2000

⌐ $1 714 - €1 841 - **£1 147** - FF12 074
Ohne Titel Object (35x25cm 13x9in) Köln 2000

⌐ $4 356 - €4 090 - **£2 699** - FF26 831
Messerschnitt Collage (102x72cm 40x28in)
München 1999

▥ $1 451 - €1 380 - **£901** - FF9 055
Grace Kelly Farbserigraphie (105x75cm 41x29in)
Hamburg 1999

▣ $23 107 - €25 179 - **£16 000** - FF165 164
Untitled Photograph (22.5x29.5cm 8x11in) London
2001

KNOOP August Hermann 1856-1900 **[56]**

⌐ $809 - €920 - **£561** - FF6 037
Gelehrter in einem historischen Interieur
Oil/panel (26.5x21cm 10x8in) Hamburg 2000

KNOPF Hermann 1870-1928 **[18]**

⌐ $2 417 - €2 728 - **£1 700** - FF17 893
Die fürsorgliche Mutter Öl/Leinwand (63x63cm
24x24in) Bern 2001

$435 - €416 - **£274** - FF2 727
Portrait of a Woman Oil/panel (18x26cm 7x10in)
Vancouver, BC. 1999

KNOPP Imre, Emerich 1867-1934 **[8]**
$3 700 - €3 887 - **£2 300** - FF25 500
Petits enfants Huile/toile (110x81cm 43x31in)
Budapest 2000

KNÖPPEL Arvid 1892-1970 **[77]**
$804 - €769 - **£506** - FF5 045
Smygande lodjur Bronze (H15cm H5in) Stockholm
1999

KNORR Hugo 1834-1904 **[12]**
$2 647 - €2 490 - **£1 639** - FF16 335
Mellem to floder ved Köningsberg, Preussen
Oil/canvas (66x114cm 25x44in) Viby J, Århus 1999

KNOTT Ralph 1878-1929 **[1]**
$1 730 - €1 912 - **£1 200** - FF12 543
**Design for the Council Chamber, County Hall,
London** Watercolour (69.5x60cm 27x23in) London
2001

KNOWLES Davidson 1879-1909 **[15]**
$777 - €767 - **£500** - FF5 032
Angler on a jetty, watching a Kingfisher Oil/canvas (61x51cm 24x20in) London 1999

KNOWLES Dorothy Elsie 1927 **[66]**
$5 103 - €4 878 - **£3 198** - FF31 998
A Road through the Fields Oil/canvas (122x116cm 48x45in) Vancouver, BC. 1999
$2 177 - €2 081 - **£1 364** - FF13 652
Rainy Day at Tweedsmuir Oil/canvas (60x91cm 23x35in) Vancouver, BC. 1999
$3 638 - €3 906 - **£2 471** - FF25 620
Heading North Oil/canvas (24x29cm 9x11in) Calgary, Alberta 2001
$1 089 - €1 077 - **£680** - FF7 063
The Bull Rushes of the Spruce River Reservoir
Watercolour/paper (56x76cm 22x29in) Calgary, Alberta 1999

KNOWLES Farquhar McGillivr. 1859-1932 **[28]**
$1 678 - €1 432 - **£1 000** - FF9 393
Beneath Autumn's Glory Oil/canvas (76.5x74cm 30x29in) Vancouver, BC. 1998

KNOWLES Frederick James 1874-? **[67]**
$542 - €595 - **£350** - FF3 903
The Woodland Farm Oil/canvas (48x33cm 19x13in) Woodford, Cheshire 2000
$280 - €326 - **£200** - FF2 136
Shropshire farmstead Watercolour/paper (41x55cm 16x22in) Bristol, Avon 2001

KNOWLES George Sheridan 1863-1931 **[60]**
$8 000 - €7 456 - **£4 835** - FF48 911
Mother and Child in Garden Oil/canvas (91x60cm 36x24in) Norwalk CT 1999
$2 080 - €1 972 - **£1 300** - FF12 938
Fireside Reverie Oil/panel (24x35cm 9x13in) Crewkerne, Somerset 1999
$2 064 - €2 134 - **£1 300** - FF14 001
Musical Accompaniment Watercolour/paper (39x53cm 15x20in) Bath 2000

KNOWLES Joseph 1907-1980 **[1]**
$7 500 - €7 774 - **£4 755** - FF50 995
Indians on Horseback Oil/canvas (51x91cm 20x35in) New-York 2000

KNOWLES Joseph Edward Sr. 1869-1942 **[1]**
$3 300 - €3 899 - **£2 338** - FF25 577
Pair of Brook Trout/Bear at River's Edge Oil/canvas (56x43cm 22x16in) Boston MA 2000

KNOX Archibald 1864-1933 **[22]**
$2 324 - €2 550 - **£1 500** - FF16 727
Skyscape Watercolour/paper (43x55cm 17x22in) Isle-of-Man 2000

KNOX George James 1810-1897 **[34]**
$499 - €427 - **£300** - FF2 804
**West country coastal view with Fisher folk on a
Beach at Sunset** Watercolour/paper (20x30cm 8x12in) Aylsham, Norfolk 1998

KNOX Jack 1936 **[13]**
$1 148 - €1 291 - **£800** - FF8 471
Bowl of Cherries Oil/board (24x29cm 9x11in) Edinburgh 2001

KNOX John 1778-1845 **[27]**
$9 938 - €9 389 - **£6 200** - FF61 586
**View of Ben Lomond, the Campsies and
Dumgoyne** Oil/canvas (90x125cm 35x49in) Perthshire 1999
$13 304 - €11 367 - **£8 050** - FF74 563
The Shepherd and his Dog Oil/panel (28x37cm 11x14in) Edinburgh 1998

KNOX Juliana, Lady 1825-1906 **[1]**
$7 930 - €8 327 - **£5 000** - FF54 623
**Sketches from Nature: Views of Madeira, Crow
Hall, Suffolk, Pyrenees** Watercolour/paper (54.5x39.5cm 21x15in) London 2000

KNOX Susan Richer 1875-1959 **[28]**
$1 500 - €1 688 - **£1 033** - FF11 074
Moutainous Desert Landscape Oil/canvas (76x96.5cm 29x37in) Washington 2000

KNOX Wilfred 1884-1966 **[27]**
$1 208 - €1 361 - **£850** - FF8 930
Sailing Ships in full Sail on a Choppy Ocean
Oil/canvas (50x75cm 19x29in) Lichfield, Staffordshire 2001
$568 - €641 - **£400** - FF4 202
Evening on the Thames Watercolour/paper (25x36cm 9x14in) Lichfield, Staffordshire 2001

KNOX William 1862-1925 **[66]**
$650 - €637 - **£419** - FF4 178
St. Georges Island, Venice Gouache/paper (30.5x45.5cm 12x17in) New-York 1999

KNOX William Dunn 1880-1945 **[44]**
$1 164 - €1 272 - **£749** - FF8 342
Moonrise Oil/canvas (35.5x46cm 13x18in) Melbourne 2000
$1 517 - €1 672 - **£1 009** - FF10 969
Little Dock Oil/board (21x30cm 8x11in) Melbourne 2000

KNUDSEN Dagfinn 1953 **[5]**
$287 - €322 - **£199** - FF2 110
Profilen Drypoint (49x68cm 19x26in) Oslo 2001

KNUDSEN Peder 1868-1944 **[74]**
$451 - €431 - **£274** - FF2 825
Havparti, Bornholm Oil/canvas (72x84cm 28x33in) Viby J, Århus 1999

KNUDSON Robert L. 1929 **[3]**
$1 600 - €1 880 - **£1 139** - FF12 335
Pride of her People Pastel (35.5x28cm 13x11in) Beverly-Hills CA 2000

K

$11 797 - €10 737 - **£7 371** - FF70 431
Der Ziegenhirte mit zwei jungen Zicklein vorn
Öl/Papier (26.4x34.8cm 10x13in) München 1999

$1 734 - €1 972 - **£1 189** - FF12 933
Jagdszene Pencil/paper (11x20cm 4x7in) Zürich 2000

$257 - €256 - **£161** - FF1 676
La Diligence, nach Jacques d'Artbois Radierung
(8.5x9.5cm 3x3in) München 1999

KOBELT K. XX [1]
$1 700 - €1 635 - **£1 049** - FF10 723
«Akademie, Techn-Hochschule» Poster
(104x72.5cm 40x28in) New-York 1999

KOBERLING Bernd 1938 [28]
$10 592 - €10 478 - **£6 604** - FF68 728
Untergrund Öl/Leinwand (225x301cm 88x118in)
Berlin 1999

$2 489 - €2 940 - **£1 767** - FF19 284
Ohne Titel Acryl/Leinwand (60x50cm 23x19in) Berlin
2001

KOBINGER Hans 1892-1974 [34]
$855 - €1 017 - **£610** - FF6 673
Zirkuswägen Mischtechnik (50x53cm 19x20in) Linz
2000

$632 - €581 - **£391** - FF3 813
Häuser im Winter Mischtechnik/Papier (57x59.5cm
22x23in) Wien 1999

$232 - €276 - **£165** - FF1 811
Kitzbühel i.T. Woodcut in colors (41x37cm 16x14in)
Linz 2000

KØBKE Christen 1810-1848 [58]
$85 525 - €74 037 - **£51 920** - FF485 650
Parti fra Capri i naerheden af Marina Picola
Oil/canvas (38x53cm 14x20in) Köbenhavn 1998

$20 215 - €17 500 - **£12 272** - FF114 790
**Portraet af Antoinette Köbke, födt Uldall, kunst-
nerens kusine** Oil/canvas (27.5x22.5cm 10x8in)
Köbenhavn 1998

$570 - €538 - **£355** - FF3 532
Studie af et antikt hoved Pencil/paper (32x26cm
12x10in) Köbenhavn 1999

$783 - €740 - **£488** - FF4 857
Parti i Aarhus Domkirke Etching (20x30cm 7x11in)
Köbenhavn 1999

KOBLIHA Frantisek 1877-1962 [26]
$504 - €477 - **£315** - FF3 130
Erwachen Charcoal/paper (41x28cm 16x11in) Praha
1999

$187 - €178 - **£117** - FF1 165
«Temptation» Woodcut (47x35cm 18x13in) Praha
2001

KOCH Anton Joseph 1768-1839 [45]
$288 420 - €318 710 - **£200 000** - FF2 090 600
Tiberlandschaft mit fröhlichen Landleuten
Oil/canvas (52.5x74cm 20x29in) London 2001

$3 339 - €3 068 - **£2 051** - FF20 123
**Szene aus der Hermanns Schlacht nach
Klopstock** Gouache/paper (27.5x22.5cm 10x8in)
Stuttgart 1999

$636 - €663 - **£400** - FF4 348
Les Argonautes Etching (21.5x25.5cm 8x10in)
London 2000

KOCH Fred XX [3]
$1 286 - €1 534 - **£917** - FF10 061
Sonnenblume Photograph (23.4x17.2cm 9x6in)
München 2000

KOCH Georg 1878-? [5]
$8 000 - €9 514 - **£5 701** - FF62 408
Full Cry/The Kill Watercolour (54x83.5cm 21x32in)
New-York 2000

KOCH Georg Karl 1857-1936 [24]
$3 313 - €3 068 - **£2 028** - FF20 123
Parforcejagd Öl/Leinwand (66x49cm 25x19in)
Hamburg 1999

KOCH Hermann 1856-1939 [22]
$1 112 - €1 278 - **£785** - FF8 384
Stilleben mit Weintrauben Öl/Leinwand (38.5x48cm
15x18in) Bremen 2001

$978 - €847 - **£600** - FF5 558
The Musician Oil/panel (29x39cm 11x15in)
Billingshurst, West-Sussex 1999

KOCH John 1909-1978 [65]
$6 000 - €7 173 - **£4 138** - FF47 052
Louging in the Park Oil/canvas (52x65cm 20x25in)
Milford CT 2000

$1 100 - €948 - **£653** - FF6 218
Study of Standing Female Model Pencil (30x23cm
11x9in) New-York 1998

KOCH Josef XX [19]
$346 - €409 - **£245** - FF2 683
Winterlandschaft Öl/Leinwand (50x71cm 19x27in)
München 2000

KOCH Ludwig 1866-1934 [93]
$5 780 - €6 573 - **£3 965** - FF43 113
Bosnisches Bauernrennen Öl/Leinwand
(165x300cm 64x118in) Zürich 2000

$1 346 - €1 453 - **£930** - FF9 534
Sanktus Florianus Oil/canvas (105x75cm 41x29in)
Wien 2001

$930 - €872 - **£574** - FF5 720
Ausfahrt mit den Schimmeln Pencil (35x49.5cm
13x19in) Wien 1999

KOCH Max Friedrich 1859-1930 [9]
$214 - €230 - **£143** - FF1 509
**Studie für eine Teil der Kuppel der Kapelle am
Nicolausberg** Mischtechnik (30x49cm 11x19in)
Berlin 2000

KOCH Pyke 1901-1991 [21]
$41 976 - €49 916 - **£29 920** - FF327 426
Cypress Oil/canvas (55x30cm 21x11in) Amsterdam
2000

$282 384 - €335 797 - **£201 280** - FF2 202 684
Daphne Tempera (28x28cm 11x11in) Amsterdam 2000

KOCH Walter 1875-1915 [25]
$2 245 - €2 263 - **£1 400** - FF14 845
«Davos 27 & 28 Januar» Poster (90x64cm 35x25in)
London 2000

KOCHANOWSKI Roman 1856/57-1945 [109]
$2 104 - €1 943 - **£1 294** - FF12 744
Dorfansicht mit Gänseliesel Oil/panel (10x17cm
3x6in) München 1999

$171 - €197 - **£118** - FF1 291
Femme dans le vent - trois dessins Crayon/papier
(700x1200cm 275x472in) Warszawa 2000

KOCHERSCHEIDT Kurt, Kappa 1943-1992 [30]
$41 950 - €36 321 - **£25 450** - FF238 250
«Grosse Weihe» Öl/Leinwand (125.5x140cm
49x55in) Wien 1998

$865 - €872 - **£540** - FF5 720
Erweiterte Naturkunde, 2.Lieferung Radierung
(53x41cm 20x16in) Wien 2000

K

KÖCKERT Julius 1827-1918 **[18]**
- $2 492 - €2 907 - £1 760 - FF19 068
  Sonnwendfeuer im Hochgebirge Öl/Leinwand (105x78cm 41x30in) Salzburg 2000
- $2 531 - €2 454 - £1 603 - FF16 098
  Stille Andacht bei einem Marterl unter der Wettertanne im Gebirge Oil/canvas (27x20cm 10x7in) München 1999

KODRA Ibrahim 1918 **[38]**
- $640 - €829 - £480 - FF5 440
  Natura morta nel cesto Tecnica mista/tela (55x65cm 21x25in) Vercelli 2001

KOECHL Manfred 1956 **[39]**
- $342 - €327 - £208 - FF2 145
  Nach vorne Gebeugter Pencil (45x34.3cm 17x13in) Wien 1999

KOEHLER & ANCONA Karl & Victor XX **[1]**
- $3 200 - €2 807 - £1 943 - FF18 412
  This is the Enemy Poster (86x60cm 34x24in) New-York 1999

KOEHLER Henry 1927 **[70]**
- $8 000 - €8 587 - £5 353 - FF56 328
  Brown Chesterfield Oil/canvas (38x62cm 14x24in) New-York 2000
- $5 250 - €4 883 - £3 250 - FF32 028
  Jockey trying on Cap Oil/canvas/panel (36x26cm 14x10in) Nantucket MA 1999
- $2 300 - €2 736 - £1 639 - FF17 945
  Cooling Out Black chalk/paper (45.5x58.5cm 17x23in) New-York 2000

KOEHLER Paul R. 1866-1909 **[18]**
- $600 - €559 - £362 - FF3 668
  Winter Landscape with Bundled Wheat Pastel/paper (28x43cm 11x17in) New-Orleans LA 1999

KOEKE Hugo 1874-1956 **[4]**
- $700 - €758 - £466 - FF4 975
  «Hamburg-American Line, Express Service to Europe, The Famous Tour» Poster (75x49cm 29x19in) New-York 2000

KOEKKOEK Barend-Cornelis 1803-1862 **[160]**
- $89 410 - €98 800 - £62 000 - FF648 086
  Figures and cattle on a path in wooded landscape with a castle beyond Oil/panel (35.5x47cm 13x18in) London 2001
- $8 417 - €9 909 - £5 915 - FF65 000
  Paysage au promeneur près d'un rocher Huile/panneau (19x17.5cm 7x6in) Argenteuil 2000
- $2 895 - €3 403 - £2 007 - FF22 324
  Conversing Figures by a Ruin Watercolour/paper (18x27cm 7x10in) Amsterdam 2000

KOEKKOEK Hendrik Barend 1849-1909 **[40]**
- $5 853 - €5 899 - £3 649 - FF38 695
  Winter Landscape witn youngsters putting on their Skates Oil/canvas (77x64cm 30x25in) Amsterdam 2000
- $2 311 - €2 496 - £1 580 - FF16 371
  A Peasant Woman and a Boy in a Wooded Landscape Oil/canvas (31x47cm 12x18in) Amsterdam 2001

KOEKKOEK Hendrik Pieter 1843-c.1890 **[75]**
- $4 500 - €4 319 - £2 821 - FF28 329
  Pulling the Wagon Oil/canvas (61x91.5cm 24x36in) New-York 1999
- $3 215 - €2 949 - £1 981 - FF19 347
  Traveller in a Landscape Oil/panel (21x34cm 8x13in) Amsterdam 1999

KOEKKOEK Hermanus I 1815-1882 **[175]**
- $23 771 - €24 958 - £14 987 - FF163 713
  Zeeuws Beurtschip in a Stiff Breeze, a Frigat in the Distance Oil/panel (40x54cm 15x21in) Amsterdam 2000
- $15 481 - €14 521 - £9 568 - FF95 251
  Beurtschepen en vissers op de rivier Oil/canvas (30x45cm 11x17in) Rotterdam 1999

KOEKKOEK Hermanus II 1836-1909 **[221]**
- $2 671 - €2 266 - £1 611 - FF14 867
  Molenlandschap Oil/canvas (60x90cm 23x35in) Rotterdam 1998
- $1 474 - €1 687 - £1 014 - FF11 067
  Marine, Segelschiffe und Dreimaster auf See Oil/panel (11x14cm 4x5in) München 2000
- $546 - €524 - £342 - FF3 440
  View of a Dutch Harbour Watercolour/paper (37x52cm 14x20in) Montréal 1999

KOEKKOEK Hermanus Willem 1867-1929 **[58]**
- $4 756 - €5 419 - £3 287 - FF35 548
  Troops Returning Home Oil/canvas (43x53.5cm 16x21in) Montréal 2000
- $2 183 - €2 454 - £1 533 - FF16 098
  Die alte Mühle Oil/panel (43x36cm 16x14in) Düsseldorf 2001
- $368 - €431 - £263 - FF2 827
  Soldier in the Snow Gouache/paper (38x26.5cm 14x10in) Amsterdam 2001

KOEKKOEK Jan Hermanus Barend 1840-1912 **[152]**
- $9 987 - €11 344 - £7 007 - FF74 415
  A River Landscape with Figures in a rowing Boat Oil/panel (35.5x51.5cm 13x20in) Amsterdam 2001
- $8 539 - €9 166 - £5 800 - FF60 125
  Salvaging off a Coastline at Sunset Oil/panel (30x44cm 11x17in) London 2001

KOEKKOEK Johannes Hermanus 1778-1851 **[62]**
- $16 116 - €18 185 - £11 337 - FF119 288
  Marine, Schiffe im Sturm Oil/panel (36x47cm 14x18in) Bern 2001
- $16 042 - €16 165 - £10 000 - FF106 036
  Looking Offshore from the Dock Oil/panel (21x26.5cm 8x10in) London 2000

KOEKKOEK Marinus Adrianus 1807-1868 **[84]**
- $10 127 - €11 344 - £7 037 - FF74 415
  Bommrijk landschap met bergbeek en herders met vee Oil/canvas (47x62cm 18x24in) Rotterdam 2001
- $2 895 - €3 343 - £2 025 - FF21 927
  Grönskande landskap med figurer och byggnader, sommardag Oil/panel (32.5x41cm 12x16in) Stockholm 2001

KOEKKOEK Marinus Adrianus II 1873-1944 **[32]**
- $1 935 - €1 815 - £1 196 - FF11 906
  Flamingo's Oil/canvas (50x63cm 19x24in) Rotterdam 1999
- $625 - €726 - £432 - FF4 762
  Eendjes aan de wallekant Oil/canvas (25x34cm 9x13in) Rotterdam 2000

KOEKKOEK Stephen Robert 1887-1934 **[39]**
- $3 400 - €3 326 - £2 159 - FF21 817
  Barca pesquera Oleo/tabla (46.5x58.5cm 18x23in) Buenos-Aires 1999
- $950 - €1 104 - £667 - FF7 240
  Entrando al templo Oleo/tabla (16x21cm 6x8in) Buenos-Aires 2001

KOEKKOEK Willem 1839-1895 [103]

$51 203 - €50 836 - **£32 000** - FF333 462
Stadsgezicht met figuren bij een oude kerk
Oil/canvas (55x70.5cm 21x27in) London 1999

$16 216 - €19 059 - **£11 243** - FF125 017
A View in a City with Villagers Conversing in a Street Oil/panel (23.5x16cm 9x6in) Amsterdam 2000

$2 808 - €2 949 - **£1 777** - FF19 347
Figures in a Dutch Town Watercolour/paper (20.5x27cm 8x10in) Amsterdam 2000

KOELLA Heinrich 1757-1789 [1]

$1 669 - €1 968 - **£1 178** - FF12 908
Zwei Frauen in Umarmung Charcoal (67.5x56cm 26x22in) Bern 2000

KOELMAN Johan Daniël 1831-1857 [18]

$2 197 - €2 496 - **£1 541** - FF16 371
A Landscape with Farmhouses along a River Oil/panel (17.5x36cm 6x14in) Amsterdam 2001

KOELMAN Johan Philip 1818-1893 [6]

$7 826 - €8 690 - **£5 454** - FF77 500
Enfants chevauchant une statue en Italie Huile/panneau (42x54cm 16x21in) Paris 2001

KOEMPOEL 1912-1987 [23]

$1 721 - €1 955 - **£1 178** - FF12 823
Flower Market Oil/canvas (60x88cm 23x34in) Singapore 2000

$1 836 - €2 085 - **£1 257** - FF13 678
Satay seller Oil/canvas (30x40.5cm 11x15in) Singapore 2000

KOENIGER Walter 1881-1943 [58]

$2 600 - €2 867 - **£1 760** - FF18 808
Winter Dawn Oil/canvas (51x61cm 20x24in) New-York 2000

$500 - €485 - **£309** - FF3 179
Winter Snow Oil/board (27x22cm 11x9in) Englewood NJ 1999

KOEPCKE XIX [1]

$12 922 - €12 782 - **£8 057** - FF83 847
Das Belvedere auf dem Pfingstberg in Potsdam, Projekt Öl/Leinwand (62x96cm 24x37in) Berlin 1999

KOEPKE Robert 1893-1968 [33]

$273 - €256 - **£165** - FF1 676
Zinnien und Mohnkapseln Öl/Karton (20x20cm 7x7in) Bremen 1999

KOERNER Ernst Carl 1846-1927 [63]

$6 800 - €7 049 - **£4 080** - FF46 240
Jerusalem Olio/tela (100x50cm 39x19in) Venezia 2000

$645 - €716 - **£448** - FF4 695
Uferszene am Nil Öl/Leinwand/Karton (20x40cm 7x15in) Köln 2001

KOERNER Jean Jules 1833-1909 [3]

$602 - €656 - **£397** - FF4 300
Brick mixte vu par le trois-quart avant Aquarelle/papier (31x22.5cm 12x8in) Paris 2000

KOERNER William H. Dethlef 1878-1938 [35]

$21 000 - €17 942 - **£12 606** - FF117 692
The Wrangler Oil/canvas (61x91.5cm 24x36in) New-York 1998

KOESTER Alexandre Max 1864-1932 [335]

$38 650 - €36 336 - **£23 400** - FF238 350
Enten am Ufer Öl/Leinwand (50x72cm 19x28in) Wien 1999

$6 951 - €6 647 - **£4 232** - FF43 600
Schlossgartenbrunnen in Karlsruhe Öl/Leinwand (33x24cm 12x9in) Stuttgart 1999

$1 427 - €1 235 - **£866** - FF8 104
Enten auf offenem Wasser Pencil/paper (12.2x21cm 4x8in) München 1998

KOETS Roelof I c.1592-1655 [8]

$8 554 - €9 447 - **£5 928** - FF61 971
Stilleben mit Weintrauben und einem Korb mit Granatäpeln Oil/panel (44x65cm 17x25in) Wien 2001

KOETS Roelof II c.1655-1725 [6]

$13 000 - €12 994 - **£7 941** - FF85 234
Grapes on a Stone Ledge Oil/panel (42x64.5cm 16x25in) New-York 2000

KOGAN Moissey 1879-1942 [91]

$2 149 - €2 147 - **£1 344** - FF14 086
Stehender weiblicher Akt Bronze (29.5x9.3x9.5cm 11x3x3in) Hamburg 1999

$560 - €481 - **£337** - FF3 152
Mädchenakt, sitzend Red chalk/paper (30x23cm 11x9in) Hamburg 1998

$465 - €460 - **£290** - FF3 018
Zwei hockende Mädchenakte Linocut (24.8x18.8cm 9x7in) Berlin 1999

KOGAN Nina Osipovna 1887-1942 [70]

$3 500 - €3 628 - **£2 100** - FF23 800
Senza titolo Tecnica mista/cartone (35x23.5cm 13x9in) Milano 1999

$1 371 - €1 278 - **£846** - FF8 384
Suprematistische Komposition Indian ink (29x20.2cm 11x7in) Hamburg 1999

KOGANOWSKY Jakob 1874-1926 [32]

$617 - €727 - **£434** - FF4 767
Am Wienfluss Öl/Karton (50x40cm 19x15in) Wien 2000

KÖGEL Benno 1892-1969 [1]

$2 146 - €2 250 - **£1 414** - FF14 757
Katzenidyll Oil/panel (21x26cm 8x10in) Köln 2000

KOGELNIK Kiki 1935-1997 [31]

$14 263 - €12 349 - **£8 653** - FF81 005
«Solo in Grau» Acryl/Leinwand (70x100cm 27x39in) Wien 1998

$2 817 - €3 270 - **£1 980** - FF21 451
«Robots» Indian ink (58.5x39.5cm 23x15in) Wien 2001

$1 324 - €1 453 - **£880** - FF9 534
Multi Farbserigraphie (71x50cm 27x19in) Wien 2000

KOGEVINAS Lykourgos / Lic 1887-1940 [7]

$2 295 - €2 553 - **£1 530** - FF16 745
Greek harbour Oil/canvas (33.5x40.5cm 13x15in) Athens 2000

$3 933 - €3 331 - **£2 294** - FF21 850
Mount Athos Gouache/paper (23.5x34.5cm 9x13in) Athens 1998

KÖGL Benedikt Paul, Benno 1892-1973 [93]

$1 081 - €1 278 - **£766** - FF8 384
Spielende Katzen Oil/panel (9x12cm 3x4in) Ahlden 2000

KOGLER Peter 1959 [29]

$1 001 - €1 163 - **£691** - FF7 627
Ohne Titel Watercolour (50x70cm 19x27in) Wien 2000

$877 - €872 - **£530** - FF5 720
Ohne Titel Lithographie (70x50cm 27x19in) Wien 2000

K

KOGYO Terazaki 1866-1919 **[2]**
⟋ $12 250 - €11 948 - **£7 500** - FF78 375
Buddha Tree and Cranes Drawing (167x63.5cm 65x25in) Tokyo 1999

KOGYO Tsukioka 1869-1927 **[15]**
⟋ $20 000 - €19 374 - **£12 474** - FF127 084
Zeppo saiu sansui zu (Landscape with Rain from the Top of Mountain) Ink (133.5x56cm 52x22in) New-York 1999
▥ $2 634 - €2 556 - **£1 640** - FF16 769
Nôgaku zue (Bilder aus Nô-Strücken) zokuhen (Ergänzung) Woodcut in colors (24x36cm 9x14in) Köln 1999

KOHL Kliment / Clemens 1754-1807 **[2]**
▥ $807 - €920 - **£563** - FF6 037
Das Schloss im Garten zu Wörlitz, nach G.M.Kraus Radierung (33.5x47cm 13x18in) Berlin 2001

KOHL Ludwig 1746-1821 **[10]**
⟋ $3 468 - €3 280 - **£2 160** - FF21 516
Interior of a Corinthian Temple Pencil (59.7x75cm 23x29in) Praha 1999

KOHL Pierre Ernest 1897-1987 **[35]**
⌕ $575 - €534 - **£359** - FF3 500
Femme en bleu Huile/toile (81x60cm 31x23in) Paris 1999

KOHL Robert 1891-1944 **[20]**
⌕ $6 170 - €7 267 - **£4 340** - FF47 670
Blumenstilleben Öl/Leinwand (75x94cm 29x37in) Wien 2000

KOHLBRENNER Beat 1948 **[2]**
⌖ $2 399 - €2 199 - **£1 466** - FF14 424
Kopf, Nr. Q Sculpture bois (37x20x17cm 14x7x6in) Zürich 1999

KOHLER Albert Stefan 1883-1946 **[10]**
⌕ $2 965 - €3 323 - **£2 065** - FF21 800
Château Brabant Öl/Leinwand (61x74.5cm 24x29in) Berlin 2001

KOHLER Fritz 1887-1971 **[60]**
⌕ $545 - €613 - **£375** - FF4 024
Winterwald mit Jäger bei Tauwetter Öl/Leinwand (60x80cm 23x31in) Bremen 2000

KOHLER Gustav 1859-1922 **[10]**
⌕ $4 624 - €4 373 - **£2 880** - FF28 688
Still Life Oil/canvas (85x110cm 33x43in) Praha 2001
⌕ $1 540 - €1 329 - **£917** - FF8 719
Bauer in Tracht Oil/panel (18x14cm 7x5in) München 1998

KÖHLER Mela 1885-1960 **[4]**
▥ $1 034 - €872 - **£610** - FF5 718
«Mode» Farblithographie (19x16cm 7x6in) Wien 1998

KOHLHOFF Walter 1906-1981 **[7]**
⟋ $900 - €1 022 - **£625** - FF6 707
Lastschiff auf dem Landwehrkanal in Berlin Aquarell/Papier (39x58cm 15x22in) Berlin 2001

KOHLHOFF Wilhelm 1893-1971 **[98]**
⌕ $5 223 - €5 113 - **£3 214** - FF33 539
Villa am Meer im Mondenschein Öl/Leinwand (85.5x65cm 33x25in) Bremen 2000
⟋ $1 118 - €1 227 - **£759** - FF8 049
Südliche Hafenarbeiter Aquarell (38x49.1cm 14x19in) Berlin 2000

KOHLMANN Ejnar 1888-1968 **[134]**
⌕ $725 - €774 - **£492** - FF5 074
Tjäderpar Oil/canvas (50x61cm 19x24in) Helsinki 2001
⌕ $360 - €336 - **£222** - FF2 202
Kustlandskap Oil/canvas (35x23cm 13x9in) Stockholm 1999

KOHLMEYER Ida 1912-1997 **[51]**
⌕ $14 000 - €13 049 - **£8 461** - FF85 594
Abstract Composition Oil/masonite (200x93cm 79x37in) New-Orleans LA 1999
⌕ $1 568 - €1 499 - **£955** - FF9 836
Cloistered No.10 Oil/canvas (68x68cm 27x27in) New-Orleans LA 1999
⟋ $1 700 - €1 453 - **£998** - FF9 529
«79-2» Pastel/paper (76x55cm 30x22in) New-Orleans LA 1998
▥ $650 - €695 - **£428** - FF4 562
Markings Serigraph (76x101cm 30x40in) New-Orleans LA 2000

KOHLSCHEIN Josef II 1884-1958 **[14]**
⌕ $1 289 - €1 534 - **£919** - FF10 061
Eifellandschaft mit blühendem Ginster Öl/Leinwand (72x75cm 28x29in) Köln 2000

KOHLSTÄDT Fritz 1921 **[14]**
⌕ $1 496 - €1 662 - **£1 043** - FF10 900
«Vorfrühling auf der Reutlinger Alb» Öl/Leinwand (80x100cm 31x39in) Stuttgart 2001

KOHRL Ludwig Dominik 1858-1927 **[18]**
⌕ $479 - €460 - **£297** - FF3 018
Junge Bayerin in festlicher Tracht Oil/panel (24.5x17cm 9x6in) Ahlden 1999

KOIDE Narashige 1887-1931 **[1]**
⟋ $3 200 - €3 753 - **£2 283** - FF24 615
Village Street Watercolour (20x31cm 7x12in) New-York 2000

KOISO Ryohei 1903-1988 **[8]**
⌕ $122 500 - €119 482 - **£75 000** - FF783 750
Two Ladies Oil/canvas (72.5x60.5cm 28x23in) Tokyo 1999
▥ $6 468 - €6 309 - **£3 960** - FF41 382
Working Woman Etching (37.5x22.5cm 14x8in) Tokyo 1999

KOISTINEN Unto 1917-1994 **[151]**
⌕ $3 600 - €4 036 - **£2 445** - FF26 476
Sittande dam Oil/canvas (52x37cm 20x14in) Helsinki 2000
⌕ $2 868 - €2 691 - **£1 772** - FF17 651
Strand Oil/panel (28x40cm 11x15in) Helsinki 1999
⟋ $1 640 - €1 850 - **£1 152** - FF12 135
«Prana, ihmisen olemuksen ydin No.3» Indian ink (50x37cm 19x14in) Helsinki 2001
▥ $345 - €353 - **£216** - FF2 316
Mor och dotter Etching (35x30cm 13x11in) Helsinki 2000

KOITSU Tsuchiya 1870-1949 **[20]**
▥ $150 - €168 - **£104** - FF1 101
Sunset Glow at Seta Bay Woodcut (38x26cm 15x10in) Cleveland OH 2001

KOIVISTO Aukusti 1886-1962 **[30]**
⌕ $457 - €538 - **£317** - FF3 530
Bron Oil/canvas (50x70cm 19x27in) Helsinki 2000

KOIVU Rudolf 1890-1946 **[17]**
⌕ $1 435 - €1 208 - **£847** - FF7 925
Landskap med hus Oil/canvas (75x110cm 29x43in) Stockholm 1998

$1 167 - €1 261 - £807 - FF8 274
Glöm inte mig Mixed media (17x36cm 6x14in)
Helsinki 2001

KOJEWNIKOW Anatoly Iwanowitsch 1917 [21]
$533 - €461 - £316 - FF3 022
Hafen am Fluss Öl/Karton (13x26cm 5x10in)
Hildrizhausen 1998

KOJIMA Torajiro 1881-1929 [1]
$11 000 - €10 656 - £6 860 - FF69 896
Garden Oil/canvas (80.5x65.5cm 31x25in) New-York
1999

KOJIMA Zenzaburo 1893-1962 [3]
$151 900 - €148 158 - £93 000 - FF971 850
Roses Oil/canvas (45.5x37.5cm 17x14in) Tokyo 1999
$20 000 - €19 374 - £12 474 - FF127 084
Rafu to sammenkyo (Nude and Vanity Mirror)
Oil/canvas (33.5x26cm 13x10in) New-York 1999

KOK Johannes Cornelis 1826-1890 [1]
$4 127 - €4 084 - £2 526 - FF26 789
**View of a Town with numerous Townsfolk on a
Quay/Town/Woodland** Oil/panel (22x26cm 8x10in)
Amsterdam 2000

KOKAN Shiba 1747-1818 [4]
$19 000 - €20 996 - £13 176 - FF137 725
Meeting of Japan, China and the West Ink
(102x49.5cm 40x19in) New-York 2001
$3 250 - €2 809 - £1 929 - FF18 426
Seiyu Ryotan Woodcut (26x18cm 10x7in) New-York
1998

KOKEN Gustav 1850-1910 [14]
$1 656 - €1 534 - £1 027 - FF10 061
Getreideernte Öl/Leinwand (38x57cm 14x22in)
Stuttgart 1999

KOKIETEK Tadeusz 1920-1982 [3]
$2 234 - €2 421 - £1 547 - FF15 881
Attaque des hussards Aquarelle (69.5x98cm
27x38in) Warszawa 2001

KOKINE Mikhail 1921 [112]
$742 - €694 - £450 - FF4 550
Sword Lilies in the Garden Oil/canvas (73x60cm
28x23in) Fernhurst, Haslemere, Surrey 1999

KOKKEN Henri 1860-1941 [26]
$1 147 - €1 115 - £711 - FF7 317
Vase aux roses Huile/toile (49x69cm 19x27in)
Antwerpen 1999
$694 - €793 - £489 - FF5 203
Nature morte aux fleurs et aux fruits Huile/pan-
neau (28x29cm 11x11in) Antwerpen 2001

KOKO Demeter 1891-1929 [15]
$3 831 - €4 506 - £2 746 - FF29 555
Wandernde Zigeuner Öl/Karton (34x48.5cm
13x19in) Wien 2001

KOKO-MIKOLETSKY Friedrich Albin 1887-1981
[61]
$925 - €799 - £557 - FF5 243
«Ohwieshorn 2558 m» Oil/panel (70x100cm
27x39in) Wien 1999

KOKOSCHKA Oskar 1886-1980 [1072]
$410 312 - €472 399 - £280 000 - FF3 098 732
London with the Houses of Parliament Oil/canvas
(92x137cm 36x53in) London 2000
$132 480 - €123 453 - £80 000 - FF809 800
Carl Leo Schmidt Oil/canvas (98x68cm 38x26in)
London 1998

$8 844 - €9 702 - £6 007 - FF63 640
Schiffe in der Bucht von Neapel Chalks/paper
(23.3x27.2cm 9x10in) Berlin 2000
$450 - €511 - £308 - FF3 353
Das jüngste Gericht Lithographie (32x28.5cm
12x11in) Hamburg 2000

KOLAR Jiri 1914 [446]
$1 011 - €957 - £630 - FF6 275
Kliny Collage/panneau (50x35cm 19x13in) Praha 2000
$750 - €777 - £450 - FF5 100
Faust a Marketka Tecnica mista (40x30cm 15x11in)
Vercelli 1999
$500 - €518 - £300 - FF3 400
Van Dyck - Portratit d'Alexandre Triest Collage
(33x26cm 12x10in) Milano 2000
$197 - €184 - £121 - FF1 207
Venus, nach Botticelli Offset (66.5x26.8cm 26x10in)
Hamburg 1999

KÖLARE Nils 1930 [78]
$1 011 - €949 - £625 - FF6 222
Komposition I Acrylic/canvas (80x35cm 31x13in)
Stockholm 1999
$632 - €601 - £384 - FF3 940
Geometrisk komposition Oil/panel (40x35cm
15x13in) Stockholm 1999

KOLB Alois 1875-1942 [53]
$102 - €118 - £70 - FF771
**Sitzender weiblicher Akt, bei Lampenschein
lesend** Radierung (39x28cm 15x11in) Heidelberg 2000

KOLBE Carl Wilhelm I 1757-1835 [181]
$386 - €460 - £275 - FF3 018
Die Kuh im Schilfe Radierung (30.3x41.2cm
11x16in) Berlin 2000

KOLBE Ernst 1876-1945 [44]
$440 - €511 - £309 - FF3 353
**Hafen mit Segelschiffen an der pommerschen
Ostseeküste** Öl/Leinwand (81x69cm 31x27in) Berlin
2001

KOLBE Georg 1877-1947 [270]
$117 012 - €101 694 - £70 505 - FF667 067
Aufsteigender Jüngling Bronze (247x87x94cm
97x34x37in) Berlin 1998
$29 980 - €29 655 - £18 693 - FF194 526
Porträt Max Liebermann Bronze (30x16x20cm
11x6x7in) Berlin 1999
$4 223 - €4 076 - £2 666 - FF26 734
Kniender Akt, den Kopf am Boden Aquarelle
(31x29.5cm 12x11in) Bern 1999
$378 - €378 - £236 - FF2 481
Hockender nach rechts geneigter Akt Radierung
(43.5x34.6cm 17x13in) Hamburg 1999

KOLBE Heinrich Christoph 1771-1836 [8]
$42 400 - €45 735 - £28 500 - FF300 000
**Portrait de trois jeunes hommes, l'un en unifor-
me de hussard** Huile/toile (105.5x128cm 41x50in)
Paris 2000

KOLESNIKOV Ivan Feodorovich 1887-1929 [4]
$4 545 - €4 368 - £2 800 - FF28 653
Still Life with Iznik Vase and Peacock Feathers
Oil/canvas/board (73x60cm 28x23in) London 1999
$3 000 - €3 220 - £2 007 - FF21 123
Winter Landscape with Figure Gouache/panel
(22x28cm 9x11in) Cedar-Falls IA 2000

K

KOLESNIKOV Sergei 1889-c.1930 **[36]**

🖼 **$3 309** - €2 820 - **£1 972** - FF18 500
L'église orthodoxe d'Iskov où le Tsar Nicolas II à abdiqué le 15 mars Huile/toile (75x94cm 29x37in) Paris 1998

🖼 **$2 759** - €2 652 - **£1 700** - FF17 396
The Hunter and his Dog Oil/cardboard (24x28cm 9x11in) London 1999

✏ **$1 623** - €1 372 - **£965** - FF9 000
Vue d'istambul sous la lune Aquarelle, gouache/papier (22x34cm 8x13in) Vittel 1998

KOLESNIKOV Stepan Feodorovich 1879-1955 **[9]**

🖼 **$2 500** - €2 672 - **£1 699** - FF17 524
Stones Oil/board (43.5x52cm 17x20in) Kiev 2001

KÖLIG Anton 1886-1950 **[28]**

🖼 **$246 800** - €290 690 - **£173 600** - FF1 906 800
Begrüssung Oil/canvas (180x104cm 70x40in) Wien 2000

🖼 **$38 725** - €37 239 - **£23 860** - FF244 275
Liegender Akt mit Krug Öl/Leinwand (79x95.5cm 31x37in) München 1999

✏ **$3 096** - €2 907 - **£1 912** - FF19 068
Zwei liegende männliche Akte Pencil/paper (35x49cm 13x19in) Wien 1999

KOLITZ Louis 1845-1914 **[13]**

🖼 **$6 863** - €7 794 - **£4 800** - FF51 124
Louise, gennant Wiwi (portrait of Louise, also known as Wiwi) Oil/canvas (100.5x75cm 39x29in) London 2001

KOLLAR François 1904-1979 **[95]**

📷 **$591** - €512 - **£358** - FF3 356
Hochzeitskleid von Elsa Schiaparelli Photograph (29.4x21.1cm 11x8in) München 1998

KØLLE Claus Anton 1827-1872 **[38]**

🖼 **$393** - €336 - **£235** - FF2 201
Naturstudie med skraeppeblade Oil/board (27x36cm 10x14in) Viby J, Arhus 1998

KOLLE Helmut von Hügel 1899-1931 **[20]**

🖼 **$10 954** - €11 760 - **£7 332** - FF77 139
Herr in der Bar Öl/Leinwand (78.2x50cm 30x19in) Hamburg 2000

🖼 **$4 087** - €3 835 - **£2 525** - FF25 154
Jockey und Pferd Öl/Leinwand (27x22cm 10x8in) Stuttgart 1999

✏ **$523** - €562 - **£350** - FF3 689
Zouave assis, profil Indian ink/paper (30.9x22.7cm 12x8in) Köln 2000

KOLLER Ben-Ami 1948 **[47]**

✏ **$544** - €610 - **£378** - FF4 000
Sans titre Crayon (48x133cm 18x52in) Versailles 2001

KOLLER Julius 1939 **[3]**

🖼 **$3 270** - €3 068 - **£2 020** - FF20 123
Transformacia Mixed media/panel (61x61cm 24x24in) Stuttgart 1999

KOLLER Oskar 1925 **[41]**

✏ **$386** - €460 - **£275** - FF3 018
Kubische Häuser Collage (28.5x29cm 11x14in) Köln 2000

KOLLER Rudolf Johann 1828-1905 **[103]**

🖼 **$16 665** - €19 819 - **£11 877** - FF130 005
Kühe und Wäscherin am Bach Öl/Leinwand (142x114cm 55x44in) Zürich 2000

🖼 **$9 637** - €9 380 - **£5 922** - FF61 531
Bauernmädchen mit zwei Kühen am Seeufer Öl/Leinwand (45x60cm 17x23in) Zürich 1999

🖼 **$2 698** - €2 626 - **£1 658** - FF17 228
Fliehendes Pferd Öl/Leinwand (47x33.5cm 18x13in) Zürich 1999

KOLLER Wilhelm 1829-1884 **[11]**

🖼 **$8 218** - €7 846 - **£5 135** - FF51 465
Das neue Schmuckstück, junge Frau in Boudoir sitzend vor Tischspiegel Oil/panel (80x62cm 31x24in) Zofingen 1999

KOLLER-PINELL Broncia 1863-1934 **[103]**

🖼 **$3 289** - €3 270 - **£1 989** - FF21 451
Stilleben mit Ananas Öl/Leinwand (45.5x40cm 17x15in) Wien 2000

🖼 **$2 547** - €2 181 - **£1 491** - FF14 307
Selbstporträt Öl/Leinwand (38x38cm 14x14in) Wien 1998

📖 **$400** - €363 - **£250** - FF2 383
Mödling-Breite Föhre Woodcut in colors (37x39cm 14x15in) Wien 1999

KÖLLIKER David 1807-1875 **[3]**

✏ **$4 818** - €4 690 - **£2 961** - FF30 765
Muraltengut, mit Blick auf den Zürichsee Gouache/papier (29.5x42cm 11x16in) Zürich 1999

KOLLMANN Karl Ivanovitch 1788-1846 **[15]**

🖼 **$9 248** - €10 746 - **£6 500** - FF70 487
Russian Types Miniature (6.5x5cm 2x1in) London 2001

✏ **$4 980** - €5 786 - **£3 500** - FF37 954
Russian Genre Scenes Watercolour (6x8cm 2x3in) London 2001

KOLLWITZ Käthe 1867-1945 **[1890]**

🗿 **$11 062** - €10 737 - **£6 889** - FF70 431
Abschied Bronze (17.5x9x10.3cm 6x3x4in) Berlin 1999

✏ **$14 608** - €12 270 - **£8 587** - FF80 484
«Zu Opfer» Charcoal/paper (50x40cm 19x15in) Stuttgart 1998

📖 **$1 000** - €1 135 - **£684** - FF7 448
Die Witwe I, from «Sieben Holzschnitte zum Kreig» Woodcut (37.5x25cm 14x9in) New-York 2000

KOLMSPERGER Waldemar I 1852-1943 **[13]**

🖼 **$1 014** - €1 125 - **£702** - FF7 378
«Der Künstler mit seinen beiden Söhnen» Öl/Karton (77x52.5cm 30x20in) Kempten 2001

✏ **$775** - €818 - **£512** - FF5 366
Entwurf zum Deckengemälde, Begrüssung des Heilige Hubertus Pencil (60x43cm 23x16in) Kempten 2000

KOLMSPERGER Waldemar II 1881-1954 **[23]**

✏ **$339** - €358 - **£224** - FF2 347
Zwei Damen in Tracht Red chalk/paper (38x33cm 14x12in) Kempten 2000

KOLNIK Arthur 1890-1972 **[15]**

🖼 **$2 400** - €2 488 - **£1 581** - FF16 322
Landscape in Provence Oil/cardboard (52x68cm 20x26in) Herzelia-Pituah 2000

KOLOZSVARY Lajos 1871-1937 **[36]**

🖼 **$811** - €818 - **£506** - FF5 366
Zecherpaar im Weinkeller Öl/Leinwand (52x42cm 20x16in) Erlangen 2000

🖼 **$443** - €409 - **£275** - FF2 683
Die Mostprobe Oil/panel (32x22cm 12x8in) Rudolstadt-Thüringen 1999

KOLOZSVARY Sigismond 1899-1983 **[321]**

🖼 **$1 167** - €1 372 - **£809** - FF9 000
Courbe dans l'existence Huile/toile (97x130cm 38x51in) Paris 2000

$1 102 - €1 296 - **£764** - FF8 500
L'étoile du berger Huile/toile (90x116cm 35x45in)
Paris 2000

$203 - €229 - **£142** - FF1 500
Composition Aquarelle/papier (13x23cm 5x9in) Paris
2001

KOLSKI Gan 1899-1932 [3]
$900 - €865 - **£550** - FF5 672
Provincetown, Mass Woodcut (20x25cm 8x10in)
Provincetown MA 1999

KOLSTØ Fredrik 1860-1945 [18]
$25 980 - €22 120 - **£15 520** - FF145 100
Lirekassegutt med ape Oil/canvas (166x100cm
65x39in) Oslo 1999
$8 400 - €9 988 - **£5 984** - FF65 520
Vinterfiske fra land Oil/canvas (68x125cm 26x49in)
Oslo 2000

KOMAROMI-KACZ Endre 1880-1969 [76]
$650 - €707 - **£446** - FF4 640
The tired Musician Oil/canvas (79x59cm 31x23in) St.
Louis MO 2001

KOMJATI Julius 1894-1958 [20]
$112 - €111 - **£70** - FF729
Landscape with Trees Etching (19.5x27cm 7x10in)
London 1999

KOMLOSY Irma 1850-1894 [2]
$3 666 - €4 360 - **£2 616** - FF28 602
Dahlien Oil/panel (54x35cm 21x13in) Wien 2000

KOMPOCZI-BALOGH Endre 1911-1977 [10]
$1 016 - €870 - **£600** - FF5 708
Summer Flowers in a Vase Oil/canvas (62x80cm
24x31in) London 1998

KONARSKI Jan 1900 [5]
$5 378 - €4 925 - **£3 278** - FF32 304
Departure for Hunting Oil/canvas (49x61cm
19x24in) Warszawa 1999

KONARZ-KONARZEWSKI Stanislaw 1914 [1]
$5 944 - €5 880 - **£3 706** - FF38 569
In der Synagoge Aquarell/Papier (48.5x36.5cm
19x14in) Ahlden 1999

KONCHALOVSKY Piotr Petrovich 1876-1956 [14]
$194 796 - €187 207 - **£120 000** - FF1 227 996
Portrait of a Frenchman Oil/canvas (114x129cm
44x50in) London 1999
$10 551 - €10 140 - **£6 500** - FF66 516
Young Breton Girl in traditionnal Costume
Oil/canvas (91x65.5cm 35x25in) London 1999

KONDEK Waclaw Jozef 1917-1976 [5]
$175 - €199 - **£121** - FF1 306
Ballade sur une vieille maison I Lithographie
(50x70cm 19x27in) Lódz 2000

KONDRACKI Henry 1953 [3]
$4 930 - €4 685 - **£3 000** - FF30 733
Cattle Watering Oil/canvas/board (38.5x56cm
15x22in) London 1999

KONDRATENKO Gavriil Pavlovich 1854-1924 [22]
$4 869 - €4 680 - **£3 000** - FF30 699
Street Scene in Italy Oil/canvas (32x54cm 12x21in)
London 1999

KONEBERG Johann Michael XVIII [4]
$1 126 - €1 308 - **£792** - FF8 580
Christus an der Geisselsäule Öl/Kupfer
(17.5x14.5cm 6x5in) Wien 2001

KONECNY Josef 1907-1989 [39]
$1 251 - €1 431 - **£860** - FF9 390
Blumenstilleben Öl/Karton (71x53cm 27x20in)
München 2000
$2 086 - €1 787 - **£1 232** - FF11 721
«Blumenstilleben mit Insekten» Oil/panel
(32.5x25cm 12x9in) München 1998

KONGSRUD Anders 1866-1938 [10]
$4 620 - €5 494 - **£3 291** - FF36 036
Dompaper i nysne Oil/canvas (50x69cm 19x27in)
Oslo 2000

KONI Nicolaus 1911 [6]
$2 200 - €2 541 - **£1 540** - FF16 671
Standing Figure of a Woman Bronze (H71cm
H28in) Delray-Beach FL 2001

KONICEK Oldrich 1886-1932 [29]
$622 - €578 - **£387** - FF3 790
To Olsany Oil/panel (61x77cm 24x30in) Praha 1999

KÖNIG Franz Niklaus 1765-1832 [72]
$3 236 - €2 792 - **£1 944** - FF18 315
Bildnisse der Schwestern Öl/Kupfer (16.5x13.5cm
6x5in) Bern 1998
$2 848 - €2 477 - **£1 716** - FF16 247
Une fête civique dans le Canton de Vaud
Aquarell, Gouache/Papier (13x20.6cm 5x8in) Bern 1998
$173 - €162 - **£106** - FF1 063
Berne/Argovie/Lucerne/Ohne Titel Lithographie
(24.8x19cm 9x7in) Bern 1999

KÖNIG Friedrich 1857-1941 [43]
$10 847 - €12 385 - **£7 647** - FF81 240
Amazonenkampf Öl/Leinwand (157x106cm 61x41in)
Bern 2001
$1 656 - €1 892 - **£1 166** - FF12 412
«Hexentanz» Öl/Leinwand (109x109cm 42x42in)
Bern 2001
$716 - €716 - **£448** - FF4 695
Der Garten (Frühling) Farblithographie (30.3x29cm
11x11in) Hamburg 1999

KÖNIG Fritz 1924 [66]
$25 845 - €25 565 - **£16 115** - FF167 695
Zwei VIII Bronze (168x95x26cm 66x37x10in) Berlin
1999
$9 693 - €9 408 - **£6 035** - FF61 711
Zwei V (Paolo und Francesca) Bronze
(61x35.7x14.3cm 24x14x5in) Berlin 1999
$739 - €869 - **£529** - FF5 701
Ohne Titel Charcoal/paper (44.5x57cm 17x22in)
Dettelbach-Effeldorf 2001

KÖNIG Hugo 1856-1899 [5]
$3 500 - €3 274 - **£2 116** - FF21 474
Picking Wildflowers Oil/panel (42.5x30.5cm
16x12in) New-York 1999

KÖNIG Johann 1586-1642 [18]
$6 524 - €6 102 - **£4 000** - FF40 028
The Temptation of Christ Oil/copper (13x9.5cm
5x3in) London 1998

KÖNIG von Leo 1871-1944 [33]
$11 978 - €12 271 - **£7 392** - FF80 493
Vor dem Tanz Öl/Leinwand (158.5x92cm 62x36in)
Düsseldorf 2000
$4 869 - €5 113 - **£3 070** - FF33 539
Porträt Generaloberst Hans von Seeckt
Öl/Leinwand (74.5x59cm 29x23in) Stuttgart 2000

KÖNIG-INGENHEIM Marie 1849-? [4]
$1 388 - €1 599 - **£948** - FF10 487
Stürmische Küstenlandschaft bei Abbazzia
Öl/Leinwand (48x70cm 18x27in) Wien 2000

KONIJNENBURG van Willem 1868-1943 **[111]**

☞ **$4 322** - €4 538 - **£2 725** - FF29 766
Bridge crossing the Thames, Londen Oil/canvas (60x90cm 23x35in) Amsterdam 2000

✎ **$222** - €199 - **£133** - FF1 303
A Head of a Man Charcoal (54.5x45cm 21x17in) Amsterdam 1998

KONINCK Christian II c.1600-1642/43 **[1]**

☞ **$44 689** - €44 210 - **£27 869** - FF290 000
Paysage de port fluvial animé de personnages Huile/toile (47x27cm 18x10in) Rouen 1999

KONINCK de Daniel 1668-c.1730 **[8]**

☞ **$27 805** - €26 319 - **£17 289** - FF172 642
Portrait of a Man, Bust length, wearing a Chain of Office on a Cloak Oil/panel (87.5x70.5cm 34x27in) Amsterdam 1999

KONINCK Jacob c.1616-1708 **[5]**

☞ **$14 251** - €16 186 - **£10 000** - FF106 175
An Open Landscape with Huntsmen on a Track before a Village Oil/canvas (52.5x67cm 20x26in) London 2001

KONINCK Philips 1619-1688 **[29]**

☞ **$23 083** - €21 781 - **£14 241** - FF142 876
Isaac Meeting Rebecca Oil/canvas (146x172cm 57x67in) Amsterdam 1999

☞ **$30 000** - €35 334 - **£20 748** - FF231 777
Three Men at Dinner with a Servant Nearby Oil/canvas (54x60.5cm 21x23in) New-York 2000

☞ **$16 113** - €15 824 - **£10 000** - FF103 799
Doctor in his Study Oil/panel (23.5x22cm 9x8in) London 1999

✎ **$7 359** - €6 350 - **£4 440** - FF41 654
Zadok the priest anointing Solomon King (1 Kings 1,38-39) Ink (13.7x24.1cm 5x9in) Amsterdam 1998

KONINCK Salomon 1609-1656 **[17]**

☞ **$48 933** - €45 767 - **£30 000** - FF300 210
The Descent from the Cross Oil/canvas (107x88.5cm 42x34in) London 1998

▥ **$1 200** - €1 403 - **£843** - FF9 202
Man with a Penknife, Shapening a Quill Etching (17x13cm 6x5in) New-York 2000

KONING Arnold Hendrik 1860-1945 **[9]**

☞ **$1 547** - €1 841 - **£1 103** - FF12 074
Bewaldete Berglandschaft Öl/Leinwand (50x70cm 19x27in) Köln 2000

KONING Edzard 1869-1954 **[17]**

☞ **$3 152** - €3 403 - **£2 155** - FF22 324
Onder moeder's paraplu Oil/canvas (40x61cm 15x24in) Amsterdam 2001

KONING Elisabeth Joanna 1816-1888 **[5]**

☞ **$2 114** - €2 269 - **£1 414** - FF14 883
Still life with an orange Oil/panel (18x24cm 7x9in) Amsterdam 2000

KONINGH de Arie Ketting 1815-1867 **[8]**

☞ **$5 775** - €6 445 - **£3 579** - FF35 719
Woman Riding a Donkey in an Italianate Landscape Oil/panel (50x42.5cm 19x16in) Amsterdam 1998

KONINGH de Leendert, Jnr. 1810-1887 **[13]**

☞ **$6 844** - €7 381 - **£4 594** - FF48 415
Kortspelare Oil/panel (55x66cm 21x25in) Stockholm 2000

KONINGH de Leendert, Snr. 1777-1849 **[39]**

☞ **$3 284** - €3 630 - **£2 278** - FF23 812
A Milkmaid walking along a waterway Oil/panel (40x51.5cm 15x20in) Amsterdam 2001

☞ **$7 613** - €7 994 - **£4 800** - FF52 438
Shipping Offshore in Breezy Weather Oil/panel (29.5x41.5cm 11x16in) London 2000

KONINGSBRUGGEN van Rob 1948 **[12]**

☞ **$19 530** - €22 689 - **£13 725** - FF148 830
Untitled Oil/canvas (60x60cm 23x23in) Amsterdam 2001

KONINGSVELD van Jacobus 1824-1866 **[6]**

☞ **$8 642** - €9 076 - **£5 468** - FF59 532
The Little Eavesdroppers Oil/canvas (50x60cm 19x23in) Amsterdam 2000

KONO Miçao 1900-1979 **[127]**

☞ **$7 045** - €7 622 - **£4 825** - FF50 000
Femme alanguie Huile/toile (41.5x59.5cm 16x23in) Granville 2001

☞ **$5 208** - €5 336 - **£3 213** - FF35 000
La sieste Huile/toile (35x27cm 13x10in) Troyes 2000

✎ **$196** - €168 - **£118** - FF1 100
Jeunes femmes au chat Crayon/papier (20x17cm 7x6in) Paris 1998

KONOPA Rudolf 1864-1938 **[27]**

✎ **$514** - €581 - **£347** - FF3 813
Frauen am Feld, vorne zwei Wiegenkinder Mischtechnik/Papier (61x79cm 24x31in) Wien 2000

KONSTANTINOPOLSKI Adolf M. 1923 **[5]**

☞ **$5 394** - €6 134 - **£3 700** - FF40 234
The Funeral of Stalin Oil/canvas (228.5x396cm 89x155in) London 2000

KONTI Isidore 1862-1938 **[25]**

⚒ **$1 250** - €1 342 - **£836** - FF8 804
Allegorical Figure, a Bookend Bronze (H25cm H10in) Bolton MA 2000

KONTOPOULOS Alecos, Alex 1905-1975 **[6]**

☞ **$6 594** - €7 592 - **£4 500** - FF49 801
Geometric Composition Mixed media/board (32.5x21.5cm 12x8in) London 2000

KONTULY Béla 1904-1983 **[5]**

☞ **$1 665** - €1 859 - **£1 162** - FF12 195
Naakt Huile/toile (80x60cm 31x23in) Antwerpen 2001

KOOGH van der Adrianus 1792-1831 **[6]**

☞ **$6 268** - €5 301 - **£3 748** - FF34 770
A Wooded Landscape with a Cowherd and Cattle by a Cottage Oil/panel (56x74.5cm 22x29in) Amsterdam 1998

KOOL Sipke, Spkee 1836-1902 **[16]**

☞ **$4 753** - €4 991 - **£3 007** - FF32 742
The Morning Coffee Oil/panel (38x50cm 14x19in) Amsterdam 2000

☞ **$1 219** - €1 361 - **£815** - FF8 929
Peasant Woman Preparing a Meal Oil/panel (20.5x27cm 8x10in) Amsterdam 2000

KOOL Willem Gillesz. 1608-1666 **[11]**

☞ **$18 912** - €21 474 - **£13 141** - FF140 863
Eisvergnügen vor einer holländischen Kleinstadt Oil/panel (45x65cm 17x25in) Köln 2001

☞ **$8 149** - €7 714 - **£5 067** - FF50 602
Beach Scene at Egmond aan Zee with Fishermen selling Fish Oil/panel (30.5x43cm 12x16in) Amsterdam 1999

KOOLEN Jacobus ?-1666 **[2]**
- $5 517 - €5 793 - **£3 648** - FF38 000
  Place de marché animée de personnages
  Huile/panneau (46.5x60cm 18x23in) Paris 2000

KOONING de Elaine Marie 1920-1989 **[22]**
- $2 000 - €1 785 - **£1 224** - FF11 712
  Reindeer, Cave Wall Charcoal/paper (76x101.5cm
  29x39in) New-York 1999

KOONING de Willem 1904-1997 **[452]**
- $640 000 - €714 544 - **£427 776** - FF4 687 104
  Brown Derby Road Oil/canvas (159.5x125cm
  62x49in) New-York 2000
- $110 000 - €123 208 - **£76 428** - FF808 192
  Study for Nude with red Hair Mixed media
  (73x58cm 28x22in) New-York 2001
- $40 692 - €39 605 - **£25 000** - FF259 790
  Standing Woman Mixed media (44.5x18cm 17x7in)
  London 1999
- $88 440 - €94 296 - **£60 000** - FF618 540
  Head II Bronze (35.5x33x10cm 13x12x3in) London
  2001
- $55 000 - €52 065 - **£34 160** - FF341 522
  «Woman» Charcoal (47x48cm 18x18in) New-York
  1999
- $2 500 - €2 366 - **£1 552** - FF15 523
  Woman in Amagansett Lithograph (71x101.5cm
  27x39in) New-York 1999

KOONS Jeff 1955 **[119]**
- $330 000 - €382 896 - **£227 832** - FF2 511 630
  Red Butt (Distance) Silkscreen/canvas (229x152.5cm
  90x60in) New-York 2000
- $24 000 - €26 882 - **£16 675** - FF176 332
  Untitled Mixed media (14.5x16.5cm 5x6in) New-York
  2001
- $440 000 - €425 735 - **£271 348** - FF2 792 636
  Winter Bears Sculpture, wood (122x112x39.5cm
  48x44x15in) New-York 2000
- $34 000 - €29 434 - **£20 505** - FF193 072
  Fisherman Golfer Metal (26.5x20.5x15cm 10x8x5in)
  New-York 1998
- $8 000 - €9 050 - **£5 596** - FF59 364
  Drawing for Vacuum Cleaner Ink/paper
  (16.5x20.5cm 6x8in) New-York 2001
- $14 000 - €16 244 - **£9 665** - FF106 554
  Stormin Norman Offset (91.5x56cm 36x22in) New-
  York 2000
- $30 000 - €32 914 - **£19 929** - FF215 904
  Moses Photograph (105.5x83cm 41x32in) New-York
  2000

KOOP Andreas Ludvig 1792-1849 **[4]**
- $11 913 - €12 732 - **£8 094** - FF83 514
  Portraet af Bertel Thorvaldsen Oil/canvas
  (100x75cm 39x29in) København 2000

KOOPMAN Augustus B. 1869-1914 **[12]**
- $5 000 - €5 537 - **£3 391** - FF36 322
  The Blue Coffee Stand Oil/canvas (96x111cm
  38x44in) New-York 2000

KOOPMAN J. XVIII **[1]**
- $6 134 - €5 899 - **£3 779** - FF38 695
  **The smalchip «De Jonge Anna» and other
  Sailing Vessels Stormy Waters** Oil/panel
  (38.5x49cm 15x19in) Amsterdam 1999

KOORNSTRA Metten 1912-1978 **[31]**
- $1 597 - €1 724 - **£1 092** - FF11 311
  A Still Life with a Rose Oil/board (30x32cm
  11x12in) Amsterdam 2001

KOPALLIK Franz 1860-1931 **[15]**
- $881 - €946 - **£589** - FF6 204
  Strasse in Eisenerz Watercolour (31x45cm 12x17in)
  Stuttgart 2000

KÖPCKE Arthur 1928-1977 **[137]**
- $1 466 - €1 478 - **£914** - FF9 693
  Thachistisk komposition Oil/board (42x57cm
  16x22in) København 2000
- $585 - €681 - **£411** - FF4 464
  Untitled Collage/paper (27.5x12cm 10x4in)
  Amsterdam 2001
- $2 068 - €2 352 - **£1 434** - FF15 427
  Continue Multiple (26x36x21cm 10x14x8in) Hamburg
  2000

KÖPF Josef 1873-1953 **[10]**
- $6 721 - €7 994 - **£4 796** - FF52 437
  Nähende Frau mit schlafendem Kind
  Öl/Leinwand (133x80cm 52x31in) Wien 2000
- $1 647 - €1 599 - **£1 016** - FF10 487
  **Interieur, das Atelier des Künstlers, er selbst im
  Malerkittel** Aquarell/Karton (75x60cm 29x23in) Wien
  1999

KOPF Maxim 1892-? **[8]**
- $4 335 - €4 100 - **£2 700** - FF26 895
  Torbole Huile/toile (67x88cm 26x34in) Praha 2001

KOPF von Joseph 1827-1903 **[4]**
- $14 000 - €15 919 - **£9 604** - FF104 424
  Woman and Putto, Emblematic of Winter Marble
  (H502cm H198in) New-York 2000

KOPFERMANN Sigrid 1925 **[33]**
- $2 434 - €2 556 - **£1 535** - FF16 769
  Blaue Schatten Öl/Leinwand (66x44cm 25x17in)
  Stuttgart 2000
- $1 391 - €1 636 - **£997** - FF10 732
  Morgennebel Öl/Leinwand (12x10.5cm 4x4in)
  Düsseldorf 2001

KOPMAN Katherine 1870-1950 **[1]**
- $2 200 - €2 262 - **£1 395** - FF14 840
  Spring Landscape Watercolour/paper (25x36cm
  10x14in) New-Orleans LA 2000

KOPP Dieter 1939 **[6]**
- $1 680 - €1 651 - **£1 120** - FF9 520
  Fiori Acquarello/carta (34x46.5cm 13x18in) Prato 1998

KOPP Mathilde 1836-? **[5]**
- $1 298 - €1 534 - **£920** - FF10 061
  Blumenstilleben an einem Bachlauf Öl/Leinwand
  (46x67cm 18x26in) Stuttgart 2000

KOPPAY Joszi Árpád, Jan 1859-c.1920 **[8]**
- $3 806 - €3 997 - **£2 398** - FF26 218
  Erzherzogin Maria Josepha Pastell/Papier
  (70x44cm 27x17in) Wien 2000

KOPPENOL Cornelis 1865-1946 **[60]**
- $3 021 - €3 403 - **£2 082** - FF22 324
  Happy Family Oil/canvas (62x75cm 24x29in)
  Amsterdam 2000
- $854 - €971 - **£592** - FF6 372
  **Drei Mädchen und ein Junge Badende und
  Segelschiffe** Oil/panel (19x24cm 7x9in) Staufen 2000

KOPPITZ Rudolf 1884-1936 **[65]**
- $2 558 - €2 543 - **£1 589** - FF16 684
  Winterlandschaft Photograph (36.8x38cm 14x14in)
  Wien 1999

KORAB Karl 1937 **[407]**
- $4 551 - €4 368 - **£3 210** - FF35 215
  Ohne Titel Öl/Karton (58.5x44cm 23x17in) Köln 2001

K

$865 - €872 - £540 - FF5 720
Landschaft im Waldviertel Mixed media
(30x22.5cm 11x8in) Wien 2000

$563 - €654 - £396 - FF4 290
Kopf im Profil Charcoal/paper (39.5x55cm 15x21in)
Wien 2001

$182 - €182 - £110 - FF1 191
Dorfplatz Farblithographie (50x66cm 19x25in) Wien
2000

KORDA Alberto 1928-2001 [4]

$998 - €1 163 - £691 - FF7 631
El guerrillero heroico Photo (33.5x27.5cm 13x10in)
Caracas ($) 2000

KORDA Vince 1897-1977 [1]

$4 070 - €4 276 - £2 538 - FF28 050
Homme à la cigarette Huile/toile (55.5x46.5cm
21x18in) Budapest 2000

KORDIAN Roch 1950 [132]

$999 - €1 143 - £695 - FF7 500
Marine Huile/toile (50x61cm 19x24in) Romorantin-
Lanthenay 2000

$275 - €305 - £191 - FF2 000
Les bateaux à marée basse Huile/panneau
(13x18cm 5x7in) Soissons 2001

KOREC Karl Johann 1937 [5]

$1 833 - €2 180 - £1 308 - FF14 301
Korec Johann Indian ink (30x21.5cm 11x8in) Wien
2000

KORECKI Wiktor 1890-1980 [93]

$1 552 - €1 542 - £967 - FF10 118
Le moulin au coucher du soleil Oil/canvas
(50x81cm 19x31in) Warszawa 1999

$837 - €976 - £587 - FF6 404
Ferme en hiver Huile/carton (24.5x35cm 9x13in)
Warszawa 2000

KORFF Alexander H. Bakker 1824-1882 [28]

$5 912 - €4 985 - £3 509 - FF32 699
The Letter Oil/panel (14x12cm 5x4in) Amsterdam
1998

$2 376 - €2 496 - £1 503 - FF16 371
Three Interior Scene Ink/paper (27x40cm 10x15in)
Amsterdam 2000

KORIN Ogata 1658-1716 [1]

$70 000 - €67 289 - £43 652 - FF441 385
Hotei Ink/paper (26.5x35.5cm 10x13in) New-York
1999

KORNBECK Julius 1839-1920 [63]

$1 211 - €1 431 - £858 - FF9 390
Birken und Tannen am See Öl/Leinwand
(67x96.5cm 26x37in) Stuttgart 2000

$1 243 - €1 075 - £738 - FF7 051
Neckarlandschaft Öl/Karton (24x42.5cm 9x16in)
Hildrizhausen 1998

KORNBECK Peter 1837-1894 [52]

$3 634 - €3 500 - £2 256 - FF22 960
Den protestantiske kirkegård i Rom Oil/canvas
(45x62cm 17x24in) København 1999

$2 399 - €2 418 - £1 495 - FF15 861
Parti i kirken S.Maria ai Frari i Venedig Oil/canvas
(30x43cm 11x16in) København 2000

KORNECK Albert Friedrich 1813-1905 [4]

$1 506 - €1 608 - £1 026 - FF10 548
Jagtselskab foran hovedbygning Oil/canvas
(61x77cm 24x30in) Vejle 2001

KÖRNER Magnus Peter 1808-1864 [10]

$199 - €202 - £125 - FF1 323
Frigilla spinus/Frigilla coelebs Lithograph
(25x17cm 9x6in) Helsinki 2000

KORNERUP Valdemar 1865-1924 [53]

$778 - €831 - £530 - FF5 449
Parti fra Kvarberg, Guldbrandsdalen Oil/canvas
(64x89cm 25x35in) Vejle 2001

KÖRNIG Hans 1905-1989 [51]

$143 - €123 - £86 - FF804
Selbst und Frau im Atelier Etching (16.2x14.1cm
6x5in) Berlin 1998

KORNISS Dezsö 1908-1984 [5]

$17 760 - €18 660 - £11 040 - FF122 400
Femme et girafe Huile/toile (70x100cm 27x39in)
Budapest 2000

$2 220 - €2 332 - £1 380 - FF15 300
Hommage à Bartok Huile/toile (20x28.5cm 7x11in)
Budapest 2000

$2 220 - €2 332 - £1 380 - FF15 300
Composition géométrique Pastel/papier (16x15cm
6x5in) Budapest 2000

KOROCHANSKY Michel 1866-1925 [60]

$1 393 - €1 220 - £844 - FF8 000
L'écluse Huile/toile (49x58cm 19x22in) Paris 1998

KOROLKIEWICZ Lukasz 1948 [3]

$7 470 - €8 328 - £5 190 - FF54 630
Limitrophe Huile/toile (116x147cm 45x57in)
Warszawa 2001

KOROMPAY Giovanni 1904-1988 [19]

$2 000 - €2 592 - £1 500 - FF17 000
Composizione Olio/tela (60x72cm 23x28in) Prato
2000

KOROMPAY von Gustav 1833-1907 [4]

$1 832 - €1 817 - £1 147 - FF11 917
Hoher Markt Aquarell/Papier (22.3x31.5cm 8x12in)
Wien 1999

KOROVIN Alexei Konstantinov. 1897-1950 [2]

$7 257 - €8 006 - £4 800 - FF52 519
Still Life with Bottle of Chianti and Fruit Oil/can-
vas (65x81cm 25x31in) London 2000

KOROVIN Alexis 1928 [26]

$2 512 - €2 287 - £1 570 - FF15 000
Fêtes russes Huile/carton (37.5x46cm 14x18in)
Saint-Dié 1999

KOROVIN Constantin Alexeiev. 1861-1939 [214]

$15 795 - €15 036 - £9 882 - FF98 631
Ung kvinna på parkbänk Oil/canvas (81x55cm
31x21in) Stockholm 1999

$4 482 - €4 812 - £3 000 - FF31 564
Landscape: before the Storm Oil/panel (27x35cm
10x13in) London 2000

$1 700 - €1 549 - £1 025 - FF11 000
Prince Igor Watercolour (28.5x23cm 11x9in) New-
York 1998

KORSCHMANN Charles 1872-? [21]

$816 - €793 - £502 - FF5 203
Bergère et ses moutons Bronze (H32cm H12in)
Bruxelles 1999

KORTHALS Claude Frédérique XX [4]

$1 390 - €1 524 - £944 - FF10 000
L'enfant et les oies Bronze (H23.5cm H9in) Soissons
2000

KORTHALS Jan 1916-1973 **[79]**
$999 - €1 089 - £688 - FF7 143
   Streetscene with People and the Silhouette of a Church Oil/canvas (60x50cm 23x19in) Amsterdam 2001

KORTMAN Johan 1858-1923 **[6]**
$1 652 - €1 850 - £1 147 - FF12 135
   Sommardag Oil/canvas (31x48.5cm 12x19in) Helsinki 2001

KORWAN Franz 1865-? **[11]**
$2 005 - €2 301 - £1 371 - FF15 092
   Winterlandschaft auf Sylt Öl/Karton (28x39cm 11x15in) Berlin 2000

KORYUSAI Isoda XVIII **[25]**
$1 764 - €1 745 - £1 100 - FF11 447
   Lady and Gentleman beside a tethered Horse with Mount Fuji Print in colors (68x11cm 26x4in) London 1999

KORZUKHIN Alexei Ivanovich 1835-1894 **[4]**
$48 312 - €45 618 - £29 400 - FF299 235
   The Abduction of Ivan Naryshkin: Scene from the Revolt of the Streltsy Oil/canvas (97.5x152cm 38x59in) London 1999
$3 023 - €3 336 - £2 000 - FF21 883
   Two Peasants Oil/canvas (35x26cm 13x10in) London 2000

KOSA Emil, Jr. 1903-1968 **[80]**
$8 000 - €6 835 - £4 840 - FF44 835
   «Whispering Silver» Oil/canvas (76x101.5cm 29x39in) San-Francisco CA 1998
$3 200 - €3 022 - £1 987 - FF19 820
   Rainy Day on the Farm Watercolour/paper (56x76cm 22x29in) Beverly-Hills CA 1999

KOSAREK Adolf 1830-1859 **[4]**
$50 575 - €47 835 - £31 500 - FF313 775
   Krajina po desti s cikany Oil/canvas (100x127.5cm 39x50in) Praha 1999
$34 680 - €32 801 - £21 600 - FF215 160
   Chapel in the Forest (Chapel in Winter) Oil/canvas (78.5x119cm 30x46in) Praha 1999

KOSEL Hermann 1896-1983 **[26]**
$370 - €400 - £255 - FF2 621
   «Südbahnhotel Semmering» Poster (95x61cm 37x24in) Wien 2001

KOSHIRO Onchi 1891-1955 **[25]**
$3 500 - €4 111 - £2 485 - FF26 964
   Figure Woodcut (60x45cm 23x17in) New-York 2000

KOSKAS George 1926 **[9]**
$4 687 - €5 445 - £3 294 - FF35 719
   Traits couleurs Oil/canvas (74x60cm 29x23in) Amsterdam 2001

KOSKULL Anders Gustaf 1831-1904 **[22]**
$1 324 - €1 428 - £889 - FF9 370
   Vallkulla Oil/canvas (72x60cm 28x23in) Stockholm 2000

KOSLER Franz Xaver 1864-? **[32]**
$4 000 - €4 637 - £2 833 - FF30 420
   Crossing the Desert Oil/panel (53x37.5cm 20x14in) New-York 2000
$3 055 - €3 634 - £2 180 - FF23 835
   Orientale mit seinem Esel vor einem Ruinenhintergrund Oil/panel (25x32.5cm 9x12in) Wien 2000

KOSNICK-KLOSS Jeanne Freundlich 1892-1966 **[72]**
$541 - €610 - £380 - FF4 000
   Composition Aquarelle/papier (31.5x23cm 12x9in) Paris 2001

KOSOLAPOV Aleksander 1943 **[11]**
$721 - €654 - £444 - FF4 290
   «Malevich» Farbserigraphie (57x76cm 22x29in) Wien 1999

KOSON Ohara 1877-1945 **[56]**
$300 - €260 - £182 - FF1 703
   Egret/Fish Woodcut in colors (33x17cm 13x7in) Mystic CT 1998

KOSSAK Jerzy 1886-1955 **[188]**
$8 757 - €10 180 - £6 146 - FF66 776
   Retour de Moscou en flammes Huile/toile (96x129cm 37x50in) Warszawa 2001
$2 290 - €2 260 - £1 411 - FF14 826
   Fuite devant les loups Oil/board (49x69cm 19x27in) Warszawa 1999
$1 269 - €1 319 - £805 - FF8 654
   Soldat avec son cheval Huile/carton (21x18.5cm 8x7in) Warszawa 2000

KOSSAK Juliusz 1824-1899 **[83]**
$26 724 - €31 193 - £18 864 - FF204 612
   Chevaux vers l'abreuvoir Huile/toile (55.5x68.5cm 21x26in) Warszawa 2000
$44 955 - €42 062 - £27 250 - FF275 909
   Konie kozackie Oil/panel (36.5x28.5cm 14x11in) Warszawa 1999
$7 830 - €7 892 - £4 883 - FF51 769
   Berek Joselewicz vers Kocko Watercolour/paper (45.5x35cm 17x13in) Warszawa 2000

KOSSAK Wojciech, Adalbert 1857-1942 **[195]**
$11 340 - €10 865 - £7 150 - FF71 271
   Portrait of a Woman with a Horse Oil/canvas (120x100cm 47x39in) Warszawa 1999
$7 504 - €6 659 - £4 485 - FF43 678
   Portret Madame Rity Sacchetto Oil/canvas (88x62cm 34x24in) Warszawa 1998
$2 863 - €2 668 - £1 771 - FF17 500
   La chasse à courre Huile/panneau (18.5x24.5cm 7x9in) Paris 2001
$1 379 - €1 622 - £988 - FF10 639
   Uhlans en route Gouache/papier (30x22cm 11x8in) Warszawa 2001

KOSSOFF Leon 1926 **[102]**
$78 930 - €76 536 - £50 000 - FF502 045
   Outside the Booking Hall, Kilburn Underground Station Oil/canvas (183x152.5cm 72x60in) London 1999
$56 969 - €55 447 - £35 000 - FF363 706
   Portrait of Philip II Oil/panel (143x77cm 56x30in) London 1999
$42 500 - €39 691 - £26 231 - FF260 355
   Fidelma in red Chair Oil/board (18.5x60cm 7x23in) New-York 1999
$2 467 - €2 778 - £1 700 - FF18 225
   Head of a Girl Charcoal/paper (76x56.5cm 29x22in) London 2000
$576 - €570 - £360 - FF3 738
   Going Home Etching, aquatint (40.5x51cm 15x20in) London 1999

KOSSONOGI Joseph 1908-1981 **[29]**
$7 500 - €8 114 - £5 138 - FF53 223
   Rider and Figures Oil/canvas (32x45cm 12x17in) Tel Aviv 2001

K

K

$700 - €751 - £468 - FF4 928
Landscape from the Balcony Watercolour/paper (35.5x23.5cm 13x9in) Tel Aviv 2000

KOSSOWSKI Henryk II 1855-1921 **[17]**
$1 740 - €1 859 - £1 185 - FF12 195
Patria Bronze (65x29cm 25x11in) Lokeren 2001

KOSSUTH Egon Josef 1874-? **[7]**
$1 600 - €1 856 - £1 104 - FF12 177
Self Portrait Oil/panel (34x34cm 13x13in) New-York 2000

KOSTA Josef Alexander 1879-1961 **[8]**
$1 211 - €1 163 - £760 - FF7 627
Häuser in der Sonnenfelsgasse Aquarell/Papier (32x25cm 12x9in) Wien 1999

KOSTABI Mark 1960 **[240]**
$3 250 - €3 369 - £1 950 - FF22 100
Spaghetti 3000 Olio/tela (137x163cm 53x64in) Prato 1999
$2 100 - €2 177 - £1 260 - FF14 280
«**The lure**» Acrilico/tela (60.5x45.5cm 23x17in) Vercelli 2001
$800 - €1 037 - £600 - FF6 800
«**Confronto dell'anima**» Acrilico/tela (20x25cm 7x9in) Vercelli 2001
$350 - €363 - £210 - FF2 380
Untitled Matita/carta (18.5x20.5cm 7x8in) Vercelli 2001
$189 - €204 - £129 - FF1 341
Ohne Titel Farbserigraphie (100x70cm 39x27in) Stuttgart 2001

KOSTANDI Kiriak Konstantinov. 1852-1921 **[5]**
$3 300 - €3 273 - £2 053 - FF21 471
Monastery Gates Wood Oil/canvas (23x30cm 9x11in) Kiev 1999

KOSTER Anton Louise 1859-1937 **[30]**
$157 - €173 - £106 - FF1 138
Havenzicht met molen (Vue sur un port fluvial avec un moulin) Huile/panneau (40x50cm 15x19in) Antwerpen 2000
$610 - €681 - £417 - FF4 464
Boerderijgezicht met bloembollenvelden in bloei Oil/panel (18x27cm 7x10in) The Hague 2000
$2 473 - €2 212 - £1 481 - FF14 512
A View of'te Spaarne, Haarlem Pastel/paper (52x62cm 20x24in) Amsterdam 1998

KOSTER Antonius H., Toon 1913-1990 **[50]**
$782 - €908 - £540 - FF5 953
Gezicht op de Nieuwkoopse plassen met visser bij zijn bunnen Oil/panel (38x59cm 14x23in) Rotterdam 2000
$452 - €499 - £295 - FF3 274
Polderlandschap Nieuwkoop Oil/canvas (30x40cm 11x15in) Den Haag 2000

KÖSTER Carl Georg 1812-1893 **[26]**
$890 - €955 - £595 - FF6 266
Teichlandschaft mit Blick auf ein Dorf Oil/panel (24x34cm 9x13in) Zürich 2000

KOSTER Everhardus 1817-1892 **[67]**
$50 000 - €48 525 - £31 505 - FF318 300
Amsterdam Man-of-War firing a Salute across the bows of a Ferry Oil/canvas (90x150.5cm 35x59in) New-York 1999
$4 782 - €4 457 - £2 951 - FF29 237
Sailboats and Ship Off Pier Oil/canvas (42x84cm 16x33in) New-Orleans LA 1999
$4 743 - €4 573 - £2 925 - FF30 000
Marine Huile/panneau (17.5x27cm 6x10in) Paris 1999

$2 701 - €2 723 - £1 684 - FF17 859
Townscape with a moored Hay-barge and a City Castle towering Watercolour (27x34.5cm 10x13in) Amsterdam 2000

KÖSTER Paul 1855-1931 **[21]**
$1 575 - €1 789 - £1 102 - FF11 738
Dorflandschaft Öl/Leinwand (65x86cm 25x33in) München 2001

KOSTER VAN HATTUM Jo 1869-1944 **[29]**
$2 671 - €2 266 - £1 611 - FF14 867
Herenportret Oil/canvas (46x46cm 18x18in) Den Haag 1998
$185 - €204 - £123 - FF1 341
Stilleben mit Wasserkanne Öl/Karton (38x27cm 14x10in) Satow 2000

KOSTKA Josef Alexander 1879-1961 **[75]**
$1 046 - €1 163 - £700 - FF7 627
Haarhof Aquarell/Papier (31.5x22cm 12x8in) Wien 2000

KOSTRZESKI Franciszek 1826-1911 **[15]**
$8 524 - €8 503 - £5 320 - FF55 778
Landscape with Figures, Capel and Farmhouse in the Background Oil/canvas (57x73cm 22x28in) Warszawa 1999

KOSUTH Joseph 1945 **[73]**
$55 000 - €61 406 - £36 762 - FF402 798
Five Works in Violet Neon Sculpture (7.5x146x6.5cm 2x57x2in) New-York 2000
$3 400 - €4 406 - £2 550 - FF28 900
The Ninth Investigation Collage (35x60cm 13x23in) Prato 2000
$1 101 - €1 296 - £789 - FF8 500
Texte, contexte Sérigraphie (80x120cm 31x47in) Paris 2001
$1 408 - €1 346 - £883 - FF8 830
«**Ice. is; bedaekke med is**» Photograph (97x97cm 38x38in) Köbenhavn 1999

KOSVANEC Vlastimil 1887-? **[15]**
$1 156 - €1 093 - £720 - FF7 172
Au bord d'un étang Huile/toile (70x100cm 27x39in) Praha 2000

KÖSZEGI-FANGH Dezsö 1876-? **[12]**
$1 191 - €1 308 - £766 - FF8 580
Dürnstein an der Donau Gouache/paper (20x30cm 7x11in) Wien 2000

KOSZKOL Jenö, Eugene 1868-1935 **[22]**
$356 - €333 - £220 - FF2 183
Interior of a Study Pastel/paper (81x61cm 31x24in) London 1999

KOSZTA József 1861-1941 **[8]**
$12 600 - €13 940 - £8 280 - FF91 440
Little Girl with Cock Oil/cardboard (69x50cm 27x19in) Budapest 2000
$2 355 - €2 543 - £1 627 - FF16 684
Am Feld Öl/Leinwand/Karton (31.5x41.5cm 12x16in) Wien 2001

KOT Pawel XX **[4]**
$4 058 - €3 900 - £2 500 - FF25 583
Lion Oil/canvas (55x67.5cm 21x26in) London 1999
$2 559 - €2 808 - £1 700 - FF18 420
Leopard Oil/canvas (24x43.5cm 9x17in) London 2000

KOTARBINSKY Wilhelm 1849-1921 **[8]**
$2 672 - €3 119 - £1 886 - FF20 461
Béatitude Encre (50.5x86.5cm 19x34in) Warszawa 2000

KÖTHE Fritz 1916 **[93]**
- $4 543 - €4 410 - £2 829 - FF28 927
  «72» Öl/Leinwand (100.5x75.4cm 39x29in) Berlin 1999
- $571 - €613 - £382 - FF4 024
  Mund, Auge Pencil (48.8x53cm 19x20in) Köln 2000
- $104 - €112 - £70 - FF737
  Elf Farbserigraphie (40x50.5cm 15x19in) Köln 2000

KOTIK Jan 1916 **[30]**
- $2 601 - €2 460 - £1 620 - FF16 137
  Figurative Composition Oil/canvas (105x80.5cm 41x31in) Praha 2001

KOTIK Pravoslav 1889-1970 **[113]**
- $2 167 - €2 050 - £1 350 - FF13 447
  Bouquet de fleurs Huile/toile (55x45cm 21x17in) Praha 2000
- $838 - €793 - £522 - FF5 199
  Venkovska idylle Huile/carton (25.5x25cm 10x9in) Praha 2000
- $260 - €246 - £162 - FF1 613
  Ombrelles sur la plage Tempera/papier (44x61cm 17x24in) Praha 2000

KOTONDO Torii 1900-1977 **[27]**
- $2 000 - €2 210 - £1 387 - FF14 497
  Ohishi Yoshio, Kuranosuke Ink (114x32.5cm 44x12in) New-York 2001
- $1 961 - €2 292 - £1 400 - FF15 034
  «Beauty applying Powder» Print (46.5x30cm 18x11in) London 2001

KOTOWSKI Jan Erazm 1885-1960 **[15]**
- $684 - €740 - £473 - FF4 852
  Course de traîneaux Crayon (46.5x66.5cm 18x26in) Warszawa 2001

KOTSCHENREITER G. Hugo 1854-1908 **[65]**
- $8 000 - €7 630 - £4 869 - FF50 047
  The Town Meeting Oil/canvas (87.5x131cm 34x51in) New-York 1999
- $1 211 - €1 308 - £837 - FF8 580
  Gemütliches Gespräch Oil/panel (16.5x12cm 6x4in) Wien 2001

KOTSIS Aleksander 1836-1877 **[14]**
- $9 380 - €10 660 - £6 478 - FF69 925
  Piège Huile/carton (38.5x31.5cm 15x12in) Warszawa 2000

KOTTLER Moses 1896-1977 **[6]**
- $2 723 - €3 051 - £1 892 - FF20 013
  Mother and Child Bronze (H24cm H9in) Johannesburg 2001

KOUDELKA Josef 1938 **[50]**
- $1 223 - €1 362 - £800 - FF8 935
  Ireland Gelatin silver print (34x53cm 13x21in) London 2000

KOUNELLIS Jannis 1936 **[164]**
- $86 610 - €93 706 - £60 000 - FF614 670
  Untitled «S» Mixed media (235x130cm 92x51in) London 2001
- $16 000 - €18 565 - £11 046 - FF121 776
  Ohne Titel Mixed media (70x93.5cm 27x36in) New-York 2000
- $5 769 - €6 781 - £4 000 - FF44 480
  Untitled Oil/paper (34x24cm 13x9in) London 2000
- $43 398 - €44 989 - £26 039 - FF295 108
  Senza titolo Fer (200x180cm 78x70in) Roma 1999
- $11 500 - €11 922 - £6 900 - FF78 200
  Senza titolo Inchiostro/carta (53x70cm 20x27in) Milano 2000

- $750 - €777 - £450 - FF5 100
  Ascolta Litografia (61x37cm 24x14in) Roma 2001

KOUPETSIAN Aram 1928 **[101]**
- $714 - €742 - £450 - FF4 868
  The Music Score Oil/canvas (40x60cm 15x23in) Fernhurst, Haslemere, Surrey 2000

KOUTACHY Joseph 1907 **[18]**
- $248 - €229 - £149 - FF1 500
  «Les Quatre Filles du Docteur March» Affiche (120x160cm 47x62in) Paris 1999

KOUWENBERGH van Philip 1671-1729 **[7]**
- $29 571 - €29 068 - £19 000 - FF190 676
  Still Life of Roses, Hollyocks, Daffodils, Peonies, Tulips, Irises Oil/canvas (101x78cm 39x30in) London 1999

KOVACIC Mijo 1946 **[2]**
- $4 052 - €4 602 - £2 816 - FF30 185
  Winter auf dem Berg Painting (87.5x112cm 34x44in) München 2001

KOVACS Ferenc P. 1911-1983 **[10]**
- $595 - €658 - £391 - FF4 318
  Church Tower of Nagybánya Oil/canvas (75x60cm 29x23in) Budapest 2001

KOVALIEVSKI Pavel 1843-1970 **[10]**
- $13 874 - €12 706 - £8 456 - FF83 344
  Cossacks at Rest in a Mountainous Landscape Oil/canvas (50x76cm 19x29in) Amsterdam 1999
- $3 000 - €2 976 - £1 866 - FF19 519
  Horseman Oil/cardboard (25.5x49cm 10x19in) Kiev 2001

KOVERECH Aleardo 1948 **[2]**
- $2 400 - €3 110 - £1 800 - FF20 400
  «Riflessi della città» Olio/tela (60x80cm 23x31in) Milano 2001

KOVO Philippe 1952 **[127]**
- $236 - €274 - £166 - FF1 800
  Le kiosque au personnage Huile/papier (25x33cm 9x12in) Neuilly-sur-Seine 2000
- $263 - €244 - £160 - FF1 600
  Les ouvriers Gouache (19x23.5cm 7x9in) Paris 1998

KOW Alexis Kogeynikow 1900-1978 **[43]**
- $500 - €438 - £303 - FF2 876
  Air France -Sports d'hiver Poster (98x59cm 38x23in) New-York 1999

KOWALCZEWSKI Karl P. 1876-? **[17]**
- $300 - €318 - £203 - FF2 088
  Field Workers Bronze (H15cm H6in) Delray-Beach FL 2001

KOWALCZEWSKI Paul Ludwig 1865-1910 **[47]**
- $368 - €409 - £255 - FF2 683
  «Stehender Schmied» Bronze (H27.5cm H10in) Berlin 2001

KOWALSKI Ivan Ivanovitch XIX-XX **[21]**
- $1 722 - €1 952 - £1 170 - FF12 805
  Vista de ciudad Oleo/lienzo (34x41cm 13x16in) Madrid 2000

KOWALSKY Hermann 1813-? **[4]**
- $3 483 - €4 141 - £2 413 - FF27 166
  Gefechtspause Öl/Leinwand (55x67cm 21x26in) München 2000

KOWALSKY Léopold-François 1856-1931 **[31]**
- $9 000 - €9 069 - £5 610 - FF59 490
  The Water Carrier Oil/canvas (146x97cm 57x38in) New-York 2000

K

$12 000 - €13 630 - **£8 420** - FF89 404
Bucolique Oil/canvas (82x100.5cm 32x39in) New-York 2001

KOYANAGUI Sei 1896-? **[58]**
$1 244 - €1 220 - **£802** - FF8 000
Petit chien dans un fauteuil Huile/toile (73x92cm 28x36in) Versailles 1999
$397 - €427 - **£266** - FF2 800
L'oiseau Technique mixte/toile (24x30cm 9x11in) Paris 2000

KOZAKIEWICZ Anton 1841-1929 **[43]**
$30 632 - €36 432 - **£21 840** - FF238 980
Aiguisement de sabres avant la bataille Huile/toile (94x151cm 37x59in) Warszawa 2000
$8 792 - €10 123 - **£6 000** - FF66 401
The Photographers Admirers Oil/canvas (85x120cm 33x47in) London 2000
$5 870 - €6 341 - **£4 058** - FF41 594
Au camp de Tziganes Huile/panneau (26.5x37cm 10x14in) Kraków 2001

KOZLENKO Nicolas 1952 **[15]**
$750 - €901 - **£525** - FF5 910
Frutas en lebrillo azul Oleo/lienzo (30x60cm 11x23in) Madrid 2000

KOZLOWSKI Jaroslaw 1910-1987 **[18]**
$949 - €1 017 - **£648** - FF6 673
«Okolice Ciechanowca» Oil chalks/paper (26.7x39.5cm 10x15in) Wien 2001

KOZLOWSKI Wladislaw 1910-1987 **[15]**
$619 - €727 - **£439** - FF4 767
Tanz Öl/Leinwand (45x36cm 17x14in) Wien 2000

KOZMAN Myron 1916 **[11]**
$5 000 - €5 687 - **£3 467** - FF37 301
Abstraction No.12 Oil/canvas (91x76cm 36x30in) Chicago IL 2000

KOZUCHOWSKI Jerzy 1893-1967 **[8]**
$438 - €490 - **£306** - FF3 213
Cavalier légionnaire Aquarelle, gouache/papier (33x25cm 12x9in) Warszawa 2001

KRABBÉ Heinrich Martin 1868-1931 **[38]**
$3 736 - €4 011 - **£2 500** - FF26 308
The New Doll Oil/canvas (65.5x53cm 25x20in) London 2000
$1 156 - €998 - **£698** - FF6 548
Mending the doll's dress Oil/canvas (33.5x25.5cm 13x10in) Amsterdam 1999
$2 523 - €2 178 - **£1 523** - FF14 287
An Interior Scene with a Woman knitting Watercolour (70x48cm 27x18in) Amsterdam 1999

KRACHKOVSKY Iosif Yevstafievich 1854-1914 **[16]**
$4 781 - €5 133 - **£3 200** - FF44 159
Tranquil River across flowering Fields Oil/canvas (40x60cm 15x23in) London 2000
$1 400 - €1 496 - **£951** - FF9 813
Stacks Oil/canvas (27x42.5cm 10x16in) Kiev 2001

KRAEMER Hermann 1808-? **[12]**
$3 443 - €3 997 - **£2 420** - FF26 218
Blick auf Riva am Gardasee Öl/Leinwand (68x97cm 26x38in) Wien 2001

KRAEMER Peter II 1857-1939 **[89]**
$893 - €1 022 - **£614** - FF6 707
Vier Bauern beim Kartenspiel Watercolour (21.2x26.4cm 8x10in) München 2000

KRAER Charles 1822-1878 **[2]**
$4 148 - €4 346 - **£2 743** - FF28 508
Ansicht von San Marco und Dogenpalast in Venedig Öl/Leinwand (27x37cm 10x14in) München 2000

KRAFFT Albert XVIII **[1]**
$3 500 - €3 860 - **£2 370** - FF25 322
A Putto Holding an Arrow Oil/canvas (24x21cm 9x8in) New-York 2000

KRAFFT Carl Rudolph 1884-1938 **[64]**
$3 250 - €3 293 - **£2 040** - FF21 598
Autumn Landscape Oil/canvas (60x76cm 24x30in) Cincinnati OH 2000
$1 200 - €1 197 - **£749** - FF7 852
Illinois Landscape Oil/board (25x35cm 10x14in) Cincinnati OH 1999
$2 500 - €2 763 - **£1 751** - FF18 124
Mountain Landscape Print (63x76cm 25x30in) Chicago IL 2001

KRAFFT Johann Peter 1780-1856 **[9]**
$61 840 - €58 138 - **£37 440** - FF381 360
Theseus und Peirithoos um Helena losend Öl/Leinwand (94.2x120cm 37x47in) Wien 1999

KRAFFT Per I 1724-1793 **[11]**
$10 884 - €9 267 - **£6 500** - FF60 788
Portrait of a young Lady, half-Length Oil/canvas (64x53.5cm 25x21in) London 1998

KRAFFT von David 1655-1724 **[3]**
$28 704 - €30 952 - **£19 266** - FF203 034
Karl XII klädd i blå rock och harnesk Oil/canvas (80x67cm 31x26in) Stockholm 2000

KRAFFT-STEINER Barbara 1764-1825 **[7]**
$5 000 - €5 600 - **£3 474** - FF36 736
Portrait of a General, said to be Baron Menziau Oil/canvas (58x47cm 22x18in) New-York 2001

KRAFT Frederik 1823-1854 **[21]**
$1 241 - €1 074 - **£738** - FF7 042
Skovbryn ved marker Oil/paper (19x28cm 7x11in) Köbenhavn 1998

KRAHE Peter Joseph 1758-1840 **[2]**
$1 079 - €1 125 - **£708** - FF7 378
Theil des Circus Maximus in Rom Black chalk/paper (19.2x27cm 7x10in) Hamburg 2000

KRAITZ Gustav 1926 **[7]**
$1 876 - €2 059 - **£1 246** - FF13 503
Utan titel Ceramic (11.5x24cm 4x9in) Stockholm 2000

KRAITZ Ulla 1936 **[8]**
$1 876 - €2 059 - **£1 246** - FF13 503
Utan titel Ceramic (11.5x24cm 4x9in) Stockholm 2000

KRAITZ Ulla & Gustav 1936/26 **[9]**
$1 275 - €1 428 - **£886** - FF9 370
Liggande häst Sandstone (17.5x28.5cm 6x11in) Stockholm 2001

KRAJEWSKY Max 1892-1972 **[15]**
$384 - €332 - **£233** - FF2 181
Olympiade Berlin Photograph (22.4x29cm 8x11in) München 1998

KRAKAUER Leopold 1890-1954 **[28]**
$1 500 - €1 675 - **£960** - FF10 988
Thorns Charcoal/paper (66x46cm 25x18in) Tel Aviv 2000

KRAL Jaroslav 1883-1942 **[38]**
$16 184 - €15 307 - **£10 080** - FF100 408
Dans un jardin Huile/carton (50x66cm 19x25in) Praha 2001

☞ **$1 502** - €1 421 - **£936** - FF9 323
Nature morte au poisson et citrons Technique mixte/carton (23x31cm 9x12in) Praha 2000
✑ **$288** - €291 - **£180** - FF1 906
Zwei Frauen Pencil/paper (11.5x19cm 4x7in) Wien 2000

KRALIK Hanns 1900-1971 **[4]**
☞ **$8 155** - €7 669 - **£5 050** - FF50 308
Aus meinem Fenster Öl/Leinwand (67x55cm 26x21in) Köln 1999

KRAMER Jacob 1892-1962 **[108]**
☞ **$2 108** - €2 040 - **£1 300** - FF13 379
Mother and child, Study in Red Oil/canvas (51x41cm 20x16in) West-Yorshire 1999
✑ **$347** - €408 - **£250** - FF2 674
Study of a Woman's Head Pastel/paper (26x24cm 10x9in) London 2001
▥ **$209** - €194 - **£130** - FF1 271
Portrait Head of Jacob Epstein Lithograph (46x31cm 18x12in) Cheshire 1999

KRAMER James 1927 **[7]**
✑ **$800** - €690 - **£480** - FF4 527
Maxwell House Watercolour/paper (34x52cm 13x20in) Santa-Fe NM 1998

KRÄMER Johann Viktor 1861-1949 **[43]**
☞ **$6 721** - €7 994 - **£4 796** - FF52 437
Arabische Schule Öl/Leinwand (100x136cm 39x53in) Linz 2000
☞ **$733** - €872 - **£523** - FF5 720
Geflügel und Früchte bewacht von einem Hund, nach Jan Fyt Öl/Leinwand (61x105cm 24x41in) Linz 2000
▥ **$3 605** - €3 634 - **£2 250** - FF23 835
«X.I Ausstellung d.Vereinigung bildender Künstler» Poster (180x90cm 70x35in) Wien 2000

KRAMPE Fritz 1913-1966 **[9]**
☞ **$7 543** - €6 516 - **£4 548** - FF42 743
«Serengeti» Mixed media (64x99cm 25x38in) Johannesburg 1998
✑ **$3 592** - €3 103 - **£2 166** - FF20 354
A Seated Man with a Stick Ink (100x68cm 39x26in) Johannesburg 1998

KRAMSZTYK Roman 1885-1942 **[16]**
☞ **$12 871** - €14 178 - **£8 556** - FF93 000
Village au bord de mer Huile/toile (92x73cm 36x28in) Aurillac 2000
✑ **$1 149** - €1 242 - **£794** - FF8 145
Nu allongé Sanguine/papier (27x33cm 10x12in) Warszawa 2001

KRANEWITTER Franz Josef 1893-1974 **[3]**
◈ **$3 600** - €4 165 - **£2 548** - FF27 319
Nude Balancing on a Ball Bronze (34x36cm 13x14in) Cleveland OH 2000

KRANTZ Nils Michael 1886-1954 **[1]**
☞ **$3 306** - €3 069 - **£2 304** - FF24 069
Stilleben med flaske, frukt og blomster Oil/canvas (55x65cm 21x25in) Oslo 2001

KRASILNIKOV Yuri XX **[18]**
☞ **$222** - €231 - **£140** - FF1 514
Copse Oil/canvas (20x30cm 7x11in) Fernhurst, Haslemere, Surrey 2000

KRASNER Lee 1908-1984 **[36]**
☞ **$160 000** - €182 966 - **£111 792** - FF1 193 616
Blue Spot Oil/masonite (101.5x122cm 39x48in) Beverly-Hills CA 2000

☞ **$8 500** - €8 001 - **£5 251** - FF52 486
Untitled, Still Life Oil/paper (48x63.5cm 18x25in) New-York 1999
✑ **$32 000** - €35 842 - **£22 233** - FF235 110
Untitled, Ahab Gouache (57.5x78.5cm 22x30in) New-York 2001
▥ **$240** - €280 - **£166** - FF1 835
P.S 1 A painting Show Screenprint in colors (100x68cm 39x26in) New-York 2000

KRASNOW Peter 1886-1979 **[3]**
☞ **$4 200** - €3 966 - **£2 608** - FF26 014
Market Scene, New York Oil/canvas (81x96.5cm 31x37in) Beverly-Hills CA 1999

KRASSILNIKOV Youri XX **[11]**
☞ **$189** - €210 - **£133** - FF1 379
Un remanso Oleo/lienzo (40x30cm 15x11in) Madrid 2001

KRASSOULINE Valery 1947 **[93]**
☞ **$518** - €442 - **£312** - FF2 900
La neige à Paris Huile/toile (46x55cm 18x21in) Enghien 1998

KRASZEWSKA Otolia 1859-1945 **[11]**
☞ **$10 526** - €12 242 - **£7 516** - FF80 299
Elegant Couple in an Interior Oil/canvas (65.5x88.5cm 25x34in) Toronto 2001

KRATKÉ Louis 1848-1921 **[32]**
☞ **$3 872** - €3 719 - **£2 400** - FF24 395
Arrestation d'émigrés Oil/canvas (65x81cm 25x31in) London 1999
☞ **$1 987** - €1 840 - **£1 200** - FF12 070
Dandy Oil/board (21x14cm 8x5in) Little-Lane, Ilkley 1999

KRATOCHWIL Marian 1906-1997 **[4]**
☞ **$1 761** - €1 886 - **£1 199** - FF12 374
Nu Huile/panneau (20x22.5cm 7x8in) Warszawa 2001

KRATSCHKOWSKI Iossif J. 1854-1914 **[8]**
☞ **$3 092** - €3 027 - **£1 902** - FF19 857
Kaislikkoranta Oil/canvas (25x51cm 9x20in) Helsinki 1999

KRATZER von Carl 1827-1903 **[14]**
☞ **$1 427** - €1 308 - **£873** - FF8 580
Blick auf Goisern Oil/panel (26x16cm 10x6in) Wien 1999

KRAUS August 1868-1934 **[7]**
◈ **$19 991** - €23 519 - **£14 112** - FF154 274
Bocciaspieler Bronze (152x92x86cm 59x36x33in) Berlin 2001
◈ **$684** - €665 - **£426** - FF4 360
Büste Heinrich Zille Plaster (14.6x6.9x6.9cm 5x2x2in) Berlin 1999

KRAUS Georg Melchior 1737-1806 **[22]**
☞ **$5 760** - €6 541 - **£3 942** - FF42 903
Der kleine Bildhauer vor der Büste des Seneca Öl/Leinwand (58.5x42.5cm 23x16in) Wien 2000
☞ **$13 000** - €10 913 - **£7 624** - FF71 585
Turkish Woman playing the Lute at a Window Oil/canvas (43x33.5cm 16x13in) New-York 1998
✑ **$581** - €665 - **£404** - FF4 360
Bildnis einer Frau mit Haube Pencil/paper (25x20cm 9x7in) Rudolstadt-Thüringen 2000
▥ **$719** - €818 - **£498** - FF5 366
Paulinzella Lithographie (32x50cm 12x19in) Rudolstadt-Thüringen 2000

K

KRAUS Gustav Wilhelm 1804-1852 **[34]**

✏ **$3 646** - €3 579 - **£2 260** - FF23 477
Spaziergang auf einem Wiesenweg oberhalb von St. Maria in Thalkirchen Aquarell/Papier (23x38cm 9x14in) München 1999

〰 **$544** - €613 - **£377** - FF4 024
Ansicht der Karlstrasse in München Lithographie (27x40cm 10x15in) München 2000

KRAUSE Emil Axel 1871-1945 **[106]**

✏ **$518** - €483 - **£320** - FF3 170
Lakeland Scenes Watercolour/paper (23x35cm 9x14in) Birmingham 1999

KRAUSE Francis 1823-1878 **[4]**

☞ **$2 738** - €2 724 - **£1 700** - FF17 869
Figures on a Clifftop Oil/canvas (20.5x30.5cm 8x12in) London 1999

KRAUSE Franz Emil 1836-1900 **[28]**

☞ **$1 182** - €1 023 - **£713** - FF6 713
Südliche Landschaft mit Viadukt und Burgruine Öl/Leinwand (63x89cm 24x35in) München 1998

☞ **$1 362** - €1 534 - **£939** - FF10 061
Italienische Landschaft Öl/Karton (31x24cm 12x9in) Satow 2000

KRAUSE George 1937 **[8]**

📷 **$4 000** - €3 735 - **£2 422** - FF24 499
George Krause Gelatin silver print (18x12cm 7x4in) New-York 1999

KRAUSE Heinrich 1885-1985 **[28]**

☞ **$1 358** - €1 163 - **£795** - FF7 630
Donaukanal Öl/Leinwand (58x85cm 22x33in) Wien 1998

KRAUSE Karl Heinz 1924 **[25]**

⚒ **$1 777** - €1 533 - **£1 068** - FF10 056
Albertus Magnus Bronze (H28.6cm H11in) Köln 1998

KRAUSE Lina 1857-1916 **[18]**

☞ **$1 384** - €1 278 - **£862** - FF8 384
Blumenstilleben Oil/panel (36x23cm 14x9in) Hildrizhausen 1999

KRAUSE Wilhelm August 1803-1864 **[19]**

☞ **$10 980** - €10 901 - **£6 855** - FF71 505
Stürmische See mit Segelschiffen in der Nähe eines Leuchtturmes Öl/Leinwand (98x136.5cm 38x53in) Wien 1999

☞ **$2 858** - €3 323 - **£2 006** - FF21 800
Bewegte See mit Mole Öl/Leinwand (33x58cm 12x22in) Hamburg 2001

☞ **$956** - €998 - **£603** - FF6 548
Marine Oil/canvas (26x39cm 10x15in) Amsterdam 2000

KRAUSKOPF Bruno 1892-1960 **[254]**

✏ **$4 728** - €5 624 - **£3 370** - FF36 892
Mutter mit Kind in der Landschaft Öl/Leinwand (89.5x73cm 35x28in) München 2000

☞ **$1 461** - €1 431 - **£941** - FF9 390
Dächer einer Stadt Mischtechnik/Karton (48x31cm 18x12in) Hildrizhausen 1999

✏ **$1 635** - €1 534 - **£1 010** - FF10 061
Badeinsel Indian ink (41x54cm 16x21in) Stuttgart 1999

〰 **$394** - €460 - **£276** - FF3 018
«Das geschriebene Buch» Lithographie (29x24.5cm 11x9in) Köln 2001

KRAUSZ Simon Andreas 1760-1825 **[12]**

☞ **$4 031** - €3 399 - **£2 392** - FF22 295
Animals Fleeing a Forest Fire Oil/panel (52.5x57cm 20x22in) Amsterdam 2000

✏ **$30 260** - €30 490 - **£18 860** - FF200 000
La plage de Schevengen à marée montante Encre (41.5x53.5cm 16x21in) Paris 2000

KRAUSZ Wilhelm Victor 1878-1959 **[30]**

✏ **$1 324** - €1 453 - **£880** - FF9 534
Hof in Heiligenkreuz Pencil (33x39cm 12x15in) Wien 2000

〰 **$1 121** - €1 308 - **£801** - FF8 580
«Künstlerhaus - 39.Jahresausstellung» Poster (95x126cm 37x49in) Wien 2000

KRAY Wilhelm 1828-1889 **[23]**

☞ **$1 927** - €2 147 - **£1 346** - FF14 086
Des Fischers Traum Öl/Leinwand (74x111cm 29x43in) München 2001

KRCHA Emil 1894-1972 **[32]**

✏ **$881** - €1 033 - **£628** - FF6 778
Nature morte aux bananes Aquarelle/papier (31x41.5cm 12x16in) Warszawa 2000

KREBS Fredrik 1845-1925 **[4]**

✏ **$6 000** - €6 408 - **£4 088** - FF42 031
Konig von Preussen (king of Prussia) Watercolour (39.5x32cm 15x12in) New-York 2001

KREBS Walter 1900-1965 **[122]**

☞ **$575** - €649 - **£404** - FF4 260
Dörfliche Szene Oil/panel (76x85cm 29x33in) Bern 2001

✏ **$302** - €280 - **£185** - FF1 836
Gebirgslandschaft Gouache/papier (63x81cm 24x31in) Bern 1999

KREGTEN van Fedor 1871-1937 **[95]**

☞ **$1 166** - €1 271 - **£803** - FF8 334
Watering Cow Oil/canvas (40.5x60cm 15x23in) Amsterdam 2001

☞ **$586** - €681 - **£405** - FF4 464
Roodbonte koe aan slootwal in polderland-schap Oil/panel (25.5x35cm 10x13in) Groningen 2000

KREIDOLF Ernst 1863-1956 **[130]**

✏ **$759** - €833 - **£515** - FF5 464
Augentrost Gouache/paper (21x28cm 8x11in) Luzern 2000

〰 **$111** - €94 - **£65** - FF615
Alpenblumen Farblithographie (21x29cm 8x11in) Bern 1998

KREITMAYR Johann Baptist 1819-1879 **[6]**

☞ **$2 596** - €2 710 - **£1 643** - FF17 775
Ansicht von Hohenschwangau Öl/Leinwand (56x44cm 22x17in) München 2001

KREITZ Willy 1903-1982 **[45]**

⚒ **$2 637** - €2 230 - **£1 575** - FF14 625
Le sculpteur Plâtre (225x60x60cm 88x23x23in) Antwerpen 1998

⚒ **$532** - €595 - **£369** - FF3 902
Fillette aux cheveux courts Plâtre (H30cm H11in) Antwerpen 2001

KREJCAR Anton 1923 **[6]**

☞ **$3 396** - €3 060 - **£1 988** - FF19 076
«Die Erweckung Plutos» Oil/panel (65x45cm 25x17in) Wien 1998

KRELL Hans c.1500-1586 **[1]**

☞ **$3 116** - €2 907 - **£1 880** - FF19 068
Bildnis des Herzogs Heinrich zu Gotha (1472-1541) Oil/panel (14x11cm 5x4in) Wien 1999

KREMEGNE Pinchus 1890-1981 **[464]**

☞ **$3 005** - €3 354 - **£1 966** - FF22 000
Vase de fleurs Huile/panneau (61x45cm 24x17in) Le Touquet 2000

$1 500 - €1 778 - £1 092 - FF11 664
Still Life with Fruit Oil/canvas (33.5x41cm 13x16in)
Tel Aviv 2001

$532 - €579 - £350 - FF3 798
Porträt eines Mädchens in blauem Kleid
Pastell/Papier (65x50cm 25x19in) Bern 2000

KREMER Petrus 1801-1888 [16]
$2 849 - €3 312 - £2 000 - FF21 728
The Flower Seller Oil/canvas (59.5x51cm 23x20in)
Billingshurst, West-Sussex 2001

KREMLICKA Rudolf 1886-1932 [25]
$5 780 - €5 467 - £3 600 - FF35 860
Landschaft Öl/Leinwand (52x60cm 20x23in) Praha
2001

$3 468 - €3 280 - £2 160 - FF21 516
At the Shoemaker's Oil/cardboard (26x35cm
10x13in) Praha 2000

$722 - €683 - £450 - FF4 482
Reaper Watercolour (15x9cm 5x3in) Praha 2000

KREMP Erminio XIX-XX [7]
$4 500 - €4 665 - £2 700 - FF30 600
Palermo, pescatori sulla spiaggia Olio/tela
(65x120cm 25x47in) Trieste 2001

KRENEK Carl 1880-1948 [40]
$546 - €472 - £329 - FF3 096
Oktober (Weinernte) Mischtechnik/Papier
(16.2x11.4cm 6x4in) Wien 2001

$258 - €291 - £180 - FF1 906
Mädchen, aus dem Fenster blickend Woodcut
(13.5x8cm 5x3in) Wien 2001

KRENN Edmund 1846-1902 [10]
$2 000 - €2 417 - £1 396 - FF15 857
Boy Asleep Oil/panel (20.5x15.5cm 8x6in) Bethesda
MD 2000

KRENZ Alfred Frederick 1899-1980 [20]
$969 - €838 - £584 - FF5 495
Mediterranean Harbour Oil/board (56x85cm
22x33in) Johannesburg 1998

KRESTIN Lazar 1868-1938 [16]
$52 500 - €48 154 - £32 340 - FF315 871
The Lesson Oil/canvas (104x119.5cm 40x47in) New-
York 1999

$35 000 - €34 065 - £21 504 - FF223 454
Three Boys at Study Oil/canvas (74.5x82.5cm
29x32in) Tel Aviv 1999

KRETSCHMER Robert 1818-1872 [6]
$8 500 - €9 882 - £5 966 - FF64 821
Rodents Watercolour/paper (36x36cm 14x14in) New-
York 2001

KRETZSCHMAR Bernhard 1889-1972 [117]
$3 523 - €3 773 - £2 398 - FF24 749
Nature morte à la bouteille et aux fruits
Huile/toile (71x76.5cm 27x30in) Warszawa 2001

$394 - €460 - £276 - FF3 018
Flieder Aquarell, Gouache/Papier (42x35cm 16x13in)
Köln 2001

$521 - €613 - £378 - FF4 024
Innenraum mit Figuren Radierung (26.5x30.5cm
10x12in) Hamburg 2001

KRETZSCHMER Johann Hermann 1811-1890 [24]
$8 092 - €9 203 - £5 612 - FF60 370
Nächtlicher Überfall der Beduinen Öl/Leinwand
(45x69cm 17x27in) Hamburg 2000

$3 991 - €3 748 - £2 473 - FF24 583
Junge Italienerin am Strand Öl/Karton (37x29cm
14x11in) Luzern 1999

KREUGER Nils 1858-1930 [162]
$5 063 - €4 416 - £3 062 - FF28 970
**«Mellby lada» - sommarlandskap med väg och
röd byggnad** Oil/canvas (118x104.5cm 46x41in)
Stockholm 1998

$4 825 - €5 571 - £3 375 - FF36 545
Högalidsgatan Oil/panel (75x75cm 29x29in)
Stockholm 2000

$1 866 - €1 794 - £1 151 - FF11 770
Kalv på Öland Mixed media/panel (23x30.5cm
9x12in) Malmö 1999

$475 - €444 - £292 - FF2 914
Sommarhage Chalks/paper (22x44.5cm 8x17in)
Stockholm 1999

KREUL Johann Fr. Karl 1804-1867 [4]
$20 786 - €18 918 - £12 987 - FF124 094
**Das Bäckermädchen steht mit ihren Backwaren
in der Eingangstür** Oil/panel (47.5x40.5cm 18x15in)
München 1999

$2 990 - €2 559 - £1 800 - FF16 785
A Young Woman selling Bread Oil/copper
(32x27cm 12x10in) London 1998

KREUL Johann Lorenz 1765-1840 [15]
$4 594 - €4 207 - £2 800 - FF27 595
**Portrait of a Mother and Child in a wooded
Landscape** Pastel (80x66cm 31x25in) London 1999

KREUTZ Heinz 1932 [69]
$1 366 - €1 278 - £827 - FF8 384
81 Quadrate über Rosa und Braun Tempera
(96x97cm 37x38in) Stuttgart 1999

$940 - €823 - £569 - FF5 398
Ohne Titel Watercolour (28x19cm 11x7in) Berlin 1998

$210 - €245 - £147 - FF1 609
Ultramarinblau, rotbraun Woodcut in colors
(49x24.5cm 19x9in) Berlin 2000

KREUTZER Felix 1835-1876 [24]
$916 - €869 - £557 - FF5 701
Bäuerin mit Kind in weiter Auenlandschaft
Öl/Leinwand (22.5x27.5cm 8x10in) Köln 1999

KREUZER Conrad 1810-1861 [3]
$6 434 - €6 177 - £4 037 - FF40 519
Blick auf deb Plabutsch Öl/Karton (29.4x41.5cm
11x16in) Wien 1999

KREUZER Vincenz 1809-1888 [13]
$1 622 - €1 817 - £1 127 - FF11 917
Waldstück mit Bach und Rotwild Oil/panel
(20.5x15cm 8x5in) Klagenfurt 2001

KREYDER Alexis 1839-1912 [73]
$5 412 - €4 573 - £3 219 - FF30 000
Panier de prunes Huile/toile (59x73cm 23x28in)
Auvers sur Oise 1998

KREYENKAMP August 1875-1950 [42]
$545 - €511 - £336 - FF3 353
Schmetterlingsflügel Vintage gelatin silver print
(39.7x29.8cm 15x11in) Köln 1999

KREYSSIG Hugo 1873-1939 [37]
$468 - €460 - £290 - FF3 018
Im Frühling Öl/Leinwand (44x65cm 17x25in)
München 1999

KRICHELDORF Carl 1863-1934 [17]
$1 659 - €1 861 - £1 127 - FF12 205
Der Schatzbrief Öl/Leinwand (62x47cm 24x18in)
Zürich 2000

K

KRICKE Norbert 1922-1986 **[52]**
- $97 533 - €82 280 - **£57 203** - FF539 720
  Space Sculpture Metal (118x128x128cm
  46x50x50in) Berlin 1998
- $8 105 - €9 203 - **£5 547** - FF60 370
  Flächenbahn Metal (27.5x58x6cm 10x22x2in) Berlin
  2000
- $1 143 - €1 227 - **£765** - FF8 049
  Im schwarzen Walde Felt pen (43.1x61cm 16x24in)
  Hamburg 2000

KRIEGER Eduard XIX **[3]**
- $6 191 - €5 635 - **£3 800** - FF36 962
  Hansel and Gretel hiding in the Forest Oil/canvas
  (95.5x75cm 37x29in) London 1999

KRIEGER Emil 1902-1979 **[4]**
- $2 739 - €2 300 - **£1 610** - FF15 090
  Marabu Bronze (H28cm H11in) Stuttgart 1998

KRIEGER Joseph 1848-1914 **[8]**
- $9 390 - €10 901 - **£6 600** - FF71 505
  Bären in einer Höhle am Eismeer Öl/Leinwand
  (126x110cm 49x43in) Wien 2001

KRIEGHOFF Cornelius David 1815-1872 **[111]**
- $34 140 - €33 035 - **£21 055** - FF216 695
  Indian Encampment on the River Oil/canvas
  (36x53.5cm 14x21in) Toronto 1999
- $27 312 - €26 428 - **£16 844** - FF173 356
  Bilking the Toll Oil/canvas/board (33.5x47cm
  13x18in) Toronto 1999
- $603 - €648 - **£404** - FF4 251
  **The Lee Cone at the Falls of Montmorency near
  Quebec, Lower Canada** Lithographie couleurs
  (46x61cm 18x24in) Montréal 2000

KRIEHUBER Josef 1801-1876 **[80]**
- $1 348 - €1 308 - **£831** - FF8 580
  Bildnis eines jungen Offiziers mit blondem Haar
  Aquarell/Papier (25x20cm 9x7in) Wien 1999

KRIGE François 1913-1995 **[27]**
- $6 260 - €7 022 - **£4 380** - FF46 060
  Still life of Proteas Oil/canvas (52x45.5cm 20x17in)
  Cape Town 2001
- $4 704 - €5 270 - **£3 268** - FF34 568
  Tulip Tree Flowers in a Vase Oil/canvas (48x31cm
  18x12in) Johannesburg 2001
- $290 - €342 - **£200** - FF2 241
  Barrydale Ink (36x51cm 14x20in) Cape Town 2000

KRIKHATZKIJ Wladimir G. 1877-1942 **[31]**
- $751 - €872 - **£518** - FF5 720
  Lenin am Flussufer Öl/Karton (20x31cm 7x12in)
  Wien 2000

KRIKI Christian Vallée dit 1965 **[127]**
- $3 318 - €3 049 - **£2 038** - FF20 000
  La famille Acrylique (97x130cm 38x51in) Paris 1999
- $1 472 - €1 677 - **£1 039** - FF11 000
  Sans titre Acrylique/toile (61x46cm 24x18in)
  Versailles 2001
- $882 - €1 067 - **£616** - FF7 000
  Microcosmos Plastique (54.5x37.5x17cm 21x14x6in)
  Paris 2000
- $255 - €305 - **£182** - FF2 000
  Fuzz Feutre/papier (18x26cm 7x10in) Paris 2000

KRILLÉ Jean 1923 **[28]**
- $1 345 - €1 162 - **£811** - FF7 622
  Blumenstrauss Acrylic/panel (60x73.5cm 23x28in)
  Wien 1998

KRIMMEL John Lewis 1787-1821 **[2]**
- $240 000 - €237 890 - **£150 120** - FF1 560 456
  **View of the Parade of the Victuallers from
  Fourth and Chesnut Streets** Watercolour
  (44x65.5cm 17x25in) New-York 1999

KRIMOV Nikolai Petrovich 1884-1958 **[7]**
- $1 494 - €1 604 - **£1 000** - FF10 521
  View of a Building Watercolour/paper (17.5x23.5cm
  6x9in) London 2000

KRINNER Michaela 1915 **[107]**
- $1 550 - €1 278 - **£913** - FF8 383
  **Stilleben mit Obstschale, roter Kanne und grü-
  ner Karaffe** Öl/Leinwand (50.5x40.5cm 19x15in)
  Lindau 1998
- $472 - €511 - **£323** - FF3 353
  Männerporträt Charcoal/paper (38x27cm 14x10in)
  Stuttgart 2001
- $246 - €230 - **£149** - FF1 509
  Der Löwe von Mykene Etching (61x47.5cm
  24x18in) Stuttgart 1999

KRISANAMIS Udomsak 1966 **[2]**
- $10 000 - €11 603 - **£6 904** - FF76 110
  Starry Mixed media/canvas (120x120cm 47x47in)
  New-York 2000

KRISTENSEN Esben Hanefelt 1952 **[12]**
- $831 - €807 - **£513** - FF5 293
  Komposition Oil/panel (55x100cm 21x39in) Vejle
  1999

KRISTO de Bela 1920 **[44]**
- $1 551 - €1 829 - **£1 090** - FF12 000
  Les trois modèles Huile/toile (32x55cm 12x21in)
  Paris 2000
- $580 - €610 - **£364** - FF4 000
  Nu à l'atelier Huile/carton (24x33cm 9x12in) Paris
  2000

KRISTUPAS Richard David 1954 **[10]**
- $1 600 - €1 528 - **£1 000** - FF10 022
  A Woodcock in the Snow Pencil (32x42cm
  12x16in) London 1999

KRIWET Ferdinand 1942 **[13]**
- $1 333 - €1 431 - **£892** - FF9 390
  Poem Print Print (135x135cm 53x53in) Königstein
  2000

KRIZE Yehiel 1909-1968 **[63]**
- $1 250 - €1 327 - **£846** - FF8 706
  Figures in a Landscape Mixed media (36x46cm
  14x18in) Tel Aviv 2001
- $950 - €1 127 - **£692** - FF7 391
  Untitled Oil/canvas (35x24cm 13x9in) Tel Aviv 2001
- $1 000 - €1 037 - **£659** - FF6 801
  A Mother and her Son in the Alley Gouache/paper
  (47x67cm 18x26in) Herzelia-Pituah 2000

KRIZHITSKY Konstantin Yiakovlev 1858-1911 **[4]**
- $9 095 - €10 824 - **£6 500** - FF71 000
  Outside the Monastery at Sunset Oil/canvas
  (69x90cm 27x35in) London 2000

KROCK Heinrich 1671-1738 **[8]**
- $3 864 - €3 226 - **£2 296** - FF21 163
  Den hellige familie holder hvil på rejsen Oil/can-
  vas (98x73cm 38x28in) København 1998

KROGH von Charlotte S. 1827-1914 **[1]**
- $3 763 - €4 295 - **£2 614** - FF28 176
  Ung pige ved havet Oil/canvas (52x47cm 20x18in)
  København 2000

KROHA Jiri 1893-1974 **[3]**
- $5 202 – €4 920 – **£3 240** – FF32 274
  Composition abstraite Pastel/papier (33.5x28cm 13x11in) Praha 2001

KROHG Christian 1852-1925 **[80]**
- $48 093 – €50 166 – **£30 340** – FF329 066
  Ellen Hvide Bang Oil/canvas (178x111cm 70x43in) Oslo 2000
- $5 597 – €6 596 – **£3 933** – FF43 268
  Flickor i dörröppning Oil/canvas (62x52cm 24x20in) Malmö 2001
- $9 333 – €10 563 – **£6 528** – FF69 292
  «Mann overbord!» Oil/canvas (33x46cm 12x18in) Oslo 2001

KROHG Othilia, Oda 1860-1935 **[4]**
- $5 615 – €4 884 – **£3 385** – FF32 037
  Italienergut Oil/canvas (55x46cm 21x18in) Oslo 1998

KROHG Per Lasson 1889-1965 **[79]**
- $6 385 – €6 000 – **£3 848** – FF39 358
  Från Bolognerskogen Oil/panel (60x90cm 23x35in) Stockholm 1999
- $345 – €399 – **£243** – FF2 618
  De prøver nybåten Watercolour/paper (24x15cm 9x5in) Oslo 2000
- $519 – €442 – **£310** – FF2 902
  «Schous Öl er Godt» Lithograph (72x59cm 28x23in) Oslo 1998

KROHN Xan 1882-1959 **[17]**
- $844 – €719 – **£504** – FF4 715
  Interiör med figurer Oil/canvas (60x68cm 23x26in) Oslo 1998

KRØJER Tom 1942 **[123]**
- $1 422 – €1 608 – **£961** – FF10 549
  Valpri Oil/canvas (144x99cm 56x38in) København 2000
- $621 – €697 – **£434** – FF4 573
  Blomstrende landskab Oil/canvas (74x50cm 29x19in) København 2001
- $215 – €241 – **£149** – FF1 581
  Parklandskab Gouache/paper (76x57cm 29x22in) Viby J, Århus 2001

KROKFORS Kristian 1952 **[32]**
- $976 – €1 093 – **£678** – FF7 170
  Kullar Oil/board (71x103.5cm 27x40in) Helsinki 2001
- $167 – €185 – **£116** – FF1 213
  Blå karta Color lithograph (51x38cm 20x14in) Helsinki 2001

KROL Abraham 1919 **[13]**
- $1 215 – €1 372 – **£855** – FF9 000
  Le baiser Burin (22x30cm 8x11in) Paris 2001

KROLL Leon A. 1884-1974 **[108]**
- $11 000 – €12 708 – **£7 702** – FF83 359
  Woman reading on Rocks Oil/canvas (40.5x61cm 15x24in) New-York 2001
- $15 000 – €17 587 – **£10 791** – FF115 366
  Low Tide, Gloucester Oil/board (23x28cm 9x11in) New-York 2001
- $750 – €698 – **£463** – FF4 577
  Portrait of a young Woman Crayon (46x27cm 18x11in) Portland ME 1999
- $210 – €226 – **£140** – FF1 481
  Monique Lithograph (28x23cm 11x9in) Cleveland OH 2000

KROLLMAN Gustav 1888-? **[8]**
- $1 400 – €1 624 – **£982** – FF10 654
  «Montana» Poster (101x76cm 40x30in) New-York 2001

KRÖN Paul 1869-1936 **[51]**
- $1 092 – €1 220 – **£740** – FF8 000
  Scène de basse-cour en Bretagne Huile/toile (62x82cm 24x32in) Paris 2000

KRONBERG Julius 1850-1921 **[50]**
- $54 648 – €51 094 – **£33 672** – FF335 156
  Vilande Bacchant Oil/canvas (199x131cm 78x51in) Stockholm 1999
- $3 199 – €3 602 – **£2 204** – FF23 625
  Friherrinnan Anna Elisabeth Lisinka Leuhusen, född Sörenen Oil/canvas (125x91cm 49x35in) Stockholm 1999
- $736 – €868 – **£517** – FF5 693
  Operasångerskan Matilda Jungstedt-Reutersvärd som Orphius Oil/panel (34x39cm 13x15in) Malmö 2000

KRONBERG Louis 1872-1965 **[119]**
- $3 750 – €3 741 – **£2 341** – FF24 537
  The Curtain call Oil/canvas (91x73cm 36x29in) Watertown MA 1999
- $1 000 – €1 120 – **£696** – FF7 349
  Girl with Hat Oil/canvas (33x22cm 13x9in) Watertown MA 2001
- $425 – €476 – **£295** – FF3 123
  Fan Study Pastel/paper (23x46cm 9x18in) Watertown MA 2001

KRONBERGER Carl 1841-1921 **[81]**
- $2 973 – €2 723 – **£1 812** – FF17 859
  Dornröschen Oil/canvas (91x120.5cm 35x47in) Amsterdam 1999
- $4 187 – €3 835 – **£2 552** – FF25 154
  Der Geniesser Oil/panel (17.5x12.4cm 6x4in) München 1999

KRONENBERG Fritz 1901-1960 **[25]**
- $237 – €220 – **£143** – FF1 442
  Am Watt Indian ink (31.5x41cm 12x16in) Heidelberg 1999

KRÖNER Christian Johann 1838-1911 **[114]**
- $2 739 – €3 068 – **£1 903** – FF20 123
  Hirschfamilie auf Waldlichtung an einem schönen Frühlingstag Öl/Leinwand (85x124cm 33x48in) Staufen 2001
- $913 – €1 074 – **£654** – FF7 043
  Winterlandschaft Öl/Leinwand (29x38cm 11x14in) München 2001
- $381 – €409 – **£255** – FF2 683
  Fasane am Waldrand Aquarell/Papier (12x17cm 4x6in) Köln 2000

KRÖNER Karl 1887-1972 **[14]**
- $4 653 – €5 624 – **£3 248** – FF36 892
  Ischia, Ponte mit Castello Aragonese Öl/Leinwand (80.5x105cm 31x41in) Berlin 2000
- $526 – €613 – **£368** – FF4 024
  Weingärten vor Torbole Aquarell/Papier (50x68cm 19x26in) Berlin 2000

KROP Hildo Hildebrand L. 1884-1970 **[37]**
- $4 516 – €4 311 – **£2 822** – FF28 277
  Zuidfranse boerin - Peasanwoman from the South of France Glazed ceramic (H29.5cm H11in) Amsterdam 1999

KROPFF Joop 1892-1979 **[100]**
- $834 – €817 – **£535** – FF5 357
  A Townview in Autumn Oil/canvas (60.5x40cm 23x15in) Amsterdam 1999
- $445 – €499 – **£309** – FF3 274
  Melktijd Oil/panel (12.5x21.5cm 4x8in) Rotterdam 2001

K

KROTOV Youri 1964 **[176]**
$3 885 - €4 170 - £2 600 - FF27 356
Watching the Water Lilies Oil/canvas (61x46cm 24x18in) Fernhurst, Haslemere, Surrey 2000

KROTOWSKI Stephan 1881-? **[6]**
$1 800 - €2 008 - £1 178 - FF13 172
«Söhnlein Rheingold» Poster (58x87.5cm 22x34in) New-York 2000

KROUTHÉN Johan 1858-1932 **[317]**
$6 014 - €6 721 - £4 077 - FF44 085
Höst Oil/canvas (100x148cm 39x58in) Stockholm 2000
$4 439 - €5 125 - £3 105 - FF33 621
Sommarlandskap med stugor och pickande höns Oil/canvas (50x74.5cm 19x29in) Stockholm 2001
$816 - €987 - £570 - FF6 473
Havsvik Oil/canvas (25x35cm 9x13in) Stockholm 2000

KRØYER Peder Severin 1851-1909 **[224]**
$80 500 - €67 215 - £47 850 - FF440 900
Augustaften i Thy Oil/canvas (124x226cm 48x88in) Köbenhavn 1998
$48 541 - €46 462 - £30 153 - FF304 773
Söstudie Oil/canvas (42x63cm 16x24in) Köbenhavn 1999
$27 683 - €25 452 - £17 100 - FF166 953
Nögen ung pige, Friluftsstudie Oil/panel (40x32cm 15x12in) Vejle 1998
$8 820 - €10 067 - £6 127 - FF66 037
Buste af Holger Drachmann Bronze (H44.5cm H17in) Köbenhavn 2000
$1 762 - €1 748 - £1 102 - FF11 464
Italienske markarbejdere Pencil/paper (15x22cm 5x8in) Köbenhavn 1999
$239 - €268 - £165 - FF1 760
Selvportraet Etching (22.5x18cm 8x7in) Köbenhavn 2000

KRUCHEN Julius 1855-1912 **[7]**
$2 607 - €3 068 - £1 840 - FF20 122
Blick über den Rhein mit Rolandsbogen links Öl/Leinwand (41x51cm 16x20in) Köln 2001

KRUCK Christian 1925-1985 **[135]**
$579 - €665 - £396 - FF4 360
Tropea, süditalienische Landschaft Watercolour (31.5x50cm 12x19in) Heidelberg 2000
$119 - €128 - £81 - FF838
Château Sud Farblithographie (50x64cm 19x25in) Satow 2001

KRUG Edouard 1829-1901 **[2]**
$9 500 - €11 172 - £6 811 - FF73 282
Motherhood Oil/canvas (97x195cm 38x76in) New-York 2001

KRUG Karl Heinz 1915-1967 **[38]**
$763 - €716 - £471 - FF4 695
Komposition Mischtechnik/Papier (49x60cm 19x23in) Stuttgart 1999

KRUG Ludwig 1490-1532 **[14]**
$224 - €256 - £155 - FF1 676
Die Geburt Christi Kupferstich (16.3x12.5cm 6x4in) Berlin 2000

KRÜGER Andreas Ludwig 1743-1805 **[2]**
$1 480 - €1 687 - £1 032 - FF11 067
Vorstellung der West-Seite des Garten-Portals zu Sans-Souci Radierung (26.5x44cm 10x17in) Berlin 2001

KRUGER Barbara 1945 **[78]**
$3 800 - €3 567 - £2 347 - FF23 395
Untitled Color lithograph (52x52cm 20x20in) New-York 1999

$15 000 - €17 404 - £10 356 - FF114 165
Untitled, You are Getting What You Paid For Photograph (183x122cm 72x48in) New-York 2000

KRUGER Dolf 1923 **[7]**
$234 - €272 - £164 - FF1 786
Bruggebouwers Gelatin silver print (20x20cm 7x7in) Amsterdam 2001

KRÜGER Franz 1797-1857 **[58]**
$19 557 - €23 008 - £13 806 - FF150 921
Porträt des Zaren Nikolaus I Öl/Leinwand (98x79cm 38x31in) Köln 2001
$792 - €767 - £497 - FF5 030
Mädchen in weissem, dekolletiertem Musselinkleid und Schneckenfrisur Aquarell/Papier (25x19cm 9x7in) Berlin 1999

KRÜGER Hermann 1834-1908 **[3]**
$2 391 - €2 812 - £1 714 - FF18 446
Blick auf die italienische Küste Öl/Leinwand (38x54cm 14x21in) Düsseldorf 2001

KRÜGER Johann Conrad 1733-1791 **[2]**
$4 484 - €5 298 - £3 177 - FF34 752
Agnes Eleonore von Thun auf Tribohm/Joachim Friedrich von Thun Öl/Leinwand (78x59cm 30x23in) Zürich 2000

KRUGER Richard 1880-? **[14]**
$700 - €774 - £485 - FF5 074
Desert Landscape Oil/canvas (76x60cm 30x24in) Felton CA 2001

KRUIJFF de Cornelis 1774-1828 **[3]**
$9 571 - €10 732 - £6 500 - FF70 399
Amsterdam, a View of the New Round Lutheran Church on the Singel Oil/panel (31x45.5cm 12x17in) London 2000

KRUIJSEN Johannes 1874-1938 **[7]**
$1 045 - €1 089 - £662 - FF7 143
Boslaan Oil/canvas (44x56cm 17x22in) Maastricht 2000

KRUIS Ferdinand 1869-1944 **[13]**
$1 292 - €1 061 - £750 - FF6 961
A Dutch Town on a Canal Watercolour (35x28cm 13x11in) London 1998

KRULL Germaine 1897-1985 **[212]**
$953 - €1 067 - £646 - FF7 000
«Le Sphinx» Tirage argentique (21.5x18cm 8x7in) Paris 2000

KRUMLINDE Olof 1856-1945 **[104]**
$932 - €1 099 - £655 - FF7 211
Skånska gårdar Oil/canvas (48x59cm 18x23in) Malmö 2000
$1 016 - €1 065 - £643 - FF6 983
Äppleplockning på gård vid Kullens fot Oil/canvas (27x37cm 10x14in) Malmö 2000

KRUMMACHER Karl 1867-1955 **[25]**
$3 618 - €3 579 - £2 256 - FF23 477
Gehöft am Nachmittag Oil/panel (47.5x65cm 18x25in) Ahlden 1999

KRUSE Max 1854-1942 **[17]**
$877 - €818 - £541 - FF5 366
Marathonläufer Bronze (H45cm H17in) Köln 1999

KRUSE von Ingrid 1935 **[10]**
$1 288 - €1 534 - £921 - FF10 061
«Leonard Bernstein, Salzau» Gelatin silver print (45.7x37.1cm 17x14in) Berlin 2000

KRUSEMAN Frederik Marianus 1816-1882 **[100]**
- **$50 193** - €58 991 - **£34 801** - FF386 958
  Wood Gatherers and skaters in a Wintry Landscape Oil/panel (58.5x79cm 23x31in)
  Amsterdam 2000
- **$9 085** - €10 460 - **£6 200** - FF68 614
  A Summer Landscape with Harvesting Farmers Oil/panel (28.5x38cm 11x14in) London 2000

KRUSEMAN Jan Adam Jansz. 1804-1862 **[12]**
- **$6 043** - €6 807 - **£4 165** - FF44 649
  A Woman in the Regional Costume of Gouda Holding a Child Oil/canvas/board (119x89.5cm 46x35in) Amsterdam 2000

KRUSEMAN Jan Theodoor 1835-1895 **[9]**
- **$21 717** - €20 420 - **£13 446** - FF133 947
  Plage de Scheveningen Oil/canvas (101x152cm 39x59in) Amsterdam 1999
- **$2 422** - €2 816 - **£1 700** - FF18 469
  Vessels at Anchor Oil/canvas (30x42cm 11x16in) Billingshurst, West-Sussex 2001

KRÜSI Hans 1920-1995 **[106]**
- **$2 308** - €2 611 - **£1 614** - FF17 129
  Menschengruppe mit Tierfiguren Öl/Papier (52x91cm 20x35in) St. Gallen 2001
- **$386** - €374 - **£238** - FF2 453
  Tiere Technique mixte (29.5x42cm 11x16in) Zürich 1999
- **$430** - €450 - **£284** - FF2 953
  Paysage animé Technique mixte/papier (51x70cm 20x27in) Genève 2000

KRUTAK Joseph XX **[2]**
- **$13 000** - €12 365 - **£7 893** - FF81 107
  «Happy Birthday (Suit)» Ink (44x28cm 17x11in) New-York 1999

KRUYDER Herman 1881-1953 **[65]**
- **$20 737** - €19 966 - **£12 966** - FF130 970
  Doorvallend Licht Oil/canvas/panel (121x85cm 47x33in) Amsterdam 1999
- **$3 680** - €3 630 - **£2 266** - FF23 812
  Paddestoelen Oil/canvas/board (34x25.5cm 13x10in) Amsterdam 1999
- **$1 026** - €888 - **£622** - FF5 828
  A farmer and his pigs Pencil/paper (16x16cm 6x6in) Amsterdam 1998

KRUYS Cornelius c.1620-c.1660 **[11]**
- **$26 406** - €27 441 - **£16 560** - FF180 000
  Nature morte à la tourte et au vase Rohmer sur un entablement Huile/panneau (44.5x67.5cm 17x26in) Paris 2000

KRUYSEN Antoon 1898-1977 **[89]**
- **$1 677** - €1 452 - **£1 018** - FF9 525
  A mill Oil/canvas (40x50cm 19x15in) Amsterdam 1999

KRYSTUFEK Elke 1970 **[4]**
- **$2 929** - €2 851 - **£1 800** - FF18 704
  I can see the whole Room!...and there's nobody in it Acrylic (76x79cm 29x31in) London 1999

KRYZHITSKII Konstantin Iakovlev. 1858-1911 **[13]**
- **$6 803** - €7 506 - **£4 509** FF49 236
  Coastal Scene with Sailboat Oil/canvas (42x60cm 16x23in) London 2000
- **$3 984** - €4 629 - **£2 800** - FF30 363
  Gone to Pick Mushrooms Watercolour/paper (36x52cm 14x20in) London 2001

KRZYZANOWSKA Michalina 1883-1962 **[5]**
- **$854** - €998 - **£585** - FF6 544
  Vistule vers Lomianki Huile/panneau (64.5x67.5cm 25x26in) Warszawa 2000

KRZYZANOWSKI Konrad 1872-1922 **[9]**
- **$3 633** - €4 274 - **£2 614** - FF28 034
  Portrait d'Aleksander Mazaraki Huile/panneau (41x31.5cm 16x12in) Warszawa 2001

KRZYZANSKI Józef 1898-1987 **[2]**
- **$3 735** - €3 668 - **£2 317** - FF24 059
  En lisant Oil/canvas (81x64.5cm 31x25in) Warszawa 1999

KUBA Ludvík 1863-1956 **[77]**
- **$1 618** - €1 531 - **£1 008** - FF10 040
  Fleurs Huile/toile (47x35.5cm 18x13in) Praha 2001
- **$809** - €765 - **£504** - FF5 020
  Charrettes Huile/panneau (10.5x15cm 4x5in) Praha 2000
- **$162** - €184 - **£111** - FF1 207
  Bildnis eines bärtigen Mannes Chalks/paper (54x32.5cm 21x12in) München 2000

KUBARKKU Mick 1922 **[9]**
- **$1 202** - €1 274 - **£801** - FF8 354
  Namangwarri - The Salt Water Crocodile Pregnant with Eggs Mixed media (125x60cm 49x23in) Melbourne 2000

KUBAT Milan 1945 **[6]**
- **$3 820** - €3 270 - **£2 299** - FF21 451
  «Drei Grazien» Oil/panel (83.5x109cm 32x42in) Wien 1998

KUBBOS Eva 1928 **[21]**
- **$2 401** - €2 578 - **£1 607** - FF16 910
  Dark Summer Watercolour, gouache (99.5x75.5cm 39x29in) Melbourne 2000

KUBEL Otto 1868-1951 **[15]**
- **$1 436** - €1 329 - **£879** - FF8 720
  Bayrische Wirtsstube Öl/Leinwand (54.5x66cm 21x25in) Hamburg 1999

KUBERT Joe 1926 **[2]**
- **$2 750** - €2 952 - **£1 840** - FF19 362
  Page 11 from The Brave & The Bold No.35 Ink (47x33.5cm 18x13in) New-York 1999

KUBICEK Janus 1927-1993 **[15]**
- **$1 127** - €1 166 - **£702** - FF6 992
  Nature morte à l'assiette et feuilles Tempera (50x65cm 19x25in) Praha 2001

KUBIERSCHKY Erich 1854-1944 **[43]**
- **$1 184** - €1 023 - **£715** - FF6 709
  Winterliche Flusslandschaft mit Bäumen Öl/Leinwand (32.5x40.5cm 12x15in) Frankfurt 1998
- **$588** - €562 - **£358** - FF3 689
  Landschaft mit Bäumen an einem Bach Pencil/paper (24.1x34cm 9x13in) Stuttgart 1999

KUBIN Alfred 1877-1959 **[931]**
- **$1 974** - €2 325 - **£1 388** - FF15 254
  Der Galan vor dem Stier Ink (18x26.5cm 7x10in) Wien 2000
- **$240** - €245 - **£150** - FF1 609
  Seegespenst Lithographie (22x24cm 8x9in) Hamburg 2000

KUBINYI Kalman 1906-1973 **[18]**
- **$140** - €150 - **£93** - FF985
  The Farm Lithograph (18x25cm 7x10in) Cleveland OH 2000

KUBISTA Bohumil 1884-1918 **[26]**
- **$6 360** - €7 158 - **£4 382** - FF46 954
  Kubistisches Stilleben mit Tassen, Kanne und Gefässen Öl/Leinwand (40x57cm 15x22in) Zwiesel 2000

K

$722 - €683 - **£450** - FF4 482
Prière Gravure bois (25.5x15.5cm 10x6in) Praha 2001

KÜCHENMEISTER Rainer 1926 **[69]**
$8 835 - €7 649 - **£5 362** - FF50 172
«Saturn» Mixed media/panel (110x92.5cm 43x36in) München 1998
$419 - €460 - **£284** - FF3 018
Figuration Indian ink (65x50cm 25x19in) Berlin 2000

KÜCHLER Albert 1803-1886 **[22]**
$2 842 - €2 691 - **£1 768** - FF17 654
En familie fra landet i faerd med at rejse bort fra Rom Oil/canvas (38x47cm 14x18in) Köbenhavn 1999
$583 - €670 - **£404** - FF4 397
Josef med Jesusbarnet Oil/canvas (34x27cm 13x10in) Köbenhavn 2000

KUCKEI Peter 1938 **[6]**
$5 260 - €6 135 - **£3 693** - FF40 246
Ohne Titel Öl/Leinwand (100x95cm 39x37in) Köln 2000

KUDER René 1882-1962 **[4]**
$511 - €438 - **£307** - FF2 875
Bauer mit zwei Pferden und Pflug auf dem Feld Aquarell/Papier (41x45cm 16x17in) St. Gallen 1998

KUDO Tetsumi 1935-1990 **[17]**
$29 082 - €28 203 - **£18 426** - FF185 000
Your Idol Construction (85x134x13cm 33x52x5in) Paris 1999
$810 - €762 - **£505** - FF5 000
Champignon vénéneux phallus Assemblage (14x10cm 5x3in) Nantes 1999

KUDRIASHEV Ivan 1896-1972 **[19]**
$6 610 - €5 648 - **£4 000** - FF37 050
Untitled Watercolour (19.5x13cm 7x5in) London 1998

KUDRYASHOV Oleg 1932 **[1]**
$850 - €817 - **£527** - FF5 357
Untitled Monotype (31x24cm 12x9in) Washington 1999

KUEHL Gotthard Johann 1850-1915 **[49]**
$6 424 - €5 623 - **£3 890** - FF36 884
Diele mit Kartofelschälerin Öl/Karton (45.2x35.5cm 17x13in) Berlin 1998
$1 740 - €2 045 - **£1 206** - FF13 415
Rufender Bauer Oil/panel (22x16cm 8x6in) Stuttgart 2000
$2 358 - €2 812 - **£1 681** - FF18 446
«Travemünde» Gouache (34x46.5cm 13x18in) Königstein 2000

KUEHNE Max 1880-1968 **[107]**
$6 000 - €6 661 - **£4 173** - FF43 694
Still Life with Window View Oil/masonite (74x59cm 29x23in) Milford CT 2001
$1 700 - €1 857 - **£1 094** - FF12 178
Haystacks Oil/board (22x31cm 9x12in) Mystic CT 2000
$850 - €773 - **£512** - FF5 068
Houses Along an Inlet, Possibly New England Watercolour (36x45cm 14x18in) Bethesda MD 1998

KÜGELGEN von Franz Gerhard 1772-1820 **[11]**
$7 883 - €8 181 - **£5 001** - FF53 662
Der Genius des Guten Öl/Leinwand (75x57cm 29x22in) Leipzig 2000

KUGHLER Francis Vandiveer 1901 **[5]**
$1 700 - €1 625 - **£1 035** - FF10 662
Thursday at Fulton Street Oil/masonite (59x73cm 23x29in) Cleveland OH 1999

KUGLER Franz Theodor 1808-1858 **[1]**
$5 365 - €6 135 - **£3 684** - FF40 246
Dreiviertelportrait des Adolph von Menzel Pencil/paper (32x26cm 12x10in) Lindau 2000

KUGLMAYR Max 1863-? **[27]**
$553 - €613 - **£384** - FF4 024
Kornernte in Oberbayern Öl/Leinwand (13.5x24.5cm 5x9in) Köln 2001

KUHBEIL Carl Ludwig 1770-1823 **[2]**
$4 500 - €4 973 - **£3 152** - FF32 624
The Great Vista Oil/canvas (74x112cm 29x44in) Chicago IL 2001

KUHFELD Peter 1952 **[18]**
$4 252 - €3 630 - **£2 500** - FF23 809
Jemima and Florence, Aged 3 & 5 Oil/canvas/board (53x38.5cm 20x15in) London 1998
$1 276 - €1 090 - **£750** - FF7 147
Catherine Reading Oil/board (38x32.5cm 14x12in) London 1998

KUHFUSS Paul 1883-1960 **[84]**
$1 595 - €1 534 - **£982** - FF10 061
Blumenstrauss vor rotem Grund Oil/panel (100x67cm 39x26in) Köln 1999
$634 - €767 - **£443** - FF5 030
Entenpaar Pastell (42x55.8cm 16x21in) Berlin 2000
$360 - €409 - **£250** - FF2 683
Am Zeughaus Lithographie (31x41cm 12x16in) Berlin 2001

KUHLER Otto August 1894-1977 **[24]**
$300 - €307 - **£188** - FF2 012
The Base of the Chrysler Etching (24x18cm 9x7in) Cleveland OH 2000

KUHLMANN-REHER Emil 1886-1957 **[28]**
$309 - €307 - **£193** - FF2 012
Pfeifenraucher mit Bierkrug am Tisch Öl/Leinwand (30.5x25.5cm 12x10in) München 1999

KUHN Charles 1903-? **[8]**
$1 400 - €1 517 - **£933** - FF9 951
«Restaurant Locanda, Singerhaus Basel» Poster (127x90cm 50x35in) New-York 2000

KUHN Friedrich 1926-1972 **[39]**
$5 186 - €4 482 - **£3 078** - FF29 399
Ohne Titel Öl/Leinwand (100x80cm 39x31in) Zollikon 1998
$926 - €1 026 - **£628** - FF6 733
Komposition Coloured pencils/paper (76.5x52cm 30x20in) Zürich 2000
$206 - €199 - **£127** - FF1 308
Palmensessel Farbserigraphie (50x65cm 19x25in) Zürich 1999

KUHN Hans 1905-1991 **[74]**
$1 139 - €1 329 - **£800** - FF8 720
Blaues Meer, Roter Himmel Mischtechnik (50x65cm 19x25in) Köln 2000

KÜHN Heinrich 1866-1944 **[141]**
$4 500 - €5 112 - **£3 157** - FF33 530
Still Life Bromoil print (38x28cm 14x11in) New-York 2001

KUHN Johann Baptist 1810-1861 **[2]**
$3 061 - €3 579 - **£2 151** - FF23 477
Ansicht vom Karolinenplatz mit reicher Personenstaffage Aquarell/Papier (21x15cm 8x5in) München 2000

KUHN John 1949 [10]
- 🎨 **$3 750** – €3 428 – **£2 294** – FF22 483
  Four Glass Vessels Sculpture, glass (14x28cm 5x11in) New-York 1999

KUHN Max 1838-1888 [5]
- ✏️ **$1 987** – €1 698 – **£1 202** – FF11 139
  Schloss Berg am Starnberger See Aquarell/Papier (18x25cm 7x9in) München 1998

KUHN Robert, Bob 1920 [21]
- **$30 000** – €27 272 – **£18 609** – FF178 890
  Running Wild Acrylic/board (50x106cm 20x42in) Hayden ID 1998
- **$6 000** – €5 454 – **£3 613** – FF35 778
  Dueces Wild Acrylic (39x30cm 15x12in) Hayden ID 1998
- 🎨 **$4 500** – €4 091 – **£2 710** – FF26 833
  Ursine Bliss Bronze (H30cm H12in) Hayden ID 1998

KÜHN Walter 1895-1970 [11]
- 🖼️ **$216** – €218 – **£135** – FF1 430
  «**8.Kriegsanleihe**» Poster (95x63cm 37x24in) Wien 2000

KUHN Walter, Walt 1880-1949 [177]
- **$55 000** – €60 192 – **£37 930** – FF394 834
  Bananas Oil/canvas (101.5x76cm 39x29in) New-York 2001
- **$6 000** – €5 139 – **£3 542** – FF33 708
  Raggedy Pants Comedian Oil/masonite (29x20.5cm 11x8in) New-York 1998
- ✏️ **$1 600** – €1 367 – **£968** – FF8 967
  Santa with his Dog/Cowboys toasting/Cowboys Singing/Cowboys and Dog Watercolour (14.5x20.5cm 5x8in) San-Francisco CA 1998
- 🖼️ **$950** – €1 079 – **£650** – FF7 079
  Edith Lithograph (38.5x26cm 15x10in) New-York 1998

KÜHNE Leberecht 1803-? [3]
- **$6 906** – €7 414 – **£4 622** – FF48 631
  Tal in den italienischen Alpen Öl/Leinwand (47.5x39.2cm 18x15in) Hamburg 2000

KÜHNEN Pieter Lodewijk 1812-1877 [12]
- **$3 216** – €3 835 – **£2 293** – FF25 154
  Romantische Landschaft Öl/Leinwand (40.5x56cm 15x22in) Köln 2000
- **$854** – €818 – **£537** – FF5 366
  Weite Flusslandschaft mit Fischern, Abendlicht Oil/panel (20.5x22cm 8x8in) Köln 1999

KUHNERT Wilhelm 1865-1926 [284]
- **$59 426** – €67 491 – **£41 566** – FF442 714
  Kaffernbüffelherde und Jungtiere an Wasserstelle Öl/Leinwand (130x233cm 51x91in) Berlin 2001
- **$18 174** – €17 640 – **£11 316** – FF115 709
  Elefanten vorm Steppenbrand flüchtend Öl/Leinwand (41.5x62.5cm 16x24in) Berlin 1999
- **$8 274** – €9 047 – **£5 800** – FF63 279
  Siberian Tiger Oil/board (27x37.5cm 10x14in) London 2000
- ✏️ **$1 211** – €1 329 – **£823** – FF8 720
  Ente Pencil (31.5x21.4cm 12x8in) Berlin 2000
- 🖼️ **$463** – €383 – **£272** – FF2 513
  Wildschweine Etching (21.5x32cm 8x12in) Heidelberg 1998

KUHNLE H. XIX [1]
- **$1 900** – €2 161 – **£1 317** – FF14 174
  Hudson River Landscape with Cows Oil/canvas (25x40cm 10x16in) Cincinnati OH 2000

KUHR Fritz 1899-1975 [16]
- **$1 186** – €1 329 – **£824** – FF8 720
  Figuren Mischtechnik (27.3x27.5cm 10x10in) Berlin 2001
- 📷 **$2 419** – €2 710 – **£1 681** – FF17 775
  Fotogramm, Dessau Photograph (18x16cm 7x6in) Köln 2001

KÜHRNER Georg Heinrich 1875-1940 [4]
- **$15 000** – €14 230 – **£9 112** – FF93 343
  The Indian Braves Oil/canvas (183x124.5cm 72x49in) New-York 1999

KUHSTOSS Paul 1870-1898 [26]
- **$10 617** – €9 983 – **£6 573** – FF65 485
  Vente de poissons, Katwijk aan Zee Oil/canvas (183x301cm 72x118in) Amsterdam 1999
- **$1 677** – €1 611 – **£1 033** – FF10 569
  Paysage animé au crépuscule Huile/toile (36.5x57cm 14x22in) Bruxelles 1999
- **$582** – €644 – **£408** – FF4 227
  Etang en hiver Huile/toile (18x27cm 7x10in) Bruxelles 2001

KUIJL J. XVII [1]
- **$3 835** – €3 630 – **£2 384** – FF23 812
  A Gentleman, seated half-length at a Table in Front of a Curtain Oil/panel (34x27.5cm 13x10in) Amsterdam 1999

KUIJPERS Theo 1939 [6]
- ✏️ **$1 392** – €1 487 – **£948** – FF9 756
  Compositie Collage (123x98cm 48x38in) Lokeren 2001

KUINDZHI Arkhip Ivanovich c.1842-1910 [4]
- **$27 986** – €33 305 – **£20 000** – FF218 464
  View of Mount Elbrus Oil/paper/board (32.5x46.5cm 12x18in) London 2000

KUITCA Guillermo David 1961 [74]
- **$70 000** – €67 731 – **£43 169** – FF444 283
  Corona de espinas (Kindertotenlieder) Acrylic/canvas (190x240cm 74x94in) New-York 1999
- **$30 000** – €28 887 – **£18 672** – FF189 489
  «**Coming**» Acrylic/canvas (99x88.5cm 38x34in) New-York 1999
- **$3 800** – €3 697 – **£2 338** – FF24 252
  No.17 Oil/canvas (30x23cm 12x9in) New-York 1999
- 🎨 **$18 000** – €20 885 – **£12 427** – FF136 998
  Sin título Construction (59x112x35cm 23x44x13in) New-York 2001

KUJASALO Matti 1946 [29]
- **$1 073** – €1 177 – **£690** – FF7 722
  Utan titel Oil/canvas/panel (63x120cm 24x47in) Helsinki 2000
- 🖼️ **$143** – €168 – **£99** – FF1 103
  Geometrisk komposition Serigraph (50x70cm 19x27in) Helsinki 2000

KUJAU Konrad 1938-2000 [14]
- **$507** – €434 – **£305** – FF2 850
  «**Mann mit weissem Kragen**» nach Jan Steen Öl/Leinwand (70x53cm 27x20in) Stuttgart 1998

KUKLA Reinhold 1877-1965 [8]
- **$686** – €654 – **£419** – FF4 290
  Weg durchs verschneite Tal Öl/Leinwand (80x62cm 31x24in) Wien 1999

KUKUK Willy 1875-1944 [23]
- **$874** – €818 – **£529** – FF5 366
  An der Wüttach Öl/Leinwand (60x70cm 23x27in) Düsseldorf 1999

KULISIEWICZ Tadeusz 1899-1988 [16]

🖎 $660 - €775 - £471 - FF5 083
Famille lisant une lettre Encre/papier (19.5x16cm 7x6in) Warszawa 2000

▥ $454 - €486 - £309 - FF3 188
Femme aux roses Gravure bois (28x15.5cm 11x6in) Kraków 2001

KULLE Jakob 1838-1898 [15]

👁 $5 331 - €6 191 - £3 746 - FF40 611
Allmogeinteriör Oil/canvas (61x84cm 24x33in) Stockholm 2001

KULMALA George Arthur 1896-1940 [25]

👁 $298 - €330 - £202 - FF2 165
Sunlight Shadows Oil/canvas/board (30.5x25.5cm 12x10in) Toronto 2000

KULMBACH von Hans c.1480-1522 [2]

🖎 $30 000 - €26 081 - £18 156 - FF171 078
The Holy Family with Angels on a Tree, after Durer Ink (26x18.5cm 10x7in) New-York 1999

KULOVESI Erkki 1895-1971 [21]

👁 $496 - €471 - £304 - FF3 089
Skog Oil/canvas (55x48cm 21x18in) Helsinki 1999

KULSTRUNK Franz 1861-1944 [22]

👁 $1 114 - €1 308 - £790 - FF8 580
Blick auf die Festung Hohensalzburg Öl/Karton (49x69cm 19x27in) Wien 2000

👁 $336 - €400 - £239 - FF2 621
Blick ins Gebirge Aquarell/Papier (25x35cm 9x13in) Linz 2000

KUMALO Sydney 1935-1988 [24]

🖎 $1 711 - €1 908 - £1 115 - FF12 516
Mother and Child Bronze (H32cm H12in) Johannesburg 2000

KUMAR Ram 1924 [25]

👁 $4 500 - €5 218 - £3 188 - FF34 226
New Zealand Series Oil/canvas (61x92cm 24x36in) New-York 2000

👁 $220 - €234 - £149 - FF1 536
Untitled #1 Ink/paper (54x74.5cm 21x29in) Miami FL 2001

KUMLIEN Akke 1884-1949 [41]

👁 $1 285 - €1 492 - £903 - FF9 790
Stilleben med frukt och krus Oil/canvas (39x50cm 15x19in) Stockholm 2001

👁 $627 - €724 - £438 - FF4 750
Waxholmsbåtar vid Blasieholmen-Stockholm Tempera/panel (26x32cm 10x12in) Stockholm 2001

KUMMER Robert 1818-1889 [15]

👁 $9 550 - €8 692 - £5 967 - FF57 016
Die Plassenburg bei Kulmbach Öl/Karton (36.5x46cm 14x18in) München 1999

👁 $1 367 - €1 431 - £859 - FF9 390
Kilkern, Castel in Schottland Oil/panel (20.5x31.5cm 8x12in) Bremen 2000

🖎 $438 - €409 - £265 - FF2 683
Hochgebirgsmassiv Pencil/paper (39x60cm 15x23in) Stuttgart 1999

KUMPF Gottfried 1930 [183]

🖎 $1 377 - €1 599 - £968 - FF10 487
Stier Bronze (H15.5cm H6in) Wien 2001

▥ $948 - €799 - £559 - FF5 241
«Wintersonne» Farblithographie (50x65cm 19x25in) Wien 1998

KUNA Henryk, Henri 1879-1945 [6]

🖎 $880 - €915 - £554 - FF6 000
Tête de jeune femme Bronze (H51cm H20in) Nîmes 2000

KUNC Milan 1944 [42]

👁 $2 250 - €2 332 - £1 350 - FF15 300
Tourists Nr.2 Acrilico/carta/tela (99x70.5cm 38x27in) Prato 2000

KUNDERA Rudolf 1911 [27]

👁 $744 - €762 - £467 - FF5 000
Place à Marseille Huile/toile (58x58cm 22x22in) Lyon 2000

KÜNDIG Reinhold 1888-1984 [136]

👁 $1 949 - €2 219 - £1 369 - FF14 554
Sonnenblumen Öl/Leinwand (54.5x45cm 21x17in) Zürich 2001

👁 $1 437 - €1 240 - £867 - FF8 133
Haus zwischen Bäumen in Frühlingslandschaft Öl/Leinwand (34x45cm 13x17in) St. Gallen 1998

KUNDMÜLLER Hans 1837-1893 [4]

👁 $1 818 - €1 943 - £1 235 - FF12 744
Lausbube mit Grossmutter Öl/Leinwand (33x26cm 12x10in) Satow 2001

KUNICHIKA Toyohara 1835-1900 [120]

▥ $128 - €144 - £89 - FF942
Acteur Gravure bois (37x24cm 14x9in) Montréal 2001

KUNIMASA Utagawa 1773-1810 [5]

▥ $30 000 - €35 181 - £21 408 - FF230 772
Matsumoto Yonesaburo Print in colors (38x25cm 14x9in) New-York 2000

KUNISADA II 1823-1880 [23]

▥ $175 - €166 - £106 - FF1 091
Portrait of a Lady with Parasol Woodcut (35x23cm 14x9in) South-Natick MA 1999

KUNIYASU Ipposai Yasugoro 1794-1832 [9]

▥ $78 - €92 - £56 - FF603
Gedächtnisbild des Schauspielers Bando Mitsugoro Woodcut in colors (38x26cm 14x10in) Frankfurt 2001

KUNIYOSHI Ichiyusai 1798-1861 [57]

▥ $256 - €240 - £160 - FF1 576
Seichu Gishi de, Crónicas del Loyal Ronin Woodcut (36x24.5cm 14x9in) Madrid 1999

KUNIYOSHI Yasuo 1889-1953 [136]

👁 $45 080 - €43 969 - £27 600 - FF288 420
Landscape Oil/board (38x46cm 14x18in) Tokyo 1999

🖎 $3 200 - €3 310 - £2 022 - FF21 709
Provincetown Cemetery Pencil (29x38cm 11x14in) New-York 2000

🖎 $1 700 - €1 472 - £1 025 - FF9 653
«Tightrope Performer» Lithograph (32.5x22.5cm 12x8in) New-York 1998

KUNST Carl 1884-1912 [23]

▥ $649 - €570 - £394 - FF3 737
Bilgeri-Ski Ausrustung Poster (50x76cm 20x30in) New-York 1999

KÜNSTLER Morton, Mort 1931 [13]

👁 $9 000 - €10 219 - £6 253 - FF67 032
Moonlight Riders Oil/canvas (71x96cm 28x38in) Dallas TX 2001

▥ $305 - €361 - £216 - FF2 369
«It's all my Fault»/«Lee's Surrender» Print in colors (66x97cm 26x38in) Cleveland OH 2001

KUNTZ Karl 1770-1830 **[11]**
- **$2 025** - €2 250 - **£1 408** - FF14 757
  Viehweide mit Baum Oil/panel (40x51cm 15x20in)
  Heidelberg 2001

KUNTZ Roger Edward 1926-1975 **[6]**
- **$3 500** - €3 757 - **£2 342** - FF24 643
  Boatyard Newport Oil/canvas (63x76cm 25x30in)
  Altadena CA 2000

KUNZ Emma 1892-1963 **[18]**
- **$3 339** - €3 932 - **£2 346** - FF25 792
  Ohne Titel Coloured pencils (63x63cm 24x24in)
  Zürich 2000

KUNZ Karl Friedrich 1905-1971 **[17]**
- **$2 896** - €2 812 - **£1 789** - FF18 446
  Kreuzigung Pencil (85x122cm 33x48in) München
  1999

KUNZ Ludwig Adam 1857-1929 **[66]**
- **$6 720** - €6 672 - **£4 200** - FF43 766
  Collection of Fruit and Game on a Table Oil/canvas (100.5x163.5cm 39x64in) London 1999
- **$2 679** - €2 454 - **£1 633** - FF16 098
  Das Asam-Schlössl «Maria Einsiedel» in München-Thalkirchen Öl/Karton (75x64cm 29x25in)
  München 1999

KUPELWIESER Leopold 1796-1862 **[11]**
- **$2 019** - €2 180 - **£1 395** - FF14 301
  Porträt des Mutter des Künstlers Öl/Leinwand (64.5x54cm 25x21in) Wien 2001

KUPER Yuri 1940 **[183]**
- **$10 703** - €10 367 - **£6 732** - FF68 000
  Les deux malles Peinture (200x200cm 78x78in) Paris
  2001
- **$842** - €991 - **£603** - FF6 500
  Composition au marteau et crochet Technique
  mixte/panneau (47x81cm 18x31in) Paris 2001
- **$1 217** - €1 006 - **£714** - FF6 600
  Les cerises Acrylique/papier (24x24cm 9x9in) Paris
  1998
- **$4 710** - €4 573 - **£2 910** - FF30 000
  Table encrier Bronze (74.5x82x60.5cm 29x32x23in)
  Paris 1999

KUPETZKY Johann 1667-1740 **[17]**
- **$4 392** - €4 602 - **£2 905** - FF30 185
  Bildnis der Baronin Huldenberg, Kniestück, sitzend Öl/Leinwand (116x95cm 45x37in) München
  2000

KUPFER Johann Michael 1859-1917 **[8]**
- **$37 432** - €38 307 - **£23 100** - FF251 542
  Im Biergarten Öl/Leinwand (74x108cm 29x42in)
  Düsseldorf 2000

KUPFERMAN Lawrence Edward 1909 **[31]**
- **$375** - €405 - **£256** - FF2 655
  Saragota Springs, Victorian House Drypoint
  (35x24.5cm 13x9in) New-York 2001

KUPFERMAN Moshe 1926 **[64]**
- **$13 500** - €12 513 - **£8 394** - FF82 081
  Untitled Acrylic/canvas (130x162.5cm 51x63in) Tel
  Aviv 1999
- **$3 917** - €4 421 - **£2 755** - FF29 000
  Sans titre Huile/papier (55x77cm 21x30in) Paris 2001
- **$700** - €683 - **£443** - FF4 482
  Untitled Acrylic (27x31.5cm 10x12in) Tel Aviv 1999
- **$1 400** - €1 660 - **£1 019** - FF10 887
  Untitled Mixed media/paper (56.5x75cm 22x29in) Tel
  Aviv 2001

- **$878** - €991 - **£617** - FF6 500
  Sans titre Lithographie (121x80.5cm 47x31in) Paris
  2001

KUPKA Frank, Frantisek 1871-1957 **[470]**
- **$31 020** - €29 145 - **£19 140** - FF191 180
  Cheminée Oil/canvas (38x46cm 14x18in) Praha 1999
- **$7 225** - €6 834 - **£4 500** - FF44 825
  The last Dream of the Dying Heinrich Heine
  Gouache/paper (37.6x48.8cm 14x19in) Praha 2000
- **$277** - €275 - **£173** - FF1 803
  Ohne Titel Farbserigraphie (64x49cm 25x19in) Luzern
  1999

KURAMATA Shiro 1934-1991 **[9]**
- **$48 000** - €51 523 - **£32 121** - FF337 968
  Miss Blanche Metal (91x63x61cm 35x24x24in) New-York 2000
- **$15 000** - €14 838 - **£9 352** - FF97 333
  Stool with Feathers Metal (H54cm H21in) New-York 1999

KURCHÉ Michel 1900-1973 **[2]**
- **$3 580** - €4 027 - **£2 500** - FF26 417
  Mountain Road with Figures Oil/wood (34x50.5cm
  13x19in) London 2001
- **$3 580** - €4 027 - **£2 500** - FF26 417
  Street Scene with Mosque Oil/canvas (34.5x39cm
  13x15in) London 2001

KURELEK William 1927-1977 **[147]**
- **$5 477** - €4 726 - **£3 282** - FF30 999
  Stooking Hay Mixed media/board (32x52cm 12x20in)
  Nepean, Ont. 1998
- **$4 692** - €4 558 - **£2 933** - FF29 899
  Misty Afternoon, Renfrew County Mixed
  media/board (24x24cm 9x9in) Toronto 1999
- **$430** - €477 - **£292** - FF3 128
  Geese Behind a Fence Indian ink (37x58.5cm
  14x23in) Toronto 2000
- **$267** - €288 - **£179** - FF1 888
  Map of Canada Color lithograph (54.5x57cm
  21x22in) Calgary, Alberta 2000

KURELLA von Ludwig 1834-1902 **[4]**
- **$21 411** - €20 134 - **£13 260** - FF132 073
  In a small Town Oil/canvas (66.5x118cm 26x46in)
  Warszawa 1999

KURENNOY Aleksandr Avvkumonih 1865-1944 **[2]**
- **$14 692** - €17 485 - **£10 500** - FF114 693
  Rabbit at Prayer Oil/canvas (76x56cm 29x22in)
  London 2000

KURODA Aki 1944 **[22]**
- **$2 143** - €2 592 - **£1 497** - FF17 000
  Personnage blanc Gouache/papier (75x54cm
  29x21in) Paris 2000
- **$192** - €229 - **£137** - FF1 500
  Composition Lithographie couleurs (80.5x61.5cm
  31x24in) Paris 2000

KURODA Seiki 1866-1924 **[1]**
- **$40 000** - €38 748 - **£24 948** - FF254 168
  Fields Oil/canvas (39.5x30.5cm 15x12in) New-York
  1999

KURON Herbert 1888-? **[32]**
- **$405** - €409 - **£253** - FF2 683
  Sommerliche Blick auf See Öl/Leinwand (37x47cm
  14x18in) Leipzig 2000

KURPERSHOEK Theo 1914-1998 **[12]**
- **$3 906** - €4 538 - **£2 745** - FF29 766
  Vondelpark, Amsterdam Oil/canvas (95x50cm
  37x19in) Amsterdam 2001

K

KURTZ Helmut 1903-1959 **[4]**

🎨 **$865** - **€958** - **£600** - FF6 285
«Parsenn Bahn, Davos» Poster (127x91cm 50x35in)
London 2001

KURTZMAN Harvey XX **[10]**

✎ **$900** - **€966** - **£602** - FF6 336
Page 25 from Christmas Carol, by Charles
Dickens Ink (35x23cm 13x9in) New-York 2000

KURZ & ALLISON XIX **[6]**

🎨 **$325** - **€301** - **£201** - FF1 977
Washington Closing the Lodge Lithograph
(61x45cm 24x18in) New-York 1999

KURZBAUER Eduard 1840-1879 **[10]**

🖼 **$31 460** - **€28 633** - **£19 656** - FF187 818
Vor dem Begräbnis eines schwäbischen
Bauern Öl/Leinwand (116x175cm 45x68in) München
1999

🖼 **$2 521** - **€2 556** - **£1 565** - FF16 769
Porträt eines Dirndls Oil/panel (19.5x14cm 7x5in)
München 2000

KÜRZINGER Marianna 1770-1809 **[1]**

🎨 **$823** - **€715** - **£496** - FF4 692
Teseus als Theaterkostümfigur Radierung
(17.1x10.5cm 6x4in) Berlin 1998

KURZWEIL Maximilian 1867-1916 **[50]**

🎨 **$790** - **€767** - **£492** - FF5 030
Der Polster (Die Gattin des Künstlers) Woodcut in
colors (28.5x25.8cm 11x10in) Berlin 1999

KUSAMA Yayoi 1929 **[100]**

🖼 **$15 000** - **€16 969** - **£10 494** - FF111 307
«Infinity-Nets» Oil/canvas (53.5x45.5cm 21x17in)
New-York 2001

🖼 **$6 000** - **€6 824** - **£4 192** - FF44 760
Untitled Oil/canvas (18x24cm 7x9in) Beverly-Hills CA
2000

🗿 **$20 920** - **€22 456** - **£14 000** - FF147 302
Flower Chair Sculpture (86.5x67.5x76cm
34x26x29in) London 2000

🖼 **$7 000** - **€6 537** - **£4 320** - FF42 882
Untitled Construction (30x15x11cm 11x5x4in) New-
York 1999

✎ **$8 500** - **€7 559** - **£5 198** - FF49 583
Star Pastel (36x26cm 14x10in) New-York 1999

KUSCHEL Max 1862-1935 **[20]**

🖼 **$778** - **€920** - **£552** - FF6 037
Die Toteninsel nach einem Motiv von Arnold
Böcklin Öl/Leinwand (100x100cm 39x39in) Stuttgart
2000

KÜSEL Matthäus 1629-1681 **[2]**

🎨 **$3 205** - **€3 811** - **£2 285** - FF25 000
Il Pomo d'Oro Eau-forte (16.5x27cm 6x10in)
Cherbourg 2000

KÜSEL Melchior 1626-1683 **[12]**

🎨 **$142** - **€153** - **£95** - FF1 006
Unterschiedliche Meer Porten und Pallazzia,
nach Johann Wilhelm Baur Radierung (14.5x21cm
5x8in) Berlin 2000

KUSHNER Robert 1949 **[33]**

✎ **$621** - **€558** - **£370** - FF3 660
Rustles of Spring Mixed media/paper (76x170cm
29x66in) Stockholm 1998

🎨 **$250** - **€279** - **£170** - FF1 827
Tryst Color lithograph (29x63cm 11x24in) Philadelphia
PA 2000

KÜSS Ferdinand 1800-1886 **[12]**

🖼 **$1 844** - **€2 045** - **£1 280** - FF13 415
Varastilleben mit erlegten Vögeln und Korb
Öl/Leinwand (50x39cm 19x15in) Köln 2001

🖼 **$2 400** - **€2 360** - **£1 500** - FF15 480
Girl with a white Rabbit Oil/board (20x16cm 7x6in)
Budapest 1999

KUSTER Friederich act.1811-1822 **[2]**

✎ **$3 500** - **€3 809** - **£2 405** - FF24 987
Lucern County, with central Heart surmounted
by two Birds Watercolour (32x39cm 12x15in)
Downington PA 2001

KUSTER Johann Caspar 1747-1818 **[7]**

🖼 **$1 542** - **€1 656** - **£1 032** - FF10 861
Waldlandschaft mit Figurenstaffage und Bach
Oil/panel (38x28.5cm 14x11in) Zürich 2000

🎨 **$1 803** - **€2 103** - **£1 266** - FF13 797
Vue de Secheiron au bord du lac de Genève
Gravure (22.5x36cm 8x14in) Genève 2000

KÜSTNER Carl 1861-1934 **[45]**

🖼 **$836** - **€716** - **£503** - FF4 694
Flusslandschaft im Winter Öl/Leinwand (70x95cm
27x37in) München 1998

🖼 **$271** - **€256** - **£168** - FF1 676
Bäume Öl/Karton (25x32cm 9x12in) München 1999

KUSTODIEV Boris Mikhailovich 1878-1927 **[59]**

🖼 **$117 808** - **€132 090** - **£80 000** - FF866 456
Celebration at Shrovetide Oil/canvas (80x94cm
31x37in) London 2000

🖼 **$56 815** - **€54 602** - **£35 000** - FF358 165
Horse Fair in Astrakhan Oil/board (34.5x40cm
13x15in) London 2000

✎ **$3 258** - **€2 791** - **£1 958** - FF18 310
Peasant with Speckled Hen Watercolour (31x18cm
12x7in) Cedar-Falls IA 1998

KUTALEK Jan 1917-1987 **[13]**

🗿 **$462** - **€437** - **£288** - FF2 868
Saint Jiri Céramique (H37cm H14in) Praha 2000

KUWASSEG Charles Euphrasie 1838-1904 **[259]**

🖼 **$6 000** - **€5 176** - **£3 606** - FF33 955
Travelers on the River Path/An Alpine View
Oil/canvas (129.5x96.5cm 50x37in) Boston MA 1998

🖼 **$4 500** - **€4 203** - **£2 777** - FF27 567
Village Along the River in the Alps Oil/canvas
(64.5x54.5cm 25x21in) Boston MA 1999

🖼 **$3 479** - **€3 735** - **£2 327** - FF24 500
Vue présumée de Grenoble Huile/toile (19x31cm
7x12in) Grenoble 2000

KUWASSEG Karl Josef 1802-1877 **[25]**

🖼 **$24 000** - **€22 659** - **£14 920** - FF148 634
Shepards near an Alpine River Oil/canvas
(130x97cm 51x38in) Milford CT 1999

🖼 **$3 500** - **€4 058** - **£2 479** - FF26 621
Fisherman on a Rocky Coast Oil/canvas
(65.5x51.5cm 25x20in) New-York 2000

🖼 **$9 571** - **€10 732** - **£6 500** - FF70 399
View in the Amazonian Forest Oil/canvas
(36.5x42cm 14x16in) London 2000

KUYCK van Frans Pieter 1852-1915 **[17]**

🖼 **$3 228** - **€2 975** - **£1 944** - FF19 512
La traversée du troupeau Huile/panneau
(36x69.5cm 14x27in) Antwerpen 1999

KUYCK van Jean-Louis 1821-1871 **[13]**

🖼 **$1 982** - **€2 068** - **£1 250** - FF13 566
The Farmyard Oil/panel (36.5x45cm 14x17in) Bristol,
Avon 2000

KUYCK van Martha 1884-1923 **[1]**
- 📇 **$2 116** - €2 222 - **£1 400** - FF14 577
  «Vlie Olympiade Anvers Antwerpen» Poster (84x61cm 33x24in) London 2001

KUYL van der Gysbrecht 1604-1673 **[3]**
- 🖎 **$81 870** - €75 921 - **£50 000** - FF498 010
  Portrait of Two Girls and Boy of the D'Arenberg Family Mine plomb (109x145cm 42x57in) London 1998

KUYPERS Cornelis 1864-1932 **[88]**
- 📇 **$6 043** - €6 807 - **£4 165** - FF44 649
  Moored Boats on a River at Daown, Renkum Oil/canvas (84x150cm 33x59in) Amsterdam 2000
- 📇 **$2 083** - €2 269 - **£1 434** - FF14 883
  Chickens near a Haystack with a Farmhouse in the Background Oil/canvas (44x75.5cm 17x29in) Amsterdam 2001
- 📇 **$986** - €908 - **£610** - FF5 953
  In the Kitchen-Garden Oil/canvas (25x54cm 9x21in) Amsterdam 1999

KUYPERS Jan 1819-1892 **[1]**
- 📇 **$3 623** - €3 993 - **£2 366** - FF26 194
  Ijsgezicht met schaatsenrijders en koek en zopie Oil/canvas (59x76cm 23x29in) Rotterdam 2000

KUYTEN Harrie 1883-1952 **[76]**
- 📇 **$2 022** - €2 269 - **£1 401** - FF14 883
  Still Life with Flowers Oil/canvas (96x66.5cm 37x26in) Amsterdam 2000
- 📇 **$1 953** - €2 269 - **£1 372** - FF14 883
  Portrait of Asta Nielsen Oil/board (47x21.5cm 18x8in) Amsterdam 2001

KUZNETSOV Pavel Varfolomeevich 1878-1968 **[9]**
- 📇 **$22 414** - €24 060 - **£15 000** - FF157 824
  Summer - Harvest Oil/board (44.5x53cm 17x20in) London 2000

KVAPIL Charles 1884-1957 **[542]**
- 📇 **$9 798** - €10 519 - **£6 555** - FF69 000
  Le peintre, son modèle et sa femme Huile/toile (131x196cm 51x77in) Bayeux 2000
- 📇 **$1 896** - €2 231 - **£1 372** - FF14 636
  Nature morte aux fleurs Huile/toile (60x82cm 23x32in) Sion 2001
- 📇 **$1 060** - €951 - **£630** - FF6 000
  Nu allongé au drapé vert Huile/panneau (27x32cm 10x12in) Vernon 1998
- 🖎 **$552** - €610 - **£374** - FF4 000
  Autoportrait à la tête bandée Aquarelle (31x22cm 12x8in) Paris 2000

KVIUM Michael 1955 **[49]**
- 📇 **$5 910** - €6 705 - **£4 165** - FF43 980
  Outline painting Oil/canvas (200x150cm 78x59in) København 2001
- 📇 **$597** - €670 - **£416** - FF4 393
  Fantasifostre Oil/canvas (33x40cm 12x15in) Viby J, Århus 2001
- 🖎 **$647** - €671 - **£410** - FF4 403
  Siddende kvinde Watercolour/paper (34x25cm 13x9in) Viby J, Århus 2000
- 📇 **$187** - €214 - **£128** - FF1 407
  Competition Color lithograph (50x66cm 19x25in) København 2000

KWIATKOWSKI Jean 1886-1971 **[10]**
- 📇 **$27 594** - €27 441 - **£17 118** - FF180 000
  Sculpture dans un jardin Huile/toile (97x130cm 38x51in) Paris 1999

- 📇 **$23 580** - €22 867 - **£14 835** - FF150 000
  Fleurs mexicaines Huile/toile (81x65cm 31x25in) Paris 1999

KWIATKOWSKI Ludwik 1880-1953 **[2]**
- 📇 **$9 312** - €9 971 - **£6 338** - FF65 408
  La cour Huile/toile (72x82cm 28x32in) Warszawa 2001

KWIATKOWSKI Teofil Antoni Antar 1809-1891 **[10]**
- 🖎 **$1 420** - €1 524 - **£950** - FF10 000
  Portrait d'un jeune homme Encre (38x29cm 14x11in) Paris 2000

KWIRYNSKI Zygmunt XX **[15]**
- 📇 **$457** - €491 - **£306** - FF3 222
  Composition, énergiquement positive Huile/toile (65x75cm 25x29in) Lódz 2000

KYHN Knud 1880-1967 **[98]**
- 📇 **$294** - €329 - **£204** - FF2 159
  Häst Sandstone (39x38cm 15x14in) Stockholm 2001

KYHN Vilhelm Peter C. 1819-1903 **[195]**
- 📇 **$7 139** - €6 564 - **£4 410** - FF43 056
  Landskab ved solnedgang med graessende koer i dis på engen Oil/canvas (122x184cm 48x72in) Vejle 1998
- 📇 **$2 984** - €2 826 - **£1 856** - FF18 536
  Sommerlandskab med hvid udsigt Oil/canvas (38x50cm 14x19in) København 1999
- 📇 **$1 304** - €1 184 - **£814** - FF7 768
  Kystparti med stejle skraenter, i vandkanten store sten, sommerdag Oil/canvas (23.5x32cm 9x12in) København 1999

KYLBERG Carl 1878-1952 **[233]**
- 📇 **$12 637** - €14 664 - **£8 725** - FF96 187
  Kvällens återsken Oil/canvas (41x51cm 16x20in) Stockholm 2000
- 📇 **$2 408** - €2 315 - **£1 486** - FF15 188
  Tulpan i vas Oil/panel (40x33cm 15x12in) Malmö 1999
- 🖎 **$297** - €330 - **£206** - FF2 166
  Djurstudier Pencil/paper (15x9cm 5x3in) Stockholm 2001

KYLBERG Maria Wilhelmina 1828-1864 **[3]**
- 📇 **$2 979** - €3 302 - **£2 064** - FF21 660
  Motiv från Tun, Västergötland Oil/canvas (71.5x85.5cm 28x33in) Malmö 2001

KYLE Georgina Moutray 1865-1950 **[9]**
- 📇 **$4 196** - €3 940 - **£2 600** - FF25 844
  Still Life with a Doll Oil/canvas/panel (73.5x54cm 28x21in) London 1999

KYOSAI Kawanabe 1831-1889 **[8]**
- 🖎 **$523 005** - €561 403 - **£350 000** - FF3 682 560
  Yamato Bijin No Zu (Japanese Beauties) Ink (182x177x2.5cm 71x69xin) London 2000

KYYHKYNEN Juho 1875-1909 **[13]**
- 📇 **$3 985** - €4 373 - **£2 566** - FF28 683
  Strandlandskap Oil/canvas (47x136cm 18x53in) Helsinki 2000
- 📇 **$1 750** - €1 934 - **£1 213** - FF12 686
  Renar i vinterlandskap Oil/canvas (27x39.5cm 10x15in) Helsinki 2001

K

L

L'ALLEMAND Friedrich, Fritz 1812-1866 [8]
- **$69 200** - €72 672 - **£43 600** - FF476 700
  General Franz Fürst von und zu Liechtenstein
  Öl/Leinwand (130x188cm 51x74in) Wien 2000

L'ALLEMAND Sigmund 1840-1910 [7]
- **$10 140** - €9 447 - **£6 305** - FF61 971
  Kaiser Franz Joseph I von Österreich
  Öl/Leinwand (66x53cm 25x20in) Wien 1999

L'AUBINIERE de Georgina M. Steple 1848-1930 [49]
- **$1 231** - €1 128 - **£750** - FF7 396
  A Field of Haystacks on the Jersey Coast
  Oil/paper/panel (29x38cm 11x14in) London 1999

L'ENGLE William Johnson II 1884-1957 [4]
- **$1 300** - €1 389 - **£884** - FF9 112
  Shimmering Spring garden Landscape with Fountain, Garden in Brittany Oil/canvas (79x64cm 31x25in) New-Orleans LA 2001

L'ÉPLATTENIER Charles 1874-1946 [136]
- **$14 257** - €12 202 - **£8 582** - FF80 037
  Le Riffelhorn et le Cervin Huile/toile (114x146cm 44x57in) Zürich 1998
- **$3 556** - €3 101 - **£2 150** - FF20 340
  Le bassin du Doubs Huile/toile (116x89cm 45x35in) Genève 1998
- **$321** - €312 - **£199** - FF2 044
  La Brévine Pastel/papier (28.5x41.5cm 11x16in) Genève 1999

L'HERMINEZ Théo 1921-1997 [4]
- **$2 734** - €3 176 - **£1 921** - FF20 836
  «Lily» Oil/canvas (45x50cm 17x19in) Amsterdam 2001

LA BELLA Vincenzo 1872-1954 [9]
- **$1 800** - €1 555 - **£1 200** - FF10 250
  La processione Olio/legno (57x70cm 22x27in) Roma 1998

LA BERE de Stephen Baghot 1877-1927 [8]
- **$427** - €442 - **£270** - FF2 899
  In the Trenches Watercolour (31x23cm 12x9in) Dorchester, Dorset 2000

LA BRÉLY de Auguste 1838-1906 [15]
- **$4 800** - €4 147 - **£2 400** - FF27 200
  Nudo Olio/tavoletta (54x30cm 21x11in) Genova 1999

LA CAVE de François Morellon XVIII [1]
- **$998** - €855 - **£600** - FF5 608
  Portrait of Antonio Vivaldi Engraving (29x21cm 11x8in) London 1998

LA CHAMBRE de Jean II 1648-1685 [2]
- **$7 000** - FF7 488 - **£4 772** - FF49 116
  Peacocks, Doves, a Deer, an Eagle, a Pheasant & a Horse at a Fountain Black chalk (24x20cm 9x7in) New-York 1998

LA COGNATA Giovanni 1954 [5]
- **$1 250** - €1 296 - **£750** - FF8 500
  Paesaggio di campagna Olio/tela (60x70cm 23x27in) Vercelli 2000

LA CORBIERE de Roger 1893-? [17]
- **$360** - €424 - **£250** - FF2 780
  Brittany Coastline in Moonlight Oil/canvas (45x53cm 18x21in) Carlisle, Cumbria 2000

LA COUR Janus Andreas 1837-1909 [287]
- **$8 595** - €7 806 - **£5 370** - FF51 202
  Skovsö en tidlig morgen over det nyud-sprungne lövvaerk, rosa himmel Oil/canvas (99x153cm 38x60in) Köbenhavn 1999
- **$1 279** - €1 235 - **£809** - FF8 100
  Paysage de montagne Huile/toile (45x47.5cm 17x18in) Paris 1999
- **$461** - €537 - **£329** - FF3 521
  Landskab Oil/canvas (30x43cm 11x16in) Aarhus 2001

LA COURT de Martin 1640-1710 [3]
- **$6 915** - €7 778 - **£4 827** - FF51 018
  Bewaldete Landschaft mit Bauer und Vieh in einer Furt Öl/Leinwand (59x83cm 23x32in) Luzern 2001

LA FARGE John 1835-1910 [57]
- **$1 900 000** - €2 259 584 - **£1 354 130** - FF14 821 900
  The Last Valley - Paradise Rocks Oil/canvas (83x107.5cm 32x42in) New-York 2000
- **$47 500** - €40 583 - **£28 514** - FF266 209
  Still Life with Rose Oil/panel (15x25.5cm 5x10in) New-York 1998
- **$22 000** - €20 461 - **£13 622** - FF134 213
  Full-Length Portrait of a Japanese Noh Dancer as a Shojo Watercolour/paper (18x15cm 7x6in) East-Dennis MA 1999

LA FARGUE Karel 1742-1783 [5]
- **$4 275** - €4 856 - **£3 000** - FF31 852
  Tollbridge over the Canal de Vliet Oil/panel (32x46cm 12x18in) London 2001

LA FARGUE Maria Margaretha 1743-1813 [4]
- **$10 119** - €11 785 - **£7 000** - FF77 303
  Domestic interior with a Husband, his Wife and Their Baby Oil/panel (23x26cm 9x10in) London 2000

LA FARGUE Paulus Constantin 1732-1782 [26]
- **$8 658** - €7 927 - **£5 278** - FF52 050
  Vue de ville, Nimègue Huile/toile (24.5x32cm 9x12in) Paris 1999
- **$2 933** - €3 403 - **£2 025** - FF22 324
  View of Leidschendam, Seen from The Hague, with tow Boats Mooring Ink (17.5x26cm 6x10in) Amsterdam 2000

LA FONTAINE Charles XIX [1]
- **$9 331** - €9 404 - **£5 817** - FF61 684
  Ung pige i klassiske gevandter dekorerer en graesk vase Oil/canvas (120x75cm 47x29in) Köbenhavn 2000

LA FONTAINE Thomas Sherwood 1915 [17]
- **$2 806** - €3 337 - **£2 000** - FF21 890
  Scotch Dew by Warpath out of Elspeth Ann Oil/canvas (63.5x76cm 25x29in) London 2000

LA FRESNAYE de Roger 1885-1925 [311]
- **$325 540** - €316 838 - **£200 000** - FF2 078 320
  Paysage de la Ferté-Sous-Jouarre, version définitive Oil/canvas (95x127cm 37x50in) London 1999
- **$7 000** - €7 559 - **£4 837** - FF49 587
  Femme nue Oil/canvas (72.5x49.5cm 28x19in) New-York 2001
- **$15 000** - €15 115 - **£9 351** - FF99 150
  Les maisons blanches à Audierne Oil/board (24x34cm 9x13in) New-York 2000
- **$14 701** - €13 805 - **£9 109** - FF90 555
  Eva Bronze (31.5x44.5x20cm 12x17x7in) München 1999
- **$1 008** - €1 220 - **£704** - FF8 000
  Portrait d'Irène Lagut Crayon/papier (27x20cm 10x7in) Paris 2000

$1 217 - €1 372 - **£843** - FF9 000
Le palefrenier Lithographie (26x17.5cm 10x6in) Paris 2000

LA GANDARA de Antonio 1861-1917 [23]

$14 200 - €16 573 - **£10 023** - FF108 713
Retrato de Leonor Uriburu de Anchirena y su hijo Emilio Oleo/lienzo (190x132cm 74x51in) Buenos-Aires 2000

$5 373 - €4 573 - **£3 198** - FF30 000
Caricatures d'artiste du «Chat noir»: Salis, Goudeau, Moreas, Javy Huile/toile (71x92cm 27x36in) Paris 1998

$796 - €762 - **£501** - FF5 000
Scène animée dans le Parc de Versailles Pastel/papier (17.5x25.5cm 6x10in) Paris 1999

LA HAYE de Reinier c.1640-c.1695 [13]

$86 304 - €74 456 - **£51 864** - FF488 400
Die Lautenspielerin Öl/Leinwand (47.5x36cm 18x14in) Bern 1998

$2 884 - €3 390 - **£2 000** - FF22 240
Young Hunter, Small three-quarter-length, in a Brown Coat Oil/panel (18x15cm 7x5in) London 2000

LA HOESE de Jean 1846-1917 [19]

$646 - €762 - **£454** - FF5 000
Esquisse du portrait de Monsieur Soupard Huile/toile (38x18cm 14x7in) Paris 2000

LA HYRE de Laurent 1606-1656 [22]

$16 320 - €18 294 - **£11 076** - FF120 000
Céphale et Procris Huile/toile (102x97cm 40x38in) Paris 2000

$388 - €457 - **£278** - FF3 000
Apollon et Coronis/Apollon er Clytie/Vénus et Adonis/Le supplice Eau-forte (16.5x24cm 6x9in) Paris 2001

LA LYRE Adolphe Lalire, dit 1850-1935 [49]

$20 000 - €18 973 - **£12 150** - FF124 458
Song of the Seas Oil/canvas (145x193cm 57x75in) New-York 1999

$2 779 - €3 278 - **£1 954** - FF21 500
Groupe de femmes Huile/toile (52x91cm 20x35in) Garches 2000

$1 220 - €1 220 - **£763** - FF8 000
Nu de dos, allongé Huile/panneau (23x38cm 9x14in) Paris 1999

LA NEZIERE de Jacques Davial 1873-1944 [27]

$668 - €762 - **£464** - FF5 000
«Simplon Orient Express» Affiche (79x108cm 31x42in) Paris 2001

LA NOUE Terence 1941 [12]

$2 000 - €2 331 - **£1 384** - FF15 293
Prosperous Voyage Etching, aquatint (201x109cm 79x42in) New-York 2000

LA PATELLIERE de Amédée 1890-1932 [119]

$2 000 - €1 860 - **£1 215** - FF12 000
Scène de ferme Huile/toile (38x46cm 14x18in) Paris 1998

$1 811 - €1 677 - **£1 122** - FF11 000
Les coquillages Huile/toile (41x33cm 16x12in) Paris 1999

$465 - €457 - **£298** - FF3 000
Le repos des moissonneurs Sanguine/papier (31x27cm 12x10in) Paris 1999

LA PIRA XIX-XX [23]

$4 200 - €3 628 - **£2 800** - FF23 800
Veduta di Napoli da Camaldoli/Veduta di Napoli da Posillipo Gouache/carta (30x44cm 11x17in) Napoli 1998

LA PIRA Gioacchino 1860-1910 [16]

$5 676 - €6 005 - **£3 600** - FF39 390
View of the Blue Grotto, Capri/Moonlit View of Naples with Vesuvius Bodycolour (32x45.5cm 12x17in) London 2000

LA RIVA Y CALLOL DE MUÑOZ de Maria Luisa 1859-1926 [6]

$4 593 - €5 172 - **£3 200** - FF33 929
Still Life of Roses in a glass Vase and Bowl on a Tabletop Oil/canvas (92x65cm 36x25in) Newbury, Berkshire 2001

LA RIVE de Pierre Louis 1753-1817 [24]

$23 206 - €26 925 - **£16 022** - FF176 619
Landschaft bei Grand Saconnex gegen den Mont Blanc Öl/Leinwand (69.5x91.5cm 27x36in) Zürich 2000

$3 963 - €4 598 - **£2 781** - FF30 163
Bergers et vaches à la montagne Huile/panneau (27.5x34.5cm 10x13in) Genève 2000

$2 399 - €2 199 - **£1 466** - FF14 424
Drei Mönche Fusain (43.6x57cm 17x22in) Zürich 1999

LA RIVIERE Adriaan Philippus 1857-1941 [49]

$992 - €927 - **£600** - FF6 082
Leaving the Barge Oil/canvas (58.5x38cm 23x14in) London 1999

$1 050 - €998 - **£639** - FF6 548
Personen bij kraampjes Oil/canvas (29x39cm 11x15in) Rotterdam 1999

LA ROCHE de Charles Ferdinand XIX [1]

$2 031 - €2 288 - **£1 428** - FF15 008
Mythologische und allegorische Darstellung der Gerechtigkeit Miniature (38.5x30cm 15x11in) Zürich 2001

LA ROCHE Maria 1870-1952 [11]

$1 839 - €2 164 - **£1 333** - FF14 195
«Ansicht von Oltingen» Indian ink (65x70cm 25x27in) Zofingen 2001

LA SERNA de Ismaël 1897-1968 [558]

$32 430 - €28 203 - **£19 554** - FF185 000
Le coin de la cheminée Huile/panneau (123x100cm 48x39in) Paris 1998

$5 490 - €5 406 - **£3 420** - FF35 460
Naturaleza muerta Oleo/tabla (61x50cm 24x19in) Madrid 1999

$2 157 - €2 134 - **£1 345** - FF14 000
Femme au chapeau Huile/isorel (32x23cm 12x9in) Paris 1999

$816 - €915 - **£553** - FF6 000
Composition surréaliste aux joueurs d'échec Encre Chine (31x21cm 12x8in) Paris 2000

$405 - €427 - **£267** - FF2 800
Nature morte à la guitare Lithographie couleurs (58.5x74cm 23x29in) Paris 2000

LA THANGUE Henry Herbert 1859-1929 [34]

$179 316 - €192 481 - **£120 000** - FF1 262 592
Back from the Common, Heyshott, West Sussex Oil/canvas (68x76.5cm 26x30in) London 2000

$65 399 - €66 871 - **£41 000** - FF438 646
The Young Fisherman Oil/canvas (40x25cm 16x10in) Newton-Abbot, Devon 2000

LA TOUCHE Gaston 1854-1913 [155]

$16 128 - €13 720 - **£9 621** - FF90 000
L'enterrement d'un enfant Huile/toile (130x164cm 51x64in) Paris 1998

$6 966 - €6 541 - **£4 302** - FF42 903
Mutter mit Kind Oil/panel (65x55cm 25x21in) Wien 1999

L

$517 - €579 - **£362** - FF3 800
Étude de lustre/Étude de tabouret Huile/panneau
(14.5x15cm 5x5in) Paris 2001

$1 491 - €1 601 - **£997** - FF10 500
Ruines dans un paysage Pastel/papier (56x45cm
22x17in) Bayeux 2000

LA TOUR de Maurice Quentin 1704-1788 [26]
$14 960 - €16 769 - **£10 417** - FF110 000
Portrait de Crébillon Pastel/papier (46x39cm
18x15in) Paris 2001

LA TROBE Julian XX [21]
$3 200 - €3 100 - **£1 995** - FF20 333
Colony Club Bedroom Oil/canvas (45.5x61cm
17x24in) Beverly-Hills CA 1999
$2 800 - €2 712 - **£1 746** - FF17 791
Elsie de Wolfe en jardin Oil/canvas (30.5x23cm
12x9in) Beverly-Hills CA 1999

LA VEGA de Jorge 1930-1971 [7]
$300 000 - €324 340 - **£210 840** - FF2 286 360
Prueba de nuevo, de la serie Los Monstruos
Oil/panel (130x200cm 51x78in) New-York 2001

LA VERTEVILLE de Christian 1949 [23]
$583 - €686 - **£418** - FF4 500
Le rallye nomade Aquarelle, gouache/papier
(15x21.5cm 5x8in) Dijon 2001

LA VERTEVILLE de Jean 1919-1940 [5]
$1 152 - €1 265 - **£742** - FF7 830
Le départ des chevaux Aquarelle/papier (14x26cm
5x10in) Senlis 2000

LA VIGNE Robert 1928 [17]
$2 250 - €2 102 - **£1 360** - FF13 788
It is Difficult to Say the Truth Oil/masonite
(68.5x19.5cm 26x7in) New-York 1999
$900 - €841 - **£544** - FF5 514
Portrait of Peter Orlovsky Ink/paper (19x12cm
7x4in) New-York 1999

LA VILLEGLÉ de Jacques Mahé 1926 [210]
$8 812 - €10 367 - **£6 317** - FF68 000
Gaîté-Montparnasse Affiche lacérée, arrachage
(250x217cm 98x85in) Paris 2001
$5 295 - €5 336 - **£3 300** - FF35 000
Sans titre Affiche lacérée, arrachage (74x92cm
29x36in) Paris 2000
$459 - €534 - **£322** - FF3 500
Sans titre Collage/carton (18x11cm 7x4in) Paris 2001
$3 800 - €4 924 - **£2 850** - FF32 300
Éric Satie Collage (83x45cm 32x17in) Prato 2000
$2 795 - €2 897 - **£1 772** - FF19 000
«Boulevards Rochechouart» Affiche (51x64cm
20x25in) Paris 2000

LA VILLÉON de Emmanuel 1858-1944 [376]
$15 000 - €16 462 - **£9 658** - FF107 982
Les palmiers Oil/canvas (115x150cm 45x59in) New-
York 2000
$4 000 - €4 726 - **£2 834** - FF31 003
Figures in the Park Oil/canvas (38x46cm 14x18in)
Boston MA 2000
$1 229 - €1 220 - **£764** - FF8 000
Pommier en fleurs Huile/panneau (30x20cm 11x7in)
Deauville 1999
$441 - €488 - **£306** - FF3 200
Deux femmes jouant au jaquet Pastel/papier
(22x27cm 8x10in) Paris 2001

LA VOLPE Alessandro 1819-1887 [56]
$10 400 - €13 476 - **£7 800** - FF88 400
Pescatori a Sorrento Olio/tela (75x140cm 29x55in)
Napoli 2000

$5 073 - €5 624 - **£3 522** - FF36 892
Fischer an der Küste vor Sorrent Öl/Leinwand
(22.5x39cm 8x15in) Köln 2001

LAABS Hans 1915 [55]
$1 499 - €1 764 - **£1 058** - FF11 570
«Liegende (Grau-grün)» Öl/Papier (47x63cm
18x24in) Berlin 2001
$805 - €705 - **£488** - FF4 627
Stilleben mit Krug Acrylic (23.8x33.8cm 9x13in)
Berlin 1998
$514 - €613 - **£367** - FF4 024
Stehender weiblicher Akt Gouache/paper
(28.4x16.6cm 11x6in) Berlin 2000

LAAGE Wilhelm 1868-1930 [153]
$378 - €419 - **£262** - FF2 750
«Das Tal» Woodcut in colors (27x35.5cm 10x13in)
Heidelberg 2001

LAAN van der Adolf c.1690-1742 [5]
$1 495 - €1 738 - **£1 049** - FF11 403
**Holländischer Dreimaster und Herringsbüse auf
See** Ink (9.5x12.5cm 3x4in) Hamburg 2001

LAAN van der Dirk Jan 1759-1829 [4]
$10 536 - €10 226 - **£6 560** - FF67 078
**Holländische Landschaft mit reicher figürlicher
Staffage** Aquarell, Gouache/Papier (26.2x31cm
10x12in) Berlin 1999

LAAN van der Gerard 1844-1915 [18]
$3 124 - €3 403 - **£2 151** - FF22 324
«Scheveningen onder de wal» Oil/canvas
(76.5x111cm 30x43in) Amsterdam 2001
$511 - €499 - **£315** - FF3 274
Visbom op volle zee Watercolour, gouache/paper
(34.5x48cm 13x18in) Dordrecht 1999

LAAN van der Kees 1903-1983 [12]
$750 - €813 - **£500** - FF5 334
«Graf Zeppelin, Landing, Zaterdag 18 juni»
Poster (110x80cm 43x31in) New-York 2000

LAANEN van der Jasper c.1592-c.1626 [50]
$33 875 - €38 112 - **£23 325** - FF250 000
Paysage de forêt avec la chasse au cerf
Huile/panneau (49x74cm 19x29in) Paris 2000
$17 671 - €19 813 - **£12 000** - FF129 968
**Wooded Landscape with Diana and her
Nymphs** Oil/copper (28.5x35cm 11x13in) London
2000

LAAR van de Jan Hendrik 1807-1874 [13]
$8 218 - €8 822 - **£5 500** - FF57 868
A Safe Return Oil/panel (59.5x49.5cm 23x19in) Bath
2000

LAASIO Mikko 1913-1997 [15]
$1 277 - €1 092 - **£750** - FF7 160
Stilleben med kanna Oil/canvas (50x73cm 19x28in)
Helsinki 1998

LABARTA Francesc 1883-1963 [8]
$7 650 - €9 010 - **£5 399** - FF59 100
Anecs Oleo/lienzo (65.5x81.5cm 25x32in) Barcelona
2000

LABAS Alexander Arkadyev. 1900-1983 [2]
$56 761 - €55 474 - **£36 000** - FF363 888
Composition Oil/canvas (79x71cm 31x27in) London
1999

LABATUT Jules Jacques 1851-1935 [5]
$24 000 - €27 259 - **£16 840** - FF178 809
The Birth of Venus Marble (H113cm H44in) New-
York 2001

LABHART Emanuel 1810-1874 **[13]**
- $4 214 - €4 912 - £2 917 - FF32 222
  Vue de Lausanne Gouache/paper (32x46cm 12x18in)
  Bern 2000

LABILLE-GUIARD Adélaïde 1749-1803 **[19]**
- $2 839 - €3 048 - £1 900 - FF19 991
  **Marie-Thérèse Louise de Savoie-Carignan,
  Princesse de Lamballe** Oil/canvas (73x60cm
  28x23in) London 2000

LABINO Dominick 1910-1987 **[4]**
- $5 500 - €5 698 - £3 500 - FF37 374
  Veiled Emergence Sculpture, glass (15.5x10x5.5cm
  6x3x2in) New-York 2000

LABISSE Félix 1905-1982 **[513]**
- $7 900 - €7 622 - £4 995 - FF50 000
  Hommage à Gilles de Rais Huile/toile (130x162cm
  51x63in) Paris 1999
- $3 016 - €3 222 - £2 054 - FF21 138
  Le mauvais présage Huile/panneau (55x46cm
  21x18in) Lokeren 2001
- $2 120 - €1 983 - £1 304 - FF13 008
  Le poisson funesto Huile/toile (32x40cm 12x15in)
  Bruxelles 1999
- $554 - €595 - £376 - FF3 902
  Visage de femme Gouache (45x35cm 17x13in)
  Bruxelles 2001
- $148 - €161 - £97 - FF1 056
  Femme rouge Color lithograph (60.6x44.8cm
  23x17in) Lokeren 2000

LABITTE Eugène Léon 1858-1937 **[58]**
- $22 017 - €20 123 - £13 477 - FF132 000
  Les rateleuses Huile/toile (131x163cm 51x64in)
  Dijon 1999
- $4 233 - €5 002 - £3 000 - FF32 809
  Fenaison au bord de la mer Oil/canvas
  (35.5x46.5cm 13x18in) London 2000
- $1 316 - €1 113 - £783 - FF7 300
  La lande Lanriec à Concarneau Huile/carton
  (33x40cm 12x15in) Quimper 1998

LABITTE G. XIX-XX **[1]**
- $2 130 - €2 287 - £1 425 - FF15 000
  Portrait de l'aviateur E.Gauthier Fusain (95x58cm
  37x22in) Paris 2000

LABO' Savinio 1899-1976 **[19]**
- $1 300 - €1 348 - £780 - FF8 840
  Notturno di periferia Olio/tela (40x60cm 15x23in)
  Torino 2001

LABOR Charles Labord 1813-1900 **[13]**
- $6 177 - €5 336 - £3 731 - FF35 000
  Le printemps Huile/toile (32.5x55.5cm 12x21in)
  Barbizon 2000
- $2 874 - €2 897 - £1 791 - FF19 000
  Le port de Cannes près de la douane Huile/toile
  (21x36cm 8x14in) Aubagne 2000

LABORNE Edmé Emile 1837-1913 **[40]**
- $997 - €921 - £621 - FF6 500
  Le retour des lavandières Huile/panneau (41x33cm
  16x12in) Paris 1999

LABOTS Gerrit David 1869-1959 **[12]**
- $187 - €218 - £129 - FF1 428
  Schaal met pruimen Oil/canvas (32x45cm 12x17in)
  Rotterdam 2000

LABOULAYE de Paul 1849-1926 **[20]**
- $4 386 - €4 214 - £2 703 - FF27 642
  Jeune femme pensive Huile/toile (46x37.5cm
  18x14in) Bruxelles 1999

LABOULAYE de Paul 1902 **[5]**
- $7 000 - €7 951 - £4 911 - FF52 152
  The Messenger Oil/canvas (91x72cm 35x28in) New-
  York 2001

LABOURET Auguste 1871-1964 **[105]**
- $181 - €213 - £130 - FF1 400
  Chemin sous les arbres Pastel (41x17cm 16x6in)
  Brest 2001

LABOUREUR Jean Émile 1877-1943 **[882]**
- $1 500 - €1 265 - £879 - FF8 301
  Marchand de fleurs de Picadilli Watercolour
  (13x11cm 5x4in) Mystic CT 1998
- $454 - €503 - £308 - FF3 300
  Jeune fille au verre de liqueur Burin (16.5x14cm
  6x5in) Paris 2000

LABRADA Fernando 1888-1977 **[20]**
- $1 980 - €1 802 - £1 200 - FF11 820
  Paisaje con árbol Oleo/lienzo/tabla (10.5x20.5cm
  4x8in) Madrid 1999

LABROUCHE Pierre 1876-1956 **[22]**
- $2 705 - €2 531 - £1 658 - FF16 600
  Port de Pasajes Huile/panneau (30x63cm 11x24in)
  Bordeaux 1998
- $926 - €991 - £610 - FF6 500
  Maison à Ciboure Huile/panneau (24x19cm 9x7in)
  Biarritz 2000

LABRUZZI Carlo 1747/48-1817 **[28]**
- $24 655 - €23 375 - £15 000 - FF153 333
  **Capriccio Landscape of the Roman Campagna
  with Shepherd driving Flock** Oil/canvas
  (50.5x79cm 19x31in) London 1999
- $7 565 - €7 622 - £4 715 - FF50 000
  Paysage animé Huile/panneau (28x40cm 11x15in)
  Chartres 2000
- $1 680 - €1 451 - £1 120 - FF9 520
  La Tomba di Cecilia Metella Matita (33.5x53cm
  13x20in) Roma 1998

LABRUZZI Tommaso Pietro 1739-1805 **[4]**
- $9 000 - €7 775 - £6 000 - FF51 000
  Architetto Giacomo Giustini Olio/tela (98.5x73cm
  38x28in) Milano 1998

LACAMERA Fortunato 1887-1951 **[4]**
- $4 200 - €4 628 - £2 801 - FF30 359
  Riachuelo Oleo/cartón (24x30cm 9x11in) Montevideo
  2000

LACASSE Joseph 1894-1975 **[96]**
- $4 992 - €5 031 - £3 111 - FF33 000
  Etude pour Carrière, jaune, vert Huile/toile
  (38x55cm 14x21in) Paris 2000
- $426 - €457 - £285 - FF3 000
  Du pain, du travail Gouache/papier (25x18.5cm
  9x7in) Paris 2000

LACAZE Germaine 1908-1994 **[41]**
- $792 - €884 - £553 - FF5 800
  Nature morte Huile/toile (55x46cm 21x18in) Lons-
  Le-Saunier 2001

LACAZE Julien 1886-1971 **[74]**
- $343 - €381 - £238 - FF2 500
  **«Plm, le Majeur par Dijon-Vallorbe et le
  Simplon»** Affiche (108x78cm 42x30in) Paris 2001

LACCETTI Valerio 1836-1909 **[12]**
- $1 120 - €1 145 - £840 - FF9 520
  Accanto al focolare Olio/tela (28x40cm 11x15in)
  Roma 2001

L

LACEPEDE de Amélie Kautz 1796-1860 **[5]**
- **$871** - €971 - **£609** - FF6 372
  Damenporträt, Halbfigur, frontal Aquarell, Gouache (9.8x8.1cm 3x3in) München 2001

LACH Andreas 1817-1882 **[39]**
- **$3 756** - €4 360 - **£2 640** - FF28 602
  Rosen und Weintrauben Öl/Leinwand (41x52.5cm 16x20in) Wien 2001
- **$4 983** - €4 265 - **£3 000** - FF27 975
  A rabbit in Long Grass Oil/canvas (32x39.5cm 12x15in) London 1998

LACH Fritz 1868-1933 **[71]**
- **$3 130** - €3 634 - **£2 200** - FF23 835
  Rose von Stiefmütterchen umgeben Öl/Karton (14x17.5cm 5x6in) Wien 2001
- **$2 167** - €2 050 - **£1 350** - FF13 447
  Perasto Aquarell/Papier (38x52cm 14x20in) Praha 2000

LACHAISE Eugène A. 1857-1925 **[2]**
- **$19 000** - €22 330 - **£13 172** - FF146 478
  The Geisha Girl Oil/canvas (79x91cm 31x35in) New-York 2000

LACHAISE Gaston 1882-1935 **[91]**
- **$160 000** - €158 593 - **£100 080** - FF1 040 304
  The Peacocks Bronze (H142cm H55in) New-York 1999
- **$25 000** - €23 899 - **£15 670** - FF156 767
  Untitled, Dancer Gilded bronze (H51cm H20in) New-York 1999
- **$3 400** - €3 516 - **£2 148** - FF23 065
  Femme nue debout Crayon (26.5x20cm 10x7in) New-York 2000

LACHANCE Georges 1888-1964 **[5]**
- **$9 000** - €10 614 - **£6 348** - FF69 625
  The Shaded Pool Oil/canvas (81x91cm 32x36in) New-Orleans LA 2001
- **$5 000** - €4 847 - **£3 096** - FF31 796
  Landscape Oil/canvas (63x76cm 25x30in) Mystic CT 1999

LACHAPELLE David 1964 **[7]**
- **$3 000** - €2 840 - **£1 865** - FF18 626
  Breakfast was Never Like this Before Type C color print (50x60cm 20x24in) New-York 1999

LACHASSAGNE XX [1]
- **$4 107** - €3 811 - **£2 562** - FF25 000
  Jungle Huile/toile (82x138cm 32x54in) Biarritz 1999

LACHENAL Raoul 1885-1956 **[3]**
- **$314** - €305 - **£199** - FF2 000
  Vase boule à col ourlé Céramique (H19cm H7in) Paris 1999

LACHEVRE Bernard 1885-1950 **[37]**
- **$656** - €610 - **£402** - FF4 000
  Bateaux de bois entrant à Honfleur Aquarelle/papier (36x51.5cm 14x20in) Honfleur 1998

LACHIEZE-REY Henri 1927-1974 **[15]**
- **$8 970** - €9 909 - **£6 220** - FF65 000
  Fillette au gilet jaune Huile/isorel (88x40cm 34x15in) Paris 2001
- **$2 900** - €3 049 - **£1 914** - FF20 000
  Fleurs Huile/toile (41x27cm 16x10in) Paris 2000

LACHMAN Harry B. 1886-1974 **[43]**
- **$4 750** - €4 059 - **£2 874** - FF26 623
  Notre Dame et les Quais Vendu Oil/canvas (38x45.5cm 14x17in) San-Francisco CA 1998

- **$2 200** - €2 464 - **£1 528** - FF16 163
  «Venice» Oil/board (40x30cm 16x12in) Cincinnati OH 2001

LACHMAN Zvi 1950 **[2]**
- **$8 000** - €9 031 - **£5 572** - FF59 240
  My Father in a Robe Bronze (H57cm H22in) Tel Aviv 2001

LACHNIT Max 1900-1972 **[4]**
- **$228** - €256 - **£158** - FF1 676
  Lesende Lithographie (34x23cm 13x9in) Berlin 2001

LACHNIT Wilhelm 1899-1962 **[58]**
- **$6 844** - €7 669 - **£4 767** - FF50 308
  Am Strand Öl/Leinwand (76x110.5cm 29x43in) Berlin 2001
- **$317** - €383 - **£221** - FF2 515
  Zu Hemingway Der alte Mann und das Meer Ink/paper (16.5x24.2cm 6x9in) Berlin 2000
- **$136** - €153 - **£95** - FF1 006
  Figurenszene Radierung (24.5x32cm 9x12in) Berlin 2001

LACINA Bohdan 1912-1971 **[18]**
- **$3 468** - €3 280 - **£2 160** - FF21 516
  Antennes Huile/toile (64x67cm 25x26in) Praha 2001
- **$317** - €301 - **£198** - FF1 972
  Composition Fusain (40x29cm 15x11in) Praha 2001

LACOMA Francisco José Pablo 1784-1849 **[3]**
- **$14 524** - €13 596 - **£9 000** - FF89 181
  Bunch of White Grapes on the Vine Oil/canvas (32.5x24.5cm 12x9in) London 1999

LACOMBE Georges 1868-1916 **[136]**
- **$32 428** - €34 575 - **£22 000** - FF226 798
  Portrait de Paul Ranson Oil/canvas (65.5x50cm 25x19in) London 2001
- **$10 912** - €11 434 - **£7 245** - FF75 000
  Paysage Huile/panneau (33x41cm 12x16in) Paris 2000
- **$216 673** - €232 581 - **£145 000** - FF1 525 632
  La danse bretonne Bas-relief (74x211cm 29x83in) London 2000

LACOSTE Charles 1870-1959 **[66]**
- **$4 102** - €4 878 - **£2 844** - FF32 000
  Paris, les Gobelins Huile/toile (53.5x44cm 21x17in) Paris 2000
- **$1 352** - €1 448 - **£920** - FF9 500
  La Garonne à Bordeaux Huile/toile (27x36cm 10x14in) Avignon 2001

LACOUR Charles 1853-1941 **[35]**
- **$981** - €838 - **£594** - FF5 500
  Le bateau-lavoir Huile/panneau (51x60cm 20x23in) Nantes 1998
- **$776** - €838 - **£536** - FF5 500
  L'entrée du Village Huile/panneau (36x25cm 14x9in) Lyon 2001

LACROIX DE MARSEILLE Charles-François c.1720-c.1782 **[90]**
- **$37 800** - €42 045 - **£25 900** - FF275 800
  Vista de un puerto mediteraneo Oleo/lienzo (101x130cm 39x51in) Madrid 2000
- **$42 500** - €39 344 - **£25 657** - FF258 081
  Mediterranean Port with Elegante Figures on a Quai Oil/canvas (80x115.5cm 31x45in) New-York 1999
- **$37 840** - €40 033 - **£24 000** - FF262 600
  Port Scene with Fishermen and Women beside a Ruined Portal Oil/panel (27.5x34cm 10x13in) London 2000

📄 **$1 985** - €1 906 - **£1 245** - FF12 500
Scène de port imaginaire animé de person-nages, bateaux à voile Gouache/panneau (19x24cm 7x9in) Paris 1999

LACROIX Paul 1827-1869 [18]
🖐 **$2 000** - €2 391 - **£1 379** - FF15 684
River Landscape Oil/canvas/board (54x76cm 21x30in) Milford CT 2000
🖐 **$20 000** - €20 731 - **£12 682** - FF135 988
Strawberries Oil/board (20.5x25.5cm 8x10in) New-York 2000

LACROIX Pierre 1912-1994 [15]
📄 **$143** - €137 - **£87** - FF900
Bibi Fricotin Encre Chine/papier (28x21cm 11x8in) Paris 1999
🎞 **$600** - €558 - **£370** - FF3 659
«Pâtes Supralta» Poster (115x159cm 45x62in) New-York 1999

LACROIX Tristan 1849-1914 [21]
🖐 **$6 971** - €6 151 - **£4 200** - FF40 345
Beagles Oil/canvas (96x130cm 37x51in) London 1998
🖐 **$1 025** - €1 220 - **£731** - FF8 000
La mare aux fées, Fontainebleau Huile/toile (54x73cm 21x28in) Neuilly-sur-Seine 2000
🖐 **$2 382** - €2 058 - **£1 439** - FF13 500
Le relais de chien Huile/panneau (24.5x32.5cm 9x12in) Barbizon 1998

LADA Josef 1887-1957 [46]
📄 **$1 184** - €1 121 - **£738** - FF7 351
Conversation Gouache (30x22cm 11x8in) Praha 2001

LADATTE François 1706-1787 [2]
🔨 **$16 437** - €17 644 - **£11 000** - FF115 737
Judith and the Head of Holofernes Marble (H90.5cm H35in) London 2000
🔨 **$27 150** - €22 867 - **£16 035** - FF150 000
Allégories des quatre Saisons: Le Printemps, l'Été, l'Automne, l'Hiver Bronze (30.5x18x18cm 12x7x7in) Paris 1998

LADBROOKE Henry 1800-1870 [11]
🖐 **$1 030** - €1 156 - **£700** - FF7 581
Norfolk River Landscape with Sheep Watering at a Stream Oil/canvas (30x20cm 12x8in) Aylsham, Norfolk 2000

LADBROOKE John Berney 1803-1879 [68]
🖐 **$5 263** - €4 984 - **£3 200** - FF32 695
The Ford Oil/canvas (40.5x56cm 15x22in) London 1999
🖐 **$1 138** - €1 322 - **£800** - FF8 675
Drover with Cattle watering by a Lane Oil/canvas (26x31cm 10x12in) London 2001

LADBROOKE Robert 1770-1842 [13]
🖐 **$11 295** - €10 847 - **£7 000** - FF71 152
River Landscape with Cattle Oil/canvas (70.5x98cm 27x38in) Suffolk 1999
🖐 **$804** - €816 - **£500** - FF5 354
A Wooded Landscape with a Cottage Beyond Oil/board (23x28cm 9x11in) London 2000

LADD Laura D. Stroud 1863-1943 [1]
🖐 **$5 500** - €6 033 - **£3 735** - FF39 572
Model in Pink Oil/canvas (39x44cm 15x17in) Thomaston ME 2000

LADDEY Ernest 1843-1874 [4]
🖐 **$3 360** - €3 997 - **£2 398** - FF26 218
Hundewelpen im Stroh Öl/Leinwand (65x86cm 25x33in) Wien 2000

LADELL Edward 1821-1886 [113]
🖐 **$11 354** - €10 946 - **£7 000** - FF71 799
Still Life with a Pheasant, Grapes, Hazelnuts and a Hock Glass Oil/canvas (53x43cm 20x16in) London 1999
🖐 **$23 851** - €28 366 - **£17 000** - FF186 068
Still Life with Fruit, Flowers and Butterfly Oil/canvas (43x35.5cm 16x13in) London 2000

LADELL Edwin 1914-1970 [14]
🎞 **$280** - €261 - **£173** - FF1 714
Amaryllis Aquatint in colors (54.5x42cm 21x16in) London 1999

LADELL Ellen c.1853-? [13]
🖐 **$8 965** - €9 624 - **£6 000** - FF63 129
Still Life with Vase, Birdnest and Fruit Oil/canvas (35.5x30.5cm 13x12in) London 2000

LADOU Robert 1929 [13]
🖐 **$3 820** - €3 687 - **£2 400** - FF24 182
Nu allongé Oil/canvas (89x129.5cm 35x50in) London 1999

LADREYT Eugène 1832-? [8]
📄 **$233** - €274 - **£167** - FF1 800
Courtisane chuchotant à l'oreille de son com-pagnon Aquarelle (24.5x16cm 9x6in) Entzheim 2001

LADURNER Adolf Ignatievich 1798-1856 [10]
🖐 **$2 415** - €2 281 - **£1 500** - FF14 961
Military Camp Oil/canvas (20x25cm 7x9in) London 1999

LADWIG Roland 1935 [19]
🖐 **$675** - €767 - **£472** - FF5 030
«Rousset, Eingang» Öl/Leinwand (55x45cm 21x17in) Berlin 2001

LAECK van der Reynier ?-c.1658 [3]
🖐 **$4 835** - €4 417 - **£3 000** - FF29 367
Dune Landscape with Figures by a Track Oil/panel (52x81cm 20x31in) London 1999

LAENEN Jean-Paul 1931 [9]
🖐 **$457** - €396 - **£278** - FF2 600
Chambre dans l'abbaye de Tongres Huile/toile (80x65cm 31x25in) Antwerpen 1998

LAER van Alexander Theobald 1857-1920 [21]
🖐 **$3 250** - €3 016 - **£1 951** - FF19 784
The old Mill Oil/canvas (60x91cm 24x36in) Milford CT 1999
🖐 **$3 750** - €4 282 - **£2 644** - FF28 090
Connecticut Winter Oil/board (25.5x30.5cm 10x12in) Boston MA 2001

LAER van Pieter, il Bamboccio 1582/1613-1642 [25]
🎞 **$269** - €307 - **£187** - FF2 012
Sitzende Frau Radierung (4.5x4.5cm 1x1in) Berlin 2001

LAERMANS Eugène 1864-1940 [105]
🖐 **$22 040** - €23 549 - **£15 010** - FF154 470
L'automne Huile/toile (151x111cm 59x43in) Lokeren 2001
🖐 **$16 146** - €17 104 - **£10 902** - FF112 194
Paysan fumant sa pipe accoudé Huile/toile (99x75cm 38x29in) Bruxelles 2001
🖐 **$3 836** - €3 506 - **£2 348** - FF23 000
La petite église Huile/toile (28x42cm 11x16in) Calais 1999
📄 **$522** - €446 - **£316** - FF2 926
Réfugiers Crayon/papier (22x29cm 8x11in) Antwerpen 1998

L

LAESSØE Augusta Charlotte D. 1851-1926 **[5]**
- $7 889 - €8 758 - **£5 500** - FF57 451
  Grapes and Peaches in a Tazza with wild Berries on a marble Ledge Oil/canvas (45x55.5cm 17x21in) London 2001

LAESSØE Thorald 1816-1878 **[79]**
- $5 016 - €5 361 - **£3 408** - FF35 164
  Udsigt fra skyggefuld Pergola Oil/canvas (39x52cm 15x20in) Köbenhavn 2001
- $1 633 - €1 680 - **£1 036** - FF11 020
  Landskab med hus Oil/canvas (30x42cm 11x16in) Vejle 2000
- $186 - €188 - **£116** - FF1 233
  Studie af grene Ink/paper (11x15cm 4x5in) Köbenhavn 2000

LAET de Alois 1866-1949 **[69]**
- $149 - €173 - **£103** - FF1 138
  Dunes au Zoute Huile/panneau (26x35cm 10x13in) Bruxelles 2000

LAETHEM van Jef 1912 **[3]**
- $3 783 - €3 222 - **£2 275** - FF21 138
  L'exposition Huile/toile (80x100cm 31x39in) Bruxelles 1998

LAEUGER Max 1864-1952 **[20]**
- $2 099 - €1 789 - **£1 251** - FF11 737
  «Kopfstudie mit Bäumen» Porcelain (15x15cm 5x5in) München 1998

LAEZZA Giuseppe ?-1905 **[29]**
- $8 000 - €9 330 - **£5 616** - FF61 203
  «Pagliaro near Salerno» Oil/canvas (61x125.5cm 24x49in) Boston MA 2001
- $1 600 - €2 073 - **£1 200** - FF13 600
  Sosta a Paestum Olio/cartone/tela (21x31cm 8x12in) Roma 2001
- $2 029 - €2 250 - **£1 408** - FF14 757
  Belebte neapoletanische Uferpromenade Aquarell, Gouache/Papier (8.5x19cm 3x7in) Köln 2001

LAFAGE de Raymond 1656-1690 **[39]**
- $2 061 - €2 287 - **£1 425** - FF15 000
  Le jugement de Paris Encre (34x23cm 13x9in) Paris 2001

LAFENESTRE Gaston Ernest 1841-1877 **[12]**
- $1 956 - €1 982 - **£1 216** - FF13 000
  Les merinos au pâturage Huile/toile (32.5x46cm 12x18in) Soissons 2000

LAFFON Carmen 1934 **[16]**
- $13 490 - €11 412 - **£8 170** - FF74 860
  Pequeñas flores Oleo/lienzo (41x33cm 16x12in) Madrid 1998
- $10 980 - €10 812 - **£6 840** - FF70 920
  Bodegón de macetas, terraza de la pintora Pastel (24.5x34cm 9x13in) Madrid 1999
- $621 - €541 - **£387** - FF3 546
  Fachada Grabado (27.5x39.5cm 10x15in) Madrid 1999

LAFITE Carl 1830-1900 **[29]**
- $1 597 - €1 817 - **£1 122** - FF11 917
  Bauernhofidylle Öl/Karton (23x34cm 9x13in) Wien 2001

LAFITE Ernst 1826-1885 **[12]**
- $874 - €945 - **£604** - FF6 197
  Portrait eines Herrn mit Schnurrbart Öl/Leinwand (71.5x58.5cm 28x23in) Wien 2001

LAFITTE Alphonse 1863-? **[22]**
- $112 - €107 - **£69** - FF700
  Thoniers au pied des remparts de Concarneau Aquatinte couleurs (21.5x31.5cm 8x12in) Paris 1999

LAFITTE Louis 1770-1828 **[30]**
- $378 - €381 - **£235** - FF2 500
  Portrait de femme Crayon/papier (35.5x27cm 13x10in) Paris 2000

LAFON François 1846-? **[19]**
- $3 884 - €4 147 - **£2 652** - FF27 200
  Jeunes femmes près d'une fontaine Huile/panneau (37x29cm 14x11in) Paris 2001

LAFOND Simon Daniel 1763-1831 **[11]**
- $640 - €706 - **£423** - FF4 631
  Vue sur le Lac de Brientz et le petit Lac de Goldswil Radierung (14.7x22.6cm 5x8in) Bern 2000

LAFONTAINE Marie-Jo 1950 **[22]**
- $10 000 - €11 381 - **£7 027** - FF74 652
  «Blut und Boden», in five parts Oil/wood (140x280.5cm 55x110in) New-York 2001
- $6 588 - €6 124 - **£4 000** - FF40 172
  Untitled Mixed media/board (62.5x187.5cm 24x73in) London 1998
- $126 248 - €122 158 - **£80 000** - FF801 304
  Les larmes d'acier Installation (420x730x180cm 165x287x70in) London 1999
- $1 000 - €1 138 - **£702** - FF7 465
  Untitled Photograph (40x30cm 15x11in) New-York 2001

LAFORESTERIE Louis Edmond 1837-1894 **[1]**
- $74 661 - €83 691 - **£52 000** - FF548 979
  La vigne, l'ormeau et bacchante Marble (H200cm H78in) London 2001

LAFOSSE de Charles 1636-1716 **[28]**
- $50 000 - €44 007 - **£30 440** - FF288 665
  Christ in the House of Martha and Mary Oil/canvas (90x117cm 35x46in) New-York 1999
- $6 000 - €6 408 - **£4 088** - FF42 031
  Bacchus and Ariadne: Allegory of Autumn Black chalk (28x21.5cm 11x8in) New-York 2001

LAFOSSE Jean-Baptiste A. 1814-1879 **[4]**
- $4 800 - €4 363 - **£2 891** - FF28 622
  Portrait of Andrew Jackson Pastel/paper (112x84cm 44x33in) New-Orleans LA 1998

LAFRENSEN Niklas I Lavreince 1698-1756 **[9]**
- $2 574 - €2 450 - **£1 610** - FF16 073
  Regentlängd från Gustav vasa till Gustaf III Akvarell/papper (26.5x19.5cm 10x7in) Stockholm 1999

LAFRENSEN Niklas II Lavreince 1737-1807 **[43]**
- $16 000 - €15 053 - **£9 984** - FF98 742
  Classical Landscape with Washerwomen beside Ruins on a Riverbank Oil/canvas (97x74.5cm 38x29in) New-York 1999
- $4 092 - €3 964 - **£2 574** - FF26 000
  La confidence/Ha, le petit chien Aquarelle (15.2x11.4cm 5x4in) Paris 1999
- $375 - €421 - **£260** - FF2 760
  Le billet doux/Qu'en dit l'Abbe, after Launay Engraving (47x36cm 18x14in) London 2000

LAFRÉRY Antonio 1512-1577 **[20]**
- $600 - €676 - **£428** - FF4 695
  Arco di Costantino Kupferstich (29.8x43.4cm 11x17in) Berlin 2000

LAFUENTE Antonio Fuente Gomez 1925 [47]
- $168 - €180 - **£114** - FF1 182
  Paisaje con río Oleo/lienzo (60x100cm 23x39in) Barcelona 2001

LAFUGIE madame Léa 1890-1972 [178]
- $967 - €1 098 - **£671** - FF7 200
  «Meo blanc Lai Chan», jeune femme et son bébé Aquarelle, gouache/papier (33x25.5cm 12x10in) Reims 2001

LAGAGE Pierre César 1911-1977 [110]
- $12 179 - €14 483 - **£8 683** - FF95 000
  Composition Huile/toile (125x98cm 49x38in) Paris 2000
- $1 664 - €1 677 - **£1 037** - FF11 000
  Scène de marché Huile/toile (61x50cm 24x19in) Paris 2000

LAGAR Celso 1891-1966 [566]
- $24 000 - €22 524 - **£15 000** - FF147 750
  Le Bois Oleo/lienzo (114.5x145cm 45x57in) Madrid 1999
- $13 660 - €15 245 - **£8 940** - FF100 500
  La Corrida Huile/panneau (49x49cm 19x19in) Le Touquet 2000
- $10 066 - €8 446 - **£5 905** - FF55 400
  Les saltimbanques Huile/toile (27x35cm 10x13in) Troyes 1998
- $665 - €572 - **£389** - FF3 752
  Desnudo femenino Aguada/papel (38.5x27.5cm 15x10in) Madrid 1998
- $96 - €90 - **£60** - FF591
  Pase taurino Litografía (32.5x44cm 12x17in) Madrid 1999

LAGARIO Lew 1827-1905 [2]
- $4 130 - €3 997 - **£2 546** - FF26 218
  Abenstimmung über einer Küstenlandschaft Oil/panel (26x31.5cm 10x12in) Wien 1999

LAGARTO Andres 1589-1667 [1]
- $5 175 - €4 571 - **£2 957** - FF29 625
  Santísima Trinidad, Santos Parientes, S.Jerónimo y Santa Paula Técnica mixta (67.5x49cm 26x19in) Madrid 1998

LAGATTA John 1894-1977 [8]
- $9 000 - €8 619 - **£5 560** - FF56 537
  Couple in Passionate Embrace, Tophat and Coat in Foreground Oil/board (67x51cm 26x20in) New-York 1999
- $3 000 - €3 360 - **£2 084** - FF22 041
  Standing partially-draped Woman from behind Charcoal (81x39cm 32x15in) New-York 2001

LAGE Leif 1933 [20]
- $296 - €322 - **£205** - FF2 110
  Portraet Watercolour/paper (40x30cm 15x11in) Köbenhavn 2001

LAGERSTAM Berndt 1868-1930 [29]
- $517 - €572 - **£358** - FF3 750
  Vinterlandskap Oil/canvas (55x45cm 21x17in) Helsinki 2001
- $437 - €370 - **£261** - FF2 426
  Strandlandskap Oil/canvas (32x36cm 12x14in) Helsinki 1998

LAGET Denis 1958 [7]
- $3 720 - €3 811 - **£2 315** - FF25 000
  Mélancolie Huile/bois (62x62cm 24x24in) Paris 2000

LAGLENNE Jean-François 1899-1962 [25]
- $1 207 - €1 296 - **£807** - FF8 500
  La ballerine Aquarelle/papier (63x47cm 24x18in) Compiègne 2000

LAGNEAU Nicolas Lanneau c.1590-1666 [37]
- $3 749 - €3 260 - **£2 269** - FF21 382
  Old Man with a Long Beard, Head and Shoulders Black chalk (26x19.5cm 10x7in) New-York 1999

LAGO Darren 1965 [4]
- $2 166 - €2 361 - **£1 500** - FF15 484
  Sopa Box Marbre Carrare (45x30x10.5cm 17x11x4in) London 2001

LAGO RIVERA Antonio 1916-1990 [111]
- $2 592 - €2 553 - **£1 615** - FF16 745
  Paisaje Oleo/lienzo (60x73cm 23x28in) Madrid 1999
- $1 080 - €1 201 - **£740** - FF7 880
  Paisaje con montaña roja Oleo/tabla (22x27cm 8x10in) Madrid 2000
- $239 - €276 - **£165** - FF1 812
  La hamaca Acuarela/papel (16.5x12cm 6x4in) Madrid 2001

LAGOOR Johannes XVII [17]
- $9 002 - €10 174 - **£6 706** - FF66 738
  Flusslandschaft mit Kahnfahrern Oil/panel (36.5x47.5cm 14x18in) Wien 2000

LAGORIO Leon Felixowitsch 1827-1905 [32]
- $21 343 - €24 798 - **£15 000** - FF162 663
  Shipping of the High Seas Oil/canvas (52.5x65cm 20x25in) London 2001
- $2 920 - €2 859 - **£1 796** - FF18 754
  Merellä Oil/canvas (20x31cm 7x12in) Helsinki 1999

LAGOUTTE Claude 1935-1990 [12]
- $270 - €229 - **£161** - FF1 500
  Projet espace 1 Technique mixte/papier (32.5x40cm 12x15in) Paris 1998

LAGRANGE André 1889-1958 [14]
- $13 000 - €11 881 - **£7 953** - FF77 932
  Summer Picnic Oil/canvas (113x145cm 44x57in) New-York 1999
- $355 - €396 - **£248** - FF2 600
  Prairie en Vendôme Huile/panneau (45x36.5cm 17x14in) Entzheim 2001
- $1 361 - €1 534 - **£942** - FF10 061
  Sommerterrasse mit luftig gekleideter Familie und Kindern Oil/panel (26x35cm 10x13in) Berlin 2000

LAGRANGE Jacques 1917-1995 [141]
- $1 390 - €1 372 - **£856** - FF9 000
  Les sept dons Huile/toile (100x81cm 39x31in) Versailles 1999
- $333 - €351 - **£219** - FF2 300
  Les toits Gouache/papier (50x65cm 19x25in) Paris 2000

LAGRENÉE Anthelme-François 1774-1832 [21]
- $4 170 - €4 857 - **£2 913** - FF31 862
  Brustbild eines Herren in blauer Uniform mit breitem Pelzkragen Miniature (7.2x6cm 2x2in) München 2000

LAGRENÉE Jean-Jacques, Jeune 1739-1821 [45]
- $108 948 - €107 094 - **£70 000** - FF702 492
  Allegory of Charity Oil/canvas (227x173cm 89x68in) London 1999
- $5 000 - €5 486 - **£3 321** - FF35 984
  Minerva and Urania Oil/paper/canvas (33.5x50cm 13x19in) New-York 2000
- $4 000 - €4 389 - **£2 657** - FF28 787
  Saint John the Baptist in the Wilderness Oil/panel (23x18cm 9x7in) New-York 2000

L

$2 331 - €2 744 - **£1 638** - FF18 000
Hermine et Tancrede Pierre noire (31x39cm 12x15in) Paris 2000

LAGRENÉE Louis J-Fr. l'Aîné 1725-1805 [44]
$59 736 - €57 931 - **£37 582** - FF380 000
La Peinture aimée des Grâces Huile/toile (59.5x48.5cm 23x19in) Paris 1999
$11 507 - €9 927 - **£6 915** - FF65 120
Landschaft mit Venus und Amor Öl/Leinwand (41.5x32.5cm 16x12in) Bern 1998
$13 000 - €13 883 - **£8 858** - FF91 068
Young Girl Resting her Head on the Lap of Another Girl Black & white chalks/paper (37x56cm 14x22in) New-York 2001

LAGUNAS MAYANDIA Santiago 1912-1995 [6]
$3 750 - €4 505 - **£2 625** - FF29 550
Luz de gas Oleo/tabla (29x38cm 11x14in) Madrid 2000

LAGYE Victor 1825-1896 [8]
$8 000 - €8 794 - **£5 126** - FF57 683
The Pet Squirrel Oil/panel (70x55cm 27x21in) New-York 2000

LAHALLE Charles D.O. 1832-1909 [9]
$21 516 - €23 885 - **£15 000** - FF156 673
Leaving Blois Oil/canvas (60.5x92cm 23x36in) London 2001

LAHARRAGUE RODRIGUEZ-BAUZA Carlos 1936 [51]
$2 280 - €2 403 - **£1 440** - FF15 760
Bodegón rojo Oleo/lienzo (65x46cm 25x18in) Madrid 2000
$1 008 - €1 081 - **£666** - FF7 092
Membrillos Oleo/cartón (32.5x24cm 12x9in) Madrid 2000
$270 - €300 - **£190** - FF1 970
Calle de Madrid Acuarela (19.5x24cm 7x9in) Madrid 2001

LAHEY Frances Vida 1882-1968 [18]
$4 529 - €4 300 - **£2 825** - FF28 207
Still Life with Flowers Oil/canvas/board (43.5x37cm 17x14in) Sydney 1999
$3 565 - €3 278 - **£2 204** - FF21 505
«Surfers Paradise» Oil/canvas (20x21cm 7x8in) Melbourne 1998

LAHNER Émile 1893-1980 [46]
$2 975 - €3 291 - **£1 955** - FF21 590
Still Life with Banana and Grapes Oil/canvas (27x35cm 10x13in) Budapest 2000

LAHS Curt 1893-1953 [15]
$24 645 - €28 633 - **£17 320** - FF187 818
Abstrakte Komposition Öl/Leinwand (100x80cm 39x31in) Hamburg 2001
$1 701 - €1 636 - **£1 049** - FF10 732
Schlafende mit rotem Hund Indian ink (35.7x47cm 14x18in) Köln 1999

LAHUERTA Genaro 1905-1985 [41]
$6 400 - €6 006 - **£4 000** - FF39 400
Castillo en Africa Occidental española Oleo/lienzo (73x100cm 28x39in) Madrid 1999

LAI FONG OF CALCUTTA XIX-XX [21]
$3 308 - €3 670 - **£2 200** - FF24 073
The Woll Clipper Holmsdale in Chinese Waters Oil/canvas (44.5x58.5cm 17x23in) London 2000
$7 000 - €6 548 - **£4 241** - FF42 953
The Ship «Sam Skolfield»/American Ship at Sea Oil/canvas (20x5cm 8x2in) Bolton MA 1999

LAI SUNG [2]
$32 500 - €31 122 - **£20 029** - FF204 145
Hong Kong Harbor Oil/canvas (45x58cm 18x23in) Portsmouth NH 1999

LAIB Wolfgang 1950 [29]
$16 248 - €15 906 - **£10 000** - FF104 335
Milkstone Carrare marble (6x29x25cm 2x11x9in) London 1999

LAINE Olavi 1922 [51]
$400 - €471 - **£277** - FF3 089
Landskap från Södern Oil/canvas (54x65cm 21x25in) Helsinki 2000

LAINÉ Victor 1830-? [12]
$2 988 - €3 208 - **£2 000** - FF21 043
Proud Mother Oil/canvas (48x60cm 18x23in) London 2000

LAING Annie Rose 1869-1946 [5]
$7 343 - €6 570 - **£4 400** - FF43 094
A Helensburgh Breakfast Oil/canvas (55x46cm 21x18in) Perthshire 1998
$19 797 - €21 336 - **£13 500** - FF139 952
At the Breakfast Table Oil/canvas (26x23.5cm 10x9in) London 2001

LAING Gerald 1936 [9]
$653 - €770 - **£450** - FF5 049
C T Strokers/AA-D/Swamp Rat/Deceleration II Screenprint in colors (89x58.5cm 35x23in) London 2000

LAING James Garden 1852-1915 [37]
$647 - €756 - **£450** - FF4 956
Evening at Scheveningen Watercolour/paper (35.5x53.5cm 13x21in) Toronto 2000

LAING Tomson act.1890-1904 [28]
$1 424 - €1 217 - **£862** - FF7 984
Highland Cattle on the Shore Oil/canvas (30x51cm 11x20in) Edinburgh 1998

LAING William Wardlaw XIX-XX [4]
$1 355 - €1 487 - **£900** - FF9 754
The Water Carrier Watercolour (53.5x30.5cm 21x12in) London 2000

LAIRESSE de Gérard 1641-1711 [54]
$77 820 - €76 496 - **£50 000** - FF501 780
Mars and Venus, an Allegory of Strife overcome by Love Oil/canvas (178x168cm 70x66in) London 1999
$733 - €818 - **£493** - FF5 366
Die Entdeckung der Schwangerschaft der Nymphe Callisto Red chalk/paper (13.1x16.8cm 5x6in) Köln 2000
$59 - €64 - **£39** - FF422
Le jugement du Roi Salomon Burin (50x38cm 19x14in) Liège 2000

LAIS Otto 1897-? [7]
$227 - €256 - **£156** - FF1 676
Der Männerchor Radierung (17.2x21.1cm 6x8in) München 2000

LAISSEMENT Henri Adolphe 1854-1921 [26]
$7 222 - €7 013 - **£4 462** - FF46 000
Nu à la cheminée Huile/toile (97.5x79cm 38x31in) Paris 1999

LAIT Edward Beecham XIX [43]
$316 - €355 - **£220** - FF2 326
River near Lewes, Sussex Watercolour/paper (12x29cm 4x11in) London 2001

LAJALLET de Hélène 1858-? **[1]**
- $13 000 - €13 100 - £8 104 - FF85 930
  Vase of Wild Flowers and Mimosas Oil/canvas
  (130x80.5cm 51x31in) New-York 2000

LAJOÜE de Jacques 1687-1761 **[42]**
- $30 000 - €30 602 - £20 844 - FF220 416
  **Couple seated on the Steps of a Fountain in a
  wooded Grove** Oil/canvas (103.5x137cm 40x53in)
  New-York 2001
- $40 000 - €43 886 - £26 572 - FF287 872
  Optics/Astronomy Oil/canvas (48x61.5cm 18x24in)
  New-York 2000
- $8 155 - €7 628 - £5 000 - FF50 035
  **Scene on a Stage set in a Theatre - «The
  Triumph of the Harlequin»** Oil/canvas (31x39cm
  12x15in) London 1998
- $3 846 - €4 573 - £2 846 - FF50 035
  Projet de cartouche avec armoiries royales
  Encre (38.5x29cm 15x11in) Paris 2000

LAKHOWSKII Arnold Borisovich 1880-1937 **[18]**
- $594 - €563 - £361 - FF3 690
  Paysage urbain Huile/toile (71x61cm 27x24in)
  Genève 1999
- $3 250 - €3 755 - £2 275 - FF24 628
  **Russian Town in Winter/Russian Town bathed in
  Sunlight** Oil/board (16x23cm 6x9in) New-York 2001
- $2 777 - €3 187 - £1 900 - FF20 903
  Eastern Market Scene Watercolour/paper
  (46x56.5cm 18x22in) London 2000

LAKOS Alfred 1870-? **[17]**
- $1 500 - €1 702 - £1 049 - FF11 164
  Rabbi at Study Oil/wood (8.5x13.5cm 3x5in) Tel
  Aviv 2001

LALAISSE Hippolyte 1812-1884 **[36]**
- $25 115 - €27 136 - £17 390 - FF178 000
  L'orage Huile/toile (137x196cm 53x77in) Limoges
  2001
- $3 709 - €4 421 - £2 644 - FF29 000
  Cavaliers arabes Huile/toile (73x59cm 28x23in)
  Clermont-Ferrand 2000
- $771 - €915 - £562 - FF6 000
  Étude chevaux et palefreniers Pierre noire
  (56x43cm 22x16in) Paris 2000

LALANDA Josechu XX **[16]**
- $257 - €276 - £174 - FF1 812
  Macho montés Bronze (H20.5cm H8in) Madrid 2001

LALANNE Claude 1927 **[12]**
- $653 - €686 - £429 - FF4 500
  Buisson d'or, Chandelier bas Métal
  (16.5x42x16.5cm 6x16x6in) Paris 2000

LALANNE François-X. & Claude 1924/1927 **[4]**
- $15 912 - €14 483 - £9 747 - FF95 000
  Tortue Topiaire Métal (45x120x85cm 17x47x33in)
  Monte-Carlo 1998

LALANNE François-Xavier 1924 **[43]**
- $8 411 - €8 080 - £5 215 - FF53 000
  Mouton Bronze (90x100x35cm 35x39x13in) Paris
  1999
- $3 888 - €4 573 - £2 787 - FF30 000
  Roitelet Bronze (13x15.5cm 5x6in) Paris 2001
- $1 721 - €1 906 - £1 167 - FF12 500
  Balançoire Encre (22x21cm 8x8in) Paris 2000

LALANNE Maxime 1827-1886 **[58]**
- $6 816 - €7 318 - £4 560 - FF48 000
  Le quai des Chartrons à Bordeaux Huile/panneau
  (17x28cm 6x11in) Paris 2000

- $348 - €351 - £216 - FF2 300
  Paysage boisé Crayon (17x27.5cm 6x10in) Paris
  2000
- $90 - €102 - £61 - FF671
  Richmond Engraving (20x27cm 8x11in) Columbia SC
  2000

LALAU Maurice 1881-? **[3]**
- $1 357 - €1 296 - £848 - FF8 500
  «Notre Dame de Paris» Affiche couleur (160x120cm
  62x47in) Paris 1999

LALAUZE Alphonse 1872-? **[40]**
- $20 160 - €22 867 - £14 205 - FF150 000
  **Le canonier Baraillier, défendant sa pièce d'ar-
  tillerie** Huile/toile (200x170cm 78x66in) Paris 2001
- $408 - €457 - £286 - FF3 000
  Trompette de dragons 1er Empire
  Aquarelle/papier (19x31cm 7x12in) Paris 2001

LALIA Alfredo 1907 **[5]**
- $303 - €315 - £182 - FF2 063
  «2.Settimana del libro» Affiche couleur (140x100cm
  55x39in) Torino 2000

LALIBERTÉ Alfred 1878-1953 **[112]**
- $1 502 - €1 442 - £942 - FF9 460
  «L'erminette» Bronze (H38cm H14in) Montréal 1999

LALIQUE René 1860-1945 **[220]**
- $120 000 - €101 421 - £71 820 - FF665 280
  **«Femme Ailée», for the Exposition Universelle,
  Paris** Bronze (103x78.5x61cm 40x30x24in) New-York
  1998
- $7 461 - €6 860 - £4 612 - FF45 000
  Cinq chevaux, bouchon de radiateur Sculpture
  verre (11.5x15cm 4x5in) Deauville 1998
- $900 - €771 - £541 - FF5 057
  Two Studies for Perfume Bottles Watercolour,
  gouache (16x11cm 6x4in) New-York 1998

LALIQUE Suzanne 1899 **[4]**
- $1 771 - €2 058 - £1 244 - FF13 500
  «Les petits fours» Huile/toile (33x41cm 12x16in)
  Paris 2001

LALLEMAND Adèle 1807-? **[1]**
- $20 385 - €22 867 - £14 265 - FF150 000
  **Bouquets de fleurs et fruits avec des mouches
  et papillons** Aquarelle, gouache/papier (39x31cm
  15x12in) Paris 2001

LALLEMAND Charles 1826-1904 **[29]**
- $370 - €412 - £258 - FF2 700
  Femme et enfant Aquarelle/papier (20.5x15.5cm
  8x6in) Paris 2001
- $452 - €534 - £318 - FF3 500
  Syrie, vieilles femmes, servantes du harem
  Tirage albuminé (11x8.5cm 4x3in) Paris 2000

LALLEMAND Jean-Baptiste c.1710-c.1803/05 **[148]**
- $8 723 - €9 909 - £6 103 - FF65 000
  Le repos après la chasse Huile/toile (92x132cm
  36x51in) Paris 2001
- $13 539 - €15 378 - £9 500 - FF100 870
  **Capriccio of a Mediterranean Port with oriental
  Figures** Oil/canvas (58.5x74.5cm 23x29in) London
  2001
- $6 455 - €6 042 - £4 000 - FF39 636
  **Coastal Landscape with Fishermen and
  Beached Boats by a Farmhouse** Oil/canvas
  (32.5x41cm 12x16in) London 1999
- $2 743 - €2 568 - £1 700 - FF16 845
  **Extensive View of Saint Peter's and the Vatican
  from the Tiber** Black chalk (25x38.5cm 9x15in)
  London 1999

L

LALLEMANT Georges c.1575-1636 [6]

📖 **$2 397** - €2 820 - **£1 718** - FF18 500
La décollation de St Jean Baptiste Eau-forte
(21.5x29.5cm 8x11in) Paris 2001

LALOUETTE XIX [3]

🖼 **$1 385** - €1 296 - **£839** - FF8 500
Les jockeys Bronze (H18.5cm H7in) Lille 1999

LAM QUA XIX [7]

🖼 **$1 500** - €1 408 - **£929** - FF9 236
Portrait of Woman in Black Dress Seated on
Red Sofa, after Chinnery Oil/panel (23x17cm
9x7in) Portsmouth NH 1999

🖼 **$8 500** - €9 365 - **£5 670** - FF61 432
View of the Whampoa Anchorage with
American and Other Shipping Watercolour/paper
(10x18cm 4x7in) Portsmouth NH 2000

LAM Wifredo 1902-1982 [1073]

🖼 **$550 000** - €529 795 - **£341 495** - FF3 475 230
Sans titre Oil/canvas (145x115cm 57x45in) New-York
1999

🖼 **$66 614** - €57 931 - **£40 166** - FF380 000
Visage cubiste Huile/toile (73x60cm 28x23in) Paris
1998

🖼 **$11 250** - €11 662 - **£6 750** - FF76 500
Totem Tecnica mista/tela (45x35cm 17x13in) Prato
1999

🖼 **$2 105** - €2 455 - **£1 503** - FF16 105
Figura Bronze (41x19x10cm 16x7x3in) Caracas ($)
2000

🖼 **$10 650** - €11 434 - **£7 125** - FF75 000
Personnage et oiseau Pastel/papier (62x47cm
24x18in) Douai 2000

📖 **$529** - €457 - **£319** - FF3 000
Le regard vertical III, IV Lithographie couleurs
(64.7x49.8cm 25x19in) Paris 1998

LAM Wladyslaw 1893-1984 [7]

🖼 **$1 057** - €1 233 - **£741** - FF8 089
Arbres à l'ombre Huile/toile (45x51cm 17x20in)
Warszawa 2000

🖼 **$2 127** - €2 065 - **£1 325** - FF13 546
Child with her Doll in an Interior Pastel/board
(80x59cm 31x23in) Warszawa 1999

LAMA Giovan Battista c.1673-1748 [8]

🖼 **$5 991** - €6 339 - **£3 800** - FF41 578
The Madonna Oil/canvas (88.5x70cm 34x27in)
London 2000

LAMA Giovanni Bernardo 1508-1579 [4]

🖼 **$90 000** - €96 272 - **£61 362** - FF631 503
The Pietà Oil/panel (107x76cm 42x29in) New-York
2001

LAMASURE Edwin (Morton), Jr. 1866-1916 [18]

🖼 **$531** - €599 - **£368** - FF3 930
Farmhouse in a Fall Landscape Watercolour/paper
(35.5x66cm 13x25in) Toronto 2000

LAMB Charles Vincent 1893-1964 [80]

🖼 **$6 686** - €7 872 - **£4 698** - FF51 639
Driving Home the Cows Oil/canvas (40.5x51cm
15x20in) Dublin 2000

🖼 **$6 001** - €5 841 - **£3 686** - FF38 313
Bridge in Portadown Oil/board (28x40cm 11x16in)
Dublin 1999

LAMB Frederick Mortimer 1861-1936 [46]

🖼 **$600** - €644 - **£401** - FF4 224
The Road in Autumn Oil/canvas (44x35cm 17x14in)
Bolton MA 2000

📖 **$350** - €409 - **£240** - FF2 683
Summer Field Pastel/paper (18x51cm 7x20in) Bolton
MA 2000

LAMB Henry 1883-1960 [147]

🖼 **$1 488** - €1 392 - **£900** - FF9 132
The Artist's Daughter, tea time Oil/canvas
(40.5x51cm 15x20in) London 1999

🖼 **$1 973** - €1 869 - **£1 200** - FF12 260
Wet Crossing Oil/board (37.5x29cm 14x11in)
Lymington 1999

📖 **$756** - €718 - **£460** - FF4 712
Cadgwith, Cornwall Ink (20x27cm 7x10in) London
1999

LAMB Oscar Hermann 1876-1947 [8]

📖 **$2 350** - €2 436 - **£1 410** - FF15 980
Giovane donna con collana di perle Tecnica
mista/carta (94x63cm 37x24in) Trieste 2001

LAMBA Jacqueline 1910-1993 [1]

🖼 **$18 000** - €19 439 - **£12 439** - FF127 510
«Behind the Sun» Oil/canvas (66x61.5cm 25x24in)
New-York 2001

LAMBART Alfred 1902 [5]

📖 **$2 114** - €1 981 - **£1 300** - FF12 992
«Withernsea» Poster (102x64cm 40x25in) London
1999

LAMBDIN George Cochran 1830-1896 [27]

🖼 **$11 000** - €10 155 - **£6 765** - FF66 614
Woman with Roses Oil/canvas (77x51cm 30x20in)
New-York 1999

🖼 **$6 500** - €5 617 - **£3 857** - FF36 847
Lazy Bones Oil/canvas (35x45cm 13x17in)
Washington 1998

LAMBEAUX Jef 1852-1908 [353]

🖼 **$4 590** - €4 214 - **£2 822** - FF27 642
Les Lutteurs Bronze (H108cm H42in) Bruxelles 1999

🖼 **$1 274** - €1 372 - **£845** - FF9 000
Les lutteurs Bronze (H56cm H22in) Corbeil-Essonnes
2000

LAMBERT André 1884-1967 [7]

📖 **$545** - €534 - **£335** - FF3 500
L'Étoile, la Belle Poule Aquarelle/papier (45x59.5cm
17x23in) Paris 1999

LAMBERT Camille Nicolas 1876-? [45]

🖼 **$637** - €531 - **£374** - FF3 480
A Summer Landscape Oil/canvas/board (41x51cm
16x20in) Amsterdam 1998

🖼 **$765** - €818 - **£521** - FF5 365
Jonge ruiter Huile/toile (40x30cm 15x11in) Lokeren
2001

LAMBERT E.F. c.1790-1846 [3]

🖼 **$2 520** - €2 931 - **£1 800** - FF19 227
The Birmingham to Warwick Royal Mail Coach
Oil/canvas (51x76.5cm 20x30in) London 2001

LAMBERT Edwin J. XIX-XX [3]

📖 **$750** - €852 - **£513** - FF5 589
Temples of the Dollar Woodcut (19.5x13cm 7x5in)
New-York 2000

LAMBERT Eugène C. XIX-XX [4]

🖼 **$8 310** - €7 622 - **£5 165** - FF50 000
Les Eaux-Douces - Constantinople Huile/panneau
(60x81cm 23x31in) Paris 1999

LAMBERT George 1700/10-1765 [30]

🖼 **$23 000** - €23 906 - **£14 494** - FF156 816
Landscape Oil/canvas (124x129cm 49x51in)
Asheville NC 2000

$28 979 - €24 848 - **£17 000** - FF162 990
View of Dover Castle and Bay Oil/canvas
(63.5x119.5cm 25x47in) Leicestershire 1998

LAMBERT George Washington 1873-1930 **[65]**
$47 685 - €46 396 - **€29 347** - FF304 335
**Portrait of Annie, Wife of John Proctor Esqr.,
Barrister at Law** Oil/canvas (73x60cm 28x23in)
Malvern, Victoria 1996
$2 740 - €3 028 - **€1 900** - FF19 860
Liphook Oil/board (36x44cm 14x17in) London 2001
$875 - €743 - **£528** - FF4 871
The Couple Watercolour/paper (65x55cm 25x21in)
Sydney 1998

LAMBERT Georges 1919-1998 **[39]**
$350 - €350 - **€219** - FF2 296
Les tuileries Oil/canvas (53x64cm 21x25in) Chicago
IL 1999

LAMBERT James, Snr, of Lewes 1725-1788 **[6]**
$1 339 - €1 601 - **£920** - FF10 500
Cattle and Pigs Outside a Threshing Barn
Oil/canvas (54.5x66cm 21x25in) Billingshurst, West-
Sussex 2000

LAMBERT Léon Eugène 1865-? **[3]**
$5 500 - €4 712 - **£3 306** - FF30 908
Urn Bronze (H37cm H14in) New-York 1998

LAMBERT Louis Eugène 1825-1900 **[111]**
$3 250 - €3 313 - **£2 036** - FF21 731
Up to Mischief Oil/canvas (38x46.5cm 14x18in) New-
York 2000
$923 - €991 - **£617** - FF6 500
Le panier de chatons Huile/papier/panneau
(24x20cm 9x7in) Cherbourg 2000
$595 - €625 - **£375** - FF4 100
Pie et chatons Crayons couleurs/papier (26x35cm
10x13in) Besançon 2000

LAMBERT Maurice 1901-1964 **[8]**
$2 881 - €2 616 - **£1 800** - FF17 161
Woman with Child on her Shoulders Terracotta
(H41cm H16in) London 1999

LAMBERT Michel c.1748-? **[1]**
$29 574 - €27 441 - **£17 748** - FF180 000
Antigone implorant le pardon de son frère
Huile/toile (115x147cm 45x57in) Paris 1999

LAMBERT Theodore Roosevelt 1905-1960 **[7]**
$25 000 - €23 778 - **£15 180** - FF155 975
The Burial Mound Oil/canvas (40.5x51cm 15x20in)
Beverly-Hills CA 1999

LAMBERT-RUCKI Jean 1888-1967 **[606]**
$6 152 - €6 098 - **£3 848** - FF40 000
La ruelle ténébreuse Huile/carton (73x54cm
28x21in) Paris 1999
$3 133 - €3 735 - **£2 234** - FF24 500
Personnages Huile/panneau (19x33cm 7x12in) Paris
2000
$7 440 - €7 622 - **£4 630** - FF50 000
Le songeur Bronze (80x46x27cm 31x18x10in) Paris
2000
$1 502 - €1 677 - **£983** - FF11 000
Le pèlerin Bronze (H12.5cm H4in) Le Touquet 2000
$802 - €777 - **£504** - FF5 100
La confession Mine plomb (28x23cm 11x9in) Paris
1999

LAMBERTI Lamberto 1925 **[21]**
$325 - €195 - **£195** - FF2 240
«**Vegetazione con case**» Olio/tela (60x80cm
23x31in) Vercelli 2001

LAMBERTS Gerrit 1776-1850 **[8]**
$794 - €818 - **£501** - FF5 366
Kanallandschaft bei Purmerend Aquarell/Papier
(23.5x37cm 9x14in) Berlin 2000

LAMBIL Willy Lambillotte 1936 **[5]**
$872 - €930 - **£591** - FF6 100
Tuniques bleues Gouache/papier (27x20cm 10x7in)
Paris 2001

LAMBINET Émile Charles 1815-1877 **[106]**
$5 750 - €5 429 - **£3 574** - FF35 610
River Landscape Oil/panel (45x60cm 18x24in)
Milford CT 1999
$2 747 - €2 668 - **£1 697** - FF17 500
Troupeau au bord de la rivière Huile/panneau
(25.5x35cm 10x13in) Melun 1999

LAMBRÉ Sylvain 1889-1958 **[37]**
$437 - €446 - **£273** - FF2 926
Portrait Huile/toile (70x50cm 27x19in) Bruxelles 2000
$190 - €198 - **£120** - FF1 300
Femmes dans une étable Technique mixte/papier
(50x60cm 19x23in) Antwerpen 2000

LAMBRECHT Constant 1915-1993 **[30]**
$399 - €446 - **£277** - FF2 926
Femme devant le miroir Huile/panneau (74x54cm
29x21in) Antwerpen 2001
$422 - €397 - **£260** - FF2 601
Deux figures Fusain/papier (52x36cm 20x14in)
Antwerpen 1999

LAMBRECHT William Adolphe 1876-1940 **[6]**
$6 437 - €6 250 - **£3 977** - FF41 000
Souk El Attarine, Tunis Huile/toile (43x55cm
16x21in) Paris 1999

LAMBRECHTS Jan Baptist 1680-c.1731 **[72]**
$4 688 - €3 992 - **£2 800** - FF26 185
A Tavern Interior with Figures at a Table Oil/can-
vas (59.5x51cm 23x20in) London 1998
$3 315 - €3 718 - **£2 310** - FF24 390
**Intérieur de taverne avec homme tenant une
cruche** Huile/panneau (14x12cm 5x4in) Bruxelles
2001

LAMBRICHS Edmond 1830-1887 **[6]**
$1 217 - €1 431 - **£872** - FF9 390
Blumenstilleben mit Vase und Schale Oil/panel
(69.5x95cm 27x37in) Düsseldorf 2001

LAMEN van der Christoffel Jacobsz. c.1606-c.1651
[53]
$14 782 - €13 805 - **£9 123** - FF90 555
Ein häusliches Konzert Oil/panel (51x69cm
20x27in) Köln 1999

LAMEYER Y BERENGUER Francisco, Frederico
1825-1917 **[10]**
$2 080 - €2 403 - **£1 440** - FF15 760
Escena andaluza Oleo/lienzo (35x42cm 13x16in)
Madrid 2001
$208 - €240 - **£144** - FF1 576
Tienda morisca Dibujo (20.5x23.5cm 8x9in) Madrid
2001

LAMI Eugène 1800-1890 **[132]**
$2 005 - €2 211 - **£1 334** - FF14 500
**Manoeuvre de la Garde Royale arrivée du Roi
Louis Philipppe en calèche** Huile/toile (32x67cm
12x26in) Biarritz 2000
$7 350 - €8 676 - **£5 180** - FF56 910
Paris, église St.Paul Huile/cuivre (36.5x22.5cm
14x8in) Liège 2000

L

LAMI

$5 000 - €4 915 - **£3 212** - FF32 239
Portrait of Michael Ney, Fils Watercolour,
gouache/paper (30.5x19cm 12x7in) New-York 1999

LAMI Stanislas 1858-1944 **[8]**
$11 207 - €12 030 - **£7 500** - FF78 912
Great Dane Observing a Snail Bronze (42x41.5cm
16x16in) London 2000

LAMME Arie Johannes 1812-1900 **[19]**
$2 417 - €2 723 - **£1 666** - FF17 859
A Sign of Admiration Oil/panel (58x41cm 22x16in)
Amsterdam 2000

LAMMERS Wilhelmus Albertus 1857-1913 **[16]**
$802 - €808 - **£500** - FF5 301
Chickens in a Farmyard Oil/canvas (21x30.5cm
8x12in) London 2000

LAMMEYER Ferdinand 1899-1995 **[8]**
$1 826 - €2 069 - **£1 268** - FF13 415
Das Forsthaus Öl/Leinwand (46x60cm 18x23in)
Staufen 2001
$285 - €327 - **£195** - FF2 146
Apfelbäume Gouache/Karton (36x49.5cm 14x19in)
Heidelberg 2000

LAMMI Ilkka 1976-2000 **[6]**
$5 888 - €6 727 - **£4 144** - FF44 128
Den sömnloses Natt Oil/canvas (130x110cm
51x43in) Helsinki 2001
$4 671 - €5 045 - **£3 234** - FF33 096
Flicka med kvist Oil/canvas (102x70cm 40x27in)
Helsinki 2001

LAMOND William Bradley 1857-1924 **[58]**
$4 641 - €4 004 - **£2 800** - FF26 266
The Blacksmith Oil/canvas (35.5x46cm 13x18in)
London 1998
$2 619 - €3 115 - **£1 804** - FF20 432
Shepherd and his Flock Oil/canvas (14x18cm
5x7in) Calgary, Alberta 2000
$1 759 - €1 694 - **£1 100** - FF11 111
Auchmithe Watercolour/paper (51x77cm 20x30in)
Billingshurst, West-Sussex 1999

LAMONICA Giuseppe 1862-1919 **[6]**
$5 355 - €5 551 - **£3 213** - FF36 414
Due bambini sugli scogli Olio/tela (33x46.5cm
12x18in) Milano 1999

LAMONT Joseph XX **[171]**
$423 - €396 - **£259** - FF2 600
Marine Huile/panneau (13x18cm 5x7in) Paris 1998
$282 - €335 - **£201** - FF2 260
Marine Aquarelle/papier (15x27cm 5x10in) Blois 2000

LAMORE Chet 1908-1980 **[12]**
$80 - €83 - **£52** - FF544
«Little red riding Hood» Silkscreen in colors
(15x40cm 6x16in) Cleveland OH 2000

LAMORINIERE François J.-P. 1828-1911 **[70]**
$1 693 - €1 450 - **£1 000** - FF9 514
Paysage de Marais Oil/canvas (40.5x73cm 15x28in)
London 1998
$1 041 - €1 022 - **£645** - FF6 707
Belgische Dünenlandschaft Oil/panel (22x39cm
8x15in) München 1999
$1 830 - €2 181 - **£1 311** - FF14 308
Paysages Dessin (30x36cm 11x14in) Bruxelles 2000

LAMOTTE Bernard 1903-1983 **[77]**
$1 500 - €1 733 - **£1 050** - FF11 367
**Fragment of a Dream, inspired by Gustave
Charpentier's Louise** Oil/canvas (91x132cm
36x52in) New-York 2001

$1 800 - €1 747 - **£1 134** - FF11 458
St. Patrick's Cathedral Oil/canvas (73x54cm
29x21in) New-York 1999
$4 250 - €4 910 - **£2 975** - FF32 206
**Between Two Worlds, inspired by Giacomo
Puccini's La vie de Boheme** Oil/canvas (25x25cm
10x10in) New-York 2001

LAMOUR Fritzner 1948 **[10]**
$959 - €1 143 - **£684** - FF7 500
Mariage religieux Huile/panneau (40x30cm 15x11in)
Paris 2000

LAMPI Franciszek 1782-1852 **[3]**
$8 435 - €8 282 - **£5 232** - FF54 327
Portrait d'une femme Oil/canvas (76.5x63.5cm
30x25in) Warszawa 1999

LAMPI Giovanni Battista I 1751-1830 **[21]**
$4 914 - €5 488 - **£3 330** - FF36 000
**Portrait de jeune femme sortant du bain dans
un ovale peint** Huile/toile (100.5x76cm 39x29in)
Paris 2000

LAMPI Giovanni Battista II 1775-1837 **[19]**
$10 212 - €9 584 - **£6 308** - FF62 864
Portrait d'une dame Oil/canvas (100x76.5cm
39x30in) Warszawa 1999

LAMPI Vilho 1898-1936 **[16]**
$8 349 - €9 418 - **£5 868** - FF61 779
Limingo å Oil/panel (37x49cm 14x19in) Helsinki 2001
$2 069 - €2 270 - **£1 332** - FF14 893
Det skymmer Oil/panel (26.5x28cm 10x11in)
Helsinki 2000

LAMPISUO Antti 1926 **[28]**
$569 - €521 - **£346** - FF3 419
Pioner i vas Oil/canvas (50x61cm 19x24in) Helsinki
1999

LAMPITT Ronald 1906 **[11]**
$1 355 - €1 296 - **£849** - FF8 499
**«Ireland, British Railways, Vale of Clara, County
Wicklow»** Poster (102x127cm 40x50in) London 1999

LAMPLOUGH Augustus Osborne 1877-1930 **[354]**
$903 - €991 - **£600** - FF6 499
A Camel Rider in the Desert Watercolour
(22.5x60.5cm 8x23in) London 2000

LAMPRADOS Emmanuel c.1580-c.1647 **[1]**
$873 495 - €809 504 - **£539 496** - FF5 310 000
Le Thrène, mise au tombeau Tempera/panneau
(30.5x68cm 12x26in) Paris 1999

LAMPRECHT Anton 1901-1984 **[39]**
$1 096 - €1 278 - **£768** - FF8 384
Boote Öl/Leinwand (75x100cm 29x39in) München
2000

LAMSWEERDE van Clotildis 1848-1913 **[2]**
$6 175 - €6 807 - **£4 033** - FF44 649
Vruchtenstilleven met druiven en peren Oil/can-
vas (42.5x62cm 16x24in) Den Haag 2000

LAMSWEERDE van Inez 1963 **[4]**
$12 000 - €13 166 - **£7 971** - FF86 361
Thank You Thighmaster Cibachrome print
(185.5x120.5cm 73x47in) New-York 2000

LAMY Aline 1862-? **[2]**
$4 075 - €3 555 - **£2 465** - FF23 317
«Le Soir» - Aftonstämning Pastel/paper
(105x105cm 41x41in) Stockholm 1998

LAMY John Peter c.1791-1839 **[17]**
🎨 **$278** - €328 - **£191** - FF2 151
Vue de la vallée, et des glaciers du Schwartzwaldalp Aquatinta (20x29.5cm 7x11in) Bern 2000

LAMY Pierre Lambert, dit 1921 **[23]**
🖋 **$1 385** - €1 296 - **£849** - FF8 500
«Paysage fantastique» Technique mixte/panneau (55x33cm 21x12in) Paris 1998

LAN YINDING Lan Yin-ting 1903-1979 **[34]**
✏ **$27 880** - €29 687 - **£17 680** - FF194 735
Valley after Rain Ink (59x94cm 23x37in) Taipei 2000

LAN YING 1585-c.1664 **[33]**
✏ **$12 179** - €14 315 - **£8 445** - FF93 898
Landscape Ink (128x49cm 50x19in) Hong-Kong 2000

LAN-BAR David Lan-Berg, dit 1912-1987 **[61]**
🖋 **$514** - €564 - **£349** - FF3 700
Composition abstraite Huile/toile (73x50cm 28x19in) Pontoise 2000
$1 739 - €1 601 - **£1 043** - FF10 499
Composition Gouache/paper (105x75cm 41x29in) Tel Aviv 1999

LANA DA MODENA Lodovico 1597-1656 **[4]**
🖋 **$32 445** - €32 703 - **£20 250** - FF214 515
Die Magdalena mit einem Engel Öl/Leinwand (117x97cm 46x38in) Wien 2000

LANCASTER Hume 1773-1850 **[3]**
🖋 **$2 346** - €2 510 - **£1 545** - FF16 466
Coastal Scene with Sailing Boat Oil/canvas (36x55cm 14x21in) Sydney 2000

LANCASTER Osbert 1908-1986 **[45]**
🖋 **$1 736** - €1 875 - **£1 200** - FF12 299
The Professor Oil/canvas (71x91.5cm 27x36in) London 2001
✏ **$705** - €690 - **£450** - FF4 527
Let us not forget, Lady Littlehampton Ink (19x13.5cm 7x5in) London 1999

LANCASTER Percy 1878-1951 **[126]**
🖋 **$1 964** - €1 875 - **£1 200** - FF15 323
Quiet Moment in a Breton Market Oil/canvas (29x34cm 11x13in) Bath 2000
✏ **$768** - €645 - **£450** - FF4 233
Haymakers Watercolour/paper (22x31.5cm 8x12in) Billingshurst, West-Sussex 1998

LANCE George 1802-1864 **[54]**
🖋 **$3 666** - €3 951 - **£2 500** - FF23 728
Apples, Pineapple, and Grapes in a wicker Basket Oil/canvas (51x68.5cm 20x26in) London 2001
🖋 **$4 782** - €5 280 - **£3 300** - FF34 637
Still Life with Grapes and a Peach/Still Life with an Apple and a Plum Oil/panel (19x24cm 7x9in) Crewkerne, Somerset 2001

LANCELEY Colin 1938 **[54]**
🖋 **$11 493** - €10 021 - **£6 949** - FF65 736
South Coast Mixed media/canvas (135x167.5cm 53x65in) Melbourne 1998
✏ **$2 070** - €1 966 - **£1 291** - FF12 895
Cyclists Circle Coloured pencils (76x109.5cm 29x43in) Sydney 2000

LANCERAY Evgeni Alexandrovich 1848-1886 **[178]**
🗿 **$3 200** - €3 639 - **£2 219** - FF23 872
Two Military Figures Bronze (49x40cm 19x16in) St. Louis MO 2000

LANCEROTTO Egisto 1848-1916 **[24]**
🖋 **$4 200** - €3 628 - **£2 100** - FF23 800
Contadinella Olio/tela (60x48cm 23x18in) Genova 1999

LANCI Baldassare c.1510-1571 **[1]**
✏ **$12 000** - €12 836 - **£8 181** - FF84 200
Capriccio of Florence: Design for the Stage Black chalk (22.5x32.5cm 8x12in) New-York 2001

LANCKOW Ludwig act.1870-1892 **[31]**
🖋 **$1 822** - €1 687 - **£1 100** - FF11 064
A Winter Landscape at Sunset Oil/canvas (30.5x53.5cm 12x21in) London 1999

LANÇON Auguste André 1836-1887 **[20]**
🖋 **$3 020** - €3 354 - **£2 105** - FF22 000
Lion léchant sa lionne/Ourse et ses petits Huile/toile (32.5x42.5cm 12x16in) Paris 2001

LANCRET Nicolas 1690-1743 **[96]**
🖋 **$97 866** - €91 533 - **£60 000** - FF600 420
Fête champêtre with Figures Conversing in a Parkland Setting Oil/canvas (41.5x55cm 16x21in) London 1998
✏ **$8 188** - €7 607 - **£5 000** - FF49 900
Study of a Standing Gallant and the Hand of Another Figure Red chalk/paper (23x11.5cm 9x4in) London 1998

LANCY Bernard Blanc-Percy 1894-1950 **[40]**
🎨 **$828** - €762 - **£497** - FF5 000
«La Kermesse Héroïque» Affiche (120x160cm 47x62in) Paris 1999

LANDACRE Paul Hambleton 1893-1963 **[71]**
🎨 **$1 200** - €1 363 - **£821** - FF8 938
Jungle Storm Woodcut (21.5x15.5cm 8x6in) New-York 2000

LANDALUZE Víctor Patricio 1828-1889 **[32]**
🖋 **$20 000** - €23 237 - **£14 056** - FF152 424
Preparativos de fiesta Oil/canvas (35.5x26cm 13x10in) New-York 2001

LANDARA Benjamin 1921-1985 **[45]**
✏ **$175** - €193 - **£116** - FF1 265
Ghost Gum Shade Watercolour/paper (24.5x35.5cm 9x13in) Melbourne 2000

LANDAU Ergy 1896-1967 **[51]**
📷 **$757** - €793 - **£475** - FF5 200
Femme photographiant un zébre Tirage argentique (16.5x22.5cm 6x8in) Paris 2000

LANDAU Sigmund 1898-1962 **[51]**
🖋 **$2 709** - €2 493 - **£1 625** - FF16 354
Paysage d'été avec bottes de foin Oil/canvas (65.5x88.5cm 25x34in) Warszawa 1999
🖋 **$1 490** - €1 677 - **£1 026** - FF11 016
Portrait de femme Huile/toile (46x27cm 18x10in) Paris 2000
✏ **$294** - €305 - **£186** - FF2 000
Jeune homme Aquarelle (45x33cm 17x12in) Paris 2000

LANDEA Carolina XX **[1]**
🖋 **$6 500** - €6 324 - **£4 000** - FF41 484
Mujer Oil/canvas (81x100cm 31x39in) New-York 1999

LANDECK Armin 1905-1984 **[121]**
🎨 **$700** - €776 - **£465** - FF5 093
Approaching Storm, Manhattan Drypoint (23x21cm 9x8in) New-York 2000

L

LANDELLE Charles Zacharie 1821-1908 **[101]**
- **$65 000** - €74 834 - **£44 356** - FF490 880
  Algérienne jouant de la Darbouka Oil/canvas
  (137.5x96.5cm 54x37in) New-York 2000
- **$5 439** - €6 403 - **£3 822** - FF42 000
  Garçon à la fontaine Huile/toile (65x49cm 25x19in)
  Paris 2000
- **$3 364** - €3 659 - **£2 217** - FF24 000
  Femme au foulard Huile/toile/carton (23.5x16cm
  9x6in) Paris 2000

LANDENBERGER Christian Adam 1862-1927 **[57]**
- **$5 678** - €6 391 - **£3 912** - FF41 923
  **Bildnis einer jungen Dame, die vor einer
  Staffelei sitzt** Öl/Leinwand (99x89cm 38x35in)
  Stuttgart 2000
- **$3 134** - €3 559 - **£2 209** - FF23 477
  Stürmische Dünenlandschaft Öl/Leinwand/Karton
  (25x30cm 9x11in) Stuttgart 2001
- **$122** - €112 - **£75** - FF737
  Ohne Titel Radierung (15x21cm 5x8in) Stuttgart 1999

LANDER Cyril George 1892-1983 **[7]**
- **$855** - €795 - **£527** - FF5 215
  Freshwater Bay Watercolour/paper (27x36cm
  10x14in) Melbourne 1999

LANDER John St. Helier 1869-1944 **[23]**
- **$11 664** - €13 720 - **£8 361** - FF90 000
  Portrait du Captain Sinclair G.Traill Huile/toile
  (166x105cm 65x41in) Paris 2001
- **$1 989** - €1 723 - **£1 200** - FF11 299
  **F.H Thornton, Three-quarter-length, in a Black
  Suit and White Shirt** Oil/canvas (91.5x71cm
  36x27in) London 1998

LANDERS Sean 1962 **[14]**
- **$40 000** - €46 412 - **£27 616** - FF304 440
  Worry Wart Oil/canvas (213x305cm 83x120in) New-
  York 2000
- **$13 835** - €13 466 - **£8 500** - FF88 328
  Ich Mache Mich Bronze (57x38x56cm 22x14x22in)
  London 1999

LANDERSET de Joseph 1753-1824 **[8]**
- **$1 344** - €1 444 - **£900** - FF9 469
  **Northern Wooded Landscape, with a Bear in the
  Foreground** Watercolour, gouache/paper (27.5x41cm
  10x16in) London 2000

LANDESIO Eugenio 1809-1879 **[5]**
- **$35 202** - €34 950 - **£22 000** - FF229 255
  Goats watering by a Lake Oil/canvas (75x89.5cm
  29x35in) London 1999

LANDHEER Hugo 1896-1995 **[4]**
- **$860** - €998 - **£594** - FF6 548
  Drie herten in een landschap Oil/canvas (56x68cm
  22x26in) Rotterdam 2000

LANDI XX **[7]**
- **$218** - €186 - **£130** - FF1 220
  «Bullitt» Poster (160x120cm 62x47in) London 1998

LANDI Bruno 1941 **[51]**
- **$900** - €933 - **£540** - FF6 120
  Parigi Olio/tela (50x60cm 19x23in) Vercelli 2000

LANDI Gaspare 1756-1830 **[10]**
- **$39 984** - €34 541 - **£26 656** - FF226 576
  Ettore rimprovera Paride Olio/tela (124x177cm
  48x69in) Venezia 1999
- **$9 200** - €11 922 - **£6 900** - FF78 200
  **Probabile ritratto di Marianna Waldstein di
  Santa Cruz** Olio/tela (54x45cm 21x17in) Prato 2000

LANDINI Andrea 1847-1912 **[28]**
- **$34 538** - €32 710 - **£21 000** - FF214 561
  The Cardinal's Pleasure Oil/canvas (45.5x37.5cm
  17x14in) London 1999
- **$11 736** - €13 720 - **£8 379** - FF90 000
  Le plaisir du Cardinal Huile/toile (27x22cm 10x8in)
  Angers 2001

LANDIS John 1805-? **[3]**
- **$2 000** - €1 725 - **£1 211** - FF11 318
  Noah's Ark Watercolour (29x40cm 11x15in) New-
  York 1999

LANDOIS Michel XVII-XVIII **[3]**
- **$33 243** - €32 014 - **£20 643** - FF210 000
  «Le Glorieux» Huile/toile (53x65cm 20x25in) Paris
  1999

LANDOLT Karl 1925 **[13]**
- **$1 879** - €1 877 - **£1 174** - FF12 314
  S'Pastorebirebäumli im Herbst Öl/Leinwand
  (74x81cm 29x31in) Zofingen 1999

LANDOLT Otto 1889-1951 **[21]**
- **$611** - €616 - **£380** - FF4 038
  «Rigi-Kaltbad» Poster (128x90cm 50x35in) London
  2000

LANDOLT Salomon 1741-1818 **[2]**
- **$4 022** - €4 336 - **£2 697** - FF28 441
  Schloss Greifensee bei Vollmond Gouache/papier
  (23x26cm 9x10in) Zürich 2000

LANDON Charles Paul 1760-1826 **[5]**
- **$44 178** - €50 177 - **£31 000** - FF329 142
  Interior with a Mother and Child Oil/panel
  (46x37.5cm 18x14in) London 2001

LANDON Edward August 1911-1984 **[20]**
- **$400** - €429 - **£267** - FF2 816
  On the Beach by the Sea Silkscreen in colors
  (28x51cm 11x20in) Cleveland OH 2000

LANDOWSKI Paul 1875-1961 **[73]**
- **$3 892** - €4 269 - **£2 643** - FF28 000
  L'envol Bronze (H81.5cm H32in) Soissons 2000
- **$3 952** - €3 659 - **£2 419** - FF24 000
  Le voleur d'oranges Bronze (H33cm H12in)
  Soissons 1999

LANDOZZI Lando 1887-1959 **[3]**
- **$2 000** - €2 592 - **£1 500** - FF17 000
  Cucitrici Olio/faesite (49x68.5cm 19x26in) Prato 2000

LANDRÉ Louise Amélie 1852-? **[13]**
- **$1 380** - €1 524 - **£957** - FF10 000
  Petite fille au cerceau Huile/toile (134x78cm
  52x30in) Autun 2001

LANDRIESVE de Jacques XVIII **[1]**
- **$25 570** - €29 824 - **£18 000** - FF195 634
  Verdure chinoise à oiseaux Tapestry (255x345cm
  100x135in) London 2001

LANDRY Pierre c.1630-? **[1]**
- **$1 525** - €1 738 - **£1 064** - FF11 403
  **Madonna mit Kind und dem hl.Joseph, nach
  Pierre Mignard** Kupferstich (38.5x35.5cm 15x13in)
  Berlin 2001

LANDSDALE Robert XIX-XX **[1]**
- **$8 500** - €8 089 - **£5 316** - FF53 060
  Indian Encampment Oil/canvas (76x116cm 30x46in)
  New-York 1999

LANDSEER Charles 1799-1879 **[16]**
- **$170 320** - €163 574 - **£105 000** - FF1 072 974
  The Merry Monks of Melrose Oil/canvas
  (107x156cm 42x61in) London 1999

LANDSEER Edwin Henry 1802-1873 **[134]**
- $220 000 - €255 606 - **£154 616** - FF1 676 664
  Refreshment Oil/panel (99x127cm 38x50in) New-York 2001
- $125 000 - €106 798 - **£75 037** - FF700 550
  Retriever and Woodcock Oil/canvas (72x49.5cm 28x19in) New-York 1998
- $21 636 - €25 428 - **£15 000** - FF166 800
  Figures Resting by a river in a Highland Landscape Oil/panel (23.5x32.5cm 9x12in) Edinburgh 2000
- $2 694 - €2 799 - **£1 700** - FF18 362
  Stag and Deer Hounds Ink (21.5x30.5cm 8x12in) London 2001
- $937 - €1 052 - **£650** - FF6 901
  Midsummer Night's Dream Engraving (66x95cm 25x37in) London 2001

LANDSEER George 1834-1878 **[2]**
- $10 564 - €12 407 - **£7 500** - FF81 387
  Sir Chamarajendra Wodyar, Maharajah of Mysore, in a White Costume Oil/canvas (39x31cm 15x12in) London 2000

LANDSEER John 1763/69-1852 **[4]**
- $120 - €116 - **£75** - FF758
  Panoply of Ottoman and Crusader Armour Engraving (30x25cm 12x10in) London 1999

LANDSEER Thomas 1795-1880 **[10]**
- $448 - €428 - **£280** - FF2 805
  The Stag at Bay, After Sir Edwin Landseer Engraving (52x92cm 20x36in) Cheshire 1999

LANDT Frantz 1885-1976 **[135]**
- $496 - €511 - **£315** - FF3 350
  Marine med motor-og sejlskibe udfor en kyst Oil/canvas (67x100cm 26x39in) Vejle 2000

LANDUYT Octave (Octaaf 1922-1996 **[59]**
- $1 320 - €1 239 - **£815** - FF8 130
  Infrastructure Huile/panneau (80x60cm 31x23in) Antwerpen 1999
- $2 532 - €2 975 - **£1 752** - FF19 512
  Onvermijdelijk V Céramique (64x54cm 25x21in) Antwerpen 2000
- $266 - €297 - **£184** - FF1 951
  Étude Fusain/papier (31x23cm 12x9in) Antwerpen 2001

LANDUYT van Charles Joseph 1854-1934 **[14]**
- $802 - €892 - **£561** - FF5 853
  Travailleur de dos Huile/toile (110x90cm 43x35in) Bruxelles 2001

LANDWEHR Johan XVII **[1]**
- $789 - €767 - **£493** - FF5 030
  ABBILD Der Weiterberühmten Kayserlichen Freyen Reichs und Ansee Stadt Kupferstich (21x59cm 8x23in) Bremen 1999

LANDY Art 1904 **[3]**
- $1 000 - €1 167 - **£696** - FF7 653
  Harbor Watercolour/paper (36x54cm 14x21in) Altadena CA 2000

LANE Abigail 1967 **[9]**
- $8 666 - €9 303 - **£5 800** - FF61 025
  Ink Pad I Mixed media (244x305x2.5cm 96x120xin) London 2000
- $6 973 - €8 201 - **£5 000** - FF53 793
  Blue Print Installation (122x46x91cm 48x18x35in) London 2001
- $10 742 - €9 178 - **£6 500** - FF60 206
  Misfit Plaster (60x85x192cm 23x33x75in) London 1998

LANE Fitz Hugh 1804-1865 **[22]**
- $700 000 - €598 070 - **£420 210** - FF3 923 080
  «Star Light» in Harbor Oil/canvas (62x91.5cm 24x36in) New-York 1998

LANE Leonard ?-1978 **[5]**
- $1 200 - €1 285 - **£819** - FF8 431
  Moonlit shoreline Oil/canvas (63x76cm 25x30in) Cleveland OH 2001

LANE Samuel 1780-1859 **[5]**
- $4 286 - €4 725 - **£2 888** - FF30 991
  Portrait of Sir Thomas Sherlock Gooch, 5th Bt. (1767-1851) Oil/canvas (72.5x61cm 28x24in) London 2000

LANFANT DE METZ François-Louis 1814-1892 **[298]**
- $9 000 - €8 591 - **£5 623** - FF56 354
  The Days Bounty Oil/canvas (64x76cm 25x30in) Dedham MA 1999
- $3 718 - €3 964 - **£2 355** - FF26 000
  Les petits mariés Huile/carton (13.5x9cm 5x3in) Bayeux 2000

LANFRANCO Giovanni 1582-1647 **[28]**
- $54 000 - €46 649 - **£27 000** - FF306 000
  San Francesco di Paola portato in Gloria dagli angeli Olio/tavola (60x43cm 23x16in) Firenze 1999
- $26 506 - €29 720 - **£18 000** - FF194 952
  Christ at the Column Oil/copper (32x26cm 12x10in) London 2000
- $8 219 - €8 823 - **£5 500** - FF57 873
  Angel Adoration With Studies of the Head of a Child/Saint Lucy Black, red & white chalks/paper (29x21cm 11x8in) London 2000

LANG Albert 1847-1933 **[38]**
- $1 696 - €1 892 - **£1 140** - FF12 409
  Bewaldete Landschaft Öl/Leinwand (70x107.5cm 27x42in) Ahlden 2001

LANG Fritz 1877-1961 **[105]**
- $97 - €102 - **£61** - FF670
  Goldfasan nach rechts Woodcut in colors (25x57.5cm 9x22in) Stuttgart 2000

LANG Gary 1950 **[29]**
- $1 900 - €2 039 - **£1 271** - FF13 377
  Rain in Olivenhain Oil/masonite (61x76cm 24x29in) San-Francisco CA 2000
- $1 500 - €1 753 - **£1 070** - FF11 499
  Early Spring, San Pasqual Oil/canvas/board (27x35cm 11x14in) Altadena CA 2001

LANG Hans 1914-1986 **[11]**
- $1 639 - €1 534 - **£993** - FF10 061
  Blick auf den Bodensee durch einen Obstgarten Öl/Leinwand (65x80cm 25x31in) Stuttgart 1999

LANG Heinrich 1838-1891 **[17]**
- $3 242 - €3 681 - **£2 252** - FF24 148
  Patrouille des 4.bayerischen Chevaulegers-Regiments König Öl/Leinwand (62.5x72.5cm 24x28in) München 2001
- $1 260 - €1 227 - **£774** - FF8 049
  Friedensverhandlung Oil/panel (23.5x30cm 9x11in) Berlin 1999

LANG JINSHAN (Long Chin San) 1892-1995 **[2]**
- $4 264 - €4 540 - **£2 704** - FF29 783
  Old Pavilion Gelatin silver print (41x61cm 16x24in) Taipei 2000

LANG Josef Adolf 1873-1936 **[5]**

$2 298 – €2 211 – £1 416 – FF14 500
«Düsseldorf, exposition internationale des
Beaux-Arts, exposition...» Affiche (97x64cm
38x25in) Poitiers 1999

LANG Louis 1814-1893 **[26]**

$1 600 – €1 772 – £1 085 – FF11 623
Meditation Oil/canvas (63x76cm 25x30in) New-York
2000

$1 112 – €1 311 – £781 – FF8 601
Landschaften mit Bauernhof am Wasser
Öl/Leinwand (24x32cm 9x12in) Bern 2000

LANG SHINING (Gius. Castiglione) 1688-1766 **[4]**

$70 000 – €60 945 – £41 734 – FF399 770
Imperial Journey to the South Ink (54x647.5cm
21x254in) New-York 1998

LANG Stephen 1944 **[1]**

$8 000 – €9 119 – £5 581 – FF59 815
Truce between Fighting Men Huile/métal
(55x101cm 22x40in) Dallas TX 2001

LANGASKENS Maurice 1884-1946 **[280]**

$1 883 – €1 735 – £1 134 – FF11 382
Le batelier Huile/toile (93x70cm 36x27in) Antwerpen
1999

$1 351 – €1 438 – £922 – FF9 430
Paysan Huile/panneau (39x29.5cm 15x11in) Bruxelles
2001

$372 – €421 – £251 – FF2 764
Les vainqueurs Technique mixte/papier
(13.5x20.5cm 5x8in) Bruxelles 2000

$93 – €111 – £66 – FF731
Le meunier Gravure bois (97x65cm 38x25in)
Bruxelles 2000

LANGE Dorothea 1895-1965 **[113]**

$5 500 – €5 193 – £3 415 – FF34 066
Serenity Gelatin silver print (24x23cm 9x9in) New-
York 1999

LANGE Edward XIX-XX **[4]**

$25 000 – €29 540 – £17 717 – FF193 770
Residence of Selah Bunce Watercolour (28x43cm
11x17in) East-Moriches NY 2000

LANGE Fritz 1851-1922 **[18]**

$6 500 – €6 366 – £4 188 – FF41 761
A Popular watering Hole for Fowl Oil/panel
(66x77.5cm 25x30in) New-York 1999

$1 530 – €1 431 – £927 – FF9 390
Enten am schilfgesäumten Ufer Oil/panel
(16x12cm 6x4in) Bremen 1999

LANGE Gustav Johann 1811-1887 **[26]**

$14 720 – €14 395 – £9 091 – FF94 424
Die Jagdpartie Öl/Leinwand (94x135cm 37x53in)
Zürich 1999

$1 367 – €1 534 – £947 – FF10 061
Winterlandschaft bei Mondlicht Öl/Leinwand
(93x75cm 36x29in) München 2000

LANGE Julius 1817-1878 **[29]**

$2 731 – €2 556 – £1 692 – FF16 769
Obersee bei Berchtesgaden Öl/Leinwand
(84x114cm 33x44in) Heidelberg 1999

LANGE Ludwig 1808-1868 **[62]**

$220 – €204 – £134 – FF1 341
Der Platz der alten Accademie bei Athen
Pencil/paper (27.8x34.2cm 10x13in) München 1999

LANGE Otto 1879-1944 **[140]**

$934 – €1 035 – £634 – FF6 792
Stilleben med figurin, Skål och trädocka Oil/can-
vas (55x43cm 21x16in) Stockholm 2000

$770 – €742 – £481 – FF4 864
Berglandschaft mit Matterhorn Ink (22x28cm
8x11in) München 1999

$849 – €736 – £515 – FF4 825
Nizza Monotype (34.5x45.5cm 13x17in) München
1998

LANGE Richard W. XIX-XX **[7]**

$446 – €409 – £272 – FF2 683
Mädchenakt am Brunnen Bronze (H20cm H7in)
München 1999

LANGELER Freddie 1899-1948 **[3]**

$1 471 – €1 588 – £1 005 – FF10 418
A Masquerade Oil/canvas (61.5x52cm 24x20in)
Amsterdam 2001

LANGENDYK Dirk 1748-1805 **[76]**

$1 282 – €1 107 – £772 – FF7 263
A Battle Scene with Cavalrymen and Infantry by
a Waterway Wash (23.5x28.5cm 9x11in) Amsterdam
1998

LANGENDYK Jan Anthonie 1780-1818 **[27]**

$897 – €1 067 – £622 – FF7 000
Militaire à cheval Encre (22.5x30cm 8x11in) Paris
2000

LANGENEGGER Johannes 1879-1951 **[2]**

$7 502 – €8 487 – £5 248 – FF55 671
Alpfahrt in Landschaft mit Zwei Bauernhöfen
und Alphütten Öl/Papier (37x48cm 14x18in) St.
Gallen 2001

LANGENMANTEL von Ludwig 1854-1922 **[7]**

$3 239 – €3 068 – £1 969 – FF20 123
Spanische Flamenco-Tänzerinnen Öl/Leinwand
(83.5x140.5cm 32x55in) München 1999

LANGER Karel 1878-1947 **[29]**

$722 – €683 – £450 – FF4 482
A la montagne Huile/toile (72x100cm 28x39in) Praha
1999

LANGER Klàra 1912-1973 **[24]**

$241 – €229 – £146 – FF1 500
Le blaireau Photo (21x15.5cm 8x6in) Paris 1999

LANGER Olaf Viggo Peter 1860-1942 **[330]**

$514 – €549 – £350 – FF3 603
Skovparti ved sö Oil/canvas (67x71cm 26x27in)
Vejle 2001

$373 – €323 – £225 – FF2 118
Landskab med kvaeg, efterår Oil/canvas
(43.5x35.5cm 17x13in) Vejle 1998

LANGERFELD von Rutger 1635-1695 **[1]**

$2 107 – €2 045 – £1 312 – FF13 415
Allegorie der vier Erdteile: Europa, Amerika,
Asien und Afrika Indian ink (28.5x19.5cm 11x7in)
Berlin 1999

LANGEROCK Henri 1830-1915 **[31]**

$8 946 – €10 411 – £6 384 – FF68 292
Lavandière dans un cours d'eau Huile/toile
(164x113cm 64x44in) Bruxelles 2000

$4 806 – €4 430 – £2 879 – FF29 059
«Boers avant l'attaque dans le Transvaal»
Oil/canvas (61x74cm 24x29in) Amsterdam 1998

$450 – €526 – £316 – FF3 449
Ruhende Schafe in Landschaft Oil/panel
(18.5x24cm 7x9in) Luzern 2000

LANGETTI Giovanni-Battista 1625-1676 **[12]**
- **$85 343** - €83 592 - **£55 000** - FF548 328
  Lot and his Daughters Oil/canvas (137x181.5cm 53x71in) London 1999

LANGEVELD Frans 1877-1939 **[50]**
- **$3 861** - €4 558 - **£2 677** - FF29 766
  A View of an Amsterdam Canal Oil/canvas (41.5x61cm 16x24in) Amsterdam 2000

LANGEVIN Claude 1942 **[129]**
- **$1 066** - €1 151 - **£715** - FF7 553
  Début de l'hiver Oil/canvas (50.5x61cm 19x24in) Calgary, Alberta 2000
- **$509** - €504 - **£318** - FF3 309
  Vers Ste. Émilie, Laurentides Oil/canvas (20.5x25.5cm 8x10in) Calgary, Alberta 1999

LANGEWEG Ger 1891-1970 **[72]**
- **$2 148** - €2 496 - **£1 509** - FF16 371
  Sailing Boats on a Lake Oil/canvas (50x70.5cm 19x27in) Amsterdam 2001
- **$317** - €340 - **£212** - FF2 232
  Haven van Blankenberghe Pencil (74x57.5cm 29x22in) Amsterdam 2000

LANGHAMMER Arthur 1854-1901 **[11]**
- **$4 857** - €5 238 - **£3 240** - FF34 359
  Med blicken mot horisonten Oil/canvas (90x121cm 35x47in) Stockholm 2000
- **$1 687** - €1 636 - **£1 068** - FF10 732
  Bauernkinder am sonnigen Wiesenhang Oil/panel (24x13.5cm 9x5in) München 1999

LANGHAMMER Carl 1868-1941 **[26]**
- **$609** - €562 - **£379** - FF3 689
  Ziegen am Steinbruch Öl/Leinwand (55x42cm 21x16in) Rudolstadt-Thüringen 1999

LANGHARD Adolf 1845-? **[3]**
- **$15 000** - €14 854 - **£9 339** - FF97 437
  The Muse Oil/canvas (161.5x121cm 63x47in) New-York 1999

LANGKER Erik 1898-1982 **[124]**
- **$423** - €441 - **£266** - FF2 892
  Seascape Oil/board (39x49.5cm 15x19in) Melbourne 2000
- **$297** - €309 - **£187** - FF2 026
  Into the Light Oil/board (35.5x43cm 13x16in) Sydney 2000

LANGLAIS Bernard 1921-1977 **[9]**
- **$3 600** - €3 413 - **£2 248** - FF22 385
  Forenoon Sculpture, wood (71x99cm 28x39in) Mystic CT 1999
- **$1 600** - €1 713 - **£1 088** - FF11 236
  «Sunrise» Collage (58x58cm 23x23in) Lambertville NJ 2001

LANGLANDS & BELL 1955/1959 **[16]**
- **$16 527** - €14 121 - **£10 000** - FF92 625
  Maisons de force Installation (92x42x40cm 36x16x15in) London 2000
- **$7 221** - €7 869 - **£5 000** - FF51 614
  U.N.Security Council, New York Assemblage (68x60x18cm 26x23x7in) London 2001

LANGLET Alexander 1870-1953 **[50]**
- **$424** - €505 - **£292** - FF3 314
  Hästar på grönbete Oil/canvas (46x59cm 18x23in) Stockholm 2000

LANGLEY Charles Dickinson 1799-1873 **[1]**
- **$8 000** - €8 713 - **£5 509** - FF57 153
  A Spaniel and a Black-Tan Terrier in the Grounds of a Country House Oil/canvas (43x53.5cm 16x21in) New-York 2001

LANGLEY Walter 1852-1922 **[155]**
- **$67 500** - €75 382 - **£43 227** - FF494 471
  Motherless Oil/canvas (122x153.5cm 48x60in) New-York 2000
- **$22 708** - €21 892 - **£14 000** - FF143 599
  At Polperro, Cornwall Oil/canvas (76x56cm 29x22in) London 1999
- **$5 983** - €6 956 - **£4 200** - FF45 630
  Breton Peasant Girl Watercolour/paper (34.5x24cm 13x9in) Billinghurst, West-Sussex 2001

LANGLEY William XIX-XX **[239]**
- **$568** - €550 - **£360** - FF3 605
  Highland Sheep Resting by a Loch Oil/canvas (51x76.5cm 20x30in) London 1999
- **$962** - €970 - **£600** - FF6 362
  Portrait of a Lady in Hayfield Oil/canvas (39.5x19.5cm 15x7in) London 2000
- **$541** - €564 - **£340** - FF3 697
  A Highland River Landscape Watercolour/paper (49.5x75cm 19x29in) Billinghurst, West-Sussex 2000

LANGLIN Victoriano Corina 1844-1971 **[5]**
- **$1 028** - €1 154 - **£720** - FF7 571
  Cavalier and Serving Maid in an Interior Oil/panel (23x16cm 9x6in) London 2001

LANGLOIS Chris 1969 **[2]**
- **$4 409** - €4 945 - **£3 061** - FF32 434
  Landsape Oil/canvas (152x196cm 59x77in) Melbourne 2001

LANGLOIS DE SÉZANNE Claude Louis 1757-1845 **[4]**
- **$3 406** - €3 506 - **£2 164** - FF23 020
  Paysage avec temple en ruine et villageoises Pierre noire (43.5x54.5cm 17x21in) Paris 2000

LANGLOIS J. XIX **[24]**
- **$1 927** - €1 871 - **£1 200** - FF12 271
  A Terrier with a dead Hare/A Spaniel with a dead Pheasant Oil/canvas (51x76cm 20x29in) London 1999
- **$896** - €962 - **£600** - FF6 313
  Terriers/Terrier ratting/Spaniel with Pheasant Oil/board (16.5x24cm 6x9in) Billinghurst, West-Sussex 2000

LANGLOIS Mark W. ?-c.1890 **[118]**
- **$1 443** - €1 455 - **£900** - FF9 543
  Interior scene with Children/The Schoolmaster Oil/canvas (52x42cm 20x16in) London 2000
- **$1 143** - €1 295 - **£800** - FF8 495
  Peeling vegetable/The Card Game Oil/panel (24x29cm 9x11in) Billinghurst, West-Sussex 2001
- **$967** - €902 - **£600** - FF5 915
  At the Cottage Door Watercolour/paper (75.5x62cm 29x24in) Billinghurst, West-Sussex 1999

LANGLON Edmond Philibert XVIII **[1]**
- **$3 749** - €3 887 - **£2 249** - FF25 498
  Natura morta Olio/tela (80x134cm 31x52in) Milano 1999

LANGMAID Rowland 1897-1956 **[151]**
- **$2 757** - €2 648 - **£1 700** - FF17 372
  H.M.S Howe in the Suez Canal/Nelson in the Mediterranean/Cruisers Watercolour (25.5x35.5cm 10x13in) London 1999

L

$390 - €356 - £240 - FF2 336
H.M.S Dreadnought Leaves Portsmouth Harbour Etching (17x35cm 6x13in) London 1998

LANGMAN Eleazar 1895-1940 [4]
$3 546 - €3 070 - £2 152 - FF20 136
Der ertse Fünfjahresplan, Moskau Photograph (17.5x23.7cm 6x9in) München 1998

LANGSCHMIDT Wilhelm Heinrich 1805-1866 [1]
$15 266 - €13 187 - £9 205 - FF86 504
Canteen Scene During the Frontier Wars Oil/canvas (47x61cm 18x24in) Johannesburg 1998

LANIAU Jean 1931 [92]
$1 690 - €1 677 - £1 051 - FF11 000
Femme agenouillée Bronze (H36cm H14in) L'Isle-Adam 1999

LANINO Bernardino c.1512-c.1583 [10]
$55 000 - €58 737 - £37 477 - FF385 291
The Head of a Bearded Man Black & white chalks/paper (39.5x29cm 15x11in) New-York 2001

LANMAN Charles 1819-1895 [9]
$2 700 - €2 962 - £1 742 - FF19 428
Fall landscape scene Oil/board (13x28cm 5x11in) Wallkill NY 2000

LANOOY Christiaan Johannes 1881-1948 [9]
$3 220 - €3 176 - £1 983 - FF20 836
Still Life with Mushrooms Oil/canvas/board (33.5x50cm 13x19in) Amsterdam 1999

LANOUE Félix Hippolyte 1812-1872 [9]
$1 013 - €1 180 - £707 - FF7 739
Female Figures in a Mediterranean Landscape Pencil (14.5x21cm 5x8in) Amsterdam 2000

LANSDOWNE James Fenwick 1940 [23]
$1 363 - €1 288 - £847 - FF8 447
Short-eared Owl, Asio Flammeus Watercolour (52x48cm 20x18in) Nepean, Ont. 1999

LANSIL Walter Franklin 1846-1925 [40]
$2 200 - €2 566 - £1 544 - FF16 830
Off the Grand Banks Oil/canvas (71x102cm 27x40in) Boston MA 2000

LANSKOY André 1902-1976 [1448]
$25 000 - €23 348 - £15 430 - FF153 150
Tourbillon Oil/canvas (97x146cm 38x57in) New-York 1999
$7 187 - €8 690 - £5 021 - FF57 000
Sans raison Huile/toile (81x65cm 31x25in) Paris 2000
$2 269 - €2 287 - £1 414 - FF15 000
Rayon craintif Huile/toile (14x18cm 5x7in) Paris 2000
$2 574 - €2 744 - £1 632 - FF18 000
Sans titre Gouache/papier (22x31cm 8x12in) Paris 2000
$140 - €136 - £87 - FF893
Cette créature perifide qui est la femme Color lithograph (67x44cm 26x17in) Amsterdam 1999

LANSON Alfred Désiré 1851-1938 [28]
$14 943 - €16 040 - £10 000 - FF105 216
Jason enlevant la toison d'or (jason Holding the Golden Fleece) Bronze (H102cm H40in) London 2000
$3 810 - €3 354 - £2 321 - FF22 000
L'orage Bronze (H69cm H27in) Dieppe 1999

LANSYER Emmanuel 1835-1893 [51]
$2 762 - €2 553 - £1 700 - FF16 745
Playa rocosa Oleo/lienzo (44x65cm 17x25in) Madrid 1999
$2 750 - €2 744 - £1 717 - FF18 000
Un matin à Pierrefonds, forêt de Compiègne Huile/toile (35.5x24.5cm 13x9in) Fontainebleau 1999

LANTARA Simon Mathurin 1729-1778 [51]
$2 840 - €3 049 - £1 900 - FF20 000
Paysage fluvial au moulin Huile/toile (38x46cm 14x18in) Troyes 2000
$4 640 - €4 878 - £2 912 - FF32 000
Paysages Huile/cuivre (16x22cm 6x8in) Paris 2000
$682 - €762 - £462 - FF5 000
Paysage Pierre noire (37x54cm 14x21in) Paris 2000

LANTERI Edouard 1848-1917 [5]
$33 168 - €36 652 - £23 000 - FF240 419
Two ladies in classical robes, reading a book Marble (H120cm H47in) London 2001

LANTERNIER Léon Raoul 1870-? [5]
$2 502 - €2 287 - £1 531 - FF15 000
Sous les voûtes, Fès Huile/toile (73x60cm 28x23in) Paris 1999

LANTOINE Fernand 1876/78-1944/46/55 [187]
$10 212 - €11 403 - £7 084 - FF74 796
Côte rocheuse Huile/panneau (130x175cm 51x68in) Antwerpen 2001
$2 568 - €2 975 - £1 776 - FF19 512
Bord de rivière Huile/toile (60x72cm 23x28in) Bruxelles 2000
$466 - €503 - £322 - FF3 300
Voiliers au Port Huile/papier (23.5x29cm 9x11in) Lyon 2001

LANTS Gerard 1927-1998 [47]
$416 - €486 - £290 - FF3 189
Wading in the Water Watercolour/paper (14x54cm 5x21in) Melbourne 2000

LANYON Peter George 1918-1964 [106]
$126 018 - €146 560 - £90 000 - FF961 371
«Porthmeor Mural» Oil/canvas (107x965cm 42x379in) London 2001
$16 436 - €15 617 - £10 000 - FF102 444
Harvey's Pool Oil/masonite (98x59cm 38x23in) London 1999
$4 141 - €3 834 - £2 500 - FF25 147
Landscape with a Path Oil/panel (33x40cm 13x16in) Par, Cornwall 1999
$8 921 - €8 600 - £5 500 - FF56 414
Composition Charcoal (13.5x22cm 5x8in) London 1999
$1 293 - €1 212 - £800 - FF7 948
A Cornish Landscape Screenprint (53x40cm 21x16in) Penzance, Cornwall 1999

LANZA Giovanni 1827-1889 [36]
$7 140 - €7 402 - £4 284 - FF48 552
Barche di pescatori sulla spiaggia di fronte a Procida Olio/tela (30x42cm 11x16in) Roma 2001
$2 890 - €2 733 - £1 800 - FF17 930
Landschaft mit antikem Dome Aquarell/Papier (43x73cm 16x28in) Praha 2000

LANZA Luigi 1860-? [29]
$1 500 - €1 555 - £900 - FF10 200
Il Canal Grande Olio/tela (37x56cm 14x22in) Roma 1999

LANZA Vincenzo 1822-1902 [10]
$5 940 - €6 607 - £3 960 - FF43 340
The british Consulate at Patras Oil/panel (45x74cm 17x29in) Athens 2000
$7 601 - €8 722 - £5 200 - FF57 210
The Parthenon, Athens Watercolour/paper (35x54cm 13x21in) London 2000

LANZIROTTI Antonio Giovanni 1839-? [9]
- $16 652 - €18 923 - **£11 500** - FF124 127
  Blind Love Marble (H106.5cm H41in) London 2000

LAPA Eduarda 1896-1976 [11]
- $5 375 - €6 231 - **£3 750** - FF40 875
  Ramo de rosas Oleo/lienzo (46x54.5cm 18x21in) Lisboa 2001
- $2 024 - €2 293 - **£1 426** - FF15 042
  Jarra com flores Oleo/tablex (37.5x28cm 14x11in) Lisboa 2001
- $1 760 - €1 990 - **£1 200** - FF13 080
  Marinha Pastel/papier (33.5x47cm 13x18in) Lisboa 2000

LAPARRA William J.E.E. 1873-1920 [17]
- $1 491 - €1 601 - **£997** - FF10 500
  Scène d'intérieur avec fileuse et son enfant Huile/toile (61x46cm 24x18in) Paris 2000
- $2 100 - €2 439 - **£1 481** - FF16 000
  Fillette devant la mer Huile/toile (46x33cm 18x12in) Paris 2001

LAPAYESE DEL RIO José 1896-2000 [34]
- $915 - €901 - **£585** - FF5 910
  «Rincón de puerto» Oleo/lienzo (38x55cm 14x21in) Madrid 1999

LAPCHINE Georges 1885-1951 [49]
- $5 600 - €4 798 - **£3 366** - FF31 470
  Russian Spring Oil/canvas (105x145cm 41x57in) Cedar-Falls IA 1998
- $2 006 - €1 852 - **£1 200** - FF12 151
  Mars en Russie (dernière neige), soleil couchant Oil/canvas (89x116cm 35x45in) London 1999

LAPERRIERE de Gaston 1848-? [11]
- $2 024 - €1 982 - **£1 245** - FF13 000
  Environs du Caire Huile/toile (58x77cm 22x30in) Paris 1999

LAPEYRE Lucien XIX-XX [15]
- $1 132 - €991 - **£685** - FF6 500
  Vue d'istambul Huile/panneau (18x36cm 7x14in) Montpellier 1998

LAPICQUE Charles 1898-1988 [1217]
- $5 127 - €4 726 - **£3 072** - FF31 000
  Avant l'orage Acrylique/toile (60.5x73cm 23x28in) Paris 1998
- $1 916 - €1 829 - **£1 197** - FF12 000
  Lagune bretonne Huile/papier/panneau (25.5x16cm 10x6in) Douai 1999
- $448 - €534 - **£310** - FF3 500
  Portrait Aquarelle (50x32cm 19x12in) Paris 2000
- $97 - €107 - **£64** - FF700
  Rome Lithographie (50x65cm 19x25in) Douai 2000

LAPIERRE-RENOUARD Paul Marie 1854-? [5]
- $14 000 - €13 864 - **£8 756** - FF90 941
  Feeding Time Oil/canvas (145.5x114cm 57x44in) New-York 1999

LAPINI Cesare 1848-? [42]
- $8 500 - €8 565 - **£5 298** - FF56 185
  After the Bath Marbre (H84cm H33in) New-York 2000
- $1 500 - €1 429 - **£950** - FF9 376
  Bust of Young Gypsy with Flowers trimmed Clothing Rests Alabaster (H55cm H22in) St. Petersburg FL 1999

LAPIRA P. XIX-XX [5]
- $6 136 - €6 445 - **£3 874** - FF42 276
  Isola Di Nisita Gouache/papier (44x64cm 17x25in) Bruxelles 2000

LAPIS Hieronymus XVIII [1]
- $1 500 - €1 655 - **£1 016** - FF10 854
  The Good Samarittan Ink (13x18.5cm 5x7in) New-York 2000

LAPITO Louis Auguste 1803-1874 [25]
- $12 520 - €14 534 - **£8 800** - FF95 340
  Blick auf Corte in korsika Öl/Leinwand (115x162.5cm 45x63in) Wien 2001
- $11 052 - €11 582 - **£7 000** - FF75 970
  Vue d'Unterseen, Berne Oil/canvas (89.5x116.5cm 35x45in) London 2000
- $4 075 - €3 811 - **£2 467** - FF25 000
  Palais au bord de la mer Huile/papier (32x44cm 12x17in) Vierzon 1999

LAPLAGNE Guillaume XIX-XX [5]
- $9 013 - €9 983 - **£6 113** - FF65 485
  Wizard (male) named Melimassikini/Yazocota woman Plaster (H60cm H23in) Amsterdam 2000

LAPLANCHE Pierre 1826-1873 [15]
- $1 013 - €1 021 - **£631** - FF6 700
  Sanglier courant Bronze (7.5x15cm 2x5in) Paris 2000

LAPLANCHE Pierre Albert 1854-? [7]
- $1 176 - €992 - **£696** - FF6 504
  Deux cerfs Bronze (44.5x44cm 17x17in) Antwerpen 1998

LAPORTE Émile 1858-1907 [44]
- $1 554 - €1 735 - **£1 085** - FF11 382
  Deux Gaulois Bronze (H80cm H31in) Bruxelles 2001
- $344 - €1 444 - **£900** - FF9 469
  Warrior and his Son Bronze (H61cm H24in) Billingshurst, West-Sussex 2000

LAPORTE George Henry 1799-1873 [29]
- $56 147 - €56 578 - **£35 000** - FF371 126
  The Horse Fair Oil/canvas (143.5x297cm 56x116in) London 2000
- $6 075 - €5 782 - **£3 800** - FF37 925
  «Well Over», jumping a five Bar Gate Oil/canvas (70x90cm 27x35in) Channel-Islands 1999

LAPORTE Georges 1926-2000 [204]
- $1 666 - €1 982 - **£1 187** - FF13 000
  Ferme à Cercot, Bourgogne Öl/Leinwand (72x98cm 28x38in) Zürich 2000
- $819 - €915 - **£536** - FF6 000
  Marine Huile/papier (31x44cm 12x17in) Le Touquet 2000

LAPORTE John 1761-1839 [27]
- $9 540 - €11 346 - **£6 800** - FF74 427
  Ullswater with Martindale Beyond/Elterwater, Westmoreland Oil/panel (26.5x38cm 10x14in) London 2000
- $1 298 - €1 249 - **£800** - FF8 190
  River Landscape with Figures Watercolour (26x34cm 10x13in) London 1999

LAPORTE-BLAISIN Léo L.-Blairsy 1865-1923 [29]
- $1 708 - €1 448 - **£1 013** - FF9 500
  Enfant à la lanterne Bronze (H27cm H10in) Paris 1998

LAPOSTOLET Charles 1824-1890 [47]
- $6 863 - €8 080 - **£4 823** - FF53 000
  Le port Huile/toile (38.5x55.5cm 15x21in) Argenteuil 2000
- $2 074 - €2 333 - **£1 448** - FF15 305
  Hafenmole Öl/Leinwand (40.5x27cm 15x10in) Luzern 2001

L

LAPOUJADE Robert 1921-1993 **[66]**
- $491 - €579 - £345 - FF3 800
  Nu assis Huile/toile (95x34cm 37x13in) Paris 2000

LAPP Henry XIX **[4]**
- $4 500 - €4 194 - £2 776 - FF27 509
  Bunch of pansies Watercolour/paper (13x18cm 5x7in) Ephrata PA 1999

LAPPAS George 1950 **[2]**
- $10 800 - €12 013 - £7 200 - FF78 800
  Large Letter in Envelope Plastic (100x190x30cm 39x74x11in) Athens 2000

LAPRADE Pierre 1875-1931 **[291]**
- $3 933 - €3 354 - £2 373 - FF22 000
  Roses dans un vase blanc sur une assiette Huile/carton (68x50cm 26x19in) Paris 1998
- $2 050 - €2 302 - £1 328 - FF15 100
  Fleurs des champs dans un verre Huile/toile (41x33cm 16x12in) Paris 2000
- $508 - €534 - £321 - FF3 500
  Le bassin dans le parc Aquarelle, gouache/papier (30x36cm 11x14in) Paris 2000

LAQUY Joseph Willem 1738-1798 **[12]**
- $19 000 - €21 281 - £13 201 - FF139 596
  Family in an Interior Oil/panel (43x53.5cm 16x21in) New-York 2001
- $9 671 - €8 954 - £6 000 - FF58 734
  Kitchen Maid at a Window Plucking a Duck Oil/panel (44.5x33cm 17x12in) London 1999
- $2 430 - €2 710 - £1 634 - FF17 775
  Musikgesellschaft Aquarell/Papier (47x52.5cm 18x20in) Ahlden 2000

LARA Clever XX **[4]**
- $1 350 - €1 449 - £903 - FF9 507
  Muñeca Oleo/lienzo (61x50cm 24x19in) Montevideo 2000

LARA Ernest William 1870-1940 **[2]**
- $3 273 - €3 826 - £2 300 - FF25 100
  Farm Labourers and Horses in busy Farmyard/Untitled Oil/canvas (44x34cm 17x13in) Oxfordshire 2000

LARA Georgina XIX **[57]**
- $5 213 - €4 745 - £3 200 - FF31 126
  Village Life Oil/canvas (35.5x53.5cm 13x21in) London 1999
- $4 029 - €4 518 - £2 800 - FF29 634
  Figures on Horseack and a Horse and Cart before a Cottage Oil/canvas (23x38cm 9x15in) Little-Lane, Ilkley 2001

LARCHÉ Raoul François 1860-1912 **[225]**
- $61 636 - €59 420 - £38 000 - FF389 769
  La tempête et les Nuées Bronze (H87cm H34in) London 1999
- $3 424 - €3 659 - £2 328 - FF24 000
  La Sève - Métamorphose de Daphné Bronze (H63cm H24in) La Rochelle 2001

LARCHER André Emile XIX **[1]**
- $3 200 - €3 772 - £2 248 - FF24 741
  Canal and Gondolas, Venice Oil/canvas (56x46cm 22x18in) New-Orleans LA 2000

LARD Maurice 1864-1908 **[3]**
- $19 549 - €22 497 - £13 477 - FF147 571
  Nach dem Ball Öl/Leinwand (179x110cm 70x43in) Saarbrücken 2000

LARDERA Berto 1911 **[28]**
- $329 - €307 - £198 - FF2 012
  Bildern in Astres égarés Farblithographie (76x57cm 29x22in) Hamburg 1999

LARESCHE A. XIX **[1]**
- $4 396 - €4 269 - £2 716 - FF28 000
  Palerme Tirage papier salé (25x32.5cm 9x12in) Paris 1999

LARGILLIERE de Nicolas 1656-1746 **[88]**
- $98 338 - €103 258 - £62 000 - FF677 331
  Allegorical Portrait of Marie-Thérèse de Bourbon, Princess de Conti Oil/canvas (137.5x107.5cm 54x42in) London 2000
- $26 000 - €30 557 - £18 025 - FF200 444
  Gentleman, said to be the Chamberlain de Montargu, Half-Length Oil/canvas (82x64.5cm 32x25in) New-York 2000
- $17 620 - €14 531 - £10 380 - FF95 320
  Bildnis eines Knaben im Harnisch mit einem roten Mantel Öl/Leinwand (27.5x22.5cm 10x8in) Wien 1998

LARGUES XVIII **[1]**
- $7 261 - €6 973 - £4 500 - FF45 741
  Vue Perspective de la Place Montarcher de la Ville du Cap Watercolour/paper (27x42.5cm 10x16in) London 1999

LARIJ Roeland 1855-1932 **[31]**
- $716 - €681 - £435 - FF4 464
  Boerenbinnenhuis met vrouw aan een spinne-wiel Oil/canvas (51x60cm 20x23in) Den Haag 1999
- $159 - €181 - £110 - FF1 190
  Zeeuwsche boerin Oil/panel (22x17cm 8x6in) Dordrecht 2000

LARIONOV Michel 1881-1964 **[204]**
- $28 702 - €32 777 - £20 188 - FF215 000
  Arbres Huile/toile (60x55cm 23x21in) Château-Thierry 2001
- $7 072 - €7 927 - £4 799 - FF52 000
  Promeneuses en conversation Huile/toile (41x32.5cm 16x12in) Paris 2000
- $1 644 - €1 765 - £1 100 - FF11 578
  The Alcoholic Watercolour (21.5x16cm 8x6in) London 2000
- $711 - €818 - £502 - FF5 366
  Selbstportrat Lithographie (11.5x9.2cm 4x3in) Hamburg 2001

LARIVE-GODEFROY de Pierre Louis 1735-1817 **[8]**
- $5 768 - €5 814 - £3 600 - FF38 136
  Rastende Hirten mit ihrer Herde Öl/Leinwand (64x93cm 25x36in) Wien 2000

LARKINS William Martin 1901-1974 **[3]**
- $1 374 - €1 484 - £950 - FF9 737
  Gardens at Antibes Gouache (31x45.5cm 12x17in) London 2001

LARMESSIN Nicolas III le Jeune c.1640-1725 **[5]**
- $1 545 - €1 524 - £952 - FF10 000
  Les quatre évangiles Encre/papier (39x29cm 15x11in) Neuilly-sur-Seine 2000

LARMESSIN Nicolas IV 1684-1753 **[10]**
- $719 - €762 - £479 - FF5 000
  Le matin/Le midi/L'après-midi/La soirée, d'après Nicolas Lancret Eau-forte (29.5x36cm 11x14in) Paris 2000

LAROCHE Ernersto 1879-1940 **[7]**
- $10 000 - €8 618 - £5 941 - FF56 529
  Paisaje del Río Santa Lucía Oleo/lienzo (101x101cm 39x39in) Montevideo 1998

$1 450 - €1 508 - £915 - FF9 893
Poema nativo Oleo/tabla (20x20cm 7x7in)
Montevideo 2000

LARONZE Jean 1852-1937 [4]
$3 821 - €3 700 - £2 400 - FF24 270
Washerwomen by the River Oil/canvas (61x32cm
24x12in) London 1999

LAROT Dina 1943 [21]
$841 - €726 - £507 - FF4 764
Liegender Halbakt Black chalk (42x58.5cm 16x23in)
Wien 1998

LARPENTEUR Balthasar Charles XIX [2]
$1 822 - €1 982 - £1 201 - FF13 000
Portrait de jeune homme Huile/toile (60x48.5cm
23x19in) Paris 2000

LARRAGA Y MONTANER Andrés 1862-1931 [21]
$4 320 - €4 805 - £2 960 - FF31 520
Paisaje costero Oleo/lienzo (43x69cm 16x27in)
Barcelona 2001

LARRAMET Hilaire Z. XX [1]
$900 - €1 050 - £631 - FF6 885
«**Fayard**» Poster (59x80.5cm 23x31in) New-York 2000

LARRAZ Julio 1944 [72]
$80 000 - €69 757 - £48 368 - FF457 576
Partial Eclipse Oil/canvas (170x211cm 66x83in)
New-York 1998
$18 000 - €21 194 - £12 648 - FF139 021
Puente Oil/canvas (58.5x81.5cm 23x32in) New-York
2000

LARREGIEU Fulbert Pierre ?-1886 [3]
$6 555 - €7 496 - £4 500 - FF49 168
A Brooding Bloodhound Bronze (22x28.5cm
8x11in) London 2000

LARROCHA GONZALEZ de José 1859-1933 [7]
$3 900 - €4 505 - £2 700 - FF29 550
Bodegón con frutero Oleo/lienzo (111x75cm
43x29in) Madrid 2000
$1 140 - €1 141 - £703 - FF7 486
Granja Oleo/cartón (22x27cm 8x10in) Madrid 2000

LARROUX Antonin 1859-1913 [12]
$1 000 - €935 - £605 - FF6 136
Peasant Woman Bronze (H51cm H20in) Chicago IL
1999

LARRUMBIDE Alberto 1909-? [13]
$1 122 - €1 321 - £792 - FF8 668
Gitana Miniature (8x10.5cm 3x4in) Bilbao 2000

LARSEN Adolph 1856-1942 [44]
$855 - €740 - £519 - FF4 856
Bygevejr fra egnen ved Jonstrup Oil/canvas
(45x69cm 17x27in) København 1998

LARSEN Alfred Valdemar 1860-1946 [45]
$532 - €571 - £361 - FF3 743
Paisaje con ovejas Oleo/lienzo (67x99cm 26x38in)
Madrid 2001

LARSEN Emanuel 1823-1859 [44]
$8 965 - €9 624 - £6 000 - FF63 129
Shipping Off a Baltic Port Oil/canvas (55.5x86.5cm
21x34in) London 2000
$1 740 - €1 878 - £1 167 - FF12 318
Marine med hjuldamper Oil/canvas (32x39cm
12x15in) København 2000

LARSEN Erik 1902-1965 [55]
$175 - €161 - £109 - FF1 059
Jomfruen og enhjörningen Watercolour/paper
(62x48cm 24x18in) Viby J, Århus 1999

LARSEN Johannes 1867-1961 [264]
$6 578 - €7 374 - £4 598 - FF48 372
Havbillede med edderfugle og böje Oil/canvas
(94x134cm 37x52in) København 2001
$2 511 - €2 815 - £1 749 - FF18 465
To spurve bader Oil/canvas (48x59cm 18x23in)
København 2001
$973 - €1 073 - £659 - FF7 040
Kystparti med store sten Oil/canvas (27x39cm
10x15in) Vejle 2000
$564 - €603 - £383 - FF3 955
Udsigt over landskab Watercolour (27x42cm
10x16in) Vejle 2001
$144 - €161 - £101 - FF1 055
«**Et staerepar**» Woodcut (24.5x19cm 9x7in) Vejle
2001

LARSEN Karl 1897-1977 [153]
$410 - €377 - £252 - FF2 473
Blomsteropstilling med lupiner Oil/canvas
(74x60cm 29x23in) København 1999

LARSEN Knud Erik 1865-1922 [63]
$1 137 - €1 077 - £708 - FF7 063
To kvinder i hvide kjoler siddende vel söbred
Oil/canvas (49x71cm 19x27in) Vejle 1999
$273 - €295 - £188 - FF1 935
Portraet af stiftamtmand Steemann i uniform
Oil/canvas (28x24cm 11x9in) København 2001

LARSEN Oskar 1882-1972 [167]
$948 - €872 - £586 - FF5 720
Bacchanal Mischtechnik/Karton (67.5x98cm 26x38in)
Wien 1999
$489 - €511 - £321 - FF3 353
Frauenraub Mischtechnik (31x44cm 12x17in)
München 2000
$609 - €654 - £415 - FF4 290
Sklavenhändler Aquarell/Papier (34.5x49cm 13x19in)
Wien 2001

LARSEN STEVNS Niels 1864-1941 [83]
$2 370 - €2 680 - £1 602 - FF17 582
Laesende kvinde Oil/canvas (51x64cm 20x25in)
København 2000
$613 - €618 - £382 - FF4 290
Den fortabte sön Watercolour (20x13cm 7x5in)
København 2000

LARSEN-SAERSLØV Frederik 1870-1942 [19]
$157 - €148 - £97 - FF971
Töjret bödes Oil/panel (35x43cm 13x16in) Viby J,
Århus 1999

LARSON Gary 1950 [2]
$1 900 - €2 128 - £1 320 - FF13 959
**Daily Comic Panel, Two old Men poised for
eating Contest** Ink (22x15cm 9x6in) New-York 2001

LARSON Harold Magnus 1865-1952 [3]
$6 000 - €6 408 - £4 088 - FF42 031
The Melting Pot Oil/panel (70x85cm 27x33in) New-
York 2001

LARSSON Albert 1869-1952 [28]
$240 - €231 - £148 - FF1 518
Brygga vid lövskog Oil/canvas (27x31cm 10x12in)
Malmö 1999

LARSSON Bo 1945 [12]
$1 560 - €1 782 - £1 099 - FF11 691
Skeppsbron Oil/canvas (82x126cm 32x49in)
Stockholm 2001
$253 - €244 - £154 - FF1 601
Motiv från Nytorget Color lithograph (38x54cm
14x21in) Stockholm 1999

L

LARSSON Carl Olof 1855-1919 [315]

- $358 150 – €312 389 - £216 630 – FF2 049 140
  «Sagor» Oil/canvas (100x164cm 39x64in) Stockholm
  1998
- $53 460 – €49 983 - £32 940 – FF327 870
  Rosorna Oil/canvas (92x71cm 36x27in) Stockholm
  1999
- $116 677 – €135 561 - £82 000 – FF889 224
  Porträtt av Elise Fürstenberg, gift meyer Oil/canvas (51x25.5cm 20x10in) London 2001
- $13 999 – €15 643 - £9 490 – FF102 613
  Min strand, Vårstudier/Landskapsvyer från Sundborn Coloured crayons/paper (66x56cm 25x22in) Stockholm 2000
- $508 – €461 - £313 – FF3 023
  Lektyr Etching (19.7x14.9cm 7x5in) Stockholm 1999

LARSSON Carl Oscar 1887-1962 [58]

- $240 – €231 - £148 – FF1 518
  Kanalen, Malmö, vid Södra Promenaden Oil/canvas (30x39cm 11x15in) Malmö 1999

LARSSON Marcus 1825-1864 [69]

- $17 290 – €15 081 - £10 458 – FF98 924
  «Vattenfall i Norrland» Oil/canvas (96x130cm 37x51in) Stockholm 1998
- $4 305 – €4 643 - £2 889 – FF30 455
  Skeppsbrott i storm Oil/canvas (76x102cm 29x40in) Stockholm 2000
- $1 420 – €1 239 - £859 – FF8 125
  Skogslandskap Oil/canvas (17x23cm 6x9in) Stockholm 1998

LARTER Richard Charles 1929 [50]

- $4 144 – €4 628 - £2 653 – FF30 359
  Untitled Pop Painting Acrylic (145.5x91cm 57x35in) Malvern, Victoria 2000
- $1 828 – €1 715 - £1 129 – FF11 249
  The Girl Oil/board (91.5x61cm 36x24in) Melbourne 1999

LARTIGUE Dany 1921 [73]

- $496 – €579 - £348 – FF3 800
  Fleurs Huile/panneau (84x60cm 33x23in) Versailles 2000

LARTIGUE Jacques Henri 1894-1986 [437]

- $3 213 – €3 506 - £2 180 – FF23 000
  Renée au collier de perles Tirage argentique (14x8.5cm 5x3in) Paris 2000

LARUE de Louis Félix 1720/31-1765/77 [81]

- $737 – €732 - £458 – FF4 800
  Allégorie de la vigilance entourée de Putti et signes du zodiaque Encre (23.6x29cm 9x11in) Paris 1999

LARUE de Philibert Benoît 1718-1780 [17]

- $6 465 – €7 622 - £4 545 – FF50 000
  Bal masqué et saltimbanques Lavis (28.5x38cm 11x14in) Lyon 2000

LARUS Eliane 1944 [77]

- $1 073 – €1 235 - £739 – FF8 100
  Scène de rue à la grue Acrylique (50x65cm 19x25in) Paris 2000
- $856 – €915 - £582 – FF6 000
  Paysage au loup-garou Acrylique/papier (35x27cm 13x10in) Paris 2000
- $1 200 – €1 037 - £724 – FF6 800
  Le chien fidèle Bronze (26x25x18cm 10x9x7in) Paris 1998

LARWILL David 1956 [40]

- $5 823 – €6 359 - £3 748 – FF41 712
  Untitled No.1 Oil/canvas (180.5x175cm 71x68in) Melbourne 2000
- $2 437 – €2 734 - £1 692 – FF17 934
  «The Madina» Oil/canvas (106x89cm 41x35in) Melbourne 2001

LAS CASAS de Jesus María 1854-1926 [7]

- $1 757 – €1 854 - £1 161 – FF12 163
  Paisaje Huile/bois (15x25cm 5x9in) Caracas ($) 2000

LASALLE Charles Louis XX [5]

- $2 000 – €2 331 - £1 384 – FF15 293
  Hunter, Boy and Retriever Watching Older Man Painting Duck Decoy Gouache/board (41x28cm 16x11in) New-York 2000

LASANSKY Mauricio 1914 [15]

- $900 – €700 - £613 – FF6 362
  Spring Engraving (60.5x22cm 23x8in) New-York 2001

LASAR C. XIX [2]

- $6 500 – €7 381 - £4 448 – FF48 417
  Along the Riverbank Oil/canvas (28.5x38.5cm 11x15in) New-York 2000

LASCH Hermann 1861-1926 [6]

- $1 423 – €1 483 - £902 – FF9 726
  Heuernte im Flusstal Gouache/paper (100x134cm 39x52in) München 2001

LASELLAZ Gustave François 1848-1910 [4]

- $8 000 – €7 922 - £4 980 – FF51 966
  The young Seamstress Oil/canvas (40x31cm 15x12in) New-York 1999

LASH Lee 1864-1935 [5]

- $13 000 – €12 177 - £7 992 – FF79 873
  42nd Street, New York Oil/canvas (63.5x75.5cm 25x29in) New-York 1999

LASINIO Carlo 1750-1838 [21]

- $450 – €388 - £267 – FF2 546
  Portraits of Artists Engraving (24x18cm 9x7in) New-York 2000

LASKA Lotte 1924 [13]

- $570 – €665 - £394 – FF4 360
  An der RheinbrÜcke in Köln Vintage gelatin silver print (22.7x16cm 8x6in) Köln 2000

LASKE Oskar 1874-1951 [500]

- $59 580 – €65 405 - £39 600 – FF429 030
  Die Kreuzigung Tempera (114.5x139.5cm 45x54in) Wien 2000
- $18 419 – €20 783 - £12 956 – FF136 329
  Hafen von Istanbul Öl/Leinwand (55x68cm 21x26in) Bern 2001
- $1 278 – €1 453 - £898 – FF9 534
  Orientalische Szene Painting (16x16cm 6x6in) Wien 2001
- $2 339 – €2 325 - £1 414 – FF15 254
  Blumenstrauss Gouache/paper (16x18.5cm 6x7in) Wien 2000
- $185 – €218 - £132 – FF1 430
  «Konzert» Farblithographie (18x16cm 7x6in) Wien 2001

LASKER Jonathan 1948 [29]

- $31 772 – €34 621 - £22 000 – FF227 101
  «The Metaphysics of Matter» Oil/canvas (183x137.5cm 72x54in) London 2001
- $11 553 – €12 590 - £8 000 – FF82 582
  «Suburban Theories» Oil/canvas (61x76.5cm 24x30in) London 2001

$8 500 - €9 863 - **£5 868** - FF64 696
Give Me Measles Oil/canvas (30.5x40.5cm 12x15in)
New-York 2001

$4 332 - €4 721 - **£3 000** - FF30 968
Untitled Pencil (77x56cm 30x22in) London 2001

LASKER-SCHÜLER Else 1876-1945 [6]
$3 348 - €3 938 - **£2 401** - FF25 831
«**Matrose aus Cameroun**» Charcoal (28x22cm
11x8in) Bern 2001

LASKOWSKI François, Franz 1869-1918 [8]
$1 200 - €1 300 - **£799** - FF8 529
«**Mose, D.Lorenzo Perosi, Edizoni Ricordi**»
Poster (124x89cm 49x35in) New-York 2000

LASSALLE Louis 1810-? [40]
$7 003 - €8 232 - **£5 076** - FF54 000
Jeunes femmes cueillant des fleurs Huile/pan-
neau (45x40cm 17x15in) Lyon 2001

$1 800 - €1 814 - **£1 122** - FF11 898
Tending the Turkeys Oil/board (32x24cm 12x9in)
New-York 2000

LASSAW Ibram 1913 [7]
$4 200 - €3 927 - **£2 589** - FF25 760
Untitled Metal (43x16x12cm 16x6x4in) New-York
1999

LASSEN Hans August 1857-1938 [26]
$1 689 - €1 892 - **£1 173** - FF12 409
Kellermeister bei der Weinprobe Öl/Leinwand
(38x58cm 14x22in) Bamberg 2001

$883 - €1 017 - **£603** - FF6 673
Die Weinprobe Öl/Leinwand (24x36cm 9x14in) Wien
2000

LASSENCE de Paul 1886-1962 [26]
$747 - €823 - **£495** - FF5 400
Côte bretonne, Ile aux moines Huile/toile
(60x74cm 23x29in) Morlaix 2000

LASSERE François 1960 [1]
$5 024 - €4 878 - **£3 104** - FF32 000
Composition aux potiches bleues de Chine
Huile/toile (116x89cm 45x35in) Clermont-Ferrand 1999

LASSNIG Maria 1919 [61]
$4 535 - €47 217 - **£33 085** - FF309 725
«**Gespenstertruhe**» Öl/Leinwand (81.5x100cm
32x39in) Wien 1998

$5 299 - €5 087 - **£3 325** - FF33 369
Aufgestützte Pencil (47.4x64.9cm 18x25in) Wien
1999

$503 - €472 - **£311** - FF3 098
Ohne Titel Farblithographie (27.5x25cm 10x9in) Wien
2000

LASTMAN Pieter Pieterz 1583-1633 [7]
$1 025 - €1 125 - **£696** - FF7 378
Die Befreiung Petri, nach Jan Pinas Kupferstich
(38x29.9cm 14x11in) Berlin 2000

LASZCZKA Konstanty 1865-1956 [10]
$2 446 - €2 642 - **£1 691** - FF17 331
Tête de femme Terracotta (H22cm H8in) Kraków
2001

LASZENKO Aleksander 1883-1944 [23]
$734 - €740 - **£457** - FF4 853
Rodos Oil/canvas/panel (35x49.5cm 13x19in)
Warszawa 2000

$2 299 - €2 522 - **£1 527** - FF16 544
Caravane dans le désert Oil/board (23x33cm
9x12in) Warszawa 2000

LASZLO DE LOMBOS Philip Alexius 1869-1937 [90]
$5 306 - €5 435 - **£3 300** - FF35 653
Portrait of a Lady Oil/board (89.5x64cm 35x25in)
Billingshurst, West-Sussex 2000

$1 600 - €1 573 - **£1 000** - FF10 320
Village in Tyrol Oil/cardboard (21x26cm 8x10in)
Budapest 1999

$1 760 - €1 731 - **£1 100** - FF11 352
Self-Portrait with Beer Pot Pencil/paper (32x26cm
12x10in) Budapest 1999

LATAPIE Louis 1891-1972 [455]
$1 084 - €1 220 - **£746** - FF8 000
Nature morte au tournesol Huile/papier/toile
(56x75cm 22x29in) Paris 2000

$687 - €686 - **£429** - FF4 560
Muguet dans un vase Huile/panneau (42x25cm
16x9in) La Varenne-Saint-Hilaire 1999

$274 - €305 - **£191** - FF2 000
Portrait de jeune fille Mine plomb (47x30cm
18x11in) Douai 2001

LATASTER Ger, Gerard 1920 [107]
$5 964 - €6 403 - **£3 990** - FF42 000
Croissant à côté du bleu Huile/toile (120x150cm
47x59in) Paris 2000

$3 124 - €3 630 - **£2 196** - FF23 812
Abstract Composition Acrylic/canvas (120x90cm
47x35in) Amsterdam 2001

$930 - €998 - **£622** - FF6 548
Abstract Composition Pencil (50x69.5cm 19x27in)
Amsterdam 2000

$247 - €250 - **£154** - FF1 637
Zelfportret met bril Lithograph (57x78cm 22x30in)
Amsterdam 2000

LATENAY de Gaston 1859-1943 [11]
$225 - €206 - **£137** - FF1 348
Waterlilys by Moonlight Aquatint (49x58cm
19x23in) Pittsburgh PA 1999

LATHAM James 1696-1747 [9]
$29 475 - €26 956 - **£18 000** - FF176 817
**Portrait of a Gentleman, in a Blue Coat and a
Red Undercoat** Oil/canvas (125x99.5cm 49x39in)
London 1998

LATHAM Molly M. c.1900-1987 [13]
$2 608 - €2 880 - **£1 800** - FF18 893
«**Steady Aim**», **Winner of the Oaks** Oil/canvas
(61.5x87.5cm 24x34in) Crewkerne, Somerset 2001

LATHAM O'Neill XIX [1]
$2 269 - €2 634 - **£1 600** - FF17 279
Young Swag Ink (57x54.5cm 22x21in) London 2001

LATHROP Dorothy 1891-? [1]
$9 500 - €8 795 - **£5 815** - FF57 691
**Girl and lamb pausing at stream, Dutch Cheese
frontispice ill.** Watercolour/paper (34x25cm 13x10in)
New-York 1999

LATHROP William Langson 1859-1938 [23]
$10 000 - €8 661 - **£6 133** - FF56 815
Autumn Landscape Oil/canvas (39.5x53cm 15x20in)
New-York 1999

$5 250 - €5 824 - **£3 491** - FF38 205
Dusk, Montauk Oil/canvas (35x30cm 14x12in)
Milford CT 2000

LATIMER Lorenzo Palmer 1857-1941 [21]
$950 - €1 080 - **£663** - FF7 087
River Landscape Oil/paper (27x22cm 11x9in) Mystic
CT 2000

$1 100 - €1 056 - **£689** - FF6 925
Telegraph Canyon - Claremont-Berkeley, CA
Watercolour/paper (13x17cm 5x7in) Altadena CA 1999

LATOIX de Gaspard XIX-XX [15]
$20 000 - €17 088 - **£12 006** - FF112 088
Two Indians on Horseback Oil/canvas (65x89cm 25x35in) New-York 1998

LATOUR René XIX [1]
$4 367 - €4 274 - **£2 800** - FF28 034
Fête Champêtre, Copy after Lancret's Le Jeu du Colin-Maillard Gouache (27.5x32cm 10x12in) London 1999

LATRI Mikhail Pelopidovich 1875-1942 [1]
$3 400 - €3 300 - **£2 099** - FF21 649
Elopement Watercolour, gouache/paper (61x46cm 24x18in) Cedar-Falls IA 1999

LATROBE Benjamin Henry 1764-1820 [2]
$37 000 - €34 486 - **£22 362** - FF226 214
View of the Principal Gates of Chartres and Levee Street Ink (27x54cm 11x21in) New-Orleans LA 1999

LAUBI Hugo 1888-1959 [37]
$1 400 - €1 399 - **£855** - FF9 179
«2nd Olympic Winter Games» Poster (102x64cm 40x25in) New-York 1998

LAUBIES René 1924 [52]
$969 - €1 143 - **£681** - FF7 500
Composition Huile/toile (43x64.5cm 16x25in) Paris 2000

$462 - €427 - **£287** - FF2 800
Composition Encre/papier (50x65cm 19x25in) Douai 1999

LAUBSER Maggie 1886-1973 [116]
$13 897 - €13 391 - **£8 585** - FF87 839
Fisherman and Boats Oil/board (44.5x49.5cm 17x19in) Johannesburg 1999

$4 116 - €4 777 - **£2 842** - FF31 334
Lake Garda Oil/board (33.5x43.5cm 13x17in) Johannesburg 2000

$593 - €699 - **£410** - FF4 585
Fields and Trees in a Mountainous Landscape Pencil (19x25.5cm 7x10in) Cape Town 2000

$451 - €524 - **£311** - FF3 436
A crane near a Lake Linocut (20.5x15.5cm 8x6in) Johannesburg 2000

LAUCHERT Richard 1823-1869 [6]
$14 217 - €16 361 - **£9 817** - FF107 324
Malteserhündchen Öl/Leinwand (35.5x48.5cm 13x19in) München 2000

LAUDER Charles James 1841-1920 [58]
$4 027 - €3 784 - **£2 500** - FF24 822
In the European Lakes Oil/canvas (76x123cm 29x48in) London 1999

$2 160 - €2 536 - **£1 524** - FF16 634
Segelfartyg vid kaj Oil/canvas (51x31cm 20x12in) Stockholm 1999

$752 - €812 - **£520** - FF5 329
Fishing Boats and Figures, Venice Watercolour/paper (16x24cm 6x9in) Cheshire 2001

LAUDER Robert Scott 1803-1869 [6]
$15 021 - €13 438 - **£9 000** - FF88 148
The Last Farewell of Burns and Highland Mary Oil/canvas (93x71cm 36x27in) Perthshire 1998

LAUDIN Jacques II c.1665-1729 [3]
$1 693 - €1 906 - **£1 166** - FF12 500
Saint Jean-Baptiste Email (11x9cm 4x3in) Limoges 2000

LAUDIN Noël I 1586-1681 [2]
$2 240 - €2 543 - **£1 533** - FF16 684
Die Verkündigung an Maria Enamel (18x16cm 7x6in) Wien 2000

LAUDY Jean 1877-1956 [218]
$10 297 - €11 434 - **£7 177** - FF75 000
Le modèle endormi Huile/toile (98x149cm 38x58in) Paris 2001

$1 055 - €1 239 - **£755** - FF8 130
Vase de fleurs Huile/toile (70x56cm 27x22in) Bruxelles 2000

$166 - €173 - **£109** - FF1 138
Notre-Dame Aquarelle/papier (32.5x47.5cm 12x18in) Bruxelles 2000

LAUER Josef 1818-1881 [53]
$24 440 - €29 069 - **£17 440** - FF190 680
Grosses Stilleben mit einem Kamelienstrauss, Früchten, Goldfischen Oil/canvas/panel (74x90cm 29x35in) Wien 2000

$3 130 - €3 634 - **£2 200** - FF23 835
Frühlingsblumen Öl/Karton (12x14.8cm 4x5in) Wien 2001

$2 706 - €2 621 - **£1 700** - FF17 191
Melon with Grapes and Apples in a Basket Watercolour (59x47.5cm 23x18in) London 1999

LAUER Nikolaus XVIII-XIX [4]
$342 - €331 - **£211** - FF2 174
Portrait de Louise Königin Pastel (28x23cm 11x9in) Montréal 1999

LAUGÉ Achille 1861-1944 [193]
$12 328 - €14 025 - **£8 556** - FF92 000
Bouquet de fleurs Huile/panneau (101x205cm 39x80in) Paris 2000

$12 070 - €12 958 - **£8 075** - FF85 000
Les toits rouges à Cailhau Huile/toile (50x73cm 19x28in) Paris 2000

$12 416 - €12 196 - **£7 704** - FF80 000
La cueillette des fruits Huile/toile (52.5x29cm 20x11in) Paris 1999

$1 106 - €1 311 - **£761** - FF8 600
Portrait de Madame Laugé Crayon/papier (44x35cm 17x13in) Toulouse 2000

LAUGÉE Georges 1853-? [90]
$3 600 - €3 296 - **£2 183** - FF21 621
Portrait of a peasant Woman in a Farm Field Oil/canvas (45x38cm 18x15in) East-Dennis MA 1998

$2 948 - €3 354 - **£2 046** - FF22 000
La faneuse Huile/toile (22.2x27.2cm 8x10in) Fontainebleau 2000

LAUGHLIN Clarence John 1905-1985 [116]
$2 200 - €2 055 - **£1 329** - FF13 419
The Dead Eye Silver print (28x45cm 11x18in) New-York 1999

LAUMANS Fanny XIX [3]
$7 024 - €7 808 - **£4 914** - FF51 219
Chien et chat dans un intérieur de musicien Huile/toile (47x56cm 18x22in) Bruxelles 2001

LAUNAY de E. XIX [1]
$4 200 - €4 573 - **£2 772** - FF30 000
Halteau fondouk Huile/toile (39x65cm 15x25in) Paris 2000

LAUNAY de Fernand XIX-XX **[9]**
- $1 406 - €1 677 - £1 003 - FF11 000
  Nu allongé Pastel/papier (52x93cm 20x36in) Soissons 2000

LAUNAY de Gustave 1864-? **[21]**
- $175 - €207 - £124 - FF1 361
  Villa on Coast Watercolour/paper (22x30cm 9x12in) New-Orleans LA 2000

LAUNAY de Nicolas 1739-1792 **[40]**
- $227 - €244 - £152 - FF1 640
  Le billet doux, d'après N.Lavreince Eau-forte (27x35cm 10x13in) Paris 2000

LAUNOIS Jean 1898-1942 **[54]**
- $1 654 - €1 448 - £1 002 - FF9 500
  Barques et bateaux à Saint-Tropez Aquarelle/papier (47.5x61.5cm 18x24in) Saumur 1998

LAUPHEIMER Anton 1848-1927 **[13]**
- $11 372 - €12 815 - £7 876 - FF84 064
  The Toast Oil/canvas (110.5x132cm 43x51in) Toronto 2000
- $9 921 - €8 180 - £5 843 - FF53 656
  Blick in eine Stube, Stehender und sitzender Jäger an einem Tisch Öl/Leinwand (81x88cm 31x34in) Lindau 1998
- $2 104 - €2 009 - £1 314 - FF13 175
  Schäferstündchen im Boudoir Oil/panel (25.5x18cm 10x7in) Zofingen 1999

LAUR Yvonne Marie, Yo 1879-1943 **[21]**
- $15 929 - €16 578 - £10 000 - FF108 746
  The Proud Mother Oil/canvas (62x81cm 24x31in) London 2000
- $308 - €366 - £212 - FF2 400
  Chat et escargot Huile/panneau (8.5x12cm 3x4in) Toulouse 2000

LAURÉN Per Åke 1879-1951 **[21]**
- $286 - €336 - £198 - FF2 206
  Bykdag Oil/canvas (41x49cm 16x19in) Helsinki 2000

LAURENCE XIX **[7]**
- $1 911 - €2 134 - £1 295 - FF14 000
  Nature morte au chaudron et aux poires Huile/toile (65x92cm 25x36in) Saint-Germain-en-Laye 2000

LAURENCE (Laurence Fish) 1919 **[5]**
- $2 001 - €2 148 - £1 339 - FF14 093
  Periodic Table Series - Alchemical Pages Mixed media (45x30cm 17x11in) Sydney 2000
- $900 - €865 - £550 - FF5 672
  «Portsmouth and Southsea, British Railways, Southern Region» Poster (102x64cm 40x25in) London 1999

LAURENCE Sydney Mortimer 1865-1940 **[99]**
- $20 000 - €23 342 - £14 178 - FF153 112
  At the Campfire Oil/canvas (61x51cm 24x20in) New-York 2001
- $7 500 - €6 408 - £4 538 - FF42 033
  Alaskan Landscape Oil/canvas (30.5x40.5cm 12x15in) San-Francisco CA 1998
- $800 - €744 - £493 - FF4 879
  «Alaska» Poster (100x73cm 39x29in) New-York 1999

LAURENCEAU Lyonel 1942 **[10]**
- $1 060 - €1 220 - £748 - FF8 000
  Portrait d'enfant Huile/toile (25x20cm 9x7in) Paris 2001

LAURENCIN de H. XX **[7]**
- $209 - €244 - £147 - FF1 600
  «Princeless-Oil» Affiche (160x120cm 62x47in) Chartres 2001

LAURENCIN Marie 1885-1956 **[2057]**
- $75 000 - €82 309 - £48 292 - FF539 910
  Trois jeunes filles devant un Pont Oil/canvas (50x61cm 19x24in) New-York 2000
- $33 456 - €31 252 - £20 213 - FF205 000
  Femme à la guitare Huile/toile (41x33cm 16x12in) Paris 1999
- $3 834 - €4 116 - £2 565 - FF27 000
  Jeune fille à la fleur Crayons couleurs/papier (21x18cm 8x7in) Paris 2000
- $1 082 - €1 220 - £749 - FF8 000
  Jeune fille à la fleur Lithographie (18x13.5cm 7x5in) Paris 2000

LAURENS Henri 1885-1954 **[301]**
- $530 000 - €509 011 - £326 745 - FF3 338 894
  Le grand Amphion Bronze (H274.5cm H108in) New-York 1999
- $75 136 - €69 253 - £45 000 - FF454 270
  Femme-fleur Bronze (H27.5cm H10in) London 1998
- $9 200 - €11 922 - £6 900 - FF78 200
  Le coureur Matita/carta (27x21.5cm 10x8in) Milano 2000
- $1 000 - €1 174 - £710 - FF7 704
  Le Jockey Etching (32.5x22cm 12x8in) New-York 2000

LAURENS Jean-Paul 1838-1921 **[40]**
- $3 909 - €3 659 - £2 421 - FF24 000
  Jeune femme assise lisant un antiphonaire Huile/toile (46x37.5cm 18x14in) Paris 1999
- $2 441 - €2 439 - £1 526 - FF16 000
  Jeune fille rêveuse Huile/toile/carton (24x20cm 9x7in) Pontoise 1999
- $800 - €732 - £490 - FF4 800
  L'apparition Lavis/papier (35x27cm 13x10in) Paris 1999

LAURENS Jules 1825-1901 **[39]**
- $57 482 - €62 504 - £37 884 - FF410 000
  Une halte à la porte de Téhéran Huile/toile (86x126.5cm 33x49in) Paris 2000
- $2 500 - €2 370 - £1 562 - FF15 549
  Guerrier Afghan Aquarelle (41x31cm 16x12in) Luzern 1999

LAURENS Paul-Albert 1870-1934 **[20]**
- $2 366 - €2 211 - £1 429 - FF14 500
  Elégante au châle bleu Huile/toile (54x45cm 21x17in) Paris 1999
- $1 100 - €1 041 - £683 - FF6 830
  «Ramses» Poster (91.5x53cm 36x20in) New-York 1999

LAURENT Bruno Émile 1928 **[207]**
- $502 - €572 - £345 - FF3 750
  Le Lapin Agile sous la neige Huile/toile (46x55cm 18x21in) Provins 2000
- $284 - €305 - £188 - FF2 000
  Le Lapin Agile Huile/toile (22x27cm 8x10in) Provins 2000
- $265 - €229 - £160 - FF1 500
  Montmartre Gouache/papier (43x58cm 16x22in) Arles 2000

LAURENT Élie Joseph 1841-1926 **[5]**
- $4 750 - €4 118 - £2 903 - FF27 014
  Still Lifes of Fruit Oil/panel (27x35cm 10x13in) New-York 1999

LAURENT Ernest Joseph 1859-1929 **[96]**
$2 320 - €2 211 - **£1 470** - FF14 500
Marché aux chevaux en Bretagne Huile/toile (55x65cm 21x25in) Douarnenez 1999
$1 092 - €1 220 - **£740** - FF8 000
Dame de qualité Fusain (32x23.5cm 12x9in) Pontoise 2000

LAURENT Eugène 1832-1898 **[17]**
$1 045 - €991 - **£635** - FF6 500
Jeune femme revenant de la pêche Bronze (H61cm H24in) Nîmes 1999

LAURENT François Nicolas ?-1828 **[2]**
$8 000 - €8 960 - **£5 558** - FF58 777
Flowers in a vase resting on a marble ledge Oil/paper/canvas (49x40cm 19x15in) New-York 2001

LAURENT Georges H. XX **[12]**
$914 - €1 067 - **£642** - FF7 000
Le coq Sculpture bois (15.5x11x7.5cm 6x4x2in) Pontoise 2000

LAURENT Henri Adolphe Louis 1840-? **[1]**
$26 000 - €26 200 - **£16 208** - FF171 860
The End of the Day's Work/The Fisherman's Family Oil/canvas (65x93.5cm 25x36in) New-York 2000

LAURENT Jean 1898-1988 **[31]**
$2 000 - €1 995 - **£1 248** - FF13 086
Still Life of Fruit and Flowers on a Ledge Oil/panel (66x55cm 26x22in) St. Louis MO 1999

LAURENT Jean Antoine 1763-1832 **[18]**
$112 750 - €104 543 - **£68 000** - FF685 759
The Meeting of Eleanor of Guyenne and the Sultan of Iconia Oil/canvas (66x55cm 25x21in) London 1999
$4 029 - €4 514 - **£2 800** - FF29 607
Young Gentleman seated, facing right in blue Coat, beige Trousers Miniature (14x11cm 5x4in) London 2001

LAURENT Jean Émile 1906 **[8]**
$2 868 - €3 354 - **£2 048** - FF22 000
Place du gouvernement, Alger Huile/toile (46x61cm 18x24in) Paris 2001

LAURENT Juan / Jean 1816-1892 **[12]**
$500 - €570 - **£345** - FF3 736
Spain Albumen print (23x34cm 9x13in) New-York 2000

LAURENT Marcel XX **[12]**
$1 457 - €1 677 - **£1 004** - FF11 000
Troménie de Locronan, la procession attaquant le chemin Huile/carton (46x38cm 18x14in) Toulon 2000
$1 126 - €1 296 - **£776** - FF8 500
Procession au pardon de Pen-Mons (Finistère) Huile/carton (20x32.5cm 7x12in) Toulon 2000

LAURENT Marie-P., née Laurent 1805-1860 **[4]**
$4 261 - €4 857 - **£2 973** - FF31 862
Bildnis der Kaiserin Eugénie v.Frankreich Miniature (10.5x14.5cm 4x5in) Köln 2001

LAURENT-DESROUSSEAUX Henri 1862-1906 **[12]**
$4 000 - €4 755 - **£2 771** - FF31 189
Children Waving from a Dock Oil/canvas (64x92cm 25x36in) Pittsburgh PA 2000
$1 584 - €1 753 - **£1 100** - FF11 500
Ramasseuses de coquillages Huile/toile (35.5x27.5cm 13x10in) Aubagne 2001

$3 766 - €3 470 - **£2 268** - FF22 764
L'écosseuse de petits pois Pastel/papier (60x45cm 23x17in) Bruxelles 1999

LAURENTI Cesare 1854-1936 **[8]**
$5 856 - €6 135 - **£3 873** - FF40 246
Vorbereitung zur Fiesta Öl/Leinwand (66x50cm 25x19in) München 2000

LAURET Emmanuel Joseph 1809-1882 **[8]**
$1 822 - €1 982 - **£1 201** - FF13 000
Jeune algéroise buvant du thé Aquarelle (25x20cm 9x7in) Paris 2000

LAURET François 1820-1868 **[19]**
$2 414 - €2 592 - **£1 615** - FF17 000
Danseuse orientale Huile/toile (24.5x19cm 9x7in) Paris 2000
$5 000 - €5 550 - **£3 485** - FF36 407
Tomb of the Syphax Gouache/paper (46.5x58.5cm 18x23in) New-York 2000

LAUREUS Alexander Lauroeus 1783-1823 **[32]**
$2 988 - €3 364 - **£2 058** - FF22 064
Hemfärd Oil/canvas (39x31.5cm 15x12in) Helsinki 2000

LAURI Filippo 1623-1694 **[38]**
$6 500 - €6 738 - **£3 900** - FF44 200
Tritone e nereide/Alfeo e Aretusa Olio/tavola (20x28.5cm 7x11in) Roma 2001

LAURIA Giuseppe 1940 **[15]**
$700 - €726 - **£420** - FF4 760
Giardino con villa Olio/tela (50x40cm 19x15in) Vercelli 1999

LAURITZ Paul 1889-1976 **[106]**
$3 750 - €3 348 - **£2 296** - FF21 960
«Laguna Tide Pools» Oil/canvas (50x60cm 20x24in) Altadena CA 1999
$600 - €576 - **£376** - FF3 777
Carmel Coastal Oil/board (20x25cm 8x10in) Altadena CA 1999

LAURO Maurice 1878-? **[9]**
$900 - €1 004 - **£589** - FF6 586
«Bigorno et le bon sirop» Poster (120.5x53cm 47x20in) New-York 2000

LAUSTINO Emanuele 1916 **[25]**
$140 - €133 - **£87** - FF873
Tropical Overlook with Palm Tree Oil/canvas (35x40cm 14x16in) Pittsburgh PA 1999

LAUTENBACHER Walter E. XX **[19]**
$643 - €767 - **£458** - FF5 030
«Nicole de Lamarché, Modeporträt» Photograph (29.5x39.4cm 11x15in) München 2000

LAUTENSACK Hans Sebald 1524-1563 **[40]**
$943 - €1 125 - **£672** - FF7 378
Landschaft mit Bauernkate und Stadt am Fluss Radierung (16.4x11cm 6x4in) Berlin 2000

LAUTERBURG Martin 1891-1960 **[66]**
$561 - €655 - **£389** - FF4 296
Stilleben mit Topfpflanzen und Malerutensilien Oil/panel (43.5x37cm 17x14in) Bern 2000
$690 - €779 - **£485** - FF5 112
Ansicht von Genf Öl/Karton (24.5x32.5cm 9x12in) Bern 2001
$201 - €187 - **£123** - FF1 224
Balkon zum Hinterhof Mischtechnik/Papier (61x46.5cm 24x18in) Bern 1999

LAUTERS Paul 1806-1875 **[33]**
$920 - €768 - **£539** - FF5 040
Landschap Oil/panel (30.5x41cm 12x16in) Lokeren 1998

$143 - €149 - **£91** - FF975
Bosgezicht met jagers Pencil/paper (34x27.5cm 13x10in) Lokeren 2000

LAUTERWASSER Siegfried 1913-2000 **[67]**
$729 - €869 - **£519** - FF5 701
Badende Photograph (40x30.3cm 15x11in) München 2000

LAUTTER J.R. XVIII **[1]**
$6 877 - €7 669 - **£4 624** - FF50 308
Küchenstilleben Oil/panel (22x34cm 8x13in) Köln 2000

LAUVERGNE Barthélémy 1805-1875 **[13]**
$3 871 - €3 934 - **£2 431** - FF26 000
Bateau battant pavillon français devant un port Huile/carton (34x43cm 13x16in) Lille 2000

LAUVERNAY-PETITJEAN Jeanne 1875-1955 **[38]**
$512 - €610 - **£355** - FF4 000
Vaison la Romaine Huile/carton (37.5x45cm 14x17in) Paris 2000

LAUVRAY Abel 1870-1950 **[154]**
$1 794 - €2 134 - **£1 279** - FF14 000
Villeneuve les Avignons Huile/toile (50x65cm 19x25in) Nantes 2000

LAUWERIER Rudolphus 1796-1883 **[4]**
$1 007 - €1 134 - **£694** - FF7 441
Travellers Conversing on a Path in a Wooded Landscape Oil/panel (22.5x18cm 8x7in) Amsterdam 2000

LAUWICH Alexandre 1823-? **[1]**
$21 601 - €21 446 - **£13 500** - FF140 679
Les Premiers pas de l'enfant Oil/canvas (95x83cm 37x32in) London 1999

LAUX August 1847-1921 **[63]**
$3 500 - €2 953 - **£2 053** - FF19 369
Farmyard Animals Oil/canvas (50x91cm 20x36in) Mystic CT 1998

$2 200 - €1 904 - **£1 335** - FF12 491
Apples in a Pail Oil/canvas (25x35cm 10x14in) Mystic CT 1998

LAUZERO Albert 1909 **[18]**
$1 083 - €1 220 - **£760** - FF8 000
«Vallon des Auffes et Notre Dame de la Garde» Huile/toile (55.5x46cm 21x18in) Paris 2001

LAUZIER Gérard 1932 **[4]**
$1 021 - €991 - **£635** - FF6 500
Tranches de vie, pl.2 Encres couleurs (50x35cm 19x13in) Paris 1999

LAVAGNA Francesco XVII-XVIII **[21]**
$26 152 - €23 900 - **£16 000** - FF156 772
Still Life with Watermelons, figs, Pomegranates, Flowers, Porcelain Oil/canvas (74.5x99cm 29x38in) London 1999

$134 029 - €122 487 - **£82 000** - FF803 460
Still Lifes of Fruits, Flowers in Landscapes, Architectural Fragments Oil/canvas (24x32cm 9x12in) London 1999

LAVAGNA Giuseppe 1684-c.1724 **[8]**
$10 906 - €10 174 - **£6 580** - FF62 963
Blumenstrauss in einer silbernen Prunkvase Öl/Leinwand (31x24cm 12x9in) Wien 1999

LAVAL Charles 1862-1894 **[8]**
$87 564 - €94 060 - **£60 000** - FF616 992
Paysage de la Martinique Oil/canvas (92x71cm 36x27in) London 2001

$60 000 - €51 186 - **£35 760** - FF335 760
Landscape with strolling Brittany Women Watercolour, gouache/paper (38x58cm 14x22in) New-York 1998

LAVAL Fernand 1886/95-1966 **[196]**
$597 - €579 - **£371** - FF3 800
La maison de Mimi Pinson à Montmartre Huile/toile (32.5x50cm 12x19in) La Varenne-Saint-Hilaire 1999

LAVALLÉE de Geeraert 1605-1666 **[15]**
$5 830 - €6 607 - **£3 960** - FF43 340
Calvario Oleo/cobre (54.5x73.5cm 21x28in) Madrid 2000

$26 944 - €28 121 - **£17 050** - FF184 464
Venus and Adonis Öl/Kupfer (24x30.5cm 9x12in) Köln 2000

LAVALLÉE-POUSSIN de Étienne 1733-1793 **[20]**
$1 300 - €1 390 - **£886** - FF9 121
View of S.Maria Maggiore, Rome Watercolour (17.5x30cm 6x11in) New-York 2001

LAVALLEY Jonas Joseph 1858-1930 **[39]**
$2 000 - €2 301 - **£1 378** - FF15 096
The Call of the Hills Oil/canvas (63x76cm 25x30in) New-Orleans LA 2000

$2 800 - €3 266 - **£1 970** - FF21 421
Under Summer Skies Oil/canvas (23x43cm 9x17in) South-Deerfield MA 2001

LAVEAUX de Ludwik 1868-1894 **[10]**
$4 046 - €3 929 - **£2 500** - FF25 772
Paysage nocturne Oil/board (18x24cm 7x9in) Warszawa 1999

$1 321 - €1 516 - **£943** - FF10 167
Paysage avec vue sur la forêt Pastel/papier (21x31.5cm 8x12in) Warszawa 2000

LAVENSON Alma 1897-1989 **[14]**
$20 000 - €20 796 - **£12 628** - FF136 416
Standard Oil Co. Photograph (34x25.5cm 13x10in) New-York 2000

LAVERGNE Adolphe Jean XIX **[32]**
$655 - €595 - **£405** - FF3 902
Jeune pêcheur Bronze (H30cm H11in) Bruxelles 1999

LAVERGNE Georges Aug. Elie 1863-1942 **[30]**
$9 615 - €12 460 - **£7 211** - FF81 729
Giovane donan con cappello Olio/tela (172x93cm 67x36in) Napoli 2001

LAVERY John 1856-1941 **[272]**
$432 720 - €508 570 - **£300 000** - FF3 336 000
Ariade Oil/canvas (127x101.5cm 50x39in) Edinburgh 2000

$96 834 - €90 922 - **£60 000** - FF596 412
The Southern Sea Oil/canvas (63.5x75cm 25x30in) London 1999

$33 116 - €36 333 - **£22 000** - FF238 326
Evening, Tangier Oil/canvas/board (25.5x35.5cm 10x13in) London 2000

$431 - €484 - **£300** - FF3 172
Alfresco meal, seated outside, a man in a blue hat Watercolour/paper (17x26cm 6x10in) Burton-on-Trent, Staffs 2001

LAVIE Raffi 1937 **[117]**
- $5 500 - €6 142 - **£3 522** - FF40 290
  Composition Oil/canvas (60.5x74cm 23x29in) Tel Aviv 2000
- $550 - €584 - **£372** - FF3 832
  Untitled Mixed media/paper (24.5x17cm 9x6in) Tel Aviv 2001

LAVIEILLE Eugène 1820-1889 **[108]**
- $4 924 - €5 793 - **£3 568** - FF38 000
  Chemin à la Ferté-Milon Huile/toile (57x74cm 22x29in) Soissons 2001
- $2 277 - €2 211 - **£1 418** - FF14 500
  Les hêtres Huile/carton (39x23cm 15x9in) Fontainebleau 1999
- $321 - €366 - **£223** - FF2 400
  Jeune femme en forêt à Lardy, Seine-et-Oise Mine plomb (27.2x18.5cm 10x7in) Fontainebleau 2000

LAVIER Bertrand 1949 **[21]**
- $6 649 - €6 418 - **£4 200** - FF42 100
  Paragon Mixed media/board (136x113cm 53x44in) London 1999
- $7 221 - €7 869 - **£5 000** - FF51 614
  Ventilateur Acrylic (185x40x50cm 66x15x19in) London 2001
- $5 337 - €4 878 - **£3 286** - FF32 000
  Zenit EM Objet (9x14x11cm 3x5x4in) Paris 1999

LAVIES Jan 1902-? **[25]**
- $163 - €191 - **£111** 250
  «Wereld Jamboree Nederland» Poster (60x44.5cm 23x17in) Hoorn 2000

LAVILLE Joy 1923 **[16]**
- $4 000 - €3 892 - **£2 462** - FF25 529
  Mujer en un interior gris/Pequeño paisaje Oil/canvas (35x40.5cm 13x15in) New-York 1999

LAVOINE Robert L.P. 1916-1999 **[678]**
- $588 - €686 - **£407** - FF4 500
  Environs de Camaret Huile/toile (50x65cm 19x25in) Le Havre 2000
- $392 - €457 - **£271** - FF3 000
  Honfleur, la Grève Huile/toile (22x33cm 8x12in) Calais 2000
- $261 - €305 - **£181** - FF2 000
  Chemin sous la neige Aquarelle/papier (33x50cm 12x19in) Le Havre 2000

LAVONEN Ahti 1928-1970 **[33]**
- $11 338 - €11 100 - **£6 976** - FF72 811
  Korosteita hopealle Mixed media/canvas (110x110cm 43x43in) Helsinki 1999
- $728 - €757 - **£456** - FF4 964
  Stilleben Mixed media (76x55cm 29x21in) Helsinki 2000

LAVONEN Kuutti 1961 **[4]**
- $197 - €219 - **£137** - FF1 434
  I tankar Etching (23.5x17.5cm 9x6in) Helsinki 2001

LAVOS Joseph 1807-1848 **[2]**
- $10 900 - €10 226 - **£6 734** - FF67 078
  Die beiden kleinen Schwestern im Blumengarten Öl/Leinwand (94x71cm 37x27in) Ahlden 1999

LAVRILLIER Carol-Marc XX **[3]**
- $4 412 - €4 269 - **£2 721** - FF28 000
  Rodin, la porte de l'enfer Photo (36x46cm 14x18in) Paris 1999

LAVROFF Georges 1895-? **[58]**
- $1 022 - €1 098 - **£684** - FF7 200
  Guépard Bronze (17x46x8cm 6x18x3in) Nice 2000

LAW Andrew 1873-1967 **[10]**
- $4 279 - €4 446 - **£2 700** - FF29 164
  Blossoms Oil/canvas (76x63.5cm 29x25in) London 2000

LAW Bhavani Charan 1880-1946 **[1]**
- $2 600 - €3 014 - **£1 841** - FF19 773
  Portrait of the Maharaja of Patiala Watercolour (35x25cm 13x9in) New-York 2000

LAW Charles Anthony 1916-1996 **[21]**
- $705 - €824 - **£496** - FF5 456
  Goose Rocks, Maine Oil/board (60x76cm 24x30in) Waverley NS 2000
- $388 - €453 - **£270** - FF2 974
  «Mountain Peek» Oil/panel (34x40cm 13x15in) Toronto 2000

LAW David 1831-1901 **[52]**
- $460 - €420 - **£280** - FF2 755
  Corn Stooks Watercolour/paper (25x35cm 9x13in) Leyburn, North Yorkshire 1998
- $317 - €356 - **£220** - FF2 335
  View of st Pauls Etching (29x41.5cm 11x16in) London 2000

LAW Denys 1907-1981 **[57]**
- $911 - €843 - **£550** - FF5 532
  The Valley in Springtime Oil/board (50x60cm 20x24in) Par, Cornwall 1999
- $358 - €385 - **£240** - FF2 525
  River scene Oil/board (27x38cm 11x15in) Birmingham 2000

LAWES Harold XIX-XX **[109]**
- $587 - €519 - **£350** - FF3 402
  «The Harvesters»/«On the Lyn, Devon» Watercolour (34x24.5cm 13x9in) London 1998

LAWFORD Valentine XX **[2]**
- $5 500 - €6 394 - **£3 860** - FF41 943
  Roses Watercolour/paper (66.5x61.5cm 26x24in) New-York 2001

LAWLER Louise A. 1947 **[52]**
- $6 185 - €6 020 - **£3 800** - FF39 488
  Arranged by Donald Marron, Susan Brundage, Cheryl Bishop at Paine Photograph (75x84.5x4cm 29x33x1in) London 1999

LAWLESS Carl E. 1896-1934 **[24]**
- $1 900 - €2 157 - **£1 320** - FF14 151
  Winter Landscape Oil/canvas (38x38cm 15x15in) Detroit MI 2001

LAWLESS Matthew James 1837-1864 **[1]**
- $37 200 - €31 718 - **£22 442** - FF208 055
  The Dinner Party Oil/canvas (21x30cm 8x12in) Dublin 1998

LAWLEY John Douglas 1906-1971 **[34]**
- $984 - €1 121 - **£680** - FF7 354
  Cab Stand, Sherbrooke Street, Montreal Oil/panel (50.5x61cm 19x24in) Montréal 2000
- $717 - €832 - **£495** - FF5 457
  On Sable Island, NS Oil/canvas/board (20.5x25.5cm 8x10in) Vancouver, BC. 2000

LAWLOR Adrian 1889-1969 **[7]**
- $5 839 - €5 551 - **£3 644** - FF36 414
  Still Life Oil/canvas (65x55cm 25x21in) Melbourne 1999
- $3 237 - €3 034 - **£2 002** - FF19 900
  Red House Oil/board (30x29.5cm 11x11in) Melbourne 1999

LAWRENCE David Herbert 1885-1930 **[5]**
- $2 527 - €2 176 - **£1 500** - FF14 272
  Mother Standing on a Beach Holding a Small Child Oil/canvas (19x14cm 7x5in) London 1998
- $2 022 - €1 741 - **£1 200** - FF11 417
  Harvesting Scene, a Horse-Drawn Wagon Full of Corn Below Tall Trees Watercolour/paper (15.5x37cm 6x14in) London 1998

LAWRENCE George Feather 1901-1981 **[231]**
- $1 883 - €1 707 - **£1 142** - FF11 200
  Hyde Park, Sidney Oil/canvas/board (40x50cm 15x19in) Sydney 1998
- $673 - €697 - **£424** - FF4 569
  Snow at Bath Oil/board (30x38cm 11x14in) Sydney 2000
- $152 - €140 - **£93** - FF917
  Landscape Ink (20x32cm 7x12in) Sydney 1999

LAWRENCE Jacob 1917-2000 **[35]**
- $20 000 - €19 857 - **£12 500** - FF130 252
  Wedding party Tempera/panel (23x30.5cm 9x12in) New-York 1999
- $62 500 - €74 328 - **£44 543** - FF487 562
  Harlem Series, No.5: Three Family Toilet Gouache/paper (57x40.5cm 22x15in) New-York 2000
- $1 400 - €1 212 - **£844** - FF7 950
  «Morning Still Life» Silkscreen in colors (61x44.5cm 24x17in) New-York 1998

LAWRENCE John C. XX **[2]**
- $9 119 - €10 846 - **£6 500** - FF71 143
  Disconsolate Oil/canvas (127x92cm 50x36in) London 2000

LAWRENCE Sydney 1858-1940 **[14]**
- $5 500 - €5 904 - **£3 680** - FF38 725
  The Northern Lights Anchorage, Alaska Oil/canvas/panel (25x20cm 10x8in) Altadena CA 2000
- $451 - €421 - **£280** - FF2 760
  Scottish Loch Watercolour (42x67cm 16x26in) Billingshurst, West-Sussex 1999

LAWRENCE Thomas 1769-1830 **[153]**
- $98 014 - €113 991 - **£70 000** - FF747 733
  Portrait of Charles Binny with his Daughters Oil/canvas (239x184cm 94x72in) London 2001
- $42 500 - €37 279 - **£25 806** - FF244 536
  Mrs Hart Davis Oil/canvas (76x63.5cm 29x25in) New-York 1999
- $3 806 - €3 997 - **£2 400** - FF26 219
  Portrait of a Young Officer Pastel/paper (28.5x23cm 11x9in) London 2000

LAWRENCE William Roderick 1829-1856 **[1]**
- $9 000 - €10 397 - **£6 301** - FF68 202
  Mount Etna Oil/canvas (92x137cm 36x53in) New-York 2001

LAWRENSON Edward Louis 1868-1934 **[17]**
- $1 419 - €1 524 - **£949** - FF9 994
  Landscape Including Man with Firewood Oil/canvas (46x81cm 18x31in) Dublin 2000
- $323 - €381 - **£227** - FF2 498
  Cumulus Clouds Watercolour/paper (28x38cm 11x14in) Dublin 2000

LAWRIE Hamish 1919-1987 **[19]**
- $486 - €469 - **£300** - FF3 077
  Figure on a Roadway Oil/board (34x44cm 13x17in) Edinburgh 1999
- $305 - €290 - **£190** - FF1 899
  River Landscape Watercolour (27x38.5cm 10x15in) Glasgow 1999

LAWSON Alexander 1773-1846 **[3]**
- $800 - €861 - **£530** - FF5 648
  Red-Winged Starling, Female/Little Owl/Winter Falcon, After A.Wilson Copper engraving in colors (33x23cm 13x9in) New-Orleans LA 2000

LAWSON Cecil Gordon 1851-1882 **[13]**
- $2 611 - €2 941 - **£1 800** - FF19 292
  Barden Towers, Yorkshire Oil/canvas (28x38cm 11x14in) London 2000

LAWSON Ernest 1873-1939 **[126]**
- $36 000 - €35 742 - **£22 500** - FF234 453
  Plowing Oil/canvas (127x152.5cm 50x60in) New-York 1999
- $30 000 - €33 602 - **£20 844** - FF220 416
  Florida Mangroves Oil/canvas (51x63.5cm 20x25in) New-York 2001
- $12 000 - €10 068 - **£7 072** - FF66 043
  A Study for «Snow Crop» Oil/panel (25x33cm 10x13in) Greenwich CT 1998

LAWSON Francis Wilfred 1842-1935 **[4]**
- $7 000 - €6 443 - **£4 201** - FF42 261
  Doubtful Coin Oil/canvas (99x73cm 39x29in) Chicago IL 1999

LAWSON Frederick, Fred 1888-1968 **[108]**
- $301 - €352 - **£210** - FF2 309
  Study of Horse and Rider in a Dales Landscape Watercolour/paper (25x36.5cm 9x14in) West-Yorkshire 2000

LAWSON Sonia 1934 **[17]**
- $1 182 - €1 226 - **£750** - FF8 042
  Goodbye Eden Mixed media (60x42cm 23x16in) West-Yorkshire 2000

LAXEIRO José Otero Abeledo 1908-1996 **[235]**
- $16 320 - €19 221 - **£11 200** - FF126 080
  El cartel Oleo/lienzo (138x105cm 54x41in) Madrid 2000
- $7 420 - €8 409 - **£5 040** - FF55 160
  Distinguido muñeco Oleo/lienzo (61x38cm 24x14in) Madrid 2000
- $2 280 - €2 403 - **£1 440** - FF15 760
  Vanitas Oleo/lienzo (25x30.5cm 9x12in) Madrid 2000
- $728 - €841 - **£504** - FF5 516
  La Romería Lápiz/papel (20x28cm 7x11in) Madrid 2000

LAYCOCK Donald, Don 1931 **[12]**
- $1 342 - €1 479 - **£892** - FF9 703
  «Over White Cliffs of Ova» Acrylic/board (137x152cm 53x59in) Melbourne 2000

LAYRAUD Joseph Fortuné 1834-1912 **[10]**
- $5 835 - €6 555 - **£4 063** - FF43 000
  Nu au seau, Rome Huile/toile (71x78cm 27x30in) Honfleur 2001

LAÿS Jean-Pierre 1825-1887 **[18]**
- $32 000 - €37 945 - **£22 016** - FF248 905
  Wild Flowers and Butterflies Oil/canvas (143.5x107cm 56x42in) New-York 2000
- $16 078 - €14 724 - **£9 800** - FF96 584
  Fleurs de printemps Oil/canvas (102x73.5cm 40x28in) London 1999

LAZARE-LÉVY 1867-1933 **[61]**
- $2 147 - €2 439 - **£1 507** - FF16 000
  Campement dans le désert Huile/toile (46x61cm 18x24in) Paris 2001
- $747 - €686 - **£464** - FF4 500
  Marchand de poteries Huile/panneau (24x33cm 9x12in) Paris 1999

L

LAZARO FERRE Isidoro 1949 **[27]**
$648 - €721 - £432 - FF4 728
Jardín Oleo/lienzo (54.5x73cm 21x28in) Barcelona 2000

LAZERGES Hippolyte 1817-1887 **[67]**
$5 935 - €5 793 - £3 758 - FF38 000
Jeune femme fumant près du puits Huile/panneau (56x37cm 22x14in) Calais 1999
$1 104 - €1 220 - £765 - FF8 000
Jeune femme à sa fenêtre Huile/panneau (34.5x24cm 13x10in) Paris 2001

LAZERGES Paul J.-Bapt. 1845-1902 **[84]**
$4 346 - €4 726 - £2 864 - FF31 000
Orientaux se reposant sous les eucalyptus Huile/toile (47x66cm 18x25in) Paris 2000
$1 910 - €1 829 - £1 177 - FF12 000
Chamelier conversant avec un touareg Huile/toile (19x12.5cm 7x4in) La Varenne-Saint-Hilaire 1999

LAZI Adolf 1884-1955 **[69]**
$343 - €409 - £245 - FF2 683
Sektglas/Besteck Pott Solingen, Doppelbelichtung Vintage gelatin silver print (11x16cm 4x6in) Berlin 2000

LAZI Franz 1922-1998 **[46]**
$386 - €460 - £275 - FF3 018
Lokomotive Photograph (21x16.9cm 8x6in) München 2000

LAZZARI Sebastiano XVIII **[3]**
$39 000 - €40 429 - £23 400 - FF265 200
Ritorno dalla caccia Olio/tela (133x158cm 52x62in) Roma 2001
$20 000 - €23 026 - £13 648 - FF151 040
Trompe l'oeil Still Life with a Parrot on a Book, Figs Oil/canvas (49x63cm 19x24in) New-York 2000

LAZZARINI Gregorio 1655-1730 **[22]**
$10 906 - €10 174 - £6 580 - FF66 738
Bildnis eines Edelmannes Öl/Leinwand (97x73cm 38x28in) Wien 1999

LAZZARO di Umberto XX **[3]**
$2 179 - €2 259 - £1 307 - FF14 817
«Crociera Aerea Transatlantica» Affiche couleur (100x70cm 39x27in) Torino 2000

LAZZARO Walter 1914-1989 **[23]**
$5 000 - €5 183 - £3 000 - FF34 000
«Bocca di Magra» Olio/tela (40x60cm 15x23in) Prato 2001
$3 750 - €3 887 - £2 250 - FF25 500
La mia barca Olio/faesite (18x24cm 7x9in) Prato 2000

LAZZELL Blanche 1878-1956 **[81]**
$1 700 - €2 022 - £1 211 - FF13 261
Woodstock Mountains Oil/canvas (40.5x46cm 15x18in) New-York 2000
$900 - €771 - £531 - FF5 056
Provincetown Dunes Oil/board (20.5x28.5cm 8x11in) New-York 1998
$1 600 - €1 537 - £978 - FF10 084
Provincetown Watercolour/paper (28x33cm 11x13in) Provincetown MA 1999
$5 000 - €5 547 - £3 325 - FF36 383
Waitman T.Willey House, Morgantown, W.Va Woodcut in colors (30.5x35.5cm 12x13in) New-York 2000

LAZZERINI Giuseppe 1831-1895 **[5]**
$33 168 - €36 652 - £23 000 - FF240 419
Two children Marble (H198cm H77in) London 2001

LE BAIL Louis 1866-1929 **[12]**
$997 - €991 - £621 - FF6 500
Au bord de l'eau Huile/toile (81x130cm 31x51in) Paris 1999

LE BARBIER Louis 1743-? **[1]**
$2 200 - €2 287 - £1 452 - FF15 000
Vue d'un pont aux environs de Rome Aquarelle (28.5x43cm 11x16in) Paris 1997

LE BARON Maice XX **[19]**
$191 - €213 - £133 - FF1 400
Cadaques Huile/toile (89x130cm 35x51in) Évreux 2001

LE BAS Edward 1904-1966 **[50]**
$3 597 - €3 199 - £2 200 - FF20 982
Afternoon, Eygalieres Oil/board (43x51cm 16x20in) London 1999
$2 524 - €2 107 - £1 500 - FF13 824
Bedside Table Oil/board (26x36.5cm 10x14in) London 1998

LE BAS Jacques Philippe 1707-1783 **[75]**
$259 - €274 - £172 - FF1 800
Embarquement des vivres d'après Berghem Gravure (18.5x23cm 7x9in) Paris 2000

LE BEAU Alcide 1872-1943 **[68]**
$4 614 - €4 573 - £2 886 - FF30 000
Les voiliers roses Huile/toile (46x55cm 18x21in) Paris 1999
$538 - €640 - £383 - FF4 200
Paysage près du lac Pastel/papier (22x15cm 8x5in) Brest 2000

LE BERGER Robert 1905-1972 **[141]**
$919 - €793 - £546 - FF5 200
Quai des Orfèvres Huile/toile (48x59cm 18x23in) Vernon 1998
$533 - €511 - £329 - FF3 353
Gesicht eines Clowns Öl/Leinwand (35x27cm 13x10in) Kempten 1999

LE BEUZE Gaston XX **[14]**
$1 504 - €1 753 - £1 041 - FF11 500
Élégantes au lévrier dans le parc Huile/toile (60x81cm 23x31in) Calais 2000

LE BIHAN Alexandre 1839-? **[14]**
$2 374 - €2 287 - £1 485 - FF15 000
Ramasseurs en forêt Huile/toile (81x130cm 31x51in) Toulouse 1999

LE BLAN J.R. XVIII **[1]**
$7 340 - €6 865 - £4 500 - FF45 031
Still Life of a Thistle and Convulvulus, with Butterflies, Moths Oil/panel (39.5x31.5cm 15x12in) London 1998

LE BLANT Julien 1851-1936 **[7]**
$18 000 - €21 155 - £12 479 - FF138 769
The Revolution Oil/canvas (149x229cm 58x90in) New-York 2000

LE BLOND XIX **[35]**
$116 - €134 - £80 - FF880
Snowballing Print (13x16cm 5x6in) Little-Lane, Ilkley 2000

LE BLOND Jean 1635-1709 **[10]**
$289 - €274 - £180 - FF1 795
The Soldiers Return/The Cherry Seller Print (10x16cm 4x6in) Little-Lane, Ilkley 1999

LE BOEUFF Pierre XIX-XX **[51]**
- $1 473 - €1 350 - **£900** - FF8 855
  A Market Scene in Ghent Oil/canvas (61x91.5cm 24x36in) London 1999
- $426 - €486 - **£300** - FF3 187
  Bruges Market Place and Belfrey Watercolour (26x36.5cm 10x14in) London 2001

LE BOURGEOIS Gaston Étienne 1880-1956 **[24]**
- $849 - €991 - **£596** - FF6 500
  Le louveteau Bas-relief (24x18cm 9x7in) Pontoise 2000

LE BOUTEUX Joseph Barthélémy 1744-? **[2]**
- $21 000 - €22 427 - **£14 309** - FF147 111
  The Death of Patroclus, with the Body of Hector Brought by Achilles Black chalk (38.5x50cm 15x19in) New-York 2001

LE BOZEC Jean-Pierre 1942 **[7]**
- $1 976 - €2 134 - **£1 366** - FF14 000
  Nu couché dans l'atelier Pastel/papier (154x200cm 60x78in) Paris 2001

LE BRETON Louis XX **[5]**
- $20 772 - €19 089 - **£12 661** - FF125 218
  View of Hobart-Town, Van Diemen's Land Pencil/paper (20.7x39.2cm 8x15in) Melbourne 1998

LE BROCQUY Louis 1916 **[173]**
- $267 030 - €298 581 - **£180 000** - FF1 958 562
  Lazarus Oil/canvas (175.5x119.5cm 69x47in) London 2000
- $77 932 - €83 803 - **£53 110** - FF549 714
  Entrance of the dark Wind (Khyber Pass, Dalkey) Oil/board (60x36cm 23x14in) Dublin 2001
- $21 588 - €24 180 - **£15 000** - FF158 611
  Bird in Flight Oil/canvas (25.5x30.5cm 10x12in) London 2001
- $11 290 - €12 387 - **£7 500** - FF81 252
  Wood, Tipperary Watercolour (18x25.5cm 7x10in) London 2001
- $4 529 - €5 333 - **£3 182** - FF34 981
  Study Towards an Image of W.B.Yeats Lithograph (49x44cm 19x17in) Dublin 2000

LE BRUN Charles 1619-1690 **[30]**
- $627 120 - €548 816 - **£379 800** - FF3 600 000
  Suzanne devant ses juges justifiée par le témoignage du jeune Daniel Huile/toile (233x190cm 91x74in) Paris 1998
- $39 480 - €43 603 - **£27 360** - FF286 020
  Die Heilige Familie in Ägypten mit dem Jesusknaben Öl/Kupfer (52x42.5cm 20x16in) Wien 2001
- $5 646 - €5 513 - **£3 600** - FF36 165
  Mercury and Pegasus Black chalk (17x14cm 6x5in) London 1999
- $983 - €991 - **£613** - FF6 500
  Les heures du jour Eau-forte (18.5x23cm 7x9in) Paris 2000

LE BRUN Christopher 1951 **[22]**
- $9 000 - €10 181 - **£6 296** - FF66 784
  Victory Oil/canvas (259x442cm 101x174in) New-York 2001

LE BRUN Jean Baptiste 1748-1813 **[1]**
- $6 820 - €6 403 - **£4 212** - FF42 000
  Couple dans une calèche et cavalier le précédant Pierre noire (55.5x76cm 21x29in) Paris 1999

LE CAIN Errol John 1941-1990 **[11]**
- $1 492 - €1 292 - **£900** - FF8 474
  Grumpy Bear Being pulled in a Sled by a Reindeer Ink (16x29.5cm 6x11in) London 1998

LE CAPELAIN John c.1814-1848 **[56]**
- $651 - €593 - **£400** - FF3 890
  Bay with Fishing Boat, Woman with Dog on the Beach Watercolour (30x42cm 11x16in) Channel-Islands 1999

LE CAVE Peter 1769-c.1815 **[62]**
- $1 364 - €1 375 - **£850** - FF9 017
  Figures and Cattle on a Frozen Lake Oil/panel (16.5x21.5cm 6x8in) London 2000
- $643 - €652 - **£400** - FF4 276
  Figures and Sheep on a River Bank Watercolour (14.5x19.5cm 5x7in) Suffolk 2000

LE CITOL Anne XX **[11]**
- $579 - €534 - **£347** - FF3 500
  La ruelle Huile/toile (46x55cm 18x21in) Grenoble 1999

LE CORBUSIER 1887-1965 **[604]**
- $160 094 - €191 391 - **£110 000** - FF1 255 441
  «Taureau I Ter» from: Les Taureaux Oil/panel (161x87cm 63x34in) London 2000
- $198 720 - €185 180 - **£120 000** - FF1 214 700
  Naissance Oil/canvas (81x99.5cm 31x39in) London 1998
- $12 850 - €12 388 - **£7 922** - FF81 258
  Ohne Titel Oil/panel (27.5x22cm 10x8in) Bern 1999
- $668 - €6 284 - **£4 080** - FF41 223
  Deux nus féminins debout Pastell/Papier (21x27cm 8x10in) Zürich 1999
- $890 - €955 - **£595** - FF6 266
  La main ouverte I Farblithographie (69.5x51.5cm 27x20in) Zürich 2000

LE DIEN & LE GRAY XIX **[6]**
- $20 625 - €22 867 - **£14 325** - FF150 000
  Aqueducs Tirage papier salé (33x24cm 12x9in) Paris 2001

LE FAGUAYS Pierre 1892-1935 **[165]**
- $3 967 - €4 123 - **£2 500** - FF27 045
  Athletic Man Bronze (H110cm H43in) Doncaster, South-Yorkshire 2000
- $2 470 - €2 317 - **£1 526** - FF15 200
  Pierrot assis Bronze (30.5x29x21cm 12x11x8in) Enghien 1999

LE FAUCONNIER Henri 1881-1946 **[112]**
- $1 765 - €1 524 - **£1 066** - FF10 000
  Les Dahlias Huile/toile (77x51cm 30x20in) Paris 1998
- $2 739 - €3 176 - **£1 941** - FF20 836
  Still Life with Flowers and Pipe Oil/canvas (51x31cm 20x12in) Amsterdam 2000
- $964 - €1 125 - **£676** - FF7 378
  Stilleben mit Blumen, Tabakstopf und Tonpfeife Gouache/Karton (100x61cm 39x24in) München 2000

LE FORESTIER René 1903-1972 **[117]**
- $261 - €274 - **£173** - FF1 800
  Concarneau Huile/panneau (22x22cm 8x8in) Quimper 2000
- $177 - €152 - **£107** - FF1 000
  Intérieur de l'église de Locronan Aquarelle/papier (38x28.5cm 14x11in) Morlaix 1998

LE GAC Jean 1936 **[51]**
- $3 458 - €3 354 - **£2 191** - FF22 000
  La sieste du peintre, avec jumelles, diptyque Technique mixte (127x187cm 50x73in) Paris 1999
- $2 956 - €3 201 - **£2 024** - FF21 000
  Sans titre Pastel/papier (61x61cm 24x24in) Paris 2001
- $129 - €137 - **£81** - FF900
  Le délassement du peintre I et II Lithographie couleurs (65x48cm 25x18in) Paris 2000

LE GALL Philippe 1951 [31]
- $361 - €381 - £238 - FF2 500
  Le jean bleu Huile/toile/carton (36x24.5cm 14x9in)
  Soissons 2000

LE GENTIL Gérard 1948 [9]
- $1 128 - €1 052 - £696 - FF6 900
  Un pastis bien frais Huile/toile (61x50cm 24x19in)
  Melun 1999

LE GRAS August Johannes 1864-1915 [24]
- $2 912 - €3 403 - £2 079 - FF22 324
  Camels before a North-African Dessert Village
  Oil/canvas (43x61.5cm 16x24in) Amsterdam 2001

LE GRAY Gustave 1820-1882 [236]
- $8 214 - €9 147 - £5 772 - FF60 000
  Mosquée du sultan Barbouk. 6 Photo (31x42cm
  12x16in) Paris 2001

LE GROUMELLEC Loïc 1958 [51]
- $4 789 - €4 726 - £2 951 - FF31 000
  Maison Peinture (120x120cm 47x47in) Versailles 1999
- $2 914 - €3 267 - £2 038 - FF21 430
  Untitled Painting (65x55cm 25x21in) Melbourne 2001
- $1 092 - €1 220 - £730 - FF8 000
  Sans titre Peinture (25x25cm 9x9in) Paris 2000

LE GULUCHE Joseph 1849-? [32]
- $1 705 - €1 982 - £1 215 - FF13 000
  Buste de femme kabyle Terracotta (H39cm H15in)
  Paris 2001

LE JEUNE Henry 1819-1904 [32]
- $2 561 - €2 976 - £1 800 - FF19 519
  Dipping his Toes Oil/board (33x22cm 12x8in)
  London 2001

LE JEUNE James 1910-1983 [52]
- $7 900 - €8 253 - £5 184 - FF54 138
  Pembroke Lane in Summer with Figures
  Oil/panel (38x48cm 14x18in) Dublin 2000
- $2 959 - €3 174 - £2 017 - FF20 822
  Children at the Beach Oil/canvas/board (25x34.5cm
  9x13in) Dublin 2001
- $1 538 - €1 651 - £1 049 - FF10 827
  The Royal Exchange, London Watercolour/paper
  (29x38cm 11x14in) Dublin 2001

LE LORRAIN Claude Gellée, dit 1600-1682 [198]
- $29 273 - €26 705 - £18 000 - FF175 172
  **Father of Psyches sacrificing at the Milesian
  temple of Apollo** Oil/canvas (98x127cm 38x50in) Co.
  Kilkenny 1999
- $1 900 000 - €2 032 409 - £1 295 420 -
  FF13 331 730
  Pastoral River Landscape with Figures Oil/can-
  vas (75x99.5cm 29x39in) New-York 2001
- $10 000 - €10 712 - £6 829 - FF70 266
  Two Figures Milking a Goat Ink (12x18cm 4x7in)
  New-York 2001
- $633 - €610 - £391 - FF4 000
  Mercure et Argus Eau-forte (16x21.5cm 6x8in) Brest
  1999

LE MARE Georges 1866-1942 [4]
- $12 009 - €10 976 - £7 351 - FF72 000
  Le café des Nattes, Sidi bou Saïd Huile/carton
  (35x51cm 13x20in) Paris 1999
- $4 710 - €4 573 - £2 910 - FF30 000
  La place Bab el Souikha, Tunis Huile/toile
  (27x41cm 10x16in) Paris 2000
- $3 885 - €4 573 - £2 730 - FF30 000
  Marché en Tunisie Aquarelle, gouache/papier
  (22x33cm 8x12in) Paris 2000

LE MAYEUR DE MERPRES Adrien 1844-1923 [31]
- $1 808 - €1 983 - £1 200 - FF13 008
  Le port de pêche avant l'orage Huile/toile
  (51x73cm 20x28in) Bruxelles 2000
- $969 - €908 - £603 - FF5 953
  Couchant de soleil Oil/panel (27x36cm 10x14in)
  Amsterdam 2001

LE MAYEUR DE MERPRES Adrien Jean 1880-1958
[317]
- $160 326 - €134 515 - £94 068 - FF882 360
  Gathering Flowers Oil/canvas (100x120cm 39x47in)
  Singapore 1998
- $59 380 - €49 820 - £34 840 - FF326 800
  Balinese Women dancing in an Interior Oil/can-
  vas (90x75cm 35x29in) Singapore 1998
- $2 862 - €3 099 - £1 975 - FF20 325
  Marine Huile/toile (30x41cm 11x16in) Bruxelles 2001
- $10 041 - €9 359 - £6 069 - FF61 392
  Weaving Pastel (51x61cm 20x24in) Singapore 1999

LE MERDY Jean 1928 [31]
- $992 - €945 - £628 - FF6 200
  Nature morte aux pommes coupées Huile/papier
  (37x45cm 14x17in) Douarnenez 1999
- $2 113 - €2 287 - £1 447 - FF15 000
  Barques échouées Gouache/papier (44x61cm
  17x24in) Granville 2001

LE MESLE Hervé XX [27]
- $57 - €69 - £40 - FF450
  Sanglier et teckel Gravure (50x70cm 19x27in) Dijon
  2000

LE MOAL Jean 1909 [144]
- $5 748 - €5 628 - £3 537 - FF36 914
  Le quai le soir Öl/Leinwand (48x55cm 18x21in)
  Zürich 2000
- $2 255 - €2 515 - £1 516 - FF16 500
  Voiliers à quai Huile/toile (27x46cm 10x18in) Paris
  2000
- $970 - €1 067 - £617 - FF7 000
  Composition Aquarelle/papier (22x31.5cm 8x12in)
  Paris 2000

LE MOINE Elisabeth Bocquet XVIII [4]
- $8 865 - €8 208 - £5 500 - FF53 839
  Portrait of a Lady Oil/canvas (83x65cm 32x25in)
  London 1999

LE MONNIER Henry 1893-1978 [71]
- $630 - €601 - £380 - FF3 940
  Caballeros charlando Aguada (14x10cm 5x3in)
  Madrid 1999
- $212 - €222 - £127 - FF1 445
  «Camembert Georges Bisson c'est le meilleur»
  Affiche couleur (150x98cm 59x38in) Torino 2000

LE MORE Paul 1863-1914 [37]
- $2 130 - €2 287 - £1 425 - FF15 000
  Le cheval Huile/toile (65x80cm 25x31in) Paris 2000
- $574 - €549 - £361 - FF3 600
  Poules, dindons dans la cour de la ferme
  Huile/toile (31x42cm 12x16in) Deauville 1999

LE MOYNE François 1688-1737 [61]
- $24 000 - €20 158 - £14 109 - FF132 230
  Diana and Callisto Oil/canvas (79.5x98.5cm
  31x38in) New-York 1998
- $5 500 - €5 892 - £3 755 - FF38 646
  **Two Studies of Heads of a Young Boy, One in
  Profile** Chalks (28.5x23cm 11x9in) New-York 2001

LE NAIL Marie Joseph Ernest XIX [6]
$1 025 – €1 220 – £731 – FF8 000
Aurore et sa pouliche dans la pâture Huile/toile
(40x54cm 15x21in) Calais 2000

LE NAIN Mathieu 1607-1677 [2]
$110 000 – €120 686 – £73 073 – FF791 648
A Young Man Playing Guitar and an Old Man
Playing Pipe in an Interior Oil/canvas (54x65cm
21x25in) New-York 2001

LE PAON Louis, Jean-Baptiste 1736/38-1785 [10]
$2 352 – €2 297 – £1 500 – FF15 069
French artillery approaching a besieged town in
the Low Countries Black chalk (37.5x53cm 14x20in)
London 1999

LE PARC Julio 1928 [53]
$3 200 – €4 147 – £2 400 – FF27 200
Serie 3 nº13 Acrilico/tela (97x130cm 38x51in) Milano
2000
$7 943 – €8 655 – £5 500 – FF56 775
Untitled Metal (100x100x17cm 39x39x6in) London
2001

LE PETIT Bernardus c.1600-c.1669 [2]
$4 050 – €4 462 – £2 646 – FF29 268
La traversée de la rivière Huile/toile (36x45.5cm
14x17in) Bruxelles 2000

LE PHO 1907 [236]
$11 000 – €12 834 – £7 656 – FF84 185
«Le jardin fleuri» Oil/canvas (113x145cm 44x57in)
Delray-Beach FL 2000
$7 000 – €7 840 – £4 863 – FF51 430
La jeune fille au bouquet de pivoines Oil/canvas
(65x92cm 25x36in) New-York 2001
$3 500 – €2 958 – £2 087 – FF19 401
Still Life with Daisies and other Flowers in a
Vase Oil/canvas (35x24cm 13x9in) San-Francisco CA
1998
$6 312 – €7 168 – £4 320 – FF47 020
Le peintre et sa muse (The Artist and His Muse)
Gouache (64x50cm 25x19in) Singapore 2000

LE POITTEVIN Eugène 1806-1870 [82]
$4 605 – €4 573 – £2 868 – FF30 000
Terrasse aux environs d'Amalfi Huile/toile
(38x66cm 14x25in) Paris 1999
$1 469 – €1 646 – £1 022 – FF10 800
Cheval de trait à l'écurie Huile/toile (24.5x31.5cm
9x12in) Soissons 2001
$1 017 – €1 125 – £706 – FF7 378
Fischer am Ufer Aquarell/Papier (23x28cm 9x11in)
München 2001

LE POITTEVIN Louis 1847-1909 [33]
$1 298 – €1 296 – £810 – FF8 500
Jeunes femmes à la rivière Huile/toile (60x81cm
23x31in) Fontainebleau 1999

LE RALLIC Étienne 1891-1968 [31]
$376 – €351 – £232 – FF2 300
Zanzibar, Trompette et Scoubidou Encre
Chine/papier (27x18.5cm 10x7in) Paris 1999
$150 – €168 – £101 – FF1 100
Le Cadre noir, figures équestres Lithographie cou-
leurs (44x30cm 17x11in) Deauville 2000

LE RICHE XVIII [8]
$4 841 – €4 378 – £3 017 – FF32 000
Nature morte à la gerbe de fleurs et au vase de
bronze Huile/toile (37x46cm 14x18in) Paris 2000

LE ROUX Constantin ?-1909 [8]
$3 662 – €3 546 – £2 300 – FF23 258
Preparing the Dinner Table Oil/canvas (80.5x125cm
31x49in) London 1999

LE ROY J. XVIII-XIX [2]
$20 979 – €19 638 – £13 000 – FF128 818
Roses, Narcissi, Morning Glory, a Parrot
Tulip/Hyacints and Irises Oil/panel (65.5x48.5cm
25x19in) London 1999

LE ROY Jules Gustave 1856-1921 [193]
$3 246 – €3 049 – £1 956 – FF20 000
Chatons à la tasse de lait Huile/toile (50x65cm
19x25in) Toulouse 1999
$1 858 – €2 211 – £1 325 – FF14 500
Chatte et ses chatons Huile/panneau (35x27cm
13x10in) Grenoble 2000

LE ROY Sylvie XX [2]
$5 187 – €5 793 – £3 515 – FF38 000
Provence Huile/toile (38x46cm 14x18in) Paris 2000
$4 231 – €4 726 – £2 867 – FF31 000
Régate Huile/toile (33x41cm 12x16in) Paris 2000

LE ROYER Léon 1858-1939 [24]
$255 – €274 – £171 – FF1 800
Paysage de Provence Huile/panneau (32x25cm
12x9in) Paris 2000
$213 – €229 – £142 – FF1 500
Les Hauts de Cannes Aquarelle/papier (34x24cm
13x9in) Paris 2000

LE SAEC René 1935-1999 [13]
$401 – €457 – £283 – FF3 000
Coiffes II, personnages Acrylique/panneau
(61x50cm 24x19in) Rennes 2001

LE SAUTEUR Claude 1926 [35]
$2 872 – €2 785 – £1 778 – FF18 268
L'aventurière Huile/toile (61x51cm 24x20in) Montréal
1999
$782 – €760 – £488 – FF4 983
The des bois Oil/canvas (20.5x25.5cm 8x10in)
Toronto 1999

LE SCOUÉZEC Maurice 1881-1940 [142]
$27 225 – €22 867 – £16 005 – FF150 000
Femmes dans une rizière Huile/papier/toile
(114x160cm 44x62in) Le Mans 1998
$3 846 – €4 573 – £2 742 – FF30 000
Village en Bretagne Huile/papier/toile (54x80cm
21x31in) Brest 2000
$675 – €762 – £470 – FF5 000
Portrait d'André MAre Peinture (33x31cm 12x12in)
Bayeux 2001
$1 288 – €1 082 – £757 – FF7 100
L'arbre solitaire Aquarelle/papier (43.5x57cm
17x22in) Le Mans 1998

LE SECQ Henri 1818-1882 [37]
$4 629 – €4 373 – £2 800 – FF28 684
La Porte Rouge, Notre-Dame, Paris Salt print
(32x23cm 12x9in) London 1999

**LE SÉNÉCHAL DE KERDREORET Gustave
Édouard** 1840-1920 [29]
$14 665 – €15 397 – £9 241 – FF101 000
Départ des pêcheurs après la tempête Huile/toile
(129x162cm 50x63in) Paris 2000
$5 492 – €6 098 – £3 820 – FF40 000
Bateaux de pêche sur la grève Huile/toile
(38x56cm 14x22in) Chateauroux 2001

L

LE SIDANER Henri 1862-1939 **[499]**

$28 391 - €30 476 - **£19 000** - FF199 910
La rentrée du troupeau Oil/canvas (90x150cm
35x59in) London 2000

$80 892 - €95 128 - **£58 000** - FF623 998
La table, harmonie grise Oil/canvas (92.5x73.5cm
36x28in) London 2001

$11 000 - €9 239 - **£6 466** - FF60 605
Street in Paris Oil/panel (18.5x24cm 7x9in) New-
York 1998

$4 108 - €3 964 - **£2 594** - FF26 000
Portrait de Louis Le Sidaner, enfant Crayons cou-
leurs/papier (18x10.5cm 7x4in) Paris 1999

$210 - €173 - **£123** - FF1 136
Ronde de femmes Lithographie (35x25.5cm
13x10in) Liège 1998

LE SUEUR Nicolas 1691-1764 **[8]**

$992 - €1 125 - **£693** - FF7 378
Venus und Amor Woodcut (19.1x16cm 7x6in)
München 2001

LE SUEUR Pierre Étienne c.1750-c.1820 **[4]**

$33 975 - €38 112 - **£23 550** - FF250 000
Paysage antique Huile/toile (130x179cm 51x70in)
Paris 2000

LE TAN Pierre 1950 **[4]**

$1 652 - €1 829 - **£1 120** - FF12 000
Sous l'eau Aquarelle/papier (20.5x16cm 8x6in) Paris
2000

LE THI LUU 1911-1988 **[4]**

$32 488 - €30 280 - **£19 635** - FF198 621
Woman and Children Mixed media (95x70cm
37x27in) Singapore 1999

LE TOULLEC Jean-Louis 1908 **[139]**

$426 - €457 - **£285** - FF3 000
Vues des Plomarch Huile/toile (54x72cm 21x28in)
Douarnenez 2000

$283 - €259 - **£172** - FF1 700
Chaumière près du phare Huile/toile (24x33cm
9x12in) Douarnenez 1998

$217 - €198 - **£132** - FF1 300
Pommiers en fleurs Aquarelle/papier (19x29cm
7x11in) Douarnenez 1998

LE TOURNEUR DU BREUIL Raymond 1876-1950
[27]

$512 - €610 - **£365** - FF4 000
La nuit à Pont d'Ain/Paysage de l'Ain Huile/pan-
neau (38x53cm 14x20in) Grenoble 2000

$448 - €534 - **£319** - FF3 500
Lune sur la rivière Huile/carton (30x40cm 11x15in)
Grenoble 2000

LE TOURNIER Joseph Marie 1892-1972 **[30]**

$185 - €183 - **£114** - FF1 200
Port du Nord, bateaux de pêche au mouillage
Aquarelle/papier (31x31cm 12x12in) Paris 1999

LE TRIVIDIC Pierre 1898-1960 **[136]**

$1 777 - €1 982 - **£1 240** - FF13 000
Vue panoramique de la ville de Rouen Huile/toile
(54x65cm 21x25in) Versailles 2001

$317 - €305 - **£195** - FF2 000
Barry, l'épagneul Aquarelle/papier (50x61cm
19x24in) Le Havre 1999

LE VA Barry 1941 **[24]**

$4 000 - €3 756 - **£2 478** - FF24 636
Exterior Plan View - Expanding Foundations
Coloured pencils (178x132cm 70x51in) New-York 1999

$3 000 - €2 802 - **£1 851** - FF18 378
**Diagrammatic Silhouettes: Sculptured
Activities, Mercury Stress** Ink (154x246cm
60x96in) New-York 1999

LE VERRIER Max 1891-1973 **[80]**

$25 920 - €24 392 - **£16 032** - FF160 000
Clarté, sculpture éclairante Bronze (H170cm
H66in) Deauville 1999

$980 - €942 - **£611** - FF6 178
Le roi de la jungle Métal (27x58cm 10x22in)
Bruxelles 1999

LE VILAIN Ernest 1834-1916 **[55]**

$18 000 - €15 530 - **£10 859** - FF101 867
The Normandy coast at Omaha Beach Oil/canvas
(175.5x241.5cm 69x95in) New-York 1998

$585 - €613 - **£390** - FF4 024
Weite südfranzösische Landschaft Öl/Leinwand
(36x55cm 14x21in) Köln 2000

LE VUONG 1952 **[5]**

$3 248 - €3 028 - **£1 963** - FF19 862
Still Life Oil/canvas (68x79cm 26x31in) Singapore
1999

LE YAOUANC Alain 1940 **[133]**

$492 - €579 - **£353** - FF3 800
Personnage devant des formes volantes
Aquarelle, gouache (21x18cm 8x7in) Paris 2001

LE ZHENWEN 1956 **[1]**

$5 148 - €4 882 - **£3 132** - FF32 024
Landscape Ink (132x68.5cm 51x26in) Hong-Kong
1999

LEA Tom 1907-1976 **[3]**

$3 500 - €3 020 - **£2 103** - FF19 807
Deer Hunters Oil/masonité (44x34cm 17x13in) Santa-
Fe NM 1998

LEACH Bernard Howell 1887-1979 **[38]**

$2 800 - €3 126 - **£1 871** - FF20 506
Untiled Ceramic (H15cm H5in) New-York 2000

$1 138 - €983 - **£680** - FF6 445
«The Man who Fished with an Unbent Pin» Ink
(15x25.5cm 5x10in) London 1998

$325 - €363 - **£217** - FF2 381
Untitled Print (16x10.5cm 6x4in) New-York 2000

LEACH Ethel Penewill Brown 1878-1960 **[2]**

$2 600 - €2 380 - **£1 577** - FF15 615
Christmas Cactus and Freesia Oil/board (25x35cm
10x14in) East-Dennis MA 1998

LEADER Benjamin Williams 1831-1923 **[321]**

$60 000 - €51 765 - **£36 198** - FF339 558
Tintern Abbey Oil/canvas (122x184cm 48x72in)
New-York 1998

$10 830 - €12 204 - **£7 500** - FF80 052
Clearing Up After Rain, Ullswater Oil/board
(40.5x61cm 15x24in) Ipswich 2000

$4 866 - €4 691 - **£3 000** - FF30 771
Reed Gatherers at Streatley on Thames Oil/board
(31.5x43.5cm 12x17in) London 1999

LEADER Charles XIX-XX **[21]**

$1 211 - €1 248 - **£750** - FF8 185
River Landscape Oil/canvas (71.5x91cm 28x35in)
London 2000

LEAKE Gerald 1885-1975 **[8]**

$1 800 - €1 631 - **£1 108** - FF10 700
Family Outing Oil/canvas (63x101cm 25x40in)
Mystic CT 1999

LEAKEY James 1775-1865 **[26]**
- $38 990 - €37 937 - **£24 000** - FF248 851
  Colonel Sir James jackson, Major George Lee, Major General B.Wakeford Oil/canvas (158x131cm 62x51in) London 1999

LÉANDRE Charles Lucien 1862-1930 **[139]**
- $9 795 - €11 434 - **£6 930** - FF75 000
  Jeune femme au bouquet Huile/toile (93x39cm 36x15in) Paris 2001
- $1 602 - €1 906 - **£1 142** - FF12 500
  Le bal Technique mixte (32x28cm 12x11in) Neuilly-sur-Seine 2000
- $690 - €762 - **£478** - FF5 000
  Monsieur Combes, Procureur de la République assisté de messieurs Pastel gras (59.5x48.5cm 23x19in) Orléans 2001
- $178 - €183 - **£111** - FF1 200
  Noël: le retour de la messe de minuit Lithographie (23x33cm 9x12in) Deauville 2000

LEAR Charles Hutton 1818-1903 **[4]**
- $7 500 - €8 050 - **£5 019** - FF52 807
  The Merchant of Venice Oil/canvas (44x86cm 17x34in) Chicago IL 2000

LEAR Edward 1812-1888 **[512]**
- $15 409 - €14 855 - **£9 500** - FF97 442
  Study of Palm Trees Oil/canvas (51.5x40.6cm 20x15in) London 1999
- $35 741 - €34 776 - **£22 000** - FF228 113
  The Gardens of the Villa Borghese Oil/canvas (35x25cm 13x9in) London 1999
- $3 640 - €4 234 - **£2 600** - FF27 772
  Karnak, Upper Egypt Watercolour (9.5x24.5cm 3x9in) London 2001
- $246 - €266 - **£170** - FF1 742
  «Platycercus Tabuesis» Lithograph (48x34cm 18x13in) Newbury, Berkshire 2001

LEAR John B. XX **[33]**
- $375 - €400 - **£255** - FF2 627
  Checks Graphite (24x34cm 9x13in) Philadelphia PA 2001

LEASON Percival Alexander 1889-1959 **[31]**
- $421 - €491 - **£297** - FF3 223
  Seated Nude on Yellow Throw Oil/canvas/board (25.5x20.5cm 10x8in) Malvern, Victoria 2000
- $194 - €184 - **£117** - FF1 206
  Eltham Farm Etching (24.5x17.5cm 9x6in) Sydney 1999

LEAVER Charles XIX **[43]**
- $2 898 - €3 200 - **£2 000** - FF20 992
  Church in a Winter Landscape Oil/canvas (62x74cm 24x29in) Hockley, Birmingham 2001
- $1 740 - €1 976 - **£1 100** - FF11 013
  Village in Winter Oil/canvas (33x48cm 12x18in) London 1999

LEAVER Noel Harry 1889-1951 **[224]**
- $2 452 - €2 181 - **£1 500** - FF14 306
  View of the Rialto Bridge, Venice Watercolour (44x28cm 17x11in) London 1999

LEAVERS Lucy Ann XIX-XX **[11]**
- $8 861 - €8 813 - **£5 500** - FF57 811
  Startled! Oil/canvas (63.5x87.5cm 25x34in) London 1999
- $3 623 - €3 449 - **£2 300** - FF22 625
  Tit-Bits Oil/canvas (37x32cm 14x12in) Billingshurst, West-Sussex 1999

LEAVITT Edward Chalmers 1842-1904 **[62]**
- $4 000 - €4 145 - **£2 534** - FF27 192
  Still-Life with Red and White Grapes Oil/canvas (38x55cm 15x22in) Portsmouth NH 2000
- $2 000 - €2 026 - **£1 255** - FF13 291
  Roses Still Life Oil/board (30x43cm 12x17in) Detroit MI 2000

LEBADANG 1921 **[66]**
- $914 - €1 022 - **£616** - FF6 707
  Le lac bleu Öl/Leinwand (73.5x60.5cm 28x23in) München 2000
- $130 - €150 - **£91** - FF985
  Coolios Etching in colors (40.5x59.5cm 15x23in) Bethesda MD 2001

LEBAILLIF Alexandre Gabriel XIX **[1]**
- $4 303 - €3 627 - **£2 554** - FF23 793
  Romantiska par i landskap Oil/canvas (32x23cm 12x9in) Stockholm 1998

LEBARBIER Jean-Jacques, l'Aîné 1738-1826 **[56]**
- $126 700 - €106 714 - **£74 830** - FF700 000
  L'hommage à la déesse Diane Huile/toile (130x188.5cm 51x74in) Paris 1998
- $4 387 - €4 421 - **£2 734** - FF29 000
  Amour pleurant Huile/toile (49.5x38cm 19x14in) Tours 2000
- $1 104 - €1 220 - **£765** - FF8 000
  Télémaque dans le temple de Vénus Gouache/papier (20x15cm 7x5in) Lille 2001

LEBARON-DESVES Augusta 1804-? **[3]**
- $1 475 - €1 677 - **£1 012** - FF11 000
  Portrait de jeune femme Pastel/papier (59x48cm 23x18in) Provins 2000

LEBAS Hippolyte 1782-1867 **[18]**
- $828 - €838 - **£506** - FF5 500
  Paysage forestier animé Aquarelle/papier (58x37cm 22x14in) Corbeil-Essonnes 2000

LEBAS Hippolyte Gabriel 1812-1880 **[37]**
- $1 335 - €1 524 - **£939** - FF10 000
  Femmes de pêcheurs devant l'océan Huile/toile (43x56.5cm 16x22in) Versailles 2001
- $638 - €610 - **£398** - FF4 000
  Paysage orientaliste animé Aquarelle/papier (10.5x31cm 4x12in) Paris 1999

LEBASQUE Henri 1865-1937 **[1399]**
- $62 761 - €73 806 - **£45 000** - FF484 137
  Danse dans la prairie Oil/canvas (89x191cm 35x75in) London 2001
- $55 000 - €51 775 - **£33 979** - FF339 619
  La Marne à Lagny Oil/canvas (63x51cm 24x20in) New-York 1999
- $14 668 - €16 007 - **£9 954** - FF105 000
  Maison à travers les arbres Huile/toile (33x41cm 12x16in) Paris 2000
- $1 496 - €1 677 - **£1 015** - FF11 000
  Terrasse sur Cannes Crayon/papier (28x42cm 11x16in) Paris 2000

LEBDUSKA Lawrence H. 1894-1966 **[56]**
- $1 600 - €1 859 - **£1 124** - FF12 193
  Territorial Dispute Oil/canvas (60x76cm 24x30in) New-York 2001

LEBEAU Chris 1878-1945 **[19]**
- $305 - €363 - **£217** - FF2 381
  Duinlandschap Linocut (80x120cm 31x47in) Amsterdam 2000

L

L

LEBECK Robert 1929 **[79]**

📷 **$584** - €647 - **£396** - FF4 242
Auf dem Bahnhof von Hiroshima Vintage gelatin silver print (30.4x20.5cm 11x8in) Berlin 2000

LEBEDA Otakar 1877-1901 **[7]**

🖼 **$1 734** - €1 640 - **£1 080** - FF10 758
Lac de montagne Huile/toile (60x48cm 23x18in) Praha 2001

LEBEDEV Klavdii Vasil'evich 1852-1916 **[13]**

🖼 **$4 200** - €4 896 - **£2 943** - FF32 118
The Seamstress Oil/canvas (83x97cm 33x38in) Cleveland OH 2000

LEBEDEV Vladimir Vasil'evich 1891-1967 **[108]**

🖼 **$908** - €1 022 - **£626** - FF6 707
Mann mit Hut und Stock Mixed media (29.5x21.5cm 11x8in) Bremen 2000

🖼 **$645** - €767 - **£447** - FF5 030
Figürliche Komposition (Familie) Gouache (42x29.8cm 16x11in) Bremen 2000

🖼 **$1 000** - €1 121 - **£694** - FF7 356
«Long Live the Vanguard of the Revolution, the red Fleet» Poster (68x48cm 27x19in) New-York 2001

LEBEDEW Wladimir W. 1875-1946 **[27]**

🖼 **$1 236** - €1 227 - **£772** - FF8 049
Abstrakte Figur mit Springseil Mixed media (34x24.2cm 13x9in) Hamburg 1999

LEBEL Edmond 1834-1908 **[4]**

🖼 **$2 290** - €2 672 - **£1 636** - FF17 526
Vendeuses de figues et noix Huile/panneau (20x26cm 7x10in) Montréal 2000

LEBEL Jean-Jacques 1936 **[11]**

🖼 **$5 228** - €6 098 - **£3 672** - FF40 000
Portrait Huile/toile (73.5x100cm 28x39in) Paris 2000

🖼 **$3 250** - €3 036 - **£1 964** - FF19 916
Hard Labor Gouache (49x32cm 19x12in) New-York 1999

LEBELLE XVIII-XIX **[2]**

🖼 **$10 053** - €9 739 - **£6 325** - FF63 886
The Place de la Concorde looking the Palais-Bourbon with Figures Miniature (5x8cm 1x3in) London 1999

LEBENSTIEN Jean 1930-1999 **[60]**

🖼 **$1 457** - €1 363 - **£902** - FF8 943
L'apothéose Aquarelle (48x59cm 18x23in) Lokeren 1999

🖼 **$537** - €492 - **£327** - FF3 230
Horsemen Lithograph (30x50cm 11x19in) Warszawa 1999

LEBLANC A. XIX **[1]**

🖼 **$11 060** - €10 671 - **£6 993** - FF70 000
Réunion de famille dans un intérieur Huile/toile (81x100cm 31x39in) Paris 1999

LEBLANC Alexandre 1793-1866 **[1]**

🖼 **$7 225** - €6 834 - **£4 500** - FF44 825
Landscape in the Northern Italy Oil/canvas (75x94cm 29x37in) Praha 2000

LEBLANC Walter 1932-1986 **[50]**

🖼 **$4 822** - €5 624 - **£3 385** - FF36 892
«100 F Nox 36» Acrylic (130x162cm 51x63in) Köln 2000

🖼 **$1 326** - €1 537 - **£917** - FF10 081
Torsions Acrylique/panneau (40x40cm 15x15in) Bruxelles 2000

🖼 **$728** - €868 - **£521** - FF5 691
Torsions schématiques Ink/paper (55x73cm 21x28in) Lokeren 2000

LEBLING Max 1851-? **[3]**

🖼 **$952** - €1 022 - **£637** - FF6 707
Viehtrieb, die Rast im Dorf Öl/Leinwand (80x120cm 31x47in) Köln 2000

LEBON Charles 1906-1957 **[81]**

🖼 **$590** - €595 - **£367** - FF3 902
Chassepierre en Ardennes Huile/toile (50x60cm 19x23in) Liège 2000

LEBON Leon G. 1846-? **[3]**

🖼 **$16 000** - €14 987 - **£9 836** - FF98 305
The Artsit's Studio Oil/canvas (86x131cm 33x51in) New-York 1999

LEBOURG Albert 1849-1928 **[1247]**

🖼 **$95 170** - €94 518 - **£59 520** - FF620 000
La Seine et les Quais, au Pont Marie, déclin du jour Huile/toile (150x260cm 59x102in) Paris 1999

🖼 **$16 000** - €17 279 - **£11 057** - FF113 342
«Saint Maurice(Valais)» Oil/canvas (51x73.5cm 20x28in) New-York 2000

🖼 **$3 892** - €4 269 - **£2 643** - FF28 000
Bord de rivière Huile/panneau (14x24cm 5x9in) Calais 2000

🖼 **$463** - €457 - **£285** - FF3 000
Paysage à Hondouville Fusain (29x15cm 11x5in) Paris 1999

LEBOURG Charles Auguste 1829-1906 **[6]**

🖼 **$1 754** - €1 894 - **£1 200** - FF12 426
Bust of Woman Wearing a Low Cut, Roses Terracotta (H71cm H27in) Billingshurst, West-Sussex 2001

LEBOVICI Yonel 1937 **[10]**

🖼 **$14 791** - €14 483 - **£9 101** - FF95 000
Saturne quatre feux Sculpture (H200cm H78in) Paris 1999

🖼 **$5 820** - €6.098 - **£3 684** - FF40 000
Pyramide pantographe, lampe articulée Métal (55x20x41cm 21x7x16in) Versailles 2000

LEBRET Frans 1820-1909 **[78]**

🖼 **$5 590** - €6.353 - **£3 861** - FF41 672
De stalknecht Oil/canvas (74x98cm 29x38in) Dordrecht 2000

🖼 **$2 500** - €2 683 - **£1 673** - FF17 602
Sheep in a landscape Oil/canvas (30x40cm 11x15in) Philadelphia PA 2000

🖼 **$67** - €63 - **£41** - FF416
Mopshondje Ami Etching (13.6x10.8cm 5x4in) Dordrecht 1999

LEBRETON Louis 1818-1866 **[24]**

🖼 **$35 428** - €33 453 - **£22 000** - FF219 439
The Astrolabe/Zélée in a Swell in the Antarctic Oil/canvas (79.5x128cm 31x50in) London 1999

🖼 **$288** - €277 - **£180** - FF1 820
Naval Engagement between the Kearsarge and the Alasana Color lithograph (43x55cm 17x22in) London 1999

LEBRUN Georges Le Brun 1873-1914 **[6]**

🖼 **$4 515** - €5 206 - **£3 150** - FF34 146
La petite couturière Huile/toile (65x50cm 25x19in) Bruxelles 2001

LEBRUN Marcel XIX-XX **[15]**

🖼 **$16 000** - €18 562 - **£11 382** - FF121 756
Street scene Oil/canvas (55x99cm 22x39in) Chicago IL 2000

🖼 **$2 130** - €2 287 - **£1 425** - FF15 000
Paris, Porte Saint-Martin Huile/toile (46x32.5cm 18x12in) Paris 2000

LEBRUN Rico 1900-1964 **[35]**
- $11 000 - €10 592 - **£6 878** - FF69 479
  Night Figures No.1 Oil/canvas (233.5x188cm 91x74in) Beverly-Hills CA 1999
- $7 000 - €7 961 - **£4 890** - FF52 220
  Woman with Lantern, Cartoon from Flood Charcoal (183x86.5cm 72x34in) Beverly-Hills CA 2000
- $700 - €734 - **£467** - FF4 812
  Three Penny Opera Lithograph (56.5x76.5cm 22x30in) New-York 2001

LEBRUN Théodore XIX **[1]**
- $24 000 - €26 579 - **£16 276** - FF174 348
  An Artist Working in His Studio Oil/canvas (64x80cm 25x31in) New-York 2000

LEBSCHÉE Carl August 1800-1877 **[17]**
- $3 000 - €3 023 - **£1 870** - FF19 830
  Sun-Dappled-Steps/An Entrence to an Estate Oil/panel (19x9cm 7x3in) New-York 2000
- $257 - €256 - **£161** - FF1 676
  Sillo, der Hund in Uniform Watercolour (17x9.5cm 6x3in) München 1999

LECHESNE Auguste 1815-1888 **[9]**
- $2 500 - €2 286 - **£1 526** - FF14 997
  Pheasants Bronze (H71cm H28in) New-York 1998

LECHEVALLIER XIX **[1]**
- $5 562 - €5 488 - **£3 427** - FF36 000
  Ruines romaines animées Aquarelle/papier (83x65cm 32x25in) Versailles 1999

LECHNER Alf 1925 **[14]**
- $4 791 - €4 602 - **£2 953** - FF30 185
  Ohne Titel Metal (70x12x10cm 27x4x3in) München 1999

LECHTER Melchior 1865-1936 **[12]**
- $1 734 - €1 943 - **£1 205** - FF12 744
  Capri Oil chalks/paper (33x52cm 12x20in) Berlin 2001

LECK van der Bart 1876-1958 **[58]**
- $161 636 - €154 285 - **£101 014** - FF1 012 044
  De Maaier - The Reaper Oil/canvas (80x96cm 31x37in) Amsterdam 1999
- $19 966 - €19 059 - **£12 478** - FF125 017
  Het zieke meisje Oil/canvas (33x39cm 12x15in) Amsterdam 1999
- $5 281 - €6 135 - **£3 711** - FF40 246
  Konstruktivistische Komposition Gouache (32.5x24.5cm 12x9in) Hamburg 2001

LECLAIR Jean 1919-1996 **[78]**
- $76 - €76 - **£47** - FF500
  Le havre Crayon/papier (23x47cm 9x18in) Ourville-en-Caux 1999

LECLAIRE Victor 1830-1885 **[19]**
- $10 000 - €9 367 - **£6 148** - FF61 441
  Still Life of Roses Oil/canvas (87x59cm 34x23in) New-York 1999

LECLERC DES GOBELINS Sébastien Jacques 1734-1785 **[41]**
- $19 396 - €18 998 - **£12 500** - FF124 620
  Diana and her Nymphs with captured Satyr Oil/copper (51.5x62cm 20x25in) London 1999
- $11 279 - €11 077 - **£7 000** - FF72 659
  Fête Champêtre with Skittle Players Oil/panel (25x33.5cm 9x13in) London 1999
- $3 586 - €3 849 - **£2 400** - FF25 251
  The Burning of the Books Red chalk (14x20.5cm 5x8in) London 2000

LECLERC Félix August 1838-1896 **[4]**
- 📷 $1 422 - €1 677 - **£999** - FF11 000
  Dakar, vue de Dakar, Sénégal, mars Tirage albuminé (19.5x24cm 7x9in) Paris 2000

LECLERC Léon 1866-1930 **[10]**
- $2 148 - €1 997 - **£1 316** - FF13 100
  Le Vieux Bassin et la Lieutenance Huile/toile (23.5x30cm 9x11in) Honfleur 1998

LECLERC Sébastien I 1637-1714 **[28]**
- $4 391 - €4 288 - **£2 800** - FF28 128
  The Reception of Monsieur de Saint-Alon, Franch Ambassador Red chalk (18x15cm 7x5in) London 1999
- $484 - €488 - **£301** - FF3 200
  Les douzes paysages, dédiés à M. de Béringhen Eau-forte (10x18cm 3x7in) Paris 2000

LECLERCQ Lucien, Luc 1895-1955 **[79]**
- $544 - €457 - **£320** - FF3 000
  Les falaises, Normandie Huile/panneau (21.5x27cm 8x10in) Paris 1998

LECLERCQ Maurice 1919 **[22]**
- $364 - €372 - **£228** - FF2 439
  La flûtiste Huile/toile (52x62cm 20x24in) Bruxelles 2000

LECOEUR Jean-Baptiste 1795-1838 **[7]**
- $1 140 - €1 159 - **£716** - FF7 600
  Malheur d'un français Huile/toile (40x32cm 15x12in) Dieppe 2000

LECOMTE DU NOÜY Jean Jules Ant. 1842-1923 **[52]**
- $55 000 - €65 219 - **£37 840** - FF427 806
  Mademoiselle de Maupin Oil/canvas (107x86cm 42x33in) New-York 2000
- $754 - €732 - **£474** - FF4 800
  Étude, la danse de Salomé Huile/toile (27.5x44cm 10x17in) Toulouse 1999

LECOMTE Emile 1866-1938 **[63]**
- $350 - €347 - **£214** - FF2 276
  Le Château de Papenkasteel à Uccle Huile/toile (90x100cm 35x39in) Bruxelles 2000

LECOMTE Hippolyte 1781-1857 **[28]**
- $7 467 - €8 080 - **£5 172** - FF53 000
  Cinq Mars prend congé de sa mère pour se rendre au siège de Perpignan Huile/toile (44x58cm 17x22in) Paris 2001
- $6 201 - €5 831 - **£3 900** - FF38 252
  French Military taking refreshments outside an Inn Oil/canvas (33x40cm 12x15in) Co. Kilkenny 1999

LECOMTE Paul 1842-1920 **[222]**
- $1 146 - €1 143 - **£715** - FF7 500
  Les bords du Cher Huile/carton (38x55cm 14x21in) Fontainebleau 1999
- $1 170 - €1 220 - **£736** - FF8 000
  Paysage Huile/panneau (26x34cm 10x13in) Nantes 2000
- $770 - €762 - **£480** - FF5 000
  Sentier du moulin Aquarelle/papier (28x38cm 11x14in) Paris 1999

LECOMTE Paul-Émile 1877-1950 **[338]**
- $3 631 - €4 269 - **£2 632** - FF28 000
  L'abreuvoir dans le village Huile/toile (73x92cm 28x36in) Calais 2001
- $1 503 - €1 677 - **£1 049** - FF11 000
  Antibes Huile/panneau (33x41cm 12x16in) Versailles 2001

L

$621 - €686 - **£430** - FF4 500
Le café Maure à l'Exposition Coloniale
Aquarelle/papier (33x41cm 12x16in) Paris 2001

$135 - €126 - **£83** - FF828
Country Lane with Cottage Aquatint (50x59cm 20x23in) Charlottesville VA 1999

LECOMTE Victor 1856-1920 **[23]**

$1 611 - €1 829 - **£1 119** - FF12 000
Entrée de Barbizon côté forêt, l'auberge Diaz
Huile/toile (38x46cm 14x18in) Barbizon 2001

$2 496 - €2 897 - **£1 776** - FF19 000
Nature morte à la lampe et au nécessaire à thé
Huile/panneau (17x23cm 6x9in) Paris 2001

LECOMTE-CHERPIN Alexina 1834 **[1]**

$29 610 - €27 441 - **£18 414** - FF180 000
Recueil d'aquarelles de vignoble Aquarelle
(26.6x18cm 10x7in) Paris 1999

LECOMTE-VERNET Émile Charles H. 1821-1900 **[15]**

$38 000 - €32 785 - **£22 925** - FF215 053
A young Greek Girl Oil/canvas (125x86.5cm 49x34in) New-York 1998

LECOQUE Alois 1891-1981 **[33]**

$1 200 - €1 162 - **£748** - FF7 625
French Village Oil/canvas (50x60cm 20x24in) Delray-Beach FL 1999

LECORNU Geneviève XX **[5]**

$1 400 - €1 302 - **£864** - FF8 539
«L'Habitation» Poster (119x79cm 47x31in) New-York 1999

LECOSSOIS Victor 1897-1976 **[21]**

$964 - €992 - **£612** - FF6 504
Estaminet de campagne Huile/toile (60x80cm 23x31in) Bruxelles 2000

LECOSTY J. XIX **[7]**

$2 581 - €2 479 - **£1 600** - FF16 263
Still Life of Roses Oil/canvas (60x71cm 23x27in) London 1999

LECOULTRE Jean 1930 **[27]**

$1 319 - €1 127 - **£798** - FF7 392
Personnage riant Huile/toile (116x89cm 45x35in) Genève 1998

LECOURT Raymond Louis 1882-1946 **[151]**

$1 552 - €1 677 - **£1 074** - FF11 000
Pommiers en fleurs Huile/toile (50x73cm 19x28in) Le Havre 2001

$582 - €503 - **£351** - FF3 300
Scène de labours Huile/panneau (32x45cm 12x17in) Le Havre 1998

$4 539 - €4 573 - **£2 829** - FF30 000
Vaches et chevaux s'abreuvant dans la vallée d'Iton Pastel/papier (90x105cm 35x41in) Évreux 2000

LECOURTIER Prosper 1855-1924/25 **[121]**

$4 182 - €4 878 - **£2 908** - FF32 000
La fantasia arabe Bronze (H85cm H33in) Toulouse 2000

$1 987 - €1 852 - **£1 200** - FF12 147
An Otter Hound by a Log Bronze (16.5x20cm 6x7in) London 1998

LECUONA de Antonio Maria 1830-1907 **[2]**

$16 500 - €18 019 - **£10 500** - FF118 200
Bendición de la mesa en un caserío Oleo/lienzo (78x100cm 30x39in) Madrid 2000

LECURIEUX Jacques Joseph 1801-? **[16]**

$4 249 - €3 886 - **£2 595** - FF25 492
Summer fruits/Autumn fruits Oil/canvas (31x39cm 12x15in) New-York 1998

LEDELI Moritz 1856-1920 **[16]**

$2 057 - €2 325 - **£1 388** - FF15 254
Armenwesen in Wien: ein Ausspeiseraum des Wiener Volksküchenvereins Grisaille (33x48cm 12x18in) Wien 2000

LEDOUX Claude Nicolas 1736-1806 **[1]**

$6 007 - €7 013 - **£4 241** - FF46 000
L'oeil réfléchissant le théâtre de Besançon/Coup d'oeil du théâtre Eau-forte (25.5x39cm 10x15in) Paris 2000

LEDOUX Jeanne-Philiberte 1767-1840 **[18]**

$9 834 - €9 909 - **£6 129** - FF65 000
Portrait d'une jeune femme au fichu rose Huile/toile (45.5x37.5cm 17x14in) Paris 2000

$3 500 - €3 361 - **£2 157** - FF22 049
Pensive child with spinning toy Oil/canvas (40x31cm 16x12in) Cambridge MA 1999

LEDRAY Charles 1960 **[2]**

$14 000 - €15 360 - **£9 300** - FF100 755
Chuck Plastic (79x28x25cm 31x11x9in) New-York 2000

LEDRU Auguste 1860-1902 **[10]**

$2 984 - €2 897 - **£1 858** - FF19 000
Encrier, femme au coquillage et aux poissons Bronze (H13cm H5in) Paris 1999

LEDUC Arthur Jacques 1848-1918 **[25]**

$3 875 - €4 293 - **£2 598** - FF28 160
Trois enfants montant sur un cheval Bronze (H69cm H27in) Vejle 2000

LEDUC Charles 1831-1911 **[18]**

$5 256 - €6 250 - **£3 747** - FF41 000
Trois mâts, le long de la côte de Belle-Ile Huile/toile (70x118cm 27x46in) Nantes 2000

LEDUC Fernand 1916 **[19]**

$1 053 - €1 176 - **£713** - FF7 715
Jaune, vert, bleu Gouache/papier (48.5x62.5cm 19x24in) Montréal 2000

LEDUC Georges 1906-1968 **[36]**

$166 - €152 - **£102** - FF1 000
Port de Cherbourg Fusain (38x28.5cm 14x11in) Cherbourg 1999

LEDUC Ozias 1864-1955 **[50]**

$53 388 - €56 077 - **£35 273** - FF367 839
Paysage à l'automne, lac Saint-Hilaire Huile/toile (51x66cm 20x25in) Montréal 2000

$1 476 - €1 584 - **£987** - FF10 393
Rose Buds Oil/board (8x16cm 3x6in) Montréal 2000

$478 - €464 - **£296** - FF3 044
Portrait de Madame Bindof Graphite (22.5x15.5cm 8x6in) Montréal 1999

LEDUC Paul 1876-1943 **[166]**

$10 200 - €9 915 - **£6 280** - FF65 040
Le Dijver à Bruges Huile/toile (70x80cm 27x31in) Bruxelles 1999

$3 960 - €3 718 - **£2 445** - FF24 390
Vers le soir à Villefranche sur mer Huile/panneau (24x31.5cm 9x12in) Bruxelles 1999

$4 480 - €4 958 - **£3 120** - FF32 520
Port de pêche méditerranéen Aquarelle, gouache/papier (24x31.5cm 9x12in) Bruxelles 2001

LEDY Cheïk 1962-1998 **[2]**
- $6 333 - €6 112 - **£4 000** - FF40 095
  Comme à l'école (Just Like in School)
  Acrylic/canvas (131.5x198cm 51x77in) London 1999

LEE & TYNDALL Robert & Robert XX **[20]**
- $902 - €1 001 - **£600** - FF6 565
  Parp-parp-parp!: said the car, and Big-Ears looked out of his window Watercolour (17.5x12.5cm 6x4in) London 2000

LEE Anthony ?-1767 **[1]**
- $21 074 - €23 121 - **£14 000** - FF151 662
  Henry Boyle (d.1756), Captain of Horse, three-quarter-length Oil/canvas (127x101.5cm 50x39in) London 2000

LEE Arthur 1881-1961 **[3]**
- $27 500 - €32 095 - **£19 494** - FF210 529
  «Rhythm» Bronze (H92.5cm H36in) New-York 2001

LEE Bertha Stringer 1873-1937 **[21]**
- $5 500 - €5 904 - **£3 680** - FF38 725
  Eucalyptus in the Mist Oil/canvas (101.5x76cm 39x29in) San-Francisco CA 2000

LEE Catherine 1950 **[6]**
- $934 - €1 065 - **£645** - FF6 985
  Study for No.36 Charcoal (110x75cm 43x29in) Zürich 2000

LEE Doris Emrick 1905-1983 **[41]**
- $52 500 - €49 253 - **£32 439** - FF323 079
  Planting the Commemoration Tree Oil/canvas (55x85cm 21x33in) New-York 1999
- $3 100 - €3 458 - **£2 029** - FF22 686
  Three Still Lives Oil/canvas (35x35cm 14x14in) Chicago IL 2000
- $2 500 - €2 843 - **£1 733** - FF18 650
  Untitled, Child's Room Gouache/board (29x20cm 11x8in) Chicago IL 2000
- $400 - €429 - **£267** - FF2 816
  Girl on Swing Lithograph (22x30cm 9x12in) Cedar-Falls IA 2000

LEE Frederick Richard 1798-1879 **[69]**
- $5 509 - €5 133 - **£3 400** - FF33 671
  Cattle in a Landscape at Dusk, after Thomas Sidney Cooper Oil/canvas (95x152.5cm 37x60in) London 1999
- $2 069 - €2 004 - **£1 300** - FF13 146
  Highland Valley Oil/canvas (71x91cm 28x36in) Par, Cornwall 1999
- $1 436 - €1 676 - **£1 000** - FF10 996
  Gentleman Fishing in a Stream with a Pike on his Line Oil/board (21x14.5cm 8x5in) West-Yorkshire 2000

LEE Henry, Jnr. XIX-XX **[7]**
- $650 - €605 - **£401** - FF3 967
  «Speed» Poster (90x142cm 35x56in) New-York 1999

LEE John Theophilus 1787-c.1827 **[2]**
- $7 500 - €8 263 - **£5 003** - FF54 204
  The Engagement Between the Chesapeake and the Shannon Oil/canvas (55x78cm 22x31in) Portsmouth OH 1999
- $4 050 - €4 505 - **£2 700** - FF29 550
  The Naval Battle of Navarino Aquatint in colors (49.5x63cm 19x24in) Athens 2000

LEE Lindy 1954 **[10]**
- $2 429 - €2 722 - **£1 698** - FF17 858
  Fortune Acrylic (165.5x135.5cm 65x53in) Melbourne 2001

- $3 885 - €3 653 - **£2 406** - FF23 965
  Night and Day Series Acrylic (42x30cm 16x11in) Melbourne 1999

LEE MAN FONG 1913-1988 **[166]**
- $135 861 - €126 624 - **£82 110** - FF830 599
  Bali Life Oil/board (75x175cm 29x68in) Singapore 1999
- $10 904 - €12 381 - **£7 463** - FF81 217
  Rojak Seller Oil/board (123.5x61cm 48x24in) Singapore 2000
- $4 090 - €4 282 - **£2 569** - FF28 090
  Seated Woman Ink (61.5x42cm 24x16in) Singapore 2000

LEE MING CHUN 1961 **[2]**
- $4 195 - €3 934 - **£2 608** - FF25 806
  Dream World Oil/canvas (82x100cm 32x39in) Taipei 1999

LEE Philip XIX-XX **[6]**
- $789 - €734 - **£487** - FF4 814
  The Bush Hut Oil/board (29.5x45cm 11x17in) Melbourne 1999

LEE Russell 1903-1986 **[23]**
- $2 000 - €2 220 - **£1 391** - FF14 564
  Father and Son Photograph (26.5x35cm 10x13in) New-York 2001

LEE SANGBOM 1897-1972 **[2]**
- $20 000 - €19 304 - **£12 392** - FF126 626
  Spring Landscape/Summer Landscape Coloured inks/paper (127.5x31.5cm 50x12in) New-York 1999

LEE Sydney 1866-1949 **[23]**
- $127 - €148 - **£90** - FF968
  «Snowdon, LMS, Snowdon from Llyn Llydaw North Wales» Poster (102x64cm 40x25in) London 2000

LEE William 1810-1865 **[21]**
- $680 - €650 - **£417** - FF4 266
  The Rosary Watercolour/paper (41.5x33cm 16x12in) London 1999

LEE-HANKEY William 1869-1952 **[346]**
- $8 067 - €7 410 - **£5 000** - FF48 606
  A Brittany Fishing Port Oil/canvas (51.5x61cm 20x24in) London 1999
- $4 325 - €3 732 - **£2 600** - FF24 482
  Sailing Boats near a Harbour Oil/board (20x25cm 7x9in) Leyburn, North Yorkshire 1998
- $1 419 - €1 524 - **£950** - FF9 995
  A Study of Two Breton Girls in a Flower Market Watercolour (28x23cm 11x9in) West-Yorshire 2000
- $278 - €258 - **£170** - FF1 693
  The Two Sisters Etching (10x12cm 4x5in) Penzance, Cornwall 1999

LEE-JOHNSON Eric 1908-1993 **[12]**
- $1 007 - €1 129 - **£704** - FF7 409
  Waihau Bay, Cape Runaway Watercolour/paper (29.5x44cm 11x17in) Auckland 2001

LEE-SMITH Hughie 1915-1999 **[15]**
- $22 000 - €24 576 - **£14 909** - FF161 205
  Study of Cityscape with Figures in Foreground Oil/canvas (45x60cm 18x24in) Detroit MI 2000

LEECH John 1817-1864 **[87]**
- $5 673 - €6 586 - **£4 000** - FF43 199
  Very friendly bathing woman Teach you to swim? Lor bless you my love Oil/canvas (37.5x48cm 14x18in) London 2001

L

✏ **$400** - €387 - **£251** - FF2 540
«The See Serpent again» Ink (13x14cm 5x5in)
New-York 1999

🎨 **$467** - €502 - **£320** - FF3 290
Sketches from oil Lithograph (32x58cm 12x22in)
Stansted Mountfitchet, Essex 2001

LEECH William John 1881-1968 [66]
🖼 **$35 980** - €40 300 - **£25 000** - FF264 352
The Garden Oil/board (38x46cm 14x18in) London
2001

🖼 **$11 110** - €9 515 - **£6 732** - FF62 416
Harbour Scene, near Concarneau Oil/panel
(16x20cm 6x8in) Dublin 1998

✏ **$1 182** - €1 270 - **£791** - FF8 329
Young Girl's Head Pencil/paper (36x25cm 14x9in)
Dublin 2000

LEEFLANG Arie 1906-1956 [18]
🖼 **$469** - €544 - **£324** - FF3 571
Botter op de helling te Urk Oil/board (38x43cm
14x16in) Rotterdam 2000

LEEKE Ferdinand 1859-1923 [60]
🖼 **$4 728** - €4 094 - **£2 852** - FF26 854
Hl.Hubertus auf der Jagd im Wald, gegen den
rechten Bildrand Öl/Leinwand (120x160cm 47x62in)
München 1998

🖼 **$1 707** - €1 789 - **£1 081** - FF11 738
Süditalienischer Friedhof mit hohen Zypressen
Öl/Leinwand (101x76cm 39x29in) Köln 2000

🖼 **$1 738** - €1 562 - **£1 037** - FF10 249
Flickporträtt Oil/panel (32x21cm 12x8in) Stockholm
1998

LEEMANS Antonius 1631-1673 [5]
🖼 **$41 392** - €39 637 - **£26 052** - FF260 000
Nature morte en trompe-l'oeil aux objets de fau-
connerie Huile/toile (120x156cm 47x61in) Paris 1999

🖼 **$53 826** - €50 343 - **£33 000** - FF330 231
A Trompe l'oeil Still Life of a Caged Bird and
Hunting Equipment Oil/canvas (95.5x106cm
37x41in) London 1998

LEEMANS Johannes c.1633-c.1688 [19]
🖼 **$34 826** - €33 339 - **£21 626** - FF220 000
Trompe l'oeil aux instruments de chasse
Huile/toile (115x132cm 45x51in) Paris 1999

🖼 **$13 020** - €14 521 - **£8 496** - FF95 251
A Trompe L'oeil Still Life of a Birdcage and
Hunting Paraphernalia Oil/panel (51.5x67cm
20x26in) Amsterdam 2000

🖼 **$5 960** - €5 820 - **£3 800** - FF38 174
Trompe L'oeil, a Powder Horn, a Gunpowder
Pouch, beside a Birdcage Oil/panel (28.5x30.5cm
11x12in) London 1999

LEEMANS Thomas XVIII [5]
🖼 **$6 246** - €6 975 - **£4 000** - FF45 755
The Morning Gun Oil/canvas (49.5x65cm 19x25in)

LEEMPOELS Jef 1867-1935 [28]
🖼 **$1 105** - €1 239 - **£750** - FF8 130
Le pensionné Huile/toile (62x45cm 24x17in)
Bruxelles 2000

🖼 **$1 617** - €1 735 - **£1 085** - FF11 382
Portrait d'homme au chapeau Huile/toile
(43.5x33.5cm 17x13in) Bruxelles 2000

LEEMPUT van Remigius, Remi 1607-1675 [2]
🖼 **$6 528** - €6 198 - **£4 000** - FF40 653
Portrait of Catherine Bridges, Countess of
Bedford Oil/panel (38.5x30.5cm 15x12in) London
1999

LEEMPUTTEN van Antoon 1875-1906 [3]
🖼 **$972** - €892 - **£601** - FF5 853
Vaches au pâturage Huile/toile (36x47.5cm
14x18in) Bruxelles 1999

LEEMPUTTEN van Cornelis 1841-1902 [145]
🖼 **$6 000** - €5 612 - **£3 627** - FF36 813
Nestling Sheep Oil/canvas (45.5x68.5cm 17x26in)
New-York 1999

🖼 **$1 900** - €1 645 - **£1 145** - FF10 789
Two Sheep and a Lamb Resting in a Field
Oil/panel (16.5x24cm 6x9in) San-Francisco CA 1998

LEEMPUTTEN van Frans 1850-1914 [92]
🖼 **$4 128** - €4 857 - **£2 914** - FF31 861
Bauer mit Pferden an der Schelde Öl/Leinwand
(56x82cm 22x32in) Köln 2001

🖼 **$1 047** - €1 125 - **£701** - FF7 378
Heimkehrender Bauer mit seinen Pferden in
deutscher Küstenlandschaft Oil/panel (37x25cm
14x9in) München 2000

LEEMPUTTEN van Jef Louis 1865-1948 [152]
🖼 **$1 315** - €1 239 - **£795** - FF8 130
Bergère et moutons dans une prairie devant un
village Huile/panneau (38x58cm 14x22in) Antwerpen
1999

🖼 **$828** - €942 - **£570** - FF6 178
Moutons dans un paysage/Retour à la bergerie
Huile/toile (19x24cm 7x9in) Bruxelles 2000

LEEN van Willem 1753-1825 [19]
🖼 **$110 000** - €123 208 - **£76 428** - FF808 192
Flowers in an urn, a basket of fruit and a
flute/Flowers in an urn Oil/canvas (193.5x115.5cm
76x45in) New-York 2001

🖼 **$16 437** - €17 644 - **£11 000** - FF115 737
Peaches, grapes and plums in a sculpted urn
on a pedestal Oil/panel (61x46cm 24x18in) London
2000

LEENE van de Jules 1887-1962 [57]
🖼 **$764** - €694 - **£473** - FF4 552
La tour ensoleillée à Bruges Huile/toile (80x65cm
31x25in) Bruxelles 1999

✏ **$350** - €384 - **£232** - FF2 520
Mare en été Gouache/papier (34x26.5cm 13x10in)
Bruxelles 2000

LEES Charles 1800-1880 [3]
🖼 **$16 690** - €14 931 - **£10 000** - FF97 943
«Moonlit Scene in Yorkshire» Oil/canvas
(53x76.5cm 20x30in) Perthshire 1998

LEES Derwent 1885-1931 [28]
🖼 **$606** - €644 - **£400** - FF4 225
Mercedes Ceret - Portrait of the Artist's Wife as
a Young Woman Oil/canvas (42.5x26.5cm 16x10in)
Penzance, Cornwall 2000

✏ **$4 641** - €3 960 - **£2 800** - FF25 973
Reclining Nude Watercolour (25x35cm 9x13in)
London 1998

LEESE Gertrude XIX-XX [6]
🖼 **$2 735** - €3 063 - **£1 900** - FF20 095
Woman chopping Carrots in an Interior Oil/can-
vas (45.5x35cm 17x13in) London 2001

LEET Gerald 1913-1998 [15]
🖼 **$5 647** - €5 187 - **£3 500** - FF34 024
The Balloon and the Elephant Tempera
(122x152.5cm 48x60in) London 1999

🖼 **$5 163** - €4 742 - **£3 200** - FF31 107
The Schoolboy Oil/board (61.5x45.5cm 24x17in)
London 1999

$2 307 - €2 550 - **£1 600** - FF16 724
Eton Scholars Pencil (32x24cm 12x9in) London 2001

LEEUW de Alexis act.c.1848-c.1883 **[76]**

$2 949 - €3 266 - **£2 000** - FF21 424
A Winter Ride Oil/canvas (75x103cm 29x40in) Billingshurst, West-Sussex 2000

$2 600 - €2 808 - **£1 796** - FF18 418
Returning Home Oil/panel (22.5x30.5cm 8x12in) New-York 2001

LEEUW de Bert 1926 **[21]**

$2 940 - €2 480 - **£1 750** - FF16 270
L'Interrogation Bronze poli (44x66x35cm 17x25x13in) Antwerpen 1998

$761 - €793 - **£480** - FF5 203
Studie Craies (125x85cm 49x33in) Antwerpen 2000

LEEUW van der Pieter 1647-1679 **[7]**

$2 500 - €2 761 - **£1 732** - FF18 114
Eine Kuh und zwei Schafe mit einem Hirtenhund auf der Weide Oil/panel (30x35cm 11x13in) Wien 2001

LEEUWEN van Hendrik, Henk 1890-1962 **[73]**

$648 - €726 - **£450** - FF4 762
Akker met ploegende boeren Oil/canvas (59x99cm 23x38in) Rotterdam 2001

$532 - €499 - **£328** - FF3 274
Polderlandschap met man in roeiboot Oil/board (23.5x30.5cm 9x12in) Rotterdam 1999

LEEWENS Will 1923-1986 **[44]**

$1 902 - €2 042 - **£1 273** - FF13 394
Abstract Composition Oil/board (47x67cm 18x26in) Amsterdam 2000

LEFEBVRE Charles V.E. 1805-1882 **[10]**

$1 923 - €2 287 - **£1 371** - FF15 000
Scène biblique Huile/toile (100x80cm 39x31in) Dreux 2000

LEFEBVRE Claude 1632-1675 **[6]**

$6 822 - €7 927 - **£4 794** - FF52 000
Portrait de Benjamin Prioli Huile/toile (47x43.5cm 18x17in) Paris 2001

LEFEBVRE Ernest Eugène 1850-1889 **[9]**

$2 471 - €2 134 - **£1 492** - FF14 000
La jardinière fleurie Huile/toile (46x55.5cm 18x21in) Soissons 1998

LEFEBVRE Jules 1836-1911 **[48]**

$20 000 - €22 201 - **£13 942** - FF145 630
The Painter's Studio Oil/canvas (54x65cm 21x25in) New-York 2001

$8 000 - €7 922 - **£4 980** - FF51 966
Diana and her Companions bathing Oil/panel (21.5x27cm 8x10in) New-York 1999

$3 500 - €3 848 - **£2 243** - FF25 239
A Lady in Profile Charcoal/paper (31.5x23cm 12x9in) New-York 2000

LEFEBVRE Maurice Jean 1873-1954 **[38]**

$506 - €496 - **£314** - FF3 252
La danseuse à la coiffe royale Huile/toile (75x50.5cm 29x19in) Bruxelles 1999

LEFEBVRE Pierre ?-1669 **[1]**

$90 000 - €93 299 - **£54 000** - FF612 000
La Sacra Famiglia con Sant'Anna e San Giovannino Tapisserie (111x88cm 43x34in) Venezia 2000

LEFEBVRE René 1914-1975 **[10]**

$538 - €640 - **£373** - FF4 200
«Le fantôme de l'Opéra, The Phantom of the Opera, Arthur Lubin» Affiche (60x80cm 23x31in) Paris 2000

LEFEBVRE Valentin c.1642-1682 **[33]**

$61 308 - €59 455 - **£38 571** - FF390 000
La naissance de Saint Jean Baptiste Huile/toile (113x282cm 44x111in) Paris 1999

$1 613 - €1 601 - **£1 003** - FF10 500
Étude de fresque, d'après Véronèse Encre (54x40cm 21x15in) Paris 1999

LEFEUBURE Karl 1847-1911 **[19]**

$1 003 - €1 125 - **£681** - FF7 378
Rehe im Isartal Oil/panel (16x25cm 6x9in) München 2000

LEFEUBURE Karl Friedrich 1805-1885 **[5]**

$14 045 - €12 782 - **£8 775** - FF83 847
Felslandschaft mit antiken Ruinen Öl/Leinwand (35x49cm 13x19in) München 1999

LEFEUVRE Albert L. XIX-XX **[14]**

$3 503 - €2 897 - **£2 055** - FF19 000
Femme et enfants partageant du pain Bronze (H75cm H29in) Chaumont 1998

LEFEUVRE Arsène XIX-XX **[2]**

$10 199 - €9 452 - **£6 342** - FF62 000
«Savon Cadum» Email/panneau (73x58cm 28x22in) Paris 1999

LEFEVRE act.1753-1774 **[1]**

$3 744 - €4 345 - **£2 664** - FF28 500
Portrait d'homme à la veste brodée tenant ses gants Pastel/papier (74x60cm 29x23in) Paris 2001

LEFEVRE Adolphe Marie 1834-1868 **[13]**

$10 800 - €11 964 - **£6 960** - FF78 480
Pintor e os seu modelos num interior de palácio Oleo/lienzo (71.5x90.5cm 28x35in) Lisboa 2000

$1 671 - €1 601 - **£1 030** - FF10 500
Nu dans la forêt Huile/toile (46x33cm 18x12in) Calais 1999

LEFEVRE François c.1747-1817 **[1]**

$8 000 - €6 955 - **£4 841** - FF45 620
Design for a High Altar with a «Baldachino» Ink (76x81cm 29x31in) New-York 1999

LEFEVRE Géo 1876-1953 **[25]**

$442 - €488 - **£299** - FF3 200
«Quinquina Montalivet dans tous les cafés» Affiche couleur (65x84cm 25x33in) Nice 2000

LEFEVRE Lucien c.1850-? **[29]**

$1 015 - €1 067 - **£637** - FF7 000
«Electricine, éclairage de luxe» Affiche (240x87cm 94x34in) Lyon 2000

LEFEVRE Robert J. Fr. Faust 1755-1830 **[31]**

$7 123 - €6 860 - **£4 432** - FF45 000
Antoine-Ch.-Horace, dit Carle Vernet (1758-1836) à la boucle d'oreille Huile/toile (63x52cm 24x20in) Montfort L'Amaury 1999

LEFFEL David A. 1931 **[4]**

$1 500 - €1 364 - **£903** - FF8 944
Still Life with Onion Oil/board (22x25cm 9x10in) Hayden ID 1998

LEFLER Franz 1831-1898 **[21]**

$3 002 - €2 761 - **£1 801** - FF18 114
Die kleinen Glasbläser Öl/Leinwand (51x113cm 20x44in) Wien 1999

L

LEFLER Heinrich 1863-1919 **[17]**
- $1 188 - €1 380 - **£835** - FF9 055
  Nymphen in einer Grotte Watercolour (27.5x20cm
  10x7in) Hamburg 2001
- $216 - €218 - **£135** - FF1 430
  «Zeichnet 4.Kriegsanleihe» Poster (126x95cm
  49x37in) Wien 2000

LEFORT Jean Louis 1875-1954 **[46]**
- $1 717 - €1 601 - **£1 038** - FF10 500
  La Fête-Dieu à Molsheim, Alsace Huile/toile
  (53x72cm 20x28in) Bergerac 1999
- $850 - €814 - **£525** - FF5 339
  Scene with Church Watercolour/paper (15x20cm
  6x8in) Portsmouth NH 1999
- $750 - €777 - **£450** - FF5 100
  Ritratto di Edgar Allan Poe Acquaforte (34.5x24cm
  13x9in) Milano 2000

LEFRANC Jules 1887-1972 **[25]**
- $1 804 - €1 524 - **£1 073** - FF10 000
  Le boxer Youkia Huile/toile (32x29cm 12x11in)
  Calais 1998

LEFRANC Louis 1912 **[29]**
- $372 - €381 - **£233** - FF2 500
  Chemin longeant la forêt Huile/panneau (27x35cm
  10x13in) Troyes 2001

LEFRANC Roland 1931-2000 **[46]**
- $2 317 - €2 134 - **£1 414** - FF14 000
  Le hameau Huile/toile (60x73cm 23x28in) Bayeux
  1998

LEFRANCQ Marcel G. XX **[3]**
- $2 412 - €2 287 - **£1 467** - FF15 000
  Aux mains de la lumière Photo (22.5x16.5cm 8x6in)
  Paris 1999

LEFTWICH George R. XIX-XX **[2]**
- $7 500 - €8 714 - **£5 271** - FF57 162
  «The Prince's Derby» Oil/canvas (51x76cm 20x29in)
  New-York 2001

LEGA Silvestro 1826-1895 **[20]**
- $18 000 - €18 660 - **£10 800** - FF122 400
  Paesaggio lungo il fiume Olio/tavoletta (14.5x26cm
  5x10in) Roma 2000
- $5 000 - €5 183 - **£3 000** - FF34 000
  Ritratto femminile di profilo Carboncino/carta
  (46x34cm 18x13in) Milano 1999

LEGAE Ezrom K.S. 1938-1999 **[12]**
- $309 - €347 - **£215** - FF2 274
  Seated Figure and a Goat Ink (23.5x17.5cm 9x6in)
  Johannesburg 2001

LEGAGNEUR Jean-Claude XX **[7]**
- $3 182 - €3 659 - **£2 246** - FF24 000
  Casa Azul, portrait de Fryda Kalho Huile/toile
  (55x45cm 21x17in) Paris 2001

LEGANGER Nicolay Tysland 1832-1894 **[9]**
- $1 400 - €1 592 - **£978** - FF10 444
  Ship off the Coast Oil/board (76x63cm 30x25in)
  Mystic CT 2000

LÉGAT Léon 1829-? **[21]**
- $18 000 - €20 723 - **£12 283** - FF135 936
  Paysage de montagne Oil/canvas (91x117cm
  35x46in) New-York 2000

LEGENDRE Guy 1946 **[56]**
- $299 - €259 - **£178** - FF1 700
  Barques au sec Huile/toile (27x35cm 10x13in)
  Quimper 1998

LEGENTILE Louis Victor 1815-1889 **[9]**
- $12 191 - €11 891 - **£7 503** - FF78 000
  Paysage de campagne, troupeaux s'abreuvant
  Huile/toile (81x116cm 31x45in) Nantes 1999
- $1 355 - €1 524 - **£933** - FF10 000
  Chemin aux vaches Huile/toile (28x41cm 11x16in)
  Barbizon 2000

LÉGER Fernand 1881-1955 **[1882]**
- $380 000 - €417 031 - **£244 682** - FF2 735 544
  «Composition sur fond bleu», le cordage
  Oil/canvas (97.5x130x38x51in) New-York 2000
- $400 728 - €369 350 - **£240 000** - FF2 422 776
  Peinture Oil/canvas (73x92cm 28x36in) London 1998
- $84 640 - €82 378 - **£52 000** - FF540 363
  Composition Oil/canvas (33x41cm 12x16in) London
  1999
- $22 000 - €25 526 - **£15 188** - FF167 442
  Maquette pour: La fleur qui marche Ceramic
  (61x49cm 24x19in) New-York 2000
- $17 400 - €18 591 - **£11 850** - FF121 950
  Composition, étude pour sculpture
  Gouache/papier (47.5x31cm 18x12in) Lokeren 2001
- $807 - €920 - **£563** - FF6 037
  L'oiseau magique Serigraph in colors (55.5x36.5cm
  21x14in) Hamburg 2001
- $3 478 - €3 964 - **£2 389** - FF26 000
  Sans titre Photo (6.5x6.5cm 2x2in) Paris 2000

LÉGER Jean XX **[13]**
- $385 - €388 - **£240** - FF2 544
  «Sports d'hiver en France» Poster (99x64cm
  38x25in) London 2000

LEGGE Arthur J. 1859-1942 **[5]**
- $1 411 - €1 219 - **£850** - FF7 999
  Tending the Sheep Watercolour (33.5x50cm
  13x19in) Billingshurst, West-Sussex 1999

LEGGETT Alexander 1828-1884 **[37]**
- $1 643 - €1 500 - **£1 000** - FF9 842
  Music Hath Charms, Stolen Moments Oil/canvas
  (61x50.5cm 24x19in) London 1998
- $4 167 - €3 937 - **£2 600** - FF25 826
  The Winnings of the Herring Oil/board (30x41cm
  11x16in) Perthshire 1999

LEGNANI IL LEGNANINO Stefano Maria 1660-1715
[5]
- $12 000 - €12 440 - **£7 200** - FF81 600
  Salomone adora gli idoli Olio/tela (55.5x71cm
  21x27in) Venezia 2000
- $1 020 - €881 - **£510** - FF5 780
  Madonna col Bambino e San Giovannino
  Inchiostro/carta (13.5x11.5cm 5x4in) Milano 1999

LEGOLEC Yann XX **[8]**
- $602 - €610 - **£374** - FF4 000
  Fermes marines Huile/toile (50x61cm 19x24in)
  Strasbourg 2000

LEGOUT-GÉRARD Fernand 1856-1924 **[345]**
- $10 759 - €10 671 - **£6 692** - FF70 000
  **Landerneau, lavandières devant les maisons
  sur les ponts** Huile/toile (38x46cm 14x18in) Brest
  1999
- $4 342 - €3 964 - **£2 641** - FF26 000
  **Scène de marché devant les Halles de
  Concarneau** Huile/panneau (22x27cm 8x10in)
  Douarnenez 1998
- $3 674 - €3 354 - **£2 235** - FF22 000
  L'attente des pêcheurs Pastel/papier (38x45cm
  14x17in) Douarnenez 1998

📖 **$294** - €335 - **£207** - FF2 200
«Le retour des sardiniers» Eau-forte (65x54cm
25x21in) Provins 2001

LEGRAIN Pierre 1889-1929 **[7]**
✏️ **$3 454** - €3 354 - **£2 134** - FF22 000
Dessin préparatoire figurant un tabouret curulle
Crayon (32.5x23.5cm 12x9in) Paris 1999

LEGRAND Alexandre 1822-1901 **[11]**
🖼️ **$2 126** - €1 982 - **£1 311** - FF13 000
Nature morte à l'autoportrait Huile/toile (34x41cm
13x16in) Nantes 1999

LEGRAND Auguste Claude 1765-1815 **[11]**
📖 **$395** - €436 - **£258** - FF2 860
Beauty and Prudence, after Giovanni Battista
Cipriani Print in colors (39x35cm 15x13in) Wien 2000

LEGRAND DE LÉRANT Scott Pierre Nicolas 1758-1829 **[4]**
🖼️ **$6 741** - €6 696 - **£4 200** - FF43 926
Drunken Cobbler Returning to his Family
Oil/panel (53.5x65cm 21x25in) London 1999

LEGRAND François 1951 **[5]**
🖼️ **$4 367** - €4 726 - **£2 991** - FF31 000
Les deux amies Huile/toile (62x80cm 24x31in) Paris 2001

LEGRAND Louis Auguste M. 1863-1951 **[435]**
🖼️ **$7 848** - €9 147 - **£5 502** - FF60 000
Deux femmes s'habillant Huile/carton (73x69cm
28x27in) Paris 2000
✏️ **$1 482** - €1 707 - **£1 012** - FF11 200
La glace à la main Fusain (40x31cm 15x12in)
Avignon 2000
📖 **$304** - €320 - **£201** - FF2 100
Ballerines au repos Pointe sèche (35x54cm 13x21in)
Paris 2000

LEGRAND Mercédès 1893-1945 **[38]**
🖼️ **$1 332** - €1 220 - **£812** - FF8 000
Femme à la robe bleue Huile/toile (72x58.5cm
28x23in) Paris 1999

LEGRAND Paul Emmanuel 1860-1936 **[13]**
🖼️ **$540** - €534 - **£333** - FF3 500
Vieux pont à l'entrée de Tolède Huile/panneau
(15x23cm 5x9in) Calais 1999

LEGRAND René 1847-? **[4]**
🖼️ **$2 563** - €2 439 - **£1 593** - FF16 000
La halte Huile/panneau (11.5x18.5cm 4x7in) Paris
1999

LEGRAS Auguste J. Fr. 1817-1887 **[4]**
🖼️ **$3 285** - €3 811 - **£2 337** - FF25 000
Nature morte au chandelier, pichet en grès, cali-
ce et livre ouvert Huile/toile (38x46.5cm 14x18in)
Paris 2001

LEGROS Alphonse 1837-1911 **[116]**
✏️ **$1 663** - €1 409 - **£1 000** - FF9 242
Portrait of a Draughtsman Pencil/paper (22x29cm
8x11in) London 1998
📖 **$107** - €123 - **£74** - FF804
La mort du vagabond Radierung (53.5x37.5cm
21x14in) Hamburg 2000

LEGUEULT Raymond 1898-1971 **[117]**
🖼️ **$8 090** - €8 385 - **£5 131** - FF55 000
Le parc en Octobre Huile/toile (81x100cm 31x39in)
Paris 2000
🖼️ **$840** - €991 - **£590** - FF6 500
Intérieur aux vases de fleurs Crayon/papier
(40x52cm 15x20in) Paris 2000

LEHERB Helmut 1933-1997 **[38]**
📖 **$255** - €276 - **£176** - FF1 811
Die Supermatic Nähmschine Radierung (29x19cm
11x7in) Wien 2001

LEHEUTRE Gustave 1861-1932 **[56]**
📖 **$216** - €244 - **£149** - FF1 600
Les pins de Saint-Clet Eau-forte (32x22.5cm
12x8in) Paris 2000

LEHMAN Acy R. XX **[2]**
📖 **$994** - €1 148 - **£700** - FF7 530
«Blow-Up» Poster (76x101.5cm 29x39in) London
2000

LEHMANN Alfred 1899-1979 **[14]**
🖼️ **$850** - €920 - **£582** - FF6 037
Blumenstilleben Öl/Karton (50x48cm 19x18in)
Stuttgart 2001
✏️ **$1 323** - €1 431 - **£906** - FF9 390
Sommertag am See Pencil (33.5x48.5cm 13x19in)
Stuttgart 2001

LEHMANN Arno 1905-1973 **[4]**
🏺 **$769** - €727 - **£479** - FF4 767
Elefant Glazed ceramic (H11.5cm H4in) Wien 1999

LEHMANN Carl Peter 1794-1876 **[12]**
🖼️ **$785** - €922 - **£554** - FF6 048
Porträtt av turkisk man Oil/canvas (68.5x51cm
26x20in) Stockholm 2000

LEHMANN Edvard 1815-1892 **[51]**
🖼️ **$1 207** - €1 144 - **£751** - FF7 503
Den unge pige spås i hånden, medens ungers-
venden ser nysgerrigt på Oil/canvas (50x41cm
19x16in) København 1999
🖼️ **$406** - €404 - **£254** - FF2 649
Et vejalter på italiensk bjergvej Oil/canvas
(32x25cm 12x9in) København 1999

LEHMANN Henri 1814-1882 **[72]**
🖼️ **$110 000** - €102 075 - **£67 210** - FF669 570
Portrait of Léo Faustine Oil/canvas (100x81.5cm
39x32in) New-York 1999
🖼️ **$6 437** - €6 250 - **£3 977** - FF41 000
Jeune fille de Mente Huile/toile (41x33cm 16x12in)
Paris 1999
✏️ **$495** - €457 - **£296** - FF3 000
Étude de femme encapuchonnée Crayon
(30x20.5cm 11x8in) Paris 1999

LEHMANN Léon 1873-1953 **[32]**
🖼️ **$502** - €442 - **£306** - FF2 900
L'ange exterminateur Huile/panneau (18x24cm
7x9in) Saint-Dié 1999

LEHMANN Rudolf W.A. 1819-1905 **[17]**
🖼️ **$45 105** - €47 259 - **£28 551** - FF310 000
La lavandière Huile/toile (155x106cm 61x41in) Paris
2000
🖼️ **$2 132** - €1 953 - **£1 300** - FF12 812
At the Convent Door Oil/canvas (96.5x76cm
37x29in) London 1999

LEHMANN Wilhelm Ludwig 1861-1932 **[36]**
🖼️ **$1 217** - €1 022 - **£715** - FF6 707
Ziehende Wetterwolken über einem See,
Chiemsee Oil/panel (45.5x64cm 17x25in) Köln 1998

LEHMANN-BRAUNS Paul 1885-1970 **[38]**
🖼️ **$488** - €511 - **£306** - FF3 353
Sonnenbeschienene Rheinlandschaft mit
Burgruine Öl/Leinwand (70.5x95cm 27x37in) Bremen
2000

L

LEHMBRUCK Wilhelm 1881-1919 **[230]**

- $767 085 - €902 076 - **£550 000** - FF5 917 230
  Torso eines jungen Weibes Stone (H118cm H46in)
  London 2001
- $45 000 - €49 919 - **£29 925** - FF327 447
  Badende (Bathing Woman) Bronze (H64cm H25in)
  New-York 2000
- $8 650 - €10 173 - **£6 203** - FF66 732
  Stehender weiblicher Akt mit Akt Handtuch
  Coloured chalks/paper (43.5x29cm 17x11in) Bern 2001
- $710 - €614 - **£429** - FF4 025
  Weib und Kind Lithograph (63x44.3cm 24x17in)
  Köln 1998

LEHMDEN Anton 1929 **[125]**

- $1 698 - €1 454 - **£994** - FF9 538
  Ohne Titel Indian ink (25x10cm 9x3in) Wien 1998
- $168 - €182 - **£116** - FF1 191
  Spitze des Stephansturms Radierung (39x29cm 15x11in) Wien 2001

LEHNARTZ Klaus 1936 **[45]**

- $300 - €358 - **£214** - FF2 347
  «**New York: Feuerfluchtleitern in Manhattan**»
  Vintage gelatin silver print (22.7x28.4cm 8x11in) Berlin 2000

LEHNEN Jakob 1803-1847 **[4]**

- $17 564 - €18 407 - **£11 124** - FF120 740
  Herbstliches Obststilleben Öl/Leinwand (45.5x54.5cm 17x21in) Köln 2000

LEHNERT & LANDROCK Rudolf & Ernest 1878-1948/66 **[111]**

- $553 - €579 - **£347** - FF3 800
  Profil d'homme Tirage argentique (22x16.5cm 8x6in) Paris 2000

LEHNERT Hildegard 1857-1943 **[14]**

- $766 - €716 - **£463** - FF4 695
  Herbstlandschaft mit Birken, auf dem Feld arbeitender Landarbeiter Öl/Leinwand (68x100cm 26x39in) Berlin 1999

LEHTINEN Kauko 1925 **[27]**

- $28 347 - €27 750 - **£17 440** - FF182 028
  Muotokuvia Mixed media (143x100cm 56x39in) Helsinki 1999
- $1 051 - €1 177 - **£730** - FF7 722
  Från Paris Mixed media (16x21cm 6x8in) Helsinki 2001
- $773 - €841 - **£509** - FF5 516
  Självporträtt Pencil/paper (33x23cm 12x9in) Helsinki 2000

LEHTO Nikolai 1905-1994 **[142]**

- $763 - €774 - **£479** - FF5 074
  Trondheim Oil/panel (59x73.5cm 23x28in) Helsinki 2000
- $443 - €504 - **£304** - FF3 309
  Tillsammans Oil/panel (28x33cm 11x12in) Helsinki 2000

LEIBERG Helge 1954 **[13]**

- $15 000 - €17 071 - **£10 540** - FF111 978
  Zuritt Acrylic/canvas (199.5x299.5cm 78x117in) New-York 2001

LEIBL Wilhelm 1844-1900 **[198]**

- $9 888 - €8 181 - **£5 616** - FF53 662
  Maria Becker, die Tochter des Malers und Hermann Becker (1817-1885) Öl/Leinwand (43.5x38cm 17x14in) München 1999
- $12 477 - €12 782 - **£7 700** - FF83 847
  Studie eines Kopfes (Der Maler Sperl?) Öl/Leinwand (27.5x20.5cm 10x8in) Düsseldorf 2000

- $3 818 - €3 272 - **£2 295** - FF21 461
  Männlicher Akt (Selbstbildnis) Chalks/paper (43x29cm 16x11in) Köln 1998
- $429 - €368 - **£258** - FF2 414
  Bäuerin in karierter Jacke Radierung (14.2x10.9cm 5x4in) Hamburg 1998

LEIBOVITCH Moni 1946 **[3]**

- $6 000 - €6 753 - **£4 133** - FF44 296
  The Artist Atelier Oil/canvas (80x100cm 31x39in) Herzelia-Pituah 2000

LEIBOVITZ Annie 1949 **[45]**

- $2 500 - €2 843 - **£1 746** - FF18 650
  David Lynch and Isabella Rosselini Cibachrome print (23x28cm 9x11in) Chicago IL 2000

LEICHT William Leighton 1804-1883 **[10]**

- $1 421 - €1 607 - **£1 000** - FF10 541
  Travellers in an italianate Landscape, a ruined aquaduct Watercolour/paper (21x33.5cm 8x13in) Near Ely 2001

LEICKERT Charles Henri Joseph 1818-1907 **[364]**

- $32 084 - €32 330 - **£20 000** - FF212 072
  Figures on a frozen River Oil/canvas (37x49.5cm 14x19in) London 2000
- $10 568 - €9 983 - **£6 593** - FF65 485
  Summer Landscape with Washerwomen Oil/panel (19x25cm 7x9in) Amsterdam 1999
- $2 665 - €3 068 - **£1 840** - FF20 123
  Flusslandschaft mit Figuren und einer Burg Aquarell/Papier (31x48cm 12x18in) München 2000

LEIDA DI Luca 1489-1533 **[4]**

- $400 - €415 - **£240** - FF2 720
  La Tentazione di Cristo Burin (17.5x14cm 6x5in) Milano 2001

LEIDENBACH Ludwig 1908-1975 **[1]**

- $1 000 - €962 - **£617** - FF6 308
  «**Grock**» Poster (128x90cm 50x35in) New-York 1999

LEIDL Anton 1900-1976 **[20]**

- $566 - €485 - **£334** - FF3 181
  «**Die Donau bei Osterhofen**» Öl/Leinwand (33x61cm 12x24in) München 1998

LEIFER Neil 1938 **[1]**

- $5 866 - €6 807 - **£4 050** - FF44 651
  The Knockout, Muhammad Ali vs.Sonny Liston, Lewiston, Maine Type C color print (49x49cm 19x19in) Vancouver, BC. 2000

LEIGH George Leonard 1857-1942 **[1]**

- $3 365 - €3 199 - **£2 100** - FF20 986
  Low Tide Oil/panel (12.5x25.5cm 4x10in) London 1999

LEIGH William Robinson 1866-1955 **[78]**

- $38 500 - €41 326 - **£25 764** - FF271 078
  Paradise Valley Oil/canvas (50x71cm 20x28in) Houston TX 2000
- $37 500 - €34 089 - **£22 586** - FF223 612
  Robbing an eagle's Nest Oil/board (30x25cm 12x10in) Hayden ID 1998
- $22 000 - €24 654 - **£15 334** - FF161 717
  Risky Business Charcoal (58.5x89cm 23x35in) Beverly-Hills CA 2001
- $5 400 - €5 186 - **£3 329** - FF34 018
  Walpi-First Mesa Etching (30.5x37.5cm 12x14in) New-York 1999

LEIGHTON Alfred Crocker 1901-1965 **[86]**
- $570 - €636 - £372 - FF4 172
  The Fire Hills, Fairlight, Hastings
  Watercolour/paper (29x37cm 11x14in) Calgary, Alberta 2000
- $203 - €194 - £126 - FF1 275
  The Outlaw/Winter Wonderland Lithograph (21.5x28cm 8x11in) Calgary, Alberta 1999

LEIGHTON Barbara Barleigh 1911-1986 **[22]**
- $188 - €181 - £117 - FF1 186
  Evening Bow Lake Woodcut (30x38cm 12x15in) Calgary, Alberta 1999

LEIGHTON Clare Veronica Hope 1901-1988 **[72]**
- $425 - €407 - £259 - FF2 667
  All Days singing in the Moutains/Old Herb Gatherers Woodcut (17.5x12.5cm 6x4in) Boston MA 1999

LEIGHTON Edmund Blair 1853-1922 **[64]**
- $172 569 - €205 236 - £123 000 - FF1 346 259
  King and a Beggar Maid Oil/canvas (163x123cm 64x48in) London 2000
- $17 637 - €17 085 - £11 000 - FF112 071
  A Stolen Interview Oil/canvas (76x56cm 29x22in) Billingshurst, West-Sussex 1999
- $2 561 - €2 976 - £1 800 - FF19 519
  The Musical Suitor Oil/canvas (30.5x15.5cm 12x6in) London 2001

LEIGHTON Frederick, Lord 1830-1896 **[161]**
- $16 000 - €16 586 - £9 600 - FF108 800
  Cervada, studio dal vero Olio/tavola (47x36cm 18x14in) Roma 2000
- $5 691 - €6 613 - £4 000 - FF43 376
  Study for Lostephane Oil/canvas/board (15.5x8cm 6x3in) London 2001
- $7 471 - €8 020 - £5 000 - FF52 608
  Needless Alarms Bronze (H56cm H22in) London 2000
- $2 276 - €2 645 - £1 600 - FF17 350
  Study for And the Sea gave up the Dead which were in it Black & white chalks (23.5x33cm 9x12in) London 2001

LEIGHTON Kathryn Woodman 1876-1952 **[13]**
- $4 250 - €3 667 - £2 554 - FF24 052
  Anatomi Oil/canvas (76x63cm 30x25in) Santa-Fe NM 1998
- $2 750 - €2 952 - £1 840 - FF19 362
  Laguna Oil/masonite (30x40cm 12x16in) Altadena CA 2000

LEIGHTON Mary, née Parker XIX-XX **[2]**
- $5 646 - €5 542 - £3 500 - FF36 352
  Portrait of Sir Baldwin Leighton in Egyptian Costume Watercolour (38x39cm 14x15in) London 1999

LEIGHTON Nicholas W. Scott 1847-1898 **[8]**
- $1 550 - €1 357 - £938 - FF8 899
  Figures on Horseback in Landscape Oil/canvas (50x86cm 20x34in) Columbia SC 1998

LEIGHTON Scott 1849-1898 **[58]**
- $2 600 - €2 593 - £1 623 - FF17 012
  Before the Hunt Oil/canvas (59x44cm 23x17in) Watertown MA 1999
- $900 - €934 - £571 - FF6 126
  Portrait of a Dog Oil/canvas (23x35.5cm 9x13in) Boston MA 2000

LEIGHTON-BARLEY Alfred & Barbara 1901/11-1965/86 **[6]**
- $238 - €202 - £142 - FF1 326
  Lunenette Peak, Mt. Assiniboine Woodcut (40x48cm 15x18in) Calgary, Alberta 1998

LEINBERGER Hans XVI **[1]**
- $1 361 - €1 534 - £942 - FF10 061
  «Drei Engel mit Arma Christi» Kupferstich (13.5x9.5cm 5x3in) München 2000

LEINWEBER Heinrich 1836-1908 **[1]**
- $7 000 - €6 932 - £4 358 - FF45 470
  Mosque Interior Oil/panel (44x33cm 17x12in) New-York 1999

LEIPOLD Karl 1864-1943 **[16]**
- $1 315 - €1 534 - £923 - FF10 061
  Piaza San Marco mit Dogenpalast bei heller Mondnacht Oil/panel (76x67cm 29x26in) Köln 2001

LEIPZIG Arthur 1918 **[5]**
- $900 - €1 041 - £637 - FF6 829
  Divers, East River Silver print (25x33cm 10x13in) New-York 2000

LEIRNER Jac 1961 **[5]**
- $18 000 - €17 339 - £11 176 - FF113 734
  The One Hundred, love Mixed media (116x116cm 45x45in) New-York 1999
- $18 000 - €20 885 - £12 427 - FF136 998
  Necessaire, Corpus Di Licti Assemblage (122x122x15cm 48x48x5in) New-York 2000
- $36 000 - €34 833 - £22 201 - FF228 488
  «To and From», Moma Oxford Accumulation (46x325x33cm 18x127x12in) New-York 1999

LEIRNER Nelson 1932 **[1]**
- $16 000 - €18 565 - £11 046 - FF121 776
  Homenagem a Fontana II Mixed media (180x125cm 70x49in) New-York 2000

LEIRO Francisco 1957 **[9]**
- $19 938 - €20 717 - £12 500 - FF135 896
  Outro de Vilanova Sculpture, wood (H230cm H90in) London 2000
- $3 520 - €3 304 - £2 090 - FF21 670
  Figura recostada Sculpture bois (54x31x22cm 21x12x8in) Madrid 1999

LEISTIKOW Walter 1865-1908 **[177]**
- $14 993 - €17 639 - £10 584 - FF115 706
  Schwäne Öl/Leinwand (48x64cm 18x25in) Berlin 2001
- $16 493 - €19 403 - £11 643 - FF127 276
  «Breege» Oil/paper/board (31.5x47cm 12x18in) Berlin 2001
- $2 381 - €2 556 - £1 594 - FF16 769
  Märkische Landschaft mit Bäumen und Gewässer Aquarell/Papier (33x40cm 12x15in) Zwiesel 2000
- $220 - €256 - £152 - FF1 676
  Kraniche Print (21.8x28cm 8x11in) München 2000

LEITCH Richard Principal c.1800-c.1880 **[40]**
- $300 - €345 - £206 - FF2 264
  Northern Coast Watercolour/paper (16x23.5cm 6x9in) Philadelphia PA 2000

LEITCH William Leighton 1804-1883 **[182]**
- $700 - €815 - £500 - FF5 345
  Figure and a Dog in a Wooded Landscape with a Tower in the Distance Watercolour (13.5x22cm 5x8in) London 2001

L

LEITGEB Franz 1911-1997 **[21]**
- $481 - €485 - **£300** - FF3 181
  Old Bavarians Oil/board (25.5x20.5cm 10x8in)
  London 2001

LEITH-ROSS Harry 1886-1973 **[55]**
- $6 500 - €6 156 - **£3 952** - FF40 378
  Bearsville Valley Oil/canvas (51x61.5cm 20x24in)
  New-York 1999
- $2 700 - €2 561 - **£1 652** - FF16 396
  The Harbour, Evening Rockport, Mass. Oil/canvas/board (21x26cm 8x10in) Chicago IL 1999
- $500 - €475 - **£306** - FF3 113
  Landscape with Arcadia Train Station
  Watercolour/paper (15x27cm 6x11in) Hatfield PA 1999

LEITHNER VON SCHWATZ Johann Joseph XVIII **[1]**
- $10 759 - €11 549 - **£7 200** - FF75 755
  Female Figures Sculpture, wood (H55cm H21in)
  London 2000

LEITNER Robert 1888-? **[4]**
- $1 151 - €1 273 - **£799** - FF8 349
  Blomsteropstilling Oil/canvas (80x62cm 31x24in)
  Vejle 2001

LEITNER Thomas 1876-1948 **[52]**
- $3 520 - €3 997 - **£2 469** - FF26 218
  Landschaft Oil/Leinwand (131x170cm 51x66in) Wien 2001
- $1 442 - €1 453 - **£900** - FF9 534
  Herbst am Weiher, Waldviertel Öl/Leinwand (68x90cm 26x35in) Wien 2000
- $8 179 - €7 669 - **£5 055** - FF50 308
  Weite Landschaft mit Vogelflug Öl/Karton (25x33.5cm 9x13in) Graz 1999

LEIVA Nicolás 1958 **[16]**
- $20 000 - €17 439 - **£12 092** - FF114 394
  Sin Título Oil/canvas (230x199cm 90x78in) New-York 1998

LEIZELT Balthazar Frederic XVIII **[12]**
- $118 - €128 - **£81** - FF838
  Palais Corsini, la Place de St. Jean de Lateran, nach Barbault Kupferstich (32.5x44cm 12x17in)
  München 2001

LEJEUNE A.A. XVIII **[1]**
- $22 000 - €22 256 - **£13 433** - FF145 989
  Trompe l'oeil of Assignats and other Revolutionary Papers Ink (81x54.5cm 31x21in)
  New-York 2000

LEJEUNE Eugène 1818-1897 **[7]**
- $7 500 - €8 376 - **£4 803** - FF54 941
  Minding the Rabbits Oil/canvas (52x60.5cm 20x23in) New-York 2000
- $2 747 - €2 668 - **£1 697** - FF17 500
  Le badinage Huile/toile (41.5x31.5cm 16x12in)
  Melun 1999

LEJEUNE Louis Aimé 1884-1969 **[6]**
- $4 520 - €3 811 - **£2 682** - FF25 000
  Buste de femme Bronze (H63cm H24in) Chinon 1998

LELAND Miss XIX **[1]**
- $6 000 - €6 908 - **£4 094** - FF45 312
  A Curly-haired Boy Elegantly dressed seated with a Horse Pull Toy Miniature (11.5x10cm 4x3in)
  New-York 2000

LELÉE Léopold, Léo 1872-1947 **[72]**
- $4 051 - €3 400 - **£2 377** - FF22 300
  Les Trois Arlésiennes Huile/toile (51x73cm 20x28in) Aubagne 1998
- $1 274 - €1 220 - **£792** - FF8 000
  Arlésienne vue de dos Fusain/papier (56x34.5cm 22x13in) Rennes 1999
- $247 - €274 - **£171** - FF1 800
  «Plm, Nimes, Autocars Plm pour Uzès, Pont du Gard» Affiche (106x76cm 41x29in) Paris 2001

LELEUX Adolphe 1812-1891 **[16]**
- $10 000 - €9 903 - **£6 226** - FF64 958
  Setting off the Hunt Oil/canvas (96.5x129.5cm 37x50in) New-York 2000

LELEUX Armand 1818-1885 **[13]**
- $2 665 - €3 095 - **£1 873** - FF20 305
  Patience Oil/canvas (57x46cm 22x18in) Stockholm 2001
- $2 345 - €1 982 - **£1 398** - FF13 000
  Les abords de Rome Huile/toile (27.5x46.5cm 10x18in) Paris 1998

LELIE de Adriaen 1755-1820 **[13]**
- $1 598 - €1 825 - **£1 127** - FF11 972
  Porträt einer Frau Öl/Leinwand (28x23cm 11x9in)
  Bern 2001

LELIENBERGH Cornelis 1626-1676 **[15]**
- $7 117 - €6 647 - **£4 392** - FF43 600
  Jagdstilleben mit erlegtem Geflügel Öl/Leinwand (60x50cm 23x19in) Köln 1999
- $12 153 - €13 613 - **£8 445** - FF89 298
  Dead Birds hanging from a Rope with a Shotgun, above a Stone Ledge Oil/panel (37.5x31cm 14x12in) Amsterdam 2001

LELLI Giovan Battista 1827-1887 **[9]**
- $3 000 - €3 887 - **£2 250** - FF25 500
  Paesaggio di Canobbio Olio/tela (56x85cm 22x33in) Milano 2000

LELLOUCHE Jules 1903-1963 **[66]**
- $2 355 - €2 287 - **£1 455** - FF15 000
  Place Halfaouine, Tunis Huile/toile (60x73cm 23x28in) Paris 1999
- $1 173 - €1 372 - **£837** - FF9 000
  Sidi Mahrez Huile/carton (18x13cm 7x5in) Paris 2001

LELLOUCHE Ofer 1947 **[43]**
- $12 000 - €12 881 - **£8 030** - FF84 492
  Near Bar-em Oil/canvas (127.5x180.5cm 50x71in) Tel Aviv 2000
- $8 500 - €9 196 - **£5 823** - FF60 319
  Still Life in Violet Oil/canvas (89x108cm 35x42in) Tel Aviv 2000
- $800 - €781 - **£506** - FF5 122
  Jaffa, View of the Sea Watercolour/paper (76x56cm 29x22in) Tel Aviv 1999

LELOIR Louis-Alexandre 1843-1884 **[31]**
- $10 101 - €11 510 - **£6 938** - FF75 500
  Chasse et pêche Huile/toile (237x98cm 93x38in)
  Neuilly-sur-Seine 1998
- $14 000 - €13 303 - **£8 517** - FF87 260
  Battledore and Shuttlecock Oil/panel (47.5x60.5cm 18x23in) New-York 1999
- $652 - €686 - **£409** - FF4 500
  Clitandre Encre (22x31cm 8x12in) Paris 2000

LELOIR Maurice 1853-1940 **[101]**
- $14 000 - €13 113 - **£8 607** - FF86 017
  Musical Outing Oil/canvas (37.5x82.5cm 14x32in)
  New-York 1999

$644 - €726 - **£444** - FF4 762
The Merry Drinkers Watercolour (17x21.5cm 6x8in)
Amsterdam 2000

$700 - €781 - **£458** - FF5 122
«Théâtre national de l'opéra-comique: Cigale»
Poster (89x55cm 35x21in) New-York 2000

LELONG XIX [25]
$5 080 - €5 641 - **£3 540** - FF37 000
**Assiette de fruits, perroquet, urne
fleurie/Corbeille de fruits** Gouache/papier
(16x21.5cm 6x8in) Paris 2001

LELONG Paul XVIII-XIX [3]
$4 713 - €4 573 - **£2 934** - FF30 000
Natures mortes Gouache/papier (15x20cm 5x7in)
Paris 1999

LELONG René 1871-1938 [39]
$8 500 - €8 417 - **£5 292** - FF55 214
Spring Day by Seashore Oil/canvas (47.5x33cm
18x12in) New-York 2000

$361 - €412 - **£251** - FF2 700
Le couple dans le cloître du Mont St Michel
Aquarelle/papier (40x50cm 15x19in) Paris 2001

$1 220 - €1 143 - **£750** - FF7 500
«Kodak» Poster (63.5x46cm 25x18in) London 1999

LELU Pierre 1741-1810 [28]
$1 498 - €1 677 - **£1 016** - FF11 000
Le char de Vénus titré par des cygnes Encre
(20x53cm 7x20in) Paris 2000

LELY Pieter 1618-1680 [117]
$22 448 - €26 697 - **£16 000** - FF175 123
**Portrait of Thomas Osborne, 1st Earl of Danby,
Later 1st Duke of Leeds** Oil/canvas (232.5x142cm
91x55in) London 2000

$9 747 - €9 484 - **£6 000** - FF62 212
**Julia Fasey, Lady Crewe, seated, wearing a
black Dress** Oil/canvas (124.5x93cm 49x36in)
London 1999

$8 500 - €8 812 - **£5 100** - FF57 800
**Ritratto allegorico della Duchessa di
Cleveland/Duchessa di Crammont** Olio/cartone
(28.5x23.5cm 11x9in) Imbersago (Lecco) 2001

LEMAIRE Casimir XIX [8]
$8 500 - €9 996 - **£6 094** - FF65 568
Warming up by the Fire Oil/canvas (50x61cm
19x24in) New-York 2001

LEMAIRE Hector 1846-1880 [5]
$3 500 - €3 034 - **£2 138** - FF19 903
Susanah Bronze (H78.5cm H30in) New-York 1999

LEMAIRE Jean Lemaire Poussin 1598-1659 [11]
$107 854 - €113 251 - **£68 000** - FF742 879
Theseus Recovering his Father's Sword Oil/canvas (66.5x85cm 26x33in) London 2000

LEMAIRE Louis Marie 1824-1910 [16]
$2 937 - €2 744 - **£1 812** - FF18 000
Bouquet de fleurs dans un vase bleu Huile/toile
(55.5x47cm 21x18in) Melun 1999

$1 025 - €1 192 - **£720** - FF7 817
**Rooster and hens by a farm building/Poultry on
a country track** Oil/canvas (40.5x30.5cm 15x12in)
London 2001

LEMAIRE Madeleine, née Coll 1845-1928 [155]
$2 218 - €2 523 - **£1 539** - FF16 548
Ålandskap Oil/canvas (61x50cm 24x19in) Helsinki
2000

$1 278 - €1 067 - **£749** - FF7 000
**Nature morte aux faisans et au panier
d'oranges** Aquarelle/papier (78x56cm 30x22in) Tours
1998

LEMAIRE R. XIX-XX [2]
$2 800 - €2 854 - **£1 754** - FF18 722
Life is Good Pastel/paper (54x66.5cm 21x26in) New-York 2000

LEMAITRE Albert 1886-1975 [58]
$904 - €992 - **£584** - FF6 504
Vallée de l'Aveyron Huile/toile (92x73cm 36x28in)
Liège 2000

$723 - €793 - **£467** - FF5 203
Paysage à Ferrière Huile/panneau (30x44cm
11x17in) Liège 2000

LEMAITRE André 1909-1995 [90]
$2 072 - €1 906 - **£1 280** - FF12 500
L'entrée du port à Honfleur Huile/toile (65x100cm
25x39in) Honfleur 1998

$1 359 - €1 524 - **£942** - FF10 000
**Le temple d'Ankor à l'exposition coloniale de
Paris, Vincennes** Gouache (75x200cm 29x78in) Paris
2000

LEMAÎTRE Églantine Robert-H. 1852-1920 [4]
$2 000 - €2 100 - **£1 352** - FF13 773
«Au coup de fusil» Bronze (H26cm H10in) Detroit
MI 2001

LEMAÎTRE Gustave 1850-1920 [18]
$1 946 - €2 134 - **£1 321** - FF14 000
Cimetière et marabout en orient Huile/toile
(78x110cm 30x43in) Calais 2000

$977 - €945 - **£602** - FF6 200
Portrait de jeune fille Huile/panneau (22.5x14.5cm
8x5in) Paris 1999

LEMAÎTRE Ivanna XX [1]
$1 359 - €1 524 - **£942** - FF10 000
**Le temple d'Ankor à l'exposition coloniale de
Paris, Vincennes** Gouache (75x200cm 29x78in) Paris
2000

LEMAÎTRE Léon Jules 1850-1905 [36]
$8 041 - €9 452 - **£5 828** - FF65 000
Animation sur les quais de Rouen Huile/panneau
(19x38cm 7x14in) Rouen 2001

LEMAÎTRE Maurice 1929 [296]
$1 795 - €1 677 - **£1 107** - FF11 000
Rue à Meyssac Huile/toile (38x45cm 14x17in) Le
Touquet 1999

$1 626 - €1 829 - **£1 119** - FF12 000
Maraichers à St Omer Huile/toile (33x46cm
12x18in) La Varenne-Saint-Hilaire 2000

LEMAÎTRE Nathanaël 1831-1897 [25]
$1 174 - €1 324 - **£813** - FF8 682
Environs d'Artemare, Ain Öl/Leinwand (39.5x59cm
15x23in) Zürich 2000

$1 017 - €903 - **£608** - FF5 921
**Sommerliche Flusslandschaft mit fernen
Gebäuden** Öl/Leinwand (24x35cm 9x13in) Frankfurt
1998

LEMAN Robert 1799-1863 [16]
$569 - €528 - **£340** - FF3 462
Old Barns Watercolour/paper (23x33cm 9x13in)
Aylsham, Norfolk 2000

LEMAN Ulrich XX [9]
$4 585 - €5 133 - **£3 083** - FF33 539
Weg mit Olivenbäumen Öl/Leinwand (72x96cm
28x37in) Satow 2000

L

$1 238 - €1 329 - £828 - FF8 720
Ermita de Valldemosa (Mallorca) Aquarell/Papier
(49.5x65cm 19x25in) Bremen 2000

LEMARCHAND David 1674-1726 [2]
$10 860 - €12 341 - £7 500 - FF80 952
Susanna and the Elders Sculpture (H10cm H3in)
London 2000

LEMAY Olivier 1734-1797 [12]
$29 820 - €32 014 - £19 950 - FF210 000
L'embarquement des marchandises Huile/toile
(67x100cm 26x39in) Paris 2000
$1 180 - €1 372 - £829 - FF9 000
**Deux femmes guidant leur troupeau dans la
campagne italienne** Gouache/papier (43x58cm
16x22in) Paris 2001

LEMBERGER Georg c.1490-c.1540 [1]
$56 783 - €60 950 - £38 000 - FF399 820
**Portrait of a Man, Aged Thirty, in Fur-Trimmed
Robes, Holding a Hat** Oil/panel (41.5x27cm
16x10in) London 2000

LEMBESSIS Polychronis 1849-1913 [8]
$8 640 - €9 610 - £5 760 - FF63 040
Laundry by the River Oil/panel (24x39cm 9x15in)
Athens 2000

LEMBKE Johann Philipp 1631-1711 [8]
$672 - €767 - £469 - FF5 030
Die Verkündigung an die Hirten Radierung
(9.5x12cm 3x4in) Berlin 2001

LEMERCIER Alfred Léon XIX [5]
$153 - €180 - £108 - FF1 182
Le fandango Litografía a color (27x21cm 10x8in)
Madrid 2000

LEMEUNIER Alfred Léon XIX [16]
$3 126 - €3 201 - £1 963 - FF21 000
Scène de chasse aux canards Huile/panneau
(34x29cm 13x11in) Lille 2000
$383 - €427 - £260 - FF2 800
**Orphée aux enfers, projet de décor, le boudoir
de Pluton** Aquarelle (36.5x51cm 14x20in) Paris 2000

LEMEUNIER Basile 1852-1922 [26]
$3 066 - €3 049 - £1 902 - FF20 000
Femme au parc Huile/toile (75x54cm 29x21in)
Neuilly-sur-Seine 1999
$2 749 - €2 384 - £1 680 - FF15 636
Portrait of a Writer Oil/canvas (25x21cm 9x8in) New-
York 1999

LEMIEUX Annette 1957 [20]
$2 000 - €2 321 - £1 380 - FF15 222
See No Evil/Seein Evil Gelatin silver print
(117x139.5x5.5cm 46x54x2in) New-York 2000

LEMIEUX Jean-Paul 1904-1990 [128]
$161 925 - €148 915 - £112 700 - FF1 239 200
La fête Oil/canvas (89x176.5cm 35x69in) Toronto 2000
$18 584 - €17 901 - £11 539 - FF117 425
Le parc Oil/canvas (35x131cm 13x51in) Toronto 1999
$9 709 - €11 287 - £6 814 - FF74 040
Le nuage Huile/toile (27.5x35.5cm 10x13in) Montréal
2001
$669 - €643 - £416 - FF4 215
Near Everson's Place near Sumpra Beach
Encre/papier (34.5x41cm 13x16in) Montréal 1999
$167 - €180 - £112 - FF1 181
La dame de coeur Sérigraphie (71.5x28cm 28x11in)
Montréal 2000

LEMIRE Charles Gab. Sauvage 1741-1827 [17]
$2 769 - €2 973 - £1 852 - FF19 500
Amour mettant une corde à son arc Sculpture
(H40cm H15in) La Flèche 2000

LEMIRE Élisa Émilie Navarre 1807-1868 [5]
$28 875 - €29 097 - £18 000 - FF190 864
Bouquet of Bourbon Roses Watercolour
(62x54.5cm 24x21in) London 2000

LEMIRE Noël Le Mire 1724-1800 [3]
$2 000 - €1 982 - £1 213 - FF12 998
Le Général Washington Engraving (42x32cm
16x12in) New-York 2000

LEMIRE Sophie Brinisholtz 1785-? [1]
$16 000 - €17 719 - £10 851 - FF116 232
**Madame de la Vallière Giving Instructions in
Piety to her Daughter** Oil/canvas (53x47cm 20x18in)
New-York 2000

LEMMEN Georges 1865-1916 [473]
$10 246 - €11 798 - £6 994 - FF77 391
La baigneuse avec son chien Oil/panel
(44.5x53.5cm 17x21in) Amsterdam 2000
$8 840 - €9 915 - £6 160 - FF65 040
**Le petit Pierre au jardin en compagnie d'une
dame** Huile/carton (28x35cm 11x13in) Bruxelles 2001
$788 - €843 - £537 - FF5 528
Zittend naakt Sanguine/papier (43.5x43cm 17x16in)
Lokeren 2001
$150 - €124 - £88 - FF812
Nu, femme assise Lithographie couleurs (31x20cm
12x7in) Bruxelles 1998

LEMMENS Émile Théophile V. 1821-1867 [31]
$1 690 - €1 972 - £1 187 - FF12 935
Sommerliche Flusslandschaft Öl/Leinwand
(16.5x21.5cm 6x8in) Luzern 2000

LEMMERS Georges 1871-1944 [88]
$2 288 - €2 727 - £1 639 - FF17 886
Canal en Flandre Oil/canvas (60x75cm 23x29in)
Lokeren 2000
$379 - €421 - £253 - FF2 764
Vue d'un village breton animé Huile/toile
(44x33cm 17x12in) Bruxelles 2000
$268 - €297 - £187 - FF1 951
«Le Baptieu», Les Contamines, Hte Savoie
Technique mixte/papier (38x46cm 14x18in) Liège 2001

LEMMI Angiolo XIX-XX [2]
$13 000 - €11 235 - £7 715 - FF73 695
The Annunciation Oil/canvas (133x96cm 52x38in)
Houston TX 1998

LEMOINE Jacques Antoine M. 1751-1824 [21]
$6 798 - €6 600 - £4 200 - FF43 296
Les deux filles de l'auteur avec leur mère
Miniature (29.5x19cm 11x7in) London 1999
$22 000 - €23 495 - £14 990 - FF154 116
**Portrait of Elizabeth-Louise Vigée-Lebrun
Reading a Letter** Black chalk/paper (49.5x41.5cm
19x16in) New-York 2001

LEMOINE Marie-Victoire 1754-1820 [11]
$55 405 - €53 357 - £34 405 - FF350 000
Portrait de jeune fille à la gerbe de fleurs
Huile/toile (160.5x130cm 63x51in) Paris 1999
$9 936 - €10 976 - £6 890 - FF72 000
**Portrait de Raoul Cyresme au château de
Corbuon à Parigné l'Évêque** Huile/toile (116x89cm
45x35in) Orléans 2001

LEMON Arthur 1850-1912 **[10]**
$625 – €716 – £430 – FF4 695
Zwei Ochsen vor Bruschwerk und Bäumen
Öl/Leinwand (105x53cm 41x20in) München 2000

LEMONIER A. XIX-XX **[7]**
$629 – €686 – £412 – FF4 500
La mosquée Validé Aquarelle/papier (26x19.5cm 10x7in) Louviers 2000

LEMONNIER Robert 1883-? **[4]**
$2 168 – €1 982 – £1 327 – FF13 000
Rue du Diable, Alger Huile/panneau (21.5x16.5cm 8x6in) Paris 2000

LEMORDANT Jean-Julien 1878/82-1968 **[161]**
$3 484 – €3 964 – £2 436 – FF26 000
La criée Huile/carton (46x38cm 18x14in) Rennes 2000
$1 491 – €1 753 – £1 081 – FF11 500
Scène de marché en Bretagne Huile/panneau (33x41cm 12x16in) Nancy 2001
$832 – €838 – £518 – FF5 500
Paquebot à quai au port de Nantes
Aquarelle/papier (36x51cm 14x20in) Quimper 2000
$308 – €351 – £214 – FF2 300
«**Finistère**» Affiche (73x103cm 28x40in) Paris 2001

LEMOS de Pedro J. 1882-1954 **[16]**
$1 600 – €1 473 – £960 – FF9 659
The Path to the Sea Woodcut in colors (25x18cm 10x7in) Pasadena CA 1999

LEMOYNE Jean-Baptiste II 1704-1778 **[11]**
$53 352 – €59 455 – £36 309 – FF390 000
«**Andromède enchaînée**» Bronze (H63cm H24in) Nice 2000

LEMOYNE Serge 1941-1998 **[55]**
$1 801 – €2 012 – £1 256 – FF13 197
Triangulation noir, blanc, rouge Acrylique/toile (211x152.5cm 83x60in) Montréal 2001
$514 – €575 – £359 – FF3 500
Sans titre, série Next menu Acrylique/toile (66x81cm 25x31in) Montréal 2001

LEMPAD I. Gusti Nyoman 1865-1978 **[26]**
$3 516 – €3 543 – £2 191 – FF23 239
Diperbcat Oleh Watercolour (25x35cm 9x13in) Singapore 2000

LEMPICKA de Tamara 1898-1980 **[239]**
$168 000 – €145 131 – £112 000 – FF952 000
La belle Rafaella au fond lilas avec écharpe de paon Olio/tela (102x153cm 40x60in) Prato 1998
$50 000 – €48 020 – £30 825 – FF314 990
Still Life with pink Fabric and Lily Oil/canvas (65x54cm 25x21in) New-York 1999
$29 153 – €28 508 – £18 008 – FF187 000
Portrait de jeune fille Huile/toile (25.5x20.5cm 10x8in) Paris 1999
$8 000 – €8 587 – £5 353 – FF56 328
Portrait of Du Pierre de Moutaut Charcoal/paper (78.5x58.5cm 30x23in) New-York 2000
$4 117 – €3 811 – £2 550 – FF25 000
Jeune fille au turban orange Aquatinte (49x35cm 19x13in) Paris 1999

LENARDI Giovanni Battista 1656-1704 **[5]**
$22 414 – €24 060 – £15 000 – FF157 824
The Martyrdom of the Jewish Chief Scribe, Eleazar Oil/canvas (171x245cm 67x96in) London 2000
$963 – €957 – £600 – FF6 275
God the Father Chastizing a Cabalist Black chalk (27x21cm 10x8in) London 1999

LENBACH von Franz Seraph 1836-1904 **[190]**
$2 720 – €2 701 – £1 700 – FF17 715
Mountainous River Landscape Oil/canvas (92.5x136.5cm 36x53in) London 1999
$3 564 – €4 060 – £2 462 – FF26 632
Portrait einer Dame Öl/Karton (56.5x48.8cm 22x19in) Zürich 2000
$2 159 – €2 045 – £1 313 – FF13 415
Bildnis eines Mannes in Trachtenjacke Öl/Leinwand/Karton (18.1x15.9cm 7x6in) München 1999
$2 761 – €2 556 – £1 713 – FF16 769
Porträt Christine von Kalckreuth Pastell/Papier (46x35cm 18x13in) Stuttgart 1999

LENCI Marino 1874-1939 **[13]**
$575 – €596 – £345 – FF3 910
Volpino Pastelli/cartone (32.5x23cm 12x9in) Roma 1999

LENDVAI-DIRCKSEN Erna 1883-1962 **[27]**
$694 – €665 – £428 – FF4 360
Alter Kunsttischler von der Insel Falster Vintage gelatin silver print (38.1x28.7cm 14x11in) Köln 1999

LENEPVEU Jules Eugène 1819-1898 **[8]**
$4 398 – €5 107 – £3 132 – FF33 500
Portrait d'Italien Huile/toile (50x37cm 19x14in) Laval 2001

LENEPVEU V. XIX-XX **[1]**
$7 000 – €8 164 – £4 914 – FF53 552
«**Musée des horreurs**» Poster (50x65cm 19x25in) New-York 2000

LENFANT Albert XIX-XX **[2]**
$4 335 – €3 718 – £2 625 – FF24 390
Jeux d'enfants/Le cadeau Huile/panneau (17.5x13cm 6x5in) Bruxelles 1998

LENGELLE Paul 1908 **[25]**
$507 – €579 – £357 – FF3 800
Potez 62 Gouache/papier (60x62cm 23x24in) Paris 2001
$499 – €581 – £350 – FF3 809
«**Air Algérie, Caravelle**» Poster (97x62cm 38x24in) London 2001

LENGO MARTINEZ Horacio 1840-1890 **[14]**
$1 823 – €2 169 – £1 300 – FF14 228
Elle a de la chance, Dandie Dinmont with a Bouquet of Flowers Oil/canvas (73x54cm 28x21in) Bath 2000
$1 550 – €1 502 – £950 – FF9 850
La casa de antigüedades Oleo/tabla (18x10cm 7x3in) Madrid 1999

LENHARD Josef XX **[2]**
$800 – €945 – £567 – FF6 200
Untitled Watercolour/paper (40x28cm 16x11in) Provincetown MA 2000

LENHART Franz 1898-1992 **[36]**
$1 200 – €1 199 – £733 – FF7 867
«**Cortina**» Poster (99x60cm 39x24in) New-York 2000

LENICA Alfred 1899-1977 **[40]**
$2 202 – €2 220 – £1 373 – FF14 560
Mère avec son enfant en deuil Oil/canvas (89x116cm 35x45in) Warszawa 2000
$511 – €442 – £309 – FF2 900
Paysage fantastique Gouache/papier (63x49cm 24x19in) Saint-Dié 1998

LENICA Jan 1929 [7]

📖 $256 - €296 - £180 - FF1 939
«Repulsion» Poster (76x101.5cm 29x39in) London 2000

LENK Franz 1898-1968 [117]

🖼 $13 439 - €13 294 - £8 379 - FF87 201
Weiden mit Krähe Tempera (50.2x50.6cm 19x19in) Berlin 1999

🖼 $9 738 - €10 226 - £6 140 - FF67 078
Abendlandschaft Oberschwaben Tempera (40x31cm 15x12in) Stuttgart 2000

✎ $1 477 - €1 687 - £1 041 - FF11 067
Blumenstilleben Aquarell/Papier (60x48cm 23x18in) Stuttgart 2001

📖 $309 - €307 - £193 - FF2 012
Fachwerkhäuser mit Strommasten Woodcut (9.7x9.7cm 3x3in) München 1999

LENK Kaspar Thomas 1933 [43]

🖼 $1 213 - €1 227 - £740 - FF8 049
Modell II Metal (28x25x48cm 11x9x18in) Stuttgart 2000

📖 $65 - €71 - £42 - FF469
Ohne Titel Serigraph (60x60cm 23x23in) Lindau 2000

LENKEWICZ Robert O. 1941 [86]

🖼 $2 566 - €2 586 - £1 600 - FF16 965
The Grep Family Oil/canvas (152x152cm 59x59in) London 2000

🖼 $2 514 - €2 415 - £1 550 - FF15 839
Myriam Acrylic/canvas (47x47cm 18x18in) London 1999

🖼 $1 867 - €2 088 - £1 300 - FF13 696
Study of Anna Navs, St.Anthony Theme, Project 182 Oil/board (39.5x39.5cm 15x15in) Penzance, Cornwall 2001

🖼 $533 - €491 - £320 - FF3 218
Study of Ruti Watercolour/paper (39x28cm 15x11in) London 1999

LENNON John 1940-1980 [72]

✎ $2 800 - €2 626 - £1 730 - FF17 226
Peace, Let Your Hair Grow, Love Drawing (43x55cm 17x22in) New-York 1999

📖 $1 069 - €999 - £660 - FF6 555
I Do Lithograph (49x71cm 19x28in) Aylsham, Norfolk 1999

LENNOX-WRIGHT Charles 1876-? [3]

🖼 $5 000 - €5 831 - £3 510 - FF38 252
Sweet Dreams, Portrait of a Setter Oil/canvas (35.5x48.5cm 13x19in) Boston MA 2000

LENOBLE Émile 1875-1940 [5]

🖼 $6 562 - €5 793 - £4 035 - FF38 000
Vase à corps ovoïde Grès (H29.5cm H11in) Paris 2000

LENOIR A. XIX [7]

🖼 $584 - €686 - £412 - FF4 500
Paysage d'hiver animé Huile/panneau (12.5x15cm 4x5in) Paris 2000

LENOIR Charles Amable 1861-1940 [35]

🖼 $26 000 - €22 432 - £15 685 - FF147 141
The Seamstress Oil/canvas (147.5x97cm 58x38in) New-York 1998

🖼 $32 500 - €29 912 - £19 506 - FF196 212
Meditation Oil/canvas (114x73cm 45x29in) Chicago IL 1999

🖼 $3 685 - €3 125 - £2 187 - FF20 500
La Victoire Huile/toile (44.5x31.5cm 17x12in) Angers 1998

LENOIR Maurice 1872-1931 [14]

🖼 $4 689 - €5 399 - £3 200 - FF35 414
A Parisian Boulevard Oil/board (39.5x61.5cm 15x24in) London 2000

🖼 $1 646 - €1 815 - £1 075 - FF11 906
Parijse boulevard met wandelaars Oil/board (31x36cm 12x14in) Den Haag 2000

LENOIR Paul-Marie 1843-1881 [7]

🖼 $35 000 - €39 177 - £24 409 - FF256 987
Le roi Cambyse au siège de Peluse Oil/canvas (71x92cm 27x36in) New-York 2001

LENOIR Pierre Charles 1879-? [7]

🖼 $10 050 - €11 434 - £7 027 - FF75 000
Sans titre Bronze (H60.5cm H23in) Paris 2000

LENOIR Simon Bernard 1729-1791 [10]

✎ $12 749 - €14 483 - £8 949 - FF95 000
Portrait d'homme Pastel/papier (62x53cm 24x20in) Paris 2001

LENORDEZ Pierre 1815-1892 [109]

🖼 $4 079 - €3 735 - £2 486 - FF24 500
L'étalon Bronze (H31cm H12in) Paris 1999

LENS Andries Cornelis 1739-1822 [23]

🖼 $9 998 - €11 662 - £7 145 - FF76 500
Vénus puissant Cupidon Huile/toile (111x137cm 43x53in) Versailles 2000

🖼 $2 835 - €3 176 - £1 970 - FF20 836
Mercury and Herse Oil/canvas (82.5x104cm 32x40in) Amsterdam 2001

LENS Bernard II, Snr. 1659-1725 [6]

✎ $5 259 - €4 573 - £3 171 - FF30 000
Sainte Hélène rêvant à la vraie croix, d'après Véronèse Gouache (35x24.5cm 13x9in) Paris 1998

LENSON Michael 1903-1971 [5]

🖼 $7 000 - €7 961 - £4 854 - FF52 221
See Sally Oil/canvas (76x91cm 30x36in) Chicago IL 2000

LENTREIN Jules 1875-1943 [12]

🖼 $1 199 - €1 363 - £825 - FF8 943
Enfant jouant au bord de l'eau Huile/toile (25x35cm 9x13in) Bruxelles 2000

LENTULOV Aristarkh Vasilievic 1882-1943 [21]

✎ $3 500 - €3 112 - £2 140 - FF20 416
The Church, Novodevichy Monastery Watercolour/paper (29x23cm 11x9in) New-York 1999

LENTZ Stanislas 1863-1920 [12]

🖼 $20 100 - €18 561 - £12 519 - FF121 750
Three persons drinking wine Oil/canvas (78x112cm 30x44in) Warszawa 1999

LENZ Maximilian, Max 1860-1948 [35]

🖼 $7 730 - €7 267 - £4 680 - FF47 670
Blick in den Blumengarten Öl/Leinwand (119x119cm 46x46in) Wien 1999

🖼 $2 459 - €2 812 - £1 688 - FF18 446
Prachtvolles Stilleben mit Pfauenfedern, Armbrust, Foliant, Figurine Öl/Leinwand (99x73cm 38x28in) Lindau 2000

LEON de XIX [1]

🖼 $19 000 - €22 371 - £13 351 - FF146 744
Puerto de la Guaira Watercolour/paper (41x79cm 16x31in) New-York 2000

LÉON de Gerónimo XIX-XX [1]

🖼 $6 000 - €5 232 - £3 627 - FF34 318
San Gerónimo Doctor/San Rafael Arcángel Oil/panel (35.5x25.5cm 13x10in) New-York 1998

LÉON Maurits 1838-1865 [3]
$19 000 - €21 558 - £13 298 - FF141 411
Preparation for the Priestly Blessing Oil/wood (20x16cm 7x6in) Tel Aviv 2001

LÉON Y ESCOSURA de Ignacio 1834-1901 [52]
$13 208 - €11 561 - £8 000 - FF75 833
The Moorish Gate Oil/canvas (92x61cm 36x24in) London 1998
$3 820 - €3 630 - £2 324 - FF23 812
Elegant geklede heer met een duif bij het geopend venster Oil/panel (19.5x15cm 7x5in) Rotterdam 1999
$4 160 - €4 805 - £2 960 - FF31 520
Interior Acuarela/papel (31x25cm 12x9in) Madrid 2001

LÉONARD Agathon v.Weydeveldt 1841-1923 [61]
$5 179 - €4 876 - £3 200 - FF31 982
Naked Nymph Standing Holding Aloft of Tazza Alabaster (H34cm H13in) London 1999

LEONARD Charly 1894-1953 [37]
$145 - €161 - £102 - FF1 056
Maison de pêcheurs Huile/panneau (27x35cm 10x13in) Bruxelles 2001

LEONARD John Henry 1834-1904 [12]
$384 - €349 - £240 - FF2 288
Sheep on a Country Lane Watercolour (24.5x33.5cm 9x13in) London 1999

LEONARD Patrick 1918 [35]
$3 424 - €3 682 - £2 333 - FF24 154
Circus Ladies Oil/board (65x57cm 25x22in) Dublin 2001
$1 097 - €1 016 - £679 - FF6 663
A Garden in Cyprus Oil/board (34x44cm 13x17in) Dublin 1999

LEONARD Robert 1879-? [3]
$1 600 - €1 539 - £987 - FF10 093
«Luna Ballhaus» Poster (70.5x94.5cm 27x37in) New-York 1999

LEONARD Zoe 1961 [11]
$3 200 - €3 511 - £2 125 - FF23 029
Trophies, Museo di Storia Naturale, Venice Gelatin silver print (75.5x108.5cm 29x42in) New-York 2000

LEONARDI Achille XIX [9]
$2 500 - €2 974 - £1 729 - FF19 509
Child's Bed Time Oil/canvas (97x74cm 38x29in) Portland OR 2000

LEONARDI Vincenzo c.1600-c.1660 [2]
$2 407 - €2 391 - £1 500 - FF15 687
Serinus serinus, Serin/Carduelis Chloris, Greenfinch Black chalk (32.5x8.5cm 12x3in) London 1999

LEONARDO GRAZZI Leonardo da Pistoia 1505-? [1]
$18 000 - €15 550 - £9 000 - FF102 000
Sacra Famiglia Olio/tavola (123x88cm 48x34in) Milano 1999

LEONARDUS Giacomo c.1723-1775 [1]
$2 278 - €2 218 - £1 400 - FF14 548
The masked Ball Etching (36x58cm 14x22in) London 1999

LEONCILLO Leoncillo Leonardi 1915-1968 [39]
$6 800 - €6 810 - £4 250 - FF44 605
Elemento per camino Céramique (148x30x25cm 58x11x9in) Milano 2001

$9 500 - €9 848 - £5 700 - FF64 600
Senza titolo Grès (H64cm H25in) Prato 2000
$1 560 - €1 348 - £1 040 - FF8 840
Corpo dolente Gouache/carta (70x50cm 27x19in) Prato 1998

LEONE di Andrea 1596/1610-1685 [17]
$27 600 - €23 843 - £13 800 - FF156 400
Accampamento militare/Battaglia tra cavalieri turchi e cristiani Olio/tela (63x76cm 24x29in) Roma 1999

LEONE John 1929 [10]
$2 970 - €3 188 - £1 987 - FF20 911
Throw'd A Shoe Oil/canvas (76x101cm 30x40in) Houston TX 2000

LEONE Romolo 1883-1958 [31]
$1 920 - €1 659 - £1 280 - FF10 880
Ballo in maschera Olio/tela (44.5x55cm 17x21in) Milano 1998
$1 040 - €1 348 - £780 - FF8 840
Veduta di casolare di campagna Olio/tavola (39x29cm 15x11in) Firenze 2000

LEONEL XIX [1]
$3 500 - €3 628 - £2 100 - FF23 800
Mercato di terraglie Olio/tavola (24x35.5cm 9x13in) Venezia 2000

LEONHARD Johannes 1858-1913 [6]
$3 321 - €3 659 - £2 215 - FF24 000
A la terrasse du café Aquarelle (48x38cm 18x14in) Deauville 2000

LEONHARDI Eduard Emil August 1826-1905 [9]
$922 - €1 022 - £638 - FF6 707
«Alte Mühle in Loschwitzgrund bei Dresden» Aquarell/Papier (47x28cm 18x11in) Kempten 2001

LEONI Ippolito 1616-1694 [3]
$5 548 - €5 183 - £3 423 - FF34 000
Portrait de femme Crayons couleurs (20.5x13.5cm 8x5in) Paris 1999

LEONI Ottavio Maria 1578-1630 [32]
$4 878 - €5 488 - £3 358 - FF36 000
Portrait du marquis Giovanni Paolo Pezoli Pierre noire (21x14.5cm 8x5in) Paris 2000

LÉONNEC Georges 1881-1940 [13]
$211 - €229 - £146 - FF1 500
«Cigarettes Naja, tabac d'Orient» Affiche (59.5x39.5cm 23x15in) Paris 2001

LEONORI R.G.L. XIX [2]
$500 - €5 429 - £3 344 - FF35 612
Seascape - Bull's Creek, New Jersey Oil/canvas (54.5x73cm 21x28in) New-York 2000

LEOPOLD Curt 1860-1946 [11]
$775 - €716 - £476 - FF4 695
Bauern auf dem Feld Öl/Leinwand (19x47cm 7x18in) München 1999

LEOPOLSKI Wilhelm 1830-1892 [4]
$5 577 - €6 279 - £3 914 - FF41 186
Repos de laboureur Huile/toile (40x50cm 15x19in) Warszawa 2001

LEPAGE Céline 1882-1928 [14]
$40 114 - €47 259 - £27 745 - FF310 000
Chevaux Métal (H114cm H44in) Paris 2000
$2 614 - €2 897 - £1 753 - FF19 000
Tête de femme aux chevaux tressés Terracotta (44x20cm 17x7in) Paris 2000

L

LEPAPE Georges 1887-1971 **[123]**

- $17 136 - €19 209 - **£11 982** - FF126 000
  Arlequin Huile/isorel (110x47.5cm 43x18in) Paris 2001
- $287 - €320 - **£200** - FF2 100
  Claudine Crayon/papier (14x10cm 5x3in) Paris 2001
- $382 - €434 - **£265** - FF2 850
  Der Handspiegel Lithographie (24.5x17.5cm 9x6in) Berlin 2000

LÉPAULLE François Gabriel G. 1804-1886 **[13]**

- $3 175 - €3 735 - **£2 300** - FF24 500
  Chien Huile/toile (65x93cm 25x36in) Angoulême 2001

LEPAUTRE Jean Le Paultre 1618-1682 **[35]**

- $102 - €120 - **£70** - FF788
  Lucha de animales y putti Grabado (16x23.5cm 6x9in) Madrid 2000

LEPAUTRE Pierre 1660-1744 **[5]**

- $6 541 - €6 311 - **£4 106** - FF41 400
  Enée portant Anchise Bronze (H62cm H24in) Monte-Carlo 1999
- $2 388 - €2 324 - **£1 470** - FF15 244
  Plan général de la ville et du château de Versailles Etching (95x128cm 37x50in) Stockholm 1999

LEPCKE Ferdinand 1866-1909 **[21]**

- $1 392 - €1 361 - **£859** - FF8 929
  Artemis Bronze (H64cm H25in) Amsterdam 1999

LEPELTIER Robert 1913-1996 **[29]**

- $3 294 - €3 062 - **£2 000** - FF20 086
  La modiste Oil/canvas (61x50cm 24x19in) London 1998

LEPERE Auguste Louis 1849-1918 **[283]**

- $3 205 - €3 811 - **£2 285** - FF25 000
  Montmartre, la rue de l'abreuvoir Huile/toile (38x60cm 14x23in) Grenoble 2000
- $3 530 - €3 811 - **£2 440** - FF25 000
  Tournant de chemin, paysage d'automne Huile/panneau (32x41cm 12x16in) Paris 2001
- $635 - €686 - **£439** - FF4 500
  Étude: Le chemin du Moulin, Marais de Saint-Jean, pleine lune Fusain (27x40cm 10x15in) Paris 2001
- $181 - €213 - **£127** - FF1 400
  Les pêcheurs en barque Gravure bois (34x25cm 13x9in) Brest 2000

LEPERE Jean-Baptiste 1761-1844 **[2]**

- $10 000 - €11 738 - **£6 087** - FF65 451
  Procession in Honor of Horus in the Temple at Philae Watercolour/paper (52x80cm 20x31in) New-York 2000

LEPERLIER Antoine 1953 **[9]**

- $4 179 - €4 878 - **£2 956** - FF32 000
  Still Life, Still alive Sculpture verre (65x55x13.5cm 25x21x5in) Paris 2001

LEPERLIER Étienne XX **[4]**

- $2 130 - €2 287 - **£1 425** - FF15 000
  La clé des champs Sculpture verre (31x27x12cm 12x10x4in) Paris 2000

LEPIC Ludovic Napoléon 1839-1889 **[41]**

- $3 502 - €3 354 - **£2 158** - FF22 000
  Plage de Berck et son marégraphe Huile/toile/panneau (129x49cm 50x19in) Calais 1999
- $2 824 - €2 439 - **£1 705** - FF16 000
  Le panier de fleurs Pastel/papier (78x72cm 30x28in) Paris 1998

LÉPICIÉ François Bernard 1698-1755 **[7]**

- $314 - €305 - **£198** - FF2 000
  Le déjeuner, d'après Boucher Gravure (38x27cm 14x10in) Paris 1999

LÉPICIÉ Nicolas Bernard 1735-1784 **[55]**

- $7 078 - €6 860 - **£4 383** - FF45 000
  La dame au bonnet blanc Huile/panneau (10.5x8.5cm 4x3in) Paris 1999
- $3 658 - €3 201 - **£2 215** - FF21 000
  Étude de jeune fille debout, préparatoire pour «La réponse désirée» Pierre noire (44x25.5cm 17x10in) Paris 1998

LEPIÉ Ferdinand 1824-1883 **[66]**

- $2 019 - €2 180 - **£1 395** - FF14 301
  Blick auf Gmunden Öl/Leinwand (56x70cm 22x27in) Wien 2001

LEPINARD Paul XX **[14]**

- $1 854 - €2 161 - **£1 283** - FF14 177
  Herbsttag am Genfersee Öl/Leinwand (50x65cm 19x25in) Bern 2000

LÉPINE Joseph 1867-1943 **[45]**

- $1 619 - €1 738 - **£1 083** - FF11 403
  Près de Cavalaire, Var Öl/Karton (58x70.5cm 22x27in) Hamburg 2000
- $917 - €2 058 - **£1 282** - FF13 500
  Paysage au pont Huile/carton (35x41cm 13x16in) Toulouse 2000

LÉPINE Stanislas 1835-1892 **[172]**

- $200 000 - €170 715 - **£119 600** - FF1 119 820
  La Marne à Chennevières Oil/canvas (180.5x234cm 71x92in) New-York 1998
- $34 050 - €38 112 - **£23 100** - FF250 000
  La Seine à Paris Huile/toile (52x84cm 20x33in) Paris 2000
- $12 607 - €12 233 - **£8 000** - FF80 246
  Cour de ferme en Normandie Oil/canvas (40x36cm 15x14in) London 1999

LEPPIEN Jean 1910-1991 **[101]**

- $2 233 - €1 906 - **£1 347** - FF12 500
  Composition Huile/toile (70x40cm 27x15in) Saint-Germain-en-Laye 1998
- $1 164 - €994 - **£694** - FF6 517
  Composition Öl/Karton (50x21cm 19x8in) Zürich 1998
- $1 027 - €1 074 - **£674** - FF7 043
  Komposition IX Pastell/Karton (41x28.5cm 16x11in) München 2000
- $241 - €274 - **£170** - FF1 800
  Sans titre Sérigraphie (56x45cm 22x17in) Paris 2001

LEPRI Stanislas 1905-1980 **[65]**

- $850 - €881 - **£510** - FF5 780
  Jeux d'enfants Olio/tela (73x60cm 28x23in) Torino 1999
- $1 300 - €1 348 - **£780** - FF8 840
  Il figliol prodigo Olio/tela (45.5x26.5cm 17x10in) Torino 1999
- $412 - €389 - **£260** - FF2 553
  Study of Two Dancers Wash (40x32cm 15x12in) London 1999

LEPRIN Marcel 1891-1933 **[247]**

- $9 220 - €7 622 - **£5 410** - FF50 000
  Nature morte au bouquet de roses, soupière et tapis Huile/toile (64.5x81cm 25x31in) Paris 1998
- $3 110 - €3 659 - **£2 229** - FF24 000
  Un Farol Huile/carton (27x35cm 10x13in) Paris 2001

L

📖 **$5 966** - €5 793 - **£3 686** - FF38 000
Le vieux port, Notre-Dame de la Garde, vus de l'Hôtel Dieu à Marseille Technique mixte/papier (29x43cm 11x16in) Melun 1999

LEPRINCE Jean-Baptiste 1734-1781 **[109]**
🗣 **$22 000** - €20 698 - **£13 728** - FF135 770
A Halt at an Inn Oil/canvas (43x58cm 16x22in) New-York 1999
🗣 **$4 970** - €5 336 - **£3 325** - FF35 000
L'esclave Huile/toile (41x32.5cm 16x12in) Paris 2000
📖 **$3 856** - €3 634 - **£2 325** - FF22 500
Bord de rivière Encre (19x26.5cm 7x10in) Paris 1998
📺 **$187** - €183 - **£118** - FF1 200
O fortunatos nimium Gravure (35x49cm 13x19in) Paris 1999

LEPRINCE Robert Léopold 1800-1847 **[15]**
🗣 **$1 161** - €1 296 - **£781** - FF8 500
Paysanne assise Huile/toile (26x20cm 10x7in) Versailles 2000

LEPRINCE Xavier 1799-1826 **[47]**
🗣 **$24 000** - €28 207 - **£16 639** - FF185 025
View of the Coast at Le Havre by La Hève Oil/canvas (46x54cm 18x21in) New-York 2000
🗣 **$4 784** - €5 336 - **£3 216** - FF35 000
Le repos des moissonneurs Huile/toile (27x21cm 10x8in) Versailles 2000
📺 **$1 775** - €1 662 - **£1 100** - FF10 900
Seated Young Man Turned to the Right Pencil/paper (10x9cm 3x3in) London 1999

LEQUESNE Eugène Louis 1815-1887 **[30]**
🗣 **$4 590** - €5 095 - **£3 200** - FF33 423
The huntress Oil/canvas (40.5x27cm 15x10in) London 2001
🏺 **$884** - €991 - **£600** - FF6 500
La faune dansant Bronze (H15cm H5in) Paris 2000

LEQUESNE Fernand 1856-? **[21]**
📺 **$1 179** - €1 306 - **£809** - FF8 569
«Cie.Gle.Transatlantique Havre-New York» Poster (99x68cm 38x26in) London 2000

LERAY Prudent Louis 1820-1879 **[11]**
🗣 **$17 000** - €14 683 - **£10 247** - FF96 316
Le passage difficile Oil/canvas (81.5x65cm 32x25in) New-York 1998

LERBERGHE van Karel 1899-1953 **[41]**
🗣 **$403** - €372 - **£243** - FF2 439
Vue à Sint Martens Latem au printemps Huile/toile (65x80cm 25x31in) Antwerpen 1999

LERCH Franz 1895-1977 **[23]**
📖 **$934** - €1 090 - **£660** - FF7 150
Badeszene Pencil (35.5x42.5cm 13x16in) Salzburg 2000

LERCHE Vincent Stoltenberg 1837-1892 **[16]**
🗣 **$5 865** - €5 611 - **£3 700** - FF40 130
To munker i kirkeinteriör Oil/canvas (38x49cm 14x19in) Oslo 2000

LERFELDT Hans Henrik 1946-1990 **[116]**
🗣 **$1 164** - €1 208 - **£738** - FF7 925
En ung pige med croqetkölle Oil/canvas (95x81cm 37x31in) Viby J, Arhus 2000
🗣 **$1 337** - €1 212 - **£834** - FF7 948
Magisk figur og kriger Oil/canvas (35x27cm 13x10in) Köbenhavn 1999
📖 **$478** - €536 - **£334** - FF3 518
Endelös nat Collage (23x18cm 9x7in) Köbenhavn 2001

📺 **$116** - €108 - **£72** - FF706
En lille pige Color lithograph (50x40cm 19x15in) Viby-J, Arhus 1999

LERGAARD Niels 1893-1982 **[64]**
🗣 **$6 360** - €5 377 - **£3 804** - FF35 272
Gudhjem i forårslys Oil/canvas (92x105cm 36x41in) Köbenhavn 1998

LERMITTE Jean-Pierre 1920-1977 **[37]**
📖 **$6 742** - €7 860 - **£4 668** - FF51 555
A la Brévine Pastel (33x54cm 12x21in) Bern 2000
📺 **$236** - €275 - **£163** - FF1 806
Abstrahierter Landschaft Farblithographie (23.5x61cm 9x24in) Bern 2000

LERMONTOFF E. XIX **[4]**
🗣 **$6 394** - €6 055 - **£3 978** - FF39 721
Parklandskab med spadserende en vinterdag Oil/canvas (78x102cm 30x40in) Köbenhavn 1999

LEROLLE Henri 1848-1929 **[12]**
🗣 **$1 036** - €1 220 - **£743** - FF8 000
Paysanne partant à la pêche Huile/toile (46.5x61cm 18x24in) Paris 2001

LEROUX André Paul 1870-? **[7]**
🗣 **$5 251** - €6 033 - **£3 636** - FF39 577
Spansk flamencodanserinde foran spejlet Oil/canvas (80x65cm 31x25in) Köbenhavn 2000

LEROUX Auguste 1871-1954 **[193]**
🗣 **$9 404** - €10 367 - **£6 256** - FF68 000
La ballerine Huile/toile (98x139cm 38x54in) Biarritz 2000
🗣 **$1 255** - €1 403 - **£851** - FF9 200
Portrait de Madeleine Leroux à la mandoline Huile/toile (80.5x81cm 31x31in) Nogent-sur-Marne 2000
🗣 **$544** - €610 - **£378** - FF4 000
Madame Leroux dans une barque sur le lac d'Annecy Huile/panneau (27x35.5cm 10x13in) Paris 2001
📖 **$249** - €290 - **£175** - FF1 900
Maternité Fusain/papier (26x20cm 10x7in) Coulommiers 2001
📺 **$190** - €178 - **£117** - FF1 165
«3e Emprunt de la Défense Nationale» Poster (114x78cm 45x31in) Philadelphia PA 1999

LEROUX Gaston Veuvenot 1854-1942 **[56]**
🏺 **$10 000** - €11 513 - **£6 842** - FF75 520
Aida Bronze (H149cm H58in) New-York 2000
🏺 **$2 799** - €2 820 - **£1 744** - FF18 500
Rebecca Bronze (H74cm H29in) Brest 2000

LEROUX Georges Paul 1877-1957 **[82]**
🗣 **$5 680** - €6 098 - **£3 800** - FF40 000
Les ruines Huile/toile (54x81cm 21x31in) Paris 2000
📺 **$342** - €332 - **£211** - FF2 180
«La grande lunette de 1900, Paris» Poster (126x89.4cm 49x35in) München 1999

LEROUX Louis Eugène 1833-1905 **[16]**
🗣 **$1 567** - €1 372 - **£949** - FF9 000
L'amateur d'art Huile/toile (55x37.5cm 21x14in) Paris 1998
🗣 **$7 889** - €8 758 - **£5 500** - FF57 451
The Flower Seller Oil/panel (45x28cm 17x11in) London 2001

LEROUX-REVAULT Laura XIX **[1]**
🗣 **$6 500** - €7 253 - **£4 521** - FF47 579
The Spinner Oil/canvas (120.5x90cm 47x35in) New-York 2001

LEROY DE LIANCOURT François 1741/42-1835 [7]

🖎 **$2 496** - €2 515 - **£1 555** - FF16 500
Paysages classiques Gouache/papier (15.5x20.5cm 6x8in) Paris 2000

LEROY Eugène 1910-2000 [164]

⌒ **$19 712** - €21 343 - **£13 496** - FF140 000
«Pour un corps de femme n°1» Huile/toile (165x130cm 64x51in) Paris 2001

⌒ **$9 000** - €9 915 - **£5 880** - FF65 040
Autoportrait Huile/toile (73x60cm 28x23in) Bruxelles 2000

⌒ **$1 325** - €1 239 - **£820** - FF8 130
Figuur Fusain/papier (62x46cm 24x18in) Lokeren 1999

LEROY Jean-François XX [18]

🖎 **$961** - €1 143 - **£685** - FF7 500
Saut d'obstacle Bronze (12.5x15cm 4x5in) Paris 2000

LEROY Patrick 1948 [199]

⌒ **$786** - €793 - **£490** - FF5 200
Le village Huile/panneau (63x49cm 24x19in) Calais 2000

LEROY Paul Alexandre Alfr. 1860-1942 [41]

⌒ **$25 000** - €29 399 - **£17 925** - FF192 847
Les filles d'Atlas Oil/canvas (211x261.5cm 83x102in) New-York 2001

⌒ **$1 550** - €1 451 - **£960** - FF9 517
Arab Market Huile/canvas (40x50cm 16x20in) Detroit MI 1999

⌒ **$1 800** - €2 098 - **£1 261** - FF13 765
Bather on Rocks, Morocco Oil/canvas (53x25cm 21x10in) Cleveland OH 2000

LEROY-SAINT-AUBER Charles 1856-c.1907 [3]

⌒ **$7 000** - €8 232 - **£5 019** - FF53 997
Afternoon Tea Oil/canvas (53.5x88.5cm 21x34in) New-York 2001

LERPINIERE Daniel c.1745-1785 [4]

▥ **$3 461** - €3 824 - **£2 400** - FF25 087
View in the Island of Jamaica, after George Robertson Engraving (35.5x51.5cm 13x20in) London 2001

LERSKI Helmar Schmuklerski 1871-1956 [10]

📷 **$1 285** - €1 431 - **£840** - FF9 390
Handstudie mit Hammer Vintage gelatin silver print (16.8x18cm 6x7in) Köln 2000

LERSY Roger 1920 [99]

⌒ **$278** - €290 - **£175** - FF1 900
Table dressée Huile/toile (50x100cm 19x39in) Le Havre 2000

LERTCHAIPRASERT Kamin 1964 [1]

⌒ **$5 844** - €6.118 - **£3 671** - FF40 129
A.B.C Oil/canvas (30.5x30.5cm 12x12in) Singapore 2000

LESAGE Augustin 1876-1954 [18]

⌒ **$14 915** - €14 483 - **£9 215** - FF95 000
Sans titre Huile/toile (127x95cm 50x37in) Paris 1999

⌒ **$8 844** - €9 147 - **£5 568** - FF60 000
Composition Huile/toile (75x60cm 29x23in) Paris 2000

LESBROS Alfred 1873-1940 [65]

⌒ **$801** - €915 - **£563** - FF6 000
Paysage au cygne Huile/panneau (38x53cm 14x20in) Marseille 2001

LESCURE Jean 1934 [75]

⌒ **$328** - €381 - **£233** - FF2 500
Les poules Huile/toile (27x35cm 10x13in) Coutances 2001

LESIEUR Pierre 1922 [93]

⌒ **$1 156** - €1 314 - **£793** - FF8 622
Une plage animée Öl/Leinwand (38x46cm 14x18in) Zürich 2000

⌒ **$1 052** - €1 060 - **£656** - FF9 534
Une plage Öl/Leinwand (31x40cm 12x15in) Zürich 2000

🖎 **$357** - €381 - **£226** - FF2 500
Paysage Pastel/papier (25x24.5cm 9x9in) Paris 2000

LESIRE Paul, Paulus 1611-1656 [6]

⌒ **$11 673** - €11 474 - **£7 500** - FF75 267
Portrait of a Gentleman, wearing a black Jacket with a white Ruff Oil/panel (68.5x55cm 26x21in) London 1999

LESKOSCHEK von Axel 1889-1976 [35]

⌒ **$1 280** - €1 453 - **£898** - FF9 534
Das Kalb auf der Fazenda Oil/panel (46x65cm 18x25in) Wien 2001

▥ **$1 236** - €1 453 - **£886** - FF9 534
Wäscherin aus Rio Pochoir (65.5x44.5cm 25x17in) Wien 2001

LESLIE Alfred 1927 [19]

🖎 **$1 800** - €1 742 - **£1 110** - FF11 424
Untitled Gouache (46x61cm 18x24in) New-York 1999

LESLIE Charles c.1835-1890 [150]

⌒ **$791** - €915 - **£560** - FF6 004
The Rainbow Oil/canvas (45.5x81.5cm 17x32in) Glasgow 2000

⌒ **$563** - €531 - **£341** - FF3 480
Highland Loch Scenes Oil/board (14x19cm 5x7in) Cape Town 1999

LESLIE Charles Robert 1794-1859 [27]

⌒ **$7 242** - €8 403 - **£5 000** - FF55 120
Sancho Panza and the Duchess Oil/canvas (61x76.5cm 24x30in) London 2000

⌒ **$5 128** - €5 962 - **£3 600** - FF39 111
Preparing for the Ball Oil/board (25.5x20.5cm 10x8in) London 2001

LESLIE DUNLOP George 1835-1921 [29]

⌒ **$480 000** - €414 122 - **£289 584** - FF2 716 464
The Garland Oil/canvas (110x110cm 43x43in) New-York 1998

⌒ **$11 119** - €11 024 - **£6 953** - FF72 315
Kökkenpigen Oil/canvas (61x50cm 24x19in) Köbenhavn 1999

⌒ **$8 652** - €9 561 - **£6 000** - FF62 718
Ten Minutes to decide Oil/canvas (27x47cm 10x18in) London 2001

LESLIE Peter 1877-? [8]

⌒ **$3 984** - €4 629 - **£2 800** - FF30 363
Elegant Interior Oil/canvas (61x51cm 24x20in) London 2001

LESOURD DE BEAUREGARD Ange Louis Guillaume 1800-c.1875 [18]

⌒ **$7 000** - €7 849 - **£4 753** - FF51 483
Still Life of Fruit, Cheese, Fish and Wine Oil/canvas (45x54cm 17x21in) New-York 2000

⌒ **$37 500** - €44 168 - **£25 935** - FF289 721
Bouquet of Primroses and Other Flowers Oil/canvas (32.5x24cm 12x9in) New-York 2000

LESPINASSE de Louis-Nicolas 1734-1803 **[10]**
- $12 089 - €11 192 - £7 500 - FF73 417
  Paris, Rive droite of the River Seine, Ile St.Louis, La Salpetriere Oil/canvas (38x46cm 14x18in) London 1999
- $39 742 - €47 259 - £28 334 - FF310 000
  Vues de Saint-Petersbourg Aquarelle (21.5x65.5cm 8x25in) Paris 2000

LESREL Adolphe Alexandre 1839-1929 **[92]**
- $56 000 - €49 574 - £34 238 - FF325 186
  The Connoisseurs Oil/panel (48.5x58.5cm 19x23in) New-York 1999
- $7 033 - €8 098 - £4 800 - FF53 121
  Refreshments Oil/panel (25x17.5cm 9x6in) London 2000

LESSARD Réal 1939 **[14]**
- $1 468 - €1 363 - £913 - FF8 943
  «Portrait de Madame Alan Bott, hommage à Tamara Lempicka» Huile/toile (120x65cm 47x25in) Liège 1999

LESSI Jean, Giovanni 1852-1922 **[3]**
- $4 892 - €5 488 - £3 391 - FF36 000
  Rue animée Huile/panneau (22x27cm 8x10in) Paris 2000

LESSI Tito Giovanni 1858-1917 **[20]**
- $8 578 - €9 742 - £6 000 - FF63 905
  Prima dell'udienza (before the audience) Oil/canvas (84x65cm 33x25in) London 2001
- $4 000 - €4 320 - £2 764 - FF28 335
  The Moneylender Oil/panel (17x11.5cm 6x4in) New-York 2001
- $2 280 - €1 970 - £1 520 - FF12 920
  Vecchio con ombrello Acquarello/carta (27x17cm 10x6in) Milano 1998

LESSIEUX Ernest Louis 1848-1925 **[89]**
- $820 - €752 - £500 - FF4 935
  Panoramic View of Nice Watercolour/paper (26x45cm 10x18in) Woking, Surrey 1998
- $402 - €457 - £279 - FF3 000
  «San Salvadour» Affiche (105x75cm 41x29in) Paris 2001

LESSIEUX Louis Ernest 1874-1925 **[18]**
- $795 - €854 - £532 - FF5 600
  Entrée de ville arabe animée Aquarelle/papier (28x46cm 11x18in) Cherbourg 2000
- $668 - €762 - £464 - FF5 000
  «Venise» Affiche (76x105cm 29x41in) Paris 2001

LESSING Carl Friedrich 1808-1880 **[40]**
- $3 334 - €3 579 - £2 231 - FF23 477
  Räuberischer Überfall Öl/Leinwand (49x64.5cm 19x25in) Kempten 2000
- $3 211 - €3 579 - £2 244 - FF23 477
  Gotische Waldkapelle in einem Gebirgstal Öl/Leinwand (36x26.5cm 14x10in) München 2001
- $1 782 - €2 045 - £1 219 - FF13 415
  Leicht nach rechts gewandter Männerkopf mit buschigem Schnurrbart Pencil (27x32.5cm 10x12in) Heidelberg 2000

LESSING Konrad Ludwig 1852-1916 **[17]**
- $2 047 - €2 045 - £1 280 - FF13 415
  Im Hof der Burg Taufers Öl/Karton (62x44cm 24x17in) Köln 1999

LESSON Madeleine XVIII-XIX **[1]**
- $2 988 - €3 208 - £2 000 - FF21 043
  Dasyrure tacheté - Marsupial Cat - dasyrus sp. Drawing (9x15.5cm 3x6in) London 2000

LESSORE Jules 1849-1892 **[36]**
- $409 - €425 - £260 - FF2 788
  Low Tide Watercolour/paper (13x25cm 5x9in) Cheshire 2000

LESSORE Thérèse 1884-1945 **[33]**
- $1 429 - €1 478 - £900 - FF9 693
  View from a Theatre Box Oil/canvas (56x51cm 22x20in) Bath 2000
- $929 - €1 020 - £600 - FF6 690
  The Fish Market, Marseilles Watercolour/paper (32.5x45.5cm 12x17in) London 2000

LESTIN de Jacques 1597-1661 **[4]**
- $12 000 - €13 166 - £7 971 - FF86 361
  The Road to Emmaus Oil/canvas (141x124cm 55x48in) New-York 2000

LESUEUR Blaise Nicolas 1716-1783 **[1]**
- $21 000 - €18 141 - £10 500 - FF119 000
  Banchetto dopo la caccia Olio/tela (73x60cm 28x23in) Firenze 1999

LESUEUR Charles-Alexandre 1778-1846 **[6]**
- $493 - €572 - £346 - FF3 752
  Nouvelle Hollande: Nlle Galles du Sud, vue d'une partie de Sydney Engraving (23.5x20cm 9x7in) Sydney 2000

LESUR Henri Victor 1863-1900 **[51]**
- $3 589 - €4 269 - £2 559 - FF28 000
  Au couchant, Bretonne ramassant du bois Huile/toile (61x46cm 24x18in) Brest 2000
- $1 491 - €1 448 - £921 - FF9 500
  Place de la Concorde Huile/panneau (12.5x22cm 4x8in) Paris 1999

LESY Désiré Lesij 1806-1859 **[9]**
- $3 024 - €3 176 - £1 913 - FF20 836
  Paysage vallonnée avec bergère Oil/panel (57.5x79cm 22x31in) Amsterdam 2000

LETELLIER XVII **[1]**
- $24 000 - €28 207 - £16 639 - FF185 025
  A Violin, a Pocket Violin, Lutes, a Musical Score and books Oil/canvas (62.5x81cm 24x31in) New-York 2000

LETELLIER Pierre 1928 **[50]**
- $211 - €251 - £150 - FF1 644
  Le pont Neuf, Paris Color lithograph (46x57cm 18x22in) London 2001

LETENDRE Rita 1929 **[67]**
- $1 057 - €1 234 - £724 - FF8 095
  L'éclatement serait possible Huile/toile (38x46cm 14x18in) Montréal 2000

LETH de Hendrick II 1703-c.1766 **[3]**
- $1 252 - €1 452 - £887 - FF9 525
  Gesigt van de Haringpakkers Toren, Nevens de Haarlemmersluis en Niewe Etching (57.5x95.5cm 22x37in) Amsterdam 2000

LETH Harald 1899-1986 **[73]**
- $870 - €808 - £522 - FF5 297
  Villa Aurora, Lemvig Oil/canvas (80x120cm 31x47in) København 1999
- $527 - €485 - £324 - FF3 179
  Vinteraften, sne og frost Oil/masonite (31x45cm 12x17in) København 1999

LETHBRIDGE Julian 1947 **[21]**
- $156 - €175 - £108 - FF1 145
  Thoor Ballylee Mixed media (47x42cm 18x16in) Stockholm 2001

L

LETHIERE

🏛 $300 - €353 - £213 - FF2 314
Untitled Lithograph (84.5x68.5cm 33x26in) New-York 2000

LETHIERE Guillaume 1760-1832 [23]
🖼 $788 - €884 - £549 - FF5 800
Offrande aux Dieux Huile/toile (41.5x61cm 16x24in) Paris 2001
✏ $290 - €305 - £182 - FF2 000
Abbé prêchant devant un auditoire Encre (12x16.5cm 4x6in) Paris 2000

LETI Bruno 1941 [10]
🏛 $115 - €111 - £70 - FF725
Landscape Section Etching, aquatint in colors (21.5x23cm 8x9in) Melbourne 1999

LETO Antonino 1844-1913 [48]
🖼 $40 034 - €45 464 - £28 000 - FF298 225
Vecchia Parigi (parisian view) Oil/canvas (107x150cm 42x59in) London 2001
🖼 $4 500 - €4 665 - £2 700 - FF30 600
Rocce e mare Olio/tela (39x64cm 15x25in) Torino 2000
🖼 $3 750 - €3 887 - £2 250 - FF25 500
Barche in secco Olio/cartone (30x40cm 11x15in) Roma 2000
✏ $14 994 - €12 953 - £7 497 - FF84 966
La Sciabica Pastelli/cartone (53.5x38cm 21x14in) Milano 1999

LETOURNEAU Édouard 1851-1907 [10]
🗿 $2 291 - €1 889 - £1 349 - FF12 392
A Saddled Stallion Bronze (16x16cm 6x6in) London 1998

LETOVSKY Nathan 1925 [49]
🖼 $193 - €226 - £137 - FF1 484
«Virtuosity» Huile/isorel (81.5x61cm 32x24in) Montréal 2001

LETSCH Louis 1856-1940 [25]
🖼 $1 025 - €1 125 - £660 - FF7 378
Korb mit Chrysanthemenblüten, sonnig beleuchtet Öl/Leinwand (59x81cm 23x31in) Lindau 2000

LETT-HAINES Arthur 1894-1978 [10]
✏ $1 047 - €969 - £650 - FF6 359
Les nuages - Triptych Watercolour (25.5x33cm 10x12in) London 1999

LETTICK Birney 1919-1986 [35]
🖼 $20 000 - €21 468 - £13 384 - FF140 820
Valley Girl Oil/board (71x53cm 28x21in) Beverly-Hills CA 2000
🖼 $7 000 - €7 514 - £4 684 - FF49 287
Escape from Alcatraz - Warner Brothers Pictures Oil/paper (38x30cm 15x12in) Beverly-Hills CA 2000

LETUAIRE Pierre Le Tuaire 1798-1884 [37]
✏ $574 - €640 - £386 - FF4 200
Les quatre saisons Aquarelle/papier (13x10cm 5x3in) Blois 2000

LETURCQ Arnaud 1961 [8]
🖼 $17 065 - €17 695 - £11 255 - FF116 071
Scène de bistrot, le P.M.U Huile/panneau (64x54cm 25x21in) Genève 2000
🖼 $5 172 - €6 098 - £3 636 - FF40 000
Scène de bar Huile/toile (33x41cm 12x16in) Garches 2000

LEU August Wilhelm 1819-1897 [44]
🖼 $7 744 - €6 704 - £4 700 - FF43 973
Extensive Alpine Lake Landscape Oil/canvas (101x124cm 39x48in) London 1998
🖼 $6 375 - €5 449 - £3 825 - FF35 745
Blick ins Isartal Öl/Leinwand (41x60cm 16x23in) Wien 1998

LEU de Thomas 1560-1612 [8]
🏛 $273 - €275 - £170 - FF1 807
Plates from Imago Bonitatis Illius Engraving (23.5x16cm 9x6in) London 2000

LEU Oskar 1864-1942 [61]
🖼 $612 - €716 - £430 - FF4 695
Moorlandschaft Öl/Leinwand (69x98cm 27x38in) München 2000

LEU Otto Friedrich 1855-1922 [18]
🖼 $4 635 - €4 857 - £2 935 - FF31 862
Im Hafen von Portofino Öl/Leinwand (72x54cm 28x21in) Köln 2000

LEUENBERGER Charles XX [1]
🏛 $5 294 - €4 945 - £3 200 - FF32 439
«Grand Prix Monaco XVIIe» Poster (156x120cm 61x47in) London 1999

LEUNG JUNLING 1944 [1]
🖼 $10 320 - €9 685 - £6 376 - FF63 528
Memories of Jiangnan Oil/canvas (59.5x75cm 23x29in) Hong-Kong 1999

LEUPIN Herbert 1916-1999 [121]
🏛 $233 - €272 - £159 - FF1 786
«Salem, milder virgin» Poster (118.5x84cm 46x33in) Hoorn 2000

LEUPPI Leo 1893-1972 [39]
🖼 $7 047 - €7 942 - £4 880 - FF52 093
Stilisiertes Bildnis Öl/Karton (65x53cm 25x20in) Zürich 2000
✏ $1 104 - €1 316 - £787 - FF8 634
Komposition Gouache/Karton (49x69cm 19x27in) Luzern 2000
🏛 $104 - €115 - £70 - FF757
Komposition Farblithographie (55x76.2cm 21x29in) Zürich 2000

LEURS Johannes Karel 1865-1938 [43]
🖼 $1 173 - €1 361 - £810 - FF8 929
Boerderij aan het water Oil/canvas (39.5x49cm 15x19in) Rotterdam 2000

LEUSDEN van Willem 1886-1974 [23]
🖼 $4 197 - €4 991 - £2 992 - FF32 742
Homme machine Oil/canvas (66x50cm 25x19in) Amsterdam 2000
🖼 $1 691 - €1 815 - £1 131 - FF11 906
Bosgezicht Oil/canvas/board (27x35cm 10x13in) Amsterdam 2000

LEUTERITZ Franz Wilhelm 1817-1902 [3]
🖼 $10 222 - €11 270 - £6 921 - FF73 928
Folkeliv i Dresden Oil/canvas (43x69cm 16x27in) Vejle 2000

LEUTERITZ Paul 1867-1919 [25]
✏ $195 - €204 - £128 - FF1 341
Drüber und Drunter, zahlreiche Hunde zeigen Zirkusdarbietungen Mischtechnik/Papier (55x45cm 21x17in) Augsburg 2000

LEUTZE Emmanuel Gottlieb 1816-1868 [19]
🖼 $26 000 - €22 432 - £15 685 - FF147 141
Queen Elizabeth I and Sir Walter Raleigh Oil/canvas (122x168.5cm 48x66in) New-York 1998

$5 500 - €6 347 - **£3 872** - FF41 633
Young Girl Before a Court Cupboard Oil/canvas (53x43cm 21x17in) Norwalk CT 2000

LEUW de Friedrich August 1817-1888 **[7]**

$4 167 - €4 090 - **£2 583** - FF26 831
Hirschjagd Öl/Leinwand (94x126cm 37x49in) München 1999

$4 761 - €4 573 - **£2 937** - FF30 000
Halte de soldats devant la masure en hiver Huile/panneau (43x34cm 16x13in) Bayeux 1999

LEUZE-HIRSCHFELD Emmy 1884-? **[17]**

$726 - €686 - **£439** - FF4 500
Femme de l'Atlas Aquarelle, gouache/papier (65x50cm 25x19in) Paris 1999

LEUZINGER Alfred 1899-1977 **[4]**

$394 - €463 - **£278** - FF3 037
Wanduhr Coloured pencils/paper (41x29cm 16x11in) St. Gallen 2000

LEUZINGER G. XIX **[3]**

$3 844 - €4 269 - **£2 679** - FF28 000
Rio de Janeiro da ilha das cobras/Puerto do livramento/Botafogo Photo (18.5x73cm 7x28in) Paris 2001

LEVACHEZ Charles Fr. Gabriel act.1760-1820 **[15]**

$273 - €305 - **£184** - FF2 000
Bonaparte 1er Consul, d'après Boilly Eau-forte (42x25cm 16x9in) Dijon 2000

LEVALLOIS Pierre Ernest XIX **[1]**

$4 303 - €5 031 - **£3 022** - FF33 000
Singe curieux Huile/toile (69x96cm 27x37in) Paris 2000

LEVANON Mordechai 1901-1968 **[146]**

$9 000 - €9 736 - **£6 165** - FF63 867
Portrait Oil/canvas (54x70cm 21x27in) Tel Aviv 2001

$1 500 - €1 688 - **£1 033** - FF11 074
The Kinnereth Oil/canvas (23x29cm 9x11in) Herzelia-Pituah 2000

$1 250 - €1 482 - **£910** - FF9 724
Interior Watercolour/paper (26x17.5cm 10x6in) Tel Aviv 2001

LEVASSEUR Henri Louis 1853-1934 **[59]**

$12 656 - €13 462 - **£8 000** - FF88 304
Jupiter and Hebe Marble (H101cm H39in) London 2000

$1 286 - €1 296 - **£801** - FF8 500
Diane chasseresse Bronze (54x25x18cm 21x9x7in) Paris 2000

LEVASSEUR Léon Gustave XIX-XX **[2]**

$3 500 - €3 318 - **£2 186** - FF21 763
Peasants in a Landscape Oil/canvas (30x50cm 12x20in) Portsmouth NH 1999

LEVASTI Filli 1883-1966 **[16]**

$5 750 - €5 961 - **£3 450** - FF39 100
La piscina Olio/tela (61x75cm 24x29in) Prato 1999

$960 - €829 - **£540** - FF5 440
Arrigo alla finestra Olio/cartone (34.5x24.5cm 13x9in) Prato 1998

$240 - €207 - **£160** - FF1 360
Chiosco tra gli alberi Matita/carta (21x29.5cm 8x11in) Prato 1998

LEVAVASSEUR Henri 1887-1962 **[21]**

$340 - €366 - **£228** - FF2 400
Couple Huile/isorel (41x33cm 16x12in) Bayeux 2000

LEVCHENKO Petr Alekseevich 1859-1917 **[6]**

$5 500 - €4 745 - **£3 305** - FF31 126
Cloister in Putivl Oil/canvas (35x45cm 13x17in) Kiev 1998

LEVEILLÉ André 1880-1963 **[63]**

$4 144 - €3 580 - **£2 503** - FF23 482
Heuhocken bei einer Pappelallee Öl/Leinwand (116.7x89.5cm 45x35in) Köln 1998

$624 - €610 - **£395** - FF4 000
La petite chapelle Huile/toile (14x22cm 5x8in) Calais 1999

$352 - €335 - **£223** - FF2 200
Jeune bigoudenne Fusain/papier (38x22cm 14x8in) Douarnenez 1999

LEVENE Ben 1938 **[11]**

$1 024 - €891 - **£620** - FF5 842
Dead Clematis in Ironstone Plate Oil/canvas (91.5x101.5cm 36x39in) London 1999

LEVENSON Silvia 1957 **[1]**

$6 000 - €5 595 - **£3 721** - FF36 699
The Major Deegan Oil/canvas (71x94.5cm 27x37in) New-York 1999

LEVENTSEV Nikolaï 1930 **[13]**

$5 325 - €4 985 - **£3 300** - FF32 700
On the Deck Oil/canvas (72x120cm 28x47in) Fernhurst, Haslemere, Surrey 1999

LÉVÊQUE Auguste 1866-1921 **[16]**

$14 859 - €13 006 - **£9 000** - FF85 312
La Musique Sacrée Oil/canvas (125x225cm 49x88in) London 1998

$3 424 - €3 966 - **£2 416** - FF26 016
Jeune fille nue se mirant Huile/toile (70.5x40.5cm 27x15in) Bruxelles 2000

LEVEQUE Edmond 1814-1874 **[9]**

$5 592 - €5 296 - **£3 400** - FF34 738
The Two Slave Girls Bronze (H53.5cm H21in) London 1999

LEVEQUE Henri 1769-1832 **[12]**

$3 000 - €2 806 - **£1 813** - FF18 406
View of Rome Watercolour/paper (53.5x75.5cm 21x29in) New-York 1999

LEVEQUE J.C. XVIII-XIX **[1]**

$8 170 - €8 232 - **£5 092** - FF54 000
M. DeSaussure son fils, ses guides, arrivant au glacier du Grand Tacul Gravure (25x34.5cm 9x13in) Paris 2000

LEVEQUE Yves 1937 **[15]**

$402 - €457 - **£279** - FF3 000
«L'échelle espacée et les fuseaux» Pastel (100x100cm 39x39in) Douai 2000

LEVER Charles XIX **[2]**

$5 172 - €6 035 - **£3 600** - FF39 586
Fingle Mill, Teign, Devon Oil/canvas (76x128cm 29x50in) London 2000

LEVER Noel Harry **[2]**

$2 522 - €2 958 - **£1 800** - FF19 403
Old Florence, Town Square with Figures, Shops, Church Spire Watercolour/paper (35x25cm 13x9in) Manchester 1999

LEVER Richard Hayley 1876-1958 **[292]**

$5 627 - €5 700 - **£3 500** - FF37 392
St. Ives Oil/canvas (35x45cm 14x18in) Par, Cornwall 2000

$2 750 - €2 350 - **£1 664** - FF15 414
Sunset on the Sea Oil/canvas/board (23x32cm 9x12in) San-Francisco CA 1998

L

L

LEVERD
$600 - €680 - **£419** - FF4 459
Man in an Elevated Train Car Watercolour
(12x19.5cm 4x7in) New-York 2001

LEVERD René 1872-1938 **[213]**
$422 - €503 - **£301** - FF3 300
Chartres, les abords de la cathédrale
Aquarelle/papier (21x31cm 8x12in) Paris 2000
$2 074 - €1 983 - **£1 300** - FF13 006
«Cycles & Automobiles Clément» Poster
(119x159cm 46x62in) London 1999

LEVERETT H.F. XIX **[1]**
$3 516 - €3 916 - **£2 300** - FF25 689
View of Freston, Suffolk Photograph (30x40.5cm
11x15in) Devon 2000

LEVI Carlo 1902-1975 **[208]**
$3 420 - €2 954 - **£1 710** - FF19 380
Amanti Olio/tela (40x60cm 15x23in) Prato 1999
$5 400 - €4 665 - **£3 600** - FF30 600
Il pittore e la modella Olio/cartone (25x40cm
9x15in) Roma 1998
$640 - €829 - **£480** - FF5 440
Maternità Matita (70x50cm 27x19in) Milano 2000

LEVI Vassilij 1878-1954 **[18]**
$843 - €975 - **£596** - FF6 398
Bulevarden på vintern Oil/canvas (50x58cm
19x22in) Helsinki 2000

LEVICK Edwin 1868-1929 **[3]**
$2 600 - €2 620 - **£1 620** - FF17 186
«C» Class Schooners Racing Gelatin silver print
(41x51cm 16x20in) New-York 2000

LEVIER Adolfo 1873-1953 **[20]**
$2 000 - €2 073 - **£1 200** - FF13 600
Sull'uscio Olio/tela (76x67cm 29x26in) Trieste 1999
$600 - €622 - **£360** - FF4 080
La Villa Rossa Acquarello/carta (40x50cm 15x19in)
Trieste 1999

LEVIER Charles 1920 **[452]**
$1 335 - €1 143 - **£840** - FF7 500
Avignon Huile/toile (76x102cm 29x40in) Paris 1998
$190 - €183 - **£117** - FF1 200
La plage Aquarelle/papier (73x53.5cm 28x21in) Paris
1999

LEVIEUX Renaud, Reynaud 1613-1699 **[6]**
$19 078 - €17 532 - **£11 718** - FF115 000
Nature morte avec ara, épagneul et écureuil
Huile/toile (81x111.5cm 31x43in) Versailles 1999

LÉVIGNE Théodore 1848-1912 **[212]**
$2 184 - €2 592 - **£1 589** - FF17 000
Berger et son troupeau avant l'orage Huile/toile
(99x130cm 38x51in) Lyon 2001
$1 618 - €1 601 - **£1 009** - FF10 500
**Nature morte aux poissons, bouteille de vin et
cuivre** Huile/toile (45x63cm 17x24in) Lyon 1999
$954 - €936 - **£591** - FF6 141
Two Dogs Portraits: Brutus and Miss Oil/panel
(35x26cm 13x10in) Toronto 1999

LEVIGNES Amélie XVIII-XIX **[3]**
$20 000 - €18 973 - **£12 150** - FF124 458
**Peonies, Roses, Tulips and other Flowers in a
Terracotta Urn** Oil/canvas (87x67.5cm 34x26in) New-
York 1999

LEVINE Jack 1915 **[96]**
$40 000 - €38 238 - **£25 072** - FF250 828
Orpheus in Vegas Oil/canvas (101.5x152.5cm
39x60in) New-York 1999

$11 000 - €10 578 - **£6 789** - FF69 390
Aileen Oil/canvas (61x53.5cm 24x21in) Boston MA
1999
$1 700 - €1 999 - **£1 218** - FF13 113
Study for a Gangster's Funeral Charcoal/paper
(45x53.5cm 17x21in) Philadelphia PA 2001
$324 - €280 - **£195** - FF1 837
Warsaw Ghetto Lithograph (47x64cm 18x25in) New-
York 1998

LEVINE Les 1935 **[12]**
$142 - €153 - **£95** - FF1 006
**Chou En-Lai's View of the back of Richard
Nixon's Chopsticks** Etching in colors (101.7x75.9cm
40x29in) Hamburg 2000

LEVINE Sherrie 1947 **[74]**
$7 500 - €7 042 - **£4 647** - FF46 193
Thin Stripe #4 Mixed media/panel (61x50.5cm
24x19in) New-York 1999
$6 000 - €6 583 - **£3 985** - FF43 180
After Joan Miro Acrylic (35.5x28cm 13x11in) New-
York 2000
$2 064 - €2 349 - **£1 450** - FF15 410
Untitled Watercolour (41x31cm 16x12in) Zürich 2001
$1 400 - €1 309 - **£846** - FF8 589
After Edward Weston Photograph (49.55x37.5cm
19x14in) New-York 1999

LEVINSEN Sophus Theobald 1869-1943 **[34]**
$928 - €892 - **£583** - FF5 853
Les barques Huile/carton (50x60cm 19x23in)
Bruxelles 1999
$501 - €545 - **£330** - FF3 577
Gezicht te Alger Oil/panel (35.5x27cm 13x10in)
Lokeren 2000

LEVINSTEIN Leon 1913-1990 **[35]**
$2 600 - €2 504 - **£1 626** - FF16 422
New York Gelatin silver print (28x35.5cm 11x13in)
New-York 1999

LEVINTHAL David 1949 **[13]**
$3 200 - €3 327 - **£2 020** - FF21 826
Untitled from the Wild West Series Polaroid
(61x49.5cm 24x19in) New-York 2000

LEVIS Giuseppe Augusto 1873-1926 **[9]**
$1 250 - €1 296 - **£750** - FF8 500
Campagna solitaria Olio/tavola (45x31.5cm
17x12in) Vercelli 1999

LÉVIS Maurice 1860-1940 **[213]**
$4 275 - €3 994 - **£2 583** - FF26 200
Paysage de bord de Marne Huile/toile (53x71cm
20x27in) Paris 1999
$3 927 - €3 811 - **£2 445** - FF25 000
Château au bord d'une rivière Huile/panneau
(24x34cm 9x13in) Cheverny 1999
$764 - €732 - **£470** - FF4 840
Lavandière à la rivière près du village
Aquarelle/papier (29x38cm 11x14in) La Varenne-Saint-
Hilaire 1999

LEVIS Max 1863-1930 **[17]**
$5 133 - €5 173 - **£3 200** - FF33 931
Contemplation Oil/panel (37.5x30cm 14x11in)
London 2000
$1 822 - €2 045 - **£1 263** - FF13 415
Damenbildnis Pastell/Papier (80x55cm 31x21in)
München 2000

LEVIT Herschel 1912-1986 **[2]**
$1 315 - €1 158 - **£939** - FF10 037
Take it Away Lithograph (34.5x25cm 13x9in) Toronto
2001

LEVITAN Isaak Il'ich 1861-1900 **[70]**
- $19 000 - €16 144 - **£11 476** - FF105 898
  Landscape Oil/canvas (70.5x54.5cm 27x21in) Tel Aviv 1999
- $4 754 - €3 920 - **£2 800** - FF25 711
  Study of a Clearing Oil/canvas (22x13.5cm 8x5in) London 1998
- $30 784 - €36 635 - **£22 000** - FF240 310
  Dacha in Spring Watercolour, gouache (61.5x75.5cm 24x29in) London 2000

LEVITSKY Dimitri Gregoriovitc 1735-1822 **[3]**
- $24 948 - €23 326 - **£15 372** - FF153 006
  Porträtt av kejsarinnan Katarina II av Ryssland,after Alexander Roslin Oil/canvas (80x66cm 31x25in) Stockholm 1999

LEVITT Helen 1918 **[66]**
- $4 000 - €4 174 - **£2 530** - FF27 382
  Portrait of Walker Evans with Curtain Photograph (11x7cm 4x2in) New-York 2001

LEVKOVITCH Léon 1936 **[8]**
- $1 027 - €1 208 - **£739** - FF7 926
  Eux Gouache/papier (37x19.5cm 14x7in) Warszawa 2001

LEVOLI Nicola 1778-1801 **[2]**
- $8 568 - €7 402 - **£4 284** - FF48 552
  Nature morte Olio/tela (98.5x73cm 38x28in) Venezia 1999

LEVORATI Ernesto XIX-XX **[6]**
- $2 491 - €2 132 - **£1 500** - FF13 987
  A country Girl Oil/canvas (35.5x25.5cm 13x10in) London 1998

LEVRAC-TOURNIERES Robert 1667/68-1752 **[34]**
- $4 993 - €5 793 - **£3 553** - FF38 000
  Portrait de Grégoire de Saint Geniez Huile/panneau (51x38.5cm 20x15in) Paris 2001

LEVRERO Beppe 1901-1986 **[5]**
- $1 500 - €1 555 - **£900** - FF10 200
  Neve Acrilico/faesite (50x70cm 19x27in) Vercelli 2000

LEVY Alexander Oscar 1881-1947 **[13]**
- $5 000 - €5 551 - **£3 477** - FF36 412
  «Vanity» Oil/canvas (91x91cm 36x36in) Milford CT 2001
- $500 - €578 - **£353** - FF3 794
  Near Porteville Oil/masonite (30x40cm 12x16in) Cleveland OH 2000

LEVY Alphonse, dit Saïd 1843-1918 **[80]**
- $345 - €335 - **£217** - FF2 200
  Homme assis Fusain/papier (28x41cm 11x16in) Paris 1999
- $2 126 - €1 887 - **£1 300** - FF12 379
  «Exposition d'oeuvres d'Alphone Lévy» Affiche couleur (62x43cm 24x16in) London 1999

LÉVY Charles XIX-XX **[31]**
- $419 - €366 - **£253** - FF2 400
  «Folies Bergères. H. Abdy charmeur de perroquets» Affiche (120.5x89cm 47x35in) Paris 1998

LÉVY Charles Octave ?-1899 **[53]**
- $4 014 - €4 462 - **£2 808** - FF29 268
  Judith Bronze (H80cm H31in) Bruxelles 2001
- $1 392 - €1 361 - **£859** - FF8 929
  The Flaneur Bronze (H58cm H22in) Amsterdam 1999

LEVY Edgar 1907-1975 **[1]**
- $20 000 - €23 105 - **£14 004** - FF151 562
  Still Life, African Mask Oil/canvas (71x91.5cm 27x36in) New-York 2001

LEVY Émile 1826-1890 **[86]**
- $45 000 - €50 371 - **£31 383** - FF330 412
  The Dizzy Spell Oil/canvas (110x58cm 43x22in) New-York 2001
- $10 000 - €10 992 - **£6 408** - FF72 104
  The Elopement Oil/canvas (55x29cm 21x11in) New-York 2000
- $244 - €213 - **£148** - FF1 400
  «Nouma-Hawa. Ses tigres et ses lions» Affiche (59x40cm 23x15in) Paris 1998

LEVY Henri Léopold 1840-1904 **[46]**
- $2 812 - €3 099 - **£1 837** - FF20 325
  Femme orientale pensive Huile/toile (45x37.5cm 17x14in) Bruxelles 2000
- $460 - €427 - **£286** - FF2 800
  Étude de tête Fusain (26.7x21cm 10x8in) Paris 1999

LEVY Laure 1866-1954 **[12]**
- $461 - €511 - **£313** - FF3 353
  Die Ruhepause des Küchenmädchens Painting (21.5x15cm 8x5in) Hamburg 2000

LÉVY Léopold 1882-1966 **[57]**
- $1 705 - €1 982 - **£1 198** - FF13 000
  Bouquet de fleurs Huile/carton (85x74cm 33x29in) Paris 2001
- $393 - €457 - **£276** - FF3 000
  Paysage Huile/toile (24x33cm 9x12in) Paris 2001

LÉVY Lucien XIX-XX **[5]**
- $1 673 - €1 968 - **£1 200** - FF12 910
  Pierrot and Pierrette Oil/panel (24x14cm 9x5in) Channel-Islands 2001
- $24 833 - €28 965 - **£17 271** - FF190 000
  Vue de Fès Pastel/papier (75x62cm 29x24in) Paris 2000

LEVY Michel 1949 **[21]**
- $6 755 - €7 622 - **£4 750** - FF50 000
  Cantiques des Cantiques Bronze (46x51x15cm 18x20x5in) Paris 2001

LEVY Moses 1885-1968 **[61]**
- $7 800 - €6 738 - **£3 900** - FF44 200
  Alla veranda Olio/tela (37x45cm 14x17in) Firenze 1999
- $3 900 - €3 369 - **£2 600** - FF22 100
  «La pittrice» Olio/faesite (40.5x33cm 15x12in) Prato 1998
- $250 - €259 - **£150** - FF1 700
  Donne Acquarello/carta (16.5x25cm 6x9in) Prato 1999
- $316 - €291 - **£190** - FF1 911
  Under Parasols on the Beach Etching (30x18cm 11x7in) London 1999

LEVY Ra'anan 1954 **[24]**
- $1 800 - €1 932 - **£1 204** - FF12 673
  Reflection Pastel/paper (48x46cm 18x18in) Tel Aviv 2000

LEVY Rudolf 1875-1943 **[29]**
- $28 180 - €27 099 - **£17 362** - FF177 756
  Seine Ufer bei St.Gervais-St.Protais Öl/Leinwand (50x61cm 19x24in) München 1999
- $2 476 - €2 812 - **£1 695** - FF18 446
  Celia-Pflanze Watercolour (63x46cm 24x18in) Hamburg 2000

LÉVY-DHURMER Lucien 1865-1953 **[181]**
- $16 000 - €13 657 - **£9 568** - FF89 585
  A Vase of Flowers Oil/canvas (54.5x46cm 21x18in) New-York 1998
- $3 925 - €4 269 - **£2 587** - FF28 000
  Portrait d'homme au turban Pastel/papier (40x32cm 15x12in) Paris 2000

L

LEWANDOWSKI Edmund D. 1914 [10]
- $43 500 - €49 781 - **£29 919** - FF326 545
  A Tribute to Industry of Miwaukee for the War Effort Oil/canvas (261x168cm 103x66in) Milwaukee WI 2000

LEWERS Margo (Hetty Marg.) 1908-1978 [12]
- $7 433 - €7 979 - **£4 975** - FF52 340
  Something to Come Oil/board (123.5x184.5cm 48x72in) Melbourne 2000

LEWICKI Jan Nepomucen 1802-1871 [1]
- $684 - €719 - **£453** - FF4 714
  Illustrations pour les mémoires de Jan Chryzostom Pasek Eau-forte, aquatinte (63x45cm 24x17in) Warszawa 2000

LEWICKI Leopold 1906-1973 [14]
- $114 - €111 - **£72** - FF729
  Intellectuals Etching (10x8cm 3x3in) Warszawa 1999

LEWIN Stephen act.1890-1910 [23]
- $5 678 - €6 095 - **£3 800** - FF39 982
  The Toast Oil/canvas (49.5x63cm 19x24in) London 2000

LEWIS Alfred Neville 1895-1972 [9]
- $1 126 - €1 264 - **£788** - FF8 290
  Pondo man Oil/panel (34x24cm 13x9in) Cape Town 2001

LEWIS Charles George 1808-1880 [25]
- $344 - €386 - **£240** - FF2 533
  The Melton Breakfast, after Francis Grant Engraving (46x72cm 18x28in) Leyburn, North Yorkshire 2001

LEWIS Charles James 1830/36-1892 [57]
- $4 243 - €4 028 - **£2 600** - FF26 424
  The Cottage Door Oil/board (84.5x63.5cm 33x25in) London 1999
- $4 400 - €5 104 - **£3 130** - FF33 483
  Home Sweet Home Oil/panel (17x11cm 7x4in) Chicago IL 2000
- $1 823 - €1 903 - **£1 150** - FF12 481
  Waiting, Country Landscape with young Girl Watercolour/paper (58x43cm 23x17in) Canterbury, Kent 2000

LEWIS Edmonia c.1843/45-? [6]
- $65 000 - €77 302 - **£48 525** - FF507 065
  Hiawatha Marble (H36.5cm H14in) New-York 2000

LEWIS Edmund Darch 1835-1910 [242]
- $18 000 - €20 439 - **£12 319** - FF134 071
  In the Valley Oil/canvas (100.5x157.5cm 39x62in) New-York 2000
- $5 500 - €6 354 - **£3 851** - FF41 679
  Lake Scene Oil/canvas (61x107cm 24x42in) New-York 2001
- $3 500 - €3 479 - **£2 117** - FF22 824
  Hudson River Landscape with figure, bridge, house and boats Oil/canvas/panel (50x25cm 20x10in) Hampden MA 2000
- $1 200 - €1 039 - **£736** - FF6 817
  New Jersey Coast Watercolour (25x53.5cm 9x21in) New-York 1999

LEWIS Frederick Christ. II 1813-1875 [4]
- $47 766 - €46 249 - **£30 000** - FF303 375
  The Darbar at Udaipur Oil/canvas (119.5x178cm 47x70in) London 1999
- $1 924 - €1 864 - **£1 200** - FF12 226
  The Durbar, on the Reception by His Highness the Maha Raja Engraving (94x61cm 37x24in) London 1999

LEWIS Frederick Christian 1779-1856 [14]
- $1 070 - €1 250 - **£756** - FF8 200
  The Quorn Hunt: Drawing Cover, Talli, Ho! and Away, Full'Cry Eau-forte, aquatinte couleurs (42.5x61cm 16x24in) Paris 2000

LEWIS Harry Emerson 1892-1958 [61]
- $468 - €533 - **£327** - FF3 498
  Village, Provence Oil/board (48x41cm 18x16in) Dublin 2000
- $401 - €457 - **£280** - FF2 998
  French Village Oil/board (38x41cm 14x16in) Dublin 2000
- $850 - €992 - **£591** - FF6 505
  «California Hills Meet the Sea» Ink/paper (60x76cm 24x30in) Altadena CA 2000

LEWIS Henry 1819-1904 [7]
- $4 377 - €4 346 - **£2 735** - FF28 508
  Indianer am Mississippi Ol/Leinwand (32x51cm 12x20in) München 1999

LEWIS J. XIX [12]
- $394 - €375 - **£240** - FF2 458
  View from Richmond Hill Oil/board (22x30cm 8x11in) London 1999

LEWIS Jeanette Maxfield 1894-1982 [4]
- $4 250 - €4 562 - **£2 844** - FF29 927
  Sun Down in Mexico Oil/canvas/board (38x48cm 14x18in) San-Francisco CA 2000

LEWIS John XVIII [8]
- $26 782 - €23 120 - **£16 000** - FF151 659
  Portrait of Bridget Vaughan of Derllys, Mrs Bevan (1698-1779) Oil/canvas (124.5x99cm 49x38in) Llandeilo, Carmarthenshire 1998
- $33 478 - €28 900 - **£20 000** - FF189 574
  Portrait of a young girl, said to be Eleanor LLoyd of Derwydd Oil/canvas (74x61cm 29x24in) Llandeilo, Carmarthenshire 1998

LEWIS John 1942 [8]
- $7 000 - €6 397 - **£4 282** - FF41 963
  Waterfall Table Sculpture, glass (54.5x61cm 21x24in) New-York 1999

LEWIS John Frederick 1805-1876 [112]
- $175 219 - €182 360 - **£110 000** - FF1 196 206
  Deer-Shooting, Winsor Park Oil/panel (62.5x75.5cm 24x29in) London 2000
- $67 344 - €80 092 - **£48 000** - FF525 369
  The End of the Day, a Game Keeper with his Dog Oil/panel (32x37cm 12x14in) London 2000
- $10 460 - €11 228 - **£7 000** - FF73 651
  Lady gazing from a Window over the Bay of Naples Watercolour (41x30.5cm 16x12in) London 2000
- $112 - €128 - **£78** - FF838
  In der Moschee von Cordoba Lithographie (36x25.5cm 14x10in) Berlin 2001

LEWIS Josephine Miles 1865-1959 [2]
- $7 000 - €8 087 - **£4 901** - FF53 046
  Haystacks in Butry, France Oil/canvas (46x55cm 18x21in) New-York 2001

LEWIS Lennard 1826-1913 [88]
- $294 - €273 - **£180** - FF1 792
  Fishermen on a Wooden Jetty with Steamers Watercolour (23x52cm 9x20in) London 1998

LEWIS Martin 1881-1962 [249]
- $2 400 - €2 248 - **£1 475** - FF14 745
  Snowy Morn, 5th Avenue at Madison Square Oil/board (31x23.5cm 12x9in) New-York 1999

🖊 **$2 200** - €2 545 - **£1 557** - FF16 695
Nocturnal Scene, New York Street Corner Pencil
(30.5x23cm 12x9in) New-York 2000

📷 **$5 200** - €5 768 - **£3 458** - FF37 838
Building a Babylon, Tudor City, N.Y.C Drypoint
(33x20.5cm 12x8in) New-York 2000

LEWIS Maud 1903-1970 [68]

🖊 **$2 815** - €3 118 - **£1 909** - FF20 453
Ploughing with oxen Oil/board (23x30.5cm 9x12in)
Toronto 2000

🖊 **$1 490** - €1 651 - **£1 010** - FF10 828
Four Winter Scenes Gouache/paper (11.5x16.5cm
4x6in) Toronto 2000

LEWIS Morland 1903-1943 [8]

🖊 **$2 524** - €2 107 - **£1 500** - FF13 824
Country Lane Oil/board (22x26cm 8x10in) London
1998

LEWIS Norman Wilfred 1909-1979 [1]

🖊 **$2 900** - €3 369 - **£2 038** - FF22 101
Rolling Landscape Watercolour/paper (33x50cm
13x20in) Cincinnati OH 2001

LEWIS Percy Wyndham 1884-1957 [74]

🖐 **$50 806** - €54 536 - **£34 000** - FF357 734
Red Portrait Oil/canvas (91.5x61cm 36x24in) London
1998

🖊 **$6 163** - €5 942 - **£3 800** - FF38 977
Lebensraum II: The Empty Tunic Watercolour
(34.5x24cm 13x9in) London 1999

LEWIS Wyndham XX [1]

🖐 **$16 375** - €14 975 - **£10 000** - FF98 232
Harbour Oil/canvas (40x50cm 16x20in) London 1998

LEWIS-BROWN John 1829-1890 [15]

🖐 **$6 640** - €6 098 - **£4 056** - FF40 000
L'allée cavalière Huile/toile (98x68cm 38x26in)
Deauville 1998

LeWITT Sol 1928 [628]

🖐 **$13 000** - €14 795 - **£9 135** - FF97 047
Complex Form #63 Enamel (150x99x86cm
59x38x33in) New-York 2001

🖐 **$1 876** - €2 134 - **£1 302** - FF14 000
Sans titre Technique mixte (40x40.5cm 15x15in) Paris
2000

🖐 **$1 400** - €1 451 - **£840** - FF9 520
Cubo piramide Tempera (15x21.5cm 5x8in) Milano
2000

🖐 **$34 000** - €38 016 - **£22 919** - FF249 369
Folding Screen Installation (183x383.5cm 72x150in)
New-York 2000

🖐 **$3 906** - €3 802 - **£2 400** - FF24 939
Untitled Glazed ceramic (26.5x132cm 10x51in)
London 1999

🖐 **$4 000** - €4 480 - **£2 779** - FF29 388
Untitled Gouache/paper (28.5x37.5cm 11x14in) New-
York 2001

📷 **$1 428** - €1 387 - **£889** - FF9 097
**Horizontal colour band and vertical colour
band** Etching, aquatint in colors (61x105.5cm 24x41in)
Luzern 1999

LEWITT Vivienne Shark 1956 [5]

🖐 **$4 440** - €4 959 - **£2 843** - FF32 527
The Elder's Oil/panel (24.5x33cm 9x12in) Malvern,
Victoria 2000

LEWITT-HIM (J. Lewitt & G. Him) 1907/00-1991/82 [11]

📷 **$369** - €409 - **£250** - FF2 680
«Aoa USA» Poster (97x61cm 38x24in) London 2000

LEWKOWICZ Leon 1888-1950 [11]

🖐 **$976** - €1 015 - **£619** - FF6 657
Tête de garçon Huile/toile (40x31cm 15x12in)
Warszawa 2000

LEWY Kurt 1898-1963 [54]

🖊 **$355** - €397 - **£246** - FF2 601
Composition Dessin (23x30cm 9x11in) Antwerpen
2001

LEX Franz 1895-1959 [21]

🖐 **$925** - €799 - **£557** - FF5 240
«Blick aux meinem Fenster» Oil/panel (63x79cm
24x31in) Wien 1998

LEX Isidore 1631-1708 [5]

🖐 **$23 579** - €25 916 - **£14 994** - FF170 000
Vaisseaux de haut bord par temps calme
Huile/panneau (72.5x107.5cm 28x42in) Paris 2000

LEY Hans Christian 1828-1875 [9]

🖐 **$1 740** - €1 878 - **£1 167** - FF12 318
**Måneskinslandskab med nisser, der danser ved
gravhöjen til violinspil** Oil/canvas (17.5x25cm
6x9in) Köbenhavn 2000

LEY van der Sophie 1859-1918 [20]

🖐 **$2 088** - €1 962 - **£1 258** - FF12 868
Street Corner, Winter, Amsterdam Oil/panel
(24.5x19.5cm 9x7in) Sydney 1999

LEYBOLD Johann Friedrich 1755-1838 [4]

🖐 **$4 600** - €4 769 - **£2 760** - FF31 280
**Gentiluomo a mezza figura, seduto presso un
tavolo** Olio/tela/tavola (106x84cm 41x33in) Roma
1999

LEYDA de Luca 1494-1533 [2]

📷 **$500** - €518 - **£300** - FF3 400
La flagellazione Acquaforte (11.5x7.5cm 4x2in)
Firenze 2000

LEYDE Kurt 1881-1941 [9]

🖐 **$1 598** - €1 585 - **£1 000** - FF10 394
**Two Women in a South American Landscape
Believed to be Guatemala** Oil/canvas (70.5x60.5cm
27x23in) London 1999

LEYDE Otto Theodore 1835-1897 [17]

🖐 **$6 412** - €6 057 - **£4 000** - FF39 733
Mending the Basket Oil/canvas (56x46cm 22x18in)
Perthshire 1999

🖐 **$12 022** - €11 357 - **£7 500** - FF74 499
Solitude Oil/canvas (37x31cm 14x12in) Perthshire
1999

🖐 **$807** - €918 - **£560** - FF6 024
An Old Cottage Garden Watercolour/paper
(28.5x24.5cm 11x9in) Edinburgh 2000

LEYDEN van Aertgen, Aert Claesz 1498-1564 [4]

🖊 **$18 000** - €19 223 - **£12 265** - FF126 095
The Adoration of the Shepherds Black chalk/paper
(25x19cm 9x7in) New-York 2001

LEYDEN van Ernest 1892-1969 [49]

🖐 **$2 145** - €1 993 - **£1 309** - FF13 070
At the Market Oil/panel (48x56cm 18x22in)
Amsterdam 1998

🖊 **$970** - €1 134 - **£693** - FF7 441
«L'aurore des villes» Collage/paper (40x48cm
15x18in) Amsterdam 2001

LEYDEN van Lucas 1494-1533 [416]

📷 **$583** - €665 - **£406** - FF4 360
Der Heilige Lukas Kupferstich (11.5x9cm 4x3in)
Berlin 2001

LEYDENFROST Alexander 1889-1961 **[4]**
$1 600 - €1 481 - £979 - FF9 716
Prisoner of war rescue in icy fjord, Ill. for Life Magazine Grisaille (44x39cm 17x15in) New-York 1999

LEYDET Victor 1861-1904 **[3]**
$2 546 - €2 397 - £1 767 - FF19 000
«Absinthe supérieure» Affiche (114x140cm 44x55in) Paris 2000

LEYENDECKER Francis Xavier 1877-1924 **[10]**
$7 500 - €6 943 - £4 590 - FF45 546
Cover for Life Magazine: circus bear playing drum, woman tamer Oil/canvas (81x64cm 32x25in) New-York 1999

LEYENDECKER Joseph Christian 1874-1951 **[68]**
$19 800 - €16 891 - £11 943 - FF110 800
Baby lying on back, with bottle, for an Amoco advertisement Oil/canvas (43x81cm 17x32in) New-York 1998
$9 000 - €8 332 - £5 508 - FF54 655
Grandfather and boy dunking doughnuts, sketch for advertisement Oil/canvas (23x26cm 9x10in) New-York 1999
$350 - €390 - £235 - FF22 558
Dutch Girl Gouache/paper (49x36cm 19x14in) East-Moriches NY 2000
$1 100 - €996 - £673 - FF6 536
«Downed» Poster (68x52cm 27x20in) New-York 1998

LEYENDECKER Paul Joseph 1842-? **[16]**
$2 500 - €2 347 - £1 549 - FF15 394
Court Scene Oil/canvas (60x73cm 24x29in) South-Deerfield MA 1999
$2 500 - €2 347 - £1 549 - FF15 394
Court Scene Oil/canvas (35x26cm 14x10in) South-Deerfield MA 1999

LEYMAN Alfred 1856-1933 **[48]**
$800 - €768 - £495 - FF5 039
South Devon, England Watercolour/paper (35x48cm 14x19in) Detroit MI 1999

LEYMARIE Auguste XIX-XX **[25]**
$2 508 - €2 134 - £1 496 - FF14 000
Femme au cygne Huile/toile (46x33cm 18x12in) Paris 1998
$1 395 - €1 601 - £954 - FF10 500
Charlot, projet d'affiche pour l'Agence Cinématographique, Paris Encre (56.5x42cm 22x16in) Paris 2000
$398 - €457 - £272 - FF3 000
«Agence Cinémato Diamant présente Maurice Chevalier» Affiche (157x115cm 61x45in) Paris 2000

LEYPOLD Carl Julius 1806-1874 **[5]**
$6 550 - €6 135 - £4 027 - FF40 246
Abendliche Elblandschaft mit angelegten Fischerkähnen Öl/Leinwand (57x80cm 22x31in) Lindau 1999

LEYRITZ de Léon Albert Marie 1888-1976 **[11]**
$9 732 - €9 382 - £6 000 - FF61 542
Buste de femme Metal (H53.5cm H21in) London 1999

LEYS Henri 1815-1869 **[97]**
$4 752 - €4 462 - £2 934 - FF29 268
Furie espagnole Huile/toile/panneau (65x54cm 25x21in) Antwerpen 1999
$1 094 - €1 190 - £720 - FF7 804
Studie naar een oude meester Oil/canvas (28.5x36.5cm 11x14in) Lokeren 2000

$214 - €256 - £152 - FF1 676
Christus am Ölberg Ink (20.5x16.5cm 8x6in) Königstein 2000

LEYSING Piet 1885-1933 **[13]**
$1 316 - €1 227 - £812 - FF8 049
Ankernde Binnenfischer am Niederrhein Öl/Leinwand (45x51cm 17x20in) Köln 1999

LEYSTER Judith c.1600/10-1660 **[7]**
$140 000 - €131 715 - £87 360 - FF863 996
Portrait of bearded Gentleman, wearing a coat and white ruff Oil/canvas (68.5x56.5cm 26x22in) New-York 1999
$62 760 - €67 368 - £42 000 - FF441 907
Youth Asleep, and a Young Mother and her Child at a Fireside Oil/panel (40x30cm 15x11in) London 2000

LEYTENS Gysbrecht 1586-1643/56 **[12]**
$50 843 - €58 991 - £35 100 - FF386 958
Winter Landscape with Sportsmen on a Forest track near a Village Oil/panel (47.5x76.5cm 18x30in) Amsterdam 1999
$4 337 - €5 050 - £3 000 - FF33 129
A Wooded Landscape with travellers Oil/panel (19.5x24cm 7x9in) London 2000

LHARDY Y GARRIGUES Agustín 1848-1918 **[24]**
$19 950 - €21 023 - £13 300 - FF137 900
Paisaje Oleo/lienzo (112x200cm 44x78in) Madrid 2000
$2 400 - €2 252 - £1 462 - FF14 775
Lago en el bosque Oleo/tabla (19x27cm 7x10in) Madrid 1999

LHERMITTE Léon Augustin 1844-1925 **[361]**
$560 000 - €664 045 - £385 280 - FF4 355 848
The Little Goose Girl of Mézy Oil/canvas (160x85cm 62x33in) New-York 2000
$27 000 - €29 631 - £17 385 - FF194 367
Puiseuses d'eau Oil/canvas (53x39cm 20x15in) New-York 2000
$2 759 - €2 592 - £1 662 - FF17 000
Paysanne au champs Huile/toile/carton (20x27cm 7x10in) Toulouse 1999
$6 000 - €6 440 - £4 015 - FF42 246
At Home by the Hearth Charcoal/paper (31x41cm 12x16in) New-York 2000

LHOMME Victor XX **[3]**
$3 500 - €3 440 - £2 248 - FF22 567
La lecture au jardin Oil/panel (40.5x33cm 15x12in) New-York 1999

LHOTAK Kamil 1912-1990 **[118]**
$10 115 - €9 567 - £6 300 - FF62 755
U-Boot und Vulkan Öl/Karton (110x135cm 43x53in) Praha 2001
$5 635 - €5 330 - £3 510 - FF34 963
Pristani balonu Huile/toile (39x47cm 15x18in) Praha 2000
$2 601 - €2 460 - £1 620 - FF16 137
Ballon au-dessus de stade Huile/toile (41x32cm 16x12in) Praha 2001
$260 - €246 - £162 - FF1 613
Sous-marin sur la surface Encre (11x15.5cm 4x6in) Praha 2001
$109 - €104 - £68 - FF681
«Pf 1955-C.Moravek» Pointe sèche (5x6cm 1x2in) Praha 2000

LHOTE André 1885-1962 **[1913]**
$117 825 - €114 337 - £73 350 - FF750 000
Les baigneuses Huile/papier/toile (130x311cm 51x122in) Paris 1999

⌐ **$14 217** - €16 007 - **£9 901** - FF105 000
Les tulipes Huile/toile (38x46cm 14x18in) Paris 2001

⌐ **$6 500** - €7 134 - **£4 185** - FF46 795
Portrait d'Anne à la robe rouge Oil/canvas
(35x22cm 13x8in) New-York 2000

⌐ **$2 500** - €2 098 - **£1 466** - FF13 759
Landscape with Church in the Hills
Gouache/paper (29x39.5cm 11x15in) New-York 1998

▥ **$186** - €198 - **£125** - FF1 300
Le nu jaune Lithographie (44x30cm 17x11in) Cannes
2000

LI FANGYING 1699-1755 **[7]**
✍ **$16 000** - €14 683 - **£9 830** - FF96 315
Bamboo and Rock Ink/paper (184x75cm 72x29in)
New-York 1999

LI FUYUAN 1942 **[2]**
✍ **$2 307** - €2 600 - **£1 612** - FF17 058
Lotus and Dragonfly Ink (66x66.5cm 25x26in)
Hong-Kong 2001

LI GENG 1949 **[3]**
⌐ **$24 529** - €20 719 - **£14 725** - FF135 907
Pilgrimage Oil/canvas (88x176cm 34x69in) Hong-
Kong 1998

LI HUASHENG 1944 **[3]**
⌐ **$1 400** - €1 628 - **£1 000** - FF10 681
Two Birds perched upon a fruiting Vine Branch
Ink (89.5x67cm 35x26in) London 2001

LI HUAYI 1948 **[11]**
✍ **$20 640** - €19 465 - **£12 800** - FF127 680
Landscape Ink (137.5x69cm 54x27in) Hong-Kong
1999

LI HUIFANG Lee Hui-fang 1948 **[8]**
⌐ **$6 292** - €5 832 - **£3 912** - FF38 253
Candlestand Oil/canvas (52x64cm 20x25in) Taipei
1999

LI JIAN 1747-1799 **[9]**
✍ **$13 482** - €14 722 - **£8 673** - FF96 568
Landscape Ink (25.5x529cm 10x208in) Hong-Kong
2000

LI KERAN 1907-1989 **[107]**
✍ **$22 269** - €18 811 - **£13 368** - FF123 389
Pavilion in Plum Blossom Grove Ink (57x49.5cm
22x19in) Hong-Kong 1998

LI KUCHAN 1898-1983 **[7]**
✍ **$1 680** - €1 954 - **£1 200** - FF12 818
Standing Heron amongst Banana Leaves Ink
(69x50cm 27x19in) London 2001

LI LIUFANG 1575-1629 **[7]**
✍ **$7 000** - €6 043 - **£4 181** - FF39 637
Landscape Ink (20.5x92.5cm 8x36in) New-York 1998

LI MING TAIO (Lee Ming Taio) 1922 **[1]**
⌾ **$2 624** - €2 794 - **£1 664** - FF18 328
Shepherd Boys besides the Tamsui River Gelatin
silver print (40.5x51cm 15x20in) Taipei 2000

LI MU 1958 **[2]**
⌐ **$3 861** - €3 664 - **£2 346** - FF24 033
Girl with Headscarf Oil/canvas (79x58.5cm 31x23in)
Hong-Kong 1999

LI PAI XIX **[1]**
⌐ **$20 984** - €19 426 - **£13 000** - FF127 424
**George Chinnery, Half-length, Wearing a Frock
Coat at his Easel** Oil/canvas (27x23cm 10x9in)
London 1999

LI QIUJUN 1899-1973 **[2]**
✍ **$1 282** - €1 445 - **£896** - FF9 477
Plum Blossoms and Camellia Ink (70.5x27cm
27x10in) Hong-Kong 2001

LI QUANWU 1957 **[7]**
⌐ **$6 177** - €5 862 - **£3 753** - FF38 452
Morning Oil/canvas (100x75cm 39x29in) Hong-Kong
1999

LI RIUHA 1565-1635 **[1]**
✍ **$3 870** - €3 632 - **£2 391** - FF23 823
Ink Plum after Wang Mian (1287-1359) Ink
(202.5x96.5cm 79x37in) Hong-Kong 1999

LI SHAN 1686-1756 **[7]**
✍ **$2 564** - €3 014 - **£1 778** - FF19 768
Shellfish and Vegetable Ink (26x30cm 10x11in)
Hong-Kong 2000

LI SHANGDA 1885-1949 **[2]**
✍ **$4 157** - €3 524 - **£2 485** - FF23 116
Landscape Coloured inks/paper (185x38cm 72x14in)
Hong-Kong 1998

LI SHIH-CH'IAO 1908-1995 **[18]**
⌐ **$36 080** - €38 419 - **£22 880** - FF252 010
Vase of Roses Oil/canvas (44x37cm 17x14in) Taipei
2000

⌐ **$7 925** - €9 250 - **£5 425** - FF60 675
Country Road Oil/canvas (41x32cm 16x12in) Taipei
2000

LI XIONGCAI 1912 **[17]**
✍ **$7 746** - €6 543 - **£4 650** - FF42 918
Travelling in Autumn Landscape Coloured
inks/paper (137x68cm 53x26in) Hong-Kong 1998

LI XUBAI 1940 **[3]**
✍ **$2 078** - €1 756 - **£1 247** - FF11 516
Misty Landscape Ink (16.5x246.5cm 6x97in) Hong-
Kong 1998

LI YANSHAN 1898-1961 **[1]**
✍ **$29 693** - €25 172 - **£17 756** - FF165 117
Poolside Studio Coloured inks/paper (26x207cm
10x81in) Hong-Kong 1998

LI YIHONG 1941 **[6]**
✍ **$7 998** - €7 543 - **£4 960** - FF49 476
Red Wall Ink (178x15cm 70x5in) Hong-Kong 1999

LI YIN XVII-XVIII **[1]**
✍ **$10 384** - €9 793 - **£6 440** - FF64 239
Thatch Hut by a Clear River Ink (195.5x54cm
76x21in) Hong-Kong 1999

LI YONG 678-747 **[2]**
✍ **$17 948** - €20 389 - **£12 600** - FF133 742
12th-13th century rubbing of the Yuhui Lixiu Bei
Ink (27x29cm 10x11in) Hong-Kong 2001

LI YOUSONG 1968 **[3]**
⌐ **$8 391** - €7 088 - **£5 037** - FF46 494
Old Dreams in Shanghai Oil/canvas (80x100cm
31x39in) Hong-Kong 1998

LI ZHONGLIANG 1944 **[21]**
⌐ **$12 870** - €12 213 - **£7 820** - FF80 110
Scenery of a Water Village Oil/canvas (112x99cm
44x38in) Hong-Kong 1999

LI ZHONGSHENG Li Chun-shan 1912-1984 **[20]**
⌐ **$146 880** - €166 767 - **£103 200** - FF1 093 920
«No.35» Oil/canvas (60x90cm 23x35in) Taipei 2001

✍ **$8 528** - €9 081 - **£5 408** - FF59 566
Abstract II Watercolour/paper (26.5x38.5cm 10x15in)
Taipei 2000

L

LI ZONGWAN 1705-1759 [1]
✍ **$23 166** – €21 969 - **£14 094** – FF144 108
Summer Landscape After Wu Zhen (1280-1354)
Ink/paper (15x91cm 5x35in) Hong-Kong 1999

LIAGNO di Theodoro Filippo XVII [2]
👁 **$23 200** – €30 063 - **£17 400** – FF197 200
Enea e la Sibilla nell'Ade Olio/tela (68x105cm 26x41in) Roma 2000

LIANG QICHAO 1873-1928 [6]
✍ **$6 666** – €7 928 - **£4 591** – FF52 005
Calligraphy Couplet in Kai Shu Ink/paper (233x45cm 91x17in) Hong-Kong 2000

LIANG SHUMING 1893-1988 [1]
✍ **$3 217** – €3 051 - **£1 957** – FF20 015
Calligraphy in Xing Shu Ink/paper (142x37cm 55x14in) Hong-Kong 1999

LIANG ZHUOSHU 1953 [2]
👁 **$8 346** – €9 159 - **£5 375** – FF60 079
Paper Cutting Oil/canvas (117x86.5cm 46x34in) Hong-Kong 2000

LIAO CHI-CH'UN Liao Jichun 1902-1976 [8]
👁 **$198 900** – €225 850 - **£139 750** – FF1 481 350
The Bridge Oil/canvas (65x53cm 25x20in) Taipei 2001

LIAO DEZHENG 1920 [2]
👁 **$44 380** – €51 799 - **£30 380** – FF339 780
Kuan Yin Mountain Oil/canvas (38x45.5cm 14x17in) Taipei 2000

LIARDO Filippo 1840-1917 [4]
👁 **$34 000** – €37 970 - **£21 773** – FF249 067
The skating Party Oil/canvas (50x64.5cm 19x25in) New-York 2000

LIAUSU Camille 1894-1975 [194]
👁 **$2 392** – €2 744 - **£1 636** – FF18 000
La grande baigneuse Huile/toile (195x97cm 76x38in) Paris 2000
👁 **$1 742** – €1 524 - **£1 055** – FF10 000
Port Huile/toile (48x55cm 18x21in) Paris 1998
$130 – €152 - **£91** – FF1 000
Pierrot et l'Arlequin, scène romantique Gouache/papier (12x26cm 4x10in) Paris 2000

LIBAL Franta 1896-1974 [32]
👁 **$404** – €383 - **£252** – FF2 510
Wald im Fruehlingssonnenschein Öl/Leinwand/Karton (42x53cm 16x20in) Praha 2001

LIBALT Gottfried XVII [7]
👁 **$35 342** – €39 627 - **£24 000** – FF259 936
Still Life with a Plate of Apples, Peaches, Pears, Cabbages and Grapes Oil/canvas (71.5x94cm 28x37in) London 2000

LIBBRECHT Marc XX [1]
🎞 **$700** – €785 - **£486** – FF5 149
«L'affiche» Poster (61x42cm 24x16in) New-York 2001

LIBENSKY Stanislav 1921 [2]
🔨 **$22 000** – €21 000 - **£13 747** – FF137 753
Cross Head Sculpture, glass (36x26x14cm 14x10x5in) New-York 1999

LIBERAKI Aglae XX [4]
🔨 **$4 764** – €4 573 - **£2 988** – FF30 000
Solstice d'été No.2 Bronze (20x31cm 7x12in) Vannes 1999

LIBERATORE Fausto Maria 1922 [31]
👁 **$420** – €363 - **£210** – FF2 380
Volto Tecnica mista/cartone (50x37cm 19x14in) Prato 1999

✍ **$480** – €415 - **£240** – FF2 720
Pittore e modella Pastelli (30x40cm 11x15in) Prato 1999

LIBERATORE Tanino 1953 [3]
✍ **$2 847** – €3 201 - **£1 999** – FF21 000
«Ranxeros à New York» Encres couleurs/papier (32x25cm 12x9in) Paris 2001

LIBERI Marco 1640-1725 [13]
👁 **$19 992** – €17 271 - **£13 328** – FF113 288
Venere fustiga Amore Olio/tela (172x115.5cm 67x45in) Venezia 1998
👁 **$18 000** – €15 110 - **£10 557** – FF99 118
Venus and Cupid Oil/canvas (97x118cm 38x46in) New-York 1998

LIBERI Pietro Libertino 1614-1687 [36]
👁 **$14 000** – €18 141 - **£10 500** – FF119 000
Venere e amore Olio/tela (155.5x130cm 61x51in) Milano 2001
👁 **$24 000** – €21 123 - **£14 611** – FF138 559
Venus and Cupid Oil/canvas (83x106cm 32x41in) New-York 1999
👁 **$18 400** – €19 074 - **£11 040** – FF125 120
Le tre Parche Olio/tela (31x42cm 12x16in) Roma 1999
✍ **$2 760** – €3 049 - **£1 914** – FF20 000
Études de personnages Encre (44x30cm 17x11in) Paris 2001

LIBERMAN Alexander 1912 [40]
🔨 **$5 500** – €5 940 - **£3 801** – FF38 964
Untitled Metal (44.5x28x28cm 17x11x11in) New-York 2001

LIBERT Georg Emil 1820-1908 [189]
👁 **$8 606** – €9 554 - **£6 000** – FF62 669
The Konigsee Oil/canvas (122x152.5cm 48x60in) London 2001
👁 **$908** – €875 - **£565** – FF5 741
Ved Balestrand, Sognefjord, Norge Oil/canvas (45x64cm 17x25in) København 1999
👁 **$541** – €603 - **£378** – FF3 957
Fra en sydlandskab bjergsö Oil/canvas/panel (32x48cm 12x18in) København 2001

LIBERTS Ludolf 1895-1959 [18]
👁 **$1 321** – €1 263 - **£831** – FF8 284
Rådhusplatsen i Riga Oil/canvas (74x92cm 29x36in) Stockholm 1999

LIBESKI Robert 1892-1988 [24]
👁 **$721** – €727 - **£450** – FF4 767
Stilleben Mixed media (52x71cm 20x27in) Wien 2000

LIBESNY Kurt 1892-? [15]
🎞 **$195** – €182 - **£121** – FF1 191
«Zeichnet 8. Kriegsanleihe» Poster (63x96cm 24x37in) Wien 1999

LIBIS XX [1]
🎞 **$9 601** – €9 677 - **£6 000** – FF63 474
«Valais, le pays du soleil» Poster (128x92cm 50x36in) London 2000

LIBISZEWSKI Herbert 1897-1985 [6]
🎞 **$178** – €209 - **£122** – FF1 369
«Die Alpenpost» Poster (100x62cm 39x24in) Hoorn 2000

LICATA Riccardo 1929 [130]
👁 **$2 500** – €2 592 - **£1 500** – FF17 000
Composizione Tempera/tela (61x50cm 24x19in) Vercelli 2001

$1 560 - €1 348 - £780 - FF8 840
Composizione Tempera/tela (33x46cm 12x18in)
Prato 1999
$900 - €777 - £600 - FF5 100
Composizione Tecnica mista/carta (50x50cm
19x19in) Milano 1998

LICHANSKY Batia 1901-1992 [31]
$1 100 - €1 181 - £736 - FF7 745
Landscape Oil/canvas (20.5x25.5cm 8x10in) Tel Aviv
2000
$1 100 - €1 304 - £801 - FF8 554
Modesty Bronze (H48cm H18in) Tel Aviv 2001

LICHT Hans 1876-1935 [55]
$541 - €604 - £370 - FF3 959
Efterårsparti fra en landsby Oil/board (60x72cm
23x28in) Viby J, Århus 2000

LICHTENAUER Joseph Mortimer 1876-? [3]
$7 000 - €5 997 - £4 208 - FF39 337
Untitled Egyptian Scene Oil/canvas (122x91.5cm
48x36in) New-York 1998

LICHTENBERGER Hermann Julius ?-1897 [3]
$22 414 - €24 060 - £15 000 - FF157 824
Honeymoon to the Schreckenstein Oil/canvas
(69x142cm 27x55in) London 2000

LICHTENHELD Wilhelm 1817-1891 [12]
$1 619 - €1 534 - £984 - FF10 061
**Mondscheinlandschaft mit einer Burg auf
Bergeskuppe über einem See** Öl/Leinwand
(57x46cm 22x18in) München 1999
$1 341 - €1 483 - £930 - FF9 726
Der Blick in die Ferne Aquarell/Papier (20x17cm
7x6in) München 2001

LICHTENSTEIN Roy 1923-1997 [1626]
$410 000 - €459 230 - £284 868 - FF3 012 352
Woman II Oil/canvas (203x142.5cm 79x56in) New-
York 2001
$90 000 - €100 807 - £62 532 - FF661 248
Lemon and Apple Acrylic/canvas (51x61cm 20x24in)
New-York 2000
$18 000 - €20 885 - £12 427 - FF136 998
Seascape Mixed media/board (23.5x50cm 9x19in)
New-York 2000
$26 000 - €29 569 - £18 166 - FF193 962
Modern Sculpture with Intersecting Arches
Metal (80x36.5x36.5cm 31x14x14in) Beverly-Hills CA
2000
$17 000 - €16 003 - £10 502 - FF104 973
Untitled Head I Metal (62.5x23x1cm 24x9xin) New-
York 1999
$20 000 - €19 220 - £12 320 - FF126 078
Seascape Pencil (15x18cm 5x7in) New-York 1999
$5 000 - €4 973 - £3 103 - FF32 622
Haystack Screenprint (48x66cm 18x25in) Beverly-
Hills CA 1999

LICHTNER-AIX Werner 1939-1987 [15]
$166 - €153 - £102 - FF1 006
Marktplatz von Vaison la Romaine I Lithographie
(50x65cm 19x25in) Bielefeld 1999

LICINI Osvaldo 1894-1958 [77]
$32 500 - €33 691 - £19 500 - FF221 000
Paesaggio Olio/tela (36x49.5cm 14x19in) Prato 1999
$45 000 - €46 649 - £27 000 - FF306 000
Studio per angelo su fondo giallo Olio/carta
(28x22.5cm 11x8in) Milano 1999
$3 600 - €4 060 - £2 700 - FF30 600
Angelo ribelle, amalassunta Matita/carta
(24.5x33cm 9x12in) Milano 2000

LICINIO Bernardino c.1490-c.1565 [12]
$150 000 - €132 020 - £91 320 - FF865 995
**«Sacra Conversazione» with Sts Joseph, the
Infant St John the Baptism** Oil/canvas
(110.5x153.5cm 43x60in) New-York 1999
$86 520 - €87 207 - £54 000 - FF572 040
**Sacra conversazione, Madonna con bambino e
i Santi Pietro e Gerolamo** Oil/panel (60.5x82.5cm
23x32in) Wien 2000

LIDDELL T. Hodgson 1860-1925 [10]
$449 - €461 - £280 - FF3 022
Beer Watercolour (24x40cm 9x15in) London 2000

LIDDELL William F. ?-c.1927 [2]
$1 746 - €2 088 - £1 200 - FF13 695
Westminster Abbey Watercolour (23.5x34cm
9x13in) Billingshurst, West-Sussex 2000

LIDDERDALE Charles Sillem 1831-1895 [125]
$8 779 - €8 106 - £5 400 - FF53 170
A Moment's Contemplation Oil/canvas (76.5x51cm
30x20in) London 1999
$1 409 - €1 226 - £849 - FF8 039
Deep in Thought Oil/panel (16.5x14cm 6x5in)
London 1998
$1 610 - €1 719 - £1 100 - FF11 278
Portrait of a Lady Watercolour/paper (39x31cm
15x12in) Billingshurst, West-Sussex 2001

LIDWINE Dominique 1960 [1]
$1 898 - €2 134 - £1 332 - FF14 000
La quête de l'oiseau du temps Encres
couleurs/papier (30x30cm 11x11in) Paris 2001

LIE Emil 1897-1976 [2]
$1 671 - €1 851 - £1 134 - FF12 145
Stående akt Bronze (H58cm H22in) Oslo 2000

LIE Jonas 1880-1940 [68]
$50 000 - €59 463 - £35 635 - FF390 050
Sapphires and Amethysts Oil/canvas
(127x152.5cm 50x60in) New-York 2000
$16 000 - €18 484 - £11 203 - FF121 249
Clouds Shadows Oil/canvas (63.5x76.5cm 25x30in)
New-York 2001
$2 100 - €1 812 - £1 262 - FF11 884
«Boat at the End of a Jetty» Oil/canvas (29x24cm
11x9in) Boston MA 1998
$2 500 - €2 625 - £1 690 - FF17 216
Dawn Watercolour/paper (25x35cm 10x14in) Fairfield
ME 2001
$800 - €744 - £493 - FF4 879
«On the Job for Victory» Poster (99x139cm
39x55in) New-York 2001

LIE-JØRGENSEN Thorbjørn 1900-1961 [15]
$779 - €864 - £529 - FF5 667
Landskap fra Valesvaer Oil/panel (46x55cm
18x21in) Oslo 2000

LIEBENWEIN Maximilian 1869-1926 [14]
$2 159 - €1 994 - £1 344 - FF13 080
Portrait der Dora Rauch mit gelbem Hut
Pastell/Papier (60x47cm 23x18in) Frankfurt 1999

LIEBERICH Nicolaï Ivanovitch 1828-1883 [12]
$3 033 - €3 573 - £2 097 - FF23 437
**Group of Wolf Hunters dismounted to take the
Wolf Alive** Bronze (25x41.5cm 9x16in) Cape Town
2000

LIEBERMANN Ernst 1869-1960 [134]
$765 - €893 - £540 - FF5 856
Study of a nude Oil/canvas (75x65cm 29x25in)
Stansted Mountfitchet, Essex 2000

L

🖋 **$121** - €112 - **£75** - FF737
Herzog Wittekind Gouache/paper (32x25cm 12x9in)
Stuttgart 1999

▥ **$58** - €61 - **£38** - FF402
«Augsburger Ansichten» Lithographie (42x23cm
16x9in) München 2000

LIEBERMANN Ferdinand 1883-1941 **[43]**
🖌 **$549** - €654 - **£392** - FF4 290
Faun mit Krokodil Porcelain (H35.2cm H13in) Wien
2000

LIEBERMANN Max 1847-1935 **[1588]**
👓 **$75 057** - €89 477 - **£53 515** - FF586 932
**Sitzende Frau nach Vorne, Studie zu den
Netzflickerinnen** Öl/Karton (59x78.7cm 23x30in)
Berlin 2000
👓 **$21 445** - €25 565 - **£15 290** - FF167 695
**Muttersau und Ferkel, Studien zum
Schweinekoben** Öl/Leinwand (26x35cm 10x13in)
Berlin 2000
👓 **$3 937** - €3 822 - **£2 451** - FF25 070
Gemüsemarkt in Delft Chalks/paper (20.3x33.7cm
7x13in) Berlin 1999
▥ **$545** - €529 - **£339** - FF3 471
Der Barmherzige Samariter Lithographie
(6.5x10.8cm 2x4in) Berlin 1999

LIEBERT Alphonse J. 1827-1913 **[6]**
📷 **$4 265** - €4 813 - **£3 000** - FF31 568
Les ruines de Paris et des environs Albumen
print (19x25cm 7x9in) London 2001

LIEBHART R. XX **[23]**
🖋 **$309** - €368 - **£214** - FF2 414
Rumänischer Matrose Charcoal (62x48cm 24x18in)
München 2000

LIEBKNECHT Robert 1903-1994 **[10]**
▥ **$174** - €164 - **£108** - FF1 073
Strassenszene in Paris Lithographie (38.9x49.8cm
15x19in) Berlin 1999

LIEBMANN Werner 1951 **[4]**
👓 **$4 100** - €3 822 - **£2 478** - FF25 070
Zu Zweit (Künstlerportraits) Mixed media
(70.3x94cm 27x37in) München 1999

LIEBSCHER Adolf 1857-1919 **[19]**
👓 **$1 069** - €1 011 - **£666** - FF6 634
Repose among the Ruins Oil/canvas (57.5x40.5cm
22x15in) Praha 2001

LIEBSCHER Karl 1851-1906 **[23]**
👓 **$990** - €919 - **£616** - FF6 030
Trees Oil/canvas (26.5x30cm 10x11in) Praha 1999

LIEDEL Oscar XX **[4]**
🖋 **$4 445** - €4 311 - **£2 797** - FF28 277
Mangbetu WOman/Batetela juju priest
Watercolour (50x34.5cm 19x13in) Amsterdam 1999

LIEDER Friedrich G., Franz 1780-1859 **[20]**
👓 **$3 002** - €3 579 - **£2 140** - FF23 477
**Bildnis einer vornehmen Empiredame und ihres
Sohnes** Miniature (48.5x31.7cm 19x12in) Köln 2000

LIEGEOIS Paul XVII **[9]**
👓 **$22 086** - €20 581 - **£13 621** - FF135 000
Pêches et prunes sur un entablement de pierre
Huile/toile (33.5x44.5cm 13x17in) Paris 1999

LIEGI Ulvi 1859-1939 **[63]**
👓 **$6 000** - €6 220 - **£3 600** - FF40 800
Paesaggio Olio/tavola (15x19.5cm 5x7in) Milano
2000

LIENDER van Jacobus 1696-1759 **[7]**
🖋 **$1 402** - €1 633 - **£979** - FF10 715
View of a Dutch Town Watercolour (13x23cm 5x9in)
Amsterdam 2000

LIENDER van Paulus 1731-1797 **[27]**
🖋 **$1 145** - €944 - **£674** - FF6 195
Dorfstrasse an einem Fluss Ink (17.2x23.6cm
6x9in) Wien 1998

LIENDER van Pieter Jacobsz. 1727-1779 **[13]**
👓 **$18 228** - €20 452 - **£12 636** - FF134 156
Holländische Kirche und Kapelle am Wasser
Öl/Leinwand (48x69.5cm 18x27in) München 2000
👓 **$779** - €908 - **£544** - FF5 953
Boatmen Before a Ruined Castle Ink (17x23.5cm
6x9in) Amsterdam 2000

LIER Adolf 1826-1882 **[89]**
👓 **$4 763** - €5 113 - **£3 188** - FF33 539
Pärchen beim Rendez-vous am Waldrand
Öl/Leinwand (55x41.5cm 21x16in) Kempten 2000
👓 **$2 146** - €2 250 - **£1 594** - FF14 757
Chiemseelandschaft mit Blick auf die Alpen
Oil/canvas/panel (22x46.5cm 8x18in) Köln 2000

LIERNUR Willem Adrianus Al. 1856-1917 **[1]**
👓 **$4 247** - €4 991 - **£2 944** - FF32 742
Differents Interests Oil/canvas (56x63cm 22x24in)
Amsterdam 2000

LIES Joseph Hendrik H. 1821-1865 **[14]**
👓 **$4 000** - €4 031 - **£2 493** - FF26 440
The Approaching of the Enemy Oil/canvas
(91x126.5cm 35x49in) New-York 2000

LIESEGANG Helmut 1858-1945 **[107]**
👓 **$2 149** - €2 556 - **£1 532** - FF16 769
**Schäfer mit seiner Herde auf einer frühlingshaf-
ten Allee** Öl/Leinwand (51x40cm 20x15in) Köln 2000
👓 **$952** - €1 022 - **£637** - FF6 707
**Schäfer mit seiner Herde auf einer Dorfstrasse
am Niederrhein** Öl/Leinwand (33x43cm 12x16in)
Köln 2000

LIESKE Karl 1816-1878 **[5]**
👓 **$1 367** - €1 534 - **£947** - FF10 061
Das Saumpferd am Brunnen vor der Almhütte
Öl/Leinwand (26x22cm 10x8in) München 2000

LIESLER Josef 1912 **[42]**
🖋 **$317** - €301 - **£198** - FF1 972
Surgeon Watercolour (47x20cm 18x7in) Praha 2000

LIESTE Cornelis 1817-1861 **[34]**
👓 **$3 810** - €4 386 - **£2 600** - FF28 773
Cattle Watering in an Extensive Landscape
Oil/panel (49.5x65cm 19x25in) London 2000

LIEVENS Jan 1607-1674 **[74]**
👓 **$28 945** - €31 765 - **£18 634** - FF208 362
**Couple in Shepherd Costume by a Tree in a
Landscape** Oil/canvas (146x120cm 57x47in)
Amsterdam 2000
👓 **$106 021** - €99 161 - **£65 000** - FF650 455
Head of a Bearded Man Oil/panel (60x49cm
23x19in) London 1998
🖋 **$16 044** - €15 428 - **£9 883** - FF101 204
**The Rollerbridge to the Slopolder, Near
Amsterdam** Ink (13.5x23cm 5x9in) Amsterdam 1999
▥ **$565** - €665 - **£406** - FF4 360
**Jacques Gaultier, französischer Musiker in
London** Radierung (26.5x21cm 10x8in) Hamburg
2001

LIEVRE Édouard 1829-1886 **[2]**
- **$4 127** - €4 400 - **£2 800** - FF28 865
  Les lavandières au bord de Loing Oil/canvas
  (33x45.5cm 12x17in) London 2001

LIFSHITZ Uri 1936 **[111]**
- **$3 800** - €4 277 - **£2 617** - FF28 054
  Untitled Oil/canvas (73x92cm 28x36in) Herzelia-
  Pituah 2000
- **$700** - €692 - **£428** - FF4 538
  Untitled Mixed media/paper (274.5x106.5cm
  108x41in) Tel Aviv 2000

LIGABUE Antonio 1899-1965 **[22]**
- **$25 800** - €22 288 - **£17 200** - FF146 200
  Paesaggio Olio/tela (50x60cm 19x23in) Prato 1998
- **$19 500** - €16 846 - **£9 750** - FF110 500
  Alci Olio/cartone (30x40cm 11x15in) Milano 1999

LIGARE David 1945 **[5]**
- **$3 000** - €2 535 - **£1 789** - FF16 629
  Cobalt Blue and White, Study Pencil (76x57cm
  29x22in) San-Francisco CA 1998

LIGARI Pietro 1686-1752 **[3]**
- **$17 500** - €18 141 - **£10 500** - FF119 000
  La Carità Olio/tela (134x105cm 52x41in) Milano 1999

LIGETI Antal 1823-1890 **[9]**
- **$10 000** - €9 833 - **£6 250** - FF64 500
  By the River Bank Oil/canvas (77.5x127.5cm
  30x50in) Budapest 1999

LIGHT John Henry XIX **[1]**
- **$2 300** - €2 523 - **£1 484** - FF16 550
  Rooster, a Peacock and two Ducks
  Watercolour/paper (17x26cm 7x10in) Philadelphia PA
  2000

LIGNON Bernard 1921 **[64]**
- **$443** - €479 - **£297** - FF3 139
  Paris Huile/toile (46x55cm 18x21in) Genève 2000

LIGON Glenn 1960 **[12]**
- **$46 000** - €53 373 - **£31 758** - FF350 106
  «Invisible man» Oil/canvas (76x51cm 29x20in) New-
  York 2001
- **$8 000** - €7 688 - **£4 928** - FF50 431
  I am an Invisible Man Soft pencil/paper (82x41.5cm
  32x16in) New-York 1999

LIGORIO Pirro 1513-1583 **[19]**
- **$8 500** - €7 456 - **£5 161** - FF48 907
  **Allegory of Music, Draped Woman Seated befo-
  re a Portative** Ink (20.5x17cm 8x6in) New-York 1999

LIGOZZI Bartolomeo 1630-1695 **[10]**
- **$11 400** - €12 949 - **£8 000** - FF84 940
  **A Stemma celebrating the Marriage of Antonio
  di Francesco Michelozzi** Oil/canvas/panel
  (228x194cm 89x76in) London 2001

LIGOZZI Jacopo, Giacomo 1547-1626 **[21]**
- **$20 000** - €20 733 - **£12 000** - FF136 000
  Il trionfo di Davide Olio/tela (165x103cm 64x40in)
  Milano 2000
- **$20 000** - €17 543 - **£12 144** - FF115 076
  Saint Catherine of Alexandria Oil/copper
  (51x35.5cm 20x13in) New-York 1999
- **$8 500** - €9 078 - **£5 792** - FF59 548
  Death Breaking his Scythe and Two Putti Red
  chalk (28.5x22cm 11x8in) New-York 2001

LIGTELIJN Evert Jan 1893-1977 **[72]**
- **$727** - €681 - **£452** - FF4 464
  Haymaking in Summer Oil/panel (50x40cm
  19x15in) Amsterdam 1999

- **$435** - €431 - **£266** - FF2 827
  Curaçao Oil/panel (20x40cm 7x15in) Amsterdam
  2000

LIIPOLA Yrjö 1881-1971 **[17]**
- **$457** - €437 - **£278** - FF2 868
  Såningsman Terracotta (H32cm H12in) Helsinki 1999

LILANGA DI NYAMA Georges 1944 **[18]**
- **$11 399** - €11 002 - **£7 200** - FF72 171
  **Maintain Good Relations with your Neighbours
  and they will Help You...** Acrylic (140x120cm
  55x47in) London 1999
- **$2 437** - €2 386 - **£1 500** - FF15 650
  Nimechoka Sana Hata Kutembea Siwezi
  Acrylic/panel (61x61cm 24x24in) London 1999
- **$1 850** - €1 918 - **£1 110** - FF12 580
  Usikate Miti Kwasa Babu Kivuli Kina Oil/masonite
  (30x40cm 11x15in) Prato 2000
- **$3 750** - €3 887 - **£2 250** - FF25 500
  Senza titolo Sculpture bois (H71cm H27in) Prato
  2000

LILIEN Ephraim Moshe 1874-1925 **[34]**
- **$4 257** - €3 997 - **£2 629** - FF26 218
  Illustration zu «Das Hohe Lied Salomo» Ink
  (49x34cm 19x13in) Wien 1999
- **$731** - €727 - **£442** - FF4 767
  Exlibris Leo M.Brown Radierung (37x24cm 14x9in)
  Wien 2000

LILIO Andrea 1555-1610 **[2]**
- **$3 899** - €3 816 - **£2 500** - FF25 030
  St. Nicholas Black chalk (20x15.5cm 7x6in) London
  1999

LILJEBLADH Birgitta 1924 **[41]**
- **$491** - €579 - **£345** - FF3 795
  2 Nerium Oil/panel (65x55cm 25x21in) Malmö 2000

LILJEFORS Bruno 1860-1939 **[685]**
- **$39 472** - €41 363 - **£25 000** - FF271 322
  **Duvhök Med Orre Mobbad Av Kråkor (Goshawk
  with Black Game)** Oil/canvas (122x200cm 48x78in)
  London 2000
- **$15 934** - €18 126 - **£11 129** - FF118 900
  Räv i vinterlandskap Oil/canvas (40x50cm 15x19in)
  Stockholm 2000
- **$8 537** - €9 919 - **£6 000** - FF65 065
  Räv i vinterlandskap (snow landscape with fox)
  Oil/panel (33x41.5cm 12x16in) London 2001
- **$3 096** - €3 485 - **£2 133** - FF22 863
  Landskap med sittande örn Akvarell/papper
  (60x35cm 23x13in) Stockholm 2000
- **$384** - €358 - **£237** - FF2 349
  Katt Woodcut (8.3x11.3cm 3x4in) Stockholm 1999

LILJEFORS Lindorm 1909-1985 **[378]**
- **$1 693** - €1 690 - **£1 057** - FF11 085
  Älgar och gråhund i höstfärger Oil/canvas
  (50x61cm 19x24in) Uppsala 1999
- **$1 220** - €1 041 - **£729** - FF6 829
  Jägare med vildsvin Oil/panel (32x45cm 12x17in)
  Stockholm 1998

LILJELUND Arvid 1844-1899 **[31]**
- **$18 825** - €16 477 - **£11 407** - FF108 084
  Torp i kuru Oil/canvas (72x119cm 28x46in) Helsinki
  1998
- **$1 932** - €2 102 - **£1 273** - FF13 790
  Flicka Oil/panel (22x16cm 8x6in) Helsinki 2000

LILLE Ludwig 1897-1957 **[9]**
- **$6 633** - €5 806 - **£4 018** - FF38 083
  A Table Oil/canvas (65x81cm 25x31in) Warszawa 1998

L

$1 887 - €2 021 - **£1 284** - FF13 258
Scène d'intérieur Huile/toile (27x35cm 10x13in)
Warszawa 2001

LILLIS Richard XX [2]
$5 500 - €5 267 - **£3 397** - FF34 550
**Cowboy at Watering Hole Returning Gunfire,
Pulp Magazine Cover** Oil/canvas (76x51cm 30x20in)
New-York 1999

LILLONI Umberto 1898-1980 [175]
$8 249 - €8 552 - **£4 949** - FF56 098
Paesaggio con case a Medole Olio/tela/cartone
(46x56cm 18x22in) Milano 1999
$6 250 - €6 479 - **£3 750** - FF42 500
S. Maria delle Grazie Olio/tela (33x46cm 12x18in)
Roma 2000
$1 800 - €1 866 - **£1 080** - FF12 240
Vaso di fiori Pastelli/carta (40x50cm 15x19in) Milano
1999

LILLY Marjorie 1891-1980 [4]
$2 305 - €2 166 - **£1 400** - FF14 209
The Visitor Oil/canvas (38x30.5cm 14x12in) London
1999

LILLYWHITE Raphael 1891-1980 [7]
$4 500 - €5 289 - **£3 119** - FF34 692
Herding Cattle Oil/board (45x60cm 18x24in)
Cincinnati OH 2000
$1 700 - €1 983 - **£1 214** - FF13 006
**Cowboy with Horse overlooking mountainous
western Landscape** Oil/masonite (30x38cm
12x15in) St. Louis MO 2001

LIM H.H. 1954 [2]
$1 800 - €2 332 - **£1 350** - FF15 300
Grazie al cielo Tecnica mista (92x125cm 36x49in)
Milano 2001

LIM TZE PENG 1923 [1]
$2 295 - €2 607 - **£1 571** - FF17 098
Village by The River Ink (70x70cm 27x27in)
Singapore 2000

LIMA CRUZ Maria Adelaide 1908-1985 [4]
$10 750 - €12 463 - **£7 500** - FF81 750
Casa de quinta Oleo/lienzo (30x40cm 11x15in)
Lisboa 2001

LIMBACH Hans Jörg 1928-1990 [4]
$11 132 - €13 107 - **£7 822** - FF85 974
Tänzerin Bronze (H206cm H81in) Zürich 2000

LIMBACH Russell 1904-1975 [17]
$200 - €186 - **£123** - FF1 222
Student and Master Etching, aquatint (24x30cm
9x12in) Cleveland OH 1999

LIMBORCH van Hendrick 1681-1759 [10]
$22 000 - €24 137 - **£14 614** - FF158 329
The Golden Age Oil/panel (60.5x83cm 23x32in)
New-York 2000
$7 471 - €8 020 - **£5 000** - FF52 608
Artemisia II, Queen of Caria Oil/panel (31x24.5cm
12x9in) London 2000

LIMOUSE Roger 1894-1990 [276]
$3 600 - €3 497 - **£2 250** - FF22 938
La commode verte Oil/canvas (132x126cm 51x49in)
New-York 1999
$2 900 - €2 817 - **£1 812** - FF18 478
Nature morte avec des pipes Oil/canvas
(53.5x65cm 21x25in) New-York 1999
$268 - €305 - **£186** - FF2 000
Femme pensive Crayon gras/papier (43x36cm
16x14in) Douai 2000

LIMPACH Maximilien XVIII [3]
$3 080 - €3 304 - **£2 035** - FF21 670
Vista desde el balcón/Calle del pueblo Oleo/tabla
(39.5x29cm 15x11in) Madrid 2000
$448 - €481 - **£296** - FF3 152
Ornamentos, Según Joan Giardini Grabado
(29x20cm 11x7in) Madrid 2000

LIN FENGMIAN 1900-1991 [258]
$96 150 - €113 010 - **£66 675** - FF741 300
Opera Figures Oil/canvas (54x45cm 21x17in) Hong-
Kong 2000
$19 230 - €21 845 - **£13 500** - FF143 295
Beach Hut Ink (67x69cm 26x27in) Hong-Kong 2001

LIN HUIKUI 1945 [6]
$8 333 - €9 466 - **£5 850** - FF62 094
Monkeys Ink (65x127cm 25x50in) Hong-Kong 2001

LIN Richard, Lin Shouyu 1933 [29]
$54 900 - €46 101 - **£32 220** - FF302 400
Gwynfryn Oil/canvas (127x127cm 50x50in) Taipei
1998
$12 240 - €13 897 - **£8 600** - FF91 160
Rise Oil/canvas (88.5x101cm 34x39in) Taipei 2001

LIN SHU 1862-1924 [5]
$405 - €5 126 - **£3 288** - FF33 625
Green Landscape Ink (133.5x67.5cm 52x26in)
Hong-Kong 1999

LIN van Hermann c.1630-c.1670 [7]
$121 035 - €113 297 - **£75 000** - FF743 182
Cavalry Battle in an Extensive Landscape
Oil/canvas (118x174cm 46x68in) London 1999
$18 574 - €22 105 - **£13 267** - FF145 000
**Le repos des chevaux/L'arrivée chez le maré-
chal-ferrant** Huile/panneau (27x29.5cm 10x11in)
Orléans 2000

LIN WENJIE Dominic Man-kit Lam 1947 [2]
$5 164 - €4 362 - **£3 100** - FF28 612
Snowy Night Mixed media (62.5x128.5cm 24x50in)
Hong-Kong 1998

LIN ZHIZHU Lin Chih-chu 1917 [2]
$12 236 - €11 339 - **£7 607** - FF74 382
Paddy Field Mixed media (24x30cm 9x11in) Taipei
1999

LINARD Jacques c.1600-1645 [17]
$34 857 - €41 161 - **£24 759** - FF270 000
Assiette remplie de cerises et de fraises
Huile/panneau (24x32cm 9x12in) Paris 2001

LINCK Jean Antoine 1766-1843 [33]
$5 533 - €5 488 - **£3 441** - FF36 000
**Paysage animé vu à travers une arche de
rochers** Aquarelle (28.5x44cm 11x17in) Paris 1999
$2 506 - €2 438 - **£1 542** - FF15 995
Vue de la Dent du Midi, et du Château de Panex
Farbradierung (36x47.7cm 14x18in) Bern 1999

LINCOLN Edwin Hale XIX-XX [27]
$6 000 - €5 595 - **£3 621** - FF36 699
**Wild Flowers of New England, Photographed
from Nature, Part VII** Platinum print (24x19cm 9x7in)
New-York 1999

LIND Andreas 1815-1885 [2]
$3 500 - €3 887 - **£2 436** - FF25 499
Skibsportraet Oil/canvas (51x77cm 20x30in)
Köbenhavn 2001

LIND Christian Georg 1800-1856 [4]
$1 913 - €2 147 - **£1 326** - FF14 084
Prospekt af Hirschholm Slot Oil/canvas
(21x27.5cm 8x10in) Köbenhavn 2000

LINDAU Dietrich Wilhelm 1799-1862 **[13]**
✏ **$1 864** - €2 045 - **£1 266** - FF13 415
Briganten mit ihren Familien nach dem Raubzug in den Bergen Pencil/paper (22.5x26.5cm 8x10in) Berlin 2000

LINDAUER Gottfried 1830-1926 **[7]**
⌐ **$13 542** - €15 176 - **£9 440** - FF99 545
Hinepare of the Ngat Kahungunu Tribe of taakitimu Fame Oil/canvas (84x66cm 33x25in) Wellington 2001

LINDBERG Alf 1905-1990 **[101]**
⌐ **$1 159** - €1 271 - **£769** - FF8 340
Hustak och grönskande träd Oil/panel (50x64cm 19x25in) Stockholm 2000

LINDBERG Frans 1858-1944 **[4]**
✏ **$2 683** - €3 021 - **£1 848** - FF19 814
Tiondemöte på Österlen i Skåne på 1820-talet Akvarell/papper (32x48cm 12x18in) Uppsala 2000

LINDBERG Gustaf 1852-1932 **[5]**
🖎 **$1 104** - €1 190 - **£741** - FF7 809
Vågen Bronze (9x26.5cm 3x10in) Stockholm 2000

LINDBERGH Harald 1901-1976 **[113]**
⌐ **$1 036** - €896 - **£625** - FF5 880
Trälastad skuta Oil/panel (38x46cm 14x18in) Stockholm 1999
⌐ **$392** - €411 - **£248** - FF2 698
Tallriken Oil/panel (33x41cm 12x16in) Malmö 2000

LINDBERG Maria 1958 **[3]**
⌐ **$1 174** - €1 310 - **£816** - FF8 592
Utan titel Painting (60x80cm 23x31in) Stockholm 2001

LINDBERG Stig 1916-1981 **[46]**
🖎 **$678** - €807 - **£483** - FF5 291
Horse Ceramic (H25cm H9in) Stockholm 2000
✏ **$505** - €586 - **£349** - FF3 847
Komposition i grått Watercolour/panel (61.5x30cm 24x11in) Stockholm 2000

LINDBERGH Peter 1945 **[6]**
📷 **$2 987** - €3 528 - **£2 121** - FF23 141
«Linda Evangelista, Naomi Campbell, Christy Turlington, Vogue Italy» Gelatin silver print (36x24cm 14x9in) Berlin 2001

LINDE van der Jan 1864-1945 **[32]**
⌐ **$1 146** - €1 134 - **£701** - FF7 462
Montelbaanstoren, Amsterdam Oil/canvas (72x47cm 28x18in) Amsterdam 2000

LINDE-WALTHER Heinrich 1868-1939 **[8]**
⌐ **$1 236** - €1 453 - **£858** - FF9 534
Mädchen mit ihren drei Brüdern Öl/Leinwand (76x94cm 29x37in) Wien 2000

LINDEGREN Amalia 1814-1891 **[5]**
✏ **$3 326** - €3 104 - **£2 049** - FF20 400
Fiske i solnedgången, par i eka Akvarell/papper (38x54cm 14x21in) Stockholm 1999

LINDELL Lage 1920-1980 **[149]**
⌐ **$4 912** - €4 616 - **£2 960** - FF30 276
Utan titel Mixed media/canvas (70x89cm 27x35in) Stockholm 1999
⌐ **$1 516** - €1 760 - **£1 047** - FF11 542
Två figurer Oil/canvas (23x35cm 9x13in) Stockholm 2000
✏ **$897** - €1 025 - **£632** - FF6 722
Utan titel Watercolour, gouache/paper (13x17cm 5x6in) Stockholm 2001

LINDAU

🎞 **$347** - €315 - **£213** - FF2 064
Figurer i svart Serigraph in colors (77x105cm 30x41in) Stockholm 1999

LINDEMANN Emil 1864-1945 **[21]**
⌐ **$266** - €311 - **£190** - FF2 041
Coquetterie Huile/papier (21x27.5cm 8x10in) Lódz 2000

LINDEMANN Kai 1931 **[54]**
⌐ **$780** - €872 - **£522** - FF5 719
Portraet Oil/canvas (66x78cm 25x30in) Köbenhavn 2000

LINDEMANN-FROMMEL Karl August 1819-1891 **[26]**
⌐ **$17 200** - €22 288 - **£12 900** - FF146 200
Il golfo di Napoli Olio/tela (60x135cm 23x53in) Napoli 2000
⌐ **$1 251** - €1 431 - **£860** - FF9 390
Castel Gandolfo Aquarell/Papier (50.4x43cm 19x16in) München 2000

LINDEMANN-FROMMEL Manfred Alfred 1852-? **[6]**
⌐ **$19 000** - €19 696 - **£11 400** - FF129 200
Porte Saint Marin Olio/tela (59x73.5cm 23x28in) Venezia 2000

LINDEN Helge 1897-1961 **[12]**
⌐ **$1 356** - €1 613 - **£967** - FF10 582
Hamnen Oil/panel (37.5x45.5cm 14x17in) Stockholm 2000

LINDEN VAN DYKE van der Philip XVIII **[2]**
⌐ **$6 460** - €6 075 - **£4 000** - FF39 849
Portrait of Captain Thomas Durell/Portrait of his Wife Oil/canvas (75x62.5cm 29x24in) London 1999

LINDENAU Martin XX **[64]**
⌐ **$1 734** - €1 672 - **£1 069** - FF10 969
Golfpartie in sommerlicher Gebirgslandschaft Öl/Leinwand (65x92cm 25x36in) Bern 1999

LINDENEG Thor 1941 **[26]**
⌐ **$433** - €404 - **£261** - FF2 649
Vemodigt sindbillede Oil/panel (80x60cm 31x23in) Köbenhavn 1999

LINDENFELD Emil 1905 **[6]**
⌐ **$1 500** - €1 390 - **£932** - FF9 120
The Encampment Oil/canvas (76x91cm 30x36in) New-Orleans LA 1999

LINDENMUTH Arlington N. 1867-? **[13]**
⌐ **$275** - €263 - **£172** - FF1 724
Near Red Hill, Landscape with Bridge Oil/board (27x35cm 11x14in) Hatfield PA 1999

LINDENMUTH Tod 1885-1976 **[63]**
⌐ **$425** - €404 - **£259** - FF2 678
Hazy August Morning Oil/board (30x40cm 12x16in) Provincetown MA 1999
🎞 **$900** - €843 - **£553** - FF5 529
«In the Weir» Woodcut in colors (23x18cm 9x7in) New-York

LINDENSCHMIT Hermann 1857-1939 **[34]**
⌐ **$1 157** - €1 363 - **£943** - FF8 942
Tischlermeister bei der Arbeit Öl/Leinwand (48.5x65cm 19x25in) Zofingen 1998

LINDER Philippe Jacques 1835-? **[16]**
⌐ **$529** - €569 - **£360** - FF3 735
Skaters Oil/panel (40x25.5cm 15x10in) Billingshurst, West-Sussex 2001
✏ **$942** - €915 - **£582** - FF6 000
Jeune élégante à l'éventail Aquarelle, gouache/papier (34x23cm 13x9in) Melun 1999

LINDER Richard 1901-1978 **[2]**
📷 **$4 326** - €4 920 - **£3 000** - FF32 272
    Untitled Lithograph (72x52cm 28x20in) London 2000

LINDERUM Richard 1851-? **[21]**
🖼 **$1 127** - €1 328 - **£780** - FF8 713
    The Recital Oil/panel (26x20cm 10x7in) Devon 2000

LINDFORS Anton 1881-? **[51]**
🖼 **$236** - €269 - **£162** - FF1 765
    Solnedgång Oil/canvas (41x41cm 16x16in) Helsinki 2000
✏ **$72** - €84 - **£51** - FF551
    Landskap Watercolour/paper (33x45cm 12x17in) Helsinki 2000

LINDGREN Emil 1866-1940 **[30]**
🖼 **$454** - €540 - **£313** - FF3 545
    Musselplockerskor på strand Oil/canvas (81x116cm 31x45in) Stockholm 2000

LINDH Bror 1877-1941 **[24]**
🖼 **$1 852** - €1 616 - **£1 120** - FF10 599
    «Arvika från Kyrkviken» Oil/canvas (39x44cm 15x17in) Stockholm 1998

LINDHOLM Berndt Adolf 1841-1914 **[208]**
🖼 **$37 275** - €42 045 - **£26 200** - FF275 800
    Kust Oil/canvas (130x100cm 51x39in) Helsinki 2001
🖼 **$20 916** - €23 545 - **£14 406** - FF154 448
    Segling i hård vind Oil/canvas (62x95cm 24x37in) Helsinki 2000
🖼 **$7 709** - €7 232 - **£4 764** - FF47 437
    Den ensamma seglaren Oil/canvas (31x25cm 12x9in) Helsinki 1999
✏ **$460** - €387 - **£270** - FF2 536
    Afton Drawing (10x17cm 3x6in) Helsinki 1998

LINDI Albert Lindegger 1904-1991 **[80]**
🖼 **$806** - €747 - **£493** - FF4 897
    Stilleben mit Fisch, Melone und Kanne Öl/Leinwand (54x73cm 21x28in) Bern 1999
✏ **$172** - €203 - **£125** - FF1 333
    «Sitzender Frauenakt am Meeresstrand» Indian ink/paper (32x24cm 12x9in) Zofingen 2001

LINDIN Carl Olaf Eric 1869-1942 **[8]**
🖼 **$446** - €495 - **£309** - FF3 249
    Landscape Oil/canvas (39x47cm 15x18in) Malmö 2001

LINDLAR Johann Wilhelm 1816-1896 **[11]**
🖼 **$2 147** - €2 250 - **£1 420** - FF14 757
    Gischtender Gebirgsbach Öl/Leinwand (106x86cm 41x33in) München 2000

LINDMAN Axel 1848-1930 **[47]**
🖼 **$933** - €808 - **£566** - FF5 298
    Kystparti med stejle klipper Oil/canvas (48x62cm 18x24in) København 1998
🖼 **$1 071** - €1 051 - **£664** - FF6 894
    Visby Oil/canvas (34x23cm 13x9in) Stockholm 1999

LINDNER Ernest 1897-1988 **[65]**
🖼 **$169** - €197 - **£119** - FF1 294
    Portrait of a Gentleman Oil/canvas (61x45.5cm 24x17in) Calgary, Alberta 2000
✏ **$1 039** - €1 160 - **£678** - FF7 606
    Untitled - Woman in White Pastel/paper (38x25cm 14x9in) Calgary, Alberta 2000
📷 **$244** - €287 - **£172** - FF1 884
    «Deadfall #2» Lithograph (57x42.5cm 22x16in) Calgary, Alberta 2000

LINDNER Peter Moffat 1852-1949 **[24]**
🖼 **$7 172** - €7 699 - **£4 800** - FF50 503
    A View of Arundel Castle at Dusk Oil/canvas (59x120cm 23x47in) London 2000
🖼 **$270** - €308 - **£190** - FF2 018
    «In Harbour, Concarneau» Watercolour/paper (27x37cm 10x14in) London 2001

LINDNER Richard 1901-1978 **[323]**
🖼 **$240 000** - €225 926 - **£148 272** - FF1 481 976
    The Walk Oil/canvas (152.5x101.5cm 60x39in) New-York 1999
🖼 **$4 118** - €4 857 - **£2 905** - FF31 862
    Busenengel Mixed media (109x55.6cm 42x21in) Köln 2001
🖼 **$15 645** - €18 407 - **£11 325** - FF120 740
    Portrait of Rand Öl/Leinwand (38x42cm 14x16in) Hamburg 2001
✏ **$2 000** - €2 147 - **£1 338** - FF14 082
    Deux Profils Pencil (21x16cm 8x6in) New-York 2000
📷 **$543** - €471 - **£330** - FF3 087
    Der Rosenkavalier Farblithographie (76.2x56cm 29x22in) München 1998

LINDO F. XVIII **[3]**
🖼 **$1 843** - €2 042 - **£1 250** - FF13 394
    Mrs.Binning, Mrs Stuart of Torrens, Sister of Countess of Dundonald Oil/panel (19.5x15cm 7x5in) Billingshurst, West-Sussex 2000

LINDQVIST Axel Hjalmar 1843-1917 **[31]**
🖼 **$386** - €358 - **£240** - FF2 349
    Sommarlandskap med kvarn vid å Oil/canvas (38x58cm 14x22in) Malmö 1999

LINDQVIST Herman 1868-1923 **[23]**
🖼 **$4 084** - €4 405 - **£2 741** - FF28 893
    Utsikt mot strandvägen, Stockholm Oil/canvas (31x41cm 12x16in) Stockholm 2000

LINDSAY Coutts, Bt. 1824-1907 **[5]**
🖼 **$2 108** - €2 025 - **£1 300** - FF13 284
    Highland Cattle watering in a mountainous Landscape Oil/canvas (30.5x45.5cm 12x17in) London 1999

LINDSAY Daryl Earnest 1890-1976 **[54]**
✏ **$273** - €265 - **£169** - FF1 740
    Ballerina Ink (30x37cm 11x14in) Sydney 1999

LINDSAY Lionel Arthur 1874-1961 **[573]**
✏ **$624** - €581 - **£385** - FF3 811
    Mending the Fence Crayon (37x43.5cm 14x17in) Melbourne 1999
📷 **$179** - €172 - **£110** - FF1 128
    The Hermitage, Cordoba Etching (21x29.5cm 8x11in) Melbourne 1999

LINDSAY Norman Alfred W. 1879-1969 **[754]**
🖼 **$66 040** - €77 886 - **£46 579** - FF510 900
    The Woman I am, the Woman I was, the Woman I will be Oil/canvas (199x119.5cm 78x47in) Woollahra, Sydney 2001
🖼 **$17 754** - €20 079 - **£12 495** - FF131 712
    Gypsy Girl Oil/canvas/board (50.5x35.5cm 19x13in) Malvern, Victoria 2001
🖼 **$7 696** - €8 595 - **£4 928** - FF56 381
    Nude in Landscape with Rabbits Oil/canvas (35.5x25cm 13x10in) Malvern, Victoria 2000
🗿 **$6 483** - €7 271 - **£4 502** - FF47 697
    Female Figure Bronze (H29cm H11in) Melbourne 2001
✏ **$2 826** - €3 131 - **£1 895** - FF20 539
    Frivolity Pencil/paper (39x28cm 15x11in) Melbourne 2000

🎨 **$2 302** - €2 141 - **£1 421** - FF14 042
«The Ambush» Etching (28x20cm 11x7in)
Melbourne 1999

LINDSAY Percival Ch., Percy 1870-1952 [51]
🎨 **$3 026** - €3 150 - **£1 900** - FF20 662
Cattle Grazing Oil/canvas (49.5x39.5cm 19x15in)
Melbourne 2000
🎨 **$1 518** - €1 694 - **£1 056** - FF11 114
Bush Summer Oil/canvas/board (23x31cm 9x12in)
Sydney 2001

LINDSAY Raymond 1904-1960 [14]
🎨 **$767** - €738 - **£472** - FF4 838
Bathing Belle Oil/canvas/board (37.5x28cm 14x11in)
Melbourne 1999

LINDSAY Thomas Corwin 1839-1907 [6]
🎨 **$800** - €870 - **£527** - FF5 707
The Cottage on the River Oil/canvas (40.5x61cm
15x24in) Boston MA 2000

LINDSTRAND Vicke 1904-1983 [36]
🎨 **$2 964** - €2 585 - **£1 792** - FF16 958
«Inga Tidblad» Oil/canvas (81x65cm 31x25in)
Stockholm 1998
⚱ **$943** - €1 062 - **£650** - FF6 969
Seated Male and Female Nudes Ceramic
(H20.5cm H8in) London 2000
✏ **$1 296** - €1 131 - **£784** - FF7 419
Man och kvinna Pencil (45x26.5cm 17x10in)
Stockholm 1998

LINDSTRÖM Arvid Mauritz 1849-1923 [56]
🎨 **$1 729** - €1 508 - **£1 045** - FF9 892
Insjölandskap i skymning Oil/canvas (37x65cm
14x25in) Stockholm 1998

LINDSTRÖM Bengt 1925 [933]
🎨 **$7 963** - €7 318 - **£4 891** - FF48 000
La joie de vivre Huile/toile (146x89cm 57x35in) Paris
1999
🎨 **$2 452** - €2 747 - **£1 705** - FF18 020
Mannen med ros Oil/canvas (46x38cm 18x14in)
Stockholm 2001
🎨 **$1 349** - €1 141 - **£806** - FF7 484
«Romantisk par» Oil/canvas (33x41cm 12x16in)
Stockholm 1998
⚱ **$449** - €488 - **£284** - FF3 198
Tängen Metal (H38cm H14in) Stockholm 2000
🎨 **$952** - €893 - **£588** - FF5 856
Figurkomposition Gouache/paper (76x35cm
29x22in) Stockholm 1999
🎨 **$189** - €161 - **£113** - FF1 059
Ohne Titel Farblithographie (76x53.5cm 29x21in)
Zürich 1998

LINDSTRÖM Fritz 1874-1962 [18]
🎨 **$1 954** - €2 230 - **£1 358** - FF14 626
Värmländskt sommarlandskap Oil/canvas
(33x48cm 12x18in) Stockholm 2001

LINDSTRÖM Rikard 1882-1943 [87]
🎨 **$868** - €787 - **£534** - FF5 161
Kustlandskap med båtar - Mariehamn Oil/panel
(46x42cm 18x16in) Stockholm 1998

LINDSTRÖM Tuija 1950 [2]
📷 **$1 517** - €1 692 - **£1 054** - FF11 098
Ur the Girl at Bull's Pond Gelatin silver print
(60x60cm 23x23in) Stockholm 2001

LINDT John William 1845-1926 [5]
📷 **$2 937** - €2 561 - **£1 776** - FF16 799
Sixty-eight Albumen Paper Photographs, Views
of Sydney Harbour... Albumen print (23.5x15cm
9x5in) Melbourne 1998

LINER Carl August 1871-1946 [92]
🎨 **$12 162** - €13 056 - **£8 138** - FF85 640
Appenzeller Winterlandschaft, Blick vom
Unterrain gegen den Dorfkern Öl/Leinwand
(43x55cm 16x21in) St. Gallen 2000
🎨 **$4 662** - €4 564 - **£2 869** - FF29 941
Winterliche Landschaft mit Blick auf den
Bodensee Öl/Leinwand/Karton (27x38.5cm 10x15in)
Zürich 1999
✏ **$2 308** - €2 611 - **£1 614** - FF17 129
Drei Stickerinnen am Fenster Pencil (21x27cm
8x10in) St. Gallen 2001
🎨 **$486** - €470 - **£305** - FF3 080
Senn beim Butterkneten Gravure bois couleurs
(21x16cm 8x6in) St. Gallen 1999

LINER Carl Walter 1914-1997 [402]
🎨 **$11 255** - €10 632 - **£7 009** - FF69 740
Komposition gelb-weiss-schwarz-grau
Öl/Leinwand (161x97cm 63x38in) St. Gallen 1999
🎨 **$5 160** - €5 873 - **£3 626** - FF38 526
Ohne Titel Öl/Leinwand (65x100cm 25x39in) Zürich
2001
🎨 **$1 745** - €1 926 - **£1 154** - FF12 631
Komposition blau-schwarz Huile/panneau
(40x29cm 15x11in) St. Gallen 2000
✏ **$1 388** - €1 190 - **£834** - FF7 804
Bootshafen auf Korsika Pencil (24x32cm 9x12in)
St. Gallen 1998

LINES Samuel 1778-1863 [4]
🎨 **$9 540** - €11 346 - **£6 800** - FF74 427
The Vale of the Conway Oil/canvas (62.5x90.5cm
24x35in) London 2000

LINET Octave 1870-1962 [33]
🎨 **$331** - €320 - **£209** - FF2 100
Rue à Montmartre Huile/isorel (29x19cm 11x7in)
Paris 1999

LINFORD Alan Carr 1926 [5]
🎨 **$988** - €1 146 - **£700** - FF7 519
«Oxford, British Railways, Western Region, See
Britain by Train» Poster (102x126cm 40x49in)
London 2000

LINGELBACH Johannes 1622-1674 [78]
🎨 **$18 634** - €17 895 - **£11 550** - FF117 386
Türkischer Händler in einem italienischen
Hafen Öl/Leinwand (41.5x53cm 16x20in) Ahlden 1999
🎨 **$12 000** - €13 290 - **£8 138** - FF87 174
Soldiers Resting in a Temporary Encampment
Oil/panel (44.5x34cm 17x13in) New-York 2000
✏ **$8 000** - €8 569 - **£5 463** - FF56 212
An Oriental Getleman Talking to Seamen on a
Mediterranean Quay Ink (15.5x23cm 6x9in) New-
York 2001

LINGEMANN Lambertus 1829-1894 [8]
🎨 **$4 447** - €3 760 - **£2 659** - FF24 665
A Cavalrist Reading in a Seventeenth Century
Interior Oil/panel (36x28cm 14x11in) Amsterdam 1998

LINGENFELDER Eugen 1862-? [7]
🎨 **$1 503** - €1 687 - **£1 042** - FF11 067
Alter Mann bei der Zeitungslektüre Oil/panel
(21x16cm 8x6in) München 2000

LINGNER Otto 1856-? [7]
🎨 **$3 732** - €4 353 - **£2 622** - FF28 437
Nu aux cheveux roux Huile/toile (70.5x99.5cm
27x39in) Warszawa 2001

L

LINGSTRÖM Freda XX [4]

📺 **$1 355** – €1 296 – **£849** – FF8 499
«**Norwegen**» Poster (102x64cm 40x25in) London
1999

LINGUET Henri 1881-1914 [22]

🐦 **$1 098** – €1 250 – **£774** – FF8 200
Les bords de Marne à La Ferté-sous-Jouarre
Huile/toile (90.5x121.5cm 35x47in) Paris 2001

LINK Carl 1887-1968 [4]

✐ **$1 800** – €1 540 – **£1 083** – FF10 103
Sun Dance Pastel (44x38cm 17x14in) New-York 1998

LINK Ogle Winston 1914-2001 [112]

📷 **$3 500** – €3 274 – **£2 116** – FF21 474
Train Engines Gelatin silver print (26.5x36cm
10x14in) New-York 1999

LINNELL James Thomas 1820-1905 [25]

🐦 **$35 857** – €32 603 – **£22 000** – FF213 859
Harvest Time Oil/canvas (76x122cm 29x48in) London
1999

LINNELL John 1792-1882 [165]

🐦 **$16 437** – €17 644 – **£11 000** – FF115 737
The emigrants, Derwent Water, Cumberland
Oil/canvas (91.5x145cm 36x57in) London 2000

🐦 **$4 623** – €4 914 – **£3 100** – FF32 232
The Morning Walk Oil/canvas (76.5x63.5cm 30x25in)
West-Midlands 2001

🐦 **$4 251** – €3 780 – **£2 600** – FF24 797
Figures Resting in a Wooded Landscape
Oil/panel (30x43cm 11x16in) London 1999

✐ **$2 877** – €3 242 – **£1 992** – FF21 268
Scenes in North Wales: Balcombe/North End
Hampstead Charcoal (37x56cm 14x22in) Toronto
2000

📺 **$608** – €602 – **£380** – FF3 946
Sheep in a Landscape, Windsor Forest Etching
(14x23cm 5x9in) London 1999

LINNELL William 1826-1906 [32]

🐦 **$2 564** – €2 981 – **£1 800** – FF19 555
Summer Evening Oil/panel (36x47cm 14x18in)
London 2001

🐦 **$1 434** – €1 601 – **£1 000** – FF10 504
Harvesting Oil/panel (30x45cm 11x17in) Bath 2001

✐ **$473** – €462 – **£300** – FF3 032
Dancing Faun Drawing (55x71cm 22x28in) Send-
Woking, Surrey 1999

LINNERHJELM Jonas Carl 1758-1829 [5]

✐ **$693** – €672 – **£428** – FF4 411
Landskab med bygninger ved söbred
Watercolour/paper (36x52cm 14x20in) Vejle 1999

LINNIG Egide 1821-1860 [22]

🐦 **$20 273** – €19 059 – **£12 272** – FF125 017
The Threemaster, Hoop being caulked on a
River Bank, Antwerp Oil/canvas (56x77.5cm
22x30in) Amsterdam 1999

🐦 **$4 007** – €3 400 – **£2 217** – FF22 301
Vissersschip in Zuiderzee Oil/panel (31.5x44.5cm
12x17in) Den Haag 1998

LINNIG Willem Jr. 1842-1890 [38]

🐦 **$710** – €843 – **£516** – FF5 528
Fleurs Huile/panneau (35x45cm 13x17in) Antwerpen
2001

LINNIG Willem Sr. 1819-1885 [25]

🐦 **$6 517** – €5 931 – **£4 000** – FF38 908
A shered Meal Oil/panel (53x41.5cm 20x16in)
London 1999

🐦 **$1 100** – €1 015 – **£685** – FF6 661
Scolding the Child Oil/panel (33x40cm 13x16in)
Norwalk CT 1999

LINNOVAARA Juhani 1934 [70]

🐦 **$7 510** – €8 409 – **£5 215** – FF55 160
Amerikafestern I Oil/canvas (130x100cm 51x39in)
Helsinki 2001

🐦 **$3 905** – €4 373 – **£2 711** – FF28 683
Tidsmaskin Oil/canvas (50x66cm 19x25in) Helsinki
2001

✐ **$232** – €235 – **£144** – FF1 544
Utan titel Mixed media (27x36cm 10x14in) Helsinki
2000

✐ **$1 200** – €1 345 – **£815** – FF8 825
Lav Gouache/paper (52x73cm 20x28in) Helsinki 2000

📺 **$304** – €336 – **£211** – FF2 206
Untitled Serigraph (69x48cm 27x18in) Helsinki 2001

LINNQVIST Hilding 1891-1984 [176]

🐦 **$3 112** – €2 656 – **£1 860** – FF17 422
Modellen i trappan Oil/canvas (135x97cm 53x38in)
Stockholm 1998

🐦 **$8 511** – €8 138 – **£5 336** – FF53 384
En vårdag i Stockholm Oil/canvas (73x92cm
28x36in) Stockholm 1999

🐦 **$1 912** – €2 143 – **£1 329** – FF14 055
Motiv från Chinon Oil/panel (31.5x41cm 12x16in)
Stockholm 2001

✐ **$510** – €484 – **£310** – FF3 176
Vårdag i parken Akvarell/papper (26x33cm 10x12in)
Stockholm 1999

LINO Gustave 1893-1961 [46]

🐦 **$6 674** – €6 411 – **£4 410** – FF46 000
Le marché arabe Huile/toile (59x90cm 23x35in)
Paris 2000

🐦 **$1 120** – €1 239 – **£780** – FF8 130
Scène de marché arabe Huile/carton (24x18cm
9x7in) Bruxelles 2001

🐦 **$1 482** – €1 448 – **£939** – FF9 500
La baie d'Alger Gouache/papier (21x30cm 8x11in)
Paris 1999

LINOSSIER Claudius 1893-1953 [6]

🏺 **$6 581** – €6 403 – **£4 048** – FF42 000
Vase sphérique à décor motifs de triangles
Métal (18.5x16.5cm 7x6in) Paris 1999

LINS Adolf 1856-1927 [47]

🐦 **$4 386** – €4 857 – **£2 974** – FF31 862
Flusstal im Frühling Öl/Leinwand (62x86cm
24x33in) Hamburg 2000

🐦 **$1 171** – €1 227 – **£774** – FF8 049
Schwälmer Bauernkinder auf dem Heimweg
von der Heuernte Öl/Leinwand (26.5x35.5cm
10x13in) München 2001

LINSON Corwin Knapp 1864-1959 [25]

🐦 **$1 000** – €1 137 – **£698** – FF7 460
Mt.Vesuvius Oil/board (13x22cm 5x9in) Mystic CT
2000

LINT van Frans XIX-XX [1]

🐦 **$31 500** – €30 032 – **£19 000** – FF197 000
Molino junto a un lago en Holanda Oleo/lienzo
(124x200cm 48x78in) Madrid 1999

LINT van Giacomo 1723-1790 [21]

🐦 **$25 000** – €29 445 – **£17 290** – FF193 147
View of the Piazza del Popolo, Rome Oil/canvas
(69x108.5cm 27x42in) New-York 2000

🐦 **$19 680** – €22 867 – **£13 830** – FF150 000
Vue de la place Saint-Pierre à Rome Huile/toile
(21x36.5cm 8x14in) Paris 2001

LINT van Hendrik Frans 1684-1763 **[60]**
- $85 000 - €90 776 - **£57 919** - FF595 450
  Capricci of Roman Ruins with Figures Oil/canvas (68x50cm 26x19in) New-York 2001
- $11 529 - €12 801 - **£7 717** - FF83 968
  Italienskt landskap med byggnader och figurer Oil/canvas (24x29cm 9x11in) Stockholm 2000
- $6 000 - €5 183 - **£4 000** - FF34 000
  Veduta della Piramide di Caio Cestio con la porta Ostiense Gouache/tavola (15x10cm 5x3in) Roma 1998

LINT van Louis 1909-1986 **[126]**
- $10 608 - €11 898 - **£7 392** - FF78 048
  Etrange métamorphose Huile/toile (132x196cm 51x77in) Bruxelles 2001
- $4 350 - €3 714 - **£2 550** - FF24 360
  Composition Huile/toile (74x145cm 29x57in) Bruxelles 2000
- $2 650 - €2 479 - **£1 610** - FF16 260
  Compositie Oil/panel (25x42.5cm 9x16in) Lokeren 1999
- $670 - €644 - **£413** - FF4 227
  Campagne Gouache/papier (24x16cm 9x6in) Bruxelles 1999

LINT van Peter 1609-1690 **[33]**
- $31 722 - €33 309 - **£20 000** - FF218 494
  The Education of the Virgin Oil/canvas (238.5x205cm 93x80in) London 2000
- $17 460 - €14 873 - **£10 380** - FF97 560
  David agenouillé démontre sa foi au roi Saul Huile/cuivre (87x105cm 34x41in) Antwerpen 1998
- $30 673 - €29 496 - **£18 895** - FF193 479
  Venus and Cupid/Cupid and Jupiter/Venus in her Chariot Black chalk (41.5x28cm 16x11in) Amsterdam 1999

LINTHEIMER Catharina XVIII **[1]**
- $69 523 - €80 669 - **£48 000** - FF529 156
  Flowers and Fruit Watercolour/paper (33x21cm 12x8in) London 2000

LINTHORST Jacobus 1745/55-1815 **[6]**
- $134 487 - €144 361 - **£90 000** - FF946 944
  Crown Imperial Lily, Tulips, Hydrangea/Grapes, Plums, Daisies, Roses Oil/panel (77x60.5cm 30x23in) London 2000

LINTON Frank B. Ashley 1871-1943 **[4]**
- $1 100 - €1 258 - **£764** - FF8 253
  Three quarter length portrait of a young gentleman in evening attire Oil/canvas (101x76cm 40x30in) Philadelphia PA 2000

LINTON James Dromgole, Sir 1840-1916 **[59]**
- $434 - €469 - **£300** - FF3 075
  The Bravo Watercolour/paper (50x41cm 20x16in) Little-Lane, Ilkley 2001

LINTON William 1791-1876 **[28]**
- $2 490 - €2 607 - **£1 565** - FF17 104
  Mediterrane Ideallandschaft mit Ziegenhirten Öl/Leinwand (44x66cm 17x25in) Bremen 2000
- $13 176 - €12 532 - **£8 000** - FF82 205
  Edinburgh & Calton Hill with Figures and Sheep/Stirling from the Forth Oil/canvas (34x46cm 13x18in) Edinburgh 1999
- $299 - €276 - **£184** - FF1 812
  Templo de Vesta en Tivoli Acuarela/papel (34x25cm 13x9in) Madrid 1999

LINTON William Evans 1878-? **[21]**
- $414 - €357 - **£250** - FF2 345
  Bullocks on the Water's Edge Watercolour/paper (26x38cm 10x14in) Bristol, Avon 1998

LINTOTT Edward Barnard 1875-1951 **[49]**
- $1 500 - €1 399 - **£930** - FF9 174
  Mountain Laurel Oil/canvas (76x63.5cm 29x25in) New-York 1999

LINTZ Ferdinand Ernst 1833-1909 **[16]**
- $349 - €408 - **£249** - FF2 678
  Forest Scene with a Malle Jan Oil/panel (27.5x33cm 10x12in) Amsterdam 2001
- $113 - €127 - **£78** - FF833
  Rustende paarden bij ploeg Watercolour/paper (29x39cm 11x15in) Rotterdam 2001

LINVILLE Marlin 1950 **[11]**
- $1 800 - €1 538 - **£1 089** - FF10 087
  «Texas Wildflowers» Oil/canvas (51x61cm 20x24in) San-Francisco CA 1998

LINZELL Ernest **[1]**
- $4 441 - €4 663 - **£2 800** - FF30 589
  Attacked by Killer Whales Oil/board (47x62cm 18x24in) London 2000

LION Alexandre Louis 1823-1852 **[7]**
- $2 264 - €2 627 - **£1 563** - FF17 231
  Paysage animé Huile/toile (65x54cm 25x21in) Genève 2000

LION de Noël XVII **[1]**
- $3 475 - €3 811 - **£2 360** - FF25 000
  La Crucifixion Huile/panneau (36.5x29.5cm 14x11in) Lille 2000

LIONNE Enrico 1865-1921 **[13]**
- $11 400 - €9 848 - **£7 600** - FF64 600
  Fiori Olio/tela (82.5x60cm 32x23in) Prato 1998

LIOTARD Jean Étienne 1702-1789 **[43]**
- $79 640 - €90 502 - **£55 000** - FF593 653
  Willem Bentick, 1st Count Bentinck (1704-1774), Half-Length,Red Velvet Oil/canvas (60x49.5cm 23x19in) London 2000
- $20 454 - €17 161 - **£12 000** - FF112 570
  Prince Ch. Edward Stuart (1720-1788) & Prince H.B. Stuart (1725-1807) Miniature (5x7cm 1x2in) London 1998
- $49 131 - €45 643 - **£30 000** - FF299 400
  Portrait of Monsieur Jean Dassier (1676-1763) Pastel/paper (55x44cm 21x17in) London 1998
- $5 410 - €3 833 - **£2 625** - FF25 140
  Erzherzogin Maria von Oesterreich im Costüm einer Dame von Galata Radierung (30.8x24.8cm 12x9in) Berlin 2000

LIPCHITZ Jacques 1891-1973 **[301]**
- $48 895 - €53 357 - **£33 180** - FF350 000
  Composition à la guitare Huile/carton (20.5x28cm 8x11in) Paris 2000
- $560 000 - €621 214 - **£372 400** - FF4 074 896
  Baigneuse assise Bronze (H83.5cm H32in) New-York 2000
- $36 800 - €34 290 - **£22 904** - FF224 929
  Hebrew Letters, Variations on a Chisel Bronze (H22cm H8in) Tel Aviv 1999
- $4 966 - €4 378 - **£3 081** - FF32 000
  Etude pour une sculpture «Femme» Fusain/papier (31x24cm 12x9in) Paris 1999
- $279 - €307 - **£190** - FF2 012
  Hommage à Picasso Farblithographie (64x44.2cm 25x17in) Berlin 2000

LIPHART von Ernest Friedrich 1847-1934 **[10]**
- $16 000 - €18 805 - **£11 092** - FF123 350
  String of Pearls Oil/canvas (233x127.5cm 91x50in) New-York 2000

$2 898 - €2 737 - **£1 800** - FF17 954
The Park at the Palace of Pavlosk Oil/canvas
(33x24.5cm 12x9in) London 1999

LIPINSKI Hipolit 1846-1884 **[8]**
$5 564 - €6 539 - **£3 858** - FF42 894
Marchand juif Huile/toile (56.5x38.5cm 22x15in)
Warszawa 2000

LIPOFSKY Marvin 1938 **[7]**
$4 000 - €3 818 - **£2 499** - FF25 046
Haystack Summer Series Sculpture, glass
(26x34x27cm 10x13x10in) New-York 1999

LIPOT Herman 1884-1972 **[13]**
$619 - €727 - **£439** - FF4 767
Badende in Landschaft Öl/Leinwand (40x50cm
15x19in) Wien 2000

LIPP Maren 1926 **[7]**
$1 201 - €1 125 - **£744** - FF7 378
**Weiblicher Halbakt, mit hinter den Kopf erhobe-
nen Armen** Bronze (31.5x12x8.5cm 12x4x3in)
Heidelberg 1999

LIPPERT Aage XX **[1]**
$1 000 - €1 166 - **£702** - FF7 650
«Kobenhavn Zoo, Okapi» Poster (62.5x87.5cm
24x34in) New-York 2000

LIPPI Lorenzo 1606-1665 **[9]**
$650 000 - €695 298 - **£443 170** - FF4 560 855
**Group Portrait of Vittoria Della Rovere and
Companions** Oil/canvas (129x121cm 50x47in) New-
York 2001
$24 105 - €23 910 - **£15 000** - FF156 837
The Muse Euterpe, holding a double Clarinet
Oil/canvas (71x58.5cm 27x23in) London 1999

LIPPINCOTT William Henry 1849-1920 **[35]**
$9 622 - €11 164 - **£6 643** - FF73 232
**Porträt der Laura Jayne Bucknell (1871-1958)
als Mädchen** Öl/Leinwand (65x54.5cm 25x21in)
Luzern 2000
$2 500 - €2 705 - **£1 712** - FF17 741
**Farmyard Scenes with Boy and Girl feeding a
Goat/Woman with Children** Oil/canvas (25x20cm
10x8in) Delaware OH 2001
$2 500 - €2 368 - **£1 520** - FF15 530
Spring Blossoms, Morris, Connecticut
Watercolour/paper (35.5x51cm 13x20in) New-York
1999

LIPPS Richard 1857-1926 **[31]**
$1 043 - €1 074 - **£657** - FF7 043
**Hof in Verona, zwei Frauen mit Kind auf dem
Arm im Gespräch** Öl/Leinwand (95x75cm 37x29in)
Berlin 2000

LIPS H.J. 1918 **[6]**
$2 642 - €2 450 - **£1 594** - FF16 073
Markt met marktkramen te Maastricht Oil/canvas
(67x108cm 26x42in) Maastricht 1999

LIPS Johann Heinrich 1758-1817 **[23]**
$2 247 - €2 232 - **£1 400** - FF14 642
**Gentleman Said to be Johann Kaspar
Lavaterre, half-length** Oil/panel (18.5x13.5cm 7x5in)
London 1999
$864 - €983 - **£609** - FF6 449
Tageszeiten Aquatint (20.4x26.5cm 8x10in) Zürich
2001

LIPSCOMBE Guy XIX-XX **[6]**
$450 - €516 - **£310** - FF3 383
**Hill Climb, an Open Top Racing Car, Possibly a
Scout on a Hill Road** Watercolour/paper (28x42.5cm
11x16in) West-Midlands 2000
$1 121 - €1 204 - **£750** - FF7 897
Three Tennis Cartoons Color lithograph (28x43cm
11x16in) London 2000

LIPSHITZ Lippy 1903-1980 **[20]**
$132 - €154 - **£91** - FF1 010
Portrait of Wolf Kibel Monotype (19x18cm 7x7in)
Johannesburg 2000

LIPSZYC Samuel ?-1935 **[17]**
$1 902 - €2 058 - **£1 302** - FF13 500
Femme debout, mains derrière le dos
Chryséléphantine (H25cm H9in) Paris 2001

LIRA Armando 1903-1959 **[22]**
$1 292 - €1 523 - **£907** - FF9 989
Caracas Oleo/lienzo (48.5x53cm 19x20in) Caracas ($)
2000

LIRA Pedro francesco 1850-? **[7]**
$5 861 - €6 748 - **£4 000** - FF44 267
Le repas des ouvriers Oil/canvas (90x115.5cm
35x45in) London 2000

LISA Esteban 1895-1983 **[4]**
$2 000 - €2 203 - **£1 334** - FF14 454
Composición Técnica mixta/papel (34.5x22cm
13x8in) Montevideo 2000

LISA Mario 1908-1992 **[22]**
$750 - €777 - **£450** - FF5 100
Natura morta Olio/tela (24x50cm 9x19in) Vercelli
2000

LISAERT Pieter XVI-XVII **[10]**
$15 644 - €18 151 - **£10 800** - FF119 064
The Five Wise Virgins Oil/panel (61x52.5cm
24x20in) Amsterdam 2000
$11 016 - €12 958 - **£7 896** - FF85 000
L'Annonciation Huile/cuivre (42x37cm 16x14in)
Saint-Germain-en-Laye 2001

LISIEWSKA Anna Rosina 1713-1783 **[1]**
$7 432 - €6 807 - **£4 530** - FF44 649
**Elisabeth-Friederike Sophie, Duchess of
Württemberg (1732-1780)** Oil/canvas (82.5x65.5cm
32x25in) Amsterdam 1999

LISIEWSKI Christian Friedrich 1725-1794 **[4]**
$14 990 - €13 879 - **£9 300** - FF91 037
Portrait of a Man writting by a Candlelight
Oil/canvas (94x115cm 37x45in) London 1999

LISKA Emanuel Krescenc 1852-1903 **[4]**
$2 764 - €2 516 - **£1 729** - FF16 501
Hagar and Ishmael Oil/panel (14x20.5cm 5x8in)
Praha 1999

LISKA Hans 1907 **[9]**
$958 - €1 062 - **£650** - FF6 965
«Mercedes-Benz, Grand Prix of Switzerland»
Poster (84x60cm 33x23in) London 2000

LISLE de Édith Fortunée Tita 1866-1911 **[2]**
$1 845 - €1 628 - **£1 100** - FF10 679
Lady Holding Hydrangeas Pastel/paper
(125x63.5cm 49x25in) London 1998

LISMANN Hermann 1878-1943 **[18]**
$3 721 - €3 579 - **£2 296** - FF23 477
Idyll Öl/Leinwand (55.3x46.3cm 21x18in) Köln 1999

LISMER Arthur 1885-1969 **[157]**
- **$10 899** - €10 474 - **£6 713** - FF68 704
  Westcoat Forest Oil/canvas (63.5x43cm 25x16in) Vancouver, BC. 1999
- **$5 843** - €6 610 - **£4 087** - FF43 361
  Sketch at Quidi Vidi near st.John, Newfoundland Oil/panel (30.5x40.5cm 12x15in) Toronto 2001
- **$701** - €755 - **£470** - FF4 955
  Untitled, Garden Sketch Ink/paper (21.5x26.5cm 8x10in) Calgary, Alberta 2000
- **$356** - €416 - **£247** - FF2 726
  Island of Spruce Copper engraving (12.5x17.5cm 4x6in) Toronto 2000

LISMONDE Jules 1908-2001 **[55]**
- **$754** - €843 - **£523** - FF5 528
  Sanctuaires interdits I Fusain/papier (50x63cm 19x24in) Antwerpen 2001

LISS Johann 1597-1631 **[2]**
- **$6 142** - €6 860 - **£4 162** - FF45 000
  Étude de vieillard barbu Huile/toile (61x50.5cm 24x19in) Paris 2000

LISSAC Pierre 1878-1955 **[1]**
- **$1 682** - €1 829 - **£1 108** - FF12 000
  Marché devant les murailles, Maroc Aquarelle/papier (49x64cm 19x25in) Paris 2000

LISSE van der Dirck c.1600-1669 **[26]**
- **$6 000** - €5 183 - **£4 000** - FF34 000
  Pan e Siringa Olio/rame (32x40.5cm 12x15in) Roma 1998

LISSITZKY El, Lazar Markovitch 1890-1941 **[106]**
- **$90 100** - €102 110 - **£61 200** - FF669 800
  Sin título Acuarela (17.5x32.5cm 6x12in) Madrid 2000
- **$14 000** - €16 367 - **£9 837** - FF107 363
  Proun II Color lithograph (65x53cm 25x20in) New-York 2000
- **$1 352** - €1 175 - **£814** - FF7 709
  Kurt Schwitters Gelatin silver print (20x15cm 7x5in) Berlin 1999

LIST Herbert 1903-1975 **[316]**
- **$1 388** - €1 329 - **£857** - FF8 720
  Colette, Paris Vintage gelatin silver print (29.5x22.7cm 11x8in) Köln 1999

LISTER William Lister 1859-1943 **[107]**
- **$836** - €787 - **£526** - FF5 160
  The Reach of the River Oil/canvas (33x76cm 12x29in) Sydney 1999
- **$517** - €570 - **£350** - FF3 740
  Coastal Scene Watercolour/paper (26.5x56.5cm 10x22in) Woollahra, Sydney 2000

LISZEWSKA Anna Rosina de Gasc 1716-1783 **[4]**
- **$5 000** - €4 573 - **£3 053** - FF29 994
  Portrait of a lady/Portrait of a gentleman Oil/canvas (77x63cm 30x25in) New-York 1998

LISZEWSKA-THERBUSCH Anna Dorothea 1721/22-1782 **[11]**
- **$5 270** - €5 852 - **£3 528** - FF38 385
  Dianas nymf överraskas av satyr Oil/canvas (87x71cm 34x27in) Stockholm 2000

LITH van Jean-Paul 1940 **[66]**
- **$1 090** - €915 - **£639** - FF6 000
  L'homme andalou Sculpture verre (73.5x28x16cm 28x11x6in) Paris 1998

LITT Arthur 1905-1961 **[109]**
- **$39** - €46 - **£27** - FF300
  Les rectangles Gouache/papier (22.5x17.5cm 8x6in) Paris 2000

LITTECKY Endre 1880-1953 **[5]**
- **$2 220** - €2 332 - **£1 380** - FF15 300
  Personne rêvant sur une terrasse Huile/toile (87x66cm 34x25in) Budapest 2000

LITTEN Sydney Mackenzie 1887-1934 **[10]**
- **$403** - €342 - **£243** - FF2 246
  Venetian Nights Etching (22.5x30cm 8x11in) London 1998

LITTLE A. Platte XIX **[4]**
- **$4 250** - €4 591 - **£2 942** - FF30 115
  Preparing Strawberries Oil/canvas (35x45cm 14x18in) Cincinnati OH 2001

LITTLE ANGEL II L.A.II 1959 **[37]**
- **$11 000** - €11 403 - **£6 600** - FF74 800
  Senza titolo Tecnica mista (85x205cm 33x80in) Prato 1999
- **$7 000** - €7 257 - **£4 200** - FF47 600
  Senza titolo Tecnica mista (110x53cm 43x20in) Prato 1999
- **$42 000** - €46 080 - **£27 900** - FF302 265
  Vase Sculpture (H62cm H24in) New-York 2000

LITTLE James XIX-XX **[7]**
- **$679** - €674 - **£424** - FF4 422
  Antwerp Watercolour/paper (34.5x24cm 13x9in) Toronto 1999

LITTLE John G. Caruthers 1928 **[70]**
- **$3 255** - €2 785 - **£1 959** - FF18 270
  Sic Transit: Quebec Oil/board (45.5x61cm 17x24in) Toronto 1998
- **$1 875** - €1 825 - **£1 154** - FF11 969
  Patinoire rue du Collège St.Henri, Montréal Oil/canvas (30x40cm 12x16in) Nepean, Ont. 1999

LITTLE Philip 1857-1942 **[26]**
- **$1 000** - €934 - **£617** - FF6 126
  Arrangement in Black and Grey Oil/canvas (63.5x76cm 25x29in) Boston MA 1999
- **$300** - €259 - **£178** - FF1 696
  Opening the Season Etching (24x19cm 9x7in) Cambridge MA 1998

LITTLECHILD George 1958 **[1]**
- **$1 434** - €1 664 - **£990** - FF10 914
  Auntie Mary Jane, She Had T.B. Mixed media/paper (76x76cm 30x30in) Calgary, Alberta 2000

LITTLEJOHN William 1929 **[2]**
- **$1 004** - €1 130 - **£700** - FF7 412
  Lemons and Fish Watercolour, gouache/paper (57x124cm 22x48in) Edinburgh 2001

LITTLEJOHNS John 1874-? **[6]**
- **$817** - €786 - **£500** - FF5 153
  «Dunoon, LNER» Poster (99x124cm 38x48in) London 1999

LITTLETON Harvey K. 1920 **[19]**
- **$7 500** - €7 769 - **£4 773** - FF50 964
  Implied Movement Sculpture, glass (76x86.5x112cm 29x34x44in) New-York 1998

LITTLEWOOD Edward XIX **[17]**
- **$1 031** - €1 033 - **£650** - FF7 101
  The old Fish Market, Norwich Oil/canvas (17x30cm 7x12in) Aylsham, Norfolk 2000

L

LITTROW von Lea 1860-1914 **[36]**
- **$1 835** - €2 045 - **£1 282** - FF13 415
  Die dalmatinische Küste bei Ragusa Öl/Leinwand (65x85cm 25x33in) München 2001
- **$133** - €153 - **£92** - FF1 006
  Dalmatinische Küste Gouache/paper (13.5x17cm 5x6in) München 2000

LITVINOVSKY Pinchas 1894-1985 **[104]**
- **$7 500** - €8 891 - **£5 463** - FF58 324
  Mother and Child Oil/canvas (162x114cm 63x44in) Tel Aviv 2001
- **$1 100** - €1 304 - **£801** - FF8 554
  Figures Oil/paper/canvas (46x69cm 18x27in) Tel Aviv 2001
- **$900** - €878 - **£570** - FF5 762
  Figures Oil/paper (29x27cm 11x10in) Tel Aviv 1999
- **$1 200** - €1 020 - **£724** - FF6 688
  «Shabat Kodesh» Mixed media/paper (72x102cm 28x40in) Tel Aviv 1999

LIU GUOSONG 1932 **[21]**
- **$15 300** - €12 646 - **£8 950** - FF82 950
  Life Pattern Mixed media (74x102cm 29x40in) Taipei 1998
- **$3 496** - €3 240 - **£2 173** - FF21 252
  White All Over When Sun Set II Ink (55.5x86.5cm 21x34in) Taipei 1999

LIU HAISU 1895-1994 **[18]**
- **$13 230** - €12 172 - **£7 938** - FF79 842
  Les gorges de a Morge, St. Gingolph Oil/canvas (79.5x59.5cm 31x23in) Taipei 1999
- **$10 000** - €10 734 - **£6 692** - FF70 410
  Mount Huang at Sunset Ink (98x164cm 38x64in) San-Francisco CA 2000

LIU HEUNG SHING 1951 **[1]**
- **$3 000** - €3 407 - **£2 105** - FF22 351
  A Hair Salon in Bejing/Worker's removing the Portrait of Mao/Youths Gelatin silver print (36.5x56cm 14x22in) New-York 1999

LIU JIESAN XVIII-XIX **[1]**
- **$1 595** - €1 534 - **£984** - FF10 061
  Ohne Titel Indian ink/paper (120x246cm 47x96in) Stuttgart 1999

LIU JUE 1410-1472 **[1]**
- **$135 135** - €128 153 - **£82 215** - FF840 630
  Autumn Landscape Ink (118.5x45cm 46x17in) Hong-Kong 1999

LIU KANG 1911 **[7]**
- **$11 478** - €13 033 - **£7 856** - FF85 492
  A View of the Kampung Oil/canvas (119x85cm 46x33in) Singapore 2000

LIU KUILING 1885-1968 **[28]**
- **$23 754** - €20 137 - **£14 204** - FF132.093
  «Camels by the Great Wall» Coloured inks/paper (170x76.5cm 66x30in) Hong-Kong 1998

LIU LINGCAMP 1906-1989 **[1]**
- **$1 400** - €1 503 - **£936** - FF9 857
  Two Military Figures Ink (101.5x67.5cm 39x26in) San-Francisco CA 2000

LIU QIWEI Max Liu Ch'i-wei 1912 **[9]**
- **$2 272** - €2 106 - **£1 412** - FF13 813
  Child Fun Mixed media/paper (27.5x46cm 10x18in) Taipei 1999

LIU TONGCHENG 1956 **[2]**
- **$3 870** - €3 632 - **£2 391** - FF23 823
  Landscape Ink (230x92cm 90x36in) Hong-Kong 1999

LIU WEI 1965 **[3]**
- **$8 524** - €7 117 - **£5 000** - FF46 685
  Swimming No.1 Oil/canvas (100x100cm 39x39in) London 1998

LIU XIAODONG 1963 **[7]**
- **$4 504** - €4 274 - **£2 737** - FF28 038
  Milk Drinker Oil/canvas (100x73cm 39x28in) Hong-Kong 1999

LIU XUN 1958 **[6]**
- **$14 835** - €13 990 - **£9 200** - FF91 770
  Mountain Ranges Amid Clouds Ink/paper (68x136.5cm 26x53in) Hong-Kong 1999

LIU YIN 1618-1664 **[3]**
- **$17 976** - €19 629 - **£11 564** - FF128 758
  Famous Sights in Jiangnan Ink (23.5x31.5cm 9x12in) Hong-Kong 2000

LIU YINGZHAO 1956 **[13]**
- **$8 385** - €7 869 - **£5 180** - FF51 616
  Harmonious Beauty Oil/canvas (120x110cm 47x43in) Hong-Kong 1999
- **$7 722** - €7 328 - **£4 692** - FF48 066
  Moonlight through the Window Oil/canvas (114x100cm 44x39in) Hong-Kong 1999

LIU YONG 1719-1805 **[4]**
- **$5 000** - €4 316 - **£2 987** - FF28 312
  Calligraphy in Running-cursive Script Ink (114.5x41cm 45x16in) New-York 1998

LIU YUANQI XVI-XVII **[2]**
- **$27 027** - €25 631 - **£16 443** - FF168 126
  Snowy Landscape Ink (127.5x55.5cm 50x21in) Hong-Kong 1999

LIVENS Henry J. XIX-XX **[28]**
- **$1 575** - €1 501 - **£998** - FF9 849
  Landscape with Fisherman Oil/canvas (39x59cm 15x23in) Cleveland OH 1999

LIVENS Horace Mann 1862-1936 **[78]**
- **$928** - €1 040 - **£645** - FF6 822
  Chickens Oil/canvas (51.5x36.5cm 20x14in) Johannesburg 2001
- **$179** - €175 - **£110** - FF1 147
  Figures in an Eastern Town Charcoal (38x28cm 14x11in) London 1999

LIVESAY Frances XIX **[3]**
- **$1 440** - €1 397 - **£906** - FF9 161
  By the Fireside Co. Mayo Watercolour/paper (34.5x49.5cm 13x19in) Dublin 1999

LIVESAY I. XX **[6]**
- **$367** - €356 - **£226** - FF2 332
  Two Pont-Aven Ladies Watercolour/paper (17.5x11.5cm 6x4in) Dublin 1999

LIVESAY John XVIII-XIX **[2]**
- **$2 487** - €2 413 - **£1 565** - FF15 825
  Set of 4 Early 19th Century Landscapes Watercolour/paper (24x34.5cm 9x13in) Dublin 1999

LIVESAY Richard c.1750-c.1823 **[17]**
- **$1 604** - €1 616 - **£1 000** - FF10 603
  Portrait of Admiral James Cranstoun, 8th Lord Cranstoun (1755-1796) Oil/canvas (23x20cm 9x7in) London 2000

LIVINGSTON Charlotte act.1929-1981 **[1]**
- **$9 864** - €11 760 - **£7 033** - FF77 139
  Mädchen mit Sonnenschirm Öl/Leinwand (79x64cm 31x25in) Ahlden 2000

LIX Frédéric Théodore 1830-1897 **[32]**
- $9 179 - €8 080 - £5 591 - FF53 000
  Les pêcheurs sur les bords du Rhin Huile/toile
  (75.5x105.5cm 29x41in) Saint-Dié 1999

LIZARS William Home 1788-1859 **[17]**
- $1 800 - €1 783 - £1 092 - FF11 698
  **Yellow-Billed Cuckoo (Plate 2), After J.J
  Audubon** Etching in colors (53.5x67cm 21x26in)
  New-York 2000

LIZCANO Y MONEDERO Angel 1846-1929 **[50]**
- $5 220 - €5 406 - £3 330 - FF35 460
  El numismático Oleo/lienzo (81x130cm 31x51in)
  Madrid 2001
- $2 015 - €1 952 - £1 235 - FF12 805
  Labores del pueblo Oleo/lienzo (49x27.5cm
  19x10in) Madrid 1999

LJUBA Ljuba Popovitch, dit 1934 **[185]**
- $6 044 - €7 013 - £4 301 - FF46 000
  «Le lac sacré ou le lieu de l'enterrement»
  Acrylique/toile (200x300cm 78x118in) Paris 2001
- $2 686 - €2 820 - £1 692 - FF18 500
  Les miroirs et les fantômes Huile/toile (54x81cm
  21x31in) Paris 2000
- $863 - €838 - £533 - FF5 500
  Sans titre Huile/toile (36x27cm 14x10in) Paris 1999
- $268 - €274 - £168 - FF1 800
  Sans titre Encre (29x21cm 11x8in) Versailles 2000

LJUNGBERG Sven 1913 **[33]**
- $760 - €816 - £508 - FF5 353
  Landskap med hus vid älv Oil/canvas (62x99cm
  24x38in) Stockholm 2000

LJUNGGREN Reinhold 1920 **[69]**
- $2 701 - €2 538 - £1 628 - FF16 651
  Motiv från Karlstad Oil/panel (39x55cm 15x21in)
  Stockholm 1999
- $794 - €758 - £495 - FF4 974
  Pojke på brygga Oil/panel (34x25cm 13x9in)
  Stockholm 1999
- $2 415 - €2 682 - £1 617 - FF17 593
  Carlsson och Madame Flod på roddtur
  Akvarell/papper (25.5x23cm 10x9in) Stockholm 2000
- $312 - €263 - £184 - FF1 723
  Från Slottet till Slussen Color lithograph (43x53cm
  16x20in) Stockholm 1998

LJUNGQUIST Birger 1894-1965 **[77]**
- $498 - €552 - £334 - FF3 623
  Kvinnoporträtt Oil/canvas (46x38cm 18x14in)
  Stockholm 1999
- $552 - €519 - £333 - FF3 406
  Panflöjten Mixed media (32.5x25.5cm 12x10in)
  Stockholm 1999
- $1 428 - €1 339 - £883 - FF8 785
  Alvefärd Akvarell/papper (24x36cm 9x14in)
  Stockholm 1999

LLABRES GRIMALT Miquel 1930-1983 **[3]**
- $12 960 - €14 416 - £9 120 - FF94 560
  «Atardecer, puerto de Pollensa» Técnica
  mixta/lienzo (65x100cm 25x39in) Madrid 2001

LLACER Teresa 1932 **[27]**
- $540 - €601 - £360 - FF3 940
  Pirineu Català Oleo/lienzo (50.5x61cm 19x24in)
  Barcelona 2000

LLACER Y VALDERMONT Francisco 1781-1857 **[1]**
- $22 950 - €25 528 - £15 300 - FF167 450
  **Merienda campestre, la cartuja de Porta
  Coeli/Paisaje imaginario** Oleo/lienzo (45.5x66cm
  17x25in) Madrid 2000

LLANECES José San Bartolomé 1863-1919 **[25]**
- $1 000 - €1 201 - £700 - FF7 880
  El tabernero Oleo/lienzo (120x64cm 47x25in) Madrid
  2000
- $7 105 - €7 445 - £4 500 - FF48 838
  Conversation in the Park Oil/panel (29.5x48x4cm
  11x18x1in) London 2000

LLEWELLYN John Dillwyn 1810-1882 **[2]**
- $2 990 - €2 559 - £1 800 - FF16 785
  **Rhubarb Leaves and Basket Under a Hornbeam
  Hedge** Calotype (16x20cm 6x8in) London 1998

LLEWELLYN William Samuel Henry 1858-1941 **[13]**
- $15 651 - €18 185 - £11 000 - FF119 286
  Waterbaby Oil/canvas (63x47.5cm 24x18in) London
  2001
- $1 431 - €1 570 - £980 - FF10 298
  Beside the Water Pump Watercolour (30.5x15cm
  12x5in) London 2000

LLIMONA Rafael 1896-1957 **[13]**
- $2 178 - €1 982 - £1 320 - FF13 002
  Paisaje con aldea Oleo/lienzo (65x81cm 25x31in)
  Barcelona 1999

LLONA Ramiro 1947 **[13]**
- $28 000 - €24 415 - £16 928 - FF160 151
  Self Portrait Lying Under the Sun Acrylic/canvas
  (182.5x172cm 71x67in) New-York 1998

LLORENS DíAZ Francisco 1874-1948 **[12]**
- $31 800 - €36 039 - £21 600 - FF236 400
  La gruta de las gaviotas Oleo/lienzo (138x188.5cm
  54x74in) Madrid 2000
- $18 360 - €20 422 - £12 580 - FF133 960
  «La Ribera», Galicia Oleo/lienzo (90x117cm
  35x46in) Madrid 2001

LLORENS POY Vicente 1937 **[4]**
- $1 122 - €1 021 - £680 - FF6 698
  Desnudo femenino Oleo/lienzo (81x54cm 31x21in)
  Madrid 1999

LLOVERA BOFILL Josep 1846-1896 **[19]**
- $1 722 - €1 952 - £1 202 - FF12 805
  Dama en un fondo nevado Oleo/lienzo (59x41cm
  23x16in) Barcelona 2000
- $864 - €961 - £608 - FF6 304
  Escena de cacería Acuarela/papel (55x44cm
  21x17in) Madrid 2001

LLOVERAS HERRERAS Federico 1912-1983 **[94]**
- $1 430 - €1 652 - £990 - FF10 835
  Puerto Oleo/lienzo (65x81cm 25x31in) Barcelona
  2001
- $504 - €541 - £342 - FF3 546
  Ramo de flores Oleo/tabla (40x20cm 15x7in)
  Barcelona 2001
- $360 - €360 - £222 - FF2 364
  Edificios de París Acuarela/papel (27x50cm 10x19in)
  Madrid 2000

LLOYD James 1905-1974 **[27]**
- $630 - €537 - £380 - FF3 521
  Among the Grasses Gouache/paper (35.5x39.5cm
  13x15in) London 1999

LLOYD Llewelyn 1879-1949 **[20]**
- $10 500 - €10 885 - £6 300 - FF71 400
  Soffioni a Santa Barbara nel Valdarno Olio/carto-
  ne (49.5x37cm 19x14in) Prato 2000
- $9 250 - €9 589 - £5 550 - FF62 900
  Barche sulla spiaggia Olio/tavola (27x36cm
  10x14in) Milano 2000

LLOYD Norman 1897-1985 **[140]**
- $380 - €408 - £260 - FF2 675
  Normandy House Oil/canvas (61.5x36cm 24x14in) London 2001
- $625 - €601 - £385 - FF3 942
  Impression Landscape with Cottages and Haystacks Oil/canvas (33x40cm 13x16in) Pittsburgh PA 1999

LLOYD Robert Malcolm ?-1907 **[96]**
- $736 - €790 - £500 - FF5 183
  Fisherfolk Heading Out to Sea Watercolour (31x49cm 12x19in) London 2001

LLOYD Stanley 1881-1954 **[7]**
- $1 513 - €1 575 - £950 - FF10 330
  The Worst Crime in the World Pencil (30x25cm 11x9in) London 2000

LLOYD Thomas Ivester 1873-1942 **[58]**
- $2 242 - €2 407 - £1 500 - FF15 786
  Rattler, a Chestnut Hunter/Menelk, a Dark Brown hunter in a Loose Box Oil/canvas (40.5x50.5cm 15x19in) London 2000
- $1 288 - €1 211 - £800 - FF7 943
  Beagling Oil/panel (20x31cm 7x12in) Salisbury, Wiltshire 1998
- $1 051 - €1 222 - £750 - FF8 018
  Duck shooting Watercolour (28x52cm 11x20in) London 2001

LLOYD Thomas James, Tom 1849-1910 **[52]**
- $7 376 - €7 091 - £4 600 - FF46 513
  Figures and cattle on a punt in an open river landscape Oil/canvas (74x149cm 29x59in) Guildford, Surrey 1999
- $948 - €990 - £600 - FF6 491
  Extensive Country Landscape, with Sheep grazing in the Foreground Oil/canvas (16x37cm 6x14in) London 2000
- $2 440 - €2 037 - £1 450 - FF13 364
  Children in the Sand Dunes Watercolour/paper (33x58cm 12x22in) Salisbury, Wiltshire 1998

LLOYD Walter Stuart act.1875-1929 **[183]**
- $1 891 - €1 835 - £1 200 - FF12 037
  Fishermen Sorting the Nets with an Extensive River Scene Beyond Oil/canvas (50x75cm 19x29in) West-Yorkshire 1999
- $1 666 - €1 533 - £1 000 - FF10 058
  Chepstow Watercolour/paper (30.5x66cm 12x25in) Glamorgan 1999

LO A NJOE Guillaume 1937 **[22]**
- $728 - €726 - £442 - FF4 762
  Zonder titel Oil/canvas (50x60cm 19x23in) Amsterdam 2000

LO MEDICO Thomas Gaetano 1904-1985 **[1]**
- $4 200 - €4 769 - £2 874 - FF31 283
  Shoeshine Boy Sculpture, wood (H34.5cm H13in) New-York 2000

LO SAVIO Francesco 1935-1963 **[6]**
- $3 294 - €3 062 - £2 000 - FF20 086
  «Progetto per metallo parasferico» Ink (19x22.5cm 7x8in) London 1998

LOAN van Dorothy 1904-1999 **[23]**
- $750 - €801 - £511 - FF5 254
  Yachting off the Coast Oil/canvas (71x81cm 28x32in) Philadelphia PA 2001
- $350 - €377 - £238 - FF2 463
  Davis Farm House, Chester Springs, PA Watercolour/paper (33x22cm 13x9in) Hatfield PA 2001

- $150 - €176 - £107 - FF1 157
  Bathers Monotype (30x26cm 12x10in) Hatfield PA 2001

LOATES Glen, Martin 1945 **[28]**
- $1 869 - €1 586 - £1 128 - FF10 405
  White Tailed Deer in the Forest Watercolour/paper (56x42cm 22x16in) Calgary, Alberta 1998

LOBBEDEZ Charles Auguste R. 1825-1882 **[20]**
- $8 700 - €8 842 - £5 469 - FF58 000
  Repos de la famille sur la grève Huile/toile (50.5x75.5cm 19x29in) Lyon 2000
- $2 400 - €2 330 - £1 482 - FF15 282
  Village Scene with Mother and Child on Horseback Oil/panel (17x12cm 7x5in) New-Orleans LA 1999

LOBEL P.H. XIX-XX **[2]**
- $3 600 - €4 199 - £2 527 - FF27 541
  «Salon des Cent» Poster (39.5x59.5cm 15x23in) New-York 2000

LOBEL-RICHE Alméry 1880-1950 **[106]**
- $361 - €335 - £225 - FF2 200
  Estrella Pastel/papier (36x23cm 14x9in) Arles 1999
- $600 - €629 - £400 - FF4 125
  Prostitutes, Paris/Femme fatale Etching (33x23cm 12x9in) New-York 2001

LOBISSER Switbert 1878-1943 **[155]**
- $258 - €291 - £180 - FF1 906
  «Im Mühlgraben» Woodcut (31.5x25.5cm 12x10in) Wien 2001

LOBO CASUERO Balthazar 1910-1993 **[72]**
- $3 179 - €3 007 - £1 980 - FF19 723
  Assis Tempera/carton (66x20.5cm 25x8in) Praha 2001
- $79 488 - €74 072 - £48 000 - FF485 880
  Jeune fille assise de face Bronze (H195cm H76in) London 1998
- $16 020 - €18 294 - £11 268 - FF120 000
  Femme se coiffant Bronze (H21cm H8in) Château-Thierry 2001
- $1 440 - €1 351 - £900 - FF8 865
  Maternidad Aguada/papel (49x64cm 19x25in) Madrid 1999

LOBO F.S. XIX **[1]**
- $6 452 - €6 126 - £3 954 - FF40 184
  Dom Pedro II. von Brasilien mit dem Imperial Orden do Cruceiro Öl/Leinwand (93x73cm 36x28in) Zürich 1999

LOBRE Maurice 1862-1951 **[17]**
- $9 500 - €9 202 - £5 925 - FF60 364
  Coffret en lacque rouge Oil/canvas (53.5x63.5cm 21x25in) Beverly-Hills CA 1999

LOBRICHON Timoléon 1831-1914 **[49]**
- $5 237 - €4 800 - £3 200 - FF31 485
  A Child's Dinner Party Oil/panel (32x61.5cm 12x24in) London 1999
- $8 000 - €8 934 - £5 123 - FF58 604
  Tug-of-War Oil/panel (30.5x40cm 12x15in) New-York 2000

LOCATELLI Andrea 1693-1741 **[63]**
- $80 692 - €86 616 - £54 000 - FF568 166
  An Italianate Landscape with Drovers and Fishermen on the Banks Oil/canvas (101.5x138.5cm 39x54in) London 2000
- $24 446 - €22 883 - £15 000 - FF150 105
  Phaeton's Sisters Mourning the Death of their Brother Oil/canvas (73.5x99cm 28x38in) London 1998

$10 161 - €10 907 - **£6 800** - FF71 546
Italianate wooded Landscape with Figures resting near a Path, Hilltop Oil/canvas (21.5x34.5cm 8x13in) London 2000

$4 991 - €4 884 - **£3 200** - FF32 039
Man Resting by a Country Road with Building beyond Ink (28x42cm 11x16in) London 1999

LOCATELLI Gian Francesco 1810-1882 [5]
$10 000 - €11 753 - **€6 933** - FF77 094
The Rich and Poor Oil/canvas (68.5x58cm 26x22in) New-York 2000

LOCATELLI Pietro c.1634-1710 [4]
$3 275 - €3 043 - **£2 000** - FF19 960
Design for a Frontispiece, Hercules Before the Portrait of a Cardinal Black chalk (27x20cm 10x7in) London 1998

LOCATELLI Romualdo 1905-1943 [15]
$42 390 - €46 839 - **€29 392** - FF307 245
Portrait of a Young Boy Oil/canvas (105x115cm 41x45in) Singapore 2001

$3 400 - €3 525 - **£2 040** - FF23 120
Signora che ride Olio/tavola (64x51cm 25x20in) Milano 2000

LOCCI Bruno 1937 [15]
$250 - €259 - **£150** - FF1 700
Freeze Frame N.809 Olio/tela (30x40cm 11x15in) Vercelli 2001

LOCHARD Félix 1874-1951 [7]
$334 - €381 - **£232** - FF2 500
«Chaines Darbilly» Affiche (120x78cm 47x30in) Paris 2000

LOCHBAUM Joseph XVIII [2]
$2 500 - €2 721 - **£1 718** - FF17 848
Nine Hearts Artist Watercolour/paper (30x36cm 12x14in) Downington PA 2001

LOCHER Carl 1851-1915 [281]
$4 750 - €4 939 - **£2 999** - FF32 398
Man O'War on the High Seas Oil/canvas (93.5x131cm 36x51in) New-York 2000

$2 165 - €2 414 - **£1 481** - FF15 838
Marine med sejlskibe Oil/canvas (60x81cm 23x31in) Viby J, Århus 2000

$1 208 - €1 144 - **£752** - FF7 504
Skibsportraet af Fregatten Jylland Oil/canvas/panel (25x38cm 9x14in) Vejle 1999

$223 - €241 - **£152** - FF1 583
Den en «Flatholm og Lysholm ved Cardiff»/Den anden «Cardiffs Rhed» Pencil (17.5x30cm 6x11in) København 2001

$87 - €81 - **£54** - FF529
Sejlskibe på havet Etching (28x43cm 11x16in) Viby J, Århus 1999

LOCHER Jens Thielsen 1825-1869 [4]
$8 588 - €9 591 - **£5 500** - FF62 913
Sailing off Kronberg Castle Oil/canvas (52.5x78.5cm 20x30in) London 2000

LÖCHERER Alois 1815-1862 [2]
$1 801 - €2 147 - **£1 284** - FF14 086
Grosses Familienbild Photograph (28.5x34.5cm 11x13in) München 2001

LOCHHEAD John 1866-1921 [25]
$8 500 - €9 357 - **£5 126** - FF48 268
«The Summer Garden» Oil/canvas (76x127cm 29x50in) San-Francisco CA 1998

LOCHHEAD Kenneth Campbell 1926 [11]
$787 - €668 - **£475** - FF4 381
Early Fall Oil/masonite (46x61cm 18x24in) Calgary, Alberta 1998

LOCHORE Brad 1960 [13]
$12 353 - €11 483 - **£7 500** - FF75 324
Shadow No.68 Oil/canvas (230x130cm 90x51in) London 1998

$9 661 - €8 255 - **£5 800** - FF54 147
Shadow No.4 Oil/canvas (100x115cm 39x45in) London 1998

LOCK Freida 1902-1962 [12]
$8 764 - €9 831 - **£6 132** - FF64 484
«Hall interior» Oil/canvas (59.5x49.5cm 23x19in) Cape Town 2001

$1 752 - €1 966 - **£1 226** - FF12 896
Interior of a Room Oil/canvas (34.5x24.5cm 13x9in) Cape Town 2001

LOCKE Charles Wheeler 1899-1983 [30]
$270 - €294 - **£187** - FF1 926
Waterfront Lithograph (21x30cm 8x12in) Cleveland OH 2001

LOCKE Walter Ronald 1883-? [27]
$110 - €118 - **£73** - FF777
Washingtonian Palms, Fla Etching (22x26cm 8x10in) Cleveland OH 2000

LOCKER Edward Hawker 1777-1848 [11]
$2 817 - €3 308 - **£2 000** - FF21 702
«Views of Ghazipur and Lucknow: Gateway to the Chalis Satun/Naubat...» Watercolour (19.5x31cm 7x12in) London 2000

LOCKERBY Mabel Irene 1887-1976 [3]
$8 212 - €7 977 - **£5 133** - FF52 324
In Montreal Oil/board (30.5x35.5cm 12x13in) Toronto 1999

LOCKEY Nicholas act.1600-1624 [1]
$23 462 - €25 286 - **£16 000** - FF165 864
Portrait of John King (1559-1621), half-length Oil/panel (79x62.5cm 31x24in) London 2001

LOCKHART William Ewart 1846-1900 [21]
$33 175 - €38 990 - **£23 000** - FF255 760
«Il Piccolo Cardinale col suo Candatario, John and Reginald, Sons...». Oil/canvas (168.5x115.5cm 66x45in) Edinburgh 2000

$4 000 - €4 308 - **£2 476** - FF25 437
Young Girl Carrying Laundry Oil/canvas (67x46cm 26x18in) Mystic CT 1999

$595 - €555 - **£360** - FF3 641
The Bass Watercolour/paper (24.5x34.5cm 9x13in) Edinburgh 1999

LOCKHEAD John 1866-1921 [4]
$642 - €730 - **£440** - FF4 788
Vessels on the Beach at Dusk Oil/canvas (25.5x35.5cm 10x13in) Bury St. Edmunds, Suffolk 2000

LOCKWOOD John Ward 1894-1963 [8]
$24 000 - €20 706 - **£14 424** - FF135 823
Siesta Oil/masonite (66x81cm 26x32in) Santa-Fe NM 1998

LOCKWOOD Wilton 1862-1914 [11]
$3 000 - €3 407 - **£2 105** - FF22 351
The Chronicle Oil/canvas (30.5x61cm 12x24in) Miami FL 2001

LODE de Gustav 1694-1742 **[1]**
- $4 043 - €3 500 - **£2 454** - FF22 958
«Sophia-Amalia (1628-1685)»/«Charlotta-Amalia (1650-1714)»/«Louisa» Gouache/paper (26x19cm 10x7in) Köbenhavn 1998

LODER OF BATH Edwin 1827-c.1885 **[30]**
- $659 - €704 - **£450** - FF4 618
Study of Three Hounds Oil/board (30x22cm 11x8in) Billingshurst, West-Sussex 2001

LODER OF BATH James c.1800-c.1860 **[38]**
- $3 885 - €4 170 - **£2 600** - FF27 356
Charlatan, a Chesnut Charger and Kate, a Black & White Dog Oil/canvas (63.5x76cm 25x29in) London 2000

LODGE George Edward 1860-1954 **[393]**
- $4 817 - €5 285 - **£3 200** - FF34 665
Gyr Falcon Oil/board (59x39cm 23x15in) London 2000
- $1 402 - €1 672 - **£1 000** - FF10 968
A Pregrine Falcon on a Rocky Outcrop Oil/canvas/board (31x46cm 12x18in) Leyburn, North Yorkshire 2000
- $1 218 - €1 163 - **£750** - FF7 632
Blackgame Amongst stubble Watercolour (29.5x44.5cm 11x17in) Edinburgh 1999

LODI da Gilardo XVII-XVIII **[6]**
- $51 200 - €48 784 - **£32 448** - FF320 000
Nature morte aux raisins, melon, pêches et corbeille Huile/toile (97x12.5cm 38x4in) Clermont-Ferrand 1999

LODI da Giovanni Agostino XV-XVI **[1]**
- $15 000 - €15 174 - **£9 159** - FF99 538
Head of a Male Saint (Saint Peter?) Oil/canvas (38x30cm 14x11in) New-York 2000

LODOLA Marco 1955 **[56]**
- $1 440 - €1 244 - **£960** - FF8 160
«Gara di ballo» Tecnica mista (76x52cm 29x20in) Prato 1998
- $1 320 - €1 710 - **£990** - FF11 220
«Videocan - can» Scultura (115x110cm 45x43in) Prato 2000
- $1 900 - €1 970 - **£1 140** - FF12 920
«Deposizione della modella» Scultura (38.5x76cm 15x29in) Prato 2001
- $200 - €259 - **£150** - FF1 700
Sciatori/Donna della lampada Feutre (33x24cm 12x9in) Prato 2000

LODS Marcel 1891-1978 **[2]**
- $2 600 - €3 032 - **£1 825** - FF19 891
«Paris, exposition internationale» Poster (60.5x96cm 23x37in) New-York 2000

LOEB Pierre 1920 **[12]**
- $3 782 - €4 269 - **£2 660** - FF28 000
Devant le mur Huile/toile (73x60cm 28x23in) Paris 2001

LOEB Sidonia 1871-1944 **[2]**
- $1 400 - €1 576 - **£964** - FF10 335
Louisiana Bayou Scene Oil/canvas (30x40cm 12x16in) New-Orleans LA 2000

LOEBER Lou, Louise 1894-1983 **[67]**
- $4 016 - €4 311 - **£2 687** - FF28 277
Openstaande deur Oil/board (49x39cm 19x15in) Amsterdam 2000
- $3 124 - €3 630 - **£2 196** - FF23 812
«Witte Wolk», White Cloud Oil/board (41.5x31cm 16x12in) Amsterdam 2001

LOEDING Harmen c.1637-c.1673 **[3]**
- $10 602 - €9 916 - **£6 500** - FF65 045
Peaches and Grapes with a Roemer Upon a Ledge with a Brown Cloth Oil/panel (36.5x31cm 14x12in) London 1998

LOEMANS Alexander Francis ?-1894 **[27]**
- $19 000 - €19 695 - **£12 047** - FF129 188
In the Tropics Oil/canvas (86.5x142cm 34x55in) New-York 2000
- $3 500 - €3 883 - **£2 327** - FF25 468
River Landscape Oil/board (43x60cm 17x24in) Milford CT 2000
- $837 - €723 - **£503** - FF4 741
Mountain Waterfall Oil/board (45.5x31cm 17x12in) Nepean, Ont. 1998

LOENEN van Cor 1943 **[42]**
- $738 - €862 - **£514** - FF5 655
Village near Pieterburen Oil/canvas (70x80cm 27x31in) Amsterdam 2000

LOESCH Ernst 1860-1946 **[5]**
- $1 366 - €1 431 - **£903** - FF9 390
Gebirgsdorf Watercolour (42.5x30.5cm 16x12in) München 2000

LOESCHIN Hermann ?-1872 **[2]**
- $7 100 - €7 622 - **£4 750** - FF50 000
Bal campagnard/Le retour du bal Huile/toile (60x73cm 23x28in) Paris 2000

LOEW Michael 1907-1985 **[2]**
- $9 000 - €9 661 - **£6 022** - FF63 369
Rainbow Minuet Oil/canvas (152x114cm 60x45in) Portland ME 2000

LOEWENSBERG Verena 1912-1986 **[47]**
- $28 795 - €26 387 - **£17 593** - FF173 090
Ohne Titel Acryl/Leinwand (121x80cm 47x31in) Zürich 1999
- $6 481 - €7 530 - **£4 555** - FF49 395
Ohne Titel Öl/Leinwand (30x30cm 11x11in) Luzern 2001
- $127 - €141 - **£86** - FF925
Farbkomposition Farbserigraphie (50x50cm 19x19in) Zürich 2000

LOEWY Maurice 1833-1907 **[6]**
- $475 - €472 - **£295** - FF3 098
Photographie lunaire, Petavius Pyrénées-Messier Heliogravure (76x50cm 29x22in) Wien 1999

LOEWY Raymond 1893-1986 **[93]**
- $2 000 - €2 240 - **£1 389** - FF14 694
«Greyhound Interior», Bus Gouache (32x47.5cm 12x18in) Beverly-Hills CA 2001
- $500 - €560 - **£347** - FF3 676
Concept Car Design Lithograph (61.5x76.5cm 24x30in) Beverly-Hills CA 2001

LÖFDAHL Eva 1953 **[21]**
- $704 - €823 - **£483** - FF5 397
Utan titel Mixed media (60x60cm 23x23in) Stockholm 2000

LÖFDAHL Oscar Magnus 1811-1895 **[6]**
- $2 877 - €2 852 - **£1 800** - FF18 709
Fishing in an Extensive Landscape Oil/canvas (32x43.5cm 12x17in) London 1999

LÖFFLER August 1822-1866 **[23]**

$3 750 - €3 887 - £2 250 - FF25 500
Veduta di Napoli dal Vomero Olio/tela (34.5x54cm 13x21in) Venezia 2000

$3 161 - €2 673 - £1 890 - FF17 533
«Salamis, Greece» Oil/cardboard (18x27cm 7x10in) Amsterdam 1998

$1 842 - €1 687 - £1 123 - FF11 067
Insel Rhodos Aquarell/Papier (16.8x25.9cm 6x10in) München 1999

LÖFFLER Bertold 1874-1960 **[90]**

$1 527 - €1 817 - £1 090 - FF11 917
Vogerl als Dose Ceramic (H10cm H3in) Wien 2000

$534 - €509 - £326 - FF3 336
Steinhaus am Semmering Pencil/paper (24x24cm 9x9in) Wien 1999

$195 - €182 - £121 - FF1 191
«Wiener Volksmusik» Poster (53x84cm 20x33in) Wien 1999

LØFFLER Emma 1843-1929 **[12]**

$288 - €336 - £206 - FF2 201
En skovsti Oil/canvas (54x46cm 21x18in) Aarhus 2001

LÖFFLER Franz 1875-1955 **[25]**

$1 211 - €1 329 - £780 - FF8 720
Blick vom Malerwinkel auf die Halbinsel Wasserburg Öl/Karton (23x34cm 9x13in) Lindau 2000

LOFFLER Hendrick 1723-1796 **[2]**

$12 341 - €10 652 - £7 353 - FF69 875
Natures mortes aux fleurs et insectes Huile/panneau (37x29.5cm 14x11in) Bruxelles 1998

LÖFFLER-RADYMNO Leopold 1827-1898 **[11]**

$10 685 - €12 472 - £7 320 - FF81 810
Baiser pendant le moisson Huile/toile (45x36.5cm 17x14in) Warszawa 2000

$13 703 - €13 811 - £8 545 - FF90 596
Un verre de vin, une gorgée pour le réconfort Oil/canvas (33.5x25.5cm 13x10in) Warszawa 2000

LOFFREDO Silvio 1932 **[54]**

$720 - €622 - £480 - FF4 080
Battistero Tempera/cartone (102.5x75cm 40x29in) Prato 1998

$330 - €285 - £220 - FF1 870
Ritratto Tecnica mista/tela (36x25cm 14x9in) Prato 1998

LÖFGREN Clara 1843-1923 **[13]**

$5 106 - €5 718 - £3 546 - FF37 508
Diskussion Oil/canvas (46x55cm 18x21in) Helsinki 2001

$842 - €728 - £508 - FF4 777
Kustlandskap med sittande flicka på klippa Oil/canvas (33x27cm 12x10in) Stockholm 1999

LOFVENS Pieter 1710-1788 **[1]**

$3 542 - €2 957 - £2 105 - FF19 399
Marine med det hollandske skib «Landman» ud for kysten Oil/canvas (23x25cm 9x9in) Köbenhavn 1998

LOGAN Maurice 1886-1977 **[48]**

$5 000 - €5 367 - £3 346 - FF35 205
The Red School House Oil/canvas (66x106.5cm 25x41in) San-Francisco CA 2000

$15 000 - €14 681 - £9 076 - FF84 066
The Island Fisherman Oil/canvas/board (43x35.5cm 16x13in) San-Francisco CA 1998

$800 - €864 - £552 - FF5 667
Decaying Ferryboat Watercolour/paper (53x71cm 21x28in) Altadena CA 2001

$1 800 - €1 674 - £1 111 - FF10 979
«Southern Pacific» Poster (58x40cm 23x16in) New-York 1999

LOGELAIN Henri 1889-1968 **[127]**

$450 - €496 - £312 - FF3 252
Maisons au bord du canal Huile/panneau (37x45cm 14x17in) Bruxelles 2001

$337 - €397 - £233 - FF2 601
Paysage Huile/panneau (29x39cm 11x15in) Antwerpen 2000

$248 - €273 - £165 - FF1 788
Le chantier naval Pastel/papier (61.5x46.5cm 24x18in) Bruxelles 2000

LOGSDAIL William 1859-1944 **[37]**

$10 000 - €11 201 - £6 948 - FF73 472
Duck Hunter returns Home Oil/canvas (76x54cm 30x21in) St. Louis MO 2001

LOHE Yves XX **[23]**

$1 775 - €1 789 - £1 107 - FF11 738
Violin Bronze (H78cm H30in) Hildrizhausen 2000

LOHMANN Adolf 1928 **[34]**

$256 - €293 - £181 - FF1 924
Zwei sitzende Stoffbären mit Ball im Blumengarten Oil/panel (10x13cm 3x5in) Bern 2001

LOHMANN Mogens 1918-1985 **[29]**

$1 307 - €1 238 - £794 - FF8 122
Komposition Oil/canvas (82x61cm 32x24in) Köbenhavn 1999

$3 127 - €3 488 - £2 139 - FF22 877
Komposition Oil/canvas (46x33cm 18x12in) Köbenhavn 2000

$1 855 - €2 011 - £1 285 - FF13 191
Punkter og pinde Relief (70x83cm 27x32in) Köbenhavn 2001

LOHMANN VAN DER FEER LADER Else 1897-1984 **[9]**

$5 097 - €4 413 - £3 093 - FF28 945
Frau mit Hut, Portrait von Frau Schmidt-Gregor Öl/Karton (70.5x62cm 27x24in) München 1998

LOHR August 1843-1919 **[83]**

$4 788 - €4 358 - £2 939 - FF28 586
Die Achsenstrasse am Vierwaldstättersee Öl/Leinwand (66x92cm 25x36in) Zürich 1999

$263 - €307 - £182 - FF2 012
«Süddeutsche Landschaft mit einem vom Wald umstandenen See» Oil/panel (24x32cm 9x12in) Buxtehude 2000

$6 732 - €5 802 - £4 000 - FF38 058
The Gateway to an Estate in Mexico with an Avenue of Palms Watercolour/paper (46.5x34cm 18x13in) London 1998

LÖHR Emil 1809-1876 **[21]**

$2 492 - €2 907 - £1 760 - FF19 068
Gasteinertal mit Blick auf Bad Gastein Öl/Leinwand (44x56cm 17x22in) Salzburg 2000

$2 125 - €1 816 - £1 275 - FF11 915
Blick auf Salzburg Öl/Karton (26.5x35cm 10x13in) Wien 1998

$2 127 - €1 816 - £1 272 - FF11 915
«Das Böcksteiner Tahl bey Sonnenuntergang» Pencil (21x27cm 8x10in) Wien 1998

LOHSE Karl 1895-1965 [13]

$1 269 – €1 534 – **£885** – FF10 061
Ohne Titel (Drei Fischer mit Boot vor Meereslandschaft) Mixed media/board (48.7x62cm 19x24in) Berlin 2000

$876 – €818 – **£530** – FF5 366
Hamburger Hafen Aquarell/Papier (35.6x41.7cm 14x16in) Berlin 1999

LOHSE Richard Paul 1902-1988 [117]

$19 874 – €19 290 – **£12 374** – FF126 537
Vier farbfelder an weissem Kreuz Öl/Leinwand (48x48cm 18x18in) Luzern 1999

$6 391 – €7 049 – **£4 328** – FF46 236
Farbgruppen um ein rotes Zentrum Acryl/Leinwand (30x30cm 11x11in) Zürich 2000

$10 626 – €9 738 – **£6 493** – FF63 878
Elemente zu zehn gleichen Themen Gouache/papier (48.5x34.5cm 19x13in) Zürich 1999

$222 – €263 – **£156** – FF1 726
Ohne Titel Farbserigraphie (70x70cm 27x27in) Zürich 2000

LOHSE-WÄCHTER Elfriede 1899-1940 [11]

$55 685 – €64 111 – **£38 000** – FF420 542
Lissy - Self-Portrait Watercolour (69x51cm 27x20in) London 2000

LOILIER Hervé 1948 [8]

$954 – €1 098 – **£673** – FF7 200
Carnaval à Cavareggio Huile/toile (55x46cm 21x18in) Barbizon 2001

LOIR Luigi 1845-1916 [404]

$22 414 – €24 060 – **£15 000** – FF157 824
Un bras arrête de la Seine Oil/canvas (77x122cm 30x48in) London 2000

$6 434 – €7 307 – **£4 500** – FF47 929
La mer à Trouville Oil/board (22x33cm 8x12in) London 2001

$1 971 – €1 677 – **£1 175** – FF11 000
Quai des Augustins Gouache/papier (12x26cm 4x10in) Paris 1998

$450 – €460 – **£282** – FF3 018
Pariser Strassenszene Etching, aquatint in colors (39.2x54.5cm 15x21in) Hamburg 2000

LOIR Nicolas 1624-1679 [16]

$3 614 – €3 278 – **£2 218** – FF21 500
Vierge à l'enfant avec Saint-Jean Baptiste et Sainte Elisabeth Huile/toile (65x81cm 25x31in) Aurillac 1998

LOISEAU Gustave 1865-1935 [700]

$46 400 – €48 784 – **£29 120** – FF320 000
Le quai de Neynac à Bordeaux Huile/toile (60x73cm 23x28in) Paris 2000

$13 221 – €11 296 – **£8 000** – FF74 100
Effet de neige, Pontoise Oil/canvas (33x41cm 12x16in) London 1998

$402 – €457 – **£279** – FF3 000
Rue animée à St Ouen Fusain (19x24cm 7x9in) Barbizon 2001

LOISEAU Jacques 1920 [5]

$51 590 – €55 006 – **£35 000** – FF360 815
Les meules Oil/canvas (60x73cm 23x28in) London 2001

LOISEAU-ROUSSEAU Paul Louis 1861-1927 [15]

$1 180 – €1 372 – **£841** – FF9 000
Jeune fille Kabyle Plâtre (H46cm H18in) Paris 2001

LOISEL Régis 1951 [30]

$408 – €457 – **£284** – FF3 000
La métamorphose du Marsupilami Encre Chine (34x25cm 13x9in) Paris 2001

LOISON Pierre 1816-1886 [4]

$1 755 – €1 952 – **£1 202** – FF12 805
Busto de dama Marbre (H58cm H22in) Madrid 2001

LOJACONO Francesco 1841-1915 [45]

$14 750 – €15 291 – **£8 850** – FF100 300
Veduta di Napoli Olio/tela (46x92cm 18x36in) Napoli 2000

$4 943 – €4 279 – **£3 000** – FF28 068
Corner of the Courtyard Oil/canvas (40.5x24.5cm 15x9in) London 1998

$4 750 – €4 924 – **£2 850** – FF32 300
Eruzione del Vesuvio Gouache/carta (33x62.5cm 12x24in) Milano 2000

LOKHORST van Dirk 1818-1893 [21]

$1 633 – €1 906 – **£1 136** – FF12 501
Horseriders on a Field Oil/panel (14x19cm 5x7in) Amsterdam 2000

LOKHORST van Dirk Peter 1848-? [18]

$1 612 – €1 360 – **£957** – FF8 918
Cows in a Landscape Oil/panel (54.5x39.5cm 21x15in) Amsterdam 1998

LOKHORST van Jan, Johan Nicolaas 1837-? [24]

$782 – €862 – **£510** – FF5 655
Winterse boerderij Oil/canvas (48.5x68.5cm 19x26in) Den Haag 2001

$2 384 – €2 843 – **£1 700** – FF18 647
A Dutch Canal Scene Oil/panel (23x31cm 9x12in) Leyburn, North Yorkshire 2000

LØKKE Marie 1876-1948 [8]

$2 800 – €3 293 – **£2 014** – FF21 600
Farm landscape with bales of hay Oil/canvas (55x76cm 22x30in) Hatfield PA 2001

LOLEK Stanislav 1873-1936 [24]

$1 040 – €984 – **£648** – FF6 454
Fin d'été Huile/toile (49x55cm 19x21in) Praha 2001

$404 – €383 – **£252** – FF2 510
Dans le champ Huile/carton (18x27cm 7x10in) Praha 2000

LOLLI Lorenzo 1612-1691 [12]

$257 – €307 – **£183** – FF2 012
Amor zerbricht seinen Bogen Radierung (18.5x13.8cm 7x5in) Berlin 2000

LOMAX John Arthur 1857-1923 [53]

$10 960 – €12 111 – **£7 600** – FF79 442
The Huntman's Story Oil/panel (35.5x45.5cm 13x17in) London 2000

$5 678 – €6 095 – **£3 800** – FF39 982
After the Hunt Oil/panel (31.5x26cm 12x10in) London 2000

LOMBARD Lambert 1505-1566 [11]

$15 880 – €14 534 – **£9 680** – FF95 340
Der wunderbare Fischzug Oil/panel (85x79cm 33x31in) Wien 1999

LOMBARDI Giovanni Battista 1823-1880 [20]

$33 376 – €36 301 – **£22 000** – FF238 119
Suzanna Marble (H218cm H85in) London 2000

LOMBARDI OMINO Giovanni Domenico 1682-1752 [2]

$12 000 – €10 367 – **£6 000** – FF68 000
Adorazione dei Pastori Olio/tela (150x100cm 59x39in) Roma 1999

$4 800 - €6 220 - £3 600 - FF40 800
Allegoria della fede e della carità/Allegoria della giustizia Olio/tela (56x40.5cm 22x15in) Milano 2001

LOMER Heinrich 1875-? [2]
$4 327 - €4 497 - £2 714 - FF29 500
Le mariage du Maharadjah de Mysore Aquarelle, gouache (175x175cm 68x68in) Paris 2000

LOMI Aurelio 1556-1622 [6]
$28 391 - €30 476 - £19 000 - FF199 170
Venus and Adonis Oil/canvas (149.5x121cm 58x47in) London 2000
$1 000 - €884 - £611 - FF5 797
Study of a Kneeling Page Black & white chalks/paper (23x31cm 9x12in) New-York 1999

LOMI Giovanni 1889-1969 [115]
$5 100 - €4 406 - £2 550 - FF28 900
Buoi maremmanai lungo la costa Olio/tela (50x70cm 19x27in) Milano 1999
$1 520 - €1 300 - £1 140 - FF12 920
Nei pressi della chiesa Olio/tavola (29x36cm 11x14in) Roma 2001

LOMIKIN Constantin 1924-1994 [33]
$1 081 - €1 271 - £750 - FF8 340
Dancers in yellow Pastel/paper (66x50cm 26x20in) Carlisle, Cumbria 2000

LOMMEN Wilhelm 1838-1895 [15]
$3 858 - €4 141 - £2 582 - FF27 166
Ausbrechende Pferdeheide Öl/Leinwand (62x85cm 24x33in) Berlin 2000
$3 334 - €3 579 - £2 231 - FF23 477
Feldgottesdienst Öl/Leinwand/Karton (22x28.5cm 8x11in) Königstein 2000

LONCIN Louis 1875-1946 [23]
$1 046 - €1 123 - £700 - FF7 369
A Dog in an Extensive Landscape Oil/canvas (96.5x61cm 37x24in) London 2000

LONDERSEEL van Jan 1570/75-1624/25 [10]
$337 - €383 - £233 - FF2 515
Landschaft mit Christus, der die Besessene heilt, nach G.van Coninxloo Kupferstich (48.5x33cm 19x12in) Berlin 2001

LONDONIO Francesco 1723-1783 [37]
$22 000 - €22 806 - £13 200 - FF149 600
Pastore con armenti Olio/tela (46x35cm 18x13in) Milano 2000
$6 000 - €6 220 - £3 600 - FF40 800
Pastore con armenti Olio/tela (45x35cm 17x13in) Milano 2000
$714 - €740 - £428 - FF4 855
Pastore con capra Inchiostro (10.5x13.5cm 4x5in) Venezia 2000
$298 - €256 - £179 - FF1 676
Ein alter Hirt mit seiner Herde Radierung (19.1x24.5cm 7x9in) Berlin 1998

LONDOT Léon 1878-1953 [37]
$402 - €471 - £286 - FF3 089
Le sas à Ostende Huile/toile (61x65cm 24x25in) Bruxelles 2001
$289 - €320 - £200 - FF2 099
By the Quayside Oil/panel (32.5x40cm 12x15in) London 2001

LONECHILD Michael 1955 [18]
$684 - €766 - £475 - FF5 027
The Wolf Spirits Acrylic/canvas (50x40cm 20x16in) Calgary, Alberta 2001

LONG Charles 1958 [13]
$5 288 - €4 519 - £3 200 - FF29 640
Legs Sculpture (152.5x61x48cm 60x24x18in) London 1998
$8 000 - €7 741 - £4 933 - FF50 775
Untitled (Black) Plastic (58.5x77.5x63.5cm 23x30x25in) New-York 1999

LONG Edwin Longsden 1829-1891 [58]
$200 000 - €223 353 - £128 080 - FF1 465 100
Sacred to Pasht Oil/canvas (101.5x152.5cm 39x60in) New-York 2000
$20 839 - €19 686 - £13 000 - FF129 132
Scotland «Rose Bradivous Zaine» Oil/canvas (125x86.5cm 49x34in) Perthshire 1999

LONG Frank Weathers 1906-? [4]
$9 000 - €10 236 - £6 241 - FF67 141
Untitled, Mountain Madonna Oil/canvas (83x71cm 33x28in) Chicago IL 2000

LONG L. XIX [4]
$6 254 - €6 845 - £4 323 - FF44 900
Cavaliers arabes Huile/toile (39x64cm 15x25in) Aurillac 2001

LONG Leonard Hugh 1911 [57]
$538 - €506 - £333 - FF3 319
Motiv från Australien Oil/canvas (55x64cm 21x25in) Stockholm 1999

LONG Richard 1945 [83]
$1 397 - €1 294 - £855 - FF8 485
Fingerprints Mixed media (21.3x16.6cm 8x6in) München 1999
$15 157 - €16 399 - £10 500 - FF107 571
Black Line Installation (991x148cm 390x58in) London 2001
$3 659 - €3 410 - £2 211 - FF22 370
Fossil Line Stone (5x3.8cm 1x1in) München 1999
$957 - €1 125 - £663 - FF7 378
Fossil line Gouache/paper (25x29cm 9x11in) Stuttgart 2000
$534 - €635 - £380 - FF4 167
Throwing Snow into a Circle Offset (35x46.5cm 13x18in) Amsterdam 2000

LONG Shorty XIX [8]
$750 - €715 - £455 - FF4 690
B&O Railroad/Pennsylvania Farm Landscape Oil/board (30x40cm 12x16in) New-York 1999

LONG Sydney 1871-1955 [209]
$5 404 - €5 258 - £3 326 - FF34 491
Narrabeen shoreline Oil/board (43x53.5cm 16x21in) Melbourne 1999
$4 469 - €3 897 - £2 702 - FF25 564
Tall Gums Oil/wood (31x38.5cm 12x15in) Melbourne 1998
$3 795 - €4 236 - £2 640 - FF27 785
Sydney Harbour Watercolour/paper (39x54cm 15x21in) Sydney 2001
$243 - €230 - £147 - FF1 510
Boyds, Narrabeen Etching (17.5x27cm 6x10in) Sydney 1999

LONGA Louis 1809-1869 [5]
$59 600 - €68 602 - £42 075 - FF450 000
Musiciens arabes sur la palce de la Brèche à Constantine Huile/toile (123x178.5cm 48x70in) Paris 2001

LONGABAUGH Charles Oglesby 1885-1944 [16]
$175 - €205 - £124 - FF1 346
Cloth Market Watercolour/paper (20x27cm 8x11in) Cedar-Falls IA 2001

LONGANESI Leo 1905-1957 **[10]**
$4 000 – €4 147 – **£2 400** – FF27 200
Pesci Olio/tela (75x120cm 29x47in) Milano 2000

LONGARETTI Trento 1916 **[39]**
$2 800 – €3 628 – **£2 100** – FF23 800
«Madre su fondi verdi» Olio/tela (50x40cm 19x15in) Torino 2000
$1 250 – €1 296 – **£750** – FF8 500
«Famiglia di viandanti» Olio/cartone (20x30cm 7x11in) Vercelli 2001

LONGCHAMP de Henriette 1818-? **[8]**
$2 888 – €3 254 – **£2 000** – FF21 347
Roses in a Bowl on a Table Oil/canvas (33.5x47cm 13x18in) London 2000

LONGE W.V. XIX-XX **[17]**
$150 – €161 – **£100** – FF1 056
Catching a Loose Horse Watercolour (30.5x45.5cm 12x17in) London 2000

LONGEN-PITTERMANN Emil Artur 1885-1936 **[18]**
$2 077 – €1 943 – **£1 258** – FF12 744
Flaneure im Parc Öl/Karton (68.5x89.5cm 26x35in) Düsseldorf 1999

LONGHI Allessandro 1733-1813 **[15]**
$11 789 – €10 933 – **£7 200** – FF71 713
Portrait of Alesio Foscari seated at a Table Wearing the Red Robes Oil/canvas (95.5x72cm 37x28in) London 1998
$882 – €767 – **£531** – FF5 028
Bildnis Giovanni Battista Piazzettas Radierung (19.3x14.7cm 7x5in) Berlin 1998

LONGHI Giuseppe 1766-1831 **[7]**
$225 – €263 – **£159** – FF1 726
Blessing from the Child Jesus Engraving (53x38cm 21x15in) Cedar-Falls IA 2001

LONGHI Luca 1507-1580 **[12]**
$31 380 – €33 684 – **£21 000** – FF220 953
Pietà with Two Angels and a Bishop and a Nun Kneeling Oil/panel (94x72.5cm 37x28in) London 2000
$12 560 – €12 196 – **£7 760** – FF80 000
Sainte Véronique Huile/toile (28.5x22cm 11x8in) Paris 1999

LONGHI Pietro 1702-1785 **[26]**
$52 000 – €67 382 – **£39 000** – FF442 000
Lo svenimento Olio/tela (61x50cm 24x19in) Milano 2001
$17 000 – €15 994 – **£10 608** – FF104 913
Portrait of a Gentleman, holding a glove Oil/copper (9x7cm 3x2in) New-York 1999
$17 931 – €19 248 – **£12 000** – FF126 259
Man Playing the Colascione by a River Black chalk/paper (23x15.5cm 9x6in) London 2000

LONGI Carlantonio 1921-1980 **[10]**
$787 – €816 – **£472** – FF5 355
«L'avventura» Affiche couleur (197x139cm 77x54in) Torino 2000

LONGLEY Stanislaus Soutten 1884-1966 **[9]**
$3 116 – €3 638 – **£2 200** – FF23 861
Autumn Watercolour/paper (44x31cm 17x12in) London 2000

LONGMIRE William Taylor 1841-1914 **[63]**
$319 – €366 – **£220** – FF2 401
Grasmere and Helm Crag Watercolour/paper (24.5x34.5cm 9x13in) Penrith, Cumbria 2000

LONGO Robert 1953 **[163]**
$60 000 – €56 337 – **£37 176** – FF369 546
Corporate Wars: Walls of Influence (center sec.) Relief (213.5x274.5x40.5cm 84x108x15in) New-York 1999
$7 000 – €6 773 – **£4 316** – FF44 428
Study, Love Hurts Charcoal (137x244cm 53x96in) New-York 1999
$2 250 – €2 520 – **£1 563** – FF16 531
Rick Lithograph (117x76.5cm 46x30in) New-York 1999
$6 775 – €7 622 – **£4 665** – FF50 000
Série Men in the Cities Photo couleurs (102x68cm 40x26in) Paris 2000

LONGOBARDI Xavier 1923 **[23]**
$284 – €274 – **£179** – FF1 800
Saint-Sébastien Gouache (50x34.5cm 19x13in) Paris 1999

LONGONI Baldassare 1876-1956 **[17]**
$18 000 – €18 660 – **£10 800** – FF122 400
Riflessi e sorrisi Olio/tela (136x136cm 53x53in) Venezia 2000
$30 000 – €31 100 – **£18 000** – FF204 000
Madre e figlio in un paesaggio Olio/tela (70x120cm 27x47in) Milano 2000
$2 400 – €2 073 – **£1 600** – FF13 600
Porto di Camogli Olio/tela (24.5x30cm 9x11in) Milano 1998

LONGONI Emilio 1859-1932 **[26]**
$44 000 – €57 016 – **£33 000** – FF374 000
Ortensie Olio/tavola (34x64cm 13x25in) Milano 2001
$17 500 – €18 141 – **£10 500** – FF119 000
Ghiacciaio Olio/tavola (24.5x38cm 9x14in) Prato 2000

LONGPRÉ de Paul 1855-1911 **[72]**
$3 558 – €3 323 – **£2 150** – FF21 800
Sumpfiger See mit bewachsenem Ufer unter bewölktem Himmel Öl/Leinwand/Karton (43x58cm 16x22in) Berlin 1999
$10 000 – €8 545 – **£5 874** – FF56 054
Roses in Pinks and Yellows/Daisies, Poppies and Cornflowers Oil/canvas (36x24cm 14x9in) Boston MA 1998
$7 000 – €6 432 – **£4 300** – FF42 189
Queen Anne's Lace and Other Summer Flowers Watercolour/paper (41x27cm 16x11in) Portsmouth NH 1999
$750 – €875 – **£522** – FF5 739
Red Roses with Bumble Bees Color lithograph (76x43cm 30x17in) Altadena CA 2000

LONGPRÉ de Raoul Maucherat 1859-c.1920 **[27]**
$8 500 – €10 043 – **£6 024** – FF65 881
Still Life with White Lilacs and Pink Roses Gouache/paper (70x52cm 27x20in) Boston MA 2000

LONGSTAFF John Campbell 1862-1941 **[17]**
$4 167 – €4 862 – **£2 900** – FF31 892
The Entombment of Christ, after Titian Oil/board (35.5x53cm 13x20in) Melbourne 2000
$1 244 – €1 396 – **£864** – FF9 157
Woman and Trees Oil/canvas (23x36cm 9x14in) Melbourne 2001

LONGSTAFF William Francis 1879-1953 **[85]**
$391 – €361 – **£240** – FF2 366
Harvesting on Bury Hill, Amberley, Sussex Oil/canvas (38x49.5cm 14x19in) London 1998
$317 – €299 – **£200** – FF1 964
On the River Thames Watercolour/paper (16.5x18cm 6x7in) Godalming, Surrey 1999

LONGSTAFFE Edgar 1849-1912 **[62]**
- $899 - €953 - **£600** - FF6 254
  Laindon, Essex, scene of a Farmyard with horse and cart Oil/canvas (36x51cm 14x20in) Stansted Mountfitchet, Essex 2000
- $971 - €1 043 - **£650** - FF6 841
  View of Balmoral Castle Oil/board (16.5x26.5cm 6x10in) London 2000

LONGUET Alexandre Marie 1805-1851 **[7]**
- $2 300 - €2 512 - **£1 480** - FF16 476
  Draped Woman Oil/canvas (39x23cm 15x9in) Mystic CT 2000

LØNNBERG William 1887-1949 **[32]**
- $1 034 - €874 - **£617** - FF5 735
  Sveaborg Oil/canvas (37x45cm 14x17in) Helsinki 1998

LØNNING Terkel Eriksen 1762-1823 **[4]**
- $2 398 - €2 799 - **£1 700** - FF18 362
  The Gunboat War 1807-14: Prins Christian Frederik Ink (51x64cm 20x25in) London 2001

LONZA Antonio 1846-1918 **[16]**
- $10 000 - €10 367 - **£6 000** - FF68 000
  Domenica all'aperto Olio/tela (150.5x206cm 59x81in) Milano 2000
- $4 800 - €6 220 - **£3 600** - FF40 800
  Processione sull'acqua Olio/tela (63.5x106cm 25x41in) Milano 2000

LOO van Carle 1705-1765 **[83]**
- $250 000 - €249 883 - **£152 725** - FF1 639 125
  Venus Requesting Vulcan to Make Arms for Aeneas Oil/canvas (129x98.5cm 50x38in) New-York 2000
- $24 840 - €22 867 - **£14 910** - FF150 000
  La remise de la dot Huile/toile (70x108cm 27x42in) Lyon 1999
- $4 777 - €5 336 - **£3 237** - FF35 000
  Adam et Eve à qui Dieu reproche leur désobéissance Sanguine (95.5x30cm 37x11in) Paris 2000

LOO van Charles Amédée Ph. 1719-1795 **[13]**
- $26 000 - €28 526 - **£17 271** - FF187 116
  Dodo's Banquet Oil/canvas (66x82cm 25x32in) New-York 2000

LOO van François 1708-1732 **[3]**
- $7 011 - €6 541 - **£4 230** - FF42 903
  Jupiter and Lo Öl/Leinwand (67x90cm 26x35in) Wien 1999

LOO van Jacob c.1614-1670 **[10]**
- $14 373 - €14 483 - **£8 958** - FF95 000
  Portrait d'homme au col blanc Huile/toile (78x65cm 30x25in) Paris 2000

LOO van Jean-Baptiste 1684-1745 **[37]**
- $11 808 - €13 720 - **£8 298** - FF90 000
  Monsieur de Germain, surintendant de Provence Huile/toile (130.5x97cm 51x38in) Paris 2001
- $24 912 - €24 392 - **£15 328** - FF160 000
  Diane et Endymiom Huile/toile (81.5x74cm 32x29in) Paris 1999
- $8 594 - €7 470 - **£5 179** - FF49 560
  Louise Charlotte de Foix, Comtesse de Sabran et de Forcalquier Pastel/papier (63.5x52.5cm 25x20in) Paris 1998

LOO van Jules César Denis 1749-1821 **[25]**
- $31 600 - €30 490 - **£19 840** - FF200 000
  Femmes et enfants sortant du bain, près de la grotte Huile/toile (178x190cm 70x74in) Rouen 1999

- $14 490 - €16 007 - **£10 048** - FF105 000
  Incendie au clair de lune Huile/toile (55x74cm 21x29in) Paris 2001

LOO van Louis-Michel 1707-1771 **[49]**
- $100 000 - €109 715 - **£66 430** - FF719 680
  Man, said to be Monsieur de Boulogne, in a orange Velvet Costume Oil/canvas (145x113cm 57x44in) New-York 2000
- $19 000 - €20 846 - **£12 621** - FF136 739
  La Sculpture Oil/canvas (92x73cm 36x28in) New-York 2000

LOO van Pieter van Loon 1731-1784 **[16]**
- $1 161 - €1 380 - **£804** - FF9 055
  Dorf mit Kirche unter hohen Bäumen, mit Gespann und Bauern Watercolour (27x34.4cm 10x13in) Köln 2000

LOOBY Keith 1940 **[62]**
- $2 292 - €2 726 - **£1 633** - FF17 882
  «Snob Sport» Oil/canvas (75x100.5cm 29x39in) Melbourne 2000
- $624 - €602 - **£386** - FF3 950
  P P Mc Guinness Ink/paper (100x67cm 39x26in) Sydney 1999

LOOF de Aurel 1901 **[4]**
- $2 068 - €2 269 - **£1 374** - FF14 883
  Wagenia Woman and Children in a River Oil/canvas (75x120cm 29x47in) Amsterdam 2000

LOOMIS Andrew 1892-1959 **[18]**
- $3 500 - €3 898 - **£2 289** - FF25 572
  Illustration: Fighter pilot in cockpit Oil/canvas (46x74cm 18x29in) New-York 2000

LOOMIS Helen 1920 **[1]**
- $3 900 - €3 729 - **£2 375** - FF24 462
  Cottage Garden Watercolour/paper (47x70cm 18x27in) Boston MA 1999

LOON van Theodoor 1581/82-1667 **[7]**
- $224 480 - €266 974 - **£160 000** - FF1 751 232
  The Adoration of the Shepherds Oil/canvas (250x167cm 98x65in) London 2000
- $6 142 - €6 860 - **£4 162** - FF45 000
  La Sainte Famille avec Sainte Anne, saint Joachim et saint J.Baptiste Huile/toile (37x27.5cm 14x10in) Paris 2000

LOOS Friedrich 1797-1890 **[14]**
- $11 978 - €12 271 - **£7 392** - FF80 493
  Blick auf den Traunsee mit Schloss Orth im Salzkammergut Öl/Leinwand (62.5x96.5cm 24x37in) Düsseldorf 2000
- $9 178 - €8 692 - **£5 581** - FF57 016
  Bruck an der Mur, von der Filialkirche St. Nikolaus aus gesehen Watercolour, gouache (12.8x18.2cm 5x7in) München 1999

LOOS Henry XIX **[11]**
- $5 729 - €4 932 - **£3 400** - FF32 350
  Three-masted Barque Sailing Off a Coastline, Flying the Red Ensign Oil/canvas (60x90cm 23x35in) London 1998

LOOS John Frederick act.1861-c.1895 **[18]**
- $7 500 - €8 263 - **£5 003** - FF54 204
  The British Ship Norseman Under Sail Oil/canvas (60x91cm 24x36in) Portsmouth NH 2000

LOOSCHEN Hans 1859-1923 **[17]**
- $2 251 - €2 250 - **£1 408** - FF14 757
  Tanzende Menschen auf dem Kostümball Öl/Leinwand (96x82cm 37x32in) Staufen 1999

LOOSE de Basile 1809-1885 **[40]**

- **$40 660** - €47 098 - **£28 120** - FF308 940
  Le portrait d'une laitière Huile/toile (101x122cm
  39x48in) Bruxelles 2000
- **$6 305** - €7 260 - **£4 304** - FF47 625
  The Teacher's Pet Oil/panel (57x44.5cm 22x17in)
  Amsterdam 2000
- **$5 200** - €6 197 - **£3 725** - FF40 650
  In de klas (dans la classe) Huile/toile (35x28cm
  13x11in) Antwerpen 2000

LOOSER Hans 1897-1984 **[6]**

- **$802** - €808 - **£500** - FF5 301
  «Coca-Cola» Poster (127x90cm 50x35in) London
  2000

LOOTEN Jan c.1618-1681 **[21]**

- **$30 572** - €29 090 - **£19 000** - FF190 817
  **An elegant Gentleman on Horseback with two
  Lady Companions on a Path** Oil/canvas
  (246.5x370.5cm 97x145in) London 1999
- **$7 822** - €9 076 - **£5 400** - FF59 532
  **Extensive Wooded Landscape with Travellers
  on a Path** Oil/canvas (99.5x118.5cm 39x46in)
  Amsterdam 2000

LOOY van Jacobus, Jac 1855-1930 **[19]**

- **$56 826** - €63 529 - **£39 550** - FF416 724
  «Augustus, Oostindische kers» Oil/canvas
  (100x140cm 39x55in) Amsterdam 2001
- **$30 442** - €34 033 - **£21 187** - FF223 245
  Lilies Oil/canvas (53x137cm 20x53in) Amsterdam
  2001
- **$10 089** - €9 983 - **£6 175** - FF65 485
  **Asters, Michaelmas daisies and Pears against a
  Garden Fence** Oil/panel (50x25cm 19x9in)
  Amsterdam 2000
- **$1 605** - €1 588 - **£982** - FF10 418
  African Water-carrier Pencil/paper (17x12.5cm
  6x4in) Amsterdam 2000

LOOY van Jan 1882-1971 **[68]**

- **$809** - €716 - **£495** - FF4 695
  «Stilleben mit Fisch, Wein» Oil/panel (50x60.5cm
  19x23in) München 1999

LOPES Joaquim 1886-1956 **[2]**

- **$2 200** - €2 493 - **£1 550** - FF16 350
  Marinha Oleo/cartón (31x23cm 12x9in) Lisboa 2001

LOPÉZ Andrés Joseph c.1750-c.1812 **[1]**

- **$6 000** - €5 232 - **£3 627** - FF34 318
  Shepherds with their Flocks Oil/copper (22x32cm
  8x12in) New-York 1998

LOPEZ Antonio 1943-1988 **[33]**

- **$1 600** - €1 504 - **£971** - FF9 863
  Fashion Sketches Pencil/paper (45x58cm 18x23in)
  New-York 1999

LOPEZ ARMENTIA Gustavo 1949 **[1]**

- **$10 000** - €10 734 - **£6 692** - FF70 410
  Desde el Interior Mixed media (123x101cm 48x39in)
  New-York 2000

LOPEZ CABRERA Ricardo 1864-1950 **[55]**

- **$1 620** - €1 802 - **£1 140** - FF11 820
  Junto al lar Oleo/lienzo (56.5x66cm 22x25in) Madrid
  2001
- **$1 518** - €1 321 - **£924** - FF8 368
  Vista de ciudad Oleo/tabla (9x14cm 3x5in) Madrid
  1999

LOPEZ DE LEAO LAGUNA Baruch 1864-1943 **[43]**

- **$2 781** - €2 468 - **£1 700** - FF16 188
  Pansies in a Vase Oil/canvas (64.5x51cm 25x20in)
  London 1999

- **$1 296** - €1 361 - **£820** - FF8 929
  Peasant by the Fire Oil/canvas/panel (22x30cm
  8x11in) Amsterdam 2000

LOPEZ DEI FIORI Gasparo 1650-1732 **[43]**

- **$12 500** - €13 813 - **£8 668** - FF90 608
  Still Life with Flowers and Fruit, Birds Oil/canvas
  (105x134cm 41x53in) New-Orleans LA 2001
- **$15 858** - €13 078 - **£9 342** - FF85 788
  **Blumenstrauss in einer vergoldeten Prunkvase
  bei einem Brunnen** Öl/Leinwand (75x102cm
  29x40in) Wien 1998
- **$16 000** - €17 719 - **£10 851** - FF116 232
  **Flowers in a Blue and White Porcelain Vases
  Resting on a Ledges** Oil/canvas (26.5x39.5cm
  10x15in) New-York 2000

LOPEZ ENGUIDANOS José 1760-1812 **[2]**

- **$19 143** - €21 465 - **£13 000** - FF140 799
  Still Life of Figs in a ceramic Bowl Oil/canvas
  (36x46cm 14x18in) London 2000

LOPEZ ENGUIDANOS Tomas 1773-1814 **[7]**

- **$162** - €180 - **£105** - FF1 182
  **Vista del real Monasterio de San Lorenzo del
  Escorial** Grabado (41x55cm 16x21in) Madrid 2000

LOPEZ GARCIA Antonio 1936 **[13]**

- **$89 937** - €83 468 - **£54 000** - FF547 516
  Street of Mud Mixed media (52x73cm 20x28in)
  London 1999
- **$7 800** - €9 010 - **£5 400** - FF59 100
  Estudio de anatomía Lápiz (40x30cm 15x11in)
  Madrid 2001

LOPEZ MÉNDEZ Luis Alfredo 1901-1996 **[68]**

- **$2 880** - €2 909 - **£1 980** - FF19 080
  Marina Oleo/tabla (38x45.5cm 14x17in) Caracas 1999
- **$1 508** - €1 777 - **£1 059** - FF15 460
  Muchacha visitiéndose Oleo/lienzo (25x20cm
  9x7in) Caracas ($) 2000

LOPEZ MEZQUITA José María 1883-1954 **[13]**

- **$5 400** - €6 006 - **£3 600** - FF39 400
  Mujer con mantón Oleo/lienzo (52x33cm 20x12in)
  Madrid 2000

LOPEZ PIQUER Luis 1802-1865 **[4]**

- **$3 640** - €4 205 - **£2 520** - FF27 700
  Remisión de las almas del purgatorio Oleo/tabla
  (94x80cm 37x31in) Madrid 2001

LOPEZ Tomas XVIII **[9]**

- **$585** - €541 - **£360** - FF3 546
  Mapa del Reyno de Aragon Grabado (79x77cm
  31x30in) Madrid 1999

LOPEZ TORRES Antonio 1902-1987 **[4]**

- **$5 760** - €5 406 - **£3 600** - FF35 460
  «La foradada de Mallorca» Oleo/tabla (21x31cm
  8x12in) Madrid 1999

LOPEZ Y PORTAÑA Vicente 1772-1850 **[25]**

- **$33 600** - €36 039 - **£22 200** - FF236 400
  **Retrato del Obispo Gregorio Ceruelo de la
  Fuente** Oleo/lienzo (93x77.5cm 36x30in) Madrid 2000
- **$4 320** - €4 805 - **£2 800** - FF31 520
  La Inmaculada Oleo/tabla (23.5x18.5cm 9x7in)
  Madrid 2000
- **$3 080** - €3 304 - **£2 035** - FF21 670
  Moisés y San Bartolomé Lápiz (30.5x21.5cm
  12x8in) Madrid 2000

LOPIENSKI Ignacy 1865-1944 **[3]**

- **$449** - €511 - **£311** - FF3 349
  Shylock et Jessyka, d'après Maurice Gottlieb
  Eau-forte (50.5x38cm 19x14in) Lódz 2000

LOPPÉ Gabriel 1825-1913 **[24]**
- [photo] **$2 120** - €2 439 - **£1 460** - FF16 000
  Paris, Bords de Seine, Place de la Concorde
  Photo (13x18cm 5x7in) Paris 2000

LORAN Erle 1905-1999 **[54]**
- **$4 750** - €5 099 - **£3 179** - FF33 447
  America at War Oil/canvas (76x91.5cm 29x36in) San-Francisco CA 2000
- **$1 700** - €1 452 - **£1 028** - FF9 527
  View of Golden Gate from Point Richmond
  Watercolour, gouache/paper (28x37.5cm 11x14in) San-Francisco CA 1998

LORANT-HEILBRONN Vincent 1874-? **[38]**
- **$839** - €838 - **£524** - FF5 500
  «L'hiver à Pau» Affiche (115x74cm 45x29in) Orléans 1999

LORCA DI CORCIA Philip 1953 **[26]**
- [photo] **$12 000** - €13 441 - **£8 337** - FF88 166
  Brian Photograph (42x58.5cm 16x23in) New-York 2001

LORCH Melchior Lorick 1527-c.1595 **[10]**
- **$482** - €562 - **£339** - FF3 689
  Bildnis Suleiman II Radierung (37.5x31.5cm 14x12in) Berlin 2001

LÖRCHER Alfred 1875-1962 **[35]**
- **$2 434** - €2 556 - **£1 535** - FF16 769
  Sitzender mit Weinkrug Terracotta (H9cm H3in) Stuttgart 2000

LORCK Karl 1828-1882 **[6]**
- **$2 521** - €2 723 - **£1 724** - FF17 859
  A Young Woman in an Interior Feeding Chicken
  Oil/canvas (63x50.5cm 24x19in) Amsterdam 2001

LORD Andrew 1950 **[9]**
- **$7 000** - €8 133 - **£4 919** - FF53 348
  Palm Bronze (73.5x51x42cm 28x20x16in) Beverly-Hills CA 2001

LORD Elyse Ashe 1900-1971 **[248]**
- **$304** - €307 - **£190** - FF2 014
  Still Life of Flowers in an oriental Vase Etching in colors (23x18cm 9x7in) London 2000

LORD Harriet 1879-1958 **[1]**
- **$8 500** - €8 174 - **£5 246** - FF53 619
  South-West Blow, View of Nantucket Oil/canvas (82x102cm 32x40in) Boston MA 1999

LORENTZ Alcide Joseph 1813-1891 **[4]**
- **$1 948** - €2 317 - **£1 389** - FF15 200
  Mlle de Montpensier/La Chevalière d'Eon/Théoroigne de Méricourt Aquarelle (46.5x34.5cm 18x13in) Grenoble 2000

LORENTZEN Christian August 1746-1828 **[45]**
- **$4 746** - €4 705 - **£2 968** - FF30 866
  Portraet af Frederikke von Staffeldt (1746-1828) Oil/canvas (71x56cm 27x22in) Köbenhavn 1999

LORENTZEN Ida 1951 **[6]**
- **$3 689** - €4 389 - **£2 551** - FF28 787
  Draperi Oil/canvas (100x80cm 39x31in) Oslo 2000

LORENTZON Waldemar 1899-1984 **[152]**
- **$10 806** - €10 154 - **£6 512** - FF66 607
  Idag skall du vara med mig Oil/canvas (200x160cm 78x62in) Stockholm 1999
- **$4 357** - €3 718 - **£2 604** - FF24 391
  Storkyrkan, Stockholm Oil/canvas (55.5x33cm 21x12in) Stockholm 1998

- **$2 318** - €2 543 - **£1 539** - FF16 680
  Tyst kväll Oil/canvas (33x46cm 12x18in) Stockholm 2000
- **$1 042** - €1 156 - **£722** - FF7 581
  Löparna Pencil/paper (9x13cm 3x5in) Stockholm 2001

LORENZ Richard 1858-1915 **[17]**
- **$35 000** - €29 903 - **£21 010** - FF196 154
  The Last Glow of a Passing Nation Oil/canvas (107x153cm 42x60in) New-York 1998
- **$20 000** - €21 943 - **£13 286** - FF143 936
  Going it Alone Oil/canvas (50.5x76cm 19x29in) New-York 2000

LORENZ Willy 1901-1981 **[35]**
- **$941** - €869 - **£563** - FF5 701
  Rehbock am Waldrand Öl/Leinwand (60x73.5cm 23x28in) München 1999

LORENZ-MUROWANA Ernst 1872-? **[62]**
- **$686** - €665 - **£431** - FF4 360
  Havel bei Ketzin, stakende Fischer in ihrem Boot Oil/panel (36x48cm 14x18in) Berlin 1999

LORENZALE Y SUGRANES Claudio 1816-1889 **[5]**
- **$1 650** - €1 802 - **£1 110** - FF11 820
  Luna Oleo/tabla (30.5x20.5cm 12x8in) Madrid 2000

LORENZETTI Pietro XIV **[1]**
- **$975 000** - €1 010 737 - **£585 000** - FF6 630 000
  Crocifissione tra due sante martiri Tempera (47.5x47.5cm 18x18in) Firenze 2001

LORENZINI Gian Antonio 1665-1740 **[4]**
- **$144** - €137 - **£90** - FF896
  Adoration of the Shepherds Copper engraving (37x46cm 14x18in) Praha 2000

LORENZL Josef 1892-1950 **[127]**
- **$1 211** - €1 431 - **£858** - FF9 390
  Gefangener Vogel, Figurenlampe Porcelain (H77.5cm H30in) Ahlden 2000

LORENZO DI BICCI c.1350-1427 **[2]**
- **$25 000** - €25 916 - **£15 000** - FF170 000
  Dormitio Virginis Tempera/tavola (22x49cm 8x19in) Roma 2001

LORIA Vincenzo 1849-1939 **[84]**
- **$575** - €596 - **£345** - FF3 910
  Antica fontana medioevale Olio/legno (29x41cm 11x16in) Roma 1999
- **$690** - €715 - **£414** - FF4 692
  Pescatore di vongole Acquarello/cartone (26x35cm 10x13in) Roma 1999

LORIMER John Henry 1856-1936 **[16]**
- **$43 272** - €50 857 - **£30 000** - FF333 600
  Kellie Castle Garden Oil/canvas (132x91.5cm 51x36in) Edinburgh 2000

LORIOT Bernard 1925-1998 **[94]**
- **$1 109** - €1 098 - **£691** - FF7 200
  Entrée du port Honfleur Huile/toile (50x61cm 19x24in) Provins 1999
- **$462** - €496 - **£316** - FF3 252
  Honfleur, les barques rouges Huile/toile (22x27cm 8x10in) Luxembourg 2001
- **$529** - €457 - **£319** - FF3 000
  Bateaux de pêche à Honfleur Aquarelle/papier (22x29cm 8x11in) Le Havre 1998

LORJOU Bernard 1908-1986 **[421]**
- **$6 124** - €6 860 - **£4 257** - FF45 000
  Le guitariste Acrylique/toile (131x97cm 51x38in) Paris 2001

L

$3 125 - €2 897 - **£1 930** - FF19 000
Bateau de pêche à quai Huile/toile (55x65cm
21x25in) Paris 1999

$2 680 - €2 287 - **£1 617** - FF15 000
Le clown Huile/papier/toile (40x23cm 15x9in) Calais
1998

$748 - €838 - **£520** - FF5 500
Projet d'affiche électorale Fusain (64x49cm
25x19in) Blois 2001

$221 - €183 - **£129** - FF1 200
Personnage et enfant Lithographie couleurs
(70x50cm 27x19in) Paris 1998

LORMIER Edouard 1847-1919 **[6]**
$8 172 - €8 842 - **£5 660** - FF58 000
Incroyable Chryséléphantine (H63cm H24in)
Armentières 2001

LORMIER J. XX **[6]**
$3 868 - €3 608 - **£2 400** - FF23 664
**Figure of a Venetian Reveller, Woman in fancy
dress with tricorn hat** Bronze (H33.5cm H13in)
London 1999

LORTA Jean-Pierre François 1752-1837 **[1]**
$11 592 - €10 671 - **£6 958** - FF70 000
Amour endormi Terracotta (31x95x45cm
12x37x17in) Paris 1999

LORTET Leberecht 1826-1901 **[29]**
$2 750 - €2 381 - **£1 658** - FF15 618
**Alpine Landscape with an Abandoned Cottage
on the Lake's Edge** Oil/canvas (45x65.5cm 17x25in)
San-Francisco CA 1999

$411 - €396 - **£257** - FF2 600
Paysage maritime Huile/papier (15.5x26.5cm
6x10in) Lyon 1999

LORY Gabriel I 1760-1840 **[79]**
$1 542 - €1 487 - **£950** - FF9 751
Blick von Thierachern auf den Thunersee Encre
Chine (38x53cm 14x20in) Bern 1999

$489 - €466 - **£297** - FF3 059
**La vallée de Lauterbrounnen avec la chute du
Staubbach** Radierung (34.5x49.6cm 13x19in) Bern
1999

LORY Gabriel II 1784-1846 **[139]**
$1 851 - €1 610 - **£1 115** - FF10 560
«Andromaque» Aquarell/Papier (58x47cm 22x18in)
Bern 1998

$445 - €374 - **£261** - FF2 453
**«Vue prise dans le petit bois nommé
Bächihölzli près...»** Aquatinta (19.3x27.6cm 7x10in)
Bern 1998

LOS COBOS de José Luis 1944 **[45]**
$302 - €288 - **£182** - FF1 891
Carrer de Petritxol Oleo/lienzo (81x65cm 31x25in)
Barcelona 1999

LOS Waldemar 1849-1888 **[9]**
$14 000 - €12 126 - **£8 586** - FF79 541
Soldiers Resting by the Windmills Oil/canvas
(70.5x106cm 27x41in) New-York 1999

LOSADA Manuel 1865-1949 **[7]**
$14 000 - €15 016 - **£9 500** - FF98 500
Tonadillera y torero Oleo/lienzo (81x65.5cm
31x25in) Madrid 2001

$825 - €901 - **£570** - FF5 910
Vista de una ciudad costera Pastel/papier
(32.5x25.5cm 12x10in) Madrid 2001

LOSERT Heribert 1913 **[23]**
$267 - €256 - **£162** - FF1 676
Reflexe Aquarell, Gouache/Papier (24x26cm 9x10in)
Bielefeld 1999

$139 - €133 - **£84** - FF872
Gesellschaft am Tisch Offset (60x71cm 23x27in)
Bielefeld 1999

LOSI Carolus XVIII **[6]**
$201 - €145 - **£175** - FF1 553
Palazzo Farnese Engraving (34x53cm 13x20in)
Stockholm 2001

LOSQUES de Daniel Thouroude 1880-1915 **[32]**
$1 197 - €1 143 - **£748** - FF7 500
«Les cendres de Rigadin» Affiche couleur
(160x120cm 62x47in) Paris 1999

LOSSOW Heinrich 1843-1897 **[25]**
$2 400 - €2 027 - **£1 441** - FF13 296
Statue in the Park Oil/panel (42x30.5cm 16x12in)
New-York 1998

LOT Henri, Hendrik 1822-1876 **[11]**
$626 - €613 - **£385** - FF4 024
**Niederrheinische Landschaft mit Weidevieh im
Vordergrund** Öl/Leinwand (47x65cm 18x25in)
Stuttgart 1999

LOTAR Eli 1905-1969 **[24]**
$1 279 - €1 444 - **£900** - FF9 470
«Lendemain» Silver print (15.5x22cm 6x8in) London
2001

LOTH Johan Karl, Carlo 1632-1698 **[38]**
$11 866 - €13 518 - **£8 200** - FF88 674
Saint Bartholomew Oil/canvas (142.5x121cm
56x47in) London 2000

$3 805 - €4 269 - **£2 637** - FF28 000
Tarquin et Lucrèce Huile/toile (70.5x68.5cm
27x26in) Paris 2000

$1 400 - €1 451 - **£840** - FF9 520
**Studio di decorazione parietale con un miraco-
lo di San Francesco** Inchiostro (13x21cm 5x8in)
Milano 2001

LOTH Onofrio c.1640-1717 **[2]**
$3 600 - €4 665 - **£2 700** - FF30 600
Natura morta con ortaggi Olio/tela (36.5x48.5cm
14x19in) Milano 2000

LOTH Wilhelm 1920-1993 **[74]**
$2 696 - €3 144 - **£1 893** - FF20 626
Kopf der Braut Bronze (H50cm H19in) Köln 2000

LOTICHIUS Ernest XIX-XX **[2]**
$2 500 - €2 989 - **£1 724** - FF19 605
Farmstead with a River View Oil/canvas (30x45cm
12x18in) Milford CT 2000

LOTIRON Robert 1886-1966 **[216]**
$1 854 - €1 829 - **£1 142** - FF12 000
Paris, le Pont des Invalides Huile/toile (60x92cm
23x36in) Calais 1999

$1 422 - €1 677 - **£999** - FF11 000
Bouquet de fleurs Huile/toile (40x32cm 15x12in)
Paris 2000

$859 - €915 - **£543** - FF6 000
Les charrettes, la moisson Aquarelle,
gouache/papier (19.5x23cm 7x9in) Paris 2000

LOTTER Heinrich 1875-1941 **[16]**
$2 871 - €3 068 - **£1 910** - FF20 123
**Der Hohentwiel mit Blick auf den See, im
Zentrum die Reichenau** Öl/Leinwand (70x101cm
27x39in) Konstanz 2000

$3 202 - €3 068 - **£2 015** - FF20 123
Säntis II, Morgenstimmung am Bodensee
Öl/Karton (30x37cm 11x14in) Stuttgart 1999

LOTTER Tobias Konrad 1717-1777 [8]
$392 - €360 - **£240** - FF2 361
Terra Sancta sive Palestina Engraving (48x57.5cm 18x22in) London 1999

LOTTI Vincenzo 1855-1926 [1]
$4 741 - €5 316 - **£3 220** - FF34 873
Die Schulklasse Öl/Leinwand (100x72cm 39x28in) Zürich 2000

LOTTIER Louis 1815-1892 [19]
$7 845 - €7 622 - **£4 905** - FF50 000
La Baie de Beyrouth Huile/toile (37.5x46cm 14x18in) Paris 1999
$3 007 - €2 897 - **£1 871** - FF19 000
Personnages se reposant devant un château
Huile/toile (27x40cm 10x15in) Montfort L'Amaury 1999

LOTTO Lorenzo 1480-1556 [7]
$192 840 - €191 277 - **£120 000** - FF1 254 696
Young Man, in a brown Mantle and a dark cap, a Letter in his Hands Oil/panel (33x26cm 12x10in) London 1999

LOTZ Károly 1833-1904 [22]
$48 100 - €50 537 - **£29 900** - FF331 500
Ouragan dans le désert Huile/toile (116x190cm 45x74in) Budapest 2000
$518 - €1 725 - **£1 058** - FF11 316
Scène Huile/toile/carton (58x47cm 22x18in) Budapest 2001
$2 640 - €3 000 - **£1 840** - FF19 680
Rive Huile/toile/carton (21x33cm 8x12in) Budapest 2001
$2 000 - €1 967 - **£1 250** - FF12 900
Nude Mixed media/paper (42x27cm 16x10in) Budapest 1999

LOTZ Marie 1877-1970 [15]
$449 - €511 - **£311** - FF3 353
Bildnis einer auf einem Ruhekissen liegenden jnugen Dame Öl/Leinwand (84x89cm 33x35in) Staufen 2000

LOTZ Matilda 1858/61-1923 [10]
$4 200 - €4 804 - **£2 920** - FF31 514
Sheep at Rest Oil/canvas (49x71cm 19x28in) New-Orleans LA 2000
$750 - €866 - **£525** - FF5 683
Sheep Oil/canvas (27.5x38.5cm 10x15in) Bethesda MD 2001

LOU BO'AN Lao Pakon 1947 [7]
$8 346 - €9 159 - **£5 375** - FF60 079
Sound of the River Ink (45x68cm 17x26in) Hong-Kong 2000

LOUBCHANSKY Marcelle 1917-1988 [68]
$858 - €838 - **£547** - FF5 500
Sans titre Huile/toile (131x81cm 51x31in) Paris 1999

LOUBON Émile 1809-1863 [44]
$21 375 - €22 867 - **£14 085** - FF150 000
Transhumance Huile/toile (91x174cm 35x68in) Roquevaire 2000
$8 665 - €10 062 - **£6 171** - FF66 000
Jeune pâtre jouant de la flûte Huile/toile (47x55cm 18x21in) Marseille 2001
$2 204 - €2 058 - **£1 335** - FF13 500
Carrière à l'Estaque Huile/toile (17x29cm 6x11in) Marseille 1999

LOUCHE Constant 1880-1965 [59]
$1 884 - €1 829 - **£1 164** - FF12 000
Col de Zenaga, Figuig, Algérie Huile/toile (34x99.5cm 13x39in) Paris 1999

LOUCHET Paul 1854-1936 [68]
$2 435 - €2 363 - **£1 515** - FF15 500
En forêt de Fontainebleau Huile/toile (82x60cm 32x23in) Fontainebleau 1999
$619 - €665 - **£414** - FF4 360
Zwei Mönche in karger Landschaft Öl/Karton (27x33cm 10x12in) Kempten 2000

LOUD May Hallowell 1860-1916 [2]
$18 700 - €16 939 - **£11 188** - FF111 111
Young swordsman in puffy shirt and wielding a homemade wooden sword Oil/canvas (149x89cm 59x35in) Thomaston ME 1998

LOUDEN Albert 1942 [31]
$1 786 - €1 762 - **£1 100** - FF11 558
All for the Ball Charcoal (40.5x58cm 15x22in) London 1999

LOUDERBACK Walt S. 1887-1941 [13]
$3 250 - €3 620 - **£2 125** - FF23 745
Illustration: Pastor listening at entrance to open-air beer garden Oil/canvas (66x48cm 26x19in) New-York 2000

LOUDET Alfred 1836-1895 [3]
$7 103 - €7 927 - **£4 940** - FF52 000
La mort d'Abel et la fuite de Caïn Huile/toile (75x107cm 29x42in) Paris 2001

LOUDON Terence XX [26]
$2 474 - €2 958 - **£1 700** - FF19 402
Green and Silver, Still Life of Mixed Flowers
Oil/canvas (75.5x50.5cm 29x19in) Billingshurst, West-Sussex 2000

LOUGHEED Robert Elmer 1901-1982 [35]
$14 000 - €15 896 - **£9 727** - FF104 273
Stranges in Cochiti Country Oil/canvas (33x63cm 13x25in) Dallas TX 2001
$4 200 - €4 936 - **£2 911** - FF32 379
Buffalo #3 Oil/board (20.5x25.5cm 8x10in) Beverly-Hills CA 2000
$1 300 - €1 476 - **£903** - FF9 682
Illustration from Margerita Henry's Mustang Ink (35x28cm 14x11in) Dallas TX 2001

LOUIS Brigitte 1953 [9]
$641 - €762 - **£457** - FF5 000
Cheval ardenais violette Bronze (14x15cm 5x5in) Paris 2000

LOUIS Morris 1912-1962 [71]
$300 000 - €348 087 - **£207 120** - FF2 283 300
Atomic Crest Acrylic (268x198cm 105x77in) New-York 2000
$4 500 - €3 845 - **£2 643** - FF25 224
Bird Oil/canvas (38x51cm 14x20in) Boston MA 1998

LOUISE OF DENMARK H.M. Queen 1817-1898 [8]
$6 907 - €7 779 - **£4 761** - FF51 028
Opstilling med lyseröde roser, hvide, röde og blå snerler Oil/canvas (38x50cm 14x19in) Köbenhavn 2000

LOUISE Ruth Harriet 1906-1944 [10]
$500 - €537 - **£334** - FF3 520
Greta Garbo Silver print (24x18cm 9x7in) New-York 2000

L

LOUND Thomas 1802-1861 **[57]**

➣ **$5 977** - €6 416 - **£4 000** - FF42 086
Great Yarmouth Beach & Jetty Oil/canvas
(40.5x63cm 15x24in) Reepham, Norwich 2000

➣ **$3 243** - €3 129 - **£2 050** - FF20 525
The End of the Day Oil/panel (40.5x33cm 15x12in)
London 1999

➣ **$360** - €331 - **£220** - FF12 000
**View of Yarmouth Along the Coast,
Approaching Storm** Watercolour/paper (22x30cm
9x12in) Aylsham, Norfolk 1998

LOUPOT Charles 1892-1960 **[102]**

➣ **$8 500** - €8 174 - **£5 246** - FF53 619
«Oreal» Gouache (47.5x32cm 18x12in) New-York
1999

▥ **$4 000** - €3 417 - **£2 420** - FF22 417
«Fourrures Canton» Poster (129.5x90cm 50x35in)
New-York 1998

LOUPPE Léo 1869-? **[6]**

➣ **$2 230** - €2 321 - **£1 400** - FF15 224
**Still Life of Pink and White Carnations in a
Green Vase and Violets** Oil/canvas (55x38cm
21x14in) London 2000

LOUREIRO Arthur José de Souza 1853-1932 **[16]**

➣ **$8 360** - €9 472 - **£5 890** - FF62 130
Erva Fresca, porquinhos da India Oleo/tabla
(30x58cm 11x22in) Lisboa 2001

➣ **$3 520** - €3 988 - **£2 480** - FF26 160
Paisagem com montanha Huile/bois (14x18cm
5x7in) Lisboa 2000

LOURENÇO Armand 1925 **[204]**

➣ **$397** - €427 - **£266** - FF2 800
Paris, Montmartre Huile/toile (46x55cm 18x21in)
Provins 2000

➣ **$267** - €274 - **£165** - FF1 800
Paris, la Madeleine Huile/toile (22x27cm 8x10in)
Provins 2000

LOUSTAL de Jacques 1956 **[19]**

➣ **$756** - €762 - **£471** - FF5 000
Saxophone Encre/papier (37x32cm 14x12in) Paris
2000

LOUSTAU Jacques J. Leopold 1815-1894 **[3]**

➣ **$4 651** - €5 183 - **£3 250** - FF34 000
La lettre Huile/toile (56x47cm 22x18in) Paris 2001

LOUSTAU Marie Euphrosine 1831-? **[3]**

➣ **$6 019** - €6 433 - **£4 089** - FF42 196
Syrener og hvide roser i glas Oil/canvas (61x50cm
24x19in) København 2001

LOUSTAUNAU Louis Auguste 1846-1898 **[13]**

➣ **$10 000** - €11 168 - **£6 404** - FF73 255
Raising the Balloon Oil/canvas (88.5x61cm 34x24in)
New-York 2000

LOUTCHANSKY Jacob, Jacques 1876-1978 **[24]**

➣ **$2 400** - €2 845 - **£1 748** - FF18 663
Horse and Rider Bronze (H47cm H18in) Tel Aviv
2001

LOUTHERBOURG de Philip Jakob I 1698-1768 **[3]**

➣ **$1 503** - €1 753 - **£1 074** - FF11 500
Le retour des paysans Lavis/papier (31x42cm
12x16in) Versailles 2000

LOUTHERBOURG de Philip Jakob II 1740-1812
[99]

➣ **$460 000** - €386 369 - **£270 434** - FF2 534 416
Winter Morning with Skating in Hyde Park
Oil/canvas (187.5x123cm 73x48in) New-York 1998

➣ **$6 498** - €6 323 - **£4 000** - FF41 475
**Milkmaid and Cowherd with Cattle, with a
Village beyond** Oil/canvas (82x116cm 32x45in)
London 1999

➣ **$5 685** - €6 065 - **£3 600** - FF39 785
**Travellers conversing at the Side of a Path, a
Horseman Cart behind** Oil/canvas (33.5x46.5cm
13x18in) London 2000

➣ **$2 303** - €2 134 - **£1 432** - FF14 000
Scène de naufrage Gouache/papier (35x47cm
13x18in) Paris 1999

▥ **$426** - €486 - **£297** - FF3 186
La bonne petite soeur Radierung (27x21.5cm
10x8in) Berlin 2001

LOUTREUIL Maurice Albert 1885-1925 **[50]**

➣ **$2 414** - €2 592 - **£1 615** - FF17 000
Femme au fauteuil Huile/toile (81.5x65cm 32x25in)
Paris 2000

➣ **$596** - €640 - **£399** - FF4 200
Jeune fille à la lecture Aquarelle/papier (39x29cm
15x11in) Compiègne 2000

LOUVET Henri Eug. 1866-? **[6]**

➣ **$753** - €845 - **£522** - FF5 545
Fårehyrden med sin hund Oil/canvas (100x76cm
39x29in) København 2000

LOUVRIER Maurice 1878-1954 **[105]**

➣ **$2 488** - €2 287 - **£1 528** - FF15 000
La rue animée Huile/panneau (53x72cm 20x28in)
Paris 1999

➣ **$1 320** - €1 448 - **£896** - FF9 500
Les moissons Huile/toile (33x45cm 12x17in) Calais
2000

LOUYOT Edmond Loujot 1860-1918 **[24]**

➣ **$1 700** - €1 748 - **£1 078** - FF11 467
Children with Kitten Oil/canvas (39x49cm 15x19in)
Detroit MI 2000

➣ **$1 100** - €1 178 - **£748** - FF7 729
Children brushing Kittens Oil/panel (11x8cm
4x3in) Chicago IL 2001

LOUYS Pierre 1870-1925 **[15]**

▥ **$2 200** - €2 566 - **£1 544** - FF16 830
«Citroën» Poster (117x159.5cm 46x62in) New-York
2000

◙ **$5 112** - €4 269 - **£2 998** - FF28 000
Nus d'adolescentes Photo (8.6x8.6cm 3x3in) Paris
1998

LOVATTI E. Augusto 1816-? **[21]**

➣ **$3 120** - €4 043 - **£2 340** - FF26 520
Veduta con il convento dei cappuccini Olio/tela
(61x49cm 24x19in) Napoli 2000

➣ **$7 027** - €7 503 - **£4 800** - FF49 214
Route de Tragara/Una casa di Capri Oil/panel
(24x14.5cm 9x5in) Billingshurst, West-Sussex 2001

LOVATTI Matteo 1861-? **[5]**

➣ **$7 750** - €8 034 - **£4 650** - FF52 700
In attesa del treno Olio/tavola (49x26cm 19x10in)
Roma 2000

LOVE Ralph 1907 **[3]**

➣ **$3 000** - €3 526 - **£2 079** - FF23 128
Borrego Desert Oil/canvas/board (20.5x25.5cm
8x10in) Beverly-Hills CA 2000

LOVELL Tom 1909-1997 **[66]**

➣ **$6 500** - €6 018 - **£3 978** - FF39 473
**Boy seated accross from father at dining table,
story illustration** Oil/board (47x68cm 18x27in) New-
York 1999

$6 050 - €5 650 - **£3 734** - FF37 062
Coronado's Expedition Oil/board (13x20cm 5x8in)
Dallas TX 1999

$5 500 - €5 136 - **£3 394** - FF33 693
Four Times to the Sun Study Pastel/paper
(25x19cm 10x7in) Dallas TX 1999

LOVEN Frank W. 1869-1941 **[22]**
$300 - €253 - **£176** - FF1 660
Landscape Oil/board (20x25cm 8x10in) Mystic CT
1998

LOVER Samuel 1797-1868 **[9]**
$5 756 - €6 448 - **£4 000** - FF42 296
Portrait of the Artist Oil/canvas (77.5x64cm
30x25in) London 2001

$1 992 - €1 905 - **£1 222** - FF12 493
The Colleen Bawn and The Colleen Dhu
Watercolour/paper (76x63cm 30x25in) Dublin 1999

LOVERIDGE Clinton 1824-1902 **[34]**
$3 000 - €2 569 - **£1 771** - FF16 854
Cows in a Wooded Landscape Oil/canvas
(45.5x61cm 17x24in) New-York 1998

$1 000 - €952 - **£632** - FF6 244
Cows by a River Oil/board (11x20cm 4x8in) New-
York 1999

LOVERING Ida XIX-XX **[1]**
$5 815 - €6 655 - **£4 000** - FF43 656
Chase Over the Common, Mitcham
Watercolour/paper (44.5x63.5cm 17x25in) Lymington
2000

LOVEROFF Frederick Nicholas 1894-1960 **[18]**
$4 399 - €5 106 - **£3 037** - FF33 490
Winter Landscape Oil/canvas (50x60cm 20x24in)
Calgary, Alberta 2000

$1 173 - €1 361 - **£810** - FF8 930
Untitled - The Old Barns Oil/panel (25x30cm
10x12in) Calgary, Alberta 2000

LOVET-LORSKI Boris 1894-1973 **[127]**
$2 750 - €3 141 - **£1 936** - FF20 606
Sun-crowned Madonna and Child Relief
(128x73cm 50x29in) Morris-Plains NJ 2001

$1 600 - €1 828 - **£1 126** - FF11 989
Young woman Bronze (H28cm H11in) Morris-Plains
NJ 2001

$500 - €571 - **£352** - FF3 746
Figure and sculpture studies Drawing (23x15cm
9x6in) Morris-Plains NJ 2001

LOVING Eugene E. 1892-1967 **[36]**
$150 - €171 - **£103** - FF1 122
The Cabildo Alley - Old New Orleans Etching
(22x15cm 9x6in) New-Orleans LA 2000

LØVMAND Christine Marie 1803-1872 **[23]**
$3 000 - €3 119 - **£1 894** - FF20 462
Spilled Milk Oil/canvas (43x54.5cm 16x21in) New-
York 2000

$1 515 - €1 393 - **£936** - FF9 138
Jordbaerplante Oil/canvas (24.5x34cm 9x13in) Vejle
1998

LOW Bet 1924 **[4]**
$430 - €399 - **£260** - FF2 615
Light Night Watercolour/paper (49x36cm 19x14in)
Edinburgh 1999

LOW Charles c.1860-c.1920 **[14]**
$3 939 - €3 823 - **£2 500** - FF25 077
The Horse Trough Watercolour/paper (36x53cm
14x20in) London 1999

LOW David 1891-1963 **[13]**
$313 - €364 - **£220** - FF2 385
**Dr.Stephenson with Wings and Halo
kicking/Prisoner in his Cell/Woman** Ink/paper
(28x24.5cm 11x9in) London 2001

LÖW Fritzi, Lazar 1892-1975 **[10]**
$810 - €920 - **£563** - FF6 037
Im Kaffee-Haus Pencil (30x21cm 11x8in) Berlin 2001

LOW William Hicok 1853-1932 **[12]**
$15 000 - €16 381 - **£9 657** - FF107 454
The Spring Oil/canvas (71x54cm 28x21in) Mystic CT
2000

$11 500 - €13 286 - **£8 052** - FF87 148
Children's Playground Oil/canvas (22.5x54.5cm
8x21in) Bethesda MD 2001

LOWCOCK Charles Frederick 1878-1922 **[35]**
$1 348 - €1 402 - **£850** - FF9 195
**The Entrance Hall of Woodsome Hall,
Huddersfield with a Cavalier** Oil/canvas (47x61cm
18x24in) Leyburn, North Yorkshire 2000

$2 480 - €2 740 - **£1 720** - FF17 970
Välklädd dam i trädgård Oil/panel (47x20cm
18x7in) Stockholm 2001

LOWE Arthur XIX-XX **[4]**
$5 436 - €5 966 - **£3 500** - FF39 134
**Children on a Wooded Lane in the Park,
Nottingham** Oil/canvas (85x126cm 33x49in) London
2000

LOWE Robin 1959 **[8]**
$3 000 - €3 360 - **£2 084** - FF22 041
«Finger Sucker» Oil/metal (87.5x94.5cm 34x37in)
New-York 2001

LOWELL Nat 1880-1956 **[40]**
$150 - €161 - **£100** - FF1 056
New York Harbor Etching (23x30cm 9x12in) Altadena
CA 2000

LOWELL Orson Byron 1871-1956 **[29]**
$1 350 - €1 449 - **£903** - FF9 505
Behind the Screen Huile/papier/toile (55x55cm
21x21in) Philadelphia PA 2000

$250 - €292 - **£175** - FF1 915
The Onlooker Ink/paper (77x53cm 30x21in)
Cleveland OH 2000

LOWENGRUND Margaret 1905-1957 **[1]**
$2 000 - €2 338 - **£1 405** - FF15 337
Factory Scene Color lithograph (38x27.5cm 14x10in)
New-York 2000

LÖWITH Wilhelm 1861-1931 **[35]**
$1 060 - €971 - **£646** - FF6 372
Der Geniesser Oil/panel (13.5x9cm 5x3in) München
1999

LOWNDES Alan 1921-1978 **[75]**
$4 482 - €4 812 - **£3 000** - FF31 564
Hill in Snow Oil/board (61x66cm 24x25in) London
2000

$1 534 - €1 761 - **£1 050** - FF11 552
Cornish Harbour Oil/board (27x20cm 11x8in) Par,
Cornwall 2000

LOWRY Lawrence Stephen 1887-1976 **[950]**
$228 897 - €221 955 - **£145 000** - FF1 455 930
Fairground at Daisy Nook Oil/canvas (35.5x51cm
13x20in) London 1999

$53 794 - €57 744 - **£36 000** - FF378 777
The Gossips, Two Ladies Oil/board (48x31cm
18x12in) London 2000

L

✍ **$11 346** - €11 802 - **£7 500** - FF77 418
Figures and Dog on a Street Pencil/paper
(19x12cm 7x4in) Manchester 2000

▥ **$793** - €890 - **£550** - FF5 839
Two Brothers Color lithograph (60x30cm 23x11in)
London 2000

LÖWSTÄDT-CHADWICK Emma 1855-1932 [20]

👝 **$36 000** - €31 059 - **£21 718** - FF203 734
Off to Sea Oil/canvas (292x213cm 114x83in) New-
York 1998

✍ **$2 157** - €1 904 - **£1 300** - FF12 487
The Young Mother Oil/canvas (60.5x57cm 23x22in)
London 1998

✍ **$1 018** - €915 - **£607** - FF6 003
Landskap med metande pojke Oil/panel (20x25cm
7x9in) Stockholm 1998

LOXTON John Samuel 1903-1971 [69]

👝 **$729** - €851 - **£507** - FF5 581
Still Life and Porcelain Oil/canvas/board (60.5x41cm
23x16in) Melbourne 2000

✍ **$484** - €504 - **£304** - FF3 305
Mt.Muller from Merrijig Watercolour/paper
(25.5x49cm 10x19in) Melbourne 2000

LOY (marines) XIX [1]

👝 **$6 798** - €6 399 - **£4 200** - FF41 976
**The full-rigged Ship «Sea King» entering
Harbour** Oil/canvas (52.5x79cm 20x31in) London
1999

LOYEUX Charles 1823-1898 [9]

👝 **$35 794** - €33 539 - **£21 516** - FF220 000
L'Abandon Huile/toile (112x180cm 44x70in) Paris
1999

👝 **$7 150** - €7 808 - **£4 810** - FF51 220
Audición musical Oleo/lienzo (58x75cm 22x29in)
Madrid 2000

LOZANO Lázaro 1906 [5]

👝 **$11 800** - €9 970 - **£7 000** - FF65 400
Varinas de Nazaré Oleo/lienzo (54.5x45cm 21x17in)
Lisboa 1998

✍ **$1 305** - €1 446 - **£841** - FF9 483
Mulher da Nazaré Tinta china (42.5x25cm 16x9in)
Lisboa 2000

LOZANO SANCHIS Francisco 1912-2000 [48]

✍ **$7 980** - €8 409 - **£5 040** - FF55 160
Paisaje Oleo/lienzo (60x81cm 23x31in) Madrid 2000

✍ **$5 250** - €4 505 - **£3 225** - FF29 550
Arrozal Oleo/tablex (27x35cm 10x13in) Madrid 1998

✍ **$992** - €961 - **£608** - FF6 304
Betera, mi jardin Técnica mixta/papel (27.5x22.5cm
10x8in) Madrid 1999

▥ **$530** - €601 - **£370** - FF3 940
Paisaje Serigrafía (73x92cm 28x36in) Madrid 2001

LOZOWICK Louis 1892-1973 [205]

👝 **$120 000** - €102 526 - **£72 036** - FF672 528
Detroit Oil/canvas (76x56cm 29x22in) New-York 1998

✍ **$500** - €567 - **£349** - FF3 716
The Capitol Building, Washington, DC Ink
(12.5x16cm 4x6in) New-York 2001

✍ **$1 600** - €1 542 - **£986** - FF10 118
Hudson Bridge Lithograph (36.5x22cm 14x8in)
New-York 1999

LU FU & GU LU XIV [1]

✍ **$10 256** - €12 054 - **£7 112** - FF79 072
**Ink Blossoms and Record of the Plum Blossom
Villa in Cerical Script** Ink/paper (23x93.5cm 9x36in)
Hong-Kong 2000

LU FUSHENG 1949 [5]

✍ **$4 128** - €3 874 - **£2 550** - FF25 411
Lady and Horse in Tang Style Ink (135.5x66cm
53x25in) Hong-Kong 1999

LU HUI 1851-1920 [27]

✍ **$1 669** - €1 832 - **£1 075** - FF12 015
Pine Shade in Moonlight Ink (108x37.5cm 42x14in)
Hong-Kong 2000

LU JIANJUN 1960 [3]

✍ **$10 965** - €10 290 - **£6 774** - FF67 498
Weatherworn Oil/canvas (120x110cm 47x43in) Hong-
Kong 1999

👝 **$8 365** - €7 938 - **£5 083** - FF52 071
Paper Fan Oil/canvas (100x90cm 39x35in) Hong-
Kong 1999

LU PUSHI Lu P'u-shih 1911-1989 [3]

✍ **$41 648** - €39 056 - **£25 893** - FF256 190
Still Life Oil/canvas (31.5x40.5cm 12x15in) Taipei
1999

LÜ SHOUKUN 1919-1975 [15]

✍ **$14 743** - €16 615 - **£10 304** - FF108 985
Zen Ink (27.5x24cm 10x9in) Hong-Kong 2001

LU VAN SIN 1905-1983 [1]

👝 **$4 912** - €4 878 - **£3 059** - FF32 000
Portrait de femme Huile/toile (44.5x31cm 17x12in)
Paris 1999

LU WEI XVII-XVIII [1]

✍ **$16 666** - €19 588 - **£11 557** - FF128 492
Landscape Ink (135x60.5cm 53x23in) Hong-Kong
2000

LU YANSHAO 1909-1993 [98]

✍ **$12 840** - €14 021 - **£8 260** - FF91 970
Calligraphy in Xing Shu Ink/paper (25x33cm
9x12in) Hong-Kong 2000

LU YONGQI 1938 [4]

✍ **$3 333** - €3 918 - **£2 311** - FF25 698
Thrush on a Tree Branch Ink (96x51.5cm 37x20in)
Hong-Kong 2000

LU YUAN XVII [1]

✍ **$5 418** - €5 084 - **£3 347** - FF33 352
Peach Blossom Spring Ink (137x59.5cm 53x23in)
Hong-Kong 1999

LÜ YUANXUN XVIII [1]

✍ **$10 272** - €11 217 - **£6 608** - FF73 576
Entertainment in the Palace Ink (44.5x686cm
17x270in) Hong-Kong 2000

LU ZHI 1496-1576 [10]

✍ **$230 760** - €262 142 - **£162 000** - FF1 719 540
Landscape, after Wang Meng Ink (135x37cm
53x14in) Hong-Kong 2001

LUARD Lowes Dalbiac 1872-1944 [9]

👝 **$9 169** - €8 503 - **£5 600** - FF55 777
Building a Rick Oil/canvas (40x95cm 15x37in)
Taunton 1998

LUBBERS Adriaan 1892-1954 [41]

👝 **$6 487** - €7 714 - **£4 624** - FF50 602
South Ferry, Forestudy Rapsody in Blue Oil/can-
vas (59x72cm 23x28in) Amsterdam 2000

▥ **$664** - €771 - **£473** - FF5 060
«Brooklyn Bridge, New York» Lithograph (30x30cm
11x11in) Amsterdam 2001

LÜBBERS Holger P. S. 1850/55-1928/31 [240]

👝 **$4 392** - €4 690 - **£2 992** - FF30 765
Marine med sejl-og motorskibe Oil/canvas
(95x132cm 37x51in) Vejle 2001

$2 414 - €2 288 - **£1 468** - FF15 009
Fiskere ordner deres fangst i strandkanten
Oil/canvas (80x110cm 31x43in) København 1999
$575 - €591 - **£364** - FF3 879
Marine med skibe udfor kyst Oil/canvas
(14.5x22.5cm 5x8in) Vejle 2000

LUBBERT Ernst 1879-1916 **[3]**
$1 300 - €1 109 - **£784** - FF7 274
«**Cardinal**» Poster (94x70cm 37x27in) New-York 1998

LÜBEN Adolf 1837-1905 **[19]**
$1 674 - €1 534 - **£1 020** - FF10 061
Vor dem Stadttor reicht die Bäuerin dem Reiter einen Erfrischungstrunk Öl/Leinwand (52x38cm 20x14in) München 1999

LUBIENIECKI Christoffel 1660/61-c.1730 **[5]**
$30 123 - €25 526 - **£18 000** - FF167 441
A Doctor Working in his Study, an Assistant Preparing Medicine beyond Oil/panel (42x36cm 16x14in) London 1998

LUBIN Aryeh 1897-1980 **[124]**
$4 200 - €4 508 - **£2 810** - FF29 572
Wood Oil/canvas (53.5x63.5cm 21x25in) Tel Aviv 2000
$700 - €743 - **£473** - FF4 874
Portrait of a Girl Oil/canvas/board (16.5x16.5cm 6x6in) Tel Aviv 2000
$400 - €429 - **£267** - FF2 816
View of Jerusalem Watercolour (26x34cm 10x13in) Tel Aviv 2000

LUBIN Jules Désiré 1854-? **[5]**
$1 092 - €1 189 - **£751** - FF7 800
Nature morte aux fraises, pêches et pruneaux Huile/toile (38x56cm 14x22in) Clermont-Ferrand 2001

LUBITCH Ossip 1896-1990 **[54]**
$2 600 - €2 209 - **£1 570** - FF14 491
Figures in a Suburb Oil/canvas (51x61.5cm 20x24in) Tel Aviv 2000
$1 000 - €1 073 - **£669** - FF7 041
Vase of Flowers and Apple Oil/canvas (43x30cm 16x11in) Tel Aviv 2000

LUC Jean XX **[9]**
$737 - €817 - **£500** - FF5 360
«**Aquarium Monaco**» Poster (100x62cm 39x24in) London 2000

LUC-DÉJÉ L. XX **[9]**
$1 554 - €1 724 - **£949** - FF9 457
«**Hyères son golf**» Poster (100x62cm 39x24in) Glasgow 2000

LUCA DI TOMME 1330-c.1389 **[3]**
$283 917 - €304 761 - **£190 000** - FF1 999 104
The Archangel Michael Tempera/panel (114x29cm 44x11in) London 2000
$120 000 - €128 363 - **£81 816** - FF842 004
Christ Blessing, a Pinnacle Tempera/panel (40x27cm 15x10in) New-York 2001

LUCAN Margaret, Countess act.1760-1814 **[48]**
$846 - €914 - **£585** - FF5 996
Madame de Chateauroux/Madame de Flavacour Miniature (4x3.5cm 1x1in) Dublin 2001

LUCANA (Ana L. Perez Tobón) 1960 **[6]**
$811 - €898 - **£550** - FF5 891
Serie Formas, Aubergine Gelatin silver print (39x38cm 15x14in) Zürich 2000

LUCANDER Anitra 1918-2000 **[64]**
$3 372 - €3 700 - **£2 171** - FF24 270
Kupolen Oil/panel (38x43cm 14x16in) Helsinki 2000

$1 632 - €1 429 - **£989** - FF9 374
Blommor Oil/panel (42x38cm 16x14in) Helsinki 1998

LUCANO Pietro 1878-1972 **[25]**
$1 325 - €1 227 - **£822** - FF8 049
Fischerboot bei Nacht mit Lagerfeuer im Hgr. Silhouette von Triest Öl/Leinwand (46x56cm 18x22in) Stuttgart 1999

LUCARINI Adolfo 1890-1959 **[5]**
$4 249 - €4 405 - **£2 549** - FF28 898
Nudo femminile Bronzo (H60cm H23in) Genova 2000

LUCAS Albert Durer 1828-1918 **[57]**
$4 819 - €4 641 - **£3 000** - FF30 444
Orchids Oil/canvas (76x63.5cm 29x25in) London 1999
$2 770 - €2 344 - **£1 500** - FF15 374
Cross leaved Heather, white, Sundew, Peacock Butterfly, Horsetail Oil/canvas (20x15cm 7x5in) Cheshire 1999

LUCAS Arthur XIX-XX **[4]**
$561 - €530 - **£350** - FF3 476
Ponte Vecchio, Florence Watercolour/paper (41x31cm 16x12in) Fernhurst, Haslemere, Surrey 1999

LUCAS August 1803-1863 **[10]**
$11 044 - €10 226 - **£6 852** - FF67 078
Wäscherinnen am Brunnen von Subiaco Öl/Leinwand (58x48cm 22x18in) Stuttgart 1999
$44 919 - €46 017 - **£27 720** - FF301 851
Villa Mattei bei Rom Öl/Leinwand (31x42cm 12x16in) Düsseldorf 2000
$1 947 - €2 045 - **£1 228** - FF13 415
Landschaft bei Olevano mit Figurengruppe im Vordergrund Pencil (24.6x32.1cm 9x12in) Heidelberg 2000

LUCAS David 1802-1881 **[19]**
$199 - €184 - **£120** - FF1 210
Arundel Mill and Castle, after John Constable Mezzotint (18x23cm 7x9in) London 1999

LUCAS Edward George Handel 1861-1936 **[16]**
$15 986 - €15 846 - **£10 000** - FF103 940
Still Life with Roses Oil/canvas (46x36cm 18x14in) London 1999
$5 601 - €5 347 - **£3 500** - FF35 071
«**Loved Ones**» Oil/panel (30x25cm 11x9in) London 1999

LUCAS George ?-c.1899 **[1]**
$5 280 - €4 805 - **£3 200** - FF31 520
La siega Oleo/lienzo (76x127cm 29x50in) Barcelona 1999

LUCAS Jean 1823-? **[4]**
$11 954 - €12 832 - **£8 000** - FF84 172
The Piazza degli Schiavoni, Venice Oil/canvas (45.5x72.5cm 17x28in) London 2000
$4 942 - €5 488 - **£3 445** - FF36 000
Place Saint Marc à Venise Aquarelle/papier (39.5x64cm 15x25in) Paris 2001

LUCAS John 1807-1874 **[9]**
$14 002 - €16 284 - **£10 000** - FF106 819
Portrait of the Hon.Ralph Nevill, full-length, in red Jacket Oil/canvas (239x147.5cm 94x58in) London 2001
$8 666 - €9 303 - **£5 800** - FF61 025
Mrs John Lucas and Her Two Eldest Sons, Three-Quarter-Length Oil/canvas (114.5x96.5cm 45x37in) London 2000

L

L

LUCAS John Seymour 1849-1923 **[73]**
- **$2 953** - €2 704 - **£1 800** - FF17 740
  Portrait of His Royal Highness George, Prince of Wales Oil/canvas (73.5x52cm 28x20in) London 1999
- **$1 000** - €960 - **£619** - FF6 299
  In His Study Oil/canvas (37x30.5cm 14x12in) Washington 1999

LUCAS John Templeton 1836-1880 **[13]**
- **$6 191** - €5 635 - **£3 800** - FF36 962
  Caught Out! Oil/canvas (71x91.5cm 27x36in) London 1999
- **$1 643** - €1 764 - **£1 100** - FF11 573
  The Travelling Musician Oil/canvas (35.5x25.5cm 13x10in) London 2000

LUCAS Sarah 1962 **[22]**
- **$34 729** - €33 676 - **£22 000** - FF220 899
  Monster Hooker Mixed media/panel (223.5x143.5cm 87x56in) London 1999
- **$42 320** - €41 189 - **£26 000** - FF270 181
  You Know What Construction (85x78.5x94cm 33x30x37in) London 1999
- **$13 835** - €13 466 - **£8 500** - FF88 328
  Boots Sculpture (15.5x11.5x26.5cm 6x4x10in) London 1999
- **$7 311** - €7 157 - **£4 500** - FF46 950
  The Shop Ink/paper (75x80cm 29x31in) London 1999
- **$34 867** - €41 003 - **£25 000** - FF268 965
  Fat, Forty and Fabulous Print (215x313cm 84x123in) London 2001
- **$20 000** - €22 401 - **£13 896** - FF146 944
  Got a Salmon on Prawn Cibachrome print (55x55cm 21x21in) New-York 2001

LUCAS VELASQUEZ Eugenio 1817-1870 **[124]**
- **$81 200** - €84 091 - **£51 800** - FF551 600
  La Ciencia del Bien y del Mal Oleo/lienzo (122x202cm 48x79in) Madrid 2000
- **$13 500** - €15 016 - **£9 000** - FF98 500
  La tienta Oleo/tabla (42x58cm 16x22in) Madrid 2000
- **$4 524** - €5 226 - **£3 132** - FF34 278
  Fraile incitando a los españoles contra Napoleón Oleo/lienzo (36.5x26cm 14x10in) Madrid 2000
- **$1 567** - €1 652 - **£1 045** - FF10 835
  Escenas goyescas Aguada/papel (18x28cm 7x11in) Madrid 2000

LUCAS Wilhelm, Willi 1884-1918 **[27]**
- **$3 228** - €3 579 - **£2 241** - FF23 477
  Bauerngehöft am Wasser bei Paderborn Öl/Leinwand (34x47.5cm 13x18in) Köln 2001

LUCAS William 1840-1895 **[24]**
- **$1 122** - €1 017 - **£700** - FF6 670
  The Flower Seller Watercolour (44.5x33.5cm 17x13in) Glasgow 1999

LUCAS Y PADILLA Eugenio 1824-1870 **[23]**
- **$7 733** - €7 692 - **£4 800** - FF50 453
  A Peasant Oil/canvas (55.5x41.5cm 21x16in) London 1999
- **$8 280** - €9 147 - **£5 742** - FF60 000
  Vue de la rade de Cadix Huile/toile (18.5x29cm 7x11in) Paris 2001

LUCAS Y VILLAAMIL Eugenio 1840/58-1918 **[146]**
- **$9 820** - €9 000 - **£6 000** - FF59 034
  Marriage Vows Oil/canvas (80.5x105.5cm 31x41in) London 1999
- **$3 952** - €4 655 - **£2 790** - FF30 535
  Cortesano en el járdin Oleo/tabla (15x24cm 5x9in) Bilbao 2000

- **$884** - €1 021 - **£612** - FF6 698
  Personajes Dibujo (9.5x14.5cm 3x5in) Madrid 2001

LUCAS-LUCAS Henry Frederick 1848-1943 **[83]**
- **$3 640** - €4 234 - **£2 600** - FF27 772
  «Merlin», a saddled liver chesnut Hunter in a Stable Oil/canvas (51x66cm 20x25in) London 2001
- **$1 764** - €1 745 - **£1 100** - FF11 447
  «Friz-Hill» a Chesnut Polo Pony Oil/canvas (28x37cm 11x14in) London 1999

LUCAS-ROBIQUET Marie E. Aimée 1858-1959 **[27]**
- **$97 125** - €114 337 - **£68 250** - FF750 000
  Beauté orientale Huile/toile (127.5x90cm 50x35in) Paris 2000

LUCASSEN Reinier 1939 **[51]**
- **$6 930** - €5 999 - **£4 205** - FF39 351
  «Lente in Tirol» Acrylic/canvas (200x120cm 78x47in) Amsterdam 1998
- **$3 906** - €4 538 - **£2 745** - FF29 766
  «Huis van de wow-ipits» Oil/canvas (70x60cm 27x23in) Amsterdam 2001
- **$1 183** - €1 271 - **£792** - FF8 334
  Steentijd Collage/board (20.5x15cm 8x5in) Amsterdam 2000
- **$970** - €1 134 - **£693** - FF7 441
  Drawing for the Heineken Hoek Cafe in Amsterdam Ink (33x40cm 12x15in) Amsterdam 2001

LUCCHESI Bruno 1926 **[27]**
- **$2 000** - €2 188 - **£1 383** - FF14 353
  Mother with Baby in a Rocker Bronze (35x20cm 14x8in) Morris-Plains NJ 2001

LUCCHESI Giorgio 1855-1941 **[15]**
- **$30 000** - €28 506 - **£18 252** - FF186 987
  The day's Hunt Oil/canvas (137x188cm 53x74in) New-York 1999
- **$12 000** - €11 883 - **£7 471** - FF77 949
  Grapevine with a Lizard Oil/canvas (129x84cm 50x33in) New-York 1999

LUCCHESI Michel 1539-? **[2]**
- **$790** - €767 - **£492** - FF5 030
  Das Boot der Verdammten, nach Michelangelo Radierung (11.7x25.4cm 4x10in) Berlin 1999

LUCE Alain 1947 **[53]**
- **$633** - €595 - **£393** - FF3 902
  Fleur Huile/toile (22x27cm 8x10in) St.Idesbald 1999

LUCE Frédéric 1896-1974 **[28]**
- **$426** - €457 - **£285** - FF3 000
  Paysage vallonné aux nuages Huile/panneau (25.5x34.5cm 10x13in) Paris 2000
- **$994** - €1 067 - **£665** - FF7 000
  Portrait de Maximilien Luce, projet pour l'affiche de l'exposition Gouache (40x32cm 15x12in) Paris 2000

LUCE Jean 1895-1964 **[3]**
- **$4 710** - €4 573 - **£2 910** - FF30 000
  Vase fuselé à décor géométrique givré Sculpture verre (H29cm H11in) Paris 1999

LUCE Louis René c.1695-1774 **[1]**
- **$29 808** - €35 063 - **£21 367** - FF230 000
  La Science couronnée par la Gloire Bas-relief (36.5x26cm 14x10in) Paris 2001

LUCE Maximilien 1858-1941 **[2339]**
- **$62 500** - €70 005 - **£43 425** - FF459 200
  Mericourt: baigneurs et plongeurs Oil/canvas (115x150.5cm 45x59in) New-York 2001

$8 102 - €8 842 - **£5 498** - FF58 000
Le chemin de l'église à Rolleboise Huile/toile
(54x65cm 21x25in) Paris 2000

$4 152 - €4 573 - **£2 769** - FF30 000
Péniche sur la Seine, mai Huile/panneau
(28.5x37.5cm 11x14in) Deauville 2000

$489 - €457 - **£296** - FF3 000
Bouquet Pastel (27x17cm 10x6in) Bourges 1999

$589 - €579 - **£365** - FF3 800
Une rue de Paris, mai 71 Estampe (29x43.5cm
11x17in) Paris 1999

LUCE Molly 1896-1986 **[58]**

$800 - €857 - **£546** - FF5 621
A Strong Breeze II Oil/masonite (60x50cm 24x20in)
Cleveland OH 2001

LUCEBERT (L.J. Swaansijk) 1924-1994 **[683]**

$14 500 - €15 031 - **£8 700** - FF98 600
De Wennoten Olio/tela (145x115cm 57x45in) Milano
2000

$5 200 - €5 900 - **£3 665** - FF38 702
Grotesk ansigt Oil/canvas (40x60cm 15x23in)
Köbenhavn 2001

$1 512 - €1 309 - **£917** - FF8 585
Portrait of Tony Pencil/paper (19.5x13cm 7x5in)
Amsterdam 1998

$147 - €174 - **£107** - FF1 140
Der Geisterseher Etching, aquatint (29.6x24cm
11x9in) Hamburg 2001

LUCERNI Ugo 1900-1989 **[8]**

$4 200 - €4 022 - **£2 588** - FF26 381
Donatella Ceramic (55x30x4cm 22x12x1in) Chicago
IL 1999

LUCERO Michael 1953 **[9]**

$7 000 - €8 325 - **£4 988** - FF54 607
Camel Rock Ceramic (64x43cm 25x16in) New-York
2000

LUCHESI Michele 1539-? **[1]**

$900 - €933 - **£540** - FF6 120
Prospettive e antichità di Roma Burin
(21.5x16.5cm 8x6in) Roma 1999

LUCIANI Ascanio c.1621-1706 **[12]**

$12 000 - €10 367 - **£8 000** - FF68 000
Il convito di Baldassare Olio/tela (100x152cm
39x59in) Roma 1998

$9 000 - €9 330 - **£5 400** - FF61 200
Capriccio architettonico con astanti vari Olio/tela
(63x50cm 24x19in) Roma 2001

LUCINI Giovanni Battisti 1639-1686 **[1]**

$10 460 - €11 228 - **£7 000** - FF73 651
**Lot and his Daughters/Joseph interpreting the
Dreams** Oil/paper/canvas (38.5x27cm 15x10in)
London 2000

LUCIONI Luigi 1900-1988 **[248]**

$13 000 - €12 122 - **£8 063** - FF79 514
Yellows and Browns Oil/canvas (57x63.5cm
22x25in) New-York 1999

$6 750 - €6 294 - **£4 187** - FF41 289
Reflective Mood Oil/canvas (43x35.5cm 16x13in)
New-York 1999

$3 600 - €3 846 - **£2 395** - FF25 229
Trees and Shadows No.2 Watercolour/paper
(18x16cm 7x6in) Cleveland OH 2000

$150 - €175 - **£104** - FF1 151
The Portrait of a Woman in Profile Etching
(24x19cm 9x7in) Bloomfield-Hills MI 2000

LÜCKER Eugène 1876-1943 **[15]**

$465 - €454 - **£286** - FF2 976
Wandelaar op berkenlaar bij avond Oil/canvas
(96x70cm 37x27in) Dordrecht 1999

LÜCKEROTH Jupp Johannes 1919-1993 **[49]**

$969 - €1 125 - **£669** - FF7 378
Mauerspinne Mixed media/canvas (61x77cm
24x30in) Köln 2000

LUCKHARDT Karl 1886-1970 **[70]**

$684 - €767 - **£471** - FF5 030
Hintertaunus mit Schäfer im Hohlweg
Öl/Leinwand (50x65cm 19x25in) Frankfurt 2000

$945 - €1 125 - **£674** - FF7 378
Burgruine Königsstein im Taunus Öl/Karton
(20x29.5cm 7x11in) Köln 2000

LUCKX Frans Josef 1802-1849 **[9]**

$10 400 - €12 394 - **£7 450** - FF81 300
Enfants jouant avec des coccinelles Huile/pan-
neau (68x53cm 26x20in) Bruxelles 2000

LUCOP Thomas XIX-XX **[26]**

$1 304 - €1 513 - **£900** - FF9 926
The Fishing Fleet at Sea Oil/canvas (46x76cm
18x29in) London 2000

$2 403 - €2 285 - **£1 500** - FF14 990
Fishing Smacks in a Swell Oil/board (30.5x48cm
12x18in) London 1999

LUCY Adrien ?-1875 **[7]**

$7 500 - €7 622 - **£4 715** - FF50 000
**Desmaclage des chêne-liège de la forêt de
Fenduck par les Kabyles** Huile/toile (99x150cm
38x59in) Lyon 2000

LUCY Charles 1814-1873 **[7]**

$5 286 - €4 970 - **£3 200** - FF32 598
The Imminent Parting Oil/canvas (84.5x106cm
33x41in) London 1999

LUDBY Max 1858-1943 **[53]**

$261 - €295 - **£181** - FF1 933
Village Scene, Dusk Watercolour/paper (25x35cm
9x13in) Toronto 2000

LÜDDERS Heinrich P. 1826-1897 **[2]**

$1 597 - €1 789 - **£1 100** - FF11 738
Agathe von Estebrügge Capt.l.Albers Aquarell,
Gouache/papier (45x62cm 17x24in) Hamburg 2000

LÜDECKE-CLEVE August 1868-1957 **[33]**

$1 514 - €1 687 - **£991** - FF11 067
Kuhherde mit zwei Bäuerinnen beim Melken
Öl/Leinwand (80x119.5cm 31x47in) Leipzig 2000

LUDIKINS F. XX **[1]**

$4 200 - €3 735 - **£2 568** - FF24 499
American Presidents Line Oceanliner Oil/canvas
(71x91cm 27x35in) New-York 1999

LUDOVICI Albert, Jnr. 1852-1932 **[69]**

$2 611 - €2 479 - **£1 600** - FF16 261
Shepherds conversing with an old Man Oil/can-
vas (96.5x114.5cm 37x45in) London 1999

$990 - €1 133 - **£680** - FF7 429
Beach Scene with Figures by Beach Huts
Oil/board (29x39cm 11x15in) Sudbury, Suffolk 2000

$582 - €535 - **£360** - FF3 512
The Chaperon Watercolour (26x37cm 10x14in)
Billingshurst, West-Sussex 1999

LUDOVICI Albert, Snr. 1820-1894 **[33]**

$89 818 - €88 848 - **£56 000** - FF582 803
The Four-in-Hand, Hyde Park Oil/canvas
(103.5x114.5cm 40x45in) London 1999

$4 009 - €3 966 - **£2 500** - FF26 018
Knightsbridge Barracks Oil/panel (17x26.5cm 6x10in) London 1999

LUEGER Michael 1804-1883 [16]

$2 648 - €2 907 - **£1 760** - FF19 068
Bauern beim Almabtrieb Öl/Leinwand (60x78cm 23x30in) Wien 2000

$2 191 - €2 543 - **£1 540** - FF16 684
Kpuhe in einer Landschaft Öl/Karton (30x42.5cm 11x16in) Wien 2001

$1 275 - €1 329 - **£837** - FF8 720
Gebirgslandschaft mit Viehweide vor Bauernhaus Watercolour (17.5x28.5cm 6x11in) München 2000

LUGARDON Albert 1827-1909 [70]

$33 441 - €32 419 - **£20 706** - FF212 654
La Jungfrau Huile/toile (98x143cm 38x56in) Genève 1999

$1 123 - €1 310 - **£778** - FF8 592
Greyerzer Hirte mit Kuh vor dem Dent de Broc Öl/Leinwand (37x50cm 14x19in) Bern 2000

$476 - €407 - **£288** - FF2 669
Vache Huile/toile (32x46cm 12x18in) Genève 1998

LUGARDON Jean Léonard 1801-1884 [25]

$9 986 - €11 586 - **£7 106** - FF76 000
Couple de personnages en costume italien Technique mixte (21x28cm 8x11in) Paris 2001

LÜGERTH Ferdinand 1885-1915 [35]

$800 - €861 - **£550** - FF5 651
Child in a Clown Costume Ivory, bronze (H16cm H6in) New-York 2001

LUGINBÜHL Bernhard 1929 [159]

$16 665 - €19 819 - **£11 877** - FF130 005
Zyklop Iron (80x62x49cm 31x24x19in) Zürich 2000

$9 900 - €9 976 - **£6 171** - FF65 441
Kehrichtengel Fer (37x37x24cm 14x14x9in) Zürich 2000

$241 - €224 - **£147** - FF1 471
Drem Radierung (31.9x24.7cm 12x9in) Bern 1999

LUGO Emil 1840-1902 [46]

$5 475 - €5 113 - **£3 379** - FF33 539
Blick auf Tivoli mit dem Sibyllentempel Öl/Leinwand (111x89cm 43x35in) Köln 1999

$3 270 - €3 068 - **£2 020** - FF20 123
Die Pilzsammler Öl/Karton (31x25cm 12x9in) Staufen 1999

$1 447 - €1 372 - **£904** - FF9 002
Felsige Landschaft mit Pan und Ziegen Aquarell/Papier (10.5x19cm 4x7in) Luzern 1999

LUGRIS GONZALEZ Urbano 1908-1973 [5]

$486 - €441 - **£324** - FF3 546
Luces en la meseta Oleo/tablex (19x30cm 7x11in) Madrid 2000

$1 272 - €1 442 - **£864** - FF9 456
Plaza platerías Gouache/papier (14x10.5cm 5x4in) Madrid 2000

$975 - €901 - **£585** - FF5 910
Nostalgia Grabado (60x45cm 23x17in) Madrid 1999

LUGRIS VADILLO Urbano 1942 [14]

$1 767 - €1 862 - **£1 178** - FF12 214
El violinista de Su Majestad Oleo/tabla (45x40cm 17x15in) Madrid 2000

$572 - €661 - **£396** - FF4 334
Los observatores de Chichen-Itza Oleo/tablex (18x27cm 7x10in) Madrid 2000

LUHN Joachim 1640-1717 [3]

$10 384 - €12 271 - **£7 360** - FF80 493
Die junge Frau und die Vergänglichkeit der Schönheit Öl/Leinwand (91x81cm 35x31in) München 2000

LUI SHOU-KWAN 1919 [4]

$4 800 - €5 110 - **£3 269** - FF33 518
Moving a Mountain Mixed media (175.5x81.5cm 69x32in) Miami FL 2001

$950 - €1 011 - **£647** - FF6 633
Imaginary Conception of a Lotus Ink (58.5x82cm 23x32in) Miami FL 2001

LUIGI de Mario 1901-1978 [25]

$2 856 - €2 467 - **£1 428** - FF16 184
Grattage Olio/tela (53x45cm 20x17in) Venezia 1999

LUIGINI Ferdinand 1870-1943 [42]

$1 699 - €1 982 - **£1 193** - FF13 000
Paysage avec canaux Aquarelle, gouache/carton (34x42cm 13x16in) Paris 2000

LUIJT Arie Martinus 1879-1951 [8]

$311 - €363 - **£219** - FF2 381
Hornblowing French Cavalry Man on Horseback Pencil (34.8x27.2cm 13x10in) Haarlem 2000

LUINI Aurelio 1530-1593 [10]

$1 587 - €1 753 - **£1 100** - FF11 500
Sainte Madeleine pénitente dans le désert Encre (24.5x17.5cm 9x6in) Paris 2001

LUINI Bernardino c.1480/85-1532 [5]

$11 763 - €11 248 - **£7 163** - FF73 785
Kopf eines Mädchens von äusserster Schönheit und Lieblichkeit Painting (57x47cm 22x18in) Stuttgart 1999

$46 925 - €39 926 - **£28 000** - FF261 895
Head of the Virgin Black, red & white chalks/paper (29.5x21cm 11x8in) London 1998

LUINI Giovanni Paolo XVI [1]

$4 000 - €4 279 - **£2 727** - FF28 066
Studies for the Mocking of Christ, the Baptist, the Magdalene Ink (17x23cm 6x9in) New-York 2001

LUINO Bernardino 1951 [1]

$3 200 - €4 147 - **£2 400** - FF27 200
Nudo Olio/tavola (77x69cm 30x27in) Milano 2000

LUISADA Avigdor 1905-1987 [12]

$10 000 - €11 168 - **£6 404** - FF73 255
Figure Oil/canvas (130x100.5cm 51x39in) Tel Aviv 2000

$1 500 - €1 555 - **£988** - FF10 201
Composition Oil/canvas (44x56cm 17x22in) Herzelia-Pituah 2000

LUKA Madeleine Kula, dite 1894-1989 [158]

$974 - €1 021 - **£617** - FF6 700
Maternité No.30 Huile/toile (65x54cm 25x21in) Versailles 2000

$475 - €513 - **£328** - FF3 365
Portrait of a Woman holding Flowers, an Alley of Trees Oil/canvas (31x40cm 12x16in) Holmdel, NJ 2001

$176 - €152 - **£106** - FF1 000
Petite fille au chien Dessin (24x16cm 9x6in) Paris 1998

LUKANIN Dmitri 1967 [3]

$4 500 - €3 883 - **£2 723** - FF25 472
A Girl with Rollers in her Hair Oil/canvas (60x60cm 23x23in) Tel Aviv 1999

LUKE Alexandra 1901 **[4]**

$571 - €671 - £405 - FF4 403
Untitled Composition Watercolour/paper (23x30.5cm 9x12in) Toronto 2000

LUKE John 1906-1975 **[20]**

$28 784 - €32 240 - £20 000 - FF211 482
Carnival Oil/panel (40.5x52cm 15x20in) London 2001

$14 078 - €13 332 - £8 559 - FF87 454
Cavehill, Belfast Oil/board (23x33cm 9x13in) Dublin 1999

$1 532 - €1 439 - £949 - FF9 438
A Sketch for «Shaw's Bridge» Pencil/paper (32.5x45cm 12x17in) London 1999

LUKER William, Jnr. 1867-1948 **[29]**

$5 600 - €6 514 - £4 000 - FF42 727
Poodle with a pink Bow Oil/canvas (45.5x37cm 17x14in) London 2001

$1 700 - €1 505 - £1 039 - FF9 871
Yorkshire Terrier with Bone Oil/canvas (30.5x46cm 12x18in) New-York 1999

LUKER William, Snr. 1828-1905 **[31]**

$19 464 - €18 764 - £12 000 - FF123 085
Autumnal Landscape Oil/canvas (91.5x153.5cm 36x60in) London 1999

$3 590 - €3 409 - £2 200 - FF22 359
Highland Cattle resting in a mountainous Landscape Oil/canvas (45.5x81.5cm 17x32in) London 1999

$1 200 - €1 223 - £751 - FF8 024
A Gordon Setter Oil/paper (21x32.5cm 8x12in) New-York 2000

LUKI Mani c.1905-? **[8]**

$7 235 - €6 980 - £4 572 - FF45 786
Bima Sculpture (H48cm H18in) Melbourne 1999

LUKITS Theodore N. 1897-1992 **[7]**

$1 200 - €1 360 - £838 - FF8 919
Jazz Bar Gouache (37x32cm 14x12in) New-York 2001

LUKKOW Frédéric XIX **[1]**

$3 511 - €4 040 - £2 419 - FF26 500
Portraits-charge Tirage argentique (36x27cm 14x10in) Chartres 2000

LUKS George Benjamin 1867-1933 **[110]**

$15 000 - €16 542 - £10 158 - FF108 511
Cafe Scene - Study of a Young Woman in a Pink Dress Oil/canvas (63.5x76cm 25x29in) New-York 2000

$6 000 - €5 985 - £3 745 - FF39 259
The Boy Scout Oil/panel (35x25cm 14x10in) Cincinnati OH 1999

$3 000 - €2 797 - £1 860 - FF18 349
Seated Woman Watercolour (40.5x30.5cm 15x12in) New-York 1999

LUM Bertha Boynton 1879-1954 **[66]**

$4 705 - €4 525 - £2 903 - FF29 680
Kyoto Oil/board (46x28cm 18x11in) Cleveland OH 1999

$600 - €648 - £415 - FF4 251
Young Asian female among swirling Waves Woodcut in colors (6x23cm 2x9in) Cincinnati OH 2001

LUM KWONG (Lin Ji-Kwan) 1939 **[1]**

$7 872 - €8 382 - £4 992 - FF54 984
Flower Basket Oil/canvas (63.5x81cm 25x31in) Taipei 2000

LUMIERE Auguste & Louis 1862/64-1954/48 **[6]**

$1 715 - €2 045 - £1 223 - FF13 415
Blumenstrauss, nach Léon Didier Photograph (14.4x10.8cm 5x4in) München 2000

LUMIKANGAS Pentti 1926 **[14]**

$105 - €101 - £64 - FF661
Tornet Etching (23x24cm 9x9in) Helsinki 1999

LUMINAIS Evariste 1822-1896 **[54]**

$1 210 - €1 220 - £754 - FF8 000
Guerrier gaulois sonnant de la trompe Huile/toile (46x65cm 18x25in) Paris 2000

$1 200 - €1 296 - £829 - FF8 500
An Afternoon Ride Oil/canvas (28.5x24.5cm 11x9in) New-York 2001

LUMIS Harriet Randall 1867-1953 **[27]**

$14 000 - €14 678 - £8 771 - FF96 283
Farm Landscape Oil/canvas (48x58cm 19x23in) Norwalk CT 2000

$2 700 - €2 329 - £1 622 - FF15 280
«Evening at Gloucester» Oil/board (30x25cm 11x9in) Boston MA 1998

LUMLEY Augustus Savile XIX **[5]**

$1 200 - €1 116 - £740 - FF7 319
«Daddy, what did You do in the Geat War?» Poster (76x50cm 30x20in) New-York 1999

LUMSDEN Ernest Stephen 1883-1945 **[50]**

$971 - €911 - £600 - FF5 979
Breakers on the Shore Oil/canvas (63.5x76cm 25x29in) London 1999

$208 - €193 - £130 - FF1 264
Boats and Palace Etching (25x30cm 9x11in) Edinburgh 1999

LUNA Luis 1958 **[2]**

$10 000 - €8 697 - £6 029 - FF57 050
Sin título Mixed media/canvas (142x150cm 55x59in) New-York 1998

LUNA Y NOVICIO Juan 1857-1900 **[25]**

$10 880 - €10 211 - £6 800 - FF66 980
En bueno compañia Oleo/lienzo (92.5x73cm 36x28in) Madrid 1999

$1 650 - €1 652 - £1 017 - FF10 835
Que se cae la carga! Oleo/tabla (20x25cm 7x9in) Madrid 2000

$960 - €961 - £592 - FF6 304
Desnudo masculino Carboncillo (32.5x55.5cm 12x21in) Madrid 2000

LUND Aage 1892-1972 **[11]**

$1 634 - €1 743 - £1 088 - FF11 434
Interiör med lille pige i lyseröd kjole i faerd med at sy Oil/canvas (56x53cm 22x20in) København 2000

LUND Bernt 1812-1885 **[5]**

$1 890 - €2 247 - £1 346 - FF14 742
Utsigt fra Framnes til Balestrand ved Sognefjorden Oil/canvas (37x55cm 14x21in) Oslo 2000

$1 192 - €1 418 - £850 - FF9 303
Surroundings of Oslow, Norway Oil/canvas (30x41cm 11x16in) Bath 2000

LUND Emil Carl 1855-1928 **[39]**

$424 - €390 - £261 - FF2 561
Parti fra Svendborgsund i baggrunden Tåsinge Oil/canvas (38x63cm 14x24in) Vejle 1999

LUND Frederick Christian 1826-1901 **[86]**

$8 050 - €6 721 - £4 785 - FF44 090
«Dronning Caroline Mathildes Arrestation Natten...» Oil/canvas (145x124cm 57x48in) København 1998

$1 005 - €1 073 - £669 - FF7 036
Den danske kommandant overraekker svens-kerne nöglerne til Kronborg Oil/canvas (62x46cm 24x18in) København 2000

L

LUND

$1 090 - €1 206 - £756 - FF7 910
Portraet af Italienerinde Oil/canvas (45x34cm
17x13in) København 2001

LUND Henrik 1879-1935 [34]
$3 306 - €3 669 - £2 304 - FF24 069
Kvinne i gronn hatt Oil/canvas (120x96cm 47x37in)
Oslo 2001
$6 820 - €5 762 - £4 095 - FF37 795
Strykersken Pastel/paper (53x68cm 20x26in) Oslo
1998

LUND Johan Ludvig G. 1777-1867 [13]
$3 810 - €4 090 - £2 550 - FF26 831
Kopenhagen Junge Frau mit Weidenkorb am
Eingang des Waldes Öl/Leinwand (52.5x45.5cm
20x17in) Bremen 2000

LUND V.C. XX [2]
$5 073 - €5 445 - £3 394 - FF35 719
Keukenstilleven pet asperges, groenten en
kreeft Oil/canvas (42x49cm 16x19in) Dordrecht 2000

LUNDAHL Amélia H. 1850-1914 [33]
$20 616 - €20 182 - £12 684 - FF132 384
Tyyni päivä öresundissä Oil/canvas (34x50cm
13x19in) Helsinki 1999
$4 048 - €4 373 - £2 797 - FF28 683
Linneor Oil/canvas (23x25cm 9x9in) Helsinki 2001
$1 423 - €1 261 - £873 - FF8 274
Sorrento Watercolour/paper (26x50cm 10x19in)
Helsinki 1999

LUNDAHL Nadine 1958 [14]
$1 194 - €1 093 - £727 - FF7 170
Stilleben med nötter Oil/panel (19.5x29cm 7x11in)
Helsinki 1999

LUNDBERG Gustaf 1695-1786 [34]
$49 215 - €56 827 - £34 425 - FF372 759
Porträtt stående i helfigur i interiör av den unge
kronprins Gustav Oil/canvas (213x160cm 83x62in)
Stockholm 2001
$5 253 - €5 113 - £3 234 - FF33 536
Porträtt föreställande Adolf Frederik/Porträtt
Lovisa Ulrica Oil/canvas (77x64cm 30x25in)
Stockholm 1999
$8 659 - €7 530 - £5 222 - FF49 392
Porträtt av Carl Gustaf Tessin/Porträtt av Hans
Maka Lovisa Ulrica Chalks (25.5x21cm 10x8in)
Stockholm 1999

LUNDBERG Robert 1861-1903 [14]
$7 077 - €7 927 - £4 919 - FF52 000
Restauration d'une mosquée à Tanger Huile/toile
(139x92cm 54x36in) Paris 2001

LUNDBERG Sture 1900-1930 [15]
$6 492 - €7 721 - £4 629 - FF50 645
Skogsinteriör Oil/canvas (57x44cm 22x17in)
Stockholm 2000
$1 213 - €1 408 - £837 - FF9 234
Positano Pencil/paper (25x20cm 9x7in) Stockholm
2000

LUNDBERG Theodor 1852-1926 [12]
$843 - €960 - £578 - FF6 297
Sittande naken kvinna Bronze (H45cm H17in)
Stockholm 2000

LUNDBOHM Sixten 1895-1982 [128]
$1 025 - €949 - £627 - FF6 225
Fjällterräng Grövelsjön Oil/canvas (66x81cm
25x31in) Uppsala 1999
$639 - €593 - £384 - FF6 295
Blommor i vas Oil/panel (39x32cm 15x12in) Malmö
1999

LUNDBORG Karl 1893-1972 [45]
$369 - €318 - £222 - FF2 089
Utsikt över skånsk by, i bakgrunden
Romeleåsen Oil/panel (20x40cm 7x15in) Malmö
1998

LUNDBYE Johan Thomas 1818-1848 [137]
$9 626 - €8 744 - £5 967 - FF57 356
Skovbund med et par faeldede traestammer
Oil/canvas (18x35cm 7x13in) København 1999
$855 - €807 - £533 - FF5 296
En bonde Watercolour/paper (22x13cm 8x5in)
København 1999
$140 - €121 - £84 - FF793
Sydsiden af Refnaes Etching (12x15cm 4x5in) Viby
J, Århus 1998

LUNDE Anders Christian 1809-1886 [36]
$1 118 - €1 077 - £694 - FF7 064
Parti fra Brede Oil/canvas (25x35cm 9x13in)
København 1999

LUNDEBY Alf 1870-1961 [9]
$981 - €1 146 - £700 - FF7 519
Blomsterstilleben Oil/canvas (64x56cm 25x22in)
Oslo 2001

LUNDEGÅRD Justus 1860-1924 [40]
$1 302 - €1 180 - £802 - FF7 742
Utsikt över Anticoli Oil/canvas (69x98cm 27x38in)
Stockholm 1999

LUNDENS Gerrit 1622-1683 [30]
$18 876 - €18 151 - £11 628 - FF119 064
Milkmaid Waylaid by a Sportsman Under a Tree
in a Meadow Oil/canvas (42.5x38.5cm 16x15in)
Amsterdam 1999
$6 840 - €7 769 - £4 800 - FF50 964
Peasants merrymaking in a Tavern Interior
Oil/panel (16x13.5cm 6x5in) London 2001

LUNDGREN Egron Sillif 1815-1875 [114]
$12 000 - €12 440 - £7 200 - FF81 600
Contadini sullo sfondo del Vesuvio Olio/tela
(90x136cm 35x53in) Roma 2000
$1 317 - €1 463 - £882 - FF9 596
Exteriör med förnämt par samt spåkvinna
Oil/canvas (54x43cm 21x16in) Stockholm 2000
$1 872 - €1 782 - £1 171 - FF11 689
Två italienskor Oil/canvas (34.5x24.5cm 13x9in)
Stockholm 1999
$702 - €668 - £439 - FF4 383
Två indiska kvinnor Akvarell/papper (22x14cm
8x5in) Stockholm 1999

LUNDGREN Tyra Carolina 1897-1979 [59]
$556 - €645 - £383 - FF4 232
Fisk Stone (H25cm H9in) Stockholm 2000
$544 - €523 - £330 - FF3 428
Fågelunge Pastel/paper (67x52cm 26x20in)
Stockholm 1999

LUNDH Theodor 1812-1896 [16]
$1 989 - €1 842 - £1 217 - FF12 084
Skjutna småfåglar, jaktstilleben Oil/canvas
(54x40cm 21x15in) Uppsala 1999

LUNDMARK Leon 1875-1942 [31]
$900 - €771 - £541 - FF5 057
Surf of the Breakers Oil/canvas (73x91cm 29x36in)
Chicago IL 1998

LUNDQVIST Evert 1904-1994 [333]
$29 094 - €31 931 - £18 746 - FF209 456
Kvinnorna vid brunnen Oil/canvas (116x104cm
45x40in) Stockholm 2000

$10 472 - €10 278 - £6 494 - FF67 416
Kärven Oil/canvas (92x60cm 36x23in) Stockholm 1999

$2 056 - €1 739 - £1 228 - FF11 404
«Röda Frukterna» Oil/panel (18.5x25.5cm 7x10in) Stockholm 1998

$510 - €485 - £310 - FF3 182
Sorg Charcoal/paper (44x58cm 17x22in) Stockholm 1999

LUNDQVIST Jan 1935 [28]
$249 - €210 - £147 - FF1 378
Djurgårdsbron - Stockholm Watercolour/paper (32x47cm 12x18in) Stockholm 1998

LUNDQVIST John 1882-1972 [13]
$7 966 - €9 391 - £5 600 - FF61 600
Svaevende kvinde Bronze (83x133cm 32x52in) Vejle 2000

LUNDSTRÖM Knut 1892-1945 [40]
$1 059 - €1 017 - £658 - FF6 673
Landskap med hus Oil/panel (90x71cm 35x27in) Stockholm 1999

$25 024 - €27 598 - £16 951 - FF181 033
Evolution rythmique Oil/canvas (32x23cm 12x9in) Stockholm 2000

LUNDSTRÖM Vilhelm 1893-1950 [167]
$35 550 - €40 205 - £24 030 - FF263 730
Opstilling med orange, krukke og gul kande Oil/canvas (146x105cm 57x41in) København 2000

$11 362 - €12 737 - £7 942 - FF83 552
Selvportraet i blå jakke Oil/canvas (119x94cm 46x37in) København 2001

$1 384 - €1 609 - £973 - FF10 557
Landskab fra Amager Oil/canvas (28x43cm 11x16in) København 2001

$733 - €739 - £457 - FF4 846
Rygvendt model Pencil/paper (45x30cm 17x11in) København 2000

LUNEL Ferdinand 1857-? [19]
$1 297 - €1 296 - £810 - FF8 500
Un aprés-midi à la Grenouillère Crayon (57x85cm 22x33in) Pontoise 1999

$656 - €656 - £410 - FF4 300
«Société du Gaz Acétylène» Affiche (126x92cm 49x36in) Orléans 1999

LUNGREN Fernand Harvey 1859-1932 [7]
$10 000 - €11 255 - £6 889 - FF73 827
Cafe Scene Oil/canvas (72.5x61cm 28x24in) Philadelphia PA 2000

LUNIOT Edmond 1851-? [6]
$1 672 - €1 994 - £1 192 - FF13 080
Bewaldete Landschaft in der Umgebung von Barbizon Öl/Leinwand (33x41cm 12x16in) Köln 2000

LUNOIS Alexandre 1863-1916 [69]
$3 002 - €2 744 - £1 837 - FF18 000
Café Hamoud Pacha, Brousse Pastel/papier (53.5x44.5cm 21x17in) Paris 1999

$388 - €381 - £240 - FF2 500
Femme espagnole remettant son soulier Estampe couleurs (47x39cm 18x15in) Paris 1999

LUNS Hubert Marie, Huib 1881-1942 [12]
$145 - €136 - £90 - FF893
«Amsterdam Rijks-Museum Stedelijk-Museum» Poster (54x89cm 21x35in) Oostwoud 1999

LUNTESCHÜTZ Jules 1822-1893 [3]
$7 139 - €7 927 - £4 976 - FF52 000
Nu aux roses Huile/panneau (58x41cm 22x16in) Paris 2001

LUNY Thomas 1759-1837 [210]
$12 962 - €12 466 - £8 000 - FF81 771
Men O'War off a Coast, with a Lighthouse beyond Oil/canvas (89x148.5cm 35x58in) London 1999

$8 418 - €10 011 - £6 000 - FF65 671
Boats in an Estuary with Figures Disembarking in the Foreground Oil/canvas (51x68.5cm 20x26in) London 2000

$6 183 - €5 641 - £3 800 - FF37 001
Dutch Barges Lying Offshore Oil/panel (25.5x35.5cm 10x13in) London 1998

LUO PING 1733-1799 [12]
$4 622 - €5 073 - £2 977 - FF33 274
Fu Sheng Reciting the Classics Ink (79x32cm 31x12in) Hong-Kong 2000

LUO ZHONGLI 1948 [21]
$19 305 - €18 319 - £11 730 - FF120 165
Dong Shui Tian Oil/canvas (53x72cm 20x28in) Hong-Kong 1999

LUONG XUAN NHI 1913 [6]
$3 888 - €4 573 - £2 817 - FF30 000
Paysage du Viet-Nam Huile/toile (50x70cm 19x27in) Lorient 2001

$6 547 - €7 318 - £4 555 - FF48 000
Deux jeunes femmes Peinture (38x32cm 14x12in) Toulouse 2001

LUOSTARINEN Leena 1949 [16]
$901 - €1 009 - £625 - FF6 619
Tillsammans Oil/canvas (44x62cm 17x24in) Helsinki 2001

$232 - €235 - £145 - FF1 544
Lotus Color lithograph (60x42cm 23x16in) Helsinki 2000

LÜPERTZ Markus 1941 [348]
$34 792 - €32 443 - £21 000 - FF212 811
From the small Street 2 Tempera/canvas (215x137cm 84x53in) London 1999

$5 699 - €6 647 - £4 401 - FF43 600
Ohne Titel Tempera (80x59.7cm 31x23in) Köln 2000

$181 481 - €175 602 - £115 000 - FF1 151 874
Standbein-Spielbein Bronze (320x100x100cm 125x39x39in) London 1999

$16 797 - €19 992 - £12 003 - FF131 137
Clitunno Bronze (48.8x21.5x16.5cm 19x8x6in) Berlin 2000

$2 216 - €1 940 - £1 342 - FF12 725
Ohne Titel Chalks (70.4x49.8cm 27x19in) Berlin 1998

$399 - €470 - £282 - FF3 085
«Hirte», kleine Fassung Radierung (31x25cm 12x9in) Berlin 2001

LUPIAC André Pierre 1873-1956 [15]
$1 424 - €1 677 - £1 001 - FF11 000
Léda et le cygne Huile/toile (71x90cm 27x35in) Toulouse 2000

LUPIAÑEZ Y CARRASCO José 1864-1933 [52]
$3 840 - €3 604 - £2 400 - FF23 640
Paisaje de Guadarrama Oleo/lienzo (50x60.5cm 19x23in) Madrid 1999

$972 - €1 081 - £648 - FF7 092
Paisaje Oleo/tabla (14.5x32.5cm 5x12in) Madrid 2000

LUPLAU Marie 1848-1925 [27]
$202 - €188 - £122 - FF1 236
Kystparti ved Svendborg Oil/canvas (22x33cm 8x12in) København 1999

L

LUPO Alessandro 1876-1953 **[82]**
- $6 000 – €6 220 – **£3 600** – FF40 800
  Chioggia Olio/legno (40x50cm 15x19in) Roma 1999
- $1 725 – €1 788 – **£1 035** – FF11 730
  Lavoro nei campi Olio/legno (21x30cm 8x11in)
  Roma 1999

LUPO Dom XX **[3]**
- $2 200 – €2 397 – **£1 523** – FF15 725
  «**Dartmouth Winter Carnival**» Poster (86x55cm
  34x22in) New-York 2001

LUPPEN van Joseph G. 1834-1891 **[49]**
- $1 671 – €1 636 – **£1 028** – FF10 732
  Wiesenlandschaft mit weidenden Kühen Oil/can-
  vas/panel (89x63cm 35x24in) Stuttgart 1999
- $358 – €397 – **£243** – FF2 601
  Vue à Brasschaat Huile/panneau (28.5x43.5cm
  11x17in) Antwerpen 2000

LUPPENS H. XIX-XX **[5]**
- $2 119 – €2 167 – **£1 400** – FF14 927
  Grenadier Guard of 1889 Bronze (H58cm H22in)
  Billingshurst, West-Sussex 2000

LUPTON Thomas Goff 1791-1873 **[6]**
- $459 – €515 – **£320** – FF3 378
  The Meet at Blagdon, after John Wray Snow
  Engraving (46.5x75cm 18x29in) Leyburn, North
  Yorkshire 2001

LURÇAT Jean 1892-1966 **[664]**
- $7 952 – €8 537 – **£5 320** – FF56 000
  Voile Huile/toile (106x168cm 41x66in) Compiègne
  2000
- $9 940 – €10 671 – **£6 650** – FF70 000
  Pêcheur du lac Huile/toile (100x65cm 39x25in)
  Compiègne 2000
- $3 266 – €3 506 – **£2 185** – FF23 000
  Les mâts Huile/bois (24x33cm 9x12in) Compiègne
  2000
- $805 – €740 – **£495** – FF4 857
  Untitled Ceramic (H22cm H8in) Köbenhavn 1999
- $1 846 – €1 982 – **£1 235** – FF13 000
  Paysage mirifique Gouache/papier (21.5x44cm
  8x17in) Compiègne 2000
- $1 518 – €1 296 – **£916** – FF8 500
  Le scorpion Tapisserie (63x81cm 24x31in) Calais
  1998

LURIE Nan XX **[3]**
- $450 – €521 – **£318** – FF3 418
  Barred Lithograph (43.5x33.5cm 17x13in) New-York
  2000

LUSIERI Giovanni Battista c.1755-1821 **[2]**
- $70 000 – €74 757 – **£47 698** – FF490 371
  **Extensive View of Rome from the Orti della
  Pineta Sacchetti** Black chalk (30x43cm 11x16in)
  New-York 2001

LUSK Doris 1916 **[4]**
- $827 – €972 – **£587** – FF6 376
  Cabbage Tree, Port Hills Watercolour (37x53.5cm
  14x21in) Auckland 2000

LUSKINA Wlodzimierz 1849-1894 **[4]**
- $12 034 – €14 313 – **£8 580** – FF93 885
  **Mademoiselle de Cazotte, épisode de la révolu-
  tion française** Huile/toile (80.5x153.5cm 31x60in)
  Warszawa 2000

LUSSANET de Paul 1940 **[26]**
- $388 – €454 – **£270** – FF2 976
  Untitled Mixed media/paper (32x23.5cm 12x9in)
  Amsterdam 2000

LUSSO Paola (Lupa) 1962 **[17]**
- $250 – €259 – **£150** – FF1 700
  Il bene e il male Tecnica mista (50x60cm 19x23in)
  Vercelli 2001

LUST de Abraham XVII **[2]**
- $11 733 – €13 613 – **£8 100** – FF89 298
  **Still Life of Grapes, Peaches, a Melon, a
  Pomegranate and a Wine-Glass** Oil/canvas
  (53x63cm 20x24in) Amsterdam 2000

LUST de Antoni Adriaan XVII **[5]**
- $14 524 – €14 635 – **£9 052** – FF96 000
  Nature morte aux raisins et autres fruits
  Huile/toile (51x63cm 20x24in) Paris 2000

LUSZCZKIEWICZ Wladyslaw 1828-1900 **[1]**
- $4 574 – €5 100 – **£3 130** – FF33 454
  Tailleur de pierre Huile/toile (61x74cm 24x29in)
  Warszawa 2000

LÜTGENDORFF von Ferdinand 1785-1858 **[7]**
- $1 329 – €1 257 – **£828** – FF8 247
  Portrait of a Girl in a Hat Oil/canvas (54.5x41.5cm
  21x16in) Praha 1999
- $1 076 – €920 – **£632** – FF6 032
  Biedermeierporträt einer Dame mit Strickzeug
  Watercolour (29x23cm 11x9in) Stuttgart 1998

LUTGERS Petrus Josephus 1808-1874 **[14]**
- $9 652 – €11 344 – **£6 692** – FF74 415
  A View of Loenen ann de Vecht Oil/canvas
  (27.5x35.5cm 10x13in) Amsterdam 2000
- $1 510 – €1 452 – **£942** – FF9 525
  View of a Villa Wash/paper (13.5x18cm 5x7in)
  Amsterdam 1999

LUTHER Adolf 1912-1990 **[94]**
- $4 240 – €4 116 – **£2 640** – FF26 998
  Ohne Titel Mixed media/panel (35x49.7cm 13x19in)
  Berlin 1999
- $1 657 – €1 432 – **£1 001** – FF9 392
  Hohlspiegelobjekt Object (46.3x46.3cm 18x18in)
  Köln 1998
- $192 – €225 – **£134** – FF1 475
  Ohne Titel Offset (60x59cm 23x23in) Köln 2000

LUTHI Ernest 1906-1983 **[11]**
- $517 – €602 – **£364** – FF3 950
  «**Windy June Morning looking over Lake
  Katepwa from Highway No.56 Hill**» Oil/board
  (30.5x40.5cm 12x15in) Calgary, Alberta 2001

LÜTHI Urs 1947 **[66]**
- $1 859 – €2 050 – **£1 259** – FF13 450
  Selbstporträt, aus der Serie der reinen Hingabe
  Acryl/Leinwand (30x40cm 11x15in) Zürich 2000
- $226 – €263 – **£156** – FF1 723
  Frauenakt in Wohnzimmer Radierung (32.5x49cm
  12x19in) Zürich 2000
- $438 – €511 – **£303** – FF3 353
  Ohne Titel Photograph in colors (8.8x17.6cm 3x6in)
  Köln 2000

LÜTHY Oskar Wilhelm 1882-1945 **[51]**
- $908 – €872 – **£563** – FF5 723
  Stilleben mit Rosen Öl/Papier (47x39cm 18x15in)
  Zürich 1999
- $1 109 – €1 316 – **£807** – FF8 632
  Rote Rose Öl/Karton (33x25cm 12x9in) Zürich 2001
- $464 – €528 – **£322** – FF3 465
  Tessiner Landschaft Aquarell/Papier (37x48cm
  14x18in) Zofingen 2000

LUTI Benedetto 1666-1724 **[25]**
- $5 400 - €6 997 - **£4 050** - FF45 900
  Atalanta e Ippomene Olio/tela (59x71cm 23x27in)
  Roma 2000
- $35 880 - €39 637 - **£24 882** - FF260 000
  Dieu poursuivant Caïn après le meurtre d'Abel
  Sanguine (50x33cm 19x12in) Paris 2001

LÜTKEN Mathias 1841-1905 **[32]**
- $426 - €404 - **£265** - FF2 648
  Amerikansk kystparti Oil/canvas (41x61cm 16x24in)
  København 1999

LUTMA Johannes II 1624-1685/89 **[6]**
- $391 - €460 - **£281** - FF3 018
  Selbstportrait Radierung (29.5x20.5cm 11x8in)
  Hamburg 2001

LUTSCHER Fernand c.1850 **[32]**
- $1 672 - €1 942 - **£1 156** - FF12 500
  La place du village Huile/toile (88x128cm 34x50in)
  Angers 2000
- $2 868 - €3 201 - **£1 877** - FF21 000
  Vaches près de la rivière/Rencontre avec le chasseur Huile/panneau (21.5x41.5cm 8x16in)
  Fontainebleau 2000
- $400 - €457 - **£281** - FF3 000
  Chemin dans la campagne Aquarelle/papier
  (18x27cm 7x10in) Fontainebleau 2001

LUTTERELL Edward Luttrel c.1650-c.1725 **[7]**
- $965 - €1 114 - **£675** - FF7 309
  Porträtt av man iklädd svart rock med spetskrage/Man iklädd svart hatt Pastel/paper (29x21.5cm 11x8in) Stockholm 2001

LUTTEROTH Ascan 1842-1923 **[54]**
- $1 920 - €1 789 - **£1 184** - FF11 738
  Baumblüte an der Este bei Hamburg
  Öl/Leinwand (64.5x100cm 25x39in) Bremen 1999
- $1 854 - €1 943 - **£1 226** - FF12 744
  Südliche Küstenlandschaft mit zwei Frauen unter Palmen Öl/Leinwand (23x33cm 9x12in)
  München 2001

LUTTICHUYS Isaak 1616-1673 **[11]**
- $6 624 - €7 143 - **£4 446** - FF46 854
  Porträtt av en dam Oil/canvas (117x90cm 46x35in)
  Stockholm 2000

LUTTICHUYS Simon 1612-1662 **[9]**
- $215 020 - €235 965 - **£138 424** - FF1 547.832
  Lobster, Bun and a Knife on a pewter Plate, a Roemer, a Wine Glass Oil/canvas (58.5x67.5cm 23x26in) Amsterdam 2000

LUTWIDGE R.W.Skeffington XIX **[1]**
- $6 620 - €7 415 - **£4 600** - FF48 640
  Study of Knowle, Kent, taken in the Rain
  Albumen print (15.5x17cm 6x6in) London 2001

LUTYENS Charles Henry Aug. 1829-1915 **[36]**
- $1 270 - €1 363 - **£850** - FF8 943
  Putti in the clouds Oil/canvas (36x90cm 14x35in)
  London 2000
- $1 204 - €1 321 - **£800** - FF8 666
  Frolicking Putti Oil/canvas (28x23cm 11x9in)
  Billingshurst, West-Sussex 2000
- $5 858 - €5 241 - **£3 500** - FF34 381
  «Jorrocks» Bronze (36.5x31.5cm 14x12in) Perthshire 1998

LUTZ Anton 1894-1976 **[7]**
- $4 277 - €5 087 - **£3 052** - FF33 369
  Meeresbrandung Öl/Leinwand (79x96cm 31x37in)
  Linz 2000

LUVONI Luigi 1859-1904 **[16]**
- $325 - €337 - **£195** - FF2 210
  Marina con barca Olio/cartone (15x9cm 5x3in)
  Vercelli 2001

LUXARDO Lazzaro 1865-1949 **[8]**
- $5 000 - €5 183 - **£3 000** - FF34 000
  L'annegato Olio/tela (73x113cm 28x44in) Milano 1999
- $400 - €415 - **£240** - FF2 720
  Lago di Massaciuccoli Olio/tavola (16x52cm 6x20in) Firenze 2001

LUXORO Alfredo 1859-1918 **[1]**
- $1 950 - €2 021 - **£1 170** - FF13 260
  La strada nel bosco Carboncino/carta (102x82cm 40x32in) Genova 2000

LUXORO Tammar 1825-1899 **[2]**
- $4 800 - €6 220 - **£3 600** - FF40 800
  «Passeggiata nel bosco» Olio/tavola (35.5x26.5cm 13x10in) Vercelli 2000

LUYCKS Frans c.1604-1668 **[1]**
- $31 128 - €30 598 - **£20 000** - FF200 712
  Nobleman, probably Johan Andreas, Graf von Liebenberg, holdinf a Hat Oil/canvas (163x135cm 64x53in) London 1999

LUYCKX Christiaan 1623-c.1653 **[21]**
- $24 000 - €28 267 - **£16 598** - FF185 421
  Still Life of Flowers in a Glass Vase with an Orange on a Pewter Plate Oil/panel (49x38.5cm 19x15in) New-York 2000

LUYCKX Frans 1802-1849 **[4]**
- $93 - €111 - **£63** - FF731
  De toekomst en het verleden? (Le futur et le passé) Huile/toile (50x60cm 19x23in) Antwerpen 2001

LUYKEN Jan 1649-1712 **[44]**
- $1 948 - €1 683 - **£1 174** - FF11 039
  A Spanish Horseman being robbed of his Horse by a Woman Wash (10.5x15cm 4x5in)
  Amsterdam 1998
- $100 - €107 - **£68** - FF703
  Murder of King of Scotland, August 1600
  Engraving (43x30cm 17x12in) Thomaston ME 2001

LUYTEN Henri Jean 1859-1945 **[60]**
- $1 800 - €2 088 - **£1 242** - FF13 699
  Lineke Oil/canvas (101x51cm 39x20in) New-York 2000
- $1 110 - €1 239 - **£770** - FF8 130
  Fillette près de la ferme Huile/carton (23x33cm 9x12in) Antwerpen 2001

LUZURIAGA Juan Ramón 1938 **[77]**
- $1 045 - €1 141 - **£665** - FF7 486
  Remolcador y gasolino Oleo/lienzo (81x65cm 31x25in) Madrid 2001
- $303 - €264 - **£189** - FF1 733
  Pareja Tinta (32x25cm 12x9in) Madrid 1999

LUZZI Cleto XIX-XX **[12]**
- $5 208 - €5 625 - **£3 600** - FF36 899
  The Cardinal's Visit Oil/canvas (46x68cm 18x26in)
  London 2001
- $20 568 - €19 843 - **£13 000** - FF130 162
  The Harem Watercolour (54x76cm 21x29in) London 1999

LUZZO Antonio 1855-1907 **[13]**
- $1 283 - €1 287 - **£804** - FF8 049
  Brig Richard Owen Portmadoc William Williams
  Indian ink (46x60cm 18x23in) Hamburg 1999

L

LUZZO Giovanni, John XIX-XX [8]
- $800 - €829 - £480 - FF5 440
  Nave Radium Acquarello/carta (45x61cm 17x24in)
  Trieste 1999

LYBAERT Théophile M.F. 1848-1927 [9]
- $645 - €716 - £448 - FF4 695
  Nordafrikanische Palastwache Öl/Leinwand
  (62x36.5cm 24x14in) Köln 2001

LYCETT Joseph 1774-c.1825 [37]
- $25 104 - €21 683 - £15 163 - FF142 233
  **Cape Pillar near the Entrance to the Derwent,
  van Diemens Land** Watercolour/paper (16.5x27cm
  6x10in) Malvern, Victoria 1998
- $543 - €528 - £335 - FF3 461
  View of Captain Piper Naval Villa Aquatint
  (30x22cm 11x8in) Sydney 1999

LYCKE Oscar 1877-1927 [41]
- $515 - €571 - £349 - FF3 747
  Vinterdag, motiv från Liden Oil/canvas (72x86cm
  28x33in) Stockholm 2000

LYDEN Edvin 1879-1956 [7]
- $1 226 - €1 345 - £789 - FF8 825
  Frostdag Oil/canvas (43x53cm 16x20in) Helsinki 2000

LYDIS Mariette 1890-1970 [262]
- $194 - €229 - £139 - FF1 500
  «Veuve Moscove» Crayons couleurs (35x50cm
  13x19in) Paris 2000
- $107 - €114 - £67 - FF750
  Petite danseuse Lithographie couleurs (42x34.5cm
  16x13in) Paris 2000

LYLE David XIX [1]
- $4 684 - €5 231 - £3 000 - FF34 316
  Four Masted Steamer «Glasgow» at Sea Oil/can-
  vas (71x101.5cm 27x39in) London 2000

LYMAN John Goodwin 1886-1967 [40]
- $5 790 - €5 564 - £3 566 - FF36 499
  Lake Massawippi, The Coming Storm Oil/canvas
  (40.5x51cm 15x20in) Vancouver, BC. 1999
- $1 619 - €1 889 - £1 127 - FF12 392
  Massawippi XV Oil/board (14x18cm 5x7in) Toronto
  2000
- $651 - €730 - £452 - FF4 786
  Reclining Nude Graphite (23x34cm 9x13in) Calgary,
  Alberta 2001

LYMAN Stephen 1957-1996 [1]
- $17 500 - €15 908 - £10 540 - FF104 352
  Raptor's Watch Acrylic/board (71x91cm 28x36in)
  Hayden ID 1998

LYMBURNER Francis 1916-1972 [118]
- $2 743 - €2 580 - £1 698 - FF16 925
  The Stumble Oil/canvas (50x60cm 19x23in)
  Melbourne 1999
- $1 308 - €1 226 - £809 - FF8 040
  Artist at Easel Oil/masonite (30x21cm 11x8in)
  Sydney 1999
- $446 - €430 - £275 - FF2 820
  Monkey Ink (16x19cm 6x7in) Sydney 1999

LYNAS-GRAY John Abernethy 1869-c.1940 [62]
- $416 - €383 - £250 - FF2 514
  Scafell and Wastwater Watercolour (35x25cm
  13x9in) London 1999

LYNCH Albert 1851-? [84]
- $14 000 - €13 588 - £8 716 - FF89 132
  La tasse de thé Oil/canvas (73x93cm 28x36in) New-
  York 1999

- $3 376 - €3 125 - £2 091 - FF20 500
  La cueillette des fleurs Huile/panneau (45x33cm
  17x12in) Paris 1999
- $1 956 - €2 287 - £1 396 - FF15 000
  La servante Aquarelle/papier (47.5x32.5cm 18x12in)
  Paris 2001

LYNCH Frederick XX [11]
- $300 - €272 - £183 - FF1 782
  Untitled Watercolour/paper (22x17cm 9x7in) Portland
  ME 1998

LYNCH Justo 1870-1953 [4]
- $12 000 - €10 220 - £7 233 - FF67 039
  Puerto de mar del plata Oleo/cartón (59x72cm
  23x28in) Buenos-Aires 1998

LYNDE Raymond XIX-XX [21]
- $4 718 - €5 226 - £3 200 - FF34 278
  Portrait of a Lady Oil/canvas (59x49.5cm 23x19in)
  Billingshurst, West-Sussex 2000

LYNDSAY Roy XX [2]
- $3 450 - €4 063 - £2 425 - FF26 652
  Find a Quiet Place Oil/canvas (45.5x61cm 17x24in)
  Dublin 2000

LYNE Michael 1912-1989 [138]
- $19 568 - €21 469 - £13 000 - FF140 829
  Flat Racing Oil/canvas (101.5x127cm 39x50in)
  London 2000
- $5 848 - €4 943 - £3 500 - FF32 424
  Vignettes -Flat Racing Oil/canvas (61x76cm
  24x29in) London 1998
- $1 200 - €1 037 - £712 - FF6 802
  **«Buccleugh Hunt, Chapel Hill»/«Dumfries Hunt,
  Burns Wark»** Watercolour, gouache/paper (28x38cm
  11x14in) Washington 1998
- $128 - €122 - £80 - FF797
  The Cotswold near Shipton Ollife Print in colors
  (38x53cm 15x21in) Northampton 1999

LYNEN Amédée Ernest 1852-1938 [162]
- $691 - €768 - £461 - FF5 040
  Hameau animé dans les environs de Bruxelles
  Technique mixte (31x87cm 12x34in) Bruxelles 2000
- $337 - €397 - £243 - FF2 601
  La buveuse d'absinthe Encre/papier (12.5x8cm
  4x3in) Bruxelles 2001
- $241 - €274 - £167 - FF1 800
  «Fédération Belge des cercles d'escrime»
  Affiche (120x90cm 47x35in) Paris 2000

LYNES George Platt 1907-1955 [151]
- $1 278 - €1 431 - £888 - FF9 390
  Männlicher Rückenakt Vintage gelatin silver print
  (23.5x19cm 9x7in) Köln 2001

LYNKER Anna 1834-1893 [1]
- $2 512 - €2 301 - £1 531 - FF15 092
  Orientalische Strasse mit einer Moschee
  Öl/Leinwand (39x24cm 15x9in) München 1999

LYNN Elwyn Augustus 1917-1997 [62]
- $3 217 - €3 548 - £2 179 - FF23 273
  Thaw Mixed media/canvas (150x150cm 59x59in)
  Woollahra, Sydney 2000
- $1 800 - €1 052 - £665 - FF6 898
  River, Rainbow and Red Mountain Acrylic
  (85.5x113.5cm 33x44in) Malvern, Victoria 1999
- $2 884 - €3 204 - £1 932 - FF21 019
  «Fading Track» Mixed media (31x41cm 12x16in)
  Nedlands 2000
- $1 044 - €981 - £629 - FF6 434
  Harvard Blues Mixed media/paper (84x115cm
  33x45in) Sydney 1999

LYNN John XIX [18]
- $27 997 - €27 298 - £17 000 - FF179 062
  The East Indiaman «Madagascar» off Berry Head Oil/canvas (53.5x81.5cm 21x32in) London 2000
- $8 965 - €9 624 - £6 000 - FF63 129
  Bermudan-Rigged Racing Cutter/Frigate Off the Bishop's Rock Lighthouse Oil/canvas (21x28.5cm 8x11in) New-York 1999

LYNTON Henry Stanton Act.1886-1904 [38]
- $600 - €581 - £370 - FF3 808
  Oasis in Egypt Watercolour/paper (25x63cm 9x24in) London 1999

LYON Danny 1942 [84]
- $1 500 - €1 411 - £928 - FF9 253
  87 North Moore Street, from The Destruction of Lower Manhattan Series Gelatin silver print (17x22cm 6x8in) New-York 1999

LYON Harold Lloyd 1930 [24]
- $586 - €688 - £414 - FF4 516
  Cool Water Oil/canvas (35.5x45.5cm 13x17in) Calgary, Alberta 2000
- $556 - €662 - £383 - FF4 342
  Easy Rider Oil/canvas (14x18cm 5x7in) Calgary, Alberta 2000

LYON John Howard ?-1921 [13]
- $1 457 - €1 652 - £1 017 - FF10 835
  Vista in un puerto Oleo/lienzo (51x68.5cm 20x26in) Barcelona 2000

LYONS William XIX [1]
- $1 522 - €1 432 - £950 - FF9 396
  Norham Castle on the Tweed Watercolour/paper (25.5x18.5cm 10x7in) London 1999

LYTH Harald 1937 [39]
- $9 960 - €8 499 - £5 952 - FF55 752
  In natura Oil/canvas (135x115cm 53x45in) Stockholm 1998
- $2 056 - €1 739 - £1 228 - FF11 404
  «Snittet» Mixed media (85x72cm 33x28in) Stockholm 1998

LYTRAS Nicholaos 1883-1927 [9]
- $51 289 - €59 050 - £35 000 - FF387 341
  The Artist and His Wife Oil/canvas (69x56cm 27x22in) London 2000

LYTTLETON Thomas Hamilton 1826-1876 [1]
- $8 300 - €7 238 - £5 019 - FF47 476
  Nimblefoot Oil/board (23x29.5cm 9x11in) Melbourne 1998

LYVÉE de Charles XVIII [1]
- $10 919 - €10 684 - £7 000 - FF70 085
  An Armadillo Watercolour (13.5x19cm 5x7in) London 1999

LYYTIKÄINEN Olli 1949-1987 [16]
- $1 870 - €1 850 - £1 166 - FF12 135
  Förlovning Watercolour/paper (16x15.5cm 6x6in) Helsinki 1999

M

MA CHENGKUAN Ma Singfoon 1940 [7]
- $14 800 - €14 045 - £8 993 - FF92 126
  Fall from Heaven Ink (135x67.5cm 53x26in) Hong-Kong 1999

MA JIN 1900-1971 [19]
- $5 938 - €5 034 - £3 551 - FF33 023
  Two Horses Coloured inks/paper (124.5x64.5cm 49x25in) Hong-Kong 1998

MA XIAOGUANG 1956 [5]
- $7 100 - €5 997 - £4 262 - FF39 341
  Harvest Season Oil/canvas (34.5x149cm 13x58in) Hong-Kong 1998

MA YUANYU 1669-1722 [4]
- $10 384 - €9 793 - £6 440 - FF64 239
  Flowers Ink (30x22cm 11x8in) Hong-Kong 1999

MAAR Dora 1907-1997 [652]
- $638 - €610 - £400 - FF4 000
  Composition géométrique Huile/toile (130x195cm 51x76in) Paris 1999
- $788 - €686 - £475 - FF4 500
  Composition à la Nativité Huile/toile (81x65cm 31x25in) Paris 1999
- $561 - €488 - £338 - FF3 200
  Paysage abstrait, bleu et brun Huile/isorel (33x24cm 12x9in) Paris 1998
- $788 - €686 - £475 - FF4 500
  Autoportrait au manteau Fusain (104x73cm 40x28in) Paris 1998
- $3 000 - €2 592 - £1 812 - FF17 000
  Paul et Nusch Éluard enlacés dans l'éblouissement du soleil Tirage argentique (27.8x21.7cm 10x8in) Paris 1998

MAAREL van der Marinus 1847-1921 [17]
- $500 - €6 977 - £4 349 - FF45 766
  In the Garden Oil/panel (48x36cm 19x14in) Portland ME 2000
- $2 223 - €2 450 - £1 452 - FF16 073
  Strandvermaak Oil/panel (20x25.5cm 7x10in) Rotterdam 2000

MAARNI Elvi 1907 [69]
- $2 272 - €1 934 - £1 357 - FF12 689
  Kvinna med violin Oil/canvas (48x42cm 18x16in) Helsinki 1998
- $2 174 - €1 850 - £1 298 - FF12 137
  Två kvinnor Oil/canvas (43x37cm 16x14in) Helsinki 1998
- $976 - €1 093 - £678 - FF7 170
  Stadsvy Pastel/paper (33x25cm 12x9in) Helsinki 2001

MAAS Christian 1951 [133]
- $1 934 - €2 134 - £1 279 - FF14 000
  Tête de cerf Bronze (100x90cm 39x35in) Paris 2000
- $553 - €610 - £368 - FF4 000
  Taureau chargeant Bronze (30x48cm 11x18in) Biarritz 2000

MAAS Henri Franz, Harry 1906-1982 [34]
- $1 152 - €1 271 - £752 - FF8 334
  Liggend naakt Oil/canvas (44x74cm 17x29in) Den Haag 2000

MAAS Paul 1890-1962 [107]
- $1 491 - €1 735 - £1 064 - FF11 382
  Toits à Salo, Lombardie Huile/toile (50x70cm 19x27in) Bruxelles 2001
- $291 - €322 - £204 - FF2 113
  Portrait d'homme fumant la pipe Huile/toile (44x34cm 17x13in) Bruxelles 2001
- $537 - €620 - £367 - FF4 065
  Jeune femme bleue Technique mixte/papier (45.5x31cm 17x12in) Bruxelles 2000

MAASS David XX [2]
$13 000 - €11 818 - **£7 829** - FF77 519
Canadas Landing Oil/board (66x106cm 26x42in)
Hayden ID 1998

MAASS Ernst 1904-1971 [31]
$1 986 - €2 179 - **£1 349** - FF14 292
Erscheinung des Engels Öl/Leinwand (61x80cm 24x31in) Luzern 2000

MAASS Harro 1939 [5]
$5 681 - €5 460 - **£3 500** - FF35 816
Run the Gauntlet Acrylic/board (79x98.5cm 31x38in)
London 1999

MAASS Johann Gottfried XIX [2]
$2 608 - €3 068 - **£1 870** - FF20 123
Neapolitaner mit Laute Öl/Leinwand (57x44cm 22x17in) München 2001

MAATEN van der Jacob Jan 1820-1879 [20]
$3 225 - €2 719 - **£1 914** - FF17 836
The «Doesburgermolen», Ede Oil/canvas (33x53cm 12x20in) Amsterdam 1998
$7 990 - €9 076 - **£5 606** - FF59 532
Dusk, Cattle returning home on a Path along a River, a Village beyond Oil/panel (20.5x31cm 8x12in) Amsterdam 2001

MAATSCH Thilo 1900-1983 [35]
$3 500 - €3 372 - **£2 162** - FF22 116
Frauenbild Oil/canvas (69x71cm 27x27in) New-York 1999
$855 - €817 - **£534** - FF5 357
Abstract Composition Gouache (28.5x20cm 11x7in)
Amsterdam 1999

MABE Manabu 1924-1997 [22]
$11 000 - €11 807 - **£7 361** - FF77 451
Dama do Céu Oil/canvas/panel (129.5x129.5cm 50x50in) New-York 2000
$7 500 - €6 540 - **£4 534** - FF42 897
Energía Oil/canvas (63.5x71cm 25x27in) New-York 1998

MABERRY Philip XX [5]
$3 500 - €3 626 - **£2 227** - FF23 783
Two Nudes Glazed ceramic (38x36x25cm 14x14x9in)
New-York 2000

MAC (Macario Gomez) XX [3]
$727 - €702 - **£450** - FF4 602
«El Hombre que sabia Demasiado» Poster (197x67cm 77x26in) London 1999

MAC AVOY Édouard 1905-1991 [123]
$2 345 - €2 363 - **£1 461** - FF15 500
Vue d'un port Huile/toile (81x116cm 31x45in) Paris 2000
$1 082 - €1 006 - **£657** - FF6 600
Fillette assise Huile/toile (27x22cm 10x8in) Calais 1998
$1 000 - €1 102 - **£667** - FF7 227
Steamship Approaching Harbor Watercolour/paper (36x54cm 14x21in) Portsmouth NH 2000

MACALLISTER Therese XX [8]
$1 544 - €1 778 - **£1 053** - FF11 660
Bowl of Fruit Oil/canvas/board (30x38cm 11x14in)
Dublin 2000

MACALLUM John Thomas Hamilton 1841-1896 [23]
$1 615 - €1 379 - **£900** - FF9 047
Girl with Shrimping Net Watercolour/paper (33.5x59cm 13x23in) Lymington 1998

McALPINE William XIX [43]
$2 116 - €2 470 - **£1 500** - FF16 203
The battle of Trafalgar, 21st October 1805 Oil/canvas (76x127cm 29x50in) London 2001

MACARA Andrew 1944 [44]
$877 - €1 006 - **£600** - FF6 601
Vegetable Garden, San Bartolmeo, Italy Oil/canvas (40x55cm 16x22in) Par, Cornwall 2000
$410 - €439 - **£280** - FF2 880
Green Gate, Cyprus Oil/canvas (30x40cm 11x15in)
London 2001

MACARDELL James 1710/28-1765 [15]
$998 - €855 - **£600** - FF5 608
Portrait of the young Benjamin Hallet (b.1742) with cello Engraving (47x23cm 18x9in) London 1998

MACARRON JAIME Ricardo 1926 [23]
$1 982 - €1 952 - **£1 235** - FF12 805
Niña Oleo/lienzo (46x38cm 18x14in) Madrid 1999
$671 - €661 - **£418** - FF4 334
Paisaje Oleo/tablex (27x35cm 10x13in) Madrid 1999

MACARTHUR Charles M. XIX [12]
$582 - €551 - **£360** - FF3 612
View of Henrietta Street, St. Mary's Church with Fisherfolk Watercolour/paper (28x43cm 11x17in)
Whitby, Yorks 1999

MACAULAY Kate act.1872-1896 [5]
$866 - €930 - **£580** - FF6 102
A Quiet Day in Loch Tarbert Watercolour/paper (39.5x75cm 15x29in) London 2000

McAULEY Charles J. 1910-1999 [28]
$4 800 - €4 766 - **£3 000** - FF31 262
Blue Waters, Cushendun Oil/canvas (40x60cm 16x24in) Belfast 1999

McAULIFFE James J. 1848-1921 [19]
$1 800 - €1 983 - **£1 200** - FF13 009
Clipper Ship on High Seas with Lookout in Crow's Nest Oil/canvas (50x76cm 20x30in)
Portsmouth NH 2000
$4 500 - €5 352 - **£3 100** - FF35 105
Goldsmith Maid, BM 2:14 Oil/board (27x37cm 11x14in) Bolton MA 2000

McAULIFFE John 1830-1931 [3]
$6 000 - €5 957 - **£3 750** - FF39 075
Count Weeks with Trotter in Old Fleetwood Park Oil/canvas (61x91cm 24x35in) New-York 1999

McBEAN Angus 1904-1990 [62]
$391 - €454 - **£270** - FF2 976
Self Portrait with Third Eye Gelatin silver print (24x18cm 9x7in) Vancouver, BC. 2000

MACBETH Robert Walker 1848-1910 [51]
$8 252 - €9 588 - **£5 800** - FF62 896
The Ballad Seller Oil/board (28x43cm 11x16in)
London 2001
$107 - €120 - **£75** - FF790
Two seated fisherman Pencil/paper (25.5x21.5cm 10x8in) Penzance, Cornwall 2001
$272 - €233 - **£160** - FF1 526
Bacchus and Ariadne, after Titian Engraving (64.5x71cm 25x27in) Glasgow 1998

MACBETH-RAEBURN Henry 1860-1947 [43]
$153 - €129 - **£90** - FF849
Portrait of General Hay MacDowell Mezzotint (67x41cm 26x16in) Oxford 1998

McBEY James 1883-1959 [208]
$2 561 - €2 533 - **£1 600** - FF16 615
Antibes Oil/canvas (46x61cm 18x24in) Glasgow 1999

🖼 **$1 327** – €1 483 - **£900** – FF9 730
The Lock Gates Watercolour (28x27.5cm 11x10in)
Edinburgh 2000

📷 **$425** – €446 - **£284** – FF2 923
Portrait of George W.Davison/Portrait of Dr.ASW Rosenbach/ Etching (24x16cm 9x6in) New-York 2001

MACBRIDE Will 1931 [30]

📷 **$899** – €767 - **£542** – FF5 030
Studie, München Gelatin silver print (37.6x55.9cm 14x22in) Köln 1998

MacBRIDE William ?-1913 [11]

📷 **$1 600** – €1 583 - **£1 000** – FF10 384
End of the Day Oil/canvas (65x105.5cm 25x41in)
Glasgow 1999

MacBRYDE Robert 1913-1966 [37]

📷 **$8 235** – €7 833 - **£5 000** – FF51 378
A Wee Glasgow Buddy Oil/canvas (76x102cm 29x40in) Edinburgh 1999

📷 **$460** – €525 - **£320** – FF3 447
Seated Woman with Fish Lithograph (38x30cm 14x11in) London 2000

MacCABE Gladys 1918 [71]

📷 **$2 010** – €2 159 - **£1 345** – FF14 159
Clown with Black Puppy Oil/canvas (48x38cm 18x14in) Dublin 2000

📷 **$1 774** – €1 905 - **£1 187** – FF12 493
Clown Oil/board (41x28cm 16x11in) Dublin 2000

📷 **$618** – €564 - **£380** – FF3 698
Riverside Houses Watercolour/paper (41x62cm 16x24in) Co. Kilkenny 1999

MACCAHON Colin 1919-1987 [31]

📷 **$57 932** – €68 041 - **£41 132** – FF446 320
South Canterbury Landscape Oil/board (60x59cm 23x23in) Auckland 2000

📷 **$27 544** – €28 621 - **£17 270** – FF187 742
Waterfall Enamel (30.5x30.5cm 12x12in) Auckland 2000

📷 **$19 946** – €22 725 - **£13 785** – FF149 065
«Northland» Ink (63x50cm 24x19in) Auckland 2000

📷 **$725** – €813 - **£507** – FF5 334
North Otago Landscape Screenprint (47x57.5cm 18x22in) Auckland 2001

McCAIG Norman J. 1929 [62]

📷 **$1 787** – €2 032 - **£1 234** – FF13 326
Corrib Fishing Boats Oil/board (45x60cm 18x24in)
Dublin 2000

📷 **$938** – €1 105 - **£659** – FF7 246
Sunset, Cliffs of Moher Oil/canvas/board (38x29cm 14x11in) Dublin 2000

MACCAIN Buck 1943 [4]

📷 **$1 800** – €2 112 - **£1 270** – FF13 856
Night Scene with India Oil/board (31.5x34.5cm 12x13in) New-York 2000

McCALL Charles James 1907-1989 [71]

📷 **$1 656** – €1 533 - **£1 000** – FF10 058
Full Length Portrait of a Man in Dark Coast and Fedora Oil/canvas (60x40cm 23x15in) Edinburgh 1999

📷 **$987** – €928 - **£600** – FF6 089
Woman at a Dressing-Table Oil/board (51x25cm 20x9in) London 1999

McCALL Robert 1919 [10]

📷 **$1 066** – €1 230 - **£750** – FF8 070
«2001: A Space Odyssey» Poster (104x68.5cm 40x26in) London 2000

McCALLIEN William J. act.1899-1913 [2]

📷 **$4 596** – €5 140 - **£3 200** – FF33 713
Washing the Net, Tarbet, Loch Fyn Oil/canvas (45.75x84cm 17x33in) Penzance, Cornwall 2001

McCANCE William 1894-1970 [8]

📷 **$1 001** – €896 - **£600** – FF5 876
Standing Nude/Standing Woman Pencil (47x30cm 18x11in) Perthshire 1998

MACCARI Mino 1898-1989 [729]

📷 **$4 000** – €5 183 - **£3 000** – FF34 000
I fidanzati Olio/tavola (40x61cm 15x24in) Prato 2000

📷 **$1 800** – €1 866 - **£1 080** – FF12 240
Tartaruga Olio/cartone/tela (25x34.5cm 9x13in) Roma 2001

📷 **$3 520** – €4 561 - **£2 640** – FF29 920
Il pittore e la modella Terracotta (34x24x20cm 13x9x7in) Roma 2001

📷 **$714** – €617 - **£476** – FF4 046
Il furto Carboncino/carta (25x34cm 9x13in) Milano 1998

📷 **$198** – €171 - **£99** – FF1 122
Autoritratto Acquaforte (25x16cm 9x6in) Prato 1999

MacCARTAN Edward 1879-1947 [14]

📷 **$700 000** – €775 226 - **£474 740** – FF5 085 150
Diana Bronze (H210.5cm H82in) New-York 2000

📷 **$500** – €8 794 - **£5 395** – FF57 686
Pan Bronze (H38.5cm H15in) New-York 2001

📷 **$16 000** – €15 515 - **£10 136** – FF101 772
Figural Fountain Pan Bronze (H77.5cm H30in) New-York 1999

MACCARTER Henry Bainbridge 1866-1942 [13]

📷 **$9 000** – €7 593 - **£5 279** – FF49 806
Cathedral Mill University Oil/canvas (103x87.5cm 40x34in) New-York 1998

McCARTHY Brian XX [2]

📷 **$2 316** – €2 666 - **£1 580** – FF17 490
Gerberas Oil/canvas (46x61cm 18x24in) Dublin 2000

McCARTHY Doris Jean 1910 [24]

📷 **$2 129** – €1 929 - **£1 328** – FF12 655
Bull Rushes, Haliburton Oil/canvas (61x76cm 24x29in) Toronto 1999

📷 **$5 425** – €5 823 - **£3 685** – FF38 197
Boatson the Beach Oil/canvas (24x27cm 9x10in) Calgary, Alberta 2001

📷 **$521** – €605 - **£360** – FF3 969
Early Spring Broughton Island, NWT Watercolour/paper (38x55cm 15x22in) Calgary, Alberta 2000

McCARTHY Frank C. 1924 [57]

📷 **$30 000** – €27 272 - **£18 069** – FF178 890
Warriors of the Neartooth Oil/canvas (60x101cm 24x40in) Hayden ID 1998

📷 **$4 950** – €4 623 - **£3 055** – FF30 323
The Scout Oil/board (30x22cm 12x9in) Dallas TX 1999

📷 **$375** – €444 - **£265** – FF2 910
Big Medicine Color lithograph (49x81cm 19x32in) Portland OR 2001

McCARTHY Helen Kiner 1884-? [2]

📷 **$2 000** – €2 352 - **£1 434** – FF15 427
Gathering Flowers Oil/canvas (30.5x40.5cm 12x15in) Philadelphia PA 2001

McCARTHY Justin 1891-1977 [43]

📷 **$2 500** – €2 087 - **£1 466** – FF13 691
Fashion Fare Oil/panel (51.5x43cm 20x16in) New-York 1998

McCARTHY Paul 1945 [8]

✏️ **$16 437** - €17 644 - **£11 000** - FF115 737
Man Fucking a Tree, Garden Felt pen/paper (220x150cm 86x59in) London 2000

📷 **$4 800** - €5 266 - **£3 188** - FF34 544
Hot Dog Cibachrome print (103.5x78cm 40x30in) New-York 2000

MACCARTNEY Linda 1942-1998 [58]

📷 **$390** - €459 - **£280** - FF3 012
Jimi Hendrix at Miami Pop Photograph (25.5x20cm 10x7in) London 2001

MACCAW Dan 1942 [7]

🖼 **$3 400** - €3 860 - **£2 362** - FF25 323
Ideal Day Oil/canvas (60x76cm 24x30in) Dallas TX 2001

McCAW Terence 1913-1978 [58]

🖼 **$1 516** - €1 786 - **£1 048** - FF11 718
Elim Mission, Cape Oil/canvas/board (60x75cm 23x29in) Cape Town 2000

🖼 **$438** - €491 - **£306** - FF3 224
Farm Cottages Oil/canvas/board (34.5x44.5cm 13x17in) Cape Town 2001

McCAY Winsor 1871-1934 [37]

✏️ **$20 900** - €17 830 - **£12 606** - FF116 956
Little Nemo in Slumberland, August 22 Ink/paper (70x54cm 27x21in) New-York 1998

MACCHERONI Henri 1932 [13]

📷 **$505** - €488 - **£319** - FF3 200
Sans titre Photo (24x17.5cm 9x6in) Paris 1999

McCHESNEY Clara Taggart 1860-1928 [4]

🖼 **$1 900** - €1 754 - **£1 168** - FF11 506
Dutch Girl by Fireplace Oil/board (91x78cm 36x31in) Hatfield PA 1999

MACCHIATI Serafino 1860-1916 [43]

🖼 **$4 800** - €6 220 - **£3 600** - FF40 800
Paesaggio Olio/tela (46x55cm 18x21in) Milano 2000

🖼 **$1 800** - €2 332 - **£1 350** - FF15 300
La spiaggia Olio/tavola (18x22.5cm 7x8in) Milano 2000

✏️ **$1 750** - €1 814 - **£1 050** - FF11 900
Bretagna Pastelli/tela (38x61cm 14x24in) Vercelli 1999

MACCIO Romulo 1931 [25]

🖼 **$15 000** - €17 428 - **£10 542** - FF114 318
Marina Taborski en el Boulmich Acrylic/canvas (161.5x130cm 63x51in) New-York 2001

🖼 **$7 500** - €7 297 - **£4 616** - FF47 867
La fuerza de la costumbre Oil/canvas (104x84cm 40x33in) New-York 1999

MACCIOTTA Giovanni 1927-1993 [13]

🖼 **$500** - €518 - **£300** - FF3 400
Figure Olio/cartone (43x32cm 16x12in) Torino 2001

McCLEAN Bruce XX [2]

📶 **$595** - €705 - **£420** - FF4 627
Untitled Screenprint in colors (115x142cm 45x55in) London 2000

McCLELLAN John Ward 1908-1986 [9]

📶 **$200** - €186 - **£123** - FF1 222
Nude with Tulips Lithograph (34x23cm 13x9in) Cleveland OH 1999

McCLELLAND Suzanne 1959 [17]

🖼 **$3 800** - €3 242 - **£2 292** - FF21 264
«Someday» Mixed media/canvas (101.5x101.5cm 39x39in) New-York 1998

MACCLINTOCK Herbert 1906-1985 [5]

🖼 **$6 298** - €7 392 - **£4 444** - FF48 486
Men in the Wheatfield Oil/board (61x72cm 24x28in) Nedlands 2000

McCLOSKEY Alberta Binford 1863-1911 [4]

🖼 **$42 500** - €44 054 - **£26 949** - FF288 974
Still Life with Fruit and Flowers on a Tabletop Oil/canvas (61x82cm 24x32in) New-York 2000

McCLOSKEY William Joseph 1859-1941 [9]

🖼 **$185 000** - €158 061 - **£111 943** - FF1 036 814
Wrapped Oranges Oil/canvas (30x61cm 11x24in) San-Francisco CA 1998

🖼 **$120 000** - €140 051 - **£85 068** - FF918 672
Wrapped Lemons Oil/canvas (25.5x43cm 10x16in) New-York 2001

MACCLOY Samuel 1831-1904 [17]

🖼 **$11 476** - €12 063 - **£7 200** - FF79 125
Hide and Go Seek Oil/canvas (35.5x31cm 13x12in) Dublin 2000

✏️ **$4 731** - €5 079 - **£3 166** - FF33 316
St.Catherine's Point Watercolour (46x76cm 18x29in) Dublin 2000

McCLURE David 1926-1998 [56]

🖼 **$13 885** - €15 482 - **£9 500** - FF101 552
Still Life with Flags Oil/panel (127x101.5cm 50x39in) Perthshire 2000

🖼 **$4 303** - €4 777 - **£3 000** - FF31 334
Maltese Fishing boats Oil/canvas/board (40.5x51cm 15x20in) London 2001

🖼 **$2 210** - €2 316 - **£1 400** - FF15 194
Flowers and Gourd Oil/paper (29x34cm 11x13in) Edinburgh 2000

✏️ **$1 447** - €1 236 - **£850** - FF8 110
Dundee Magnolia Watercolour (48x33cm 18x12in) Glasgow 1998

McCLYMONT John I. XIX-XX [12]

🖼 **$4 482** - €4 812 - **£3 000** - FF31 564
Still Life Oil/canvas (35.5x48.5cm 13x19in) London 2000

MACCO Georg 1863-1933 [82]

🖼 **$2 835** - €2 592 - **£1 735** - FF17 000
Halte devant les ruines de Palmyre Huile/toile (52.5x76.5cm 20x30in) Paris 1999

🖼 **$507** - €562 - **£352** - FF3 689
Madonna di Campiglio bei Bozen Öl/Karton (31x42cm 12x16in) Köln 2001

McCOLLUM Allan 1944 [87]

🖼 **$22 414** - €24 060 - **£15 000** - FF157 824
144 Plaster Surrogates No.1 Enamel (174.5x335.5cm 68x132in) London 2000

🖼 **$8 500** - €9 862 - **£5 868** - FF63 693
Eight Plaster Surrogates Enamel (139x24.5cm 54x9in) New-York 2000

🖼 **$4 200** - €4 039 - **£2 587** - FF26 492
Four Surrogates Enamel/panel (15x11cm 5x4in) New-York 1999

🗝 **$13 000** - €11 090 - **£7 841** - FF72 748
Perfect Vehicle Object (198x91.5x91.5cm 77x36x36in) New-York 1998

McCOMAS Francis John 1875-1938 [28]

✏️ **$3 750** - €3 607 - **£2 314** - FF23 658
The Village Road Watercolour (36x39cm 14x15in) Boston MA 1999

M

McCOMAS Gene Francis 1886-1982 [8]
  $2 750 - €2 350 - £1 664 - FF15 414
  The Sun Goes Down in Tahiti/Tahitian House
  Oil/canvas/board (28x35cm 11x13in) San-Francisco CA
  1998

McCOMBE Leonard 1923 [1]
  $3 500 - €3 291 - £2 167 - FF21 590
  Swimming Champion Keith Carter Gelatin silver
  print (35x28.5cm 13x11in) New-York 1999

McCONNELL George 1852-1929 [16]
  $518 - €476 - £319 - FF3 122
  River Landscapes Oil/canvas (34x22cm 13x9in)
  New-York 1998

MACCONNICO Hilton XX [1]
  $1 514 - €1 677 - £1 027 - FF11 000
  Terre 2000 (texte de l'auteur) Aquarelle (76x60cm
  29x23in) Paris 2000

McCORD George Herbert 1848-1909 [80]
  $2 600 - €2 462 - £1 580 - FF16 151
  Venice Oil/canvas (77x51cm 30x20in) New-York 1999
  $2 500 - €2 775 - £1 738 - FF18 206
  Sunset Glow Oil/canvas (15x25cm 6x10in) Milford
  CT 2001

MacCORD Mary Nicholena 1864-1955 [13]
  $650 - €696 - £442 - FF4 564
  Hillside Farm Gouache/paper (50x66cm 20x26in)
  Portsmouth NH 2001

McCORMICK Arthur David 1860-1943 [59]
  $14 669 - €13 337 - £9 000 - FF87 488
  The Temptation of Monmouth Oil/canvas
  (129x102cm 50x40in) London 1999
  $3 075 - €3 301 - £2 058 - FF21 655
  Cavaliers in an Inn Oil/canvas (41x56cm 16x22in)
  Dublin 2000
  $1 231 - €1 429 - £850 - FF9 372
  Nelson in Chase of the French Fleet Watercolour
  (44x31cm 17x12in) London 2000

McCORMICK Katherine Hood 1882-1960 [3]
  $1 200 - €1 037 - £712 - FF6 802
  Lobster Shacks, Mensha, Martha's Vineyard
  Woodcut (21x27cm 8x11in) Provincetown MA 1998

McCORMICK S. Barret 1890-? [1]
  $220 000 - €205 935 - £136 334 - FF1 350 844
  King Kong Poster (206x104cm 81x40in) New-York
  1999

McCOUCH Gordon Mallet 1885-1956 [8]
  $3 333 - €3 964 - £2 375 - FF26 001
  Stadtlandschaft Oil/canvas/panel (49x66cm 19x25in)
  Zürich 2000
  $6 188 - €6 531 - £3 886 - FF40 901
  Gebirgslandschaft Öl/Karton (30x42cm 11x16in)
  Zürich 2000

MACCOY Ann Wyeth 1882-1945 [1]
  $4 000 - €4 294 - £2 676 - FF28 164
  Still Life Watercolour/paper (33x48cm 13x19in)
  Portland ME 2000

McCOY John W. 1909 [4]
  $1 500 - €1 645 - £1 018 - FF10 792
  Boat in estuary Delaware on Single Trawler
  Watercolour/paper (48x34cm 19x13in) Thomaston ME
  2000

MACCOY Wilton Charles 1902-1986 [16]
  $2 600 - €2 788 - £1 720 - FF18 286
  Smoke Tree Oil/board (30x40cm 12x16in) New-
  Orleans LA 2000

McCRACKEN Francis 1879-1959 [6]
  $200 - €235 - £138 - FF1 541
  Melons and Grapes Serigraph in colors (27x35cm
  11x14in) Cincinnati OH 2000

McCRACKEN Francis 1879-1959 [6]
  $8 488 - €9 670 - £5 866 - FF63 432
  Landscape in Spain Oil/canvas (44x54cm 17x21in)
  Auckland 2000
  $1 485 - €1 692 - £1 026 - FF11 100
  Boat Harbour Watercolour/paper (23x26.5cm 9x10in)
  Auckland 2000

McCRACKEN James XX [9]
  $2 100 - €2 402 - £1 460 - FF15 757
  Migrating Herons Oil/board (81x81cm 32x32in)
  Cincinnati OH 2000

McCRACKEN John Harvey 1934 [31]
  $24 000 - €23 222 - £14 800 - FF152 325
  Untitled Acrylic (244x38x9cm 96x14x3in) New-York
  1999
  $17 000 - €19 725 - £11 736 - FF129 387
  «Portal» Sculpture, wood (292x46x4cm 114x18x1in)
  New-York 2000
  $15 000 - €17 404 - £10 356 - FF114 165
  «Cherokee» Sculpture (16.5x244x31cm 6x96x12in)
  New-York 2000

McCRADY John 1911-1968 [60]
  $46 000 - €39 409 - £27 655 - FF258 506
  Mississippi Storm Mixed media/canvas (58x76cm
  23x30in) New-Orleans LA 1998
  $2 900 - €2 433 - £1 701 - FF15 960
  Five O'Clock at Norco Watercolour/paper (36x56cm
  14x22in) New-Orleans LA 1998
  $1 050 - €881 - £616 - FF5 778
  «Steamboat Round the Bend» Lithograph
  (26x39cm 10x15in) New-Orleans LA 1998

MACCREA Harold Wellington 1887-1969 [11]
  $1 464 - €1 253 - £881 - FF8 221
  «The End of the Day» Oil/canvas (51x61cm
  20x24in) Toronto 1998

MACCREA Joel XX [1]
  $5 000 - €4 680 - £3 098 - FF30 701
  «The Palm Beach Story» Poster (206x104cm
  81x40in) New-York 1999

MACCRICKARD Kate 1974 [2]
  $4 000 - €3 452 - £2 420 - FF22 642
  Infanta Watercolour (182x182cm 71x71in) Tel Aviv
  1999

McCROSSAN Mary 1865-1934 [36]
  $5 268 - €4 951 - £3 200 - FF32 478
  Amalfi Oil/canvas (61x51cm 24x20in) London 1999

MACCRUM George Herbert 1888-? [1]
  $14 000 - €11 980 - £8 428 - FF78 586
  Snow and stream Oil/canvas (91x101cm 36x40in)
  New-York 1998

McCUBBIN Frederick 1855-1917 [65]
  $1 246 350 - €1 142 558 - £771 120 - FF7 494 690
  Bush Idyll Oil/canvas (119.5x221.5cm 47x87in)
  Melbourne 1998
  $54 714 - €47 258 - £33 048 - FF309 995
  The Sheltered Pool Oil/canvas (50x60.8cm 19x23in)
  Malvern, Victoria 1998
  $17 642 - €19 761 - £12 257 - FF129 625
  The Country Lane/Farm House Oil/board
  (23.5x34.5cm 9x13in) Melbourne 2001

M

MACCUBBIN Louis 1890-1952 **[17]**
- **$1 086** - €1 045 - **£669** - FF6 853
  Grey and Silver Oil/canvas (45x60cm 17x23in)
  Melbourne 1999

McCULLOCH Horatio 1805-1867 **[68]**
- **$358 835** - €321 023 - **£215 000** - FF2 105 774
  Kilchurn Castle, Loch Awe Oil/canvas
  (115.5x184cm 45x72in) Perthshire 1998
- **$3 451** - €3 832 - **£2 400** - FF25 139
  On the Banks of Loch Lomond Oil/canvas
  (45.5x60cm 17x24in) Glasgow 2001
- **$3 221** - €3 027 - **£2 000** - FF19 858
  View of a Loch Oil/panel (28x23cm 11x9in) London
  1999

MacCULLOCH James c.1850-1915 **[14]**
- **$415** - €427 - €260 - FF2 798
  Figures in an Extensive Highland Landscape
  Watercolour (21x37cm 8x14in) London 2000

McCURRY Steve 1950 **[3]**
- **$8 500** - €9 655 - **£5 964** - FF63 331
  Afghan Refugee Dye-transfer print (68x45cm
  26x17in) New-York 2001

MACDANIEL Henry XX **[7]**
- **$1 900** - €1 774 - **£1 172** - FF11 639
  Where the Mohawk River Joins Watercolour
  (56x76cm 22x30in) Detroit MI 1999

McDERMITT William Thomas 1884-1961 **[5]**
- **$1 900** - €2 220 - **£1 356** - FF14 565
  Stage in atmospheric landscape Oil/canvas
  (63x76cm 25x30in) Altadena CA 2001

McDERMOTT & McGOUGH David & Peter
1952/1958 **[40]**
- **$3 200** - €2 993 - **£1 934** - FF19 633
  Tea Pot of Sixty Years Ago Photograph (35.5x28cm
  13x11in) New-York 1999

McDERMOTT David 1952 **[2]**
- **$2 750** - €2 586 - **£1 703** - FF16 966
  **The World, Seen and Unseen, of McDermott and
  McGough** Gelatin silver print (24x20cm 9x7in) New-
  York 1999

MACDONALD Grant 1944 **[17]**
- **$22 000** - €21 356 - **£13 587** - FF140 085
  Sunset at Santa Fe Oil/canvas (101x152cm 40x60in)
  Dallas TX 1999
- **$9 000** - €10 219 - **£6 253** - FF67 032
  Morning in Luxembourg Garden Oil/canvas
  (60x91cm 24x36in) Dallas TX 2001

MACDONALD Harold L. 1861-? **[1]**
- **$5 500** - €5 234 - **£3 440** - FF34 333
  Still Life with Roses in a Pitcher Oil/canvas
  (60x45cm 24x18in) New-York 1999

MACDONALD J. Tim XIX-XX **[21]**
- **$540** - €632 - **£380** - FF4 147
  Unloading the Catch Watercolour/paper (14.5x24cm
  5x9in) Oxfordshire 2000

MacDONALD James Edward Hervey 1873-1932
[144]
- **$2 700** - €2 898 - **£1 806** - FF19 010
  River View, Autumn Oil/canvas (63x76cm 25x30in)
  Bolton MA 2000
- **$7 487** - €7 104 - **£4 549** - FF46 598
  In the Barn Oil/board (23x18cm 9x7in) Calgary,
  Alberta 1999
- **$682** - €661 - **£421** - FF4 333
  Word to us all Ink (27.5x20.5cm 10x8in) Toronto
  1999

- **$113** - €132 - **£78** - FF867
  Georgian Bay Etching in colors (6x7.5cm 2x3in)
  Toronto 2000

MACDONALD James W.G., Jock 1897-1960 **[22]**
- **$6 518** - €7 563 - **£4 500** - FF49 613
  Jardin, Riviera Garden Oil/canvas (81x99.5cm
  31x39in) Vancouver, BC. 2000
- **$5 449** - €5 237 - **£3 356** - FF34 352
  Glacier, Garibaldi park Oil/panel (30.5x38cm
  12x14in) Vancouver, BC. 1999
- **$1 785** - €2 019 - **£1 256** - FF13 243
  «Fish and Shrimps» Watercolour/paper (24x34cm
  9x13in) Vancouver, BC. 2001

MacDONALD John Blake 1829-1901 **[33]**
- **$11 221** - €10 600 - **£7 000** - FF69 533
  Prince Charles Stuart's Flight Oil/canvas
  (100x140cm 39x55in) Perthshire 1999
- **$1 339** - €1 275 - **£850** - FF5 863
  Mother and Child in a Cottage Interior Oil/canvas
  (41x52cm 16x20in) Billingshurst, West-Sussex 1999
- **$1 006** - €1 080 - **£673** - FF7 086
  Cattle watering in the Shallows of the Lock
  Oil/canvas (30x45.5cm 11x17in) Montréal 2000

MacDONALD Lawrence 1799-1878 **[11]**
- **$2 332** - €2 652 - **£1 600** - FF17 396
  Bust of a Gentleman Marble (H61cm H24in)
  London 2000

MacDONALD Manly Edward 1889-1971 **[96]**
- **$2 577** - €2 224 - **£1 549** - FF14 588
  Streamside Mill in Winter Oil/canvas (71x91.5cm
  27x36in) Nepean, Ont. 1998
- **$973** - €823 - **£582** - FF5 399
  Fall River Scene Oil/canvas/board (30.5x40.5cm
  12x15in) Toronto 1998

MacDONALD Murray act.1889-1910 **[15]**
- **$1 157** - €1 284 - **£800** - FF8 423
  After the Days Toil Oil/canvas/board (35.5x25.5cm
  13x10in) London 2001

MacDONALD Thoreau 1901-1989 **[55]**
- **$233** - €252 - **£156** - FF1 652
  Mac Donald House, Thornhill Ink/paper
  (14.5x20.5cm 5x8in) Calgary, Alberta 2000
- **$115** - €107 - **£70** - FF704
  Deer Silkscreen (20x24cm 8x9in) Toronto 1998

MACDONALD William Alister 1861-1948 **[80]**
- **$583** - €565 - **£360** - FF3 705
  York Minster from the Roman Wall
  Watercolour/paper (26.5x36cm 10x14in) West-Yorkshire
  1999

MACDONALD-WRIGHT Stanton 1890-1973 **[37]**
- **$40 000** - €38 066 - **£25 020** - FF249 696
  L'Age D'Or Oil/panel (244x122cm 96x48in) New-York
  1999
- **$13 000** - €14 785 - **£9 083** - FF96 981
  «Première Enfance» Oil/canvas (122x91.5cm
  48x36in) Beverly-Hills CA 2000
- **$4 200** - €4 769 - **£2 874** - FF31 283
  Spring Stream Watercolour (30x48cm 11x18in) New-
  York 2000
- **$550** - €466 - **£329** - FF3 056
  **From Kyoto Series: No. 8 Buson/No. 18 «In the
  Hand the Firefly...»** Woodcut in colors (45.5x54.5cm
  17x21in) San-Francisco CA 1998

McDONNELL Hector 1947 **[20]**
- **$5 249** - €5 079 - **£3 236** - FF33 316
  Mary's Bathroom Oil/canvas (76x38cm 29x14in)
  Dublin 1999

$3 276 - €2 795 - **£1 952** - FF18 333
Sawmills Arch, St. James Market Oil/board (30x16cm 11x6in) Dublin 1998

McDOUGAL John act.1877-c.1941 [46]
$866 - €817 - **£540** - FF5 360
The Majesty of Sea and Rock Cemaes Bay Anglesey Watercolour/paper (41x64cm 16x25in) Birmingham 1999

MACDOWELL William 1888-1950 [20]
$1 599 - €1 830 - **£1 100** - FF12 005
Shipping on the Thames Watercolour/paper (30x48cm 12x19in) Bournemouth, Dorset 2000

MACDUFF Frederick H. 1931 [29]
$2 600 - €3 049 - **£1 855** - FF20 000
Figures on the Beach Oil/canvas (53x64cm 21x25in) Delray-Beach FL 2000
$2 395 - €2 301 - **£1 476** - FF15 092
Badewagen am Strand Öl/Leinwand (28x35.5cm 11x13in) München 1999

MACDUFF William ?-c.1876 [2]
$13 176 - €12 532 - **£8 000** - FF82 205
Christmas Morning in an English Cottage Oil/canvas (60.5x83cm 23x32in) Edinburgh 1999

MACE John Edmund 1889-? [26]
$1 820 - €2 118 - **£1 300** - FF13 891
On the Scent/Gone to Ground Oil/canvas (51x61cm 20x24in) London 2001
$988 - €1 146 - **£700** - FF7 519
«The English Lakes, Scafell and Wastwater, LMS» Poster (102x127cm 40x50in) London 2000

McELCHERAN William Hadd 1927-1999 [42]
$4 020 - €4 435 - **£2 658** - FF29 091
Businessman Walking Bronze (38x28x12.5cm 14x11x4in) Vancouver, BC. 2000

McELHENY Josiah 1966 [1]
$22 000 - €25 076 - **£15 349** - FF164 491
Studies in the Search for Infinity Installation (51x366x20.5cm 20x144x8in) New-York 2001

McENTAGART Brett 1939 [17]
$1 304 - €1 270 - **£801** - FF8 329
Boats on the Canal, towards Baggot Street, Dublin Oil/board (60x45cm 24x18in) Dublin 1999

McENTEE Jervis 1828-1891 [47]
$24 000 - €20 509 - **£14 097** - FF134 529
Figures by a Woodland Shack in Autumn Oil/canvas (40.5x81cm 15x31in) Boston MA 1998
$1 800 - €1 728 - **£1 115** - FF11 338
Farmhouse in the Valley Oil/board (20x30cm 8x12in) Detroit MI 1999

MACENTYRE Eduardo 1929 [6]
$1 100 - €1 089 - **£684** - FF7 145
Bandas violetas Acrilico/papel (80x80cm 31x31in) Buenos-Aires 1999

McEVOY Arthur Ambrose 1878-1927 [71]
$6 488 - €6 255 - **£4 000** - FF41 028
Lydia Lopokova in spanish Costume Oil/canvas (76x63.5cm 29x25in) London 1999
$2 440 - €2 736 - **£1 700** - FF17 947
Early Morning, Dieppe Oil/paper (22.5x30.5cm 8x12in) London 2001
$506 - €590 - **£350** - FF3 872
Bedside Vigil Ink (25.5x24cm 10x9in) London 2000

McEWAN Tom 1846-1914 [64]
$5 208 - €4 468 - **£3 148** - FF29 305
Watching Grannie Spin Oil/canvas (58.5x44.5cm 23x17in) Toronto 1998

$1 549 - €1 731 - **£1 050** - FF11 352
Granny Oil/canvas (24.5x19.5cm 9x7in) Edinburgh 2000

McEWEN Jean Albert 1923-1999 [59]
$12 892 - €14 109 - **£8 894** - FF92 550
«Blason de Chevalier Rouge» Acrylic/canvas (190x287cm 75x113in) Vancouver, BC. 2001
$3 198 - €3 087 - **£1 981** - FF20 249
De ma main à la couleur Huile/toile (117x89cm 46x35in) Montréal 1999
$297 - €347 - **£210** - FF22 277
Abstract Watercolour/paper (35x25cm 13x9in) Channel-Islands 2000
$196 - €215 - **£135** - FF1 413
Abstraction Lithographie (63x46cm 24x18in) Montréal 2001

McEWEN Rory 1932-1982 [8]
$1 111 - €1 239 - **£750** - FF8 127
Chicory Watercolour, gouache/vellum (61x67cm 24x26in) Edinburgh 2000
$1 555 - €1 735 - **£1 050** - FF11 378
Lobster Etching (34x42.5cm 13x16in) Edinburgh 2000

MacEWEN Walter 1860-1943 [24]
$32 000 - €34 349 - **£21 414** - FF225 312
An Ancester Oil/canvas (190x85.5cm 74x33in) New-York 2000
$22 000 - €21 945 - **£13 734** - FF143 952
The Chess Players Oil/canvas (55x45cm 22x18in) Cincinnati OH 1999

McFALL David 1919-1988 [6]
$9 373 - €9 173 - **£6 000** - FF60 172
Bust of Winston Churchill «The Rocquebrune Head» Bronze (H38.5cm H15in) London 1999

MACFARLANE Alasdair ?-c.1940 [9]
$1 116 - €1 068 - **£700** - FF7 003
«The Clyde Coast, British Railways» Poster (100x127cm 39x50in) London 1999

McFARLANE Duncan XIX [5]
$80 000 - €88 144 - **£53 368** - FF578 184
American Ship Clara Wheeler, Pilot Schonner the Duke Off Point Lyras Oil/canvas (60x91cm 24x36in) Portsmouth NH 2000

McFAYDEN Jock 1950 [8]
$1 540 - €1 801 - **£1 100** - FF11 812
Second Away, Round 6 Oil/canvas (101x101cm 39x39in) London 2001

McFEE Henry Lee 1886-1953 [13]
$5 000 - €5 367 - **£3 346** - FF35 205
Landscape Oil/canvas (61.5x76.5cm 24x30in) New-York 2000

McGARRY Pip 1955 [21]
$2 419 - €2 198 - **£1 500** - FF14 420
Siberian Tiger Cubs Oil/canvas (50x75cm 19x29in) Billingshurst, West-Sussex 1999

MACGARY Dave 1958 [8]
$8 000 - €9 084 - **£5 558** - FF59 584
Touch the Clouds Bronze (H69cm H27in) Dallas TX 2001

McGEEHAN Jessie M. ?-1913 [23]
$5 983 - €6 956 - **£4 200** - FF45 630
The young Flowersellers Oil/canvas (89.5x69.5cm 35x27in) Billingshurst, West-Sussex 2001
$4 384 - €4 468 - **£3 000** - FF32 069
First Steps Oil/canvas (30.5x45.5cm 12x17in) Perthshire 2000

M

MACGEHEE Paul XX [1]

$5 500 - €5 282 - £3 408 - FF34 646
End of the Line Oil/board (58x88cm 23x35in) Detroit MI 1999

MacGEORGE William Stewart 1861-1931 [63]

$90 619 - €101 037 - £62 000 - FF662 761
See-Saw Oil/canvas (127x192cm 50x75in) Perthshire 2000

$10 900 - €10 297 - £6 800 - FF67 546
Host of Golden Daffodils Oil/canvas (61.5x51cm 24x20in) Perthshire 1999

$2 087 - €1 867 - £1 250 - FF12 247
«In the Lake Wood, Kirkcudbright» Oil/canvas (30.5x40.5cm 12x15in) Perthshire 1998

McGHIE John 1867-1941 [53]

$5 706 - €5 928 - £3 600 - FF38 885
By the Sea Oil/canvas (36x46cm 14x18in) London 2000

$1 841 - €2 065 - £1 250 - FF13 543
Boats in the Harbour at Low Tide Oil/canvas (35x44.5cm 13x17in) Billingshurst, West-Sussex 2000

MacGILCHRIST John 1893-1977 [1]

$1 300 - €1 248 - £801 - FF8 189
Zooming over Manhattan Etching (30x20cm 11x7in) New-York 1999

McGILL Donald Fraser Gould 1875-1962 [88]

$485 - €455 - £300 - FF2 986
Drunken Bride and Groom stepping towards a Vicar Watercolour/paper (27x17.5cm 10x6in) London 1999

MACGILLIVRAY James Pittendrigh 1856-1938 [8]

$5 450 - €5 149 - £3 400 - FF33 773
Sir George Reid (1841-1913), a Bust Bronze (H35cm H13in) Perthshire 1999

MACGILVARY Norwood Hodge 1874-1949 [24]

$500 - €572 - £347 - FF3 751
In the Meadows Oil/canvas/board (15x16cm 6x6in) Philadelphia PA 2000

McGINNIS Robert E. 1926 [27]

$4 500 - €5 012 - £2 943 - FF32 878
Movie poster design: man at gallows surrounded by beautiful women Tempera (64x41cm 25x16in) New-York 2000

$3 000 - €2 873 - £1 853 - FF18 845
Woman Lounging on Modern Couch Holding Sandal and Emeralds, Book Cover Tempera drawing (38x26cm 15x10in) New-York 1999

$4 750 - €4 549 - £2 934 - FF29 839
Montage of Cast of Mainly Black Characters, Movie Poster Design Gouache/paper (44x49cm 17x19in) New-York 1999

$455 - €418 - £280 - FF2 743
On Her Majesty's Secret Service Poster (76x101.5cm 29x39in) London 1999

MACGINTY Mick 1952 [8]

$6 500 - €6 977 - £4 350 - FF45 769
Jaws II - Universal Pictures Acrylic/board (60x48cm 24x19in) Beverly-Hills CA 2000

McGLAUCHLIN Tom 1934 [2]

$7 500 - €7 159 - £4 686 - FF46 961
Fantasy Figural Vessels Sculpture, glass (H51cm H20in) New-York 1999

McGLYNN Thomas Arnold 1878-1966 [14]

$5 500 - €4 749 - £3 355 - FF31 150
Blossom Time Oil/canvas (40x50cm 16x20in) Oakland CA 1999

MacGONIGAL Maurice Joseph 1900-1979 [95]

$12 164 - €12 697 - £7 698 - FF83 290
The Dingle Horsefair Oil/canvas (127x101.5cm 50x39in) Dublin 2000

$7 055 - €7 365 - £4 464 - FF48 308
Farmyard, Dingle, Peninsula Oil/board (30.5x61cm 12x24in) Dublin 2000

$5 075 - €4 698 - £3 143 - FF30 817
Farmyard, Inverin, Connemara Oil/board (30x40cm 12x16in) Dublin 1999

$887 - €952 - £593 - FF6 246
Fishing Boats Watercolour (23x33cm 9x12in) Dublin 2000

MACGORAN Kieran ?-1990 [21]

$800 - €794 - £500 - FF5 210
Windy Day Charcoal/paper (39x29cm 15x11in) Belfast 1999

McGOUGH Peter 1958 [3]

$2 750 - €2 586 - £1 703 - FF16 966
The World, Seen and Unseen, of McDermott and McGough Photograph (24x20cm 9x7in) New-York 1999

MacGOUN Hannah Clarke Prest. 1864-1913 [17]

$829 - €721 - £500 - FF4 731
Children Picking Blackberries Watercolour/paper (27.5x18.5cm 10x7in) Solihull, West-Midlands 1998

MACGRATH Raymond 1903 [7]

$1 135 - €1 219 - £759 - FF7 995
Farmyard Watercolour/paper (30.5x44.5cm 12x17in) Dublin 2000

McGREGOR Harry XIX-XX [4]

$2 503 - €2 240 - £1 500 - FF14 691
A Walk in the Woods Oil/canvas (64x77cm 25x30in) Perthshire 1998

McGREGOR Robert 1848-1922 [66]

$8 293 - €7 213 - £5 000 - FF47 314
Clearing Potato Field Oil/canvas (54.5x91.5cm 21x36in) Glasgow 1998

$3 060 - €2 876 - £1 900 - FF18 865
Loading the Haycart Oil/canvas (25.5x41cm 10x16in) London 1999

$593 - €570 - £370 - FF3 739
Les ramasseuses de pommes de terre Aquarelle/papier (21.5x31.5cm 8x12in) Bruxelles 1999

MACGREGOR Sara ?-c.1919 [3]

$25 648 - €24 229 - £16 000 - FF158 932
The Lavender Beads Oil/canvas (102x58.5cm 40x23in) Perthshire 1999

MACGREGOR William York 1855-1923 [17]

$639 - €609 - £400 - FF3 992
Ludlow Castle Watercolour/paper (33x49cm 12x19in) Channel-Islands 1999

McGREW Ralph Brownell 1916-1994 [16]

$300 000 - €340 637 - £208 440 - FF2 234 430
Miles to go Oil/canvas (106x182cm 42x72in) Dallas TX 2001

$4 000 - €4 542 - £2 779 - FF29 792
Dry River Bed Oil/board (45x60cm 18x24in) Dallas TX 2001

McGUINNESS Norah Allison 1903-1980 [88]

$11 297 - €10 608 - £7 000 - FF69 581
The Last of the Shelley Banks Oil/canvas (84x99cm 33x38in) London 1999

$3 276 - €2 795 - £1 818 - FF18 333
Moths Around a Lamp Oil/board (41x20.5cm 16x8in) Dublin 1998

✏ **$2 803** - €3 301 - **£1 970** - FF21 655
Summer Table Gouache/paper (24.5x38cm 9x14in)
Dublin 2000

MacGUINNESS William Bingham 1848-1928 **[104]**
🖎 **$1 092** - €1 270 - **£768** - FF8 329
Still Moorning Watercolour/paper (33x55cm 12x21in)
Dublin 2001

MACGUIRE Edward 1932-1986 **[3]**
🖎 **$9 289** - €10 793 - **£6 528** - FF70 796
Blackbird on a Plate II Oil/canvas/board (61x51cm
24x20in) Dublin 2001
🖎 **$3 227** - €3 031 - **£2 000** - FF19 880
Bird and Skull Oil/canvas (33x23cm 12x9in) London
1999

MACH David 1956 **[17]**
🖎 **$4 418** - €4 275 - **£2 800** - FF28 045
Mask Construction (31x22x20cm 12x8x7in) London
1999

MACHARD Jules Louis 1839-1900 **[20]**
🖎 **$7 000** - €8 251 - **£4 918** - FF54 121
Bust Portrait of a Beautiful Young Girl Oil/canvas
(55x45cm 22x18in) New-Orleans LA 2000
🖎 **$1 786** - €1 982 - **£1 235** - FF13 000
Vénus bandant son arc Huile/toile (47x31cm
18x12in) Paris 2001
🖎 **$2 034** - €2 231 - **£1 350** - FF14 634
Jeune femme nue à la rêverie Pastel/toile
(85x113cm 33x44in) Bruxelles 2001

MACHEK Anton 1775-1844 **[6]**
🖎 **$2 601** - €2 460 - **£1 620** - FF16 137
Portrait of Johann Bartosch Oil/canvas (45x34cm
17x13in) Praha 2001

MACHELL Christopher 1747-1827 **[6]**
✏ **$260** - €253 - **£160** - FF1 662
Dovedale Watercolour/paper (32x27cm 12x10in)
London 1999

MACHELL Reginald XIX **[2]**
🖎 **$6 704** - €7 618 - **£4 630** - FF49 974
**Portrait of a Young Woman Wearing a Red Irish
Shawl** Oil/canvas (68x50cm 27x20in) Dublin 2000

MACHEN William H. 1832-1911 **[23]**
🖎 **$2 200** - €1 848 - **£1 293** - FF12 121
Still Life, Game Oil/canvas (74x55cm 29x22in)
Cleveland OH 1998
🖎 **$700** - €832 - **£485** - FF5 458
Portrait of Girl Oil/canvas (45x27cm 18x11in) Detroit
MI 2000

MACHEREN van Philip XVII **[3]**
🖎 **$10 818** - €12 715 - **£7 500** - FF83 404
Naval Engagement Oil/canvas (80x114cm 31x44in)
London 2000

MACHEROT Raymond 1924 **[25]**
✏ **$597** - €579 - **£371** - FF3 800
Sibylline en danger, pl.38 Encre Chine/papier
(46x38cm 18x14in) Paris 1999

MACHETANZ Fred 1908 **[14]**
🖎 **$9 000** - €8 181 - **£5 420** - FF53 667
Old Veteran Oil/board (48x38cm 19x15in) Hayden ID
1998

MACHNIEWICZ Franciszek 1859-1897 **[2]**
🖎 **$8 923** - €10 140 - **£6 162** - FF66 514
Odalisque Huile/toile (140x95cm 55x37in) Warszawa
2000
🖎 **$2 774** - €2 970 - **£1 888** - FF19 484
Portrait de fille Huile/toile (31.5x23cm 12x9in)
Kraków 2001

MacIAN Ronald Robert 1803-1856 **[1]**
🖎 **$14 616** - €16 296 - **£10 000** - FF106 897
Gilli Challum Oil/canvas (85x120cm 33x47in)
Perthshire 2000

MACIEJEWSKI Zbyslaw Marek 1946-1999 **[8]**
🖎 **$4 744** - €5 249 - **£3 296** - FF34 431
Coquelicots Huile/toile (73x60cm 28x23in) Warszawa
2001

McILHENNEY Charles Morgan 1858-1904 **[5]**
🖎 **$22 000** - €20 857 - **£13 384** - FF136 813
**Landscape with Young Woman Amid Flowers
and Blossoms** Oil/canvas (55x83cm 22x33in)
Amesbury MA 1999

McILVAINE William 1813-1867 **[3]**
✏ **$525** - €612 - **£368** - FF4 016
Scenic Landscape with Town in the Distance
Watercolour/paper (21x43cm 8x17in) Cleveland OH
2000

McINNERNEY Michael, Mike XX **[8]**
🎞 **$504** - €554 - **£320** - FF3 636
«Legalise Pot Rally» Poster (76x51cm 29x20in)
London 2000

MACINNES Robert 1801-1886 **[6]**
🖎 **$72 990** - €70 366 - **£45 000** - FF461 569
Return from the Vineyard Oil/canvas (96x120.5cm
37x47in) London 1999

McINNES William Beckwith 1889-1939 **[49]**
🖎 **$3 237** - €3 034 - **£2 002** - FF19 900
Old Farm Oil/canvas (49.5x59.5cm 19x23in)
Melbourne 1999
🖎 **$1 437** - €1 351 - **£889** - FF8 865
Summer Landscape Oil/panel (17x60.5cm 6x23in)
Melbourne 1999

McINNIS Robert Ford M. 1942 **[71]**
🖎 **$407** - €389 - **£253** - FF2 550
Blue Beads Oil/canvas (61x61cm 24x24in) Calgary,
Alberta 1999
🖎 **$408** - €404 - **£255** - FF2 648
South of Cayley, AB Oil/canvas (30.5x40.5cm
12x15in) Calgary, Alberta 1999

MacINTIRE Kenneth Stevens 1891-1979 **[67]**
🖎 **$650** - €594 - **£397** - FF3 896
Autumn Landscape Oil/board (48x63cm 19x25in)
Columbia SC 1999

MACINTOSH John Macintosh 1847-1913 **[23]**
✏ **$286** - €322 - **£200** - FF2 113
River running Through a Wooded Landscape
Watercolour (27.5x18cm 10x7in) London 2001

McINTYRE Donald 1923 **[153]**
🖎 **$1 952** - €2 296 - **£1 400** - FF15 062
Camaes Harbour Oil/board (49.5x75cm 19x29in)
London 2001
🖎 **$921** - €1 081 - **£650** - FF7 090
Dutchman's Cap off Mull Oil/board (16x25.5cm
6x10in) London 2000

McINTYRE James ?-c.1898 **[11]**
🖎 **$10 063** - €9 677 - **£6 200** - FF63 478
Mending the Nets Oil/canvas (93x128cm 36x50in)
London 1999
✏ **$1 578** - €1 636 - **£1 000** - FF10 730
Accordian Player Watercolour/paper (35x48cm
14x19in) Belfast 2000

McINTYRE Joseph Wrightson 1841-1897 **[20]**
🖎 **$10 057** - €11 734 - **£7 000** - FF76 972
The East Prospect of Sheffield Oil/canvas
(100x163cm 39x64in) West-Yorkshire 1999

M

$4 370 - €4 263 - **£2 691** - FF27 964
Low Wood, Windermere Oil/canvas (60x105cm
24x41in) Chicago IL 1999

MACINTYRE Peter 1910-1995 **[38]**
$3 683 - €4 156 - **£2 590** - FF27 260
Abandoned Stockyard, Anthony's Lagoon,
Northern Territory Oil/board (61x86.5cm 24x34in)
Malvern, Victoria 2001
$1 363 - €1 288 - **£824** - FF8 447
The Auckland Club, New Zealand Ink (37x47cm
14x18in) Sydney 1999

McINTYRE Raymond Francis 1879-1933 **[3]**
$7 036 - €7 394 - **£4 632** - FF48 499
After the Bath Oil/board (28x18.5cm 11x7in)
Auckland 2000

MACINTYRE Robert Finlay XIX-XX **[14]**
$11 577 - €10 095 - **£7 000** - FF66 218
Arundel Castle, Sussex Oil/canvas (56.5x92cm
22x36in) London 1998
$1 012 - €1 192 - **£700** - FF7 819
Old Racehorse, Hersal Moor Oil/cardboard
(28.5x45.5cm 11x17in) Devon 2000

MACINTYRE-CROXFORD Agnes XIX **[5]**
$1 846 - €1 792 - **£1 149** - FF11 755
Curious Friends Oil/canvas (40.5x61cm 15x24in)
London 1999

MACIP Vicente Juan c.1555-1622 **[2]**
$28 000 - €29 903 - **£19 079** - FF196 148
Saint Ignatius of Loyola giving a Disciple a
Letter Oil/panel (57x50cm 22x24in) New-York 2001

MACK Heinz 1931 **[190]**
$12 800 - €16 586 - **£9 600** - FF108 800
«Schleier zu Sais» Olio/tela (130x120cm 51x47in)
Milano 2001
$7 600 - €9 848 - **£5 700** - FF64 600
«Silber auf schwarz» Tecnica mista (80x100cm
31x39in) Milano 2001
$3 906 - €4 538 - **£2 745** - FF29 766
Pyramid Mixed media (34x45cm 13x17in) Amsterdam
2001
$7 476 - €6 472 - **£4 537** - FF42 453
Luftsteele mit Waben Sculpture (200x85x4cm
78x33x1in) München 1998
$2 067 - €2 045 - **£1 289** - FF13 415
Lichtrelief Metal (20.5x40.5cm 8x15in) Berlin 1999
$1 863 - €1 792 - **£1 148** - FF11 738
Weisse Struktur Mixed media/paper (64x49cm
25x19in) München 1999
$210 - €245 - **£147** - FF1 609
Lichtstern Serigraph (18x22cm 7x8in) Köln 2001

MACK Leal 1892-1962 **[6]**
$3 750 - €3 599 - **£2 350** - FF23 608
Home from the Mill Oil/canvas (81x101cm 32x40in)
Altadena CA 1999

McKAIN Bruce 1900-? **[9]**
$1 900 - €2 245 - **£1 346** - FF14 726
Higgins Wharf Oil/canvas/board (40x50cm 16x20in)
Provincetown MA 2000

MACKAY Thomas Hope act.1907-1923 **[9]**
$1 449 - €1 362 - **£900** - FF8 936
October Morning Oil/canvas (46x61cm 18x24in)
London 1999

MACKAY Thomas, Tom 1851-1920 **[72]**
$385 - €436 - **£269** - FF2 862
Cavalrymen Oil/board (22x30cm 8x11in)
Billingshurst, West-Sussex 2001

$1 705 - €1 433 - **£1 000** - FF9 398
Picking Flowers by the River Watercolour/paper
(16x25cm 6x9in) Billingshurst, West-Sussex 1998

McKAY William Darling 1844-1924 **[78]**
$4 751 - €4 060 - **£2 875** - FF26 629
The Potato Gatherers Oil/canvas (44x76.5cm
17x30in) Edinburgh 1998
$2 111 - €2 017 - **£1 300** - FF13 230
Distant View of Arthur's Seat from the East
Lothian Coast Oil/canvas (25.5x38cm 10x14in)
Edinburgh 1999

MACKE August 1887-1914 **[192]**
$579 075 - €540 897 - **£350 000** - FF3 548 055
Stilleben mit Sonnenblumen II Oil/board
(81x103cm 31x40in) London 1999
$29 107 - €33 234 - **£20 520** - FF218 003
«Allegorische Szene» Oil/panel (15.5x22cm 6x8in)
Stuttgart 2001
$18 760 - €20 580 - **£12 743** - FF134 994
Grosser Araberkopf Charcoal/paper (23.8x18.6cm
9x7in) Berlin 2000
$1 333 - €1 431 - **£892** - FF9 390
Drei Akte Woodcut (25.7x19.8cm 10x7in) Hamburg
2001

MACKE Helmut 1891-1936 **[44]**
$2 175 - €2 556 - **£1 508** - FF16 769
Landschaft mit Reitern Watercolour (25.5x33.5cm
10x13in) Stuttgart 2000

McKEEVER Ian 1946 **[9]**
$749 - €799 - **£500** - FF5 241
That Which Appears Woodcut (50.5x38cm 19x14in)
London 2000

MACKELDEY Bernhard Carl 1826-1890 **[3]**
$4 499 - €4 488 - **£2 808** - FF29 438
Vue sur le Château Chillon Oil/canvas (78x105cm
30x41in) Warszawa 1999
$2 316 - €2 761 - **£1 651** - FF18 111
Blick auf Neapel Aquarell/Papier (53x63cm 20x24in)
Köln 2000

MACKELLAR Duncan 1849-1908 **[14]**
$466 - €530 - **£320** - FF3 479
Rowboat on Loch Katrine Watercolour/paper
(24.5x34.5cm 9x13in) London 2000

McKELVEY Frank 1895-1974 **[175]**
$21 593 - €18 421 - **£12 868** - FF120 832
Farmhouse, Mourne Mountains Oil/canvas
(51x66cm 20x25in) Dublin 1998
$6 844 - €5 836 - **£4 129** - FF38 282
Cows Grazing by a Sunlit River Oil/board
(30x43cm 12x17in) Dublin 1998
$2 217 - €2 159 - **£1 362** - FF14 159
To Mahee Island Watercolour/paper (28x38cm
11x15in) Dublin 1999

MACKEN Mark 1913-1977 **[10]**
$12 936 - €10 914 - **£7 700** - FF71 588
Femme de Loth Bronze poli (190x50x44cm
74x19x17in) Antwerpen 1998

MacKENDRICK Lilian 1906-1987 **[6]**
$3 500 - €4 043 - **£2 450** - FF26 523
In the Orchard Oil/canvas (50.5x76cm 19x29in) New-
York 2001

MACKENNA Noel Vincent Joseph 1956 **[10]**
$777 - €871 - **£543** - FF5 714
Dog in Landscape» Watercolour (29x32cm 11x12in)
Melbourne 2001

McKENNA Stephen 1939 **[16]**
- **$8 313** – €7 872 – **£5 054** – FF51 639
  Still Life with Fish Oil/canvas (59x54cm 23x21in)
  Dublin 1999
- **$4 596** – €5 079 – **£3 187** – FF33 316
  St Johns Point Lighthouse and Cliffs Oil/board
  (32x46cm 12x18in) Dublin 2001

MacKENNAL Edgar Bertram 1863-1931 **[43]**
- **$3 015** – €3 380 – **£2 100** – FF22 170
  Head of a young Woman Bronze (H51cm H20in)
  London 2001

MACKENSEN Fritz 1866-1953 **[80]**
- **$3 212** – €2 811 – **£1 945** – FF18 442
  Herbstpark Öl/Karton (43.5x59.3cm 17x23in) Berlin
  1998
- **$6 360** – €7 158 – **£4 382** – FF46 954
  Auf der Weide bei Worpswede Öl/Karton
  (30.5x46.5cm 12x18in) Bremen 2000
- **$726** – €818 – **£500** – FF5 366
  Torfkahn auf der Hamme Chalks/paper (40x30cm
  15x11in) Bremen 2000
- **$329** – €307 – **£203** – FF2 012
  Flett Etching, aquatint (24.2x39.4cm 9x15in) Bremen
  1999

MacKENZIE Alexander 1923 **[44]**
- **$5 614** – €5 658 – **£3 500** – FF37 112
  Granite Tower Oil/board (61x38cm 24x14in) London
  2000
- **$827** – €802 – **£520** – FF5 258
  Litton, Derbyshire Mixed media (15x19cm 6x7in)
  Par, Cornwall 1999
- **$406** – €439 – **£280** – FF2 878
  Green Abstract Watercolour (16x24cm 6x9in)
  London 2001

MACKENZIE Alison 1907-1982 **[2]**
- **$1 195** – €1 143 – **£749** – FF7 499
  «St. Andrews, British Railways» Poster (102x64cm
  40x25in) London 1999

MacKENZIE James Hamilton 1875-1926 **[32]**
- **$1 452** – €1 619 – **£980** – FF10 620
  Dutch idyll Oil/canvas (34.5x52.5cm 13x20in)
  Edinburgh 2000

MACKENZIE Jim 1953 **[10]**
- **$613** – €589 – **£377** – FF3 864
  Sturdies Bay Pastel/paper (40.5x61cm 15x24in)
  Vancouver, BC. 1999

MACKENZIE Marie Henri 1878-1961 **[103]**
- **$2 574** – €2 859 – **£1 791** – FF18 752
  Stadsgezicht Amsterdam Oil/board (63x76cm
  24x29in) Groningen 2001
- **$821** – €908 – **£569** – FF5 953
  A Portrait of a lady in red Oil/canvas/board
  (24x19cm 9x7in) Amsterdam 2001

McKENZIE Queenie, Nakarra c.1930-1999 **[26]**
- **$12 579** – €13 503 – **£8 419** – FF88 576
  Duluyn Country Mixed media (90x160cm 35x62in)
  Melbourne 2000
- **$3 144** – €3 326 – **£2 104** – FF22 144
  Jootal (Tick Dreaming) Mixed media/canvas
  (60x90cm 23x35in) Melbourne 2000

McKENZIE Robert Tait 1867-1938 **[16]**
- **$4 370** – €4 997 – **£3 000** – FF32 778
  **After a Hop, Twist and Change of Feet, the
  Moment before Delivery** Bronze (H29cm H11in)
  London 2000

MacKENZIE Roderick D. 1865-1914 **[6]**
- **$5 600** – €6 660 – **£3 991** – FF43 685
  In Giverny Oil/canvas (38x30.5cm 14x12in) New-York
  2000

MACKENZIE Thomas Blakeley 1887-1944 **[3]**
- **$1 824** – €1 579 – **£1 100** – FF10 357
  **«He saw Carilin, Ni Murrachu walking a little
  way in front»** Watercolour (38x28cm 14x11in)
  London 1999

MACKENZIE William Gibbs 1857-1924 **[9]**
- **$2 829** – €2 414 – **£1 686** – FF15 833
  Belfast Lough Oil/canvas (37x53.5cm 14x21in)
  Dublin 1998

MACKEPRANG Adolf Heinrich 1833-1911 **[159]**
- **$12 936** – €14 765 – **£8 987** – FF96 855
  Kronhjort med sin rudel ved en skovso Oil/can-
  vas (140x107cm 55x42in) København 2000
- **$1 350** – €1 208 – **£806** – FF7 922
  Dådyr i Dyrehaven Oil/canvas (74x53cm 29x20in)
  København 1998
- **$910** – €861 – **£566** – FF5 650
  Skovparti med hare Oil/canvas (40x29cm 15x11in)
  Vejle 1999

McKEWAN David Hall 1816-1873 **[53]**
- **$791** – €724 – **£480** – FF4 752
  A River Landscape with a Castle Beyond
  Watercolour (18x27cm 7x10in) London 1998

McKIBBIN XX [1]
- **$1 635** – €1 571 – **£1 000** – FF10 306
  «Ulster Invites» Poster (102x64cm 40x25in) London
  1999

MACKIE Charles Hodge 1862-1920 **[24]**
- **$805** – €894 – **£560** – FF5 865
  **River Scene with a Man rowing and a Woman
  on the Shore** Oil/panel (35.5x51cm 13x20in)
  Glasgow 2001
- **$622** – €694 – **£420** – FF4 551
  The Bridge of Nomentano, Near Rome Oil/panel
  (23.5x32cm 9x12in) Edinburgh 2000

MACKIE Hamish 1973 **[5]**
- **$3 710** – €3 371 – **£2 300** – FF22 111
  A Running Hare Bronze (H53cm H20in)
  Billingshurst, West-Sussex 1999

MACKIE Helen Madeleine ?-1957 **[19]**
- **$6 352** – €7 366 – **£4 500** – FF48 315
  «Waterloo Station, Southern Railway» Poster
  (102x127cm 40x50in) London 2000

MACKIE Kathleen Isabella 1899-? **[3]**
- **$1 080** – €1 210 – **£750** – FF7 937
  Near Glenveagh Co.Donegal Oil/canvas/board
  (25.5x35.5cm 10x13in) London 2001
- **$1 583** – €1 774 – **£1 100** – FF11 636
  The Poison Glen from Ferry's House, Donegal
  Watercolour (12.5x17.5cm 4x6in) London 2001

MACKIEWICZ Konstanty 1894-1985 **[16]**
- **$1 590** – €1 494 – **£987** – FF9 801
  Pierrot Oil/canvas (65x64cm 25x25in) Warszawa 1999

MACKINNON Sine 1901-1996 **[35]**
- **$624** – €611 – **£400** – FF4 011
  Rocky Coast Oil/board (38x45.5cm 14x17in) London
  1999

MACKINSTRY Cherith 1928 **[4]**
- **$863** – €967 – **£600** – FF6 344
  Donegal Landscape Oil/board (16x30.5cm 6x12in)
  London 2001

M

McKINSTRY George A. XIX [1]

$3 800 - €4 191 - £2 573 - FF27 489
Indian Village, Dakota Oil/board (29x39.5cm 11x15in) New-York 2000

MACKINTOSH Charles Rennie 1868-1928 [53]

$12 807 - €12 665 - £8 000 - FF83 079
Pine Cones Watercolour (25.5x19cm 10x7in) Glasgow 1999

MACKLEY Evan 1940 [18]

$958 - €922 - £590 - FF6 047
Flowerscape Oil/canvas/board (60.5x50.5cm 23x19in) Melbourne 1999

MACKLIN Thomas Eyre 1867-1943 [12]

$2 441 - €2 243 - £1 500 - FF14 716
The Fisherman's Family Oil/canvas/board (38.5x29cm 15x11in) Oxfordshire 1999

MacKNIGHT Dodge 1860-1950 [44]

$5 500 - €6 162 - £3 829 - FF40 422
Mexican Village Scene with Children Watercolour/paper (37x53.5cm 14x21in) Washington 2001

McKNIGHT Thomas 1941 [43]

$300 - €334 - £209 - FF2 192
Dog on the Patio Lithograph (40x45cm 16x18in) Delray-Beach FL 2001

MACKOWIAK Erwin 1926 [16]

$1 421 - €1 685 - £986 - FF11 056
Le repos de la danseuse Huile/toile (87x107cm 34x42in) Maisieres-Mons 2000

MACKRILL Martyn R. 1961 [67]

$40 599 - €45 340 - £26 000 - FF297 411
First-Class Yachting - The Royal Clyde Yatch Club Regatta 1895 Oil/canvas (91.5x152.5cm 36x60in) London 2000

$12 819 - €12 188 - £8 000 - FF79 947
Two Giants «Neck and Neck» Oil/canvas (66x106.5cm 25x41in) London 1999

$2 977 - €2 546 - £1 800 - FF16 699
The Wool Clipper «Golden Fleece» and Tug «Cambria» Watercolour/paper (37.5x56cm 14x22in) London 1999

MACLAGAN Philip Douglas 1901-1972 [2]

$3 406 - €3 284 - £2 100 - FF21 539
The Attic Room Oil/panel (40.5x30.5cm 15x12in) London 1999

MacLAREN Walter XIX-XX [4]

$4 184 - €4 491 - £2 800 - FF29 460
The Flute Player Oil/canvas (42.5x30cm 16x11in) London 2000

MacLAUGHLIN Donald Shaw 1876-1938 [34]

$133 - €120 - £83 - FF790
Chicago, Michigan Avenue No.2 Etching (27.5x37cm 10x14in) Toronto 1999

McLAUGHLIN John 1898-1976 [47]

$16 000 - €15 406 - £10 004 - FF101 060
#3 Acrylic (152.5x122cm 60x48in) Beverly-Hills CA 1999

$4 000 - €4 641 - £2 761 - FF30 444
Untitled Oil/masonite (58.5x71cm 23x27in) New-York 1999

MACLEA J.W. XIX [4]

$1 761 - €2 042 - £1 247 - FF13 394
Shipping by White Chalk Cliffs Oil/panel (30.5x42.5cm 12x16in) Amsterdam 2000

MacLEAN Alexander 1840-1877 [12]

$156 933 - €131 817 - £92 000 - FF864 662
Covent Garden Market Oil/canvas (119.5x243cm 47x95in) London 1998

McLEAN Bruce 1944 [80]

$426 - €392 - £260 - FF2 574
The 2nd International Screenprint (77.5x63.5cm 30x25in) London 1998

MACLEAN George 1939 [7]

$2 597 - €2 496 - £1 600 - FF16 373
Bald Eagle Pencil/paper (35.5x44.5cm 13x17in) London 1999

McLEAN James Augustus 1904-1989 [32]

$14 000 - €16 922 - £9 774 - FF111 000
Wash Day Oil/canvas (107.5x128.5cm 42x50in) Bethesda MD 2000

$650 - €751 - £455 - FF4 925
Outside the Hotel Oil/panel (50x59.5cm 19x23in) Bethesda MD 2000

$4 250 - €5 138 - £2 967 - FF33 700
«Shore Leave, Charleston, South Carolina» Oil/canvas (21x18cm 8x7in) Bethesda MD 2000

$1 700 - €2 055 - £1 186 - FF13 478
«Sunday Quartet» Watercolour/paper (23x27.5cm 9x10in) Bethesda MD 2000

MacLEARY Bonnie 1898-1971 [6]

$5 500 - €6 543 - £3 805 - FF42 921
Fountain Bronze (H41cm H16in) Detroit MI 2000

MACLEAY Kenneth 1802-1878 [37]

$2 600 - €2 785 - £1 769 - FF18 269
St.Fillans Oil/canvas (40x60cm 16x24in) Chicago IL 2001

$640 - €633 - £400 - FF4 154
Dunkeld Watercolour, gouache/paper (31.5x47cm 12x18in) Glasgow 1999

McLECHLAN M. XIX [1]

$3 500 - €3 753 - £2 315 - FF24 616
The British Ship «Balmacarra» with Sails Furled and Men on Deck Oil/canvas (60x91cm 24x36in) East-Dennis MA 2000

McLELLAN Alexander Matheson 1872-1957 [9]

$224 - €209 - £135 - FF1 368
The World Powers, The Chinese and Roman Armies Meeting on Lake Baikal Watercolour/paper (20x39cm 8x15in) Carlisle, Cumbria 1999

$2 118 - €2 456 - £1 500 - FF16 108
«Aberdeen, LMS & LNER, The Silver City by the Sea»op Poster (102x127cm 40x50in) London 2000

MACLEOD Pegi Nicol 1904-1949 [13]

$7 287 - €8 070 - £4 942 - FF52 937
Forest landscape Oil/canvas (73.5x66.5cm 28x26in) Toronto 2000

MACLEOD William Douglas 1892-1963 [48]

$239 - €257 - £160 - FF1 683
Tangiers Etching (18x32cm 7x12in) London 2000

MACLET Élisée 1881-1962 [1398]

$3 224 - €3 430 - £2 038 - FF22 500
L'entrée du funiculaire de Montmartre Huile/toile (65x50cm 25x19in) Paris 2000

$2 500 - €2 232 - £1 531 - FF14 640
Montmartre Oil/canvas/board (27x19.5cm 10x7in) New-York 1999

$512 - €579 - £358 - FF3 800
Rivière à Ornans Aquarelle/papier (17x24cm 6x9in) Paris 2001

MACLIAMMOIR Michael 1899-1978 **[3]**
- $1 537 - €1 651 - **£1 029** - FF10 827
  Mythological Figure Watercolour (28.5x21.5cm 11x8in) Dublin 2000

MACLISE Daniel 1806-1870 **[55]**
- $512 096 - €488 832 - **£320 000** - FF3 206 528
  King Cophetua and the Beggar Maid Oil/canvas (120x181.5cm 47x71in) London 1999
- $20 113 - €22 855 - **£13 890** - FF149 922
  Dear Harp of my Country Oil/canvas (53x43cm 21x17in) Dublin 2000
- $4 315 - €3 728 - **£2 600** - FF24 455
  Young Girl Carrying a Bowl of Fruit Oil/canvas (35x29.5cm 13x11in) Billingshurst, West-Sussex 1999
- $805 - €757 - **£500** - FF4 964
  Mrs Robert Small, seated in black Dress, red embroidered Shawl Watercolour (26x20cm 10x7in) London 1999

MacMASTER James 1856-1913 **[39]**
- $790 - €922 - **£550** - FF6 047
  Winter Watercolour/paper (25x34cm 9x13in) West-Yorkshire 2000

McMEIN Neysa 1890-1949 **[4]**
- $11 000 - €12 823 - **£7 616** - FF84 111
  Woman in Costume Pausing at Masquerade Ball Pastel/paper (89x71cm 35x28in) New-York 2000

MACMIADHACHAIN Padraig 1924 **[12]**
- $1 442 - €1 619 - **£1 000** - FF10 617
  St.Aldhelm's Head Oil/canvas (63.5x76cm 25x29in) London 2000

McMILLEN Mildred 1884-1940 **[1]**
- $1 300 - €1 536 - **£921** - FF10 076
  Fifth Annual Exhibition Ink/paper (40x30cm 16x12in) Provincetown MA 2000

MacMONNIES Frederick William 1863-1937 **[79]**
- $22 000 - €23 615 - **£14 722** - FF154 902
  Monsieur Cardin (Le Raseur) Oil/canvas (177.5x106.5cm 69x41in) New-York 2000
- $12 500 - €12 005 - **£7 706** - FF78 747
  Bacchante and Infant Faun Bronze (H88cm H35in) Cambridge MA 1999
- $9 000 - €8 606 - **£5 481** - FF56 450
  Pan of Rohallion Bronze (H75.5cm H29in) Boston MA 1999

MACMONNIES LOW Mary L. Fairchild 1858-1946 **[19]**
- $1 200 - €1 007 - **£707** - FF6 604
  Coastal Rocks Oil/canvas (54x73cm 21x29in) Greenwich CT 1998
- $2 250 - €1 923 - **£1 361** - FF12 612
  Plattekill Creek Oil/board (30.5x40.5cm 12x15in) San-Francisco CA 1998
- $1 700 - €1 893 - **£1 194** - FF12 418
  Spanish Lady playing Guitar Watercolour/paper (43x27cm 17x11in) Cleveland OH 2001

MacMORRIS LeRoy Daniel 1893-1985 **[5]**
- $2 000 - €2 161 - **£1 384** - FF14 172
  On the Loma Oil/board (27x33cm 11x13in) Cincinnati OH 2001

MACMUNN Charles 1840-1903 **[4]**
- $1 792 - €2 080 - **£1 237** - FF13 645
  Skow-Wash Bridge/100 Feet Span/Quoi-Eek Bridge/Place/4 Mile/Trestle Vintage gelatin silver print (19x15cm 7x5in) Vancouver, BC. 2000

MACNAB Iain 1890-1967 **[46]**
- $463 - €500 - **£320** - FF3 280
  Study of a Female seated Nude Gouache/paper (55.5x36cm 21x14in) London 2001
- $313 - €337 - **£210** - FF2 209
  Drying Sails, Lake Garda Etching (22x20cm 9x8in) Par, Cornwall 2000

MACNAB Peter ?-1900 **[8]**
- $2 031 - €2 287 - **£1 400** - FF15 005
  Mending the ets Oil/canvas (49x75cm 19x29in) London 2000

MACNAIR Frances MacDonald 1873-1921 **[4]**
- $19 295 - €16 462 - **£11 500** - FF107 981
  Three Girls Reminiscent of the Three Graces Pencil/paper (32x25cm 12x9in) London 1998

MacNALLY Matthew James 1874-1943 **[93]**
- $657 - €612 - **£406** - FF4 012
  Up the Garden Path Oil/canvas/board (21.5x29cm 8x11in) Melbourne 1999
- $404 - €452 - **£281** - FF2 963
  Lorne Watercolour/paper (23x26cm 9x10in) Sydney 2001

McNALLY Tony 1953 **[2]**
- $1 311 - €1 524 - **£921** - FF9 994
  Wild Ponies on Beach, West of Ireland Acrylic/canvas (30x41cm 11x16in) Dublin 2001

MACNEE Daniel 1806-1882 **[18]**
- $4 340 - €4 688 - **£3 000** - FF30 749
  Young Boy Holding a Dragoons Cap and Standing in a Landscape Oil/canvas (124x99cm 49x39in) Bristol, Avon 2001

MacNEE Robert Russell 1880-1952 **[99]**
- $2 090 - €1 786 - **£1 265** - FF11 717
  A Woodland Stream Oil/canvas (51x61cm 20x24in) Edinburgh 1998
- $1 363 - €1 533 - **£950** - FF10 059
  «Near Loch Etive» Oil/canvas (29.5x40cm 11x15in) Edinburgh 2001
- $4 312 - €3 751 - **£2 600** - FF24 603
  A Cockerel with Hens in a Farmyard Watercolour (48.5x38.5cm 19x15in) Glasgow 1998

McNEIL George 1908-1995 **[18]**
- $1 800 - €2 088 - **£1 242** - FF13 699
  Torrent Oil/board (30.5x38cm 12x14in) New-York 2000

MacNEIL Hermon Atkins 1866-1947 **[29]**
- $50 000 - €54 857 - **£33 215** - FF359 840
  The Sun Vow Bronze (H89cm H35in) New-York 2000
- $4 000 - €3 656 - **£2 447** - FF23 979
  Night, pair of Bookends Bronze (H23cm H9in) Boston MA 1999

MACNICOL Bessie 1869-1904 **[7]**
- $21 541 - €24 136 - **£15 000** - FF158 322
  Portrait of Mary Oil/canvas (52x41cm 20x16in) Edinburgh 2001

McNICOLL Helen Galloway 1879-1915 **[6]**
- $21 625 - €20 831 - **£13 427** - FF136 640
  Feeding the Ducks Oil/canvas (40.5x45.5cm 15x17in) Toronto 1999
- $325 - €345 - **£219** - FF2 263
  Lady in White Dress Oil/board (30x13cm 12x5in) Portland OR 2001

McNULTY William Charles 1884-1963 **[24]**
- $600 - €620 - **£379** - FF4 070
  In the Fifties (The Whirlpool) Drypoint (34.5x18.5cm 13x7in) New-York 2000

M

MACOMBER Mary Lizzie 1861-1916 [10]
🖼 **$3 054** - €2 617 - **£1 836** - FF17 165
The Prayer Oil/canvas (25x20cm 10x8in) Cedar-Falls
IA 1998

MACOUILLARD Louis 1917-1987 [5]
✎ **$325** - €303 - **£200** - FF1 990
Tide Pools at Dillon Beach, CA Watercolour
(34x45cm 13x18in) Detroit MI 1999

MACOUN Gustav 1892-1934 [63]
🖼 **$549** - €519 - **£342** - FF3 406
Hameau Huile/carton (50x60cm 19x23in) Praha 2001
🖼 **$289** - €273 - **£180** - FF1 793
Regard sur Trosky Huile/carton (29.5x38.5cm
11x15in) Praha 2000

MACPHAIL Rodger 1953 [58]
🖼 **$4 545** - €4 368 - **£2 800** - FF28 653
Muscovy Ducks Oil/board (65x49.5cm 25x19in)
London 1999
🖼 **$2 419** - €2 198 - **£1 500** - FF14 420
Grouse in Winter Watercolour (37x52cm 14x20in)
Billingshurst, West-Sussex 1999

MACPHERSON Earl ?-1993 [1]
✎ **$2 000** - €1 851 - **£1 224** - FF12 145
Woman in uniform seated on airplane's fusela-
ge, calendar ill. Pastel/paper (81x61cm 32x24in)
New-York 1999

MACPHERSON John act.1865-1884 [35]
✎ **$985** - €1 088 - **£680** - FF7 137
Farmyard Scene Watercolour/paper (30.5x20cm
12x7in) Hockley, Birmingham 2001

MACPHERSON Robert 1811-1872 [43]
🖼 **$1 942** - €2 085 - **£1 300** - FF13 678
The Theatre of Marcellus, Via de Sugherari
Albumen print (40x26.5cm 15x10in) London 2000

MACPHERSON Robert 1937 [6]
🖼 **$29 148** - €32 670 - **£20 382** - FF214 302
Scale from the Tool Acrylic (176x10x6cm 69x3x2in)
Melbourne 2001

MacQUEEN Kenneth Robertson 1897-1960 [46]
✎ **$2 221** - €2 089 - **£1 375** - FF13 701
Pin Cushion Rock, Maroochydore
Watercolour/paper (37x45cm 14x17in) Melbourne 1999

MacQUEEN Mary McCartney 1912-1994 [24]
🖼 **$106** - €110 - **£67** - FF724
Sand and Sails Lithograph (11.5x24cm 4x9in)
Melbourne 2000

MACQUOID Percy Thomas 1852-1925 [14]
✎ **$2 678** - €2 549 - **£1 700** - FF16 723
Black Cat in an Interior Watercolour (18.5x34cm
7x13in) Billingshurst, West-Sussex 1999

MACQUOID Thomas Robert 1820-1912 [18]
✎ **$882** - €889 - **£550** - FF5 832
Il Frontone, The Porta S.Pietro, Perugia
Watercolour/paper (24x32cm 9x12in) London 2000

MacRAE Elmer Livingston 1875-1953 [25]
🖼 **$4 000** - €4 549 - **£2 794** - FF29 840
Bouquet of Flowers in a Blue and White Teapot
Oil/canvas (68x68cm 27x27in) New-York 2000
✎ **$1 500** - €1 285 - **£885** - FF8 427
Flower and Fruit Studies Watercolour/paper
(40.5x33cm 15x12in) New-York 1998

MacRAE Emma Fordyce 1887-1974 [24]
🖼 **$6 500** - €6 977 - **£4 350** - FF45 769
Anemonies and Freesia Oil/masonite (40.5x50.5cm
15x19in) New-York 2000

🖼 **$1 700** - €1 886 - **£1 130** - FF12 370
Fishing in Central Park Oil/board (19x25cm 7x10in)
Milford CT 2000

McRAE Tommy c.1830-1901 [2]
✎ **$10 737** - €11 452 - **£7 165** - FF75 117
Hunting Figures Ink/paper (24.5x31cm 9x12in)
Melbourne 2000

MacRAE Wendell 1896-1980 [8]
📷 **$1 800** - €1 733 - **£1 125** - FF11 369
Valves, Merchant's Refrigeration Plant Gelatin silver print (21.5x16.5cm 8x6in) New-York 1999

MACRÉAU Michel 1935-1997 [101]
🖼 **$4 020** - €3 659 - **£2 512** - FF24 000
«Le cri du crucifié» Huile/toile (130x96cm 51x37in)
Enghien 1999
🖼 **$1 117** - €1 067 - **£696** - FF7 000
Portrait de chevalier au vitrail
Acrylique/carton/toile (80x60cm 31x23in) Paris 1999
✎ **$1 071** - €1 098 - **£666** - FF7 192
«Cécille je temps brasse» Fusain (65x50cm
25x19in) Paris 2000

MACRET Adrien Ch., André 1751-1789 [2]
🃏 **$949** - €920 - **£601** - FF6 037
La fuite à dessein, nach J.-H. Fragonard
Farbradierung (35.7x25.7cm 14x10in) München 1999

MACRET Jean César 1768-c.1789 [2]
🃏 **$686** - €818 - **£489** - FF5 366
Marie-Antoinette d'Autriche, Königin von
Frankreich, nach Lebrun Farbradierung (32x22cm
12x8in) Berlin 2001

MACRITCHIE Alexina XIX-XX [2]
✎ **$1 674** - €2 002 - **£1 150** - FF13 130
Schmma: a Study of a Turkish Musician
Watercolour (51x32.5cm 20x12in) Billingshurst, West-
Sussex 2000

MACSWEENEY Sean 1935 [20]
🖼 **$3 412** - €3 301 - **£2 103** - FF21 655
Maggie's Wall Oil/board (58.5x78.5cm 23x30in)
Dublin 1999
🖼 **$1 932** - €2 012 - **£1 212** - FF13 326
The Field Toor Oil/canvas (30x40cm 11x15in) Dublin
2000

MacSWINEY Eugene Joseph 1866-? [15]
🖼 **$2 000** - €2 079 - **£1 260** - FF13 636
In the Garden Oil/canvas (58x30cm 23x12in) Detroit
MI 2000
🖼 **$1 204** - €1 168 - **£758** - FF7 662
Gypsies Oil/canvas (30.5x51cm 12x20in) Dublin 1999

MacTAGGART William II, Sir 1903-1981 [83]
🖼 **$6 223** - €6 939 - **£4 200** - FF45 515
Cornfield and Sky Oil/board (49x58cm 19x22in)
Edinburgh 2000
🖼 **$3 952** - €3 760 - **£2 400** - FF24 661
View of Craig Ney, Drumnadrochit Oil/board
(20x27cm 7x10in) Edinburgh 1999
🖼 **$364** - €337 - **£220** - FF2 213
Crowd Scene Pastel (24x33cm 9x12in) Edinburgh
1999

MacTAGGART William, sir 1835-1910 [154]
🖼 **$39 919** - €34 199 - **£24 000** - FF224 332
Cockenzie, afternoon Oil/canvas (107x124cm
42x48in) Edinburgh 1998
🖼 **$51 739** - €46 287 - **£31 000** - FF303 623
West Wind, Machrihanish Oil/canvas (78x103.5cm
30x40in) Perthshire 1998

$5 881 - €5 445 - **£3 600** - FF35 715
On the Foreshore Oil/canvas (30x46cm 11x18in)
Edinburgh 1999

$6 653 - €5 700 - **£4 000** - FF37 388
The Bass Rock and Berwick Law from Crail
Watercolour/paper (25x35cm 9x13in) Edinburgh 1998

McVICKER J. Jay 1911 [16]
$650 - €748 - **£448** - FF4 909
«**Wintry Vigil**» Aquatint (27x39cm 10x15in) Cleveland
OH 2000

MACWEENEY Leslie XX [8]
$297 - €330 - **£207** - FF2 165
Distracted Girl Watercolour/paper (30x35cm 11x13in)
Dublin 2001

MacWHIRTER John 1839-1911 [185]
$10 453 - €8 931 - **£6 325** - FF58 585
My Lady of the Wood Oil/canvas (142.5x99cm
56x38in) Edinburgh 1998
$3 731 - €4 197 - **£2 668** - FF27 532
«**Fair Strathspey**» Oil/canvas (72x46cm 28x18in)
Edinburgh 2001
$3 989 - €4 637 - **£2 800** - FF30 420
Golden October Oil/canvas (23.5x33.5cm 9x13in)
Billingshurst, West-Sussex 2001
$535 - €634 - **£390** - FF4 162
Taw Marsh, Dartmoor/Dartmoor Watercolour
(33x46.5cm 12x18in) London 2001

MACWILLIAM Frederick Edward 1909-1992 [56]
$25 612 - €29 757 - **£18 000** - FF195 195
Mother and Daughter Bronze (H114.5cm H45in)
London 2001
$7 935 - €8 903 - **£5 500** - FF58 397
Seated Woman Bronze (H50cm H19in) London 2000
$1 309 - €1 270 - **£824** - FF8 329
Woman of Belfast Watercolour (27.5x40cm 10x15in)
Dublin 1999

MACY William Ferdinand 1852-1901 [7]
$2 900 - €3 154 - **£1 911** - FF20 689
Sunset Marsh, Nantucket Landscape Oil/canvas
(23x56cm 9x22in) Boston MA 2000

MACY William Starbuck 1853-1945 [8]
$1 500 - €1 364 - **£903** - FF8 944
Figures Along the Riverbank Oil/canvas (46x74cm
18x29in) Bethesda MD 1998
$6 000 - €6 753 - **£4 133** - FF44 296
Hunter with Hounds in Marsh Landscape
Oil/panel (20.5x33.5cm 8x13in) Washington 2000

MAD-JAROVA Antoinette 1937 [6]
$4 422 - €4 192 - **£2 689** - FF27 500
Connivence Huile/toile (55x46cm 21x18in) Paris
1999

MADAN Fred 1885-? [3]
$2 200 - €2 552 - **£1 543** - FF16 743
«**Niagara Falls**» Poster (102x67cm 40x26in) New-
York 2000

MADARASZ von Viktor 1830-1917 [1]
$11 220 - €12 751 - **£7 820** - FF83 640
«**Zrinyi et Frangepan**» Huile/toile (25.5x32.5cm
10x12in) Budapest 2001

MADDEN Anne 1932 [10]
$7 334 - €7 872 - **£4 907** - FF51 639
Triptych Oil/canvas (71x117cm 27x46in) Dublin 2000

MADDOCK Beatrice Louise, Bea 1934 [6]
$686 - €736 - **£459** - FF4 831
Four Aquatint (17x59cm 6x23in) Sydney 2000

MADDOX Allen 1948 [9]
$11 689 - €13 103 - **£8 175** - FF85 950
Untitled Grid Oil/canvas (173.5x244cm 68x96in)
Auckland 2001
$1 273 - €1 450 - **£879** - FF9 514
Cross Oil/canvas (45.5x45.5cm 17x17in) Auckland
2000

MADDOX Conroy 1912 [84]
$903 - €1 060 - **£650** - FF6 951
Landscape of the Mind Oil/board (25.5x17.5cm
10x6in) London 2001
$329 - €309 - **£200** - FF2 029
Inscription in the Desert Watercolour (38x51cm
14x20in) London 1999

MADELAIN Gustave 1867-1944 [305]
$2 435 - €2 058 - **£1 488** - FF13 500
**Débarquement des péniches sur la Seine à
Paris** Huile/toile (45.5x65cm 17x25in) Neuilly-sur-
Seine 1998
$1 412 - €1 524 - **£932** - FF10 000
Le remorqueur quai du Louvre Huile/panneau
(21.5x32cm 8x12in) Soissons 2001
$329 - €366 - **£229** - FF2 400
Le Pont Neuf et le Vert Galant Aquarelle/papier
(19.5x30.5cm 7x12in) Neuilly-sur-Seine 2001

MADELINE Paul 1863-1920 [293]
$4 463 - €4 497 - **£2 781** - FF29 500
Promenade en bord de rivière Huile/toile
(38x46cm 14x18in) Calais 2000
$2 263 - €2 058 - **£1 363** - FF13 500
Paysage de la Creuse Huile/carton (41.5x30.5cm
16x12in) Soissons 1998

MADERSON Arthur Karl 1942 [21]
$4 090 - €3 432 - **£2 400** - FF22 514
Lismore River Pool, Midday Sun Oil/panel
(114x112cm 45x44in) Co. Kilkenny 1998
$1 708 - €1 778 - **£1 079** - FF11 660
By the Water Oil/board (46x41cm 18x16in) Dublin
2000

MADIAI Mario 1944 [31]
$440 - €570 - **£330** - FF3 740
Senza titolo Olio/tela (70x100cm 27x39in) Prato 2000

MADIOL Adrien Jean Madyol 1845-1892 [26]
$2 167 - €2 107 - **£1 334** - FF13 821
Lecture de la lettre Huile/toile (80x64cm 31x25in)
Bruxelles 1999

MADIOL Jacques, Jakob 1871-1950 [95]
$1 265 - €1 239 - **£785** - FF8 130
Le port de Nice Huile/toile (80x100cm 31x39in)
Bruxelles 1999
$583 - €545 - **£360** - FF3 577
Jardin au Cap Ferrat Huile/panneau (33x41cm
12x16in) Lokeren 1999

MADLENER Josef 1881-1967 [24]
$1 158 - €1 125 - **£715** - FF7 378
Schafe im Allgäuer Hochgebirge Öl/Karton
(28x34cm 11x13in) Augsburg 1999
$693 - €784 - **£481** - FF5 103
Das Christkind kommt Pastell/Papier (32x38cm
12x14in) Luzern 2001

MADOU Jean-Baptiste 1796-1877 [136]
$12 960 - €11 891 - **£7 872** - FF78 000
Les Fiancés Huile/panneau (40x60cm 15x23in)
Bruxelles 1998
$5 791 - €6 807 - **£4 015** - FF44 649
Le Bon Verre Oil/panel (39x31cm 15x12in)
Amsterdam 2000

M

$355 - €372 - **£235** - FF2 439
Le trouble fête, dessin préparatoire Crayon/papier (12x20cm 4x7in) Bruxelles 2000

MADRASSI Luca 1848-1919 [85]

$3 921 - €4 573 - **£2 754** - FF30 000
La mère heureuse Bronze (H85cm H33in) Bayeux 2000

$1 400 - €1 495 - **£954** - FF9 807
Amourous Couple Bronze (H74cm H29in) Chester NY 2001

MADRAZO de Tito Livio 1899-1979 [15]

$2 800 - €2 389 - **£1 689** - FF15 668
«Saint-Clair and Day» Poster (56x80cm 22x31in) New-York 1998

MADRAZO Y GARRETA de Raimundo 1841-1920 [85]

$44 324 - €42 686 - **£27 524** - FF280 000
Portrait de femme assise Huile/toile (152x110.5cm 59x43in) Paris 1999

$69 000 - €60 065 - **£42 000** - FF394 000
Pórtico de la iglesia de San Ginés Oleo/lienzo (62x82cm 24x32in) Madrid 1999

$2 435 - €2 897 - **£1 736** - FF19 000
Gare animée à Madrid Huile/carton (20x31cm 7x12in) Calais 2000

MADRAZO Y GARRETA de Ricardo 1852-1917 [23]

$21 000 - €19 670 - **£12 910** - FF129 026
Arab Warrior by a Fountain Oil/panel (73.5x42cm 28x16in) New-York 1999

MADRAZO Y KUNTZ de Federigo 1815-1894 [28]

$14 040 - €15 617 - **£9 360** - FF102 440
Retrato de dama Oleo/lienzo (68x60cm 26x23in) Madrid 2000

$6 360 - €7 208 - **£4 320** - FF47 280
La Virgen con el niño y San Agustín Oleo/tabla (33x15.5cm 12x6in) Madrid 2000

$3 080 - €3 304 - **£2 090** - FF21 670
Felipe IV de Austria Pastel/papier (47x36.5cm 18x14in) Madrid 2001

MADRAZO Y OCHOA de Federico 1875-1934 [9]

$10 132 - €11 700 - **£7 087** - FF76 744
Porträtt på dam i blommig klänning Oil/canvas (60x92cm 23x36in) Stockholm 2001

MADSEN Andreas Peter 1822-1911 [43]

$1 152 - €1 142 - **£699** - FF7 492
Liggende hund Oil/canvas (52x71cm 20x27in) Vejle 2000

MADSEN-OHLSEN Jeppe 1891-1948 [123]

$1 758 - €1 616 - **£1 080** - FF10 598
Påskemorgen på guds Ageren, påske Litani Oil/canvas (41x41cm 16x16in) Vejle 1999

$1 165 - €1 072 - **£720** - FF7 029
Mor og barn på kirkegården, Allinge Kirke Oil/canvas (32x38cm 12x14in) Vejle 1998

MADVIG Einar 1882-1952 [20]

$825 - €738 - **£494** - FF4 841
Tvaersnit/Laengdesnit/Gavl Interieur - udkast til en sportshal Pencil (78x108cm 30x42in) København 2000

MAEDA Josaku 1926 [11]

$9 059 - €8 421 - **£5 500** - FF55 237
Paysage humain Oil/canvas (100x65.5cm 39x25in) London 1998

MAEDA Seison 1886-1977 [14]

$11 760 - €11 470 - **£7 200** - FF75 240
A Shrike Painting (115.5x35.5cm 45x13in) Tokyo 1999

$45 080 - €43 969 - **£27 600** - FF288 420
Plum Blossoms and a Bird Drawing (56x67.5cm 22x26in) Tokyo 1999

MAEGHT A. XX [2]

$481 - €485 - **£300** - FF3 181
«La Clusaz, Gd.Bornand, PLM» Poster (99x62cm 38x24in) London 2000

MAEHLY Johann Friedrich 1805-1848 [1]

$1 619 - €1 583 - **£1 000** - FF10 386
Plan der Stadt Basel Lithographie (61x38cm 24x14in) Zürich 1999

MAELLA Mariano Salvador 1738-1819 [25]

$45 900 - €54 058 - **£32 400** - FF354 600
Purísima Oleo/lienzo (158x104cm 62x40in) Madrid 2000

$35 200 - €33 036 - **£22 000** - FF216 700
Adoración de los pastores Oleo/lienzo (58x37cm 22x14in) Madrid 1999

$4 240 - €4 805 - **£2 960** - FF31 520
La Sagrada Familia y la Trinidad Oleo/lienzo (40x27.5cm 15x10in) Barcelona 2000

$1 984 - €1 862 - **£1 240** - FF12 214
Venerable Tomas de Las Virgen Lápiz (38.5x24cm 15x9in) Madrid 1999

MÄENPÄÄ Arvi 1899-1976 [8]

$915 - €773 - **£546** - FF5 073
Hem från byn Oil/canvas (9x9cm 3x3in) Helsinki 1998

MAENTEL Jacob 1763-1863 [31]

$11 000 - €9 490 - **£6 660** - FF62 252
Portrait of a Gentleman in a Windsor Chair Watercolour/paper (28x22cm 11x8in) New-York 1999

MAERTELAERE de Edmond 1876-1938 [10]

$233 - €273 - **£160** - FF1 788
Monnik (moine) Huile/toile (69x58cm 27x22in) Antwerpen 2000

MAERTELAERE de Lodewyk 1819-1864 [2]

$6 924 - €5 759 - **£4 065** - FF37 778
The Ruins of the Monastry of the Sint Baafs-Cathedral, Ghent Oil/canvas (72.5x86cm 28x33in) Amsterdam 1998

MAERTENS Médard 1875-1946 [68]

$1 608 - €1 588 - **£978** - FF10 418
Table Still Life Oil/canvas (47x55cm 18x21in) Amsterdam 2000

$560 - €620 - **£392** - FF4 065
Jeune femme nue de dos Huile/toile/panneau (27x40cm 10x15in) Bruxelles 2001

$261 - €223 - **£158** - FF1 463
Auguste Oleffe à table Fusain/papier (30x22cm 11x8in) Antwerpen 1998

MAES Dirk 1659-1717 [44]

$5 247 - €6 135 - **£3 687** - FF40 246
Heimkehr des Jägers, junge Frau begrüsst den Mann Ol/Leinwand (53x70cm 20x27in) München 2000

$857 - €920 - **£573** - FF6 032
Überfall auf einen Reisewagen, im Vordergrund ein Reiterkampf Ink (20x30.5cm 7x12in) Hamburg 1998

MAES Eugène Rémy 1849-1931 [69]

$10 500 - €10 411 - **£6 552** - FF68 292
Dans le poulailler Huile/toile (56x91cm 22x35in) Antwerpen 1999

MAES Godfried 1649-1700 **[19]**
- $1 117 - €971 - £673 - FF6 369
  Ceres überreicht Triptolemos die Zügel ihres Zweigespanns Ink (6.8x23.8cm 2x9in) Berlin 1998

MAES J.-Baptist Lodewijk 1794-1856 **[17]**
- $11 802 - €11 344 - £7 360 - FF74 415
  The Cow-Pox Vaccination Oil/canvas (60x71cm 23x27in) Amsterdam 1999

MAES Jacques 1905-1968 **[105]**
- $369 - €397 - £251 - FF2 601
  Nature morte au panier et cruche Huile/toile (80x62cm 31x25in) Bruxelles 2001

MAES Karel 1900-1974 **[7]**
- $813 - €762 - £500 - FF4 997
  «New York» Poster (99x62cm 38x24in) London 1999

MAES Nicolaes 1634-1693 **[132]**
- $24 500 - €25 398 - £14 700 - FF166 600
  Ritratto di due bambini di una nobile casa Olio/tela (123x104cm 48x40in) Imbersago (Lecco) 2001
- $15 374 - €13 279 - £9 267 - FF87 102
  Portrait of a Gentleman Oil/canvas (64.7x55.5cm 25x21in) Amsterdam 1998
- $10 195 - €9 955 - £6 500 - FF65 299
  Lady, said to be Princess of the House of Orange, white Dress Oil/canvas (45.5x35cm 17x13in) London 1999
- $7 792 - €9 076 - £5 444 - FF59 532
  Bust Length Study of an Old Woman, Wearing a Cap Red chalk (9x6.5cm 3x2in) Amsterdam 2000

MAESTOSI F. XIX-XX **[3]**
- $11 207 - €12 030 - £7 500 - FF78 912
  Palazzo Pitti, Florence Oil/canvas (100x150cm 39x59in) London 2000

MAESTRI Michelangelo ?-c.1812 **[67]**
- $4 760 - €4 934 - £2 856 - FF32 368
  Putto ebbro e satirelli con un asino Tempera/carta (31x47cm 12x18in) Roma 1999
- $7 200 - €9 330 - £5 480 - FF61 200
  L'Aurora da Guido Reni/Dal Guercino Gravure (24.5x47cm 9x18in) Venezia 2000

MAESTRO RUDOLFINO XVI **[1]**
- $21 600 - €18 660 - £14 400 - FF122 400
  «Sine Baccho et Cerere friget Venus» Olio/tela (137x200cm 53x78in) Roma 1998

MAETZEL Emil 1877-1955 **[146]**
- $382 - €434 - £262 - FF2 850
  Badender Knabe Watercolour (36x28cm 14x11in) Hamburg 2000
- $249 - €276 - £172 - FF1 811
  Schweigen Linocut (24x17cm 9x6in) Heidelberg 2001

MAETZEL-JOHANNSEN Dorothea 1886-1930 **[102]**
- $463 - €460 - £289 - FF3 018
  Nacktes Paar im Grünen, sitzend Pencil (18.5x11.8cm 7x4in) Hamburg 1999
- $713 - €665 - £431 - FF4 360
  Mutter und Kind Radierung (15.8x21.6cm 6x8in) Hamburg 1999

MAEXMONTAN Frans 1847-1901 **[12]**
- $2 366 - €2 691 - £1 641 - FF17 651
  Fartyg utanför Helsingfors Oil/canvas (95x72cm 37x28in) Helsinki 2000

MAEYER de Lode 1903-1981 **[66]**
- $155 - €173 - £107 - FF1 138
  Dame à la jupe verte Huile/panneau (60x40cm 23x15in) Antwerpen 2001

MAEZTU WHITNEY de Gustavo 1887-1947 **[57]**
- $18 525 - €19 521 - £12 350 - FF128 050
  Barco de Avila Oleo/lienzo (100x120cm 39x47in) Madrid 2000
- $9 690 - €10 211 - £6 460 - FF66 980
  Castillo de Briones Oleo/lienzo (60x80cm 23x31in) Madrid 2000
- $1 344 - €1 442 - £888 - FF9 456
  Retrato de joven Carbón/papel (26x21cm 10x8in) Madrid 2000
- $130 - €150 - £90 - FF985
  A la feria de Osuna Litografía (88x64cm 34x25in) Madrid 2000

MAFAI Antonietta Raphaël 1900-1975 **[11]**
- $10 200 - €8 812 - £6 800 - FF57 800
  Cappello rosso Olio/tavola (80x54cm 31x21in) Prato 1998
- $6 250 - €6 479 - £3 750 - FF42 500
  Le tre sorelle Bronzo (H25cm H9in) Roma 2001

MAFAI Mario 1902-1965 **[93]**
- $9 600 - €12 440 - £7 200 - FF81 600
  Mazzo di fiori Olio/tela (40x50cm 15x19in) Prato 2000
- $5 750 - €5 961 - £3 450 - FF39 100
  Donnine allegre Tecnica mista (34x44cm 13x17in) Roma 2001
- $1 400 - €1 451 - £840 - FF9 520
  Nudo all'aperto Tecnica mista/carta (33.5x47cm 13x18in) Roma 1999

MAFFEI Francesco c.1620-1660 **[12]**
- $3 353 - €2 834 - £2 000 - FF18 587
  Allegory of the East Wind Oil/panel (36x29cm 14x11in) London 1998
- $9 000 - €9 641 - £6 146 - FF63 239
  Studies for St.Sebastian and Three other Male Figures Ink (23.5x34cm 9x13in) New-York 2001

MAFFEI Ricardo 1953 **[3]**
- $16 000 - €18 803 - £11 243 - FF123 574
  Sin título Pastel/paper (68.5x106cm 26x41in) New-York 2000

MAFFEI von Guido 1838-c.1898 **[13]**
- $779 - €716 - £478 - FF4 695
  Herbstlicher Waldrand mit Holzstapel Öl/Karton (49x72cm 19x28in) Stuttgart 1999

MAFLI Walter 1915 **[65]**
- $666 - €793 - £475 - FF5 200
  Paysage d'hiver Huile/toile (50x60cm 19x23in) Genève 2000
- $252 - €295 - £175 - FF1 933
  Stilles Seeufer Öl/Leinwand (32.5x46cm 12x18in) Bern 2000

MAGAARD Valdemar 1864-1937 **[34]**
- $250 - €236 - £155 - FF1 549
  Köksinteriör med mor och barn Oil/canvas (36x34cm 14x13in) Stockholm 1999

MAGAÑA Mardonio 1866-1947 **[2]**
- $3 303 - €3 874 - £2 376 - FF25 410
  El juicio Sculpture bois (28.5x20cm 11x7in) México 2001

MAGANZA Alessandro 1556-1630 **[32]**
- $8 400 - €7 257 - £4 200 - FF47 600
  Ritratto di gentiluomo con cane Olio/tela (101x86cm 39x33in) Milano 1999

M

$1 338 - €1 131 - **£800** - FF7 421
Rebecca and Eliezer at the Well Ink (21x19cm
8x7in) London 1998

MAGATTI Pietro Antonio 1687-1768 [7]
$5 558 - €5 087 - **£3 388** - FF33 369
Kain und Abel Öl/Leinwand (73.5x89.5cm 28x35in)
Wien 1999

MAGAUD Dominique Antoine 1817-1899 [6]
$4 991 - €5 336 - **£3 398** - FF35 000
Le jeune baron assis sur son fauteuil Huile/toile
(110x82cm 43x32in) Lyon 2001

MAGAZZINI Salvatore 1955 [42]
$800 - €1 037 - **£600** - FF6 800
«Tunisi» Olio/tavola (60x80cm 23x31in) Vercelli 2000
$650 - €674 - **£390** - FF4 420
Meknès Olio/cartone (31.5x41cm 12x16in) Prato 1999

MAGE Édouard Mathurin ?-1904 [4]
$4 890 - €4 573 - **£2 961** - FF30 000
Marché en Saintonge, effet de brouillard
Huile/toile (81x131cm 31x51in) Lille 1999

MAGGI Cesare 1881-1961 [131]
$15 000 - €15 550 - **£9 000** - FF102 000
Al pascolo Olio/tela (100x140cm 39x55in) Milano
2000
$10 000 - €10 367 - **£6 000** - FF68 000
Novembre a Forno Alpi Graie Olio/cartone
(69.5x76cm 27x29in) Vercelli 2001
$2 000 - €2 592 - **£1 500** - FF17 000
Case tra il verde Olio/tavola (20x27.5cm 7x10in)
Vercelli 2000
$10 000 - €10 367 - **£6 000** - FF68 000
Montagna innevata Pastelli/cartone (37.5x56cm
14x22in) Milano 2000

MAGGIONI Piero 1931-1995 [6]
$1 280 - €1 659 - **£960** - FF10 880
Le brianze Olio/tavola (64x50.5cm 25x19in) Vercelli
2001

MAGGIORANI Luigi XIX-XX [6]
$3 207 - €3 083 - **£2 000** - FF20 223
**Elegant Gentleman with a Young Girl Holding a
Posy of Flowers** Oil/panel (39.5x26.5cm 15x10in)
West-Yorkshire 1999

MAGGIOTTO Francesco 1750-1805 [10]
$3 900 - €4 043 - **£2 340** - FF26 520
Ritratto femminile Olio/tela (54x40cm 21x15in)
Milano 2000
$8 516 - €7 911 - **£5 200** - FF51 896
**Portraits of Doge Bartolomeo Gradonico/Doge
Alvise Pisani/...** Oil/copper (14.5x12cm 5x4in)
London 1998

MAGGS John Charles 1819-1896 [102]
$5 768 - €6 374 - **£4 000** - FF41 812
Unicorn Coach on a winter's Day Oil/canvas
(36x67cm 14x26in) London 2001
$2 763 - €3 213 - **£1 973** - FF21 078
**Bath to London Coach/By Stonehenge in
Winter** Oil/canvas (20.5x40.5cm 8x15in) Toronto 2001
$1 400 - €1 493 - **£932** - FF9 795
Coaching Scenes Pencil (10x15cm 4x6in) Cleveland
OH 2000

MAGHELLI R. XIX-XX [8]
$579 - €564 - **£356** - FF3 699
Gypsi Girl Watercolour/paper (49x32cm 19x12in)
Nepean, Ont. 1999

MAGIASSIS Vassilis 1880-1926 [3]
$1 350 - €1 502 - **£900** - FF9 850
Hadrian Gate, Athens Oil/cardboard (30.5x24cm
12x9in) Athens 2000

MAGINI Carlo 1720-1806 [6]
$80 000 - €82 932 - **£48 000** - FF544 000
**Zucca, melanzane, pomodori, formaggi su piat-
to e lettere** Olio/tela (62x80.5cm 24x31in) Prato 1999

MAGLIOLI Giovanni Andrea XVI-XVII [1]
$897 - €1 022 - **£626** - FF6 707
**Nereide mit einem Seepferd/Putto mit Dreizack
auf Seepferd reitend** Kupferstich (9.5x13.5cm 3x5in)
Berlin 2001

MAGLIONE André 1838-1923 [15]
$705 - €732 - **£446** - FF4 800
La balançoire Huile/toile (20x40cm 7x15in) Nantes
2000

MAGNASCO IL LISSANDRO Alessandro c.1667-
1749 [70]
$47 817 - €51 328 - **£32 000** - FF336 691
**Wooded Landscapes with Washerwomen and
Anglers** Oil/canvas (129.5x100cm 50x39in) London
2000
$31 034 - €30 397 - **£20 000** - FF199 392
**Capuchin Friar tending a Companion's foot by
a Fire** Oil/canvas (54.5x40cm 21x15in) London 1999
$1 527 - €1 605 - **£1 005** - FF10 530
Femme allaitant Huile/toile/panneau (17.5x17.5cm
6x6in) Genève 2000
$9 713 - €10 427 - **£6 500** - FF68 394
Amorous Couple Wash (23.5x17cm 9x6in) London
2000

MAGNASCO Stefano c.1635-1674 [7]
$48 210 - €47 819 - **£30 000** - FF313 674
The Adoration of the Shepherds Oil/canvas
(174x165.5cm 68x65in) London 1999
$15 767 - €16 681 - **£10 000** - FF109 417
The Judgment of Solomon Oil/canvas (84.5x107cm
33x42in) London 1999

MAGNE Désiré Alfred 1855-1936 [23]
$4 541 - €4 650 - **£2 851** - FF30 500
**Chocolatière, plateau de pâtisserie et coupe de
fruits** Huile/toile (63x90cm 24x35in) Lyon 2000

MAGNELLI Alberto 1888-1971 [347]
$56 344 - €66 532 - **£40 000** - FF436 420
«Détermination» Oil/canvas (130x162cm 51x63in)
London 2001
$19 440 - €22 867 - **£13 935** - FF150 000
A travers l'espace Huile/toile (60x81cm 23x31in)
Paris 2001
$13 395 - €12 998 - **£8 500** - FF85 261
Peinture Oil/canvas (35x27cm 13x10in) London 1999
$5 865 - €5 067 - **£3 910** - FF33 235
Composizione Tecnica mista/carta (49x64cm
19x25in) Milano 1998
$225 - €233 - **£135** - FF1 530
Composizione Linogravure couleurs (35x49.5cm
13x19in) Prato 2000

MAGNI Giuseppe 1869-1956 [48]
$12 000 - €14 226 - **£8 742** - FF93 319
The Proposal Oil/canvas (59x47cm 23x18in) Chicago
IL 2001
$680 - €881 - **£510** - FF5 780
Paesaggio Olio/tavoletta (16x24cm 6x9in) Milano
2000

MAGNI Pietro 1817-1877 [5]
- $104 601 - €112 281 - **£70 000** - FF736 512
  La leggitrice (The Reading Girl) Marble (H173.5cm H68in) London 2001
- $3 250 - €3 585 - **£2 149** - FF23 519
  Bus of a Woman, slightly turned to the sinister Marble (H75cm H29in) New-York 2000

MAGNUS Camille 1850-? [85]
- $1 340 - €1 524 - **£930** - FF10 000
  Femme à la source Huile/toile (46x61cm 18x24in) Fontainebleau 2000
- $1 590 - €1 487 - **£960** - FF9 756
  Paysannes à l'orée du bois Huile/toile/panneau (30x40cm 11x15in) Liège 1999

MAGNUS Edouard 1799-1872 [3]
- $19 491 - €22 931 - **£13 760** - FF150 417
  «Zwei Kinder mit Blumen spielend» Oil/canvas/panel (91.5x92.5cm 36x36in) Berlin 2001

MAGRANER Amador 1957 [1]
- $5 048 - €5 578 - **£3 500** - FF36 589
  «L'homme i la ciutat» Mixed media (60x90cm 23x35in) London 2001

MAGRATH William 1838-1918 [5]
- $6 500 - €5 627 - **£3 920** - FF36 910
  «Admiring her Dance» Oil/canvas (77.5x40cm 30x15in) San-Francisco CA 2001
- $3 200 - €3 071 - **£2 006** - FF20 145
  The Student Watercolour (46.5x77cm 18x30in) New-York 1999

MAGRITTE René 1898-1967 [805]
- $1 031 800 - €1 100 118 - **£700 000** - FF7 216 300
  Ceci n'est pas une pomme Oil/panel (142x100cm 55x39in) London 2001
- $744 570 - €638 651 - **£450 000** - FF4 189 275
  «La nuit d'amour» Oil/canvas (54x64cm 21x25in) London 1998
- $224 480 - €266 974 - **£160 000** - FF1 751 232
  Ceci est un morceau de fromage Oil/masonite (14x17.5cm 5x6in) London 2000
- $75 000 - €71 104 - **£45 630** - FF466 410
  Les fanatiques Gouache/paper (25x19cm 9x7in) New-York 1999
- $1 800 - €1 525 - **£1 075** - FF10 005
  Untitled Etching (28x22cm 11x8in) New-York 1998
- $188 - €204 - **£124** - FF1 341
  L'Amour/La descente de la courtille Gelatin silver print (40x30cm 15x11in) Hamburg 2000

MAGROTTI Ercole 1890-1967 [39]
- $784 - €756 - **£484** - FF4 960
  Fishing Village with Boats Oil/canvas/board (49.5x69cm 19x27in) Johannesburg 1999
- $570 - €492 - **£380** - FF3 230
  Paesaggio costiero con barche a riva Olio/tela (30x40cm 11x15in) Roma 1998

MAGSAYSAY-HO Anita 1914 [11]
- $45 912 - €52 133 - **£31 424** - FF341 968
  Ginger Tea Oil/canvas (51x41cm 20x16in) Singapore 2000

MAGUES Isidore XIX [2]
- $2 249 - €2 317 - **£1 392** - FF15 200
  Jeune femme Pastel/paper (70x55cm 27x21in) Toulouse 2000

MAGUIRE Cecil 1930 [21]
- $3 226 - €3 682 - **£2 242** - FF24 154
  Old Lane Oil/board (49x58cm 19x23in) Blackrock, Co.Dublin 2000

- $3 472 - €3 599 - **£2 200** - FF23 606
  Regatta Morning, Roundstone Oil/board (30x40cm 12x16in) Belfast 2000

MAGUIRE Helena J. 1860-1909 [23]
- $1 331 - €1 280 - **£820** - FF8 395
  In the Highlands Watercolour/paper (32.5x47cm 12x18in) London 2000

MAGUIRE Robert 1921 [5]
- $1 500 - €1 748 - **£1 038** - FF11 469
  Woman Standing by Tree, Castle in Background Oil/masonite (101x59cm 40x23in) New-York 2000

MAGUIRE Timothy, Tim 1958 [25]
- $13 723 - €14 731 - **£9 184** - FF96 628
  Orange Column or Corinth Oil/canvas (151x214cm 59x84in) Sydney 2000
- $2 859 - €3 069 - **£1 913** - FF20 131
  Column Oil/canvas (60x90cm 23x35in) Sydney 2000
- $6 861 - €7 365 - **£4 592** - FF48 314
  Hollyhock Pastel (68x83cm 26x32in) Sydney 2000
- $684 - €798 - **£483** - FF5 237
  «Poppies» Color lithograph (63.5x90cm 25x35in) Malvern, Victoria 2000

MAGUIRE William Henry act.1830-1840 [1]
- $24 466 - €27 404 - **£17 000** - FF179 759
  View of Donegall Square Oil/panel (28.5x49cm 11x19in) London 2001

MAGYAR-MANNHEIMER Gusztáv 1859-1937 [16]
- $770 - €852 - **£506** - FF5 588
  Clouds swirling Oil/cardboard (69x97cm 27x38in) Budapest 2000

MAHER Georges Washington 1846-1926 [1]
- $4 000 - €3 427 - **£2 404** - FF22 478
  Study for Blinn Residence, Pasadena, California Watercolour (89x30.5cm 35x12in) New-York 1998

MAHIAS Robert 1890-? [6]
- $1 371 - €1 518 - **£950** - FF9 958
  «L'hiver au Mont-Doré» Poster (105x76cm 41x29in) London 2001

MAHLANGU Speelman 1958 [10]
- $1 471 - €1 418 - **£909** - FF9 300
  Woman seated on a Bench Bronze (H35cm H13in) Johannesburg 1999

MAHLER Sepp 1901-1975 [1]
- $1 217 - €1 022 - **£715** - FF6 707
  «Das Paar»/«Einsam» Lithographie (16.5x11.5cm 6x4in) Stuttgart 1999

MAHLKNECHT Edmund 1820-1903 [63]
- $6 292 - €5 448 - **£3 817** - FF35 737
  Auf dem Weg zur Alm Öl/Karton (36.5x58cm 14x22in) Wien 1998
- $916 - €998 - **£631** - FF6 548
  Mountainous Landscape with a Woman on a Path Oil/panel (17x21cm 6x8in) Amsterdam 2001

MAHOKIAN Wartan 1869-1937 [56]
- $2 630 - €3 068 - **£1 849** - FF20 123
  Segelschiffe bei Sonnenuntergang vor der Insel Krim Öl/Leinwand (108x160cm 42x62in) Kempten 2000
- $2 200 - €2 476 - **£1 515** - FF16 241
  Mondnacht bei Metone (Moon Night near Metone) Oil/canvas (81.5x116cm 32x45in) Washington 2000
- $2 106 - €2 058 - **£1 335** - FF13 500
  Marine Huile/toile (33x42.5cm 12x16in) Paris 1999

M

MAHONEY James 1810-1879 **[9]**
🖋 **$595 - €635 - £396 -** FF4 164
Rue aux Ours, Rouen Watercolour (36x25cm
14x10in) Dublin 2000

MAHONEY James Owen 1907-1987 **[10]**
👁 **$1 500 - €1 671 - £1 048 -** FF10 964
«Evening» Oil/board (40x50cm 16x20in) New-York
2001

MAHOOD Marguerite Henriette 1901-1989 **[10]**
▥ **$986 - €917 - £609 -** FF6 018
Fury Linocut in colors (27.5x36.5cm 10x14in)
Melbourne 1999

MAHRINGER Anton 1902-1974 **[29]**
🖋 **$2 289 - €2 543 - £1 533 -** FF16 684
Drei Zinnen Pastell/Papier (49.5x42cm 19x16in) Wien
2000
▥ **$770 - €872 - £538 -** FF5 720
«Gebirgslandschaft» Farbserigraphie (48x35.5cm
18x13in) Klagenfurt 2001

MAHU Cornelis c.1613-1689 **[38]**
👁 **$22 025 - €18 164 - £12 975 -** FF119 150
**Stilleben mit einem Flötenglas, einem
umgestürzten Zinnkrug** Oil/panel (48x64cm
18x25in) Wien 1998

MAHU Victor c.1665-1700 **[13]**
👁 **$11 576 - €13 189 - £8 000 -** FF86 511
**Tavern Scene with Topers drinking, smoking
and playing Cards** Oil/canvas (56x82.5cm 22x32in)
London 2000

MAHUET XIX **[7]**
🖎 **$4 538 - €4 269 - £2 811 -** FF28 000
François Ier et Claude de France à Cheval
Bronze (43x46cm 16x18in) Paris 1999

MAï TRUNG THU 1906-1980 **[77]**
👁 **$1 661 - €1 906 - £1 136 -** FF12 500
La jeune femme au paravent Peinture
(61.5x45.5cm 24x17in) Soissons 2000
👁 **$6 312 - €7 168 - £4 320 -** FF47 020
**Femme couchée à l'éventail (Reclining Lady
with a Fan)** Oil/canvas (23x53cm 9x20in) Singapore
2000
🖋 **$3 544 - €3 303 - £2 142 -** FF21 667
Femme Gouache (34x17.5cm 13x6in) Singapore 1999

MAIA Celeste 1941 **[2]**
👁 **$13 200 - €14 955 - £9 000 -** FF98 100
Two for Tango Oleo/lienzo (130x145cm 51x57in)
Lisboa 2000

MAIANO da Benedetto 1442-1497 **[1]**
🖎 **$50 000 - €51 833 - £30 000 -** FF340 000
Madonna col Bambino Terracotta (110x40cm
43x15in) Firenze 2001

MAIDEN Joseph 1813-1843 **[2]**
👁 **$305 609 - €24 447 - £16 000 -** FF160 360
**A Bay Hunter and a Spaniel in a wooded
Landscape** Oil/canvas (80x108cm 31x42in) London
1999

MAIDMENT Henry XIX-XX **[80]**
👁 **$1 644 - €1 765 - £1 100 -** FF11 578
**Figures on the Edge of a Riverbank/A farm by a
Wooded Pool** Oil/canvas (30.5x61cm 12x24in)
London 2000
👁 **$896 - €962 - £600 -** FF6 313
**Shepherd, shepherdess and Sheep by bridge
over Pond** Oil/canvas (27x37cm 10x14in) Burton-on-
Trent, Staffs 2000

MAIER Emil 1845-? **[1]**
👁 **$4 820 - €3 960 - £2 800 -** FF25 973
Arabs near Steps leading to a Mosque Oil/canvas
(62x41cm 24x16in) London 1998

MAIGNAN Albert Pierre René 1845-1908 **[30]**
👁 **$1 497 - €1 677 - £1 049 -** FF11 000
Tête de jeune homme Huile/panneau (35x23.5cm
13x9in) Paris 2001
👁 **$1 500 - €1 316 - £910 -** FF8 630
Exposition Franco-Britannique Poster (160x119cm
63x47in) New-York 1999

MAIGRET Georges Edmond XIX-XX **[7]**
👁 **$945 - €933 - £582 -** FF6 119
Strandlandskap med musselplockerskor Oil/can-
vas (70x110cm 27x43in) Stockholm 1999

MAIJLER Ede XIX-XX **[1]**
👁 **$4 290 - €3 997 - £2 667 -** FF26 218
Kaiser Franz Joseph I von Österreich
Öl/Leinwand (142x78cm 55x30in) Wien 1999

MAILAND Henri Ange Eugène XIX **[18]**
📷 **$1 457 - €1 677 - £1 004 -** FF11 000
**Cour du Cloître de Saint-Bertrand de
Comminges** Tirage albuminé (26x36cm 10x14in)
Paris 2000

MAILLARD Émile 1846-1926 **[28]**
👁 **$1 280 - €1 082 - £761 -** FF7 100
Tempête dans le port de Dieppe Huile/toile
(40x50cm 15x19in) Amiens 1998
👁 **$745 - €793 - £471 -** FF5 200
Temps gris sur Venise Huile/toile (33x46cm
12x18in) Paris 2000

MAILLART Diogène 1840-1926 **[41]**
👁 **$10 840 - €12 196 - £7 464 -** FF80 000
Le retour du fils Huile/toile (112x166cm 44x65in)
Nancy 2000
👁 **$2 051 - €2 362 - £1 400 -** FF15 493
**Lady, Said to Alice Dorchy, Wearing a Blue
Dress and Blue Head-Band** Oil/canvas (63x47cm
24x18in) London 2000
👁 **$552 - €610 - £374 -** FF4 000
Autoportrait à l'âge de cinquante-neuf ans
Huile/toile (35x27cm 13x10in) Paris 2000

MAILLAUD Fernand 1862-1948 **[301]**
👁 **$3 832 - €3 354 - £2 321 -** FF22 000
Ane sous les arbres près du pont Huile/toile
(54x67cm 21x26in) La Varenne-Saint-Hilaire 1998
👁 **$1 308 - €1 524 - £906 -** FF10 000
Charrette et paysans au bord de l'eau Huile/pan-
neau (27x35cm 10x13in) Besançon 2000
🖋 **$788 - €884 - £551 -** FF5 800
Un couple assis sur un banc Crayons couleurs
(28.5x23cm 11x9in) Paris 2001

MAILLET Leo 1902-1990 **[16]**
▥ **$269 - €307 - £187 -** FF2 012
Zwei weibliche Akte Drypoint (49.6x24.5cm 19x9in)
Berlin 2000

MAILLOL Aristide 1861-1944 **[806]**
👁 **$480 000 - €455 064 - £292 032 -** FF2 985 024
Méditerranée (Deux baigneuses) Oil/canvas
(98x130cm 38x51in) New-York 1999
🖎 **$650 000 - €713 342 - £418 535 -** FF4 679 220
Torse de Vénus Bronze (H113.5cm H44in) New-York
2000
🖎 **$55 000 - €51 775 - £33 979 -** FF339 619
Jeune fille accroupie Bronze (H20cm H7in) New-
York 1999

🖼 $4 251 - €5 039 - **£3 000** - FF33 054
Femme nue debout en mouvement Pastel/paper (34x23cm 13x9in) London 2000

▥ $390 - €455 - **£275** - FF2 987
Nude Seen from Behind Lithograph (14x9cm 5x3in) Toronto 2000

MAINCENT Gustave 1850-1887 [45]

👝 $30 000 - €25 883 - **£18 099** - FF169 779
La grenouillère Oil/canvas (90x150cm 35x59in) New-York 1998

👝 $2 966 - €2 567 - **£1 800** - FF16 841
Figures in a Wood Beside a River Oil/canvas (54x73cm 21x28in) London 1998

🖼 $2 641 - €2 897 - **£1 753** - FF19 000
Élégants en bord de mer Huile/toile (32.5x46cm 12x18in) Melun 2000

MAINELLA Raffaele 1858-1907 [58]

🖼 $1 054 - €1 020 - **£650** - FF6 689
On the Venetian Lagoon Watercolour/paper (30.5x15cm 12x5in) London 1999

MAINERI de Gian Francesco XV-XVI [3]

👝 $95 000 - €105 209 - **£64 429** - FF690 127
Madonna and Child Oil/panel (49.5x35.5cm 19x13in) New-York 2000

MAINO de Giovanni Angelo 1475-c.1539 [1]

👝 $280 000 - €290 263 - **£168 000** - FF1 904 000
Angeli reggicandelabro con stemmi Sculpture bois (82x32x20cm 32x12x7in) Firenze 2001

MAINOLFI Luigi 1949 [20]

👝 $600 - €622 - **£360** - FF4 080
Composizione Acrilico/cartone (69x48cm 27x18in) Vercelli 2000

👝 $320 - €415 - **£240** - FF2 720
Composizione Tecnica mista (15x15cm 5x5in) Vercelli 2000

👝 $13 000 - €13 476 - **£7 800** - FF88 400
Chiome nere Terracotta (110x62cm 43x24in) Vercelli 2000

👝 $1 680 - €2 177 - **£1 260** - FF14 280
Taso Terracotta (21x40x23cm 8x15x9in) Roma 2000

MAINSSIEUX Lucien 1885-1958 [457]

👝 $1 060 - €1 143 - **£711** - FF7 500
Les Alpilles Huile/toile/panneau (46x55cm 18x21in) Grenoble 2000

👝 $426 - €457 - **£285** - FF3 000
Nature morte aux pommes Huile/toile (25x33cm 10x13in) Grenoble 2000

🖼 $166 - €198 - **£118** - FF1 300
Femme d'Afrique du Nord Encre/papier (27x21cm 10x8in) Grenoble 2000

MAIOLI Luigi 1819-1897 [1]

👝 $5 500 - €4 910 - **£3 368** - FF32 209
Réveil du Printemps Marble (H66cm H25in) New-York 1999

MAIRE André 1898-1984 [377]

👝 $7 083 - €6 860 - **£4 455** - FF45 000
Les bûcherons, projet de couverture pour la revue L'Illustration Huile/toile (151x96cm 59x37in) Paris 1999

👝 $3 053 - €3 430 - **£2 126** - FF22 500
Les Tahitiennes Huile/panneau (62x93cm 24x36in) Cannes 2001

🖼 $871 - €762 - **£527** - FF5 000
Femme d'Afrique Fusain (56x44cm 22x17in) Paris 1998

MAIRE Edmond 1862-1914 [6]

👝 $26 000 - €24 796 - **£15 826** - FF162 653
Freshly Picked Flowers with a Watering Can Oil/canvas (89.5x117cm 35x46in) New-York 1999

MAIROVITCH Zvi 1911-1974 [141]

👝 $2 200 - €2 281 - **£1 449** - FF14 962
A Girl Oil/canvas (46x38cm 18x14in) Herzelia-Pituah 2000

👝 $700 - €683 - **£443** - FF4 482
Head of a Woman Oil/canvas (32.5x23.5cm 12x9in) Tel Aviv 1999

🖼 $2 600 - €2 570 - **£1 591** - FF16 856
House Drawing (31x33.5cm 12x13in) Tel Aviv 2000

MAISSEN Fernand 1873-? [27]

🖼 $478 - €457 - **£301** - FF3 000
La chasse sous la neige à Saint-Cyr-du Vexin Aquarelle, gouache/papier (23x32cm 9x12in) Deauville 1999

▥ $478 - €564 - **£336** - FF3 700
Braque du Bourbonnais/Braque d'Auvergne Gravure (40x56cm 15x22in) Neuilly-sur-Seine 2000

MAISTRE de Roy 1894-1968 [108]

👝 $45 325 - €42 733 - **£28 091** - FF280 308
The Footballers Oil/canvas (90.5x134.5cm 35x52in) Melbourne 1999

👝 $13 998 - €13 234 - **£8 687** - FF86 807
Scene Two from a Film Ballet in Colour Oil/board (48.5x58.5cm 19x23in) Malvern, Victoria 1999

👝 $5 844 - €6 424 - **£3 745** - FF42 136
Portrait of Bethia Foot Oil/wood (43x33cm 16x12in) Melbourne 2000

🖼 $625 - €729 - **£435** - FF4 783
Study for Crucifixion Wash (57.5x40cm 22x15in) Melbourne 2000

MAISTRE Louis 1862-? [2]

🖼 $3 729 - €4 024 - **£2 502** - FF26 397
Portraet af en russisk dreng Pastel/paper (56x47cm 22x18in) København 2000

MAITLAND Paul 1863-1909 [30]

👝 $5 304 - €4 576 - **£3 200** - FF30 018
Sunset behind the Trees, Kensington Gardens Oil/cardboard (11.5x18cm 4x7in) London 1998

MAITRE DE L'AUTEL DE MAILKAMMER XV [1]

👝 $75 750 - €76 987 - **£47 621** - FF505 000
«Le Christ au jardin des Oliviers»/«Le Christ couronné d'épines» Huile/panneau (143x54.5cm 56x21in) Granville 2000

MAITRE DE LA COUR DE BOURGOGNE (Jean Lorny/Lormy) XVI [1]

🖼 $3 743 - €3 663 - **£2 400** - FF24 029
The Deposition Ink (20x33cm 7x12in) London 1999

MAITRE DE LA PASSION DE KARLSRUHE XV [1]

👝 $4 703 400 - €4 116 123 - **£2 848 500** - FF27 000 000
La Flagellation du Christ Technique mixte/panneau (66.5x46.5cm 26x18in) Paris 1998

MAITRE DES JEUX XVII [3]

👝 $17 000 - €14 962 - **£10 349** - FF98 146
The Poullain Family and their Servants Gathered Around a Table Oil/canvas (89x115.5cm 35x45in) New-York 1999

MAITRE DU RETABLE BRABANÇON XV [1]

👝 $227 970 - €259 163 - **£156 400** - FF1 700 000
Retable de la Passion Sculpture bois (194x215x28cm 76x84x11in) Louviers 2000

MAITRE L.D. (Léon Davent?) act.1540-1556 **[3]**
🏛 **$5 146** - €6 135 - **£3 669** - FF40 246
Sacra Conversazione, nach Parmigianino
Etching (24.1x18.4cm 9x7in) Berlin 2000

MAITRE M.Z. XV-XVI **[2]**
🏛 **$1 207** - €1 250 - **£768** - FF8 200
La Décollation de Sainte Catherine Burin
(25x31cm 9x12in) Paris 2000

MAJANI Augusto 1867-1959 **[10]**
✏ **$480** - €622 - **£360** - FF4 080
La preda Tecnica mista/carta (32x24cm 12x9in) Torino
2000

MAJO de Paolo 1703-1784 **[3]**
◔ **$4 320** - €3 732 - **£2 880** - FF24 480
San Gennaro Olio/rame (28.5x22cm 11x8in) Napoli
1998

MAJOR Ernest Lee 1864-1951 **[10]**
◔ **$7 000** - €8 164 - **£4 914** - FF53 552
Robed Women in a Woodland View Oil/canvas
(95x68.5cm 37x26in) Boston MA 2001
✏ **$2 000** - €1 909 - **£1 249** - FF12 523
Woman with a Ring, Melisande Pastel/paper
(64x50cm 25x20in) Dedham MA 1999

MAJOR Henry A. XIX-XX **[12]**
◔ **$1 058** - €973 - **£650** - FF6 383
A Bunch of Grapes hanging from a Vine Oil/canvas (30.5x35.5cm 12x13in) London 1998

MAJOR Theodore 1908 **[6]**
◔ **$3 542** - €4 157 - **£2 500** - FF27 269
Portrait of a Young Woman Oil/board (62x75cm
24x29in) Manchester 2000

MAJORE Frank 1948 **[13]**
📷 **$2 400** - €2 311 - **£1 500** - FF15 159
April in Paris Cibachrome print (157.5x122cm
62x48in) New-York 1999

MAJOREL Fernand 1898-1965 **[36]**
◔ **$1 111** - €1 296 - **£779** - FF8 500
Rivage du Midi Huile/toile (72x116cm 28x45in) Paris
2000
✏ **$338** - €366 - **£234** - FF2 400
Jeune femme allongée Sanguine (32x44.5cm
12x17in) Lyon 2001

MAJORELLE Jacques 1886-1962 **[219]**
◔ **$21 907** - €25 611 - **£15 640** - FF168 000
Scène de marché en Afrique Huile/toile/carton
(63.5x52.5cm 25x20in) Paris 2001
◔ **$1 409** - €1 601 - **£989** - FF10 500
Tolède, temps gris (septembre) Huile/panneau
(24x33cm 9x12in) Paris 2001
⬧ **$3 505** - €3 811 - **£2 310** - FF25 000
Vase marocain Céramique (55x40cm 21x15in) Paris
2000
✏ **$17 667** - €19 818 - **£12 246** - FF130 000
Scène de marché Pastel gras (65x50cm 25x19in)
Paris 2000
🏛 **$2 305** - €1 906 - **£1 352** - FF12 500
«Le Maroc, le Grand Atlas» Affiche (105x75cm
41x29in) Paris 1998

MAJORELLE Louis 1859-1926 **[5]**
⬧ **$2 791** - €3 170 - **£1 940** - FF20 794
Kerzenhalter Bronze (H15cm H5in) München 2001

MAJZNER Victor 1945 **[21]**
◔ **$4 670** - €5 231 - **£3 244** - FF34 312
«Stalking out Paradise» Oil/canvas (198.5x168cm
78x66in) Melbourne 2001

✏ **$817** - €900 - **£543** - FF5 906
«Road to Paraburdoo, Pilbara» Watercolour/paper
(55x75.5cm 21x29in) Melbourne 2000

MAK Paul, Pavel Ivanov 1885-c.1960 **[17]**
✏ **$1 432** - €1 611 - **£1 000** - FF10 567
Le coiffeur du village Gouache (28.5x17.5cm
11x6in) London 2001

MAKAROV Ivan Kuzmich 1822-1897 **[2]**
◔ **$7 172** - €7 699 - **£4 800** - FF50 503
Portrait of a Boy in soldier's Cap Oil/canvas
(53.5x43cm 21x16in) London 2000

MAKART Hans 1840-1884 **[94]**
◔ **$14 499** - €12 179 - **£8 500** - FF79 887
**An elegant Lady, possibly Baroness
Teschenberg** Oil/canvas (235x123cm 92x48in)
London 1998
◔ **$15 480** - €14 534 - **£9 600** - FF95 340
Der Falke Öl/Leinwand (63x47.5cm 24x18in) Wien
2001
◔ **$5 021** - €5 624 - **£3 489** - FF36 892
«Halbportrait einer vornehmen Dame» Oil/panel
(33x24cm 12x9in) Bamberg 2001
✏ **$1 123** - €1 090 - **£693** - FF7 150
Satyrkinder beim Spielen Pencil/paper (18x18.5cm
7x7in) Wien 1999

MÄKELÄ Juho 1885-1943 **[11]**
✏ **$295** - €320 - **£204** - FF2 096
Landskap Watercolour/paper (32x25cm 12x9in)
Helsinki 2001

MÄKELÄ Jukka 1949 **[21]**
◔ **$843** - €925 - **£542** - FF6 067
Snöslask Acrylic (70x100cm 27x39in) Helsinki 2000
◔ **$587** - €655 - **£408** - FF4 296
Komposition Acrylic (22x37.5cm 8x14in) Stockholm
2001

MÄKELÄ Marika 1947 **[20]**
◔ **$6 240** - €6 059 - **£3 853** - FF39 743
Utan titel Oil/canvas (230x300cm 90x118in)
Stockholm 1999
◔ **$1 664** - €1 856 - **£1 156** - FF12 172
Guardian Oil/wood (41x30cm 16x11in) Stockholm
2001

MAKHAIEFF Michaïl Ivanovitch 1718-1770 **[1]**
🏛 **$2 582** - €2 121 - **£1 500** - FF13 914
**Vue des bords de la Neva en remontant la riviè-
re** Engraving (53x140cm 20x55in) London 1998

MAKI Haku 1924 **[13]**
🏛 **$150** - €144 - **£93** - FF947
Persimmons Color lithograph (21x23cm 8x9in)
Chicago IL 1999

MAKIELSKI Leon A. 1885-? **[8]**
◔ **$2 500** - €2 320 - **£1 501** - FF15 219
Fall Colors Oil/canvas (63x76cm 25x30in) Milford CT
1999

MÄKILÄ Otto 1904-1955 **[45]**
◔ **$747** - €841 - **£514** - FF5 516
Ensamt träd Oil/canvas/panel (28x16cm 11x6in)
Helsinki 2000
✏ **$284** - €252 - **£174** - FF1 654
Kvinnofigurer Drawing (10.5x15.5cm 4x6in) Helsinki
1999

MAKIN Jeffrey T. 1943 **[54]**
◔ **$4 675** - €5 139 - **£2 996** - FF33 708
The Three Sisters Oil/canvas (120.5x150cm 47x59in)
Melbourne 2000

$1 104 - €1 036 - £682 - FF6 794
Pathway Sherbrooke Forest Oil/canvas (87x113cm 34x44in) Sydney 1999

MAKLOTH Johann XIX [5]
$1 777 - €2 045 - £1 227 - FF13 415
Kinderbildnis Öl/Leinwand (43x36cm 16x14in) München 2000

MAKOS Christopher 1948 [19]
$1 281 - €1 180 - £769 - FF7 739
Altered Image Silkscreen (101.5x81.5cm 39x32in) Amsterdam 1999
$730 - €818 - £507 - FF5 366
Andy Warhol Gelatin silver print (29.5x19.5cm 11x7in) Köln 2001

MAKOVSKI Aleksandr Vladimir. 1869-1924 [25]
$4 980 - €4 586 - £3 037 - FF37 954
Gaggle of Geese Oil/canvas (45x63cm 17x24in) London 2001
$4 058 - €3 900 - £2 500 - FF25 583
Landscape with River Oil/canvas/board (19x29cm 7x11in) London 1999
$2 920 - €2 859 - £1 796 - FF18 754
Musiikkihetki Akvarell/papper (27x21cm 10x8in) Helsinki 1999

MAKOVSKI Konstantin Egorovich 1839-1915 [113]
$44 777 - €53 287 - £32 000 - FF349 542
Olenka and Kolya on the Balcony of the Dacha, the Artist's Children Oil/canvas (135x102cm 53x40in) London 2000
$13 517 - €15 705 - £9 500 - FF103 019
Spring Bacchanale Oil/board (44.5x60cm 17x23in) London 2001
$13 253 - €14 860 - £9 000 - FF97 476
Portrait of a Child Oil/panel (35x26.5cm 13x10in) London 2000
$2 845 - €3 306 - £2 000 - FF21 688
Birch in the Glade Watercolour/paper (51x35cm 20x13in) London 2001

MAKOVSKI Vladimir Egorovitch 1846-1920 [100]
$7 470 - €8 409 - £5 145 - FF55 160
Interior Oil/canvas (60x50cm 23x19in) Helsinki 2000
$8 138 - €9 447 - £5 616 - FF61 971
Die alte Uniform Oil/panel (23.8x17.8cm 9x7in) Wien 2000
$2 988 - €3 208 - £2 000 - FF21 043
Portrait of a Violinist Watercolour/paper (44x33cm 17x12in) London 2000

MAKOWSKI Tadeusz, Tadé 1882-1932 [60]
$51 383 - €42 480 - £30 143 - FF278 651
Deux enfants au drapeau et au lampion Oil/canvas (81x60cm 31x23in) Warszawa 1998
$8 321 - €8 385 - £5 186 - FF55.000
Pommiers en fleurs Huile/toile (16x27cm 6x10in) Paris 2000
$10 966 - €12 247 - £7 650 - FF80 338
Quatre enfants au drapeau, ballon et chien Aquarelle (25.5x30cm 10x11in) Warszawa 2001

MAKOWSKI Zbigniew 1930 [13]
$1 379 - €1 622 - £988 - FF10 639
Spirale, 2e version Encre/papier (50x68cm 19x26in) Warszawa 2001

MAKS Kees 1876-1967 [136]
$50 400 - €54 630 - £30 585 - FF286 195
Danse de gitanes Oil/canvas (124x162cm 48x63in) Amsterdam 1998
$21 549 - €18 654 - £13 077 - FF122 365
Circus Oil/board (40x50cm 15x19in) Amsterdam 1998

$6 488 - €5 899 - £3 980 - FF38 695
«Vrijheidsdressur» Oil/board (32x47cm 12x18in) Amsterdam 1999
$2 036 - €1 906 - £1 267 - FF12 501
Elegant Lady Watercolour/paper (19x15.5cm 7x6in) Amsterdam 1999

MAL Nidha XVIII [1]
$18 000 - €19 891 - £12 483 - FF130 476
Ruler on Terrace Painting (26.5x37.5cm 10x14in) New-York 2001

MALACARNE Claudio 1956 [15]
$850 - €881 - £510 - FF5 780
Mattino d'estate Olio/tela (60x80cm 23x31in) Vercelli 2000

MALACHOWSKI Soter Jaxa 1867-1952 [33]
$2 111 - €2 463 - £1 508 - FF16 157
Kapryjska noc Huile/toile (100x70cm 39x27in) Lódz 2000
$965 - €1 098 - £669 - FF7 200
Promenade en barque Aquarelle, gouache/papier (35.5x52cm 13x20in) Lódz 2000

MALACREA Francesco 1812-1886 [20]
$2 622 - €2 897 - £1 818 - FF19 000
Grappes de raisins Huile/toile (41.5x31.5cm 16x12in) Paris 2001

MALAGODI Giuseppe 1890-1968 [22]
$700 - €726 - £420 - FF4 760
Nel paese Olio/tavola (55.5x65cm 21x25in) Roma 1999

MALAGOLI Francesco XVIII [6]
$28 380 - €30 025 - £18 000 - FF196 950
Grapes, Figs, Apples, Pears, Pomegranates, Black Currants and Fennel Oil/canvas (41x56.5cm 16x22in) London 2000

MALAINE Joseph Laurent 1745-1809 [7]
$11 242 - €10 671 - £7 014 - FF70 000
Panier de fleurs et de fruits Huile/panneau (31x27.5cm 12x10in) Deauville 1999

MALANCA José 1897-1967 [10]
$3 200 - €3 549 - £2 129 - FF23 278
Paisaje serrano Oleo/lienzo (37x50cm 14x19in) Buenos-Aires 2000
$2 900 - €3 240 - £2 038 - FF22 101
Calle de pueblo Oleo/lienzo (38x38cm 14x14in) Buenos-Aires 2000

MALANGA Gérard 1943 [6]
$520 - €488 - £321 - FF3 200
Jonas Mekas Print (50.5x40.5cm 19x15in) Paris 1999

MALANGI David 1927-1999 [16]
$1 315 - €1 269 - £831 - FF8 324
Gunmirringu Mortuary Rites Mixed media (69.5x40cm 27x15in) Melbourne 1999

MALANI Nalini 1946 [11]
$1 000 - €1 137 - £698 - FF7 460
Media Material (Betrayal) Mixed media/paper (51x71cm 20x27in) New-York 2000

MALARDOT Charles André 1817-1879 [8]
$240 - €272 - £162 - FF1 786
Landschap met vissers bij een meer naar Etching (36x26cm 14x10in) Dordrecht 2000

MALASSIS Edmond act.c.1885-c.1940 [18]
$170 - €183 - £114 - FF1 200
Indiscrétion Aquarelle/papier (28x19cm 11x7in) Paris 2000

M

MALATESTA Adeodato 1806-1891 [2]
- $17 500 - €18 141 - **£10 500** - FF119 000
  Al mercato Olio/tela (100x82cm 39x32in) Firenze 2000

MALATESTA Narciso 1835-1896 [5]
- $4 500 - €3 887 - **£3 000** - FF25 500
  Natura morta con cacciagione Olio/tela (82x57cm 32x22in) Firenze 1998

MALAUSSENA Jean-Pierre 1935 [58]
- $669 - €686 - **£413** - FF4 500
  Amoureux II Bronze (21x18x10cm 8x7x3in) Paris 2000

MALAVAL Robert 1937-1980 [172]
- $2 163 - €2 134 - **£1 332** - FF14 000
  Souvenir de Chine Acrylique/papier (75x55cm 29x21in) Versailles 1999
- $598 - €686 - **£409** - FF4 500
  Dissipation d'un rideau noir Huile/panneau (20x26cm 7x10in) Paris 2000
- $392 - €457 - **£275** - FF3 000
  «Deux pieds» Sculpture (H27cm H10in) Versailles 2000
- $1 081 - €1 067 - **£666** - FF7 000
  Les bielles Encre (48x62.5cm 18x24in) Versailles 1999
- $215 - €229 - **£135** - FF1 500
  Sans titre Lithographie (50x65cm 19x25in) Paris 2000

MALBET Aurélie Léontine XIX-XX [4]
- $11 000 - €9 738 - **£6 725** - FF63 875
  A Feast for the Hungry Ones Oil/canvas (65.5x100.5cm 25x39in) New-York 1999

MALBON William 1805-1877 [25]
- $3 150 - €2 999 - **£2 000** - FF19 674
  Chat amoung the Ruins Oil/panel (44x59cm 17x23in) Billingshurst, West-Sussex 1999
- $733 - €789 - **£500** - FF5 175
  Creswell Crags Oil/panel (31x46cm 12x18in) West-Yorkshire 2001

MALBONE Edward Green 1777-1807 [8]
- $6 000 - €6 613 - **£3 991** - FF43 376
  Portrait of Gentleman in Black Coat Miniature (6x5cm 2x2in) Portsmouth NH 2000

MALBRANCHE Louis Claude 1790-1838 [12]
- $2 408 - €2 744 - **£1 654** - FF18 000
  Villages sous la neige Huile/toile (28x41cm 11x16in) Paris 2000

MALCHAIR John Baptiste 1731-1812 [26]
- $2 689 - €2 887 - **£1 800** - FF18 938
  Brewhouse at the back of Brewers Lane with tom Tower beyond, Oxford Watercolour (21x32.5cm 8x12in) London 2000

MALCHIN Karl 1838-1923 [5]
- $11 352 - €11 248 - **£6 888** - FF73 785
  Blick auf Brunshaupten und Arendsee Öl/Leinwand (68x119cm 26x46in) Satow 2000

MALCHUS von Carl Freiherr 1835-1889 [6]
- $10 760 - €9 915 - **£6 480** - FF65 040
  Retour des pêcheurs Huile/toile (80x129cm 31x50in) Bruxelles 1999

MALCLES Jean-Denis 1912 [42]
- $1 845 - €1 574 - **£1 100** - FF10 328
  «La Belle et la Bête» Poster (159x114.5cm 62x45in) London 1998

MALCZEWSKI Jacek 1854-1929 [283]
- $50 578 - €56 717 - **£34 342** - FF372 042
  Tobiasz avec un ange Huile/toile (156x120cm 61x47in) Warszawa 2000
- $26 652 - €29 700 - **£17 928** - FF194 820
  Tête de cheval Huile/toile (87x73cm 34x28in) Warszawa 2000
- $10 315 - €9 846 - **£6 445** - FF64 587
  Autoportrait Oil/board (26.8x21.5cm 10x8in) Warszawa 1999
- $888 - €990 - **£597** - FF6 494
  Parki et Minerwa Crayon (22x28cm 8x11in) Warszawa 2000
- $617 - €684 - **£410** - FF4 487
  Portrait de Feliks Manghi Jasienski Lithographie (59x43cm 23x16in) Warszawa 2000

MALCZEWSKI Rafal 1892-1965 [54]
- $811 - €852 - **£535** - FF5 587
  Paysage au lac Huile/panneau (51x61cm 20x24in) Montréal 2000
- $555 - €621 - **£376** - FF4 073
  Hiver Aquarelle (37x55.5cm 14x21in) Warszawa 2000

MALDARELLI Frederico 1826-1893 [6]
- $13 420 - €14 404 - **£8 980** - FF94 486
  Two Women of Pompeii Oil/canvas (155x137cm 61x53in) Toronto 1999

MALEAS Konstantinos 1879-1928 [24]
- $32 400 - €36 039 - **£21 600** - FF236 400
  Alexander's Gate Oil/cardboard (55x50cm 21x19in) Athens 2000
- $13 188 - €15 184 - **£9 000** - FF99 602
  The Bridge at Lipio Oil/board (22x30.5cm 8x12in) London 2000

MALECKI Wladyslaw Aleksander 1836-1900 [16]
- $5 778 - €6 624 - **£3 549** - FF36 892
  Polnische Kavallerie und Planwagen auf Waldlichtung Öl/Leinwand (27.5x41cm 10x16in) Berlin 1999

MALECY de Alexis Joseph Louis 1799-1842 [2]
- $272 - €305 - **£184** - FF2 000
  Portrait d'homme Huile/toile (81x65cm 31x25in) Paris 2000

MALESCI Giovanni 1884-1969 [22]
- $1 250 - €1 296 - **£750** - FF8 500
  Le colline di Santa Margherita Ligure Olio/tavola (19x27.5cm 7x10in) Milano 2000

MALESPINA Louis-Ferdinand 1874-1940 [80]
- $2 014 - €2 287 - **£1 399** - FF15 000
  Course de trotteurs Huile/isorel (46x61cm 18x24in) Dijon 2001
- $2 050 - €2 287 - **£1 384** - FF15 000
  Course à Chantilly Huile/panneau (27x34.5cm 10x13in) Deauville 2000
- $413 - €396 - **£255** - FF2 600
  Le saut de la hale Aquarelle, gouache (22x17.5cm 8x6in) Senlis 1999
- $355 - €396 - **£239** - FF2 600
  «Auteuil, course d'obstacle» Affiche (102x119cm 40x46in) Orléans 2000

MALESPINE Émile 1892-1952 [20]
- $191 - €183 - **£119** - FF1 200
  Composition Gouache/papier (36.5x25.5cm 14x10in) Paris 1999

MALET Albert 1905-1986 [390]
- $1 479 - €1 403 - **£924** - FF9 200
  Panorama de Rouen Huile/toile (51x65cm 20x25in) Ourville-en-Caux 1999

$454 - €534 - £329 - FF3 500
Vue de Rouen Huile/toile (19x33cm 7x12in) Calais
2001

$260 - €274 - £171 - FF1 800
Sous-bois Gouache/papier (24x32cm 9x12in) Paris
2000

MALEVITCH Kasimir Sevrinovitch 1878-1935 [35]

$15 500 000 - €17 194 312 - £10 307 500 -
FF112 787 300
Suprematist Composition Oil/canvas (80.5x80.5cm
31x31in) New-York 2000

$40 994 - €40 065 - £26 000 - FF262 808
Trees Oil/cardboard (31x19cm 12x7in) London 1999

$63 600 - €72 078 - £43 200 - FF472 800
Composición suprematista Lápiz/papel
(21x29.5cm 8x11in) Madrid 2000

$2 500 - €2 366 - £1 552 - FF15 523
**Peasant Woman goes for Water/Death of a Man
in an Aero Plane** Lithograph (9.5x14cm 3x5in) New-
York 1999

MALFAIT Hubert 1898-1971 [127]

$11 136 - €11 898 - £7 584 - FF78 048
Meisje bij de woonwagen Huile/toile (120x100cm
47x39in) Lokeren 2001

$9 520 - €9 915 - £6 000 - FF65 040
Paysannes sur un champ de navets Huile/toile
(51x68cm 20x26in) Antwerpen 2000

$649 - €694 - £442 - FF4 552
Wandelaars Pierre noire/papier (26x34cm 10x13in)
Lokeren 2001

$111 - £130 - £78 - FF850
La moisson Lithographie couleurs (48x58cm
18x22in) Paris 2000

MALFRAY Charles Alexandre 1887-1940 [98]

$3 048 - €2 668 - £1 846 - FF17 500
Femme nue debout, bras levés Plâtre (H63cm
H24in) Orléans 1998

$314 - €305 - £194 - FF2 000
Nu féminin Sanguine/papier (20x26.5cm 7x10in)
Entzheim 1999

MALFROY XIX-XX [33]

$5 102 - €4 955 - £3 152 - FF32 500
Port de Martigues, Port de Bouc Huile/toile
(45x63cm 17x24in) Narbonne 1998

$3 581 - €3 506 - £2 203 - FF23 000
Les deux mâts à Martigues Huile/toile (33x46cm
12x18in) Aix-en-Provence 1999

MALFROY Charles 1862-? [82]

$4 901 - €5 717 - £3 442 - FF37 500
Port animé à Berre en Provence Huile/toile
(60x92cm 23x36in) Bayeux 2000

$3 618 - €4 116 - £2 511 - FF27 000
Les Martigues Huile/toile (23x28cm 9x11in)
Versailles 2000

MALFROY Henri 1895-1944 [192]

$4 441 - €4 116 - £2 762 - FF37 500
Port de pêche Huile/toile (60x93cm 23x36in) Paris
1999

$2 658 - €3 125 - £1 927 - FF20 500
Paris, Notre-dame Huile/toile (30x40cm 11x15in)
Calais 2001

$5 396 - €5 793 - £3 610 - FF38 000
Le port des Martigues Lavis/papier (65x54cm
25x21in) Paris 2000

MALHERBE William 1884-1951 [86]

$1 800 - €1 788 - £1 116 - FF11 727
Vase with Anemones Resting on a Table
Oil/panel (45x35cm 18x14in) Norwalk CT 2000

$1 076 - €976 - £652 - FF6 400
Mountain Stream Oil/panel (34x27cm 13x10in)
Sydney 1998

MALHOA José 1855-1933 [19]

$184 800 - €209 373 - £126 000 - FF1 373 400
Adelaide, personagem de O.Fado Huile/toile
(50.5x65.5cm 19x25in) Lisboa 2000

$64 500 - €74 776 - £45 000 - FF490 500
Estudo para «A Beira-Mar» Oleo/lienzo (41x33cm
16x12in) Lisboa 2001

$22 360 - €25 922 - £15 600 - FF170 040
Estudo para «Basta, meu Pai!» Carbón/papel
(59x46.5cm 23x18in) Lisboa 2001

MALI Christian Friedrich 1832-1906 [113]

$8 644 - €9 076 - £5 450 - FF59 532
Homeward Bound Oil/canvas (61x79.5cm 24x31in)
Amsterdam 2000

$1 987 - €1 841 - £1 233 - FF12 074
**Hirtenbub und Hirtenmädchen mit Schafen im
Gebirge** Öl/Karton (22x14cm 8x5in) Stuttgart 1999

MALIAVINE Philippe Andreevitch 1869-1940 [254]

$67 166 - €79 931 - £48 000 - FF524 313
Portrait of Alexandra Balachova Oil/canvas
(171x193cm 67x75in) London 2000

$8 654 - €8 261 - £5 407 - FF54 191
Dancing Girl in Colorful Scarf Oil/canvas (72x92cm
28x36in) Cedar-Falls IA 1999

$1 791 - €1 677 - £1 109 - FF11 000
Couple de danseurs Russes Huile/carton
(35x27cm 13x10in) Troyes 1999

$1 600 - €1 717 - £1 070 - FF11 265
Russian Beauty Graphite (65x49cm 25x19in) Cedar-
Falls IA 2000

MALICKI Adam 1896-1949 [2]

$2 203 - €2 583 - £1 572 - FF16 946
Paysage d'hiver dans les Tatras Huile/carton
(70x98cm 27x38in) Warszawa 2000

MALICOAT Philip Cecil 1908-1981 [10]

$1 600 - €1 383 - £949 - FF9 070
Harbor Scene Oil/canvas (50x66cm 20x26in)
Provincetown MA 1998

$2 400 - €2 836 - £1 700 - FF18 601
Saint Germain Paris Oil/board (35x40cm 14x16in)
Provincetown MA 2000

$1 700 - €2 009 - £1 204 - FF13 176
Reclining Nude Graphite (27x35cm 11x14in)
Provincetown MA 2000

MALIE Thomas 1700-1789 [1]

$2 988 - €3 208 - £2 000 - FF21 043
**«Land Crab/Nodde/Boody/Corals, sponges,
Pargo caught/Butterflies...»** Ink (48x40cm 18x15in)
London 2000

MALIKITA Maurus M. 1964 [2]

$1 800 - €1 866 - £1 080 - FF12 240
The Stage of Marriage Olio/tela (49x75cm 19x29in)
Prato 2000

MALINCONICO Nicola 1663-1721 [9]

$15 620 - €16 769 - £10 450 - FF110 000
**Nature morte au vase de fleurs et fruits ou l'al-
légorie de l'été** Huile/toile (44.5x58cm 17x22in) Paris
2000

MALINOVSKII Wiktor Adam 1829-1892 [9]

$5 717 - €6 375 - £3 912 - FF41 817
Au coucher de soleil Huile/toile (45x60cm 17x23in)
Warszawa 2000

M

$2 600 – €2 227 – £1 563 – FF14 611
Travelling Salesman Oil/canvas (27x20.5cm 10x8in)
Warszawa 1998

MALINOVSKY Lise 1957 **[39]**
$2 266 – €2 284 – £1 412 – FF14 980
Blomsterbillede Oil/canvas (200x150cm 78x59in)
Köbenhavn 2000
$466 – €470 – £290 – FF3 084
Jesper Olsen Pastel (63x90cm 24x35in) Köbenhavn
2000

MALINVERNI Angelo 1877-1947 **[13]**
$1 000 – €1 037 – £600 – FF6 800
Baite ai piedi dei monti Olio/carta (50x60.5cm
19x23in) Vercelli 2001
$500 – €518 – £300 – FF3 400
Paesaggio della Val Susa Olio/cartone (35x44cm
13x17in) Vercelli 1999

MALISSARD Georges 1877-1942 **[35]**
$13 465 – €13 568 – £8 392 – FF89 000
Le tamdem Bronze (90x42cm 35x16in) Nice 2000
$2 847 – €3 029 – £1 800 – FF19 868
Dolly, a standing Mare Bronze (39.5x31cm 15x12in)
London 2000

MALKINE Georges 1898-1970 **[10]**
$35 510 – €40 399 – £24 645 – FF265 000
«Scandale» Huile/toile (55x38cm 21x14in) Paris 2000

MALKNECHT Ferdinand XVIII **[1]**
$1 824 – €2 180 – £1 254 – FF14 301
Stadtansicht von Gmunden Indian ink/paper
(18.5x26.5cm 7x10in) Salzburg 2000

MALKOWSKI Bronislaw 1883-c.1936 **[1]**
$4 649 – €4 809 – £2 937 – FF31 545
Pêcheur Oil/canvas (96.5x56cm 37x22in) Warszawa
2000

MALKOWSKY Heiner 1920-1988 **[58]**
$1 749 – €1 636 – £1 059 – FF10 732
Konstruktivistische Landschaft Öl/Leinwand
(76.5x101cm 30x39in) Stuttgart 1999
$1 093 – €1 022 – £662 – FF6 707
Grüner Stuhl Mischtechnik/Papier (57x40cm
22x15in) Stuttgart 1999

MALLE Charles 1935 **[201]**
$1 023 – €1 220 – £729 – FF8 000
Le Pont Neuf sous la neige Huile/toile (46x55cm
18x21in) Soissons 2000
$833 – €991 – £594 – FF6 500
Paris, le manège au quai d'Orsay Huile/toile
(33x46cm 12x18in) Calais 2000

MALLEBRANCHE Louis-Claude 1790-1838 **[45]**
$1 970 – €1 677 – £1 172 – FF11 000
Paysage romantique Huile/toile (59x48cm 23x18in)
Joigny 1998
$2 320 – €2 592 – £1 572 – FF17 000
Rue de village sous la neige Huile/toile (32x48cm
12x18in) Saint-Dié 2000

MALLERY van Karel 1571-1635 **[5]**
$1 516 – €1 770 – £1 017 – FF11 608
Vermis Sericus, after J.Stradanus Engraving
(20.6x26.5cm 8x10in) Haarlem 2000

MALLET Jean Baptiste 1759-1835 **[62]**
$6 800 – €7 622 – £4 615 – FF50 000
Jeunes femmes au bain Huile/toile (46x66.5cm
18x26in) Paris 2000
$6 354 – €6 403 – £3 960 – FF42 000
Le retour du père de famille Huile/toile (40.5x33cm
15x12in) Paris 2000

$9 065 – €10 671 – £6 370 – FF70 000
Scènes d'intérieurs paysans Aquarelle,
gouache/papier (24x31.5cm 9x12in) Paris 2000

MALLET-STEVENS Robert 1886-1945 **[9]**
$9 352 – €10 671 – £6 503 – FF70 000
«St.Jean de Luz» Affiche couleur (160x120cm
62x47in) Paris 2001

MALLETT Robert **[44]**
$355 – €396 – £240 – FF2 600
Cross Farm, Back River, Whitard Mill Oil/canvas
(43x55cm 17x22in) Aylsham, Norfolk 2000

MALLEYN Gerrit Mallein 1753-1816 **[14]**
$7 078 – €6 807 – £4 360 – FF44 649
Two Men Leading Horses out of a Stable
Oil/canvas (48x48cm 14x18in) Amsterdam 1999

MALLINA Erich 1873-1954 **[49]**
$2 377 – €2 035 – £1 430 – FF13 347
Dreifaltigkeit Drawing (62.5x45cm 24x17in) Wien
1998

MALLO GONZALEZ Cristino 1905-1989 **[65]**
$7 540 – €7 808 – £4 810 – FF51 220
Desnudo femenino Bronze (21x17x11cm 8x6x4in)
Madrid 2000
$170 – €168 – £109 – FF1 103
Collage azul Collage (17.5x12cm 6x4in) Madrid 1999

MALLO GONZALEZ Maruja 1908-1995 **[14]**
$12 800 – €12 013 – £8 000 – FF78 800
Grajo y excrementos Oleo/cartón (45x58cm
17x22in) Madrid 1999
$15 000 – €12 797 – £8 940 – FF83 940
Naturalez Viva Oil/canvas/board (42.5x37cm 16x14in)
New-York 1998

MALLOL SUAZO Josep Maria 1910-1986 **[46]**
$6 160 – €6 607 – £4 070 – FF43 340
Figura en rojo Oleo/lienzo (65x50cm 25x19in)
Madrid 2000
$1 173 – €1 021 – £731 – FF6 698
Paisaje Oleo/cartón (21x21cm 8x8in) Madrid 1999
$3 410 – €3 304 – £2 090 – FF21 670
Mujer posando Pastel (43x59cm 16x23in) Barcelona
1999

MALMSTRÖM August 1829-1901 **[56]**
$5 712 – €6 633 – £4 014 – FF43 512
«Polisen kommer» Oil/canvas (38x61cm 14x24in)
Stockholm 2001
$408 – €390 – £257 – FF2 560
Landskap med barn på klippa Oil/canvas
(16x19cm 6x7in) Stockholm 1999

MALMSTRÖM Henning 1890-1968 **[13]**
$725 – €813 – £504 – FF5 333
Blomsterstilleben Pastel/paper (108x71cm 42x27in)
Malmö 2001

MALNOVITZER Zvi 1945 **[16]**
$24 000 – €25 918 – £16 586 – FF170 013
Tashlich Oil/canvas (139.5x178cm 54x70in) New-York
2001
$8 000 – €8 960 – £5 558 – FF58 777
The Jazz Singer Oil/canvas (115.5x97cm 45x38in)
New-York 2001

MALO-RENAULT Émile A. 1870-1938 **[118]**
$303 – €259 – £183 – FF1 700
La petite sirène Gravure (25x38cm 9x14in) Rennes
1998

MALOMBRA Pietro 1556-1618 **[1]**
- 🖊 **$3 929** - €3 644 - **£2 400** - FF23 904
  Christ Among the Doctors Ink (17.5x26cm 6x10in)
  London 1998

MALONEY Martin 1961 **[2]**
- 😊 **$3 736** - €4 011 - **£2 500** - FF26 308
  Portrait Lilac Oil/canvas (56x86.5cm 22x34in)
  London 2000

MALSKAT Lothar 1913-1988 **[79]**
- 🖊 **$514** - €613 - **£367** - FF4 024
  Herbststimmung im Laubwald Coloured chalks
  (54x44cm 21x17in) Köln 2000

MALTA Eduardo 1900-1967 **[10]**
- 🖊 **$1 364** - €1 545 - **£961** - FF10 137
  Retrato de senhora Lápiz/papel (60x45.5cm
  23x17in) Lisboa 2001

MALTBY Peggy, Peg 1899-1984 **[12]**
- 🖊 **$511** - €492 - **£315** - FF3 225
  Jack and the Beanstalk/The Giant
  Watercolour/paper (18x14cm 7x5in) Melbourne 1999

MALTESE Jean-Pierre 1946 **[28]**
- 😊 **$1 990** - €1 829 - **£1 222** - FF12 000
  Nature morte à la cruche Huile/toile (61x46cm
  24x18in) Paris 1999
- 😊 **$384** - €457 - **£266** - FF3 000
  Les voiliers Huile/toile (25x37cm 9x14in) Albi 2000

MALTHOUSE Eric 1914-1997 **[36]**
- 🖊 **$333** - €307 - **£200** - FF2 011
  Men Fishing, Ogmore Gouache (23x36cm 9x14in)
  Glamorgan 1999
- 📰 **$436** - €497 - **£300** - FF3 263
  Façade Jix Screenprint in colors (56x76cm 22x29in)
  London 2000

MALTMAN William 1901-1971 **[45]**
- 🖊 **$162** - €190 - **£114** - FF1 244
  Afternoon, Lake Ontario Watercolour/paper
  (25.5x35cm 10x13in) Calgary, Alberta 2000

MALTON James 1761-1803 **[22]**
- 📰 **$483** - €475 - **£300** - FF3 114
  **Views in the City of Dublin: View from Capel
  Street looking over Essex** Aquatint in colors
  (49.5x37cm 19x14in) London 1999

MALTON Thomas I 1726-1801 **[6]**
- 📰 **$880** - €874 - **£550** - FF5 731
  College in the University of Cambridge Aquatint
  (36x49cm 14x19in) London 1999

MALTON Thomas II 1748-1804 **[12]**
- 🖊 **$3 177** - €2 712 - **£1 900** - FF17 790
  **The Transept of St. Pauls Cathedral from the
  north Entrance** Watercolour (46.5x61.5cm 18x24in)
  London 1998
- 📰 **$348** - €396 - **£240** - FF2 599
  **North View of the Rock of Gibraltar from the
  Spanish Lines** Aquatint (35.5x77.5cm 13x30in)
  London 2000

MALUDA (Maria de Lurdes R.) 1934-1999 **[9]**
- 😊 **$17 100** - €14 910 - **£10 200** - FF97 800
  Vista de Lisboa Oleo/lienzo (73x92cm 28x36in)
  Lisboa 1998
- 📰 **$427** - €474 - **£285** - FF3 106
  Casario do Algarve Serigrafia (35x43.5cm 13x17in)
  Lisboa 2000

MALVANO Ugo 1878-1952 **[6]**
- 🖊 **$8 400** - €7 255 - **£4 200** - FF47 600
  La piazza del paese Olio/tela (82x116cm 32x45in)
  Torino 1999

MALY von August 1835-? **[2]**
- 🖊 **$1 920** - €2 180 - **£1 347** - FF14 301
  **Erzherzog Karl leitet ein Gefecht gegen franzö-
  sische Truppen** Aquarell/Papier (68x43cm 26x16in)
  Wien 2001

MAMBOR Renato 1936 **[22]**
- 😊 **$800** - €1 037 - **£600** - FF6 800
  Senza titolo Tecnica mista (70x100cm 27x39in) Prato
  2000

MAMBOUR Auguste 1896-1968 **[158]**
- 😊 **$11 316** - €11 403 - **£7 038** - FF74 796
  Toilette Huile/toile (55x55cm 21x21in) Liège 2000
- 😊 **$3 315** - €3 222 - **£2 028** - FF21 138
  Buste de jeune fille Huile/panneau (36x27cm
  14x10in) Liège 1999
- 🖊 **$1 441** - €1 329 - **£863** - FF8 716
  African dancing Charcoal/paper (74x54.5cm
  29x21in) Amsterdam 1998
- 📰 **$246** - €273 - **£171** - FF1 788
  Jeune fille debout/Jeune homme au tam-tam
  Lithographie (77x56cm 30x22in) Liège 2001

MAMMEN Jeanne 1890-1976 **[51]**
- 🖊 **$5 502** - €5 336 - **£3 461** - FF35 000
  Portrait de femme Crayon/papier (48.5x36.5cm
  19x14in) Paris 1999
- 📰 **$822** - €767 - **£497** - FF5 030
  Erotische Szene Farblithographie (44x34cm 17x13in)
  Hamburg 1999

MAMMERI Azouaoui 1890-1954 **[17]**
- 🖊 **$3 912** - €4 573 - **£2 793** - FF30 000
  Palabres sur la place, Maroc Huile/toile
  (55.5x65cm 21x25in) Paris 2001
- 🖊 **$3 912** - €4 573 - **£2 793** - FF30 000
  Marocaine devant un mausolée Gouache/papier
  (33x50cm 12x19in) Paris 2001

MAMPASO BUENO Manuel 1924 **[32]**
- 🖊 **$1 485** - €1 652 - **£990** - FF10 835
  Composición abstracta Oleo/lienzo (117x89cm
  46x35in) Madrid 2000
- 🖊 **$520** - €601 - **£360** - FF3 940
  Jinete en la playa Acrílico/papel (27x37cm 10x14in)
  Madrid 2000
- 🖊 **$427** - €420 - **£273** - FF2 758
  Noche en el puerto Gouache/papier (64x128cm
  25x50in) Madrid 1999

MAN de L.J. XVIII **[2]**
- 😊 **$22 634** - €19 127 - **£13 500** - FF125 465
  A Calm with British Shipping at Anchor Oil/can-
  vas (99.5x129.5cm 39x50in) London 1998
- 😊 **$19 368** - €17 966 - **£12 000** - FF117 850
  **Barge coming alongside a Royal Yacht with
  Numerous other Vessels** Oil/canvas (61.5x77cm
  24x30in) London 1998

MAN Felix (Hans Baumann) 1893-1985 **[23]**
- 📷 **$523** - €562 - **£350** - FF3 689
  Reichspräsident Hindenburg Photograph
  (17.6x23.8cm 6x9in) München 2000

MAN RAY (Emmanuel Radnitsky) 1890-1976 **[2077]**
- 😊 **$211 601** - €205 945 - **£130 000** - FF1 350 908
  The Rug Oil/canvas (47x52cm 18x20in) London 1999
- 😊 **$26 000** - €22 457 - **£15 704** - FF147 308
  Le Pont d'Avignon Oil/panel (24.5x35cm 9x13in)
  New-York 1998
- 🖌 **$11 056** - €9 287 - **£6 500** - FF60 918
  «Ballet Français II» Bronze (H82cm H32in) London
  1998

MANAGO
- $5 953 - €5 001 - **£3 500** - FF32 802
  La Jurassienne Assemblage (38x28cm 14x11in) London 1998
- $5 800 - €6 251 - **£3 955** - FF41 003
  La main Ink (35.5x25.5cm 13x10in) New-York 2001
- $800 - €727 - **£500** - FF4 767
  Ohne Titel Farbradierung (18x14cm 7x5in) Wien 1999
- $4 087 - €3 964 - **£2 571** - FF26 000
  Autoportrait à l'étoile de mer Photo (11.5x8.3cm 4x3in) Paris 1999

MANAGO Dominique 1902 [10]
- $863 - €808 - **£534** - FF5 300
  Marché provençal Huile/panneau (27x35cm 10x13in) Paris 1999

MANAGO Vincent 1880-1936 [141]
- $1 828 - €2 134 - **£1 293** - FF14 000
  Rue Saussier, Kairouan Huile/toile (46x55cm 18x21in) Paris 2001
- $1 564 - €1 829 - **£1 117** - FF12 000
  Devant le magasin Huile/panneau (33x41cm 12x16in) Paris 2001
- $775 - €793 - **£488** - FF5 300
  Scène orientaliste, les lanciers Gouache/papier (31x48cm 12x18in) Toulouse 2000

MANAI Piero 1951-1988 [3]
- $1 360 - €1 762 - **£1 020** - FF11 560
  Carbone (coal) Carboncino/carta (65x240cm 25x94in) Milano 2000

MAÑANOS Asterio 1865-1935 [6]
- $4 000 - €4 805 - **£2 800** - FF31 520
  Alfonso XIII de niño Oleo/lienzo (89x63cm 35x24in) Madrid 2000

MANANSALA Vicente Silva 1910-1981 [10]
- $34 434 - €39 100 - **£23 568** - FF256 476
  Carabaos (Cows) Oil/canvas/board (74x83cm 29x32in) Singapore 2000
- $31 564 - €35 841 - **£21 604** - FF235 103
  Sabungero (Cock Fighter) Oil/canvas (28x36cm 11x14in) Singapore 2000
- $25 434 - €28 104 - **£17 635** - FF184 347
  Still Life Watercolour/paper (64x98cm 25x38in) Singapore 2001

MANARA de Horacio 1804-? [1]
- $5 590 - €5 869 - **£3 707** - FF38 500
  Portrait de jeune femme devant un paysage Huile/toile (86x111cm 33x43in) Paris 2000

MANARA Milo 1945 [22]
- $703 - €640 - **£439** - FF4 200
  Strip de Giuseppe Bergmann Encre Chine/papier (16x48cm 6x18in) Paris 1999

MANARESI Paolo 1908-1991 [5]
- $4 500 - €3 887 - **£3 000** - FF25 500
  Figure sul mare Olio/tavoletta (11x22.5cm 4x8in) Firenze 1998

MANARESI Ugo 1851-1917 [26]
- $4 462 - €4 626 - **£2 677** - FF30 345
  Giovane gabbrigiana Olio/tela (50x35cm 19x13in) Milano 1999
- $2 640 - €2 281 - **£1 760** - FF14 960
  Marina livornese con barca Olio/tavola (12.5x20.5cm 4x8in) Milano 1998

MANASSÉ (O.& A. v.Wlassics) 1896/93-1969/46 [93]
- $638 - €727 - **£441** - FF4 767
  Die Tänzerin Erny Weltoen Vintage gelatin silver print (20.8x13.5cm 8x5in) Wien 2000

MANAURE Mateo 1926 [54]
- $1 428 - €1 293 - **£924** - FF8 484
  Desnudo Oleo/cartón (40x50cm 15x19in) Caracas 1999
- $645 - €662 - **£430** - FF4 343
  Sin título Técnica mixta/cartón (35x35cm 13x13in) Caracas 2000
- $442 - €381 - **£260** - FF2 496
  Sin título Tinta china (48.5x39cm 19x15in) Caracas 1998

MANCANDAN Jacobus Sibrandi 1602-1680 [19]
- $7 913 - €7 080 - **£4 741** - FF46 440
  Cincinnatus Called from the Plough Oil/panel (38x50.5cm 14x19in) Amsterdam 1998
- $1 943 - €2 086 - **£1 300** - FF13 682
  Ruined Tower on a Rocky Cliff by the Sea Black chalk/paper (17x28.5cm 6x11in) London 2000

MANCHON Raphaël 1884-1975 [14]
- $133 - €137 - **£90** - FF900
  Vue de l'église à Caen Eau-forte (39x24cm 15x9in) Deauville 2000

MANCINI Antonio 1852-1930 [124]
- $62 500 - €64 791 - **£37 500** - FF425 000
  In giardino Olio/tela (150x115cm 59x45in) Roma 2000
- $20 000 - €25 916 - **£15 000** - FF170 000
  Ritratto di ragazzo seduto Olio/tela (76.5x50.5cm 30x19in) Milano 2001
- $30 247 - €31 765 - **£19 138** - FF208 362
  Children on a Sunny Beach Oil/panel (15x24cm 5x9in) Amsterdam 2001
- $2 100 - €1 814 - **£1 400** - FF11 900
  L'amatore di stampe Carboncino (20x16cm 7x6in) Milano 1998

MANCINI Bartolomeo XVII-XVIII [5]
- $7 000 - €5 876 - **£4 105** - FF38 546
  La Madonna del Dito Oil/copper (26.5x21.5cm 10x8in) New-York 1998

MANCINI Carlo 1829-1910 [8]
- $4 800 - €6 220 - **£3 600** - FF40 800
  Paesaggio con armenti Olio/tela (47x83cm 18x32in) Roma 2000

MANCINI Francesco 1679-1758 [12]
- $21 947 - €25 916 - **£15 487** - FF170 000
  Le triomphe de Bacchus Huile/toile (119x173cm 46x68in) Paris 2001
- $16 000 - €14 812 - **£9 600** - FF97 160
  Holy Family Oil/canvas (123x93cm 48x36in) New-York 1999
- $1 547 - €1 604 - **£928** - FF10 519
  Betsabea al bagno Olio/tela (33.5x42cm 13x16in) Venezia 1999

MANCINI Francesco Longo 1880-1954 [31]
- $2 880 - €2 488 - **£1 920** - FF16 320
  La Primavera Olio/tela (96x101cm 37x39in) Trieste 1998
- $9 141 - €8 385 - **£5 681** - FF55 000
  La présentation des étoffes Aquarelle/papier (34.5x52cm 13x20in) Paris 1999

MANCINI Francesco, Lord 1829-1905 [30]
- $5 140 - €6 661 - **£3 855** - FF43 696
  Nascondino Olio/tela (62x39cm 24x15in) Napoli 2001
- $2 000 - €2 073 - **£1 200** - FF13 600
  Donna sul prato Olio/tela (26x18cm 10x7in) Milano 2000

🖊 **$1 200** - €1 555 - **£900** - FF10 200
Carica di cavalleria Acquarello/cartone (33x23cm 12x9in) Torino 2000

MANCIOLI Corrado 1904-1958 **[7]**
▨ **$1 587** - €1 757 - **£1 100** - FF11 527
«Coppa Katana» Poster (102x68cm 40x26in) London 2001

MANCOBA Ernest 1910 **[9]**
🐾 **$10 425** - €10 090 - **£6 427** - FF66 187
Komposition Oil/canvas (61x50cm 24x19in) København 1999
🐾 **$5 838** - €5 651 - **£3 599** - FF37 065
Komposition Oil/canvas (33x24cm 12x9in) København 1999

MANDARRK Wally 1915-1987 **[8]**
🐾 **$721** - €764 - **£480** - FF5 012
Namarden (Lightning Spirit) Mixed media (92x33cm 36x12in) Melbourne 2000

MANDEKER OF NEW YORK XIX-XX **[2]**
📷 **$14 138** - €12 112 - **£8 500** - FF79 451
Autographed portrait of Rakhmaninov Photograph (25x20cm 9x7in) London 1998

MANDELBAUM Audrey 1966 **[6]**
🐾 **$600** - €583 - **£366** - FF3 827
Swim Thy Waters Mixed media (8.5x25.5x2.5cm 3x10xin) Tel Aviv 2000

MANDELBERG Johan Edvard 1730-1786 **[14]**
🐾 **$11 040** - €11 905 - **£7 410** - FF78 090
Bataljscener Oil/canvas (36x46cm 14x18in) Stockholm 2000
🐾 **$1 432** - €1 394 - **£882** - FF9 146
Sjöstycke Oil/panel (17x25cm 6x9in) Stockholm 1999

MANDELLI Pompilio 1914 **[12]**
🐾 **$1 500** - €1 555 - **£900** - FF10 200
Autunno nel paesaggio Olio/tela (50x60cm 19x23in) Vercelli 1999

MANDELSLOH Ernst August 1886-1962 **[10]**
🐾 **$691** - €799 - **£484** - FF5 243
«Gosausee mit Dachstein» Aquarell/Papier (46x63cm 18x24in) Linz 2001

MANDER van Carel I 1548-1606 **[11]**
🐾 **$32 666** - €36 813 - **£22 622** - FF241 480
Abendmahl, Christus reicht Judas ein Stück Brot Oil/panel (124x186cm 48x74in) Berlin 2000

MANDER William Henry 1850-1922 **[113]**
🐾 **$2 919** - €2 804 - **£1 800** - FF18 393
On the Mawddach, Wales Oil/canvas (51x76.5cm 20x30in) London 1999
🐾 **$1 298** - €1 457 - **£900** - FF9 556
On the Conway Oil/canvas (20.5x30.5cm 8x12in) London 1999

MANDEVARE Alphonse N. Michel 1759-1829 **[28]**
🖊 **$5 366** - €4 878 - **£3 292** - FF32 000
Paysage de forêt avec une cascade et des promeneurs Gouache/papier (59.5x87cm 23x34in) Paris 1999

MANDL Josef 1874-? **[10]**
🐾 **$1 567** - €1 652 - **£1 045** - FF10 835
Hada niña Oleo/lienzo (67x39cm 26x15in) Madrid 2000

MANÉ-KATZ 1894-1962 **[818]**
🐾 **$44 000** - €47 229 - **£29 444** - FF309 804
Boy with Donkey Oil/canvas (145x96cm 57x37in) Tel Aviv 2000

🐾 **$9 802** - €11 434 - **£6 877** - FF75 000
Jeune enfant assis Huile/toile (99x79cm 38x31in) Paris 2001
🐾 **$5 578** - €6 560 - **£4 000** - FF43 034
Trois garçons Oil/canvas (24x35.5cm 9x13in) London 2001
🐾 **$3 408** - €3 659 - **£2 280** - FF24 000
L'homme au tambour Bronze (29x19x21cm 11x7x8in) Cannes 2000
🖊 **$2 145** - €2 363 - **£1 430** - FF15 500
Le port, bateaux à marée basse Gouache/papier (46x61cm 18x24in) Deauville 2000
▨ **$250** - €259 - **£158** - FF1 700
Le tambour Color lithograph (64x49cm 25x19in) Johannesburg 2000

MANERA Domenico XIX **[1]**
🐾 **$15 000** - €15 550 - **£9 000** - FF102 000
Ritratto di Anna Pichler Plâtre (H72cm H28in) Roma 2000

MANERA Enrico 1947 **[78]**
🐾 **$600** - €777 - **£450** - FF5 100
«Batman» Tecnica mista (100x100cm 39x39in) Vercelli 2000

MANERO MIGUEL Luis 1876-1937 **[11]**
🐾 **$5 795** - €5 706 - **£3 705** - FF37 430
Vista de Burgos Oleo/lienzo (43x78cm 16x30in) Madrid 1999

MANES Antonin 1784-1843 **[52]**
🐾 **$9 482** - €9 715 - **£5 852** - FF63 724
Felslandschaft mit Hirsch Öl/Leinwand (74.5x57.5cm 29x22in) Düsseldorf 2000
🐾 **$14 450** - €13 667 - **£9 000** - FF89 650
Landscape with a wooded Hill Oil/cardboard (31x44cm 12x17in) Praha 2001
🖊 **$144** - €137 - **£90** - FF896
Tree, Study Pencil/paper (22.7x31.8cm 8x12in) Praha 2000

MANES Josef 1820-1871 **[11]**
🖊 **$303** - €287 - **£180** - FF1 882
Landscape with a Ruin Ink (7.5x9.6cm 2x3in) Praha 2000

MANES Pablo Curatella 1891-1963 **[7]**
🐾 **$37 500** - €36 487 - **£23 081** - FF239 336
Los Acróbatas Bronze (42.5x20.5x13cm 16x8x5in) New-York 1999

MANES Václav 1793-1858 **[7]**
🐾 **$15 895** - €15 034 - **£9 900** - FF98 615
Fille à fleur Huile/toile (70.5x54.5cm 27x21in) Praha 2001

MANESOVA Amalie 1817-1883 **[21]**
🖊 **$216** - €205 - **£135** - FF1 344
Lilac, Study Watercolour (35x26.5cm 13x10in) Praha 2000

MANESSIER Alfred 1911-1993 **[420]**
🐾 **$26 365** - €22 146 - **£15 500** - FF145 267
Orage sur les blés Oil/canvas (130x195cm 51x76in) London 1998
🐾 **$12 004** - €11 891 - **£7 277** - FF78 000
Montagnes bleues Huile/toile (33x55cm 12x21in) Paris 2000
🐾 **$7 445** - €6 386 - **£4 500** - FF41 892
Femme à la lampe Oil/canvas (33x24cm 12x9in) London 1998
🖊 **$2 600** - €2 298 - **£1 589** - FF15 074
Cavalry Watercolour/paper (28x41cm 11x16in) New-York 1999

MANET

📹 $133 - €153 - £94 - FF1 006
Thème de pacques Farblithographie (31.2x24cm 12x9in) Hamburg 2001

MANET Édouard 1832-1883 **[476]**
🔲 $19 000 000 - €22 045 499 - £13 117 600 - FF144 609 000
Jeune fille dans un jardin Oil/canvas (154x117cm 60x46in) New-York 2000
🔲 $600 000 - €567 979 - £372 660 - FF3 725 700
Panier fleuri Oil/canvas (65x81cm 25x31in) New-York 1999
✏️ $21 180 - €19 277 - £13 000 - FF126 451
Couple espagnol Pencil/paper (11.5x10cm 4x3in) London 1999
📹 $630 - €716 - £438 - FF4 695
Le gamin Radierung (21x14.5cm 8x5in) Berlin 2001

MANET Julie 1878-1966 **[28]**
✏️ $506 - €549 - £347 - FF3 600
Enfant près de la clôture Dessin (31x21cm 12x8in) Paris 2001

MANETAS Miltos 1964 **[2]**
🔲 $11 548 - €12 494 - £8 000 - FF81 950
Vanessa Beecroft Oil/canvas (198x162.5cm 77x63in) London 2001

MANFREDI Alberto 1930 **[69]**
🔲 $2 340 - €2 021 - £1 170 - FF13 260
Anna con le bracia alzate Olio/tela (60x50cm 23x19in) Prato 1999
🔲 $1 800 - €1 555 - £900 - FF10 200
Autoritratto con Ida Olio/faeste (35x25cm 13x9in) Prato 1999

MANFREDI Bartolomeo c.1580-c.1620 **[6]**
🔲 $40 180 - €34 682 - £24 220 - FF227 500
Les quatre âges de la vie d'un homme Huile/toile (125x155cm 49x61in) Bruxelles 1998
🔲 $27 600 - €23 843 - £13 800 - FF156 400
Coronazione di spine Olio/tela (80x113cm 31x44in) Prato 1999

MANGE Joseph C., José 1866-1935 **[92]**
🔲 $1 401 - €1 372 - £862 - FF9 000
Fleurs sur un entablement Huile/panneau (46x54cm 18x21in) Toulon 1999
🔲 $780 - €762 - £497 - FF5 000
Femme au bord de l'eau Huile/toile (46x33cm 18x12in) Paris 1999
🔲 $487 - €412 - £289 - FF2 700
Fort St Louis à Toulon Gouache/panneau (17x24cm 6x9in) Aubagne 1998

MANGIN Marcel 1852-1915 **[130]**
🔲 $342 - €290 - £205 - FF1 900
Baigneuse surprise Huile/toile (33x53cm 12x20in) Neuilly-sur-Seine 1998
🔲 $180 - €152 - £108 - FF1 000
Bain de soleil/Etude de femme drapée Huile/toile (46x29cm 18x11in) Neuilly-sur-Seine 1998
🔲 $108 - €91 - £64 - FF600
Académies féminines Pierre noire/papier (62x47cm 24x18in) Neuilly-sur-Seine 1998

MANGINI Pier Lorenzo XVIII **[5]**
📹 $896 - €961 - £608 - FF6 304
«Pórtico de Santa María la Mayor», según Francesco Pannini Grabado (48x70cm 18x27in) Madrid 2001

MANGITAK Kelly Palik 1940 **[1]**
📹 $1 173 - €1 361 - £810 - FF8 930
Blue Geese on Snow Pochoir (25x16cm 10x6in) Calgary, Alberta 2000

MANGLARD Adrien 1695-1760 **[46]**
🔲 $240 000 - €242 793 - £146 544 - FF1 592 616
Mediterranean Harbor Scene with Sailors, others Figures on the Docks Oil/canvas (138.5x259cm 54x101in) New-York 2000
🔲 $36 000 - €31 578 - £21 859 - FF207 136
Shipwreck in Stormy Seas Oil/canvas (50x95cm 19x37in) New-York 1999
🔲 $44 829 - €48 120 - £30 000 - FF315 648
Estuary with Fisherfolk on a Cliff/Capriccio of a Mediterranean Port Oil/panel (25x31cm 9x12in) London 2000
✏️ $4 350 - €4 573 - £2 730 - FF30 000
Port animé de personnages Encre (35x47.5cm 13x18in) Paris 2000
📹 $579 - €562 - £360 - FF3 689
L'Eclaircie Radierung (22.4x31.1cm 8x12in) Berlin 1999

MANGO de Leonardo 1843-? **[10]**
🔲 $32 375 - €38 112 - £22 750 - FF250 000
La cérémonie du Dossèh, au Caire Huile/toile/carton (69x92cm 27x36in) Paris 2000
🔲 $12 698 - €14 179 - £8 580 - FF93 007
Séance chez le coiffeur Huile/toile (43x31.51cm 16x12in) Luxembourg 2000

MANGOLD Burkhard 1873-1950 **[72]**
✏️ $614 - €648 - £405 - FF4 250
Männer im Ruderboot Gouache/Karton (56x78cm 22x30in) Zürich 2000
📹 $597 - €504 - £350 - FF3 306
«Somer-Terrasse Stadt-Casino» Poster (127x90cm 50x35in) London 1998

MANGOLD Josef 1884-1942 **[20]**
🔲 $1 834 - €2 045 - £1 233 - FF13 415
Burg Eltz Öl/Leinwand (99x70cm 38x27in) Koblenz 2000
🔲 $1 850 - €1 943 - £1 166 - FF12 744
Stilleben mit Rose in einer Glasvase Coloured pencils (38x31.5cm 14x12in) Heidelberg 2000

MANGOLD Robert 1937 **[130]**
🔲 $70 000 - €79 187 - £48 972 - FF519 435
«Irregular Gray Area with a Drawn Ellipse» Acrylic (249x152.5cm 98x60in) New-York 2001
🔲 $13 000 - €14 706 - £9 094 - FF96 466
«Study for Irregular Area #1» Acrylic (76x56cm 29x22in) New-York 2001
🔲 $17 000 - €16 337 - £10 472 - FF107 166
Double Circle (Blue) Acrylic (38x38cm 14x14in) New-York 1999
✏️ $6 500 - €7 268 - £4 381 - FF47 673
Untitled Graphite (76x56cm 29x22in) New-York 2000
📹 $1 072 - €1 278 - £764 - FF8 384
Five color Frame Woodcut in colors (53.2x44.5cm 20x17in) Berlin 2000

MANGOLD Sylvia Plimack 1938 **[13]**
📹 $1 300 - €1 220 - £803 - FF8 003
The Pin Oak at the Pond Etching, aquatint in colors (66x74cm 25x29in) New-York 1999

MANGRAVITE Peppino Gino 1896-1978 **[16]**
🔲 $5 500 - €6 255 - £3 814 - FF41 031
The Senate in Session Oil/canvas (86x73cm 34x29in) Chicago IL 2000

MANGUIN Henri Charles 1874-1949 **[395]**
🔲 $30 000 - €28 241 - £18 534 - FF185 247
Iris et tulipes Oil/canvas (65x46cm 25x18in) New-York 1999

MANHART Eduard 1880-1945 **[14]**

🖼️ **$1 661** - €1 534 - **£993** - FF10 061
Stadt am Fluss Öl/Leinwand (27x38.5cm 10x15in)
München 1999

✏️ **$519** - €581 - **£360** - FF3 813
«Beschädigtes Haus aus der Zeit des 1.Weltkriegs» Charcoal (34.5x24cm 13x9in)
Klagenfurt 2001

MANIATTY Stephen George 1910-? **[29]**

🖼️ **$1 700** - €1 839 - **£1 177** - FF12 065
Little Brown House, Old Albany Road Oil/board
(49x39cm 19x15in) South-Deerfield MA 2001

MANIQUET Frédéric Marius 1822-1896 **[12]**

🖼️ **$2 154** - €2 363 - **£1 463** - FF15 500
Chemin en sous-bois Huile/toile (46x38cm 18x14in) Mâcon 2000

MANIT POO-AREE 1935 **[6]**

🖼️ **$1 785** - €1 920 - **£1 197** - FF12 593
Three Friends Pencil/paper (38x53cm 14x20in)
Bangkok 2000

📜 **$1 201** - €1 116 - **£742** - FF7 321
Young Maiden Print (34x20cm 13x7in) Bangkok 1999

MANJEANS & THEURIER A. & Charles XIX **[1]**

✏️ **$1 420** - €1 524 - **£950** - FF10 000
Vue de Tours Dessin (69x98cm 27x38in) Bordeaux 2000

MANJIRO Terauchi 1890-1964 **[3]**

🖼️ **$15 190** - €14 816 - **£9 300** - FF97 185
Nude Woman Oil/board (11.5x16cm 4x6in) Tokyo 1999

MANJUWI Charlie 1934 **[3]**

🖼️ **$2 624** - €2 799 - **£1 751** - FF18 362
Sacred Wurrkadi Associated with the Morning Star Ceremony Mixed media (127x40cm 50x15in)
Melbourne 2000

MANKES Jan 1889-1920 **[59]**

🖼️ **$146 272** - €145 210 - **£91 392** - FF952 512
Woudsterweg in Avondschemering Oil/canvas
(41x59cm 16x23in) Amsterdam 1999

🖼️ **$83 952** - €99 832 - **£59 840** - FF654 852
Lezende jongen in interieur Oil/canvas (41x24cm 16x9in) Amsterdam 2000

📜 **$387** - €408 - **£256** - FF2 678
Landscape with a Pond Etching (9x6.5cm 3x2in)
Amsterdam 2000

MANLIO (Manlio Parrini) 1901-1968 **[2]**

📜 **$641** - €746 - **£450** - FF4 891
«Second International Aircraft Exhibition» Poster
(99x69cm 38x27in) London 2001

MANLY Eleanor E. XIX-XX **[7]**

🖼️ **$12 833** - €12 932 - **£8 000** - FF84 828
The Young Admirer's Gift Oil/canvas (56x43cm 22x16in) London 2000

MANN Alexander 1853-1908 **[32]**

🖼️ **$2 689** - €2 887 - **£1 800** - FF18 938
Portrait of a Girl with Long Hair Oil/canvas
(53.5x43cm 21x16in) London 2000

🖼️ **$1 600** - €1 855 - **£1 133** - FF12 168
Along the Shore, Tangier Oil/panel (14x23.5cm 5x9in) New-York 2000

MANN Cathleen S. 1896-1959 **[26]**

🖼️ **$815** - €706 - **£500** - FF4 632
Still Life of Flowers, Including Daffodils, Poppies and Tulips Oil/canvas (61x71cm 24x27in)
Bayswater, London 1999

MANN Cyril 1911-1980 **[17]**

🖼️ **$2 156** - €1 837 - **£1 300** - FF12 048
Daffodils Oil/canvas (56x40.5cm 22x15in) London 1998

✏️ **$1 394** - €1 640 - **£1 000** - FF10 758
Peonies Still Life Gouache/paper (35.5x48.5cm 13x19in) London 2001

MANN David 1948 **[18]**

🖼️ **$18 000** - €20 517 - **£12 558** - FF134 584
To the West Wind Oil/canvas (76x101cm 30x40in)
Dallas TX 2001

MANN Harrington 1864-1937 **[39]**

🖼️ **$211** - €1 012 - **£720** - FF6 636
Meditteranean Harbour Oil/canvas (30x34.5cm 11x13in) London 1998

MANN James Scrimgeour 1883-1946 **[17]**

✏️ **$689** - €631 - **£420** - FF4 139
SS Lancashire in the Far East Watercolour/paper
(18x23.5cm 7x9in) Manchester 1999

📜 **$900** - €1 050 - **£631** - FF6 885
«Allan Line, Canada» Poster (63.5x100cm 25x39in)
New-York 2000

MANN Joshua Hargrave Sams act.1849-1884 **[26]**

🖼️ **$2 070** - €2 155 - **£1 300** - FF14 137
Silent Prayer Oil/board (26x21.5cm 10x8in) London 2000

MANN Sally 1951 **[87]**

📷 **$6 000** - €6 908 - **£4 094** - FF45 312
One Big Snake Gelatin silver print (47.5x58cm 18x22in) New-York 2000

MANNERS William 1865-c.1940 **[212]**

🖼️ **$1 153** - €1 367 - **£840** - FF8 966
Timber Wagon at Sunset/Shepherd on Horseback driving his Flock Oil/canvas (40x60cm 15x23in) Newcastle-upon-Tyne 2001

🖼️ **$1 008** - €979 - **£640** - FF6 419
Wandering Sheep Oil/board (23x30cm 9x11in) West-Yorkshire 1999

✏️ **$781** - €918 - **£560** - FF6 024
Children picking Flowers, with a Wagon and Horse in the Foreground Watercolour/paper
(16x24.5cm 6x9in) West-Yorkshire 2001

MANNFELD Bernhard K.J. 1848-1925 **[32]**

📜 **$63** - €77 - **£44** - FF503
Kircheninterieur Radierung (58x39cm 22x15in) Bad-Vilbel 2000

MANNHEIM Jean 1863-1945 **[64]**

🖼️ **$5 000** - €4 756 - **£3 036** - FF31 195
The Music Lesson Oil/canvas (86.5x99cm 34x38in)
Beverly-Hills CA 1999

🖼️ **$3 500** - €3 780 - **£2 418** - FF24 793
«Belgium» Oil/board (28x38cm 11x15in) Altadena CA 2001

MANNING Constance Tempe 1896-1960 **[25]**

🖼️ **$456** - €429 - **£275** - FF2 815
View of the Harbour Oil/board (35x39cm 13x15in)
Sydney 1999

MANNIX Max 1939 **[48]**

🖼️ **$415** - €482 - **£291** - FF3 159
At the Crossroad Oil/board (31x45cm 12x17in)
Sydney 2000

M

MANNO Francesco 1754-1831 **[3]**
- $16 437 - €17 644 - **£11 000** - FF115 737
  Hercules and the Lernaean Hydra Oil/canvas (134x158cm 52x62in) London 2000

MANNOZZI Giovanni di San Giov 1592-1636 **[6]**
- $110 000 - €109 949 - **£67 199** - FF721 215
  Portrait of a Young Man in a Light Brown Jacket and Lace Collar Tempera (53x38cm 20x14in) New-York 2000
- $3 600 - €4 665 - **£2 700** - FF30 600
  Adorazione dei Magi Craies/papier (32x25cm 12x9in) Milano 2001

MANNUCCI Cipriano 1882-1970 **[58]**
- $1 500 - €1 555 - **£900** - FF10 200
  Sera nebbiosa, Venezia Olio/tavola (45x60.5cm 17x23in) Prato 2000
- $1 000 - €1 037 - **£600** - FF6 800
  Viale parigino Olio/cartone/tela (35x45cm 13x17in) Vercelli 1999

MANOLO (Manuel Hugué) 1872-1945 **[120]**
- $630 - €601 - **£380** - FF3 940
  Retrato Lápices de color/papel (18x13cm 7x5in) Madrid 1999
- $2 160 - €2 403 - **£1 480** - FF15 760
  Figura femenina Bronze (H36cm H14in) Madrid 2000
- $767 - €915 - **£547** - FF6 000
  Paysages Gouache (10.5x22cm 4x8in) Madrid 1999
- $112 - €120 - **£74** - FF788
  Torero y gitana Litografía a color (35x30cm 13x11in) Madrid 2000

MANOS Constantine 1934 **[5]**
- $3 200 - €3 635 - **£2 245** - FF23 841
  Selected Works from Greek Portfolio Gelatin silver print (18x26cm 7x10in) New-York 2001

MANRIQUE CABRERA César 1919-1992 **[28]**
- $3 975 - €4 505 - **£2 700** - FF29 550
  Sin título Técnica mixta (64x49cm 25x19in) Madrid 2000
- $896 - €841 - **£546** - FF5 516
  Pez tropical Gouache (10.5x22cm 4x8in) Madrid 1999

MANSARAY Abu-Bakarr 1970 **[2]**
- $2 058 - €1 986 - **£1 300** - FF13 030
  The Most Dangerous and Destructive Object Ballpoint pen (44.5x64cm 17x25in) London 1999

MANSER Albert 1937 **[26]**
- $2 264 - €2 627 - **£1 563** - FF17 231
  Oberefahre im Winter Oil/panel (41x61cm 16x24in) St. Gallen 2000
- $2 150 - €2 495 - **£1 485** - FF16 369
  Oberefahre im Winter Oil/panel (20x30cm 7x11in) St. Gallen 2000

MANSER Percy L. 1886-? **[7]**
- $750 - €892 - **£534** - FF5 850
  Pastoral Landscape with Country Home Oil/canvas (45x55cm 18x22in) Portland OR 2000

MANSFELD August H. 1816-1901 **[10]**
- $1 184 - €1 308 - **£820** - FF8 580
  Die lustige Mädchenklasse Öl/Leinwand (73x100cm 28x39in) Wiener Neustadt 2001

MANSFELD Josef 1819-1894 **[26]**
- $2 347 - €2 761 - **£1 683** - FF18 111
  Illustres Frühstücks-Stilleben Oil/panel (40x31cm 15x12in) Hamburg 2001

MANSFELD Moritz c.1850-c.1890 **[21]**
- $4 319 - €3 696 - **£2 600** - FF24 245
  Bottles of Wine, a Coffee Pot, Cups and Saucers, Newspaper on a table Oil/panel (26x21cm 10x8in) London 1998

MANSHIP Paul Howard 1885-1966 **[70]**
- $140 000 - €154 396 - **£94 808** - FF1 012 774
  Atalanta Bronze (H167.5cm H65in) New-York 2000
- $65 000 - €71 314 - **£43 179** - FF467 792
  Europa and the Bull Bronze (H28.5cm H11in) New-York 2000

MANSION André Léon Larue 1785-c.1840 **[25]**
- $1 004 - €973 - **£632** - FF6 383
  Sarah Mary Bulkeley, full face in white dress Miniature (13x9cm 5x3in) London 1999

MANSKIRCH Bernhard Gottfried 1736-1817 **[15]**
- $2 830 - €3 284 - **£1 954** - FF21 539
  Waldlandschaft mit Bach und Staffagefiguren Öl/Leinwand (42x58.5cm 16x23in) Luzern 2000

MANSKIRCH Jakob c.1750-c.1810 **[4]**
- $3 954 - €3 835 - **£2 505** - FF25 154
  Hügellandschaft mit Wald Oil/panel (42.5x62cm 16x24in) München 1999

MANSKIRSCH Franz Joseph 1768-1830 **[17]**
- $8 118 - €8 181 - **£5 060** - FF53 662
  Romantisierte Landschaften mit Bauernkate unter mächtigen Bäumen Oil/panel (46x63cm 18x24in) Stuttgart 2000
- $7 665 - €7 158 - **£4 730** - FF46 954
  Bewaldete Flusslandschaft mit zwei Jägern Oil/panel (26.5x33cm 10x12in) Köln 1999

MANSON James Bolivar 1879-1945 **[53]**
- $2 469 - €2 321 - **£1 500** - FF15 224
  Portrait of Jenny Oil/canvas (61x51cm 24x20in) London 1999
- $2 179 - €2 441 - **£1 514** - FF16 012
  Flowers, Château de Nanteuil Oil/board (44.5x34cm 17x13in) Melbourne 2001

MANSON Tom XX **[7]**
- $811 - €758 - **£500** - FF4 974
  Study of Calves Oil/board (39x50cm 15x19in) Co. Kilkenny 1999

MANSOUROFF Paul 1896-1983 **[100]**
- $4 252 - €4 878 - **£2 908** - FF32 000
  Sans titre Acrylique/bois (105x21.5cm 41x8in) Paris 2000
- $288 - €335 - **£202** - FF2 200
  Sans titre Crayons couleurs/papier (27x11cm 10x4in) Paris 2001

MÅNSSON Per 1896-1949 **[23]**
- $1 641 - €1 839 - **£1 144** - FF12 062
  Sill, bröd och vin Oil/panel (46x54cm 18x21in) Stockholm 2001

MANTA Abel 1888-1982 **[2]**
- $11 970 - €10 437 - **£7 140** - FF68 460
  A caminho da igreja Oleo/tabla (32.5x23.5cm 12x9in) Lisboa 1998

MANTEGANI Roger 1957 **[4]**
- $15 000 - €16 101 - **£10 038** - FF105 615
  Una historia en común Oil/canvas (120x99.5cm 47x39in) New-York 2000

MANTEGAZZA Giacomo 1853-1920 **[36]**
- $21 600 - €18 660 - **£14 400** - FF122 400
  La visita della Regina Margherita Olio/tela (100x150cm 39x59in) Milano 1998

$11 400 - €9 848 - £5 700 - FF64 600
La processione del Corpus Domini Olio/tela
(80x120cm 31x47in) Milano 1999
$1 857 - €2 091 - £1 279 - FF13 717
Rokokointeriör med ung flicka omsvärmad av äldre herrar Oil/canvas (40x28cm 15x11in) Uppsala 2000
$999 - €863 - £499 - FF5 664
Ballerina orientale Acquarello/carta (18x32cm 7x12in) Milano 1999

MANTEGNA Andrea 1431-1506 [16]
$5 000 - €5 615 - £3 242 - FF36 830
The Entombment Engraving (31x43.5cm 12x17in) New-York 2000

MANTON George Grenville 1855-1932 [9]
$11 989 - €11 884 - £7 500 - FF77 955
Quiet Read Oil/canvas (115.5x68cm 45x26in) London 1999

MANTOVANI Guido Antonio 1916-? [4]
$3 000 - €3 110 - £1 800 - FF20 400
Scorcio di Venezia Olio/tavola (33x41.5cm 12x16in) Venezia 2000

MANTOVANI Luigi 1880-1957 [36]
$900 - €777 - £600 - FF5 100
Iris Olio/tela (70x50cm 27x19in) Milano 1998
$650 - €674 - £390 - FF4 420
Naviglio Olio/tavoletta (19x24cm 7x9in) Milano 1999

MÄNTYNEN Jussi 1886-1978 [182]
$2 223 - €1 939 - £1 344 - FF12 718
«Gammelhusbond» Bronze (H23cm H9in) Stockholm 1998

MANTZ Werner 1901-1983 [78]
$3 185 - €3 528 - £2 160 - FF23 141
Häuserblock in Köln-Bickendorf II Vintage gelatin silver print (16.9x22.5cm 6x8in) Berlin 2000

MANUEL Víctor 1897-1969 [127]
$22 000 - €21 184 - £13 692 - FF138 958
Paisaje Guajiro Oil/canvas (61x50cm 24x19in) New-York 1999
$7 000 - €6 088 - £4 220 - FF39 935
Mujer en Rojo Oil/canvas/board (40.5x34cm 15x13in) New-York 1998
$1 068 - €1 143 - £726 - FF7 500
«Autour d'un étang» Aquarelle/papier (50x60cm 19x23in) Provins 2001

MANZ Curt 1900-1989 [8]
$432 - €374 - £258 - FF2 450
Blumenstilleben mit Iris in einer weissen Vase Öl/Leinwand (65x46cm 25x18in) Zürich 1998

MANZ Emil 1880-1945 [3]
$1 619 - €1 738 - £1 083 - FF11 403
Athlet als Bogenschütze Bronze (H67cm H26in) Stuttgart 2000

MANZANA-PISSARRO Georges 1871-1961 [243]
$3 412 - €3 811 - £2 312 - FF25 000
Le jardin de l'artiste à Monsseau Huile/panneau (51x63cm 20x24in) Aix-en-Provence 2000
$2 420 - €2 439 - £1 508 - FF16 000
Château de Beynac Huile/panneau (34x24cm 13x9in) Paris 2000
$161 - €183 - £111 - FF1 200
Félix, fils de l'auteur Crayon gras/papier (27x21cm 10x8in) Paris 2000
$560 - €555 - £350 - FF3 642
Peacocks Pochoir (31x49cm 12x19in) London 1999

MANZANET Ricardo XIX [17]
$1 178 - €1 141 - £741 - FF7 486
Paisaje Oleo/lienzo (75x40cm 29x15in) Madrid 1999

MANZONE Giuseppe 1887-1983 [25]
$1 300 - €1 348 - £780 - FF8 840
«Giochi nel parco» Olio/tavola (48x35cm 18x13in) Vercelli 1999
$880 - €1 140 - £660 - FF7 480
Marina presso Sorin Olio/tavola (26x36cm 10x14in) Vercelli 2000

MANZONI Piero 1933-1963 [156]
$190 620 - €164 672 - £127 080 - FF1 080 180
Achrome Tecnica mista/tela (80x60cm 31x23in) Milano 1998
$47 168 - €50 291 - £32 000 - FF329 888
Achrome Mixed media (30x40cm 11x15in) London 2001
$828 800 - €706 632 - £500 000 - FF4 635 200
Achrome Assemblage (85x90cm 33x35in) London 1998
$22 448 - €26 697 - £16 000 - FF175 123
«Linea m.0,78» Object (15x5.5cm 5x2in) London 2000
$29 000 - €30 063 - £17 400 - FF197 200
Achrome Tecnica mista/carta (25x20cm 9x7in) Milano 1999
$13 500 - €13 995 - £8 100 - FF91 800
Tavole di accertamento Litografia (49.5x35cm 19x13in) Milano 2001

MANZONI Ridolfo 1675-1743 [4]
$19 764 - €18 798 - £12 000 - FF123 308
The Rape of the Sabines Tempera (23.5x31cm 9x12in) London 1999

MANZU Giacomo 1908-1991 [337]
$5 100 - €4 406 - £2 550 - FF28 900
Fanciullo con drappo Tecnica mista/cartone (42x55.5cm 16x21in) Prato 1999
$5 500 - €5 702 - £3 300 - FF37 400
Il vescovino Olio/tavola (30x20.5cm 11x8in) Milano 1999
$130 000 - €144 210 - £86 450 - FF945 958
Cardinale Seduto Bronze (H86.5cm H34in) New-York 2000
$31 000 - €34 722 - £21 538 - FF227 763
Bozzeto per Donna seduta Bronze (H47.5cm H18in) New-York 2001
$2 700 - €2 332 - £1 350 - FF15 300
Uomo di spalle Matita/carta (34x25.5cm 13x10in) Prato 1999
$500 - €518 - £300 - FF3 400
Ulisse Acquaforte, acquatinta a colori (36x25cm 14x9in) Milano 2001

MANZUOLI Egisto XIX [7]
$3 200 - €3 718 - £2 249 - FF24 387
Cherubs with Tambourine, Panpipes, Bow & Arrows Oil/canvas (61x50cm 24x20in) New-Orleans LA 2001

MANZUOLI MASO DA SAN FRIANO Tommaso 1532-c.1571 [11]
$28 000 - €28 326 - £17 096 - FF185 805
The Resurrection: Design for a frescoed altarpiece Ink (28x35cm 11x13in) New-York 2000

MAO JIKUN 1954 [4]
$500 - €518 - £300 - FF3 400
Innocenza Inchiostro (34x34cm 13x13in) Prato 1999

M

MAO XIANG 1611-1693 **[8]**

✏️ $8 901 - €8 394 - **£5 520** - FF55 062
Calligraphy in Xing, Cao Shu Ink/paper (112x59cm
44x23in) Hong-Kong 1999

MAPPLETHORPE Robert 1946-1989 **[552]**

📷 $3 099 - €3 601 - **£2 178** - FF23 624
America Print in colors (66x55.5cm 25x21in) Zürich
2001

📷 $6 500 - €6 759 - **£4 104** - FF44 338
Poppy Gelatin silver print (38x38cm 14x14in) New-
York 2000

MAR de la David 1832-1898 **[17]**

✏️ $499 - €538 - **£340** - FF3 526
Women Feeding Chickens Watercolour/paper
(26x32cm 10x12in) Great Dunwow, Essex 2001

MARA Fabien XX **[3]**

📷 $1 513 - €1 829 - **£1 057** - FF21 180
Sans titre Photo couleur (145x95cm 57x37in) Paris
2000

MARA LO SCARPETTA Antonio 1680-c.1750 **[11]**

✏️ $35 810 - €32 591 - **£21 980** - FF213 785
Trompe-l'oeil Öl/Leinwand (57x73cm 22x28in) Zürich
1999

MARA Pol 1920-1998 **[274]**

$3 010 - €3 470 - **£2 072** - FF22 764
Goal Oil/canvas (146x146cm 57x57in) Lokeren 2000

$1 200 - €1 154 - **£740** - FF7 569
The Girl behind a Wave of Silk Mixed media
(91.5x72.5cm 36x28in) Washington 2000

✏️ $844 - €793 - **£521** - FF5 203
«Denkt ge?» Aquarelle/papier (110x73cm 43x28in)
Antwerpen 1999

MARAGALL Julio XX **[5]**

$4 680 - €4 360 - **£2 860** - FF28 600
Figura con caballo Bronze (50x40x68cm
19x15x26in) Caracas 1998

MARAGLIANO Federico 1873-1952 **[14]**

$2 070 - €1 789 - **£1 035** - FF11 733
Paesaggio Olio/tavola (13.5x34.5cm 5x13in) Milano
1999

MARAIS Adolphe 1856-1940 **[15]**

$27 000 - €31 513 - **£19 059** - FF206 709
La sortie de troupeau Oleo/lienzo (120x147cm
47x57in) Buenos-Aires 2000

$2 725 - €2 675 - **£1 689** - FF17 548
Sheep and Cattle in a Pasture Oil/canvas
(38x47cm 14x18in) Toronto 1999

MARAIS Jean 1913-1998 **[91]**

$949 - €1 067 - **£666** - FF7 000
Buste de Jean Cocteau Sculpture (H43cm H16in)
Limoges 2001

✏️ $262 - €290 - **£181** - FF1 900
**Maquette de costume antique d'homme pou
Britannicus** Gouache/carton (24x33.5cm 9x13in) Paris
2001

MARAIS-MILTON Victor 1872-1968 **[99]**

$10 747 - €10 151 - **£6 500** - FF66 588
A Cardinal reading in an Interior Oil/canvas
(44.5x37.5cm 17x14in) Billingshurst, West-Sussex 1999

$4 854 - €4 553 - **£3 000** - FF29 863
A Closer Inspection Oil/board (35x27cm 13x10in)
London 1999

✏️ $2 455 - €2 256 - **£1 508** - FF14 800
La lettre amusante Aquarelle, gouache/papier
(43x34.5cm 16x13in) Soissons 1999

MARAK Julius Eduard 1832-1899 **[27]**

$11 560 - €10 934 - **£7 200** - FF71 720
Morning in the Forest Oil/panel (66x49.5cm
25x19in) Praha 2000

$3 757 - €3 553 - **£2 340** - FF23 309
Vieil arbre Huile/carton (22.5x20.5cm 8x8in) Praha
1999

$635 - €601 - **£396** - FF3 944
Trees Pencil/paper (39.5x54cm 15x21in) Praha 2000

MARANIELLO Giuseppe 1945 **[16]**

$1 500 - €1 555 - **£900** - FF10 200
Teatrino Assemblage (73x103cm 28x40in) Prato 1999

MARASCO Antonio 1896-1975 **[58]**

$3 507 - €4 090 - **£2 462** - FF26 831
Les baigneuses Öl/Leinwand (73.5x60.7cm 28x23in)
Köln 2000

$950 - €985 - **£570** - FF6 460
Notturno lunare Olio/cartone (18x13cm 7x5in) Prato
2000

MARASTONI Giuseppe 1834-1895 **[6]**

$1 283 - €1 308 - **£802** - FF8 580
Frauenbildnis Öl/Metall (26x22cm 10x8in) Wien
2000

MARATKA Josef 1874-1937 **[15]**

$534 - €506 - **£333** - FF3 317
Eve Bronze (H12cm H4in) Praha 2000

MARATTA Carlo 1625-1713 **[99]**

$250 000 - €274 286 - **£166 075** - FF1 799 200
Saint Andrew Led to the Cross of Martyrdom
Oil/canvas (120x160cm 47x62in) New-York 2000

$380 000 - €334 451 - **£231 344** - FF2 193 854
**Physician, Probably Giovanni Guglielmo Riva
(1627-1677)** Oil/canvas (100x75cm 39x29in) New-
York 1999

$3 782 - €3 811 - **£2 357** - FF25 000
**Etudes de Putti avec reprises des mains et des
pieds** Sanguine/papier (40x26cm 15x10in) Paris 2000

$144 - €164 - **£100** - FF1 073
Die Heilige Familie mit den Engeln Radierung
(17.5x13cm 6x5in) München 2001

MARAZZANI-VISCONTI Agostino, Count 1853-
1914 **[1]**

$4 482 - €4 812 - **£3 000** - FF31 564
Stallion Pursed by Two Dogs Bronze (33x55cm
12x21in) London 2000

MARC Franz 1880-1916 **[212]**

$7 621 280 - €7 106 554 - **£4 600 000** -
FF46 615 940
The Waterfall: Women beneath a Waterfall
Oil/canvas (164x158cm 64x62in) London 1999

$140 828 - €131 317 - **£85 000** - FF861 381
Small Study of Stones Oil/canvas (58x83cm
22x32in) London 1999

$37 521 - €41 159 - **£25 486** - FF269 988
Frauentorso Bronze (24x15.7x12cm 9x6x4in) Berlin
2000

$32 238 - €37 117 - **£22 000** - FF243 471
Drei Pferde in hügeliger Landschaft Pencil/paper
(17x20.5cm 6x8in) London 2000

$999 - €1 176 - **£705** - FF7 713
«Eidechsen» Woodcut (8.5x8.5cm 3x3in) Berlin 2001

MARC Robert 1943-1993 **[238]**

$4 974 - €4 573 - **£3 075** - FF30 000
Composition cubiste Huile/toile (99x188cm
38x74in) Deauville 1998

$1 745 - €2 058 - **£1 227** - FF13 500
Abstrait Huile/bois (90x47cm 35x18in) Cabestany
2000

$621 - €686 - **£430** - FF4 500
Nature morte à la bouteille Huile/toile (41x33cm 16x12in) Paris 2001

$315 - €300 - **£195** - FF1 970
Composición con personaje Crayon gras/papier (20x11cm 7x4in) Madrid 1999

MARCA della Giovanni Battista 1532-1592 [1]

$1 680 - €1 451 - **£840** - FF9 520
Scena storica Matita (17x24cm 6x9in) Milano 1999

MARCA-RELLI Conrad 1913-2000 [79]

$18 000 - €16 007 - **£11 008** - FF104 999
Figure Mixed media/canvas (166.5x140cm 65x55in) New-York 1999

$4 000 - €4 549 - **£2 794** - FF29 840
Seated Figure Outdoors Oil/canvas (53x38cm 21x15in) Chicago IL 2000

$3 500 - €3 628 - **£2 100** - FF23 800
Composizione Olio/tela (22x30cm 8x11in) Milano 2000

$10 000 - €9 610 - **£6 160** - FF63 039
«FI-2-67» Collage (176.5x146cm 69x57in) New-York 1999

MARÇAL Matilde 1946 [2]

$2 250 - €2 493 - **£1 450** - FF16 350
Figura - Sequència Oleo/lienzo (116x88.5cm 45x34in) Lisboa 2000

MARCASE 1946 [4]

$1 129 - €1 041 - **£676** - FF6 829
Meditatieve compositie I Pastel/papier (110x110cm 43x43in) Antwerpen 1999

MARCEL-BERONNEAU Pierre Amédée 1869-1937 [59]

$3 611 - €3 506 - **£2 231** - FF23 000
Visage Huile/toile (38.5x46.5cm 15x18in) Paris 1999

MARCEL-CLÉMENT Amédée Julien 1873-? [74]

$3 619 - €3 403 - **£2 241** - FF22 324
Plages roses Oil/canvas (50x61cm 19x24in) Amsterdam 1999

$2 930 - €3 374 - **£2 000** - FF22 133
Boats at Concarneau Watercolour (45x54cm 17x21in) London 2000

MARCEL-LENOIR Jules Oury, dit 1872-1931 [120]

$12 935 - €11 281 - **£7 821** - FF74 000
L'écharpe blanche Huile/toile (78x90cm 30x35in) Toulouse 1998

$1 538 - €1 524 - **£962** - FF10 000
Couple à l'antique Huile/toile (49x25cm 19x9in) Toulouse 1999

$1 048 - €915 - **£634** - FF6 000
Portrait de jeune fille Crayon/papier (40x32cm 15x12in) Toulouse 1998

$310 - €353 - **£215** - FF2 314
«Invocation à la Madone d'onyx vert» Farblithographie (38x27cm 14x10in) München 2001

MARCELLI Giorgio XIX [3]

$12 618 - €13 720 - **£8 316** - FF90 000
Nubien et flamants roses Huile/toile (54x65cm 21x25in) Paris 2000

MARCH Charlotte 1934 [37]

$787 - €764 - **£490** - FF5 014
Donyale mit Modeschmuck Vintage gelatin silver print (30.6x30cm 12x11in) Berlin 1999

MARCH Giovanni 1894-1974 [77]

$2 070 - €1 788 - **£1 035** - FF11 730
Paesaggio Olio/tela (50x65cm 19x25in) Prato 1999

$1 200 - €1 555 - **£900** - FF10 200
Natura morta con pesci e limoni Olio/cartone (24x33cm 9x12in) Prato 2000

MARCH Y MARCO Vicente 1859-1914 [19]

$15 600 - €18 019 - **£10 800** - FF118 200
Pintora en el jardín Oleo/lienzo (42x60cm 16x23in) Madrid 2001

$448 - €420 - **£273** - FF2 758
Vista de un jardín Oleo/tabla (40x29cm 15x11in) Madrid 1999

MARCHAIS DES GENTILS XIX [2]

$4 189 - €4 497 - **£2 802** - FF29 500
Paysage à la rivière avec un bateau Huile/panneau (28.5x45cm 11x17in) Paris 2000

MARCHAIS Pierre-Antoine 1763-1859 [4]

$14 963 - €16 995 - **£10 500** - FF111 483
Classical Landscape with Belisarius amongst Peasant Oil/canvas (55x73cm 21x28in) London 2001

MARCHAL Achille XIX-XX [4]

$1 400 - €1 520 - **£969** - FF9 970
Still Life Oil/wood (22x17cm 9x7in) Cleveland OH 2001

MARCHAL Charles François 1825-1877 [6]

$13 646 - €11 462 - **£8 000** - FF75 188
The Visiting Dignitary Oil/canvas (73x116cm 28x45in) London 1998

MARCHAND André 1877-1951 [46]

$2 541 - €2 668 - **£1 718** - FF17 500
Veneur et ses chiens Huile/toile (57x73cm 22x28in) Evreux 2001

$613 - €686 - **£427** - FF4 500
Les haras de Meautry à Touques Huile/panneau (26.5x35cm 10x13in) Toulouse 2001

MARCHAND André 1907-1998 [244]

$1 876 - €2 134 - **£1 302** - FF14 000
Belle Ile en Mer, Respiration marine aux falaises Huile/toile (81x65cm 31x25in) Paris 2000

$1 186 - €1 281 - **£820** - FF8 404
Foxhound on a Riverbank Oil/panel (23x26cm 9x10in) Cheshire 2001

$439 - €427 - **£271** - FF2 800
Environ d'Aix Aquarelle/carton (26x34cm 10x13in) Paris 1999

MARCHAND Jean XVIII [2]

$3 858 - €4 360 - **£2 604** - FF28 602
Stilleben mit Früchten und erlegtem Federwild Öl/Leinwand (44.5x37cm 17x14in) Wien 2000

MARCHAND Jean Hippolyte 1883-1940 [126]

$8 606 - €9 554 - **£6 000** - FF62 669
Paysans à la source d'eau Oil/canvas (162.5x130cm 63x51in) London 2001

$4 303 - €4 777 - **£3 000** - FF31 334
Petite cascade dans une forêt Oil/canvas (92.5x66.5cm 36x26in) London 2001

$712 - €838 - **£511** - FF5 500
Femme assise au châle gris Huile/panneau (26.5x22cm 10x8in) Paris 2001

$287 - €277 - **£180** - FF1 818
Plante à la fenêtre Watercolour (23.5x19.5cm 9x7in) London 1999

MARCHAND John Norval 1875-1921 [4]

$2 500 - €2 914 - **£1 731** - FF19 116
Townsman Letting Horses Out of their Corral, Racing Away on Horse Oil/canvas (66x45cm 26x18in) New-York 2000

M

MARCHANT DUBOIS D'HAULT Jehan XIX [1]
- $25 000 - €27 919 - **£16 010** - FF183 137
  The Sunday Market at the Grand-Place, Brussels Oil/panel (77.5x104cm 30x40in) New-York 2000

MARCHÉ Ernest G. 1864-1932 [13]
- $489 - €457 - **£296** - FF3 000
  Le Moulin Rouge Huile/toile (40x69cm 15x27in) Orléans 1999

MARCHESI DA COTIGNOLA Girolamo c.1490-c.1559 [3]
- $220 000 - €234 949 - **£149 908** - FF1 541 166
  Madonna and Child with Saint Mary Magdalen and Augustine Oil/panel (212x147.5cm 83x58in) New-York 2001
- $48 000 - €41 466 - **£32 000** - FF272 000
  La Pietà con le tre Marie, Sant'Anna, Nicodemo, Giuseppe d'Arimatea Olio/tavola (77x67cm 30x26in) Roma 1999

MARCHESI IL SANSONE Giuseppe 1699-1771 [4]
- $850 - €881 - **£510** - FF5 780
  Madonna con Bambino e San Francesco de Sales Craies/papier (40x25.5cm 15x10in) Roma 1999

MARCHESINI Alessandro 1664-1738 [2]
- $50 298 - €42 504 - **£30 000** - FF278 811
  A Young Man Offering a Sacrifice to Appollo/The Toilet of Venus Oil/copper (42.5x58cm 16x22in) London 1998

MARCHET Lucien XIX-XX [4]
- $488 - €562 - **£336** - FF3 689
  Französische Artillerie, Offiziere im Manöver Öl/Leinwand (46x38cm 18x14in) Saarbrücken 2000

MARCHETTI Ludovico 1853-1909 [54]
- $5 500 - €6 487 - **£3 879** - FF42 549
  Italian Soldiers marching Oil/canvas (53x83cm 21x33in) New-Orleans LA 2001
- $2 173 - €2 556 - **£1 534** - FF16 769
  Musketier mit gezücktem Schwert in der Stube Oil/panel (27x18cm 10x7in) Köln 2001
- $2 558 - €2 149 - **£1 500** - FF14 097
  Arab Boy in a Courtyard Watercolour/paper (37x26.5cm 14x10in) Billingshurst, West-Sussex 1998

MARCHI Vincenzo 1818-1894 [7]
- $8 000 - €6 955 - **£4 841** - FF45 620
  Apostolic Library, Vatican Watercolour/paper (38x53.5cm 14x21in) New-York 1999

MARCHIG Giannino 1897-1983 [25]
- $5 750 - €5 961 - **£3 450** - FF39 100
  Modella in piedi Olio/tela (100x50cm 39x19in) Trieste 1999
- $550 - €570 - **£330** - FF3 740
  Studio per il nostromo Inchiostro (35x50cm 13x19in) Trieste 2000

MARCHIONI Elisabetta XVII-XVIII [30]
- $8 960 - €10 174 - **£6 132** - FF66 738
  Blumenstrauss Öl/Leinwand (60x50cm 23x19in) Wien 2000

MARCHIS de Alessio 1684-1752 [25]
- $6 426 - €5 551 - **£3 213** - FF36 414
  Due paesaggi Olio/tela (32.5x47cm 12x18in) Milano 1999
- $4 000 - €4 285 - **£2 731** - FF28 106
  View of a Ruined Chapel with a Beam of Sunlight/Steps Leading Gouache/paper (23.5x18cm 9x7in) New-York 2001

MARCHISIO Andrea 1850-1927 [15]
- $15 000 - €17 640 - **£10 755** - FF115 708
  The Dance Continues Oil/canvas (178x472.5cm 70x186in) New-York 2001
- $3 500 - €4 135 - **£2 480** - FF27 127
  Peasant Herding Horses Oil/canvas (44x63cm 17x25in) Austinburg OH 2000
- $12 500 - €12 958 - **£7 500** - FF85 000
  Non basta l'arte a sollevar chi soffre Olio/tavola (35x26.5cm 13x10in) Vercelli 1999

MARCIL René 1917 [17]
- $469 - €456 - **£293** - FF2 990
  Still Life Watercolour/paper (40.5x57cm 15x22in) Toronto 1999

MARCIUS-SIMONS Pinkney 1867-1909 [19]
- $11 638 - €13 873 - **£8 299** - FF91 000
  Arlésiens au rouet Huile/toile (73x92cm 28x36in) Saint-Martin-de-Crau 2000

MARCKE DE LUMMEN van Émile 1827-1890 [91]
- $2 466 - €2 269 - **£1 525** - FF14 883
  Cows near a ditch Oil/canvas (60x86cm 23x33in) Amsterdam 1999
- $2 000 - €2 251 - **£1 377** - FF14 765
  Country Landscape with Cows Oil/canvas (25x35cm 10x14in) New-Orleans LA 2000

MARCKE DE LUMMEN van Jean 1875-1918 [10]
- $1 538 - €1 829 - **£1 096** - FF12 000
  Le jockey Fusain (45x63cm 17x24in) Calais 2000

MARCKE van Emile 1797-c.1850 [9]
- $2 750 - €2 743 - **£1 717** - FF17 996
  Coastal Landscape with Cows Oil/canvas (55x82cm 22x32in) Dedham MA 1999

MARCKS Alexander 1864-1909 [3]
- $755 - €828 - **£512** - FF5 433
  Dorfansicht mit Fachwerkhaus und Bogenbrücke Öl/Leinwand (60x73cm 23x28in) Saarbrücken 2000

MARCKS Gerhard 1889-1981 [617]
- $11 844 - €14 316 - **£8 268** - FF93 909
  Hella Bronze (H93cm H36in) Düsseldorf 2000
- $5 079 - €4 857 - **£3 093** - FF31 862
  Sinnende Bronze (H60cm H23in) Bielefeld 1999
- $482 - €398 - **£282** - FF2 613
  Stehender nackter Jüngling Pencil/paper (42x24.2cm 16x9in) Heidelberg 1998
- $217 - €256 - **£150** - FF1 676
  Frauenkopf Woodcut (21x16.5cm 8x6in) Braunschweig 2000

MARCOLA Giovan Battista 1711-1780 [12]
- $703 - €599 - **£420** - FF3 927
  Diana with her Dog and two Nymphs Black chalk (19.5x26.5cm 7x10in) London 1998

MARCOLA Marco 1740-1793 [20]
- $26 418 - €22 822 - **£13 209** - FF149 702
  Festa di ballo Olio/tela (88x79cm 34x31in) Venezia 1999
- $4 879 - €5 058 - **£2 927** - FF33 177
  Compagnia elegante sotto un portico Olio/tavoletta (26x21cm 10x8in) Venezia 2000
- $600 - €622 - **£360** - FF4 080
  Suicidio di una donna, con un uomo alle sue spalle Matita (28x19.5cm 11x7in) Roma 1999

MARCON Charles 1920 [40]
- $437 - €427 - **£278** - FF2 800
  Pêcheur Huile/carton (39.5x94cm 15x37in) Paris 1999

$698 - €686 - **£448** - FF4 500
Trois personnages Huile/papier/panneau (16.5x45.5cm 6x17in) Paris 1999

$296 - €274 - **£183** - FF1 800
Personnages Encre/papier (48x62cm 18x24in) Paris 1999

MARCONI Gaudenzio 1841-1885 [8]

$756 - €838 - **£525** - FF5 500
Nu feminin Tirage albuminé (26.5x17cm 10x6in) Paris 2001

MARCOUSSIS Louis 1883-1941 [229]

$84 760 - €79 273 - **£51 324** - FF520 000
Intérieur au balcon (ou «Composition à la fenêtre») Huile/toile (73x94cm 28x37in) Chartres 1999

$15 584 - €18 349 - **£10 950** - FF120 363
Paysage de Kerity Oil/panel (33x41cm 12x16in) Zürich 2000

$4 366 - €5 220 - **£3 000** - FF34 239
Nature morte Watercolour (8.5x13.5cm 3x5in) London 2001

$1 500 - €1 519 - **£933** - FF9 967
Alcools: nuit Rhénane Etching (15.5x9.5cm 6x3in) New-York 2000

MARCUCCI Giuseppe 1807-1876 [1]

$900 - €933 - **£540** - FF6 120
Teologia, Giustizia, Poesia e Filosofia, vda Raffaello Gravure (52x46cm 20x18in) Firenze 2000

MARCUCCI Lucia 1933 [5]

$2 100 - €1 814 - **£1 400** - FF11 900
«Prrrr!!» Collage/cartone (48.5x66.5cm 19x26in) Prato 1998

MARCUCCI Mario 1910-1992 [92]

$1 200 - €1 244 - **£720** - FF8 160
Vaso con fiori secchi Olio/cartone (69.5x49.5cm 27x19in) Prato 2000

$720 - €622 - **£360** - FF4 080
Figura maschile Olio/carta (20x30cm 7x11in) Firenze 1999

MARCUS Elli 1899-1977 [7]

$1 643 - €1 940 - **£1 166** - FF12 727
Marlene Dietrich Vintage gelatin silver print (21x15.5cm 8x6in) Berlin 2001

MARCUS Kaete Ephraim 1892-1970 [49]

$4 700 - €4 518 - **£3 097** - FF31 964
Sisters Oil/canvas (65x55cm 25x21in) Herzelia-Pituah 2000

$2 600 - €2 760 - **£1 759** - FF18 103
Man Singing Bronze (H24cm H9in) Tel Aviv 2001

$1 200 - €1 288 - **£803** - FF8 449
Tiberias, Landscape and Figures Pastel/paper (39.5x61cm 15x24in) Tel Aviv 2000

MARCUS Otto 1863-1952 [2]

$4 940 - €5 445 - **£3 226** - FF35 719
Auf der Mole (Concarneau, Bretagne) Oil/canvas (112x91cm 44x35in) Den Haag 2000

MARCUSE Rudolf 1878-1929 [49]

$776 - €731 - **£480** - FF4 797
Pierrot Seated playing a Guitar Ceramic (H34cm H13in) London 1999

MARCZYNSKI Adam 1908-1985 [12]

$5 720 - €6 140 - **£3 827** - FF40 275
Relief variable 06 Acrylique/panneau (87.5x70cm 34x27in) Kraków 2000

MARDEN Brice 1938 [174]

$1 400 000 - €1 563 066 - **£935 760** - FF10 253 040
Rain Forest Mixed media (153x267cm 60x105in) New-York 2000

$62 928 - €58 640 - **£38 000** - FF384 655
Composition Mixed media (55.5x76.5cm 21x30in) London 1998

$38 000 - €42 489 - **£25 615** - FF278 707
Car Drawing (Counting) #13 Gouache (15x15cm 5x5in) New-York 1999

$4 500 - €4 354 - **£2 775** - FF28 561
Focus I-V, New York, Brooke Alexander Etching, aquatint in colors (39.5x28cm 15x11in) New-York 1999

MARE André 1885-1932 [35]

$4 115 - €4 878 - **£2 905** - FF32 000
Sans titre Tapisserie (215x165cm 84x64in) Paris 2000

MARECHAL Charles 1865-? [13]

$1 544 - €1 753 - **£1 072** - FF11 500
La basse cour Huile/toile (49x65cm 19x25in) Mayenne 2001

MARECHAL Francis XX [6]

$640 - €762 - **£443** - FF5 000
Paysage provençal au printemps Huile/toile (65x81cm 25x31in) Thonon-les-Bains 2000

MARÉCHAL François 1861-1945 [76]

$881 - €967 - **£569** - FF6 341
Paysage Huile/panneau (24x32.5cm 9x12in) Liège 2000

$225 - €223 - **£140** - FF1 463
Tête d'homme Encre (13.5x11.5cm 5x4in) Liège 1999

$100 - €111 - **£70** - FF731
«Arbre mort» Eau-forte (21x12.5cm 8x4in) Liège 2001

MARECHAL Olivier XIX-XX [4]

$127 - €150 - **£90** - FF984
Apples and Grapes on the Vine in a Basket Oil/canvas (73.5x60.5cm 28x23in) London 2001

MAREES von Hans 1837-1887 [29]

$4 775 - €4 346 - **£2 983** - FF28 508
Rosalie Lier (1826-1914), die Frau des Malers Adolf Lier (1826-1882) Öl/Leinwand (57.5x47.5cm 22x18in) München 1999

$3 860 - €4 602 - **£2 752** - FF30 185
Parklandschaft mit Kindern am Brunnen Öl/Leinwand (11x23.5cm 4x9in) Berlin 2000

$2 528 - €2 454 - **£1 574** - FF16 098
Komposition mit vier Figuren in Orangenhain/Komositionskizze Black chalk/paper (24.6x32cm 9x12in) Berlin 1999

MAREMBERT Jean 1900-1970 [9]

$2 417 - €2 820 - **£1 681** - FF18 500
Deux sauts Mine plomb (44x31cm 17x12in) Paris 2000

MARESCA G. XIX [3]

$1 770 - €1 877 - **£1 200** - FF12 314
A Matter of Taste Oil/canvas (25.5x39.5cm 10x15in) London 2001

MARESCALCO LO SPADA Pietro 1503/20-1584/89 [5]

$5 981 - €5 793 - **£3 762** - FF38 000
La décollation de Saint Jean-Baptiste Huile/toile/panneau (65.5x90.5cm 25x35in) Paris 1999

MARET Jacques 1901-1975 [18]

$1 120 - €1 250 - **£782** - FF8 200
Composition surréaliste Huile/toile (73x92cm 28x36in) Évreux 2001

M

M

MAREVNA Marie Vorobieff 1892-1984 [78]

$5 485 - €5 445 - £3 427 - FF35 719
Still Life with Flowers Oil/canvas (80x60cm 31x23in) Amsterdam 1999

$6 593 - €6 187 - £4 074 - FF40 583
Portrait de femme Oil/panel (21x30cm 8x11in) Lódz 1999

$771 - €762 - £472 - FF5 000
Femme assise Aquarelle/papier (35x25cm 13x9in) Paris 2000

MAREY Etienne Jules 1830-1904 [21]

$8 267 - €7 809 - £5 000 - FF51 222
Vagues de l'eau Silver print (9.5x7cm 3x2in) London 1999

MARFAING André 1925-1987 [111]

$6 390 - €6 860 - £4 275 - FF45 000
Sans titre Huile/toile (162x130cm 63x51in) Paris 2000

$3 909 - €4 726 - £2 731 - FF31 000
Composition Huile/toile (73x60cm 28x23in) Paris 2000

$1 365 - €1 524 - £913 - FF10 000
Sans titre Huile/toile (18x14cm 7x5in) Paris 2000

$1 427 - €1 524 - £951 - FF10 000
Composition Lavis/papier (63.5x48.5cm 25x19in) Paris 2000

MARFFY Ödön 1878-1959 [10]

$15 200 - €14 946 - £9 500 - FF98 040
Piping Man with a Book Oil/canvas (84x68cm 33x26in) Budapest 1999

$1 056 - €1 200 - £736 - FF7 872
Vue de Balatoni Aquarelle/papier (33x43.5cm 12x17in) Budapest 2001

MARFURT Leo 1894-1977 [16]

$1 010 - €1 180 - £692 - FF7 739
«Belgische Spoorwegen, De Groote Verkeerswegen» Poster (107.5x72.5cm 42x28in) Hoorn 2000

MARGANTIN Louis A. 1900-1965 [19]

$7 810 - €8 385 - £5 225 - FF55 000
Le peintre et son modèle Huile/toile (80x120cm 31x47in) Paris 2000

MARGARITIS Ph. XIX [3]

$2 272 - €1 982 - £1 374 - FF13 000
Costume d'attica Tirage albuminé (14.4x11cm 5x4in) Paris 1998

MARGAT André 1903-1999 [115]

$3 848 - €3 964 - £2 381 - FF26 000
Les oiseaux lyres et les singes capucins Huile/panneau (70x50cm 27x19in) Caen 2000

$2 960 - €3 049 - £1 832 - FF20 000
Deux panthères à l'affût Huile/panneau (30x28cm 11x11in) Caen 2000

$1 184 - €1 037 - £717 - FF6 800
Jeune gorille Fusain (65x49cm 25x19in) Paris 1998

MARGETSON William Henry 1861-1940 [36]

$5 500 - €6 167 - £3 735 - FF40 451
Lady in White Oil/canvas (79x35.5cm 31x13in) New-York 2000

$3 040 - €2 902 - £1 900 - FF19 038
The Angel Appearing to the Shepherds Oil/panel (50.5x28.5cm 19x11in) London 1999

$563 - €561 - £358 - FF3 678
Cavalier Talking to a Young Woman Watercolour/paper (40x30cm 16x12in) Manchester 1999

MARGETTS Mary ?-1886 [5]

$2 270 - €2 197 - £1 400 - FF14 409
Dog Roses on a Mossy Bank Watercolour (33x25.5cm 12x10in) London 1999

MARGO Boris 1902-1995 [23]

$700 - €673 - £428 - FF4 412
Untitled Oil/canvas (60x40cm 24x16in) Provincetown MA 1999

$2 750 - €2 565 - £1 706 - FF16 823
Abstract Figure Ink (72.5x57cm 28x22in) New-York 1999

$2 500 - €2 954 - £1 771 - FF19 377
The Alchemist Print in colors (86x58cm 34x23in) Provincetown MA 2000

MARGOLIES John 1940 [2]

$100 - €108 - £68 - FF707
«Richfield Gas, Goleta, California» Photograph in colors (32.5x48cm 12x18in) Beverly-Hills CA 2001

MARGOLIES Samuel L. 1897-1974 [48]

$420 - €456 - £290 - FF2 991
The Lone Traveler Etching (24x19cm 9x7in) Cleveland OH 2001

MARGRETHE II Queen of Denmark 1940 [6]

$12 940 - €13 425 - £8 210 - FF88 060
En ballerina på scenen Pastel (33x24cm 12x9in) Viby J, Arhus 2000

MARGRY Antoine XIX [3]

$15 000 - €13 718 - £9 160 - FF89 982
Bouquet of flowers Oil/canvas (72x59cm 28x23in) New-York 1998

MARGUERAY Michel 1938 [62]

$855 - €793 - £532 - FF5 200
Rue de Vire enneigée Huile/toile (54x65cm 21x25in) Corbeil-Essonnes 1999

$359 - €335 - £216 - FF2 200
Neige à Besnardière Huile/toile (22x27cm 8x10in) Maubeuge 1999

MARGULIES Joseph 1896-1984 [60]

$1 300 - €1 504 - £920 - FF9 865
«Frustated Fisherman» Oil/canvas (60x45cm 24x18in) Cleveland OH 2000

MARI RIBAS Antoni 1906-1974 [23]

$291 - €330 - £198 - FF2 167
Figuras Aguada/papel (17x23cm 6x9in) Madrid 2000

MARIA ANNA Erzherzogin 1738-1789 [1]

$1 647 - €1 817 - £1 077 - FF11 917
Die Heilige Maria Magdalena als Büsserin Aquarell (15x19cm 5x7in) Wien 2000

MARIA de Mario 1852-1924 [5]

$1 800 - €1 866 - £1 080 - FF12 240
Effetto di luna sulle antiche architetture Acquarello/cartone (67x40cm 26x15in) Roma 1999

MARIA-BERGLER de Ettore 1851-1938 [7]

$7 000 - €7 257 - £4 200 - FF47 600
La venditrice di cocomeri Olio/tela (70x38cm 27x14in) Napoli 1999

MARIAGE Louis François XVIII-XIX [6]

$936 - €915 - £593 - FF6 000
La moisson/La vendange, d'après l'Albane Eau-forte couleurs (52x59cm 20x23in) Paris 1999

MARIANI XX [4]

$1 671 - €1 906 - £1 166 - FF12 500
«Boudu sauvé des eaux, film de Jean Renoir avec Michel Simon» Affiche (159x235cm 62x92in) Paris 2001

MARIANI Carlo Maria 1931 **[67]**
- $18 900 - €16 327 - **£12 600** - FF107 100
  «**Quarto sogno**» Olio/tela (140x121cm 55x47in)
  Prato 1998
- $4 800 - €6 220 - **£3 600** - FF40 800
  «**Frammento di corpo di donna 7**» Olio/tela
  (116x90.5cm 45x35in) Milano 2001
- $3 428 - €3 403 - **£2 142** - FF22 324
  Transformazione Coloured chalks (66x48cm
  25x18in) Amsterdam 1999

MARIANI Mario 1907 **[1]**
- $2 200 - €2 599 - **£1 559** - FF17 051
  Paris Street Scene Oil/canvas (24x36cm 9x14in)
  Boston MA 2000

MARIANI Pompeo 1857-1927 **[222]**
- $8 800 - €11 403 - **£6 600** - FF74 800
  Paesaggio fluviale Olio/tavola (74x48.5cm 29x19in)
  Venezia 2000
- $3 900 - €3 369 - **£2 600** - FF22 100
  Pescatori che escono in mare Tecnica mista/tavola
  (20x30cm 7x11in) Milano 1998
- $1 327 - €1 470 - **£900** - FF9 640
  Huntsman and Dog in a Wood at Sunset
  Gouache/paper (14x9cm 5x3in) Billingshurst, West-
  Sussex 2000
- $2 200 - €2 851 - **£1 650** - FF18 700
  Signora in poltrona Monotype (41x31.5cm 16x12in)
  Prato 2000

MARIANNECCI C. XIX **[1]**
- $11 865 - €11 344 - **£7 280** - FF74 415
  The Madonna del Granduca, after Raphael
  Watercolour (85x56cm 33x22in) Amsterdam 1999

MARIAUD Léon Joseph 1879-1955 **[2]**
- $402 - €457 - **£279** - FF3 000
  «**Citroën**» Affiche (77x104cm 30x40in) Paris 2001

MARIE Adrien E. 1848-1891 **[36]**
- $5 715 - €6 708 - **£4 034** - FF44 000
  L'artiste dans son atelier Huile/panneau (46x37.5cm
  18x14in) Paris 2000
- $7 250 - €8 129 - **£4 923** - FF53 322
  Moment of Beauty Oil/panel (40.5x31cm 15x12in)
  New-York 2000
- $320 - €366 - **£223** - FF2 400
  Touristes anglais devant Notre-Dame de Paris
  Crayon/papier (39x52cm 15x20in) Paris 2001

MARIE Gustave XIX-XX **[14]**
- $600 - €512 - **£361** - FF3 357
  «**Edmond Sagot - Etrennes aux Dames**» Poster
  (64x88.5cm 25x34in) New-York 1998

MARIE Jacques XIX-XX **[6]**
- $1 611 - €1 602 - **£1 000** - FF10 511
  French Village Oil/canvas (61x45.5cm 24x17in)
  London 2000

MARIE Jean-Jacques 1949 **[9]**
- $487 - €457 - **£301** - FF3 000
  Les genêts Huile/toile (60x60cm 23x23in) Brides-les-
  Bains 1999

MARIE P. XX **[3]**
- $414 - €396 - **£257** - FF2 600
  «**Edmond Sagot, Étrennes aux Dames**» Affiche
  (120x81cm 47x31in) La Varenne-Saint-Hilaire 1999

MARIE Raoul E. XIX **[8]**
- $1 817 - €1 753 - **£1 147** - FF11 500
  Les pêcheurs à la ligne Huile/toile (46x32.5cm
  18x12in) Paris 1999

MARIE-ALIX Alice XX **[2]**
- $6 000 - €6 440 - **£4 015** - FF42 246
  Porrait of Paul Poiret Oil/canvas (115.5x81cm
  45x31in) New-York 2000

MARIëN Marcel 1920-1993 **[105]**
- $4 425 - €4 421 - **£2 766** - FF29 000
  **Les seins et la main d'une femme nue, se reflé-
  tant dans un miroir** Technique mixte (8x10.5cm
  3x4in) Paris 1999
- $885 - €884 - **£553** - FF5 800
  Maquette originale de l'affiche des Lèvres Nues
  Technique mixte, dessin (27x42.5cm 10x16in) Paris
  1999
- $587 - €644 - **£379** - FF4 227
  La Lettre volée Photo (24x18cm 9x7in) Liège 2000

MARIENHOF Jan A. c.1610-c.1650/60 **[8]**
- $12 550 - €12 394 - **£7 750** - FF81 300
  **Homme barbu assis portant un bonnet de four-
  rure et une chaîne en or** Huile/toile (45.3x34.5cm
  17x13in) Antwerpen 1999

MARIESCHI Jacopo di Paolo 1711-1794 **[11]**
- $18 965 - €22 313 - **£13 729** - FF146 366
  Intérieur d'église, Venise Huile/toile (35.5x55.5cm
  13x21in) Sion 2001

MARIESCHI Michele 1696-1743 **[72]**
- $155 170 - €151 986 - **£100 000** - FF996 960
  **Capricci of the Venetian Lagoon, with Boatmen
  and Peasants** Oil/canvas (37.5x56cm 14x22in)
  London 1999
- $27 979 - €31 371 - **£19 000** - FF205 783
  **Capricci of the venetian Lagoon with Peasants
  resting before Houses** Oil/canvas (23.5x35cm
  9x13in) London 2000
- $2 400 - €3 110 - **£1 800** - FF20 400
  Veduta della Chiesa della Salute China
  (12.5x20cm 4x7in) Milano 2000
- $1 435 - €1 636 - **£1 001** - FF10 732
  Campo San Giovanni e Paolo Radierung
  (31x44.5cm 12x17in) Berlin 2001

MARIETTE Pierre I ?-1657 **[1]**
- $901 - €826 - **£550** - FF5 415
  Palestine Engraving (39x53.5cm 15x21in) London
  1999

MARIJAC (Jacques Dumas) 1908-1994 **[11]**
- $261 - €244 - **£161** - FF1 600
  Jim Boum Encre Chine (24.5x16.5cm 9x6in) Paris
  1999

MARIKA Mathaman c.1920-c.1970 **[6]**
- $6 289 - €6 752 - **£4 209** - FF44 288
  Marrana Mixed media (114x61cm 44x24in)
  Melbourne 2000

MARIKA Mawalan 1908-1967 **[19]**
- $4 288 - €4 603 - **£2 870** - FF30 196
  Untitled Mixed media (118x45cm 46x17in) Melbourne
  2000

MARILHAT Prosper Georges Ant. 1811-1847 **[41]**
- $410 312 - €472 399 - **£280 000** - FF73 098 732
  **Vue de la Place de l'Esbekieh et du quartier
  Copte, au Caire** Oil/canvas (107x161cm 42x63in)
  London 2000
- $8 037 - €6 860 - **£4 806** - FF45 000
  Caravane près d'une source Huile/toile (30x41cm
  11x16in) Paris 1998
- $877 - €884 - **£555** - FF5 800
  Bédouins au bord du désert Crayon (16x25.5cm
  6x10in) Paris 2000

M

MARIN Claude 1924 [54]
- $402 - €457 - **£281** - FF3 000
  Le port de Saint Cast Huile/carton (22x27cm 8x10in) Rennes 2000

MARIN Émile 1876-1940 [58]
- $1 123 - €1 310 - **£778** - FF8 592
  Sonniger Hof mit maurischer Loggia Watercolour (34x26cm 13x10in) Bern 2000

MARIN Enrique 1935-1992 [18]
- $293 - €316 - **£200** - FF2 070
  Segoria Fetching Water from a Fountain Watercolour/paper (37x52cm 14x20in) London 2001

MARIN Giovanni XIX [1]
- $4 170 - €4 203 - **£2 600** - FF27 569
  A Market Boat in Venice Oil/panel (22x33cm 8x12in) London 2000

MARIN HIGUERO Enrique 1876-1940 [36]
- $1 080 - €1 201 - **£760** - FF7 880
  Jardín granadino Acuarela/papel (46x31cm 18x12in) Madrid 2001

MARIN Jacques 1877-1950 [16]
- $1 334 - €1 139 - **£782** - FF7 470
  Buste de femme Bronze (H51cm H20in) Bruxelles 1998

MARíN Javier 1962 [6]
- $1 600 - €1 750 - **£1 106** - FF11 482
  Nude Male Figure seated on Horse Bronze (139x60x157cm 55x24x62in) Morris-Plains NJ 2001
- $18 000 - €19 321 - **£12 045** - FF126 738
  Muler blanca Bronze (77x42cm 30x16in) New-York 2000

MARIN John 1870-1953 [210]
- $170 000 - €168 783 - **£106 250** - FF1 107 142
  Morning Scene: Sea and Ledges Oil/canvas (61x73.5cm 24x28in) New-York 1999
- $80 000 - €95 140 - **£57 016** - FF624 080
  Weehawken Sequence Oil/canvas/board (35.5x25.5cm 13x10in) New-York 2000
- $22 500 - €26 758 - **£16 035** - FF175 522
  Downtown New York Watercolour (19.5x25cm 7x9in) New-York 2000
- $1 100 - €1 309 - **£761** - FF8 584
  Rue St.Jacques, Paris Etching (12x17cm 5x7in) Plainville CT 2000

MARIN Joseph Charles 1759-1834 [10]
- $20 065 - €22 410 - **£13 597** - FF147 000
  La source Terracotta (H29cm H11in) Paris 2000

MARIN RAMOS Eustaquio 1873-1959 [17]
- $10 627 - €11 434 - **£7 230** - FF75 000
  Flamenco Huile/carton (105x82cm 41x32in) Paris 2001

MARIN Ricardo 1874-1942 [53]
- $160 - €144 - **£98** - FF945
  El preso Tinta/papel (17.5x25cm 6x9in) Madrid 1999

MARIN SEVILLA Enrique ?-1940 [2]
- $2 240 - €2 403 - **£1 520** - FF15 760
  Rincón de Granada Oleo/lienzo (100x71cm 39x27in) Madrid 2001

MARIN-MARIE 1901-1987 [206]
- $9 352 - €10 671 - **£6 496** - FF70 000
  Calme plat Gouache/papier (50x70cm 19x27in) Paris 2000
- $268 - €290 - **£185** - FF1 900
  Agression de Merz-El-Kebir/Defense de Dakar Lithographie (50x82cm 19x32in) Soissons 2001

MARINARI Onorio 1627-1715 [14]
- $20 472 - €20 452 - **£12 800** - FF134 156
  Madonna mit Kind und fliegenden Engeln Öl/Leinwand (123x101cm 48x39in) Köln 1999
- $20 616 - €23 116 - **£14 000** - FF151 629
  Apollo, Half-Length, holding a Lyre Oil/canvas (88x74.5cm 34x29in) London 2000

MARINELLI Vincenzo 1820-1892 [12]
- $6 250 - €6 479 - **£3 750** - FF42 500
  Il ballo dell'Ape Olio/tela (81x121cm 31x47in) Napoli 1999
- $3 234 - €3 042 - **£2 000** - FF19 957
  Figures in a ruined Courtyard Oil/canvas (55.5x26.5cm 21x10in) London 1999

MARINI Antonio 1788-1861 [5]
- $15 484 - €14 940 - **£9 790** - FF98 000
  Scène de tempête Huile/toile (96x133cm 37x52in) Paris 1999

MARINI Antonio Maria 1668-1725 [15]
- $24 000 - €25 631 - **£16 353** - FF168 127
  Coastal Landscape with Ships in a Storm Oil/canvas (200x294cm 78x115in) New-York 2001
- $8 000 - €10 367 - **£6 000** - FF68 000
  Marina in burrasca Olio/tela (32x45cm 12x17in) Milano 2000

MARINI Marino 1901-1980 [1409]
- $383 065 - €355 514 - **£230 000** - FF2 332 016
  Presentazione dei Giocolieri Oil/canvas (150x121cm 59x47in) London 1999
- $26 500 - €27 471 - **£15 900** - FF180 200
  Cavallo e cavaliere Tecnica mista/cartone (64.5x44.5cm 25x17in) Prato 1999
- $12 613 - €12 328 - **£8 000** - FF80 864
  Cavallo e cavaliere Tempera (32.5x24cm 12x9in) London 1999
- $92 000 - €119 215 - **£69 000** - FF782 000
  Danzatrice Terracotta (126x32x29cm 49x12x11in) Milano 2000
- $83 275 - €77 286 - **£50 000** - FF506 960
  Piccolo Cavaliere Ceramic (H39cm H15in) London 1999
- $12 000 - €12 440 - **£7 200** - FF81 600
  Figure China/carta (55x34.5cm 21x13in) Milano 2000
- $1 041 - €1 010 - **£660** - FF6 623
  Figurkomposition Color lithograph (64.5x49.5cm 25x19in) København 1999

MARINKO George J. 1908-1990 [60]
- $850 - €882 - **£539** - FF5 788
  Starboard Track Mixed media (28x31.5cm 11x12in) Boston MA 2000

MARINO DI TEANA Francisco 1920 [12]
- $737 - €838 - **£519** - FF5 500
  Développement dans l'espace Métal (12.5x19cm 4x7in) Paris 2001

MARINO Nino 1929 [6]
- $964 - €1 125 - **£677** - FF7 378
  Chevaux et Cavaliers IV Farblithographie (37x50.5cm 14x19in) Köln 2000

MARINOT Maurice 1882-1960 [13]
- $7 272 - €7 699 - **£4 812** - FF50 500
  Flacon rond à col droit Sculpture verre (H18cm H7in) Neuilly-sur-Seine 2000

MARINSKY Harry 1909-? [5]
- $21 462 - €23 915 - **£15 000** - FF156 873
  Studing Form Bronze (H131cm H51in) Near Ely 2001

MARINUS Ferdinand 1808-1890 **[33]**
- **$17 245** - €15 092 - **£10 444** - FF99 000
  La danse Huile/toile (182x287cm 71x112in) Paris 1998
- **$2 070** - €2 231 - **£1 386** - FF14 634
  Vaches au clair de lune Huile/toile (50x90cm 19x35in) Antwerpen 2000

MARIO DEI FIORI Mario Nuzzi 1603-1673 **[53]**
- **$26 897** - €28 872 - **£18 000** - FF189 388
  Variegated Tulips, Daffodils, Convulvuli, Carnations and other flowers Oil/canvas (96x135cm 37x53in) London 2000
- **$31 200** - €26 953 - **£15 600** - FF176 800
  Vaso di fiori Olio/tela (76x61cm 29x24in) Milano 1999

MARIOTON Claudius 1844-1919 **[17]**
- **$291** - €322 - **£204** - FF2 113
  Le travail Bronze (H41cm H16in) Bruxelles 2001

MARIOTON Eugène 1854-1933 **[139]**
- **$3 250** - €3 275 - **£2 226** - FF21 482
  Farewell Gilded bronze (H91cm H36in) Delray-Beach FL 2000
- **$1 723** - €1 452 - **£1 018** - FF9 523
  «Fascinator» Bronze (H55cm H21in) Amsterdam 1998

MARIOTTI Leopoldo XIX-XX **[4]**
- **$2 280** - €1 970 - **£1 522** - FF12 920
  Pastorella con gregge Acquarello/carta (64x97cm 25x38in) Milano 1998

MARIS Frits, Ferdinand J. 1873-1935 **[18]**
- **$3 906** - €4 538 - **£2 745** - FF29 766
  Summer day in the field Oil/canvas (35x28.5cm 13x11in) Amsterdam 2001

MARIS Jacob 1837-1899 **[117]**
- **$19 305** - €22 689 - **£13 385** - FF148 830
  Zandkruiers Oil/canvas (40.5x60cm 15x23in) Amsterdam 2000
- **$6 256** - €5 899 - **£3 877** - FF38 695
  «Annie» Oil/canvas/panel (14x11.5cm 5x4in) Amsterdam 1999
- **$2 702** - €3 176 - **£1 873** - FF20 836
  Drinking from the Kitten's Bowl Watercolour (28x14.5cm 11x5in) Amsterdam 2000

MARIS Matthijs 1839-1917 **[39]**
- **$96 260** - €90 756 - **£59 660** - FF595 320
  The Bridal Veil Oil/canvas (67x57.5cm 26x22in) Amsterdam 1999
- **$2 700** - €2 306 - **£1 650** - FF15 653
  Woman Trussing a Fowl Oil/panel (34x26.5cm 13x10in) New-York 1999
- **$3 140** - €2 949 - **£1 892** - FF19 347
  Peasant and a Goat by a Watermill Watercolour (23x14.5cm 9x5in) Amsterdam 1999

MARIS Simon Wzn. 1873-1935 **[96]**
- **$1 125** - €1 134 - **£701** - FF7 441
  Double-portrait of the Artist's Children/Lady wearing a Bonnet Oil/canvas (55x46cm 21x18in) Amsterdam 2000
- **$975** - €861 - **£587** - FF5 646
  Lady in a Sunhat Oil/canvas (38.5x26.5cm 15x10in) Amsterdam 1998

MARIS Willem 1844-1910 **[139]**
- **$11 583** - €13 613 - **£8 031** - FF89 298
  Milking Time Oil/canvas (51x41cm 20x16in) Amsterdam 2000

- **$1 527** - €1 817 - **£1 090** - FF11 917
  Bauer mit einem Karren aus Heimweg Oil/panel (22x17.8cm 8x7in) Wien 2000
- **$307** - €272 - **£185** - FF1 783
  Sheets Depicting Studies of Landscapes, Animals and Farms Black chalk/paper (13x28cm 5x11in) Amsterdam 1998

MARIS Willem Matthijs 1872-1929 **[19]**
- **$765** - €818 - **£521** - FF5 365
  De drie gebroeders Maris Lithographie (21.4x28.8cm 8x11in) Lokeren 2001

MARISALDI Falco Elena 1902-1990 **[20]**
- **$1 320** - €1 140 - **£660** - FF7 480
  Ragazzi pastori Olio/cartone (34.5x49.5cm 13x19in) Vercelli 1999
- **$200** - €259 - **£150** - FF1 700
  Carretto siciliano Olio/carta (30x41cm 11x16in) Vercelli 2000

MARISCAL Javier 1950 **[19]**
- **$1 890** - €2 102 - **£1 260** - FF13 790
  Café Oleo/papel (105x75cm 41x29in) Madrid 2000
- **$496** - €579 - **£348** - FF3 800
  Bar Pastel/papier (65x50cm 25x19in) Versailles 2000
- **$456** - €524 - **£325** - FF3 500
  Sans titre Sérigraphie (76x55.5cm 29x21in) Paris 2001

MARISOL Escobar 1930 **[28]**
- **$80 000** - €92 823 - **£55 232** - FF608 880
  Person with Poodle Sculpture, wood (118x59.5x45.5cm 46x23x17in) New-York 2000

MARISTANY Vives XX **[99]**
- **$231** - €228 - **£144** - FF1 497
  Playa Oleo/tabla (14.5x25cm 5x9in) Madrid 1999

MARIUS-ERAUD Gerarda Hermina 1854-1919 **[17]**
- **$1 923** - €1 632 - **£1 160** - FF10 704
  «Vruchten» Oil/canvas (21.5x37cm 8x14in) Den Haag 1998

MARJORAM Gerard XX **[15]**
- **$880** - €978 - **£614** - FF6 413
  The twelve Pins near Cashel, Connemara Oil/canvas (44.5x89.5cm 17x35in) Dublin 2001
- **$437** - €483 - **£292** - FF3 165
  West of Ireland Landscapes Acrylic/canvas (34x44cm 13x17in) Dublin 2000

MARK Mary Ellen 1941 **[22]**
- **$1 100** - €1 253 - **£760** - FF8 220
  «Mother Teresa, Calcutta» Silver print (30x20cm 12x8in) New-York 2001

MARKAU Franz 1881-1967 **[4]**
- **$485** - €460 - **£295** - FF3 018
  Türkische Familie bei der Mittagsruhe Gouache/paper (44x33cm 17x12in) Köln 1999

MARKELBACH Alexandre 1824-1906 **[5]**
- **$3 486** - €3 470 - **£2 170** - FF22 764
  Repas en temps de guerre Huile/toile (40x50cm 15x19in) Bruxelles 1999

MARKES Albert Ernest 1865-1901 **[55]**
- **$583** - €494 - **£350** - FF3 238
  «Long Reach, Dartford» Watercolour (34x51cm 13x20in) London 1998

MARKES Richmond XIX **[66]**
- **$418** - €449 - **£280** - FF2 946
  Fishing Vessels off a Coastline Watercolour (19x35cm 7x13in) Suffolk 2000

M

MARKHAM Kyra 1891-1967 **[88]**
〓 **$800** – €745 - **£493** - FF4 890
 «**The Silver Trumpets of the Rain**» Lithograph
 (34x26cm 13x10in) Cleveland OH 1999

MARKINO Yoshiko XIX-XX **[16]**
 $13 326 – €11 386 - **£8 000** - FF74 686
 Spring mists at Westminster Bridge Oil/canvas
 (51x76cm 20x29in) London 1998
 $10 702 – €10 057 - **£6 500** - FF65 972
 The booking Office Watercolour/paper (28x17.5cm
 11x6in) London 1999

MARKKULA Mauno 1905-1959 **[33]**
 $727 – €841 - **£514** - FF5 516
 Storm Oil/canvas (35x50cm 13x19in) Helsinki 2000
 $913 – €1 009 - **£633** - FF6 619
 Kvällsbelysning Oil/canvas (22x27cm 8x10in)
 Helsinki 2001

MARKO Andreas 1824-1895 **[74]**
 $17 400 – €15 031 - **£11 600** - FF98 600
 Pastori laziali Olio/tela (106x177cm 41x69in) Milano
 1998
 $8 514 – €7 994 - **£5 280** - FF52 437
 Landschaft mit heimkehrender Fischerfamilie
 Öl/Leinwand (76x102cm 29x40in) Wien 1999
 $3 500 – €3 628 - **£2 100** - FF23 800
 Riposo al pascolo Olio/tela (30x42.5cm 11x16in)
 Venezia 2000

MARKO C 1902-1986 **[9]**
 $7 293 – €7 775 - **£4 625** - FF51 000
 Nature morte à la carafe Huile/toile (92x73cm
 36x28in) Deauville 2000

MARKO Ferenc 1832-1874 **[3]**
 $5 180 – €5 442 - **£3 220** - FF35 700
 La foire aux pastèques Huile/toile (21x29cm
 8x11in) Budapest 2000

MARKO Henry 1855-1921 **[48]**
 $2 100 – €1 814 - **£1 050** - FF11 900
 Paraggi Olio/tela (110x40cm 43x15in) Vercelli 1999
 $720 – €622 - **£360** - FF4 080
 Paesaggio montano con baita Olio/tela (25x35cm
 9x13in) Vercelli 1999

MARKO Karl I 1791-1860 **[36]**
 $32 300 – €27 610 - **£19 380** - FF181 108
 Landschaft mit Ruth und Boas im Vordergrund
 Öl/Leinwand (106.5x137.5cm 41x54in) Wien 1998
 $12 000 – €12 440 - **£7 200** - FF81 600
 Veduta di Tivoli con il Tempio di Vesta Olio/tela
 (46x60cm 18x23in) Roma 2000
 $3 860 – €4 063 - **£2 752** - FF30 185
 Bewaldete Landschaft mit badenden Nymphen
 Öl/Karton (19.8x25.3cm 7x9in) Köln 2000
 $374 – €363 - **£231** - FF2 383
 Ideale Landschaft mit figürlicher Staffage Ink
 (21x17.5cm 8x6in) Wien 1999

MARKO Karl II 1822-1891 **[51]**
 $14 561 – €13 805 - **£8 858** - FF90 555
 Hirten auf dem Weg zum Markt in weiter italieni-
 scher Berglandschaft Öl/Leinwand (97x132cm
 38x51in) Köln 1999
 $7 075 – €8 209 - **£4 885** - FF53 847
 Val di Nievole-Autumno Öl/Leinwand (72x98cm
 28x38in) Luzern 2000
 $1 404 – €1 637 - **£927** - FF10 740
 Abendstimmung am See Öl/Leinwand
 (28.5x46.5cm 11x18in) Bern 2000

MARKOFF Natacha 1911 **[10]**
 $1 491 – €1 601 - **£997** - FF10 500
 Villa à Gammarth Huile/toile (46x54cm 18x21in)
 Paris 2000

MARKOS Lajos 1917-1993 **[18]**
 $4 400 – €4 723 - **£2 944** - FF30 980
 Winter Sleigh Oil/canvas (60x76cm 24x30in) Houston
 TX 2000

MARKOV Léonid 1926 **[91]**
 $178 – €152 - **£107** - FF1 000
 Seringa Huile/carton (28x29cm 11x11in) Enghien
 1998
 $2 768 – €2 659 - **£1 716** - FF17 440
 Abendstimmung am Quai Notre-Dame
 Pastell/Papier (48x64cm 18x25in) Ahlden 1999

MARKOV-GRINBERG Mark 1907 **[8]**
 $4 286 – €4 602 - **£2 869** - FF30 185
 Parade auf dem Roten Platz Vintage gelatin silver
 print (53.9x20.8cm 21x8in) Hamburg 2000

MARKOWICZ Artur 1872-1934 **[53]**
 $9 500 – €10 277 - **£6 508** - FF67 415
 The Chess Players, Krakow Oil/paper/board
 (49.5x35cm 19x13in) Tel Aviv 2001
 $2 059 – €2 210 - **£1 377** - FF14 499
 Juif lisant Pastel/papier (44x32.5cm 17x12in)
 Warszawa 2000

MARKOWSKI Eugeniusz 1912 **[4]**
 $1 550 – €1 799 - **£1 070** - FF11 801
 L'étreinte de deux personnes Gouache (36x26cm
 14x10in) Warszawa 2000

MARKS Claude ?-c.1915 **[15]**
 $690 – €762 - **£456** - FF4 997
 Orchard Landscape Gouache/paper (26x36cm
 10x14in) Dublin 2000

MARKS George 1857-1933 **[23]**
 $1 319 – €1 422 - **£900** - FF9 329
 Rabbits amidst the Gorse Watercolour (24.5x55cm
 9x21in) Bury St. Edmunds, Suffolk 2001

MARKS Hans 1946 **[13]**
 $303 – €320 - **£200** - FF2 100
 Deux guepards Mine plomb (49.5x65cm 19x25in)
 Versailles 2000

MARKS Henry Stacy 1829-1898 **[76]**
 $56 783 – €60 952 - **£38 000** - FF399 820
 The Bookworm Oil/canvas (86.5x145cm 34x57in)
 London 2000
 $48 378 – €56 208 - **£34 000** - FF368 702
 The Seven Ages/The School Boy/The Lover/The
 Soldier/The Justice Oil/panel (64x81cm 25x31in)
 London 2001
 $651 – €634 - **£400** - FF4 156
 Lancing Downs Watercolour/paper (19x49cm 7x19in)
 Newbury, Berkshire 1999

MARKUS Ans 1947 **[3]**
 $7 030 – €8 168 - **£4 941** - FF53 578
 Ruimte (Space) Oil/canvas (70x160cm 27x62in)
 Amsterdam 2001

MARKUS Antoon 1870-1955 **[13]**
 $524 – €487 - **£320** - FF3 197
 De Zonsondergang Oil/canvas (30x48cm 11x18in)
 Amsterdam 1998

MARKWICK H.W. XIX-XX **[1]**
 $2 395 – €2 813 - **£1 700** - FF18 451
 A Shikara on a Lake, Kashmir Watercolour
 (37x48.5cm 14x19in) London 2000

M

MARLATT H. Irving 1860-1929 **[17]**
- **$35 000** - €30 196 - **£21 035** - FF198 075
  Indians Crossing a River Oil/canvas (106x152cm 42x60in) Santa-Fe NM 1998
- **$2 500** - €2 325 - **£1 543** - FF15 249
  Halloween Moon Oil/canvas (60x45cm 24x18in) Portland ME 1999

MARLET Jean Henri 1771-1847 **[16]**
- **$2 580** - €3 049 - **£1 828** - FF20 000
  Le montreur de marionnettes rue de Verneuil Huile/toile (24x39cm 9x15in) Béziers 2000

MARLIAVE de François Marie 1874-1953 **[86]**
- **$1 205** - €1 368 - **£824** - FF8 976
  Actor Watercolour, gouache/paper (35x24cm 13x9in) Singapore 2000

MARLIER de Philips c.1600-c.1669 **[12]**
- **$32 874** - €35 288 - **£22 000** - FF231 475
  Garland of Fruit and Flowers Surrounding a Personification of Charity Oil/canvas (184x131cm 72x51in) London 2000
- **$75 075** - €83 847 - **£50 875** - FF550 000
  Vase de fleurs sur un entablement Huile/panneau (107x76.5cm 42x30in) Paris 2000
- **$100 000** - €106 795 - **£68 140** - FF700 530
  Carnations in a Glass Vase on a Stone Table Oil/panel (45x34cm 17x13in) New-York 2001

MARLOW William 1740-1813 **[42]**
- **$4 989** - €5 329 - **£3 400** - FF34 954
  The Pont du Gard, Nîmes Oil/canvas (38x56cm 14x22in) London 2001
- **$28 119** - €27 519 - **£18 000** - FF180 516
  Elegant Figures walking in the Gardens at Kew by the Pagoda Oil/copper (23x53cm 9x20in) London 1999
- **$2 878** - €2 772 - **£1 800** - FF18 182
  Lyons from the Saone, France Pencil (29x51cm 11x20in) London 1999

MARMA Rodolfo 1923 **[51]**
- **$900** - €933 - **£540** - FF6 120
  Isola d'Elba - Procchio Olio/tela (50x70cm 19x27in) Prato 2000
- **$380** - €492 - **£285** - FF3 230
  «Monachina» Olio/tavola (35x25cm 13x9in) Prato 2000

MARNEFFE Ernest 1866-1921 **[52]**
- **$3 727** - €4 338 - **£2 572** - FF28 455
  Jeune femme à l'éventail Huile/panneau (45x36cm 17x14in) Liège 2000
- **$894** - €843 - **£554** - FF5 528
  Tête de jeune femme au chapeau Huile/toile (24x19.5cm 9x7in) Liège 1999

MARNY Paul 1829-1914 **[158]**
- **$1 010** - €956 - **£625** - FF6 271
  Continental Street and Market Scene with Figures in foreground Watercolour/paper (45x33cm 18x13in) Whitby, Yorks 1999

MAROCHETTI Charles, Carlo 1805-1867 **[16]**
- **$1 959** - €1 804 - **£1 200** - FF11 834
  Bust of The Duke of Wellington Bronze (H34.5cm H13in) London 1998

MARÖHN Ferdinand Maronnio XIX **[39]**
- **$6 588** - €6 541 - **£4 113** - FF42 903
  Almabtrieb Öl/Leinwand (37x60cm 14x23in) Wien 1999
- **$2 975** - €2 543 - **£1 785** - FF16 681
  Das Vogelnest Oil/panel (32.5x24.5cm 12x9in) Wien 1998

$886 - €994 - **£620** - FF6 520
  Gentleman chassing a Dog from a Tavern Watercolour/paper (34.5x46cm 13x18in) London 2001

MAROLA 1905-1986 **[21]**
- **$378** - €420 - **£259** - FF2 758
  Getino y otras nostalgias Serigrafia (25x18cm 9x7in) Madrid 2001

MAROLD Ludwig, Ludek 1865-1898 **[53]**
- **$5 491** - €5 193 - **£3 420** - FF34 067
  Portrait of a young Girl Oil/cardboard (74x50.7cm 29x19in) Praha 1999
- **$843** - €768 - **£527** - FF5 037
  In Love Ink/paper (33.6x26.9cm 13x10in) Praha 1999

MARON von Anton 1733-1808 **[13]**
- **$2 250** - €2 631 - **£1 593** - FF17 255
  Portrait of an Artist Oil/canvas (78x101cm 31x40in) Cedar-Falls IA 2001
- **$1 312** - €1 524 - **£922** - FF10 000
  Décoration de fresque romaine Aquarelle, gouache (50x63cm 19x24in) Paris 2001

MARONIEZ Georges Philibert 1865-1933 **[189]**
- **$24 649** - €23 367 - **£15 400** - FF153 276
  «L'heure dorée» Oil/canvas (96x140cm 37x55in) Doncaster, South-Yorkshire 1999
- **$3 389** - €4 040 - **£2 416** - FF26 500
  Coucher de soleil Huile/panneau (73x117cm 28x46in) Poitiers 2000
- **$1 008** - €991 - **£647** - FF6 500
  Chevaux au bord de l'eau Huile/toile (32x40cm 12x15in) Paris 1999
- **$476** - €473 - **£296** - FF3 100
  Cour de ferme Aquarelle/papier (18x24cm 7x9in) Brest 1999

MAROT Daniel I 1663-1752 **[7]**
- **$8 000** - €8 569 - **£5 463** - FF56 212
  Design for a Garden: A Fountain Under a Rotunda Leading to a Pool Watercolour (32x45cm 12x17in) New-York 2001
- **$1 242** - €1 059 - **£749** - FF6 948
  The Celebration of the Birth of the Prince of Orange Engraving (80x56cm 31x22in) London 1998

MAROT François 1666-1719 **[5]**
- **$25 704** - €22 205 - **£12 852** - FF145 656
  Allegoria della Musica Olio/tela (76x138cm 29x54in) Milano 1999

MARPLES George 1869-1939 **[9]**
- **$230** - €255 - **£160** - FF1 672
  Canada Geese in Flight Etching (21x31cm 8x12in) London 2001

MARQUARD Otto 1881-1969 **[16]**
- **$1 764** - €1 687 - **£1 074** - FF11 067
  Kopfweiden am Seeufer, bei Hegne, im Hintergrund der Reichenauer Damm Öl/Leinwand (95x68cm 37x26in) Konstanz 1999

MARQUES Bernardo 1899-1962 **[3]**
- **$1 364** - €1 545 - **£961** - FF10 130
  Casario Tinta china/papel (30x22cm 11x8in) Lisboa 1999

MARQUÉS GARCIA José María 1862-1936 **[16]**
- **$420** - €420 - **£259** - FF2 758
  Paisaje con río Tinta (41x30cm 16x11in) Madrid 2000

MARQUES Guilherme 1887-? **[33]**
- **$310** - €271 - **£824** - FF8 334
  Congolese village Oil/canvas/board (40.5x55.5cm 15x21in) Amsterdam 1999

M

$864 - €797 - £518 - FF5 228
Village of Bafwatutavele Oil/board (29x35cm
11x13in) Amsterdam 1998

MARQUES PUIG Josep M. 1890-1950 [10]
$480 - €450 - £292 - FF2 955
Paisaje con huertos y carretera Oleo/lienzo
(38x55cm 14x21in) Barcelona 1999

MARQUESTE Laurent Honoré 1848-1920 [4]
$3 016 - €2 949 - £1 862 - FF19 347
Hebe Bronze (H78cm H30in) Amsterdam 1999

MARQUET Albert 1875-1947 [1007]
$85 000 - €95 206 - £59 058 - FF624 512
Le port de Bougie Oil/canvas (50x61cm 19x24in)
New-York 2001
$36 600 - €36 039 - £22 800 - FF236 400
Le Parc Oleo/lienzo (26x35cm 10x13in) Madrid 1999
$1 937 - €2 134 - £1 292 - FF14 000
Portrait d'homme au monocle Encre Chine/papier
(20.5x17cm 8x6in) Deauville 2000
$243 - €290 - £173 - FF1 900
Bord de rivière Lithographie couleurs (45x55cm
17x21in) Paris 2000

MARQUET René Paul 1875-? [18]
$3 000 - €3 485 - £2 108 - FF22 863
German Shepherd Bronze (H44.5cm H17in) New-
York 2001

MARQUEZ ALCALA José 1937 [22]
$424 - €481 - £296 - FF3 152
El pez Oleo/tabla (81x65cm 31x25in) Madrid 2001

MARQUIS James Richard ?-1885 [14]
$7 510 - €6 719 - £4 500 - FF44 074
The Bass Rock Oil/canvas (81x112cm 31x44in)
Perthshire 1998
$2 700 - €2 540 - £1 684 - FF16 662
A Valley in County Wicklow Ireland Oil/canvas
(30.5x46cm 12x18in) New-York 1999

MARQUIS Richard 1945 [2]
$8 000 - €7 311 - £4 894 - FF47 958
Teapot Sculpture, glass (H20cm H7in) New-York 1999

MARR Joseph Heinrich L. 1807-1871 [24]
$21 635 - €25 565 - £15 335 - FF167 695
Nach dem Kirchgang Oil/panel (54x74cm 21x29in)
Ahlden 2000
$1 511 - €1 431 - £919 - FF9 390
**Alm im Hochgebirge, vorn Ziegen, rechts die
Almhütte** Öl/Leinwand (20x27.5cm 7x10in) München
1999

MARR von Carl 1858-1936 [61]
$65 000 - €61 763 - £39 546 - FF405 138
The Gossips Oil/canvas (104x166.5cm 40x65in)
New-York 1999
$1 955 - €1 687 - £1 184 - FF11 067
«Putto mit Rosen» Öl/Karton (48x34cm 18x13in)
Kempten 1999
$1 305 - €1 278 - £841 - FF8 384
Im Gras liegender weiblicher Akt Oil/panel
(7x21cm 2x8in) Kempten 1999
$536 - €511 - £340 - FF33 353
Tod und Leben Charcoal (45.5x38.5cm 17x15in)
Zwiesel 1999

MARRABLE Madeline F. Cockburn ?-1916 [4]
$1 303 - €1 454 - £880 - FF9 536
**River Landscape with Boats by Timber
Buildings** Watercolour/paper (43x71cm 17x28in)
Aylsham, Norfolk 2000

MARRALWANGA Peter 1916-1987 [10]
$12 498 - €12 056 - £7 898 - FF79 085
Salwater Crocodile Mixed media (210x90cm
82x35in) Melbourne 1999

MARRANI A. XIX [2]
$1 491 - €1 636 - £1 013 - FF10 732
Blick auf den Innenhof des Bargello in Florenz
Aquarell/Papier (41x28cm 16x11in) Berlin 2000

MARRE Henri 1858-1927 [20]
$871 - €991 - £598 - FF6 500
Jardin fleuri Huile/panneau (32.5x40.5cm 12x15in)
Toulouse 2000

MARREL Jacob 1614-1681 [31]
$50 000 - €53 398 - £34 070 - FF350 265
**Parrot, Parakeet, Melon, Bunches of Grapes,
Peaches, other Fruit** Oil/canvas (77x96cm 30x37in)
New-York 1998
$302 549 - €304 862 - £188 579 - FF1 999 766
**Ein Blumenstrauss in einer Nische mit
Eidechse und Kirschen** Öl/Kupfer (20x14.5cm
7x5in) Zürich 2000

MARSA CASAS Xavier 1944 [2]
$3 245 - €3 304 - £2 035 - FF21 670
Venecia Acuarela/papel (52x68cm 20x26in) Madrid
2000

MARSANS Luis 1930 [6]
$1 950 - €1 802 - £1 170 - FF11 820
Caballero Tinta/papel (25.5x22cm 10x8in) Barcelona
1999

MARSH Reginald 1898-1954 [489]
$24 000 - €26 882 - £16 675 - FF176 332
Striptease Tempera/board (45.5x61cm 17x24in) New-
York 2001
$3 750 - €4 153 - £2 543 - FF27 241
Seated Girl Oil/masonite (12x10cm 5x4in) New-York
2000
$11 000 - €12 038 - £7 587 - FF78 966
Railway Tank Car, Jersey City Watercolour/paper
(35.5x51cm 13x20in) New-York 2001
$1 300 - €1 148 - £799 - FF7 528
Locomotive Lehigh Valley Etching (17.5x27.5cm
6x10in) New-York 1999
$4 000 - €4 399 - £2 774 - FF28 856
«Reginald Marsh, Photographs of New York»
Silver print (12x17cm 5x7in) New-York 2001

MARSHAL Alexander XVII [1]
$25 254 - €30 034 - £18 000 - FF197 013
**Still-Life Centifolia (cabbage rose), Dianthus
Caryophyllus** Watercolour (25.5x19.5cm 10x7in)
London 2000

MARSHALL Benjamin 1767-1835 [47]
$140 000 - €119 614 - £84 042 - FF784 616
**Mr.Thornhill's Sailor being Rubbed Down at
Epsom** Oil/canvas (101x126.5cm 39x49in) New-York
1998
$23 324 - €21 467 - £14 000 - FF140 814
**Griffith Owen, Harpist to the Corbet Family of
Tywyn** Oil/canvas (90x70cm 35x27in) Glamorgan 1999
$300 000 - €281 447 - £185 370 - FF1 846 170
**Mr. Richard Prince, Colonel Mellish's Trainer,
with Mr. J.Frost** Oil/canvas (43x33cm 16x12in) New-
York 1999

MARSHALL Brent 1957 [2]
$3 400 - €3 933 - £2 406 - FF25 801
Tidal Pool Sculpture, glass (24x29cm 9x11in)
Cleveland OH 2000

MARSHALL Clark Summers 1861-1944 **[5]**
🖉 **$10 000** - €11 028 - **£6 772** - FF72 341
First Snow Oil/canvas (51.5x77cm 20x30in) New-York 2000

MARSHALL Francis 1901-1980 **[9]**
▥ **$2 884** - €3 187 - **£2 000** - FF20 906
«The Red Shoes» Poster (76x104.5cm 29x41in) London 2001

MARSHALL Frank Howard 1866-1945 **[7]**
🖉 **$2 000** - €2 178 - **£1 377** - FF14 288
«The Gabilans» Oil/board (22x30cm 9x12in) Altadena CA 2001

MARSHALL Herbert Menzies 1841-1913 **[104]**
🖉 **$1 816** - €1 912 - **£1 200** - FF12 545
Market Place, Norwich Watercolour (20x30cm 7x11in) London 2000

MARSHALL John Fitz 1859-1932 **[37]**
🖉 **$6 654** - €5 636 - **£4 000** - FF36 968
Dog Days Oil/canvas (36x61cm 14x24in) London 1998
🖉 **$519** - €499 - **£320** - FF3 270
Apple Blossom on a mossy Bank Oil/canvas (20.5x40.5cm 8x15in) London 1999

MARSHALL John Miller act.1881-1927 **[29]**
🖉 **$402** - €380 - **£250** - FF2 494
Shipping at Dusk Watercolour (24.5x59.5cm 9x23in) Billingshurst, West-Sussex 1999

MARSHALL Lambert 1810-1870 **[9]**
🖉 **$8 279** - €9 084 - **£5 500** - FF59 586
The Badger Bait Oil/paper (51x61cm 20x24in) London 2000

MARSHALL Roberto Ang.Kitterm. 1849-c.1923 **[35]**
🖉 **$1 345** - €1 571 - **£950** - FF10 303
Looking Towards the Sea, Hastings Watercolour/paper (21.5x35cm 8x13in) London 2000

MARSHALL Roberto Angelo Kitt. 1818-1878 **[22]**
🖉 **$953** - €995 - **£601** - FF6 525
Sheep on the Road, near Horsebridge, Hampshire Watercolour/paper (44x88cm 17x34in) Sydney 2000

MARSHALL Thomas Falcon 1818-1878 **[18]**
🖉 **$11 156** - €10 217 - **£6 800** - FF67 018
The Storyteller Oil/canvas (71x106.5cm 27x41in) Ipswich 1999

MARSHALL Willis Elstob XIX-XX **[17]**
🖉 **$2 381** - €2 299 - **£1 475** - FF15 079
The Old Keeper Huile/toile (41x56cm 16x22in) Montréal 1999

MARSILLACH CODONY Joaquim 1905-1986 **[13]**
🖉 **$1 740** - €1 802 - **£1 110** - FF11 820
Campo florido Oleo/lienzo (54x73cm 21x28in) Barcelona 2000

MARSTBOOM Antoon 1905-1960 **[46]**
🖉 **$142** - €149 - **£90** - FF975
Composition Encre/papier (29x19cm 11x7in) Antwerpen 2000

MARSTON Freda, née Clulow 1895-1949 **[29]**
🖉 **$762** - €877 - **£520** - FF5 754
The Boathouse Oil/canvas (40.5x50.5cm 15x19in) Billingshurst, West-Sussex 2000
▥ **$1 129** - €1 309 - **£800** - FF8 588
«North West England, LMS» Poster (102x64cm 40x25in) London 2000

MARSTON George Edward 1882-1940 **[21]**
🖉 **$35 499** - €34 091 - **£22 000** - FF223 623
«S.Y Endurance» trapped in the ice in the Weddell Sea Oil/board (42x71cm 16x27in) London 1999
🖉 **$3 489** - €3 664 - **£2 200** - FF24 034.
New Coastline West of Cape North, taken from the Nimrod, 8 March Watercolour/paper (21.5x54cm 8x21in) London 2000

MARSTRAND Wilhelm 1810-1873 **[401]**
🖉 **$2 820** - €3 353 - **£2 010** - FF21 997
Tiggermunkene stiger i land med deres bytte Oil/canvas (38x53cm 14x20in) København 2000
🖉 **$3 194** - €2 818 - **£1 923** - FF18 486
Portraet af en italienerinde Oil/canvas (38.5x29cm 15x11in) København 1998
🖉 **$363** - €350 - **£226** - FF2 296
Natdram og en pibe tobak, mand siddende i seng/Den strenge krovaert Pencil/paper (10.9x9cm 4x3in) København 1999

MARSZALKIEWICZ Stanislaw 1789-1872 **[4]**
🖉 **$2 215** - €2 069 - **£1 341** - FF13 572
Portret Elzulii Sierakowskiej Watercolour, gouache/paper (7.5x6cm 2x2in) Warszawa 1999

MARTAZ XIX **[1]**
🖉 **$3 929** - €3 887 - **£2 450** - FF25 500
Paysage des Pyrénées Gouache/papier (61x83cm 24x32in) Versailles 1999

MARTEL Jan & Joël 1896-1966 **[79]**
🖉 **$42 752** - €48 784 - **£29 728** - FF320 000
Trinité Bronze (105.5x17.5x21cm 41x6x8in) Paris 2001
🖉 **$2 451** - €2 744 - **£1 663** - FF18 000
Lapin Bronze (13.5x14.5cm 5x5in) Paris 2000

MARTEL Joël 1896-1966 **[2]**
🖉 **$5 750** - €5 336 - **£3 452** - FF35 003
Accordian Player Bronze (H28cm H11in) Milford CT 1999

MARTEL Paul Jean 1879-1944 **[27]**
🖉 **$1 392** - €1 636 - **£991** - FF10 731
Portrait d'une élégante au chapeau Pastel/papier (60x50cm 23x19in) Bruxelles 2000

MARTELLI Ugo 1881-1921 **[1]**
🖉 **$5 700** - €4 924 - **£3 800** - FF32 300
Paesaggio romantico al calar del sole Olio/tela (60x65cm 23x25in) Prato 1998

MARTEN Elliot Henry XIX-XX **[65]**
🖉 **$471** - €452 - **£300** - FF2 968
Sheep Grazing on the Downs Watercolour/paper (23x32cm 9x12in) London 1999

MARTENS Conrad 1801-1878 **[113]**
🖉 **$34 118** - €40 038 - **£24 076** - FF262 632
View from Craigend Oil/canvas (48x67cm 18x26in) Melbourne 2000
🖉 **$25 945** - €29 061 - **£18 025** - FF190 625
Spencer Lodge, Miller's Point, Sydney Oil/board (34x44cm 13x17in) Melbourne 2001
🖉 **$6 152** - €5 785 - **£3 809** - FF37 944
From Norton's Crossing, Nepean River Watercolour (16.5x25cm 6x9in) Melbourne 1999

MARTENS Dino XX **[5]**
🖉 **$1 700** - €1 985 - **£1 200** - FF13 018
«Reticello» Sculpture, glass (H12.5cm H4in) New-York 2000

M

MARTENS Ditlev 1795-1864 **[3]**
$13 772 - €15 988 - **£9 680** - FF104 874
In der Akademie Öl/Leinwand (50x66.5cm 19x26in)
Wien 2001

MARTENS George 1894-1979 **[13]**
$5 520 - €5 445 - **£3 399** - FF35 719
Still Life with Fruit Oil/canvas (51x50.5cm 20x19in)
Amsterdam 1999
$1 877 - €2 178 - **£1 296** - FF14 287
Havengezicht Watercolour/paper (26.5x36.5cm
10x14in) Groningen 2000

MARTENS Henry ?-1860 **[14]**
$1 347 - €1 572 - **£962** - FF10 309
**The 11th Prince Albert's Own Hussards (Officer
1845)** Huile/toile (29x25.5cm 11x10in) Montréal 2000
$1 224 - €1 350 - **£800** - FF8 854
The Relief, 2nd Life Guards Watercolour (11x19cm
4x7in) London 2000
$921 - €1 027 - **£600** - FF6 736
**The Capture of Fort Armstrong/The Battle of
the Gwanga** Aquatint in colors (41.5x60.5cm 16x23in)
Johannesburg 2000

MÄRTENS Max 1887-1970 **[27]**
$558 - €460 - **£328** - FF3 018
**Fischer im Kahn auf dem Chiemsee im sonni-
gen Licht** Aquarell/Papier (42x58cm 16x22in) Lindau
1998

MARTENS von Friedrich 1809-1875 **[9]**
$11 243 - €10 620 - **£6 800** - FF69 661
Tête Noire: paysage des Alpes, Dauphiné
Albumen print (26.5x32.5cm 10x12in) London 1999

MARTENS VON SVENHOVEN Jacob Constantyn
c.1793-1861 **[1]**
$4 804 - €4 538 - **£2 906** - FF29 766
Figures and Cattle in a Yard Oil/canvas (69.5x92cm
27x36in) Amsterdam 1999

MARTENS Willy 1856-1927 **[18]**
$3 000 - €2 806 - **£1 813** - FF18 406
Tending the Garden Oil/canvas (57.5x67.5cm
22x26in) New-York 1999
$201 - €230 - **£139** - FF1 509
Impressionistischer Blick auf kleines Haus
Öl/Leinwand (66x24cm 25x9in) Rudolstadt-Thüringen
2000
$14 306 - €16 698 - **£10 098** - FF109 529
Mother and Child with Goatkid in a Landscape
Watercolour (52x34.5cm 20x13in) Toronto 2000

MARTI AGUILO Ricardo 1868-1936 **[16]**
$12 760 - €13 214 - **£7 920** - FF86 680
Paisaje con campesinos (Argentina) Oleo/lienzo
(90x171cm 35x67in) Barcelona 2000
$2 379 - €2 343 - **£1 482** - FF15 366
Composición floral Oleo/lienzo (60x106cm 23x41in)
Barcelona 1999
$1 485 - €1 652 - **£1 017** - FF10 835
Pescadores en la playa Oleo/tabla (24x34cm
9x13in) Madrid 2001

MARTI Joan 1922 **[34]**
$662 - €751 - **£462** - FF4 925
Desnudo Oleo/tablex (47x37cm 18x14in) Barcelona
2000
$812 - €871 - **£536** - FF5 713
Muchacha en un interior Pastel/papier (49.5x32cm
19x12in) Barcelona 2000

MARTI Marcel 1925 **[11]**
$976 - €931 - **£604** - FF6 107
Pausia I Bronze (41x20x18cm 16x7x7in) Barcelona
1999

MARTI Ramon 1915 **[1]**
$5 800 - €6 006 - **£3 700** - FF39 400
Riera de argentona Oleo/lienzo (50x100cm 19x39in)
Barcelona 2000

MARTI Y ALSINA Ramón 1826-1894 **[59]**
$14 766 - €13 522 - **£9 000** - FF88 700
The Tiger Oil/canvas (87.5x210cm 34x82in) London
1999
$2 700 - €2 258 - **£1 612** - FF14 812
Bodegón de frutas Oleo/tabla (47.5x52cm 18x20in)
Madrid 1998
$1 120 - €1 201 - **£740** - FF7 880
Paisaje con acantilado Oleo/lienzo (42.5x34cm
16x13in) Barcelona 2000

MARTI Y MONSO José 1840-1912 **[1]**
$2 762 - €2 553 - **£1 657** - FF16 745
Mujer con sombrilla Oleo/tabla (32x47cm 12x18in)
Madrid 1999

MARTIGNONI Joseph XIX **[2]**
$3 174 - €3 591 - **£2 220** - FF23 553
Fischerhaus am Bodensee Öl/Leinwand (27x35cm
10x13in) St. Gallen 2001

MARTIKAINEN Olavi 1920-1979 **[60]**
$232 - €235 - **£144** - FF1 544
Landskap Oil/canvas (55x70cm 21x27in) Helsinki
2000
$220 - €202 - **£134** - FF1 323
Två fjäll Oil/canvas (30x41cm 11x16in) Helsinki 1999

MARTIN Agnes 1912 **[83]**
$1 100 000 - €1 276 318 - **£759 440** - FF8 372 100
Untitled #6 Mixed media/canvas (183x183cm 72x72in)
New-York 2000
$70 000 - €81 220 - **£48 328** - FF532 770
David Oil/canvas (63x63cm 25x25in) New-York 2000
$120 000 - €134 409 - **£83 376** - FF881 664
«Untitled #10» Acrylic (30.5x30.5cm 12x12in) New-
York 2001
$210 000 - €197 099 - **£129 738** - FF1 292 886
The Laws Sculpture, wood (237x46x5cm 93x18x1in)
New-York 1999
$195 000 - €183 021 - **£120 471** - FF1 200 537
Kali Sculpture, wood (28x29x12cm 11x11x4in) New-
York 1999
$75 000 - €84 006 - **£52 110** - FF551 040
Untitled Ink/paper (20.5x20.5cm 8x8in) New-York
2001
$2 500 - €2 800 - **£1 737** - FF18 368
Untitled Color lithograph (23x23cm 9x9in) New-York
2001

MARTIN Alfred 1888-1950 **[108]**
$114 - €124 - **£79** - FF813
Nu Aquarelle/papier (30x44cm 11x17in) Maisieres-
Mons 2001
$41 - €45 - **£27** - FF292
Nu Gravure (21.5x15.5cm 8x6in) Liège 2000

MARTIN André Denis Othon 1898-1960 **[1]**
$12 268 - €11 272 - **£7 536** - FF73 942
Stehender Frauenakt Bronze (H182cm H71in)
Zürich 1999

MARTIN Andreas 1720-1767 **[21]**
$4 530 - €4 360 - **£2 832** - FF28 602
Reisende in einer bewaldeten Landschaft
Oil/panel (25.5x35cm 10x13in) Wien 1999

MARTIN Anson A. c.1830-c.1870 **[10]**
$4 254 - €4 529 - £2 800 - FF29 710
Huntsman with Chestnut Hunter, the Hunt digging out in the Background Oil/canvas (76x63.5cm 29x25in) Billingshurst, West-Sussex 2000

MARTIN Bernice Fenwick 1921 **[9]**
$193 - €209 - £129 - FF1 369
Summer Landscape Oil/board (21.5x26.5cm 8x10in) Calgary, Alberta 2000

MARTIN Charles 1848-1934 **[13]**
$2 800 - €3 034 - £1 866 - FF19 902
«Je sais tout» Poster (152x111cm 60x44in) New-York 2000

MARTIN Charles E. 1910-1995 **[1]**
$5 000 - €5 600 - £3 474 - FF36 736
Magazine Cover, Two Sunday Painters and Abstractionist on Dock Gouache/paper (45x33cm 18x13in) New-York 2001

MARTIN David 1736-1798 **[29]**
$850 000 - €843 914 - £531 250 - FF5 535 710
Portrait of Benjamin Franklin Oil/canvas (127x101.5cm 50x39in) New-York 1999
$4 500 - €5 228 - £3 162 - FF34 295
Feeding the Pet Deer Oil/canvas (76x62cm 29x24in) New-York 2001

MARTIN David ?-c.1935 **[6]**
$2 081 - €2 058 - £1 300 - FF13 500
On the Clyde Watercolour/paper (44x74cm 17x29in) Glasgow 1999

MARTIN David Stone 1913-1992 **[3]**
$1 200 - €1 149 - £741 - FF7 538
Classical Spanish Guitarist, Probably Record Album Cover Ink (32x25cm 12x10in) New-York 1999

MARTIN DES BATAILLES Jean-Baptiste 1659-1735 **[14]**
$35 544 - €36 588 - £22 392 - FF240 000
Portrait équestre d'un militaire devant une ville assiégée Huile/toile (144x112cm 56x44in) Paris 2000
$20 587 - €19 581 - £12 500 - FF128 446
Cavalry Skirmish Oil/canvas (73x92.5cm 28x36in) London 1999

MARTIN DES GOBELINS Pierre Denis c.1663-1742 **[5]**
$115 704 - €114 766 - £72 000 - FF752 817
The Reception of François Pidou de Saint Olon, Ambassador of Louis XIV Oil/canvas (69x87.5cm 27x34in) London 1999

MARTIN Elias 1739-1818 **[55]**
$15 420 - €17 542 - £10 770 - FF115 065
Romantiskt landskap Oil/canvas (70.5x110.5cm 27x43in) Stockholm 2000
$1 523 - €1 769 - £1 070 - FF11 603
Strandbild med gamal ek, figurer och båtar Indian ink (26x36cm 10x14in) Stockholm 2001

MARTIN Étienne Philippe 1858-1945 **[16]**
$5 120 - €5 946 - £3 646 - FF39 000
La colline Puget à Marseille Huile/toile (71x120cm 27x47in) Aix-en-Provence 2001
$2 184 - €2 287 - £1 372 - FF15 000
Marseille, promenade de la plage Huile/panneau (23.5x33.5cm 9x13in) Aubagne 2000

MARTIN Eugène Louis 1880-1954 **[46]**
$289 - €341 - £210 - FF2 236
Bord de l'Aubonne Huile/toile (55x46cm 21x18in) Sion 2001

MARTIN Fletcher 1904-1979 **[59]**
$2 700 - €3 132 - £1 920 - FF20 546
Summer Day Oil/canvas (46x66cm 18x25in) Washington 2000
$500 - €466 - £310 - FF3 058
Seated Woman Pencil/paper (39x47cm 15x18in) New-York 1999
$250 - €269 - £167 - FF1 763
Bronco Buster Lithograph (31x21cm 12x8in) Cleveland OH 2000

MARTIN Fritz 1859-? **[2]**
$18 091 - €17 895 - £11 280 - FF117 386
Allegorie des Handels Öl/Leinwand (120x273cm 47x107in) Ahlden 1999

MARTIN Gilbert 1924 **[1]**
$7 750 - €7 970 - £4 916 - FF52 282
Still Life of Wildflowers Oil/canvas (59x72cm 23x28in) New-Orleans LA 2000

MARTIN Gilbert XIX **[4]**
$2 115 - €1 982 - £1 271 - FF13 000
Vase de fleurs et bouquet de violettes Huile/toile (41x32.5cm 16x12in) Paris 1999

MARTIN Henri 1860-1943 **[543]**
$108 843 - €108 239 - £67 521 - FF710 000
Vue de la bastide - Terrasse de Marquayrol Huile/toile (100x140cm 39x55in) Paris 1999
$55 547 - €64 791 - £39 015 - FF425 000
Remparts à Collioure Huile/toile (85x61cm 33x24in) Versailles 2000
$8 872 - €8 232 - £5 535 - FF54 000
Les Catalanes dans le port de Collioure Huile/panneau (33x40cm 12x15in) Deauville 1999
$1 544 - €1 601 - £979 - FF10 500
Homme marchant (étude pour les bords de la Garonne) Crayon (78x54cm 30x21in) Paris 2000
$757 - €838 - £513 - FF5 000
Tête de femme couronnée d'épines Lithographie couleurs (49x32cm 19x12in) Paris 2000

MARTIN Henry 1835-1908 **[43]**
$1 559 - €1 414 - £950 - FF9 277
Shipping in a Cornish Harbour Oil/panel (13x23cm 5x9in) Penzance, Cornwall 1998

MARTIN Homer Dodge 1836-1897 **[44]**
$6 000 - €7 035 - £4 316 - FF46 146
Cows adn Sheep grazing in an Autumn River Landscape Oil/canvas (51x91.5cm 20x36in) New-York 2001
$4 500 - €5 352 - £3 207 - FF35 104
Misty Morning on the Hudson River Oil/canvas (25.5x51cm 10x20in) New-York 2000

MARTIN Jacques 1844-1919 **[63]**
$1 746 - €1 829 - £1 105 - FF12 000
La branche de cerisier Huile/panneau (100x35.5cm 39x13in) Paris 2000

MARTIN Jacques 1921 **[22]**
$1 830 - €2 058 - £1 285 - FF13 500
Enak dans différentes attitudes Encre Chine/papier (50x37cm 19x14in) Paris 2001

MARTIN Jason 1970 **[17]**
$18 179 - €15 533 - £11 000 - FF101 887
Untitled Oil/canvas (244x244cm 96x96in) London 1998
$6 000 - €5 634 - £3 717 - FF36 954
Pilgrim Oil/panel (51x51cm 20x20in) New-York 1999

M

MARTIN Johan Fredrik 1755-1816 **[52]**
📖 **$2 649** - €2 857 - **£1 778** - FF18 741
Stora och lilla toppö fallen vid trollhättan
Akvarell/papper (40x54cm 15x21in) Stockholm 2000
📖 **$626** - €672 - **£418** - FF4 408
Romantiskt landskap Etching (50x36.5cm 19x14in)
Stockholm 2000

MARTIN John 1789-1854 **[81]**
📖 **$3 647** - €4 338 - **£2 600** - FF28 457
Cephalus and Procris Watercolour (8.5x15cm
3x5in) London 2000
📖 **$644** - €633 - **£400** - FF4 152
**Illustrations of the Bible: Adam and Eve
Hearing the Judgement** Mezzotint (37.5x28cm
14x11in) London 1999

MARTIN John, Jack 1904-1965 **[35]**
📖 **$1 235** - €1 161 - **£750** - FF7 616
Deserted Farm Oil/board (49.5x40.5cm 19x15in)
London 1999

MARTIN Kenneth 1905-1984 **[14]**
📖 **$5 692** - €6 702 - **£4 000** - FF43 965
Abstract Oil/board (36x26.5cm 14x10in) London 2000
📖 **$588** - €549 - **£365** - FF3 601
Chalk Farm Color lithograph (46x33.5cm 18x13in)
London 1999

MARTIN Louis XIX **[1]**
📖 **$5 648** - €5 488 - **£3 531** - FF36 000
La ronde des enfants Huile/panneau (36x45cm
14x17in) Lyon 1999

MARTIN Louis-Auguste XIX **[2]**
📷 **$59 526** - €56 223 - **£36 000** - FF368 798
**Portraits parlementaires, O.Barrot, E.Cavaignac,
Lamartine, Ledru** Daguerreotype (30x30cm 11x11in)
London 1999

MARTIN Martin 1792-1865 **[31]**
📖 **$200** - €230 - **£137** - FF1 509
**Schwarzer Ort und Halstein von der Schönau
aus** Ink (20.6x26.8cm 8x10in) Heidelberg 2000

MARTIN Maurice 1894-1978 **[126]**
📖 **$744** - €762 - **£459** - FF5 000
Hiver sur le Loing Huile/toile (54x65cm 21x25in)
L'Isle-Adam 2000

MARTIN Peter 1959 **[3]**
📖 **$1 650** - €1 710 - **£990** - FF11 220
Mercato Olio/tela (50x75cm 19x29in) Prato 2000

MARTIN Philip 1927 **[25]**
📖 **$1 400** - €1 814 - **£1 050** - FF11 900
«Offering» Olio/tela (100x80cm 39x31in) Milano
2000

MARTIN Raymond 1910-1992 **[19]**
📖 **$139** - €137 - **£85** - FF900
Nu allongé Mine plomb (28x38cm 11x14in) Paris
1999

MARTIN REBOLLO Tomás 1858-1919 **[15]**
📖 **$1 020** - €1 021 - **£629** - FF6 698
Pueblo de serranía Oleo/tabla (17x24cm 6x9in)
Madrid 2000

MARTIN René 1891-? **[12]**
📖 **$1 922** - €2 134 - **£1 339** - FF14 000
Jeune fille aux arbouses Pastel/papier (58x42.5cm
22x16in) Paris 2001

MARTIN Robert Wallace 1843-1923 **[2]**
📖 **$6 500** - €6 963 - **£4 438** - FF45 672
Edwin Martin Terracotta (33.5x33.5cm 13x13in) New-
York 2001

MARTIN Sylvester act.1856-1906 **[38]**
📖 **$7 000** - €8 133 - **£4 919** - FF53 348
«All but who Whoop, the road to Baddinton»
Oil/canvas (45.5x127cm 17x50in) New-York 2001
📖 **$1 200** - €1 394 - **£843** - FF9 145
Two Setters/Two Pointers Oil/panel (20x25.5cm
7x10in) New-York 2001

MARTIN Thomas act.1764-1789 **[1]**
📖 **$10 944** - €12 196 - **£7 448** - FF80 000
Coquillages des mers du Sud Aquarelle, gouache
(24.5x21cm 9x8in) Paris 2000

MARTIN Thomas Mower 1838-1934 **[165]**
📖 **$586** - €657 - **£407** - FF4 307
Old Mill Oil/canvas (51x34cm 20x13in) Calgary,
Alberta 2001
📖 **$360** - €306 - **£217** - FF2 008
Rocky Mountain Vista Watercolour/paper (24x35cm
9x13in) Calgary, Alberta 1998

MARTIN Vicente 1911 **[26]**
📖 **$650** - €698 - **£435** - FF4 579
Perfil de mujer Acrílico/lienzo (72.5x72.5cm 28x28in)
Montevideo 2000

MARTIN-FERRIERES Jacques, Jac 1893-1972
[257]
📖 **$3 500** - €4 061 - **£2 416** - FF26 641
Village à rivière Oil/canvas (54.5x81cm 21x31in)
New-York 2000
📖 **$1 887** - €1 982 - **£1 193** - FF13 000
Barque à Collioure Huile/panneau (27.5x35.5cm
10x13in) Paris 2000

MARTIN-GOURDAULT Marie 1881-1938 **[3]**
📖 **$10 297** - €11 434 - **£7 177** - FF75 000
Fiançailles, golfe de Carthage Huile/toile
(310x214cm 122x84in) Senlis 2001

MARTIN-KAVEL François 1861-1931 **[72]**
📖 **$2 480** - €2 343 - **£1 500** - FF15 366
Gitane Oil/canvas (80x63.5cm 31x25in) Billingshurst,
West-Sussex 1999
📖 **$960** - €953 - **£600** - FF6 252
The Courtesan seated on a Couch Oil/canvas
(34.5x25cm 13x9in) London 1999
📖 **$445** - €442 - **£277** - FF2 900
Portrait de femme Fusain (45.5x32cm 17x12in) Paris
1999

MARTINA Piero 1912-1982 **[5]**
📖 **$840** - €726 - **£420** - FF4 760
Fiori Olio/tela (70x80cm 27x31in) Prato 1999

MARTINATI Luigi 1893-1984 **[40]**
📖 **$787** - €816 - **£472** - FF5 355
«Voi assassini» Affiche couleur (195x140cm
76x55in) Torino 2000

MARTINE MARTINE 1932 **[6]**
📖 **$3 132** - €3 506 - **£2 125** - FF23 000
Livre sur fond vert Huile/toile (91x73cm 35x28in)
Paris 2000

MARTINEAU Edith 1842-1909 **[33]**
📖 **$4 685** - €5 002 - **£3 200** - FF32 809
Empty (a Little Highland Girl) Watercolour/paper
(37.5x20cm 14x7in) Billingshurst, West-Sussex 2001

MARTINEAU Gertrude XIX-XX **[11]**
📖 **$1 087** - €928 - **£650** - FF6 090
«Lochanmore, Rothiemurchus, Aviemore»
Watercolour (38x28.5cm 14x11in) London 1998

MARTINELLI Giovanni 1600/04-c.1659/68 **[21]**
📷 **$8 383** – €7 084 - **£5 000** - FF46 468
    Allegory of Painting Oil/canvas (43x37.5cm
    16x14in) London 1998

MARTINELLI IL TROMETTA Niccolo c.1540-1611 **[8]**
✏️ **$16 000** – €17 087 - **£10 902** - FF112 084
    The Resurrection/The Ascension of
    Christ/Madonna and Child Seated Black
    chalk/paper (38.5x13.5cm 15x5in) New-York 2001

MARTINELLI Onofrio 1900-1966 **[7]**
📷 **$7 750** – €8 034 - **£4 650** - FF52 700
    Natura morta con frutta e ramo di magnolie
    Olio/tela (60x70cm 23x27in) Roma 2001

MARTINET François Nicolas 1731-? **[43]**
🎟️ **$287** – €277 - **£180** - FF1 818
    Histoire naturelle des oiseaux Etching (48x31.5cm
    18x12in) London 1999

MARTINETTI Maria 1864-? **[28]**
✏️ **$3 500** – €3 628 - **£2 100** - FF23 800
    Giocatori di morra Acquarello/carta (65x100cm
    25x39in) Roma 2000

MARTINEZ & DA Maria & Popovi 1887/1921-1980/71 **[6]**
🦅 **$5 500** – €6 141 - **£3 676** - FF40 282
    San Ildefonso blackware Jar Ceramic (H14.5cm
    H5in) New-York 2000

MARTINEZ ABADES Juan 1862-1920 **[74]**
📷 **$8 960** – €9 610 - **£5 920** - FF63 040
    Vapor en el muelle Oleo/lienzo (30x60cm 11x23in)
    Madrid 2000
📷 **$4 240** – €4 805 - **£2 880** - FF31 520
    Pareja a la sombra de un árbol Oleo/lienzo
    (25x19cm 9x7in) Madrid 2000

MARTINEZ ALCOVER Manuel 1927 **[4]**
📷 **$975** – €901 - **£585** - FF5 910
    Mariscadoras Oleo/lienzo (65x81cm 25x31in) Madrid
    1999

MARTINEZ ANDREO Ramón XX **[4]**
📷 **$8 204** – €8 266 - **£5 114** - FF54 224
    A Village by the River Oil/panel (24x33cm 9x12in)
    Singapore 2000

MARTINEZ CHECA Fernando 1858-? **[29]**
📷 **$754** – €781 - **£481** - FF5 122
    Melón partido Oleo/lienzo (40.5x60cm 15x23in)
    Madrid 2000

MARTINEZ CUBELLS Salvador 1845-1914 **[5]**
📷 **$25 500** – €30 032 - **£18 000** - FF197 000
    Joven aguadora en el corral Oleo/lienzo (60x88cm
    23x34in) Madrid 2000
📷 **$8 640** – €9 610 - **£5 760** - FF63 040
    La lechera Oleo/tabla (43x31cm 16x12in) Madrid
    2000

MARTINEZ CUBELLS Y RUIZ Enrique 1874-1947 **[76]**
📷 **$26 100** – €27 029 - **£16 650** - FF177 300
    Puerto Oleo/lienzo (42x60cm 16x23in) Madrid 2000
📷 **$3 864** – €3 364 - **£2 352** - FF22 064
    Jarrón de rosas Oleo/tabla (33x24cm 12x9in)
    Madrid 1999

MARTINEZ DE LA VEGA Joaquín 1846-1905 **[5]**
📷 **$18 900** – €21 023 - **£12 600** - FF137 900
    Escena de Carnaval Oleo/lienzo (76x43cm 29x16in)
    Madrid 2000
📷 **$1 120** – €1 201 - **£740** - FF7 880
    El piropo Oleo/tabla (25x34.5cm 9x13in) Madrid 2000

MARTINEZ DEL MAZO Juan Bautista c.1612-1667 **[3]**
📷 **$23 500** – €24 361 - **£14 100** - FF159 800
    Mercurio Olio/tela (185x105cm 72x41in) Imbersago
    (Lecco) 2001

MARTINEZ DIAZ Rafael 1915-1991 **[8]**
📷 **$1 885** – €1 952 - **£1 202** - FF12 805
    Paisaje con caminantes y burros Oleo/cartón
    (49x64cm 19x25in) Madrid 2000
📷 **$1 800** – €1 802 - **£1 110** - FF11 820
    Paisaje castellano Oleo/tabla (33.5x41cm 13x16in)
    Madrid 2000

MARTINEZ Domingo 1688-1749 **[2]**
📷 **$7 000** – €6 006 - **£4 200** - FF39 400
    La Virgen con el niño Oleo/cobre (64x43.5cm
    25x17in) Madrid 1998

MARTINEZ HOWARD Julio 1932-1999 **[12]**
✏️ **$1 500** – €1 653 - **£1 000** - FF10 844
    Desnudo de espalda Tempera/papier (48x64cm
    18x25in) Montevideo 2000

MARTINEZ Julian 1879-1943 **[14]**
🦅 **$945** – €1 015 - **£632** - FF6 660
    Carlos IV, según una obra de Tolsá Bronze
    (H52cm H20in) México 2000
📷 **$1 600** – €1 867 - **£1 129** - FF12 249
    Deer Dancer Watercolour/paper (20.5x25.5cm 8x10in)
    New-York 2000

MARTINEZ Julian 1904-1987 **[2]**
📷 **$2 250** – €2 142 - **£1 407** - FF14 048
    Deer Dancer Watercolour/paper (24x30.5cm 9x12in)
    New-York 2000

MARTINEZ LOZANO Josep 1923 **[53]**
📷 **$1 584** – €1 442 - **£984** - FF9 456
    Chiringuito y barcas Oleo/lienzo (38x46cm 14x18in)
    Barcelona 1999
📷 **$858** – €781 - **£520** - FF5 122
    Nocturno portuario Oleo/tabla (24x29.5cm 9x11in)
    Barcelona 1999
✏️ **$169** – €156 - **£104** - FF1 024
    Figura femenina sentada de espaldas Acuarela
    (20.5x14.5cm 8x5in) Barcelona 1999

MARTINEZ Maria 1887-1980 **[15]**
🦅 **$7 500** – €8 386 - **£5 055** - FF55 008
    Water jar, with raised concentric bowl Ceramic
    (16x15cm 6x5in) New-York 2000

MARTINEZ MOYANO Sebastián 1956 **[124]**
📷 **$693** – €661 - **£418** - FF4 334
    Amsterdam Oleo/tablex (55x46cm 21x18in) Madrid
    1999
📷 **$330** – €330 - **£203** - FF2 167
    Copa y naranja Oleo/lienzo (24x19cm 9x7in) Madrid
    2000

MARTINEZ NOVILLO Cirilo 1921 **[64]**
📷 **$7 040** – €6 607 - **£4 400** - FF43 340
    Paisaje Manchego Oleo/lienzo (84x100cm 33x39in)
    Madrid 1999
✏️ **$828** – €721 - **£516** - FF4 728
    Paisaje Acuarela (21x30cm 8x11in) Madrid 1999
🎟️ **$114** – €120 - **£74** - FF788
    Paisaje con figuras Litografía (43x50cm 16x19in)
    Madrid 2000

MARTINEZ ORTIZ DE ZARATE Nicolás 1907-1990 **[26]**
📷 **$6 480** – €7 208 - **£4 320** - FF47 280
    Arrantzales de Ondárroa Oleo/lienzo (73x60cm
    28x23in) Madrid 2000

M

$390 - €450 - **£270** - FF2 955
Iglesia del Carmen de Sestao Carbón/papel
(17x23cm 6x9in) Madrid 2001

MARTINEZ PADILLA Rafael 1878-1961 **[8]**
$3 500 - €3 754 - **£2 312** - FF24 625
Mujer ante el espejo Oleo/lienzo (115x88cm
45x34in) Barcelona 2000

MARTINEZ PEDRO Luis 1910-1990 **[22]**
$8 500 - €7 339 - **£5 185** - FF48 142
Untitled Oil/canvas (81.5x61cm 32x24in) Miami FL
1999

$175 - €171 - **£111** - FF1 123
Abstract Gouache/paper (53x22cm 21x9in) Norwalk
CT 1999

MARTINEZ Prospero 1885-? **[17]**
$2 196 - €2 318 - **£1 451** - FF15 202
Marina Huile/masonite (63x67cm 24x26in) Caracas ($)
2000

MARTINEZ Raoul 1876-1973 **[55]**
$1 384 - €1 361 - **£889** - FF8 929
An Interior with Books, Flowers and Fruits on a
Table Oil/board (46x35cm 18x13in) Amsterdam 1999

MARTINEZ Raymond 1944 **[10]**
$640 - €610 - **£398** - FF4 000
Masque Sculpture verre (23x17cm 9x6in) Paris 1999

MARTINEZ Raymundo 1938 **[7]**
$4 573 - €4 270 - **£2 822** - FF28 009
Valle de México Oleo/lienzo (70x140cm 27x55in)
México 1999

MARTINEZ Ricardo 1918 **[61]**
$42 000 - €40 442 - **£26 140** - FF265 284
«Pareja blanca» Oil/canvas (130x150cm 51x59in)
New-York 1999
$18 000 - €21 194 - **£12 648** - FF139 021
Músico Oil/canvas (54.5x100.5cm 21x39in) New-York
2000
$7 156 - €8 393 - **£5 148** - FF55 055
Mujer con los brazos en alto Oleo/papel (30x24cm
11x9in) México 2001
$1 691 - €1 464 - **£1 020** - FF9 605
Mujer Tinta/papel (20.5x14.5cm 8x5in) México 1998

MARTINEZ Richard 1898-1987 **[4]**
$500 - €534 - **£340** - FF3 504
Deer Watercolour/paper (22x33cm 9x13in) Cloudcroft
NM 2001

MARTINEZ Sebastiano 1602-1667 **[3]**
$18 011 - €16 703 - **£11 000** - FF109 562
The Lamentation Oil/panel (23x28.5cm 9x11in)
London 1998

MARTINEZ TARRASSO Casimir 1900-1979 **[37]**
$3 780 - €4 205 - **£2 660** - FF27 580
Paisaje Oleo/lienzo (40.5x40cm 15x15in) Madrid 2001
$1 080 - €1 201 - **£760** - FF7 880
Paisaje Oleo/tabla (27x33cm 10x12in) Barcelona 2001

MARTINEZ VAZQUEZ Eduardo 1886-1971 **[26]**
$9 920 - €9 610 - **£6 080** - FF63 040
Sierra de Madrid Oleo/lienzo (100x188cm 39x74in)
Madrid 1999
$4 575 - €4 505 - **£2 850** - FF29 550
Paisaje con horreos Oleo/lienzo (54.5x65.5cm
21x25in) Madrid 1999
$1 081 - €1 185 - **£1 740** - FF7 880
Camino de Piedralaves Oleo/cartón (10x14cm
3x5in) Madrid 2000

MARTINEZ Xavier 1869-1943 **[25]**
$7 500 - €8 050 - **£5 019** - FF52 807
A Farm House at Dusk Oil/board (23x30.5cm
9x12in) San-Francisco CA 2000

MARTINI Alberto 1876-1954 **[107]**
$1 900 - €1 970 - **£1 140** - FF12 920
Al bar dei cacciatori Olio/cartone (30x40cm
11x15in) Prato 1999
$1 560 - €1 348 - **£1 040** - FF8 840
Corte dei miracoli, n.5 China/carta (13x9cm 5x3in)
Roma 1998

MARTINI Arturo 1885-1947 **[83]**
$4 600 - €5 961 - **£3 450** - FF39 100
Lavandaia Olio/tela (35x44.5cm 13x17in) Milano
2000
$78 500 - €81 377 - **£47 100** - FF533 800
Figure nella grotta Terracotta (145x47x9cm
57x18x3in) Roma 2000
$15 600 - €13 476 - **£7 800** - FF88 400
Vittoria del fascismo Bronzo (H78cm H30in) Milano
1999
$1 200 - €1 555 - **£900** - FF10 200
Figura femminile allegorica e Attesa Inchiostro
(17.5x29.5cm 6x11in) Milano 2001

MARTINI Bruno 1911-1979 **[86]**
$159 - €159 - **£105** - FF1 139
Ansicht von Venedig Gouache/paper (39.5x63.5cm
15x25in) Bern 2000

MARTINI de Gaetano 1840-1917 **[4]**
$9 000 - €9 330 - **£5 400** - FF61 200
Il guardiano dell'harem Olio/tavola (22.5x36.5cm
8x14in) Milano 1999

MARTINI Martinus 1566-1610 **[3]**
$1 691 - €1 973 - **£1 177** - FF12 945
Warhaffte und Eigentliche Abconterfactur
Kupferstich (48.6x114.6cm 19x45in) Bern 2000

MARTINI Pietro Antonio 1739-1797 **[9]**
$1 200 - €1 555 - **£900** - FF10 200
The Exhibition of the Royal Academy, after
J.H.Ramberg Gravure (37x52cm 14x20in) Venezia
2000

MARTINI Quinto 1908-1990 **[22]**
$2 280 - €1 970 - **£1 140** - FF12 920
Natura morta con porro Tempera/cartone
(60x73.5cm 23x28in) Prato 1999
$3 250 - €3 369 - **£1 950** - FF22 100
Ritratto di bimbo Stone (H45cm H17in) Prato 1999

MARTINI Sandro 1941 **[34]**
$1 200 - €1 037 - **£800** - FF6 800
Il drago Egoro Tempera/carta (138.5x144cm 54x56in)
Prato 1998

MARTINI Vivaldo 1908-1989 **[19]**
$1 846 - €2 165 - **£1 317** - FF14 202
Nu Huile/toile (81x65cm 31x25in) Genève 2000

MARTINO Antonio Pietro 1902-1989 **[71]**
$5 400 - €6 351 - **£3 885** - FF41 657
Manayunk Country Oil/canvas (66x101cm 26x40in)
Hatfield PA 2001
$4 000 - €4 704 - **£2 868** - FF30 855
Winter Manayunk Oil/board (29x49.5cm 11x19in)
Philadelphia PA 2001
$1 000 - €984 - **£624** - FF6 261
Rocky Seascape Chalks (26x43cm 10x17in) Hatfield
PA 1999

MARTINO de Eduardo Federico 1838-1912 [46]
- $12 000 - €13 308 - £7 984 - FF87 295
  Marina, corbeta con bandera argentina Oleo/lienzo (69x118cm 27x46in) Buenos-Aires 2000
- $1 217 - €1 169 - £750 - FF7 668
  Chilean Gunboat firing a Salute Oil/canvas (23x38cm 9x14in) London 1999
- $684 - €767 - £471 - FF5 030
  Die königliche Yacht «Victoria and Albert» Indian ink (12x23cm 4x9in) Hamburg 2000

MARTINO de Giovanni 1870-1935/38 [27]
- $780 - €674 - £520 - FF4 420
  Busto di ragazzo Bronzo (H33cm H12in) Napoli 1998

MARTINO de Giovanni 1908-? [27]
- $2 800 - €2 673 - £1 749 - FF17 532
  Price Street with Figures Oil/canvas (76x91cm 30x36in) Hatfield PA 1999
- $1 500 - €1 735 - £1 061 - FF11 383
  Impressionistic View of Manayunk Oil/board (29x39cm 11x15in) Hatfield PA 2000

MARTINOTTI Evangelista Giovanni 1634-1694 [1]
- $2 946 - €3 068 - £1 866 - FF20 123
  Flusstal in Gebirgslandschaft Oil/panel (18.3x26.3cm 7x10in) München 2000

MARTINS Gomes 1914 [1]
- $4 080 - €4 237 - £2 635 - FF27 795
  Setúbal Oleo/tablex (70x110cm 27x43in) Lisboa 2000

MARTINS Maria 1900-1973 [4]
- $210 000 - €202 212 - £130 704 - FF1 326 423
  Brouillard noir (Black Fog) Bronze (88.5x76x37cm 34x29x14in) New-York 1999

MARTINZ Fritz 1924 [8]
- $680 - €799 - £482 - FF5 243
  Weiblicher Akt Black chalk (60x84cm 23x33in) Wien 2000

MARTON Lajos 1891-1952 [17]
- $800 - €769 - £493 - FF5 046
  «Robbialac» Poster (118.5x78.5cm 46x30in) New-York 1999

MARTORI SAVINI Filippo 1877-1952 [13]
- $300 - €311 - £180 - FF2 040
  Marina Olio/tavola (19x23cm 7x9in) Prato 1999

MARTOS Manuel 1950 [32]
- $168 - €168 - £103 - FF1 103
  Ondárroa Oleo/papel (35x25cm 13x9in) Madrid 2000

MARTSZEN Jan II 1609-1647 [27]
- $6 627 - €7 431 - £4 500 - FF48 742
  A Cavalry Engagement Oil/panel (48.5x63.5cm 19x25in) London 2000
- $7 951 - €9 259 - £5 500 - FF60 738
  A Cavalry Engagement Oil/panel (31.5x48cm 12x18in) London 2000

MARTTINEN Veikko 1917 [32]
- $2 130 - €2 354 - £1 477 - FF15 444
  Morgon Oil/canvas (81x60cm 31x23in) Helsinki 2001

MARTY André Edouard 1882-1974 [19]
- $235 - €229 - £145 - FF1 500
  La lecture Crayon/papier (22x17cm 8x6in) Paris 1999
- $1 800 - €2 099 - £1 263 - FF13 770
  «Toilettes d'hiver» Poster (76.5x119cm 30x46in) New-York 2000

MARUGAN Amal 1934 [53]
- $239 - €252 - £159 - FF1 654
  El rastro de Madrid Oleo/tabla (22x27cm 8x10in) Madrid 2000

MARULLO Giuseppe c.1615-c.1685 [6]
- $27 398 - €27 616 - £17 100 - FF181 146
  Christus und die Samariterin am Brunnen Öl/Leinwand (126x137.5cm 49x54in) Wien 2000

MARUSSIG Anton 1868-1925 [2]
- $2 900 - €2 812 - £1 796 - FF18 446
  Bergdorf in Südtirol Aquarell/Papier (13x20.5cm 5x8in) Graz 1999

MARUSSIG Guido 1885-1972 [11]
- $2 000 - €2 073 - £1 200 - FF13 600
  Parco vendramin Olio/tela (76x55cm 29x21in) Milano 2000

MARUSSIG Piero 1879-1937 [99]
- $10 350 - €10 885 - £6 300 - FF71 400
  Natura morta con cesto e pipa Olio/tela (60x50cm 23x19in) Milano 2000
- $9 000 - €9 330 - £5 400 - FF61 200
  Bambino Olio/cartone (32x24.5cm 12x9in) Torino 2001

MARUYAMA Banka (kensako) 1867-1942 [2]
- $4 500 - €4 362 - £2 786 - FF28 616
  Mountain Village Watercolour/paper (49x33cm 19x13in) Mystic CT 1999

MARVAL Jacqueline 1866-1932 [152]
- $10 350 - €11 434 - £7 177 - FF75 000
  Le matin dans la roseraie Huile/toile (192x97cm 75x38in) Lyon 2001
- $3 834 - €4 116 - £2 565 - FF27 000
  Grand bouquet aux roses et mimosas Huile/toile (89x116cm 35x45in) Grenoble 2000
- $804 - €915 - £558 - FF6 000
  Bouquet de fleurs Huile/toile (37.5x32.5cm 14x12in) Paris 2000
- $307 - €259 - £181 - FF1 700
  Jeune femme à la fleur Lithographie (73x53cm 28x20in) Grenoble 1998

MARVASI Duccio XX [7]
- $441 - €381 - £266 - FF2 500
  «Napoléon», d'Abel Gance Affiche couleur (120x160cm 47x62in) Argenteuil 1999

MARVILLE Charles 1816-1879 [180]
- $1 099 - €1 067 - £684 - FF7 000
  Route Tirage albuminé (43.3x62.3cm 17x24in) Paris 1999

MARWAN 1934 [13]
- $18 252 - €20 452 - £12 712 - FF134 156
  Liegender I Öl/Leinwand (130.5x162cm 51x63in) Berlin 2001
- $1 825 - €2 045 - £1 271 - FF13 415
  Rotes Kleid Aquarell/Karton (60x48.5cm 23x19in) Berlin 2001

MARX Alphonse XIX [13]
- $9 125 - €10 367 - £6 296 - FF68 000
  Jeune femmes aux fleurs Huile/toile (32x41.5cm 12x16in) Paris 2000

MARX Franz 1889-1960 [36]
- $802 - €767 - £502 - FF5 030
  Stierkampf Öl/Leinwand (49x60cm 19x23in) Hamburg 1999

M

MARXEN Herbert 1900-1954 **[6]**
- $5 861 - €6 748 - **£4 000** - FF44 267
  The Seamstress Oil/canvas (51.5x47.5cm 20x18in)
  London 2000

MARXER Alfred 1876-1945 **[81]**
- $792 - €919 - **£547** - FF6 030
  Lotte Marxer mit Kind Öl/Leinwand (93x70cm
  36x27in) Zürich 2000
- $1 600 - €1 539 - **£987** - FF10 093
  «Winter Sport» Poster (97x77.5cm 38x30in) New-
  York 1999

MARY Benjamin 1792-1846 **[5]**
- $38 029 - €44 664 - **£27 000** - FF292 977
  Bresil, Vue de Rio de Janeiro Watercolour
  (30.5x312.5cm 12x123in) London 2000

MARY Joséphine XIX **[8]**
- $680 - €762 - **£473** - FF5 000
  Marines Huile/panneau (16x11cm 6x4in) Coutances
  2001

MARYAN (M.Pinchas Burstein) 1927-1977 **[192]**
- $5 128 - €6 098 - **£3 656** - FF40 000
  Sans titre Huile/toile (130x97cm 51x38in) Paris 2000
- $3 804 - €4 421 - **£2 673** - FF29 000
  Personnage Huile/toile (100x81cm 39x31in) Paris
  2001
- $900 - €762 - **£541** - FF5 000
  Visage Crayon gras/papier (76.5x56.5cm 30x22in)
  Paris 1998

MARZELLE Jean 1916 **[103]**
- $532 - €624 - **£380** - FF4 096
  Woodland Landscape Oil/canvas (59.5x73cm
  23x28in) London 2000
- $398 - €457 - **£272** - FF3 000
  Paysage Huile/toile (22x27cm 8x10in) Paris 2000
- $167 - €183 - **£110** - FF1 200
  Paysage Aquarelle/papier (38x59cm 14x23in) Douai
  2000

MARZOCCHI DE BELLUCI Numa XIX-XX **[14]**
- $3 018 - €3 598 - **£2 152** - FF23 600
  La baie d'Alger Huile/toile (38x55cm 14x21in)
  Noyon 2000
- $2 590 - €3 049 - **£1 820** - FF20 000
  Jeune femme sur la terrasse Huile/toile (34x25cm
  13x9in) Valenciennes 2000

MARZOHL Johann Baptist 1792-1863 **[7]**
- $964 - €936 - **£595** - FF6 142
  Innerschweizer Landschaften Aquarell/Papier
  (45x58cm 17x22in) Luzern 1999

MAS Y FONDEVILLA Arturo, Arcadio 1852-1934
[57]
- $18 480 - €16 818 - **£11 200** - FF110 320
  Puerto con barcos Oleo/lienzo (45.5x49.5cm
  17x19in) Barcelona 1999
- $2 772 - €2 523 - **£1 680** - FF16 548
  L'avi de la pipa Oleo/lienzo (37.5x28cm 14x11in)
  Madrid 1999
- $2 010 - €1 802 - **£1 230** - FF11 820
  Escena de interior Gouache (45.5x65cm 17x25in)
  Madrid 1999

MASALIN Ebba 1873-1942 **[1]**
- $6 460 - €6 391 - **£4 028** - FF41 921
  Vid pianot Oil/canvas (48x29cm 18x11in) Helsinki
  1999

MASANAO XVIII-XIX **[2]**
- $61 685 - €59 282 - **£38 000** - FF388 865
  Recumbent Cow Sculpture (H5cm H1in) London
  1999

MASANOBU Okumura 1686-1764 **[13]**
- $14 000 - €16 418 - **£9 990** - FF107 693
  Erotic Scenes Ink (35.5x56.5cm 13x22in) New-York
  2000
- $1 500 - €1 374 - **£914** - FF9 010
  Shoki the Demon Queller Woodcut (70.5x25.5cm
  27x10in) New-York 1999

MASAYOSHI 1764-1824 **[8]**
- $159 - €153 - **£99** - FF1 006
  Landschaften Woodcut in colors (25.5x33cm
  10x12in) München 1999

MASCART Gustave 1834-1914 **[192]**
- $2 613 - €2 287 - **£1 582** - FF15 000
  Port méditerranéen Huile/toile (38x61cm 14x24in)
  Paris 1998
- $2 403 - €2 058 - **£1 408** - FF13 500
  Village au bord du fleuve Huile/toile (33x41cm
  12x16in) Paris 1998

MASCART Paul 1874-1958 **[55]**
- $1 181 - €1 372 - **£841** - FF9 000
  Ile de Bréhat Huile/toile (50x65cm 19x25in) Pont-
  Audemer 2001
- $192 - €229 - **£132** - FF1 500
  Waea (mare), indigène des îles Loyauté
  Huile/toile (41x33cm 16x12in) Blois 2000

MASCHERINI Marcello 1906-1983 **[21]**
- $2 800 - €2 903 - **£1 680** - FF19 040
  Fauno che suona il flauto Bronzo (H18.5cm H7in)
  Trieste 1999

MASCII Jean 1936 **[70]**
- $185 - €213 - **£131** - FF1 400
  «L'esclave libre» Affiche (120x160cm 47x62in) Paris
  2001

MASEFIELD John 1875-? **[1]**
- $7 489 - €7 872 - **£4 699** - FF51 639
  Here is Much Rum Watercolour (29x23cm 11x9in)
  Dublin 2000

MASELLI Titina 1924 **[23]**
- $5 000 - €5 183 - **£3 000** - FF34 000
  «Fili e scritte II» Olio/tavola (73x95cm 28x37in)
  Roma 2001

MASEREEL Frans 1889-1972 **[1034]**
- $5 466 - €5 113 - **£3 311** - FF33 539
  Mädchen im Hafenbezirk Öl/Karton (48x63cm
  18x24in) Stuttgart 1999
- $1 731 - €2 045 - **£1 222** - FF13 415
  Hambourg Dock flottant Oil/paper/panel (32x40cm
  12x15in) Köln 2001
- $730 - €767 - **£460** - FF5 030
  Mutter mit Kind Indian ink/paper (25.5x20cm 10x7in)
  Stuttgart 2000
- $162 - €184 - **£111** - FF1 209
  Voisins Woodcut (26.8x42.5cm 10x16in) Zürich 2000

MASI Roberto 1940 **[6]**
- $1 560 - €1 348 - **£780** - FF8 840
  Cavalli in riva al fiume Olio/tela (40x50cm 15x19in)
  Prato 1999

MASIDE GARCIA Carlos 1897-1958 **[3]**
- $4 888 - €5 646 - **£3 384** - FF37 036
  Poleiras Gouache/papier (29.5x22.5cm 11x8in) Madrid
  1999

MASKELL Christopher Mark 1846-1933 **[24]**
- $349 - €383 - **£237** - FF2 515
  Suffolk Village Oil/panel (18x22cm 7x8in)
  Saarbrücken 2000

MASKELYNE Nevil Story 1823-1911 **[3]**
📷 **$2 590** - €2 902 - **£1 800** - FF19 033
    Broad Street, Oxford, from the Gateway of the Sheldonian Theatre Calotype (16x20.5cm 6x8in) London 2001

MASLOWSKI Stanislaw 1853-1926 **[28]**
✎ **$2 490** - €2 776 - **£1 730** - FF18 210
    Chaumière Aquarelle (68x100cm 26x39in) Warszawa 2001

MASO DE FALP Felip 1851-1929 **[5]**
🖼 **$5 320** - €5 706 - **£3 610** - FF37 430
    Pescadores Oleo/lienzo (85x136cm 33x53in) Madrid 2001

MASON Alice Trumbull 1904-1971 **[4]**
▥ **$1 900** - €1 925 - **£1 192** - FF12 626
    Dark Woodland Woodcut (31x40cm 12x16in) Cincinnati OH 2000

MASON Barry 1947 **[38]**
🖼 **$1 419** - €1 524 - **£950** - FF9 995
    Clipper in Full Sail Oil/canvas (71x91.5cm 27x36in) Suffolk 2000
🖼 **$1 729** - €1 686 - **£1 050** - FF11 059
    The Pool of London Oil/canvas (30.5x45.5cm 12x17in) London 2000

MASON Concetta 1956 **[3]**
🗿 **$3 000** - €2 864 - **£1 874** - FF18 784
    Coral Motion Sculpture, glass (H26.5cm H10in) New-York 1999

MASON Finch 1850-1915 **[48]**
✎ **$798** - €762 - **£502** - FF5 000
    Wife of his chest/Pretty soul Aquarelle/papier (23.5x34cm 9x13in) Deauville 1999

MASON Frank Henry 1876-1965 **[380]**
🖼 **$2 464** - €2 459 - **£1 500** - FF16 128
    The red Duster Oil/canvas (38x54cm 14x21in) London 2000
🖼 **$891** - €863 - **£550** - FF5 660
    Steam Ship in a Rough Sea Oil/board (34x23.5cm 13x9in) West-Yorkshire 1999
✎ **$1 319** - €1 473 - **£920** - FF9 664
    Staithes Watercolour/paper (27.5x20cm 10x7in) Bath 2001
▥ **$777** - €901 - **£550** - FF5 911
    «Boatbuilding, LNER, East Coast Occupations» Poster (102x62cm 40x24in) London 2000

MASON George Frederick 1904 **[7]**
✎ **$375** - €403 - **£255** - FF2 645
    Works of Bears Watercolour (35x43cm 13x16in) Boston MA 2001

MASON John 1927 **[2]**
🗿 **$9 000** - €9 323 - **£5 728** - FF61 157
    Vessel Ceramic (40.5x34.5x34.5cm 15x13x13in) New-York 2000

MASON Mary Townsend 1882-1964 **[3]**
🖼 **$2 200** - €2 042 - **£1 320** - FF13 392
    Fountain in the Park Oil/canvas (45x30cm 18x12in) Milford CT 1999

MASON Roy Martell 1886-1972 **[39]**
🖼 **$4 800** - €4 050 - **£2 815** - FF26 563
    Setting Decoys Oil/canvas (45x53cm 18x21in) Mystic CT 1998
🖼 **$1 000** - €1 181 - **£708** - FF7 750
    Untitled Oil/canvas (38x38cm 15x15in) Crossville TN 2000

✎ **$1 000** - €971 - **£610** - FF6 372
    Three Mallards feeding in a Pond Watercolour/paper (25x35cm 10x14in) Kennebunk ME 2000

MASON William Sanford 1824-1864 **[5]**
🖼 **$3 500** - €3 726 - **£2 384** - FF24 443
    Portrait of a Gentleman Reading a Book Oil/board (49x37.5cm 19x14in) New-York 2001

MASQUERIER John James 1778-1855 **[12]**
🖼 **$3 500** - €4 091 - **£2 478** - FF26 836
    Self Portrait Oil/canvas (86x109cm 34x43in) Cedar-Falls IA 2001

MASRELIER Louis 1748-1810 **[32]**
✎ **$1 507** - €1 283 - **£900** - FF8 416
    Satyrs and Bacchant making an offering to an herm near a Grotto Black chalk/paper (33x28.5cm 12x11in) London 1998

MASRIERA Lluis 1872-1958 **[18]**
🖼 **$5 365** - €5 556 - **£3 330** - FF36 445
    Figuras en una iglesia Oleo/lienzo (89x116cm 35x45in) Barcelona 2000
🖼 **$630** - €601 - **£400** - FF3 940
    Paisaje con árboles Oleo/cartón (25x32cm 9x12in) Barcelona 1999

MASRIERA Y MANOVENS Francisco 1842-1902 **[40]**
🖼 **$12 100** - €13 214 - **£7 700** - FF86 680
    Retrato de dama Oleo/lienzo (180x100cm 70x39in) Madrid 2001
🖼 **$3 456** - €2 890 - **£2 064** - FF18 960
    Romantica Oleo/lienzo (60x43cm 23x16in) Madrid 1998
🖼 **$2 700** - €3 003 - **£1 750** - FF19 700
    Descanso después de la faena Oleo/tabla (10x16.5cm 3x6in) Madrid 2000

MASRIERA Y MANOVENS José 1841-1912 **[9]**
🖼 **$5 124** - €5 045 - **£3 192** - FF33 096
    Zingara Oleo/lienzo (61.5x43.5cm 24x17in) Madrid 1999

MASSA de André de Gronau XIX **[5]**
📷 **$3 437** - €3 811 - **£2 387** - FF25 000
    Château de Franconville Tirage albuminé (31x25cm 12x9in) Paris 2001

MASSANI Pompeo 1850-1920 **[81]**
🖼 **$9 000** - €10 434 - **£6 375** - FF68 445
    Beautiful Music Oil/canvas (46x75cm 18x29in) New-York 2000
🖼 **$1 250** - €1 296 - **£750** - FF8 500
    Case con ponte Olio/tavoletta (17x23cm 6x9in) Formigine, Mo 2000

MASSARI Lucio 1569-1633 **[3]**
🖼 **$45 000** - €48 058 - **£30 663** - FF315 238
    Venus and Adonis Oil/canvas (95.5x132cm 37x51in) New-York 2001
✎ **$7 500** - €8 010 - **£5 110** - FF52 542
    The Flagellation of Christ Black chalk (34.5x23cm 13x9in) New-York 2001

MASSAUX Léon 1845-1926 **[4]**
🖼 **$3 375** - €3 718 - **£2 205** - FF24 390
    La vachère Huile/toile/panneau (110x81cm 43x31in) Bruxelles 2000

MASSÉ Emmanuel Auguste 1818-1881 **[5]**
🖼 **$3 957** - €3 811 - **£2 462** - FF25 000
    Les enfants de troupe du 1er Grenadier de la Garde Impériale Huile/toile (50.5x61.5cm 19x24in) Montfort L'Amaury 1999

M

$3 018 - €3 354 - **£2 021** - FF22 000
La marchande de fruits/La marchande de fleurs
Huile/panneau (23x18cm 9x7in) Toulouse 2000

MASSÉ Jean Baptiste 1687-1767 [35]
$536 - €610 - **£370** - FF4 000
Portrait d'homme Pierre noire (21.5x16.5cm 8x6in)
Paris 2000

MASSÉ Jean Eugène 1856-1950 [119]
$1 335 - €1 524 - **£939** - FF10 000
Pêcheurs au bord du fleuve Huile/toile (55x46.5cm
21x18in) Fontainebleau 2001
$773 - €920 - **£551** - FF6 037
Die Rue de Saules am Montmartre in Paris
Oil/panel (23.5x25.5cm 9x10in) Köln 2000
$1 802 - €2 058 - **£1 267** - FF13 500
Barque sur l'étang Pastel/papier (61x81cm 24x31in)
Fontainebleau 2001

MASSÉ René Charles 1855-1913 [19]
$4 899 - €5 488 - **£3 405** - FF36 000
Les Japonais Terracotta (H53cm H20in) Argenteuil
2001

MASSEN Daniel 1896-1972 [6]
$6 000 - €6 824 - **£4 161** - FF44 761
Construction Oil/masonite (40x45x5cm 16x18x2in)
Chicago IL 2000

MASSERIA Franceso 1927 [2]
$2 750 - €2 546 - **£1 660** - FF16 699
Julie Pastel/paper (60x50cm 24x20in) Detroit MI 1999

MASSIER Clément 1845-1917 [25]
$497 - €562 - **£336** - FF3 689
**Reliefkopf eines jungen Mädchens im Profil von
links** Ceramic (23x17cm 9x6in) Lindau 2000

MASSIEU Lola 1921 [4]
$171 - €180 - **£111** - FF1 182
El volcán Grabado (44x31cm 17x12in) Madrid 2000

MASSMANN Hans 1887-1973 [55]
$915 - €872 - **£575** 720
Berglandschaft im Winter Oil/panel (92x80cm
36x31in) Wien 1999

MASSON Alexandre, Alex XX [6]
$1 771 - €2 058 - **£1 244** - FF13 500
Pen'sardines devant la baie de Douarnenez
Huile/toile (50x61cm 19x24in) Rennes 2001

MASSON André 1896-1987 [1672]
$41 272 - €44 005 - **£28 000** - FF288 652
«Les fleurs de déchaînement» Oil/canvas
(114x146cm 44x57in) London 2001
$34 000 - €32 694 - **£20 947** - FF214 461
Après le déluge Oil/canvas (73x91.5cm 28x36in)
New-York 1999
$8 000 - €7 693 - **£4 928** - FF50 461
Les musiciens Oil/canvas (23x56cm 9x22in) New-
York 1999
$30 647 - €32 921 - **£21 000** - FF215 947
Amazone, femme et cheval Bronze (H123cm
H48in) London 2001
$7 471 - €8 020 - **£5 000** - FF52 608
Répulsion Bronze (H8.5cm H3in) London 2000
$3 128 - €3 506 - **£2 122** - FF23 000
Fragement d'un féminaire Encre (31x24cm 12x9in)
Paris 2000
$257 - €307 - **£183** - FF2 012
Figürliche Szene Farblithographie (48.5x63cm
19x24in) Berlin 2000

MASSON Antoine 1636-1700 [12]
$385 - €335 - **£232** - FF2 200
**Gaspard Charrier, lieutenant particulier au
Présidial de Lyon** Burin (34x26.5cm 13x10in) Paris
1998

MASSON Benedict 1819-1893 [27]
$11 000 - €10 452 - **£6 692** - FF68 561
Cupid and Psyche Oil/canvas (81.5x65cm 32x25in)
New-York 1999

MASSON Clovis Edmond 1838-1913 [138]
$877 - €942 - **£596** - FF6 178
Lion, lionne et deux lionceaux Bronze
(34x49x20cm 13x19x7in) Bruxelles 2001

MASSON Edouard 1881-1950 [74]
$380 - €421 - **£265** - FF2 764
L'arbre Huile/toile (38.5x46.5cm 15x18in) Liège 2001
$582 - €644 - **£405** - FF4 227
Vase de fleurs Pastel/papier (50x93cm 19x36in)
Bruxelles 2001

MASSON François 1745-1807 [1]
$3 707 - €4 116 - **£2 583** - FF27 000
Buste de André Massena, duc de Rivoli Marbre
(H64cm H25in) Paris 2001

MASSON Georges Armand 1892-1977 [8]
$4 960 - €4 805 - **£3 040** - FF31 520
Puerto de paisajes Oleo/tabla (33x24cm 12x9in)
Madrid 1999

MASSON Henri Léopold 1907-1996 [241]
$2 115 - €1 810 - **£1 273** - FF11 875
«Nature morte aux fleurs et fruits» Oil/canvas
(40.5x51cm 15x20in) Toronto 1998
$1 285 - €1 217 - **£801** - FF7 980
Les pêcheurs Huile/toile (30.5x40.5cm 12x15in)
Montréal 1999
$444 - €430 - **£273** - FF2 818
Venice Watercolour/paper (35.5x42cm 13x16in)
Toronto 1999
$205 - €199 - **£127** - FF1 304
**Quand les humains/La montagne/Restez
enfant/Bonheur toujours** Lithographie (55x44.5cm
21x17in) Montréal 1999

MASSON Jules Edmond 1871-1932 [47]
$1 466 - €1 646 - **£950** - FF10 799
Figure of Napoleon, Third-Quarter Bronze (H33cm
H12in) London 2000

MASSON Marcel 1911-1988 [73]
$473 - €515 - **£311** - FF3 376
Montmartre, Rue des Norvins Öl/Leinwand
(73x54cm 28x21in) Bern 2000

MASSONET Armand 1892-1979 [54]
$1 197 - €1 115 - **£738** - FF7 317
Fumées Huile/toile (60x50cm 23x19in) Bruxelles
1999
$467 - €534 - **£325** - FF3 500
«Bruxelles, foire commerciale» Affiche (70x100cm
27x39in) Paris 2001

MASSOT de Pierre XX [2]
$2 646 - €2 744 - **£1 744** - FF18 000
Marcel Duchamp Photo (9.5x6.5cm 3x2in) Paris 2000

MASSOT Firmin 1766-1849 [12]
$141 958 - €152 381 - **£95 000** - FF999 552
**Portraits of Karl-David de Bonstetten and his
wife Sophie-Elisabeth** Oil/canvas (69x58cm
27x22in) London 2000

$29 000 - €29 337 - **£17 707** - FF192 441
Lady with a Hunting Dog in the Valley of l'Arve, Geneva Oil/canvas (38x34.5cm 14x13in) New-York 2000

$7 000 - €7 081 - **£4 274** - FF46 451
Young Lady seated under a Tree with a Portfolio of Drawings Black chalk (26.5x21.5cm 10x8in) New-York 2000

MASSYS Cornelis c.1510-c.1565 [12]

$1 072 - €1 278 - **£764** - FF8 384
Samson bringt den Tempel zum Einsturz Kupferstich (8.1x10.4cm 3x4in) Berlin 2000

MASSYS Jan c.1510-c.1575 [4]

$244 770 - €227 535 - **£150 000** - FF1 492 530
Susannah and the Elders Oil/panel (131x111cm 51x43in) London 1999

$45 000 - €48 136 - **£30 681** - FF315 751
Peasants Making Music Oil/panel (70x100cm 27x39in) New-York 2001

MASTENBROEK Albert 1946 [9]

$4 659 - €5 445 - **£3 326** - FF35 719
Nieuwehaven, Rotterdam Oil/panel (17.5x24cm 6x9in) Amsterdam 2001

MASTENBROEK van Johann Hendrik 1875-1945 [202]

$27 965 - €31 765 - **£19 621** - FF208 362
«Dordrecht» Oil/canvas (121x170cm 47x66in) Amsterdam 2001

$14 755 - €17 244 - **£10 533** - FF113 110
Canalscene at Dusk, Rotterdam Oil/canvas (40.5x61cm 15x24in) Amsterdam 2001

$4 300 - €3 625 - **£2 552** - FF23 781
A rainbow over Kralingse veer Oil/canvas (27x44cm 10x17in) Amsterdam 1998

$1 261 - €1 180 - **£762** - FF7 739
Spoorhaven Rotterdam Black chalk/paper (21x34.5cm 8x13in) Dordrecht 1999

MASTENBROEK van Johannes Hendrikus 1827-1909 [3]

$1 797 - €2 042 - **£1 261** - FF13 394
«De Roonie vaart, Moerdijk, Figures by a Sluice in Summer» Watercolour (35x49cm 13x19in) Amsterdam 2001

MASTER OF 1416 XV [3]

$81 000 - €69 974 - **£40 500** - FF459 000
Madonna col Bambino e Santi Tempera/tavola (106x162cm 41x63in) Prato 1999

$97 129 - €104 260 - **£65 000** - FF683 904
The Madonna and Child with a Goldfinch with Saints John the Baptist Oil/panel (73.5x46cm 28x18in) London 2000

MASTER OF BORGO ALLA COLLINA XV [2]

$59 772 - €64 160 - **£40 000** - FF420 864
The Madonna & Child with Saints John the Baptist and Nicholas of Bari Oil/panel (89x43cm 35x16in) London 2000

MASTER OF CARMIGNANO XV [2]

$27 405 - €26 679 - **£16 835** - FF175 000
Vierge à l'Enfant entourée de St Jean-Baptiste et St Antoine abbé Tempera/panneau (59x46cm 23x18in) Paris 1999

MASTER OF CHARLES OF DURAZZO XV [1]

$62 760 - €67 368 - **£42 000** - FF441 907
Royal Banquet with Other Figures and Two Ladies in a Garden Oil/panel (30x104cm 11x40in) London 2000

MASTER OF COETIVY XV [1]

$37 991 - €39 384 - **£22 794** - FF258 342
Le ore delle Vergine, codice Disegno (18x13cm 7x5in) Milano 1999

MASTER OF FONTANAROSA XVII [1]

$12 000 - €11 290 - **£7 488** - FF74 056
Christ among the Doctors - a Fragment Oil/canvas (51x88cm 20x34in) New-York 1999

MASTER OF FRANKFURT 1460-c.1515 [7]

$194 259 - €208 521 - **£130 000** - FF1 367 808
Allegory of Love Oil/panel (25x128.5cm 9x50in) London 2000

MASTER OF GIOVANNI BARRILE XIV [1]

$1 858 320 - €1 768 409 - **£1 155 360** - FF11 600 000
La Crucifixion Peinture (136x118cm 53x46in) Paris 1999

MASTER OF GÜSTROW XVI [1]

$37 357 - €40 100 - **£25 000** - FF263 040
The Dormition of the Virgin Oil/panel (70.5x56cm 27x22in) London 2000

MASTER OF HOVINGHAM XVII [2]

$11 452 - €10 671 - **£7 063** - FF70 000
Le repos pendant la fuite en Égypte Huile/toile (21.5x42.5cm 8x16in) Paris 1999

MASTER OF JATIVA XV [3]

$23 346 - €22 949 - **£15 000** - FF150 534
King David endorsing the Succession of Solomon (?) Oil/panel (76x51cm 29x20in) London 1999

MASTER OF LAVAGNOLA XIV [1]

$184 600 - €198 184 - **£123 500** - FF1 300 000
Crucifixion Tempera (99x53cm 38x20in) Paris 2000

MASTER OF MARRADI act.c.1475-c.1500 [5]

$132 294 - €130 043 - **£85 000** - FF853 026
Cassone Panel with a Subject from Roman History Oil/panel (68x165.5cm 26x65in) London 1999

$20 000 - €20 733 - **£12 000** - FF136 000
La visione di San Tommaso d'Aquino Olio/tavoletta (33x22cm 12x8in) Venezia 2000

MASTER OF PEREA act.c.1490-c.1510 [3]

$105 080 - €112 812 - **£70 300** - FF740 000
L'Adoration des rois mages Huile/panneau (202.5x154cm 79x60in) Neuilly-sur-Seine 2000

MASTER OF PONTEROSSO XVI [1]

$67 236 - €79 273 - **£47 268** - FF520 000
Vierge et Enfant entre deux anges Huile/panneau (58.5x44cm 23x17in) Versailles 2000

MASTER OF POPIGLIO XV [1]

$25 056 - €24 392 - **£15 392** - FF160 000
Madone à l'Enfant Tempera/panneau (44x24cm 17x9in) Paris 1999

MASTER OF RABENDEN XVII [1]

$291 180 - €272 268 - **£179 520** - FF1 785 960
South German Bavarian Late Gothic Polychrome Sculpture (H86cm H33in) Amsterdam 1999

MASTER OF SAINT IVO c.1370-c.1420 [7]

$55 000 - €57 016 - **£33 000** - FF374 000
Madonna in trono con Gesú Bambino ed i Santi Caterina d'Alessandria Tempera/tavola (80x50cm 31x19in) Roma 2000

$31 796 - €26 944 - **£19 000** - FF176 743
Saint Paul Oil/panel (41x24.5cm 16x9in) London 1998

M

MASTER OF SAN GAGGIO XIII-XIV [1]
- $150 000 - €129 582 - £100 000 - FF849 999
  Madonna col Bambino, Flagellazione, Crocifissione, Trittico Tempera/tavola (46x68.5cm 18x26in) Milano 1998

MASTER OF SAN JACOPO A MUCCIANA XIV-XV [2]
- $105 515 - €103 350 - £68 000 - FF677 932
  Mystic Marriage of St Catherine with St Luke the Evangelist Tempera (53x36cm 20x14in) London 1999

MASTER OF SAN LUCCHESE XIV [1]
- $59 736 - €57 931 - £37 582 - FF380 000
  La Vierge adorant l'Enfant/La Vierge d'humilité allaitant/Le Christ Tempera/panneau (80x71cm 31x27in) Paris 1999

MASTER OF SAN MINIATO XV [9]
- $120 000 - €105 259 - £72 864 - FF690 456
  The Madonna Adoring the Christ Child in a Landscape Mixed media/panel (98.5x57cm 38x22in) New-York 1999
- $131 109 - €148 914 - £92 000 - FF976 810
  The Madonna and Child Tempera/panel (43x32cm 16x12in) London 2001

MASTER OF SANTA CATERINA GUALINO XIV [1]
- $425 000 - €440 578 - £255 000 - FF2 890 000
  Santa Caterina d'Alessandria Sculpture bois (139x31x20cm 54x12x7in) Firenze 2001

MASTER OF SANTA VERDIANA XIV [2]
- $29 886 - €32 080 - £20 000 - FF210 432
  Saints Stephen and Abbot, and Evangelist in the Gable Above Oil/panel (132x59cm 51x23in) London 2000

MASTER OF SANTO SPIRITO XV-XVI [3]
- $20 000 - €16 634 - £11 740 - FF109 110
  Saint Anthony Abbot (?) Oil/panel (66.5x49cm 26x19in) New-York 1998

MASTER OF SHELDON XVI-XVII [1]
- $22 448 - €26 697 - £16 000 - FF175 123
  King Richard III (1452-1485), Half-Length, in a Dark-Blue Robe Oil/panel (84x56cm 33x22in) London 2000

MASTER OF THE ACQUAVELLA STILL LIFE XVII [4]
- $150 000 - €160 193 - £102 210 - FF1 050 795
  Pomegranates, Melons, Grapes, Peaches, Figs and other Fruits Oil/canvas (72x85cm 28x33in) New-York 2001

MASTER OF THE ANTWERP ADORATION XVI [1]
- $70 000 - €61 401 - £42 504 - FF402 766
  Christ and the Centurion of Capernaum and the Last Supper Oil/panel (128x75.5cm 50x29in) New-York 1999

MASTER OF THE ANTWERP CRUCIFIXION act.c.1520 [1]
- $30 000 - €32 091 - £20 454 - FF210 501
  Abraham and Melchisedek Oil/panel (120x50cm 47x19in) New-York 2001

MASTER OF THE BARGELLO XIV [1]
- $53 628 - €45 629 - £32 000 - FF299 308
  Madonnna and Child enthroned with Saint Bartholomew, a male Martyr. Tempera/panel (37.5x18.5cm 14x7in) London 1998

MASTER OF THE BORGHESE TONDO XV-XVI [5]
- $54 309 - €53 195 - £35 000 - FF348 936
  Nativity with the Infant St John the Baptist, the Annunciation Oil/panel (87x84cm 34x33in) London 1999

MASTER OF THE CAMPANA CASSONI XVI [1]
- $9 862 - €10 586 - £6 600 - FF69 442
  Saint John the Baptist in a Landscape Oil/panel (99.5x56cm 39x22in) London 2000

MASTER OF THE CESPO DI GAROFANI XV [1]
- $20 000 - €20 733 - £12 000 - FF136 000
  Cristo in pietà con i simboli della Passione Tempera/tavola (65.5x58cm 25x22in) Milano 2000

MASTER OF THE COBURG RONDELS XV [1]
- $2 700 - €2 820 - £1 712 - FF18 378
  Sketch of a Kneeling Apostle/Kneeling Donor Dressed in Armor Ink (19x9cm 7x3in) Boston MA 2000

MASTER OF THE CORSI CRUCIFIX XIV [1]
- $90 000 - €96 272 - £61 362 - FF631 503
  The Flagellation Tempera/panel (20x16cm 7x6in) New-York 2001

MASTER OF THE DEATH OF SAINT NICHOLAS OF MUNSTER XV [1]
- $3 200 000 - €3 198 502 - £1 954 880 - FF20 980 800
  Calvary Oil/panel (129x200cm 50x78in) New-York 2000

MASTER OF THE FIESOLE EPIPHANY XV [4]
- $22 500 - €26 501 - £15 561 - FF173 832
  Madonna and Child with the Infant Saint John and Saint Francis Tempera/panel (68.5x42.5cm 26x16in) New-York 2000

MASTER OF THE GHISLIERI APSE XVI [3]
- $11 000 - €9 649 - £6 679 - FF63 291
  The Flagellation Ink (29x17cm 11x6in) New-York 1999

MASTER OF THE GROTESQUE VASES XVII [4]
- $68 841 - €69 364 - £42 906 - FF455 000
  Natures mortes aux vases de fleurs sur des entablements Huile/toile (91.5x67cm 36x26in) Paris 2000

MASTER OF THE GUARDESCHI FLOWERS XVIII [4]
- $21 500 - €22 288 - £12 900 - FF146 200
  Fiori Olio/tela (105x78.5cm 41x30in) Milano 1999

MASTER OF THE HALF-LENGTH (FEMALE) FIGURES XVI [11]
- $15 517 - €15 199 - £10 000 - FF99 696
  Lucretia Oil/panel (69x51cm 27x20in) London 1999
- $190 000 - €189 911 - £116 071 - FF1 245 735
  The Virgin and Child Oil/panel (36x26.5cm 14x10in) New-York 2000

MASTER OF THE HARTFORD STILL LIFE XVII [2]
- $56 000 - €72 566 - £42 000 - FF476 000
  Natura morta con fiori entro una zuppiera, fragole e pesche Olio/tela (51x65.5cm 20x25in) Firenze 2000

MASTER OF THE JOHNSON NATIVITY c.1470-c.1500 [4]
- $5 657 - €6 095 - £3 800 - FF39 982
  The Symbols of the Passion Oil/panel (42x33.5cm 16x13in) London 2000

MASTER OF THE JOHNSON TABERNACLE XV [2]
- $19 000 - €16 518 - £11 498 - FF108 349
  Virgin and Child Enthroned Between Saints John The Baptist and Michael Mixed media/panel (66x35cm 26x14in) New-York 1999

MASTER OF THE KRESS LANDSCAPES (G. di L. Larciani) XV-XVII [5]
- $110 000 - €111 280 - £67 166 - FF729 949
  The Madonna and Child with the Infant Saint John the Baptist Oil/panel (74x56.5cm 29x22in) New-York 2000

MASTER OF THE KURPFÄLZISCHEN SKETCH-BOOK XVI-XVII [1]
- $2 925 - €2 813 - £1 802 - FF18 454
  River Landscape with Hunters in a Boat Passing a Farmstead Ink (15x27cm 5x10in) Amsterdam 1999

MASTER OF THE LANGMATT FOUNDATION VIEWS XVIII [25]
- $55 000 - €57 016 - £33 000 - FF374 000
  Veduta della piazzetta e Santa Maria della Salute, Venezia Olio/tela (77x130cm 30x51in) Milano 1999
- $18 000 - €23 325 - £13 500 - FF153 000
  Veduta del Bacino di San Marco con la piazzetta, Venezia Olio/tela (25.5x38.5cm 10x15in) Milano 2000

MASTER OF THE LAUTENBACH HIGH ALTAR XVI [1]
- $37 162 - €34 033 - £22 650 - FF223 245
  Saints Dorothea, Apollonia and Agatha, Wing of an Altarpiece Mixed media/panel (192.5x123cm 75x48in) Amsterdam 1999

MASTER OF THE LEGEND OF SAINT CATHERINE XV [4]
- $400 000 - €427 876 - £272 720 - FF2 806 680
  Virgin and Child Enthroned Oil/panel (45x32.5cm 17x12in) New-York 2001

MASTER OF THE LEGEND OF SAINT JOHN THE EVANGELIST act.c.1500 [1]
- $26 400 - €22 806 - £17 600 - FF149 600
  Cristo al calvario Olio/tavola (107x89cm 42x35in) Roma 1998

MASTER OF THE LEGEND OF THE MAGDALENE c.1483-c.1530 [7]
- $448 290 - €481 202 - £300 000 - FF3 156 480
  The Virgin and Child Oil/panel (42x31cm 16x12in) London 2000

MASTER OF THE LILLE ADORATION XVI [2]
- $281 977 - €276 921 - £175 000 - FF1 816 482
  Biblical Figure, probably Pontius Pilate Oil/panel (56.5x42.5cm 22x16in) London 1999

MASTER OF THE LIVERPOOL MADONNA act.c.1495-c.1500 [2]
- $55 000 - €63 942 - £38 604 - FF419 430
  The Birth of the Virgin Oil/panel (159x115.5cm 62x45in) New-York 2001

MASTER OF THE LOMBARD FRUITBOWL XVII [3]
- $59 854 - €67 982 - £42 000 - FF445 935
  Sweetmeats and Pastries in a Wicker Basket with Cherries Oil/canvas (75.5x100cm 29x39in) London 2001

MASTER OF THE MISERICORDIA c.1350-c.1390 [7]
- $78 000 - €101 074 - £58 500 - FF663 000
  Cristo crocefisso fra la Vergine e San Giovanni Evangelista Olio/tavola (65x34cm 25x13in) Firenze 2000
- $59 000 - €61 163 - £35 400 - FF401 200
  Vergine annunciata Tempera/tavola (15x24cm 5x9in) Firenze 2000

MASTER OF THE PANZANO TRIPTYCH act.1380-1400 [1]
- $50 000 - €53 484 - £34 090 - FF350 835
  The Annunciation Oil/panel (112x92cm 44x36in) New-York 2001

MASTER OF THE PARROT XVI [6]
- $37 240 - €36 476 - £24 000 - FF239 270
  Virgin and Child enthroned, a Hilly Landscape with a Castle beyond Oil/panel (57.5x48cm 22x18in) London 1999

MASTER OF THE PAU SUPPER AT EMMAUS XVII [2]
- $13 721 - €15 995 - £9 500 - FF104 918
  Saint Andrew Led to Martyrdom Oil/canvas (100x130cm 39x51in) London 2000

MASTER OF THE PORTIUNCULA c.1500 [1]
- $44 088 - €50 308 - £30 624 - FF330 000
  La légende de Chevalier de Cologne Huile/panneau (167x133cm 65x52in) Paris 2000

MASTER OF THE PRODIGAL SON c.1500-c.1560 [9]
- $195 816 - €182 028 - £120 000 - FF1 194 024
  Healing of the Sick of the Palsy (Matthew IX,1-8,Mark II,3-12,Luke V) Oil/panel (99x142.5cm 38x56in) London 1998
- $62 510 - €57 931 - £37 316 - FF380 000
  Le bon Samaritain Huile/panneau (94x125cm 37x49in) Paris 1999

MASTER OF THE RETABLO DE LOS SANTOS JUANES act.c.1525 [2]
- $36 117 - €40 840 - £25 416 - FF267 894
  The Lamentation Oil/panel (53.5x38cm 21x14in) Amsterdam 2001

MASTER OF THE RIFLESSI XVIII [2]
- $35 700 - €30 840 - £17 850 - FF202 300
  Il risveglio della dama Olio/tela (68.5x57.5cm 26x22in) Venezia 1999

MASTER OF THE RINUCCINI CHAPEL act.1359-1394 [1]
- $138 000 - €178 823 - £103 500 - FF1 173 000
  Cristo incorona la Vergine fra i Santi Pietro, Lucia Tempera/tavola (64x37.5cm 25x14in) Roma 2000

MASTER OF THE RUGS XVII [2]
- $40 000 - €41 466 - £24 000 - FF272 000
  Tappeti, cuscini tendaggi e vaso di fiori e argenteria su un tavolo Olio/tela (115x145cm 45x57in) Milano 1999

MASTER OF THE SEYFRIEDSBERGER ALTAR XVI [1]
- $29 359 - €27 460 - £18 000 - FF180 126
  The Nativity/The Coronation of the Virgin Oil/panel (94x72cm 37x28in) London 2000

MASTER OF THE STOCKHOLM PIETA XVI [2]
- $9 600 - €8 293 - £6 400 - FF54 400
  Madonna col Bambino Olio/tavola (47x33.5cm 18x13in) Milano 1998

M

MASTER OF THE TIBURTINE SIBYL active Bruges c.1480-1495 [1]
- $26 097 - €24 409 - **£16 000** - FF160 112
  The Crucifixion Oil/panel (91x71cm 35x27in)
  London 1998

MASTER OF THE WEILHEIM ROSENKRANZFEST XVI [1]
- $18 757 - €17 544 - **£11 500** - FF115 080
  Pentecost Oil/panel (47x39cm 18x15in) London 1998

MASTER OF VOLTERRA XVI [1]
- $13 000 - €14 967 - **£8 871** - FF98 176
  The Madonna and Child with the Infant Saint John the Baptist Oil/panel (66x50cm 25x19in) New-York 2000

MASTERS Edward XIX [9]
- $4 311 - €3 732 - **£2 600** - FF24 482
  Busy Village Lane Oil/canvas (51x76cm 20x29in) London 1998
- $616 - €661 - **£418** - FF4 334
  Perros en un jardín Oleo/lienzo (29x36cm 11x14in) Madrid 2000

MASTERS Edwin XIX-XX [13]
- $2 824 - €2 417 - **£1 700** - FF15 852
  A Farmyard Oil/canvas (25.5x45.5cm 10x17in) London 1998

MASTERS Thomas XIX-XX [2]
- $4 000 - €3 463 - **£2 412** - FF22 714
  Country Scene with a Horsedrawn Cart/Figures Oil/canvas (25.5x45.5cm 10x17in) San-Francisco CA 1998

MASTRO-VALERIO Alessandro 1889-1953 [5]
- $229 - €219 - **£143** - FF1 434
  Morning Paper Lithograph (15x23cm 6x9in) Cedar-Falls IA 1999

MASTROIANNI Umberto 1910-1998 [216]
- $1 500 - €1 555 - **£900** - FF10 200
  Senza titolo Tecnica mista/cartone (51x101cm 20x39in) Roma 2001
- $1 000 - €1 037 - **£600** - FF6 800
  Composizione Tecnica mista/cartone (22.5x22.5cm 8x8in) Vercelli 2001
- $3 000 - €3 887 - **£2 250** - FF25 500
  Salto Bronzo (111x87x25cm 43x34x9in) Milano 2000
- $1 320 - €1 710 - **£990** - FF11 220
  Salto Bronzo (H30.5cm H12in) Vercelli 2001
- $400 - €518 - **£300** - FF3 400
  Senza titolo Collage (49x31cm 19x12in) Milano 2001
- $160 - €207 - **£120** - FF1 360
  Composizione Serigrafia (70x100cm 27x39in) Torino 2000

MASTURZIO Marzio XVII [14]
- $11 500 - €11 922 - **£6 900** - FF78 200
  Battaglia Olio/tela (76x100cm 29x39in) Milano 1999
- $6 600 - €5 702 - **£4 400** - FF37 400
  Battaglia tra cavalieri Olio/rame (15.5x21.5cm 6x8in) Milano 1998

MASUCCI Agostino Masucco 1691-1758 [9]
- $4 000 - €3 703 - **£2 414** - FF24 290
  The Penitent Magdalene Oil/canvas (63.5x47.5cm 25x18in) New-York 1999
- $5 732 - €5 325 - **£3 500** - FF34 930
  Portrait of a Cleric, Half-Length, in Clerical Robes Oil/copper (16x12.5cm 6x4in) London 1998
- $7 799 - €7 632 - **£5 000** - FF50 061
  Design for an Illustration for an old Testament Scene Red chalk/paper (23x16.5cm 9x6in) London 1999

MASUI Paul Auguste 1888-1981 [60]
- $688 - €793 - **£483** - FF5 203
  Le labour Huile/toile (55x60cm 21x23in) Bruxelles 2000
- $937 - €1 091 - **£668** - FF7 154
  Rentrée au port d'Ostende Pastel/papier (70x60cm 27x23in) Bruxelles 2001

MASURÉ Jules 1819-? [4]
- $8 734 - €7 535 - **£5 200** - FF49 429
  Evening Seascape, with Sailing Ships Off the Beach Oil/canvas (77x109cm 30x42in) Glamorgan 1998
- $1 584 - €1 795 - **£1 116** - FF11 772
  Marinha com barcos Oleo/tabla (26.5x35cm 10x13in) Lisboa 2001

MASWIENS Joseph 1828-1880 [14]
- $3 690 - €3 718 - **£2 295** - FF24 390
  Intérieur d'église Huile/toile (60x75.5cm 23x29in) Bruxelles 2000

MASZKOWSKI Marceli 1837-1862 [3]
- $1 468 - €1 480 - **£915** - FF9 706
  Portrait de fille avec poupée/Petite fille Pencil (26x20.5cm 10x8in) Warszawa 2000

MATA Carles Vazquez 1949 [13]
- $858 - €781 - **£520** - FF5 122
  Toro Bronze (48x50x10cm 18x19x3in) Barcelona 1999

MATAL Bohumír 1922-1988 [45]
- $1 300 - €1 230 - **£810** - FF8 068
  Eine Figur Öl/Leinwand (70x35cm 27x13in) Praha 2000
- $578 - €547 - **£360** - FF3 586
  «Female Nude» Mixed media/board (44x25cm 17x9in) Praha 2001
- $578 - €547 - **£360** - FF3 586
  Avion au-dessus de la ville Crayon/papier (23.5x31cm 9x12in) Praha 2001

MATALONI Giovanni 1869-1944 [13]
- $2 400 - €2 272 - **£1 490** - FF14 902
  «La Tribuna» Poster (244x110cm 96x43in) New-York 1999

MATANIA Eduardo 1847-1929 [5]
- $3 327 - €2 818 - **£2 000** - FF18 484
  Young Boy and Fisherman Oil/canvas (39x19.5cm 15x7in) London 1998

MATANIA Fortunino 1881-1963 [91]
- $3 168 - €3 477 - **£2 040** - FF22 806
  Vor dem prachtvollen Kirchenportal an der Piazza dell'Gesu Öl/Leinwand (76x50.5cm 29x19in) Lindau 1999
- $4 134 - €3 888 - **£2 600** - FF25 501
  The Doctors Visit Oil/board (18x27cm 7x10in) Co. Kilkenny 1999
- $561 - €523 - **£349** - FF3 432
  Marozia on the Throne, with Anastasio III kneeling at her Feet Watercolour (30x21cm 11x8in) London 1999
- $8 993 - €8 641 - **£5 500** - FF56 684
  «Southport, LMS» Poster (102x127cm 40x50in) London 1999

MATANIA Franco XIX-XX [70]
- $149 - €138 - **£90** - FF905
  Portrait of a Woman Reading Chalks/paper (60x40cm 24x16in) Billingshurst, West-Sussex 1999

MATANIA Ugo 1888-1979 [7]
- $9 985 - €8 202 - **£5 800** - FF53 803
  A young Girl beside a Venetian Canal Pastel (31x35.5cm 12x13in) London 1998

MATARÉ Ewald 1887-1965 [291]
- $11 252 - €13 294 - **£7 948** - FF87 201
Waschtisch Öl/Leinwand (63x83cm 24x32in) Köln 2001
- $13 618 - €11 762 - **£8 224** - FF77 155
Stiere an der Weide Mixed media/panel (26.6x33.6cm 10x13in) Köln 1998
- $14 048 - €12 002 - **£8 500** - FF78 731
Small Standing Cow Bronze (H.4.5cm H1in) London 1998
- $3 462 - €4 090 - **£2 445** - FF26 831
Poststrasse im Nebel Aquarell/Papier (29x39.5cm 11x15in) Köln 2001
- $3 029 - €3 579 - **£2 139** - FF23 477
Zeichen einer Weide Woodcut in colors (23x57.5cm 9x22in) Köln 2001

MATAS GARCIA Manuel 1928 [11]
- $520 - €601 - **£360** - FF3 549
Combarro Acuarela/papel (35x49cm 13x19in) Madrid 1999

MATEGOT Mathieu 1910-2001 [25]
- $800 - €854 - **£506** - FF5 600
Maquette réalisée pour un mobilier de chambre à coucher Gouache (46.5x46.5cm 18x18in) Paris 2000
- $2 516 - €2 592 - **£1 557** - FF17 000
Zircon Tapisserie (151x195cm 59x76in) Argenteuil 2000

MATEJKO Jan 1838-1893 [46]
- $28 000 - €32 348 - **£19 605** - FF212 186
Male Figures Study Oil/board (61x33cm 24x13in) New-York 2001
- $1 911 - €1 898 - **£1 190** - FF12 453
Étude d'un personnage historique Oil/board (31.5x20.5cm 12x8in) Warszawa 1999
- $1 257 - €1 402 - **£860** - FF9 199
Copernic Crayon/papier (18x22cm 7x8in) Warszawa 2000

MATEJKO Theo 1893-1946 [30]
- $302 - €327 - **£209** - FF2 145
«Wien - Die Brücke zwischen Ost und West» Poster (126x96cm 49x37in) Wien 2001

MATELDI Filberto 1882-1942 [1]
- $1 800 - €2 008 - **£1 178** - FF13 172
«Birra Metzger Torino» Poster (101x138cm 39x54in) New-York 2000

MATEOS GONZALEZ Francisco 1894-1976 [146]
- $5 100 - €5 106 - **£3 145** - FF33 490
Caín Oleo/lienzo (81x100cm 31x39in) Madrid 2000
- $455 - €390 - **£279** - FF2 561
Personaje Acuarela (16.5x23cm 6x4in) Madrid 1998

MATET Jean 1870-? [17]
- $570 - €488 - **£342** - FF3 200
«Griffon Bicyclettes Motocyclettes» Affiche (157x119cm 61x46in) Paris 2001

MATHAM Jacob 1571-1631 [90]
- $4 468 - €3 855 - **£2 696** - FF25 290
Dog, looking up to the right Black chalk (13.3x12.8cm 5x5in) Amsterdam 1998
- $538 - €653 - **£375** - FF4 024
Die Madonna mit Kind, nach Hendrick Goltzius Kupferstich (5.5x4cm 2x1in) Berlin 2001

MATHAM Jan 1600-1648 [1]
- $27 942 - €26 492 - **£17 000** - FF173 777
Peaches, Apple, Apricot, Plums, Cherries on Ledge with a Wasp Oil/panel (30x43cm 11x16in) London 1999

MATHAM Theodor Dirck 1606-1676 [6]
- $5 640 - €4 872 - **£3 400** - FF31 956
View of the Cathedral of Notre-Dame, Paris seen from the Back Wash (20x33cm 7x12in) Amsterdam 1998

MATHELOT Christian 1923 [10]
- $245 - €229 - **£151** - FF1 500
La Bataille d'Angleterre, paru dans «Coq Hardi» Nos.134 & 141 Encre Chine (29x29cm 11x11in) Paris 1999

MATHER John Robert 1848-1916 [43]
- $6 529 - €6 125 - **£4 034** - FF40 177
The Treasury Gardens, Melbourne Oil/canvas (41x61cm 16x24in) Melbourne 1999
- $312 - €365 - **£217** - FF2 392
Near Ivanhoe Oil/board (14x19cm 5x7in) Melbourne 1999
- $708 - €666 - **£445** - FF4 366
Cattle in the Shadows of the Derelict Farm Buildings Watercolour/paper (24x34cm 9x13in) Sydney 1999

MATHER Margrethe 1885-1952 [14]
- $20 000 - €22 295 - **£13 896** - FF146 244
Max Eastman, Poet Platinum, palladium print (19x23.5cm 7x9in) New-York 2001

MATHEWS Lucia Kleinhans 1870-1955 [3]
- $2 000 - €1 709 - **£1 210** - FF11 208
«Menlo» Pastel/paper (30x35.5cm 11x13in) San-Francisco CA 1998

MATHEWS Terry O. 1931 [9]
- $1 089 - €1 074 - **£700** - FF7 045
Fish swimming on a naturalistic Base Bronze (13x21cm 5x8in) London 1999

MATHEWSON Frank Convers 1862-1941 [20]
- $10 000 - €11 553 - **£7 002** - FF75 781
Garden in June Oil/canvas (38x51cm 14x20in) New-York 2001
- $1 400 - €1 523 - **£922** - FF9 988
October Afternoon, Matunuck, Rhode Island Watercolour, gouache/paper (36x49.5cm 14x19in) Boston MA 2000

MATHEY Georg Alexander 1884-1968 [13]
- $296 - €276 - **£182** - FF1 811
Cirque de Paris Woodcut (25.3x22.3cm 9x8in) Hamburg 1999

MATHEY Paul 1891-1970 [25]
- $1 174 - €1 324 - **£813** - FF8 682
Sommerlandschaft Öl/Leinwand (50x61cm 19x24in) Zürich 2000

MATHEY Paul 1844-1929 [24]
- $2 844 - €3 049 - **£1 882** - FF20 000
L'entrée de la ville close à Concarneau Huile/toile (33x46cm 12x18in) Douarnenez 2000

MATHEY-DORET Émile A. 1854-? [1]
- $2 937 - €2 744 - **£1 774** - FF18 000
Fâcheuse aventure d'après Charles Delort Eau-forte (68x91cm 26x35in) Paris 1999

MATHIESEN Egon 1907-1976 [118]
- $499 - €536 - **£334** - FF3 517
Fête for Else Oil/canvas (100x78cm 39x30in) København 2000
- $243 - €229 - **£147** - FF1 500
Paysage Watercolour/paper (55x42cm 21x16in) København 1999

M

MATHIEU Gabriel 1848-1921 **[54]**
- 🐟 **$2 641** - €2 897 - **£1 753** - FF19 000
  Le bateau lavoir Huile/toile (37.5x57.5cm 14x22in) Melun 2000
- 🐟 **$900** - €858 - **£570** - FF5 625
  River Landscape Oil/canvas (31x44cm 12x17in) Cleveland OH 1999

MATHIEU Georges 1921 **[584]**
- 🐟 **$25 154** - €21 495 - **£15 101** - FF141 000
  Composition Huile/toile (97x161cm 38x63in) Paris 1998
- 🐟 **$10 500** - €10 885 - **£6 300** - FF71 400
  Ames exilées Olio/tela (100x81cm 39x31in) Milano 2000
- ✒ **$2 483** - €2 897 - **£1 744** - FF19 000
  Elanion Technique mixte/papier (48x63.5cm 18x25in) Versailles 2000
- 🎞 **$240** - €276 - **£169** - FF1 811
  Komposition in Rot und Schwartz Farblithographie (13x20.5cm 5x8in) Hamburg 2001

MATHIEU Hubert Jean 1897 **[2]**
- 🎞 **$362** - €418 - **£250** - FF2 740
  «Téléphérique de Béout, Lourdes» Poster (100x62cm 39x24in) London 2000

MATHIEU Jean 1749-1815 **[2]**
- 🎞 **$657** - €726 - **£455** - FF4 762
  Le Serment d'Armour, after Fragonard Etching (58.5x44cm 23x17in) Amsterdam 2001

MATHIEU Paul 1872-1932 **[141]**
- 🐟 **$17 760** - €19 831 - **£12 320** - FF130 080
  Estacade à Ostende Huile/toile (101x140cm 39x55in) Antwerpen 2001
- 🐟 **$4 633** - €5 031 - **£2 930** - FF33 000
  Port de Zeebrugge Huile/toile (40x55cm 15x21in) Chinon 2000
- 🐟 **$1 048** - €992 - **£652** - FF6 504
  Polders Huile/panneau (27x40cm 10x15in) Bruxelles 1999

MATHON Émile Louis act.1868-1887 **[22]**
- 🐟 **$3 155** - €2 744 - **£1 902** - FF18 000
  Entrée du port à marrée basse Huile/toile (40x68cm 15x26in) Paris 1998

MATHONIERE de Nicolas XVII **[14]**
- 🎞 **$112** - €120 - **£74** - FF788
  Spongia fel funci talus fert hasta cruorem Grabado (19x14.5cm 7x5in) Madrid 2001

MATIFAS Louis Rémy 1847-1896 **[25]**
- 🐟 **$949** - €941 - **£593** - FF6 173
  Landskab med blomsterende frugttraeer Oil/canvas (38x55cm 14x21in) Köbenhavn 1999

MATIGNON Albert 1869-1937 **[22]**
- 🐟 **$5 000** - €4 915 - **£3 212** - FF32 239
  An Elegant Lady with her Poodle/A Lady with her Hound Oil/canvas (35x27cm 13x10in) New-York 1999
- 🎞 **$1 600** - €1 539 - **£987** - FF10 093
  «Chaussures Incroyable» Poster (120x159.5cm 47x62in) New-York 1999

MATILLA Y MARINA Segundo 1862-1937 **[105]**
- 🐟 **$10 800** - €12 013 - **£7 200** - FF78 800
  Barcas en la playa Oleo/lienzo (74x121cm 29x47in) Madrid 2000
- 🐟 **$4 480** - €4 205 - **£2 800** - FF27 580
  Figuras en la playa Oleo/cartón (19x17cm 7x6in) Madrid 1999

- ✒ **$305** - €300 - **£190** - FF1 970
  Fachada con balcones Lápiz/papel (31x21.5cm 12x8in) Barcelona 1999

MATINO Vittorio 1943 **[27]**
- 🐟 **$3 927** - €4 071 - **£2 356** - FF26 703
  Malí Acrilico/tela (93x57cm 36x22in) Milano 2000

MATISSE Auguste 1866-1931 **[14]**
- 🎞 **$2 341** - €1 998 - **£1 400** - FF13 108
  «Chamonix, Mont-Blanc» Poster (107x78cm 42x30in) London 1998

MATISSE Camille XIX-XX **[37]**
- 🐟 **$840** - €982 - **£600** - FF6 443
  Still Life of Flower Oil/canvas (69x51cm 27x20in) London 2001

MATISSE Henri 1869-1954 **[2376]**
- 🐟 **$4 500 000** - €5 221 303 - **£3 106 800** - FF34 249 500
  Les glaïeuls Oil/canvas (154x102cm 60x40in) New-York 2000
- 🐟 **$1 900 000** - €1 801 295 - **£1 155 960** - FF11 815 720
  Femme lisant devant une table et bouquet, Nice Oil/canvas (66x54.5cm 25x21in) New-York 1999
- 🐟 **$200 000** - €186 781 - **£123 440** - FF1 225 200
  Portrait de madame Girbe Oil/canvas (40.5x27.5cm 15x10in) New-York 1999
- 🐾 **$1 255 230** - €1 476 124 - **£900 000** - FF9 682 740
  Nu couché III Bronze (18.5x46.5cm 7x18in) London 2001
- ✒ **$50 000** - €60 020 - **£30 825** - FF314 990
  Tête cubiste Pencil (32.5x25.5cm 12x10in) New-York 1999
- 🎞 **$6 494** - €7 318 - **£4 497** - FF48 000
  Visage de profil reposant sur un bras, paravent Louis XIV Lithographie (30x24cm 11x9in) Paris 2000
- 📷 **$1 806** - €2 058 - **£1 240** - FF13 500
  Sans titre Photo (31x23cm 12x9in) Paris 2000

MATIUSHIN Mikhail 1861-1934 **[3]**
- 🐟 **$9 827** - €10 842 - **£6 500** - FF71 119
  Coloured Wheels Mixed media (22x22cm 8x8in) London 2000

MATIZ Leo 1917-1998 **[9]**
- 📷 **$1 440** - €1 430 - **£900** - FF9 378
  Freida Kahlo in her Studio, Coyoacán, Mexico/Freida Kahlo and Rivera Gelatin silver print (25x25cm 10x10in) London 1999

MATOSSY Pierre 1891-1969 **[20]**
- ✒ **$664** - €762 - **£454** - FF5 000
  Le chercheur d'or, Niafunke Gouache/papier (51x41cm 20x16in) Soissons 2000

MATOUSCHEK Richard 1920-1976 **[5]**
- ✒ **$1 538** - €1 453 - **£958** - FF9 534
  Der Traum einer Hausmeisterin Pencil (37.5x17.5cm 14x6in) Wien 1999

MATSCH von Franz 1861-1942 **[55]**
- 🐟 **$1 692** - €1 817 - **£1 155** - FF11 917
  Stilleben mit Marillen und Ribisel Öl/Leinwand (39.5x47.7cm 15x18in) Wien 2001
- 🐟 **$677** - €727 - **£462** - FF4 767
  Berglandschaft Öl/Leinwand (14.4x48cm 5x18in) Wien 2001
- ✒ **$1 692** - €1 817 - **£1 155** - FF11 917
  Bacchus Mischtechnik/Papier (43.5x51.8cm 17x20in) Wien 2001

MATSCHEK Alain 1948 [2]
$1 343 - €1 524 - **£919** - FF10 000
Le peintre Claude Becq préparant une toile
Pastel gras/papier (57x48.5cm 22x19in) Verdun 2000

MATSCHINSKY-DENNINGHOFF Brigitte 1923 [19]
$2 671 - €3 176 - **£1 904** - FF20 836
Untitled Sculpture (H35cm H13in) Amsterdam 2000

MATSCHINSKY-DENNINGHOFF Martin & Brigitte 1921/1923 [16]
$2 367 - €2 761 - **£1 662** - FF18 111
Sekunde I Metal (H97.5cm H38in) Köln 2000
$6 968 - €7 644 - **£4 733** - FF50 140
65-7 Metal (44x16x14cm 17x6x5in) Berlin 2000

MATTA Federica XX [21]
$1 377 - €1 524 - **£919** - FF10 000
Silence Technique mixte/papier (46x61cm 18x24in)
Paris 2000

MATTA Roberto 1911 [1547]
$90 000 - €78 477 - **£54 414** - FF514 773
L'engin dans l'éminence Oil/canvas (114.5x146cm 45x57in) New-York 1998
$20 000 - €23 237 - **£14 056** - FF152 424
«Entre deux sol des transfigures» Oil/canvas (62x77cm 24x30in) New-York 2001
$65 000 - €75 520 - **£45 682** - FF495 378
Sin título Oil/canvas (26.5x22cm 10x8in) New-York 2001
$12 000 - €11 871 - **£7 482** - FF77 866
Margarita, Cast Bronze Armchair Bronze (140x95x21cm 55x37x8in) New-York 1999
$4 500 - €4 665 - **£2 700** - FF30 600
Personaggio Bronze (H55.5cm H21in) Milano 2000
$14 960 - €16 769 - **£10 153** - FF110 000
Tiene el miedo muchos ojos, Don Qui, cap XX Pastel/papier (122x152.5cm 48x60in) Paris 2000
$324 - €360 - **£210** - FF2 364
Les automoviles II Litografía a color (41x54.5cm 16x21in) Madrid 2000

MATTA-CLARK Gordon 1943-1978 [20]
$16 000 - €18 209 - **£11 243** - FF119 443
E'tant d'Art pour locataire, Comical intersect Type C color print (60.5x46cm 23x18in) New-York 2001

MATTAS Åke 1920-1962 [19]
$1 236 - €1 345 - **£815** - FF8 825
Modell Oil/panel (53x31cm 20x12in) Helsinki 2000
$398 - €404 - **£247** - FF2 647
Skiss Oil/canvas (26x38cm 10x14in) Helsinki 2000

MATTEIS de Francesco 1852-1917 [8]
$19 051 - €22 410 - **£13 656** - FF147 000
Les enfants musiciens Bronze (101x27x32cm 39x10x12in) Paris 2001
$1 920 - €1 659 - **£1 280** - FF10 880
I fidanzati Terracotta (33x12.5x17cm 12x4x6in) Milano 1998

MATTEIS de Paolo 1662-1728 [59]
$66 984 - €57 029 - **£40 000** - FF374 084
A Pastoral Scene with Peasants and Farm Animals Oil/canvas (209x310cm 82x122in) London 1998
$7 842 - €7 658 - **£5 000** - FF50 230
St-Ignatius of Loyola healing the Sick Oil/canvas (73.5x50.5cm 28x19in) London 1999
$6 600 - €5 702 - **£4 400** - FF37 400
Maddalena/Maria Egiziaca Olio/tavola (19.5x28.5cm 7x11in) Napoli 1998

MATTENHEIMER Andreas Theodor 1752-1810 [1]
$4 101 - €4 602 - **£2 843** - FF30 185
Der Heilige Johannes von Nepomuk in Betrachtung des Kruzifixes Öl/Leinwand (92.5x70cm 36x27in) München 2000

MATTENHEIMER Andreas Theodor 1787-1856 [14]
$9 273 - €10 000 - **£6 224** - FF65 595
Fruktstilleben Oil/panel (47x43cm 18x16in) Stockholm 2000
$14 407 - €16 203 - **£10 057** - FF106 287
Früchtestilleben Oil/panel (32.5x25.4cm 12x10in) Luzern 2001

MATTER Herbert 1907-1984 [36]
$1 400 - €1 561 - **£913** - FF10 240
«Engelberg - Trubsee» Poster (99x64cm 39x25in) New-York 2000
$1 400 - €1 560 - **£981** - FF10 336
Giacometti/Man walking/Head of a Man/City Square/Standing Woman Silver print (33x45cm 13x18in) New-York 2001

MATTERN Walter I. 1891-1946 [17]
$650 - €752 - **£460** - FF4 932
Winter Landscape with Cabins on Lake, Strong Reflections in Water Oil/board (63x76cm 25x30in) Hatfield PA 2000
$250 - €282 - **£173** - FF1 848
Winter Landscape with Village Houses and Frozen Pond Oil/board (30x35cm 12x14in) Hatfield PA 2000

MATTESON Tompkins H. 1813-1884 [3]
$6 000 - €5 620 - **£3 688** - FF36 864
Playing in the Snow Oil/canvas (64x77cm 25x30in) New-York 1999

MATTHEUER Wolfgang 1927 [81]
$9 693 - €9 408 - **£6 035** - FF61 711
Gartenbild Oil/hardboard (85x70cm 33x27in) Berlin 1999
$220 - €266 - **£153** - FF1 744
Mit Feuer und Schwert Woodcut (46x32cm 18x12in) Berlin 2000

MATTHEWS James XIX-XX [67]
$800 - €711 - **£489** - FF4 662
«At Fittleworth Sussex» Watercolour/paper (51x33cm 20x13in) New-Orleans LA 1999

MATTHEWS Marmaduke 1837-1913 [87]
$335 - €370 - **£221** - FF2 424
Panoramic View Watercolour/paper (16x26.5cm 6x10in) Vancouver, BC. 2000

MATTHEWS Michael 1954 [32]
$753 - €832 - **£520** - FF5 458
The Frigate Neptune Outward Bound in the Solent Oil/board (65x45.5cm 25x17in) Hockley, Birmingham 2001
$727 - €781 - **£494** - FF5 124
Flat Panorama, The Prairie Acrylic/canvas (18x53cm 7x20in) Calgary, Alberta 2001

MATTHEWS Rodney 1946 [3]
$2 487 - €2 153 - **£1 500** - FF14 124
In search of forever Watercolour (55x108.4cm 21x42in) London 1998

MATTHEY Gill Julien 1889-c.1956 [3]
$2 471 - €2 744 - **£1 722** - FF18 000
Vue de Fez Huile/toile (60x73cm 23x28in) Paris 2001

M

MATTHIESEN Oscar Adam Otto 1861-1957 **[64]**
- $615 - €531 - £370 - FF3 482
  Kustparti med roddbåtar Oil/canvas (36x55cm 14x21in) Malmö 1998

MATTHIEU Cornelis c.1610-c.1660 **[7]**
- $23 466 - €27 227 - £16 200 - FF178 596
  Extensive Wooded River Landscape with a Stone Bridge and Travellers Oil/canvas (102x140cm 40x55in) Amsterdam 2000
- $7 359 - €6 350 - £4 440 - FF41 654
  Wooded River Landscape with an Angler Oil/panel (37x50cm 14x19in) Amsterdam 1998

MATTHIEU Georg David 1737-1778 **[11]**
- $128 830 - €117 983 - £78 520 - FF773 916
  Ulrike Sophie, Princess of Mecklenburg-Schwerin (1723-1813) Oil/canvas (127.5x103.5cm 50x40in) Amsterdam 1999
- $35 676 - €32 672 - £21 744 - FF214 315
  Friedrich, Duke of Mecklenburg-Schwerin (1717-1785) Oil/canvas (87x70cm 34x27in) Amsterdam 1999
- $1 007 - €1 134 - £694 - FF7 441
  Portrait of Luise, Duchess of Mecklenburg-Schwerin (1756-1808) Oil/canvas (27.9x22cm 10x8in) Amsterdam 2000
- $1 470 - €1 278 - £885 - FF8 380
  Interieur mit zwei Damen beim Brettspiel Radierung (17.9x22.7cm 7x8in) Berlin 1998

MATTHIS Leonie 1883-1952 **[2]**
- $5 200 - €5 730 - £3 458 - FF37 585
  Figura femenina a frente al mar Gouache/papier (55x60cm 21x23in) Buenos-Aires 2000

MATTHISON William 1853-1926 **[45]**
- $631 - €752 - £456 - FF4 936
  View of Milurn Across the Lake, with a Figure Fishing from a Punt Watercolour (53x36cm 20x14in) Leyburn, North Yorkshire 2000

MATTIA Alphonse 1947 **[1]**
- $16 000 - €16 575 - £10 184 - FF108 724
  Architect's Valet Chair Sculpture, wood (198x56x44cm 77x22x17in) New-York 2000

MATTIACCI Eliseo 1940 **[16]**
- $20 000 - €20 733 - £12 000 - FF136 000
  Le tavole della Legge Metal (H215cm H84in) Prato 1999

MATTINEN Seppo 1930 **[43]**
- $1 432 - €1 211 - £855 - FF7 943
  Spillemand Oil/canvas (85x100cm 33x39in) Köbenhavn 1998
- $380 - €350 - £234 - FF2 296
  Lille mand der kigger på malerier Oil/masonite (30x20cm 11x7in) Köbenhavn 1999

MATTIOLI Carlo 1911-1994 **[115]**
- $24 000 - €24 880 - £14 400 - FF163 200
  Paesaggio Olio/tela (136x105cm 53x41in) Prato 2000
- $21 500 - €22 288 - £12 900 - FF146 200
  Spiaggia d'estate Olio/tela (100x70cm 39x27in) Milano 1999
- $4 250 - €4 406 - £2 550 - FF28 900
  La spiaggia estiva Tecnica mista/cartone (46x32cm 18x12in) Vercelli 2000
- $3 900 - €3 369 - £1 950 - FF22 100
  Nudo Matita/carta (44x29cm 17x11in) Prato 1999
- $300 - €311 - £180 - FF2 040
  Albero Multiplo (68x99cm 26x38in) Prato 2000

MATTIS-TEUTSCH Hans Janos 1884-1960 **[23]**
- $7 000 - €7 744 - £4 600 - FF50 800
  Composition with five Figures Oil/canvas (81x71cm 31x27in) Budapest 2000
- $28 000 - €30 978 - £18 400 - FF203 200
  Sense Oil/cardboard (29x36cm 11x14in) Budapest 2000
- $15 750 - €17 425 - £10 350 - FF114 300
  Motherhood Sculpture, wood (21x16x4.5cm 8x6x1in) Budapest 2000
- $2 450 - €2 711 - £1 610 - FF17 780
  Draft of fresco Mixed media/paper (71x51cm 27x20in) Budapest 2000
- $354 - €383 - £242 - FF2 515
  Figur Linocut (23.5x15cm 9x5in) Stuttgart 2001

MATTO Francisco 1911-1995 **[50]**
- $4 392 - €5 120 - £3 041 - FF33 583
  Sin título Oleo/cartón (50x41cm 19x16in) Caracas ($) 2000
- $8 102 - €7 720 - £5 064 - FF50 640
  Bautismo Oleo/cartón (45x35cm 17x13in) Caracas 1999
- $2 532 - €2 413 - £1 582 - FF15 825
  Constructivo Gouache (43x49cm 16x19in) Caracas 1999

MATTON Arsène 1873-1953 **[18]**
- $25 812 - €28 660 - £17 991 - FF188 000
  Les porteurs d'ivoire Bronze (H102cm H40in) Paris 2001
- $3 897 - €3 532 - £2 400 - FF23 171
  Native African Fisherman Bronze (H52cm H20in) London 1999

MATULKA Jan 1890-1972 **[106]**
- $13 000 - €14 785 - £9 015 - FF96 982
  Old Boat and Houses Oil/canvas (45x55cm 18x22in) Chicago IL 2000
- $1 800 - €1 862 - £1 137 - FF12 211
  Tree Study Watercolour (45.5x30cm 17x11in) New-York 2000
- $850 - €966 - £582 - FF6 334
  Woman Washing/Evening Cassis Lithograph (25.5x32.5cm 10x12in) New-York 2000

MATUSHEVSKI Yuri 1930-1999 **[41]**
- $802 - €913 - £550 - FF5 987
  Huts by the River Oil/board (28x77.5cm 11x30in) London 2000

MATUSZCZAK Edward 1906-1965 **[8]**
- $2 508 - €2 492 - £1 562 - FF16 345
  Le marché Oil/board (29.5x23.5cm 11x9in) Warszawa 2000

MAUBERT James 1666-1746 **[6]**
- $51 952 - €44 203 - £31 000 - FF289 955
  Portrait of Elizabeth (1714-1788) and Catherine (c.1716-178) Sancroft Oil/canvas (122x145cm 48x57in) London 1998

MAUCH Richard 1874-1921 **[11]**
- $846 - €725 - £500 - FF4 757
  Landscape of River Valley with Traditional Dressed Young Boy and Girl Oil/canvas (100x110cm 39x43in) Leamington-Spa, Warwickshire 1998

MAUDER Josef 1884-1969 **[32]**
- $2 015 - €2 301 - £1 420 - FF15 092
  Ansicht von München Öl/Karton (23.5x33.5cm 9x13in) Stuttgart 2001

MAUFRA Maxime 1861-1918 **[448]**
- $18 000 - €16 007 - **£11 008** - FF104 999
  L'anse Cap Suzon Oil/canvas (58.5x73cm 23x28in)
  New-York 1999
- $2 844 - €3 049 - **£1 882** - FF20 000
  La vallée du Vénéon Huile/toile (24.5x33cm 9x12in)
  Douarnenez 2000
- $2 335 - €2 287 - **£1 437** - FF15 000
  La calanque Aquarelle/papier (25x18cm 9x7in)
  Soissons 1999
- $375 - €432 - **£258** - FF2 835
  Village Color lithograph (38x30cm 15x12in) Cleveland
  OH 1999

MAUGENDRE Adolphe 1809-1895 **[16]**
- $248 - €229 - **£151** - FF1 500
  Creully/Maisons/Argoues/Longues Lithographie
  couleurs (18x25cm 7x9in) Bayeux 1998

MAULBERTSCH Frans Anton 1724-1796 **[15]**
- $2 280 - €1 970 - **£1 461** - FF12 920
  Annunciazione Inchiostro (24x15.5cm 9x6in) Milano
  1999
- $3 222 - €3 579 - **£2 241** - FF23 477
  **Jesus reicht den Gläubigen das Abendmahl,
  rechts der heilige Petrus** Radierung (42x32cm
  16x12in) Heidelberg 2001

MAUNY Jacques 1893-1962 **[3]**
- $679 - €788 - **£468** - FF5 169
  Amica America de Giraudoux Jean Gravure
  (28.5x19.5cm 11x7in) Genève 2000

MAURA Y MONTANER Bartolome 1842-1926 **[15]**
- $161 - €156 - **£101** - FF1 024
  La Familia de Carlos IV de Goya Grabado
  (60x67cm 23x26in) Madrid 1999

MAURER Albert 1878 **[2]**
- $5 142 - €4 726 - **£3 158** - FF31 000
  Visage de femme Crayons couleurs (28x19cm
  11x7in) Paris 1999

MAURER Alfred Henry 1868-1932 **[68]**
- $55 000 - €54 606 - **£34 375** - FF358 193
  Lady with Muff Oil/canvas (91.5x73.5cm 36x28in)
  New-York 1999
- $18 000 - €17 130 - **£11 259** - FF112 363
  Woman in a Green Dress with White Collar
  Tempera/board (45.5x33cm 17x12in) New-York 1999
- $4 316 - €5 031 - **£3 026** - FF33 400
  Étude de femme assise Pastel/papier (62x48cm
  24x18in) Paris 2000

MAURER Hubert 1738-1818 **[6]**
- $5 556 - €6 485 - **£3 806** - FF42 541
  Portrait de Zofia Potocka Huile/toile (72.5x55.5cm
  28x21in) Warszawa 2000

MAURER Jacob 1826-1887 **[10]**
- $2 528 - €2 454 - **£1 561** - FF16 098
  Abendstimmung im Taunus Öl/Leinwand
  (53.5x42cm 21x16in) Frankfurt 1999

MAURER John XVIII **[2]**
- $505 - €528 - **£320** - FF3 462
  **Perspective View of Temple Barr and St.
  Dunstans Church** Etching (18.5x28cm 7x11in)
  London 2000

MAURER Louis 1832-1932 **[26]**
- $1 700 - €2 055 - **£1 186** - FF13 478
  Four-in-hand Lithograph (55x81cm 22x32in) Bolton
  MA 2000

MAURER Sascha 1897-1961 **[31]**
- $1 700 - €1 852 - **£1 177** - FF12 151
  «Smuggler's Notch Attic and Barn» Poster
  (93x60cm 37x24in) New-York 2001

MAURI Emilio 1855-1908 **[2]**
- $7 040 - €7 110 - **£4 840** - FF46 640
  Figura Oleo/lienzo (113x94cm 44x37in) Caracas 1999

MAURICE Charles XIX-XX **[3]**
- $974 - €1 039 - **£650** - FF6 814
  Hawk Attacking a Heron Etching (43x54.5cm
  16x21in) London 2000

MAURIÉ Gaston 1873-1912 **[5]**
- $2 522 - €3 049 - **£1 762** - FF20 000
  Élégantes aux courses Aquarelle, gouache/papier
  (28.5x14cm 11x5in) Granville 2000
- $1 100 - €1 227 - **£720** - FF8 050
  **«Autosoap Chambat , hygiène, propreté, sou-
  plesse de la peau...»** Poster (90x146.5cm 35x57in)
  New-York 2000

MAURIK van Justus 1807-1890 **[2]**
- $1 724 - €1 906 - **£1 196** - FF12 501
  Children feeding Chicken on a Village Square
  Oil/panel (41.5x32.5cm 16x12in) Amsterdam 2001

MAURIN Charles 1856-1914 **[125]**
- $3 618 - €3 125 - **£2 185** - FF20 500
  La Communiante Huile/toile (81x45cm 31x17in)
  Paris 1998
- $423 - €366 - **£255** - FF2 400
  Maison blanche et arbres Huile/carton (21x30cm
  8x11in) Paris 1998
- $3 290 - €3 049 - **£2 046** - FF20 000
  Jeune fille faisant sa toilette Pastel/papier
  (44x28cm 17x11in) Versailles 1999
- $239 - €229 - **£145** - FF1 500
  La République Eau-forte (79.5x49cm 31x19in)
  Troyes 1999

MAURIN Nicolas Eustache 1799-1850 **[7]**
- $177 - €180 - **£111** - FF1 182
  Tancredo vencedor de antioquia Grabado
  (29x40cm 11x15in) Barcelona 2000

MAURUS Edmond XX **[23]**
- $467 - €534 - **£325** - FF3 500
  «Air France AEF AOF» Affiche (62x100cm 24x39in)
  Paris 2001

MAURUS Hans 1901-1942 **[121]**
- $1 147 - €1 278 - **£801** - FF8 384
  Das Matterhorn mit den Winkelmatten vorn
  Öl/Leinwand (61x81cm 24x31in) München 2001

MAURY François 1861-1933 **[54]**
- $13 524 - €13 050 - **£8 491** - FF85 600
  La belle Odalisque Huile/toile (130x153cm 51x60in)
  Lons-Le-Saunier 2000
- $1 804 - €1 524 - **£1 073** - FF10 000
  Écrivain public à Istanbul Huile/toile (21x27cm
  8x10in) Paris 1998

MAURY Georges Sauveur 1872-? **[22]**
- $4 402 - €4 726 - **£2 945** - FF31 000
  Rue Souika, Rabat Huile/toile (60x44cm 23x17in)
  Paris 2000

MAUVE Anton 1838-1888 **[191]**
- $13 476 - €12 706 - **£8 352** - FF83 344
  Sheep on a Moor Oil/panel (39.5x61cm 15x24in)
  Amsterdam 1999
- $1 720 - €2 045 - **£1 192** - FF13 415
  Jäger in verschneiter Marschlandschaft Oil/panel
  (21x26cm 8x10in) Bremen 2000

M

$1 498 - €1 724 - **£1 034** - FF11 311
Schaapskude (Flock of Sheep) Charcoal/paper
(29x42cm 11x16in) Maastricht 2000

MAUVE Anton Rudolf 1876-1962 **[49]**
$1 245 - €1 380 - **£862** - FF9 055
**«Bewaldete holländische Landschaft mit
Person»** Öl/Leinwand (40x62.5cm 15x24in) Kempten
2001

$1 047 - €1 180 - **£722** - FF7 739
A Picnic in the Park Oil/board (23x32cm 9x12in)
Amsterdam 2000

MAUZAISSE Jean-Baptiste 1784-1844 **[9]**
$4 871 - €5 793 - **£3 355** - FF38 000
**Le duc d'Orléans dans le costume porté au
sacre de Charle X** Fusain (35x23cm 13x9in) Paris
2000

MAUZAN Achille L. 1883-1952 **[152]**
$2 000 - €2 231 - **£1 309** - FF14 636
«Tonsa» Poster (129x92.5cm 50x36in) New-York
2000

MAVIGNIER Almir de Silva 1925 **[34]**
$11 707 - €13 294 - **£8 013** - FF87 201
Abstrakte Komposition Öl/Leinwand
(100.5x50.5cm 39x19in) Berlin 2000

$7 709 - €7 414 - **£4 757** - FF48 631
Konvex hälfte Öl/Leinwand (30.5x30.5cm 12x12in)
Köln 1999

$141 - €143 - **£86** - FF939
Serielle Reihungen Farbserigraphie (90x35cm
35x13in) Stuttgart 2000

MAVROGORDATO Alexander James XIX-XX **[26]**
$433 - €511 - **£300** - FF3 351
Old Gateway, Perugia Watercolour/paper (54x37cm
21x14in) Devon 2000

MAX Corneille 1875-1924 **[10]**
$4 433 - €3 838 - **£2 673** - FF25 176
Dame mit Hund im Boot Öl/Leinwand (95x100cm
37x39in) München 1998

MAX Peter 1937 **[127]**
$7 000 - €7 452 - **£4 768** - FF48 881
Statue of Liberty Oil/panel (183x91cm 72x35in)
Miami FL 2001

$4 250 - €4 833 - **£2 969** - FF31 705
Elton John Mixed media (81x71cm 32x28in) Chicago
IL 2000

$3 400 - €3 426 - **£2 119** - FF22 474
The Lady in colors Oil/canvas (40x30cm 16x12in)
Chicago IL 2000

$500 - €504 - **£311** - FF3 305
The Lady Watercolour/paper (15x23cm 6x9in)
Chicago IL 2000

$375 - €405 - **£259** - FF2 656
Somewhere in Space Screenprint (52.5x72cm
20x28in) Bethesda MD 2001

MAX von Gabriel 1840-1915 **[96]**
$3 416 - €3 579 - **£2 259** - FF23 477
**Bildnis eines jungen Mädchens mit rotem
Haarband** Öl/Leinwand (48x39cm 18x15in) München
2000

$2 726 - €2 352 - **£1 622** - FF15 426
Durch Nacht zum Licht Öl/Leinwand (28x36cm
11x14in) München 1998

$567 - €562 - **£355** - FF3 689
Paar im Wald Aquarell/Papier (12.5x17cm 4x6in)
München 1999

MAX-EHRLER Louise 1850-? **[5]**
$3 326 - €3 123 - **£2 061** - FF20 486
Ein böser Verdacht Öl/Leinwand (96x64cm 37x25in)
Luzern 1999

MAXENCE Edgard 1871-1954 **[135]**
$4 000 - €3 741 - **£2 418** - FF24 542
Vase of Queen Anne's lace and Poppies
Oil/panel (65x45.5cm 25x17in) New-York 1999

$1 755 - €1 884 - **£1 193** - FF12 357
Bouquet de coquelicots Huile/panneau (33x23cm
12x9in) Bruxelles 2001

$579 - €640 - **£401** - FF4 200
«Le livre de chevalerie» Fusain/papier (44x25cm
17x9in) Paris 2001

MAXFIELD Douglas E. XX **[17]**
$540 - €607 - **£350** - FF3 983
«Flower's» Poster (51x33cm 20x12in) London 2000

MAXIM Ora Inge 1895-1982 **[5]**
$300 - €288 - **£183** - FF1 890
Hollyhock Lane Print (10x13cm 4x5in) Provincetown
MA 1999

MAXIMOV Vasily Maximovich 1844-1911 **[3]**
$1 968 - €2 076 - **£1 300** - FF13 617
Portrait of a Maiden in a White Shawl Oil/canvas
(50x42cm 19x16in) London 2000

MAXWELL Donald 1877-1936 **[14]**
$5 712 - €5 937 - **£3 600** - FF38 946
The Empires Loom Oil/canvas (127x101cm 50x39in)
Leyburn, North Yorkshire 2000

$478 - €457 - **£300** - FF3 001
«The Uplands of Dorset, Southern Railway»
Poster (100x127cm 39x50in) London 1999

MAXWELL Jack XX **[5]**
$1 046 - €1 123 - **£700** - FF7 369
«Le Golf de Chiberta est ouvert» Poster
(120x80cm 47x31in) London 2000

MAXWELL John 1905-1962 **[15]**
$7 933 - €9 324 - **£5 500** - FF61 164
Seeds and Cones Oil/panel (60x49.5cm 23x19in)
Edinburgh 2000

$1 647 - €1 566 - **£1 000** - FF10 275
Policeman arresting the Hens Ink (31x24cm
12x9in) Edinburgh 1999

MAXWELL John A. XX **[4]**
$6 588 - €6 266 - **£4 000** - FF41 102
White Vase with Flowers Watercolour (54x38cm
21x14in) Edinburgh 1999

MAXWELL-LYTE Farnham 1828-1906 **[6]**
$5 000 - €5 756 - **£3 412** - FF37 760
A Chateau in Pau Albumen print (26x35cm 10x13in)
New-York 2000

MAY Arthur Dampier act.1873-1914 **[7]**
$637 - €544 - **£380** - FF3 568
Carriage and Pair Leaving the Residence
Oil/canvas (22.5x12cm 8x4in) London 1998

MAY Heinz 1878-1954 **[16]**
$681 - €716 - **£429** - FF4 695
Fruchtschale, abstrakt Aquarell (50.3x72.5cm
19x28in) Heidelberg 2000

MAY Henrietta Mabel 1884-1971 **[22]**
$7 000 - €7 099 - **£4 347** - FF46 566
Knitting Oil/canvas (91x102cm 36x40in) New-York
2000

MAY Nicholas 1962 [3]
🖋 **$21 652** - €23 426 - **£15 000** - FF153 667
Untitled Oil/canvas (276.5x244cm 108x96in) London 2001

MAY Philip W., Phil May 1864-1903 [70]
🖋 **$298** - €321 - **£200** - FF2 104
Head of a contorted man Pencil/paper (17x13cm 6x5in) London 2000

MAY Walter William 1831-1896 [37]
🖋 **$495** - €466 - **£300** - FF3 056
Shipping Barge at the Harbour's Entrance Watercolour/paper (25x18cm 9x7in) London 1999

MAYALL John Jabez Edwin 1810-1901 [17]
📷 **$1 709** - €1 875 - **£1 100** - FF12 302
Portrait of David Livingstone Albumen print (25x19cm 10x7in) London 2000

MAYAN Théophile 1860-c.1937 [11]
🖋 **$1 748** - €1 524 - **£1 057** - FF10 000
Au printemps Pastel/papier (45x52cm 17x20in) Paris 1998

MAYBERY Edgard James 1887-? [26]
🖋 **$128** - €156 - **£90** - FF1 022
Heathland Landscapes with Birch Trees Watercolour/paper (18x39cm 7x15in) Cirencester, Gloucestershire 2000

MAYBURGER Joseph 1813-1908 [20]
🖋 **$10 522** - €12 514 - **£7 500** - FF82 089
Drover on Horseback with his Cattle in a Mountainous Landscape Oil/canvas (89.5x143cm 35x56in) London 2000
🖋 **$5 525** - €4 723 - **£3 315** - FF30 979
Partie am Königssee Öl/Leinwand (68x117cm 26x46in) Wien 1998

MAYDELL von Ernst, Baron 1888-? [10]
🖋 **$2 600** - €2 222 - **£1 527** - FF14 574
Lizard and Moth Watercolour (16x18.5cm 6x7in) Boston MA 1998

MAYER & PIERSON Ernest & Louis 1817/22-c.1865/1913 [15]
📷 **$2 912** - €3 049 - **£1 830** - FF20 000
Costumes de bal Tirage papier salé (29x22cm 11x8in) Paris 2000

MAYER Albrecht 1875-1952 [6]
📜 **$1 200** - €1 053 - **£728** - FF6 904
Basler Elektrizitats Poster (99x69cm 39x27in) New-York 1999

MAYER Auguste 1805-1890 [31]
🖋 **$23 883** - €23 125 - **£15 000** - FF151 687
View of Constantinople from Tophane looking towards the Sea of Marmara Oil/canvas (39.5x58.5cm 15x23in) London 1999
🖋 **$641** - €762 - **£441** - FF5 000
Quatre hussards de différents grades, du 4e Régiment Aquarelle/papier (23.5x31cm 9x12in) Paris 2000

MAYER Casper 1871-1931 [1]
🖎 **$3 500** - €3 975 - **£2 395** - FF26 072
Making a Searpoint Bronze (H30.5cm H12in) New-York 2000

MAYER Erich 1876-1960 [138]
🖋 **$1 208** - €1 347 - **£787** - FF8 838
Die Vaal Rivier by Parys Oil/canvas (37x57.5cm 14x22in) Johannesburg 2000
🖋 **$461** - €544 - **£319** - FF3 566
Early View of Gordon's Bay Oil/board (13x18cm 5x7in) Cape Town 2000

🖋 **$143** - €160 - **£93** - FF1 051
Farmhouse among Trees Watercolour/paper (13x17cm 5x6in) Johannesburg 2000

MAYER Friedrich 1825-1875 [4]
🖋 **$3 441** - €3 835 - **£2 405** - FF25 154
Sommerlandschaft bei aufziehendem Gewitter Oil/panel (79x120cm 31x47in) München 2001

MAYER Henry, Hy 1858-1953 [3]
📜 **$1 285** - €1 349 - **£850** - FF8 852
Scribner's Color lithograph (46x36cm 18x14in) London 2000

MAYER LA MARTINIERE Constance Marie 1775-1821 [9]
🖋 **$4 968** - €5 488 - **£3 445** - FF36 000
Portrait d'ange Lucie Scholastique Anceaume (1771-1846) Huile/toile (74x60cm 29x23in) Paris 2001
🖋 **$1 990** - €1 829 - **£1 222** - FF12 000
Portrait de femme assise Pierre noire (47x37cm 18x14in) Paris 1999

MAYER Lou XX [3]
📜 **$750** - €698 - **£463** - FF4 577
«Jewish War Sufferers» Poster (76x53cm 30x21in) New-York 1999

MAYER Ludwig 1834-1917 [3]
🖋 **$18 986** - €18 317 - **£12 000** - FF120 150
Roman Beauty Oil/canvas (143x104cm 56x40in) London 2000

MAYER Luigi c.1750-1803 [33]
🖋 **$21 749** - €21 633 - **£13 500** - FF141 901
Ancien Building believed to be Troflo in Val di Noto, Villesmondo Oil/canvas (45x65cm 17x25in) London 1999
🖋 **$912** - €1 085 - **£650** - FF7 114
Gothic Tomb in Erwaton Church, Suffolk Watercolour (41x28.5cm 16x11in) London 2000
📜 **$5 000** - €4 629 - **£3 102** - FF30 366
Views in Egypt, Palestine, and other Parts of the Ottoman Empire Aquatint (46.5x33cm 18x12in) New-York 1999

MAYER Martin 1931 [12]
🖎 **$2 063** - €2 045 - **£1 290** - FF13 415
Schlafende Bronze (20x63cm 7x24in) München 1999

MAYER Nicolas 1852-1929 [8]
🖎 **$11 000** - €10 893 - **£6 848** - FF71 453
Le duel Bronze (H58.5cm H23in) New-York 1999

MAYER Peter Bela 1888-1954 [22]
🖋 **$3 000** - €2 841 - **£1 824** - FF18 636
Lake Dunmore, Vermont Oil/canvas/board (61x51cm 24x20in) New-York 1999

MAYER Ralph 1895-? [6]
🖋 **$7 000** - €7 092 - **£4 393** - FF46 519
The Firehouse Oil/canvas (66x83cm 26x33in) Cincinnati OH 2000

MAYER-MARTON Georg 1897-1960 [9]
🖋 **$6 478** - €7 631 - **£4 557** - FF50 053
«Forest Walkers» Öl/Leinwand (76.9x102cm 30x40in) Wien 2000
🖋 **$2 880** - €3 270 - **£2 020** - FF21 451
Klabund-Kreidekreis Aquarell/Papier (50.5x35.5cm 19x13in) Wien 2001

MAYES William Edward 1861-1952 [68]
🖋 **$241** - €244 - **£150** - FF1 602
Norfolk River Landscape with Sheep in Foreground Watercolour/paper (15x30cm 6x12in) Aylsham, Norfolk 2000

MAYMURA Narritjin 1922-1982 [16]
- $972 - €1 043 - **£650** - FF6 844
  Langgalili Story Mixed media (85x50.5cm 33x19in)
  Melbourne 2000

MAYNARD George Willoughby 1843-1923 [6]
- **$6 000** - €6 761 - **£4 155** - FF44 352
  «The Alarm» Oil/canvas (71x127cm 28x50in) Hatfield
  PA 2000
- $1 300 - €1 477 - **£890** - FF9 686
  The Bowl of Porridge Watercolour/paper (22x17cm
  8x6in) New-York 2000

MAYNARD Richard Field 1875-? [5]
- $1 800 - €1 721 - **£1 096** - FF11 290
  Frolicking Mermaids Pastel/paper (60x44.5cm
  23x17in) Boston MA 1999

MAYNÉ Jean 1850-1905 [15]
- $624 - €744 - **£447** - FF4 878
  Herberginterieur Oil/canvas (54.5x67cm 21x26in)
  Lokeren 2000

MAYNE Roger 1929 [18]
- $1 205 - €990 - **£700** - FF6 493
  Clarendon Cres Gelatin silver print (18x13cm 7x5in)
  London 1998

MAYNO Juan Bautista 1569-1649 [2]
- **$232 755** - €227 978 - **£150 000** - FF1 495 440
  The Penitent Magdalen in the Desert Oil/canvas
  (117.5x89cm 46x35in) London 1999

MAYO Antoine Malliakaris 1905-1990 [24]
- $796 - €762 - **£490** - FF5 000
  Sous-bois Huile/toile (45x55cm 17x21in) Calais 1999
- $775 - €762 - **£498** - FF5 000
  Silence Gouache/papier (14x22.5cm 5x8in) Paris 1999

MAYO Eileen Rosemary 1906 [8]
- $300 - €290 - **£190** - FF1 904
  Prowling Cat Linocut (11.5x16cm 4x6in) Ipswich
  1999

MAYODON Jean 1893-1967 [49]
- $5 827 - €5 336 - **£3 552** - FF35 000
  Sirène et triton Grès (H55cm H21in) Paris 1999

MAYOR Hannah 1871-1947 [1]
- $1 293 - €1 509 - **£900** - FF9 896
  Still Life of Flowers Watercolour/paper (23.5x26.5cm
  9x10in) West-Yorshire 2000

MAYOR Igor 1946-1991 [6]
- $533 - €613 - **£376** - FF4 024
  Weibliche akte Aquarell/Papier (36.3x24.5cm 14x9in)
  Hamburg 2001

MAYOR William Frederick 1868-1916 [7]
- $8 921 - €8 600 - **£5 500** - FF56 414
  Cassis Oil/canvas (81x112cm 31x44in) London 1999

MAYR-GRAETZ Karl 1850-1929 [19]
- $4 650 - €4 991 - **£3 111** - FF32 742
  Märchenstunde: Telling a story Oil/panel
  (40x54cm 15x21in) Amsterdam 2000
- $544 - €613 - **£383** - FF4 024
  Lesender Kavalier im Studuerzimmer Oil/panel
  (15.5x11cm 6x4in) München 2001

MAYRHOFER Johann Nepomuk 1764-1832 [6]
- **$26 000** - €23 017 - **£15 896** - FF150 979
  Still Life with Fruit, Flowers and Butterflies
  Oil/canvas (64x50cm 25x19in) New-York 1999
- $31 774 - €37 039 - **£22 000** - FF242 957
  **Grapes, Peaches and a Nasturtium, with a
  Month on a Ledge** Oil/panel (29x23cm 11x9in)
  London 2000

MAYRSHOFER Max 1875-1950 [248]
- $813 - €716 - **£495** - FF4 695
  Halbporträt eines Herren im Profil Öl/Karton
  (59.5x49.5cm 23x19in) Stuttgart 1999
- $554 - €562 - **£344** - FF3 689
  Zwei Frauenakte in Landschaft Oil/panel
  (21x27cm 8x10in) München 2000
- $157 - €164 - **£100** - FF1 073
  Vier Akte unter Bäumen Charcoal/paper (30x40cm
  11x15in) Zwiesel 2000

MAYS Douglas Lionel 1900-1991 [6]
- $1 129 - €1 309 - **£800** - FF8 588
  **«Teignmouth is Devon, British
  Railways,Western Region,Travel by Train»** Poster
  (102x64cm 40x25in) London 2000

MAYS Maxwell 1918 [2]
- $1 200 - €1 165 - **£741** - FF7 642
  New England Village in Winter Watercolour
  (48x63cm 19x25in) Portsmouth NH 1999

MAYWALD Willy 1907-1985 [105]
- $593 - €665 - **£412** - FF4 360
  Kurt Seligmann, «Feu Follet» Vintage gelatin silver
  print (23x17.5cm 9x6in) Köln 2001

MAZARD Alphonse 1865-1939 [42]
- $863 - €838 - **£533** - FF5 500
  Le marais en hiver Huile/toile (38x55cm 14x21in)
  Melun 1999
- $203 - €229 - **£139** - FF1 500
  Le peintre Gustave Guignery à son chevalet
  Huile/carton (27x35cm 10x13in) Barbizon 2000

MAZE Paul 1887-1979 [569]
- $3 669 - €3 919 - **£2 500** - FF25 706
  Albert Bridge Oil/canvas (38x56cm 14x22in) London
  2001
- $1 623 - €1 602 - **£1 000** - FF10 507
  Wooded Lane Oil/canvas (35x27.5cm 13x10in)
  London 1999
- $1 445 - €1 683 - **£1 000** - FF11 043
  Still Life with Tulips Pastel/paper (26.5x30cm
  10x11in) London 2000

MAZELL Peter XVIII-XIX [5]
- $1 946 - €1 735 - **£1 200** - FF11 380
  **Golden Eagle/Magpie/Black Cock/Male
  Grouse/Osprey/Cock of the Wood** Engraving
  (38x55cm 14x21in) London 1999

MAZEROLLE Alexis Joseph 1826-1889 [13]
- $5 136 - €5 102 - **£3 200** - FF33 467
  Sketch for a Ceiling Decoration Oil/canvas
  (64.5x64.5cm 25x25in) London 1999
- $1 800 - €1 954 - **£1 246** - FF12 819
  Cupid stealing Arrows from sleeping Venus
  Oil/canvas (30x17cm 12x7in) Cleveland OH 2001

MAZIARSKA Jadwiga 1913 [3]
- $2 516 - €2 702 - **£1 684** - FF17 721
  Composition Huile/toile (80x125cm 31x49in)
  Kraków 2000

MAZONE Giovanni 1433-? [1]
- **$30 000** - €28 637 - **£18 744** - FF187 848
  Blessed Augustinian Monk Tempera/panel
  (30x20cm 11x7in) New-York 1999

MAZUMDAR Hemendranath 1894-1948 [20]
- **$36 385** - €34 034 - **£22 000** - FF223 247
  Lady in Blue and Gold Sari Oil/board (122x66cm
  48x25in) London 1999
- $4 482 - €4 812 - **£3 000** - FF31 564
  Portrait of a Young Woman Oil/canvas (33x25.5cm
  12x10in) London 2000

$4 034 - €4 331 - **£2 700** - FF28 408
Pujarini Coloured pencils/paper (26x20cm 10x7in)
London 2000

MAZUMDAR Kshistindranath 1891-1975 [9]
$14 885 - €13 923 - **£9 000** - FF91 328
Chaitanya Watercolour (35.5x25cm 13x9in) London
1999

MAZUR Michael 1935 [26]
$1 200 - €1 063 - **£736** - FF6 975
Palette Monotype (90.5x121.5cm 35x47in) New-York
1999

MAZZA Aldo 1880-1964 [13]
$1 100 - €1 227 - **£720** - FF8 050
«Fiera de Milano» Poster (139x99cm 54x38in) New-
York 2000

MAZZA Giuseppe 1817-1884 [3]
$20 825 - €21 588 - **£12 495** - FF141 610
Episodio delle cinque giornate di Milano
Olio/tela (74.5x59cm 29x23in) Milano 1999

MAZZACURATI Marino 1907-1969 [12]
$3 000 - €3 110 - **£1 800** - FF20 400
Lotta Bronzo (63x26cm 24x10in) Milano 1999

MAZZANOVICH Lawrence 1872-1946 [23]
$5 000 - €5 603 - **£3 485** - FF36 754
Billowing Clouds Oil/canvas (76x76cm 29x29in)
Beverly-Hills CA 2001
$3 200 - €2 700 - **£1 877** - FF17 708
Autumn Day Oil/panel (30x40cm 12x16in) Mystic CT
1998

MAZZANTI Ludovico 1686-1775 [3]
$10 000 - €12 958 - **£7 500** - FF85 000
**San Domenico distribuisce il rosario con Santa
Caterina da Siena** Olio/tela (255x158cm 100x62in)
Milano 2000

MAZZELLA J. XIX [7]
$6 454 - €6 708 - **£4 048** - FF44 000
**Port à marée basse/Bord de mer par gros
temps** Huile/toile (35x65cm 13x25in) Paris 2000

MAZZETTI Emo 1870-1955 [17]
$1 666 - €1 727 - **£999** - FF11 328
Paesaggio lacustre Olio/tavola (40x53cm 15x20in)
Milano 1999
$600 - €622 - **£360** - FF4 080
Frassene d'Acosto Olio/tavoletta (28x41cm
11x16in) Firenze 2001

MAZZOLA BEDOLI Girolamo c.1500-1569 [8]
$21 000 - €18 256 - **£12 709** - FF119 754
**Half-Length Study of a Putto and a Study of the
Head of Another Putto** Red chalk/paper (9x11cm
3x4in) New-York 1999
$11 000 - €12 352 - **£7 132** - FF81 026
Madonna and Child Etching (9x5.5cm 3x2in) New-
York 2000

MAZZOLA DI VALDUGGIA Giuseppe 1748-1838 [7]
$10 802 - €11 248 - **£6 844** - FF73 785
**Amoretto auf der Jagd (Amor auf der
Hasenjagd)** Öl/Leinwand (105x88cm 41x34in)
München 2001
$1 900 - €1 970 - **£1 140** - FF12 920
L'Abbazia di Chiaravalle Acquarello/carta (21x29cm
8x11in) Venezia 2000

MAZZOLARI Ugo 1873-1946 [3]
$2 480 - €3 214 - **£1 860** - FF21 080
Contadina con gerla Olio/legno (50x32cm 19x12in)
Roma 2001

MAZZOLINI Giuseppe 1806-1876 [29]
$2 000 - €2 275 - **£1 410** - FF14 920
Madonna and Child Oil/canvas (100x74cm 39x29in)
Philadelphia PA 2001

MAZZOLINO Ludovico c.1480-c.1528 [5]
$70 000 - €74 878 - **£47 726** - FF491 169
**The Madonna and Saint Joseph Adoring the
Infant Christ** Oil/panel (32.5x27cm 12x10in) New-
York 2001

MAZZON Galliano 1896-1978 [9]
$440 - €570 - **£330** - FF3 740
«Fantasia n.96» Olio/tela (92x65.5cm 36x25in)
Milano 2001

MAZZONI Franco 1930 [8]
$1 038 - €872 - **£610** - FF5 723
**Provenzalische Landschaft mit baumbestande-
nen Hügeln** Öl/Leinwand (65x79.5cm 25x31in) Bern
1998

MAZZONI Sebastiano c.1611-1678 [10]
$44 000 - €45 613 - **£26 400** - FF299 200
Venere che allatta Amore Olio/tela (80x96cm
31x37in) Milano 2001

MAZZOTTA Federico XIX [15]
$10 008 - €11 366 - **£7 000** - FF74 556
Ai piedi del vulcano (by the volcano) Oil/canvas
(68x97cm 26x38in) London 2001

MAZZUOLI Giuseppe 1727-1781 [2]
$3 000 - €3 110 - **£1 800** - FF20 400
Santo Pellegrino Terracotta (27x33cm 10x12in)
Firenze 2000

MAZZUOLI IL BASTAROLO Giuseppe c.1536-1589
[2]
$40 000 - €35 086 - **£24 288** - FF230 152
Seated Woman and her Young Son Oil/canvas
(90x73.5cm 35x28in) New-York 1999

MB XX [4]
$476 - €415 - **£288** - FF2 724
Look for the Nex Noddy Book Watercolour
(17x14.5cm 6x5in) London 1998

MBUNO Kivuthi 1947 [3]
$1 650 - €1 710 - **£990** - FF11 220
Caccia tribale Pastel gras (48x73.5cm 18x28in) Prato
2000

MEACCI Ricciardo 1856-1940 [35]
$2 335 - €2 508 - **£1 600** - FF16 453
Medieval Flower Procession Watercolour
(8.5x15cm 3x5in) London 2001

MEAD Larkin Goldsmith 1835-1910 [11]
$5 450 - €5 113 - **£3 367** - FF33 538
Venezia Marble (H60cm H24in) Cleveland OH 1999

MEAD Roderick Fletcher 1900-1971 [5]
$650 - €682 - **£434** - FF4 472
Out of the garden Woodcut (23.5x20.5cm 9x8in)
New-York 2001

MEADE Arthur 1863-c.1947 [15]
$1 608 - €1 776 - **£1 110** - FF11 650
**Cornish coastal Scene with Fishermen coming
to the Shore** Oil/canvas (60x45cm 23x17in) Hockley,
Birmingham 2001

MEADE Charles 1827-1858 [2]
$5 000 - €4 701 - **£3 096** - FF30 838
Portrait of L.J.M Daguerre Salt print (19x13cm
7x5in) New-York 1999

M

MEADMORE Clement 1929 **[22]**

$17 000 - €14 667 - **£10 256** - FF96 208
Fling Bronze (86.5x132x101.5cm 34x51x39in) New-York 1998

$4 130 - €4 550 - **£2 772** - FF29 848
Wall sculpture Bronze (44x85x17cm 17x33x6in) Malvern, Victoria 2000

MEADOWS Arthur Gordon 1868-? **[13]**

$4 217 - €4 050 - **£2 600** - FF26 568
On the Thames at Putney Oil/canvas (51x76.5cm 20x30in) London 1999

$2 422 - €2 496 - **£1 500** - FF16 371
St. Columba Canal/Looking to St. Marks Oil/canvas/board (14x22.5cm 5x8in) London 2000

MEADOWS Arthur Joseph 1843-1907 **[162]**

$10 427 - €10 507 - **£6 500** - FF68 923
The Gulf of Salerno, Amalfi Coast Oil/canvas (127x115.5cm 50x45in) London 2000

$6 638 - €5 736 - **£4 000** - FF37 624
«The First Boat in Morning» Oil/canvas (34.5x59.5cm 13x23in) Billingshurst, West-Sussex 1999

$6 249 - €5 919 - **£3 800** - FF38 825
Venice, the Pigeons of St Mark's Oil/panel (30.5x25.5cm 12x10in) London 1999

MEADOWS Bernard 1915 **[49]**

$1 333 - €1 431 - **£892** - FF9 390
Stürzender Vogel Bronze (38x37x27.7cm 14x14x10in) Hamburg 2000

$1 256 - €1 084 - **£750** - FF7 113
Two Drawings for a Sculpture Watercolour (26x21cm 10x8in) London 1998

MEADOWS Christopher XIX-XX **[6]**

$2 200 - €2 113 - **£1 363** - FF13 858
Sailing vessels along a Rocky Coast Watercolour/paper (24x34cm 9x13in) St. Louis MO 1999

MEADOWS Edwin Long act.1854-? **[45]**

$3 529 - €3 556 - **£2 200** - FF23 327
Cattle Watering in Epping Forest Oil/canvas (76x126.5cm 29x49in) London 2000

$717 - €805 - **£500** - FF5 278
Ploughing Scene, with a Hunt in the Distance Oil/canvas (31x46cm 12x18in) Leyburn, North Yorkshire 2001

MEADOWS James Edwin 1828-1888 **[97]**

$6 132 - €5 333 - **£3 696** - FF34 981
Rural Landscape with Farmers and Haywagon Oil/canvas (77.5x127cm 30x50in) Toronto 1998

MEADOWS James M., Snr. 1798-1864 **[8]**

$4 170 - €4 203 - **£2 600** - FF27 569
Herring Boats off Flamborough Head Oil/canvas (30x55cm 11x21in) London 2000

$2 701 - €2 587 - **£1 700** - FF16 971
Shipping off Flamborough Head/Untitled Oil/canvas (30x48cm 12x19in) Aylsham, Norfolk 1999

MEADOWS Robert Mitchell ?-1812 **[5]**

$210 - €224 - **£140** - FF1 470
Fluellen Makeing Pistol Eat the Leek, After Henry Bunbury Engraving (40x46cm 15x18in) Leyburn, North Yorkshire 2000

MEADOWS W.G. XIX **[15]**

$2 116 - €2 059 - **£1 300** - FF13 509
Plough Team Drinking from a Pond, Ducks, Pigs and Chickens Beyond Oil/canvas (76x127cm 29x50in) Newbury, Berkshire 1999

MEADOWS William Ed./ W. Jos. act.1870-1895 **[76]**

$3 797 - €3 663 - **£2 400** - FF24 030
Venetian Scenes Oil/canvas (35.5x56cm 13x22in) London 1999

$2 429 - €2 725 - **£1 700** - FF17 877
The Grand canal, Venice Oil/board (20.5x26cm 8x10in) London 2001

MEALL G. XVII **[1]**

$6 033 - €5 133 - **£3 600** - FF33 672
Portrait of a gentleman seated on a stone block holding a flute Oil/panel (40.5x32cm 15x12in) London 1998

MEARNS Fanny XIX **[16]**

$325 - €393 - **£227** - FF2 578
Picking Wild Flowers Watercolour (29.5x47cm 11x18in) Bethesda MD 2000

MEARS George act.1870-c.1900 **[24]**

$2 162 - €1 832 - **£1 300** - FF12 014
The Diamond Jubilee Fleet Review of 1897 Oil/canvas (30.5x61cm 12x24in) London 1998

MEASHAM Henry 1844-1922 **[15]**

$439 - €422 - **£280** - FF2 770
Cows Grazing with Cottages in the distance Watercolour/paper (27x39.5cm 10x15in) London 1999

MEATYARD Ralph Eugene 1925-1972 **[37]**

$6 000 - €5 009 - **£3 565** - FF32 859
Boy with Bones Gelatin silver print (17.5x19cm 6x7in) New-York 1998

MEAUZÉ Pierre 1913-1978 **[6]**

$4 211 - €4 084 - **£2 650** - FF26 789
Mother and Child Bronze (H62.5cm H24in) Amsterdam 1999

MECATTI Dario 1909-1976 **[12]**

$2 750 - €3 195 - **£1 932** - FF20 958
«Montmartre»/«Boulevard Hausman» Oil/panel (29x39cm 11x15in) New-York 2001

MECHANICUS Philip 1936 **[11]**

$496 - €590 - **£353** - FF3 869
Poppies Silver print (26.5x24cm 10x9in) Amsterdam 2000

MECHAU Jacob Wilhelm 1745-1808 **[34]**

$4 126 - €4 602 - **£2 774** - FF30 185
Flusslandschaft mit mythologischer Staffage Öl/Leinwand (70x102cm 27x40in) Köln 2000

$1 120 - €1 203 - **£750** - FF7 891
The Latomia dei Cappuccini at Acradina (Syracuse) Black chalk (41.5x33.5cm 16x13in) London 2000

$134 - €153 - **£93** - FF1 006
Arco della Toretta Radierung (38x28cm 14x11in) Berlin 2000

MECHEL von Christian / Chrétien 1737-1817 **[39]**

$198 - €230 - **£136** - FF1 507
Ansicht von Basel Radierung (35.5x45.5cm 13x17in) Zürich 2000

MECHELAERE Léon 1880-1964 **[21]**

$727 - €620 - **£435** - FF4 065
Béguinage à Bruges Huile/toile (50x50cm 19x19in) Brugge 1998

MECINA-KRZESZ Jozef 1860-1934 **[3]**

$4 066 - €4 779 - **£2 819** - FF31 346
Portrait d'une petite fille, orpheline Huile/toile (63x46cm 24x18in) Warszawa 2000

MECKEL VON HEMSBACH Adolf 1856-1893 [7]
🖐 **$6 230** – €7 267 - **£4 400** - FF47 670
Abendstimmung über Oase Öl/Leinwand
(94x132cm 37x51in) Salzburg 2000

MECKENEM van Israhel c.1445-1503/17 [41]
▥ **$4 277** - €4 090 - **£2 604** - FF26 831
Die heilige Barbara Kupferstich (16.1x10.7cm 6x4in)
Stuttgart 1999

MECKLENBURG Ludwig 1820-1882 [7]
🖐 **$5 508** - €6 586 - **£3 800** - FF43 200
**Venetian Waterfront Looking Towards the
Doge's Palace** Oil/canvas (50x69cm 19x27in)
Cambridge 2000
🖐 **$3 919** - €4 090 - **£2 490** - FF26 831
Stadt im Veneto bei Sonnenuntergang Oil/panel
(27.5x23cm 10x9in) München 2000

MECKSEPER Friedrich 1936 [309]
▥ **$381** - €434 - **£266** - FF2 850
Physik Etching, aquatint in colors (39.5x49.5cm
15x19in) Hamburg 2001

MÉCOU André Joseph c.1771-1837 [6]
▥ **$127** - €137 - **£85** - FF900
**Oh! Quelle douleur/Oh! Quel plaisir, d'après
Sicardi** Gravure (36x31cm 14x12in) Blois 2000

MEDARD Eugène 1847-1887 [5]
🖐 **$4 400** - €5 004 - **£3 051** - FF32 824
**French Troops preparing for Battle behind a
Stone Wall** Oil/canvas (68x99cm 27x39in) East-Dennis
MA 2000

MÉDARD Jules Ferdinand 1855-c.1925 [20]
🖐 **$9 000** - €7 774 - **£5 425** - FF50 991
Still Life with Roses and Daisies Oil/canvas
(46x61cm 18x24in) New-York 1998
🖐 **$3 160** - €3 049 - **£1 984** - FF20 000
Bouquet de roses et fleurettes Huile/carton
(40x32cm 15x12in) Senlis 1999

MEDEK Mikulas 1926-1974 [8]
🖐 **$31 790** - €30 068 - **£19 800** - FF197 230
Untitled Oil/canvas (140x95cm 55x37in) Praha 2001
🖐 **$23 120** - €21 867 - **£14 400** - FF143 440
Croisement des oiseaux Email (115.5x74.5cm
45x29in) Praha 2001

MEDINA Henrique 1901-1984 [9]
✏ **$1 806** - €2 094 - **£1 260** - FF13 734
Nú femenino Lápiz/papel (32.5x23.5cm 12x9in)
Lisboa 2001

MEDINA John Baptist 1655/60-1710 [7]
🖐 **$20 918** - €19 904 - **£13 000** - FF130 559
**Helen Hope, Countess of Haddington, seated, in
a dark yellow Dress** Oil/canvas (127x101.5cm
50x39in) London 1999

MEDINA SERRANO Antonio 1944 [25]
🖐 **$3 135** - €3 304 - **£2 090** - FF21 670
El pelele Oleo/tabla (40x70cm 15x27in) Madrid 2000
🖐 **$810** - €901 - **£555** - FF5 910
Carnaval Oleo/tabla (19x27cm 7x10in) Madrid 2000

MEDINA VERA Inocencio 1876-1918 [17]
🖐 **$6 300** - €5 406 - **£3 780** - FF35 460
Escena rural Oleo/lienzo (48x59cm 18x23in) Madrid
1999
✏ **$1 575** - €1 351 - **£945** - FF8 865
Mujer con manto Acuarela/papel (49x34cm 19x13in)
Madrid 1998

MEDINI Giulio XX [3]
🖐 **$3 491** - €4 116 - **£2 454** - FF27 000
Marrakech Porte El Monassin Huile/toile (59x80cm
23x31in) Aubagne 2000

MEDIZ Karl 1868-1944 [81]
🖐 **$3 070** - €2 863 - **£1 853** - FF18 781
**Portrait der Frau von Birkenreuth,
Spitzenbesetztes Seidenkleid** Öl/Leinwand
(160x181cm 62x71in) Lindau 1999
🖐 **$2 102** - €1 816 - **£1 267** - FF11 910
Bub mit Apfel Öl/Leinwand (62x50cm 24x19in) Wien
1998
✏ **$438** - €436 - **£265** - FF2 860
Die Tochter beim Betrachten grösserer Blätter
Pencil (39.3x29cm 15x11in) Wien 2000

MEDIZ-PELIKAN Emilie 1861-1908 [150]
🖐 **$9 390** - €10 901 - **£6 600** - FF71 505
«Trudi in Weiss» Öl/Leinwand (201x135cm 79x53in)
Wien 2001
🖐 **$2 031** - €2 180 - **£1 386** - FF14 301
«Felsenbogen bei Duino» Öl/Leinwand (89x122cm
35x48in) Wien 2001
✏ **$468** - €400 - **£280** - FF2 621
Störche im Wasser Ink (22x25.5cm 8x10in) Wien
1998
▥ **$421** - €363 - **£250** - FF2 380
Karl Mediz Lithographie (47x28cm 18x11in) Wien
1998

MEDLAND Thomas 1755-1822 [5]
▥ **$507** - €577 - **£350** - FF3 784
**East Front of Hertford Castle/West Front of
Hertford Castle** Aquatint (42x56cm 16x22in) London
2000

MEDLYCOTT Hubert James, Bt. 1841-1920 [40]
🖐 **$632** - €750 - **£460** - FF4 919
Bridge Scene on the Thames Watercolour/paper
(17.5x26cm 6x10in) Billingshurst, West-Sussex 2001

MEDNYANSZKY László 1852-1919 [54]
🖐 **$48 000** - €47 198 - **£30 000** - FF309 600
Landscape of Mountains Oil/canvas (115x200cm
45x78in) Budapest 1999
🖐 **$6 720** - €6 464 - **£4 160** - FF42 400
Tramp Oil/canvas (100x70cm 39x27in) Budapest 1999
🖐 **$2 805** - €3 188 - **£1 955** - FF20 910
Lumière du soir Huile/toile (34.5x42.5cm 13x16in)
Budapest 2001
🖐 **$1 815** - €2 063 - **£1 265** - FF13 530
La vallée d'Arva Technique mixte/papier (36x51.5cm
14x20in) Budapest 2001

MEDUNETSKY Konstantin 1899-1935 [2]
▥ **$4 000** - €4 486 - **£2 777** - FF29 427
«Theatre Kamerny de Moscou» Poster (71x45cm
28x18in) New-York 2001

MEDVECZKY Jenö 1902-1969 [4]
✏ **$18 150** - €20 626 - **£12 650** - FF135 300
Jeune femme portant des gants noirs
Pastel/papier (76.5x50cm 30x19in) Budapest 2001

MEE Anne, née Foldstone 1770/75-1851 [37]
🖐 **$1 223** - €1 371 - **£850** - FF8 990
**Maddalina and Henry Trant as Children, seated
on a red Sofa** Miniature (15x11cm 5x4in) London
2001

MEEGAN Harry Halsey XIX-XX [6]
🖐 **$561** - €530 - **£350** - FF3 476
The Gate of London (Tower Bridge)
Oil/canvas/board (22x30cm 9x12in) Fernhurst,
Haslemere, Surrey 1999

M

MEEGAN Walter 1859-1944 **[55]**
- **$1 135** - €1 177 - **£720** - FF7 720
  Bridlington Harbour by Moonlight Oil/canvas (51x66cm 20x25in) West-Yorshire 2000
- **$881** - €798 - **£549** - FF5 237
  Returning Home Oil/canvas (43x33cm 16x12in) London 1999

MEEGEREN van Hans 1899-1947 **[111]**
- **$27 426** - €27 227 - **£17 136** - FF178 596
  Christ and the Scribes in the Temple Oil/canvas (157x202cm 61x79in) Amsterdam 1999
- **$1 260** - €1 361 - **£862** - FF8 929
  Two Children Playing Oil/canvas (80x64cm 31x25in) Amsterdam 2001
- **$1 100** - €956 - **£665** - FF6 272
  Head of Christ Oil/canvas (31x23cm 12x9in) New-York 1999
- **$587** - €499 - **£354** - FF3 270
  Bijbelse voorstelling Pastel/paper (58x48cm 22x18in) Rotterdam 1998

MEEKER Joseph Rusling 1827-1887 **[50]**
- **$15 000** - €15 383 - **£9 376** - FF100 906
  Louisiana Bayou Landscape Oil/canvas (41x76cm 16x30in) New-Orleans LA 2000

MEENAN Anton XX **[4]**
- **$1 008** - €1 129 - **£700** - FF7 406
  Lighthouse, Tory island Oil/canvas/board (20x25.5cm 7x10in) London 2001

MEER van der Barend 1659-1690/1702 **[22]**
- **$13 650** - €15 245 - **£9 250** - FF100 000
  Nature morte au panier de fraises, plat de pêches et raisins Huile/toile (63.5x76.5cm 25x30in) Paris 2000

MEER van der Jan III 1656-1705 **[27]**
- **$14 426** - €12 239 - **£8 702** - FF80 284
  Arcadisch landschap met personen en vee Oil/canvas (112x131cm 44x51in) Rotterdam 1998
- **$5 575** - €6 647 - **£3 975** - FF43 600
  Südliche Landschaft mit Hirten und Vieh Öl/Leinwand (57x67cm 22x26in) Köln 2000

MEERE Charles 1898-1961 **[10]**
- **$7 652** - €7 372 - **£4 729** - FF48 358
  The Young Model Oil/board (55x31.5cm 21x12in) Sydney 1999
- **$3 420** - €3 992 - **£2 414** - FF26 189
  «Symphony in Green» Oil/canvas/board (25x30.5cm 9x12in) Malvern, Victoria 2000

MEERHOUT Jan ?-1677 **[10]**
- **$10 322** - €9 447 - **£6 292** - FF61 971
  Am Fluss Oil/panel (27x40cm 10x15in) Wien 1999

MEERKÄMPER Emil 1873-1948 **[3]**
- **$1 760** - €1 774 - **£1 100** - FF11 636
  «Weisshorn, Davos, Suizzera-Suisse-Suiza» Poster (100x66cm 39x25in) London 2000

MEERMANN Arnold 1829-1908 **[17]**
- **$2 400** - €2 681 - **£1 620** - FF17 586
  City Scene with Street Vendors Oil/panel (38x28cm 15x11in) Columbia SC 2000

MEERTS Franz 1836-1896 **[57]**
- **$290** - €248 - **£176** - FF1 626
  La petite tricoteuse Huile/panneau (40x30cm 15x11in) Antwerpen 1998

MEESER Lillian Burk 1864-1942 **[9]**
- **$1 300** - €1 097 - **£762** - FF7 194
  On the Street Oil/board (27x33cm 11x13in) Mystic CT 1998

- **$200** - €192 - **£122** - FF1 260
  Untitled Linocut (13x9cm 5x3in) Provincetown MA 1999

MEESON Dora 1869-1955 **[25]**
- **$1 632** - €1 549 - **£1 000** - FF10 163
  Barges before Battersea Bridge Oil/board (25.5x35.5cm 10x13in) London 1999

MEESTER DE BETZENBROECK de Raymond 1904-1995 **[84]**
- **$3 146** - €3 594 - **£2 189** - FF23 577
  Mouflon sur son rocher Bronze (H60cm H23in) Bruxelles 2001

MEESTERS Dirk 1899-1950 **[11]**
- **$2 063** - €2 042 - **£1 263** - FF13 394
  Woodloggers in the Snow Oil/board (31x41cm 12x16in) Amsterdam 2000

MEETEREN BROUWER van Menno Simon Jacobus 1882-1974 **[34]**
- **$1 096** - €1 022 - **£676** - FF6 702
  Sungkem Oil/canvas (50.5x40cm 19x15in) Singapore 1999

MEGAN Renier 1637-1690 **[2]**
- **$1 100** - €1 286 - **£773** - FF8 435
  Mountainous Landscapes Etching (18x24cm 7x9in) New-York 2000

MEGE Isabelle 1878-1966 **[5]**
- **$1 051** - €1 250 - **£724** - FF8 200
  Enfant au chapeau blanc Huile/toile (12x12cm 4x4in) Chambéry 2000

MEGE Salvator XIX **[5]**
- **$17 000** - €14 548 - **£10 234** - FF95 426
  Schuylkill River, Philadelphia Oil/canvas (27x40cm 11x16in) New-York 1998

MEGERT Christian 1936 **[30]**
- **$2 734** - €3 176 - **£1 921** - FF20 836
  Spiegelrelïef Relief (25x20x4cm 9x7x1in) Amsterdam 2001

MÉGUIN Régine 1938 **[115]**
- **$373** - €396 - **£250** - FF2 600
  Nature morte à la gourde Huile/toile (19x24cm 7x9in) Cannes 2000

MEHEDIN Léon 1828-1905 **[7]**
- **$2 221** - €2 592 - **£1 558** - FF17 000
  Entrée du château de Solférino, porte ouest Tirage albuminé (28x38.5cm 11x15in) Paris 2001

MÉHEUT François XX **[29]**
- **$2 898** - €2 668 - **£1 739** - FF17 500
  Le skieur Bronze (H47.5cm H18in) Soissons 1999

MÉHEUT Mathurin 1882-1958 **[1047]**
- **$13 611** - €11 586 - **£8 101** - FF76 000
  La grande Troménie de Locronan Huile/toile (100x137cm 39x53in) Brest 1998
- **$2 115** - €2 515 - **£1 508** - FF16 500
  Étude de biche et de cerf couchés Technique mixte (72x100cm 28x39in) Brest 2000
- **$1 538** - €1 677 - **£1 008** - FF11 000
  Composition aux pivoines Huile/panneau (48x33cm 18x12in) Brest 2000
- **$3 550** - €3 811 - **£2 375** - FF25 000
  Marin portant des raies Céramique (H44cm H17in) Douarnenez 2000
- **$1 107** - €1 169 - **£741** - FF7 800
  Arbustes dans le jardin Aquarelle, gouache/papier (25x42cm 9x16in) Douarnenez 2000

〰 $166 – €168 – **£103** – FF1 100
Jeune femme de Locronan Gravure (20.5x25.5cm 8x10in) Rennes 2000

MEHEUT-JUDE Maryvonne XX **[10]**
✎ $922 – €915 – **£573** – FF6 000
Brest, la base sous marine et le port de Guerre Gouache/papier (30x82cm 11x32in) Brest 1999

MEHNERT Wilhelm 1823-1878 **[1]**
🖌 $9 765 – €11 248 – **£6 736** – FF73 785
Statue des Zar Nicholas I Bronze (H78cm H30in) München 2000

MEHOFFER József 1869-1946 **[64]**
🖌 $8 844 – €9 701 – **£6 008** – FF63 636
Joueuse de tennis Huile/toile (50x37cm 19x14in) Warszawa 2000
🖌 $870 – €797 – **£530** – FF5 230
Study of a Man's Head Oil/paper (13.5x10cm 5x3in) Warszawa 1999
✎ $1 687 – €1 594 – **£1 020** – FF10 456
Personnage de femme, esquisse pour «un jardin étrange» Fusain (61.5x39.5cm 24x15in) Warszawa 1999
〰 $790 – €956 – **£552** – FF6 268
Jardinier audacieux II Gravure cuivre (21x30cm 8x11in) Kraków 2000

MEHTA Tyeb 1925 **[16]**
☞ $22 000 – €25 020 – **£15 371** – FF164 122
Untitled Oil/canvas (169.5x118.5cm 66x46in) New-York 2000
☞ $14 885 – €13 923 – **£9 000** – FF91 328
Diagonal Series Oil/canvas (90x115cm 35x45in) London 1999
☞ $2 250 – €2 559 – **£1 572** – FF16 785
Untitled Charcoal/paper (72x53.5cm 28x21in) New-York 2000

MEHUS Lieven 1630-1691 **[14]**
☞ $12 500 – €12 958 – **£7 500** – FF85 000
Il carro della vittoria Olio/tela (36.5x55.5cm 14x21in) Prato 2000
✎ $87 354 – €85 476 – **£56 000** – FF560 683
Self-Portrait Red chalk/paper (21.5x17cm 8x6in) London 1999

MEI Paolo XIX **[6]**
☞ $3 507 – €4 171 – **£2 500** – FF27 363
The Lovers' Tiff Oil/panel (34.5x26cm 13x10in) London 2000

MEID Hans 1883-1957 **[299]**
✎ $548 – €511 – **£338** – FF3 353
Stehender Frauenakt Charcoal (47.8x35.7cm 18x14in) Hamburg 1999
〰 $124 – €138 – **£86** – FF905
Frankfurt III, Schwanheimer Eichen Drypoint (22x32.5cm 8x12in) Heidelberg 2001

MEIDNER Ludwig 1884-1966 **[389]**
☞ $21 267 – €23 008 – **£14 571** – FF150 925
Moses am brennenden Dornbusch Öl/Karton (60x70cm 23x27in) Stuttgart 2001
☞ $7 014 – €8 181 – **£4 924** – FF53 662
Bildnis Else Meidner Öl/Karton (40x31.7cm 15x12in) Köln 2000
✎ $17 217 – €14 142 – **£10 000** – FF92 764
Porträt des Kunsthistorikers Leopold Reidemeister Crayon (72.5x57cm 28x22in) London 1998
〰 $279 – €307 – **£190** – FF2 012
Alte Frau (Kuba Meidner II) Radierung (19.8x15.8cm 7x6in) Berlin 2000

MEIER Emil 1877-? **[19]**
🖌 $1 342 – €1 162 – **£814** – FF7 624
«Sommer» Ceramic (H29.8cm H11in) Wien 1998

MEIER Theo 1908-1984 **[122]**
☞ $11 814 – €11 011 – **£7 140** – FF72 226
Woman and Bird Oil/canvas (100x135cm 39x53in) Singapore 1999
☞ $10 688 – €8 968 – **£6 271** – FF58 824
Gunung Agung: The Agung Mountain Oil/canvas (66x81cm 25x31in) Singapore 1998
☞ $4 591 – €5 213 – **£3 142** – FF34 196
Nude by the Pond Oil/canvas (45x35cm 17x13in) Singapore 2000

MEIER-DENNINGHOFF Brigitte 1923 **[9]**
🖌 $5 468 – €6 353 – **£3 843** – FF41 672
«Nr.50» Sculpture (H64cm H25in) Amsterdam 2001

MEIER-MICHEL Johanna 1876-? **[73]**
🖌 $1 202 – €1 125 – **£728** – FF7 378
Figur Frühling Ceramic (H25.5cm H10in) Köln 1999

MEIERHANS Joseph 1890-1981 **[36]**
☞ $450 – €529 – **£323** – FF3 471
Spring Oberiberg-Drusberg Oil/board (76x60cm 30x24in) Hatfield PA 2001

MEIFRÉN ROIG Eliseo 1859-1940 **[145]**
☞ $79 200 – €72 078 – **£48 000** – FF472 800
Playa de Pals Oleo/lienzo (107x150cm 42x59in) Madrid 1999
☞ $24 940 – €25 828 – **£15 480** – FF169 420
Pueblo junto al mar Oleo/lienzo (46x65cm 18x25in) Barcelona 2000
☞ $2 680 – €2 403 – **£1 640** – FF15 760
Vista costera Oleo/lienzo (18x27cm 7x10in) Madrid 1999
✎ $1 215 – €1 351 – **£855** – FF8 865
Paisaje con lago Crayon gras/papier (13x17.5cm 5x6in) Barcelona 2001

MEIJER Christoffel 1776-1813 **[4]**
✎ $8 022 – €7 714 – **£4 941** – FF50 602
Large Crowd of people, a Wedding Scene in a Town Square Ink (43.5x58cm 17x22in) Amsterdam 1999

MEIJER Jan 1927-1995 **[103]**
☞ $821 – €882 – **£550** – FF5 786
Dieudonne Oil/canvas (74x115cm 29x45in) London 2000
〰 $322 – €276 – **£193** – FF1 810
Komposition Etching, aquatint in colors (59.5x49.5cm 23x19in) Hamburg 1998

MEIJER Johan 1885-1970 **[76]**
☞ $1 430 – €1 328 – **£825** – FF8 713
Lente Oil/canvas (40.5x60cm 15x23in) Amsterdam 1998
☞ $727 – €681 – **£452** – FF4 464
«Nevelstemming» Oil/canvas (25.5x45.5cm 10x17in) Amsterdam 1999

MEIJER Louis Johan Hendrik 1809-1866 **[54]**
☞ $12 266 – €13 805 – **£8 451** – FF90 555
Preussische Bark in Seenot vor der Küste Öl/Leinwand (143x175cm 56x68in) Bremen 2000
☞ $12 000 – €13 290 – **£8 138** – FF87 174
Loading the Boat Oil/panel (45.5x57.5cm 17x22in) New-York 2000
☞ $5 424 – €5 384 – **£3 388** – FF35 320
Marine med sejlskibe i oprört hav, i forgrunden fiskerbåd med net Oil/panel (20.5x29.5cm 8x11in) København 1999

M

MEIJER Salomon 1877-1965 **[71]**

🦢 **$3 906** - €4 538 - **£2 745** - FF29 766
Seringen Oil/board (46x43.5cm 18x17in) Amsterdam 2001

🦢 **$1 030** - €998 - **£642** - FF6 548
Canal in Amsterdam Oil/cardboard (20x15.5cm 7x6in) Amsterdam 1999

▥ **$321** - €318 - **£195** - FF2 083
Op de heide/Browersgracht Etching (23x31cm 9x12in) Amsterdam 2000

MEIJI Hashimoto 1904-1991 **[1]**

✏ **$6 076** - €5 926 - **£3 720** - FF38 874
Maiko Girl Drawing (53x44cm 20x17in) Tokyo 1999

MEIJIER de Anthony Andreas 1806-1867 **[5]**

🦢 **$5 937** - €6 632 - **£4 141** - FF43 500
Bord de mer animé de bateaux et personnages Huile/panneau (46.5x63cm 18x24in) Tours 2001

MEILERTS-KRASTINS Ludmilla 1908-1998 **[55]**

🦢 **$1 041** - €1 215 - **£725** - FF7 973
Christmas Lillies Oil/canvas (75.5x59cm 29x23in) Melbourne 1999

MEILI Conrad 1895-1969 **[158]**

🦢 **$1 123** - €1 310 - **£778** - FF8 592
Tulipes variées Öl/Leinwand (64.5x54cm 25x21in) Bern 2000

✏ **$166** - €198 - **£118** - FF1 300
Nu sur le dos Crayon (21.5x36cm 8x14in) Paris 2000

MEINECKE Tristan XX **[1]**

🦢 **$3 750** - €4 265 - **£2 600** - FF27 975
Untitled Oil/canvas/board (60x45cm 24x18in) Chicago IL 2000

MEINERS Claas Hendrik 1819-1894 **[21]**

🦢 **$1 854** - €1 815 - **£1 189** - FF11 906
Dutch Pasture Oil/panel (38x52cm 14x20in) Amsterdam 1999

🦢 **$1 383** - €1 534 - **£960** - FF10 061
Wanderer an einem Gebirgsbach Oil/panel (27x36cm 10x14in) Köln 2001

MEINERS Piet 1857-1903 **[20]**

✏ **$4 247** - €4 991 - **£2 909** - FF32 742
Peasantwomen Nursing their Children in an Interior in Laage Vuursche Pencil (32.5x48.5cm 12x19in) Amsterdam 2000

MEINZOLT Georg M. 1863-1948 **[20]**

🦢 **$1 096** - €1 278 - **£759** - FF8 384
Landschaft im Mondlicht Oil/panel (36x50cm 14x19in) Satow 2000

MEIRELES Cildo 1948 **[4]**

🦢 **$15 000** - €14 563 - **£9 267** - FF95 527
Estojo Geometrico Iron (5x29x54cm 1x11x21in) New-York 1999

MEIREN van der Jan Baptiste 1664-c.1708 **[20]**

🦢 **$15 708** - €14 836 - **£9 500** - FF97 321
The Garden of Eden/Teh Deluge Oil/copper (21.5x27.5cm 8x10in) London 1999

MEISEL Ernst 1838-1895 **[10]**

🦢 **$4 141** - €3 834 - **£2 500** - FF25 147
A Couple in a Wine Cellar Oil/canvas (64.5x75.5cm 25x29in) London 2001

🦢 **$2 997** - €3 323 - **£2 081** - FF21 800
Mönche beim Wein Oil/panel (16x21cm 6x8in) Köln 2001

MEISEL Hugo 1887-1966 **[12]**

🦢 **$346** - €409 - **£245** - FF2 683
Sitzender Kakadu in roséfarbenem, gelbem Gefieder mit Flügeln Ceramic (H49cm H19in) Stuttgart 2000

MEISELAS Susan 1948 **[5]**

📷 **$5 000** - €5 679 - **£3 508** - FF37 252
Lena on the Bully Box, Essex Junction, VT from Carnival Strippers Gelatin silver print (19.5x29cm 7x11in) New-York 2001

MEISENBACH Karl 1898-1976 **[16]**

🦢 **$568** - €665 - **£399** - FF4 360
Der Kaiser von Sachrang aus gesehen Öl/Leinwand (75x95cm 29x37in) München 2000

MEISSEL Ernst 1838-1895 **[8]**

🦢 **$32 500** - €32 750 - **£20 260** - FF214 825
The Engagement Ring Oil/canvas (63.5x78.5cm 25x30in) New-York 2000

MEISSER Leonhard 1902-1977 **[85]**

🦢 **$1 660** - €1 626 - **£1 022** - FF10 664
Frühlingslandschaft Öl/Leinwand (73x100cm 28x39in) St. Gallen 1999

🦢 **$1 680** - €1 555 - **£1 028** - FF10 202
Winterabend Öl/Leinwand (33x40.5cm 12x15in) Bern 1999

▥ **$62** - €63 - **£39** - FF410
Eisfeld mit Schlittschuhläuferin Farblithographie (27.5x15.5cm 10x6in) Zofingen 1999

MEISSNER Ernst Adolf 1837-1902 **[46]**

🦢 **$2 748** - €2 352 - **£1 654** - FF15 425
«Schafe hinter dem Gehöft» Öl/Leinwand (52x73cm 20x28in) Stuttgart 1998

🦢 **$893** - €1 022 - **£614** - FF6 707
Hüterbub am Wiesengatter links, in die Landschaft blickend Öl/Leinwand/Karton (21x41cm 8x16in) München 2001

MEISSNER Leo 1895-1977 **[27]**

▥ **$270** - €276 - **£169** - FF1 813
Star Ridge, No Car Woodcut (21x26cm 8x10in) Cleveland OH 2000

MEISSONIER Ernest 1815-1891 **[220]**

🦢 **$4 500** - €3 901 - **£2 749** - FF25 590
The Dragoon Oil/panel (25.5x20cm 10x7in) New-York 1999

🦢 **$9 380** - €9 076 - **£5 944** - FF59 532
Napolenon during the «Campagne de France» Bronze (39x37x16.5cm 15x14x6in) Amsterdam 1999

✏ **$592** - €549 - **£368** - FF3 600
Portrait équestre Encre (18x15.5cm 7x6in) Paris 1999

MEISSONIER Jean-Charles 1848-1917 **[29]**

🦢 **$4 170** - €4 573 - **£2 832** - FF30 000
Matin d'Avril; bergère filant sa grenouille à la tête de ses moutons Huile/toile (57x41cm 22x16in) Orléans 2000

🦢 **$4 034** - €4 537 - **£2 816** - FF29 760
Der Page (38.5x32cm 15x9in) Luzern 2001

✏ **$4 499** - €5 107 - **£3 125** - FF33 500
Le poète Aquarelle, gouache/papier (46x35cm 18x13in) Barbizon 2001

MEISSONIER Joseph François Xav. 1864-1943 **[18]**

🦢 **$1 540** - €1 652 - **£1 045** - FF10 835
Paisaje nevado Oleo/lienzo (38x56cm 14x22in) Madrid 2000

MEISTER Otto 1887-1969 **[19]**
- $570 - €652 - £402 - FF4 275
  «Camoghé» Öl/Leinwand (64.5x81cm 25x31in) Bern 2001

MEISTERMANN Georg 1911-1990 **[176]**
- $26 304 - €30 678 - £18 468 - FF201 234
  Ohne Titel Öl/Leinwand (100x140cm 39x55in) Köln 2000
- $15 424 - €17 895 - £10 647 - FF117 386
  Ohne Titel, Schwinge Öl/Leinwand (45.5x62.5cm 17x24in) Köln 2000
- $5 239 - €5 624 - £3 506 - FF36 892
  Miniatur Öl/panel (14.2x20.9cm 5x8in) Köln 2000
- $1 143 - €1 227 - £765 - FF8 049
  Zwei Mädchen Indian ink (38.5x49cm 15x19in) Köln 2000
- $252 - €235 - £155 - FF1 542
  Violinschlüssel Farblithographie (12.5x27cm 4x10in) Hamburg 1999

MEIXMORON DE DOMBASLE de Charles 1839-1912 **[21]**
- $2 930 - €2 693 - £1 800 - FF17 664
  Sommerlandskab med to kvinder der nyder udsigten Oil/canvas (50x73cm 19x28in) Vejle 1999

MEJIAZ Mauro 1930 **[10]**
- $986 - €928 - £638 - FF6 090
  Viceras Oleo/lienzo (79.5x58.5cm 31x23in) Caracas 1999

MEKKINK Johan 1904-1991 **[6]**
- $8 899 - €9 983 - £6 166 - FF65 485
  Stilleven met Aardappels Oil/panel (44x60cm 17x23in) Amsterdam 2000

MELARA Sonia 1960 **[1]**
- $2 400 - €2 545 - £1 627 - FF16 697
  La Annunciation (the Annunciation) Red chalk/paper (192x132cm 75x51in) Tel Aviv 2001

MELBYE Anton 1818-1875 **[159]**
- $9 408 - €10 739 - £6 536 - FF70 440
  Lodsen saettes Oil/canvas (96x143cm 37x56in) København 2000
- $3 853 - €4 394 - £2 585 - FF27 276
  Skibe på havet Oil/canvas (67x91cm 26x35in) København 2000
- $1 167 - €1 341 - £808 - FF8 795
  Indsejling til Dover Oil/canvas (16x24cm 6x9in) København 2000
- $431 - €404 - £268 - FF2 647
  Aftenstemning med fiskerskibe ved mole Chalks (13x22cm 5x8in) København 1999

MELBYE Fritz Siegfried G. 1826-1896 **[19]**
- $30 000 - €25 971 - £18 093 - FF170 358
  View of the Blue Hole of Jamaica Oil/canvas (76x112cm 29x44in) San-Francisco CA 1998
- $2 261 - €2 126 - £1 400 - FF13 947
  Mount Fiji, Japan Oil/board (26x47cm 10x18in) London 1999

MELBYE Vilhelm 1824-1882 **[127]**
- $14 475 - €16 714 - £10 125 - FF109 635
  Segelfartyg på stormigt hav, kustvy med Bambours slott, Northumberland Oil/canvas (87x152cm 34x59in) Stockholm 2001
- $3 731 - €4 380 - £2 633 - FF28 731
  Artiskt vatyten Oil/canvas (86x138cm 33x54in) Stockholm 2000
- $1 676 - €1 810 - £1 158 - FF11 876
  Fransk fregat og eskadre ved Bosporus Oil/canvas (34x44cm 13x17in) København 2001

MELCHER Jakob 1816-1882 **[3]**
- $1 716 - €1 842 - £1 148 - FF12 082
  Fille de Nuremberg Crayon (45x43cm 17x16in) Warszawa 2000

MELCHER TILMES Jan Hermanus 1847-1920 **[9]**
- $3 362 - €3 176 - £2 097 - FF20 836
  Doorwertsche Bosch Oil/canvas (65x93cm 25x36in) Amsterdam 1999

MELCHERS Julius, Gari 1860-1932 **[33]**
- $17 000 - €15 695 - £10 455 - FF102 950
  New York Harbor Oil/canvas (69x89.5cm 27x35in) New-York 1999
- $14 000 - €13 505 - £9 494 - FF101 703
  The Wedding Oil/canvas (35.5x28cm 13x11in) New-York 2000
- $16 000 - €17 279 - £11 057 - FF113 342
  Camp Meeting Watercolour/paper (31x50cm 12x19in) Bethesda MD 2001

MELCHIOR Wilhelm 1817-1860 **[23]**
- $6 500 - €6 756 - £4 096 - FF44 317
  Hunter with Dogs and Game Oil/canvas (73.5x88.5cm 28x34in) New-York 2000
- $1 009 - €1 180 - £720 - FF7 739
  Fox chasing the Ducks Oil/canvas (28.5x36.5cm 11x14in) Amsterdam 2001

MELDRUM Duncan Max 1875-1955 **[52]**
- $4 151 - €4 650 - £2 884 - FF30 500
  Misty Landscape Oil/canvas (65x92.5cm 25x36in) Melbourne 2001
- $781 - €929 - £557 - FF6 096
  Eltham Oil/wood (22x30.5cm 8x12in) Woollahra, Sydney 2000

MELÉ Juan N. 1923 **[4]**
- $9 500 - €8 284 - £5 743 - FF54 337
  Relief No.53 Relief (70x84cm 27x33in) New-York 1998

MELENDEZ Bill Melendez Studio **[5]**
- $600 - €644 - £401 - FF4 224
  Lucy and Linus in Yard (animation cel) Gouache (22x28cm 9x11in) New-York 2000

MELENDEZ Luis 1716-1780 **[8]**
- $256 000 - €240 260 - £156 000 - FF1 576 000
  La Sagrada Familia Tempera (34x44cm 13x17in) Madrid 1999

MELGAARD Bjarne XX **[2]**
- $10 469 - €11 619 - £7 296 - FF76 218
  «Uten tittel» Oil/canvas (202x349cm 79x137in) Oslo 2001

MELGERS Henk Johan 1899-1973 **[9]**
- $3 640 - €4 084 - £2 522 - FF26 789
  Zieunerkamp Oil/canvas (70x85cm 27x33in) Amsterdam 2000

MELIDA Y ALINARI Enrique 1834-1892 **[10]**
- $2 307 - €2 744 - £1 645 - FF18 000
  Espagnole au balcon Huile/panneau (36x22cm 14x8in) Paris 2000

MÉLIES Georges 1861-1938 **[7]**
- $7 420 - €7 927 - £5 059 - FF52 000
  A la conquête du Pôle Mine plomb (17x21.5cm 6x8in) Argenteuil 2001
- $2 283 - €2 439 - £1 556 - FF16 000
  Le modèle irascible Tirage argentique (6x16cm 2x6in) Argenteuil 2001

MELIK Edgar 1904-1976 **[61]**
- **$1 393** - €1 220 - **£844** - FF8 000
  Femme et ange Huile/carton (76x54cm 29x21in)
  Paris 1998

MELIN Joseph Urbain 1814-1886 **[11]**
- **$24 000** - €27 884 - **£16 867** - FF182 908
  The Staghounds and Huntsman Oil/canvas
  (132x91.5cm 51x36in) New-York 2001

MÉLINGUE Étienne Marin 1808-1875 **[6]**
- **$1 428** - €1 361 - **£866** - FF8 929
  Seated Scolar Bronze (H41cm H16in) Amsterdam
  1999

MELINI Carlo Domenico c.1740-1795 **[1]**
- **$842** - €818 - **£524** - FF5 366
  **Die Söhne des Prinzen von Turin in savoyardi-
  schen Kostümen** Etching (36.9x49.3cm 14x19in)
  Berlin 1999

MELISSI Agostino 1616-1683 **[3]**
- **$8 400** - €7 257 - **£5 600** - FF47 600
  Ritratto di un farmacista a mezza figura Olio/tela
  (101x77cm 39x30in) Roma 1998

MELLA Henri 1935 **[47]**
- **$299** - €320 - **£203** - FF2 100
  Promenade Huile/carton (45x55cm 17x21in)
  Montauban 2001
- **$156** - €168 - **£103** - FF1 100
  Scène de plage Huile/carton (35x24cm 13x9in)
  Cahors 2000

MELLAN Claude 1598-1688 **[47]**
- **$649** - €545 - **£380** - FF3 575
  Portrait de Dreux d'Aubray Eau-forte (34x25.5cm
  13x10in) Liège 1998

MELLE 1908-1976 **[53]**
- **$5 485** - €5 445 - **£3 427** - FF35 719
  Two Crickets in a Landscape Oil/panel
  (36.5x85.5cm 14x33in) Amsterdam 1999
- **$4 296** - €4 991 - **£3 019** - FF32 742
  Het schilderij (The Picture) Oil/panel (40x29.5cm
  15x11in) Amsterdam 2001
- **$321** - €318 - **£195** - FF2 083
  Surrealistic Figures Ink (63x51cm 24x20in)
  Amsterdam 2000

MELLÉ Léon Auguste 1816-1889 **[73]**
- **$345** - €381 - **£239** - FF2 500
  Rochers à Fontainebleau Huile/panneau
  (21.5x32.5cm 8x12in) Paris 2001

MELLE van Henri 1859-1930 **[9]**
- **$1 911** - €1 735 - **£1 183** - FF11 382
  La dentellière Huile/toile (51x71cm 20x27in)
  Bruxelles 1999

MELLENCAMP John Cougar XX **[1]**
- **$7 000** - €5 957 - **£4 166** - FF39 078
  Self portrait Oil/canvas (53.5x43cm 21x16in) New-
  York 1998

MELLERY Xavier 1845-1921 **[75]**
- **$4 729** - €5 445 - **£3 228** - FF35 719
  Marken, la sainte famille Mixed media/board
  (75.5x53cm 29x20in) Amsterdam 2000
- **$2 561** - €2 949 - **£1 748** - FF19 347
  Two Women from Marken Watercolour (42x29.5cm
  16x11in) Amsterdam 1999

MELLI Roberto 1885-1958 **[14]**
- **$5 400** - €4 665 - **£3 600** - FF30 600
  Ombrelloni Olio/tela (43x63.5cm 16x25in) Roma
  1998

MELLING Antoine-Ignace 1763-1831 **[32]**
- **$18 235** - €17 684 - **£11 472** - FF116 000
  Vue de Kadi-Kieuï Aquarelle (36x63.5cm 14x25in)
  Toulouse 1999

MELLING Henry XIX **[3]**
- **$85 595** - €80 493 - **£53 000** - FF528 001
  **The Opening Cruise of the Royal Mersey Yacht
  Club, 1847-The «Ariel!»..** Oil/canvas (66x140cm
  25x55in) London 1999

MELLIS de Alfredo 1845 **[1]**
- **$7 686** - €7 260 - **£4 649** - FF47 625
  Camellias in a Tin Vase Oil/canvas (37x30.5cm
  14x12in) Amsterdam 1999

MELLO de Tomáz XIX-XX **[2]**
- **$4 320** - €4 487 - **£2 790** - FF29 430
  O Barbeiro Oleo/lienzo (90.5x51.5cm 35x20in) Lisboa
  2000

MELLON Campbell A. 1876-1955 **[169]**
- **$5 248** - €5 969 - **£3 700** - FF39 156
  Early June, Gorleston Oil/canvas (50x58cm
  20x23in) Aylsham, Norfolk 2001
- **$2 700** - €2 579 - **£1 700** - FF16 919
  Beach Scene at Gorleston with Figures Oil/can-
  vas (20x27cm 8x11in) Aylsham, Norfolk 1999

MELLOR Dawn XX **[1]**
- **$6 610** - €5 648 - **£4 000** - FF37 050
  **Love me Love my Dog Series : «Jean and
  Cookie»/«Sophia and Blossom»...** Oil/board
  (42x29.5cm 16x11in) London 1998

MELLOR Everett Watson 1878-1965 **[24]**
- **$2 759** - €2 355 - **£1 650** - FF15 449
  «Ullswater» Oil/canvas (34x75cm 13x29in) Leeds
  1998
- **$2 728** - €2 581 - **£1 700** - FF16 931
  Peep at Windermere Oil/board (24.5x34.5cm 9x13in)
  London 1999
- **$919** - €1 073 - **£640** - FF7 037
  «Friar's Crag, Derwentwater» Watercolour
  (29.5x45cm 11x17in) West-Yorshire 2000

MELLOR William 1851-1931 **[300]**
- **$5 698** - €6 625 - **£4 000** - FF43 457
  On the Wharfe, Yorkshire Oil/canvas (74x48.5cm
  29x19in) Billingshurst, West-Sussex 2001
- **$4 548** - €4 426 - **£2 800** - FF29 032
  River Landscape, Cumberland Oil/canvas
  (30.5x51cm 12x20in) London 1999
- **$557** - €656 - **£400** - FF4 303
  The Strid, Bolton Abbey Watercolour/paper
  (20x30cm 7x11in) Cheshire 2001

MELLSTRÖM Rolf 1896-1953 **[55]**
- **$434** - €464 - **£295** - FF3 046
  Räv med byte Oil/canvas (74x87cm 29x34in)
  Stockholm 2001

MELNIKOV Avraham 1892-1960 **[1]**
- **$2 000** - €1 643 - **£1 161** - FF10 775
  Jerusalem Watercolour (23x29cm 9x11in) Tel Aviv
  1998

MELO E CASTRO Maria de Lourdes 1903-? **[2]**
- **$3 960** - €4 487 - **£2 790** - FF29 430
  Castelo dos templários em tomar Oleo/cartón
  (22x27cm 8x10in) Lisboa 2001

MELONE Altobello Meloni 1497-c.1530 **[4]**
- **$6 274** - €6 126 - **£4 000** - FF40 184
  Leda and the Swann Red chalk (12x15.5cm 4x6in)
  London 1999

MÉLOTTE Antoine Marie 1722-1795 **[2]**
- $20 110 - €17 111 - **£12 000** - FF112 240
  Equestrian Battle Scene Sculpture (85x172cm
  33x67in) London 1998

MELOTTI Fausto 1901-1986 **[168]**
- $6 000 - €6 220 - **£3 600** - FF40 800
  Senza titolo Tecnica mista/cartone (43x57cm 16x22in)
  Prato 2000
- $1 500 - €1 555 - **£900** - FF10 200
  Senza titolo Tempera (35x25.5cm 13x10in) Milano
  2001
- $30 000 - €25 916 - **£20 000** - FF170 000
  Scultura C-Infinito Metal (278x116x80cm
  109x45x31in) Milano 1998
- $3 800 - €4 924 - **£2 850** - FF32 300
  Bestia Céramique (14.5x33x25cm 5x12x9in) Milano
  2001
- $1 980 - €1 710 - **£1 320** - FF11 220
  «**Progetto per una decorazione in ceramica**»
  Acquarello/carta (48x33.5cm 18x13in) Milano 1998
- $250 - €259 - **£150** - FF1 700
  «**12 variazioni**» Acquaforte (50x70cm 19x27in)
  Milano 2001

MELROSE Andrew W. 1836-1901 **[52]**
- $3 400 - €3 765 - **£2 305** - FF24 699
  **Sheep Grazing in an Extensive Mountain
  Landscape** Oil/canvas (86x125cm 34x49in) New-York
  2000
- $5 000 - €5 249 - **£3 381** - FF34 433
  **Berkshire Hills, Mass, the Ledge/The Mohawk
  near Littlefalls** Oil/canvas (49x23cm 19x9in) Fairfield
  ME 2001

MELS Jacques 1899-1974 **[23]**
- $179 - €204 - **£126** - FF1 339
  Winter Landscape Watercolour/paper (32x52cm
  12x20in) Amsterdam 2001

MELSEN Marten 1870-1947 **[33]**
- $6 688 - €7 932 - **£4 864** - FF52 032
  Chaumière en automne Huile/toile (52x70cm
  20x27in) Antwerpen 2001
- $541 - €545 - **£336** - FF3 577
  Paysanne à la porte Aquarelle/papier (17x10.5cm
  6x4in) Antwerpen 2000

MELTSNER Paul R. 1905-1966 **[24]**
- $1 300 - €1 290 - **£797** - FF8 465
  Backstage at the Follies Oil/canvas (76x60cm
  30x24in) Mystic CT 2000
- $1 300 - €1 125 - **£784** - FF7 382
  «**The Lockout**»/«**The Outcast**» Lithograph
  (29.5x26cm 11x10in) New-York 1998

MELTZER Arthur 1893-1989 **[38]**
- $31 000 - €29 591 - **£19 371** - FF194 106
  Abandoned Quarry Oil/canvas (106x116cm 42x46in)
  Hatfield PA 1999
- $5 000 - €4 773 - **£3 124** - FF31 307
  Melting Snow, Landscape with Stone Barn
  Oil/canvas (63x76cm 25x30in) Hatfield PA 1999
- $650 - €698 - **£435** - FF4 576
  Summer landscape Oil/canvas (33x35cm 13x14in)
  Altadena CA 2000
- $275 - €294 - **£187** - FF1 926
  Driftwood Charcoal/paper (49x38cm 19x15in)
  Philadelphia PA 2001

MELVILLE Arthur 1855-1904 **[45]**
- $15 000 - €17 787 - **£10 320** - FF116 674
  Sandhills Valley Oil/canvas (112x143cm 44x56in)
  New-York 2000

- $1 600 - €1 934 - **£1 117** - FF12 685
  Old Memories Oil/canvas (51x76.5cm 20x30in)
  Bethesda MD 2000
- $2 631 - €3 019 - **£1 800** - FF19 803
  Market in Cairo Oil/canvas (24x33cm 9x12in) London
  2000
- $2 090 - €1 938 - **£1 300** - FF12 711
  Lachlan Castle, Argyll Watercolour/paper (17x25cm
  6x9in) London 1999

MELVILLE Eliza Anne XIX **[1]**
- $5 202 - €4 803 - **£3 200** - FF31 508
  **Portrait of William Henry Hunt (1790-1864), sket-
  ching at a desk** Oil/board (28x25.5cm 11x10in)
  London 1999

MELVILLE Harden Sidney XIX-XX **[40]**
- $1 158 - €1 344 - **£800** - FF8 819
  The Plough Team/The Logger Oil/canvas
  (46x81.5cm 18x32in) London 2000

MELVILLE John 1902-1986 **[44]**
- $239 - €231 - **£150** - FF1 515
  The Sea Tenby Watercolour/paper (15x25cm 5x9in)
  London 1999

MELZER Franciscus 1808-? **[8]**
- $1 095 - €1 022 - **£675** - FF6 707
  Die schlafende Grossmutter am Fenster
  Oil/panel (33x27cm 12x10in) Köln 1999

MELZER Moritz 1877-1966 **[64]**
- $885 - €971 - **£601** - FF6 372
  Lanzenkämpferin Monotype (46.3x33.5cm 18x13in)
  Berlin 2000

MELZI Francesco 1493-c.1570 **[1]**
- $17 920 - €20 348 - **£12 264** - FF133 476
  Die Geburt Christi Öl/Leinwand (142x110cm
  55x43in) Wien 2000

MENA Daniel 1949 **[105]**
- $1 400 - €1 502 - **£950** - FF9 520
  Bodegón cubista Oleo/lienzo (46x55cm 18x21in)
  Barcelona 2001
- $1 140 - €1 201 - **£740** - FF7 880
  La Tribune Oleo/lienzo (33x42cm 12x16in) Madrid
  2000
- $1 680 - €1 802 - **£1 140** - FF11 820
  Copa con naranjas y periódico Acuarela/papel
  (50x65cm 19x25in) Madrid 2000

MENA de Pedro 1628-1688 **[3]**
- $10 080 - €10 812 - **£6 660** - FF70 920
  Dolorosa Sculpture bois (H26cm H10in) Madrid 2000

MENABONI Athos 1895-1990 **[6]**
- $4 000 - €4 701 - **£2 773** - FF30 837
  Valley Quail Oil/panel (82.5x42.5cm 32x16in)
  Beverly-Hills CA 2000

MÉNAGEOT François-Guillaume 1744-1816 **[9]**
- $12 406 - €14 788 - **£8 846** - FF97 000
  Scène mythologique Huile/toile (60x50cm 23x19in)
  Lyon 2000

MENARD Émile René 1862-1930 **[169]**
- $2 491 - €2 744 - **£1 661** - FF18 000
  Le passage du gué Huile/toile (71x90cm 27x35in)
  Deauville 2000
- $486 - €534 - **£323** - FF3 500
  Les meules à Barbizon Huile/panneau (28x38cm
  11x14in) Melun 2000
- $409 - €457 - **£285** - FF3 000
  Etude de ciel Technique mixte/papier (22.5x37.5cm
  8x14in) Paris 2001

M

MÉNARD René Joseph 1827-1887 **[18]**
- $5 254 - €5 641 - **£3 515** - FF37 000
  Le retour du troupeau Huile/toile (48x73cm
  18x28in) Louviers 2000

MENARDEAU Maurice 1897-1977 **[66]**
- $907 - €915 - **£565** - FF6 000
  Thonier dans le calme plat Huile/panneau
  (37x45cm 14x17in) Quimper 2000

MENASCO Milton XX **[2]**
- $65 000 - €60 980 - **£40 163** - FF400 003
  «La Troienne» and her Foals Oil/panel (84x110cm
  33x43in) New-York 1999
- $3 000 - €3 485 - **£2 108** - FF22 863
  **Greentree Farm's Shut out, a Chesnut
  Racehorse** Watercolour/paper (34.5x52cm 13x20in)
  New-York 2001

MENATO Giuseppe 1876-? **[3]**
- $8 500 - €8 812 - **£5 100** - FF57 800
  Notturni in città Olio/tela (76x100cm 29x39in)
  Milano 2000

MENDE Carl Adolf 1807-1857 **[7]**
- $2 313 - €2 556 - **£1 604** - FF16 769
  Dirndl mit Andachtsbuch vor der Hütte
  Öl/Leinwand (65x55cm 25x21in) München 2001
- $2 074 - €2 301 - **£1 437** - FF15 092
  **«Vor Bildstock knieendes Dirndl im
  Hochgebirge»** Oil/panel (36x34cm 14x13in) Kempten
  2001

MENDELSON Marc 1915 **[63]**
- $5 274 - €4 462 - **£3 132** - FF29 268
  Interieur Oil/canvas (73x50cm 28x19in) Lokeren 1998
- $2 280 - €2 479 - **£1 560** - FF16 260
  Stilleven met citroenen Oil/canvas (36.5x28.5cm
  14x11in) Lokeren 2000
- $1 290 - €1 487 - **£888** - FF9 756
  Compositie Ink/paper (20.5x29.5cm 8x11in) Lokeren
  2000

MENDES DA COSTA Joseph 1863/64-1939 **[31]**
- $4 650 - €4 991 - **£3 111** - FF32 742
  Grotesque Heads (Inkstand) Grès (H7.5cm H2in)
  Amsterdam 2000

MENDES DA COSTA Samuel Henri 1845-1923 **[9]**
- $2 311 - €2 496 - **£1 580** - FF16 371
  A View of the Koppelpoort, Amersfoort Oil/canvas
  (35x50cm 13x19in) Amsterdam 2001

MENDEZ BRINGA Narciso 1868-1933 **[5]**
- $363 - €330 - **£214** - FF2 167
  Charla en el patio Gouache/papier (39x23.5cm
  15x9in) Madrid 1999

MÉNDEZ Leopoldo 1902-1969 **[24]**
- $180 - €207 - **£124** - FF1 358
  Village Scene Lithograph (34x28cm 13x11in)
  Cleveland OH 2000

MENDIETA Ana 1948-1985 **[1]**
- $2 800 - €3 186 - **£1 967** - FF20 902
  Sandwomen Gelatin silver print (20.5x25.5cm
  8x10in) New-York 2001

MENDILAHARZU Graciano XIX-XX **[3]**
- $3 100 - €3 602 - **£2 178** - FF23 625
  Un negrito, cabeza Oleo/tabla (34x26cm 13x10in)
  Buenos-Aires 2001

MENDIVE Manuel 1944 **[25]**
- $16 000 - €15 567 - **£9 848** - FF102 116
  La traición Oil/canvas (118x192cm 46x75in) New-
  York 1999

- $2 299 - €2 317 - **£1 433** - FF15 200
  El pensamento Huile/toile (81x105cm 31x41in) Paris
  2000
- $1 815 - €1 829 - **£1 131** - FF12 000
  Personnages fantastiques Pastel/papier (69x93cm
  27x36in) Paris 2000

MENDJISKY Maurice 1889-1951 **[23]**
- $1 063 - €1 143 - **£724** - FF7 500
  Bouquet de fleurs Huile/panneau (50x80cm 19x31in)
  Paris 2001

MENDJISKY Serge 1929 **[213]**
- $1 160 - €1 220 - **£728** - FF8 000
  Le Baou de Saint-Jeannet en été Huile/toile
  (30x60cm 11x23in) Nice 2000
- $412 - €457 - **£285** - FF3 000
  Coucher de soleil au Cap Ferrat Huile/toile
  (33x41cm 12x16in) Troyes 2001

MENDLICK Oscar 1871-1963 **[22]**
- $960 - €944 - **£600** - FF6 192
  Young Woman in Black Dress Oil/canvas
  (50.5x34cm 19x13in) Budapest 1999

MENDOLA Rosolino 1949 **[22]**
- $500 - €518 - **£300** - FF3 400
  «Sintesi» Olio/tela (50x70cm 19x27in) Vercelli 2001

MENDONÇA Antonio Higino XIX-XX **[3]**
- $9 120 - €7 952 - **£5 440** - FF52 160
  Fragatas no Tejo Oleo/lienzo (33x42cm 12x16in)
  Lisboa 1998

MENDOZA Ryan 1971 **[1]**
- $4 200 - €5 442 - **£3 150** - FF35 700
  La famiglia Olio/tela (90x30cm 35x11in) Milano 2001

MENE Pierre-Jules 1810-1879 **[1756]**
- $2 577 - €2 422 - **£1 600** - FF15 886
  Chien au piquet Bronze (23x31cm 9x12in) London
  1999

MENEGAZZI Carlo XIX **[11]**
- $750 - €907 - **£524** - FF5 949
  Venice Watercolour (38x68.5cm 14x26in) Bethesda
  MD 2000

MENEGHELLI Enrico 1853-c.1895 **[10]**
- $3 750 - €4 374 - **£2 633** - FF28 692
  Country Landscape with Peasants Oil/canvas
  (35.5x61cm 13x24in) Boston MA 2000
- $7 500 - €8 050 - **£5 019** - FF52 807
  Street Scene Oil/board (30x23cm 12x9in) Bolton MA
  2000

MENEGHETTI Renato 1947 **[31]**
- $8 400 - €7 257 - **£4 200** - FF47 600
  **Condizionatrice superautomatica per la borghe-
  sia** Olio/tela (100x119cm 39x46in) Milano 1999
- $5 806 - €6 468 - **£3 798** - FF42 426
  Studio Rx Mischtechnik (21.5x18.5cm 8x7in)
  München 2000

MENENDEZ Cesar 1954 **[5]**
- $12 000 - €11 676 - **£7 386** - FF76 587
  Acajutla Oil/canvas (150.5x150.5cm 59x59in) New-
  York 1999

MENENDEZ PIDAL Luis 1864-1932 **[8]**
- $14 400 - €13 515 - **£9 000** - FF88 650
  Vino y filosofía Oleo/lienzo (58x46cm 22x18in)
  Madrid 2001

MENESCARDI Giustino XVIII **[5]**
- $13 448 - €14 436 - **£9 000** - FF94 694
  Joseph's Dream Oil/canvas (44.5x31cm 17x12in)
  London 2000

MENESES Jesús XX **[13]**

$259 - €217 - **£154** - FF1 422
Puerto de Alicante Acuarela/papel (50x70cm 19x27in) Madrid 1998

MENESES OSORIO Francisco 1630-1705 **[4]**

$7 200 - €7 208 - **£4 440** - FF47 280
San Jerónimo Oleo/lienzo (168x108cm 66x42in) Madrid 2000

MENEZ Maria Iñes 1926-1994 **[3]**

$6 820 - €7 727 - **£4 650** - FF50 685
Composição abstracta Technique mixte/papier (73x54cm 28x21in) Lisboa 2000

MENEZES de Visconde Luiz 1820-1878 **[4]**

$1 848 - €2 094 - **£1 260** - FF13 734
Cena da vida de S.Sebastião Oleo/lienzo (25x40cm 9x15in) Lisboa 2000

$1 376 - €1 595 - **£960** - FF10 464
«Retrato da filha Maria» Lápiz/papel (20x13.5cm 7x5in) Lisboa 2001

MENG Siew Hock 1942 **[12]**

$9 962 - €10 038 - **£6 210** - FF65 844
Resting Beauty Oil/canvas (46x61cm 18x24in) Singapore 2000

$3 730 - €4 236 - **£2 553** - FF27 784
Seated Nude Pastel/paper (64.5x49cm 25x19in) Singapore 2000

MENGARDI Giovanni Battista c.1738-1796 **[1]**

$1 176 - €1 022 - **£708** - FF6 704
Die Opferung Isaaks Radierung (11x15.9cm 4x6in) Berlin 1998

MENGE Charles 1920 **[17]**

$2 809 - €3 275 - **£1 945** - FF21 481
Getreideernte bei Prolins, Val d'Hérémence Tempera (40.5x50cm 15x19in) Bern 2000

$1 103 - €1 255 - **£764** - FF8 229
Le vieux pont à Monthery Huile/panneau (29x36cm 11x14in) Sion 2000

MENGELATTE François 1920 **[8]**

$317 - €320 - **£198** - FF2 100
Village de Bigorre Huile/panneau (44x31cm 17x12in) Tarbes 2000

MENGELBERG Otto 1817-1890 **[1]**

$7 204 - €8 181 - **£5 006** - FF53 662
Die Rückkehr des Verlorenen Sohnes Öl/Leinwand (97x121cm 38x47in) Köln 2001

MENGIN Paul Eugène 1853-1937 **[14]**

$1 325 - €1 387 - **£832** - FF9 100
La joueuse de mandoline Bronze (H55cm H21in) Toulouse 2000

MENGOTTI Enrique 1899-1988 **[3]**

$2 655 - €2 703 - **£1 665** - FF17 730
Retrato femenino de perfil Oleo/lienzo (17x11cm 6x4in) Madrid 2000

MENGOZZI-COLONNA Girolamo 1688-c.1766 **[1]**

$380 000 - €411 099 - **£260 338** - FF2 696 632
The Interior of a Church/The Interior of a Classical Library Oil/canvas (211x146cm 83x57in) New-York 2001

MENGS Anton Rafael 1728-1779 **[34]**

$41 000 - €42 503 - **£24 600** - FF278 800
Ritratto di Papa Clemente XIII Olio/tela (152x111cm 59x43in) Roma 1999

$45 600 - €39 393 - **£30 400** - FF258 400
La consegna delle chiavi Olio/tela (100x57cm 39x22in) Roma 1998

$6 471 - €5 999 - **£4 000** - FF39 351
Portrait of a Father John Gahagan, in a Van Dyck costume, head study Oil/paper/canvas (42x28cm 16x11in) London 1999

$1 212 - €1 431 - **£861** - FF9 390
Das Urteil des Paris Ink (56x33cm 22x12in) Köln 2001

MENGUY Frédéric 1927 **[149]**

$1 311 - €1 448 - **£909** - FF9 500
Femme au bouquet Huile/toile (73x54cm 28x21in) Orléans 2001

$120 - €137 - **£83** - FF900
Nature morte Lithographie (66x51cm 25x20in) Avignon 2000

MENINSKY Bernard 1891-1950 **[230]**

$2 025 - €2 187 - **£1 400** - FF14 349
Still Life of Apples and Pears Oil/canvas (51x76cm 20x29in) London 2001

$1 280 - €1 163 - **£800** - FF7 627
Portrait of a Lady Oil/canvas (40.5x33cm 15x12in) London 1999

$1 079 - €1 209 - **£750** - FF7 930
Study of a Female Nude from behind Crayon (53x20cm 20x7in) London 2001

MENKEN Johann Heinrich 1766-1839 **[7]**

$1 135 - €1 278 - **£782** - FF8 384
Flusslandschaft mit rastender Hirtin vor dem Gewitter Öl/Leinwand (24x34cm 9x13in) Bremen 2000

MENKES Zygmunt, Joseph 1896-1986 **[183]**

$88 440 - €97 012 - **£60 080** - FF636 360
Homme jouant de la flûte Huile/toile (163x127cm 64x50in) Warszawa 2000

$7 000 - €8 164 - **£4 914** - FF53 552
Woman with cigarette Oil/canvas (73x60cm 29x24in) Cambridge MA 2000

$7 761 - €7 093 - **£4 749** - FF46 530
Still Life Oil/canvas (37.5x41.5cm 14x16in) Warszawa 1999

$800 - €776 - **£495** - FF5 087
Coming to America Watercolour/paper (45x23cm 18x9in) Mystic CT 1999

MENN Barthélemy 1815-1893 **[39]**

$2 475 - €2 494 - **£1 542** - FF16 360
Madame Darier Öl/Leinwand (70x56cm 27x22in) Zürich 2000

$2 968 - €2 493 - **£1 744** - FF16 353
Galante Szene mit jungem Edelmann und Damen unter Bäumen Öl/Karton (20x28.5cm 7x11in) Bern 1998

MENNES J. XIX **[1]**

$15 000 - €12 941 - **£9 082** - FF84 889
Springtime in the Country Oil/canvas (61.5x77cm 24x30in) New-York 1999

MENNET Louis 1829-1875 **[30]**

$963 - €929 - **£594** - FF6 094
La Sarine près de Fribourg Huile/panneau (57x33.5cm 22x13in) Bern 1999

$377 - €429 - **£261** - FF2 815
Frühlingserwachen Öl/Karton (30.5x21cm 12x8in) Zofingen 1999

MENNYEY Francesco 1889-1950 **[11]**

$2 500 - €2 592 - **£1 500** - FF17 000
Paesaggio invernale Olio/cartone (47x62.5cm 18x24in) Vercelli 1999

$1 000 - €1 296 - **£750** - FF8 500
Rodi Olio/cartone/tela (33.5x44.5cm 13x17in) Vercelli 2000

MENOCAL [illegible] $1 200 - €1 244 - **£720** - FF8 160
Torino, San Carlo e Santa Cristina Gravure
(50x39.5cm 19x15in) Torino 2001

MENOCAL Armando G. 1863-1942 **[9]**
$6 000 - €5 181 - **£3 660** - FF33 982
Soldados Oil/canvas (38x27cm 14x10in) Miami FL
1999

MENON Anjolie Ela 1940 **[30]**
$15 000 - €17 391 - **£10 626** - FF114 076
Mother and Child Oil/canvas (178.5x82cm 70x32in)
New-York 2000
$10 254 - €9 591 - **£6 200** - FF62 915
Portrait of a Young Woman Oil/masonite
(61x45.5cm 24x17in) London 1999
$3 980 - €3 854 - **£2 500** - FF25 281
Pundit Oil/board (23x15cm 9x5in) London 1999

MENPES Mortimer L. 1860-1938 **[197]**
$4 184 - €4 491 - **£2 800** - FF29 460
English Rose Oil/panel (35.5x26.5cm 13x10in)
London 2000
$741 - €865 - **£520** - FF5 673
Asian Vilage, Huts and Figures Pencil/paper
(13.5x24.5cm 5x9in) Crewkerne, Somerset 2000
$198 - €185 - **£120** - FF1 214
«A Quiet Game of Draughts» Etching (23x27cm
9x10in) London 1998

MENS van Isidore 1890-1985 **[110]**
$10 700 - €12 394 - **£7 400** - FF81 300
Scène de rue à Batavia Huile/toile (100x120cm
39x47in) Bruxelles 2000
$1 994 - €1 829 - **£1 239** - FF12 000
Rue à Rabat Huile/panneau (65x60cm 25x23in) Paris
1999
$514 - €545 - **£327** - FF3 577
Souk des étoffes à Tunis Huile/panneau (26x21cm
10x8in) Bruxelles 2000
$476 - €496 - **£300** - FF3 252
Djerba Aquarelle/papier (27x37cm 10x14in)
Antwerpen 2000

MENSE Carlo 1886-1965 **[123]**
$2 842 - €2 455 - **£1 716** - FF16 102
Portrait Hertha Mense Oil/panel (85x57cm 33x22in)
Köln 1998
$1 491 - €1 636 - **£1 013** - FF10 732
Sonnenuntergang am Rhein Aquarell/Papier
(26.7x34.6cm 10x13in) Düsseldorf 2000
$162 - €189 - **£113** - FF1 240
Südlicher Park Woodcut (18.3x25cm 7x9in) Berlin
2000

MENTA Édouard J. 1858-1915 **[35]**
$2 570 - €2 477 - **£1 584** - FF16 251
Alter Kesselflicker am Strassenrand Öl/Leinwand
(50x65cm 19x25in) Bern 1999
$2 130 - €2 287 - **£1 425** - FF15 000
Hiver, la patineuse Huile/panneau (40.5x32.5cm
15x12in) Paris 2000

MENTOR Blasco 1918 **[203]**
$8 854 - €8 156 - **£5 403** - FF53 500
Duel au modèle blond Huile/toile (96x144cm
37x56in) Les Baux-de-Provence 1998
$2 222 - €2 643 - **£1 583** - FF17 334
Paysage Huile/toile (61x73cm 24x28in) Genève 2000
$1 200 - €1 296 - **£829** - FF8 500
Le peintre à la fenêtre Huile/toile (33x46cm
12x18in) La Varenne-Saint-Hilaire 2001
$541 - €579 - **£356** - FF3 411
Sans titre Bronze (H13.5cm H5in) Albi 2000

$233 - €229 - **£143** - FF1 500
Étude pour un portrait de femme en buste Mine
plomb (46x33cm 18x12in) Toulon 1999

MENTZEL Vincent 1945 **[9]**
$634 - €681 - **£424** - FF4 464
Riccardo Chailly Cibachrome print (100x105cm
39x41in) Amsterdam 2000

MENUSIER Jean Pierre 1783-? **[7]**
$5 373 - €5 793 - **£3 602** - FF38 000
**Portraitsde Napoléon Ier et de sa deuxième
femme, Marie-Louise** Miniature (3.5x2.5cm 1xin)
Paris 1999

MENZ Willy 1890-1969 **[26]**
$157 - €153 - **£98** - FF1 006
**Die Freie Hansestadt Bremen vor dem grossen
Kriege im Jahre** Woodcut in colors (40x110cm
15x43in) Bremen 1999

MENZEL von Adolph 1815-1905 **[259]**
$249 032 - €293 988 - **£176 870** - FF1 928 435
«Borussia» Öl/Leinwand (112.5x61.5cm 44x24in)
Berlin 2001
$26 897 - €25 949 - **£17 000** - FF170 212
Soldier seen from the Back Oil/canvas (32x26cm
12x10in) London 1999
$7 916 - €9 203 - **£5 556** - FF60 370
Specht in den Zweien eines Baums
Gouache/paper (30x16cm 11x3in) Hamburg 2001
$248 - €215 - **£147** - FF1 410
«Die Näherin am Fenster» Radierung (22x17cm
8x6in) Rudolstadt-Thüringen 1998

MENZIES John ?-1939 **[3]**
$36 718 - €32 849 - **£22 000** - FF215 474
At Noontide Heat Oil/canvas (68.5x89cm 26x35in)
Perthshire 1998

MENZIES William A. XIX-XX **[4]**
$11 608 - €13 072 - **£8 000** - FF85 746
**Coronation Portrait of King George V, after Sir
Luke Fildes** Oil/canvas (187x122cm 73x48in) London
2000

MENZIO Francesco 1899-1979 **[67]**
$11 000 - €11 403 - **£6 600** - FF74 800
Paesaggio delle Langhe Olio/tela (100x160cm
39x62in) Vercelli 2001
$6 000 - €6 220 - **£3 600** - FF40 800
Nudo disteso Olio/tela (47x61cm 18x24in) Vercelli
2001
$1 800 - €1 866 - **£1 080** - FF12 240
Frammento Olio/tavola (43x28cm 16x11in) Vercelli
2000
$2 250 - €2 332 - **£1 350** - FF15 300
Modella nello studio, Carla Tempera/carta
(52x36cm 20x14in) Vercelli 1999

MENZLER Wilhelm 1846-1926 **[34]**
$4 250 - €4 064 - **£2 588** - FF26 660
**The Harem Garden - Portrait of a Mother and
child** Oil/canvas (101.5x67cm 39x26in) Boston MA
1999
$1 386 - €1 278 - **£830** - FF8 383
**Damenporträt, Brustbild, im Profil nach rechts
gewendet** Öl/Leinwand (44x36cm 17x14in) Dresden
1998

MÉRAC du Agnès 1951 **[26]**
$1 558 - €1 372 - **£949** - FF9 000
Le réveil Bronze (H24.5cm H9in) Villeneuve-les-
Avignon 1999

MERAGA Carlo XIX [1]
- $2 301 - €2 592 - £1 603 - FF17 000
Le port de Villefranche Huile/panneau (31.5x40.5cm 12x15in) Nice 2001

MERANO Giovan Battista 1632-1698 [8]
- $14 000 - €14 513 - £8 400 - FF95 200
Il transito di San Giuseppe Olio/tela (122x150cm 48x59in) Roma 2000
- $15 600 - €13 476 - £10 400 - FF88 400
Allegoria dell'inverno Olio/tela (124x94cm 48x37in) Milano 1998
- $2 728 - €2 710 - £1 700 - FF17 779
Christ Brandishing Arrows, with Saint Roch/The Madona and Child Black chalk (26x19cm 10x7in) London 1999

MÉRARD Pierre XVIII-XIX [1]
- $10 196 - €11 660 - £7 000 - FF76 484
Bust of Claude François Moreau, Facing Slightly to Sinister Terracotta (H84.5cm H33in) London 2000

MERCADE Benet 1821-1897 [4]
- $9 230 - €7 808 - £5 460 - FF51 220
Coro de Sta María Novella Oleo/lienzo (88x120cm 34x47in) Madrid 1998

MERCADE Jaume 1922 [12]
- $8 625 - €7 508 - £5 375 - FF49 250
Bosc de Valls Oleo/lienzo (70x91cm 27x35in) Madrid 1999

MERCADÉ QUERALT Jaime 1889-1967 [34]
- $3 564 - €3 244 - £2 160 - FF21 276
Paisaje Tarragona Oleo/lienzo (63x51cm 24x20in) Madrid 1999

MERCATOR Gerardus, G. Kremer 1512-1594 [32]
- $244 - €262 - £163 - FF1 720
Map of Ins.Ceilan Engraving (34x49cm 13x19in) London 2000

MERCER Edward Stanley XX [1]
- $1 966 - €1 982 - £1 225 - FF13 000
Merce Cunningham I Sérigraphie couleurs (76x51cm 29x20in) Paris 2000

MERCER Frederick ?-c.1937 [22]
- $252 - €244 - £160 - FF1 602
Cottage at Slapton, South Devon with a Figure and Pony Trap Watercolour/paper (16x26cm 6x10in) Devon 1999

MERCIÉ Marius Jean Antonin 1845-1916 [223]
- $11 132 - €9 604 - £6 690 - FF63 000
Gloria Victis Bronze (H100cm H39in) Belfort 1998
- $3 622 - €3 069 - £2 164 - FF20 134
Corpus Christi Sculpture (H33cm H12in) Bremen 1998

MERCIER Charles 1832-1909 [26]
- $3 160 - €3 049 - £1 998 - FF20 000
Vue des ruines de Pompéi Huile/panneau (25x46.5cm 9x18in) Paris 1999

MERCIER Georges XX [8]
- $795 - €915 - £561 - FF6 000
«Le plombier amoureux» Affiche (120x160cm 47x62in) Paris 2001

MERCIER Jean Adrien 1899-1995 [553]
- $3 341 - €3 125 - £2 023 - FF20 500
La Baule Huile/papier (27.5x18.5cm 10x7in) Paris 1999
- $2 073 - €1 906 - £1 274 - FF12 500
La mouette Aquarelle/papier (28.5x22cm 11x8in) Angers 1999

- $456 - €427 - £276 - FF2 800
Rêverie de Loire Lithographie (50x50cm 19x19in) Paris 1999

MERCIER Philippe 1689-1760 [63]
- $24 369 - €23 711 - £15 000 - FF155 532
Woman taking off her Stocking Oil/canvas (127x100cm 50x39in) London 1999
- $11 932 - €10 231 - £7 000 - FF67 113
Portrait of Thomas Samwell Oil/canvas (73.5x59.5cm 28x23in) Leicestershire 1998
- $13 101 - €12 172 - £8 000 - FF79 840
Study of a Standing Woman her Head Turned in Profile Black & white chalks/paper (52x31cm 20x12in) London 1998

MERCIER Ruth act.1880-1913 [7]
- $9 910 - €9 076 - £6 040 - FF59 532
Rose Splendour Oil/canvas (65x105cm 25x41in) Amsterdam 1999
- $926 - €994 - £620 - FF6 523
Boats at Anchor - South of France Watercolour (35x52cm 13x20in) Bath 2000

MERCK van der Jacob Fransz. 1610-1664 [20]
- $47 600 - €55 278 - £33 450 - FF362 600
Landskap med förnämt jaktsällskap Oil/canvas (103x133cm 40x52in) Stockholm 2001
- $5 662 - €5 249 - £3 500 - FF34 432
Portrait of Lady, in a black Dress/Portrait of a Gentleman, black coat Oil/canvas (76x64.5cm 29x25in) London 1998
- $7 343 - €6 826 - £4 500 - FF44 775
Portrait of a Lady, small full-length, in a black Dress Oil/panel (45.5x29cm 17x11in) London 1998

MERCKAERT Jules 1872-1924 [51]
- $795 - €917 - £543 - FF6 016
Matin sur la Dendre Huile/toile (56x45cm 22x17in) Bruxelles 2000
- $441 - €488 - £306 - FF3 200
Paysage Huile/panneau (15x24cm 5x9in) Paris 2001

MERCKER Erich 1891-1973 [162]
- $893 - €1 022 - £614 - FF6 707
Pinnistal, Stubai, Tirol Öl/Leinwand (65.5x85.5cm 25x33in) München 2000

MERCULIANO Giacomo 1859-1935 [13]
- $1 501 - €1 677 - £1 017 - FF11 000
Lionne rugissant Bronze (64x26cm 25x10in) Paris 1999

MEREILES Cildo 1948 [1]
- $13 000 - €11 335 - £7 859 - FF74 356
«To:L.C» Assemblage (41x60cm 16x23in) New-York 1998

MÉRET Émile-Louis XIX-XX [18]
- $1 134 - €1 081 - £684 - FF7 092
St Jean de Pied de Porc Oleo/lienzo (54x65cm 21x25in) Madrid 1999

MERHO (Pierre Merhottein) 1948 [1]
- $1 980 - €1 859 - £1 222 - FF12 195
Kiekeboe Encre/papier (46x35cm 18x13in) Antwerpen 1999

MERIAN Maria Sybilla 1647-1717 [21]
- $40 557 - €39 685 - £26 000 - FF260 317
A Surinam Hawk Moth at various Stages of its Life-Cycle Watercolour, gouache (28.5x37cm 11x14in) London 1999
- $270 - €307 - £188 - FF2 012
Insectes de Surinem/Lycium Kupferstich (40x30cm 15x11in) München 2001

MERIAN Matthäus I 1593-1650 **[188]**
- $7 012 - €8 168 - **£4 899** - FF53 578
  Landscape with a Peasant in the Foreground Three Bridges over a Stream Ink (12x15.5cm 4x6in) Amsterdam 2000
- $126 - €143 - **£88** - FF936
  «Bienna Biel» Kupferstich (21x32cm 8x12in) Bern 2001

MERIAN Matthäus II 1621-1687 **[11]**
- $167 - €169 - **£104** - FF1 106
  Blick von Nordosten auf die befestigte Stadt Strassburg Kupferstich (24x38cm 9x14in) Staufen 2000

MÉRIDA Carlos 1891-1984 **[216]**
- $28 000 - €30 055 - **£18 737** - FF197 148
  Abstract Mixed media/panel (84x183cm 33x72in) New-York 2000
- $30 000 - €29 189 - **£18 465** - FF191 469
  El Exodo de las Siete Tribus Oil/masonite (47x86.5cm 18x34in) New-York 1999
- $15 000 - €14 444 - **£9 336** - FF94 744
  Remembranza de Talavera Oil/masonite (40x30cm 15x11in) New-York 1999
- $1 890 - €1 637 - **£1 140** - FF10 735
  Reproducción de un boceto Bronze (20x27x3cm 7x10x1in) México 1998
- $17 000 - €14 785 - **£10 249** - FF96 985
  «Duo» Mixed media/paper (78x57cm 30x22in) New-York 1998
- $1 089 - €1 017 - **£672** - FF6 669
  Sin título Litografía (57x38cm 22x14in) México 1999

MÉRIEL-BUSSY André 1902-1985 **[70]**
- $776 - €762 - **£481** - FF5 000
  Vénus Huile/toile (81x54cm 31x21in) Lyon 1999
- $384 - €457 - **£274** - FF3 000
  Marine, le paysage des barques Gouache/papier (21x26cm 8x10in) Brest 2000

MERIGOT J. 1760-1824 **[4]**
- $5 768 - €6 374 - **£4 000** - FF41 812
  Dry Harbour in the Parish of St Ann/The Bridge/Port Antonio Aquatint (47x66.5cm 18x26in) London 2001

MÉRIMÉE Jean 1757-1836 **[2]**
- $1 554 - €1 829 - **£1 092** - FF12 000
  :L'ombre de Polinure se présente à Enée Crayon (22x15.5cm 8x6in) Paris 2000

MERINO Daniel 1941 **[48]**
- $728 - €841 - **£504** - FF5 516
  Menina Oleo/tabla (45x37cm 17x14in) Madrid 2001

MÉRITE Édouard Paul 1867-1941 **[104]**
- $749 - €686 - **£456** - FF4 500
  Perdrix Huile/carton (26.5x35cm 10x13in) Paris 1999
- $270 - €305 - **£188** - FF2 000
  Étude de chevreuils Crayon/papier (31x24cm 12x9in) Paris 2001

MERK Eduard 1816-1888 **[18]**
- $3 554 - €4 090 - **£2 454** - FF26 831
  Mutter mit Kindern in der guten Stube Öl/Leinwand (53x41cm 20x16in) München 2000
- $670 - €767 - **£461** - FF5 030
  Fröhliche Tafelrunde niederländischer Herren und einer Dame Oil/panel (24x32.5cm 9x12in) München 2000

MERKE Henri XVIII-XIX **[15]**
- $725 - €702 - **£460** - FF4 607
  The Tiger at Bay Aquatint (46x55.5cm 18x21in) London 1999

MERKEL Georg, Jerzy 1881-1976 **[52]**
- $7 730 - €7 267 - **£4 680** - FF47 670
  Hirte und Nymphe Öl/Leinwand (56.5x44.5cm 22x17in) Wien 1999
- $947 - €1 067 - **£660** - FF7 000
  Femme et enfant Huile/panneau (24x19cm 9x7in) Paris 2001

MERKER Max 1861-1928 **[28]**
- $778 - €920 - **£552** - FF6 037
  Harzlandschaft Öl/Leinwand/Karton (60x45cm 23x17in) Ahlden 2000

MERKESTEIJN van Gerrit Arnoldus 1825-1858 **[3]**
- $1 544 - €1 815 - **£1 070** - FF11 906
  A Lady in an Interior Making Lace by the Light of an Oil Lamp Oil/panel (52x40cm 20x15in) Amsterdam 2000

MERLE Hugues 1823-1881 **[30]**
- $13 065 - €11 891 - **£8 166** - FF78 000
  La jeune mendiante Huile/toile (100x80cm 39x31in) Fontainebleau 1999
- $7 043 - €8 080 - **£4 817** - FF53 000
  Les deux amis Huile/toile (26x34cm 10x13in) Soissons 2000

MERLIN C. XIX **[10]**
- $30 000 - €32 039 - **£20 442** - FF210 159
  View of the Gardens of a Country House Oil/canvas (70x102.5cm 27x40in) New-York 2001
- $368 - €366 - **£229** - FF2 000
  Les grappes de raisin Aquarelle/papier (23.5x37cm 9x14in) Paris 1999

MERLIN Daniel 1861-1933 **[39]**
- $5 000 - €5 380 - **£3 585** - FF38 569
  Playtime Oil/canvas (51x62cm 20x24in) New-York 2001
- $2 688 - €2 975 - **£1 800** - FF19 512
  Jeunes chats Huile/toile (22.5x27cm 8x10in) Antwerpen 2000

MERLO Camillo 1856-1931 **[30]**
- $1 000 - €1 296 - **£750** - FF8 500
  Neve Olio/cartone (30x41cm 11x16in) Vercelli 2001

MERLO Metello 1886-1964 **[82]**
- $1 000 - €1 296 - **£750** - FF8 500
  Paesaggio londinese Olio/cartone (40x50cm 15x19in) Vercelli 2000
- $840 - €726 - **£420** - FF4 760
  Mattino di aprile (Oggebbio) Olio/cartone (24x30cm 9x11in) Torino 1999

MERME Charles ?-1869 **[2]**
- $2 948 - €3 506 - **£2 044** - FF23 000
  Promeneurs dans la fôret amazonienne Huile/toile (64x88cm 25x34in) Paris 2000

MÉRODACK-JEANNEAU Alexis 1873-1919 **[63]**
- $260 - €305 - **£186** - FF2 000
  Espagnole à la robe fleurie Crayons couleurs/papier (37x21cm 14x8in) Angers 2001

MERODE von Carl Freiherr 1853-1909 **[14]**
- $2 163 - €2 180 - **£1 350** - FF14 301
  Stilleben mit Hummer Öl/Leinwand (37x90cm 14x35in) Wien 2000
- $1 474 - €1 555 - **£974** - FF10 201
  Auf dem Markt Oil/panel (22.5x17.5cm 8x6in) Zürich 2000

MERRICK Emily M. XIX **[2]**
- $25 896 - €24 294 - **£16 000** - FF159 358
  Primrose day Oil/canvas (154x122cm 60x48in) Leyburn, North Yorkshire 1999

MERRIFIELD Tom 1932 **[73]**

- **$1 811** - €1 702 - **£1 100** - FF11 164
  Wayne Sleep Bronze (H30.5cm H12in) London 1999
- **$408** - €342 - **£240** - FF2 243
  Dancer Resting Crayon (39.5x28.5cm 15x11in)
  London 1998

MERRILD Knut 1894-1954 **[6]**

- **$3 318** - €3 752 - **£2 242** - FF24 614
  Aroma of birth Oil/panel (19x16cm 7x6in)
  København 2000

MERRIOTT Jack 1901-1968 **[57]**

- **$245** - €271 - **£170** - FF1 777
  Sunlit Valley Watercolour/paper (34x50cm 13x19in)
  London 2001
- **$777** - €901 - **£550** - FF5 911
  «Service to the Fishing Industry, Hull, British Railways» Poster (102x127cm 40x50in) London 2000

MERSHIMER Frederic W. 1945 **[16]**

- **$425** - €398 - **£261** - FF2 612
  The Arch Mezzotint (30x45cm 11x17in) New-York 1999

MERSON Luc Olivier 1846-1920 **[39]**

- **$30 000** - €28 460 - **£18 225** - FF186 687
  Springtime Awakening Oil/canvas (65x92cm 25x36in) New-York 1999
- **$1 035** - €1 143 - **£717** - FF7 500
  Fillette nue courant Mine plomb (47x55cm 18x21in) Nantes 2001

MERSSEMAN de Auguste Joseph M. 1808-c.1880 **[6]**

- **$5 446** - €5 488 - **£3 394** - FF36 000
  Élégante à l'éventail Huile/panneau (40x34cm 15x13in) Paris 2000

MERTENS Charles 1865-1919 **[46]**

- **$1 276** - €1 220 - **£800** - FF8 004
  Two Racing Pigeons on a Jetty with a Continental Town beyond Oil/canvas (61x80cm 24x31in) London 1999

MERTENS Wouter XVII **[4]**

- **$17 677** - €17 534 - **£11 000** - FF115 013
  Peaches, grapes and other Fruit in a Basket, a partly peeled Lemon Oil/canvas (40x55cm 15x21in) London 1999

MERTZ Albert 1920-1991 **[106]**

- **$397** - €403 - **£246** - FF2 645
  Röd, blå komposition med stole Gouache/paper (24x32cm 9x12in) København 2000

MERTZ Johannes Cornelis 1819-1891 **[19]**

- **$2 015** - €2 259 - **£1 409** - FF14 819
  Welcome Intelligence Oil/panel (50x38.5cm 19x15in) Auckland 2001
- **$1 642** - €1 815 - **£1 139** - FF11 906
  Portrait of a young Lady Oil/panel (28.5x23.5cm 11x9in) Amsterdam 2001

MERWART Paul 1855-1902 **[18]**

- **$6 057** - €7 158 - **£4 293** - FF46 954
  Portrait einer jungen Dame Oil/panel (55x33cm 21x12in) Ahlden 2001

MÉRYON Charles 1821-1868 **[279]**

- **$700** - €805 - **£482** - FF5 283
  La Rue des Chantres Etching (29x14cm 11x5in) Cleveland OH 2000

MERZ Albert 1942 **[28]**

- **$399** - €470 - **£282** - FF3 085
  Badende Farbserigraphie (62.5x47.5cm 24x18in) Berlin 2001

MERZ Gerhard 1947 **[38]**

- **$6 719** - €7 925 - **£4 739** - FF51 985
  Milano Mixed media (90x280x24.5cm 35x110x9in) Köln 2001
- **$12 309** - €11 910 - **£7 800** - FF78 127
  Roma Relief (91.5x189.5x15cm 36x74x5in) London 1999
- **$262** - €281 - **£175** - FF1 844
  Hamburg Farbserigraphie (35x70cm 13x27in) Köln 2000

MERZ Karl 1890-1970 **[11]**

- **$539** - €613 - **£374** - FF4 024
  Partie auf der Baar Öl/Leinwand (79x98cm 31x38in) Staufen 2001

MERZ Mario 1925 **[107]**

- **$32 942** - €30 622 - **£20 000** - FF200 864
  Untitled Acrylic (185x286cm 72x112in) London 1998
- **$5 768** - €6 374 - **£4 000** - FF41 812
  Untitled Painting (77x104cm 30x40in) London 2001
- **$68 868** - €56 567 - **£40 000** - FF371 056
  Lance Construction (282x70x35.5cm 111x27x13in) London 1998
- **$3 952** - €4 704 - **£2 824** - FF30 855
  Ohne Titel Pencil (62.4x87.5cm 24x34in) Berlin 2000
- **$1 008** - €1 176 - **£707** - FF7 714
  Ohne Titel Farbradierung (27.6x35.6cm 10x14in) Köln 2000
- **$35 000** - €39 832 - **£24 594** - FF261 282
  Two Lances Photograph (269x76x40.5cm 105x29x15in) New-York 2001

MESCHIS Renzo 1945 **[25]**

- **$175** - €181 - **£105** - FF1 190
  Paesaggio siciliano Olio/tela (30x20cm 11x7in) Vercelli 2001

MESDACH Salomon XVII **[1]**

- **$7 940** - €7 267 - **£4 840** - FF47 670
  Bildnis einer Dame mit Halskrause und Perlenschmuck im Haar Oil/panel (54.5x43.5cm 21x17in) Wien 1999

MESDAG Hendrick Willem 1831-1915 **[188]**

- **$259 260** - €272 268 - **£164 040** - FF1 785 960
  Bomschuiten at Sea Oil/canvas (100x157.5cm 39x62in) Amsterdam 2000
- **$73 700** - €81 308 - **£48 741** - FF533 346
  At the Coast Oil/canvas (49.5x78.5cm 19x30in) Vancouver, BC. 2000
- **$20 745** - €21 781 - **£13 080** - FF142 876
  Le soleil couchant en hiver Oil/panel (28x42cm 11x16in) Amsterdam 2000
- **$15 699** - €13 275 - **£9 388** - FF87 076
  Een binnenkomende bomschuit Watercolour (61x80cm 24x31in) Amsterdam 1998

MESDAG Taco 1829-1902 **[11]**

- **$1 481** - €1 543 - **£938** - FF10 120
  Winterlandschap met boerderij achter de duinen Oil/canvas (38.5x48.5cm 15x19in) Den Haag 2000

MESDAG VAN HOUTEN Sientje, Sina 1834-1909 **[70]**

- **$3 362** - €3 630 - **£2 299** - FF23 812
  A Still Life with a Jar Oil/canvas (140x100cm 55x39in) Amsterdam 2001
- **$2 657** - €2 496 - **£1 601** - FF16 371
  Paul Joseph Constantin Gabriël (1828-1903) Oil/canvas (51x40cm 20x15in) Amsterdam 1999
- **$1 015** - €861 - **£612** - FF5 649
  Stilleven met bloemen en gemberpotten Oil/board (41.5x34cm 16x13in) Den Haag 1998

M

$401 - €386 - £250 - FF2 530
Farmhouses in Drenthe Watercolour (20x29cm 7x11in) Amsterdam 1999

MESECK Felix 1883-1955 [36]

$5 997 - €7 056 - £4 233 - FF46 282
Vier Personen Öl/Leinwand (93x78cm 36x30in) Berlin 2001

$123 - €138 - £83 - FF905
Penthesilea Drypoint (36.8x27.7cm 14x10in) Koblenz 2000

MESEGUER José 1900-1957 [7]

$650 - €601 - £400 - FF3 940
Los mártires del Coliseo Oleo/tabla (16.5x21.5cm 6x8in) Madrid 1999

MESENS Edouard Léon Théod. 1903-1971 [88]

$500 - €518 - £300 - FF3 400
«I Love You Free» Tecnica mista/carta (31.5x33cm 12x13in) Milano 1999

MESGRINY de Claude François A. 1836-1884 [8]

$7 500 - €6 502 - £4 583 - FF42 651
River Landscape Oil/canvas (36.5x56.5cm 14x22in) New-York 1999

MESHERSKY Arseny Ivanovitch 1834-1902 [23]

$5 997 - €6 661 - £4 000 - FF43 692
Mountain View Oil/canvas (49x70cm 19x27in) London 2001

$3 750 - €4 483 - £2 586 - FF29 407
Fisherman on a Mountain Lake Oil/canvas (32x43cm 12x17in) Milford CT 2000

MESLÉ Joseph Paul 1855-1929 [12]

$921 - €1 071 - £657 - FF7 026
Village in Brittany Oil/canvas (46.5x65cm 18x25in) Toronto 2001

MESLY David 1918 [102]

$3 400 - €3 125 - £2 088 - FF20 500
Igor, l'ours Bronze (8x22cm 3x8in) Bourges 1999

MESNAGER Jérôme 1961 [269]

$1 452 - €1 677 - £1 016 - FF11 000
«L'éternelle idole» Acrylique/toile (130x97cm 51x38in) Paris 2001

$1 000 - €854 - £603 - FF5 600
«A nous deux pour la vie» Acrylique (76x57.5cm 29x22in) Paris 1998

$412 - €457 - £276 - FF3 000
Dominique Acrylique (40x33cm 15x12in) Paris 2000

$1 173 - €1 098 - £710 - FF7 200
Monsieur Vie René Encre (65x50cm 25x19in) Paris 1999

$447 - €534 - £319 - FF3 500
La ballade de l'amour Lithographie couleurs (37x115cm 14x45in) Paris 2000

MESNIER Patrice 1945 [18]

$1 670 - €1 524 - £1 016 - FF10 000
L'arrivée de course Fer (35x55x30cm 13x21x11in) Versailles 1998

MESPLES Paul Eugène 1849-? [10]

$3 200 - €3 177 - £2 000 - FF20 841
The Pagan Procession Oil/board (37.5x77cm 14x30in) London 1999

MESQUIDA Guillermo 1765-1747 [1]

$19 200 - €18 019 - £12 000 - FF118 200
La expulsión del jardín del Edén Oleo/lienzo (63.5x48.5cm 25x19in) Palma de Mallorca 1999

MESQUITA de Samuel Jessurun 1868-1944 [73]

$412 - €386 - £249 - FF2 530
Muziekkapel «Artis» Pastel/paper (17x29cm 6x11in) Dordrecht 1999

$598 - €681 - £415 - FF4 464
Heron Etching (29.8x17.7cm 11x6in) Haarlem 2000

MESS George Jo 1898-1962 [14]

$3 750 - €4 200 - £2 605 - FF27 552
«Adirondacks, Near Lake Placid» Oil/canvas (53x73cm 21x29in) Cincinnati OH 2001

MESSAGER Annette 1943 [20]

$28 000 - €26 290 - £17 348 - FF172 454
Mes trophées Acrylic (80x185.5cm 31x73in) New-York 1999

$21 421 - €23 630 - £14 508 - FF155 000
La Reine de la Nuit, série des Chimères Technique mixte (170x26cm 66x10in) Paris 2000

$16 896 - €18 294 - £11 568 - FF120 000
Histoire des robes Assemblage (130x30x8.5cm 51x11x3in) Paris 2001

$18 000 - €17 416 - £11 100 - FF114 244
L'Histoire des Robes Construction (30x139x8.5cm 11x54x3in) New-York 1999

$16 653 - €19 818 - £11 895 - FF130 000
Les variétés No.74 Photo (230x40cm 90x15in) Paris 2000

MESSAGIER Jean 1920-1999 [528]

$4 363 - €4 116 - £2 691 - FF27 000
Weilmesterschaft Acrylique/toile (125x195cm 49x76in) Paris 1999

$1 254 - €1 448 - £877 - FF9 500
«Printemps d'hiver» Acrylique/toile (69.5x124cm 27x48in) Paris 2001

$714 - €686 - £448 - FF4 500
Composition Huile/toile (28.5x41cm 11x16in) Vannes 1999

$832 - €838 - £518 - FF5 500
Aile brisée Bronze (H17cm H6in) Paris 2000

$445 - €427 - £280 - FF2 800
Printemps de Buster Brown Pastel/paper (57x87.5cm 22x34in) Belfort 1999

$116 - €117 - £71 - FF700
Le nez dans l'été/Mai cousu par les fleurs de pommiers Lithographie couleurs (54.5x76cm 21x29in) Paris 1999

MESSEG Aharon 1942 [85]

$7 000 - €6 918 - £4 284 - FF45 381
Figure Oil/canvas (180x160cm 70x62in) Tel Aviv 2000

$3 600 - €4 268 - £2 622 - FF27 995
House in a Landscape Oil/canvas (77x92.5cm 30x36in) Tel Aviv 2001

$1 250 - €1 342 - £836 - FF8 804
Trees in Landscape Oil/canvas (25.5x21cm 10x8in) Tel Aviv 2000

$300 - €322 - £200 - FF2 112
Figure and Flags Mixed media/paper (19x30cm 7x11in) Tel Aviv 2000

MESSELL Oliver 1904-1978 [33]

$840 - €977 - £600 - FF6 409
Costume Design for Tough at the Top Watercolour (50x35.5cm 19x13in) London 2001

MESSENSEE Jürgen 1937 [83]

$2 166 - €2 543 - £1 536 - FF16 684
Ohne Titel Acryl/Karton (95x70cm 37x27in) Wien 2000

$2 097 - €1 816 - £1 272 - FF11 912
Ohne Titel Mischtechnik/Papier (29x20.5cm 11x8in) Wien 1998

MESSER Abraham Jozef 1886-1931 **[3]**
- $8 000 - €7 338 - **£4 928** - FF48 132
  Jewish Taylor Mixed media/board (61x44.5cm 24x17in) New-York 1999
- $6 000 - €5 503 - **£3 696** - FF36 099
  The Scribe Oil/board (25.5x30cm 10x11in) New-York 1999
- $6 000 - €5 840 - **£3 686** - FF38 306
  Jewish Chess Players Pastel (62x45cm 24x17in) Tel Aviv 1999

MESSER Ken XX **[6]**
- $324 - €314 - **£200** - FF2 058
  Tranquil Summer River Scene Windrush Valley, Gloucestershire Watercolour/paper (30x43cm 12x17in) Tunbridge-Wells, Kent 1999

MESSERER Stephan 1798-1865 **[12]**
- $126 - €123 - **£79** - FF804
  Bremen: die Hachenburg Indian ink (10x19cm 3x7in) Bremen 1999
- $200 - €194 - **£125** - FF1 274
  Bremen: St. Petri Dom Kirche/St. Ansgarii Kirche/St. Stephani Kirche Copper engraving (15x10cm 5x3in) Bremen 1999

MESSICK Benjamin, Ben 1901-1981 **[32]**
- $3 750 - €3 504 - **£2 336** - FF22 982
  Young Girl holding Flower Oil/canvas (60x45cm 24x18in) Mystic CT 1999

MESSINA Francesco 1900-1995 **[98]**
- $24 000 - €20 733 - **£16 000** - FF136 000
  Nudo femminile Bronze (H80.5cm H31in) Prato 1998
- $4 100 - €4 250 - **£2 460** - FF27 880
  Mussolini Bronze (H61cm H24in) Roma 1999
- $960 - €1 244 - **£720** - FF8 160
  Volto femminile Sanguina/carta (20x16.5cm 7x6in) Milano 2000

MESSMER Otto 1892-1983 **[6]**
- $1 300 - €1 254 - **£821** - FF8 226
  Sunday Page to Felix The Cat Ink (41x52cm 16x20in) New-York 1999

MESTRE BOSCH Juan 1824-1893 **[2]**
- $3 060 - €2 703 - **£1 890** - FF17 730
  Paisaje de Mallorca Oleo/lienzo (24x32cm 9x12in) Madrid 1999

MESTRES BORRELL Félix 1872-1933 **[11]**
- $10 825 - €10 047 - **£6 500** - FF65 904
  The proud Mother Oil/canvas (106.5x125.5cm 41x49in) London 1999

MESTROVICH Ivan 1883-1962 **[13]**
- $2 391 - €2 812 - **£1 714** - FF18 446
  Sitzender Akt Bronze (H39cm H15in) Düsseldorf 2001

MESZAROS Andor 1900-1972 **[9]**
- $3 373 - €3 778 - **£2 343** - FF24 782
  Spitting Boy, Fountain Bronze (32x50cm 12x19in) Melbourne 2001

MESZLENYI Attila XX **[11]**
- $319 - €347 - **£219** - FF2 276
  Tétra Aquarelle/papier (20x18cm 7x7in) Bruxelles 2001

MESZÖLY Géza 1844-1887 **[12]**
- $18 150 - €20 626 - **£12 650** - FF135 300
  Ruisseau Huile/toile (61x101cm 24x39in) Budapest 2001
- $2 625 - €2 904 - **£1 725** - FF19 050
  Shore of Lake Balaton Oil/canvas (26x35cm 10x13in) Budapest 2000

METCALF Conger 1914-1998 **[29]**
- $4 000 - €4 676 - **£2 832** - FF30 670
  Woman in flowered Hat Oil/paper (35x45cm 14x18in) Cedar-Falls IA 2001
- $650 - €648 - **£405** - FF4 253
  Portrait of a Young Man Pencil/paper (27x25cm 11x10in) Watertown MA 1999

METCALF Eliab 1785-1834 **[8]**
- $7 000 - €8 170 - **£4 941** - FF53 591
  Self Portrait, Havana, Cuba Oil/canvas (76x60cm 30x24in) New-York 2000

METCALF Willard Leroy 1858-1925 **[50]**
- $50 000 - €53 670 - **£33 460** - FF352 050
  Mountain Lakes Oil/canvas (46.5x55cm 18x21in) New-York 2000
- $17 000 - €19 303 - **£11 634** - FF126 622
  Souvenir de Printemps Oil/panel (23x15cm 9x5in) New-York 2000
- $3 750 - €3 205 - **£2 203** - FF21 022
  «At Campton N.H» Mixed media/paper (28x43cm 11x16in) Boston MA 1998

METEIN-GILLIARD Valentine 1891-1969 **[6]**
- $3 066 - €3 607 - **£2 222** - FF23 658
  Saviésan à la channe Huile/toile (100x73cm 39x28in) Sion 2001

METELLI Orneore 1872-1938 **[4]**
- $3 500 - €3 628 - **£2 100** - FF23 800
  Il Santuario Olio/tela (48.5x71.5cm 19x28in) Milano 2001

METEREAU Florimond 1888-? **[6]**
- $2 484 - €2 744 - **£1 722** - FF18 000
  Casbah à Skoura Gouache/papier (60x50cm 23x19in) Paris 2001

METEYARD Sidney Harold 1868-1947 **[20]**
- $5 440 - €5 106 - **£3 400** - FF33 490
  Retrato de joven Oleo/lienzo (43x33cm 16x12in) Madrid 1999
- $9 821 - €11 680 - **£7 000** - FF76 616
  Sibyl Red chalk/paper (34.5x22.5cm 13x8in) London 2000

METEYARD Thomas Bredford 1865-1928 **[4]**
- $3 736 - €4 011 - **£2 500** - FF26 308
  Scituate, Landscape, Maryland Oil/canvas (36.5x54.5cm 14x21in) London 2000

METHER-BORGSTRÖM Ernst 1917-1996 **[40]**
- $4 610 - €4 035 - **£2 793** - FF26 469
  April Oil/canvas (111x146cm 43x57in) Helsinki 1998
- $600 - €673 - **£417** - FF4 412
  Ytor Gouache/paper (49x69cm 19x27in) Helsinki 2001
- $330 - €303 - **£201** - FF1 985
  Untitled Lithograph (39x50cm 15x19in) Helsinki 1999

METHEY André 1871-1920 **[11]**
- $628 - €610 - **£398** - FF4 000
  Vase boule à col évasé à décor floral Céramique (H14.5cm H5in) Paris 1999

METHUEN Paul Ayshford, Lord 1886-1974 **[86]**
- $889 - €993 - **£620** - FF6 512
  Collanges, Lot, France Oil/canvas (45x65cm 17x25in) Bath 2001
- $1 701 - €1 452 - **£1 000** - FF9 523
  Nude and Cat Oil/board (24x34.5cm 9x13in) London 1998
- $353 - €328 - **£220** - FF2 151
  Isle Abbots, Somerset Ink (39x29cm 15x11in) London 1999

M

METIVET

METIVET Lucien M. Fr., Luc 1863-1937 **[49]**
- $899 - €838 - £540 - FF5 431
  Street Singer Color lithograph (139x154cm 54x60in) London 1999

METLICOVITZ Leopoldo 1868-1944 **[57]**
- $2 233 - €2 135 - £1 400 - FF14 007
  «Fleurs de mousse» Poster (109x79cm 42x31in) London 1999

METMAN Philip 1892-1967 **[10]**
- $789 - €920 - £554 - FF6 037
  Ohne Titel Gouache/paper (24.8x15.7cm 9x6in) Köln 2000

METSU Gabriel 1629-1667 **[12]**
- $10 752 - €11 898 - £7 536 - FF78 048
  Place du marché Huile/toile (54x62.5cm 21x24in) Bruxelles 2001
- $1 431 888 - €1 407 524 - £920 000 - FF9 232 752
  Officer paying court to young Woman in an Interior Oil/canvas (40.5x35.5cm 15x13in) London 1999

METTENHOVEN Marcel 1891-1979 **[43]**
- $978 - €838 - £588 - FF5 500
  Environ d'Auray Huile/toile (50x73cm 19x28in) Pontivy 1998
- $581 - €610 - £385 - FF4 000
  Ile aux Moines Aquarelle/papier (24x17cm 9x6in) Vannes 2000

METTES Franz 1909-1984 **[35]**
- $124 - €145 - £85 - FF952
  «Reist per spoor Week-eind retours» Poster (100x61.5cm 39x24in) Hoorn 2000

METTHEY André 1871-1920 **[17]**
- $1 739 - €1 753 - £1 084 - FF11 500
  Oiseaux dressés sur fond de feuillage (plat) Céramique (8x36.5cm 3x14in) Paris 2000

METTLER Ernest 1903-1933 **[2]**
- $1 000 - €947 - £621 - FF6 209
  «Fach-Ausstellung» Poster (127.5x91cm 50x35in) New-York 1999

METZ Cäsar 1823-1895 **[13]**
- $390 - €415 - £262 - FF2 725
  Hojlandskab med graessende koer Oil/board (46x63cm 18x24in) Viby J, Århus 2001

METZ Friedrich 1820-1901 **[6]**
- $2 440 - €2 556 - £1 614 - FF16 769
  Gebirgslandschaft mit Hirten und weidenden Ziegen am Wasser vorn Öl/Leinwand (30x43cm 11x16in) München 2000

METZ Gerry Michael 1943 **[8]**
- $1 550 - €1 687 - £1 065 - FF11 065
  «The Intruder» Watercolour/paper (50x76cm 20x30in) St. Louis MO 2001

METZ Johann Martin 1717-c.1790 **[9]**
- $4 599 - €5 336 - £3 272 - FF35 000
  Coupe de raisins et de roses sur un entablement Huile/toile (38x30cm 14x11in) Paris 2001

METZINGER Jean 1883-1956 **[349]**
- $106 844 - €117 691 - £71 255 - FF772 000
  Le chat sur la table Huile/toile (162x130cm 63x51in) Deauville 2000
- $46 368 - €43 209 - £28 000 - FF283 430
  Nu couché à la persienne Oil/canvas (81x116cm 31x45in) London 1998
- $17 359 - €16 797 - £11 000 - FF110 179
  Nu au collier Oil/canvas (35x24cm 13x9in) London 1999

- $2 502 - €2 287 - £1 540 - FF15 000
  La maison rouge Aquarelle/papier (19x13cm 7x5in) Paris 1999

METZKER Ray K. 1931 **[10]**
- $2 200 - €2 442 - £1 533 - FF16 019
  City Whispers, Philadelphia Gelatin silver print (28.5x20.5cm 11x8in) New-York 2001

METZKES Harald 1929 **[48]**
- $2 965 - €3 323 - £2 065 - FF21 800
  Jahrmarkt auf dem Dorf Öl/Leinwand (60x70cm 23x27in) Berlin 2001
- $1 343 - €1 176 - £813 - FF7 712
  Kafeetafel Öl/Leinwand (24x30cm 9x11in) Berlin 1998
- $71 - €87 - £50 - FF570
  Stilleben mit Geige und Wasserglas Farblithographie (26x35cm 10x13in) Berlin 2000

METZLER Kurt Laurenz 1941 **[27]**
- $14 525 - €16 020 - £9 837 - FF105 082
  Der Anwalt Sculpture (H270cm H106in) Zürich 2000
- $4 746 - €5 095 - £3 176 - FF33 420
  Frau Bronze (H58cm H22in) Zürich 2000
- $655 - €559 - £390 - FF3 666
  Two Figures Collage/paper (75.5x55.5cm 29x21in) Zürich 1998

METZMACHER Émile Pierre 1815-? **[16]**
- $13 000 - €12 352 - £7 909 - FF81 027
  Glass of Cognac Oil/panel (57x47.5cm 22x18in) New-York 1999
- $2 476 - €2 759 - £1 730 - FF18 100
  Jeune femme au chapeau Huile/toile (21.5x18.5cm 8x7in) Paris 2001
- $4 540 - €4 393 - £2 800 - FF28 818
  L'Indiscret Watercolour/paper (34x24cm 13x9in) London 1999

MEUCCI Michelangelo c.1840-c.1905 **[185]**
- $960 - €1 244 - £720 - FF8 160
  Cacciagione Olio/tela (100x50cm 39x19in) Prato 2001
- $938 - €819 - £567 - FF5 370
  Stilleben med fåglar Oil/panel (47x34cm 18x13in) Stockholm 1998

MEULEN van der Adam Frans 1632-1690 **[60]**
- $34 650 - €33 036 - £21 450 - FF216 700
  Militares ante la ciudad de Dole, en Bélgica Oleo/lienzo (104x141cm 40x55in) Madrid 1999
- $32 874 - €35 288 - £22 500 - FF231 475
  Landscape with a cavalry skirmish Oil/canvas (58.5x76.5cm 23x30in) London 2000
- $3 750 - €4 153 - £2 543 - FF27 241
  A Cavalry Skirmish Oil/canvas (34.5x43.5cm 13x17in) New-York 2000
- $4 913 - €4 564 - £3 000 - FF29 940
  Three Riders Red chalk/paper (34.5x25cm 13x9in) London 1998

MEULEN van der Cornelis 1642-1692 **[2]**
- $16 000 - €13 307 - £9 392 - FF87 288
  A Vanitas Still Life of a Skull, a guttering Candle, tortoiseshell.. Oil/canvas (58.5x47.5cm 23x18in) New-York 1998

MEULEN van der Edmond 1841-1905 **[19]**
- $1 270 - €1 363 - £852 - FF8 943
  Portrait de chien (Dogue) Huile/toile (55x46.5cm 21x18in) Bruxelles 2000

1058

MEULENAERE de Edmond 1884-1963 **[92]**
$286 - €273 - **£173** - FF1 788
Vue de ville Huile/panneau (50x62cm 19x24in)
Bruxelles 1999

MEULENER Pieter 1602-1654 **[47]**
$9 576 - €10 671 - **£6 517** - FF70 000
**L'arrivée d'un carosse dans la porte d'une
ville flamande** Huile/toile (89x163cm 35x64in) Paris
2000
$9 552 - €9 296 - **£5 880** - FF60 976
Ryttarbatalj Oil/panel (50x84cm 19x33in) Stockholm
1999

MEUNIER Constantin 1831-1905 **[304]**
$7 266 - €6 807 - **£4 368** - FF44 649
Poissonnier avec pipe Oil/canvas (179.5x80cm
70x31in) Amsterdam 1999
$4 526 - €3 765 - **£2 657** - FF24 697
Le Chemin de Fer Oil/canvas (37.5x52.5cm 14x20in)
Amsterdam 1998
$3 162 - €3 099 - **£1 950** - FF20 325
Le puddleur Oil/panel (32.5x24.5cm 12x9in) Lokeren
1999
$10 400 - €12 394 - **£7 450** - FF81 300
L'abreuvoir Bronze (84.6x65.5cm 33x25in) Lokeren
2000
$1 435 - €1 380 - **£885** - FF9 055
Mineur Bronze (H45.6cm H17in) Köln 1999
$602 - €520 - **£359** - FF3 414
Portrait de Violette Verlant enfant Fusain/papier
(57x40cm 22x15in) Bruxelles 1998

MEUNIER Georges 1869-1942 **[66]**
$1 601 - €1 372 - **£963** - FF9 000
**Lox «Kina-Lox, Coca, Kola» Toni-apéritif par
excellence** Affiche (124x87cm 48x34in) Orléans 1998

MEUNIER Henri Georges 1873-1922 **[37]**
$326 - €305 - **£201** - FF2 000
Les chaumières de Bréhat Lithographie couleurs
(32x48cm 12x18in) Brest 1999

MEUNIER Jean-Baptiste 1786-1858 **[2]**
$2 988 - €3 208 - **£2 000** - FF21 043
**Basset à jambes torses/Chiens de
bergers/Chien turc** Drawing (15x9cm 5x3in) London
2000

MEUNIER Philippe XVIII **[1]**
$8 717 - €10 367 - **£6 045** - FF68 000
**Charles Philippe d'Artois sortant de la
Chambre des Aides de Paris** Encre (18x27cm
7x10in) Paris 2000

MEURER Charles Alfred 1865-1955 **[38]**
$6 000 - €7 113 - **£4 371** - FF46 659
**Still Life with Tankard, Newspaper, Books and
Pipe** Oil/canvas (55x66cm 22x26in) Chicago IL 2001
$2 600 - €2 768 - **£1 771** - FF18 155
**Still Life of a Pipe, Spectacles, Pack of
Cigarettes, Matches** Oil/canvas (25.5x20cm 10x7in)
New-York 2001

MEURIS B. XIX **[11]**
$2 500 - €2 592 - **£1 500** - FF17 000
Il golfo di Sorrento Gouache/carta (37x54cm
14x21in) Napoli 1999

MEURIS Emmanuel 1894-1969 **[41]**
$1 432 - €1 611 - **£1 000** - FF10 567
**Fishermen in rowing Boats with Capri
beyond/Figure on a Track** Bodycolour (45.5x57cm
17x22in) London 2001

MEURON de Maximilien 1785-1868 **[4]**
$9 981 - €11 845 - **£7 266** - FF77 695
Zwei ruhende Hirten Oil/panel (49x51cm 19x20in)
Zürich 2001

MEURS Harmen Hermanus 1891-1964 **[76]**
$1 753 - €2 045 - **£1 231** - FF13 415
Blumenstilleben Öl/Leinwand (81.7x65.5cm
32x25in) Köln 2000
$845 - €908 - **£565** - FF5 953
The Montelbaanstoren, Amsterdam Watercolour
(49x35cm 19x13in) Amsterdam 2000

MEUSNIER Philippe 1656-1734 **[4]**
$24 000 - €22 524 - **£15 000** - FF147 750
Capricho arquitectónico Oleo/lienzo (71x87cm
27x34in) Madrid 1999

MEUTTMAN William 1869-1948 **[3]**
$1 600 - €1 820 - **£1 117** - FF11 936
Two Strike Souix, Pine Ridge Oil/canvas (35x25cm
14x10in) Chicago IL 2000

MEVIUS Hermann 1820-1864 **[18]**
$4 776 - €5 368 - **£3 353** - FF35 215
«Mittag auf der Rhede von Dordrecht»
Öl/Leinwand (53.5x76cm 21x29in) Hamburg 2001
$995 - €860 - **£600** - FF5 643
Rowing into Harbour Oil/canvas (30x29.5cm
11x11in) Billingshurst, West-Sussex 1999

MEW Thomas Hillier XIX **[7]**
$289 - €341 - **£200** - FF2 234
Huntsman Smoking on a Grey Horse
Watercolour/paper (15x22cm 5x8in) Devon 2000

MEYENDORFF de Th. XX **[2]**
$13 593 - €13 416 - **£8 668** - FF88 000
Vues d'intérieurs: salon bleu et bureau vert
Aquarelle/papier (23.5x30cm 9x11in) Montfort
L'Amaury 1999

MEYER Carl Theodor 1860-1932 **[79]**
$1 086 - €921 - **£649** - FF6 040
Herbststimmung Öl/Leinwand (94x79cm 37x31in)
Bremen 1998
$285 - €307 - **£191** - FF2 012
Sommerliche Almlandschaft Pastell/Papier
(29.8x36cm 11x14in) Hamburg 2000

MEYER Claus 1856-1919 **[39]**
$1 334 - €1 534 - **£942** - FF10 061
Vater und Sohn rauchen am offenen Fenster
Oil/panel (51x40.5cm 20x15in) Bremen 2001
$2 251 - €2 556 - **£1 564** - FF16 769
Grossmutter den Enkel Lesen lehrend Oil/panel
(17.5x24.5cm 6x9in) Köln 2001

MEYER Conrad 1618-1689 **[9]**
$2 632 - €2 495 - **£1 644** - FF16 367
Ohne Titel aus Lieber Amicorum Encre Chine
(14.5x16cm 5x6in) Luzern 1999

MEYER de Hendrick I c.1600-c.1690 **[20]**
$19 475 - €18 168 - **£11 750** - FF119 175
Grosse Strandlandschaft bei Scheveningen
Oil/panel (91x154cm 35x60in) Wien 1998
$7 856 - €8 622 - **£5 057** - FF56 555
Travellers halting outside the Swan Inn Oil/panel
(72.5x107.5cm 28x42in) Amsterdam 2000
$3 021 - €3 403 - **£2 082** - FF22 324
A Horse Fair Outside a Town Oil/panel (33x39cm
12x15in) Amsterdam 2000

M

MEYER de Hendrick II 1737-1793 **[37]**
📖 **$1 651** - €1 588 - **£1 017** - FF10 418
Autumn Landscape with Peasants Transporting Hay on a Barge, Cottages Ink (10x13.5cm 3x5in)
Amsterdam 1999

MEYER de Maurice 1911-1999 **[70]**
📖 **$636** - €595 - **£391** - FF3 902
Le moulin à aubes Huile/toile (40x50cm 15x19in)
Bruxelles 1999
📖 **$177** - €186 - **£117** - FF1 219
La Grand-Place à Bruxelles Huile/panneau
(18x23cm 7x9in) Bruxelles 2000

MEYER Edgar 1853-1925 **[7]**
📖 **$943** - €971 - **£594** - FF6 372
Abend in der römischen Campagna
Aquarell/Papier (31x47cm 12x18in) Berlin 2000

MEYER Elias 1763-1809 **[8]**
📖 **$1 250** - €1 341 - **£852** - FF8 796
Prospekt fra herregården Lovenborg ved Holbaek Gouache/paper (41x52cm 16x20in)
København 2001

MEYER Émile XIX-XX **[14]**
📖 **$18 000** - €19 321 - **£12 045** - FF126 738
The Folly of Love Oil/canvas (165x125.5cm 64x49in)
New-York 2000

MEYER Emmy 1866-1940 **[10]**
📖 **$976** - €1 022 - **£613** - FF6 707
Bote auf der Hamme Öl/Karton (45x63cm 17x24in)
Bremen 2000

MEYER Ernst 1797-1861 **[41]**
📖 **$606** - €670 - **£420** - FF4 394
Parti fra Capri med dreng siddende i skygge af fiskerbåd Oil/canvas (26x30cm 10x11in) Vejle 2001
📖 **$204** - €228 - **£139** - FF1 495
Interiörscene med en munk Watercolour,
gouache/paper (28x25cm 11x9in) Viby J, Århus 2000

MEYER F. XIX **[2]**
📖 **$1 684** - €1 636 - **£1 052** - FF10 732
Bremen: Ansicht von der Westseite der freien Hansestadt Lithograph (36x68cm 14x26in) Bremen 1999

MEYER Felix 1653-1713 **[18]**
📖 **$155** - €184 - **£107** - FF1 204
Prospect des Obern Theils von dem Genffer See Kupferstich (20.5x32cm 8x12in) Bern 2000

MEYER Franz Anton 1710-1782 **[1]**
📖 **$4 035** - €3 811 - **£2 440** - FF25 000
Le repos des chasseurs Huile/toile (46x35cm 18x13in) Paris 1999

MEYER Frederick William ?-c.1922 **[12]**
📖 **$5 206** - €4 750 - **£3 200** - FF31 158
Coastal Scene at Dusk Oil/canvas (61x101.5cm 24x39in) London 1998

MEYER Friedrich Elias 1723-1785 **[2]**
📖 **$8 240** - €8 181 - **£5 148** - FF53 662
Mann mit Zwei Papageien/Frau mit hochgebundener Frisur Terracotta (H34cm H13in) München 1999

MEYER Georg Friedrich 1735-1779 **[2]**
📖 **$3 050** - €3 477 - **£2 128** - FF22 806
Landschaft mit einer Herde an der Tränke
Öl/Leinwand (36x29.5cm 14x11in) Berlin 2001

MEYER Heinrich 1760-1832 **[4]**
📖 **$1 600** - €1 711 - **£1 090** - FF11 220
Landscape with a Tree lined Road and a Farmhouse Ink (14x23.5cm 5x9in) New-York 2001

MEYER Johann Friedrick 1728-c.1789 **[1]**
📖 **$112 490** - €111 578 - **£70 000** - FF731 906
View of Prague from the East Oil/canvas
(162x286cm 63x112in) London 1999

MEYER Johann Jakob 1787-1858 **[25]**
📖 **$1 618** - €1 815 - **£1 123** - FF11 907
Blick auf Como mit Villa Olmo im Vordergrund
Aquarell/Papier (19x28cm 7x11in) Luzern 2001
📖 **$1 687** - €1 628 - **£1 059** - FF10 678
Vue prise près de l'auberge du Corbeau à Zurich Radierung (32.8x45.8cm 12x18in) Zürich 1999

MEYER John 1942 **[8]**
📖 **$3 698** - €3 287 - **£2 266** - FF21 564
The Lighthouse, Umhlanga Oil/board (42x49.5cm 16x19in) Johannesburg 1999
📖 **$5 160** - €5 753 - **£3 364** - FF37 740
Karoo Farmer Acrylic/board (19x34.5cm 7x13in)
Johannesburg 2000

MEYER Julia XIX-XX **[2]**
📖 **$4 037** - €4 431 - **£2 600** - FF29 067
Lost in Thought Oil/canvas (53.5x43cm 21x16in)
London 2000

MEYER Lazare XIX **[1]**
📖 **$7 000** - €7 257 - **£4 200** - FF47 600
In campagna Olio/tavola (26.5x35cm 10x13in)
Venezia 2000

MEYER Rudolf 1803-1857 **[3]**
📖 **$3 267** - €3 233 - **£2 000** - FF21 208
Panoramic View of the Swiss Alps Aquatint
(16.5x110cm 6x43in) London 2000

MEYER Siri 1898-? **[9]**
📖 **$1 270** - €1 423 - **£885** - FF9 334
Der Verrückte Schwerpunkt Watercolour
(16.5x12cm 6x4in) Stockholm 2001

MEYER VON BREMEN Johann Georg 1813-1886 **[107]**
📖 **$16 000** - €14 632 - **£9 771** - FF95 980
An artist and his family in the atelier Oil/canvas
(51x41cm 20x16in) New-York 1998
📖 **$10 478** - €11 248 - **£7 013** - FF73 785
Stubeninterieur, eine junge Frau in Tracht hält liebevoll ihr Kind Öl/Leinwand (31x26cm 12x10in)
Stuttgart 2000
📖 **$970** - €920 - **£590** - FF6 037
Kind mit Schürze und Blasebalg am Kachelofen
Aquarell/Papier (18x11cm 7x4in) Köln 1999
📖 **$1 000** - €915 - **£612** - FF6 000
Composition, d'après Der Grossvater Besuch
Lithographie (35x45cm 13x17in) Dijon 1999

MEYER-AMDEN Otto 1885-1933 **[38]**
📖 **$6 526** - €7 005 - **£4 367** - FF45 953
Amdener Landschaft V, Gebirgslandschaft mit jungem Baum Öl/Leinwand (27.5x19.2cm 10x7in)
Bern 2000
📖 **$7 471** - €7 211 - **£4 788** - FF47 299
Stehender Knabenakt von vorn, die Hände erhoben Crayon (20.8x13cm 8x5in) Bern 1999

MEYER-EBERHARDT Kurt 1895-1977 **[50]**
📖 **$142** - €133 - **£86** - FF872
Romantische Bootsfahrt Radierung (24x17.5cm 9x6in) Hamburg 1999

MEYER-ELBING Oscar Edwin Adalbert 1866-? **[2]**
📖 **$2 331** - €2 744 - **£1 638** - FF18 000
Le derviche Cheik Iskender/Femme turque d'Ali Pacha Huile/toile (27x21.5cm 10x8in) Paris 2000

MEYER-WALDECK Kunz 1859-1953 [18]
- $292 - €307 - **£193** - FF2 012
  Kopfstudien Oil/panel (27x34.5cm 10x13in) München 2000

MEYER-WISMAR Ferdinand 1833-1917 [10]
- $2 143 - €2 301 - **£1 434** - FF15 092
  Der gelehrige Schüler Öl/Leinwand (51.5x41cm 20x16in) Bremen 2000

MEYERHEIM Friedrich Edouard 1808-1879 [28]
- $8 573 - €9 203 - **£5 738** - FF60 370
  Versteckspielen Öl/Leinwand (51x42cm 20x16in) Bremen 2000
- $9 086 - €10 226 - **£6 260** - FF67 078
  Die Stiftskirche von Gernrode am Harz Öl/Leinwand (30.5x37.5cm 12x14in) Bremen 2000

MEYERHEIM Hermann 1815-1880 [15]
- $9 785 - €11 248 - **£6 910** - FF73 785
  Holländisches Stadtidyll am Ende des 19.Jahrhunderts Öl/Leinwand (68x96cm 26x37in) Bremen 2001

MEYERHEIM Paul Friedrich 1842-1915 [86]
- $16 236 - €18 151 - **£11 300** - FF119 064
  Rotkäppchen im Walde (Little Red Ridinghood) Oil/canvas (190x217cm 74x85in) Amsterdam 2001
- $2 980 - €3 323 - **£2 003** - FF21 800
  Löwen im Zoo Öl/Leinwand (58x81cm 22x31in) Köln 2000
- $1 734 - €1 972 - **£1 189** - FF12 933
  Morgentoilette Oil/panel (24x37.8cm 9x14in) Zürich 2000
- $402 - €460 - **£276** - FF3 018
  Vivat hoch, Entwurf für eine Glückwunschkarte Coloured pencils (28.5x36.5cm 11x14in) München 2000

MEYERHEIM Paul Wilhelm XIX [11]
- $8 427 - €7 669 - **£5 265** - FF50 308
  Aus der Kirche schreitet die junge Dorfschönheit und ihr Verehrer Öl/Leinwand (63.5x58cm 25x22in) München 1999
- $2 049 - €1 943 - **£1 246** - FF12 744
  Ankernde Boote vor einer befestigten Stadt Öl/Leinwand/Karton (40x32.5cm 15x12in) Köln 1999

MEYERHEIM Robert Gustave 1847-1920 [8]
- $3 585 - €3 260 - **£2 200** - FF21 386
  Coming from their Last Pastures Watercolour/paper (39.5x67cm 15x26in) London 1999

MEYERHEIM Wilhelm Alexander 1815-1882 [65]
- $7 105 - €6 647 - **£4 304** - FF43 600
  Reges Treiben an der Kaimauer einer alten Hafenstadt Öl/Leinwand (70x93cm 27x36in) Bremen 1999
- $4 048 - €4 346 - **£2 709** - FF28 508
  Eisvergnügen nach der Schule Öl/Leinwand (19.5x79cm 7x31in) Berlin 2000
- $404 - €434 - **£271** - FF2 850
  König Wilhelm von Preussen Aquarell/Papier (25x18cm 9x7in) Berlin 2000

MEYERINGH Aelbert 1645-1714 [16]
- $1 398 - €1 534 - **£949** - FF10 061
  Ein Mann mit Planwagen vor einer weiten italienischen Hügellandschaft Black chalk (25.1x38.2cm 9x15in) Berlin 2000

MEYEROWITZ Joel 1938 [28]
- $1 600 - €1 717 - **£1 086** - FF11 264
  Images of Provincetown Photograph in colors (49.5x39.5cm 19x15in) Beverly-Hills CA 2001

MEYEROWITZ William 1898-1981 [54]
- $1 800 - €1 966 - **£1 158** - FF12 894
  Off to Picnic Oil/board (37x47cm 14x18in) Mystic CT 2000
- $700 - €641 - **£426** - FF4 204
  The Dancers Oil/board (41x30cm 16x12in) Bloomfield-Hills MI 1999
- $1 200 - €1 370 - **£846** - FF8 987
  Mt.Pleasant Street, Gloucester Watercolour/paper (37x55.5cm 14x21in) Boston MA 2001
- $400 - €463 - **£283** - FF3 035
  View of Central Park Lake Etching (24x18cm 9x7in) New-York 2000

MEYERS Frank Harmon 1899-1956 [10]
- $3 000 - €2 879 - **£1 880** - FF18 886
  Fishing Boats at Dock - Reflections (probably Monterey) Oil/board (24x30cm 9x12in) Altadena CA 1999

MEYERS Isidoor 1836-1917 [89]
- $691 - €644 - **£429** - FF4 227
  Prairies près de la ferme Huile/toile (40x50cm 15x19in) Antwerpen 1999
- $743 - €644 - **£452** - FF4 225
  Paysanne et sa vache au crépuscule Huile/panneau (24x37cm 9x14in) Antwerpen 1998

MEYERS Jerome 1867-1940 [4]
- $425 - €493 - **£302** - FF3 235
  The New Arrival Graphite (30.5x46.5cm 12x18in) Washington 2000

MEYERS Ralph W. 1885-1948 [3]
- $4 250 - €4 045 - **£2 658** - FF26 532
  Standing Twenty Oil/canvas (40x30cm 16x12in) New-York 1999

MEYNET Félix 1961 [7]
- $406 - €457 - **£285** - FF3 000
  Double M, projet de couverture du chamois blanc Encre Chine (32x33cm 12x12in) Paris 2001

MEYNIER Charles 1768-1832 [20]
- $3 944 - €4 421 - **£2 746** - FF29 000
  Allégorie de la naissance du roi de Rome Huile/toile (46.5x56cm 18x22in) Paris 2001
- $7 435 - €8 842 - **£5 156** - FF58 000
  Le philosophe Bias rachetant les esclaves Lavis (39x59cm 15x23in) Paris 2000

MEYRET Louis Alfred XIX [1]
- $2 162 - €2 058 - **£1 344** - FF13 500
  La porte des Allemands à Metz Aquarelle/papier (56x86cm 22x33in) Saint-Dié 1999

MEYS Marcel XIX-XX [15]
- $620 - €613 - **£387** - FF4 024
  Am Wildbach Photograph (40.2x30.3cm 15x11in) München 1999

MEYSSENS Johannes 1612-1670 [3]
- $11 000 - €9 649 - **£6 679** - FF63 291
  Marguerite of Constantinople, Countess of Flanders Ink (17.5x12cm 6x4in) New-York 1999

MEYTENS van Martin c.1695-1770 [15]
- $23 370 - €21 802 - **£14 100** - FF143 010
  Ganzfigurenbildnis der Füstin Elisabeth Esterhazy de Galantha Öl/Leinwand (289x160cm 113x62in) Wien 1999
- $8 000 - €7 584 - **£4 867** - FF49 750
  Portrait of a Gentleman, wearing a red velvet brocade jacket Oil/canvas (125x94cm 49x37in) New-York 1999

M

MEZA Guillermo 1917 [27]
$3 200 - €3 718 - £2 249 - FF24 387
Mujer desnuda Oil/paper (41x45.5cm 16x17in) New-York 2001
$3 853 - €4 519 - £2 772 - FF29 645
Leopardo Oleo/tabla (35x25cm 13x9in) México 2001

MÉZIERES Jean-Claude 1938 [11]
$1 266 - €1 143 - £780 - FF7 500
Les Héros de l'Équinoxe Encre Chine/papier (46x37cm 18x14in) Neuilly-sur-Seine 1999

MEZZADRI Antonio XVII [3]
$9 600 - €8 293 - £6 400 - FF54 400
Vaso di fiori Olio/tela (75x60cm 29x23in) Milano 1998

MGM STUDIO [16]
$1 500 - €1 441 - £924 - FF9 455
Tom and Jerry: Tom, Jerry and Leo take a stroll Gouache (38x43cm 15x17in) Beverly-Hills CA 1999

MGUDLANDLU Gladys 1925-1979 [11]
$2 723 - €3 051 - £1 892 - FF20 013
Leaf Forms Oil/board (90x29cm 35x11in) Johannesburg 2001
$4 006 - €4 494 - £2 803 - FF29 478
Two Girls running through a Forest Gouache/paper (54.5x73.5cm 21x28in) Cape Town 2001

MHALER XX [46]
$247 - €270 - £171 - FF1 773
Playa y casas Oleo/lienzo (60x73cm 23x28in) Barcelona 2001

MHLABA Zwelidumile Mxgazi 1942-1991 [10]
$215 - €240 - £140 - FF1 576
Mother and Child Charcoal/paper (70x40cm 27x15in) Johannesburg 2000

MI CHUNMAO 1983 [1]
$3 852 - €4 227 - £2 481 - FF27 729
Serenade Ink (59x80cm 23x31in) Hong-Kong 2000

MI HANWEN c.1640-c.1700 [4]
$6 000 - €5 224 - £3 577 - FF34 266
Calligraphy in Xing Shu Ink/paper (209.5x72.5cm 82x28in) New-York 1998

MI WANZHONG 1570-1628 [4]
$12 179 - €14 315 - £8 445 - FF93 898
Landscape Ink (133x52cm 52x20in) Hong-Kong 2000

MIASOEDOV Grigori Grigorievich 1834-1911 [5]
$68 035 - €75 061 - £45 000 - FF492 367
Grand Prince Vladimir Receiving Instructions on Christianity Oil/canvas (145x205cm 57x80in) London 2000

MICBERTH Sotère 1969 [5]
$870 - €915 - £574 - FF6 000
Elégie Bronze (H15.5cm H6in) Blangy-sur-Bresle 2000

MICCINI Eugenio 1925 [18]
$2 000 - €2 592 - £1 500 - FF17 000
Rizómata Tecnica mista (64x100cm 25x39in) Prato 2000

MICH Michel Liebaux, dit 1881-1923 [104]
$411 - €427 - £271 - FF2 800
«Pneu Continental, qu'importe le moteur» Affiche (119x157cm 46x61in) Corbeil-Essonnes 2000

MICHA Maurice 1890-1969 [53]
$751 - €843 - £510 - FF5 528
Le violoniste Huile/toile (90x57cm 35x22in) Bruxelles 2000

MICHAEL Arthur C. XX [6]
$2 754 - €3 173 - £1 900 - FF20 814
«White Star Line, The Big Ship Route USA & Canada» Poster (92x61cm 36x24in) London 2000

MICHAELIS Alice, née Priester 1875-? [2]
$2 386 - €2 045 - £1 434 - FF13 413
Blumengarten Gouache/paper (70.5x70cm 27x27in) Hamburg 1998

MICHAELIS Gerrit Jan 1775-1857 [5]
$1 038 - €998 - £647 - FF6 548
Cowherd by a Farm in a Summer Landscape Oil/canvas (55x68cm 21x26in) Amsterdam 1999

MICHAELIS von Heinrich H.J. 1912-? [6]
$2 921 - €3 390 - £2 017 - FF22 237
Karretjiemense around a Fire, Northern Cape Oil/board (75x100.5cm 29x39in) Johannesburg 2000

MICHAHELLES XX [3]
$837 - €927 - £580 - FF6 080
«Italie» Poster (100x64cm 39x25in) London 2001

MICHAHELLES Ruggero 1898-1977 [13]
$1 200 - €1 244 - £720 - FF8 160
Ritratto di vecchio Olio/tela (66x49cm 25x19in) Prato 1999
$800 - €1 037 - £600 - FF6 800
Natura morta Olio/tavola (32.5x44.5cm 12x17in) Prato 2000

MICHALIK Marian 1947-1997 [12]
$561 - €544 - £355 - FF3 568
Landscape before the Rain Pastel/paper (41x62cm 16x24in) Warszawa 1999

MICHALLON Achille Etna 1796-1822 [19]
$76 740 - €91 469 - £54 720 - FF600 000
Sans titre Huile/toile (65x54cm 25x21in) Arles 2000
$9 950 - €9 528 - £6 143 - FF62 500
Paysage animé avec bergère/Paysage au ruisseau avec bergère Huile/toile (24x32.5cm 9x12in) Besançon 2000
$625 - €732 - £446 - FF4 800
Vue d'en face des fortifications regardant les Buttes Saint-Chaumont Crayon (13x18cm 5x7in) Paris 2001

MICHALLON Claude 1751-1799 [1]
$24 408 - €27 361 - £17 000 - FF179 474
The dying Gaul Marble (32x62cm 12x24in) London 2001

MICHALOWSKI Piotr 1801-1855 [58]
$172 458 - €189 174 - £117 156 - FF1 240 902
Cavalier sur un cheval Huile/toile (61x46cm 24x18in) Warszawa 2000
$32 212 - €29 745 - £20 062 - FF195 112
Equestrian portrait of Napoleon Bronze (H48cm H18in) Warszawa 1999
$7 222 - €6 187 - £4 342 - FF47 600
Retour à la ferme Watercolour/paper (20.5x28.7cm 8x11in) Warszawa 1998

MICHALS Duane 1932 [125]
$2 500 - €2 134 - £1 495 - FF13 997
Narcissus Gelatin silver print (12.5x20cm 4x7in) San-Francisco CA 1998

MICHAU Theobald 1676-1765 [77]
$56 520 - €60 980 - £37 720 - FF400 000
Réunion de paysans devant l'auberge Huile/panneau (35.5x49.5cm 13x19in) Monaco 2000

$17 931 - €19 248 - £12 000 - FF126 259
View of a riverside village with fishermen and travellers on a Path Oil/canvas (23.5x29cm 9x11in) London 2001

MICHAUD Hérick 1954 [24]
$718 - €838 - £492 - FF5 500
La petite marchande de ballons Huile/toile (50x61cm 19x24in) Paris 2000
$334 - €320 - £206 - FF2 100
Le cycliste Huile/toile (19x27cm 7x10in) Marseille 1999

MICHAUD Hippolyte 1831-1886 [2]
$3 651 - €4 269 - £2 606 - FF28 000
Jeunes femmes à la coiffe rouge Huile/toile (32.5x24.5cm 12x9in) Paris 2001

MICHAUD R. XX [8]
$2 886 - €2 615 - £1 800 - FF17 152
«Mégève à Rochebrune» Poster (96x69cm 37x27in) London 1999

MICHAUX Henri 1899-1984 [510]
$5 884 - €6 098 - £3 732 - FF40 000
Sans titre Acrylique/toile (52.5x63cm 20x24in) Paris 2000
$5 054 - €5 946 - £3 623 - FF39 000
«Composition K250» Huile/toile (27x35cm 10x13in) Paris 2001
$4 568 - €4 904 - £3 056 - FF32 167
Encre de Chine sur toile Indian ink (27x38cm 10x14in) Bern 2000
$420 - €363 - £253 - FF2 383
Ohne Titel Lithographie (50x33cm 19x12in) Wien 1999

MICHAUX John 1876-1956 [125]
$444 - €496 - £308 - FF3 252
L'attaque de la poulpe Huile/papier (42x51cm 16x20in) Antwerpen 2001
$660 - €694 - £417 - FF4 552
Matinée de septembre sur l'Escaut Huile/panneau (27x40cm 10x15in) Bruxelles 2000
$301 - €297 - £187 - FF1 951
Tunis Crayon gras (44x53cm 17x20in) Liège 1999

MICHEL A. XIX-XX [11]
$1 900 - €1 845 - £1 183 - FF12 100
Promeneurs et bateaux de pêche sur la grève Huile/panneau (18x36cm 7x14in) La Varenne-Saint-Hilaire 1999

MICHEL Charles 1874-1940 [36]
$582 - €694 - £417 - FF4 552
Zeegezicht (marine) Huile/toile (17x27cm 6x10in) Antwerpen 2000

MICHEL Eugène ?-c.1905 [1]
$18 071 - €17 235 - £11 000 - FF113 052
Rare Carved Glass Vase, with Triton and Sea Creatures Sculpture, glass (H26cm H10in) London 1999

MICHEL Georges 1763-1843 [122]
$5 775 - €5 445 - £3 579 - FF35 719
«Aux environs de Montmartre» Oil/paper/canvas (50.5x73cm 19x28in) Amsterdam 1999
$1 912 - €2 134 - £1 330 - FF14 000
Personnage près d'une chaumière Huile/toile (24x33cm 9x12in) Paris 2001
$493 - €457 - £306 - FF3 000
Vue de Montmartre Crayon (9x16cm 3x6in) Paris 1999

MICHEL Gustave Frédéric 1851-1924 [15]
$3 033 - €3 573 - £2 097 - FF23 437
Pair of Wrestlers beside a Shell-shaped Pool Gilded bronze (26x41cm 10x16in) Cape Town 2000

MICHEL Marius 1853-? [10]
$1 161 - €991 - £700 - FF6 500
Rue de village Huile/panneau (64.5x44cm 25x17in) Pontoise 1998

MICHEL Paul XX [50]
$269 - €252 - £162 - FF1 650
Cheval au pas Bronze (11x15cm 4x5in) La Varenne-Saint-Hilaire 1999

MICHEL Pierre Aug. 1889-1969 [6]
$2 020 - €2 236 - £1 400 - FF14 665
«Barcelonette, PLM» Poster (107x79cm 42x31in) London 2001

MICHEL Robert 1897-1983 [57]
$2 207 - €1 943 - £1 344 - FF12 744
«Knick-porträt» Mixed media (48x60.5cm 18x23in) Stuttgart 1999
$7 445 - €6 954 - £4 500 - FF45 617
Schloss No.3 Watercolour (32x21cm 12x8in) London 1999

MICHEL-HENRY 1928 [145]
$3 250 - €3 055 - £1 967 - FF20 040
Roses d'Indes Oil/canvas (114x145cm 45x57in) Delray-Beach FL 1999
$1 900 - €1 639 - £1 146 - FF10 752
«Rose Manille» Oil/canvas (59x72cm 23x28in) Delray-Beach FL 1998
$573 - €637 - £400 - FF4 178
Still Life of Flowers in a Vase by a Window Oil/canvas (46.5x33cm 18x12in) Godalming, Surrey 2001

MICHELACCI Luigi 1879-1959 [38]
$840 - €1 088 - £630 - FF7 140
Vecchia e bambina Olio/faesite (18x11cm 7x4in) Prato 2000

MICHELANGELO (M.-A. Buonarroti) 1475-1564 [9]
$11 057 820 - €11 869 656 - £7 400 000 - FF77 859 840
The Risen Christ: Three-Quarter Nude/Study of the Same Figure Black chalk (23.5x20.5cm 9x8in) London 2000

MICHELE DA VERONA c.1470-1536/44 [1]
$90 000 - €96 272 - £61 362 - FF631 503
Soldiers Outside a City Oil/canvas (102x103cm 40x40in) New-York 2001

MICHELE DI MATTEO DA BOLOGNA XV [1]
$23 000 - €21 955 - £14 370 - FF144 016
Female Saint Holding a Book Tempera/tavola (25.5x9cm 10x3in) New-York 1999

MICHELENA Arturo 1863-1898 [12]
$500 000 - €486 488 - £307 750 - FF3 191 150
El Panteón de Los Héroes Oil/canvas (135.5x169cm 53x66in) New-York 1999
$105 000 - €101 106 - £65 352 - FF663 211
Flores Oil/canvas (64x80cm 25x31in) New-York 1999
$6 400 - €6 464 - £4 400 - FF42 400
Desnudo femenino en el taller Oleo/lienzo (42x33cm 16x12in) Caracas 1999
$3 367 - €3 533 - £2 225 - FF23 309
Fragmento de Pentesiléa Carboncillo (35x25cm 13x9in) Caracas ($) 2000

M

MICHELET Georges C. 1873-? **[11]**
- $35 050 - €38 112 - **£23 100** - FF250 000
  Le retour du mahmal au Caire, Triptyque
  Huile/toile (134x147cm 52x57in) Paris 2000
- $3 810 - €4 269 - **£2 648** - FF28 000
  Jeune syrienne aux boucles d'oreilles Huile/panneau (41x32.5cm 16x12in) Paris 2001

MICHELETTI Mario 1892-1975 **[38]**
- $1 000 - €1 037 - **£600** - FF6 800
  Covone Olio/cartone (65x50cm 25x19in) Vercelli 1999

MICHELI Guglielmo 1866-1926 **[8]**
- $3 300 - €2 851 - **£2 200** - FF18 700
  Barca all'ormeggio nel porto di Livorno
  Olio/tavola (18x33cm 7x12in) Milano 1998

MICHELINO di Domenico 1417-1491 **[12]**
- $161 986 - €181 624 - **£110 000** - FF1 191 377
  The Madonna and Child Tempera/panel (73x52cm 28x20in) London 2000
- $19 467 - €19 622 - **£12 128** 709
  Die Grablegung Christi, Predella eines Altars
  Tempera/panel (23.5x40.5cm 9x15in) Wien 2000

MICHELOZZI Corrado 1883-1965 **[46]**
- $3 750 - €3 887 - **£2 250** - FF25 500
  Lavoratore del ferro Olio/tela (145x94cm 57x37in) Prato 2000
- $640 - €829 - **£480** - FF5 440
  Natura morta Olio/tavola (60x44cm 23x17in) Prato 2001
- $660 - €570 - **£330** - FF3 740
  Natura morta di frutta Olio/tavola (16x25cm 6x9in) Prato 1999

MICHELSON Gustav XX **[2]**
- $2 000 - €1 915 - **£1 235** - FF12 563
  Two Standing Herons, Setting Sun, Illustration
  Gouache/paper (55x43cm 22x17in) New-York 1999

MICHETTI Francesco Paolo 1851-1929 **[169]**
- $8 400 - €7 257 - **£4 200** - FF47 600
  Contadinella con buoi e capretta Olio/tela/cartone (40x50cm 15x19in) Prato 1999
- $6 042 - €5 368 - **£3 700** - FF35 215
  Hirtenmädchen Öl/Karton (30x23.5cm 11x9in) Hamburg 1999
- $1 120 - €1 451 - **£840** - FF9 520
  Contadinello Bronzo (H22cm H8in) Roma 2001
- $3 000 - €3 110 - **£1 800** - FF20 400
  Pastorella con armenti Tecnica mista/carta (46x61.5cm 18x24in) Venezia 2000

MICHIE Alastair 1921 **[11]**
- $486 - €471 - **£300** - FF3 087
  Enigma II Acrylic (51x61cm 20x24in) London 1999

MICHIE David Alan Redpath 1928 **[22]**
- $1 094 - €1 036 - **£680** - FF6 797
  Figure at Window Oil/canvas (35x50cm 13x19in) Glasgow 1999

MICHIE James Coutts 1861-1919 **[10]**
- $980 - €1 104 - **£675** - FF7 240
  Twilight Oil/canvas (68x51cm 26x20in) Uppsala 2000
- $1 738 - €2 017 - **£1 200** - FF13 228
  A Glade in a Birch Wood Oil/canvas (40.5x30.5cm 15x12in) London 2000

MICHIELI VICENTINO Andrea c.1542-c.1617 **[7]**
- $24 466 - €22 883 - **£15 000** - FF150 105
  David Victorious Over Goliath, the Fighting Armies of the Istraelites Oil/canvas (151x217cm 59x85in) London 1998

MICHIS Pietro 1836-1903 **[5]**
- $16 200 - €13 995 - **£8 100** - FF91 800
  Betrice Cenci condotta al patibolo Olio/tela (135x174cm 53x68in) Prato 1999

MICHL Ferdinand 1877-1951 **[13]**
- $171 - €203 - **£122** - FF1 334
  Hundekartenspiel Radierung (29x34cm 11x13in) Linz 2000

MICHONZE Grégoire 1902-1982 **[302]**
- $3 304 - €3 041 - **£1 983** - FF19 949
  Still Life Oil/paper/panel (32.5x50cm 12x19in) Tel Aviv 1999
- $1 809 - €1 677 - **£1 125** - FF11 000
  La ferme Huile/toile (35x27cm 13x10in) Paris 1999
- $295 - €274 - **£180** - FF1 800
  Le village Feutre (21x19cm 8x7in) Paris 1998

MICKER Jan Christiansz. c.1598-1664 **[13]**
- $4 704 - €4 033 - **£2 800** - FF26 260
  Nimrod overseeing the Building of the Tower of Babel Oil/panel (57.5x82.5cm 22x32in) London 1998

MIDDENDORF Helmut 1953 **[162]**
- $8 500 - €7 251 - **£5 127** - FF47 566
  Caligari Oil/canvas (185.5x236cm 73x92in) New-York 1998
- $2 286 - €2 198 - **£1 410** - FF14 421
  Ohne Titel (Gesicht) Acryl/Papier (52.5x39.5cm 20x15in) Köln 1999
- $1 213 - €1 227 - **£740** - FF8 049
  Paris-Rodin, Rainer & Me Mixed media/paper (43x30.5cm 16x12in) Stuttgart 2000
- $425 - €409 - **£262** - FF2 683
  Ohne Titel Farblithographie (99.5x130cm 39x51in) München 1999

MIDDLEDITCH Edward 1923-1987 **[36]**
- $630 - €654 - **£400** - FF4 290
  Kensington Gardens Pastel (38x32cm 14x12in) Cheshire 2000

MIDDLETON Colin 1910-1983 **[154]**
- $20 148 - €22 568 - **£14 000** - FF148 037
  The Visitation Oil/board (122x122cm 48x48in) London 2001
- $10 736 - €10 412 - **£6 756** - FF68 297
  Moneycaragh Oil/canvas (51x73.5cm 20x28in) Dublin 1999
- $4 561 - €5 206 - **£3 169** - FF34 148
  Bogland, Meenatinney Oil/canvas (30x30cm 12x12in) Blackrock, Co.Dublin 2000
- $537 - €577 - **£360** - FF3 787
  Seated Model Pencil/paper (25x15cm 10x6in) Belfast 2000

MIDDLETON James Charles 1894-? **[25]**
- $1 932 - €2 311 - **£1 333** - FF15 158
  Pudding Bag Lane St.Ives Oil/canvas (30.5x40.5cm 12x15in) Penzance, Cornwall 2000
- $143 - €161 - **£100** - FF1 053
  The Harbour Herm, Guernsey Watercolour/paper (29x35cm 11x15in) Penzance, Cornwall 2001

MIDDLETON John 1828-1856 **[42]**
- $5 149 - €4 899 - **£3 200** - FF32 137
  A Scene near Intwood Oil/canvas (25.5x46cm 10x18in) London 1999
- $2 351 - €2 297 - **£1 500** - FF15 066
  Wooded Landscape with Quarry Watercolour (32.5x51cm 12x20in) London 1999

MIDDLETON Max 1922 **[61]**

$1 608 – €1 867 – **£1 129** – FF12 244
Sunlight and Shadows Oil/canvas (40x50cm 15x19in) Sydney 2000

$337 – €391 – **£236** – FF2 567
Candlenight Oil/canvas (20x15cm 7x5in) Sydney 2000

MIDDLETON Sam 1927 **[59]**

$301 – €303 – **£187** – FF1 990
Untitled Mixed media/paper (47x62cm 18x24in) Stockholm 2000

MIDELFART Willie 1904-1975 **[25]**

$630 – €602 – **£397** – FF3 952
Gård i fjellandskap Oil/panel (38x46cm 14x18in) Oslo 1999

MIDJAW Midjaw c.1897-1985 **[6]**

$1 973 – €1 904 – **£1 247** – FF12 487
Nawarran (The Rock Python) Mixed media (78x41.5cm 30x16in) Melbourne 1999

MIDWOOD William Henry XIX **[34]**

$9 617 – €8 326 – **£5 800** – FF54 614
The New Arrival Oil/canvas (71x91.5cm 27x36in) London 1998

MIDY Arthur 1887-1944 **[92]**

$1 196 – €1 372 – **£818** – FF9 000
Paysan au panier Huile/toile (42x39cm 16x15in) Paris 2000

$536 – €579 – **£370** – FF3 800
Marée basse en Bretagne Huile/panneau (27x35cm 10x13in) Quimper 2001

MIDY Ernest 1878-1938 **[12]**

$1 320 – €1 289 – **£811** – FF8 455
Champs de genêts Huile/toile (71x112cm 27x44in) Bruxelles 1999

MIEG Peter 1906-1990 **[14]**

$385 – €414 – **£258** – FF2 715
Malven, Bauernrosen Aquarell/Papier (27.5x20.5cm 10x8in) Zofingen 2000

MIEGHEM van Eugeen 1875-1930 **[646]**

$16 660 – €17 352 – **£10 500** – FF113 820
Vers le soir (Anvers) Huile/toile (39x50cm 15x19in) Antwerpen 2000

$1 935 – €2 231 – **£1 332** – FF14 634
Spaanse vrouw Oil/paper (23x17cm 9x6in) Lokeren 2000

$946 – €1 091 – **£651** – FF7 154
Zittende man/Figuren Red chalk (25x24.5cm 9x9in) Lokeren 2000

$621 – €744 – **£426** – FF4 878
Nature morte au vase de fleurs Monotype (20x15cm 7x5in) Antwerpen 2000

MIEHE Walter 1883-1972 **[16]**

$1 688 – €1 738 – **£1 064** – FF11 403
Fünf-Uhr-Tee Öl/Karton (35.5x49cm 13x19in) Berlin 2000

MIEL Jan 1599-1663 **[33]**

$85 000 – €90 776 – **£57 919** – FF595 450
Laban looking for the Idols hidden by Rachel Oil/canvas (147.5x194cm 58x76in) New-York 2001

$10 815 – €10 901 – **£6 750** – FF71 505
Fröhliche Gesellschaft vor einer Trattoria Öl/Leinwand (49x66.5cm 19x26in) Wien 2000

$1 195 – €1 283 – **£800** – FF8 417
Man and a Donkey Ink (19x17.5cm 7x6in) London 2000

MIELATZ Charles F. 1864-1919 **[42]**

$280 – €261 – **£172** – FF1 711
Old Tom's on Thames Street Etching (24x15cm 9x6in) Cleveland OH 1999

MIELICH Alphons Leopold 1863-1929 **[29]**

$6 626 – €6 134 – **£4 000** – FF40 235
A Family Meal in an Arabian Town Oil/panel (38.5x50cm 15x19in) London 1999

$2 303 – €2 543 – **£1 596** – FF16 684
Ein Esel am Markt, Ägypten Mixed media (20.5x26.5cm 8x10in) Wien 2001

$2 504 – €2 907 – **£1 760** – FF19 068
Portrait einer Orientalin Pastell/papier (36x27cm 14x10in) Wien 2001

MIEREVELT van Michiel Jansz. 1567-1641 **[21]**

$8 823 – €8 891 – **£5 500** – FF58 319
Petronella Borres, three-quarter-length, in a Black Dress Oil/panel (109x86cm 42x33in) London 2000

$3 376 – €3 131 – **£2 036** – FF20 538
Portret van een adellijke dame met familiewapen Miniature (14x11cm 5x4in) Maastricht 1999

MIERIS van Frans I 1635-1681 **[21]**

$575 000 – €636 793 – **£389 965** – FF4 177 087
Child's Lesson (Possibly Hannah Bringing Her Son to High Priest Eli) Oil/panel (29x21.5cm 11x8in) New-York 2000

$89 369 – €77 109 – **£53 924** – FF505 801
Study of a standing old woman Black chalk/paper (225x117cm 88x46in) Amsterdam 1998

MIERIS van Frans II 1689-1763 **[18]**

$26 518 – €25 948 – **£17 000** – FF170 207
Man making Advances to a Maid in a Kitchen Interior Oil/panel (29x24.5cm 11x9in) London 1999

$500 – €583 – **£351** – FF3 825
Head of a Saint Crayon/papier (9x8cm 3x3in) Portsmouth NH 2000

MIERIS van Willem 1662-1747 **[78]**

$87 216 – €73 176 – **£51 168** – FF480 000
Le repos de Diane Huile/panneau (54.5x45.5cm 21x17in) Besançon 1998

$114 199 – €119 913 – **£72 000** – FF786 578
The Death of Cleopatra Oil/panel (23x20cm 9x7in) London 2000

$6 703 – €5 704 – **£4 000** – FF37 413
Bacchanalian Scene, Allegory of Autumn Black chalk/paper (25.5x35cm 10x13in) London 1998

MIERLO van Eugene Victor Joseph 1880-1972 **[34]**

$548 – €644 – **£384** – FF4 227
Paysage avec tour ensoleillée Huile/toile (80x100cm 31x39in) Bruxelles 2000

MIERZEJEWSKI Jacek 1884-1925 **[4]**

$15 919 – €17 462 – **£10 814** – FF114 544
Autoportrait/esquisse du parc Huile/toile/carton (57x46cm 22x18in) Warszawa 2000

MIESENBERGER Maria 1965 **[4]**

$4 702 – €4 885 – **£2 980** – FF32 041
Utan titel (Heimat) Photograph (81x75cm 31x29in) Stockholm 2000

MIETH Hansel 1912 **[12]**

$1 000 – €973 – **£614** – FF6 384
Mad Monkey, Puerto Rico Silver print (33x26cm 13x10in) New-York 1999

M

MIETH Hugo 1865-? **[13]**
- $876 - €920 - £592 - FF6 037
  Alte Fachwerkhäuser am Dorfbach mit Personen Oil/panel (60x70cm 23x27in) Kempten 2001

MIETTINEN Olli 1899-1969 **[16]**
- $901 - €1 009 - £625 - FF6 619
  Granar Oil/canvas (50x61cm 19x24in) Helsinki 2001

MIGLIARA Giovanni 1785-1837 **[44]**
- $18 000 - €15 550 - £12 000 - FF102 000
  Scala interna della Sacra di San Michele Olio/tela (51.5x36.5cm 20x14in) Milano 1998
- $11 954 - €12 832 - £8 000 - FF84 172
  Italian Piazza with Elegant Figures conversing, a woman drawing Oil/canvas (16.5x25cm 6x9in) London 2000
- $1 400 - €1 451 - £840 - FF9 520
  Veduta dell'abside di Santa Maria Maggiore a Bergamo con frate Matita/carta (26x21.5cm 10x8in) Milano 2001

MIGLIARO Vincenzo 1858-1938 **[85]**
- $24 982 - €23 186 - £15 000 - FF152 088
  The Afternoon Meeting Oil/canvas (61.5x40cm 24x15in) London 1999
- $4 983 - €4 265 - £3 000 - FF27 975
  Young Girl in a Neapolitan Market Oil/board (34.5x21.5cm 13x8in) London 1998
- $2 000 - €2 439 - £1 500 - FF17 000
  Profilo di signora Acquarello/carta (23x13cm 9x5in) Roma 2000

MIGNARD Nicolas d'Avignon 1606-1668 **[58]**
- $12 820 - €15 245 - £8 830 - FF100 000
  La Fuite en Égypte Huile/toile (154x125cm 60x49in) Bernay 2000
- $38 000 - €41 691 - £25 243 - FF273 478
  Saint Roseline of Villeneuve Oil/canvas (109x90.5cm 42x35in) New-York 2000
- $2 896 - €2 439 - £1 710 - FF16 000
  Étude pour Saint Éloi Sanguine (28.3x20.5cm 11x8in) Paris 1998

MIGNARD Paul 1638/40-1691 **[2]**
- $96 420 - €95 639 - £60 000 - FF627 348
  Vittorio Amedeo II, Duke of Savoy, later King of Sardinia (1666-1732) Oil/canvas (191x135cm 75x53in) London 1999
- $5 057 - €5 243 - £3 034 - FF34 391
  La Sacra Famiglia Tempera (34x28cm 13x11in) Venezia 2000

MIGNARD Pierre I le Romain 1612-1695 **[22]**
- $16 437 - €17 644 - £11 000 - FF115 737
  The Presentation of the Virgin in the Temple Oil/canvas (117.5x165.5cm 46x65in) London 2000
- $5 918 - €6 641 - £4 433 - FF43 560
  Retrato de caballero Oleo/lienzo (82x65cm 32x25in) México 2000

MIGNECO Giuseppe 1908-1997 **[358]**
- $12 000 - €12 440 - £7 200 - FF81 600
  Uomo con scialle Olio/tela (60x60cm 23x23in) Torino 2001
- $6 000 - €6 220 - £3 600 - FF40 800
  Cactus Olio/tela (40x30cm 15x11in) Milano 2000
- $1 400 - €1 451 - £840 - FF9 520
  Figura di donna China (29.5x21.5cm 11x8in) Prato 2001
- $200 - €207 - £120 - FF1 360
  Paesaggio Acquaforte (65x85cm 25x33in) Vercelli 2000

MIGNERY Herb 1937 **[11]**
- $3 300 - €3 542 - £2 208 - FF23 235
  Horse Catcher Bronze (H38cm H15in) Houston TX 2000

MIGNON Abraham 1640-1679 **[18]**
- $972 022 - €827 032 - £580 000 - FF5 424 972
  Forest floor still life with Grapes, Plums, Rosehips, blackberries Oil/canvas (92x71cm 36x27in) London 1998
- $217 525 - €213 625 - £135 000 - FF1 401 286
  Grapes, Pomegranates and Vine Leaves Hung before a Niche Oil/panel (43.5x36cm 17x14in) London 1999

MIGNON Jean XVI **[9]**
- $4 741 - €4 602 - £2 952 - FF30 185
  Satyr mit verschlungenen Beinen Radierung (24.4x13.1cm 9x5in) Berlin 1999

MIGNON Léon 1847-1898 **[40]**
- $923 - €942 - £577 - FF6 178
  Combat de taureaux romains Bronze (54x67cm 21x26in) Bruxelles 2000

MIGNON Lucien 1865-1944 **[108]**
- $873 - €915 - £552 - FF6 000
  Vase de fleurs Huile/toile (55x37.5cm 21x14in) Paris 2000
- $801 - €945 - £563 - FF6 200
  Esterel Huile/carton (24x29cm 9x11in) Garches 2000

MIGNOT Louis Rémy 1831-1870 **[14]**
- $165 000 - €157 022 - £103 207 - FF1 029 996
  Tropical Landscape Oil/canvas (60.5x90cm 23x35in) New-York 1999

MIGONNEY Jules 1876-1929 **[10]**
- $8 374 - €7 775 - £5 247 - FF51 000
  Trois femmes Huile/toile (56x75cm 22x29in) Paris 1999
- $4 567 - €4 421 - £2 894 - FF29 000
  Jeune femme nue Fusain (77.5x62cm 30x24in) Paris 1999
- $1 417 - €1 372 - £898 - FF9 000
  «Vénus mauresque» Gravure bois (30x41.5cm 11x16in) Paris 1999

MIHR ALI XIX **[1]**
- $47 583 - €49 964 - £30 000 - FF327 741
  Fath Ali Shah Qajar Seated on a Jewelled Throne Watercolour, gouache (33x21cm 12x8in) London 2000

MIJARES José Maria 1921 **[40]**
- $3 500 - €3 022 - £2 135 - FF19 823
  Payaso Mixed media/paper (47x34.5cm 18x13in) Miami FL 1999

MIKESCH Fritz / Friderike 1853-1891 **[4]**
- $8 500 - €10 147 - £6 273 - FF67 393
  Tabletop Still Life of Barrel, Pot, Lantern, Duck and Vegetables Oil/panel (30.5x23cm 12x9in) Bethesda MD 2000

MIKKELSEN Sven Havsteen 1912-1999 **[15]**
- $2 060 - €2 149 - £1 297 - FF14 097
  Udsigt over huse Oil/canvas (46x55cm 18x21in) København 2000

MIKL Josef 1929 **[96]**
- $3 360 - €3 997 - £2 398 - FF26 218
  Vase mit Blumen Öl/Leinwand (54.5x43.5cm 21x17in) Wien 2000
- $1 548 - €1 453 - £956 - FF9 534
  Ohne Titel Tempera/Karton (33x29.7cm 12x11in) Wien 1999

✏ **$1 033** - €1 022 - **£644** - FF6 707
«**35**» Aquarell, Gouache/Papier (49.8x37.9cm 19x14in)
Berlin 1999

▥ **$336** - €363 - **£232** - FF2 383
Ohne Titel Farblithographie (42x38cm 16x14in) Wien
2001

MIKLOS Gustave 1888-1967 **[44]**
✺ **$27 810** - €27 441 - **£17 136** - FF180 000
Vitesse contraste de forme Huile/toile (93x73cm
36x28in) Paris 1999
✍ **$2 298** - €2 211 - **£1 418** - FF14 500
Portrait Métal (38x24cm 14x9in) Fontainebleau 1999
✏ **$2 057** - €2 439 - **£1 452** - FF16 000
Inérieur, escalier Gouache (14x9.5cm 5x3in) Paris
2000

MIKOLA Andréas Armas 1884-1970 **[8]**
✺ **$875** - €968 - **£575** - FF6 350
Afternoon in the Park Oil/canvas (96x110cm
37x43in) Budapest 2000

MIKOLA Armas 1901-1983 **[47]**
✺ **$1 296** - €1 214 - **£799** - FF7 943
Gatuvy från Paris Oil/canvas (82x50cm 32x19in)
Helsinki 1999

MIKOLA Nandor 1911 **[31]**
✏ **$447** - €508 - **£306** - FF3 335
Kardborras Akvarell/papper (70x48cm 27x18in)
Stockholm 2000

MIKULSKI Kazimierz 1918-1998 **[8]**
✺ **$6 645** - €7 710 - **£4 587** - FF50 577
Flamme bleue Huile/toile (46x38cm 18x14in)
Warszawa 2000

MILAN Pierre c.1500-1557 **[4]**
▥ **$936** - €786 - **£550** - FF5 158
The Dance of the Dryads, after Rosso Engraving
(28x40cm 11x15in) London 1998

MILANI Aureliano 1675-1749 **[22]**
✺ **$75 415** - €64 166 - **£45 000** - FF420 903
Mars and venus at the Forge of Vulcan Oil/canvas
(190x261cm 74x102in) London 1998
✏ **$1 472** - €1 651 - **£1 000** - FF10 830
The Flagellation Black chalk (31x24cm 12x9in)
London 2000
▥ **$1 400** - €1 451 - **£840** - FF9 520
Gesù condotto al Calvario Acquaforte (64x120cm
25x47in) Milano 2000

MILANI F. XIX **[1]**
✺ **$6 588** - €6 541 - **£4 113** - FF42 903
Heimkehr von der Feldarbeit Öl/Leinwand
(62.5x50.5cm 24x19in) Wien 1999

MILANI Umberto 1912-1969 **[20]**
✺ **$3 000** - €3 110 - **£1 800** - FF20 400
Senza titolo Olio/masonite (91.5x109cm 36x42in)
Milano 2000
✎ **$1 800** - €1 866 - **£1 080** - FF12 240
Testa di donna Bronzo (H30.5cm H12in) Milano
1999
✏ **$600** - €518 - **£400** - FF3 400
Composizione Tecnica mista/carta (28x34cm
11x13in) Milano 1998

MILANO da Giulio 1895-1990 **[37]**
✺ **$1 000** - €1 037 - **£600** - FF6 800
Nudo di schiena seduto Tempera/cartone (50x35cm
19x13in) Vercelli 2001
✺ **$1 200** - €1 244 - **£720** - FF8 160
Odalisca Olio/tavola (20x26.5cm 7x10in) Torino 1999

✏ **$325** - €337 - **£195** - FF2 210
Ussaro Acquarello/cartone (25.5x18.5cm 10x7in)
Vercelli 2000

MILATZ Franciscus Andreas 1764-1808 **[6]**
✏ **$3 076** - €2 657 - **£1 854** - FF17 430
A View of the Voldersgracht in Haarlem, with a
man crossing a Bridge Watercolour (36x46cm
14x18in) Amsterdam 1998

MILBOURNE Henry 1781-1826 **[16]**
✺ **$5 421** - €6 320 - **£3 800** - FF41 458
River Landscape with Cattle and Figures
Oil/canvas (96x111cm 38x44in) Buckie, Banffshire
2000

MILBURN Oliver 1883-1932 **[2]**
✺ **$4 000** - €4 667 - **£2 784** - FF30 612
Cityscape, Waterway, Trees Oil/canvas (76x91cm
30x36in) Altadena CA 2000

MILCENDEAU Charles 1872-1919 **[77]**
✏ **$1 231** - €1 448 - **£882** - FF9 500
Portrait de fillette Crayon/papier (19.5x15.5cm 7x6in)
Paris 2001

MILDNER Johann Josef 1765-1808 **[1]**
✏ **$15 498** - €13 073 - **£9 090** - FF85 752
Alter Mann Aquarell/Papier (16.2x12.2cm 6x4in) Wien
1998

MILEHAM Harry Robert 1873-1957 **[11]**
✺ **$5 113** - €5 807 - **£3 500** - FF38 090
Mary Livock Mileham, Saeted, Wearing a White
Dress, Holding her Violin Oil/canvas (81x81cm
31x31in) Bury St. Edmunds, Suffolk 2000

MILES Maurice A. XX **[2]**
▥ **$1 411** - €1 637 - **£1 000** - FF10 735
«For the Zoo, London Transport» Poster
(102x64cm 40x25in) London 2000

MILES OF NORTHLEACH John XVIII-XIX **[7]**
✺ **$12 354** - €12 846 - **£7 800** - FF84 265
The Noted Sheep Killing Dog Oil/canvas
(48x68.5cm 18x26in) Newbury, Berkshire 2000

MILES Thomas Rose ?-c.1906 **[125]**
✺ **$3 308** - €2 829 - **£2 000** - FF18 555
Running out of Whitby in Heavy Seas Oil/canvas
(110.5x86.5cm 43x34in) London 1999
✺ **$1 600** - €1 882 - **£1 147** - FF12 342
Ship off Coast Oil/canvas (20x40cm 8x16in) San
Rafael CA 2001

MILESI Alessandro 1856-1945 **[77]**
✺ **$9 400** - €12 181 - **£7 050** - FF79 900
Ritratto femminile Olio/tela (74x53.5cm 29x21in)
Milano 2001

MILET-MUREAU Iphigénie 1780-? **[6]**
✺ **$67 779** - €63 447 - **£42 000** - FF416 182
Pink Roses in a Glass Vase on a Marble Edge
Oil/panel (46x37.5cm 18x14in) London 1999

MILEY R.A. XIX **[3]**
✺ **$3 086** - €3 671 - **£2 200** - FF24 079
Chestnut Hunter in a Stable Oil/canvas (61.5x76cm
24x29in) London 2000

MILGATE Rodney Armour 1934 **[40]**
✺ **$647** - €609 - **£401** - FF3 994
«Experiment in Depth» Oil/board (182x122.5cm
71x48in) Melbourne 1999

MILHAZES Beatriz 1960 **[3]**
✺ **$23 000** - €22 155 - **£14 280** - FF145 327
«Com título» Acrylic/canvas (162x190cm 63x74in)
New-York 1999

M

MILI Gjon 1904-1984 **[16]**

📷 **$3 861 – €4 345 – £2 696 –** FF28 500
Vase aux fleurs, Picasso peignant avec de la lumière Tirage argentique (34x26.5cm 13x10in) Paris 2001

MILIADIS Stelios 1881-1965 **[8]**

$5 275 – €6 074 – £3 600 – FF39 840
Athenian Ruins Oil/board (34x45cm 13x17in) London 2000

MILIAN Raúl 1914-1986 **[11]**

$7 000 – €6 794 – £4 358 – FF44 566
Abstracto/Rostro Rojo/Rostro Azul/Florero Ink (38x28cm 14x11in) New-York 1999

MILICH Abram Adolphe 1884-1964 **[42]**

$2 620 – €2 235 – £1 561 – FF14 663
Portrait Madame René Clair Öl/Leinwand (92x67cm 36x26in) Zürich 1998

$2 157 – €1 861 – £1 296 – FF12 210
Weiblicher Halbakt Öl/Leinwand (29x25cm 11x9in) Bern 1998

MILIUS Félix Augustin 1843-1894 **[6]**

$4 249 – €3 886 – £2 559 – FF25 492
Première entrevue Oil/canvas (50x38cm 20x15in) New-York 1998

MILLAIS John Everett 1829-1896 **[99]**

$1 195 440 – €1 283 206 – £800 000 – FF8 417 280
«The brown Boy» - Master Liddell, Son of Charles Liddell esq. Oil/canvas (161.5x105.5cm 63x41in) London 2000

$164 373 – €176 441 – £110 000 – FF1 157 376
Marry Oil/canvas (92x71.5cm 36x28in) London 2000

$209 202 – €224 561 – £140 000 – FF1 473 024
Alice Gray Oil/canvas (30.5x20.5cm 12x8in) London 2000

$1 200 – €1 231 – £750 – FF8 072
Young Maidens Sleeping Watercolour/paper (8x13cm 3x5in) New-Orleans LA 2000

MILLAIS John Guille 1865-1931 **[20]**

$586 – €538 – £360 – FF3 531
Mallard Ducks on a Pond Grisaille (23x39cm 9x15in) Billingshurst, West-Sussex 1999

MILLAIS Raoul 1901-1999 **[95]**

$5 602 – €5 348 – £3 500 – FF35 078
Horses in a Landscape Oil/canvas (51x61cm 20x24in) London 1999

$2 314 – €2 186 – £1 400 – FF14 342
A Stable Boy with a dappled grey Horse and Dog Oil/board (20x24cm 7x9in) Billingshurst, West-Sussex 1999

$513 – €508 – £320 – FF3 330
Open Landau and Figures in Parkland Pastel/paper (15x17.5cm 5x6in) Leyburn, North Yorkshire 1999

MILLAIS William Henry 1828-1899 **[17]**

$1 048 – €963 – £649 – FF6 314
Old Weir, Tynmouth Watercolour (37.5x59cm 14x23in) London 1999

MILLAN Victor 1909 **[39]**

$510 – €480 – £330 – FF3 150
Virgen del Valle Acrílico/lienzo (119.5x63cm 47x24in) Caracas 1999

MILLAR Addison Thomas 1860-1913 **[88]**

$500 – €4 814 – £3 331 – FF31 578
Rug Merchant, Alger Oil/canvas (45x60cm 18x24in) Felton CA 1998

$3 500 – €4 104 – £2 518 – FF26 922
Rug Merchant Oil/board (18x23cm 7x9in) New-York 2001

$525 – €576 – £338 – FF3 777
Harbor scene with fishing boat Watercolour/paper (23x25cm 9x10in) Wallkill NY 2000

MILLAR James H.C. act.1884-1903 **[18]**

$786 – €893 – £550 – FF5 858
The Arch Rock, Gulls on a Rocky Coastline Oil/canvas (91x60cm 35x23in) Devon 2001

MILLARD Frederick, Fred 1857-1919 **[9]**

$1 115 – €1 294 – £770 – FF8 488
A View of Chipping Campden, Glos/The Companion View Oil/canvas (25x33cm 10x13in) Bourton-on-the-Water, Glos. 2000

MILLARES Manolo 1926-1972 **[132]**

$102 000 – €90 097 – £63 000 – FF591 000
Composición Técnica mixta (131x97.5cm 51x38in) Madrid 1999

$20 000 – €24 026 – £14 000 – FF157 600
Negro, rojo y blanco Oleo/papel (48.5x69cm 19x27in) Madrid 2000

$8 800 – €9 610 – £5 920 – FF63 040
Composición Oleo/tabla (30.5x23cm 12x9in) Madrid 2000

$8 520 – €7 208 – £5 040 – FF47 280
Sin título Gouache/papier (55x76cm 21x29in) Madrid 2000

$686 – €676 – £438 – FF4 432
Torquemada Serigrafia (49.5x69.5cm 19x27in) Barcelona 1999

MILLASSON Anne XX **[11]**

$1 844 – €1 829 – £1 147 – FF12 000
La plage rose Pastel/papier (30x39cm 11x15in) Brest 1999

MILLECAMPS Yves 1930 **[8]**

$1 608 – €1 829 – £1 134 – FF12 000
«Ediotrope» Tapisserie (208x164cm 81x64in) Paris 2001

MILLER Alfred Jacob 1810-1874 **[49]**

$190 000 – €188 639 – £118 750 – FF1 237 394
Deer by the River, Wyoming Oil/canvas (77.5x63.5cm 30x25in) New-York 1999

$40 000 – €34 175 – £24 012 – FF224 176
«Schim-a-co-che» Oil/paper (29x26cm 11x10in) New-York 1998

$38 000 – €37 666 – £23 769 – FF247 072
Indian with the Scalp Lock of his Enemy Watercolour, gouache (24x20.5cm 9x8in) New-York 1999

MILLER Barse 1904-1973 **[17]**

$3 200 – €3 586 – £2 230 – FF23 522
Farmyard Watercolour/paper (53.5x65cm 21x25in) Beverly-Hills CA 2001

MILLER Charles Henry 1842-1922 **[15]**

$2 000 – €2 164 – £1 370 – FF14 192
Landscape with Watermill and Figures Oil/canvas (26x41cm 10x16in) East-Moriches NY 2001

$1 700 – €1 894 – £1 143 – FF12 427
Long Island Scene with Mill Watercolour/paper (23x33cm 9x13in) Portsmouth NH 2000

MILLER Charles Keith, Capt. XIX-XX **[20]**

$4 184 – €4 491 – £2 800 – FF29 500
Britannia - White Cliffs of Dover in Background Oil/canvas (69x104cm 27x40in) Edinburgh 2000

MILLER Evylena Nunn 1888-1966 **[19]**
🐦 **$1 200** - €1 152 - **£752** - FF7 554
Sierras Landscape Oil/canvas/board (50x40cm
20x16in) Altadena CA 1999

MILLER Frederick XIX-XX **[18]**
✎ **$345** - €332 - **£220** - FF2 176
**Sheep Grazing on Top of the Seven Sisters,
Sussex** Watercolour (23x42cm 9x16in) London 1999

MILLER Garry Fabian 1957 **[2]**
📷 **$4 332** - €4 721 - **£30** - FF30 968
Sections of England: The Sea Horizon
Photograph (48x48cm 18x18in) London 2001

MILLER George XIX **[4]**
🐦 **$11 000** - €12 131 - **£7 449** - FF79 575
Fly Fishing in the Adirondacks Oil/canvas
(23x30.5cm 9x12in) New-York 2000

MILLER Godfrey Clive 1893-1964 **[88]**
🐦 **$13 057** - €11 970 - **£8 078** - FF78 515
«Landscape Series» Oil/canvas (42.5x60cm
16x23in) Melbourne 1998
🐦 **$3 885** - €3 663 - **£2 407** - FF24 026
Table Arrangement Mixed media/canvas (26x36cm
10x14in) Melbourne 1999
🔨 **$5 660** - €5 906 - **£3 570** - FF38 743
Figure Bronze (H18cm H7in) Sydney 2000
✎ **$550** - €518 - **£341** - FF3 396
Figure Study Pencil/paper (38x27cm 14x10in)
Melbourne 1999

MILLER Harriette G. 1892-1971 **[3]**
🔨 **$14 000** - €12 925 - **£8 610** - FF84 782
Innocence Marbre (H47.5cm H18in) New-York 1999

MILLER Iris Marie Andrews 1881-1981 **[8]**
🐦 **$700** - €720 - **£444** - FF4 722
Fisherman's Wife, Vollendam Oil/canvas (99x66cm
39x26in) Detroit MI 2000

MILLER James XVIII-XIX **[8]**
✎ **$2 258** - €2 619 - **£1 600** - FF17 177
**A House Situated on the Banks of the Thames,
Near Hammersmith** Watercolour (26x39cm 10x15in)
London 2000

MILLER James Robertson ?-1912 **[6]**
✎ **$679** - €638 - **£420** - FF4 183
Barges, Volendam Watercolour (36x26cm 14x10in)
Leyburn, North Yorkshire 1999

MILLER John 1931 **[83]**
🐦 **$1 012** - €1 179 - **£700** - FF7 735
Summer Garden, St Crede Oil/canvas (71x76cm
27x29in) London 2000
🐦 **$641** - €647 - **£400** - FF4 241
Horizon XXII - Lelant 8 Oil/canvas (35.5x30.5cm
13x12in) London 2000
✎ **$248** - €272 - **£160** - FF1 784
Cliffs in Winter Haze, Cornwall Watercolour/paper
(29.5x40cm 11x15in) London 2000

MILLER Joseph XIX **[7]**
🐦 **$5 755** - €5 704 - **£3 600** - FF37 418
The Latest Acquisition Oil/canvas (73x60.5cm
28x23in) London 1999

MILLER Kenneth Hayes 1876-1952 **[22]**
🍸 **$325** - €369 - **£222** - FF2 422
Leaving the Shop Etching (20.5x25.5cm 8x10in)
New-York 2000

MILLER Lee 1907-1977 **[33]**
📷 **$9 241** - €10 427 - **£6 500** - FF68 398
Self-Portrait Silver print (23x17.5cm 9x6in) London
2001

MILLER Lewis 1796-1882 **[24]**
✎ **$800** - €854 - **£545** - FF5 604
**Ludwig miller Home and Lot, South King St.,
Shows the House and Yard** Watercolour/paper
(10x20cm 4x8in) York PA 2001

MILLER Lilian May 1895-1943 **[14]**
🍸 **$700** - €751 - **£476** - FF4 929
«Rain Blossom, Japan» Woodcut in colors
(25x37cm 9x14in) Boston MA 2001

MILLER Mildred Bunting 1892-1964 **[18]**
🐦 **$350** - €323 - **£215** - FF2 119
Summer Afternoon Oil/board (45x60cm 18x24in)
Hatfield PA 1999

MILLER Ralph Davidson 1858-1945 **[21]**
🐦 **$700** - €756 - **£483** - FF4 958
Stream in Forest Interior Oil/canvas (50x76cm
20x30in) Altadena CA 2001

MILLER Richard Edward 1875-1943 **[82]**
🐦 **$55 000** - €60 911 - **£37 301** - FF399 547
Bather Oil/board (91.5x96.5cm 36x37in) New-York
2000
🐦 **$21 000** - €20 815 - **£13 135** - FF136 539
Lamplight Oil/masonite (26.5x35.5cm 10x13in) New-
York 1999
✎ **$500** - €5 551 - **£3 477** - FF36 412
Covered Wagon Gouache (25x25cm 10x10in)
Milford CT 2001

MILLER Roy 1938 **[53]**
🐦 **$1 445** - €1 403 - **£900** - FF9 203
Through the Fog Oil/canvas (61x76cm 24x29in)
London 1999

MILLER William G. act.1891-1908 **[3]**
✎ **$1 046** - €1 123 - **£700** - FF7 365
**Full Length Portrait of Lady Clad in Sailing Club
Uniform on Balcony** Watercolour/paper (63x38cm
24x14in) London 2000

MILLER William Rickarby Jnr 1850-1923 **[1]**
🐦 **$3 600** - €3 949 - **£2 323** - FF25 905
Country scene Oil/canvas (45x76cm 18x30in)
Wallkill NY 2000

MILLER William Rickarby Snr 1818-1893 **[64]**
🐦 **$13 000** - €11 125 - **£7 826** - FF72 972
View of New York Harbor from Castle Point
Oil/canvas (36x58cm 14x23in) New-York 1998
🐦 **$2 250** - €2 457 - **£1 448** - FF16 118
Figures by Cottage Oil/board (20x15cm 8x6in)
Mystic CT 2000
🐦 **$2 000** - €2 175 - **£1 318** - FF14 268
Walk along the Wood Lane Watercolour/paper
(30.5x24cm 12x9in) Boston MA 2000

MILLER-DIFLO Otto 1878-1949 **[43]**
🐦 **$996** - €920 - **£613** - FF6 037
**Blick auf die Fraueninsel im Chiemsee und die
Kampenland** Öl/Karton (45x64cm 17x25in)
München 1999
🐦 **$213** - €256 - **£146** - FF1 676
Flusslandschaft Öl/Karton (29x42cm 11x16in)
München 2000
✎ **$257** - €256 - **£160** - FF1 676
Stilles Wasser Aquarell/Papier (11x14cm 4x5in)
München 1999

MILLER-PARKER Agnes 1895-1980 **[4]**
🍸 **$182** - €213 - **£126** - FF1 395
Wulf and Rammes Woodcut (11x12.5cm 4x4in)
Melbourne 2000

M

MILLER-RANSON Elie XX **[2]**
- $3 072 - €3 403 - **£2 084** - FF22 324
  Portrait of a woman Oil/board (50.5x31cm 19x12in) Amsterdam 2000

MILLES Carl 1875-1955 **[281]**
- $25 000 - €27 360 - **£17 245** - FF179 470
  Orpheus Girl Bronze (H106.5cm H41in) New-York 2001
- $4 636 - €5 000 - **£3 112** - FF32 797
  Ikaros Bronze (H58.5cm H23in) Stockholm 2000

MILLES Ruth 1873-1941 **[95]**
- $1 107 - €1 189 - **£741** - FF7 800
  Yvonne, jeune bretonne Bronze (H24cm H9in) Menton 2000

MILLESON Royal Hill 1849-1926 **[22]**
- $2 000 - €2 079 - **£1 260** - FF13 636
  Fall Landscape with Stream Oil/canvas (30x45cm 12x18in) Detroit MI 2000

MILLET Aimé 1819-1891 **[8]**
- $1 471 - €1 413 - **£915** - FF9 268
  Flora Bronze (H68cm H26in) Stockholm 1999

MILLET Clarence 1897-1959 **[65]**
- $11 000 - €12 708 - **£7 702** - FF83 359
  «Sunday Morning, New Orleans» Oil/canvas (66x66cm 26x26in) New-York 2001
- $3 400 - €3 091 - **£2 047** - FF20 274
  «Jakson Square» Oil/canvas/board (25x20cm 10x8in) New-Orleans LA 1998
- $160 - €148 - **£99** - FF972
  «Pirate's Alley, Old New Orleans» Woodcut (17x14cm 7x5in) New-Orleans LA 1999

MILLET Francis David, Frank 1846-1912 **[18]**
- $4 200 - €4 471 - **£2 861** - FF29 328
  Portrait of a Classical Woman Oil/panel (40x22cm 15x8in) New-York 2001

MILLET Francisque J-Fr. I 1642-1679/80 **[27]**
- $7 228 - €8 418 - **£5 000** - FF55 216
  An Arcadian Landscape with Harvesters Oil/canvas (43x72.5cm 16x28in) London 2000
- $8 861 - €8 813 - **£5 500** - FF57 811
  Italianate Landscape with Fishermen drawing in their Nets, Villa Oil/canvas (34.5x44.5cm 13x17in) London 1999

MILLET Francisque J-Fr. II 1666-1723 **[6]**
- $15 000 - €17 667 - **£10 374** - FF115 888
  Two Figures on a Path in a Wooded Classical Landscape with Buildings Oil/canvas (75x92.5cm 29x36in) New-York 2000
- $17 000 - €14 279 - **£9 994** - FF93 663
  Landscape with Figures and Classical Buildings Oil/canvas (33x47cm 12x18in) New-York 1998

MILLET François 1851-1917 **[14]**
- $1 373 - €1 957 - **£957** - FF10 000
  Gardienne de dindons Pastel/papier (26x38cm 10x14in) Paris 2001

MILLET Frédéric 1786-1859 **[14]**
- $1 342 - €1 524 - **£926** - FF10 000
  Jeune fille vêtue d'une robe rose et écharpe de soie blanche Miniature (14x10cm 5x3in) Paris 2000

MILLET Jean-Baptiste 1831-1906 **[51]**
- $839 - €793 - **£522** - FF5 200
  Les toits de chaume Pierre noire/papier (15x21cm 5x8in) Paris 1999

MILLET Jean-Charles 1892-1944 **[35]**
- $1 099 - €1 067 - **£679** - FF7 000
  Les glaneuses Encre Chine/papier (21.5x36.5cm 8x14in) Melun 1999

MILLET Jean-François 1814-1875 **[606]**
- $110 000 - €102 075 - **£67 210** - FF669 570
  Portrait of M. Troyan Oil/canvas (73x59.5cm 28x23in) New-York 1999
- $100 000 - €95 371 - **£60 870** - FF625 590
  Wood Cutter in the Forest/young Woman Taking Linenes from a Shelf Oil/panel (17x29cm 6x11in) New-York 1999
- $2 201 - €2 363 - **£1 472** - FF15 500
  Femme assise sur un banc Crayon/papier (13x9cm 5x3in) Rennes 2000
- $1 841 - €1 821 - **£1 150** - FF11 942
  Woman Carding Etching (25.5x17.5cm 10x6in) London 1999

MILLIERE Maurice 1871-1946 **[130]**
- $400 - €397 - **£248** - FF2 606
  Portrait of a Lady in a Plumed Hat Drypoint (55x38cm 22x15in) Norwalk CT 2000

MILLIKEN James W. ?-c.1930 **[80]**
- $589 - €653 - **£400** - FF4 284
  Morning Glow, Rufford Watercolour/paper (16.5x28cm 6x11in) Billingshurst, West-Sussex 2000

MILLIKEN Robert W. 1920 **[45]**
- $886 - €805 - **£549** - FF5 283
  Wigeon over Strangford Louch, Northern Ireland Watercolour (53x73cm 20x28in) Billingshurst, West-Sussex 1999

MILLINGTON John 1891-1948 **[12]**
- $600 - €650 - **£400** - FF4 265
  The Red Jacket: White Star Clipper/The Slieve Roe Watercolour (36x26.5cm 14x10in) Billingshurst, West-Sussex 2000

MILLIOUD-MELAY Gabrielle 1875-1931 **[3]**
- $16 000 - €14 164 - **£9 782** - FF92 910
  Still Life of Hollyhocks and red Flowers in a Baroque Vase Oil/canvas (210x134cm 82x52in) New-York 1999

MILLMAN Edward 1907-1964 **[3]**
- $700 - €724 - **£442** - FF4 748
  Flophouse Lithograph (22.5x32.5cm 8x12in) New-York 2000

MILLNER Carl 1825-1895 **[100]**
- $25 448 - €28 121 - **£17 649** - FF184 464
  Tiefe Landschaft mit Fels und Personenstaffage Öl/Leinwand (100x130cm 39x51in) München 2001
- $3 132 - €3 068 - **£2 018** - FF20 123
  Almhütte und Kühe im Hochgebirge Öl/Leinwand (37x49cm 14x19in) Kempten 1999
- $1 473 - €1 534 - **£933** - FF10 061
  Voralpenlandschaft, vorn zwei Rehe am Ufer des Teiches Oil/paper/canvas (16x25.5cm 6x10in) München 2000

MILLNER William Edward act.1845-1891 **[19]**
- $5 612 - €6 674 - **£4 000** - FF43 780
  The Orange Seller Oil/canvas (46x61cm 18x24in) London 2000
- $2 416 - €2 404 - **£1 500** - FF15 766
  Wandering Thoughts Oil/board (29x19cm 11x7in) London 1999

MILLOT Henri ?-1756 **[6]**
- $14 480 - €12 196 - **£8 552** - FF79 800
  Portrait d'homme à la cape rouge Huile/toile (80.5x65.5cm 31x25in) Paris 1998

MILLS Arthur George 1907 [1]

$2 118 - €2 456 - **£1 500** - FF16 108
«Fishguard-Rosslare, British Railways, Western Region, Express Train» Poster (102x63cm 40x24in) London 2000

MILLS John Fitzmaurice ?-1991 [10]

$390 - €406 - **£246** - FF2 665
Castle Leslie, County Mohaghan Watercolour/paper (30x42cm 11x16in) Dublin 2000

MILLS Reginald XX [17]

$302 - €358 - **£220** - FF2 348
Two Horses in a Stable Oil/canvas (51x60.5cm 20x23in) Newcastle-upon-Tyne 2001

MILLWARD Clem 1929 [37]

$1 429 - €1 340 - **£883** - FF8 793
Mallee Scrub Oil/canvas (92x183cm 36x72in) Sydney 1999

$528 - €629 - **£365** - FF4 125
Inland Waters Oil/canvas (90x120cm 35x47in) Sydney 2000

MILNE David Brown 1882-1953 [90]

$84 630 - €72 418 - **£50 947** - FF475 033
Ollie Matson's Yard, Winter/Gate and Barns Oil/canvas (46.5x56.5cm 18x22in) Toronto 1998

$20 484 - €19 821 - **£12 633** - FF130 017
From an upper Window, Ottawa II Oil/canvas/board (30.5x41.5cm 12x16in) Toronto 1999

$9 559 - €9 250 - **£5 895** - FF60 674
Balsam Tree #1 Watercolour/paper (37x54.5cm 14x21in) Toronto 1999

$1 092 - €1 057 - **£673** - FF6 934
Painting Place Drypoint in colors (12x17cm 4x6in) Toronto 1999

MILNE John Erskine 1931-1978 [45]

$1 314 - €1 249 - **£800** - FF8 195
Landscape Form II Bronze (H21.5cm H8in) London 1999

MILNE John Maclauchlan 1885-1957 [116]

$11 221 - €10 600 - **£7 000** - FF69 533
Early Spring Oil/canvas (71x92cm 27x36in) Perthshire 1999

$32 390 - €33 812 - **£20 500** - FF221 791
River Scene Oil/canvas (35x44cm 13x17in) Knutsford, Cheshire 2000

$1 432 - €1 644 - **£980** - FF10 782
An East Neuk Fishing Village Watercolour/paper (21.5x17.5cm 8x6in) Edinburgh 2000

MILNE Joseph 1861-1911 [47]

$2 241 - €2 216 - **£1 400** - FF14 538
Ferryden, Arbroath Oil/board (38x54.5cm 14x21in) Glasgow 1999

$1 915 - €1 670 - **£1 158** - FF10 956
Red Rooves Oil/board (22x28.5cm 8x11in) Melbourne 1998

MILNE Malcolm 1887-1954 [21]

$560 - €513 - **£340** - FF3 366
Still Life Oil/board (40.5x33cm 15x12in) London 1998

MILNE William Watt 1873-1951 [85]

$3 022 - €3 385 - **£2 100** - FF22 205
On the Riverbank Oil/board (40x56cm 15x22in) Bury St. Edmunds, Suffolk 2001

$2 531 - €2 442 - **£1 600** - FF16 020
In a Cottage Garden Oil/canvas/board (30.5x25.5cm 12x10in) London 1999

MILO Jean van Gindertael 1906-1993 [196]

$799 - €770 - **£500** - FF5 050
Yachts in Harbour, a Promenade in the South of France Oil/canvas (33x51cm 12x20in) London 1999

$440 - €471 - **£300** - FF3 089
Stilleven met vruchten Aquarelle/papier (30x46cm 11x18in) Lokeren 2001

MILON Joseph 1868-1947 [10]

$2 232 - €2 287 - **£1 377** - FF15 000
Baigneuses à l'étang de Berre Huile/panneau (38x46cm 14x18in) Aubagne 2000

MILONE Antonio XIX-XX [30]

$1 680 - €1 451 - **£1 120** - FF9 520
Pastorello con gregge Olio/tavola (34x46cm 13x18in) Napoli 1998

MILPURRURRU George 1934-1998 [12]

$4 860 - €5 217 - **£3 252** - FF34 222
Gumang - The Goose Dancing Ceremony Mixed media (120x95cm 47x37in) Melbourne 2000

MILROY Lisa 1959 [20]

$13 448 - €14 436 - **£9 000** - FF94 694
Butterflies Oil/canvas (190.5x221cm 75x87in) London 2000

MILSHTEIN Zwy 1934 [83]

$662 - €686 - **£419** - FF4 500
Nature morte Huile/toile (61x50cm 24x19in) Paris 2000

MILTHON XX [3]

$1 742 - €1 829 - **£1 101** - FF12 000
Couple Bronze (H50cm H19in) Paris 2000

MILTON JENSEN Carl 1855-1928 [125]

$459 - €417 - **£287** - FF2 736
Skovparti, vinter Oil/canvas (65x90cm 25x35in) Viby J, Århus 1999

MILTON Peter 1930 [38]

$600 - €672 - **£418** - FF4 405
«Bruegelscape #1»/«Les belles et la bête I: the Reheasal» Etching (50x91cm 19x35in) New-York 2001

MIMNAUGH Terry XX [3]

$13 000 - €11 818 - **£7 829** - FF77 519
Fishing the blackfoot Oil/board (66x91cm 26x36in) Hayden ID 1998

MIMRAN Patrick 1956 [3]

$60 000 - €67 087 - **£40 446** - FF440 064
Number 53 Oil/board (148.5x122cm 58x48in) New-York 2000

MIN de Giovanni 1786-1859 [2]

$2 640 - €2 281 - **£1 320** - FF14 960
Rappresentazione allegorica della disfatta di Napoleone alla Beresina Inchiostro (27.5x40cm 10x15in) Milano 1999

MIN Jaap 1914-1987 [33]

$4 650 - €4 991 - **£3 111** - FF32 742
Boerderij Het Sluisje Te Bergen Oil/canvas (65x86cm 25x33in) Amsterdam 2000

MINAMI Keiko 1911 [10]

$1 400 - €1 509 - **£954** - FF9 897
Standing Bird Crayon (24x28.5cm 9x11in) New-York 2001

MINARDI Tommaso 1787-1871 [18]

$650 - €671 - **£390** - FF4 420
Studio di Madonna seduta Matita/carta (18.5x13cm 7x5in) Milano 2000

M

MINARTZ Antoine G., dit Tony 1870-1944 **[52]**
- $4 983 - €4 265 - **£3 000** - FF27 975
  La danse Oil/canvas (46.5x55cm 18x21in) London 1998
- $313 - €294 - **£193** - FF1 928
  Woman on a Sofa Watercolour (40.5x30.5cm 15x12in) Melbourne 1999

MINAUX André 1923-1986 **[131]**
- $770 - €701 - **£481** - FF4 600
  Homme assis Huile/toile (130x80cm 51x31in) Enghien 1999
- $775 - €915 - **£545** - FF6 000
  Portrait de femme Huile/toile (46x34cm 18x13in) Fontainebleau 2000
- $113 - €122 - **£76** - FF800
  Sans titre Lithographie couleurs (87x60cm 34x23in) Paris 2000

MIND Gottfried 1768-1814 **[29]**
- $732 - €855 - **£510** - FF5 609
  Zwei Katzen Pencil (10x12.5cm 3x4in) Bern 2000
- $163 - €183 - **£104** - FF1 200
  Chat attrapant une souris Lithographie (13.5x20cm 5x7in) Paris 2000

MINDERHOUT van Hendrik 1632-1696 **[16]**
- $24 390 - €27 441 - **£16 794** - FF180 000
  Navires près d'un port méditerranéen Huile/toile (173x184cm 68x72in) Lille 2000
- $10 526 - €11 677 - **£7 000** - FF76 597
  The Dutch Flagship Eendracht in Action at The Battle of Lowestoft Oil/canvas (72x105.5cm 28x41in) London 2000

MINERBI Arrigo 1881-1960 **[4]**
- $4 249 - €4 405 - **£2 549** - FF28 898
  Busto d'Angelo Bronzo (52x50x32cm 20x19x12in) Genova 2000

MINET Louis Émile 1850-1920 **[19]**
- $8 000 - €7 922 - **£4 980** - FF51 966
  Gentle Stream Oil/canvas (118x162cm 46x63in) New-York 1999
- $4 458 - €4 317 - **£2 800** - FF28 315
  Vase of Summer Flowers Oil/canvas (100.5x70.5cm 39x27in) London 1999

MINGELMANGANU Alec ?-1981 **[5]**
- $12 579 - €13 503 - **£8 419** - FF88 576
  Wandjina and Snake Mixed media/canvas (51x40.5cm 20x15in) Melbourne 2000

MINGORANCE ACIEN Manuel 1920 **[20]**
- $1 450 - €1 502 - **£925** - FF9 850
  La llamada Oleo/lienzo (60x45cm 23x17in) Madrid 2000

MINGOZZI Giovanni XIX-XX **[2]**
- $810 - €840 - **£486** - FF5 508
  «Barbisio» Affiche couleur (125x89cm 49x35in) Torino 2000

MINGUILLON IGLESIAS Julia 1906-1965 **[4]**
- $2 080 - €1 952 - **£1 300** - FF12 805
  París Acuarela/papel (34x48cm 13x18in) Madrid 1999

MINGUZZI Luciano 1912 **[52]**
- $3 900 - €3 369 - **£2 600** - FF22 100
  Pescatore Bronzo (H32cm H12in) Milano 1998
- $520 - €674 - **£390** - FF4 420
  Studio di costume per Ernani di Verdi Inchiostro (70x50cm 27x19in) Milano 2001
- $180 - €155 - **£120** - FF1 020
  Personaggi Acquaforte (20.5x24.5cm 8x9in) Prato 1998

MINIAM van John XVIII-XIX **[1]**
- $7 000 - €6 039 - **£4 238** - FF39 615
  Gentleman and Lady with Flowers, Birth Letter for Elisabeth Schuman Watercolour (42x30.5cm 16x12in) New-York 1999

MINIER Suzanne 1884-? **[16]**
- $871 - €991 - **£604** - FF6 500
  Jeune fille à l'eventail Huile/toile (91.5x73.5cm 36x28in) Fontainebleau 2000

MINKKINEN Arno Rafael 1945 **[3]**
- $1 198 - €1 022 - **£723** - FF6 707
  Fosters Pond Gelatin silver print (50x39.9cm 19x15in) Köln 1998

MINKOWSKI Maurice 1889-1930 **[12]**
- $9 000 - €8 760 - **£5 529** - FF57 459
  Naomi and Ruth Watercolour, gouache/paper (100x68cm 39x26in) Tel Aviv 1999

MINNE B. XX **[2]**
- $3 800 - €4 118 - **£2 533** - FF27 010
  «Monaco, 1e et 2e juin» Poster (119x79cm 47x31in) New-York 2000

MINNE Georges 1866-1941 **[186]**
- $4 140 - €4 958 - **£2 840** - FF32 520
  Baadster III (Baigneuse III) Bronze (H80cm H31in) Antwerpen 2000
- $7 722 - €6 445 - **£4 524** - FF42 276
  De metser Plaster (75.8x63cm 29x24in) Lokeren 1998
- $2 476 - €2 659 - **£1 657** - FF17 440
  Résurrection Pencil/paper (17.5x11.8cm 6x4in) Hamburg 2000
- $857 - €1 022 - **£611** - FF6 707
  Taufe Christi Woodcut (61.2x50.6cm 24x19in) Berlin 2000

MINNE Joris 1897-1988 **[103]**
- $102 - €99 - **£63** - FF650
  Cables Linogravure (24x21cm 9x8in) Bruxelles 1999

MINNS Benjamin Edwin 1864-1937 **[145]**
- $2 452 - €2 254 - **£1 494** - FF14 784
  Lady Sewing Watercolour/paper (43x33.5cm 16x13in) Melbourne 1998
- $107 - €112 - **£67** - FF735
  Aboriginal Hunting Etching (19.5x16.5cm 7x6in) Sydney 2000

MINOLI Paolo 1942 **[14]**
- $1 521 - €1 768 - **£1 069** - FF11 597
  Poema «leggenda Indiana» Acryl/Leinwand (80x80x3cm 31x31x1in) Luzern 2001

MINOR Ferdinand 1814-1883 **[3]**
- $7 266 - €8 447 - **£5 100** - FF55 008
  Idle moments Oil/canvas (110x87.5cm 43x34in) London 2001

MINOR Robert Crannell 1839-1904 **[26]**
- $2 750 - €2 939 - **£1 872** - FF19 279
  Impressionistic Woodland and Field Landscape Oil/canvas (71x96cm 28x38in) New-Orleans LA 2001

MINORU Niizuma 1930-1998 **[10]**
- $8 000 - €9 382 - **£5 708** - FF61 539
  Untitled Marble (167x34x34cm 65x13x13in) New-York 2000
- $3 500 - €3 390 - **£2 182** - FF22 239
  Untitled Marble (78.5x26.5x23cm 30x10x9in) New-York 2001

MINOTT Joseph Otis ?-1909 **[1]**
- $7 500 - €8 664 - **£5 251** - FF56 835
  The launching of the Defender Watercolour (49x66.5cm 19x26in) New-York 2001

MINOZZI Bernardino 1699-1769 [1]
- $3 235 - €2 999 - **£2 000** - FF19 675
  Wooded Landscapes with Classical Figures
  Wash (45.5x34.5cm 17x13in) London 1999

MINOZZI Flaminio Innocenzo 1735-1817 [6]
- $5 164 - €5 793 - **£3 613** - FF38 000
  Décor de théâtre Encre (33.5x46.5cm 13x18in) Paris 2001

MINSHULL R.T. XIX-XX [17]
- $3 787 - €4 244 - **£2 600** - FF27 836
  Barefoot Girl on a Rocky Mountain Path Oil/canvas (48x38cm 19x15in) Leominster, Herefordshire 2000
- $549 - €640 - **£380** - FF4 196
  Her First Lesson Oil/board (8x11cm 3x4in) Cheshire 2000

MINSK 1923 [23]
- $594 - €610 - **£372** - FF4 000
  Inoudations Huile/toile (46x55cm 18x21in) L'Isle-Adam 2000

MINTCHINE Abraham 1898-1931 [83]
- $3 400 - €3 319 - **£2 153** - FF21 770
  Village on the Hilltop Oil/paper/board (49.5x65.5cm 19x25in) Tel Aviv 1999
- $2 750 - €2 308 - **£1 613** - FF15 137
  Irene Gouache/board (53x48cm 20x18in) New-York 1998

MINTCHINE Isaac 1900-1941 [132]
- $625 - €686 - **£424** - FF4 500
  Projet d'illustration pour un conte ou légende russe Aquarelle, gouache (24.5x32cm 9x12in) Pontoise 2000

MINTON John 1917-1957 [220]
- $63 452 - €70 116 - **£44 000** - FF459 932
  Blitzed city with self-portrait Oil/board (30.5x40cm 12x15in) London 2001
- $807 - €759 - **£500** - FF4 981
  Self-Portrait Pencil/paper (30.5x21cm 12x8in) London 1999
- $313 - €337 - **£210** - FF2 209
  Jungle Foliage Color lithograph (27x37cm 10x14in) Swindon, Wiltshire 2000

MINUJIN Marta XX [3]
- $7 000 - €6 811 - **£4 308** - FF44 676
  Sin título Bronze (29x43x28cm 11x16x11in) New-York 1999

MIOLÉE Adrianus 1879-1961 [14]
- $400 - €431 - **£273** - FF2 827
  View of a Backyard Oil/cardboard (30x42cm 11x16in) Amsterdam 2000

MIOT Paul Émile 1827-1900 [47]
- $1 939 - €2 287 - **£1 363** - FF15 000
  Baie de Juan Fernandez, Ile de Robinson Crusoe, Chili Tirage albuminé (17x24.5cm 6x9in) Paris 2000

MIOTTE Jean 1926 [184]
- $4 236 - €4 269 - **£2 640** - FF28 000
  Elan Acrylique/toile (130x97cm 51x38in) Paris 2000
- $1 680 - €1 451 - **£1 120** - FF9 520
  Composizione Olio/tela (115x90cm 45x35in) Milano 1998
- $487 - €427 - **£295** - FF2 800
  Composition Gouache/papier (34x25cm 13x9in) Douai 1998
- $142 - €168 - **£102** - FF1 100
  Elan Lithographie couleurs (65x50cm 25x19in) Paris 2001

MIR TRINXET Joaquín 1873-1940 [94]
- $328 746 - €352 882 - **£220 000** - FF2 314 752
  El Abismo (The Abyss) Oil/canvas (172x95cm 67x37in) London 2000
- $48 000 - €45 049 - **£30 000** - FF295 500
  Invierno Oleo/lienzo (113x74cm 44x29in) Madrid 1999
- $10 070 - €11 412 - **£7 030** - FF74 860
  Jardines Oleo/lienzo/tabla (26x36cm 10x14in) Madrid 2001
- $1 190 - €1 024 - **£697** - FF6 715
  Paisaje con figuras Lápiz/papel (23x32cm 9x12in) Madrid 1998

MIRA Alfred S. XX [23]
- $5 200 - €5 165 - **£3 224** - FF33 879
  Industrial Wharf Landscape Oil/canvas (50x63cm 20x25in) Norwalk CT 2000
- $3 700 - €3 839 - **£2 347** - FF25 184
  View of the 1939 World's Fair, New York Oil/canvas/board (30x40.5cm 11x15in) Boston MA 2000

MIRA Víctor 1949 [111]
- $1 540 - €1 682 - **£980** - FF11 032
  Sillas de filósofos Oleo/cartón (54.5x31.5cm 21x12in) Madrid 2000
- $650 - €601 - **£390** - FF3 940
  Pinturas de la noche Tempera/carton (38x11cm 14x4in) Madrid 1999
- $512 - €481 - **£320** - FF3 152
  «Hombre y árbol» Acuarela/papel (29x23.5cm 11x9in) Madrid 1999
- $141 - €153 - **£97** - FF1 006
  Stuhl Radierung (24x32.5cm 9x12in) Stuttgart 2001

MIRABELLA Sabatino XIX [1]
- $6 325 - €6 557 - **£3 795** - FF43 010
  Da Borgo Paradiso, Palermo Olio/tela (86x120cm 33x47in) Roma 1999

MIRABELLA Saro 1914 [6]
- $2 400 - €2 488 - **£1 440** - FF16 320
  Veduta di Borgo Maggiore, San Marino Olio/tela (60x75.5cm 23x29in) Roma 2000

MIRABENT GATELL Josep 1831-1899 [7]
- $7 800 - €7 808 - **£4 810** - FF51 220
  Bodegón Oleo/lienzo (68x98cm 26x38in) Madrid 2000

MIRAGLIA Ermogene 1907-1964 [13]
- $1 600 - €2 073 - **£1 200** - FF13 600
  Mercato Olio/tela (50x70cm 19x27in) Roma 2001

MIRALLES DARMANIN Enrique 1855-? [6]
- $8 540 - €8 409 - **£5 460** - FF55 160
  La partida de cartas Oleo/lienzo (48x38cm 18x14in) Madrid 2000
- $1 794 - €2 134 - **£1 279** - FF14 000
  Le déjeuner solitaire Huile/toile (32x24cm 12x9in) Calais 2000

MIRALLES DARMANIN José 1850-1900 [34]
- $39 032 - €43 753 - **£26 490** - FF287 000
  La collation/La danse Huile/toile (196x168cm 77x66in) Paris 2000
- $8 000 - €6 929 - **£4 906** - FF45 452
  Moment of Rest Oil/canvas (101.5x66cm 39x25in) New-York 1999

MIRALLES Enrique ?-1883 [11]
- $3 859 - €3 859 - **£2 347** - FF24 000
  Après le spectacle Huile/toile (41x33cm 16x12in) Paris 1999

MIRALLES Y GALUP Francisco 1848-1901 **[89]**
- **$21 600** - €24 026 - **£15 200** - FF157 600
  El careo Oleo/lienzo (61x50cm 24x19in) Madrid 2001
- **$12 800** - €12 013 - **£8 000** - FF78 800
  Terraza del Parque Monceau, París Oleo/tabla (32x18cm 12x7in) Madrid 1999
- **$1 450** - €1 502 - **£925** - FF9 850
  La florista Tinta/papel (58x42cm 22x16in) Madrid 1999

MIRANDA Celso 1954 **[40]**
- **$336** - €360 - **£222** - FF2 364
  París Oleo/tabla (28x41cm 11x16in) Madrid 2000

MIRANDA REDON Manuel XIX **[1]**
- **$7 980** - €8 409 - **£5 040** - FF55 160
  Alto en el camino Oleo/cobre (32x42cm 12x16in) Madrid 2000

MIRAT Paul 1885-1966 **[4]**
- **$956** - €915 - **£582** - FF6 000
  Visite de Napoléon III au Lycée de Pau Gouache/papel (48x57cm 18x22in) Pau 1999

MIRBEL de A. Lizinka, née Rue 1796-1849 **[18]**
- **$1 849** - €1 829 - **£1 153** - FF12 000
  Homme en redingote, sur fond de nuages Miniature (22x18cm 8x7in) Paris 1999

MIRER Rudolf 1937 **[27]**
- **$694** - €687 - **£433** - FF4 509
  Wassermann Farblithographie (61x51cm 24x20in) St. Gallen 1999

MIRKO (Mirko Basaldella) 1910-1969 **[52]**
- **$14 800** - €19 178 - **£11 100** - FF125 800
  Personaggio totem Bronzo (H277cm H109in) Milano 2001
- **$1 900** - €1 970 - **£1 140** - FF12 920
  Guerriero Bronzo (H22cm H8in) Milano 1999
- **$1 440** - €1 244 - **£960** - FF8 160
  Studio per scultura Acquarello/carta (57x45cm 22x17in) Milano 1998

MIRO Joan 1893-1983 **[5585]**
- **$446 304** - €524 844 - **£320 000** - FF3 442 752
  «Paysage» Oil/canvas (215x173cm 84x68in) London 2001
- **$472 770** - €458 756 - **£300 000** - FF3 009 240
  Danseuse Enamel (106x73.5cm 41x28in) London 1999
- **$66 945** - €78 727 - **£48 000** - FF516 412
  Tête Oil/canvas (16x72cm 6x28in) London 2001
- **$240 000** - €266 235 - **£159 600** - FF1 746 384
  Personnages dans la nuit Bronze (H100.5cm H39in) New-York 2000
- **$60 000** - €56 034 - **£37 032** - FF367 560
  Femme Bronze (31x27x23cm 12x10x9in) New-York 1999
- **$31 800** - €36 039 - **£21 600** - FF236 400
  Constelaciones Acuarela (20x28cm 7x11in) Madrid 2000
- **$2 286** - €2 454 - **£1 530** - FF16 098
  Le corbeau Vizir Farblithographie (89.4x61.8cm 35x24in) Hamburg 2000

MIRO Joaquín 1849-1914 **[33]**
- **$4 350** - €4 505 - **£2 775** - FF29 550
  Caravana árabe Oleo/lienzo (36x49.5cm 14x19in) Madrid 2000
- **$3 112** - €3 049 - **£2 006** - FF20 000
  La rue Chenavard à Lyon Huile/carton (16x24cm 6x9in) Amiens 1999

MIRO LLEO Gaspar 1859-1930 **[51]**
- **$4 249** - €3 886 - **£2 595** - FF25 492
  Paris, la porte Saint-Denis Oil/canvas (53x72cm 21x28in) New-York 1998
- **$1 920** - €1 802 - **£1 200** - FF11 820
  Médicos ante el Hospital de la Santa Cruz de Barcelona Oleo/cartón (24x16cm 9x6in) Madrid 1999

MIROU Anton 1584-c.1661 **[31]**
- **$99 960** - €116 084 - **£70 245** - FF761 460
  Landskap med figurer och byggnader Oil/copper (39.5x65.5cm 15x25in) Stockholm 2001
- **$42 753** - €48 559 - **£30 000** - FF318 525
  Landscape with elegant Figures and a Hunting Party on a Boat Oil/copper (25x34cm 9x13in) London 2001

MIRZA Bashir 1941 **[2]**
- **$2 988** - €3 208 - **£2 000** - FF21 043
  Man with Bird Felt pen/paper (70x50.5cm 27x19in) London 2001

MIRZA Sayyid XIX **[1]**
- **$112 602** - €106 311 - **£70 000** - FF697 354
  Full-length Portrait of Sultan Muhammad Mirza Sayf al Dawlah Oil/canvas (151.5x73.5cm 59x28in) London 1999

MISKY Ludwik 1884-1938 **[9]**
- **$5 537** - €5 929 - **£3 768** - FF38 891
  Sur la plage polonaise Huile/panneau (49x68.5cm 19x26in) Warszawa 2001

MISONNE Léonard 1870-1943 **[69]**
- **$1 548** - €1 829 - **£1 092** - FF12 000
  Le chemin creux Photo (29x39cm 11x15in) Chartres 2001

MISRACH Richard 1949 **[56]**
- **$5 000** - €5 367 - **£3 396** - FF35 202
  Hawaii Dye-transfer print (38x45.5cm 14x17in) Beverly-Hills CA 2001

MISTI Ferdinand Mifliez 1865-1923 **[97]**
- **$1 108** - €935 - **£650** - FF6 136
  «Bougie à 5 trous» Poster (140x100cm 55x39in) London 1998

MITACQ Michel Tacq, dit 1927 **[8]**
- **$825** - €793 - **£511** - FF5 200
  La Patrouille des Castors, pl.27 Encre Chine/papier (50x36cm 19x14in) Paris 1999
- **$800** - €793 - **£486** - FF5 203
  Patrouille des Castors Sérigraphie (50x70cm 19x27in) Bruxelles 2000

MITCHELL Alfred R. 1888-1972 **[100]**
- **$12 000** - €11 044 - **£7 202** - FF72 447
  Nocturnal, Indian Palace, Sesquincentiennial Expo Oil/board (40x50cm 16x20in) Pasadena CA 1999
- **$5 500** - €4 910 - **£3 368** - FF32 209
  «Aliotto's Novo» Oil/board (20x25cm 8x10in) Altadena CA 1999

MITCHELL Denis 1912-1993 **[50]**
- **$2 551** - €2 178 - **£1 500** - FF14 285
  «Widdon No. 2» Bronze (H58cm H22in) London 1998

MITCHELL Ernest Gabriel 1859-? **[7]**
- **$4 113** - €3 969 - **£2 600** - FF26 032
  A Rest by the Way Oil/canvas (51x71cm 20x27in) London 1999
- **$1 240** - €1 342 - **£850** - FF8 804
  A Moonlit River Landscape Pencil (36.5x52cm 14x20in) Lenton-Lane, Nottingham 2001

MITCHELL Flora H. 1890-1973 [17]
🖋 **$1 774** - €1 905 - **£1 187** - FF12 493
Site of James Joyce Bloomsday Dublin-Now
Demolished Watercolour (28x24cm 11x9in) Dublin
2000

MITCHELL George Bertrand 1872-1966 [10]
😊 **$800** - €690 - **£480** - FF4 527
«A Fisherman's Haven» Oil/masonite (30.5x40.5cm
12x15in) Boston MA 1998

MITCHELL Hutton 1872-1939 [24]
🖋 **$427** - €358 - **£250** - FF2 351
Milkmaid and Cow Watercolour (36x53.5cm
14x21in) London 1998

MITCHELL J.A. XIX [1]
😊 **$18 239** - €21 692 - **£13 000** - FF142 287
The Warwickshire Hunt at Edgehill Huile/toile
(94x131cm 37x51in) London 2000

MITCHELL Janet 1912-1998 [79]
😊 **$1 207** - €1 346 - **£787** - FF8 830
They Should Have Been Here By Now Oil/canvas
(51x61cm 20x24in) Calgary, Alberta 2000
🖋 **$965** - €913 - **£640** - FF5 992
The Hills are Alive with Music Watercolour/paper
(36x55cm 14x21in) Calgary, Alberta 1999

MITCHELL Joan 1926-1992 [200]
😊 **$250 000** - €279 531 - **£168 525** - FF1 833 600
Untitled Oil/canvas (259.5x199.5cm 102x78in) New-
York 2000
😊 **$60 000** - €69 617 - **£41 424** - FF456 660
Untitled Oil/canvas (35x99cm 13x38in) New-York
2000
🖋 **$16 000** - €16 696 - **£10 091** - FF109 520
Untitled Oil/canvas (34x22cm 13x8in) New-York 2000
🖋 **$13 000** - €15 084 - **£8 975** - FF98 943
Untitled Pastel/paper (38x28cm 14x11in) New-York
2000
🍷 **$700** - €823 - **£497** - FF5 396
Composition Lithograph (76x56cm 29x22in) New-
York 2000

MITCHELL John 1837-1929 [6]
🖋 **$706** - €819 - **£500** - FF5 372
The Dee at Aberdeen with Lochnargar in the
Distance Watercolour (18x26cm 7x10in) London 2000

MITCHELL John Campbell 1865-1922 [32]
😊 **$3 492** - €2 992 - **£2 100** - FF19 629
On Duchray Water Oil/canvas (45x75cm 17x29in)
Edinburgh 1998
😊 **$1 037** - €1 156 - **£700** - FF7 585
At Benderloch Oil/board (29.5x34.5cm 11x13in)
Edinburgh 2000
🖋 **$7 212** - €8 476 - **£5 000** - FF55 600
Sheep on the Hill Road,
Aberdeenshire/Benachie from kemnay
Watercolour (47x62cm 18x24in) Edinburgh 2000

MITCHELL Neil 1858-1934 [9]
🖋 **$500** - €583 - **£357** - FF3 825
Seascape with a Distant Sailing Ship
Watercolour/paper (20x34cm 8x13in) St. Louis MO
2000

MITCHELL OF MARYPORT William c.1806-1900
[18]
😊 **$2 331** - €2 164 - **£1 400** - FF14 194
The Old Graving Bank & Bridge, Maryport as it
was in the year 1837 Oil/canvas (50x86cm 20x34in)
Carlisle, Cumbria 1999

😊 **$896** - €962 - **£600** - FF6 313
Maryport Pier, Fresh Southerly Breeze, Half Tide
Oil/board (29x44cm 11x17in) Carlisle, Cumbria 2000

MITCHELL Philip 1814-1896 [58]
🖋 **$868** - €840 - **£550** - FF5 509
Devonshire Wooded River Landscape with
Cattle Watering Watercolour/paper (50x76cm
19x29in) Devon 1999

MITCHELL Samuel Augustus 1792-1868 [13]
🍷 **$300** - €320 - **£200** - FF2 099
Mitchell's New National Map, Exhibiting the
United States Engraving (160x152cm 63x60in)
Baltimore MD 2000

MITCHELL Thomas 1735-1790 [3]
😊 **$6 313** - €7 509 - **£4 500** - FF49 253
View of Chatam Oil/canvas (60x105cm 23x41in)
London 2000

MITCHELL Thomas Livingstone 1792-1855 [2]
🖋 **$1 370** - €1 430 - **£864** - FF9 380
Portrait of Baby Blanche Mitchell
Watercolour/paper (33x24cm 12x9in) Sydney 2000

MITCHELL Willard Morse 1881-1953 [35]
🖋 **$164** - €187 - **£113** - FF1 225
Evangeline's Well/Summer Landscape
Watercolour/paper (4.5x5cm 1x1in) Montréal 2000

MITCHELL William Frederick c.1845-1914 [97]
🖋 **$408** - €449 - **£260** - FF2 946
Evening shipping on the Thames, towards St
Pauls, London Watercolour/paper (15x28cm 6x11in)
Whitby, Yorks 2000

MITELLI Agostino 1609-1660 [12]
🖋 **$851** - €791 - **£520** - FF5 189
An Architectural Design, Possibly for the
Palazzo Pitti, Florence Ink (19x13cm 7x5in) London
1998

MITELLI Giuseppe Maria 1634-1718 [19]
😊 **$10 000** - €10 367 - **£6 000** - FF68 000
La scuola del nudo Olio/tela (99x146cm 38x57in)
Milano 1999
🖋 **$720** - €818 - **£500** - FF5 366
Der Tod des Hl.Joseph Ink (41x29cm 16x11in) Köln
2001
🍷 **$171** - €194 - **£117** - FF1 274
Masken, Architekturteile, Vasen Radierung
(19x14cm 7x5in) München 2000

MITFORD Bertram Osbaldeston 1777-1842 [1]
😊 **$3 638** - €3 173 - **£2 200** - FF20 811
Elegant figures in an interior Watercolour
(30.5x52cm 12x20in) London 1998

MITI ZANETTI Giuseppe 1860-1946 [24]
😊 **$2 400** - €3 110 - **£1 800** - FF20 400
Venezia Olio/tela (117x69cm 46x27in) Milano 2001
😊 **$1 500** - €1 555 - **£900** - FF10 200
Veduta del Palazzo Ducale dalla riva degli
Schiavoni Olio/cartone (15.5x20.5cm 6x8in) Milano
1999

MITORAJ Igor 1944 [65]
🔨 **$26 000** - €30 557 - **£18 025** - FF200 444
Eros Portanova Marble (H234cm H92in) New-York
2000
🔨 **$1 020** - €1 143 - **£700** - FF7 500
Torse Bronze (31x24x5cm 12x9x1in) Versailles 2001

MITSCHEK Alois XX [7]
🍷 **$196** - €400 - **£247** - FF2 621
«Wählt christlichsozial» Poster (95x126cm 37x49in)
Wien 2000

MITSUNARI Tosa 1646-1710 **[1]**

$4 750 - €4 350 - £2 895 - FF28 535
Book-Washing Komachi Ink (88x37.5cm 34x14in) New-York 1999

MITSUYOSHI Tosa 1700-1772 **[1]**

$2 000 - €2 081 - £1 272 - FF13 648
Four Seasons Painting (25x21.5cm 9x8in) New-York 2000

MITTERFELLNER Andreas 1912-1972 **[27]**

$1 003 - €1 125 - £681 - FF7 378
Bockarspitze Oil/panel (50x70cm 19x27in) München 2000

$2 003 - €1 943 - £1 269 - FF12 744
Chiemseelandschaft mit Heufuhrwerk vorne links Oil/panel (20x45cm 7x17in) München 1999

MITTERTREINER Johannes Jacobus 1851-1890 **[6]**

$3 474 - €4 084 - £2 409 - FF26 789
A Bleachfield in a Village Oil/canvas (25.5x35.5cm 10x13in) Amsterdam 2000

MITTEY Joseph 1853-1936 **[14]**

$1 698 - €1 970 - £1 172 - FF12 923
Rosenstudie Watercolour, gouache (84x57cm 33x22in) Luzern 2000

MIU GUYING 1875-1955 **[2]**

$14 846 - €12 586 - £8 878 - FF82 558
Chrysanthemum Coloured inks (173.5x41cm 68x16in) Hong-Kong 1998

MIYAJIMA Tatsuo 1957 **[11]**

$14 080 - €15 245 - £9 640 - FF100 000
Opposite hexagone Sculpture (100x100x10cm 39x39x3in) Paris 2001

$11 954 - €12 832 - £8 000 - FF84 172
«Opposite Harmony - 89927/38735» Construction (11x26x3cm 4x10x1in) London 2001

MIYAMOTO Saburo 1905-1974 **[2]**

$75 000 - €82 744 - £49 605 - FF542 767
Nude (Rafu) Oil/canvas (68x33cm 26x12in) New-York 2000

MIYAO c.1868-1912 **[11]**

$11 076 - €11 891 - £7 410 - FF78 000
Statuettes de moines debout Bronze (H32cm H12in) Paris 2000

MIZEN Frederick Kimball 1888-1965 **[15]**

$14 500 - €12 510 - £8 714 - FF82 059
Navajo Portrait Oil/canvas (137x91cm 54x36in) Santa-Fe NM 1998

$2 600 - €2 227 - £1 563 - FF14 611
Colorado Landscape Oil/canvas (88x106cm 35x42in) Cincinnati OH 1998

$1 400 - €1 645 - £970 - FF10 793
Montana Watercolour, gouache/paper (17x22cm 6x8in) Beverly-Hills CA 2000

$2 000 - €1 923 - £1 234 - FF12 616
«Chevrolet» Poster (92.5x59cm 36x23in) New-York 1999

MIZRACHI Menachem 1951 **[1]**

$3 800 - €4 034 - £2 571 - FF26 459
Nude in Front of a Television Oil/canvas (90x110cm 35x43in) Tel Aviv 2001

MLECKO Martin 1951 **[4]**

$429 - €511 - £307 - FF3 353
Zeichen, Berlin-Mitte Gelatin silver print (21x28cm 8x11in) Berlin 2000

MNISZECH Comte Andrzej Jerzy 1823-1905 **[4]**

$7 000 - €8 232 - £5 019 - FF53 997
The Mating Call Oil/panel (84x86.5cm 33x34in) New-York 2001

MOBERLY Mariquita Jenny 1855-c.1935 **[9]**

$490 - €570 - £350 - FF3 738
Boy with his Dog Watercolour/paper (28x22cm 11x9in) Par, Cornwall 2001

MOCHTAR But 1930 **[1]**

$7 679 - €7 157 - £4 641 - FF46 946
Penari-penari: Dancers Oil/canvas (65x95cm 25x37in) Singapore 1999

MODEL Lisette 1906-1983 **[61]**

$1 963 - €2 198 - £1 367 - FF14 421
«Promenade d'anglais» Gelatin silver print (50x39cm 19x15in) Köln 2001

MODELL Elisabeth 1820-1865 **[5]**

$4 983 - €4 265 - £3 000 - FF27 975
A Gentleman's Study Oil/canvas (40x44.5cm 15x17in) London 1998

MODERSOHN Otto 1865-1943 **[190]**

$85 780 - €102 260 - £61 160 - FF670 780
Feierabend Öl/Leinwand (90.5x150.5cm 35x59in) Berlin 2000

$15 782 - €18 407 - £11 080 - FF120 740
Mondlandschaft bei Fischerhude Öl/Leinwand (60.5x85cm 23x33in) Köln 2000

$8 229 - €7 669 - £5 077 - FF50 308
In den Feldern bei Fischerhude Oil/panel (32x18cm 12x7in) Bremen 1999

$1 117 - €1 278 - £777 - FF8 384
Abenddämmerung über norddeutschem Gehöft Pastel/paper (35x49cm 13x19in) Zwiesel 2000

MODERSOHN-BECKER Paula 1876-1907 **[101]**

$123 602 - €117 599 - £76 797 - FF771 397
Kind am Schafstall Öl/Karton (50.4x70.3cm 19x27in) Hamburg 1999

$139 458 - €164 633 - £99 047 - FF1 079 923
«Kopf eines blonden Mädchens» Tempera (29.5x27cm 11x10in) Berlin 2001

$7 621 - €7 056 - £4 665 - FF46 283
Die Frau mit der Kuh/Birkenstämme, Sitzende Bäuerin mit Kind im Arm Pencil/paper (21x26cm 8x10in) München 1999

$3 006 - €2 812 - £1 821 - FF18 446
Zwei Bauernmädchen Etching (14x10cm 5x3in) Bremen 1999

MODESITT John 1955 **[8]**

$2 500 - €2 683 - £1 673 - FF17 602
Landscape Oil/canvas (76x101cm 30x40in) Altadena CA 2000

MODIGLIANI Amedeo 1884-1920 **[441]**

$2 862 500 - €3 206 210 - £1 988 865 - FF21 031 360
Portrait de Minoutcha Oil/canvas (55.5x33cm 21x12in) New-York 2001

$167 364 - €196 817 - £120 000 - FF1 291 032
Portrait de femme Oil/canvas (46x33cm 18x12in) London 2001

$25 280 - €24 392 - £15 872 - FF160 000
Tête de jeune fille à la frange Bronze (H51cm H20in) Paris 1999

$36 180 - €41 161 - £25 110 - FF270 000
Nu féminin Crayon (51x27.5cm 20x10in) Paris 2000

$312 - €335 - £209 - FF2 200
Portrait de femme Estampe (15x10cm 5x3in) Cannes 2000

MODOTTI Tina 1896-1942 **[88]**
📷 **$6 000** - €6 688 - **£4 168** - FF43 873
Velvety green Frog, Pottery of Ozumpa, Oaxaca
Gelatin silver print (19x18.5cm 7x7in) New-York 2001

MOE Louis 1857-1945 **[87]**
$865 - €740 - **£519** - FF4 852
«**På kanten af Helvede sidder en lille Djaevel og fryser**» Oil/canvas (25x13.5cm 9x5in) København 1998

$281 - €295 - **£177** - FF1 938
To grønlaenderbørn spejder ud over fjorden
Indian ink (15x15cm 5x5in) København 2000

$190 - €161 - **£114** - FF1 059
En nøgen pige i et trae Etching (45x28cm 17x11in)
Viby J, Arhus 1998

MOELLER Arnold 1886-1963 **[26]**
$1 021 - €869 - **£609** - FF5 699
Bauer mit Pferdekarren Öl/Karton (33x46cm 12x18in) München 2001

MOELLER Louis Charles 1855-1930 **[76]**
$20 000 - €17 088 - **£12 006** - FF112 088
Sign Here Oil/canvas (51x101.5cm 20x39in) New-York 1998

$6 000 - €6 824 - **£4 192** - FF44 760
The Discussion Oil/canvas (20x25cm 8x10in) Chicago IL 2000

MOER van Jean Baptiste 1819-1884 **[38]**
$17 749 - €17 045 - **£11 000** - FF111 811
Racing at Schevening Oil/canvas (147x207cm 57x81in) Billingshurst, West-Sussex 1999

$1 032 - €1 190 - **£710** - FF7 804
Gezicht in de San Marco-Basiliek te Venetië
Oil/panel (47x65cm 18x25in) Lokeren 2000

$763 - €868 - **£535** - FF5 691
Chevet d'église à Venise Huile/panneau (26x34.5cm 10x13in) Bruxelles 2001

MOERENHOUT Edward XIX **[18]**
$2 104 - €1 983 - **£1 304** - FF13 008
La rade Huile/panneau (60x107cm 23x42in) Antwerpen 1999

$669 - €595 - **£410** - FF3 902
Paysage marin Huile/panneau (15x29cm 5x11in) Antwerpen 1999

MOERENHOUT Jozef Jodocus 1801-1874 **[57]**
$28 093 - €29 496 - **£17 712** - FF193 479
The Falconry Oil/panel (61x77cm 24x30in) Amsterdam 2000

$2 619 - €3 115 - **£1 804** - FF20 432
Travellers reting before an Inn Oil/panel (9x12cm 3x4in) Calgary, Alberta 2000

$385 - €454 - **£266** - FF2 976
Battlescene Pencil (23x33.5cm 9x13in) Amsterdam 2000

MOERKERK Herman 1879-1949 **[36]**
$388 - €454 - **£277** - FF2 976
Elegant Lady Oil/panel (29x19cm 11x7in) Amsterdam 2001

$348 - €363 - **£220** - FF2 381
Carnaval Ink/paper (16.5x13cm 6x5in) Maastricht 2000

MOERKERK Johan Marie 1903-1988 **[11]**
$197 - €200 - **£122** - FF1 309
«**Erres Radio**» Poster (55x39.5cm 21x15in) Haarlem 2000

MOERKERKEN van Emil 1915-1995 **[20]**
📷 **$676** - €726 - **£452** - FF4 762
Het Maanmeisje Silver print (38x26cm 14x10in) Amsterdam 2000

MOERMAN Albert Edouard 1808-1856 **[12]**
$24 168 - €28 259 - **£16 644** - FF185 364
Paysage hivernal animé de personnes devant un village Huile/panneau (56x70cm 22x27in) Antwerpen 2000

$18 785 - €21 070 - **£13 090** - FF138 210
Paysage d'hiver avec patineurs Huile/toile (26.5x39.5cm 10x15in) Bruxelles 2001

MOERMAN Jan Lodewijk 1850-1896 **[21]**
$2 325 - €2 496 - **£1 555** - FF16 371
Cardplayers Oil/panel (25x18cm 9x7in) Amsterdam 2000

MOES Wally 1856-1918 **[14]**
$4 203 - €4 538 - **£2 874** - FF29 766
A Lady from Laren Wearing her Sunday Costume Oil/panel (74.5x62cm 29x24in) Amsterdam 2001

MOESCHLIN Walter Johann 1902-1961 **[9]**
$2 220 - €2 435 - **£1 507** - FF15 974
Artistenmädchen Öl/Leinwand (92x74cm 36x29in) Luzern 2000

MOESMAN Johannes H., Joop 1909-1988 **[10]**
$1 508 - €1 452 - **£943** - FF9 525
Seated Female Nude Black chalk/paper (31.5x50cm 12x19in) Amsterdam 1999

MOEST Hermann 1868-1945 **[12]**
$1 550 - €1 278 - **£913** - FF8 383
Stehender weiblicher Rückenakt Öl/Leinwand (115x70cm 45x27in) Lindau 1998

MOEYAERT Claes Cornelisz. c.1590/93-1655 **[37]**
$42 240 - €39 643 - **£26 400** - FF260 040
San Antonio Abad Oleo/lienzo (186.5x110.5cm 73x43in) Palma de Mallorca 1999

$5 138 - €5 031 - **£3 161** - FF33 000
Mercure et Argus Huile/panneau (48.5x68cm 19x26in) Paris 1999

$1 651 - €1 588 - **£1 017** - FF10 418
Two Angels at a Tomb with Five Women Bringing Sacrifices Red chalk (18x27cm 7x10in) Amsterdam 1999

$529 - €460 - **£318** - FF3 016
Die Landschaft mit Merkur und Argus Radierung (10.8x18.8cm 4x7in) Berlin 1998

MOFFAT Curtis 1887-1949 **[7]**
📷 **$2 776** - €3 117 - **£1 800** - FF20 448
Sir Thomas Beecham Silver print (28.5x23cm 11x9in) London 2000

MOFFATT Tracey 1960 **[42]**
$874 - €980 - **£611** - FF6 429
«**Up in the Sky #25**» Offset (61x76cm 24x29in) Melbourne 2001

📷 **$4 000** - €4 641 - **£2 761** - FF30 444
Guapa (Good Looking) Photograph in colors (76x101.5cm 29x39in) New-York 2000

MOFFETT Donald XX **[1]**
$4 250 - €4 959 - **£2 958** - FF32 526
«**Lot 020396**» Mixed media/canvas (61x51cm 24x20in) New-York 2000

MOFFETT Ross E. 1888-1971 **[14]**
$2 900 - €2 708 - **£1 789** - FF17 765
Being Neighborly Oil/board (30.5x41cm 12x16in) Boston MA 1999

MOGANO Phoshoko David 1932 [10]
$619 - €693 - **£430** - FF4 548
«Christian City, Lebowa, N.TVL» Watercolour/paper (52x71cm 20x27in) Johannesburg 2001

MOGFORD John 1821-1885 [93]
$3 216 - €3 690 - **£2 200** - FF24 204
Figures on a Beach, Recovering a Barrel from a Choppy Sea Oil/canvas (42x74.5cm 16x29in) Leamington-Spa, Warwickshire 2000
$1 917 - €2 123 - **£1 300** - FF13 925
Figures on a Beach at Low Tide Oil/canvas (29x53.5cm 11x21in) Billingshurst, West-Sussex 2000
$1 780 - €1 732 - **£1 095** - FF11 361
Mount St Michael, Normandy Watercolour/paper (33x49.5cm 12x19in) Malvern, Victoria 1999

MOGFORD OF EXETER Thomas 1809-1868 [7]
$11 946 - €12 434 - **£7 500** - FF81 559
B.Kerr Esquire with His Day's Bag, His Setters Boris, Carl, and Mouse Oil/canvas (50.5x69cm 19x27in) London 2000

MOGGIOLI Umberto 1886-1919 [13]
$36 000 - €31 100 - **£24 000** - FF204 000
La primavera nel veronese Olio/tela (53x63cm 20x24in) Milano 1998
$2 200 - €2 281 - **£1 320** - FF14 960
Volto femminile Pastelli/cartone (14x9cm 5x3in) Milano 2000

MOGISSE Robert 1931 [235]
$482 - €518 - **£323** - FF3 400
Village de pêche Breton Huile/toile (54x65cm 21x25in) Provins 2000
$253 - €229 - **£156** - FF1 500
Les gondoles à Venise Huile/toile (22x27cm 8x10in) Provins 1999

MOHIDIN Latiff 1938 [7]
$20 783 - €17 437 - **£12 194** - FF114 380
Pago-Pago Oil/board (74x104cm 29x40in) Singapore 1998

MOHIMAN Henry XIX [1]
$5 480 - €4 575 - **£3 213** - FF30 008
Skibsportraet af «Dante» Oil/canvas (60x80cm 23x31in) København 1998

MOHL John Koenakeefe 1903-1985 [3]
$1 062 - €1 024 - **£656** - FF6 717
Old Orchard at the Foot of the Magaliesberg near Lady Selbourne Oil/canvas/board (34.5x24cm 13x9in) Johannesburg 1999

MOHLER Gustave 1836-? [9]
$800 - €855 - **£544** - FF5 617
Still Life oF fruit in Basket Oil/canvas (37x45cm 14x18in) New-Orleans LA 2001

MOHLITZ Philippe 1941 [67]
$278 - €274 - **£171** - FF1 800
Sieste en Égypte Burin (30x40cm 11x15in) Paris 1999

MOHN Victor Paul 1842-1911 [30]
$18 965 - €19 429 - **£11 704** - FF127 448
Osterprozession römische Landleute Öl/Leinwand (52x90.5cm 20x35in) Düsseldorf 2000
$540 - €613 - **£375** - FF4 024
Campagnalandschaft mit Mädchen am Brunnen Pencil/paper (26.5x32cm 10x12in) Köln 2001

MOHOLY Lucia 1894-1989 [39]
$1 063 - €921 - **£645** - FF6 040
Bauhaus Dessau, Dach des Atelierhauses Photograph (12.2x21.1cm 4x8in) München 1998

MOHOLY-NAGY László 1895-1946 [298]
$971 295 - €1 042 605 - **£650 000** - FF6 839 040
«A X.I» Oil/canvas (132.5x115cm 52x45in) London 2000
$11 127 - €10 737 - **£6 990** - FF70 431
Zeichnung aus gekreuzten Linien, Kreisen und Bogen Indian ink (41.5x32cm 16x12in) München 1999
$5 595 - €6 141 - **£3 605** - FF40 280
Konstruktion, ur Kestnermappe 6 Lithograph (59x41.8cm 23x16in) Stockholm 2000
$3 000 - €2 505 - **£1 782** - FF16 429
«Film Still Study from Aus dem Lichtspielfilm, schwarz-weis-grau» Gelatin silver print (12.5x18cm 4x7in) New-York 1999

MOHR Arno 1910-2001 [55]
$570 - €665 - **£398** - FF4 360
Berlin, Chausseestrasse mit Dorothenstädtischem Friedhof Pastel (31x48cm 12x18in) Berlin 2000
$153 - €179 - **£107** - FF1 173
Spaziergang mit Hund Drypoint (12.3x16.1cm 4x6in) Berlin 2000

MOHR Johann Georg Paul 1808-1843 [12]
$5 073 - €5 624 - **£3 522** - FF36 892
Sommerliche Waldlandschaft Öl/Karton (46x57cm 18x22in) Köln 2001
$286 - €242 - **£171** - FF1 588
Landskab med klipper Watercolour/paper (36x56cm 14x22in) Viby J, Århus 1998

MOHR Paul XIX-XX [8]
$959 - €984 - **£600** - FF6 457
«Bicyclettes Dainty» Poster (121x80cm 47x31in) London 2000

MOHRMANN John Henry 1857-1916 [33]
$5 179 - €4 876 - **£3 200** - FF30 281
The German Cargo Steamer «Nicaria» Oil/canvas (59.5x100.5cm 23x39in) London 1999

MOIGNIEZ Jules 1835-1894 [581]
$1 645 - €1 601 - **£1 012** - FF10 500
Chien de chasse à l'arrêt Bronze (25x42cm 9x16in) Paris 1999

MOILLIET Louis René 1880-1962 [43]
$8 306 - €8 916 - **£5 558** - FF58 486
Zuckerrohrpflanzung in Andalusien Aquarell/Papier (23.5x31cm 9x12in) Bern 2000

MOILLON Louyse 1610-1696 [7]
$459 900 - €533 572 - **£327 250** - FF3 500 000
Le panier d'abricots Huile/panneau (40x52cm 15x20in) Paris 2001
$82 186 - €88 220 - **£55 000** - FF578 688
Plums on a White Dish on a Table Oil/panel (25x34.5cm 9x13in) London 2000

MOINE Antonin Marie 1796-1849 [7]
$1 636 - €1 524 - **£1 012** - FF10 000
Chactas Bronze (16x32x12cm 6x12x4in) Paris 1999

MOIRIGNOT Edmond 1913 [29]
$1 246 - €1 296 - **£782** - FF8 500
Noé foulant le vin Bronze (H63cm H24in) Paris 2000

MOISE Theodore Sidney 1808-1885 [6]
$2 000 - €2 288 - **£1 390** - FF15 007
Portrait of Catherine Elizabeth Boush Levy Oil/canvas/board (76x64cm 30x25in) New-Orleans LA 2000

MOISÉS Julio 1888-1968 **[18]**
- $1 331 - €1 568 - **£939** - FF10 283
  Naturalez muerta Oleo/lienzo (81x60cm 31x23in)
  Madrid 2000

MOISSET Raymond 1906-1994 **[61]**
- $216 - €244 - **£152** - FF1 600
  Sans titre Huile/toile (38x61cm 14x24in) Paris 2001

MOITTE Alexandre 1750-1829 **[8]**
- $777 - €915 - **£557** - FF6 000
  Portrait de vieille femme avec bonnet Pierre noire
  (47x39cm 18x15in) Paris 2001

MOITTE Jean Guillaume 1746-1810 **[21]**
- $44 072 - €42 686 - **£27 720** - FF280 000
  Tête de Prêtre sacrificateur Terracotta
  (58.5x34.5x24cm 23x13x9in) Paris 1999
- $8 218 - €8 822 - **£5 500** - FF57 868
  A Classical Scene Ink (42x75.5cm 16x29in) London
  2000

MOIX SOLE Josep 1907 **[8]**
- $290 - €300 - **£185** - FF1 970
  Corbeta Coloma, Capitán D.Camilo Pagés
  Técnica mixta/papel (50x70cm 19x27in) Barcelona
  2000

MOJA Frederico Moia 1802-1885 **[27]**
- $35 000 - €30 805 - **£21 308** - FF202 065
  The Courtyard of the Doge's Palace, Venice
  Oil/paper/canvas (43x54.5cm 16x21in) New-York 1999
- $8 400 - €10 885 - **£6 300** - FF71 400
  Venezia Olio/cartone (27x35cm 10x13in) Vercelli 2000
- $2 124 - €1 835 - **£1 062** - FF12 036
  Castello Acquarello/cartone (22.5x30cm 8x11in)
  Milano 1999

MOJE Klaus 1936 **[3]**
- $3 250 - €3 367 - **£2 068** - FF22 087
  Untitled Sculpture (44x43.5cm 17x17in) New-York
  2000

MOKADY Moshe 1902-1975 **[142]**
- $10 000 - €11 168 - **£6 404** - FF73 255
  Interior Oil/canvas (100x81.5cm 39x32in) Tel Aviv
  2000
- $2 300 - €2 441 - **£1 556** - FF16 014
  Untitled Oil/board (25x27cm 9x10in) Tel Aviv 2001
- $40 000 - €42 936 - **£26 768** - FF281 640
  Figures in the Forest Watercolour (59x48.5cm
  23x19in) Tel Aviv 2000

MOKE 1950 **[9]**
- $1 335 - €1 524 - **£939** - FF10 000
  Nuits de Matongué Huile/toile (135x86cm 53x33in)
  Paris 2001

MOKETARINJA Richard 1916-1983 **[18]**
- $126 - €139 - **£85** - FF914
  Central Australian Watercolour/paper (26.5x36cm
  10x14in) Sydney 2000

MOKOH I Dewa Putu 1934 **[2]**
- $2 295 - €2 607 - **£1 571** - FF17 098
  Chidren Playing Badminton in a Countyard
  Watercolour (99x199cm 38x78in) Singapore 2000

MOKWA Marian 1889-1987 **[27]**
- $2 091 - €1 779 - **£1 247** - FF11 672
  Shoal Oil/canvas (50x62cm 19x24in) Warszawa 1998
- $655 - €764 - **£459** - FF5 012
  Voilliers au bord Huile/carton (35x38cm 13x14in)
  Torun 2000

$2 587 - €2 364 - **£1 583** - FF15 510
Cottage and and fishing Boats on the See bank
Watercolour/board (53.5x75cm 21x29in) Warszawa
1999

MOLA Pier Francesco 1612-1666 **[56]**
- $24 655 - €23 375 - **£15 000** - FF153 333
  Saint Jerome in the Wilderness Oil/canvas
  (66.5x53.5cm 26x21in) London 1999
- $8 188 - €7 607 - **£5 000** - FF49 900
  **A Design for a Ceiling Decoration: an Allegory
  of Painting** Ink (19x25cm 7x9in) London 1998
- $329 - €354 - **£220** - FF2 319
  **The Holy Family with Angels presenting the
  Instruments of the Passions** Etching (46.5x31cm
  18x12in) London 2000

MOLANUS Mattheus c.1590-1645 **[13]**
- $12 064 - €14 377 - **£8 642** - FF94 308
  **Paysage boisé animé d'un personnage près
  d'un pont** Huile/cuivre (18x26.5cm 7x10in)
  Antwerpen 2000

MOLCHANOVA Natalia 1962 **[4]**
- $1 200 - €1 035 - **£726** - FF6 792
  Recollecting Crete Watercolour/paper (60x77cm
  23x30in) Tel Aviv 1999

MOLDOVAN Kurt 1918-1977 **[171]**
- $1 527 - €1 817 - **£1 090** - FF11 917
  Träume Indian ink (45x31cm 17x12in) Wien 2000
- $215 - €182 - **£127** - FF1 191
  «Zyklus Krieg» Radierung (8x10cm 3x3in) Wien
  1998

MOLE Jean-Baptiste 1616-1661 **[1]**
- $3 897 - €4 346 - **£2 620** - FF28 508
  **Madonna mit Kind, der Heilige Elisabeth und
  dem Johannesknaben** Öl/Kupfer (36.8x28.8cm
  14x11in) Köln 2000

MOLE John Henry 1814-1886 **[136]**
- $1 621 - €1 569 - **£1 000** - FF10 292
  Gathering Firewood Watercolour (28x44.5cm
  11x17in) London 1999

MOLENAAR Johannes Petrus 1914-1989 **[39]**
- $565 - €590 - **£356** - FF3 869
  Harbour Scene Oil/canvas (40x60cm 15x23in)
  Amsterdam 2000
- $382 - €363 - **£232** - FF2 381
  Havengezicht Oil/canvas (29x39cm 11x15in)
  Rotterdam 2000
- $283 - €295 - **£179** - FF1 934
  Rotterdamse haven met de Caltex Naples
  Charcoal (45x75cm 17x29in) Den Haag 2000

MOLENAER Bartholomeus c.1600-1650 **[37]**
- $13 104 - €11 152 - **£7 800** - FF73 155
  Peasants merrymaking in a Barn Oil/canvas
  (110.5x131.5cm 43x51in) London 1998
- $11 393 - €12 706 - **£7 434** - FF83 344
  **A School Interior with Children reading, playing
  and teacher entering** Oil/panel (39x50.5cm 15x19in)
  Amsterdam 2000
- $7 000 - €6 088 - **£4 220** - FF39 935
  **Peasants Gaming and Eating Mussels in an
  Interior** Oil/panel (28x32.5cm 11x12in) New-York
  1998

MOLENAER Cornelis c.1540-1589 **[2]**
- $13 451 - €12 706 - **£8 391** - FF83 344
  David and Abigail Oil/canvas/panel (102x153.5cm
  40x60in) Amsterdam 1999

M

MOLENAER Jan Jacobsz. 1654-c.1690 **[17]**
- $6 076 - €6 807 - **£4 222** - FF44 649
  Monks merrymaking in a Tavern Oil/panel
  (34x42cm 13x16in) Amsterdam 2001

MOLENAER Jan Miense 1609/10-1668 **[156]**
- $17 000 - €14 912 - **£10 322** - FF97 814
  Figures Making Merry in an Inn by a Fireplace
  Oil/panel (56.5x51.5cm 22x20in) New-York 1999
- $5 500 - €5 702 - **£3 300** - FF37 400
  Il fumatore Olio/tavola (23.5x18.5cm 9x7in) Milano
  1999

MOLENAER Klaes / Nicolaes c.1630-1676 **[136]**
- $22 232 - €20 348 - **£13 552** - FF133 476
  Eisvergnügen Öl/Leinwand (35.5x52cm 13x20in)
  Wien 1999
- $7 790 - €7 267 - **£4 700** - FF47 670
  Windmühle in einer Landschaft Oil/panel
  (28x35cm 11x13in) Wien 1999

MOLES Francisco XIX-XX **[3]**
- $3 135 - €3 304 - **£1 980** - FF21 670
  Pastora con ovejas Oleo/lienzo (40x22cm 15x8in)
  Madrid 2000

MOLES Pascal Pierre 1741-1797 **[7]**
- $500 - €601 - **£354** - FF3 940
  La caza del cocodrilo, según François Boucher
  Grabado (65.5x46cm 25x18in) Madrid 2000

MOLFENTER Hans 1884-1979 **[25]**
- $13 292 - €12 782 - **£8 190** - FF83 847
  Cannstatter Wasen Öl/Leinwand (89x112cm
  35x44in) München 1999
- $1 111 - €1 125 - **£678** - FF7 378
  Landschaft mit Häusern Öl/Leinwand (27x30.5cm
  10x12in) Stuttgart 2000
- $1 213 - €1 227 - **£740** - FF8 049
  Marktszene Gouache/paper (13x23cm 5x9in) Stuttgart
  2000

MOLIJN Petrus Marius 1819-1849 **[5]**
- $9 430 - €7 974 - **£5 639** - FF52 303
  **Backgammon Players in a Kitchen with
  Gentleman Admiring a Kitchen Maid** Oil/panel
  (40.5x52.5cm 15x20in) Amsterdam 1998

MOLIN da Oreste 1856-1921 **[11]**
- $3 000 - €3 887 - **£2 475** - FF25 500
  Ritratto di donna (La bella Helena) Olio/tela
  (51x63cm 20x24in) Milano 2000
- $11 000 - €9 490 - **£6 636** - FF62 252
  The Competition Pastel/paper (53x77.5cm 20x30in)
  New-York 1998

MOLIN Lei 1927-1990 **[13]**
- $564 - €635 - **£388** - FF4 167
  Jardin Charcoal (68x102cm 26x40in) Amsterdam 2000

MOLINA CAMPOS Florencio 1891-1959 **[66]**
- $12 500 - €13 773 - **£8 337** - FF90 344
  Pretendiente Tempera (35x50cm 13x19in)
  Montevideo 2000
- $11 000 - €11 807 - **£7 361** - FF77 451
  Jineteando Oil/board (30x39.5cm 11x15in) New-York
  2000
- $7 000 - €7 613 - **£4 614** - FF49 940
  Gaucho Gouache/paper (31x45.5cm 12x17in) Boston
  MA 2000

MOLINARI Alexander 1772-1831 **[9]**
- $11 000 - €12 354 - **£7 881** - FF81 039
  Porträt einer jungen, adeligen Dame im Park
  Öl/Leinwand (55x37cm 21x14in) Wien 2000

MOLINARI Antonio 1655/65-1728/34 **[20]**
- $43 499 - €43 265 - **£27 000** - FF283 802
  Bacchus and Ariadne with Cupid Oil/canvas
  (159x124.5cm 62x49in) London 1999
- $35 166 - €29 940 - **£21 000** - FF196 394
  Lot and his Daughters Oil/canvas (100.5x83.5cm
  39x32in) London 1998

MOLINARI Guido 1933 **[21]**
- $4 857 - €5 667 - **£3 381** - FF37 176
  Verticalité en bruns Acrylic (152.5x63.5cm 60x25in)
  Toronto 2000
- $396 - €463 - **£271** - FF3 035
  Sans titre Lithographie (38x32cm 14x12in) Montréal
  2000

MOLINAROLO Jakob Gabriel c.1721-1780 **[1]**
- $272 370 - €267 736 - **£175 000** - FF1 756 230
  **Adonis taking leave of Venus/Venus Mourning
  the Dead Adonis** Relief (104x68cm 40x26in) London
  1999

MOLINARY Andres 1847-1915 **[10]**
- $3 500 - €4 027 - **£2 412** - FF26 418
  Black Boy with Watermelon/Black Girl Studying
  Oil/canvas (27x17cm 11x7in) New-Orleans LA 2000

MOLINE de Alfred XIX **[8]**
- $2 159 - €1 982 - **£1 327** - FF13 000
  Cavaliers à la croisée des chemins Huile/panneau
  (21.5x29cm 8x11in) Paris 1999

MOLINER Manes Fernandez 1921 **[81]**
- $207 - €204 - **£132** - FF1 339
  Pañando manzanas Oleo/lienzo/tabla (12x14.5cm
  4x5in) Madrid 1999
- $144 - €144 - **£88** - FF945
  Escena de carnaval en Asturias Crayon
  gras/papier (25x32cm 9x12in) Madrid 2000

MOLINERO Santos 1939 **[12]**
- $513 - €541 - **£342** - FF3 546
  Bodegón de libros Oleo/lienzo (65x81cm 25x31in)
  Madrid 2000

MOLINIER Pierre 1900-1976 **[218]**
- $6 480 - €7 622 - **£4 695** - FF50 000
  Les toits de Valenciennes Huile/isorel (37x47cm
  14x18in) Paris 2001
- $11 850 - €11 434 - **£7 485** - FF75 000
  Poupée Plâtre (H93cm H36in) Paris 1999
- $6 480 - €7 622 - **£4 695** - FF50 000
  Femme nue debout Crayon/papier (26x17cm
  10x6in) Paris 2001
- $751 - €884 - **£544** - FF5 800
  Le temps de la mort Lithographie (24.5x33.5cm
  9x13in) Paris 2001
- $1 231 - €1 448 - **£892** - FF9 500
  Molinier avec l'éperon d'amour Photo (8.5x12cm
  3x4in) Paris 2001

MOLINO Walter 1915-1997 **[5]**
- $2 000 - €2 073 - **£1 200** - FF13 600
  **Giornata VIII, novella III, Bruno Buffalmacco
  Calandrino e moglie** Tempera/cartone (47x34cm
  18x13in) Vercelli 2000
- $1 105 - €1 220 - **£748** - FF8 000
  «Santa Margherita Ligure» Affiche couleur
  (70x100cm 27x39in) Nice 2000

MOLINS H. XX **[2]**
- $14 009 - €13 416 - **£8 817** - FF88 000
  Danseuse Chryséléphantine (H68cm H26in) La
  Varenne-Saint-Hilaire 1999

MOLITOR von Martin 1759-1812 **[21]**
- $921 - €1 017 - **£638** - FF6 673
  Klassizistische Landschaft mit einem Tempel
  Gouache/paper (23x28cm 9x11in) Wien 2001

MOLITOR VON MUHLFELD Joseph 1856-1890 **[1]**
- $82 500 - €78 391 - **£50 193** - FF514 214
  Master of all he surveys Oil/canvas (139.5x104cm
  54x40in) New-York 1999

MÖLK van Joseph Adam c.1714-1794 **[4]**
- $12 800 - €14 534 - **£8 760** - FF95 340
  Die Speizung der Zehntausend Öl/Kupfer
  (49x66cm 19x25in) Wien 2000

MOLKENBOER Theodore 1871-1920 **[4]**
- $1 127 - €1 316 - **£772** - FF8 632
  «Elias P van Bommel Boekbinder» Poster
  (85.5x62.5cm 33x24in) Hoorn 2000

MOLL Carl 1861-1945 **[90]**
- $69 874 - €71 582 - **£43 120** - FF469 546
  **Im Empfangssalon der französischen Botschaft
  zu Wien** Öl/Leinwand (120.5x120.5cm 47x47in)
  Düsseldorf 2000
- $52 960 - €58 138 - **£35 200** - FF381 360
  Dahlien Öl/Leinwand (60x60cm 23x23in) Wien 2000
- $13 584 - €11 628 - **£8 176** - FF76 272
  Selbstportrait Oil/panel (34x24.5cm 13x9in) Wien
  1998
- $508 - €545 - **£347** - FF3 575
  Winter Woodcut in colors (43x43cm 16x16in) Wien
  2001

MOLL Evert 1878-1955 **[319]**
- $2 374 - €2 124 - **£1 422** - FF13 931
  A Windmill along the Maas Oil/canvas (80x60cm
  31x23in) Amsterdam 1998
- $988 - €1 089 - **£645** - FF7 143
  Zeehaven Oil/panel (20x25cm 7x9in) Den Haag 2000
- $526 - €590 - **£366** - FF3 869
  Binnenhaven Watercolour/paper (11x18cm 4x7in)
  Rotterdam 2001

MOLL Margarete 1884-1977 **[20]**
- $3 146 - €2 658 - **£1 876** - FF17 438
  Weiblicher Torso Bronze (H29cm H11in) Düsseldorf
  1998

MOLL Oskar 1875-1947 **[79]**
- $53 289 - €46 026 - **£32 184** - FF301 914
  **Stilleben mit Matisse-Plastik, Blumenvasen und
  Wandschirm** Öl/Leinwand (142.5x119.5cm 56x47in)
  Köln 1998
- $15 507 - €15 339 - **£9 669** - FF100 617
  Sonnige Landschaft Öl/Leinwand (37.5x46cm
  14x18in) Berlin 1999
- $11 842 - €10 228 - **£7 152** - FF67 092
  Waldbach mit Felsen Watercolour (49x56.5cm
  19x22in) Köln 1998

MØLLBACK Christian 1853-1921 **[14]**
- $2 362 - €2 686 - **£1 650** - FF17 618
  **Silkepaeoner i en vase, ved vasens fod grene af
  lilla** Oil/canvas (83x67cm 32x26in) København 2000
- $25 000 - €29 645 - **£17 200** - FF194 457
  Cactus with Scarlet Blossoms Oil/canvas
  (43x35cm 16x13in) New-York 2000

MOLLENHAUER Ernst 1892-1963 **[9]**
- $16 194 - €17 384 - **£10 839** - FF114 032
  Collioure Öl/Leinwand (75.5x95.5cm 29x37in) Köln
  2000
- $17 014 - €16 361 - **£10 487** - FF107 324
  Beladenes Ochsenfuhrwerk am Abend
  Tempera/paper (58.3x71.7cm 22x28in) Köln 1999

MØLLER Carl H.K. 1845-1920 **[38]**
- $502 - €536 - **£342** - FF3 516
  Skovsti Oil/canvas (53x77cm 20x30in) Vejle 2001
- $277 - €269 - **£171** - FF1 764
  Bådebro ved Fagerstrand Oil/canvas (25x42cm
  9x16in) Vejle 1999

MØLLER Carl Heinrich 1802-1882 **[1]**
- $6 351 - €7 158 - **£4 398** - FF46 954
  **Theodor Hildebrand, der Begründer der
  Berliner Schokoladenfirma** Marble (H64cm H25in)
  Berlin 2000

MØLLER Jens Peter 1783-1854 **[51]**
- $3 179 - €3 488 - **£2 160** - FF22 877
  **Slottet Landeck ved Innfloden oplyst ved den
  dalende sol** Oil/canvas (76x100cm 29x39in)
  København 2000
- $1 203 - €1 341 - **£823** - FF8 799
  **Sydtysk bjerglandskab med en borg på en
  bjergtop** Oil/panel (26x36cm 10x14in) Viby J, Århus
  2000
- $399 - €403 - **£249** - FF2 643
  Parti fra Genf Indian ink (15.5x17cm 6x6in)
  København 2000

MØLLER Johan Frederik 1797-1871 **[18]**
- $888 - €807 - **£550** - FF5 294
  Lille pige, der leger med dukkestueinventar
  Oil/canvas (41x33cm 16x12in) København 1999

MÖLLER Niels Björnson 1827-1887 **[10]**
- $3 237 - €3 626 - **£2 250** - FF23 786
  Slott vid insjö, motiv från Schweiz Oil/canvas
  (49x84cm 19x33in) Uppsala 2001

MØLLER Otto 1883-1964 **[13]**
- $82 641 - €67 881 - **£48 000** - FF445 267
  Sancho Panza Oil/canvas (71x51cm 27x20in)
  London 1998
- $100 - €102 - **£62** - FF670
  Der Redner Woodcut (21.5x15,9cm 8x6in) Hamburg
  2000

MÖLLER Sigurd 1895-1984 **[47]**
- $603 - €565 - **£362** - FF3 705
  Frukt och blomsterstilleben Oil/canvas (80x99cm
  31x38in) Stockholm 1999

MÖLLGAARD Christian 1919 **[40]**
- $344 - €336 - **£209** - FF2 204
  Sejlskibe udfor Kronborg Oil/canvas (71x102cm
  27x40in) Viby J, Århus 2000

MOLLICA Achille ?-1887 **[18]**
- $42 000 - €46 167 - **£26 913** - FF302 836
  On the Veranda Oil/canvas (122.5x164.5cm 48x64in)
  New-York 2000
- $3 800 - €4 924 - **£2 850** - FF32 300
  Giovane popolana Olio/tela (65x40cm 25x15in)
  Roma 2000

MOLLIET Clémence XIX-XX **[5]**
- $4 000 - €4 782 - **£2 759** - FF31 368
  Young Girl in a Pasture Oil/canvas (91x67cm
  36x26in) Milford CT 2000

MOLLINAROLO Jakob Gabriel 1717-1780 **[1]**
- $1 153 - €974 - **£690** - FF6 392
  Louise Elisabeth Vigée le Brun Etching (43x32cm
  16x12in) London 1999

MÖLLINGER Franziska XIX **[4]**
- $714 - €767 - **£475** - FF5 030
  Ansicht von Thun Lithographie (30.8x40.2cm
  12x15in) München 2000

M

MOLLINGER Gerrit Alexander G. 1836-1867 [6]

$2 895 - €3 403 - **£2 007** - FF22 324
An Extensive Landscape with Travellers on a Sandy Track Oil/panel (15x22cm 5x8in) Amsterdam 2000

$3 362 - €3 630 - **£2 299** - FF23 812
Doing the Laundry Watercolour/paper (29x58cm 11x22in) Amsterdam 2001

MOLLOY Sylvia 1914 [1]

$9 681 - €9 298 - **£6 000** - FF60 988
Looking Downtown, Cape Town Oil/canvas/board (98.5x61.5cm 38x24in) London 1999

MOLNAR C. Pál 1894-1981 [31]

$990 - €1 125 - **£690** - FF7 380
Visite d'un cloître Huile/panneau (60x50cm 23x19in) Budapest 2001

$1 850 - €1 944 - **£1 150** - FF12 750
Paysage italien Huile/panneau (33x41cm 12x16in) Budapest 2000

$2 035 - €2 138 - **£1 265** - FF14 025
Avez-vous du feu? Encre/papier (33x23cm 12x9in) Budapest 2000

MOLNAR George 1953 [4]

$18 000 - €20 438 - **£12 506** - FF134 065
Time for a Chew Oil/canvas (96x78cm 38x31in) Dallas TX 2001

MOLNAR János Z. 1880-1960 [58]

$529 - €509 - **£326** - FF3 341
Stilleben med rosor och kopp Oil/canvas (66x53cm 25x20in) Malmö 1999

MOLNÉ Hector 1935/37 [39]

$19 000 - €18 486 - **£11 694** - FF121 263
Lechón Asao Oil/canvas (117x107cm 46x42in) New-York 1999

$8 000 - €8 587 - **£5 353** - FF56 328
Secuestro de la mujer de Antonio Oil/canvas (61.5x51.5cm 24x20in) New-York 2000

MOLOCH B. Colomb 1849-1909 [11]

$915 - €915 - **£572** - FF6 000
«Nous apportons le meilleur de nous-mêmes» Affiche (80x120cm 31x47in) Orléans 1999

MOLONY Miss Freda XIX-XX [1]

$19 344 - €16 493 - **£11 670** - FF108 188
The Blessing of the Fishing Fleet, Etaples, Brittany Oil/canvas (88x68cm 35x27in) Dublin 1998

MOLS Florent 1815-1892 [11]

$4 794 - €5 445 - **£3 363** - FF35 719
View of Antwerp Oil/panel (21x30cm 8x11in) Amsterdam 2001

MOLS Niels Pedersen 1859-1921 [116]

$2 361 - €2 017 - **£1 417** - FF13 233
Marsklandskab med køer Oil/canvas (125x175cm 49x68in) København 1998

$721 - €804 - **£504** - FF5 276
Sydlandsk sölandskab Oil/canvas (40x49cm 15x19in) København 2001

$433 - €430 - **£263** - FF2 820
Køer på marken Oil/canvas (32x47cm 12x18in) Vejle 2000

MOLS Robert 1848-1903 [63]

$2 347 - €2 439 - **£1 472** - FF16 000
Le port Huile/toile (37x52cm 14x20in) Paris 2000

$2 030 - €1 982 - **£1 285** - FF13 000
Petit port breton Huile/panneau (14x23cm 5x9in) Calais 1999

MØLSTED Christian 1862-1930 [80]

$2 856 - €3 216 - **£1 968** - FF21 098
Solnedgang ved Kullen, september Oil/canvas (95x140cm 37x55in) København 2000

$1 629 - €1 480 - **£1 009** - FF9 706
Kuttere ud for kysten Oil/canvas (53x75cm 20x29in) København 1999

$868 - €1 005 - **£615** - FF6 591
Sejlskibe på åbent hav, solnedgang Oil/paper/panel (23.5x35cm 9x13in) København 2000

MOLTENI Giuseppe 1800-1867 [6]

$18 000 - €18 660 - **£10 800** - FF122 400
La zingara Olio/tela (157x123cm 61x48in) Torino 2000

$9 902 - €10 265 - **£5 941** - FF67 337
Spazzacamino Olio/cartone (30x26cm 11x10in) Milano 1999

MOLTINO Francis 1818-1874 [28]

$1 448 - €1 681 - **£1 000** - FF11 024
On Westminster Bridge Oil/canvas (51x76cm 20x29in) London 2000

$825 - €861 - **£520** - FF5 650
Near Ramsgate Oil/canvas (19x40cm 7x15in) Cambridge 2000

MOLTKE Harald 1871-1960 [67]

$691 - €737 - **£460** - FF4 837
Smilende grönlaenderinde ved en fjord Oil/canvas (77x68cm 30x26in) København 2000

$364 - €346 - **£221** - FF2 268
Jakt av isbjörn Oil/panel (32x40cm 12x15in) Stockholm 1999

MOLVIG Jon 1923-1970 [70]

$16 296 - €17 955 - **£10 819** - FF117 776
Ballad of a Native Stockman Oil/board (121x138.5cm 47x54in) Woollahra, Sydney 2000

$4 149 - €4 654 - **£2 881** - FF30 526
Woman with Mirror Oil/board (106.5x61cm 41x24in) Melbourne 2001

$394 - €461 - **£278** - FF3 021
Nude Ink/paper (72x48.5cm 28x19in) Malvern, Victoria 2000

MOLYN Pieter 1595-1661 [75]

$12 280 - €11 388 - **£7 500** - FF74 701
A Family resting in a Wooded Dune Landscape Oil/panel (49x61cm 19x24in) London 1998

$10 579 - €9 983 - **£6 527** - FF65 485
Travellers in the Dunes, a Town in the Distance Oil/panel (26.5x33cm 10x12in) Amsterdam 1999

$12 701 - €13 634 - **£8 500** - FF89 433
Riders, Another Figure Descending a Road from House with Square Tower Black chalk (15.5x26cm 6x10in) London 2000

MOLZAHN Johannes 1892-1965 [38]

$103 302 - €84 851 - **£60 000** - FF556 584
Schöpfung I Oil/canvas (97x87.5cm 38x34in) London 1998

$16 727 - €19 941 - **£11 926** - FF130 802
Welten Watercolour (26.2x29.2cm 10x11in) Berlin 2000

$913 - €869 - **£567** - FF5 701
Opus XXXIII Woodcut (37.4x27.7cm 14x10in) Hamburg 1999

MOMBELLO Lucas 1520-1588/96 [3]

$14 251 - €16 186 - **£10 000** - FF106 175
The Wedding Feast at Cana Oil/canvas (118x105.5cm 46x41in) London 2001

$10 041 - €8 509 - **£6 000** - FF55 813
  The Coronation of the Virgin Oil/canvas (73x73cm
  28x28in) London 1998

MOMEN Karl 1935 **[12]**
$2 325 - €2 766 - **£1 658** - FF18 141
  Metaphor - livets träd Bronze (H42.5cm H16in)
  Stockholm 2000

MOMMERS Hendrick 1623-1693 **[57]**
$8 000 - €9 408 - **£5 736** - FF61 711
  Vegetable Market in Rome Oil/canvas (65x88cm
  25x34in) New-York 2001
$3 038 - €3 462 - **£2 100** - FF22 709
  Vegetable Market in an Italian Piazza Oil/panel
  (28x37cm 11x14in) London 2001

MOMPER de Frans 1603-1660 **[40]**
$60 765 - €68 067 - **£42 225** - FF446 490
  View of a Town by a River Oil/panel (69.5x117.5cm
  27x46in) Amsterdam 2001
$5 044 - €6 098 - **£3 524** - FF40 000
  Moines en prière dans une grotte/Pélerins dans
  un paysage montagneux Huile/panneau
  (27.5x26cm 10x10in) Paris 2000

MOMPER de Jan III, Monsu X 1614-c.1688 **[14]**
$7 951 - €9 259 - **£5 606** - FF60 738
  An Italianate Coastal Landscape with Travellers
  in the Foreground Oil/canvas (45.5x64cm 17x25in)
  London 2000
$9 000 - €10 600 - **£6 224** - FF69 533
  Landscapes with Peasants and Animals Oil/cop-
  per (15.5x21cm 6x8in) New-York 2000

MOMPER de Joos II Jodocus 1564-1635 **[132]**
$124 136 - €121 588 - **£80 000** - FF797 568
  Peasants harvesting, an extensive Landscape
  with Church beyond Oil/canvas (131x101.5cm
  51x39in) London 1999
$28 800 - €32 703 - **£19 710** - FF214 515
  Gebirgslandschaft mit Reisenden Oil/panel
  (39x56.5cm 15x22in) Wien 2001
$16 488 - €15 882 - **£10 188** - FF104 181
  Fallen Tree by a Waterfall in a Mountainous
  Landscape, a Valley Beyond Oil/panel (40.5x33cm
  15x12in) Amsterdam 1999

MOMPER de Philippe I c.1585-1634 **[10]**
$49 410 - €46 996 - **£30 000** - FF308 271
  Townscape with Peasants Unloading a Cart by
  a Canal Oil/canvas (60x120cm 23x47in) London 1999

MOMPER de Philippe II ?-1675 **[1]**
$10 248 - €10 842 - **£6 500** - FF71 121
  Extensive River Landscape with a Church,
  Cattle Grazing an a Traveller Oil/panel (48x64.5cm
  18x25in) London 2000

MOMPO Manuel Hernández 1927-1992 **[168]**
$9 720 - €10 812 - **£6 840** - FF70 920
  El Sena, París Oleo/lienzo (121x181cm 47x71in)
  Madrid 2001
$6 600 - €6 607 - **£4 070** - FF43 340
  Composición Técnica mixta (46x55cm 18x21in)
  Madrid 2000
$3 500 - €3 003 - **£2 100** - FF19 700
  Composición Oleo/tabla (25x36cm 9x14in) Madrid
  1999
$1 960 - €2 102 - **£1 330** - FF13 790
  Composición Acuarela/papel (26x34cm 10x13in)
  Madrid 2001
$768 - €721 - **£468** - FF4 728
  Composición Serigrafía (69x49cm 27x19in) Madrid
  1999

MOMPOU DENCAUSE Josep 1888-1968 **[15]**
$5 950 - €5 118 - **£3 485** - FF33 575
  Puerto mediterráneo Oleo/lienzo (50x70cm
  19x27in) Madrid 1998
$6 035 - €5 106 - **£3 655** - FF33 490
  Port de la Selva Oleo/papel (32.5x41.5cm 12x16in)
  Madrid 1998

MONA Domenico c.1550-1602 **[3]**
$2 267 - €2 381 - **£1 500** - FF15 618
  Rebecca and Eliezer at the Well Ink (27.5x38cm
  10x14in) London 2000

MONACHESI Sante 1910-1991 **[157]**
$1 750 - €1 814 - **£1 050** - FF11 900
  Muri ciechi Olio/tela (60x50cm 23x19in) Prato 2001
$900 - €933 - **£540** - FF6 120
  Muri ciechi Olio/tavola (40x30cm 15x11in) Milano
  1999
$550 - €570 - **£330** - FF3 740
  Muri ciechi Tempera/carta (60x45cm 23x17in) Torino
  1999

MONACO Pietro 1707/10-1772 **[6]**
$540 - €466 - **£270** - FF3 060
  Riposo dalla fuga in Egitto/Partenza d Abramo
  da Aran verso Cana Gravure (35.5x47.5cm 13x18in)
  Firenze 1999

MONAFO Janet 1940 **[1]**
$3 600 - €3 111 - **£2 136** - FF20 408
  Self Portrait with Rose Pastel/paper (117x117cm
  46x46in) Washington 1998

MONAHAN Hugh 1914-1970 **[44]**
$1 500 - €1 420 - **£932** - FF9 313
  Wetland Landscape with Mallards in Flight
  Oil/canvas (50x60cm 20x24in) Portland OR 1999

MONALDI Paolo 1697-1773 **[26]**
$30 800 - €39 911 - **£23 100** - FF261 800
  Paesaggio con scena campestre Olio/tela
  (97x146cm 38x57in) Roma 2001
$32 500 - €35 993 - **£22 041** - FF236 096
  Peasant girl Playing a Lute/Peasant Couple
  Seated in Wooded Landscape Oil/canvas
  (52x42cm 20x16in) New-York 2000
$7 799 - €7 632 - **£5 000** - FF50 061
  Peasants conversing before a Ruined Arch
  Oil/canvas (35x28cm 13x11in) London 1999

MONAMI Pierre 1814-1857 **[4]**
$20 400 - €26 435 - **£15 300** - FF173 400
  L'Arco di Costantino, con la Meta Sudante e il
  tempio di Venere Olio/tela (38x57cm 14x22in) Roma
  2001

MONAMY Peter 1670/89-1749 **[66]**
$21 230 - €19 545 - **£13 000** - FF128 204
  The Morning Gun Oil/canvas (75x61.5cm 29x24in)
  London 1998
$6 500 - €6 486 - **£3 956** - FF42 543
  Shipping off the Coast Oil/canvas (34x39cm
  13x15in) New-York 2000

MONANTEUIL Jean J. 1785-1860 **[4]**
$40 986 - €45 277 - **£28 422** - FF297 000
  Portrait d'un jeune garçon Huile/toile (65x54cm
  25x21in) Tarbes 2001

MONASTERIOS Rafael 1884-1961 **[8]**
$9 900 - €9 223 - **£6 050** - FF68 000
  Desnudo Oleo/lienzo (73.5x97.5cm 28x38in) Caracas
  1998
$3 001 - €3 167 - **£1 983** - FF20 775
  Paisaje Huile/bois (30x22cm 11x8in) Caracas ($) 2000

MONCADA CALVACHE José 1895-? [3]

$3 600 - €4 260 - **£2 220** - FF23 640
Bodegón Oleo/lienzo (30x46cm 11x18in) Madrid 2000

MONCHABLON Alphonse Xavier 1835-1907 [3]

$4 553 - €4 421 - **£2 813** - FF29 000
Les deux amies et le chaton Huile/toile (61x46cm 24x18in) Paris 1999

MONCHABLON Jean Ferdinand, Jan 1855-1904 [46]

$4 000 - €4 376 - **£2 766** - FF28 707
European Landscape Oil/canvas (45x60cm 18x24in) Morris-Plains NJ 2001

$12 000 - €11 402 - **£7 300** - FF74 794
Bords de la Sâone Oil/panel (33x44.5cm 12x17in) New-York 1999

MONCHAUX de Kathy 1960 [3]

$14 442 - €15 737 - **£10 000** - FF103 228
Vent Construction (26x145x10cm 10x57x3in) London 2001

MONDAINI Giacinto 1903-1979 [3]

$908 - €942 - **£545** - FF6 177
«13a fiera di Milano» Affiche couleur (98x69cm 38x27in) Torino 2000

MONDINO Aldo 1938 [102]

$3 250 - €3 369 - **£1 950** - FF22 100
Mon-Dine Olio/tavola (189x140cm 74x55in) Firenze 2001

$900 - €933 - **£540** - FF6 120
Esquela Olio/carta (40x50cm 15x19in) Prato 2000

$550 - €570 - **£330** - FF3 740
Il colore della musica Pastelli/cartone (67x48cm 26x18in) Vercelli 2001

MONDO Domenico 1723-1806 [19]

$2 760 - €2 384 - **£1 380** - FF15 640
Scena classica Inchiostro (33.5x48cm 13x18in) Milano 1999

MONDON Jean act.1736-1745 [1]

$80 000 - €85 575 - **£54 544** - FF561 336
Animals, Musicians, Fruits, Coat-of-Arms, Trades Bodycolour (25.5x29cm 10x11in) New-York 2001

MONDRIAN Piet 1872-1944 [161]

$173 698 - €172 436 - **£108 528** - FF1 131 108
Sailboat moored in a River Oil/canvas (66x102cm 25x40in) Amsterdam 2000

$55 000 - €46 947 - **£32 890** - FF307 950
Dusk (Schemering) Oil/canvas/board (27.5x44cm 10x17in) New-York 1998

$94 686 - €91 619 - **£60 000** - FF600 978
Isolated Tree on the Gein Pastel (46x62cm 18x24in) London 1999

MONDZAIN Simon 1890-1979 [64]

$3 846 - €3 735 - **£2 376** - FF24 500
La rue de la Marine, Alger Huile/toile (73x60cm 28x23in) Paris 1999

$452 - €525 - **£312** - FF3 446
Stilleben mit Blumenstrauss in Vase auf gemustertem Tuch Öl/Leinwand (35x27cm 13x10in) Luzern 2000

MONET Claude 1840-1926 [374]

$5 000 000 - €4 313 774 - **£3 005 000** - FF28 296 500
Vue du bassin aux nymphéas avec saule Oil/canvas (140x150cm 55x59in) New-York 1998

$2 199 400 - €2 134 286 - **£1 369 200** - FF14 000 000
Étretat, la falaise d'Aval au coucher du soleil Huile/toile (60x81cm 23x31in) Cheverny 1999

$189 722 - €203 796 - **£130 000** - FF1 336 816
Meule, soleil couchant Oil/paper/board (11.5x19cm 4x7in) London 2001

$56 012 - €59 721 - **£38 000** - FF391 742
Honfleur, la grève en aval Pastel (32x48.5cm 12x19in) London 2001

$5 258 - €6 135 - **£3 660** - FF40 246
Ravin de la petite Creuse Farblithographie (39.8x56.8cm 15x22in) Köln 2000

MONEY Fred 1882-1956 [35]

$3 589 - €4 269 - **£2 559** - FF28 000
Massif d'hortensias près de la chaumière Huile/toile (70x100cm 27x39in) Calais 2000

MONFALLET Adolphe François 1816-1900 [10]

$5 966 - €5 793 - **£3 686** - FF38 000
Représentation théâtrale de Turlupin au temps de Louis XIII Huile/toile (55x66cm 21x25in) Paris 1999

$5 509 - €4 525 - **£3 200** - FF29 684
The Game of Dice Oil/panel (32x25cm 12x9in) London 1998

MONFORT Octavianus XVII [7]

$65 000 - €67 382 - **£39 000** - FF442 000
Primavera/Estate/Autunno/Inverno Tempera (26.5x32.5cm 10x12in) Milano 2000

$5 699 - €4 924 - **£2 849** - FF32 298
Natura morta con canestro di frutta Tempera/paper (58x77cm 23x30in) Milano 1999

MONFREID de Georges Daniel 1856-1929 [29]

$115 689 - €98 844 - **£70 000** - FF648 375
Le cheval blanc Oil/canvas (141.5x94cm 55x37in) London 1998

$8 114 - €8 842 - **£5 318** - FF58 000
Sur le chemin en bordure de mer Huile/toile (59x81cm 23x31in) Brest 2000

$13 597 - €16 007 - **£9 555** - FF105 000
Étude pour un calvaire Bas-relief (74.5x59x19cm 29x23x7in) Paris 2000

MONGE Jules 1855-1934 [39]

$4 336 - €3 964 - **£2 654** - FF26 000
La poignée de braves à Saint-Cloud Huile/toile (65x100cm 25x39in) Paris 1999

$691 - €778 - **£482** - FF5 101
Beim Hufschmied Öl/Leinwand (24x35cm 9x13in) Luzern 2001

MONGIN Antoine Pierre 1762-1827 [22]

$3 531 - €3 508 - **£2 200** - FF23 008
Extensive Wooded Landscape with Huntsmen Pausing on a Track Bodycolour (65.5x102.5cm 25x40in) London 1999

MONGINOT Charles 1825-1900 [25]

$12 627 - €15 017 - **£9 000** - FF98 506
Hawking Oil/canvas (244x165cm 96x64in) London 2000

$3 249 - €3 326 - **£2 004** - FF20 500
Vase de fleurs Huile/toile (116x78cm 45x30in) Troyes 1999

MONGRELL MUÑOZ Bartolome 1890-1938 [3]

$3 780 - €3 604 - **£2 340** - FF23 640
Luna sobre la playa de La Malvarrosa Oleo/lienzo (53x94cm 20x37in) Madrid 1999

$2 111 - €2 439 - **£1 461** - FF15 996
El haren Oleo/lienzo (29x41cm 11x16in) Barcelona 2000

MONGRELL Y TORRENT José 1874-1937 **[15]**
$19 125 - €22 524 - **£13 875** - FF147 750
Mujeres en la playa Oleo/lienzo (78x64cm 30x25in)
Madrid 2001

MONGUZZI Bruno 1941 **[3]**
$1 000 - €962 - **£617** - FF6 308
«Typographic posters» Poster (128x91cm 50x35in)
New-York 1999

MONI de Louis 1698-1771 **[15]**
$3 457 - €3 933 - **£2 437** - FF25 796
Lesende Frau am Fenster Oil/panel (26x21.2cm
10x8in) Zürich 2001

MONIER Émile Adolphe 1883-? **[9]**
$4 428 - €4 462 - **£2 754** - FF29 268
Négresse portant un panier de fruits Céramique
(H67cm H26in) Bruxelles 2000

MONIER Julien XIX-XX **[6]**
$1 200 - €1 037 - **£712** - FF6 802
«Ingenue» Marble (H58.5cm H23in) Washington 1998

MONIES David 1812-1894 **[77]**
$14 278 - €13 128 - **£8 820** - FF86 112
Interior med portraet af malerens dotre Oil/can-
vas (158x152cm 62x59in) Vejle 1998
$993 - €1 073 - **£686** - FF7 037
Portraet af en dame med hvid kyse Oil/canvas
(75x60cm 29x23in) København 2001
$933 - €940 - **£581** - FF6 168
Söndagsudflugt i skoven Oil/canvas (27x38cm
10x14in) København 2000

MÖNIG Anton c.1840 **[5]**
$5 792 - €5 015 - **£3 493** - FF32 896
Stadt am Niederrhein mit Blick auf einen Dom
Öl/Leinwand (56x68cm 22x26in) München 1998

MONIN Guillaume 1908 **[10]**
$383 - €427 - **£260** - FF2 800
Les otages, projet de décor Aquarelle/papier
(46.5x62.5cm 18x24in) Paris 2000

MONINOT Bernard 1949 **[15]**
$3 026 - €3 049 - **£1 886** - FF20 000
Voiture bâchée II Assemblage (75.5x105.5cm
29x41in) Paris 2000

MONIUSZKO Jan Czeslaw 1853-1908 **[12]**
$1 781 - €2 079 - **£1 257** - FF13 640
A la cour de nobles Huile/toile (49x66cm 19x25in)
Warszawa 2000

MONK William 1863-1937 **[159]**
$318 - €308 - **£200** - FF2 022
Windsor Races/Regatta with the Castle beyond
Pastel/paper (25x35cm 10x14in) Leominster,
Herefordshire 1999
$91 - €78 - **£55** - FF514
The Pool of London Etching (17x25cm 7x10in)
Aylsham, Norfolk 1998

MONKS John Austin Sands 1850-1917 **[12]**
$1 500 - €1 638 - **£965** - FF10 745
Farm Animals by the Shore Oil/canvas (55x81cm
22x32in) Mystic CT 2000
$650 - €697 - **£442** - FF4 570
Sheep in meadow by Stream Watercolour/paper
(32x48cm 12x19in) Thomaston ME 2001

MONKS Robert Hatton XX **[3]**
$20 000 - €17 275 - **£12 080** - FF113 314
Marsh Landscape Oil/canvas (99x200cm 39x79in)
Watertown MA 1998

$4 200 - €4 995 - **£2 993** - FF32 764
Spring Trees in Blossom, Boston Oil/canvas
(58x43.5cm 22x17in) New-York 2000

MONLÉON Manuel XX **[1]**
$1 800 - €1 704 - **£1 118** - FF11 177
«Valencia, festividad de las fallas» Poster
(98.5x69cm 38x27in) New-York 1999

MONLÉON Y TORRES Rafael 1847-1900 **[16]**
$1 890 - €2 102 - **£1 260** - FF13 790
Vista de Londres desde el Támesis con la
Catedral de San Pablo Oleo/tabla (20.5x21cm
8x8in) Madrid 2000
$166 - €192 - **£115** - FF1 260
Marinas Tinta (8x12cm 3x4in) Madrid 2000

MONNET Charles 1732-1808 **[14]**
$660 - €610 - **£395** - FF4 000
Scène de sacrifice humain à une divinité Encre
(12x8.5cm 4x3in) Paris 1999

MONNET-LAVERPILIERE Estelle XIX **[2]**
$241 - €259 - **£161** - FF1 700
Jeté de fleurs Huile/toile (38x46cm 14x18in)
Cherbourg 2000

MONNICKENDAM Martin 1874-1943 **[41]**
$2 882 - €2 723 - **£1 743** - FF17 859
L'Arc du Caroussel avec l'église St.Germain
Oil/panel (49x40.5cm 19x15in) Amsterdam 1999
$577 - €547 - **£360** - FF3 585
Sacré-Coeur Oil/board (38x29cm 14x11in) London
1999
$652 - €681 - **£411** - FF4 464
Noordermarkt, Amsterdam Pastel (21.5x29cm
8x11in) Amsterdam 2000

MONNIER A. XIX **[4]**
$2 199 - €2 134 - **£1 358** - FF14 000
Rivière et sous-bois Tirage papier salé (14x18cm
5x7in) Paris 1999

MONNIER Henry Bonaventure 1799-1877 **[83]**
$350 - €337 - **£219** - FF2 213
Landpartie Ink (18.5x24cm 7x9in) München 1999
$5 000 - €5 686 - **£3 493** - FF37 300
«Loterie nationale» Poster (153x114cm 60x45in)
Chicago IL 2000

MONNOT Maurice Louis 1869-1937 **[37]**
$1 831 - €1 829 - **£1 144** - FF12 000
L'astiquage des cuivres Huile/toile (61x46cm
24x18in) Pontoise 1999
$1 268 - €1 361 - **£848** - FF8 929
Souvenir de mes bons amis Mme et Ms Cortès:
a Still Life Oil/panel (19x27cm 7x10in) Amsterdam
2000

MONNOYER Antoine 1670-1747 **[16]**
$16 119 - €14 923 - **£10 000** - FF97 890
Still Life of Carnations, Lilies, Roses,
Hollyhocks, Delphiniums Oil/canvas (150x102cm
59x40in) London 1999
$7 860 - €7 622 - **£4 980** - FF50 000
Nature morte au vase de fleurs sur un entable-
ment Huile/toile (47.5x38cm 18x14in) Paris 1999

MONNOYER Jean-Baptiste 1636-1699 **[117]**
$68 160 - €73 176 - **£45 600** - FF480 000
Nature morte de fleurs dans un vase sculpté
Huile/toile (125x152cm 49x59in) Paris 2000
$28 490 - €24 240 - **£17 000** - FF159 007
Grapes, Peaches, Plums, Roses, Hyacinth,
Hydrangea and other Flowers Oil/canvas
(115x96.5cm 45x37in) London 1998

M

MONOD
- $950 - €1 054 - £632 - FF6 915
  Nature morte Etching in colors (50.5x44.5cm 19x17in) New-York 2000

MONOD Claude 1944-1990 [8]
- $592 - €564 - £368 - FF3 700
  Vase globulaire à décor interne de poudres colorées Sculpture verre (H22.5cm H8in) Paris 1999

MONOGRAMME: A.P. XIX [1]
- $3 453 - €4 116 - £2 462 - FF27 000
  Gardien de troupeaux Huile/toile (80x132cm 31x51in) Strasbourg 2000

MONOGRAMME: A.Q.F. (Augustin Quesnel ?) 1595-1651 [1]
- $2 495 - €2 442 - £1 600 - FF16 019
  Portrait of a Gentleman, Head and Shoulders, wearing black, black Cap Oil/panel (17x14cm 6x5in) London 1999

MONOGRAMME: A.W. [3]
- $5 029 - €4 250 - £3 000 - FF27 881
  The Vision of Saint-Anthony of Padua Oil/copper (71x88.5cm 27x34in) London 1998

MONOGRAMME: B.B. XVII [1]
- $28 800 - €37 320 - £21 600 - FF244 800
  Arpa, due liuti, un violino, frutta, volumi/Chitarra, liuti, violino Olio/tela (93x143cm 36x56in) Roma 2000

MONOGRAMME: C.V.M. XVII [1]
- $15 000 - €16 542 - £10 158 - FF108 511
  A Coastal Scene with Peasants and Elegant Figures on the Shore Oil/panel (33.5x43.5cm 13x17in) New-York 2000

MONOGRAMME: D.F. XVII [1]
- $6 606 - €6 353 - £4 069 - FF41 672
  Wooded Landscape with Figures Oil/panel (19.5x28cm 7x11in) Amsterdam 1999

MONOGRAMME: E.L. XIX [1]
- $13 672 - €15 314 - £9 500 - FF100 454
  Mexique Albumen print (16.5x20.5cm 6x8in) London 2001

MONOGRAMME: F.I.T. XVIII [1]
- $2 737 - €3 176 - £1 890 - FF20 836
  Figures Playing Skittles in Front of an Inn Oil/panel (16.4x22cm 6x8in) Amsterdam 2000

MONOGRAMME: I.D. XVII [1]
- $16 426 - €19 059 - £11 340 - FF125 017
  Still Life with a Bun, Cheese and a Knife on a Pewter Plate, with Mice Oil/panel (26x31.5cm 10x12in) Amsterdam 2000

MONOGRAMME: I.S. act.1633-1658 [1]
- $186 927 - €207 522 - £130 000 - FF1 361 256
  An old Man standing beside a table with Books, a Candle and a Skull Oil/canvas (63.5x52cm 25x20in) London 2001

MONOGRAMME: P.M. XVII [3]
- $42 090 - €50 058 - £30 000 - FF328 356
  Portrait of Elizabeth Coffin Oil/canvas (98x76cm 38x29in) London 2000

MONOGRAMME: S.B. XVII [1]
- $13 999 - €13 315 - £8 500 - FF87 343
  Still Life of Ham, Hard Cheese, Salami, Bread, Song Birds Oil/canvas (72x91cm 28x35in) London 1999

MONOGRAMME: S.G. XVII [1]
- $3 128 - €3 630 - £2 160 - FF23 812
  Hilly Landscape with Travellers on a Path near a Waterfall Oil/panel (27x32.5cm 10x12in) Amsterdam 2000

MONOGRAMME: S.K. act.c.1660 [4]
- $25 000 - €29 064 - £17 547 - FF190 650
  The Return of the Prodigal Son Oil/canvas (160x239cm 62x94in) New-York 2001

MONOGRAMME: S.L.V. XVI-XVII [2]
- $19 992 - €17 271 - £9 996 - FF113 288
  La Battaglia di Anversa del 17 agosto 1585 Olio/tela (108.5x188cm 42x74in) Milano 1999

MONORY Jacques 1934 [176]
- $8 484 - €9 147 - £5 688 - FF60 000
  Luchess of Florida, Technicolor No.9 Huile/toile (150x150cm 59x59in) Paris 2000
- $5 170 - €4 726 - £3 183 - FF31 000
  Bertinoro, analyse et décomposition d'un instant de plaisir, No.266 Huile/toile (52x190cm 20x74in) Paris 1999
- $3 276 - €3 659 - £2 191 - FF24 000
  Sans titre Acrylique/toile (24x19cm 9x7in) Paris 2000
- $260 - €244 - £157 - FF1 600
  Tanatorolls Lithographie (119x96cm 46x37in) Paris 1999

MONROE Lanford ?-2000 [1]
- $8 000 - €9 084 - £5 558 - FF59 584
  River Run Oil/board (71x101cm 28x40in) Dallas TX 2001

MONS Karl 1890-1947 [2]
- $5 267 - €5 113 - £3 253 - FF33 539
  Schwälmerin in Abendmahlshaube Oil/panel (65x55cm 25x21in) Frankfurt 1999

MONSAGRATI Alessandro 1884-? [6]
- $600 - €518 - £300 - FF3 400
  Il mercato del pesce a Venezia Olio/tavola (10.5x14.5cm 4x5in) Prato 1999

MONSÉGUR Alexandre 1849-? [1]
- $5 060 - €5 013 - £3 069 - FF32 886
  Tranquil Countryside with Fisherman Oil/canvas (140x71cm 55x28in) New-Orleans LA 2000

MONSEN Frederick 1865-1929 [11]
- $4 000 - €3 340 - £2 376 - FF21 906
  Man Beneath Perched Rock Gelatin silver print (45x35cm 17x13in) New-York 1998

MONSIAUX Nicolas André 1755-1837 [16]
- $2 059 - €2 287 - £1 435 - FF15 000
  Satyre et Bacchante en sous-bois Aquarelle/papier (28x21cm 11x8in) Paris 2001

MØNSTED Peder Mork 1859-1941 [903]
- $36 995 - €42 983 - £26 000 - FF281 949
  Late evening sunshine Oil/canvas (94x138cm 37x54in) London 2001
- $11 592 - €9 679 - £6 890 - FF63 489
  Forårsdag ved Lugano Oil/canvas (38x49cm 14x19in) København 1998
- $4 319 - €3 696 - £2 600 - FF24 245
  A sunlit Garden on Capri Oil/canvas (33x45cm 12x17in) London 1998
- $1 244 - €1 077 - £755 - FF7 064
  Mand, der fisker i en sø Grisaille (36x28cm 14x11in) København 1998

MONTAG Carl 1880-1956 **[7]**
- **$2 484** - €2 678 - **£1 666** - FF17 566
  Blumenstilleben Öl/Leinwand (60.5x59cm 23x23in) Zürich 2000

MONTAGNA Benedetto c.1481-c.1558 **[12]**
- **$848** - €991 - **£599** - FF6 500
  La Vierge à l'enfant, d'après Bartoloméo Montagna Burin (20.5x15.5cm 8x6in) Paris 2000

MONTAGNÉ Agricol Louis 1879-1960 **[155]**
- **$3 517** - €2 973 - **£2 092** - FF19 500
  Avignon au soleil couchant Huile/toile (81x101cm 31x39in) Neuilly-sur-Seine 1998
- **$686** - €686 - **£429** - FF6 500
  Pierrot Huile/panneau (35x26.5cm 13x10in) Paris 1999
- **$826** - €869 - **£518** - FF5 700
  Avignon, le Pont Saint-Benezet Aquarelle/papier (43x29cm 16x11in) Paris 2000

MONTAGNE Pierre Marius 1828-1879 **[4]**
- **$1 823** - €2 073 - **£1 251** - FF13 600
  Personnage mythologique assis Bronze (H70cm H27in) Toulouse 2000

MONTAGU Domenico ?-1750 **[5]**
- **$450** - €389 - **£225** - FF2 550
  Vedute di Roma: Il Colosseo, Chiesa del Gesú Gravure (15.5x26.5cm 6x10in) Firenze 1999

MONTAGU Henry ?-c.1883 **[1]**
- **$2 434** - €2 341 - **£1 500** - FF15 357
  Rydal Mount, Cumbria Pencil (19x27cm 7x10in) London 2000

MONTAGUE Alfred ?-c.1883/88 **[138]**
- **$2 200** - €2 371 - **£1 500** - FF15 554
  Rotterdam Oil/canvas (76.5x63.5cm 30x25in) London 2001
- **$1 717** - €1 483 - **£1 037** - FF9 728
  «Auf dem Weg zum Markt» Öl/Karton (45x34cm 17x13in) Konstanz 1998

MONTAGUE Arthur XIX **[2]**
- **$4 644** - €4 360 - **£2 880** - FF28 602
  Fischerboote vor der Küste Öl/Leinwand (56x75cm 22x29in) Wien 1999

MONTAGUE Clifford act.1883-1901 **[28]**
- **$1 673** - €1 968 - **£1 200** - FF12 910
  «Ponti Sesio, Roma» Oil/canvas (31x61cm 12x24in) West-Yorshire 2001
- **$823** - €783 - **£500** - FF5 137
  Dutch Sailing Barges off the Coast Oil/panel (18.5x38.5cm 7x15in) Penzance, Cornwall 1999

MONTALANT de Julius O. XIX **[7]**
- **$7 900** - €6 846 - **£4 563** - FF44 910
  Valley of the Temples, Argregento, Sicily Oil/canvas (56x101cm 22x40in) New-Orleans LA 1998

MONTALBA Clara 1842-1929 **[30]**
- **$1 197** - €1 094 - **£750** - FF7 176
  At Chioggia, near Venice, a View of the Lagoon Watercolour (22x15cm 9x6in) Fernhurst, Haslemere, Surrey 1999

MONTALD Constant 1862-1944 **[107]**
- **$4 576** - €5 453 - **£3 278** - FF35 772
  Allégories des genres littéraires Huile/toile (91x187cm 35x73in) Liège 2000
- **$5 328** - €4 991 - **£3 203** - FF32 742
  La sortie du bain Oil/canvas (91x70.5cm 35x27in) Amsterdam 1999
- **$1 056** - €992 - **£652** - FF6 504
  L'îlot Robinson Aquarelle/carton (55x72cm 21x28in) Bruxelles 1999

MONTAN Anders 1845-1917 **[35]**
- **$547** - €613 - **£371** - FF4 024
  Zwei Männer im Bierkeller Öl/Leinwand (47x48cm 18x18in) München 2000
- **$748** - €694 - **£465** - FF4 551
  Gårdsidyll med figurer Oil/canvas (35x45cm 13x17in) Malmö 1999

MONTANA Bob XX **[7]**
- **$5 500** - €5 904 - **£3 680** - FF38 725
  Page No.17 from Archie Comics No.1 Ink (45.5x33cm 17x12in) New-York 2000

MONTANARI Giuseppe 1889-1970 **[13]**
- **$12 500** - €12 958 - **£7 500** - FF85 000
  Pugilatori Olio/tela (130x113cm 51x44in) Milano 2000
- **$720** - €933 - **£540** - FF6 120
  San Franceso e gli uccelli Olio/tavola (75x65cm 29x25in) Milano 2000

MONTANARINI Luigi 1906-1998 **[102]**
- **$750** - €777 - **£450** - FF5 100
  «Nuove variazioni n.23» Olio/tela (60x50cm 23x19in) Roma 1999
- **$300** - €311 - **£180** - FF2 040
  Musicista Gouache/carta (29x21cm 11x8in) Roma 1999

MONTANI Carlo 1868-1936 **[13]**
- **$1 300** - €1 348 - **£780** - FF8 840
  Vaso di fiori in interno Olio/cartone (49x60cm 19x23in) Roma 2000
- **$2 100** - €2 177 - **£1 260** - FF14 280
  Veduta del Lago di Nemi Olio/cartone (33x48cm 12x18in) Roma 2000

MONTANINI Pietro 1626-1689 **[9]**
- **$10 240** - €11 628 - **£7 008** - FF76 272
  Gebirgige Landschaft mit Figuren Öl/Leinwand (73x98cm 28x38in) Wien 2000

MONTARDIER ?-c.1848 **[2]**
- **$22 000** - €24 239 - **£14 676** - FF159 000
  The United States and the Macedonian/The Constitution and the Java Watercolour/paper (43x53cm 17x21in) Portsmouth NH 2000

MONTASSIER Henri 1880-1946 **[35]**
- **$1 618** - €1 519 - **£1 000** - FF9 965
  Street Scene, Algiers Oil/panel (37.5x45.5cm 14x17in) Billingshurst, West-Sussex 1999

MONTAUT Ernest 1879-1936 **[107]**
- **$471** - €534 - **£318** - FF3 500
  «Le pneu Michelin a vaincu le rail» Affiche (72x50.5cm 28x19in) Blois 2000

MONTEFORTE Edoardo 1849-1932 **[13]**
- **$21 000** - €21 770 - **£12 600** - FF142 800
  Scena agreste Olio/tela (76x132cm 29x51in) Vercelli 2001
- **$3 000** - €2 592 - **£2 000** - FF17 000
  Paesaggio Olio/tavola (21x34cm 8x13in) Milano 1998

MONTEFUSCO Vincenzo 1852-1912 **[13]**
- **$960** - €1 244 - **£720** - FF8 160
  Il pastorello Olio/tavola (19x24cm 7x9in) Milano 2001

MONTELATICCI, CECCO BRAVO Francesco 1607-1661 **[19]**
- **$10 110** - €8 572 - **£6 000** - FF56 226
  Elegant Youth Being Attended by Servants with Food and Wine in Prison Oil/canvas (73.5x101cm 28x39in) London 1998

M

M

$35 000 - €37 378 - **£23 849** - FF245 185
The Head of a Devil/Study of a Flower
Chalks/paper (13.5x15.5cm 5x6in) New-York 2001

MONTELATICI Mario 1894-1974 **[3]**
$20 000 - €19 207 - **£12 394** - FF125 988
Young Boy in tattered clothes with a puppy at his side Mixed media (45x25cm 18x10in) St. Louis MO 1999

MONTEMEZZANO Francesco c.1540-c.1605 **[6]**
$11 249 - €11 158 - **£7 000** - FF73 190
Lady, said to be the Contarini Family, in an elaborate Dress, Jewels Oil/canvas (57x47cm 22x18in) London 1999

MONTEMEZZO Antonio Matteo 1841-1898 **[24]**
$13 127 - €11 246 - **£7 891** - FF73 772
Ein Hirtenhund hat eine Gänseschar am Weiher überrascht Oil/panel (34x65cm 13x25in) Stuttgart 1998
$1 750 - €1 814 - **£1 050** - FF11 900
Aratura al tramonto Olio/tela (33x41cm 12x16in) Milano 2001

MONTEN Heinrich M. Dietrich 1799-1843 **[12]**
$2 087 - €2 454 - **£1 496** - FF16 098
Prinz Carl von Bayern in Uniform des Schwererreiter-Regiments Öl/Leinwand (41x30.5cm 16x12in) München 2001

MONTENARD Frédéric 1849-1926 **[57]**
$3 328 - €3 354 - **£2 074** - FF22 000
Rivage Méditerranéen Huile/toile (38x56cm 14x22in) Calais 2000
$783 - €686 - **£474** - FF4 500
Paysanne en Provence Huile/panneau (23.5x32.5cm 9x12in) Paris 1998

MONTENEGRO Roberto 1881-1968 **[58]**
$70 000 - €61 037 - **£42 322** - FF400 379
Tehuanas en tehuantepec Oil/canvas (255x325cm 100x127in) New-York 1998
$3 500 - €3 405 - **£2 154** - FF22 338
Retrato de dama Oil/canvas (75.5x59.5cm 29x23in) New-York 1999
$3 200 - €2 730 - **£1 907** - FF17 907
Peach and Lemon Oil/canvas/board (25.5x35cm 10x13in) New-York 1998
$842 - €956 - **£588** - FF6 272
La pareja del cuarto rojo Gouache/papier (28x35cm 11x13in) México 2001

MONTENEGRO Y CAPELL José 1855-1929 **[31]**
$2 810 - €3 310 - **£1 983** - FF21 709
Patio andaluz Oleo/lienzo (50x61cm 19x24in) Madrid 2000
$648 - €721 - **£432** - FF4 728
Patio del Antiguo Convento de la Merced Oleo/tabla (28x46cm 11x18in) Madrid 2000
$624 - €721 - **£432** - FF4 728
Patio de los leones Acuarela/papel (30.5x21cm 12x8in) Sevilla 2000

MONTESANO Gian Marco 1939 **[37]**
$2 000 - €2 073 - **£1 309** - FF13 660
«Combattere comunque» Olio/tela (100x120cm 39x47in) Milano 1999
$780 - €674 - **£390** - FF4 420
Grande marine rose Olio/tela (95x110cm 37x43in) Prato 1999

MONTESINOS Ricardo 1942 **[23]**
$702 - €781 - **£494** - FF5 122
«Barcas deportivas (Gijón)» Oleo/lienzo (61x74cm 24x29in) Madrid 2001

$205 - €216 - **£136** - FF1 418
Paisaje rocoso Oleo/tabla (46x27cm 18x10in) Madrid 2000

MONTEYN Jan Baptist 1695-1722 **[2]**
$5 289 - €5 899 - **£3 451** - FF38 695
A Cobbler and other Figures on a Town Square Oil/canvas (99x120.5cm 38x47in) Amsterdam 2000

MONTEZEMOLO di Guido 1878-1941 **[4]**
$1 300 - €1 348 - **£780** - FF8 840
Natura morta Olio/tela (65x54cm 25x21in) Vercelli 2001
$2 500 - €2 592 - **£1 500** - FF17 000
Autunno dorato Olio/tavola (41x35cm 16x13in) Vercelli 1999

MONTEZIN Pierre Eugène 1874-1946 **[654]**
$17 000 - €16 347 - **£10 473** - FF107 230
Promeneurs en bord de Seine à Veneux les Sablons Oil/paper/canvas (96.5x130cm 37x51in) New-York 1999
$13 000 - €12 501 - **£8 009** - FF82 000
Untitled Oil/canvas (60.5x73cm 23x28in) New-York 1999
$2 178 - €2 287 - **£1 372** - FF15 000
Bord de Seine à Veneux-les-Sablons Huile/panneau (24x19cm 9x7in) Fontainebleau 2000
$1 562 - €1 524 - **£989** - FF10 000
Poules picorant près de la petite ferme Gouache/papier (17x25cm 6x9in) Calais 1999

MONTFORT Antoine Alphonse 1802-1884 **[15]**
$4 206 - €4 573 - **£2 772** - FF30 000
Dromadaire/Cheval Mine plomb (23x30.5cm 9x12in) Paris 2000

MONTFORT van Franz 1889-1960 **[47]**
$647 - €644 - **£403** - FF4 227
La mariée Huile/toile (51x36cm 20x14in) Bruxelles 1999
$832 - €992 - **£596** - FF6 504
Silhouette III Huile/carton (36.5x27cm 14x10in) Bruxelles 2000
$227 - €235 - **£150** - FF1 544
Nu cubiste Mine plomb (17x13.5cm 6x5in) Bruxelles 2000

MONTGOMERY Alfred 1857-1922 **[15]**
$2 500 - €2 136 - **£1 512** - FF14 011
Sheep and Chickens in the Barn Oil/board (112x36cm 44x35in) San-Francisco CA 1998

MONTGOMERY Anne 1908-1991 **[11]**
$1 894 - €2 116 - **£1 213** - FF13 878
Family Group Oil/board (50x61.5cm 19x24in) Malvern, Victoria 2000
$1 157 - €1 306 - **£814** - FF8 567
Three Women Oil/board (37x28cm 14x11in) Malvern, Victoria 2001
$736 - €831 - **£518** - FF5 452
Summer Cottage Gouache/paper (23.5x35.5cm 9x13in) Malvern, Victoria 2001

MONTHOLON de François Richard 1856-1940 **[60]**
$13 000 - €14 290 - **£8 330** - FF93 735
Washerwomen Along the River Oil/canvas (114.5x162.5cm 45x63in) New-York 2000
$2 121 - €1 982 - **£1 309** - FF13 660
Vase de fleurs Huile/toile (46.5x55.5cm 18x21in) Melun 1999
$674 - €767 - **£467** - FF5 030
Haus mit roten und weissen Rosen an einem sonnigen Tag Öl/Karton (24x32.5cm 9x12in) Lindau 2000

MONTI Cesare 1891-1959 **[31]**
- $2 280 - €1 970 - £1 520 - FF12 920
  Venezia Olio/tela (60x80cm 23x31in) Milano 1998

MONTI DI RAVENNA Gaetano 1776-1847 **[2]**
- $3 750 - €3 887 - £2 250 - FF25 500
  Testa di cavallo Plâtre (H75cm H29in) Prato 2000

MONTI IL BOLOGNESE Francesco 1685-1768 **[13]**
- $15 767 - €16 681 - £10 000 - FF109 417
  St. Geminianus exorcising Devils from the Daughter of the Emperor Oil/canvas (53x35cm 20x13in) London 2000
- $963 - €957 - £600 - FF6 275
  Madonna handing Rosaries to St. Dominic and Catherine Black & white chalks (27.5x19cm 10x7in) London 1999

MONTI IL BRESCIANINO Francesco 1646-1712 **[18]**
- $35 884 - €33 562 - £22 000 - FF220 154
  The Defeat of the Turks before Vienna Oil/canvas (95x194.5cm 37x76in) London 1998
- $14 943 - €16 040 - £10 000 - FF105 216
  Cavalry Battle near a Tower Oil/canvas (42.5x65cm 16x25in) London 2000
- $5 154 - €6 760 - £3 500 - FF37 912
  Turkish Troops and Artillery by Tent of a General/Christian General Black chalk (51x36cm 20x14in) London 1999

MONTI Nicolà 1780-1854 **[4]**
- $3 952 - €4 710 - £2 831 - FF30 894
  La nouvelle pantoufle Huile/toile (52x66cm 20x25in) Antwerpen 2000

MONTI Piero 1910-1994 **[37]**
- $275 - €285 - £165 - FF1 870
  Kilimangiaro Olio/cartone (36x50cm 14x19in) Vercelli 2000

MONTI Rafaello 1818-1881 **[3]**
- $30 479 - €30 714 - £19 000 - FF201 468
  Bust of a Veiled Lady Marble (H71cm H27in) London 2000

MONTICELLI Adolphe 1824-1886 **[380]**
- $15 000 - €16 488 - £9 612 - FF108 156
  The Music Party Oil/canvas (103x150cm 40x59in) New-York 2000
- $19 891 - €16 959 - £12 000 - FF111 244
  Rendez-vous sous la vasque fleurie Oil/panel (47x64cm 18x25in) London 1998
- $8 585 - €7 927 - £5 345 - FF12 500
  Elégante et Fiston Huile/bois (31x20cm 12x7in) Marseille 1999
- $2 865 - €2 439 - £1 705 - FF16 000
  Enfants aux armures Gouache/papier (26x22cm 10x8in) Marseille 1998

MONTIGNY Jenny 1875-1937 **[52]**
- $17 544 - €16 856 - £10 812 - FF110 568
  Jardin ensoleillé Huile/toile (41x44.5cm 16x17in) Bruxelles 1999
- $6 534 - €5 453 - £3 828 - FF35 772
  Bij de hoeve Oil/canvas (32x47cm 12x18in) Lokeren 1998
- $772 - €644 - £452 - FF4 227
  Meisjeshoofd Charcoal/paper (28x33.5cm 11x13in) Lokeren 2000

MONTIGNY Jules 1840-1899 **[29]**
- $2 024 - €1 983 - £1 256 - FF13 008
  Le vieux marché aux poissons à Furnes Huile/toile (50x60cm 19x23in) Bruxelles 1999

MONTINI Giovani XVII **[2]**
- $48 210 - €47 819 - £30 000 - FF313 674
  The Archangel Michael appearing to Hagar and Ishmael and Wildnerness Oil/canvas (127x171.5cm 50x67in) London 1999

MONTINI Umberto 1897-1978 **[12]**
- $1 100 - €1 140 - £660 - FF7 480
  Fiume d'inverno Olio/tela (45x70cm 17x27in) Milano 1999
- $780 - €674 - £390 - FF4 420
  Lago lombardo Olio/tavola (30x44cm 11x17in) Milano 1999

MONTJOYE de L. XVIII-XIX **[2]**
- $2 727 - €2 748 - £1 700 - FF18 026
  General Kléber Wounded at Alexandria in 1799 Ink (29x41cm 11x16in) London 2000

MONTLEVAULT Charles Joly, dit 1835-1897 **[25]**
- $1 528 - €1 753 - £1 045 - FF11 500
  Paysage marocain animé Huile/panneau (26x42cm 10x16in) Paris 2000

MONTMÉJA de A. XIX **[3]**
- $408 - €457 - £284 - FF3 000
  Maladies de peaux Tirage albuminé (12x9cm 4x3in) Paris 2001

MONTOBIO Guillaume 1883-1962 **[40]**
- $844 - €992 - £608 - FF6 504
  Paysage flamand Huile/toile (60x80cm 23x31in) Bruxelles 2001

MONTOYA Gustavo 1925 **[53]**
- $2 000 - €2 183 - £1 357 - FF14 317
  Nina en Azul Oil/canvas (54.5x44cm 21x17in) New-York 2000
- $1 600 - €1 511 - £993 - FF9 910
  Man in the Shadows Color lithograph (77x57.5cm 30x22in) Los-Angeles CA 1999

MONTPEZAT de Henri d'Ainecy, Cte 1817-1859 **[30]**
- $22 806 - €21 343 - £14 126 - FF140 000
  La promenade Huile/toile (104x131cm 40x51in) Paris 1999
- $38 000 - €40 789 - £25 429 - FF267 558
  The Morning Ride Oil/canvas (66x81.5cm 25x32in) New-York 2000
- $3 588 - €3 964 - £2 488 - FF26 000
  Cavalier en costume d'apparat Huile/bois (11x10cm 4x3in) Vernou en Sologne 2001

MONTVALLON de Valérie XX **[13]**
- $927 - €1 067 - £639 - FF7 000
  Ciel cousu II Technique mixte/toile (100x100cm 39x39in) Paris 2000

MONTYN Jean 1924-1988 **[45]**
- $108 - €109 - £67 - FF714
  Thailand Etching (65x50cm 25x19in) Amsterdam 2000

MONTZAIGLE de Edgard de St-Pierre 1867-? **[12]**
- $5 416 - €6 098 - £3 772 - FF40 000
  La loge Gouache (21x26cm 8x10in) Paris 2001

MONVOISIN Raymond A. Quinsac 1794-1870 **[12]**
- $33 956 - €39 637 - £23 972 - FF260 000
  L'âtre endormi Huile/toile (147x185cm 57x72in) Paris 2000
- $22 000 - €19 363 - £13 393 - FF127 012
  «Le 9 Thermidor» Oil/canvas (40x63.5cm 15x25in) New-York 1999
- $1 500 - €1 764 - £1 075 - FF11 570
  Portrait of a Lady Oil/canvas (35.5x27.5cm 13x10in) New-York 2001

M

MONY Luc XIX-XX **[1]**
🖼 **$4 676** - €4 116 - **£2 848** - FF27 000
Femme au rocher Bronze (H73cm H28in) Saint-Dié 1999

MOODY Barbara XX **[2]**
😊 **$1 400** - €1 654 - **£992** - FF10 851
Reincarnation I: Hollywood/A Diptych Oil/board (15x15cm 5x5in) Boston MA 2000

MOODY Fannie 1861-c.1948 **[32]**
😊 **$6 659** - €6 949 - **£4 200** - FF45 584
The Triumvirate (English Bulldog, Scottis Terrier, Welsh Terrier) Oil/canvas (40x61cm 16x24in) Canterbury, Kent 2000
😊 **$2 100** - €2 443 - **£1 500** - FF16 027
The stolen Bone Oil/canvas (31.5x42.5cm 12x16in) London 2001
✏ **$1 838** - €1 553 - **£1 100** - FF10 190
Terriers rabbiting Pastel/paper (55x45.5cm 21x17in) London 1998

MOODY John Charles 1884-1962 **[25]**
✏ **$476** - €457 - **£300** - FF2 995
Richmond, yorkshire Watercolour (40x53cm 16x21in) Aylsham, Norfolk 1999

MOOKHERJEA Sailoz 1907-1960 **[6]**
😊 **$600** - €709 - **£425** - FF4 650
Village Scene Watercolour/paper (14.5x12.5cm 5x4in) New-York 2000

MOON Carl 1879-1948 **[79]**
📷 **$1 800** - €1 980 - **£1 248** - FF12 985
«The Hunter» Silver print (48x33cm 19x13in) New-York 2001

MOON Sarah M. Hadengue 1938 **[20]**
📷 **$775** - €767 - **£484** - FF5 030
Rückenakt Photograph (60.5x40cm 23x15in) München 1999

MOONEY Carmel XX **[3]**
😊 **$2 841** - €3 301 - **£1 997** - FF21 655
Cattle and Sunlight Oil/canvas (25x25cm 9x9in) Dublin 2001

MOONEY John A. 1843-1918 **[1]**
😊 **$5 500** - €6 538 - **£3 810** - FF42 885
Basket of Apples Spilled Oil/canvas (56x91.5cm 22x36in) New-York 2000

MOONEY Martin 1960 **[11]**
😊 **$2 045** - €2 032 - **£1 274** - FF13 326
Huband Bridge, Dublin Oil/board (31x44cm 12x17in) Dublin 1999

MOONY Robert James Enraght 1879-1946 **[19]**
😊 **$3 041** - €2 598 - **£1 840** - FF17 043
The Young Laird Oil/canvas (137x77cm 53x30in) Edinburgh 1998

MOOR de Bob 1925-1992 **[23]**
✏ **$422** - €397 - **£260** - FF2 601
Meester Mus Crayon/papier (37x25cm 14x9in) Antwerpen 1999

MOOR de Carel 1656-1738 **[17]**
😊 **$17 724** - €17 406 - **£11 000** - FF114 178
Young Lady Playing the Theorbo-lute with a Negro Page Oil/panel (33.5x31cm 13x12in) London 1999

MOOR de Christiaan 1899-1981 **[23]**
😊 **$436** - €408 - **£271** - FF2 678
Madonna and Child Oil/canvas (100x80cm 39x31in) Amsterdam 1999

MOOR Karl 1904-1991 **[48]**
😊 **$814** - €813 - **£509** - FF5 336
Am Bahnübergang in Laufen, wartendes Mädchen mit Fahrrad Öl/Leinwand (53x54cm 20x21in) Zofingen 1999
😊 **$373** - €424 - **£259** - FF2 778
Stilleben mit blühendem Zweig Oil/panel (28x39cm 11x15in) Basel 2001

MOORE A. Harvey ?-1905 **[4]**
😊 **$289** - €347 - **£200** - FF2 273
Open Seascape with Tender to the Foreground and Fishing Vessels Oil/board (20x36cm 7x14in) Cambridge 2000

MOORE Abel Buel 1806-1879 **[1]**
😊 **$3 750** - €3 849 - **£2 354** - FF25 250
Adelson Early/His Wife Oil/canvas (71x59cm 28x23in) Bolton MA 2000

MOORE Albert Joseph 1841-1893 **[42]**
😊 **$57 523** - €68 412 - **£41 000** - FF448 753
Standing Female Figure Holding a Glass Pitcher Oil/canvas (27x10cm 10x3in) London 2000
✏ **$5 678** - €6 095 - **£3 800** - FF39 982
Study for «The Last Supper» in St.Alban's Church, Rochdale Pencil (24.5x60cm 9x23in) London 2000

MOORE Barlow 1834-1897 **[25]**
✏ **$1 260** - €1 200 - **£800** - FF7 869
In Full Sail/Nearing the Coast Watercolour (20x13cm 7x5in) Billingshurst, West-Sussex 1999

MOORE Benson Bond 1882-1974 **[37]**
😊 **$1 600** - €1 848 - **£1 120** - FF12 125
November Afternoon, Soldier's Home, D.C. Oil/board (45.5x35.5cm 17x13in) Bethesda MD 2001
😊 **$800** - €967 - **£568** - FF6 342
«Four Mile Run, Virginia»/«Villa Park, Washington, D.C.» Oil/board (10x14.5cm 3x5in) Bethesda MD 2000

MOORE Charles Bennette 1879-1939 **[24]**
📷 **$180** - €207 - **£122** - FF1 359
Brulatour Courtyard Photograph (34x23cm 13x9in) New-Orleans LA 2000

MOORE Claude T. Stanfield 1853-1901 **[44]**
😊 **$9 437** - €8 610 - **£5 800** - FF56 475
Frigate Outward Bound Off Shoeburyness Oil/canvas (51x76cm 20x29in) London 1998
😊 **$796** - €703 - **£480** - FF4 610
«The Dromede Passing the Recruiter's Ship» Oil/canvas (31x51.5cm 12x20in) Retford, Nottinghamshire 1998

MOORE David 1927 **[19]**
📷 **$836** - €870 - **£552** - FF5 705
Aboriginal Couple S.A Gelatin silver print (60x60cm 23x23in) Sydney 2001

MOORE Ernest 1865-? **[2]**
😊 **$2 800** - €2 479 - **£1 711** - FF16 259
A Pug Oil/canvas/board (28x21.5cm 11x8in) New-York 1999

MOORE Frank Montague 1877-1967 **[27]**
😊 **$1 600** - €1 903 - **£1 140** - FF12 481
Carmel Pines and Flowers Oil/masonite (49x74cm 19x29in) Portland OR 2000

MOORE Henry 1831-1895 **[163]**
😊 **$9 981** - €8 454 - **£6 000** - FF55 452
«Calming Down» Oil/canvas (89.5x135cm 35x53in) London 1998

$3 885 – €4 170 – **£2 600** – FF27 356
Fishing Fleet Returning to Whitby Oil/canvas
(50x74cm 19x29in) West-Yorkshire 2000
$1 341 – €1 555 – **£950** – FF10 198
Off the Yorkshire Coast Oil/canvas (28x48cm
11x19in) Tunbridge-Wells, Kent 2000
$1 416 – €1 653 – **£1 000** – FF10 846
Highland Valley Watercolour/paper (37x54.5cm
14x21in) London 2000

MOORE Henry 1898-1986 **[2001]**
$14 547 – €15 966 – **£9 373** – FF104 728
Ideas for Sculpture Mixed media (29.2x24cm
11x9in) Stockholm 2000
$760 000 – €729 903 – **£468 540** – FF4 787 848
Mother with Child on Lap Bronze (H81.5cm H32in)
New-York 1999
$35 000 – €33 656 – **£21 563** – FF220 769
Draped reclining Figure Bronze (9.5x17.5x7.5cm
3x6x2in) New-York 1999
$13 947 – €16 401 – **£10 000** – FF107 586
Mother and Child Wax crayon (24x26.5cm 9x10in)
London 2001
$1 000 – €1 037 – **£600** – FF6 800
Stone reclining Figure Litografia a colori (51x76cm
20x29in) Milano 2001

MOORE Henry P. XIX **[1]**
$5 200 – €4 346 – **£3 078** – FF28 509
**Contrabands Aboard the U.S.S Vermont, Port
Royal** Albumen print (12x20cm 5x8in) New-York 1998

MOORE John XIX **[1]**
$11 362 – €10 926 – **£7 000** – FF71 668
Blackshore, Southwold Oil/canvas (45.5x60.5cm
17x23in) London 1999

MOORE Leslie L. Hardy 1907-1997 **[33]**
$372 – €450 – **£260** – FF2 952
Norfolk Marsh, River Bure Watercolour/paper
(38x50cm 15x20in) Aylsham, Norfolk 2000

MOORE Nelson Augustus 1824-1902 **[22]**
$4 200 – €4 570 – **£2 810** – FF29 572
Boating on the Lake Oil/canvas (36.5x62.5cm
14x24in) New-York 2000
$1 100 – €1 148 – **£731** – FF7 531
Landscape, Cows grazing in Pasture Oil/canvas
(36x28cm 14x11in) Plainville CT 2001
$3 000 – €3 305 – **£2 001** – FF21 681
Along the Hudson Pencil/paper (21x38cm 8x15in)
Portsmouth NH 2000

MOORE OF IPSWICH John 1820-1902 **[78]**
$4 572 – €3 916 – **£2 700** – FF25 689
The Fishing Fleet on a Calm Sea Oil/canvas
(35.5x51cm 13x20in) Ipswich 1998
$2 411 – €2 443 – **£1 500** – FF16 025
View of Tantallon Castle Oil/canvas (15x30cm
6x12in) Aylsham, Norfolk 2000

MOORE R.H. XIX **[1]**
$9 713 – €10 427 – **£6 500** – FF68 394
Champion Bourbon, a Basser Hound Oil/canvas
(47x61cm 18x24in) London 2000

MOORE Rubens Arthur XIX-XX **[13]**
$3 048 – €3 071 – **£1 900** – FF20 146
A Venetian Backwater Oil/canvas (51x35.5cm
20x13in) London 2000

MOORE Thomas Cooper 1827-1901 **[4]**
$17 642 – €17 452 – **£11 000** – FF114 479
Pool of London Oil/canvas (63.5x114.5cm 25x45in)
London 1999

MOORE William XIX **[7]**
$13 000 – €14 327 – **£8 648** – FF93 982
Street Scene Oil/board (61x88cm 24x35in)
Portsmouth NH 2000

MOORE William, Snr. 1790-1851 **[7]**
$1 079 – €1 209 – **£750** – FF7 930
**Study of a Man and Wife seated in a Drawing
Room reding a Newspaper** Watercolour
(35.5x29.5cm 13x11in) Newbury, Berkshire 2001

MOORE-PARK Carlton 1877-1956 **[8]**
$607 – €607 – **£380** – FF3 983
The Dispute Ink (34.5x25cm 13x9in) London 1999

MOORMAN Charlotte 1933-1991 **[3]**
$1 680 – €1 451 – **£1 120** – FF9 520
Elm Cello Multiplo (105x75cm 41x29in) Prato 1998

MOORMANS Frans 1831-1893 **[32]**
$32 500 – €28 039 – **£19 607** – FF183 927
Dutch Gallery at the Louvre, Paris Oil/canvas
(114x146cm 44x57in) New-York 1998
$3 996 – €4 573 – **£2 748** – FF30 000
Troubadours Huile/panneau (54x45cm 21x17in)
Bordeaux 2000
$2 159 – €1 848 – **£1 300** – FF12 122
The Violonist Oil/panel (41.5x32cm 16x12in) London
1998

MOOS Carl Franz 1878-1959 **[40]**
$1 100 – €1 199 – **£761** – FF7 862
«Kandersteg» Poster (100x64cm 39x25in) New-York
2001

MOOS Friedrich 1822-1895 **[6]**
$5 131 – €5 087 – **£3 133** – FF33 369
Orchideen im Wald Öl/Karton (90x70cm 35x27in)
Wien 1999
$2 122 – €1 817 – **£1 242** – FF11 922
Pendants, Feldhasen, Fasane Oil/panel (8x12.3cm
3x4in) Wien 1999

MOOS von Max 1903-1979 **[241]**
$5 569 – €5 612 – **£3 471** – FF36 810
Der Denker Tempera (57x43cm 22x16in) Zürich 2000
$1 895 – €1 875 – **£1 181** – FF12 297
Ohne Titel Tempera (42x30cm 16x11in) Luzern 1999
$407 – €407 – **£254** – FF2 668
Komposition Schlacht Indian ink/paper (59x41.5cm
23x16in) Zofingen 1999

MOOY Jaap 1915-1987 **[19]**
$3 803 – €3 630 – **£2 376** – FF23 812
Animal Gouache/paper (48.5x63.5cm 19x25in)
Amsterdam 1999

MOOY Jan 1776-1847 **[4]**
$2 902 – €2 723 – **£1 794** – FF17 859
The «Abel Tasman» under Full Sail Watercolour
(37.5x52.5cm 14x20in) Amsterdam 1999

MOPOPE Stephen (Kiowa) 1898-1974 **[6]**
$500 – €534 – **£340** – FF3 504
Indian Warrior with Peyote Rattle
Watercolour/paper (26x21cm 10x8in) Cloudcroft NM
2001

MORA Francis Luis 1874-1940 **[133]**
$14 000 – €15 028 – **£9 368** – FF98 574
**When Play and Fancy Rule the Board'Tis Joy to
Dine** Oil/canvas (91.5x141cm 36x55in) New-York 2000
$4 000 – €4 549 – **£2 794** – FF29 840
Tale of Cinderella Oil/canvas (121x91cm 48x36in)
Mystic CT 2000

M

$15 000 - €17 587 - **£10 791** - FF115 366
«In the Shadow of the Main Sail» Oil/canvas/board
(19x23.5cm 7x9in) New-York 2001

$700 - €654 - **£436** - FF4 290
Rescue at Sea Pastel/paper (28x50cm 11x20in)
Mystic CT 1999

$500 - €467 - **£311** - FF3 064
Picnic Scene Monotype (18x26cm 7x10in) Mystic
CT 1999

MORA Joseph Jacinto 1876-1947 [6]

$3 000 - €3 501 - **£2 055** - FF22 968
Portrait Navajo on Horse in Traditional Dress
Watercolour/paper (45x27cm 18x11in) Cloudcroft NM
2000

MORA Mirka Madeleine 1928 [17]

$317 - €377 - **£219** - FF2 475
Angelic Child Watercolour/paper (57.5x40cm
22x15in) Sydney 2000

MORACH Otto 1887-1973 [51]

$12 376 - €12 471 - **£7 714** - FF81 802
Bei Marseille Öl/Leinwand (58x68cm 22x26in) Zürich
2000

$17 920 - €20 944 - **£12 793** - FF137 385
Selbstbildnis Öl/Leinwand (40x32cm 15x12in)
Zürich 2001

$479 - €557 - **£336** - FF3 651
Tanzende Figuren Woodcut (40.5x28.5cm 15x11in)
Luzern 2001

MORADO José Chavez 1909 [30]

$3 980 - €3 445 - **£2 400** - FF22 600
Bodegón con peras y plátano Oleo/lienzo
(30x40cm 11x15in) México 1998

$2 752 - €3 228 - **£1 980** - FF21 175
Máscaras Acuarela (35.5x40cm 13x15in) México
2001

MORAGAS Y TORRES Tomás 1837-1906 [12]

$10 257 - €11 810 - **£7 000** - FF77 468
Guarding the City Watercolour, gouache/paper
(77x57cm 30x22in) London 2000

MORAIN Pierre 1821-1893 [4]

$4 481 - €4 812 - **£3 000** - FF31 564
**Grapes in a Basket with a Dish of
Peaches/Wine Flask on a Table** Oil/canvas
(54x65cm 21x25in) London 2000

MORAIS Graça 1948 [1]

$2 728 - €3 091 - **£1 922** - FF20 274
Sem título Pastel (63x74cm 24x29in) Lisboa 2001

MORAÏTES Petros c.1835-1905 [2]

$2 573 - €3 068 - **£1 834** - FF20 123
Griechenland Albumen print (36x49cm 14x19in)
München 2000

MORALES Armando 1927 [227]

$60 000 - €58 379 - **£36 930** - FF382 938
Seated Nude Oil/canvas (165x131cm 64x51in) New-
York 1999

$65 000 - €69 771 - **£43 498** - FF457 665
Rapido en aguas azules, México Oil/canvas
(54x72.5cm 21x28in) New-York 2000

$16 000 - €13 951 - **£9 673** - FF91 515
Figuras Oil/paper (38.5x30.5cm 15x12in) New-York
1998

$48 000 - €46 703 - **£29 544** - FF306 350
Mujeres Pastel/paper (51x76cm 20x29in) New-York
1999

MORALES Darío 1944-1988 [26]

$39 000 - €41 862 - **£26 098** - FF274 599
Mujer lavandose los pies Bronze (H34.5cm H13in)
New-York 2000

$4 000 - €3 882 - **£2 490** - FF25 466
Desnudo Graphite (43.5x54.5cm 17x21in) New-York
1999

MORALES de Luis, El Divino 1509-1586 [17]

$350 000 - €374 391 - **£238 630** - FF2 455 845
Christ as the Man of Sorrows Oil/panel (49x33cm
19x12in) New-York 2001

$412 328 - €462 316 - **£280 000** - FF3 032 596
The Pietà Oil/panel (43.5x31cm 17x12in) London
2000

MORALES Eduardo 1868-1938 [18]

$6 500 - €6 366 - **£4 188** - FF41 761
Quitrín y Jinete Oil/canvas (43.5x56cm 17x22in)
New-York 1999

$4 000 - €3 454 - **£2 440** - FF22 655
Paisaje Oil/canvas (27x40cm 10x15in) Miami FL 1999

MORALES Rodolfo 1925-2001 [34]

$42 500 - €37 058 - **£25 695** - FF243 087
Sin Título Oil/canvas (148x117cm 58x46in) New-York
1998

$10 000 - €10 734 - **£6 692** - FF70 410
Sin título Oil/canvas (80x100cm 31x39in) New-York
2000

$990 - €1 162 - **£712** - FF7 623
Las musas de la música Litografía (52x72cm
20x28in) México 2001

MORALES Ruiz XIX-XX [3]

$5 055 - €5 509 - **£3 500** - FF36 134
The Musician Oil/canvas (58x37cm 22x14in) London
2001

MORALT Willy 1884-1947 [139]

$9 182 - €8 436 - **£5 641** - FF55 339
**Der Sonntagsspaziergang/Mutter mit zwei
Kindern und Hund** Oil/panel (37x54cm 14x21in)
Konstanz 1999

$7 482 - €8 443 - **£5 263** - FF55 383
Begrüssungsszene in einer Landschaft Oil/panel
(27x38cm 10x14in) Bern 2001

$1 251 - €1 431 - **£860** - FF9 390
Schloss Karneid (?) in Südtirol Gouache/paper
(73x51.5cm 28x20in) München 2000

MORAN Earl 1893-1984 [7]

$4 000 - €4 578 - **£2 751** - FF30 027
Portrait of Rita Hayworth, Nude Oil/canvas
(44x89cm 17x35in) Milwaukee WI 2000

MORAN Edward 1829-1901 [124]

$13 200 - €13 093 - **£8 214** - FF85 887
Marine Sunset Oil/canvas (49x73cm 19x29in)
Timonium MD 1999

$8 000 - €7 493 - **£4 918** - FF49 152
«Sunset Marine» Oil/board (25.5x46cm 10x18in)
New-York 1999

$1 500 - €1 654 - **£1 015** - FF10 851
Looking Out to Sea Watercolour/paper (38x54cm
14x21in) New-York 2000

MORAN Edward Percy 1862-1935 [68]

$2 400 - €2 576 - **£1 606** - FF16 898
**Farewell to his Officers-Leaving NY for
Mt.Vernon** Oil/panel (49x34cm 19x13in) Chicago IL
2000

$1 700 - €1 501 - **£1 040** - FF10 191
Heading for Home on a Winter Evening Oil/can-
vas (25.5x21cm 10x8in) Boston MA 1999

MORAN John 1831-1903 **[9]**
📷 **$24 000** - €22 566 - **£14 860** - FF148 024
Photographs from the Darien Expedition
Albumen print (20x27cm 8x11in) New-York 1999

MORAN Leon John 1864-1941 **[26]**
🖎 **$3 250** - €3 696 - **£2 270** - FF24 245
Dutch Woman at the Shore Oil/canvas (76x51cm 30x20in) Chicago IL 2000

MORAN Mary Nimmo 1842-1899 **[9]**
▦ **$200** - €233 - **£142** - FF1 530
California Forest after T.Moran Etching (28x20cm 11x8in) St. Louis MO 2000

MORAN Patricia XX **[1]**
🖎 **$4 568** - €4 291 - **£2 753** - FF28 150
Still life of Sunflowers Oil/canvas (75x90cm 29x35in) Sydney 1999

MORAN Peter 1841-1914 **[47]**
🖎 **$4 500** - €4 091 - **£2 710** - FF26 833
Heading Home Oil/canvas (33x58cm 13x23in) Hayden ID 1998
🖎 **$4 620** - €4 294 - **£2 831** - FF28 170
Couple of Surprised Cows in a Stream Oil/canvas (40x30cm 16x12in) Portland ME 1998
🖎 **$1 450** - €1 548 - **£988** - FF10 157
River Landscape Pencil (31x23cm 12x9in) Philadelphia PA 2001
▦ **$70** - €82 - **£49** - FF539
The Returning Herd, after Voltz F.J Etching (28x22cm 11x8in) Philadelphia PA 2000

MORAN Thomas Sydney 1837-1926 **[204]**
🖎 **$130 000** - €123 714 - **£81 315** - FF811 512
The Cavern, California Coast Oil/canvas (35.5x51cm 13x20in) New-York 1999
🖎 **$12 000** - €10 253 - **£7 261** - FF74 252
Autumn Oil/canvas (23x33cm 9x12in) San-Francisco CA 1999
🖎 **$6 000** - €6 720 - **£4 168** - FF44 083
River Scene based on Hiawathan Story by Longfellow Indian ink (18x25cm 7x10in) St. Louis MO 2001
▦ **$1 900** - €1 825 - **£1 171** - FF11 969
Sailboat in the Waves, After Chase Etching (61x44cm 24x17in) New-York 1999

MORANDI Giorgio 1890-1964 **[762]**
🖎 **$350 000** - €362 829 - **£210 000** - FF2 380 000
Paesaggio Olio/tela (62x44cm 24x17in) Milano 2000
🖎 **$280 000** - €265 057 - **£173 908** - FF1 738 660
Natura morta Oil/canvas (26x35cm 10x13in) New-York 1999
🖎 **$11 720** - €13 783 - **£8 404** - FF90 411
Fiori Pencil (24x16.5cm 9x6in) Bern 2001
▦ **$13 357** - €12 312 - **£8 000** - FF80 759
Natura morta Etching (35.5x35cm 13x13in) London 1998

MORANDINI IL POPPI Francesco 1544-1597 **[3]**
🖎 **$2 400** - €2 633 - **£1 594** - FF17 272
The Annunciation to Zacharias, after Andrea del Sarto Black chalk (27.5x30.5cm 10x12in) New-York 2000

MORANDO Pietro 1892-1980 **[114]**
🖎 **$2 100** - €2 177 - **£1 260** - FF14 280
Riviera Ligure Olio/tela (40x50cm 15x19in) Vercelli 2000
🖎 **$1 800** - €1 866 - **£1 080** - FF12 240
Paesaggio urbano Olio/tavola (40.5x24cm 15x9in) Vercelli 2001

🖎 **$800** - €829 - **£480** - FF5 440
Pifferaio Tecnica mista/carta (70x50cm 27x19in) Vercelli 1999
▦ **$250** - €259 - **£150** - FF1 700
Fratelloni/Cantastorie con chitarra/Cantastorie Litografia (78x53cm 30x20in) Vercelli 1999

MORANG Alfred G. 1901-1958 **[7]**
🖎 **$2 600** - €2 227 - **£1 563** - FF14 611
Cafe Scene Watercolour (23x22cm 9x9in) Cincinnati OH 1998

MORANG Dorothy 1906-? **[5]**
🖎 **$3 750** - €3 581 - **£2 308** - FF23 491
Space Motion Oil/canvas (55x78cm 22x31in) Cincinnati OH 1999

MORANI Vincenzo 1809-1870 **[12]**
🖎 **$3 000** - €3 110 - **£1 800** - FF20 400
Dama pensierosa Olio/tela (72x61cm 28x24in) Roma 1999
🖎 **$3 000** - €3 110 - **£1 800** - FF20 400
Ester e Assuero Olio/tela (30x37.5cm 11x14in) Roma 1999
🖎 **$450** - €466 - **£270** - FF3 060
Il banchetto di Erode (da Rubens) Acquarello/carta (22x28cm 8x11in) Roma 1999

MORAS Walter 1854-1925 **[107]**
🖎 **$2 179** - €1 791 - **£1 265** - FF11 745
Frühling in Thüringen Öl/Leinwand (81x60cm 31x23in) Berlin 1999
🖎 **$821** - €767 - **£496** - FF5 030
Spreewaldhäuser und Schuppen Oil/panel (25x40cm 9x15in) Berlin 1999

MORAT Johann Martin 1805-1867 **[10]**
🖎 **$2 989** - €2 554 - **£1 756** - FF16 756
Blick auf Schönau im Schwarzwald Mixed media (31x43cm 12x16in) Staufen 1999
🖎 **$2 673** - €2 556 - **£1 628** - FF16 769
Blick auf Lenzkirch, im Vordergrund Schäferszene Mischtechnik/Papier (22.5x36cm 8x14in) Staufen 1999

MORATH-MILLER Inge 1923 **[39]**
📷 **$1 151** - €1 117 - **£716** - FF7 328
Wien, Strudelhofstiege Gelatin silver print (32.8x22.6cm 12x8in) Berlin 1999

MORAZZONE Pier Francesco 1571/73-1626 **[15]**
🖎 **$271 000** - €304 898 - **£186 600** - FF2 000 000
Saint Pierre/Saint Paul Huile/panneau (75x32cm 29x12in) Lille 2000
🖎 **$23 000** - €20 115 - **£13 965** - FF132 337
Angel in Flight, Hands Raised in Grief Red chalk (42x28cm 16x11in) New-York 1999

MORBELLI Angelo 1853-1919 **[56]**
🖎 **$432 027** - €428 929 - **£270 000** - FF2 813 589
La prima messa a Burano Oil/canvas (71x101cm 27x39in) London 1999
🖎 **$37 500** - €38 874 - **£22 500** - FF255 000
Il capitello Olio/tela (31x48cm 12x18in) Roma 2000
🖎 **$92 500** - €95 890 - **£55 500** - FF629 000
Sogno e realtà Carboncino (80x336cm 31x132in) Milano 2000

MORBELLI Marc 1936 **[7]**
🖎 **$1 278** - €1 372 - **£855** - FF9 000
La fourmi Sculpture (15x10cm 5x3in) Monte-Carlo 2000

M

MORBY Walter J. XIX [3]
- ✎ $2 380 – €2 769 – **£1 700** – FF18 163
  Over the Brook/Through the Brook/Lost the Scent/Going into Cover Watercolour (36x53.5cm 14x21in) London 2001

MORCAY Charles XX [1]
- ☞ $4 027 – €4 006 – **£2 500** – FF26 278
  The Laundry Woman Oil/panel (39x30.5cm 15x12in) Billingshurst, West-Sussex 1999

MORCHAIN Paul 1876-1939 [219]
- ☞ $594 – €686 – **£415** – FF4 500
  Bateaux à marée basse Huile/toile (50x65cm 19x25in) Paris 2001
- ☞ $277 – €320 – **£194** – FF2 100
  Le mouillage Huile/carton (15.5x18.5cm 6x7in) Paris 2001
- ✎ $198 – €229 – **£138** – FF1 500
  Paysage de campagne Gouache/carton (13.5x16cm 5x6in) Paris 2001

MORCILLO RAYA Gabriel 1888-1973 [25]
- ☞ $41 400 – €36 130 – **£25 200** – FF237 000
  La vendimia Oleo/lienzo (115x111cm 45x43in) Madrid 1998
- ☞ $2 280 – €2 403 – **£1 440** – FF15 760
  Odalisca Oleo/lienzo (70x60cm 27x23in) Madrid 2000

MORDEN Robert XVII [168]
- ▥ $95 – €103 – **£65** – FF673
  England Engraving (37x43cm 14x16in) Swindon, Wiltshire 2001

MORDT Gustaf Adolf 1826-1856 [15]
- ☞ $6 552 – €7 258 – **£4 446** – FF47 610
  Gutt ved fossefall i fjellandskap Oil/canvas (76x90cm 29x35in) Oslo 2000
- ☞ $998 – €942 – **£620** – FF6 181
  Norsk fjeldlandskab Oil/canvas (24x32cm 9x12in) København 1999

MORÉ CORS Mariano 1899-1974 [1]
- ☞ $14 025 – €16 518 – **£9 900** – FF108 350
  Valle de Teberga, Peña de Sobía Oleo/lienzo (85.5x119cm 33x46in) Madrid 2001

MORE Germaine XX [38]
- ✎ $212 – €198 – **£130** – FF1 300
  Vue du balcon Pastel/papier (24x32cm 9x12in) Vannes 1999

MORE Jacob c.1740-1793 [15]
- ☞ $14 726 – €16 511 – **£10 000** – FF108 307
  View of Lake Albano Oil/canvas (66x89cm 25x35in) London 2000
- ☞ $3 250 – €3 369 – **£1 950** – FF22 100
  Veduta di Terracina/Il lago di Averno Acquarello/carta (34x44.5cm 13x17in) Roma 2000

MOREA Nicola 1943 [2]
- ☞ $500 – €518 – **£300** – FF3 400
  «Percorso stellare» Smalto/tela (41x53cm 16x20in) Prato 2001

MOREAU & LECOURTIER Hippolyte & Prosper 1832/55-1927/24 [2]
- ⚘ $11 913 – €12 577 – **£7 870** – FF82 500
  Piqueur au relais Bronze (H78cm H30in) Soissons 2000

MOREAU Achille c.1800-c.1845 [2]
- ▥ $1 248 – €1 220 – **£791** – FF8 000
  Air/Eau/Feu/Terre Aquatinte (26.5x36.5cm 10x14in) Paris 1999

MOREAU Adrien 1843-1906 [66]
- ☞ $31 000 – €26 745 – **£18 702** – FF175 438
  Day of Sporting Oil/panel (71x91.5cm 27x36in) New-York 1998
- ☞ $3 884 – €3 735 – **£2 397** – FF24 502
  Dame am Flussufer Öl/Leinwand (33x20cm 12x7in) Bern 1999
- ✎ $561 – €640 – **£391** – FF4 200
  Le malaise du gentilhomme Encre (26x18cm 10x7in) Paris 2001

MOREAU Auguste 1834-1917 [226]
- ⚘ $7 263 – €8 537 – **£5 264** – FF56 000
  Jeune femme à l'oiseau Marbre (H84cm H33in) Vendôme 2001
- ⚘ $1 384 – €1 611 – **£975** – FF10 569
  L'Aurore Bronze (H49cm H19in) Bruxelles 2001

MOREAU Auguste, Louis 1855-1919 [70]
- ⚘ $6 700 – €7 622 – **£4 650** – FF50 000
  «Pris dans les filets» Bronze (H96cm H37in) Royan 2000
- ⚘ $1 260 – €1 201 – **£760** – FF7 880
  El Día/La Noche, jarrones Metal (H49cm H19in) Madrid 1999
- ✎ $4 325 – €4 116 – **£2 689** – FF27 000
  Le jeune Alcibiade rentrant à Athènes victorieux Lavis (62x97cm 24x38in) Rouen 1999

MOREAU Charles 1830-1891 [13]
- ☞ $4 009 – €3 854 – **£2 500** – FF25 279
  Cottage Interior with a Lady Spinning Wool Oil/panel (46x37.5cm 18x14in) West-Yorkshire 1999
- ☞ $2 840 – €3 049 – **£1 900** – FF20 000
  Élégante au miroir Huile/toile (46x24cm 18x9in) Blois 2000

MOREAU Clément 1903-1988 [15]
- ▥ $456 – €511 – **£317** – FF3 353
  Ohne Titel Woodcut (28x22cm 11x8in) Berlin 2001

MOREAU DE TOURS Georges 1848-1901 [48]
- ☞ $100 000 – €95 020 – **£60 840** – FF623 290
  Heinrich Heine and the Muse of Poetry Oil/canvas (152.4x195.5cm 59x76in) New-York 1999
- ☞ $5 214 – €5 031 – **£3 296** – FF33 000
  La joueuse de mandoline Huile/toile (93x65cm 36x25in) Paris 1999
- ☞ $701 – €793 – **£473** – FF5 200
  Homme assis à l'oiseau Huile/panneau (30x18cm 11x7in) Toulouse 2000
- ✎ $1 091 – €1 220 – **£759** – FF8 000
  L'assassinat d'Henri IV Grisaille (28x23cm 11x9in) Toulouse 2001

MOREAU Gustave 1826-1898 [70]
- ☞ $25 920 – €30 490 – **£18 580** – FF200 000
  Break à quatre chevaux Huile/toile (34x50.5cm 13x19in) Paris 2001
- ☞ $192 012 – €190 635 – **£120 000** – FF1 250 484
  La Naissance de Vénus Oil/canvas (21x26cm 8x10in) London 1999
- ⚘ $4 402 – €4 726 – **£2 945** – FF31 000
  Jeune fille à l'oiseau Bronze (H62cm H24in) Bordeaux 2000
- ✎ $280 959 – €240 050 – **£170 000** – FF1 574 625
  L'Enlèvement de Ganymède Watercolour, gouache/paper (58.5x45.5cm 23x17in) London 1998

MOREAU Henri 1869-1943 [20]
- ☞ $949 – €1 041 – **£630** – FF6 829
  Jeune femme en déshabillé Huile/toile (52x41cm 20x16in) Bruxelles 2000

MOREAU Hippolyte, Hip. 1832-1927 **[164]**
- $5 295 - €5 336 - **£3 300** - FF35 000
  Jeune femme tenant un oiseau Marbre (H33cm H84in) Lyon 2000
- $2 920 - €2 479 - **£1 740** - FF16 260
  Cupidon, d'après Bouguereau Marbre (H75cm H29in) Bruxelles 1998

MOREAU Jacques Gaston 1903-1994 **[34]**
- $365 - €351 - **£227** - FF2 300
  Bateaux échoués, Concarneau Aquarelle/papier (25x33cm 9x12in) Paris 1999

MOREAU Jean-Michel le jeune 1741-1814 **[79]**
- $3 000 - €2 949 - **£1 927** - FF19 343
  A Sacrificial Procession Ink (28.5x37cm 11x14in) New-York 1999
- $223 - €215 - **£139** - FF1 413
  Le Bal masqué, after P.-L. Moreau Engraving (51x40cm 20x15in) Haarlem 1999

MOREAU Louis Gabriel l'Aîné 1740-1806 **[82]**
- $11 502 - €12 348 - **£7 695** - FF81 000
  Paysage de rivière avec un moulin à eau et des lavandières Huile/toile (37x46.5cm 14x18in) Paris 2000
- $2 661 - €2 973 - **£1 803** - FF19 500
  Paysage fluvial avec berger et troupeau sur un bac Huile/panneau (15.5x19.5cm 6x7in) Paris 2000
- $3 397 - €3 811 - **£2 377** - FF25 000
  Pêcheurs au bord d'un fleuve, au pied d'une montagne Aquarelle (19x27.5cm 7x10in) Paris 2001

MOREAU Mathurin 1822-1912 **[451]**
- $8 500 - €9 378 - **£5 621** - FF61 513
  Figural Group, Les Armes d'Achilles Bronze (H107cm H42in) New-York 2000
- $2 250 - €2 652 - **£1 550** - FF17 393
  «La Rosée» Bronze (H67cm H26in) New-York 2000

MOREAU Max 1902-1992 **[93]**
- $2 220 - €2 479 - **£1 549** - FF16 260
  Nature morte au panier de fruits Huile/toile (92x73cm 36x28in) Bruxelles 2001
- $3 260 - €3 811 - **£2 327** - FF25 000
  Portrait d'homme Aquarelle (59x45cm 23x17in) Paris 2001

MOREAU-NÉLATON Étienne Adolphe 1859-1927 **[45]**
- $6 830 - €7 622 - **£4 750** - FF50 000
  Barque sur la plage Huile/toile (65x81cm 25x31in) Paris 2001
- $1 571 - €1 844 - **£1 108** - FF12 097
  Ung dam med apa Pastel/paper (63x48cm 24x18in) Stockholm 2000
- $800 - €892 - **£523** - FF5 854
  «Les Arts de la Femme» Poster (118.5x80cm 46x31in) New-York 2000

MOREAU-VAUTHIER Augustin Edme 1831-1893 **[21]**
- $10 506 - €10 367 - **£6 473** - FF68 000
  Allégorie de la fortune Bronze (H128cm H50in) Paris 1999
- $2 435 - €2 897 - **£1 736** - FF19 000
  Allégorie de la Fortune Bronze (H65cm H25in) Chambéry 2000

MOREAU-VAUTHIER Paul G. 1871-1936 **[22]**
- $1 711 - €1 601 - **£1 048** - FF10 500
  Lampe, femme tenant un abat-jour formant réflecteur Bronze (H42cm H16in) Neuilly-sur-Seine 1998

MOREELSE Paulus 1571-1638 **[33]**
- $23 346 - €22 949 - **£15 000** - FF150 534
  Portrait of a Gentleman, Head and Shoulders, wearing a Lace Collar Oil/canvas (55.5x46cm 21x18in) London 1999
- $340 - €366 - **£228** - FF2 400
  Amour dansant avec deux nymphes Estampe (21.5x29.5cm 8x11in) Paris 2000

MOREL Casparus Johannes 1798-1861 **[11]**
- $2 902 - €2 723 - **£1 794** - FF17 859
  Low Tide, Moored Fishing Pinks by a Landing Stage Oil/panel (31x41cm 12x16in) Amsterdam 1999

MOREL DE TANGRY XIX-XX **[31]**
- $301 - €257 - **£180** - FF1 685
  «La Côte d'Azur» Poster (108x78cm 42x30in) London 1998

MOREL Émile 1918 **[44]**
- $301 - €305 - **£187** - FF2 000
  Trouville, scène de plage Huile/panneau (19x27cm 7x10in) Soissons 2000

MOREL François c.1768-c.1840 **[12]**
- $4 192 - €3 811 - **£2 572** - FF25 000
  Marchande de fleurs à Venise Huile/panneau (42x21cm 16x8in) Paris 1999

MOREL Henriette XX **[7]**
- $3 872 - €3 201 - **£2 272** - FF21 000
  Femmes à l'éventail noir Huile/toile (88x115cm 34x45in) Lyon 1998

MOREL Jan Baptiste 1662-1732 **[7]**
- $16 374 - €15 184 - **£10 000** - FF99 602
  Garland of Tulipes, Irises, Roses, Surrounding the Madonna and Child Oil/panel (104x73cm 40x28in) London 1998
- $23 591 - €20 000 - **£14 000** - FF131 194
  Poppy, a Rose, a Crocus and Other Flowers Oil/panel (36x30cm 14x11in) London 1998

MOREL Jan Evert 1777-1808 **[11]**
- $2 400 - €2 032 - **£1 436** - FF13 326
  Sheep Grazing Under a Tree Oil/canvas (28x37.5cm 11x14in) New-York 1998

MOREL Jan Evert II 1835-1905 **[109]**
- $5 523 - €5 206 - **£3 339** - FF34 146
  Ramasseurs de bois mort dans un paysage hivernal Huile/toile (55x77cm 21x30in) Antwerpen 1999
- $4 179 - €3 534 - **£2 499** - FF23 182
  Travellers with a Donkey in a Wooded River Landscape Oil/panel (14x18cm 5x7in) Amsterdam 1998

MOREL Louis Fernand 1887-1975 **[8]**
- $12 000 - €13 169 - **£7 726** - FF86 385
  Danseuse au tambourin II Bronze relief (60x43cm 23x16in) New-York 1999

MOREL Louise 1898-1974 **[9]**
- $1 732 - €1 677 - **£1 097** - FF11 000
  «Aïcha» Huile/toile (54x65cm 21x25in) Paris 1999

MOREL-FATIO Antoine Léon 1810-1871 **[51]**
- $63 216 - €53 540 - **£38 000** - FF351 199
  L'arrivée sur la Rade de Toulon du Prince Président, Napoléon III Oil/canvas (129.5x227cm 50x89in) London 1998
- $6 669 - €6 403 - **£4 183** - FF42 000
  Visite de l'Escadre Huile/toile (55x80cm 21x31in) Lyon 1999

M

MORELL

$2 940 - €3 356 - **£2 042** - FF22 012
Mariner Oil/canvas (24x37cm 9x14in) København 2000

$414 - €457 - **£287** - FF3 000
Trois mâts français en mer Aquarelle/papier (25x34cm 9x13in) Nantes 2001

MORELL Abelardo 1948 **[6]**

$3 600 - €3 363 - **£2 175** - FF22 057
Camera Obscura Image of the Sea in Attic/Dictionnary Silver print (45x56cm 18x22in) New-York 1999

MORELL Josep Marcia 1899-1949 **[14]**

$547 - €625 - **£380** - FF4 100
«Playas de Levante» Affiche (100x62.5cm 39x24in) Paris 2000

MORELL Pit 1939 **[74]**

$73 - €77 - **£46** - FF503
3.Mai in Hepstedt Etching, aquatint in colors (45.5x32cm 17x12in) Bremen 2000

MORELL Y ORLANDIS Fausto XIX-XX **[2]**

$16 896 - €15 857 - **£10 560** - FF104 016
Angeles jugando con cabras, conejos, párajos, bolas de nieve y carros Oleo/lienzo (80x467.5cm 31x184in) Palma de Mallorca 1999

MORELLET François 1926 **[85]**

$3 278 - €3 964 - **£2 290** - FF26 000
Géométrie 56 Technique mixte (50x39cm 19x15in) Paris 2000

$4 514 - €5 368 - **£3 217** - FF35 215
«2 trames 2+2» Sculpture (60x60cm 23x23in) München 2000

$2 760 - €3 049 - **£1 914** - FF20 000
Projet pi piquant n° 7 Encre (36x36cm 14x14in) Paris 2001

$317 - €340 - **£212** - FF2 232
Untitled Screenprint (61.5x61.5cm 24x24in) Amsterdam 2000

MORELLI Domenico 1826-1901 **[53]**

$5 500 - €5 702 - **£3 300** - FF37 400
Ritratto di giovane donna Olio/tavola (41x21.5cm 16x8in) Milano 2000

$720 - €933 - **£540** - FF6 120
Donna araba Inchiostro/carta (30x21cm 11x8in) Torino 2000

MORELLI F. XIX **[1]**

$12 000 - €11 444 - **£7 304** - FF75 070
Dancing Girl Marble (H95.5cm H37in) New-York 1999

MORELLO Federico 1885-? **[5]**

$1 040 - €1 348 - **£780** - FF8 840
«Riposo» Olio/tavola (68x59cm 26x23in) Torino 2000

MORENI Mattia 1920-1999 **[91]**

$34 200 - €29 545 - **£17 100** - FF193 800
«Ancora un'immagine lanciata» Olio/tela (130x130cm 51x51in) Milano 1999

$7 200 - €9 330 - **£5 400** - FF61 200
Regressito consapevole «Le cose, gli oggetti pensano in silenzio» Olio/tela (46x65cm 18x25in) Milano 2000

$2 250 - €2 332 - **£1 350** - FF15 300
L'identikit artificato, Perche? Tecnica mista/tela (36.5x31cm 14x12in) Prato 2000

$2 500 - €2 592 - **£1 500** - FF17 000
L'identi Kit artificato Tecnica mista/carta (70x50cm 27x19in) Prato 2000

MORENO CAPDEVILLA Francisco 1926 **[4]**

$3 912 - €3 659 - **£2 368** - FF24 000
Le jeune peintre/Fillette et ses lapins Huile/toile (46x38cm 18x14in) Reims 1999

MORENO CARBONERO José 1858-1942 **[27]**

$23 040 - €21 623 - **£14 400** - FF141 840
Flores y frutas Oleo/lienzo (180x165cm 70x64in) Madrid 1999

$16 775 - €16 518 - **£10 450** - FF108 350
Alfonso XIII; Gran Masetro de «La órdenes militares» Oleo/lienzo (76.5x52.5cm 30x20in) Madrid 1999

$5 500 - €6 060 - **£3 658** - FF39 754
Jinete y caballos en un parque Oleo/lienzo (44x34cm 17x13in) Buenos-Aires 2000

MORENO Matias 1840-? **[2]**

$972 - €1 081 - **£648** - FF7 092
Dama con mantón Acuarela/papel (36.5x23cm 14x9in) Madrid 2000

MORENO MEYERHOFF Pedro 1951 **[9]**

$5 185 - €5 106 - **£3 230** - FF33 490
Viejo garage, el jardinero Oleo/tabla (35x50cm 13x19in) Madrid 1999

$1 950 - €1 802 - **£1 170** - FF11 820
La vieja Lápiz/papel (47x33cm 18x12in) Barcelona 1999

MORENO Michel 1945 **[149]**

$676 - €754 - **£441** - FF4 949
Unloading the Boats Oil/board (63x78.5cm 24x30in) Johannesburg 2000

$296 - €305 - **£188** - FF2 000
Post'Art Gouache (32x31cm 12x12in) Paris 2000

MORENO Rafael 1887-1955 **[2]**

$17 000 - €18 132 - **£11 323** - FF118 938
Traspatio en marianao Oil/canvas/board (58.5x77cm 23x30in) New-York 2000

MORENO TÉJADA J. XIX **[2]**

$12 612 - €13 537 - **£8 436** - FF88 800
Pueblo fronterizo de México Oleo/lienzo (44x74cm 17x29in) México 2000

MORENO VILLA José 1887-1955 **[10]**

$2 062 - €2 252 - **£1 387** - FF14 775
Personajes surrealistas Tinta (22.5x15.5cm 8x6in) Madrid 2000

MORERA Y GALICIA Jaime 1855-1927 **[21]**

$4 160 - €4 805 - **£2 880** - FF31 520
Nieves de estudio de Algorta Oleo/lienzo (57x62cm 22x24in) Madrid 1999

$2 790 - €2 703 - **£1 710** - FF17 730
El jardinero Oleo/tabla (23x36cm 9x14in) Madrid 1999

$832 - €961 - **£576** - FF6 304
El cercado guadarrama Lápiz/papel (28x36cm 11x14in) Seville 2000

MORET Henry 1856-1913 **[453]**

$36 636 - €39 332 - **£24 510** - FF258 000
Belle-Ile-en-Mer, les Aiguilles Huile/toile (81x100cm 31x39in) Paris 2000

$15 223 - €12 958 - **£9 061** - FF85 000
Barques au sec séchant leurs voiles rouges Huile/toile (45x31cm 17x12in) Brest 1998

$307 - €351 - **£211** - FF2 300
Voiles au port Fusain/papier (13x18cm 5x7in) Paris 2000

MORETH J. XVIII-XIX **[4]**
$6 039 - €6 860 - £4 167 - FF45 000
Vue du lac d'Ermenonville Gouache/papier
(35x48cm 13x18in) Paris 2000

MORETTI Alessandro XVIII **[3]**
$4 712 - €5 284 - £3 200 - FF34 658
The Colosseum Black chalk (50x67cm 19x26in)
London 2000

MORETTI Antonio 1881-1965 **[19]**
$450 - €466 - £270 - FF3 060
Toilette mattutina Olio/tavola (32x39cm 12x15in)
Firenze 2000
$950 - €985 - £570 - FF6 460
Natura morta con mele, pere e teiera
Acquarello/carta (56x74cm 22x29in) Firenze 2000

MORETTI FOGGIA Mario 1882-1954 **[41]**
$2 700 - €2 799 - £1 620 - FF18 360
Gregge in alta montagna Olio/tavola (40x50cm
15x19in) Vercelli 1999
$1 760 - €2 281 - £1 320 - FF14 960
«Giornata piovosa a Chioggia» Olio/tela/cartone
(34.5x44.5cm 13x17in) Vercelli 2000

MORETTI Giuseppe c.1730-c.1790 **[2]**
$20 000 - €17 543 - £12 144 - FF115 076
View of the Piazzetta, Venice Oil/canvas
(52.5x70cm 20x27in) New-York 1999

MORETTI Lucien-Philippe 1922 **[278]**
$3 140 - €3 049 - £1 940 - FF20 000
Le repos du graveur Huile/toile (60x73cm 23x28in)
Paris 1999
$952 - €1 067 - £662 - FF7 000
Le violoniste Huile/toile (27x22cm 10x8in) Le
Touquet 2001
$863 - €838 - £533 - FF5 500
La jeune violoniste Aquarelle (49x41cm 19x16in)
Paris 1999

MORETTI Luigi 1884-1950 **[29]**
$697 - €727 - £439 - FF4 767
Venezianische Nacht Öl/Leinwand (45x54cm
17x21in) Wien 2000

MORETTI R., Professor XIX **[10]**
$2 292 - €2 674 - £1 595 - FF17 541
The Chess Game Watercolour/paper (35x53cm
13x20in) Melbourne 2000

MORETTI Raymond 1931 **[147]**
$2 129 - €2 073 - £1 308 - FF13 600
Composition (La ville) Huile/toile (100x81cm
39x31in) Paris 1999
$453 - €457 - £282 - FF3 000
Composition Encre Chine (74.5x104cm 29x40in)
Paris 2000
$124 - €122 - £76 - FF800
Composition IV Lithographie (75x53cm 29x20in)
Paris 1999

MORGAN Alfred ?-c.1904 **[9]**
$8 836 - €8 509 - £5 500 - FF55 814
Medea by her Wiles restored to Youthfulness
Oil/canvas (61.5x112.5cm 24x44in) London 1999

MORGAN Alfred George XIX-XX **[7]**
$643 - €607 - £400 - FF3 984
Fishermen and Fleet by the Fish Quay, Whitby
Oil/canvas (69x121cm 27x48in) Whitby, Yorks 1999

MORGAN Ann XIX **[3]**
$2 336 - €2 090 - £1 400 - FF13 712
Off the Coast Oil/canvas (26x36cm 10x14in)
Perthshire 1998

MORGAN Barbara Brooks J. 1900-1992 **[104]**
$1 200 - €1 128 - £743 - FF7 401
Martha Graham, El Penitente Silver print (48x38cm
19x15in) New-York 1999

MORGAN Baxter XIX-XX **[4]**
$1 129 - €1 037 - £700 - FF6 804
The Last Load Watercolour/paper (23.5x39.5cm
9x15in) Devon 1999

MORGAN Charlotte Elizabeth 1867-1947 **[1]**
$1 700 - €1 983 - £1 183 - FF13 010
«Carmel Mission» Oil/canvas/board (25x35cm
10x14in) Altadena CA 2000

MORGAN Cole 1950 **[15]**
$9 765 - €11 344 - £6 862 - FF74 415
«Stripes» Mixed media (160x190cm 62x74in)
Amsterdam 2001
$5 859 - €6 807 - £4 117 - FF44 649
Three up four down Mixed media/board
(100x100cm 39x39in) Amsterdam 2001

MORGAN de Evelyn née Pickering 1855-1919 **[25]**
$41 440 - €35 753 - £25 000 - FF234 522
«The Vision» Oil/canvas (61x78.5cm 24x30in)
London 1998

MORGAN de William 1839-1917 **[14]**
$1 520 - €1 441 - £950 - FF9 455
Iznik, Two-handled Vase Ceramic (H14cm H5in)
Edinburgh 1999

MORGAN Franklin Townsend 1883-? **[4]**
$4 400 - €4 485 - £2 757 - FF29 421
Tug Pulling a Barge, Skyline Cityscape Oil/can-
vas (50x40cm 20x16in) Altadena CA 2000

MORGAN Frederick 1847-1927 **[76]**
$426 870 - €495 956 - £300 000 - FF3 253 260
Apple-gathering Oil/canvas (97x152.5cm 38x60in)
London 2001
$84 180 - €100 115 - £60 000 - FF656 712
Feeding the Ducks Oil/canvas (40.5x51cm 15x20in)
London 2000
$157 - €175 - £110 - FF1 148
Hunting Scene Watercolour/paper (20x31cm 8x12in)
Driffield, East Yorkshire 2001

MORGAN Gertrude, Sister 1900-1980 **[21]**
$2 500 - €2 157 - £1 513 - FF14 148
Lord I cant' Make this Journey Watercolour/paper
(21x9cm 8x3in) New-York 1999

MORGAN Howard 1949 **[27]**
$542 - €595 - £349 - FF3 900
Landscape with Boats on a River
Watercolour/paper (55x36.5cm 21x14in) London 2000

MORGAN Jane 1832-1899 **[3]**
$2 739 - €2 666 - £1 683 - FF17 490
The Dirty Boy Oil/canvas (40x30cm 16x12in) Dublin
1999

MORGAN Jenny XX **[4]**
$2 810 - €3 139 - £1 800 - FF20 590
**Hauling the Traul in Heavy Weather - Grimsby
Trawler «Grimsby Town»** Oil/canvas (51x76cm
20x29in) London 2000

MORGAN John 1823-1886 **[37]**
$149 430 - €160 401 - £100 000 - FF1 052 160
The Auction Oil/canvas (118x177cm 46x69in) London
2000
$18 000 - €17 104 - £10 951 - FF112 192
Find the Timble Oil/canvas (91.5x61cm 36x24in)
New-York 1999

M

$5 009 - €4 670 - **£3 100** - FF30 631
Breton Lovers, being a young Lady spinning in company of a young Man Oil/canvas (33x27cm 13x11in) Tavistock, Devon 1999

MORGAN Mary DeNeale 1868-1948 [59]
$12 000 - €10 253 - **£7 261** - FF67 252
Carmel Mission (No. 380) Oil/board (50x60.5cm 19x23in) San-Francisco CA 1998
$4 750 - €4 786 - **£2 961** - FF31 397
Monastery Bay, Carmel Oil/board (30x45cm 12x18in) Oakland CA 2000

MORGAN Matt 1839-1890 [3]
$56 120 - €66 743 - **£40 000** - FF437 808
Day at Boulogne Oil/canvas (118x251cm 46x98in) London 2000

MORGAN Michèle 1920 [15]
$424 - €488 - **£299** - FF3 200
Sans titre Gouache/papier (56x76cm 22x29in) Barbizon 2001

MORGAN Sally 1951 [31]
$129 - €122 - **£80** - FF800
Corroboree Spirit Silkscreen (56x40cm 22x15in) Sydney 1999

MORGAN Walter Jenks 1847-1924 [29]
$191 - €220 - **£124** - FF1 443
Figures in a Tavern Interior Watercolour (8x13cm 3x5in) Billingshurst, West-Sussex 2000

MORGAN William 1826-1900 [13]
$3 400 - €2 905 - **£1 997** - FF19 058
«Reverie, Gypsy Girl» Oil/canvas (91x61cm 36x24in) New-Orleans LA 1998
$11 000 - €12 131 - **£7 449** - FF79 575
The Village Pump Oil/canvas (38x30.5cm 14x12in) New-York 2000

MORGARI Luigi 1857-1935 [14]
$2 400 - €2 073 - **£1 200** - FF13 600
Interno con figure Olio/cartone (22x26cm 8x10in) Vercelli 1999
$570 - €492 - **£380** - FF3 230
Re Salomone Sanguina/carta (27x41cm 10x16in) Firenze 1998

MORGARI Pietro 1843/52-1885 [5]
$2 500 - €2 592 - **£1 500** - FF17 000
La convalescente Olio/tela (42.5x29cm 16x11in) Vercelli 1999
$2 495 - €2 113 - **£1 500** - FF13 863
Portrait of a Girl in Profile Pastel/paper (56.5x47cm 22x18in) London 1998

MORGARI Rodolfo 1827-1909 [10]
$1 000 - €1 037 - **£600** - FF6 800
Allegoria della Primavera Olio/tela (49x42cm 19x16in) Vercelli 1999

MORGENSTERN Carl 1811-1893 [22]
$12 009 - €14 316 - **£8 562** - FF93 909
An der ligurischen Küste Öl/Leinwand (60.5x85cm 23x33in) Köln 2000
$7 725 - €6 386 - **£4 532** - FF41 890
Morgenstimmung über dem Canale di San Marco in Venedig Öl/Leinwand (27.5x41cm 10x16in) Heidelberg 1998

MORGENSTERN Carl Ernst 1847-1928 [22]
$2 634 - €2 556 - **£1 640** - FF16 769
Abendliche Isarlandschaft mit Burg Schwaneck sowie Tierstaffage Öl/Leinwand (85x104cm 33x40in) Frankfurt 1999

MORGENSTERN Christian Bernhard 1805-1867 [43]
$16 207 - €18 407 - **£11 336** - FF120 740
Abendlandschaft mit Fischerhütte unter mächtigen Bäumen Öl/Leinwand (89x107cm 35x42in) Berlin 2001
$14 971 - €14 316 - **£9 116** - FF93 909
Blick über den Starnberger See an einem Sommerabend Öl/Leinwand (26.5x37.5cm 10x14in) Stuttgart 1999
$962 - €1 125 - **£676** - FF7 378
Mitterndorff (bei Dachau) Pencil (39.5x60.2cm 15x23in) München 2001

MORGENSTERN Friedrich Ernst 1853-1919 [28]
$2 737 - €3 068 - **£1 887** - FF20 123
Am Strand von Nieuport Öl/Leinwand (40x59.5cm 15x23in) Hamburg 2000
$710 - €716 - **£442** - FF4 695
Gehöft an einer belgischen Kirche Öl/Leinwand (28x41cm 11x16in) Frankfurt 2000

MORGENSTERN Johann Ludwig Ernst 1738-1819 [15]
$32 397 - €36 325 - **£22 000** - FF238 275
The Interior of a Cathedral Oil/copper (40.5x51.5cm 15x20in) London 2000
$2 386 - €2 045 - **£1 434** - FF13 413
Kircheninterieur Oil/panel (23x31cm 9x12in) Stuttgart 1998

MORGENTHALER Ernst 1887-1962 [232]
$7 425 - €7 482 - **£4 628** - FF49 081
Ausblick ins Limmattal Öl/Leinwand (117x180cm 46x70in) Zürich 2000
$2 366 - €2 550 - **£1 586** - FF16 730
Blick aus dem Atelier über Limmat und Uetliberg Öl/Leinwand (50x73.5cm 19x28in) Zürich 2000
$1 326 - €1 312 - **£827** - FF8 608
Herbstliche Hügellandschaft Öl/Papier (25x32cm 9x12in) St. Gallen 1999
$342 - €391 - **£241** - FF2 565
Landhaus mit Garten Aquarell/Papier (24.5x22cm 9x8in) Bern 2001
$102 - €102 - **£64** - FF670
Kamelmarkt in Fes Lithographie (23x31cm 9x12in) Lindau 1999

MORGHEN Filippo 1730-1807 [9]
$330 - €360 - **£228** - FF2 364
Carlos III, Rey de España Grabado (45x38.5cm 17x15in) Madrid 2001

MORGHEN Raphael 1758-1833 [28]
$217 - €216 - **£135** - FF1 415
Francinini de Moncada, on Horseback, after Anthony Van Dyke Engraving (63x43cm 25x17in) Dublin 1999

MORGNER Michael 1942 [76]
$423 - €511 - **£295** - FF3 353
Ahrenshoop Indian ink/paper (21x29.4cm 8x11in) Berlin 2000
$89 - €102 - **£62** - FF670
Ohne Titel Serigraph (52.5x38.5cm 20x15in) Hamburg 2001

MORGNER Wilhelm 1891-1917 [99]
$30 296 - €35 791 - **£21 399** - FF234 773
Allee Öl/Karton (61x69.5cm 24x27in) Köln 2001
$3 399 - €2 810 - **£1 994** - FF18 431
Kampf am Kreuz Watercolour (23x30.2cm 9x11in) Heidelberg 1998

$611 - €665 - **£402** - FF4 360
Die Geschwister Woodcut (21.6x17.5cm 8x6in)
Hamburg 2000

MORI Henri 1933-1994 [6]
$1 097 - €1 296 - **£779** - FF8 500
Ours sur la banquise Bronze (14.5x16x13cm
5x6x5in) Neuilly-sur-Seine 2001

MORI Mariko 1967 [19]
$32 000 - €30 962 - **£19 734** - FF203 100
Mirage (Miko no Inori) Mixed media (61x75.5cm
24x29in) New-York 1999
$5 000 - €5 400 - **£3 455** - FF35 419
Miko no Inori Sculpture (29.5x16.5x11cm 11x6x4in)
New-York 2001
$48 000 - €55 694 - **£33 139** - FF365 328
Warrior Photograph (122x152.5cm 48x60in) New-York
2000

MORI Neno 1898-1970 [18]
$1 900 - €1 970 - **£1 140** - FF12 920
Venezia Olio/tela (60x42.5cm 23x16in) Venezia 1999

MORICCI Giuseppe 1806-1880 [9]
$9 373 - €10 671 - **£6 615** - FF70 000
Venise Huile/toile (73x124cm 28x48in) Rennes 2001

MORIER David 1704/05-1770 [13]
$10 943 - €13 015 - **£7 800** - FF85 372
**Equestrian Portrait of Augustus, Duke of
Cumberland, with an Aide-Camp** Oil/canvas
(125x99cm 49x38in) London 2000
$13 328 - €15 851 - **£9 500** - FF103 979
**Equestrian Portrait of George III with a Review
of Troops Beyond** Oil/canvas (52x42cm 20x16in)
London 2000

MORIERA Ruben XX [1]
$1 700 - €1 825 - **£1 137** - FF11 969
Tarzan Sunday Page Ink (67x50cm 26x19in) New-
York 2000

MORIKANE [2]
$2 500 - €2 289 - **£1 523** - FF15 017
**Twenty Four Beauties, two prints from the
Series** Woodcut (42x28.5cm 16x11in) New-York 1999

MORIMOTO SOSUKE 1937 [1]
$120 000 - €140 724 - **£85 632** - FF923 088
Young Woman Oil/canvas (117x95cm 46x37in) New-
York 2000

MORIMURA Yasumasa 1951 [23]
$5 000 - €5 690 - **£3 513** - FF37 326
Marilyn Monroe Gelatin silver print (54.5x45cm
21x17in) New-York 2001

MORIN Edmond 1824-1882 [7]
$1 069 - €1 220 - **£746** - FF8 000
Le réveillon Gouache/papier (22x29.5cm 8x11in) Paris
2001

MORIN Georges 1874-? [21]
$697 - €803 - **£480** - FF5 266
Dancer Gilded bronze (H21cm H8in) Billingshurst,
West-Sussex 2000

MORIN Louis 1855-1938 [24]
$1 200 - €1 136 - **£745** - FF7 451
«La Cire à Cacheter à Mèche, I.Lambert» Poster
(123x92.5cm 48x36in) New-York 1999

MORINET G. XIX-XX [5]
$1 200 - €1 339 - **£785** - FF8 781
**«Appareils & accessoires photographie, ouver-
ture le 15 juillet»** Poster (125.5x97cm 49x38in) New-
York 2000

MORIS Louis Marie 1818-1883 [18]
$9 000 - €10 456 - **£6 325** - FF68 590
Napoleon on Horseback Gilded bronze (H77.5cm
H30in) New-York 2001

MORISE Max 1900-? [1]
$21 045 - €25 029 - **£15 000** - FF164 178
Cadavre exquis (Exquisite Corpse) Coloured
crayons (30x24.5cm 11x9in) London 2000

MORISOT Berthe 1841-1895 [204]
$130 000 - €145 610 - **£90 324** - FF955 136
Petite fille dans un jardin Oil/canvas (81x58cm
31x22in) New-York 2001
$75 000 - €72 120 - **£46 207** - FF473 077
Jeune fille accoudée Oil/canvas (39x32cm 15x12in)
New-York 1999
$18 170 - €17 532 - **£11 477** - FF115 000
Fillette dans le jardin à Cimiez Pastel/papier
(28x44cm 11x17in) Paris 1999
$316 - €307 - **£196** - FF2 012
Jeune fille au chat Etching (14.9x12cm 5x4in) Berlin
2001

MORISOT Henriette XIX-XX [5]
$1 623 - €1 372 - **£965** - FF9 000
Scène galante dans le parc Huile/toile (27x41cm
10x16in) Calais 1998

MORITZ Friedrich Wilhelm 1783-1855 [19]
$438 - €438 - **£274** - FF2 873
**Bauernfamilie vor Haus versammelt mit
Hühnerschar, Kühen und Ziegen** Aquarell/Papier
(19x27.5cm 7x10in) Zofingen 1999

MORITZ Karl 1896-1963 [15]
$494 - €409 - **£290** - FF2 681
«Waldlichtung mit Wasserstelle» Aquarell/Papier
(23x35cm 9x13in) Radolfzell 1998

MORITZ William 1816-1860 [10]
$1 827 - €1 768 - **£1 157** - FF11 600
Patio d'une maison mauresque algéroise
Aquarelle/papier (30x24cm 11x9in) Paris 1999

MORIYAMA Daido 1938 [6]
$2 200 - €2 533 - **£1 501** - FF16 614
Pig Gelatin silver print (23.5x34.5cm 9x13in) New-
York 2000

MORIZOT Edma 1839-1921 [9]
$908 - €876 - **£570** - FF5 749
Landschaft mit Bauernhaus und Hühnern
Öl/Leinwand (46.5x55cm 18x21in) Zürich 1999

MORLAND George 1763-1804 [250]
$60 000 - €70 668 - **£41 496** - FF463 554
The Fox Inn Oil/canvas (126x162.5cm 49x63in) New-
York 2000
$6 500 - €6 977 - **£4 349** - FF45 766
A Peasant Family in a Cart Stopped by a Road
Oil/canvas (45.5x61cm 17x24in) New-York 2000
$4 061 - €3 952 - **£2 500** - FF25 922
Gypsies around a Camp-fire in a Clearing
Oil/canvas (29.5x37cm 11x14in) London 1999
$900 - €1 022 - **£625** - FF6 707
Landschaft mit Pferdekarren Chalks (26.5x41cm
10x16in) Köln 2001
$147 - €143 - **£90** - FF939
Visit to the Child at Nurse Mezzotint (45x55cm
17x21in) London 1999

MORLAND Henry Robert 1730-1797 [17]
$18 239 - €21 692 - **£13 000** - FF142 287
Stealing the Letter Oil/canvas (111.5x92.5cm
43x36in) London 2000

$4 035 - €3 736 - **£2 500** - FF24 504
Servant Ironing Pastel/paper (55.5x43.5cm 21x17in)
London 1999

MORLAND James Smith 1846-1921 **[15]**

$241 - €223 - **£150** - FF1 466
The Sexton's Nap - Dolywyddelan Church
Watercolour/paper (51x64cm 20x25in) Cheshire 1999

MORLE Stuart 1960 **[8]**

$1 268 - €1 460 - **£865** - FF9 578
Ballet Shoes III Oil/board (36x36cm 14x14in) Dublin
2000

MORLETTE Y RUIZ Juan Patricio 1715-1780 **[4]**

$4 749 - €4 610 - **£2 957** - FF30 238
**San Emigdio de Ascoli, Patrón de Los
Terremotos** Oil/copper (58x45cm 22x17in) New-York
1999

$20 000 - €23 237 - **£14 056** - FF152 424
Virgen de Guadalupe Oil/copper (42x32.5cm
16x12in) New-York 2001

MORLEY Eugene 1909 **[2]**

$750 - €837 - **£491** - FF5 488
Hymn to the Rising Sun Lithograph (23x35cm
9x14in) Chicago IL 2000

MORLEY Harry 1881-1943 **[105]**

$9 625 - €9 699 - **£6 000** - FF63 621
The Night Passeth and the Day Cometh Tempera
(91.5x183cm 36x72in) London 2000

$1 764 - €1 778 - **£1 100** - FF11 664
Endymion II Oil/canvas (63.5x76cm 25x29in) London
2000

$320 - €323 - **£200** - FF2 120
The garden Fence, Wool, Dorset Watercolour/paper
(24x35cm 9x13in) London 2000

MORLEY Henry 1869-1937 **[10]**

$3 037 - €3 387 - **£2 050** - FF22 215
View of Stirling Castle from the South Oil/panel
(25x35cm 9x13in) Edinburgh 2000

MORLEY Malcolm 1931 **[184]**

$140 000 - €130 746 - **£86 408** - FF857 640
Arizonac Oil/canvas (203x267cm 79x105in) New-York
1999

$11 000 - €12 321 - **£7 642** - FF80 819
A Variety of Catastrophes Oil/canvas (53x60.5cm
20x23in) New-York 2001

$14 000 - €15 654 - **£9 437** - FF102 681
H.M.S Hood Acrylic (23x30.5cm 9x12in) New-York
2000

$13 000 - €12 141 - **£8 023** - FF79 638
Sentinel Bronze (159.5x42x28cm 62x16x11in) New-
York 1999

$4 500 - €4 476 - **£2 793** - FF29 359
Plymouth Watercolour/paper (49.5x79cm 19x31in)
Beverly-Hills CA 1999

$569 - €648 - **£400** - FF4 249
Untitled Color lithograph (59x86cm 23x33in) London
2001

MORLEY Ralph XIX-XX **[5]**

$728 - €854 - **£520** - FF5 605
Glengarry Castle, Loch Oich/On Ullswater
Watercolour/paper (23x35cm 9x13in) Manchester 2000

MORLEY Thomas William 1859-1925 **[119]**

$701 - €805 - **£480** - FF5 281
A Sunlit Street Oil/board (21x28cm 8x11in) Par,
Cornwall 2000

$412 - €400 - **£260** - FF2 626
A white Pony on Moorland Watercolour/paper
(36x53cm 14x21in) London 1999

MORLON Antony, Paul 1835-? **[24]**

$3 108 - €2 758 - **£1 900** - FF18 092
A Broken Silence Oil/canvas (45.5x33cm 17x12in)
London 1999

MORLOTTI Ennio 1910-1992 **[288]**

$40 800 - €35 246 - **£27 200** - FF231 200
Rocce Olio/tela (150x150cm 59x59in) Prato 1998

$20 000 - €20 733 - **£12 000** - FF136 000
Foglie Olio/tela/tavola (44x61cm 17x24in) Vercelli
2000

$8 500 - €8 812 - **£5 100** - FF57 800
Bosco di ulivi Olio/tela (30x40cm 11x15in) Milano
2000

$1 750 - €1 814 - **£1 050** - FF11 900
Vegetazione Pastel gras/papier (24x29cm 9x11in)
Milano 1999

$150 - €155 - **£90** - FF1 020
Fiori Litografia (42.5x30.5cm 16x12in) Torino 2000

MORMILE Gaetano 1839-1890 **[21]**

$4 114 - €3 835 - **£2 538** - FF25 154
**Italienische Bäuerin mit ihren Kindern und zwei
Eseln vor der Scheune** Öl/Leinwand (79x90cm
31x35in) Köln 1999

MÖRNER Axel Otto 1774-1852 **[4]**

$36 828 - €34 433 - **£22 692** - FF225 866
**Stockholmspanorama med människor, utsikt
från Mosebacke** Oil/canvas (225x140cm 88x55in)
Stockholm 1999

MÖRNER Hjalmar 1794-1837 **[17]**

$51 342 - €49 965 - **£31 605** - FF327 746
**Italiensk skördefest vid monte testaccio utanför
Rom** Oil/canvas (93x136cm 36x53in) Stockholm 1999

$494 - €547 - **£335** - FF3 591
Resminnen från Frankrike, Tyskland och Italien
Color lithograph (35x24.5cm 13x9in) Stockholm 2000

MÖRNER Stellan 1896-1979 **[275]**

$2 631 - €2 474 - **£1 630** - FF16 251
Figur vid vas Oil/canvas (54x65cm 21x25in)
Stockholm 1999

$2 593 - €2 262 - **£1 568** - FF14 838
Stolen-landskap med kyrka Oil/canvas (22x27cm
8x10in) Stockholm 1998

$487 - €499 - **£301** - FF3 275
Landskap med figurer Akvarell/papper (14x26cm
5x10in) Stockholm 2000

MORNET Pierre 1972 **[10]**

$378 - €381 - **£235** - FF2 500
Louise Acrylique (20x11.5cm 7x4in) Paris 2000

MORO dal Marco Angolo c.1537-c.1590 **[4]**

$3 002 - €3 579 - **£2 140** - FF23 477
**Tiburtinische Sibylle zeigt Kaiser August die
Erscheinung der Madonna** Radierung (27x39.7cm
10x15in) Berlin 2000

MORO Giacomo XVIII **[1]**

$4 145 - €3 843 - **£2 500** - FF25 211
**The Port of Marsamucetto/The Castello Ricasoli
and San Angiolo** Watercolour (33x62cm 12x24in)
London 1999

MORO Marco 1817-1885 **[1]**

$3 570 - €3 084 - **£1 785** - FF20 230
Vedute di Venezia Litografia (49x56cm 19x22in)
Venezia 1999

MORO Pietro XIX **[1]**

$20 358 - €19 818 - **£12 506** - FF130 000
Trompe l'oeil au jeu d'enfants Huile/toile
(96.5x58cm 37x22in) Paris 1999

MORO Vala act.1933 **[2]**
📖 **$406** - €472 - **£289** - FF3 098
Fesche Mädchen Farbradierung (35x25cm 13x9in)
Wien 2000

MORODER Otto XVIII-XIX **[1]**
📖 **$12 426** - €13 808 - **£8 322** - FF90 573
Das letzte Aufgebot, Tirol Woodcut (81x106cm 31x41in) Wien 2000

MORODER-LUSENBERG Josef 1846-1939 **[16]**
🖐 **$4 148** - €4 346 - **£2 743** - FF28 508
Alter Bauer mit Filzhut Öl/Leinwand (62x46cm 24x18in) München 2000
🖐 **$5 551** - €5 087 - **£3 395** - FF33 369
Im Herrgottswinkel Oil/panel (20.5x16cm 8x6in) Wien 1999

MOROMASA Furuyama c.1671-1751 **[1]**
✏ **$2 410** - €2 525 - **£1 600** - FF16 566
Courtesan Writing a Letter Ink (42x54.5cm 16x21in) London 2000

MORONEY Ken 1949 **[123]**
🖐 **$1 793** - €1 925 - **£1 200** - FF12 625
Afternoon on the Beach Oil/board (48x58.5cm 18x23in) London 2000
🖐 **$557** - €656 - **£400** - FF4 303
Moored Boats Oil/cardboard (13.5x18cm 5x7in) London 2001

MORONI Adrien 1943 **[2]**
🖐 **$2 468** - €2 439 - **£1 528** - FF16 000
Les peupliers et mas de Vence Huile/toile (65x54cm 25x21in) Cannes 2000

MORONI Giovan Battista c.1525-1578 **[6]**
🖐 **$254 031** - €272 681 - **£170 000** - FF1 788 672
Portrait of a Nobleman, Bust-Length, in Black Costume and a Ruff Oil/canvas/board (44.5x34.5cm 17x13in) London 2000

MOROSINI George ?-1882 **[2]**
✏ **$1 974** - €2 075 - **£1 300** - FF13 612
Portrait of Miss Dillon, Half-Length, Wearing a Blue Gown Coloured chalks/paper (33.5x26.5cm 13x10in) Suffolk 2000

MOROT Aimé 1850-1913 **[31]**
🖐 **$3 022** - €3 506 - **£2 150** - FF23 000
Fillette accoudée au bras d'un fauteuil Huile/toile (46x55cm 18x21in) Paris 2001
🖐 **$9 246** - €10 214 - **£6 411** - FF67 000
La mort du lion, esquisse d'après Gérôme Huile/toile (23x29cm 9x11in) Chartres 2001

MORPHY Garret act.1680-1716 **[4]**
🖐 **$13 480** - €15 872 - **£9 472** - FF104 112
Portrait of a Gentleman Wearing Damascened Armour Oil/canvas (56x48cm 22x18in) Dublin 2000

MORRELL Geoffrey F. XIX-XX **[3]**
✏ **$3 047** - €3 014 - **£1 900** - FF19 773
If London were on Saturn Grisaille (46.5x75.5cm 18x29in) London 1999

MORRELL Wayne Beam 1923 **[30]**
🖐 **$1 200** - €1 340 - **£802** - FF8 788
Palm Beach Courtyard Oil/masonite (60x91cm 24x36in) Delray-Beach FL 2000
🖐 **$1 100** - €1 155 - **£743** - FF7 575
Gloucester Harbor with Ship «Gloucester» Oil/board (28x39cm 11x15in) Fairfield ME 2001

MORREN Georges 1868-1941 **[38]**
🖐 **$4 600** - €4 538 - **£2 839** - FF29 766
Femme nue assise au chapeau rouge Oil/canvas (55x46.5cm 21x18in) Amsterdam 1999

🖐 **$1 878** - €2 107 - **£1 309** - FF13 821
Coin de jardin à Bandol Huile/toile (32x24cm 12x10in) Bruxelles 2001
✏ **$524** - €496 - **£326** - FF3 252
Vue de la baie de Nice Pastel/papier (23x30cm 9x11in) Bruxelles 1999

MORRICE James Wilson 1865-1924 **[43]**
🖐 **$87 854** - €92 278 - **£58 045** - FF605 306
Paysage aux Antilles Huile/toile (59.5x81.5cm 23x32in) Montréal 2000
🖐 **$6 581** - €7 352 - **£4 460** - FF48 223
«Port de Bretagne» Huile/panneau (12.5x15.5cm 4x6in) Montréal 2000

MORRIS (Maurice De Bevere) 1923-2001 **[16]**
✏ **$628** - €610 - **£391** - FF4 000
Lucky Luke jouant avec son revolver Feutre/papier (48x31cm 18x12in) Paris 1999

MORRIS Alfred XIX **[18]**
🖐 **$3 000** - €2 729 - **£1 836** - FF17 899
Sheep Resting on a Rocky Hillside Oil/canvas (100x74cm 39x29in) New-Orleans LA 1998

MORRIS Cedric Lockwood 1889-1982 **[120]**
🖐 **$6 489** - €7 171 - **£4 500** - FF47 038
The Minton Pot Oil/canvas (76x51cm 29x20in) London 2001
🖐 **$6 939** - €8 081 - **£4 800** - FF53 007
Snipes at Low Tide Oil/board (29x25.5cm 11x10in) London 2000
✏ **$1 250** - €1 151 - **£750** - FF7 548
Man playing a Guitar Ink (44.5x28.5cm 17x11in) Glamorgan 1999

MORRIS Charles Greville 1861-1922 **[17]**
🖐 **$700** - €644 - **£420** - FF4 226
Cottage by the Stream Oil/board (28x23cm 11x9in) Chicago IL 1999

MORRIS Charles, Snr. 1898-? **[6]**
🖐 **$748** - €688 - **£460** - FF4 513
Cologne Cathedral Oil/canvas (29.5x24cm 11x9in) Oxfordshire 1999

MORRIS Franklin E. 1938 **[4]**
🖐 **$7 000** - €6 609 - **£4 351** - FF43 351
Looking towards Washington Street, Brooklyn, New York Oil/canvas (50x76cm 20x30in) Milford CT 1999
🖐 **$2 000** - €2 219 - **£1 330** - FF14 553
Park Row at Broadway, New York Oil/canvas (35x27cm 14x11in) Milford CT 2000

MORRIS Garman XIX-XX **[71]**
✏ **$193** - €180 - **£120** - FF1 183
Vessels in calm Waters Watercolour (28x71cm 11x27in) Billingshurst, West-Sussex 1999

MORRIS George L.K. 1905-1975 **[28]**
🖐 **$24 000** - €22 729 - **£14 592** - FF149 090
Airplane Factory Oil/canvas (61x41cm 24x16in) New-York 1999

MORRIS J.C. act.1851-1863 **[6]**
🖐 **$4 489** - €5 339 - **£3 200** - FF35 024
A Spaniel with the Day's Bag Oil/canvas (70.5x91.5cm 27x36in) London 2000

MORRIS J.W. XIX **[19]**
🖐 **$1 503** - €1 271 - **£900** - FF8 337
Stags before a Loch in a Highland Landscape Oil/canvas (61x106.7cm 24x42in) London 1998

M

MORRIS James Charles XIX **[7]**
🕊 **$2 600** – €2 218 – **£1 565** – FF14 551
Shepherd boy playing flute with dog to flock
Huile/toile (60x137cm 24x54in) Norwalk CT 1999

MORRIS John XIX **[32]**
🕊 **$12 000** – €11 914 – **£7 500** – FF78 151
Full Cry Oil/canvas (101.5x127cm 39x50in) New-York 1999
🕊 **$3 500** – €3 274 – **£2 116** – FF21 474
The day's Bag Oil/canvas/board (91.5x70.5cm 36x27in) New-York 1999

MORRIS John W. XIX **[12]**
🕊 **$1 466** – €1 580 – **£1 000** – FF10 366
A Shepherd and his Flock in a Highland Landscape Oil/canvas (61x107cm 24x42in) London 2001
🕊 **$953** – €1 028 – **£650** – FF6 740
Sheep resting in a Highland Landscape Oil/panel (20.5x30cm 8x11in) London 2001

MORRIS Kathleen Moir 1893-1986 **[18]**
🕊 **$13 912** – €15 407 – **£9 435** – FF101 062
Old Horse, Richelieu, Quebec Oil/canvas (56.5x61.5cm 22x24in) Toronto 2000
🕊 **$1 810** – €1 946 – **£1 245** – FF12 765
Lake Reflections Oil/panel (30.5x35.5cm 12x13in) Toronto 2001

MORRIS Margaret 1891-1990 **[8]**
🕊 **$5 737** – €6 369 – **£4 000** – FF41 779
Spring in Carlyle square Oil/board (24x19cm 9x7in) London 2001

MORRIS Mary XIX-XX **[4]**
🕊 **$986** – €1 148 – **£704** – FF7 528
Coastal view with Sailboats in Distance Oil/canvas (56x81.5cm 22x32in) Toronto 2001

MORRIS Philip Richard 1838-1902 **[48]**
🕊 **$6 053** – €6 300 – **£3 800** – FF41 323
A Shepherd with His Flock with a Rough Sea Beyond Oil/canvas (122x221cm 48x87in) London 2000
🕊 **$4 594** – €4 207 – **£2 800** – FF27 595
The Harvest Oil/board (44x53cm 17x20in) Cambridge 1999
🕊 **$652** – €757 – **£450** – FF4 963
Bury, Sussex Oil/board (9x13.5cm 3x5in) London 2000
🖉 **$510** – €599 – **£360** – FF3 926
Spring Watercolour (7.5x12cm 2x4in) London 2000

MORRIS Robert 1931 **[64]**
🕊 **$50 000** – €56 004 – **£34 740** – FF367 360
Untitled Sculpture (274.5x183x20.5cm 108x72x8in) New-York 2001
🕊 **$17 305** – €19 123 – **£12 000** – FF125 436
Silver Brain Plaster (12.5x15x17.5cm 4x5x6in) London 2001
🕊 **$2 400** – €2 592 – **£1 658** – FF17 001
Untitled, Drawing for Timber Piece Ink (49x63.5cm 19x25in) New-York 2001
📖 **$400** – €409 – **£250** – FF2 683
Ohne Titel Offset (45x57.5cm 17x22in) Hamburg 2000

MORRIS Sarah 1967 **[6]**
🕊 **$8 965** – €9 624 – **£6 000** – FF63 129
Sorry Mixed media/canvas (152.5x244cm 60x96in) London 2000

MORRIS W. Walker c.1820-c.1880 **[9]**
🕊 **$34 000** – €29 049 – **£20 410** – FF190 549
The Day's Bag Oil/canvas (102x153.5cm 40x60in) New-York 1998

🕊 **$5 613** – €5 553 – **£3 500** – FF36 425
The Gamekeeper's Son Oil/canvas (61x51cm 24x20in) London 1999

MORRIS William 1957 **[9]**
🕊 **$131 000** – €151 554 – **£92 721** – FF994 132
Canopic Jar, Fallow Deer Sculpture, glass (H107cm H42in) Cleveland OH 2000
🕊 **$12 000** – €11 455 – **£7 498** – FF75 138
Standing STone Sculpture, glass (65x58x11cm 25x22x4in) New-York 1999

MORRIS William Bright 1834-1896 **[21]**
🕊 **$10 852** – €11 720 – **£7 500** – FF76 878
The Patio Oil/canvas (102.5x79cm 40x31in) London 2001

MORRIS Wright 1910-1992 **[28]**
📷 **$4 000** – €4 605 – **£2 729** – FF30 208
Tenant Farmer Dwelling, near Culpepper Gelatin silver print (19.5x23.5cm 7x9in) New-York 2000

MORRISH Sydney S. XIX-XX **[8]**
🕊 **$5 787** – €6 250 – **£4 000** – FF40 999
«Hush!» Oil/board (40x30cm 15x11in) West-Midlands 2001

MORRISH William Sidney 1844-1917 **[38]**
🖉 **$468** – €438 – **£290** – FF2 873
Cattle and Sheep in Landscape Watercolour/paper (48x20cm 19x8in) Petersfield, Hampshire 1999

MORRISON James 1932 **[25]**
🕊 **$545** – €5 496 – **£3 400** – FF36 052
From the Barravourish Oil/board (86.5x147cm 34x57in) London 2000
🕊 **$1 942** – €2 085 – **£1 300** – FF13 678
Snow, Kingairloch Oil/cardboard (30.5x86.5cm 12x34in) London 2000

MORRISON Robert Edward 1852-1925 **[17]**
🕊 **$985** – €1 064 – **£680** – FF6 978
Loch Scene Oil/panel (24.5x33.5cm 9x13in) Billingshurst, West-Sussex 2001

MORRISSEAU Norval H. 1932 **[97]**
🕊 **$912** – €1 022 – **£633** – FF6 701
Watergod Acrylic/paper (44x73cm 17x29in) Calgary, Alberta 2001
🖉 **$873** – €1 026 – **£620** – FF6 731
Loons and Dragonflies Coloured inks/paper (28.5x39.5cm 11x15in) Toronto 2000
🗐 **$437** – €513 – **£310** – FF3 368
Shaman Conjuring/Dawn/Shaman and Apprentice/Composition with Loons Serigraph in colors (61.5x46cm 24x18in) Toronto 2000

MORROCCO Alberto 1917-1999 **[52]**
🕊 **$12 917** – €14 529 – **£9 000** – FF95 304
«Red Hill, Anticoli II» Oil/canvas (122x108cm 48x42in) Edinburgh 2001
🕊 **$15 201** – €15 092 – **£9 500** – FF98 996
Dog in the Kitchen Oil/canvas (43x53.5cm 16x21in) London 1999
🕊 **$7 894** – €8 272 – **£5 000** – FF54 264
Golden Sand, Donmouth Oil/panel (25.5x46cm 10x18in) Edinburgh 2000
🖉 **$12 465** – €13 434 – **£8 500** – FF88 119
Woman on a Divan Watercolour (63.5x76cm 25x30in) Edinburgh 2000

MORROCCO Leon Francesco 1942 **[18]**
🕊 **$4 327** – €5 086 – **£3 000** – FF33 360
Plaice with Fruit Oil/canvas (63.5x81cm 25x31in) Edinburgh 2000

📖 **$2 697** - €2 528 - **£1 669** - FF16 583
Flowers on Purple Ground Pastel/paper
(170x110cm 66x43in) Melbourne 1999

MORROW Albert George 1863-1927 [9]

📜 **$800** - €933 - **£561** - FF6 120
«Illustrated Bits» Poster (49x72.5cm 19x28in) New-York 2000

MORSE Auguste Achille XIX [1]

📜 **$1 007** - €931 - **£604** - FF6 107
Le cortège de la Mariée/Le nouveau né, d'après A.Moreau Grabado (50x68.5cm 19x26in) Madrid 1999

MORSE Jonathan Bradley 1834-1898 [11]

🖼 **$1 050** - €1 183 - **£727** - FF7 761
Seascape with Rocky Coast Oil/canvas (43x71cm 17x28in) Hatfield PA 2000

MORSING Ivar 1919 [101]

🖼 **$1 062** - €919 - **£641** - FF6 027
Vilande kvinna Oil/canvas (69x64cm 27x25in) Stockholm 1999

📖 **$465** - €438 - **£288** - FF2 876
Fågelmannen Oil/panel (20x43cm 7x16in) Stockholm 1999

MORSTADT Anna 1874-? [11]

🖼 **$16 991** - €19 818 - **£11 817** - FF130 000
Caïds de Kérouan Huile/toile (100x80cm 39x31in) Paris 2000

🖼 **$2 326** - €2 134 - **£1 446** - FF14 000
Mustapha le cavalier Pastel/paper (46x45cm 18x17in) Paris 1999

MORTEL Jan c.1650-1719 [13]

🖼 **$39 672** - €44 210 - **£27 550** - FF290 000
Nature morte aux fruits Huile/toile (78x64cm 30x25in) Paris 2001

🖼 **$16 426** - €19 059 - **£11 340** - FF125 017
Stilleven van fruit, bloemen en insecten Oil/panel (41x34cm 16x13in) Rotterdam 2000

MORTELEQUE F. XIX [2]

🖼 **$4 104** - €4 573 - **£2 793** - FF30 000
Paysage au cours d'eau et un château Technique mixte (79x91cm 31x35in) Paris 2000

MORTELMANS Frank 1898-1986 [28]

📖 **$230** - €248 - **£154** - FF1 626
Coup de vent sur Anvers Pastel/papier (30x40cm 11x15in) Antwerpen 2000

MORTELMANS Frans 1865-1936 [125]

🖼 **$14 365** - €16 112 - **£10 010** - FF105 690
Table garnie auc chrysanthème, pêches et raisins Huile/toile (100x150cm 39x59in) Bruxelles 2001

🖼 **$6 096** - €5 949 - **£3 744** - FF39 024
Nature morte aux fruits Huile/toile (45x73cm 17x28in) Antwerpen 1999

📖 **$1 855** - €1 735 - **£1 148** - FF11 382
Rozen Huile/panneau (22.5x12.5cm 8x4in) Lokeren 1999

📖 **$37** - €45 - **£26** - FF292
Jozef vinck uit mijn schetsboeck Crayon/papier (25x18cm 9x7in) Antwerpen 2000

MORTENSEN Richard 1910-1993 [542]

🖼 **$41 737** - €42 340 - **£25 924** - FF277 735
Carré sans merci Oil/canvas (150x150cm 59x59in) Köbenhavn 2000

🖼 **$9 977** - €9 909 - **£6 240** - FF65 000
Mont Valérien II Huile/toile (81x65cm 31x25in) Paris 1999

📖 **$1 664** - €1 677 - **£1 037** - FF11 000
Composition Huile/toile (14x18cm 5x7in) Paris 2000

📖 **$502** - €536 - **£342** - FF3 516
Figurkomposition Watercolour (31x48cm 12x18in) Vejle 2001

📜 **$433** - €404 - **£261** - FF2 649
Candalicia Serigraph in colors (105x131cm 41x51in) Köbenhavn 1999

MORTENSEN William 1897-1965 [29]

📷 **$1 480** - €1 382 - **£894** - FF9 068
Scene from Decameron Of Boccaccio Photograph (25.5x29cm 10x11in) New-York 1999

MORTIER Antoine 1908-1999 [67]

🖼 **$9 315** - €11 155 - **£6 390** - FF73 170
L'évasion Huile/toile (162x114cm 63x44in) Antwerpen 2000

🖼 **$3 094** - €3 222 - **£1 950** - FF21 138
Homuncule 2000 Huile/toile (110x80cm 43x31in) Antwerpen 2000

📖 **$301** - €322 - **£205** - FF2 113
Compositie Fusain/papier (27x21.5cm 10x8in) Lokeren 2001

MORTIER Pierre 1611-1711 [9]

📜 **$360** - €311 - **£180** - FF2 040
Cremone, Amsterdam Gravure (53.5x65cm 21x25in) Milano 1999

MORTIMER Geoffrey E. XIX-XX [51]

🖼 **$166** - €180 - **£115** - FF1 178
Extensive Norfolk Landscape with Fishermen and Ponies in foreground Oil/canvas (22x27cm 9x11in) Aylsham, Norfolk 2001

MORTIMER John Hamilton 1741-1779 [33]

🖼 **$4 054** - €4 607 - **£2 800** - FF30 222
Reclining Male Nude Black chalk/paper (31.5x49cm 12x19in) London 2000

📜 **$325** - €317 - **£200** - FF2 078
Bardolph/Cassandra/Ophelia/York Etching (40x32cm 15x12in) London 1999

MORTIMER Lewis XX [28]

📖 **$329** - €366 - **£230** - FF2 402
Fisherfolk conversing outside a cottage Watercolour/paper (36x24cm 14x9in) Birmingham 2001

MORTIMER Thomas XIX-XX [88]

📖 **$253** - €246 - **£160** - FF1 616
Vessels at a Harbour at Dusk Watercolour/paper (25x53cm 10x21in) London 1999

MÖRTL Michael XIX-XX [7]

🎨 **$1 377** - €1 599 - **£968** - FF10 487
Gänsereigen Ceramic (H11.5cm H4in) Wien 2001

MORTON Alastair 1910-1963 [21]

📖 **$807** - €759 - **£500** - FF4 981
Abstract Composition Watercolour, gouache (49x61.5cm 19x24in) London 1999

MORTON Cavendish 1911 [41]

📖 **$221** - €203 - **£135** - FF1 331
Blythburgh Church Watercolour (15x25cm 6x10in) Aylsham, Norfolk 1998

MORTON Constance 1900 [24]

📖 **$548** - €606 - **£380** - FF3 972
The Barbican, Plymouth Gouache/paper (27.5x38cm 10x14in) London 2001

MORTON Gary 1951 [1]

📖 **$3 500** - €3 974 - **£2 431** - FF26 068
Fresh Mounts for the Fall Roundsup Watercolour/paper (48x73cm 19x29in) Dallas TX 2001

M

MORTON George ?-1904 **[4]**
- $4 750 - €5 402 - **£3 318** - FF35 435
  The Reluctant Encounter Oil/canvas (24x35cm 9x14in) Chicago IL 2000

MORTON Thomas Corsan 1859-1928 **[6]**
- $5 439 - €5 433 - **£3 400** - FF35 639
  By the River Oil/panel (16x25cm 6x9in) Edinburgh 1999

MORVAN Hervé 1917-1980 **[72]**
- $267 - €290 - **£185** - FF1 900
  «Graines Delbard» Affiche (154x115cm 60x45in) Paris 2001

MORYCINSKI Grzegorz 1936 **[19]**
- $457 - €510 - **£313** - FF3 345
  Masque de Venise Pastel/papier (100x70cm 39x27in) Warszawa 2000

MOSBACHER Alois 1954 **[134]**
- $728 - €799 - **£484** - FF5 243
  Ohne Titel Öl/Leinwand (55x70cm 21x27in) Wien 2000
- $309 - €363 - **£219** - FF2 383
  Ohne Titel Charcoal/paper (75x50cm 29x19in) Wien 2000

MOSBRUGGER Friedrich 1804-1930 **[2]**
- $7 108 - €8 181 - **£4 908** - FF53 662
  Junge Italienerin Öl/Leinwand (62x49cm 24x19in) München 2000

MOSCARDO José 1953 **[26]**
- $1 404 - €1 562 - **£988** - FF10 244
  Paisaje nevado Oleo/lienzo (54x65cm 21x25in) Madrid 2001
- $928 - €871 - **£580** - FF5 713
  Mercadillo en Cadaqués Técnica mixta/papel (50x63cm 19x24in) Barcelona 1999

MOSCARDO Ramón 1953 **[25]**
- $744 - €721 - **£468** - FF4 728
  La Frontera, Cadaqués Oleo/lienzo (50x65cm 19x25in) Madrid 1999
- $715 - €661 - **£429** - FF4 334
  Puente sobre el Sena, Paris Oleo/lienzo (24x19cm 9x7in) Barcelona 1999
- $616 - €661 - **£418** - FF4 334
  Vista portuaria Gouache/carton (52x62cm 20x24in) Madrid 2000

MOSCHER van Jacob 1635-1655 **[2]**
- $6 342 - €6 647 - **£4 017** - FF43 600
  Holländische Flusslandschaft mit Gehöft und Anglern am Ufer Oil/panel (35x46cm 13x18in) Köln 2000

MOSCONI A. XIX **[11]**
- $700 - €726 - **£420** - FF4 760
  Veduta della Zecca, Firenze Acquarello/carta (10x16cm 3x6in) Firenze 2000

MOSELEY R.S. XIX-XX **[14]**
- $1 129 - €1 220 - **£780** - FF8 003
  Snowed Out Oil/board (17.5x30cm 6x11in) Billingshurst, West-Sussex 2001

MOSELY Zack XX **[4]**
- $1 600 - €1 717 - **£1 070** - FF11 265
  Smilin' Jack Daily Strips Ink (15x49.5cm 5x19in) New-York 2000

MOSENGEL Adolf 1837-1885 **[19]**
- $887 - €920 - **£562** - FF6 037
  Alpenlandschaft mit Ziegenhirte Öl/Karton (28.5x23cm 11x9in) Rudolstadt-Thüringen 2000

MOSER Carl 1873-1939 **[78]**
- $2 355 - €2 543 - **£1 627** - FF16 684
  Tiroler Bauernmädchen Woodcut in colors (23.7x23.7cm 9x9in) Wien 2001

MOSER Julius 1832-1916 **[1]**
- $3 660 - €3 930 - **£2 449** - FF25 776
  Psyche Bronze (H73cm H28in) Warszawa 2000

MOSER Koloman, Kolo 1868-1918 **[121]**
- $60 259 - €49 496 - **£35 000** - FF324 674
  Plomberg Oil/canvas (50x50cm 19x19in) London 1998
- $989 - €1 125 - **£686** - FF7 378
  «Mein Lied» Ink (34x20.5cm 13x8in) Hamburg 2000
- $193 - €218 - **£135** - FF1 430
  Kopf eines jungen Mädchens vor Föhre Radierung (8x10cm 3x3in) Wien 2001

MOSER Richard 1874-1924 **[31]**
- $3 509 - €3 997 - **£2 425** - FF26 218
  «Stadttor in Dürnstein» Gouache/paper (32.1x25.8cm 12x10in) Wien 2000

MOSER Wilfrid 1914-1997 **[81]**
- $9 017 - €10 477 - **£6 337** - FF68 724
  Dans le métro Öl/Leinwand (97x130cm 38x51in) Luzern 2001
- $3 832 - €4 453 - **£2 693** - FF29 208
  Ohne Titel Öl/Leinwand (65x54cm 25x21in) Luzern 2001
- $2 285 - €2 201 - **£1 429** - FF14 437
  Vorstadtgatren Öl/Karton (32.5x40.5cm 12x15in) Zürich 1999
- $15 083 - €13 822 - **£9 215** - FF90 666
  Skulptur Sculpture (43x21x14cm 16x8x5in) Zürich 1999
- $662 - €790 - **£472** - FF5 180
  Der weisse Berg Gouache (24x31.5cm 9x12in) Luzern 2000

MOSES Ed 1926 **[19]**
- $7 000 - €7 514 - **£4 684** - FF49 287
  Untitled Acrylic/canvas (109x137cm 42x53in) Beverly-Hills CA 2000
- $5 000 - €4 814 - **£3 126** - FF31 581
  Untitled Acrylic (64x53.5cm 25x21in) Beverly-Hills CA 1999
- $3 500 - €2 958 - **£2 087** - FF19 401
  Cubist Studies, BI Charcoal (76x61cm 29x24in) San-Francisco CA 1998

MOSES Forrest K. 1893-1974 **[7]**
- $2 000 - €2 311 - **£1 400** - FF15 156
  Scholl Recess Oil/masonite (40.5x61cm 15x24in) Bethesda MD 2001

MOSES Grandma 1860-1961 **[142]**
- $55 000 - €52 578 - **£34 474** - FF344 888
  «The Old Automobile» Oil/board (40.5x51cm 15x20in) New-York 1999
- $16 000 - €17 559 - **£10 302** - FF115 180
  Over the Hills and Through the Snow Oil/masonite (20.5x25.5cm 8x10in) Beverly-Hills CA 2000
- $18 000 - €19 699 - **£12 416** - FF129 218
  The Roses Garden Gouache (23x18cm 9x7in) New-York 2001

MOSES Stefan 1928 **[122]**
- $550 - €613 - **£360** - FF4 024
  Strassenfeger Gelatin silver print (40.3x30.5cm 15x12in) Köln 2000

MOSKOWITZ Ira 1912-1985 **[21]**
🎨 **$130** - €150 - **£89** - FF984
Famryard Scene Lithograph (18x22cm 7x9in)
Cleveland OH 2000

MOSKOWITZ OF SAFED Shalom 1896-1980 **[11]**
✏️ **$3 400** - €3 827 - **£2 342** - FF25 101
The Story of David and Bath-Sheba
Gouache/paper (49.5x48.5cm 19x19in) Herzelia-Pituah
2000

MOSLER Henry 1841-1920 **[22]**
🐎 **$3 560** - €3 338 - **£2 200** - FF21 899
Teaching the Koran Oil/canvas (64x48cm 25x18in)
London 1999
🐎 **$4 250** - €4 833 - **£2 969** - FF31 705
Tambourine Player Oil/panel (32x23cm 12x9in)
New-York 2000

MOSNIER Jean Laurent 1743/44-1808 **[15]**
🐎 **$15 000** - €17 629 - **£10 399** - FF115 641
**Marquise d'Aramon, seated Half-Length, in a
grey Dress** Oil/canvas (76.5x64cm 30x25in) New-
York 2000

MOSNIER Pierre Meunier 1641-1703 **[3]**
🐎 **$5 230** - €5 615 - **£3 500** - FF36 830
Moses and the Daughters of Jethro Black chalk
(25.5x33cm 10x12in) London 2000

MOSNY Henry XIX **[22]**
🐎 **$490** - €584 - **£350** - FF3 830
**Figures by a Grounded Fishing Boat on a Sunlit
Rocky Coastline** Oil/canvas (34.5x60cm 13x23in)
London 2000

MOSQUITO John c.1920 **[2]**
🐎 **$3 430** - €3 683 - **£2 296** - FF24 157
Untitled Mixed media/canvas (99.5x49cm 39x19in)
Sydney 2000

MOSS Bill XX **[5]**
✏️ **$550** - €514 - **£339** - FF3 369
Shipbuilders, City Island, NY Watercolour/paper
(48x73cm 19x29in) Detroit MI 1999

MOSS Marlow Marjor.Jewell 1890-1958 **[11]**
🐎 **$23 659** - €28 133 - **£16 864** - FF184 549
Composition in Blue, Red, Black and White
Oil/canvas (92x69cm 36x27in) Amsterdam 2000

MOSSA Alexis 1844-1926 **[169]**
✏️ **$454** - €488 - **£304** - FF3 200
Projet de chars pour bataille de fleurs
Aquarelle/papier (14x17cm 5x6in) Nice 2000

MOSSA Gustave-Adolphe 1883-1971 **[169]**
🐎 **$18 190** - €21 648 - **£13 000** - FF142 001
La blonde aux poissons Oil/canvas (48x99cm
18x38in) London 2000
✏️ **$710** - €762 - **£475** - FF5 000
**Projet de plafond aux oiseaux avec aux angles,
symboles de la musique** Aquarelle/papier
(18.5x40.5cm 7x15in) Nice 2000

MOSSET Olivier 1944 **[63]**
🐎 **$4 734** - €4 581 - **£3 000** - FF30 048
N.T.C Acrylic/canvas (400x400cm 157x157in) London
1999
🐎 **$2 168** - €1 982 - **£1 335** - FF13 000
Monochrome blanc Acrylique/toile (61x61cm
24x24in) Paris 2000

MÖSSMER Joseph 1780-1845 **[13]**
✏️ **$1 498** - €1 453 - **£924** - FF9 534
Parklandschaft mit Skulptur Aquarell/Papier
(34x25cm 13x9in) Wien 1999

MÖSSMER Raimund 1813-1874 **[8]**
🐎 **$3 565** - €3 634 - **£2 230** - FF23 835
Blick auf den Traunsee und den Traunstein
Öl/Karton (30.5x25.5cm 12x10in) Wien 2000

MOSSON Georges 1851-1933 **[15]**
🐎 **$2 640** - €2 556 - **£1 658** - FF16 769
**Gladiolen in hoher Glasvase und ungeordnete
bunte Gartenblumen** Öl/Leinwand (80x60cm
31x23in) Berlin 1999

MOSTAERT Gillis I c.1534-1598 **[27]**
🐎 **$13 451** - €12 706 - **£8 391** - FF83 344
David and Abigail Oil/canvas (102x153.5cm 40x60in)
Amsterdam 2000
🐎 **$5 789** - €6 353 - **£3 726** - FF41 672
The Adoration of the Shepherds Oil/panel
(36x50cm 14x19in) Amsterdam 2000
🐎 **$5 130** - €5 827 - **£3 600** - FF38 223
The Arrival at Bethlehem Oil/panel (24x36.5cm
9x14in) London 2001

MOSTAERT Jan c.1472/73-1555/56 **[3]**
🐎 **$70 000** - €74 878 - **£47 726** - FF491 169
**Portrait of a Lady, presumably Anne of
Bretagne** Oil/panel (42x32.5cm 16x12in) New-York
2001

MOSTYN Marjorie 1893-1979 **[44]**
🐎 **$252** - €293 - **£180** - FF1 922
Flowers in a Bowl Oil/board (35x45cm 14x18in) Par,
Cornwall 2001

MOSTYN Thomas Edwin, Tom 1864-1930 **[130]**
🐎 **$2 406** - €2 425 - **£1 500** - FF15 905
Figures Before a Thatched Cottage Oil/canvas
(63.5x30cm 25x11in) London 2000
🐎 **$438** - €429 - **£280** - FF2 814
Woodland Stream Oil/canvas (25x36cm 9x14in)
Leyburn, North Yorkshire 1999

MOTA Y MORALES Vicente 1869-? **[24]**
🐎 **$2 160** - €2 403 - **£1 480** - FF15 760
Paisaje con vacas Oleo/lienzo (49x60cm 19x23in)
Madrid 2001

MOTAU Julian 1948-1968 **[13]**
✏️ **$418** - €466 - **£272** - FF3 057
The Scream Charcoal (69x42cm 27x16in)
Johannesburg 2000

MOTE George William 1832-1909 **[48]**
🐎 **$2 595** - €2 868 - **£1 800** - FF18 815
A Rough Field in Surrey Oil/canvas (61x91.5cm
24x36in) London 2001

MOTELEY Georges 1865-1923 **[35]**
🐎 **$1 916** - €1 677 - **£1 160** - FF11 000
L'abreuvoir Huile/toile (63x72cm 24x28in) Paris 1998
🐎 **$1 598** - €1 464 - **£974** - FF9 600
L'Eglise de Thaon, Calvados Huile/panneau
(26.5x35cm 10x13in) Paris 1999

MOTHERWELL Robert 1915-1991 **[817]**
🐎 **$160 000** - €179 212 - **£111 168** - FF1 175 552
«Altamira #1» Mixed media (182.5x91.5cm 71x36in)
New-York 2000
🐎 **$30 000** - €28 241 - **£18 534** - FF185 247
«Fusains supérieurs» Mixed media/canvas
(73.5x58.5cm 28x23in) New-York 1999
🐎 **$40 000** - €37 356 - **£24 688** - FF245 040
Spanish Elegy XV Oil/canvas/board (30.5x40.5cm
12x15in) New-York 1999
✏️ **$6 000** - €6 480 - **£4 146** - FF42 503
Untitled, from VVV Portfolio Indian ink (42.5x33cm
16x12in) New-York 2001

M

M

⊞ **$2 500** - €2 360 - **£1 554** - FF15 482
Untitled from Africa Suite Silkscreen (102.5x72.5cm
40x28in) San-Francisco CA 1999

MOTI Kaïko 1921-1981 **[29]**
⊞ **$228** - €265 - **£157** - FF1 738
«Owl II» Etching in colors (56x43cm 22x17in) Calgary,
Alberta 2000

MOTLEY Wilton XIX-XX **[5]**
👁 **$1 200** - €1 108 - **£747** - FF7 267
Noonday Heat Oil/canvas (60x86cm 24x34in)
Chicago IL 1999

MOTONAGA Sadamasa 1922 **[3]**
👁 **$6 900** - €5 961 - **£4 600** - FF39 100
Senza titolo Tecnica mista/carta (79x40cm 31x15in)
Milano 2000

MOTSWAI Tommy 1963 **[4]**
✎ **$561** - €626 - **£366** - FF4 108
And New South African Red Nose's Day Party
Pastel/paper (75x55cm 29x21in) Johannesburg 2000

MOTT-SMITH May 1879-1952 **[14]**
👁 **$900** - €853 - **£562** - FF5 596
Harbour Scene/Chickens Feeding Oil/board
(25x33cm 10x13in) Mystic CT 1999
👁 **$600** - €569 - **£374** - FF3 730
Pasadena Garden/San Rafael Heights
Gouache/paper (81x55cm 32x22in) Mystic CT 1999

MOTTA Raffaello 1550-1578 **[10]**
✎ **$21 959** - €21 441 - **£14 000** - FF140 644
**The Holy Ghost surrounded by music-making
angels** Black chalk (26.5x34cm 10x13in) London 1999

MOTTET J. XIX **[1]**
✎ **$4 929** - €4 497 - **£3 032** - FF29 500
Portrait de femme assise Huile/toile (118.5x89cm
46x35in) Paris 1999

MOTTET Johann Daniel 1754-1822 **[8]**
👁 **$1 681** - €1 987 - **£1 191** - FF13 032
Bildnis von C.F.Freudenreich Öl/Leinwand
(83x66cm 32x25in) Zürich 2001

MOTTOLA Xavero XVIII **[1]**
✎ **$4 841** - €4 532 - **£3 000** - FF29 727
**Dido and Aeneas Hunting, Below Juno and
Putti** Ink (60.5x80cm 23x31in) London 1999

MOTTRAM Charles 1807-1876 **[12]**
⊞ **$2 750** - €3 030 - **£1 834** - FF19 875
Boston, After J.W.Hill Engraving (83x114cm
33x45in) Portsmouth NH 2000

MOTTRAM Charles Sim act.1876-1919 **[94]**
✎ **$427** - €376 - **£260** - FF2 465
Fishermen Going Out to Sea Watercolour
(34x44cm 13x17in) London 1999

MOTTU Luc Henri 1815-1859 **[9]**
✎ **$535** - €624 - **£375** - FF4 096
Paysages de montagne Gouache/papier (9x12.5cm
3x4in) Genève 2001

MOTZ Wim 1900-1977 **[25]**
👁 **$3 236** - €3 630 - **£2 242** - FF23 812
Musical Still Life Oil/canvas (80x70cm 31x27in)
Amsterdam 2000

MOTZER August Ferdinand 1844-? **[2]**
👁 **$17 367** - €18 200 - **£11 000** - FF119 381
**Vienna Townhall/Natural History Museum,
Vienna** Tempera (65x94cm 25x37in) London 2000

MOUALLA Fikret M. Saygi 1903-1967 **[507]**
👁 **$6 572** - €6 098 - **£4 092** - FF40 000
Terrasse du café Huile/toile (38x46cm 14x18in)
Paris 1999
👁 **$3 721** - €4 269 - **£2 545** - FF28 000
Bouquet de fleurs et théière Huile/toile (33x24cm
12x9in) Paris 2000
✎ **$1 497** - €1 677 - **£1 040** - FF11 000
Jeune fille allongée Aquarelle, gouache/papier
(20x25cm 7x9in) Le Touquet 2001

MOUCHERON de Frédéric 1633-1686 **[65]**
👁 **$32 977** - €31 765 - **£20 377** - FF208 362
**Shepherds with Cattle and Sheep by a
Fountain, at Sunset** Oil/panel (117.5x190.5cm
46x75in) Amsterdam 1999
👁 **$6 500** - €6 738 - **£3 900** - FF44 200
Paesaggio con cavalieri Olio/tela (77x109cm
30x42in) Roma 2000
👁 **$5 375** - €5 899 - **£3 460** - FF38 695
**Birch Trees by a Torrent in an italianate
Landscape** Oil/panel (40.5x34cm 15x13in)
Amsterdam 2000
✎ **$1 877** - €2 178 - **£1 296** - FF14 287
**An Italianate Landscape with Travellers on a
Road, a Village on a Hill** Ink (31.5x43cm 12x16in)
Amsterdam 2000

MOUCHERON de Isaac 1667-1744 **[66]**
👁 **$93 102** - €91 191 - **£60 000** - FF598 176
**Italianate Landscapes with Figures and classi-
cal buildings** Oil/canvas (263x150cm 103x59in)
London 1999
👁 **$54 153** - €61 508 - **£38 000** - FF403 465
**Extensive Italiamate Landscape with
Shepherds and Shepherds** Oil/panel (43x55cm
16x21in) London 2001
✎ **$4 000** - €4 046 - **£2 442** - FF26 543
**Classical Landscape with a Sacrifice offered to
Pan** Ink (24x34cm 9x13in) New-York 2000

MOUCHOT Hippolyte Louis 1846-1893 **[7]**
👁 **$4 200** - €4 607 - **£2 852** - FF30 219
Portrait of a Lady in Blue Oil/canvas (54x38cm
21x15in) New-Orleans LA 2000

MOUCHOT Louis Claude 1830-1891 **[14]**
👁 **$1 065** - €1 220 - **£732** - FF8 000
Célébration de la messe dans une église
Huile/panneau (60x49cm 23x19in) Paris 2000

MOUDARRES Fateh 1922-1999 **[3]**
👁 **$4 296** - €4 833 - **£3 000** - FF31 701
Red Maaloula Oil/canvas (68.5x48cm 26x18in)
London 2001

MOUFFE Michel 1957 **[8]**
👁 **$6 725** - €7 219 - **£4 500** - FF47 351
Antre V Graphite (186x186cm 73x73in) London 2000

MOUGIN Joseph 1876-1961 **[1]**
🏺 **$7 869** - €8 156 - **£4 986** - FF53 500
Vase avec en décor le corps d'une femme
Céramique (H67cm H26in) Poitiers 2000

MOUILLARD Lucien 1842-1912 **[2]**
👁 **$22 304** - €25 916 - **£15 895** - FF170 000
Le bain turc Huile/toile (65x55cm 25x21in) Paris
2001

MOULE Thomas 1785-1851 **[8]**
⊞ **$206** - €219 - **£140** - FF1 436
Dorsetshire Engraving (18.5x25cm 7x9in) Crewkerne,
Somerset 2001

MOULENE Jean-Luc 1955 **[1]**
📷 **$3 139** - €3 506 - **£2 127** - FF23 000
Michael Faraday, Paris Hiver Cibachrome print (100x80cm 39x31in) Paris 2000

MOULIN Charles Lucien XIX-XX **[9]**
🖐 **$9 000** - €10 584 - **£6 453** - FF69 425
At the Spring Oil/canvas (172x71cm 67x27in) New-York 2001
✏ **$1 638** - €1 911 - **£1 150** - FF12 534
Deep in thought Pastel/paper (80x61cm 31x24in) Godalming, Surrey 2001

MOULIN Félix Jacques Ant. 1802-c.1875 **[20]**
📷 **$3 595** - €3 067 - **£2 169** - FF20 121
Weiblicher Akt Albumen print (12.4x16.9cm 4x6in) Köln 1998

MOULINET Antoine Edouard J. 1833-1891 **[11]**
🖐 **$4 160** - €4 878 - **£2 992** - FF32 000
La salle de classe Huile/toile (62x56cm 24x22in) Paris 2001

MOULINNEUF Étienne XVIII **[7]**
🖐 **$68 069** - €65 553 - **£42 269** - FF430 000
Trompe-l'oeil aux coquillages, instruments scientifiques, gravure Huile/toile (75.5x62.5cm 29x24in) Paris 1999
🖐 **$3 546** - €3 283 - **£2 200** - FF21 535
Trompe l'oeil: Le Bénédicté Oil/canvas (41x32.5cm 16x12in) London 1999

MOULY Marcel 1918 **[114]**
🖐 **$832** - €884 - **£558** - FF5 800
La clairière jaune Huile/toile (60x73cm 23x28in) Cannes 2000
🖐 **$588** - €503 - **£345** - FF3 300
Le verger rouge Huile/toile (27x41cm 10x16in) Avignon 1998

MOUNCEY William 1852-1901 **[25]**
🖐 **$12 081** - €11 353 - **£7 500** - FF74 468
Golden Autumn, Galloway Oil/canvas (100.5x126cm 39x49in) London 2001
🖐 **$3 801** - €3 248 - **£2 300** - FF21 303
On the Edge of the Road Oil/canvas (40.5x51cm 15x20in) Edinburgh 1998
🖐 **$4 327** - €5 086 - **£3 000** - FF33 360
Girls, Senwick Wood, Kirkcudbright Oil/canvas (30.5x40.5cm 12x15in) Edinburgh 2000

MOUNT PLEASANT ARTIST (the) (Samuel Benz) XIX **[1]**
✏ **$14 000** - €11 688 - **£8 211** - FF76 671
Birth Letter for Maria Anna Martin Watercolour (24x19.5cm 9x7in) New-York 1998

MOUNT Reginald XX **[3]**
📜 **$613** - €592 - **£380** - FF3 882
«Ladykillers» Poster (56x43cm 22x16in) London 1999

MOUNT Rita 1888-1967 **[44]**
🖐 **$507** - €480 - **£316** - FF3 150
Bateaux de pêche, Gaspé Huile/carton/toile (23x28cm 9x11in) Montréal 1999

MOUNT Shepard Alonzo 1804-1868 **[6]**
🖐 **$1 500** - €1 706 - **£1 040** - FF11 190
Gentleman Oil/canvas (68x55cm 27x22in) East-Moriches NY 2001

MOUNT William Sidney 1807-1868 **[20]**
🖐 **$20 000** - €21 888 - **£13 796** - FF143 576
John Crary/His Wife Henrietta & their Daughter Phebe Oil/canvas (91.5x73.5cm 36x28in) New-York 2001

$22 000 - €24 981 - **£15 056** - FF163 864
Portrait of Maria Seabury Oil/panel (20.5x17cm 8x6in) New-York 2000

MOUNTAIN Robert Frederick 1821-1871 **[8]**
✏ **$709** - €681 - **£440** - FF4 466
Une troïka Aquarelle (11.5x23.5cm 4x9in) Montréal 1999

MOUNTFORD Arnold 1878-? **[6]**
🖐 **$11 536** - €12 748 - **£8 000** - FF83 624
Olivia Monckton, Wife of Reginald Monkton, of Le Moigne's, Wrington Oil/canvas (102x127cm 40x50in) London 2001

MOUR van Jan Baptiste 1671-1737 **[16]**
🖐 **$83 940** - €91 469 - **£55 020** - FF600 000
Concert donné par un ambassadeur à la cour du Sultan Ahmed III Huile/toile (75x102cm 29x40in) Louviers 2000
🖐 **$5 800** - €5 697 - **£3 600** - FF37 367
Lady in Elegant Costume, holding a Scroll Oil/canvas (34.5x27cm 13x10in) London 1999

MOUREN Henri Laurent 1844-1926 **[93]**
🖐 **$1 189** - €1 326 - **£830** - FF8 700
Paysage des Alpes dans la vallée du Glaizin Huile/toile (46.5x55.5cm 18x21in) Versailles 2001
✏ **$362** - €305 - **£213** - FF2 000
La Marne à Charenton Aquarelle/papier (25x21cm 9x8in) Grenoble 1998

MOURIER Claude 1930 **[127]**
🖐 **$707** - €701 - **£429** - FF4 600
Coucher de soleil Huile/toile (46x55cm 18x21in) Toulouse 2000
🖐 **$387** - €457 - **£272** - FF3 000
Pêcheur Huile/toile (33x41cm 12x16in) Nîmes 2000

MOURIER-PETERSEN Christian 1858-1945 **[24]**
🖐 **$39 984** - €45 639 - **£27 778** - FF299 370
Strygestuen på Holbaekgård Oil/canvas (65x50cm 25x19in) København 2000

MOURLOT Maurice 1906-1983 **[162]**
🖐 **$393** - €335 - **£234** - FF2 200
Nature morte aux harengs saurs et à la bouteille Huile/isorel (55x46cm 21x18in) Paris 1998
🖐 **$232** - €198 - **£138** - FF1 300
Buffet briard et souris Huile/carton (40x28cm 15x11in) Paris 1998
📜 **$749** - €716 - **£468** - FF4 695
Fleurs coquillages, nach Max Ernst Print (43x51.5cm 16x20in) Köln 1999

MOUTTE Alphonse 1840-1913 **[5]**
🖐 **$4 125** - €4 505 - **£2 625** - FF29 550
Desnudo Oleo/lienzo (115x90cm 45x35in) Madrid 2000

MOWBRAY Henry Siddons 1858-1928 **[8]**
🖐 **$2 500** - €2 266 - **£1 539** - FF14 862
Pan playing Flute Oil/panel (11x15cm 4x6in) Mystic CT 1999

MOXHAM Miriam 1885-1971 **[2]**
🖐 **$14 273** - €13 570 - **£8 907** - FF89 012
Sport of Kings - The Preliminary Oil/canvas/board (55x113cm 21x44in) Melbourne 1999

MOY Seong 1921 **[17]**
📜 **$180** - €193 - **£120** - FF1 267
Spring Moon Color lithograph (33x45cm 13x18in) Cleveland OH 2000

M

MOYERS John 1958 **[7]**
- **$35 200** - €34 169 - **£21 739** - FF224 136
  Descending Taos Mountain Oil/canvas (101x127cm 40x50in) Dallas TX 1999
- **$19 000** - €21 574 - **£13 201** - FF141 513
  The Ones who came before Oil/canvas (111x76cm 44x30in) Dallas TX 2001

MOYERS Terri Kelly 1953 **[3]**
- **$4 000** - €4 542 - **£2 779** - FF29 792
  Appaloosa Autumn Oil/board (35x45cm 14x18in) Dallas TX 2001

MOYERS William 1916 **[13]**
- **$3 300** - €3 542 - **£2 208** - FF23 235
  Up to No Good Oil/canvas (30x22cm 12x9in) Houston TX 2000

MOYNAN Richard Thomas 1856-1906 **[13]**
- **$31 662** - €35 464 - **£22 000** - FF232 630
  What shall I say Oil/canvas (35.5x46cm 13x18in) London 2001
- **$7 886** - €7 301 - **£4 761** - FF47 891
  Evening near Dalkey Oil/panel (25.5x35cm 10x13in) Dublin 1999

MOYNET Jean-Pierre 1819-1876 **[3]**
- **$5 133** - €5 173 - **£3 200** - FF33 931
  A Summer Evening on the Canal Oil/canvas (95x122cm 37x48in) London 2000

MOYNIHAN Rodrigo 1910-1991 **[37]**
- **$2 891** - €2 785 - **£1 800** - FF18 266
  Landscape at Bruén Oil/canvas (76x76cm 29x29in) London 1999

MOYREAU Jean 1690-1762 **[33]**
- **$150** - €161 - **£100** - FF1 056
  L'Enfance, after J. Raoux Etching (40.5x30.5cm 15x12in) London 2000

MOZIER Joseph 1812-1870/76 **[11]**
- **$34 000** - €32 356 - **£21 267** - FF212 241
  Pocahantas Marble (H121cm H48in) New-York 1999

MOZIN Charles Louis 1806-1862 **[49]**
- **$3 408** - €3 659 - **£2 280** - FF24 000
  Paysage de cascades dans les Alpes Huile/toile (100x79.5cm 39x31in) Paris 2000
- **$4 102** - €4 878 - **£2 825** - FF32 000
  Le fort de Socoa Huile/panneau (28.5x40cm 11x15in) Paris 2000
- **$1 829** - €2 134 - **£1 272** - FF14 000
  Vue de la Seine près du Palais Bourbon Aquarelle/papier (14x21cm 5x8in) Nice 2000

MOZLEY Charles 1915-1991 **[26]**
- **$1 022** - €863 - **£600** - FF5 660
  «You can be sure of Shell, These Men Use Shell» Poster (75x113cm 29x44in) London 1998

MOZOS MARTINEZ Pedro 1915-1982 **[76]**
- **$2 415** - €2 102 - **£1 505** - FF13 790
  Concierto de piano Oleo/lienzo (60.5x60.5cm 23x23in) Madrid 1999
- **$517** - €450 - **£322** - FF2 955
  Nuestras cualidades Acuarela/papel (24x31cm 9x12in) Madrid 1999

MOZYN Michiel c.1630-? **[2]**
- **$20 608** - €21 343 - **£13 118** - FF140 000
  «Stipendi Peccati Morti», d'après Jean-Baptiste Corneille Burin (72.5x51.5cm 28x20in) Paris 2000

MRKUSICH Milan 1925 **[16]**
- **$14 914** - €16 718 - **£10 430** - FF109 660
  Orange Achromatic Acrylic (160x122.5cm 62x48in) Auckland 2001

- **$10 077** - €11 296 - **£7 047** - FF74 095
  Untitled Painting Oil/board (60x48cm 23x18in) Auckland 2001
- **$1 876** - €1 972 - **£1 235** - FF12 933
  Abstract Composition Indian ink (32x23.5cm 12x9in) Auckland 2000

MRKVICKA Otakar 1898-1957 **[7]**
- **$462** - €437 - **£288** - FF2 868
  Portrait de femme Huile/panneau (49x32cm 19x12in) Praha 2000

MROCZKOWSKI Aleksander 1850-1927 **[13]**
- **$5 295** - €4 873 - **£3 177** - FF31 966
  Coquetteries au bord de l'étang Oil/canvas (44x76cm 17x29in) Warszawa 1999

MROZEK Erich 1907 **[9]**
- **$7 000** - €7 279 - **£4 419** - FF47 745
  Bauhaus Study, Bauhaus, Dessau Photograph (16.5x21cm 6x8in) New-York 2000

MUAFANGEJO John Ndevasia 1943-1987 **[42]**
- **$371** - €431 - **£256** - FF2 830
  Me Are Working in Town Linocut (59.5x41.5cm 23x16in) Johannesburg 2000

MUBIN Othon 1924-1981 **[14]**
- **$4 239** - €4 116 - **£2 619** - FF27 000
  Composition abstraite Huile/toile (89x115cm 35x45in) Paris 1999

MUCCHI Gabriele 1899-? **[31]**
- **$800** - €829 - **£480** - FF5 440
  Natura morta con caffettiera Olio/tela/cartone (25x30cm 9x11in) Milano 2000

MUCCINI Marcello 1926-1978 **[17]**
- **$1 000** - €1 037 - **£600** - FF6 800
  Tetti di Roma Olio/tela (35x50cm 13x19in) Roma 2001

MUCHA Alphonse 1860-1939 **[1192]**
- **$320 000** - €351 184 - **£206 048** - FF2 303 616
  Winter Tale Oil/canvas (124x99cm 48x38in) New-York 2000
- **$19 652** - €18 587 - **£12 240** - FF121 924
  Moravska Madona Huile/toile (89x60.5cm 35x23in) Praha 2000
- **$2 600** - €2 241 - **£1 544** - FF14 697
  Wooded Landscape Oil/board (42x33.5cm 16x13in) New-York 1998
- **$2 888** - €3 354 - **£2 037** - FF22 000
  Tête byzantine Bronze (11.5x8cm 4x3in) Neuilly-sur-Seine 2001
- **$2 500** - €2 683 - **£1 673** - FF17 662
  Prostitute Soliciting near the Arc de Triomphe Watercolour, gouache/paper (21.5x16.5cm 8x6in) Los-Angeles CA 2000
- **$3 953** - €4 497 - **£2 743** - FF29 500
  «Le laurier» Affiche couleur (58.5x43.5cm 23x17in) Paris 2000
- **$2 500** - €2 351 - **£1 548** - FF15 422
  Alphonse Marie Mucha: Settings and Models Gelatin silver print (13x17cm 5x6in) New-York 1999

MUCHA Reinhard 1950 **[4]**
- **$52 992** - €49 381 - **£32 000** - FF323 920
  Untitled Sculpture (145x253x32cm 57x99x12in) London 1998

MUCHA Willy 1905-1995 **[40]**
- **$193** - €195 - **£120** - FF1 281
  La Rade de Tangers Watercolour/paper (48.5x64.5cm 19x25in) Billingshurst, West-Sussex 2000

$884 - €980 - **£600** - FF6 427
«Oustreham Riva Bella, SNCF» Poster (100x62cm 39x24in) London 2000

MUCHE Georg 1895-1987 [30]

$12 275 - €14 316 - **£8 618** - FF93 909
Am Ufer Öl/Leinwand (100.5x80.5cm 39x31in) Köln 2000

$1 112 - €1 278 - **£785** - FF8 384
«Schon wieder Scheuchen über dem Horizont» Pencil/paper (42.5x62cm 16x24in) Hamburg 2001

$2 044 - €1 789 - **£1 237** - FF11 735
Hand-Herz Radierung (15x13.5cm 5x5in) Berlin 1998

MÜCKE Karl Emil 1847-1923 [14]

$2 251 - €2 556 - **£1 564** - FF16 769
Mutterglück, Holländische Interieur Öl/Leinwand (46.5x35cm 18x13in) Köln 2001

$11 383 - €13 225 - **£8 000** - FF86 753
Feeding Time/Watching the Pot Oil/panel (30.5x23.5cm 12x9in) London 2001

MUCKLEY William Jabez 1837-1905 [23]

$4 366 - €5 220 - **£3 000** - FF34 239
Vase of Roses and Butterfly on a Ledge, a Landscape beyond Oil/canvas (49x39.5cm 19x15in) Billingshurst, West-Sussex 2000

$2 766 - €2 338 - **£1 650** - FF15 334
Still Life with Grapes Watercolour/paper (43x57cm 16x22in) Leamington-Spa, Warwickshire 1998

MUDD James 1821-1906 [7]

$709 - €810 - **£500** - FF5 316
«On the Llugway, North Wales» Albumen print (43x49cm 16x19in) London 2001

MUECK Ron 1958 [2]

$59 497 - €50 834 - **£36 000** - FF333 450
Big Baby 2 Sculpture (85x71x70cm 33x27x27in) London 1998

MUEHLHAUS Daan 1907-1981 [29]

$599 - €681 - **£413** - FF4 464
Amsterdamse gracht Oil/canvas (60x80cm 23x31in) Dordrecht 2000

MUELLER Alexander 1872-1935 [1]

$3 750 - €4 084 - **£2 582** - FF26 790
Landscape «Lily Pond» Oil/canvas (50x63cm 20x25in) Altadena CA 2000

MUELLER Otto 1874-1930 [374]

$613 016 - €571 614 - **£370 000** - FF3 749 543
Reclining Girl Tempera (60x105cm 23x41in) London 1999

$18 462 - €20 963 - **£12 828** - FF137 509
Landschaft Watercolour (18x23cm 7x9in) München 2001

$4 328 - €4 856 - **£3 000** - FF31 853
Russisches Haus Mit Sonnenblumen Lithograph (29x39.5cm 11x15in) London 2000

MUENIER Jules Alexis 1863/69-1942 [33]

$125 000 - €116 557 - **£77 537** - FF764 562
The Best Days Oil/canvas (131x137cm 51x53in) New-York 1999

$4 000 - €4 430 - **£2 712** - FF29 058
The One That Got Away Oil/canvas (54.5x66cm 21x25in) New-York 2000

MUGNAINI Joseph Anthony 1912 [1]

$900 - €1 022 - **£616** - FF7 180
Views of the Moon with Ray Bradbury Color lithograph (66x50.5cm 25x19in) New-York 2000

MUHAMMAD BABA XVIII [1]

$9 513 - €9 927 - **£6 000** - FF65 120
Portrait of Shah Sulayman Safavi Gouache (11.5x6.5cm 4x2in) London 2000

MUHEIM Jost Anton 1808-1880 [4]

$4 250 - €3 680 - **£2 563** - FF24 136
Extensive Landscape with a Rustic Cottage Oil/canvas (64x84.5cm 25x33in) San-Francisco CA 1998

MÜHL Otto 1925 [173]

$12 735 - €10 901 - **£7 665** - FF71 505
«Parndorfer Heide» Öl/Leinwand (100x130cm 39x51in) Wien 1998

$3 641 - €3 997 - **£2 420** - FF26 218
Mai Acryl/Leinwand (80x100cm 31x39in) Wien 2000

$1 702 - €1 599 - **£1 051** - FF10 487
Kreuzigung Indian ink (43x61cm 16x24in) Wien 1999

$869 - €726 - **£515** - FF4 764
«12 Aktionen» Farbserigraphie (104x73cm 40x28in) Wien 1998

MÜHL Roger 1929 [240]

$4 750 - €3 986 - **£2 787** - FF26 144
Oliviers Oil/canvas (150x160cm 59x62in) New-York 1998

$2 750 - €2 324 - **£1 640** - FF15 246
Village sous la neige Oil/canvas (63x92cm 24x36in) San-Francisco CA 1998

$1 478 - €1 723 - **£1 023** - FF11 300
Les cyprès Huile/toile (39x40cm 15x15in) Calais 2000

$177 - €168 - **£110** - FF1 100
Les barques Lithographie (56x76cm 22x29in) Saint-Dié 1999

MÜHLBACHER Ferdinand 1844-1921 [2]

$7 320 - €7 267 - **£4 580** - FF47 670
Schwarzstrasse mit Blick auf Festung Öl/Karton (29x45cm 11x17in) Salzburg 1999

MÜHLBECK Josef 1878-1948 [40]

$878 - €920 - **£581** - FF6 037
Bei Aubing auf einem Hohlweg eine Bäuerin mit Vieh Öl/Leinwand (30x40cm 11x15in) München 2000

MÜHLENEN von Max Rudolf 1903-1971 [51]

$1 642 - €1 625 - **£1 024** - FF10 657
Ohne Titel Huile/papier/toile (74x110cm 29x43in) Luzern 1999

$2 958 - €3 217 - **£1 949** - FF21 102
Gelb-blauer Akt Öl/Karton (32x41cm 12x16in) Bern 2000

MÜHLENFELD Otto 1871-1907 [3]

$7 000 - €7 054 - **£4 363** - FF46 270
The American Schooner Amy Oil/canvas (51x60.5cm 20x23in) New-York 2000

MUHLENHAUPT Curt 1921 [146]

$1 193 - €1 022 - **£717** - FF6 706
Else B. Öl/Leinwand (35x25cm 13x9in) Berlin 1998

$314 - €358 - **£218** - FF2 347
«Die Blücherkirche am Landwehrkanal» Coloured pencils/paper (50x35.5cm 19x13in) Berlin 2000

$125 - €143 - **£87** - FF939
Ali aus Plönjeshausen Lithographie (28x33.8cm 11x13in) Berlin 2000

MÜHLENWEG Elisabeth 1910-1961 [14]

$282 - €332 - **£202** - FF2 180
Der Heilige Georg zu Pferde Painting (20x16cm 7x6in) Konstanz 2001

MUHLHOFER Mary Elizabeth 1877-1950 [14]
- $500 - €443 - £306 - FF2 906
  White Flowers in a Vase Watercolour/paper
  (38x27cm 15x11in) Cincinnati OH 1999

MÜHLIG Bernhard 1829-1910 [100]
- $1 313 - €1 368 - £832 - FF8 974
  Maskenball der Münchner Künstlergesellschaft
  Öl/Leinwand (37.5x52cm 14x20in) Zürich 2000
- $952 - €1 022 - £622 - FF8 156
  Partie in der Sächsischen Schweiz Öl/Leinwand
  (17x26.5cm 6x10in) Köln 2000

MÜHLIG Hugo 1854-1929 [145]
- $10 733 - €11 248 - £6 798 - FF73 785
  Auf dem Felde Öl/Karton (39.3x57.5cm 15x22in)
  Köln 2000
- $4 840 - €4 090 - £2 886 - FF26 828
  Bei der Feldarbeit Oil/panel (18x28cm 7x11in)
  Düsseldorf 1998
- $859 - €1 022 - £612 - FF6 707
  Ein Pferdekarren Aquarell/Papier (24x40cm 9x15in)
  Köln 2000

MÜHLIG Meno 1823-1873 [42]
- $10 315 - €9 846 - £6 445 - FF64 587
  Banquet Scene Oil/canvas (130x163.5cm 51x64in)
  Warszawa 1999
- $2 956 - €2 761 - £1 786 - FF18 111
  **Auf der Pirsh, Jäger, seinen Hund zur Ruhe
  ermahnend** Öl/Leinwand (48.5x38.5cm 19x15in)
  Berlin 1999
- $1 639 - €1 534 - £993 - FF10 061
  Besuch beim Waffenschmied Öl/Leinwand
  (30x38.5cm 11x15in) Düsseldorf 1999

MÜHLMANN Joseph 1805-1865 [1]
- $3 970 - €3 634 - £2 420 - FF23 835
  Maria mit dem Kind in einer Landschaft
  Öl/Leinwand (30x25cm 11x9in) Wien 1999

MUHLSTOCK Louis 1904 [64]
- $263 - €294 - £178 - FF1 928
  Portrait de femme Encre/papier (20x15cm 7x5in)
  Montréal 2000

MUIR Anne Davidson ?-1951 [10]
- $1 231 - €1 177 - £749 - FF7 722
  Nejlikor i vas Oil/canvas (46x35.5cm 18x13in)
  Helsinki 1999

MUIR James N. 1945 [6]
- $3 000 - €3 406 - £2 084 - FF22 344
  «Southern Steel 1» Bronze (H18cm H7in) Dallas TX
  2001

MUIRHEAD David Thomson 1867-1930 [30]
- $253 - €264 - £160 - FF1 730
  Near Huntingdon Watercolour/paper (24x34cm
  9x13in) Leyburn, North Yorkshire 2000

MUIRHEAD John 1863-1927 [20]
- $448 - €481 - £300 - FF3 156
  Stonehaven Watercolour/paper (24.5x35cm 9x13in)
  Billingshurst, West-Sussex 2000

MUJEZINOVIC Ismar 1947 [6]
- $722 - €728 - £450 - FF4 776
  «Xiv Olympic Winter Games Sarjevo» Poster
  (68x48cm 26x18in) London 2000

MUKERJI Roma 1910 [2]
- $7 000 - €8 116 - £4 958 - FF53 235
  Buddha and Amrapali Watercolour/paper
  (38.5x28.5cm 15x11in) New-York 2000

MUKHERJEE Binod Behari 1904-1980 [11]
- $2 866 - €2 775 - £1 800 - FF18 202
  Landscape Tempera (49.5x28cm 19x11in) London
  1999
- $2 977 - €2 784 - £1 800 - FF18 265
  Trees Ink (33x20.5cm 12x8in) London 1999

MUKUH Ida Bagus XX [1]
- $2 630 - €2 753 - £1 652 - FF18 059
  Temple Festival with a Divine Presence Ink
  (45x91cm 17x35in) Singapore 2000

MULARD François Henri 1769-1850 [2]
- $100 000 - €88 013 - £60 880 - FF577 330
  **Lady, Seated three-quarter length, Wearing a
  White Dress with a Shawl** Oil/canvas (100x80.5cm
  39x31in) New-York 1999

MULAS Maria XX [3]
- $3 000 - €3 110 - £1 800 - FF20 400
  I sassi di Ravenna Tirage argentique (100x150cm
  39x59in) Milano 2001

MULCAHY Michael 1952 [14]
- $1 201 - €1 333 - £837 - FF8 745
  Kilkenny Reflections IV Mixed media (65x55cm
  25x21in) Dublin 2001
- $944 - €1 016 - £643 - FF6 663
  «1+2=0» (Series) Mixed media/paper (56x76cm
  22x29in) Dublin 2001

MULDERS Marc 1958 [5]
- $3 885 - €3 857 - £2 427 - FF25 301
  5 gevilde konijnen III Oil/canvas (70x70cm 27x27in)
  Amsterdam 1999

MULERTT Carl Eugene 1869-1915 [7]
- $3 000 - €2 593 - £1 780 - FF17 006
  The End of the Day Oil/canvas (117x101.5cm
  46x39in) Washington 1998

MULET Y CLAVER Vicente 1897-1945 [5]
- $3 010 - €2 779 - £1 800 - FF18 227
  Man making Twine/A Fishing Village Oil/canvas
  (41x49.5cm 16x19in) London 1999

MULHAUPT Frederick 1871-1938 [53]
- $7 500 - €7 082 - £4 657 - FF46 454
  Cape Ann Pastureland Oil/canvas (45.5x61cm
  17x24in) Beverly-Hills CA 1999
- $7 600 - €6 345 - £4 457 - FF41 621
  «Gloucester Fishing Dock» Oil/board (30x39cm
  12x15in) Nantucket MA 1998

MULHOLLAND Craig 1969 [7]
- $574 - €646 - £400 - FF4 235
  «Child 1» Charcoal/paper (73.5x53cm 28x20in)
  Edinburgh 2001

MULHOLLAND Sydney A. XIX [17]
- $300 - €280 - £185 - FF1 839
  Seascape with crashing Surf and Sailboats
  Watercolour (26x56cm 10x22in) New-Orleans LA 1999

MULIER IL CAVALIER TEMPESTA Pietro 1637-1701
[51]
- $18 000 - €18 660 - £10 800 - FF122 400
  Tempesta con costa marina e barche Olio/tela
  (147.5x223cm 58x87in) Milano 1999
- $17 000 - €15 994 - £10 608 - FF104 913
  **Wooded Landscape at Sunset with
  Shepherdesses by a Stream** Oil/canvas
  (73.5x98cm 28x38in) New-York 1999

MULIER Pieter I 1615-1670 **[24]**
$5 671 - €6 353 - £3 941 - FF41 672
**Threemaster and other Shipping in choppy
Waters on a cloudy Day** Oil/panel (39.5x46cm
15x18in) Amsterdam 2001
$6 510 - €7 260 - £4 248 - FF47 625
Sailing Ships in Rough Seas Oil/panel (26x53.5cm
10x21in) Amsterdam 2001

MÜLLER Adam 1811-1844 **[15]**
$7 597 - €7 272 - £4 719 - FF47 703
**Portraet af maleren C.A. Lorentzen i sit atelier,
Kopi efter M. Rörbye** Oil/canvas (71x58cm 27x22in)
Köbenhavn 1999
$2 392 - €2 684 - £1 658 - FF17 606
Hans Tausen, beskytter biskop Ronnow Oil/can-
vas (35x29cm 13x11in) Köbenhavn 2000

MULLER Adolf, Willy 1889-1953 **[13]**
$394 - €463 - £278 - FF3 037
Villette, Paris Öl/Karton (19x24cm 7x9in) St. Gallen
2000

MÜLLER Albert 1884-1963 **[13]**
$2 392 - €2 301 - £1 474 - FF15 092
Konstruktivistische Komposition Collage/paper
(20.5x14.5cm 8x5in) München 1999

MÜLLER Albert 1897-1926 **[246]**
$20 568 - €18 848 - £12 567 - FF123 636
Kleiner sitzender Akt Öl/Leinwand (60x50cm
23x19in) Zürich 1999
$5 423 - €6 192 - £3 823 - FF40 620
«Brissago» Öl/Karton (28x36.5cm 11x14in) Bern
2001
$701 - €769 - £476 - FF5 044
Wohnhaus von Albert Müller in Orbino Oil chalks
(17x22cm 6x8in) Basel 2000
$225 - €264 - £159 - FF1 735
Maske Woodcut (15x14cm 5x5in) St. Gallen 2000

MÜLLER Alfredo 1869-1940 **[72]**
$2 463 - €2 287 - £1 543 - FF15 000
Étang dans un sous-bois Huile/toile (84x65cm
33x25in) Paris 1999
$6 417 - €6 403 - £4 006 - FF42 000
La ronde Pastel/papier (65x81cm 25x31in) Nice 1999
$850 - €817 - £527 - FF5 357
Cleo de Merode Aquatint in colors (36.5x35cm
14x13in) New-York 1999

MÜLLER Andreas Johann Jakob 1811-1890 **[1]**
$5 702 - €5 190 - £3 504 - FF34 044
Madonna and Child Oil/panel (69x34cm 27x14in)
London 1999

MÜLLER Anton 1853-1897 **[14]**
$7 488 - €6 902 - £4 484 - FF45 272
**Alte Freunde, Ein Förster und sein Hund in der
Stube am Tisch** Oil/panel (45x36.5cm 17x14in)
Dresden 1998

MÜLLER Archibald Herman 1878-1952 **[6]**
$6 200 - €7 188 - £4 392 - FF47 151
Sita Abandoned Oil/canvas/board (86.5x58.5cm
34x23in) New-York 2000

MÜLLER August 1836-1885 **[17]**
$3 569 - €4 200 - £2 584 - FF27 551
Scène d'intérieur, grand-père et son petit-fils
Huile/toile (45x36.5cm 17x14in) Sion 2001
$1 478 - €1 458 - £950 - FF9 565
Young Girl in traditional Costume Oil/canvas
(41x33cm 16x12in) London 1999

MÜLLER C. XIX **[2]**
$5 643 - €5 717 - £3 510 - FF37 500
Dame orientale Chryséléphantine (H38cm H14in)
Aubagne 2001

MÜLLER Carl 1862-1938 **[10]**
$1 316 - €1 453 - £912 - FF9 534
**Belebte Strasse vor der Kalvarienbergkirche bei
Regen** Aquarell/Papier (39x29cm 15x11in) Wien 2001

MÜLLER Charles Louis Lucien 1815-1892 **[38]**
$42 894 - €48 712 - £30 000 - FF319 527
La ronde du mai Oil/canvas (156x214cm 61x84in)
London 2001
$3 294 - €3 270 - £2 056 - FF21 451
Romantische Begegnung Öl/Leinwand (91x117cm
35x46in) Wien 1999

MÜLLER David 1834-1913 **[2]**
$2 648 - €2 502 - £1 649 - FF16 409
Müllheim, Kt. Thurgau Gouache/paper (20x35cm
7x13in) St. Gallen 1999

MÜLLER Dorette 1898-1973 **[2]**
$3 736 - €4 011 - £2 500 - FF26 308
«Golf Club d'Alsace» Poster (105x74cm 41x29in)
London 2000

MULLER Edmund Gustavus XIX **[15]**
$695 - €640 - £430 - FF4 195
The Top of Nant Frangon Pass, North Wales
Watercolour/paper (66x89cm 25x35in) Bristol, Avon
1999

MULLER Émile ?-1899 **[3]**
$4 038 - €4 747 - £2 800 - FF31 136
**Plaque from the Series Les Heures, after
Eugène Grasset** Ceramic (45.5x18cm 17x7in)
London 2000

MÜLLER Erich Martin 1888-1972 **[37]**
$592 - €665 - £402 - FF4 346
Gänse am Bach Oil/panel (41x50cm 16x19in)
München 2000
$3 192 - €3 579 - £2 167 - FF23 477
Andacht im Spital in Dinkelsbühl Aquarell/Papier
(46x54cm 18x21in) München 2000

MÜLLER Ernst Emmanuel 1844-1915 **[15]**
$994 - €920 - £616 - FF6 037
Früchtestilleben mit Zinn Öl/Leinwand (50x60cm
19x23in) Stuttgart 1999

MULLER Eugène Robert XIX **[2]**
$2 572 - €2 592 - £1 603 - FF17 000
Jeune fille à l'oiseau Pastel/papier (73x58cm
28x22in) Paris 2000

MÜLLER Franz 1843-1929 **[9]**
$2 875 - €2 761 - £1 782 - FF18 111
Kaukasier Öl/Leinwand (152x70cm 59x27in) Ahlden
1999

MÜLLER Friedrich 1749-1825 **[31]**
$448 - €511 - £313 - FF3 353
Rastender Bauer mit Pferd, Esel und Hund
Radierung (18x20.5cm 7x8in) Berlin 2001

MÜLLER Fritz 1867-1926 **[10]**
$550 - €630 - £382 - FF4 130
Lakeside Fall Landscape Oil/canvas (40x50cm
16x20in) New-Orleans LA 2000

MULLER Fritz 1897-? **[13]**
$700 - €711 - £437 - FF4 665
A Monk tasting Wine Oil/masonite (17x23cm 7x9in)
Portland OR 2000

M

MÜLLER Hans 1873-? **[20]**
- $600 - €587 - **£383** - FF3 853
  Bishop and Child Bronze (H27cm H11in) Boston MA 1999

MÜLLER Hans Alexander 1888-1962 **[16]**
- $60 - €67 - **£41** - FF439
  Don Quixote Woodcut in colors (32x23cm 12x9in) Cleveland OH 2001

MÜLLER Heinrich 1810-1841 **[1]**
- $13 419 - €11 484 - **£8 077** - FF75 329
  Am Zugersee mit Blick gegen die Rigi/Bergansicht bei Grindelwald Gouache/paper (31.5x46.5cm 12x18in) Zürich 1998

MÜLLER Heinrich, Haiggi 1885-1960 **[42]**
- $1 169 - €1 002 - **£703** - FF6 572
  Herrenporträt Öl/Leinwand (34.5x26cm 13x10in) Zürich 1998

MÜLLER Heinz 1872-? **[11]**
- $511 - €511 - **£320** - FF3 353
  Maria mit Kind Bronze (H37cm H14in) Lindau 1999

MULLER Jacques 1930-1997 **[16]**
- $850 - €991 - **£588** - FF6 500
  Paris, la porte Saint Martin Huile/toile (24x33cm 9x12in) Calais 2000

MULLER Jan Harmensz. 1571-1628 **[61]**
- $1 200 - €1 129 - **£741** - FF7 409
  The Banquet of Belshazzar Engraving (35.5x40cm 13x15in) New-York 1999

MÜLLER Johann Georg 1913-1986 **[38]**
- $22 869 - €21 474 - **£14 170** - FF140 863
  Blaue Blumen Öl/Leinwand (149x160cm 58x62in) München 1999
- $12 434 - €10 739 - **£7 509** - FF70 446
  Maschinenteil II Öl/Leinwand (100.5x100.5cm 39x39in) Köln 1998
- $9 526 - €10 226 - **£6 376** - FF67 078
  Weiblicher Kopf Watercolour (53.8x75.5cm 21x29in) Hamburg 2000

MÜLLER Johannes Emil XX **[2]**
- $1 395 - €1 585 - **£955** - FF10 397
  «Sports-Montana-Vermala» Poster (110x80cm 43x31in) Hannover 2000

MÜLLER Josef Felix 1955 **[33]**
- $6 058 - €6 647 - **£4 024** - FF43 600
  Drei kriechende Figuren Sculpture, wood (66x350x60cm 25x137x23in) München 2000
- $394 - €459 - **£272** - FF3 010
  Fragender Kopf Gouache/paper (41.5x29cm 16x11in) Bern 2000
- $173 - €196 - **£121** - FF1 284
  Kopfüber Woodcut in colors (65x51cm 25x20in) Zürich 2001

MÜLLER Karl 1818-1893 **[11]**
- $1 489 - €1 391 - **£900** - FF9 123
  Harvest Beauty Oil/canvas (66x54.5cm 25x21in) London 1999

MÜLLER Leopold Carl 1834-1892 **[74]**
- $52 998 - €62 325 - **£38 000** - FF408 826
  Cairo Marketplace Oil/canvas (135x213cm 53x83in) London 2001
- $2 648 - €2 907 - **£1 760** - FF19 068
  Porträt eines Afrikaners Öl/Leinwand (63.5x50cm 25x19in) Wien 2000
- $4 634 - €5 087 - **£3 080** - FF33 369
  Stadtmotiv aus dem Orient Oil/panel (21x35cm 8x13in) Wien 2000

MÜLLER Maria 1847-c.1902 **[7]**
- $2 191 - €2 543 - **£1 540** - FF16 684
  Portrait eines Orientalen Öl/Leinwand (31.5x21.5cm 12x8in) Wien 2001

MÜLLER Max 1911-1991 **[35]**
- $1 144 - €1 077 - **£714** - FF7 063
  Interiör med kunstneren med sin familie Oil/canvas (61x73cm 24x28in) Vejle 1999
- $666 - €672 - **£415** - FF4 406
  Interiör med kvinde og blomstervase Oil/masonite (41x32cm 16x12in) København 2000

MULLER Mic 1928 **[35]**
- $857 - €732 - **£517** - FF4 800
  La coupe de fruits Huile/toile (38x46cm 14x18in) Strasbourg 1998

MÜLLER Michael ?-1642 **[1]**
- $4 080 - €3 867 - **£2 548** - FF25 369
  Stammbuchblatt des Michael Müller Indian ink (8.5x13.5cm 3x5in) Luzern 1999

MÜLLER Moritz 1841-1899 **[60]**
- $1 674 - €1 534 - **£1 020** - FF10 061
  Waldweiher im Mondlicht mit Rehen am Ufer Öl/Leinwand (63.5x79cm 25x31in) München 1999
- $1 156 - €1 093 - **£727** - FF7 172
  Aufscheuchener Rehbock Öl/Leinwand (34x42cm 13x16in) Praha 2000

MÜLLER Moritz I Feuermüller 1807-1865 **[22]**
- $6 267 - €6 135 - **£3 856** - FF40 246
  Im Schein einer Kerze spielt ein Bauernbursche auf der Zitter Öl/Leinwand (74x61cm 29x24in) Stuttgart 1999
- $10 495 - €12 271 - **£7 375** - FF80 493
  Junges Paar bei Kerzenlicht Öl/Leinwand (29x27cm 11x10in) München 2000

MÜLLER Moritz II XIX-XX **[24]**
- $458 - €511 - **£320** - FF3 353
  Jagdhund, einen Hasen apportierend Öl/Leinwand (50.5x66cm 19x25in) München 2001

MÜLLER Morten 1828-1911 **[58]**
- $3 208 - €2 791 - **£1 934** - FF18 307
  To kvinner i furuskog Oil/canvas (50x60cm 19x23in) Oslo 1998
- $1 134 - €1 084 - **£714** - FF7 113
  Vandfald Oil/canvas (29x48cm 11x18in) Oslo 1999

MÜLLER Otto 1905-1973 **[3]**
- $9 900 - €9 976 - **£6 171** - FF65 441
  Kopf Métal (16x17x27cm 6x6x10in) Zürich 2000

MÜLLER Paul Jakob 1894-1983 **[208]**
- $354 - €340 - **£219** - FF2 229
  Strauss mit Sonnenblumen in einer Vase Öl/Karton (63x52.5cm 24x20in) Bern 1999
- $336 - €311 - **£205** - FF2 040
  Fünfbogige Brücke über die Seine Huile/panneau (24.5x41cm 9x16in) Bern 1999

MÜLLER Paul Lothar 1869-? **[33]**
- $447 - €460 - **£281** - FF3 018
  Arm, aber zufrieden, ältlicher Musikus im Schlafrock Oil/panel (21x16cm 8x6in) Berlin 2000

MÜLLER Peter Paul 1853-1915 **[40]**
- $1 015 - €860 - **£603** - FF5 700
  Waldweiher im Herbst Öl/Leinwand (48x76cm 18x29in) München 1998

MULLER René 1929-1993 **[2]**
🔲 **$6 474** - €6 226 - **£3 995** - FF40 837
**Reiter und Figuren vor grünem und gelbem
Hintergrund** Öl/Leinwand (88x116cm 34x45in) Bern
1999

MÜLLER Richard 1874-1954 **[278]**
🔲 **$3 504** - €3 067 - **£2 122** - FF20 118
«Die Stärkere» Öl/Leinwand (46x65.5cm 18x25in)
Berlin 1998
🔲 **$3 429** - €3 681 - **£2 295** - FF24 148
**Zwei Mäuschen, genussvoll an einer aufgesch-
nittenen Melone knabbernd** Öl/Leinwand
(33x43cm 12x16in) Berlin 2000
✏️ **$424** - €411 - **£264** - FF2 699
Ruine Habstein Pencil/paper (43.7x30.2cm 17x11in)
Berlin 1999
🔲 **$215** - €245 - **£149** - FF1 609
Mein Hund Boy Radierung (15.8x13.7cm 6x5in)
Berlin 2000

MÜLLER Robert 1920 **[38]**
🔲 **$6 514** - €6 403 - **£4 183** - FF42 000
Insecte Fer (31x40x18cm 12x15x7in) Paris 1999
✏️ **$821** - €812 - **£512** - FF5 329
Ohne Titel Gouache/papier (34x21.5cm 13x8in)
Luzern 1999

MÜLLER Robert Antoine XIX **[14]**
🔲 **$1 943** - €2 086 - **£1 300** - FF13 682
Rest in the Woods Oil/panel (40.5x30.5cm 15x12in)
London 2000

MÜLLER Rodolphe, Jean R. c.1741-c.1815 **[1]**
✏️ **$1 509** - €1 790 - **£1 100** - FF11 741
Extensive italianate Landscape with Ruins
Watercolour/paper (40x55.5cm 15x21in) Billingshurst,
West-Sussex 2001

MÜLLER Rudolf 1802-1885 **[43]**
✏️ **$1 443** - €1 455 - **£900** - FF9 543
**Figures in a rowing BOat on a Lake in a
Mountainous Landscape** Watercolour (35x52cm
13x20in) London 2000

MÜLLER Rudolf, Rudi 1895-1972 **[128]**
🔲 **$161** - €155 - **£99** - FF1 020
Au Parc Huile/panneau (16x22.5cm 6x8in) Bern 1999

MÜLLER VOM SIEL Georg Bernhard 1865-1939
[17]
🔲 **$382** - €358 - **£231** - FF2 347
Die Dorfstrasse (Winter) Etching, aquatint
(38x58.5cm 14x23in) Bremen 1999

MÜLLER von Emma 1859-1925 **[44]**
🔲 **$7 655** - €8 692 - **£5 319** - FF57 016
Der erste Liebesbrief Öl/Leinwand (60x63cm
23x24in) Köln 2001
🔲 **$1 093** - €1 227 - **£758** - FF8 049
Bildnis eines jungen Mädchens Oil/panel
(16x11.8cm 6x4in) München 2000

MULLER William James 1812-1845 **[274]**
🔲 **$4 517** - €4 433 - **£2 800** - FF29 081
View on the River Medway Oil/canvas (32.5x61cm
12x24in) London 1999
🔲 **$1 472** - €1 396 - **£920** - FF9 156
Welsh Village Oil/panel (19.5x16.5cm 7x6in)
Crewkerne, Somerset 1999
✏️ **$2 581** - €2 533 - **£1 600** - FF16 618
Purfleet, Essex Watercolour (34.5x46.5cm 13x18in)
London 1999

MÜLLER Wout 1946 **[31]**
🔲 **$1 131** - €1 089 - **£707** - FF7 143
«Ada (Nabakov)» Oil/board (33x29cm 12x11in)
Amsterdam 1999

MÜLLER-BAUMGARTEN Karl 1879-1946 **[84]**
🔲 **$425** - €434 - **£266** - FF2 850
Landschaft mit Blick über den Chiemsee
Öl/Leinwand (81x100cm 31x39in) Berlin 2000
🔲 **$500** - €511 - **£313** - FF3 353
Porträt eines alten Bauern Öl/Karton (38x28cm
14x11in) Augsburg 2000

MÜLLER-BRITTNAU Willy 1938 **[45]**
🔲 **$2 505** - €2 416 - **£1 544** - FF15 845
Ohne Titel Öl/Leinwand (100x100cm 39x39in) Bern
1999
🔲 **$150** - €170 - **£105** - FF1 113
Ohne Titel Farbserigraphie (69x59cm 27x23in) Zürich
2001

MÜLLER-BROCKMANN Josef 1914-1996 **[6]**
🔲 **$1 400** - €1 570 - **£972** - FF10 299
«Schutz das Kind!, Watch that Child» Poster
(127x89cm 50x35in) New-York 2001

MÜLLER-CORNELIUS Ludwig 1864-1943 **[112]**
🔲 **$2 251** - €2 250 - **£1 408** - FF14 757
Der Pferdemarkt Öl/Karton (34x48.5cm 13x19in)
Köln 1999
🔲 **$1 773** - €1 535 - **£1 069** - FF10 070
Bauern bei der Heuernte Oil/panel (15x20cm
5x7in) München 1998

MÜLLER-EIBENSTOCK Otto 1898-1985 **[4]**
✏️ **$1 825** - €2 045 - **£1 271** - FF13 415
Abstrakte Komposition Gouache/paper
(44.5x28.5cm 17x11in) Berlin 2001

MÜLLER-GOSSEN Franz 1871-1946 **[29]**
🔲 **$660** - €625 - **£401** - FF4 100
Bord de mer Huile/toile (70x97cm 27x38in) Genève
1999

MÜLLER-HOFSCHMIED Willy 1890-1966 **[17]**
✏️ **$696** - €818 - **£482** - FF5 366
Ohne Titel Indian ink/paper (37.5x23cm 14x9in)
Stuttgart 2001

MÜLLER-KAEMPFF Paul 1861-1941 **[97]**
🔲 **$3 894** - €4 602 - **£2 760** - FF30 185
Darsser Sommerlandschaft Öl/Leinwand
(78x118cm 30x46in) Satow 2000
🔲 **$1 258** - €1 431 - **£873** - FF9 390
Ahrenshoop Oil/panel (19x26cm 7x10in) Rudolstadt-
Thüringen 2000
✏️ **$1 868** - €1 535 - **£1 085** - FF10 067
Blühende Obstbäume bei Ahrenshoop
Aquarell/Papier (25x32cm 9x12in) Berlin 1998

MÜLLER-KRAUS Erich 1911-1967 **[7]**
🔲 **$525** - €460 - **£318** - FF3 017
«Strandkomposition» Linocut in colors
(28.4x36.6cm 11x14in) Berlin 1998

MÜLLER-KURZWELLY Konrad Alexander 1855-
1914 **[43]**
🔲 **$1 291** - €1 329 - **£814** - FF8 720
Alte Weiden am See Öl/Leinwand (70x99cm
27x38in) Berlin 2000
🔲 **$893** - €869 - **£548** - FF5 701
Ebbe, auf Land liegende Fischkutter Öl/Karton
(22x32cm 8x12in) Berlin 1999

M

MÜLLER-LANDAU Rolf 1903-1956 **[25]**

🔲 **$4 369** - €4 090 - **£2 708** - FF26 831
Bildnis einer am Fenster sitzenden Frau
Öl/Leinwand (92x73cm 36x28in) Heidelberg 1999

🔲 **$442** - €437 - **£275** - FF2 869
Sanrum Monotype (46x54cm 18x21in) Luzern 1999

MÜLLER-LANDECK Fritz 1865-1942 **[32]**

🔲 **$793** - €799 - **£495** - FF5 243
Vorfrühling Öl/Leinwand (70x100cm 27x39in) Wien 2000

MÜLLER-LINGKE Albert 1844-c.1900 **[30]**

🔲 **$2 187** - €2 454 - **£1 516** - FF16 098
Zwei kleine Reisigsammler Öl/Leinwand (76x62cm 29x24in) München 2000

🔲 **$982** - €1 022 - **£622** - FF6 707
Die Jahreswende: Fahrende Musikanten in verschneiter Gebirgslandschaft Oil/panel (27x19cm 10x7in) München 2000

MÜLLER-LINOW Bruno 1909-1997 **[47]**

🔲 **$408** - €460 - **£281** - FF3 018
Stilleben mit Weinflaschen Indian ink (33.5x46.5cm 13x18in) München 2000

🔲 **$84** - €97 - **£57** - FF637
Liegender weiblicher Akt Drypoint (14.8x20.7cm 5x8in) Heidelberg 2000

MÜLLER-MASSDORF Julius 1863-? **[9]**

🔲 **$15 163** - €12 822 - **£9 067** - FF84 104
Tea Room Tango Oil/canvas (64.5x78.5cm 25x30in) Amsterdam 1998

MÜLLER-SCHNUTTENBACH Hans 1889-1974 **[11]**

🔲 **$2 193** - €2 556 - **£1 537** - FF16 769
Dorfstrasse Öl/Karton (34.5x49cm 13x19in) München 2000

🔲 **$1 117** - €1 278 - **£777** - FF8 384
Uferlandschaft Gouache/paper (30x42.5cm 11x16in) Rudolstadt-Thüringen 2000

MÜLLER-SCHÖNHAUSEN A. 1838-c.1872 **[2]**

🔲 **$5 474** - €5 113 - **£3 308** - FF33 539
Kaffetafel mit zahlreichen, sonntäglich gewandeten Gästen im Garten Oil/panel (29x39.5cm 11x15in) Berlin 1999

MÜLLER-WERLAU Peter Paul 1864-1949 **[24]**

🔲 **$1 704** - €1 431 - **£1 001** - FF9 389
Frohenleichamsprozession in einem Städchen am Rhein Öl/Leinwand (47x66cm 18x25in) Köln 1998

🔲 **$730** - €613 - **£429** - FF4 024
Alte Häuser in St.Goar Oil/canvas/board (38x32cm 14x12in) Köln 1998

MÜLLER-WISCHIN Anton 1865-1949 **[49]**

🔲 **$768** - €872 - **£538** - FF5 720
Fischerboote im Hafen Öl/Leinwand (80x100cm 31x39in) Wien 2001

🔲 **$505** - €589 - **£354** - FF3 866
Waldstück am frühen Morgen Öl/Karton (28x46cm 11x18in) Bern 2000

MULLEY Oskar 1891-1949 **[119]**

🔲 **$13 035** - €10 894 - **£7 725** - FF71 460
Voralpenlandschaft Öl/Leinwand (100x135cm 39x53in) Wien 1998

🔲 **$3 785** - €3 634 - **£2 375** - FF23 835
Winterlandschaft Öl/Karton (58x51.5cm 22x20in) Wien 1999

🔲 **$2 928** - €2 812 - **£1 805** - FF18 446
An der Brücke Öl/Leinwand (28x29.5cm 11x11in) München 1999

🔲 **$1 276** - €1 431 - **£884** - FF9 390
Gebirgshof Black chalk (36.7x26.5cm 14x10in) München 2000

🔲 **$881** - €945 - **£601** - FF6 197
«Tirol, Kufstein, ein Alpenparadies des Wilden Kaisers» Poster (86x54cm 33x21in) Wien 2001

MULLICAN Matt 1951 **[35]**

🔲 **$7 212** - €8 476 - **£5 000** - FF55 600
Untitled Oil/canvas (183x244cm 72x96in) London 2000

🔲 **$3 500** - €3 481 - **£2 172** - FF22 835
Untitled Etching, aquatint in colors (56x38cm 22x14in) Beverly-Hills CA 1999

MULLIKEN Jonathan 1746-1782 **[1]**

🔲 **$7 500** - €7 773 - **£4 752** - FF50 986
Boston Massacre Engraving (24x21cm 9x8in) Portsmouth NH 2000

MULLIN Charles Edward 1885-? **[1]**

🔲 **$4 500** - €5 040 - **£3 126** - FF33 062
Magazine cover, Elegant Woman walking leashed Panther Gouache/paper (48x34cm 19x13in) New-York 2001

MULLIN Willard 1902-1978 **[8]**

🔲 **$10 000** - €9 470 - **£6 080** - FF62 121
Lou Gehrig Watercolour/paper (59x48cm 23x18in) New-York 1999

MULLINEUX Mary 1875-1965 **[1]**

🔲 **$1 500** - €1 441 - **£917** - FF9 454
Flowers Woodcut in colors (20x25cm 8x10in) Provincetown MA 1999

MULLINS Edwin Roscoe 1849-1907 **[5]**

🔲 **$5 805** - €5 049 - **£3 500** - FF33 120
The Conquerors Bronze (11x60cm 4x23in) London 1998

MULLOCK James Flewitt 1818-1892 **[1]**

🔲 **$16 613** - €16 027 - **£10 500** - FF105 131
Lady Rosamund Morgan's Dapple grey Mare/Groom with grey Carriage Horse Oil/canvas (44.5x61cm 17x24in) London 1999

MULREADY Augustus E. ?-1886 **[47]**

🔲 **$7 787** - €8 605 - **£5 400** - FF56 446
Street Flower Seller Oil/canvas (53x38cm 21x15in) Bexhill-on-Sea, East-Sussex 2001

🔲 **$3 307** - €2 884 - **£2 000** - FF18 919
The Flower Girl Oil/canvas (36.5x25cm 14x9in) London 1998

MULREADY William 1786-1863 **[35]**

🔲 **$1 185** - €1 329 - **£805** - FF8 718
Die Heilige Fmilie auf der Flucht nach Ägypten Öl/Leinwand (46x55cm 18x21in) Zürich 2000

🔲 **$946** - €1 029 - **£623** - FF6 752
Junge mit leerem Milchkrug Oil/panel (44x30cm 17x11in) Bern 2000

🔲 **$824** - €866 - **£520** - FF5 680
Seated Nude Pencil (26.5x20cm 10x7in) London 2000

MULTRUS Josef 1898-1957 **[40]**

🔲 **$1 300** - €1 230 - **£810** - FF8 068
Vendeur de nouvelles Huile/toile (59.5x75cm 23x29in) Praha 1999

🔲 **$619** - €727 - **£439** - FF4 767
Kartoffelschälende Öl/Karton (17.5x18cm 6x7in) Wien 2000

MULVAD Emma 1838-1903 **[25]**
☞ **$1 631 - €1 742 - £1 111** - FF11 427
Opstilling med liljer Oil/canvas (42x35cm 16x13in)
Vejle 2001

MULVANEY John 1844-1906 **[2]**
✎ **$7 436 - €7 238 - £4 580** - FF47 475
View of Reginalds Tower, Waterford
Watercolour/paper (50x76cm 20x30in) Dublin 1999

MULVANY John George c.1766-1838 **[3]**
☞ **$25 468 - €20 998 - £15 000** - FF137 740
A Country Scene in Ireland Oil/canvas (117x155cm
46x61in) Newbury, Berkshire 1998

MULVANY Thomas Joseph 1779-1845 **[4]**
☞ **$3 447 - €3 809 - £2 390** - FF24 987
The Sea Roamer Oil/canvas (75x62cm 29x24in)
Dublin 2001

MULVEY Charles 1918 **[8]**
✎ **$170 - €201 - £120** - FF1 319
Beached Boat, Chinook Watercolour/paper
(47x32cm 18x12in) Portland OR 2001

MULVEY Matilda 1882-c.1947 **[4]**
☞ **$6 807 - €7 903 - £4 808** - FF51 839
Grey and Gold Oil/canvas (61x51cm 24x20in)
London 2001

MUMPRECHT Walter Rudolf 1918 **[192]**
☞ **$3 996 - €4 563 - £2 817** - FF29 930
Komposition auf weissem Grund Tempera/canvas
(62.5x162cm 24x63in) Bern 2001
✎ **$652 - €701 - £436** - FF4 595
**Du, ich, wir, wachsen verzweigen erweitern
bewegen** Indian ink/paper (24.5x31cm 9x12in)
Zofingen 2000
▥ **$179 - €199 - £119** - FF1 306
Chat Aquatinta (41.5x19cm 16x7in) Bern 2000

MUNAKATA Shiko 1903-1975 **[165]**
✎ **$8 500 - €9 968 - £6 065** - FF65 388
Bamboo Oil/paper (70.5x35.5cm 27x13in) New-York
2000
▥ **$4 200 - €4 232 - £2 618** - FF27 762
Saain no saku (festival note) Woodcut (31x26cm
12x10in) New-York 2000

MUNARI Bruno 1907-1998 **[42]**
☞ **$4 249 - €4 405 - £2 549** - FF28 898
«Negativo, positivo» Olio/masonite (40x40cm
15x15in) Milano 1999
☞ **$1 900 - €1 970 - £1 140** - FF12 920
Composizione rosso e nero Olio/faesite (34x34cm
13x13in) Roma 1999
✎ **$650 - €674 - £390** - FF4 420
Composizione Matita/carta (48x33cm 18x12in)
Milano 1999

MUNARI Cristoforo 1667-1720 **[18]**
☞ **$48 000 - €49 759 - £28 800** - FF326 400
Natura morta di frutta e ortaggi Olio/tela
(86x71cm 33x27in) Roma 2000

MUNCASTER Claude Graham 1903-1974 **[110]**
☞ **$1 240 - €1 172 - £750** - FF7 687
A View of the South Downs from Tillington
Oil/board (44x79.5cm 17x31in) Billingshurst, West-
Sussex 2001
☞ **$1 135 - €1 090 - £700** - FF7 153
**Unloading at the Quayside, Bridgetown,
Barbados** Oil/board (30.5x46cm 12x18in) London
1999
✎ **$322 - €296 - £200** - FF1 944
Evening at Lancing Watercolour (35x50.5cm
13x19in) London 1999

MUNCH Edvard 1863-1944 **[736]**
☞ **$627 615 - €738 062 - £450 000** - FF4 841 370
Sommer ved kysten, Krager Oil/canvas
(111x120cm 43x47in) London 2001
☞ **$247 905 - €211 809 - £150 000** - FF1 389 375
The Gothic Girl Oil/canvas (80.5x65cm 31x25in)
London 1998
☞ **$55 000 - €52 888 - £33 885** - FF346 923
Vinterlandskap i Skymning Oil/board (18x23cm
7x9in) New-York 1999
☞ **$14 293 - €13 795 - £9 026** - FF90 486
Die Landungsbrücke und das grosse Haus
Craies/papier (36x25cm 14x9in) Bern 1999
▥ **$8 306 - €8 916 - £5 558** - FF58 486
Portrait August Strindberg Lithographie (58x41cm
22x16in) Bern 2000

MÜNCH-K'HE Willi 1885-1960 **[51]**
▥ **$78 - €92 - £56** - FF603
«Fahrendes Volk» Radierung (28x22cm 11x8in)
Konstanz 2001

MUNDELL Jock 1818-1875 **[10]**
☞ **$822 - €883 - £550** - FF5 793
**Figures Boating on a Lake with Mountains
Beyond** Oil/canvas (25.5x45.5cm 10x17in) London
2000

MUNDO MARCET Ignasi 1918 **[126]**
☞ **$1 024 - €961 - £624** - FF6 304
Barcelona alta Oleo/lienzo (73x60cm 28x23in)
Barcelona 1999
☞ **$549 - €541 - £351** - FF3 546
Arlequin Oleo/tablex (61x23cm 24x9in) Barcelona
1999
▥ **$120 - €139 - £83** - FF914
El puerto de Tarragona Lápiz (30x18.5cm 11x7in)
Barcelona 2000

MUNDT Caroline Emilie 1842-1922 **[72]**
☞ **$2 116 - €2 019 - £1 288** - FF13 243
Paa Stranden, Gl. Skagen Oil/canvas (47x36cm
18x14in) Viby J, Arhus 1999
☞ **$1 011 - €943 - £611** - FF6 183
**Sommerlandskab med tre drenge, der bygger
modelskib** Oil/canvas (36x24cm 14x9in) København
1999

MUNDUWALAWALA Ginger Riley 1937 **[11]**
☞ **$26 312 - €25 382 - £16 628** - FF166 496
Garimala and Bulukbun Acrylic/canvas
(170x317.5cm 66x125in) Melbourne 1999
☞ **$5 718 - €6 138 - £3 827** - FF40 262
Limmem Bight Country Acrylic (64.5x56cm
25x22in) Melbourne 2000

MUNG MUNG George, Jambin 1924-1991 **[6]**
☞ **$17 102 - €16 498 - £10 808** - FF108 222
Tewas Country Mixed media (54x12.5cm 21x4in)
Melbourne 1999

MUNGER Anne Wells 1862-1945 **[8]**
☞ **$3 250 - €3 740 - £2 240** - FF24 534
Pass Christian Cottage Oil/canvas (45x60cm
18x24in) New-Orleans LA 2000

MUNGER Gilbert Davis 1837-1903 **[18]**
☞ **$6 500 - €7 198 - £4 408** - FF47 219
**Entrance to the Grand canal with the Church of
the Salute & St.Mark's** Oil/canvas (68x91cm
27x36in) New-York 1999
☞ **$2 200 - €2 100 - £1 374** - FF13 775
Homage to Corot Huile/toile (30x25cm 12x10in) Bel
Air MD 1999

M

MUNGITOK Kellipilak 1940 [2]

📺 **$504** - €592 - **£358** - FF3 886
Thoughts of Birds Print in colors (56x44.5cm 22x17in) Toronto 2000

MUNIER Émile 1810-1895 [34]

🖼 **$300 000** - €336 187 - **£209 100** - FF2 205 240
Le sauvetage (the Rescue) Oil/canvas (101.5x187.5cm 39x73in) New-York 2001

🖼 **$65 000** - €60 704 - **£40 118** - FF398 190
La Petite Fille Oil/canvas (64.5x52.5cm 25x20in) Boston MA 1991

$512 - €610 - **£354** - FF4 000
La belle emmitouflée - L'Hiver Aquarelle/papier (16x25.5cm 6x10in) Saint-Dié 2000

MUNILL Antoni 1939-1977 [19]

$156 - €168 - **£106** - FF1 103
Paisaje con casas Gouache/carton (28x35.5cm 11x13in) Barcelona 2001

MUNIZ Vik 1961 [42]

📷 **$7 500** - €7 799 - **£4 735** - FF51 158
Hands, from the Eries Pictures of soil Gelatin silver print (58.5x48.5cm 23x19in) New-York 2000

MUNKACSI Martin Marmorstein 1896-1963 [63]

📷 **$2 926** - €2 404 - **£1 700** - FF15 769
Summer Camp near Bad Kissingen, Germany Gelatin silver print (29x23cm 11x9in) London 1998

MUNKACSY Mihály 1844-1900 [72]

🖼 **$74 715** - €80 200 - **£50 000** - FF526 080
La brodeuse Oil/panel (95x130cm 37x51in) London 2000

🖼 **$19 000** - €21 218 - **£12 167** - FF139 184
Tending the Garden Oil/canvas (35x50.5cm 13x19in) New-York 2000

🖼 **$7 894** - €8 272 - **£5 000** - FF54 264
Disturbing News Oil/canvas (39x29cm 15x11in) London 2000

MUNN George Frederick 1852-1907 [7]

🖼 **$2 200** - €2 362 - **£1 498** - FF15 491
Still Life with Fan Oil/board (28x38.5cm 11x15in) Boston MA 2001

MUNN Paul Sandby 1773-1845 [48]

✏ **$1 211** - €1 121 - **£750** - FF7 355
The Ferry at Barnmouth, North Wales Wash (24x39.5cm 9x15in) London 1999

MUNNINGER Ludwig XX [20]

🖼 **$5 000** - €4 895 - **£3 194** - FF32 112
Bavarian Mountain Snow Scene with Figures on Road and on frozen Lake Oil/canvas (99x73cm 39x29in) Detroit MI 1999

MÜNNINGHOF Xeno 1873-1944 [31]

🖼 **$875** - €908 - **£555** - FF5 953
Farm in a Forest Oil/canvas (46x35cm 18x13in) Amsterdam 2000

🖼 **$615** - €544 - **£371** - FF3 566
Farm in a Landscape Oil/board (21.5x32.5cm 8x12in) Amsterdam 1998

MUNNINGS Alfred James 1878-1959 [585]

🖼 **$1 600 000** - €1 384 969 - **£971 040** - FF9 084 800
A Winner at Epsom Oil/canvas (99x121.5cm 38x47in) New-York 1998

🖼 **$225 795** - €247 722 - **£150 000** - FF1 624 950
Portrait of Sir John Frecheville Ramsden, Bt., on a Bay Hunter Oil/canvas (63.5x76cm 25x29in) London 2000

🖼 **$40 000** - €42 936 - **£26 768** - FF281 640
Exmoor Ponies Oil/panel (17x24.5cm 6x9in) New-York 2000

✏ **$6 488** - €6 255 - **£4 000** - FF41 028
Green Pastures and still Waters Watercolour/paper (33x17cm 12x6in) London 1999

📺 **$600** - €672 - **£416** - FF4 408
Hounds gathering for the Box Hunt Lithograph (47x66cm 18x26in) St. Louis MO 2001

MUNNS John Bernard 1869-1942 [8]

🖼 **$3 750** - €3 823 - **£2 349** - FF25 075
A Pekingese Oil/canvas (43x51cm 16x20in) New-York 2000

MUÑOZ BARBERAN Manuel 1921 [5]

🖼 **$3 360** - €3 604 - **£2 280** - FF23 640
«Tejados y torre, Murcia» Oleo/lienzo (82x65.5cm 32x25in) Madrid 2001

MUNOZ CONDADO Pedro 1903-1988 [7]

🖼 **$2 880** - €2 703 - **£1 800** - FF17 730
«Mercado» Oleo/lienzo (100x82cm 39x32in) Madrid 1999

MUÑOZ DEGRAIN Antonio Gomez 1843-1927 [60]

🖼 **$64 800** - €72 078 - **£43 200** - FF472 800
Ecos de Roncesvalles Oleo/lienzo (248x200cm 97x78in) Madrid 2000

🖼 **$8 550** - €9 010 - **£5 400** - FF59 100
Montañas nevadas Oleo/lienzo (57x86cm 22x33in) Madrid 2000

🖼 **$1 920** - €1 802 - **£1 170** - FF11 820
Rincón de Sevilla Oleo/cartón (16x23cm 6x9in) Madrid 1999

MUÑOZ DIAZ María XIX [2]

🖼 **$5 490** - €5 406 - **£3 420** - FF35 460
Puerto de Malalga Oleo/lienzo (64x96.5cm 25x37in) Madrid 1999

MUÑOZ Juan 1953 [43]

🖼 **$20 000** - €22 625 - **£13 992** - FF148 410
Study for Positive Corner, Documenta IX Oil/paper (94x66cm 37x25in) New-York 2001

🗿 **$56 811** - €54 971 - **£36 000** - FF360 586
Greek Conversation Piece Bronze (130x50x50cm 51x19x19in) London 1999

🗿 **$32 000** - €27 702 - **£19 299** - FF181 715
Balcony Construction (71x105.5x35.5cm 27x41x13in) New-York 1998

MUÑOZ LUCENA Tomas 1860-1943 [22]

🖼 **$6 400** - €6 006 - **£4 000** - FF39 400
Granadinas cantando en el patio Oleo/lienzo (38.5x28cm 15x11in) Madrid 1999

MUÑOZ Lucio 1929-1998 [120]

🖼 **$22 950** - €25 528 - **£15 300** - FF167 450
Situación Oleo/tabla (146x114cm 57x44in) Madrid 2000

🖼 **$10 560** - €9 610 - **£6 560** - FF63 040
Composición Oleo/tabla (92x73cm 36x28in) Madrid 1999

📺 **$244** - €240 - **£156** - FF1 576
Composición Grabado (56x76cm 22x29in) Barcelona 1999

MUÑOZ OTERO Manuel 1850-? [10]

🖼 **$3 929** - €3 354 - **£2 349** - FF22 000
Vue de Tanger Huile/toile (42.5x64cm 16x25in) Paris 1998

🖼 **$1 030** - €1 022 - **£643** - FF6 707
Ansicht von Venedig Oil/panel (22.5x34cm 8x13in) München 1999

MUÑOZ REYES Ana 1947 [7]

🖼 **$1 885** - €1 952 - **£1 202** - FF12 805
Soledad Oleo/tablex (83x109cm 32x42in) Madrid 2000

MUÑOZ RUBIO Ramón XIX-XX **[19]**
- $4 250 - €5 106 - **£2 975** - FF33 490
  Galantería Oleo/lienzo (98x65cm 38x25in) Madrid 2000
- $286 - €330 - **£198** - FF2 167
  Oliendo las flores Acuarela/papel (24x17.5cm 9x6in) Madrid 2001

MUÑOZ Y CUESTA Domingo 1850-1912/35 **[64]**
- $14 720 - €13 815 - **£9 200** - FF90 620
  La rabieta Oleo/lienzo (200x110cm 78x43in) Madrid 1999
- $25 500 - €25 528 - **£15 725** - FF167 450
  Revisando papeles Oleo/lienzo (96x93cm 37x36in) Madrid 2000
- $1 620 - €1 802 - **£1 110** - FF11 820
  Mujer andaluza Oleo/tabla (23.5x18cm 9x7in) Madrid 2001

MUÑOZ-VERA Guillermo 1949 **[37]**
- $45 000 - €52 984 - **£31 621** - FF347 553
  Cuesta salobre Oil/canvas/panel (192x100cm 75x39in) New-York 2000
- $16 000 - €15 529 - **£9 961** - FF101 865
  Membrillos Oil/canvas/panel (52x106.5cm 20x41in) New-York 2000
- $5 415 - €5 706 - **£3 610** - FF37 430
  Ancianas Lápiz/papel (34.5x60cm 13x23in) Madrid 2000

MUNRO Hugh 1873-1928 **[16]**
- $13 625 - €12 872 - **£8 500** - FF84 433
  Blue Morn on the Mull Oil/canvas (55x76.5cm 21x30in) Perthshire 1999

MUNRO Patrick 1954 **[11]**
- $1 195 - €1 283 - **£800** - FF8 417
  Woodcock Oil/canvas (45.5x63.5cm 17x25in) London 2000

MUNROE Sarah Sewell XX **[4]**
- $19 000 - €17 272 - **£11 443** - FF113 297
  Lady with Parasol Oil/canvas (101x101cm 40x40in) Bethesda MD 1998

MUNSCH Josef 1832-1896 **[7]**
- $25 777 - €25 639 - **£16 000** - FF168 179
  An Interesting Book/The Discussion Oil/panel (30.5x40.5cm 12x15in) London 1999

MUNSCH Leopold 1826-1888 **[47]**
- $1 682 - €1 817 - **£1 162** - FF11 917
  Auf der Alm Öl/Karton (35x43cm 13x16in) Wien 2001

MUNSON K.O. XX **[1]**
- $7 700 - €6 569 - **£4 644** - FF43 089
  Lounging woman with stockings, calendar illustration Pastel (74x51cm 29x20in) New-York 1998

MÜNSTER Mia 1894-1970 **[4]**
- $2 105 - €2 352 - **£1 426** - FF15 427
  Elegante Dame in den Spiegel blickend Watercolour (38x27.5cm 14x10in) Saarbrücken 2000

MÜNSTER Sebastian 1489-1552 **[20]**
- $213 - €196 - **£130** - FF1 283
  Tabula Asiae IIII Woodcut (25x34.5cm 9x13in) London 1999

MÜNSTERFELD F. XIX-XX **[8]**
- $1 025 - €949 - **£627** - FF6 225
  Strandlandskap med kvinnor och korgar Oil/canvas (66x105cm 25x41in) Uppsala 1999

MUNSTERHJELM Ali 1873-1944 **[104]**
- $1 890 - €2 186 - **£1 337** - FF14 341
  Aura å Oil/canvas (54x69cm 21x27in) Helsinki 2000

MUNSTERHJELM Hjalmar 1840-1905 **[142]**
- $112 050 - €126 136 - **£77 175** - FF827 400
  Fiskarpar på stranden Oil/canvas (118x192cm 46x75in) Helsinki 2000
- $22 530 - €25 227 - **£15 645** - FF165 480
  Kor på strandstig Oil/canvas (42x61cm 16x24in) Helsinki 2001
- $8 261 - €9 250 - **£5 736** - FF60 676
  Sommarkväll Oil/board (13x25cm 5x9in) Helsinki 2001
- $431 - €437 - **£270** - FF2 868
  Strandlandskap Drawing (9.5x16.5cm 3x6in) Helsinki 2001

MUNTANÉ MUNS Lluís 1899-1987 **[8]**
- $3 500 - €3 428 - **£2 255** - FF22 486
  Muchacha en el palco Oil/canvas (92.5x73.5cm 36x28in) New-York 1999

MUNTANYA J. XIX-XX **[1]**
- $4 200 - €4 686 - **£2 749** - FF30 736
  «Copa Catalunya 3ª Año, 29 de Mayo 1910, Mataro-Barcelona» Poster (104x145cm 40x57in) New-York 2000

MÜNTER Gabriele 1877-1962 **[219]**
- $53 987 - €49 979 - **£33 049** - FF327 843
  Prozession in Murnau Öl/Leinwand (46.3x38.3cm 18x15in) München 1999
- $90 997 - €84 998 - **£55 000** - FF557 551
  Blick aus der Bonner Wohnung Oil/board (47x33.5cm 18x13in) London 1999
- $8 481 - €8 232 - **£5 280** - FF53 997
  Blick auf des Murnauer Moos Indian ink/paper (25.5x37cm 10x14in) Berlin 1999
- $2 140 - €1 789 - **£1 267** - FF11 733
  Mme Vernot Linocut in colors (18x12.3cm 7x4in) Hamburg 1998

MUNTHE Gerhard Peter Frantz 1849-1929 **[54]**
- $10 540 - €12 539 - **£7 290** - FF82 250
  Storvask på landet Oil/panel (47x74cm 18x29in) Oslo 2000
- $3 513 - €3 977 - **£2 457** - FF26 086
  Vaskeplassen Oil/canvas (30x53cm 11x20in) Oslo 2001
- $1 050 - €901 - **£645** - FF5 910
  Barco en la playa Acuarela/papel (33x27cm 12x10in) Madrid 1998
- $648 - €748 - **£456** - FF4 909
  Hvem er det der tramper på min bru? Color lithograph (73x49cm 28x19in) Oslo 2000

MUNTHE Ludwig 1841-1896 **[86]**
- $5 695 - €5 495 - **£3 600** - FF36 045
  Winter Oil/canvas (42x56.5cm 16x22in) London 1999
- $3 439 - €4 090 - **£2 451** - FF26 831
  Abendstimmung am Meer, im Hintergrund die Silhouette einer Stadt Öl/Leinwand (41x33cm 16x12in) Köln 2000

MUNTHE MORGENSTJERNE Gerhard Arij Ludwig 1875-1927 **[119]**
- $19 216 - €18 151 - **£11 624** - FF119 064
  Shellfisher on the Beach Oil/canvas (97x165cm 38x64in) Amsterdam 1999
- $12 449 - €10 983 - **£7 500** - FF72 045
  Unloading the Catch from a Sailing Boat Oil/canvas (45x74cm 17x29in) London 1998
- $5 564 - €5 445 - **£3 567** - FF35 719
  A Bomschuit in the Breakers Oil/canvas/panel (22x15.5cm 8x6in) Amsterdam 1999

M

M

🖋 **$4 623** - €4 991 - **£3 161** - FF32 742
Fisherwomen on the Beach of Katwijk
Watercolour, gouache (16.5x10.5cm 6x4in) Amsterdam
2001

MUNTHE-NORSTEDT Anna 1854-1936 **[31]**
🖼 **$6 208** - €6 042 - **£3 822** - FF39 634
Namnsdagsbord Oil/panel (49.5x65cm 19x25in)
Stockholm 1999
🖼 **$1 632** - €1 800 - **£1 105** - FF11 806
**Stilleben med remmare, krus, vinglas, äpple
och blåsippor i vas** Oil/canvas (31x39cm 12x15in)
Stockholm 2000

MUNTZ Johann Heinrich 1727-1798 **[7]**
🖋 **$471** - €562 - **£336** - FF3 689
Ideallandschaft mit Ruinen Ink (6.4x9.6cm 2x3in)
Berlin 2000

MUNTZ-ADAMS Josephine 1862-1952 **[19]**
🖼 **$1 917** - €1 844 - **£1 181** - FF12 095
Portrait of a Girl Oil/canvas/board (26x20cm 10x7in)
Melbourne 1999

MÜNZER Adolf 1870-1952 **[40]**
🖼 **$1 202** - €1 125 - **£728** - FF7 378
Tanz Tempera/canvas (37.5x65.5cm 14x25in) Stuttgart
1999
🖼 **$629** - €716 - **£439** - FF4 695
Fjord-Landschaft Watercolour (36x49cm 14x19in)
München 2000
▭ **$396** - €400 - **£247** - FF2 621
«**Scholle München - 25.Ausstellung der
Secession**» Poster (95x66cm 37x25in) Wien 2000

MÜNZNER Rolf 1942 **[12]**
▭ **$105** - €123 - **£73** - FF804
Mädchen und alter Leuchtturm Print (33x25.5cm
12x10in) Berlin 2000

MURA de Francesco Francesch. 1696-1782 **[74]**
🖼 **$16 800** - €21 770 - **£12 600** - FF142 800
Adorazione dei pastori Olio/tela (192x102cm
75x40in) Milano 2001
🖼 **$17 253** - €16 847 - **£11 000** - FF110 506
The Madonna and Child Oil/canvas (70x57cm
27x22in) London 1999
🖼 **$4 184** - €4 491 - **£2 800** - FF29 460
Female Saint with a Putto Oil/copper (25x20.5cm
9x8in) London 2001
🖋 **$8 500** - €7 456 - **£5 161** - FF48 907
**Design for an Allegorical Ceiling with the Four
Continents** Ink (68.5x44.5cm 26x17in) New-York
1999

MURA della Angelo 1867-1922 **[10]**
🖼 **$3 750** - €3 887 - **£2 250** - FF25 500
Marina Tecnica mista/tela (20x36cm 7x14in) Torino
2001

MURADO Antonio 1964 **[5]**
🖼 **$1 102** - €1 141 - **£703** - FF7 486
Pétalos Oleo/cartulina (49.5x70cm 19x27in) Madrid
2000

MURAKAMI Kagaku 1888-1939 **[1]**
🖋 **$26 000** - €30 168 - **£17 950** - FF197 886
Mukozan no zu (Mount Muko) Ink (23.5x33cm
9x12in) New-York 2000

MURAKAMI Takashi 1962 **[4]**
🖌 **$1 900** - €2 204 - **£1 311** - FF14 460
Project Ko2 (Perfect Edition) Plastic
(52.5x21.5x14.5cm 20x8x5in) New-York 2000

MURANT Emanuel 1622-c.1700 **[32]**
🖼 **$14 157** - €13 613 - **£8 721** - FF89 298
**Village Street with a man Feeding His Sheep,
view of a Church Tower** Oil/canvas (61.5x85.5cm
24x33in) Amsterdam 1999

MURATA Hiroshi XX **[1]**
▭ **$2 400** - €2 048 - **£1 444** - FF13 432
Fan Study Color lithograph (69x99cm 27x39in)
Norwalk CT 1999

MURATON Euphémie,née Duhanot 1840-1914 **[25]**
🖼 **$16 575** - €19 818 - **£11 440** - FF130 000
Vase de fleurs et petit chien Huile/toile
(125x97.5cm 49x38in) Bordeaux 2000
🖼 **$2 626** - €3 049 - **£1 870** - FF20 000
**Nature morte au bouquet de fleurs et écuelle en
cuivre** Huile/toile (90x67cm 35x26in) La Varenne-
Saint-Hilaire 2001

MURAWJOFF Wladimir L., Graf 1861-1914 **[5]**
🖼 **$6 823** - €7 669 - **£4 791** - FF50 308
**Grosse Winterlandschaft mit wandernden
Elchen** Tempera (67x102cm 26x40in) Hamburg 2001

MURAY Nickolas 1892-1965 **[34]**
📷 **$900** - €841 - **£544** - FF5 514
New York Street Scene Vintage gelatin silver print
(22x17cm 9x7in) New-York 1999

MURCH Arthur James 1902-1989 **[139]**
🖼 **$2 376** - €2 016 - **£1 433** - FF13 222
Reclining Nude with Cat Oil/canvas (45x65cm
17x25in) Sydney 1998
🖼 **$1 636** - €1 799 - **£1 048** - FF11 798
Still Life (Crooked-Neck Squash) Oil/canvas
(29x36cm 11x14in) Melbourne 2000
🖼 **$2 886** - €3 388 - **£2 037** - FF22 222
At the Well, Kneeling Figure Bronze (H26cm
H10in) Melbourne 2000
🖋 **$718** - €676 - **£445** - FF4 432
Reclining Nude Pastel/paper (29.5x52.5cm 11x20in)
Melbourne 1999

MURCH Walter Tandy 1907-1967 **[38]**
🖼 **$18 000** - €15 379 - **£10 805** - FF100 879
Violin Oil/masonite (35x51cm 19x20in) New-York
1998
🖼 **$3 000** - €3 466 - **£2 100** - FF22 734
Study for Caliper of the World Oil/paper
(22x27.5cm 8x10in) Bethesda MD 2001
🖋 **$4 000** - €3 426 - **£2 361** - FF22 472
Measures of Time Graphite (30.5x36cm 12x14in)
New-York 1998

MURDOCH Helen Messinger 1862-1956 **[3]**
📷 **$2 600** - €2 859 - **£1 653** - FF16 000
Aviation at Boston Airport Autochrome (8x10cm
3x4in) New-York 2001

MURER Augusto 1922-1985 **[50]**
🗿 **$32 500** - €33 691 - **£19 500** - FF221 000
Fauno Bronzo (H190cm H74in) Prato 2000
🗿 **$1 650** - €1 710 - **£990** - FF11 220
Fanciulla Bronzo (H32cm H12in) Prato 2000
🖋 **$700** - €726 - **£420** - FF4 760
Cavallo Acquarello (69.5x50cm 27x19in) Prato 2001

MURET Albert 1874-1955 **[10]**
▭ **$2 647** - €2 473 - **£1 600** - FF16 219
Chemin de fer, Martigny-Orsières Poster
(100x71cm 39x27in) London 1999

MURI Roland 1959 **[3]**
🖼 **$2 956** - €2 737 - **£1 810** - FF17 756
Schwarzer Jazzmusiker am Kontrabass
Mischtechnik (49x34.5cm 19x13in) Bern 1999

MURILLO Bartolomé Esteban 1618-1682 **[38]**
- $360 000 - €315 778 - **£218 592** - FF2 071 368
  The Penitent Magdalen in Prayer in a Mountainous Landscape Oil/canvas (196x145cm 77x57in) New-York 1999
- $90 000 - €79 212 - **£54 792** - FF519 597
  Allegory of Spring, a Young Girl Holding Flowers Oil/canvas (89x66cm 35x25in) New-York 1999
- $60 000 - €64 072 - **£40 974** - FF421 596
  Studies of putti among Clouds Ink (32.5x22.5cm 12x8in) New-York 2001

MURILLO Y BRACHO José María 1827-1882 **[22]**
- $6 080 - €5 706 - **£3 705** - FF37 430
  Bodegón de frutas y flores Oleo/tabla (54.5x46cm 21x18in) Madrid 1999

MURNOT Félix 1924 **[600]**
- $461 - €457 - **£286** - FF3 000
  Plage Huile/carton (15x25cm 5x10in) L'Isle-Adam 1999
- $330 - €351 - **£221** - FF2 300
  Marine Aquarelle/papier (19x27cm 7x10in) Ourville-en-Caux 2000

MURPHY Ada Clifford XIX-XX **[5]**
- $2 300 - €2 616 - **£1 607** - FF17 158
  Young Girl Picking Flowers Oil/canvas (25x20cm 10x8in) Mystic CT 2000

MURPHY Christopher P.H. Jr. 1902-1969 **[7]**
- $1 750 - €1 870 - **£1 164** - FF12 267
  Savannah Street Scene Oil/board (30x27cm 12x11in) Cleveland OH 2000

MURPHY Hermann Dudley 1867-1945 **[68]**
- $24 000 - €22 949 - **£14 616** - FF150 535
  Portrait of Mrs. Sarah Skinner Oil/canvas (129.5x101.5cm 50x39in) Boston MA 1999
- $10 000 - €8 661 - **£6 133** - FF56 815
  Monadnock from Troy Road Oil/canvas (63.5x76cm 25x29in) New-York 1999
- $1 500 - €1 416 - **£932** - FF9 289
  The Sinking Schooner Oil/panel (40x30cm 16x12in) Milford CT 1999
- $1 500 - €1 813 - **£1 047** - FF11 892
  Venetian Boats Watercolour/paper (28x22cm 11x8in) Bethesda MD 2000

MURPHY John Francis 1853-1921 **[122]**
- $9 000 - €8 225 - **£5 506** - FF53 953
  Arkville Landscape Oil/canvas (40.5x56cm 15x22in) Boston MA 1999
- $4 250 - €3 631 - **£2 571** - FF23 821
  Morning Glow Oil/panel (21x15cm 8x5in) San-Francisco CA 1998
- $4 250 - €3 884 - **£2 600** - FF25 480
  November Day Watercolour/paper (13.6x18.5cm 5x7in) Boston MA 1999

MURPHY John J.A. XIX-XX **[3]**
- $1 600 - €1 655 - **£1 011** - FF10 854
  Adam, Eve and Apple Woodcut (17.5x19.5cm 6x7in) New-York 2000

MURPHY Nellie Littlehale 1867-1941 **[8]**
- $800 - €830 - **£507** - FF5 445
  Still Life with Freesia Watercolour/paper (37x37cm 14x14in) Boston MA 2000

MURPHY Stephen 1962 **[4]**
- $2 974 - €2 542 - **£1 800** - FF16 672
  Hell/Inferno/Skull, Crossbones/Swarm Mixed media/board (12x18cm 4x7in) London 1998

$11 655 - €12 511 - **£7 800** - FF82 068
  Submarine Type C color print (183x220cm 72x86in) London 2000

MURPHY Todd 1962 **[1]**
- $2 688 - €2 288 - **£1 600** - FF15 006
  «Care for Elton John» Coloured chalks/paper (112x75cm 44x29in) London 1998

MURRAMURRA Dick Ngulei Ngulei 1920-1988 **[2]**
- $2 761 - €2 672 - **£1 750** - FF17 527
  Two Kangaroos Mixed media/board (71.5x45cm 28x17in) Malvern, Victoria 1999

MURRAY Alexander H. Hallam 1854-1934 **[11]**
- $318 - €344 - **£220** - FF2 255
  Coastal Landscape Watercolour (30x40cm 11x15in) London 2001

MURRAY Charles Fairfax 1849-1919 **[22]**
- $4 309 - €3 718 - **£2 600** - FF24 390
  Guilia Oil/canvas (52x40cm 20x15in) London 1998
- $1 345 - €1 402 - **£850** - FF9 195
  Portrait of Henry Harby Sentence Tempera/paper (29.5x24cm 11x9in) Leyburn, North Yorkshire 2000

MURRAY David 1849-1933 **[116]**
- $19 642 - €23 360 - **£14 000** - FF153 232
  In Dartmouth Harbour Oil/canvas (100x150cm 39x59in) London 2000
- $2 810 - €2 655 - **£1 700** - FF17 415
  Ludlow Oil/panel (37x45cm 14x17in) Billingshurst, West-Sussex 1999
- $851 - €727 - **£500** - FF4 771
  Poplars, Evening Oil/panel (12.5x21cm 4x8in) Glasgow 1998
- $606 - €670 - **£420** - FF4 394
  Collecting the Boats for a Tow-out Watercolour (28x42cm 11x16in) London 2001

MURRAY Ebenezer H. XIX **[7]**
- $1 000 - €919 - **£614** - FF6 027
  Gypsy Life Oil/canvas (45x60cm 18x24in) Detroit MI 1999

MURRAY Eileen 1885-1962 **[7]**
- $648 - €736 - **£447** - FF4 830
  The Italian Shepherd Oil/cardboard (39x28cm 15x11in) Dublin 1998

MURRAY Elizabeth 1940 **[93]**
- $52 000 - €60 335 - **£35 900** - FF395 772
  Picture - Crack Up Oil/canvas (274x320x26.5cm 107x125x10in) New-York 2000
- $35 000 - €39 134 - **£23 500** - FF256 704
  Untitled Sculpture (124.5x143.5x50.5cm 49x56x19in) New-York 2000
- $3 200 - €3 713 - **£2 209** - FF24 355
  Point Pastel (90x118cm 35x46in) New-York 2000
- $1 500 - €1 762 - **£1 065** - FF11 559
  Undoing Lithograph (73.5x58.5cm 28x23in) New-York 2000

MURRAY George 1875-1933 **[11]**
- $452 - €523 - **£320** - FF3 430
  Lochranza, Isle of Arran Oil/canvas (42x61cm 16x24in) Glasgow 2000

MURRAY H. XIX **[14]**
- $1 000 - €1 099 - **£640** - FF7 210
  The End of the Day Watercolour, gouache/paper (28.5x44cm 11x17in) New-York 2000

MURRAY John Philip 1952 **[5]**
- $1 180 - €1 270 - **£804** - FF8 329
  Looking beneath Oil/paper (30x41cm 11x16in) Dublin 2001

M

MURRAY John Reed 1861-1906 [2]
- $2 565 - €2 324 - **£1 600** - FF15 246
  Moonrise Oil/board (30x40.5cm 11x15in) Glasgow 1999

MURRAY John, Dr 1809-1901 [166]
- $2 388 - €2 304 - **£1 500** - FF15 114
  The Taj Mahal from the East Albumen print (35x43.5cm 13x17in) London 1999

MURRAY Thomas 1663-1734 [19]
- $23 073 - €25 497 - **£16 000** - FF167 248
  Portrait of a Lady Oil/canvas (124.5x100.5cm 49x39in) London 2001
- $4 877 - €4 503 - **£3 000** - FF29 539
  Portrait of Gentleman, traditionally identified as Thomas Wharton Oil/canvas (76.5x62cm 30x24in) London 1999

MURRAY William XVIII-XIX [2]
- $10 500 - €12 488 - **£7 483** - FF81 913
  A Foxhound Outside a Kennel Oil/panel (16.5x20cm 6x7in) New-York 2000

MURRAY William Grant 1877-1950 [11]
- $563 - €486 - **£340** - FF3 189
  «The Old House, Bamff» Watercolour/paper (45x30.5cm 17x12in) London 1998

MURTEIRA Jaime Augusto 1910-1986 [9]
- $3 520 - €3 988 - **£2 480** - FF26 160
  Paisagem Oleo/lienzo (50.5x65.5cm 19x25in) Lisboa 2001
- $880 - €997 - **£620** - FF6 540
  Costa do Estoril (?) Oleo/tabla (20x12cm 7x4in) Lisboa 2001

MURUA Mario 1952 [33]
- $12 000 - €10 463 - **£7 255** - FF68 636
  Desde mi casa Acrylic/canvas (199x200cm 78x78in) New-York 1998

MUS Italo 1892-1967 [42]
- $35 000 - €36 283 - **£21 000** - FF238 000
  Interno di casa con personaggi Olio/tela (99x141cm 38x55in) Torino 2000
- $3 800 - €4 204 - **£2 850** - FF32 300
  Baite di Valtournanche Olio/tela (40x50cm 15x19in) Torino 2000
- $1 800 - €1 555 - **£900** - FF10 200
  Paesaggio Valdostano Olio/tavola (25x15cm 9x5in) Vercelli 1999

MUSANTE Franc./Gruppo Aperto 1950 [31]
- $1 000 - €1 037 - **£600** - FF6 800
  Il signor Chicco in equilibrio instabile sul filo della notte Tecnica mista (70x50cm 27x19in) Vercelli 2000
- $500 - €518 - **£300** - FF3 400
  «Il banchetto degli Dei pagani» Tecnica mista/tavola (15x63cm 5x24in) Vercelli 1999

MUSATI XX [3]
- $1 040 - €1 049 - **£650** - FF6 880
  «Vallée d'Aoste, Gressoney-Breuil-Courlmayeur-La Thuile-Pilaz» Poster (100x70cm 39x27in) London 2000

MUSATOV Grigorij 1889-1941 [11]
- $13 872 - €13 120 - **£8 640** - FF86 064
  Famille juive Huile/toile (61x104cm 24x40in) Praha 2000

MUSCHAMP Francis Sydney 1851-1929 [68]
- $3 500 - €3 628 - **£2 100** - FF23 800
  «Veduta di Torno sul lago di Como» Olio/tela (44x66cm 17x25in) Milano 2000

- $2 322 - €2 020 - **£1 400** - FF13 248
  An Amourous Advance Oil/canvas (40.5x30.5cm 15x12in) London 1998
- $687 - €629 - **£420** - FF4 125
  A Doubtful Customer Watercolour/paper (41x61cm 16x24in) Oxford 1998

MUSCHERT Michel 1952 [1]
- $2 706 - €2 727 - **£1 683** - FF17 886
  La veillée de la malade Huile/panneau (28x22cm 11x8in) Bruxelles 2000

MUSFELD Ernest Max 1900-1964 [8]
- $694 - €687 - **£433** - FF4 509
  Tessiner Landschaft Aquarell/Papier (48x71cm 18x27in) Luzern 1999

MUSGRAVE Arthur Franklin 1876-? [12]
- $3 800 - €4 519 - **£2 708** - FF29 643
  The Sunlit Garden Oil/canvas (51x61cm 20x24in) New-York 2000

MUSGRAVE Mary Ann, Mrs. W. XIX [2]
- $3 613 - €3 506 - **£2 249** - FF23 000
  Portrait de famille Aquarelle (46x54cm 18x21in) Montfort L'Amaury 1999

MUSIC Zoran Antoni 1909 [992]
- $37 422 - €31 433 - **£22 000** - FF206 186
  Motif Vegetal Acrylic/canvas (202x147.5cm 79x58in) London 1998
- $18 047 - €16 527 - **£11 000** - FF108 411
  Paysage Italien Acrylic/canvas (81x116cm 31x45in) London 1999
- $13 600 - €17 623 - **£10 200** - FF115 600
  Paesaggio senese Olio/tela (22.5x32cm 8x12in) Prato 2000
- $2 912 - €3 049 - **£1 830** - FF20 000
  Éclat d'été Aquarelle, gouache/papier (33x68cm 12x26in) Versailles 2000
- $404 - €457 - **£282** - FF2 997
  Paysage Dalmate Farblithographie (28.5x38cm 11x14in) Zürich 2001

MUSIKISTY Gregory ?-1737 [3]
- $37 315 - €43 460 - **£26 069** - FF285 081
  Brustbild Zar Peters des Grossen in Rüstung Miniature (4x3.5cm 1x1in) München 2000

MUSIN Auguste 1852-1923 [98]
- $6 237 - €6 693 - **£4 239** - FF43 902
  Coucher de soleil sur l'Escaut calme Huile/toile (44x68cm 17x26in) Bruxelles 2001
- $2 007 - €2 231 - **£1 341** - FF14 634
  Bateaux à la panne Huile/panneau (23x39cm 9x15in) Bruxelles 2000
- $616 - €595 - **£387** - FF3 901
  Marine Aquarell/Papier (31x50cm 12x19in) Zürich 1999

MUSIN François Etienne 1820-1888 [161]
- $29 150 - €27 267 - **£17 710** - FF178 860
  Schepen in de storm voor Oostende Oil/canvas (136x179cm 53x70in) Lokeren 1999
- $5 520 - €5 952 - **£3 705** - FF39 045
  Fiskeskutor till sjöss Oil/canvas (57x80.5cm 22x31in) Stockholm 2000
- $4 097 - €4 497 - **£2 637** - FF29 500
  Combat naval Huile/panneau (45.5x31.5cm 17x12in) Sens 2000
- $2 270 - €2 181 - **£1 400** - FF14 306
  Barges preparing to set sail Watercolour (30.5x44.5cm 12x17in) London 1999

MUSIN Maurice 1939 [49]
$1 068 - €992 - £664 - FF6 504
Le joueur de pipeau Huile/panneau (49x74.5cm 19x29in) Liège 1999

MUSLER Jay 1949 [4]
$11 000 - €10 000 - £6 873 - FF68 876
Untitled Sculpture, glass (11x55cm 4x21in) New-York 1999

MUSS-ARNOLT Gustav 1858-1927 [16]
$6 000 - €5 483 - £3 670 - FF35 968
Welsh Terrier Oil/canvas (56x71cm 22x27in) Boston MA 1999
$5 365 - €4 534 - £3 200 - FF29 739
On the Scent Oil/canvas (32.5x40.5cm 12x15in) Glasgow 1998
$1 533 - €1 473 - £950 - FF9 660
Two Poodles Watercolour (58x46cm 22x18in) London 1999

MUSSARD Robert 1713-1777 [3]
$7 284 - €7 072 - £4 500 - FF46 389
William IV Charles Henry Friso, Prince of Orange-Nassau (1711-1751) Miniature (5.5x7.5cm 2x2in) London 1997

MUSSAT SARTON Paolo 1947 [2]
$1 600 - €1 659 - £960 - FF10 880
Rovesciare i propri occhi - Giuseppe Penone Photo (8.5x20cm 3x7in) Milano 2000

MUSSCHER van Michiel 1645-1705 [28]
$32 408 - €36 302 - £22 520 - FF238 128
Lawyer in Study Oil/panel (46.5x38.5cm 18x15in) Amsterdam 1999
$32 874 - €35 288 - £22 000 - FF231 475
Portrait of a Young Lady, head and shoulders, wearing red dress Oil/copper (15.5x13cm 6x5in) London 2000

MUSSINI Cesar 1804-1879 [2]
$4 881 - €4 838 - £2 962 - FF31 734
Ungt par i renaissancedragter Oil/canvas (120x90cm 47x35in) Vejle 2000

MUSSO Carlo 1907-1968 [63]
$1 440 - €1 866 - £1 080 - FF12 240
Tramonto sul porto di Savona Olio/tavola (49x60cm 19x23in) Torino 2000
$650 - €674 - £390 - FF4 420
«Diano marina» Olio/cartone (19x29cm 7x11in) Vercelli 2001
$180 - €155 - £90 - FF1 020
Fontana Angelica China/carta (26x16cm 10x6in) Vercelli 1999

MUT TORROJA Antoni 1921-1990 [38]
$243 - €252 - £151 - FF1 654
Paisaje con campesina Oleo/lienzo (60x73cm 23x28in) Barcelona 2000

MUTER Mela 1876-1967 [128]
$30 000 - €33 302 - £20 913 - FF218 445
Famille de musiciens Oil/panel (153x117cm 60x46in) Tel Aviv 2001
$6 603 - €7 089 - £4 417 - FF46 500
Nature morte au journal/Vue de Village Huile/panneau (46x55cm 18x21in) Avignon 2000
$3 194 - €3 579 - £2 201 - FF23 477
Alpenveilchen auf Tisch Öl/Karton (42x33.5cm 16x13in) Frankfurt 2000
$3 957 - €3 634 - £2 416 - FF23 836
Pejzaz z Saint Paul de Vence/Port na poludniu Francji Watercolour/paper (50x35cm 19x13in) Warszawa 1998

MUTRIE Annie Feray 1826-1893 [21]
$13 197 - €14 223 - £9 000 - FF93 298
Margret's Corner Oil/canvas (83.5x63.5cm 32x25in) London 2001
$8 021 - €8 083 - £5 000 - FF53 018
Hyacinths Oil/panel (45.5x33cm 17x13in) London 2000
$385 - €449 - £270 - FF2 945
Posy of Spring Flowers Watercolour (10.5x19cm 4x7in) Crewkerne, Somerset 2000

MUTRIE Martha Darlay 1824-1885/86 [13]
$7 184 - €8 382 - £5 000 - FF54 980
Still Life of Fruit and Other Objets on a Marble Top Table Oil/canvas (81x61cm 31x24in) West-Yorshire 2000
$1 665 - €1 715 - £1 050 - FF11 248
Still Life of Rhododendrons/Still Life of Wild Roses with Tufted Vetch Gouache/paper (10x20cm 4x8in) Carlisle, Cumbria 2000

MÜTZNER Sammys 1869-1958 [9]
$2 550 - €2 401 - £1 650 - FF15 750
Sin título, paisaje, Caracas Oleo/tabla (32x27.5cm 12x10in) Caracas 1999

MUUKKA Elias 1853-1938 [77]
$3 722 - €3 187 - £2 196 - FF20 907
Stig Oil/canvas (30x61cm 11x24in) Helsinki 1998
$1 293 - €1 430 - £896 - FF9 377
Frostdag Oil/canvas (41x37cm 16x14in) Helsinki 2001

MUXART DOMENECH Jaime 1922 [43]
$812 - €751 - £487 - FF4 925
Testa Oleo/tabla (59x43cm 23x16in) Barcelona 1999

MUYBRIDGE Eadweard 1830-1904 [144]
$2 800 - €3 121 - £1 963 - FF20 472
Untitled from «Animal Locomotion» Photograph (20x38cm 8x15in) New-York 2001

MUYDEN van Jacques Alfred 1818-1898 [28]
$1 700 - €1 823 - £1 124 - FF11 956
Mother and Child Oil/panel (17x14cm 7x5in) New-Orleans LA 2000

MUYS Nicolaes 1740-1808 [8]
$56 783 - €60 952 - £38 000 - FF399 820
Group Portrait of a Family in an Ornamental Garden Oil/panel (86.5x70cm 34x27in) London 2000

MUZIANO Girolamo 1528-1592 [10]
$42 500 - €36 948 - £25 721 - FF242 360
St. Roch in a Landscape Ink (50x36cm 19x14in) New-York 1999

MUZIKA Frantisek 1900-1974 [21]
$13 005 - €12 300 - £8 100 - FF80 685
Forêt Huile/carton (33x46cm 12x18in) Praha 2001
$2 312 - €2 187 - £1 440 - FF14 344
Personnage allongée Encre (23.5x36cm 9x14in) Praha 2001

MUZZIOLI Giovanni 1854-1894 [16]
$125 000 - €125 961 - £77 925 - FF826 250
By the Fountain Oil/canvas (94x183cm 37x72in) New-York 1999
$9 000 - €7 775 - £6 000 - FF51 000
Due ragazze in una villa Pompeiana Olio/tela (62x33cm 24x12in) Roma 1998

MWAI Cheff 1931 [2]
$2 500 - €2 592 - £1 500 - FF17 000
Majenuru kutoka kwa kampu (5) Acrilico/tavola (56x14cm 22x5in) Prato 1999

MY van der Hieronymus 1687-1761 **[9]**
- **$36 107** - €42 089 - **£25 000** - FF276 087
  Double portrait of boy and a Girl, Small Full-Lenght, with a Greyhood Oil/panel (54x46cm 21x18in) London 2000

MYDANS Carl 1907 **[5]**
- **$6 000** - €6 239 - **£3 788** - FF40 924
  New York City Skyline Gelatin silver print (24.5x33.5cm 9x13in) New-York 2000

MYERS Frank Harmon 1899-1956 **[35]**
- **$2 750** - €2 952 - **£1 840** - FF19 365
  Cypress Point (No. 330) Oil/masonite (45.5x61cm 17x24in) San-Francisco CA 2000
- **$550** - €506 - **£330** - FF3 320
  Great Rock, Point Lobos Oil/board (30x40cm 12x16in) Pasadena CA 1999

MYERS Harry 1886-1961 **[4]**
- **$1 600** - €1 861 - **£1 141** - FF12 207
  Young Ballerinas/Ballerina Oil/masonite (40x30cm 16x12in) New-York 2000

MYERS Jerome 1867-1940 **[60]**
- **$26 000** - €29 523 - **£17 794** - FF193 658
  The Playground Oil/canvas (41x56cm 16x22in) New-York 2000
- **$2 900** - €3 249 - **£2 019** - FF21 313
  Children at Play Oil/board (22x30cm 9x12in) Watertown MA 2001
- **$1 700** - €1 933 - **£1 187** - FF12 682
  Street Scene with Mothers and Their Children Charcoal (22x32cm 9x12in) New-York 2000
- **$200** - €216 - **£137** - FF1 419
  Elderly Woman in Babushka standing Etching (21x8cm 8x3in) Thomaston ME 2001

MYERS Joel Philip 1934 **[6]**
- **$4 000** - €3 818 - **£2 499** - FF25 046
  Untitled Sculpture, glass (25x22x10cm 9x8x3in) New-York 1999

MYGATT Robertson K. 1861-1919 **[11]**
- **$5 000** - €5 946 - **£3 563** - FF39 005
  Landscape Oil/canvas (45.5x66cm 17x25in) New-York 2000
- **$1 200** - €1 435 - **£827** - FF9 410
  Sailing on a Summer Day Oil/panel (24x35cm 9x14in) Milford CT 2000

MYLIUS Carl Friedrich 1827-1916 **[11]**
- **$582** - €562 - **£366** - FF3 689
  Königstein im Taunus mit Burgruine Albumen print (23.4x17.9cm 9x7in) München 1999

MYN van der Frans, Francis 1719-1783 **[29]**
- **$6 836** - €7 279 - **£4 500** - FF47 748
  Portrait of a Lady, said to be Agnus Tolson of Giggleswick Oil/canvas (74x61.5cm 29x24in) Billingshurst, West-Sussex 2000

MYN van der Herman 1684-1741 **[22]**
- **$25 242** - €29 667 - **£17 500** - FF194 600
  Portrait of Hon. Henry Howard, Lady Arabella Howard, Lady Diana Howard Oil/canvas (170x142cm 67x56in) Carlisle, Cumbria 2000
- **$4 674** - €4 360 - **£2 820** - FF28 602
  Bildnis einer Dame Öl/Kupfer (18.5x15.5cm 7x6in) Wien 1999

MYNTTI Eemu 1890-1943 **[36]**
- **$2 020** - €1 850 - **£1 230** - FF12 135
  Landskap Oil/canvas (46x60cm 18x23in) Helsinki 1999
- **$450** - €420 - **£277** - FF2 758
  Modellen Mixed media (24x36cm 9x14in) Helsinki 1999
- **$600** - €673 - **£417** - FF4 412
  Konstnären Aimo Kanerva Pastel/paper (60x46cm 23x18in) Helsinki 2001

MYRAH Newman 1921 **[2]**
- **$5 000** - €4 545 - **£3 011** - FF29 815
  Pulled up Lame Oil/canvas (55x76cm 22x30in) Hayden ID 1998

MYRBACH-REINFELD von Felician 1853-1940 **[37]**
- **$200** - €229 - **£139** - FF1 500
  L'enfant bibelot Encre Chine (19x12cm 7x4in) Paris 2001

MYSLIVE Frank Richard 1908 **[3]**
- **$1 500** - €1 706 - **£1 040** - FF11 190
  Calamity Junction Oil/canvas (91x93cm 36x37in) Chicago IL 2000

MYTENS Daniel 1590-1648 **[6]**
- **$56 783** - €60 952 - **£38 000** - FF399 820
  Portrait of King Charles I, wearing a red silver-embroidered doublet Oil/canvas (203x131cm 79x51in) London 2000
- **$8 608** - €9 659 - **£5 968** - FF63 360
  Caballero con gola Oleo/lienzo (118x86cm 46x33in) México 2000

MYTENS Daniel II 1636-1688 **[1]**
- **$23 495** - €26 319 - **£16 327** - FF172 642
  Mercury and Herse Oil/canvas (89.5x113cm 35x44in) Amsterdam 2001

MYTENS Jan c.1614-1670 **[17]**
- **$58 000** - €51 048 - **£35 310** - FF334 851
  Venus and Adonis Oil/canvas (225.5x171.5cm 88x67in) New-York 1999
- **$19 284** - €19 128 - **£12 000** - FF125 469
  Portrait Histoire of a young Man and Lady as Meleager and Atalanta Oil/canvas (57.5x96.5cm 22x37in) London 1999
- **$11 673** - €11 474 - **£7 500** - FF75 267
  Portrait of Christaen Huygens in a Landscape, Country House beyond Oil/panel (43.5x32cm 17x12in) London 1999

MYTENS van Marten I 1648-1736 **[7]**
- **$6 679** - €5 809 - **£4 028** - FF38 102
  Porträtt av Överstelöjtnant Magnus Fleming/Hans Maka Wendela Christin Oil/canvas (108x84cm 42x33in) Stockholm 1998
- **$30 875** - €26 930 - **£18 675** - FF176 650
  Porträtt av sexårig gosse med hund Oil/panel (42x32.5cm 16x12in) Stockholm 1998

MYTENS van Marten II 1695-1770 **[11]**
- **$10 248** - €10 842 - **£6 500** - FF71 121
  The Emperor Joseph II (1741-1790) as a Boy seated on a Throne Oil/canvas (126x94cm 49x37in) London 2000

N

N.A.S.A. XX **[14]**
📷 **$3 000** - €3 454 - **£2 047** - FF22 656
Unmanned Space Craft on the Moon Gelatin silver print (76x36cm 29x14in) New-York 2000

NABERT Wilhelm J. August 1830-1904 **[21]**
✎ **$1 714** - €1 841 - **£1 147** - FF12 074
Gebirgslandschaft mit Bachlauf Öl/Leinwand (74x110cm 29x43in) Stuttgart 2000

NACERADSKY Jiri 1939 **[16]**
✎ **$10 115** - €9 567 - **£6 300** - FF62 755
Lac des cygnes Huile/toile (163x130cm 64x51in) Praha 2001

NACHT-SAMBORSKI Artur 1898-1974 **[12]**
✎ **$14 279** - €13 334 - **£8 647** - FF87 464
Half-naked Woman in foliage Ornament Oil/canvas (80x63cm 31x24in) Warszawa 1999
✎ **$5 493** - €6 078 - **£3 817** - FF39 868
Fleurs et fruits Gouache (65x47cm 25x18in) Warszawa 2001

NACHTMANN Franz Xaver 1799-1846 **[8]**
✎ **$26 360** - €25 565 - **£16 590** - FF167 695
Die Zeichenstunde Indian ink (48x69.5cm 18x27in) München 1999

NACKAERTS Frans 1884-1948 **[7]**
✎ **$2 381** - €2 556 - **£1 594** - FF16 769
Tulpenfelder Coloured chalks (40.4x63.4cm 15x24in) Köln 2000

NADAL Carlos 1917-1998 **[143]**
✎ **$7 320** - €7 208 - **£4 680** - FF47 280
«El interior verde» Oleo/lienzo (73x92cm 28x36in) Madrid 1999
✎ **$4 170** - €4 203 - **£2 600** - FF27 569
Fanatico de Miro Oil/canvas (27.5x40.5cm 10x15in) London 2000
✎ **$793** - €781 - **£507** - FF5 122
Plaże Gouache (31x24.5cm 12x9in) Madrid 1999

NADAR Adrien A. Tournachon 1825-1903 **[25]**
📷 **$2 590** - €2 902 - **£1 800** - FF19 033
Fig. 55 from Mecanisme de la physionomie humaine Albumen print (12x9cm 4x3in) London 2001

NADAR Félix Tournachon dit 1820-1910 **[107]**
✎ **$2 158** - €2 454 - **£1 507** - FF16 098
«Les Omnibus de Londres» Pencil (11x10cm 4x3in) München 2000
📷 **$1 677** - €1 555 - **£1 043** - FF10 200
Monseigneur Dreux-Brézé (sic), évêque de Moulins Tirage albuminé (23.1x17.4cm 9x6in) Paris 1999

NADAR Paul 1856-1939 **[20]**
📷 **$1 693** - €1 906 - **£1 182** - FF12 500
Jean Cocteau Tirage argentique (25x17.5cm 9x6in) Paris 2001

NADELMAN Elie 1882-1946 **[72]**
🗿 **$270 000** - €299 016 - **£183 114** - FF1 961 415
Horse Bronze (H92cm H36in) New-York 2000
🗿 **$46 000** - €47 574 - **£29 067** - FF312 068
Classical Head Marble (H40.5cm H15in) New-York 2000
✎ **$3 800** - €3 242 - **£2 264** - FF21 264
Standing Woman Ink (25x14.5cm 9x5in) New-York 1998

NADERA Ida Bagus Made 1910-1998 **[12]**
✎ **$2 295** - €2 607 - **£1 571** - FF17 098
Going to the Temple Acrylic/canvas (96.5x62cm 37x24in) Singapore 2000

NADJAMERREK Lofty Bardayal c.1926 **[11]**
✎ **$2 386** - €2 545 - **£1 592** - FF16 692
Fresh Water Crocodile and Catfish Mixed media (63.5x38cm 25x14in) Melbourne 2000

NADORP Franz Joh. Heinr. 1794-1876 **[13]**
✎ **$474** - €460 - **£295** - FF3 018
Athena und ihre Gefährtinnen zu Gast in einem Kerker Indian ink (25x20.2cm 9x7in) Berlin 1999

NAEF Hermann 1892-1964 **[9]**
✎ **$2 132** - €2 051 - **£1 313** - FF13 451
Alpfahrt, drei Sennen mit Ziegen und Kühen vor Berglandschaft Huile/panneau (26x35cm 10x13in) St. Gallen 1999

NAEF Milo 1908-1991 **[3]**
✎ **$2 206** - €2 129 - **£1 385** - FF13 963
Senn mit Ziege vor Toggenburger Landschaft Aquarell/Papier (54x35cm 21x13in) St. Gallen 1999

NAEGELE Otto Ludwig 1880-1952 **[7]**
🖼 **$1 474** - €1 633 - **£1 000** - FF10 712
«Forstenriederpark» Poster (120x89cm 47x35in) London 2000

NAEGELI Harald 1939 **[7]**
✎ **$1 609** - €1 824 - **£1 124** - FF11 963
Ohne Titel Collage (15.5x22cm 6x8in) Zürich 2001

NAEKE Gustav Heinrich 1786-1835 **[20]**
✎ **$419** - €460 - **£284** - FF3 018
Studienblatt mit Maria der Verkündigung und einer weiteren Heiligen Pencil/paper (20.8x25.7cm 8x10in) Berlin 2000

NAFTEL Isabel XIX **[19]**
✎ **$4 017** - €3 468 - **£2 400** - FF22 748
Under the Whispering Trees Watercolour/paper (25x34cm 9x13in) Llandeilo, Carmarthenshire 1998

NAFTEL Maud 1856-1890 **[8]**
✎ **$4 718** - €5 226 - **£3 200** - FF34 278
Landscape near the Sea Watercolour (34.5x52cm 13x20in) Billingshurst, West-Sussex 2000

NAFTEL Paul Jacob 1817-1891 **[63]**
✎ **$1 423** - €1 229 - **£850** - FF8 061
Chickens in a Landscape Watercolour/paper (34x25cm 13x9in) Llandeilo, Carmarthenshire 1998

NAGAI Kazumasa 1929 **[10]**
🖼 **$272** - €318 - **£186** - FF2 083
«A Genealogy of Japanese Contemporary Sculpture» Poster (103x72.5cm 40x28in) Hoorn 2000

NAGAOKA Kunito 1940 **[8]**
🖼 **$233** - €256 - **£158** - FF1 676
Horizonte Farbradierung (28.8x23cm 11x9in) Berlin 2000

NAGASAWA Hidetoshi 1940 **[5]**
✎ **$3 750** - €3 887 - **£2 250** - FF25 500
Senza titolo Tecnica mista/carta (150x72cm 59x28in) Prato 1999

NAGEL Andrés 1947 **[13]**
✎ **$13 500** - €15 016 - **£9 250** - FF98 500
El partido que perdió la Real Acrilico (195x195cm 76x76in) Madrid 2001

NAGEL Bill 1888-1967 **[33]**
$124 - €143 - £87 - FF939
Wiesenbude Aquarell/Papier (24.5x33.7cm 9x13in)
Hamburg 2001

NAGEL Hanna 1907-1975 **[91]**
$309 - €286 - £186 - FF1 878
Lesende Indian ink (31.3x21.3cm 12x8in) Heidelberg
1999

NAGEL Johan Friedrich 1765-1825 **[4]**
$733 - €872 - £523 - FF5 720
**Helle Landschaft mit Bauernhaus und
Wanderern** Gouache/paper (19x29cm 7x11in) Wien
2000

NAGEL Otto 1894-1967 **[31]**
$1 822 - €1 687 - £1 115 - FF11 067
**Auf eienem Tisch vor ockerfarbender Wand
grosse Hortensienblüte** Öl/Karton (49x39cm
19x15in) Merzhausen 1999
$4 165 - €4 039 - £2 638 - FF26 495
**Blüte in Wasserglas neben aufgeschlagenem
Buch** Öl/Karton (38.5x29.5cm 15x11in) Lindau 1999

NAGEL Peter 1941 **[42]**
$56 - €66 - £39 - FF436
Pulcini Colorati Etching in colors (25x18.5cm 9x7in)
Braunschweig 2001

NAGEL Wilhelm 1866-1944 **[102]**
$670 - €665 - £417 - FF4 360
**Auf einem Tisch mit gefaltetem Tuch Tonvase
mit Wiesenblumenstrauss** Öl/Karton (69x55cm
27x21in) Merzhausen 1999
$245 - €289 - £176 - FF1 894
Winterlandschaft mit Wald und Bächlein
Gouache/paper (39x51cm 15x20in) Zürich 2001

NÄGELE Reinhold 1884-1972 **[220]**
$7 620 - €8 181 - £5 100 - FF53 662
Prozession in Schwäbisch Gmünd Tempera
(47.5x38cm 18x14in) Stuttgart 2000
$2 686 - €3 068 - £1 894 - FF20 123
Sommernacht Painting (25x20cm 9x7in) Stuttgart
2001
$5 847 - €5 010 - £3 515 - FF32 862
Stofftiere spielen mit einer Puppe im Tigerfell
Pastell/Papier (49x63cm 19x24in) Stuttgart 1998
$407 - €460 - £286 - FF3 018
Esslinger Dächer Radierung (19.5x15cm 7x5in)
Stuttgart 2001

NAGLE Ron 1939 **[5]**
$9 500 - €9 841 - £6 046 - FF64 555
Untitled Ceramic (18x19x16.5cm 7x7x6in) New-York
2000

NAGLER Fred 1891-1983 **[2]**
$12 000 - €13 863 - £8 402 - FF90 937
On a Far Hill Oil/canvas (76x102cm 30x40in) New-
York 2001

NAGORNOV Vladislav 1974 **[25]**
$1 080 - €1 081 - £666 - FF7 092
**Un ángel dormido (copia de William Adolphe
Bouguereau)** Oleo/lienzo (52x65cm 20x25in) Madrid
2000
$405 - €450 - £277 - FF2 955
Desnudo tumbado Oleo/lienzo (27x35cm 10x13in)
Madrid 2001

NAGY Gabor L. 1945 **[24]**
$454 - €524 - £317 - FF3 440
Monday, six stems Oil/canvas (76x60cm 30x24in)
Calgary, Alberta 2001

NAGY István 1873-1937 **[15]**
$770 - €852 - £506 - FF5 588
Cemetery Pastel/paper (23x31cm 9x12in) Budapest
2000

NAGY Oszkar 1883-1965 **[28]**
$2 200 - €2 163 - £1 375 - FF14 190
Sisters Oil/canvas (55x45cm 21x17in) Budapest 1999

NAGY Peter 1959 **[15]**
$1 611 - €1 881 - £1 104 - FF12 336
Industrial Culture Etching (51x51cm 20x20in)
Stockholm 2000

NAGY Vilmos 1874-1953 **[38]**
$822 - €883 - £550 - FF5 793
A Lady with a Parasol Walking her Dog Oil/can-
vas (70x56.5cm 27x22in) London 2000

NAHA Raymond 1933-1974/76 **[17]**
$1 100 - €1 262 - £752 - FF8 279
Snake Priest Painting (50x40cm 20x16in) Cloudcroft
NM 2000
$3 000 - €3 305 - £2 002 - FF21 681
Mudhead Ceremony Watercolour/paper (60x81cm
24x32in) St. Ignatius MT 2000

NAHL Johann August II 1752-1825 **[7]**
$2 153 - €2 454 - £1 502 - FF16 098
Bildnis einer Dame in antikisierender Tracht
Aquarell/Papier (45.5x38.5cm 17x15in) Berlin 2001

NAHL Karl 1818-1878 **[19]**
$3 700 - €3 659 - £2 311 - FF24 000
Fillette au perroquet Huile/toile (70x56cm 27x22in)
Tours 1999
$2 000 - €1 902 - £1 214 - FF12 478
Floral Still Life Oil/wood (40.5x23cm 15x9in)
Beverly-Hills CA 2000
$1 136 - €1 092 - £700 - FF7 163
Bar-Tailed Trogon Watercolour (8.5x22.5cm 3x8in)
London 1999

NÄHR Moritz 1859-c.1937 **[1]**
$42 799 - €42 335 - £26 686 - FF277 702
Portrait Gustav Klimt Vintage gelatin silver print
(49.4x27.1cm 19x10in) Berlin 1999

NAIDITCH Vladimir 1903-1980 **[69]**
$1 063 - €991 - £657 - FF6 500
Nature morte au gibier Huile/toile/carton (46x56cm
18x22in) Paris 1999

NAIDOO R. Ramishamy XIX **[2]**
$17 365 - €16 243 - £10 500 - FF106 549
Portrait of a Young Priest Oil/canvas (48.5x38cm
19x14in) London 1999

NAIGEON Jean Guillaume Els. 1797-1867 **[3]**
$4 413 - €5 336 - £3 083 - FF35 000
**Portrait présumé de la reine Marie Amélie et de
sa fille** Huile/toile (101x81.5cm 39x32in) Paris 2000

NAILLOD Charles 1876-? **[12]**
$86 - €82 - £54 - FF537
Summer Afternoon Etching in colors (38.5x29cm
15x11in) Praha 2000

NAILOR Gerald Lloyde 1917-1952 **[6]**
$420 - €493 - £296 - FF3 236
Eagle and Deer Tempera/paper (48x43cm 18x16in)
New-York 2000

NAIRN James McLachlan 1859-1904 **[7]**
$4 655 - €5 217 - £3 245 - FF34 218
«Ma belle, portrait of Mabel Hill» Oil/board
(35x25cm 13x9in) Wellington 2001

🖋 **$10 480** - €11 747 - **£7 329** - FF77 058
Country Road with Woodgatherer
Watercolour/paper (52x73.5cm 20x28in) Auckland 2001

NAIRN Margaret, Mrs XX **[4]**
🖋 **$3 560** - €3 340 - **£2 200** - FF21 911
Winston Churchill Sketching in the South of France Ink/paper (66x48cm 25x18in) Leyburn, North Yorkshire 1999

NAISH John George 1824-1905 **[14]**
🖋 **$2 821** - €3 163 - **£1 973** - FF20 746
Midhurst from the West, County Suffolk
Watercolour/paper (34.5x44cm 13x17in) Auckland 2001

NAIVEU Matthijs 1647-1721 **[32]**
👁 **$45 696** - €53 067 - **£32 112** - FF348 096
Stilleben med druvklase, granatäpple och insekter Oil/canvas (57x46.5cm 22x18in) Stockholm 2001

NAIWINCX Herman c.1624-c.1655 **[9]**
🗐 **$210** - €204 - **£131** - FF1 841
Die zwei grossen Bäume Radierung (13.4x12.3cm 5x4in) Berlin 1999

NAKACHE Armand 1894-1976 **[57]**
👁 **$3 942** - €4 573 - **£2 805** - FF30 000
Le clown rouge à la cravate blanche Huile/toile (54x45cm 21x17in) Paris 2001

NAKAGAWA Hachiro 1877-1922 **[4]**
🖋 **$400** - €468 - **£283** - FF3 067
Bamboo Forest with Building Watercolour/paper (48x31cm 19x12in) Columbia SC 2001

NAKAGAWA Kikuto 1888-? **[1]**
🗐 **$1 000** - €1 022 - **£626** - FF6 707
Interior Scene Print (44x34cm 17x13in) Cleveland OH 2000

NAKAMURA Fusetsu 1866-1943 **[1]**
👁 **$70 000** - €77 732 - **£48 678** - FF509 887
Preparing for the Ritual Oil/canvas (167.5x97cm 65x38in) New-York 2001

NAKAMURA Katzuo 1926 **[16]**
👁 **$1 302** - €1 114 - **£783** - FF7 308
Summer Landscape Oil/board (48.5x61cm 19x24in) Toronto 1998

NAKAMURA Munehiro 1950 **[3]**
🖋 **$5 488** - €5 353 - **£3 360** - FF35 112
Trees Drawing (45.5x60.5cm 17x23in) Tokyo 1999

NAKAMURA Naondo 1905-1981 **[13]**
🖋 **$3 200** - €3 225 - **£1 994** - FF21 152
Figure in red Gouache/paper (46.5x34.5cm 18x13in) New-York 2000

NAKAMURA Tsune 1887-1924 **[2]**
👁 **$38 000** - €36 810 - **£23 700** - FF241 459
Still Life with Mandarin Oranges Oil/panel (21.5x26cm 8x10in) New-York 1999

NAKANE Hiroshi 1925 **[2]**
👁 **$9 408** - €9 716 - **£5 760** - FF60 192
Statue of Buddha Oil/canvas (100x80.5cm 39x31in) Tokyo 1999

NAKANISHI Manabu 1959 **[1]**
🐾 **$4 432** - €3 701 - **£2 600** - FF24 276
Rambling Rose Bronze (35x24.5x45cm 13x9x17in) London 1998

NAKANISHI Toshio 1900-1948 **[1]**
🖋 **$7 840** - €7 647 - **£4 800** - FF50 160
Still Life Watercolour/paper (36x51cm 14x20in) Tokyo 1999

NAKASHIMA George 1905-1990 **[15]**
🐾 **$5 500** - €5 904 - **£3 680** - FF38 728
Lounge Chair Sculpture, wood (84.5x82x47cm 33x32x18in) New-York 2000
🐾 **$6 500** - €5 940 - **£3 976** - FF38 966
Two Doors Cabinet Sculpture, wood (68.5x183x33cm 26x72x12in) New-York 1999

NAKHALOV Boris Pavlovich 1925 **[24]**
👁 **$526** - €598 - **£360** - FF3 923
Thoughtful Moment Oil/canvas (99.5x80cm 39x31in) London 2000

NAKIAN Reuben 1897-1986 **[63]**
🐾 **$15 000** - €14 367 - **£9 439** - FF94 242
Goat and Nymph Bronze (H203cm H80in) Houston TX 1999
🐾 **$3 250** - €3 131 - **£2 008** - FF20 539
Leda and the Swan Bronze (33x41x18cm 13x16x7in) Chicago IL 1999
🖋 **$300** - €277 - **£186** - FF1 816
Nymph and Faun Ink (28x18.5cm 11x7in) Washington 1999

NAKKEN William Carel 1835-1926 **[90]**
👁 **$8 730** - €9 147 - **£5 526** - FF60 000
Chevaux devant le maréchal-ferrant Huile/toile (44x75cm 17x29in) Paris 2000
👁 **$2 214** - €2 087 - **£1 372** - FF13 692
Horse and a Dog in a Stable Oil/panel (31.5x40cm 12x15in) Amsterdam 1999
🖋 **$2 927** - €3 068 - **£1 854** - FF20 123
Bauern auf dem Weg zum Markt Aquarell/Papier (40x60cm 15x23in) Köln 2000

NALDINI Giovanni Battista 1537-1591 **[15]**
👁 **$2 375** - €2 853 - **£1 662** - FF18 715
La caridad Oleo/tabla (36x28cm 14x11in) Madrid 2000
🖋 **$10 195** - €9 955 - **£6 500** - FF65 299
Group of Figures fighting/Study after Michelangelo Black chalk (106x149cm 41x58in) London 1999

NALECZ Wlodzimierz 1865-1946 **[16]**
👁 **$1 221** - €1 256 - **£774** - FF8 321
Bateaux à la rade Huile/carton (39.5x27cm 15x10in) Warszawa 2000

NALLARD Louis 1918 **[22]**
🖋 **$924** - €800 - **£560** - FF5 247
Abstract composition Watercolour, gouache/paper (32.5x41cm 12x16in) Amsterdam 1998

NAM Jacques Lehmann, dit 1881-1974 **[81]**
👁 **$3 026** - €3 049 - **£1 886** - FF20 000
Chat Siamois et chat blanc sur une table Huile/panneau (60x73cm 23x28in) Paris 2000
👁 **$2 723** - €2 744 - **£1 697** - FF18 000
Le lapin Bronze (12.5x16.5cm 4x6in) Pontoise 2000
🖋 **$486** - €534 - **£330** - FF3 500
L'éléphant d'Afrique Fusain (27x21.5cm 10x8in) Soissons 2000
🗐 **$3 000** - €2 999 - **£1 832** - FF19 669
«Cats» Poster (44x104cm 17x41in) New-York 2000

NAM Kwan 1911-1990 **[3]**
👁 **$7 000** - €8 209 - **£4 995** - FF53 846
La porte historique Oil/canvas (45x25cm 17x9in) New-York 2000

NAM SON 1890-1973 **[2]**
👁 **$4 134** - €3 854 - **£2 499** - FF25 279
Old Flower Market in Hanoi Oil/canvas (49.5x73cm 19x28in) Singapore 1999

N

NAMATBARA Paddy Compass c.1890-1973 [3]

🐦 **$2 684** - €2 863 - **£1 791** - FF18 779
Spirit Figures Mixed media (94x42cm 37x16in)
Melbourne 2000

NAMATJIRA Albert 1902-1959 [174]

✍ **$8 655** - €7 954 - **£5 275** - FF52 174
Ghost Gum and Hermannsburg Ranges
Watercolour/paper (36x52.5cm 14x20in) Melbourne
1998

NAMATJIRA Albert, Jnr. 1955 [12]

✍ **$180** - €174 - **£111** - FF1 143
Toward Mt Chappel Watercolour/paper (18x24cm
7x9in) Sydney 1999

NAMATJIRA Enos 1920-1966 [15]

✍ **$467** - €515 - **£310** - FF3 375
Dusk, Central Australia Watercolour/paper
(27x38cm 10x14in) Melbourne 2000

NAMATJIRA Ewald 1930-1984 [37]

✍ **$261** - €245 - **£157** - FF1 608
The MacDonnell Ranges Watercolour/paper
(34x51cm 13x20in) Sydney 1999

NAMATJIRA Gabriel 1941-1969 [17]

✍ **$137** - €152 - **£93** - FF997
Treed Gully Central Australia Watercolour/paper
(37x52cm 14x20in) Sydney 2000

NAMATJIRA Keith 1938-1977 [26]

✍ **$182** - €213 - **£126** - FF1 395
Across to the Mountains Watercolour/paper
(23x33cm 9x12in) Melbourne 2000

NAMATJIRA Maurice 1938-1977 [13]

✍ **$229** - €253 - **£155** - FF1 662
Central Australian Landscape Watercolour/paper
(51x72cm 20x28in) Sydney 2000

NAMATJIRA Oscar 1922-1991 [26]

✍ **$263** - €254 - **£166** - FF1 665
Ghost Gum Watercolour/paper (25x37cm 9x14in)
Sydney 1999

NAMCHEONG XIX [2]

🐦 **$3 500** - €4 082 - **£2 457** - FF26 776
**Balcksmith Stall at Macao, After George
Chinnery** Oil/canvas (51x39cm 20x15in) Portsmouth
NH 2000

NAMPITJIN Eubena c.1930 [8]

🐦 **$1 143** - €1 228 - **£765** - FF8 052
Artist's Country Acrylic (90x60cm 35x23in)
Woollahra, Sydney 2000

NAMUR Émile Jean Fr. 1852-1908 [8]

🐦 **$672** - €744 - **£468** - FF4 878
Buste de garçonnet Terracotta (H31cm H12in)
Bruxelles 2001

NAMUTH Hans 1915-1990 [7]

📷 **$1 200** - €1 128 - **£743** - FF7 401
Mark Rothko in his Studio Dye-transfer print
(33x49cm 13x19in) New-York 1999

NANGERONI Carlo 1922 [21]

🐦 **$900** - €933 - **£540** - FF6 120
Seriale Percosi Acrilico/tela (60x60cm 23x23in)
Prato 1999

NANI Giacomo 1701-1770 [8]

🐦 **$89 776** - €102 020 - **£62 000** - FF669 209
Vases of Flowers in a Landscape Oil/canvas
(76x101.5cm 29x39in) London 2000

NANI Mariano c.1725-1804 [3]

🐦 **$10 704** - €12 196 - **£7 400** - FF80 000
**Nature morte au gibier sur un
entablement/Nature morte au gibier** Huile/toile
(117.5x78cm 46x30in) Toulouse 2000

🐦 **$5 525** - €5 106 - **£3 400** - FF33 490
Florero con frutas sobre una mesa Oleo/lienzo
(33x24cm 12x9in) Madrid 1999

NANI Napoleone 1841-1899 [4]

🐦 **$84 000** - €72 566 - **£56 000** - FF476 000
In assenza della maestra Olio/tela (92x132cm
36x51in) Milano 1998

NANMEI Haruki 1795-1878 [1]

✍ **$2 800** - €2 712 - **£1 746** - FF17 791
**Courtesan and Attendants under Cherry
Blossoms** Coloured inks (103x60.5cm 40x23in) New-
York 1999

NANNINGA Jaap 1904-1962 [71]

🐦 **$3 327** - €3 176 - **£2 079** - FF20 836
Icarus (Witte Driehoek) Oil/canvas (40x50.5cm
15x19in) Amsterdam 1999

🐦 **$3 052** - €3 630 - **£2 176** - FF23 812
Tulips in vase Oil/canvas (20.5x26.5cm 8x10in)
Amsterdam 1999

✍ **$3 565** - €3 403 - **£2 228** - FF22 324
Compositie blauw/bruin Gouache/paper (25x31cm
9x12in) Amsterdam 1999

NANNINI Raffaello XIX-XX [19]

🐦 **$1 500** - €1 456 - **£926** - FF9 552
Beauty Gilded bronze (H30cm H12in) Cedar-Falls IA
1999

NANO (Campeggi Silvano) 1923 [14]

🎫 **$364** - €377 - **£218** - FF2 475
«Scaramouche» Affiche couleur (195x140cm
76x55in) Torino 2000

NANOGAK Agnes 1925 [13]

🎫 **$228** - €265 - **£157** - FF1 738
Two Boys Spear Fishing Print (33x34cm 13x13in)
Calgary, Alberta 2000

NANSEN Fridtjof 1861-1930 [13]

🎫 **$404** - €434 - **£271** - FF2 850
Selbstbildnis im Profil Lithographie (37x33cm
14x12in) Königstein 2000

NANTEI Nishimura 1775-1834 [4]

✍ **$3 500** - €3 868 - **£2 427** - FF25 370
Tiger Ink (87x33.5cm 34x13in) New-York 2001

NANTEUIL Célestin François 1813-1873 [37]

✍ **$881** - €1 037 - **£631** - FF6 800
Rome, sur les marches de la maison Aquarelle,
gouache/papier (27x18cm 10x7in) Paris 2001

NANTEUIL Robert 1623-1678 [43]

🐦 **$13 099** - €12 147 - **£8 000** - FF79 681
**Miniature Portrait of Jean François Paul de
Gondy** Miniature (6x4cm 2x1in) London 1998

🐦 **$8 626** - €8 423 - **£5 500** - FF55 253
**Portrait of the Duc de Nemours, wearing a lace
Collar** Mixed media drawing (17x12.5cm 6x4in)
London 1999

🎫 **$104** - €122 - **£73** - FF800
**Ferdinand de Neufville, d'après Philippe de
Champaigné** Burin (36.5x26.5cm 14x10in) Paris 2000

NAPALTJARRI Milliga c.1920-1993 [1]

🐦 **$6 249** - €6 028 - **£3 949** - FF39 542
Purrunga Acrylic/canvas (100x50cm 39x19in)
Melbourne 1999

NAPANGARDI Eunice c.1945 [6]
- $14 082 - €16 014 - £9 661 - FF105 042
  Uparli Dreaming (Bush Banana) Synthetic polymer silkscreened/canvas (382x133cm 150x52in) Sydney 2000

NAPANGARDI Pansy c.1948 [19]
- $1 052 - €1 018 - £666 - FF6 677
  Untitled Acrylic/canvas (119.5x119.5cm 47x47in) Malvern, Victoria 1999

NAPIER George Alexander 1823-1869 [1]
- $14 030 - €16 686 - £10 000 - FF109 452
  Shipping off Gibraltar Oil/canvas (71x91.5cm 27x36in) London 2000

NAPIER William Henry Edward 1830-1894 [9]
- $1 490 - €1 459 - £917 - FF9 572
  Lower Fort Garry Watercolour/paper (25.5x35.5cm 10x13in) Toronto 1999

NAPOLETANO Filippo d'Angeli c.1587-c.1640 [9]
- $68 000 - €88 116 - £51 000 - FF578 000
  Natura morta con conchiglie e vasetto con fiori Olio/tavola (39x51cm 15x20in) Firenze 2000
- $20 891 - €20 722 - £13 000 - FF135 925
  Soldiers storming a Town Oil/panel (14.5x24cm 5x9in) London 1999
- $1 690 - €1 982 - £1 215 - FF13 000
  Le moulin Encre (21.5x30.5cm 8x12in) Paris 2001

NAPPELBAUM Ida 1900-? [4]
- $515 - €613 - £368 - FF4 024
  Männerportrait Photograph (14.7x11.2cm 5x4in) Berlin 2000

NAPPER John 1916-2001 [37]
- $3 402 - €2 904 - £2 000 - FF19 047
  Big City Girl Oil/canvas (61x38cm 24x14in) London 1998
- $921 - €1 092 - £650 - FF7 161
  Still Life Oil/canvas (41x33cm 16x12in) London 2000
- $1 276 - €1 090 - £750 - FF7 147
  Notes for a Modern Mythology No.7: Starters Watercolour/paper (36x27cm 14x10in) London 1998

NAPPI Rudy XX [6]
- $4 500 - €5 012 - £2 943 - FF32 878
  Paperback book cover: three lounging women Oil/board (61x39cm 24x15in) New-York 2000
- $2 800 - €3 136 - £1 945 - FF20 572
  Woman loitering in Hotel Hallway as Man with Key approaches Oil/board (42x30cm 16x12in) New-York 2001

NAQSH Jamil 1938 [4]
- $6 687 - €6 475 - £4 200 - FF42 472
  Woman with Pigeon Oil/canvas (76.5x107cm 30x42in) London 1999
- $1 942 - €2 085 - £1 300 - FF13 678
  Nude with Pigeon Ink (38x51cm 14x20in) London 2000

NARA Yoshimoto 1959 [2]
- $1 900 - €2 085 - £1 262 - FF13 677
  No Pain No Gain Gouache/paper (30x46.5cm 11x18in) New-York 2000

NARAHA Tajashi 1930 [12]
- $1 270 - €1 423 - £885 - FF9 334
  Pyramid Stone (17x20cm 6x7in) Stockholm 2001

NARANJO Adolph 1916 [2]
- $1 900 - €2 218 - £1 341 - FF14 546
  Hunting Buffalo Gouache/paper (45.5x38cm 17x14in) New-York 2000

NARANJO Eduardo 1944 [57]
- $79 350 - €69 250 - £48 300 - FF454 250
  El Mundo Gris de Marina Oleo/lienzo (115.5x81cm 45x31in) Madrid 1998
- $2 400 - €2 403 - £1 480 - FF15 760
  Desnudo Oleo/tablex (24x33cm 9x12in) Madrid 2000
- $44 850 - €39 141 - £27 300 - FF256 750
  Retrato de las hijas de Miguel Fisac Lápiz (80x60cm 31x23in) Madrid 1998
- $710 - €601 - £430 - FF3 940
  Asesinado por el cielo Aquatinta (60x51cm 23x20in) Madrid 1998

NARAY Aurel 1883-1948 [57]
- $490 - €473 - £303 - FF3 100
  Girl with a Violin Oil/canvas (69x49cm 27x19in) Johannesburg 1999

NARAYAN Badri 1929 [14]
- $952 - €924 - £600 - FF6 061
  Vibhasha Ragini Ink (56x76cm 22x29in) London 1999

NARDI Enrico 1864-1947 [25]
- $619 - €563 - £380 - FF3 693
  The Bosco Sacro near Rome, Italy Pastel/paper (27x47.5cm 10x18in) London 1999

NARDI François 1861-1936 [38]
- $3 361 - €3 964 - £2 363 - FF26 000
  Venise Huile/toile (38x56cm 14x22in) Coulommiers 2000

NARDO DI CIONE ?-1365 [1]
- $7 995 - €7 622 - £4 865 - FF50 000
  Sainte-Catherine Tempera (18x15cm 7x5in) Toulouse 1999

NARDO di Mariotto c.1360-c.1425 [3]
- $101 150 - €104 857 - £60 690 - FF687 820
  La Madonna col Bambino fra una santa e il Battista e due angeli Tempera/tavola (83x48cm 32x18in) Venezia 2000

NARDONE Vincent 1937 [2]
- $2 400 - €2 246 - £1 487 - FF14 736
  Tribute to Mt St Helena Pastel (36x58cm 14x23in) Philadelphia PA 1999

NARICI Francesco c.1719-1785 [1]
- $7 518 - €6 364 - £4 500 - FF41 743
  The Apotheosis of Hercules - a Bozzetto Oil/canvas (90.5x71.5cm 35x28in) London 1998

NARJOT Ernest 1826-1898 [4]
- $4 000 - €4 621 - £2 800 - FF30 312
  Attempting to Escape Oil/canvas (68.5x110cm 26x43in) Bethesda MD 2001

NARODITSKY Mikhail 1946 [46]
- $357 - €371 - £225 - FF2 434
  Two Westies Oil/board (16x23cm 6x9in) Fernhurst, Haslemere, Surrey 2000

NARTOWSKI Tadeusz 1892-1971 [11]
- $480 - €560 - £337 - FF3 676
  Szczecin Aquarelle/papier (48x66cm 18x25in) Torun 2000

NARVAEZ Francisco 1905-1982 [76]
- $6 545 - €6 104 - £4 235 - FF40 040
  Girasoles Oleo/lienzo (73x60cm 28x23in) Caracas 1999
- $6 280 - €5 106 - £3 489 - FF33 496
  Torso femenino Bronze (52x17x18.5cm 20x6x7in) Caracas 1998
- $1 870 - €1 694 - £1 210 - FF11 110
  Sin título Gouache (43x50.5cm 16x19in) Caracas 1999

N

NASH David 1945 **[26]**

$3 000 – €3 481 – **£2 071** – FF22 833
Burr Shrine Sculpture, wood (58x58.5x18cm
22x23x7in) New-York 2000

$1 197 – €1 448 – **£837** – FF9 500
Treshold column, septembre Fusain (35x24cm
13x9in) Paris 2000

NASH Frederick 1782-1856 **[33]**

$1 683 – €2 002 – **£1 200** – FF13 134
Prince of Wales Lodge, Hyde Park Watercolour
(23x34cm 9x13in) London 2000

NASH John Northcote 1893-1977 **[175]**

$8 218 – €8 822 – **£5 500** – FF57 868
Green Landscape Oil/canvas (61x45.5cm 24x17in)
London 2000

$2 334 – €2 161 – **£1 450** – FF14 176
Mine, Bugle, Cornwall Watercolour/paper (35x72cm
13x28in) Cheshire 1999

NASH Joseph 1808-1878 **[92]**

$2 646 – €2 307 – **£1 600** – FF15 135
The Great Hall, Crewe Hall, Cheshire Watercolour
(36.5x50.5cm 14x19in) London 1998

$402 – €460 – **£280** – FF3 016
Views of the great Exhibitions Color lithograph
(42x28cm 16x11in) London 2000

NASH Paul 1889-1946 **[179]**

$68 299 – €79 353 – **£48 000** – FF520 521
Trees beside a Pond Oil/canvas (76x63cm 30x25in)
Lewes, Sussex 2001

$6 276 – €6 737 – **£4 200** – FF44 190
Russell Square Watercolour (38x28cm 14x11in)
London 2000

$1 191 – €1 111 – **£739** – FF7 287
Sea Wall Woodcut (7.5x11cm 2x4in) London 1999

$5 692 – €6 702 – **£4 000** – FF43 965
A Private World Photograph (19.5x30cm 7x11in)
London 2000

NASH Tom 1891-1968 **[14]**

$3 607 – €4 047 – **£2 500** – FF26 549
The Miraculous Draught of Fisches Oil/canvas
(76x91.5cm 29x36in) London 2000

NASH Willard 1898-1943 **[8]**

$2 500 – €2 157 – **£1 502** – FF14 148
Landscape with Adobes Lithograph (24x35cm
9x14in) Santa-Fe NM 1998

NASHAR 1928-1994 **[4]**

$2 543 – €2 811 – **£1 763** – FF18 436
Ship Scene Oil/canvas (64x89cm 25x35in) Singapore
2001

NASINI Giuseppe Nicola 1657-1736 **[24]**

$1 440 – €1 244 – **£720** – FF8 160
Disegno per soffitto, l'Adorazione dei pastori
Inchiostro (30x21.5cm 11x8in) Milano 1999

$198 – €198 – **£124** – FF1 300
La Sainte Vierge Eau-forte (16.7x12.5cm 6x4in) Paris
1999

NASKE Frantisek 1884-1959 **[23]**

$867 – €820 – **£540** – FF5 379
Nue Huile/panneau (82x101.5cm 32x39in) Praha 1999

$165 – €154 – **£102** – FF1 012
«P.V.V. Internationale Jaarbeurs te Praag» Poster
(62.5x95cm 24x37in) Oostwoud 1999

NASMYTH Alexander 1758-1840 **[77]**

$8 235 – €7 833 – **£5 000** – FF51 378
**Lake Landscape, traditionally identifield as
Lake Geneva** Oil/canvas (45.5x61cm 17x24in)
Edinburgh 1999

$14 497 – €13 623 – **£9 000** – FF89 361
Barskimming Bridge Oil/paper/panel (28.5x29cm
11x11in) London 1999

NASMYTH Charlotte 1804-c.1866 **[13]**

$13 000 – €12 325 – **£7 909** – FF80 844
**Mountainous River Landscape, Travellers on a
Path, a Ferry Boat beyond** Oil/canvas (71x91cm
27x35in) New-York 1999

$6 157 – €5 921 – **£3 800** – FF38 841
Near Chiddingstone, Kent Oil/panel (25.5x35.5cm
10x13in) London 1999

NASMYTH Elizabeth 1793-1862 **[2]**

$4 999 – €4 892 – **£3 200** – FF32 091
Driving Cattle by a Loch Oil/canvas (41x55cm
16x21in) London 1999

NASMYTH Jane 1778-1866 **[13]**

$5 769 – €6 781 – **£4 000** – FF44 480
Furness Abbey, Lancashire Oil/canvas (46x61cm
18x24in) Edinburgh 2000

$864 – €1 017 – **£620** – FF6 670
Cottage in Kent Oil/canvas (26x34cm 10x13in)
Cheshire 2001

NASMYTH Patrick, Peter 1787-1831 **[104]**

$6 385 – €5 567 – **£3 861** – FF36 520
Wooded landscape with Gypsies Oil/canvas
(70x99.5cm 27x39in) Melbourne 1998

$3 253 – €2 872 – **£2 000** – FF18 841
**Wooded Landscape with Figures and Cattle by
a Brook** Oil/panel (25.5x29cm 10x11in) Godalming,
Surrey 1999

NASON Peter c.1612-1688/90 **[28]**

$9 500 – €8 361 – **£5 783** – FF54 846
**Gentleman, Standing Three-quarter length,
Wearing a Breastplate** Oil/canvas (118x93cm
46x36in) New-York 1999

NASON Thomas Willoughby 1889-1971 **[42]**

$200 – €189 – **£124** – FF1 243
Lyme Farm Woodcut (10x22cm 4x9in) Mystic CT
1999

NAST Gustave L. 1826-? **[3]**

$41 520 – €45 735 – **£27 690** – FF300 000
La danseuse orientale Bronze (H188cm H74in)
Deauville 2000

NAST Thomas 1840-1902 **[16]**

$939 – €1 022 – **£645** – FF6 707
Damenporträt mit rotem Hut Pastel/canvas
(35x25.5cm 13x10in) Leipzig 2001

NAT van der Willem Hendrik 1864-1929 **[87]**

$1 251 – €1 452 – **£864** – FF9 525
Schaapherder met kudde Oil/panel (33x53cm
12x20in) Rotterdam 2000

$1 726 – €1 588 – **£1 067** – FF10 418
Goats in a shed Oil/canvas/panel (25x31cm 9x12in)
Amsterdam 1999

$1 198 – €1 361 – **£840** – FF8 929
Cows in a polder Landscape Watercolour/paper
(28x48cm 11x18in) Amsterdam 2001

NATALI Renato 1883-1979 **[366]**

$3 737 – €3 874 – **£2 242** – FF25 415
«Vecchia ardenza» Olio/faesite (37x54cm 14x21in)
Roma 1999

$1 800 – €2 332 – **£1 350** – FF15 300
Sera al porto Olio/tavola (19.5x25cm 7x9in) Prato
2001

$400 – €415 – **£240** – FF2 720
Foglio di studi: scene sacre Matita/carta (16x21cm
6x8in) Prato 1999

NATHAN M.H. XIX-XX [6]
$8 000 - €9 408 - £5 736 - FF61 711
The Snake Charmer Oil/canvas (63.5x76cm 25x29in) New-York 2001

NATHAN Max 1880-1973 [18]
$327 - €362 - £227 - FF2 373
Vinterandskab, i baggrunden fjord Oil/canvas (71x90cm 27x35in) Vejle 2001

NATHAN-GARAMOND Jacques 1910-? [15]
$218 - €244 - £147 - FF1 600
«Exposition agricole du plan Marshall» Affiche (118x75cm 46x29in) Orléans 2000

NATHE Christoph 1753-1808 [28]
$2 470 - €2 710 - £1 678 - FF17 775
Waldige Landschaft mit Wassermühle Ink/paper (18x23.6cm 7x9in) Berlin 2000
$269 - €307 - £187 - FF2 012
Baumbestandene Landschaft mit liegendem Knaben Radierung (16.5x22.2cm 6x8in) Berlin 2000

NATIVI Gualtiero 1921-1997 [55]
$1 500 - €1 555 - £900 - FF10 200
Forma penetrata Tempera/tela (80x60cm 31x23in) Vercelli 2000
$1 800 - €1 866 - £1 080 - FF12 240
Costellazione pluridimensionale Tempera/carta (34x24cm 13x17in) Prato 1999

NATKIN Robert 1930 [154]
$4 000 - €3 356 - £2 346 - FF22 014
Dibbuk Acrylic/canvas (106.5x127cm 41x50in) New-York 1998
$1 500 - €1 280 - £894 - FF8 394
«Bath» Acrylic/canvas (61x101.5cm 24x39in) New-York 1998
$1 000 - €1 044 - £630 - FF6 845
Untitled Tempera (42x33.5cm 16x13in) New-York 2000
$750 - €882 - £537 - FF5 785
Untitled Gouache/paper (91x71cm 36x28in) Chicago IL 2001

NATOIRE Charles-Joseph 1700-1777 [106]
$9 030 - €10 671 - £6 398 - FF70 000
Le sommeil d'Endymion Huile/toile (19x36cm 7x14in) Béziers 2000
$4 903 - €5 488 - £3 326 - FF36 000
Diane et Endymion Pierre noire (32.5x21cm 12x8in) Paris 2000

NATON Avraham 1906-1959 [57]
$4 400 - €4 671 - £2 977 - FF30 637
Forms Oil/canvas (61.5x46cm 24x18in) Tel Aviv 2001
$12 000 - €12 442 - £7 908 - FF81 612
The Artist's Wife Oil/cardboard (45x32cm 17x12in) Herzelia-Pituah 2000
$500 - €488 - £316 - FF3 201
Cubist Composition Pencil (47.5x33cm 18x12in) Tel Aviv 1999

NATTERO Louis 1875-1915 [87]
$2 269 - €2 592 - £1 596 - FF17.000
Tartane en haute mer Huile/toile (60x92cm 23x36in) Marseille 2001
$1 921 - €1 906 - £1 195 - FF12 500
Goélettes dans le port Huile/toile (19x24cm 7x9in) Marseille 1999

NATTES John Claude c.1765-1822 [20]
$1 129 - €1 046 - £700 - FF6 861
Telescope in the Garden at North Mimms Place/Brewery at N.Mimms Place Ink (23.5x32.5cm 9x12in) London 1999

NATTIER Jean-Baptiste 1678-1726 [2]
$24 000 - €20 158 - £14 109 - FF132 230
The Death of Adonis Oil/canvas (87.5x106cm 34x41in) New-York 1998

NATTIER Jean-Marc 1685-1766 [29]
$580 000 - €681 668 - £402 114 - FF4 471 452
La Force: Personification of Fortitude, said to portray M.A.de Mailly Oil/canvas (131x113.5cm 51x44in) New-York 2000
$120 000 - €105 259 - £72 864 - FF690 456
Manon Balletti Oil/canvas (84.5x73cm 33x28in) New-York 1999
$2 400 - €2 855 - £1 660 - FF18 729
Peter Paul Reubens (1577-1640) Graphite (47x34cm 18x13in) New-Orleans LA 2000

NATTINI Amos 1892-? [2]
$7 500 - €7 775 - £4 500 - FF51 000
L'energia idroelettrica Olio/tavola (237x194cm 93x76in) Milano 2001

NATTINO Girolamo 1842-1913 [4]
$2 062 - €2 421 - £1 455 - FF15 878
Sittande ung kvinna med tamburin Oil/canvas (40x28cm 15x11in) Stockholm 2000

NATTINO V. 1890-1971 [3]
$4 850 - €5 028 - £2 910 - FF32 980
Venezia Olio/tela (40x113cm 15x44in) Genova 2000

NATTRESS George c.1840-c.1890 [7]
$3 507 - €4 171 - £2 500 - FF27 363
Sport at the Mill Pool Watercolour (33.5x56cm 13x22in) London 2000

NATUREL G. XIX [1]
$2 124 - €2 058 - £1 336 - FF13 500
Vue du temple d'Hercule Victor (dit à tord «de Vesta») Mine plomb (20x27.5cm 7x10in) Paris 1999

NATUS Johannes act.1658-1662 [4]
$55 000 - €58 737 - £37 477 - FF385 291
Peasants smoking and making Music in an Inn Oil/panel (51.5x41cm 20x16in) New-York 2001
$2 214 - €2 033 - £1 361 - FF13 333
Le calepin Huile/panneau (31x26cm 12x10in) Bruxelles 1999

NATZLER Gertrude & Otto act.c.1935-1971 [4]
$4 000 - €3 656 - £2 447 - FF23 979
Vase Glazed ceramic (H20cm H7in) New-York 1999

NAUDÉ Hugo Pieter 1868-1941 [115]
$8 608 - €9 599 - £5 613 - FF62 964
Mountain Landscape Oil/canvas (41x55cm 16x21in) Johannesburg 2000
$3 984 - €4 623 - £2 751 - FF30 324
River Landscape, Cape Oil/board (28.5x39cm 11x15in) Johannesburg 2000
$742 - €832 - £516 - FF5 458
Groote Schuur Watercolour (25.5x35.5cm 10x13in) Johannesburg 2001

NAUDET Françoise 1928 [19]
$5 351 - €5 313 - £3 366 - FF34 000
La mouette Bronze (48x21x32.5cm 18x8x12in) Paris 1999

NAUDET Thomas Charles 1773/78-1810 [7]
$883 - €991 - £600 - FF6 498
Three Peasants Women with a Child one Holding a Distaff/Peasant Family Watercolour (9.5x15.5cm 3x6in) London 2000

N

NAUDIN Bernard 1876-1946 **[34]**
- $200 - €193 - £125 - FF1 265
«Journée Nationale des Orphelins» Poster
(119x79cm 47x31in) Columbia SC 1999

NAUEN Heinrich 1880-1941 **[119]**
- $34 278 - €32 723 - £21 414 - FF214 649
Herbst(wald) Öl/Karton (177x90.5cm 69x35in) Köln
1999
- $13 972 - €13 294 - £8 681 - FF87 201
Levkojen und Sonnenblumen Öl/Leinwand
(90x75.5cm 35x29in) Hamburg 1999
- $958 - €920 - £590 - FF6 037
Zwei Frauen (Engländerin) Indian ink (27.5x33cm
10x12in) München 1998
- $358 - €409 - £250 - FF2 683
Weg am Niederrhein Radierung (25x18cm 9x7in)
Hamburg 2001

NAUER Adolf 1886-? **[10]**
- $3 889 - €4 175 - £2 602 - FF27 387
Scène d'auberge Huile/toile (70x85cm 27x33in)
Warszawa 2000

NAULEAU André-Charles XX **[62]**
- $254 - €213 - £149 - FF1 400
Marais de Saint-Jean de Monts Huile/toile
(54x65cm 21x25in) La Roche-sur-Yon 1998

NAUMAN Bruce 1941 **[227]**
- $290 000 - €323 778 - £193 836 - FF2 123 844
Second Poem Piece Metal (152.5x152.5x1.5cm
60x60xin) New-York 2000
- $240 000 - €278 469 - £165 696 - FF1 826 640
Labrea-Art Tips-Art Split-Tar Pits Construction
(62x58.5x5cm 24x23x1in) New-York 2000
- $28 000 - €30 720 - £18 600 - FF201 510
Hand and Shrunken hand Ink (69x84cm 27x33in)
New-York 2000
- $1 800 - €2 332 - £1 350 - FF15 300
Senza titolo Litografia a colori (80x112cm 31x44in)
Milano 2001
- $1 715 - €2 045 - £1 223 - FF13 415
Rooster Woodcut in colors (19.5x50.5cm 7x19in)
Berlin 2000
- $480 000 - €535 908 - £320 832 - FF3 515 328
Light Trap for Henry Moore, No.1 Photograph
(162.5x101.5cm 63x39in) New-York 2000

NAUMANN August Franz 1749-1795 **[3]**
- $2 196 - €2 180 - £1 371 - FF14 301
Hauptansicht der Stadt Salzburg Farbradierung
(30.5x57cm 12x22in) Salzburg 1999

NAUMANN Hermann 1930 **[60]**
- $245 - €256 - £155 - FF1 676
Bildnis einer jungen Frau mit Hut Watercolour
(73x50.7cm 28x19in) Berlin 2000
- $142 - €133 - £86 - FF872
Dem Dichter Henry Miller gewidmet Lithographie
(72.5x53cm 28x20in) Berlin 1999

NAUMER Helmuth 1907-1990 **[2]**
- $3 800 - €3 278 - £2 283 - FF21 505
Chimayo Creek Watercolour (35x53cm 14x21in)
Santa-Fe NM 1998

NAUR Albert 1889-1973 **[131]**
- $461 - €390 - £275 - FF2 559
Landskab med vej og trae Oil/canvas (67x86cm
26x33in) København 1998

NAUTA Max 1896-1957 **[6]**
- $46 - €54 - £32 - FF357
Nettenboeters Watercolour/paper (39.5x51.5cm
15x20in) Amsterdam 2000

NAVARETTE Y FOS Ricardo Maria 1834-1909 **[1]**
- $27 600 - €24 026 - £17 200 - FF157 600
El Embajador de España Oleo/lienzo (84x170cm
33x66in) Madrid 1999

NAVARRA PRUNA Carme 1933 **[16]**
- $378 - €360 - £240 - FF2 364
Niña con sombrero Oleo/lienzo (61x50cm 24x19in)
Barcelona 1999

NAVARRE Henri 1885-1971 **[16]**
- $1 259 - €1 220 - £791 - FF8 000
Visage de Flore Sculpture verre (H37cm H14in) Paris
1999

NAVARRETE de Juan Fernandez c.1526-1579 **[1]**
- $3 852 - €3 826 - £2 400 - FF25 100
Seated Nude Male Red chalk/paper (41.5x26cm
16x10in) London 1999

NAVARRO Enrique 1924-1997 **[27]**
- $1 242 - €1 381 - £874 - FF9 062
Bailarina y máscara Grisaille (50x67cm 19x26in)
Madrid 2001

NAVARRO GARCIA Roman 1854-1928 **[2]**
- $1 620 - €1 802 - £1 110 - FF11 820
Tribunal militar Aguada/papel (24x28cm 9x11in)
Madrid 2001

NAVARRO J. Elizalde 1924 **[1]**
- $10 173 - €11 241 - £7 054 - FF73 738
«The Mind is a Series of Boxes and Doors»
Acrylic/canvas (116x90cm 45x35in) Singapore 2001

NAVARRO LLORENS José 1867-1923 **[111]**
- $66 000 - €72 078 - £42 000 - FF472 800
La cala de Granaella-Alicante Oleo/lienzo
(125x140cm 49x55in) Madrid 2000
- $23 680 - €22 224 - £14 430 - FF145 780
Zoco árabe Oleo/lienzo (64.5x50.5cm 25x19in)
Barcelona 1999
- $6 500 - €6 006 - £4 000 - FF39 400
Mercado marroquí Oleo/lienzo (31x41cm 12x16in)
Madrid 1999

NAVARRO Luis XX **[1]**
- $11 096 - €12 196 - £7 056 - FF80 000
Homenaje a Dali (Hommage à Salvador Dali)
Huile/toile (80x64cm 31x25in) Paris 2000

NAVARRO Miquel 1945 **[7]**
- $12 460 - €13 364 - £8 455 - FF87 665
Sin título Pintura (154x107cm 60x42in) Barcelona
2001

NAVARRO Pascual 1923 **[9]**
- $485 - €509 - £321 - FF3 338
Figuras Gouache (23x32.5cm 9x12in) Caracas ($)
2000

NAVARRO VIVES Josep 1931 **[40]**
- $2 560 - €2 403 - £1 560 - FF15 760
Barca Oleo/lienzo (97x130cm 38x51in) Barcelona
1999
- $660 - €721 - £456 - FF4 728
Composición Técnica mixta/lienzo (60x92cm
23x36in) Barcelona 2001

NAVAZIO de Walter 1887-1921 **[3]**
- $9 000 - €9 917 - £6 003 - FF65 052
Paisaje serrano Oleo/lienzo (53x65cm 20x25in)
Montevideo 2000

NAVELLIER Edouard 1865-1944 **[14]**
- $4 402 - €4 726 - £2 945 - FF31 000
Le touareg Bronze (H37.5cm H14in) Soissons 2000

NAVEZ Arthur 1881-1931 **[41]**
- $828 - €992 - £568 - FF6 504
  Stilleven (Nature morte) Huile/toile (50x66cm 19x25in) Antwerpen 2000

NAVEZ François Joseph 1787-1869 **[49]**
- $4 022 - €4 604 - £2 766 - FF30 200
  Intérieur d'église Huile/toile (95x63cm 37x24in) Bordeaux 2000
- $521 - €456 - £315 - FF2 994
  La mère et l'enfant Mine plomb (35.5x28cm 13x11in) Montréal 1998

NAVEZ Léon 1900-1967 **[58]**
- $1 485 - €1 239 - £870 - FF8 130
  La cruche jaune Huile/toile (51x61cm 20x24in) Bruxelles 1998
- $1 935 - €1 859 - £1 215 - FF12 195
  Le chapeau fleuri Huile/carton (35x28cm 13x11in) Bruxelles 1999

NAVIASKY Philip 1894-1982 **[185]**
- $535 - €520 - £340 - FF3 410
  A Portrait Study of a Lady wearing a blue Dress and colourful Scarf Oil/canvas (60x50cm 23x19in) West-Yorkshire 1999
- $434 - €371 - £260 - FF2 434
  A Market Scene with Figures, Buildings beyond Oil/board (23.5x28.5cm 9x11in) Leeds 1998
- $184 - €157 - £110 - FF1 030
  A Study of a Lady Seated Charcoal/paper (35x23.5cm 13x9in) Leeds 1998

NAVLET Joseph 1821-1889 **[41]**
- $2 076 - €2 229 - £1 389 - FF14 621
  «Noroda» Leaving the Fleet off Dartmouth Reiterschlacht um ein Kastell Öl/Leinwand (65x81cm 25x31in) Zürich 2000
- $321 - €381 - £227 - FF2 500
  Scène de bataille Aquarelle (18x28cm 7x11in) Paris 2000

NAVRATIL Josef 1798-1865 **[31]**
- $3 323 - €3 143 - £2 070 - FF20 619
  Coupe de fruits Huile/panneau (23x24cm 9x9in) Praha 2000
- $1 134 - €1 033 - £709 - FF6 774
  Mountain Landscape Tempera/paper (19.2x23.3cm 7x9in) Praha 1999

NAWROCKI Boleslaw 1877-1946 **[2]**
- $4 752 - €5 307 - £3 315 - FF34 813
  Portrait de chanteuse Janina Smotrycka Huile/toile (101x84cm 39x33in) Warszawa 2001

NAY Ernst Wilhelm 1902-1968 **[449]**
- $149 419 - €176 393 - £106 122 - FF1 157 061
  «Mit Tropfenketten» Öl/Leinwand (100.5x124cm 39x48in) Berlin 2001
- $119 614 - €112 486 - £74 074 - FF737 858
  Pelote Öl/Leinwand (80x130cm 31x51in) Köln 1999
- $15 440 - €18 407 - £11 008 - FF120 740
  Ohne Titel Tempera/Karton (37.9x33.1cm 14x13in) Berlin 2000
- $21 920 - €25 565 - £15 390 - FF167 695
  Ohne Titel Aquarell/Papier (31.6x47.6cm 12x18in) Köln 2000
- $1 285 - €1 227 - £803 - FF8 049
  Farblitho 1967 - 1 (Rythmen und Kadenzen) Farblithographie (76x56cm 29x22in) Köln 1999

NAYA Carlo 1816-1882 **[22]**
- $953 - €847 - £663 - FF7 000
  Palais Grimani, Venise Tirage albuminé (53x42cm 20x16in) Paris 2001

NAYLOR John 1960 **[7]**
- $811 - €780 - £500 - FF5 116
  Canada Geese Pastel/paper (51.5x35.5cm 20x13in) London 1999

NAYWINCK Harman 1624-1651 **[3]**
- $316 - €281 - £193 - FF1 844
  Der hochstämmige Wald auf einer Landzunge Radierung (13.5x12.3cm 5x4in) Pforzheim 1999

NEAGLE John 1796-1865 **[12]**
- $1 800 - €2 079 - £1 260 - FF13 640
  Portrait of Mrs.Neagle and Her Son, Garrett Oil/panel (53x41cm 21x16in) New-York 2001

NEAL James 1918 **[45]**
- $1 481 - €1 392 - £900 - FF9 134
  The Harbour, Whitstable Oil/board (40x50cm 15x19in) London 1999
- $936 - €799 - £550 - FF5 242
  «The Garden Urn» Oil/board (37x27cm 14x10in) London 1998

NEALE John Preston 1771/80-1847 **[21]**
- $491 - €497 - £300 - FF3 260
  Gallow Hill Nottingham Pencil (15x22cm 5x8in) Lenton-Lane, Nottingham 1998

NEAVE David S. XX **[2]**
- $6 723 - €6 649 - £4 200 - FF43 616
  In the Park Oil/panel (21.5x16.5cm 8x6in) Glasgow 1999

NEAVE Vincent XX **[2]**
- $3 903 - €4 360 - £2 500 - FF28 597
  «Noroda» Leaving the Fleet off Dartmouth Oil/canvas (83.5x121.5cm 32x47in) London 2000

NEBBIA Cesare c.1536-1614 **[17]**
- $14 400 - €18 660 - £10 800 - FF122 400
  Lucrezia romana Olio/tela (143x105cm 56x41in) Roma 2000
- $2 783 - €2 581 - £1 700 - FF16 932
  A Priest Giving a Communion to a Kneeling Priest Ink (34.5x24cm 13x9in) London 1998

NEBEKER Bill 1942 **[6]**
- $15 400 - €16 530 - £10 305 - FF108 431
  The Legend Lives Bronze (H91cm H36in) Houston TX 2000

NEBEL Carl, Carlos 1805-1855 **[17]**
- $476 - €559 - £340 - FF3 665
  El Hacendado y su Mayordomo Litografía a color (31x40cm 12x15in) México 2000

NEBEL Kay Heinrich 1888-1953 **[13]**
- $4 132 - €4 857 - £2 865 - FF31 862
  Bergschafe Öl/Karton (49x59cm 19x23in) Stuttgart 2000
- $2 126 - €2 301 - £1 457 - FF15 092
  Zwei Stieglitze Tempera/panel (36x25cm 14x9in) Stuttgart 2001

NEBEL Otto 1892-1973 **[271]**
- $5 180 - €5 845 - £3 644 - FF38 342
  «Blaues Geschehnis» Öl/Karton (55x50cm 21x19in) Bern 2000
- $2 412 - €2 066 - £1 450 - FF13 554
  «Maiblatt B/1965» Mixed media (22x15cm 8x5in) Zürich 1998
- $994 - €1 067 - £663 - FF7 000
  «K6.68» Gouache (23x19cm 9x7in) Paris 2000
- $127 - €141 - £84 - FF927
  Abstrakte Formen Farblithographie (55x40.5cm 21x15in) Bern 2000

N

N

NEBOT Balthasar c.1700-c.1770 **[12]**
- $3 142 - €2 740 - **£1 900** - FF17 973
  «Shoveha'Penny» Oil/canvas (41x51cm 16x20in)
  London 1998

NECHITA Alexandra 1985 **[1]**
- $92 326 - €80 798 - **£55 915** - FF530 000
  Whishes from earth Acrylique (60x90cm 23x35in)
  Paris 1998

NECK van der Jan 1635-1714 **[11]**
- $7 471 - €8 020 - **£5 000** - FF52 608
  Young boy, full length, wearing a Crimson Tunic
  Oil/canvas (112x87cm 44x34in) London 2000
- $15 861 - €16 655 - **£10 000** - FF109 247
  Putti and a Faun Cavorting with a Goat Oil/panel
  (42.5x33cm 16x12in) London 2000

NEDELKOPOULOS Nicholas, Nick 1955 **[16]**
- $686 - €736 - **£459** - FF4 831
  Couple of Eager Beavers Pastel/paper (18x38cm
  7x14in) Sydney 2000
- $857 - €921 - **£574** - FF6 041
  Spiritual Warfare Etching (100.5x50cm 39x19in)
  Sydney 2000

NEDER Johann Michael 1807-1882 **[47]**
- $28 947 - €29 655 - **£17 864** - FF194 526
  Familienbild Öl/Leinwand (36x44.5cm 14x17in)
  Düsseldorf 2000
- $4 257 - €4 724 - **£2 964** - FF30 985
  Knabe mit Bernhardiner vor Stiegenaufgang
  Oil/panel (41x33.5cm 16x13in) Salzburg 2001
- $1 316 - €1 453 - **£912** - FF9 534
  Bildnis der Kinder Munsch Pencil/paper
  (35.8x24cm 14x9in) Wien 2001

NEDERGAARD Niels 1944-1987 **[27]**
- $1 263 - €1 476 - **£892** - FF9 680
  Komposition Gouache (135x78cm 53x30in)
  Köbenhavn 2000

NEDHAM OF LEICESTER William c.1790-c.1850 **[4]**
- $7 295 - €8 677 - **£5 200** - FF56 915
  **Gentleman on a Grey Hunter in an Open
  Landscape** Oil/canvas (77x97cm 30x38in) London
  2000

NEEDELL Philip G. 1886-1974 **[29]**
- $269 - €288 - **£180** - FF1 887
  The Anchorage, Bosham Woodcut in colors
  (16x22cm 6x8in) London 2000

NEEF de Mathilde XIX **[2]**
- $3 864 - €3 659 - **£2 349** - FF24 000
  **Jonquilles, pois de senteur, hortensias/Roses
  trémières, marguerites** Gouache/papier (34x26cm
  13x10in) Paris 1999

NEEFS Jacobus 1610-1660 **[2]**
- $11 400 - €12 949 - **£8 000** - FF84 940
  **The Interior of a Gothic Cathedral at Night with
  a Procession** Oil/panel (26x38.5cm 10x15in) London
  2001

NEEFS Pieter I 1578-1656/61 **[52]**
- $30 142 - €25 663 - **£18 000** - FF168 337
  A Church Interior with Many Figures Oil/panel
  (73.5x104.5cm 28x41in) London 1998
- $3 805 - €4 269 - **£2 637** - FF28 000
  Intérieur d'église gothique Huile/panneau
  (24x18.5cm 9x7in) Paris 2000

NEEFS Pieter II 1620-1675 **[30]**
- $41 232 - €46 232 - **£28 000** - FF303 259
  **The Interior of a Cathedral with Figures atten-
  ding a Sermon** Oil/panel (35.5x51.5cm 13x20in)
  London 2000
- $13 755 - €15 339 - **£9 249** - FF100 617
  Kircheninterieur Oil/panel (27.5x19.6cm 10x7in)
  Köln 2000

NEEL Alice 1900-1984 **[16]**
- $1 500 - €1 813 - **£1 047** - FF11 892
  Sam Lithograph (87x61cm 34x24in) Bethesda MD
  2000

NEELMEYER Ludwig 1814-1870 **[7]**
- $4 393 - €4 346 - **£2 739** - FF28 508
  Zwei Alpenlandschaften Öl/Leinwand (26.5x37cm
  10x14in) Ahlden 1999

NEER van der Aert I c.1603-1677 **[49]**
- $100 000 - €94 082 - **£62 400** - FF617 140
  **Winter Landscape with Figures playing on a
  frozen River** Oil/canvas (136x173cm 53x68in) New-
  York 1999
- $200 000 - €176 027 - **£121 760** - FF1 154 660
  **Winter Landscape with Skaters and Townsfolk
  on a Frozen Waterway** Oil/canvas (61x85cm
  24x33in) New-York 1999
- $35 000 - €30 805 - **£21 308** - FF202 065
  **Moonlit River Landscape with a Fisherman
  Tending his Nets** Oil/canvas (33x39cm 12x15in)
  New-York 1999

NEER van der Eglon Hendrick 1634-1703 **[16]**
- $810 - €901 - **£555** - FF5 910
  El dúo (lección de música) Oleo/tabla (60x50cm
  23x19in) Madrid 2001
- $67 326 - €63 529 - **£41 538** - FF416 724
  **Youth, Standing Small Three Quarter Length by
  a Table in an Interior** Oil/panel (30x24.5cm 11x9in)
  Amsterdam 1999

NEERGARD Hermania Sigvardine 1799-1874 **[18]**
- $37 000 - €41 416 - **£25 803** - FF271 672
  Lily Pond Oil/canvas (67x62cm 26x24in) New-York
  2001

NEERVOORT Jan C. 1863-1940 **[17]**
- $725 - €620 - **£440** - FF4 065
  Nature morte aux lièvres Huile/toile (50x75cm
  19x29in) Bruxelles 1998

NEFF Sibylle 1929 **[5]**
- $21 187 - €20 013 - **£13 193** - FF131 276
  Lueg is Land Öl/Papier (28x55cm 11x21in) St. Gallen
  1999
- $930 - €1 027 - **£615** - FF6 736
  Hausfassade mit Katze auf Fenstersims
  Crayon/papier (17x25cm 6x9in) St. Gallen 2000

NEFF von Timoléon Carl Nehf 1805-1876 **[11]**
- $42 447 - €34 997 - **£25 000** - FF229 567
  Female nude with Draperies in a Landscape
  Oil/canvas (125x86cm 49x33in) London 1998

NEFFLEN Paul XIX **[2]**
- $4 539 - €4 791 - **£3 000** - FF31 425
  **Still Life with, Compote , Gobler and Decanter
  on Table** Oil/canvas (99x71cm 39x28in) Belfast 2001

NEFKENS Martinus Jacobus 1866-1941 **[43]**
- $718 - €634 - **£433** - FF4 160
  Farm on the Moor Oil/canvas (60x80cm 23x31in)
  Amsterdam 1998

NEGRE Charles 1820-1880 **[40]**
📷 **$3 500** - €3 653 - **£2 214** - FF23 959
Piefferari rentrant au logis Albumen print (16x12cm 6x4in) New-York 2000

NÉGRÉANU Matei 1942 **[17]**
✍ **$1 567** - €1 829 - **£1 108** - FF12 000
Sans titre Sculpture verre (53x25.5x15.5cm 20x10x6in) Paris 2001

NEGRI Mario 1916 **[20]**
✍ **$2 100** - €2 177 - **£1 260** - FF14 280
Figura Bronzo (H43cm H16in) Milano 2000

NEGRI Pietro 1628/35-c.1679 **[11]**
🖼 **$33 600** - €32 014 - **£21 294** - FF210 000
Suzanne et les vieillards Huile/toile (108x182cm 42x71in) Clermont-Ferrand 1999

NEGULESCU Jean 1900-1993 **[11]**
✎ **$1 400** - €1 505 - **£954** - FF9 875
Seated Nude Ink/paper (73.5x49cm 28x19in) Beverly-Hills CA 2001

NEHER Michael 1798-1876 **[16]**
🖼 **$37 640** - €34 257 - **£23 517** - FF224 711
Platz in einer mittelitalienischen Stadt Öl/Leinwand (58x47cm 22x18in) München 1999
🖼 **$7 561** - €8 692 - **£5 339** - FF57 016
«Ansicht von Donauwörth mit Hl.Kreuz-Kirche» Oil/panel (30x25cm 11x9in) Bremen 2001

NEHLIG Victor 1830-1910 **[13]**
🖼 **$700** - €663 - **£437** - FF4 352
The Scholar/The Soldier Oil/canvas (40x30cm 16x12in) Mystic CT 1999

NEHRING Maciej 1901-1977 **[8]**
✎ **$1 135** - €1 067 - **£705** - FF7 001
Vue sur Mnich du côté Morskie Oko Watercolour/paper (78x63cm 30x24in) Warszawa 1999

NEIIMBURRA XX **[3]**
🖼 **$8 551** - €8 249 - **£5 404** - FF54 111
Three Dancing Mimihs Mixed media (78x47cm 30x18in) Melbourne 1999

NEILLOT Louis 1898-1973 **[106]**
🖼 **$1 500** - €1 339 - **£918** - FF8 784
The Orchard at Saulcet Oil/canvas (61x50cm 24x19in) New-York 1999
🖼 **$672** - €793 - **£472** - FF5 200
Les écolières Huile/toile (22x27cm 8x10in) Fontainebleau 2000
✎ **$465** - €549 - **£327** - FF3 600
Paysage Aquarelle/papier (31x48cm 12x18in) Paris 2000

NEILSON Raymond P. Rodgers 1881-1964 **[10]**
🖼 **$400** - €366 - **£242** - FF2 402
Still Life of a Porcelain Bust of Marie Antoinette as a Baby Oil/canvas (76x63cm 30x25in) East-Dennis MA 1998

NEIMAN LeRoy 1927 **[128]**
🖼 **$20 000** - €23 711 - **£14 570** - FF155 532
«High Seas sailing» Oil/canvas (91x91cm 36x36in) Chicago IL 2001
🖼 **$1 200** - €1 371 - **£844** - FF8 991
Matedor Oil/board (48x23cm 19x9in) Chicago IL 2001
🖼 **$5 500** - €6 354 - **£3 851** - FF41 679
Three piece horse racing suite Bronze (41x60cm 16x24in) Delray-Beach FL 2001
✎ **$1 250** - €1 260 - **£779** - FF8 262
Golf Winner's Pencil/paper (71x111cm 28x44in) St. Petersburg FL 2000

🎨 **$700** - €604 - **£415** - FF3 959
Opening Ceremonies for the XIII Olympiad Screenprint in colors (71x106cm 28x42in) Bethesda MD 1998

NÉJAD Néjad Devrim 1923-1994 **[35]**
🖼 **$1 535** - €1 524 - **£960** - FF10 000
Composition en jaune Huile/toile (30x87cm 11x34in) Paris 1999

NEJEDLY Otakar 1883-1957 **[53]**
🖼 **$15 895** - €15 034 - **£9 900** - FF98 615
An der Elbe Öl/Leinwand (110x120cm 43x47in) Praha 2001
🖼 **$2 520** - €2 386 - **£1 575** - FF15 651
Dorf in Südböhmen Tempera (75x90cm 29x35in) Praha 1999
🖼 **$1 098** - €1 039 - **£684** - FF6 813
Czech Landscape Oil/cardboard (22x39cm 8x15in) Praha 2000

NELIMARKKA Eero 1891-1977 **[247]**
🖼 **$1 768** - €1 511 - **£1 038** - FF9 914
Landskap från lappland Oil/canvas (38x87cm 14x34in) Helsinki 1998
🖼 **$1 201** - €1 009 - **£706** - FF6 616
Interiör från lada Oil/board (39x29cm 15x11in) Helsinki 1998
✎ **$243** - €286 - **£168** - FF1 875
Från borgå Watercolour/paper (30x46cm 11x18in) Helsinki 2000

NELIMARKKA Tuomas 1925-1997 **[25]**
🖼 **$330** - €370 - **£224** - FF2 427
Landskap Oil/canvas (37x56cm 14x22in) Helsinki 2000

NELLENS Roger 1937 **[37]**
🖼 **$1 100** - €1 155 - **£693** - FF7 576
Machine Volante III Oil/canvas (91x72cm 36x28in) Cleveland OH 2000

NELLI DI Ottaviano 1370/75-1445/50 **[1]**
🖼 **$114 000** - €98 482 - **£76 000** - FF646 000
Madonna dell'umiltà fra due angeli musicanti con l'Eterno in gloria Tempera/tavola (170x115cm 66x45in) Milano 1998

NELLIUS Martinus N. c.1660-c.1710 **[12]**
🖼 **$22 276** - €22 447 - **£13 885** - FF147 243
Stilleben mit geschälter Zitrone, Auster und Pfeife Huile/marouflage (43x38cm 16x14in) Zürich 2000
🖼 **$20 920** - €22 456 - **£14 000** - FF147 302
Still Life of a roemer, an orange, lemon, a medlar, an apple Oil/panel (28x23cm 11x9in) London 2000

NELSON A. XVIII **[2]**
🖼 **$2 810** - €2 655 - **£1 700** - FF17 415
Rural Landscapes Oil/canvas/panel (28.5x44cm 11x17in) Billingshurst, West-Sussex 1999
🖼 **$2 576** - €2 433 - **£1 600** - FF15 959
View of hospital Hill, Grenada Watercolour/paper (31.5x49cm 12x19in) London 1999

NELSON Alphonse Henri 1854-? **[19]**
✍ **$450** - €453 - **£280** - FF2 974
Bust of a Woman Bronze (H45cm H18in) Scottsdale AZ 2000

NELSON Arthur XX **[1]**
🖼 **$12 840** - €12 755 - **£8 000** - FF83 668
View of Canterbury Cathedral with Figures Fishing in the Foreground Oil/canvas (47.5x58.5cm 18x23in) London 1999

N

NELSON Carl Gustaf Simon 1898-1988 **[6]**
- $4 000 - €3 712 - **£2 401** - FF24 350
  Under the Big Top Oil/canvas (58x71cm 23x28in)
  Milford CT 1999

NELSON E.M. XIX-XX **[3]**
- $2 200 - €2 243 - **£1 378** - FF14 710
  Holywood Ping Oil/canvas (35.5x40.5cm 13x15in)
  New-York 2000

NELSON Ernest Bruce 1888-1952 **[3]**
- $5 500 - €5 606 - **£3 446** - FF36 776
  April in the Park Oil/canvas (60x76cm 24x30in)
  Altadena CA 2000

NELSON George Laurence 1887-1978 **[26]**
- $1 000 - €1 069 - **£680** - FF7 013
  Camp Scene Oil/board (22x24cm 9x9in) New-
  Orleans LA 2001

NELSON Joan 1958 **[50]**
- $10 000 - €11 312 - **£6 996** - FF74 205
  Untitled Tempera (101.5x122cm 39x48in) New-York
  2001
- $13 000 - €11 561 - **£7 950** - FF75 832
  Untitled (No.186) Oil/wood (53.5x40.5cm 21x15in)
  New-York 1999
- $6 500 - €5 545 - **£3 920** - FF36 374
  Untitled Mixed media/panel (10x20cm 3x7in) New-
  York 1998

NELSON Leonard 1912-1993 **[4]**
- $2 000 - €2 254 - **£1 385** - FF14 784
  «The color Field» Acrylic (50x45cm 20x18in)
  Hatfield PA 2000
- $2 000 - €2 254 - **£1 385** - FF14 784
  «Figure #1» Oil/masonite (22x25cm 9x10in) Hatfield
  PA 2000

NEMES Andrej, Endre 1909-1985 **[150]**
- $2 511 - €2 362 - **£1 556** - FF15 491
  Urholkad Oil/canvas (160x130cm 62x51in) Stockholm
  1999
- $1 501 - €1 786 - **£1 071** - FF11 716
  Cirkus Tempera/panel (65x50cm 25x19in) Stockholm
  2000
- $600 - €583 - **£370** - FF3 821
  Komposition Mixed media (31.5x23.5cm 12x9in)
  Stockholm 1999
- $556 - €645 - **£383** - FF4 232
  Inträng Tempera/paper (17x22cm 6x8in) Stockholm
  2000

NEMES LAMPÉRTH Jozsef 1891-1924 **[6]**
- $3 700 - €3 887 - **£2 300** - FF25 500
  Nu couché Encre/papier (31x41cm 12x16in) Budapest
  2000

NÉMETH Miklos 1934 **[2]**
- $1 980 - €2 250 - **£1 380** - FF14 760
  La journée des mères Tempera (62x122cm 24x48in)
  Budapest 2001

NEMETHY Albert, Jnr. XX **[8]**
- $900 - €987 - **£580** - FF6 476
  Hudson river scene Oil/canvas (40x50cm 16x20in)
  Wallkill NY 2000

NEMETHY Albert, Snr. XX **[5]**
- $1 350 - €1 278 - **£838** - FF8 382
  Dayliner «New York» Oil/canvas (66x101cm
  26x40in) Wallkill NY 1999

NEMON Oscar 1906-1985 **[18]**
- $1 163 - €1 140 - **£722** - FF7 479
  Buste de pasteur Bronze (H36cm H14in) Bruxelles
  1999

NEMOURS Aurélie 1910 **[27]**
- $16 563 - €19 745 - **£11 808** - FF129 516
  Rythme du millimètre Öl/Leinwand (120x120x4.5cm
  47x47x1in) Luzern 2000
- $7 839 - €6 860 - **£4 747** - FF45 000
  «Structure au silence» Huile/toile (79x79cm
  31x31in) Besançon 1998
- $871 - €961 - **£590** - FF6 305
  Ohne Titel Oil/panel (15x15cm 5x5in) Zürich 2000
- $2 038 - €1 739 - **£1 214** - FF11 405
  Composition Gouache/paper (50x50cm 19x19in)
  Zürich 1998
- $115 - €122 - **£76** - FF800
  Composition Sérigraphie (60x60cm 23x23in) Paris
  2000

NEMUKHIN Vladimir 1925 **[9]**
- $4 477 - €5 329 - **£3 200** - FF34 954
  Composition with Playing Cards Oil/canvas
  (72x79.5cm 28x31in) London 2000

NEOGRADY Antal, Laszlo 1861-1942 **[116]**
- $1 081 - €1 090 - **£675** - FF7 150
  Ein Nachmittag am Flussufer Öl/Leinwand
  (40x50cm 15x19in) Wien 2000
- $2 923 - €2 689 - **£1 753** - FF17 637
  Bauernhofidylle Öl/Papier (31.5x30cm 12x11in)
  Wien 1999
- $313 - €359 - **£218** - FF2 356
  Mezöre indulo leány Watercolour/paper (45x60cm
  17x23in) Budapest 2000

NEOGRADY László 1896-1962 **[176]**
- $28 000 - €26 606 - **£17 035** - FF174 521
  Springtime Oil/canvas (101.5x152.5cm 39x60in)
  New-York 1999
- $1 521 - €1 309 - **£901** - FF8 584
  Gänseliesl Öl/Leinwand (60x80cm 23x31in) Wien
  1998

NEPO Ernst 1895-1971 **[12]**
- $4 905 - €5 450 - **£3 285** - FF35 752
  Blumenstilleben Öl/Karton (32x31.5cm 12x12in)
  Wien 2000

NEPOMNYASHY Boris Abramovich 1921 **[1]**
- $3 556 - €4 194 - **£2 508** - FF27 510
  Ironing Oil/canvas (61x81.5cm 24x32in) Woollahra,
  Sydney 2001

NEPPEL Heinrich 1874-1936 **[31]**
- $449 - €511 - **£311** - FF3 353
  Kühe an einem bayerischen See Oil/panel
  (20x27cm 7x10in) Hamburg 2000

NEPVEU Marie-Edwige 1800-1867 **[4]**
- $30 000 - €28 637 - **£18 744** - FF187 848
  **Roses, Morning Glories, Primroses and other
  Flowers** Oil/canvas (48.5x59cm 19x23in) New-York
  1999
- $14 000 - €13 364 - **£8 747** - FF87 662
  Narcissus, Zinnias and various other Flowers
  Oil/canvas (38.5x30.5cm 15x12in) New-York 1999

NERDRUM Odd 1944 **[31]**
- $4 360 - €5 067 - **£3 064** - FF33 240
  Himmel og hav Oil/canvas/panel (22x26cm 8x10in)
  Oslo 2001
- $1 582 - €1 708 - **£1 093** - FF11 205
  Mor og datter i landskap Lithograph (50x59cm
  19x23in) Oslo 2001

NÉRÉE TOT BABBERICH de Chistoph Karel Henri
1880-1909 **[9]**
🖋 **$2 052** - €1 777 - **£1 245** - FF11 657
Symbolistic figures Ink (54.5x39cm 21x15in)
Amsterdam 1998

NERENZ Wilhelm 1804-1871 **[8]**
🖼 **$10 776** - €9 309 - **£6 498** - FF61 062
Family Resting Before an Italian Lake Oil/canvas
(81x124cm 31x48in) Johannesburg 1998

NÉRI Paul 1910-1965 **[34]**
🖼 **$2 608** - €3 049 - **£1 862** - FF20 000
Marocaines dans l'oued à Tiznit Huile/toile
(50x65cm 19x25in) Paris 2001
🖋 **$667** - €610 - **£408** - FF4 000
Casbah de Tarahaout, Maroc Aquarelle,
gouache/papier (38x30cm 14x11in) Paris 1999

NERLI Girolamo Pieri Ball. 1860/63-1926 **[45]**
🖼 **$5 232** - €4 903 - **£3 236** - FF32 162
Portrait Study of a Young Girl Oil/canvas (62x47cm
24x18in) Sydney 1999
🖼 **$1 664** - €1 732 - **£1 045** - FF11 364
The Blue Scarf Oil/canvas/board (44.5x30.5cm
17x12in) Melbourne 2000
🖋 **$583** - €643 - **£388** - FF4 219
Village Women Watercolour/paper (24.5x16.5cm
9x6in) Melbourne 2000

NERLINGER Oskar 1893-1969 **[28]**
🖋 **$846** - €1 022 - **£590** - FF6 707
Kleine Stadt im Frühling Watercolour (48.5x62.2cm
19x24in) Berlin 2000
📷 **$262** - €281 - **£175** - FF1 844
Untitled Photograph (29.7x23.3cm 11x9in) München
2000

NERLY Friedrich I 1807-1878 **[53]**
🖼 **$24 066** - €23 008 - **£15 084** - FF150 925
**Schlucht mit Wildbach, Ziegenhirte unterhalb
Cervaras im Aequergebirge** Öl/Karton (47x51cm
18x20in) Hamburg 1999
🖋 **$1 842** - €2 045 - **£1 284** - FF13 415
«Marktszene in ital.Altstadt» Watercolour
(50x48cm 19x18in) Stuttgart 2001
📠 **$174** - €164 - **£107** - FF1 073
Säugende Ziege Radierung (20x23cm 7x9in) Lindau
1999

NERLY Friedrich II 1824-1919 **[23]**
🖼 **$65 000** - €72 590 - **£41 626** - FF476 157
Santa Maria della Salute, Venice Oil/canvas
(152.5x106.5cm 60x41in) New-York 2000
🖼 **$14 654** - €16 871 - **£10 000** - FF110 669
**The Bay of Naples with Vesuvius in the
Distance** Oil/canvas (48x91.5cm 18x36in) London
2000
🖼 **$3 300** - €3 016 - **£2 018** - FF19 782
**Venetian Canal Scene Towards the Church
of the Salute at Dusk** Oil/canvas (18x26cm 7x10in)
Pittsburgh PA 1999
🖋 **$1 947** - €2 301 - **£1 380** - FF15 092
Venedig, Dogenpalast Watercolour (40x54.5cm
15x21in) Stuttgart 2000

NERMAN Einar 1888-1983 **[63]**
🖼 **$468** - €539 - **£322** - FF3 538
Stilleben med sommarblomster Oil/panel
(38x47cm 14x18in) Stockholm 2000
🖼 **$536** - €604 - **£369** - FF3 962
Askungen Oil/panel (39x32cm 15x12in) Stockholm
2000

🖋 **$234** - €267 - **£164** - FF1 753
Madonna Akvarell/pappper (23x13cm 9x5in)
Stockholm 2001

NERONI Bartolomeo il Riccio c.1500-c.1571 **[10]**
🖼 **$23 462** - €19 963 - **£14 000** - FF130 947
Ecce Homo Oil/panel (84x67cm 33x26in) London
1998
🖼 **$5 459** - €5 342 - **£3 500** - FF35 042
The Martyrdom of a Saint Ink (19.5x40.5cm
7x15in) London 1999

NEROSLOW Alexander 1891-1971 **[57]**
🖋 **$142** - €153 - **£97** - FF1 006
Fischersfrau Aquarell/Papier (38x46cm 14x18in)
Rudolstadt-Thüringen 2001

NERUD Josef Karl 1900-1982 **[27]**
🖋 **$630** - €716 - **£440** - FF4 695
Hügelige Landschaft mit Dorf Ink (44.5x57.5cm
17x22in) München 2001

NERY Ismael 1900-1934 **[2]**
🖋 **$21 000** - €20 432 - **£12 925** - FF134 028
Surrealist Composition Watercolour (33.5x24cm
13x9in) New-York 1999

NESBITT Frances E. c.1864-1934 **[35]**
🖋 **$488** - €475 - **£300** - FF3 117
Figures at a Harbour Pencil (18.5x24.5cm 7x9in)
London 1999

NESBITT Jackson Lee 1913 **[57]**
🖼 **$9 000** - €10 295 - **£6 258** - FF67 531
Charging Hot Steel Oil/canvas/board (30x22cm
12x9in) Cincinnati OH 2001
🖼 **$2 200** - €2 498 - **£1 505** - FF16 386
Over 50 Years of Service - Omaha Steel Works
Gouache (35.5x50cm 13x19in) New-York 2000
📠 **$1 100** - €1 056 - **£681** - FF6 929
The Goose Etching (30x23.5cm 11x9in) New-York
1999

NESBITT Lowell 1933-1993 **[140]**
🖼 **$3 639** - €4 223 - **£2 512** - FF27 702
Violet Iris Oil/canvas (183x160cm 72x62in) Stockholm
2000
🖼 **$924** - €800 - **£560** - FF5 247
«Rose» Acrylic/canvas (96.5x76.5cm 37x30in)
Amsterdam 1998
🖋 **$590** - €549 - **£350** - FF3 270
Flor Lápiz/papel (102x76cm 40x29in) Lisboa 1998
📠 **$125** - €143 - **£88** - FF936
Yellow Rose Lithograph (63x63cm 25x25in) Chicago
IL 2001

NESCH Rolf 1893-1975 **[272]**
🖼 **$7 953** - €9 459 - **£5 668** - FF62 047
Stilleben mit Sommerblumen in einer Vase
Öl/Leinwand (58x51cm 22x20in) München 2000
🖋 **$1 433** - €1 431 - **£896** - FF9 390
Zwei Reiter Chalks/paper (19.7x27.2cm 7x10in)
Hamburg 1999
📠 **$2 597** - €3 088 - **£1 800** - FF20 255
Kater mit dem Mond Linocut (50x40cm 19x15in)
London 2000

NESFIELD William Andrew 1793-1881 **[13]**
🖋 **$1 168** - €1 327 - **£820** - FF8 706
Naworth Castle, Cumberland Watercolour/paper
(28x36cm 11x14in) Cambridge 2001

NESHAT Shirin 1957 **[46]**
📷 **$21 652** - €23 426 - **£15 000** - FF153 667
«Rapture» Gelatin silver print (115.5x177cm 45x69in)
London 2001

N

NESPOLO Ugo 1941 [241]

🍷 **$4 000** - €4 147 - **£2 400** - FF27 200
Leopardeggiando Alcatraz Tecnica mista
(155x90cm 61x35in) Prato 1999

🍷 **$2 000** - €2 073 - **£1 200** - FF13 600
Senza titolo Acrilico/cartone (70x100cm 27x39in)
Prato 1999

🍷 **$1 440** - €1 244 - **£960** - FF8 160
Fairy Tale Acrilico/tavola (40x30cm 15x11in) Milano
1998

🍷 **$1 100** - €1 140 - **£660** - FF7 480
Senza titolo Tecnica mista/carta (70x50.5cm 27x19in)
Prato 2000

▥ **$250** - €259 - **£150** - FF1 700
Guardar Marilyn Serigrafia (75x75cm 29x29in)
Vercelli 2001

NESSELTHALER Andreas 1748-1821 [6]

🍷 **$8 965** - €9 624 - **£6 000** - FF63 129
**View of a Country House, with figures and catt-
le** Oil/canvas (56.5x75cm 22x29in) London 2000

NESSI Marie-Lucie Valtat 1900-1992 [199]

🍷 **$900** - €990 - **£625** - FF6 496
«Bouquet de printemps» Oil/canvas (73x60cm
29x23in) Delray-Beach FL 2001

🍷 **$109** - €130 - **£77** - FF850
Jardin Huile/toile (35x24cm 13x9in) Toulouse 2000

NESTE van Alfred 1874-1969 [115]

🍷 **$968** - €892 - **£583** - FF5 853
Petite ruelle à Bruges Huile/panneau (36x45cm
14x17in) Antwerpen 1999

NESTEL Hermann 1858-? [13]

🍷 **$6 457** - €6 647 - **£4 070** - FF43 600
**Bordighera, Gartenterrasse über der Küste mit
blühenden Sträuchern** Öl/Leinwand (55x81cm
21x31in) Berlin 2000

NESTEROV Mikhail Vasilievich 1862-1942 [15]

🍷 **$25 187** - €29 974 - **£18 000** - FF196 617
The Mother and Child Oil/copper (31.5x18.5cm
12x7in) London 2000

🍷 **$3 054** - €2 617 - **£1 836** - FF17 165
The Archangel Michael Watercolour/paper (13x8cm
5x3in) Cedar-Falls IA 1998

NESTEROVA Natalia 1944 [9]

🍷 **$9 960** - €11 572 - **£7 000** - FF75 909
Evening Oil/canvas (150x180cm 59x70in) London
2001

NET van 't Gerrit 1910-1971 [16]

✎ **$234** - €227 - **£146** - FF1 488
Compositie Pastel (65x50cm 25x19in) Amsterdam
1999

▥ **$5 655** - €5 445 - **£3 536** - FF35 719
Siesta Tapestry (168x228cm 66x89in) Amsterdam
1999

NETER de Laurentius c.1600-1650 [8]

🍷 **$10 123** - €11 281 - **£7 030** - FF74 000
Couple galant Huile/panneau (29x25.5cm 11x10in)
Paris 2001

NETHERWOOD Arthur 1864-1930 [28]

✎ **$169** - €183 - **£117** - FF1 200
Handelssted ved fjorden Watercolour/paper
(20x32cm 7x12in) Oslo 2001

NETO Ernest 1964 [5]

🗝 **$30 000** - €34 809 - **£20 712** - FF228 330
Apolo Metal (335.5x335.5x274.5cm 132x132x108in)
New-York 2000

NETSCHER Caspar 1635/39-1684 [62]

🍷 **$31 220** - €30 490 - **£19 900** - FF200 000
**Portrait de groupe des trois enfants de l'Élec-
teur de Bavière** Huile/toile (123x98cm 48x38in) Paris
1999

🍷 **$8 479** - €8 168 - **£5 239** - FF53 578
**Lady, Seated Small three Quarter Length on a
Draped Balcony** Oil/canvas (49x39.5cm 19x15in)
Amsterdam 1999

✎ **$8 494** - €8 168 - **£5 232** - FF53 578
**Portrait of a Woman on a Terrace Holding a
Mask** Ink (15x12cm 5x4in) Amsterdam 1999

NETSCHER Constantin c.1668-c.1723 [40]

🍷 **$4 277** - €4 724 - **£2 964** - FF30 985
**Bildnis einer Dame mit Hund in einer
Landschaft** Öl/Leinwand (48.5x38.5cm 19x15in)
Wien 2001

🍷 **$9 684** - €8 983 - **£6 000** - FF58 925
**Lady Wearing a Brown Brocade Dress,
Standing by a Curtain** Oil/panel (31x25cm 12x9in)
London 1999

NETTI Francesco 1832-1894 [4]

🍷 **$22 000** - €22 806 - **£13 200** - FF149 600
Riposo in mietitura Olio/tela (60x81.5cm 23x32in)
Milano 2000

NETTLESHIP John Trivett 1841-1902 [18]

✎ **$451** - €410 - **£280** - FF2 691
Black Bear Pastel/paper (46x60cm 18x23in)
Billingshurst, West-Sussex 1999

NEU Paul 1881-1940 [5]

▥ **$1 200** - €1 154 - **£740** - FF7 569
«La Bougie Eyquem» Poster (153x102cm 60x40in)
New-York 1999

NEUBAUER Max 1890-1920 [58]

✎ **$361** - €400 - **£250** - FF2 621
«Wien VI Ratzenstadl, Magdalenstr.74»
Aquarell/Papier (18x28cm 7x11in) Wien 2001

NEUBERT Ludwig, Louis 1846-1892 [33]

🍷 **$1 384** - €1 278 - **£851** - FF8 384
Norddeutsche Landschaft Oil/panel (20x38cm
7x14in) München 1999

NEUBÖCK Maximilian 1893-1960 [17]

🍷 **$13 424** - €11 623 - **£8 144** - FF76 240
«Badende» Oil/panel (110x160cm 43x62in) Wien
1998

🍷 **$2 607** - €2 179 - **£1 545** - FF14 292
Stilleben mit Fischen Öl/Leinwand (40x50cm
15x19in) Wien 1998

NEUBURGER Elie 1891-1972 [5]

🍷 **$1 094** - €1 134 - **£694** - FF7 441
Garden Scene Oil/board (56x45cm 22x17in)
Amsterdam 2000

NEUCKENS Piet J. XIX [9]

🍷 **$426** - €421 - **£263** - FF2 764
Le taste-vin Huile/panneau (38x31cm 14x12in)
Antwerpen 1999

NEUDECKER Marielle 1965 [4]

🗝 **$3 635** - €3 106 - **£2 200** - FF20 377
Landscape Construction (20x20x61cm 7x7x24in)
London 1998

📷 **$2 163** - €2 543 - **£1 500** - FF16 680
The infinity of Infantile Senility Type C color print
(135x415cm 53x163in) London 2000

NEUENSCHWANDER Albert 1902-1984 **[84]**
- $792 - €919 - £547 - FF6 030
  Stilleben mit Rittersporn und Sommerblumen
  Öl/Leinwand (90x79.5cm 35x31in) Luzern 2000

NEUGEBAUER Josef 1810-1895 **[22]**
- $4 515 - €5 335 - £3 200 - FF34 997
  **Portrait of the Artist's Daughter Marie Playing
  Piano** Oil/panel (47.5x36cm 18x14in) London 2000

NEUHAUS Werner 1897-1934 **[29]**
- $58 600 - €68 915 - £42 021 - FF452 056
  Emmentaler Landschaft Oil/canvas/panel
  (99.5x120cm 39x47in) Bern 2001
- $723 - €690 - £451 - FF4 528
  Knabenportrait, Stalder Köbeli Charcoal (46x30cm
  18x11in) Zofingen 1999

NEUHOF Waltère Joseph 1904-? **[22]**
- $367 - €340 - £221 - FF2 232
  Winterlandschap Oil/canvas (40x50cm 15x19in)
  Maastricht 1999
- $435 - €454 - £276 - FF2 976
  Jeker Oil/canvas (49x23cm 19x9in) Maastricht 2000

NEUHUYS Albertus Johan 1844-1914 **[89]**
- $1 479 - €1 588 - £990 - FF10 418
  De priktol: the top Oil/canvas (60.5x47.5cm 23x18in)
  Amsterdam 2000
- $2 500 - €2 482 - £1 533 - FF16 279
  Serving the Meal Oil/canvas (38x30cm 15x12in)
  Mystic CT 2000
- $3 750 - €3 495 - £2 266 - FF22 927
  Mother and Children Watercolour/paper (26x20cm
  10x8in) New-Orleans LA 2000

NEUHUYS Jan Antoon 1832-1891 **[6]**
- $11 087 - €9 313 - £6 500 - FF61 090
  Emigration of the Huguenots Oil/canvas
  (82x133cm 32x52in) London 1998

NEUMANN Abraham 1873-1942 **[30]**
- $2 093 - €1 926 - £1 256 - FF12 637
  Paysage de Bretagne Oil/canvas (46x55cm 18x21in)
  Kraków 1999
- $2 307 - €2 019 - £1 397 - FF13 246
  Paysage de Palestine Pastel/panel (34x39cm
  13x15in) Warszawa 1998

NEUMANN Carl Johan 1833-1891 **[129]**
- $1 867 - €2 145 - £1 296 - FF12 601
  Råkold dag på stranden ved Hornbaek Oil/canvas
  (37x51cm 14x20in) København 2000
- $750 - €671 - £449 - FF4 401
  **Klitter med marehalm, i baggrunden blikstille
  hav. Skagen** Oil/canvas (25x38cm 9x14in) København
  1998

NEUMANN Ernst 1871-1954 **[1]**
- $4 910 - €5 351 - £3 400 - FF35 097
  «Sosa» Poster (138x91cm 54x35in) London 2001

NEUMANN Ernst 1907-1956 **[119]**
- $1 287 - €1 437 - £897 - FF9 426
  Étude pour portrait de femme Huile/panneau
  (66x61cm 25x24in) Montréal 2001
- $203 - €198 - £125 - FF1 299
  Redpath Library, Montréal Etching (12.5x16cm
  4x6in) Montréal 1999

NEUMANN Fritz XIX-XX **[18]**
- $878 - €818 - £530 - FF5 367
  Kroatischer Reiterkampf Oil/panel (60x40cm
  23x15in) München 1998

NEUMANN Hans 1888-1960 **[31]**
- $274 - €254 - £169 - FF1 668
  «Ambor Zigaretten» Poster (63x95cm 24x37in) Wien
  1999

NEUMANN Hans 1873-1957 **[57]**
- $398 - €384 - £249 - FF2 516
  Tigerpaar Woodcut in colors (22.5x32cm 8x12in)
  München 1999

NEUMANN Johan Jens 1860-1940 **[230]**
- $703 - €673 - £437 - FF4 417
  Marine med fiskekuttere ud for Kullen Oil/canvas
  (55x92cm 21x36in) København 1999
- $364 - €403 - £241 - FF2 641
  Marine ved Kronborg Oil/canvas (32x44cm 12x17in)
  Viby J, Århus 2000

NEUMANN Max 1949 **[41]**
- $8 963 - €10 583 - £6 363 - FF69 423
  «G.N.» Öl/Leinwand (160x124.5cm 62x49in) Berlin
  2001
- $903 - €869 - £557 - FF5 701
  Ohne Titel Mixed media/paper (18x15.5cm 7x6in)
  Köln 1999

NEUMANN von Robert 1888-1976 **[32]**
- $800 - €910 - £554 - FF5 968
  Farmhouse Oil/board (50x60cm 20x24in) Cincinnati
  OH 2000
- $175 - €200 - £120 - FF1 313
  The Four Net Menders Woodcut (36x25cm 14x10in)
  Milwaukee WI 2000

NEUMONT Maurice 1868-1930 **[29]**
- $535 - €457 - £321 - FF3 000
  «Théâtre National de l'Opéra. Bal Directoire»
  Affiche (115x155cm 45x61in) Paris 1998

NEUQUELMAN Lucien 1909-1988 **[177]**
- $1 990 - €1 906 - £1 252 - FF12 500
  Port de la Rochelle Huile/toile (55x81cm 21x31in)
  La Rochelle 1999
- $1 309 - €1 372 - £828 - FF9 000
  Au jardin des Tuileries Huile/toile (27x41cm
  10x16in) Versailles 2000
- $568 - €610 - £380 - FF4 000
  Le golfe de Saint-Tropez Aquarelle/papier (28x38cm
  11x14in) Lyon 2000

NEURAC de L. XIX-XX **[6]**
- $1 122 - €1 131 - £700 - FF7 422
  «Luchon-Superbagnères» Poster (99x64cm
  38x25in) London 2000

NEUREUTHER Eugen Napoleon 1806-1882 **[63]**
- $2 064 - €2 301 - £1 443 - FF15 092
  Madonna mit Kind in Frühlingslandschaft
  Öl/Leinwand (68.5x42.5cm 26x16in) München 2001
- $2 584 - €2 352 - £1 614 - FF15 427
  **Waldinneres mit Fluss und mythologischer
  Szene** Öl/Papier (37.8x27.8cm 14x10in) München
  1999
- $855 - €971 - £594 - FF6 372
  Mutter mit ihren Kindern in der Kinderstube
  Pencil/paper (23.5x17.5cm 9x6in) Berlin 2001
- $292 - €256 - £176 - FF1 676
  **Die Verleihung des Künstlerwappens an
  Albrecht Dürer** Radierung (60.5x47cm 23x18in)
  Berlin 1998

NEUREUTHER Ludwig c.1770-1832 **[5]**
- $2 298 - €2 250 - £1 414 - FF14 757
  Stadtansicht von Bamberg Pencil (28x37cm
  11x14in) Bamberg 1999

NEUSCHUL Ernst 1895-1968 **[13]**
$807 - €868 - £550 - FF5 692
«Mann und Frau» Oil/canvas (100x70cm 39x27in)
London 2001

NEUSER William 1833-1902 **[3]**
$4 200 - €4 727 - £2 893 - FF31 007
Husband and Wife, Probably Mr.and Mrs.Linser
Oil/canvas (76x63cm 30x25in) New-Orleans LA 2000

NEUSTÄDTL Otto 1878-1962 **[9]**
$511 - €509 - £309 - FF3 336
Abtenau Öl/Leinwand/Karton (43.5x58cm 17x22in)
Wien 2000

NEUSTÄTTER Ludwig, Louis 1829-1899 **[7]**
$5 500 - €6 377 - £3 896 - FF41 831
Picking Wildflowers Oil/panel (29x22cm 11x8in)
New-York 2000

NEUSÜSS Floris M. 1937 **[26]**
$472 - €562 - £337 - FF3 689
«München» Vintage gelatin silver print (34.1x25.4cm
13x10in) Berlin 2000

NEUTRA Richard Joseph 1892-1970 **[1]**
$3 500 - €3 652 - £2 207 - FF23 957
Neutra House/Sunset Plaza/Los Angeles Pastel
(61x91.5cm 24x36in) New-York 2000

NEUVILLE de Alphonse Marie 1835-1885 **[83]**
$6 428 - €7 470 - £4 517 - FF49 000
La bataille de Rezonville Huile/toile (120x320cm
47x125in) Dieppe 2001
$2 246 - €2 302 - £1 386 - FF15 100
Scène militaire Huile/toile (60x60cm 23x23in) Noyon
2000
$1 068 - €1 143 - £726 - FF7 500
Portrait de militaire Huile/toile (13x10cm 5x3in)
Marseille 2001
$214 - €244 - £147 - FF1 600
Le départ du bataillon Crayon/papier (39x30cm
15x11in) Paris 2000

NEUVONEN Antti 1937 **[3]**
$1 050 - €1 177 - £713 - FF7 722
Bandlek Sculpture (H50cm H19in) Helsinki 2000

NEUWEILER Arnold 1895-1983 **[9]**
$1 840 - €1 611 - £1 114 - FF10 568
La Maison de pêcheur Pastell/Papier (58x40cm
22x15in) Zofingen 1998

NEVE de Franz 1606-1681 **[3]**
$15 580 - €14 534 - £9 400 - FF95 340
Neptun und Ceres tauschen Perlen und Früchte
aus Öl/Leinwand (89x139.5cm 35x54in) Wien 1999

NEVELSON Louise 1900-1988 **[357]**
$5 706 - €6 726 - £4 009 - FF44 813
Sin título Collage/panneau (55x44.5cm 21x17in)
Caracas ($) 2000
$1 300 - €1 442 - £864 - FF9 459
Voyage Mixed media (23x19x5cm 9x7x1in) New-York
2000
$24 000 - €22 414 - £14 812 - FF147 024
Maquette for Shadows and Flags Column Metal
(198x33x30.5cm 77x12x12in) New-York 1999
$9 500 - €8 028 - £5 866 - FF52 660
Promenade (Three-part sculpture) Stone
(H78.5cm H30in) San-Francisco CA 1998
$2 000 - €1 713 - £1 202 - FF11 239
«Night Tree» Collage (76x63cm 30x25in) St. Louis
MO 1998
$1 200 - €1 152 - £743 - FF7 559
Untitled, No.4 Aquatint (70.5x54.5cm 27x21in) New-
York 1999

NEVIL Edward XIX **[26]**
$285 - €317 - £190 - FF2 077
Coastal View with Fisherfolk and Their Boats at
Evening Watercolour/paper (23x48cm 9x19in)
Leominster, Herefordshire 2000

NEVINSON Christopher R. Wynne 1889-1946 **[194]**
$27 266 - €26 972 - £17 000 - FF176 922
From Southwark Bridge Oil/canvas (46.5x35cm
18x13in) London 1999
$4 265 - €3 906 - £2 600 - FF25 624
The Torn Cornfield Oil/canvas (32x40cm 12x15in)
London 1999
$20 521 - €19 899 - £13 000 - FF130 531
War wounded Ink (21x13.5cm 8x5in) London 1999
$1 366 - €1 257 - £820 - FF8 247
View of the Thames, London Drypoint (25x35cm
9x13in) London 1999

NEWBERRY Francis Henry 1855-1946 **[3]**
$3 259 - €3 863 - £2 340 - FF25 341
Looking Towards Southwold from Walberswick
Oil/board (24x34.5cm 9x13in) London 2000

NEWBOTT John c.1805-1867 **[12]**
$8 730 - €9 579 - £5 800 - FF62 831
Lake Albano with the Castel Gandolfo
Beyond/Lake Nemi Oil/canvas (47.5x63.5cm
18x25in) London 2000

NEWBOULD Frank 1887-1951 **[36]**
$706 - €819 - £500 - FF5 372
«Camping Coaches in England and Scotland,
LNER» Poster (102x64cm 40x25in) London 2000

NEWBURY Albert Ernest 1891-1941 **[13]**
$836 - €787 - £526 - FF5 160
White Camellias Oil/canvas/board (42x32cm
16x12in) Sydney 1999

NEWBURY Francis H. 1885-1946 **[4]**
$90 377 - €102 770 - £62 000 - FF674 126
Summers Day (Looking Across the Estuary
from Walberswick to Southwold) Oil/canvas
(113x75.5cm 44x29in) London 2000

NEWCOMB Mary 1922 **[59]**
$38 500 - €38 796 - £24 000 - FF254 486
Gate to a Descending Garden Oil/canvas
(112x127cm 44x50in) London 2000
$18 323 - €15 655 - £11 000 - FF102 693
French Barges coming and Going Oil/board
(76.5x101cm 30x39in) London 1998
$799 - €770 - £500 - FF5 050
The Lighthouse, Corran Ferry, Scotland Coloured
pencils/paper (18x22cm 7x8in) London 1999

NEWCOMB Rock 1945 **[5]**
$4 355 - €3 957 - £2 700 - FF25 956
Bluff? Acrylic/board (90x60cm 35x23in) Billingshurst,
West-Sussex 1999

NEWCOMBE Frederick Clive 1847-1894 **[22]**
$7 332 - €7 902 - £5 000 - FF51 832
On a Welsh River Oil/canvas (51x76.5cm 20x30in)
London 2001
$347 - €404 - £240 - FF250
The pillar Rock, Ennerdale, Cumberland
Watercolour/paper (41x71cm 16x27in) Cheshire 2000

NEWCOMBE Warren 1894-? **[4]**
$1 000 - €960 - £619 - FF6 299
Anna Karenina in Hollywood/New England
Meeting House Lithograph (26.5x39.5cm 10x15in)
New-York 1999

NEWCOMBE William John Bertram 1907-1969 **[29]**

✏ **$1 000** - €853 - **£596** - FF5 596
Picnic Watercolour/paper (56x74cm 22x29in) New-York 1998

NEWELL George Glenn 1870-1947 **[15]**

◯ **$5 000** - €5 367 - **£3 346** - FF35 205
Driving the Ox-Team at Midnight Oil/canvas (76x101.5cm 29x39in) New-York 2000

◯ **$2 500** - €2 301 - **£1 500** - FF15 093
Cows Grazing in Sunny Pasture Oil/panel (35x40cm 14x16in) Pasadena CA 1999

NEWELL Hugh 1830-1915 **[42]**

◯ **$1 200** - €1 025 - **£726** - FF6 725
The Old Wheelbarrow Oil/canvas (38x61cm 14x24in) San-Francisco CA 1998

✏ **$150** - €134 - **£92** - FF877
Man Drinking at a Well Charcoal (40x27cm 16x11in) Bloomfield-Hills MI 1999

NEWENHAM Frederick 1807-1859 **[2]**

◯ **$3 276** - €2 795 - **£1 952** - FF18 333
A lady of the Court Oil/panel (33.5x30.5cm 13x12in) Dublin 1998

NEWLING Edward XX **[2]**

◯ **$5 103** - €5 841 - **£3 510** - FF38 313
Portrait of Chester Beatty Oil/canvas (91x76cm 36x30in) Dublin 2000

NEWMAN Arnold 1918 **[92]**

📷 **$2 750** - €2 565 - **£1 660** - FF16 823
Igor Stravinsky Photograph (17.5x32.5cm 6x12in) New-York 1999

NEWMAN Barnett 1905-1970 **[32]**

◯ **$2 800** - €2 696 - **£1 750** - FF17 685
The Moment, from Four on Plexiglas Mixed media (124.5x12.5cm 49x4in) Beverly-Hills CA 1999

▥ **$15 000** - €14 199 - **£9 316** - FF93 142
Untitled Etching #2 Etching (59x37cm 23x14in) New-York 1999

NEWMAN Benjamin Tupper 1859-1940 **[9]**

◯ **$2 700** - €2 307 - **£1 586** - FF15 134
Tired Out Oil/canvas (32x45.5cm 12x17in) Boston MA 1998

NEWMAN George Allen 1875-1940 **[13]**

◯ **$525** - €502 - **£328** - FF3 290
Landscape with Canal and Boat Oil/board (38x28cm 15x11in) Hatfield PA 1999

NEWMAN Henry Roderick 1843-1917 **[22]**

✏ **$22 000** - €24 981 - **£15 056** - FF163 864
Temple of Philae, Nubia Watercolour/paper (66x51cm 25x20in) New-York 2000

NEWMAN John 1952 **[30]**

◈ **$2 750** - €3 063 - **£1 798** - FF20 092
Hanging in Air (At The End of a Rope) Sculpture (79x34x24cm 31x13x9in) New-York 2000

▥ **$2 000** - €1 695 - **£1 195** - FF11 117
Sotto Voce/Auto da Fe Lithograph (146x146cm 57x57in) New-York 1998

NEWMAN Robert Loftin 1827-1912 **[21]**

◯ **$8 000** - €9 084 - **£5 475** - FF59 587
Walking Tiger Oil/canvas (35.5x61cm 13x24in) New-York 2000

◯ **$1 000** - €866 - **£613** - FF5 681
The Bather Oil/canvas (20x25.5cm 7x10in) New-York 1999

NEWSON Marc 1963 **[2]**

⬧ **$90 000** - €99 977 - **£60 273** - FF655 803
Lockheed Lounge Metal (89x63.5x152.5cm 35x25x60in) New-York 2000

NEWTON Alfred Pizzey 1830-1883 **[3]**

✏ **$11 143** - €12 501 - **£7 798** - FF82 000
Paysage pris à Glencoe dans les Highlands Aquarelle, gouache (78.5x134.5cm 30x52in) Paris 2001

NEWTON Algernon 1880-1968 **[40]**

◯ **$1 205** - €1 161 - **£750** - FF7 615
Canford Cliffs Oil/canvas (46x61cm 18x24in) London 1999

◯ **$1 016** - €994 - **£650** - FF6 523
Nocturne Oil/canvas/board (35.5x30.5cm 13x12in) London 1999

✏ **$2 390** - €2 566 - **£1 600** - FF16 834
The End of a perfect Day Watercolour, gouache/paper (53x75cm 20x29in) Billingshurst, West-Sussex 2000

NEWTON Gilbert Stuart 1794-1835 **[4]**

◯ **$4 841** - €4 878 - **£3 017** - FF32 000
Elégant et élégantes se promenant dans le parc d'un château Collage/panneau (34x27.5cm 13x10in) Paris 2000

NEWTON Helmut 1920 **[163]**

📷 **$3 500** - €4 030 - **£2 388** - FF26 435
Piscine Deligny, Paris Gelatin silver print (44x30cm 17x11in) New-York 2000

NEWTON Kenneth 1933-1984 **[12]**

◯ **$2 738** - €2 573 - **£1 700** - FF16 879
Still Life with Onions, Mushrooms and Corn on the Cob Oil/canvas (76x101.5cm 29x39in) Salisbury, Wiltshire 1999

NEWTON Lilias Torrance 1896-1980 **[5]**

◯ **$41 613** - €44 724 - **£28 628** - FF293 368
«Nude» Oil/canvas (203x91.5cm 79x36in) Toronto 2001

NEWTON Marshall XIX **[1]**

📷 **$3 637** - €3 436 - **£2 200** - FF22 537
Helen Kellerer and Annie Sullivan Gelatin silver print (20x15cm 7x5in) London 1999

NEWTON Richard c.1777-1798 **[3]**

▥ **$926** - €994 - **£620** - FF6 523
Over Weight - The Sinking Fund - The Dowfall of Faro Etching in colors (27.5x37.5cm 10x14in) Suffolk 2000

NEWTON William John, Sir 1785-1869 **[26]**

◯ **$908** - €956 - **£600** - FF6 268
Lady Frances Theodosia Jocelyn, facing left in white dress Miniature (13x9.5cm 5x3in) London 2000

NEY Lloyd Raymond 1893-1964 **[12]**

✏ **$425** - €457 - **£284** - FF2 995
Modernist Watercolour/paper (44x59cm 17x23in) Hatfield PA 2000

NEYDHART Francis 1860-? **[5]**

◯ **$5 000** - €5 872 - **£3 550** - FF38 521
Samison Concert Oil/canvas (36x46cm 14x18in) New-York 2000

NEYMARK Gustave Mardoché 1850-? **[14]**

◯ **$2 001** - €1 829 - **£1 225** - FF12 000
Le pesage Huile/toile (54x65cm 21x25in) Dijon 1999

N

NEYN de Pieter Pietersz. 1597-1639 **[38]**

🕭 **$9 666** - €9 615 - **£6 000** - FF63 067
River Landscape with Peasants on a Bank beside a Barn, Sailing Vessels Oil/panel (77.5x118cm 30x46in) London 1999

🕭 **$26 299** - €24 934 - **£16 000** - FF163 555
Dune Landscape with Travellers resting by a Fence and Dogs playing Oil/panel (18x24.5cm 7x9in) London 1999

NEYT Bernard 1825-1880 **[4]**

🕭 **$3 480** - €3 718 - **£2 370** - FF24 390
Kerkinterieur Huile/toile (84x68cm 33x26in) Lokeren 2001

NEYTS Gillis 1623-1687 **[35]**

🕭 **$4 970** - €5 336 - **£3 325** - FF35 000
Le repos du chasseur au point d'eau Huile/toile (37x56.5cm 14x22in) Paris 2000

✎ **$2 050** - €1 771 - **£1 236** - FF11 618
An Italianate fortified Villa on an Outcrop Ink (17x24.5cm 6x9in) Amsterdam 1998

▥ **$1 264** - €1 227 - **£787** - FF8 049
Die Landschaft mit dem Reiter und den drei Reisenden Radierung (12.9x17.4cm 5x6in) Berlin 1999

NGATANE Ephraim 1938-1971 **[25]**

🕭 **$2 228** - €2 496 - **£1 548** - FF16 374
Pimville, Johannesburg Acrylic/board (44.5x61.5cm 17x24in) Johannesburg 2001

NGUYEN ANH 1914-2000 **[51]**

✎ **$290** - €274 - **£180** - FF1 800
Les porteurs Technique mixte/papier (17.5x25.5cm 6x10in) Paris 1999

NGUYEN GIA TRI 1908-1993 **[6]**

🕭 **$51 651** - €58 649 - **£35 352** - FF384 714
Landscape of Vietnam Mixed media/panel (160x120cm 62x47in) Singapore 2000

✎ **$3 751** - €3 496 - **£2 314** - FF22 930
Ladies in the Garden Mixed media/paper (51x76cm 20x29in) Singapore 1999

NGUYEN PHAN CHANH 1882-1984 **[12]**

🕭 **$20 674** - €19 269 - **£12 495** - FF126 395
Dreaming by the Pond Oil/canvas (52x40.5cm 20x15in) Singapore 1999

✎ **$31 740** - €29 579 - **£19 585** - FF194 023
Les chanteuses à la campagne Gouache (65.5x49.5cm 25x19in) Singapore 1999

NGUYEN PHUOC 1943 **[4]**

🕭 **$14 921** - €16 943 - **£10 212** - FF111 139
Preparing for Wedding Oil/canvas (119.5x160cm 47x62in) Singapore 2000

NGUYEN SANG 1923-1988 **[11]**

🕭 **$22 446** - €20 920 - **£13 566** - FF137 229
Portrait of Miss Nhung Painting (81x61cm 31x24in) Singapore 1999

🕭 **$4 645** - €4 329 - **£2 866** - FF28 398
Musicians Mixed media (30x26cm 11x10in) Singapore 1999

NGUYEN THANH LE 1919 **[9]**

🕭 **$4 313** - €4 020 - **£2 661** - FF26 369
Young Lady in the Garden Oil/panel (100x70cm 39x27in) Singapore 1999

NGUYEN TRUNG 1940 **[14]**

🕭 **$2 969** - €2 491 - **£1 742** - FF16 340
Me va Con Oil/canvas (100x85cm 39x33in) Singapore 1998

NGUYEN TU NGHIEM 1922 **[11]**

🕭 **$4 304** - €4 888 - **£2 946** - FF32 061
Goat Oil/board (31x29cm 12x11in) Singapore 2000

NHULMARMAR c.1910-c.1977 **[1]**

🕭 **$3 287** - €3 181 - **£2 083** - FF20 866
Ganalbingu Language Group Witji - The Rainbow Serpent Mixed media/board (32.5x25cm 12x9in) Malvern, Victoria 1999

NI TIAN 1855-1919 **[9]**

✎ **$4 157** - €3 511 - **£2 495** - FF23 032
Portrait of Li Quingzhao Ink (102x26.5cm 40x10in) Hong-Kong 1998

NI YUANLU 1593-1644 **[8]**

✎ **$8 751** - €8 299 - **£5 324** - FF54 440
Letter Ink/paper (23.5x31.5cm 9x12in) Hong-Kong 1999

NIBBRIG Hart Ferdinand 1866-1915 **[41]**

🕭 **$39 100** - €38 571 - **£24 080** - FF253 011
Philemon and Baucis Oil/canvas (100x120cm 39x47in) Amsterdam 1999

🕭 **$14 262** - €13 613 - **£8 913** - FF89 298
Panoramic View of Veere at High Tide Oil/canvas (37.5x57.5cm 14x22in) Amsterdam 1999

🕭 **$5 724** - €6 807 - **£4 080** - FF44 649
Eiffel Landscape in Spring Oil/canvas (30x40cm 11x15in) Amsterdam 2000

▥ **$436** - €454 - **£273** - FF2 976
Gezicht op Zoutelande Color lithograph (69x100cm 27x39in) Dordrecht 2000

NIBBS Richard Henry c.1816-1893 **[97]**

🕭 **$9 681** - €10 812 - **£6 200** - FF70 921
Plymouth Oil/canvas (76x157cm 29x61in) London 2000

🕭 **$1 622** - €1 558 - **£1 000** - FF10 218
Fishing Boats in Shoreham Harbour Oil/canvas (40.5x25.5cm 15x10in) London 1999

🕭 **$915** - €776 - **£550** - FF5 087
Dutch Barge at Anchor Watercolour (57x48cm 22x18in) London 1998

NIBLETT Gary 1943 **[19]**

🕭 **$9 500** - €8 636 - **£5 721** - FF56 648
Winter Supplies Oil/canvas (60x91cm 24x36in) Hayden ID 1998

🕭 **$3 960** - €4 251 - **£2 650** - FF27 882
Mexican Moonlight Oil/canvas (30x40cm 12x16in) Houston TX 2000

NICCOLO DA SIENA act.1428-1470 **[2]**

🕭 **$120 000** - €129 821 - **£82 212** - FF851 568
The Transfiguration Tempera (111x61cm 43x24in) New-York 2001

NICCOLO di Lorenzo c.1380-c.1415 **[7]**

🕭 **$140 000** - €141 629 - **£85 484** - FF929 026
Saints Benedict(?) and Peter, The Angel of the Annunciation in roundel Tempera/panel (66x38.5cm 25x15in) New-York 2000

NICHOLAS J.T. XIX-XX **[1]**

🕭 **$5 500** - €6 291 - **£3 824** - FF41 269
Stepping Stone Bridge Oil/canvas (76x91cm 30x36in) Cincinnati OH 2000

NICHOLAS Thomas Andrew 1934 **[17]**

🕭 **$1 000** - €1 080 - **£691** - FF7 083
Island Cove, Maine Oil/canvas (25x35cm 10x14in) Detroit MI 2001

NICHOLL Agnes Rose 1842-? **[10]**

🖅 **$867** - €825 - **£550** - FF5 414
Cherry-Pickers Watercolour (41.5x33.5cm 16x13in)
Billingshurst, West-Sussex 1999

NICHOLL Andrew 1804-1886 **[155]**

🖅 **$4 605** - €5 158 - **£3 200** - FF33 837
**Steamer off the Coast with Dunluce Castle,
Co.Antrim beyond** Watercolour (40.5x56cm 15x22in)
London 2001

NICHOLLS Alfred XIX-XX **[1]**

▥ **$1 798** - €1 728 - **£1 100** - FF11 336
«**The most interesting Route to Scotland,
Midland Railway**» Poster (99x61cm 38x24in) London
1999

NICHOLLS Bertram 1883-1974 **[36]**

☞ **$1 381** - €1 275 - **£849** - FF8 365
A castle of the Scaligeri Oil/canvas (33x51cm
12x20in) London 1999

🖅 **$255** - €299 - **£180** - FF1 963
Classical Landscape Watercolour/paper (28x37cm
11x14in) London 2000

NICHOLLS Burr H. 1848-1915 **[16]**

☞ **$7 000** - €5 990 - **£4 214** - FF39 293
Gate of Justice Oil/canvas (60x50cm 24x20in) New-
York 1998

☞ **$2 400** - €2 193 - **£1 468** - FF14 387
Venetian Red Gate/Entrance to a Campo, Venice
Oil/canvas/board (35.5x24.5cm 13x9in) Boston MA
1999

NICHOLLS Charles George XVIII-XIX **[21]**

🖅 **$1 408** - €1 654 - **£1 000** - FF10 851
**Part of the Fort of Monghyr/The Tea Works at
Kanpur** Watercolour (20x25cm 7x9in) London 2000

NICHOLLS Charles Wynne 1831-1903 **[15]**

☞ **$3 800** - €3 633 - **£2 314** - FF23 834
Figures in the Interiors of a Gun Ship Oil/canvas
(23x72cm 9x28in) Columbia SC 1999

☞ **$570** - €612 - **£381** - FF4 015
Young Beauty Oil/canvas (20.5x15cm 8x5in)
Vancouver, BC. 2000

🖅 **$1 331** - €1 524 - **£915** - FF9 994
Interiors with Young Woman with her Maid
Watercolour/paper (25x35cm 10x14in) Dublin 2000

NICHOLLS George F. 1885-1937 **[19]**

🖅 **$187** - €209 - **£130** - FF1 374
Extensive Landscape with Farmhouse beyond
Watercolour (28.5x45.5cm 11x17in) Newbury,
Berkshire 2001

▥ **$895** - €839 - **£550** - FF5 501
«**Shap Fell**» Poster (127x101.5cm 50x39in) London
1999

NICHOLLS John E. act.1922-1955 **[25]**

☞ **$3 327** - €2 818 - **£2 000** - FF18 484
Still Life of Flowers Oil/canvas (59.5x49cm 23x19in)
London 1998

NICHOLLS Joseph 1692-1760 **[5]**

☞ **$67 666** - €67 302 - **£42 000** - FF441 470
**The Thames, from South Bank, looking, North-
West of London & St Paul** Oil/canvas (61x101.5cm
24x39in) London 1999

☞ **$67 363** - €66 636 - **£42 000** - FF437 102
View of Westminster from Lambeth Oil/canvas
(61x12cm 24x4in) London 1999

NICHOLLS W.A. XIX **[2]**

🖅 **$4 961** - €4 326 - **£3 000** - FF28 379
**Putney Church/Lower Richmond Road looking
toward Putney Church** Watercolour (32x47cm
12x18in) London 1998

NICHOLS Audley Dean 1886-1941 **[5]**

☞ **$8 000** - €7 980 - **£4 994** - FF52 346
Texas Landscape Oil/canvas (40x60cm 16x24in)
Cincinnati OH 1999

NICHOLS Ben XX **[3]**

▥ **$1 819** - €1 756 - **£1 148** - FF11 516
Composition avec cinq Cercles Gravure bois
(15.8x20cm 6x7in) Bern 1999

NICHOLS Dale William 1904-1995 **[80]**

☞ **$2 100** - €1 961 - **£1 296** - FF12 864
Fort Gains, Dauphin Island, AL Oil/paper
(34x47cm 13x18in) Detroit MI 1999

☞ **$11 000** - €9 490 - **£6 611** - FF62 252
«**Pair of Western Landscapes with Cow Boys!**»
Acrylic/masonite (35x40cm 14x16in) Santa-Fe NM
1998

▥ **$350** - €336 - **£217** - FF2 207
Grain Elevator Lithograph (24x31.5cm 9x12in) New-
York 1999

NICHOLS Edward W. 1819-1871 **[7]**

☞ **$13 000** - €12 035 - **£7 957** - FF78 946
New Hampshire fall Landscape Oil/canvas/board
(72x112cm 28x44in) Wethersfield CT 1999

NICHOLS Henry Hobart 1869-1962 **[37]**

☞ **$3 000** - €3 220 - **£2 007** - FF21 123
Garth Shore, Georgian Way Oil/canvas (45.5x56cm
17x22in) New-York 2000

NICHOLSON Alice Hogarth XIX-XX **[6]**

☞ **$22 709** - €21 810 - **£14 000** - FF143 063
Children playing on the Beach Oil/canvas
(86.5x112cm 34x44in) London 1999

NICHOLSON Ben 1894-1982 **[539]**

☞ **$220 738** - €215 734 - **£140 000** - FF1 415 120
Greek Island Oil/board (97x192.5cm 38x75in)
London 1999

☞ **$90 234** - €107 875 - **£62 000** - FF707 612
«**July**» Oil/canvas/board (54x61cm 21x24in) London
2000

☞ **$49 619** - €53 300 - **£34 000** - FF349 628
«**Urbino**» Tempera (48.5x30.5cm 19x12in) London
2001

◆ **$41 840** - €44 912 - **£28 000** - FF294 604
Celestial Relief (68x78cm 26x30in) London 2000

🖅 **$11 157** - €13 121 - **£8 000** - FF86 068
«**Gythian Theatre**» Watercolour (53x66cm 20x25in)
London 2001

▥ **$1 730** - €1 968 - **£1 200** - FF12 908
Fragment of Tuscan Cathedral Etching (20x15cm
7x5in) London 2000

NICHOLSON Charles A., Sir XIX-XX **[2]**

🖅 **$1 740** - €1 851 - **£1 100** - FF12 141
The new Screen, Blisland in Cornwall
Watercolour (40.5x33cm 15x12in) London 2000

NICHOLSON Edward Horace 1901-1966 **[23]**

☞ **$1 200** - €1 339 - **£785** - FF8 781
Indiana Dunes Oil/board (45x55cm 18x22in) Chicago
IL 2000

NICHOLSON Emily act.1842-1869 **[8]**

🖅 **$202** - €227 - **£140** - FF1 486
Cliburn Road Looking Towards Winderwath
Watercolour/paper (33x23.5cm 12x9in) Penrith,
Cumbria 2000

NICHOLSON Francis 1753-1844 **[114]**
- $5 292 – €4 615 – £3 200 – FF30 271
  View of Tintern Abbey, with a herdsman and livestock in the foreground Oil/panel (31x44cm 12x17in) London 1998
- $1 024 – €1 019 – £620 – FF25 681
  At the Falls Watercolour/paper (35.5x51cm 13x20in) London 2000

NICHOLSON George Washington 1832-1912 **[86]**
- $4 000 – €3 730 – £2 481 – FF24 466
  The Market in the Center of Town Oil/canvas (64x51cm 25x20in) New-York 1999
- $1 900 – €1 886 – £1 165 – FF12 372
  Caravan Oil/panel (30x25cm 12x10in) Mystic CT 2000

NICHOLSON John Hobson 1911-1988 **[35]**
- $538 – €465 – £320 – FF3 053
  On the Coast, near Laxey, Isle of Man Watercolour/paper (20x37cm 7x14in) Chester 1998

NICHOLSON John Miller XIX **[8]**
- $1 487 – €1 736 – £1 050 – FF11 388
  Still Life Fruit Watercolour/paper (25x40cm 10x16in) Isle-of-Man 2000

NICHOLSON Kate 1928 **[19]**
- $2 241 – €2 406 – £1 500 – FF15 782
  Quarry Beck Oil/board (91.5x71cm 36x27in) London 2000

NICHOLSON Lillie May 1884-1964 **[9]**
- $1 500 – €1 750 – £1 044 – FF11 479
  «Boy in Blue Jumper, Red Trim» Oil/board (30x40cm 12x16in) Altadena CA 2000

NICHOLSON William, Sir 1872-1949 **[169]**
- $24 001 – €23 829 – £15 000 – FF156 310
  The Enchanted Journey Enamel (188x170cm 74x66in) London 1999
- $48 378 – €56 208 – £34 000 – FF368 702
  The blue Shawl Oil/canvas/board (91.5x71cm 36x27in) London 2001
- $25 616 – €23 256 – £16 000 – FF152 547
  A Game of Pelota Oil/canvas/board (33x40cm 12x15in) London 1999
- $1 297 – €1 246 – £800 – FF8 175
  Portrait of Ben Nicholson as a Baby Ink/paper (15x16cm 5x6in) London 1999
- $143 – €164 – £100 – FF1 077
  Under the Arch of the Bridge Color lithograph (29x44cm 11x17in) London 2000

NICHOLSON Winifred 1893-1981 **[88]**
- $25 816 – €23 712 – £16 000 – FF155 539
  Flowers, Bankshead Oil/canvas (71x41cm 27x16in) London 1999
- $27 747 – €32 238 – £19 500 – FF211 466
  Iris, Tindle Tarn Oil/canvas (37.5x38.5cm 14x15in) London 2001
- $2 430 – €2 588 – £1 600 – FF16 977
  The Hebrides on a Sunny Day Pastel/paper (31.5x49cm 12x19in) Billingshurst, West-Sussex 2000

NICKEL Hans 1916-1977 **[19]**
- $730 – €767 – £424 – FF5 030
  Bauer beim Tränken seiner Pferde Öl/Leinwand (60x70cm 23x27in) Kempten 2001

NICKELE van Isaack Nikkelen c.1640-1703 **[11]**
- $17 931 – €19 248 – £12 000 – FF126 259
  Capriccio of a Renaissance style colonnade, an ornamental lake Oil/panel (49.5x68.5cm 19x26in) London 1999

NICKERSON Reginald Eugene 1915-? **[20]**
- $4 750 – €5 346 – £3 272 – FF35 067
  The Four Masted Schooner Marie Palmer Oil/canvas (54x92cm 21x36in) Philadelphia PA 2000

NICKLESS Will XX **[13]**
- $244 – €238 – £150 – FF1 558
  Game of Blind Man's Buff at a Family Party Watercolour/paper (49.5x38cm 19x14in) London 1999

NICKOLLS Trevor 1949 **[14]**
- $1 710 – €1 650 – £1 080 – FF10 822
  Untitled (Self-Portrait) Acrylic/canvas (60.5x45.5cm 23x17in) Melbourne 1999

NICOL Erskine 1825-1904 **[92]**
- $48 660 – €46 911 – £30 000 – FF307 713
  Interviewing the Member Oil/canvas (105.5x142cm 41x55in) London 1999
- $10 794 – €12 091 – £7 500 – FF79 310
  Interior of an Irish Homestead Oil/canvas (46.5x63cm 18x24in) London 2001
- $2 964 – €2 916 – £1 900 – FF19 126
  Derravaragh from Clonave, Co Westmeath Oil/canvas (26.5x58.5cm 10x23in) Bath 1999
- $4 078 – €3 809 – £2 517 – FF24 987
  The Old Ghillie Oil/canvas (36x26cm 14x10in) Dublin 1999
- $782 – €889 – £540 – FF5 830
  Study of a Group of Figures Gouache/paper (18x25cm 7x10in) Dublin 2000

NICOLA PISANO c.1470-c.1540 **[2]**
- $73 399 – €68 650 – £45 000 – FF450 315
  The Holy Family with Saint John the Baptist in a Landscape Oil/panel (66x53cm 25x20in) London 1998

NICOLAI Olaf 1962 **[4]**
- $4 552 – €4 346 – £2 844 – FF28 508
  Die zwei Seiten des Buches Mixed media/board (66x94x9.6cm 25x37x3in) Köln 1999

NICOLAIDES Kimon 1892-1938 **[7]**
- $2 600 – €2 483 – £1 650 – FF16 287
  Death of Lincoln Oil/canvas (111x137cm 44x54in) Cincinnati OH 1999

NICOLAU Francisco Sebastian 1956 **[3]**
- $2 750 – €2 851 – £1 650 – FF18 700
  Rosales Olio/tavola (58x94.5cm 22x37in) Prato 2000

NICOLAUS Martin 1870-1945 **[39]**
- $577 – €562 – £355 – FF3 689
  Flusswehr im Enztal Öl/Leinwand (60x75cm 23x29in) Stuttgart 1999
- $524 – €486 – £325 – FF3 186
  Schäfer mit Herde auf der Ebinger Alb Öl/Karton (30x39cm 11x15in) Stuttgart 1999

NICOLAY Helen 1866-1954 **[11]**
- $3 200 – €2 899 – £1 958 – FF19 013
  Donkeys on Parade Watercolour, gouache/paper (23x35cm 9x14in) Portland ME 1998

NICOLET P. XVIII **[2]**
- $26 440 – €22 806 – £13 200 – FF149 600
  Amore prigioniero/Amore trionfante Olio/tela (87x141cm 34x55in) Prato 1999

NICOLI Claudio 1958 **[47]**
- $1 200 – €1 244 – £720 – FF8 160
  Nudo femminile Bronzo (H30cm H11in) Torino 2001

NICOLITCH Obrad 1898-1976 **[8]**
- $1 038 – €991 – £648 – FF6 500
  «Nijni et Stone» Affiche (138.5x99cm 54x38in) Orléans 1999

NICOLL Archibald Frank 1886-? **[7]**
- $579 - €680 - **£411** - FF4 463
  Wharf Scene Oil/canvas (18x26cm 7x10in) Auckland 2000

NICOLL Gordon William 1888-? **[3]**
- $765 - €732 - **£480** - FF4 802
  «**Bristol, Clifton Suspension Bridge, British Railways**» Poster (102x64cm 40x25in) London 1999

NICOLL Marion Florence 1909-1985 **[73]**
- $1 618 - €1 882 - **£1 138** - FF12 345
  «**Hyacinth**» Oil/canvas (91.5x51cm 36x20in) Calgary, Alberta 2001
- $623 - €529 - **£376** - FF3 468
  West of the Rockies Watercolour/paper (33x37cm 12x14in) Calgary, Alberta 1998
- $260 - €306 - **£184** - FF2 007
  «**Sun Dogs**» Print in colors (41.5x48.5cm 16x19in) Calgary, Alberta 2000

NICOLL Émile Frédéric 1830-1894 **[3]**
- $2 916 - €3 430 - **£2 112** - FF22 500
  Le port de Saint-Valéry en Caux Huile/panneau (35x26.5cm 13x10in) Soissons 2001

NICOLLE Victor Jean 1754-1826 **[328]**
- $1 643 - €1 764 - **£1 100** - FF11 573
  Facade of a Roman Palace from Beneath an Archway in a Sunken Courtyard Watercolour (6x9cm 2x3in) London 2001

NICOLO DI BARTOLOMEO DE BRUSIS XV-XVI **[1]**
- $74 100 - €76 816 - **£44 460** - FF503 880
  Madonna con Bambino in gloria d'angeli e i Santi Giovanni Evangelista Olio/tavola (30x18cm 11x7in) Roma 1999

NICOLO di Piero Lamberti ?-1456 **[1]**
- $100 000 - €103 665 - **£60 000** - FF680 000
  Madonna col Bambino Sculpture/bois (105x34x26cm 41x13x10in) Firenze 2001

NICZ-BOROWIAKOWA Maria 1896-1944 **[1]**
- $3 218 - €3 609 - **£2 185** - FF23 675
  Paysage à l'église Huile/panneau (32.5x44cm 12x17in) Warszawa 2000

NICZKY Eduard 1850-1919 **[15]**
- $3 017 - €2 812 - **£1 861** - FF18 446
  Junge Frau im Empirekostüm auf einer Bank im Park sitzend Oil/panel (26x17.5cm 10x6in) Köln 1999

NIDZGORSKI Adam XX **[19]**
- $308 - €313 - **£188** - FF2 050
  Sans titre Technique mixte/papier (41x29cm 16x11in) Paris 2000

NIE OU 1948 **[14]**
- $6 420 - €7 045 - **£4 135** - FF46 215
  Harvest Time Oil/canvas (50x60cm 19x23in) Hong-Kong 2000
- $4 879 - €5 328 - **£3 138** - FF34 948
  Residents in a Mountain Village Ink (16x22cm 6x8in) Hong-Kong 2000

NIEDERÉE Johann 1830-1853 **[2]**
- $2 149 - €2 147 - **£1 344** - FF14 086
  Studienkopf eines bärtigen Mannes Oil/panel (43x37cm 16x14in) Köln 1999

NIEDERER Gen 1881-1957 **[4]**
- $6 250 - €6 153 - **£3 874** - FF40 246
  Frau im Kosmos Öl/Papier (41x25cm 16x9in) München 1999

NIEDERHÄUSERN de Auguste, dit Rodo 1863-1913 **[7]**
- $2 800 - €3 272 - **£1 999** - FF21 466
  Les races humaines Bronze (H4.5cm H1in) Zürich 2001

NIEDERMAYER Wilhelm 1899-1965 **[5]**
- $626 - €613 - **£385** - FF4 024
  Späte Heimkehr, der Kellner Charcoal (59.5x47cm 23x18in) Zwiesel 1999

NIEDERMAYR Walter 1952 **[8]**
- $6 280 - €5 366 - **£3 800** - FF35 197
  Passo pordoi I (1-4) Photograph in colour (88x108.5cm 34x42in) London 1998

NIEDMANN August Heinrich 1826-1910 **[7]**
- $24 395 - €25 565 - **£15 450** - FF167 695
  Toast auf das Brautpaar Öl/Leinwand (73.5x86cm 28x33in) Köln 2000

NIEGELSSOHN August XIX **[1]**
- $17 305 - €19 123 - **£12 000** - FF125 436
  View of the Schloßplatz, Berlin Watercolour, gouache/paper (59x91.5cm 23x36in) London 2001

NIEHAUS Kasper 1889-1974 **[28]**
- $1 575 - €1 363 - **£955** - FF8 943
  Three People with a Horse Oil/canvas/board (100x92cm 39x36in) Amsterdam 1998

NIEKERK Maurits 1871-1940 **[13]**
- $827 - €817 - **£503** - FF5 357
  Interior with a Piano and Roses in a Chinese Vase Oil/canvas (80x56cm 31x22in) Amsterdam 2000
- $6 494 - €7 260 - **£4 520** - FF47 625
  Roses in a Vase Oil/board (33x24cm 12x9in) Amsterdam 2001

NIELSEN Amaldus Clarin 1838-1932 **[29]**
- $14 076 - €14 683 - **£8 880** - FF96 312
  Udenfor Oil/canvas (88x162cm 34x63in) Oslo 2000
- $10 428 - €9 070 - **£6 286** - FF59 498
  Fra Stavenes, Söndfjord Oil/panel (33x55cm 12x21in) Oslo 1998
- $5 460 - €6 492 - **£3 889** - FF42 588
  Sponga i Mandal Oil/panel (28x41cm 11x16in) Oslo 2001

NIELSEN Ejnar 1872-1956 **[25]**
- $1 665 - €1 616 - **£1 048** - FF10 597
  Opstilling med markblomster Oil/canvas (83x56cm 32x22in) Köbenhavn 1999

NIELSEN Kai 1882-1924 **[170]**
- $3 049 - €2 959 - **£1 883** - FF19 410
  Sabinerindernes rov Oil/canvas (59x59cm 23x23in) Vejle 1999
- $796 - €673 - **£475** - FF4 413
  Pige med kat Bronze (H20cm H7in) Köbenhavn 1998

NIELSEN Kay Rasmus 1886-1957 **[55]**
- $4 200 - €4 979 - **£3 059** - FF32 661
  Deserted moment Gouache/board (21x15cm 8x5in) New-York 2001

NIELSEN Kehnet 1947 **[46]**
- $1 186 - €1 273 - **£794** - FF8 353
  Figur i rum Oil/canvas (79x59cm 31x23in) Köbenhavn 2000

NIELSEN Knud 1916 **[130]**
- $4 812 - €5 366 - **£3 292** - FF35 196
  Hilsen til Botticelli Oil/canvas (130x120cm 51x47in) Köbenhavn 2000
- $1 060 - €1 075 - **£658** - FF7 053
  Komposition Oil/canvas (46x55cm 18x21in) Köbenhavn 2000

N

NIELSEN Niels Daniel XIX **[1]**
🖌 $4 260 - €4 038 - **£2 592** - FF26 487
  Skibsportraet af fregatten «Den danske Eeg»
  Gouache/paper (43x55cm 16x21in) København 1999

NIELSEN Poul 1920-1998 **[66]**
🖼 $776 - €805 - **£492** - FF5 283
  Interiør med kvinde Oil/canvas (76x40cm 29x15in)
  Viby J, Århus 2000

NIELSSEN Clementine/Clemence 1850-1911 **[8]**
🖼 $5 962 - €5 624 - **£3 716** - FF36 892
  Zwei Katzen Öl/Leinwand (64x50cm 25x19in)
  Hamburg 1999
🖼 $1 024 - €1 090 - **£648** - FF7 150
  Katze im Korb und Blumentöpfe Öl/Leinwand
  (35x44cm 13x17in) Salzburg 2000

NIEMANN A. XIX **[1]**
🖌 $4 187 - €3 953 - **£2 600** - FF225 933
  Interior of Grand Duke Constantine
  Nicholaevich's Bedroom Watercolour/paper
  (44x54cm 17x21in) London 1999

NIEMANN Edmund John 1813-1876 **[227]**
🖼 $2 600 - €2 788 - **£1 720** - FF18 286
  Welsh Landscape Oil/canvas (76x101cm 30x40in)
  New-Orleans LA 2000
🖼 $1 148 - €1 193 - **£720** - FF7 827
  View over the Swale, with Richmond Beyond
  Oil/board (20.5x31cm 8x12in) Suffolk 2000

NIEMANN Edmund John, Jnr. XIX **[12]**
🖼 $8 500 - €9 876 - **£5 973** - FF64 780
  The Castle Oil/canvas (76x127cm 29x50in) New-York
  2001

NIEMANN Edward H. XIX-XX **[115]**
🖼 $1 659 - €1 861 - **£1 150** - FF12 210
  View of a River Valley Oil/canvas (45.5x35.5cm
  17x13in) London 2000
🖼 $735 - €698 - **£450** - FF4 577
  Near Sandown, Isle of Wight Oil/board (30.5x47cm
  12x18in) London 1999

NIEMANTSVERDRIET Jan Frank 1885-1945 **[12]**
🖌 $1 590 - €1 487 - **£978** - FF9 756
  Porteurs d'eau/Mendiant Aquarelle/papier
  (23x33cm 9x12in) Bruxelles 1999

NIEMEYER Jo 1946 **[5]**
🖼 $1 932 - €2 304 - **£1 377** - FF15 110
  «Laanica» Oil/canvas (100x38x5cm 39x14x1in)
  Luzern 2000
🖼 $1 803 - €2 095 - **£1 267** - FF13 745
  «Lahti» Oil/canvas (12x80x3cm 4x31x1in) Luzern
  2001

NIEMEYER John Henry 1839-1932 **[5]**
🖼 $1 200 - €1 418 - **£850** - FF9 301
  A Path Through the Elms Oil/canvas (64x79cm
  25x31in) Boston MA 2000

NIEMEYER-HOLSTEIN Otto 1896-1984 **[48]**
🖼 $1 905 - €2 045 - **£1 275** - FF13 415
  Garten mit Blumenkübeln Oil/panel (35x48cm
  13x18in) Zwiesel 2000
🖼 $1 031 - €1 022 - **£643** - FF6 707
  Blumenstilleben Oil/panel (39.5x29.6cm 15x11in)
  Hamburg 1999
🖌 $456 - €511 - **£317** - FF3 353
  «Verschneiter Taxus» Watercolour (56x39cm
  22x15in) Berlin 2001
🖼 $159 - €179 - **£111** - FF1 173
  Tor-Mond Etching, aquatint in colors (31.5x23.5cm
  12x9in) Berlin 2001

NIEPCE DE SAINT-VICTOR Claude Félix A. 1805-
1870 **[2]**
📷 $20 668 - €19 522 - **£12 500** - FF128 055
  Portrait of Mallarmé/Portrait of a Mother and
  Child Photograph (9.5x7.5cm 3x2in) London 1999

NIEPCE Nicéphore 1765-1833 **[1]**
🖼 $36 377 - €34 358 - **£22 000** - FF225 376
  Le Cardinal d'Amboise Heliogravure (16x13cm
  6x5in) London 1999

NIERMAN Leonardo 1932 **[131]**
🖼 $1 400 - €1 351 - **£879** - FF8 860
  Biblical Fire Oil/board (91x121cm 36x48in) Chicago
  IL 1999
🖼 $800 - €792 - **£489** - FF5 192
  Magic fire Oil/masonite (29x39cm 11x15in) Delray-
  Beach FL 2000
🖼 $96 - €107 - **£64** - FF101
  Sin título Poster (59x79cm 23x31in) México 2000

NIESIOLOWSKI Tymon 1882-1965 **[32]**
🖼 $5 493 - €6 078 - **£3 817** - FF39 868
  Après le bain Huile/toile (65.5x54cm 25x21in)
  Warszawa 2001
🖌 $436 - €509 - **£306** - FF3 341
  Nature morte Aquarelle/papier (58x42cm 22x16in)
  Torun 2000

NIESSMANN Adolf 1899-? **[2]**
🖌 $978 - €1 125 - **£691** - FF7 378
  Französischer Bootshafen mit Angler Aquarell,
  Gouache/Papier (56x72cm 22x28in) Bremen 2001

NIESTLÉ Henry 1876-1966 **[28]**
🖼 $320 - €358 - **£215** - FF2 347
  Disteln im Topf Öl/Leinwand (42x34cm 16x13in)
  München 1999

NIESTLÉ Jean Bloé 1884-1942 **[2]**
🖼 $21 433 - €23 008 - **£14 346** - FF150 925
  Grasmücke in einer Brombeerhecke Öl/Leinwand
  (79.5x105.5cm 31x41in) Bremen 2000

NIETO Anselmo Miguel 1881-1964 **[21]**
🖼 $4 050 - €4 505 - **£2 775** - FF29 550
  Laura de San Telmo fumando Oleo/lienzo
  (90x66cm 35x25in) Madrid 2001
🖼 $1 417 - €1 351 - **£900** - FF8 865
  Retrato de joven Oleo/lienzo (40x29cm 15x11in)
  Madrid 1999
🖌 $353 - €348 - **£220** - FF2 285
  Retrato femenino Pastel (40x28cm 15x11in) Madrid
  1999

NIETO Rodolfo 1936-1988 **[32]**
🖼 $1 431 - €1 679 - **£1 029** - FF11 011
  Personaje Lápices de color/papel (69.5x49cm
  27x19in) México 2001
🖼 $696 - €773 - **£463** - FF5 068
  Sin título Serigrafia (84x60cm 33x23in) México 2000

NIETSCHE Paul 1885-1950 **[20]**
🖼 $1 345 - €1 444 - **£900** - FF9 473
  Nine Dahlias Oil/canvas (50.5x61cm 19x24in) London
  2000

NIEULANDT van Adriaen I 1587-1658 **[18]**
🖼 $10 532 - €11 798 - **£7 319** - FF77 391
  The Annunciation Oil/panel (106x74.5cm 41x29in)
  Amsterdam 2001
🖼 $4 636 - €4 269 - **£2 783** - FF28 000
  Guerriers sur le pont Huile/cuivre (15.5x20.5cm
  6x8in) Lyon 1999

NIEULANDT van Will. II G.Terranova 1584-1635/36 **[41]**
- $32 221 - €27 605 - **£19 369** - FF181 078
  Heroische Landschaft aus dem Albanerbergen Oil/panel (50x65cm 19x25in) Stuttgart 1998
- $32 356 - €29 995 - **£20 000** - FF196 756
  Forum, Rome with the Temple of Castor and Pollux Oil/panel (21x27.5cm 8x10in) London 1999

NIEUWENHOVEN van Willem 1879-1973 **[48]**
- $1 375 - €1 361 - **£842** - FF8 929
  Mother and Child in an Interior Lit by an Oil-lamp Oil/canvas (66x55cm 25x21in) Amsterdam 2000
- $1 335 - €1 240 - **£814** - FF8 134
  Red Roses in a ginger Jar Oil/canvas (45.5x35cm 17x13in) Amsterdam 1998

NIEUWENHUIS Theodorus 1866-1951 **[2]**
- $989 - €953 - **£615** - FF6 250
  Advertising poster for «Jacques Perk/Gedichten/2de Druk» Poster (38.2x25.8cm 15x10in) Haarlem 1999

NIEUWENHUIZEN Adrianus Wilhelmus 1814-1859 **[7]**
- $2 165 - €2 042 - **£1 342** - FF13 394
  People Attending Mass in a Church Interior Oil/panel (17.5x22cm 6x8in) Amsterdam 1999

NIEUWENHUS Jan 1922-1986 **[11]**
- $1 691 - €1 815 - **£1 131** - FF11 906
  Textiel ontwerp XVI Ballpoint pen (50x65.5cm 19x25in) Amsterdam 2000

NIEUWENHUYSE van Jean W. 1900-1980 **[9]**
- $4 921 - €5 793 - **£3 458** - FF38 000
  Bateaux sur le Bosphore Huile/toile (73x92cm 28x36in) Paris 2000

NIEUWERKERKE de Alfred Emilien 1811-1892 **[19]**
- $3 069 - €3 659 - **£2 188** - FF24 000
  Guillaume ler dit le Taciturne, prince d'Orange Bronze (H16cm H6in) Compiègne 2000

NIEWEG Jaap 1877-1955 **[73]**
- $910 - €908 - **£553** - FF5 953
  Een stilleven met een schedel en drie flessen Oil/canvas (46x55cm 18x21in) Amsterdam 2000
- $919 - €908 - **£559** - FF5 953
  The Seafront Oil/canvas (30x40cm 11x15in) Amsterdam 2000

NIGG Joseph 1782-1863 **[15]**
- $25 000 - €30 218 - **£17 455** - FF198 215
  Blumenstilleben Oil/canvas (64.5x54.5cm 25x21in) Bethesda MD 2000
- $8 890 - €10 174 - **£6 272** - FF66 738
  Blumenstrauss in Vase Öl/Kupfer (29.5x23cm 11x9in) Wien 2001
- $1 272 - €1 487 - **£906** - FF9 756
  Composition aux fleurs, fruits et insectes Aquarelle/papier (44x32cm 17x12in) Bruxelles 2001

NIGHTINGALE Basil 1864-1940 **[56]**
- $6 030 - €6 760 - **£4 289** - FF44 340
  Huntsman jumping a Stream Oil/canvas (77x127cm 30x50in) Leyburn, North Yorkshire 2001
- $1 203 - €1 190 - **£750** - FF7 809
  The Open Hunter's Plate at the Rugby Hunt Steeplechase Pencil (39.5x70.5cm 15x27in) London 1999

NIGHTINGALE Robert 1815-1895 **[22]**
- $32 012 - €30 558 - **£20 000** - FF200 450
  Miss Florence Nickalls with her Parents Mr and Mrs Tom Nickalls Oil/canvas (109x183cm 42x72in) London 1999

- $6 000 - €7 052 - **£4 159** - FF46 256
  Vandercken, Winner of the Liverpool Cup with Jeffrey up, on racecourse Oil/canvas (72x92cm 28x36in) New-York 2000

NIGRO Adolfo 1942 **[20]**
- $13 000 - €11 335 - **£7 859** - FF74 356
  Agua y raíces Oil/canvas (100x100cm 39x39in) New-York 1998
- $1 500 - €1 743 - **£1 054** - FF11 431
  Dominios naturales I y II Tinta/papel (48x66cm 18x25in) Buenos-Aires 2001

NIGRO Mario 1917-1992 **[121]**
- $5 000 - €5 183 - **£3 000** - FF34 000
  Satanico Acrilico/tela (125x100cm 49x39in) Venezia 1999
- $4 000 - €4 147 - **£2 400** - FF27 200
  Senza titolo Tempera (56x48x5cm 22x18x1in) Prato 2000
- $1 000 - €1 296 - **£750** - FF8 500
  Composizione Olio/tela (30x24cm 11x9in) Milano 2000
- $650 - €674 - **£390** - FF4 420
  Senza titolo Tecnica mista/carta (17x24cm 6x9in) Prato 1999

NIJLAND Dirk 1881-1955 **[57]**
- $495 - €499 - **£308** - FF3 274
  River Landscape with Bridge Oil/canvas/board (23.5x35.5cm 9x13in) Amsterdam 2000
- $328 - €363 - **£227** - FF2 381
  A Still Life with roses in a vase and a coffee set on a table Pastel/paper (48x38cm 18x14in) Amsterdam 2001

NIJMEGEN van Dionys 1705-1798 **[8]**
- $2 593 - €2 917 - **£1 810** - FF19 131
  Porträt des Dionys Elisasz Nijmegen, Enkel des Künstlers Oil/panel (38x30cm 14x11in) Luzern 2001

NIJMEGEN van Willem 1636-1698 **[2]**
- $8 038 - €6 843 - **£4 800** - FF44 890
  Trompe l'Oeil of an Engraved Portrait of the Painter Hendrick Goltzius Oil/canvas (87.5x76.5cm 34x30in) London 1998
- $14 178 - €15 882 - **£9 852** - FF104 181
  Engraving of a Head of a young Man hanging on a wooded Partition Oil/canvas (44x36cm 17x14in) Amsterdam 2001

NIKEL Lea 1918 **[143]**
- $14 000 - €16 597 - **£10 199** - FF108 872
  Untitled Acrylic/canvas (121x121cm 47x47in) Tel Aviv 2001
- $6 000 - €6 660 - **£4 182** - FF43 689
  Composition Acrylic/canvas (80x50cm 31x19in) Tel Aviv 2001
- $1 300 - €1 380 - **£879** - FF9 051
  Untitled Oil/paper/canvas (26x21.5cm 10x8in) Tel Aviv 2001
- $900 - €889 - **£550** - FF5 834
  Untitled Mixed media/paper (32x24cm 12x9in) Tel Aviv 2001

NIKIFOR (Epifan Drowniak) 1895-1968 **[125]**
- $590 - €552 - **£357** - FF3 619
  Street in Nomy Sacz Watercolour/panel (13.5x12.6cm 5x4in) Warszawa 1999

NIKODEM Arthur 1870-1940 **[17]**
- $21 700 - €20 348 - **£13 412** - FF133 476
  Landschaft Öl/Leinwand (50.5x54cm 19x21in) Wien 1999

$10 815 - €11 952 - **£7 500** - FF78 397
Landsxape with Crocuses/Hill Town Oil/board
(36x36cm 14x14in) London 2001

NIKOS 1930 [13]
$3 250 - €3 608 - **£2 265** - FF23 664
«Paesaggio» Oil/canvas (80x101cm 31x39in) New-York 2001

NIKUTOWSKI Arthur Johan Severin 1830-1888 [7]
$28 000 - €24 157 - **£16 892** - FF158 460
At the Fair Oil/canvas (75x102cm 29x40in) New-York 1998

NILOUSS Peter Alexandrovitch 1869-1943 [22]
$1 373 - €1 372 - **£858** - FF9 000
Femmes devant une sculpture dans un parc
Huile/toile (80.5x100cm 31x39in) Paris 1999
$393 - €457 - **£276** - FF3 000
Rue de Paris Huile/carton (15.5x22cm 6x8in) Paris 2001

NILS-UDO 1937 [7]
$388 - €366 - **£242** - FF2 400
Autel de neige Multiple (100x70cm 39x27in) Nantes 1999

NILSON Johann Esaias 1721-1788 [40]
$839 - €920 - **£569** - FF6 037
Die Anbetung der Könige Ink (11.4x7.8cm 4x3in) Berlin 2000
$175 - €204 - **£123** - FF1 341
L'Amour triomphant/Colombine se sauve du Moulin Radierung (21.5x16cm 8x6in) Berlin 2001

NILSON Severin 1846-1918 [458]
$3 958 - €3 442 - **£2 387** - FF22 579
Höbärgning Oil/canvas (96x132cm 37x51in) Stockholm 1998
$2 296 - €2 701 - **£1 664** - FF17 720
Sommarlandskap med skördeflicka Oil/canvas (48x68cm 18x26in) Stockholm 2001
$1 207 - €1 341 - **£808** - FF8 796
Gripsholms slott Oil/panel (33x24.5cm 12x9in) Stockholm 2000
$1 105 - €1 264 - **£760** - FF8 294
Mother and Child Pastel/papier (81x65cm 31x25in) Lymington 2000

NILSSON Algoth 1887-1993 [9]
$844 - €783 - **£525** - FF5 138
«Briggen Amazone av Malmö» Oil/canvas (27x40cm 10x15in) Malmö 1999

NILSSON Axel 1889-1981 [188]
$2 824 - €2 654 - **£1 702** - FF17 408
Flox och lejongap Oil/canvas (75x60cm 29x23in) Stockholm 1999
$2 224 - €2 581 - **£1 535** - FF16 929
Alhommor Oil/panel (27x42cm 10x16in) Stockholm 2000
$900 - €874 - **£555** - FF5 732
Vy över Stockholm Pastel/paper (23x36cm 9x14in) Stockholm 1999

NILSSON Ernst 1892-1937 [86]
$229 - €212 - **£140** - FF1 391
Slottet och svandammen Woodcut (23x17cm 9x6in) Uppsala 1999

NILSSON Gunnar 1904-1995 [14]
$1 465 - €1 642 - **£1 021** - FF10 770
Stående flicka Bronze (H56cm H22in) Stockholm 2001

NILSSON Johan Alfred 1864-1942 [3]
$1 685 - €1 621 - **£1 040** - FF10 631
Köpenhamnsfärjan Malmö Gouache/paper (28x43cm 11x16in) Malmö 1999

NILSSON Karl-Gustaf 1942 [53]
$1 413 - €1 195 - **£844** - FF7 840
Utan titel Oil/panel (41x100cm 16x39in) Stockholm 1998
$687 - €810 - **£483** - FF5 313
Färgbygge Gouache/paper (48x80cm 18x31in) Malmö 2000

NILSSON Lars 1956 [21]
$586 - €657 - **£408** - FF4 308
Dandy Mixed media (71x49cm 27x19in) Stockholm 2001
$1 668 - €1 935 - **£1 151** - FF12 696
Madonna Mixed media/paper (109x80cm 42x31in) Stockholm 2000

NILSSON Nils 1901-1949 [82]
$1 485 - €1 273 - **£892** - FF8 348
Hovs hallar, utsikt från konstnärens ateljé Oil/canvas (79x95cm 31x37in) Uppsala 1998

NILSSON Olof Walfrid 1868-1956 [75]
$1 432 - €1 394 - **£882** - FF9 146
Smedjan, älvlandskap i vinterskrud Värmland Oil/canvas (63x78cm 24x30in) Stockholm 1999

NILSSON Vera 1888-1979 [89]
$5 771 - €5 423 - **£3 478** - FF35 574
Palmer Oil/canvas (57x60cm 22x23in) Stockholm 1999
$2 618 - €2 569 - **£1 623** - FF16 854
Flicka på pall Oil/paper (31x19cm 12x7in) Stockholm 1999
$313 - €264 - **£185** - FF1 730
Sovande flicka Pencil/paper (29x18cm 11x7in) Stockholm 1999

NILSSON Wiwen 1897-1974 [2]
$10 836 - €10 419 - **£6 687** - FF68 346
Komposition Sculpture (H53cm H20in) Malmö 1999

NILUS Petr Alexandrovich 1869-1943 [22]
$6 156 - €7 327 - **£4 400** - FF48 062
An Evening Rendez vous in the park Oil/canvas (63x91cm 24x35in) London 2000
$4 000 - €3 971 - **£2 500** - FF26 051
Girl on a Terrace overlooking the Sea Oil/panel (34.5x44cm 13x17in) London 1999

NINAS Paul 1903-1964 [8]
$2 000 - €2 357 - **£1 405** - FF15 463
Abstract with Fowl and Nude Oil/panel (30x40cm 12x16in) New-Orleans LA 2000

NINNES Bernard 1899-1971 [47]
$480 - €479 - **£300** - FF3 144
Figures Driving Horse, and Cart in Moorland Landscape Oil/canvas (63x76cm 25x30in) Rotherham 1999

NINO Carmelo 1951 [15]
$3 060 - €2 881 - **£1 980** - FF18 900
Sin título, figuras Oleo/lienzo (120x99.5cm 47x39in) Caracas 1999
$967 - €1 067 - **£655** - FF7 000
«La Réserve de Nice grand restaurant sur la mer» Affiche couleur (80x118cm 31x46in) Nice 2000

NIPON PRITAKOMOL 1932 [9]
$2 805 - €3 017 - **£1 881** - FF19 789
Nude Acrylic/canvas (79x59cm 31x23in) Bangkok 2000

$1 869 - €1 736 - **£1 155** - FF11 389
Rural Scene Acrylic/board (25.5x35.5cm 10x13in)
Bangkok 1999

$1 020 - €1 097 - **£684** - FF7 196
The Buddha Among Ruins Watercolour/paper
(38x28cm 14x11in) Bangkok 2000

NISBET Noel Laura 1887-1956 [45]

$421 - €501 - **£300** - FF3 288
Birth of Draupadi Ink (53.5x40.5cm 21x15in)
London 2000

NISBET Pollok Sinclair 1848-1922 [42]

$1 363 - €1 533 - **£950** - FF10 059
Calla St.Anna, Toledo Oil/canvas (56x35.5cm
22x13in) Edinburgh 2001

$560 - €626 - **£380** - FF4 108
At the Well Granada Oil/canvas (24.5x19cm 9x7in)
Edinburgh 2001

NISBET Robert Buchan 1857-1942 [25]

$2 099 - €2 498 - **£1 500** - FF16 389
Sunset in the Bay Oil/canvas (35.5x45.5cm 13x17in)
London 2000

$1 657 - €1 430 - **£1 000** - FF9 380
A scottish Harbour Oil/panel (25.5x36cm 10x14in)
London 1998

$844 - €812 - **£520** - FF5 324
Near Abinger, Surrey Watercolour (19x33.5cm
7x13in) London 1999

NISBET Robert Hogg 1879-1961 [63]

$2 300 - €1 961 - **£1 366** - FF13 001
Lake Landscape with Fisherman in Boat Oil/canvas (45x61cm 18x24in) Hatfield PA 1998

$800 - €880 - **£555** - FF5 774
Macedonia Brook Oil/canvas/board (25x20cm
10x8in) Delray-Beach FL 2001

NISBET Tom 1909 [36]

$519 - €485 - **£320** - FF3 183
Canal Side Watercolour/paper (38x28cm 14x11in) Co.
Kilkenny 1999

NISBET Veronica 1887-? [4]

$3 019 - €2 892 - **£1 900** - FF18 968
The Seven Cosolations Watercolour (34x69cm
13x27in) Sighthill 1999

NISHIMURA Shigenobu XVIII [1]

$7 000 - €8 209 - **£4 995** - FF53 846
**Portrait of the Actor Bando Hikosaburo I
Removing his Grey Wig** Print in colors (30.5x15cm
12x5in) New-York 2000

NISHIZAWA Luis 1920 [26]

$4 183 - €4 907 - **£3 009** - FF32 186
Los volcanes desde el mirador Oleo/lienzo
(15x33cm 5x12in) México 2001

$842 - €842 - **£514** - FF5 521
Iztaccíhuatl Grabado (54x80cm 21x31in) México
2000

NISS Thorvald 1842-1905 [146]

$1 005 - €1 073 - **£669** - FF7 036
Efterårslandskab, solen bryder gennem skyerne Oil/canvas (80x97cm 31x38in) Köbenhavn 2000

$457 - €444 - **£282** - FF2 911
Sejlbåde ved bådebro Oil/canvas (36x23cm 14x9in)
Vejle 1999

NISSL Rudolf 1870-1955 [31]

$1 704 - €1 789 - **£1 152** - FF11 738
Sitzender weiblicher Akt Öl/Leinwand (58x72cm
22x28in) Kempten 2001

NISTRI Giuliano 1926 [8]

$1 211 - €1 255 - **£726** - FF8 234
«My Fair Lady» Affiche couleur (198x140cm
77x55in) Torino 2000

NISTRI Lorenzo, Enzo 1923 [8]

$303 - €315 - **£182** - FF2 063
«Il servo» Affiche couleur (140x100cm 55x39in)
Torino 2000

NITSCH Hermann 1938 [284]

$18 474 - €20 580 - **£12 087** - FF134 994
Schütt-Bild mit Malhemd Acrylic (200.5x300cm
78x118in) München 2000

$2 691 - €2 543 - **£1 676** - FF16 684
Ohne Titel Mixed media (68.5x65cm 26x25in) Wien
1999

$603 - €562 - **£364** - FF3 689
Schüttbild mit Resten organischer Fasern Acryl
(29.5x21cm 11x8in) Hamburg 1999

$1 742 - €1 817 - **£1 097** - FF11 917
Ohne Titel Felt pen (52.5x44cm 20x17in) Wien 2000

$483 - €487 - **£301** - FF3 193
Entwurf einer unterirdischen Stadt Sérigraphie
(161x396cm 63x155in) Zürich 2000

NITSCH Richard 1866-1945 [25]

$2 101 - €2 269 - **£1 452** - FF14 883
An old Lady in Local costume with a Songbook
Oil/panel (93.5x64cm 36x25in) Amsterdam 2001

$1 008 - €1 125 - **£678** - FF7 378
Ein alter Bauer/Eine alte pommersche Bäuerin
Oil/panel (18.4x13.8cm 7x5in) Köln 2000

NITSCHE Erik 1908-1998 [5]

$925 - €885 - **£580** - FF5 802
«General Dynamics, the Energetic Sea» Poster
(127x90cm 50x35in) London 1999

NITSCHE Julius Edmond Robert 1882-1965 [1]

$2 400 - €2 272 - **£1 490** - FF14 902
«Grosse Allgemeine Hunde Ausstelung» Poster
(85x67cm 33x26in) New-York 1999

NITSCHKE Detlev 1934 [5]

$3 291 - €3 068 - **£2 031** - FF20 123
Viktualienmarkt Oil/panel (22.5x28cm 8x11in)
Bremen 1999

NITZSCHKE Ludwig 1822-1850 [5]

$5 215 - €6 135 - **£3 681** - FF40 245
Gehöft im Plauenschen Grund bei Dresden
Öl/Leinwand (68x99cm 26x38in) Köln 2001

NIVA Jussi 1966 [1]

$1 370 - €1 528 - **£952** - FF10 024
Untitled Color lithograph (51x52cm 20x20in)
Stockholm 2001

NIVARD Charles François 1739-1821 [7]

$3 847 - €4 116 - **£2 535** - FF27 000
Paysage au château Huile/toile (38x46cm 14x18in)
Roquevaire 2000

NIVELT Roger R. 1899-1962 [51]

$22 218 - €24 544 - **£15 407** - FF161 000
Chasseurs de panthère Huile/panneau (129x94.5cm
50x37in) Boulogne-sur-Seine 2001

$2 343 - €2 287 - **£1 483** - FF15 000
«Le chef féticheur Bagondo» Huile/toile (60x81cm
23x31in) Calais 1999

$834 - €762 - **£510** - FF5 000
**Portrait de femme Lobi/Chasseur à l'arc Lobi,
Haute Volta** Lavis (52.5x34.5cm 20x13in) Paris 1999

NIVIAKSIAK 1908-1959 [3]
📖 **$2 246** - €2 622 - **£1 539** - FF17 202
The Archer Gravure (59x30cm 23x11in) Montréal 2000

NIVOULIES de PIERREFORT Marie-Anne 1879-1968 [16]
📖 **$3 894** - €3 364 - **£1 947** - FF22 066
Scorcio di giardino/Statua e giardino Olio/tela (40x35cm 15x13in) Milano 1999

NIXON John Nixion c.1760-1818 [48]
✎ **$1 405** - €1 225 - **£849** - FF8 036
Spectators in a Carriage at Brighton Races, Sussex Watercolour (9.5x13cm 3x5in) London 1998
📖 **$4 216** - €4 079 - **£2 600** - FF26 759
Country Dance (published London William Holland 1789) Etching in colors (37.5x237cm 14x93in) London 1999

NIXON Kay 1895-1988 [35]
✎ **$430** - €480 - **£300** - FF3 151
Leopard in a Tree with Gazelle beyond Gouache/paper (51x36cm 20x14in) Bath 2001

NIXON Mima XIX-XX [4]
✎ **$383** - €425 - **£260** - FF2 785
Arab Market Scene Watercolour/paper (26x18cm 10x7in) Lymington 2000

NIXON Nicholas 1947 [34]
📷 **$849** - €941 - **£576** - FF6 171
View of Boston and Cambridge from Boston University Gelatin silver print (20.3x25.2cm 7x9in) Berlin 2000

NIZZOLI Marcello 1887-1969 [8]
📖 **$799** - €908 - **£555** - FF5 953
«Bergamo» Poster (70x100.5cm 27x39in) Hoorn 2001

NOACK Auguste 1822-1905 [3]
☞ **$4 502** - €5 113 - **£3 149** - FF33 539
Die Traumdeutung des ägyptischen Josef im Gefängnis Öl/Leinwand (98x112cm 38x44in) München 2001

NOAILLY Francisque 1855-1942 [6]
☞ **$118** - €137 - **£84** - FF900
La fontaine Huile/toile/carton (30x20cm 11x7in) Senlis 2001

NOAK Helene 1864-1895 [2]
☞ **$1 639** - €1 671 - **£1 025** - FF10 964
Stiefmütterchen in einer Schale Öl/Karton (25x36cm 9x14in) Wien 2000

NOAKOWSKI Stanislaw 1867-1928 [9]
✎ **$768** - €703 - **£468** - FF4 614
Gothic Church Indian ink (35x25.5cm 13x10in) Warszawa 1999

NØBBE Jacob 1850-1919 [12]
☞ **$1 643** - €1 841 - **£1 141** - FF12 074
Landschaft mit Steinbrücke, Boot im Schilf, Weiden und Erlen Öl/Leinwand (45x32cm 17x12in) Oersberg-bei Kappeln 2001

NOBELE de Henry A. 1820-1870 [7]
☞ **$1 157** - €1 091 - **£717** - FF7 154
La bataille Huile/panneau (61x56cm 24x22in) Antwerpen 1999

NOBILLET Auguste Michel 1850-1914 [6]
☞ **$34 000** - €31 846 - **£20 903** - FF208 899
In the Greenhouse Oil/canvas (118x161cm 46x63in) New-York 1999

NOBLE Edwin XIX-XX [8]
✎ **$470** - €549 - **£330** - FF3 600
Changing Pasture Watercolour (33x35.5cm 12x13in) Crewkerne, Somerset 2000

NOBLE James 1919-1989 [33]
☞ **$690** - €656 - **£420** - FF4 302
The Nautilus Oil/canvas (25.5x31cm 10x12in) London 1999

NOBLE James Campbell 1846-1913 [48]
☞ **$2 841** - €2 947 - **£1 800** - FF19 331
Coldingham Old Harbour Oil/canvas (59x110.5cm 23x43in) Penzance, Cornwall 2000
☞ **$2 377** - €2 470 - **£1 500** - FF16 202
Kirkaldy Harbour Oil/canvas (30.5x51cm 12x20in) London 2001

NOBLE John Sargent 1848-1896 [42]
☞ **$124 238** - €148 525 - **£85 363** - FF974 263
A Christmas Carol Oil/canvas (138x152cm 54x59in) Billingshurst, West-Sussex 2000
☞ **$28 000** - €29 103 - **£17 645** - FF190 906
The Sportsman's Friends Oil/canvas (64x76.5cm 25x30in) New-York 2000
✎ **$867** - €825 - **£550** - FF5 414
The Fallen Stag Watercolour (39.5x53.5cm 15x21in) Billingshurst, West-Sussex 1999

NOBLE Matthew 1818-1876 [11]
🏺 **$727** - €827 - **£511** - FF5 428
Figure of Purity Ceramic (H43.5cm H17in) Woollahra, Sydney 2001

NOBLE Paul 1963 [2]
✎ **$6 873** - €7 378 - **£4 600** - FF48 399
Paul's Palace Pencil/paper (167.5x150cm 65x59in) London 2000

NOBLE Richard Pratchett act.c.1829-c.1861 [18]
✎ **$866** - €820 - **£540** - FF5 378
Landscape with Cottage Watercolour (58x38cm 22x14in) Leicestershire 1999

NOBLE Robert 1857-1917 [52]
☞ **$1 629** - €1 817 - **£1 100** - FF11 920
Figures by The Tyne, East Lothian Oil/canvas (69x89cm 27x35in) Edinburgh 2000
☞ **$590** - €659 - **£400** - FF4 324
Cottage at Polwarth Oil/board (27x35cm 10x13in) Edinburgh 2000

NOBLE Thomas Satterwhite 1835-1907 [11]
☞ **$17 000** - €18 605 - **£11 726** - FF122 039
View of Gravesand Bay Waterfront Oil/canvas (45.5x35.5cm 17x13in) New-York 2001

NOCI Arturo 1874-1953 [16]
☞ **$8 800** - €11 403 - **£6 600** - FF74 800
Tornando dall'orto Olio/tela (113.5x101cm 44x39in) Milano 2000
✎ **$1 800** - €2 098 - **£1 261** - FF13 765
Child with Grapes Pastel/paper (87x60cm 34x24in) Cleveland OH 2000

NOCKEN Wilhelm Theodor 1830-1905 [57]
☞ **$1 189** - €1 090 - **£727** - FF7 150
Aufziehendes Unwetter Öl/Leinwand (47.5x67cm 18x26in) Wien 1999

NODE-VERAN Charles 1811-1886 **[3]**
- **$129 648** - €120 823 - **£80 000** - FF792 544
  Roses, Tulips, Morning Glory, Delphinium and Primrose Peerless Oil/panel (46.5x37cm 18x14in) London 1999

NOÉ Luis Felipe 1933 **[17]**
- **$40 000** - €38 517 - **£24 896** - FF252 652
  «Eroticón» Mixed media/canvas (140x117cm 55x46in) New-York 1999

NOEH Anna T. 1926 **[67]**
- **$387** - €322 - **£227** - FF2 114
  Cleaning the Sealskin Huile/carton/toile (30.5x40.5cm 12x15in) Montréal 1998

NOËL Alexandre Jean 1752-1834 **[42]**
- **$76 800** - €72 078 - **£46 800** - FF472 800
  Vista del Puerto de Cartagena Oleo/lienzo (60x73cm 23x28in) Madrid 1999
- **$8 099** - €9 081 - **£5 500** - FF59 568
  Paris, a View of the Pantheon/Paris, a View of Les Invalides Oil/canvas (16x21.5cm 6x8in) London 2000
- **$6 000** - €5 216 - **£3 631** - FF34 215
  Mountainous Landscape with Fishermen in the foreground Watercolour/paper (34x53cm 13x20in) New-York 1999

NOEL Edmé Antony, Tony 1845-1909 **[9]**
- **$6 030** - €6 760 - **£4 200** - FF44 340
  Les gladiateurs (the gladiators) Bronze (H47cm H18in) London 2001

NOEL Georges 1924 **[172]**
- **$4 241** - €4 116 - **£2 640** - FF27 000
  Hola, Monet Technique mixte/toile (97x130cm 38x51in) Paris 1999
- **$2 613** - €2 744 - **£1 647** - FF18 000
  Palimpseste efface Technique mixte (50x65cm 19x25in) Paris 2000
- **$1 268** - €1 372 - **£868** - FF9 000
  Composition Encre (54x76cm 21x29in) Paris 2001

NOËL Guy-Gérard XX **[40]**
- **$255** - €244 - **£159** - FF1 600
  «Fahrenheit 451» Affiche couleur (120x160cm 47x62in) Paris 1999

NOEL John Bates XIX-XX **[117]**
- **$1 142** - €1 187 - **£720** - FF7 789
  Bracebridge Pool, Sutton Park Oil/canvas (45.5x35.5cm 17x13in) Cirencester, Gloucesterhire 2000
- **$727** - €730 - **£500** - FF5 706
  Beach Scenes with fishing Smacks and Figures Oil/canvas (40x30cm 16x12in) Carmarthen, Wales 2000
- **$407** - €397 - **£269** - FF2 602
  Kempsey Common Pencil (35.5x45cm 13x17in) London 1999

NOEL Jules Achille 1815-1881 **[391]**
- **$8 236** - €8 842 - **£5 510** - FF58 000
  Le produit de la pêche sur la grève Huile/toile (54x38cm 21x14in) Granville 2000
- **$5 259** - €5 107 - **£3 249** - FF33 500
  La descente des vaches vers la rivière Huile/toile (32.5x46.5cm 12x18in) Melun 1999
- **$764** - €701 - **£469** - FF4 642
  Pêcheur en barque/Paysannes près de la vieille tour Mine plomb (13x21cm 5x8in) Paris 1999

NOËL Léon 1807-1884 **[20]**
- **$158** - €183 - **£110** - FF1 200
  Une tireuse de cartes, d'après Marguerite Gérard Lithographie (32x26cm 12x10in) Paris 2001

NOëL Louis 1839-1925 **[7]**
- **$820** - €861 - **£544** - FF5 650
  Pêcheur au bord d'un étang Huile/toile (65x53cm 25x20in) Quimper 2000

NOEL Martin 1956 **[16]**
- **$114** - €128 - **£75** - FF838
  Bebeto Woodcut in colors (50x40cm 19x15in) Köln 2000

NOEL Peter Paul Joseph 1789-1822 **[5]**
- **$6 500** - €6 738 - **£3 900** - FF44 200
  Scena di mercato Olio/tavola (44x53.5cm 17x21in) Venezia 2000
- **$2 304** - €2 147 - **£1 421** - FF14 086
  Der ungebetene Gast Pencil (28.5x34.5cm 11x13in) Köln 1999

NOEL Pol XX **[21]**
- **$748** - €717 - **£461** - FF4 700
  Les quais à Quimper Huile/toile (30x65cm 11x25in) La Varenne-Saint-Hilaire 1999

NOEL R. XIX **[1]**
- **$2 665** - €2 744 - **£1 679** - FF18 000
  La Bretagne, le jour de la fête de la République Aquarelle, gouache/papier (47x71cm 18x27in) Paris 2000

NOELSMITH Thomas ?-1900 **[43]**
- **$600** - €508 - **£358** - FF3 335
  Cottage scene with woman picking flowers, chickens on road, church Watercolour/board (25x35cm 10x14in) Asheville NC 1998

NOERR Julius 1827-1897 **[40]**
- **$3 235** - €3 068 - **£1 968** - FF20 123
  Lagernde Bauernfamilie am Dachauer Moos Öl/Leinwand (45x76cm 17x29in) Köln 1999
- **$3 682** - €3 835 - **£2 333** - FF25 154
  Ein Bauer und sein Sohn beim Pflügen oberhalb eines Gebirgssees Öl/Leinwand (29x39cm 11x15in) München 2000

NOGARI Giuseppe 1699-1763 **[36]**
- **$163 180** - €151 690 - **£100 000** - FF995 020
  Equestrian Portrait of Field Marshal Count J.M. von der Schulenburg Oil/canvas (198x143.5cm 77x56in) London 1998
- **$7 093** - €7 662 - **£4 903** - FF50 259
  Portrait de vieillard Huile/toile (53.5x43.5cm 21x17in) Warszawa 2001
- **$17 493** - €15 112 - **£8 746** - FF99 127
  Ritratto di vecchia Pastelli/carta (58x42cm 22x16in) Milano 1999

NOGARI Paris c.1536-1601 **[1]**
- **$32 500** - €33 691 - **£19 500** - FF221 000
  Matrimonio mistico di santa Caterina Olio/rame (29.5x24cm 11x9in) Milano 2000

NOGARO Carlo 1837-1961 **[3]**
- **$2 500** - €2 592 - **£1 500** - FF17 000
  Il gatto e l'uccellino Olio/tela (25x46cm 9x18in) Vercelli 1999

NOGUCHI Isamu 1904-1988 **[87]**
- **$115 000** - €133 433 - **£79 396** - FF875 265
  Dress, Cave of the Heart Bronze (228.5x203.5x51cm 89x80x20in) New-York 2000
- **$50 000** - €58 092 - **£35 140** - FF381 060
  Untitled Relief (45.5x174cm 17x68in) New-York 2001
- **$4 250** - €3 626 - **£2 533** - FF23 785
  Female Nude Ink (49.5x58.5cm 19x23in) New-York 1998

N

NOGUES Xavier 1873-1940 **[12]**
- **$18 300** - €18 019 - **£11 400** - FF118 200
  Chica de la sombrilla Oleo/tabla (27x35cm 10x13in)
  Barcelona 1999
- **$441** - €420 - **£273** - FF2 758
  Cazadores con su jauría Aguafuerte (15.5x22cm
  6x8in) Barcelona 1999

NOIRDEMANGE XVIII **[1]**
- **$10 934** - €11 739 - **£7 315** - FF77 000
  **Vive l'Amour, enfants encadrant l'autel de
  l'Amour** Miniature (12.5x11cm 4x4in) Paris 2000

NOIRÉ Maxime 1861-1927 **[153]**
- **$2 048** - €1 982 - **£1 263** - FF13 000
  Route de Laghouart Huile/toile (32x70cm 12x27in)
  Paris 1999
- **$849** - €991 - **£590** - FF6 500
  El-Abiod, Biskra Huile/toile (27x46.5cm 10x18in)
  Paris 2000

NOIROT Émile 1853-1924 **[132]**
- **$1 927** - €2 134 - **£1 307** - FF14 000
  La gardienne de dindons Huile/toile (61x45cm
  24x17in) Lyon 2000
- **$1 422** - €1 601 - **£979** - FF10 500
  Coin de mare en Forez Huile/toile (25x18cm 9x7in)
  Lyon 2000
- **$579** - €640 - **£401** - FF4 200
  Mare dans un bois Fusain (21x30.5cm 8x12in) Lyon
  2001

NOIROT Louis 1820-1902 **[8]**
- **$961** - €1 143 - **£685** - FF7 500
  Au Perron, près de Villerest, Loire Huile/toile
  (55x37.5cm 21x14in) Grenoble 2000

NOIZEUX Henri 1871-? **[25]**
- **$269** - €259 - **£166** - FF1 700
  Pouldavid Aquarelle/papier (13.5x30.5cm 5x12in) Le
  Havre 1999

NOLAN Sidney Robert 1917-1992 **[1024]**
- **$24 263** - €21 156 - **£14 671** - FF138 776
  Horse Oil/board (140.5x99.5cm 55x39in) Melbourne
  1998
- **$6 606** - €7 286 - **£4 474** - FF47 792
  African Head - African Series Oil/board
  (124x93.5cm 48x36in) Woollahra, Sydney 2000
- **$2 717** - €2 580 - **£1 695** - FF16 924
  Hidra Oil/paper/board (25x30.5cm 9x12in) Sydney
  1999
- **$2 173** - €1 852 - **£1 294** - FF12 147
  Central Australia Mixed media/paper (51x76cm
  20x29in) Sydney 1998
- **$406** - €482 - **£286** - FF3 159
  Salome Serigraph in colors (81x61cm 31x24in)
  Sydney 2000

NOLAND Cady 1956 **[23]**
- **$6 348** - €6 098 - **£3 936** - FF40 000
  Trashed Mailbox Métal (51x61x41cm 20x24x16in)
  Paris 1999
- **$2 250** - €2 611 - **£1 553** - FF17 124
  Lincoln Years Silkscreen (123x305cm 48x120in)
  New-York 2000

NOLAND Kenneth 1924 **[246]**
- **$50 000** - €48 051 - **£30 800** - FF315 195
  Via Media (Suddenly) Acrylic/canvas (259x330cm
  101x129in) New-York 1999
- **$13 000** - €14 039 - **£8 984** - FF92 090
  «Eastline» Acrylic/canvas (15x175cm 5x68in) New-
  York 2001

$4 000 - €4 077 - **£2 506** - FF26 746
  Job Oil/masonite (89.5x14.5cm 35x5in) New-York
  2000
- **$1 442** - €1 695 - **£1 000** - FF11 120
  Untitled Gouache/paper (24x33cm 9x12in) London
  2000
- **$2 200** - €2 361 - **£1 472** - FF15 490
  Circle I Series, from Handmade Paper Project
  Print in colors (50.5x40.5cm 19x15in) Beverly-Hills CA
  2000

NOLAU François Joseph 1804-1883 **[6]**
- **$3 432** - €3 811 - **£2 392** - FF25 000
  Arc de Triomphe près d'un palais Aquarelle/papier
  (21x26cm 8x10in) Paris 2001

NOLDE Emil Hansen 1867-1956 **[1035]**
- **$723 114** - €593 955 - **£420 000** - FF3 896 088
  Junges Paar Oil/canvas (53.5x63.5cm 21x25in)
  London 1998
- **$72 913** - €86 921 - **£51 986** - FF570 163
  Vase mit Rosen Öl/Leinwand (44x27.5cm 17x10in)
  Berlin 2000
- **$69 489** - €64 908 - **£42 000** - FF425 766
  Marschlandschaft mit Windmühle
  Watercolour/paper (25x35cm 9x13in) London 1999
- **$5 403** - €6 135 - **£3 698** - FF40 246
  Frau N., Frau Ada Nolde Drypoint (50.5x39.7cm
  19x15in) Hamburg 2000

NOLET A. XIX **[11]**
- **$2 815** - €2 592 - **£1 689** - FF17 000
  Village du Nord au bord de la mer Huile/toile
  (92x73cm 36x28in) Marseille 1999

NÖLKEN Franz 1884-1918 **[35]**
- **$10 338** - €10 226 - **£6 446** - FF67 078
  Landschaft mit Lorenzug Öl/Leinwand (44x
  56.6x45cm 22x17in) Berlin 1999
- **$15 697** - €17 384 - **£10 645** - FF114 032
  Frauen mit rotem Schirm am Ostseestrand
  Öl/Karton (31.5x39.8cm 12x15in) Hamburg 2000
- **$792** - €869 - **£538** - FF5 701
  Stehender weiblicher Akt Watercolour
  (39.5x26.4cm 15x10in) Berlin 2000
- **$298** - €256 - **£179** - FF1 676
  Max Reger (VII) Radierung (23.6x28.8cm 9x11in)
  Hamburg 1998

NOLL Alexandre 1890-1970 **[38]**
- **$1 207** - €1 372 - **£847** - FF9 000
  Sans titre Huile/panneau (41x27cm 16x10in) Paris
  2001
- **$5 440** - €6 098 - **£3 804** - FF40 000
  Hippopotame Sculpture bois (H11cm H4in) Paris
  2001

NOLLÉ Lambert XIX **[2]**
- **$9 814** - €9 452 - **£6 094** - FF62 000
  Paris, l'église et le boulevard de la Madeleine
  Huile/toile (55.5x79.5cm 21x31in) Paris 1999

NOLLEKENS Jan 1695-1783 **[2]**
- **$6 000** - €7 775 - **£4 500** - FF51 000
  Tre giocatori di carte in un interno Olio/tela
  (38x40cm 14x15in) Roma 2001

NOLLET Paul 1911-1996 **[72]**
- **$1 406** - €1 189 - **£840** - FF7 800
  Nu au guéridon Huile/toile (150x140cm 59x55in)
  Liège 1998
- **$468** - €396 - **£280** - FF2 600
  «Fillette au bouquet» Huile/panneau (90.5x79cm
  35x31in) Liège 1998

NOLLI Giovanni Battista 1692-1756 **[6]**
- 📖 $424 - €492 - **£293** - FF3 230
  Roma Kupferstich (40.8x68.6cm 16x27in) Luzern 2000

NOLPE Pieter c.1613-c.1652 **[9]**
- ✏️ $5 286 - €4 359 - **£3 114** - FF28 596
  Flusslandschaft mit einem Schloss und Booten Öl/Leinwand (30x36.5cm 11x14in) Wien 1998

NOLTEE Cornelis, Cor 1903-1967 **[379]**
- ✏️ $1 325 - €1 363 - **£836** - FF8 943
  Jeune fille à la poupée Huile/toile (80x80cm 31x31in) Antwerpen 2000
- ✏️ $559 - €635 - **£386** - FF4 167
  Boerenpaard op het land Oil/board (25x39cm 9x15in) Dordrecht 2000
- ✏️ $79 - €91 - **£55** - FF595
  Café Felt pen/paper (9x14cm 3x5in) Dordrecht 2000

NOMÉ, MONSU DESIDERIO François c.1593-c.1640 **[20]**
- ✏️ $18 525 - €19 521 - **£11 700** - FF128 050
  El Colíseo de Roma Oleo/lienzo (120x194cm 47x76in) Madrid 2000
- ✏️ $11 808 - €12 501 - **£7 814** - FF82 000
  Paysages avec ruines Huile/toile (34x55cm 13x21in) Madrid 2000

NOMELLINI Plinio 1866-1943 **[50]**
- ✏️ $72 000 - €93 299 - **£54 000** - FF612 000
  Il polledro Olio/tela (163x125.5cm 64x49in) Milano 2001
- ✏️ $22 800 - €19 696 - **£15 200** - FF129 200
  «Filari di olivi» Olio/tela (36x69cm 14x27in) Roma 1998
- ✏️ $9 500 - €9 848 - **£5 700** - FF64 600
  Marina Olio/tavola (24x33cm 9x12in) Roma 2000
- ✏️ $4 920 - €4 353 - **£3 280** - FF27 880
  Maestrale Elbano Acquarello/carta (65x96cm 25x37in) Firenze 1998
- 📖 $2 800 - €2 389 - **£1 689** - FF15 668
  «Oli Sasso» Poster (136.5x197cm 53x77in) New-York 1998

NONELL Y MONTURIOL Isidro 1872-1911 **[41]**
- ✏️ $179 200 - €192 208 - **£118 400** - FF1 260 800
  Gitana de perfil Oleo/cartón (50x40.5cm 19x15in) Madrid 2000
- ✏️ $6 160 - €6 607 - **£4 070** - FF43 340
  Mendigo Técnica mixta/cartón (41x32cm 16x12in) Madrid 2000
- ✏️ $4 615 - €3 904 - **£2 730** - FF25 610
  Dos mujeres hablando Lápiz/papel (48x31cm 18x12in) Madrid 1998

NONN Carl 1876-1949 **[23]**
- ✏️ $1 522 - €1 687 - **£1 056** - FF11 067
  «Wolkenschatten» Öl/Leinwand (50x61cm 19x24in) Köln 2001

NONNENBRUCH Max 1857-1922 **[14]**
- ✏️ $8 596 - €8 366 - **£5 292** - FF54 878
  Kvinna vid svandamm Oil/canvas (122x87cm 48x34in) Stockholm 1999

NONO Luigi 1850-1918 **[12]**
- ✏️ $31 000 - €32 136 - **£18 600** - FF210 800
  Paesaggio di campagna Olio/tela (32x56cm 12x22in) Milano 2000

NONOTTE Donat, Donatien 1708-1785 **[21]**
- ✏️ $30 000 - €29 986 - **£18 327** - FF196 695
  Portrait of the Marquise de Gast Oil/canvas (100.5x80.5cm 39x31in) New-York 2000

NOORDE van Cornelis 1731-1795 **[17]**
- ✏️ $1 251 - €1 452 - **£864** - FF9 525
  Fishermen Loading their Catch on a Cart on the Beach at Katwijk aan Black chalk (16x23.5cm 6x9in) Amsterdam 2000

NOORDIJK Willem 1887-1970 **[55]**
- ✏️ $698 - €817 - **£499** - FF5 357
  View of Amersfoort in Winter» Oil/canvas (56x40cm 22x15in) Amsterdam 2001
- ✏️ $582 - €681 - **£415** - FF4 464
  Boerderij te Eemenes, Voorjaar Oil/canvas (30x40cm 11x15in) Amsterdam 2001

NOORT van Adam 1562-1641 **[5]**
- ✏️ $2 390 - €2 479 - **£1 580** - FF16 260
  La fuite en Egypte Lavis (23x17.5cm 9x6in) Bruxelles 2000

NOORT van Adrianus Cornelis 1914 **[162]**
- ✏️ $1 385 - €1 271 - **£853** - FF8 334
  The Little Indian Oil/canvas (60x41cm 23x16in) Amsterdam 1999
- ✏️ $583 - €545 - **£354** - FF3 577
  Strandgezicht te zandvoort Oil/panel (30x40cm 11x15in) Lokeren 1999

NOORT van Jan c.1620-c.1676 **[23]**
- ✏️ $40 000 - €35 086 - **£24 288** - FF230 152
  Cimon and Iphigenia Oil/canvas (105x149cm 41x58in) New-York 1998
- ✏️ $14 679 - €13 730 - **£9 000** - FF90 063
  A Boy, half length, Wearing a Plumed Hat, Holding a Falcon Oil/canvas (83x66.5cm 32x26in) London 1998
- 📖 $279 - €307 - **£190** - FF2 012
  Landschaft mit dem Sibyllentempel von Tivoli, nach P.Lastman Radierung (16.3x21.2cm 6x8in) Berlin 2000

NOORT van Pieter 1602-1648 **[8]**
- ✏️ $11 954 - €12 832 - **£8 000** - FF84 172
  Huntsman with dead game and a spaniel in a landscape Oil/panel (99.5x158cm 39x62in) London 2000

NOOTEBOOM Jacobus Hendricus J. 1811-1878 **[17]**
- ✏️ $3 049 - €2 632 - **£1 840** - FF17 264
  A Seascape with a Fishing Fleet Oil/canvas (17x27cm 6x10in) Amsterdam 1999

NOQUET Jean-Michel 1950 **[167]**
- ✏️ $1 333 - €1 372 - **£846** - FF9 000
  Honfleur Huile/toile (60x73cm 23x28in) Bernay 2000
- ✏️ $510 - €473 - **£317** - FF3 100
  Voile sur la Côte Huile/toile (33x41cm 12x16in) Corbeil-Essonnes 1999
- 📖 $370 - €381 - **£235** - FF2 500
  Venise Lithographie (42x54cm 16x21in) Bernay 2000

NORBERTO Proietti Norberto 1927 **[34]**
- ✏️ $6 250 - €6 479 - **£3 750** - FF42 500
  Pronto si gira Olio/tavola (50x80cm 19x31in) Roma 1999
- ✏️ $3 480 - €3 006 - **£2 320** - FF19 720
  «La stireria» Tecnica mista/tavola (30x40cm 11x15in) Roma 1998

NORBLIN DE LA GOURDAINE Jean-Pierre 1745-1830 **[104]**
- ✏️ $5 693 - €5 737 - **£3 548** - FF37 632
  Portrait einer Dame Öl/Leinwand (47x37.5cm 18x14in) Zürich 2000

N

$13 280 – €14 178 – **£9 067** – FF93 000
Jeunes femmes au bain Huile/panneau
(40.5x31.5cm 15x12in) Paris 2001
$3 475 – €3 811 – **£2 360** – FF25 000
La promenade publique Lavis (23x22.5cm 9x8in)
Paris 2000
$241 – €281 – **£168** – FF1 844
Bettler mit Hund Radierung (9.6x7.2cm 3x2in) Berlin
2000

NORBLIN DE LA GOURDAINE Sébastien 1796-
1884 **[16]**
$4 000 – €3 811 – **£2 425** – FF25 000
**Destruction d'Herculanum par l'éruption du
Vésuve en l'An 79** Huile/toile (66x97cm 25x38in)
Paris 1999
$5 227 – €5 173 – **£3 200** – FF33 933
**The Chariot of Aurora, within a decorated
mount** Watercolour (68.5x45.5cm 26x17in) London
2000

NORBLIN Stefan Juliusz 1892-1952 **[17]**
$1 310 – €1 528 – **£919** – FF10 025
Petite tête Pastel/papier (36x46cm 14x18in) Torun
2000
$425 – €461 – **£283** – FF3 022
«Wilnochemins de fer de l'état polonais» Poster
(99x61cm 39x24in) New-York 2000

NØRBYE Anna L. Vilhelmine 1851-1924 **[1]**
$4 569 – €4 088 – **£2 738** – FF26 818
Blumenstilleben Öl/Leinwand (34.5x47cm 13x18in)
Hamburg 1998

NORCIA da Paolo 1953 **[23]**
$180 – €233 – **£135** – FF1 530
Notturno Tecnica mista/tela (80x120cm 31x47in)
Vercelli 2000

NORDAHL-GROVE Fritz 1822-1885 **[92]**
$1 321 – €1 144 – **£802** – FF7 505
**«Kjaempegrav ved Jyllinde, i baggrunden
Roskilde Fjord», vinterdag** Oil/canvas (34x66cm
13x25in) København 1998
$945 – €1 005 – **£633** – FF6 593
Strandparti med fiskere ved båd Oil/wood
(29x39cm 11x15in) Viby J, Århus 2001

NORDBERG Olle 1905-1986 **[261]**
$588 – €659 – **£409** – FF4 324
**Interiör med längtande kvinna och svävande
mansfigur** Oil/canvas (38x34cm 14x18in) Landskrona
2001
$453 – €465 – **£280** – FF3 047
Man vid hus Oil/panel (32x23cm 12x9in) Stockholm
2000

NORDENBERG Bengt 1822-1902 **[112]**
$91 492 – €104 080 – **£63 902** – FF682 719
Efter björnjakten Oil/canvas (110x141cm 43x55in)
Stockholm 2000
$6 664 – €7 739 – **£4 683** – FF50 764
**«Storebror på Julbesök», motiv från Norra
Skåne** Oil/canvas (66x95cm 25x37in) Stockholm 2001
$3 142 – €3 689 – **£2 217** – FF24 195
Allmogeinteriör med familj Oil/canvas (24x31cm
9x12in) Stockholm 2000
$1 098 – €1 219 – **£735** – FF7 997
Exteriör med tre män och en häst Akvarell/papper
(26x35.5cm 10x13in) Stockholm 2000

NORDENBERG Henrik 1857-1928 **[41]**
$1 505 – €1 517 – **£938** – FF9 950
Interiör Oil/canvas (60x46cm 23x18in) Stockholm
2000

$773 – €743 – **£470** – FF4 876
Interiör med läsande man Oil/canvas (47x34cm
18x13in) Stockholm 1999

NORDENCREUTZ Brita 1899-1982 **[24]**
$301 – €312 – **£189** – FF2 045
Fiasko/Clowner Akvarell/papper (20x13cm 7x5in)
Stockholm 2000

NORDFELDT Bror Julius Olsson 1878-1955 **[81]**
$5 000 – €5 876 – **£3 466** – FF38 547
Callalilies in a Purple Vase Oil/canvas (51x40.5cm
20x15in) Beverly-Hills CA 2000
$3 300 – €3 753 – **£2 305** – FF24 618
Still Life Oil/board (30x40cm 12x16in) Mystic CT
2000
$1 400 – €1 562 – **£916** – FF10 245
Farm Scene Watercolour/paper (30x40cm 12x16in)
Chicago IL 2000
$3 250 – €3 070 – **£2 024** – FF20 140
Asian Landscape by the Sea Woodcut in colors
(32.5x25cm 12x9in) San-Francisco CA 1999

NORDGREN Anna 1847-1916 **[31]**
$1 130 – €1 286 – **£789** – FF8 438
På hemväg Oil/canvas (67x50cm 26x19in) Stockholm
2000
$673 – €731 – **£426** – FF4 798
Dam med bricka Oil/panel (28x18cm 11x7in)
Stockholm 2000

NORDGREN Axel Wilhelm 1828-1888 **[69]**
$7 140 – €7 064 – **£4 452** – FF46 334
På stranden Oil/canvas (100x135cm 39x53in)
Helsinki 1999
$1 281 – €1 486 – **£911** – FF9 750
Skymning över fiskeläge Oil/canvas (57x87cm
22x34in) Stockholm 2000

NORDIN Alice 1871-1948 **[28]**
$561 – €616 – **£362** – FF4 038
Sittande flicka Bronze (H21cm H8in) Lund 2000

NORDLING Adolf 1840-1888 **[17]**
$823 – €969 – **£596** – FF6 354
Segelskutor på upprört hav Oil/canvas/panel
(77x101cm 30x39in) Stockholm 2001
$1 074 – €1 046 – **£661** – FF6 859
**Svenska linieskeppet Stockholm utanför tra-
vemünde 1857** Oil/canvas (44x29cm 17x11in)
Stockholm 1999

NORDLUND Elin Alfhild 1861-1941 **[4]**
$4 174 – €4 709 – **£2 934** – FF30 889
Landskap i Åland, Eckerö Storby Oil/canvas
(51x101cm 20x39in) Helsinki 2001
$3 401 – €3 868 – **£2 359** – FF25 373
Posthuset på Åland Oil/canvas/panel (25x35cm
9x13in) Helsinki 2000

NORDSTRÖM Karl Fr. 1855-1923 **[71]**
$5 345 – €6 081 – **£3 733** – FF39 889
Roslagsgaten, Stockholm Oil/canvas (95x70cm
37x27in) Stockholm 2000
$300 – €335 – **£210** – FF2 198
Västgötaslätten Pastel (69x100cm 27x39in)
Köbenhavn 2001

NORDSTRÖM Lars Gunnar 1924 **[28]**
$10 159 – €11 436 – **£6 997** – FF75 017
Kontraster Oil/panel (90x140cm 35x55in) Helsinki
2000
$3 805 – €4 205 – **£2 637** – FF27 580
Komposition Acrylic/paper (89x61cm 35x24in)
Helsinki 2001

$2 943 - €3 297 - **£2 046** - FF21 624
Komposition Painting (24.5x33cm 9x12in) Stockholm 2001

$1 609 - €1 766 - **£1 036** - FF11 583
Komposition Gouache/paper (29.5x29.5cm 11x11in) Helsinki 2000

$257 - €303 - **£178** - FF1 985
Grön-svart komposition Serigraph (68x48cm 26x18in) Helsinki 2000

NORELIUS Einar 1900-1984 **[35]**
$449 - €378 - **£265** - FF2 481
Tomtenissar med paket Watercolour/paper (27x28cm 10x11in) Stockholm 1998

NORFINI Luigi 1825-1909 **[12]**
$553 - €573 - **£431** - FF3 760
Cane e beccaccina/Merlo/Capinere/Allodola Acquarello/carta (30x25cm 11x9in) Milano 1999

NØRGAARD Bjorn 1947 **[19]**
$458 - €377 - **£266** - FF2 471
Komposition Color lithograph (105x143cm 41x56in) København 1998

NØRGÅRD Lars 1956 **[43]**
$2 224 - €2 153 - **£1 371** - FF14 120
Komposition Oil/canvas (205x180cm 80x70in) København 1999

NORIE Orlando 1832-1901 **[154]**
$818 - €762 - **£504** - FF5 000
Déchargement de la charrette Aquarelle/papier (17x23.5cm 6x9in) Lille 1999

NORIERI August 1860-1898 **[4]**
$2 800 - €3 124 - **£1 832** - FF20 491
Lake Pontchartrain Oil/board (35x40cm 14x16in) Chicago IL 2000

NORLIND Ernst 1877-1952 **[37]**
$735 - €697 - **£456** - FF4 570
Flygande storkpar Oil/panel (70x61cm 27x24in) Malmö 1999

NORMAN Dorothy 1905-1997 **[25]**
$2 000 - €2 303 - **£1 475** FF15 104
Alfred Stieglitz - Hand on Coat Gelatin silver print (9.5x7.5cm 3x2in) New-York 2000

NORMAN George Parsons 1840-1914 **[15]**
$21 188 - €19 265 - **£13 000** - FF126 371
Contentment/A Corner on a Norfolk Broad Oil/canvas (71.5x127cm 28x50in) London 1999

NORMAND Alfred Nicolas 1822-1909 **[31]**
$2 043 - €2 287 - **£1 422** - FF15 000
Chapiteau à Pompei Tirage albuminé (21x15.5cm 8x6in) Paris 2001

NORMANN Adelsteen 1848-1918 **[221]**
$12 806 - €14 879 - **£9 000** - FF97 597
Over fjorden (across the fjord) Oil/canvas (112.5x150cm 44x59in) London 2001

$6 792 - €5 925 - **£4 108** - FF38 863
Fjordlandskap Oil/canvas (90x120cm 35x47in) Stockholm 1998

$1 890 - €2 247 - **£1 346** - FF14 742
Fra Nord-Norge Oil/panel (27x44cm 10x17in) Oslo 2000

NORMANN Emma Pastor 1871-1954 **[17]**
$1 500 - €1 743 - **£1 054** - FF11 431
Mountain Lake with fishing Cottages Oil/canvas (60x79cm 24x31in) New-Orleans LA 2001

$1 260 - €1 466 - **£897** - FF9 828
Et vestlandsk gårdsbruk Oil/panel (31x40cm 12x15in) Oslo 2000

NORONHA DA COSTA Luís Mário 1942 **[4]**
$4 136 - €4 686 - **£2 820** - FF30 738
Paisagem com figura feminina e vela Acrylique/toile (54x75cm 21x29in) Lisboa 2000

NOROY L. XX **[2]**
$641 - €746 - **£450** - FF4 891
«Cie.belge maritime du Congo, Thysville» Poster (100x56cm 39x22in) London 2001

NØRREGAARD Asta Eline J. 1853-1933 **[3]**
$12 300 - €10 698 - **£7 415** - FF70 177
Oppstilling med kobberfat og grønnsaker Oil/canvas (101x120cm 39x47in) Oslo 1998

NORRIE Susan 1953 **[13]**
$34 308 - €36 827 - **£22 962** - FF241 572
Objet d'Art Enamel (100x346.5cm 39x136in) Sydney 2000

$1 554 - €1 742 - **£1 087** - FF11 429
Untitled, Chairs Oil/canvas/board (16x11.5cm 6x4in) Melbourne 2001

NORRIS Joe 1925-1996 **[23]**
$1 619 - €1 889 - **£1 127** - FF12 392
Untitled Oil/panel (81.5x122cm 32x48in) Toronto 2000

$1 040 - €1 218 - **£733** - FF7 988
Untitled, Winter Village Oil/panel (30.5x40.5cm 12x15in) Calgary, Alberta 2001

NORRMAN Gunnar 1912-1996 **[50]**
$337 - €324 - **£208** - FF2 126
Träd med hus Charcoal/paper (47x25cm 18x9in) Malmö 1999

NORRMAN Herman 1864-1906 **[8]**
$1 130 - €1 286 - **£789** - FF8 438
Stilleben med kanna och glas Oil/canvas/panel (21x31cm 8x12in) Stockholm 2000

NORTH John William 1842-1924 **[23]**
$36 095 - €36 372 - **£22 500** - FF238 585
Among the galtees: Galtee Castle, County Cork, Ireland Oil/canvas (132x183cm 51x72in) London 2000

$8 823 - €8 891 - **£5 500** - FF58 324
Wooded River Valley with Bathers by a Fallen Tree Oil/canvas (67.5x97.5cm 26x38in) London 2000

$20 053 - €20 207 - **£12 500** - FF132 549
Beyond the Blue Hills, Somerset Watercolour (66x94cm 25x37in) London 2000

NORTH Noah 1809-1880 **[1]**
$12 000 - €14 103 - **£8 692** - FF92 508
Portraits Oil/panel (70x58cm 27x23in) Bolton MA 2001

NORTHCOTE H.B. XIX **[3]**
$400 - €443 - **£277** - FF2 909
Working the Lochs Oil/board (22x30cm 9x12in) St. Petersburg FL 2001

NORTHCOTE James 1746-1831 **[59]**
$15 446 - €14 260 - **£9 500** - FF93 540
Portrait of Charlotte Leycester, in a white dress, holding a ducking Oil/canvas (134.5x112cm 52x44in) London 1999

$4 010 - €4 041 - **£2 500** - FF26 509
Maternal Affection Oil/canvas (64.5x48.5cm 25x19in) London 2000

NORTHFIELD Issac James 1868-1973 **[6]**
$750 - €871 - **£526** - FF5 711
«Australia for Sunshine & Romance» Poster (49x63cm 19x25in) New-York 2000

NORTON Benjamin Cam XIX [24]
- $5 599 - €5 460 - £3 400 - FF35 812
  Voluptuary, Winner of the Grand National in 1883, with G.P.Wilson Oil/canvas (71x90cm 27x35in) London 2000

NORTON Charles William c.1870-1946 [5]
- $322 - €347 - £220 - FF2 277
  Cottage at Church Cove, the Lizard Watercolour/paper (22.5x27.5cm 8x10in) London 2001

NORTON Elizabeth 1887-? [13]
- $3 000 - €3 022 - £2 007 - FF21 123
  Cat and Dog Bookends Bronze (H16cm H6in) New-York 2000

NORTON Jim C. 1953 [7]
- $6 000 - €6 813 - £4 168 - FF44 688
  The blue Coat Oil/canvas (45x60cm 18x24in) Dallas TX 2001

NORTON Larry 1963 [4]
- $5 110 - €4 250 - £3 000 - FF27 881
  Big Beach Bums, Hippo Oil/canvas (46x62cm 18x24in) London 1998

NORTON Louis Doyle 1867-1940 [10]
- $1 000 - €1 073 - £669 - FF7 041
  On the Lock, Kennebunkport Watercolour/paper (23x35cm 9x14in) Portland ME 2000

NORTON William Edward 1843-1916 [68]
- $4 250 - €3 570 - £2 498 - FF33 418
  Gaff-Rigged Sloop in Boston Harbour Oil/canvas (39x66cm 15x26in) Bolton MA 1998
- $2 400 - €2 745 - £1 669 - FF18 008
  Three Male Figure Studies Oil/canvas (40x30cm 16x12in) Cincinnati OH 2000
- $1 600 - €1 842 - £1 091 - FF12 083
  Ships on a Beach Watercolour/paper (44x58.5cm 17x23in) New-York 2000

NORTVEDT Therese 1954 [1]
- $3 294 - €3 711 - £2 280 - FF24 342
  Dinner at eight Oil/canvas (120x90cm 47x35in) Oslo 2000

NORWELL Graham Noble 1901-1967 [192]
- $146 - €172 - £104 - FF1 125
  View of a Snow covered Bridge leading to the Village Aquarelle/papier (30.5x40.5cm 12x15in) Montréal 2000

NOSKOWIAK Sonya 1900-1975 [18]
- $7 000 - €5 916 - £4 189 - FF38 808
  Fruit Blossom Gelatin silver print (21.5x15.5cm 8x6in) Beverly-Hills CA 1998

NOTER de David Emil Joseph 1825-1912 [85]
- $15 980 - €18 151 - £11 212 - FF119 064
  Preparing for the Banquet Oil/canvas (64x90cm 25x35in) Amsterdam 2001
- $1 574 - €1 524 - £991 - FF10 000
  Nature morte aux bouvreuils et sansonnet Huile/toile (24x31cm 9x12in) Paris 1999
- $7 890 - €7 436 - £4 770 - FF48 780
  Nature morte au homard Aquarelle/papier (19x30cm 7x11in) Antwerpen 1999

NOTER de Pierre François 1779-1843 [23]
- $14 285 - €16 790 - £9 904 - FF110 134
  Figures on a square, ghent Oil/canvas (91.5x74.5cm 36x29in) Amsterdam 2000
- $2 805 - €3 344 - £2 000 - FF21 937
  Winter Landscape with Figures on a Frozen Canal Oil/panel (27x36.5cm 10x14in) Leyburn, North Yorkshire 2000

- $686 - €644 - £423 - FF4 227
  L'arrivée du carrosse Lavis (28x40cm 11x15in) Bruxelles 1999

NOTERMAN Emmanuel 1808-1863 [40]
- $2 955 - €3 403 - £2 017 - FF22 324
  Verbode Jagt: Chasse privée Oil/panel (61.5x51cm 24x20in) Amsterdam 2000
- $1 130 - €1 329 - £810 - FF8 720
  Jagdgesellschaft vor der erlegten Beute Oil/panel (22x27cm 8x10in) Stuttgart 2001
- $174 - €181 - £109 - FF1 190
  Declamerende herbergier Ink/paper (26.5x19cm 10x7in) Dordrecht 2000

NOTERMAN Zacharie 1820-1890 [75]
- $3 473 - €3 201 - £2 081 - FF21 000
  Chiens et chat dans la grange Huile/toile (73x93cm 28x36in) Paris 1998
- $2 413 - €2 363 - £1 542 - FF15 500
  Les singes musiciens Huile/bois (24.5x19cm 9x7in) Montpellier 1999

NOTHNAGEL August Friedrich W. 1822-1899 [2]
- $5 548 - €4 856 - £3 360 - FF31 854
  Der Golf von Neapel mit Vesuv Öl/Leinwand (47x66cm 18x25in) Berlin 1999

NOTKIN Richard 1948 [1]
- $4 000 - €4 144 - £2 546 - FF27 181
  Oval Curbside Teapot Ceramic (10x21.5x10cm 3x8x3in) New-York 2000

NOTT Raymond 1888-1948 [18]
- $700 - €817 - £487 - FF5 357
  Barn in Landscape Pastel/paper (46x60cm 18x24in) Altadena CA 2000

NOTTE Emilio 1891-1982 [42]
- $7 800 - €6 738 - £5 200 - FF44 200
  Dormiente con cagnolino Olio/tela (100x140cm 39x55in) Napoli 1998
- $2 700 - €2 332 - £1 800 - FF15 300
  Sulla spiaggia Olio/tavola (50x60cm 19x23in) Napoli 1998

NOTZ Johannes 1802-1862 [8]
- $518 - €602 - £370 - FF3 952
  Portrait of Archibald Little Esq of Shabden Park, Surrey Watercolour (34x27cm 13x10in) Oxfordshire 2001

NOUAILHER Couly 1514-? [2]
- $14 819 - €14 500 - £9 500 - FF95 115
  The Lamentation Enamel (21.5x16.5cm 8x6in) London 1999

NOURRISSON René c.1610-c.1650 [1]
- $106 027 - €118 881 - £72 000 - FF779 810
  Still Life of Apples in a wicker Basket with Pears on a Ledge Oil/panel (34.5x44.5cm 13x17in) London 2000

NOURSE Elisabeth 1859-1938 [32]
- $12 152 - €11 891 - £7 776 - FF78 000
  Portrait de femme Huile/toile (46x55cm 18x21in) Bayeux 1999
- $5 500 - €6 060 - £3 669 - FF39 750
  On the Margin of the Bay Gouache (48x73cm 19x29in) Detroit MI 2000

NOURY Gaston 1866-? [38]
- $2 600 - €2 901 - £1 702 - FF19 027
  «Pour les Pauvres, Grandes Fêtes des Tuileries du 13 au 21 Août» Poster (139x90cm 54x35in) New-York 2000

NOUVEAU Henri Neugeboren 1901-1959 **[124]**
- $1 666 - €1 982 - **£1 188** - FF13 000
  Composition Huile/papier (29x44.5cm 11x17in) Paris 2000
- $1 532 - €1 464 - **£955** - FF9 600
  Der urwald Embryo Collage (21x14.5cm 8x5in) Paris 1999

NOVAK Ladislav 1925-1999 **[13]**
- $289 - €273 - **£180** - FF1 793
  Ceinture de chasteté Technique mixte/papier (30x21cm 11x8in) Praha 2000

NOVARO Jean-Claude 1941 **[43]**
- $576 - €549 - **£358** - FF3 600
  Vase de forme cylindrique à décors d'oxydes Sculpture verre (H24.5cm H9in) Paris 1999

NOVATI Marco 1895-1975 **[54]**
- $3 100 - €3 214 - **£1 860** - FF21 080
  Ritratto della madre Olio/tela (80x60cm 31x23in) Venezia 2000
- $1 285 - €1 110 - **£642** - FF7 282
  Ritratto Olio/tavola (40x30cm 15x11in) Venezia 1999
- $650 - €674 - **£390** - FF4 420
  Fiori Acquarello/carta (45x28.5cm 17x11in) Venezia 2000

NOVELIERS Pierre XVI-XVII **[1]**
- $34 894 - €36 640 - **£22 000** - FF240 343
  Portrait of Isabel de Valois, Consort of Kings Philip II of Spain Oil/canvas (208.5x94cm 82x37in) London 2000

NOVELLI Gastone 1925-1968 **[87]**
- $93 756 - €110 190 - **£65 000** - FF722 800
  Attenti al Sergente Bond Mixed media (200x180cm 78x70in) London 2000
- $15 000 - €15 550 - **£9 000** - FF102 000
  Ekaris Tecnica mista/tela (50x61cm 19x24in) Milano 1999
- $10 500 - €9 071 - **£7 000** - FF59 500
  Composizione Tecnica mista/tavola (26.5x35cm 10x13in) Prato 1998
- $1 400 - €1 814 - **£1 050** - FF11 900
  Monte con rifugio Bronzo (6x12cm 2x4in) Milano 2001
- $3 300 - €2 851 - **£2 200** - FF18 700
  «Accorstarsi è difficile» Tecnica mista/carta (49x69cm 19x27in) Milano 1998

NOVELLI IL MONREALESE Pietro 1603-1647 **[25]**
- $41 238 - €43 302 - **£26 000** - FF284 042
  The Martyrdom of Saint Bartholomew Oil/canvas (211x156.5cm 83x61in) London 2000
- $20 497 - €21 685 - **£13 000** - FF142 242
  Gentleman, three-quarter length, standing beside a pedestal Oil/canvas (101.5x75.5cm 39x29in) London 2000

NOVELLI Pier Antonio III 1729-1804 **[80]**
- $55 335 - €47 803 - **£36 890** - FF313 565
  Ercole e Onfale attorniati dalle ancelle/La gara tra Apollo e Pan Olio/tela (78x95.5cm 30x37in) Venezia 1998
- $1 988 - €2 230 - **£1 350** - FF14 628
  Two girls Seated by an Urn Black chalk (21.5x15.5cm 8x6in) London 2000

NOVER XX **[1]**
- $2 400 - €2 677 - **£1 571** - FF17 563
  «Absinthe Vichet, 1ère marque de Pontarlier» Poster (95.5x136cm 37x53in) New-York 2000

NOVI Nathalie 1963 **[4]**
- $574 - €579 - **£358** - FF3 800
  La princesse se déguise en sorcière Pastel/papier (60x42cm 23x16in) Paris 2000

NOVICE William XVIII-XIX **[3]**
- $10 267 - €9 568 - **£6 200** - FF62 759
  Tom Oldacre and his Hounds Oil/canvas (72x92cm 28x36in) London 1998

NOVION de Charles, comte XIX **[1]**
- $8 673 - €7 927 - **£5 309** - FF52 000
  Le port et la rade de Tanger, Afrique Huile/toile (45.5x54.5cm 17x21in) Paris 1999

NOVKOUNSKI Oleg XX **[8]**
- $165 - €152 - **£100** - FF1 000
  Hiver russe Aquarelle/papier (19x13cm 7x5in) Morlaix 1998

NOVO Stefano 1862-1927 **[45]**
- $3 600 - €3 110 - **£2 400** - FF20 400
  Nel Campiello a Venezia Olio/tela (84x51cm 33x20in) Roma 1998
- $2 560 - €2 695 - **£1 560** - FF17 680
  Paesaggi arcadici Olio/tavoletta (24x33cm 9x12in) Venezia 2000

NOVOA GARCIA Leopoldo 1919 **[12]**
- $3 780 - €4 205 - **£2 520** - FF27 580
  Espacio negro con desgarradura y relieve Oleo/lienzo (105x85cm 41x33in) Madrid 2000
- $145 - €168 - **£100** - FF1 103
  Sin título Grabado (61x45.5cm 24x17in) Madrid 2000

NOVOA Glexis 1964 **[1]**
- $16 000 - €17 065 - **£10 657** - FF111 942
  El país de los muertos Mixed media/canvas (208.5x559cm 82x220in) New-York 2000

NOVOA Gustavo 1939 **[22]**
- $2 400 - €2 199 - **£1 466** - FF14 426
  Remote Places Oil/masonite (99x80cm 39x31in) Delray-Beach FL 1999

NOVOPACKY Johann 1821-1908 **[27]**
- $346 - €328 - **£216** - FF2 151
  White Bull and Poultry, Study Oil/cardboard (26x38cm 10x14in) Praha 2000

NOVOTNY Elmer Ladislaw 1909-1997 **[24]**
- $700 - €657 - **£432** - FF4 307
  Portrait, Woman wearing a Cloche Oil/canvas (55x44cm 22x17in) Cleveland OH 1999

NOWAK Bretislav, Jnr. 1952 **[1]**
- $7 500 - €7 159 - **£4 686** - FF46 961
  Two-Part Construction Sculpture, glass (33x30x11cm 12x11x4in) New-York 1999

NOWAK Ernst 1853-1919 **[49]**
- $1 265 - €1 329 - **£837** - FF8 720
  Bruder Kellermeister Öl/Leinwand (50x63cm 19x24in) München 2000
- $2 356 - €2 454 - **£1 493** - FF16 098
  Schuster bei seiner Arbeit am Fenster Öl/Leinwand (39.5x32cm 15x12in) München 2000

NOWAK Vilém, Willi 1886-1977 **[48]**
- $3 468 - €3 280 - **£2 160** - FF21 516
  Shepherd Oil/canvas (51x71.5cm 20x28in) Praha 2000
- $433 - €410 - **£270** - FF2 689
  Maedchen mit Vogel Oil/panel (26x17cm 10x6in) Praha 2001
- $404 - €383 - **£252** - FF2 521
  «Horsemen» Watercolour/paper (26x33cm 10x12in) Praha 2001

N

NOWEY Adolf c.1835-? **[29]**
- $667 - €767 - £471 - FF5 030
  Ziegen und Schafe im Stall Oil/panel (26x39.5cm 10x15in) Bremen 2001

NOWICKA-KWIATKOWSKA Michalina 1877-1932 **[2]**
- $2 604 - €2 598 - £1 625 - FF17 043
  Petite filles nourrissant des oiseaux dans la forêt Pastel/paper (46x58cm 18x22in) Warszawa 1999

NOWOSIELSKI Jerzy 1923 **[67]**
- $8 694 - €9 033 - £5 817 - FF61 218
  Nu Huile/toile (81x65cm 31x25in) Warszawa 2000
- $2 403 - €2 334 - £1 485 - FF15 311
  Paysage à l'église orthodoxe Huile/toile (36x24.5cm 14x9in) Warszawa 1999
- $1 025 - €1 133 - £711 - FF7 434
  Nu Encre (34.5x24cm 13x9in) Warszawa 2001
- $593 - €623 - £390 - FF4 087
  Nu Sérigraphie couleurs (59.5x50cm 23x19in) Warszawa 2000

NOYER Philippe 1940 **[5]**
- $1 100 - €1 251 - £754 - FF8 204
  Girl on the Pier Acrylic/canvas (63x51cm 25x20in) Chicago IL 2000

NOYER Philippe Henri 1917-1985 **[70]**
- $1 200 - €1 292 - £826 - FF8 467
  Luncheon on the Grass Oil/canvas (38x45cm 15x18in) New-York 2001
- $743 - €833 - £520 - FF5 462
  French ladies beside fishing nets, seascapes beyond Watercolour/paper (64.5x48cm 25x18in) West-Sussex 2001

NOYES George Loftus 1864-1954 **[85]**
- $7 500 - €6 408 - £4 538 - FF42 033
  Spring Landscape Oil/canvas (45.5x56cm 17x22in) San-Francisco CA 1998
- $3 750 - €4 374 - £2 633 - FF28 692
  «A Blue Day» Oil/canvas/board (23.5x40cm 9x15in) Boston MA 2000
- $1 000 - €952 - £625 - FF6 242
  Trees by the Sea Watercolour/paper (62x38cm 24x15in) New-York 1999

NOZAL Alexandre 1852-1929 **[105]**
- $1 335 - €1 524 - £939 - FF10 000
  Bord de lac animé Huile/toile (50x65cm 19x25in) Fontainebleau 2001
- $1 152 - €1 098 - £698 - FF7 302
  Vue de Louviers Huile/toile (46x32.5cm 18x12in) Paris 1999
- $636 - €549 - £378 - FF3 600
  «Pisco(?) Paysage de montagne» Pastel/papier (30x47cm 11x18in) Vernon 1998

NUBLAT Marc 1948 **[108]**
- $424 - €396 - £261 - FF2 600
  Forme N°2 Gouache (34x26cm 13x10in) Paris 1999

NÜCKEL Otto 1888-1956 **[34]**
- $6 229 - €6 687 - £4 168 - FF43 864
  Promenade Öl/Leinwand (110x90cm 43x35in) Zürich 2000

NUCUM Edgar S. XX **[4]**
- $1 593 - €1 849 - £1 100 - FF12 131
  After the Battle of Trafalgar Oil/canvas (70.5x114cm 27x44in) London 2000

NUDERSCHER Frank Bernard 1880-1959 **[34]**
- $1 200 - €1 197 - £749 - FF7 852
  The Missouri River from Olive Street Road Oil/board (38x45cm 15x18in) St. Louis MO 1999

NUFFEL van Georges XIX **[13]**
- $1 700 - €1 696 - £1 061 - FF11 123
  The Old House Oil/board (35x43cm 14x17in) Cincinnati OH 1999

NUFFEL van Georges XIX **[13]**
- $23 881 - €20 059 - £14 000 - FF131 579
  The young Artist Oil/canvas (53.5x70.5cm 21x27in) London 1998

NUGLISCH Friedrich Christian XVII-XVIII **[1]**
- $3 412 - €3 811 - £2 312 - FF25 000
  Neptune sur son char/Cérès sur son char Huile/toile (46x38cm 18x14in) Paris 2000

NUIJEN Wijnandus J.J. 1813-1839 **[11]**
- $53 750 - €45 319 - £31 900 - FF297 270
  Farm in a Landscape Oil/panel (69.5x86cm 27x33in) Amsterdam 1998
- $18 289 - €17 244 - £11 335 - FF113 110
  Shipping in a Calm Oil/panel (29x37cm 11x14in) Amsterdam 1999
- $89 - €100 - £61 - FF654
  Houten bruggetje in park Drawing (24x16cm 9x6in) Rotterdam 2001

NUMAN Hermanus 1744-1820 **[10]**
- $782 - €726 - £485 - FF4 762
  Vissers bij ruine Watercolour/paper (25.5x40cm 10x15in) Dordrecht 1999

NUMBULMOORE Charlie 1907-1971 **[4]**
- $18 491 - €19 722 - £12 341 - FF129 369
  Wandjina Spirit Mixed media (62x38.5cm 24x15in) Melbourne 1998
- $8 947 - €9 543 - £5 971 - FF62 598
  Wandjina Spirit Mixed media (40.5x26cm 15x10in) Melbourne 2000

NUMKENA Dennis 1941 **[1]**
- $6 500 - €6 445 - £4 065 - FF42 262
  Badger Kachinas Oil/canvas (93x117cm 36x46in) New-York 1999

NUNAMAKER Alfred R. 1915-1988 **[3]**
- $6 250 - €5 933 - £3 829 - FF38 921
  Delaware River Winter Landscape with Houses on Far Riverbank Oil/board (20x25cm 8x10in) Hatfield PA 1999

NUNAMAKER Kenneth Rollin 1890-1957 **[11]**
- $32 500 - €32 267 - £20 312 - FF211 659
  The Old Farm Oil/canvas (56x61cm 22x24in) New-York 1994
- $13 000 - €13 954 - £8 699 - FF91 533
  Farm Scene Oil/canvas (35.5x35.5cm 13x13in) New-York 2000

NUNES VAIS Italo 1860-1932 **[7]**
- $9 000 - €8 643 - £5 577 - FF56 694
  The Letter Oil/canvas (68x50cm 27x20in) Oakland CA 1999

NUÑEZ DE VILLAVICENCIO Pedro 1644-1700 **[3]**
- $53 628 - €45 629 - £32 000 - FF299 308
  Portrait of the Archbishop of Seville, Don Ambroio de Spinola (d.1684) Oil/canvas (90x65.5cm 35x25in) London 1998

NUÑEZ DEL PRADO Marina 1910-1995 **[9]**
- $6 000 - €6 440 - £4 015 - FF42 246
  Danza de cholos Terracotta (H31.5cm H12in) New-York 2000

NUÑEZ LOSADA Francisco 1889-1973 **[18]**
- $2 880 - €2 703 - £1 800 - FF17 730
  Arenas de San Pedro Oleo/lienzo (53x67cm 20x26in) Madrid 1999

NUÑEZ SEGURA Jordi 1932 [54]
$243 - €276 - £165 - FF1 812
El Moll de la Fusta (Puerto de Barcelona)
Oleo/lienzo (65x81cm 25x31in) Barcelona 2000

NUNGURRAYI Gabriella Possum 1967 [11]
$287 - €277 - £177 - FF1 814
Bush Fire Dreaming Silkscreen (63x90cm 24x35in)
Melbourne 1999

NUNNEY John ?-1966 [3]
$847 - €982 - £600 - FF6 441
«Holidays by Lms, On Sale at Any Lms Station or Bokkstall» Poster (102x64cm 40x25in) London 2000

NUNZIO 1954 [25]
$7 800 - €10 107 - £5 850 - FF66 300
Confine Tecnica mista (214x103cm 84x40in) Roma 2000
$2 250 - €2 332 - £1 350 - FF15 300
Senza titolo Tecnica mista (103x72cm 40x28in) Prato 1999
$4 000 - €4 147 - £2 400 - FF27 200
Discesa Sculpture bois (120x34x12cm 47x13x4in) Prato 1999
$4 250 - €4 406 - £2 550 - FF28 900
«Bolero» Sculpture bois (23.5x45x10cm 9x17x3in) Firenze 2001
$1 400 - €1 451 - £840 - FF9 520
Senza titolo Tecnica mista/carta (72x52cm 28x20in) Roma 2001

NUPEN Kjell 1955 [6]
$14 326 - €15 900 - £9 984 - FF104 299
Komposisjon Oil/canvas (160x115cm 62x45in) Oslo 2001
$583 - €674 - £410 - FF4 418
Studie av dyr Color lithograph (54x40cm 21x15in) Oslo 2000

NUSE Roy Cleveland 1885-1975 [3]
$2 500 - €2 940 - £1 792 - FF19 284
«Rush Valley: Autumn» Oil/canvas (23.5x33cm 9x12in) Philadelphia PA 2001

NUSS Fritz 1907-1999 [35]
$1 635 - €1 573 - £1 007 - FF10 316
Sich entkleidende Bronze (H12cm H4in) München 1999

NUSS Karl Ulrich 1943 [13]
$655 - €613 - £397 - FF4 024
Sitzender weiblicher Akt Bronze (H12cm H4in) Stuttgart 1999

NUSSBAUM Felix 1904-1944 [44]
$95 260 - €102 260 - £63 760 - FF670 780
Atelier-Stilleben mit Maske und Uhr Öl/Leinwand (47x65cm 18x25in) Köln 2000
$33 350 - €31 075 - £20 757 - FF203 841
Portrait of a Man Oil/canvas (43.5x35cm 17x13in) Tel Aviv 1999
$13 800 - €12 859 - £8 589 - FF84 348
Piazza in Rapallo Gouache/paper (50x35cm 19x13in) Tel Aviv 1999

NUSSI Arnaldo 1902-1977 [11]
$2 160 - €1 866 - £1 440 - FF12 240
Paesaggio a Cortina Olio/tela/tavola (50x70cm 19x27in) Trieste 1998

NUSSIO Oskar 1899-1976 [29]
$704 - €592 - £414 - FF3 883
«Piz Linard und Inn» Öl/Leinwand/Karton (30x24cm 11x9in) Bern 1998

NUTTER William 1754-1802 [10]
$280 - €334 - £200 - FF2 193
The Farm-Yard, after Henry Singleton Engraving (36x26cm 14x10in) Leyburn, North Yorkshire 2000

NUTTER William Henry 1821-1872 [15]
$1 662 - €1 605 - £1 050 - FF10 525
Wetheral Ferry Watercolour/paper (20x28cm 8x11in) Carlisle, Cumbria 1999

NUTTING Wallace 1861-1941 [98]
$225 - €253 - £157 - FF1 662
«Warm Spring Day»/«Russet and Gold» Photograph (15x23cm 6x9in) Portland OR 2001

NUVOLONE Carlo Fr. il Panfilo 1608-1661/65 [30]
$25 377 - €26 647 - £16 000 - FF174 795
Saint Antony of Padua and the Infant Christ Oil/canvas (205x126cm 80x49in) London 2000
$9 500 - €9 848 - £5 700 - FF64 600
San Francesco in estasi Olio/tela (99x78cm 38x30in) Milano 2000
$5 894 - €5 466 - £3 600 - FF35 856
Madonna and Child Oil/panel (21.5x15cm 8x5in) London 1998

NUVOLONE Giuseppe il Panfilo 1619-1703 [13]
$18 920 - €20 017 - £12 000 - FF131 300
Christ and the Woman Taken in Adultery Oil/canvas (124.5x102cm 49x40in) London 2000
$7 500 - €7 775 - £4 500 - FF51 000
Santa in meditazione Olio/tavola (58x45cm 22x17in) Milano 2001

NUVOLONE Panfilo c.1581-c.1651 [3]
$60 000 - €77 749 - £45 000 - FF510 000
Natura morta con pesche, uva bianca, uva nera, pampini su un'alzata Olio/tela (36x48.5cm 14x19in) Milano 2001

NYBERG Frans 1882-1962 [53]
$249 - €252 - £154 - FF1 654
Borgå Akvarell/papper (24x18cm 9x7in) Helsinki 2000

NYBO Poul Friis 1869-1929 [138]
$512 - €471 - £315 - FF3 091
Interiör med kvinde Oil/canvas (45x37cm 17x14in) Vejle 1999
$264 - €295 - £181 - FF1 935
Interiör med kvinde, der arrangerer blomster Oil/canvas (35x29cm 13x11in) Viby J, Århus 2000

NYBORG Peter 1937 [119]
$450 - €431 - £282 - FF2 825
Komposition Oil/canvas (40x55cm 15x21in) Köbenhavn 1999

NYE Edgar Hewitt 1879-1943 [37]
$950 - €842 - £582 - FF5 522
Rocky Coast Oil/canvas (83x71cm 33x28in) Cincinnati OH 1999

NYEL Robert 1930 [51]
$301 - €347 - £210 - FF2 276
Les coupeurs d'herbe Huile/toile (46x55cm 18x21in) Bruxelles 2001

NYFELER Albert 1883-1969 [117]
$1 028 - €991 - £633 - FF6 500
Winter auf der Alp Öl/Leinwand (45x60cm 17x23in) Bern 1999
$171 - €196 - £120 - FF1 284
Gebirgslandschaft bei Anbruch der Dämmerung Watercolour (21.5x27cm 8x10in) Bern 2001

NYHOLM Arvid Frederick 1866-1927 **[9]**
📖 **$4 885** - €5 574 - **£3 395** - FF36 565
    Metande pojke Akvarell/papper (26x36cm 10x14in)
    Stockholm 2001

NYILASY Sándor 1873-1934 **[10]**
☁ **$910** - €1 007 - **£598** - FF6 604
    Summer Landscape Oil/canvas (48.5x74.5cm
    19x29in) Budapest 2000

NYL-FROSCH Marie 1857-1914 **[12]**
☁ **$5 500** - €6 377 - **£3 896** - FF41 831
    An Oppulent Still Life in a Oriental Vase Oil/can-
    vas (105x75.5cm 41x29in) New-York 2000

NYLUND Gunnar 1904-1996 **[16]**
🏺 **$481** - €485 - **£300** - FF3 181
    A Glazed Stoneware Vase Porcelain (H16cm H6in)
    London 2000

NYMAN Björn 1927 **[12]**
☁ **$1 200** - €1 165 - **£741** - FF7 643
    Stilleben med spelkort och dödskalle Oil/panel
    (39.5x50.5cm 15x19in) Stockholm 1999
☁ **$737** - €755 - **£455** - FF4 951
    Lerkärl och plunta Oil/panel (36x44cm 14x17in)
    Stockholm 2000

NYMAN Hilding 1870-1937 **[12]**
☁ **$1 235** - €1 077 - **£747** - FF7 066
    Skymningslandskap Oil/canvas (110x94cm
    43x37in) Stockholm 1998

NYMAN Olle 1909-1999 **[100]**
☁ **$950** - €1 020 - **£635** - FF6 692
    Stadsbild med palmer Oil/panel (44x54cm 17x21in)
    Stockholm 2000
☁ **$467** - €466 - **£291** - FF3 058
    Fruktstilleben Oil/canvas (31x23cm 12x9in) Uppsala
    1999
📖 **$448** - €512 - **£316** - FF3 361
    Figur mot blå fond Akvarell/papper (22x15cm 8x5in)
    Stockholm 2001

NYROP Børge C. 1881-1948 **[64]**
☁ **$356** - €336 - **£222** - FF2 207
    Fiskere traekker nettene ind Oil/canvas (54x68cm
    21x26in) København 1999

NYRS de XIX-XX **[2]**
🖼 **$1 778** - €1 982 - **£1 196** - FF13 000
    **«Corsets N.D. Busc Eynedé changeable et
    interchangeable»** Affiche (158x113cm 62x44in)
    Orléans 2000

NYS Francis 1863-1900 **[3]**
📖 **$1 622** - €1 588 - **£1 040** - FF10 418
    Elegant Lady on the Beach of Boulogne
    Watercolour, gouache (28.5x35cm 11x13in) Amsterdam
    1999

NYSTRÖM Jenny 1854-1946 **[424]**
☁ **$37 807** - €44 378 - **£26 680** - FF291 098
    Det röda parasollet Oil/canvas (136x91cm 53x35in)
    Stockholm 2000
☁ **$21 420** - €24 875 - **£15 052** - FF163 170
    Flicka med rött parasoll Oil/canvas (92x65cm
    36x25in) Stockholm 2000
☁ **$1 638** - €1 689 - **£1 015** - FF11 076
    I segelbåten Mixed media (29.5x20cm 11x7in)
    Stockholm 2000
📖 **$2 474** - €2 151 - **£1 492** - FF14 112
    Två dalkullor Akvarell, gouache/papper (28x18cm
    11x7in) Stockholm 1998

NZAU John 1964 **[2]**
☁ **$1 500** - €1 555 - **£900** - FF10 200
    El Nino Scandal IV Olio/tela (31x51cm 12x20in)
    Prato 2000

O

O'BRADY Gertrude Allen 1904 **[55]**
📖 **$299** - €335 - **£203** - FF2 200
    **Exhibition of Portraits by O'Brady, Reading
    Room May, 29 May 30** Gouache (32x24cm 12x9in)
    Paris 2000

O'BRIEN Dermod William 1865-1945 **[28]**
☁ **$2 905** - €3 301 - **£2 016** - FF21 655
    Extensive Landscape Oil/canvas (38x45cm
    15x18in) Dublin 2000
☁ **$3 505** - €3 046 - **£2 112** - FF19 981
    **Harvesting at Cahirmoyle, a Team of Horses
    and a Reaper and Binder** Oil/canvas (35x44cm
    13x17in) Dublin 1998

O'BRIEN Frank Morgan 1877-1919 **[1]**
☁ **$3 600** - €3 988 - **£2 413** - FF26 162
    Summer House Oil/canvas (69x69cm 27x27in)
    Dedham MA 2000

O'BRIEN Geraldine 1922 **[8]**
☁ **$572** - €635 - **£398** - FF4 164
    Willow Pattern Oil/canvas (35x42.5cm 13x16in)
    Dublin 2001

O'BRIEN John 1831-1891 **[2]**
☁ **$1 943** - €2 267 - **£1 352** - FF14 870
    Sailing by the Coast Oil/canvas (30.5x40.5cm
    12x15in) Toronto 2000

O'BRIEN Justin Maurice 1917-1996 **[70]**
☁ **$23 292** - €25 436 - **£14 992** - FF166 848
    Portrait of a Boy Oil/board (80.5x53.5cm 31x21in)
    Melbourne 2000
☁ **$10 360** - €9 767 - **£6 420** - FF64 070
    Boys in a Landscape Oil/wood (40x39cm 15x15in)
    Melbourne 1999
📖 **$1 544** - €1 452 - **£971** - FF9 527
    Herod Washing his Hands Watercolour/paper
    (38x31cm 14x12in) Sydney 1999

O'BRIEN Kitty Wilmer 1910-1982 **[23]**
☁ **$7 916** - €8 867 - **£5 500** - FF58 162
    The Aasleigh Valley, Co.Sligo Oil/board (51x61cm
    20x24in) London 2001
☁ **$4 832** - €5 079 - **£3 031** - FF33 316
    Peter's Street, Westport Oil/board (25x62cm
    9x24in) Dublin 2000
📖 **$615** - €660 - **£411** - FF4 331
    St. Brigid's Cathedral, Kildare Watercolour/paper
    (42x30cm 16x11in) Dublin 2000

O'BRIEN Lucius Richard 1832-1899 **[49]**
☁ **$5 121** - €4 955 - **£3 158** - FF32 504
    Sunrise on the Saguenay Oil/canvas/board
    (41x59cm 16x23in) Toronto 1999
📖 **$1 536** - €1 487 - **£947** - FF9 753
    Sailboats on a River Watercolour/paper (24x35cm
    9x13in) Toronto 1999

O'BRIEN Lucy XX **[1]**
📖 **$2 142** - €2 286 - **£1 427** - FF14 992
    Room in Fitzwilliam Square Watercolour/paper
    (46x35cm 18x14in) Dublin 2000

O'CEALLACAIN Diarmuid XX **[9]**
- $4 317 - €4 836 - **£3 000** - FF31 722
  Oig Bean (Young Woman) Oil/canvas (61x45.5cm 24x17in) London 2001
- $5 037 - €5 642 - **£3 500** - FF37 009
  Carraroe, Connemara Oil/board (28x39cm 11x15in) London 2001

O'COLMAIN Seamus 1925-1990 **[15]**
- $1 003 - €1 079 - **£684** - FF7 079
  Darby Court Oil/board (46x56cm 18x22in) Dublin 2001
- $409 - €483 - **£288** - FF3 165
  Scrapyard Sympathy Oil/board (33x22.5cm 12x8in) Dublin 2000

O'CONNOR Andrew 1874-1941 **[4]**
- $13 547 - €14 863 - **£9 000** - FF97 497
  Pro Patria, Victory Bronze (H63cm H24in) London 2000

O'CONNOR Frank XX **[1]**
- $6 130 - €6 792 - **£4 110** - FF44 551
  Nude Oil/canvas (91x60cm 36x24in) New-York 2000

O'CONNOR James Arthur 1792-1841 **[98]**
- $21 588 - €24 180 - **£15 000** - FF158 611
  Oncoming Storm, Windswept Trees Oil/canvas (35.5x46cm 13x18in) London 2001
- $5 407 - €6 282 - **£3 800** - FF41 208
  Figure resting by a ruined Tower Oil/canvas (23.5x30cm 9x11in) London 2001
- $1 925 - €1 940 - **£1 200** - FF12 724
  Lough Derg Wash/paper (21x28cm 8x11in) London 2000

O'CONNOR John 1830-1889 **[9]**
- $5 449 - €6 085 - **£3 800** - FF39 916
  The Ghetto, Rome Oil/canvas (55x38cm 21x14in) Bath 2001
- $1 731 - €1 650 - **£1 050** - FF10 821
  St. Paul's Cathedral Watercolour (20x38cm 8x15in) Stratford-upon-Avon, Warwickshire 1999

O'CONNOR Kathleen Letitia 1876-1968 **[12]**
- $11 640 - €12 825 - **£7 728** - FF84 126
  Luxembourg Gardens, Paris, Girl Sketching Oil/board (42x59cm 16x23in) Woollahra, Sydney 2000
- $2 624 - €3 080 - **£1 852** - FF20 202
  Woman in a Hat Oil/cardboard (21.5x31cm 8x12in) Nedlands 2000

O'CONNOR Patrick XX **[1]**
- $3 860 - €4 444 - **£2 634** - FF29 151
  Jack B.Yeats Oil/canvas (60x50cm 23x19in) Dublin 2000

O'CONNOR Roderic 1908-2001 **[5]**
- $929 - €1 079 - **£652** - FF7 079
  Portrait of a young Man Oil/canvas (74x60cm 29x23in) Dublin 2001

O'CONNOR Sandy 1954 **[1]**
- $5 049 - €4 352 - **£3 000** - FF28 544
  Sir Richard Francis Burton Bronze (H45.5cm H17in) London 1998

O'CONNOR Sean XX **[24]**
- $536 - €609 - **£370** - FF3 997
  The Gap of Dunloe, Killarney Oil/board (40x50cm 16x20in) Dublin 2000
- $173 - €180 - **£110** - FF1 160
  The 18th Green Watercolour/paper (26x36cm 10x14in) Belfast 2000

O'CONNOR Victor George 1918 **[81]**
- $1 253 - €1 417 - **£882** - FF9 297
  The Thames, towards Westminster, London Oil/canvas (45.5x61cm 17x24in) Malvern, Victoria 2001
- $526 - €594 - **£370** - FF3 894
  Study for Characters in an Emigré Group based on a Story by I.B.Singer Oil/paper (23.5x33cm 9x13in) Malvern, Victoria 2001

O'CONOR Roderick 1860-1940 **[122]**
- $115 136 - €128 961 - **£80 000** - FF845 928
  Basket of Roses on a white Cloth Oil/canvas (46x55cm 18x21in) London 2001
- $14 123 - €17 074 - **£9 867** - FF112 000
  Nature morte à la pipe Huile/toile (33x41cm 12x16in) Granville 2000
- $1 320 - €1 570 - **£941** - FF10 300
  Femme au diadème Encre (47x28cm 18x11in) Brest 2000

O'DONOGHUE Hughie 1953 **[12]**
- $11 083 - €10 697 - **£7 000** - FF70 166
  Fires II Oil/canvas (104x180cm 40x70in) London 1999
- $1 725 - €1 640 - **£1 050** - FF10 756
  Fabric of Memory Mixed media (104x72cm 40x28in) London 1999
- $3 193 - €3 428 - **£2 137** - FF22 488
  Face Mixed media/paper (38x58.5cm 14x23in) Dublin 2000

O'GALOP Marius Rossillon 1869-1946 **[40]**
- $1 424 - €1 656 - **£1 000** - FF10 864
  «Pneu vélo Michelin» Poster (100x79cm 39x31in) London 2001

O'GORMAN Juan 1905-1982 **[29]**
- $120 000 - €128 807 - **£80 304** - FF844 920
  Paisaje de Patzcuaro Tempera (46x57cm 18x22in) New-York 2000

O'HALLORAN James XX **[1]**
- $614 - €724 - **£431** - FF4 747
  Crowded Table Top Oil/board (30.5x40.5cm 12x15in) Dublin 2000

O'HARA Helen 1846-1920 **[30]**
- $2 743 - €2 576 - **£1 700** - FF16 898
  Cliffs, Co.Derry Watercolour (31x26cm 12x10in) London 1999

O'HIGGINS Pablo Esteban 1904-1983 **[31]**
- $250 - €253 - **£155** - FF1 661
  Portrait of an Old Man with Hat Lithograph (43x34cm 17x13in) Chester NY 2000

O'KEEFE Daniel 1740-1787 **[4]**
- $75 000 - €82 286 - **£49 822** - FF539 760
  Flower Pastel/paper (21.5x16.5cm 8x6in) New-York 2000

O'KEEFFE Georgia 1887-1986 **[52]**
- $3 700 000 - €4 144 272 - **£2 570 760** - FF27 184 640
  Black Cross with Stars and Blue Oil/canvas (101.5x76cm 39x29in) New-York 2001
- $225 000 - €214 930 - **£141 660** - FF1 409 850
  Reddish purple barn from the front-end view Oil/canvas (17x17cm 7x7in) Fairfield ME 1999
- $20 000 - €21 949 - **£12 878** - FF143 976
  Grapes and Oranges Watercolour (14x33cm 5x12in) Beverly-Hills CA 2000
- $1 153 - €1 312 - **£800** - FF8 605
  Le grand arbre Color lithograph (46x57cm 18x22in) London 2000

O

O'KEEFFE Margaret XX [1]
$4 518 – €4 243 – **£2 800** – FF27 832
The Girl in the Scarlet Shawl Oil/canvas
(40.5x51cm 15x20in) London 1999

O'KELLY Aloysius C. 1853-1926 [26]
$15 440 – €17 776 – **£10 536** – FF116 606
Breton Girl holding a Daffodil Oil/canvas (55x40cm
22x16in) Blackrock, Co.Dublin 2000
$9 785 – €10 735 – **£6 500** – FF70 419
Fishing Vessels at Concarneau, Brittany
Oil/panel (25.5x31cm 10x12in) London 2000

O'LYNCH VAN TOWN Karl 1869-1942 [49]
$2 163 – €2 180 – **£1 350** – FF14 301
Landschaftsmotiv Öl/Leinwand (56x70cm 22x27in)
Wien 2000

O'MALLEY Power 1878-1946 [11]
$3 571 – €3 045 – **£2 154** – FF19 973
Afternoon Light Oil/canvas (60x76cm 24x30in)
Dublin 1998

O'MALLEY Tony 1913 [68]
$7 196 – €8 060 – **£5 000** – FF52 870
Maguez Acrylic/canvas (76x55.5cm 29x21in) London
2001
$2 588 – €3 047 – **£1 818** – FF19 989
Samhain No.3 Acrylic/board (76x10cm 29x3in)
Dublin 2000
$2 295 – €2 666 – **£1 613** – FF17 490
«Self Portrait» Wash (34x24cm 13x9in) Dublin 2001
$1 818 – €2 032 – **£1 232** – FF13 326
Lanzarote Carborundum (152x10cm 59x3in) Dublin
2000

O'MEARA Frank 1853-1888 [2]
$726 255 – €681 918 – **£450 000** – FF4 473 090
Rêverie (Dreaming) Oil/canvas (180x129.5cm
70x50in) London 1999
$75 265 – €82 574 – **£50 000** – FF541 650
Autumnal Greys (Forest of Fontainebleau)
Oil/canvas (71x32cm 27x12in) London 2000

O'NEIL Henry Nelson 1817-1880 [30]
$493 119 – €529 323 – **£330 000** – FF3 472 128
Before Waterloo Oil/canvas (183x140cm 72x55in)
London 2000
$11 926 – €14 184 – **£8 500** – FF93 038
Rosalind, As You Like It Oil/panel (52x41cm
20x16in) London 2000
$6 823 – €5 731 – **£4 000** – FF37 594
**Naomi with her Daughters-in-law, Ruth and
Orpah/Esther in royal Robes** Oil/canvas
(39.5x29.5cm 15x11in) London 1998
$1 342 – €1 397 – **£848** – FF9 161
Bray, Co Wicklow Watercolour/paper (12x18cm
4x7in) Dublin 2000

O'NEILL Daniel 1920-1974 [173]
$15 433 – €16 565 – **£10 327** – FF108 658
Shark Coast Oil/board (50x68cm 19x26in) Toronto
2000
$6 021 – €6 606 – **£4 000** – FF43 332
Solitude Oil/board (41x32cm 16x12in) London 2000
$1 656 – €1 778 – **£1 108** – FF11 660
Lands at Gortahook Watercolour/paper
(16.5x25.5cm 6x10in) Dublin 2000

O'NEILL George Bernard 1828-1917 [53]
$23 620 – €27 719 – **£16 668** – FF181 822
The Task Oil/canvas (60x50cm 23x19in) Melbourne
2000
$9 244 – €7 920 – **£5 558** – FF51 952
«Cicho, sza!» Oil/panel (30.5x25cm 12x9in)
Warszawa 1998

O'NEILL LATHOM Rose Cecil 1875-1944 [17]
$2 700 – €2 500 – **£1 652** – FF16 396
**Children at the scene of a doll and car mishap,
for Puck Magazine** Ink (38x56cm 15x22in) New-
York 1999

O'NEILL Mark XX [15]
$2 840 – €3 047 – **£1 937** – FF19 989
Ramgarth Rest Oil/board (40.5x42cm 15x16in)
Dublin 2001
$1 617 – €1 905 – **£1 136** – FF12 493
The Knife and Fork Oil/board (19x30.5cm 7x12in)
Dublin 2000

O'NEILL Terry 1938-1997 [17]
$513 – €510 – **£320** – FF3 343
Steve McQueen in his Hollywood Office Gelatin
silver print (34x23cm 13x9in) London 1999

O'NEILLE Joan 1828-1907 [1]
$19 200 – €18 019 – **£11 700** – FF118 200
La Gola, Pollenca, Mallorca/Formentor, Mallorca
Oleo/lienzo (55x100cm 21x39in) Barcelona 1999

O'REILLY Joseph ?-1893 [5]
$9 465 – €8 986 – **£5 800** – FF58 947
Head and Shoulders of a Woman Oil/canvas
(51x38cm 20x14in) London 1999

O'RYAN Fergus 1911-1989 [75]
$1 420 – €1 651 – **£998** – FF10 827
Reflections at Roundstone Oil/board (38x56cm
14x22in) Dublin 2001
$1 278 – €1 072 – **£750** – FF7 035
Market Marrakesh Oil/board (26x35cm 10x14in) Co.
Kilkenny 1998
$601 – €698 – **£422** – FF4 581
Rothamburg, the Marquis Gateway
Watercolour/paper (43x33cm 16x12in) Dublin 2001

O'SHEE G. Poer XIX-XX [1]
$1 903 – €1 960 – **£1 200** – FF12 855
Study of a Bay Mare and Two Terrier Puppies
Oil/canvas (30x40cm 11x15in) Lichfield, Staffordshire
2000

O'SICKEY Joseph Benjamin 1918 [6]
$9 000 – €9 560 – **£5 936** – FF62 708
Autumn Garden with Table and Wicker Chairs
Oil/canvas (175x234cm 69x92in) Cleveland OH 2000

O'SULLIVAN Sean 1904-1964 [21]
$692 – €787 – **£475** – FF5 164
Portrait of a Gentleman Oil/canvas (75x63cm
29x24in) Dublin 2000
$2 513 – €2 920 – **£1 766** – FF19 156
Landscape Oil/canvas/board (25x29cm 9x11in)
Dublin 2001
$869 – €729 – **£510** – FF4 785
**Portrait of Kevin O'Sullivan (The Artist's
Brother)** Pastel/paper (55x40cm 22x16in) Blackrock,
Co.Dublin 1998

O'SULLIVAN Timothy 1840-1882 [44]
$2 400 – €2 763 – **£1 637** – FF18 124
**View on Apache Lake, Sierra Blanca Range,
Arizona** Albumen print (26.5x20cm 10x7in) New-York
2000

OAKES John Wright 1820-1887 [30]
$2 321 – €2 010 – **£1 400** – FF13 182
«On the Stockgill River, Ambleside» Oil/canvas
(61x50.5cm 24x19in) London 1998

OAKLEY Juliana XIX **[3]**
🖙 **$2 639** – €2 845 – **£1 800** – FF18 659
  Young Girl with a Doll Oil/canvas (40.5x33cm
  15x12in) London 2001

OAKLEY Octavius 1800-1867 **[49]**
🖊 **$1 254** – €1 163 – **£780** – FF7 626
  The little Gleaner Watercolour (49x33cm 19x12in)
  London 1999

OAKLEY Thornton 1881-1953 **[18]**
🖊 **$3 500** – €4 080 – **£2 423** – FF26 762
  Immigrants Arriving in Industrialized New York
  Charcoal (67x41cm 26x16in) New-York 2000

OAKLEY Violet 1874-1960 **[16]**
🖙 **$16 000** – €18 008 – **£11 022** – FF118 123
  **The Creation and Preservation of the Union,
  George Washington** Oil/canvas (101x61cm 39x24in)
  Philadelphia PA 2000
🖊 **$2 900** – €3 380 – **£2 008** – FF22 174
  Elizabethan Woman Seated in Chair Watercolour
  (60x54cm 24x21in) New-York 2000

OATES Bennett XX **[6]**
🖙 **$2 420** – €2 324 – **£1 500** – FF15 247
  Bure Bank - Horstead, Norfolk Oil/board
  (34x44.5cm 13x17in) London 1999

OBE (Josef Oberberger) 1905-1994 **[7]**
🖊 **$213** – €245 – **£146** – FF1 609
  **Wissenschaft ist der heutige Stand unseres
  Irrtums** Gouache (47.7x42cm 18x16in) Heidelberg
  2000

OBERHAUSER Emanuel 1854-1919 **[8]**
🖙 **$4 471** – €5 113 – **£3 070** – FF33 539
  Das Bad der Venus Öl/Leinwand (64.5x110cm
  25x43in) Lindau 1999

OBERHUBER Oswald 1931 **[176]**
🖊 **$549** – €647 – **£388** – FF4 242
  Ohne Titel Felt pen (44x60cm 17x23in) Berlin 2001

OBERLÄNDER Adolf 1845-1923 **[60]**
🖊 **$137** – €158 – **£91** – FF1 006
  «Feueralarm in Krähwinkel» Ink (20.8x17.2cm
  8x6in) München 2001

OBERLIN O. XIX **[1]**
▥ **$4 713** – €4 573 – **£2 934** – FF30 000
  Rouen le Havre, le lancement de la ligne
  Lithographie couleurs (180x75cm 70x29in) Montfort
  L'Amaury 1999

OBERMAN Antonie 1781-1845 **[35]**
🖙 **$12 963** – €13 613 – **£8 202** – FF89 298
  A Summer Landscape/A Winter Landscape
  Oil/panel (36.5x48cm 14x18in) Amsterdam 2000
🖙 **$2 417** – €2 723 – **£1 666** – FF17 859
  Milking Time Oil/panel (37x30cm 14x11in)
  Amsterdam 2000

OBERMÜLLNER Adolf 1833-1898 **[20]**
🖙 **$1 279** – €1 278 – **£800** – FF8 384
  Aufziehendes Gewitter Öl/Leinwand (30.5x45.5cm
  12x17in) München 2000

OBEROLINI Riccardo XIX-XX **[1]**
🖎 **$40 000** – €34 510 – **£24 132** – FF226 372
  Seated Allegorical Lady Marble (H142cm H55in)
  New-York 1998

OBERTEUFFER George 1878-1937 **[30]**
🖙 **$2 700** – €3 024 – **£1 876** – FF19 837
  Ohne Titel Oil/canvas (50x38cm 20x15in) Cincinnati
  OH 2001

🖙 **$2 000** – €2 240 – **£1 389** – FF14 694
  «Summer House» Oil/board (35x43cm 14x17in)
  Cincinnati OH 2001

OBERTHÜR Joseph 1872-1956 **[9]**
🖊 **$1 037** – €1 037 – **£648** – FF6 800
  Bert et biche Aquarelle, gouache/papier (16.5x25cm
  6x9in) Soissons 1999

OBIN Philomé 1892-1986 **[41]**
🖙 **$7 335** – €6 860 – **£4 441** – FF45 000
  Les bourgeois en calèche Huile/toile (51x46cm
  20x18in) Paris 1999

OBIN Sénèque 1893-1977 **[12]**
🖙 **$978** – €915 – **£592** – FF6 000
  La cérémonie Huile/panneau (50x60cm 19x23in)
  Paris 1999

OBIOLS DELGADO Mariano c.1860-? **[41]**
🖙 **$3 840** – €3 613 – **£2 400** – FF23 700
  Romería Oleo/lienzo (35.5x52cm 13x21in) Madrid
  1998
🖙 **$5 490** – €5 406 – **£3 420** – FF35 460
  Romería Oleo/lienzo (28x48cm 11x18in) Madrid 1999

OBREGON Alejandro 1920-1992 **[73]**
🖙 **$65 000** – €62 589 – **£40 456** – FF410 559
  Sin Título Oil/canvas (130x150cm 51x59in) New-York
  1999
🖙 **$18 000** – €17 513 – **£11 079** – FF114 881
  Barracudas Oil/canvas (70x80cm 27x31in) New-York
  1999
🖙 **$12 000** – €11 676 – **£7 386** – FF76 587
  Huracan Oil/board (35.5x41cm 13x16in) New-York
  1999

OBROVSKY Jakub 1882-1949 **[35]**
🖙 **$3 468** – €3 280 – **£2 160** – FF21 516
  Golden Shoe Oil/canvas (142x112cm 55x44in) Praha
  2001
🖙 **$953** – €902 – **£594** – FF5 916
  Liseuse de nouvelles Huile/toile (86x68cm 33x26in)
  Praha 2001

OBST Adolf 1869-1945 **[13]**
🖙 **$592** – €613 – **£375** – FF4 024
  Winter im Riesengebirge Öl/Leinwand (69x95cm
  27x37in) Rudolstadt-Thüringen 2000

OCAMPO Galo 1913-1985 **[1]**
🖙 **$6 312** – €7 168 – **£4 320** – FF47 020
  Igorot Dance Mixed media (84x61cm 33x24in)
  Singapore 2000

OCAMPO Manuel 1965 **[26]**
🖙 **$8 000** – €7 688 – **£4 928** – FF50 431
  El tirano de Europa/El tirano de America Oil/can-
  vas (244x305cm 96x120in) New-York 1999
🖙 **$1 420** – €1 524 – **£950** – FF10 000
  Tromba di Culo Sanita di Corpo Sculpture
  (71x57x18cm 27x22in) Paris 2000

OCARANZA Manuel 1841-1882 **[4]**
🖙 **$26 800** – €29 720 – **£17 825** – FF194 950
  Hombre con pipa Oleo/lienzo (60x47cm 23x18in)
  México 2000

OCHOA Y MADRAZO de Rafael 1858-? **[23]**
🖊 **$5 238** – €5 488 – **£3 315** – FF36 000
  Portrait de femme Pastel/papier (66x52.5cm 25x20in)
  Paris 2000
▥ **$260** – €290 – **£181** – FF1 900
  **«Ciwl & Grands Express Européens, sud-
  express, Paris-Madrid»** Affiche (105x76cm 41x29in)
  Paris 2001

OCHS Jacques 1883-1971 **[50]**
- $1 020 - €842 - **£598** - FF5 521
  Le couple sur le balcon Huile/toile (60x70cm 24x27in) Antwerpen 1998

OCHTERVELT Jacob c.1634-1708/10 **[22]**
- $24 000 - €26 579 - **£16 276** - FF174 348
  Elegant Company Making Music Oil/canvas (79.5x63.5cm 31x25in) New-York 2000
- $44 999 - €44 076 - **£29 000** - FF289 118
  Lucretia Oil/panel (28.5x24cm 11x9in) London 1999

OCHTMAN Dorothy 1892-1971 **[11]**
- $3 000 - €3 587 - **£2 069** - FF23 526
  Iris with Copper Oil/canvas (76x63cm 30x25in) Milford CT 2000

OCHTMAN Leonard 1854-1934 **[40]**
- $4 000 - €4 782 - **£2 759** - FF31 368
  Autumn on the Farm Oil/canvas (41x55cm 16x22in) Milford CT 2000
- $1 900 - €1 801 - **£1 186** - FF11 814
  Snow Scene Oil/canvas (27x35cm 11x14in) Mystic CT 1999

OCIEPKA Teofil 1891-1978 **[11]**
- $342 580 - €345 285 - **£213 640** - FF2 264 920
  L'esprit de la forêt Oil/canvas (55.4x67cm 21x26in) Warszawa 2000

OCKEL Eduard 1834-1910 **[6]**
- $4 250 - €3 912 - **£2 550** - FF25 658
  Stag in a Woodland Setting Oil/canvas (76x96cm 30x38in) Freehold NY 1999
- $1 112 - €1 278 - **£785** - FF8 384
  «**Normanninnen von der Feldarbeit heimkehrend**» Öl/Leinwand (29x44.5cm 11x17in) Bremen 2001

OCKELMAN Robert 1849-1915 **[3]**
- $2 003 - €2 325 - **£1 408** - FF15 254
  Badende Porcelain (H44.5cm H17in) Wien 2001

OCKER Adriaen Jansz. 1621/22-c.1670 **[3]**
- $8 569 - €7 994 - **£5 170** - FF52 437
  Ideale italienische Landschaft mit Wasserfall Öl/Leinwand (60x72cm 23x28in) Wien 1999

OCKER Dirk 1882-1958 **[9]**
- $749 - €817 - **£516** - FF5 357
  Mother and Child Oil/canvas (100.5x70.5cm 39x27in) Amsterdam 2001

OCTAVIEN François 1695-1732/40 **[4]**
- $59 772 - €64 160 - **£40 000** - FF420 864
  Fête champêtre with elegant figures/Fête champêtre with figures Oil/canvas (43.5x63cm 17x24in) London 2000

OCTOBRE Aimé Jérémie D. 1868-1943 **[2]**
- $1 934 - €1 982 - **£1 193** - FF13 000
  Jeune femme pensive Bronze (H68cm H26in) Chartres 1999

ODA Hiroki 1914 **[3]**
- $7 448 - €7 265 - **£4 560** - FF47 652
  Bride of Boulogne Oil/canvas (45.5x53cm 17x20in) Tokyo 1999
- $2 548 - €2 485 - **£1 560** - FF16 302
  Girl Oil/canvas (23x16cm 9x6in) Tokyo 1999

ODDIE Walter Mason 1808-1865 **[7]**
- $17 000 - €14 781 - **£11 376** - FF119 697
  Fishing at a River's Bend Oil/canvas (91.5x127cm 36x50in) New-York 2000

ODELMARK Frans Wilhelm 1849-1937 **[336]**
- $16 055 - €14 004 - **£9 711** - FF91 858
  Palatsinteriör - Alhambra Oil/canvas (161x116cm 63x45in) Stockholm 1998
- $1 435 - €1 548 - **£963** - FF10 151
  Utsikt från dogepalatset Oil/canvas (90x63cm 35x24in) Stockholm 2000
- $577 - €650 - **£398** - FF4 267
  En gård i Venedig Oil/panel (31x24cm 12x9in) Stockholm 2000
- $747 - €714 - **£465** - FF4 682
  Orientalisk exteriör Watercolour/paper (45x35cm 17x13in) Stockholm 1999

ODETS Clifford XX **[1]**
- $8 000 - €7 609 - **£4 857** - FF49 912
  Portrait of Marilyn Monroe Pastel (19x11cm 7x4in) New-York 1999

ODIERNA Guido 1913-1991 **[42]**
- $400 - €457 - **£278** - FF3 001
  Capri Oil/canvas (68x96cm 27x38in) Philadelphia PA 2000

ODIN Blanche 1865-1957 **[121]**
- $1 916 - €1 860 - **£1 193** - FF12 200
  Fleurs dans un vase Aquarelle/papier (25x30cm 9x11in) Biarritz 1999

ODIORNE William 1881-1978 **[6]**
- $527 - €579 - **£337** - FF3 800
  Epicerie Chocolat Morand, Paris Tirage argentique (18x22cm 7x8in) Paris 2000

ODJIG Daphne 1928 **[22]**
- $277 - €310 - **£192** - FF2 035
  New Love Silkscreen in colors (50x40cm 20x16in) Calgary, Alberta 2001

ODLE Alan Elsden 1888-1948 **[7]**
- $516 - €427 - **£303** - FF2 800
  Scène fantastiques Encre/papier (28x38cm 11x14in) Paris 1998

OECHS Anton XVIII **[1]**
- $2 193 - €2 125 - **£1 380** - FF13 939
  The 5th Prince of Thurn und Taxis and his wife Miniature (6x5cm 2x1in) London 1999

OECONOMO Aristide 1821-1887 **[10]**
- $10 767 - €9 967 - **£6 500** - FF65 382
  A greek Beauty Oil/canvas (84x68.5cm 33x26in) London 1999

OECONOMO Georg Aristides 1860-? **[2]**
- $3 500 - €3 857 - **£2 300** - FF25 300
  Little Girl with a Bunch of Flowers Oil/canvas (90x50.5cm 35x19in) Budapest 2000

OEFELE-PIEKARSKI Franz Ignaz 1721-1797 **[3]**
- $5 466 - €6 391 - **£3 841** - FF41 923
  Zwei Mädchen, die ein kleines Kätzchen füttern/Zwei Jungen mit Hund Oil/canvas/panel (69x52cm 27x20in) München 2000

OEHLEN Albert 1954 **[41]**
- $19 532 - €19 010 - **£12 000** - FF124 699
  Untitled 16/89 Oil/canvas (239x198cm 94x77in) London 1999

OEHLEN Markus 1956 **[24]**
- $4 144 - €3 580 - **£2 503** - FF23 482
  Ohne Titel Acrylic (150x120cm 59x47in) Köln 1998

OEHLER Christoph 1881-1964 **[14]**
- $151 - €177 - **£105** - FF1 160
  «**Niesen von Beatenberg**» Öl/Leinwand (56x40cm 22x15in) Bern 2000

OEHLER Max 1881-1943 **[14]**
$670 - €767 - £466 - FF5 030
Der ehemalige Marstall des Weimarer Schlosses Öl/Leinwand (48x66cm 18x25in)
Rudolstadt-Thüringen 2000

OEHME Ernst Erwin 1831-1907 **[37]**
$2 737 - €2 556 - £1 689 - FF16 769
Am Chiemsee Öl/Leinwand (40x51cm 15x20in) Köln 1999
$93 - €97 - £59 - FF637
Brand (Sächsische Schweiz) Pencil/paper (20.5x27cm 8x10in) Leipzig 2000

OEHMICHEN Hugo 1843-1933 **[60]**
$5 922 - €7 158 - £4 134 - FF46 954
Der Apfeljunge Öl/Leinwand (51x40.5cm 20x15in) Düsseldorf 2000
$1 240 - €1 176 - £754 - FF7 714
In der Kirche Öl/Leinwand/Karton (43x34cm 16x13in) Köln 1999

OEHRING Hedwig 1855-? **[31]**
$607 - €562 - £376 - FF3 689
Paar alte Bauern Oil/panel (16x12cm 6x4in) Stuttgart 1999

OELMAN Paul H. 1890-1975 **[6]**
$1 800 - €2 073 - £1 241 - FF13 600
Female Nudes Vintage gelatin silver print (21x16cm 8x6in) New-York 2001

OELTZJEN Jan 1880-1968 **[25]**
$236 - €281 - £163 - FF1 844
Fluss mit Dampfer Aquarell/Papier (37x51cm 14x20in) Bremen 2000
$165 - €174 - £104 - FF1 140
Kleiner Hafen Woodcut (15x17.3cm 5x6in) Heidelberg 2000

OENICKE Karl 1862-1924 **[14]**
$686 - €665 - £431 - FF4 360
Bispingen, Feldweg auf einer Bergkuppe und Bauernhaus Öl/Leinwand/Karton (43x57cm 12x22in) Berlin 1999

OEPTS Willem, Wim 1904-1988 **[85]**
$3 816 - €4 538 - £2 720 - FF29 766
Le palmier Oil/canvas (37x45cm 14x17in) Amsterdam 2000
$2 148 - €2 496 - £1 509 - FF16 371
Untitled Oil/canvas (16x25cm 6x9in) Amsterdam 2001
$551 - €544 - £335 - FF3 571
Landscape Pencil/paper (25x40cm 9x15in) Amsterdam 2000
$169 - €181 - £113 - FF1 190
Cafe Woodcut (31.5x32.5cm 12x12in) Amsterdam 2000

OERDER Frans David 1866-1944 **[133]**
$1 998 - €2 228 - £1 303 - FF14 618
Still Life of Flowers in a Green Vase Oil/canvas (54x44cm 21x17in) Johannesburg 2000
$1 470 - €1 524 - £931 - FF9 999
The Donkey Oil/canvas (24x32cm 9x12in) Johannesburg 2000
$495 - €555 - £344 - FF3 638
Sheep in a Vlei Pastel/paper (47.5x58cm 18x22in) Johannesburg 2000

OERTLE Hans 1897-? **[1]**
$1 518 - €1 724 - £1 055 - FF11 311
«Philips» Poster (101.5x152.5cm 39x60in) Hoorn 2001

OERTLI Max 1921 **[11]**
$679 - €788 - £469 - FF5 169
Stilleben mit Flasche und Peperoni Öl/Leinwand (50x39cm 19x15in) St. Gallen 2000

OESCH Albert Sebastian 1893-1920 **[29]**
$1 363 - €1 252 - £837 - FF8 215
Zwei musizierende Trachtenmänner Crayons couleurs/papier (27x25.5cm 10x10in) Zürich 1999
$145 - €144 - £90 - FF942
Wohlbeleibter Mann, einem Tanzpaar zuschauend Lithographie (10x6cm 3x2in) St. Gallen 1999

OESER Adam Friedrich 1717-1799 **[9]**
$407 - €486 - £290 - FF3 186
Eine in einem Baum sitzende nackte Nymphe erscheint einem Mann Indian ink (18.8x12.3cm 7x4in) Köln 2000
$897 - €1 022 - £626 - FF6 707
Amor und Psyche Radierung (28x20cm 11x7in) Berlin 2001

OESTERLE Wilhelm 1876-1928 **[23]**
$405 - €460 - £281 - FF3 018
Im Winter Linocut (14.5x24.5cm 5x9in) Berlin 2001

OESTERLEY Carl August H. 1839-1930 **[31]**
$1 085 - €971 - £650 - FF6 369
Partie aus dem Norheimsund/Norwegen Öl/Leinwand (70x41cm 27x16in) Hamburg 1998
$853 - €807 - £528 - FF5 295
Parti fra Norge Oil/canvas (29x39cm 11x15in) København 1999

OFEK Avraham 1935-1990 **[25]**
$5 500 - €5 702 - £3 624 - FF37 405
Two Men and a Bull Oil/canvas (70x97cm 27x38in) Herzelia-Pituah 2000
$1 900 - €2 138 - £1 308 - FF14 027
Man and Animal Drawing (43x62cm 16x24in) Herzelia-Pituah 2000

OFFERMANS Anthony Jacobus 1796-1872 **[15]**
$5 115 - €5 070 - £3 200 - FF33 260
Figures on a Frozen River Oil/panel (40x52cm 15x20in) London 1999

OFFERMANS Tony Lodewijk George 1854-1911 **[35]**
$2 623 - €2 437 - £1 601 - FF15 983
Idle Hours Oil/canvas (73x59cm 28x23in) Amsterdam 1998
$1 347 - €1 271 - £835 - FF8 334
Woman by the Fire Watercolour/paper (56.5x39.5cm 22x15in) Amsterdam 1999

OFFNER Alfred 1879-? **[9]**
$140 - €131 - £87 - FF858
«Zeichnet 7. Kriegsanleihe» Poster (95x63cm 37x24in) Wien 1999

OFFORD Gertrude E. XIX-XX **[2]**
$6 105 - €5 879 - £3 800 - FF38 562
The Art Class Oil/canvas (76x56cm 29x22in) London 1999

OFILI Chris 1968 **[20]**
$105 000 - €121 830 - £72 492 - FF799 155
Popcorn Mixed media (195.5x122x14.5cm 76x48x5in) New-York 2000
$78 000 - €90 503 - £53 851 - FF593 658
Cupid's Wings Mixed media/canvas (122x91.5x13cm 48x36x5in) New-York 2000
$5 052 - €5 467 - £3 500 - FF35 860
Untitled Oil/canvas (9x7cm 3x2in) London 2001

O

🖋 **$7 000** - €7 919 - **£4 897** - FF51 943
Untitled Watercolour/paper (24.5x16cm 9x6in) New-York 2001

ÖFVERSTRÖM Hugo 1900-1973 **[72]**
🖼 **$423** - €407 - **£263** - FF2 669
Bâtar vid sjöbodar Oil/canvas (44x57cm 17x22in) Stockholm 1999

OGATA GEKKO Tai Masanosuke, dit 1859-1920 **[43]**
🖋 **$1 400** - €1 547 - **£970** - FF10 148
Courtesan looking at an ornamental Scent Bag (Kusudama) Ink (109x38cm 42x14in) New-York 2001
🗂 **$224** - €256 - **£155** - FF1 676
Sage in the Clouds Woodcut (24x25cm 9x9in) Köln 2000

OGÉ Eugène 1861-1936 **[83]**
🗂 **$766** - €732 - **£479** - FF4 800
«Au tribunal de La Hay, La Menthe Pastille» Affiche couleur (130x197cm 51x77in) Orléans 1999

OGÉ Pierre Marie Fr. 1849-1912 **[9]**
🖼 **$1 200** - €1 063 - **£736** - FF6 975
Marguerite Bronze (H60cm H24in) Detroit MI 1999

OGGI I. XVII-XVIII **[1]**
🖋 **$16 331** - €15 034 - **£10 000** - FF98 619
Portsmouth Harbour from Gosport with the Anchor Park in the Foreground Oil/canvas (64.5x126cm 25x49in) London 1998

OGGIONO d' Marco c.1475-1549 **[9]**
🌀 **$68 000** - €88 116 - **£51 000** - FF578 000
Madonna col Bambino Olio/tavola (49x41cm 19x16in) Milano 2000
🌀 **$18 000** - €21 200 - **£12 448** - FF139 066
The Christ Child with the Infant Baptist Oil/panel (44x36cm 17x14in) New-York 2001

OGILVIE Clinton 1838-1900 **[10]**
🌀 **$3 417** - €3 297 - **£2 146** - FF21 625
Landscape with Cows Oil/canvas (58x111cm 23x44in) Kingston, Ontario 1999
🌀 **$6 000** - €6 813 - **£4 106** - FF44 690
Cows by a Stream Oil/canvas (15x26cm 5x10in) New-York 2000

OGILVY Charles 1832-1890 **[4]**
🌀 **$7 798** - €7 587 - **£4 800** - FF49 770
Ship in full Sail Oil/canvas (50x77cm 19x30in) London 1999

OGISU Takanori 1901-1986 **[1]**
🌀 **$4 000** - €3 845 - **£2 494** - FF25 222
Ballerina Oil/canvas (11x9cm 4x3in) New-York 1999

OGUISS Takanori 1901-1986 **[253]**
🌀 **$125 000** - €120 200 - **£77 012** - FF788 462
Modern Restaurant Oil/canvas (97x131cm 38x51in) New-York 1999
🌀 **$69 717** - €60 217 - **£42 107** - FF395 000
Kiosque à journaux Huile/toile (73x60cm 28x23in) Moulins 1998
🌀 **$9 065** - €10 661 - **£6 500** - FF69 930
Maisons dans un paysage Oil/board (27x35cm 10x13in) London 2001
🖋 **$8 187** - €7 165 - **£4 958** - FF47 000
Rue de Paris Aquarelle/papier (31x23.5cm 12x9in) Paris 1998
🗂 **$716** - €762 - **£453** - FF5 000
Cartes de voeux Lithographie couleurs (18x25cm 7x9in) Paris 2000

OHL Frits Lucien N. 1904-1976 **[63]**
🌀 **$2 193** - €2 044 - **£1 353** - FF13 405
Boats Oil/canvas (58x78cm 22x30in) Singapore 1999
🌀 **$1 130** - €1 249 - **£783** - FF8 193
Labouring under a Flamboyant Oil/board (20x30cm 7x11in) Singapore 2001

OHLSON Alfred 1868-1940 **[13]**
🖼 **$776** - €755 - **£477** - FF4 954
Dalkarl spänner armborst Bronze (H51cm H20in) Stockholm 1999

OHLSON Oscar 1847-1912 **[4]**
🌀 **$739** - €697 - **£458** - FF4 573
Marinmotiv Oil/panel (17x25cm 6x9in) Stockholm 1999

OHM Wilhelm 1905-1965 **[22]**
🌀 **$4 544** - €5 368 - **£3 209** - FF35 215
Stilleben Öl/Leinwand (49x63.5cm 19x25in) Köln 2001

ÖHRSTRÖM Alma 1897-1987 **[25]**
🌀 **$1 267** - €1 175 - **£788** - FF7 708
Glasverandan Oil/panel (48x40cm 18x15in) Malmö 1999

ÖHRSTRÖM Edvin 1906-1994 **[22]**
🖼 **$735** - €697 - **£456** - FF4 500
Morgontoalett Bronze (H26cm H10in) Stockholm 1999

OINONEN Mikko 1883-1956 **[77]**
🌀 **$1 369** - €1 514 - **£949** - FF9 928
Blomsterstilleben Oil/canvas (66x81cm 25x31in) Helsinki 2001

OITICICA Hélio 1937 **[2]**
🌀 **$42 500** - €49 378 - **£29 869** - FF323 901
«Transdimensional» Oil/canvas (19x27cm 7x10in) New-York 2001
🖋 **$14 000** - €13 592 - **£8 649** - FF89 159
Mataesquema 19 Gouache/board (45.5x53.5cm 17x21in) New-York 1999

OITTINEN Mauno 1896-1970 **[13]**
🖼 **$1 195** - €1 345 - **£823** - FF8 825
Kubistisk kvinna Bronze (H20cm H7in) Helsinki 2000

OJA Onni 1909 **[82]**
🌀 **$2 448** - €2 097 - **£1 445** - FF13 755
Halkia Oil/canvas (56x81cm 22x31in) Helsinki 1998
🌀 **$1 045** - €1 177 - **£720** - FF7 722
Landskap från Nummi Oil/canvas (27x41cm 10x16in) Helsinki 2000
🗂 **$266** - €252 - **£161** - FF1 654
Vintermotiv från Halikko Color lithograph (35x55cm 13x21in) Helsinki 1999

OJEDA Y SILES de Manuel c.1835-1904 **[3]**
🌀 **$4 761** - €4 144 - **£2 898** - FF27 186
Retrato del Marqués de Molins Oleo/lienzo (70x56cm 27x22in) Madrid 1999
🌀 **$2 520** - €2 403 - **£1 520** - FF15 760
Pelando la pava Oleo/tabla (32.5x25cm 12x9in) Madrid 1999

OJEN van Evert Marinus 1886-1964 **[1]**
📷 **$4 481** - €5 292 - **£3 181** - FF34 711
Reihenhäuser am Strand von Hoek van Holland, Architekt J.J.P.Oud Vintage gelatin silver print (22.5x17cm 8x6in) Berlin 2001

OJSTERSEK Peter 1961 **[2]**
🌀 **$2 000** - €2 121 - **£1 356** - FF13 914
Red Hill Oil/wood (100x106x12cm 39x41x4in) Tel Aviv 2001

OKA Shikanosuke 1898-1978 **[2]**
- $470 400 - €458 811 - **£288 000** - FF3 009 600
  Chapel Oil/canvas (73x91cm 28x35in) Tokyo 1999

OKADA Kenzo 1902-1982 **[33]**
- $18 000 - €20 926 - **£12 634** - FF137 268
  Island Oil/canvas (185.5x124cm 73x48in) New-York 2001
- $8 000 - €7 688 - **£4 928** - FF50 431
  Untitled Collage/canvas (100.5x105.5cm 39x41in) New-York 1999
- $5 400 - €6 132 - **£3 695** - FF40 221
  Kimi sleeping Pencil/paper (15x14.5cm 5x5in) New-York 2000

OKADA Saburosuke 1869-1939 **[8]**
- $28 000 - €27 123 - **£17 463** - FF177 917
  Rafu (Nude) Oil/canvas/board (33x24cm 12x9in) New-York 1999
- $15 680 - €15 294 - **£9 600** - FF100 320
  Potted Flowers Pastel/board (40x25cm 15x9in) Tokyo 1999

OKAMOTO Taro XX **[3]**
- $5 488 - €5 353 - **£3 360** - FF35 112
  The Sun Ceramic (25.5x22cm 10x8in) Tokyo 1999

OKASHY Avshalom 1916-1980 **[44]**
- $6 000 - €6 491 - **£4 110** - FF42 578
  Composition Oil/canvas (130x97cm 51x38in) Tel Aviv 2001
- $3 800 - €4 290 - **£2 646** - FF28 139
  Composition Oil/canvas (50x60cm 19x23in) Tel Aviv 2001
- $1 600 - €1 659 - **£1 054** - FF10 881
  Cafe in Acre Gouache/paper (50x70cm 19x27in) Herzelia-Pituah 2000

OKUHARA Tetsu 1942 **[4]**
- $17 000 - €15 901 - **£10 278** - FF104 305
  South American Journey Gelatin silver print (153.5x192cm 60x75in) New-York 1999

OKUMURA Toghyu 1889-1990 **[1]**
- $16 000 - €16 123 - **£9 974** - FF105 760
  Higoi (red carp) Mixed media (42x58.5cm 16x23in) New-York 2000

OKUN Edward, Edouard 1872-1945 **[19]**
- $8 466 - €9 715 - **£5 791** - FF63 724
  Tal in den Sabbiner Bergen mit hochgelegenem Ort Anticoli Öl/Leinwand (73x93cm 28x36in) Berlin 2000
- $2 140 - €2 515 - **£1 484** - FF16 498
  Grotte à Sorrento Huile/panneau (18x24cm 7x9in) Warszawa 2000

OLAFSSON Tove 1909-1992 **[29]**
- $1 246 - €1 076 - **£752** - FF7 060
  Liggende nögenmodel Bronze (19x31cm 7x12in) Vejle 1998

OLALDE Gastón 1925 **[8]**
- $1 026 - €1 081 - **£648** - FF7 092
  Sin título Técnica mixta (27.5x30cm 10x11in) Madrid 2000

OLARIA Federico 1849-1898 **[11]**
- $10 000 - €9 903 - **£6 226** - FF64 958
  Patroling the Garden Oil/canvas (103.5x125cm 40x49in) New-York 1999
- $18 000 - €18 709 - **£11 343** - FF122 725
  Straight from the Crate Oil/canvas (54x64.5cm 21x25in) New-York 2000

OLBRICH Joseph Maria 1867-1908 **[2]**
- $585 - €665 - **£400** - FF4 360
  «**Darmstadt**» Poster (31x20cm 12x7in) Hannover 2000

OLBRICHT Alexander 1876-1942 **[28]**
- $206 - €204 - **£128** - FF1 341
  Rankenornament Woodcut (17.4x13.9cm 6x5in) Berlin 1999

OLDE Hans 1895-1987 **[14]**
- $1 197 - €1 125 - **£742** - FF7 378
  Gehöft am See Öl/Leinwand (55.5x70cm 21x27in) München 1999

OLDE Hans, Joh. Wilhelm 1855-1917 **[20]**
- $202 - €174 - **£122** - FF1 140
  Friedrich Nietzsche auf dem Krankenbett Radierung (18x12.7cm 7x5in) Berlin 1998

OLDENBURG Claes Thure 1929-1997 **[609]**
- $14 000 - €16 244 - **£9 665** - FF106 554
  Pat Standing in a Radish Patch Oil/canvas (166.5x128.5cm 65x50in) New-York 2000
- $85 000 - €72 554 - **£50 830** - FF475 923
  Street Fragment with Car and Girl walking Oil/board (80.5x52cm 31x20in) New-York 1998
- $8 000 - €6 902 - **£4 826** - FF45 274
  Untitled Enamel (45x30.5cm 17x12in) New-York 1998
- $180 000 - €193 211 - **£120 456** - FF1 267 380
  Alphabet, Good humor Sculpture (365.5x172.5x76cm 143x67x29in) Beverly-Hills CA 2000
- $6 000 - €6 902 - **£3 619** - FF33 388
  «**Profiterole**» Sculpture (H15cm H5in) New-York 1998
- $11 500 - €12 823 - **£7 732** - FF84 115
  Study for a Sculpture of a Torn Notebook Charcoal (73.5x58.5cm 28x23in) New-York 2000
- $897 - €759 - **£536** - FF4 981
  «**Apple core-autumn**» Color lithograph (104x79cm 40x31in) Stockholm 1998

OLDEROCK Max 1895-1972 **[29]**
- $2 191 - €2 301 - **£1 486** - FF15 092
  Rote Sichel Mixed media/panel (52x76cm 20x29in) Stuttgart 2000
- $335 - €383 - **£233** - FF2 515
  Heilige Pastell/Papier (21x12cm 8x4in) Rudolstadt-Thüringen 2000

OLDERT Johan 1912-1984 **[47]**
- $346 - €384 - **£225** - FF2 532
  Swellendam Region, C.P Oil/board (34.5x49.5cm 13x19in) Johannesburg 2000

OLDEWELT Ferdinand Gustaaf W. 1857-1935 **[11]**
- $1 933 - €2 178 - **£1 333** - FF14 287
  A Bouquet of Yellow Roses and Daffodils Watercolour/paper (51x35.5cm 20x13in) Amsterdam 2000

OLDFIELD John Edwin c.1790-c.1860 **[5]**
- $161 - €162 - **£100** - FF1 064
  Figures in a Continental Mountainous Landscape Watercolor (12x16.5cm 4x6in) London 2000

OLDFIELD Otis 1890-1969 **[13]**
- $5 000 - €5 876 - **£3 466** - FF38 547
  Oasis Oil/canvas (46x56cm 18x22in) Beverly-Hills CA 2000

OLDS Elizabeth 1897-1991 **[12]**
- $350 - €327 - **£216** - FF2 142
  Sunday Fisherman Lithograph (29x41cm 11x16in) Cleveland OH 1999

O

OLEFFE Auguste 1867-1931 **[82]**
- $1 689 - €1 588 - **£1 022** - FF10 418
  The Harbour of Ostend Oil/canvas (60x76cm 23x29in) Amsterdam 1999
- $214 - €223 - **£135** - FF1 463
  Femme à la canne Encre/papier (28x21cm 11x8in) Antwerpen 2000

OLEG Kedria XIX-XX **[1]**
- $6 453 - €7 675 - **£4 000** - FF50 347
  French Bulldog Bronze (27x38cm 10x14in) London 2000

OLEN Hank XX **[2]**
- $2 750 - €2 870 - **£1 739** - FF18 825
  Maxie Rosenbloom vs. Abie Bain, New York City Photograph (20.5x26cm 8x10in) New-York 2000

OLERE David 1902-1985 **[7]**
- $662 - €610 - **£397** - FF4 000
  «Tchin Tchin» Affiche (240x160cm 94x62in) Paris 1999

OLGA ALEKSANDROVNA Grand Duchess 1882-1960 **[27]**
- $784 - €806 - **£497** - FF5 289
  Haveexteriør med kornblomster og margueritter Watercolour/paper (36x48cm 14x18in) Vejle 2000

OLGA NIKOLAJEWNA v.WÜRTTEMBERG (Königin) 1822-1892 **[2]**
- $3 776 - €4 346 - **£2 607** - FF28 508
  Katharinenpalast in Zarskoje selo Oil/panel (27x36.5cm 10x14in) München 2000

OLGYAY Ferenc 1872-1939 **[19]**
- $396 - €454 - **£276** - FF2 976
  Margitsziget Oil/canvas (80x100cm 31x39in) Budapest 2000

OLIBEECK Jacob XVII **[2]**
- $10 919 - €10 684 - **£7 000** - FF70 085
  Dutch Man-of-War and other Vessels in a Stiff Breeze Oil/canvas (47x64.5cm 18x25in) London 1999

OLINSKY Ivan Gregorevitch 1878-1962 **[31]**
- $5 500 - €6 575 - **£3 793** - FF43 131
  Young Woman with Lilies Oil/canvas (76x63cm 30x25in) Milford CT 2000
- $4 000 - €3 776 - **£2 486** - FF24 772
  The Green Bow Oil/panel (40x30cm 16x12in) Milford CT 1999

OLINSKY Tosca 1909-1983 **[5]**
- $1 100 - €1 188 - **£761** - FF7 794
  Portrait of a young Lady Oil/canvas (45x35cm 18x14in) Cincinnati OH 2001

OLIS Jan c.1610-1676 **[26]**
- $16 113 - €15 824 - **£10 000** - FF103 799
  Elegant Figures Drinking and Smoking in an Interior Oil/panel (36x49cm 14x19in) London 1999
- $14 463 - €14 346 - **£9 000** - FF94 102
  Kitchen Interior with a Hare and a Mallard on a Table by a Basket Oil/panel (28.5x34cm 11x13in) London 1999

OLITSKY Jules 1922 **[126]**
- $7 943 - €8 655 - **£5 500** - FF56 775
  «Cythera 7» Mixed media/canvas (168x122cm 66x48in) London 2001
- $1 900 - €2 205 - **£1 312** - FF14 464
  Blue sky and Winter Dusk Oil/paper/board (20.5x25.5cm 8x10in) New-York 2000
- $1 800 - €1 734 - **£1 112** - FF11 374
  Untitled Pastel (28x25cm 11x10in) Chicago IL 1999

OLIVA Pedro Pablo 1949 **[28]**
- $14 000 - €16 266 - **£9 839** - FF106 696
  Leonora, el gato y sus tristezas Acrylic/canvas (120x110cm 47x43in) New-York 2001
- $4 500 - €4 368 - **£2 801** - FF28 649
  Ismael y el lagarto verde Acrylic/canvas (60x49.5cm 23x19in) New-York 1999

OLIVA Victor 1861-1928 **[25]**
- $4 624 - €4 373 - **£2 880** - FF28 688
  View of Prague Seen from Charles Bridge Oil/canvas (82x103cm 32x40in) Praha 2000
- $8 000 - €8 925 - **£5 236** - FF58 545
  «Zlatá, Praja» Poster (108.5x38.5cm 42x15in) New-York 2000

OLIVA Y RODRIGO Eugenio 1857-1925 **[31]**
- $714 - €841 - **£518** - FF5 516
  Retrato del padre del artista Oleo/lienzo (53x37cm 20x14in) Madrid 2001
- $858 - €781 - **£520** - FF5 122
  Mora Oleo/lienzo (32x25cm 12x9in) Madrid 1999

OLIVARES de Alfonso XX **[1]**
- $5 555 - €6 250 - **£3 825** - FF41 000
  Composition Huile/toile (80x63cm 31x24in) Paris 2000

OLIVARES VELENCIAGA Juan Benito 1909 **[8]**
- $1 260 - €1 351 - **£855** - FF8 865
  Paisaje de Vizcaya Oleo/lienzo (54x66cm 21x25in) Madrid 2001

OLIVARI Eugenio 1863-1917 **[2]**
- $2 400 - €2 488 - **£1 440** - FF16 320
  Le Ferriere di Pra Olio/tela (18x24cm 7x9in) Genova 2000

OLIVE Ceferino 1907-1995 **[97]**
- $612 - €721 - **£432** - FF4 728
  Locomotora Acuarela/papel (25.5x33cm 10x12in) Barcelona 2000

OLIVE DES MARTIGUES Henri 1898-1980 **[10]**
- $542 - €610 - **£373** - FF4 000
  Vue des Martigues Huile/panneau (23.5x33cm 9x12in) La Varenne-Saint-Hilaire 2000

OLIVE FONT Jacint 1896-1967 **[26]**
- $1 080 - €1 201 - **£720** - FF7 880
  Vista de Cadaqués Oleo/lienzo (65x92cm 25x36in) Barcelona 2000

OLIVE Jean-Baptiste 1848-1936 **[210]**
- $17 771 - €19 818 - **£11 947** - FF130 000
  La côte à Saint-Honorat Huile/toile (110x157cm 43x61in) Saint-Martin-de-Crau 2000
- $20 590 - €22 105 - **£13 775** - FF145 000
  Sortie du port de Marseille, au fond la Major en construction Huile/toile (31.5x59.5cm 12x23in) Marseille 2000
- $7 476 - €8 537 - **£5 258** - FF56 000
  Bord de corniche Huile/panneau (33x41.5cm 12x16in) Marseille 2001

OLIVE Josep 1944 **[29]**
- $134 - €132 - **£83** - FF866
  Pueblo costeño Acuarela/papel (50x65cm 19x25in) Barcelona 2000

OLIVECRONA Eliza 1858-1902 **[3]**
- $2 540 - €2 899 - **£1 765** - FF19 013
  «Alskar, älskar inte...» Oil/canvas (38x30cm 14x11in) Stockholm 2000

OLIVEIRA Nathan 1928 [34]

  $13 000 - €10 913 - £7 624 - FF71 585
    Head Oil/canvas (91.5x71cm 36x27in) Beverly-Hills CA 1998

  $25 000 - €29 007 - £17 260 - FF190 275
    Yucatan Figure No.3 Bronze (101.5x56x76cm 39x22x29in) New-York 2000

  $5 500 - €6 382 - £3 797 - FF41 860
    Seated Figure Pencil (32x26.5cm 12x10in) New-York 2000

OLIVER Alfred XIX-XX [33]

  $962 - €970 - £600 - FF6 362
    Snowy Track leading into a Pine Wood Oil/canvas (50x101cm 20x40in) Fernhurst, Haslemere, Surrey 2000

OLIVER AZNAR Mariano 1863-1927 [2]

  $2 805 - €3 304 - £1 980 - FF21 670
    Diversión de maños Oleo/lienzo (44x33.5cm 17x13in) Madrid 2000

OLIVER E. [4]

  $90 - €80 - £55 - FF524
    «Plantation Home, New Orleans» Etching (8x12cm 3x5in) New-Orleans LA 1999

OLIVER Emma, née Eburne 1819-1885 [10]

  $457 - €445 - £280 - FF2 918
    Oxley, Herts Watercolour (24x34cm 9x13in) London 1999

OLIVER Myron 1891-1967 [2]

  $3 575 - €3 644 - £2 240 - FF23 905
    Fishing Boat, Monterey, CA Oil/canvas/board (30x40cm 12x16in) Altadena CA 2000

OLIVER Peter c.1594-1647 [12]

  $10 550 - €10 145 - £6 500 - FF66 549
    The Family of Cain, after Paolo Veronese Pencil (18.5x27.5cm 7x10in) London 1999

OLIVER William c.1840-c.1897 [23]

  $5 202 - €4 803 - £3 200 - FF31 508
    The Love Letter Oil/canvas (91.5x71cm 36x27in) London 1999

  $2 110 - €1 936 - £1 300 - FF12 697
    Portrait of a Woman Oil/canvas (44x35cm 17x13in) London 1999

OLIVER William 1804-1853 [41]

  $7 801 - €7 189 - £4 698 - FF47 154
    Trois personnages au bord de mer Huile/toile (85x110cm 33x43in) Bruxelles 1999

OLIVERO Matteo 1879-1932 [8]

  $2 750 - €2 851 - £1 650 - FF18 700
    Ritratto di Gino Olio/tela (90x65cm 35x25in) Vercelli 2001

  $4 000 - €4 147 - £2 400 - FF27 200
    Paesaggi di mare Olio/tela/cartone (13x18cm 5x7in) Milano 2000

OLIVET LEGARES José 1885-1956 [8]

  $2 120 - €2 403 - £1 480 - FF15 760
    Paisaje con pastor Oleo/lienzo (74x96cm 29x37in) Barcelona 2000

  $680 - €601 - £420 - FF3 940
    Paisaje de Olot Oleo/tabla (15x21.5cm 5x8in) Madrid 1999

OLIVETTI Giorgio 1908 [15]

  $848 - €898 - £508 - FF5 766
    «Rancho Notorious» Affiche couleur (195x140cm 76x55in) Torino 2000

OLIVIÉ-BON Léon 1863-1901 [3]

  $12 000 - €14 229 - £8 256 - FF93 339
    The Apprentice Oil/canvas (135x82cm 53x32in) New-York 2000

OLIVIER d' Louis Camille XIX [4]

  $2 976 - €2 515 - £1 770 - FF16 500
    Nu féminin assis Tirage albuminé (16.6x11.3cm 6x4in) Chartres 1998

OLIVIER Friedrich 1791-1859 [13]

  $2 336 - €2 045 - £1 414 - FF13 412
    «Aus dem Garten der Villa Palumbara» Pencil/paper (13.2x18.4cm 5x7in) Berlin 1998

OLIVIER Jean XX [7]

  $2 800 - €3 124 - £1 832 - FF20 491
    «Orient, envoyer vos lettres par hydravion - Naples-Corfou-Athenes..» Poster (71x98cm 27x38in) New-York 2000

OLIVIER von Ferdinand 1785-1841 [4]

  $1 464 - €1 534 - £968 - FF10 061
    Dienstag, Bergfeste Salzburg von der Mittagseite Lithographie (19.7x27.1cm 7x10in) München 2000

OLIVIERA Nathan 1928 [8]

  $40 000 - €45 491 - £27 948 - FF298 404
    Bubbelgum Man Oil/canvas (127x101.5cm 50x39in) Beverly-Hills CA 2000

  $5 000 - €4 464 - £3 062 - FF29 281
    Standing Woman Watercolour/paper (76x56.5cm 29x22in) New-York 1999

OLIVIERI Claudio 1934 [38]

  $700 - €726 - £420 - FF4 760
    Fatuo Acrilico/tela (90x70cm 35x27in) Prato 2000

OLIVIERO Domenico 1679-1755 [13]

  $22 080 - €19 074 - £14 720 - FF125 120
    Rissa presso un' osteria rurale Olio/tela (68x95cm 26x37in) Pavia 1998

OLLEROS Y QUINTANA Blas 1851-1919 [8]

  $1 235 - €1 470 - £880 - FF9 641
    Kelp Gatherers Watercolour (61x92.5cm 24x36in) London 2000

OLLERS Edvin 1888-1959 [114]

  $381 - €329 - £229 - FF2 158
    «Hård vind, Gullholmen» Oil/paper/panel (40x53cm 15x20in) Malmö 1998

  $345 - €302 - £209 - FF1 978
    «Sommardag, Småland» Oil/canvas (26x35cm 10x13in) Stockholm 1998

OLLEY Margaret Hannah 1923 [103]

  $18 166 - €17 271 - £11 337 - FF113 288
    Dry Still Life Oil/canvas (100x75cm 39x29in) Melbourne 1999

  $2 402 - €2 716 - £1 690 - FF17 819
    Portrait of Nini, Wau Papua New Guinea Oil/board (38x30.5cm 14x12in) Malvern, Victoria 2001

  $1 226 - €1 187 - £756 - FF7 786
    Sketch of Notre-Dame Ink (39.5x52.5cm 15x20in) Woollahra, Sydney 1999

  $2 337 - €2 569 - £1 498 - FF16 854
    Still life and Rushcutter's Bay Screenprint (75.5x59.5cm 29x23in) Melbourne 2000

ØLLGAARD Hans 1911-1969 [118]

  $329 - €375 - £231 - FF2 461
    Opstilling med frugter Oil/canvas (77x100cm 30x39in) Vejle 2001

O

OLLILA Yrjö 1887-1932 **[28]**
- $1 546 - €1 682 - **£1 019** - FF11 032
  Stilleben Oil/canvas (46x46cm 18x18in) Helsinki 2000
- $1 199 - €1 177 - **£744** - FF7 722
  Skog Oil/canvas (39x39cm 15x15in) Helsinki 1999

OLLIVIER Michel Barthélémy 1712-1784 **[12]**
- $4 368 - €4 878 - **£2 960** - FF32 000
  Un banquet champêtre Huile/panneau (27x21cm 10x8in) Paris 2000
- $4 119 - €4 573 - **£2 871** - FF30 000
  Etude de femme assise Pierre noire (18x20.5cm 7x8in) Paris 2001

OLLSON Julius 1864-1942 **[1]**
- $4 170 - €4 203 - **£2 600** - FF27 569
  Seascape by Moonlight Oil/canvas (61x76.5cm 24x30in) London 2001

OLMEDO Onib 1936-1996 **[2]**
- $2 123 - €1 979 - **£1 310** - FF12 981
  Music of a Clown Pastel/paper (71x56cm 27x22in) Singapore 1999

OLMO PASCUAL del Gregorio 1921-1977 **[11]**
- $2 025 - €2 252 - **£1 425** - FF14 775
  Paisaje imaginario Oleo/lienzo (72x53cm 28x20in) Madrid 2001

OLOFSSON Pierre 1921-1996 **[125]**
- $1 846 - €2 026 - **£1 189** - FF13 292
  Jalusi Tempera (50x39cm 19x15in) Stockholm 2000
- $775 - €922 - **£552** - FF6 047
  Näckens Polska IV Mixed media (48x30cm 18x11in) Stockholm 2000
- $721 - €781 - **£457** - FF5 521
  Utan titel Gouache/paper (24x40cm 9x15in) Stockholm 2000
- $201 - €216 - **£134** - FF1 417
  Komposition Serigraph in colors (38x54cm 14x21in) Stockholm 2000

OLON XX **[4]**
- $546 - €610 - **£370** - FF4 000
  «Aéromaritime pour l'Afrique Occidentale» Affiche (99x62cm 38x24in) Paris 2000

OLORUNTOBA Z.O. 1934 **[6]**
- $588 - €685 - **£420** - FF4 491
  Traditional African Musicians Tapestry (50x50cm 20x20in) London 2000

OLOVSON Per Gudmar 1936 **[13]**
- $950 - €888 - **£585** - FF5 828
  Gosshuvud Bronze (H34cm H13in) Stockholm 1999

OLPINSKI Jan Kazimierz 1875-1936 **[11]**
- $2 403 - €2 334 - **£1 485** - FF15 311
  Portrait de femme Oil/wood (61x49cm 24x19in) Warszawa 1999

OLRIK Balder 1966 **[17]**
- $3 058 - €2 960 - **£1 885** - FF19 415
  Intruder Oil/canvas (165x125cm 64x49in) København 1999

OLRIK Henrik 1830-1890 **[25]**
- $5 731 - €5 776 - **£3 573** - FF37 891
  Jeftas datter sörger med sine veninder Oil/canvas (195x160cm 76x62in) København 2000
- $2 280 - €2 153 - **£1 422** - FF14 124
  Portraet af Maria Pugaard i hvid kjole med blonder, koralhalskaede Oil/canvas (78x64cm 30x25in) København 1999

OLSEN Alfred Theodor 1854-1932 **[78]**
- $568 - €538 - **£353** - FF3 530
  Parti fra Möens klint med udsigt over vandet Oil/canvas (41x118cm 16x46in) København 1999

OLSEN Carl 1818-1878 **[51]**
- $1 999 - €2 282 - **£1 388** - FF14 968
  Skibsportraet af Briggen Trident af Bjorneborg Oil/canvas (42x68cm 16x26in) København 2000
- $700 - €804 - **£484** - FF5 277
  Fiskerbåde på havet, solnedgang Oil/canvas (22x30cm 8x11in) København 2000

OLSEN Christian Benjamin 1873-1935 **[211]**
- $1 178 - €1 143 - **£727** - FF7 499
  Marine med sejlskibe udfor Københavns havn, solnedgang Oil/canvas (41x52cm 16x20in) Vejle 1999
- $461 - €537 - **£329** - FF3 521
  Marine med sejlskib Oil/canvas (26x41cm 10x16in) Aarhus 2000

OLSEN Gudmund 1913-1985 **[63]**
- $379 - €376 - **£230** - FF2 468
  La Guitare Oil/canvas (100x81cm 39x31in) Vejle 2000

OLSEN John Henry 1928 **[541]**
- $42 624 - €47 604 - **£27 295** - FF312 264
  Landscape Hanging on to an Edge Oil/canvas (152.5x137cm 60x53in) Malvern, Victoria 2000
- $9 712 - €9 157 - **£6 019** - FF60 066
  Drilling Oil/canvas (75x90cm 29x35in) Melbourne 1999
- $1 984 - €2 244 - **£1 396** - FF14 720
  «The Rain kept falling...» Ceramic (19.5x37cm 7x14in) Malvern, Victoria 2001
- $5 844 - €6 424 - **£3 745** - FF42 136
  Escaping Mouse Mixed media/paper (79.5x103.5cm 31x40in) Melbourne 2000
- $1 062 - €1 170 - **£713** - FF7 675
  Cat Kitchen Lithograph (73.5x96cm 28x37in) Malvern, Victoria 2000

OLSEN Jörgen Peter 1815-1869 **[4]**
- $1 167 - €1 341 - **£808** - FF8 795
  Skibsportraet af Briggen Una af Montrose fört af Capt.W.Murray Gouache/paper (46x67cm 18x26in) København 2000

OLSHAUSEN-SCHÖNBERGER Käthe 1881-? **[10]**
- $225 - €250 - **£156** - FF1 643
  Alle auf einen Ink (36.5x47cm 14x18in) Heidelberg 2001

OLSKY XX **[5]**
- $4 000 - €3 847 - **£2 468** - FF25 232
  «Chapeaux Mossant» Poster (158x118cm 62x46in) New-York 1999

OLSOMMER Charles Clos 1883-1966 **[66]**
- $1 496 - €1 689 - **£1 052** - FF11 076
  «La lecture» Watercolour (30.5x37.5cm 12x14in) Bern 2001

OLSON Axel 1899-1986 **[343]**
- $4 665 - €4 702 - **£2 908** - FF30 842
  Drabbad av rymden Oil/canvas (116x89cm 45x35in) København 2000
- $1 155 - €1 232 - **£783** - FF8 079
  De utbombade Oil/canvas (24x35cm 9x13in) Stockholm 2000
- $595 - €558 - **£368** - FF3 660
  Caféinteriör/Modellstudie Indian ink/paper (20.5x20cm 8x7in) Stockholm 1999
- $173 - €179 - **£108** - FF1 148
  Hamn i skymning Color lithograph (35x51.5cm 13x20in) Stockholm 2000

OLSON Bengt 1930 [80]
- $480 - €466 - £296 - FF3 057
  Komposition i grönt Oil/canvas (81x81cm 31x31in)
  Stockholm 1999

OLSON Benjamin 1873-1935 [2]
- $7 495 - €8 370 - £4 800 - FF54 906
  Returning to Harbour Oil/canvas (60.5x84.5cm 23x33in) London 2000

OLSON Erik 1901-1986 [250]
- $5 911 - €4 998 - £3 532 - FF32 788
  «Det är vackrast när det skymmer» Oil/canvas (68x97cm 26x38in) Stockholm 1998
- $2 540 - €2 846 - £1 770 - FF18 668
  Brunnen i St.Paul Mixed media (26x29cm 10x11in) Stockholm 2001
- $1 255 - €1 181 - £778 - FF7 745
  Tyngdlyftaren Akvarell/papper (29x20cm 11x7in) Stockholm 1999
- $143 - €121 - £85 - FF793
  Sydländskt landskap med ansikte Color lithograph (34.5x47.5cm 13x18in) Stockholm 1998

OLSON Erik H. 1909-1995 [89]
- $510 - €528 - £321 - FF3 461
  Stadsbild Oil/panel (34x25cm 13x9in) Stockholm 2000
- $1 700 - €1 437 - £1 014 - FF9 423
  Optochromi Construction (H55cm H21in) San-Francisco CA 1998

OLSON Victor XX [7]
- $2 000 - €1 915 - £1 235 - FF12 563
  Boys Trying to Sell Cold Drinks to Construction Crew, Magazine Cover Oil/board (69x60cm 27x24in) New-York 1999

OLSSON Emil 1890-1964 [27]
- $442 - €382 - £266 - FF2 507
  «Samtal» Oil/canvas (39x37cm 15x14in) Malmö 1998

OLSSON HAGALUND Olle 1904-1972 [166]
- $49 827 - €55 824 - £34 731 - FF366 180
  Begravning i Grundsund Oil/canvas (114x140cm 44x55in) Stockholm 2001
- $37 486 - €41 142 - £24 153 - FF269 876
  Färghandeln, Hagalund Oil/canvas (38x46cm 14x18in) Stockholm 1999
- $14 280 - €13 393 - £8 832 - FF87 852
  Flicka med gul hatt Oil/panel (27x22cm 10x8in) Stockholm 1999
- $5 373 - €6 020 - £3 745 - FF39 490
  Kollastning i Gdynia Gouache/paper (31x38cm 12x14in) Stockholm 2001
- $313 - €352 - £218 - FF2 306
  Motiv från Hagalund Color lithograph (55x84cm 21x33in) Malmö 2001

OLSSON Julius 1864-1942 [150]
- $12 944 - €11 185 - £7 800 - FF73 366
  «Bleak North Westerly» Oil/canvas (115x151cm 45x59in) Billingshurst, West-Sussex 1999
- $3 315 - €2 860 - £2 000 - FF18 761
  Breaking the Waves Oil/canvas (45x60cm 17x23in) Bristol, Avon 1998
- $934 - €1 048 - £650 - FF6 877
  On the Scotch Coast Oil/canvas (30.5x46.5cm 12x18in) London 2001
- $1 059 - €1 228 - £750 - FF8 058
  «Dunluce Castle, LMS, Nothern Ireland» Poster (102x127cm 40x50in) London 2000

OLSSON Sigvard 1936 [4]
- $509 - €513 - £317 - FF3 367
  Indigo Akvarell/papper (139x102cm 54x40in) Stockholm 2000

ØLSTED Peter 1824-1887 [27]
- $373 - €376 - £232 - FF2 467
  Vinterlandskab Oil/canvas (29x39cm 11x15in) Köbenhavn 2000

OLSZEWSKI Karl Ewald 1884-1965 [28]
- $1 112 - €920 - £652 - FF6 032
  «Störche» Öl/Leinwand (70.5x90cm 27x35in) Heidelberg 1998

OLTMANS Alexander 1814-1853 [1]
- $6 547 - €6 000 - £4 000 - FF39 356
  Street Scene in Amsterdam Oil/canvas (72x56cm 28x22in) London 1999

OLZON Nils 1891-1953 [33]
- $399 - €336 - £235 - FF2 205
  Vinter, Ljusnedalen Oil/canvas (64x99cm 25x38in) Stockholm 1998

OMAN Valentin 1935 [55]
- $437 - €472 - £302 - FF3 098
  «Tihozilje XIII»/«Tihozilje XV» Mischtechnik/Papier (20.5x28.5cm 8x11in) Wien 2001
- $275 - €327 - £194 - FF2 145
  2.XI.Vence Farblithographie (73x27cm 28x10in) Klagenfurt 2000

OMEGNA Filippo 1881-1948 [2]
- $5 750 - €5 961 - £3 450 - FF39 100
  Baccanale Olio/tela (75x142cm 29x55in) Torino 2000

OMERTH Georges act.c.1895-c.1925 [56]
- $893 - €838 - £552 - FF5 500
  Sans titre Sculpture (H55cm H21in) Nice 1999

OMICCIOLI Giovanni 1901-1975 [217]
- $1 400 - €1 451 - £840 - FF9 520
  Vaso di fiori Olio/cartone/tela (55x40cm 21x15in) Roma 1999
- $1 000 - €1 037 - £600 - FF6 800
  Fiori di marzo Olio/cartone/tela (38x25cm 14x9in) Roma 2001
- $654 - €678 - £392 - FF4 450
  Fiori nel vaso etrusco Acquarello/cartone (29x20cm 11x7in) Venezia 1999

OMMEGANCK Balthazar Paul 1755-1826 [102]
- $4 176 - €4 462 - £2 844 - FF29 268
  Personnages, moutons et chèvres dans un paysage vallonné avec ruine Huile/panneau (48x65cm 18x25in) Antwerpen 2001
- $1 433 - €1 451 - £896 - FF9 390
  Flusslandschaft mit einer Viehherde Oil/panel (20.5x29cm 8x11in) Köln 1999
- $360 - €305 - £216 - FF2 000
  Bergers conduisant leurs troupeaux Lavis (25.5x39.5cm 10x15in) Paris 1998

ONDERDONK Julian Robert 1882-1922 [24]
- $135 000 - €128 402 - £81 972 - FF842 265
  A Blue Bonnet Field at Sunset Oil/canvas (76x101.5cm 29x39in) Beverly-Hills CA 1999
- $6 500 - €7 771 - £4 483 - FF50 973
  A Tranquil Brook Oil/board (30x21cm 12x8in) Milford CT 2000
- $5 500 - €5 332 - £3 405 - FF34 976
  Cactus in Bloom Pastel/paper (12x18cm 5x7in) Mystic CT 1999

O

ONDERDONK Robert Jenkins 1853-1917 **[1]**

🖼 **$3 250** - €3 696 - **£2 253** - FF24 245
Scene near San Antonio, Texas Oil/panel
(25x27cm 10x11in) Cincinnati OH 2000

ONG Jimmy 1964 **[3]**

✏ **$2 180** - €2 476 - **£1 492** - FF16 243
Self Portrait Charcoal/paper (145x79cm 57x31in)
Singapore 2000

ONG KIM SENG 1945 **[13]**

🖼 **$4 090** - €4 282 - **£2 569** - FF28 090
Kampong Scene Oil/canvas (56x71cm 22x27in)
Singapore 2000

✏ **$2 953** - €2 753 - **£1 785** - FF18 056
Balinese Serenity Watercolour/paper (38x54cm
14x21in) Singapore 1999

ONGANIA Umberto XIX **[88]**

🖼 **$479** - €492 - **£300** - FF3 228
**A Figure in a Gondola with St Marks Square
Beyond** Watercolour (39.5x20cm 15x7in) London
2000

ONGARO Athos 1947 **[5]**

🗿 **$4 200** - €3 628 - **£2 800** - FF23 800
Cavallino Bronze (H33cm H12in) Prato 1998

🖼 **$650** - €674 - **£390** - FF4 420
Composizione con statua e coniglio Matita/carta
(49x63.5cm 19x25in) Prato 2000

ONGENAE Joseph 1921-1993 **[10]**

🖼 **$3 236** - €3 630 - **£2 242** - FF23 812
Untitled Oil/board (72x122cm 28x48in) Amsterdam
2000

ONISHI Shigeru 1928 **[2]**

🖼 **$1 800** - €1 866 - **£1 080** - FF12 240
Senza titolo Gouache/carta (81.5x69.5cm 32x27in)
Prato 1999

ONKEN Carl Eduard 1846-1934 **[19]**

🖼 **$2 444** - €2 907 - **£1 744** - FF19 068
Motiv aus Volocca bei Abbazia Öl/Leinwand
(37x48cm 14x18in) Wien 2000

ONLEY Norman Anthony, Toni 1928 **[85]**

🖼 **$778** - €881 - **£548** - FF5 778
«Collage #5» Oil/paper (89x114.5cm 35x45in)
Vancouver, BC. 2001

🖼 **$661** - €710 - **£449** - FF4 658
Mount Garibaldi Watercolour/paper (10.5x12cm
4x4in) Calgary, Alberta 2001

🖼 **$119** - €116 - **£73** - FF758
Iceflow Silkscreen (20.5x38cm 8x14in) Toronto 1999

ONNES Harm Kamerlingh 1893-1985 **[110]**

🖼 **$1 539** - €1 359 - **£928** - FF8 915
Children Playing, Terschelling Oil/canvas
(50x60.5cm 19x23in) Amsterdam 1998

🖼 **$2 769** - €2 723 - **£1 779** - FF17 859
An Angler at the Waterside Oil/board (34x40cm
13x15in) Amsterdam 1999

🖼 **$582** - €681 - **£415** - FF4 464
Droomeiland Gouache/paper (17.5x26cm 6x10in)
Amsterdam 2001

ONNES Menso Kamerlingh 1860-1925 **[2]**

🖼 **$27 218** - €23 015 - **£16 276** - FF150 967
Poppies in a Vase Watercolour (50.5x33.5cm
19x13in) Amsterdam 1998

ONO Yoko 1933 **[12]**

🖼 **$2 800** - €2 626 - **£1 730** - FF17 226
Peace, Let your Hair grow, Love Drawing
(43x55cm 17x22in) New-York 1999

🖼 **$888** - €1 053 - **£626** - FF6 904
John Lennon Farbserigraphie (71x54.5cm 27x21in)
Zürich 2000

ONOFRIO d' Crescenzio c.1632-1698 **[17]**

🖼 **$22 800** - €19 696 - **£11 400** - FF129 200
Paesaggio con figure Olio/tela (95x133cm 37x52in)
Milano 1999

🖼 **$6 274** - €6 126 - **£4 000** - FF40 184
**Extensive wooded Landscape with a Church
and a Lake in the distance** Black chalk (35.5x46cm
13x18in) London 1999

🖼 **$305** - €297 - **£190** - FF1 945
Die Landschaft mit Mars und Adonis Radierung
(31.4x44.3cm 12x17in) Berlin 1999

ONOSATO Toshinobu 1912-1986 **[7]**

🖼 **$19 600** - €19 117 - **£12 000** - FF125 400
Four Circle Oil/canvas (100x100cm 39x39in) Tokyo
1999

🖼 **$7 498** - €8 286 - **£5 200** - FF54 355
Abstract Oil/canvas (24x33.5cm 9x13in) London 2001

ONSAGER Søren 1878-1946 **[22]**

🖼 **$4 200** - €3 790 - **£2 588** - FF24 863
Sarrsborg River Oil/canvas (44x44cm 17x17in)
Asheville NC 1999

ONSI Omar 1901-1969 **[4]**

🖼 **$5 180** - €6 098 - **£3 640** - FF40 000
Les hauteurs de Beyrouth Huile/panneau (38x55cm
14x21in) Paris 2000

🖼 **$5 729** - €6 444 - **£4 000** - FF42 268
Village Watercolour/paper (32.5x45cm 12x17in)
London 2001

ONSLOW Edouard Amable 1843-? **[7]**

🖼 **$7 045** - €7 622 - **£4 880** - FF50 000
Foire de village, Basse-Auvergne Huile/toile
(60x88cm 23x34in) Romorantin-Lanthenay 2001

ONSLOW-FORD Gordon Max 1912 **[13]**

🖼 **$7 500** - €8 100 - **£5 183** - FF53 132
Amorous Landscape Watercolour, gouache/paper
(35x49.5cm 13x19in) New-York 2001

ONTANI Luigi 1943 **[51]**

🖼 **$12 627** - €15 017 - **£9 000** - FF98 506
Salinuntefebo Mixed media (200x100cm 78x39in)
London 2000

🖼 **$2 760** - €2 384 - **£1 840** - FF15 640
Senza titolo Acquarello/cartone (98x98cm 38x38in)
Milano 1998

🖼 **$5 200** - €6 738 - **£3 900** - FF44 200
Indiband Photo couleurs (13.5x8.5cm 5x3in) Milano
2001

ONTAÑON FERNANDEZ Santiago 1903-1989 **[12]**

🖼 **$867** - €1 021 - **£612** - FF6 698
Boceto para el telón del ballet de Chinitas
Gouache/papier (27x43cm 10x16in) Madrid 2000

ONUS Lin 1948-1996 **[9]**

🖼 **$32 380** - €30 446 - **£20 050** - FF199 710
Barmah Forest Oil/canvas (182.5x182.5cm 71x71in)
Melbourne 1999

🖼 **$933** - €1 029 - **£621** - FF6 750
Silver Seas Oil/canvas/board (44x59cm 17x23in)
Melbourne 2000

🖼 **$783** - €886 - **£551** - FF5 810
**«Wiradjuri Language group Gumbirri
Garginingi»** Screenprint in colors (50x75cm 19x29in)
Malvern, Victoria 2001

OOLEN van Adriaen ?-1694 **[7]**
🖙 **$31 805** - €37 038 - **£22 000** - FF242 952
An Extensive Landscape with Various Fowl in a Parkland Setting Oil/canvas (98x129cm 38x50in) London 2000

OOMS Karel 1845-1900 **[10]**
🖙 **$7 155** - €6 693 - **£4 347** - FF43 902
De verboden lectuur Oil/panel (61x46cm 24x18in) Lokeren 2000

OONARK Jessie 1906-1985 **[14]**
▥ **$839** - €698 - **£493** - FF4 580
Shaman Helping Spirits Gravure bois (94x64cm 37x25in) Montréal 1998

OORSCHOT van Dorus, Théo 1910-1989 **[34]**
🖙 **$488** - €570 - **£344** - FF3 736
Still Life with Pink Roses Oil/canvas (80x60.5cm 31x23in) Toronto 2000

OORT van Hendrik 1775-1847 **[6]**
🖙 **$3 457** - €3 630 - **£2 180** - FF23 812
View of the Nieuwegracht (?), Utrecht Oil/panel (34x28.5cm 13x11in) Amsterdam 2000

OORTHUYS Cas 1908-1975 **[17]**
📷 **$781** - €908 - **£549** - FF5 953
Win in friesland bij grouw Silver print (25x24cm 9x9in) Amsterdam 2001

OOST van Dominique Joseph 1667-1738 **[1]**
🖙 **$14 670** - €15 245 - **£9 240** - FF100 000
Portrait de Louis de la Verdure, chevalier Huile/toile (117x88.5cm 46x34in) Tours 2000

OOST van Jacob I 1601-1671 **[8]**
🖙 **$177 500** - €190 561 - **£118 750** - FF1 250 000
Réunion de personnages auprès d'une sculpture Huile/toile (187x240cm 73x94in) Angers 2000
🖙 **$35 178** - €39 637 - **£24 752** - FF260 000
Les musiciens Huile/toile (108.5x104cm 42x40in) Paris 2001

OOST van Jacob II 1637-1713 **[3]**
🖙 **$13 386** - €14 788 - **£9 282** - FF97 000
Joseph et ses frères Huile/toile (141x188cm 55x74in) Lille 2001

OOSTEN van Izaack 1613-1661 **[50]**
🖙 **$30 533** - €30 286 - **£19 000** - FF198 660
Extensive wooded Landscape with a Falconer and his Hoop on a Path Oil/canvas (75x121cm 29x47in) London 1999
🖙 **$67 243** - €72 180 - **£45 000** - FF473 472
Landscape with Sportsmen on a Path by a Lake/Landscape with a Rider Oil/panel (34x47cm 13x18in) London 2000

OOSTERDIJCK van Wybrand XVII **[2]**
🖙 **$1 000** - €1 070 - **£681** - FF7 016
Head of a Youth wearing a Cap Oil/paper (21x16.5cm 8x6in) New-York 2001

OOSTERLYNCK Jean Émile 1915-1995 **[23]**
🖙 **$688** - €793 - **£473** - FF5 203
Een huis bij de zee Oil/canvas (30x40cm 11x15in) Lokeren 2000

OOSTERWYCK van Maria 1630-1693 **[9]**
🖙 **$57 708** - €54 454 - **£35 604** - FF357 192
Roses, a Tulip, a Poppy, Ears of Corn, Forget-me-not, an Amaranth Oil/panel (40x30.5cm 15x12in) Amsterdam 1999

OPALKA Roman 1931 **[58]**
🖙 **$64 992** - €63 623 - **£40 000** - FF417 340
«1965/1 -oo: Detail 336249-358364» Acrylic/canvas (196x135cm 77x53in) London 1999
✏ **$220** - €257 - **£154** - FF1 685
Train Encre/papier (25.5x17cm 10x6in) Warszawa 2000
▥ **$856** - €832 - **£529** - FF5 457
Création du monde Lithographie (67x50cm 26x19in) Warszawa 1999

OPDAHL Ørnulf 1944 **[13]**
🖙 **$4 774** - €4 033 - **£2 866** - FF26 456
Komposisjon Oil/canvas (90x120cm 35x47in) Oslo 1998
▥ **$221** - €247 - **£153** - FF1 623
Fra Rosmersholm Lithograph (72x51cm 28x20in) Oslo 2001

OPDENHOFF George Wilhelm 1807-1873 **[56]**
🖙 **$8 456** - €9 076 - **£5 658** - FF59 532
A vis hoeker and other Dutch fishing ships riding at anchor Oil/canvas (63x88.5cm 24x34in) Amsterdam 2000
🖙 **$5 019** - €5 899 - **£3 480** - FF38 695
Sailors in Moored Barges on a River Estuary Oil/panel (23.5x31cm 9x12in) Amsterdam 2000

OPHEY Walter 1882-1930 **[61]**
🖙 **$17 312** - €20 452 - **£12 228** - FF134 156
Park am Benrather Schloss Öl/Leinwand (71x71cm 27x27in) Köln 2001
🖙 **$4 144** - €3 580 - **£2 503** - FF23 482
Niederrheinische Landschaft unter hohem Himmel Öl/Karton (32.8x32.5cm 12x12in) Köln 1998
✏ **$2 256** - €2 454 - **£1 487** - FF16 059
Landschaftskomposition Coloured chalks (32.5x41.6cm 12x16in) Hamburg 2000
▥ **$253** - €276 - **£167** - FF1 811
Landschaft Woodcut (12.7x18.8cm 5x7in) Hamburg 2000

OPIE Catherine 1961 **[5]**
📷 **$4 000** - €4 641 - **£2 761** - FF30 444
Bo and Chicken (from the Being and Having Series) Photograph in colors (40x50cm 15x19in) New-York 2000

OPIE John 1761-1807 **[50]**
🖙 **$3 765** - €4 369 - **£2 600** - FF28 662
The Shepherd Boy Oil/canvas (135x101.5cm 53x39in) London 2000
🖙 **$8 941** - €9 880 - **£6 200** - FF64 808
Portrait of a Girl Oil/canvas (72x60cm 28x23in) London 2001
🖙 **$5 460** - €6 351 - **£3 900** - FF41 659
Self Portrait as a Young Man Oil/canvas (41x33cm 16x13in) Par, Cornwall 2001

OPIE Julian 1958 **[38]**
🗇 **$6 056** - €6 693 - **£4 200** - FF43 902
«Soviet Frost (White II)» Metal (90x90x141cm 35x35x55in) London 2001
🗇 **$6 137** - €5 124 - **£3 600** - FF33 613
«W» Construction (25.5x53x10.5cm 10x20x4in) London 1998

OPISSO CARDONA Alfredo 1907-1980 **[66]**
🖙 **$1 200** - €1 201 - **£740** - FF7 880
La toilette Oleo/tabla (38.5x46cm 15x18in) Madrid 2000
🖙 **$1 885** - €1 952 - **£1 202** - FF12 805
Tomando café Oleo/tabla (17x22.5cm 6x8in) Barcelona 2000

O

✒ **$552** - €511 - **£331** - FF3 349
Composición abstracta Aguada/papel (63x46cm 24x18in) Barcelona 1999

OPISSO SALA Ricardo 1880-1960 **[100]**
✒ **$585** - €541 - **£351** - FF3 546
Dama con perros Tinta/papel (34.5x19cm 13x7in) Barcelona 1999

OPITZ Franz Karl 1916-1998 **[73]**
▥ **$112** - €113 - **£70** - FF738
Komposition Etching, aquatint in colors (36x28cm 14x11in) Zofingen 1999

OPITZ Georg Emanuel 1775-1841 **[70]**
✒ **$2 521** - €2 447 - **£1 600** - FF16 049
Bedroom Scene with Woman Asleep Watercolour/paper (20x16.5cm 7x6in) London 1999

OPIZ Georg Emanuel 1775-1841 **[5]**
▥ **$1 368** - €1 475 - **£932** - FF10 669
Opstilling med den danske haer og Frederik VI til hest foran Aquatint in colors (50x65cm 19x25in) Köbenhavn 2001

OPPEGARD Sandra F. 1941 **[1]**
✒ **$1 400** - €1 626 - **£983** - FF11 158
Going to the Track, Keeneland (Study 1) Watercolour/paper (19x29cm 7x11in) New-York 2001

OPPEL Gustav 1891-1978 **[19]**
⬥ **$438** - €509 - **£310** - FF3 336
Scherzo Porcelain (H19.8cm H7in) Wien 2000

OPPEL Liesel 1897-1960 **[19]**
⬥ **$6 137** - €7 158 - **£4 309** - FF46 954
Zinnien Oil/panel (50x70cm 19x27in) Köln 2000
⬥ **$4 919** - €4 602 - **£2 979** - FF30 185
Spätsommer an der Hamme, Abendstimmung/Mädchen mit Zöpfen Öl/Karton (31x40cm 12x15in) Bremen 1999

OPPENHEIM Alfred Nathaniel 1873-1953 **[10]**
▥ **$667** - €741 - **£464** - FF4 863
Zeppelin über dem Frankfurter Dom Farblithographie (88.5x58.5cm 34x22in) Heidelberg 2001

OPPENHEIM Dennis 1938 **[119]**
⬥ **$4 249** - €4 084 - **£2 617** - FF26 788
Untitled Metal (51x51x51cm 20x20x20in) New-York 1999
✒ **$2 948** - €3 354 - **£2 046** - FF22 000
Study for toe to hell Aquarelle (96x127cm 37x50in) Bordeaux 2000
▥ **$375** - €420 - **£261** - FF2 753
Projects Color lithograph (96.5x127cm 37x50in) New-York 2001
◉ **$800** - €859 - **£543** - FF5 632
«Crystal Recorder, Stroking the Throat of Tornado Diane...» Photograph in colors (28x35.5cm 11x13in) Beverly-Hills CA 2001

OPPENHEIM Louis 1879-1936 **[17]**
▥ **$398** - €372 - **£245** - FF2 440
«Liebesgaben S. Adam» Poster (95x70.5cm 37x27in) Oostwoud 1999

OPPENHEIM Méret 1913-1985 **[118]**
⬥ **$10 969** - €10 052 - **£6 702** - FF65 939
Strand, drei Hütten und Felsen Öl/Karton (34x50cm 13x19in) Zürich 1999
⬥ **$922** - €832 - **£574** - FF5 720
L'écureuil Assemblage (H24cm H9in) Wien 1999
⬥ **$2 752** - €3 132 - **£1 933** - FF20 547
Frau mit Locken, ihre Halskette haltend Ink (32x43cm 12x16in) Zürich 2001

OPPENHEIMER Charles 1875-1961 **[38]**
⬥ **$10 705** - €10 182 - **£6 500** - FF66 792
Galloway woodlands in Winter Oil/canvas (51.5x61cm 20x24in) Edinburgh 1999
✒ **$665** - €570 - **£400** - FF3 738
On the Ken, Galloway Watercolour/paper (31x45cm 12x17in) Edinburgh 1998
▥ **$959** - €984 - **£600** - FF6 457
«South-west Scotland - See Scotland by Rail» Poster (102x127cm 40x50in) London 2000

OPPENHEIMER Johnny 1923 **[7]**
⬥ **$1 682** - €1 739 - **£1 058** - FF11 405
Stilleben med böcker och ljusstake Oil/canvas (52x64cm 20x25in) Stockholm 2000

OPPENHEIMER Joseph 1876-1966 **[50]**
⬥ **$625** - €734 - **£450** - FF4 812
Portrait of a Lady Oil/canvas (91.5x76cm 36x29in) London 2001
⬥ **$4 410** - €4 940 - **£3 064** - FF32 407
Wansee Oil/board (25.5x32.5cm 10x12in) Melbourne 2001

OPPENHEIMER Max, Mopp 1885-1954 **[105]**
⬥ **$29 320** - €29 069 - **£18 360** - FF190 680
Blumenbeet Öl/Leinwand (90x85cm 35x33in) Wien 1999
✒ **$748** - €844 - **£526** - FF5 538
Frauenkopf Charcoal/paper (27x25cm 10x9in) Bern 2001
▥ **$1 236** - €1 227 - **£772** - FF8 043
Malerei und Musik Farblithographie (75x64cm 29x25in) Hamburg 1999

OPPENOORDT Gilles Marie 1672-1742 **[16]**
⬥ **$10 000** - €8 772 - **£6 072** - FF57 538
Design for a Frontispiece with an Alleogory of Time Ink (47x29cm 18x11in) New-York 1999

OPPENOORTH Willem J. 1847-1905 **[38]**
⬥ **$1 049** - €975 - **£640** - FF6 393
Summer Landscape with a sailing Barge on a River Oil/canvas/panel (39.5x60cm 15x23in) Amsterdam 1998
⬥ **$557** - €635 - **£385** - FF4 167
Forest Landscape with Ducks on a Riverbank Oil/panel (27.5x17.5cm 10x6in) Amsterdam 2000

OPPI Ubaldo 1889-1942 **[24]**
⬥ **$58 800** - €50 796 - **£29 400** - FF333 200
Studio per la figlia di Jefte Olio/cartone (41x66.5cm 16x26in) Milano 1999
✒ **$1 800** - €2 332 - **£1 350** - FF15 300
Nudo maschile China (42.5x20cm 16x7in) Prato 2000

OPPLER Ernst 1867-1929 **[112]**
⬥ **$3 136** - €3 470 - **£2 184** - FF22 764
Couple au piano Huile/toile (88x103cm 34x40in) Bruxelles 2001
▥ **$221** - €185 - **£130** - FF1 215
Pavlova Dancing the Dying Swan Drypoint (31x24cm 12x9in) London 1998

OPPLIGER Ernst 1950 **[1]**
✒ **$1 266** - €1 429 - **£890** - FF9 372
Jagdmotiv Silhouette (40x49.5cm 15x19in) Bern 2001

OPRANDI Giorgio 1883-1962 **[8]**
⬥ **$28 294** - €26 221 - **£16 890** - FF172 000
La belle orientale Huile/toile (134x115cm 52x45in) Paris 1999

$3 311 - €3 781 - £2 334 - FF24 799
Fischerboote auf dem Meer vor Ischia Oil/panel (55x64.5cm 21x25in) Bern 2001

$3 600 - €3 110 - £2 400 - FF20 400
«Case somali, Mogadiscio» Olio/tavola (36x39cm 14x15in) Roma 1998

OPSOMER Isidore 1878-1967 **[85]**
$4 991 - €5 701 - £3 473 - FF37 398
Ferme au bord d'un cours d'eau Huile/toile (100x127cm 39x50in) Bruxelles 2001

$2 080 - €2 479 - £1 490 - FF16 260
De oude molen Oil/panel (65x80cm 25x31in) Lokeren 2001

$1 590 - €1 487 - £966 - FF9 756
Portret van Koning Albert I Oil/panel (42x33cm 16x12in) Lokeren 1999

$295 - €321 - £183 - FF1 951
L'Escaut à Anvers Aquarelle (33x44cm 12x17in) Antwerpen 2000

OPSTAL Andreas Johannes 1792-1858 **[1]**
$6 360 - €5 949 - £3 936 - FF39 024
Plaisirs d'hiver Huile/panneau (37.5x46.5cm 14x18in) Antwerpen 1999

ORANGE Maurice 1867-1916 **[51]**
$1 509 - €1 753 - £1 075 - FF11 500
Chasseurs à pied dans une tranchée Huile/toile (45.5x65cm 17x25in) La Rochelle 2001

$1 373 - €1 538 - £954 - FF10 091
Porträtt av fransk officer Oil/canvas (32x20cm 12x7in) Landskrona 2001

$448 - €488 - £308 - FF3 200
Officier en tenue rouge Gouache/papier (37x18cm 14x7in) Coutances 2001

ORANJE-NASSAU van Wilhelmina 1880-1962 **[7]**
$27 203 - €24 337 - £16 297 - FF159 640
View of Oud Loo Oil/canvas (46x35cm 18x13in) Amsterdam 1998

$8 332 - €9 076 - £5 738 - FF59 532
«Lente» Oil/panel (32.5x39.5cm 12x15in) Amsterdam 2001

ORANT Marthe 1874-1957 **[346]**
$1 025 - €1 143 - £715 - FF7 500
Nature morte aux choux Huile/carton (64x81cm 25x31in) Versailles 2001

$575 - €686 - £410 - FF4 500
L'après-midi au luxembourg Gouache/papier (21.5x29.5cm 8x11in) Paris 2001

ORAZI Manuel 1860-1934 **[43]**
$2 576 - €2 668 - £1 639 - FF17 500
Hop Frog, Edgar Poe Gouache (47x62cm 18x24in) Neuilly-sur-Seine 2000

$2 563 - €2 744 - £1 744 - FF18 000
Palais de la danse Affiche (160x60cm 62x23in) Romans-sur-Isère 2001

ORBAN Dezsö, Desiderious 1884-1986 **[125]**
$2 400 - €2 360 - £1 500 - FF15 480
Landscape with Hills Oil/canvas (39x51cm 15x20in) Budapest 1999

$356 - €371 - £225 - FF2 431
Sydney Harbour and Bridge Mixed media (28x38cm 11x14in) Sydney 2000

$358 - €337 - £216 - FF2 211
The Breakfast Table Pastel/paper (43x56cm 16x22in) Sydney 1999

ORCHARDSON William Quiller 1832-1910 **[24]**
$8 219 - €8 823 - £5 500 - FF57 873
The Letter Oil/canvas (68x51cm 26x20in) London 2000

$3 448 - €3 297 - £2 100 - FF21 628
Portrait of a Lady, head and shoulders Mixed media (15.5x12cm 6x4in) Sighthill 1999

ORCHART Stanley XIX-XX **[59]**
$199 - €223 - £140 - FF1 460
Norfolk Landscape with Church Watercolour/paper (35x47cm 13x18in) Leamington-Spa, Warwickshire 2001

ORD Joseph Biyas 1805-1865 **[8]**
$26 000 - €28 794 - £17 633 - FF188 877
Still Life with Fruit and Tankard Oil/canvas (43x53cm 17x21in) New-York 2000

ORDAZ Luis 1912-1976 **[28]**
$672 - €679 - £462 - FF4 452
Paisaje Oleo/cartón (30x46cm 11x18in) Caracas 1999

ORDNER Paul 1900-1969 **[39]**
$900 - €1 004 - £589 - FF6 586
«Mont-Revard, téléphérique, téleski» Poster (99.5x62cm 39x24in) New-York 2000

ORDOÑEZ Sylvia 1956 **[5]**
$14 000 - €12 207 - £8 464 - FF80 075
Plato, arco y cielo Oil/canvas (120x100cm 47x39in) New-York 1998

ORDWAY Alfred 1819-1897 **[14]**
$3 000 - €3 306 - £1 995 - FF21 688
Mount Washington at Intervale Oil/canvas (38x63cm 15x25in) Portsmouth NH 2000

$425 - €456 - £289 - FF2 994
«Trees» Oil/board (37.5x30cm 14x11in) Boston MA 2001

ORELL Argio 1884-1942 **[9]**
$2 350 - €2 436 - £1 410 - FF15 980
Notturno veneziano Tecnica mista/carta (35x32cm 13x12in) Trieste 2001

ORFEI Orfeo 1836-1915 **[7]**
$3 415 - €3 579 - £2 163 - FF23 477
Der Obsthändler Oil/panel (37x25cm 14x9in) Köln 2000

ORGAN Bryan 1935 **[28]**
$1 149 - €1 341 - £800 - FF8 796
Bees and Flowers Oil/canvas (126.5x101cm 49x39in) London 2000

ORGEIX d' Christian 1927 **[39]**
$1 136 - €1 220 - £760 - FF8 000
Sans titre Crayon (41x29cm 16x11in) Paris 2000

ORI Luciano 1926 **[14]**
$1 500 - €1 555 - £900 - FF10 200
Poesia visiva, La rivoluzione Tecnica mista (95x70cm 37x27in) Prato 1999

ORIANI Pippo 1909-1972 **[121]**
$1 400 - €1 451 - £840 - FF9 520
Spazio Pintura (50x40cm 19x15in) Prato 2001

$600 - €777 - £450 - FF5 100
Arlecchini Tempera/cartone (32x47cm 12x18in) Milano 2001

$1 455 - €1 242 - £867 - FF8 146
Immortale Eroina Collage (60x70cm 23x27in) Zürich 1998

ORIENT Joseph 1677-1747 **[7]**
$12 800 - €14 534 - £8 760 - FF95 340
Winterlandschaft Öl/Leinwand (38x47.5cm 14x18in) Wien 2000

$5 286 - €4 359 - **£3 114** - FF28 596
Gebirgige Landschaft mit rastenden Reitern vor einem Bauerngehöft Oil/panel (26x21cm 10x8in) Wien 1998

ORIOLI degli Pietro di Francesco 1458-1496 [6]
$30 330 - €35 355 - **£21 000** - FF231 913
A female Saint in a Landscape Oil/panel (89x47cm 35x18in) London 2001
$23 660 - €21 903 - **£14 283** - FF143 675
Saint John the Baptist and three Saints, a fragment from an Assumption Tempera/panel (40.5x37cm 15x14in) Dublin 1999

ORKIN Ruth 1921-1985 [59]
$5 000 - €4 662 - **£3 018** - FF30 582
American Girl In Italy Photograph (20.5x30.5cm 8x12in) New-York 1999

ORLAN 1947 [8]
$2 844 - €2 744 - **£1 796** - FF18 000
L'origine de la guerre Cibachrome print (87.5x102cm 34x40in) Paris 1999

ORLANDO Joe 1927 [3]
$1 700 - €1 825 - **£1 137** - FF11 969
Artwork for Seven Page Story «Who's Next?» Ink (45.5x33cm 17x12in) New-York 2000

ORLÉANS d' (duc d') Philippe XIXe [11]
$2 091 - €2 439 - **£1 454** - FF16 000
Remorquage après un accident d'automobile/Voyage en Espagne du Sud Tirage argentique (10x32cm 3x12in) Paris 2000

ORLÉANS d' Marie, princesse 1813-1839 [9]
$1 092 - €1 075 - **£660** - FF7 052
Jeanne d'Arc Bronze (H35cm H13in) Vejle 2000
$1 410 - €1 677 - **£971** - FF11 000
Louise d'Orléans reine des Belges et son fils Crayon (21x28cm 8x11in) Paris 2000

ORLÉANS d', duc de Chartres Ferdinand Philippe 1810-1842 [6]
$20 512 - €24 392 - **£14 128** - FF160 000
Animaux, paysage et personnages Crayon (29x44cm 11x17in) Paris 2000

ORLÉANS d', duch. de Chartres Françoise 1844-1925 [3]
$705 - €838 - **£485** - FF5 500
Nature morte aux cèpes Aquarelle/papier (35x55cm 13x21in) Paris 2000

ORLEY van Richard 1663-1732 [17]
$5 019 - €4 901 - **£3 200** - FF32 147
The Madonna and Child Oil/panel (65.5x55cm 25x21in) London 1999
$2 500 - €2 173 - **£1 513** - FF14 785
Diana Returning from the Hunt Ink (12.5x16cm 4x6in) New-York 1999

ORLIK Emil 1870-1932 [833]
$8 034 - €6 641 - **£4 713** - FF43 565
Pfälzer Landschaft bei Neukastel im Mondschein Öl/Leinwand (63x83cm 24x32in) Heidelberg 1998
$1 800 - €1 529 - **£1 087** - FF10 032
Landscape Oil/paper/canvas (22x28cm 8x11in) Tel Aviv 1999
$574 - €491 - **£347** - FF3 219
Rosen in chinesischer Porzellanvase Aquarell/Papier (32x22.5cm 12x8in) München 1998
$242 - €235 - **£150** - FF1 542
Porträt Alfred Döblin Radierung (18.8x7.8cm 7x3in) Berlin 1999

$995 - €1 176 - **£707** - FF7 713
Lillian Gish Vintage gelatin silver print (12x9cm 4x3in) Berlin 2001

ORLOFF Chana 1888-1968 [164]
$41 947 - €38 874 - **£26 086** - FF255 000
L'Accordéoniste Per Krogh Bronze (91x60x40cm 35x23x15in) Versailles 1999
$18 000 - €14 785 - **£10 454** - FF96 982
Danseuse orientale Bronze (H61.5cm H24in) Tel Aviv 1998
$454 - €488 - **£304** - FF3 200
Mère et enfants Mine plomb (30x22.5cm 11x8in) Versailles 2000

ORLOVSKII Vladimir Donatovich 1842-1914 [26]
$2 500 - €2 266 - **£1 539** - FF14 862
Summer Landscape with Figures Oil/canvas (56x40cm 22x16in) Mystic CT 1999
$2 434 - €2 340 - **£1 500** - FF15 350
Summer Landscape with Figure Oil/canvas/board (19x40cm 7x15in) London 1999

ORLOWSKY Alexander Ossipovich 1777-1832 [49]
$1 754 - €1 943 - **£1 189** - FF12 744
Kutschfahrten Watercolour, gouache (17x24.5cm 6x9in) Hamburg 2000

ORLOWSKY Hans 1894-1967 [35]
$161 - €153 - **£100** - FF1 006
Zwei Harlekine Woodcut (17x12cm 6x4in) Berlin 1999

ORME Daniel c.1766-1832 [21]
$159 - €168 - **£105** - FF1 100
Stanislaw August Poniatowski, roi de Pologne, d'après Le Brun Gravure cuivre (20x15.5cm 7x6in) Warszawa 2000

ORME Edward XIXe [6]
$1 203 - €1 335 - **£800** - FF8 754
Battle of Trafalguar, Death of Lord Viscount Nelson/Battle of the Nile Engraving (51x60.5cm 20x23in) London 2000

ORMEA Willem c.1610-c.1680 [7]
$11 337 - €9 713 - **£6 815** - FF63 712
Fische, Krabben und andere Seetiere sind wie ein Stilleben ausgelegt Öl/Leinwand (69x101cm 27x39in) Stuttgart 1998

OROÑO Dumas XXe [1]
$7 020 - €6 540 - **£4 290** - FF42 900
Montevideo Oleo/cartón (43x54cm 16x21in) Caracas 1998

OROZCO Gabriel 1962 [17]
$35 000 - €40 610 - **£24 164** - FF266 385
Arbol Lunar (Moon Tree) Sculpture (254x200x200cm 100x78x78in) New-York 2000
$75 000 - €87 022 - **£51 780** - FF570 825
Horses Running Endlessly Sculpture, wood (2x88x88cm x34x34in) New-York 2000
$4 800 - €5 463 - **£3 373** - FF35 833
Buiding and Birds Type C color print (40.5x51cm 15x20in) New-York 2001

OROZCO José Clemente 1893-1949 [150]
$55 000 - €53 382 - **£34 243** - FF350 163
Successful People Oil/canvas (46x38cm 18x14in) New-York 1999
$10 000 - €9 730 - **£6 155** - FF63 823
Mujer prostitua Graphite (40x9cm 15x3in) New-York 1999
$1 400 - €1 221 - **£846** - FF8 007
Prometeo Drypoint (16.5x22cm 6x8in) New-York 1998

OROZCO ROMERO Carlos 1898-1984 **[34]**
- **$20 000** - €23 237 - **£14 056** - FF152 424
  Valle de México Oil/canvas (46x61cm 18x24in) New-York 2001

OROZCO Trino 1915 **[51]**
- **$576** - €538 - **£360** - FF3 528
  Paisaje Oleo/tabla (39.5x59.5cm 15x23in) Caracas 1999
- **$515** - €540 - **£341** - FF3 544
  Paisaje Oleo/cartón (34x45cm 13x17in) Caracas ($) 2000

ORPEN Bea 1913-1980 **[16]**
- **$650** - €698 - **£435** - FF4 581
  Sharp's Cottage, Clooney, Co.Donegal Gouache/paper (33x48cm 12x18in) Dublin 2000

ORPEN Richard Caulfield 1863-1938 **[10]**
- **$939** - €914 - **£577** - FF5 996
  Is it worth it? Watercolour/paper (33x22cm 13x9in) Dublin 1999

ORPEN William 1878-1931 **[196]**
- **$34 540** - €38 688 - **£24 000** - FF253 778
  Vivian Hugh Smith (1867-1956), Later 1st Baron Bicester of Tusmore Oil/canvas (127x101.5cm 50x39in) London 1999
- **$88 764** - €83 346 - **£55 000** - FF546 711
  The Normandy Cider Press/The Cyder Press Oil/canvas (53.5x76.5cm 21x30in) London 1999
- **$4 461** - €4 997 - **£3 100** - FF32 779
  Interior, the Artist's Studio, Chelsea Ink (22x21cm 8x8in) London 2001
- **$327** - €330 - **£204** - FF2 165
  On the Cliff Print (20x28cm 7x11in) Dublin 1999

ORPI Arcadi 1933 **[38]**
- **$196** - €210 - **£129** - FF1 379
  Fonda de Ibiza Oleo/lienzo (46x55cm 18x21in) Barcelona 2000

ORR Joseph Charles 1949 **[2]**
- **$4 950** - €5 313 - **£3 312** - FF34 852
  Red Barn Morning Acrylic (60x76cm 24x30in) Houston TX 2000

ORR Louis 1879-1961 **[27]**
- **$127** - €137 - **£85** - FF900
  Le Pont-Neuf (vu de l'écluse de la Monnaie) Eau-forte (73x105cm 28x41in) Paris 2000

ORRENTE IL BASSANO SPAGNOLO Pietro c.1570-1644 **[18]**
- **$15 000** - €15 016 - **£9 250** - FF98 500
  Abraham rechaza los dones del rey de Sodoma Oleo/lienzo (99x162cm 38x63in) Madrid 2001
- **$10 600** - €12 013 - **£7 400** - FF78 800
  Los pastores Oleo/lienzo (76x102cm 29x40in) Madrid 2001

ORROCK James 1829-1913 **[119]**
- **$911** - €844 - **£550** - FF5 536
  Castle from the River/Landscape with Castle Watercolour (23.5x35cm 9x13in) Billingshurst, West-Sussex 1999

ORSAY d' Alfred, Comte 1801-1852 **[9]**
- **$26 025** - €28 685 - **£17 000** - FF188 161
  Portrait of Arthur Wellesley, 1st Duke of Wellington (1759-1852) Oil/canvas (229x146cm 90x57in) London 2000
- **$10 115** - €9 567 - **£6 300** - FF62 755
  Gallantry Scene Oil/canvas (73x59cm 28x23in) Praha 2000

- **$13 490** - €14 483 - **£9 025** - FF95 000
  Autoportrait en pied Bronze (68x32x26.5cm 26x12x10in) Paris 2000

ORSI 1889-1947 **[17]**
- **$3 000** - €2 840 - **£1 863** - FF18 628
  «Jeux Olympiques, Paris» Poster (117x79cm 46x31in) New-York 1999

ORSI Carlo XIX **[2]**
- **$10 000** - €10 992 - **£6 408** - FF72 104
  A Game of Chess Oil/canvas (53.5x75.5cm 21x29in) New-York 2000

ORSI d' Achille 1845-1929 **[20]**
- **$1 080** - €933 - **£540** - FF6 120
  La nassa Bronzo (H44cm H17in) Vercelli 1999

ORSI Lelio c.1508/11-1587 **[14]**
- **$13 332** - €13 018 - **£8 500** - FF85 391
  Design for a Section of painted façade decorated with the Sacrifice... Black chalk (30x25.5cm 11x10in) London 1999

ORSZAG Lili 1926-1978 **[8]**
- **$1 480** - €1 555 - **£920** - FF10 200
  Fragment Technique mixte (41x25cm 16x9in) Budapest 2000

ORTEGA Aurélien XX **[14]**
- **$918** - €930 - **£571** - FF6 100
  Paysage varois Huile/toile (46x55cm 18x21in) Bergerac 2000

ORTEGA José 1921-1991 **[64]**
- **$5 250** - €5 442 - **£3 150** - FF35 700
  L'arrestato Olio/tela (130x130cm 51x51in) Milano 2001
- **$1 150** - €1 192 - **£690** - FF7 820
  Maschera Tempera/cartone (67x50cm 26x19in) Venezia 2000
- **$660** - €601 - **£400** - FF3 940
  Personajes Técnica mixta/papel (66x68cm 25x26in) Madrid 1999
- **$160** - €207 - **£120** - FF1 360
  Senza titolo Acquatinta (66.5x50.5cm 26x19in) Torino 2000

ORTEGA MUÑOZ Godofredo 1905-1982 **[23]**
- **$21 700** - €21 023 - **£13 650** - FF137 900
  «El pozo» Oleo/lienzo (66x83cm 25x32in) Madrid 1999
- **$15 000** - €15 016 - **£9 250** - FF98 500
  Castaños Oleo/lienzo (33x41cm 12x16in) Madrid 1999

ORTEGO Y VEREDA Francisco Javier 1833-1881 **[38]**
- **$1 525** - €1 502 - **£950** - FF9 850
  Fiesta asturiana Oleo/lienzo (25x41cm 9x16in) Madrid 1999

ORTELIUS Abraham Oertel 1527-1598 **[53]**
- **$626** - €597 - **£380** - FF3 916
  Russia Engraving (35.5x44.5cm 13x17in) London 1999

ORTH XX **[1]**
- **$12 776** - €12 196 - **£7 984** - FF80 000
  «Le Gosse» Affiche couleur (240x160cm 94x62in) Paris 1999

ORTH Emil Cordius 1833-1919 **[2]**
- **$1 794** - €2 013 - **£1 243** - FF13 204
  Gammel fiskerhytte ved Strandhusene ved Svendborg Oil/canvas (24x32cm 9x12in) København 2000

O

ORTIZ ALFAU Rafael 1935 **[6]**
- $560 - €601 - £370 - FF3 940
  Jardines de Albia Acuarela/papel (48x64cm 18x25in)
  Madrid 2000

ORTIZ Angeles Manuel 1895-1984 **[93]**
- $6 240 - €7 208 - £4 320 - FF47 280
  Cabezas Oleo/lienzo (100x65cm 39x25in) Seville
  2000
- $1 540 - €1 652 - £1 017 - FF10 835
  Paisaje Oleo/lienzo (15.5x22.5cm 6x8in) Madrid 2000
- $1 088 - €961 - £672 - FF6 304
  Dos cabezas Dibujo (25x32cm 9x12in) Madrid 1999

ORTIZ DE ZARATE Manuel 1886-1946 **[158]**
- $1 219 - €1 067 - £738 - FF7 000
  Nu Huile/toile (92x65cm 36x25in) Versailles 1998
- $641 - €762 - £457 - FF5 000
  A l'heure du thé Aquarelle/papier (32x22cm 12x8in)
  Calais 2000

ORTIZ ECHAGÜE José 1886-1980 **[6]**
- $2 200 - €2 054 - £1 332 - FF13 474
  Murallas de Avila Gelatin silver print (22x16.5cm
  8x6in) New-York 1999

ORTLIEB Friedrich 1839-1909 **[31]**
- $3 208 - €3 068 - £1 953 - FF20 123
  **In ein Bauernstube liest ein Mädchen ihren
  Eltern einen Brief vor** Öl/Leinwand (58x70cm
  22x27in) Stuttgart 1999
- $1 348 - €1 534 - £935 - FF10 061
  **Mutter bei der Handarbeit in malerischer
  Bauernstube** Oil/canvas/panel (25x27.5cm 9x10in)
  Lindau 2000

ORTMANN Theo 1902-1941 **[1]**
- $1 941 - €2 178 - £1 345 - FF14 287
  Surrealist Scene Oil/canvas (39x30cm 15x11in)
  Amsterdam 2000

ORTMANS François Auguste 1827-1884 **[44]**
- $4 471 - €5 031 - £3 078 - FF33 000
  Vaches à l'étang au crépuscule Huile/toile
  (56x87cm 22x34in) Paris 2000
- $1 206 - €1 372 - £837 - FF9 000
  Le vieux chêne Huile/panneau (11x15cm 4x5in) Paris
  2000
- $4 800 - €4 856 - £2 930 - FF31 852
  The Forest of Fontainbleau Watercolour
  (17.5x26cm 6x10in) New-York 2000

ORTOLANI Augusto 1873-? **[1]**
- $4 400 - €5 702 - £3 300 - FF37 400
  Prime luci Olio/tela (78x114cm 30x44in) Milano 2000

ORTUÑO PASCUAL Roberto 1953 **[35]**
- $1 134 - €1 081 - £702 - FF7 092
  Figura sentada en un sofá Oleo/lienzo (100x100cm
  39x39in) Barcelona 1999
- $578 - €536 - £356 - FF3 515
  Florero sobre fondo fucsia Gouache/papier
  (50x50cm 19x19in) Madrid 1998

ORTVAD Erik 1917 **[89]**
- $3 885 - €3 364 - £2 342 - FF22 065
  «Landliv» Oil/canvas (70x80cm 27x31in) Köbenhavn
  1998
- $768 - €838 - £521 - FF5 500
  Composition Huile/papier (21x30cm 8x11in) Paris
  2000
- $262 - €295 - £183 - FF1 932
  Degerhamn Watercolour/paper (23x32cm 9x12in)
  Viby J, Århus 2001

ORUP Bengt 1916-1996 **[49]**
- $496 - €520 - £314 - FF3 412
  Efter fiestan Oil/canvas (73x92cm 28x36in) Malmö
  2000

OS van Georgius Jacobus J. 1782-1861 **[72]**
- $21 648 - €20 452 - £13 504 - FF134 156
  Blumen Fruchtstilleben Öl/Leinwand (90x70cm
  35x27in) Hamburg 1999
- $3 122 - €2 949 - £1 888 - FF19 347
  Still Life with Fruit Oil/panel (13.5x18.5cm 5x7in)
  Amsterdam 1999
- $1 695 - €1 982 - £1 210 - FF13 000
  Bouquet de fleurs sur un entablement
  Aquarelle/papier (25x19.5cm 9x7in) Angers 2001

OS van Giorgius Jacobus J. 1805-1841 **[2]**
- $2 135 - €2 045 - £1 343 - FF13 415
  **Stilleben mit Pflaumen, weissen und roten
  Trauben** Öl/Leinwand (26.5x21cm 10x8in) Köln 1999

OS van Jan 1744-1808 **[51]**
- $51 720 - €60 980 - £36 360 - FF400 000
  **Nature morte de fleurs et de fruits sur un enta-
  blement** Huile/panneau (58x44.5cm 22x17in) Paris
  2000
- $8 921 - €8 568 - £5 500 - FF56 203
  Crowded Ferry Oil/panel (21.5x28cm 8x11in)
  London 1999

OS van Pieter Frederick 1808-1892 **[14]**
- $4 936 - €5 368 - £3 253 - FF35 215
  Stallinterieur mit Fuhrwerk und Personen
  Oil/panel (60.5x80.5cm 23x31in) Heidelberg 2000
- $1 978 - €1 770 - £1 185 - FF11 608
  A Lady on a Horseback and a Beggar Oil/panel
  (22x18.5cm 8x7in) Amsterdam 1998

OS van Pieter Gerardus 1776-1839 **[49]**
- $5 073 - €5 445 - £3 394 - FF35 719
  **Shepherdess and cattle resting by a wooded
  pond** Oil/canvas (47x62.5cm 18x24in) Amsterdam
  2000
- $2 796 - €3 176 - £1 962 - FF20 836
  The little Shepherds Oil/panel (22x31cm 8x12in)
  Paris 2001
- $1 983 - €1 982 - £1 240 - FF13 000
  Harde de daims dans la neige Gouache (19x24cm
  7x9in) Soissons 1999

OS van Pim 1910-1954 **[8]**
- $1 908 - €2 269 - £1 360 - FF14 883
  Solarised Nude Silver print (39.5x29.5cm 15x11in)
  Amsterdam 2000

OS van Tony 1886-1945 **[31]**
- $927 - €868 - £563 - FF5 691
  Winterlandschap Oil/canvas (45x75cm 17x29in)
  Lokeren 1999

OS-DELHEZ van Henri 1880-1976 **[67]**
- $493 - €454 - £305 - FF2 976
  Dijkherstel Oil/canvas (40x50.5cm 15x19in)
  Amsterdam 1999
- $499 - €454 - £306 - FF2 976
  «Montmartre» Oil/canvas (30.5x40.5cm 12x15in)
  Amsterdam 1999

OSBERT Alphonse 1857-1939 **[66]**
- $3 243 - €3 583 - £2 248 - FF23 500
  Chant du soir Huile/carton (35x27cm 13x10in) Paris
  2001
- $1 306 - €1 296 - £812 - FF8 500
  **Etude pour la décoration du Hall des Bains de
  Vichy** Fusain (63x24.5cm 24x9in) Paris 1999

OSBORNE James 1940-1992 **[22]**
$1 683 - €2 002 - **£1 200** - FF13 134
Greyhounds Coursing Bronze (30.5x43cm 12x16in)
London 2000

OSBORNE Malcolm 1880-1963 **[44]**
$129 - €143 - **£90** - FF940
The Donchon - Loches Castle Etching (21.5x19cm
8x7in) Godalming, Surrey 2001

OSBORNE Russell Sallye XVIII **[1]**
$3 000 - €2 859 - **£1 819** - FF18 752
Theorem Still Life Drawings Watercolour (23x20cm
9x8in) New-York 1999

OSBORNE Walter Frederick 1859-1903 **[69]**
$528 240 - €450 392 - **£318 683** - FF2 954 381
Dorothy and Irene Falkiner Oil/canvas (149x114cm
59x45in) Dublin 1998
$445 051 - €497 636 - **£300 000** - FF3 264 280
A New Arrival Oil/canvas/board (45.5x35.5cm
17x13in) London 2000
$22 408 - €21 243 - **£14 000** - FF139 342
Portrait of Miss Armstrong Oil/canvas (33x25.5cm
12x10in) London 1999
$1 509 - €1 778 - **£1 060** - FF11 660
The Horserguards Pencil/paper (25.5x36cm 10x14in)
Dublin 2000

OSBORNE William 1823-1901 **[13]**
$14 392 - €16 120 - **£10 000** - FF105 741
**Stealing the milk, Two Terriers in the Artist's
Studio** Oil/canvas (46x35.5cm 18x13in) London 2001
$2 188 - €2 539 - **£1 511** - FF16 658
**Portrait of a Seated Jack Russel wearing a
White Cravat and Collar** Oil/canvas (35x45cm
13x17in) Dublin 2000

OSCARSSON Bernhard 1894-1971 **[50]**
$741 - €646 - **£448** - FF4 239
«Miguel» Oil/canvas (81x65cm 31x25in) Stockholm
1998
$475 - €492 - **£299** - FF3 225
Stickande kvinna vid eldstad Oil/panel (26x34cm
10x13in) Stockholm 2000

OSEN Erwin Dominik 1891-1970 **[9]**
$620 - €581 - **£383** - FF3 813
Blick nur Klosterneuburg Aquarell/Papier
(48.5x34cm 19x13in) Wien 1999

OSHIVER Harry James 1888-1974 **[15]**
$850 - €807 - **£520** - FF5 293
**Portrait of a Young Woman seated in Windsor
Chair** Oil/canvas (76x60cm 30x24in) Hatfield PA 1999
$1 050 - €1 002 - **£656** - FF6 574
Lounging Nude Oil/board (28x38cm 11x15in)
Hatfield PA 1999

OSIECKI Stefan 1902-1939 **[3]**
$558 - €522 - **£344** - FF3 423
«Polen Zakopane Kasprowy» Poster (70x100cm
27x39in) Oostwoud 1999

OSIPOV Alexander 1946 **[2]**
$675 - €647 - **£425** - FF4 242
Choosing Flowers Oil/canvas (46x38cm 18x14in)
Fernhurst, Haslemere, Surrey 1999
$336 - €361 - **£225** - FF2 367
Rainy Day Oil/canvas/board (24x33cm 9x12in)
Fernhurst, Haslemere, Surrey 1999

OSIPOW Paul 1939 **[27]**
$398 - €404 - **£250** - FF2 647
Komposition Oil/canvas (37x37cm 14x14in) Helsinki
2000

OSMENT Philip, Phil XIX-XX **[37]**
$134 - €144 - **£90** - FF946
Sailboats on the High Seas Watercolour/paper
(25x40cm 10x16in) Little-Lane, Ilkley 2000

OSNAGHI Josefine XIX-XX **[9]**
$405 - €438 - **£280** - FF2 870
**Still Life of a Ewer, Strawberries and other
Objects on a Table** Oil/panel (20.5x25.5cm 8x10in)
London 2001

OSPINA Nadin 1960 **[4]**
$15 000 - €15 999 - **£9 991** - FF104 946
Centinela Terracotta (H113cm H44in) New-York 2000
$2 400 - €2 788 - **£1 686** - FF18 290
Retador Terracotta (35.5x24cm 13x9in) New-York
2001

OSSANI Gogliardo XX **[1]**
$1 141 - €1 183 - **£684** - FF7 758
«Riviera di Rimini» Affiche couleur (99x69cm
38x27in) Torino 2000

OSSENBECK van Jan c.1624-1674 **[19]**
$6 600 - €5 702 - **£4 400** - FF37 400
Sosta di viandanti Olio/tela (53x77cm 20x30in)
Milano 1998

OSSIAO Paulo 1952 **[2]**
$528 - €598 - **£372** - FF3 924
Jovens Acuarela/papel (28x37.5cm 11x14in) Lisboa
2001

OSSIPOV Alexandre 1892-1981 **[18]**
$821 - €793 - **£515** - FF5 200
Au marché aux fleurs Huile/toile (46x38cm
18x14in) L'Isle-Adam 1999
$241 - €259 - **£161** - FF1 700
Marché aux fleurs Huile/toile/carton (22x30cm
8x11in) L'Isle-Adam 1999

OSSLUND Erik 1913 **[5]**
$1 865 - €2 190 - **£1 316** - FF14 365
Fjällandskap i höstfärger Oil/paper/panel (32x41cm
12x16in) Stockholm 2000

OSSLUND Helmer 1866-1938 **[368]**
$6 403 - €6 905 - **£4 297** - FF45 292
Norrländskt kustlandskap Oil/canvas/panel
(43.5x69cm 17x27in) Stockholm 2000
$2 340 - €2 228 - **£1 464** - FF14 612
Normandie om våren Oil/canvas/panel (21.5x32cm
8x12in) Stockholm 1999
$1 207 - €1 341 - **£808** - FF8 796
Fjällandskap Tempera/paper (30.5x58cm 12x22in)
Stockholm 2000

OSSORIO Alfonso 1916-1990 **[32]**
$18 000 - €19 754 - **£11 590** - FF129 578
Her and Now Mixed media (198x96.5cm 77x37in)
New-York 2000
$3 287 - €3 529 - **£2 200** - FF23 147
Untitled Mixed media/board (91.5x83cm 36x32in)
London 2000
$9 616 - €9 452 - **£6 175** - FF62 000
Sans titre Aquarelle (101x75.5cm 39x29in) Paris 1999

OSSWALD Eugen 1879-1960 **[60]**
$539 - €613 - **£374** - FF4 024
Hund und totes Reh Öl/Leinwand (70x104cm
27x40in) Rudolstadt-Thüringen 2000
$403 - €332 - **£237** - FF2 179
Glucke mit Kühen Aquarell/Papier (20x37cm 7x14in)
Lindau 1998
$1 200 - €1 199 - **£733** - FF7 867
«Stay Young Playing Golf in Germany» Poster
(100x62cm 39x24in) New-York 2000

O

OSSWALD Fritz 1878-1966 **[115]**
- $447 - €511 - £310 - FF3 353
  Blumenstrauss Öl/Leinwand (77x70cm 30x27in) Rudolstadt-Thüringen 2000

OSSWALD Karl 1925-1972 **[2]**
- $918 - €844 - £564 - FF5 533
  Landschaft mit Hohentwiel Aquarell/Papier (30x40cm 11x15in) Radolfzell 1999

OSSWALD-TOPPI Margherita 1897-1971 **[53]**
- $913 - €1 043 - £644 - FF6 841
  Stilleben mit Blumensträussen und Krügen Öl/Karton (43x57cm 16x22in) Bern 2001

OST Alfred 1884-1945 **[236]**
- $344 - €397 - £236 - FF2 601
  De bibliothecaris Ink/paper (25x32.5cm 9x12in) Lokeren 2000
- $234 - €198 - £139 - FF1 300
  Vluchtelingen Color lithograph (19x28cm 7x11in) Lokeren 2000

OSTADE van Adriaen Jansz. 1610-1685 **[526]**
- $44 020 - €47 259 - £29 450 - FF310 000
  Scène d'intérieur paysan: une famille dans une grange Huile/panneau (36.5x46.5cm 14x18in) Paris 2000
- $50 680 - €42 686 - £29 932 - FF280 000
  La réunion à l'auberge Huile/panneau (23.5x20.5cm 9x8in) Paris 1998
- $9 229 - €7 972 - £5 563 - FF52 291
  A Hurdy-Gurdy Player at the Door of a House Wash (10x9cm 3x3in) Amsterdam 1998
- $400 - €384 - £246 - FF2 519
  The barn Etching (15.5x19cm 6x7in) New-York 1999

OSTADE van Isaac Jansz. 1621-1649 **[32]**
- $81 555 - €76 278 - £50 000 - FF500 350
  Peasants Resting and Smoking by an Inn Oil/panel (62x60cm 24x23in) London 1998
- $1 095 - €1 271 - £756 - FF8 334
  A Man, Seen from behind Black chalk (8x4cm 3x1in) Amsterdam 2000

OSTAIJEN van Paul 1896-1928 **[1]**
- $4 541 - €4 710 - £3 002 - FF30 894
  Compositie Crayons couleurs/papier (23x35cm 9x13in) Bruxelles 2000

OSTENDORFER Martin XVI **[2]**
- $11 934 - €10 224 - £7 174 - FF67 066
  Mariä Verkündigung Oil/panel (88x64cm 34x25in) Köln 1998

OSTERIDER Adolf A. 1924 **[11]**
- $2 817 - €3 270 - £1 944 - FF21 451
  Nach dem Kostümfest Öl/Leinwand (120x80cm 47x31in) Graz 2000

ÖSTERLIN Anders 1926 **[65]**
- $784 - €879 - £545 - FF5 766
  Landskap Oil/canvas (61x80cm 24x31in) Malmö 2001

ÖSTERLIND Allan 1855-1938 **[105]**
- $926 - €933 - £577 - FF6 123
  Mme Gösta Olson Oil/canvas (58x71cm 22x27in) Stockholm 2000
- $344 - €323 - £207 - FF2 117
  Dansande och sjungande spanjorskor Akvarell/papper (52x35cm 20x13in) Stockholm 1999

OSTERLIND Anders 1887-1960 **[225]**
- $1 391 - €1 363 - £858 - FF8 943
  Parkgezicht Oil/canvas (92x74cm 36x29in) Lokeren 1999

OSTERLUND Herman 1873-1964 **[55]**
- $485 - €508 - £307 - FF3 333
  Kapellet i Arild Oil/canvas (57x70cm 22x27in) Malmö 2000

OSTERROTH Gustav 1836-1875 **[7]**
- $2 673 - €2 556 - £1 628 - FF16 769
  Blick von erhöhter Warte auf den Kochelsee Öl/Leinwand (34x27cm 13x10in) Stuttgart 1999

OSTERSETZER Carl 1865-1914 **[80]**
- $1 367 - €1 534 - £947 - FF10 061
  Jäger und Dirndl am Ufer des Gebirgssees Öl/Leinwand (50.5x78.5cm 19x30in) München 2000
- $1 943 - €2 086 - £1 300 - FF13 682
  Pause for Thought Oil/canvas (30x19.5cm 11x7in) London 2000

OSTERTAG Georg 1906-1980 **[5]**
- $2 071 - €1 943 - £1 279 - FF12 744
  Komposition Pastell/Papier (70x50cm 27x19in) Stuttgart 1999

OSTERWALD d' Rose 1795-1831 **[6]**
- $332 - €312 - £204 - FF2 044
  Ansichten des Berner Oberlandes Aquatinta (14.2x20.6cm 5x8in) Bern 1999

OSTHAUS Edmund Henry 1858-1928 **[106]**
- $30 000 - €29 785 - £18 750 - FF195 378
  Setter in a Landscape Oil/canvas (61x76cm 24x29in) New-York 2000
- $9 000 - €10 703 - £6 414 - FF70 209
  A Setter Retrieving Watercolour (29x44.5cm 11x17in) New-York 2000

OSTIER André 1906 **[18]**
- $1 202 - €1 431 - £859 - FF9 390
  Pablo Picasso devant «La Flute de Pan» Gelatin silver print (20.4x20cm 8x7in) Berlin 2000

OSTOJA-KOTKOWSKI Stanislaus Joseph 1922-1994 **[17]**
- $255 - €246 - £157 - FF1 612
  Study in Form Watercolour/paper (78.5x55cm 30x21in) Melbourne 1999

OSTRANDER William Cheesbrough 1858-? **[1]**
- $1 900 - €2 012 - £1 257 - FF13 196
  «Study for the Fairy's Hammock» Watercolour/paper (30.5x36.5cm 12x14in) New-York 2000

OSTROUKHOV Ilya Semenovich 1858-1929 **[3]**
- $4 026 - €3 801 - £2 500 - FF24 936
  Woodland Pond Oil/canvas (30x40.5cm 11x15in) London 1999

OSTROWSKY Abbo 1889-? **[5]**
- $1 800 - €2 104 - £1 264 - FF13 803
  Bracing Subway Excavation, New York Etching (35.5x28cm 13x11in) New-York 2000

OSTROWSKY Sam 1886-? **[13]**
- $700 - €801 - £486 - FF5 252
  Still Life with Fruit Oil/canvas (25x30cm 10x12in) Cincinnati OH 2000

OSWALD Charles W. XIX-XX **[66]**
- $651 - €558 - £393 - FF3 663
  Highland River Scenes Oil/canvas (48.5x75cm 19x29in) Toronto 1998

$579 - €537 - **£360** - FF3 523
Höstplöjning Oil/canvas (31x41cm 12x16in) Malmö
1999

OSWALD John H. 1843-1895 **[21]**
$1 213 - €1 029 - **£720** - FF6 747
St Michael's Mount Oil/canvas (65x100.5cm
25x39in) Billingshurst, West-Sussex 1998

OTEIZA de Jorge 1908 **[11]**
$6 700 - €6 006 - **£4 100** - FF39 400
Provecto para un monumento Bronze
(14x12.5x10cm 5x4x3in) Madrid 1999

OTÉMAR d' Edouard Modérat XIX-XX **[6]**
$2 413 - €2 744 - **£1 656** - FF18 000
Massif de fleurs et arrosoir Huile/toile (46x31cm
18x12in) Lyon 2000

OTERO Alejandro 1921-1990 **[43]**
$20 000 - €17 439 - **£12 092** - FF114 394
Máscara Oil/canvas (54x65cm 21x25in) New-York
1998
$5 000 - €5 276 - **£3 024** - FF34 608
Acompter sur mer honorares Collage/carton
(31x24.5cm 9x12in) Caracas 2000
$8 000 - €9 419 - **£5 621** - FF61 787
Héctor Gouache (51x43cm 20x16in) New-York 2000

OTERO Carlos 1888-1977 **[20]**
$5 026 - €5 924 - **£3 531** - FF38 859
Puente cannaregio, Venezia Oleo/lienzo
(73.5x100.5cm 28x39in) Caracas ($) 2000
$1 190 - €1 078 - **£770** - FF7 070
Paisaje Oleo/lienzo (33.5x30cm 13x11in) Caracas
1999

OTERO Manuel 1921 **[14]**
$226 - €252 - **£155** - FF1 654
Plantas y peces Email (28.5x21.5cm 11x8in) Madrid
2001

OTHO Otto T. XIX **[1]**
$3 168 - €3 068 - **£1 990** - FF20 123
**Zwei Winterlandschaften im Abendlicht mit
Mühlen, Wehrturm, Eisläufer** Öl/Leinwand
(24.5x32cm 9x12in) Berlin 1999

OTHONIEL Jean-Michel 1964 **[16]**
$693 - €838 - **£484** - FF5 500
Le peuplier Assemblage (71.5x53.5x6cm 28x21x2in)
Paris 2000

OTIS George Demont 1879-1962 **[67]**
$4 250 - €4 959 - **£2 958** - FF32 526
Storm Over Mojave Oil/canvas (66x81cm 26x32in)
Altadena CA 2000
$5 500 - €5 904 - **£3 680** - FF38 725
La Brea Fields Oil/canvas (29x39cm 11x15in)
Altadena CA 2000

OTT Johann Nepomuk 1804-1870 **[13]**
$9 114 - €10 226 - **£6 318** - FF67 078
Italienische Küstenlandschaft nach dem Sturm
Öl/Leinwand (42.5x58.5cm 16x23in) München 2000

OTT Lucien ?-1927 **[11]**
$653 - €701 - **£437** - FF4 600
Loguivy, barques au sec Aquarelle/papier (25x39cm
9x15in) Douarnenez 2000

OTTAVIANI Giovanni 1735-1808 **[14]**
$960 - €901 - **£600** - FF5 910
**«Deduta della Scala Reggia ordinata da
Alesandro VII** Grabado (49x72cm 19x28in) Madrid
1999

OTTE William Louis 1871-1957 **[20]**
$6 500 - €7 640 - **£4 506** - FF50 114
West Wind, Carmel Oil/board (23x30.5cm 9x12in)
Beverly-Hills CA 2000
$3 500 - €4 083 - **£2 436** - FF26 786
«La Cumbre-the Top» Pastel/board (11x15cm 4x6in)
Altadena CA 2000

OTTENFELD von Rudolf Otto 1856-1913 **[14]**
$11 941 - €11 562 - **£7 500** - FF75 843
An Arab Warrior Oil/panel (18.5x13cm 7x5in)
London 1999

OTTERBEEK Jacobus Hermanus 1839-1902 **[3]**
$1 742 - €1 724 - **£1 066** - FF11 311
**Fisherfolk at the Beach looking at a Hot-air
Balloon** Watercolour/paper (27x37cm 10x14in)
Amsterdam 2000

OTTERNESS Tom 1952 **[20]**
$24 000 - €27 153 - **£16 790** - FF178 092
Podium Figure Bronze (183x56x56cm 72x22x22in)
New-York 2001
$4 000 - €4 460 - **£2 689** - FF29 257
Untitled Bronze (9.5x20x14cm 3x7x5in) New-York
2000

OTTESEN Otto Didrik 1816-1892 **[108]**
$5 076 - €6 036 - **£3 618** - FF39 595
**Dueslag med åben dör, hvori ses talrige duer,
omgivet af voksende efeu** Oil/wood (51x69.5cm
20x27in) Köbenhavn 2000
$2 820 - €3 353 - **£2 010** - FF21 997
Röde roser Oil/canvas (26.5x21.5cm 10x8in)
Köbenhavn 2000

OTTEWELL Benjamin John ?-1937 **[34]**
$316 - €355 - **£220** - FF2 326
The Littleworth Road, Burnham Beeches
Watercolour/paper (51.5x34cm 20x13in) London 2001

OTTINGER George Morton 1833-1917 **[2]**
$50 000 - €42 719 - **£30 015** - FF280 220
The Last Ride of the Pony Express of 1861
Oil/canvas (51x58.5cm 20x23in) New-York 1998

OTTINO Pasquale 1570/80-1630 **[5]**
$5 029 - €4 250 - **£3 000** - FF27 881
The Adoration of the Shepherds Oil/panel
(21.5x24cm 8x9in) London 1998

OTTLER Otto 1891-1965 **[5]**
$540 - €613 - **£383** - FF4 024
«Strandhotel Staffelsee» Poster (120x84cm
47x33in) Hannover 2000

OTTMANN Henri 1877-1927 **[174]**
$15 513 - €14 483 - **£9 395** - FF95 000
Chez la modiste Huile/toile (171x148cm 67x58in)
Versailles 1999
$3 155 - €3 503 - **£2 200** - FF22 978
Au bord de la rivière Oil/canvas (50x73.5cm
19x28in) London 2001
$566 - €534 - **£343** - FF3 500
La Seine Huile/toile (33x46cm 12x18in) Paris 1999
$246 - €274 - **£165** - FF1 800
Portrait d'homme Pastel/papier (38x26cm 14x10in)
Paris 2000

OTTO Heinrich 1858-1923 **[54]**
$161 - €138 - **£96** - FF905
Bäume Radierung (29x36.7cm 11x14in) Hamburg
1998

O

OTTO Johann Heinrich act.1762-1797 **[1]**
- $3 100 - €3 374 - £2 130 - FF22 131
  Lancaster County, with Central Script surrounded by Profuse Block Watercolour (33x41cm 13x16in) Downington PA 2001

OTTO Waldemar 1929 **[13]**
- $1 074 - €940 - £650 - FF6 169
  Liegende Bronze (5.2x12.8x5.3cm 2x5x2in) Berlin 1998

OTTOLENGHI-WEDEKIND Herta 1885-1953 **[1]**
- $8 188 - €8 181 - £5 120 - FF53 662
  Klassische Tanzszene Relief (79x102cm 31x40in) München 1999

OUBORG Pieter, Piet 1893-1956 **[120]**
- $1 144 - €1 361 - £816 - FF8 929
  Abstract Composition Oil/board (27.5x33cm 10x12in) Amsterdam 2000
- $2 310 - €2 000 - £1 401 - FF13 117
  Untitled Collage (10.5x15.5cm 4x6in) Amsterdam 1998

OUD Jacobus J. Peter XIX-XX **[1]**
- $13 000 - €13 954 - £8 699 - FF91 533
  Giso No.404, a Piano Lamp Metal (11x19x30cm 4x7x11in) New-York 2000

OUDART Paul Louis 1796-1850 **[15]**
- $2 875 - €3 354 - £2 019 - FF22 000
  Phaseanus Pucrasca, Fragopan d'Hastings/Trois oiseaux huppés Aquarelle, gouache (16.5x10cm 6x3in) Paris 2000

OUDENHOVEN van Joseph c.1825-c.1900 **[10]**
- $4 833 - €4 807 - £3 000 - FF31 533
  New Admirer Oil/panel (40.5x49cm 15x19in) London 1999

OUDERAA van der Piet 1841-1915 **[61]**
- $10 925 - €11 325 - £6 555 - FF74 290
  La strage degli innocenti Olio/tela (143x220cm 56x86in) Roma 1999
- $4 011 - €3 812 - £2 441 - FF25 003
  De zwaard slijper Oil/panel (95x69cm 37x27in) Rotterdam 1999
- $946 - €1 091 - £651 - FF7 154
  Portret van een dame Oil/panel (40x31cm 15x12in) Lokeren 2000

OUDES Dirk 1895-1969 **[3]**
- $2 748 - €2 949 - £1 838 - FF19 347
  Boer Ontmoet Koe Oil/board (42x52cm 16x20in) Amsterdam 2000

OUDINOT Achille François 1820-1891 **[22]**
- $6 000 - €6 046 - £3 740 - FF39 660
  Figures Along a Wooded canal Oil/canvas (73x54.5cm 28x21in) New-York 2000

OUDOT Georges 1928 **[74]**
- $14 343 - €16 007 - £9 387 - FF105 000
  La Vouivre (statue) Bronze (H100cm H39in) Besançon 2000
- $1 745 - €2 058 - £1 227 - FF13 500
  Le Torrent Bronze (H17cm H6in) Fontainebleau 2000
- $430 - €454 - £284 - F2 975
  Frauenkopf, la Pensée Pastell/Papier (32.5x22cm 12x8in) Zürich 2000

OUDOT Roland 1897-1981 **[564]**
- $3 249 - €2 901 - £1 990 - FF19 030
  Fleurs Oil/canvas (54x50cm 21x25in) New-York 1999
- $1 072 - €915 - £646 - FF6 000
  Coucher de soleil en Provence Huile/toile (27x41cm 10x15in) Calais 1998

- $455 - €427 - £273 - FF2 800
  Nu Fusain/papier (32.5x52.5cm 12x20in) Paris 1999
- $132 - €134 - £83 - FF882
  Skördefest Color lithograph (36x43cm 14x16in) Helsinki 2000

OUDRY Jacques-Charles 1720-1778 **[37]**
- $16 000 - €14 830 - £9 948 - FF97 281
  Deer at a Stream and a Wolf fighting over a Basket of Birds, Landscape Oil/canvas (192x98cm 75x38in) New-York 1999
- $16 000 - €18 845 - £11 065 - FF123 614
  Black Hunting Dog with a Game Bird/White and Tan Dog with a Hare Oil/canvas (48.5x59cm 19x23in) New-York 2000
- $1 025 - €1 085 - £650 - FF7 114
  Tree and a Cottage Black & white chalks/paper (36.5x26cm 14x10in) London 2000

OUDRY Jean-Baptiste 1686-1755 **[142]**
- $480 000 - €479 775 - £293 232 - FF3 147 120
  Le retour de chasse: a Hunting Dog Guarding Dead Game Oil/canvas (263x189cm 103x74in) New-York 2000
- $44 996 - €44 631 - £28 000 - FF292 762
  Dead Hare, a Pheasant, a young Partridge, a Jay and other Game Oil/canvas (81.5x100.5cm 32x39in) London 1999
- $4 902 - €5 793 - £3 473 - FF38 000
  Dispute de Ragotin Huile/toile (33.5x43cm 13x16in) Béziers 2000
- $6 000 - €6 427 - £4 097 - FF42 159
  The Head and the Tail of the Snake, from the Fables of La Fontaine Ink (31x26cm 12x10in) New-York 2001
- $111 - €131 - £76 - FF860
  A Bois du cerf Radierung (50x35.5cm 19x13in) Bern 2000

OUDRY Marie Marguerite ?-1780 **[1]**
- $3 227 - €3 201 - £2 007 - FF21 000
  Portrait de Jean Baptiste Oudry Pastel/papier (19x16cm 7x6in) Paris 1999

OUHEL Ivan 1945 **[16]**
- $895 - €847 - £558 - FF5 558
  Paysage Huile/toile (55x60cm 21x23in) Praha 2001

OULESS Philip John 1817-1885 **[39]**
- $16 995 - €15 998 - £10 500 - FF104 942
  The Screw Steamer «Lady Bird» entering St. Helier, Jersey Oil/canvas (48.5x75cm 19x29in) London 1999
- $1 062 - €1 240 - £750 - FF8 134
  Elizabeth Castle Oil/canvas (26.5x43cm 10x16in) Channel-Islands 2000

OULINE A. 1918-1940 **[36]**
- $632 - €701 - £437 - FF4 600
  Le pêcheur Bronze (40x52cm 15x20in) Moulins 2001

OULTON Therese 1953 **[35]**
- $4 326 - €4 781 - £3 000 - FF31 359
  Germination V Oil/canvas (57x45.5cm 22x17in) London 2001

OURSLER Tony 1957 **[16]**
- $29 993 - €29 084 - £19 000 - FF190 777
  Give it back Sculpture (H190cm H74in) London 1999
- $23 000 - €19 621 - £13 873 - FF128 708
  Instant Suckling Assemblage (20x60x20cm 7x23x7in) New-York 1998
- $1 875 - €2 072 - £1 300 - FF13 593
  Poetics Country Screenprint in colors (88x91cm 34x35in) London 2001

OURY Léon Louis 1846-? [21]

📖 $638 - €610 - **£400** - FF4 002
«Exposition Internationale de Bruxelles» Poster (121x76cm 47x29in) London 1999

OUSLEY William, Will 1866/70-1953 [18]

🖌 $950 - €977 - **£602** - FF6 411
Creek Winding through a Meadow of blue Bonnets Oil/canvas (40x60cm 16x24in) New-Orleans LA 2000

✏ $1 700 - €1 453 - **£998** - FF9 529
«West Fork of Calcasieu River, LA No.490, Mist» Pencil/paper (46x85cm 18x33in) New-Orleans LA 1998

OUTCAULT Richard Felton 1863-1928 [4]

✏ $8 500 - €9 468 - **£5 559** - FF62 104
Gag cartoon: Black parson takes a fall to amusement Ink (34x55cm 13x22in) New-York 2000

OUTER Nestor 1865-1930 [16]

🖌 $972 - €992 - **£608** - FF6 504
Neige en forêt Aquarelle/papier (56x38cm 22x14in) Bruxelles 1999

OUTERBRIDGE Paul, Jnr. 1896-1958 [178]

📷 $22 000 - €20 544 - **£13 285** - FF134 763
Pierrot Platinum print (11.5x9cm 4x3in) New-York 1999

OUTHWAITE Ida Sherbourne Rent. 1888-1960 [29]

✏ $5 108 - €4 454 - **£3 088** - FF29 216
Wattle Fairy Watercolour/paper (44.5x33.5cm 17x13in) Melbourne 1998

OUTIN Pierre 1840-1899 [19]

🖌 $21 313 - €22 497 - **£14 084** - FF147 571
Galantes Paar auf einer Parkbank Öl/Leinwand (80x60.5cm 31x23in) Heidelberg 2000

🖌 $20 173 - €21 654 - **£13 542** - FF142 041
Les bonbons de Madame Oil/canvas (47x31cm 18x12in) London 2000

OUTRAM George 1863-1936 [18]

🖌 $332 - €387 - **£230** - FF2 540
On the Derwent, Derbyshire Watercolour/paper (30x46cm 11x18in) Cheshire 2000

OUVRIÉ Justin Pierre 1806-1879 [115]

🖌 $15 727 - €17 861 - **£11 000** - FF117 159
Capriccio de Dordrecht Oil/canvas (70x100cm 27x39in) London 2001

🖌 $3 058 - €3 354 - **£2 076** - FF22 000
La Commanderie Huile/toile (32x24.5cm 12x9in) Pontoise 2000

✏ $897 - €838 - **£553** - FF5 500
Le tombeau d'Héloïse Aquarelle (17x14.5cm 6x5in) Paris 1999

OUWATER Isaak 1750-1793 [21]

🖌 $74 234 - €69 489 - **£46 000** - FF455 818
View of St.Bavo's Cathedral, Haarlem, with Elegant Company Oil/canvas (43.5x55cm 17x21in) London 1999

🖌 $10 897 - €9 209 - **£6 500** - FF60 409
Landscape with Figures Relaxing in Front of a Farmhouse Oil/canvas (34.5x39cm 13x15in) London 1998

OVADYAHU Samuel 1892-1963 [71]

🖌 $3 300 - €3 421 - **£2 174** - FF22 443
An Alley Oil/canvas (66x59cm 25x23in) Herzelia-Pituah 2000

🖌 $900 - €1 067 - **£655** - FF6 998
Eagle Oil/paper/board (33x26.5cm 12x10in) Tel Aviv 2001

🖌 $1 200 - €1 288 - **£803** - FF8 449
Rural Scene Watercolour/paper (32.5x45cm 12x17in) Tel Aviv 2000

OVCACEK Eduard 1933 [17]

🖌 $1 329 - €1 257 - **£828** - FF8 247
Choses secretes Huile/carton (29.5x44cm 11x15in) Praha 2001

OVENDEN Graham 1943 [19]

🖌 $6 163 - €5 942 - **£3 800** - FF38 977
Ophelia Oil/canvas/board (89.5x68.5cm 35x26in) London 1999

✏ $404 - €379 - **£250** - FF2 488
Young Girl standing looking over her right Shoulder Pencil/paper (37.5x26cm 14x10in) London 1999

OVENS Jurgen 1623-1678 [17]

🖌 $9 975 - €11 330 - **£7 000** - FF74 322
Portrait of a Lady, as Minerva, standing, wearing a purple Dress Oil/canvas (205x132.5cm 80x52in) London 2001

🖌 $15 144 - €17 895 - **£10 734** - FF117 386
Schlafendes Kind und Cherubine Öl/Leinwand (65x77cm 25x30in) München 2000

OVERBECK Friedrich Theodor 1897-1972 [4]

✏ $27 500 - €27 439 - **£16 739** - FF179 990
The Madonna and Child with Angels Black chalk (45.5x46cm 17x18in) New-York 2000

OVERBECK Fritz 1869-1909 [98]

🖌 $8 896 - €10 226 - **£6 282** - FF67 078
«Das Tal des Schweigens» Öl/Leinwand (101.5x155cm 39x61in) Bremen 2001

🖌 $4 253 - €4 090 - **£2 624** - FF26 831
Abend Öl/Karton (34.9x46.9cm 13x18in) Köln 1999

🖌 $4 372 - €4 090 - **£2 648** - FF26 831
Rheinauen im Vorfrühling Oil/canvas/panel (30.5x41.5cm 12x16in) Bremen 1999

📖 $401 - €332 - **£235** - FF2 178
Die Windmühle Etching, aquatint (18x24cm 7x9in) Heidelberg 1998

OVERBECK Johann Friedrich 1789-1869 [21]

✏ $424 - €409 - **£265** - FF2 683
Männlicher Rückenakant Pencil/paper (24x29cm 9x11in) München 1999

📖 $300 - €281 - **£186** - FF1 844
Ein betender Pilger mit dem Kreuze Radierung (11.3x7.6cm 4x2in) Heidelberg 1999

OVERBEEK Leendert c.1752-1815 [10]

🖌 $2 922 - €3 403 - **£2 041** - FF22 324
Scene at the Edge of a Village, with Various Resting Figures Watercolour (27x35cm 10x13in) Amsterdam 2000

OVERBEEK van Gijsbertus Johannes 1882-1947 [47]

🖌 $1 313 - €1 452 - **£911** - FF9 525
A horse-drawn carriage along the Maas, Rotterdam Oil/canvas (50x90cm 19x35in) Amsterdam 2001

OVERBEEKE van Olav Cleofas 1946 [10]

🖌 $5 859 - €6 807 - **£4 117** - FF44 649
Stilleven met glaasje water Oil/canvas (75x75cm 29x29in) Amsterdam 2001

OVERSCHIE van Pieter c.1620-c.1672 [15]

🖌 $18 822 - €18 378 - **£12 000** - FF120 552
Still Life of a Lobster in a Wan-li kraak Porcelain Bowl, Grapes Oil/panel (35.5x46cm 13x18in) London 1999

O

OVERSTRAETEN van War 1891-1981 [82]

$577 - €644 - £400 - FF4 227
Le sentier de St Rémy de Provence Huile/toile
(80x65cm 31x25in) Antwerpen 2001

$164 - €161 - £101 - FF1 056
Twee vrouwen aan de wastafel Gouache/paper
(32x39.5cm 12x15in) Lokeren 1999

OWEN Bill 1942 [19]

$14 500 - €16 464 - £10 074 - FF107 997
Below the Rim Oil/canvas (40x50cm 16x20in) Dallas
TX 2001

$2 750 - €2 568 - £1 697 - FF16 846
Cowpuncher of 1977 Charcoal (50x76cm 20x30in)
Dallas TX 1999

OWEN George O. act.1884-1926 [9]

$392 - €463 - £276 - FF3 036
På hemväg frå₃n skörden Akvarell/papper
(42x56cm 16x22in) Malmö 2000

OWEN Hugh XIX [7]

$3 166 - €3 546 - £2 200 - FF23 263
Street Scene, Bristol Calotype (10x8cm 3x3in)
London 2001

OWEN Joel XIX-XX [81]

$483 - €457 - £300 - FF3 001
Landskab med bjergsö og graessende får
Oil/canvas (51x76cm 20x29in) Vejle 1999

OWEN Robert Emmett 1878-1957 [104]

$3 900 - €3 272 - £2 288 - FF21 464
«Newfound Lake» Oil/canvas (38x53cm 15x21in)
Hannover MA 1998

$2 200 - €2 116 - £1 357 - FF13 878
Autumn Woods Oil/canvas (30.5x40.5cm 12x15in)
Boston MA 2000

OWEN Samuel 1768/69-1857 [77]

$1 614 - €1 494 - £1 000 - FF9 801
Busy Fishing Port Watercolour (14x11cm 5x4in)
London 1999

OWEN Will 1869-1957 [4]

$3 300 - €3 542 - £2 208 - FF23 235
The Strays Pencil/paper (40x50cm 16x20in) Houston
TX 2000

OWEN William 1769-1825 [24]

$8 823 - €8 891 - £5 500 - FF58 319
**Mrs Shaw of Greens Norton, Towncester, full-
length in Black Dress** Oil/canvas (248x146cm
97x57in) London 2000

$1 600 - €1 755 - £1 062 - FF11 514
**Portrait of a Gentleman, Half-Length, Wearing a
Brown Jacket** Oil/canvas (77.5x63.5cm 30x25in)
New-York 2000

OWENS Laura 1970 [1]

$7 500 - €8 703 - £5 178 - FF57 085
Chicago Oil/canvas (50.5x45.5cm 19x17in) New-York
2000

OXMAN Katja XX [5]

$400 - €415 - £253 - FF2 722
Unforeseen Directions Etching, aquatint in colors
(77.5x60cm 30x23in) Boston MA 2000

OXTOBY David 1938 [33]

$140 - €149 - £95 - FF977
Mr.Upton Mixed media (51x35.5cm 20x13in) Miami
FL 2001

OYENS David 1842-1902 [44]

$2 824 - €2 823 - £1 994 - FF21 799
Schlafendes Mädchen im Interieur Öl/Karton
(50x33cm 19x12in) Köln 2001

OYENS Pieter 1842-1894 [22]

$4 770 - €4 462 - £2 898 - FF29 268
L'amateur d'Art Oil/canvas (50x35cm 19x13in)
Lokeren 1999

$2 064 - €1 983 - £1 272 - FF13 008
La toilette Huile/panneau (33x27cm 12x10in)
Bruxelles 1999

OYSTON George XIX-XX [186]

$288 - €354 - £210 - FF2 241
**Country Lane with Sheep in the foreground,
and a Mother** Watercolour/paper (48x31cm 18x12in)
Newcastle-upon-Tyne 2001

OZANNE Nicolas Marie 1728-1811 [40]

$182 390 - €216 916 - £130 000 - FF1 422 876
**The Departure of the French Fleet from Toulon
on an Expedition** Oil/canvas (162x293cm 63x115in)
London 2001

$1 771 - €1 673 - £1 100 - FF10 972
Sierra Leone Wash/paper (8x14.5cm 3x5in) London
1999

OZANNE Pierre 1737-1813 [23]

$1 105 - €1 296 - £794 - FF8 500
Jeune homme poussant un bateau Crayon
(26x22cm 10x8in) Paris 2001

$65 - €61 - £40 - FF400
**Figure de proue au chien porté par un aigle et
aux Amours** Gravure (23x20.5cm 9x8in) Versailles
1999

OZENFANT Amédée 1886-1966 [122]

$18 590 - €19 818 - £11 791 - FF130 000
La belle vie Huile/toile (130x97cm 51x38in) Paris
2000

$8 512 - €9 452 - £5 933 - FF62 000
«Pacifique III» Huile/toile (80x100cm 31x39in) Paris
2001

$2 078 - €2 017 - £1 294 - FF13 232
Paysage Gouache/papier (22x29cm 8x11in) Luzern
1999

OZOLS Auzeklis 1941 [4]

$4 500 - €5 181 - £3 070 - FF33 984
Paradis Oil/canvas (60x60cm 24x24in) New-Orleans
LA 2000

P

PAAL László 1846-1879 [9]

$34 000 - €33 432 - £21 250 - FF219 300
**Forest Scene of Barbizon, Sunshine in the
Forest** Oil/canvas (61.5x50.5cm 24x19in) Budapest
1999

$12 043 - €12 653 - £7 943 - FF83 000
Sous-bois Huile/panneau (24x32cm 9x12in) Calais
2000

PAALEN Wolfgang 1905-1959 [27]

$23 000 - €24 001 - £14 506 - FF157 435
Mother of Agate Oil/canvas (129.5x59.5cm 50x23in)
New-York 2000

✏️ **$5 685** - €6 632 - **£3 954** - FF43 500
Variétés de la pluie Encre Chine (37x51cm 14x20in) Paris 2000

PAAPE Eddy 1920 **[20]**
✏️ **$496** - €457 - **£298** - FF3 000
Luc Orient Encre Chine/papier (38x29cm 14x11in) Paris 1999

PAATELA Oskari 1888-1952 **[26]**
🖐 **$630** - €630 - **£428** - FF4 633
Vid grinden Oil/canvas (60x45cm 23x17in) Helsinki 2000

PABEL Hilmar XX **[43]**
📷 **$619** - €665 - **£414** - FF4 360
Pablo Picasso, 80.Geburtstag, Nizza Photograph (28x36.3cm 11x14in) München 2000

PABST Camille Alfred 1821-1898 **[14]**
🖐 **$5 611** - €5 461 - **£3 454** - FF35 823
Midsommarkransarna bindas Oil/canvas (68x90cm 26x35in) Stockholm 1999

PACE DA CAMPIDOGLIO Michelangelo c.1610-c.1670 **[14]**
🖐 **$32 900** - €30 490 - **£20 460** - FF200 000
Nature morte aux raisins, melons, pommes et prunes sur une entablement Huile/toile (73x96cm 28x37in) Versailles 1999

PACE Nicholas 1957 **[13]**
🖐 **$1 957** - €2 148 - **£1 300** - FF14 087
Scarlet Macaw Oil/canvas (54x43.5cm 21x17in) London 2000

PACENZA Onofrio A. 1904-1971 **[1]**
🖐 **$4 000** - €3 909 - **£2 536** - FF25 644
Trovador del riachuelo Oleo/lienzo (62x80cm 24x31in) Buenos-Aires 1999

PACHECO ALTAMIRANO Arturo 1905 **[17]**
🖐 **$1 980** - €1 845 - **£1 210** - FF12 100
Sin título Oleo/lienzo (60x73cm 23x28in) Caracas 1998

PACHECO Ana Maria 1943 **[6]**
▥ **$1 947** - €2 078 - **£1 300** - FF13 628
The Three Graces Etching (17.5x16cm 6x6in) London 2000

PACHECO Francesco 1564-1654 **[3]**
🖐 **$62 400** - €72 078 - **£43 200** - FF472 800
Vida de San Juan Evangelista Oleo/tabla (124.5x38cm 49x14in) Seville 2000
✏️ **$15 400** - €16 518 - **£10 175** - FF108 350
Santa Ana, La Virgen y el Niño Aguada (31x17.5cm 12x6in) Madrid 2000

PACHER Ferdinand 1852-1911 **[6]**
🖐 **$3 742** - €3 579 - **£2 279** - FF23 477
In einem bayrischen Wirtshaus wird ein Chevauxleger beobachtet Oil/panel (26x35cm 10x13in) Stuttgart 1999

PACHT Vilhelm 1843-1912 **[43]**
🖐 **$515** - €511 - **£322** - FF3 351
Portraet af kunstnerens sön Knud med faderens palet Oil/canvas (110x62cm 43x24in) Köbenhavn 1999

PACHTER Charles 1942 **[10]**
🖐 **$5 068** - €4 882 - **£3 147** - FF32 025
The painted Flag Acrylic/canvas (152.5x76cm 60x29in) Toronto 1999

PACKARD Emmy Lou XX **[2]**
✏️ **$1 500** - €1 706 - **£1 040** - FF11 190
Mural Study Gouache (19x91cm 7x36in) Chicago IL 2000

PADAMSEE Akbar 1928 **[18]**
🖐 **$13 000** - €15 072 - **£9 209** - FF98 866
Metascape Oil/canvas (136.5x136.5cm 53x53in) New-York 2000
🖐 **$11 577** - €10 829 - **£7 000** - FF71 033
Head VI Oil/canvas (91.5x61cm 36x24in) London 1999

PADDAY Charles Murray 1868-1954 **[16]**
🖐 **$19 425** - €20 852 - **£13 000** - FF136 780
Dividing the Spoil Oil/canvas (91.5x128cm 36x50in) London 2000
🖐 **$2 514** - €2 125 - **£1 500** - FF13 940
Woman with Barrel on the Quayside Oil/panel (16x21cm 6x8in) Penzance, Cornwall 1998

PADERLIK Arnost 1919-1999 **[19]**
🖐 **$809** - €765 - **£504** - FF5 020
Stilleben mit Klarinette Öl/Leinwand/Karton (35x48cm 13x18in) Praha 2000

PADILLA J. XVIII **[6]**
🖐 **$3 424** - €3 857 - **£2 360** - FF25 301
Mixed Flowers in Baskets in a wan-li bowl, fish and vegetables Oil/canvas (89.2x130.2cm 35x51in) Amsterdam 2000

PADUA Paul Mathias 1903-1984 **[115]**
🖐 **$3 028** - €3 579 - **£2 146** - FF23 477
Portrait des Prinzen Ferdinand Ludwig von Bayern Öl/Leinwand (116x104cm 45x40in) München 2000
🖐 **$4 621** - €4 346 - **£2 861** - FF28 508
Bunter Strauss in blauer Vase Öl/Leinwand (73x53cm 28x20in) Köln 1999
🖐 **$1 714** - €1 789 - **£1 085** - FF11 738
Junge Frau mit weissem Kopftuch Oil/panel (18x15cm 7x5in) München 2000
🖐 **$254** - €291 - **£174** - FF1 906
Bildnis einer Zigeunerfrau Charcoal (47x34cm 18x13in) Salzburg 2000

PADURA Miguel 1957 **[7]**
🖐 **$20 000** - €19 460 - **£12 310** - FF127 646
Song of Firefly Oil/canvas (132x173.5cm 51x68in) New-York 1999

PAEDE Paul 1868-1929 **[82]**
🖐 **$1 535** - €1 789 - **£1 075** - FF11 738
Mädchenporträt Öl/Leinwand (55x61cm 21x24in) München 2000
🖐 **$1 418** - €1 228 - **£855** - FF8 056
Sitzender Frauenakt Öl/Karton (36x25cm 14x9in) München 2000

PAEFFGEN Claus Otto 1933 **[64]**
🖐 **$9 526** - €10 226 - **£6 376** - FF67 078
Geisha, Maus und Zahnbürste Öl/Leinwand (115x135cm 45x53in) Köln 2000
🖐 **$13 824** - €13 294 - **£8 530** - FF87 201
Elvis Acryl (100.3x55.3cm 39x21in) Köln 1999
🖐 **$857** - €920 - **£573** - FF6 037
Ohne Titel Oil chalks (32x24cm 12x9in) Köln 2000
▥ **$237** - €204 - **£142** - FF1 340
«Nur wenig Zeit für protokollarische Auftritte...» Serigraph (33.5x46cm 13x18in) Köln 1998

PAELINCK Joseph 1781-1839 **[10]**
🖐 **$24 000** - €26 331 - **£15 943** - FF172 723
The Emperor Augustus Ordering the Adornment of Rome Oil/canvas (50x95.5cm 19x37in) New-York 2000

P

PAEMEL van Jules 1896-1968 **[41]**

▦ **$129** - €124 - **£80** - FF813
    Ruisseau près de la chaumière Gravure
    (27.5x20.5cm 10x8in) Bruxelles 1999

PAEP de Thomas c.1628-1670 **[3]**

🖎 **$23 542** - €21 986 - **£14 529** - FF144 217
    Früchtestilleben Oil/panel (28.5x21cm 11x8in) Köln
    1999

PAERELS Willem 1878-1962 **[218]**

🖎 **$3 016** - €3 222 - **£2 054** - FF21 138
    Portret van een schilder Huile/toile (80x60cm
    31x23in) Lokeren 2001

    $488 - €545 - **£338** - FF3 577
    Les bords de la Seine Fusain/papier (40x53cm
    15x20in) Antwerpen 2001

PAESCHKE Paul 1875-1943 **[179]**

✐ **$540** - €613 - **£375** - FF4 024
    Blankenese Pastell/Karton (25.5x33cm 10x12in)
    Berlin 2001

▦ **$182** - €204 - **£127** - FF1 341
    Hafenmotiv Radierung (20.5x27cm 8x10in) Berlin
    2001

PAEZ de José 1720-1790 **[27]**

🖎 **$19 000** - €20 394 - **£12 714** - FF133 779
    Coronación de la Virgen Oil/canvas (169x124cm
    66x48in) New-York 2000

🖎 **$8 400** - €9 010 - **£5 550** - FF59 100
    La Coronación de la Virgen Oleo/cobre (64.5x48cm
    25x18in) Madrid 2000

🖎 **$16 800** - €18 019 - **£11 100** - FF118 200
    La Virgen de Guadalupe Oleo/cobre (34x43cm
    13x16in) Madrid 2000

PAGAN Luigi 1907-? **[10]**

🖎 **$900** - €933 - **£540** - FF6 120
    Mercato di Chioggia Olio/tavola (30x40cm 11x15in)
    Venezia 2000

PAGANI DA MONTERUBBIANO Vicenzo 1490-1568
[2]

🖎 **$73 399** - €68 650 - **£45 000** - FF450 315
    The Lamentation Oil/panel (77x184cm 30x72in)
    London 1998

PAGANI Paolo 1661-1716 **[7]**

✐ **$1 793** - €1 925 - **£1 200** - FF12 625
    Simiramide Ink (16x14cm 6x5in) London 2000

PAGANO Michele c.1697-c.1732 **[7]**

🖎 **$8 800** - €11 403 - **£6 600** - FF74 800
    **Una fonte con un viandante ed un cane/Due
    astanti presso un ponte** Olio/tela (35.5x25.5cm
    13x10in) Roma 2000

PAGANS MONSALVATJE Jordi 1932 **[27]**

🖎 **$476** - €511 - **£323** - FF3 349
    «Paisatje Cap de Creus» Oleo/lienzo (73x60cm
    28x23in) Barcelona 2001

🖎 **$266** - €276 - **£170** - FF1 812
    Cadaqués, S'Arenella/Cadaqués, Cementiri
    Oleo/lienzo (22x27cm 8x10in) Barcelona 2000

PAGE Edward A. 1850-1928 **[27]**

🖎 **$3 000** - €3 425 - **£2 115** - FF22 469
    Cottages by the Sea Oil/canvas (51x76cm 20x29in)
    Boston MA 2001

🖎 **$900** - €822 - **£550** - FF5 395
    The Harbor, Marblehead Oil/canvas/board
    (20.5x31.5cm 8x12in) Boston MA 1999

PAGE Evelyn 1899-1988 **[3]**

🖎 **$70 365** - €73 937 - **£46 320** - FF484 995
    Recumbent Nude Oil/canvas/board (70.7x91cm
    27x35in) Auckland 2000

🖎 **$16 025** - €16 652 - **£10 048** - FF109 232
    Summer's Day, Oriental Parade, Wellington
    Oil/board (31x49cm 12x19in) Auckland 2000

PAGE Fred Hutchison 1908-1984 **[63]**

🖎 **$3 737** - €3 873 - **£2 367** - FF25 408
    The Milk Sippers and the Mural Mixed media
    (80x75cm 31x29in) Johannesburg 2000

🖎 **$3 106** - €2 993 - **£1 919** - FF19 634
    The Area Acrylic/paper (30x18.5cm 11x7in)
    Johannesburg 1999

✐ **$422** - €497 - **£291** - FF3 260
    Southend P.E Ink (32x53cm 12x20in) Cape Town
    2000

▦ **$117** - €122 - **£74** - FF797
    The Wake Linocut (19x22cm 7x8in) Johannesburg
    2000

PAGE Marie Danforth 1869-1940 **[2]**

🖎 **$47 500** - €46 338 - **£29 250** - FF303 957
    Tommy, Young Boy with a Black Cat Oil/canvas
    (81x81cm 32x32in) New-York 1999

PAGE William 1794-1872 **[25]**

✐ **$3 316** - €3 075 - **£2 000** - FF20 169
    The Citadel, Corfu Watercolour (18.5x27cm 7x10in)
    London 1999

PAGENKOPF Ursula XX **[15]**

🖎 **$390** - €438 - **£271** - FF2 871
    Fellin' Soo Good! Oil/canvas (35x45cm 14x18in)
    Calgary, Alberta 2001

PAGES Bernard 1940 **[12]**

🖎 **$6 220** - €7 318 - **£4 459** - FF48 000
    Hommage à Gaston Bachelard Technique mixte
    (150x38x38cm 59x14x14in) Paris 2001

PAGES Jules Eugène 1867-1946 **[42]**

🖎 **$2 190** - €2 439 - **£1 539** - FF16 000
    La Seine à Nemours Huile/toile (45x61cm 17x24in)
    Paris 2001

🖎 **$669** - €640 - **£415** - FF4 200
    Bouquet de fleurs Huile/toile (34.5x26.5cm 13x10in)
    Rennes 1999

PAGES Jules François 1833-1910 **[7]**

🖎 **$9 000** - €9 719 - **£6 219** - FF63 755
    Italian Harbor Oil/canvas (45x55cm 18x22in)
    Altadena CA 2001

🖎 **$7 500** - €8 765 - **£5 354** - FF57 495
    «A bit of Brittany» Oil/wood (12x12cm 5x5in)
    Altadena CA 2001

PAGET Sidney Edward 1861-1908 **[10]**

✐ **$500** - €604 - **£349** - FF3 964
    Peasant Women Along a Track in a Landscape
    Watercolour/paper (42x62.5cm 16x24in) Bethesda MD
    2000

PAGET Walter Stanley «Wal» 1863-1935 **[8]**

✐ **$364** - €316 - **£220** - FF2 071
    Work Stops for the Hunt Wash/paper (33x50cm
    12x19in) Crewkerne, Somerset 1998

PAGGI Giovanni Battista 1554-1627 **[21]**

🖎 **$20 700** - €21 459 - **£12 420** - FF140 760
    La nascita della Vergine Olio/tela (148x154cm
    58x60in) Roma 1999

✐ **$1 645** - €1 524 - **£1 023** - FF10 000
    **Dieu intervient pour sauver une ville frappée
    par la peste** Encre (24.5x38.5cm 9x15in) Paris 1999

PAGGIARO Emile 1859-1929 [1]

📖 **$1 000** - €947 - **£621** - FF6 209
«Festeggiamenti» Poster (205.5x99cm 80x38in)
New-York 1999

PAGLIACCI Aldo 1913 [24]

🖼 **$400** - €518 - **£300** - FF3 400
Natura morta Olio/tela (100x80cm 39x31in) Milano
2001

PAGLIAI Arturo 1852-1896 [4]

🖼 **$2 800** - €3 628 - **£2 100** - FF23 800
Scorcio di parco con tempietto Olio/tela
(55x120cm 21x47in) Roma 2001

PAGLIANO Eleuterio 1826-1903 [23]

🖼 **$600** - €622 - **£360** - FF4 080
Gli addii Olio/cartone (41x28cm 16x11in) Trieste 2001
✏ **$700** - €726 - **£420** - FF4 760
Suora Acquarello/carta (22x15cm 8x5in) Milano 2000

PAGLIEI Giocchino 1852-1896 [7]

🖼 **$40 000** - €40 308 - **£24 936** - FF264 400
Gallant Dragoon Oil/canvas (95.5x141cm 37x55in)
New-York 2000
🖼 **$7 200** - €6 220 - **£4 500** - FF40 800
Guardiana di tacchini Olio/tela (35x54.5cm
13x21in) Prato 1999

PAGNI Ferruccio 1866-1935 [5]

🖼 **$12 250** - €12 699 - **£7 350** - FF83 300
Pascolo a Torre del Lago Olio/tela (48x56cm
18x22in) Milano 1999

PAGOLA Javier 1955 [27]

✏ **$384** - €360 - **£240** - FF2 364
Composición Collage/papier (50x65cm 19x25in)
Madrid 1999

PAGUENAUD Jean-Louis 1876-1952 [62]

🖼 **$44 438** - €51 833 - **£30 906** - FF340 000
Vue de Tanger Huile/panneau (123x183cm 48x72in)
Paris 2000
🖼 **$1 191** - €1 372 - **£813** - FF9 000
Croiseur en haute mer Peinture (70x100cm
27x39in) Mayenne 2000
🖼 **$1 355** - €1 487 - **£924** - FF9 500
Cuirassés en escadre Gouache/papier (48x62cm
18x24in) Paris 2001

PAICE George 1854-1925 [114]

🖼 **$1 585** - €1 487 - **£980** - FF9 755
Two Red Setters in a Higland Landscape
Oil/canvas (50x68cm 20x27in) London 1999
🖼 **$725** - €702 - **£460** - FF4 607
Colleen Oil/canvas (23x31cm 9x12in) London 2001

PAIK Nam June 1932 [121]

🖼 **$12 991** - €14 056 - **£9 000** - FF92 200
Mongolian Tartar Rite with White Line Mixed
media (201x135x23cm 79x53x9in) London 2001
🖼 **$6 336** - €7 481 - **£4 500** - FF49 069
Self-Portrait Mixed media (53.5x66x30.5cm
21x25x12in) London 2001
🔨 **$28 000** - €26 290 - **£17 348** - FF172 454
Improvisational Music Metal (178x74x51cm
70x29x20in) New-York 1999
🔨 **$3 200** - €3 100 - **£1 995** - FF20 333
Zen Drawings V Sculpture (42.5x40x15.5cm
16x15x6in) New-York 1999
✏ **$1 490** - €1 697 - **£1 047** - FF11 129
Happy Pencil/paper (25x35cm 9x13in) Zürich 2001
📖 **$400** - €439 - **£258** - FF2 878
Untitled Screenprint in colors (37.5x27.5cm 14x10in)
New-York 2000

📷 **$2 750** - €2 851 - **£1 650** - FF18 700
Performance Photo (48x35cm 18x13in) Prato 2000

PAÏL Edouard 1851-1916 [89]

🖼 **$1 880** - €2 134 - **£1 306** - FF14 000
Moutons dans un paysage de bruyères en
fleurs Huile/toile (51x65cm 20x25in) Dijon 2001
🖼 **$745** - €838 - **£513** - FF5 500
Canards près de la ferme Huile/panneau (27x35cm
10x13in) La Varenne-Saint-Hilaire 2000

PAILES Isaac 1895-1978 [127]

🖼 **$534** - €610 - **£371** - FF4 000
Portrait de femme Huile/toile (73x54cm 28x21in)
Paris 2000

PAILHES Fred 1902-1991 [258]

🖼 **$379** - €442 - **£262** - FF2 900
Le port du Havre Huile/isorel (60x74cm 23x29in) Le
Havre 2000
🖼 **$196** - €229 - **£135** - FF1 500
Le clown blanc Huile/isorel (26x21cm 10x8in) Le
Havre 2000
✏ **$230** - €229 - **£143** - FF1 500
Les respectueuses Aquarelle (28.5x39cm 11x15in)
Paris 1999

PAILLARD Henri Pierre 1844-1912 [5]

🖼 **$2 091** - €2 439 - **£1 454** - FF16 000
Promeneurs près de la Mosquée Youssef Bey à
Tunis Huile/toile (47x33cm 18x12in) Paris 2000

PAILLER Henri 1876-1954 [35]

🖼 **$1 049** - €1 220 - **£737** - FF8 000
Rue de Village Huile/toile (39.5x55cm 15x21in) Paris
2001

PAILLET Charles 1871-1937 [68]

🗿 **$2 449** - €2 287 - **£1 483** - FF15 000
Grand cerf royal Bronze (52x40cm 20x15in) La
Varenne-Saint-Hilaire 1999

PAILLOU Peter c.1745-c.1806 [30]

✏ **$4 035** - €3 736 - **£2 500** - FF24 504
Birds of Paradise Watercolour (48.5x34cm 19x13in)
London 1999

PAILOS Manuel 1918 [29]

🖼 **$850** - €913 - **£569** - FF5 989
Puerto Oleo/lienzo (35x29cm 13x11in) Montevideo
2000

PAINE Charles XX [1]

📖 **$1 835** - €2 128 - **£1 300** - FF13 961
«Boat Race 1923, Putney Bridge, Hammersmith
and Chiswick Park» Poster (29x44cm 11x17in)
London 2000

PAING Marguerite XIX-XX [53]

🖼 **$102** - €107 - **£64** - FF700
Soleil et asters Huile/toile (28x20cm 11x7in) Paris
2000

PAIROJ WANGBORN 1972 [2]

📖 **$1 275** - €1 371 - **£855** - FF8 995
Sunset at Chao Phraya River Woodcut (80x100cm
31x39in) Bangkok 2000

PAIZS-GOEBEL Jenö 1899-1944 [2]

🖼 **$4 200** - €4 647 - **£2 760** - FF30 480
Still Life of Flowers in front of the Window
Tempera/board (95x79cm 37x31in) Budapest 2000

PAJAMA XX [1]

📷 **$4 400** - €4 904 - **£3 084** - FF32 171
Untitled/Portrait Figure Study Silver print
(16x11cm 6x4in) New-York 2001

PAJDIC Predrag Sebastian 1965 **[2]**
🖋 **$5 500** - €5 833 - **£3 729** - FF38 264
    Angel Ink (200x260cm 78x102in) Tel Aviv 2001

PAJETTA Guido Paolo 1898-1987 **[18]**
😊 **$1 380** - €1 192 - **£920** - FF7 820
    Figure femminili Olio/tavola (50x70cm 19x27in)
    Milano 1998

PAJETTA Pietro 1845-1911 **[23]**
😊 **$13 000** - €13 476 - **£7 800** - FF88 400
    Il prete e la perpetua Olio/tela (57x33.5cm 22x13in)
    Milano 1999

PAJOT Gilbert 1902-1952 **[24]**
🖋 **$2 986** - €2 744 - **£1 834** - FF18 000
    «Loire» le quatre-mats barque du commerce
    Aquarelle, gouache/papier (45x61cm 17x24in) Paris
    1999

PAJOT Paul Émile 1870-1930 **[61]**
🖋 **$3 177** - €3 201 - **£1 980** - FF21 000
    Le retour du corsaire Aquarelle/papier (43x29cm
    16x11in) La Roche-sur-Yon 2000

PAJOU Augustin 1730-1809 **[28]**
🖌 **$15 672** - €18 294 - **£11 064** - FF120 000
    Portrait de A.C. Viel de Munas, marquis
    d'Espeuilles Plâtre (34x25cm 13x9in) Paris 2000
🖋 **$1 767** - €1 981 - **£1 200** - FF12 996
    Menelaus and Astyanax Black chalk (18.5x13cm
    7x5in) London 2000

PAJOU Jacques Augustin C. 1766-1828 **[4]**
🖋 **$6 080** - €6 708 - **£4 118** - FF44 000
    Portrait du sculpteur Augustin Pajou, père de
    l'artiste Crayon (30x22cm 11x8in) Paris 2000

PAL (Jean de Paleologu) 1855-1942 **[299]**
🎞 **$1 794** - €2 134 - **£1 279** - FF14 000
    «Cycles La Française» Affiche (122x81cm 48x31in)
    Orléans 2000

PALACIOS Alirio 1944 **[26]**
😊 **$16 000** - €17 174 - **£10 707** - FF112 656
    Estudio No.3 «a propósito de Vermeer» Oil/board
    (170x140cm 66x55in) New-York 2000
😊 **$6 290** - €5 923 - **£4 070** - FF38 850
    Duende en Oración dos Técnica mixta/papel
    (121x74.5cm 47x29in) Caracas 1999
🎞 **$1 500** - €1 540 - **£1 000** - FF10 105
    Sin título Serigrafía (166x66cm 65x25in) Caracas 2000

PALADINI Vinicio 1902-1971 **[18]**
😊 **$2 749** - €2 850 - **£1 649** - FF18 698
    Senza titolo Tempera (18x28cm 7x11in) Milano 2001

PALADINO Mimmo 1948 **[445]**
😊 **$30 000** - €32 914 - **£19 929** - FF215 904
    Untitled Oil/panel (198x150x10cm 77x59x3in) New-
    York 2000
😊 **$12 000** - €11 207 - **£7 406** - FF73 512
    Marcofio Oil/board (73x73cm 28x28in) New-York
    1999
😊 **$2 250** - €2 332 - **£1 350** - FF15 300
    Senza titolo Acrílico (30x39.5cm 11x15in) Prato 2000
🖌 **$50 000** - €56 562 - **£34 980** - FF371 025
    Arma da Pane Bronze (98x132x45.5cm 38x51x17in)
    New-York 2001
🖌 **$9 500** - €10 641 - **£6 600** - FF69 801
    Disco Bronze (63.5x57x26.5cm 25x22x10in) New-
    York 2001
🖋 **$1 800** - €2 332 - **£1 350** - FF15 300
    «Film» Tecnica mista/carta (30x40cm 11x15in) Prato
    2000

🎞 **$609** - €716 - **£422** - FF4 695
    Ohne Titel Farblithographie (60x79.5cm 23x31in)
    Stuttgart 2000

PALAGI Pelagio 1775-1860 **[12]**
😊 **$1 200** - €1 244 - **£720** - FF8 160
    Ottentoti Korah in viaggio Inchiostro (18x24cm
    7x9in) Milano 2001

PALAMEDES Anthonie Stevaerts 1601-1673 **[63]**
😊 **$25 340** - €21 343 - **£14 966** - FF140 000
    Le concert à l'auberge Huile/panneau (38.5x49.5cm
    15x19in) Paris 1998
😊 **$7 077** - €6 000 - **£4 200** - FF39 358
    Elegant Lovers in an Interior Oil/panel (23.5x31cm
    9x12in) London 1998
🖋 **$47 055** - €45 945 - **£30 000** - FF301 380
    Walking musketeer, seen from behind Black
    chalk (20.5x15cm 8x5in) London 1999

PALAMEDESZ. Palamedes I 1607-1638 **[32]**
😊 **$7 225** - €6 834 - **£4 500** - FF44 825
    Battle Scene Oil/panel (52x78.5cm 20x30in) Praha
    1999
😊 **$8 056** - €7 912 - **£5 000** - FF51 899
    Cavalry engagement Oil/copper (9.5x18cm 3x7in)
    London 1999
🖋 **$16 250** - €15 016 - **£10 000** - FF98 500
    Choque de caballerías Aquarelle/carton (42x65cm
    16x25in) Madrid 1999

PALANQUINOS MASTER Act.c.1500 **[4]**
😊 **$67 100** - €66 071 - **£41 800** - FF433 400
    Crucifixión Tempera (106x56cm 41x22in) Madrid
    1999

PALANTI Giuseppe 1881-1946 **[32]**
😊 **$2 640** - €2 281 - **£1 320** - FF14 960
    Ritratto femminile Olio/tela (65x50cm 25x19in) Prato
    1999

PALAU BUIXO de Juan 1919-1991 **[4]**
🖋 **$1 885** - €1 952 - **£1 202** - FF12 805
    L'estany de la pesquera, Banyoles Oleo/lienzo
    (60x73cm 23x28in) Barcelona 2000

PALAU FERRE Matías 1921-2000 **[9]**
🖋 **$682** - €661 - **£429** - FF4 334
    Maternidad Crayon gras/papier (65x52cm 25x20in)
    Barcelona 1999

PALAZUELO Pablo 1916 **[41]**
🖋 **$8 520** - €7 208 - **£5 040** - FF47 280
    Sueño dorado V Gouache/papier (65x50cm 25x19in)
    Madrid 1998
🎞 **$180** - €204 - **£122** - FF1 339
    Sin título Serigrafía (84x60cm 33x23in) Madrid 2000

PALAZZI Bernardino 1907-1987 **[23]**
😊 **$1 950** - €2 021 - **£1 170** - FF13 260
    Marina con natura morta Olio/tela (61x80cm
    24x31in) Vercelli 2001

PALDI Israel 1892-1979 **[78]**
😊 **$3 200** - €3 435 - **£2 141** - FF22 531
    Figures in Café Oil/board (40x47.5cm 15x18in) Tel
    Aviv 2000
😊 **$1 000** - €1 062 - **£676** - FF6 963
    Gipsy Woman Oil/canvas (22x18.5cm 8x7in) Tel Aviv
    2001
🖋 **$550** - €591 - **£368** - FF3 875
    Landscape Mixed media/paper (21.5x30cm 8x11in)
    Tel Aviv 2000

PALENCIA PEREZ Benjamín 1894-1980 **[460]**
- **$28 400** - €24 026 - **£16 800** - FF157 600
  Campos de Castilla Oleo/lienzo (73x116cm 28x45in) Madrid 1998
- **$3 520** - €3 304 - **£2 200** - FF21 670
  Paisaje Oleo/lienzo (18.5x26.5cm 7x10in) Madrid 1999
- **$1 120** - €1 201 - **£760** - FF7 880
  Pescadores de Altea Tinta/papel (33x41cm 12x16in) Madrid 2001
- **$915** - €901 - **£570** - FF5 910
  Desde mi rincón Litografía (50x39cm 19x15in) Madrid 1999

PALENCIA Y UBANELL Gabriel 1869-? **[8]**
- **$1 064** - €1 141 - **£722** - FF7 486
  Vista de un jardín Oleo/lienzo (35.5x50cm 13x19in) Madrid 2001

PALENSKE Reinhold H. 1884-1954 **[24]**
- **$100** - €108 - **£69** - FF708
  «The Seabiscuit» Etching (25x30cm 10x12in) Chicago IL 2001

PALERMO Blinky 1943-1977 **[106]**
- **$200 000** - €173 139 - **£120 620** - FF1 135 720
  Untitled Mixed media (200x200cm 78x78in) New-York 1998
- **$81 070** - €86 438 - **£55 000** - FF566 995
  Untitled Mixed media (40x50cm 15x19in) London 2001
- **$8 500** - €7 938 - **£5 246** - FF52 071
  Ohne Titel Gewidmet Thelonious Monk Mixed media (21.5x22.5cm 8x12in) New-York 1999
- **$17 000** - €16 449 - **£10 483** - FF107 897
  Blue Triangle Gouache/paper (48x53.5cm 18x21in) New-York 1999
- **$1 600** - €1 728 - **£1 105** - FF11 334
  Untitled, from Hommage à Picasso Aquatint in colors (48x34cm 18x13in) New-York 2001

PALET Joan 1911-1996 **[45]**
- **$405** - €450 - **£277** - FF2 955
  Figura femenina con chal Oleo/lienzo (73x60cm 28x23in) Barcelona 2001

PALEY Albert 1944 **[14]**
- **$12 000** - €11 455 - **£7 498** - FF75 138
  Table Lamp Metal (H105cm H41in) New-York 1999
- **$10 000** - €10 359 - **£6 365** - FF67 953
  Coffee Table Metal (43x91cm 16x35in) New-York 2000

PALEZIEUX de Gérard 1919 **[27]**
- **$1 854** - €2 161 - **£1 283** - FF14 177
  Stilleben mit Früchteschale und Kaffeegedeck Aquarell/Papier (19x22.5cm 7x8in) Bern 2000
- **$185** - €211 - **£128** - FF1 386
  Paysage campagnard Aquatinte couleurs (24.5x19cm 9x7in) Sion 2000

PALFFY Peter 1899-1988 **[16]**
- **$244** - €232 - **£149** - FF1 525
  Leda Monotype (40x52cm 15x20in) Wien 1999

PALIN William Mainwaring 1862-1947 **[23]**
- **$1 255** - €1 384 - **£850** - FF9 079
  The Blythe Oil/canvas (36x50.5cm 14x19in) London 2000

PALING Isaak 1630-1719 **[4]**
- **$50 000** - €55 373 - **£33 910** - FF363 225
  A Musical Concert on a Terrace with a Young Couple Oil/panel (82.5x66cm 32x25in) New-York 2000

PALING Johannes Jacobus 1844-1892 **[11]**
- **$2 600** - €3 143 - **£1 815** - FF20 614
  Mother and Child in Interior Oil/canvas (71x56cm 27x22in) Bethesda MD 2000

PALIZZI Filippo 1818-1899 **[107]**
- **$78 720** - €91 469 - **£55 320** - FF600 000
  Scène de chasse dans la campagne napolitaine Huile/toile (94x133.5cm 37x52in) Paris 2001
- **$20 800** - €26 953 - **£15 680** - FF176 800
  Bassotto, Terrier e volpino al guinzaglio Olio/tela (50x44cm 19x17in) Milano 2001
- **$6 900** - €7 153 - **£4 140** - FF46 920
  Capretta e agnello Olio/tavola (20x25cm 7x9in) Roma 1999
- **$1 120** - €1 451 - **£840** - FF9 520
  Caprette tra i cespugli Inchiostro (21x31cm 8x12in) Roma 2000

PALIZZI Giuseppe 1812-1888 **[120]**
- **$34 000** - €44 058 - **£25 500** - FF289 000
  Temporale Olio/tela (131x229cm 51x90in) Milano 2001
- **$7 021** - €6 555 - **£4 252** - FF43 000
  Vache et paysanne au pré Huile/toile (55x73cm 21x28in) Autun 1999
- **$6 112** - €6 098 - **£3 816** - FF40 000
  Veaux à l'étable Huile/toile (34x39.5cm 13x15in) Fontainebleau 2000
- **$2 100** - €2 177 - **£1 260** - FF14 280
  Pastorello con capre Tempera/carta (29x39cm 11x15in) Genova 2000

PALIZZI Nicola 1820-1870 **[33]**
- **$28 000** - €36 283 - **£21 000** - FF238 000
  Napoli, veduta del Golfo dalle colline Olio/tela (79.5x101cm 31x39in) Roma 2001
- **$1 380** - €1 192 - **£920** - FF7 820
  Pastori al guado Olio/tela (19x23.5cm 7x9in) Napoli 1998

PALKO Franz Xaver 1724-1767 **[7]**
- **$419** - €460 - **£284** - FF3 018
  Gott haucht Adam das Leben ein Radierung (24.1x17.5cm 9x6in) Berlin 2000

PALLANDRE M. XIX-XX **[9]**
- **$245** - €229 - **£151** - FF1 500
  P.O. & Grande Ceinture. Versailles, Trianon Affiche (104x74cm 40x29in) Paris 1999

PALLANDT van Charlotte 1898-1997 **[102]**
- **$3 171** - €3 403 - **£2 121** - FF22 324
  Zittende met Opgetrokken Inkeerknie Bronze (H13cm H5in) Amsterdam 2000

PALLARÉS Y ALLUSTANTE Joaquín 1858-1935 **[65]**
- **$5 092** - €5 336 - **£3 223** - FF35 000
  La partie d'échecs Huile/panneau (53.5x66cm 21x25in) Paris 2000
- **$2 100** - €2 102 - **£1 295** - FF13 790
  Odalisca Oleo/tabla (30x24cm 11x9in) Madrid 2000

PALLENBERG Joseph Franz 1882-1945 **[35]**
- **$783** - €716 - **£479** - FF4 695
  Röhrender Hirsch auf Bodenplatte Bronze (52x57cm 20x22in) München 1999

PALLIER Raymond XIX-XX **[9]**
- **$765** - €732 - **£480** - FF4 802
  «Cagnes sur Mer» Poster (100x71cm 39x27in) London 1999

P

PALLIERE Armand Julien 1784-1862 **[7]**

⌐ **$750 000** - €883 069 - **£527 025** - FF5 792 550
Panorama of the City of Sao Paulo Oil/canvas
(36.5x97cm 14x38in) New-York 2000

✎ **$1 282** - €1 524 - **£889** - FF10 000
Une femme dans un salon arrangeant un bouquet de fleurs Aquarelle (34x25.5cm 13x10in) Paris 2000

PALLIERE Jean Léon 1823-1887 **[17]**

⌐ **$28 119** - €30 642 - **£18 431** - FF201 000
Indigènes de la Terre de Feu Huile/papier
(28x22.5cm 11x8in) Louviers 2000

✎ **$7 574** - €6 527 - **£4 500** - FF42 816
Indians on the Pampas, Argentina
Watercolour/paper (23x18cm 9x7in) London 1998

PALLMANN Kurt 1886-? **[14]**

✎ **$2 317** - €2 659 - **£1 585** - FF17 440
Berlin, Landwehrkanal im Herbst mit Droschkenplatz Öl/Leinwand (51x63cm 20x24in) Berlin 2000

PALLMANN Peter Götz 1908-1966 **[66]**

⌐ **$1 809** - €1 789 - **£1 128** - FF11 738
Inneres einer Kirche Oil/panel (48x73cm 18x28in) Ahlden 1999

⌐ **$1 015** - €1 227 - **£708** - FF8 049
Vor dem Küchengebäude des Potsdamer Marmorpalais Öl/Karton (30x35cm 11x13in) Düsseldorf 2000

PALLYA Carolus 1875-1930 **[14]**

⌐ **$500** - €474 - **£312** - FF3 109
Gypsy Caravan Oil/panel (11x17cm 4x7in) Mystic CT 1999

PALM DE ROSA Anna 1859-1924 **[271]**

✎ **$1 542** - €1 754 - **£1 177** - FF11 506
Stockholms slott Akvarell/papper (15x22cm 5x8in) Stockholm 2000

PALM Gustaf Wilhelm 1810-1890 **[89]**

⌐ **$4 633** - €4 332 - **£2 854** - FF28 415
Vue af Ruinerna af Junos tempel vid Girgenti Oil/canvas (53x71cm 20x27in) Stockholm 1999

⌐ **$1 464** - €1 722 - **£1 060** - FF11 296
Gårdsinteriör i en bondgård i grannskapet av Syracusa Oil/canvas (28x39cm 11x15in) Stockholm 2001

PALM Torsten 1885-1934 **[32]**

⌐ **$882** - €989 - **£613** - FF6 487
Ruinen, motiv från Kullen Oil/canvas (46x38cm 18x14in) Stockholm 2001

⌐ **$1 260** - €1 223 - **£778** - FF8 025
Smedsudden Oil/panel (32.5x40.5cm 12x15in) Stockholm 1999

PALMA CARLOS Rui XX **[3]**

✎ **$1 320** - €1 496 - **£930** - FF9 810
Cenas da Vida Lisboeta Técnica mixta/papel (39.5x58.5cm 15x23in) Lisboa 2001

PALMA IL GIOVANE Jacopo Negretti 1544-1628 **[151]**

⌐ **$12 704** - €11 628 - **£7 744** - FF76 272
Il martirio di Santa Giustina, das Martyrium der heiligen Justina Öl/Leinwand (222x294cm 87x115in) Wien 1999

⌐ **$83 795** - €71 296 - **£50 000** - FF467 670
The Pietà Oil/canvas (112x92cm 44x36in) London 1998

⌐ **$3 239** - €3 632 - **£2 200** - FF23 827
The Madonna and Child Oil/copper (12.5x10cm 4x3in) London 2000

✎ **$2 860** - €3 354 - **£2 057** - FF22 000
Cavaliers/Deux études de personnages Encre (11.5x15cm 4x5in) Paris 2001

▦ **$246** - €281 - **£172** - FF1 844
Die Anbetung der Hirten Radierung (14.5x8cm 5x3in) Berlin 2001

PALMA IL VECCHIO Jacopo de Negreto 1480-1528 **[3]**

⌐ **$70 000** - €61 401 - **£42 504** - FF402 766
The Mystic Marriage of Saint Catherine Oil/canvas (67x82cm 26x32in) New-York 1999

PALMAROLI Y GONZALEZ Vicente 1834-1896 **[35]**

⌐ **$15 000** - €12 677 - **£8 919** - FF83 154
The Pensive Lover Oil/panel (70x54cm 27x21in) Washington 1998

⌐ **$5 791** - €6 807 - **£4 015** - FF44 649
A Ballerina Oil/panel (23x17.5cm 9x6in) Amsterdam 2000

PALMEIRO José 1903-1984 **[333]**

⌐ **$1 400** - €1 502 - **£950** - FF9 850
Bodegón Oleo/lienzo (50x61cm 19x24in) Madrid 2001

✎ **$497** - €420 - **£294** - FF2 758
Bodegón Gouache/papier (20x12.5cm 7x4in) Madrid 1998

PALMER Adelaide 1851-1911 **[2]**

⌐ **$5 200** - €6 184 - **£3 706** - FF40 565
President Carnot Roses Oil/canvas (31x46.5cm 12x18in) New-York 2000

PALMER Erastus Dow 1817-1904 **[6]**

◈ **$28 000** - €26 517 - **£17 024** - FF173 938
Good Morning Relief (41x32cm 16x12in) New-York 1999

PALMER Ethleen Mary 1906-1958 **[28]**

▦ **$292** - €276 - **£176** - FF1 810
Hill Country Linocut in colors (27x37cm 10x14in) Sydney 1999

PALMER Frances Flora /Fanny 1812-1876 **[34]**

▦ **$1 400** - €1 692 - **£977** - FF11 100
The Old Oaken Bucket Lithograph (50x66cm 20x26in) Bolton MA 2000

PALMER Franklin, Frank 1912-1990 **[13]**

✎ **$456** - €511 - **£316** - FF3 350
Venice Watercolour/paper (44x59cm 17x23in) Calgary, Alberta 2001

PALMER Harry Sutton 1854-1933 **[203]**

✎ **$2 010** - €2 059 - **£1 250** - FF13 509
A View in Windsor Forest Watercolour (44x60.5cm 17x23in) Billingshurst, West-Sussex 2000

PALMER Herbert Sidney 1881-1970 **[72]**

⌐ **$739** - €868 - **£524** - FF5 696
Breezy Morning, Beech Lake, Haliburton Oil/masonite (22x26cm 8x10in) Toronto 2000

PALMER James Lynwood 1868-1941 **[44]**

⌐ **$26 215** - €25 425 - **£16 500** - FF166 775
Royal Lancer, Winner of the Doncaster St Leger and the Irish St Leger Oil/canvas (102x127cm 40x50in) London 1999

⌐ **$8 020** - €6 779 - **£4 800** - FF44 467
A Bay Hunter before a Tree in an extensive Landscape Oil/canvas (76x101.5cm 29x39in) London 1998

✎ **$8 000** - €9 514 - **£5 701** - FF62 408
The Steeplechase Watercolour (23x38cm 9x14in) New-York 2000

PALMER John XIX [3]
  $134 - €124 - **£80** - FF814
    Second World war Dogfight with Spirfires
    Gouache/paper (38x48cm 15x19in) Aylsham, Norfolk
    1999

PALMER Maud C. 1903-1940 [2]
  $2 416 - €2 373 - **£1 500** - FF15 569
    The Leisure Hour Oil/canvas (44.5x34.5cm 17x13in)
    Penzance, Cornwall 1998

PALMER Pauline Lennards 1867-1938 [38]
  $5 500 - €5 707 - **£3 489** - FF37 436
    **The Cameo Brooch - Portrait of a Woman in a
    White Dress** Oil/canvas/board (100.5x78.5cm
    39x30in) Boston MA 2000
  $800 - €736 - **£480** - FF4 829
    Venetian Scene Oil/board (25x33cm 10x13in)
    Morris-Plains NJ 1999

PALMER Samuel 1805-1881 [130]
  $322 690 - €383 775 - **£230 000** - FF2 517 396
    Landscape, Twilight Tempera (23x28cm 9x11in)
    London 2000
  $91 013 - €105 849 - **£65 000** - FF694 323
    «Sabrina» Watercolour (16.5x23.5cm 6x9in) London
    2001
  $557 - €656 - **£400** - FF4 303
    The rising Moon Etching (14.5x22cm 5x8in) London
    2001

PALMER Stanley XX [3]
  $63 - €71 - **£44** - FF467
    «Backwater» Engraving (45x68cm 17x26in)
    Wellington 2001

PALMER Walter Launt 1854-1932 [86]
  $29 000 - €32 170 - **£19 285** - FF211 021
    Beech Leaves Oil/canvas (50x60cm 20x24in) Milford
    CT 2000
  $900 - €771 - **£541** - FF5 057
    Wooded Landscape Oil/canvas (30x38cm 12x15in)
    Cleveland OH 2000
  $10 000 - €11 102 - **£6 955** - FF72 824
    Snowy River Bank Gouache/paper (44x34cm
    17x13in) Milford CT 2001

PALMER William Charles 1906-1987 [8]
  $2 500 - €2 888 - **£1 750** - FF37 569
    **Rodeo, inspired by Aaron Copland's Rodeo,
    Courting at Burnt Ranch** Oil/panel (53x90cm
    21x35in) New-York 2001

PALMERO DE GREGORIO Alfredo 1901-1991 [84]
  $2 160 - €2 403 - **£1 440** - FF15 760
    Toros en el campo Oleo/lienzo (89x118cm 35x46in)
    Madrid 2000

PALMEZZANO Marco 1458-1539 [9]
  $21 812 - €20 348 - **£13 160** - FF133 476
    Der Heilige Sebastian in einer Landschaft
    Oil/panel (116.5x45.5cm 45x17in) Wien 1999
  $18 920 - €20 017 - **£12 000** - FF131 300
    The Decapitation of Saint John The Baptist
    Oil/panel (30x44cm 11x17in) London 2000

PALMIÉ Charles Joh. 1863-1911 [48]
  $4 213 - €4 090 - **£2 602** - FF26 831
    **Die französische Kanalküste nördlich von
    Rouen** Öl/Leinwand (60x92cm 23x36in) München
    1999

PALMIERI Francesco XVI [1]
  $2 500 - €2 592 - **£1 500** - FF17 000
    Figura di suonatore di ghironda Inchiostro
    (25.5x17cm 10x6in) Milano 2000

PALMIERI Pietro il Vecchio 1737-1804 [18]
  $839 - €785 - **£520** - FF5 152
    Peasant with Two Horses Drinking at a Fountain
    Black chalk (17x25cm 6x9in) London 1999

PALMIERI Pietro Jacopo 1782-c.1820 [2]
  $1 500 - €1 555 - **£900** - FF10 200
    Interno di una stalla con cavalli Inchiostro
    (21.5x28cm 8x11in) Milano 2000

PALMU Juhani 1945 [26]
  $846 - €858 - **£531** - FF5 626
    Byvägen Oil/canvas (35x60cm 13x23in) Helsinki 2000
  $672 - €572 - **£401** - FF3 751
    Stilleben med rosor och plommon Oil/canvas
    (28x30cm 11x11in) Helsinki 1998

**PALOMINO DE CASTRO Y VELASCO Agiselo
Antonio don** 1653-1726 [7]
  $13 860 - €13 214 - **£8 800** - FF86 680
    Santa Rosa Oleo/lienzo (167x121cm 65x47in) Madrid
    1999
  $3 780 - €4 205 - **£2 520** - FF27 580
    **Salvador con un cáliz rodeado de ángeles, con
    símbolos eucarísticos** Oleo/lienzo (59x44.5cm
    23x17in) Madrid 2000

PALTRONIERI IL MIRANDOLESE Pietro 1673-1741
[9]
  $68 780 - €57 931 - **£40 622** - FF380 000
    Caprices architecturaux dans les paysages
    Huile/toile (73x98cm 28x38in) Paris 1998

PALUMBO Eduardo 1932 [21]
  $650 - €674 - **£390** - FF4 420
    Giochi ardenti Olio/tela (70x100cm 27x39in) Vercelli
    1999

PALUMBO L. XIX [3]
  $4 289 - €4 871 - **£3 000** - FF31 952
    Veduta del Vesuvio da Mergellina, Napoli Oil/can-
    vas (56x71cm 22x27in) London 2001
  $2 319 - €2 147 - **£1 400** - FF14 082
    The Bay of Naples Oil/panel (19x33cm 7x12in)
    London 1999

PALUSKY Robert Clark 1942 [2]
  $6 000 - €5 727 - **£3 749** - FF37 569
    «Above all Else Confusion Reigns» Sculpture,
    glass (49.5x38x7.5cm 19x14x2in) New-York 1999

PAMBOUJIAN Gérard 1941 [197]
  $993 - €1 143 - **£684** - FF7 500
    Port Grimaud Huile/toile (60x81cm 23x31in) Toulon
    2000
  $467 - €457 - **£287** - FF3 000
    Nu féminin à genoux tenue par un gorille
    Huile/toile/carton (35x24cm 13x9in) Toulon 1999

PAN GONGSHOU 1741-1794 [6]
  $15 444 - €14 646 - **£9 996** - FF96 072
    Scholars in Studio Ink/paper (64.5x32.5cm 25x12in)
    Hong-Kong 1999

PAN HONGHAI 1942 [4]
  $12 840 - €14 091 - **£8 270** - FF92 430
    Water Village Oil/canvas (95x129.5cm 37x50in)
    Hong-Kong 2000

PAN Marta 1923 [1]
  $3 003 - €3 201 - **£1 904** - FF21 000
    Équilibre Sculpture bois (45x22.5x17cm 17x8x6in)
    Paris 2000

PAN TIANSHOU 1897-1971 [37]
  $12 900 - €12 106 - **£7 970** - FF79 410
    Lotus Ink (70x41cm 27x16in) Hong-Kong 1999

P

PAN YULIANG 1895-1977 **[43]**
- $67 100 - €56 345 - **£39 380** - FF369 600
  Lady Brushing Her Hair Oil/canvas (54x65.5cm 21x25in) Taipei 1998
- $41 648 - €39 056 - **£25 893** - FF256 190
  Girl's Profile Oil/wood (22.5x30.5cm 8x12in) Taipei 1999

PANABAKER Frank Shirley 1904-1992 **[38]**
- $1 790 - €1 532 - **£1 077** - FF10 048
  Windswept Pines on Georgian Bay Oil/board (51x61cm 20x24in) Toronto 1998
- $861 - €816 - **£535** - FF5 350
  «Fall, Georgian Bay» Oil/canvas/board (28x35cm 11x13in) Calgary, Alberta 1999

PANAMARENKO 1940 **[81]**
- $3 752 - €3 470 - **£2 338** - FF22 764
  Reis naar de Sterren Construction (22x56cm 8x22in) Lokeren 1999
- $6 864 - €6 445 - **£4 238** - FF42 276
  Het volkomen ruimteschip Crayon/papier (90x149cm 35x58in) Antwerpen 1999
- $368 - €397 - **£254** - FF2 601
  Poule Lithographie (54x38cm 21x14in) Antwerpen 2001

PANAT de A., Marquis 1886-1965 **[83]**
- $189 - €229 - **£132** - FF1 500
  Trois personnages dans un café Pastel/papier (15x15cm 5x5in) Lavaur 2000

PANCERA Enrico XX **[2]**
- $4 000 - €4 147 - **£2 400** - FF27 200
  Busto di gioinetto Bronze (H42cm H16in) Imbersago (Lecco) 2001

PANCKOUCKE Ernestine 1784-1860 **[10]**
- $1 997 - €1 724 - **£1 205** - FF11 306
  Study of a bunch of flowers with a butterfly Gouache/vellum (307x234cm 120x92in) Amsterdam 1998

PANCOAST Morris Hall 1877-1963 **[36]**
- $1 700 - €1 426 - **£1 002** - FF9 356
  Waiting in the Trees Oil/board (35x35cm 14x14in) Greenwich CT 1998

PANDEREN van Egbert c.1581-1637 **[4]**
- $2 097 - €2 301 - **£1 424** - FF15 092
  Die vier Tageszeiten, nach Tobias Verhaecht Kupferstich (18.4x22cm 7x8in) Berlin 2000

PANDIANI Antonio 1838-1928 **[9]**
- $1 828 - €1 974 - **£1 250** - FF12 948
  Children Bronze (H26cm H10in) Billingshurst, West-Sussex 2001

PANDYA Dinesh 1956 **[2]**
- $3 980 - €3 854 - **£2 500** - FF25 281
  Untitled Mixed media/canvas (101x76cm 39x29in) London 1999

PANE Gina 1939-1990 **[9]**
- $1 600 - €1 659 - **£960** - FF10 880
  Azione sentimentale Photo (29.5x20cm 11x7in) Milano 2001

PANEK Jerzy 1918-2001 **[19]**
- $7 093 - €7 662 - **£4 903** - FF50 259
  Cheval III Huile/toile (59x85cm 23x33in) Kraków 2001
- $366 - €396 - **£253** - FF2 599
  Autoportrait Pastel/papier (40.5x28.5cm 15x11in) Kraków 2001
- $1 130 - €1 284 - **£790** - FF8 423
  Fiacre I Gravure bois (71x55cm 27x21in) Warszawa 2001

PANERAI Ruggero 1862-1923 **[82]**
- $6 500 - €6 738 - **£3 900** - FF44 200
  Madre e figlio, gioie materne Olio/tela (49x63.5cm 19x25in) Prato 1999
- $2 000 - €2 073 - **£1 200** - FF13 600
  Due cavalli al pascolo Olio/tela/cartone (27x35cm 10x13in) Milano 2000

PANETTI Domenico 1460-c.1513 **[2]**
- $9 900 - €9 976 - **£6 171** - FF65 441
  Die heilige Anthonius und Stephanus Huile/panneau (83x64cm 32x25in) Zürich 2000
- $24 000 - €23 989 - **£14 661** - FF157 350
  The Madonna and Child Before a Mountainous Landscape with a Town Oil/panel (22x23.5cm 8x9in) New-York 2000

PANFIL Jozef 1958 **[14]**
- $403 - €470 - **£282** - FF3 084
  Nature morte Huile/toile (24x46cm 9x18in) Warszawa 2000

PANG XUNQIN 1906-1985 **[13]**
- $68 400 - €64 143 - **£42 525** - FF420 750
  Iris Oil/paper/board (57x51cm 22x20in) Taipei 1999
- $4 544 - €4 262 - **£2 825** - FF27 956
  Vase of Flower Ink (33.5x45cm 13x17in) Taipei 1999

PANGRAC Miroslav 1924 **[15]**
- $1 011 - €957 - **£630** - FF6 275
  Music Bronze (H73cm H28in) Praha 2000

PANINI Francesco 1745-1812 **[18]**
- $350 - €328 - **£212** - FF2 150
  Paris Oil/canvas (60x91cm 24x36in) Chicago IL 1999
- $29 886 - €32 080 - **£20 000** - FF210 432
  View of the Funerary Monument of King Joseph I of Portugal Ink (86.5x62.5cm 34x24in) London 2000
- $855 - €901 - **£570** - FF5 910
  Vista de la Basílica de San Juan Grabado (50x71cm 19x27in) Madrid 2000

PANINI Giovanni Paolo 1691-1765 **[106]**
- $162 000 - €139 948 - **£81 000** - FF918 000
  Paesaggio con architetture e figure Olio/tela (122x170cm 48x66in) Prato 1999
- $133 110 - €129 582 - **£81 770** - FF850 000
  Ruines romaines avec soldats en discussion avec un philosophe Huile/toile (81.5x108.5cm 32x42in) Paris 1999
- $4 800 - €6 220 - **£3 600** - FF40 800
  Figure tra le rovine China (18.5x13.5cm 7x5in) Milano 2000

PANITZSCH Robert 1879-1949 **[173]**
- $1 629 - €1 483 - **£1 000** - FF9 727
  Fishing Boats moored in a Harbour Oil/canvas (70.5x100.5cm 27x39in) London 1999

PANKIEWICZ Józef 1866-1940 **[53]**
- $14 943 - €16 394 - **£9 925** - FF107 536
  Paysage du Sud de la France Oil/canvas (41.4x59cm 16x23in) Warszawa 2000
- $6 606 - €6 659 - **£4 120** - FF43 680
  Nature morte aux poissons Oil/canvas (25x40cm 9x15in) Warszawa 2000
- $1 998 - €2 283 - **£1 407** - FF14 976
  Paysage de Saint Tropez Aquarelle (28.5x41cm 11x16in) Warszawa 2001
- $685 - €690 - **£427** - FF4 529
  La traversée d'un pont Drypoint (13x19.5cm 5x7in) Warszawa 2000

PANKOK Bernhard 1872-1943 **[96]**

- **$2 921** - €3 068 - **£1 842** - FF20 123
  Waldweg Öl/Leinwand (57x77cm 22x30in) Stuttgart 2000
- **$713** - €818 - **£487** - FF5 366
  Stehender weiblicher Rückenakt Red chalk (50x32.5cm 19x12in) Heidelberg 2000
- **$164** - €189 - **£112** - FF1 240
  Kühe auf der Weide Vernis mou (10x12.5cm 3x4in) Heidelberg 2000

PANKOK Otto 1893-1966 **[311]**

- **$4 519** - €4 346 - **£2 788** - FF28 508
  Nuna stehend Bronze (H48.5cm H19in) Köln 1999
- **$4 136** - €4 704 - **£2 868** - FF30 855
  Hand mit Buch Charcoal (59x41.8cm 23x16in) Hamburg 2000
- **$515** - €500 - **£320** - FF3 320
  Hahn Woodcut (32.7x29.3cm 12x11in) Berlin 1999

PANN Abel Pfeffermann 1883-1963 **[72]**

- **$10 500** - €10 250 - **£6 650** - FF67 233
  Figures on the Beach Oil/panel (41x33cm 16x12in) Tel Aviv 1999
- **$5 500** - €6 034 - **£3 549** - FF39 580
  And they shall beat their Swords into Ploughares Pastel (54x59cm 21x23in) Tel Aviv 2000
- **$2 000** - €2 167 - **£1 333** - FF14 215
  «While We Pray in Comfort and Security, They Tremble in Misery» Poster (96x64cm 38x25in) New-York 2000

PANNAGGI Ivo 1901-1981 **[5]**

- **$10 000** - €10 367 - **£6 000** - FF68 000
  Vaso, tavolozza, pennelli e solidi Olio/tavola (27.5x33cm 10x12in) Milano 1999
- **$6 500** - €5 454 - **£3 813** - FF35 773
  Self Portrait Gelatin silver print (17x12cm 6x4in) New-York 1998

PANNELL Joseph **[2]**

- **$350** - €386 - **£233** - FF2 532
  Trafalgar Square Etching (21x26cm 8x10in) East-Dennis MA 2000

PANNIER Willy 1952 **[113]**

- **$406** - €427 - **£269** - FF2 800
  Scène de plage Huile/panneau (27x22cm 10x8in) Saint-Malo 2000

PANNKA Claude 1928-1972 **[13]**

- **$197** - €183 - **£121** - FF1 203
  The Ghost Gum Watercolour/paper (25x35.5cm 9x13in) Melbourne 1999

PANSAERS Clément 1885-1922 **[1]**

- **$735** - €762 - **£484** - FF5 000
  «Bar nicanor» Affiche (32x24.5cm 12x9in) Paris 2000

PANSING Fred 1854-1912 **[12]**

- **$15 000** - €13 636 - **£9 204** - FF89 445
  Portrait of the Steamship «Nantasket» Oil/canvas (38x66cm 15x26in) Nantucket MA 1998
- **$900** - €865 - **£555** - FF5 677
  «Atlantic Transport Line, New York-London» Poster (70.5x104cm 27x40in) New-York 1999

PANT van der Theresia 1924 **[12]**

- **$5 704** - €5 445 - **£3 565** - FF35 719
  Kreet - Scream Bronze (H42cm H16in) Amsterdam 1999

PANTAZIS Périclès 1849-1884 **[40]**

- **$17 550** - €19 512 - **£11 700** - FF128 050
  Still Life with pears, apples and quinces Oil/canvas (40x50cm 15x19in) Athens 2000

- **$3 516** - €2 975 - **£2 100** - FF19 512
  Nature morte Huile/bois (21x29cm 8x11in) Bruxelles 1998
- **$5 861** - €6 748 - **£4 000** - FF44 267
  Boating on the River Watercolour, gouache/paper (25.5x23.5cm 10x9in) London 2000

PANTON Lawrence Arthur C. 1894-1954 **[84]**

- **$586** - €569 - **£366** - FF3 735
  Rock Patterns, Nova Scotia Oil/board (33x40.5cm 12x15in) Toronto 1999
- **$253** - €244 - **£157** - FF1 598
  Woman seated in an Armchair Crayon (25.5x34cm 10x13in) Toronto 1999
- **$408** - €390 - **£255** - FF2 559
  Falls Linocut in colors (22.5x25cm 8x9in) Toronto 1999

PANTON Verner 1926-1998 **[8]**

- **$24 000** - €27 847 - **£16 569** - FF182 664
  Living Tower (manufactured for Fritz Hansen EFP) Sculpture, wood (205.5x203x65cm 80x79x25in) New-York 2000

PANTORBA de Bernardino 1896-1988 **[14]**

- **$13 500** - €15 016 - **£9 500** - FF98 500
  Parque en invierno Oleo/lienzo (83x119cm 32x46in) Madrid 2001

PANUSKA Jaroslav 1872-1958 **[72]**

- **$1 069** - €1 011 - **£666** - FF6 634
  Early Spring in the Highlands Oil/cardboard (50x65cm 19x25in) Praha 2000
- **$332** - €314 - **£207** - FF2 061
  Village in Winter Oil/cardboard (25x34cm 9x13in) Praha 1999

PANYINGATO Franco XIX-XX **[4]**

- **$1 100** - €1 052 - **£692** - FF6 899
  Isle of Capri Oil/canvas (91x91cm 36x36in) Milwaukee WI 1999

PANZA Giovanni 1894-1989 **[83]**

- **$7 400** - €9 589 - **£5 550** - FF62 900
  Il girotondo Olio/tela (99.5x148cm 39x58in) Milano 2000
- **$4 956** - €4 281 - **£2 478** - FF28 084
  Mercato Olio/tavola (40x56cm 15x22in) Milano 1999
- **$1 800** - €2 332 - **£1 350** - FF15 500
  Mercato Olio/legno (25x35.5cm 9x13in) Roma 2000

PAOLETTI Antonio Ermolao 1834-1912 **[88]**

- **$13 500** - €13 995 - **£8 100** - FF91 800
  Lavandaie al fiume Olio/tela (58x73cm 22x28in) Roma 1999
- **$7 664** - €8 172 - **£5 200** - FF53 606
  The Firewood Seller Oil/panel (33x23cm 12x9in) London 2001
- **$962** - €970 - **£600** - FF6 362
  The Lazy Fish Seller Watercolour (20.5x24.5cm 8x9in) Billingshurst, West-Sussex 2000

PAOLETTI Rodolfo 1866-1940 **[26]**

- **$1 200** - €1 555 - **£900** - FF10 200
  Paesaggio lacustre con statue Olio/tela (60x100cm 23x39in) Milano 2001

PAOLETTI Silvio 1864-1921 **[11]**

- **$24 000** - €24 880 - **£14 400** - FF163 200
  Ciacole in un interno Olio/tela (66x96.5cm 25x37in) Milano 1999

PAOLI Bruno 1915 **[30]**

- **$320** - €415 - **£240** - FF2 720
  Scorcio di strada Olio/tavola (48x37cm 18x14in) Firenze 2000

P

P

☞ $300 - €389 - **£225** - FF2 550
«Lerici» Olio/tavola (25x35cm 9x13in) Prato 2001

PAOLINI Giulio 1940 **[91]**
☞ **$41 637** - €38 643 - **£25 000** - FF253 480
Cadre Mixed media/canvas (125x125cm 49x49in) London 1999
☞ **$9 600** - €12 440 - **£7 200** - FF81 600
«Diapason» Tecnica mista (107.5x100cm 42x39in) Milano 2000
☞ **$8 400** - €10 885 - **£6 300** - FF71 400
Senza titolo Collage/tela (44x32cm 17x12in) Milano 2001
✐ **$3 500** - €3 285 - **£2 162** - FF21 548
Untitled Chalks (75.5x104.5cm 29x41in) New-York 1999
▥ **$350** - €363 - **£210** - FF2 380
Belvedere Litografia a colori (44x42cm 17x16in) Milano 2000
◉ **$5 600** - €7 257 - **£4 200** - FF47 600
Bandiere Photo couleurs (32x28cm 12x11in) Milano 2000

PAOLINI Pietro 1603-1681 **[18]**
☞ **$35 000** - €36 283 - **£21 000** - FF238 000
Allegoria dell'udito e della vista Olio/tela (95x137cm 37x53in) Milano 2001

PAOLO di Giovanni 1399-1482 **[9]**
☞ **$800 000** - €855 751 - **£545 440** - FF5 613 360
Scenes from the Story of Esther: a cassone panel Tempera/panel (52.5x180.5cm 20x71in) New-York 2001
☞ **$58 611** - €49 900 - **£35 000** - FF327 323
Christ as the Man of Sorrows Tempera/panel (14x10cm 5x3in) London 1998

PAOLO VENEZIANO ?-1358/62 **[3]**
☞ **$48 000** - €41 466 - **£32 000** - FF272 000
Madonna con Bambino Tempera/tavola (96x64.5cm 37x25in) Roma 1998
☞ **$257 120** - €255 036 - **£160 000** - FF1 672 928
The Madonna and Child enthroned Oil/panel (41x29cm 16x11in) London 1999

PAOLOZZI Eduardo 1924 **[235]**
☞ **$3 736** - €4 011 - **£2 500** - FF26 308
Head Acrylic (43x33.5cm 16x13in) London 2000
▧ **$35 572** - €41 330 - **£25 000** - FF271 105
«Ag5» Bronze (H100.5cm H39in) London 2001
▧ **$3 572** - €3 835 - **£2 391** - FF25 154
Dumont Head Bronze (H22.8cm H8in) Köln 2000
✐ **$2 041** - €1 742 - **£1 300** - FF13 693
«Fairground» Indian ink (33x25.5cm 12x10in) London 1998
▥ **$329** - €319 - **£200** - FF2 090
Picture is a fact Screenprint in colors (95x64cm 37x25in) London 2000

PAP Emil 1884-? **[71]**
☞ **$1 764** - €1 778 - **£1 100** - FF11 664
Reflective Moment Oil/canvas (99x73.5cm 38x28in) London 2000

PAPALOUKAS Spyros 1892-1957 **[4]**
☞ **$4 396** - €5 061 - **£3 000** - FF33 200
Arches Oil/cardboard (19x24cm 7x9in) London 2000

PAPALUCA Louis, Luca 1890-1934 **[32]**
☞ **$2 141** - €2 087 - **£1 300** - FF13 693
The M.Y «Alice» R.T.Y.C in the Bay of Naples Gouache/paper (40x65cm 15x25in) London 2000

PAPAMICHAIL Hera 1964 **[3]**
◉ **$756** - €841 - **£504** - FF5 516
Melina in Clouds Polaroid (9x10.5cm 3x4in) Athens 2000

PAPART Max 1911-1994 **[805]**
☞ **$2 355** - €2 287 - **£1 455** - FF15 000
«Florentine deux» Technique mixte/toile (82x67cm 32x26in) Paris 1999
☞ **$525** - €610 - **£363** - FF4 001
Kvinnocollage Mixed media (33x47cm 12x18in) Stockholm 2000
▧ **$957** - €915 - **£597** - FF6 000
Tête d'homme Bronze (32x30x6cm 12x11x2in) Paris 1999
✐ **$545** - €534 - **£335** - FF3 500
Paysage aztèque Encre Chine/papier (61x50cm 24x19in) Paris 1999
▥ **$158** - €168 - **£105** - FF1 100
Composition Lithographie (36x25cm 14x9in) Saint-Dié 2000

PAPAZOFF Georges 1894-1972 **[151]**
☞ **$15 987** - €19 056 - **£11 400** - FF125 000
«Hommage au Douanier Rousseau: le rêve de la bohémienne endormie» Huile/toile (130x195cm 51x76in) Saint-Germain-en-Laye 2000
☞ **$2 278** - €2 592 - **£1 581** - FF17 000
Composition abstraite Huile/toile (54.5x65cm 21x25in) Paris 2000
☞ **$1 023** - €1 220 - **£729** - FF8 000
Composition surréaliste Huile/toile (22x33cm 8x12in) Paris 2000
✐ **$480** - €466 - **£296** - FF3 057
Surrealistisk komposition Indian ink/paper (17x30cm 6x11in) Stockholm 1999

PAPE de Abraham 1620-1666 **[6]**
☞ **$43 579** - €42 838 - **£28 000** - FF280 996
Kitchen Interior with a Mischievous Boy spraying a Scullery-Maid Oil/panel (49x41cm 19x16in) London 1999

PAPE Eduard Friedrich 1817-1905 **[15]**
☞ **$3 048** - €3 072 - **£1 900** - FF20 151
A Fisherman by a River in the South Tirol, Austria Oil/panel (45.5x67cm 17x26in) London 2000
☞ **$2 330** - €2 556 - **£1 583** - FF16 769
Märkische Landschaft mit Weiher Oil/panel (20x30.5cm 7x12in) Berlin 2000

PAPE Eric 1870-1938 **[38]**
☞ **$1 500** - €1 293 - **£890** - FF8 484
Egyptian Courtyard Oil/canvas (31x22cm 12x9in) Cambridge MA 1998
☞ **$1 300** - €1 250 - **£802** - FF8 200
Portrait of a Woman Pastel/paper (48x33.5cm 18x13in) Boston MA 1999

PAPÉ Frank Cheyne 1878-1972 **[12]**
☞ **$700** - €643 - **£430** - FF4 218
At the Mercy of the Sea Watercolour (30.5x20.5cm 12x8in) Oxfordshire 1999

PAPE Lígia 1929 **[1]**
☞ **$10 000** - €9 633 - **£6 209** - FF63 186
Untitled Mixed media (36x36cm 14x14in) New-York 1999

PAPE William 1859-1920 **[19]**
☞ **$5 852** - €6 647 - **£4 093** - FF43 600
Junges Mädchen auf Wiese sitzend, einen Strauss roter Blüten haltend Öl/Karton (83x62cm 32x24in) Berlin 2001
☞ **$2 412** - €2 812 - **£1 690** - FF18 446
Capri Öl/Karton (43x34cm 16x13in) München 2000

PAPETY Dominique Louis 1815-1849 **[22]**
- $999 - €927 - £600 - FF6 083
  La Perse Oil/canvas (29x37cm 11x14in) Carlisle, Cumbria 1999
- $1 136 - €1 220 - £760 - FF8 000
  Le couple de troubadour Aquarelle, gouache (50x34cm 19x13in) Paris 2000

PAPF Karl Ernest 1833-1910 **[1]**
- $2 537 - €2 665 - £1 600 - FF17 479
  Wild Banana Palm, Brazil Oil/board (45x35.5cm 17x13in) London 2000

PAPILLON Jean-Baptiste 1698-1776 **[1]**
- $49 350 - €45 735 - £30 690 - FF300 000
  La fabrication et la pose du papier peint Lavis (36.5x27.5cm 14x10in) Paris 1999

PAPPERITZ Fritz Georg 1846-1918 **[26]**
- $5 746 - €6 450 - £4 000 - FF42 311
  Reclining Nude with a Landscape beyond Oil/canvas (95x165cm 36x64in) London 2001
- $1 842 - €1 687 - £1 123 - FF11 067
  Nymphenreigen an einem stillen Teich Öl/Leinwand (59x49cm 23x19in) München 1999

PAPPERITZ Gustav Friedrich 1813-1861 **[31]**
- $22 360 - €21 474 - £13 860 - FF140 863
  Ansicht von Granada Öl/Leinwand (95x133cm 37x52in) Ahlden 1999
- $665 - €625 - £412 - FF4 097
  Südliche Landschaft Öl/Papier (13.5x21cm 5x8in) Luzern 1999

PAPRILL Henry A. XIX **[12]**
- $1 104 - €1 185 - £740 - FF7 774
  View of the Great Britain, an iron Steamship Aquatint in colors (39x60cm 15x23in) London 2001

PAQUIN Pauline Thibodeau 1952 **[30]**
- $678 - €648 - £422 - FF4 250
  A la sortie du village Oil/canvas (61x91.5cm 24x36in) Calgary, Alberta 1999

PARADES de Vincent XIX **[3]**
- $32 952 - €36 588 - £22 968 - FF240 000
  Cardinal et gentilhomme jouant aux échecs/Rencontre dans un salon Huile/toile (60x105cm 23x41in) Paris 2001
- $3 444 - €2 973 - £2 076 - FF19 500
  La leçon de musique Huile/toile (33x46cm 12x18in) Bruxelles 1998

PARADIES Herman Cornelis A. 1883-1966 **[23]**
- $1 560 - €1 724 - £1 082 - FF11 311
  The Harbour of Rotterdam Charcoal (38.5x78cm 15x30in) Amsterdam 2001

PARADISE Phillip Herschel 1905 **[12]**
- $700 - €751 - £468 - FF4 928
  South Pacific House in Coastal landscape Watercolour/paper (26x36cm 10x14in) Altadena CA 2000

PARANT Louis Bertin 1768-1851 **[7]**
- $4 015 - €3 811 - £2 505 - FF25 000
  Portrait présumé du Duc de Berry, en buste Miniature (15x11.5cm 5x4in) Deauville 1999
- $2 457 - €2 744 - £1 573 - FF18 000
  Projet de camée, Vénus et l'Amour Aquarelle, gouache (16x22cm 6x8in) Paris 2000

PARASACCHI Domenico XVII **[2]**
- $1 033 - €1 077 - £650 - FF7 065
  The Principle Fountains of Rome Engraving (28x42cm 11x16in) London 2000

PARAVANO Dino 1935 **[26]**
- $689 - €714 - £436 - FF4 685
  Still life of Pomegranates and a Ewer Oil/board (34x49cm 13x19in) Johannesburg 2000
- $580 - €527 - £360 - FF3 460
  Impala Pencil/paper (25x25.5cm 9x10in) Billingshurst, West-Sussex 1999

PARAVISINI Christine XX **[18]**
- $1 502 - €1 677 - £1 045 - FF11 000
  Gorille Bronze (H34cm H13in) Paris 2001

PARAYRE Henry 1887-1970 **[8]**
- $5 009 - €4 269 - £2 984 - FF28 000
  Baigneuse Bronze (27x34cm 10x13in) Paris 1998

PARCELL Malcolm 1896-1987 **[4]**
- $3 500 - €3 923 - £2 439 - FF25 730
  Locking the Gate Oil/canvas (51x76cm 20x29in) Beverly-Hills CA 2001

PARDI Gianfranco 1933 **[35]**
- $800 - €1 037 - £600 - FF6 800
  Architettura Olio/tela (50x100cm 19x39in) Vercelli 2001

PARDO Jorge 1963 **[4]**
- $10 580 - €10 297 - £6 500 - FF67 545
  «1,2,3,4,5,6,7,8,9,10» Installation (8x100x65cm 3x39x25in) London 1999
- $23 000 - €26 019 - £16 090 - FF170 671
  Untitled, 9 Ink (133.5x133.5cm 52x52in) New-York 2001

PARDO Mercedes 1921 **[11]**
- $240 - €229 - £150 - FF1 500
  Sin título Serigrafia (77x57.5cm 30x22in) Caracas 1999

PARDONNEAU Jules XIX **[5]**
- $2 267 - €2 515 - £1 567 - FF16 500
  Nature morte sucrée Huile/toile (46x38cm 18x14in) Cherbourg 2001

PAREDES Y JUAN de Vincente 1857-1903 **[56]**
- $5 850 - €6 403 - £4 048 - FF42 000
  Le concert Huile/toile (46x65cm 18x25in) Aix-en-Provence 2001
- $3 141 - €3 506 - £2 185 - FF23 000
  Piccador Huile/panneau (22x16cm 8x6in) Paris 2001
- $1 296 - €1 084 - £774 - FF7 110
  «Aurore, Rêve, Crépuscule» Aguada/papel (30x35cm 11x13in) Madrid 1998

PARELLE Marc-Antoine XVIII **[2]**
- $24 000 - €28 207 - £16 639 - FF185 025
  A Lady Holding a Dog Oil/panel (41x32.5cm 16x12in) New-York 2000

PARENT Aubert Henri J. 1753-1835 **[5]**
- $13 448 - €14 436 - £9 000 - FF94 694
  Leda and the Swan Relief (H56cm H22in) London 2000

PARENT Mimi Benoît 1924 **[6]**
- $5 396 - €5 793 - £3 610 - FF38 000
  Femme Technique mixte (46x37.5cm 18x14in) Paris 2000

PARENT Roger 1881-1986 **[88]**
- $1 819 - €2 107 - £1 258 - FF13 821
  Groupe de personnages dans un paysage Huile/toile (100x120cm 39x47in) Bruxelles 2000
- $599 - €694 - £414 - FF4 552
  Nature morte au cactus Huile/toile (90x60cm 35x23in) Bruxelles 2000

P

P

✏️ $321 - €372 - **£222** - FF2 439
La cueillette des pommes Fusain (72x99cm 28x38in) Bruxelles 2000

PARENTE Francesco 1885-1969 **[7]**
🗿 $1 700 - €1 762 - **£1 020** - FF11 560
Il broncio Bronzo (H40cm H15in) Firenze 2000

PAREROULTJA Edwin 1918-1986 **[19]**
🖌️ $176 - €169 - **£108** - FFI 110
Rock Formation Watercolour/paper (28x35.5cm 11x13in) Melbourne 1999

PAREROULTJA Otto 1914-1973 **[49]**
✏️ $607 - €584 - **£374** - FF3 830
James Range Country Watercolour/paper (32.5x51.5cm 12x20in) Melbourne 1999

PARESCE Renato, René 1866-1937 **[54]**
🖼️ $16 800 - €14 513 - **£11 200** - FF95 200
Paesaggio Olio/tela (40x60.5cm 15x23in) Prato 1998
🖼️ $10 000 - €10 367 - **£6 000** - FF68 000
Village français Olio/tela (35x27.5cm 13x10in) Milano 2000
🖼️ $2 600 - €2 695 - **£1 560** - FF17 680
«Londres, la descente de Frogal» China (32x23.5cm 12x9in) Milano 2001

PARESSANT Jules 1917 **[45]**
🖼️ $1 818 - €1 982 - **£1 192** - FF13 000
Les arbres rouges, l'étang du Pont de Fer Huile/toile/panneau (55x48cm 21x18in) Brest 2000
🖼️ $433 - €473 - **£284** - FF3 100
Palette sans titre sur fond de peau de serpent Huile/toile (30x23cm 11x9in) Brest 2000
〰️ $222 - €221 - **£138** - FFI 450
Dolmen et Menhir Eau-forte (12x30cm 4x11in) Brest 1999

PARET Y ALCAZAR Luis 1746-1799 **[13]**
🖼️ $120 000 - €121 396 - **£73 272** - FF796 308
Portrait of Gentleman seated at a Desk reading Cicero's Treatise Oil/panel (49x38cm 19x14in) New-York 2000
🖼️ $6 361 - €7 407 - **£4 400** - FF48 590
Putti Adorning themselves With Flowers Oil/canvas (38.5x26cm 15x10in) London 2000

PARIGI Giulio 1571-1635 **[8]**
✏️ $11 763 - €11 486 - **£7 500** - FF75 345
The galley of Calai and Zeti propelled by Boreas and Oreithyia Black chalk (13.5x19cm 5x7in) London 1999

PARIN Gino F. 1876-1944 **[20]**
🖼️ $2 750 - €2 851 - **£1 650** - FF18 700
Fra i pensieri Olio/cartone (30x40cm 11x15in) Trieste 2001

PARIS Pierre Adrien 1745-1819 **[14]**
✏️ $3 506 - €3 049 - **£2 114** - FF20 000
Les Bains de la Belle Gabrielle Pierre noire/papier (32x44.5cm 12x17in) Paris 1998

PARIS René 1881-1970 **[19]**
🗿 $1 712 - €1 677 - **£1 053** - FF11 000
Le chevreau Bronze (H15.5cm H6in) Soissons 1999

PARIS Roland 1894-1945 **[28]**
🗿 $601 - €562 - **£364** - FF3 689
Pierrette Porcelaine (H37cm H14in) Köln 1999

PARIS Walter 1842-1906 **[21]**
✏️ $1 400 - €1 194 - **£842** - FF7 835
Southern garden scene Watercolour/paper (28x44cm 11x17in) Norwalk CT 1999

PARISATI Jacopo di Paride 1440/43-1499 **[1]**
🖼️ $10 800 - €9 330 - **£7 200** - FF61 200
San Domenico Olio/tavola (55.5x39cm 21x15in) Milano 1998

PARISH Maxfield XX **[3]**
🎞️ $357 - €348 - **£220** - FF2 286
Stars Print in colors (65x42.5cm 25x16in) London 1999

PARISON Gaston 1889-? **[10]**
🖼️ $2 624 - €3 049 - **£1 870** - FF20 000
A la fontaine , Maroc Huile/toile (46x55cm 18x21in) Paris 2001

PARISY Eugène Ferdinand XIX **[16]**
🖼️ $732 - €769 - **£485** - FF5 043
Stilleben mit einer Languste und zwei Steingutflaschen Oil/panel (14.5x21cm 5x8in) Zürich 2000

PARIZEAU Philippe Louis 1740-1801 **[31]**
✏️ $1 800 - €1 928 - **£1 229** - FF12 647
Figures near a Well Surrounded by a Ruined Wall Red chalk (26x42cm 10x16in) New-York 2001

PARK David 1911-1960 **[35]**
🖼️ $450 000 - €511 778 - **£314 415** - FF3 357 045
The Flower Seller Oil/canvas (132x121.5cm 51x47in) Beverly-Hills CA 2000
🖼️ $17 000 - €16 909 - **£10 551** - FF110 914
Flying Trapeze Oil/panel (61.5x44cm 24x17in) Beverly-Hills CA 1999
✏️ $24 000 - €27 884 - **£16 867** - FF182 908
Woman ironing Ink (43x35.5cm 16x13in) Beverly-Hills CA 2001

PARK James Stuart 1862-1933 **[141]**
🖼️ $3 373 - €3 635 - **£2 300** - FF23 847
Roses on Ledge Oil/canvas (51.5x76.5cm 20x30in) London 2001
🖼️ $2 933 - €3 370 - **£2 030** - FF22 108
Still Life, Roses Oil/canvas (33x43cm 13x17in) Hamilton, Lanarkshire 2000

PARK John Anthony 1880-1962 **[214]**
🖼️ $3 482 - €3 921 - **£2 400** - FF25 723
Still Life with Poppies Oil/canvas (35.5x46cm 13x18in) London 2000
🖼️ $5 647 - €5 187 - **£3 500** - FF34 024
Fishing Boats Oil/board (30x40cm 11x15in) Devon 1999

PARK Madeleine Fish 1891-1960 **[38]**
🗿 $525 - €586 - **£343** - FF3 842
Ringlings, Tiger on the Ball Plaster (38x17cm 15x7in) Watertown MA 2000

PARK Richard Henry 1832-? **[3]**
🗿 $42 500 - €49 601 - **£30 128** - FF325 363
Figure of a young Girl Marble (H125.5cm H49in) New-York 2001

PARK Seung-Soon 1954 **[2]**
🖼️ $2 600 - €3 049 - **£1 855** - FF20 000
Thou to be seen Tomorrow Mixed media/canvas (60x100cm 23x39in) New-York 2000

PARK SOO-GUN 1914-1965 **[7]**
🖼️ $350 000 - €339 042 - **£218 295** - FF2 223 970
Mother and Child Mixed media (45.5x38cm 17x14in) New-York 1999
🖼️ $110 000 - €128 997 - **£78 496** - FF846 164
Mother and Child Walking Under Trees Mixed media (19.5x22cm 7x8in) New-York 2000

PARK Stuart 1862-1933 **[26]**
- $3 149 - €2 717 - **£1 900** - FF17 823
  Pale Yellow Roses in a Vase Oil/canvas (61x76cm 24x29in) London 1998
- $2 530 - €2 935 - **£1 800** - FF19 254
  Still Life Study of Red Begonia Oil/canvas (29.5x37cm 11x14in) West-Sussex 2000

PARKE Jessie Burns 1889-? **[4]**
- $750 - €840 - **£521** - FF5 510
  «**Paris**» Oil/board (20x15cm 8x6in) Cincinnati OH 2001

PARKEHARRISON Robert 1968 **[1]**
- $2 200 - €2 499 - **£1 543** - FF16 390
  «**Cloud Machine**» Gelatin silver print (77x100.5cm 30x39in) New-York 2001

PARKER A.M. XIX **[2]**
- $6 500 - €6 238 - **£4 074** - FF40 920
  Extensive Landscape with Figures on a Riverbank Oil/canvas (86x109cm 33x42in) New-York 1999

PARKER Alfred Charles 1906-1985 **[3]**
- $5 000 - €5 600 - **£3 474** - FF36 736
  Couple lounging in the Grass, Camera nearby Gouache/paper (22x67cm 9x26in) New-York 2001

PARKER Bill 1922 **[349]**
- $205 - €229 - **£143** - FF1 500
  Comoposition Acrylique/toile (57x76.5cm 22x30in) Lons-Le-Saunier 2001
- $135 - €152 - **£95** - FF1 000
  Composition sur fond jaune Pastel (56x76cm 22x29in) Paris 2001

PARKER George Waller 1888-? **[6]**
- $2 000 - €2 377 - **£1 385** - FF15 594
  European Village Street on a Sunny Day Oil/canvas (54x65cm 21x25in) Detroit MI 2000

PARKER Harold 1873-1962 **[3]**
- $3 915 - €3 678 - **£2 360** - FF24 129
  Daphne Bronze (H47cm H18in) Sydney 1999

PARKER Harry Hanley 1916-1917 **[1]**
- $2 092 - €2 358 - **£1 449** - FF15 467
  «**A Surrey Cornfield**» Oil/canvas (30.5x45.5cm 12x17in) Toronto 2000

PARKER Henry H. 1858-1930 **[303]**
- $9 373 - €10 358 - **£6 500** - FF67 944
  Silent Stream Oil/canvas (60.5x91.5cm 23x36in) London 2001
- $3 220 - €3 457 - **£2 155** - FF22 676
  On the River Conway, North Wales Oil/canvas (30.5x45.5cm 12x17in) Toronto 2000
- $828 - €909 - **£550** - FF5 965
  A River Landscape/Figures and a Dog on a Bank with a River Below Watercolour (35x24.5cm 13x9in) London 2000

PARKER Henry Perlee 1795-1873 **[44]**
- $1 867 - €2 005 - **£1 250** - FF13 152
  Smugglers Landing Cargo Oil/canvas (61x76cm 24x29in) West-Yorshire 2000
- $870 - €980 - **£600** - FF6 431
  Fisherman Oil/canvas (44x34cm 17x13in) London 2000

PARKER James 1915-1987 **[4]**
- $3 500 - €4 010 - **£2 388** - FF26 435
  Selected Images Gelatin silver print (10.5x8.5cm 4x3in) New-York 2000

PARKER John 1839-1915 **[18]**
- $1 140 - €1 295 - **£800** - FF8 494
  Charlie is my Darling Watercolour (36.5x25cm 14x9in) West-Midlands 2001

PARKER John Adams 1827-1905 **[6]**
- $5 500 - €5 234 - **£3 440** - FF34 333
  Twilight - Hudson River Oil/canvas (60x106cm 24x42in) New-York 1999

PARKER Lawton Silas 1868-1954 **[35]**
- $16 000 - €16 652 - **£10 044** - FF109 228
  Fauvist Landscape Oil/panel (50x55cm 20x22in) Chicago IL 2000
- $24 000 - €28 542 - **£17 104** - FF187 224
  Shady Lagoon Oil/canvas/board (34.5x33cm 13x12in) New-York 2000

PARKER Olivia 1941 **[23]**
- $1 100 - €1 267 - **£750** - FF8 310
  «**Whelks**» Gelatin silver print (24.5x19cm 9x7in) New-York 2000

PARKHURST Anita (Mrs. Willcox) 1892 **[1]**
- $1 700 - €1 983 - **£1 193** - FF13 005
  «**Y.W.C.A., the friendly Road**» Poster (49.5x67cm 19x26in) New-York 2000

PARKINSON Norman 1913-1990 **[87]**
- $1 893 - €1 556 - **£1 100** - FF10 204
  Model in Lace Dress on Sofa Gelatin silver print (55x43cm 22x17in) London 1998

PARKINSON Richard 1844-1909 **[2]**
- $3 879 - €4 573 - **£2 727** - FF30 000
  Nouvelle Guinée: types et tribus Tirage albuminé (14x21cm 5x8in) Paris 2000

PARKINSON William H. XIX-XX **[6]**
- $10 383 - €11 473 - **£7 200** - FF75 261
  In the School Room Oil/canvas (76x128cm 29x50in) London 2001

PARKMAN Alfred Edward 1852-c.1930 **[49]**
- $821 - €882 - **£550** - FF5 786
  Cefn Bryn From Clyne Watercolour/paper (18x44cm 7x17in) Bath 2000

PARKS Gordon 1912 **[6]**
- $3 000 - €2 833 - **£1 863** - FF18 581
  Untitled Dye-transfer print (56.5x99.5cm 22x39in) New-York 1999

PARLBER Samuel XIX **[3]**
- $2 079 - €2 133 - **£1 300** - FF13 990
  The Town of Largs Ayrshire Watercolour (13x35cm 5x13in) London 2000

PARME de Jean Antoine Julien 1736-1799 **[8]**
- $9 660 - €10 671 - **£6 699** - FF70 000
  Vénus désarmant l'amour Encre (30x42cm 11x16in) Paris 2001

PARMEGGIANI Romano 1930 **[6]**
- $3 750 - €3 147 - **£2 200** - FF20 640
  Boy Looking at his Reflection Oil/canvas (70x50cm 27x19in) New-York 1998

PARMENTIER Jacques, James 1658-1730 **[8]**
- $11 229 - €11 316 - **£7 000** - FF74 225
  Triumph of Cupid Oil/canvas (92.5x146.5cm 36x57in) London 2000
- $6 964 - €7 843 - **£4 800** - FF51 447
  A duel Oil/panel (51x76cm 20x29in) London 2001

PARMENTIER Pol C. XX **[14]**
- $425 - €471 - **£296** - FF3 089
  «**Nature morte aux Hortensias**» Huile/panneau (80x60cm 31x23in) Liège 2001

PARMIGGIANI Claudio 1943 [12]
- $17 308 - €20 343 - **£12 000** - FF133 440
  Giovane che sogna Assemblage (70x55x20cm 27x21x7in) London 2000
- $3 000 - €3 110 - **£1 800** - FF20 400
  Senza titolo Collage (69x49cm 27x19in) Milano 2000

PARMIGIANINO Michele Rocca 1670/75-1751 [34]
- $9 790 - €9 101 - **£6 000** - FF59 701
  Acis and Galatea fleeing the Giant Polyphemus Oil/canvas (47.5x59cm 18x23in) London 1998
- $6 480 - €7 208 - **£4 320** - FF47 280
  La vocación de San pedro Oleo/papel (20.5x16.5cm 8x6in) Madrid 2000

PARMIGIANO Girolamo Fr. Mazzola 1503-1540 [60]
- $80 692 - €86 616 - **£54 000** - FF568 166
  Study for the Madonna dal Collo Lungo Ink (19x13cm 7x5in) London 2000
- $1 738 - €1 687 - **£1 082** - FF11 067
  Die zwei Liebenden Radierung (14.8x10.3cm 5x4in) Berlin 1999

PARODI Domenico 1668-1740 [10]
- $750 - €777 - **£450** - FF5 100
  Figura allegorica con due putti Matita/carta (20x28.5cm 7x11in) Milano 2000

PARODI Filippo 1630-1702 [1]
- $89 250 - €92 521 - **£53 550** - FF606 900
  Putto alato assiso su animale marino Marbre (97x90cm 38x35in) Venezia 1999

PARODI Tomaso XVIII [1]
- $6 924 - €6 784 - **£4 463** - FF44 500
  Portrait de femme tenant des fleurs/Portrait d'homme tenant un livre Huile/toile (113x85cm 44x33in) Mayenne 1999

PARPAN Ferdinand 1902 [25]
- $9 000 - €9 990 - **£6 273** - FF65 533
  Man smoking a Pipe Bronze (H92.5cm H36in) New-York 2001
- $2 130 - €2 287 - **£1 425** - FF15 000
  Femme nue agenouillée Bronze (H21cm H8in) Paris 2000

PARR Mike 1945 [16]
- $804 - €758 - **£506** - FF4 973
  Zastruga Self Portrait Charcoal/paper (100x69.5cm 39x27in) Sydney 1999
- $1 181 - €1 326 - **£766** - FF8 701
  Self Portrait Etching, aquatint (105x77.5cm 41x30in) Malvern, Victoria 2000

PARR Nuna 1949 [8]
- $5 214 - €6 051 - **£3 600** - FF39 690
  Dancing Bear Stone (51x61x20.5cm 20x24x8in) Vancouver, BC. 2000

PARR Remi, Remigius 1723-c.1760 [7]
- $334 - €394 - **£240** - FF2 582
  View of the Royal Palace of Hampton Court, after Jacques Rigaud Engraving (25.5x40cm 10x15in) London 2001

PARRA Carmen 1944 [9]
- $4 404 - €5 165 - **£3 168** - FF33 880
  Ajolote V Acrílico/papel (83x154cm 32x60in) México 2001
- $407 - €452 - **£270** - FF2 963
  Figura maya Serigrafía (68.5x49cm 26x19in) México 2000

PARRA Ginés 1895-1960 [163]
- $3 060 - €3 604 - **£2 220** - FF23 640
  Retrato de mujer de perfil Oleo/tablex (43.5x41cm 17x16in) Madrid 2001
- $2 117 - €2 192 - **£1 350** - FF14 381
  El Sena Oleo/tabla (20x39.5cm 7x15in) Madrid 2000
- $915 - €901 - **£585** - FF5 910
  Paisaje Acuarela/papel (37x41cm 14x16in) Madrid 1999

PARRA Y SOLER Miguel 1784-1846 [4]
- $10 600 - €12 013 - **£7 200** - FF78 800
  Bodegón de flores en una fuente Oleo/lienzo (77x52cm 30x20in) Madrid 2000

PARRAMON Josep M. 1919 [31]
- $294 - €276 - **£184** - FF1 812
  El Gran Canal, Venecia Oleo/lienzo (46x55cm 18x21in) Barcelona 1999

PARRÉ Mathias 1811-1849 [5]
- $3 810 - €4 090 - **£2 550** - FF26 831
  Winterlandschaft mit Haus zwischen lichten Bäumen am Kanal Öl/Leinwand (38x46cm 14x18in) Berlin 2000

PARRIS Edmund Thomas 1793-1873 [29]
- $1 800 - €2 047 - **£1 269** - FF13 428
  Allegory of the Arts and Literature Oil/canvas (51x137cm 20x54in) Philadelphia PA 2001
- $2 377 - €2 186 - **£1 469** - FF14 336
  «A Turkish Bathroom» Oil/copper (41.5x33cm 16x12in) Melbourne 1998
- $1 075 - €1 209 - **£750** - FF7 932
  The Letter Watercolour (43x31cm 16x12in) London 1998

PARRISH Jean 1920 [2]
- $4 000 - €4 757 - **£2 850** - FF31 204
  New Mexico Winter Scene Oil/masonite (40.5x51cm 15x20in) New-York 2000

PARRISH Maxfield Frederick 1870-1966 [176]
- $170 000 - €162 514 - **£106 556** - FF1 066 019
  Plum Pudding Oil/board (50x41cm 19x16in) New-York 1999
- $32 000 - €30 216 - **£19 872** - FF198 204
  «Hot Springs, Yaualpai Co., Arizona» Oil/canvas (45.5x31cm 17x12in) Beverly-Hills CA 1999
- $45 000 - €48 447 - **£27 013** - FF252 198
  Maquette for «The Tempest» Watercolour/paper (30.5x21.5cm 12x8in) New-York 1998
- $190 - €174 - **£115** - FF1 140
  Daybreak Lithograph (43x74cm 17x29in) Chicago IL 1998

PARRISH Stephen 1846-1938 [27]
- $15 000 - €17 060 - **£10 575** - FF111 906
  A Stormy Day Oil/board (40x50cm 16x20in) MT. Morris NY 2001
- $450 - €3 626 - **£2 563** - FF23 783
  Gloucester Harbour Oil/canvas (20x25cm 8x10in) Portsmouth NH 1998
- $150 - €146 - **£92** - FF955
  Gloucester Harbor Engraving (23x34cm 9x13in) East-Dennis MA 1999

PARROCEL Charles 1688-1752 [64]
- $16 000 - €15 053 - **£9 984** - FF98 742
  Battle Scene Oil/canvas (101x162cm 39x63in) New-York 1999
- $20 225 - €19 056 - **£12 250** - FF125 000
  Le passage du Rhin par Louis XIV Huile/toile (84x122cm 33x48in) Paris 1999

$2 325 - €2 592 - **£1 625** - FF17 000
Moïse sauvé des eaux Encre (20.5x29cm 8x11in)
Paris 2001

PARROCEL Étienne, le Romain 1696-1776 [46]
$4 467 - €4 573 - **£2 805** - FF30 000
Scène de bataille Huile/toile (40x57cm 15x22in)
Troyes 2000

$3 166 - €3 049 - **£1 956** - FF20 000
Saint Joseph et l'Enfant Jésus Huile/toile
(41x21.5cm 16x8in) Paris 1999

$1 600 - €1 755 - **£1 062** - FF11 514
**The Adoration of the Magi, after Francesco
Romanelli** Black & white chalks (38.5x27cm 15x10in)
New-York 2000

PARROCEL Ignace Jacques 1667-1722 [9]
$5 760 - €6 541 - **£3 942** - FF42 903
**Rastende Soldaten unter einem Baum in einer
südlichen Landschaft** Öl/Leinwand (94x109cm
37x42in) Wien 2001

$7 867 - €7 927 - **£4 903** - FF52 000
Le choc de cavalerie/L'assaut Huile/toile
(30x47.5cm 11x18in) Paris 2000

PARROCEL Joseph des Batailles 1646-1704 [42]
$16 000 - €15 053 - **£9 984** - FF98 742
Battle Scene Oil/canvas (101x162cm 39x63in) New-
York 1999

$16 290 - €13 720 - **£9 621** - FF90 000
L'attaque de la calèche Huile/toile (79x95.5cm
31x37in) Paris 1998

$941 - €793 - **£555** - FF5 200
Scène champêtre Encre (14.3x22.3cm 5x8in) Paris
1998

PARROCEL Joseph François 1704-1781 [53]
$5 700 - €4 817 - **£3 400** - FF31 598
Aurora Oil/canvas (73.5x81cm 28x31in) London 1998

$752 - €838 - **£525** - FF5 500
Agar et Ismael sesourus par l'ange Encre
(27.5x13.5cm 10x5in) Paris 2001

PARROTT William 1813-1869 [16]
$156 519 - €181 851 - **£110 000** - FF1 192 862
Fair in the Champs Elysée, Paris Oil/canvas
(114x150cm 44x59in) London 2001

PARROW Karin 1900-1984 [52]
$1 744 - €2 074 - **£1 243** - FF13 606
Stilleben Oil/panel (61x54cm 24x21in) Stockholm
2000

PARRY Roger 1905-1978 [46]
$524 - €457 - **£317** - FF3 000
Zuydersée, Hollande Tirage argentique (24x30.4cm
9x11in) Saint-Germain-en-Laye 1998

PARS William 1742-1782 [10]
$8 878 - €8 219 - **£5 500** - FF53 910
Part of the Vatican, Rome Watercolour (39.5x58cm
15x22in) London 1999

PARSHALL Dewitt 1854-1956 [12]
$2 500 - €2 922 - **£1 784** - FF19 165
«The Old Fliver» Mixed media/paper (38x49cm
15x19in) Altadena CA 2001

PARSHALL Douglas Ewell 1899-1990 [18]
$3 750 - €3 348 - **£2 296** - FF21 960
«Moorish Courtyard» Oil/board (46x41cm 18x16in)
Altadena CA 1999

$4 500 - €5 043 - **£3 136** - FF33 081
Two Horses Oil/canvas/board (30.5x39.5cm 12x15in)
Beverly-Hills CA 2001

PARSONS Alfred William 1847-1920 [56]
$7 565 - €7 165 - **£4 600** - FF46 999
Fallen Oil/canvas (68.5x151.5cm 26x59in) London
1999

$1 600 - €1 532 - **£988** - FF10 051
**Contemplative Man Walking Beneath Large
Tree, Poem Illustration** Watercolour/paper (25x33cm
10x13in) New-York 1999

PARSONS Arthur Wilde 1854-1931 [136]
$2 315 - €1 980 - **£1 400** - FF12 988
Figures in a Village Street Oil/canvas (51x76cm
20x29in) London 1999

$348 - €307 - **£210** - FF2 017
Tozers Boatyard, Newquay Oil/canvas (28x48.5cm
11x19in) Bristol, Avon 1998

$707 - €717 - **£440** - FF4 700
Lane Fear Porlock Watercolour (37.5x55cm 14x21in)
Crewkerne, Somerset 2001

PARSONS Beatrice Emma 1870-1955 [129]
$2 172 - €2 521 - **£1 500** - FF16 536
Little Orchard Garden Watercolour/paper
(24.5x17cm 9x6in) London 2000

PARSONS Charles 1821-1910 [9]
$1 100 - €1 127 - **£684** - FF7 390
Monitor and Merrimac Battle Scene
Watercolour/paper (15x27cm 6x11in) Hatfield PA 2000

$3 000 - €3 626 - **£2 094** - FF23 785
**Clipper Ship Dreadnought Off Tuskar Light,
after Mc Farlane** Lithograph (48x67cm 19x26in)
Bolton MA 2000

PARSONS Edith Barretto Stev. 1878-1956 [53]
$17 000 - €16 485 - **£10 769** - FF108 133
Figural Fountain Frog Baby Bronze (H100cm
H39in) New-York 1999

$1 000 - €854 - **£587** - FF5 605
**Puppy Bookend: Seated Puppy and Puppy
Drinking** Bronze (H15cm H5in) Boston MA 1998

PARSONS Elizabeth 1953 [1]
$3 956 - €4 092 - **£2 500** - FF26 842
The Millenium Twelve Top Flat Racehorses
Oil/canvas/paper (41x36cm 16x14in) London 2000

PARSONS Elizabeth 1831-1897 [5]
$2 204 - €2 587 - **£1 555** - FF16 970
Afternoon Walk Oil/canvas (32x47cm 12x18in)
Melbourne 2000

PARSONS John R. XIX [1]
$12 994 - €14 474 - **£8 500** - FF94 945
«Jane Morris» Albumen print (20x14cm 8x5in)
London 2000

PARSONS John Usher XIX [1]
$6 500 - €5 427 - **£3 812** - FF35 597
**Dark-haired, Blue-eyed Young Gentleman
Seated** Oil/canvas (72.5x56.5cm 28x22in) New-York
1998

PARSONS Jonathan 1970 [2]
$8 368 - €9 841 - **£6 000** - FF64 551
Carcass Sculpture (200x110x40cm 78x43x15in)
London 2001

PARSONS Sheldon 1866-1943 [25]
$5 000 - €5 487 - **£3 219** - FF35 994
Field of Yellow Oil/canvas/board (51x61cm 20x24in)
Beverly-Hills CA 2000

$4 800 - €5 708 - **£3 421** - FF37 444
#2 Red Chiles Oil/board (30.5x51cm 12x20in) New-
York 2000

P

PARTENHEIMER Jürgen 1947 **[41]**

✐ **$2 192** - €2 556 - **£1 539** - FF16 769
    Ohne Titel Collage (106x78cm 41x30in) Köln 2000

▥ **$163** - €179 - **£110** - FF1 175
    Ohne Titel Linocut in colors (60.7x42.2cm 23x16in)
    Berlin 2000

PARTHÉNIS Constantin 1878-1967 **[25]**

🖎 **$41 031** - €47 240 - **£28 000** - FF309 873
    The Sea, Poros Oil/board (43x46cm 16x18in)
    London 2000

🖎 **$8 500** - €8 565 - **£5 298** - FF56 185
    Seated Female Figure Oil/canvas (45.5x29.5cm
    17x11in) New-York 2000

🖎 **$8 039** - €9 225 - **£5 500** - FF60 511
    Reclining Beauty Red chalk/paper (28x43.5cm
    11x17in) London 2000

PARTIKEL Alfred 1888-1945 **[18]**

🖎 **$3 321** - €3 477 - **£2 086** - FF22 806
    Kleine Winterlandschaft Oil/panel (25.5x30cm
    10x11in) Bremen 2000

PARTINGTON Jack 1914-1987 **[1]**

📷 **$4 000** - €3 762 - **£2 476** - FF24 675
    **Sequin Fan Number, Roxy Theatre, New York
    City** Gelatin silver print (39.5x49.5cm 15x19in) New-
    York 1999

PARTINGTON Richard Langtry 1868-1929 **[8]**

🖎 **$7 000** - €6 658 - **£4 250** - FF43 673
    Rock in Sea, Sailing Ship on the Horizon Oil/can-
    vas (76x112cm 29x44in) Beverly-Hills CA 1999

PARTNER Jason XX **[84]**

✐ **$127** - €150 - **£90** - FF987
    **The Wherry Albion returning home/Mid Week
    Quiet, Morston/Blythburgh** Watercolour/paper
    (7x17cm 3x7in) Aylsham, Norfolk 2001

PARTON Arthur B. 1842-1914 **[66]**

🖎 **$4 500** - €3 898 - **£2 759** - FF25 566
    Cows Watering Along a Stream Oil/canvas
    (46.5x61cm 18x24in) New-York 1999

🖎 **$2 600** - €2 413 - **£1 561** - FF15 827
    Arkville Valley, Maine Oil/canvas (22x30cm 9x12in)
    Milford CT 1999

PARTON Ernest 1845-1933 **[72]**

🖎 **$20 000** - €22 412 - **£13 940** - FF147 016
    When Lingering Daylight Welcomes Night
    Oil/canvas (122x184cm 48x72in) Beverly-Hills CA
    2001

🖎 **$3 171** - €3 002 - **£1 972** - FF19 689
    Le berger et son troupeau Huile/toile (82x122cm
    32x48in) Montréal 1999

🖎 **$2 595** - €2 493 - **£1 600** - FF16 350
    On the Nadder, Wiltshire Oil/canvas/board
    (30.5x39.5cm 12x15in) London 1999

PARTOS Paul 1943 **[20]**

🖎 **$10 378** - €11 624 - **£7 210** - FF76 250
    Untitled Oil/canvas (224x197cm 88x77in) Melbourne
    2001

🖎 **$2 084** - €2 478 - **£1 485** - FF16 257
    Untitled Mixed media (73x55cm 28x21in) Melbourne
    2000

PARTRIDGE Bernard, Sir 1861-1945 **[14]**

✐ **$375** - €368 - **£240** - FF2 412
    The Good Fairy/Conservation Piece Ink
    (34x25.5cm 13x10in) London 1999

▥ **$362** - €418 - **£250** - FF2 740
    «Take up the Sword of Justice» Poster
    (152x102cm 59x40in) London 2000

PARTRIDGE Frank H. XIX-XX **[14]**

✐ **$421** - €453 - **£290** - FF2 971
    «Norfolk Coastal View Home from the Marsh»
    Watercolour/paper (26x72cm 10x28in) Leominster,
    Herefordshire 2001

PARTRIDGE John 1790-1872 **[12]**

🖎 **$29 165** - €28 048 - **£18 000** - FF183 985
    **Group Portrait of the Artist and other Members
    of the Partridge Family** Oil/canvas (110x151cm
    43x59in) London 1999

PARTRIDGE Nehemiah 1683-1737 **[1]**

🖎 **$8 500** - €7 869 - **£5 131** - FF51 616
    **John Dunbar and His Wife Jeannette Von
    Egmont Schermerhorn** Oil/canvas/board
    (110.5x99cm 43x38in) New-York 1999

PARTRIDGE Roi 1888-1984 **[30]**

▥ **$523** - €533 - **£327** - FF3 497
    Bristlecone Pine Etching (17x14cm 6x5in) Altadena
    CA 2000

PARTRIDGE William Ordway 1861-1930 **[3]**

🖎 **$9 868** - €9 346 - **£6 000** - FF61 303
    Ideal Head of a Woman Marble (H70cm H27in)
    London 1999

PARTURIER Marcel 1901-1976 **[131]**

🖎 **$1 196** - €1 372 - **£818** - FF9 000
    Bateau de pêche, Veere, Hollande Huile/toile
    (50x61cm 19x24in) Paris 2000

🖎 **$668** - €762 - **£464** - FF5 000
    La Salute Huile/isorel (21x27cm 8x10in) Paris 2000

PARVEZ Ahmed 1926-1979 **[16]**

🖎 **$4 500** - €5 317 - **£3 189** - FF34 878
    The Couple Oil/cardboard (76x62cm 29x24in) New-
    York 2000

✐ **$2 250** - €2 659 - **£1 594** - FF17 439
    Women in Purdah at the Gate Charcoal
    (28.5x38.5cm 11x15in) New-York 2000

PASCAL Léopold 1900-1957 **[34]**

🖎 **$487** - €573 - **£347** - FF3 800
    Le vase de Roses Huile/toile (50x65cm 19x25in)
    Brest 2000

PASCAL Paul 1867-? **[12]**

🖎 **$1 901** - €1 982 - **£1 196** - FF13 000
    Retour de pêche à Concarneau Huile/toile
    (51x64cm 20x25in) Nantes 2000

PASCAL Paul B. 1832-1903 **[207]**

🖎 **$1 224** - €1 372 - **£851** - FF9 000
    Sur la route d'Alger à El-Biar Aquarelle,
    gouache/papier (44x31cm 17x12in) Paris 2001

PASCALI Pino 1935-1968 **[88]**

🖎 **$5 000** - €5 183 - **£3 000** - FF34 000
    Panoramica, Villaggio lungo Tecnica mista
    (19.5x99.5cm 7x39in) Vercelli 2000

🖎 **$2 000** - €2 592 - **£1 500** - FF17 000
    Eschimesi Tecnica mista (23x30cm 9x11in) Milano
    2000

🖎 **$23 400** - €20 215 - **£15 600** - FF132 600
    La nave kitch Assemblage (100x82cm 39x32in) Prato
    1998

🖎 **$1 400** - €1 451 - **£840** - FF9 520
    Cane Matita/carta (22x26cm 8x10in) Prato 2001

PASCH Clemens 1910-1985 **[11]**

🖎 **$1 336** - €1 278 - **£814** - FF8 384
    Sitzendes Mädchen Bronze (H53cm H20in)
    Bielefeld 1999

PASCH Lorenz II 1733-1805 **[15]**
- $4 416 - €4 762 - £2 964 - FF31 236
  Porträtt föreställande Magdalena Johanna af Bagge af Söderby Oil/canvas (77x62cm 30x24in) Stockholm 2000

PASCH Ulrica 1735-1796 **[10]**
- $4 179 - €4 067 - £2 572 - FF26 677
  Poträtt av kommerserådet Fredrik Morsing Oil/canvas (74x59cm 29x23in) Stockholm 1999

PASCHKE Ed 1939 **[42]**
- $13 000 - €14 536 - £8 763 - FF95 347
  «Aragon» Oil/canvas (106.5x203cm 41x79in) New-York 2000
- $5 500 - €6 382 - £3 797 - FF41 863
  Aykroyd Acrylic/canvas (81x92cm 31x36in) New-York 2000
- $550 - €555 - £343 - FF3 638
  Bad Color lithograph (36x30cm 14x12in) Chicago IL 2000

PASCIN Jules Pincas, dit 1885-1930 **[1555]**
- $69 598 - €70 127 - £43 378 - FF460 000
  La mulatresse Huile/toile (85x71cm 33x27in) Paris 2000
- $1 800 - €2 016 - £1 250 - FF13 225
  Femme et fleurs Mixed media (18x15cm 7x6in) St. Louis MO 2001
- $1 231 - €1 448 - £882 - FF9 500
  Fille de joie Fusain (29x22.5cm 11x8in) Paris 2001
- $365 - €354 - £230 - FF2 323
  La Loge Etching (26x16.5cm 10x6in) London 1999

PASCIUTI Antonio 1937 **[12]**
- $100 - €1 140 - £660 - FF7 480
  Raccolta delle mele in Agro Romano Olio/tela (40x50cm 15x19in) Vercelli 2000
- $680 - €881 - £510 - FF5 780
  «Estate» Olio/tela (30x40cm 11x15in) Vercelli 2001

PASCUAL DUCE Antonio 1942 **[50]**
- $336 - €360 - £228 - FF2 364
  Bodegón Oleo/tabla (22x27cm 8x10in) Madrid 2001

PASCUAL RODES Ivo 1883-1949 **[12]**
- $6 000 - €7 208 - £4 200 - FF47 280
  El Poble i Puig Sacalín Oleo/lienzo (80x99cm 31x38in) Madrid 2000

PASETTI O. XIX-XX **[4]**
- $3 360 - €3 997 - £2 398 - FF26 218
  Südländische Terrasse Öl/Leinwand (68x105cm 26x41in) Wien 2001

PASETTI OF SAINT-PETERSBURG A. XIX **[1]**
- $2 881 - €2 731 - £1 800 - FF17 915
  Pyotr Tchaikovsky, Cabinet Style Photograph Photograph (16.5x10.5cm 6x4in) London 1999

PASINELLI Lorenzo 1629-1700 **[12]**
- $39 652 - €41 636 - £25 000 - FF273 117
  Cornelia Receiving the News of Pompey's Defeat Oil/canvas (61x49cm 24x19in) London 2000
- $2 160 - €1 866 - £1 080 - FF12 240
  Studio di putti che giocano Sanguina/carta (25x16.5cm 9x6in) Milano 1999

PASINETTI Antonio 1863-1940 **[3]**
- $2 150 - €2 229 - £1 290 - FF14 620
  Veduta di lago Olio/cartone (50x70cm 19x27in) Genova 2000

PASINI Alberto 1826-1899 **[171]**
- $100 000 - €94 867 - £60 750 - FF622 290
  Caserne à Istanbul Oil/canvas (66x81.5cm 25x32in) New-York 1999

- $18 000 - €19 199 - £11 989 - FF125 935
  Outside the Courtyard Oil/canvas (23x18cm 9x7in) Cleveland OH 2000
- $4 966 - €5 793 - £3 488 - FF38 000
  Oriental et son cheval Aquarelle/papier (18x14cm 7x5in) Bayeux 2001

PASINI Lazzaro 1861-1949 **[21]**
- $861 - €998 - £610 - FF6 548
  A Coastal View Oil/canvas (39x59cm 15x23in) Amsterdam 2000
- $1 407 - €1 347 - £874 - FF8 834
  Blomstrende roser ved et vindue Oil/canvas (42x32cm 16x12in) Köbenhavn 1999

PASINI V. XIX **[2]**
- $1 300 - €1 420 - £836 - FF9 312
  Figures in the Square Watercolour/paper (35x20cm 14x8in) Mystic CT 2000

PASKELL William Frederick 1866-1951 **[83]**
- $350 - €393 - £245 - FF2 576
  Schooner Under Sail Oil/canvas (59x91cm 23x36in) Bolton MA 2001
- $250 - €279 - £174 - FF1 833
  Mountain Landscape Watercolour/paper (35x25cm 14x10in) Cleveland OH 2001

PASMORE Daniel, Jnr. XIX **[8]**
- $1 561 - €1 735 - £1 043 - FF11 382
  La lettre Huile/panneau (25.5x19.5cm 10x7in) Bruxelles 2000

PASMORE Daniel, Snr. Act.1829-c.1865 **[11]**
- $2 418 - €2 540 - £1 600 - FF16 659
  Portrait of Hyacinte Rigaud Black chalk (29.5x21cm 11x8in) London 2000

PASMORE F.G., Jnr. XIX-XX **[12]**
- $1 769 - €1 960 - £1 200 - FF12 854
  The First Favourite Oil/canvas (30.5x26cm 12x10in) Manchester 2000

PASMORE John Frederick 1820-1881 **[26]**
- $1 565 - €1 532 - £1 000 - FF10 051
  «Village Gossip» Oil/canvas (31x41cm 12x16in) Leyburn, North Yorkshire 1999

PASMORE Victor 1908-1998 **[228]**
- $12 905 - €15 384 - £9 200 - FF100 913
  Linear Image Mixed media (81x81x4cm 31x31x1in) London 2000
- $30 517 - €29 620 - £19 000 - FF194 292
  Pink Roses Oil/canvas (45x25.5cm 17x10in) London 1999
- $12 806 - €14 879 - £9 000 - FF97 597
  «Abstract in white and black, Version 1» Construction (122x122x23cm 48x48x9in) London 2001
- $10 672 - €12 400 - £7 500 - FF81 336
  Linear Image Relief (77.5x77.5cm 30x30in) London 2001
- $2 092 - €2 246 - £1 400 - FF14 730
  Looking Out to Sea Ink (23.5x27.5cm 9x10in) London 2000
- $604 - €690 - £420 - FF4 524
  Brown Image Etching, aquatint (91x64.5cm 35x25in) London 2000

PASOLINI Pier Paolo 1922-1975 **[3]**
- $14 102 - €16 769 - £10 054 - FF110 000
  Portrait de Maria Callas Technique mixte/papier (25x35cm 9x13in) Paris 2000

PASQUA Philippe 1965 **[6]**
- $11 979 - €14 483 - £8 369 - FF95 000
  Anesthésie N.1 Huile/toile (160x200cm 62x78in) Paris 2000

P

$8 236 - €8 842 - **£5 510** - FF58 000
Triptyque à la jeune fille Technique mixte/papier
(181x121cm 71x47in) Paris 2000

PASQUIER Noël 1941 **[13]**
$5 256 - €6 098 - **£3 688** - FF40 000
Océane Technique mixte/toile (60x60cm 23x23in)
Neuilly-sur-Seine 2000

PASQUIERI XIX **[1]**
$7 344 - €6 860 - **£4 531** - FF45 000
Scène de bataille dans un site portuaire
Aquarelle, gouache/papier (50x80cm 19x31in) Paris
1999

PASSAGE du Arthur Marie, comte 1838-1900 **[52]**
$5 449 - €5 336 - **£3 353** - FF35 000
Jeanne d'Arc à cheval Bronze (H48.5cm H19in)
Soissons 1999

PASSANTE Bartolomeo 1618-1648 **[6]**
$251 190 - €213 858 - **£150 000** - FF1 402 815
Christ Disputing with the Doctors Oil/canvas
(99x131.5cm 38x51in) London 1998
$56 000 - €49 287 - **£34 092** - FF323 304
Philosopher Oil/canvas (99x71.5cm 38x28in) New-
York 1999

PASSARI Bernardino Passeri c.1510-c.1590 **[1]**
$3 860 - €4 602 - **£2 752** - FF30 185
**Der Heilige Antonius entdeckt den Leichnam
des Hl.Paul Eremita** Kupferstich (41.2x27.1cm
16x10in) Berlin 2000

PASSAROTTI Bartolomeo 1529-1592 **[49]**
$66 486 - €64 029 - **£41 370** - FF420 000
Portrait d'un jeune homme âgé de 19 ans
Huile/toile (57x43cm 22x16in) Montfort L'Amaury
1999
$5 693 - €4 847 - **£3 400** - FF31 797
Study for a Torso Ink (25.5x15cm 10x5in) London
1998

PASSAURO Edmondo 1893-1969 **[8]**
$1 100 - €1 140 - **£660** - FF7 480
Ritratto di giovane donna Tecnica mista/carta
(66x51cm 25x20in) Trieste 2001

PASSAVANT Johann David 1787-1861 **[1]**
$16 854 - €15 339 - **£10 530** - FF100 617
Taunuslandschaft mit Ruine Königstein
Öl/Leinwand (74x102cm 29x40in) München 1999

PASSE de Willem 1598-c.1637 **[2]**
$5 049 - €5 665 - **£3 500** - FF37 162
James I, King of England and his Family
Engraving (31.5x38cm 12x14in) London 2000

PASSE van de Crispin I c.1564-1637 **[66]**
$403 - €460 - **£283** - FF3 018
Allegorie der Völlerei Kupferstich (18.5x21.5cm
7x8in) Berlin 2001

PASSE van de Crispin II c.1593-1670 **[9]**
$2 063 - €2 352 - **£1 439** - FF15 427
Die Parabel vom schlechten Reichen Kupferstich
(26x33cm 10x12in) Berlin 2001

PASSE van de Magdalena 1600-1638 **[8]**
$131 - €153 - **£92** - FF1 006
**Strand mit Fischern und einem Wal, nach Adam
Willaerts** Kupferstich (20.5x26.5cm 8x10in) Hamburg
2001

PASSEBON Pierre XX **[1]**
$1 377 - €1 524 - **£934** - FF10 000
**Misha, texte de Danielle Digne; tiré de Misha,
l'Enfant Divorcé** Gouache/papier (42x19cm 16x7in)
Paris 2000

PASSERI Giuseppe 1654-1714 **[30]**
$6 563 - €5 623 - **£3 945** - FF36 886
Die Himmelfahrt des Hl. Nikolaus Öl/Leinwand
(49.5x32cm 19x12in) Köln 1998
$3 000 - €2 608 - **£1 815** - FF17 107
Music-Making Angels Among Clouds Ink
(18x28cm 7x11in) New-York 1999

PASSEY Charles Henry XIX **[56]**
$1 200 - €1 296 - **£830** - FF8 503
Man fishing in the River Oil/canvas (76x127cm
30x50in) Chicago IL 2001

PASSIEUX Olivier 1973 **[10]**
$2 322 - €2 592 - **£1 615** - FF17 000
Mémoire femme Huile/toile (120x120cm 47x47in)
Paris 2001
$715 - €610 - **£426** - FF4 000
L'attente Huile/toile (100x100cm 39x39in) Paris 1998

PASSIGLI Carlo 1881-1953 **[49]**
$1 440 - €1 244 - **£960** - FF8 160
Figura femminile nuda Olio/cartone (70x50cm
27x19in) Firenze 1998
$1 380 - €1 192 - **£920** - FF7 820
Sulla riva del fiume Olio/cartone (30x40cm 11x15in)
Firenze 1998

PASSINI Johann Nepomuk 1798-1874 **[7]**
$2 444 - €2 907 - **£1 744** - FF19 068
Das Missgeschick Oil/panel (48x37.5cm 18x14in)
Wien 2000
$11 996 - €11 248 - **£7 414** - FF73 785
Motiv bei Lienz, Osttirol Aquarell/Papier (25x34cm
9x13in) Graz 1999

PASSINI Ludwig Johann 1832-1903 **[32]**
$1 710 - €2 035 - **£1 220** - FF13 347
Rinderherden in der Campagna Aquarell/Karton
(16x26cm 6x10in) Wien 2000

PASSMORE John Richard 1904-1984 **[114]**
$40 026 - €42 965 - **£26 789** - FF281 834
The Baptism Oil/board (122x151cm 48x59in)
Melbourne 2000
$7 136 - €6 785 - **£4 453** - FF44 506
Non-figurative Abstract Oil/canvas/board
(39x45.5cm 15x17in) Melbourne 1999
$2 368 - €2 645 - **£1 516** - FF17 348
Interior with Figures Oil/board (32.5x25.5cm
12x10in) Malvern, Victoria 2000
$1 519 - €1 670 - **£973** - FF10 955
Unloading the Catch Ink (44.5x58.5cm 17x23in)
Melbourne 2000

PASTEGA Luigi 1858-1927 **[33]**
$8 284 - €9 459 - **£5 840** - FF62 047
Glückliche Familie Öl/Leinwand (49x71cm 19x27in)
Kassel 2001
$5 000 - €5 753 - **£3 446** - FF37 740
The Flower Vendor Oil/canvas (30x40cm 12x16in)
New-Orleans LA 2000

PASTERNAK Leonid Ossipovich 1862-1945 **[8]**
$194 - €204 - **£128** - FF1 341
Porträt eines bärtigen Mannes Öl/Leinwand
(29.5x23cm 11x9in) München 2000
$7 788 - €8 721 - **£5 412** - FF57 204
Die ersten Schritte Pencil (23.5x30.5cm 9x12in)
Wien 2001

PASTOR CALPENA Vicente 1918-1993 **[22]**
  $756 - €841 - **£532** - FF5 516
    Los cuatro postes, Avila Acuarela/papel (54x74cm 21x29in) Madrid 2001

PASTORIS Federico 1837-1884 **[2]**
  $5 000 - €4 723 - **£3 024** - FF30 978
    A royal Match Oil/canvas (35x47.5cm 13x18in) New-York 1999

PASTOUR Louis 1876-1948 **[149]**
  $2 449 - €2 592 - **£1 553** - FF17 000
    Le Paillon en été Huile/toile (46x61cm 18x24in) Cannes 2000
  $621 - €579 - **£384** - FF3 800
    «Féerie de lumière, marche de Cannes» Huile/panneau (33x24cm 12x9in) Paris 1999

PASZKOWSKA Alexandra XX **[5]**
  $476 - €511 - **£318** - FF3 353
    Buto-Tänzer auf Schloss Neuschwanstein Photograph (53x38cm 20x14in) München 2000

PATA Chérubin 1827-1899 **[59]**
  $11 360 - €12 196 - **£7 600** - FF80 000
    La vente aux enchères Huile/toile (69.5x174.5cm 27x68in) Neuilly-sur-Seine 2000
  $7 872 - €7 318 - **£4 780** - FF48 000
    Cerf courant sous bois Huile/toile (45x55cm 17x21in) Calais 1998

PATAKY VON SOSPATAK László 1857-1912 **[28]**
  $2 287 - €2 352 - **£1 450** - FF15 427
    Wildpferde Oil/panel (60x80cm 23x31in) Bamberg 2000

PATANIA Giuseppe 1780-1852 **[5]**
  $17 750 - €18 401 - **£10 650** - FF120 700
    Nudo di donna Olio/tavola (54x78cm 21x30in) Napoli 2000

PATCH Thomas 1720-1782 **[13]**
  $208 500 - €244 459 - **£150 000** - FF1 603 545
    Mediterranean Seaport, with a triumphal Arch, Figures on the Quay Oil/canvas (124x170.5cm 48x67in) London 2001
  $340 641 - €327 148 - **£210 000** - FF2 145 948
    View of the Piazza della Signorina, Florence Oil/canvas (87.5x121.5cm 34x47in) London 1999
  $5 539 - €6 299 - **£3 800** - FF41 317
    Caricatures of Florentine Individuals Etching (49x33cm 19x12in) Oxfordshire 2000

PATEL Antoine Pierre II 1648-1707 **[54]**
  $17 996 - €16 769 - **£11 099** - FF110 000
    Paysage imaginaire de ruines de Temples antiques animé de personnages Huile/toile (88x100cm 34x39in) Paris 1999
  $8 777 - €8 181 - **£5 416** - FF53 662
    Antikisierende Landschaft mit zwei Figuren bei einem Grabmal Öl/Leinwand (34x41cm 13x16in) Köln 1999
  $2 281 - €2 592 - **£1 596** - FF17 000
    Paysage imaginaire de rivière animé de barques et de promeneurs Gouache/vélin (16.5x23cm 6x9in) Paris 2001

PATEL Pierre I le Bon c.1605-1676 **[9]**
  $4 050 - €4 573 - **£2 823** - FF30 000
    Paysage lacustre animé de personnages Huile/toile (39x34cm 15x18in) Bayeux 2001
  $3 398 - €3 964 - **£2 363** - FF26 000
    Paysage avec ruines animé de personnages Gouache/papier (13.5x21cm 5x8in) Nice 2000

PATELIN Jean XIX-XX **[1]**
  $1 000 - €1 116 - **£654** - FF7 318
    «La Côte» Poster (66x94cm 25x37in) New-York 2000

PATER André 1953 **[1]**
  $30 000 - €34 855 - **£21 084** - FF228 636
    Three Hounds Pastel/paper (96.5x76cm 37x29in) New-York 2001

PATER Jean-Baptiste 1695-1736 **[44]**
  $500 000 - €440 067 - **£304 400** - FF2 886 650
    Fête Champêtre Oil/canvas (54.5x64.5cm 21x25in) New-York 1999
  $102 895 - €99 092 - **£63 895** - FF650 000
    Scène élégante dans un parc avec un joueur de cornemuse Huile/cuivre (30x36.5cm 11x14in) Paris 1999
  $4 532 - €5 336 - **£3 185** - FF35 000
    Étude de femme tenant un plat Sanguine/papier (20x10.5cm 7x4in) Paris 2001
  $1 053 - €1 022 - **£656** - FF6 707
    Repos de Troupes Radierung (17.3x22.4cm 6x8in) Berlin 1999

PATERSON Amish 1890-1955 **[2]**
  $4 384 - €4 889 - **£3 000** - FF32 069
    Tranquility Oil/canvas (76x63.5cm 29x25in) Perthshire 2000
  $4 490 - €3 847 - **£2 700** - FF25 237
    Still life of Marguerites Oil/panel (41x34cm 16x13in) Edinburgh 1998

PATERSON Caroline XIX-XX **[7]**
  $6 721 - €6 416 - **£4 200** - FF42 085
    Rin-tor, Children Playing before a Cottage Watercolour (22x32cm 8x12in) Cheshire 1999

PATERSON Emily Murray 1855-1934 **[31]**
  $462 - €402 - **£280** - FF2 638
    St Ives Oil/board (27x33cm 10x12in) London 1999
  $1 552 - €1 437 - **£950** - FF9 425
    Fishing Boats by a Quayside Watercolour (27.5x38cm 10x14in) Edinburgh 1999

PATERSON Esther 1892-1971 **[8]**
  $1 867 - €2 058 - **£1 242** - FF13 500
    Middle Park Baths Oil/board (21.5x22.5cm 8x8in) Melbourne 2000
  $1 574 - €1 848 - **£1 111** - FF12 121
    Milking Time Gouache (17x26.5cm 6x10in) Melbourne 2000

PATERSON G. XIX **[3]**
  $450 - €425 - **£280** - FF2 789
    Glimpse of an English Homestead/English Farmyard Engraving (90x114cm 35x44in) New-York 1999

PATERSON George M. XIX-XX **[3]**
  $896 - €962 - **£600** - FF6 313
    English Farmyard, After J.F.Herring Engraving (66x94cm 25x37in) London 2000

PATERSON James 1854-1932 **[99]**
  $12 937 - €11 252 - **£7 800** - FF73 810
    Autumn Morning, Evisa, Corsica Oil/canvas (71x91.5cm 27x36in) Glasgow 1998
  $3 294 - €3 133 - **£2 000** - FF20 551
    By the River, Dalwhat Glen, Moniaive Oil/canvas (25.5x35.5cm 10x13in) Edinburgh 1999
  $4 498 - €4 211 - **£2 800** - FF27 621
    «Moniaive» Watercolour (37x53cm 14x20in) London 1999

PATERSON John Ford 1851-1912 **[11]**
☞ **$5 180** – €4 884 – **£3 210** – FF32 035
In the Country Oil/canvas (71x35.5cm 27x13in)
Melbourne 1999

PATERSON Maggie, née Hamilton XIX-XX **[2]**
☞ **$5 321** – €4 547 – **£3 220** – FF29 825
Still Life Oil/canvas (39.5x39.5cm 15x15in) Edinburgh
1998

PATERSON Mary Viola 1899-1981 **[27]**
▥ **$353** – €334 – **£220** – FF2 191
Hyde Park Woodcut in colors (25x32.5cm 9x12in)
Billingshurst, West-Sussex 1999

PATERSON Tom XIX-XX **[30]**
✐ **$582** – €677 – **£410** – FF4 444
Girls at Play Watercolour/paper (21.5x31cm 8x12in)
Calgary, Alberta 2001

PATHE Moritz 1893-1956 **[4]**
▥ **$1 253** – €1 388 – **£850** – FF9 107
«Peter Pathe» Poster (125x90cm 49x35in) London
2000

PATINI Teofilo 1840-1906 **[12]**
☞ **$3 000** – €3 110 – **£1 800** – FF20 400
Paesaggio con volo d'aquila Olio/tela (23x16cm
9x6in) Roma 1999

PATIÑO PEREZ Antón 1957 **[17]**
☞ **$2 970** – €3 304 – **£1 980** – FF21 670
Deriva Oleo/lienzo (195x47cm 76x18in) Madrid 2000

PATKO Karoly, Karl 1895-1941 **[15]**
☞ **$18 400** – €18 093 – **£11 500** – FF118 680
Nude Oil/canvas (80.5x48cm 31x18in) Budapest 1999
☞ **$1 850** – €1 944 – **£1 150** – FF12 750
Les trois grâces Encre/papier (39x33cm 15x12in)
Budapest 2000

PATON Frank 1856-1909 **[137]**
☞ **$10 000** – €8 657 – **£6 031** – FF56 786
«The Naughty Puppy» Oil/canvas (40.5x51cm
15x20in) San-Francisco CA 1998
☞ **$1 604** – €1 616 – **£1 000** – FF10 603
Brief Encounter Oil/panel (30.5x25.5cm 12x10in)
London 2000
✐ **$878** – €941 – **£600** – FF6 173
The Morning's Bag Watercolour/paper (16x24cm
6x9in) London 2001
▥ **$216** – €183 – **£130** – FF1 203
Not at Home/Rough and Ready/7 Champions of
Chrisendom/Merry Christmas Etching (10.5x17cm
4x6in) London 1998

PATON Hugh 1853-1927 **[7]**
▥ **$100** – €94 – **£62** – FF615
Sailboats Moored in a City Harbor Etching
(34x28cm 13x11in) St. Petersburg FL 1999

PATON Joseph Noel 1821-1901 **[54]**
☞ **$36 540** – €40 741 – **£25 000** – FF267 242
The Ballard Singers Oil/canvas (47x42cm 18x16in)
Perthshire 2000
☞ **$28 276** – €24 224 – **£17 000** – FF158 902
Puck and the Fairy Oil/cardboard (24x28cm 9x11in)
Edinburgh 1998
✐ **$947** – €993 – **£600** – FF6 511
Study for a Battle Scene Ink/paper (15x22cm 5x8in)
Edinburgh 2000

PATON Richard 1717-1791 **[12]**
☞ **$8 364** – €9 243 – **£5 800** – FF60 627
The Battle of Doggerbank, 5th August Oil/canvas
(46.5x61cm 18x24in) London 2001

PATON Walter Hugh 1828-1895 **[111]**
☞ **$3 623** – €3 449 – **£2 300** – FF22 625
Ossian's Cairn, Moss of Connel, Argylyshire
Oil/canvas/board (89.5x143cm 35x56in) Billingshurst,
West-Sussex 1999
☞ **$40 687** – €48 389 – **£29 000** – FF317 410
Dunnottar Castle Oil/canvas (92.5x59cm 36x23in)
London 2000
✐ **$1 043** – €977 – **£649** – FF6 407
Claverhouse Tower, Angus Watercolour
(24x35.5cm 9x13in) London 1999

PATOUX Emile Joseph 1893-1985 **[81]**
☞ **$684** – €744 – **£450** – FF4 878
Le tombeau du géant Oil/canvas (71x85cm 27x33in)
Lokeren 2000

PATRIARCA Amato 1945 **[5]**
☞ **$800** – €829 – **£480** – FF5 440
Gente Olio/tela (50x50cm 19x19in) Vercelli 2001

PATRICIO António José 1827-1885 **[1]**
☞ **$10 260** – €8 946 – **£6 120** – FF58 680
Alexandre e Diogenes Oleo/lienzo (63x75cm
24x29in) Lisboa 1998

PATRICK Ann XX **[9]**
☞ **$595** – €509 – **£350** – FF3 339
«Sleeping Baby» Oil/board (30.5x25cm 12x9in)
Glasgow 1998

PATRICK James McIntosh 1907-1998 **[224]**
☞ **$39 528** – €37 596 – **£24 000** – FF246 616
Balshando in August Oil/canvas (91.5x213cm
36x83in) Edinburgh 1998
☞ **$20 028** – €17 917 – **£12 000** – FF117 531
Autumn, Carse of Gowrie from Above Millhill
Oil/canvas (64x76cm 25x29in) Perthshire 1998
☞ **$2 553** – €2 182 – **£1 500** – FF14 313
The Piazza, Assisi Oil/canvas/board (30.5x45.5cm
12x17in) Glasgow 1998
☞ **$2 042** – €1 746 – **£1 200** – FF11 450
The Harbour, Broughty Ferry Ink (18.5x27.5cm
7x10in) Glasgow 1998
▥ **$680** – €582 – **£400** – FF3 816
The Avenue, Spring Print in colors (51x61cm
20x24in) Glasgow 1998

PATROIS Isidore 1815-1884 **[13]**
☞ **$3 208** – €3 233 – **£2 000** – FF21 207
The Young Connoisseur Oil/panel (35.5x28cm
13x11in) London 2000

PATRU Émile 1877-1940 **[26]**
☞ **$921** – €965 – **£610** – FF6 328
Le printemps campagne genevoise Huile/toile
(50x60cm 19x23in) Genève 2000

PATSOGLOU Aristide 1941 **[15]**
▨ **$469** – €534 – **£330** – FF3 500
Danseuse Bronze (H40cm H15in) Paris 2001

PATTA de Margaret 1903-1964 **[1]**
▣ **$4 800** – €4 012 – **£2 842** – FF26 316
Photogram, Light Rhythm Gelatin silver print
(25.5x20cm 10x7in) New-York 1998

PATTEN Alfred Fowler 1829-1888 **[9]**
☞ **$2 149** – €2 030 – **£1 300** – FF13 317
The Pine Cone Gatherer Oil/canvas (34x28.5cm
13x11in) Billingshurst, West-Sussex 1999

PATTEN Leonard XX **[2]**
▥ **$988** – €1 146 – **£700** – FF7 519
«Swanage, Dorset, Southern Railway, For
Sunshine and Health» Poster (100x64cm 39x25in)
London 2000

PATTERSON Ambrose MacCarthy 1877-1967 **[9]**
$14 144 - €15 864 - **£9 856** - FF104 064
Elégantes dans les dunes Huile/toile (64.5x65.5cm 25x25in) Bruxelles 2001

PATTERSON Ben 1934 **[4]**
$850 - €881 - **£510** - FF5 780
What is wrong with his picture Assemblage (52x77cm 20x30in) Prato 2000

PATTERSON Howard Ashman 1891-? **[5]**
$10 000 - €11 569 - **£7 078** - FF75 888
Street Scene with Flags Oil/canvas (60x50cm 24x20in) Cleveland OH 2001

PATTERSON Margaret Jordan 1867-1950 **[227]**
$1 400 - €1 650 - **£983** - FF10 824
Still Life with Fruit, Bowl and Pichter Oil/canvas (38x45cm 15x18in) East-Dennis MA 2000
$1 100 - €923 - **£648** - FF6 054
Tug Boats Watercolour, gouache/paper (35x43cm 14x17in) Greenwich CT 1998
$250 - €216 - **£148** - FF1 414
Night on a Dutch Canal Woodcut (17x13cm 7x5in) Cambridge MA 1998

PATTERSON Margaret Worsley XIX-XX **[2]**
$3 582 - €3 009 - **£2 100** - FF19 736
Illustrations for «Rose Elf», «Snow Queen» and «Goblin Market» Watercolour (20x13cm 7x5in) Billingshurst, West-Sussex 1998

PATTERSON Robert 1898-1981 **[2]**
$2 800 - €3 264 - **£1 938** - FF21 410
Crowd Outside Toyshire At Christmas Time Gouache/paper (35x38cm 14x15in) New-York 2000

PATTERSON Simon 1967 **[14]**
$13 552 - €11 579 - **£8 200** - FF75 952
Yellow, red and blue No.2 Acrylic/canvas (162x218.5cm 63x86in) London 1998
$4 627 - €3 954 - **£2 800** - FF25 935
Time Machine Object (12x89x3cm 4x35x1in) London 1998
$14 202 - €13 743 - **£9 000** - FF90 146
The Great Bear Color lithograph (108.5x134cm 42x52in) London 1999

PATTEYN César 1850-1931 **[49]**
$16 000 - €13 820 - **£9 644** - FF90 651
Friends' Encounter Oil/canvas (58.5x80cm 23x31in) New-York 1998

PATTI Tom 1943 **[9]**
$16 000 - €15 273 - **£9 998** - FF100 184
Compound Bronze Riser From the Riser from the Riser Series Sculpture, glass (13.5x10x7.5cm 5x3x3in) New-York 1999

PATTON Eric XIX-XX **[60]**
$828 - €889 - **£554** - FF5 830
Rainfall, Hebrides Oil/canvas (40x49.5cm 15x19in) Dublin 2000

PATWARDHAN Sudhir 1949 **[9]**
$9 000 - €10 235 - **£6 288** - FF67 140
Street Corner Acrylic/canvas (152.5x182.5cm 60x71in) New-York 2000
$7 442 - €6 961 - **£4 500** - FF45 664
Running Woman Oil/canvas (139.5x85cm 54x33in) London 1999

PAUDISS Christoph c.1625-1666 **[2]**
$26 793 - €22 811 - **£16 000** - FF149 633
Portrait of an Old Man, wearing a Fur Trimmed Coat Oil/canvas (74x62.5cm 29x24in) London 1998

PAUELSEN Erik 1749-1790 **[22]**
$2 091 - €2 150 - **£1 326** - FF14 105
Portraet af ung kvinde med opsat hår Oil/canvas (62x50cm 24x19in) Vejle 2000

PAUL Celia 1959 **[2]**
$17 668 - €17 148 - **£11 000** - FF112 484
Family Group Oil/canvas (165x200cm 64x78in) London 1999

PAUL Ernst 1877-1947 **[11]**
$950 - €1 097 - **£665** - FF7 199
Haystacks Oil/canvas (49x61.5cm 19x24in) Bethesda MD 2001

PAUL Frank R. 1884-1963 **[24]**
$25 000 - €26 835 - **£16 730** - FF176 025
Cover to Science Fiction No.1 Oil/canvas (61.5x42cm 24x16in) New-York 2000
$1 600 - €1 548 - **£1 013** - FF10 155
«Science-fiction Explores de Future» Ink (47.5x36cm 18x14in) New-York 1999

PAUL Jeremy 1954 **[16]**
$4 515 - €4 954 - **£3 000** - FF32 499
A Place in the Shade Acrylic/board (50x80cm 19x31in) London 2000

PAUL John XIX **[49]**
$12 106 - €11 207 - **£7 500** - FF73 514
View of Fish Street and the Monument Oil/canvas (74x126cm 29x49in) London 1999

PAUL John c.1830-c.1890 **[4]**
$5 559 - €4 943 - **£3 400** - FF32 426
Retriever, a Bay Racehorse Held by a Groom in a Stable Yard Oil/canvas (61.5x74cm 24x29in) London 1999

PAUL John Dean 1775-1852 **[14]**
$142 - €168 - **£100** - FF1 100
Symptoms of a skurry in a Pewy country Gravure (42x76cm 16x30in) Neuilly-sur-Seine 2000

PAUL Joseph 1804-1887 **[50]**
$3 208 - €3 233 - **£2 000** - FF21 207
On the Trent Oil/canvas (68.5x125cm 26x49in) London 2000
$809 - €759 - **£500** - FF4 977
Landscape with Windmill Oil/panel (16.5x27cm 6x10in) London 1999

PAUL Maurice 1889-1965 **[6]**
$1 294 - €1 452 - **£897** - FF9 525
Harbour at Oostende Oil/canvas (41x51cm 16x20in) Amsterdam 2000

PAUL Peter 1943 **[28]**
$192 - €179 - **£116** - FF1 173
Architekturmotive Farblithographie (57x76cm 22x29in) Hamburg 1999

PAUL-BAUDRY Cécile XIX-XX **[6]**
$359 - €427 - **£248** - FF2 800
Portrait de jeune femme Huile/toile (60x50cm 23x19in) Paris 2000

PAUL-MANCEAU Georges 1872-1955 **[4]**
$4 020 - €3 811 - **£2 445** - FF25 000
Portrait d'homme Huile/panneau (27x21.5cm 10x8in) Paris 1999

PAUL-MARTIN Joseph, dit Paul 1799-? **[3]**
$1 195 - €1 283 - **£800** - FF8 417
On the River Norwich Oil/canvas (48x83cm 19x33in) Aylsham, Norfolk 2000

PAULI Fritz 1891-1968 **[169]**
- $405 - €449 - £275 - FF2 945
  Erschrockene Nonne Pencil/paper (57.5x45.5cm 22x17in) Zürich 2000
- $120 - €112 - £73 - FF735
  Einzelgänger II Eau-forte, aquatinte (45x58.3cm 17x22in) Bern 1999

PAULI Georg 1855-1935 **[181]**
- $81 510 - €87 112 - £55 380 - FF571 415
  «Haga» Oil/canvas (240x280cm 94x110in) Köbenhavn 2001
- $2 246 - €2 438 - £1 420 - FF15 994
  Liggande modell Oil/canvas (41x68cm 16x26in) Stockholm 2000
- $583 - €554 - £355 - FF3 637
  Sydländskt landskap med bro Oil/panel (32.5x24cm 12x9in) Stockholm 1999
- $768 - €904 - £556 - FF5 930
  Kubistiskt landskap Akvarell/papper (27x21cm 10x8in) Stockholm 2001

PAULI Hanna 1864-1940 **[41]**
- $1 221 - €1 330 - £799 - FF8 721
  Från Nynäshamn, flickan Bendictsson Oil/canvas (32x64cm 12x25in) Uppsala 2000
- $1 153 - €1 075 - £717 - FF7 049
  Flickporträtt Oil/canvas (40x36cm 15x14in) Stockholm 1999
- $654 - €642 - £405 - FF4 213
  Porträtt av Ellen Key Akvarell/papper (34x27cm 13x10in) Stockholm 1999

PAULIN Paul 1852-1937 **[9]**
- $1 296 - €1 448 - £878 - FF9 500
  Statuette représentant le peintre Jean-Baptiste Armand Guillaumin Bronze (19x16cm 7x6in) Paris 2000

PAULMANN Joseph XIX **[31]**
- $712 - €827 - £500 - FF5 426
  Figures resting by a Stook Oil/canvas (40.5x61cm 15x24in) London 2001
- $1 300 - €1 241 - £800 - FF8 143
  Waiting for the Ferry Oil/canvas (30x40cm 12x16in) Cincinnati OH 1999

PAULME George XIX-XX **[7]**
- $668 - €762 - £466 - FF5 000
  «Cycles & motocyclettes gladiator, pré St.Gervais, Seine» Affiche (149.5x110cm 58x43in) Paris 2001

PAULSEN Fritz 1838-1898 **[12]**
- $3 418 - €3 579 - £2 148 - FF23 477
  Frierende kleine Händler an Weihnachten Öl/Leinwand (123x94cm 48x37in) Bremen 2000
- $10 102 - €12 015 - £7 200 - FF78 816
  Ausflug des Mädchenpensionats Oil/panel (32x41cm 12x16in) Köln 2000

PAULSEN Ingwer 1883-1943 **[61]**
- $899 - €1 022 - £623 - FF6 707
  Stadttor in Franken Öl/Leinwand (81.5x65.5cm 32x25in) Hamburg 2000
- $186 - €174 - £112 - FF1 140
  Brücke in Friedrichstadt Radierung (32x29.5cm 12x11in) Berlin 1999

PAULSEN Julius 1860-1940 **[266]**
- $1 060 - €1 206 - £745 - FF7 912
  Kvindeportraet Oil/canvas (54x54cm 21x21in) Vejle 2001
- $625 - €670 - £426 - FF4 398
  Udsigt mellem hoje traeer til sydlansk by Oil/canvas (26x37cm 10x14in) Köbenhavn 2001

PAULUCCI Enrico 1901-1999 **[298]**
- $3 400 - €4 406 - £2 550 - FF28 900
  Sul mare Olio/tela (50x60cm 19x23in) Vercelli 2000
- $1 920 - €1 659 - £1 280 - FF10 880
  Paesaggio Olio/tela (34.5x44.5cm 13x17in) Prato 1998
- $640 - €829 - £480 - FF5 440
  Paesaggio nebbioso Inchiostro (34x48cm 13x18in) Prato 2000

PAULUS DU CHATELET Pierre, baron 1881-1959 **[157]**
- $3 638 - €4 214 - £2 516 - FF27 642
  Vase de fleurs Huile/toile (90x70cm 35x27in) Bruxelles 2000
- $78 - €87 - £54 - FF569
  Mijnwerker (Mineur) Dessin (23x18cm 9x7in) Antwerpen 2001
- $131 - €136 - £83 - FF894
  Cheval de halage Aquatint in colors (35x45.8cm 13x18in) Lokeren 2000

PAULUZZI Daniel 1866-1956 **[6]**
- $23 940 - €22 309 - £14 760 - FF146 340
  Le pays noir, les hiercheuses Huile/toile (200x250cm 78x98in) Bruxelles 1999
- $2 660 - €2 479 - £1 640 - FF16 260
  Paysage de dunes Huile/toile (40x50cm 15x19in) Bruxelles 1999

PAUMIER Eugène XIX **[3]**
- $1 152 - €1 143 - £717 - FF7 500
  Nègre chevauchant à cru Aquarelle (40x31.5cm 15x12in) Paris 1999

PAUPION Edouard Jérôme 1854-1912 **[29]**
- $10 591 - €10 671 - £6 400 - FF70 000
  Le napolitain charmeur de Lézard Huile/toile (69x90cm 27x35in) Calais 2000
- $287 - €320 - £193 - FF2 100
  Tête d'arabe Huile/panneau (12x10.5cm 4x4in) Dijon 2000

PAUPORTE Édouard 1868-1939 **[169]**
- $78 - €76 - £48 - FF500
  Bord de mer Aquarelle/papier (21.5x27.5cm 8x10in) Vitry-Le-François 1999

PAUQUET Hippolyte Louis Em. 1797-? **[4]**
- $1 754 - €2 013 - £1 200 - FF13 202
  Dignitaires turques Watercolour (16.5x11.5cm 6x4in) London 2001

PAUQUET Polydore Jean Ch. 1799-? **[1]**
- $4 536 - €5 336 - £3 251 - FF35 000
  Vues d'un zoo Aquarelle, gouache/papier (15x22.5cm 5x8in) Paris 2001

PAUS Herbert Andrew 1880-1946 **[11]**
- $9 750 - €11 138 - £6 864 - FF73 062
  Jack Spratt Oil/canvas (94x178cm 37x70in) Pittsfield MA 2001
- $2 600 - €2 407 - £1 591 - FF15 789
  Unloading a barge, cover for Popular Science, May Watercolour, gouache/paper (48x30cm 19x12in) New-York 1999

PAUSER Sergius 1896-1970 **[49]**
- $5 124 - €5 087 - £3 199 - FF33 369
  Dame in gestreifer Bluse Öl/Leinwand (73x61cm 28x24in) Wien 1999
- $2 971 - €2 543 - £1 788 - FF16 684
  Kaktusstock Öl/panel (20x12.5cm 7x4in) Wien 1998
- $1 234 - €1 453 - £868 - FF9 534
  Landschaft mit Brücke Aquarell/Papier (29.5x41.6cm 11x16in) Wien 2000

PAUSINGER Margarethe 1880-1956 [5]
📖 **$164** - €160 - **£101** - FF1 048
  Bäuerliche Idylle Woodcut (23x30cm 9x11in) Linz 1999

PAUSINGER von Clemens 1855-1938 [11]
🖙 **$9 820** - €11 527 - **£6 930** - FF75 610
  Spaniern Oil/canvas (151x110cm 59x43in) Stockholm 2000

PAUSINGER von Franz Xavier 1839-1915 [61]
🖙 **$6 540** - €7 267 - **£4 380** - FF47 670
  Strecke und der Hetzjagd des Fürsterzbischofs Markus Sittikus Öl/Leinwand (162.8x298cm 64x117in) Wien 2000
🖙 **$2 366** - €2 036 - **£1 402** - FF13 353
  Hirsch im Gebirge Öl/Leinwand (37.5x57.5cm 14x22in) Wien 1998
🖙 **$784** - €767 - **£497** - FF5 030
  Hirschrudel am Waldrand Oil/panel (18x38.5cm 7x15in) München 1999
✏️ **$825** - €945 - **£575** - FF6 340
  Szarvas pár Charcoal/paper (140x90cm 55x35in) Budapest 2000

PAUTROT Ferdinand 1832-1874 [119]
🐾 **$2 147** - €2 211 - **£1 352** - FF14 500
  Le renard Bronze (50x60x40cm 19x23x15in) Orléans 2000

PAUTSCH Fryderyk 1877-1950 [24]
🖙 **$11 000** - €9 373 - **£6 554** - FF61 486
  Young Girl with Flowers Oil/canvas (79x88.5cm 31x34in) New-York 1998

PAUTY Edmond XX [83]
✏️ **$151** - €152 - **£94** - FF1 000
  Rabat, au pied de la tour Hassan Fusain (38x52.5cm 14x20in) Paris 2000

PAUVERT-TISSIER Odette 1903-1966 [2]
🖙 **$11 214** - €12 806 - **£7 887** - FF84 000
  Artémis Huile/toile (140x162cm 55x63in) Reims 2001
🖙 **$4 569** - €5 199 - **£3 171** - FF34 100
  Petit garçon Huile/toile (54x65cm 21x25in) Reims 2000

PAUW de Jef 1888-1930 [86]
🖙 **$341** - €322 - **£211** - FF2 113
  Nature morte Huile/toile (80x70cm 31x27in) Antwerpen 1999

PAUW de René 1887-1946 [38]
🖙 **$406** - €471 - **£281** - FF3 089
  Hoogaert Yachts à Breskens Huile/panneau (48x63cm 18x24in) Bruxelles 2000

PAUWELS Henri Jozef 1903-1983 [220]
🖙 **$202** - €223 - **£136** - FF1 463
  Boerderij aan de stroom (Ferme au bord du fleuve) Huile/toile (62x85cm 24x33in) Antwerpen 2000

PAUWELS Jos 1818-1876 [88]
🖙 **$1 164** - €1 361 - **£831** - FF8 929
  Terrasse sur mer Oil/board (68.5x58cm 26x22in) Amsterdam 2001

PAUWELS Maximilien XVII [1]
🖙 **$13 629** - €14 334 - **£9 000** - FF94 025
  Marauders attacking a village in a forest Oil/canvas (235x435cm 92x171in) London 2000

PAVAN Angelo 1893-1945 [25]
🖙 **$3 234** - €3 369 - **£1 950** - FF22 100
  Ultimi raggi Olio/tavola (50x41cm 19x16in) Milano 2000

$1 800 - €2 332 - **£1 350** - FF15 300
  «Tenda rossa» Olio/tavola (40x31cm 15x12in) Prato 2000

PAVELIC Myfanwy Spencer 1916 [9]
🖙 **$10 137** - €9 764 - **£6 294** - FF64 050
  Red, white and blue Acrylic/canvas (51x40.5cm 20x15in) Toronto 1999

PAVESI Pietro XIX [12]
✏️ **$1 448** - €1 605 - **£982** - FF10 525
  Cardinals Playing Chess Watercolour/paper (45x33cm 17x12in) Hilton 2000

PAVIL Élie Anatole 1873-1948 [325]
🖙 **$2 042** - €2 058 - **£1 273** - FF13 500
  Notre-Dame sous la neige Huile/toile (73x92cm 28x36in) Paris 2000
🖙 **$1 441** - €1 601 - **£1 004** - FF10 500
  Joueurs de cartes Huile/panneau (15x22cm 5x8in) Paris 2001
✏️ **$162** - €183 - **£114** - FF1 200
  Discussion près de la mosquée Encre (13x18cm 5x7in) Paris 2001

PAVLIK Michael XX [4]
🗿 **$20 000** - €23 237 - **£14 056** - FF152 424
  Untitled #2127 Sculpture, glass (75x38x38cm 29x14x14in) New-York 2001

PAVLIKEVICH J. XIX-XX [5]
✏️ **$1 299** - €1 143 - **£791** - FF7 500
  Portrait de Hamal Bachir Aquarelle/papier (40x30cm 15x11in) Paris 1999

PAVLOS P. Dionyssopoulos 1930 [52]
🖙 **$8 574** - €10 367 - **£5 990** - FF68 000
  Vase de fleurs Technique mixte (137x70cm 53x27in) Lille 2000
🖙 **$1 638** - €1 829 - **£1 110** - FF12 000
  Sans titre Marbre (40x30x30cm 15x11x11in) Paris 2000
✏️ **$10 521** - €12 271 - **£7 387** - FF80 493
  Affiches Massicotées Collage (148x116cm 58x45in) Köln 2000

PAVLOVICH Alexander I XIX [1]
🖙 **$3 023** - €3 336 - **£2 000** - FF21 883
  The Classical Bust Marble (H36cm H14in) London 2000

PAVY Eugène c.1850-c.1905 [36]
🖙 **$8 668** - €8 385 - **£5 346** - FF55 000
  Marchands de fruits et légumes Huile/panneau (38x47cm 14x18in) Paris 1999
🖙 **$4 979** - €4 393 - **£3 000** - FF28 818
  By the Doorway to the Citadel Oil/panel (31x44.5cm 12x17in) London 1998

PAVY Philippe 1860-? [44]
🖙 **$3 227** - €3 027 - **£1 994** - FF19 857
  Ryttare Oil/panel (31x63cm 12x24in) Helsinki 1999
🖙 **$1 636** - €1 500 - **£1 000** - FF9 839
  The Orange Seller Oil/panel (22x15.5cm 8x6in) London 1999

PAWLE John 1915 [23]
🖙 **$641** - €647 - **£400** - FF4 241
  On the Beach Oil/canvas (96.5x81cm 37x31in) London 2000

PAWLISZAK Waclaw 1866-1905 [18]
🖙 **$98 256** - €84 150 - **£59 058** - FF551 990
  Le cadeau du cosaque Oil/canvas (124x213cm 48x83in) Warszawa 1998

P

$15 671 - €14 802 - **£9 477** - FF97 097
Garde d'hetman Oil/canvas (80x48.5cm 31x19in)
Warszawa 1999

$1 332 - €1 485 - **£896** - FF9 741
Escarmouche entre hussards et turcs Crayon
(31x46.5cm 12x18in) Warszawa 2000

PAXSON Edgar Samuel 1852-1919 **[39]**

$45 000 - €49 836 - **£30 519** - FF326 902
Return of Chief Joseph and His tribe Oil/canvas
(91.5x61cm 36x24in) New-York 2000

$27 500 - €24 999 - **£16 563** - FF163 982
Portrait of Chief Gall Oil/canvas (35x27cm 14x11in)
Hayden ID 1998

$4 500 - €4 939 - **£2 897** - FF32 397
Portrait of a Sho-Sho-Ne Watercolour/paper
(30.5x23cm 12x9in) Beverly-Hills CA 2000

PAXSON Ethel Easton 1885-1982 **[19]**

$500 - €447 - **£305** - FF2 930
Mediterranean Village by the Sea
Watercolour/paper (34x23cm 13x9in) Boston MA 1999

PAXTON William MacGregor 1869-1941 **[91]**

$18 000 - €21 407 - **£12 828** - FF140 418
Study for Phryne Oil/canvas (71.5x31cm 28x12in)
New-York 2000

$1 700 - €2 009 - **£1 204** - FF13 176
Cape Cod Study Oil/board (21x24cm 8x9in)
Provincetown MA 2000

$650 - €604 - **£402** - FF3 965
Line of Laundry Watercolour/paper (34x51cm
13x20in) East-Dennis MA 1999

PAYA SANCHIS José ?-1984 **[8]**

$2 612 - €2 853 - **£1 805** - FF18 715
Pueblo valenciano Oleo/lienzo (60x73.5cm 23x28in)
Madrid 2001

PAYEN G. XIX-XX **[5]**

$1 972 - €2 107 - **£1 343** - FF13 821
Femme dans un jardin Huile/toile (81x60cm
31x23in) Lokeren 2001

$3 051 - €3 430 - **£2 142** - FF22 500
Élégante 1900 à un bar Pastel/papier (100x80cm
39x31in) Belfort 2001

PAYER Julius J.P. 1841-1915 **[5]**

$2 208 - €2 543 - **£1 508** - FF16 684
Weiblicher Rückenakt Öl/Leinwand (92.5x72.5cm
36x28in) Wien 2000

PAYNE Albert Henry 1812-1902 **[10]**

$209 - €225 - **£140** - FF1 473
The Song of the Bell Engraving (68x54cm 26x21in)
London 2000

PAYNE David ?-1891 **[53]**

$3 177 - €3 082 - **£2 000** - FF20 215
Changing Sky, Derbyshire Oil/canvas (51x76cm
20x29in) London 1999

$900 - €874 - **£556** - FF5 732
Landschaften mit Tierstaffage Öl/Leinwand
(35.5x30.5cm 13x12in) Luzern 1999

$850 - €861 - **£533** - FF5 646
The Dining Room at Lu Shan Watercolour/paper
(49x63cm 19x25in) Morris-Plains NJ 1999

PAYNE Edgar Alwin 1882-1947 **[302]**

$26 000 - €28 534 - **£16 741** - FF187 168
Lake in the High Sierras Oil/canvas (63.5x76cm
25x29in) Beverly-Hills CA 2000

$6 000 - €7 012 - **£4 283** - FF45 996
«Pine trees» Oil/canvas/panel (24x33cm 9x13in)
Altadena CA 2001

$1 300 - €1 519 - **£928** - FF9 965
«Sails at twilight» Graphite (27x38cm 11x15in)
Altadena CA 2001

PAYNE Elsie Palmer 1884-1971 **[62]**

$5 000 - €4 272 - **£3 025** - FF28 022
My Neighbor Oil/canvas (61x45.5cm 24x17in) San-
Francisco CA 1998

$750 - €805 - **£501** - FF5 280
Mountain landscape with trees and snow
Gouache/paper (21x23cm 8x9in) Altadena CA 2000

PAYNE William 1744/45-1833 **[152]**

$799 - €820 - **£500** - FF5 381
Figures in a Stormy Coastal Landscape
Watercolour (43x64cm 16x25in) London 2000

PAYNTER Catherine 1949 **[5]**

$804 - €901 - **£559** - FF5 913
The Road to Sugar Loaf Mixed media (99x78.5cm
38x30in) Johannesburg 2001

PAYTON Bertha Manzler XX **[2]**

$553 - €645 - **£390** - FF4 234
«Winter Scene near New York» Oil/panel
(11.5x17cm 4x6in) Toronto 2000

PAYZANT Charles 1898-1980 **[12]**

$850 - €759 - **£520** - FF4 977
«Sierra Sundown» Watercolour/paper (28x41cm
11x16in) Altadena CA 1999

PAZ de Joseph XVIII **[2]**

$11 260 - €12 143 - **£7 558** - FF79 651
Den krönta Madonnan Oil/canvas (126x94cm
49x37in) Stockholm 2000

PAZOTTI XIX-XX **[3]**

$4 166 - €4 878 - **£2 940** - FF32 000
Voiliers à Venise/Caïque sur le Bosphore
Huile/toile (38x55.5cm 14x21in) Paris 2001

PAZZI Pietro Antonio 1706-c.1766 **[6]**

$260 - €266 - **£163** - FF1 744
**Brustbild mit Hermelin, nach Johann Theodor
von Bayern** Radierung (22.5x16.5cm 8x6in) Köln
2000

PAZZINI Norberto 1856-1937 **[11]**

$2 400 - €3 110 - **£1 800** - FF20 400
Contadina nelle campagna umbra Olio/tavola
(22x34.5cm 8x13in) Milano 2001

PEAK Robert, Bob 1928-1992 **[28]**

$3 750 - €4 177 - **£2 452** - FF27 399
**Story illustration: Young couple walking near
hardware store** Gouache/paper (53x55cm 21x22in)
New-York 2000

$398 - €460 - **£280** - FF3 019
«My Fair Lady» Poster (104x68.5cm 40x26in) London
2000

PEAKE Mervyn Lawrence 1911-1968 **[81]**

$24 643 - €23 502 - **£15 000** - FF154 162
Glassblower Oil/board (122x54.5cm 48x21in)
London 1999

$2 092 - €2 246 - **£1 400** - FF14 730
Windy Day on the Coast Oil/canvas (25.5x35.5cm
10x13in) London 2000

$1 153 - €1 072 - **£700** - FF7 030
Prancing Horse Wash (31.5x24cm 12x9in) London
1998

PEALE Anna Claypoole 1791-1878 **[6]**

$2 900 - €2 798 - **£1 821** - FF18 354
**Portraits of Elizabeth Brown and Reverend
Obadiah B. Brown** Miniature (8x6cm 3x2in)
Downington PA 1999

P

PEALE Charles Willson 1741-1827 [19]
* **$31 000** - €29 018 - **£19 210** - FF190 346
Joseph Sansom Oil/canvas (51x42cm 20x16in)
Philadelphia PA 1999

PEALE Harriet Cany 1800-1869 [5]
* **$16 000** - €13 858 - **£9 812** - FF90 904
Braddock's Field Oil/canvas (63.5x96.5cm 25x37in)
New-York 1999
* **$6 500** - €7 216 - **£4 520** - FF47 335
The Little Tamborine Player Oil/panel (30x24cm
12x9in) Milford CT 2001

PEALE James 1749-1831 [16]
* **$130 000** - €111 070 - **£78 039** - FF728 572
Still Life with Watermelon Oil/canvas (46x66cm
18x25in) New-York 1998

PEALE Margaretta Angelica 1795-1882 [3]
* **$15 000** - €16 059 - **£10 207** - FF105 339
**Still Life on marble-top Table with pierced oval
fruit Basket** Oil/canvas (48x68cm 19x27in)
Portsmouth NH 2001

PEALE Mary Jane 1826-1902 [13]
* **$25 000** - €27 360 - **£17 245** - FF179 470
George Washington/Martha Washington Oil/can-
vas (77.5x64cm 30x25in) New-York 2001
* **$8 500** - €9 913 - **£5 967** - FF65 028
Still Life with Fuschia and Rose Oil/canvas
(37x23cm 14x9in) Boston MA 2000

PEALE Raphaelle, Raphael 1774-1825 [8]
* **$170 000** - €145 245 - **£102 051** - FF952 748
Still Life with Watermelon Oil/panel (33x49.5cm
12x19in) New-York 1998
* **$950** - €906 - **£576** - FF5 941
Profile Portrait of George Reinicker, Jr. Miniature
(12x10cm 5x4in) New-York 1999

PEALE Rembrandt 1778-1860 [36]
* **$39 000** - €41 753 - **£26 539** - FF273 881
Boys robbing bird's Nest Oil/panel (36x45cm
14x18in) Portsmouth NH 2001

PEALE Rubens 1784-1864 [4]
* **$57 500** - €68 382 - **£40 980** - FF448 557
Still Life with Watermelon Oil/canvas (48.5x68.5cm
19x26in) New-York 2000

PÉAN DU PAVILLON Isidore 1790-1856 [2]
* **$28 494** - €27 441 - **£17 694** - FF180 000
**Portrait présumé d'Armand-Benoît Roussel
(1773-1852), buste de Molière** Huile/toile
(127x99cm 50x38in) Paris 1999

PÉAN René Louis 1875-1945 [141]
* **$784** - €717 - **£479** - FF4 700
Espagnole à la guitare Pastel/papier (53x45cm
20x17in) Paris 1999
* **$705** - €838 - **£502** - FF5 500
**«Alcazar d'été, les tableaux vivants de Robert
Paxton»** Affiche (124x88.5cm 48x34in) Orléans 2000

PEARCE Bryan 1929 [44]
* **$3 478** - €3 220 - **£2 100** - FF21 123
The Island, St Ives Oil/board (55x77cm 22x30in) Par,
Cornwall 1999
* **$1 224** - €1 464 - **£844** - FF9 600
Tankard of Anemones Pastel (32x24cm 12x9in)
Penzance, Cornwall 2000

PEARCE Charles Sprague 1851-1914 [89]
* **$20 000** - €23 026 - **£13 648** - FF151 040
The Letter Oil/canvas (56x46cm 22x18in) New-York
2000

* **$825** - €942 - **£573** - FF6 176
Landscape and Sky Study Oil/canvas (23x33cm
9x13in) Cleveland OH 2001
* **$165** - €188 - **£114** - FF1 236
La folie Pencil (27x21cm 11x8in) Cleveland OH 2001

PEARCE Stephen 1819-1904 [8]
* **$13 000** - €15 104 - **£9 136** - FF99 075
**Mr.Radclyffe, Master of the South Dorset
Hounds** Oil/canvas (56x76cm 22x29in) New-York
2001

PEARLSTEIN Philip 1924 [116]
* **$17 000** - €14 503 - **£10 254** - FF95 132
Nude with Swan Decoy and Wet Roof Oil/canvas
(152.5x152.5cm 60x60in) New-York 1998
* **$2 600** - €3 021 - **£1 827** - FF19 815
Halloween Oil/canvas (50x60cm 20x24in) New-
Orleans LA 2001
* **$1 400** - €1 503 - **£936** - FF9 857
Standing Male and Female Watercolour/paper
(35.5x43cm 13x16in) Beverly-Hills CA 2000
* **$425** - €364 - **£255** - FF2 388
Nude seated on a Rug beside a Mirror Color
lithography (76x55cm 30x22in) St. Louis MO 1998

PEARS Charles 1873-1958 [95]
* **$4 555** - €4 156 - **£2 800** - FF27 263
«Wreck Demolition» Oil/board (32x75cm 12x29in)
London 1998
* **$846** - €772 - **£520** - FF5 063
Hoisting the Boom Oil/board (42.5x29cm 16x11in)
London 1998
* **$394** - €469 - **£280** - FF3 074
At the Seaside Watercolour (26x31cm 10x12in)
London 2000
* **$1 211** - €1 408 - **£850** - FF9 237
«Bombay, the Empire Marketing Board» Poster
(51x76cm 20x29in) London 2001

PEARSALL Mike ?-1997 [14]
* **$900** - €864 - **£557** - FF5 669
Western Maryland #840 Watercolour/paper
(40x58cm 16x23in) Detroit MI 1999

PEARSE Susan Beatrice 1878-1980 [9]
* **$672** - €722 - **£450** - FF4 737
Little girl with a Candle Watercolour (37x23cm
14x9in) London 2000

PEARSON Cornelius 1805-1891 [98]
* **$883** - €890 - **£550** - FF5 836
Figures in a rowing Boat on a Lake Watercolour
(31.5x49.5cm 12x19in) London 2000

PEARSON Fred XIX-XX [2]
* **$1 901** - €1 871 - **£1 150** - FF12 273
Highland landscapes with cattle
Watercolour/paper (43x68cm 16x26in) Lichfield,
Staffordshire 2000

PEARSON John 1777-1813 [5]
* **$2 244** - €2 670 - **£1 600** - FF17 512
Distant view of Chester across the Meadows
Watercolour (37x26.5cm 14x10in) London 2000

PEARSON Marguerite Stuber 1898-1978 [106]
* **$3 000** - €3 220 - **£2 007** - FF21 123
Daisies in a Teapot Oil/board (50x60cm 20x24in)
East-Dennis MA 2000
* **$1 200** - €1 365 - **£838** - FF8 952
Harbour Scene Oil/board (20x25cm 8x10in) Mystic
CT 2000

P

PEARSON Robert ?-1891 **[1]**
🌐 **$11 000** – €12 212 – **£7 650** – FF80 106
Governor's Island, New York Oil/canvas (44x70cm 17x27in) Milford CT 2001

PEARSON William Henry XIX-XX **[48]**
✎ **$521** – €452 – **£320** – FF2 964
Evening, Dartford/With Wind and Tide, Longkeach Watercolour (27x21cm 10x8in) Billingshurst, West-Sussex 1999

PEART John 1945 **[34]**
🌐 **$647** – €614 – **£403** – FF4 029
Untitled Acrylic/paper/board (52.5x53cm 20x20in) Sydney 1999

PEAT Thomas XVIII-XIX **[11]**
🌐 **$1 088** – €1 039 – **£680** – FF6 813
William Smith, small-half-length, in a Green Coat Oil/metal (31.5x23.5cm 12x9in) London 1999

PEBBLES Frank Marion 1839-1928 **[7]**
🌐 **$500** – €554 – **£346** – FF3 636
Quiet River Morning Oil/canvas (27x38cm 11x15in) St. Petersburg FL 2001

PECCATTE Charles M. 1870-1962 **[60]**
🌐 **$606** – €640 – **£401** – FF4 200
Mère et enfants au bord d'une crique Huile/toile (45x54cm 17x21in) Saint-Dié 2000

PECHAM Georg c.1568-1604 **[4]**
🎨 **$1 480** – €1 687 – **£1 032** – FF11 067
Der Erzengel Michael vertreibt Luzifer Radierung (20.5x16cm 8x6in) Berlin 2001

PECHAN József 1875-1922 **[8]**
🌐 **$773** – €716 – **£473** – FF4 695
Junges Mädchen Öl/Leinwand (56x41cm 22x16in) Magdeburg 1999

PÉCHAUBES Eugène 1890-1967 **[277]**
✎ **$1 633** – €1 906 – **£1 147** – FF12 500
Le labour Huile/toile (55x110cm 21x43in) Paris 2000
🌐 **$1 168** – €1 008 – **£703** – FF6 615
Travhästar i kamp Oil/panel (41x33cm 16x12in) Malmö 1998
✎ **$292** – €274 – **£176** – FF1 800
Course à Saint-Cloud Aquarelle (25.5x71cm 10x27in) Paris 1999
🎨 **$205** – €229 – **£143** – FF1 500
La dilligence Gravure (49x65cm 19x25in) Entzheim 2001

PECHE Dagobert 1887-1923 **[24]**
🎨 **$358** – €400 – **£242** – FF2 621
Damenportrait Woodcut (14x14.5cm 5x5in) Wien 2000

PECHEUX Benoît 1779-c.1835 **[3]**
🌐 **$6 770** – €7 267 – **£4 530** – FF47 670
Bildnis eines kleinen Mädchen Öl/Leinwand (41x32cm 16x12in) Wien 2001

PÉCHEUX Laurent 1729-1821 **[9]**
🌐 **$4 913** – €4 564 – **£3 000** – FF29 940
Jupiter and Antiope Oil/canvas (88x128cm 34x50in) London 1998
✎ **$815** – €915 – **£570** – FF6 000
L'Annonciation Encre (29.5x21.5cm 11x8in) Paris 2001

PECHMANN von Heinrich C. Freiherr 1826-1905 **[6]**
🌐 **$3 612** – €3 964 – **£2 400** – FF25 999
Extensive Alpine Landscape Oil/canvas (62x90cm 24x35in) London 2000

PECHSTEIN Hermann Max 1881-1955 **[1183]**
🌐 **$150 084** – €164 638 – **£101 945** – FF1 079 955
Stürmische See Abends Öl/Karton (70x84cm 27x33in) Berlin 2000
🌐 **$140 832** – €163 616 – **£98 976** – FF1 073 248
Seine mit Brücke und Frachtkähnen Öl/Leinwand (33x46cm 12x18in) Köln 2001
✎ **$9 927** – €9 272 – **£6 000** – FF60 823
Varieté-Tänzerin vor dem Spiegel Coloured crayons (21x16cm 8x6in) London 1999
🎨 **$952** – €924 – **£600** – FF6 061
Segelboote Vor Der Kuste Drypoint (33x40cm 12x15in) London 1999

PECK Sheldon 1797-1869 **[5]**
🌐 **$50 000** – €57 565 – **£34 120** – FF337 600
William Botts Benjamin, Mrs. Benjamin and their Daughter Oil/panel (58.5x76cm 23x29in) New-York 2000

PECKHAM Robert Deacon 1785-1877 **[1]**
🌐 **$20 000** – €17 255 – **£12 110** – FF113 186
Mary L.Edgell Oil/canvas (96.5x73.5cm 37x28in) New-York 1999

PECNARD Maurice XX **[5]**
🎨 **$190** – €198 – **£119** – FF1 300
«Ligne de Paris à l'Afrique», carte d'Afrique avec cinq étoiles rouges Affiche (100x65cm 39x25in) Paris 2000

PECQUEREAU Alphonse 1831-c.1910 **[10]**
✎ **$1 672** – €1 859 – **£1 170** – FF12 195
Rivière et vue citadine Aquarelle/papier (38x54cm 14x21in) Antwerpen 2001

PÉCRUS Charles 1826-1907 **[160]**
🌐 **$3 337** – €3 811 – **£2 347** – FF25 000
Vapeurs et voiliers dans un bassin du Havre Huile/toile (38x55cm 14x21in) Fontainebleau 2001
🌐 **$3 160** – €2 929 – **£1 971** – FF17 560
Arranging Flowers Oil/panel (41.5x34cm 16x13in) London 1998
✎ **$269** – €305 – **£188** – FF2 000
Le chemin Pastel/papier (11x17.5cm 4x6in) Paris 2001

PECSI Joszef 1889-1956 **[9]**
📷 **$547** – €613 – **£380** – FF4 024
Weiblicher Akt Vintage gelatin silver print (22.5x16.5cm 8x6in) Köln 2001

PEDDER John 1850-1929 **[37]**
✎ **$639** – €656 – **£400** – FF4 304
Cattle in a Meadow Watercolour (24x36cm 9x14in) London 2000

PEDERSEN Carl-Henning 1913 **[581]**
🌐 **$18 400** – €16 819 – **£11 525** – FF110 325
Turquoise Bird and Red Figure Oil/canvas (127x112cm 50x44in) Köbenhavn 1999
🌐 **$13 986** – €12 110 – **£8 433** – FF79 434
«Himmeltegn over skoven» Oil/canvas (70x60cm 27x23in) Köbenhavn 2000
🌐 **$3 197** – €3 094 – **£1 971** – FF20 297
Komposition med fugle Oil/canvas (33x44cm 12x17in) Köbenhavn 1999
🖌 **$1 639** – €1 876 – **£1 127** – FF12 306
Maske Bronze (H28cm H11in) Köbenhavn 2000
✎ **$1 999** – €2 015 – **£1 244** – FF13 218
Lyksalighedens ö Indian ink/paper (69x51cm 27x20in) Köbenhavn 2000

📖 **$386** - €363 - **£241** - FF2 383
Komposition Color lithograph (70x50cm 27x19in)
Vejle 1999

PEDERSEN Finn 1944 **[349]**
🦢 **$1 243** - €1 073 - **£750** - FF7 039
Party Oil/canvas (96.5x130cm 37x51in) London 1998
🦢 **$499** - €536 - **£334** - FF3 517
Figurkomposition Oil/canvas (80x100cm 31x39in)
Köbenhavn 2000
📖 **$610** - €726 - **£435** - FF4 762
Fairy Tale Screenprint in colors (76x56cm 29x22in)
Amsterdam 2000

PEDERSEN Hugo Vilfred 1870-1959 **[199]**
🦢 **$1 203** - €1 341 - **£823** - FF8 799
**Livvagt, Java, soldat fra Javas Kejserhof i
Solrakarta** Oil/canvas (171x90cm 67x35in) Viby J,
Århus 2000
🦢 **$699** - €673 - **£434** - FF4 415
Det gyldne bassin, Madura, Indien Oil/canvas
(60x39cm 23x15in) Köbenhavn 1999
🦢 **$256** - €281 - **£174** - FF1 844
**Ansicht eines indischen Dorfes mit Lehmhütten
unter hohen Bäumen** Oil/panel (31x23cm 12x9in)
Saarbrücken 2000

PEDERSEN Ole 1856-1898 **[24]**
🦢 **$1 168** - €1 009 - **£705** - FF6 619
Hedeparti, bondepige med graessende ko
Oil/canvas (57x100cm 22x39in) Vejle 1998

PEDERSEN Thorolf 1858-1942 **[17]**
🦢 **$1 417** - €1 611 - **£990** - FF10 570
Hjuldamperen Ornen ud for kysten Oil/canvas
(81x130cm 31x51in) Köbenhavn 2000

PEDERSEN Viggo C.F.V 1854-1926 **[311]**
🦢 **$901** - €875 - **£572** - FF5 738
Solnedgang over havet Oil/canvas (47x65cm
18x25in) Viby J, Århus 1999
🦢 **$466** - €536 - **£323** - FF3 518
Graessende köer i skoven Oil/canvas (45x35cm
17x13in) Köbenhavn 2000
📖 **$298** - €296 - **£186** - FF1 942
Snelandskab med gård og hönsehus
Gouache/paper (39x58cm 15x22in) Köbenhavn 1999

PEDERZOLI P. XIX **[2]**
🦢 **$12 000** - €13 913 - **£8 500** - FF91 261
A Merry Couple Oil/canvas (49x39.3cm 19x15in)
New-York 2000

PEDON Bartolomeo 1665-1733 **[10]**
🦢 **$20 000** - €19 091 - **£12 496** - FF125 232
Ships in a Storm Off a Rocky Coast Oil/canvas
(86x156cm 33x61in) New-York 1999
🦢 **$10 000** - €10 367 - **£6 000** - FF68 000
Veduta di costiera con navi in tempesta Olio/tela
(63.5x92cm 25x38in) Milano 1999
🦢 **$8 400** - €7 257 - **£4 200** - FF47 600
Paesaggio Olio/tela (31x39cm 12x15in) Milano 1999

PEDRA A. XIX **[3]**
📷 **$728** - €762 - **£457** - FF5 000
Architecture islamique Tirage albuminé (21x27cm
8x10in) Paris 2000

PEDRAZA OSTOS José 1880-1937 **[22]**
📖 **$90** - €108 - **£63** - FF709
La tauromaquía de Goya Grabado (13x16cm 5x6in)
Madrid 2000

PEDRETTI Giulano 1924 **[3]**
🖋 **$5 581** - €6 563 - **£4 002** - FF43 053
Bündner Figur Bronze (H61cm H24in) Bern 2001

PEDRETTI Turo 1896-1964 **[19]**
🦢 **$3 774** - €3 230 - **£2 271** - FF21 186
Christolais bei Samedan Huile/toile (19x24cm
7x9in) Zürich 1998

PEDRO del Francesco 1749-1806 **[7]**
📖 **$180** - €155 - **£120** - FF1 020
**Costantinopoli presa dai Veneziani/Scena stori-
ca con Doge** Gravure (21x27cm 8x10in) Firenze 1998

PEEL James 1811-1906 **[93]**
🦢 **$9 821** - €11 680 - **£7 000** - FF76 616
Last Days of Summer Oil/canvas (91.5x145cm
36x57in) London 2000
🦢 **$2 037** - €1 806 - **£1 250** - FF11 844
**Cattle Watering, a Man Carrying Faggots on the
River Path** Oil/canvas (44x80cm 17x31in) West-
Midlands 1999
🦢 **$1 272** - €1 431 - **£876** - FF9 390
Wassermühle Öl/Leinwand (23x31cm 9x12in)
München 2000

PEEL Paul 1860/61-1892 **[20]**
🦢 **$118 299** - €131 006 - **£80 229** - FF859 345
Before the Bath Oil/canvas (87x84cm 34x33in)
Toronto 2000
🦢 **$19 530** - €16 712 - **£11 757** - FF109 623
The Young Biologist Oil/canvas (26x23cm 10x9in)
Toronto 1998
✏ **$149 430** - €160 401 - **£100 000** - FF1 052 160
The Daisy Chain Pastel (68.5x96.5cm 26x37in)
London 2000

PEELE James 1847-1905 **[22]**
🦢 **$700** - €772 - **£465** - FF5 062
Elephant Rock, Back Beach, Sorrento Oil/board
(28x45cm 11x17in) Melbourne 2000

PEELE John Thomas 1822-1897 **[15]**
🦢 **$4 800** - €4 505 - **£3 000** - FF29 550
Costureras Oleo/lienzo (92x74cm 36x29in) Madrid
1999

PEERLESS Thomas, Tom XIX **[34]**
✏ **$312** - €265 - **£188** - FF1 739
View of the Te Anau, Lake Otago
Watercolour/paper (31x50cm 12x19in) Sydney 1998

PEETERS Bonaventura 1614-1652 **[55]**
🦢 **$14 823** - €14 099 - **£9 000** - FF92 481
**Smalschips Sailing on Choppy Seas in a
Strong Breeze** Oil/panel (58.5x74cm 23x29in)
London 1999
🦢 **$30 864** - €36 588 - **£21 792** - FF240 000
**Navire hollandais et navire portant le drapeau
de St.Georges** Huile/panneau (29x42cm 11x16in)
Bordeaux 2000
📖 **$1 053** - €1 022 - **£656** - FF6 707
Der Sturm Radierung (9.6x13.8cm 3x5in) Berlin 1999

PEETERS Bonaventura II 1648-1702 **[4]**
🦢 **$4 933** - €4 538 - **£3 050** - FF29 766
**A Dutch threemaster and a «wijdschip» offsho-
re in a gale** Oil/canvas (41x58.5cm 16x23in)
Amsterdam 1999

PEETERS Clara c.1585-c.1655 **[10]**
🦢 **$162 040** - €181 512 - **£112 600** - FF1 190 640
**Pears, an Apple, an Apricot, Grapes, almonds
and walnuts** Oil/copper (26.5x22cm 10x8in)
Amsterdam 2001

PEETERS François XIX-XX **[2]**
🦢 **$261** - €297 - **£188** - FF1 951
La leçon de peinture Huile/toile (78x62cm 30x24in)
Antwerpen 2000

P

PEETERS Gillis Egidius I 1612-1653 **[18]**
🔹 **$14 501** – €14 242 – **£9 000** – FF93 419
European Vessels Landing Off the Coast of South America Oil/panel (48.5x71.5cm 19x28in) London 1999
🔹 **$4 319** – €4 284 – **£2 686** – FF28 100
Personnages et animaux près d'un hameau Huile/panneau (34x32cm 13x12in) L'Isle-Adam 1999

PEETERS Henk 1925 **[14]**
🔹 **$6 640** – €7 714 – **£4 666** – FF50 602
Do-It-Yourself-Sculpture Mixed media (53x53cm 20x20in) Amsterdam 2001
🔹 **$1 874** – €2 178 – **£1 317** – FF14 287
Automatical Drawing Felt pen/paper (30.5x22cm 12x8in) Amsterdam 2001
🔹 **$468** – €544 – **£329** – FF3 571
Wit op Wit/Wit op Wit Rond Silkscreen (70x50cm 27x19in) Amsterdam 2001

PEETERS Jacob Balthasar c.1650-c.1730 **[2]**
🔹 **$22 000** – €20 698 – **£13 728** – FF135 770
Courtyard of a fantastical Palace with Figures Oil/canvas (70.5x90cm 27x35in) New-York 1999

PEETERS Jacobus 1637-1695 **[6]**
🔹 **$2 868** – €3 079 – **£1 919** – FF20 200
Portraits équestres, scènes de siège Eau-forte (12x26cm 4x10in) Paris 2000

PEETERS Jan I 1624-1677/80 **[26]**
🔹 **$21 204** – €18 294 – **£12 792** – FF120 000
Sortie de l'estuaire par temps d'orage Huile/toile (58x86cm 22x33in) Paris 1998
🔹 **$4 367** – €4 274 – **£2 800** – FF28 034
An Estuary Scene with Sailing Vessels in Choppy Seas Oil/panel (23.5x34cm 9x13in) London 1999
🔹 **$4 719** – €4 538 – **£2 907** – FF29 766
View of Dormans Near Rheims, on the Marne Est of Paris Ink (9.5x30cm 3x11in) Amsterdam 1999

PEETERS Jozef 1895-1960 **[37]**
🔹 **$394** – €421 – **£268** – FF2 764
Hoofd van een man Pastel (31.5x24.5cm 12x9in) Lokeren 2001

PEGERON C. XIX **[39]**
🔹 **$49** – €53 – **£34** – FF350
Le temple d'Auguste et de Livie à Vienne, d'après Debelle Lithographie couleurs (21x27cm 8x10in) Grenoble 2001

PEGOT Bernard c.1830-c.1900 **[9]**
🔹 **$1 566** – €1 524 – **£962** – FF10 000
Portrait d'Adèle de Chassepot, marquise de Therisy (1815-1898) Pastel/papier (65x53cm 25x20in) Paris 1999

PÉGOT-OGIER Jean-Bertrand 1877-1915 **[158]**
🔹 **$3 287** – €3 583 – **£2 154** – FF23 500
Sur les bords de la Laïta Huile/toile (50x61cm 19x24in) Brest 2000
🔹 **$2 008** – €1 982 – **£1 237** – FF13 000
Femme au chapeau sur la terrasse Huile/toile (25x33cm 9x12in) Quimper 1999
🔹 **$512** – €610 – **£365** – FF4 000
Jeune Bretonne en bord de mer Crayon/papier (14x22cm 5x8in) Brest 2000

PEGRAM Henry Alfred 1863-1937 **[9]**
🔹 **$8 625** – €7 312 – **£5 118** – FF47 965
Bronze Bronze (H28cm H11in) New-York 1998

PEGURIER Auguste 1856-1936 **[41]**
🔹 **$483** – €534 – **£327** – FF3 500
Portrait de l'artiste par lui-même Huile/toile (42x33cm 16x12in) Paris 2000
🔹 **$311** – €351 – **£218** – FF2 300
Le port de Saint-Tropez Pastel/papier (12x17cm 4x6in) Paris 2001

PEHRSON Karl Axel 1921 **[137]**
🔹 **$3 100** – €3 687 – **£2 211** – FF24 188
Mefoittisk örnört Acrylic/canvas (90x73cm 35x28in) Stockholm 2000
🔹 **$1 079** – €1 209 – **£750** – FF7 928
Knistra Oil/canvas (24x41cm 9x16in) Stockholm 2001
🔹 **$1 566** – €1 719 – **£1 009** – FF11 278
Fladderört Gouache/paper (29x38cm 11x14in) Stockholm 2000
🔹 **$217** – €209 – **£132** – FF1 371
Exotisk fågel Color lithograph (38x45cm 14x17in) Stockholm 1999

PEI-MING Yan 1960 **[11]**
🔹 **$18 304** – €19 818 – **£12 532** – FF130 000
L'homme le plus riche Huile/toile (235x200cm 92x78in) Paris 2001

PEIFFER Auguste Joseph 1832-1886 **[23]**
🔹 **$1 500** – €1 663 – **£1 041** – FF10 908
«Psyche» Bronze (56x27x22cm 22x11x9in) New-Orleans LA 2001

PEIFFER-WATENPHUL Max 1896-1976 **[415]**
🔹 **$21 445** – €25 565 – **£15 290** – FF167 695
Landschaft bei Sorrent Oil/canvas/panel (51x89cm 20x35in) Berlin 2000
🔹 **$5 362** – €4 998 – **£3 240** – FF32 784
Venedig, Schiff vor der Dogana Watercolour (26x60cm 10x23in) München 1999
🔹 **$477** – €409 – **£287** – FF2 682
Stilleben mit Artishicken Farblithographie (29x46.5cm 11x18in) Hamburg 1998

PEIKERT Martin 1901-1975 **[77]**
🔹 **$3 800** – €4 141 – **£2 631** – FF27 162
Mob, maquette Gouache (35x22cm 14x9in) New-York 2001
🔹 **$1 084** – €1 037 – **£680** – FF6 803
«St. Moritz» Poster (102x64cm 40x25in) London 1999

PEINADO VALLEJO Joaquín 1898-1975 **[119]**
🔹 **$13 500** – €15 016 – **£9 000** – FF98 500
Bassin Boat Oleo/lienzo (114x148cm 44x58in) Madrid 2000
🔹 **$8 540** – €8 409 – **£5 320** – FF55 160
Paisaje Oleo/lienzo (46x65cm 18x25in) Madrid 1999
🔹 **$3 600** – €3 604 – **£2 220** – FF23 640
Puerto Oleo/lienzo (27x46cm 10x18in) Madrid 2000
🔹 **$901** – €1 021 – **£612** – FF6 698
Los amantes Acuarela/papel (34x23.5cm 13x9in) Madrid 2000
🔹 **$112** – €132 – **£81** – FF866
Composición Grabado (19x13cm 7x5in) Madrid 2001

PEINER Werner 1897-1984 **[41]**
🔹 **$428** – €460 – **£286** – FF3 018
Dorf auf dem Hügel Watercolour (43x58cm 16x22in) Köln 2000

PEIPERS Friedrich Eugen 1805-1885 **[22]**
🔹 **$2 191** – €2 352 – **£1 466** – FF15 427
Strassenzug mit Blick auf die Ruine Falkenstein Öl/Karton (40x28.5cm 15x11in) Frankfurt 2000
🔹 **$419** – €460 – **£284** – FF3 018
Blick über die Häuser von Capri Pencil (25.8x37.3cm 10x14in) Berlin 2000

PEIRE Luc 1916-1994 **[173]**
- 🏛 **\$3 223** - €2 727 - **£1 914** - FF17 886
  Graphie 1227 Mixed media/panel (50x60cm 19x23in)
  Lokeren 1998
- ✏ **\$605** - €579 - **£380** - FF3 800
  Composition Crayon/papier (26x34cm 10x13in)
  Versailles 1999

PEISER Kurt 1887-1962 **[328]**
- 🏛 **\$1 258** - €1 339 - **£858** - FF8 780
  Chevaux au port d'Anvers Huile/toile (80x60cm
  31x23in) Bruxelles 2001
- 🏛 **\$577** - €644 - **£400** - FF4 227
  Portrait d'homme Huile/toile (32x24cm 12x9in)
  Antwerpen 2001
- ✏ **\$780** - €644 - **£457** - FF4 222
  La solitude Pastel/papier (39x48cm 15x18in)
  Antwerpen 1998
- ▥ **\$186** - €198 - **£127** - FF1 300
  A l'auberge Eau-forte (45x35cm 17x13in) Bruxelles
  2001

PEISER Mark C. 1938 **[10]**
- ⬚ **\$3 000** - €2 864 - **£1 874** - FF18 784
  Untitled #15397 Sculpture, glass (14.5x28x8cm
  5x11x3in) New-York 1999

PEITHNER VON LICHTENFELS Eduard 1833-1912
[50]
- ✏ **\$244** - €276 - **£164** - FF1 811
  **Studie zu einem Gebirgsbächlein in steiniger
  Umgebung** Ink/paper (35x48.5cm 13x19in) Wien
  2000

PEIZEL Bart 1887-1974 **[38]**
- ✏ **\$327** - €340 - **£205** - FF2 232
  Gezicht vanaf de Merwekade te Dordrecht Black
  chalk (23x32.5cm 9x12in) Dordrecht 2000

PEKALSKI Leonard 1896-1944 **[19]**
- 🏛 **\$2 069** - €2 320 - **£1 404** - FF15 219
  Composition Huile/toile (65x60cm 25x23in)
  Warszawa 2001

PEKIK Djoko 1938 **[15]**
- 🏛 **\$17 255** - €16 080 - **£10 647** - FF105 478
  Traditional Dance in Central Java Oil/canvas
  (96x131cm 37x51in) Singapore 1999
- 🏛 **\$3 956** - €4 372 - **£2 743** - FF28 676
  Tari Anbbuk Oil/canvas (50x59cm 19x23in) Singapore
  2001
- 🏛 **\$2 922** - €3 059 - **£1 835** - FF20 064
  Street Girls Oil/canvas (25.5x30.5cm 10x12in)
  Singapore 2000
- ✏ **\$3 798** - €3 976 - **£2 386** - FF26 083
  Women Carrying Rice Coloured chalks/paper
  (76.5x97.5cm 30x38in) Singapore 1998

PELAEZ Amelia 1897-1968 **[124]**
- 🏛 **\$30 000** - €25 903 - **£18 300** - FF169 914
  Coco Oil/canvas (76.5x61cm 30x24in) Miami FL 1999
- ✏ **\$12 000** - €13 051 - **£7 910** - FF85 612
  Composition Watercolour/paper (55.5x75cm 21x29in)
  Boston MA 2000

PELAEZ LEIRENA Juan 1882-1937 **[4]**
- 🏛 **\$1 785** - €2 102 - **£1 260** - FF13 790
  Paisaje asturiano Oleo/cartón (27x34cm 10x13in)
  Madrid 2000

PELAYO ENTRIALGO Orlando 1920-1990 **[255]**
- 🏛 **\$2 970** - €3 304 - **£1 980** - FF21 670
  Sin título Oleo/lienzo (60x81cm 23x31in) Madrid
  2000
- 🏛 **\$1 920** - €1 802 - **£1 200** - FF11 820
  Pueblo Oleo/cartón (16x26.5cm 6x10in) Madrid 1999

\$970 - €1 067 - **£617** - FF7 000
  Composition Gouache/papier (48.5x64cm 19x25in)
  Paris 2000
- ▥ **\$427** - €420 - **£273** - FF2 758
  Personajes Grabado (65x50cm 25x19in) Madrid 1999

PELAYO FERNANDEZ Eduardo c.1850-1901 **[3]**
- 🏛 **\$4 750** - €5 706 - **£3 325** - FF37 430
  **Hombres de guerra saludando a un hombre de
  paz** Oleo/tabla (32.5x49cm 12x19in) Madrid 2000

PELC Antonin 1895-1967 **[28]**
- ✏ **\$317** - €301 - **£198** - FF1 972
  Black Man and a Cock Indian ink (44.2x31.3cm
  17x12in) Praha 1999

PELEGRIN Santiago 1885-1954 **[1]**
- 🏛 **\$1 960** - €2 102 - **£1 295** - FF13 790
  Paisaje Oleo/cartón (24x29cm 9x11in) Madrid 2000

PELEZ Fernand 1843-1913 **[28]**
- 🏛 **\$1 046** - €1 220 - **£733** - FF8 000
  Jeune marchand de citrons Huile/toile (73x50cm
  28x19in) Neuilly-sur-Seine 2000
- 🏛 **\$1 448** - €1 220 - **£855** - FF8 000
  Vue de Venise Aquarelle, gouache (21x27.2cm
  8x10in) Paris 1998

PELGROM Jacobus 1811-1861 **[13]**
- 🏛 **\$6 312** - €5 402 - **£3 800** - FF35 435
  The House under the Rock-face Oil/panel
  (36x45cm 14x17in) London 1998
- 🏛 **\$3 595** - €4 084 - **£2 522** - FF26 789
  Cattle-market with Factories in a Town beyond
  Oil/canvas (37.5x42cm 14x16in) Amsterdam 2001

PELHAM James II 1800-1874 **[2]**
- ✏ **\$2 632** - €3 078 - **£1 850** - FF20 189
  Portraits of Children of the Blathers Family
  Watercolour/paper (64.5x49.5cm 25x19in) Oxfordshire
  2000

PELHAM Thomas Kent XIX **[46]**
- 🏛 **\$2 012** - €2 086 - **£1 207** - FF13 685
  Fiori per il convento Olio/tela (65x40cm 25x15in)
  Roma 1999
- 🏛 **\$1 221** - €1 123 - **£750** - FF7 364
  Deep in Thought Oil/panel (25.5x20.5cm 10x8in)
  London 1998

PELISIER D. XX **[7]**
- 🏛 **\$1 033** - €1 096 - **£700** - FF7 187
  **Figures Dancing in a Square/Figures in
  Evening Dress Crossing a square** Oil/panel
  (20.5x35cm 8x13in) London 2001

PÉLISSIER-PEZOLT Agnès 1901-1997 **[19]**
- 🏛 **\$356** - €382 - **£238** - FF2 506
  Stilleben mit Hibiskusblumen Öl/Karton (41x33cm
  16x12in) Zofingen 2000

PELLAERT Guy 1934 **[18]**
- ▥ **\$781** - €717 - **£480** - FF4 702
  Taxi Driver Poster (104x68.5cm 40x26in) London
  1999

PELLAN Alfred 1906-1987 **[140]**
- 🏛 **\$7 078** - €7 904 - **£4 935** - FF51 845
  Grande Pointe, Charlevoixo Huile/toile (58.5x43cm
  23x16in) Montréal 2001
- 🏛 **\$2 296** - €1 948 - **£1 385** - FF12 778
  Nature morte, étude Oil/canvas (19x32cm 7x12in)
  Calgary, Alberta 1998
- ✏ **\$2 711** - €2 313 - **£1 616** - FF15 173
  Portrait of a Young Woman Charcoal/paper
  (61x47cm 24x18in) Vancouver, BC. 1998

P

〰️ **$244** - €211 - **£147** - FF1 384
«Fleuron» Sérigraphie (78.5x109cm 30x42in)
Montréal 1998

PELLAR Hanns 1886-1972 **[20]**
🔍 **$1 483** - €1 431 - **£936** - FF9 390
Rokokodame im park Öl/Karton (63.5x61cm
25x24in) München 1999

PELLEGRIN Charles XIX-XX **[2]**
🔍 **$3 571** - €3 659 - **£2 203** - FF24 000
Les Martigues Huile/toile (38x55cm 14x21in)
Aubagne 2000

PELLEGRIN Jacques 1944 **[56]**
🔍 **$582** - €610 - **£368** - FF4 000
Paris, rue des Francs Bourgeois Huile/toile
(54x65cm 21x25in) Castres 2000

PELLEGRIN Joseph Honoré Maxime 1793-1869
[25]
✏️ **$2 800** - €2 490 - **£1 712** - FF16 333
The Brig «Villanova» of Glasgow in the Bay of
Marseille Watercolour (43x61cm 16x24in) New-York
1999

PELLEGRINI Alfred Heinrich 1881-1958 **[110]**
🔍 **$6 531** - €6 288 - **£4 084** - FF41 249
Stilleben mit Kaffeekanne Öl/Karton (41x54cm
16x21in) Zürich 1999
🔍 **$2 254** - €2 420 - **£1 508** - FF15 874
Hering und Zibele, Stilleben Öl/panel
(10.5x30.5cm 4x12in) Zofingen 2000
✏️ **$821** - €725 - **£495** - FF4 754
Venice Watercolour/paper (36x37.5cm 14x14in)
Amsterdam 1998

PELLEGRINI Carlo 1839-1889 **[10]**
🔍 **$493** - €561 - **£342** - FF3 681
Ansicht von Davos Aquarell/Papier (18x29cm
7x11in) Zofingen 2000
〰️ **$1 443** - €1 307 - **£900** - FF8 576
Cleaning her Skis Poster (38x25cm 14x9in) London
1999

PELLEGRINI Carlo 1866-1937 **[6]**
✏️ **$771** - €749 - **£476** - FF4 913
Seilschaft in Hochalpiner Landschaft
Gouache/papier (84x35cm 33x13in) Zürich 1999
〰️ **$2 245** - €2 034 - **£1 400** - FF13 341
«Andermatt» Poster (110x66cm 43x25in) London
1999

PELLEGRINI Carlo Enrique 1800-1875 **[3]**
✏️ **$1 500** - €1 653 - **£1 001** - FF10 841
Retrato de Juan Cristomo Cardenas Lápiz
(43.5x35cm 17x13in) Buenos-Aires 2000

PELLEGRINI Domenico 1759-1840 **[6]**
🔍 **$8 100** - €6 997 - **£5 400** - FF45 900
La nascità de Venere Olio/tela (84x73cm 33x28in)
Milano 1998

PELLEGRINI Gian Antonio 1675-1741 **[44]**
🔍 **$93 384** - €91 795 - **£60 000** - FF602 136
Achilles discovered amongst the Daughters of
Lycomedes Oil/canvas (128x103cm 50x40in) London
1999
🔍 **$35 000** - €36 283 - **£21 000** - FF238 000
San Sebastiano Olio/tela (102x79cm 40x31in)
Venezia 1999
🔍 **$26 000** - €28 526 - **£17 271** - FF187 116
The Assumption of the Virgin Oil/paper/panel
(39.5x24.5cm 15x9in) New-York 2000
✏️ **$1 793** - €1 925 - **£1 200** - FF12 625
Diana Ink (25.5x13.5cm 10x5in) London 2000

PELLEGRINI Honoré c.1800-1870 **[3]**
✏️ **$3 581** - €3 506 - **£2 203** - FF23 000
Trois mâts barque devant l'entrée du port de
Marseille Aquarelle/papier (43x60cm 16x23in) Paris
1999

PELLEGRINI Riccardo 1863-1934 **[122]**
🔍 **$4 800** - €4 147 - **£3 200** - FF27 200
Gita romantica in Laguna Olio/tela (37x57cm
14x22in) Milano 1998
🔍 **$2 800** - €3 628 - **£2 100** - FF23 800
Festa a Siviglia Olio/tela (26x40cm 10x15in) Milano
2000
✏️ **$1 300** - €1 348 - **£780** - FF8 840
La portantina Acquarello/carta (30x20cm 11x7in)
Milano 2000

**PELLEGRINO DA SAN DANIELE Martino di
Battista** 1467-1546/47 **[4]**
🔍 **$32 276** - €30 213 - **£20 000** - FF198 182
The Nativity Oil/panel (63.5x43cm 25x16in) London
1999

PELLENC Léon 1819-1894 **[6]**
🔍 **$7 000** - €6 932 - **£4 358** - FF45 470
The River Seine at the Pont du Jour, Paris
Oil/panel (36x49cm 14x19in) New-York 1999

PELLETIER Antoine Jules c.1825-? **[7]**
🔍 **$28 000** - €24 787 - **£17 119** - FF162 593
Still Life of Flowers and Fruit with Medici Vase
and Mandoline Oil/canvas (130x98,5cm 51x38in)
New-York 1999
🔍 **$3 043** - €2 556 - **£1 789** - FF16 767
Variastilleben mit Obst, Trauben und
Chinaschüssel Öl/Leinwand (62x50cm 24x19in)
Köln 1998

PELLETIER Auguste XVIII-XIX **[37]**
✏️ **$7 172** - €7 699 - **£4 800** - FF50 503
Couroucou Orange (Trogon à queue blanche) -
White-Tailed Trogon Watercolour (52x39cm 20x15in)
London 2000

PELLETIER Pierre Jacques 1869-1931 **[42]**
🔍 **$752** - €701 - **£464** - FF4 600
Paris, vu du haut de Montmartre Huile/toile
(100.5x81.5cm 39x32in) Besançon 1999
✏️ **$205** - €229 - **£137** - FF1 500
Bord de rivière Pastel/papier (30x46cm 11x18in)
Versailles 2000

PELLICCIOTTI Tito 1871-1950 **[97]**
🔍 **$2 300** - €2 384 - **£1 380** - FF15 640
Al pascolo Olio/tela (47x72cm 18x28in) Roma 1999
🔍 **$1 700** - €1 762 - **£1 020** - FF11 560
Asinello mucche nella stalla Olio/tavola
(16.5x18.5cm 6x7in) Firenze 2001

PELLICER Y ROUVIERE Carlos 1865-1959 **[2]**
🔍 **$52 500** - €46 476 - **£32 098** - FF304 862
La Paloma Oil/canvas (145x75cm 57x29in) New-York
1999

PELLINI Eugenio 1864-1934 **[12]**
🔍 **$1 500** - €1 555 - **£900** - FF10 200
Testa di giovinetta Marbre (H39.5cm H15in) Milano
2001

PELLIS Napoleone 1888-1967 **[26]**
🔍 **$4 000** - €4 147 - **£2 400** - FF27 200
Bambina sulle scale Olio/tela (70x48cm 27x18in)
Trieste 2000
🔍 **$5 000** - €5 183 - **£3 000** - FF34 000
«Case carniche» Olio/cartone (20.5x29.5cm 8x11in)
Prato 1999

PELLIZZA DA VOLPEDO Giuseppe 1868-1907 **[24]**
- **$328 000** - €425 028 - **£246 000** - FF2 788 000
Aprile nei prati di Volpedo Olio/tela (53x64.5cm 20x25in) Milano 2001
- **$6 800** - €8 812 - **£5 100** - FF57 800
Studio di testa Olio/tela (38.5x28.5cm 15x11in) Milano 2001

PELLOS René Pellarin, dit 1900 **[25]**
- **$195** - €213 - **£128** - FF1 400
L'Étalon Zinc, dessin humoristique Crayon/papier (10x41cm 3x16in) Douai 2000

PELOUSE Léon Germain 1838-1891 **[153]**
- **$2 313** - €2 287 - **£1 444** - FF15 000
Paysage animé Huile/toile (146x92cm 57x36in) Tours 1999
- **$3 891** - €3 278 - **£2 298** - FF21 500
Lavandière devant la ferme en automne Huile/toile (66x93cm 25x36in) Grenoble 1998
- **$1 400** - €1 617 - **£980** - FF10 609
Hilly Landscape with Cows Oil/panel (26.5x35cm 10x13in) Bethesda MD 2001

PELS Albert 1910-1998 **[49]**
- **$825** - €705 - **£484** - FF4 624
Toast at the Bar Oil/board (40x50cm 16x20in) Chester NY 1998
- **$520** - €557 - **£355** - FF3 653
Dodger outfielder Oil/canvas (47x24cm 18x9in) Cleveland OH 2001

PELT van der Abraham 1815-1895 **[2]**
- **$8 600** - €7 251 - **£5 104** - FF47 563
A Lady Sewing/A Man Sleeping Oil/panel (23x29cm 9x11in) Amsterdam 1998

PELT van Godfried 1873-1926 **[10]**
- **$338** - €363 - **£226** - FF2 381
Still life with flowers in a vase Oil/board (75x63cm 29x24in) Amsterdam 2000

PELTON Agnes 1881-1961 **[24]**
- **$4 250** - €4 967 - **£3 034** - FF32 580
Still life, hydrangeas in ceramic pitcher Oil/canvas (55x66cm 22x26in) Altadena CA 2001
- **$8 000** - €7 609 - **£4 857** - FF49 912
West Wind Oil/canvas (30.5x40.5cm 12x15in) Beverly-Hills CA 1999
- **$975** - €1 147 - **£699** - FF7 521
Scarecrow Pastel/paper (33x49cm 13x19in) San Rafael CA 2001

PELUSO Francesco 1836-? **[71]**
- **$3 259** - €3 236 - **£2 036** - FF21 225
The unexpected Arrival Oil/canvas (58.5x42.5cm 23x16in) Toronto 1999
- **$3 088** - €2 888 - **£1 903** - FF18 943
Värdshusscen med vindrickande män Oil/panel (48x33cm 18x12in) Stockholm 1999

PELUZZI Eso 1894-1985 **[26]**
- **$2 600** - €2 695 - **£1 560** - FF17 680
Cascina langarola Olio/tela (55x69cm 21x27in) Vercelli 2001
- **$1 100** - €1 147 - **£660** - FF7 480
Marina Olio/tela/tavola (21x36cm 8x14in) Vercelli 1999

PEMBA George Mnyalaza M. 1912 **[18]**
- **$4 578** - €4 411 - **£2 828** - FF28 935
Man reading Oil/canvas/board (49x66cm 19x25in) Johannesburg 1999
- **$4 952** - €5 547 - **£3 440** - FF36 388
«Mother and Child» Oil/canvas/board (30x41.5cm 11x16in) Johannesburg 2001

- **$2 390** - €2 774 - **£1 650** - FF18 194
An Old Woman Wrapped in a Blanket Watercolour (35x24cm 13x9in) Johannesburg 2000

PEMBERTON Sophie Theresa 1869-1959 **[9]**
- **$3 403** - €3 229 - **£2 068** - FF21 181
Untitled, Portrait of a Young Woman Oil/canvas (76x43cm 29x16in) Calgary, Alberta 1999

PEÑA Alfonso X. 1903-? **[5]**
- **$3 523** - €4 132 - **£2 534** - FF27 104
Pareja de indígenas Oleo/lienzo (70x55cm 27x21in) México 2001

PENA Tonita 1895-1949 **[11]**
- **$2 500** - €2 672 - **£1 701** - FF17 524
Six Ceremonial Dancers Painting (25x38cm 10x15in) Cloudcroft NM 2001
- **$3 200** - €3 172 - **£2 001** - FF20 806
Scene from the Lightining Dance Watercolour/paper (24x32.5cm 9x12in) New-York 1999

PEÑA Y MUNOZ Maximino 1863-1940 **[83]**
- **$1 925** - €2 102 - **£1 225** - FF13 790
Retrato de caballero Oleo/lienzo (70x55cm 27x21in) Madrid 2000
- **$551** - €571 - **£351** - FF3 743
Fuente en la iglesia Gouache/papier (30x28cm 11x11in) Madrid 2000

PENAGOS ZALABARDO Rafael 1889-1954 **[23]**
- **$420** - €450 - **£277** - FF2 955
Carnaval Lápiz (17x21.5cm 6x8in) Madrid 2000
- **$600** - €600 - **£366** - FF3 933
«Valley of Aran, The Pyrénées & The Saronne Offer Beautiful Landscapes» Poster (99x70cm 39x27in) New-York 2000

PENALBA Alicia Perez 1918-1982 **[67]**
- **$14 283** - €13 720 - **£8 856** - FF90 000
Ombre habitée Bronze (H145cm H57in) Paris 1999
- **$3 568** - €3 049 - **£2 160** - FF20 000
Sans titre Bronze (26x26x18cm 10x10x7in) Paris 1998
- **$4 200** - €3 913 - **£2 592** - FF25 670
Migrateur Tapestry (185x243cm 72x95in) New-York 1999

PENCK A.R. (Ralf Winckler) 1939 **[921]**
- **$30 913** - €26 127 - **£18 500** - FF171 384
«Dumpfkopf No. 1» Oil/canvas (150x150cm 59x59in) London 1998
- **$5 260** - €6 135 - **£3 693** - FF40 246
Ohne Titel Acryl/Leinwand (50x40cm 19x15in) Köln 2000
- **$2 286** - €2 198 - **£1 410** - FF14 421
Selbstportrait Acryl/Leinwand (28x23cm 11x9in) Köln 1999
- **$1 144** - €1 361 - **£816** - FF8 929
A Male Figure Standing Metal (H60cm H23in) Amsterdam 2000
- **$999** - €1 176 - **£705** - FF7 713
Ohne Titel Aquarell, Gouache/Karton (25x33.5cm 9x13in) Berlin 2001
- **$340** - €383 - **£234** - FF2 515
Tigerkopf Farblithographie (90x64cm 35x25in) Satow 2000

PENCZ Georg 1500-1550 **[157]**
- **$328** - €383 - **£231** - FF2 515
Die Triumphe des Petrarca Kupferstich (15x21cm 5x8in) Berlin 2001

P

PENDER Jack 1918-1998 **[107]**

$414 - €401 - £260 - FF2 629
Mousehole Harbour Gaps Oil/paper (17x17cm 7x7in) Par, Cornwall 1999

PENDL Erwin 1875-1945 **[80]**

$1 692 - €1 817 - £1 155 - FF11 917
Auf der Freyung Aquarell/Papier (18.5x10cm 7x3in) Wien 2001

PENFIELD Edward 1866-1925 **[121]**

$3 500 - €3 240 - £2 142 - FF21 254
Earl postman delivering letter to young woman Gouache/board (30x74cm 12x29in) New-York 1999

$700 - €763 - £484 - FF5 003
«Harper's Spetember» Poster (33x46cm 13x18in) New-York 2001

PENFOLD Frank Crawford 1849-1920 **[14]**

$5 400 - €5 186 - £3 346 - FF34 016
Breton Women at Close of Day Oil/canvas (45x66cm 18x26in) Chicago IL 1999

$1 750 - €1 819 - £1 102 - FF11 931
Girl Visiting Black American Family Oil/canvas (10x15cm 3x5in) Batavia NY 2000

PENFOLD William XIX **[1]**

$10 000 - €9 516 - £6 255 - FF62 424
Still Life with a Basket of Fruit on a Table Oil/canvas (63x76cm 25x30in) New-York 1999

PENKOAT Pierre 1945 **[220]**

$397 - €427 - £266 - FF2 800
Sans titre Technique mixte (100x64cm 39x25in) Cannes 2000

$559 - €488 - £338 - FF3 200
La guitare Huile/toile/panneau (27x35cm 10x13in) Paris 1998

$478 - €534 - £332 - FF3 500
Violon Gouache (33x26cm 12x10in) Paris 2001

PENLEY Aaron Edwin 1807-1870 **[65]**

$533 - €495 - £320 - FF3 244
A mountainous river Landscape with a Figure carrying washing Watercolour (20.5x48cm 8x18in) London 1999

PENLEY Edwin Aaron 1830-1900 **[19]**

$502 - €486 - £310 - FF3 190
Lakeland Landscapes Watercolour/paper (11x31cm 4x12in) Kirkby-Lonsdale, Cumbria 1999

PENN Irving 1917 **[395]**

$8 000 - €7 483 - £4 836 - FF49 084
Camel Pack, New York Platinum, palladium print (75.5x57cm 29x22in) New-York 1999

PENNACHINI Domenico 1860-1910 **[16]**

$16 000 - €17 761 - £11 153 - FF116 504
«Classical Maidens» Oil/canvas (54.5x89.5cm 21x35in) New-York 2001

$17 265 - €16 180 - £10 681 - FF106 135
Companions Oil/canvas (46x26cm 18x10in) Melbourne 1999

$1 200 - €1 399 - £841 - FF9 176
The Shepherd's Flirtation Watercolour/paper (53x36cm 21x14in) Cleveland OH 2000

PENNASILICO Giuseppe 1861-1940 **[42]**

$2 000 - €2 073 - £1 200 - FF13 600
Ritratto di bambina Olio/tela (46x36cm 18x14in) Milano 2000

$1 600 - €1 659 - £960 - FF10 880
Figure nel paesaggio Olio/legno (23x30cm 9x11in) Roma 1999

PENNE de Olivier Charles 1831-1897 **[203]**

$7 019 - €7 013 - £4 388 - FF46 000
Trois chiens au terrier Huile/toile (47x68cm 18x26in) Soissons 1999

$4 403 - €4 955 - £3 032 - FF32 500
Hallali sur pied Huile/panneau (27x35cm 10x13in) Soissons 2000

$1 269 - €1 403 - £880 - FF9 200
Diligence attaquée par les loups Aquarelle, gouache/papier (12x20cm 4x7in) Paris 2001

$670 - €640 - £422 - FF4 200
Le rendez-vous/L'hallali, série Chasse à courre Lithographie couleurs (40x63cm 15x24in) Deauville 1999

PENNELL Harry 1879-1934 **[23]**

$2 363 - €2 294 - £1 500 - FF15 046
A Sussex Cornfield Oil/canvas (41x61cm 16x24in) West-Yorshire 1999

PENNELL Joseph 1860-1926 **[288]**

$8 000 - €9 408 - £5 756 - FF61 715
«Gray Day» Oil/canvas/board (30x40cm 12x16in) Hatfield PA 2001

$1 900 - €1 825 - £1 177 - FF11 968
Street View, London/View of the Statue of St.Paul Crayon (30.5x23.5cm 12x9in) New-York 1999

$381 - €409 - £255 - FF2 683
View on the Spree, Berlin Lithographie (50.5x65.3cm 19x25in) Hamburg 2000

PENNI Giovanni Francesco 1488-1528 **[3]**

$14 400 - €12 440 - £9 600 - FF81 600
San Giovanni Battista Olio/tavola (105x84cm 41x33in) Roma 1998

PENNI Luca c.1500-1556 **[3]**

$6 750 - €6 997 - £4 050 - FF45 900
Cristo e la Samaritana Olio/tavola (84x62cm 33x24in) Venezia 2000

PENNIMAN John Rilto 1782-1841 **[2]**

$4 750 - €4 978 - £3 129 - FF32 656
Portrait's of Gentleman & Woman Oil/canvas (60x71cm 24x28in) Thomaston ME 2000

PENNINGTON Harper 1854-1920 **[3]**

$18 975 - €16 374 - £11 464 - FF107 406
Nocturne, dusky scene of a harbor at nightfall Oil/canvas (59x75cm 23x29in) Bethesda MD 1999

PENNINKS IL PENNITO Johannes 1627-c.1700 **[3]**

$7 019 - €6 868 - £4 500 - FF45 054
River Landscape with drovers crossing a Bridge by a fortified town Oil/canvas (80x108cm 31x42in) London 1999

PENNOYER Albert Shelton 1888-1957 **[24]**

$1 200 - €1 142 - £750 - FF7 490
Invitation Lane Oil/canvas (56x69cm 22x27in) New-York 1999

$500 - €472 - £310 - FF3 096
Poolside Pastel/paper (58x43cm 23x17in) Milford CT 1999

PENNY Edwin 1930 **[27]**

$737 - €743 - £460 - FF4 877
Wrens Watercolour (36.5x25cm 14x9in) London 2000

PENONE Giuseppe 1947 **[32]**

$21 045 - €25 029 - £15 000 - FF164 178
Soffio Terracotta (61.5x50x47cm 24x19x18in) London 2000

$1 647 - €1 531 - £1 000 - FF10 043
Study for «Soffio Polmonare» Watercolour/paper (25.5x36.5cm 10x14in) London 1998

〽️ **$809** - €869 - **£542** - FF5 701
 Il verde del bosco (das Grün des Waldes) Print
 (59.5x44.5cm 23x17in) Köln 2000

PÉNOT Albert Joseph c.1870-? [48]
 $1 082 - €915 - **£643** - FF6 000
 Élégante en bord de rivière Huile/panneau
 (22x13cm 8x5in) Auvers sur Oise 1998
 $437 - €488 - **£304** - FF3 200
 Piqueurs de four à Montbrison Fusain
 (36.5x48.5cm 14x19in) Paris 2001

PENOT J. Valette-Falgores 1710-c.1777 [19]
 $35 904 - €33 539 - **£22 154** - FF220 000
 Nature morte aux artichauts Huile/toile (40x49cm
 15x19in) Arcachon 1999
 $8 063 - €8 385 - **£5 093** - FF55 000
 Nature morte aux pêches, raisins et figues
 Huile/toile (36x43cm 14x16in) Toulouse 2000
 $2 130 - €2 287 - **£1 425** - FF15 000
 Paysage animé devant un ruisseau et une ruine
 Gouache/papier (33.5x43.5cm 13x17in) Toulouse 2000

PENROSE Roland 1900-1984 [23]
 $1 449 - €1 601 - **£1 004** - FF10 500
 Composition à l'oiseau Collage (27.5x21.5cm
 10x8in) Paris 2001
 $1 704 - €1 829 - **£1 140** - FF12 000
 Paul Éluard, Nusch, Lee Miller Photo (9.5x14.5cm
 3x5in) Paris 2000

PENSÉE Charles 1799-1871 [35]
 $315 - €351 - **£220** - FF2 300
 Paysage rocheux au cavalier Aquarelle/papier
 (24x33.5cm 9x13in) Neuilly-sur-Seine 2001
 $361 - €335 - **£216** - FF2 300
 Orleans, vue du quai Barentin Lithographie
 (37x50cm 14x19in) Orléans 1999

PENSON James 1814-1907 [4]
 $128 - €150 - **£90** - FF982
 St.Michael's Mount Watercolour/paper (22x33cm
 8x12in) Oxfordshire 2000

PENSTONE Constance 1865-1928 [14]
 $364 - €343 - **£220** - FF2 252
 Balston's Cottage, Kalk Bay Watercolour/paper
 (32x43cm 12x16in) Cape Town 1999

PENSTONE Edward XIX-XX [7]
 $794 - €877 - **£550** - FF5 755
 Children and a Lamb beside a Blossom Tree
 Watercolour (28.5x38.5cm 11x15in) London 2001

PEPIN Raoul XX [1]
 $4 500 - €5 040 - **£3 126** - FF33 062
 **Pausing the Futuristic Cadillac/Man and Woman
 in Cadillac** Watercolour, gouache/paper (40x50cm
 16x20in) New-York 2001

PEPINO Anton Josef 1863-1921 [3]
 $12 220 - €14 534 - **£8 727** - FF95 340
 Der Bildhauer Viktor Tilgner in seiner Werkstatt
 Oil/panel (48x70cm 18x27in) Wien 2000

PEPLOE Samuel John 1871-1935 [101]
 $51 926 - €61 028 - **£36 000** - FF400 320
 Lemons and Pottery Vase on a Draped Table
 Oil/canvas (38x46cm 14x18in) Edinburgh 2000
 $32 940 - €31 330 - **£20 000** - FF205 514
 Still Life with a Bowl of Fruit, Melon and Carafe
 Oil/canvas (33x39cm 12x15in) Edinburgh 1999
 $3 199 - €3 196 - **£2 000** - FF20 964
 Study of a Golden Haired Child Mixed
 media/paper (21.5x15cm 8x5in) Edinburgh 1999

PEPPER Beverly 1924 [43]
 $14 000 - €14 108 - **£8 727** - FF92 540
 Untitled Metal (H185.5cm H73in) New-York 2000
 $4 200 - €4 777 - **£2 934** - FF31 332
 «Lxv» Metal (65x39x14.5cm 25x15x5in) Beverly-Hills
 CA 2000

PEPPER Charles Hovey 1864-1950 [15]
 $3 500 - €3 996 - **£2 467** - FF26 214
 The Fillet of Gold Oil/canvas (62x43cm 24x16in)
 Boston MA 2001
 $2 000 - €2 073 - **£1 267** - FF13 596
 In the Woods Mixed media/paper (48x30cm 19x12in)
 Portsmouth NH 2000

PEPPER George Douglas 1903-1962 [26]
 $1 251 - €1 215 - **£782** - FF7 973
 Newfoundland Harbour Oil/board (40.5x51cm
 15x20in) Toronto 1999
 $953 - €916 - **£587** - FF6 011
 Autumn Ontario Oil/panel (30.5x35.5cm 12x13in)
 Vancouver, BC. 1999

PEPYN Marten 1575-1643 [12]
 $23 908 - €25 664 - **£16 000** - FF168 345
 **The Virgin and Child in a Paradise with Angels
 gathering Flowers** Oil/panel (50x96.5cm 19x37in)
 London 2000
 $2 264 - €2 100 - **£1 400** - FF13 772
 The Last Judgement Oil/copper (28x21cm 11x8in)
 London 1999

PÉRADON Pierre-Edmond 1893-1981 [55]
 $615 - €610 - **£373** - FF4 000
 Maison à Tilly sur Seulies Huile/panneau (46x65cm
 18x25in) Toulouse 2000
 $564 - €518 - **£346** - FF3 400
 Arromanches Huile/carton (19x27cm 7x10in) Paris
 1999

PÉRAIRE Paul Emmanuel 1829-1893 [44]
 $4 065 - €4 573 - **£2 799** - FF30 000
 Pêcheur au bord de l'eau Huile/toile (38x55cm
 14x21in) Barbizon 2000
 $1 220 - €1 201 - **£780** - FF7 880
 Paseo en barca Oleo/lienzo (27x52cm 10x20in)
 Madrid 1999

PERALTA DEL CAMPO Francisco 1837-1897 [13]
 $17 000 - €15 399 - **£10 171** - FF101 010
 Matador's Wedding Oil/canvas (40x69cm 16x27in)
 Fairfield ME 1998
 $3 850 - €3 304 - **£2 365** - FF21 670
 Galanteo Oleo/tabla (33x21cm 12x8in) Madrid 1998

PERALTA Pedro 1961 [5]
 $500 - €554 - **£335** - FF3 637
 La visita al Monolito Acrilico (47x61cm 18x24in)
 Montevideo 2000

PÉRAUT R. XX [1]
 $2 512 - €2 439 - **£1 552** - FF16 000
 Vue de Kouba, Alger/Le port d'Alger Huile/toile
 (24x32cm 9x12in) Paris 1999

PERAZA Humberto 1925 [18]
 $2 000 - €1 872 - **£1 239** - FF12 280
 Manolete Bronze (H71cm H28in) Norwalk CT 1999

PERBANDT von Carl 1832-1911 [12]
 $4 000 - €4 294 - **£2 676** - FF28 164
 A River Landscape Oil/canvas (76x127cm 29x50in)
 San-Francisco CA 2000

PERBOYRE Paul Emile Léon 1851-1929 **[81]**

🕊 **$2 558** - €2 434 - **£1 600** - FF15 968
Ambush Franco Prussian War Oil/panel (36x44.5cm 14x17in) Channel-Islands 1999

🕊 **$791** - €888 - **£550** - FF5 824
French artillery Officers conversing Oil/panel (23x18cm 9x7in) London 2001

PERCEVAL de Jesús 1916 **[10]**

🕊 **$1 152** - €963 - **£688** - FF6 320
Maria de los remedios Oleo/tabla (32x25cm 12x9in) Madrid 1998

PERCEVAL Don 1908-1979 **[2]**

🕊 **$12 000** - €11 414 - **£7 286** - FF74 868
Horses of Santa Domingo Oil/canvas/board (51x61.5cm 20x24in) Beverly-Hills CA 1999

PERCEVAL John de Burgh 1923-2000 **[207]**

🕊 **$9 656** - €10 951 - **£6 802** - FF71 834
Billabong in Spring Oil/hardboard (46x61cm 18x24in) Sydney 2001

🕊 **$4 967** - €5 460 - **£3 183** - FF35 815
Murrumbeena Oil/wood (31x36.5cm 12x14in) Melbourne 2000

🖌 **$875** - €965 - **£582** - FF6 328
Teapot with Teapot Face Ceramic (H23cm H9in) Melbourne 2000

🖊 **$1 158** - €1 001 - **£699** - FF6 564
On the Road to Whittlesea Pastel (26.5x27.5cm 10x10in) Malvern, Victoria 1998

PERCEVAL Matthew 1945 **[36]**

🕊 **$739** - €697 - **£466** - FF4 575
Fishing Boat in Bamboo Oil/canvas (67x75cm 26x29in) Sydney 1999

PERCIER Charles 1764-1838 **[49]**

🖊 **$5 128** - €6 098 - **£3 532** - FF40 000
Étude d'une console à figure égyptienne et ceinture en bronze Aquarelle (19x35.5cm 7x13in) Paris 2000

PERCY Arthur Carlson 1886-1976 **[95]**

🕊 **$882** - €940 - **£598** - FF6 169
Trädgård med blå stege Oil/panel (60x40cm 23x15in) Stockholm 2001

🕊 **$920** - €1 000 - **£582** - FF6 557
Passiflora Oil/canvas (46x26.5cm 18x10in) Stockholm 2000

PERCY Herbert Sidney XIX **[20]**

🕊 **$1 100** - €1 114 - **£690** - FF7 310
Untitled Oil/panel (35x25cm 14x10in) Detroit MI 2000

🖊 **$298** - €321 - **£200** - FF2 104
Cattle, Geese and Peasant Girl on the Bank of a River Watercolour (35x50cm 13x19in) Billingshurst, West-Sussex 2000

PERCY Samuel 1750-1820 **[3]**

🕊 **$7 910** - €8 414 - **£5 000** - FF55 190
England expects every Man to do his Study Mixed media (87x80cm 34x31in) London 2000

PERCY Sidney Richard 1821-1886 **[249]**

🕊 **$37 042** - €43 063 - **£26 000** - FF282 474
Children playing in a Landscape Oil/canvas (90x151cm 35x59in) London 2001

🕊 **$32 222** - €32 048 - **£20 000** - FF210 224
On the Hill, North Wales Oil/canvas (81x119.5cm 31x47in) London 1999

🕊 **$9 639** - €9 282 - **£6 000** - FF60 888
The Ponway, Trefew, North Wales Oil/canvas (25.5x38cm 10x14in) London 1999

📷 **$11 763** - €13 720 - **£8 253** - FF90 000
Cahiers d'écoliers Tirage papier salé (21.5x17cm 8x6in) Paris 2001

PERDOMO Felix 1956 **[30]**

🕊 **$5 000** - €4 865 - **£3 077** - FF31 911
Sin título Oil/canvas (155x123cm 61x48in) New-York 1999

PEREDA Francisco XIX-XX **[1]**

🕊 **$4 030** - €3 904 - **£2 535** - FF25 610
Personajes goyescos a la puerta de la taberna Oleo/lienzo (67x50cm 26x19in) Madrid 1999

PEREDA Raimondo 1840-1915 **[4]**

🗿 **$20 000** - €22 716 - **£14 034** - FF149 008
Young Nubian Marble (H40.5cm H15in) New-York 2001

PEREDA Y SALGADO de Antonio 1608/1611-1678 **[10]**

🕊 **$25 500** - €30 032 - **£17 500** - FF197 000
Cristo crucificado Oleo/lienzo (183x119cm 72x46in) Madrid 2000

PEREHUDOFF William 1919 **[33]**

🖼 **$272** - €260 - **£170** - FF1 706
Tanagra #1, #2, #3 Silkscreen in colors (57x74cm 22x29in) Toronto 1999

PEREIRA Ezequiel 1868-1943 **[6]**

🕊 **$26 840** - €30 409 - **£18 300** - FF199 470
Pedrozas, paisagem nortenha Huile/bois (49.5x70cm 19x27in) Lisboa 2000

🕊 **$4 515** - €5 234 - **£3 150** - FF34 335
Arcos de Valdevez Oleo/tabla (12.5x20cm 4x7in) Lisboa 2001

PEREIRA Irene Rice 1907-1971 **[39]**

🕊 **$2 900** - €3 365 - **£2 002** - FF22 071
Then Sundrenched Burning Sea, from The Union of Fire and Water Oil/canvas (127x91.5cm 50x36in) New-York 2000

🖊 **$1 100** - €1 138 - **£695** - FF7 462
Gemini Gouache (89x61cm 35x24in) New-York 2000

PÉRELLE Adam 1638-1695 **[11]**

🖊 **$5 303** - €5 190 - **£3 400** - FF34 041
View of the Roman Forum, with Shepherds and their Flocks Ink (30x26.5cm 11x10in) London 1999

🖼 **$962** - €932 - **£600** - FF6 113
Diverses vues de Chantilly/Vues des belles maisons de France Etching (38x28.5cm 14x11in) London 1999

PERELLI Achille 1822-1891 **[18]**

🖊 **$4 300** - €4 506 - **£2 723** - FF29 556
Nature morte of a Green-Winged Teal Watercolour/paper (55x43cm 22x17in) New-Orleans LA 2000

PERESS Gilles 1946 **[2]**

📷 **$3 000** - €3 407 - **£2 105** - FF22 351
French Peasants Gelatin silver print (15.5x23cm 6x9in) New-York 2001

PERETTI Achille 1857/62-1923 **[6]**

🕊 **$2 250** - €2 589 - **£1 551** - FF16 986
New Orleans Tree-Lined Avenue Oil/canvas (22x29cm 9x11in) New-Orleans LA 2000

PÉREZ Alfonso 1881-1914 **[13]**

🕊 **$4 309** - €5 031 - **£3 049** - FF33 000
Le marché aux poissons Huile/toile (40.5x32.5cm 15x12in) Paris 2001

PEREZ Augusto 1929 **[13]**
$2 750 - €2 308 - **£1 613** - FF15 137
Seated Man Bronze (H39cm H15in) New-York 1998

PEREZ BARRADAS Rafael 1890-1929 **[50]**
$714 - €767 - **£478** - FF5 030
Frau mit Hut Öl/Karton (31x24cm 12x9in) Bremen 2000
$4 000 - €4 160 - **£2 525** - FF27 286
Hospitalet Acuarela/papel (47x42cm 18x16in) Montevideo 2000

PÉREZ Bartolomé 1634-1693 **[23]**
$17 550 - €19 521 - **£11 375** - FF128 050
Guirnalda de flores con la Adoración de los Pastores Oleo/lienzo (44.5x55.5cm 17x21in) Madrid 2000

PEREZ Dick XX **[3]**
$4 500 - €4 262 - **£2 736** - FF27 954
Christy Mathewson Watercolour/paper (35x25cm 13x9in) New-York 1999

PEREZ GABRIELLI Cristina 1952 **[23]**
$510 - €511 - **£314** - FF3 349
Encinas Oleo/lienzo (27x22cm 10x8in) Madrid 2000

PEREZ GIL José 1918-1998 **[12]**
$7 840 - €8 409 - **£5 180** - FF55 160
Calpe e Ifach Oleo/lienzo (120x130cm 47x51in) Madrid 2000

PEREZ RUBIO Timoteo 1896-1977 **[7]**
$3 550 - €3 003 - **£2 150** - FF19 700
Paisaje con árboles Oleo/cartón (36x43cm 14x16in) Madrid 1998

PEREZ VILLAAMIL Genaro 1807-1854 **[95]**
$270 000 - €300 325 - **£190 000** - FF1 970 000
Día de procesión en un pueblo español Oleo/lienzo (108x145cm 42x57in) Madrid 2001
$25 403 - €27 268 - **£17 000** - FF178 867
Tarde de Verano en el Lago Oil/panel (53.5x76.5cm 21x30in) London 2000
$4 860 - €5 406 - **£3 150** - FF35 460
Paisaje con barcos y ruinas Oleo/cobre (25.5x35cm 10x13in) Madrid 2000
$2 565 - €2 703 - **£1 620** - FF17 730
Interior de una iglesia Gouache (22x27cm 8x10in) Madrid 2000
$198 - €216 - **£136** - FF1 418
Escalera del Hospital de Sandra Crúz, Toledo Litografía (34.5x38cm 13x14in) Madrid 2001

PEREZ VILLALTA Guillermo 1948 **[41]**
$18 900 - €21 023 - **£12 950** - FF137 900
Visitación Oleo/lienzo (223x180cm 87x70in) Madrid 2001
$4 030 - €3 904 - **£2 470** - FF25 610
Balancing-Balancek Técnica mixta (66x72.5cm 25x28in) Madrid 1999
$249 - €288 - **£177** - FF1 891
Sin título Litografía (55x74.5cm 21x29in) Madrid 2001

PEREZZOLI Francesco ?-1772 **[2]**
$3 200 - €4 147 - **£2 400** - FF27 200
Adorazione dei pastori Olio/tela (58x73cm 22x28in) Roma 2001

PERGOLA Romolo 1890-1960 **[2]**
$4 200 - €3 628 - **£2 100** - FF23 800
La cariola Olio/tela (50x30cm 19x11in) Genova 1999

PERGOLESI Michelangelo XVIII **[2]**
$1 119 - €1 078 - **£700** - FF7 070
Architectural and Ornamental Designs Etching (39.5x54.5cm 15x21in) London 1999

PERI Lucien 1880-1948 **[46]**
$726 - €686 - **£451** - FF4 500
Le maquis de Pinarelo, Corse Huile/carton (89x129cm 35x50in) Neuilly-sur-Seine 1999
$484 - €488 - **£301** - FF3 200
Campo dell'Oro, le pont Aquarelle/papier (27.5x47.5cm 10x18in) Paris 2000
$604 - €686 - **£419** - FF4 500
«Cannes, Côte d'Azur» Affiche (100x63cm 39x24in) Paris 2001

PERICOLI Tullio 1936 **[19]**
$1 300 - €1 348 - **£780** - FF8 840
Ritratto di Pasolini Inchiostro/carta (38.5x58cm 15x22in) Milano 1999

PERIES Ivan 1921-1988 **[7]**
$6 368 - €6 167 - **£4 000** - FF40 450
Two Figures seated Oil/canvas (61x71cm 24x27in) London 1999

PERIGAL Arthur 1816-1884 **[76]**
$4 673 - €4 181 - **£2 868** - FF27 424
«Loch Lomond Side» Oil/canvas (45.5x69cm 17x27in) Perthshire 1998
$1 093 - €1 165 - **£720** - FF7 639
At Inistrymik, Scottish Landscape with Cattle Beside a Loch Oil/board (27x43.5cm 10x17in) West-Midlands 2000
$516 - €577 - **£350** - FF3 784
Fisherman on a River Watercolour/paper (22x28cm 8x11in) Edinburgh 2000

PERIGNON Alexis Joseph 1806-1882 **[7]**
$12 240 - €13 720 - **£8 523** - FF90 000
Femme en vert Huile/toile (92.5x73cm 36x28in) Paris 2001

PERIGNON Alexis N. le jeune 1785-1864 **[8]**
$4 569 - €4 269 - **£2 844** - FF28 000
L'abandon Huile/toile (81x65cm 31x25in) Cherbourg 1999

PERIGNON Alexis Nicolas 1726-1782 **[52]**
$1 452 - €1 227 - **£863** - FF8 050
Un moulin à eau Craies (10.5x17cm 4x6in) Monte-Carlo 1998
$66 - €79 - **£46** - FF516
Vue de la ville de Berne prise de la terrasse Kupferstich (14.8x22.4cm 5x8in) Bern 2000

PERILLI Achille 1927 **[223]**
$7 500 - €6 479 - **£5 000** - FF42 500
Inventario delle mirabilie Olio/tela (162x130cm 63x51in) Prato 1998
$3 300 - €3 421 - **£1 980** - FF22 440
«Interact» Olio/tela (81x65cm 31x25in) Milano 2001
$1 750 - €1 814 - **£1 050** - FF11 900
Lo spazio della víttima Tecnica mista/tela (30x40cm 11x15in) Prato 1999
$1 500 - €1 555 - **£900** - FF10 500
Senza título Tecnica mista/carta (70x100cm 27x39in) Roma 2001
$63 - €70 - **£43** - FF462
Composizione Aquatint in colors (57x50cm 22x19in) Zürich 2000

PERIN Alphonse Henri 1798-1874 **[13]**
$513 - €1 524 - **£943** - FF10 000
Portrait de femme assise coiffée d'un bonnet Mine plomb (24x18.5cm 9x7in) Paris 2000

PERIN Marcel XX **[3]**
- **$4 051** – €4 726 – **£2 817** – FF31 000
  Vue d'une villa dans le sud de l'Italie
  Aquarelle/papier (29x44cm 11x17in) Nice 2000

PÉRIN-SALBREUX Lié Louis 1753-1817 **[24]**
- **$4 680** – €4 421 – **£2 830** – FF29 000
  Portrait de Gabriel Charles de Calmesne
  Huile/toile (81.5x65.5cm 32x25in) Paris 1999

PERINO DEL VAGA Pietro Buonaccorsi 1500/01-1547 **[17]**
- **$55 000** – €48 244 – **£33 396** – FF316 459
  The Back of a Nude and Two Studies/Nude Seen from Behind Chalks (28x19cm 11x7in) New-York 1999

PERIS BRELL Julio 1866-1944 **[7]**
- **$2 030** – €2 102 – **£1 295** – FF13 790
  Fachada de la Catedral de Valencia Oleo/tabla (16x22cm 6x8in) Madrid 2000

PERIS MARCO Vicente 1943 **[4]**
- **$5 940** – €6 607 – **£3 960** – FF43 340
  Arlequín Oleo/lienzo (145.5x114cm 57x44in) Madrid 2000

PERKINS David J. 1936 **[19]**
- **$2 140** – €2 495 – **£1 500** – FF16 369
  Blue and Yellow Macaw Oil/canvas (76x66cm 29x25in) London 2000

PERKINS Grandville 1830-1895 **[50]**
- **$4 600** – €5 126 – **£3 094** – FF33 626
  The Delaware Water Gap Oil/canvas (34x53cm 13x21in) East-Moriches NY 2000
- **$4 500** – €3 839 – **£2 709** – FF25 185
  Sailboat, tugboat and Paddlewheel Boat Cliffside Harbor view Oil/canvas (30x45cm 12x18in) Norwalk CT 1999
- **$1 200** – €1 104 – **£720** – FF7 244
  Sailbaots near Rocky Shore, Dinghy with Figures Watercolour/paper (25x68cm 10x27in) Morris-Plains NJ 1999

PERKINS, THE BEARDSLEY LIMNER Sarah 1771-1831 **[2]**
- **$48 000** – €51 262 – **£32 707** – FF336 254
  Portrait of Joseph Wheeler Oil/canvas (114x76cm 45x30in) New-York 2001
- **$2 500** – €2 670 – **£1 703** – FF17 513
  Portrait of an Older Woman Pastel/paper (46.5x39.5cm 18x15in) New-York 2001

PERKO Anton 1833-1905 **[16]**
- **$578** – €654 – **£390** – FF4 290
  Das Flaggschiff Ferdinand Max vor Brioni Aquarell/Papier (16x23cm 6x9in) Wien 2000

PERL Karl 1876-? **[11]**
- **$871** – €915 – **£589** – FF6 000
  Femme nue, bras écartés Bronze (H43cm H16in) Vendôme 2001

PERLBERG Christian 1806-1884 **[4]**
- **$2 994** – €3 374 – **£2 073** – FF22 135
  Aufbruch zur Falkenjagd Oil/panel (43x29cm 16x11in) Berlin 2000

PERLBERG Friedrich 1848-1921 **[73]**
- **$18 239** – €16 911 – **£11 000** – FF110 931
  Mosques in Cairo Oil/canvas (150x101cm 59x39in) London 1999
- **$523** – €562 – **£350** – FF3 689
  Araberlager mit Schimmel Öl/Leinwand (60x90cm 23x35in) München 2000

PERLBERG Georg 1807-1884 **[9]**
- **$540** – €613 – **£375** – FF4 024
  «Ansicht von Oberburg in Österreich» Aquarell/Papier (29.5x39cm 11x15in) Berlin 2001

PERLET Aimée XIX **[2]**
- **$9 712** – €9 429 – **£6 000** – FF61 852
  Marie Clémence Isaure Boissy d'Anglas, Vicomtesse de Nisas Miniature (14.5x12cm 5x4in) London 1999

PERLIN Bernard 1918 **[14]**
- **$180 000** – €172 073 – **£112 824** – FF1 128 726
  Vacant Lots Tempera/panel (61x76cm 24x29in) New-York 1999
- **$700** – €795 – **£479** – FF5 213
  Father Coughlin speaking Lithograph (30.5x36cm 12x14in) New-York 2000

PERLMAN Herman 1904 **[1]**
- **$1 500** – €1 717 – **£1 031** – FF11 260
  Blonde Crazy Ink (36x39cm 14x15in) New-York 2000

PERLMUTTER Isaac 1866-1932 **[9]**
- **$4 290** – €4 875 – **£2 990** – FF31 980
  Fonte des neiges Huile/toile (63x75cm 24x29in) Budapest 2001
- **$300** – €303 – **£872** – **£2 300** – FF25 400
  Autumn Street Oil/board (22x12.5cm 8x4in) Budapest 2000

PERLROTT-CSABA Vilmos 1880-1955 **[24]**
- **$9 600** – €9 440 – **£6 000** – FF61 920
  View of a Town in Szepes County Oil/canvas (41.5x54cm 16x21in) Budapest 1999
- **$2 405** – €2 527 – **£1 495** – FF16 575
  Jardin printanier de Szentendren Tempera/papier (61x86cm 24x33in) Budapest 2000

PERMAN Louisa Ellen 1854-1921 **[17]**
- **$3 952** – €3 760 – **£2 400** – FF24 661
  Still Life with pink Roses in a Vase Oil/canvas (61x30.5cm 24x12in) Edinburgh 1999
- **$4 170** – €4 203 – **£2 600** – FF27 569
  Pink and Red Roses in a Vase Oil/canvas (40.5x35.5cm 15x13in) London 2000

PERMEKE Constant 1886-1952 **[320]**
- **$42 611** – €35 442 – **£25 019** – FF232 484
  «Het kiren» Oil/canvas (100x120cm 39x47in) Amsterdam 1998
- **$11 500** – €11 344 – **£7 082** – FF74 415
  Koeien Oil/canvas (49x79.5cm 19x31in) Amsterdam 1999
- **$3 726** – €4 462 – **£2 556** – FF29 268
  Vlaamse vlakte (plaine flamande) Huile/toile/car-ton (29x36cm 11x14in) Antwerpen 2000
- **$6 739** – €5 701 – **£4 002** – FF37 398
  Liggend naakt Bronze (49x22cm 19x8in) Lokeren 1998
- **$6 032** – €6 445 – **£4 108** – FF42 276
  Profiel van een vrouw Fusain/papier (51x40cm 20x15in) Lokeren 2001

PERMEKE Hendrick Lodewijk 1849-1912 **[13]**
- **$782** – €843 – **£523** – FF5 528
  Après la pluie, vient le beau temps Huile/panneau (30x54cm 11x21in) Antwerpen 2000

$752 - €892 - **£547** - FF5 853
Barques de pêches amarrées au bord de la rivière Huile/panneau (22x41cm 8x16in) Antwerpen 2001

PERMEKE Paul 1918-1990 **[216]**
$2 178 - €2 231 - **£1 377** - FF14 634
Village en hiver Huile/toile (100x120cm 39x47in) Bruxelles 2000
$1 003 - €1 091 - **£660** - FF7 154
Clown Oil/canvas (50x40cm 19x15in) Lokeren 2000
$422 - €496 - **£300** - FF3 252
Paysage à la ferme Huile/carton (30x40cm 11x15in) Antwerpen 2000

PERNES Léo ?-1960 **[30]**
$654 - €717 - **£454** - FF4 700
Marine Concarneau Huile/toile (38x46cm 14x18in) Brest 2001

PERNES Michel 1943 **[4]**
$1 987 - €1 829 - **£1 192** - FF12 000
Le Val 3 Huile/toile (41x33cm 16x12in) Chantilly 1999

PERNET Alexandre J. Henry 1763-? **[45]**
$3 461 - €3 170 - **£2 109** - FF20 794
Gotische Kapellenruine im Wasser versunken Öl/Leinwand (33x40cm 12x15in) Berlin 1999
$6 239 - €6 105 - **£4 000** - FF40 048
A Capriccio with Roman Figures by a ruined Temple Watercolour (55x40.5cm 21x15in) London 1999

PERNET Percival 1890-1977 **[10]**
$1 424 - €1 656 - **£1 000** - FF10 864
«Championnat du monde» Poster (100x65cm 39x25in) London 2001

PERNHART Marcus 1824-1871 **[5]**
$2 758 - €3 270 - **£1 948** - FF21 451
St. Ruprecht bei Klagenfurt Boxer Öl/Leinwand (29x33.5cm 11x13in) Klagenfurt 2000

PERNOT François Alexandre 1793-1865 **[37]**
$118 - €137 - **£83** - FF900
La ferme Pierre noire/papier (14.5x21cm 5x8in) Paris 2001

PÉRON Pierre 1905-1988 **[62]**
$134 - €145 - **£90** - FF950
Brets - Le château vu de Recouvrance Gravure (17x22cm 6x8in) Douarnenez 2000

PÉRON René 1904-1972 **[77]**
$600 - €664 - **£406** - FF4 358
«Pilote du Diable» Poster (119x160cm 47x63in) New-York 2000

PÉROT Roger 1908-1976 **[27]**
$448 - €534 - **£319** - FF3 500
«Corset le Furet, le rêve de la femme» Affiche (138x98cm 54x38in) Orléans 2000

PEROUX Joseph Nicolaus 1771-1849 **[6]**
$1 876 - €2 058 - **£1 274** - FF13 500
Portrait d'homme/Portrait de femme Huile/toile (24.5x20.5cm 9x8in) Lille 2000

PEROW Wassili Grigoriev. 1834-1882 **[9]**
$2 406 - €2 180 - **£1 482** - FF14 301
Portrait eines bärtigen Mannes Aquarell/Papier (31.5x23.5cm 12x9in) Wien 1999

PERRACHON André 1827-1909 **[25]**
$29 100 - €29 575 - **£18 294** - FF194 000
Chez la marchande de fleurs Huile/toile (120x172cm 47x67in) Lyon 2000

$4 968 - €4 573 - **£2 982** - FF30 000
Bouquet de roses et carafe Huile/toile (44x37cm 17x14in) Lyon 1999
$2 852 - €3 049 - **£1 942** - FF20 000
Bouquet de roses Huile/toile (21x26cm 8x10in) Lyon 1999

PERRAULT Henry 1867-1932 **[6]**
$6 208 - €5 946 - **£3 825** - FF39 000
Jeune fille lisant sur les remparts de Granville Huile/toile (88x117cm 34x46in) Calais 1999

PERRAULT Léon Jean Basile 1832-1908 **[56]**
$60 000 - €57 012 - **£36 504** - FF373 974
Love and Innocence Oil/canvas (142x113cm 55x44in) New-York 1999
$24 000 - €20 315 - **£14 366** - FF133 260
Teasing the Baby Oil/canvas (53x66cm 20x25in) New-York 1998

PERRAULT Marie XIX **[2]**
$3 800 - €4 443 - **£2 670** - FF29 141
«Evening» Woodcut in colors (39.5x31.5cm 15x12in) New-York 2000

PERRAULT-HARRY Émile 1878-1938 **[9]**
$2 847 - €3 029 - **£1 800** - FF19 868
Polar Bear Bronze (44.5x24cm 17x9in) London 2000

PERREN-BARBERINI XX **[7]**
$1 043 - €945 - **£650** - FF6 198
«Zermatt» Poster (102x65cm 40x25in) London 1999

PERRET Aimé 1847-1927 **[60]**
$4 140 - €4 573 - **£2 871** - FF30 000
Scène de moisson Huile/toile (47x56cm 18x22in) Paris 2001
$580 - €610 - **£382** - FF4 000
Paysage au faucheur Huile/toile (32.5x41cm 12x16in) Paris 2000

PERRET Henri François c.1825-? **[17]**
$1 136 - €1 220 - **£760** - FF8 000
Les lavandières au fleuve au couchant Huile/toile (49x65cm 19x25in) La Varenne-Saint-Hilaire 2000
$1 986 - €1 982 - **£1 240** - FF13 000
Coucher de soleil sur la mare Huile/panneau (26x45cm 10x17in) Fontainebleau 1999

PERRETT Galen Joseph 1875-1949 **[2]**
$4 323 - €4 030 - **£2 667** - FF26 434
Kvinna vid marmorbassäng Oil/canvas (76.5x50.5cm 30x19in) Stockholm 1999

PERRETT John Douglas 1859-1937 **[9]**
$1 758 - €2 066 - **£1 248** - FF13 549
The Pink and White Terraces Pastel/paper (28.5x47cm 11x18in) Auckland 2000

PERRI Frank XX **[41]**
$450 - €523 - **£316** - FF3 429
Mexican Village Oil/canvas (76x101cm 30x40in) Cincinnati OH 2001

PERRIAND Charlotte 1903-1999 **[1]**
$40 000 - €42 936 - **£26 768** - FF281 640
Tunisie, Bookcase Metal (160x358x52.5cm 62x140x20in) New-York 2000

PERRIER Alexandre 1862-1936 **[17]**
$3 084 - €2 973 - **£1 901** - FF19 501
Le Salève Öl/Leinwand (45.5x65cm 17x25in) Bern 1999

PERRIER LE BOURGUIGNON François 1590-1650 [26]

🖎 **$30 000** - €26 315 - **£18 216** - FF172 614
Diana and Actaeon Oil/canvas (109x152.5cm 42x60in) New-York 1999

▥ **$535** - €486 - **£330** - FF3 185
Les statues antiques de Rome Gravure (9x12cm 3x4in) Montréal 1999

PERRIGARD Hal Ross 1891-1960 [50]

🖎 **$442** - €381 - **£263** - FF2 502
Quiet Winter Day Oil/panel (20x25.5cm 7x10in) Toronto 1998

PERRIN Charles Robert 1915 [2]

🖌 **$1 900** - €1 774 - **£1 172** - FF11 639
Looking toward Sankaty Head Watercolour/board (22x54cm 9x21in) Detroit MI 1999

PERRIN Gabriel XIX [6]

🖎 **$4 735** - €4 421 - **£2 868** - FF29 000
Gerbe de fleurs Huile/toile (46x73cm 18x28in) Orléans 1999

PERRIN Ida Southwell 1860-? [1]

🖎 **$9 249** - €10 746 - **£6 500** - FF70 491
«Bluebell Wood» Oil/canvas (101.5x71.5cm 39x28in) London 2001

PERRINE van Dearing 1868-1955 [10]

🖎 **$5 000** - €4 740 - **£3 123** - FF31 090
«Autumn» Oil/canvas (63.5x76cm 25x29in) Washington 1999

PERRON Charles Clément 1893-1958 [79]

🖎 **$1 111** - €1 067 - **£697** - FF7 000
La fenêtre Huile/carton (45.5x38cm 17x14in) Lyon 1999

🖎 **$648** - €762 - **£449** - FF5 000
Nature morte au pichet en Jersey et au miroir Huile/panneau (41x33cm 16x12in) Nantes 2000

🖌 **$234** - €259 - **£162** - FF1 700
Nu alangui Fusain (24x44cm 9x17in) Nantes 2001

PERRONEAU Jean-Baptiste 1715-1783 [28]

🖎 **$34 164** - €39 637 - **£24 310** - FF260 000
Portrait de Charles de Baschi, Marquis d'Aubaïs, Baron du Caïla Huile/toile (81x64cm 31x25in) Paris 2001

🖌 **$7 268** - €7 013 - **£4 563** - FF46 000
Portrait d'homme de trois-quarts en buste Pastel/papier (46x55cm 18x21in) Nîmes 1999

PERROT Ferdinand 1808-1841 [19]

🖎 **$3 328** - €3 354 - **£2 074** - FF22 000
Embarcations près de la côte Huile/toile (49x65cm 19x25in) Paris 2000

🖎 **$2 196** - €2 345 - **£1 500** - FF15 379
Children Playing on a Bridge Oil/canvas (27x45cm 10x17in) Billingshurst, West-Sussex 2001

PERROT Pierre Josse Joseph act.1724-1735 [2]

🖌 **$951** - €1 067 - **£665** - FF7 000
Projet d'arc de triomphe Encre (39.5x28cm 15x11in) Paris 2001

PERRY Adélaïde E. 1891-1973 [15]

🖎 **$1 938** - €1 644 - **£1 169** - FF10 786
Summer Morning Oil/canvas (51x61cm 20x24in) Sydney 1998

🖎 **$1 215** - €1 446 - **£841** - FF9 488
Seascape Oil/board (25x35cm 9x13in) Sydney 2000

PERRY Arthur W. XIX-XX [13]

🖌 **$524** - €500 - **£324** - FF3 277
Fishing Boat off the Coast Watercolour/paper (28x38cm 11x14in) Bury St. Edmunds, Suffolk 1999

PERRY Enoch Wood 1831-1915 [42]

🖎 **$4 000** - €4 258 - **£2 724** - FF27 932
Mother Nursing a Child in an Interior Oil/canvas/panel (44.5x57cm 17x22in) New-York 2001

🖎 **$6 200** - €6 866 - **£4 204** - FF45 039
Quilting Oil/canvas (38x33cm 15x13in) New-York 2000

PERRY Heather ?-1962 [3]

▥ **$957** - €1 050 - **£650** - FF6 888
«Australia M.C.C. at Lords» Poster (25x33cm 9x12in) London 2000

PERRY Lilla Cabot 1848-1933 [24]

🖎 **$9 000** - €8 596 - **£5 608** - FF56 385
Theatre Posters, Ikeo Oil/canvas (55x45cm 22x18in) Cambridge MA 1999

🖎 **$4 000** - €4 294 - **£2 725** - FF28 166
Pack, Monadnock from Handcock N.H. Oil/canvas/board (30.5x38cm 12x14in) Boston MA 2001

PERRY Roy 1936 [29]

🖎 **$527** - €565 - **£360** - FF3 704
The Thames at Lambeth Oil/board (31.5x52cm 12x20in) London 2001

🖌 **$204** - €174 - **£120** - FF1 142
Monday Morning, Farnham Gouache/paper (33x45.5cm 12x17in) Godalming, Surrey 1998

PERSCHEID Nicola 1864-1930 [18]

📷 **$376** - €409 - **£247** - FF2 683
Portrait des Sozialisten Karl Kautsky Gelatin silver print (24.7x19.8cm 9x7in) Hamburg 2000

PERSÉUS Edvard 1841-1890 [6]

🖎 **$451** - €500 - **£306** - FF3 278
Gustaf II Adolf Oil/panel (27x20cm 10x7in) Stockholm 2000

PERSICALLI Pietro 1886-? [1]

🖎 **$9 600** - €8 293 - **£4 800** - FF54 400
Chiaro di luna Olio/tela (62x62cm 24x24in) Prato 1999

PERSOGLIA von Franz 1852-1912 [25]

🖎 **$7 471** - €8 020 - **£5 000** - FF52 608
Flirtation Oil/canvas (58x80cm 22x31in) London 2000

🖎 **$2 812** - €3 085 - **£1 911** - FF20 237
En ung smuk kvinde beundrer en skulptur i en kunstners atelier Oil/panel (38x30cm 14x11in) København 2000

PERSON Henri 1876-1926 [63]

🖎 **$16 919** - €14 483 - **£10 184** - FF95 000
Le port de Toulon Huile/toile (73x91cm 28x35in) Paris 1998

🖎 **$2 305** - €2 134 - **£1 428** - FF14 000
Scène de rue Huile/panneau (33.5x41cm 13x16in) Paris 1999

🖌 **$1 176** - €1 296 - **£784** - FF8 500
Voiliers à quais Aquarelle/papier (25x40cm 9x15in) Deauville 2000

PERSON Ragnar 1905-1992 [366]

🖎 **$2 975** - €2 790 - **£1 840** - FF18 302
Femtioårs, kalaset Oil/canvas (46.5x55cm 18x21in) Stockholm 1999

🖎 **$1 065** - €1 267 - **£760** - FF8 314
Vid den gamla stenmuren - landskap i aftonrodnad Oil/canvas (33x41cm 12x16in) Stockholm 2000

▥ **$258** - €242 - **£155** - FF1 588
Utvandrarna Color lithograph (49x69cm 19x27in) Stockholm 1999

PERSSON Peter Adolf 1862-1914 **[58]**
- **$1 246** - €1 180 - **£773** - FF7 739
  Solbelyst vinterlandskap Oil/canvas (55x79cm 21x31in) Malmö 1999

PERUGINI Charles Edward 1839-1918 **[18]**
- **$23 028** - €19 343 - **£13 500** - FF126 879
  «I Know a Maiden fair to see, take care» Oil/board/canvas (56x55.5cm 22x21in) Billingshurst, West-Sussex 1998
- **$9 821** - €11 680 - **£7 000** - FF76 616
  Sideways Glance Oil/canvas (46.5x30.5cm 18x12in) London 2000
- **$8 398** - €7 896 - **£5 200** - FF51 795
  Kate Perugini nee Dickens, Head and Shoulders Watercolour (45x39cm 18x15in) Guildford, Surrey 1999

PERUGINI Kate, née Dickens 1839-1929 **[4]**
- **$151 758** - €176 168 - **£107 000** - FF1 155 589
  «Flossie» Oil/board (33.5x26cm 13x10in) London 2001

PERUGINO il Pietro Vannucci 1445/46-1523 **[2]**
- **$105 000** - €104 768 - **£63 913** - FF687 235
  Head of an Apostle Drawing (24x20cm 9x7in) New-York 2000

PERUZZI Osvaldo 1907 **[6]**
- **$1 280** - €1 659 - **£960** - FF10 880
  Aereopittura Tecnica mista/carta (21.5x28cm 8x11in) Milano 2000

PERUZZINI IL PERUGINO Antonio Francesco 1643/46-1724 **[21]**
- **$32 445** - €32 703 - **£20 250** - FF214 515
  Landschaft mit Figuren Öl/Leinwand (106x156cm 41x61in) Wien 2000
- **$24 000** - €25 631 - **£16 353** - FF168 127
  Mountainous Landscape/Wooded River Landscape Oil/canvas (100x76cm 39x29in) New-York 2001

PERZEL Jean 1892-1986 **[4]**
- **$4 144** - €3 659 - **£842** - FF24 000
  Lampe de bureau Métal (45x30cm 17x11in) Paris 1999

PESARO IL TROMETTA Nicoló Martinelli da c.1540-1610/15 **[3]**
- **$3 000** - €3 485 - **£2 108** - FF22 863
  Saint Jerome knelling Black chalk (24.5x18cm 9x7in) New-York 2001

PESCE Gaetano 1939 **[18]**
- **$18 239** - €21 692 - **£13 000** - FF142 287
  Golgotha Chair Sculpture (100x52x47cm 39x20x18in) London 2000
- **$7 996** - €7 700 - **£5 000** - FF50 506
  Study for the Vittel Bottle Competition Gouache (284x161cm 111x63in) London 1999

PESCE Jean 1926 **[90]**
- **$1 216** - €1 448 - **£842** - FF9 500
  Le Bateau rouge Huile/toile (50x61cm 19x24in) Albi 2000

PESCHERET Leon R. 1892-1961 **[12]**
- **$150** - €172 - **£103** - FF1 126
  New Orleans Patio Etching in colors (34x26cm 13x10in) Milwaukee WI 2000

PESCHKA Anton Emanuel 1885-1940 **[67]**
- **$5 559** - €6 177 - **£3 723** - FF40 519
  Krumau Öl/Leinwand (73.5x103cm 28x40in) Wien 2000

- **$850** - €945 - **£569** - FF6 197
  Laxenburger Allee Mischtechnik (48x33cm 18x12in) Linz 2000
- **$896** - €1 017 - **£628** - FF6 673
  «Rauhreif» Watercolour (34.5x50cm 13x19in) Wien 2001
- **$236** - €254 - **£158** - FF1 668
  Bächlein Woodcut (15x21cm 5x8in) Wien 2000

PESCHKE Christian 1946 **[42]**
- **$1 535** - €1 789 - **£1 075** - FF11 738
  Rote Pferde Oil/panel (61x81cm 24x31in) München 2000
- **$4 230** - €4 602 - **£2 789** - FF30 185
  Kruzifix Marble (H230cm H90in) Ahlden 2000

PESELLINO Francesco di Stefano c.1422-1457 **[3]**
- **$448 000** - €580 526 - **£336 000** - FF3 808 000
  Il trionfo della Fama, del Tempo e della Religione Tempera/tavola (42x176.5cm 16x69in) Firenze 2000

PESENTI Domenico 1843-1918 **[9]**
- **$5 503** - €5 165 - **£3 400** - FF33 883
  Figures in the Interior of an Art Gallery, Florence Oil/canvas (34.5x25.5cm 13x10in) Billingshurst, West-Sussex 1999
- **$2 750** - €2 851 - **£1 650** - FF18 700
  Il coro di S. Maria Novella a Firenze Acquarello/carta (60x39cm 23x15in) Prato 2000

PESKE Geza 1859-1934 **[20]**
- **$1 327** - €1 090 - **£771** - FF7 153
  Der kleine Schneeballwerfer Öl/Leinwand (100x75cm 39x29in) Wien 1998

PESKÉ Jean 1870-1949 **[389]**
- **$2 020** - €2 409 - **£1 441** - FF15 800
  Automne méditerranéen Huile/toile (80x175cm 31x68in) Paris 2000
- **$1 800** - €1 906 - **£1 191** - FF12 500
  Paysage provençal Huile/toile (73x54cm 28x21in) Belfort 2000
- **$1 340** - €1 143 - **£808** - FF7 500
  Nature morte aux fruits Huile/panneau (20x27.5cm 7x10in) Paris 1998
- **$524** - €488 - **£321** - FF3 200
  Notre-Dame-de-Paris, le pont des Arts Aquarelle/papier (18.5x29cm 7x11in) Honfleur 1998
- **$196** - €229 - **£140** - FF1 500
  Voiliers à quai/Voiliers dans un port Lithographie (25.5x34cm 10x13in) Paris 2001

PESNE Antoine 1683-1757 **[26]**
- **$9 454** - €10 737 - **£6 612** - FF70 431
  Maturin Veïyssière de la Croze, Prediger, Orientalist und Direktor Öl/Leinwand (101x76cm 39x29in) Berlin 1998
- **$7 056** - €6 132 - **£4 251** - FF40 225
  Selbstbildnis des Künstlers in seinem Atelier Black chalk (34x25.2cm 13x9in) Berlin 1998

PETER Axel 1863-1947 **[45]**
- **$330** - €372 - **£227** - FF2 438
  Porslinsskål med frukter och blad/Tallrik med frukter och blad Oil/canvas (36x46cm 14x18in) Uppsala 2000

PETER Emanuel Thomas 1799-1873 **[37]**
- **$3 594** - €3 432 - **£2 212** - FF22 515
  Hüftbildnis einer jungen Dame im weissen, schulterfreien Kleid Miniature (10.7x8.1cm 4x3in) Zürich 1999
- **$681** - €654 - **£427** - FF4 290
  Bildnis einer Dame in grünem Kleid Aquarell/Papier (22.3x17cm 8x6in) Wien 1999

P

PETER Johann Wenzel 1745-1829 **[14]**
🖼 **$18 912** - €19 056 - **£11 787** - FF125 000
Le chien à l'arrêt devant un faisan et perroquet
Huile/toile (92x118cm 36x46in) Paris 2000

PETER Richard, Sen. 1895-1977 **[4]**
📷 **$1 014** - €881 - **£611** - FF5 782
Oberleitungsbau Vintage gelatin silver print
(39.3x48.3cm 15x19in) Berlin 1998

PETER Victor 1840-1918 **[17]**
🐾 **$781** - €665 - **£466** - FF4 359
Lioness with Cubs Bronze (21x39x18cm 8x15x7in)
Amsterdam 1998

PETERDI Gabor 1915 **[44]**
▥ **$125** - €134 - **£83** - FF877
Red Eclipse Silkscreen (36x28cm 14x11in) Cleveland
OH 2000

PÉTERELLE Adolphe 1874-1947 **[116]**
🖼 **$1 094** - €1 220 - **£764** - FF8 000
Bateaux la nuit Huile/toile (50x72.5cm 19x28in) Paris
2001
🖼 **$508** - €579 - **£349** - FF3 800
Personnages en noir Huile/carton (41x24cm
16x9in) Paris 2000
✏ **$218** - €244 - **£153** - FF1 600
Femme debout Fusain/papier (29.5x17cm 11x6in)
Paris 2001

PETERMAN Daniel 1797-1871 **[2]**
✏ **$4 250** - €4 539 - **£2 895** - FF29 772
**Fraktur Birth Letter with Female Figures,
Flowers and Birds** Watercolour (33x40cm 12x15in)
New-York 2001

PETERS Anna 1843-1926 **[113]**
🖼 **$3 574** - €4 090 - **£2 458** - FF26 831
Feldblumenstrauss in bauchiger Vase
Öl/Leinwand (55.5x69.5cm 21x27in) München 2000
🖼 **$4 759** - €5 624 - **£3 373** - FF36 531
Herbststimmung Öl/Karton (24x30cm 9x11in)
Stuttgart 2000

PETERS Bernard E. 1893-? **[30]**
🖼 **$1 000** - €997 - **£624** - FF6 543
On Kaskaskia Island Oil/board (45x60cm 18x24in)
St. Louis MO 1999
🖼 **$450** - €504 - **£312** - FF3 306
Dockside Harbor Scene Oil/board (20x25cm
8x10in) St. Louis MO 2001

PETERS Carl William 1897-1980 **[51]**
🖼 **$4 000** - €4 151 - **£2 537** - FF27 226
Jack's Place Oil/canvas (51x61cm 20x24in) Boston
MA 2000

PETERS Charles Rollo 1862-1928 **[42]**
🖼 **$5 500** - €5 279 - **£3 447** - FF34 625
Nocturnal - Casa Lagunitas Oil/canvas (48x63cm
19x25in) Altadena CA 1999
🖼 **$3 250** - €2 901 - **£1 990** - FF19 032
House in Nocturnal Landscape Oil/canvas
(22x30cm 9x12in) Altadena CA 1999

PETERS Matthew William 1741/42-1814 **[22]**
🖼 **$25 000** - €21 569 - **£15 082** - FF141 482
Charmian and the Soothsayer Oil/canvas
(155x117cm 61x46in) New-York 1998
🖼 **$32 500** - €38 279 - **£22 477** - FF251 091
**Portrait of Lady Elizabeth Compton, Half-
Length, Wearing a White Dress** Oil/canvas
(76x63cm 29x24in) New-York 2000

PETERS Otto 1882-1952 **[4]**
🖼 **$5 054** - €5 696 - **£3 500** - FF37 362
The young Shepherd's Music Oil/canvas
(87.5x98cm 34x38in) London 2000

PETERS Pieter Francis 1818-1903 **[97]**
🖼 **$5 507** - €6 459 - **£3 930** - FF42 365
Château Freudensberg en Tyrol Huile/toile
(99x157cm 38x61in) Warszawa 2000
🖼 **$5 192** - €6 135 - **£3 680** - FF40 246
**Oberitalienischer See mit alter Burganlage auf
einem mächtigen Felsen** Öl/Leinwand (78x114cm
30x44in) Stuttgart 2000
🖼 **$2 872** - €2 812 - **£1 767** - FF18 446
Flusslandschaft im Mondschein Oil/panel
(23x31cm 9x12in) Stuttgart 1999
✏ **$717** - €613 - **£421** - FF4 021
Schloss Heuschlingen an der Jagst im Winter
Aquarell/Papier (21x13cm 8x5in) Stuttgart 1998

PETERS Pietronella 1848-1924 **[24]**
🖼 **$3 954** - €3 835 - **£2 505** - FF25 154
**Vier Kinder beim Milchtrinken am Tisch vor
dem Fenster** Öl/Leinwand/Karton (44.5x37cm
17x14in) München 2000
🖼 **$4 543** - €5 113 - **£3 130** - FF33 539
**Bunter Strauss aus Iris, tränenden Herzen und
Tulpen** Öl/Karton (24x16cm 9x6in) Stuttgart 2000

PETERS Udo 1884-1964 **[27]**
🖼 **$5 486** - €5 113 - **£3 385** - FF33 539
Spätsommer im Moor Öl/Karton (37x49cm
14x19in) Bremen 1999

PETERS Wilhelm Otto 1851-1935 **[17]**
🖼 **$2 964** - €3 355 - **£2 073** - FF22 010
Fransk gatesmug Oil/canvas (60x42cm 23x16in)
Oslo 2001

PETERSEN & HOLM Lorenz et Peter Ch. 1803/23-
1870/88 **[1]**
🖼 **$4 812** - €5 338 - **£3 200** - FF35 016
The Heligoland Brig Osten off Heligoland
Oil/canvas (47x64cm 18x25in) London 2000

PETERSEN Anna Sofie 1845-1910 **[8]**
🖼 **$4 003** - €4 602 - **£2 826** - FF30 185
Laternenumzug im Schnee Öl/Leinwand (60x80cm
23x31in) Bremen 2000

PETERSEN Armand 1891-1969 **[42]**
🐾 **$4 566** - €5 183 - **£3 172** - FF34 016
Le tigre marchant Bronze (10.5x33cm 4x12in)
Pontoise 2001

PETERSEN Carl Olof 1880-1939 **[11]**
▥ **$381** - €367 - **£238** - FF2 409
Angorakatzen Woodcut in colors (26.5x25cm 10x9in)
München 1999

PETERSEN Edvard Frederik 1841-1911 **[88]**
🖼 **$1 242** - €1 341 - **£858** - FF8 797
Sommerlandskab med graessende Oil/canvas
(88x132cm 34x51in) København 2001
🖼 **$1 506** - €1 608 - **£1 026** - FF10 548
Dansk sensommerlandskab med höstarbejdere
Oil/canvas (32x48cm 12x18in) Vejle 2001

PETERSEN Emanuel A. 1894-1948 **[289]**
🖼 **$912** - €1 006 - **£609** - FF6 597
**Motiv fra Grönland med tre personer der baerer
ved** Oil/canvas (47x40cm 18x15in) Vejle 2000
🖼 **$462** - €509 - **£308** - FF3 342
Grönlandsk fjordparti Oil/canvas (27x36cm
10x14in) Vejle 2000

PETERSEN Heinrich And. Sophus 1834-1916 **[6]**
$11 000 - €12 120 - **£7 338** - FF79 500
The Barque Talisman, Captain A.Baker, Master
Oil/canvas (58x86cm 23x34in) Portsmouth NH 2000

PETERSEN Jacob 1774-1855 **[33]**
$2 363 - €2 249 - **£1 500** - FF14 755
Frigates at Seas Oil/canvas (62.5x83cm 24x32in)
Billingshurst, West-Sussex 1999
$3 424 - €3 756 - **£2 326** - FF24 637
Skibsportræt af briggen Haekla Watercolour,
gouache/paper (50x67cm 19x26in) København 2000

PETERSEN Johan 1839-1874 **[3]**
$10 000 - €11 028 - **£6 772** - FF72 341
Quartering Breeze Oil/canvas (40.5x53.5cm
15x21in) New-York 2000

PETERSEN Julius Hans Henrik 1851-1911 **[32]**
$251 - €268 - **£171** - FF1 758
**Dansk sommerlandskab med dannebrog og
hvidmalt hus** Oil/canvas (61x100cm 24x39in) Vejle
2001

PETERSEN Lorenz 1803-1870 **[8]**
$1 825 - €2 045 - **£1 258** - FF13 415
Besegelter Dampfer Hermes vor Helgoland
Oil/canvas/panel (48x64cm 18x25in) Hamburg 2000

PETERSEN Roland 1926 **[25]**
$4 250 - €3 640 - **£2 509** - FF23 878
Thursday Afternoon Oil/canvas (122x125.5cm
48x49in) New-York 1999
$4 113 - €4 084 - **£2 570** - FF26 789
Man Contemplating Woman Acrylic/canvas
(87x122cm 34x48in) Amsterdam 1999

PETERSEN Sophus 1837-1904 **[34]**
$8 267 - €9 400 - **£5 775** - FF61 663
Opstilling med stentøjskande, rodvinspokal
Oil/canvas (55x47cm 21x18in) København 2000
$1 926 - €1 852 - **£1 188** - FF12 150
Rosor Oil/canvas (25x30cm 9x11in) Malmö 1999

PETERSEN Tom 1861-1926 **[93]**
$1 492 - €1 609 - **£1 017** - FF10 554
**Parti fra Kongens Nytorv med sporvogns-hol-
depladsen** Oil/canvas (40x45cm 15x17in) København
2001
$721 - €778 - **£491** - FF5 101
Agent Plougs gård ved Vesterport i Fåborg
Oil/canvas (41x35cm 16x13in) København 2001

PETERSEN Vilhelm Peter Carl 1812-1880 **[30]**
$5 888 - €5 382 - **£3 688** - FF35 304
Parti ved Sletten strand, solnedgang Oil/canvas
(68x94cm 26x37in) København 1999
$1 217 - €1 342 - **£824** - FF8 801
Strandparti med laue fyrretraeer Oil/canvas
(25x36cm 9x14in) Vejle 2000

PETERSEN-ANGELN Heinrich 1850-1906 **[14]**
$1 891 - €1 637 - **£1 140** - FF10 741
**Segelboote und ein Dreimaster, der von einem
Schlepper gezogen wird** Oil/panel (36x50cm
14x19in) München 1998

PETERSEN-FLENSBURG Heinrich 1861-1908 **[51]**
$847 - €726 - **£509** - FF4 761
**Segelboot auf einem Strand liegend,
Abendstimmung Nordsee** Öl/Karton (24.7x30cm
9x11in) Hamburg 1998
$1 432 - €1 227 - **£860** - FF8 047
Dorf Kampen auf Sylt Gouache/paper (33x50cm
12x19in) Hamburg 1998

PETERSON Jacob 1774-1854 **[1]**
$3 123 - €3 488 - **£2 000** - FF22 877
**Scooner Saucy Jak of Dundee, Captain John
Miller** Watercolour (47.5x65.5cm 18x25in) London
2000

PETERSON Jane Philipp 1876-1965 **[273]**
$6 500 - €7 070 - **£4 284** - FF46 373
Pink Dogwood Oil/canvas (76x101.5cm 29x39in)
Boston MA 2000
$4 500 - €5 380 - **£3 104** - FF35 289
House by the Water Oil/board (30x39cm 12x15in)
Milford CT 2000
$3 000 - €3 150 - **£2 028** - FF20 660
Church in late Fall setting Watercolour,
gouache/paper (58x43cm 23x17in) Fairfield ME 2001

PETERSON John Erik Christian 1839-1874 **[1]**
$7 500 - €7 213 - **£4 629** - FF47 311
The Constitution Oil/canvas (35.5x61cm 13x24in)
Boston MA 2000

PETERSON Roger Tory 1908-1996 **[11]**
$1 925 - €1 940 - **£1 200** - FF12 724
Pink Flamingos Watercolour/paper (40x62cm
15x24in) London 2000

PETERSSEN Eilif 1852-1928 **[25]**
$131 026 - €113 962 - **£78 988** - FF747 544
Fra Pantheon-plassen, Roma Oil/canvas
(161x204cm 63x80in) Oslo 1998
$6 510 - €7 741 - **£4 637** - FF50 778
Gammel kone i interior Oil/canvas (70x80cm
27x31in) Oslo 2000
$8 728 - €10 085 - **£6 112** - FF66 152
Fra Sandö Oil/canvas (36x44cm 14x17in) Oslo 2001

PETHER Abraham 1756-1812 **[22]**
$5 331 - €6 341 - **£3 800** - FF41 591
**Crossing the Bridge with Cattle watering
beyond** Oil/canvas (64x76cm 25x29in) London 2000
$2 611 - €2 941 - **£1 800** - FF19 292
**Figures an a Parkland Track with a Country
House Beyond** Oil/canvas (36x44cm 14x17in)
London 2000

PETHER Henry c.1800-c.1870 **[35]**
$16 039 - €15 866 - **£10 000** - FF104 072
Greenwich Reach - Moonlight Oil/canvas
(61x92.5cm 24x36in) London 1999
$7 966 - €6 883 - **£4 800** - FF45 148
Moonlit River Landscape Oil/canvas (34x42.5cm
13x16in) Billingshurst, West-Sussex 1999

PETHER Sebastian 1790-1844 **[38]**
$1 741 - €1 961 - **£1 200** - FF12 862
**A Moonlit River Landscape with a Castle Ruin
in the Foreground** Oil/canvas (63.5x84cm 25x33in)
London 2000
$2 438 - €2 252 - **£1 500** - FF14 769
**Figures before a Cottage in a moonlit River
Landscape** Oil/panel (20.5x25.5cm 8x10in) London
1999

PETHER William 1731-1821 **[20]**
$544 - €456 - **£320** - FF2 990
Carlo Tessarini da Rimini Mezzotint (35x25cm
13x9in) London 1998

PETILLION Jules 1845-1899 **[25]**
$2 800 - €3 246 - **£1 983** - FF21 294
Flower Market, Paris Oil/panel (26.5x35cm 10x13in)
New-York 2000

P

PETION Françoise 1944 **[145]**
🖌 **$293** - €305 - **£184** - FF2 000
    La bretonne sur la falaise Pastel/papier (34x26cm 13x10in) Pontivy 2000

PETIT Auguste XIX-XX **[7]**
  $1 127 - €1 250 - **£783** - FF8 200
    Vase de pivoines Huile/toile (73x60cm 28x23in) Besançon 2001

PETIT Charles XIX **[22]**
  $7 502 - €8 417 - **£5 200** - FF55 212
    An Interior Scene Oil/canvas (68.5x58.5cm 26x23in) London 2000
  $5 463 - €5 899 - **£3 736** - FF38 695
    Mother's little Helpers Oil/panel (36x26.5cm 14x10in) Amsterdam 2001

PETIT Corneille XIX **[4]**
  $9 000 - €8 847 - **£5 782** - FF58 030
    Les apprêts du goûter/Le retour du marché Oil/canvas (46.5x38cm 18x14in) New-York 1999

PETIT Danielle 1921-1997 **[3]**
🖌 **$2 000** - €1 906 - **£1 267** - FF12 500
    L'arbre de la Liberté Gouache/papier (50x65cm 19x25in) Chaumont 1999

PETIT Eugène 1839-1886 **[93]**
  $3 644 - €3 374 - **£2 200** - FF22 129
    On the Scent Oil/canvas (38x46cm 14x18in) London 1999
  $1 538 - €1 829 - **£1 096** - FF12 000
    Vase de fleurs Huile/panneau (24x17cm 9x6in) Calais 2000

PETIT Georges 1879-1959 **[8]**
🗿 **$540** - €644 - **£387** - FF4 227
    Le mineur Bronze (32x21cm 12x8in) Liège 2000

PETIT John Louis 1801-1868 **[64]**
🖌 **$1 335** - €1 493 - **£900** - FF9 792
    Tipperary Watercolour (28x38cm 11x14in) London 2000

PETIT Marc 1930 **[2]**
▥ **$1 025** - €1 220 - **£731** - FF8 000
    Escapade Tapisserie (100x50cm 39x19in) Calais 2000

PETIT Philippe 1900-1945 **[2]**
▥ **$1 200** - €1 346 - **£833** - FF8 828
    «Sakharoff, Clotilde & Alexandre» Poster (68x46cm 27x18in) New-York 2001

PETIT Pierre 1832-1909 **[26]**
📷 **$545** - €457 - **£319** - FF3 000
    Portrait de l'écrivain Alphonse Karr Tirage albuminé (14.7x18.5cm 5x7in) Paris 1998

PETIT Pierre-Joseph 1768-1825 **[12]**
  $15 000 - €14 319 - **£9 372** - FF93 924
    View of the Cascade and Temple of the Sibyl at Tivoli Oil/panel (72x57cm 28x22in) New-York 1999
  $3 114 - €3 049 - **£1 916** - FF20 000
    Troupeau s'abreuvant Huile/toile (22x27cm 8x10in) Paris 1999

PETIT-GÉRARD Pierre 1852-1933 **[20]**
  $3 858 - €3 241 - **£2 268** - FF21 259
    Holländische Bäuerin auf dem Feld Öl/Leinwand (116x89cm 45x35in) Bern 1998

PETITI Filiberto 1845-1924 **[49]**
  $450 - €466 - **£270** - FF3 060
    Paesaggio collinare Olio/cartone (20x27cm 7x10in) Roma 1999

PETITJEAN Edmond Marie 1844-1925 **[387]**
  $29 646 - €27 441 - **£18 360** - FF180 000
    Le port de Fécamp Huile/toile (101.5x152.5cm 39x60in) Paris 1999
  $4 958 - €5 641 - **£3 441** - FF37 000
    Vue de village Huile/toile (66x54.5cm 25x21in) Reims 2000
  $1 988 - €2 134 - **£1 330** - FF14 000
    Maison au bord de l'étang Huile/toile (28x48cm 11x18in) Neuilly-sur-Seine 2000

PETITJEAN Hippolyte 1854-1929 **[212]**
  $15 000 - €12 585 - **£8 800** - FF82 554
    Nature morte Oil/canvas (51x61cm 20x24in) New-York 1998
  $2 211 - €2 357 - **£1 500** - FF15 463
    Maison dans un paysage de campagne Oil/board (22x36cm 8x14in) London 2001
🖌 **$905** - €838 - **£561** - FF5 500
    Baigneuse Aquarelle/papier (19x22cm 7x8in) Paris 1999

PETITOT Ennemonde Alexandre 1727-1801 **[6]**
▥ **$1 000** - €1 037 - **£600** - FF6 800
    Sacerdotesse/Mariee/Vivandiere/Bergere/Jeune moine/Epouse/Berger Acquaforte (22x16cm 8x6in) Milano 2001

PETITOT Isaac 1604-1673 **[1]**
  $4 584 - €4 251 - **£2 800** - FF27 888
    Saint Sebastian Relief (H14cm H5in) London 1998

PETITOT Joseph 1771-? **[7]**
  $826 - €762 - **£494** - FF5 000
    Des américains face à une armada Encre (13x8cm 5x3in) Paris 1999

PETITPIERRE Petra Frieda 1905-1959 **[23]**
  $681 - €626 - **£418** - FF4 107
    Petit vase Öl/Leinwand (14x20cm 5x7in) Zürich 1999

PETLEY Roy 1951 **[172]**
  $1 865 - €1 791 - **£1 150** - FF11 751
    Rue de la Préfecture, Nice Oil/board (41x61cm 16x24in) London 1999
  $688 - €656 - **£420** - FF4 301
    Waxham Beach Oil/board (25.5x35.5cm 10x13in) Bury St. Edmunds, Suffolk 1999
🖌 **$571** - €599 - **£360** - FF3 932
    The Lane, Norfolk Watercolour/paper (33x43cm 13x17in) Aylsham, Norfolk 2000

PETLEY-JONES Llewellyn 1908-1986 **[72]**
  $1 054 - €893 - **£633** - FF5 858
    Au Vieux Montmartre Oil/canvas (38x54.5cm 14x21in) Vancouver, BC. 1998
  $725 - €614 - **£435** - FF4 027
    Still Life Oil/board (30.5x38cm 12x14in) Vancouver, BC. 1998

PETLIN Irving 1934 **[18]**
  $11 000 - €10 273 - **£6 789** - FF67 386
    Marriage Oil/canvas (208.5x200cm 82x78in) New-York 1999
  $6 750 - €6 997 - **£4 050** - FF45 900
    Calcium garden Olio/tela (89x87cm 35x34in) Roma 2001
🖌 **$700** - €636 - **£433** - FF4 171
    Les cent hommes Pastel/paper (71x73cm 27x28in) New-York 1999

PETO John Frederick 1854-1907 **[49]**
  $190 000 - €180 813 - **£118 845** - FF1 186 056
    Rack Picture Oil/canvas (56x45.5cm 22x17in) New-York 1999

$28 000 - €32 483 - £19 919 - FF213 074
Still life with Pipe, Books and Tobacco Box
Oil/board (19x24cm 7x9in) Chicago IL 2000

PETRAZZI Adolfo 1579-1665 [6]
$498 170 - €494 133 - £310 000 - FF3 241 298
Tulips, Carnations, Irises, Daffodils, Hyacinths and other Flowers Oil/canvas (111x146.5cm 43x57in) London 1999

PETRELLA DA BOLOGNA Vittorio 1886-1951 [23]
$500 - €518 - £300 - FF3 400
Strada di paese Olio/tavola (40.5x30cm 15x11in) Vercelli 2001

PETRI Heinrich 1834-1872 [2]
$4 443 - €5 113 - £3 068 - FF33 539
Madonna mit Kind in der Rosenlaube
Öl/Leinwand (88x63cm 34x24in) München 2000

PETRIDES Konrad 1864-1943 [47]
$836 - €872 - £526 - FF5 720
Lauterbrunnental mit Jungfrau (Schweiz)
Öl/Leinwand (60x80cm 23x31in) Wien 2000

PETRIE George 1790-1866 [3]
$3 367 - €4 005 - £2 440 - FF26 268
The Lakes of Killarney, Co.Kerry, Ireland
Watercolour (47.5x78cm 18x30in) London 2000

PETRILLI A., Prof. XIX [8]
$75 000 - €83 757 - £48 030 - FF549 412
Stella Polare Marble (H160cm H62in) New-York 2000

PETRINI Giuseppe Antonio 1677-1758 [14]
$16 284 - €17 989 - £11 292 - FF118 000
L'astronome Huile/toile (93x73.2cm 36x28in) Paris 2001
$2 800 - €3 628 - £2 100 - FF23 800
Il sacrificio di Isacco Olio/carta (28.5x29cm 11x11in) Milano 2000

PETRIS de Giovanni 1890-1940 [4]
$1 650 - €1 710 - £990 - FF11 220
Aurora nei Roeri Olio/cartone (20x30cm 7x11in) Vercelli 1999

PETRITSKYI Anatol' 1885-1964 [4]
$11 431 - €12 271 - £7 651 - FF80 493
Tanzendes Paar Öl/Leinwand (80.2x63.9cm 31x25in) Köln 2000

PETROV-VODKIN Kuzma Sergievitch 1878-1939 [35]
$9 248 - €10 746 - £6 500 - FF70 487
Study of a Rock Oil/canvas (42x56.5cm 16x22in) London 2001
$5 037 - €5 995 - £3 600 - FF39 323
Male Head Watercolour (29.5x19cm 11x7in) London 2000

PETROVA Elena 1971 [53]
$577 - €540 - £350 - FF3 539
Flowers and Apples Oil/canvas (60x48cm 23x18in) Fernhurst, Haslemere, Surrey 1999
$290 - €272 - £180 - FF1 783
Lilies of the Valley Oil/canvas (32x27cm 12x10in) Fernhurst, Haslemere, Surrey 1999

PETROVICHEV Piotr Ivanovich 1874-1947 [12]
$14 500 - €12 510 - £8 714 - FF82 059
Golden Autumn Oil/canvas (67x156cm 26x61in) Kiev 1998
$1 600 - €1 784 - £1 075 - FF11 703
Early Autumn Oil/canvas (20.5x30cm 8x11in) Kiev 2000

PETROVITS Ladislaus Eugen 1839-1907 [22]
$2 926 - €2 404 - £1 700 - FF15 769
Melons and Grapes with a Basket Oil/canvas (48x68.5cm 18x26in) London 1998
$1 121 - €1 308 - £792 - FF8 580
Bauernhof in Vahrn Aquarell/Papier (39x56cm 15x22in) Salzburg 2000

PETROVSKY Ivan 1913 [21]
$1 445 - €1 309 - £935 - FF8 585
Sin título, figura Oleo/lienzo (65x90cm 25x35in) Caracas 1999
$561 - €483 - £330 - FF3 168
Obreros en Reposo Gouache/papier (45x59cm 17x23in) Caracas 1998

PETRUCCI Carlo Alberto 1881-? [3]
$750 - €706 - £463 - FF4 633
Still Life with Flowers Monotype (39.5x35cm 15x13in) New-York 1999

PETRUOLO Salvatore 1857-1946 [59]
$5 100 - €5 287 - £3 060 - FF34 680
Pescatori a Sorrento Olio/tela (91.5x107cm 36x42in) Venezia 2000
$1 600 - €2 073 - £1 200 - FF13 600
Scorcio costiero con barca e pescatore Olio/cartone (34.5x37cm 13x14in) Roma 2000
$1 700 - €1 554 - £1 040 - FF10 191
Walking Along the Cliffs Watercolour/paper (55x31.5cm 21x12in) Boston MA 1999

PETTENKOFEN von August Xaver Ritter 1822-1889 [123]
$10 460 - €11 228 - £7 000 - FF73 651
Travellers with their Wagon in a Landscape
Oil/panel (34x57cm 13x22in) London 2000
$6 110 - €7 267 - £4 360 - FF47 670
Marktpferde Oil/panel (10x18cm 3x7in) Wien 2000
$1 624 - €1 830 - £1 142 - FF12 006
Schlachtszene mit Pferden Aquarell/Papier (22.5x32.5cm 8x12in) Zürich 2000

PETTER Franz Xaver 1791-1866 [26]
$20 962 - €21 474 - £12 936 - FF140 863
Blumen und Früchtestilleben mit einem Vogel
Öl/Leinwand (41.5x54cm 16x21in) Düsseldorf 2000
$4 840 - €4 649 - £3 000 - FF30 494
Still Life of Flowers Oil/panel (40x31cm 15x12in) London 1999

PETTER Theodor 1822-1872 [10]
$7 282 - €7 994 - £4 840 - FF52 437
Junges Mädchen überquert einen kleinen Bach
Öl/Leinwand (43x32cm 16x12in) Wien 2000

PETTERSEN Arvid 1943 [10]
$835 - €785 - £503 - FF5 146
Utan titel Oil/canvas (56x57cm 22x22in) Stockholm 1999
$3 474 - €3 501 - £2 166 - FF22 962
Porträtt Oil/metal (41x30cm 16x11in) Stockholm 2000

PETTERSSON Gunnar 1947 [7]
$260 - €236 - £160 - FF1 548
Svanar Color lithograph (52.5x80.5cm 20x31in) Stockholm 1999

PETTERSSON Primus Mortimer 1895-1975 [33]
$170 - €174 - £105 - FF1 142
Landskap med hus Pastel/paper (18.5x28cm 7x11in) Stockholm 2000

PETTIBON Raymond 1957 [27]
$17 000 - €19 725 - £11 736 - FF129 387
Of the Moral Springs Oil/canvas (152.5x123cm 60x48in) New-York 2000

P

$3 000 - €2 883 - **£1 848** - FF18 911
Untitled (One Anvil Incus) Ink/paper (34x37cm
13x14in) New-York 1999

$1 100 - €1 262 - **£752** - FF8 279
Bloodshot Serigraph (56x43cm 22x16in) New-York
2000

PETTIBONE Richard 1938 **[25]**

$2 000 - €2 321 - **£1 380** - FF15 222
The New Age Oil/canvas (25.5x20.5cm 10x8in) New-
York 1999

$6 500 - €7 577 - **£4 500** - FF49 702
Andy Warhol, 32 Cans of Campbell's, Soup
Screenprint (17x13cm 6x5in) New-York 2000

PETTIE John 1839-1893 **[30]**

$5 664 - €5 311 - **£3 500** - FF34 840
Young Swordsman Oil/canvas (49.5x38cm 19x14in)
London 1999

$1 700 - €1 584 - **£1 027** - FF10 393
Portrait of a Man in Riding Habit Oil/canvas
(30x22cm 12x9in) New-Orleans LA 1999

PETTITT Charles 1831-1885 **[22]**

$1 625 - €1 501 - **£1 000** - FF9 846
«Sunset Glow» on the Langdale Pikes Oil/canvas
(35.5x61cm 13x24in) London 1999

$799 - €900 - **£550** - FF5 901
**Sunrise at the inlet of River Brathay, Lake
Windermere** Oil/canvas (30.5x46cm 12x18in) London
2000

PETTITT Edwin Alfred 1840-1912 **[23]**

$311 - €368 - **£220** - FF2 414
Barmouth, North Wales Oil/canvas (30x43cm
12x17in) Aylsham, Norfolk 2001

PETTITT George William 1831-1863 **[14]**

$6 276 - €6 737 - **£4 200** - FF44 190
The Vesper Hour, Lake Lugano, Italy Oil/canvas
(51x91.5cm 20x36in) London 2000

$1 300 - €1 201 - **£800** - FF7 877
Children fishing on Lake Windermere, Cumbria
Oil/board (20.5x38cm 8x14in) London 1999

PETTITT Joseph Paul ?-1882 **[26]**

$9 415 - €10 925 - **£6 500** - FF71 661
The Saw Mill, Camlaw, North Wales Oil/canvas
(152.5x112cm 60x44in) London 2000

$2 847 - €3 343 - **£2 009** - FF21 926
Rydal Water, Keswick Oil/canvas (69x123cm
27x48in) Stockholm 2000

PETTITT Wilfred Stanley 1904 **[17]**

$1 209 - €1 424 - **£850** - FF9 342
The Valley of the River Wensum, Norfolk Oil/can-
vas (51x61cm 20x24in) Suffolk 2000

PETTORUTI Emilio 1892-1971 **[42]**

$60 000 - €58 252 - **£37 068** - FF382 110
Monte Solaro Oil/canvas (39x47cm 15x18in) New-
York 1999

$15 000 - €13 079 - **£9 069** - FF85 795
Sin Título Ink/paper (21x26.5cm 8x10in) New-York
1998

PETTRICH Ferdinand 1798-1872 **[1]**

$22 000 - €26 164 - **£15 679** - FF171 622
Bust of Andrew Jackson Marble (H61cm H24in)
New-York 2000

PETTY George 1894-1975 **[12]**

$1 700 - €1 686 - **£1 057** - FF11 061
«The Petty Girl» Poster (104x68.5cm 40x26in) New-
York 1999

PETYARRE Ada Bird c.1930 **[15]**

$8 717 - €8 434 - **£5 375** - FF55 324
Atnankere Dreaming Acrylic/canvas (134x192cm
52x75in) Woollahra, Sydney 1999

PETYARRE Gloria Tamerre c.1938/45 **[25]**

$1 959 - €1 843 - **£1 213** - FF12 089
Mountain Devil Awelye Acrylic/canvas (130x158cm
51x62in) Melbourne 1999

$1 165 - €1 307 - **£815** - FF8 572
**«Awelye for Arnkerthe, the Mountain Devil
Lizard»** Acrylic (88.5x120cm 34x47in) Melbourne
2001

PETZET Hermann 1860-1935 **[11]**

$333 - €358 - **£223** - FF2 347
Der 5 eckige Turm.Nürnberg Öl/Leinwand/Karton
(66x52cm 25x20in) München 2000

PETZHOLDT Frederik Ernst Ch. 1805-1838 **[19]**

$7 949 - €8 719 - **£5 401** - FF57 193
Landskab med klipper, Italien Oil/paper/canvas
(39x47cm 15x18in) København 2000

$4 987 - €4 713 - **£3 108** - FF30 912
Fra Vemmetofte Strand med Masestenen
Oil/canvas (21x31cm 8x12in) København 1999

PETZL Joseph 1803-1871 **[6]**

$5 024 - €4 350 - **£3 030** - FF28 532
Der Schützenkönig Öl/Leinwand (35x28cm
13x11in) München 1998

PETZOLD Werner 1940 **[1]**

$1 999 - €2 301 - **£1 378** - FF15 092
Wismut I Öl/Leinwand (75x88cm 29x34in) Leipzig
2000

PEVERELLI Cesare 1922-2000 **[101]**

$850 - €881 - **£510** - FF5 780
Esce dallo spazio Olio/tela (55x46cm 21x18in)
Milano 1999

$750 - €777 - **£450** - FF5 100
Andiamo incontro al sole Olio/tela (30x20cm
11x7in) Vercelli 2000

PEVERNAGIE Erik 1939 **[47]**

$3 197 - €3 811 - **£2 280** - FF25 000
«The Moment he had Been Waiting for»
Huile/toile (100x81cm 39x31in) Paris 2000

$2 898 - €3 450 - **£1 988** - FF22 764
Als puntje bij paaltje komt Technique mixte/papier
(73x92cm 28x36in) Antwerpen 2000

PEVERNAGIE Louis 1904-1970 **[21]**

$3 180 - €2 975 - **£1 968** - FF19 512
Figuren Huile/panneau (49x59cm 19x23in) Lokeren
1999

$3 300 - €2 723 - **£1 936** - FF17 864
Nu assis Technique mixte/papier (70x50cm 27x19in)
Antwerpen 2000

PEVSNER Antoine 1884-1962 **[104]**

$106 794 - €114 637 - **£71 460** - FF751 968
Domino blanc Öl/Leinwand (94x55cm 37x21in) Bern
2000

$75 141 - €71 969 - **£47 288** - FF472 086
Construction en rond Bronze (48x49x26cm
18x19x10in) Bern 1999

$897 - €991 - **£622** - FF6 500
Composition Fusain/papier (24.5x33.5cm 9x13in)
Paris 2001

PEYNET Raymond 1908-1998 **[86]**

$214 - €244 - **£148** - FF1 600
Sous-bois animé Gouache (13.5x28cm 5x11in)
Douai 2000

$179 - €198 - £121 - FF1 300
«La Riviera» Affiche couleur (100x140cm 39x55in)
Nice 2000

PEYNOT Émile Edmond 1850-1932 **[25]**
$10 800 - €10 288 - £6 590 - FF67 487
Christopher Columbus in Period Dress with
Sword Bronze (H101cm H40in) Bloomfield-Hills MI
1999
$8 859 - €9 909 - £5 973 - FF65 000
En Champagne Bronze (57x50x32cm 22x19x12in)
Orléans 2000

PEYO (Pierre Culliford) 1928-1992 **[22]**
$496 - €457 - £298 - FF3 000
Benco et les Schtroumpfs Encre Chine/papier
(36x26cm 14x10in) Paris 1999

PEYRAUD Frank Charles 1858-1948 **[27]**
$2 000 - €1 939 - £1 238 - FF12 718
Landscape Oil/canvas (55x66cm 22x26in) Mystic CT
1999
$475 - €454 - £292 - FF2 975
Summer Landscape Oil/board (22x30cm 9x12in)
Cincinnati OH 1999

PEYRE Raphaël Charles 1872-1949 **[17]**
$12 000 - €12 799 - £7 993 - FF83 956
Group of Venus and Cupid Marble (H91cm H35in)
New-York 2000
$3 070 - €3 506 - £2 159 - FF23 000
Trois amours Sculpture (H46cm H18in) Tonnerre
2001

PEYRISSAC Jean 1895-1974 **[42]**
$5 050 - €5 793 - £3 454 - FF38 000
Nu à la balançoire Huile/toile (92x60cm 36x23in)
Paris 2000
$5 044 - €6 098 - £3 524 - FF40 000
Le Buisson ardent Fer (61x20x20cm 24x9x7in) Paris
2000
$3 432 - €3 659 - £2 176 - FF24 000
Signes magiques au soleil d'été Gouache/papier
(14x27cm 5x10in) Paris 2000

PEYRO-URREA Juan 1847-1924 **[4]**
$22 400 - €21 023 - £13 650 - FF137 900
El relato de la expedición Oleo/tabla (37x50cm
14x19in) Madrid 2001
$9 871 - €9 558 - £6 200 - FF62 697
Message à la reine Oil/panel (30x50cm 11x19in)
London 1999

PEYROL-BONHEUR Juliette 1830-1891 **[16]**
$1 200 - €1 391 - £850 - FF9 127
A Sheep and Lambs Resting in a Moorland
Landscape Oil/canvas (32.5x45cm 12x17in) London
2000

PEYRON Guido 1898-1960 **[31]**
$850 - €881 - £510 - FF5 780
Paesaggio marino Olio/tela/tavola (42x65.5cm
16x25in) Prato 2000
$1 140 - €985 - £570 - FF6 460
Dama con cappello Olio/carta (44x29cm 17x11in)
Firenze 2000
$300 - €259 - £200 - FF1 700
Natura morta con bicchieri e bottiglie
Acquarello/carta (36x27cm 14x10in) Firenze 1998

PEYRON Pierre 1744-1814 **[9]**
$2 796 - €2 592 - £1 739 - FF17 000
Étude pour Socrate détachant Alcibiade des
charmes de la volupté Encre (14x21cm 5x8in) Paris
1999

PEYROTTE Alexis 1699-1769 **[6]**
$2 886 - €3 354 - £2 028 - FF22 000
Un singe habillé en franciscain prêchant aux
dindons Gouache/papier (27.5x34.5cm 10x13in) Paris
2001

PEYTON Bertha Menzler 1871-1950 **[13]**
$6 500 - €7 280 - £4 516 - FF47 756
«Song of Youth» Oil/canvas (101x127cm 40x50in)
Cincinnati OH 2001
$2 100 - €1 772 - £1 231 - FF11 621
Western Landscape Oil/canvas (76x101cm 30x40in)
Mystic CT 1998

PEYTON Elizabeth 1965 **[12]**
$80 000 - €89 606 - £55 584 - FF587 776
«David, Victoria + Brooklyn» Oil/canvas
(152.5x101.5cm 60x39in) New-York 2001
$21 000 - €24 366 - £14 498 - FF159 831
Untitled Oil/canvas (45.5x36cm 17x14in) New-York
2000
$9 000 - €10 443 - £6 213 - FF68 499
Matthew in Tompkins Square Pencil/paper
(19x15cm 7x5in) New-York 2000

PEZ Aimé 1808-1849 **[2]**
$15 370 - €14 377 - £9 338 - FF94 308
Blindemannetje spelen Oil/panel (67.5x80cm
26x31in) Lokeren 1999

PEZANT Aymar 1846-1916 **[47]**
$1 043 - €1 227 - £748 - FF8 049
Eine Bäuerin mit Kuhen und Schafen auf einem
Feldweg Öl/Leinwand (55x65cm 21x25in) Stuttgart
2001
$784 - €860 - £520 - FF5 642
Cattle Watering Oil/canvas (16x24.5cm 6x9in)
London 2000

PEZILLA Mario XIX-XX **[11]**
$549 - €482 - £333 - FF3 162
Exposition de l'électricité Poster (102x71cm
40x28in) New-York 1999

PEZOLT Georg 1810-1878 **[3]**
$3 055 - €3 634 - £2 180 - FF23 835
Blick auf Festung Hohensalzburg und den
Untersberg Öl/Papier (20x25cm 7x9in) Wien 2000

PFAFF Hans 1875-? **[5]**
$2 800 - €2 693 - £1 728 - FF17 663
«Pianos Kaps» Poster (66x96.5cm 25x37in) New-
York 1999

PFAFF Judy 1946 **[17]**
$900 - €845 - £556 - FF5 540
Yoyogi I/Yoyogi II Woodcut in colors (80.5x91.5cm
31x36in) New-York 1999

PFAHL John 1939 **[29]**
$1 200 - €1 332 - £836 - FF8 737
«Great Salt Lake Angles, Utah»/«Shed with
Blue Dotted Lines, Penland» Photograph in colors
(36x46cm 14x18in) New-York 2001

PFAHLER Georg Karl 1926 **[203]**
$4 763 - €5 113 - £3 188 - FF33 539
Metro-Col Acryl/Leinwand (140.5x160.5cm 55x63in)
Köln 2000
$3 213 - €3 068 - £2 007 - FF20 123
Ohne Titel Mixed media (59.5x42cm 23x16in) Köln
1999
$1 161 - €1 022 - £707 - FF6 707
Ohne Titel Mischtechnik/Papier (43.5x61.5cm
17x24in) Stuttgart 1999

P

PFANHAUSER
$202 - €174 - £122 - FF1 140
Komposition Farbserigraphie (33.7x33.7cm 13x13in)
Hamburg 1998

PFANHAUSER Franciszek 1796-c.1865 **[2]**
$8 052 - €7 994 - £5 027 - FF52 437
Motiv aus einem Park Oil/panel (35.5x48cm
13x18in) Wien 1999

PFAU Konrad 1885-1954 **[24]**
$726 - €818 - £510 - FF5 366
Porträt eines Afrikaners Öl/Leinwand (58.5x48.5cm
23x19in) München 2001

PFEFFERKORN Felix Samuel 1945-1980 **[198]**
$1 136 - €1 278 - £793 - FF8 384
«Tropical Fruits» Öl/Karton (58x48cm 22x18in)
Lindau 2001
$487 - €511 - £329 - FF3 353
Liegender weiblicher Akt Oil/panel (40x30cm
15x11in) Kempten 2001

PFEIFFER Anton Heinrich 1801-1866 **[1]**
$3 977 - €4 090 - £2 522 - FF26 831
Bedeutender Becher Sculpture, glass (H14.5cm
H5in) Heilbronn 2000

PFEIFFER François Joseph II 1778-1835 **[2]**
$2 068 - €2 352 - £1 434 - FF15 427
**Bäuerin neben malerische Kate mit drei
Schafen** Watercolour (44x55cm 17x21in) Lindau 2000

PFEIFFER Gordon Edward 1899-1983 **[76]**
$132 - €154 - £90 - FF1 011
An Autumn Scene Huile/panneau (30.5x40.5cm
12x15in) Montréal 2000

PFEIFFER Harry R., Heinrich 1874-1960 **[20]**
$600 - €510 - £358 - FF3 348
Sun on Water Oil/canvas (76x76cm 30x30in) New-
York 1998
$400 - €345 - £237 - FF2 262
Bright Morning, Provincetown Acrylic/board
(30x25cm 12x10in) Cambridge MA 1998

PFEIFFER Henri 1907-1952 **[221]**
$179 - €152 - £106 - FF1 000
Sans titre Aquarelle/papier (44x32cm 17x12in) Paris
1998

PFEIFFER Wilhelm 1822-1891 **[13]**
$3 180 - €3 579 - £2 191 - FF23 477
Hindernisrennen Öl/Karton (43x52cm 16x20in)
München 2000

PFEILER Maximilian XVIII **[14]**
$75 062 - €69 777 - £46 000 - FF457 709
**Putti playing with Fruit by an upturned Urn of
Flowers** Oil/canvas (172.5x247cm 67x97in) London
1998
$8 000 - €9 422 - £5 532 - FF61 807
**Still Life of Grapes, a Melon, Figs, Plums,
Peaches and Other Fruit** Oil/canvas (54x68cm
21x26in) New-York 2000

PFENNINGER Matthias 1739-1813 **[9]**
$206 - €234 - £145 - FF1 532
**«Passage et ouverture du Hauenstein Canton
de Soleure»** Radierung (32x25cm 12x9in) Bern 2001

PFERSCHY Karl 1888-1930 **[6]**
$419 - €472 - £292 - FF3 098
«Schafmarkt» Woodcut in colors (43.5x34.5cm
17x13in) Salzburg 2001

PFEUFFER Helmut 1933 **[16]**
$412 - €409 - £257 - FF2 683
Berglandschaft Indian ink (21x29.6cm 8x11in)
Hamburg 1999

PFISTER Albert 1884-1978 **[34]**
$3 403 - €3 429 - £2 121 - FF22 495
Restaurant Kunststube in Küsnacht Öl/Karton
(45x53cm 17x20in) Zürich 2000
$4 193 - €3 589 - £2 524 - FF23 540
Stilleben mit Eichelhäher Huile/toile (33x46.5cm
12x18in) Zürich 1998
$236 - €276 - £166 - FF1 811
Abstraktion Aquarell/Papier (14x20.5cm 5x8in)
Luzern 2000

PFIZENMAIER Ed XX **[16]**
$2 000 - €2 220 - £1 394 - FF14 563
Selected New York images Gelatin silver print
(32x21cm 12x8in) New-York 2001

PFLUG Johann Baptist 1785-1865 **[7]**
$13 127 - €11 246 - £7 891 - FF73 772
Auffahrt des Brautwagens Watercolour,
gouache/paper (15.9x21cm 6x8in) Stuttgart 1998

PFLUGFELDER Johann Gottfried XIX **[1]**
$3 157 - €3 068 - £1 974 - FF20 123
Ansicht der Stadt Bremen Kupferstich (26x38cm
10x14in) Bremen 1999

PFLUGRADT Gustav 1829-1907 **[10]**
$5 000 - €4 960 - £3 111 - FF32 533
In a Small Town Oil/canvas (53.5x67.5cm 21x26in)
Kiev 1999

PFORR Heinrich 1880-1970 **[16]**
$3 564 - €4 090 - £2 438 - FF26 831
Abend im Winter Öl/Leinwand (84x112cm 33x44in)
Berlin 2000

PFORR Johann Georg 1745-1798 **[23]**
$6 610 - €7 669 - £4 702 - FF50 308
Treffen der Jäger zu Pferde im Wald Oil/panel
(59x51cm 23x20in) Erlangen 2000
$9 012 - €9 084 - £5 625 - FF59 587
Aufbruch zur Falkenjagd Öl/Leinwand (36x42.5cm
14x16in) Wien 2000
$825 - €920 - £554 - FF6 037
Reiter am Brunnen Ink (19.5x29cm 7x11in) Köln
2000

PFÜLLER Volker 1939 **[2]**
$2 000 - €1 893 - £1 242 - FF12 419
«Ghetto»/«Sex Comedy» Poster (59.5x84cm
23x33in) New-York 1999

PFUND Alois 1876-1946 **[12]**
$1 047 - €1 125 - £701 - FF7 378
Gehöft in Tirol Öl/Leinwand (78x98cm 30x38in) Köln
2000

PFYFFER Eduard 1836-1899 **[2]**
$5 461 - €5 265 - £3 366 - FF34 534
Wirtshaus Treib am Vierwaldstättersee
Öl/Leinwand (44x73cm 17x28in) Bern 1999

PFYFFER VON ALTISHOFEN-KNÖRR Niklaus
1836-1908 [8]
$1 127 - €1 315 - £791 - FF8 623
Küstenlandschaft bei Nervi Öl/Leinwand
(53.5x75cm 21x29in) Luzern 2000

PHALIBOIS J. XIX **[1]**
$15 235 - €14 025 - £9 144 - FF92 000
**Tableau animé musical: maître d'école, élèves à
leur pupitre** Construction (78x95cm 30x37in) Lyon
1999

PHELAN Charles T. 1840-? **[15]**
☞ **$2 000** - €2 334 - **£1 411** - FF15 311
   Sheep in a Meadow Oil/canvas (25x35cm 10x14in)
   New-York 2000

PHELPS William Preston 1848-1923 **[34]**
☞ **$11 000** - €11 807 - **£7 361** - FF77 451
   Wooded Landscape with Waterfall Oil/canvas
   (157x137cm 62x54in) Bolton MA 2000
☞ **$2 600** - €2 227 - **£1 563** - FF14 611
   Feeding Time Oil/canvas (59x89cm 23x35in) Dedham
   MA 1998
☞ **$3 000** - €3 220 - **£2 007** - FF21 123
   Distant View of Keene, New Hampshire Oil/can-
   vas (22x38cm 9x15in) Portland ME 2000

PHILIPAULT Julie 1780-1834 **[2]**
☞ **$13 490** - €14 483 - **£9 025** - FF95 000
   **Charles Marie Galté (1772-1830)/Angélique
   Louise Rose Galté** Huile/toile (114x87cm 44x34in)
   Paris 2000

PHILIPP Martin E. 1887-1978 **[90]**
▥ **$112** - €128 - **£77** - FF838
   «Perlhühner» Woodcut in colors (21.2x29.4cm
   8x11in) Berlin 2000

PHILIPP Robert 1895-1981 **[145]**
☞ **$2 600** - €2 957 - **£1 816** - FF19 396
   Good Read Oil/canvas (64x76cm 25x30in) New-York
   2000
☞ **$700** - €796 - **£485** - FF5 222
   Girl Sewing Oil/board (20x25cm 8x10in) Cincinnati
   OH 2000
✎ **$1 000** - €955 - **£615** - FF6 264
   Night Life Gouache/paper (20x35cm 8x14in)
   Cincinnati OH 1999

PHILIPPE Paul XIX-XX **[5]**
☞ **$2 536** - €2 515 - **£1 577** - FF16 500
   Retour des chaloupes sardinières Huile/toile
   (65x92cm 25x36in) Brest 1999

PHILIPPE Paul XIX-XX **[75]**
▦ **$6 421** - €5 959 - **£4 000** - FF39 086
   Exotic Dancer Ivory, bronze (H37.5cm H14in)
   London 1999

PHILIPPE Raoul XX **[2]**
▥ **$1 520** - €1 533 - **£950** - FF10 054
   «Bobsleigh» Poster (38x51cm 14x20in) London 2000

PHILIPPEAU Karel Frans 1825-1897 **[19]**
☞ **$3 457** - €3 889 - **£2 413** - FF25 509
   Römische Strassenszene Oil/panel (33.5x25cm
   13x9in) Luzern 2001

PHILIPPET Léon 1843-1906 **[42]**
☞ **$1 989** - €2 107 - **£1 326** - FF13 821
   Fête villageoise Huile/toile (44x69cm 17x27in)
   Bruxelles 2000
✎ **$387** - €421 - **£255** - FF2 764
   L'italienne Gouache/papier (33.5x18cm 13x7in) Liège
   2000

PHILIPPI Peter 1866-1958 **[13]**
☞ **$9 724** - €9 715 - **£6 080** - FF63 724
   Winkelweisheit Öl/Leinwand (50x57cm 19x22in)
   Hamburg 1999

PHILIPPI Robert 1877-1959 **[15]**
▥ **$180** - €179 - **£112** - FF1 173
   Kniende und sitzende weibliche Akte Woodcut
   (44x49cm 17x19in) Hildrizhausen 1999

PHILIPPOTEAUX Henri Félix Emmanuel 1815-1884
[42]
☞ **$33 602** - €33 361 - **£21 000** - FF218 834
   La rapt Oil/canvas (46x38cm 18x14in) London 1999
✎ **$2 934** - €3 049 - **£1 936** - FF20 000
   **Études de personnages, soldats, officiers,
   orientaux** Mine plomb (50x62cm 19x24in) Paris 2000

PHILIPPOTEAUX Paul Dominique 1846-1923 **[29]**
☞ **$5 231** - €4 421 - **£3 111** - FF29 000
   Scène de rue Huile/toile (60x49cm 23x19in) Paris
   1998
☞ **$2 200** - €2 085 - **£1 374** - FF13 679
   Fierce Skirmish, Civil War Oil/paper (22x30cm
   9x12in) Mystic CT 1999
☞ **$2 800** - €3 628 - **£2 100** - FF23 800
   Ritratto di arabo Inchiostro (32x24cm 12x9in)
   Venezia 2000

PHILIPS Charles 1708-1747 **[11]**
☞ **$56 010** - €53 466 - **£35 000** - FF350 714
   **Group Portrait of a Family, by a Lake and a clas-
   sical Pavilion** Oil/canvas (160x135cm 62x53in)
   London 1999
☞ **$37 357** - €40 100 - **£25 000** - FF263 040
   The edwards Family on a Terrace Oil/canvas
   (73x91.5cm 28x36in) London 2000

PHILIPS Hermann August 1844-1927 **[11]**
☞ **$15 000** - €16 488 - **£9 612** - FF108 156
   The Bather Oil/canvas (120x80.5cm 47x31in) New-
   York 2000

PHILIPSEN Sally 1879-1936 **[84]**
☞ **$401** - €429 - **£273** - FF2 812
   Mole og småbåde ved Dragör Oil/canvas
   (51x70cm 20x27in) Vejle 2001
☞ **$351** - €323 - **£216** - FF2 119
   Landskab med nögne traeer Oil/panel
   (30.5x38.5cm 12x15in) Vejle 1999

PHILIPSEN Theodore Esbern 1840-1920 **[163]**
☞ **$2 914** - €2 679 - **£1 800** - FF17 574
   Kalve ved Hollaenderbrönden, Saltholm Oil/can-
   vas (130x184cm 51x72in) Vejle 1998
☞ **$2 181** - €2 412 - **£1 513** - FF15 820
   **Interior med kunstnerens hund siddende på en
   stol ved et vindue** Oil/canvas (40x52cm 15x20in)
   Vejle 2001
☞ **$1 154** - €1 341 - **£811** - FF8 798
   Köer ved en vandlöb Oil/panel (34x43cm 13x16in)
   Köbenhavn 2001
▦ **$2 739** - €3 085 - **£1 888** - FF20 235
   Romersk tyr på stor Bronze (40x49cm 15x19in)
   Köbenhavn 2000
✎ **$300** - €349 - **£214** - FF2 289
   Staldinteriör Pastel/paper (41x53cm 16x20in) Aarhus
   2001

PHILIPSON Robin 1916-1993 **[146]**
☞ **$13 154** - €14 667 - **£9 000** - FF96 207
   Lion Oil/canvas (123x123cm 48x48in) Perthshire 2000
☞ **$9 618** - €9 086 - **£6 000** - FF59 599
   Quiet Village Oil/canvas (35.5x46cm 13x18in)
   Perthshire 1998
☞ **$5 754** - €6 428 - **£3 900** - FF42 165
   Rose Window Oil/board (36x26cm 14x10in)
   Edinburgh 2000
✎ **$3 160** - €2 707 - **£1 900** - FF17 759
   Odalisque Watercolour/paper (22x37.5cm 8x14in)
   Edinburgh 1998

P

PHILLIP John «Spanish» 1817-1867 **[42]**
- $7 230 - €7 577 - **£4 800** - FF49 699
  Senor and Senorita Oil/canvas (103x70cm 40x27in) London 2001
- $1 857 - €1 719 - **£1 150** - FF11 276
  Girl in Andalusian Dress Watercolour (51x31.5cm 20x12in) London 1999

PHILLIPS Ammi 1788-1865 **[51]**
- $12 000 - €12 815 - **£8 176** - FF84 063
  Young Man wearing a White Shirt with Wide Black Tie and Black Jacket Oil/canvas (76x61cm 29x24in) New-York 2001

PHILLIPS Bert Greer 1868-1956 **[44]**
- $210 000 - €200 752 - **£131 628** - FF1 316 847
  Pueblo Indian Girl with Wild Plum Blossoms Oil/board (168x91.5cm 66x36in) New-York 1999
- $42 500 - €40 628 - **£26 639** - FF266 504
  After the Ceremony Oil/board (62x192cm 24x75in) New-York 1999
- $7 500 - €8 231 - **£4 829** - FF53 994
  Portrait of an Indian Mixed media (32.5x24cm 12x9in) Beverly-Hills CA 2000

PHILLIPS Charles 1708-1747 **[7]**
- $18 434 - €15 685 - **£11 000** - FF102 887
  Portrait of Beleived to be of te Dashwood Family by a Classical Temple Oil/canvas (158x136cm 62x53in) London 1998

PHILLIPS Coles 1880-1927 **[7]**
- $27 500 - €30 096 - **£18 969** - FF197 417
  The Spirit of Transportation Watercolour, gouache/paper (90x71cm 35x27in) New-York 2001

PHILLIPS Frederick XX **[4]**
- $500 - €534 - **£332** - FF3 504
  The Loggia Serigraph in colors (69x50cm 27x20in) Chicago IL 2000

PHILLIPS Gordon 1927 **[14]**
- $12 100 - €11 300 - **£7 468** - FF74 124
  A helping Hand Oil/canvas (106x124cm 42x49in) Dallas TX 1999
- $13 000 - €12 365 - **£7 893** - FF81 107
  The Lost Feather Oil/canvas (76x101.5cm 29x39in) Beverly-Hills CA 1999

PHILLIPS James March 1864-? **[11]**
- $700 - €816 - **£491** - FF5 355
  Monterey Coastal Scene Watercolour/paper (50x72cm 20x28in) San Rafael CA 2000

PHILLIPS Joel 1960 **[9]**
- $4 950 - €4 623 - **£3 055** - FF30 323
  Redstone June Oil/board (66x96cm 26x38in) Dallas TX 1999
- $3 400 - €3 860 - **£2 362** - FF25 323
  Sunset Trail Oil/board (38x27cm 15x11in) Dallas TX 2001
- $2 200 - €2 361 - **£1 472** - FF15 490
  The Horseman's Doorway Watercolour/paper (38x27cm 15x11in) Houston TX 2000

PHILLIPS John XIX **[9]**
- $7 316 - €7 623 - **£4 600** - FF50 003
  Mexico Lithograph (55.5x37.5cm 21x14in) London 2000

PHILLIPS John Campbell 1873-1949 **[12]**
- $450 - €390 - **£273** - FF2 555
  Foothills in the Berkshires Oil/board (18x26cm 7x10in) Mystic CT 1998

PHILLIPS Peter 1939 **[64]**
- $789 - €917 - **£554** - FF6 013
  Small Composition #5 Öl/Leinwand (36x50cm 14x19in) Luzern 2001
- $1 452 - €1 602 - **£983** - FF10 508
  Study for Gefährliches Spiel #8 Collage (78x60cm 30x23in) Zürich 2000
- $165 - €152 - **£101** - FF1 000
  Tiger Sérigraphie (73x101cm 28x39in) Paris 1999

PHILLIPS Richard 1681-1741 **[1]**
- $8 688 - €9 873 - **£6 000** - FF64 762
  Lady Standing by a Fountain in a Landscape, Holding a Spring Oil/canvas (127x101.5cm 50x39in) London 2000

PHILLIPS S. George 1890-1965 **[5]**
- $2 500 - €2 989 - **£1 733** - FF19 605
  The Blacksmith Shop Oil/canvas (55x60cm 22x24in) Milford CT 2000
- $3 500 - €3 757 - **£2 342** - FF24 646
  Bucks Country Oil/canvas (40.5x33cm 15x12in) New-York 2000

PHILLIPS Thomas 1770-1845 **[28]**
- $15 433 - €15 017 - **£9 500** - FF98 503
  Sir Joseph Banks (1744-1820), wearing Uniform, the Order of the Garte Oil/canvas (94x73cm 37x28in) London 1999

PHILLIPS Tom 1937 **[57]**
- $6 724 - €7 218 - **£4 500** - FF47 347
  Dante Oil/canvas (48.5x38cm 19x14in) London 2000
- $337 - €286 - **£200** - FF1 874
  Diamond Construction/Dark Words Falling/Dark Words/Painter with Plane Color lithograph (75x54cm 29x21in) Billingshurst, West-Sussex 1998

PHILLIPS Walter Joseph 1884-1963 **[478]**
- $6 667 - €7 197 - **£4 473** - FF47 212
  Peggy's Cove Watercolour/paper (34.5x55.5cm 13x21in) Calgary, Alberta 2000
- $649 - €734 - **£456** - FF4 815
  Lake McArthur, canadian Rockies Woodcut in colors (19x23.5cm 7x9in) Vancouver, BC. 2001

PHILLOTT Constance 1842-1931 **[21]**
- $6 375 - €7 441 - **£4 500** - FF48 360
  A Cottage Child Watercolour/paper (23.5x18.5cm 9x7in) London 2000

PHILP James George 1816-1885 **[19]**
- $984 - €928 - **£620** - FF6 088
  Figures in a rowing Boat on an Inlet, with Harbour Side Buildings Watercolour/paper (30.5x51cm 12x20in) Godalming, Surrey 1999

PHILPOT Glyn Warren 1884-1937 **[90]**
- $13 172 - €12 378 - **£8 000** - FF81 196
  Portrait of Vivian Forbes Oil/canvas (146x97cm 57x38in) London 1999
- $7 919 - €8 235 - **£5 000** - FF54 016
  Square at Ostend, Evening Oil/canvas (63.5x76cm 25x29in) London 2000
- $2 019 - €2 266 - **£1 400** - FF14 864
  Head of a Man Oil/canvas (35.5x41cm 13x16in) London 2000
- $1 157 - €1 250 - **£800** - FF8 199
  «Vitrine, Coiffeur de Luxe, St.Paul du Val» Ink (43x27cm 16x10in) Newbury, Berkshire 2001

PHIPPEN George 1916-1966 **[21]**
- $3 960 - €4 251 - **£2 650** - FF27 882
  Cowboy and Horses Oil/canvas (50x40cm 20x16in) Houston TX 2000

P

$1 800 – €2 044 – £1 250 – FF13 406
Pack String Ink (16x34cm 6x13in) Dallas TX 2001

PHRA SORALAKLIKIT 1875-1958 [2]
$29 370 – €27 284 – £18 150 – FF178 970
King Rama III Oil/canvas (42x32cm 16x12in)
Bangkok 1999

PIACENTINO Gianni 1945 [11]
$1 000 – €1 037 – £600 – FF6 800
Progetti Inchiostro (33.5x48cm 13x18in) Milano 2001
$750 – €777 – £450 – FF5 100
Vehicles/Sculptures Litografia (49x69cm 19x27in)
Milano 2001

PIACENZA Carlo 1814-1887 [10]
$4 750 – €4 924 – £2 850 – FF32 300
I mietitori Olio/tela (65x126cm 25x50in) Torino 2000
$1 600 – €2 073 – £1 200 – FF13 600
Strada di montagna con pastorella Olio/cartone
(20x35.5cm 7x13in) Vercelli 2000

PIACESI Walter 1929 [44]
$1 300 – €1 348 – £780 – FF8 840
L'opera d'arte Tecnica mista/cartone (35x50cm
13x19in) Vercelli 1999
$640 – €829 – £480 – FF5 440
«Viale adriatico in estate» Tecnica mista/cartone
(35x25cm 13x9in) Prato 2000

PIAN Giovanni Battista 1813-1857 [1]
$4 801 – €3 996 – £2 827 – FF26 213
Am Neptunbrunnen Öl/Leinwand (52x39cm
20x15in) Wien 1998

PIANA Giuseppe Ferdinando 1864-1956 [10]
$1 640 – €2 125 – £1 230 – FF13 940
Promontorio sul mare Olio/tavola (25x35cm 9x13in)
Vercelli 2000

PIANCA Giuseppe Antonio 1703-c.1760 [10]
$7 000 – €7 257 – £4 200 – FF47 600
Sacra Famiglia Olio/tela (76x96cm 29x37in) Milano
2001

PIANE dalle, il Mulinaretto Giovanni Maria 1660-1745 [17]
$64 800 – €55 979 – £43 200 – FF367 200
Ritratto del Magnifico Clemente Doria Olio/tela
(142x120cm 55x47in) Milano 1998
$18 400 – €23 843 – £13 800 – FF156 400
Ritratto di gentildonna/Ritratto di gentiluomo
Olio/tela (119x96cm 46x37in) Milano 2000

PIANON Alessandro XX [1]
$1 545 – €1 695 – £1 026 – FF111 120
Fågel Sculpture, glass (H31cm H12in) Stockholm 2000

PIATTI Antonio 1875-1962 [32]
$16 800 – €14 513 – £11 200 – FF95 200
Corso Vittorio Emanuele, Milano Olio/tela
(155x101cm 61x39in) Milano 1998
$3 200 – €4 147 – £2 400 – FF27 200
Dolce riposo Olio/tela (73x95cm 28x37in) Roma
2000
$1 750 – €1 814 – £1 050 – FF11 900
Paesaggio comasco con contadina Olio/tavola
(33x41.5cm 12x16in) Milano 2000
$1 200 – €1 037 – £800 – FF6 800
Ragazza lombarda Pastelli/cartone (60x52cm
23x20in) Milano 1998

PIATTI Celestino 1922 [55]
$142 – €153 – £95 – FF1 006
Siegfried Lenz Lithographie (42x32.5cm 16x12in)
München 2001

PIATTOLI Giuseppe c.1740-c.1815 [20]
$2 646 – €2 300 – £1 594 – FF15 084
Durchzug durch das Rote Meer Ink (46x59.3cm
18x23in) Berlin 1998

PIAUBERT Jean 1900 [312]
$3 148 – €3 049 – £1 980 – FF20 000
Mystagogie Peinture (150x150cm 59x59in) Paris 1999
$812 – €915 – £570 – FF6 000
Petit cosmos blanc Huile/toile (50x73cm 19x28in)
Paris 2001
$1 555 – €1 586 – £972 – FF10 406
Composition bleue et noire Aquarelle/papier
(74x103cm 29x40in) Bruxelles 2000
$192 – €179 – £118 – FF1 173
Rumb Farbserigraphie (26x31.5cm 10x12in) Hamburg
1999

PIAZZA A. XIX [5]
$12 335 – €11 682 – £7 500 – FF76 629
Cupid with a Bow and Arrow Marble (H74cm
H29in) London 1999

PIAZZA Calisto c.1500-c.1561 [4]
$115 840 – €131 639 – £80 000 – FF863 496
The Coronation of the Virgin Oil/panel (131x261cm
51x102in) London 2000

PIAZZETTA Giovanni Battista 1682-1754 [47]
$16 000 – €13 307 – £9 392 – FF87 288
A Youth, half-length, holding a String of Pearls
Oil/canvas/panel (73x55.2cm 28x21in) New-York 1998
$11 000 – €10 428 – £6 692 – FF68 406
Saint Jerome Emiliani Oil/canvas (41x31cm
16x12in) New-York 1998
$22 080 – €24 392 – £15 312 – FF160 000
Le joueur de mandoline Pierre noire (35x26cm
13x10in) Paris 2001

PIAZZONI Gottardo 1872-1945 [12]
$1 900 – €2 161 – £1 327 – FF14 174
Coastal View/Mountainous Scene Oil/board
(13x16cm 5x6in) Mystic CT 2000

PIC DE LEOPOLD Andreas 1789-1860 [9]
$252 – €216 – £151 – FF1 418
«Vista general del Real Sitio de Aranjuez»
Litografía (29x46cm 11x18in) Madrid 1998

PICABIA Francis 1879-1953 [752]
$170 000 – €158 763 – £104 924 – FF1 041 420
Kalinga Oil/panel (151.5x95.5cm 59x37in) New-York
1999
$35 863 – €38 496 – £24 000 – FF252 518
Femme en rouge Oil/panel (46x38.5cm 18x15in)
London 2000
$14 708 – €17 532 – £10 488 – FF115 000
Les mouettes Huile/panneau (21x17cm 8x6in) Nice
2000
$8 040 – €9 147 – £5 670 – FF60 000
Portrait de jeune espagnole Crayon/papier
(29x22cm 11x8in) Paris 2001
$700 – €602 – £410 – FF3 950
Puerto pesquero Grabado (54x68cm 21x26in)
Madrid 1998

PICARD Georges 1857-1946 [87]
$5 004 – €5 488 – £3 322 – FF36 000
Le printemps Huile/toile (200x161cm 78x63in)
Melun 2000
$454 – €488 – £304 – FF3 200
Femme couchée Huile/toile (38x57cm 14x22in)
Paris 2000
$170 – €183 – £114 – FF1 200
Femme endormie Huile/toile (26x52cm 10x20in)
Paris 2000

P

PICARD

🖋 $567 - €640 - £395 - FF4 200
Bouquet à la rose blanche Pastel/papier (38x46cm 14x18in) Bayeux 2001

PICARD Louis 1861-1940 **[22]**
🖼 $5 176 - €6 098 - £3 580 - FF40 000
Confidences de femmes Huile/toile (126x109cm 49x42in) Bordeaux 2000
🖼 $1 069 - €1 090 - £669 - FF7 150
Leda mit dem Schwan Öl/Leinwand (74x92cm 29x36in) Wien 2000
🖼 $2 600 - €2 373 - £1 581 - FF15 568
At the Ballet Oil/panel (23x33cm 9x13in) New-Orleans LA 1998

PICART Bernard 1673-1733 **[78]**
🖼 $59 007 - €66 469 - £41 496 - FF436 007
«Ländliche Freuden» Öl/Leinwand (91x146cm 35x57in) Stuttgart 2001
🖋 $650 - €680 - £408 - FF4 463
Male Nude Figure Seated Holding a club Red chalk/paper (49x30cm 19x12in) Litchfield CT 2000
📀 $98 - €102 - £61 - FF669
Leonardo atraviesa el Helesponto Nadando Aguafuerte (35.5x26cm 13x10in) Madrid 2000

PICART Jean-Michel 1600-1682 **[16]**
🖼 $552 891 - €593 483 - £370 000 - FF3 892 992
Tulips, Roses, Lilies, Carnations, Morning Glory and Other Flowers Oil/canvas (115.5x159.5cm 45x62in) London 2000
🖼 $85 000 - €85 989 - £51 901 - FF564 051
Still Life of Flowers in a Bronze Vase Oil/canvas (50x37.5cm 19x14in) New-York 2000
🖼 $18 676 - €18 359 - £12 000 - FF120 427
Still Life of three Roses in a Glass Vase and Wild Strawberries Oil/canvas (29.5x24cm 11x9in) London 1999

PICART LE DOUX Charles Alexandre 1881-1959 **[286]**
🖼 $976 - €991 - £607 - FF6 500
Paysage du Midi Huile/toile (58.5x71cm 23x27in) Paris 2000
🖋 $134 - €152 - £92 - FF1 000
A fleur de Seine Lavis (19.5x15.5cm 7x6in) Paris 2000

PICART LE DOUX Jean 1902-1982 **[131]**
🖋 $570 - €610 - £388 - FF4 000
Coquillages sur la grève Gouache/papier (27x39cm 10x15in) Pontoise 2001
📀 $4 326 - €4 269 - £2 665 - FF28 000
Jour et nuit Tapisserie (100x150cm 39x59in) Calais 1999

PICASSO Pablo 1881-1973 **[10913]**
🖼 $3 400 000 - €3 731 330 - £2 189 260 - FF24 475 920
Le peintre au modèle Oil/canvas (129x194.5cm 50x76in) New-York 2000
🖼 $1 200 000 - €1 024 293 - £717 600 - FF6 718 920
Buste de femme Oil/canvas (101x80.5cm 39x31in) New-York 1998
🖼 $220 626 - €214 086 - £140 000 - FF1 404 312
Bol vert et tomates Tempera/panel (20.5x27cm 8x10in) London 1999
🖋 $3 500 - €4 114 - £2 426 - FF26 986
Young Wood-owl, Vase Glazed ceramic (H25.5cm H10in) New-York 2000
🖋 $48 642 - €51 863 - £33 000 - FF340 197
Homme et femme Pencil/paper (32x42cm 12x16in) London 2001

PICHHAZDE Meir 1955 **[34]**
🖼 $8 695 - €8 003 - £5 219 - FF52 498
Composition Mixed media/canvas (138x138cm 54x54in) Tel Aviv 1999

📀 $5 190 - €4 985 - £3 200 - FF32 700
Toros Vallauris Linocut in colors (65x53.5cm 25x21in) London 1999
📷 $5 900 - €4 878 - £3 462 - FF32 000
Vues de l'atelier de Horta de Ebro avec présentation des toiles, été Tirage argentique (8.5x11cm 3x4in) Paris 1998

PICAULT C.E. XIX-XX **[4]**
🖼 $15 000 - €14 253 - £9 126 - FF93 493
Landscape with a meandering Stream/At the edge of the Forest Oil/panel (37.5x54.5cm 14x21in) New-York 1999
🖼 $3 100 - €3 005 - £1 919 - FF19 713
Woodland Pond at Sunrise Oil/panel (25x35cm 10x14in) Englewood NJ 1999

PICAULT Émile Louis 1833-1915 **[353]**
🖼 $6 129 - €6 708 - £4 228 - FF44 000
L'enlèvement de Sabine Sculpture bois (H86cm H33in) Paris 2001
🖋 $1 621 - €1 389 - £950 - FF9 108
Farm Labourer Bronze (H64cm H25in) London 1998

PICAULT Pierre 1680-1711 **[7]**
📀 $915 - €899 - £568 - FF5 898
Tentation du Saint Antoine, d'après Jacquesa Callota Etching (51.5x69.5cm 20x27in) Warszawa 1999

PICCAGLIANI E., of La Scala XX **[1]**
📷 $4 161 - €3 945 - £2 600 - FF25 877
Maria Callas, Giulietta Simionato and Cesare Siepi Photograph (10x13.5cm 3x5in) London 1999

PICCINELLI IL BRESCIANINO Andrea c.1485-1525 **[8]**
🖼 $318 560 - €362 008 - £220 000 - FF2 374 614
Venus with Sacred and Prophane Love Oil/panel (68x149cm 26x58in) London 2000

PICCINELLI Raffaello ?-1545 **[1]**
🖼 $24 105 - €23 910 - £15 000 - FF156 837
The Madonna and Child with the Infant Saint John the Baptist Oil/panel (58x45cm 22x17in) London 1999

PICCIONI Gino 1873-1941 **[14]**
🖼 $27 500 - €28 508 - £16 500 - FF187 000
Colazione in giardino Olio/tela (83.5x115cm 32x45in) Milano 1999

PICCIRILLI Attilio 1866-1945 **[7]**
🖋 $18 000 - €17 871 - £11 250 - FF117 226
The Wave Marble (H117cm H46in) New-York 1999

PICENARDI Mauro 1735-1809 **[4]**
🖼 $12 413 - €12 159 - £8 000 - FF79 756
Danaë Oil/canvas (86.5x116cm 34x45in) London 1999

PICHETTE James 1920-1996 **[284]**
🖼 $1 029 - €1 067 - £653 - FF7 000
Composition Huile/toile (35x85cm 13x33in) Paris 2000
🖋 $478 - €534 - £312 - FF3 500
Festival Huile/papier (34x24cm 13x9in) Le Touquet 2000
🖋 $586 - €549 - £359 - FF3 600
«Composition abstraite» Gouache (37.5x50cm 14x19in) Paris 1998

$7 500 - €7 961 - **£5 075** - FF52 222
Boy on a Bike in a Landscape Oil/canvas
(100x74.5cm 39x29in) Tel Aviv 2001
$1 300 - €1 541 - **£947** - FF10 109
Young Woman at the Table Gouache/paper
(35x26.5cm 13x10in) Tel Aviv 2001

PICHLER Antonio 1802-? [1]
$3 750 - €3 887 - **£2 250** - FF25 500
Ritratto di gentiluomo Plâtre (H53cm H20in) Roma
2000

PICHLER Johann Peter 1765-1807 [9]
$134 - €128 - **£83** - FF838
**Bildnis Gideon Ernest Loudon, Feldmarschall,
nach Haubenstricker** Mezzotint (37.4x26.4cm
14x10in) Berlin 1999

PICHLER Rudolf 1874-1950 [19]
$578 - €654 - **£390** - FF4 290
Der Ratzenstadl im Schnee Aquarell/Papier
(17.5x29cm 6x11in) Wien 2000

PICHLER Walter 1936 [45]
$2 172 - €1 816 - **£1 287** - FF11 910
Ohne Titel Pencil/paper (30x43cm 11x16in) Wien
1998

PICHON Charles XX [5]
$2 385 - €2 211 - **£1 483** - FF14 500
Vue d'Alger et le port Aquarelle/papier (53x103cm
20x40in) Evreux 1999

PICHON Jean-Jacques XVIII-XIX [1]
$6 667 - €6 288 - **£4 200** - FF41 244
**View of the Governor General's Bodyguard at
Baloo-Gunge** Watercolour/paper (40.5x68.5cm
15x26in) Godalming, Surrey 1999

PICHON Pierre Auguste 1805-1900 [3]
$25 249 - €23 630 - **£15 639** - FF155 000
**Duc d'Orléans en pied dans un intérieur,
d'après Ingres** Huile/toile (155x120cm 61x47in) Paris
1999

PICHOT GIRONES Ramón Antonio 1872-1925 [32]
$10 240 - €9 610 - **£6 400** - FF63 040
Nu en un interior Oleo/lienzo (112x161cm 44x63in)
Madrid 1999
$2 167 - €2 553 - **£1 530** - FF16 745
Escena parisina Oleo/cartón (40x33cm 15x12in)
Madrid 2000

PICHOT Ramón 1924-1996 [37]
$1 989 - €2 343 - **£1 365** - FF15 366
Figura sentada Oleo/lienzo (47x38.5cm 18x15in)
Barcelona 2000
$1 508 - €1 562 - **£936** - FF10 244
Fruta y hortalizas Oleo/cartón (34.5x43.5cm
13x17in) Barcelona 2000

PICHOT SOLER Ramon 1925-1987 [9]
$4 080 - €4 805 - **£2 800** - FF31 520
Paris Oleo/lienzo (54x65cm 21x25in) Madrid 2000
$1 323 - €1 220 - **£792** - FF8 000
Nature morte aux fruits et aux oignons Huile/car-
ton (34x43cm 13x16in) Paris 1998

PICINELLI IL BRESCIANINO Andrea c.1487-1545
[3]
$30 000 - €32 039 - **£20 442** - FF210 159
**Christ holding the Cross, as the Man of
Sorrows** Oil/canvas (109x72.5cm 42x28in) New-York
2001
$2 470 - €2 350 - **£1 500** - FF15 413
Saint Jérôme/The Madonna Oil/panel (18x24.5cm
7x9in) London 1999

PICINNI Gennaro 1933 [17]
$1 100 - €1 140 - **£660** - FF7 480
«Natura morta con pesce viola» Olio/tavola
(75x90cm 29x35in) Vercelli 1999

PICK Anton 1840-c.1905 [50]
$1 129 - €1 108 - **£700** - FF7 270
Extensive Alpine Landscape Oil/canvas/board
(68.5x101.5cm 26x39in) London 1999

PICK Seraphine 1964 [4]
$7 658 - €8 585 - **£5 356** - FF56 312
Bad Bath Stack Oil/canvas (50.5x152.5cm 19x60in)
Auckland 2001

PICKEN Thomas XIX [7]
$236 - €227 - **£147** - FF1 488
View of Quebec, d'après Captain B.Beaufoy
Lithographie (36x52cm 14x20in) Montréal 1999

PICKERING George c.1794-1857 [4]
$867 - €931 - **£580** - FF6 107
A Landscape Near Newstead Watercolour
(26x38cm 10x14in) London 2000

PICKERING Henry c.1720-c.1775 [19]
$6 164 - €5 920 - **£3 800** - FF38 831
**Portrait of Mr.Norreys of Speke, in naval
Uniform, feigned oval** Oil/canvas (76.5x63.5cm
30x25in) London 1999

PICKERING Joseph Langsdale 1845-1912 [18]
$37 500 - €43 569 - **£26 355** - FF285 795
Where winter touches lightly Oil/canvas
(112x151cm 44x59in) New-York 2001
$2 734 - €2 775 - **£1 700** - FF18 205
The Stack-Yard Corner Oil/canvas (35.5x46cm
13x18in) London 2000
$757 - €655 - **£450** - FF4 298
«On the Pellice, Piedmont» Oil/panel (20x30.5cm
7x12in) London 1998

PICKERSGILL Frederick Richard 1820-1900 [36]
$784 - €884 - **£543** - FF5 800
The Arrest of Carrara at Ventimiglia Oil/board
(42.5x50cm 16x19in) Toronto 2000

PICKERSGILL Henry William 1782-1875 [19]
$4 837 - €5 621 - **£3 400** - FF36 870
Portrait of Thomas Cubitt (1788-1855) Oil/canvas
(76.5x63.5cm 30x25in) London 2001
$2 565 - €2 466 - **£1 600** - FF16 178
**Portrait of William, 6th Marquess of Lothian K.T
(1763-1841)** Pencil (40x30.5cm 15x12in) Billingshurst,
West-Sussex 2001

PICKETT Joseph 1848-1918 [1]
$6 750 - €6 294 - **£4 187** - FF41 289
New Hope, PA. Oil/canvas (40.5x50.5cm 15x19in)
New-York 1999

PICKETT W. XVIII-XIX [1]
$4 812 - €4 849 - **£3 000** - FF31 810
**Romantic and Picturesque Scenery of England
& Wales after Loutherbourg** Aquatint (47.5x31.5cm
18x12in) London 2000

PICKHARDT Carl E., Jr. 1908 [15]
$550 - €513 - **£339** - FF3 364
«Subway» Lithograph (25x20cm 10x8in) Cleveland
OH 1999

PICKNELL William Lamb 1853-1897 [22]
$75 000 - €71 265 - **£45 630** - FF467 467
Bleak December Oil/canvas (139.5x203cm 54x79in)
New-York 1999

P

$38 000 - €41 691 - £25 243 - FF273 478
French Landscape Oil/canvas (57.5x70.5cm
22x27in) New-York 2000

PICO MITJANS José 1904-1991 **[47]**
$150 - €156 - £93 - FF1 024
El desfile Tinta/papel (31x28.5cm 12x11in) Madrid
2000

PICOLO Y LOPEZ Manuel 1855-1912 **[16]**
$1 067 - €1 051 - £665 - FF6 895
Damas Oleo/tabla (19.5x11cm 7x4in) Madrid 1999

PICOT François Édouard 1786-1868 **[9]**
$18 986 - €18 317 - £12 000 - FF120 150
Jeune femme à l'étoile d'Hermine Oil/canvas
(92x73cm 36x28in) London 1999
$18 407 - €21 657 - £13 325 - FF142 061
Léda et le Cygne Huile/toile (22x31cm 8x12in) Sion
2001

PICOU Henri Pierre 1824-1895 **[110]**
$7 445 - €7 622 - £4 675 - FF50 000
La récolte des fleurs Huile/toile (100x71cm
39x27in) Lille 2000
$1 403 - €1 601 - £979 - FF10 500
L'amour prisonnier Huile/panneau (41x33cm
16x12in) Paris 2001

PICQUÉ Charles 1799-1869 **[8]**
$4 526 - €3 842 - £2 697 - FF25 203
«Brigand italien et sa belle» Huile/toile (120x95cm
47x37in) Bruxelles 1998

PIDDING Henry James 1797-1864 **[2]**
$29 886 - €32 080 - £20 000 - FF210 432
Figures Playing Baccarat in a Gaming Room
Oil/canvas (110.5x141cm 43x55in) London 2000
$11 954 - €12 832 - £8 000 - FF84 172
**Naval Intelligence: Greenwich Pensioners
Reading a Copy of the Times** Oil/canvas
(112x86.5cm 44x34in) London 2000

PIDELASERRA Y BRIAS Mariano 1877-1946 **[14]**
$1 071 - €1 261 - £735 - FF8 274
Els peixos del Aquarium Oleo/tabla (37.5x45.5cm
14x17in) Barcelona 2000

PIDGEON Henry Clarke 1807-1880 **[13]**
$324 - €303 - £200 - FF1 985
The Devon Coast Watercolour (37x54.5cm 14x21in)
London 1999

PIECK Anton 1895-1986 **[85]**
$11 257 - €11 344 - £7 017 - FF74 415
Still Life with Eggs and a Pharmacist Jar
Oil/panel (20x20cm 7x7in) Amsterdam 2000
$720 - €726 - £449 - FF4 762
View in a Street in East Looe Watercolour
(31.5x23cm 12x9in) Amsterdam 2000
$175 - €181 - £111 - FF1 190
Street Scene, Amersfoort Etching (19.5x19cm
7x7in) Amsterdam 2000

PIECK Henri Christiaan 1895-1972 **[27]**
$519 - €590 - £361 - FF3 869
«Nederlandsche Jaarbeurs Utrecht» Poster
(75x101cm 29x39in) Hoorn 2001

PIELER Frans Xaver 1876-1952 **[117]**
$4 277 - €5 087 - £3 052 - FF33 369
Grosses Blumenstück in altmeisterlichem Stil
Öl/Leinwand (76.5x63cm 30x24in) Wien 2000
$1 891 - €2 250 - £1 348 - FF14 757
Blumenstilleben in einer Messingvase Oil/panel
(33x33cm 12x12in) Köln 2000

PIELER van J. XVIII-XIX **[1]**
$14 000 - €12 960 - £8 451 - FF85 015
Flowers in a Terracotta Urn Resting on a Ledge
Oil/canvas (89x68.5cm 35x26in) New-York 1999

PIENE Otto 1928 **[257]**
$5 360 - €5 880 - £3 640 - FF38 569
City Armor Mixed media (100x130.5cm 39x51in)
Berlin 2000
$452 - €5 292 - £3 394 - FF34 712
Eye Ball Mixed media/canvas (40.2x50cm 15x19in)
Berlin 1999
$1 795 - €1 662 - £1 098 - FF10 900
Revelation Mixed media/canvas (30.3x40cm 11x15in)
Dettelbach-Effeldorf 1999
$2 842 - €2 812 - £1 772 - FF18 446
Ohne Titel Gouache/Karton (67x94.5cm 26x37in)
Berlin 1999
$213 - €204 - £130 - FF1 341
Sponge Farblithographie (92x64cm 36x25in) Bielefeld
1999

PIENKOWSKI Ignacy 1877-1948 **[22]**
$4 556 - €4 193 - £2 734 - FF27 505
Danseuse Oil/canvas (55.2x46.3cm 21x18in)
Warszawa 1999

PIEPENHAGEN August Bedrich 1791-1868 **[30]**
$3 179 - €3 007 - £1 980 - FF19 723
Paysage romantique à la rotonde Huile/toile
(20.5x27.5cm 8x10in) Praha 1999

PIEPENHAGENOVA Louisa 1828-1893 **[5]**
$2 852 - €2 907 - £1 784 - FF19 068
Schloss in Tirol Öl/Leinwand (38x48cm 14x18in)
Wien 2000

PIEPER Christian 1843-1934 **[4]**
$32 500 - €30 441 - £19 981 - FF199 683
The adoring Sister Oil/canvas (68.5x49cm 26x19in)
New-York 1999

PIERCE Charles Franklin 1844-1920 **[41]**
$2 300 - €2 171 - £1 429 - FF14 244
The Buggy Oil/canvas (50x76cm 20x30in) Milford CT
1999
$600 - €648 - £415 - FF4 251
Early Autumn Landscape Oil/board (30x40cm
12x16in) Cincinnati OH 2001

PIERCE Elijah 1892-1982 **[6]**
$12 000 - €10 357 - £7 242 - FF67 936
«Mother's Prayers» Sculpture, wood (45x36cm
18x14in) New-York 1999

PIERCE Joseph W. XIX **[3]**
$1 700 - €1 542 - £1 035 - FF10 113
**An American Clipper Ship and a British Bark in
an Oriental Harbour** Watercolour/paper (59x92cm
23x36in) East-Dennis MA 1999

PIERCE Waldo 1884-1970 **[54]**
$2 750 - €2 356 - £1 653 - FF15 456
«Big Blow at Searsport» Oil/canvas (66x91cm
26x36in) Dedham MA 1998

PIERDON François 1821-1904 **[19]**
$495 - €486 - £319 - FF3 186
Waldlandschaft mit Wäscherin am Fluss
Öl/Leinwand (27x22cm 10x8in) Hildrizhausen 1999

PIERI Giovanni Francesco XVIII **[1]**
$21 420 - €18 504 - £10 710 - FF121 380
Profili di regnanti Scultura (42x34cm 16x13in)
Venezia 1999

PIERNEEF Jacob Hendrik 1886-1957 **[291]**

🔄 **$24 871** - €23 320 - **£15 369** - FF152 968
Summer Rain in the Bushveld Oil/board (88x140cm 34x55in) Johannesburg 1999

🔄 **$13 323** - €12 493 - **£8 233** - FF81 947
Lowveld Vista Oil/board (44.5x59.5cm 17x23in) Johannesburg 1999

🔄 **$4 905** - €4 726 - **£3 030** - FF31 002
Landscape with a Log in the Foreground Oil/board (29.5x39.5cm 11x15in) Johannesburg 1999

✎ **$1 154** - €1 083 - **£713** - FF7 102
Thames, Battersea, London Watercolour (22x34cm 8x13in) Johannesburg 1999

📜 **$310** - €299 - **£191** - FF1 963
Huis in Rustenberg, TVL Linocut (14.5x21cm 5x8in) Johannesburg 1999

PIERO di COSIMO 1462-1521 **[2]**

✎ **$150 000** - €160 453 - **£102 270** - FF1 052 505
Study of the Madonna and another figure/Kneeling Angel Ink (10x9cm 3x3in) New-York 1999

PIERON Henri XIX **[15]**

🔄 **$1 912** - €1 983 - **£1 216** - FF13 008
Landschap med koeien Oil/canvas (120x76cm 47x29in) Lokeren 2000

PIERRAKOS Alkis 1920 **[37]**

🔄 **$907** - €1 067 - **£629** - FF7 000
Paysage Huile/toile (61x46cm 24x18in) Paris 2000

PIERRE & GILLES 1976 **[19]**

🔄 **$5 446** - €5 488 - **£3 394** - FF36 000
Patrick dans les fleurs - Le Magicien Peinture (26.5x38cm 10x14in) Paris 2000

📷 **$16 655** - €15 457 - **£10 000** - FF101 392
Le ramasseur de coquillages; Model: Kohji Kanari, Costume: Tomah Photograph in colors (106x117cm 41x46in) London 1999

PIERRE Jean-Baptiste Marie 1713-1789 **[55]**

🔄 **$25 000** - €24 988 - **£15 272** - FF163 912
River Landscape with a Peasant Family, a Man in a Boat Oil/canvas (210x119cm 82x46in) New-York 2000

🔄 **$13 608** - €16 007 - **£9 754** - FF105 000
Paysans au repos et promeneurs au tour d'une fontaine à l'obélisque Huile/toile (50x59.5cm 19x23in) Paris 2001

✎ **$6 944** - €8 232 - **£5 059** - FF54 000
Naïades Encre (23.5x32cm 9x12in) Neuilly-sur-Seine 2001

📜 **$378** - €381 - **£235** - FF2 500
Le marché de village Eau-forte (11.5x17cm 4x6in) Paris 2000

PIERRE-HENRY 1924 **[41]**

🔄 **$923** - €1 098 - **£635** - FF7 200
Enfant à l'agneau Huile/toile (130x89cm 51x35in) Biarritz 2001

🔄 **$491** - €579 - **£345** - FF3 800
Femme de profil Huile/toile (41x33cm 16x12in) Fontainebleau 2000

PIERRE-LOUIS Prosper 1947 **[23]**

🔄 **$827** - €841 - **£517** - FF5 514
Loa Huile/toile (101x76cm 39x29in) Montréal 2000

PIERSON Albert Léopold XIX-XX **[12]**

🔄 **$509** - €488 - **£313** - FF3 200
Bord de rivière à Hennebont Huile/panneau (24x33cm 9x12in) La Varenne-Saint-Hilaire 1999

PIERSON Jack 1960 **[58]**

🔄 **$20 000** - €18 779 - **£12 392** - FF123 182
Sister Honky Tonk Acrylic (183x183cm 72x72in) New-York 1999

🔄 **$17 000** - €19 347 - **£11 945** - FF126 908
Dhope Construction (117x98cm 46x38in) New-York 2001

🔄 **$32 200** - €36 066 - **£22 372** - FF236 579
Youicide Assemblage (59.5x167.5cm 23x65in) New-York 2001

📄 **$2 200** - €2 129 - **£1 356** - FF13 963
Untitled Ink (35.5x28cm 13x11in) New-York 1999

📷 **$2 600** - €2 852 - **£1 727** - FF18 711
Lights (42nd St) Cibachrome print (96.5x76cm 37x29in) New-York 2000

PIERSON Pierre L. 1822-1913 **[28]**

📷 **$3 975** - €4 573 - **£2 739** - FF30 000
La Comtesse de Castiglione, Alta, assise Tirage albuminé (18x18.5cm 7x7in) Chartres 2000

PIET Fernand 1869-1942 **[264]**

🔄 **$2 496** - €2 515 - **£1 555** - FF16 500
Le marché Huile/carton (50x73.5cm 19x28in) Cherbourg 2000

🔄 **$1 415** - €1 329 - **£877** - FF8 720
Frau am Tisch Öl/Karton (34x27cm 13x10in) München 1999

✎ **$142** - €152 - **£95** - FF1 000
La pensive Fusain (24x15cm 9x5in) Coulommiers 2000

PIETERCELIE Alfred 1879-1955 **[85]**

🔄 **$520** - €496 - **£316** - FF3 252
Vase de fleurs Huile/toile (70x60cm 27x23in) Bruxelles 1999

PIETERS Evert 1856-1932 **[204]**

🔄 **$72 500** - €81 153 - **£50 561** - FF532 331
In the Orchard Oil/canvas (131x113cm 51x44in) New-York 2001

🔄 **$4 228** - €4 538 - **£2 829** - FF29 766
Wolkamster: a peasantwoman combing wool Oil/canvas (34x51cm 13x20in) Amsterdam 2000

🔄 **$3 240** - €3 403 - **£2 050** - FF22 324
Towning the Boat Oil/panel (16x24cm 6x9in) Amsterdam 2000

✎ **$6 137** - €6 999 - **£3 827** - FF38 695
Children Plaiting a Daisy Chain Watercolour (39x54cm 15x21in) Amsterdam 1999

PIETERSZ. Pieter II 1578-1631 **[1]**

🔄 **$14 178** - €15 882 - **£9 852** - FF104 181
Christ driving the Money Changers from the Temple Oil/panel (93x124cm 36x48in) Amsterdam 2001

PIETILÄ Tuulikki 1917 **[28]**

📜 **$182** - €185 - **£113** - FF1 213
Stad Woodcut (60x50cm 23x19in) Helsinki 2000

PIETRI de Pietro Antonio 1663-1716 **[22]**

🔄 **$9 060** - €8 721 - **£5 664** - FF57 204
Der heilige Vincent de Paul verteilt Brot an die Armen Öl/Leinwand (99x73.5cm 38x28in) Wien 1999

✎ **$3 275** - €3 043 - **£2 000** - FF19 963
St Clement Giving the Veil to Flavia Domitilla Ink (11x19cm 4x7in) London 1998

PIETRI de Pietro Michele XVIII-XIX **[2]**

✎ **$1 498** - €1 586 - **£950** - FF10 401
Trompe l'Oeil of Engravings After Portraits and Landscapes Watercolour (35x49.5cm 13x19in) London 2000

P

PIETRO DA CORTONA 1596-1669 **[32]**
- **$34 825** - €38 112 - **£24 075** - FF250 000
  Sainte Dafrosa Huile/toile (187x119cm 73x46in)
  Versailles 2001
- **$23 030** - €25 435 - **£15 960** - FF166 845
  Daniel in der Löwengrube Öl/Leinwand (100x60cm
  39x23in) Wien 2001
- **$235 275** - €229 725 - **£150 000** - FF1 506 900
  **Construction of a classical temple, groups of
  Astrologers, Architects** Black chalk (25.5x42cm
  10x16in) London 1999

PIETRO DI DOMENICO 1457-c.1533 **[3]**
- **$58 000** - €75 157 - **£43 500** - FF493 000
  Madonna dell'Umiltà Tempera/tavola (61x49cm
  24x19in) Roma 2001
- **$51 765** - €53 662 - **£31 059** - FF352 002
  Madonna col Bambino e San Giovannino
  Tempera/tavola (43.5x32.5cm 17x12in) Venezia 2000

PIETRO DI RUFFOLO XV **[1]**
- **$13 000** - €14 967 - **£8 871** - FF98 176
  Saint Sebastian Oil/panel (90x40cm 35x15in) New-
  York 2000

PIETRO di Sano 1405-1481 **[7]**
- **$368 412** - €313 658 - **£220 000** - FF2 057 462
  **The Madonna and Child with Saint Bernardino
  of Siena** Tempera/panel (50x44cm 19x17in) London
  1998
- **$358 996** - €333 718 - **£220 000** - FF2 189 044
  The Madonna and Child Tempera/panel (41.5x29cm
  16x11in) London 1998

PIETRO GERINI di Niccolo c.1340-c.1415 **[2]**
- **$28 000** - €29 026 - **£16 800** - FF190 400
  Madonna con il bambino Tempera/tavola (68x50cm
  26x19in) Milano 2001

PIETTE DE MONTFOUCAULT Ludovic Piette, dit
1826-1877 **[33]**
- **$4 020** - €4 573 - **£2 790** - FF30 000
  La visite Huile/toile (54.5x38cm 21x14in) Paris 2000
- **$1 611** - €1 829 - **£1 119** - FF12 000
  Marché aux fleurs à Pontoise Pastel (47x33cm
  18x12in) Pontoise 2001

PIETZSCH Richard 1872-1960 **[19]**
- **$453** - €511 - **£314** - FF3 353
  Landschaft bei Königsdorf, Obb Oil/canvas/panel
  (37x52cm 14x20in) München 2001

PIFFARD Harold Hume XIX-XX **[29]**
- **$3 197** - €3 169 - **£2 000** - FF20 788
  Double Act Oil/canvas (76.5x64cm 30x25in) London
  1999

PIGA Bernard 1934 **[11]**
- **$530** - €610 - **£374** - FF4 000
  L'homme et le cheval Dessin (65x50cm 25x19in)
  Barbizon 2001

PIGALLE Jean-Baptiste 1714-1785 **[10]**
- **$2 937** - €2 506 - **£1 750** - FF16 436
  Mercury Bronze (H69cm H27in) Billingshurst, West-
  Sussex 1998

PIGATO Orazio 1896-1966 **[4]**
- **$3 750** - €3 887 - **£2 250** - FF25 500
  Paesaggio marino Olio/tavola (45x61cm 17x24in)
  Prato 2000

PIGEON Maurice 1883-1944 **[15]**
- **$2 711** - €3 201 - **£1 925** - FF21 000
  L'automne à Morsalines Huile/toile (100x81cm
  39x31in) Paris 2001

PIGEOT Pierre XX **[16]**
- **$1 344** - €1 128 - **£788** - FF7 400
  Couchant sur la falaise Aquarelle/papier (30x46cm
  11x18in) Grenoble 1998
- **$721** - €797 - **£500** - FF5 230
  «Foreign Correspondent, Correspondant 17»
  Poster (160x119.5cm 62x47in) London 2001

PIGHILLS Joseph 1902-1984 **[11]**
- **$190** - €200 - **£120** - FF1 311
  Maldon Essex Watercolour/paper (22x38cm 9x15in)
  Aylsham, Norfolk 2000

PIGLHEIM Bruno 1848-1894 **[14]**
- **$5 056** - €4 602 - **£3 159** - FF30 185
  Weihnachtsmorgen Öl/Leinwand (81x109cm
  31x42in) München 1999
- **$1 367** - €1 534 - **£947** - FF10 061
  **Zwei Frauen und ein Kind vor einer
  Fensterleibung** Oil/panel (26.7x35cm 10x13in)
  München 2000

PIGNATELLI Ercole 1935 **[77]**
- **$960** - €829 - **£640** - FF5 440
  Piazza d'Italia con Arianna Olio/tela (50.5x60cm
  19x23in) Prato 1998
- **$300** - €311 - **£180** - FF2 040
  Senza titolo Tecnica mista/carta (20.5x20.5cm 8x8in)
  Vercelli 2000

PIGNATELLI Luca 1962 **[3]**
- **$10 500** - €10 885 - **£6 300** - FF71 400
  Aereo con rocce e lago ghiacciato Tecnica mista
  (250x210cm 98x82in) Milano 2000
- **$3 000** - €3 887 - **£2 250** - FF25 500
  **«Ricognizione, bombardieri sul lago ghiaccia-
  to»** Tecnica mista (60x80cm 23x31in) Milano 2001

PIGNON Édouard 1905-1993 **[847]**
- **$10 350** - €11 434 - **£7 177** - FF75 000
  La ferme de Jo Huile/toile (130x195cm 51x76in)
  Paris 2001
- **$3 470** - €3 659 - **£2 292** - FF24 000
  Personnages Huile/toile (50x65cm 19x25in) Paris
  2000
- **$2 392** - €2 744 - **£1 636** - FF18 000
  Combats de coqs Huile/toile (24x35cm 9x13in)
  Paris 2001
- **$1 611** - €1 829 - **£1 119** - FF12 000
  La charge, pousseurs de blé Gouache/papier
  (48x62.5cm 18x24in) Orléans 2001
- **$89** - €102 - **£61** - FF670
  Picasso Soleil Farblithographie (53.5x75.8cm
  21x29in) Heidelberg 2000

PIGNON-ERNEST Ernest 1942 **[21]**
- **$2 168** - €2 439 - **£1 492** - FF16 000
  Salomé Encre (21x19cm 8x7in) Paris 2000
- **$271** - €305 - **£186** - FF2 000
  Regards Lithographie couleurs (48.5x40cm 19x15in)
  Paris 2000

PIGNONE Joseph c.1910-c.1990 **[1]**
- **$2 600** - €3 031 - **£1 800** - FF19 880
  **Usin an Eggbeater to Wind a Coil/Blind
  Woman/Adjusting** Gouache/paper (53x38cm
  21x15in) New-York 2000

PIGNONE Simone 1611/14-1698 **[34]**
- **$10 460** - €11 228 - **£7 000** - FF73 651
  An Allegory of Peace Oil/canvas (96.5x77cm
  37x30in) London 2000
- **$6 000** - €6 427 - **£4 097** - FF42 159
  Seted Male Nude Red chalk/paper (41x28cm
  16x11in) New-York 2001

PIGNOTTI Lamberto 1926 **[10]**
🎨 **$2 000** - €2 073 - **£1 200** - FF13 600
Arte bellisima e superlativa Tecnica mista/cartone (72x50.5cm 28x19in) Prato 1999

PIGOTT Charles XIX-XX **[25]**
🖌 **$299** - €258 - **£180** - FF1 694
Sheep in a Stormy Landscape Watercolour/paper (17x24cm 6x9in) Leyburn, North Yorkshire 1998

PIGOTT Hadrian 1961 **[5]**
🖼 **$1 442** - €1 695 - **£1 000** - FF11 120
Wash II (Self Position II), London 12 septembre Installation (8x13x8cm 3x5x3in) London 2000

PIGOTT Walter Henry c.1810-1901 **[25]**
🖌 **$704** - €703 - **£440** - FF4 611
Cattle Grazing and Drinking in Haddon Pastures Watercolour/paper (71x38cm 28x15in) Rotherham 1999

PIGUENIT William Charles 1836-1914 **[52]**
🖌 **$15 669** - €14 700 - **£9 681** - FF96 424
Scene on the Derwent River, Tasmania Oil/canvas (45x76.5cm 17x30in) Melbourne 1999
🖌 **$791** - €742 - **£489** - FF4 864
Mountain Reflections Oil/canvas (14.5x29.5cm 5x11in) Melbourne 1999
🖌 **$1 271** - €1 237 - **£782** - FF8 115
Lakeside View, Tasmania Watercolour/paper (18x27.5cm 7x10in) Malvern, Victoria 1999

PIGUET Gustave 1909-1976 **[9]**
🖼 **$1 090** - €1 233 - **£767** - FF8 087
Knabenakt Bronze (H75cm H29in) Bern 2001

PIGUET Jean-Louis 1944 **[12]**
🖌 **$685** - €782 - **£483** - FF5 131
«**Fenêtres aux Issambres**» Öl/Leinwand (65x54cm 25x21in) Bern 2001

PIGUET Rodolphe 1840-1915 **[28]**
🖌 **$470** - €435 - **£288** - FF2 856
Altes Chalet am Seeufer Pastell/Papier (23.5x31.5cm 9x12in) Bern 1999

PIHLS Hans 1903 **[4]**
🖌 **$2 018** - €2 035 - **£1 260** - FF13 347
Wien, Peterskirche Öl/Leinwand (48x64cm 18x25in) Wien 2000

PIKE Jimmy 1940 **[58]**
🖌 **$2 630** - €2 823 - **£1 760** - FF18 520
Waterhole Country Kurhuminti/Jilji Parrapara Kurkuminti Painting (35x45cm 13x17in) Woollahra, Sydney 2000
🖼 **$82** - €90 - **£54** - FF592
Untitled I Serigraph in colors (40.5x51cm 15x20in) Melbourne 2000

PIKE John 1911-1979 **[14]**
🖌 **$550** - €492 - **£336** - FF3 225
Barns in Winter Watercolour/paper (51x67cm 20x26in) Boston MA 1999

PIKE Jonathan 1949 **[4]**
🖌 **$4 545** - €4 370 - **£2 800** - FF28 667
The Villa, Soranzo at Stra Watercolour/paper (58.5x76cm 23x29in) London 1999

PIKE Sidney XIX-XX **[63]**
🖌 **$1 200** - €1 146 - **£720** - FF7 519
The Ford Oil/board (75x62cm 29x24in) London 1999
🖌 **$567** - €589 - **£360** - FF3 861
Hens in a Farmyard Oil/board (16x20cm 6x7in) Cheshire 2000

🖌 **$179** - €163 - **£110** - FF1 072
Fisherman on a Mountainous Stream Watercolour/paper (25x20cm 9x7in) Stansted Mountfitchet, Essex 1998

PIKE William Henry 1846-1908 **[46]**
🖌 **$836** - €951 - **£580** - FF6 239
«**Good Story**» Oil/panel (23x30cm 9x12in) Birmingham 2000
🖌 **$773** - €792 - **£480** - FF5 195
Hauling in the Boats/Hauling in the Catch Watercolour (33x66cm 12x25in) Billingshurst, West-Sussex 2000

PIKESLEY Richard 1951 **[9]**
🖌 **$971** - €1 043 - **£650** - FF6 839
Campo Stefano, Venice Oil/canvas (86x81cm 33x31in) London 2000

PILET Edgar 1912 **[17]**
🖌 **$1 443** - €1 677 - **£1 014** - FF11 000
Gri-gri Huile/toile (85x70cm 33x27in) Paris 2001

PILET Léon 1840-1916 **[20]**
🖼 **$625** - €625 - **£391** - FF4 100
Fillette au chat Bronze (H28cm H11in) Paris 1999

PILICHOWSKI Leopold 1869-1933 **[6]**
🖌 **$1 368** - €1 532 - **£950** - FF10 052
Study of a Girl in a blue Cloche Hat Pastel/paper (40.5x58.5cm 15x23in) London 2001

PILKINGTON George William 1879-1958 **[27]**
🖌 **$555** - €536 - **£343** - FF3 513
Shipping in a Harbour Oil/canvas/board (24x34cm 9x13in) Johannesburg 1999

PILLARD Elizabeth XIX **[1]**
🖌 **$57 000** - €49 177 - **£34 388** - FF322 580
A Studio of their Own Oil/canvas (159x159cm 62x62in) New-York 2001

PILLATI Henryk 1832-1894 **[4]**
🖌 **$6 604** - €7 134 - **£4 565** - FF46 793
Insurgé blessé Huile/toile (36x45cm 14x17in) Kraków 2001

PILLE Charles-Henri 1844-1897 **[67]**
🖌 **$71** - €69 - **£43** - FF450
Assaut d'une maison Encre/papier (22x27cm 8x10in) Troyes 1999

PILLEAU Henry 1815-1899 **[38]**
🖌 **$648** - €544 - **£380** - FF3 568
Figures and Cattle Before a River in the Italian Tyrol near Simplon Watercolour (30.5x48cm 12x18in) London 1998

PILLEMENT Jean-Baptiste 1728-1808 **[218]**
🖌 **$18 013** - €21 474 - **£12 843** - FF140 863
Südliche Landschaft mit Wäscherinnen Öl/Leinwand (49.5x70cm 19x27in) Köln 2000
🖌 **$6 500** - €6 205 - **£4 061** - FF40 700
Peasants and Goats in Hilly Landscapes Oil/metal (17.5x24.5cm 6x9in) New-York 1999
🖌 **$3 014** - €2 566 - **£1 800** - FF16 833
Two Peasants in a Landscape Black chalk/paper (18x29cm 7x11in) London 1998

PILLET Edgard 1912-1996 **[86]**
🖌 **$1 611** - €1 372 - **£959** - FF9 000
Douce amère Huile/toile (46x54cm 18x21in) Paris 1998
🖼 **$515** - €589 - **£362** - FF3 861
Parcours réels Serigraph (44x36cm 17x14in) Helsinki 2001

P

PILLHOFER Joseph 1921 **[19]**
- $4 669 - €3 999 - **£2 733** - FF26 229
«Kleiner Kuros» Bronze (H55cm H21in) Wien 1998

PILLINI Marguerita XIX-XX **[7]**
- $1 623 - €1 372 - **£965** - FF9 000
Le repas de famille Huile/toile (93x125cm 36x49in) Quimper 1998

PILLOT Lucien M. 1882-1973 **[14]**
- $1 512 - €1 677 - **£1 050** - FF11 000
Les falaises de Mouthier, Haute Pierre Huile/toile/panneau (54x126cm 21x49in) Besançon 2001

PILNY Otto 1866-1936 **[121]**
- $30 061 - €35 063 - **£20 907** - FF230 000
Vente d'esclaves dans le désert Huile/toile (110x160cm 43x62in) Paris 2000
- $4 644 - €5 283 - **£3 220** - FF34 652
An Arab Mehari Scene Öl/Leinwand (48x64cm 18x25in) Zofingen 1998
- $1 968 - €2 287 - **£1 402** - FF15 000
Rue animée, au Caire Huile/toile/carton 12x10in) Paris 2001

PILO Carl Gustav 1712-1792 **[13]**
- $15 038 - €16 873 - **£10 424** - FF110 678
König Frederik V.von Dänemark im Prachtornat Öl/Leinwand (92x66cm 36x25in) München 2000
- $2 346 - €2 221 - **£1 460** - FF14 567
Portraet af Frederik V i rustning Oil/canvas (41x31cm 16x12in) Vejle 1999

PILON Agathe XIX **[2]**
- $28 000 - €30 720 - **£18 600** - FF201 510
Roses, a Pansy, forget-me-nots in a Glass Vase and a Fly on a marble Oil/canvas (24.5x32.5cm 9x12in) New-York 2001

PILON Germain 1528-1580 **[3]**
- $717 264 - €769 924 - **£480 000** - FF5 050 368
Bust of Henri II, Crowned with Laurels in Classical Armour Bronze (H85cm H33in) London 2001

PILOT Robert Wakeham 1898-1967 **[161]**
- $12 852 - €10 885 - **£7 725** - FF71 403
Ice Floes at Levis, Quebec Oil/canvas (46.5x56cm 18x22in) Vancouver, BC. 1998
- $4 210 - €4 912 - **£2 930** - FF32 219
«Wolf's Cove, Quebec» Oil/panel (26.5x34.5cm 10x13in) Toronto 2000
- $265 - €293 - **£179** - FF1 925
The Old Fort Chambly Etching (11.5x34cm 4x13in) Toronto 2000

PILOTY Ferdinand I 1785-1844 **[4]**
- $1 928 - €1 841 - **£1 204** - FF12 074
Anbetung der Hirten, nach Pietro da Cortona Lithographie (30.5x23.5cm 12x9in) Saarbrücken 1999

PILOTY von Carl Theodor 1826-1886 **[30]**
- $1 980 - €1 995 - **£1 234** - FF13 088
Kopie nach Delaroche Huile/panneau (30x41cm 11x16in) Zürich 2000

PILS Isidore 1813-1875 **[77]**
- $12 648 - €12 958 - **£7 803** - FF85 000
Étude de tapis Huile/toile (81.5x100cm 32x39in) Vendôme 2001
- $1 918 - €2 287 - **£1 368** - FF15 000
Saint Pierre guerissant un boitteux Huile/toile (37.5x30cm 14x11in) Paris 2000

- $605 - €610 - **£377** - FF4 000
Portrait du peintre Léon Cogniet (1794-1880) à l'Académie Aquarelle/papier (22x17cm 8x6in) Paris 2000

PILSBURY Wilmot Clifford 1840-1908 **[54]**
- $584 - €562 - **£360** - FF3 685
The Ship Inn Watercolour/paper (25.5x37cm 10x14in) London 1999

PILTZ Otto 1846-1910 **[24]**
- $3 151 - €3 484 - **£2 186** - FF22 851
Kunsthandler på besog i en almuestue Oil/canvas (69x92cm 27x36in) Vejle 2001
- $2 657 - €2 275 - **£1 600** - FF14 920
A young Maid in a Doorway Oil/panel (36x28.5cm 14x11in) London 1998

PILZ Otto 1876-1934 **[27]**
- $1 100 - €1 233 - **£747** - FF8 090
Pair of Lions Attacking a Bull with one Lion on the Bull's Back Bronze (27x46cm 11x18in) Cleveland OH 2000

PIMM William Edwin 1863-1952 **[3]**
- $4 818 - €4 677 - **£3 000** - FF30 677
In the Larder Oil/canvas (45.5x61cm 17x24in) London 1999

PIMONENKO Nikolai Karnilovitch 1862-1912 **[5]**
- $23 000 - €24 578 - **£15 630** - FF161 220
Hay-makening Oil/canvas (51x71cm 20x27in) Kiev 2001

PINA Alfredo 1883-1966 **[130]**
- $2 235 - €2 515 - **£1 539** - FF16 500
Le Purgatoire Bronze (H32cm H12in) Limoges 2000

PINAL Fernand 1881-1958 **[84]**
- $1 046 - €1 220 - **£724** - FF8 000
Le bois de Clamart à l'Automne Huile/toile (46x38cm 18x14in) Calais 2000
- $1 659 - €1 861 - **£1 150** - FF12 210
Vieux Pommiers dans la Cuve à Laon Mixed media (39.5x31cm 15x12in) London 2000

PINARD René XIX-XX **[21]**
- $430 - €412 - **£267** - FF2 700
Les bords de la Loire à Nantes Crayon (30x49cm 11x19in) Rennes 1999
- $366 - €351 - **£227** - FF2 300
Le pont de chemin de fer sur la Loire à Nantes Gravure (46x55cm 18x21in) Rennes 1999

PINATEL R. XIX-XX **[7]**
- $750 - €871 - **£526** - FF5 711
«Le Maroc» Poster (106x76cm 42x30in) New-York 2000

PINAZO **[3]**
- $2 880 - €2 710 - **£1 800** - FF17 775
Mozalbete Oleo/lienzo (35x26cm 13x10in) Madrid 1998

PINAZO CAMARLENCH Ignacio 1849-1916 **[46]**
- $19 320 - €16 861 - **£11 760** - FF110 600
Cuerpo entero de mujer española con peineta, mantón y castañuelas Oleo/lienzo (117.5x65cm 46x25in) Madrid 1998
- $4 575 - €4 505 - **£2 850** - FF29 550
Amanecer en la playa Oleo/tabla (10x20cm 3x7in) Madrid 1999
- $330 - €330 - **£203** - FF2 167
Escena Lápiz/papel (11x12.5cm 4x4in) Madrid 2000

PINCAS-MORENO Moreno Pincas, dit 1936 **[23]**
- **$2 818** - €3 049 - **£1 930** - FF20 000
  Scène de cabaret Huile/toile (81x60cm 31x23in)
  Paris 2001

PINCEMIN Jean-Pierre 1944 **[181]**
- **$9 744** - €9 147 - **£6 036** - FF60 000
  Sans titre Acrylique (300x291cm 118x114in) Paris
  1999
- **$3 097** - €3 354 - **£2 120** - FF22 000
  Sans titre Peinture (75x52cm 29x20in) Paris 2001
- **$992** - €851 - **£600** - FF5 585
  Sans titre Oil/paper (21x19cm 8x7in) London 1998
- **$427** - €488 - **£298** - FF3 200
  Feuilles et arbre Gouache (32x21cm 12x8in) Paris
  2001
- **$260** - €290 - **£180** - FF1 900
  Composition Estampe couleurs (60.5x43cm 23x16in)
  Paris 2001

PINCHART Auguste Émile 1842-1924 **[58]**
- **$7 270** - €7 622 - **£4 555** - FF50 000
  Jeune bédouine au guéridon Huile/toile (84x43cm
  33x16in) Paris 2000
- **$5 250** - €5 027 - **£3 235** - FF32 977
  Springtime Reflection Oil/canvas (44x33cm
  17x13in) Portsmouth NH 1999

PINCHON Joseph Porphyre 1871-1953 **[34]**
- **$132** - €122 - **£79** - FF800
  Le voyage de M. Mitaine et d'Ernest Encre
  Chine/papier (20x25cm 7x9in) Paris 1999

PINCHON Robert Antoine 1886-1943 **[393]**
- **$7 147** - €7 318 - **£4 488** - FF48 000
  Rouen, vue de la Seine Huile/toile (54x73cm
  21x28in) Paris 2000
- **$2 312** - €1 982 - **£1 391** - FF13 000
  Bord de Seine en automne Huile/carton
  (18.5x27cm 7x10in) Deauville 1998
- **$649** - €610 - **£402** - FF4 000
  Paysage Aquarelle (15x23cm 5x9in) Deauville 1999

PINCHON Robert Henri 1889-? **[42]**
- **$102** - €122 - **£71** - FF800
  Le port de Cancale Encre Chine/papier (23x31cm
  9x12in) Paris 2000

PINDER Douglas Houzen 1886-1949 **[88]**
- **$132** - €130 - **£85** - FF855
  Trackway, Dartmoor, near Tavistock
  Watercolour/paper (8x13cm 3x5in) Tavistock, Devon
  1999

PINEDA MONTON Miguel XIX **[1]**
- **$5 467** - €5 600 - **£3 400** - FF36 733
  Valencia Lonja Oil/canvas (61x45.5cm 24x17in)
  Billingshurst, West-Sussex 2000

PINEDA-BUENO José Antonio 1950 **[30]**
- **$714** - €610 - **£420** - FF4 000
  L'ombrelle blanche Huile/toile (54x65cm 21x25in)
  Paris 1998

PINEDO Émile 1840-1916 **[52]**
- **$1 300** - €1 478 - **£901** - FF9 698
  Figure of a Nude Girl Standing on a Pillow
  Bronze (H34cm H13in) St. Louis MO 2000

PINEL Anna, née Guersant c.1830-c.1890 **[3]**
- **$21 000** - €18 118 - **£12 669** - FF118 845
  A Beauty holding a Bird Oil/canvas (81.5x65.5cm
  32x25in) New-York 1998

PINEL DE GRANDCHAMP Louis Émile 1831-1894
[45]
- **$10 452** - €9 909 - **£6 357** - FF65 000
  Odalisque au miroir Huile/toile (79x98cm 31x38in)
  Bergerac 1999
- **$13 634** - €11 271 - **£8 000** - FF73 936
  Beauté Turque à la perruche Oil/canvas
  (27.5x22.5cm 10x8in) London 1998
- **$1 017** - €1 067 - **£637** - FF7 000
  Egyptienne à la gargoulette Aquarelle/papier
  (32x23cm 12x9in) Paris 2000

PINEL Édouard 1804-1884 **[4]**
- **$4 724** - €3 964 - **£2 771** - FF26 000
  Mer et voiliers Huile/toile (42x67cm 16x26in)
  Angoulême 1998

PINEL Gustave N. 1842-1896 **[15]**
- **$4 269** - €4 573 - **£2 907** - FF30 000
  Repos du chamelier dans le sud algérien
  Huile/toile (60x92cm 23x36in) Troyes 2001

PINELLI Achille 1809-1841 **[8]**
- **$5 700** - €4 924 - **£3 800** - FF32 300
  La mungitura Terracotta (23x35cm 9x13in) Roma
  1998
- **$4 799** - €4 922 - **£3 000** - FF32 286
  **Le Vendemmiatrici in ripolo, nelle vicinanze di
  Roma** Watercolour (25.5x30.5cm 10x12in) London
  2000

PINELLI Bartolomeo 1781-1835 **[180]**
- **$1 178** - €1 321 - **£800** - FF8 664
  **Parade with Gentlemen in a Carriage and
  Figure Leading a Plumed Horse** Black chalk
  (15x25.5cm 5x10in) London 2000
- **$270** - €233 - **£180** - FF1 530
  Marinai sul molo di Napoli Acquaforte (22x32cm
  8x12in) Roma 1998

PINELLI de Auguste 1823-1892 **[8]**
- **$36 260** - €42 686 - **£25 480** - FF280 000
  L'école mauresque Huile/toile (87.5x134cm
  34x52in) Paris 2000

PINELO LLULL José 1861-1922 **[18]**
- **$5 000** - €6 006 - **£3 500** - FF39 400
  Vista de Guadalcanal Oleo/lienzo (68x100cm
  26x39in) Madrid 2000
- **$2 560** - €2 403 - **£1 600** - FF15 760
  Paseando Oleo/tabla (32x41cm 12x16in) Madrid 1999

PINET DE GAULADE Louis Charles 1920 **[4]**
- **$2 156** - €1 982 - **£1 324** - FF13 000
  Voyage dans le temps Tapisserie (72x125cm
  28x49in) Paris 1999

PINGGERA Heinz 1900 **[23]**
- **$2 800** - €2 619 - **£1 692** - FF17 179
  The Concert Oil/canvas (73.5x99cm 28x38in) New-
  York 1999

PINGRET Édouard 1788-1875 **[52]**
- **$3 397** - €3 941 - **£2 383** - FF25 854
  Joueuse de luth Huile/toile (74x61cm 29x24in)
  Genève 2000
- **$2 249** - €1 950 - **£1 374** - FF12 792
  Papal Chamberlain Oil/paper/board (37x25.5cm
  14x10in) New-York 1999

PINGUSSON G.H. XX **[4]**
- **$2 007** - €2 287 - **£1 378** - FF15 000
  «Latitude 43, St.Tropez» Affiche (79x119cm
  31x46in) Paris 2000

P

P

PINHEIRO Oscar XIX-XX **[4]**
$4 031 - €4 421 - £2 737 - FF29 000
Paris, le théâtre du Vaudeville Huile/toile (50x65cm 19x25in) Calais 2000

PINK Edmund XIX **[7]**
$11 782 - €10 153 - £7 000 - FF66 602
Two Panoramic Views of the Bay and City of Rio de Janeiro Watercolour/paper (13.5x55cm 5x21in) London 1998

PINK Lutka 1916-1998 **[18]**
$329 - €382 - £234 - FF2 509
Still Life with Apples and Pears Oil/canvas (52.5x65cm 20x25in) Toronto 2001

PINKAS von Hippolyt 1827-1901 **[9]**
$17 340 - €16 044 - £10 800 - FF107 580
Old Man and the Death Oil/canvas (41x28cm 16x11in) Praha 2000

PINKER Stanley 1924 **[8]**
$4 249 - €4 931 - £2 934 - FF32 345
Last Trump for General Rubrics Oil/canvas (229.5x51cm 90x20in) Johannesburg 2000

PINKHOF L. 1898 **[1]**
$2 400 - €2 272 - £1 490 - FF14 902
«Anti-Pogrom-Dag» Poster (107x76cm 42x29in) New-York 1999

PINNEY Eunice 1770-1849 **[4]**
$2 400 - €2 071 - £1 453 - FF13 582
Peace Watercolour (20x15cm 8x6in) New-York 1999

PINNOY Jozef 1808-1866 **[1]**
$8 098 - €7 669 - £4 924 - FF50 308
Handwerkerfamilie am Mittagstisch Öl/Leinwand (47x43cm 18x16in) München 1999

PIÑOLE Y RODRIGUEZ Nicanor 1878-1978 **[68]**
$5 400 - €6 006 - £3 600 - FF39 400
El río Viñao Oleo/cartón (22.5x30cm 8x11in) Madrid 2000
$270 - €300 - £185 - FF1 970
Apunte de cabeza Lápiz/papel (18x14cm 7x5in) Madrid 2000

PINOS SALA Juan 1862-1910 **[7]**
$2 565 - €2 853 - £1 710 - FF18 715
Campesinos Oleo/lienzo (78x118cm 30x46in) Madrid 2000

PINOT Albert 1875-1962 **[86]**
$647 - €690 - £438 - FF4 529
View in the Park Oil/canvas (50x65cm 19x25in) Cape Town 2001
$369 - €372 - £229 - FF2 439
Port animé Huile/panneau (29x45cm 11x17in) Bruxelles 2000
$218 - €242 - £151 - FF1 626
Le jardin des Tuileries Aquarelle/papier (35x53cm 13x20in) Bruxelles 2000

PINOT-GALLIZIO Giuseppe 1902-1964 **[40]**
$2 238 - €2 439 - £1 550 - FF16 000
Sans titre Huile/toile (60.5x73cm 23x28in) Paris 2001
$2 400 - €3 110 - £1 800 - FF20 400
Senza titolo Tecnica mista/carta (50x70cm 19x27in) Torino 2000

PINS Yaacov 1917 **[14]**
$240 - €284 - £174 - FF1 866
Ein Kerem Woodcut (31x18.5cm 12x7in) Tel Aviv 2001

PINTO Alberto XIX **[1]**
$25 000 - €23 416 - £15 370 - FF153 602
A Brittany Family Oil/canvas (116x148.5cm 45x58in) New-York 1999

PINTO Angelo 1908 **[7]**
$225 - €210 - £136 - FF1 375
Beach Scene Gouache/paper (36x39cm 14x15in) Norwalk CT 1999
$900 - €1 022 - £616 - FF6 703
Carousel Woodcut (17x21.5cm 6x8in) New-York 2000

PINTO Biagio 1911-1989 **[4]**
$2 000 - €2 352 - £1 434 - FF15 427
Florida Landscape Oil/canvas (40.5x51cm 15x20in) Philadelphia PA 2001

PINTO Salvatore 1905-1966 **[30]**
$190 - €212 - £129 - FF1 388
«Nude» Etching (24.5x20cm 9x7in) Philadelphia PA 2000

PINTORI Giovanni 1912-? **[7]**
$900 - €1 009 - £625 - FF6 621
«Olivetti Lettera 22» Poster (70x49cm 27x19in) New-York 2000

PINTOS FONSECA Luis 1906-1959 **[2]**
$928 - €961 - £592 - FF6 304
Paisaje rural con iglesia Crayon gras/papier (24x31.5cm 9x12in) Madrid 2000

PINTURICCHIO Bernardino di Betto c.1454-1513 **[5]**
$300 000 - €320 907 - £204 540 - FF2 105 010
Madonna and Child Tempera/panel (42x38.5cm 16x15in) New-York 2001

PINWELL George John 1842-1875 **[10]**
$9 928 - €11 525 - £7 000 - FF75 599
Study for Seat in St. James' Park, London Watercolour (20.5x30.5cm 8x12in) London 2001

PIO Angelo Gabriello 1690-1770 **[2]**
$7 200 - €6 220 - £4 800 - FF40 800
San Francesco di Paola e angiolino Terracotta (H65cm H25in) Prato 1998

PIOLA Domenico I 1627-1703 **[73]**
$15 500 - €16 068 - £9 300 - FF105 400
Putti musicanti Olio/tela (98x124cm 38x48in) Genova 2001
$4 617 - €3 988 - £2 783 - FF26 159
The Madonna and Child Oil/canvas (108.7x85.3cm 42x33in) Amsterdam 1998
$3 899 - €3 816 - £2 500 - FF25 030
St. Sebastian Ink (42.5x29.5cm 16x11in) London 1999

PIOLA Paolo Gerolamo 1666-1724 **[12]**
$1 704 - €1 829 - £1 140 - FF12 000
Saint Jean-Baptiste annonçant la venue du Christ Encre (22x31cm 8x12in) Paris 2000

PIOLA Pellegrino 1617-1640 **[3]**
$2 520 - €2 177 - £1 260 - FF14 280
San Michele Arcangelo che sconfigge Lucifero Acquarello (27.5x21cm 10x8in) Milano 1999

PIOLA Pier Francesco ?-1600 **[1]**
$28 015 - €27 538 - £18 000 - FF180 640
Holy Family with the Enfant Saint John the Baptist and St Elizabeth Oil/canvas (122x99cm 48x38in) London 1999

PIOMBANTI AMMANNANTI Giuseppe 1898-1996
[23]
- $2 400 - €2 488 - £1 440 - FF16 320
  La cura del sole Olio/cartone (36x52.5cm 14x20in)
  Torino 1999
- $4 400 - €5 702 - £3 300 - FF37 400
  La vendemmiatrice Céramique (H39cm H15in)
  Torino 2000
- $750 - €777 - £450 - FF5 100
  Gente di paese Carboncino (44x28cm 17x11in)
  Torino 2000

PION Louis 1851-1934 **[4]**
- $319 - €372 - £225 - FF2 439
  Vue de Liège Technique mixte/papier (24.5x32.5cm
  9x12in) Liège 2001

PIOT Adolphe Étienne 1850-1910 **[56]**
- $4 500 - €4 248 - £2 797 - FF27 868
  Beauty and the Book Oil/canvas (45x38cm 18x15in)
  Milford CT 1999
- $2 256 - €561 - £1 567 - FF16 800
  Profil de femme Huile/panneau (35.5x28cm 13x11in)
  Pontoise 2001

PIOT Eugène 1812-1890 **[12]**
- $3 141 - €2 967 - £1 900 - FF19 464
  **Acropole d'Athènes, le Parthénon, coupe sur la
  partie de l'Opisthodome** Salt print (32.5x22.5cm
  12x8in) London 1999

PIOT Jacques S. 1743-1812 **[1]**
- $3 918 - €3 773 - £2 450 - FF24 749
  Portrait de Cécile Cazenone (1753-1830)
  Pastell/Papier (56x45cm 22x17in) Zürich 1999

PIOT Louis [3]
- $3 783 - €3 964 - £2 394 - FF26 000
  Élégant dans le jardin Huile/toile (100x80cm
  39x31in) Paris 2000

PIOTROWSKI Antoni 1853-1924 **[26]**
- $6 678 - €6 398 - £4 210 - FF41 970
  Larks Oil/canvas (66.5x91.5cm 26x36in) Warszawa
  1999

PIOTROWSKI Maksymilian Antoni 1813-1875 **[3]**
- $11 573 - €11 047 - £7 231 - FF72 463
  Kind and Soldiers discussing Oil/canvas
  (32.5x41cm 12x16in) Warszawa 1999

PIPAL Viktor 1887-1971 **[66]**
- $1 211 - €1 163 - £760 - FF7 627
  Gärtnerei Oil/hardboard (43.5x59cm 17x23in) Wien
  1999
- $605 - €581 - £380 - FF3 813
  Rosenstilleben Oil/panel (39.2x31.1cm 15x12in)
  Wien 1999
- $336 - €363 - £232 - FF2 383
  Wien, Mölkerbastei mit dem Dreimäderlhaus
  Charcoal (32.5x24cm 12x9in) Wien 2001

PIPER Jane ?-1992 **[4]**
- $6 000 - €6 753 - £4 133 - FF44 296
  Pink Still Life Oil/canvas (107x112cm 42x44in)
  Philadelphia PA 2000

PIPER John 1903-1992 **[1007]**
- $21 897 - €21 110 - £13 500 - FF138 470
  Harlaxton Manor, Lincolnshire Oil/canvas
  (107x183cm 42x72in) London 1999
- $13 463 - €13 999 - £8 500 - FF91 827
  Portland Oil/canvas (51x61cm 20x24in) London 2000
- $2 432 - €2 617 - £1 700 - FF11 778
  Herakles tuning his Lyre, and Athena Acrylic
  (24.5x40cm 9x15in) Near Ely 2001

$2 401 - €2 180 - **£1 500** - FF14 301
Dancing Spirits Terracotta (51.5x68.5cm 20x26in)
London 1999

$3 401 - €4 031 - **£2 400** - FF26 443
Cornish Wood on an Estuary Watercolour
(56x71cm 22x27in) London 2000

$639 - €634 - **£400** - FF4 157
The Quest Screenprint in colors (64x87cm 25x34in)
London 1999

PIPPAL Hans Robert 1915-1998 **[105]**
- $286 - €2 180 - £1 392 - FF14 301
  Paris, Notre-Dame Oil/panel (36.5x56cm 14x22in)
  Wien 1999
- $2 003 - €2 325 - £1 408 - FF15 254
  Venedig Öl/Karton (17.5x25cm 6x9in) Wien 2001
- $1 462 - €1 433 - £884 - FF9 534
  Wien Ringstrasse Pastell/Papier (37x52cm 14x20in)
  Wien 2000

PIPPEL Otto Eduard 1878-1960 **[498]**
- $1 819 - €2 045 - £1 277 - FF13 415
  Herbst am Dürrensee Öl/Leinwand (98x128cm
  38x50in) Düsseldorf 2001
- $2 509 - €2 949 - £1 740 - FF19 347
  Wanderer in a Mountainous Landscape Oil/can-
  vas (100.5x80.5cm 39x31in) Amsterdam 2000
- $3 200 - €2 709 - £1 915 - FF17 768
  The Haystacks/Trees in a Landscape Oil/canvas
  (35x40cm 13x15in) New-York 1998

PIPPICH Carl 1862-1932 **[50]**
- $2 122 - €1 817 - £1 242 - FF11 922
  «Einkaufender Husar» Mischtechnik/Papier
  (36x60cm 14x23in) Wien 1998

PIPPIG Heiko 1951 **[27]**
- $3 542 - €3 323 - £2 188 - FF21 800
  **Selbst als Akt auf einem Hocker, einen Schädel
  in der Linken haltend** Acryl/Leinwand (155x130cm
  61x51in) Stuttgart 1999
- $2 236 - €2 454 - £1 440 - FF16 098
  Sitzender männlicher Akt Mixed media/canvas
  (120x90cm 47x35in) Lindau 2000

PIPPIN Horace 1888-1946 **[4]**
- $65 000 - €64 535 - £40 625 - FF423 319
  Choir Practice Oil/canvas (30.5x40.5cm 12x15in)
  New-York 1999

PIPPIN Steven 1960 **[5]**
- $6 500 - €6 247 - £4 004 - FF40 975
  **The Continued Saga of an Amateur
  Photographer #1-5** Photograph (56x84cm 22x33in)
  New-York 1999

PIQTOUKUN David Ruben 1950 **[4]**
- $228 - €256 - £158 - FF1 677
  The Shaman's Dream Silkscreen in colors (62x36cm
  24x14in) Calgary, Alberta 2001

PIRA 1954 **[1]**
- $15 052 - €16 160 - £10 070 - FF106 000
  Tenue de soirée Bronze (H178cm H70in) Paris 2000

PIRANDELLO Fausto 1899-1975 **[123]**
- $20 000 - €25 916 - £15 000 - FF170 000
  Bagnanti Olio/tavola (42x50cm 16x19in) Milano 2001
- $9 000 - €9 330 - £5 400 - FF61 200
  Natura morta Olio/tavola (40x37cm 15x14in) Prato
  1999
- $1 680 - €2 177 - £1 260 - FF14 280
  Bagnanti Pastelli (22x28cm 8x11in) Roma 2000

P

PIRANESI Francesco c.1758-1810 **[121]**

⬛ **$448** - €390 - **£279** - FF2 561
«Arco de Augusto» Grabado (13.5x27cm 5x10in)
Madrid 1999

PIRANESI Giovanni Battista 1720-1778 **[1624]**

✎ **$70 000** - €70 815 - **£42 742** - FF464 513
Man Reclining, asleep Ink (16x21.5cm 6x8in) New-York 2000

⬛ **$600** - €680 - **£415** - FF4 587
Ravine del Sisto Etching (41x64cm 16x25in) South-Natick MA 2000

PIRANESI Laura c.1755-1785 **[4]**

✎ **$7 261** - €6 136 - **£4 318** - FF40 250
Le feu d'artifice au château Saint-Ange, Rome d'après Desprez Craies (31x49cm 12x19in) Monte-Carlo 1998

PIRCHAN Emil II 1884-1957 **[7]**

⬛ **$221** - €219 - **£137** - FF1 434
Josephslegende Lithographie (47x38cm 18x14in) St. Gallen 1999

PIRE Ferdinand 1943 **[20]**

☞ **$1 338** - €1 487 - **£936** - FF9 756
La réussite ratée Huile/panneau (61x46cm 24x18in) Bruxelles 2001

☞ **$831** - €892 - **£565** - FF5 853
Personnages fantasmagoriques Peinture (23.5x17cm 9x6in) Bruxelles 2001

☞ **$258** - €297 - **£180** - FF1 951
Jeunes femmes nues Lavis/papier (38.5x28.5cm 15x11in) Bruxelles 2001

PIRE Marcel 1913-1981 **[53]**

☞ **$1 270** - €1 363 - **£852** - FF8 943
Vue du marché aux poissons à Malines Huile/toile (80x100cm 31x39in) Bruxelles 2000

PIRES Yves 1958 **[77]**

🔨 **$1 602** - €1 829 - **£1 126** - FF12 000
L'Insouciante Bronze (H26.5cm H10in) Corbeil-Essonnes 2001

PIREZ DA EVORA Alvaro XV **[4]**

☞ **$119 544** - €128 321 - **£80 000** - FF841 728
Saints-John the Evangelist and Augustine (?) Oil/panel (125x83cm 49x32in) London 2000

PIRIE George 1863-1946 **[32]**

☞ **$3 421** - €2 923 - **£2 070** - FF19 173
By the Barn Door Oil/canvas (46x61cm 18x24in) Edinburgh 1998

☞ **$687** - €630 - **£420** - FF4 132
Deerhound Puppy Drinking from a Bowl Oil/canvas (25x35cm 10x14in) London 1999

☞ **$959** - €1 071 - **£650** - FF7 027
Study of a Farm Cat Watercolour/paper (32x24cm 12x9in) Edinburgh 2000

PIRINGER Benedikt 1780-1826 **[9]**

⬛ **$726** - €732 - **£452** - FF4 800
Pont de la Mulatière sur Saône, d'après P.N.Wéry Eau-forte (42.5x61cm 16x24in) Paris 2000

PIRNER Maximilian 1854-1924 **[24]**

✎ **$2 312** - €2 187 - **£1 440** - FF14 344
Madonna mit Jesuskind und Engeln Pastell/Papier (80x105cm 31x41in) Praha 2000

PIRON Leo 1899-1962 **[22]**

☞ **$6 630** - €7 436 - **£4 620** - FF48 780
La place communale Huile/toile (70x100cm 27x39in) Bruxelles 2001

☞ **$3 165** - €3 718 - **£2 265** - FF24 390
Paysage enneigé à Etikhove Huile/toile (25x35cm 9x13in) Bruxelles 2000

⬛ **$510** - €545 - **£347** - FF3 577
Moulin sous la neige Aquatinte couleurs (47.5x54.5cm 18x21in) Lokeren 2001

PIROVANO Giovanni 1880-1959 **[6]**

☞ **$1 450** - €1 503 - **£870** - FF9 860
La lavandaia Olio/cartone (35x27cm 13x10in) Vercelli 1999

PIRRONE Luigi XX **[1]**

📷 **$18 000** - €15 044 - **£10 657** - FF98 685
Fotografia, aero-liquida di Cantania Gelatin silver print (20.5x27.5cm 8x10in) New-York 1998

PIRSCH Adolf 1858-1929 **[14]**

☞ **$17 514** - €16 958 - **£11 000** - FF111 237
The Market in front of the Forum Oil/canvas (79x114cm 31x44in) London 2001

PISA Alberto 1864-1930 **[35]**

✎ **$1 200** - €1 244 - **£720** - FF8 160
Trafalgar Square Acquarello (25x32cm 9x12in) Vercelli 2001

PISANO Eduardo 1912-1989 **[51]**

☞ **$286** - €244 - **£171** - FF1 600
Femme nue à la Mantille Huile/panneau (72x43cm 28x16in) Paris 1998

PISANO Giovanni c.1250-c.1320 **[1]**

🔨 **$20 000** - €20 733 - **£12 000** - FF136 000
Testa di giovane con elmo Marbre (22.5x5cm 8x1in) Firenze 2001

PISANO Giovanni 1875-1954 **[22]**

☞ **$1 800** - €2 332 - **£1 350** - FF15 300
Sera d'estate Olio/cartone (49.5x70cm 19x27in) Torino 2000

☞ **$600** - €777 - **£450** - FF5 100
Gregge sotto la neve Olio/tavola (20x26cm 7x10in) Vercelli 2000

PISANO Nino 1315-1368 **[1]**

🔨 **$220 000** - €228 064 - **£132 000** - FF1 496 000
Giovane Santo Sculpture bois (127x40x20cm 50x15x7in) Firenze 2001

PISEMSKY Aleksey Alexandrov. 1859-1913 **[5]**

☞ **$7 304** - €7 020 - **£4 500** - FF46 049
Summer Landscape with wooden Hut Oil/board (37.5x52cm 14x20in) London 1999

✎ **$754** - €2 263 - **£1 400** - FF14 842
Poppy Fields Watercolour/paper (33.5x51cm 13x20in) London 1998

PISIS de Filippo 1896-1956 **[619]**

☞ **$33 500** - €34 728 - **£20 100** - FF227 800
Casalecchio Olio/tela (70x80cm 27x31in) Milano 2000

☞ **$14 328** - €13 825 - **£9 000** - FF90 685
Natura morta Oil/panel (26x40cm 10x15in) London 1999

☞ **$1 520** - €1 970 - **£1 140** - FF12 920
Composizione con volti Inchiostro/carta (26.5x40cm 10x15in) Milano 2000

⬛ **$600** - €622 - **£360** - FF4 080
Figura Litografia (36x27cm 14x10in) Torino 2000

PISSARRO Camille 1830-1903 **[1357]**

☞ **$2 100 000** - €2 352 154 - **£1 459 080** - FF15 429 120
L'hiver à Montfoucault, effet de neige Oil/canvas (114.5x110cm 45x43in) New-York 2001

$900 000 - €853 245 - **£547 560** - FF5 596 920
Sente et coteaux d'Auvers Oil/canvas (61x73.5cm 24x28in) New-York 1999

$155 200 - €152 449 - **£96 300** - FF1 000 000
Soleil couchant, coteau de Bazincourt Huile/panneau (15.5x23.5cm 6x9in) Paris 1999

$9 230 - €9 909 - **£6 175** - FF65 000
Vieille et vieux paysans Aquarelle/papier (14.5x8.5cm 5x3in) Paris 2000

$2 690 - €2 274 - **£1 600** - FF14 917
Une rue à Rouen, Rue des Arpents Drypoint (14.5x10.5cm 5x4in) London 1998

PISSARRO Hugues Claude 1935 [315]

$8 500 - €9 820 - **£5 951** - FF64 413
«Le petit fils» Oil/canvas (129x161cm 51x63in) New-York 2001

$6 000 - €5 034 - **£3 520** - FF33 021
La rue des dames à Paris Oil/canvas (50x61.5cm 19x24in) New-York 1998

$6 000 - €6 975 - **£4 317** - FF45 756
«Le chemin de la Serverie» Oil/canvas (33x41cm 13x16in) New-York 2001

$3 000 - €3 466 - **£2 100** - FF22 734
Passage del Corso à San Remo Pastel/paper (35x49cm 14x19in) New-York 2001

PISSARRO Lucien 1863-1944 [139]

$37 886 - €36 737 - **£24 000** - FF240 981
Dartmouth, early Spring Oil/canvas (53.5x65cm 21x25in) London 1999

$43 359 - €40 032 - **£27 000** - FF262 591
Fishpond Village, Dorset Oil/panel (35x45cm 13x17in) London 1999

$2 769 - €3 149 - **£1 900** - FF20 658
Rye From Cadborough Watercolour (19.5x25cm 7x9in) London 2000

$292 - €274 - **£177** - FF1 800
Les lavandières Gravure bois couleurs (23.5x11cm 9x4in) Paris 1999

PISSARRO Ludovic Rodo 1878-1952 [364]

$1 528 - €1 524 - **£930** - FF10 000
Le modèle nu Huile/toile (60x93cm 23x36in) Paris 2000

$2 069 - €1 982 - **£1 275** - FF13 000
Paysage d'Angleterre Huile/panneau (33x41cm 12x16in) Calais 1999

$273 - €305 - **£183** - FF2 000
La chapelle du village Aquarelle/papier (22x31cm 8x12in) Paris 2000

PISSARRO Orovida 1893-1968 [47]

$3 638 - €3 403 - **£2 200** - FF22 324
Samoan Boy Gouache (25.5x24cm 10x9in) London 1999

$699 - €644 - **£420** - FF4 224
Seen from Above Etching, aquatint (23x13cm 9x5in) London 1999

PISSARRO Paul Émile 1884-1972 [270]

$3 749 - €3 347 - **£2 296** - FF21 958
Le clos sous la neige Oil/canvas (73.5x54.5cm 28x21in) New-York 1999

$1 900 - €1 654 - **£1 132** - FF10 850
Chaumière, Berneval Oil/canvas/board (28x37cm 11x14in) St. Louis MO 1998

$943 - €1 125 - **£672** - FF7 378
Ausblick in ein Tal Watercolour (37x26.5cm 14x10in) Berlin 2000

$154 - €137 - **£94** - FF900
Toit de chaume Gravure (21x28cm 8x11in) Avignon 1999

PISTILLI Enrico / Ulrico 1854-? [9]

$12 908 - €10 671 - **£7 574** - FF70 000
La Baie de Naples Huile/toile (72x110cm 28x43in) Paris 1998

PISTOIA da Frà Paolino 1490-1547 [3]

$5 615 - €5 495 - **£3 600** - FF36 043
The Madonna and Child Black & white chalks (10x9.5cm 3x3in) London 1999

PISTOLETTO Michelangelo 1933 [120]

$51 630 - €47 917 - **£31 000** - FF314 315
Gente di schiena Mixed media (230x125.5cm 90x49in) London 1999

$5 250 - €5 442 - **£3 150** - FF35 700
Ginnasta Olio/tavola (115x70cm 45x27in) Torino 1999

$7 000 - €9 071 - **£5 250** - FF59 500
Frattali Scultura (80x80cm 31x31in) Prato 2000

$2 250 - €2 098 - **£1 389** - FF13 760
Le bain turc Serigraph in colors (69x100cm 27x39in) Bloomfield-Hills MI 1999

PISTORIUS Eduard Karl 1796-1862 [6]

$14 424 - €16 952 - **£10 000** - FF111 200
The Donkey Seller Oil/canvas (77x71cm 30x27in) London 2000

PITATI de' Bonifacio Veronese 1487-1553 [9]

$65 000 - €62 047 - **£40 612** - FF407 004
Sacra Conversazione, Holy Family with Saints Luke, Dorothy, Peter Oil/canvas (164x197cm 64x77in) New-York 1999

$25 227 - €28 134 - **£16 461** - FF184 549
The Mystical Marriage of Saint Catharine Oil/panel (69x91.5cm 27x36in) Amsterdam 2000

$3 000 - €3 110 - **£1 800** - FF20 400
Martirio di San Pietro da Verona Olio/tavola (29x54.5cm 11x21in) Venezia 2000

PITCHER Henry XIX-XX [12]

$337 - €292 - **£205** - FF1 918
The Englishman, Scotsman and Irishman Oil/board (17x11.3cm 6x4in) Canterbury, Kent 1998

PITCHER Neville E. Sotheby XX [25]

$1 089 - €1 074 - **£700** - FF7 045
Grimsby Trawlers Oil/canvas (61x76cm 24x29in) London 1999

PITCHFORTH Roland Vivian 1895-1982 [272]

$449 - €453 - **£280** - FF2 969
Figure in a Wooded Path Watercolour/paper (43x58cm 16x22in) London 2000

PITHAWALA Manchershaw 1872-1937 [3]

$7 172 - €7 699 - **£4 800** - FF50 503
Portrait of a Parsi Gentleman Oil/board (53.5x38.5cm 21x15in) London 2000

PITLOO Antonio Sminck 1791-1837 [23]

$8 412 - €7 799 - **£5 200** - FF51 156
The Gardens of the Palazzetto Chiatamone, Naples Oil/paper/canvas (49.5x39cm 19x15in) London 1999

$9 900 - €8 552 - **£6 600** - FF56 100
Il teatro di Taormina Olio/tela (33x40.5cm 12x15in) Napoli 1998

PITT Moses ?-1696 [2]

$518 - €599 - **£365** - FF3 927
Regni Norvegiae Nova et accurata descriptio Copper engraving (42x48cm 16x18in) Oslo 2000

P

PITT William ?-c.1890 **[61]**
🖼 **$1 204** - €1 321 - **£800** - FF8 666
Long Compton Church, Warwickshire Oil/canvas (35.5x56cm 13x22in) London 2000
🖼 **$2 170** - €2 199 - **£1 350** - FF14 422
Chaddar, Somersetshire Oil/panel (7.5x25cm 2x9in) Crewkerne, Somerset 2001

PITTARA Carlo 1836-1890 **[46]**
🖼 **$15 313** - €13 034 - **£9 114** - FF85 500
Paysage alpin Huile/toile (66x80cm 25x31in) Toulouse 1998
🖼 **$5 000** - €5 183 - **£3 000** - FF34 000
Angolo di Rivara Canavese Olio/tavoletta (13x24cm 5x9in) Torino 2001
✏ **$3 500** - €3 030 - **£2 110** - FF19 875
River Scene with Two Horses and a Rider Watercolour (31x49cm 12x19in) San-Francisco CA 1998

PITTERI Giovanni Marco, Al. 1702-1786 **[38]**
🗂 **$256** - €281 - **£174** - FF1 844
Bildnis des Malers Giovanni Bettino Cignaroli im Dreiviertelprofil Radierung (46.2x35.3cm 18x13in) Berlin 2000

PITTMAN Hobson Pittman 1899-1972 **[29]**
🖼 **$2 600** - €2 926 - **£1 791** - FF19 195
Fishing Boat Entering a Harbor by Moonlight Oil/canvas (40.5x51cm 15x20in) Philadelphia PA 2000
✏ **$2 200** - €2 055 - **£1 370** - FF13 483
Still Life Watercolour/paper (53x36cm 21x14in) Mystic CT 1999
🗂 **$200** - €221 - **£141** - FF1 517
The Sideboard, Fruit Filled Compote Woodcut (26x20cm 10x8in) Hatfield PA 2000

PITTMAN Lari 1952 **[7]**
🖼 **$40 000** - €46 412 - **£27 616** - FF304 440
Where Suffering and Redemption Will Sprout From The Same Vine Acrylic/panel (244x325cm 96x127in) New-York 2000

PITTNER Olivér 1911-1971 **[4]**
🖼 **$1 386** - €1 575 - **£966** - FF10 332
Nagybanya Pastel/papier (49x69cm 19x27in) Budapest 2000

PITTO Giacomo 1872-? **[5]**
🖼 **$1 191** - €1 321 - **£825** - FF8 664
Italiensk torgmarknad Oil/canvas (50x70cm 19x27in) Malmö 2001

PITTO Giuseppe 1823-1916 **[14]**
🖼 **$1 691** - €1 815 - **£1 131** - FF11 906
Flower Market in an Italian City Oil/canvas (49x69cm 19x27in) Amsterdam 2001

PITTONI Giovanni Battista I 1520-1583 **[3]**
🗂 **$1 615** - €1 841 - **£1 126** - FF12 074
Landschaft mit antiken Ruinen, im Vordergrund eine Statue des Herkules Radierung (21.5x31.5cm 8x12in) Berlin 2001

PITTONI Giovanni Battista II 1687-1767 **[46]**
🖼 **$30 127** - €29 728 - **£18 720** - FF195 000
Le repos pendant la fuite en Égypte Huile/toile (68x48cm 26x18in) Le Puy 1999
🖼 **$52 300** - €56 140 - **£35 000** - FF368 256
Diana The Huntress: Modelli Oil/canvas (17x28.5cm 6x11in) London 2000
✏ **$4 000** - €4 285 - **£2 731** - FF28 106
Page with a Dish Bearing an Instrument of Geometry/Donkey and Goats Red chalk/paper (25x19cm 9x7in) New-York 2001

PITZ Hermann 1956 **[2]**
🏛 **$5 228** - €6 174 - **£3 711** - FF40 497
«Der Grunewald» Installation (60x60x60cm 23x23x23in) Berlin 2001

PITZNER Max Joseph 1855-1912 **[17]**
🖼 **$1 168** - €1 278 - **£808** - FF8 384
Winter im Dachauer Land Öl/Karton (32x25cm 12x9in) Hildrizhausen 2001

PIUMATI Giovanni 1850-1915 **[7]**
🖼 **$440** - €570 - **£330** - FF3 740
Giardino con statua Olio/carta (24x30.5cm 9x12in) Milano 2000

PIXIS Theodor 1831-1907 **[15]**
🖼 **$5 974** - €5 112 - **£3 596** - FF33 533
«Junges Mädchen sich in Wasser spiegelnd» Öl/Leinwand (87x57cm 34x22in) Stuttgart 1998
🖼 **$2 370** - €2 045 - **£1 411** - FF13 414
Verehrer nahen Öl/Karton (21x17.3cm 8x6in) München 1998

PIZA Arthur Luis 1928 **[72]**
🗂 **$150** - €125 - **£88** - FF823
Abstract Etching in colors (44x28cm 17x11in) Shaker-Heights OH 1998

PIZA ENSENYAT Cristobal 1850-? **[2]**
🖼 **$2 166** - €2 287 - **£1 431** - FF15 000
La marchande de fleurs Huile/panneau (41x32cm 16x12in) Soissons 2000

PIZARRO Cecilio ?-1886 **[17]**
🖼 **$1 224** - €1 442 - **£840** - FF9 456
Caballero con uniforme de gala Oleo/lienzo (33x35.5cm 12x10in) Madrid 2000

PIZIO Orest 1879-1938 **[2]**
🖼 **$9 000** - €9 822 - **£6 106** - FF64 430
Woman with Parasol Oil/canvas (98x72.5cm 38x28in) New-York 1998

PIZZELLA Edmundo 1868-? **[8]**
✏ **$1 849** - €1 982 - **£1 259** - FF13 000
Elégante aux courses Pastel/papier (113x71cm 44x27in) Calais 2001

PIZZETA Claudius c.1832-c.1899 **[3]**
🖼 **$2 624** - €3 049 - **£1 844** - FF20 000
Nature morte Huile/carton (18x23cm 7x9in) Paris 2001

PIZZI CANNELLA Piero 1955 **[65]**
🖼 **$5 681** - €4 802 - **£3 400** - FF31 497
Solitario Oil/canvas (238.5x135cm 93x53in) London 1998
🖼 **$3 750** - €3 887 - **£2 250** - FF25 500
Le perle Olio/tela (90x65cm 35x25in) Prato 2000
✏ **$1 650** - €1 710 - **£990** - FF11 431
Marina Tecnica mista/carta (55x77cm 21x30in) Prato 2000

PIZZI Carlo 1842-1908 **[6]**
🖼 **$17 931** - €19 248 - **£12 000** - FF126 259
Lake Garda/Lake Como Oil/canvas (39.5x70cm 15x27in) London 2000

PIZZINATO Armando 1910 **[14]**
🖼 **$4 749** - €4 924 - **£2 849** - FF32 298
Fiori Olio/tela (50x39.5cm 19x15in) Milano 1999

PIZZIRANI Guglielmo 1886-1971 **[2]**
🖼 **$1 600** - €2 073 - **£1 200** - FF13 600
Paesaggio fluviale Olio/cartone (16x22cm 6x8in) Roma 2001

PLA Y GALLARDO Cecilio 1860-1934 **[162]**
- $3 520 - €3 312 - £2 200 - FF21 725
  Coro de ángeles Oleo/lienzo (70x40cm 27x15in)
  Madrid 1998
- $3 190 - €3 304 - £1 980 - FF21 670
  Dama con abanico Oleo/lienzo (20x27.5cm 7x10in)
  Madrid 1998
- $598 - £731 - £361 - FF3 743
  Retrato de familia Lápiz/papel (14x22cm 5x8in)
  Madrid 1999

PLA Y RUBIO Alberto 1867-1929 **[38]**
- $8 000 - €9 402 - £5 546 - FF61 675
  The Haywagon Oil/canvas (73.5x63cm 28x24in)
  New-York 2000
- $648 - €721 - £456 - FF4 728
  Combate medieval Oleo/tabla (31x21cm 12x8in)
  Madrid 2001

PLAGEMANN Anna Augusta 1799-1888 **[9]**
- $3 763 - €4 295 - £2 439 - FF28 176
  En stor buket blomster i en vase på et marmorbord Oil/canvas (62x48cm 24x18in) Köbenhavn 2000

PLAGEMANN Arnold Abraham 1826-1862 **[9]**
- $1 314 - €1 311 - £800 - FF8 602
  Dutch Merchant Ship and Fishing Vssel in choppy Sea Oil/canvas (53x64.5cm 20x25in) London 2000

PLAGEMANN Carl Gustaf 1805-1868 **[7]**
- $7 254 - €6 905 - £4 538 - FF45 297
  Italienska med vindruvsklasar Oil/canvas (74x58cm 29x22in) Stockholm 1999

PLANAS DORIA Francisco 1879-1955 **[31]**
- $768 - €721 - £468 - FF4 728
  Suburbi Oleo/tabla (50x70cm 19x27in) Madrid 1999
- $350 - €300 - £210 - FF1 970
  Pueblo Oleo/lienzo (33x41cm 12x16in) Madrid 1999

PLANCKH Viktor 1904-1941 **[19]**
- $18 975 - €17 519 - £11 815 - FF114 918
  Bürgerliche Familie Oil/canvas (92x117cm 36x46in)
  Bethesda MD 1999
- $1 218 - €1 308 - £831 - FF8 580
  «Obsternte» Watercolour (32x60.5cm 12x23in) Wien 2001

PLANCOULAINE Franck 1960 **[6]**
- $804 - €915 - £552 - FF6 000
  Sortie de Toril Huile/toile (60x73cm 23x28in) Metz 2000

PLANELLA Ramón 1783-1819 **[1]**
- $10 800 - €12 013 - £7 200 - FF78 800
  Florero de cristal Oleo/tabla (47x34.5cm 18x13in)
  Madrid 2000

PLANELLS CRUANYES Angel 1904-1987 **[32]**
- $1 620 - €1 802 - £1 080 - FF11 820
  Cosiendo las redes Oleo/lienzo (51x80.5cm 20x31in) Madrid 2000
- $1 488 - €1 442 - £912 - FF9 456
  La mirada de l'espia que viatja Oleo/lienzo (22x27cm 8x10in) Barcelona 1999

PLANES José 1891-1974 **[7]**
- $2 430 - €2 703 - £1 620 - FF17 730
  Dos figuras Bronze (H69cm H27in) Madrid 2000

PLANQUETTE Félix 1873-1964 **[92]**
- $2 098 - €2 007 - £1 315 - FF13 163
  Le retour du troupeau Oil/canvas (71x103cm 27x40in) Stockholm 1999

- $996 - €1 098 - £664 - FF7 200
  Vue de la cathédrale de Bayeux Huile/toile (27x35cm 10x13in) Coutances 2000

PLANSON André 1898-1981 **[361]**
- $2 060 - €2 134 - £1 311 - FF14 000
  La Trinité sur Mer, août Huile/toile/carton (54x65cm 21x25in) Neuilly-sur-Seine 2000
- $551 - €640 - £387 - FF4 200
  Saint Guénolé Huile/carton (33x40.5cm 12x15in)
  Paris 2001
- $816 - €767 - £506 - FF5 030
  Liegender Frauenakt Watercolour (45.5x62cm 17x24in) München 1999
- $161 - €137 - £95 - FF900
  Scène de plage - les régates Lithographie couleurs (33x50cm 12x19in) Brest 1998

PLANSON Joseph Alphonse 1799-? **[5]**
- $6 555 - €7 446 - £4 600 - FF48 840
  Still Life of a Chocolatier, Together with Boiled Eggs, a Coffee Oil/canvas (38.5x46cm 15x18in)
  London 2001

PLANTE Ada May 1875-1950 **[7]**
- $2 625 - €2 461 - £1 624 - FF16 141
  Darebin House Ivanhoe Oil/board (64x54cm 25x21in) Melbourne 1999

PLANTEY Madeleine 1890-1985 **[35]**
- $771 - €915 - £561 - FF6 000
  Rêverie Huile/toile (46x55cm 18x21in) Lyon 2001

PLANTIER du Marc 1901-1975 **[2]**
- $12 510 - €13 720 - £8 307 - FF90 000
  Petite console Fer (60x120x32cm 23x47x12in) Paris 2000

PLAS Laurens 1828-1893 **[10]**
- $960 - €908 - £599 - FF5 953
  Livestock in a Meadow Oil/canvas (22.5x30.5cm 8x12in) Amsterdam 1999

PLAS Pieter 1810-1853 **[16]**
- $2 058 - €2 269 - £1 344 - FF14 883
  Rustend vee aan de slootkant Oil/panel (30x39cm 11x15in) Den Haag 2000

PLAS van der David 1647-1704 **[1]**
- $77 342 - €75 955 - £48 000 - FF498 235
  Group Portrait of Elegant Figures, Drinking and Playing Music Oil/canvas (71.5x59cm 28x23in)
  London 1999

PLAS van der Nicholas 1954 **[36]**
- $1 900 - €1 776 - £1 171 - FF11 653
  Children in the Beach Oil/panel (49x69cm 19x27in)
  Delray-Beach FL 1999

PLASENCIA Casto 1846-1890 **[5]**
- $2 600 - €3 003 - £1 800 - FF19 700
  Pastora Oleo/lienzo (25.5x35cm 10x13in) Seville 2000

PLASKETT Joseph Francis 1918 **[75]**
- $966 - €834 - £581 - FF5 470
  Port au persil, Quebec Oil/canvas (40.5x51cm 15x20in) Nepean, Ont. 1998
- $402 - €443 - £265 - FF2 909
  A Medici Fountain Luxembourg Gardens, Paris Pastel/papier (61x51cm 24x20in) Vancouver, BC. 2000

PLASSAN Antoine Émile 1817-1903 **[42]**
- $2 916 - €3 201 - £1 877 - FF21 000
  Vue de sablé Huile/panneau (21.5x33cm 8x12in)
  Fontainebleau 2000

P

P

PLASSE Georges 1878-? [11]
$2 572 - €3 049 - £1 874 - FF20 000
Les quais et le Pont-Neuf à Paris Huile/toile
(63x82.5cm 24x32in) Paris 2001

PLATE Carl Olaf 1909-1977 [22]
$4 860 - €5 217 - £3 252 - FF34 222
Segments on Yellow Oil/board (92x137.5cm
36x54in) Melbourne 2000

PLATEN Angelika 1942 [13]
$647 - €764 - £459 - FF5 013
«Georg Baselitz, Hamburg» Gelatin silver print
(38.5x26cm 15x10in) Berlin 2001

PLATERO Mario 1942 [76]
$217 - €229 - £143 - FF1 500
Tango Huile/toile (46x55cm 18x21in) Abbeville 2000

PLATHNER Hermann 1831-1902 [13]
$5 000 - €4 751 - £3 042 - FF31 164
Politics Oil/canvas (26.5x32cm 10x12in) New-York
1999

PLATNER von Ferdinand 1824-1896 [2]
$3 500 - €3 628 - £2 100 - FF23 800
Scena popolare romana Olio/tela (37x48cm
14x18in) Roma 2000

PLATSCHEK Hans 1923-2000 [50]
$749 - €869 - £517 - FF5 701
Ohne Titel Gouache (41.6x29.5cm 16x11in) Köln
2000

PLATT James C. ?-1882 [1]
$3 000 - €3 263 - £1 977 - FF21 403
Still Life with Fruit Oil/board (19.5x25cm 7x9in)
Boston MA 2000

PLATT John Edgar 1886-1967 [7]
$669 - €787 - £481 - FF5 164
Red Chestnut No.1 Woodcut in colors (38x22cm
14x8in) London 2001

PLATTEAU Z. XIX [10]
$727 - €843 - £503 - FF5 528
Promeneurs en sous-bois Huile/panneau (17x24cm
6x9in) Bruxelles 2000

PLATTEEL Jean-Pierre XIX [3]
$5 804 - €6 536 - £4 000 - FF42 875
Stocking the Larder Oil/panel (80.5x66cm 31x25in)
London 2000

PLATTEMONTAGNE de Nicolas 1631-1706 [9]
$5 749 - €6 403 - £4 040 - FF42 000
Étude d'anges, de bras, de mains et de jambes
Trois crayons (27x42.5cm 10x16in) Paris 2001

PLATTNER Karl 1919-1986 [72]
$44 500 - €46 131 - £26 700 - FF302 600
L'apparizione dell'Angelo Olio/tela (90x135cm
35x53in) Milano 2000
$18 387 - €20 123 - £12 685 - FF132 000
Femme aux trois perroquets Huile/toile (73x73cm
28x28in) Paris 2001
$18 660 - €18 660 - £10 800 - FF122 400
Incomunicabilità Olio/tela (30x50cm 11x19in)
Milano 2000
$2 000 - €2 073 - £1 200 - FF13 600
Paesaggio della Val Venosta Acquarello/carta
(18x22.5cm 7x8in) Roma 2001
$330 - €285 - £165 - FF1 870
Figure Litografia a colori (51x70cm 20x27in) Prato
1999

PLATZ Ernst Heinrich 1867-1940 [21]
$5 082 - €4 343 - £2 985 - FF28 485
Die Dent Blanche in den Walliser Alpen
Öl/Leinwand (62x88cm 24x34in) Bielefeld 1998

PLATZER Johann Georg 1704-1761 [39]
$64 890 - €65 405 - £40 500 - FF429 030
**Musizierende und tanzende Gesellschaft auf
einer Schlosserasse** Oil/panel (38x48cm 14x18in)
Wien 2000
$90 000 - €85 912 - £56 232 - FF563 544
**Revellers Dancing and Making Music/Port
Scene with Travellers** Oil/copper (17x24cm 6x9in)
New-York 1999

PLATZÖDER Ludwig 1898-1987 [16]
$1 009 - €1 125 - £705 - FF7 378
Stilleben mit Fayencekrug Oil/panel (40x32.5cm
15x12in) München 2001

PLAUEN E.O., Ernst Ohser 1903-1944 [30]
$320 - €307 - £195 - FF2 012
Erziehung zum Gentleman Indian ink/paper
(29.8x22.4cm 11x8in) Dettelbach-Effeldorf 1999

PLAUZEAU Alfred 1875-1918 [12]
$41 841 - €49 204 - £30 000 - FF322 758
La femme captive Oil/canvas (196.5x132cm
77x51in) London 2001

PLAYFAIR James Charles XIX-XX [12]
$511 - €429 - £300 - FF2 816
Moment's Thought Watercolour (19x26cm 7x10in)
London 1998

PLAZZOTTA Enzo (Plazota) 1921-1981 [91]
$38 339 - €42 459 - £26 000 - FF278 512
L'arrivée Bronze (H190cm H74in) Billingshurst, West-
Sussex 2000
$3 059 - €2 862 - £1 850 - FF18 773
Young Colt Bronze (32x47cm 12x18in) London 1999

PLÉ Henri Honoré 1853-1922 [40]
$15 000 - €16 549 - £9 921 - FF108 553
Figural Group, Indian Warrior and Squaw Bronze
(H112cm H44in) New-York 2000
$700 - €672 - £433 - FF4 409
David Vainqueur Bronze (H41cm H16in) Delray-
Beach FL 1999

PLEDGER Morris J. 1955 [17]
$597 - €527 - £360 - FF3 458
**«Mallard Duck by the Water's Edge»/«Wigeon
Drake in Reeds...»** Watercolour (44x35.5cm 17x13in)
London 1998

PLEISSNER Ogden Minton 1905-1983 [178]
$6 250 - €7 132 - £4 344 - FF46 782
Spring in Cape Breton Oil/canvas (67x79cm
26x31in) Cleveland OH 2001
$8 500 - €9 413 - £5 764 - FF61 748
Study for Monday Morning Oil/canvas/board
(20x25cm 8x10in) New-York 2000
$11 000 - €12 380 - £7 577 - FF81 209
The Game Trail Watercolour/paper (45.5x71cm
17x27in) Washington 2000
$450 - €471 - £282 - FF3 090
The Lye Brook Pool, Battenbill River, Vermont
Print (56x77cm 22x30in) East-Moriches NY 2000

PLENKERS Stefan 1945 [7]
$590 - €613 - £372 - FF4 024
Impressionen der Chinareise Aquarell/Papier
(48.7x63cm 19x24in) Berlin 2000

PLENSA Jaume 1955 **[78]**
- $1 760 - €1 656 - **£1 100** - FF10 862
  Composición Técnica mixta (39.5x42cm 15x16in) Madrid 1998
- $7 187 - €6 250 - **£4 333** - FF41 000
  Suite del Silenci II Bronze (106x46x37cm 41x18x14in) Paris 1998
- $7 975 - €8 287 - **£5 000** - FF54 358
  Satroc Bronze (50x124x17cm 19x48x6in) London 2000
- $3 173 - €3 730 - **£2 200** - FF24 464
  Nocturn I + II Mixed media/paper (42x29.5cm 16x11in) London 2000
- $256 - €252 - **£163** - FF1 654
  Africanos Grabado (75x55cm 29x21in) Barcelona 1999

PLESSI Fabrizio 1940 **[25]**
- $1 650 - €1 710 - €990 - FF11 220
  Una strana doccia Acrilico/tela (116x81cm 45x31in) Prato 1999
- $910 - €1 074 - **£642** - FF7 043
  Icaro Gouache (68.7x99cm 27x38in) Köln 2001

PLESSIS du Enslin H. 1894-1975 **[40]**
- $386 - €334 - **£232** - FF2 189
  View on a Bridge Oil/canvas (50x60cm 19x23in) Johannesburg 1998

PLESSNER Rudolf 1889-? **[4]**
- $2 099 - €1 831 - **£1 269** - FF12 012
  Folkliv vid Potsdammerstrasse, Berlin - kvällsljus Oil/canvas (65x92cm 25x36in) Stockholm 1998

PLETKA Paul 1946 **[4]**
- $72 500 - €62 041 - **£43 645** - FF406 964
  «Lesson in the History of Pioneers Days» Oil/canvas (152x152cm 59x59in) New-York 1998

PLETSCH Oskar 1830-1888 **[25]**
- $298 - €332 - **£208** - FF2 180
  Der Raub der Sabinerinnen Pencil (8.8x10.1cm 3x3in) München 2001

PLETSER George, Jürgen 1871-1942 **[48]**
- $310 - €295 - **£188** - FF1 934
  Gevarieerd stilleven van rozen Oil/canvas (48x42cm 18x16in) Rotterdam 1999

PLEYDENWURFF Wilhelm ?-1494 **[3]**
- $578 - €547 - **£360** - FF3 586
  The Holy Trinity Woodcut (24.5x17.5cm 9x6in) Praha

PLEYSIER Ary 1809-1879 **[22]**
- $10 802 - €11 344 - **£6 835** - FF74 415
  Tjalken on the River Schelde Oil/canvas (113x172cm 44x67in) Amsterdam 2000
- $9 387 - €8 837 - **£5 800** - FF57 968
  The Royal Yacht, Victoria & Albert II, arriving at Boulogne Oil/canvas (58.5x86.5cm 23x34in) London 1999
- $907 - €862 - **£552** - FF5 655
  Personen op een havenhoofd bij stormachtig weer Oil/panel (18x21cm 7x8in) Rotterdam 1999

PLIMER Andrew 1763-1837 **[86]**
- $3 479 - €4 159 - **£2 400** - FF27 284
  Half Length Oval Portrait of an Officer, Possibly Third Foot East Kent Miniature (5.5x4.5cm 2x1in) Cambridge 2000

PLISSON Henry 1908 **[47]**
- $5 055 - €5 509 - **£3 500** - FF36 134
  Viewing Monet's Waterlilies Oil/canvas (76.5x101cm 30x39in) London 2001
- $367 - €427 - **£258** - FF2 800
  Chevaux au pré Encre (44.5x28.5cm 17x11in) Paris 2001

PLOBERGER Herbert 1902-1977 **[1]**
- $62 600 - €72 672 - **£44 000** - FF476 700
  Stilleben, auf dem Tisch unter dem Tisch Öl/Leinwand (89x116cm 35x45in) Wien 2001

PLOCKHORST Bernhard 1825-1907 **[5]**
- $6 522 - €7 669 - **£4 675** - FF50 308
  Portrait eines Mädchens mit Blumenkorb und Labrador Öl/Leinwand (100x78cm 39x30in) München 2001

PLOMTEUX Léopold 1920 **[80]**
- $433 - €421 - **£265** - FF2 764
  Portrait de fillette Huile/panneau (46.5x40cm 18x15in) Liège 1999
- $227 - €235 - **£144** - FF1 544
  Compositie Black chalk (32x51cm 12x20in) Lokeren 2000

PLONSKI Michel 1778-1812 **[3]**
- $4 257 - €3 948 - **£2 600** - FF25 896
  A Pack of Dogs Playing Black chalk/paper (11x49.5cm 4x19in) London 1998

PLOSKY Jonas 1940 **[17]**
- $651 - €703 - **£450** - FF4 614
  Looking Out to Sea Oil/board (61x106.5cm 24x41in) London 2001

PLOTNIKOV Vladimir Alexandrov. 1853-1919 **[2]**
- $2 191 - €2 352 - **£1 466** - FF15 427
  Reigen, Ukrainische Bauernmädchen beim Tanz Aquarell/Karton (52x67.5cm 20x26in) Köln 2000

PLOZ XIX-XX **[8]**
- $1 515 - €1 448 - **£949** - FF9 500
  «Vichy, chemin de fer» Poster (108x79cm 42x31in) London 1999

PLUCHART Henri Eugène 1835-1898 **[2]**
- $3 637 - €3 964 - **£2 384** - FF26 000
  Vues de la côte napolitaine Huile/toile (50x68cm 19x26in) Versailles 2000

PLÜCKEBAUM Karl 1880-1952 **[40]**
- $410 - €383 - **£248** - FF2 515
  Der Herr Baron und sein alter Förster Öl/Karton (60x70cm 23x27in) Bremen 2000

PLÜCKEBAUM Meta 1876-1945 **[53]**
- $120 - €143 - **£85** - FF939
  Zwei kleine Kätzchen mit grünen Schleifen Radierung (37x31cm 14x12in) Merzhausen 2000

PLUM Poul August 1876-1878 **[12]**
- $1 153 - €1 073 - **£700** - FF7 036
  Interior med aeldre kvinde Oil/canvas (38x32cm 14x12in) Viby J, Århus 1998

PLUMOT André 1829-1906 **[53]**
- $7 033 - €8 098 - **£4 800** - FF53 121
  Crossing the Ford Oil/canvas (76x115cm 29x45in) London 2000

P

$547 - €595 - **£360** - FF3 902
Schapen Oil/panel (17.5x24cm 6x9in) Lokeren 2000

PLÜSCHOW Guillaume, Guglielmo 1852-1930 [64]
📷 $414 - €493 - **£296** - FF3 234
Stehender weiblicher Akt Albumen print
(22.5x16.5cm 8x6in) Zürich 2000

PO del Giacomo 1652-1726 [21]
$150 000 - €131 574 - **£91 080** - FF863 070
Rachael at the Well Oil/canvas (176.5x230cm
69x90in) New-York 1999
$14 420 - €14 534 - **£9 000** - FF95 340
Pieta mit Engeln Öl/Leinwand (95x58cm 37x22in)
Wien 2000

POBBIATI Mario 1887-1956 [26]
$2 912 - €3 019 - **£1 747** - FF19 805
Festa campestre Olio/tela (80x100cm 31x39in)
Milano 1999

POCCETTI Bernardino 1542/48-1612 [20]
$11 000 - €11 783 - **£7 511** - FF77 292
Two Heads of Little Boys Red chalk/paper
(13.5x21cm 5x8in) New-York 2001

POCHINI XIX [2]
$5 143 - €5 641 - **£3 415** - FF37 000
Buste de jeune fille Marbre Carrare (H70cm H27in)
Rouen 2000

POCHWALSKI Kazimierz 1855-1940 [22]
$1 750 - €2 082 - **£1 248** - FF13 656
Repos de chasseur Huile/carton (50.5x41cm
19x16in) Warszawa 2000
$3 786 - €3 558 - **£2 350** - FF23 337
Coquelicots Oil/panel (33.5x47cm 13x18in)
Warszawa 1999

POCHWALSKI Wladislaw 1860-1924 [2]
$3 685 - €3 790 - **£2 337** - FF24 858
Paysage hivernal dans la forêt Oil/canvas
(62x120cm 24x47in) Kraków 2000

POCIECHA Michal 1852-1908 [4]
$562 - €567 - **£351** - FF3 720
Marchand de vieilleries Watercolour, gouache/paper
(48x33cm 18x12in) Warszawa 2000

POCK Alexander 1871-1950 [36]
$2 377 - €2 036 - **£1 391** - FF13 353
Berittener Öl/Karton (35x24.8cm 13x9in) Wien 1998
$225 - €242 - **£150** - FF1 585
Mounted Cavalry Watercolour (16.5x14.5cm 6x5in)
London 2000

POCK Tobias 1609-1683 [3]
$2 989 - €2 455 - **£1 736** - FF16 107
Heilige Nacht Engraving (37x43cm 14x16in) Berlin
1998

POCOCK Lexden Lewis 1850-1919 [8]
$594 - €555 - **£366** - FF3 643
**A stile bridge over welsh River, landskap med
bro** Akvarell/papper (36x53cm 14x20in) Stockholm
1999

POCOCK Nicholas 1740-1821 [112]
$12 627 - €15 017 - **£9 000** - FF98 506
**East Indiaman, Rockingham, being Floated off a
Shoal in the Red Sea** Oil/canvas (82.5x122.5cm
32x48in) London 2000
$1 325 - €1 486 - **£900** - FF9 747
The Casada Press Watercolour (8.5x11.5cm 3x4in)
London 2000

POCOCKE Edward 1843-1901 [40]
$174 - €207 - **£120** - FF1 356
Pull's Ferry Watercolour/paper (23x34cm 9x13in)
Bexhill-on-Sea, East-Sussex 2000

PODCHERNIKOFF Alexis Matthew 1886-1933 [89]
$2 250 - €2 629 - **£1 606** - FF17 248
Near Indio, Cal Oil/canvas (40x60cm 16x24in)
Altadena CA 2001
$2 250 - €2 430 - **£1 555** - FF15 938
Flower Fields Oil/canvas (25x41cm 10x16in)
Altadena CA 2001

PODESTA Giovanni Andrea c.1620-c.1670 [18]
$1 100 - €1 140 - **£660** - FF7 480
Baccanale Gravure (26x39cm 10x15in) Milano 2000

PODESTI Francesco 1800-1895 [9]
$20 000 - €18 408 - **£12 004** - FF120 746
The Bathing Ladies Oil/canvas (53x76cm 21x30in)
Chicago IL 1999

PODESTI Vincenzo 1812-1897 [1]
$8 400 - €10 885 - **£6 300** - FF71 400
Michelangelo mostra il Mosè a Vittoria Colonna
Olio/tela (123x175cm 48x68in) Prato 2000

PODKOWINSKI Wladyslaw 1866-1895 [14]
$38 880 - €36 378 - **£23 568** - FF238 624
Szal uniesien Oil/canvas (47.3x36cm 18x14in)
Warszawa 1999
$4 614 - €4 039 - **£2 795** - FF26 492
In Front of the Opera Watercolour/paper (11.5x13cm
4x5in) Warszawa 1998

PODSADECKI Kazimierz 1904-1970 [38]
$201 - €189 - **£124** - FF1 243
Naked Woman Chalks/paper (20x29cm 7x11in)
Warszawa 1999

POEL van der Adriaen Lievensz. 1626-c.1685 [8]
$7 550 - €7 267 - **£4 720** - FF47 670
Nächtliche Feuerbrunst Oil/panel (48x62cm
18x24in) Wien 1999

POEL van der Egbert Lievensz. 1621-1664 [74]
$6 420 - €6 378 - **£4 000** - FF41 834
Night Scene with Soldiers Looting a Village
Oil/panel (38.5x49.5cm 15x19in) London 1999
$6 000 - €5 727 - **£3 748** - FF37 569
**Kitchen Interior with a Peasant Woman Peeling
Vegetables** Oil/panel (29x39.5cm 11x15in) New-York
1999

POELENBURGH van Cornelis c.1586-1667 [90]
$8 764 - €10 174 - **£6 160** - FF66 738
**Ein Wanderer beobachtet badende Nymphen im
Wald** Oil/panel (46.5x61cm 18x24in) Wien 2001
$8 000 - €9 422 - **£5 532** - FF61 807
Saints Matthew and James Oil/panel (12.5x10.5cm
4x4in) New-York 2000
$8 606 - €9 447 - **£5 538** - FF61 971
Cimon and Iphigenia Red chalk/paper (11.4x20.5cm
4x8in) Wien 2000

POELL Alfred 1867-1929 [4]
$7 428 - €8 721 - **£5 268** - FF57 204
Spitzmauer und Grosser Priel Öl/Karton (63x56cm
24x22in) Wien 2000

POERSON Charles 1609-1667 [6]
$170 000 - €149 117 - **£103 224** - FF978 146
The Dispute Between Minerva and Neptune
Oil/canvas (156x106.5cm 61x41in) New-York 1999
$104 601 - €112 281 - **£70 000** - FF736 512
Cavalry Engagement Oil/canvas (76.5x125cm
30x49in) London 2000

POERTZEL Otto 1876-1963 **[93]**
- $2 171 - €1 838 - **£1 300** - FF12 059
  Dancing Girl Ivory, bronze (H19cm H7in) London 1998

POETOEBOEN Ida Bagus XX **[1]**
- $3 565 - €3 267 - £2 178 - FF21 430
  Der Wald Gouache/papier (12.5x27cm 4x10in) Zürich 1999

POETOU Émile François 1885-1975 **[14]**
- $1 272 - €1 190 - **£772** - FF7 804
  Mensen vernietigen zichzelf Plaster (25x46cm 9x18in) Lokeren 1999

POETZELBERGER Oswald 1893-1966 **[15]**
- $5 331 - €4 599 - **£3 204** - FF30 170
  Sturm Öl/Leinwand (60x75cm 23x29in) München 1998

POGANY Willy Andrew 1882-1955 **[23]**
- $1 900 - €2 116 - **£1 242** - FF13 882
  Woman in white blown by winter winter winds, Magazine Cover Oil/board (49x39cm 19x15in) New-York 2000
- $1 600 - €1 532 - **£988** - FF10 051
  Santa Claus Holding Placard Aloft, Illustration Watercolour/paper (28x16cm 11x6in) New-York 1999

POGEDAIEFF de Georges A. 1897-1971 **[23]**
- $51 - €61 - **£37** - FF400
  Bord de rivière Aquarelle/papier (39x54cm 15x21in) Paris 2001

POGGENBEEK Geo, Jan Hendrick 1853-1903 **[91]**
- $9 169 - €8 622 - **£5 677** - FF56 555
  Ducks on a riverbank under the pollard willows Oil/canvas (33x53cm 12x20in) Amsterdam 1999
- $1 101 - €943 - **£650** - FF6 188
  Figures on a Street Oil/canvas/panel (34x25.5cm 13x10in) London 1998
- $1 166 - €1 364 - **£820** - FF8 948
  Ducks by a River Watercolour/paper (27x40cm 10x15in) Oxfordshire 2000

POGGINI Domenico 1520-1590 **[1]**
- $71 495 - €68 983 - **£44 888** - FF452 500
  Buste de François de Medicis (1541-1587) Grand Duc de Toscane Sculpture (H80cm H31in) Monte-Carlo 1999

POGLIAGHI Ludovico 1857-1950 **[5]**
- $1 650 - €1 710 - **£990** - FF11 220
  Parata in omaggio a Napoleone Tecnica mista/carta (54x71cm 21x27in) Milano 1999

POGNA Giuseppe 1845-1907 **[13]**
- $2 820 - €2 436 - **£1 880** - FF15 980
  Pescatori nel golfo Olio/tela (55x30cm 21x11in) Trieste 1998

PÖHACKER Leopold 1782-1844 **[4]**
- $1 577 - €1 817 - **£1 077** - FF11 917
  Portrait einer Dame Öl/Karton (15.5x20cm 6x7in) Wien 2000

POHL Adolf Josef 1872-? **[15]**
- $630 - €581 - **£396** - FF3 813
  Schmied Bronze (H48.5cm H19in) Wien 1999

POHL E. Henry 1874-1956 **[12]**
- $2 000 - €1 841 - **£1 200** - FF7 074
  On the Slopes of Mt. Tacoma Washington Oil/canvas (76x91cm 30x36in) Pasadena CA 1999
- $950 - €1 026 - **£656** - FF6 729
  «California Desert from Warren Well» Pastel/board (40x50cm 16x20in) Altadena CA 2001

POHL Johann Baptist XIX **[4]**
- $350 - €364 - **£221** - FF2 388
  Buttneria Scalpelata/Vaccinium Scabrum Lithograph (38x27cm 15x11in) New-York 2000

POHLE Hermann 1831-1901 **[34]**
- $17 000 - €16 213 - **£10 347** - FF106 350
  The Farm Oil/canvas (119x173cm 46x68in) New-York 1999
- $4 012 - €3 857 - **£2 502** - FF25 301
  Elegant Party embarking on a Boat, a Palatial Mansion beyond Oil/canvas (88x121cm 34x47in) Amsterdam 1999
- $1 130 - €1 329 - **£797** - FF8 719
  Alte Burguine mit Kapelle am Fluss Öl/Leinwand (33.5x47.5cm 13x18in) Köln 2001

POHLE Leon 1841-1908 **[1]**
- $4 021 - €4 602 - **£2 765** - FF30 185
  Andacht, ein junges Mädchen, das Gebetbuch auf den Knien Öl/Leinwand (63x50cm 24x19in) München 2000

POIGNANT Lucien 1905-1941 **[15]**
- $589 - €701 - **£420** - FF4 600
  Sous-bois près de Pralognan Huile/panneau (45.5x37cm 17x14in) Grenoble 2000

POILLERAT Gilbert 1902-1988 **[13]**
- $55 000 - €59 037 - **£36 806** - FF387 255
  Console Iron (89.5x130cm 35x51in) New-York 2000

POILLEUX-SAINT-ANGE Georges L. XIX-XX **[5]**
- $11 101 - €12 958 - **£7 837** - FF85 000
  L'adoration de Moïse Huile/toile (73x93cm 28x36in) Paris 2000

POILLY de François I 1622-1693 **[2]**
- $833 - €971 - **£586** - FF6 372
  Die Jungfrau hebt den Schleier über dem schlafenden Kind, nach Raffael Kupferstich (37x28.5cm 14x11in) Berlin 2001

POILLY de Nicolas II 1675-1747 **[7]**
- $2 177 - €1 853 - **£1 300** - FF12 157
  The Assumption of the Virgin Black & white chalks (49.5x31.5cm 19x12in) London 1998

POILLY Jean-Baptiste 1669-1728 **[6]**
- $1 092 - €1 067 - **£692** - FF7 000
  Les Éstrennes Royalles, présentées à Monseigneur le Dauphin Burin (83x53cm 32x20in) Paris 1999

POILPOT - XIX-XX **[6]**
- $425 - €473 - **£296** - FF3 100
  «Chemins de fer d'Orléans, Le Lioran, Hôte des touristes» Affiche (105x73cm 41x59in) Paris 2001

POINT Armand 1860-1932 **[107]**
- $9 000 - €9 069 - **£5 610** - FF59 490
  The Bather Oil/canvas (100.5x73cm 39x28in) New-York 2000
- $1 000 - €1 073 - **£669** - FF7 041
  La danse Sanguine/papier (64.5x49.5cm 25x19in) New-York 2000

POINT Rudolf 1927 **[36]**
- $421 - €409 - **£260** - FF2 683
  Kirchgang in Tirol Oil/panel (20x40cm 7x15in) Augsburg 1999

POINTELIN Auguste 1839-1933 **[56]**
- $1 120 - €1 067 - **£709** - FF7 000
  Cmbe Jurassienne Huile/toile (33x45cm 12x17in) Besançon 1999

P

P

⬨ **$168** - €198 - **£118** - FF1 300
Paysage Fusain/papier (33.5x43.5cm 13x17in) Lons-Le-Saunier 2000

POIRIER Jacques 1928 **[4]**
⬤ **$1 062** - €1 172 - **£719** - FF7 685
Le massif Oil/canvas (91x76cm 36x30in) Calgary, Alberta 2000

POIRIER Jacques 1942 **[30]**
⬤ **$651** - €756 - **£450** - FF4 961
L'automne dans le parc des grands-jardins Oil/canvas (60x76cm 24x30in) Calgary, Alberta 2000

POIRIER Narcisse 1883-1983 **[141]**
⬤ **$184** - €198 - **£123** - FF1 299
Bouquet de fleurs Oil/board (30.5x40.5cm 12x15in) Montréal 2000

POIRIER Ray 1938 **[30]**
⬤ **$875** - €838 - **£539** - FF5 500
La montagne en provence Huile/toile (54x73cm 21x28in) Strasbourg 1999

POIRSON Maurice 1850-1882 **[6]**
⬨ **$2 750** - €3 049 - **£1 904** - FF20 000
Rêverie Aquarelle/papier (40x55cm 15x21in) Coulommiers 2001

POISSON Pierre Marie 1876-1953 **[18]**
⬰ **$3 645** - €3 964 - **£2 402** - FF26 000
La fête chez les Ouled-Naïl Bas-relief (56.5x96cm 22x37in) Paris 2000

POITEVIN Louis Alphonse 1819-1882 **[27]**
📷 **$643** - €686 - **£428** - FF4 500
Autoportrait Photo (30x24cm 11x9in) Paris 2000

POITRAS Jane Ash 1951 **[11]**
⬤ **$1 298** - €1 468 - **£913** - FF9 630
«Spirit» Oil/canvas (66x56cm 25x22in) Vancouver, BC. 2001

POKHITONOV Ivan Pavlovich 1851-1924 **[36]**
⬤ **$7 131** - €5 880 - **£4 200** - FF38 567
The Return of the Hunter Oil/canvas (30.5x61cm 12x24in) London 1998
⬤ **$9 572** - €10 733 - **£6 500** - FF70 404
View of a Village in Winter Sunshine Oil/canvas/board (13.5x26cm 5x10in) London 2000

POKORNY Richard 1907-1997 **[32]**
⬨ **$770** - €727 - **£478** - FF4 767
Rochusplatz Aquarell/Papier (31x21cm 12x8in) Wien 2000

POL van Christiaen 1752-1813 **[14]**
⬤ **$35 208** - €41 161 - **£25 137** - FF270 000
Nature morte au panier de fleurs sur un entablement de marbre Huile/toile (44.5x37.5cm 17x14in) Paris 2001

POL van der Louis 1896-1982 **[27]**
⬤ **$571** - €487 - **£344** - FF3 194
Die Blumenverkäuferin Oil/panel (30x40cm 11x15in) Zürich 1998

POLACK F. Ferdinand XIX-XX **[8]**
⬤ **$1 248** - €1 159 - **£779** - FF7 600
La danseuse de flamenco Huile/panneau (39x48cm 15x18in) Biarritz 1999

POLANZANI Francesco, Felice 1700-c.1785 **[5]**
▥▥ **$384** - €457 - **£274** - FF3 000
Portrait de Piranèse, frontispice des Opere di Architectura Eau-forte (38x29cm 14x11in) Paris 2000

POLASEK Albin 1879-1965 **[10]**
⬰ **$7 500** - €7 081 - **£4 662** - FF46 448
Forest Idyll Bronze (63x50cm 25x20in) Milford CT

POLEDNE Franz 1873-1932 **[66]**
⬤ **$6 170** - €7 267 - **£4 340** - FF47 670
«Johann Nestroy zum 100.Geburtstag» Mischtechnik/Karton (74x52cm 29x20in) Wien 2000
⬤ **$1 198** - €1 163 - **£839** - FF7 627
Motiv aus Weissenkirchen, Wachau Watercolour (34x23cm 13x9in) Wien 1999

POLELONEMA Otis 1902-1981 **[1]**
⬤ **$5 000** - €4 956 - **£3 127** - FF32 509
Priest of the Snake Dance Gouache/paper (19.5x32.5cm 7x12in) New-York 1999

POLENG Ida Bagus Made 1915-1999 **[1]**
⬤ **$9 451** - €8 809 - **£5 712** - FF57 780
Harvesting Acrylic/canvas (46x62cm 18x24in) Singapore 1999

POLENOV Vasili Dimitrevich 1844-1927 **[22]**
⬤ **$35 712** - €34 321 - **£22 000** - FF225 132
The Shores of the Lake Oil/canvas/board (90x63cm 35x24in) London 1999
⬤ **$15 281** - €12 599 - **£9 000** - FF82 644
Waiting by the Woodland River Oil/canvas (45x29.5cm 17x11in) London 1998

POLEO Héctor 1918-1989 **[65]**
⬤ **$20 000** - €17 394 - **£12 058** - FF114 100
Paisaje Andino Oil/canvas (89x116cm 35x45in) New-York 1998
⬤ **$1 830** - €1 931 - **£1 209** - FF12 669
Girasoles Oleo/cartón (29x24cm 11x9in) Caracas ($) 2000
⬨ **$4 200** - €4 397 - **£2 520** - FF28 840
Figuras Crayon/papier (46x59cm 18x23in) Caracas 2000
▥▥ **$345** - €354 - **£230** - FF2 323
Sin título Serigrafia (67x87cm 26x34in) Caracas 2000

POLGARI Geza 1862-? **[2]**
⬤ **$27 460** - €30 490 - **£19 140** - FF200 000
Jeune femmme endormie dans une barque Huile/toile (120x150cm 47x59in) Paris 2001

POLI de Fabio 1947 **[14]**
⬤ **$1 680** - €1 451 - **£1 120** - FF9 520
Cabaret Tecnica mista/tela (50x100cm 19x39in) Prato 1998

POLI Flavio 1900-1984 **[3]**
⬰ **$5 281** - €6 135 - **£3 711** - FF40 246
Löwe Sculpture, glass (14x40cm 5x15in) München 2001

POLI Gherardo c.1680-c.1740 **[8]**
⬤ **$34 324** - €31 369 - **£21 000** - FF205 764
Peasants Merrymaking and Dancing/Peasants resting and Conversing Oil/canvas (60.5x87.5cm 23x34in) London 1999
⬤ **$6 600** - €5 702 - **£4 400** - FF37 400
Capriccio architettonico di rovine antiche Olio/tela (22.5x28.5cm 8x11in) Roma 1998

POLI Giuseppe 1700-1767 **[7]**
⬤ **$15 307** - €15 033 - **£9 500** - FF98 609
Architectural Capriccio with Figures and Statuary Oil/canvas (56x93.5cm 22x36in) London 1999

POLIAKOFF Nicolas 1899-1976 [64]
- 🖼️ **$2 654** - €2 439 - **£1 630** - FF16 000
  Composition abstraite Estampe couleurs (65x50cm 25x19in) Paris 1999

POLIAKOFF Serge 1900-1969 [1099]
- 🖼️ **$126 072** - €122 335 - **£80 000** - FF802 464
  Composition Oil/canvas (130x97.5cm 51x38in) London 1999
- 🖼️ **$62 760** - €67 368 - **£42 000** - FF441 907
  Composition Oil/canvas (38x46.5cm 14x18in) London 2000
- 🖼️ **$19 534** - €22 258 - **£13 417** - FF146 000
  Figure Huile/toile (22x16cm 8x6in) Paris 2000
- ✏️ **$15 552** - €18 294 - **£11 148** - FF120 000
  Composition Gouache/papier (47x63.5cm 18x25in) Versailles 2001
- 🖼️ **$2 552** - €2 915 - **£1 800** - FF19 121
  Composition bleue et rouge Color lithograph (64x48cm 25x18in) London 2001

POLIDORI Robert 1951 [3]
- 📷 **$971** - €1 043 - **£650** - FF6 841
  Galerie Basse No.3 Versaille Series Photograph in colour (79x101.5cm 31x39in) London 2000

POLIDORO DA CARAVAGGIO (Polidoro Caldara) 1492-1543 [6]
- 🖼️ **$8 965** - €9 624 - **£6 000** - FF63 129
  A Groupe of Agricultural Labourers/Sketch of Another Similar Figure Ink (11x15.5cm 4x6in) London 2000

POLIDORO DA LANCIANO 1515-1565 [12]
- 🖼️ **$6 400** - €7 267 - **£4 380** - FF47 670
  Madonna mit Kind und dem Johannesknaben in einer Landschaft Oil/panel (67x52cm 26x20in) Wien 2000

POLITI Leo 1908 [1]
- ✏️ **$2 600** - €2 227 - **£1 563** - FF14 611
  Gossip Watercolour/paper (20x15cm 8x6in) Cincinnati OH 1998

POLIZZI Franco 1954 [17]
- 🖼️ **$1 900** - €1 970 - **£1 140** - FF12 920
  Notturno Olio/tela (100x100cm 39x39in) Roma 2000
- ✏️ **$500** - €518 - **£300** - FF3 400
  Tramonto Pastelli (35x50cm 13x19in) Roma 2001

POLK Brigid 1939 [2]
- 📷 **$11 000** - €10 273 - **£6 789** - FF67 386
  Mr. and Mrs. Brigid Pork, Drella and Andy Warhol - Alice Neel Polaroid (12.5x10.5x2cm 4x4xin) New-York 1999

POLK Charles Peale 1767-1822 [7]
- 🖼️ **$390 000** - €371 143 - **£243 945** - FF2 434 536
  Portrait of George Washington Oil/canvas (94x84cm 37x33in) New-York 1999

POLKE Sigmar 1941 [479]
- 🖼️ **$275 000** - €256 823 - **£169 730** - FF1 684 650
  Untitled Oil/canvas (259.5x200cm 102x78in) New-York 1999
- 🖼️ **$40 917** - €34 162 - **£24 000** - FF224 090
  Totenkopf Mixed media/canvas (40x50cm 15x19in) London 1998
- ✿ **$209 202** - €224 561 - **£140 000** - FF1 473 024
  Zollstockpalme Installation (255x145cm 100x57in) London 2000
- ✏️ **$15 781** - €15 270 - **£10 000** - FF100 163
  Untitled (Eichhörnchen) Gouache/paper (100x70cm 39x27in) London 1999

POLL van der Daniel Herbert 1877-1963 [15]
- 🖼️ **$10 507** - €9 983 - **£6 393** - FF65 485
  Tijger Oil/canvas (80x160cm 31x62in) Den Haag 1999
- ✏️ **$1 204** - €1 321 - **£800** - FF8 666
  Tiger Pastel (35x55cm 13x21in) London 2000

POLLACK Hans 1891-1968 [18]
- 🖼️ **$503** - €581 - **£352** - FF3 813
  «Mühlviertler Landschaft» Oil/panel (47x59cm 18x23in) Linz 2001

POLLAK August 1838-? [3]
- 🖼️ **$1 682** - €1 817 - **£1 162** - FF11 917
  Stilleben mit Erdbeeren, Ribisel, Spargel und Radieschen Öl/Leinwand (55.5x70cm 21x27in) Wien 2001

POLLAK Max 1886-1950 [36]
- 🖼️ **$107** - €109 - **£67** - FF715
  Hanne Isborn Farbradierung (39.5x32cm 15x12in) Wien 2000

POLLAK Zsigmond, Siegmund 1837-1912 [4]
- 🖼️ **$12 220** - €14 534 - **£8 720** - FF95 340
  Ausgleichsversuch streikender Arbeiter Öl/Leinwand (85x120cm 33x47in) Wien 2000

POLLARD James 1792-1867 [60]
- 🖼️ **$430 000** - €367 386 - **£258 129** - FF2 409 892
  Off in Good Style/All Over but Settling Oil/canvas (38x64cm 14x25in) New-York 1998
- 🖼️ **$3 419** - €3 975 - **£2 400** - FF26 074
  Meet at the Swan/After the Hunt Oil/canvas (30.5x40.5cm 12x15in) London 2001
- 🖼️ **$436** - €499 - **£300** - FF3 274
  Royal Mail Coach Aquatint (35x49.5cm 13x19in) Lymington 2000

POLLARD Robert I 1755-1838 [13]
- 🖼️ **$558** - €557 - **£340** - FF3 655
  Battle of the Nile, after Nicholas Pocock Aquatint in colors (42x60.5cm 16x23in) London 2000

POLLARD Robert II XIX [1]
- 🖼️ **$643** - €709 - **£420** - FF4 648
  The Chelsea, after James Pollard/Phenomenon after Edwards/Champion Aquatint (25x24cm 9x9in) London 2000

POLLARD Samuel George XIX [1]
- 🖼️ **$7 700** - €7 759 - **£4 800** - FF50 897
  Evening Scene at Beer, Devon Oil/canvas (56x87cm 22x34in) London 2000

POLLENTINE Alfred 1836-c.1890 [185]
- 🖼️ **$2 586** - €3 017 - **£1 800** - FF19 793
  Santa Maria Della Salute, Venice Oil/canvas (41x61cm 16x24in) West-Yorshire 2000
- 🖼️ **$2 079** - €2 322 - **£1 450** - FF15 231
  The Ducal Palace/Canale della Guidecca Oil/canvas (29x24cm 11x9in) Bath 2001
- ✏️ **$1 751** - €2 023 - **£1 226** - FF13 271
  Procession from the Dogges Palace, Venice Watercolour/paper (55x73cm 22x29in) Calgary, Alberta 2001

POLLET Joseph Michel-Ange 1814-1870 [14]
- ⬆ **$7 500** - €7 153 - **£4 565** - FF49 919
  Nude Female Figure on Pedestal: Night Gilded bronze (H96.5cm H37in) New-York 1999

P

P

$5 384 – €6 403 – £3 838 – FF42 000
Nymphe sortant du bain Bronze (H45cm H17in)
Calais 2000

POLLIN R. XX [6]
$2 840 – €3 354 – £2 017 – FF22 000
Poisson sur la vague Bronze (33x68cm 12x26in)
Neuilly-sur-Seine 2001

POLLITT Albert act.1885-1926 [102]
$482 – €489 – £300 – FF3 205
Shepherd and Sheep on a Moorland Track
Watercolour/paper (27x43cm 11x17in) Aylsham,
Norfolk 2001

POLLOCK Jackson 1912-1956 [71]
$7 250 000 – €8 120 532 – £5 037 300 –
FF53 267 200
«Black and White, Number 6» Enamel/canvas
(142.5x115cm 56x45in) New-York 2001
$800 000 – €896 059 – £555 840 – FF5 877 760
Orange Head Oil/canvas (47.5x40cm 18x15in) New-
York 2001
$420 000 – €470 431 – £291 816 – FF3 085 824
Poured black Shape I Oil/canvas (30.5x41.5cm
12x16in) New-York 2001
$35 000 – €39 832 – £24 594 – FF261 282
«Untitled, Wysuph #61» Coloured pencils/paper
(30.5x45.5cm 12x17in) New-York 2001
$11 000 – €9 321 – £6 573 – FF61 144
Untitled Engraving (40x60cm 15x23in) New-York
1998

POLLOCK Lilla XIX [1]
$3 573 – €3 659 – £2 244 – FF24 000
Fillette dans un paysage champêtre Huile/toile
(78x60cm 30x23in) Lille 2000

POLLONERA Carlo 1849-1923 [16]
$4 000 – €4 147 – £2 400 – FF27 200
Valico del Sempione, effetto di nuvole Olio/carto-
ne (38x46.5cm 14x18in) Vercelli 1999
$3 250 – €3 369 – £1 950 – FF22 100
Paesaggio montano Olio/cartone (33x42cm
12x16in) Vercelli 2000

POLLONI Silvio 1888-1972 [43]
$960 – €829 – £480 – FF5 440
Figura distesa Olio/tela (40x51cm 15x20in) Firenze
1999
$450 – €389 – £225 – FF2 550
Paesaggio sull'Arno Olio/tela (30x40cm 11x15in)
Prato 1999

POLOS Theodore C. 1901-1976 [2]
$1 200 – €1 339 – £785 – FF8 781
Untitled Lithograph (39x28cm 15x11in) Chicago IL
2000

POLUNIN Vladimir 1880-? [3]
$1 063 – €1 022 – £650 – FF6 703
«Summer Nights, London Underground» Poster
(102x64cm 40x25in) London 1999

POLYA Tibor 1886-1937 [8]
$1 600 – €1 573 – £1 000 – FF10 320
Garden Party Oil/board (60x50cm 23x19in) Budapest
1999

POMA Silvio 1841-1932 [62]
$10 400 – €13 476 – £7 800 – FF88 400
Visita alla nutrice Olio/tela (61x37cm 24x14in) Prato
2000
$3 200 – €4 147 – £2 400 – FF27 200
Isola Madre Olio/cartone (17.5x24cm 6x9in) Prato
2000

POMAR Julio 1928 [3]
$8 360 – €9 472 – £5 890 – FF62 130
Menino do tambor Feutre/papier (109x74cm
42x29in) Lisboa 2001

POMARDI Simone 1760-1830 [17]
$4 000 – €4 147 – £2 400 – FF27 200
Giardini di Villa Romana Acquarello/carta (51x74cm
20x29in) Vercelli 2001

POMERAT Georges XIX-XX [3]
$12 150 – €14 483 – £8 664 – FF95 000
**Déchargement de marchandises sur le port de
Marseille** Huile/toile (240x190cm 94x74in) Saint-
Martin-de-Crau 2000

POMEROY Florence Walton 1890-1981 [8]
$2 750 – €2 552 – £1 651 – FF16 740
Knitting Mittens Oil/canvas (60x68cm 24x27in)
Milford CT 1999

POMEROY Frederick William 1856-1924 [10]
$17 480 – €19 988 – £12 000 – FF131 115
Perseus with the Head of Medusa Bronze
(H108.5cm H42in) London 2001
$2 871 – €3 219 – £2 000 – FF21 114
Dionysus Bronze (H44.5cm H17in) London 2001

POMEY Louis Edmond 1831-1891 [4]
$69 000 – €65 806 – £42 000 – FF431 657
The Concert Oil/panel (80.5x59cm 31x23in) New-
York 1999

POMFRET Tom 1920-1997 [11]
$301 – €260 – £180 – FF1 706
«L'Alhambra, Granada» Gouache/paper
(39.5x63.5cm 15x25in) London 1998

POMI Alessandro 1890-1976 [18]
$3 400 – €3 525 – £2 040 – FF23 120
Modella nell'atelier Olio/tavola (60x45cm 23x17in)
Milano 2001
$600 – €777 – £450 – FF5 100
Cammellino Olio/tavoletta (23x32.5cm 9x12in)
Milano 2000
$1 937 – €2 008 – £1 162 – FF13 171
«Cicli Attila» Affiche couleur (140x99cm 55x38in)
Torino 2000

POMODORO Arnaldo 1926 [263]
$5 686 – €5 567 – £3 500 – FF36 517
Bozzetto Mixed media (20.5x22.5cm 8x8in) London
1999
$32 198 – €30 480 – £20 000 – FF199 938
Cono Tronco Polished bronze (H110cm H43in)
London 1999
$6 500 – €5 608 – £3 921 – FF36 785
Untitled Bronze (18x15x15cm 7x5x5in) New-York
1998
$500 – €522 – £315 – FF3 422
Study for the Wheel Ink (21.5x27.5cm 8x10in) New-
York 2000
$360 – €311 – £180 – FF2 040
Cronaca 3-Ugo Mulas Gravure cuivre couleurs
(99x69cm 38x27in) Prato 1999

POMODORO Gió 1930 [115]
$12 000 – €15 550 – £9 000 – FF102 000
Contatti antagonisti Marbre (85x64x50cm
33x25x19in) Milano 2001
$4 416 – €4 116 – £2 668 – FF26 998
Flügel Bronze (24.3x26x4.8cm 9x10x1in) München
1999
$850 – €881 – £510 – FF5 780
Figura Tecnica mista/carta (35x50cm 13x19in) Vercelli
2001

POMPA Gaetano 1933-1998 **[25]**
- $2 000 - €2 073 - £1 200 - FF13 600
  Sigismondo Malatesta Tecnica mista (46x90cm 18x35in) Roma 2001

POMPE Walter 1703-1777 **[4]**
- $11 931 - €10 163 - £7 093 - FF66 666
  La Vierge à l'Enfant Terracotta (H60cm H23in) Antwerpen 1998

POMPIGNOLI Luigi XIX-XX **[8]**
- $3 500 - €3 998 - £2 464 - FF26 226
  Portrait of four Artistocratic Children on a Palacial Estate Oil/canvas (81x64cm 32x25in) Pittsfield MA 2001

POMPON François 1855-1933 **[199]**
- $10 717 - €12 501 - £7 527 - FF82 000
  Panthère mouchetée Plâtre (14.5x32x7cm 5x12x2in) Pontoise 2000
- $6 362 - €6 174 - £3 960 - FF40 500
  Le sanglier courant Crayon (16x31cm 6x12in) Pontoise 1999

PONÇ Joan 1927-1984 **[118]**
- $2 275 - €2 102 - £1 365 - FF13 790
  Suite instruments of torture Tempera (50x70cm 19x27in) Barcelona 1999
- $1 798 - €1 862 - £1 147 - FF12 214
  Suite Quadrada petita B Técnica mixta/papel (50x50cm 19x19in) Barcelona 2000
- $168 - €180 - £114 - FF1 182
  Juego apalafonte Serigrafia (69x49cm 27x19in) Madrid 2001

PONCE DE LEON Angel 1925 **[5]**
- $94 - €101 - £63 - FF665
  Expressionist View of a Rooster and Village Acrylic/canvas (54x71cm 21x28in) South-Natick MA 2000

PONCE DE LÉON Fidelio 1895/96-1949/57 **[51]**
- $16 000 - €13 951 - £9 673 - FF91 515
  Mujer Oil/canvas (51x61cm 20x24in) New-York 1998
- $2 745 - €2 703 - £1 710 - FF17 730
  Mujeres en el jardin Oleo/lienzo (33x40.5cm 12x15in) Madrid 1999

PONCE-CAMUS Marie Nicolas 1778-1839 **[5]**
- $1 974 - €1 845 - £1 193 - FF12 100
  Portrait présumé de Marie Amélie Huile/toile (65x54cm 25x21in) Paris 1999

PONCELET Maurice Georges 1897-1978 **[65]**
- $614 - €595 - £379 - FF3 900
  Paris Street at Night Oil/canvas (64.5x91.5cm 25x36in) Toronto 1999

PONCELET Thierry 1946 **[11]**
- $3 834 - €4 462 - £2 736 - FF29 268
  Notable à la tête de griffon et de cocker Huile/toile (115x80cm 45x31in) Bruxelles 2001

PONCET Antoine 1928 **[57]**
- $1 117 - €942 - £665 - FF6 182
  Froidamente Bronze poli (H22cm H8in) Antwerpen 1998

PONCET Jean-Baptiste 1827-1901 **[4]**
- $1 087 - €1 296 - £775 - FF8 500
  Portrait de Armance Costa de Beauregard comtesse de Musy Huile/toile (116x80cm 45x31in) Paris 2000

PONCHIN Antoine 1872-1934 **[21]**
- $31 464 - €36 588 - £22 080 - FF240 000
  Côte méditerranéenne Huile/toile (142.5x273cm 56x107in) Paris 2001

- $1 622 - €1 588 - £1 040 - FF10 418
  Coastal View Oil/canvas (54.5x64.5cm 21x25in) Amsterdam 1999

PONCHIN Louis XIX **[2]**
- $4 263 - €4 037 - £2 652 - FF26 481
  Opstilling med spillekort, jetons, pibe og karaffel med cognac Oil/canvas (38x46cm 14x18in) Köbenhavn 1999

POND Arthur c.1705-1758 **[6]**
- $1 990 - €2 193 - £1 300 - FF14 388
  Portrait of Thomas Wilson, Prebendary of St. Paul's Cathedral Pastel/paper (59.5x44.5cm 23x17in) London 2000

PONEMONE Scott 1949 **[1]**
- $5 084 - €5 976 - £3 524 - FF39 200
  Noon Today Aquarelle/papier (92x92cm 36x36in) Paris 2000

PONGRATZ Peter 1940 **[51]**
- $480 - €545 - £336 - FF3 575
  Ohne Titel Mischtechnik/Papier (44.5x63cm 17x24in) Wien 2001

PONOMAREW Serge 1911-1984 **[53]**
- $4 017 - €4 726 - £2 879 - FF31 000
  Femme nue Marbre (H44cm H17in) Paris 2001

PONS ARNAU Francisco 1886-1965 **[11]**
- $550 - €1 502 - £975 - FF9 850
  Retrato de Maria Sorolla Oleo/tabla (47x30cm 18x11in) Madrid 1999

PONS Jean 1913 **[133]**
- $121 - €137 - £85 - FF900
  Composition Gouache/papier (40x30cm 15x11in) Paris 2001

PONS Louis 1927 **[61]**
- $1 206 - €1 372 - £837 - FF9 000
  Objet rituel Technique mixte (76.5x44.5cm 30x17in) Paris 2000
- $1 219 - €1 403 - £840 - FF9 200
  Sans titre Encre/papier (49x64cm 19x25in) Marseille 2000

PONS MARTI Jaume 1885-1931 **[5]**
- $9 520 - €8 409 - £5 880 - FF55 160
  Vista de Sant Féliu de Guixols Oleo/lienzo (70x150cm 27x59in) Madrid 1999

PONSEN Tunis 1891-1968 **[26]**
- $3 500 - €3 304 - £2 175 - FF21 675
  Rockport Oil/canvas (76x91cm 30x36in) Milford CT 1999

PONSIOEN Johan 1900-1969 **[8]**
- $8 227 - €8 168 - £5 140 - FF53 578
  De Geranium Oil/canvas (60.5x51cm 23x20in) Amsterdam 1999
- $5 853 - €5 899 - £3 649 - FF38 695
  Mosterdpotje Oil/board (25x29.5cm 9x11in) Amsterdam 2000

PONSOBY David Barbazon 1910 **[2]**
- $376 - €399 - £248 - FF2 616
  Lisboa vista do Tejo Acuarela/papel (47x65.5cm 18x25in) Lisboa 2000

PONSOLD Renate 1935 **[19]**
- $413 - €460 - £270 - FF3 018
  Frank Stella Vintage gelatin silver print (19.9x25.3cm 7x9in) Köln 2000

P

PONSON Raphaël Luc 1835-1904 **[53]**
- $4 250 - €4 783 - £2 927 - FF31 376
  Fishing Boats, Ostend Oil/canvas (60.5x100.5cm 23x39in) Philadelphia PA 2000
- $1 570 - €1 343 - £949 - FF8 809
  Fishing Boat off the Coast Oil/board (27x38cm 10x14in) London 1999

PONSONE Matteo c.1580/90-1664 **[1]**
- $40 931 - €46 497 - £28 243 - FF305 000
  La mort de Lucrèce Huile/toile (101x81.5cm 39x32in) Paris 2000

PONTEGHINI Giulio Avezuti 1507-1556/57 **[1]**
- $48 933 - €45 767 - £30 000 - FF300 210
  The Lamentation Oil/panel (257x170cm 101x66in) London 1998

PONTHUS-CINIER Antoine 1812-1885 **[61]**
- $17 305 - €19 123 - £12 000 - FF125 436
  Rome at sunset with St.Peters and Castel Sant'Angelo Oil/canvas (100.5x151cm 39x59in) London 2001
- $4 005 - €4 573 - £2 817 - FF30 000
  Paysans sur le chemin débouchant vers la val- lée Huile/toile (46x39cm 18x15in) Fontainebleau 2001
- $963 - €1 143 - £701 - FF7 500
  Paysage d'Italie Huile/toile/panneau (22x32cm 8x12in) Lyon 2001

PONTI Carlo 1820-1893 **[24]**
- $987 - €915 - £609 - FF6 000
  Vues de Venise Tirage albuminé (23x29cm 9x11in) Paris 1999

PONTI Gió 1897-1979 **[20]**
- $2 200 - €2 518 - £1 513 - FF16 515
  Two Flaring Form Ginori Vases Decorated with Skiers Porcelain (H17cm H7in) New-York 2000
- $1 190 - €1 234 - £714 - FF8 092
  Bozzetto per affresco Pastelli/carta (38x27cm 14x10in) Milano 1999

PONTING Herbert George 1871-1935 **[122]**
- $2 080 - €1 972 - £1 300 - FF12 938
  Sitting Penguin Snowed Up Print (31.5x41cm 12x16in) Crewkerne, Somerset 1999
- $2 905 - €3 236 - £1 900 - FF21 226
  Death of an Iceberg Carbon print (58x73cm 23x29in) London 2000

PONTIUS Paulus 1603-1658 **[31]**
- $155 - €124 - £79 - FF813
  S.Rosalia, d'après Van Dyck Burin (44x33.4cm 17x13in) Bruxelles 2000

PONTOY Henri 1888-1968 **[261]**
- $11 681 - €11 586 - £7 265 - FF76 000
  Femme à l'oued Huile/toile (96x145cm 37x57in) Bergerac 1999
- $5 154 - €5 031 - £3 263 - FF33 000
  Les souks de la Médina de Fès Huile/toile (55x46cm 21x18in) Calais 1999
- $2 826 - €3 049 - £1 866 - FF20 000
  Port de Rabat Huile/toile (41x33cm 16x12in) Orléans 2001
- $2 001 - €1 829 - £1 225 - FF12 000
  Au fondouk Gouache/papier (42.5x60.5cm 16x23in) Paris 1999
- $1 142 - €1 067 - £690 - FF7 000
  La mosquée Sidi Mahrez, place Bab el Souika/Entrée de souk à Tunis Lithographie (32x25cm 12x9in) Paris 1999

PONTY Max 1904-1972 **[35]**
- $800 - €744 - £493 - FF4 879
  «Plages de France» Poster (99x61cm 39x24in) New-York 1999

POOKE-DUITS Marion Louise 1883-1975 **[9]**
- $75 - €84 - £49 - FF548
  Portrait of a Woman Oil/canvas (55x40cm 22x16in) Watertown MA 2000

POOLE Earle Lincoln 1891-1972 **[7]**
- $425 - €389 - £259 - FF2 550
  A Titmouse and Chickadee on a Branch in Winter Watercolour/paper (29x18cm 11x7in) Boston MA 1998

POOLE Eugene Alonzo 1841-1912 **[7]**
- $4 250 - €4 029 - £2 655 - FF26 426
  Houses by the River Oil/canvas (50x35cm 20x14in) Mystic CT 1999

POOLE Frederick Victor 1865-1936 **[6]**
- $6 100 - €6 405 - £3 846 - FF42 015
  Diana Oil/canvas/board (119x91cm 47x36in) Cleveland OH 2000

POOLE James 1804-1886 **[27]**
- $1 493 - €1 290 - £900 - FF8 465
  Figures in a River Landscape, Snowdon Oil/can- vas (40x60cm 15x23in) Billingshurst, West-Sussex 1999

POOLE Leslie Donald 1942 **[10]**
- $860 - €923 - £584 - FF6 055
  Cactus Acrylic/paper (31x31cm 12x12in) Calgary, Alberta 2001

POOLE Paul Falconer 1807-1879 **[63]**
- $2 750 - €2 645 - £1 697 - FF17 347
  Depicting a Mother and Daughter Drinking from a Well Oil/canvas (66x51cm 26x20in) Detroit MI 1999
- $1 171 - €1 250 - £800 - FF8 202
  «Sunny Hours» Oil/panel (17x21.5cm 6x8in) Billingshurst, West-Sussex 2001
- $611 - €616 - £387 - FF4 038
  The Songbird Watercolour (44.5x35cm 17x13in) London 2000

POONS Larry 1937 **[63]**
- $3 000 - €3 361 - £2 088 - FF22 048
  «Angela D» Acrylic/canvas (206.5x65cm 81x25in) Washington 2001
- $3 500 - €3 020 - £2 111 - FF19 807
  Untitled, #13 Acrylic/canvas (140x75cm 55x29in) New-York 1998

POOR Henry Varnum 1888-1970 **[32]**
- $1 400 - €1 279 - £856 - FF8 392
  Groves and Rolling Hills Oil/canvas (45.5x51cm 17x20in) Boston MA 1999

POORE Henry Rankin 1859-1940 **[18]**
- $3 500 - €3 491 - £2 185 - FF22 901
  The Old White Horse of the Dunes Oil/board (60x86cm 24x34in) Dedham MA 1999

POORTEN van Jacobus Johannes 1841-1914 **[20]**
- $3 095 - €3 323 - £2 072 - FF21 800
  Niederländisches Dorf am Wasser, Sommerstimmung mit Wäscherin Öl/Leinwand (68x100cm 26x39in) Köln 2000

POORTER de Jean Antoine 1703-? **[4]**
- $28 000 - €24 026 - £17 200 - FF157 600
  Fiesta en una aldea flamenca Oleo/lienzo (196x227cm 77x89in) Madrid 1998

POORTER de Willem 1608-c.1660 **[12]**
☞ **$130 320** - €148 094 - **£90 000** - FF971 433
    The Healing of the Blind Tobit Oil/panel (51x66cm 20x25in) London 2000
☞ **$11 840** - €13 263 - **£8 299** - FF87 000
    La présentation de Jésus au Temple Huile/panneau (37.5x30cm 14x11in) Paris 2001

POORTVLIET Rien 1932-1995 **[19]**
☞ **$2 642** - €2 496 - **£1 648** - FF16 371
    Boarhunt in a Snow-Clad Woodland Oil/canvas (30x60cm 11x23in) Amsterdam 1999
✎ **$528** - €499 - **£329** - FF3 274
    Fawn - Study Ink (39x30cm 15x11in) Amsterdam 1999

POOT Rik 1924 **[44]**
⚒ **$1 612** - €1 809 - **£1 110** - FF12 195
    Moeder en kind Terracotta (60.5x18cm 23x7in) Lokeren 2000

POOTOOGOOK Kananginak 1935 **[23]**
▥ **$260** - €302 - **£180** - FF1 984
    Hunting with the Bow Print (61x76cm 24x29in) Vancouver, BC. 2000

POPE Alexander 1849-1924 **[33]**
☞ **$28 004** - €32 569 - **£20 000** - FF213 638
    Seventeen seated King Charles and Blenheim Spaniels Oil/canvas (61x245cm 24x96in) London 2001
☞ **$11 000** - €9 398 - **£6 603** - FF61 648
    The Morning Lesson, A Lady on her Grey Horse Oil/canvas (84x105.5cm 33x41in) New-York 1998
☞ **$2 500** - €2 854 - **£1 762** - FF18 724
    Portrait of a Labrador Retriever Oil/canvas (35.5x38.5cm 13x15in) Boston MA 2001

POPE Alexander 1763-1835 **[6]**
✎ **$1 540** - €1 949 - **£969** - FF9 800
    Lady Francis Ducie, fille de Henry Herbert, Lord of Carnavon Aquarelle, gouache (36x27cm 14x10in) Neuilly-sur-Seine 1999

POPE Gustav ?-c.1895/1910 **[13]**
☞ **$5 974** - €5 162 - **£3 600** - FF33 861
    Classical Maiden Holding a Dove Oil/canvas (62.5x52cm 24x20in) Billingshurst, West-Sussex 1999

POPE Henry Martin 1843-1908 **[19]**
✎ **$305** - €252 - **£180** - FF1 652
    Harvesting Watercolour/paper (20x30cm 7x11in) Newbury, Berkshire 1999

POPHAM W. J. XX **[17]**
☞ **$617** - €596 - **£390** - FF3 909
    Ship in Full Sail off Dover Oil/canvas (43x53cm 17x21in) Carlisle, Cumbria 1999

POPINEAU François Émile 1887-? **[1]**
⚒ **$10 000** - €11 087 - **£6 944** - FF72 723
    Nude female Bronze (H79.5cm H31in) New-York 2001

POPOV Pavel XX **[4]**
☞ **$581** - €544 - **£360** - FF3 567
    Taking a Rest Oil/canvas (27x35cm 10x13in) Fernhurst, Haslemere, Surrey 1999

POPOVA Liubov Sergeevna 1889-1929 **[29]**
✎ **$26 000** - €23 121 - **£15 901** - FF151 665
    Architectonic Composition Pencil (27.5x20.5cm 10x8in) New-York 1999

POPPE Fedor 1850-? **[10]**
☞ **$1 334** - €1 534 - **£942** - FF10 061
    Patriarch mit Gefolge auf der Piazetta in Venedig Öl/Leinwand (85x62.5cm 33x24in) Bremen 2001
☞ **$2 250** - €2 363 - **£1 486** - FF15 502
    Scene of 18th Century Gentry at Summer Play Oil/wood (30x45cm 12x18in) Portland OR 2000

POPPEL van Peter 1945 **[9]**
☞ **$1 618** - €1 815 - **£1 121** - FF11 906
    Portret van Ferdinand Erfmann Oil/board (18x15cm 7x5in) Amsterdam 2000

PORAY Stanislaus Pociecha 1888-1948 **[14]**
☞ **$4 200** - €4 609 - **£2 704** - FF30 235
    Farmer's Mail Oil/canvas (58.5x71cm 23x27in) Beverly-Hills CA 2000

PORBUCHRAI Yehuda 1949 **[3]**
☞ **$14 000** - €15 804 - **£9 751** - FF103 670
    Angel Oil/canvas (170x142cm 66x55in) Tel Aviv 2001

PORCAR RIPOLLÉS Juan Bautista 1888-1974 **[30]**
☞ **$6 670** - €6 907 - **£4 140** - FF45 310
    Nubes y velas Oleo/lienzo (50x65cm 19x25in) Barcelona 2000
☞ **$2 501** - €2 463 - **£1 599** - FF16 154
    Niña con cesta de frutas Carboncillo (48x59cm 18x23in) Madrid 1999

PORCELLIS Jan c.1584-1632 **[15]**
☞ **$13 200** - €17 105 - **£9 900** - FF112 200
    Marina con velieri Olio/tela (84x120cm 33x47in) Roma 2000

PORCELLIS Julius c.1609-1645 **[14]**
☞ **$27 898** - €25 391 - **£17 124** - FF166 551
    Segelschiffe vor der Küste auf bewegter See Huile/panneau (39x56cm 15x22in) Zürich 1999

POREAU Oswald 1877-1955 **[139]**
☞ **$590** - €694 - **£425** - FF4 552
    Brise-lames à Breskens Huile/toile (48.5x65cm 19x25in) Bruxelles 2001
☞ **$344** - €322 - **£208** - FF2 113
    Vue des étangs de Tervueren Huile/panneau (25.5x32.5cm 10x12in) Liège 1999

PORET de Xavier 1894-1975 **[84]**
☞ **$3 701** - €3 430 - **£2 301** - FF22 500
    Études du chien Mirabeau Fusain/papier (56x76cm 22x29in) Paris 1999
▥ **$461** - €442 - **£284** - FF2 900
    Nature morte au brocard Lithographie couleurs (64x45cm 25x17in) Senlis 1999

PORGES Clara 1879-1963 **[64]**
☞ **$4 141** - €4 504 - **£2 729** - FF29 543
    Soglio in der Morgensonne Öl/Leinwand (102x83.5cm 40x32in) Bern 2000
✎ **$913** - €1 043 - **£644** - FF6 841
    Engadiner Seelandschaft im Abenrot Watercolour (48x55cm 18x21in) Bern 2001

PORION Charles L.E. 1814-c.1870 **[6]**
☞ **$16 500** - €16 518 - **£10 175** - FF108 350
    Baile español Oleo/lienzo (163x131cm 64x51in) Madrid 2000

PORPORA Paolo 1617-1673 **[7]**
☞ **$95 000** - €105 209 - **£64 429** - FF690 127
    Forest Floor Still Life with Porcupine, Rabbit, Ducks, Tortoise, Snail Oil/canvas (94x131.5cm 37x51in) New-York 2000

P

PORQUIER Édouard 1848-? **[42]**

✏ $622 - €732 - £431 - FF4 800
Bateau dans la tempête Aquarelle/papier (32x43cm 12x16in) Nantes 2000

PORSET Emilio XIX-XX **[3]**

🖘 $2 894 - €3 125 - £2 000 - FF20 500
La halte des cavaliers Huile/toile (30x45cm 11x17in) Lyon 2001

PORSON Josep Serra 1824-1910 **[3]**

🖘 $3 355 - €3 304 - £2 090 - FF21 670
El estudio del artista Oleo/tabla (34x26cm 13x10in) Madrid 1999

PORTA IL SALVIATI Giuseppe 1520-1580 **[4]**

🖘 $20 983 - €20 963 - £13 120 - FF137 509
Christus und die Ehebrecherin Oil/panel (118x168cm 46x66in) Köln 1999

✏ $4 600 - €4 920 - £3 136 - FF32 276
The Fall of the Children of Niobe Ink (27x19cm 10x7in) New-York 2001

PORTA Tommaso 1689-1768 **[5]**

🖘 $10 635 - €9 187 - £5 317 - FF60 266
Paesaggio fluviale con figure Olio/tela (85x115cm 33x45in) Roma 1999

PORTAELS Jean-François 1818-1895 **[83]**

🖘 $55 366 - €47 259 - £33 108 - FF310 000
Souvenir du Caire Huile/toile (131x95cm 51x37in) Paris 1998

🖘 $7 293 - €8 180 - £5 115 - FF53 658
Portrait Huile/toile (80x70cm 31x27in) Maisieres-Mons 1999

🖘 $1 682 - €1 437 - £1 003 - FF9 425
Deux anges portant un enfant au ciel Huile/panneau (42.5x29cm 16x11in) Bruxelles 1998

🖘 $1 596 - €1 735 - £1 050 - FF11 382
La veillée de Marie-Madeleine Black chalk/paper (23x48.5cm 9x19in) Lokeren 2000

PORTAIL Jacques-André 1691-1759 **[12]**

✏ $32 500 - €34 814 - £22 194 - FF228 364
Two Women Reading a Letter Chalks (34x26cm 13x10in) New-York 2001

PORTELA Severo, Jr. 1898-1985 **[2]**

🖘 $2 924 - €3 390 - £2 040 - FF22 236
Naturaleza morta com faianças e cebolas Oleo/lienzo (27x35cm 10x13in) Lisboa 2001

PORTELLI Carlo ?-1574 **[4]**

🖘 $141 958 - €152 381 - £95 000 - FF999 552
The Holy Family with the Infant Saint-John the Baptist Oil/panel (132x104cm 51x40in) London 2000

🖘 $90 000 - €91 047 - £54 954 - FF597 231
A Sybil Oil/panel (60.5x46.5cm 23x18in) New-York 2000

PORTENART Jeanne 1911-1992 **[51]**

🖘 $438 - €421 - £273 - FF2 764
Jeunes femmes dans une perspective Huile/panneau (78x98cm 30x38in) Bruxelles 1999

PORTER Allan XX **[16]**

📷 $465 - €460 - £290 - FF3 018
Carola I/Carola II Photograph (25.2x20.2cm 9x7in) München 1999

PORTER Bonnie 1959 **[3]**

📷 $1 600 - €1 556 - £976 - FF10 205
Depth Cibachrome print (203x60cm 79x23in) Tel Aviv 2000

PORTER Charles Ethan 1847-1923 **[16]**

🖘 $11 000 - €12 362 - £7 722 - FF81 092
Still Life with Vase of Mountain Laurel Blossoms Oil/canvas (50x45cm 20x18in) Windsor CT 2001

🖘 $5 000 - €5 619 - £3 510 - FF36 860
Still life Apples & Grapes Oil/canvas (30x40cm 12x16in) Windsor CT 2001

PORTER Eliot 1901-1990 **[83]**

📷 $2 200 - €1 839 - £1 302 - FF12 061
Foxtail Grass, Colorado Photograph (93x75cm 37x29in) New-York 1998

PORTER Fairfield 1907-1975 **[79]**

🖘 $200 000 - €237 851 - £142 540 - FF1 560 200
Dog at the Door Oil/canvas (166.5x137.5cm 65x54in) New-York 2000

🖘 $30 000 - €35 678 - £21 381 - FF234 030
The Parking Lot Oil/canvas (37.5x52.5cm 14x20in) New-York 2000

🖘 $18 000 - €17 485 - £11 251 - FF114 694
Johnson House - Morning Oil/masonite (28x36cm 11x14in) New-York 1998

✏ $4 000 - €3 426 - £2 361 - FF22 472
North Meadow Watercolour/paper (35x36cm 13x14in) New-York 1998

▥ $260 - €266 - £163 - FF1 743
Apple Blossoms III Color lithograph (51x64cm 20x25in) Cleveland OH 2000

PORTER Marjorie I. XX **[3]**

🖘 $1 800 - €1 960 - £1 239 - FF12 859
After the Party Pastel/paper (30.5x45.5cm 12x17in) New-York 2000

PORTER Robert Ker 1777-1842 **[6]**

🖘 $1 427 - €1 499 - £900 - FF9 832
Study of a seated Soldier wearing a Helmet and Breastplate Oil/panel (33.5x23.5cm 13x9in) London 2000

✏ $2 726 - €2 620 - £1 700 - FF17 189
Cavalry Officer Watercolour/paper (35.5x26.5cm 13x10in) Billingshurst, West-Sussex 1999

PORTIELJE Edward Antoon 1861-1949 **[158]**

🖘 $14 493 - €13 613 - £8 736 - FF89 298
Beautiful Morning Oil/canvas (83x72cm 32x28in) Amsterdam 1999

🖘 $3 082 - €2 851 - £1 920 - FF18 699
Vissersboten op het strand Oil/panel (11.5x20cm 4x7in) Lokeren 1999

PORTIELJE Gerard 1856-1929 **[100]**

🖘 $41 760 - €44 619 - £28 440 - FF292 680
Le dégustateur, cave Huile/panneau (38x46cm 14x18in) Lokeren 2001

🖘 $12 870 - €11 148 - £7 830 - FF73 125
Chez le cordonnier Huile/panneau (30x40cm 11x15in) Antwerpen 1998

▥ $3 200 - €2 730 - £1 930 - FF17 907
«Antwerpen, Semaine d'Aviation» Poster (122.5x86.5cm 48x34in) New-York 1998

PORTIELJE Jan Frederik Pieter 1829-1908 **[56]**

🖘 $6 644 - €5 686 - £4 000 - FF37 300
An Oriental Beauty Oil/panel (59x48cm 23x18in) London 1998

🖘 $2 517 - €2 355 - £1 558 - FF15 447
Spaanse schone Huile/panneau (15x10.8cm 5x4in) Lokeren 1999

PORTINARI Cándido 1903-1962 **[48]**

🖘 $55 000 - €47 958 - £33 253 - FF314 583
Retrato de Mulher Oil/canvas (46.5x38cm 18x14in) New-York 1998

🖋 $5 500 - €4 796 - **£3 325** - FF31 458
Sem Título Graphite (20.5x21cm 8x8in) New-York
1998

PORTMAN M.S.C. XIX [5]
🖋 $674 - €629 - **£420** - FF4 124
**A Sailing Boat on a Loch in a Highland
Landscape** Watercolour (37.5x54.5cm 14x21in)
London 1999

PORTO Silva 1850-1893 [6]
🗨 $36 900 - €40 878 - **£23 780** - FF268 140
Lavadeiras na margem do rio Huile/bois
(31.5x54.5cm 12x21in) Lisboa 2000
🗨 $24 750 - €27 418 - **£15 950** - FF179 850
Rua no interior de uma vila Oleo/lienzo
(35.5x25.5cm 13x10in) Lisboa 2000

PORTOCARRERO René 1912-1986 [250]
🗨 $8 500 - €9 124 - **£5 688** - FF59 848
Sin título Oil/paper (72.5x38.5cm 28x15in) New-York
2000
🗨 $8 640 - €8 049 - **£5 280** - FF52 800
Sin título Huile/bois (48x28.5cm 18x11in) Caracas
1998
🖋 $8 000 - €6 976 - **£4 836** - FF45 757
Florero Pastel/canvas (35x24cm 13x9in) New-York
1998

PORTTMANN Wilhelm 1819-1893 [6]
🗨 $1 100 - €1 278 - **£773** - FF8 384
Romantischer Gebirgssee Öl/Leinwand (85x130cm
33x51in) Rudolstadt-Thüringen 2001

PORTWAY Douglas 1922-1993 [63]
🗨 $962 - €970 - **£600** - FF6 362
The Bridge Oil/canvas (91.5x72cm 36x28in) London
2000

POSADA José Guadalupe 1852-1913 [33]
🎞 $95 - €89 - **£59** - FF587
Machaquito Grabado (17x12.5cm 6x4in) México 1999

POSCHINGER von Richard 1839-1915 [19]
🗨 $2 773 - €2 556 - **£1 661** - FF16 767
Bauer mit zwei Kühen auf dem Weg ins Dorf
Öl/Karton (36x50.5cm 14x19in) Dresden 1998

POSE Eduard Wilhelm 1812-1878 [11]
🗨 $3 244 - €3 323 - **£2 002** - FF21 800
Schloss in Tirol Öl/Leinwand (47.5x61.5cm 18x24in)
Düsseldorf 2000

POSENAER Joseph 1876-1935 [51]
🗨 $579 - €694 - **£397** - FF4 552
Wandeling in het park (promenade au parc)
Huile/toile (38x43cm 14x16in) Antwerpen 2000

POSI Paolo 1708-1776 [3]
🖋 $13 000 - €13 883 - **£8 858** - FF91 068
**Design for an Apparatus Possibly for the Festa
della Chinea of 1766** Black chalk (44.5x60.5cm
17x23in) New-York 2001

POSSART Felix 1837-1928 [50]
🖋 $933 - €1 036 - **£624** - FF6 797
**Galeria del Alberca, Alhambra, kvinna på ter-
rass** Oil/canvas (50x35cm 19x13in) Stockholm 2000
🗨 $1 333 - €1 431 - **£892** - FF9 390
Partie in Cordoba Öl/Leinwand (34x26cm 13x10in)
Köln 2000

POSSENTI Antonio 1933 [267]
🗨 $2 500 - €2 592 - **£1 500** - FF17 000
Sulla spiaggia Olio/cartone/tela (40x49.5cm 15x19in)
Prato 2000
🗨 $880 - €1 140 - **£660** - FF7 480
In giardino Olio/tavola (30x20cm 11x7in) Roma 2000

🖋 $450 - €389 - **£225** - FF2 550
Figura e conchiglie Tecnica mista, disegno (33x24cm
12x9in) Prato 1999
🎞 $300 - €259 - **£150** - FF1 700
Senza titolo Litografia a colori (35x25cm 13x9in)
Prato 1999

POSSENTI Giovanni Pietro 1618-1659 [3]
🎞 $815 - €895 - **£554** - FF5 869
Die Schmiede des Vulkan Radierung (39.6x28.9cm
15x11in) Berlin 2000

POSSIN Rudolf 1861-1922 [23]
🗨 $757 - €869 - **£518** - FF5 701
Strickendes Mädchen/Lesende Holländerin
Oil/panel (35x27cm 13x10in) Berlin 2000

POSSOZ Mily 1888-1967 [28]
🗨 $6 300 - €6 979 - **£4 060** - FF45 780
**Paisagem de Sintra com o Palácio da Vila a
Várzea e o Mar no horizonte** Oleo/lienzo
(36.5x47cm 14x18in) Lisboa 2000
🗨 $1 672 - €1 894 - **£1 178** - FF12 426
Carro de bois Acuarela/papel (39.5x49.5cm 15x19in)
Lisboa 2001
🎞 $200 - €230 - **£137** - FF1 509
Les tulipes Drypoint (47x33cm 18x13in) Cleveland
OH 2000

POST Eduard 1827-1882 [11]
🗨 $4 862 - €4 857 - **£3 040** - FF31 862
Im Atelier des Malerfürsten Öl/Leinwand (98x83cm
38x32in) Köln 1999

POST Frans Jansz. 1612-1680 [14]
🗨 $2 600 000 - €2 630 255 - **£1 587 560** -
FF17 253 340
**A Brazilian Landscape with Natives on a Road
approaching a Village** Oil/panel (25.5x40.5cm
10x15in) New-York 2000

POST George 1906 [14]
🖋 $800 - €736 - **£480** - FF4 829
San Francisco Waterfront Watercolour/paper
(43x58cm 17x23in) Pasadena CA 1999

POST William Merritt 1856-1935 [61]
🗨 $3 000 - €2 832 - **£1 865** - FF18 579
October Tints Oil/canvas (55x71cm 22x28in) Milford
CT 1999
🗨 $2 000 - €2 194 - **£1 290** - FF14 391
Fall Landscape with stream and trees Oil/canvas
(38x30cm 15x12in) Wallkill NY 2000
🖋 $500 - €427 - **£293** - FF2 802
Landscape in Autumn Watercolour/paper (30x40cm
12x16in) Portsmouth NH 1998

POSTEL Jules 1867-1955 [74]
🗨 $1 255 - €1 239 - **£765** - FF8 130
L'automne Huile/toile (59x74cm 23x29in) Bruxelles
2000

POSTIGLIONE Luca 1876-1936 [57]
🗨 $4 750 - €4 924 - **£2 850** - FF32 300
La diva ripassa la parte Olio/cartone (55x43.5cm
21x17in) Napoli 2000
🗨 $1 200 - €1 555 - **£900** - FF10 200
Le due sorelle Olio/tela (38x26cm 14x10in) Roma
2001

POSTIGLIONE Salvatore 1861-1906 [31]
🗨 $2 640 - €2 281 - **£1 760** - FF14 960
Signora con cappello Olio/tela (79x64cm 31x25in)
Napoli 1998
🗨 $1 011 - €1 049 - **£606** - FF6 878
Paesaggio Irpino Olio/tela (22x34cm 8x13in) Milano
1999

P

POSTMA Cornelius, Kor 1903-1977 **[21]**
- $919 - €908 - £559 - FF5 953
  Le canard bleu Oil/cardboard (22x33.5cm 8x13in) Amsterdam 2000

POSTMA Gerriet 1932 **[31]**
- $371 - €431 - £256 - FF2 827
  In het atelier Gouache (54x61cm 21x24in) Groningen 2000

POSTMA Gerrit 1819-1894 **[5]**
- $17 578 - €19 966 - £12 333 - FF130 970
  Before the Bull Fight, Sevilla Oil/canvas (80x170cm 31x66in) Amsterdam 2001
- $8 000 - €7 613 - £5 004 - FF49 939
  The Prize Winner Oil/canvas (73.5x101.5cm 28x39in) New-York 1999

POSTUPA Ladislav XX **[6]**
- $2 000 - €2 200 - £1 387 - FF14 428
  Untitled Silver print (39x27cm 15x11in) New-York 2001

POT Hendrick Gerritsz c.1585-1657 **[11]**
- $5 044 - €6 098 - £3 524 - FF40 000
  Portrait d'une jeune fille tenant une corbeille Huile/panneau (33x26.5cm 12x10in) Paris 2000

POTEMONT Adolphe Théodore J. 1828-1883 **[18]**
- $3 781 - €4 421 - £2 699 - FF29 000
  La promenade dans les blés Huile/panneau (24x32cm 9x12in) Paris 2001
- $1 990 - €1 906 - £1 252 - FF12 500
  La petite bourse Encre (25.7x25cm 10x9in) Paris 1999

POTHAST Bernard 1882-1966 **[121]**
- $21 739 - €20 420 - £13 104 - FF133 947
  Morining Sunshine Oil/canvas (51x61.5cm 20x24in) Amsterdam 1999
- $9 754 - €11 385 - £6 885 - FF74 679
  «Morning Sunshine» Oil/canvas (33.5x41cm 13x16in) Toronto 2000

POTHAST Wilhelm Frederik A. 1877-1917 **[1]**
- $4 277 - €4 311 - £2 666 - FF28 277
  Hendrickje Uylenburgh (1600-c.1682), wearing a gold black Dress Oil/panel (70.5x53.5cm 27x21in) Amsterdam 2000

POTHOVEN Hendrik 1726-1807 **[4]**
- $8 625 - €8 168 - £5 243 - FF53 578
  A Family Portrait: a Gentleman an his Wife seated small full Lengths Oil/canvas/panel (87.5x77.5cm 34x30in) Amsterdam 1999
- $1 651 - €1 588 - £1 017 - FF10 418
  Portrait of Sir Anthony van Dyck Black chalk (23x19cm 9x7in) Amsterdam 1999

POTIER Antoine Julien 1796-1865 **[2]**
- $2 364 - €2 134 - £1 457 - FF14 000
  Oreste et Pylate investis par les bergers Huile/toile (20.5x26cm 8x10in) Paris 1999

POTIN Jacques 1920 **[11]**
- $998 - €838 - £586 - FF5 500
  La Maison Blanche Tapisserie (297x551cm 117x217in) Paris 1998

POTRELLE Jean-Louis 1788-1824 **[1]**
- $748 - €732 - £474 - FF4 800
  Le Départ/L'Attaque Eau-forte couleurs (18x19cm 7x7in) Paris 1999

POTRITONOW XIX-XX **[2]**
- $10 240 - €9 915 - £6 440 - FF65 040
  Paysage estival au berger/Paysage estival animé de deux paysannes Huile/panneau (18x27cm 7x10in) Antwerpen 1999

POTRONAT Lucien 1889-? **[1]**
- $886 - €881 - £550 - FF5 781
  L'Esterel Oil/canvas (44x54cm 17x21in) Manchester 1999

POTRZEBOWSKI Jerzy 1921-1974 **[22]**
- $363 - €409 - £255 - FF2 686
  Moisson Aquarelle/papier (27x41cm 10x16in) Warszawa 2001

PÖTSCH Igo 1884-1943 **[29]**
- $981 - €1 090 - £657 - FF7 150
  Herbststilleben Oil/panel (75.2x49cm 29x19in) Wien 2000
- $2 943 - €2 543 - £1 774 - FF16 684
  Weingärten im Vorfrühling Gouache (68x73cm 26x28in) Wien 1999

POTT Laslett John 1837-1898 **[34]**
- $4 964 - €4 959 - £3 104 - FF32 532
  Der junge Napoleon Öl/Leinwand (61.5x51cm 24x20in) Köln 1999

POTTEAU Philippe Jacques 1807-1876 **[11]**
- $1 004 - €870 - £600 - FF5 705
  Der Gorilla des Kaisers Photograph (26.4x14.8cm 10x5in) München 1998

POTTER Beatrix H. 1866-1943 **[37]**
- $2 083 - €2 431 - £1 450 - FF15 944
  Still Life Study of a Wooden Tub, Birdcage, Sieve, Brace-and-Bit Pencil/paper (18x25.5cm 7x10in) Swindon, Wiltshire 2000

POTTER Charles ?-c.1902 **[12]**
- $292 - €269 - £180 - FF1 764
  «Pass to Llanberris» Watercolour/paper (57x88cm 22x34in) Billinghurst, West-Sussex 1999

POTTER George W. XIX-XX **[1]**
- $7 500 - €8 639 - £5 174 - FF56 670
  Calamity Jane (1852-1903) General Crook's Scout Posed in her Buckskins Photograph (13x9cm 5x3in) New-York 1999

POTTER Louis McLellan 1873-1912 **[12]**
- $4 000 - €4 542 - £2 737 - FF29 793
  Monks Reading Bronze (H24.5cm H9in) New-York 2000

POTTER Mary 1900-1981 **[92]**
- $7 748 - €8 500 - £5 000 - FF55 757
  Beachwood Oil/canvas (81x125.5cm 31x49in) London 2000
- $2 801 - €3 274 - £2 000 - FF21 477
  Abstract Composition Oil/canvas (30.5x45.5cm 12x17in) London 2001
- $811 - €782 - £500 - FF5 128
  Sun in the Water Watercolour/paper (10x10cm 3x3in) London 1999

POTTER Paulus 1625-1654 **[48]**
- $14 965 - €16 886 - £10 527 - FF110 767
  Die Offiziersstube Oil/panel (36x47.5cm 14x18in) Bern 2001
- $130 000 - €138 834 - £88 582 - FF910 089
  Cows and Sheep in a Meadow, a Farmstead beyond Oil/panel (28.5x38cm 11x14in) New-York 2001
- $2 000 - €2 139 - £1 363 - FF14 033
  Sheep Ink (14.5x22.5cm 5x8in) New-York 2001

▥ **$421** - €409 - **£262** - FF2 683
Het Boellenboekje Radierung (10.1x14cm 3x5in)
Berlin 1999

POTTER Pieter Symonsz 1597-1652 **[15]**
☞ **$6 648** - €7 714 - **£4 590** - FF50 602
Potiphar's Wife Denouncing Joseph Oil/panel
(37.5x45cm 14x17in) Amsterdam 2000

POTTHAST Edward Henry 1857-1927 **[119]**
☞ **$42 500** - €36 311 - **£25 512** - FF238 187
Souvenir of Canada Oil/canvas (61x91.5cm
24x36in) New-York 1998
☞ **$20 000** - €20 731 - **£12 682** - FF135 988
Lake Louise Oil/canvas (30.5x40.5cm 12x15in) New-
York 2000
✐ **$8 500** - €7 926 - **£5 272** - FF51 990
Moonlit Night Watercolour/board (42x52cm 16x20in)
New-York 1999

POTTHOF Hans 1911 **[71]**
☞ **$4 811** - €5 582 - **£3 321** - FF36 616
Bretagne, Pointe de Raz Oil/panel (36x53.5cm
14x21in) Zürich 2000
☞ **$4 354** - €4 952 - **£3 019** - FF32 486
Holzfuhrwerk Öl/Papier (31x26cm 12x10in) Zofingen
2000
▥ **$291** - €248 - **£174** - FF1 629
Am Ufer Farblithographie (56.5x76.5cm 22x30in)
Zürich 1998

POTTIER Gaston XIX-XX **[30]**
☞ **$641** - €762 - **£457** - FF5 000
Le port de Douarnenez Huile/toile (60x92cm
23x36in) Brest 2000

POTTIN Louis Joseph XIX-XX **[2]**
☞ **$4 140** - €3 811 - **£2 485** - FF25 000
Autoportrait de l'Artiste dans son atelier
Huile/toile (98x78cm 38x30in) Saint-Germain-en-Laye
1999

POTTNER Emil 1872-1942 **[72]**
☞ **$4 312** - €4 346 - **£2 688** - FF28 508
Sonnenbeschienene Gartenlandschaft
Öl/Leinwand (71x84cm 27x33in) Düsseldorf 2000
▥ **$80** - €77 - **£50** - FF503
Enten im Teich Woodcut in colors (41x49.5cm
16x19in) Berlin 1999

POTUYL Hendrik 1630-1660 **[8]**
☞ **$3 332** - €3 869 - **£2 341** - FF25 382
Fest i holländsk by Oil/panel (53.5x80cm 21x31in)
Stockholm 2001

POTUZNIK Heribert 1910-1984 **[26]**
✐ **$1 084** - €1 163 - **£740** - FF7 627
Mädchen mit Kappe Watercolour, gouache
(55.5x42.5cm 21x16in) Wien 2001

POTWOROWSKI Piotr 1898-1962 **[9]**
☞ **$8 089** - €6 930 - **£4 863** - FF45 458
Ogród Oil/canvas (55.5x70cm 21x27in) Warszawa
1998

POUCETTE 1935 **[25]**
☞ **$121** - €145 - **£84** - FF950
Chevaux/Arlequin musicien Huile/papier (37x34cm
14x13in) Paris 2000

POUCHOL Paul 1904-1963 **[5]**
☞ **$2 546** - €2 897 - **£1 767** - FF19 000
Sirène et oiseau Céramique (H57cm H22in) Paris
2000

POUGHÉON Eugène Robert 1886-1955 **[26]**
☞ **$80 000** - €67 614 - **£47 880** - FF443 520
«Amazons» Oil/canvas (609x609cm 240x240in) New-
York 1998

POUGIN DE SAINT-AUBIN Claude ?-1783 **[2]**
☞ **$7 500** - €6 943 - **£4 527** - FF45 543
**Portrait of a Young Boy in Blue, Standing in a
Landscape** Oil/panel (112x82cm 44x32in) New-York
1999

POUGNY Jean, Yvan Puni, dit 1894-1956 **[224]**
☞ **$7 275** - €7 622 - **£4 830** - FF50 000
La fenêtre ouverte, Côte d'Azur Huile/toile
(100x65cm 39x25in) Paris 2000
☞ **$4 722** - €4 573 - **£2 970** - FF30 000
Personnages dans un jardin Huile/toile/carton
(14x22cm 5x8in) Paris 1999
✐ **$1 482** - €1 372 - **£918** - FF9 000
Aux courses Gouache/papier (18x25cm 7x9in) Paris
1999

POUILLY de XIX-XX **[3]**
🔨 **$3 475** - €3 811 - **£2 360** - FF25 000
Cheval sautant une barrière Bronze (33x34.5cm
12x13in) Pontoise 2000

POULAKIS Theodoro 1622-1692 **[2]**
☞ **$132 090** - €114 110 - **£66 045** - FF748 510
Il diluvio universale/Il Paesaggio del Mar Rosso
Tempera/tavola (62x78.5cm 24x30in) Venezia 1999

POULBOT Francisque 1879-1946 **[112]**
✐ **$233** - €229 - **£143** - FF1 500
Titis parisiens Fusain (32.5x24.5cm 12x9in) Toulon
1999
▥ **$233** - €229 - **£144** - FF1 500
«Exposition de l'Enfance» Affiche (120x80cm
47x31in) Paris 1999

POULET Jean 1926 **[40]**
☞ **$536** - €625 - **£371** - FF4 100
Vase de fleurs Huile/toile (41x33cm 16x12in) Le
Havre 2000

POULSEN Axel 1887-1972 **[3]**
🔨 **$651** - €737 - **£440** - FF4 835
Fader og søn Relief (96x91cm 37x35in) Købennavn
2000

POUM MALAKOUL M.L. 1910-1973 **[6]**
☞ **$7 140** - €7 679 - **£4 788** - FF50 372
Walk Way in Chiangmai Oil/canvas (48x48cm
18x18in) Bangkok 2000

POUMEYROL Jean-Marie 1945 **[29]**
☞ **$6 846** - €6 403 - **£4 195** - FF42 000
«Les nasses» Acrylique/panneau (73x100cm
28x39in) Paris 1998

POUNCY Benjamin Thomas ?-1799 **[7]**
✐ **$1 534** - €1 804 - **£1 100** - FF11 834
**The Twin Towers of St.Mary's Church, Reculver,
Kent** Watercolour/paper (20x30cm 7x11in) London
2001

POURBUS Frans 1545-1581 **[5]**
☞ **$35 240** - €29 063 - **£20 760** - FF190 640
Orpheus bezaubert Bäume und Tiere Oil/panel
(75x108cm 29x42in) Wien 1999

POURBUS Frans II 1569-1622 **[9]**
☞ **$7 203** - €7 013 - **£4 425** - FF46 000
**Portrait d'une jeune femme de la famille
Dointerp portant une fraise** Huile/panneau
(41x31cm 16x12in) Paris 1999

P

P

POURBUS Pieter 1524-1584 **[5]**
- 🔍 **$65 000** – €61 154 – **£40 560** – FF401 141
  Portrait of a Lady, wearing a striped bodice and black coat Oil/panel (48x38cm 18x14in) New-York 1999

POURCELLY Jean-Baptiste act.1791-1802 **[9]**
- 🔍 **$12 000** – €10 526 – **£7 286** – FF69 045
  Village Oil/panel (25.5x51cm 10x20in) New-York 1999
- ✏️ **$1 630** – €1 829 – **£1 141** – FF12 000
  Scènes galantes au bord d'une rivière Gouache/papier (15.5x22cm 6x8in) Paris 2001

POURTALES DE PURY Edouard 1802-1885 **[4]**
- 🔍 **$7 121** – €6 848 – **£4 394** – FF44 920
  Blick auf den Neuenburgersee Öl/Leinwand (87x97cm 34x38in) Bern 1999

POURTAU Léon 1868/72-1897 **[17]**
- 🔍 **$24 450** – €22 867 – **£14 985** – FF150 000
  «Vallée au printemps» Huile/toile (73x93cm 28x36in) Paris 1998
- 🔍 **$6 368** – €6 098 – **£4 008** – FF40 000
  Le lavoir Huile/papier (33x24cm 12x9in) Nice 1999
- ✏️ **$8 150** – €7 622 – **£4 495** – FF50 000
  «Autoportrait de l'artiste» Pastel/papier (31x22cm 12x8in) Paris 1998

POUSSETTE-DART Richard 1916-1992 **[44]**
- 🔍 **$120 000** – €131 694 – **£77 268** – FF863 856
  Birds beside a Waterfall Oil/canvas (150x150cm 59x59in) New-York 2000
- 🔍 **$16 000** – €14 942 – **£9 875** – FF98 016
  Untitled Gouache (51x40.5cm 20x15in) New-York 1999

POUSSIN Nicolas 1594-1665 **[15]**
- 🔍 **$6 100 000** – €5 350 683 – **£3 703 920** – FF35 098 180
  The Agony in the Garden Oil/copper (60x47cm 23x18in) New-York 1999
- 🔍 **$50 192** – €49 008 – **£32 000** – FF321 472
  Bacchus with nymphs and Putti Ink (11x25cm 4x9in) London 2001

POUSSOVSKI Vladimir 1951 **[137]**
- 🔍 **$160** – €137 – €97 – FF900
  Voiliers en mer Huile/toile (16x31cm 6x12in) Enghien 1998

POVORINA Alexandra 1885-1963 **[12]**
- 🔍 **$1 496** – €1 738 – **£1 051** – FF11 403
  Frau aus Bayern Öl/Leinwand (65.5x50.5cm 25x19in) Hamburg 2001

POWELL Alfred XIX-XX **[20]**
- ✏️ **$838** – €782 – **£520** – FF5 127
  Sheep and Drover on a Hillside Path Watercolour/paper (52.5x77cm 20x30in) Billingshurst, West-Sussex 1999

POWELL Charles Martin 1775-1824 **[57]**
- 🔍 **$8 165** – €7 517 – **£5 000** – FF49 309
  Dutch Shipping in a Stiff Breeze Oil/canvas (56.5x89.5cm 22x35in) London 1998
- 🔍 **$4 555** – €4 156 – **£2 800** – FF27 263
  Spritsail Dutch Barge Running Before the Squall Oil/panel (20x25.5cm 7x10in) London 1998

POWELL Francis 1833-1914 **[7]**
- ✏️ **$630** – €612 – **£400** – FF4 012
  Scottish River Watercolour/paper (63.5x96.5cm 25x37in) London 1999

POWELL John XVIII **[1]**
- 🔍 **$7 332** – €7 902 – **£5 000** – FF51 832
  Portrait of Sir Joshua Reynolds, small Half-length Oil/panel (21.5x18cm 8x7in) London 2001

POWELL Joseph 1780-1834 **[17]**
- ✏️ **$364** – €390 – **£240** – FF2 561
  Paisaje con río Acuarela (36x43cm 14x16in) Madrid 2000

POWELL Lucien Whiting 1846-1930 **[36]**
- 🔍 **$1 800** – €1 932 – **£1 204** – FF12 673
  Grand Canal, Venice Oil/canvas (61x91.5cm 24x36in) New-York 2000
- 🔍 **$1 200** – €1 145 – **£749** – FF7 513
  Italian Canal Scene, Venice Watercolour/paper (49x76cm 19x30in) Hatfield PA 1999

POWELL William E. 1878-c.1955 **[58]**
- ✏️ **$1 086** – €1 200 – **£750** – FF7 872
  «The Jackdam of Rheims» Watercolour/paper (27x37cm 10x14in) Hockley, Birmingham 2001

POWER Cyril Edward 1874-1951 **[76]**
- 🗔 **$4 762** – €4 400 – **£2 800** – FF26 241
  «The Sunshine Roof» Linocut in colors (25.5x33cm 10x12in) London 1998

POWER Harold Septimus 1878-1951 **[108]**
- 🔍 **$5 226** – €4 915 – **£3 236** – FF32 239
  Hauling Timber Oil/canvas (36.5x55cm 14x21in) Melbourne 1999
- 🔍 **$937** – €1 094 – **£652** – FF7 175
  Summer Palette Oil/canvas/board (33.5x43cm 13x16in) Melbourne 2000
- ✏️ **$1 150** – €1 106 – **£708** – FF7 257
  Harbour Scene Watercolour/paper (23.5x30cm 9x11in) Melbourne 1999

POWER James P. XX **[19]**
- 🔍 **$1 013** – €1 094 – **£700** – FF7 179
  The Way to the Water, Dittisham, Devon Oil/board (43x53.5cm 16x21in) London 2001

POWER John Wardell 1881-1943 **[5]**
- 🔍 **$17 532** – €19 271 – **£11 235** – FF126 408
  A Wreck on the Shore Oil/canvas (41x61cm 16x24in) Melbourne 2000

POWERS Ken 1972 **[6]**
- 🔍 **$375** – €423 – **£260** – FF2 775
  Winter Landscape with Man on Horseback Gouache/paper (38x53cm 15x21in) Hatfield PA 2000

POWERS Asahel Lynde 1813-1843 **[5]**
- 🔍 **$13 000** – €13 883 – **£8 858** – FF91 068
  Dark-Haired Young Man reading the Genessee Farmer Oil/canvas (76x62cm 29x24in) New-York 2001

POWERS Hiram 1805-1873 **[32]**
- 🗝 **$20 305** – €18 922 – **£12 261** – FF124 120
  Frauenbüste, den Kopf nach links gewandt Marble (H62cm H24in) Dresden 1998

POWERS Marion XX **[10]**
- 🔍 **$1 200** – €1 111 – **£734** – FF7 287
  Smiling woman with basket of produce, probably unpublished mag. cover Oil/board (53x36cm 21x14in) New-York 1999

POWERS Preston 1843-? **[1]**
- 🗝 **$4 000** – €3 815 – **£2 434** – FF25 023
  Figural Group with Native American Hunter and Buffalo Bronze (H45.5cm H17in) New-York 1999

POWOLNY Michael 1871-1954 **[185]**
🖎 **$1 637 - €1 817 - £1 140** - FF11 917
Aufsatz mit einem Putto Glazed ceramic
(21.5x22cm 8x8in) Salzburg 2001

POY DALMAU Emilio 1876-1933 **[61]**
☞ **$1 620 - €1 802 - £1 050** - FF11 820
Vacas pastando entre órreos Oleo/lienzo
(43.5x70cm 17x27in) Madrid 2000
☞ **$448 - €481 - £304** - FF3 152
«Un remanso en el Cinca, Aragón» Oleo/tabla
(23x34.5cm 9x13in) Madrid 2001

POYNTER Edward John, Bt. 1836-1919 **[133]**
☞ **$98 014 - €113 991 - £70 000** - FF747 733
On Guard in the Time of the Pharaohs Oil/canvas
(82.5x52cm 32x20in) London 2001
☞ **$4 109 - €3 751 - £2 500** - FF24 606
A marble Interior Oil/panel (35.5x25cm 13x9in)
London 1998
✐ **$2 689 - €2 887 - £1 800** - FF18 938
**Study for the South Kensington Science
Certificate of 1884** Black & white chalks/paper
(36x24cm 14x9in) London 2000

POZANSKI Helga XX **[4]**
✐ **$425 - €456 - £284** - FF2 991
Still Life with Iris Watercolour/paper (99x128cm
39x50in) Bolton MA 2000

POZIER Jacinthe 1844-1915 **[25]**
☞ **$8 954 - €8 690 - £5 574** - FF57 000
**Les vieilles meules aux environs de Méry-sur-
Oise** Huile/toile (124x200cm 48x78in) Amiens 1999
☞ **$3 559 - €3 735 - £2 359** - FF24 500
Lavandières en Bretagne Huile/toile (33x46cm
12x18in) Quimper 2000

POZZATI Concetto 1935 **[60]**
☞ **$1 200 - €1 244 - £720** - FF8 160
In un piatto, da e per Morandi Tecnica mista
(80x80cm 31x31in) Firenze 2001

POZZI Carlo 1618-1688 **[4]**
✐ **$606 - €574 - £378** - FF3 765
The Vision of St.Bernard Ink (28.1x22.8cm 11x8in)
Praha 2000

POZZI Pipo 1910-1999 **[9]**
☞ **$450 - €466 - £270** - FF3 060
Il sogno Olio/cartone (30x40cm 11x15in) Torino 2000

POZZI Pompeo 1817-? **[5]**
📷 **$1 634 - €1 829 - £1 137** - FF12 000
Hôpital de Milan Tirage albuminé (28x38cm 11x14in)
Paris 2001

POZZI Stefano c.1707-1768 **[15]**
☞ **$15 000 - €15 550 - £9 000** - FF102 000
**Il Beato Gregorio Barbarigo riceve da San Carlo
Borromeo gli strumenti** Olio/tela (123x68cm
48x26in) Roma 2001
✐ **$800 - €820 - £500** - FF5 381
The Coronation of the Virgin Pencil (29.5x17.5cm
11x6in) New-York 2000

POZZI Walter 1911-1989 **[29]**
☞ **$1 000 - €1 037 - £600** - FF6 800
Paesaggio Olio/cartone (45x59cm 17x23in) Vercelli
2001

POZZO Ugo 1900-1981 **[34]**
☞ **$8 700 - €7 516 - £4 350** - FF49 300
«Charlot» Olio/tela (76x84cm 29x33in) Milano 1999

PRAAG van Alexander Salomon 1812-1865 **[3]**
☞ **$3 014 - €2 949 - £1 932** - FF19 347
A Town along a River Oil/panel (18x23cm 7x9in)
Amsterdam 1999

PRABHA B. 1933 **[22]**
☞ **$3 956 - €4 372 - £2 743** - FF28 676
Lady with Pears Oil/canvas (101x116.5cm 39x45in)
Singapore 2001
✐ **$1 576 - €1 773 - £1 100** - FF11 628
Krishna and the Gopis Gouache (46.5x61.5cm
18x24in) London 2001

PRACHE Honoré XIX **[1]**
☞ **$14 765 - €13 568 - £9 069** - FF89 000
Le sacrifice d'Abraham Huile/toile (237x160cm
93x62in) Limoges 1999

PRACHENSKY Markus 1932 **[75]**
☞ **$10 748 - €10 226 - £6 678** - FF67 078
Komposition Acryl/Leinwand (120x150cm 47x59in)
Hamburg 1999
☞ **$5 260 - €6 135 - £3 693** - FF40 246
«Rot und Violett» Öl/Leinwand (60x58.5cm 23x23in)
Köln 2000
☞ **$3 633 - €3 488 - £2 280** - FF22 881
Ohne Titel Öl/Leinwand (30x26cm 11x10in) Wien
1999
✐ **$2 686 - €2 351 - £1 627** - FF15 424
Ohne Titel Indian ink (70.3x50.1cm 27x19in) Berlin
1998
🎨 **$172 - €164 - £106** - FF1 073
Komposition Farbserigraphie (70x50cm 27x19in)
Hamburg 1999

PRACHENSKY Wilhelm Nikolaus 1898-1956 **[50]**
☞ **$8 638 - €10 174 - £6 076** - FF66 738
Der Dogenpalast in Venedig Mixed media
(61.5x85cm 24x33in) Wien 2000
☞ **$15 460 - €14 534 - £9 360** - FF95 340
Löwenzahn Öl/Karton (38x36cm 14x14in) Wien 1999
✐ **$5 077 - €5 450 - £3 465** - FF35 752
Winterliche Dorfidylle Aquarell/Papier (48x68cm
18x26in) Wien 2001

PRADA Carlo 1884-1960 **[19]**
☞ **$2 150 - €2 229 - £1 290** - FF14 620
Cittadina sul mare Olio/tela (40x55cm 15x21in)
Trieste 2001

PRADA Carlos 1944 **[13]**
🖎 **$1 350 - €1 413 - £810** - FF9 270
Figura Bronze (H68cm H26in) Caracas 2000

PRADELLES Hippolyte 1824-1913 **[2]**
☞ **$7 242 - €7 775 - £4 845** - FF51 000
Scènes de marché à Constantinople Huile/toile
(58x41cm 22x16in) Le Puy 2000

PRADES de Alfred Frank c.1820-c.1890 **[43]**
☞ **$9 373 - €9 173 - £6 000** - FF60 712
**William James Fenn Williams with his Hounds
in a River Landscape** Oil/canvas (61x74cm 24x29in)
London 1999
☞ **$1 040 - €994 - £650** - FF6 517
**Officers and Men of the Rifle Brigate on
Manoeuvres** Oil/canvas (25.5x35.5cm 10x13in)
London 1999
✐ **$375 - €441 - £260** - FF2 891
Royal Horse Guards, Royal Review at Chobham
Watercolour/paper (23x37cm 9x14in) London 2000

PRADIER James 1790-1852 **[196]**
🖎 **$2 100 - €2 240 - £1 398** - FF14 692
Atlanta, Fastening Her Sandal Bronze (H22cm
H9in) Cleveland OH 2000

P

P

$483 - €534 - **£327** - FF3 500
Pradier sculptant le buste de son fils John Lavis
(10x7cm 3x2in) Paris 2000

PRADILLA GONZALEZ Miguel 1884-1965 **[17]**
$2 268 - €2 523 - **£1 512** - FF16 548
Horreo asturiano Oleo/lienzo (55x46cm 21x18in)
Madrid 2000
$1 282 - €1 351 - **£832** - FF8 865
Día de mercado en Noya Oleo/tabla (15x26cm
5x10in) Madrid 2000

PRADILLA Y ORTIZ Francisco 1848-1921 **[109]**
$12 880 - €13 815 - **£8 510** - FF90 620
Paisaje Oleo/lienzo (41x61cm 16x24in) Madrid 2000
$2 422 - €2 553 - **£1 572** - FF16 745
Atardeciendo en el río Oleo/cartón (16x26cm
6x10in) Madrid 2000
$1 372 - €1 351 - **£877** - FF8 865
Romeo y Julieta Gouache/papier (31x47cm 12x18in)
Madrid 1999

PRAEGER Sophia Rosamund 1867-1954 **[6]**
$565 - €632 - **£380** - FF4 143
The Three Bold Babes Watercolour (35.5x23.5cm
13x9in) London 2000

PRAETORIUS Charles act.1888-1914 **[1]**
$5 040 - €5 588 - **£3 500** - FF36 654
St Ives Harbour in twilight Oil/canvas (61x75cm
24x29in) Mere, Wiltshire 2001

PRAGER Heinz-Günter 1944 **[15]**
$3 288 - €3 835 - **£2 308** - FF25 154
Stück Iron (28.5x126cm 11x49in) Köln 2000

PRAIWAN DAKLIANG 1957 **[6]**
$2 937 - €2 728 - **£1 815** - FF17 897
The Past Acrylic/canvas (88.5x118cm 34x46in)
Bangkok 1999

PRAM-HENNINGSEN Christian 1846-1892 **[15]**
$1 454 - €1 608 - **£1 009** - FF10 546
**Sommereng med pige der har fanget en som-
merfugl** Black chalk/paper (82x58cm 32x22in) Vejle
2001

PRAMPOLINI Enrico 1894-1956 **[117]**
$28 000 - €36 283 - **£21 000** - FF238 000
Senza titolo Olio/tela (129.5x95cm 50x37in) Milano
2001
$20 400 - €17 623 - **£13 600** - FF115 600
Immagini radiofoniche Tecnica mista/cartone
(57x45cm 22x17in) Prato 1998
$3 795 - €3 278 - **£2 530** - FF21 505
La Ruota Tecnica mista/cartone (32x24cm 12x9in)
Milano 1998
$950 - €985 - **£570** - FF6 460
Nudo femminile disteso Matita/carta (18.5x24.5cm
7x9in) Milano 1999

PRANGENBERG Norbert 1949 **[27]**
$3 097 - €3 657 - **£2 200** - FF23 987
Makaber 1 Watercolour (170x250cm 66x98in) London
2001

PRANISHNIKOFF Ivan ?-c.1920 **[7]**
$800 - €924 - **£560** - FF6 062
In the Courtyard Watercolour/paper (21x25cm
8x10in) Delray-Beach FL 2001

PRANTL Karl 1923 **[11]**
$2 559 - €2 556 - **£1 600** - FF16 769
Zur Meditation Stone (16x16x10cm 6x6x3in)
Hamburg 1999

PRAPHAN SRISOUTA 1939 **[7]**
$1 014 - €942 - **£627** - FF6 182
Child at Play Woodcut (73x54cm 28x21in) Bangkok
1999

PRASAD Jaggu 1963 **[5]**
$1 656 - €1 817 - **£1 100** - FF11 920
Studies of Beetles and Insects Watercolour
(49.5x34.5cm 19x13in) London 2000

PRASCHL Stefan 1910-1994 **[25]**
$1 597 - €1 817 - **£1 122** - FF11 917
Winterlandschaft Mischtechnik/Papier (44.5x66cm
17x25in) Wien 2001
$94 - €87 - **£58** - FF572
**«Erste Freisichtanlage im Tiergarten
Schönbrunn»** Poster (22x30cm 8x11in) Wien 1999

PRASONG LUEMUANG 1962 **[3]**
$892 - €960 - **£598** - FF6 296
Thai Gable Chronicles Watercolour/paper (69x98cm
27x38in) Bangkok 2000

PRASSINOS Mario 1916-1985 **[189]**
$4 854 - €4 802 - **£3 027** - FF31 500
Paysage turc No 25, La Viorne Huile/toile
(114x146cm 44x57in) Paris 1999
$2 487 - €2 744 - **£1 684** - FF18 000
Arbres Acrylique/toile (75x105cm 29x41in) Paris 2000
$582 - €625 - **£389** - FF4 100
Portrait Aquarelle/papier (25x32cm 9x12in) Versailles
2000
$129 - €155 - **£92** - FF1 014
Composition jaune-noir Farbradierung (61x43.5cm
24x17in) Hamburg 2000

PRATELLA Ada XIX-XX **[3]**
$1 360 - €1 762 - **£1 020** - FF11 560
Pescatori in barca Olio/tela (24x13cm 9x5in) Napoli
2000

PRATELLA Attilio 1856-1949 **[277]**
$18 500 - €20 385 - **£12 304** - FF133 718
Pescadores en la Bahia de Napoles Oleo/lienzo
(40.5x53cm 15x20in) Buenos-Aires 2000
$5 400 - €6 997 - **£4 050** - FF45 900
Pescatori nel golfo di Napoli Olio/tavola (22x33cm
8x12in) Roma 2001
$650 - €751 - **£455** - FF4 925
Farm Scene Watercolour/paper (53x34.5cm 20x13in)
Bethesda MD 2001

PRATELLA Fausto 1888-1964 **[59]**
$4 250 - €4 406 - **£2 550** - FF28 900
Barche sulla spiaggia al tramonto Olio/tela
(66x126.5cm 25x49in) Milano 1999
$1 450 - €1 503 - **£870** - FF9 860
Attesa dei pescatori Olio/tavola (23x35cm 9x13in)
Prato 2000

PRATERE de Edmond 1826-1888 **[20]**
$3 450 - €3 811 - **£2 392** - FF25 000
Vaches à la mare Huile/toile (71x93cm 27x36in)
Lille 2001

PRATERE de Henri 1815-1890 **[7]**
$6 555 - €7 622 - **£4 600** - FF50 000
La halte des chasseurs Huile/toile (94x124cm
37x48in) Paris 2001

PRATI Eugenio 1842-1907 **[3]**
$1 785 - €1 850 - **£1 071** - FF12 138
Ragazza veneziana in giardino Acquarello/carta
(51x34cm 20x13in) Milano 1999

PRATT Bela Lyon 1867-1917 **[6]**
$11 000 - €10 155 - £6 765 - FF66 614
Fountain Bronze (H67cm H26in) New-York 1999

PRATT Christopher 1935 **[34]**
$1 092 - €1 057 - £673 - FF6 934
March Crossing Serigraph (49.5x77.5cm 19x30in)
Toronto 1999

PRATT Claude 1860-c.1935 **[14]**
$3 998 - €4 643 - £2 809 - FF30 458
Motiv från Alger Oil/canvas (87x69cm 34x27in)
Stockholm 2001
$1 956 - €1 670 - £1 150 - FF10 952
**«The Scholar», an Elderly Man Seated at a Table
Studying his Books** Watercolour/paper (45x60cm
17x23in) Solihull, West-Midlands 1998

PRATT Henry Cheever 1803-1880 **[2]**
$25 000 - €26 835 - £16 730 - FF176 025
California Redwoods Oil/canvas (73.5x91.5cm
28x36in) San-Francisco CA 2000

PRATT Hugo 1927-1995 **[25]**
$861 - €793 - £516 - FF5 200
Corto Maltese Gouache (35x49.5cm 13x19in) Paris
1999

PRATT Jonathan 1835-1911 **[17]**
$7 731 - €7 266 - £4 800 - FF47 659
Tying a Fly for Grandfather Oil/canvas (78x63.5cm
30x25in) London 1999
$3 419 - €3 975 - £2 400 - FF26 074
Shared Meal Oil/canvas (46x32cm 18x12in) London
2001

PRATT Joseph Bishop 1854-1910 **[15]**
$196 - €230 - £140 - FF1 509
Forrard On, after Thomas Blinks Engraving
(63x92cm 24x36in) London 2000

PRATT Mary Frances 1935 **[5]**
$9 924 - €10 652 - £6 741 - FF69 873
Plum Tomatoes Oil/board (14.5x20cm 5x7in)
Calgary, Alberta 2001
$793 - €852 - £539 - FF5 589
Tied boat Color lithograph (13.5x13.5cm 5x5in)
Calgary, Alberta 2001

PRATT Matthew 1734-1805 **[2]**
$6 500 - €5 608 - £3 935 - FF36 785
Bracelet Centering a Portrait of a Young Lady
Miniature (2x1cm 1x1in) New-York 1999

PRATT Pierre 1962 **[5]**
$529 - €534 - £330 - FF3 500
Friends Acrylique (19x25cm 7x9in) Paris 2000

PRATT William 1855-c.1936 **[44]**
$2 900 - €2 884 - £1 800 - FF18 920
Fare Thee Well Oil/canvas (52x76cm 20x29in)
London 1999
$1 435 - €1 614 - £1 000 - FF10 589
Fifeshire homesteads, near Crail Oil/canvas
(25x35cm 9x13in) Edinburgh 2001

PRATUANG EMJAOEN 1935 **[14]**
$12 750 - €13 713 - £8 550 - FF89 950
Quae Noi Oil/canvas (99x129cm 38x50in) Bangkok
2000
$4 272 - €3 969 - £2 640 - FF26 032
Natural Phenomenon Oil/canvas (58x70cm 22x27in)
Bangkok 1999
$4 806 - €4 465 - £2 970 - FF29 286
Hibiscus Oil/canvas (33x40cm 12x15in) Bangkok
1999

$1 869 - €1 736 - £1 155 - FF11 389
Grass Cluster Ink (28x36cm 11x14in) Bangkok 1999

PRAX-ZADKINE Valentine 1899-1981 **[254]**
$4 158 - €3 470 - £2 436 - FF22 764
La pêche Oil/canvas (61x81cm 24x31in) Lokeren
1998
$1 673 - €1 968 - £1 200 - FF12 910
Nature morte avec pipe, livre et bouteille Oil/can-
vas (33x41cm 12x16in) London 2001
$500 - €427 - £298 - FF2 798
Fishermen off the Coast Watercolour, gouache
(44.5x61cm 17x24in) New-York 1998

PRAYAT PONGDAM 1934 **[9]**
$2 002 - €1 860 - £1 237 - FF12 202
The Water Buffaloes Charcoal/paper (32x42.5cm
12x16in) Bangkok 1999
$816 - €877 - £547 - FF5 756
Mother and Child Woodcut (63x43cm 24x16in)
Bangkok 2000

PRAYURA ULUCHADHA 1928 **[1]**
$3 060 - €3 291 - £2 052 - FF21 588
Seascaoe, Ban Bang Khao, Cha-am
Watercolour/paper (39x57cm 15x22in) Bangkok 2000

PREATONI Luigi XIX-XX **[3]**
$688 - €694 - £428 - FF4 552
Élégante à l'éventail Bronze (H28.5cm H11in)
Bruxelles 2000

PRÉAULX Michel François XVIII-XIX **[13]**
$667 - €768 - £460 - FF5 038
**Two Turks in a Ruin/Vue des Iles Cyranées
d'Europe** Watercolour (19.5x38.5cm 7x15in)
Billingshurst, West-Sussex 2000
$1 443 - €1 677 - £1 028 - FF11 000
Le Parthénon/Le temple de Thésée Lithographie
(46x64cm 18x25in) Paris 2001

PRÉAUX L'AGENT Raymond 1916 **[110]**
$232 - €198 - £140 - FF1 300
Fleurs dans un broc Huile/panneau (27x22cm
10x8in) Grenoble 1998

PRECHTL Michael Mathias 1926 **[25]**
$202 - €174 - £122 - FF1 140
«Goya»/«Bosch»/«Gruegel» Farblithographie
(15.6x14.3cm 6x5in) Berlin 1998

PRECIADO DE LA VEGA Francisco 1713-1789 **[2]**
$25 200 - €24 026 - £16 000 - FF157 600
Inmaculada Oleo/lienzo (98x73.5cm 38x28in) Madrid
1999

PREDA Ambrogio 1839-1906 **[15]**
$10 057 - €10 938 - £6 628 - FF71 748
Ansicht von Lugano Öl/Leinwand (40x70cm
15x27in) Bern 2000

PREDA Carlo c.1645-1729 **[2]**
$8 600 - €11 144 - £6 450 - FF73 100
Madonna col Bambino Olio/tela (102.5x88.5cm
40x34in) Milano 2000

PREECHA THAOTHONG 1948 **[4]**
$2 040 - €2 194 - £1 368 - FF14 392
St.Peter's Rome Watercolour/paper (38x50cm
14x19in) Bangkok 2000

PREEN von Hugo 1854-1941 **[41]**
$213 - €254 - £152 - FF1 668
Schärding Pencil/paper (20.5x15cm 8x5in) Linz 2000

P

PREETORIUS Emil 1883-1973 **[10]**
📖 $858 - €736 - £518 - FF4 828
«Preetorius Ausstellung» Poster (90x55cm
35x21in) München 1998

PREGARTBAUER Lois 1899-1971 **[52]**
$3 597 - €3 991 - £2 409 - FF26 218
Winterhafen Öl/Karton (30.4x37.4cm 11x14in) Wien
2000
$768 - €872 - £538 - FF5 720
Landschaft Oil chalks/paper (41x57cm 16x22in) Wien
2001

PREGNO Enzo 1898-1972 **[75]**
$750 - €777 - £450 - FF5 100
Porta romana Olio/tela (50x70cm 19x27in) Firenze
2001
$400 - €415 - £240 - FF2 720
Vaso di fiori Olio/tela (40x30cm 15x11in) Firenze
2000

PREGO DE OLIVER Manuel 1915-1986 **[10]**
$1 755 - €1 952 - £1 202 - FF12 805
Mendigo Técnica mixta (62x48cm 24x18in) Madrid
2001
$1 170 - €1 351 - £810 - FF8 865
Retrato de mujer Carboncillo (48x37cm 18x14in)
Madrid 2000

PREHN A. XIX-XX **[3]**
$2 400 - €2 822 - £1 726 - FF18 514
Barnyard scene with chickens Oil/canvas
(68x55cm 27x22in) Hatfield PA 2001

PREISLER Jan 1872-1918 **[20]**
$1 416 - €1 339 - £882 - FF8 785
Blue Cave in Capri Oil/canvas (24x36.5cm 9x14in)
Praha 2001
$505 - €478 - £315 - FF3 137
Study for the Painting Adam and Eve
Pencil/paper (61.3x35cm 24x13in) Praha 1999

PREISLER Johann Daniel 1666-1737 **[12]**
$579 - €658 - £400 - FF4 317
The Robbed Mother Ink (29x20cm 11x7in) London
2000

PREISS Fritz 1882-1943 **[331]**
$7 085 - €6 647 - £4 377 - FF43 600
Tennisspielerin Metal (H27.5cm H10in) Ahlden 1999

PREISSIG Vojtech Adalbert 1873-1944 **[47]**
$4 335 - €4 100 - £2 700 - FF26 895
Cavalier sur chameau Huile/toile (30x19cm 11x7in)
Praha 2000
$820 - €762 - £510 - FF4 996
Leda Watercolour/paper (31.8x23.5cm 12x9in) Praha
1999
$635 - €601 - £396 - FF3 944
Fille avec fleurs Eau-forte, aquatinte (26x20.5cm
10x8in) Praha 2000

PRÉJELAN René 1877-1968 **[12]**
$653 - €717 - £443 - FF4 700
«Ponctua, la meilleure montre de précision la
moins chère» Affiche couleur (158x118cm 62x46in)
Paris 2000

PRELL Hermann 1854-1922 **[8]**
$3 732 - €3 589 - £2 303 - FF23 541
Skyddsängeln på besök Oil/panel (39x60cm
15x23in) Malmö 1999

PRELLER Alexis 1911-1975 **[58]**
$6 540 - €6 302 - £4 040 - FF41 336
Image of the Sun Oil/canvas (101x96cm 39x37in)
Johannesburg 1999

$2 773 - €2 466 - £1 699 - FF16 173
Urn Head Oil/board (28.5x44cm 11x17in)
Johannesburg 1999

PRELLER Friedrich I 1804-1878 **[58]**
$4 814 - €5 368 - £3 237 - FF35 215
Wandernder Mönch im Gebirge Öl/Leinwand
(104.5x81cm 41x31in) Ahlden 2000
$1 053 - €1 022 - £656 - FF6 707
Doppelbildnis der Schwestern Anna und
Margarete Ludolff Pencil (25x32.5cm 9x12in) Berlin
1999
$114 - €123 - £76 - FF804
Eichengruppe am Ausgang des Webicht bei
Tiefurt Radierung (15.8x19.6cm 6x7in) Berlin 2000

PRELLER Friedrich II 1838-1901 **[21]**
$3 211 - €3 579 - £2 244 - FF23 477
Motiv aus der Gründungsgeschichte Roms
Öl/Leinwand (48.5x78cm 19x30in) München 2001

PREM Heimrad 1934-1978 **[136]**
$9 906 - €11 248 - £6 883 - FF73 785
Amazonen-Serie Öl/Leinwand (104.5x120cm
41x47in) München 2001
$6 360 - €5 377 - £3 804 - FF35 272
«Svarta Glog» Oil/canvas (60x80cm 23x31in)
Köbenhavn 1998
$1 030 - €1 154 - £716 - FF7 568
«Er + Sie» Gouache/paper (77x57cm 30x22in)
Stockholm 2001

PREMAZZI Luigi Ossipovitch 1814-1891 **[22]**
$20 500 - €21 251 - £12 300 - FF139 400
Duomo di Milano Olio/tela (62x76cm 24x29in)
Milano 2000
$2 320 - €3 006 - £1 740 - FF19 720
Paesaggio Olio/cartone (28x38cm 11x14in) Milano
2001
$813 - €945 - £561 - FF6 197
Motiv aus der Türkei Aquarell/Papier (16x11cm
6x4in) Wien 2000

PRENDERGAST Charles 1863-1948 **[7]**
$2 000 - €2 240 - £1 389 - FF14 694
Autumn Apple picking Mixed media (21x28cm
8x11in) St. Louis MO 2001

PRENDERGAST Maurice Brazil 1859-1924 **[108]**
$240 000 - €263 315 - £159 432 - FF1 727 232
Park, Naples Oil/canvas (49x61.5cm 19x24in) New-
York 2000
$50 000 - €59 463 - £35 635 - FF390 050
St.Malo Oil/panel (21.5x16cm 8x6in) New-York 2000
$95 000 - €112 979 - £67 706 - FF741 095
Summer Day, St.Cloud Watercolour (34.5x49.5cm
13x19in) New-York 2000
$80 000 - €89 549 - £55 792 - FF587 400
Recess Monotype (15x20cm 5x7in) New-York 2001

PRENDONI Attilio 1874-1942 **[5]**
$2 100 - €2 177 - £1 260 - FF14 280
Giovane donna seduta Marbre (H49cm H19in)
Milano 2000

PRENTICE Levi Wells 1851-1935 **[101]**
$45 000 - €40 907 - £27 103 - FF268 335
Autumn in the Adirondacks Oil/canvas (91x167cm
36x66in) Hayden ID 1998
$9 000 - €9 236 - £5 642 - FF60 585
Clearing off the Coast of Maine Oil/canvas
(38x66cm 15x26in) Downington PA 2000
$9 000 - €10 584 - £6 453 - FF69 425
Sunset Oil/canvas (30.5x22.5cm 12x8in) Philadelphia
PA 2001

PRENTICE Michael 1944 [2]
🔨 **$4 116** - €3 472 - **£2 450** - FF22 778
Foque Pierre (78x23x20cm 30x9x7in) Antwerpen 1998

PRENTZEL Hans 1880-1956 [34]
🖋 **$650** - €767 - **£457** - FF5 030
Junger Angler bei abziehendem Gewitter
Öl/Leinwand (33x61.5cm 12x24in) Frankfurt 2000
🖋 **$547** - €613 - **£371** - FF4 024
Am Plönlein Chalks/paper (50x60cm 19x23in)
München 2000

PRENZEL Robert XIX-XX [2]
🔨 **$4 964** - €5 469 - **£3 295** - FF35 876
Aboriginal Man Laughing/Aboriginal Woman Smoking a Pipe Relief (69x55cm 27x21in)
Woollahra, Sydney 2000

PRESAS Leopoldo 1915 [9]
🖋 **$3 600** - €4 183 - **£2 530** - FF27 436
Naturaleza muerta con pescados Oleo/lienzo
(60x80cm 23x31in) Buenos-Aires 2001

PRESCOTT-DAVIES Norman 1862-1915 [21]
🖋 **$6 000** - €6 440 - **£4 015** - FF42 246
Classical Girl with a Stringed Instrument Oil/canvas (37x19cm 14x7in) San-Francisco CA 2000

PRESSMANE Joseph 1904-1967 [173]
🖋 **$14 000** - €15 358 - **£9 034** - FF100 742
Deux femmes au balcon Oil/canvas (153.5x117.5cm 60x46in) Tel Aviv 2000
🖋 **$3 361** - €3 964 - **£2 363** - FF26 000
Le marché vu depuis l'atelier de l'artiste
Huile/toile (61x44cm 24x17in) Fontainebleau 2000
🖋 **$511** - €610 - **£364** - FF4 000
Paysage Huile/toile (27x22cm 10x8in) Paris 2000
🖋 **$195** - €183 - **£119** - FF1 200
Paysage Aquarelle/papier (26x34.5cm 10x13in) Paris 1998

PRESTEL Johann E. Gottlieb 1804-1885 [4]
🖋 **$1 498** - €1 453 - **£924** - FF9 534
Zug mit Treidelpferden an der Donau Ink
(24.5x34.5cm 9x13in) Wien 1999

PRESTEL Johann Gottlieb 1739-1808 [21]
▥ **$202** - €230 - **£140** - FF1 509
Waldlandschaft im Gebirge, nach Hans von Kulmbach Etching, aquatint (26x17.8cm 10x7in)
Berlin 2000

PRESTEL Marie Catherine 1747-1794 [13]
▥ **$179** - €179 - **£112** - FF1 173
Bukolische Landschaft mit Hirten und einem Dorf, nach Gainsborough Etching, aquatint
(48x64.5cm 18x25in) Hamburg 1999

PRESTELE Karl 1839-? [7]
🖋 **$1 521** - €1 278 - **£894** - FF8 383
Die Donnenbergklamm im Zillertal Öl/Leinwand
(58x48cm 22x18in) Köln 1998

PRESTILEO Enzo 1957 [3]
🖋 **$1 875** - €1 944 - **£1 125** - FF12 750
Natura morta con catino di frutta Olio/tela
(60x50cm 23x19in) Torino 1999

PRESTON Chloë XX [7]
🖋 **$471** - €522 - **£320** - FF3 427
Young girl in a red cape/A Narrow band with the girl crying Watercolour/paper (36x27cm 14x10in)
London 2000

PRESTON Margaret Rose 1875-1963 [93]
🖋 **$29 472** - €34 397 - **£20 804** - FF225 629
Mixed Flowers Oil/canvas (52x41.5cm 20x16in)
Malvern, Victoria 2000

🖋 **$17 166** - €16 702 - **£10 565** - FF109 560
Still Life with red and white Hibiscus
Oil/canvas/board (35.5x44cm 13x17in) Melbourne 1999
🖋 **$14 161** - €12 232 - **£8 553** - FF80 234
Aboriginal Designs Gouache/paper (14x13cm 5x5in)
Malvern, Victoria 1998
▥ **$4 533** - €4 262 - **£2 807** - FF27 959
Lorikeets Woodcut in colors (24.5x24.5cm 9x9in)
Melbourne 1999

PRESTOPINO Gregorio 1907-1984 [25]
🖋 **$600** - €514 - **£354** - FF3 370
Sleeping Infant Gouache (56x78cm 22x30in) New-York 1998

PRETE del Juan 1897-1987 [9]
🖋 **$5 000** - €5 509 - **£3 335** - FF36 136
Abstracción 2 Técnica mixta (60x70cm 23x27in)
Montevideo 2000

PRETI IL CAVALIERE CALABRESE Mattia 1613-1699 [46]
🖋 **$89 110** - €92 376 - **£53 466** - FF605 949
Mosé e le tavole della legge Olio/tela (147x197cm 57x77in) Milano 1999
🖋 **$4 206** - €3 899 - **£2 500** - FF25 578
Female Figure seated on Clouds/Four Studies of Hands Red chalk/paper (20x27.5cm 7x10in)
London 1999

PRêTRE Jean Gabriel c.1780-c.1845 [58]
🖋 **$2 875** - €3 354 - **£2 019** - FF22 000
Hirondelle fenêtre, hirondelle, Torcol fourmilier/Pigeons Aquarelle, gouache (16x10cm 6x3in)
Paris 2000

PREUDHOMME Jérôme XVIII [6]
🖋 **$3 631** - €3 659 - **£2 263** - FF24 000
Le repos de Diane Huile/toile (62x83cm 24x32in)
Paris 2000

PREUSCHEN von Hermione 1854-1898 [15]
🖋 **$998** - €971 - **£613** - FF6 372
Tempio, Bank unterm Holunder Öl/Karton
(64x46cm 25x18in) Berlin 1999
🖋 **$2 348** - €2 500 - **£1 600** - FF16 401
Still Life of Flowers, Decanter and Silver
Oil/panel (52.5x26.5cm 20x10in) Billingshurst, West-Sussex 2001

PREUSS Rudolf 1879-1961 [22]
🖋 **$1 184** - €1 308 - **£820** - FF8 580
Gerlos im Zillertal Aquarell/Papier (28x38cm 11x14in) Wien 2001

PREUSSE August 1908-1942 [4]
🖋 **$4 822** - €5 624 - **£3 385** - FF36 892
Ohne Titel Oil/canvas/panel (81x70.6cm 31x27in)
Köln 2000
🖋 **$1 211** - €1 431 - **£856** - FF9 390
«Bewachsener Schutthaufen» Gouache/paper
(34.5x22cm 13x8in) Köln 2001

PRÉVAL de Christiane 1876-? [5]
🖋 **$2 800** - €2 854 - **£1 754** - FF18 722
Three Friends Oil/panel (16.5x13.5cm 6x5in) New-York 2000

PRÉVERT Jacques 1900-1977 [58]
🖋 **$1 502** - €1 677 - **£1 045** - FF11 000
Collage Collage (24x30cm 9x11in) Paris 2001

PREVIATI Gaetano 1852-1920 [47]
🖋 **$11 207** - €12 031 - **£7 500** - FF78 916
Beduini nell'oasi Oil/canvas (40.5x67cm 15x26in)
London 2000

P

✏ **$3 203** - €3 321 - **£1 922** - FF21 783
Ragazza con capra Inchiostro/carta (17.5x29cm
6x11in) Milano 1999

PREVOST A. XIX [2]

✏ **$9 131** - €8 918 - **£5 820** - FF58 500
Dessins d'oiseaux Aquarelle, gouache (28x23cm
11x9in) Paris 1999

PRÉVOST Jean Louis, le Jeune c.1760-c.1815 [30]

⌣ **$120 000** - €114 549 - **£74 976** - FF751 392
**Lilacs, Roses, Peonies, Tulips and other
Flowers** Oil/canvas (146.5x113.5cm 57x44in) New-
York 1999

⌣ **$12 736** - €12 196 - **£8 016** - FF80 000
**Nature morte de pommes/Nature morte de rai-
sins** Huile/toile (45.5x55cm 17x21in) Paris 1999

✏ **$4 571** - €4 354 - **£3 227** - FF33 006
Nature morte au vase de fleurs et nid d'oiseau
Huile/toile (45x32.5cm 15x12in) Paris 2000

✏ **$13 259** - €12 974 - **£8 500** - FF85 103
**Still-Life with Peaches, Pears, Plums and
Grapes** Watercolour, gouache/paper (38x29cm
14x11in) London 1999

PRÉVOST Nicolas XIX [1]

⌣ **$5 128** - €6 098 - **£3 532** - FF40 000
L'approche de l'orage sur la campagne
Huile/toile (67.5x100cm 26x39in) Paris 2000

PRÉVOT-VALERI André 1890-1959 [222]

⌣ **$1 089** - €1 067 - **£702** - FF7 000
Vue de village Huile/toile (46x60cm 18x23in) Amiens
1999

⌣ **$236** - €274 - **£168** - FF1 800
La rivière Huile/toile (20x30.5cm 7x12in) Coutances
2001

PRÉVOT-VALERI Auguste 1857-1930 [33]

⌣ **$1 423** - €1 524 - **£969** - FF10 000
Bergers et ses moutons sur la lande Huile/toile
(46x65cm 18x25in) Calais 2001

⌣ **$1 200** - €1 296 - **£829** - FF8 500
Le retour du troupeau Huile/toile (33x46cm
12x18in) La Varenne-Saint-Hilaire 2001

PREY Johannes Zacharias 1744-1823 [4]

⌣ **$11 200** - €12 394 - **£7 500** - FF81 300
Ode à la Médecine Huile/toile (118x88cm 46x34in)
Antwerpen 2000

✏ **$1 700** - €1 559 - **£1 047** - FF10 228
**Rabbi Aryeh Loeb Ben Hayim Breslau (1741-
1809)** Pastel/paper (23.5x16cm 9x6in) New-York 1999

PREYER Emilie 1849-1930 [48]

⌣ **$23 114** - €20 231 - **£14 000** - FF132 708
**Still Life of Plums, a Peach, Grapes and an
Apricot** Oil/canvas (16x21cm 6x8in) London 1998

PREYER Ernest 1842-1917 [8]

⌣ **$3 000** - €3 374 - **£2 094** - FF22 135
Blick auf das antike amphiteater in Taormina
Öl/Leinwand (72.5x90cm 28x35in) Lindau 2001

PREYER Johann Wilhelm 1803-1889 [23]

⌣ **$85 000** - €98 198 - **£59 517** - FF644 138
Still Life with Fruit upon a Marble Ledge Oil/can-
vas (73x88cm 29x35in) New-York 2001

⌣ **$28 414** - €28 633 - **£17 712** - FF187 818
**Stilleben mit Pfirsichen, Wein, Mandeln und
Pflaumen auf einem Teller** Öl/Karton (12.5x17.5cm
4x6in) Düsseldorf 2000

PREZIOSI Amadeo, 5th Count 1816-1882 [90]

✏ **$4 385** - €5 032 - **£3 000** - FF33 006
Library in a Palace Interior Watercolour/paper
(39x47cm 15x18in) London 2000

PRIANISHNIKOV Hilarion Mikhaïlov. 1840-1894 [2]

⌣ **$19 590** - €23 313 - **£14 000** - FF152 924
The Hunt Oil/canvas (102.5x81cm 40x31in) London
2000

PRIANISHNIKOV Ivan Petrovich 1841-1909 [7]

⌣ **$5 093** - €4 200 - **£3 000** - FF27 548
Manoeuvres Oil/board (25x42cm 9x16in) London
1998

PRICE Chester 1885-1962 [2]

⌣ **$900** - €1 041 - **£637** - FF6 829
New York Public Library Etching (26x18cm 10x7in)
New-York 2000

PRICE Clark Kelley 1945 [1]

⌣ **$9 500** - €8 636 - **£5 721** - FF56 648
Sacajawea-Familiar Signs of Home Oil/canvas
(76x101cm 30x40in) Hayden ID 1998

PRICE Clayton S. 1874-1950 [7]

⌣ **$28 000** - €23 981 - **£16 531** - FF157 304
Deserted Cabins Oil/canvas (87x102cm 34x40in)
New-York 1998

PRICE Frank Corbyn 1862-? [13]

✏ **$499** - €460 - **£300** - FF3 017
Labourers in a Field at Aldingbourne, Sussex
Watercolour (23x43cm 9x16in) London 1999

PRICE George 1901-1995 [6]

✏ **$1 600** - €1 865 - **£1 107** - FF12 234
**Woman and Two Small Children Ask Directions
in a Department Store** Watercolour (26x26cm
10x10in) New-York 2000

PRICE James XIX [30]

✏ **$289** - €293 - **£183** - FF1 923
**Cattle and Dwelling by a Rocky River with Hills
Beyond** Watercolour/paper (36x53cm 14x21in)
Whitby, Yorks 2000

PRICE Ken 1935 [34]

⌣ **$6 000** - €5 727 - **£3 749** - FF37 569
«Specimen CJ1303.04» Sculpture (16.5x25.5x23cm
6x10x9in) New-York 1999

PRICE Mary Elizabeth 1877-1965 [4]

⌣ **$7 000** - €8 098 - **£4 954** - FF53 121
**T'ang Riders, still life with oriental figures on
horses** Oil/canvas (45x76cm 18x30in) Hatfield PA
2000

PRICE Nick XX [6]

⌣ **$950** - €843 - **£580** - FF5 531
«Camel Filters» Affiche couleur (173x120cm
68x47in) London 1999

PRICE Norman Mills 1877-1951 [15]

⌣ **$6 000** - €6 683 - **£3 924** - FF43 838
**Story illustration: Captured woman spy brought
into Union camp** Oil/canvas (45x109cm 18x43in)
New-York 2000

✏ **$1 400** - €1 559 - **£915** - FF10 229
**Story illustration: Battle scene with rapaging
officers** Gouache/paper (29x26cm 11x10in) New-York
2000

PRICE William Lake 1810-1896 [17]

⌣ **$3 808** - €3 659 - **£2 361** - FF24 000
The Spanish bull-fights Lithographie (36.5x60cm
14x23in) Paris 1999

⌣ **$2 293** - €2 554 - **£1 500** - FF16 754
**Elegant Company on Horseback/Elegant
Couple in a Curricle** Albumen print (20.5x27cm
8x10in) Devon 2000

PRIEBE Karl 1914-1976 **[30]**
🖌 **$2 000** - €2 275 - **£1 387** - FF14 920
  Dacing Figure Gouache/board (39x30cm 15x12in)
  Chicago IL 2000

PRIEBE Rudolf 1889-1964 **[43]**
🖑 **$632** - €613 - **£393** - FF4 024
  Fischerboote am Steg Öl/Leinwand (70x100cm
  27x39in) Bad-Vilbel 1999

PRIECHENFRIED Alois Heinrich 1867-1953 **[77]**
🖑 **$3 586** - €3 981 - **£2 500** - FF26 116
  Military Discussion Oil/canvas (52.5x42cm 20x16in)
  London 2001
🖑 **$1 782** - €1 817 - **£1 115** - FF11 917
  Der Brief Öl/Leinwand (31x40cm 12x15in) Wien 2000

PRIEST Alfred 1874-1929 **[15]**
🖑 **$1 592** - €1 719 - **£1 100** - FF11 279
  **Portrait of Bessie Priest, Bust-Length, Aged
  Nine Years** Oil/canvas (45.5x35.5cm 17x13in) London
  2001

PRIESTMAN Bertram Walter 1868-1951 **[104]**
🖑 **$1 945** - €1 883 - **£1 200** - FF12 350
  **Cattle Grazing in a Meadow Beside a River with
  Hills** Oil/canvas (41x61cm 16x24in) West-Yorshire
  1999
🖑 **$1 041** - €1 014 - **£640** - FF6 650
  Moonlit Estuary Oil/canvas (23x33cm 9x13in) Little-
  Lane, Ilkley 1999

PRIETO Monique 1962 **[4]**
🖑 **$12 000** - €13 923 - **£8 284** - FF91 332
  Clubfoot Acrylic/canvas (137x183cm 53x72in) New-
  York 2000

PRIETO MUNOZ Gregorio 1897-1992 **[58]**
🖑 **$3 510** - €3 904 - **£2 340** - FF25 610
  Santorini, Grecia Oleo/cartón (57x40cm 22x15in)
  Madrid 2000
🖑 **$1 732** - €1 652 - **£1 045** - FF10 835
  Escena del Quijote Oleo/papel (46x31cm 18x12in)
  Madrid 1999
🖌 **$459** - €511 - **£306** - FF3 349
  Fiestas de Delfos Tinta/papel (28x21cm 11x8in)
  Madrid 2000
📇 **$121** - €114 - **£76** - FF750
  Ilustración del Quijote Serigrafia (52x37cm
  20x14in) Madrid 1998

PRIEUR Paul 1620-? **[2]**
🖑 **$2 576** - €2 151 - **£1 531** - FF14 108
  Portraet af Christian V Enamel (2.6x2.4cm 1x1in)
  Köbenhavn 1998

PRIEUR-BARDIN François Léon 1870-1939 **[34]**
🖑 **$9 166** - €9 604 - **£5 802** - FF63 000
  Un homme sur le port Huile/toile (43x61cm
  16x24in) Arles 2000
🖑 **$3 012** - €2 973 - **£1 856** - FF19 500
  Vue du Bosphore Huile/toile (21x40cm 8x15in) Paris
  1999

PRIKING Franz 1927-1979 **[969]**
🖑 **$7 878** - €9 147 - **£5 610** - FF60 000
  La chapelle Huile/toile (146x114cm 57x44in) Aix-en-
  Provence 2001
🖑 **$2 414** - €2 592 - **£1 615** - FF17 000
  Nature morte Huile/papier/toile (49x63cm 19x24in)
  Cannes 2000
🖑 **$1 229** - €1 464 - **£851** - FF9 600
  Les arbres au coucher de soleil Huile/toile
  (27x35cm 10x13in) Albi 2000

🖌 **$928** - €884 - **£588** - FF5 800
  Les Baux de Provence Aquarelle/papier (31.5x49cm
  12x19in) Soissons 1999

PRIM GUYTO José María 1907-1973 **[27]**
🖑 **$891** - €811 - **£540** - FF5 319
  Malecon de puerto Oleo/lienzo (60x67cm 23x26in)
  Barcelona 1999
🖌 **$226** - €252 - **£155** - FF1 654
  Parejas en un bar Acuarela/papel (34.5x49cm
  13x19in) Barcelona 2001

PRIMATICCIO Francesco 1504-1570 **[7]**
🖑 **$94 110** - €91 890 - **£60 000** - FF602 760
  **Standing prophet and a Study of the Head of a
  Woman wearing a veil** Red chalk (23x10.5cm 9x4in)
  London 1999

PRIMAVESI Joh. Georg 1774-1855 **[7]**
🖑 **$8 327** - €8 436 - **£5 179** - FF55 339
  Bewaldete Flusslandschaft im Mondlicht
  Oil/canvas (19x28cm 7x11in) Hamburg 2000

PRIN René 1905-1985 **[53]**
🖑 **$544** - €635 - **£379** - FF4 167
  Rainy Day Oil/canvas (60x81cm 23x31in) Amsterdam
  2000
🖑 **$778** - €915 - **£564** - FF6 000
  Quais animés du port de Rouen Huile/panneau
  (27x35cm 10x13in) Calais 2001

PRINA André Julien 1887-1941 **[47]**
🖑 **$2 599** - €2 912 - **£1 806** - FF19 103
  «Etude Cornette de Saint-Cyr, Paris»
  Oil/paper/canvas (57x42cm 22x16in) Johannesburg
  2001
🖑 **$1 662** - €1 892 - **£1 168** - FF12 408
  Nu brun les pieds dans l'eau Oil chalks/paper
  (60x45cm 23x17in) Woollahra, Sydney 2001

PRINCE Elizabeth XIX **[1]**
🖌 **$2 415** - €2 281 - **£1 500** - FF14 961
  **The Artist's Sister, Anne King, at Buff's Bay,
  Jamaica** Watercolour/paper (30x40cm 11x15in)
  London 1999

PRINCE Richard 1949 **[146]**
🖑 **$32 500** - €36 339 - **£21 908** - FF238 368
  All I've Heard Acrylic (142x122cm 55x48in) New-
  York 2000
🖑 **$18 000** - €16 901 - **£11 152** - FF110 863
  **3 Jokes Painted to Death or 3 Jokes Really
  Painted** Mixed media (35.5x25.5cm 13x10in) New-
  York 1999
🪑 **$12 000** - €11 611 - **£7 400** - FF76 162
  «Br100» Sculpture, wood (157.5x143x24cm
  62x56x9in) New-York 1999
🖌 **$12 000** - €13 923 - **£8 284** - FF91 332
  «What was the Name...») Graphite (101.5x66cm
  39x25in) New-York 2000
📇 **$34 706** - €29 653 - **£21 000** - FF194 512
  My Parents Silkscreen (190.5x147.5cm 75x58in)
  London 1998
📷 **$22 000** - €20 657 - **£13 631** - FF135 500
  Cowboy Photograph in colour (59x40.5cm 23x15in)
  New-York 1999

PRINCE William Mead 1893-1951 **[6]**
🖑 **$4 750** - €5 099 - **£3 178** - FF33 444
  The Newsboy and the Blind Fiddler Oil/canvas
  (64x53cm 25x20in) Philadelphia PA 2001

PRINCETEAU René Pierre 1844-1914 **[43]**
🖑 **$28 152** - €25 916 - **£18 000** - FF170 000
  Sanglier au ferme en forêt de Compiègne
  Huile/toile (208x158cm 81x62in) Libourne 1999

$106 059 - €88 844 - **£62 361** - FF582 780
Dos-à-dos Oil/panel (46x54cm 18x21in) Amsterdam 1998

$2 860 - €3 201 - **£1 940** - FF21 000
Hussard Huile/toile (13.5x20cm 5x7in) Libourne 2000

PRINET René Xavier François 1861-1946 **[82]**
$21 484 - €21 648 - **£13 390** - FF142 000
Les amazones sur la plage Huile/toile (109x145cm 42x57in) Paris 2000

$4 692 - €5 183 - **£3 253** - FF34 000
Château de Montmorency, projet de fresque Huile/toile (41x100cm 16x39in) Compiègne 2001

$1 918 - €2 208 - **£1 368** - FF15 000
Étude pour: Après le bain Huile/panneau (34x22cm 13x8in) Paris 2000

$383 - €457 - **£273** - FF3 000
Étude pour, La toilette, avant le bain Fusain (63x48.5cm 24x19in) Paris 2000

PRINI Giovanni 1878-1958 **[3]**
$9 320 - €9 662 - **£5 592** - FF63 376
L'idoletto di casa Annie Bronzo (58x40x67cm 22x15x26in) Milano 1999

PRINNER Anton 1902-1983 **[56]**
$5 422 - €6 555 - **£3 788** - FF43 000
Le Sphinge Bronze (84x24x48cm 33x9x18in) Paris 2000

$3 627 - €3 811 - **£2 397** - FF27 000
Femme allongée Bronze (72x23x8cm 28x9x3in) Paris 2000

$6 700 - €7 622 - **£4 725** - FF50 000
Composition Collage (49x33cm 19x12in) Paris 2001

$566 - €657 - **£390** - FF4 307
La femme tondue Eau-forte (20x13cm 7x5in) Genève 2000

PRINS de Ferdinand 1859-1908 **[16]**
$867 - €843 - **£530** - FF5 528
Chemin forestier Huile/toile (42x66cm 16x25in) Bruxelles 1999

PRINS Johannes Huibert 1757-1806 **[40]**
$1 698 - €1 906 - **£1 188** - FF12 500
Pont sur un canal Aquarelle (24x20cm 9x7in) Paris 2001

PRINS Pierre Ernest 1838-1913 **[220]**
$4 025 - €3 811 - **£2 500** - FF25 000
Nature morte aux roses Huile/toile (61x81cm 24x31in) Paris 1999

$837 - €793 - **£520** - FF5 200
Personnages près des fortifications Pastel/papier (25x33cm 9x12in) Paris 1999

PRINSEP Emily Rebecca c.1800-c.1860 **[5]**
$2 455 - €2 920 - **£1 750** - FF19 154
Portraits of: Thomas Prinsep (1800-1830)/Augustus Prinsep (1803-1830) Watercolour/paper (18x15cm 7x5in) Bath 2000

PRINSEP James 1799-1840 **[17]**
$2 879 - €2 953 - **£1 800** - FF19 371
Arriving at a Fortified Town after Sunset Watercolour (13.5x19.5cm 5x7in) London 2000

PRINSEP Thomas, Captain 1800-1830 **[3]**
$15 712 - €14 696 - **£9 500** - FF96 402
The Esplanade at Calcutta, with Esplanade Row beyond Watercolour (21.5x31.5cm 8x12in) London 1999

PRINSEP Valentine Cameron 1838-1904 **[21]**
$22 492 - €21 659 - **£14 000** - FF142 072
Mu Lady Betty Oil/canvas (81.5x58cm 32x22in) London 1999

$12 257 - €13 545 - **£8 500** - FF88 850
The Taj Mahal, India Oil/canvas (30.5x37cm 12x14in) London 2001

PRINSEP William 1794-1874 **[38]**
$1 323 - €1 238 - **£800** - FF8 118
The Orient off the Island of Jago Watercolour (11.5x18.5cm 4x7in) London 1999

PRINSSAY Jenny XIX **[1]**
$230 000 - €232 676 - **£140 438** - FF1 526 250
View of a Bay on the Island of Martinique Oil/canvas (63.5x87cm 25x34in) New-York 2000

PRINTEMPS Léon 1871-? **[8]**
$820 - €747 - **£503** - FF4 900
«Excursions aux Iles de l'Océan» Affiche (103.5x72cm 40x28in) Saint-Cloud 1999

PRINTZENSKÖLD Carl 1864-1926 **[2]**
$6 416 - €6 466 - **£4 000** - FF42 414
At the Shoemaker's Oil/canvas (81.5x58.5cm 32x23in) London 2000

PRINZ A. Emil XIX **[1]**
$4 750 - €5 331 - **£3 306** - FF34 972
Two Greyhounds in a Park Oil/canvas (76x122cm 29x48in) New-York 2001

PRINZ Bernhard 1953 **[11]**
$1 147 - €1 278 - **£750** - FF8 384
Konvent Cibachrome print (37.7x56.8cm 14x22in) Köln 2000

PRINZ Karl Ludwig 1875-1944 **[73]**
$925 - €1 090 - **£651** - FF7 150
Grosses Ödstein-Gesäuse Oil/panel (79x99.5cm 31x39in) Wien 2000

$523 - €590 - **£362** - FF3 867
«Im Park» Oil/panel (30x32cm 11x12in) Toronto 2000

PRIOR Thomas Abiel 1809-1886 **[4]**
$1 154 - €1 295 - **£800** - FF8 494
Dido Buildings, after H M W Turner Engraving (41x63cm 16x24in) London 2000

PRIOR William Henry 1812-1882 **[4]**
$822 - €794 - **£520** - FF5 206
Boulogne, France Watercolour (15x34.5cm 5x13in) Billingshurst, West-Sussex 1999

PRIOR William Matthew 1803-1873 **[48]**
$8 000 - €8 544 - **£5 451** - FF56 042
Young Man in Beige Vest with Floral Decoration Oil/board (53x38cm 21x15in) New-York 2001

$5 500 - €6 332 - **£3 853** - FF41 536
Portrait of a Ruddy-Cheeked, dark-haired Gentleman Oil/panel (35x24cm 13x9in) New-York 2000

$45 000 - €42 217 - **£27 805** - FF276 925
Portrait of two Blonde-haired Sisters wearing red Dresses Gouache/board (52x61cm 20x24in) New-York 1999

PRIOU Louis 1845-? **[10]**
$4 887 - €4 449 - **£3 000** - FF29 181
A Cupid playing Oil/panel (40x29cm 15x11in) London 1999

PRISSE D'AVENNES Émile 1807-1879 **[2]**
$1 443 - €1 455 - **£900** - FF9 543
The Captain of the Port of Damietta Watercolour/paper (29x22.5cm 11x8in) London 2000

PRITCHARD George Thompson 1878-1962 **[47]**
$1 500 - €1 561 - **£941** - FF10 240
Sailing on the High Seas Oil/canvas (60x91cm 24x36in) Chicago IL 2000

PRITCHARD Gwilym 1931 **[23]**
$411 - €488 - £300 - FF3 202
Penman Priory in Snow Oil/panel (60x120.5cm 23x47in) Billingshurst, West-Sussex 2001

PRITCHARD Thomas XIX **[3]**
$3 067 - €3 609 - £2 220 - FF23 676
Forest near Zermatt with Dent-Blanche Aquarelle/papier (76x54cm 29x21in) Sion 2001

PRITCHETT Edward ?-1864 **[103]**
$23 206 - €20 021 - £14 000 - FF131 332
The Grand Canal with Santa Maria Della Salute, Venice Oil/canvas (43x63cm 16x24in) London 1998
$8 965 - €9 624 - £6 000 - FF63 129
Venetian Cappriccio Oil/canvas (30.5x45.5cm 12x17in) London 2000
$3 448 - €3 369 - £2 200 - FF22 097
A View of Santa Maria della Salute from the Piazzta, Venice Watercolour (23.5x38.5cm 9x15in) London 1999

PRITCHARD Robert Taylor 1823-1907 **[28]**
$402 - €378 - £250 - FF2 482
The Organist Watercolour/paper (33x23cm 12x9in) Salisbury, Wiltshire 1999

PRITT XX **[1]**
$800 - €769 - £493 - FF5 046
«Chez Torrilhon» Poster (113.5x158cm 44x62in) New-York 1999

PRITT Thomas XIX **[2]**
$2 705 - €2 833 - £1 700 - FF18 580
Landscape with Figures on a Bridge, Horses and Cottage with Woodland Oil/canvas (89x73cm 35x29in) Bury St. Edmunds, Suffolk 2000

PRITZELWITZ von Johanne act.c.1881-? **[1]**
$6 529 - €7 414 - £4 537 - FF48 631
Portraitdarstellung einer jungen Frau Oil/panel (53.5x66cm 21x25in) Eltville-Erbach 2001

PRIVAT Colette 1932 **[9]**
$1 300 - €1 318 - £807 - FF8 648
Bouquet mélangé Oil/canvas (50x60cm 20x24in) New-York 2000

PRIVAT G. XIX-XX **[2]**
$738 - €823 - £496 - FF5 400
«Dupré, champion de France et du monde sur cycles La Française» Affiche (151x106cm 59x41in) Orléans 2000

PRIVAT Gilbert Auguste 1892-1969 **[42]**
$1 274 - €1 448 - £894 - FF9 500
Femme année 1930 et son enfant Bronze (30x51cm 11x20in) Paris 2001

PRIVAT-LIVEMONT Henri 1861-1936 **[182]**
$1 047 - €1 091 - £668 - FF7 154
Autoportrait en habit de soldat Huile/panneau (55x38cm 21x14in) Bruxelles 2000
$248 - €297 - £170 - FF1 951
Nature morte au lièvre Huile/panneau (25x35cm 9x13in) Bruxelles 2000
$1 100 - €1 181 - £736 - FF7 745
The Proposal Pastel/paper (30.5x48.5cm 12x19in) New-York 2000
$3 400 - €3 219 - £2 111 - FF21 112
«La Vague» Poster (70x51.5cm 27x20in) New-York 1999

PRIVATO Cosimo 1889-1971 **[37]**
$950 - €985 - £570 - FF6 460
Chiacchiere in cucina Olio/tela (60x80cm 23x31in) Trieste 2001

$960 - €1 244 - £720 - FF8 160
Popolana Olio/cartone (40x30cm 15x11in) Milano 2000

PRIVER Aharon 1902-1979 **[7]**
$1 500 - €1 688 - £1 033 - FF11 074
Mother and Child Stone (H32cm H12in) Herzelia-Pituah 2000

PROBST Carl 1854-1924 **[25]**
$5 500 - €5 036 - £3 352 - FF33 037
Interior Scene with standing nude Female Figure Oil/canvas (68x41cm 27x16in) Bloomfield-Hills MI 1999
$1 354 - €1 453 - £906 - FF9 534
Träumereien Oil/panel (26x18cm 10x7in) Wien 2000

PROBST Georg Balthasar XVIII **[13]**
$90 - €102 - £63 - FF670
Gesicht der Kirche und Gasssen St.Petri zu Florenz Radierung (30x41cm 11x16in) Berlin 2001

PROBST Thorwald 1886-1948 **[12]**
$1 500 - €1 285 - £901 - FF8 429
Irises Oil/canvas (76x96cm 30x38in) Cincinnati OH 1998

PROBSTHAYN Carl 1770-1818 **[4]**
$4 116 - €4 698 - £2 859 - FF30 817
Mytologiske scenerier Oil/canvas (88x65cm 34x25in) Köbenhavn 2000

PROCACCINI Camillo 1551-1629 **[33]**
$1 195 - €1 283 - £800 - FF8 417
Running Apostle, seen from behind Red chalk/paper (30.5x21.5cm 12x8in) London 2000
$381 - €409 - £255 - FF2 683
Die Ruhe auf der Flucht nach Ägypten Radierung (27.6x21cm 10x8in) Berlin 2000

PROCACCINI Ercole II 1596-1676 **[8]**
$3 137 - €3 063 - £2 000 - FF20 092
Kneeling Figure by a standing Angel accompanied by a Putti Red chalk/paper (20x26cm 7x10in) London 2000

PROCACCINI Giulio Cesare 1570-1625 **[34]**
$75 000 - €64 791 - £50 000 - FF425 000
Le tentazioni di Sant'Antonio Olio/tela (95.5x80.5cm 37x31in) Milano 1998
$50 000 - €43 858 - £30 360 - FF287 690
Madonna and Child with Saint John the Baptist and Two Angels Oil/panel (44.5x33cm 17x12in) New-York 1999
$14 039 - €13 737 - £9 000 - FF90 109
Figure Studies Ink (34.5x22cm 13x8in) London 1999

PROCHAZKA Antonín 1882-1945 **[77]**
$17 340 - €16 400 - £10 800 - FF107 580
Harvest Oil/canvas (70x93cm 27x36in) Praha 2000
$24 565 - €23 234 - £15 300 - FF152 405
Nature morte aux fleurs rouges Huile/toile (40x25cm 15x9in) Praha 2000
$5 159 - €5 501 - £3 500 - FF36 081
Crouching Figure with an Ewer Bronze (H39.5cm H15in) London 2001
$1 589 - €1 503 - £990 - FF9 861
Bathing Charcoal (35x47cm 13x18in) Praha 2001

PROCHAZKA Jaro 1886-1949 **[19]**
$433 - €410 - £270 - FF2 689
Motif from the Brevnov Monastery Oil/cardboard (48x64cm 18x25in) Praha 2000

P

PROCHAZKA Josef 1909 **[21]**
- $664 – €629 – £414 – FF4 123
  Landscape and Corn Field Oil/cardboard (35x50cm 13x19in) Praha 2000

PROCHAZKOVA-SCHEITHAUEROVA Linka 1884-1960 **[14]**
- $6 358 – €6 014 – £3 960 – FF39 446
  Vintage Oil/canvas (12x16cm 4x6in) Praha 2000

PROCKTOR Patrick 1936 **[110]**
- $3 484 – €3 623 – £2 200 – FF23 767
  Peter and Sandy Oil/canvas (38x51cm 14x20in) London 2000
- $3 124 – €3 058 – £2 000 – FF20 057
  Still Life with Lily, Matchbox and Birthday Card Oil/canvas (30.5x30.5cm 12x12in) London 1999
- $373 – €401 – £250 – FF2 632
  Figure Drawing Charcoal/paper (72.5x53.5cm 28x21in) London 2000
- $104 – €116 – £72 – FF759
  Nasturtiums Wusih Aquatint in colors (59.5x45cm 23x17in) Sydney 2001

PROCOPIO Pino 1954 **[18]**
- $500 – €518 – £300 – FF3 400
  «Vaso misterioso» Olio/tavola (30x40cm 11x15in) Vercelli 1999

PROCTER Albert XIX-XX **[23]**
- $384 – €437 – £270 – FF2 866
  Old Cottage near Freshfield with Ducks in Foreground Watercolour/paper (33x48cm 13x19in) Oxford 2001

PROCTER Burt 1901-1980 **[7]**
- $8 800 – €8 218 – £5 431 – FF53 908
  Cowboy on Horse Oil/canvas (55x71cm 22x28in) Dallas TX 1999

PROCTER Dod, née Shaw 1891-1972 **[70]**
- $12 327 – €11 713 – £7 500 – FF76 833
  Bella Donna Lilies Oil/canvas (68.5x54cm 26x21in) London 2000
- $4 871 – €4 752 – £3 000 – FF31 174
  Study of a Boy Oil/panel (30.5x25.5cm 12x10in) London 1999

PROCTER Ernest 1886-1935 **[48]**
- $99 617 – €117 294 – £70 000 – FF769 398
  The Merry-Go-Round Oil/canvas (102x128cm 40x50in) London 2000
- $6 939 – €8 081 – £4 800 – FF53 007
  Girl on a Bridge Oil/canvas (51x61cm 20x24in) London 2000
- $312 – €298 – £190 – FF1 957
  Along The Path, Burma Watercolour (24x34.5cm 9x13in) London 1999

PROCTOR Adam Edwin 1864-1913 **[44]**
- $17 184 – €18 446 – £11 500 – FF120 998
  The Village Shop Oil/canvas (91.5x61cm 36x24in) London 2000
- $692 – €777 – £480 – FF5 096
  River Scenes Oil/board (25.5x20.5cm 10x8in) London 2000
- $290 – €270 – £180 – FF1 774
  Picnic on the Heath Watercolour/paper (26.5x36cm 10x14in) Billingshurst, West-Sussex 1999

PROCTOR Alexander Phimister 1862-1950 **[44]**
- $4 500 – €3 845 – £2 701 – FF25 219
  A Bronze Horse Bronze (H30cm H11in) New-York 1998

- $1 540 – €1 653 – £1 030 – FF10 843
  Big Horn Mountain Sheep Watercolour/paper (31x39cm 12x15in) Houston TX 2000

PROCTOR Althea Mary 1879-1966 **[108]**
- $953 – €928 – £587 – FF6 086
  Seated Nude Pencil (24.5x35cm 9x13in) Malvern, Victoria 1999
- $729 – €867 – £519 – FF5 690
  Before Rehearsal Lithograph (41.5x33.5cm 16x13in) Melbourne 2000

PRODAN Auriel XX **[7]**
- $800 – €831 – £504 – FF5 454
  Mediterranean Harbour Scene Oil/canvas (50.5x71cm 19x27in) Washington 2000

PROIETTI Norberto 1927 **[16]**
- $7 500 – €7 775 – £4 500 – FF51 000
  Duomo di Vicenza Olio/tavola (45x70cm 17x27in) Vercelli 1999
- $2 700 – €2 799 – £1 620 – FF18 360
  Figure Olio/tavola (30x20cm 11x7in) Vercelli 2000

PROKOFYEVA Anna 1960 **[14]**
- $930 – €901 – £570 – FF5 910
  Masaje, copia de Léon Gérôme Oleo/lienzo (61x38cm 24x14in) Madrid 1999
- $412 – €385 – £250 – FF2 527
  Crockery and Glass Oil/canvas (51x31cm 20x12in) Fernhurst, Haslemere, Surrey 1999

PROKSCH Peter 1935 **[17]**
- $2 339 – €2 325 – £1 414 – FF15 254
  Ruine Oil/panel (24x33cm 9x12in) Wien 2000
- $2 716 – €2 326 – £1 590 – FF15 260
  «Der fünfte Engel» Indian ink/paper (41.5x57cm 16x22in) Wien 1998

PRON Hector 1817-1905 **[13]**
- $14 986 – €14 025 – £9 282 – FF92 000
  Les Voisins, Mare en Brie Huile/toile (75x125cm 29x49in) Troyes 1999

PRONASZKO Andrzej 1879-1961 **[6]**
- $8 839 – €8 781 – £5 505 – FF57 597
  Nature morte au vase Oil/panel (58x46cm 22x18in) Warszawa 1999

PRONASZKO Zbigniew 1885-1958 **[45]**
- $3 786 – €3 558 – £2 350 – FF23 337
  Nature morte avec des violons Oil/panel (87x61cm 34x24in) Warszawa 1999

PRONK Cornelis 1691-1759 **[17]**
- $1 558 – €1 815 – £1 088 – FF11 906
  View of steenwijck Black chalk (14x20cm 5x7in) Amsterdam 2000

PRONTCHENKO Léonid 1956 **[68]**
- $402 – €457 – £282 – FF3 000
  Les marionnettes Huile/toile (110x100cm 43x39in) Paris 2001

PROOST Alfons 1880-1957 **[36]**
- $1 345 – €1 611 – £923 – FF10 569
  Ballerine Huile/toile (80x76cm 31x29in) Antwerpen 2000
- $492 – €545 – £343 – FF3 577
  Wandelaars op het strand (Promenade sur la plage) Huile/panneau (28x38cm 11x14in) Antwerpen 2001

PROOYEN van Albert Jurardus 1834-1898 **[77]**
- $6 304 – €6 807 – £4 311 – FF44 649
  Sailing Vessels in a Stiff Breeze Oil/panel (34.5x63cm 13x24in) Amsterdam 2001

$930 - €998 - £622 - FF6 548
Small boat in a stream by a windmill Oil/panel (9.5x14cm 3x5in) Amsterdam 2000

PROPHETER Otto 1875-1927 [4]
$2 325 - €1 990 - £1 400 - FF13 055
Portrait of a Lady wearing a yellow Dress, red ribbon in her hair Oil/board (81.5x70cm 32x27in) London 1998

PROSA Alfredo 1884-? [2]
$7 250 - €7 516 - £4 350 - FF49 300
Paesaggio alpino con mucche Olio/tela (70x104.5cm 27x41in) Milano 2000

PROSALENTIS Emilios 1859-1926 [42]
$12 455 - €14 341 - £8 500 - FF94 068
Ship at Anchor Oil/canvas (56x65cm 22x25in) London 2000

$7 016 - €7 508 - £4 800 - FF52 809
At Sea Oil/canvas (35x25.5cm 13x10in) London 2000

$6 750 - €7 508 - £4 500 - FF49 250
Constantinople Watercolour/paper (29x57cm 11x22in) Athens 2000

PROSALENTIS Pavlo 1857-1894 [4]
$3 123 - €3 583 - £2 136 - FF23 500
Portrait de jeune orientale Huile/toile (40.5x24cm 15x9in) Soissons 2000

PROSALENTIS Spyridon 1830-1895 [6]
$1 890 - €2 102 - £1 260 - FF13 790
Sailing Boat Watercolour/paper (28x20cm 11x7in) Athens 2000

PROSDOCINI Alberto 1852-? [91]
$1 320 - €1 140 - £660 - FF7 480
Veduta di Venezia Acquarello/carta (39x73cm 15x28in) Firenze 1999

PROSSER George Frederick c.1800-c.1880 [15]
$5 265 - €6 156 - £3 700 - FF40 379
«**Winton from Morestead Downs**» Watercolour (42x78cm 16x30in) Oxfordshire 2000

PROST Louis 1876-? [1]
$5 000 - €5 333 - £3 330 - FF34 982
Figure of a young Girl Bronze (H69.7cm H27in) New-York 2000

PROST Maurice 1894-1967 [69]
$4 170 - €4 573 - £2 832 - FF30 000
Panthère en furie Bronze (H26cm H10in) Calais 2000

PROT XVIII-XIX [2]
$1 799 - €2 012 - £1 213 - FF13 200
Imrudence No.1 à 3/Sagesse No.1 à 3 d'après Rullmann Ludwig Gravure (60.5x66.5cm 23x26in) Orléans 2000

PROTAIS Alexandre 1826-1890 [16]
$638 - €719 - £448 - FF4 716
Soldaten im Winter bei einer Feuerstelle Öl/Leinwand (26.5x22cm 10x8in) Zürich 2001

PROTHEAU François 1823-1865 [1]
$10 578 - €12 348 - £7 468 - FF81 000
Jeune mère portant son enfant, le visage blotti contre le sien Marbre (H177cm H69in) Paris 2000

PROTTI Alfredo 1882-1949 [5]
$19 635 - €20 355 - £11 781 - FF133 518
Interno con figura Olio/tela (69x91cm 27x35in) Milano 2000

PROUD Alastair 1954 [10]
$4 545 - €4 368 - £2 800 - FF28 653
Kruger Lion Oil/board (65x100.5cm 25x39in) London 1999

PROUD Geoffrey Robert 1946 [48]
$855 - €957 - £595 - FF6 276
Circus Grower Oil/canvas (60.5x51cm 23x20in) Sydney 2001

$792 - €943 - £548 - FF6 187
Windy Hillside Pastel/paper (54x70cm 21x27in) Sydney 2000

PROUD Liam ?-1999 [7]
$832 - €952 - £572 - FF6 246
Setting Sail Roundstone Regatta Oil/board (60x91cm 24x36in) Dublin 2000

PROUDFOOT William 1822-1901 [4]
$3 621 - €4 202 - £2 500 - FF27 564
R;W.R.Mackenzie Esq., of Stormontfield, in a Brown Suit, Gloves Oil/canvas (91.5x72cm 36x28in) London 2000

PROUT John Skinner 1806-1876 [85]
$794 - €933 - £550 - FF6 123
Figures in a Continental Street Watercolour (56.5x43cm 22x16in) London 2000

$202 - €235 - £142 - FF1 540
Sydney Cove/Woolloomooloo BAy/The Heads of Port Jackson Lithograph (18x27cm 7x10in) Sydney 2000

PROUT Margaret Fisher 1875-1963 [68]
$1 823 - €1 573 - £1 100 - FF10 319
Summer Oil/board (51x61cm 20x24in) London 1998

PROUT Samuel 1783-1852 [250]
$747 - €803 - £500 - FF5 265
The Bridge at Verona Pencil/paper (25.5x36cm 10x14in) London 2000

$419 - €463 - £280 - FF2 955
Rudiments of Landscape Soft ground (29x39.5cm 11x15in) London 2000

PROUT Samuel Gillespie 1822-1911 [55]
$852 - €716 - £500 - FF4 694
Figures in a Busy Continental Street Watercolour (42x30cm 16x11in) London 1998

PROUVÉ Jean 1901-1984 [2]
$40 000 - €42 936 - £26 768 - FF281 640
Tunisie, Bookcase Metal (160x358x52.5cm 62x140x20in) New-York 2000

PROUVÉ Victor 1858-1943 [100]
$2 099 - €2 498 - £1 500 - FF16 389
A Lady in a Field of Lillies Oil/canvas (68x92cm 26x36in) London 2000

$1 352 - €1 578 - £949 - FF10 348
Judit mit dem Haupt des Holofernes Oil/panel (46x27cm 18x10in) Luzern 2000

$903 - €915 - £567 - FF6 000
Femme nue Fusain (114x75cm 44x29in) Nancy 2000

PROVAGGI Cesare XIX [4]
$480 - €622 - £360 - FF4 080
Nello studio del pittore Acquarello/carta (21x26cm 8x10in) Milano 2000

PROVERBIO Luciano 1936 [11]
$950 - €985 - £570 - FF6 460
«**Interno**» Olio/carta/tavola (50x40cm 19x15in) Torino 2001

$1 200 - €1 244 - £720 - FF8 160
Donne e diavolo Tecnica mista/cartone (27x24cm 10x9in) Torino 2000

P

$640 - €829 - **£480** - FF5 440
Interno Pastel gras (41x60cm 16x23in) Torino 2000

PROVINO Salvatore 1943 [53]
$440 - €570 - **£330** - FF3 740
«**Movimento di un corpo**» Olio/tela (70x50cm
27x19in) Vercelli 2000
$200 - €259 - **£150** - FF1 700
Nel silenzio Olio/tela (33x22cm 12x8in) Vercelli 2001

PROVIS Alfred XIX [37]
$3 401 - €3 847 - **£2 300** - FF25 237
Interior at St.Pol de Leon Oil/canvas (34x49cm
13x19in) London 2000
$4 658 - €3 945 - **£2 800** - FF25 877
Feeding Chicks Oil/panel (23.5x32cm 9x12in)
London 1998

PROVOST Jan 1462/65-1529 [5]
$77 542 - €89 971 - **£53 539** - FF590 168
Geburt Christi Oil/panel (84x46cm 33x18in) Luzern
2000

PROWETT James Christie ?-1946 [12]
$1 933 - €1 816 - **£1 200** - FF11 914
A Country Stroll Oil/canvas (40x52cm 15x20in)
London 1999

PROWSE Ruth 1883-1967 [20]
$1 052 - €1 179 - **£731** - FF7 732
Matzikama Oil/board (38x53.5cm 14x21in)
Johannesburg 2001
$1 389 - €1 339 - **£858** - FF8 783
Cape Town Harbour Oil/board (25.5x36cm 10x14in)
Johannesburg 1999

PRUANG PLIANSAI-SUEB 1932 [4]
$1 869 - €1 736 - **£1 155** - FF11 389
Festival at Khun Yuam Oil/canvas (49x69cm
19x27in) Bangkok 1999
$2 002 - €1 860 - **£1 237** - FF12 202
Nude Watercolour (76.5x51cm 30x20in) Bangkok 1999

PRUCHA Gustav 1875-1952 [56]
$1 690 - €1 454 - **£1 002** - FF9 538
Trojka in winterlicher Landschaft Öl/Leinwand
(60x90.5cm 23x35in) Wien 1998

PRUD'HON Blaise XX [24]
$335 - €335 - **£209** - FF2 200
Bécassines en vol Mine plomb (26x39cm 10x15in)
Soissons 1999
$190 - €213 - **£132** - FF1 400
Le dix cors Eau-forte (64x49cm 25x19in) Soissons
2001

PRUD'HON Pierre-Paul 1758-1823 [85]
$14 292 - €13 081 - **£8 712** - FF85 806
Bildnis Madame Ursule Renon de François
Öl/Leinwand (63.5x54.5cm 25x21in) Wien 1999
$14 499 - €14 422 - **£9 000** - FF94 600
A Maiden in Grecian Attire Oil/canvas (42x35.5cm
16x13in) London 1999
$14 805 - €13 720 - **£9 207** - FF90 000
Clotho la fileuse Pierre noire (22x12.5cm 8x4in)
Paris 1999
$938 - €945 - **£584** - FF6 200
L'Enlèvement d'Europe Eau-forte (13.5x19cm
5x7in) Paris 2000

PRUDKVSKAYA Lyudmilla XX [1]
$3 091 - €2 862 - **£1 892** - FF18 773
Die Tennisspielerin Aquarelle (58x40cm 22x15in)
Bern 1999

PRUITT & EARLY 1964/1963 [13]
$3 200 - €3 713 - **£2 209** - FF24 355
Sculpture for Teenage Boys, Pabst Case, You're Playing with Fire Assemblage (48x22x12.5cm
18x8x4in) New-York 2000

PRUNA Pedro 1904-1977 [174]
$38 400 - €36 039 - **£24 000** - FF236 400
Retrato de la esposa del pintor Oleo/lienzo
(110x143.5cm 43x56in) Madrid 1999
$14 850 - €16 518 - **£10 450** - FF108 350
Los dos amantes Oleo/lienzo (54x65cm 21x25in)
Madrid 2001
$510 - €601 - **£370** - FF3 960
Paisaje Lápices de color/papel (40x30cm 15x11in)
Barcelona 2001
$855 - €901 - **£570** - FF5 910
Niña con flores Tinta/papel (39.5x31.5cm 15x12in)
Madrid 2000
$239 - €276 - **£165** - FF1 812
Odaliscas Litografía (28.5x21cm 11x8in) Madrid
2000

PRUNIER Gaston 1863-1927 [15]
$411 - €457 - **£287** - FF3 000
Fête ouvrière Huile/carton (50.5x74cm 19x29in) Paris
2001

PRUSAKOV Nikolai 1900-1952 [3]
$2 386 - €2 013 - **£1 400** - FF13 207
«**Two Worlds**» Poster (124x94cm 48x37in) London
1998

PRÜSSEN Clemens 1888-1966 [23]
$381 - €409 - **£255** - FF2 683
**Eifellandschaft mit Wanderin und blühendem
Ginster** Öl/Karton (40x50cm 15x19in) Köln 2000

PRUTSCHER Otto 1880-1949 [10]
$860 - €945 - **£572** - FF6 197
Entwurfszeichnung für einen Samowar
Pencil/paper (54.5x42.5cm 21x16in) Wien 2000

PRUVOST Pierre 1921 [9]
$1 341 - €1 524 - **£920** - FF10 000
Cargo à Bougie, Algérie Gouache/papier (47x61cm
18x24in) Aubagne 2000

PRYCE George Willis XIX-XX [74]
$208 - €221 - **£140** - FF1 451
Highland Landscapes Oil/board (24.5x36.5cm
9x14in) London 2001

PRYDE James Ferrier 1866-1941 [38]
$5 630 - €6 278 - **£3 800** - FF41 180
Figures by a Monument Oil/canvas (73x71cm
28x27in) Edinburgh 2000
$3 952 - €3 760 - **£2 400** - FF24 661
Romantic Landscape, a little Shade Oil/canvas
(25.5x35.5cm 10x13in) Edinburgh 1999
$2 177 - €2 452 - **£1 500** - FF16 082
Mary Queen of Scots Bed in a Bedchamber
Watercolour/paper (16.5x14cm 6x5in) London 2000

PRYN Harald 1891-1968 [348]
$1 537 - €1 481 - **£957** - FF9 716
Vinterdag i Hösterköb Oil/canvas (108x138cm
42x54in) København 1999
$832 - €698 - **£488** - FF4 581
Sommerdag i landsbygaden i Veddelev
Oil/canvas (38x60cm 14x23in) Vejle 1998
$243 - €268 - **£164** - FF1 760
Vinterlandskab med huse Oil/canvas (33x42cm
12x16in) Vejle 2000

P

PRYNNE Edward A. Fellowes 1854-1921 [5]
- $15 651 - €18 185 - **£11 000** - FF119 286
  Enthroned Oil/canvas (148.5x112cm 58x44in) London 2001

PRYSE Gerald Spencer 1882-1956 [8]
- $600 - €650 - **£400** - FF4 264
  «**London Transport**» Poster (101x63cm 40x25in) New-York 2000

PRYTHERCH Thomas 1864-? [3]
- $1 234 - €1 390 - **£850** - FF9 116
  Making New Friends Watercolour (25x33cm 9x12in) Newbury, Berkshire 2000

PRYTZ Adolf 1813-1870 [1]
- $2 106 - €2 005 - **£1 317** - FF13 150
  Utsikt af Götheborg Indian ink (51x76cm 20x29in) Stockholm 1999

PSAIER Pietro 1939 [394]
- $455 - €420 - **£287** - FF2 758
  Happy Birthday Mr President Técnica mixta/lienzo (81x66cm 31x25in) Madrid 1999
- $487 - €450 - **£307** - FF2 955
  Perfil de Manolete, Ultimo minuto Técnica mixta/papel (50x35cm 19x13in) Madrid 1999
- $399 - €420 - **£266** - FF2 758
  The Spirit of Marilyn Serigrafia (40x30.5cm 15x12in) Madrid 2000

PSEUDO ADRIAEN VAN DE VENNE (Jan van de Venne) c.1590-c.1650 [20]
- $5 820 - €4 958 - **£3 460** - FF32 520
  Saint Simon Huile/panneau (75.8x58.5cm 29x23in) Antwerpen 1998
- $3 884 - €3 506 - **£2 394** - FF23 000
  L'homme au chapeau Huile/panneau (25x31cm 9x12in) Paris 1999

PSEUDO BOSSCHAERT XVII [1]
- $644 520 - €632 962 - **£400 000** - FF4 151 960
  Still Life of Flowers in a Vase on a Stone Ledge Oil/copper (61.5x45cm 24x17in) London 2001

PSEUDO FARDELLA Pittore di C. Torre XVII [7]
- $27 293 - €30 516 - **£19 000** - FF200 174
  A Parrot, a Partridge, a Dead Hare/Turkeys, Ducks and other Game Oil/canvas (115.5x157.5cm 45x62in) London 2001
- $160 000 - €207 331 - **£120 000** - FF1 360 000
  Natura morta con ciliegie/Natura morta con fragole Olio/tavola (45x53cm 17x20in) Firenze 2000

PSEUDO GUARDI XVIII [5]
- $34 000 - €35 246 - **£20 400** - FF231 200
  Natura morta con vasi di fiori Olio/tela (93x127.5cm 36x50in) Milano 2000

PSEUDO PIER FRANCESCO FLORENTINO XV [15]
- $39 902 - €45 322 - **£28 000** - FF297 290
  The Madonna and Child Oil/panel (70.5x45cm 27x17in) London 2001

PSEUDO ROESTRATEN (Johann Kröger ?) XVII [6]
- $15 000 - €16 542 - **£10 158** - FF108 511
  A Vanitas Still Life: Ornamental Chocolate pot, a Stoneware Vase Oil/canvas (108.5x120.5cm 42x47in) New-York 2000
- $13 999 - €13 315 - **£8 500** - FF87 343
  Vanitas Still Life on a Table Draped with a Tapestry Oil/canvas (91x87.5cm 35x34in) London 1999

PSEUDO SIMONS XVII [4]
- $7 411 - €7 049 - **£4 500** - FF46 240
  Landscape with Travellers, Set within a Stone Cartouche Adorned Oil/canvas (54.5x111cm 21x43in) London 1999

PU HUA 1834-1911 [15]
- $3 096 - €2 920 - **£1 920** - FF19 152
  Bamboo Ink/paper (146x39.5cm 57x15in) Hong-Kong 1999

PU JIN 1879-1966 [4]
- $2 227 - €1 881 - **£1 336** - FF12 338
  Horse and Groom in Willow Shade Ink (20x52cm 7x20in) Hong-Kong 1998

PU QUAN 1913 [4]
- $4 200 - €4 885 - **£3 000** - FF32 045
  Chesnut, grey and dappled Horses grazing on Riverbanks Ink (89x245cm 35x96in) London 2001

PU RU 1896-1963 [205]
- $51 360 - €56 083 - **£33 040** - FF367 880
  Seven Sages in Bamboo Grove Oil/canvas/board (131.5x65.5cm 51x25in) Hong-Kong 2000
- $5 128 - €6 027 - **£3 556** - FF39 536
  «**Shou'lao**», **God of Longevity** Ink (74x38cm 29x14in) Hong-Kong 2000

PUCCI Silvio 1892-1961 [37]
- $800 - €829 - **£480** - FF5 440
  Case e pagliai Olio/tela (50x60cm 19x23in) Prato 2000
- $840 - €726 - **£420** - FF4 760
  Vaso con fiori Olio/tela (40x30cm 15x11in) Prato 1999

PUCCINELLI Antonio 1822-1897 [11]
- $23 400 - €20 215 - **£15 600** - FF132 016
  Ritratto di un uficiale e di sua moglie Olio/tela (128.5x94cm 50x37in) Prato 1998
- $7 500 - €7 775 - **£4 500** - FF51 000
  La dichiarazione Olio/tela (58x48cm 22x18in) Torino 2000
- $570 - €492 - **£285** - FF3 230
  Barche in Darsena Olio/cartone (24.5x33.5cm 9x13in) Firenze 1999

PUCCINI Mario 1869-1920 [69]
- $19 000 - €19 696 - **£11 400** - FF129 200
  Paesaggio campestre in alta Provenza Olio/cartone (44x53cm 17x20in) Milano 1999
- $25 200 - €21 770 - **£16 800** - FF142 800
  Barconi in porto Olio/tavola (18x28cm 7x11in) Roma 1998
- $2 380 - €2 467 - **£1 428** - FF16 184
  Uomo in giardino Carboncino/carta (27x29cm 10x11in) Milano 1999

PUCHEGGER Anton c.1890-1917 [10]
- $1 483 - €1 687 - **£1 045** - FF11 067
  Diana-Meerkatze Porcelain (H31cm H12in) Berlin 2001

PUCHINGER Erwin 1876-1944 [15]
- $155 - €182 - **£111** - FF1 191
  «**Zeichnet 3.Kriegsanleihe**» Poster (125x95cm 49x37in) Wien 2000

PÜCHLER Johann Michael XVII-XVIII [2]
- $940 - €818 - **£566** - FF5 363
  Doppelbildnis Kaiser Leopold I und seine Gemahlin Kupferstich (6x10.3cm 2x4in) Berlin 1998

PUDLICH Robert 1905-1962 **[63]**

▱ **$3 029** - €3 579 - **£2 139** - FF23 477
Sitzende junge Frau Öl/Leinwand (88x57cm 34x22in) Köln 2001

▱ **$837** - €715 - **£491** - FF4 691
Kleines Stilleben Oil/panel (12,5x9.5cm 4x3in) Bielefeld 1998

▱ **$110** - €102 - **£66** - FF670
Dame mit Page/Clown mit Äffchen Lithographie (25x16cm 9x6in) Heidelberg 1999

PUECH Denys 1854-1942 **[39]**

▱ **$12 500** - €11 066 - **£7 642** - FF72 586
Winged Sea Maiden Gilded bronze (H81.5cm H32in) New-York 1999

▱ **$2 401** - €2 211 - **£1 441** - FF14 500
Héro pleurant Léandre Bronze (H18cm H7in) Rodez 1999

PUENTE José XX **[15]**

▱ **$605** - €661 - **£385** - FF4 334
Escena taurina Oleo/lienzo (65x80cm 25x31in) Madrid 2000

▱ **$692** - €647 - **£427** - FF4 245
Rematando el quite al caballo Oleo/lienzo (23.5x31cm 9x12in) México 1999

PUENTE Rogelio 1936 **[8]**

▱ **$3 780** - €4 205 - **£2 520** - FF27 580
Interior de invernadero Oleo/lienzo (73x54.5cm 28x21in) Madrid 2000

PUEYRREDON Prilidiano P. 1823-1870 **[4]**

▱ **$120 000** - €132 228 - **£79 812** - FF867 360
Viejo pescador en la ribera Oleo/lienzo (80x105cm 31x41in) Buenos-Aires 2000

PUGA Antonio 1602-1648 **[1]**

▱ **$28 600** - €33 036 - **£19 800** - FF216 700
Vieja hilandera Oleo/lienzo (137x98cm 53x38in) Madrid 2000

PUGET Pierre 1620-1694 **[15]**

▱ **$97 129** - €104 260 - **£65 000** - FF683 904
Harbour Scene with a Man, Lighthouse/Harbour Scene, a Man, Elephant Oil/copper (32x42cm 12x16in) London 2000

▱ **$23 328** - €27 441 - **£16 722** - FF180 000
Navire de guerre aux armes de France Encre (27.5x41.5cm 10x16in) Paris 2001

PUGH Clifton Ernest 1924-1990 **[245]**

▱ **$5 935** - €5 441 - **£3 672** - FF35 689
The Shooting of the Wild Dogs Oil/canvas (89x242.5cm 35x95in) Melbourne 1998

▱ **$5 828** - €5 480 - **£3 609** - FF35 947
The Famous Wombat Oil/board (64.5x54.5cm 25x21in) Melbourne 1999

▱ **$627** - €712 - **£442** - FF4 669
Reclining Nude Oil/canvas (41x31cm 16x12in) Sydney 2001

▱ **$597** - €623 - **£376** - FF4 088
Shearing Quarters Watercolour, gouache/paper (53x72cm 20x28in) Sydney 2000

▱ **$146** - €138 - **£88** - FF906
Leda & the Swan I & II Color lithograph (32x52.5cm 12x20in) Sydney 1999

PUGH David Darwin 1946-1994 **[72]**

▱ **$1 029** - €865 - **£605** - FF5 671
Hector Lake Oil/canvas (91x121cm 36x48in) Calgary, Alberta 1999

PUGHE Buddig Anwylini 1857-? **[3]**

▱ **$1 179** - €1 306 - **£800** - FF8 569
Hedgerow Blossoms Watercolour (57.5x42cm 22x16in) Billingshurst, West-Sussex 2000

PUGI G. XIX-XX **[44]**

▱ **$11 819** - €13 138 - **£8 268** - FF86 178
Dame tenant un flambeau dans la main Marbre (H158cm H62in) Antwerpen 2001

▱ **$1 590** - €1 495 - **£1 000** - FF9 808
Bust of a Young Lady with Bow Bonnet Alabaster (H38cm H14in) Co. Kilkenny 1999

PUGIN Augustus Charles 1769-1832 **[11]**

▱ **$940** - €919 - **£600** - FF6 026
View of Twickenham Pencil (17x31cm 6x12in) London 1999

PUGLIESE LEVI Clemente 1855-1936 **[12]**

▱ **$2 000** - €2 073 - **£1 200** - FF13 600
Tramonto Olio/tela (54x82cm 21x32in) Vercelli 1999

▱ **$260** - €3 680 - **£2 130** - FF24 140
Prime nevi Olio/tavola (32x45.5cm 12x17in) Vercelli 1999

PUHLMANN Rico 1934-1996 **[15]**

▱ **$908** - €882 - **£565** - FF5 785
Modell Schwabe, San Francisco Vintage gelatin silver print (30x24.2cm 11x9in) Berlin 1999

PUHONNY Victor 1838-1909 **[22]**

▱ **$1 425** - €1 617 - **£1 021** - FF11 000
Chemin en sous-bois Huile/toile (37x54cm 14x21in) Paris 2001

▱ **$1 420** - €1 524 - **£950** - FF10 000
Clair de lune sur la rivière Huile/toile (24x41cm 9x16in) Epinal 2000

PUIFORCAT Jean 1897-1945 **[3]**

▱ **$35 000** - €37 569 - **£23 422** - FF246 435
Coffee and Tea Service for Tray Metal (15x86.5cm 5x34in) New-York 2000

PUIG RODA Gabriel 1865-1919 **[31]**

▱ **$25 925** - €25 528 - **£16 150** - FF167 450
Amigas pero rivales Oleo/lienzo (50x35cm 19x13in) Madrid 1999

▱ **$7 863** - €8 930 - **£5 500** - FF58 579
Recogiendo uvas (picking grapes) Oil/panel (36.5x21.5cm 14x8in) London 2001

▱ **$7 560** - €8 409 - **£5 320** - FF55 160
Dama zaragozana Acuarela/papel (65x43cm 25x16in) Madrid 2001

PUIG Y PERUCHO Bonaventura 1886-1977 **[17]**

▱ **$3 420** - €2 860 - **£2 042** - FF18 762
La pinada Oleo/lienzo (120x97.5cm 47x38in) Madrid 1998

▱ **$448** - €481 - **£296** - FF3 152
Arboles Oleo/tabla (33x24cm 12x9in) Barcelona 2000

PUIGAUDEAU du Ferdinand Loyen 1864-1930 **[259]**

▱ **$32 238** - €37 117 - **£22 000** - FF243 471
Barques de pêche au soleil couchant Oil/canvas (100x129.5cm 39x50in) London 2000

▱ **$21 534** - €19 935 - **£13 000** - FF130 765
Blowing Bubbles Oil/canvas (50x65cm 19x25in) London 1999

▱ **$6 995** - €7 622 - **£4 585** - FF50 000
Barques sous voiles près de la chaumière au soleil couchant Huile/panneau (19x60cm 7x23in) Brest 2000

▱ **$2 840** - €3 250 - **£1 900** - FF220 000
Barque en Brière, soleil couchant Aquarelle/papier (28.5x45cm 11x17in) Nantes 2000

PUIGDENGOLAS BARELLA Josep 1906-1987 **[33]**
- 🌐 **$6 050** - €6 607 - **£3 850** - FF43 340
  Costa de Mallorca Oleo/lienzo (46x55cm 18x21in) Madrid 2000
- 🌐 **$2 440** - €2 403 - **£1 520** - FF15 760
  Pollença, Mallorca Oleo/tablex (33x46cm 12x18in) Barcelona 1999
- 🎬 **$604** - €686 - **£419** - FF4 500
  «Balneario San Sebastian» Affiche (70x50cm 27x19in) Paris 2001

PUJOL de Abel 1787-1861 **[17]**
- ✏️ **$1 620** - €1 817 - **£1 100** - FF11 918
  Design for the Decoration of a Cupola in a Theatre Watercolour (29x29cm 11x11in) London 2000

PUJOL DE GUASTAVINO Clément 1850-1905 **[40]**
- 🌐 **$8 400** - €9 010 - **£5 700** - FF59 100
  Vendedor árabe Oleo/tabla (56x45cm 22x17in) Madrid 2001
- 🌐 **$4 250** - €4 178 - **£2 730** - FF27 406
  The Odalisque and the Musician Oil/panel (22x37.5cm 8x14in) New-York 1999
- ✏️ **$414** - €457 - **£287** - FF3 000
  Jeune fille au parc Aquarelle/papier (55x27.5cm 21x10in) Paris 2001

PUJOL Ernesto 1957/61 **[10]**
- 🌐 **$7 500** - €7 297 - **£4 616** - FF47 867
  Diez Indiecitos Acrylic (211x195.5cm 83x76in) New-York 1999
- 🌐 **$6 500** - €6 309 - **£4 046** - FF41 382
  Manos negras vendadas Oil/canvas (120.5x91cm 47x35in) New-York 1999
- 🌐 **$3 500** - €3 405 - **£2 154** - FF22 338
  Polyptych Oil/canvas (30x30cm 11x11in) New-York 1999

PUJOL Paul, Casimir-Paul 1848-? **[7]**
- ✏️ **$2 044** - €2 287 - **£1 378** - FF15 000
  La lettre d'amour Aquarelle, gouache/papier (56.5x39cm 22x15in) Orléans 2000

PULAKIS Teodoro c.1620-1692 **[13]**
- 🌐 **$119 000** - €123 362 - **£71 400** - FF809 200
  Mosè riceve le tavole della legge Tempera/tavola (60x78.5cm 23x30in) Venezia 1999

PULFORD Eric XX **[15]**
- 🎬 **$500** - €554 - **£339** - FF3 635
  «The Wages of Fear» Poster (101x76cm 40x30in) New-York 2000

PULHAM Peter Rose 1910-1956 **[8]**
- 📷 **$6 044** - €6 770 - **£4 200** - FF44 411
  Pablo Picasso in his Rue des Grands Augustins Studio Silver print (28.5x22.5cm 11x8in) London 2001

PULLER John Anthony XIX **[30]**
- 🌐 **$5 239** - €6 264 - **£3 600** - FF41 087
  A Spill in the Snow Oil/canvas (20x25.5cm 7x10in) Billingshurst, West-Sussex 2000

PULLICINO Alberto c.1719-c.1765 **[5]**
- 🌐 **$27 588** - €28 965 - **£17 385** - FF190 000
  Vue du fort Manoel et du port maltais de Marsamxett Huile/toile (59x128cm 23x50in) Tours 2000

PULLINEN Laila 1933 **[8]**
- 🔨 **$8 684** - €9 923 - **£6 112** - FF65 088
  Dans Bronze (H68.5cm H26in) Helsinki 2001

PULLINGER Herbert 1878-1970 **[8]**
- 🌐 **$5 000** - €4 309 - **£2 970** - FF28 264
  Bucks County Delaware River Landscape Oil/canvas (45x76cm 18x30in) Hatfield PA 1998
- 🎬 **$50** - €54 - **£33** - FF352
  Stone House on Street Corner Woodcut (16x13cm 6x5in) Hatfield PA 2000

PULZONE IL GAETANO Scipione c.1550-1598 **[5]**
- 🌐 **$30 000** - €27 175 - **£18 360** - FF178 254
  Portrait of a Noblewoman Oil/canvas (47x36cm 18x14in) Portland ME 1998

PUMMILL Robert 1936 **[11]**
- 🌐 **$17 090** - €19 406 - **£11 874** - FF127 294
  Crossing Pecos Country Oil/canvas (106x137cm 42x54in) Dallas TX 2001
- 🌐 **$6 087** - €6 911 - **£4 229** - FF45 336
  Choosin a Campsite Oil/canvas (76x116cm 30x46in) Dallas TX 2001

PÜMPIN Fritz 1901-1972 **[17]**
- 🌐 **$3 894** - €3 408 - **£2 358** - FF22 356
  Wintertag im Basler Rheinhafen Öl/Leinwand (50x60cm 19x23in) Zofingen 1998
- ✏️ **$1 676** - €1 880 - **£1 164** - FF12 332
  «Wehrwille» Chalks/paper (34x58cm 13x22in) Luzern 2001

PUN WOO XIX-XX **[3]**
- 🌐 **$9 500** - €10 796 - **£6 561** - FF70 817
  The L.Schep off Hong Kong Harbor Oil/canvas (63.5x86.5cm 25x34in) New-York 2000

PUNCT Carl Christoph ?-1765 **[1]**
- 🔨 **$3 028** - €3 579 - **£2 146** - FF23 477
  Figuren Porcelain (16x17.5cm 6x6in) Ahlden 2000

PUNT Johannes 1711-1779 **[4]**
- 🎬 **$1 000** - €1 119 - **£697** - FF7 342
  Tableaux des Galeries de l'Eglise des Jésuites d'Anvers, after Rubens Engraving (37.5x54cm 14x21in) New-York 2001

PUPINI Biagio dalle Lame 1511-1575 **[17]**
- 🌐 **$73 431** - €68 260 - **£45 000** - FF447 759
  The Madonna and Child appearing to Saint Petronius of Bologna Oil/panel (231x160cm 90x62in) London 1998
- 🌐 **$3 750** - €3 887 - **£2 250** - FF25 500
  Madonna e fedeli in preghiera Inchiostro (17x28cm 6x11in) Milano 2001

PUPPO Mario 1905-1977 **[13]**
- 🎬 **$485** - €503 - **£291** - FF3 298
  «Cesenatico» Affiche couleur (99x62cm 38x24in) Torino 2000

PURCELL Joseph Douglas 1927 **[10]**
- 🌐 **$504** - €592 - **£358** - FF3 886
  Marriots Cove, October, South Shore, Nova scotia Oil/masonite (71x91.5cm 27x36in) Toronto 2000

PURCELL Richard 1736-1766 **[2]**
- 🎬 **$1 122** - €1 257 - **£780** - FF8 247
  The Prodigal Son, Feasted on his Return/In Essex, after Le Clare Print (23.5x35.5cm 9x13in) Bury St.Edmunds, Suffolk 2001

PURCHAS Thomas James XIX-XX **[16]**
- 🌐 **$466** - €404 - **£283** - FF2 649
  Udsigt over walisisk landskab Oil/wood (23x29cm 9x11in) København 1998

PURDY Donald Roy 1924 **[30]**
- 🌐 **$600** - €503 - **£352** - FF3 302
  Woman with Violets Oil/board (50x60cm 20x24in) New-York 1998

P

PURGAU von Franz Michael 1677/78-c.1751 **[8]**
- $5 760 - €6 541 - **£3 942** - FF42 903
  Waldesgrund mit Distel, Frosch, Schnecke und Insekten Öl/Leinwand (46.5x35cm 18x13in) Wien 2000

PURICELLI GUERRA Giuseppe 1832-1894 **[11]**
- $4 800 - €6 220 - **£3 600** - FF40 800
  La solitudine del letterato Olio/tela (75x60cm 29x23in) Milano 2000

PURIFICATO Domenico 1915-1984 **[105]**
- $2 320 - €3 006 - **£1 740** - FF19 720
  La rissa Olio/tela (100x130cm 39x51in) Roma 2000
- $3 000 - €3 110 - **£1 800** - FF20 400
  Figura di profilo Olio/tela (70x50cm 27x19in) Roma 2000
- $1 440 - €1 866 - **£1 080** - FF12 240
  Natura morta Olio/tela (35x45cm 13x17in) Roma 2000
- $920 - €1 192 - **£690** - FF7 820
  Cavallo China (49.5x73cm 19x28in) Milano 2000

PURRMANN Hans 1880-1966 **[319]**
- $51 289 - €59 050 - **£35 000** - FF387 341
  Die Küste bei Sanary Oil/canvas (38x46.5cm 14x18in) London 2000
- $15 951 - €15 339 - **£9 843** - FF100 617
  Das Forum Romanum in Rom Öl/Karton (13x22.1cm 5x8in) Köln 1999
- $1 752 - €1 841 - **£1 105** - FF12 074
  Männlicher Akt beim Handstand Pencil/paper (37.5x28.5cm 14x11in) Stuttgart 2000
- $665 - €665 - **£416** - FF4 360
  Sechs badende Frauen am Strand (Badende) Etching (30.7x40.5cm 12x15in) Hamburg 1999

PURRMANN-HAUFLER Karl 1877-1966 **[42]**
- $716 - €613 - **£431** - FF4 024
  «Ecke in einem Schlosszimmer» Öl/Leinwand (61x68cm 24x26in) Stuttgart 1998

PURSALS FORMENT Joaquín c.1870-c.1942 **[3]**
- $84 000 - €72 078 - **£50 400** - FF472 800
  Purnevada de 1881, Barcelona Oleo/lienzo (121x195cm 47x76in) Madrid 1998

PURSELL Weimer 1906-1974 **[6]**
- $1 500 - €1 442 - **£925** - FF9 462
  «Chicago World's Fair» Poster (106x69.5cm 41x27in) New-York 1999

PURSER Sarah Henrietta 1848-1943 **[9]**
- $46 165 - €39 382 - **£27 512** - FF258 332
  Sitting in the Garden, Portrait in the Open Air Oil/canvas (91.5x71cm 36x27in) Dublin 1998
- $2 839 - €3 047 - **£1 899** - FF19 989
  Portrait of the Abbey Actress Helen Laird Pastel/paper (41.5x30.5cm 16x12in) Dublin 2000

PURSER William c.1790-c.1852 **[22]**
- $1 003 - €1 128 - **£700** - FF7 401
  Cape Colonna, Italy Watercolour (11x15cm 4x5in) London 2001

PURUNTATAMERI Stanislaus 1906-1987 **[5]**
- $1 709 - €1 654 - **£1 083** - FF10 850
  Purukapali Sculpture, wood (H64.5cm H25in) Malvern, Victoria 1999

PURVES-SMITH Peter Ch. Roderick 1912-1949 **[5]**
- $41 327 - €40 209 - **£25 434** - FF263 757
  Burke and Wills Oil/canvas (54x41cm 21x16in) Malvern, Victoria 1999

PURVIS John Milne 1888-1957 **[39]**
- $1 471 - €1 414 - **£900** - FF9 275
  «Camping Coaches, LNER» Poster (102x127cm 40x50in) London 1999

PURVIS Thomas G. XIX-XX **[11]**
- $2 281 - €2 556 - **£1 572** - FF16 769
  Hamburger Dampfer, Granada auf offener See Öl/Leinwand (59.5x90cm 23x35in) Hamburg 2000

PURY de Edmond Jean 1845-1911 **[36]**
- $505 - €589 - **£350** - FF3 866
  Profilporträt eines blondhaarigen Mädchens Oil/panel (34x24cm 13x9in) Bern 2000

PURYEAR Martin 1941 **[11]**
- $440 000 - €491 249 - **£294 096** - FF3 222 384
  Untitled Sculpture (147.5x147.5x24cm 58x58x9in) New-York 2000

PURYGIN Leonid 1951 **[10]**
- $5 691 - €6 613 - **£4 000** - FF43 376
  Surrealist Crucifixion Oil/canvas (43x39cm 16x15in) London 2001

PUSA Unto 1913-1973 **[21]**
- $1 718 - €1 682 - **£1 057** - FF11 032
  Kaatunut kelo Oil/canvas (60x90cm 23x35in) Helsinki 1999

PUSCH Richard 1912-1998 **[15]**
- $305 - €343 - **£212** - FF2 247
  «Der Luchberg im Osterzgebirge» Aquarell/Papier (33.3x44.5cm 13x17in) Berlin 2001

PUSHMAN Hovsep T. 1877-1966 **[61]**
- $30 000 - €27 175 - **£18 360** - FF178 254
  Charging into the Unknown Oil/panel (68x68cm 27x27in) Portland ME 1998
- $8 750 - €8 327 - **£5 473** - FF54 623
  Still Life of a Rose with an Asian Statue Oil/canvas (32x23cm 12x9in) New-York 1999
- $350 - €408 - **£243** - FF2 678
  «Meditation» Etching in colors (48x58cm 19x23in) Altadena CA 2000

PUSOLE Pierluigi 1963 **[17]**
- $3 250 - €3 369 - **£1 950** - FF22 100
  Levitobarca pac quattro Olio/tela (100x120cm 39x47in) Milano 1999
- $1 440 - €1 866 - **£1 080** - FF12 240
  Io sono Dio Olio/tavola (90x105cm 35x41in) Milano 2001

PUTHUFF Hanson Duvall 1875-1972 **[69]**
- $16 500 - €16 820 - **£10 338** - FF110 330
  Light and Air Oil/canvas (45x60cm 18x24in) Altadena CA 2000
- $6 500 - €7 584 - **£4 524** - FF49 745
  Foothill Landscape Oil/canvas/board (30x39cm 12x15in) Altadena CA 2000

PUTMAN Salliann 1937 **[7]**
- $2 678 - €2 575 - **£1 650** - FF16 893
  Red Still Life Oil/board (51x45.5cm 20x17in) London 1999
- $892 - €858 - **£550** - FF5 631
  Anemones Watercolour/paper (26.5x20.5cm 10x8in) London 1999

PUTNAM Arthur 1873-1930 **[16]**
- $8 000 - €7 609 - **£4 857** - FF49 912
  Leopard and Python Bronze (H18cm H7in) Beverly-Hills CA 1999

PUTOT Michel 1948 **[44]**
- $1 010 - €1 067 - **£668** - FF7 000
  Le trio Huile/toile (41x33cm 16x12in) Saint-Dié 2000

PUTTER de Pieter c.1600-1659 **[14]**
- $4 626 - €5 387 - £3 200 - FF35 338
A Fishmonger in his Shop Oil/panel (47x63cm 18x24in) London 2000

PÜTTNER Josef Carl Berthold 1821-1881 **[51]**
- $3 294 - €3 270 - £2 056 - FF21 451
Ruderboote im stürmischer Brandung Öl/Leinwand (69x100.5cm 27x39in) Wien 1999
- $1 641 - €1 952 - £1 170 - FF12 802
Lac au milieu de rochers Huile/panneau (19.5x31.5cm 7x12in) Warszawa 2000

PUTZ Leo 1869-1940 **[166]**
- $22 862 - €24 542 - £15 302 - FF160 987
Junges Leben Öl/Leinwand (100x130cm 39x51in) Stuttgart 2000
- $25 234 - €28 121 - £17 638 - FF184 464
Der Reigen, unter Bäumen am Seeufer spielt links ein junges Mädchen Öl/Leinwand (82x120cm 32x47in) München 2001
- $23 544 - €26 162 - £15 768 - FF171 612
Gusti Bennat II Öl/Leinwand (45x35cm 17x13in) Wien 2000
- $1 937 - €1 817 - £1 197 - FF11 917
Erotische Darstellung Charcoal (25.9x20.2cm 10x7in) Wien 1999
- $1 308 - €1 161 - £800 - FF7 617
«Moderne Galerie» Affiche couleur (108x80cm 42x31in) London 1999

PUTZ Ludwig 1866-? **[19]**
- $1 333 - €1 585 - £923 - FF10 397
Kavallerieüberfall Oil/panel (25x16cm 9x6in) München 2000

PÜTZHOFEN-HAMBÜCHEN Paul XIX-XX **[27]**
- $754 - €832 - £510 - FF5 456
Kanalparti Oil/canvas (37x50cm 14x19in) Vejle 2000

PUVIS DE CHAVANNES Pierre 1824-1898 **[249]**
- $35 958 - €29 728 - £21 099 - FF195 000
Le sommeil Huile/toile (62x103cm 24x40in) Versailles 1998
- $1 818 - €1 738 - £1 139 - FF11 403
Dorfansicht mit Ruinen Oil/panel (11.5x17.5cm 4x6in) Hamburg 1999
- $2 000 - €1 966 - £1 285 - FF12 895
A Study of Figures Charcoal/paper (26x17cm 10x6in) New-York 1999
- $355 - €305 - £214 - FF2 000
«Galerie Rapp» Affiche (145x91cm 57x35in) Paris 1998

PUY Jean 1876-1960 **[296]**
- $6 648 - €6 403 - £4 107 - FF42 000
Le port de Douëlan Huile/carton (37.5x54.5cm 14x21in) Paris 1999
- $1 482 - €1 378 - £900 - FF9 038
Nature morte avec vase bleu Oil/canvas (28x35.5cm 11x13in) London 1998
- $635 - €686 - £439 - FF4 500
Port de pêche Crayons couleurs/papier (15x21cm 5x8in) Paris 2001

PUYET José 1926 **[28]**
- $1 170 - €1 351 - £810 - FF8 865
El torero Oleo/lienzo (81x65cm 31x25in) Madrid 2001

PUYL van der Gérard, Louis Fr. 1750-1824 **[12]**
- $9 618 - €9 076 - £5 934 - FF59 532
Martinus Carolus van Beurden (1753-1788) & his Wife L.T van Beurden Oil/panel (48.5x37cm 19x14in) Amsterdam 1999

PUYO Constant Emile Joac. 1857-1933 **[33]**
- $1 233 - €1 143 - £762 - FF7 500
Femme voilée en bord de mer Photo (26.4x36cm 10x14in) Paris 1999

PY Jan 1921 **[26]**
- $2 113 - €2 287 - £1 447 - FF15 000
Allée des bordages - Rêve en forêt de Compiègne Huile/toile (65x81cm 25x31in) Compiègne 2001

PYALL Henry 1795-1833 **[3]**
- $362 - €412 - £250 - FF2 700
The Most Infernal Bad Egg Aquatint (28x21.5cm 11x8in) London 2000

PYBOURNE Thomas 1708-c.1734 **[1]**
- $41 483 - €39 657 - £26 000 - FF260 130
Racehorses watering at a Through Oil/canvas (125.5x103cm 49x40in) London 1999

PYE Patrick 1929 **[14]**
- $944 - €914 - £582 - FF5 996
At the Window Pastel/paper (32x21.5cm 12x8in) Dublin 1999

PYE William, Will XIX-XX **[36]**
- $2 706 - €3 003 - £1 800 - FF19 696
The Fishing Fleet Making Sail at Dusk Oil/canvas (67x160cm 26x62in) London 2000
- $151 - €160 - £100 - FF1 047
Flotilla in the Bay Oil/board (13x25cm 5x10in) Dorchester, Dorset 2000
- $301 - €293 - £190 - FF1 919
The Morning after the Gale Watercolour/paper (20x49cm 8x19in) London 1999

PYK Madeleine 1934 **[476]**
- $1 755 - €2 005 - £1 236 - FF13 152
Min familj Oil/canvas (100x135cm 39x53in) Stockholm 2001
- $809 - €940 - £576 - FF5 306
Tigerhuvud Oil/canvas (61x50cm 24x19in) Stockholm 2001
- $579 - €571 - £356 - FF3 748
Landskap med kvinnor och djur Oil/canvas (42x29cm 16x11in) Stockholm 1999
- $283 - €280 - £174 - FF1 835
Hästar Indian ink (51x65cm 20x25in) Stockholm 1999
- $246 - €212 - £148 - FF1 392
«Stockholm» Color lithograph (41x47cm 16x18in) Malmö 1998

PYKE Guelda 1905-1994 **[20]**
- $1 050 - €1 158 - £698 - FF7 594
Reclining Nude Watercolour (51x71cm 20x27in) Melbourne 2000

PYLE Arnold 1908 **[33]**
- $200 - €194 - £123 - FF1 273
Farmyard with Hogs Watercolour/paper (27x32cm 11x12in) Cedar-Falls IA 1999

PYLE Howard 1853-1911 **[25]**
- $37 500 - €34 621 - £23 062 - FF227 096
Colonies & Nation, Part 6 Oil/canvas (61x40.5cm 24x15in) New-York 1999
- $8 000 - €8 755 - £5 518 - FF57 430
«Sorrow» Oil/board (20.5x29cm 8x11in) New-York 2001
- $5 500 - €6 411 - £3 808 - FF42 055
Twilight Land Ink (24x33cm 9x13in) New-York 2000

PYNACKER Adam 1622-1673 **[25]**
- $22 814 - €25 916 - £15 963 - FF170 000
Vue de la côte méditerranéenne Huile/toile (85x107cm 33x42in) Paris 2001

P

$137 248 - €163 616 - £97 856 - FF1 073 248
Vor Abfahrt der Schiffe im Hafen Oil/panel
(33x46cm 12x18in) Köln 2000

PYNAS Jacob Symonsz c.1585-c.1640 **[10]**
$5 416 - €5 814 - £3 624 - FF38 136
Die Bekehrung des Saulus Oil/panel (55.5x58.5cm
21x23in) Wien 2000
$11 599 - €11 537 - £7 200 - FF75 680
**Crucifixion with the Virgin Mary and Saint John
the Evangelist** Oil/copper (25x18cm 9x7in) London
1999

PYNAS Jan Symonsz 1583/84-1631 **[11]**
$1 494 - €1 604 - £1 000 - FF10 521
Jospeh Distributing the Corn Ink (20x15cm 7x5in)
London 2000

PYNE Charles XIX-XX **[16]**
$254 - €295 - £180 - FF1 937
A Figure on a Moorland Track Watercolour
(23x39cm 9x15in) London 2000

PYNE Ganesh 1937 **[86]**
$23 908 - €25 664 - £16 000 - FF168 345
The Bird Tempera/canvas (48x46cm 18x18in) London
2000
$4 869 - €4 680 - £3 000 - FF30 699
Untitled Tempera (43x35cm 16x13in) London 1999
$5 292 - €4 950 - £3 200 - FF32 472
Festival Pencil (28.5x30cm 11x11in) London 1999

PYNE George 1800-1884 **[75]**
$1 497 - €1 453 - £950 - FF9 529
The First Court, Magdalene College, Cambridge
Watercolour/paper (23.5x32.5cm 9x13in) London 1999

PYNE James Baker 1800-1870 **[149]**
$18 497 - €21 491 - £13 000 - FF140 974
Heidelburg on the Neckar Oil/canvas (91.5x143cm
36x56in) London 2001
$3 605 - €3 984 - £2 500 - FF26 132
**Recollections of the Lago Maggiore, Market Day
at Pallanza** Oil/canvas (61x84cm 24x33in) London
2001
$725 - €817 - £500 - FF5 362
Near the Mumbles, South Wales Watercolour
(35.5x53cm 13x20in) Newbury, Berkshire 2000

PYNE Robert Lorrdine 1856-1905 **[3]**
$1 100 - €1 141 - £697 - FF7 487
The White House Across the Meadow Oil/board
(26.5x31.5cm 10x12in) Boston MA 2000

PYNE Thomas 1843-1935 **[72]**
$484 - €451 - £300 - FF2 957
Dedham Lock Watercolour/paper (17x24.5cm 6x9in)
Billingshurst, West-Sussex 1999

PYNE William Henry 1769-1843 **[20]**
$2 238 - €2 156 - £1 400 - FF14 141
**Figures in the Street, Le Puy, Clermont-Ferrand,
France** Watercolour (12x17.5cm 4x6in) London 1999
$4 800 - €4 444 - £2 977 - FF29 151
The History of the Royal Residences Aquatint
(37.5x27cm 14x10in) New-York 1999

PYYKKÖ Kimmo 1940 **[14]**
$336 - €320 - £206 - FF2 096
Ryhmäpäällikkö Bronze (H19.5cm H7in) Helsinki
1999

Q

QI BAISHI 1863-1957 **[394]**
$7 500 - €8 050 - £5 019 - FF52 807
Dragonfly and Begonia Ink (136.5x44.5cm 53x17in)
San-Francisco CA 2000

QI GONG 1912 **[6]**
$2 574 - €2 441 - £1 566 - FF16 012
Calligraphy in Xing Shu Ink/paper (28.5x86.5cm
11x34in) Hong-Kong 1999

QI KUN 1901-1944 **[5]**
$3 612 - €3 390 - £2 231 - FF22 234
Lady after Tang Yin Ink/paper (99x28cm 38x11in)
Hong-Kong 1999

QIAN DU 1763-1844 **[21]**
$3 589 - €4 219 - £2 489 - FF27 675
Boating in Autumn Ink (97.5x27cm 38x10in) Hong-
Kong 2000

QIAN FENG 1740-1795 **[2]**
$8 346 - €9 159 - £5 375 - FF60 079
Returning Home Ink/paper (120.5x73.5cm 47x28in)
Hong-Kong 1999

QIAN GU 1508-c.1574 **[2]**
$5 934 - €5 596 - £3 680 - FF36 708
Landscape Ink (29x27.5cm 11x10in) Hong-Kong
1999

QIAN HUI'AN 1833-1910 **[6]**
$2 658 - €2 556 - £1 640 - FF16 769
Zhong Kui und Drache Indian ink/paper (46.8x29cm
18x11in) Stuttgart 1999

QIAN SHOUTIE 1896-1967 **[6]**
$2 307 - €2 621 - £1 620 - FF17 195
Peony in Ink Ink/paper (68x59cm 26x23in) Hong-
Kong 2001

QIAN SONGYAN 1898-1985 **[15]**
$1 926 - €2 114 - £1 240 - FF13 864
Landscape Ink (132x46.5cm 51x18in) Hong-Kong
2000

QIAN WEICHENG 1720-1772 **[3]**
$14 190 - €13 317 - £8 767 - FF87 351
Sparrows among Magnolia Blossoms Ink
(62x289cm 24x113in) Hong-Kong 1999

QIAN XUAN 1235-c.1300 **[2]**
$51 280 - €60 272 - £35 560 - FF395 360
Two Lotus Seedpods on One Stalk Ink/paper
(25x88cm 9x34in) Hong-Kong 2000

QIAN YONG 1759-1844 **[1]**
$6 450 - €6 083 - £4 000 - FF39 900
Calligraphy Couplet in Li Shu Ink (132x29cm
51x11in) Hong-Kong 1999

QIANLONG Emperor c.1736-1796 **[39]**
$14 214 - €12 133 - £8 500 - FF79 588
**Scene of Gathering of Mandarins in a Palace
Interior** Painting (72x46cm 28x18in) London 1998
$9 713 - €10 427 - £6 500 - FF68 394
White Jade Flattened Vase and Cover Sculpture
(H17cm H6in) London 2001
$12 563 - €14 272 - £8 820 - FF93 619
Poem in running Script Calligraphy Ink
(170x52.5cm 66x20in) Hong-Kong 2001

QINNUAYUAK Lucy 1915-1982 **[21]**
$371 - €317 - £221 - FF2 077
Joyful Mothers Engraving (43x61cm 17x24in)
Vancouver, BC. 1998

QIU SHIHUA 1940 **[2]**
- $5 814 - €6 601 - **£4 085** - FF43 301
  Morning mist over the River Oil/panel (72.5x103cm 28x40in) Taipei 2001

QIU TI Schudy 1906-1958 **[3]**
- $39 360 - €41 911 - **£24 960** - FF274 920
  Tulips Oil/canvas (60x49.5cm 23x19in) Taipei 2000
- $26 569 - €24 623 - **£16 518** - FF161 515
  Camellia Oil/canvas (39.5x39.5cm 15x15in) Taipei 1999

QIU YACAI Chiu Ya-Tsai 1949 **[7]**
- $14 102 - €15 892 - **£9 856** - FF104 247
  Lady in Pink Oil/canvas (129.5x96cm 50x37in) Hong-Kong 2001

QIU YING c.1495-1552 **[10]**
- $44 870 - €50 972 - **£31 500** - FF334 355
  Playing Chess Ink (84.5x41cm 33x16in) Hong-Kong 2001

QU LEILEI 1951 **[2]**
- $3 409 - €2 847 - **£2 000** - FF18 674
  Facing the World Mixed media/paper (140x114cm 55x44in) London 1998

QU YIN-AN 1944 **[3]**
- $550 - €570 - **£330** - FF3 740
  La peonia della ricchezza Acquarello (68.5x45cm 26x17in) Prato 2000

QU ZHAOLING XIX **[3]**
- $6 435 - €6 103 - **£3 915** - FF40 030
  Spring Season Ink (119x53cm 46x20in) Hong-Kong 1999

QUADAL Martin Ferdinand 1736-1808 **[12]**
- $3 750 - €3 823 - **£2 349** - FF25 075
  A Red and White Spaniel, with Dead Game in a Landscape Oil/canvas (76x101.5cm 29x39in) New-York 2000

QUADRONE Giovanni Battista 1844-1898 **[32]**
- $24 150 - €25 035 - **£14 490** - FF164 220
  L'inverno in Sardegna Olio/tela (21.5x35cm 8x13in) Roma 1999
- $500 - €518 - **£300** - FF3 400
  Scena sarda China (16x13cm 6x5in) Vercelli 2000

QUAEDVLIEG Carel Max Gerlach 1823-1874 **[20]**
- $18 000 - €21 168 - **£12 906** - FF138 850
  Fontana del Tritone, piazza Barberini, Rome Oil/canvas (72x65cm 28x25in) New-York 2001
- $3 237 - €3 113 - **£1 997** - FF20 418
  Römische Landschaft mit Badenden Öl/Leinwand (19.9x34cm 7x13in) Bern 1999

QUAGLINO Massimo 1899-1982 **[43]**
- $1 500 - €1 555 - **£900** - FF10 200
  Fiori alla finestra Olio/tela (60x50cm 23x19in) Torino 1999
- $3 500 - €3 628 - **£2 100** - FF23 800
  Paesaggio del Monferrato Olio/tela (31.5x38cm 12x14in) Torino 2001
- $220 - €285 - **£165** - FF1 870
  Nuda sulla dormeuse Carboncino/carta (29.5x41.5cm 11x16in) Torino 2000

QUAGLIO Domenico 1787-1837 **[77]**
- $32 441 - €33 234 - **£20 020** - FF218 003
  Südwestansicht der Kathedrale in Reims Öl/Leinwand (101x136cm 39x53in) Düsseldorf 2000
- $14 606 - €13 294 - **£9 128** - FF87 201
  Innenansicht der St.Sebald-Kirche in Nürnberg Oil/panel (72.5x62cm 28x24in) München 1999

- $2 506 - €2 812 - **£1 737** - FF18 446
  Die Begegnung Oil/panel (33x28cm 12x11in) München 2000
- $911 - €1 022 - **£631** - FF6 707
  Südostansicht der Liebfrauenkirche in München Ink (17.5x12.1cm 6x4in) München 2000
- $152 - €164 - **£102** - FF1 073
  Gotischer Klosterhof Lithographie (53x43cm 20x16in) Königstein 2000

QUAGLIO Franz 1844-1920 **[89]**
- $3 826 - €3 270 - **£2 247** - FF21 447
  Vor dem Zirkus Oil/panel (27x36cm 10x14in) Stuttgart 1998
- $1 133 - €970 - **£682** - FF6 364
  Elegante Reiterin auf einem Schimmel Watercolour, gouache (9.5x7cm 3x2in) München 1998

QUAGLIO Lorenzo II 1793-1869 **[44]**
- $26 238 - €30 678 - **£18 438** - FF201 234
  Lustige Gesellschaft mit Blaskapelle vor Wirtshaus im Oberland Öl/Leinwand (43x55cm 16x21in) München 2000
- $8 904 - €8 181 - **£5 470** - FF53 662
  Der Rosenkavalier Öl/Leinwand (25x32cm 9x12in) Stuttgart 1999
- $477 - €409 - **£287** - FF2 682
  Ein Bauer aus Lenggries Pencil/paper (24.2x20.1cm 9x7in) Köln 1998

QUANTIN Henry 1865-1939 **[12]**
- $3 408 - €3 966 - **£2 432** - FF26 016
  Vue de la forêt de Soignes en été Huile/toile (60x80cm 23x31in) Bruxelles 2001

QUARENGHI Giacomo 1744-1817 **[11]**
- $6 500 - €6 738 - **£3 900** - FF44 200
  Elaborato cortile ottagono con figure Inchiostro (29.5x42.5cm 11x16in) Milano 2001

QUAREZ Michel 1938 **[4]**
- $1 000 - €853 - **£603** - FF5 596
  «St. Denis» Poster (310.5x231cm 122x90in) New-York 1998

QUARTI MARCHIO Ernesto 1907-1982 **[13]**
- $1 200 - €1 555 - **£900** - FF10 200
  La modella del pittore Olio/tela (60x50cm 23x19in) Milano 2001

QUARTLEY Arthur 1839-1886 **[28]**
- $8 000 - €8 775 - **£5 433** - FF57 560
  Beached Sailing Vessel with Ship under Sail in Background Oil/canvas (33x60cm 13x24in) Williamsburg MA 2000
- $1 200 - €1 119 - **£744** - FF7 339
  Fishermen on a Barge Oil/canvas (36.5x28.5cm 14x11in) New-York 1999

QUARTO Andrea 1959 **[45]**
- $750 - €777 - **£450** - FF5 100
  «Palme fantastiche» Olio/tela (80x70cm 31x27in) Vercelli 2001
- $375 - €389 - **£225** - FF2 550
  Villaggio fantastico Olio/tela (40x30cm 15x11in) Vercelli 2001

QUAST Pieter Jansz 1606-1647 **[80]**
- $9 188 - €7 778 - **£5 500** - FF51 020
  Elegant Company Making Music Oil/panel (45x61.5cm 17x24in) London 1998
- $2 636 - €2 496 - **£1 639** - FF16 371
  An old Lady drinking Oil/panel (16.5x12cm 6x4in) Amsterdam 1999

Q

$1 100 - €1 177 - **£750** - FF7 718
Standing Man facing Right and a standing Man facing Left Pencil (21x16cm 8x6in) New-York 2001

QUASTLER Gertrude 1909-1963 **[43]**

$55 - €47 - **£33** - FF311
«Young Bird - Old Vine» Woodcut (51x28cm 20x11in) Pittsburgh PA 1998

QUATREMAINE William Wells XIX-XX **[11]**

$150 - €152 - **£93** - FF996
Church Doorway Watercolour/paper (15x21cm 6x8in) Bloomfield-Hills MI 2000

QUATTROCIOCCHI Domenico 1874-1941 **[7]**

$4 600 - €4 769 - **£2 760** - FF31 280
Piazza Navona Olio/legno (31x37cm 12x14in) Roma 1999

QUAYLE E. Christian XIX-XX **[16]**

$1 673 - €1 968 - **£1 200** - FF12 910
The red Pier, Douglas, Isle of Man Watercolour/paper (24x34cm 9x13in) Cheshire 2001

QUEJIDO Manolo 1946 **[5]**

$5 600 - €6 006 - **£3 800** - FF39 400
«Nayade I» Oleo/lienzo (100x100cm 39x39in) Madrid 2001

QUELLINUS Erasmus I c.1584-c1640 **[1]**

$15 295 - €17 490 - **£10 500** - FF114 726
Fruitwood group of St. Joseph and The Infant Christ Sculpture, wood (H45cm H17in) London 2000

QUELLINUS Erasmus II 1607-1678 **[42]**

$15 083 - €12 833 - **£9 000** - FF84 180
Infant Pyrrhus at the Court of Glaucias/Dido Supervising the cutting Oil/copper (67.5x91.5cm 26x36in) London 1998

$5 424 - €6 098 - **£3 808** - FF40 000
Les sénateurs apprenant à Cincinnatus sa nomination de consul Huile/cuivre (31x31cm 12x12in) Grenoble 2001

$2 893 - €3 270 - **£1 953** - FF21 451
Fries mit den Allegorien des Glaubens, der Liebe Black chalk (21.4x41cm 8x16in) Wien 2000

QUELLINUS Jan Erasmus Ceder 1634-1715 **[5]**

$40 000 - €35 086 - **£24 288** - FF230 152
The Holy Family with Saint Anne Oil/canvas (202x284cm 79x111in) New-York 1999

$4 777 - €5 336 - **£3 237** - FF35 000
La Vierge à l'Enfant Huile/panneau (86x64.5cm 33x25in) Paris 2000

QUENDRAY A. XIX-XX **[14]**

$200 - €229 - **£137** - FF1 500
«Parc de la Bedoyere, Garches» Affiche (107x77cm 42x30in) Paris 2000

QUENIOUX Gustave Fr. Raoul 1865-1949 **[2]**

$9 000 - €8 583 - **£5 478** - FF56 303
Apollo and the Nine Muses Oil/canvas (120x99cm 47x38in) New-York 1999

QUENTIN Bernard 1923 **[418]**

$236 - €259 - **£156** - FF1 700
Signes épiques Gouache/papier (24x32cm 9x12in) Paris 2000

QUENTIN Laurence XX **[11]**

$132 - €152 - **£91** - FF1 000
Félin pour l'autre Aquarelle (18x24cm 7x9in) Paris 2000

QUERALT Jaume 1949 **[61]**

$487 - €452 - **£300** - FF2 962
Composición Oleo/lienzo (72x91cm 28x35in) Madrid 1998

$617 - €572 - **£380** - FF3 752
«Las III poupées» Pastel/papier (75x110cm 29x43in) Madrid 1998

QUERENA Luigi 1820-1887 **[11]**

$12 750 - €13 217 - **£7 650** - FF86 700
La Laguna di Venezia Olio/tela (22x53cm 8x20in) Genova 2000

QUERFURT August 1698-1761 **[86]**

$5 285 - €5 087 - **£3 304** - FF33 369
Reitergefecht Öl/Leinwand (37x58cm 14x22in) Wien 1999

$3 478 - €4 090 - **£2 493** - FF26 831
Ein Reiter spricht mit einem Pferdeknecht Oil/panel (23.5x32cm 9x12in) Stuttgart 2001

QUERFURT Tobias ?-c.1776 **[3]**

$6 400 - €7 267 - **£4 380** - FF47 670
«Die Befreiungsschlacht von Wien 1683» Öl/Leinwand (53.5x75cm 21x29in) Wien 2000

QUERNER Curt 1904-1976 **[63]**

$1 714 - €1 841 - **£1 147** - FF12 074
Schneeschmelze im Erzgebirge Aquarell/Papier (39x57cm 15x22in) Zwiesel 2000

QUERVAIN de Daniel 1937 **[48]**

$104 - €88 - **£61** - FF574
«Stille nach dem Sturm» Etching (32.2x49.5cm 12x19in) Bern 1998

QUESNEL François 1543-1619 **[1]**

$21 000 - €22 495 - **£14 340** - FF147 558
Portrait of a Man Wearing a Ruff Coloured chalks (30.5x20.5cm 12x8in) New-York 2001

QUEST Charles Francis 1904-1993 **[19]**

$300 - €350 - **£214** - FF2 295
Two Figures/Abstract Woodcut (30x22cm 12x9in) St. Louis MO 2000

QUESTA della Francesco c.1639-1724 **[8]**

$29 602 - €27 616 - **£17 860** - FF181 146
Natura morta con frutta e fiori Öl/Leinwand (66x81cm 25x31in) Wien 1999

QUETGLAS Matías 1946 **[3]**

$2 500 - €2 592 - **£1 500** - FF17 000
Pasión y melancolia n.3 Pastelli/carta (39x32.5cm 15x12in) Prato 2000

QUEVERDO François 1748-1797 **[11]**

$2 500 - €2 167 - **£1 527** - FF14 217
The Three Graces Carrying Cupid in a Basket Gouache/paper (32.5x23.5cm 12x9in) New-York 1999

QUIBEL Raymond 1883-1978 **[99]**

$907 - €1 021 - **£637** - FF6 700
Paysage de neige Huile/toile (65x92cm 25x36in) Garches 2001

$1 222 - €1 143 - **£740** - FF7 500
Montmartre et son moulin Huile/panneau (36x28cm 14x11in) Chartres 1999

QUIDOR John 1801-1881 **[2]**

$120 000 - €102 526 - **£72 036** - FF672 528
The Money Diggers Oil/canvas (68.5x86.5cm 26x34in) New-York 1998

QUIESSE Claude 1938 **[47]**

$617 - €534 - **£373** - FF3 500
Ange bleu Huile/toile (41x33cm 16x12in) Le Havre 1998

QUIGLEY Daniel XVIII [6]
- **$30 431** - €33 603 - **£21 000** - FF220 418
  The Godolphin Arabian Oil/canvas (100x125.5cm 39x49in) Crewkerne, Somerset 2001
- **$15 622** - €15 289 - **£10 000** - FF100 287
  A Bay Racehorse with his Jockey on a Racecourse Oil/canvas (78x110cm 30x43in) London 1999

QUIGLEY Edward B. 1895-1986 [52]
- **$1 700** - €1 683 - **£1 058** - FF11 042
  Small Town General Store Oil/canvas/board (55x71cm 22x28in) Portland OR 1999
- **$850** - €842 - **£529** - FF5 521
  John Day River about 20 Miles from Dayville Ore Oil/canvas/board (30x40cm 12x16in) Portland OR 1999
- **$200** - €211 - **£132** - FF1 385
  Two Pirates Sword Fighting on a Beach Watercolour/paper (16x23cm 6x9in) Portland OR 2000

QUIGLEY Edward W. 1898-1977 [52]
- **$2 200** - €1 846 - **£1 290** - FF12 107
  Abstraction of Wheel Spokes Gelatin silver print (16x12cm 6x4in) New-York 1998

QUIGNON Fernand 1854-1941 [39]
- **$1 028** - €991 - **£633** - FF6 500
  Dorf in hügeliger Landschaft Öl/Leinwand (42.5x46cm 16x18in) Bern 1999
- **$685** - €640 - **£422** - FF4 500
  Champ de blé Huile/toile (16x26.5cm 6x10in) Brest 1999

QUILICI Jean-Claude 1920 [45]
- **$1 579** - €1 326 - **£928** - FF8 700
  Printemps au village Huile/toile (46x61cm 18x24in) Aubagne 1998

QUILICI Pancho 1954 [18]
- **$12 076** - €11 277 - **£7 548** - FF73 970
  Sin título Oleo/lienzo (64.5x202.5cm 25x79in) Caracas 1999
- **$496** - €473 - **£310** - FF3 100
  Elucubraciones Técnica mixta (20x20cm 7x7in) Caracas 1999
- **$442** - €381 - **£260** - FF2 496
  Presencias Lineales, Agua de Mayo Aguafuerte (44.5x61cm 17x24in) Caracas 1998

QUILLERY Roger 1914-1991 [177]
- **$61** - €73 - **£42** - FF480
  Maisons aux toits rouges Huile/carton (34x42cm 13x16in) Melun 2000

QUILLIVIC Raymond Louis 1942 [31]
- **$284** - €305 - **£190** - FF2 000
  Bigouden Gouache/papier (27x27cm 10x10in) Douarnenez 2000

QUILLIVIC René 1879-1969 [53]
- **$1 153** - €1 372 - **£850** - FF480
  Le thonier blanc Huile/carton (40x52cm 15x20in) Brest 2000
- **$3 740** - €4 269 - **£2 598** - FF28 000
  Femme d'Audierne Plâtre (70x22x18cm 27x8x7in) Brest 2000
- **$345** - €335 - **£213** - FF2 200
  La prière du soir Gravure bois (31x23cm 12x9in) Brest 1999

QUILP XIX [3]
- **$8 021** - €8 083 - **£5 000** - FF53 018
  Modern Game Cocks trimmed and spurred Oil/canvas (53x43cm 20x16in) London 2000

- **$2 689** - €2 887 - **£1 800** - FF18 938
  King Henry, Champion of the Marches, Modern Game Cock Trimmed, Spurred Oil/board (33.5x24.5cm 13x9in) London 2000

QUINAUX Joseph 1822-1895 [50]
- **$1 800** - €1 781 - **£1 122** - FF11 680
  L'emblève Oleo/tabla (37x55cm 14x21in) Buenos-Aires 1999
- **$825** - €793 - **£518** - FF5 203
  Village au bord de l'église Huile/toile (25x40cm 9x15in) Bruxelles 1999

QUINET Achille 1831-1900 [38]
- **$992** - €838 - **£590** - FF5 500
  Le tonnelier Tirage albuminé (18.9x24.6cm 7x9in) Chartres 1998

QUINET Adèle XIX [1]
- **$4 457** - €4 269 - **£2 805** - FF28 000
  Nature morte aux raisins et grenades Huile/toile (24.5x32cm 9x12in) Paris 1999

QUINETTE Jean-Claude XX [69]
- **$140** - €152 - **£96** - FF1 000
  Les grandes marées au large de Granville Aquarelle/papier (18x55cm 7x21in) Coutances 2001

QUINKHARD Jan Maurits 1688-1772 [7]
- **$11 505** - €10 891 - **£7 154** - FF71 438
  Two Gentlemen and a Clerk conversing over an architectural Plan Oil/canvas (99x114cm 38x44in) Amsterdam 1999
- **$4 694** - €3 967 - **£2 800** - FF26 022
  Portrait of a Seated Gentleman, Holding a Letter Oil/panel (36.5x32cm 14x12in) London 1999

QUINN Anthony 1915 [16]
- **$90** - €95 - **£60** - FF600
  «Lady from Crete» Print in colors (66x41cm 26x16in) Portland OR 2001

QUINN Edward 1920-1997 [13]
- **$1 205** - €1 377 - **£850** - FF9 032
  Grace Kelly Gelatin silver print (24x18.5cm 9x7in) London 2001

QUINN James Peter 1870-1951 [29]
- **$3 196** - €3 073 - **£1 969** - FF20 158
  Reclining Nude Oil/canvas (41x61.5cm 16x24in) Melbourne 1999

QUINN Marc 1964 [10]
- **$29 748** - €25 417 - **£18 000** - FF166 725
  You take my Breath away Sculpture (H180cm H70in) London 1998
- **$16 000** - €18 100 - **£11 193** - FF118 728
  Six Bread Hands Sculpture (70x70x11cm 27x27x4in) New-York 2001

QUINQUAND Anna 1890-1984 [18]
- **$4 287** - €4 573 - **£2 715** - FF30 000
  Femme Foulah Grès (H40.5cm H15in) Paris 2001

QUINQUELA MARTIN Benito 1890-1977 [48]
- **$22 000** - €21 405 - **£13 541** - FF140 410
  Regreso de la pesca Oleo/tabla (60.5x69cm 23x27in) Buenos-Aires 1999
- **$5 596** - €6 098 - **£3 668** - FF40 000
  Le port de Buenos Aires Fusain/papier (103x89cm 40x35in) Louviers 2000
- **$1 600** - €1 859 - **£1 124** - FF12 193
  «Buque en reparación» Aguafuerte (70x54cm 27x21in) Buenos-Aires 2001

Q

QUINTANA CASTILLO Manuel 1928 **[39]**
- $16 000 - €15 567 - £9 848 - FF102 116
  Tabique No.2 Acrylic (190x175cm 74x68in) New-York 1999
- $2 012 - €1 879 - £1 258 - FF12 328
  Sin título Tempera (47.5x43cm 18x16in) Caracas 1999
- $1 005 - €1 185 - £706 - FF7 770
  Relieve, collage, ocho Técnica mixta (28x26cm 11x10in) Caracas ($) 2000

QUINTANILLA Isabel 1938 **[5]**
- $3 528 - €3 379 - £2 220 - FF22 167
  Stilleben auf Kommode Crayon (25x35cm 9x13in) Bern 1999

QUINTANILLA ISASI Luis 1893-1978 **[19]**
- $123 - €114 - £74 - FF748
  Taberna Grabado (38x28cm 14x11in) Madrid 1999

QUINTANILLA Luis 1918 **[3]**
- $1 512 - €1 622 - £1 026 - FF10 638
  «Turista de 1960» Oleo/lienzo (46x62cm 18x24in) Madrid 2001

QUINTAVALLE Noël 1893-? **[6]**
- $1 120 - €1 451 - £840 - FF9 520
  Il nastro rosa Olio/tela (65x45cm 25x17in) Prato 2001

QUINTE Lothar 1923-2000 **[51]**
- $2 143 - €2 301 - £1 434 - FF15 092
  Komposition Tempera/canvas (70.2x100.4cm 27x39in) Hamburg 2000
- $173 - €194 - £120 - FF1 274
  Informelle Komposition Drypoint (35x70.5cm 13x27in) Köln 2001

QUINTERO Daniel 1949 **[7]**
- $2 970 - €3 304 - £1 980 - FF21 670
  La ventana (casa de Antonio López) Lápiz/papel (94x105cm 37x41in) Madrid 2000

QUINTON Alfred Robert 1853-1934 **[28]**
- $753 - €874 - £520 - FF5 732
  In the Grounds of Warwick Castle Watercolour (24.5x34cm 9x13in) London 2000

QUINTON Clément Henri 1851-1920 **[92]**
- $1 376 - €1 189 - £831 - FF7 800
  Pâturages, le plateau aux 1000 vaches Huile/toile (51x66cm 20x25in) Barbizon 1998
- $1 058 - €1 170 - £734 - FF7 674
  Paysage Huile/toile (28x41cm 11x16in) Genève 2001
- $1 976 - €2 058 - £1 252 - FF13 500
  «Vittel Vosges. Saison du 25 mai au 25 septembre» Affiche (106x72cm 41x28in) Versailles 2000

QUINTYN Robert 1916 **[8]**
- $3 134 - €3 659 - £2 148 - FF24 000
  Moutons au pâturage/Moutons près du village Huile/toile (50x61cm 19x24in) Dijon 2000

QUIROS Antonio 1912-1984 **[21]**
- $5 040 - €5 406 - £3 330 - FF35 460
  Personaje con bastón Oleo/tablex (91x63cm 35x24in) Madrid 2000
- $2 170 - €2 102 - £1 330 - FF13 790
  Sin título Técnica mixta (17.5x35cm 6x13in) Madrid 1999

QUIROS de Cesareo Bernaldo 1881-1968 **[10]**
- $23 000 - €22 575 - £14 257 - FF148 080
  Jarrón con flores Oleo/cartón (66x54cm 25x21in) Buenos-Aires 1999

QUIRT Walter 1902-1968 **[6]**
- $12 000 - €14 070 - £8 632 - FF92 293
  I'm going away, far far into the Distance, NEver to Return, Goodbye Oil/canvas (68.5x102cm 26x40in) New-York 2001

QUITTNER Rudolf 1872-1910 **[10]**
- $15 012 - €17 049 - £10 500 - FF111 834
  View of Sacré Coeur from Montmartre Oil/canvas (112x160cm 44x62in) London 2001
- $3 750 - €3 811 - £2 357 - FF25 000
  Square d'Anvers et le Sacré-Coeur Huile/toile (73x54cm 28x21in) Amiens 2000

QUITTON Edward 1842-1921 **[21]**
- $932 - €1 041 - £651 - FF6 829
  Nature morte en trompe l'oeil Huile/panneau (36x24cm 14x9in) Bruxelles 2001

QUIZET Alphonse 1885-1955 **[409]**
- $2 317 - €2 287 - £1 428 - FF15 000
  Jardins et moulins à Montmartre Huile/panneau (35x65cm 13x25in) Paris 1999
- $961 - €1 067 - £669 - FF7 000
  Le Sacré-Coeur Huile/panneau (42x33cm 16x12in) Neuilly-sur-Seine 2001
- $715 - €671 - £441 - FF4 400
  Vue de Paris, le Pont Neuf et Notre-Dame Aquarelle/papier (30x46cm 11x18in) La Varenne-Saint-Hilaire 1999

QUOST Ernest 1844-1931 **[82]**
- $26 401 - €28 974 - £17 000 - FF190 056
  La fête au bord de la rivière Oil/canvas (96.5x132cm 37x51in) London 2000
- $2 173 - €2 058 - £1 350 - FF13 500
  Vase de fleurs et livres sur une terrasse Huile/toile (90x70cm 35x27in) Paris 1999
- $622 - €534 - £374 - FF3 500
  La cueillette des pommes Huile/toile (34x22cm 13x8in) Deauville 1998

QVIST Carl Gustaf 1787-1822 **[2]**
- $2 865 - €2 789 - £1 764 - FF18 292
  Landskap med fågel på gren Oil/panel (30x19.5cm 11x7in) Stockholm 1999

QVISTORFF Victor H.W. 1883-1953 **[116]**
- $578 - €539 - £349 - FF3 795
  Udsigt fra Liseleje Oil/canvas (36x51cm 14x20in) Köbenhavn 1999
- $437 - €404 - £272 - FF2 648
  Havneparti med motorskib Oil/canvas (27x39cm 10x15in) Viby J, Århus 1999

R

RAADSIG Peter Johann 1806-1882 **[118]**
- $1 881 - €2 148 - £1 307 - FF14 088
  To italienerinder, der holder hvil i vejkanten Oil/canvas (38x50cm 14x19in) Köbenhavn 2000
- $999 - €1 008 - £623 - FF6 609
  Udsigt mod Pavens sommerresidens, Castel Gandolfo Oil/panel (20x28cm 7x11in) Köbenhavn 2000

RAAIJ van Jozef 1898-1974 **[4]**
- $3 827 - €4 311 - £2 638 - FF28 277
  In the Artist's studio Oil/canvas (63x52cm 24x20in) Amsterdam 2000

RAALTE van Henri Benedictus 1881-1929 **[24]**
$288 - €320 - £193 - FF2 101
«An Australian Summer Day» Etching (41x44cm 16x17in) Nedlands 2000

RAAPHORST Cornelis 1875-1954 **[125]**
$4 271 - €4 991 - £3 049 - FF32 742
Kittens playing with a Sewing Kit Oil/canvas (40.5x51cm 15x20in) Amsterdam 2001
$2 626 - €2 496 - £1 598 - FF16 371
Drie jonge poesjes Oil/canvas (17.5x26.5cm 6x10in) Den Haag 2000

RAATIKAINEN Orvo XX **[27]**
$1 090 - €1 261 - £771 - FF8 274
Familj Oil/canvas (40x74cm 15x29in) Helsinki 2000

RABA Manuel Gomez 1928-1983 **[10]**
$3 920 - €4 205 - £2 660 - FF27 580
Composición Técnica mixta/tabla (60x72cm 23x28in) Madrid 2001
$1 216 - €1 141 - £741 - FF7 486
Composición Técnica mixta (33x32cm 12x12in) Madrid 1999

RABAN Zeev 1890-1970 **[19]**
$320 - €312 - £202 - FF2 049
Shepherd and Girl by the Sea of Galilee Watercolour/paper (17.5x18cm 6x7in) Tel Aviv 1999

RABAS Václav 1885-1954 **[29]**
$2 312 - €2 187 - £1 440 - FF14 344
Ein Blumenstrauss Öl/Leinwand (70x56cm 27x22in) Praha 1999
$635 - €601 - £396 - FF3 944
Paysage d'automne Huile/carton (25x35cm 9x13in) Praha 2000

RABE Johannes 1827-? **[7]**
$17 438 - €14 324 - £10 127 - FF93 959
Das Nationaldenkmal von 1848 im Invalidenpark zu Berlin Öl/Leinwand (40.5x51cm 15x20in) Berlin 1998

RABERABA Henoch 1914-1975 **[19]**
$155 - €171 - £105 - FF1 123
Outback Ranges Watercolour/paper (34.5x45cm 13x17in) Sydney 2000

RABERABA Herbert 1916-1975 **[31]**
$203 - €241 - £143 - FF1 579
Mc Donnell Ranges Watercolour/paper (25.5x35.5cm 10x13in) Sydney 2000

RABES Max Friedrich 1868-1944 **[66]**
$2 564 - €3 049 - £1 828 - FF20 000
Couple d'orientaux devant le fleuve Huile/toile (55x81cm 21x31in) Calais 2001
$1 336 - €1 534 - £914 - FF10 061
Altes Schloss in Berlin Öl/Karton (13x19cm 5x7in) Berlin 2000

RABIER Benjamin 1869-1939 **[61]**
$7 649 - €7 089 - £4 757 - FF46 500
«Savonnerie La Girafe, Marseille» Email/panneau (85x36cm 33x14in) Paris 1999
$538 - €534 - £334 - FF3 500
«Le dragon - 9 -» Encre Chine/papier (38x31cm 14x12in) Paris 1999
$857 - €838 - £529 - FF5 500
«Ch. Baret dans l'Ane de Buridon» Affiche (160x118cm 62x46in) Paris 1999

RABIN Sam 1903 **[11]**
$4 062 - €4 575 - £2 800 - FF30 011
The Third Man Oil/board (47.5x65cm 18x25in) London 2000

$1 886 - €2 125 - £1 300 - FF13 938
All Over Oil/paper (19.5x25cm 7x9in) London 2000

RABINE Oskar 1928 **[41]**
$2 837 - €3 201 - £1 995 - FF21 000
Le petit Paris Huile/toile (50x61cm 19x24in) Paris 2001

RABINOVITCH Gregor 1884-1958 **[46]**
$149 - €125 - £87 - FF820
Höhenflug des Denkers/Liebespaar am Bach Radierung (6.8x10cm 2x3in) Bern 1998

RABUS Carl 1898-1983 **[48]**
$1 074 - €1 278 - £766 - FF8 384
Sitzende Frau Öl/Leinwand (99x70cm 38x27in) München 2000
$176 - €204 - £123 - FF1 341
Konstruktion Woodcut in colors (25.5x30cm 10x11in) Berlin 2001

RABUZIN Ivan 1919 **[34]**
$3 068 - €2 897 - £1 907 - FF19 000
Paysage naïf à la route Huile/toile (92x73cm 36x28in) Neuilly-sur-Seine 1999
$845 - €986 - £593 - FF6 467
Blumenlandschaft Watercolour (56.5x76cm 22x29in) Luzern 2000
$321 - €374 - £222 - FF2 451
Wachsende Blume Farbserigraphie (65x53.5cm 25x21in) Bern 2000

RACHOU Henri 1856-1944 **[7]**
$1 004 - €1 181 - £720 - FF7 749
Les tortues Farblithographie (47.5x29.5cm 18x11in) Bern 2001

RACIM Mohammed 1896-1975 **[11]**
$5 180 - €6 098 - £3 640 - FF40 000
Enluminure Gouache (21.5x14cm 8x5in) Paris 2000

RACIM Omar 1883-1958 **[3]**
$3 780 - €3 964 - £2 368 - FF26 000
Mosquée à Alger Gouache/papier (35x24cm 13x9in) Paris 2000

RACKHAM Arthur 1867-1939 **[141]**
$12 436 - €10 766 - £7 500 - FF70 621
Peer and the Thread Balls Watercolour (27x20.5cm 10x8in) London 1998
$525 - €480 - £321 - FF3 147
Goblins Drinking in a Bell Tower Print (11x11cm 4x4in) Pittsburgh PA 1999

RACKHAM W. Leslie 1864-1944 **[152]**
$354 - €403 - £250 - FF2 645
Irstead Mill and Marshes with Cattle Oil/canvas (22x27cm 9x11in) Aylsham, Norfolk 2001
$355 - €341 - £206 - FF2 236
Near Wroxham Broad Watercolour (20x42cm 7x16in) London 1999

RACKLEY Mildred 1906 **[8]**
$950 - €913 - £589 - FF5 987
Fifth Avenue Screenprint in colors (46x38.5cm 18x15in) New-York 1999

RACOFF Rastilaw 1904 **[32]**
$549 - €518 - £341 - FF3 400
La pêche Huile/carton (32.5x26cm 12x10in) Neuilly-sur-Seine 1999

RACZ Andre 1916 **[5]**
$650 - €738 - £445 - FF4 844
Perseus Beheading Medusa IV Etching, aquatint (54x35cm 21x13in) New-York 2000

R

RADA Vlastimil 1895-1962 **[31]**
- **$1 098** - €1 039 - **£684** - FF6 813
  Paysage Huile/toile/panneau (39x66.5cm 15x26in) Praha 2001
- **$346** - €328 - **£216** - FF2 151
  Jour d'hiver Huile/carton (22x30cm 8x11in) Praha 2001

RÅDAL Erik 1905-1941 **[24]**
- **$3 447** - €4 025 - **£2 433** - FF26 400
  Kragelund Kirke Oil/canvas (80x125cm 31x49in) Köbenhavn 2000
- **$1 811** - €1 879 - **£1 149** - FF12 328
  Praesten Oil/canvas (26x30cm 10x11in) Viby J, Århus 2000

RADDA Madame 1891-1967 **[21]**
- **$681** - €590 - **£413** - FF3 869
  Still Life with Flowers Oil/canvas (46x37.5cm 18x14in) Amsterdam 1999

RADDATZ Hermann A. 1907-1983 **[8]**
- **$12 318** - €11 760 - **£7 695** - FF77 139
  Stilleben mit Ananas Öl/Leinwand (54x73cm 21x28in) Köln 2000
- **$3 190** - €3 068 - **£1 968** - FF20 123
  Ohne Titel (Stilleben mit Sommerblumen und blauer Vase) Aquarell (53.5x64.4cm 21x25in) Köln 1999

RADEMACHER Niels Grønbek 1812-1885 **[33]**
- **$419** - €404 - **£260** - FF2 649
  Blomstrende traer og buske i Lindegårdens have, Ordrup Oil/canvas (24x32cm 9x12in) Köbenhavn 1999

RADEMAKER Abraham 1675-1735 **[61]**
- **$1 333** - €1 151 - **£803** - FF7 552
  A Mountainous River Landscape with a Ferry near a Town on a Rise Wash (14x24.5cm 5x9in) Amsterdam 1998

RADEMAKER Hermanus Everhardus 1820-1885 **[10]**
- **$6 177** - €7 260 - **£4 283** - FF47 625
  Cattle Drivers in a Rhine Landscape Oil/panel (37x50cm 14x19in) Amsterdam 2000

RÄDERSCHEIDT Anton 1892-1970 **[136]**
- **$12 760** - €12 271 - **£7 862** - FF80 493
  Pferdeschau/Zwei weidende Pferde Oil/masonite (126x100cm 49x39in) Köln 1999
- **$2 120** - €2 044 - **£1 307** - FF13 407
  Porträt eines Mannes im Anzug Öl/Leinwand (55x45.5cm 21x17in) Bern 1999
- **$3 572** - €3 835 - **£2 391** - FF25 154
  Radfahrer Indian ink/paper (100x65cm 39x25in) Köln 2000
- **$147** - €153 - **£93** - FF1 006
  Brücke in Köln Farblithographie (43x57cm 16x22in) Berlin 2000

RADFORD Edward 1831-1920 **[13]**
- **$3 761** - €4 063 - **£2 600** - FF26 649
  Shared Moment Oil/canvas (51x61.5cm 20x24in) London 2001
- **$4 345** - €5 042 - **£3 000** - FF33 072
  Narcissus Watercolour/paper (39.5x50cm 15x19in) London 2000

RADICE Mario 1898-1987 **[47]**
- **$11 500** - €11 922 - **£6 900** - FF78 200
  Composizione Olio/tela (52x38cm 20x14in) Vercelli 2001
- **«Composizione CH77 Bz»** Acrilico/cartone (30x40cm 11x15in) Milano 2001
- **$1 300** - €1 348 - **£780** - FF8 840
  Composizione astratta China (33.5x47.5cm 13x18in) Milano 2000

RADIMSKY Václav 1867-1946 **[31]**
- **$2 312** - €2 187 - **£1 440** - FF14 344
  Landscape Oil/canvas (81x100cm 31x39in) Praha 2000

RADL Anton 1774-1852 **[7]**
- **$27 200** - €23 250 - **£16 320** - FF152 512
  Motiv aus dem Taunus Öl/Leinwand (65.5x95cm 25x37in) Wien 1998

RADLER Max 1904-1971 **[31]**
- **$32 238** - €37 117 - **£22 000** - FF243 471
  Urban Scene with Train Oil/canvas (55x80cm 21x31in) London 2000
- **$273** - €307 - **£190** - FF2 012
  Flusslandschaft mit Angler Charcoal (52.5x74cm 20x29in) Berlin 2001

RADOS Luigi, Lovis, comte 1773-1840 **[7]**
- **$90** - €108 - **£63** - FF709
  Santa Cena Grabado (57x102cm 22x40in) Madrid 2000

RADZIWILL Franz 1895-1983 **[228]**
- **$47 142** - €46 017 - **£29 853** - FF301 851
  Landschaft mit ockerfarbenem Haus Oil/canvas/panel (55x72cm 21x28in) Bremen 1999
- **$19 991** - €23 519 - **£14 112** - FF154 274
  «Der Goldlack» Oil/canvas/panel (42x32cm 16x12in) Berlin 2001
- **$1 408** - €1 636 - **£989** - FF10 732
  Landschaft Pencil/paper (25.5x33cm 10x12in) Hamburg 2001
- **$671** - €665 - **£420** - FF4 365
  Zwel Akte Drypoint (24x19cm 9x7in) London 1999

RAE Barbara 1943 **[11]**
- **$1 599** - €1 379 - **£950** - FF9 047
  Coastal Landscape Mixed media (57.5x82cm 22x32in) Glasgow 1998
- **$1 401** - €1 566 - **£950** - FF10 271
  Quarry Sunset Watercolour (66x95.5cm 25x37in) Edinburgh 2000

RAE Fiona 1963 **[24]**
- **$15 000** - €16 457 - **£9 964** - FF107 952
  Blue & Yellow Oil/canvas (198x183cm 77x72in) New-York 2000
- **$8 965** - €9 624 - **£6 000** - FF63 129
  Purple and Yellow Oil/canvas (54x122cm 21x48in) London 2000
- **$576** - €637 - **£400** - FF4 181
  Abstract Oil/panel (10.5x10cm 4x3in) London 2001

RAE Henrietta 1859-1928 **[18]**
- **$729 560** - €867 664 - **£520 000** - FF5 691 504
  Hylas and the Water Nymphs Oil/canvas (142x223cm 55x87in) London 2000
- **$2 566** - €2 586 - **£1 600** - FF16 965
  Spinning Oil/canvas (56.5x43cm 22x16in) London 2000

RAE John 1882-? **[2]**
- **$1 500** - €1 748 - **£1 038** - FF11 469
  Man Opening Telephone Store Watercolour/paper (28x23cm 11x9in) New-York 2000

RAEBURN Henry 1756-1823 **[105]**
- ☞ $38 944 - €45 771 - **£27 000** - FF300 240
  Margaretta Henrietta, Lady Hepburn, Seated, With a Green Shawl Oil/canvas (124.5x103cm 49x40in) Edinburgh 2000
- ☞ $14 481 - €13 779 - **£9 000** - FF90 387
  Mrs James Law, née Jane Robinson, in a black Dress, with Headdress Oil/canvas (77.5x64cm 30x25in) London 1999

RAEDECKER Anton 1861-1960 **[7]**
- ☞ $1 335 - €1 588 - **£952** - FF10 418
  A Woman standing Sculpture, wood (H31cm H12in) Amsterdam 2000

RAEDECKER John 1885-1956 **[85]**
- ☞ $5 073 - €5 445 - **£3 394** - FF35 719
  Hert in Sneeuw - Deer in Snow Oil/canvas (80x61cm 31x24in) Amsterdam 2000
- ☞ $16 912 - €18 151 - **£11 316** - FF119 064
  Standing Nude Sculpture (H104cm H40in) Amsterdam 2000
- ☞ $5 942 - €5 899 - **£3 712** - FF38 695
  Female Figure Sculpture, wood (H25.5cm H10in) Amsterdam 1999
- ✐ $1 260 - €1 361 - **£862** - FF8 929
  A Standing Nude Pencil/paper (64x39.5cm 25x15in) Amsterdam 2001
- ▥ $261 - €250 - **£163** - FF1 637
  Couple and two Birds Woodcut (16.5x24cm 6x9in) Amsterdam 1999

RAEDECKER Max 1914-1987 **[24]**
- ✐ $465 - €499 - **£311** - FF3 274
  Still life on beach Watercolour, gouache/paper (47x62.5cm 18x24in) Amsterdam 2000

RAEMAEKERS Louis 1869-1970 **[34]**
- ✐ $164 - €181 - **£107** - FF1 190
  Zeppelins bij Dover Watercolour/paper (25x34cm 9x13in) Rotterdam 2000
- ▥ $485 - €454 - **£299** - FF2 976
  «Santol Antilood, Haarlem» Poster (216x80cm 85x31in) Oostwoud 1999

RAETZ Markus 1941 **[84]**
- ☞ $12 268 - €13 458 - **£8 332** - FF88 277
  Ohne Titel Sculpture (32x25x2.5cm 12x9xin) Luzern 2000
- ✐ $1 275 - €1 183 - **£779** - FF7 763
  Die Zote Encre Chine (13.3x17.9cm 5x7in) Bern 1999
- ▥ $265 - €316 - **£189** - FF2 070
  Sicht II, aus «Sehen» Aquatint (75.5x53cm 29x20in) Zürich 2000

RAEVEN Servatius XVI **[1]**
- ▥ $1 115 - €1 329 - **£795** - FF8 720
  Trium Humani Generis Ordinum Sive Statum, nach Marten de Vos Kupferstich (23.4x29.9cm 9x11in) Berlin 2000

RAFART Pepe 1946 **[2]**
- ☜ $12 000 - €11 647 - **£7 471** - FF76 399
  Albatros I Sculpture (25x38x23cm 9x14x9in) New-York 1999

RAFFAEL Joseph 1933 **[25]**
- ☞ $13 000 - €14 785 - **£9 083** - FF96 981
  Sunset Oil/canvas (198x289.5cm 77x113in) Beverly-Hills CA 2000
- ✐ $7 000 - €7 961 - **£4 890** - FF52 220
  Three Fish, Blue Water Watercolour/paper (53.5x118cm 21x46in) Beverly-Hills CA 2000
- ▥ $3 500 - €3 980 - **£2 418** - FF26 157
  «Haiku Fish II, III, IV» Color lithograph (53.5x76cm 21x29in) Beverly-Hills CA 2000

RAFFAELE Ambrogio 1845-1928 **[4]**
- ☞ $1 547 - €1 604 - **£928** - FF10 519
  Pittore al lavoro Olio/tavoletta (29x40.5cm 11x15in) Milano 1999

RAFFAELLI Jean-François 1850-1924 **[376]**
- ☞ $31 518 - €30 584 - **£20 000** - FF200 616
  A Paris, la promenade Oil/canvas (48x37cm 18x14in) London 1999
- ☞ $8 055 - €8 012 - **£5 000** - FF52 556
  Elegant Lady on a Coastal Path Oil/canvas (25x33cm 9x12in) London 1999
- ✐ $1 661 - €1 422 - **£1 000** - FF9 325
  La Seine Pastel (23x31cm 9x12in) London 1998
- ▥ $530 - €459 - **£321** - FF3 010
  Le jardin de la vieille fille Etching in colors (32x23cm 12x9in) München 1998

RAFFAELLO SANZIO 1483-1520 **[9]**
- ☞ $4 808 - €4 421 - **£2 970** - FF28 997
  Aerkeenglen Michael i kamp med djaevlen- Hellige Frants af Assisi Oil/panel (113x77cm 44x30in) Vejle 1998
- ☞ $550 000 - €603 430 - **£365 365** - FF3 958 240
  Saint Mary of Egypt Oil/panel (37.5x14.5cm 14x5in) New-York 2000

RAFFALT Ignaz 1800-1857 **[30]**
- ☞ $1 234 - €1 453 - **£868** - FF9 534
  Rückkehr von der Jagd Öl/Leinwand (34.5x42cm 13x16in) Wien 2000

RAFFALT Johann Gualbert 1836-1865 **[10]**
- ☞ $27 055 - €25 435 - **£16 380** - FF166 845
  Markttag in Szolnok Oil/panel (42x68cm 16x26in) Wien 1999
- ☞ $2 321 - €2 761 - **£1 656** - FF18 114
  Pferde am Flussufer in der Puszta Oil/panel (21.5x42cm 8x16in) Wien 2000

RAFFET Auguste Denis 1804-1860 **[95]**
- ☞ $1 401 - €1 524 - **£963** - FF10 000
  Grenadier à cheval dans la neige Huile/toile (24x19cm 9x7in) Noyon 2001
- ✐ $457 - €427 - **£282** - FF2 800
  Louis XVI et le bonnet phrygien Crayon/papier (12.5x9.5cm 4x3in) Paris 1999

RAFFIN André 1927 **[79]**
- ☞ $927 - €793 - **£561** - FF5 200
  La sieste sur le canapé Huile/toile (54x72cm 21x28in) Paris 1998

RAFFLER Max 1902-1988 **[69]**
- ✐ $298 - €255 - **£176** - FF1 674
  «Frauen am Ammersee»/«Lüttes-Hütte» Watercolour (24x33cm 9x12in) München 1998

RAFFORT Étienne 1802-1895 **[8]**
- ☞ $9 798 - €10 519 - **£6 555** - FF69 000
  Les souks en Algérie Huile/toile (72.5x59.5cm 28x23in) Soissons 2000

RAFFY LE PERSAN Jean 1912 **[167]**
- ☞ $1 115 - €1 271 - **£770** - FF8 334
  Farm on a Riverbank Oil/canvas (60x73cm 23x28in) Amsterdam 2000
- ☞ $521 - €488 - **£322** - FF3 200
  Coucher de soleil hivernal Huile/bois (19x35cm 7x13in) La Grand'Combe 1999

RAFOLS CASAMADA Alberto 1923 **[127]**
- ☞ $2 400 - €2 287 - **£1 500** - FF15 000
  Sin título Oleo/lienzo (50x60cm 19x23in) Caracas 1999

R

$2 380 - €2 553 - **£1 572** - FF16 745
Estructura clara Oleo/lienzo (41.5x23cm 16x9in)
Madrid 2000

$1 525 - €1 502 - **£925** - FF9 850
Way Técnica mixta/papel (50x62.5cm 19x24in)
Barcelona 2000

$179 - €192 - **£121** - FF1 260
Formas Serigrafia (32x23cm 12x9in) Madrid 2001

RAFTERY Ted 1938 [19]
$651 - €765 - **£460** - FF5 018
Evening Breeze Acrylic/canvas (61x76cm 24x29in)
Calgary, Alberta 2000

RAGALZI Sergio 1951 [16]
$400 - €415 - **£240** - FF2 720
Forma Carboncino (72x101cm 28x39in) Vercelli 2000

RAGAN Leslie 1897-1972 [31]
$3 000 - €3 499 - **£2 106** - FF22 951
«Union Terminal Cleveland, New York Central»
Poster (68x102cm 26x40in) New-York 2000

RAGGI Giovanni 1712-1792/94 [7]
$44 000 - €42 001 - **£27 491** - FF275 510
Cleopatra's Banquet Oil/canvas (239x254cm
94x100in) New-York 1999

RAGGI Pietro Paolo c.1646-1724 [4]
$42 753 - €48 559 - **£30 188** - FF318 525
The Rape of the Sabine Women Oil/canvas
(180x222cm 70x87in) London 2001

RAGGIO Giuseppe 1823-1916 [35]
$22 780 - €25 916 - **£16 065** - FF170 000
Troupeau dans la campagne romaine Huile/toile
(70x129cm 27x50in) Paris 2001

$600 - €777 - **£450** - FF5 100
Montoni al pascolo Olio/tavola (19x30.5cm 7x12in)
Prato 2000

$1 000 - €1 037 - **£600** - FF6 800
Buttero Acquarello/carta (47x30cm 18x11in) Roma
2000

RAGIONE Raffaele 1851-1919 [89]
$9 000 - €7 775 - **£6 000** - FF51 000
Tre donne al parco Olio/cartone (29x37cm 11x14in)
Milano 1998

RAGN-JENSEN Leif 1911-1993 [20]
$805 - €740 - **£495** - FF4 857
Ryper i sneen Oil/canvas (30x45cm 11x17in) Vejle
1999

RAGOCZY Joachim 1895-1975 [23]
$105 - €123 - **£73** - FF804
**Weiblicher Halbakt, die Augen niedergeschla-
gen** Radierung (19.9x14.8cm 7x5in) Berlin 2000

RAGOLIA Michele ?-1686 [5]
$10 500 - €9 128 - **£6 354** - FF59 877
**God and Father Appearing Before the Holy
Family** Oil/canvas (41.5x46.5cm 16x18in) New-York
1999

$1 765 - €1 754 - **£1 100** - FF11 504
Saint James the Great Fighting the Moors Black
chalk (25x22cm 9x8in) London 1999

RAGON Adolphe ?-1924 [14]
$579 - €537 - **£360** - FF3 520
Coming up with the Tide Watercolour (29x60cm
11x23in) London 1999

RAGONEAU G. XIX [2]
$5 163 - €4 959 - **£3 200** - FF32 527
Figures in a Classical Capriccio Oil/canvas
(87.5x124.5cm 34x49in) London 1999

RAGOT Jules 1835-1912 [57]
$2 014 - €1 888 - **£1 246** - FF12 382
Still Life Oil/canvas (88.5x57cm 34x22in) Melbourne
1999

$819 - €793 - **£515** - FF5 203
Nature morte aux fleurs Huile/toile (45x30cm
17x11in) Antwerpen 1999

RAHIMAN Abalal c.1856-1931 [7]
$3 343 - €3 237 - **£2 100** - FF21 236
Boy Pencil/paper (29.5x20cm 11x7in) London 1999

RAHL Carl 1812-1865 [30]
$1 442 - €1 453 - **£900** - FF9 534
Frauenportrait Öl/Leinwand (71x51cm 27x20in)
Wien 2000

$1 286 - €1 534 - **£917** - FF10 061
**Südliche Gebirgslandschaft mit zwei Frauen an
einem Felsbrunnen** Öl/Leinwand (25.5x20cm
10x7in) Berlin 2000

RAHMBERG Ulf 1935 [17]
$837 - €787 - **£518** - FF5 163
**Skiss till «Tack farsan och morsan för vad du
gav och tog»** Mixed media (47x38cm 18x14in)
Stockholm 1999

$2 123 - €2 463 - **£1 465** - FF16 159
Generalerna våldför sig på de meniga Mixed
media (23.5x26cm 9x10in) Stockholm 2000

RAHN-HIRZEL Eduard 1801-1851 [6]
$4 992 - €5 625 - **£3 456** - FF36 899
Blick auf den Zürichsee Öl/Leinwand (41x54cm
16x21in) Zürich 2000

RAHOULT Diodore Charles 1819-1874 [18]
$7 731 - €7 165 - **£4 615** - FF47 000
Les joueurs de boules Huile/toile (60x73cm
23x28in) Paris 1999

RAIEV Vassili Iegorovich 1807-1871 [4]
$72 200 - €81 360 - **£50 000** - FF533 685
Rome Oil/canvas (96.5x138.5cm 37x54in) London
2000

RAIGHASSE Pierre XX [5]
$1 280 - €1 220 - **£811** - FF8 000
Ste-Anne-la-Palud, jour de pardon Huile/toile
(60x120cm 23x47in) Douarnenez 1999

RAIMONDI Aldo 1902-1998 [49]
$962 - €997 - **£577** - FF6 543
Due gattini in un cesto Acquarello/carta (51x38cm
20x14in) Milano 1999

RAIMONDI Marcantonio c.1480-1534 [98]
$60 000 - €64 077 - **£40 884** - FF420 318
Standing Nude Holding a Veil Ink (17x9cm 6x3in)
New-York 2001

$537 - €511 - **£333** - FF3 353
Passion Christi, nach Dürer Kupferstich
(12.6x9.6cm 4x3in) Berlin 1999

RAIN Charles 1911-1985 [2]
$26 000 - €30 485 - **£18 704** - FF199 968
The Magic Hand Oil/masonite (41x35cm 16x13in)
New-York 2001

RAINALDI Francesco 1770-1805 [1]
$858 - €838 - **£544** - FF5 500
Logge del Vaticano d'après Raphaël Burin
(49.5x37cm 19x14in) Paris 1999

RAINBIRD Victor Noble 1888-1936 [166]
$288 - €238 - **£170** - FF1 561
«A Byway at Rouen» Watercolour/paper (25x17.5cm
9x6in) Tyne & Wear 1998

RAINE Herbert 1875-1951 **[20]**
- $377 - €430 - £260 - FF2 819
  «Farm Buildings, St.Joachim, P.Q.» Etching
  (16.5x19cm 6x7in) Montréal 2000

RAINER Arnulf 1929 **[709]**
- $10 002 - €10 737 - £6 694 - FF70 431
  Ohne Titel, aus Totenmaske-Serie Acrylic
  (72.8x51cm 28x20in) Köln 2000
- $2 102 - €1 816 - £1 267 - FF11 910
  Ohne Titel Mischtechnik (23.5x17cm 9x6in) Wien
  1998
- $3 468 - €4 090 - £2 446 - FF26 831
  Ohne Titel Gouache (43.5x17.5cm 17x6in) Köln 2001
- $458 - €545 - £327 - FF3 575
  Ohne Titel Farbradierung (32x44cm 12x17in) Linz
  2000
- $2 150 - €1 817 - £1 277 - FF11 920
  Sterbender Maler, Fotopose Gelatin silver print
  (24x17.8cm 9x7in) Wien 1998

RAINERI Carlo Antonio 1765-1826 **[5]**
- $44 280 - €38 253 - £22 140 - FF250 920
  Uccelli Tempera drawing (65x58cm 25x22in) Genova
  1999
- $5 500 - €5 702 - £3 300 - FF37 400
  Un fagiano argentato, un uccello e insetti
  Tempera/carta (38x48cm 14x18in) Milano 2000
- $19 500 - €20 215 - £11 700 - FF132 600
  Spatola che affera un
  pesce/Serpentario/Gufo/Spatola e un rapace
  Acquatinta (54x69.5cm 21x27in) Milano 2000

RAINERI IL SCHIVENOGLIA Francesco Maria
1676-1758 **[4]**
- $28 000 - €29 026 - £16 800 - FF190 400
  Battaglia di cavalieri turchi e cristiani Olio/tela
  (140x185cm 55x72in) Roma 2001

RAINERI Vittorio 1797-1869 **[9]**
- $12 000 - €10 367 - £8 000 - FF68 000
  Una gru coronata e un gufo argentato posato
  su un ramo/Un uccello Acquarello/carta (59.5x74cm
  23x29in) Milano 1998
- $15 000 - €12 958 - £10 000 - FF85 000
  Un uccello del paradiso/Una Spatola e un rapa-
  ce/... Acquatinta (54x69.5cm 21x27in) Milano 1998

RAINEY Clifford XX **[3]**
- $13 000 - €12 409 - £8 123 - FF81 399
  Standing Man with Tools Sculpture, glass
  (58.5x19.5x18cm 23x7x7in) New-York 1999

RAINFORD Edward act.1850-1864 **[1]**
- $56 732 - €65 857 - £40 000 - FF431 996
  Celia telling Rosalind that Orlando is in the
  forest Oil/panel (76x53.5cm 29x21in) London 2001

RAITTILA Tapani 1921 **[40]**
- $610 - €706 - £432 - FF4 633
  Skatudden Oil/canvas (35x27cm 13x10in) Helsinki
  2000
- $286 - €336 - £198 - FF2 206
  Park Watercolour/paper (38x56cm 14x22in) Helsinki
  2000

RAJLICH Thomas 1940 **[17]**
- $3 124 - €3 630 - £2 196 - FF23 812
  Untitled Oil/canvas (100x100cm 39x39in) Amsterdam
  2001

RAKOCZY Basil 1908-1979 **[32]**
- $6 132 - €5.758 - £3 800 - FF37 772
  Nature morte aux Fruits Oil/canvas (60.5x81cm
  23x31in) London 1999

- $2 156 - €2 539 - £1 515 - FF16 658
  Fleurs dans un vase blanc Oil/canvas (26.5x35cm
  10x13in) Dublin 2000
- $1 413 - €1 205 - £852 - FF7 906
  Huntsman and the White Stag Gouache/paper
  (50x63cm 20x25in) Dublin 1998

RAKOWSKY de Mecislas 1887-1947 **[32]**
- $817 - €942 - £570 - FF6 178
  Chemin creux ensoleillé Huile/toile (54x65cm
  21x25in) Bruxelles 2001
- $1 720 - €1 983 - £1 200 - FF13 008
  Jour de marché Huile/carton (19x24cm 7x9in)
  Bruxelles 2001

RALAMBO Émile XIX-XX **[11]**
- $440 - €457 - £277 - FF3 000
  Le forgeron Aquarelle/papier (28x37.5cm 11x14in)
  Paris 2000

RALEIGH Henry P. 1880-1944 **[17]**
- $1 500 - €1 436 - £926 - FF9 422
  Couple by a French Window, Story Illustration
  Watercolour (41x37cm 16x14in) New-York 1999

RALLI Théodore Scaramanga 1852-1909 **[40]**
- $100 000 - €95 371 - £60 870 - FF625 590
  Jalousie Oil/canvas (72.5x50cm 28x19in) New-York
  1999
- $6 624 - €5 610 - £3 864 - FF36 800
  Landscape with Pine Trees Oil/canvas (30x45cm
  11x17in) Athens 1998

RAM Sita XIX **[2]**
- $14 085 - €16 542 - £10 000 - FF108 510
  «The Taj-Mahal from the south-East, Agra»
  Watercolour (37x32cm 14x12in) London 2000

RAMA Olga Carol 1918 **[16]**
- $4 000 - €4 147 - £2 400 - FF27 200
  Spazio anche più che tempo Tecnica mista
  (60x80cm 23x31in) Torino 2001
- $625 - €648 - £375 - FF4 250
  Senza titolo Acquarello/carta (17x25cm 6x9in) Torino
  2000

RAMACHANDARAN A. 1935 **[4]**
- $1 984 - €1 856 - £1 200 - FF12 177
  Mansarover Watercolour (63.5x49cm 25x19in)
  London 1999

RAMAH (Henri Raemaeker) 1887-1947 **[83]**
- $1 032 - €1 190 - £712 - FF7 804
  De wintertuin Oil/paper/panel (44x44cm 17x17in)
  Lokeren 2000
- $532 - €595 - £369 - FF3 902
  Chat endormi Huile/papier (28x22cm 11x8in)
  Antwerpen 2001
- $1 262 - €1 091 - £761 - FF7 158
  Illustrations de conte Crayon/papier (31.5x24.5cm
  12x9in) Bruxelles 1998

RAMALHO Antonio 1859-1916 **[1]**
- $13 760 - €15 952 - £9 600 - FF104 640
  Naturaleza morta, frutos na mesa Oleo/tabla
  (34.5x49cm 13x19in) Lisboa 2001

RAMANUJAM K.G. 1941-1973 **[5]**
- $3 500 - €3 980 - £2 445 - FF26 110
  Untitled Acrylic/canvas (55.5x84.5cm 21x33in) New-
  York 2000
- $2 539 - €2 464 - £1 600 - FF16 164
  Untitled Ink (28x56.5cm 11x22in) London 1999

R

RAMASSO Marco 1964 [16]
- $1 700 - €1 762 - £1 020 - FF11 560
  Messaggere di speranza Olio/tela (40x50cm 15x19in) Vercelli 2000

RAMBAUD Bernard XX [22]
- $681 - €732 - £456 - FF4 800
  Repos au lac de l'Eychauda Aquarelle/papier (17x36cm 6x14in) Grenoble 2000

RAMBERG Johann Heinrich 1763-1840 [70]
- $476 - €511 - £318 - FF3 353
  Allegorische Darstellung der Ewigkeit und der Vergänglichkeit Ink/paper (19.9x32.1cm 7x12in) Hamburg 2000
- $399 - €460 - £275 - FF3 018
  Fridericus II.Rex Lithographie (24x17cm 9x6in) Saarbrücken 2000

RAMBERG von Arthur Georg 1819-1875 [29]
- $9 268 - €9 715 - £6 106 - FF63 724
  Einzug Heinrich des Vogelers auf der Burg Püchau Öl/Leinwand (169x245cm 64x96in) Leipzig 2000
- $142 - €133 - £86 - FF872
  Eine Dame in ihrem Zimmer Pencil/paper (16.7x13cm 6x5in) Berlin 1999

RAMBO Jules XIX-XX [85]
- $206 - €198 - £128 - FF1 300
  La dentellière Huile/toile (67x43cm 26x16in) Bruxelles 1999

RAMBOUX Johan Anton Alban 1790-1866 [7]
- $3 225 - €3 835 - £2 235 - FF25 154
  Schonenburg bei Ruwer unterhalb Trier Ink/paper (15x28.5cm 5x11in) Köln 2000
- $2 926 - €3 323 - £2 033 - FF21 800
  Ansicht des Moseltals unterhalb Trier Lithographie (34x44cm 13x17in) Berlin 2001

RAME Jules Louis 1855-1927 [32]
- $2 160 - €2 439 - £1 505 - FF16 000
  La gardienne de moutons Huile/toile (46.5x61cm 18x24in) Bayeux 2001

RAMEL Jacques XX [20]
- $704 - €732 - £443 - FF4 800
  «Grand Prix Automobile de Monaco XIV°» Affiche (119x80cm 46x31in) Paris 2000

RAMENGHI IL BAGNACAVALLO Bartolomeo I 1485-1542 [7]
- $22 082 - €20 443 - £13 330 - FF134 096
  The Holy Family Oil/panel (61x52cm 24x20in) Dublin 1999

RAMENGHI IL BAGNACAVALLO Bartolomeo II XVI [3]
- $31 000 - €27 192 - £18 823 - FF178 367
  The Mystic Marriage of Saint Catherine Oil/panel (61x49cm 24x19in) New-York 1999

RAMEY Claude 1754-1838 [2]
- $78 300 - €76 225 - £48 100 - FF500 000
  Homme de qualité vêtu d'une redingote Marble (63x41cm 24x16in) Paris 1999

RAMIREZ Martin 1895-1963 [3]
- $24 000 - €27 847 - £16 569 - FF182 664
  Stag with Two Dogs Pencil (134.5x73.5cm 52x28in) New-York 2000

RAMIREZ SANCHEZ Manuel 1886-1961 [5]
- $918 - €1 021 - £612 - FF6 698
  Paisaje de Mallorca Oleo/cartón (46x55cm 18x21in) Madrid 2000

RAMIS Julio 1909-1990 [31]
- $2 950 - €3 003 - £1 850 - FF19 700
  Composición Acrílico (30x19.5cm 11x7in) Madrid 2000
- $456 - €481 - £304 - FF3 152
  Composición Técnica mixta/papel (28x24cm 11x9in) Madrid 2000

RAMOS ARTAL Manuel 1855-? [84]
- $2 700 - €2 258 - £1 612 - FF14 812
  Pastora con rebaño/Claro en el bosque Oleo/lienzo (35x51cm 13x20in) Madrid 1998
- $1 375 - €1 502 - £950 - FF9 850
  El jardín Oleo/lienzo (46x25.5cm 18x10in) Madrid 2001
- $224 - €264 - £162 - FF1 733
  Paisaje con casa Lápiz/papel (22.5x16.5cm 8x6in) Madrid 2001

RAMOS BRITO Gerardo XX [1]
- $2 144 - €2 378 - £1 426 - FF15 596
  Fósil Técnica mixta/papel (120x150cm 47x59in) México 2000

RAMOS Carlos Augusto 1912-1983 [5]
- $4 300 - €4 985 - £3 000 - FF32 700
  Paisagem com vista de Coimbra Oleo/tabla (60x72cm 23x28in) Lisboa 2001

RAMOS Domingo E. 1894-1967 [39]
- $17 000 - €14 785 - £10 249 - FF96 985
  Paisaje Oil/canvas (94.5x112cm 37x44in) New-York 1998

RAMOS Julio 1868-1945 [3]
- $6 380 - €6 607 - £3 960 - FF43 340
  Escena cotidiana Oleo/lienzo (73.5x98cm 28x38in) Madrid 2000

RAMOS MARTINEZ Alfredo 1872-1946 [80]
- $200 000 - €235 485 - £140 540 - FF1 544 680
  India Xochitl Oil/panel (67x61cm 26x24in) New-York 2000
- $946 - €1 125 - £655 - FF7 378
  Dame im Profil vor Rosengebinde Öl/Leinwand (21x27cm 8x10in) Bremen 2000
- $5 500 - €5 904 - £3 747 - FF38 728
  Mexican Church Pastel/paper (66x49cm 25x19in) Boston MA 2001

RAMOS Mel 1935 [212]
- $30 000 - €34 119 - £20 961 - FF223 803
  Statue of Liberty Oil/canvas (178x94cm 70x37in) Beverly-Hills CA 2000
- $11 000 - €10 578 - £6 777 - FF69 384
  Barbara Acrylic/canvas (46x35.5cm 18x13in) New-York 1999
- $10 000 - €9 946 - £6 207 - FF65 244
  Yum Yum Oil/canvas (35.5x30.5cm 13x12in) Beverly-Hills CA 1999
- $7 753 - €7 669 - £4 834 - FF50 308
  Ohne Titel Watercolour (58.2x58cm 22x22in) Berlin 1999
- $428 - €511 - £305 - FF3 353
  Vantage Print in colors (78.5x63.5cm 30x25in) Berlin 2000

RAMOS Y ALBERTOS Francisco Javier 1744-1817 [1]
- $34 560 - €32 435 - £21 600 - FF212 760
  San Pedro y San Juan curando al paralítico Oleo/lienzo (273x167cm 107x65in) Palma de Mallorca 1999

RAMPAZO Luciano 1936 **[79]**
- $950 - €957 - £592 - FF6 279
  Paris, le soir Oil/canvas (60x50cm 24x20in) New-York 2000
- $700 - €809 - £490 - FF5 304
  «Place du Pantheon» Oil/canvas (27x35cm 11x14in) New-York 2001

RAMSAY Allan 1713-1784 **[70]**
- $69 174 - €65 794 - £42 000 - FF431 579
  Lady Margaret Grant, in a blue-lined oyster satin Dress, blue bow Oil/canvas (127x100.5cm 50x39in) Edinburgh 1999
- $23 433 - €22 933 - £15 000 - FF150 430
  Portrait of Catherine Gale, wearing a silver Silk Dress Oil/canvas (74.5x61.5cm 29x24in) London 1999

RAMSAY Allan 1852-1912 **[21]**
- $1 288 - €1 211 - £800 - FF7 943
  Burning the Heather Oil/canvas (35.5x53.5cm 13x21in) London 1999
- $887 - €1 004 - £600 - FF6 583
  An October Day Oil/canvas (30.5x45.5cm 12x17in) London 2000

RAMSAY Dennis 1925 **[9]**
- $1 901 - €1 748 - £1 175 - FF11 469
  Still life with Pears Tempera/board (45.5x60cm 17x23in) Melbourne 1998

RAMSAY Hugh 1877-1906 **[5]**
- $2 594 - €2 906 - £1 802 - FF19 062
  Self Portrait Charcoal/paper (50x37.5cm 19x14in) Melbourne 2001

RAMSBOTTOM Amos XIX-XX **[6]**
- $1 199 - €1 280 - £800 - FF8 394
  Cricketing Subjects Watercolour (27x18.5cm 10x7in) London 2000

RAMSDELL Frederick Winthrop 1865-1915 **[6]**
- $1 407 - €1 601 - £976 - FF10 500
  «Crescent cycles» Affiche (155x106cm 61x41in) Paris 2000

RAMSEY Carolyn XX **[10]**
- $950 - €1 042 - £645 - FF6 838
  Cajun Houseboat/Cajun Man in Snapbrim Hat/Cajun Boy Casting a Net Silver print (27x35cm 11x14in) New-Orleans LA 2000

RAMSEY Charles Frederick 1875-1951 **[4]**
- $475 - €550 - £336 - FF3 608
  Abstract in White & Blue Pencil (59x44cm 23x17in) Hatfield PA 2000

RAMSEY Milne 1847-1915 **[16]**
- $54 000 - €50 115 - £32 421 - FF328 730
  Roses and an Orienatl Vase on a Brocade Tablecloth Oil/canvas (86x68cm 34x27in) Milford CT 1999

RAN Haya 1948 **[2]**
- $2 400 - €2 701 - £1 653 - FF17 718
  Rochale Tempera (80x61cm 31x24in) Herzelia-Pituah 2000

RANCILLAC Bernard 1931 **[213]**
- $6 798 - €6 708 - £4 188 - FF44 000
  Je me demande qui l'embrasse maintenant Acrylique/toile (160x114cm 62x44in) Versailles 1999
- $6 541 - €5 488 - £3 837 - FF36 000
  Cecil rouge Acrylique/toile (116x89cm 45x35in) Paris 1998
- $480 - €457 - £298 - FF3 450
  Personnage Crayons couleurs/papier (34x34cm 13x13in) Paris 1999

RANCOULET Ernest XIX-XX **[63]**
- $3 493 - €4 176 - £2 400 - FF27 391
  A Fisherwoman, the figure standing with a Basket of shell fish Bronze (H86cm H33in) Billingshurst, West-Sussex 2000
- $885 - €892 - £550 - FF5 853
  Guerrier en tenue d'apparat Bronze (H71cm H27in) Bruxelles 2000

RAND Paul 1896-1970 **[3]**
- $1 947 - €2 202 - £1 370 - FF14 445
  Bc Mountain Watercolour/paper (54.5x48cm 21x18in) Vancouver, BC. 2001

RANDAL Frank XIX-XX **[5]**
- $1 018 - €1 218 - £700 - FF7 989
  Madonna and Child with Saints, after Palma Vecchio Watercolour/paper (49.5x73cm 19x28in) Billingshurst, West-Sussex 2001

RANDALL Ted (Theodore) 1914-1985 **[1]**
- $4 200 - €4 351 - £2 673 - FF28 540
  Planter Form Ceramic (59x58.5x22cm 23x23x8in) New-York 2000

RANDOLPH Lee Fritz 1880-1956 **[7]**
- $700 - €795 - £486 - FF5 213
  Lush Forest Landscape with Figures along a Trail Oil/canvas (61x51cm 24x20in) St. Petersburg FL 2001

RANDON de Charles, Ing. géogr. XVIII-XIX **[1]**
- $30 000 - €25 198 - £17 637 - FF165 288
  Panoramic of Paris with the Dome of the Invalides Watercolour, gouache/paper (57x90cm 22x35in) New-York 1998

RANFT Richard 1862-1931 **[76]**
- $1 207 - €1 296 - £807 - FF8 500
  La carriole au printemps Huile/panneau (39x51cm 15x20in) Paris 2000
- $375 - €388 - £237 - FF2 558
  Au cirque femme au cheval Color lithograph (34.5x23.5cm 13x9in) New-York 2000

RANFT Thomas 1945 **[14]**
- $122 - €112 - £75 - FF737
  Ausbruch einer Landschaft/Horizonte/Drei Ebenen Radierung (54x39cm 21x15in) Bielefeld 1999

RANFTL Mathias Johann 1805-1854 **[58]**
- $17 468 - €17 895 - £10 780 - FF17 186
  Wäscherinnen auf dem Weg ins Gebirge Oil/panel (63x48cm 24x18in) Düsseldorf 2000
- $24 133 - €24 318 - £15 042 - FF159 513
  Mädchen mit Hund vor Wien Huile/panneau (31x39cm 12x15in) Zürich 2000
- $924 - €872 - £573 - FF5 720
  Studie zu einem aufschauenden Hund Aquarell/Papier (17.5x15cm 6x5in) Wien 1999

RANGEL Mario 1938 **[8]**
- $1 541 - €1 808 - £1 108 - FF11 858
  Sueño recurrente Acuarela (49x32cm 19x12in) México 2001

RANGER Henry Ward 1858-1916 **[66]**
- $6 000 - €5 745 - £3 697 - FF37 688
  View of Mystic, Connecticut Oil/canvas (71x91cm 28x36in) Portsmouth NH 1999
- $2 000 - €2 275 - £1 397 - FF14 920
  Country Landscape Oil/board (30x40cm 12x16in) Mystic CT 2000

R

✐ **$850 - €928 - £547 -** FF6 089
Beached Boats Watercolour/paper (26x41cm
10x16in) Mystic CT 2000

RANIERI de Aristide XIX-XX [16]
✎ **$7 500 - €6 639 - £4 585 -** FF43 551
Terpsichore Marble (H90cm H35in) New-York 1999

RANIERI DI LEONARDO DA PISA XVI [2]
☞ **$100 000 - €110 747 - £67 820 -** FF726 450
**The Madonna and Child with Saint
Bartholomew and Michael** Oil/panel (162x128.5cm
63x50in) New-York 2000

RANITZ de Elisabeth C. Maria 1880-? [12]
✐ **$204 - €220 - £140 -** FF1 442
Interieur mit Blumen Gouache/paper (64x48cm
25x18in) München 2001

RANK William XX [2]
✐ **$3 200 - €3 284 - £2 006 -** FF21 541
**Velvet of Pennsylvania Amish Farm with House,
Barn, Horse and Carriage** Watercolour/paper
(64x86cm 25x34in) Downington PA 2000

RANKEN William Bruce Ellis 1881-1941 [31]
☞ **$7 657 - €6 679 - £4 631 -** FF43 809
«Early Summer» - Stilleben med blommor i vas
Oil/canvas (135x109cm 53x42in) Stockholm 1998
☞ **$6 907 - €6 542 - £4 200 -** FF42 912
**Portrait of Violet Keppel, bust-length in white
dress** Oil/canvas (76x63.5cm 29x25in) London 1999

RANKIN David G. 1946 [112]
☞ **$3 646 - €4 254 - £2 537 -** FF27 906
Rocky Hillside Oil/board (243x156.5cm 95x61in)
Melbourne 2000
☞ **$1 461 - €1 606 - £936 -** FF10 534
Bundeena Headland Oil/canvas (76x92cm 29x36in)
Melbourne 2000
▥ **$176 - €169 - £108 -** FF1 110
Ragged Scrub I Screenprint (82x62cm 32x24in)
Melbourne 1999

RANKIN William XX [3]
☞ **$7 000 - €6 781 - £4 365 -** FF44 479
Le salon de musique de la Villa Trianon
Watercolour/paper (56x77.5cm 22x30in) Beverly-Hills
CA 1999

RANN Vollian Burr 1897-1956 [10]
☞ **$1 800 - €1 730 - £1 100 -** FF11 345
Roof Tops Provincetown Oil/board (40x50cm
16x20in) Provincetown MA 1999

RANSOM Fletcher C. XIX-XX [3]
☞ **$1 700 - €1 696 - £1 061 -** FF11 123
No Hunting Oil/canvas (55x71cm 22x28in) Cincinnati
OH 1999

RANSOM Sydney Lewis XIX-XX [3]
▥ **$1 200 - €1 339 - £785 -** FF8 781
«The Poster, an Illustred Monthly Chronicle»
Poster (75.5x50cm 29x19in) New-York 2000

RANSON Paul Élie 1861-1909 [78]
☞ **$26 043 - €25 347 - £16 000 -** FF166 265
Rochers en Eskual Heria Oil/canvas (50x61cm
19x24in) London 1999
✐ **$902 - €762 - £536 -** FF5 000
Carnaval à Venise Gouache/papier (20x15cm 7x5in)
Quimper 1998
▥ **$900 - €779 - £542 -** FF5 110
La lecture Lithograph (13x21.5cm 5x8in) New-York
1998

RANSON Pierre 1736-1786 [2]
▥ **$244 - €238 - £150 -** FF1 563
Cahier de groupes de fleurs et d'ornements
Engraving (23.5x18.5cm 9x7in) London 1999

RANSVE Bjorn 1944 [27]
☞ **$23 188 - €27 586 - £16 038 -** FF180 950
Stenansikt Oil/panel (121x100cm 47x39in) Oslo 2000
▥ **$663 - €743 - £460 -** FF4 871
Sittende akt (röd) Color lithograph (53x42cm
20x16in) Oslo 2001

RANSY Jean 1910-1991 [30]
☞ **$1 793 - €2 107 - £1 292 -** FF13 821
Vers Murano Huile/toile (53x90cm 20x35in) Bruxelles
2001
✐ **$400 - €471 - £288 -** FF3 089
**Le jardin du cardinal/La bibliothèque, projets de
décor** Gouache/papier (21x29cm 8x11in) Bruxelles
2001

RANTANEN Ulla 1938 [14]
▥ **$276 - €235 - £165 -** FF1 544
I vattnet Etching (54x74cm 21x29in) Helsinki 1998

RANTZER Philip 1956 [3]
✎ **$2 400 - €2 664 - £1 673 -** FF17 475
Untitled Construction (32.5x17.5x12.5cm 12x6x4in)
Tel Aviv 2001

RANUCCI Giuseppe XVIII [2]
☞ **$9 000 - €10 600 - £6 224 -** FF69 533
Madonna in Prayer Oil/copper (35.5x27.5cm
13x10in) New-York 2000

RANUCCI Lucio 1934 [44]
☞ **$1 569 - €1 829 - £1 087 -** FF12 000
Au balcon Huile/papier (40x50cm 15x19in)
Strasbourg 2000

RANVIER-CHARTIER Lucie 1867-1932 [9]
☞ **$1 956 - €2 287 - £1 396 -** FF15 000
«Souk aux étoffes» Huile/toile (33x41cm 12x16in)
Paris 2001
▥ **$1 145 - €1 067 - £708 -** FF7 000
**«Tunisie. La mieux située des stations hiver-
nales africaines»** Affiche couleur (107x74cm
42x29in) Paris 1999

RANWELL William act.1830-1843 [1]
✐ **$4 209 - €5 006 - £3 000 -** FF32 835
**The Launch of H.M.S.Trafalgar 120 Guns at
Woolwich Dockyard** Ink (52x74cm 20x29in) London
2000

RANZONI Daniele 1843-1889 [17]
☞ **$58 800 - €50 796 - £39 200 -** FF333 200
Lo chalet di Villa Ada sul Lago Maggiore
Olio/tela (75x100cm 29x39in) Roma 1998
✐ **$12 766 - €15 044 - £8 970 -** FF98 683
Melankoli Akvarell/papper (40.5x27cm 15x10in)
Malmö 2000

RANZONI Hans 1868-1956 [24]
☞ **$1 986 - €2 180 - £1 320 -** FF14 301
**Blühende Obstbäume in den Weingärten bei
Gumpoldskirchen** Öl/Karton (52x71cm 20x27in)
Wien 2000

RAOULT Ivan XIX [3]
▦ **$3 000 - €3 068 - £1 890 -** FF20 126
**Indigenous People of the Caucus Mountains,
the Region of Bessarabie** Albumen print (18x24cm
7x9in) New-York 2000

RAOUX Albert XIX **[14]**
📷 **$2 627** - €2 736 - **£1 665** - FF17 948
Blumenstilleben auf einem Marmorsockel
Öl/Leinwand (72x94.5cm 28x37in) Zürich 2001

RAOUX Jean 1677-1734 **[15]**
📷 **$16 746** - €14 257 - **£10 000** - FF93 521
The Judgement of Solomon Oil/canvas (63x102cm 24x40in) London 1998

RAPACKI Józef 1871-1929 **[82]**
📷 **$11 603** - €11 574 - **£7 242** - FF75 920
Paysans dans la région de Cracovie devant une chaumière Oil/canvas (92.5x134.5cm 36x52in) Warszawa 1999
📷 **$2 400** - €2 783 - **£1 700** - FF18 255
A Summer Meadow Oil/canvas (68.5x96.5cm 26x37in) London 2000
✏ **$1 495** - €1 746 - **£1 024** - FF11 453
Vieux cimetière en automne Aquarelle/papier (67.5x49.5cm 26x19in) Warszawa 2000
🗐 **$146** - €156 - **£99** - FF1 025
Maison de campagne Lithographie (33x44.5cm 12x17in) Lódz 2001

RAPENO Armand 1858-? **[12]**
🗐 **$344** - €396 - **£243** - FF2 600
«**L'esclave Reine**» Affiche (120x160cm 47x62in) Paris 2001

RAPETTI Camillo 1859-1929 **[6]**
📷 **$4 250** - €4 406 - **£2 550** - FF28 900
Sulle quai della Senna Olio/cartone (32.5x24cm 12x9in) Prato 2000

RAPHAEL Joseph Morris 1869-1950 **[100]**
📷 **$8 000** - €7 554 - **£4 968** - FF49 551
The Village Bridge Oil/panel (51x76cm 20x29in) Beverly-Hills CA 1999
📷 **$2 097** - €1 815 - **£1 273** - FF11 906
A sailing boat on the lake De Kaag near Leiden Oil/panel (19.5x31cm 7x12in) Amsterdam 1999
✏ **$1 146** - €1 134 - **£701** - FF7 441
St. Margherita Watercolour/paper (40x59.5cm 15x23in) Amsterdam 2000
🗐 **$1 048** - €908 - **£636** - FF5 953
Brussels on a rainy day Etching (12x17cm 4x6in) Amsterdam 1999

RAPHAEL William 1833-1914 **[37]**
📷 **$1 100** - €942 - **£661** - FF6 181
Trapper Before a Coal Stove Oil/canvas (27x35cm 11x14in) Cleveland OH 1998
✏ **$400** - €343 - **£240** - FF2 247
The Trapper Pencil/paper (20x30cm 8x12in) Cleveland OH 1998

RAPIN Aimé(e) 1869-1956 **[17]**
✏ **$417** - €402 - **£257** - FF2 640
Stilleben mit Blumenstrauss und Wasserglas Pastell/Papier (29x38cm 11x14in) Bern 1999

RAPIN Henri 1873-1939 **[9]**
✏ **$2 599** - €2 897 - **£1 816** - FF19 000
Temple de la victoire Acropole d'Athéne Crayon/papier (73x60cm 28x23in) Paris 2001

RAPISARDI Alfio 1929 **[13]**
📷 **$700** - €726 - **£420** - FF4 760
Natura morta Tempera/cartone (70x50cm 27x19in) Prato 1999

RAPNICKI Janusz XX **[3]**
🗐 **$1 361** - €1 429 - **£900** - FF9 375
«**Olimpiada W Tokio**» Poster (82x57cm 32x22in) London 2000

RAPOTEC Stanislaus, Stan 1913-1997 **[27]**
📷 **$15 143** - €17 127 - **£10 657** - FF112 343
Drawing at St Peter's Square Acrylic (122x183cm 48x72in) Malvern, Victoria 2001
📷 **$2 019** - €2 243 - **£1 352** - FF14 713
Bottle of Wine and Grapes Acrylic/paper (63x47.5cm 24x18in) Nedlands 2000

RAPOUS Michele Antonio 1733-1819 **[11]**
📷 **$26 400** - €24 210 - **£19 800** - FF224 400
Giuseppe spiega sogni/Si fa riconoscere dai fratelli/Incontro/Giacobbe Olio/tela (49x62cm 19x24in) Venezia 2000

RAPP Alex 1869-1927 **[38]**
📷 **$669** - €740 - **£464** - FF4 854
Vinter vid stranden, Helsingfors Oil/canvas (44x49cm 17x19in) Helsinki 2001

RAPPARD van Anthon Gerhard Alex. 1858-1892 **[10]**
📷 **$7 361** - €6 353 - **£4 442** - FF41 672
The Tile Painter - a study Oil/canvas (32x24cm 12x9in) Amsterdam 1999
✏ **$678** - €635 - **£422** - FF4 167
Tuin op Sinneveld te Santpoort Charcoal (24x45cm 9x17in) Amsterdam 1999

RAPPINI Vittorio XIX-XX **[19]**
✏ **$400** - €518 - **£300** - FF3 400
A street in Cairo Acquarello/carta (35x23.5cm 13x9in) Torino 2000

RÄSÄNEN Eino 1902-1970 **[11]**
🖎 **$425** - €404 - **£260** - FF2 647
Ropande pojke Bronze (H29cm H11in) Helsinki 1999

RASCH Heinrich 1840-1913 **[17]**
📷 **$1 528** - €1 565 - **£966** - FF10 268
Courtship Oil/panel (28x44.5cm 11x17in) Billingshurst, West-Sussex 2000

RASCHEN Henry 1854-1937 **[17]**
📷 **$14 000** - €15 610 - **£9 448** - FF102 394
Native American on Horseback with Village of Teepees Background Oil/canvas (74x100cm 29x39in) Thomaston ME 2000

RASCHKA Robert 1847-? **[5]**
✏ **$1 792** - €1 631 - **£1 100** - FF10 699
An ornate Drawing Room Gouache/paper (26x53cm 10x20in) London 1999

RASENBERGER Alfred 1885-1949 **[37]**
📷 **$1 227** - €1 431 - **£864** - FF9 390
Alpenlandschaft bei Kandersteig, Schweiz Öl/Leinwand (50x70cm 19x27in) Königstein 2001

RASER Pierre XX **[2]**
📷 **$2 031** - €2 134 - **£1 337** - FF14 000
Cafetière, framboise et coffret Huile/toile (33x41cm 12x16in) Paris 2000

RASKIN Joseph 1897-1981 **[17]**
📷 **$2 200** - €2 510 - **£1 529** - FF16 466
Around the Bend Oil/canvas (76x60cm 30x24in) Dedham MA 2001

RASKIN Saul 1878-? **[13]**
🗐 **$80** - €92 - **£55** - FF603
«**Self Drawing**» Lithograph (32x23cm 12x9in) Cleveland OH 2000

RASMUSSEN Aage 1913-1975 **[31]**
🗐 **$1 200** - €1 053 - **£728** - FF6 904
«**Storstromsbroen**» Poster (100x61cm 39x24in) New-York 1999

RASMUSSEN Carl I.E.C. 1841-1893 **[82]**
- **$2 806** - €2 422 - **£1 695** - FF15 886
  Marine med sejlskibe ved solnedgang, i forgrunden båd med tre køer Oil/canvas (42x69cm 16x27in) Vejle 1999
- **$1 366** - €1 475 - **£943** - FF9 676
  Landskab Oil/canvas (21x36cm 8x14in) København 2001

RASMUSSEN Georg Anton 1842-1914 **[103]**
- **$3 654** - €4 346 - **£2 604** - FF28 508
  Überfahrt, norwegischer Fjord an einem hellen Sommertag Öl/Leinwand (62x96cm 24x37in) Köln 2000
- **$523** - €562 - **£350** - FF3 689
  Norwegische Fjordlandschaft Öl/Karton (18x24cm 7x9in) Bremen 2000

RASMUSSEN Niels Peter 1847-1918 **[96]**
- **$887** - €1 046 - **£624** - FF6 864
  Duer der hviler sig ved foderskålen Oil/canvas (40x56cm 15x22in) Vejle 2000
- **$628** - €670 - **£418** - FF4 398
  Bogfinke på en gren omgivet af brombaerranker Oil/canvas (34x24cm 13x9in) København 2000

RASMUSSEN-EILERSEN Eiler 1827-1912 **[65]**
- **$1 066** - €1 139 - **£726** - FF7 471
  Skovparti med lille pige der vogter får Oil/canvas (69x95cm 27x37in) Vejle 2001
- **$3 387** - €3 156 - **£2 100** - FF20 702
  Monastery near Copenhagen Watercolour/paper (86x125cm 33x49in) Billingshurst, West-Sussex 1999

RASPAIL Benjamin fils 1823-1899 **[4]**
- **$2 179** - €2 134 - **£1 341** - FF14 000
  Natures mortes aux oiseaux Huile/panneau (24.5x19cm 9x7in) Besançon 1999

RASSENFOSSE Armand 1862-1934 **[719]**
- **$9 982** - €11 403 - **£6 946** - FF74 796
  Jeune femme nue de dos Huile/carton (72x53cm 28x20in) Bruxelles 2001
- **$2 422** - €2 355 - **£1 482** - FF15 447
  Portrait de Jeanne T. (étude) Huile/panneau (30x24cm 11x9in) Liège 1999
- **$1 864** - €1 550 - **£1 094** - FF10 170
  Portrait of a Miner Watercolour (27x16.5cm 10x6in) Amsterdam 1998
- **$214** - €248 - **£151** - FF1 626
  La tricoteuse Eau-forte (26x17cm 10x6in) Bruxelles 2000

RASTRUP Lars 1862-1949 **[23]**
- **$853** - €858 - **£531** - FF5 297
  Sceneri fra et fiskerleje Oil/canvas (38x54cm 14x21in) Vejle 1999

RATEAU Armand Albert 1882-1938 **[13]**
- **$600 000** - €644 036 - **£401 520** - FF4 224 600
  Armchair, Model No.1793 Bronze (92.5x61x51.5cm 36x24x20in) New-York 2000
- **$65 000** - €63 107 - **£40 157** - FF413 952
  Wall Sconce Bronze (20.5x25.5cm 8x10in) New-York 1999

RATH Alan 1959 **[3]**
- **$14 000** - €13 925 - **£8 689** - FF91 341
  Clock II (2 O'clock) Assemblage (63.5x127x33cm 25x50x12in) Beverly-Hills CA 1999

RATHBONE John 1750-1807 **[51]**
- **$1 160** - €1 278 - **£774** - FF8 384
  Schottisches Hochland Öl/Leinwand (46x55cm 18x21in) Satow 2000

RATHSMAN Siri 1895-1974 **[90]**
- **$588** - €659 - **£409** - FF4 324
  «Komposition-20» Oil/canvas (90x130cm 35x51in) Stockholm 2001

RATNAVIRA Gamini P. 1949 **[8]**
- **$4 869** - €4 680 - **£3 000** - FF30 699
  Royalty of the Canopy - Hyacinth Macaws Acrylic/canvas (90x120.5cm 35x47in) London 1999

RATTERMAN Walter G. 1887-1944 **[6]**
- **$1 400** - €1 512 - **£967** - FF9 917
  Reclining nude Oil/canvas (46x61cm 18x24in) Bethesda MD 2001

RATTI Carlo Giuseppe 1737-1795 **[4]**
- **$14 000** - €12 960 - **£8 451** - FF85 015
  Angel Liberating Peter from Prison Oil/canvas (159.5x103.5cm 62x40in) New-York 1999

RATTI Giovanni Agostino 1699-1775 **[4]**
- **$600** - €622 - **£360** - FF4 080
  San Marco evangelista Inchiostro (23x19cm 9x7in) Milano 2000

RATTNER Abraham 1895-1978 **[46]**
- **$4 000** - €3 730 - **£2 481** - FF24 466
  There was Darkness Over all the Land Oil/canvas (81x100cm 31x39in) New-York 1999
- **$650** - €625 - **£403** - FF4 097
  In the Beginning Color lithograph (66x51cm 25x20in) New-York 1999

RATTRAY Alexander Wellwood 1849-1902 **[23]**
- **$529** - €494 - **£320** - FF3 239
  Evening in the Glen Oil/canvas/board (30.5x42cm 12x16in) Glasgow 1998

RATY Albert 1889-1970 **[181]**
- **$5 060** - €5 701 - **£3 519** - FF37 398
  Le pont sur la rivière Huile/toile (38x46cm 14x18in) Bruxelles 2001
- **$1 612** - €1 859 - **£1 102** - FF12 195
  Église en Ardennes Huile/carton (32x41cm 12x16in) Bruxelles 2000
- **$378** - €446 - **£266** - FF2 926
  Village Encre Chine (20.5x14.5cm 8x5in) Liège 2000

RATZKA Arthur Ludwig 1869-? **[1]**
- **$2 061** - €1 952 - **£1 283** - FF12 802
  Portraet af pige med bold Pastel/paper (80x59cm 31x23in) Vejle 1999

RAU Ch. XX **[3]**
- **$319** - €305 - **£199** - FF2 000
  «D'où viens-tu Johnny?» Affiche couleur (160x240cm 62x94in) Paris 1999

RAU Emil 1858-1937 **[110]**
- **$9 272** - €9 715 - **£6 133** - FF63 724
  Rast im Schatten: Dirndl und Schnitter am Tisch vor dem Bauernhaus Öl/Leinwand (110x133cm 43x52in) München 2000
- **$4 779** - €4 090 - **£2 876** - FF27 828
  Hausmusik in der Bauernstube Öl/Leinwand (110x90cm 43x35in) München 1998
- **$2 322** - €2 180 - **£1 440** - FF14 301
  Profilportrait eines Mädchens in Tracht Oil/panel (38x31cm 14x12in) Wien 1999

RAU Martin Friedrich 1858-? **[1]**
- **$2 000** - €2 230 - **£1 344** - FF14 628
  Coupl Playing Cards in Tavern Oil/board (20x25cm 8x10in) Detroit MI 2000

RAU William H. 1855-1920 **[14]**
📷 $900 - €752 - **£532** - FF4 934
    Bear Creek Curve Photograph (42x51cm 16x20in)
    New-York 1998

RÄUBER Wilhelm Carl 1849-1926 **[20]**
  $762 - €818 - **£510** - FF5 366
    Falknerjagd Oil/panel (35x27cm 13x10in) Frankfurt
    2000

RAUCH Carluccio 1836-1894 **[2]**
  $2 116 - €2 501 - **£1 500** - FF16 404
    Picnic by the Fountain Watercolour, gouache/paper
    (36x54cm 14x21in) London 2000

RAUCH DE MILAN Johann Nepomuk 1804-1847
[17]
  $18 300 - €18 168 - **£11 425** - FF119 175
    Hirten auf einer Landstrasse in der Toskana
    Oil/panel (52.5x74cm 20x29in) Wien 1999
  $4 991 - €5 113 - **£3 080** - FF33 539
    Italienische Landschaft mit Staffage Öl/Karton
    (31x25.5cm 12x10in) Düsseldorf 2000

RAUCHINGER Henryk / Heinrich 1858-1942 **[15]**
  $3 078 - €3 520 - **£2 114** - FF23 091
    Portrait de Karoline des Swiecickich
    Zakrzenskiej Huile/toile (69x56cm 27x22in)
    Warszawa 2000

RAUDNITZ Albert 1814-1899 **[9]**
  $5 490 - €6 096 - **£3 675** - FF39 985
    Interiör med kvinna vid spegel Oil/panel (53x40cm
    20x15in) Stockholm 2000

RAUECKER Theodor 1854-1940 **[5]**
  $3 971 - €4 724 - **£2 834** - FF30 985
    Der Mittagsschlaf Öl/Leinwand (45x56cm 17x22in)
    Wien 2000

RAUGHT John Willard 1857-1931 **[6]**
  $2 500 - €2 433 - **£1 536** - FF15 961
    Countryside Scene with Figure on Path Oil/board
    (20x27cm 8x11in) Hatfield PA 1999

RAUH Caspar Walter 1912-1983 **[90]**
  $302 - €361 - **£215** - FF2 368
    Am Fluss Watercolour (32.6x47.4cm 12x18in)
    Hamburg 2000
  $179 - €204 - **£125** - FF1 341
    Den Fluss hinab/Drei Köpfe/Vor der Ausfahrt
    1977/Episode im Walde Radierung (39.5x53cm
    15x20in) Hamburg 2001

RAUHWERGER Jan 1942 **[1]**
  $2 600 - €2 570 - **£1 591** - FF16 856
    Woman (Lea Nikel) in Landscape
    Watercolour/paper (100x70cm 39x27in) Tel Aviv 2000

RAULINO Tobias Dyonis 1787-1838 **[3]**
  $7 908 - €7 669 - **£4 977** - FF50 308
    Blick auf Baden Baden Gouache/paper (64x90cm
    25x35in) München 1999

RAULT XX **[13]**
  $143 - €152 - **£90** - FF1 000
    La Seine à Notre-Dame Lavis/papier (46x35cm
    18x13in) Paris 2000

RAUMANN Joseph 1908 **[73]**
  $523 - €610 - **£362** - FF4 000
    La plage Huile/toile (50x62cm 19x24in) Le Havre
    2000

RAUPP Friedrich, Fritz 1871-1949 **[22]**
  $825 - €818 - **£516** - FF5 366
    Blick auf die Fraueninsel (Chiemsee)
    Öl/Leinwand (32.5x45.5cm 12x17in) München 1999

RAUPP Karl 1837-1918 **[59]**
  $17 096 - €19 875 - **£12 000** - FF130 372
    Midday Rest Oil/canvas (134.5x213cm 52x83in)
    London 2001
  $9 326 - €8 692 - **£5 754** - FF57 016
    Gewagte Überfahrt Oil/panel (50x40cm 19x15in)
    Köln 1999
  $1 749 - €1 943 - **£1 216** - FF12 744
    Uferlandschaft am Chiemsee Öl/Karton
    (29.5x38cm 11x14in) Heidelberg 2001
  $249 - €281 - **£172** - FF1 844
    Strandpartie bei Frauenchiemsee Pencil/paper
    (30.2x24.2cm 11x9in) München 2000

RAURICH Y PETRE Nicolás 1871-1945 **[14]**
  $2 240 - €2 102 - **£1 365** - FF13 790
    Cascada Oleo/cartón (49x37cm 19x14in) Madrid 1999

RAUSCHENBERG Robert 1925 **[1061]**
  $53 760 - €45 735 - **£32 070** - FF300 000
    China Proverb Acrylique (213x92cm 83x36in) Paris
    1998
  $18 000 - €20 885 - **£12 427** - FF136 998
    Untitled Acrylic (85.5x61cm 33x24in) New-York 2000
  $50 000 - €54 322 - **£32 195** - FF359 940
    On Tour (#5) Mixed media (30.5x23cm 12x9in) New-
    York 2000
  $8 500 - €9 908 - **£5 885** - FF64 995
    Bamhue, Roci Japan Sculpture (228.5x102cm
    89x40in) New-York 2000
  $3 200 - €3 761 - **£2 218** - FF24 670
    Tibetan Locks (Mountaineer) Relief (12x12x4cm
    4x4x1in) New-York 2000
  $8 327 - €7 729 - **£5 000** - FF50 696
    Untitled Watercolour, gouache (79x56cm 31x22in)
    London 1999
  $1 800 - €1 527 - **£1 085** - FF10 016
    Test Stone #2, from Booster and Seven Studies
    Lithograph (104.5x75.5cm 41x29in) New-York 1998
  $1 558 - €1 329 - **£939** - FF8 719
    Neapel Gelatin silver print (48.3x32.7cm 19x12in)
    Köln 1998

RAUSCHER August Friedrich 1754-1808 **[10]**
  $9 491 - €8 692 - **£5 785** - FF57 016
    Hirschjagd Öl/Leinwand (43.2x57.2cm 17x22in)
    München 1999
  $10 002 - €10 737 - **£6 694** - FF70 431
    Waldlandschaft Gouache/paper (22.5x28cm 8x11in)
    Hamburg 2000

RAVASCO Cesare 1875-? **[4]**
  $4 500 - €4 378 - **£2 769** - FF28 720
    Alegoria Bronze (56x50cm 22x19in) Buenos-Aires
    1999

RAVAULT Ange René 1766-1845 **[4]**
  $10 962 - €10 671 - **£6 734** - FF70 000
    Portrait de famille sur fond de paysage
    Huile/toile (73x60cm 28x23in) Paris 1999

RAVAZZI Marco 1815 **[1]**
  $4 500 - €4 407 - **£2 899** - FF28 911
    Le bal masqué Oil/canvas (68.5x57cm 26x22in)
    New-York 1999

RAVEEL Roger 1921 **[179]**
  $17 577 - €20 420 - **£12 352** - FF133 947
    De omarming Oil/canvas (195x145cm 76x57in)
    Amsterdam 2001
  $8 710 - €9 420 - **£5 624** - FF61 788
    Drie witte paaltjes Oil/canvas (80x100cm 31x39in)
    Lokeren 2000

R

$2 152 - €1 983 - £1 296 - FF13 008
Paysage Huile/papier (25x35cm 9x13in) Antwerpen 1999

$4 300 - €4 958 - £2 960 - FF32 520
Man met hoed Gouache/paper (72x54cm 28x21in) Lokeren 2000

$417 - €446 - £284 - FF2 926
Een man ten voeten uit Eau-forte (39.5x29.5cm 15x11in) Lokeren 2001

RAVEL Edouard John E. 1847-1920 [51]
$850 - €984 - £602 - FF6 453
Flusslandschaft mit einem verlassenen Boot am Ufer Öl/Leinwand (34x57cm 13x22in) Zürich 2000

$667 - €787 - £469 - FF5 160
Mädchen mit Zöpfen Oil/panel (21x17.5cm 8x6in) Bern 2000

$267 - €315 - £193 - FF2 064
«Etude pour la Fontaine de Jouvence» Pierre noire (45.5x33.5cm 17x13in) Sion 2001

RAVEL Jules Hippolyte 1826-1898 [9]
$4 670 - €4 269 - £2 858 - FF28 000
Turc rêvant des Houris Huile/panneau (55x41cm 21x16in) Paris 1999

RAVEL Marie XIX [1]
$13 000 - €12 874 - £8 093 - FF84 445
The Flower Arranger Oil/canvas (45x56cm 17x22in) New-York 1999

RAVEN John Samuel 1829-1877 [5]
$49 730 - €50 112 - £31 000 - FF328 711
The Rooks Parliament Oil/canvas (30.5x51cm 12x20in) London 2000

RAVEN Samuel 1775-1847 [23]
$2 887 - €2 856 - £1 800 - FF18 733
Snipe Shooting Oil/panel (12x17cm 4x6in) London 1999

RAVEN von Ernst 1816-1890 [8]
$1 960 - €2 045 - £1 234 - FF13 415
Königssee und der Watzmann Öl/Leinwand (84x121cm 33x47in) Stuttgart 2000

RAVEN-HILL Leonard 1867-1942 [12]
$1 100 - €1 283 - £772 - FF8 415
«Pick-me-up» Poster (49x75.5cm 19x29in) New-York 2000

RAVENET Simon François I 1706-1774 [7]
$192 - €225 - £135 - FF1 475
La marche comique, nach Pater Radierung (42x30.5cm 16x12in) Berlin 2001

RAVENSBERG Ludvig Orning 1871-1958 [4]
$702 - €811 - £494 - FF5 319
Fra Nice Mixed media/paper (36x54cm 14x21in) Oslo 2000

RAVENSTEIN von Paul 1854-1938 [12]
$1 380 - €1 278 - £833 - FF8 384
Hammerschmiede im Schwarzwald Öl/Karton (43x56cm 16x22in) Heidelberg 1999

RAVENSWAAY Huibert Antonie 1891-1972 [11]
$239 - €272 - £165 - FF1 786
De pont te Gorinchem Oil/panel (27x50cm 10x19in) Dordrecht 2000

RAVENSWAAY van Adriana 1816-1872 [8]
$27 218 - €23 015 - £16 276 - FF150 967
Peonies, Tulips, Violets, Morning Glory and Forget-me-nots Oil/canvas (60x50cm 23x19in) Amsterdam 1998

$2 969 - €2 897 - £1 827 - FF19 000
Nature morte aux fleurs sauvages Huile/panneau (19x23cm 7x9in) Nantes 1999

RAVENSWAAY van Johannes Gijsb. 1815-1849 [7]
$7 673 - €7 606 - £4 800 - FF49 891
Figures with a Horse and Sled on a Frozen River Oil/canvas (42x49.5cm 16x19in) London 1999

RAVENTOS Maria Assumpció 1930 [4]
$960 - €901 - £600 - FF5 910
Muro nomada 2 Tapisserie (270x250cm 106x98in) Madrid 1999

RAVENZWAAY van Jan 1789-1869 [39]
$4 794 - €5 445 - £3 363 - FF35 719
Cattle at Pasture Oil/canvas (51x62cm 20x24in) Amsterdam 2001

$3 850 - €3 630 - £2 386 - FF23 812
Ship in a Moonlit Bay Oil/panel (18x25cm 7x9in) Amsterdam 1999

$283 - €318 - £196 - FF2 083
Bozgezicht met rustende boer en zijn koeien Encre (17.5x18cm 6x7in) The Hague 2000

RAVERAT Gwen, née Darwin 1885-1957 [10]
$587 - €541 - £360 - FF3 550
Modern Woodcutters No.1 Woodcut (11x16.5cm 4x6in) London 1998

RAVESTEYN van Dirck de Quade 1565/70-c.1620 [6]
$107 589 - €115 489 - £72 000 - FF757 555
The Toilet of Venus Oil/canvas (163x128cm 64x50in) London 2000

$65 000 - €69 530 - £44 317 - FF456 085
The Mystic Marriage of Saint Catherine Oil/panel (44x29.5cm 17x11in) New-York 2001

RAVESTEYN van Hubert 1638-c.1690 [7]
$43 260 - €43 603 - £27 000 - FF286 020
Holländische Bauernwirtschaft Oil/panel (62x89cm 24x35in) Wien 2000

$14 500 - €15 031 - £8 700 - FF98 600
Natura morta Olio/tavola (35x45cm 13x17in) Milano 1999

RAVESTEYN van Jan Anthonisz c.1570-1657 [21]
$69 826 - €68 394 - £45 000 - FF448 632
Portrait of Joannes Ruyter, aged five, in a red Costume, Garden beyond Oil/panel (120.5x79.5cm 47x31in) London 1999

RAVET Victor 1840-1895 [11]
$1 814 - €2 132 - £1 298 - FF13 983
Intérieur animé Huile/panneau (43.5x59cm 17x23in) Bruxelles 2000

$1 379 - €1 588 - £941 - FF10 418
Jeune femme en robe rose Oil/panel (41.5x29.5cm 16x11in) Amsterdam 2000

RAVI VARMA Raja 1848-1906 [9]
$38 000 - €44 901 - £26 930 - FF294 530
Village Beauty Oil/canvas (43x28cm 16x11in) New-York 2000

RAVIER François-Auguste 1814-1895 [375]
$6 850 - €6 708 - £4 215 - FF44 000
Paysage près de Crémieu Huile/toile (46.5x37.5cm 18x14in) Lyon 1999

$2 432 - €2 668 - £1 569 - FF17 500
Paysage vallonné au ciel nuageux Huile/toile/carton (21x41cm 8x16in) Paris 2000

$1 645 - €1 524 - £1 023 - FF10 500
Soleil couchant sur un étang Aquarelle (28x20.5cm 11x8in) Paris 1999

$18 942 - €16 007 - **£11 266** - FF105 000
Ensemble de photographies Tirage papier salé
(21.5x28cm 8x11in) Chartres 1998

RAVILIOUS Eric 1903-1942 **[22]**
$1 611 - €1 582 - **£1 000** - FF10 379
The Holy Children, Apocrypha Woodcut
(21.5x29cm 8x11in) London 1999

RAVN Johannes 1922-1991 **[47]**
$308 - €351 - **£211** - FF2 304
Fiskgjusebo Oil/canvas (81x65.5cm 31x25in)
Stockholm 2000

RAVO René 1904-? **[10]**
$401 - €343 - **£240** - FF2 247
«Radiola, machine à laver...à essorage centrifuge!» Poster (154x114cm 60x44in) London 1998

RAWLINGS John XX **[7]**
$1 400 - €1 170 - **£828** - FF7 675
Nude Behind Bamboo Shade Silver print
(38x49cm 15x19in) New-York 1998

RAWLINGS Leo 1918-1984 **[23]**
$1 934 - €1 804 - **£1 200** - FF11 832
Sikhs and Garwolies of the 11th Division cutting their Retreat Watercolour/paper (47x67.5cm
18x26in) London 1999

RAWNSLEY Damon XX **[2]**
$13 772 - €12 862 - **£8 500** - FF84 368
Fountain with Seated Mermaid Holding a Conch Shell, a Merboy Bronze (H115cm H45in)
Billingshurst, West-Sussex 1998

RAWORTH William Henry 1820-1905 **[22]**
$226 - €266 - **£160** - FF1 745
Summerhill House, Gilmandyke Creek, Australia Watercolour/paper (26x36cm 10x14in)
London 2000

RAWSON Carl Wendell 1884-1970 **[11]**
$1 700 - €1 987 - **£1 213** - FF13 032
Lakeview through the trees Oil/canvas/panel
(40x50cm 16x20in) Altadena CA 2001

RAY Alphonse [3]
$668 - €762 - **£466** - FF5 000
Ghardaïa, soir Aquarelle/papier (23.5x50.5cm 9x19in)
Paris 2001

RAY Charles 1953 **[16]**
$340 000 - €319 113 - **£210 052** - FF2 093 244
Ink Drawing Technique mixte (128.5x109x3cm
50x42x1in) New-York 1999
$170 000 - €164 488 - **£104 839** - FF1 078 973
Untitled Mixed media (42x29cm 16x11in) New-York
1999
$2 000 000 - €2 320 579 - **£1 380 800** -
FF15 222 000
Male Mannequin Sculpture (187x69x47cm
73x27x18in) New-York 2000
$14 000 - €12 120 - **£8 443** - FF79 500
Untitled Sculpture, wood (29x305x4cm 11x120x1in)
New-York 1998
$260 000 - €251 570 - **£160 342** - FF1 650 194
Plank Piece I-II Photograph (100.5x68.5cm 39x26in)
New-York 1999

RAYA-SORKINE 1936 **[381]**
$2 430 - €2 897 - **£1 732** - FF19 000
Le repas du poète Huile/toile (46x55cm 18x21in)
Orléans 2000
$522 - €488 - **£316** - FF3 200
Fleurs dans un vase Huile/toile (32x24cm 12x9in)
Orléans 1999

$706 - €686 - **£436** - FF4 500
Musiciens Aquarelle/papier (23x31cm 9x12in) Paris
1999

$136 - €152 - **£89** - FF1 000
La mariée au bouquet Lithographie (14x19cm
5x7in) Eguilles 2000

RAYMOND Alex 1909-1956 **[6]**
$13 200 - €11 261 - **£7 962** - FF73 867
Flash Gordon Sunday comic strip: surviving a water explosion Ink (42x54cm 16x21in) New-York
1998

RAYMOND Casimir 1870-1965 **[36]**
$4 937 - €4 602 - **£3 046** - FF30 185
Variastilleben mit Kirschen and Reineclauden
Öl/Leinwand (50x65cm 19x25in) Köln 1999
$352 - €335 - **£223** - FF2 200
Le cabanon Aquarelle/papier (23x34cm 9x13in)
Uchaux 1999

RAYMOND Jean-Paul 1948 **[5]**
$3 082 - €3 049 - **£1 922** - FF20 000
Sans titre Sculpture verre (28x27x15.5cm 11x10x6in)
Paris 1999

RAYMOND Marie 1908-1988 **[77]**
$880 - €991 - **£618** - FF6 500
Composition sur fond jaune Huile/toile (38x46cm
14x18in) Paris 2001
$2 298 - €2 515 - **£1 595** - FF16 500
Composition Aquarelle/papier (14x10cm 5x3in)
Vannes 2001

RAYNAUD Aurélien 1970 **[17]**
$17 856 - €17 161 - **£11 000** - FF112 566
Mammals of the Deep - Whale Screen Oil/canvas
(147.5x399cm 58x157in) London 1999
$8 560 - €9 979 - **£6 000** - FF65 461
Les Faucons (Falcons) Oil/panel (82.5x94.5cm
32x37in) London 2000
$2 568 - €2 994 - **£1 800** - FF19 638
Le salut de l'éléphant Bronze (H17cm H6in)
London 2000
$4 545 - €4 345 - **£2 800** - FF28 653
Study of a Group of Primates Coloured pencils
(118x58.5cm 46x23in) London 1999

RAYNAUD Jean-Pierre 1939 **[135]**
$9 072 - €10 671 - **£6 503** - FF70 000
Bleu, blanc, rouge Technique mixte (134x135.5cm
52x53in) Paris 2001
$1 990 - €1 906 - **£1 252** - FF12 500
Métal rouge Huile/métal (60x50cm 23x19in)
Versailles 1999
$12 864 - €14 635 - **£8 928** - FF96 000
Rosier 5+5+5+5 Assemblage (92x185x25cm
36x72x9in) Paris 2000
$2 856 - €2 744 - **£1 771** - FF18 000
Archetype rouge Sculpture (16x17.5cm 6x6in) Paris
1999
$2 070 - €2 287 - **£1 435** - FF15 000
«Cm 80» Technique mixte/papier (100x65cm 39x25in)
Paris 2001
$378 - €457 - **£264** - FF3 000
Sans titre Sérigraphie (76.5x66cm 30x25in) Paris
2000

RAYNAUD Patrick 1946 **[19]**
$589 - €567 - **£368** - FF3 720
Suitcase Object (32x80x61cm 12x31x24in)
Amsterdam 1999

R

RAYNER Henry 1902-1957 **[31]**
$274 - €307 - **£190** - FF2 017
Mr Walter Sickert & the Lady Etching (11.5x18.5cm 4x7in) London 2000

RAYNER Louise J. 1829-1924 **[92]**
$6 794 - €7 913 - **£4 700** - FF51 903
Bishop Lloyd's Palace, Chester Watercolour/paper (26x12cm 10x4in) Cheshire 2000

RAYNER Margaret XIX-XX **[32]**
$350 - €402 - **£240** - FF2 640
Interior View of Hythe Church with Bearded Man at Door Watercolour, gouache/paper (39x25cm 15x10in) Leominster, Herefordshire 2000

RAYNER Samuel A. ?-c.1874/80 **[28]**
$805 - €760 - **£500** - FF4 987
A Chapel Scene Watercolour (63.5x51cm 25x20in) Billingshurst, West-Sussex 1999

RAYPER Ernesto 1840-1873 **[6]**
$3 750 - €3 887 - **£2 250** - FF25 500
Cascata Olio/cartone (30.5x40.5cm 12x15in) Milano 1999

RAYSKI von Ferdinand 1806-1890 **[21]**
$13 643 - €15 850 - **£9 588** - FF103 970
Bildnis eines Herren im Stuhl sitzend Öl/Leinwand (87x67cm 34x26in) Hamburg 2001
$2 890 - €2 733 - **£1 800** - FF17 930
Portrait of an Old Jew Oil/cardboard (32x26.5cm 12x10in) Praha 2000

RAYSSE Martial 1936 **[122]**
$7 236 - €6 860 - **£4 401** - FF45 000
L'Oeil Peinture (60x73cm 23x28in) Paris 1999
$2 923 - €2 820 - **£1 848** - FF18 500
Dessin Technique mixte (30x24cm 11x9in) Paris 1999
$23 478 - €26 221 - **£15 910** - FF172 000
«Le rayon prisunic» Accumulation (34x53cm 13x20in) Versailles 2000
$1 980 - €2 287 - **£1 386** - FF15 000
Sans titre Pastel/papier (34x31cm 13x12in) Paris 2001
$616 - €661 - **£418** - FF4 334
Camellos Litografía (54.5x75cm 21x29in) Madrid 2001

RAZA Sayed Haider 1922 **[52]**
$41 000 - €46 629 - **£28 646** - FF305 864
Satpura Acrylic/canvas (119.5x239cm 47x94in) New-York 2000
$5 652 - €6 245 - **£3 919** - FF40 966
Awakening Acrylic/canvas (150x30.5cm 59x12in) Singapore 2001
$2 155 - €2 514 - **£1 500** - FF16 494
The Fruit Shop Gouache/paper (37x34cm 14x13in) London 2000

RAZUMOV Konstantin 1974 **[143]**
$1 666 - €1 732 - **£1 050** - FF11 359
The Boating Party Oil/canvas (46x55cm 18x21in) Fernhurst, Haslemere, Surrey 2000
$635 - €609 - **£400** - FF3 993
In the Rocking Chair Oil/canvas/board (33x41cm 12x16in) Fernhurst, Haslemere, Surrey 1999

RAZZIA Gérard Courbouleix 1950 **[26]**
$192 - €195 - **£119** - FF1 279
«La Coupole brasserie-Restaurant» Poster (159x114.5cm 62x45in) Haarlem 2000

REA Cecil 1860-1935 **[6]**
$6 151 - €5 773 - **£3 800** - FF37 869
A woodland Nymph Oil/canvas (71x64.5cm 27x25in) London 1999

REA Constance XIX-XX **[3]**
$14 212 - €13 363 - **£8 800** - FF87 654
Fête champêtre Oil/canvas (94x72cm 37x28in) London 1999

REA Louis Edward 1868-1927 **[6]**
$6 000 - €5 555 - **£3 672** - FF36 436
Mont Tamalpais from Ridge above Big Lagoon Oil/canvas (45x101cm 18x40in) San Rafael CA 1999

READ Benjamin XIX **[1]**
$57 740 - €57 116 - **£36 000** - FF374 659
Summer and Winter fashions Aquatint (42x57cm 16x22in) London 1999

READ Catherine 1723-1778 **[8]**
$5 095 - €5 912 - **£3 575** - FF38 781
Portrait de Georges, Second Marquis Townshend et Lord John Townshend Pastel/papier (58.5x69cm 23x27in) Genève 2000

READ Elmer Joseph 1862-? **[7]**
$600 - €561 - **£370** - FF3 679
Nassau Cottages, Bahamas Watercolour/paper (25x37cm 10x14in) New-Orleans LA 1999

READ Katherine 1723-1778 **[6]**
$1 965 - €1 797 - **£1 200** - FF11 787
Portrait of a gentleman, half-length, wearing a blue coat Pastel/paper (60x50cm 24x20in) London 1998

READ Matthias 1669-1747 **[1]**
$14 030 - €16 686 - **£10 000** - FF109 452
St John in the Vale, Cumberland, with Threlkeld Old Bridge View Oil/canvas (59.5x99.5cm 23x39in) London 2000

READER William XVII **[2]**
$16 159 - €17 438 - **£10 842** - FF114 387
En lille falkoner med sin jagthund ved byttet Oil/canvas (148x108cm 58x42in) København 2000

READY William James Durant 1823-1873 **[12]**
$1 172 - €1 350 - **£800** - FF8 853
Coastal Scenes Oil/panel (21.5x27cm 8x14in) Billingshurst, West-Sussex 2000

REALFONZO Tommaso Masillo c.1677-c.1750 **[13]**
$19 143 - €21 465 - **£13 000** - FF140 799
Still Life of Flowers in a Terracotta Vase Oil/canvas (81x65cm 31x25in) London 2000

RÉALIER-DUMAS Maurice 1860-1928 **[30]**
$670 - €640 - **£417** - FF4 200
«Maderes Blandy» Affiche (61x164cm 24x64in) Paris 1999

REAM Carduc. Plantagenet 1837-1917 **[36]**
$3 800 - €4 519 - **£2 617** - FF29 644
Still Life of Apples Oil/canvas (50x39cm 20x15in) Holmdel, NJ 2000
$2 250 - €2 416 - **£1 506** - FF15 845
Still Life with Fruit and a wine Glass Oil/canvas (30.5x45.5cm 12x17in) San-Francisco CA 2000

REAM Morston Constantine 1840-1898 **[30]**
$5 500 - €5 656 - **£3 488** - FF37 101
Still Life with Desserts Oil/canvas (76x63cm 30x25in) Cincinnati OH 2000
$2 500 - €2 989 - **£1 717** - FF19 605
Still Life Oil/board (15x18cm 6x7in) Chicago IL 2000

REASE William H. 1818-c.1872 **[1]**
$900 - €1 070 - **£620** - FF7 021
Boston & Philadelphia Steamship Line Steamship «Saxon» Lithograph (59x89cm 23x35in) Bolton MA 2000

🖊 **$13 000** - €11 302 - **£7 867** - FF74 133
    Study of Two Camels Ink (37x26cm 14x10in) New-York 1999

▥ **$4 214** - €4 090 - **£2 624** - FF26 831
    Pastorale Landschaft Radierung (62x97cm 24x38in) Berlin 1999

ROOS William 1808-1878 **[10]**
🖌 **$1 666** - €1 533 - **£1 000** - FF10 058
    Portrait of a Gentleman/ His Wife Oil/canvas (75x62.5cm 29x24in) Glamorgan 1999

ROOSE van Charles 1883-1960 **[49]**
🖌 **$2 707** - €2 355 - **£1 615** - FF15 447
    Jeune femme nue assoupie Huile/toile (70x55cm 27x21in) Bruxelles 1998

ROOSENBOOM Albert 1845-1875 **[43]**
🖌 **$4 000** - €4 294 - **£2 678** - FF28 164
    Daydreaming Oil/canvas (66x51cm 26x20in) Portland ME 2000
🖌 **$3 860** - €3 630 - **£2 390** - FF23 812
    The young Entertainer Oil/panel (24x19cm 9x7in) Amsterdam 1999

ROOSENBOOM Margaretha 1843-1896 **[31]**
🖌 **$64 944** - €72 605 - **£45 200** - FF476 256
    Still life with Roses Oil/canvas (60x42cm 23x16in) Amsterdam 2001
🖌 **$9 246** - €9 983 - **£6 322** - FF65 485
    A Bouquet of Flowers at the Water's Edge Oil/panel (7.5x11cm 2x4in) Amsterdam 2001
🖊 **$12 355** - €14 521 - **£8 566** - FF95 251
    Yellow Roses Watercolour (24.5x18cm 9x7in) Amsterdam 1999

ROOSENBOOM Nicolaas Johannes 1805-1880 **[101]**
🖌 **$96 000** - €96 737 - **£59 843** - FF634 555
    Skaters on the 1J, Amsterdam Oil/canvas (101x126.5cm 39x49in) London 2000
🖌 **$6 465** - €5 585 - **£3 898** - FF36 637
    Winter Landscape with Loggers Oil/canvas (49.5x66cm 19x25in) Johannesburg 1998
🖌 **$5 019** - €5 899 - **£3 480** - FF38 695
    Men on a Jetty Pulling a Vessel through the Ice Oil/panel (21x28cm 8x11in) Amsterdam 2000

ROOSKENS Anton 1906-1976 **[329]**
🖌 **$22 819** - €21 781 - **£14 260** - FF142 876
    «No.430» Oil/canvas (97x130cm 38x51in) Amsterdam 1999
🖌 **$8 954** - €8 622 - **£5 599** - FF56 555
    «No. 315» Oil/canvas (100x81cm 39x31in) Amsterdam 1999
🖌 **$1 213** - €1 361 - **£840** - FF8 929
    Untitled Mixed media (27x37cm 10x14in) Amsterdam 2000
🖊 **$2 804** - €2 420 - **£1 692** - FF15 872
    «Three Stars» Gouache/paper (30x37cm 11x14in) Köbenhavn 1998
▥ **$336** - €363 - **£229** - FF2 381
    Composition Color lithograph (33x38.5cm 12x15in) Amsterdam 2001

ROOTIUS Jacob 1644-c.1681 **[12]**
🖌 **$32 660** - €35 063 - **£21 850** - FF230 000
    Bouquet de fleurs dans un vase en verre Huile/toile (75x59cm 29x23in) Paris 2000
🖌 **$7 000** - €5 822 - **£4 109** - FF38 188
    Swag of Grapes, Peaches, Plums, Balckberries, Cherries, Figs Oil/canvas (32.5x45cm 12x17in) New-York 1998

ROOTIUS Jan Albertsz. 1615-1674 **[10]**
🖌 **$8 138** - €9 076 - **£5 310** - FF59 532
    Portrait of a young Woman of Hoorn Oil/canvas (67x56.5cm 26x22in) Amsterdam 2000

ROOVER de Carlo 1900-1986 **[172]**
🖌 **$751** - €843 - **£523** - FF5 528
    Naakt met toeloupe Huile/toile (100x120cm 39x47in) Antwerpen 2001
🖌 **$495** - €545 - **£343** - FF3 577
    «Ochtendstemming aan zee» Huile/toile (80x100cm 31x39in) Antwerpen 2001

ROOWY Yves XIX-XX **[9]**
▥ **$1 372** - €1 496 - **£950** - FF9 813
    «Pneu Vélo Michelin» Poster (121x79cm 47x31in) London 2001

ROPÉLÉ Walter 1934 **[26]**
🖌 **$2 090** - €2 177 - **£1 324** - FF14 277
    Das rot gestrichene Gartenhaus Acryl/Leinwand (90x99.5cm 35x39in) Zürich 2000

ROPER Edward 1857-1891 **[9]**
🖊 **$5 839** - €5 551 - **£3 644** - FF36 414
    Chasing an Emu - Plains near Aracat, Victoria Watercolour, gouache/paper (26.5x50cm 10x19in) Melbourne 1999

ROPER Richard c.1730-c.1780 **[7]**
🖊 **$100 887** - €87 970 - **£61 000** - FF577 047
    A Hunt with Hounds on a Heath, a Country House Beyond Oil/canvas (110.5x151cm 43x59in) London 1998
🖌 **$46 443** - €40 393 - **£28 000** - FF264 961
    A Gentleman on his Chestnut Hunter Oil/canvas (85.5x109cm 33x42in) London 1998

ROPS Félicien 1833-1898 **[1379]**
🖌 **$5 716** - €5 641 - **£3 522** - FF37 000
    La Seine à Coudray-Montceau Huile/toile (40x74.5cm 15x29in) Neuilly-sur-Seine 1999
🖌 **$5 328** - €4 991 - **£3 203** - FF32 742
    Le chasseur Oil/canvas (25.5x35.5cm 10x13in) Amsterdam 1999
🖊 **$1 750** - €1 814 - **£1 050** - FF11 900
    Ecce Mulier Matita/carta (23.5x15cm 9x5in) Milano 2000
▥ **$237** - €255 - **£158** - FF1 671
    Junges Paar mit älterer Dame Etching, aquatint (72x51cm 28x20in) Zofingen 2000

ROQUE GAMEIRO Alfredo 1864-1935 **[5]**
🖊 **$3 655** - €4 237 - **£2 550** - FF27 795
    Barcos na praia Acuarela/papel (18.5x16.5cm 7x6in) Lisboa 2001

ROQUE GAMEIRO Raquel 1889-1970 **[3]**
🖊 **$3 360** - €3 490 - **£2 170** - FF22 890
    Sintra Acuarela/papel (71.5x52cm 28x20in) Lisboa 2000

ROQUEPLAN Camille 1803-1855 **[74]**
🖌 **$3 070** - €2 812 - **£1 871** - FF18 446
    Hafenschenke am Wasser mit Blick auf Segelschiffe und die Küstenfelsen Öl/Leinwand (38x61cm 14x24in) München 1999
🖌 **$2 242** - €2 134 - **£1 394** - FF14 000
    Le moulin Huile/papier/panneau (15.5x23.5cm 6x9in) Paris 1999
🖊 **$695** - €762 - **£461** - FF5 000
    La petite vendangeuse Crayon/papier (31.5x24.5cm 12x9in) Melun 2000

R

ROQUIN Robert XX **[5]**

📏 $855 - €838 - £551 - FF5 500
Projet d'affiche: Deauville, la Plage fleurie
Gouache/papier (48x29cm 18x11in) Deauville 1999

📻 $389 - €381 - £240 - FF2 500
«4e Emprunt National, Crédit Foncier» Affiche
(80x114cm 31x44in) Paris 1999

RØRBYE Martinus 1803-1848 **[72]**

🖼 $523 005 - €561 403 - £350 000 - FF3 682 560
**Turkish Notary Drawing up a Marriage Contract
in Front of the Mosque** Oil/canvas (95x130cm
37x51in) London 2000

🖼 $125 580 - €104 855 - £74 646 - FF687 804
To hyrdedrenge i den romerske Campagne
Oil/canvas (50x62cm 19x24in) København 1998

🖼 $10 397 - €10 478 - £6 481 - FF68 733
Catacomberne i Palermo Oil/canvas (36.5x25.5cm
14x10in) København 2000

📏 $1 852 - €1 763 - £1 154 - FF11 481
En liggende italiensk bonde Pencil/paper
(22x30cm 8x11in) København 1999

ROS Frans 1883-1968 **[8]**

🖼 $758 - €843 - £530 - FF5 528
Intérieur d'église Huile/toile (99x80cm 38x31in)
Antwerpen 2001

ROS Y GUELL Antoni 1873-1954 **[22]**

🖼 $840 - €901 - £570 - FF5 910
Paisaje con río Oleo/lienzo (45x55cm 17x21in)
Barcelona 2001

ROSA Costantino 1803-1878 **[2]**

🖼 $30 000 - €31 100 - £18 000 - FF204 000
Paesaggio con figure Olio/tela (150x225cm
59x88in) Venezia 1999

🖼 $4 000 - €6 183 - £3 000 - FF34 000
Paesaggio bergamasco Olio/tela (42.5x52.5cm
16x20in) Milano 2001

ROSA dalla Saverio 1745-1821 **[1]**

🖼 $11 000 - €11 403 - £6 600 - FF74 800
Sacra Famiglia Olio/tela (61x47cm 24x18in) Milano
2000

ROSA de Francesco Pacecco 1580/1607-c.1654/56
[16]

🖼 $35 500 - €38 112 - £23 750 - FF250 000
**Scène de l'ancien testament: Moïse et les filles
de Jethro** Huile/toile (153x197cm 60x77in) Paris 2000

🖼 $55 000 - €57 016 - £33 000 - FF374 000
La Madonna della Purità Olio/tela (103x102cm
40x40in) Venezia 1999

ROSA de Gaetano 1690-1770 **[15]**

🖼 $21 411 - €20 365 - £13 000 - FF133 584
**Wooded Landscape with a Bear Hunt/Wooded
Landscape with a Boor Hunt** Oil/canvas
(101x154cm 39x60in) London 1999

🖼 $2 749 - €3 132 - £1 900 - FF20 546
**Italianate Landscape with Cowherds and their
Livestock** Oil/canvas (73x98.5cm 28x38in) London
1999

ROSA de la Fabian 1869-1937 **[2]**

🖼 $367 296 - €417 061 - £251 392 - FF2 735 744
Women Working in a Rice Field Oil/canvas
(65x96cm 25x37in) Singapore 2000

🖼 $7 964 - €7 422 - £4 914 - FF48 682
Trees Oil/canvas (31x42cm 12x16in) Singapore 1999

ROSA de Raffaele 1940 **[1]**

🖼 $800 - €829 - £480 - FF5 440
La festa dei pazzi Olio/tela (50x50cm 19x19in)
Vercelli 2000

🖼 $425 - €441 - £255 - FF2 890
«Il Parnaso sede delle Muse» Olio/tela (30x25cm
11x9in) Vercelli 2001

ROSA Francesco ?-1687 **[6]**

🖼 $16 000 - €20 733 - £12 000 - FF136 000
Alessandro Magno e il re Dario Olio/tela
(215x323cm 84x127in) Milano 2000

ROSA Salvator 1615-1673 **[222]**

🖼 $150 000 - €160 193 - £102 210 - FF1 050 795
A Cavalry Battle Oil/canvas (150x289cm 59x113in)
New-York 2001

🖼 $40 442 - €34 286 - £24 000 - FF224 904
Satyrs Carousing with Maidens Oil/canvas
(107x107cm 42x42in) London 1998

🖼 $6 276 - €6 737 - £4 200 - FF44 190
Two Men Conversing Wash (14x9.5cm 5x3in)
London 2000

📻 $375 - €420 - £262 - FF2 758
Albert Etching (35x23cm 13x9in) New-York 2001

ROSAI Ottone 1895-1957 **[391]**

🖼 $13 200 - €17 105 - £9 900 - FF112 200
Pretino in strada Olio/tavola (44.5x36cm 17x14in)
Milano 2001

🖼 $7 500 - €7 775 - £4 500 - FF51 000
Quattro uomini seduti Olio/faesite (40x30cm
15x11in) Prato 2000

📏 $2 100 - €1 814 - £1 095 - FF14 190
Autoritratto Matita/carta (50x37cm 19x14in) Milano
1999

ROSAIRE Arthur Dominique 1879-1922 **[26]**

🖼 $1 238 - €1 070 - £746 - FF7 016
Scène de village Huile/panneau (21x26cm 8x10in)
Montréal 2001

ROSALBIN DE BUNCEY Marie Abraham XIX-XX
[15]

🖼 $786 - €917 - £544 - FF6 014
«Baigneuses le soir» Oil/panel (32.5x46.5cm
12x18in) Bern 2000

ROSALES MARTINEZ Eduardo 1836-1873 **[29]**

🖼 $4 200 - €3 604 - £2 580 - FF23 640
Boceto para una escena palaciega Oleo/lienzo
(47x83cm 18x32in) Madrid 1998

🖼 $2 030 - €2 102 - £1 295 - FF13 790
Calabacillas Oleo/tabla (24.5x18cm 9x7in) Madrid
2000

🖼 $570 - €571 - £351 - FF3 743
Escena Lápiz (15x20cm 5x7in) Madrid 2000

ROSALS Y CUADRADA Ramón XIX **[1]**

📏 $2 160 - €2 403 - £1 440 - FF15 760
Interior de la biblioteca de El Escorial
Acuarela/papel (30x38cm 11x14in) Madrid 2000

ROSAM Walter Alfred 1883-1916 **[4]**

🖼 $7 592 - €6 645 - £4 598 - FF43 590
Blumenstilleben Chalks (65x54cm 25x21in) Berlin
1998

ROSATI Alberto 1893-1971 **[10]**

📏 $6 957 - €6 441 - £4 200 - FF42 247
A difficult Move Watercolour (34.5x51.5cm 13x20in)
London 1999

ROSATI Giulio 1858-1917 **[79]**

🖼 $460 000 - €515 486 - £320 620 - FF3 381 368
Picking the Favorite Oil/canvas (65x104cm 25x40in)
New-York 2001

📏 $15 030 - €14 501 - £9 500 - FF95 118
The Carpet Seller Watercolour/paper (51.5x71cm
20x27in) London 1999

RÖSCH Ludwig 1865-1936 **[54]**
- $538 - €581 - £372 - FF3 813
  Vorfrühling Brienzer See (Schweiz)
  Mischtechnik/Papier (78.5x54.5cm 30x21in) Wien 2001

ROSCOE S.G. William 1852-c.1922 **[25]**
- $476 - €495 - £300 - FF3 245
  Wooded Glade with Workman resting with his Flask watching Children Watercolour/paper (29x21cm 11x8in) Cirencester, Gloucesterhire 2000

ROSE David 1936 **[44]**
- $94 - €81 - £57 - FF534
  Echidna Chasm, East Kimberleys Silkscreen (61x56cm 24x22in) Sydney 1998

ROSE Francis, Sir 1909-1979 **[33]**
- $145 - €163 - £100 - FF1 071
  Abstract in Blue and Black Watercolour (61x42.5cm 24x16in) London 2000

ROSE Georges 1895-1951 **[94]**
- $465 - €488 - £308 - FF3 200
  Vue de Paris Aquarelle/papier (32x45cm 12x17in) Toulouse 2000

ROSE Guy 1867-1925 **[34]**
- $400 000 - €441 133 - £270 880 - FF2 893 640
  Vista from Point Lobos Oil/canvas (61x61cm 24x24in) New-York 2001
- $32 000 - €37 609 - £22 185 - FF246 700
  Giverny Hillside Oil/canvas (22x32cm 8x12in) Beverly-Hills CA 2000
- $6 500 - €6 182 - £3 946 - FF40 553
  Range Talk Watercolour (44x59cm 17x23in) Beverly-Hills CA 1999

ROSE Karl Julius 1828-1911 **[42]**
- $1 913 - €2 250 - £1 371 - FF14 757
  Reissender Gebirgsfluss Öl/Leinwand (57x89cm 22x35in) München 2001

ROSE Knut 1936 **[12]**
- $19 285 - €21 404 - £13 440 - FF140 402
  «Helt viser ansikt» Oil/canvas (114x146cm 44x57in) Oslo 2001
- $302 - €349 - £213 - FF2 291
  Fra Gjengangere-mappen Color lithograph (71x52cm 27x20in) Oslo 2000

ROSÉ Manuel 1887-1961 **[34]**
- $4 860 - €5 406 - £3 420 - FF35 460
  Paisaje Oleo/lienzo (50x65cm 19x25in) Madrid 2001
- $1 000 - €1 040 - £631 - FF6 823
  Campesino Oleo/lienzo (40x24cm 15x9in) Montevideo 2000

ROSE Paul XX **[4]**
- $447 - €421 - £270 - FF2 764
  Kudu in the African Bush Oil/canvas (60x96.5cm 23x37in) Cape Town 1999

ROSE Ted XX **[5]**
- $1 300 - €1 432 - £867 - FF9 395
  Mood Indigo, Depicting a Night Scene of a Train at a Station, Santa Fe Watercolour/paper (43x43cm 17x17in) Detroit MI 2000

ROSE-INNES Alexander 1915-1996 **[28]**
- $2 352 - €2 635 - £1 634 - FF17 284
  «Still Life with red Book» Oil/canvas (40x50cm 15x19in) Johannesburg 2001
- $1 547 - €1 733 - £1 075 - FF11 371
  Oak Tree, with a Studio in the Distance Oil/canvas (45x35cm 17x13in) Johannesburg 2001

ROSEBEE XX **[9]**
- $3 000 - €2 905 - £1 884 - FF19 054
  New England Clambake Oil/panel (60.5x68.5cm 23x26in) New-York 1999
- $1 500 - €1 631 - £988 - FF10 701
  Waterfront View Oil/board (30.5x40.5cm 12x15in) Boston MA 2000

ROSELAND Harry Herman 1866/68-1950 **[122]**
- $13 000 - €12 065 - £7 805 - FF79 138
  Arguing the Point Oil/canvas (55x71cm 22x28in) Milford CT 1999
- $3 600 - €3 702 - £2 283 - FF24 284
  Night in the Swamp Oil/metal (25x35cm 10x14in) New-Orleans LA 2000

ROSELL Alexander 1859-1922 **[60]**
- $1 699 - €1 594 - £1 050 - FF10 457
  The Wheel of Life Oil/canvas (56x76cm 22x29in) Leyburn, North Yorkshire 1999
- $1 210 - €1 163 - £750 - FF7 627
  Going to Market Oil/canvas (25.5x33cm 10x12in) London 1999

ROSELLI Carlo 1939 **[67]**
- $1 250 - €1 296 - £750 - FF8 500
  Ippodromo Acrilico/tela (50x50cm 19x19in) Vercelli 2001
- $560 - €726 - £420 - FF4 760
  Figure in strada Olio/tela (30x30cm 11x11in) Roma 2000
- $125 - €130 - £75 - FF850
  Partita a biliardo Serigrafia (60x80cm 23x31in) Vercelli 2000

ROSELLI Matteo 1578-1650 **[3]**
- $10 460 - €11 228 - £7 000 - FF73 651
  The Madonna and Child with the Infant Saint John the Baptist Oil/canvas (91x73cm 35x28in) London 2000

ROSEN Charles 1878-1950 **[15]**
- $5 000 - €5 343 - £3 398 - FF35 048
  Modernist landscape with cottages and large lush trees Oil/canvas (74x61cm 29x24in) Lambertville NJ 2001

ROSEN Ernest T. 1877-1926 **[10]**
- $1 043 - €1 220 - £744 - FF8 000
  L'élégante au fauteuil Huile/toile (70x54cm 27x21in) Angers 2001

ROSEN Jan 1854-1936 **[15]**
- $5 778 - €6 791 - £4 006 - FF44 544
  Hussards devant une maison Huile/carton (24x30.5cm 9x12in) Warszawa 2000
- $2 032 - €1 680 - £1 192 - FF11 020
  Officer Piechoty Watercolour, gouache/paper (47x36cm 18x14in) Warszawa 1998
- $1 174 - €1 271 - £813 - FF8 334
  Revue de la cavalerie devant W.Ks.Konstanty Lithographie couleurs (54x87.5cm 21x34in) Bydgoszcz 2001

ROSEN Kay XX **[2]**
- $2 600 - €2 912 - £1 806 - FF19 102
  «Blood Clot» Enamel/canvas (19x73.5cm 7x28in) New-York 2000
- $1 600 - €1 817 - £1 095 - FF11 917
  The Man Etching (65x49cm 25x19in) Chicago IL 2000

ROSEN von Georg 1843-1923 **[20]**
- $1 158 - €1 337 - £810 - FF8 770
  Brudafärd Akvarell/papper (21x14cm 8x5in) Stockholm 2001

ROSENBAUM Julius 1848-1929 **[2]**
- **$2 361** - €2 744 - **£1 683** - FF18 000
  La musicienne Huile/toile (40.5x27cm 15x10in) Paris 2001

ROSENBAUM Richard 1864-? **[11]**
- **$7 000** - €5 990 - **£4 214** - FF39 293
  Carriages Racing through the Park Oil/canvas (60x91cm 24x36in) New-York 1998

ROSENBERG Edvard Axel 1858-1934 **[37]**
- **$809** - €841 - **£507** - FF5 516
  Landskap Oil/canvas (68x92cm 26x36in) Helsinki 2000
- **$4 088** - €4 079 - **£2 551** - FF26 757
  Lekande barn i sommarlandskap Oil/canvas (30.5x46cm 12x18in) Uppsala 1999

ROSENBERG Elliott 1790-1835 **[5]**
- **$404** - €379 - **£250** - FF2 488
  Hastings from the West Cliff, Beach Scene Watercolour/paper (25x38cm 10x15in) Canterbury, Kent 1999

ROSENBERG Isaac 1890-1918 **[1]**
- **$11 536** - €12 748 - **£8 000** - FF83 624
  Self Portrait Oil/canvas (51x46cm 20x18in) London 2001

ROSENBERG James N. 1874-1970 **[9]**
- **$550** - €569 - **£347** - FF3 734
  New York Cityscape Lithograph (22.5x26cm 8x10in) New-York 2000

ROSENBERG Louis Conrad 1890-1983 **[28]**
- **$236** - €248 - **£150** - FF1 627
  Grande Mosquée Etching (17x30.5cm 6x12in) Edinburgh 2000

ROSENBERG Valle 1891-1919 **[7]**
- **$1 479** - €1 682 - **£1 026** - FF11 032
  Borgå Oil/canvas (48x40cm 18x15in) Helsinki 2000

ROSENBLUET Emilio 1896-1945 **[2]**
- **$4 183** - €4 907 - **£3 009** - FF32 186
  Paisaje Oleo/lienzo (50x70cm 19x27in) México 2001

ROSENBLUM Walter 1919 **[4]**
- **$1 000** - €934 - **£605** - FF6 124
  Candy Store, Pitt Street, New York Gelatin silver print (26.5x34cm 10x13in) New-York 1999

ROSENFELD Alexander XX **[3]**
- **$1 400** - €1 633 - **£974** - FF10 714
  Ship Passengers in Deck Chairs Oil/canvas (22x30cm 9x12in) Altadena CA 2000

ROSENFELD Morris XIX-XX **[2]**
- **$3 000** - €3 145 - **£1 879** - FF20 632
  Yacht's billowing sails Silver print (34x25cm 13x10in) New-York 2000

ROSENGRAVE Harry 1899-1986 **[25]**
- **$483** - €417 - **£291** - FF2 736
  Standing Nude/Seated Nude Oil/board (49x38.5cm 19x15in) Malvern, Victoria 1998

ROSENGREN Jean 1894-1965 **[85]**
- **$301** - €289 - **£185** - FF1 898
  Skånsk gård med höns Oil/canvas (52x75cm 20x29in) Malmö 1999

ROSENHAUER Theodor 1901-1996 **[14]**
- **$9 649** - €11 248 - **£6 762** - FF73 785
  Blick aufs Meer Öl/Leinwand (98x123cm 38x48in) München 2000

ROSENQUIST James 1933 **[618]**
- **$40 000** - €38 464 - **£24 644** - FF252 308
  Gift Wrapped Dill IV Acrylic/canvas/panel (152.5x152.5cm 60x60in) New-York 1999
- **$26 000** - €23 121 - **£15 901** - FF151 665
  Leaky Neck Acrylic/canvas (52x91.5cm 20x36in) New-York 1999
- **$48 000** - €33 763 - **£33 350** - FF352 665
  Untitled Acrylic/canvas (30.5x45.5cm 12x17in) New-York 2001
- **$80 000** - €89 450 - **£53 928** - FF586 752
  Ceiling Sculpture (106.5x222.5x50.5cm 41x87x19in) New-York 2000
- **$8 000** - €7 957 - **£4 965** - FF52 195
  Study for Welcome to Water Planet II Charcoal/paper (141.5x95.5cm 55x37in) Beverly-Hills CA 1999
- **$1 300** - €1 317 - **£808** - FF8 638
  Industrial Cottage Color lithograph (68x121cm 27x48in) Bloomfield-Hills MI 2000

ROSENQVIST Hans 1913 **[1]**
- **$2 200** - €2 076 - **£1 357** - FF13 617
  Paper Clip Color lithograph (92.5x175.5cm 36x69in) New-York 1999

ROSENSOHN Lennart 1918-1994 **[54]**
- **$861** - €743 - **£518** - FF4 874
  «Rituell dans» Mixed media (65x55cm 25x21in) Malmö 1998

ROSENSTAND Emil Christian 1859-1932 **[17]**
- **$2 996** - €3 521 - **£2 077** - FF23 097
  Rencontre Gouache/papier (61x43cm 24x16in) Warszawa 2000

ROSENSTAND Vilhelm J. 1838-1915 **[72]**
- **$2 962** - €2 690 - **£1 836** - FF17 648
  Krigsscene med soldat og ung pige Oil/canvas (94x96cm 37x37in) København 1999
- **$264** - €295 - **£185** - FF1 934
  Interiör fra trappeopgang Oil/wood (27x19cm 10x7in) København 2001

ROSENSTEIN Erna 1913-? **[9]**
- **$1 340** - €1 497 - **£935** - FF9 819
  Echos larges Encre/papier (23x32cm 9x12in) Warszawa 2001

ROSENSTOCK Isidore 1880-1956 **[99]**
- **$400** - €465 - **£280** - FF3 051
  Still Life of Dahlias Watercolour/paper (44.5x37cm 17x14in) Billingshurst, West-Sussex 2001

ROSENTALIS Moshe 1922 **[37]**
- **$3 000** - €3 245 - **£2 055** - FF21 289
  Galilee Landscape Oil/canvas (55x46cm 21x18in) Tel Aviv 2001
- **$600** - €649 - **£411** - FF4 257
  Houses among the Trees Oil/paper/board (25x17cm 9x6in) Tel Aviv 2001

ROSENTHAL Albert 1863-1939 **[17]**
- **$16 000** - €17 510 - **£11 036** - FF114 860
  «The Milliner's Shop» Oil/canvas (101.5x76cm 39x29in) New-York 2001

ROSENTHAL Joe 1921 **[28]**
- **$4 000** - €4 174 - **£2 530** - FF27 382
  Flag Raising Photograph (10x12.5cm 3x4in) New-York 2000

ROSENVINGE Odin XIX-XX **[25]**
- **$1 486** - €1 687 - **£1 017** - FF11 067
  «Cunard Europe America» Poster (101x62cm 39x24in) Hannover 2000

R

ROSENZWEIG Nanette,née WINDISCH XVIII-XIX [2]
- **$4 269** - €5 027 - **£3 000** - FF32 974
Young Lady, facing left in low-cut white Dress
Miniature (6x5cm 2x1in) London 2000

ROSIER Amédée 1831-1898 [103]
- **$3 753** - €4 192 - **£2 543** - FF27 500
Village au bord de l'étang Huile/toile (38.5x55.5cm 15x21in) Coulommiers 2000
- **$2 678** - €2 820 - **£1 768** - FF18 500
Venise, l'entrée du grand canal Huile/panneau (29x44.5cm 11x17in) Neuilly-sur-Seine 2000
- **$710** - €762 - **£475** - FF5 000
Vue de Venise Aquarèle/papier (27x31cm 10x12in) Paris 2000

ROSIERSE Johannes 1818-1901 [45]
- **$85 000** - €73 334 - **£51 280** - FF481 040
Evening Market Oil/canvas (109x139cm 42x54in) New-York 1998
- **$5 500** - €5 904 - **£3 680** - FF38 725
Market Scene with Lamplight Oil/canvas (80.5x62cm 31x24in) Philadelphia PA 2000
- **$1 874** - €1 724 - **£1 159** - FF11 311
An elegant Couple reading a Poem Oil/panel (34.5x26.5cm 13x10in) Amsterdam 1999

ROSINSKI Grégor 1941 [11]
- **$896** - €992 - **£608** - FF6 504
Thorgal, Le maître des Montagnes, Pl.21 Crayon/papier (36.5x51cm 14x20in) Bruxelles 2000

RÖSLER Waldemar 1882-1916 [5]
- **$6 962** - €6 647 - **£4 349** - FF43 600
Frühlingstag Öl/Leinwand (79.5x106.5cm 31x41in) Köln 1999

ROSLIN Alexander 1718-1793 [67]
- **$15 792** - €18 780 - **£11 256** - FF123 186
Portraet af en ung mand, iført rosa frakke og vest Oil/canvas (60.5x50cm 23x19in) Köbenhavn 2000

ROSNER Charles 1894-1975 [3]
- **$1 900** - €1 777 - **£1 151** - FF11 658
Clipper Ships at Sea Gouache/paper (26x36cm 10x14in) Bolton MA 1999

ROSOMAN Leonard H. 1913-? [42]
- **$7 827** - €9 216 - **£5 500** - FF60 452
Desert Fringe No.13 Oil/canvas (122x183cm 48x72in) London 2000
- **$5 103** - €4 356 - **£3 000** - FF28 571
Girl behind Screen Oil/canvas (46x61cm 18x24in) London 1998
- **$723** - €697 - **£450** - FF4 571
Exeter Cathedral following a Baedeker Raid Watercolour (46x56cm 18x22in) London 1999

ROSS Alex 1918 [46]
- **$3 500** - €3 376 - **£2 212** - FF22 148
Superman Peace on Earth Watercolour, gouache (44.5x65cm 17x25in) New-York 1999

ROSS Alexander, Alex 1909-1990 [5]
- **$1 700** - €1 982 - **£1 177** - FF12 999
Passionate Embrace Watercolour, gouache/paper (36x26cm 14x10in) New-York 2000

ROSS Christian Meyer 1843-1904 [13]
- **$9 000** - €10 091 - **£6 111** - FF66 193
Grazing out the Window Oil/canvas (75.5x55.5cm 29x21in) New-York 2000
- **$2 293** - €2 540 - **£1 556** - FF16 663
Dame i silkekjole Oil/panel (42x23cm 16x9in) Oslo 2000

$3 900 - €3 848 - **£2 402** - FF25 241
Kvinna med solfjäder Pastel/paper (133x75cm 52x29in) Stockholm 1999

ROSS Cyril 1963 [35]
- **$20 995** - €19 744 - **£13 000** - FF129 509
Golden Memories Oil/canvas (102x152cm 40x59in) London 1999
- **$8 110** - €7 789 - **£5 000** - FF51 094
Clash of the Leviathians: Dauntless racing off the New England Coast Oil/canvas (76.5x51cm 30x20in) London 1999

ROSS Horatio 1801-1886 [20]
- **$1 400** - €1 461 - **£885** - FF9 584
Stag Brought Home - Glenfeshit Salt print (19x21cm 7x8in) New-York 2000

ROSS Joseph Halford 1866-? [53]
- **$383** - €423 - **£260** - FF2 777
Cottage garden Watercolour (28.5x38cm 11x14in) London 2000

ROSS Robert Thorburn 1816-1876 [18]
- **$8 376** - €7 871 - **£5 200** - FF51 631
The Sailors Return Oil/canvas (39x51cm 15x20in) London 1999

ROSS William Charles 1794-1860 [51]
- **$4 500** - €5 118 - **£3 144** - FF33 570
Portrait of Lady Carrington Oil/canvas (91x60cm 36x24in) Chicago IL 2000
- **$903** - €991 - **£600** - FF6 499
Young Lady, facing left in black velvet Dress Miniature (10.5x8cm 4x3in) London 2000

ROSSANO Federico 1835-1912 [41]
- **$4 000** - €5 183 - **£3 000** - FF34 000
Buvette sulla Senna Olio/tavola (34.5x55.5cm 13x21in) Vercelli 2001
- **$5 000** - €5 183 - **£3 000** - FF34 000
Le betulle Olio/tela (31x24cm 12x9in) Roma 1999
- **$2 144** - €2 436 - **£1 500** - FF15 976
Il riposo (the rest) Pastel/paper (44x58cm 17x22in) London 2001

ROSSE Franz 1858-1900 [10]
- **$423** - €511 - **£295** - FF3 353
Nymphe Bronze (H64.5cm H25in) Köln 2000

ROSSEAU Percival Leonard 1859-1937 [31]
- **$27 000** - €23 902 - **£16 507** - FF176 786
English Setter Oil/canvas (71x86.5cm 27x34in) New-York 1999
- **$10 000** - €10 671 - **£6 349** - FF70 000
Deux chiens à l'arrêt Huile/toile (40.5x27cm 15x10in) Soissons 2000

ROSSEELS Jacques 1828-1912 [27]
- **$1 008** - €1 115 - **£702** - FF7 317
Koehoudster met kudde in een Kampisch landschap (Vachère et troupeau) Huile/toile (54x94cm 21x37in) Antwerpen 2001

ROSSELLI Cosimo di Lorenzo 1439-1507 [4]
- **$489 540** - €455 069 - **£300 000** - FF2 985 060
The Crucifixion with the Madonna, Saint John the Baptist Oil/panel (207x193.5cm 81x76in) London 1998

ROSSELLI Matteo 1578-1651 [18]
- **$176 770** - €175 337 - **£110 000** - FF1 150 138
Judith and Holofernes Oil/canvas (189x140cm 74x55in) London 1999

✎ **$4 000** - €3 477 - **£2 420** - FF22 810
Study of a Draped Male Figure, Seated, Holding a Cornucopia Red chalk/paper (37.5x30cm 14x11in) New-York 1999

ROSSELLINO Antonio 1427-c.1479 **[2]**

🔨 **$180 000** - €233 247 - **£135 000** - FF1 530 000
La Madonna dei candelabri Bas-relief (81x55.5cm 31x21in) Firenze 2000

🔨 **$500 000** - €518 327 - **£300 000** - FF3 400 000
San Gerolamo penitente su sfondo di paesaggio Bas-relief (42.5x38cm 16x14in) Firenze 2001

ROSSELLO Mario 1927 **[16]**

✎ **$180** - €233 - **£135** - FF1 530
Figure Feutre (23.5x30.5cm 9x12in) Prato 2000

ROSSER Albert XX **[26]**

✎ **$313** - €337 - **£210** - FF2 209
Bassen thwaite Lake & Skiddaw Watercolour/paper (25x35cm 10x14in) Carlisle, Cumbria 2000

ROSSERT Paul 1841/51-1918 **[26]**

🔨 **$5 500** - €6 377 - **£3 896** - FF41 831
On the Beach Oil/canvas (25.5x44cm 10x17in) New-York 2000

🔨 **$1 090** - €915 - **£639** - FF6 000
Elégante à Paris Aquarelle/papier (34x24cm 13x9in) Troyes 1998

ROSSET-GRANGER Édouard 1853-? **[11]**

🔨 **$8 500** - €8 417 - **£5 292** - FF55 214
An early Departure Oil/canvas (85x53cm 33x20in) New-York 1999

ROSSETTI Dante Gabriel 1828-1882 **[61]**

✎ **$60 000** - €56 648 - **£37 302** - FF371 586
Study for «Belcolore» Red chalk/paper (25x23cm 9x9in) New-York 1999

ROSSI Alberto 1858-1936 **[42]**

🔨 **$4 750** - €5 299 - **£3 109** - FF34 761
Tending the Herd Oil/canvas (58x83cm 23x33in) Chicago IL 2000

🔨 **$4 155** - €3 811 - **£2 582** - FF25 000
Piramidi di Ghiseh Huile/carton (19.5x43cm 7x16in) Paris 1999

✎ **$750** - €777 - **£450** - FF5 100
I due fratellini a Rapallo Pastelli/cartone (50.5x71.5cm 19x28in) Vercelli 1999

ROSSI Alberto María 1879-1965 **[3]**

🔨 **$3 100** - €3 016 - **£1 908** - FF19 785
El circo Oleo/tabla (30x44.5cm 11x17in) Buenos-Aires 1999

ROSSI Aldo 1931-1997 **[4]**

✎ **$1 200** - €1 555 - **£900** - FF10 200
«La scuola di Broni» Inchiostro (29.5x20.5cm 11x8in) Milano 2001

ROSSI Alexander M. act.1870-1903 **[59]**

🔨 **$14 428** - €16 187 - **£10 000** - FF106 178
Bathers Oil/canvas (91.5x71cm 36x27in) London 2000

✎ **$410** - €439 - **£280** - FF2 880
The Curtsey Watercolour/paper (51x38cm 20x14in) London 2001

ROSSI Giacomo 1748-1817 **[5]**

🗐 **$1 179** - €1 165 - **£733** - FF7 642
Il nuovo teatro delle fabriche et edificii, in prospettiva di Roma Estampe (28x43cm 11x16in) Liège 1999

ROSSI Gino 1884-1947 **[29]**

✎ **$1 800** - €2 332 - **£1 350** - FF15 300
Nudo Matita/carta (18.5x6cm 7x2in) Prato 2000

ROSSI Giovanni Battista c.1730-1782 **[2]**

🗐 **$17 000** - €16 992 - **£10 385** - FF111 460
The Education of the Virgin Oil/canvas (112.5x100.5cm 44x39in) New-York 2000

ROSSI Giuseppe 1876-1952 **[5]**

🔨 **$26 103** - €28 169 - **£17 514** - FF184 779
Parti fra Paris med Pont du Carrousel, Louvre og Notre-Dame Oil/canvas (100x150cm 39x59in) København 2000

ROSSI Lucius 1846-1913 **[52]**

🔨 **$21 656** - €21 823 - **£13 500** - FF143 148
The Minuet Oil/canvas (56x83cm 22x33in) Dorchester, Dorset 2000

🔨 **$2 183** - €2 610 - **£1 500** - FF17 119
The Harlequin Oil/panel (40.5x32.5cm 15x12in) Billingshurst, West-Sussex 2000

ROSSI Luigi 1853-1923 **[66]**

🔨 **$2 400** - €2 739 - **£1 667** - FF17 967
Portrait de femme Oleo/tabla (35x26cm 13x10in) Buenos-Aires 2000

🔨 **$850** - €957 - **£585** - FF6 275
Two Elegant Ladies on a Terrace Watercolour/paper (34x27cm 13x11in) Chicago IL 2000

ROSSI Nicola Maria 1647/99-1702/55 **[10]**

🔨 **$15 000** - €13 040 - **£9 078** - FF85 539
The Triumph of Amphitrite Oil/canvas (75x101cm 29x39in) New-York 1999

✎ **$2 000** - €2 324 - **£1 405** - FF15 242
Pagan offering with an Angel hovering with a Cross Black chalk (31.5x22cm 12x8in) New-York 2001

ROSSI Pasqualino 1641-1725 **[7]**

🔨 **$18 000** - €15 550 - **£9 000** - FF102 000
Il violinista Olio/tela (142x79cm 55x31in) Roma 1999

🔨 **$4 222** - €3 811 - **£2 602** - FF25 000
La Vierge à l'enfant Huile/toile (31x24.5cm 12x9in) Paris 1999

ROSSI Vanni 1894-1973 **[14]**

🔨 **$3 400** - €3 525 - **£2 040** - FF23 120
Il Salice Olio/tela (50x70cm 19x27in) Milano 1999

ROSSIGLIANI Giuseppe Nicola c.1510-? **[9]**

🗐 **$1 600** - €1 511 - **£993** - FF9 910
Hercules and the Nemean Lion Woodcut (24.5x19cm 9x7in) New-York 1999

RÖSSING Karl 1897-1987 **[99]**

🔨 **$16 920** - €20 452 - **£11 812** - FF134 156
Grossstadtmusen Öl/Leinwand (86.5x119.5cm 34x47in) Berlin 2000

🗐 **$116** - €107 - **£71** - FF704
Ohne Titel Linocut in colors (23.8x26.8cm 9x10in) Dettelbach-Effeldorf 1999

ROSSINI Luigi 1790-1857 **[153]**

🗐 **$320** - €311 - **£200** - FF2 037
Veduta di fianco del Campidoglio di Roma Etching (54.5x44.5cm 21x17in) London 1999

ROSSITER Charles 1827-c.1890 **[22]**

🔨 **$1 658** - €1 435 - **£1 000** - FF9 416
Love's Lucky Hand Oil/canvas (20x25cm 7x9in) London 1998

RÖSSLER Rudolf 1864-1934 **[12]**

🔨 **$2 102** - €1 817 - **£1 267** - FF11 917
Mein süsses Hündchen Öl/Leinwand (66x53cm 25x20in) Wien 1999

RÖSSLER von Ludwig C.F.W. 1842-1910 **[6]**
$5 124 - €5 624 - £3 300 - FF36 892
Pflege im Kloster, junge Novizin pflegt einen verletzten Kreuzritter Öl/Leinwand (102x79cm 40x31in) Lindau 2000

ROSSO Medardo 1858-1928 **[50]**
$19 162 - €20 431 - £13 000 - FF134 017
Petite rieuse Plaster (H34cm H13in) London 2001

ROSSO Mino 1904-1963 **[4]**
$7 500 - €7 775 - £4 500 - FF51 000
Senza titolo Bronzo (H52cm H20in) Milano 2000

ROSSUM DU CHATTEL van Fredericus Jacobus 1856-1917 **[81]**
$4 147 - €4 309 - £2 600 - FF28 266
Figure in a Punt on a Quiet Strech of River Oil/canvas (57x39.5cm 22x15in) Suffolk 2000
$279 - €318 - £193 - FF2 083
Poldermolen met roeiboot Oil/canvas (37x28cm 14x11in) Dordrecht 2000
$2 397 - €2 723 - £1 681 - FF17 859
A River Landscape with a Washer Woman by a Farm Watercolour/paper (29x45.5cm 11x17in) Amsterdam 2001

ROSSUM van Jacob 1881-1963 **[23]**
$350 - €408 - £243 - FF2 678
Summer Landscape with Cows Oil/panel (22x37cm 8x14in) Amsterdam 2000
$1 602 - €1 360 - £966 - FF8 920
Naakt voor toilettafel Watercolour/paper (37x21cm 14x8in) Den Haag 1998

ROSSUM van Jan c.1630-c.1678 **[2]**
$8 270 - €9 076 - £5 324 - FF59 532
Elisabeth van Heemskerck/Pieter van Heemskerch (1637-1716) Oil/canvas (78.5x66.5cm 30x26in) Amsterdam 2000

ROSTRUP BØYESEN Peter 1882-1952 **[97]**
$535 - €590 - £362 - FF3 872
Badende piger Oil/canvas (68x71cm 26x27in) Vejle 2000

ROSZAK Theodore 1907-1981 **[15]**
$850 - €967 - £589 - FF6 341
Adolescence Lithograph (43x31cm 17x12in) Chicago IL 2000
$3 000 - €3 131 - £1 898 - FF20 537
Photogram Photograph (13x10cm 5x3in) New-York 2000

ROTA G. XIX **[3]**
$4 447 - €5 183 - £3 117 - FF34 000
Le chapeau à plume/Coquette cavalière Huile/panneau (35x27cm 13x10in) Neuilly-sur-Seine 2000

ROTAN Thurman 1903-1991 **[9]**
$5 000 - €5 551 - £3 477 - FF36 412
«Skyscrapers» Gelatin silver print (11.5x22cm 4x8in) New-York 2001

ROTARI Pietro Antonio 1707-1762 **[48]**
$19 920 - €23 145 - £14 000 - FF151 818
Portrait of Catherine the Great in Morning Oil/canvas (76.5x55cm 30x21in) London 2001
$15 000 - €13 157 - £9 108 - FF86 307
Young Woman, half length, Looking over her Shoulder Oil/canvas/board (43.5x34.5cm 17x13in) New-York 1998
$26 400 - €22 806 - £17 600 - FF149 600
Giovane donna con cestino di fiori Pastelli/carta (70x55.5cm 27x21in) Prato 1998

$999 - €869 - £602 - FF5 698
Bildnis einer Dame mit Haarband Radierung (8.5x6.7cm 3x2in) Berlin 1998

ROTELLA Mimmo 1918 **[493]**
$8 280 - €9 147 - £5 742 - FF60 000
«La flessione verticale» Affiche lacérée, arrachage (143x115cm 56x45in) Paris 2001
$3 617 - €4 260 - £2 542 - FF27 941
«Il bulbo giallo» Öl/Metall (50x37cm 19x14in) Zürich 2000
$2 329 - €1 987 - £1 388 - FF13 034
Senza titolo Decollage (17x22.5cm 6x8in) Zürich 1998
$720 - €622 - £360 - FF4 080
Autoritratto Collage (8x7cm 3x2in) Prato 1999
$238 - €256 - £159 - FF1 676
Pepsi Cola Offset (58.8x76.1cm 23x29in) Hamburg 2000

ROTH Andreas XX **[20]**
$440 - €449 - £275 - FF2 942
Monterey Coastal - 17 Mile Drive Oil/canvas (60x88cm 24x35in) Altadena CA 2000

ROTH Björn 1961 **[2]**
$9 475 - €9 374 - £5 908 - FF61 488
Bali, Mosfellssveit Acrylique (64x76cm 25x29in) Luzern 1999

ROTH Dieter 1930-1998 **[566]**
$50 340 - €43 585 - £30 540 - FF285 900
Gartenfenster Mixed media (195x135cm 76x53in) Wien 1998
$4 950 - €4 988 - £3 085 - FF32 720
Ace Shirt Pong Wad Technique mixte (54x41cm 21x16in) Zürich 2000
$1 504 - €1 431 - £934 - FF9 390
Grabstein Collage/board (40x30cm 15x11in) Hamburg 1999
$43 316 - €43 647 - £26 999 - FF286 307
Fernquartett Assemblage (83x70x28cm 32x27x11in) Zürich 2000
$1 955 - €2 325 - £1 395 - FF15 254
Löwen Selbstturm Sculpture (H29cm H11in) Wien 2000
$1 169 - €1 125 - £721 - FF7 378
Vogelzeichnung Indian ink (24x33cm 9x12in) Köln 1999
$247 - €288 - £171 - FF1 892
Blumenstrauss Offset (62x44cm 24x17in) Bern 2000

ROTH Ernest David 1879-1964 **[66]**
$500 - €432 - £302 - FF2 832
Landscape Oil/canvas/board (20x25cm 8x10in) Watertown MA 1998
$1 600 - €1 750 - £1 106 - FF11 482
Chelsea Piers Watercolour/paper (50x60cm 20x24in) Morris-Plains NJ 2001
$210 - €196 - £129 - FF1 286
Union Square, New York City Etching (24x18cm 9x7in) Cleveland OH 1999

ROTH George XVIII **[5]**
$14 049 - €16 298 - £10 000 - FF106 909
Portrait of Isaac Brodeau, three-quarter-length, reading a Book Oil/canvas (91.5x71cm 36x27in) London 2001

ROTH George Andries 1809-1887 **[13]**
$9 373 - €10 358 - £6 500 - FF67 944
Drover with his Cattle in a Wooded Landscape Oil/canvas (61.5x100.5cm 24x39in) London 2001

R

ROTH Harold XX **[3]**
- 📷 **$700** – €785 – **£485** – FF5 151
  Grand Central Station Gelatin silver print (26x34cm 10x13in) New-York 2000

ROTH Leo 1914 **[41]**
- 🏛 **$2 200** – €2 335 – **£1 488** – FF15 318
  The Painter Oil/canvas (56x71cm 22x27in) Tel Aviv 2001
- 🖋 **$450** – €534 – **£328** – FF3 502
  The Shearing Ink (29x19cm 11x7in) Tel Aviv 2001

RÖTH Philipp 1841-1921 **[131]**
- 🏛 **$4 543** – €5 113 – **£3 130** – FF33 539
  Kühe am Waldrand mit Weiher Öl/Leinwand (76x116cm 29x45in) München 2000
- 🏛 **$3 370** – €3 068 – **£2 106** – FF20 123
  Felder und Häuser am Rande einer Ortschaft Oil/panel (22.5x30.5cm 8x12in) München 1999
- 🖋 **$201** – €234 – **£138** – FF1 509
  Grosser Baum in Landschaft Pencil (44x49cm 17x19in) München 2000

ROTH Sanford 1906-1962 **[14]**
- 📷 **$650** – €555 – **£389** – FF3 641
  Selected Works Gelatin silver print (33.5x22cm 13x8in) San-Francisco CA 1998

ROTH Toni 1899-1971 **[14]**
- 🏛 **$273** – €281 – **£172** – FF1 844
  Bildnis einer frommen Bäuerin Oil/panel (56x39cm 22x15in) München 2000

ROTHAUG Alexander 1870-1946 **[120]**
- 🏛 **$942** – €920 – **£597** – FF6 037
  Im Dom Öl/Leinwand (45x35cm 17x13in) Bremen 1999
- 🖋 **$526** – €502 – **£328** – FF3 293
  Quo vadis, Domine/Die Taufe Indian ink/paper (19x29cm 7x11in) Zofingen 1999

ROTHAUG Leopold 1868-1959 **[49]**
- 🏛 **$832** – €767 – **£498** – FF5 030
  Alte verfallene Mühle in Steiermark zwischen wucherndem Buschwerk Öl/Karton (80x63.5cm 31x25in) Dresden 1998
- 🏛 **$1 857** – €2 180 – **£1 317** – FF14 301
  Die alten Pappeln Öl/Karton (35x27cm 13x10in) Wien 2000

ROTHBORT Samuel 1882-1971 **[30]**
- 🏛 **$1 200** – €1 288 – **£803** – FF8 449
  Harbor I Oil/canvas (61x68cm 24x27in) Portland ME 2000

ROTHE Gatja H. 1935 **[18]**
- 🏛 **$225** – €226 – **£147** – FF1 648
  Monarch Butterflies Mezzotint (88x58cm 35x23in) Chicago IL 2000

ROTHENBERG Susan 1945 **[149]**
- 🏛 **$95 000** – €91 297 – **£58 520** – FF598 870
  Goat over Dog Oil/canvas (180.5x123cm 71x48in) New-York 1999
- 🏛 **$47 500** – €53 734 – **£33 231** – FF352 473
  Untitled Acrylic (56x76cm 22x29in) New-York 2001
- 🏛 **$125 000** – €139 765 – **£84 262** – FF916 800
  Untitled Acrylic/paper (26.5x26.5cm 10x10in) New-York 2000
- 🏛 **$11 000** – €10 571 – **£6 776** – FF69 342
  Untitled Pencil/paper (99x70cm 38x27in) New-York 1999
- 🏛 **$1 100** – €1 207 – **£710** – FF7 918
  Mezzo Fist #2 Mezzotint (62.5x50cm 24x19in) New-York 2000

ROTHENBURGH Otto 1893-1992 **[4]**
- 🏛 **$4 500** – €3 854 – **£2 656** – FF25 281
  Columbus Circle Oil/canvas (91.5x76cm 36x29in) New-York 1998

ROTHENSTEIN Michael 1908-1994 **[71]**
- 🖋 **$885** – €907 – **£550** – FF5 947
  Landscape with Swans Watercolour (39x50.5cm 15x19in) Billingshurst, West-Sussex 2000
- 🏛 **$259** – €220 – **£156** – FF1 443
  Cross Form Aquatint (20.5x28.5cm 8x11in) London 1998

ROTHENSTEIN William 1872-1945 **[78]**
- 🏛 **$649** – €624 – **£400** – FF4 095
  Ypres Oil/canvas (61x102cm 24x40in) Billingshurst, West-Sussex 1999
- 🖋 **$243** – €238 – **£150** – FF1 558
  Portrait of man Chalks/paper (18.5x14.5cm 7x5in) London 1999

ROTHER Richard 1890-1980 **[16]**
- 🖋 **$386** – €358 – **£236** – FF2 347
  Teilheimer Tal Pencil/paper (16.7x17.9cm 6x7in) Dettelbach-Effeldorf 1999

ROTHKO Mark 1903-1970 **[86]**
- 🏛 **$3 000 000** – €3 480 868 – **£2 071 200** – FF22 833 000
  Black in Deep Red Oil/canvas (176x136.5cm 69x53in) New-York 2000
- 🏛 **$906 555** – €1 066 090 – **£650 000** – FF6 993 090
  Untitled Acrylic/paper/canvas (100x65.5cm 39x25in) London 2001
- 🖋 **$12 000** – €13 923 – **£8 284** – FF91 332
  Untitled Ink (46x24cm 18x9in) New-York 2000

RÖTHLISBERGER William 1862-1943 **[29]**
- 🏛 **$365** – €426 – **£252** – FF2 792
  Stille Uferpartie mit Weiden und Büschen Öl/Leinwand/Karton (28x45cm 11x17in) Bern 2000

ROTHSCHILD Judith 1921-1993 **[2]**
- 🏛 **$4 250** – €4 015 – **£2 570** – FF26 334
  Ogygia V Acrylic (118x92.5cm 46x36in) New-York 1999

ROTHSTEIN Arthur 1915-1985 **[54]**
- 📷 **$3 800** – €3 588 – **£2 359** – FF23 536
  Sharecropper's Wife and Child, Arkansas Gelatin silver print (35x25.5cm 13x10in) New-York 1999

ROTHSTÉN Carl Abraham 1826-1877 **[55]**
- 🏛 **$1 195** – €1 345 – **£823** – FF8 825
  A Cottage in the Mountains Oil/canvas (63x90cm 24x35in) Helsinki 2000
- 🏛 **$793** – €877 – **£550** – FF5 750
  Motiv över Ulvsundasjön Oil/canvas (21x22cm 8x8in) Stockholm 2001

ROTHWELL I. XIX **[2]**
- 🏛 **$1 524** – €1 508 – **£950** – FF9 891
  English Setters on Point Oil/canvas (27.5x42.5cm 10x16in) London 1999

ROTHWELL Richard 1800-1868 **[14]**
- 🏛 **$6 550** – €5 990 – **£4 000** – FF39 292
  Portrait of a Young Boy, Holding a Spaniel, in a Wooded Landscape Oil/canvas (76x63.5cm 29x25in) London 1998

RÖTIG Georges Frédéric 1873-1961 **[588]**
- 🏛 **$3 417** – €3 659 – **£2 325** – FF24 000
  Cerfs et biches aux environs de Fontainebleau Huile/toile (54x73cm 21x28in) Marseille 2001

R

$2 115 - €2 363 - **£1 433** - FF15 500
Le Colvert Huile/panneau (19x27cm 7x10in) Pontoise 2000

$763 - €709 - **£466** - FF4 654
Stags and Deer in a snowy Forest Watercolour (24x31cm 9x12in) Amsterdam 1998

$170 - €198 - **£121** - FF1 300
Chiens d'arrêt Lithographie (55x74cm 21x29in) Pont-Audemer 2001

ROTKY Carl 1891-1977 [37]
$1 752 - €2 035 - **£1 209** - FF13 347
Südsteirische Landschaft Öl/Karton (32x25cm 12x9in) Graz 2000

$4 219 - €4 090 - **£2 612** - FF26 831
Blick zum Koglberg Aquarell/Papier (32x47cm 12x18in) Graz 1999

$198 - €232 - **£142** - FF1 525
Herbstwald Linocut in colors (25x20cm 9x7in) Graz 2001

ROTTA Antonio 1828-1903 [30]
$177 862 - €206 648 - **£125 000** - FF1 355 525
Una festa veneziana (a venetian water fete) Oil/canvas (106x172cm 41x67in) London 2001

$40 000 - €41 466 - **£24 000** - FF272 000
Soldati fasciano la zampa di un cagnolino e viene dato ad una ragazza Olio/tela (62x52.5cm 24x20in) Venezia 1999

$6 400 - €8 293 - **£4 800** - FF54 400
Giocando coi bimbi Olio/tela (33x27.5cm 12x10in) Vercelli 2000

ROTTA Silvio Giulio 1853-1913 [4]
$25 216 - €28 633 - **£17 522** - FF187 818
La Nonna Öl/Leinwand (85x107cm 33x42in) Köln 2001

RÖTTEKEN Carl Johann F. 1831-1900 [3]
$17 509 - €20 581 - **£12 136** - FF135 000
Vue d'un marché dans une ville italienne Huile/toile (109x105cm 42x41in) Paris 2000

ROTTENHAMMER Hans I, Johann 1564-1625 [42]
$418 975 - €356 409 - **£250 000** - FF2 338 350
The Rape of the Sabines Oil/canvas (152.5x211cm 60x83in) London 1998

$82 560 - €79 322 - **£50 880** - FF520 320
Le baptême du Christ Huile/cuivre (33x49cm 12x19in) Bruxelles 1999

$24 207 - €22 659 - **£15 000** - FF148 636
The Adoration of the Shepherds Oil/copper (33x25cm 12x9in) London 2000

$11 954 - €12 832 - **£8 000** - FF84 172
The Muses with Pegasus on Mount Parnassus Ink (33x36.5cm 12x14in) London 2000

ROTTERMOND Peter XVII [2]
$1 510 - €1 452 - **£930** - FF9 525
Allegorical scene with Mars and Venus, two Cupids and a Horse Wash (27.5x22cm 10x8in) Amsterdam 1999

ROTTIERS Bernard-Eugène-Ant. 1771-1858 [1]
$2 689 - €2 887 - **£1 800** - FF18 938
The Fall of the Giants Black chalk (40.5x55cm 15x21in) London 2000

ROTTMANN Carl 1797/98-1850 [31]
$77 360 - €79 251 - **£48 740** - FF519 854
Gebirgslandschaft mit zwei Hirschen am Bach Oil/panel (34.5x47cm 13x18in) Düsseldorf 2000

$839 - €920 - **£569** - FF6 037
Aulis Pencil (20x26.3cm 7x10in) Berlin 2000

ROTTMANN Leopold 1812-1881 [18]
$460 - €460 - **£288** - FF3 018
Am Brunnenkopf Aquarell/Papier (36x53.5cm 14x21in) Heidelberg 1999

ROTTMANN Mozart 1874-? [50]
$1 006 - €1 104 - **£683** - FF7 244
Im Maleratelier, Zimmerecke mit Staffelei Öl/Leinwand (49x38cm 19x14in) Saarbrücken 2000

ROTTMAYR Johann Michael 1654-1730 [9]
$7 644 - €6 643 - **£4 605** - FF43 577
Dem hl. Stephan Harding erscheint die Muttergottes Ink (25.7x20cm 10x7in) Berlin 1998

ROUAN François 1943 [42]
$19 110 - €21 343 - **£12 950** - FF140 000
Fizel.Stücke.Grigio Technique mixte (151x111cm 59x43in) Paris 2000

$12 280 - €12 196 - **£7 648** - FF80 000
Buste Huile/papier/toile (117x83cm 46x32in) Paris 1999

$4 194 - €3 887 - **£2 608** - FF25 500
Composition Technique mixte/toile (29.5x23cm 11x9in) Paris 1999

$2 647 - €2 744 - **£1 679** - FF18 000
Sans titre Aquarelle, gouache (65x49cm 25x19in) Paris 2000

$298 - €274 - **£183** - FF1 800
Composition Eau-forte (66x33cm 25x12in) Paris 1999

ROUARGUE Adolphe 1810-? [15]
$3 827 - €4 269 - **£2 671** - FF28 000
Marine Huile/toile (89x130cm 35x51in) Versailles 2001

$236 - €274 - **£163** - FF1 800
La Cathédrale de Strasbourg Crayon/papier (17x12cm 6x4in) Rennes 2000

ROUART Ernest 1874-1942 [16]
$5 542 - €5 183 - **£3 355** - FF34 000
Elégantes, avenue du bois Huile/panneau (32.5x23.5cm 12x9in) Lons-Le-Saunier 1999

$145 - €152 - **£91** - FF1 000
La panthère Encre Chine/papier (34.5x16cm 13x6in) Paris 2000

ROUAULT Georges 1871-1958 [1485]
$150 000 - €129 560 - **£90 600** - FF849 855
Paysage biblique (aux sept arbres) Oil/paper/canvas (37x52cm 14x20in) New-York 1998

$40 000 - €33 802 - **£23 860** - FF221 728
Manon (Anaïs) Oil/panel (22x17cm 8x6in) San-Francisco CA 1998

$18 000 - €19 439 - **£12 439** - FF127 510
Des bouqueaux chetifs du chemin de Cythère Watercolour, gouache (33x37cm 12x14in) New-York 2001

$1 000 - €1 181 - **£708** - FF7 750
Son avocat, en phrases creuse, clame sa totale inconscience Etching, aquatint (53.5x40.5cm 21x15in) Boston MA 2000

ROUAULT Georges-Dominique 1904 [223]
$1 337 - €1 189 - **£819** - FF7 800
Place du Tertre à Montmartre Huile/toile (46x55cm 18x21in) La Varenne-Saint-Hilaire 1999

$492 - €447 - **£300** - FF2 929
Paris Street Watercolour/paper (23x18cm 9x7in) Godalming, Surrey 1998

$6 566 - €7 318 - **£4 560** - FF48 000
L'Amazone Aquatinte couleurs (44x33.5cm 17x13in) Paris 2001

R

ROUBAL Franz 1889-1967 [31]
- $2 817 - €3 270 - £1 980 - FF21 451
  Rangkampf zweier Hengste Öl/Leinwand (83x100cm 32x39in) Graz 2001
- $777 - €727 - £470 - FF4 767
  Rebhühner mit ihren Jungen Öl/Karton (47x30cm 18x11in) Wien 1999
- $406 - €472 - £286 - FF3 098
  Der Tiger Charcoal/paper (18.5x22cm 7x8in) Graz 2001

ROUBAUD Frants / Franz 1856-1928 [104]
- $12 078 - €11 404 - £7 500 - FF74 808
  Mounted Cossacks riding into Battle Oil/canvas (81x149.5cm 31x58in) London 1999
- $5 778 - €5 624 - £3 549 - FF36 892
  Morgengebet Öl/Leinwand (70.5x90.5cm 27x35in) Berlin 1999
- $2 200 - €2 217 - £1 371 - FF14 542
  Kurd's Flight with his Booty Oil/board (40.5x25cm 15x9in) New-York 2000
- $990 - €1 125 - £692 - FF7 378
  Tscherkessenreiter Aquarell/Papier (50x35cm 19x13in) München 2001

ROUBAUDO Georges 1898-1999 [153]
- $97 - €107 - £67 - FF700
  Voiliers à Antibes Huile/toile (61x50cm 24x19in) Paris 2001

ROUBICHON Alphonse 1867-? [4]
- $8 250 - €8 817 - £5 621 - FF57 796
  The Lady's Garden Oil/canvas (93x116cm 37x46in) New-Orleans LA 2001

ROUBILLAC Louis François 1702/05-1762 [3]
- $117 313 - €99 814 - £70 000 - FF654 738
  Bust of Philip Dormer Stanhope, 4th Earl of Chesterfield (1694-1773) Bronze (H62.5cm H24in) London 1998

ROUBILLE Auguste 1872-1955 [28]
- $6 000 - €6 998 - £4 212 - FF45 902
  «Spratt's Patent Ltd.» Poster (115.5x156cm 45x61in) New-York 2000

ROUBTZOFF Alexandre 1884-1949 [103]
- $16 614 - €17 837 - £11 115 - FF117 000
  Élégante Huile/toile (198x84cm 77x33in) Paris 2000
- $11 736 - €13 720 - £8 379 - FF90 000
  La partie d'échecs Huile/toile (50x65cm 19x25in) Paris 2001
- $2 908 - €3 049 - £1 822 - FF20 000
  Jardin à Tunis Huile/toile/carton (20.5x28.5cm 8x11in) Paris 2000

ROUBY Alfred 1849-1909 [55]
- $2 047 - €2 287 - £1 387 - FF15 000
  Bouquet Huile/toile (73x60cm 28x23in) Paris 2000

ROUEDE Émile XIX-XX [2]
- $4 075 - €3 811 - £2 467 - FF25 000
  Nature morte au gibier Huile/toile (73x65cm 28x25in) Reims 1999

ROUGELET Benedict, Benoît 1834-1894 [16]
- $12 725 - €12 348 - £7 921 - FF81 000
  Les amours au tambourin Marbre (62x51cm 24x20in) Pontoise 1999

ROUGEMONT de Guy 1935 [36]
- $3 244 - €3 201 - £1 999 - FF21 000
  Nuage, planche Métal (63.5x244x70cm 25x96x27in) Paris 1999
- $149 - €137 - £91 - FF900
  «Lumière des quatre Fils III» Lavis (40x30cm 15x11in) Paris 1999

- $2 800 - €2 609 - £1 728 - FF17 113
  Lumière de Villemonteix Tapestry (210x143cm 82x56in) New-York 1999

ROUGEMONT de Philippe 1891-1965 [37]
- $812 - €839 - £511 - FF5 506
  Sittande nakenmodell Oil/canvas (64x53cm 25x20in) Stockholm 2000

ROUGEOT Charles Edouard XIX [1]
- $3 772 - €3 659 - £2 373 - FF24 000
  Scènes de chasse Huile/toile (47x65cm 18x25in) Neuilly-sur-Seine 1999

ROUGET Georges 1784-1869 [7]
- $7 579 - €7 089 - £4 589 - FF46 500
  Portrait d'officier Huile/toile (65x55cm 25x21in) Noyon 1999

ROUGHT John Willard XX [1]
- $8 500 - €9 124 - £5 791 - FF59 852
  Playing Outside on a Fall Afternoon Oil/canvas (45.5x38cm 17x14in) Boston MA 2001

ROUILLARD Jean-Sébastien 1789-1852 [7]
- $7 262 - €7 318 - £4 526 - FF48 000
  Portrait de Claude Thienon et de son fils Louis Huile/toile (55.5x46cm 21x18in) Tours 2000

ROUILLARD Pierre Louis 1820-1881 [9]
- $102 528 - €97 567 - £63 744 - FF640 000
  Grand cerf Fer (250x170x60cm 98x66x23in) Lille 1999

ROUILLÉ Jean XX [13]
- $245 - €274 - £166 - FF1 800
  «A travers le monde» Affiche (59x39cm 23x15in) Paris 2000

ROULET Henry 1915-1995 [40]
- $2 881 - €3 241 - £2 018 - FF21 257
  «Arlequin bleu» Öl/Leinwand (46x38cm 18x14in) Luzern 2001
- $1 799 - €1 734 - £1 109 - FF11 376
  Triste journée Öl/Leinwand (30x50cm 11x19in) Bern 1999
- $571 - €529 - £349 - FF3 468
  Dame am Fensterplatz Gouache/panneau (16x13cm 6x5in) Bern 1999

ROULLAND Jean 1931 [38]
- $544 - €457 - £320 - FF3 000
  Sans titre, tryptique Aquarelle (32x25cm 12x9in) Lille 1998

ROULLEAU Jules P. 1855-1895 [5]
- $6 335 - €5 336 - £3 741 - FF35 000
  Hébé sur l'aigle Bronze (H74cm H29in) Paris 1998

ROULLET Gaston 1847-1925 [151]
- $2 399 - €2 761 - £1 654 - FF18 111
  Blick in die Bucht von Haiphong Öl/Leinwand (100x70cm 39x27in) Saarbrücken 2000
- $1 668 - €1 829 - £1 109 - FF12 000
  Entrée de Dakar au Sénégal, Ile de Gorée Huile/panneau (18x46cm 7x18in) Paris 2000
- $653 - €686 - £430 - FF4 500
  Etretat, bateau à marée basse Aquarelle/papier (11x21cm 4x8in) Calais 2000
- $800 - €933 - £561 - FF6 120
  «Salon des Cent» Poster (40x60cm 15x23in) New-York 2000

ROUMYANSEVA Galina Alekseyevna 1927 [20]
- $4 205 - €3 977 - £2 600 - FF26 087
  Portrait of a peasant Girl Oil/canvas (119.5x81cm 47x31in) London 1999

ROUNTREE Harry 1878-1950 **[44]**
✏ **$854** - €994 - **£600** - FF6 518
Squirrel and Duckling inspecting a Chimney
Watercolour (24.5x19.5cm 9x7in) Billingshurst, West-Sussex 2001

ROURA JUANOLA Lluis 1943 **[11]**
🖌 **$1 334** - €1 381 - **£828** - FF9 062
Plaza de pueblo con figuras Oleo/tabla (81x100cm 31x39in) Barcelona 2000

ROUSAUD Aristide 1868-1946 **[6]**
🗿 **$2 564** - €3 049 - **£1 828** - FF20 000
Cheval à l'abreuvoir Bronze (35x55cm 13x21in) Paris 2000

ROUSSE Frank act.1897-1915 **[96]**
✏ **$992** - €947 - **£620** - FF6 214
View of Whitby, Fishing Vessels in the fore-ground Watercolour/paper (26x48cm 10x19in) Driffield, East Yorkshire 1999

ROUSSE Georges 1947 **[42]**
📷 **$2 063** - €1 982 - **£1 279** - FF13 000
Sans titre Photo couleur (95x115cm 37x45in) Paris 1999

ROUSSEAU Albert 1908-1982 **[203]**
🖌 **$689** - €701 - **£431** - FF4 595
Rue petit Champlain Huile/toile (61x76cm 24x29in) Montréal 2000
🖌 **$373** - €411 - **£250** - FF2 696
Voiliers Huile/panneau (20x25.5cm 7x10in) Montréal 2000
✏ **$268** - €243 - **£165** - FF1 592
Sans titre Aquarelle (34.5x41.5cm 13x16in) Montréal 2000

ROUSSEAU Camille XX **[50]**
🖌 **$1 244** - €1 372 - **£828** - FF9 000
Élégantes et enfants en bord de mer Huile/toile/panneau (50x38cm 19x14in) Biarritz 2000
🖌 **$448** - €481 - **£304** - FF3 152
Marina Oleo/tabla (20x25cm 7x9in) Barcelona 2001

ROUSSEAU Clément 1872-1950 **[3]**
🗿 **$9 558** - €9 299 - **£5 880** - FF61 000
Pied de lampe à fût cylindrique Sculpture (H22cm H8in) Paris 1999

ROUSSEAU Eugène 1827-1891 **[3]**
🗿 **$3 420** - €2 897 - **£2 055** - FF19 000
Vase de section triangulaire Sculpture verre (H26cm H10in) Paris 1998

ROUSSEAU Gabriel XX **[11]**
✏ **$1 401** - €1 372 - **£862** - FF9 000
Rue de Marrakech animée Aquarelle/papier (37x27cm 14x10in) Toulon 1999

ROUSSEAU Helen Hoffman 1898-1992 **[15]**
🖌 **$7 000** - €7 514 - **£4 684** - FF49 287
View of Laguna Beach Hotel Oil/board (63x76cm 25x30in) Altadena CA 2000

ROUSSEAU Henri Émilien 1875-1933 **[184]**
🖌 **$16 797** - €14 330 - **£10 133** - FF94 000
Allée des peupliers en Camargue Huile/toile (73x100cm 28x39in) Arles 2000
🖌 **$2 618** - €2 973 - **£1 792** - FF19 500
Cavalier arabe Huile/panneau (22x16cm 8x6in) Saumur 2000
✏ **$14 290** - €16 007 - **£9 933** - FF105 000
La danse du foulard Aquarelle, gouache/papier (46x61cm 18x24in) Paris 2001

ROUSSEAU Henri, le Douanier 1844-1910 **[69]**
🖌 **$149 600** - €167 694 - **£101 530** - FF1 100 000
Bateaux à voile Huile/toile (99x99cm 38x38in) Paris 2000
🖌 **$58 065** - €53 357 - **£35 770** - FF350 000
La cueillette du coton (paysage exotique avec église) Huile/bois (30.4x40cm 11x15in) Deauville 1998
✏ **$35 863** - €38 496 - **£24 000** - FF252 518
Promeneurs s'acheminant vers un chalet de montagne Pencil (36x30cm 14x11in) London 2000
🖼 **$200** - €192 - **£123** - FF1 259
Chenes de Roche Etching (12.5x17cm 4x6in) New-York 1999

ROUSSEAU Jean Jacques 1861-1911 **[25]**
🖌 **$1 258** - €1 212 - **£783** - FF7 949
Brogede köer i en frugtplantage Oil/canvas (75x93cm 29x36in) Köbenhavn 1999

ROUSSEAU Léon 1829-1881 **[8]**
🖌 **$602** - €579 - **£371** - FF3 800
Nature morte au gibier Huile/toile (50x61cm 19x24in) Paris 1999

ROUSSEAU Margarite 1888-1948 **[9]**
🖌 **$19 000** - €20 396 - **£12 944** - FF133 788
The Boat Ride Oil/canvas (61.5x91cm 24x35in) Boston MA 2001

ROUSSEAU Nicolas XIX **[14]**
🖌 **$1 650** - €1 894 - **£1 129** - FF12 421
Country Landscape Oil/canvas (38x55cm 15x22in) Cleveland OH 2000

ROUSSEAU Philippe 1816-1887 **[65]**
🖌 **$43 220** - €45 378 - **£27 250** - FF297 660
Still Life with Oysters, Lemmons and Chrysantemums in a Vase Oil/canvas (100x132cm 39x51in) Amsterdam 2000
🖌 **$13 982** - €15 882 - **£9 810** - FF104 181
A Still Life of Anemones in a Silver Jug Oil/canvas (75x100cm 29x39in) Amsterdam 2001
🖌 **$1 200** - €1 386 - **£840** - FF9 093
Still Life with Lemons Oil/canvas (25x35cm 10x14in) New-York 2001

ROUSSEAU Théodore 1812-1867 **[358]**
🖌 **$271 491** - €291 440 - **£181 716** - FF1 911 723
Sonnenuntergang über Paris Öl/Leinwand (105x160cm 41x62in) Berlin 2000
🖌 **$32 991** - €32 014 - **£20 538** - FF210 000
Paysanne, au bord de la mare Huile/panneau (32x51cm 12x20in) Fontainebleau 1999
🖌 **$7 948** - €9 452 - **£5 511** - FF62 000
Sous-bois Huile/papier/toile (14x23cm 5x9in) Paris 2000
✏ **$2 208** - €2 439 - **£1 531** - FF16 000
Bergère et troupeau de moutons paissant en lisière de forêt Crayon (26x42.5cm 10x16in) Paris 2001
🖼 **$378** - €320 - **£225** - FF2 100
La mare/Paysage du Berry/Marais dans les Landes Eau-forte (21x29cm 8x11in) Auvers sur Oise 1998

ROUSSEAU Victor 1865-1954 **[97]**
🗿 **$3 458** - €3 222 - **£2 132** - FF21 138
Homme nu assis sur un rocher Bronze (H34cm H13in) Bruxelles 1999
✏ **$186** - €198 - **£127** - FF1 300
Jeune femme nue de face Technique mixte/papier (14x10cm 5x3in) Bruxelles 2001

R

ROUSSEAUX des

ROUSSEAUX des Jacques c.1600-1638 **[8]**
$11 400 - €12 949 - **£8 000** - FF84 940
Old Man reading a Book Oil/panel (42.5x36.5cm 16x14in) London 2001

ROUSSEAUX-MORRICE David 1903 **[16]**
$396 - €342 - **£239** - FF2 246
Landscape Ile Maniton, Ontario Huile/panneau (21.5x26.7cm 8x10in) Montréal 1999

ROUSSEL Alphonse 1829-1868 **[1]**
$10 656 - €11 604 - **£6 979** - FF76 118
Man och kvinna i renässansdräkter i solbelyst landskap med vattendrag Oil/canvas (139x240cm 54x94in) Uppsala 2000

ROUSSEL Charles Emmanuel 1861-1936 **[45]**
$3 988 - €4 040 - **£2 480** - FF26 500
Pêcheurs poussant la barque Huile/toile (61x108cm 24x42in) Aubagne 2000
$1 305 - €1 372 - **£861** - FF9 000
Promeneur sur la plage Huile/panneau (17x27cm 6x10in) Calais 2000

ROUSSEL Ker Xavier 1867-1944 **[196]**
$14 594 - €15 677 - **£10 000** - FF102 832
Paysage, vue d'un Parc Oil/canvas (100.5x150cm 39x59in) London 2001
$7 335 - €7 622 - **£4 620** - FF50 000
Le printemps Huile/toile (68x101cm 26x39in) Paris 2000
$3 362 - €3 125 - **£2 041** - FF20 500
Silène Huile/carton (28x40cm 11x15in) Paris 1998
$923 - €915 - **£559** - FF6 000
Faunes dans un paysage Pastel/papier (16x19.5cm 6x7in) Paris 2000
$496 - €579 - **£350** - FF3 800
Deux femmes conversant, la terrasse Lithographie (18x8.5cm 7x3in) Paris 2000

ROUSSEL Pierre 1927-1995 **[30]**
$922 - €991 - **£634** - FF6 500
Scène d'intérieur Huile/toile (80x79cm 31x31in) Paris 2001

ROUSSEL René XIX-XX **[8]**
$63 - €74 - **£44** - FF487
«Tournai, ville d'art» Affiche (87x125cm 34x49in) Liège 2000

ROUSSEL Théodore 1847-1926 **[47]**
$5 049 - €5 665 - **£3 500** - FF37 162
Pond in Hyde Park, London Oil/canvas (51x61cm 20x24in) London 2000
$2 440 - €2 736 - **£1 700** - FF17 947
The English Coast Oil/panel (11x17.5cm 4x6in) London 2001
$1 127 - €1 043 - **£700** - FF6 843
Ships moored at Rochester Watercolour/paper (16.5x21.5cm 6x8in) London 1999

ROUSSEL Theodore 1914-1989 **[2]**
$2 000 - €2 324 - **£1 405** - FF15 242
Portrait of the Countess of Manchester, Bust-length in a pink Dress Oil/panel (38.5x31cm 15x12in) New-York 2001

ROUSSELET Louis XIX **[4]**
$3 920 - €3 630 - **£2 400** - FF23 810
Mr. Louis Rousselet in Court Dress Albumen print (17x13cm 7x5in) London 1999

ROUSSELLE Georges 1924-1976 **[18]**
$550 - €610 - **£380** - FF4 000
Maisons au bord de l'eau Joinville Huile/toile (46.5x61cm 18x24in) Chaumont 2001

ROUSSELOT Lucien 1900-1992 **[125]**
$300 - €335 - **£208** - FF2 200
Chasseur d'Afrique chargeant Aquarelle/papier (31x29cm 12x11in) Paris 2001

ROUSSET Jules 1840-? **[13]**
$4 002 - €3 430 - **£2 407** - FF22 500
Le pont de St. Cloud Huile/toile (33x52.5cm 12x20in) Pontoise 1998
$2 041 - €2 287 - **£1 419** - FF15 000
Aux abords de la Mosquée Sid Abdel Rahman à Alger Huile/toile/carton (26x20.5cm 10x8in) Paris 2001

ROUSSIN Georges 1854-? **[5]**
$1 280 - €1 448 - **£865** - FF9 500
Au petit clou/Le port Gouache/papier (25x36cm 9x14in) Toulouse 2000

ROUSSIN Victor Marie 1812-1903 **[8]**
$3 705 - €3 734 - **£2 304** - FF24 492
Smärre färgbortfall Oil/canvas (87x65cm 34x25in) Stockholm 2000
$2 525 - €2 134 - **£1 502** - FF14 000
Deux Bretonnes sur un chemin portant des cruches Huile/panneau (27x21cm 10x8in) Quimper 1998

ROUVIERE Charles 1866-1924 **[9]**
$3 782 - €3 811 - **£2 357** - FF25 000
Antibes Huile/toile (46x65cm 18x25in) Saint-Étienne 2000
$1 444 - €1 677 - **£1 028** - FF11 000
Femme dans son intérieur Huile/toile (37x27cm 14x10in) Mâcon 2001

ROUX Antoine I 1765-1835 **[92]**
$4 574 - €5 336 - **£3 181** - FF35 000
Vaisseau anglais «Hannibal» à l'ancre, au loin une frégate Aquarelle/papier (42x60cm 16x23in) Nice 2001

ROUX Antoine, fils aîné 1799-1872 **[26]**
$4 192 - €3 811 - **£2 525** - FF25 000
Le brick «Herminie Capt Alex Davy» Gouache/papier (43x59cm 16x23in) La Rochelle 1998

ROUX Carl 1826-1894 **[24]**
$7 303 - €6 647 - **£4 563** - FF43 600
Zwei Kälber im Gebüsch Oil/panel (51x69.5cm 20x27in) München 1999
$1 453 - €1 534 - **£960** - FF10 061
Kuhhirte mit Kühen an einer Brücke Öl/Leinwand (25x48cm 9x18in) Heidelberg 2000

ROUX Constant 1865-1929 **[28]**
$896 - €1 067 - **£620** - FF7 000
Buste de gladiateur Bronze (32x33x28cm 12x12x11in) Strasbourg 2000

ROUX François 1811-1882 **[43]**
$3 659 - €4 269 - **£2 545** - FF28 000
Trois mâts «Alcion», Capitaine Chanielen rade de Marseille Aquarelle/papier (43x55cm 16x21in) Nice 2000

ROUX Frédéric 1805-1874 **[37]**
$5 379 - €5 336 - **£3 346** - FF35 000
Le trois mâts «Le Zampa» - Pouen Capitaine Pattin Aquarelle/papier (57x45cm 22x17in) Paris 1999

ROUX Gaston Louis 1904-1988 **[44]**
$351 - €409 - **£247** - FF2 683
Südländische Stadtansicht Öl/Karton (26.5x35cm 10x13in) Hamburg 2001

1356

ROUX Gérard 1946 [18]
🖎 $787 - €915 - £561 - FF6 000
  Le retour des pêcheurs Huile/panneau (24x35cm
  9x13in) Pont-Audemer 2001

ROUX Joël 1948 [9]
🖎 $819 - €915 - £555 - FF6 000
  Saint Jacques Sculpture bois (H51cm H20in) Pau
  2000

ROUX Louis François Fr. 1817-1903 [20]
🖎 $18 000 - €16 897 - £11 154 - FF110 836
  U.S Ship Harmonia, Flying U.S Flag Oil/canvas
  (111x179cm 44x70in) Portsmouth NH 1999
🖎 $10 241 - €10 671 - £6 440 - FF70 000
  «Amélie» Nicolas Paquet et Compagnie
  Aquarelle, gouache/papier (39x60cm 15x23in) Paris
  2000

ROUX Paul c.1845-1918 [29]
🖎 $255 - €274 - £171 - FF1 800
  Moulin de Sannois Aquarelle/papier (19x30.5cm
  7x12in) Paris 2000

ROUX Polydore 1792-1833 [1]
🖎 $16 437 - €17 644 - £11 000 - FF115 737
  **Extensive Mountainous Landscape with an
  Artist Sketching on a Hillside** Oil/canvas
  (97x129cm 38x50in) London 2000

ROUX Tony George 1894-1928 [15]
🖎 $1 443 - €1 455 - £900 - FF9 543
  «Font-Romeu» Poster (99x62cm 38x24in) London
  2000

ROUX-CHAMPION Joseph-Victor 1871-1953 [83]
🖎 $4 418 - €5 031 - £3 118 - FF33 000
  Le port de Brigneau Huile/toile (60x73cm 23x28in)
  Rennes 2001
🖎 $388 - €442 - £266 - FF2 900
  Les quais à Paris Aquarelle (24x31cm 9x12in) Paris
  2000

ROVEDATA Giovan Battista c.1570-c.1640 [2]
🖎 $12 569 - €10 694 - £7 500 - FF70 150
  The Crucifixion Oil/panel (55x39.5cm 21x15in)
  London 1998

ROVERE XVIII [1]
🖎 $4 182 - €4 878 - £2 908 - FF32 000
  **Le vaisseau «Vangarte» et la frégate «Verron»,
  devant l'île de Malte** Aquarelle/papier (39.5x55.5cm
  15x21in) Nice 2000

ROVERS Joseph, Jos 1893-1970 [30]
🖎 $1 178 - €1 134 - £736 - FF7 441
  Landscape with Bridge Oil/canvas (66x80cm
  25x31in) Amsterdam 1999
🖎 $1 010 - €1 180 - £692 - FF7 739
  «De Bijenkorf Den Haag» Poster (110x79.5cm
  43x31in) Hoorn 2000

ROVERSI Paolo 1947 [10]
📷 $1 000 - €946 - £621 - FF6 208
  Kasia e Lisa Paris Gelatin silver print (29x39cm
  11x15in) New-York 1999

ROVIRA RAMIS Antonio 1938 [13]
🖎 $549 - €541 - £351 - FF3 546
  «Puerto de Pollensa» Técnica mixta (46x55cm
  18x21in) Madrid 1999

ROVNER Michal 1957 [4]
📷 $8 000 - €9 050 - £5 596 - FF59 364
  «One Person Game against Nature III V-3/V-8»
  Photograph (81.5x106.5cm 32x41in) New-York 2001

ROWAN Marian Ellis Ryan 1848-1922 [79]
🖎 $1 250 - €1 458 - £870 - FF9 567
  Monarch Butterflies Watercolour/paper (35x19.5cm
  13x7in) Melbourne 2000

ROWBOTHAM Charles Edmund 1858-1921 [168]
🖎 $1 581 - €1 468 - £949 - FF9 627
  **Figures and Goat beside the edge of a
  Lake/Figures in a rowing Boat** Watercolour
  (12x19cm 4x7in) London 1999

ROWBOTHAM Claude Hamilton 1864-1949 [129]
🖎 $354 - €391 - £240 - FF2 563
  The Back Door Watercolour/paper (19x13cm 7x5in)
  London 2000
🖎 $111 - €108 - £70 - FF707
  A breezy Morning, Falmouth Print in colors
  (6x10cm 2x4in) Par, Cornwall 1999

ROWBOTHAM Mark Alun XX [5]
🖎 $811 - €780 - £500 - FF5 119
  Decorating Bunty's Hat Pastel/paper (24x19.5cm
  9x7in) London 1999

ROWBOTHAM Thomas Ch. Leeson 1823-1875
[149]
🖎 $5 803 - €5 024 - £3 500 - FF32 956
  Castle and Town of Heidelberg, Germany
  Oil/canvas (66x91.5cm 25x36in) London 1998
🖎 $956 - €875 - £580 - FF5 742
  Figures on a Track before an Italian Lake
  Watercolour (19x44.5cm 7x17in) London 1998

ROWBOTHAM Thomas Leeson 1783-1853 [30]
🖎 $985 - €920 - £608 - FF6 037
  Blick auf Köln Aquarell/Papier (10.5x25cm 4x9in)
  Köln 1999

RØWDE Teddy 1912 [2]
🖎 $7 378 - €8 777 - £5 103 - FF57 575
  Likhenter fra New York Oil/panel (33x24cm 12x9in)
  Oslo 2000

ROWDEN Thomas, Tom 1842-1926 [124]
🖎 $809 - €873 - £540 - FF5 728
  Highland Cattle Watercolour/paper (22x51cm 8x20in)
  Stansted Mountfitchet, Essex 2000

ROWE Clifford XX [1]
🖎 $1 219 - €1 119 - £749 - FF7 343
  Dead End Poster (76x101.5cm 29x39in) London 1999

ROWE Ernest Arthur c.1860-1922 [115]
🖎 $1 622 - €1 385 - £902 - FF9 082
  Beechives in an Orchard Watercolour/paper
  (25.5x35.5cm 10x13in) London 1998

ROWE George 1797-1864 [5]
🖎 $10 780 - €9 818 - £6 600 - FF64 400
  **Parker and Macord - Potato Salesmen and
  general Fruiterers, bendigo** Watercolour/paper
  (23.5x34cm 9x13in) Malvern, Victoria 1998

ROWE Sidney Grant 1861-1928 [26]
🖎 $520 - €459 - £320 - FF3 014
  Farmstead, with Geese by a Track
  Watercolour/paper (27x36cm 11x14in) Godalming,
  Surrey 1999

ROWE Tom Trythall 1856-? [7]
🖎 $1 314 - €1 249 - £800 - FF8 195
  Fishermen on the Harbour Beach Oil/canvas
  (38x55cm 14x21in) London 1998

ROWE Willie Reed 1914 [14]
🖎 $900 - €1 036 - £614 - FF6 796
  The Art House-633 Saint Peter Street Etching
  (13x12cm 5x5in) New-Orleans LA 2000

R

ROWLAND William XVIII-XIX **[8]**
- $1 345 - €1 444 - £900 - FF9 473
  The Start/On the Scent/Middle of the Chase/In Full Cry Oil/panel (17.5x28cm 6x11in) London 2000

ROWLANDSON George Derville 1861-1928 **[66]**
- $4 636 - €4 321 - £2 800 - FF28 343
  The Kill Oil/canvas (61x91.5cm 24x36in) London 1998
- $888 - €836 - £549 - FF5 483
  Over the Brook Oil/panel (24.5x38cm 9x14in) London 1999
- $158 - €177 - £110 - FF1 158
  Hunting scene Print (41x62cm 16x24in) Stansted Mountfitchet, Essex 2001

ROWLANDSON Thomas 1756-1827 **[787]**
- $2 821 - €2 756 - £1 800 - FF18 079
  Dr Syntax Obtruding Watercolour (12.5x21cm 4x8in) London 1999
- $190 - €204 - £130 - FF1 337
  A Picture of Misery Engraving (34x24cm 13x9in) Loughton, Essex 2001

ROWNTREE Harry 1878-1950 **[17]**
- $423 - €446 - £280 - FF2 927
  Anthony and Cleopatra Wash (35x24.5cm 13x9in) London 2000

ROWNTREE Kenneth 1915-1997 **[24]**
- $1 150 - €1 093 - £700 - FF7 171
  Cavendish Road, Clare, Suffolk Oil/canvas (41x66cm 16x25in) London 1999
- $864 - €899 - £550 - FF5 897
  Stockholm Oil/board (27x35.5cm 10x13in) London 2000

ROWORTH Edward 1880-1964 **[98]**
- $470 - €527 - £326 - FF3 456
  Extensive Landscape with a View of a Valley Oil/board (50x74.5cm 19x29in) Johannesburg 2001
- $392 - €378 - £242 - FF2 480
  Two Figures in an Extensive Landscape Oil/board (32.5x47.5cm 12x18in) Johannesburg 1999

ROWORTH Ivanonia 1920 **[12]**
- $182 - €197 - £125 - FF1 294
  Judging a Single Harness Class, Paarl Show, South Africa Oil/board (44.5x60cm 17x23in) Bristol, Avon 2001

ROY Abel XIX-XX **[8]**
- $2 749 - €2 668 - £1 711 - FF17 500
  La moisson Huile/toile (19.5x33cm 7x12in) Fontainebleau 1999

ROY de J.B. 1784-1862 **[2]**
- $2 310 - €2 479 - £1 550 - FF16 260
  Bergers et leurs troupeaux dans un paysage Huile/panneau (29x42cm 11x16in) Antwerpen 2000

ROY de Jean-Baptiste 1759-1839 **[38]**
- $5 056 - €4 878 - £3 196 - FF32 000
  Vaches au pâturage Huile/panneau (85x73.5cm 33x28in) Paris 1999
- $1 663 - €1 555 - £1 024 - FF10 200
  Landskap med boskap Oil/panel (26x35.5cm 10x13in) Stockholm 2000

ROY Félix 1824-? **[2]**
- $11 736 - €13 720 - £8 379 - FF90 000
  Le favori Huile/toile (92x73cm 36x28in) Paris 2001

ROY Jamini 1887-1972 **[136]**
- $3 250 - €3 510 - £2 246 - FF23 022
  Gopini Gouache/paper (84.5x32.5cm 33x12in) Bethesda MD 2001

ROY Louis 1862-1907 **[42]**
- $11 157 - €13 121 - £8 000 - FF86 068
  Le printemps en Franche Comté Oil/board (50.5x32.5cm 19x12in) London 2001
- $1 713 - €1 448 - £1 019 - FF9 500
  Bord de mer en Bretagne Pastel/papier (30.5x43.5cm 12x17in) Pontoise 1998

ROY Marius 1833-? **[14]**
- $1 600 - €1 717 - £1 070 - FF11 265
  Soldier in Prone Position Firing Rifle Oil/panel (13x23cm 5x9in) Asheville NC 2000

ROY Martin XX **[3]**
- $3 200 - €3 435 - £2 173 - FF22 529
  King Kong for a Day Gelatin silver print (37x25cm 14x9in) Beverly-Hills CA 2001

ROY Pierre 1880-1950 **[56]**
- $36 000 - €39 935 - £23 940 - FF261 957
  La femme peintre Oil/canvas (60x73cm 23x28in) New-York 2000
- $3 925 - €3 811 - £2 425 - FF25 000
  La Malinoise Huile/toile (32.5x24cm 12x9in) Paris 1999
- $461 - €381 - £270 - FF2 500
  «Leylands Farms» Crayon (22.5x19.6cm 8x7in) Paris 1998

ROY Pranay Ranjan XX **[2]**
- $8 620 - €10 058 - £6 000 - FF65 976
  Buddha and Sajata Watercolour (36x26.5cm 14x10in) London 2000

ROY Proshanto 1908-1973 **[8]**
- $3 592 - €4 191 - £2 500 - FF27 490
  Barge on a River Watercolour (26.5x27cm 10x10in) London 2000

ROY Rob 1909-1992 **[13]**
- $1 393 - €1 448 - £877 - FF9 500
  Grand Prix de Monaco 1930, Chiron sur Bugatti 35 Nº18 Aquarelle/papier (55x40cm 21x15in) Paris 2000

ROY van Dolf 1858-1943 **[26]**
- $488 - €545 - £338 - FF3 577
  Allongée nue dans un intérieur Huile/toile (38x47cm 14x18in) Bruxelles 2001

ROY van Leo 1921 **[8]**
- $921 - €843 - £561 - FF5 528
  La fiancée du marchant de glace Huile/panneau (70x50cm 27x19in) Bruxelles 1999

ROY-AUDY Jean-Baptiste 1778-1848 **[1]**
- $22 905 - €26 718 - £16 360 - FF175 259
  Charles-Paphnuce-Anaclet Boucher, Seigneur de Maskinongé et de Carufel Huile/toile (67x55.5cm 26x21in) Montréal 2000

ROYBAL José D. 1922-1978 **[13]**
- $600 - €568 - £374 - FF3 726
  Portrait of Two Women Watercolour/paper (17x27cm 7x11in) St. Ignatius MT 1999

ROYBET Ferdinand 1840-1920 **[241]**
- $19 933 - €23 630 - £14 523 - FF155 000
  Portrait de Carmen de Wendel Huile/toile (128x94cm 50x37in) Paris 2001
- $8 000 - €6 910 - £4 822 - FF45 325
  Seeing his Reflection Oil/panel (81.5x52cm 32x20in) New-York 1998
- $1 647 - €1 524 - £1 020 - FF10 000
  Le peintre à sa palette Huile/panneau (24x18.5cm 9x7in) Paris 1999

🖊 $483 - €534 - **£327** - FF3 500
Autoportrait et deux mousquetaires
Crayon/papier (46x31cm 18x12in) Paris 2000

ROYDS Mabel A. Lumsden 1874-1941 **[16]**
📇 $327 - €302 - **£200** - FF1 980
Boatmen Woodcut (25.5x35.5cm 10x13in) London
1998

ROYE van de Jef, Jozef 1861-1941 **[11]**
🖐 $940 - €1 115 - **£684** - FF7 317
Coquelicots Huile/toile (127x80cm 50x31in)
Antwerpen 2001

ROYEN Peter 1923 **[19]**
📇 $344 - €291 - **£205** - FF1 911
Lehnender Linocut in colors (46.7x23.2cm 18x9in)
Düsseldorf 1998

ROYEN van Willem Frederik 1645/54-1723 **[8]**
🖐 $8 089 - €7 499 - **£5 000** - FF49 189
Flowers in an urn on a Ledge Oil/panel
(23x18.5cm 9x7in) London 1999

ROYER Charles 1862-1940 **[10]**
🖐 $806 - €838 - **£506** - FF5 500
La petite blanchisseuse Huile/panneau
(36.5x24.5cm 14x9in) Paris 2000

ROYER Henri 1869-1938 **[33]**
🖊 $544 - €518 - **£344** - FF3 400
Douarnenez, marins au repos Crayon/papier
(30x40cm 11x15in) Douarnenez 1999

ROYER Lionel Noël 1852-1926 **[36]**
🖐 $32 488 - €27 288 - **£29 099** - FF179 000
«La vie de Jésus» Huile/toile (200x600cm 78x236in)
Le Mans 1998
🖐 $3 902 - €3 811 - **£2 487** - FF25 000
Cupidon à la tourterelle Huile/toile (73x60cm
28x23in) Paris 1999

ROYER Louis 1793-1868 **[3]**
🗿 $3 648 - €4 084 - **£2 475** - FF26 789
Vader des Vaderlands Bronze (H48cm H18in)
Amsterdam 2000

ROYET Henri XIX-XX **[49]**
🖐 $605 - €610 - **£377** - FF4 000
Trois personnages en fin de soirée sur le boule-
vard par temps de neige Huile/panneau (31x41cm
12x16in) Pontoise 2000

ROYET Hyacinthe XIX-XX **[1]**
🖐 $3 310 - €3 811 - **£2 260** - FF25 000
Scène de parc Huile/toile (62x92cm 24x36in)
Avignon 2000

ROYLE Herbert F. 1870-1958 **[123]**
🖐 $6 352 - €6 626 - **£4 000** - FF43 466
The Old Manor House, Nesfield Oil/canvas
(49x39cm 19x15in) Little-Lane, Ilkley 2000
🖐 $1 940 - €1 825 - **£1 211** - FF11 974
Blubberhouses Moor Oil/canvas (28x39cm 11x15in)
Little-Lane, Ilkley 1999

ROYLE Stanley 1888-1961 **[49]**
🖐 $6 650 - €6 411 - **£4 100** - FF42 054
Winter Landscape with a Shepherd feeding his
Flock Oil/board (40x50cm 15x19in) West-Sussex 1999
🖐 $1 200 - €1 157 - **£740** - FF7 590
Leintwardine Bridge, Derbyshire Oil/board
(30x40cm 11x15in) West-Sussex 1999
🖊 $796 - €927 - **£550** - FF6 080
Evening, Derbyshire Village Watercolour/paper
(24x33.5cm 9x13in) London 2000

ROYLE Tony XX **[3]**
🖊 $681 - €655 - **£420** - FF4 298
The Goddness Lakshmi by a Lily Pond
Gouache/paper (63x49cm 24x19in) London 1999

ROYO Josep 1945 **[66]**
🖐 $212 - €240 - **£148** - FF1 576
Interior con frutero Oleo/lienzo (65x80.5cm 25x31in)
Madrid 2001

ROYON Louis 1882-1968 **[21]**
📇 $1 654 - €1 545 - **£1 000** - FF10 137
Compagnie maritime Belge (Lloyd Royal), 1930
calendar Poster (54x31cm 21x12in) London 1999

ROZ André 1897-1946 **[37]**
🖐 $12 977 - €14 483 - **£8 493** - FF95 000
Fort de Joux, vallée du Doubs Huile/toile
(100x142cm 39x55in) Besançon 2000
🖐 $3 384 - €3 583 - **£2 192** - FF23 500
Neige sur le mont Chasseron Huile/toile (46x38cm
18x14in) Besançon 2000
🖐 $1 123 - €1 310 - **£778** - FF8 592
St.Simeon le petit Oil/paper/panel (49.5x32cm
19x12in) Bern 2000

ROZA José Conrado XVIII **[1]**
🖐 $237 450 - €228 674 - **£147 450** - FF1 500 000
Portrait des nains de la reine Marie Ière du
Portugal Huile/toile (263x189.5cm 103x74in) Paris
1999

ROZANOVA Olga Vladimirovna 1886-1918 **[9]**
📇 $1 700 - €1 997 - **£1 207** - FF13 100
Head, from Let's Grumble Lithograph (17x11.5cm
6x4in) New-York 2000

ROZEN George 1895-1973 **[14]**
🖐 $4 000 - €3 703 - **£2 448** - FF24 291
Soldier with grenade and pistol, pulp magazine
cover Oil/canvas (73x50cm 29x20in) New-York 1999

ROZEN Jerome 1895-1987 **[7]**
🖐 $2 800 - €2 681 - **£1 729** - FF17 589
Couple on Ship's aft Deck, Story Illustration
Oil/canvas (50x81cm 20x32in) New-York 1999
🖐 $4 250 - €4 734 - **£2 779** - FF31 052
Illustration: Women working lathes at muni-
tions factory Oil/board (27x34cm 11x13in) New-York
2000

ROZIER Dominique 1840-1901 **[45]**
🖐 $2 616 - €2 897 - **£1 774** - FF19 000
Nature morte au gibier Huile/toile (54x65cm
21x25in) Bordeaux 2000
🖐 $1 242 - €1 064 - **£747** - FF6 982
Stilleben Öl/Leinwand (33.5x41cm 13x16in) Zürich
1998

ROZIER Jules 1821-1882 **[108]**
🖐 $3 590 - €3 354 - **£2 215** - FF22 000
Les lavandières Huile/panneau (30.5x56cm 12x22in)
Melun 1999
🖐 $1 853 - €1 601 - **£1 119** - FF10 500
Effet de lumière sur le ruisseau Huile/toile
(27x46cm 10x18in) Barbizon 1998

ROZWADOWSKI Zygmunt 1870-1950 **[48]**
🖐 $5 016 - €4 984 - **£3 124** - FF32 690
Attaque des uhlans du Grand-Duché de
Varsovie Oil/canvas (80x116.5cm 31x45in) Warszawa
1999
🖐 $1 987 - €1 840 - **£1 200** - FF12 070
The Escort Oil/board (32x40.5cm 12x15in)
Billingshurst, West-Sussex 1999

R

R

$1 403 - €1 610 - £960 - FF10 562
Attelage Aquarelle/papier (33x48cm 12x18in)
Katowice 2000

RUANO LLOPIS Carlos 1879-1950 **[82]**
$2 337 - €2 553 - £1 615 - FF16 745
El Espontáneo Oleo/lienzo (42.5x70.5cm 16x27in)
Madrid 2001

$351 - €335 - £219 - FF2 200
«Beziers Toros» Affiche couleur (280x127cm
110x50in) Orléans 1999

RUBBIANI Felice 1677-1752 **[11]**
$19 460 - €21 343 - £13 216 - FF140 000
**Nature morte aux fruits, coupe de porcelaine et
petit singe** Huile/toile (84.5x143cm 33x56in) Paris
2000

$5 416 - €5.814 - £3 624 - FF38 136
Stilleben von Blumen und Früchten Öl/Leinwand
(54x44cm 21x17in) Wien 2000

RUBBO Anthony Datillo 1870-1955 **[48]**
$2 377 - €2 186 - £1 469 - FF14 336
Still Life Oil/board (44x56.5cm 17x22in) Melbourne
1998

$484 - €504 - £306 - FF3 305
Sunny Day Oil/board (24.5x29cm 9x11in) Melbourne
2000

RUBCZAK Jan 1884-1949 **[42]**
$7 243 - €6 621 - £4 432 - FF43 428
Harbour in France Oil/canvas (54.5x65cm 21x25in)
Warszawa 1999

RUBELLI de Giuseppe 1844-1916 **[5]**
$1 750 - €1 814 - £1 050 - FF11 900
**Composizione con bicchiere/Natura morta con
bottiglia** Olio/tela (29x24cm 11x9in) Milano 1999

RUBEN Franz Leo 1842-1920 **[26]**
$1 739 - €2 045 - £1 246 - FF13 415
Hirte mit vieherde in Küstenandschaft
Öl/Leinwand (39x68cm 15x26in) München 2001

RUBENS Arnold Francesco c.1687-1719 **[11]**
$9 234 - €7 976 - £5 566 - FF52 319
**Mediterranean Harbour with Merchants unloa-
ding Cargo** Oil/panel (18.8x23.2cm 7x9in)
Amsterdam 1998

RUBENS Peter Paul 1577-1640 **[105]**
$300 000 - €320 907 - £204 540 - FF2 105 010
**The Infant Christ and Saint John the Baptist in
an Extensive Landscape** Oil/canvas (117x160.5cm
46x63in) New-York 2001

$83 730 - €71 286 - £50 000 - FF467 605
«Eusebia» Oil/panel (79x72.5cm 31x28in) London
1998

$150 831 - €128 332 - £90 000 - FF841 806
A Kitchenmaid, a Boy and a Butcher by a Table
Oil/panel (20.5x28cm 8x11in) London 1998

$70 000 - €61 401 - £42 504 - FF402 766
**Two Studies for Knife Handles: Snake
Intertwined with a Man; Samson** Ink (20x15cm
7x5in) New-York 1999

$375 - €358 - £229 - FF2 347
**Maria mit dem Kind,vor Fensterausschnitt mit
Landschaft und Kirchenbau** Kupferstich
(43.7x33.4cm 17x13in) Köln 1999

RUBIN Reuven 1893-1974 **[450]**
$180 000 - €203 199 - £125 370 - FF1 332 900
The Divine Spirit Returns to Jerusalem Oil/can-
vas (163x114.5cm 64x45in) Tel Aviv 2001

$55 000 - €62 089 - £38 307 - FF407 275
Flowers in Tiberias Oil/canvas (61x50cm 24x19in)
Tel Aviv 2001

$35 000 - €37 864 - £23 978 - FF248 374
Rabbi with Torah Oil/canvas (27x36cm 10x14in) Tel
Aviv 2001

$3 200 - €3 462 - £2 192 - FF22 708
Jacob wrestling with the Angel Bronze (H43cm
H16in) Tel Aviv 2001

$5 200 - €5.772 - £3 624 - FF37 863
The Shepherd's Family Watercolour, gouache
(65.5x56cm 25x22in) Tel Aviv 2001

$275 - €243 - £168 - FF1 596
Mother and Child with Dove Color lithograph
(66x50cm 26x20in) Norwalk CT 1999

RUBIN Victor 1950 **[27]**
$1 715 - €1 841 - £1 148 - FF12 078
Autumn Mixed media/canvas (168x198.5cm 66x78in)
Sydney 2000

$1 037 - €1 162 - £721 - FF7 625
Birds Oil/board (101x75.5cm 39x29in) Melbourne
2001

RUBINCAM Barclay 1920-1978 **[3]**
$5 000 - €4 701 - £3 096 - FF30 838
Spring at the Little House Pastel/paper (81x101cm
32x40in) West-Chester PA 1999

RUBINCAM Harry C. 1871-1940 **[11]**
$5 500 - €5 128 - £3 319 - FF33 640
Portrait of a Woman Photograph (23x18cm 9x7in)
New-York 1999

RUBINO Edoardo 1871-1954 **[8]**
$2 200 - €2 851 - £1 650 - FF18 700
Volto di Bambina Marbre (34x19cm 13x7in) Milano
2001

RUBINO Peter XX **[1]**
$3 500 - €3 362 - £2 128 - FF22 055
Mickey Mantle Bronze (H35.5cm H13in) New-York
1999

RUBINSTEIN Eva 1933 **[19]**
$619 - €665 - £414 - FF4 360
Railroad Station Boston Photograph (24.2x20.3cm
9x7in) München 2000

RUBIO Louis, Luigi 1795-1882 **[9]**
$9 000 - €9 069 - £5 610 - FF59 490
Italian Beauty Holding a Basket of Flowers
Oil/canvas (91.5x71cm 36x27in) New-York 2000

RUBY Claire XX **[3]**
$4 000 - €4 294 - £2 676 - FF28 164
Pewter & Silver Oil/canvas (40x50cm 16x20in)
Altadena CA 2000

$1 700 - €1 825 - £1 137 - FF11 969
Tuckahoe Market Oil/canvas (30x40cm 12x16in)
Altadena CA 2000

RUCKER Robert M. 1932 **[28]**
$4 200 - €3 893 - £2 611 - FF25 536
**Expansive Mississippi Riverscape with
Steamboat and St.Louis Cathedral** Oil/canvas
(66x101cm 26x40in) New-Orleans LA 1999

$1 300 - €1 212 - £785 - FF7 948
Steamboat George Prince Oil/canvas (20x25cm
8x10in) New-Orleans LA 1999

$300 - €314 - £190 - FF2 062
Louisiana Bayou with Cypress Tree
Watercolour/paper (20x14cm 8x5in) New-Orleans LA
2000

RÜCKRIEM Ulrich 1938 **[37]**
- $17 084 - €19 429 - **£11 848** - FF127 448
  Exemplar I Sculpture (100x100x30cm 39x39x11in) München 2000
- $409 - €409 - **£256** - FF2 683
  Bogen Iron (1x67x6.5cm x26x2in) Hamburg 1999

RUCKTESCHELL von Walter 1882-1941 **[4]**
- $879 - €1 022 - **£617** - FF6 707
  Porträt eines Herren Öl/Leinwand (55x41cm 21x16in) Hamburg 2001

RUDAKOV Konstantin Ivanovich 1891-1949 **[35]**
- $869 - €1 022 - **£623** - FF6 707
  Dame in Blau und Herr mit Zylinder Mischtechnik (32x22cm 12x8in) Hamburg 2001
- $958 - €1 074 - **£666** - FF7 043
  Dame und Herr im besseren Etablissement Gouache/paper (30x20cm 11x7in) Oersberg-bei Kappeln 2001

RUDAUX Henri Edmond 1870-1927 **[11]**
- $374 - €427 - **£259** - FF2 800
  «Cie Havraise Péninsulaire» Affiche (106x75cm 41x29in) Paris 2000

RUDBERG Gustav 1915-1994 **[285]**
- $2 442 - €2 736 - **£1 702** - FF17 950
  Kvällsstämning, Hven Oil/canvas (102x130cm 40x51in) Stockholm 2001
- $2 452 - €2 447 - **£1 530** - FF16 054
  Hvenskutor Oil/canvas (49x65cm 19x25in) Uppsala 1999
- $576 - €559 - **£355** - FF3 668
  Landskap med kvinna Oil/panel (34x36cm 13x14in) Stockholm 1999

RUDE François 1784-1855 **[33]**
- $1 931 - €1 906 - **£1 190** - FF12 500
  Le petit pêcheur Bronze (17x18cm 6x7in) Calais 1999

RUDE Olaf 1886-1957 **[277]**
- $3 498 - €2 957 - **£2 092** - FF19 399
  Udsigt mod huse, Allinge Oil/canvas (97x130cm 38x51in) København 1998
- $3 112 - €3 352 - **£2 142** - FF21 990
  Opstilling med roser i vase Oil/canvas (46x47cm 18x18in) København 2001
- $1 105 - €1 076 - **£679** - FF7 060
  Selvportraet Oil/canvas (41.5x40cm 16x14in) København 1999
- $379 - €429 - **£256** - FF2 813
  Udsigt over klipper og hav på Bornholm Watercolour/paper (39x49cm 15x19in) København 2000

RUDE Sophie, née Frémiet 1797-1867 **[5]**
- $160 000 - €177 609 - **£111 536** - FF1 165 040
  The Death of Cenchirias, Son of Neptune Oil/canvas (206.5x254.5cm 81x100in) New-York 2001

RUDEL E. XX **[1]**
- $3 916 - €3 659 - **£2 366** - FF24 000
  Le potier marocain Huile/toile (60x81cm 23x31in) Paris 1999

RUDEL Jean Aristide 1884-1959 **[45]**
- $981 - €915 - **£605** - FF6 000
  Repos à la plage Huile/carton (16x23cm 6x9in) Lyon 1999

RÜDELL Carl 1855-1939 **[93]**
- $1 842 - €1 841 - **£1 152** - FF12 074
  Wandernde Zigeuner in der Eifel Aquarell/Papier (10.8x16cm 4x6in) Köln 1999

RUDENSCHÖLD Thure Gabriel 1799-1878 **[1]**
- $7 176 - €7 738 - **£4 816** - FF50 758
  Landskap Oil/canvas (62x76cm 24x29in) Stockholm 2000

RUDGE Bradford 1805-1885 **[9]**
- $176 - €166 - **£110** - FF1 091
  The Menai Straits Watercolour/paper (26x36cm 10x14in) Bedford 1999

RUDHART Claude Charles 1829-1895 **[2]**
- $5 217 - €5 793 - **£3 636** - FF38 000
  Famille de pêcheurs sur la grève Huile/toile (40x88cm 15x34in) Paris 2001

RÜDISÜHLI Eduard 1875-1938 **[48]**
- $476 - €562 - **£337** - FF3 689
  Frühlingslied, nackte Schöne sitzt in einer blühenden Wiese Öl/Leinwand (67x80cm 26x31in) Konstanz 2000
- $1 160 - €1 307 - **£816** - FF8 576
  Treppenaufgang zu einer Villa Öl/Karton (28x35cm 11x13in) Zürich 2001

RÜDISÜHLI Hermann Traugott 1864-1945 **[68]**
- $1 573 - €1 329 - **£938** - FF8 719
  Sichen am See Öl/Leinwand (50x78cm 19x30in) Düsseldorf 1998
- $334 - €393 - **£242** - FF2 581
  «Waldlandschaft, Bäuerin im Abendlicht» Öl/Karton (27x23cm 10x9in) Zofingen 2001

RUDNAY Gyula / Jules 1878-1957 **[18]**
- $12 600 - €12 120 - **£7 800** - FF79 500
  The Wedding in Cana Oil/canvas (121x201cm 47x79in) Budapest 1999
- $1 610 - €1 781 - **£1 058** - FF11 684
  Village Oil/cardboard (54x44.5cm 21x17in) Budapest 2000
- $770 - €852 - **£506** - FF5 588
  Party in the openair Oil/canvas/board (14.5x18.5cm 5x7in) Budapest 2000
- $910 - €1 007 - **£598** - FF6 604
  Landscape Watercolour/paper (48x35cm 18x13in) Budapest 2000

RUDOLPH Charlotte 1896-1983 **[31]**
- $654 - €613 - **£404** - FF5 023
  Tanzszene aus den «Chorischen Studien», Mary Wigman Vintage gelatin silver print (16.5x23cm 6x9in) Köln 1999

RUDOLPH Harold 1850-1884 **[4]**
- $15 000 - €17 691 - **£10 581** - FF116 043
  Dawn in the Bayou with black figures in a pirogue Oil/canvas (40x60cm 16x24in) New-Orleans LA 2001

RUDOLPH Wilhelm 1889-1982 **[107]**
- $3 194 - €3 579 - **£2 224** - FF23 477
  Blick auf Dresden Öl/Leinwand (43x66cm 16x25in) Berlin 2001
- $320 - €368 - **£226** - FF2 414
  Zurückgelehnter weiblicher Akt Graphite (41.2x31cm 16x12in) Dettelbach-Effeldorf 2001
- $171 - €204 - **£122** - FF1 341
  Wisent Woodcut (14x23cm 5x9in) Berlin 2000

RUDOMINE Albert 1892-1975 **[38]**
- $1 316 - €1 220 - **£818** - FF8 000
  Etudes pictorialistes, vues de villages Tirage argentique (17x23cm 6x9in) Paris 1999

RÜDT von August 1900-1966 **[32]**
- $270 - €307 - **£188** - FF2 012
  Weite Moorlandschaft Öl/Leinwand (33x48cm 12x18in) München 2001

R

RUDY Durs, Sr. 1766-1843 [1]
📖 **$10 000** - €10 660 - **£6 341** - FF69 924
Rare Lehigh County, Pennsylvania
Watercolour/paper (18x27cm 7x11in) Downington PA 2000

RUDZKA-CYBISOWA Hanna 1897-1988 [24]
🖼 **$3 486** - €3 887 - **£2 422** - FF25 494
Nature morte aux fruits Huile/toile (56x75cm 22x29in) Warszawa 2001
🖼 **$1 340** - €1 497 - **£935** - FF9 819
Port de pêcheurs Huile/carton (26x34.5cm 10x13in) Warszawa 2001
🖼 **$265** - €2 425 - **£1 540** - FF9 910
Gubalowka en été Gouache/papier (49x34.5cm 19x13in) Warszawa 2001

RUEDA Gerardo 1926-1996 [104]
🖼 **$4 590** - €5 106 - **£3 145** - FF33 490
«Pintura amarilla» Oleo/lienzo (40x50.5cm 15x19in) Madrid 2001
🖼 **$2 112** - €1 952 - **£1 300** - FF12 805
Composición en azul, blanco y rojo Técnica mixta (37x27cm 14x10in) Madrid 1999
🖼 **$5 040** - €5 406 - **£3 420** - FF35 460
Bodegón sorprendente Bronze (H39cm H15in) Barcelona 2001
📖 **$1 525** - €1 502 - **£950** - FF9 850
Especial verde II Collage/papier (72x65cm 28x25in) Madrid 1999
🖼 **$153** - €180 - **£111** - FF1 182
Composición en azul y rojo Pochoir (77x57cm 30x22in) Madrid 2001

RUEFF A. XIX [7]
🖼 **$2 415** - €2 287 - **£1 500** - FF15 000
Lacs des montagnes alpestres Huile/panneau (22x41cm 8x16in) Paris 1999

RÜEGG Ernst Georg 1883-1948 [39]
🖼 **$1 103** - €1 060 - **£683** - FF6 950
Ohne Titel Huile/panneau (32.5x44cm 12x17in) Zürich 1999
🖼 **$319** - €363 - **£221** - FF2 382
Lehmgrube im Zürcher Oberland Indian ink (31x47cm 12x18in) Zofingen 2000

RUELAS Julio 1870-1907 [13]
🖼 **$2 120** - €2 490 - **£1 506** - FF16 332
Implacable, Revista Moderna Vol.IV Tinta/papel (12.5x17.5cm 4x6in) México 2000

RUELLEN Andrée 1905-1966 [9]
📖 **$3 200** - €3 510 - **£2 065** - FF23 026
Shore scene and workers Watercolour/paper (26x42cm 10x16in) Wallkill NY 2000

RUELLES des Pieter XVII [1]
🖼 **$12 464** - €11 628 - **£7 520** - FF76 272
Gebirgige Flusslandschaft mit einer steinernen Bogenbrücke Öl/Leinwand (53.5x66cm 21x25in) Wien 1999

RUETER Georg 1875-1966 [87]
🖼 **$634** - €681 - **£424** - FF4 464
A Dead White Chicken hanging from a String Oil/panel (75.5x50cm 29x19in) Amsterdam 2000
🖼 **$1 522** - €1 588 - **£960** - FF10 418
Marigold Flowers in Vase Oil/canvas (30.5x40.5cm 12x15in) Amsterdam 2000

RUETZ Michael 1940 [36]
📷 **$734** - €818 - **£480** - FF5 366
Rudi Dutschke Vintage gelatin silver print (26.1x38.6cm 10x15in) Köln 2000

RUFALO Carlos Roberto XX [21]
🖼 **$3 200** - €2 758 - **£1 901** - FF18 091
Vista del Buceo Oleo/lienzo (48x68cm 18x26in) Montevideo 1998
🖼 **$520** - €449 - **£309** - FF2 943
Casona Oleo/tabla (24x31cm 9x12in) Montevideo 1998

RUFF Thomas 1958 [232]
🎞 **$3 600** - €4 131 - **£2 462** - FF27 095
Sterne: 08h24 -35°, 03h36 -35°, 20h00 -50°, 18h12 -40°, 17h12 -35° Print (89.5x64.5cm 35x25in) New-York 2001
📷 **$3 749** - €4 143 - **£2 600** - FF27 177
Niederrheinisiches Stahlkontor Type C color print (37x50cm 14x19in) London 2001

RUFFNER Ginny Martin 1952 [3]
🖼 **$5 000** - €5 946 - **£3 563** - FF39 005
Seeing Arizona Sculpture, glass (51.5x26.5x21.5cm 20x10x8in) New-York 2000

RUFFONY O. XIX-XX [10]
🖼 **$1 105** - €1 037 - **£682** - FF6 800
La conduite de balle Sculpture (H62cm H24in) Nice 1999

RUGE Willy XX [1]
📷 **$2 857** - €3 068 - **£1 912** - FF20 123
Fallschirmspringer Photograph (21.7x15.8cm 8x6in) München 2000

RUGENDAS Georg Philipp I 1666-1742 [71]
🖼 **$30 075** - €33 234 - **£20 858** - FF218 003
Lagerleben/Der Aufbruch vor der Schlacht Öl/Leinwand (102x147cm 40x57in) München 2001
🖼 **$9 855** - €9 203 - **£6 082** - FF60 370
Aufbruch zur Schlacht Öl/Leinwand (59.5x84.5cm 23x33in) Köln 1999
🖼 **$1 138** - €969 - **£680** - FF6 359
Three Hunters loading furs on two Horses Ink (12x17.5cm 4x6in) London 1998
🎞 **$265** - €256 - **£163** - FF1 676
Szenen aus der Belagerung der Stadt Augsburg Radierung (25x40cm 9x15in) München 1999

RUGENDAS Johann Lorenz 1775-1826 [13]
🎞 **$258** - €245 - **£157** - FF1 609
Bataille Victorieuse de Poplawy, 16. Mai 1807 Lithographie (49x60cm 19x23in) München 1999

RUGENDAS Johann Moritz 1802-1858 [39]
🖼 **$35 000** - €37 569 - **£23 422** - FF246 435
India Mexicana bañandose en el Rio Oil/canvas (45x37cm 17x14in) New-York 2000
🖼 **$24 840** - €27 630 - **£16 560** - FF181 240
Deteniendo la caravana Oleo/lienzo (24x32cm 9x12in) Madrid 2000
📖 **$2 000** - €1 703 - **£1 205** - FF11 173
Gaucho con Poncho Lápiz/papel (26.5x18.5cm 10x7in) Buenos-Aires 1998

RUGGERI Piero 1930 [100]
🖼 **$5 000** - €5 183 - **£3 000** - FF34 000
Prato fiorito Olio/tela (160x110cm 62x43in) Torino 2000
🖼 **$1 600** - €1 659 - **£960** - FF10 880
Napoleone Olio/tela (80x80cm 31x31in) Torino 1999
🖼 **$500** - €518 - **£300** - FF3 400
Prato e nubi Olio/tela (15x25cm 5x9in) Vercelli 2000
📖 **$475** - €492 - **£285** - FF3 230
«Giardino» Tecnica mista/carta (66x47.5cm 25x18in) Torino 2001

RUGGIERO Pasquale 1851-1916 **[13]**
$2 089 - €1 767 - **£1 249** - FF11 590
A Serenade Oil/panel (30x18.5cm 11x7in)
Amsterdam 1998

RUHLMANN Jacques-Emile 1879-1933 **[12]**
$4 425 - €4 618 - **£2 800** - FF30 293
Single Roll of Wallpaper, peacocks sitting on trees, flowering branche Tapestry (740x76cm 291x29in) London 2000

RÜHM Gerhard 1930 **[33]**
$804 - €799 - **£486** - FF5 243
Ohne Titel Coloured pencils/paper (40x29.7cm 15x11in) Wien 2000

RUILLÉ de Geoffroy, Vicomte 1842-1922 **[40]**
$3 284 - €3 125 - **£2 041** - FF20 500
Tête de chihuahua Bronze (H13cm H5in) Paris 1994

RUIN Ingrid 1881-1956 **[30]**
$428 - €488 - **£294** - FF3 199
Nomader Oil/canvas (42x60cm 16x23in) Helsinki 2000

RUISCHER Johannes c.1625-c.1675 **[14]**
$7 885 - €6 804 - **£4 758** - FF44 629
Panoramic landscape with a town by a sea shore Black chalk (24.2x42cm 9x16in) Amsterdam 1998
$442 - €486 - **£300** - FF3 186
Die Ruine (Schloss Brederode?) Radierung (8.8x10cm 3x3in) Berlin 2000

RUISDAEL van Jacob Isaaksz. 1628/29-1682 **[111]**
$250 000 - €249 883 - **£152 725** - FF1 639 125
Torrent in a Scandinavian Wooded Landscape, a Cottage Beyond Oil/canvas (99x86.5cm 38x34in) New-York 2000
$46 000 - €45 978 - **£28 101** - FF301 599
Winter Landscape with Peasants on a Road and Skaters on a Frozen River Oil/canvas (31x45cm 12x17in) New-York 2000
$42 471 - €40 840 - **£26 163** - FF267 894
Road Flanked by a Cottage and Two Large Trees with a Man Leading Dogs Black chalk (15x20cm 5x7in) Amsterdam 1999
$988 - €817 - **£580** - FF5 361
Das Haus auf der Anhöhe Radierung (19.4x27.8cm 7x10in) Berlin 1998

RUITER Jan 1942 **[8]**
$718 - €771 - **£480** - FF5 060
Deconstructions, Rietveld Chair Photograph (80x100cm 31x39in) Amsterdam 2000

RUITH van Horace 1839-1923 **[28]**
$3 652 - €4 090 - **£2 537** - FF26 831
Ärmlicher Flötenspieler mit Hund Oil/panel (53x40cm 20x15in) Staufen 2001
$4 961 - €4 641 - **£3 000** - FF30 442
Indian Tradesman, possibly a Peshwa, white Tunic and blue Turban Oil/canvas (29x21cm 11x8in) London 1999
$363 - €361 - **£220** - FF2 370
Girl Holding a Daisy Watercolour/paper (44.5x32cm 17x12in) London 2000

RUIZ BLASCO José 1841-1913 **[7]**
$9 180 - €10 211 - **£6 120** - FF66 980
La marioneta Oleo/lienzo (58x41cm 22x16in) Madrid 2000

RUIZ Graciela 1948 **[10]**
$486 - €541 - **£333** - FF3 546
Composición Oleo/lienzo (65x54cm 25x21in) Madrid 2001

$1 282 - €1 351 - **£855** - FF8 865
Composición cubista Collage (35x31.5cm 13x12in) Madrid 2001

RUIZ GUERRERO Manuel 1864-1917 **[8]**
$8 103 - €7 551 - **£5 000** - FF49 534
The Flamenco Dance Oil/canvas (53.5x70cm 21x27in) London 1999

RUIZ Juan XVIII **[3]**
$40 282 - €39 560 - **£25 000** - FF259 497
Naples, a Panoramic View of the Bay with the Molo Grande in the Centre Oil/copper (32.5x79cm 12x31in) London 1999

RUIZ LUNA Justo 1860-1926 **[18]**
$2 340 - €2 703 - **£1 620** - FF17 730
Río Oleo/lienzo (70x42cm 27x16in) Seville 2000
$2 475 - €2 703 - **£1 717** - FF17 730
Merienda Oleo/tabla (39x37cm 15x14in) Madrid 2000
$1 140 - €1 201 - **£760** - FF7 880
Marina Pastel (29x46cm 11x18in) Madrid 2000

RUIZ PIPO Manolo 1929-1998 **[203]**
$824 - €3 049 - **£1 952** - FF20 000
Paysan mangeant Huile/toile (72x52cm 28x20in) Paris 2001
$1 150 - €1 067 - **£717** - FF7 000
Le Toréro Gouache/papier (26x18.5cm 10x7in) Biarritz 1999

RUIZ SANCHEZ MORALES Manuel Bernardino 1857-1922 **[15]**
$812 - €841 - **£504** - FF5 516
Puerto de Bilbao Acuarela/papel (29x47.5cm 11x18in) Madrid 2000

RUIZ Tommaso XVIII **[7]**
$47 301 - €50 042 - **£30 000** - FF328 251
Naples, a View of the Bay seen from Posillipo with the Molo Grande Oil/copper (32x78.5cm 12x30in) London 2000

RUKLEVBSKY Yakov 1884-1965 **[1]**
$2 200 - €2 454 - **£1 440** - FF16 100
«Bezradostnaya, Ulitsa (Joyless Street)» Poster (71.5x100.5cm 28x39in) New-York 2000

RUL Henry 1862-1942 **[73]**
$1 058 - €917 - **£651** - FF6 016
Paysage à la rivière Huile/toile (54x43cm 21x16in) Bruxelles 1999
$238 - €248 - **£157** - FF1 626
Landschap met windmolen (paysage et moulin) Huile/panneau (14x24cm 5x9in) Antwerpen 2000

RULLIER Jean-Jacques 1962 **[2]**
$1 283 - €1 448 - **£902** - FF9 500
Le rêve de la fuite impossible Encre Chine (30x40cm 11x15in) Paris 2001

RULLMANN Ludwig 1765-1822 **[8]**
$2 186 - €2 592 - **£1 543** - FF17 000
Le matin et le midi/Le soir et la nuit Gouache/papier (19x25cm 7x9in) Paris 2000

RUMINE de Gabriel XIX **[6]**
$5 181 - €5 803 - **£3 600** - FF38 066
«Greece, l'Acropole et le Temple de Jupiter Olympien» Salt print (25.5x35cm 10x13in) London 2001

RUMKIN Yakov 1913-1986 **[6]**
$1 276 - €1 453 - **£882** - FF9 534
«Kosmisches Ornament» Gelatin silver print (29.3x21.8cm 11x8in) Wien 2000

R

RUMMELL Richard 1848-1924 [6]

📖 **$1 300** - €1 516 - **£912** - FF9 945
«French Line, the France» Poster (108x68cm 42x26in) New-York 2000

RUMMELSPACHER Joseph 1852-1921 [34]

👁 **$1 149** - €971 - **£687** - FF6 370
In Mecklenburg-Vorpommern Öl/Leinwand (52x78cm 20x30in) Berlin 1998

RUMOHR Knut 1916 [36]

👁 **$3 967** - €4 403 - **£2 764** - FF28 882
Komposisjon med gult Tempera/canvas (99x127cm 38x50in) Oslo 2001

👁 **$1 763** - €1 957 - **£1 228** - FF12 836
Komposisjon i rodt og blått Tempera/canvas (68x52cm 26x20in) Oslo 2001

📖 **$367** - €424 - **£258** - FF2 782
Komposisjon Woodcut in colors (50x35cm 19x13in) Oslo 2000

RUMOHR von Carl Friedrich 1785-1843 [10]

✏ **$276** - €297 - **£184** - FF1 945
Tischbein-Karikaturen Ink (21x34.7cm 8x13in) Hamburg 2000

RUMP Gotfred 1816-1880 [39]

👁 **$421** - €469 - **£294** - FF3 077
Solnedgang ved skovsö Oil/canvas (63x81cm 24x31in) Köbenhavn 2001

RUMPF Fritz Carl Georg 1888-1949 [7]

📖 **$1 846** - €2 096 - **£1 263** - FF13 751
«Söhnlein Rheingold» Poster (72x95cm 28x37in) Hannover 2000

RUMPF Peter Philip 1821-1896 [34]

👁 **$5 209** - €5 113 - **£3 229** - FF33 539
Mädchen am Brunnen vor einem Kornfeld sitzend Öl/Leinwand (45x42cm 17x16in) München 1999

👁 **$11 224** - €11 760 - **£7 424** - FF77 139
Der Liebesbrief Oil/panel (25.5x18cm 10x7in) München 2000

✏ **$1 871** - €1 789 - **£1 173** - FF11 738
Waldweg mit Dame und kleinem Jungen Watercolour (22x17.5cm 8x6in) Hamburg 1999

RUMPLER Franz 1848-1922 [47]

👁 **$1 009** - €1 090 - **£697** - FF7 150
Fackelzug Öl/Leinwand (42x57.5cm 16x22in) Wien 2001

👁 **$1 680** - €1 451 - **£1 120** - FF9 520
In taverna Oil/canvas (29x23cm 11x9in) Trieste 1998

✏ **$340** - €291 - **£203** - FF1 906
Schlafendes Mädchen Pencil/paper (19.5x25cm 7x9in) Wien 1998

RUMSEY Charles Cary 1879-1922 [5]

🗿 **$2 000** - €2 227 - **£1 405** - FF14 610
Panther Bronze (38x16cm 15x6in) Cleveland OH 2001

RUNDALTSOV Mikhaïl 1871-1935 [2]

✏ **$1 849** - €2 149 - **£1 300** - FF14 097
Crimean Landscape Watercolour/paper (49x65cm 19x25in) London 2001

RUNDT Carl Ludwig 1802-1868 [4]

👁 **$1 715** - €2 045 - **£1 223** - FF13 415
Einzug der Lords in die St.Pauls-Kathedrale Öl/Leinwand (90x71cm 35x27in) Ahlden 2000

RUNEBERG Walter 1838-1920 [3]

🗿 **$6 262** - €7 064 - **£4 401** - FF46 334
Finland Bronze (H49cm H19in) Helsinki 2001

RUNGE Ludwig Julius 1843-1922 [27]

👁 **$1 330** - €1 249 - **£824** - FF8 194
Heimkehr vom Heringfang Öl/Leinwand (40x80cm 15x31in) Luzern 1999

RUNGE Philipp Otto 1777-1810 [9]

📖 **$2 061** - €1 764 - **£1 240** - FF11 568
Die Nacht Etching (72x48cm 28x18in) München 1998

RUNGIUS Carl Clemens Moritz 1869-1959 [139]

👁 **$75 000** - €87 652 - **£53 542** - FF574 957
Along the Stream Oil/canvas (63x76cm 25x30in) Altadena CA 2001

👁 **$20 000** - €17 088 - **£12 102** - FF112 088
Lake O'Hara Oil/canvas (36x36cm 14x14in) San-Francisco CA 1998

📖 **$3 000** - €2 727 - **£1 806** - FF17 889
Antelope Etching (15x20cm 6x8in) Hayden ID 1998

RUNK Ferdinand 1764-1834 [4]

✏ **$2 310** - €2 761 - **£1 588** - FF18 114
Die Stadt Gmunden von der Seeseite Radierung (32x42cm 12x16in) Salzburg 2000

RUOFF Fritz 1906-1988 [44]

✏ **$391** - €460 - **£271** - FF3 018
Komposition Coloured pencils/paper (10.5x15cm 4x5in) Stuttgart 2000

RUOKOKOSKI Jalmari 1886-1936 [251]

👁 **$1 793** - €1 682 - **£1 108** - FF11 032
Borgå Oil/canvas (50x40cm 19x15in) Helsinki 1999

👁 **$809** - €874 - **£559** - FF5 736
Stilleben Oil/canvas (30x44cm 11x17in) Helsinki 2001

✏ **$372** - €437 - **£257** - FF2 868
Rött hus Watercolour/paper (53x34cm 9x13in) Helsinki 2000

📖 **$121** - €143 - **£84** - FF937
Borgå Etching in colors (35x37cm 13x14in) Helsinki 2000

RUOPPOLO Giovan Battista 1629-1693 [12]

👁 **$235 000** - €243 614 - **£141 000** - FF1 598 000
Natura morta con uva, meloni, cigliege, pesche, prugne e melograni Olio/tela (92.5x132.5cm 36x52in) Milano 2000

RUOPPOLO Giuseppe 1631-c.1710 [6]

👁 **$60 000** - €77 749 - **£45 000** - FF510 000
Natura morta con vaso di fiori e cestino di fragole/Pere e ciliege Olio/tela (50x63cm 19x24in) Roma 2000

RUPERTI K. XIX [1]

👁 **$5 236** - €5 453 - **£3 300** - FF35 772
Fleurs Huile/toile (75x46cm 29x18in) Antwerpen 2000

RUPPERT von Otto 1841-? [28]

👁 **$2 895** - €3 403 - **£2 007** - FF22 324
Arabs Camping in the Desert Oil/panel (33.5x53.5cm 13x21in) Amsterdam 2000

👁 **$1 112** - €1 329 - **£764** - FF8 720
Strassenszene in einer fränkischen Kleinstadt Oil/panel (40x29.5cm 15x11in) München 2000

RUPPRECHT Tini 1867-1956 [7]

✏ **$722** - €683 - **£450** - FF4 482
Porträt einer junge Dame Pastel/canvas (75x65cm 29x25in) Praha 1999

RUPRECHT Johann Christian c.1600-1654 [1]

👁 **$5 004** - €5 921 - **£3 558** - FF38 837
Porträt einer alten Frau mit Turban Oil/panel (41x28.5cm 16x11in) Luzern 2000

RUSCHA Edward, Ed 1937 **[467]**
- $95 000 - €91 477 - **£59 403** - FF600 048
  Brave Men run in my Family Acrylic (152.5x102cm 60x40in) Beverly-Hills CA 1999
- $32 000 - €30 813 - **£20 009** - FF202 121
  See Oil/canvas (76x76cm 29x29in) Beverly-Hills CA 1999
- $55 000 - €60 360 - **£35 414** - FF395 934
  Lemon Drops Oil/paper/board (28.5x25.5cm 11x10in) New-York 2000
- $23 000 - €22 877 - **£14 276** - FF150 061
  A Large Dog Pastel/paper (58.5x74cm 23x29in) Beverly-Hills CA 1999
- $2 600 - €2 904 - **£1 665** - FF19 046
  Now Color lithograph (152x101.5cm 59x39in) New-York 2000
- $2 600 - €2 993 - **£1 774** - FF19 635
  Sunset Strip Gelatin silver print (51x76cm 20x29in) New-York 2000

RUSCHEWEYH Ferdinand 1785-1846 **[11]**
- $198 - €230 - **£139** - FF1 509
  Überfahrt der Bacchanten Ink (21.5x29cm 8x11in) Hamburg 2001
- $270 - €307 - **£187** - FF2 012
  Segnender Christus, nach Thorwaldsen Radierung (13x9cm 5x3in) Berlin 2001

RUSCHI Francesco c.1605-1661 **[9]**
- $25 200 - €21 770 - **£16 800** - FF142 800
  Allegoria dell'Autunno Olio/tela (116x175cm 45x68in) Milano 1998

RUSH Olive 1873-1966 **[2]**
- $1 900 - €2 207 - **£1 335** - FF14 480
  Santa Fe Scene Oil/canvas (60x40cm 24x16in) Cincinnati OH 2001

RUSHBURY Henry George 1889-1968 **[70]**
- $578 - €543 - **£350** - FF3 565
  Falmouth Estuary Watercolour (26.5x34cm 10x13in) London 1999
- $131 - €117 - **£80** - FF767
  Fountains Abbey Drypoint (35.5x28cm 13x11in) London 1999

RUSHEN R. XIX **[1]**
- $3 849 - €3 808 - **£2 400** - FF24 977
  View of Temple Bar Oil/canvas (30.5x36cm 12x14in) London 1999

RUSHTON Emma 1965 **[1]**
- $6 610 - €5 648 - **£4 000** - FF37 050
  English Clergy 1-4 Sculpture (H51cm H20in) London 1998

RUSHTON George Robert 1869-1947 **[21]**
- $458 - €437 - **£280** - FF2 867
  On the Wye Watercolour/paper (29x40cm 11x15in) Bury St. Edmunds, Suffolk 1999

RUSHTON William Charles 1860-1921 **[20]**
- $1 005 - €1 173 - **£700** - FF7 697
  «Old Cottage, near Huthwaite, Notts» Oil/canvas (36x46cm 14x18in) West-Yorkshire 2000
- $417 - €424 - **£260** - FF2 779
  Bingley, Figuresin the Foreground Oil/canvas (34x44cm 13x17in) Little-Lane, Ilkley 2000
- $119 - €124 - **£75** - FF815
  The Beck at Windhill, Near Shipley Watercolour/paper (24x35cm 9x14in) Little-Lane, Ilkley 2000

RUSIÑOL Y PRATS Santiago 1861-1931 **[28]**
- $84 000 - €72 078 - **£50 400** - FF472 800
  Cuenca Oleo/lienzo (99x124.5cm 38x49in) Madrid 1998
- $78 000 - €78 084 - **£48 100** - FF512 200
  Jardines de España, rincón neoclásico, Valencia Oleo/lienzo (80x100cm 31x39in) Madrid 2000
- $16 200 - €18 019 - **£11 400** - FF118 200
  Paisaje de Normandía Oleo/lienzo (32x40cm 12x15in) Madrid 2001
- $1 160 - €1 220 - **£728** - FF8 000
  «Fulls de la Vida» Affiche (100x71cm 39x27in) Lyon 2000

RUSKIN John 1819-1900 **[83]**
- $11 229 - €11 316 - **£7 000** - FF74 225
  Study of a House at Horta, North Italy Watercolour (15x22cm 5x8in) London 2000

RUSLI 1922 **[7]**
- $2 543 - €2 811 - **£1 763** - FF18 436
  A House Oil/canvas (51x62cm 20x24in) Singapore 2001

RUSS Franz, Jnr. 1844-1906 **[21]**
- $3 888 - €4 084 - **£2 460** - FF26 789
  Jeune fille au chapeau des plumes/Jeune fille au corsage de roses Oil/canvas (67.5x54.5cm 26x21in) Amsterdam 2000
- $1 087 - €1 278 - **£779** - FF8 384
  Portrait einer jungen Frau Oil/panel (28.5x20.5cm 11x8in) München 2001

RUSS Karl 1779-1843 **[6]**
- $700 - €716 - **£438** - FF4 695
  Alexander in Begleitung von Soldaten besucht Diogenes in der Tonne Aquatinta (22x33.5cm 8x13in) Köln 2000

RUSS Leander 1809-1864 **[7]**
- $9 527 - €10 671 - **£6 622** - FF70 000
  Portrait de Mehemet Ali Vice-roi d'Égypte Huile/panneau (22.5x17.5cm 8x6in) Paris 2001

RUSS Robert 1847-1922 **[76]**
- $23 220 - €21 802 - **£14 400** - FF143 010
  Kanal bei Rotterdam Öl/Leinwand (98x142cm 38x55in) Wien 1999
- $11 712 - €12 271 - **£7 747** - FF80 493
  Alte Mühle bei Delft Öl/Leinwand (96x68cm 37x26in) München 2000
- $1 442 - €1 453 - **£900** - FF9 534
  S.Giovanni, Venezia Öl/Karton (17.5x30cm 6x11in) Wien 2000
- $1 607 - €1 817 - **£1 085** - FF11 917
  Terrassenhäuser im Südlichen Italien Aquarell/Papier (26x33cm 10x12in) Wien 2000

RUSSAC Michel XX **[15]**
- $332 - €305 - **£204** - FF2 000
  Vedette Géranium Gouache/papier (45.5x60cm 17x23in) Cherbourg 1999

RUSSELL Andrew Joseph 1830-1902 **[29]**
- $9 500 - €10 943 - **£6 554** - FF71 782
  Executives of the Union Pacific Railroad and Well-Wishers, Utah Albumen print (23x30cm 9x12in) New-York 2000

RUSSELL Charles Marion 1864-1926 **[181]**
- $200 000 - €237 851 - **£142 540** - FF1 560 200
  Indian Rider Oil/canvas (56x45.5cm 22x17in) New-York 2000

R

  $2 000 - €2 147 - **£1 338** - FF14 082
Nature's People Bronze (H17cm H6in) San-Francisco
CA 2000

  $47 500 - €50 930 - **£31 426** - FF334 077
The Footrace Ink (31x43cm 12x17in) Hayden ID
2000

RUSSELL Deborah 1951 **[8]**
  $2 186 - €2 450 - **£1 528** - FF16 074
Roadside, Morning Walk Acrylic/board (70x90cm
27x35in) Melbourne 2001

RUSSELL Edward John 1832-1906 **[8]**
  $3 000 - €3 305 - **£2 001** - FF21 681
**U.S.S.Constitution and Other Ships in Stormy
Seas** Watercolour/paper (50x73cm 20x29in)
Portsmouth NH 2000

RUSSELL George Horne 1861-1933 **[57]**
  $1 554 - €1 497 - **£965** - FF9 821
Breezy Day, Nova Scotia Oil/board (45.5x61cm
17x24in) Toronto 1999

  $1 022 - €966 - **£635** - FF6 335
«Sardine Boats, St Andrews» Oil/panel
(23.5x30.5cm 9x12in) Nepean, Ont. 1999

RUSSELL George William, A.E. 1867-1935 **[70]**
  $8 627 - €10 158 - **£6 062** - FF66 632
The Dreaming Pool Oil/canvas (45x64.5cm 17x25in)
Dublin 2000

  $4 959 - €5 333 - **£3 379** - FF34 981
Crows in freshly tilled Field Oil/board (30x47cm
11x18in) Dublin 2000

  $1 477 - €1 651 - **£1 001** - FF10 827
Cushendun, Co.Antrim Watercolour (9x11cm 3x4in)
Dublin 2000

RUSSELL Gyrth 1892-1970 **[114]**
  $1 629 - €1 932 - **£1 150** - FF12 670
Quayside Scene with Moored Boats Oil/canvas
(49x74cm 19x29in) Eastbourne, Sussex 2000

  $1 047 - €1 246 - **£721** - FF8 173
Old Dinant Oil/canvas (13x20cm 5x7in) Calgary,
Alberta 2000

  $494 - €464 - **£300** - FF3 044
Gypsy Caravans Watercolour/paper (30.5x40.5cm
12x15in) London 1999

  $1 635 - €1 571 - **£1 000** - FF10 306
**«Yorkshire, British Railways, North Eastern
Region»** Poster (102x127cm 40x50in) London 1999

RUSSELL James XIX **[2]**
  $4 742 - €4 061 - **£2 800** - FF26 641
**Books, a tam O'Shanter, Bird's Eggs and Nests,
in a Highland Landscape** Oil/canvas (38x76.5cm
14x30in) London 1998

RUSSELL John 1745-1806 **[83]**
  $18 669 - €18 412 - **£12 000** - FF120 774
Portrait of a Young Boy/Portrait of a Young Girl
Oil/canvas (39.5x33.5cm 15x13in) London 1999

  $5 678 - €6 095 - **£3 800** - FF39 982
**Portrait of Mrs Wilson, wearing a white muslin
dress** Pastel/paper (61x46cm 24x18in) London 2000

RUSSELL John act.1869-1918 **[44]**
  $2 500 - €2 806 - **£1 740** - FF18 406
Trout on a Riverbank Oil/canvas (36x74.5cm
14x29in) New-York 2001

RUSSELL John Bucknell 1819-1893 **[15]**
  $14 424 - €16 952 - **£10 000** - FF111 200
Salmon on a River Bank Oil/canvas (75.5x129.5cm
29x50in) Edinburgh 2000

RUSSELL John Peter 1858-1930 **[60]**
  $193 110 - €166 794 - **£116 640** - FF1 094 100
Rocher au Chien, Clos Marion, Belle-Ile Oil/can-
vas (65x81cm 25x31in) Malvern, Victoria 1998

  $29 246 - €28 456 - **£17 999** - FF186 658
Souvenir de Belle ile Oil/canvas (32x40cm 12x15in)
Melbourne 1999

  $5 180 - €4 871 - **£3 208** - FF31 953
Young Girl in an Orchard, France
Watercolour/paper (23x29cm 9x11in) Melbourne 1999

RUSSELL John Wentworth 1879-1959 **[23]**
  $413 - €408 - **£251** - FF2 678
Portrait of an Artist Charcoal (65x50cm 25x19in)
Amsterdam 2000

RUSSELL Morgan 1886-1953 **[44]**
  $1 922 - €2 134 - **£1 339** - FF14 000
Synchromie Huile/toile/carton (38x46cm 14x18in)
Paris 2001

  $23 341 - €25 916 - **£16 269** - FF170 000
Synchromie Huile/papier (27x18.5cm 10x7in) Paris
2001

RUSSELL Moses B. c.1810-1884 **[7]**
  $4 250 - €5 055 - **£2 928** - FF33 158
**Nathaniel B.Fessenden in Red in a Landscape
with his Dog Flight** Oil/canvas (76x63cm 30x25in)
Bolton MA 2000

  $550 - €524 - **£333** - FF3 440
**Gentleman in black jacket and waistcoat with
white stock and collar** Miniature (6x5cm 2x2in)
New-York 1999

RUSSELL Theodore 1614-1689 **[5]**
  $12 627 - €15 017 - **£9 000** - FF98 506
**Portrait of Catherine Howard, Lady d'Aubigny
(d.1650) Head & Shoulders** Oil/panel (39x31.5cm
15x12in) London 2000

RUSSELL Walter 1871-1963 **[9]**
  $4 750 - €4 568 - **£2 932** - FF29 966
Ipswich Willows, an autumnal landscape Oil/can-
vas (63.5x76cm 25x29in) Boston MA 1999

RUSSELL Walter Westley 1867-1949 **[47]**
  $3 854 - €3 741 - **£2 400** - FF24 542
The Square at Etaples Oil/canvas (71x91.5cm
27x36in) London 1999

  $484 - €465 - **£300** - FF3 049
Binham Priory Watercolour (18.5x25cm 7x9in)
London 1999

RUSSOLO Luigi 1885-1947 **[10]**
  $10 000 - €10 367 - **£6 000** - FF68 000
Tramonto di primavera Olio/tavola (49x56.5cm
19x22in) Prato 1999

  $118 665 - €114 480 - **£75 000** - FF750 937
Senza Titolo Crayons couleurs (19x52cm 7x20in)
London 1999

RUSSOV Alexandre Nikolaev. 1844-1928 **[2]**
  $1 765 - €1 670 - **£1 100** - FF10 955
Sunset over the City Watercolour/paper (39x75cm
15x29in) London 1999

RUST Johan Adolph 1828-1915 **[43]**
  $5 017 - €4 426 - **£3 022** - FF29 035
**Moored Craft in the Amsterdam «Y», the
Oosterkerk in the distance** Oil/canvas (54x80cm
21x31in) Amsterdam 1998

  $5 791 - €6 807 - **£4 015** - FF44 649
Peasants Unloading a Barge on a Jetty Oil/panel
(24.5x35.5cm 9x13in) Amsterdam 2000

RUSTAMADJI (Surabaya) 1921 [9]
$2 953 - €2 753 - £1 785 - FF18 056
Jamu Seller Oil/canvas (120x90cm 47x35in)
Singapore 1999

RUSTICI Francesco Rustichino c.1595-1626 [4]
$24 000 - €20 733 - £12 000 - FF136 000
Giuditta e Oloferne Olio/tela (121x92cm 47x36in)
Milano 1997

RUSTIGE von Heinrich Gaudenz 1810-1900 [20]
$4 465 - €4 346 - £2 742 - FF28 508
Aufziehendes Wetter auf dem Alpensee
Öl/Leinwand (45x55cm 17x21in) Stuttgart 1999

RUSTIN Jean 1928 [50]
$2 754 - €3 049 - £1 868 - FF20 000
La chambre verte Huile/toile (55x46cm 21x18in)
Lyon 2000
$302 - €305 - £188 - FF2 000
Composition abstraite Encre (76x56cm 29x22in)
Paris 2000

RUSZCZYC Ferdynand 1870-1936 [26]
$4 261 - €3 989 - £2 641 - FF26 169
A Village in the Evening Oil/canvas/board
(54.5x40.5cm 21x15in) Warszawa 1999
$7 712 - €8 959 - £5 418 - FF58 769
Paysage aux cyprès Huile/toile/carton (32x26.5cm
12x10in) Warszawa 2001
$4 064 - €3 360 - £2 384 - FF22 040
Communion Gouache (35.5x44.5cm 13x17in)
Warszawa 1998

RUSZKOWSKI Zdzislaw 1907-1990 [79]
$1 549 - €1 700 - £1 000 - FF11 151
Nude Standing in Interior Oil/canvas (127x83.5cm
50x32in) London 2000
$499 - €489 - £320 - FF3 209
Venice Watercolour (48x31.5cm 18x12in) London
1999

RUTHART Carl Borromäus A. 1630-1703 [25]
$74 715 - €80 200 - £50 000 - FF526 080
Lion and a Tiger Fighting over a Fallen Stag
Oil/canvas (98x114.5cm 38x45in) London 2000

RUTHENBECK Reiner 1937 [12]
$10 257 - €9 925 - £6 500 - FF65 105
Gelehnte Platte mit Weissen Ecken Oil/panel
(200x100cm 78x39in) London 1999

RUTHERSTON Albert 1881-1953 [20]
$235 - €245 - £150 - FF1 608
Portrait of Lord David Cecil Pencil/paper (26x22cm
10x8in) London 2000

RUTHS Amelie 1871-1956 [23]
$1 344 - €1 261 - £831 - FF8 274
Stilleben Oil/canvas (82x60cm 32x23in) Helsinki 1999

RUTHS Johann Valentin G. 1825-1905 [40]
$22 459 - €23 008 - £13 860 - FF150 925
Thüringer Landschaft Öl/Leinwand (99x158.5cm
38x62in) Düsseldorf 2000
$2 158 - €2 454 - £1 496 - FF16 098
Felsschlucht im Sabinergebirge Oil/board
(53x70cm 20x27in) Hamburg 2000
$946 - €869 - £581 - FF5 701
**Im Vorfrühling, reetgedeckte Kate unter blühen-
den Bäumen** Oil/panel (21x31cm 8x12in) Konstanz
1999
$733 - €716 - £464 - FF4 695
Hamburg mit Binnenalster/Strassenszene
Lithographie (36.5x57.5cm 14x22in) Bremen 1999

RUTHVEN Jerry 1947 [7]
$3 800 - €4 315 - £2 640 - FF28 302
New Mexico, early Fall Oil/canvas (101x76cm
40x30in) Dallas TX 2001

RUTTEN Johannes, Jan 1809-1884 [6]
$11 666 - €12 252 - £7 381 - FF80 368
A View of Gouda Oil/panel (54x44.5cm 21x17in)
Amsterdam 2000

RÜTTIMANN Hans 1940 [37]
$385 - €372 - £237 - FF2 437
Die sitzende Katze Crayon/papier (26x21cm 10x8in)
Bern 1999

RUTTKAY György 1898-1975 [2]
$3 145 - €3 304 - £1 955 - FF21 675
Le scieur Huile/toile/carton (33.5x29cm 13x11in)
Budapest 2000

RUTZ Viktor 1913 [11]
$389 - €427 - £264 - FF2 800
«Zodiac, la punctualidad del astro» Affiche couleur (128x93cm 50x36in) Paris 2000

RUYBAL Mercedes 1928 [7]
$2 065 - €2 102 - £1 295 - FF13 790
Muñeca Oleo/cartón (38.5x31cm 15x12in) Madrid
2000

RUYSCH Rachel 1664-1750 [20]
$89 590 - €84 736 - £55 800 - FF555 830
Still Life with Flowers, Insects and a stag Bettle
Oil/canvas (70x54cm 27x21in) Praha 2001

RUYSDAEL van Jacob Salomonsz. c.1629-1681
[44]
$10 688 - €12 140 - £7 500 - FF79 635
**Wooded Landscape with Herders resting and
Cattle and Sheep grazing** Oil/panel (52x68.5cm
20x26in) London 2001
$380 000 - €425 628 - £264 024 - FF2 791 936
**Wooded landscape with figures outside the
gates of a woodyard** Oil/canvas (33x39cm 12x15in)
New-York 2001

RUYSDAEL van Salomon 1600/03-1670 [100]
$92 294 - €79 715 - £55 637 - FF522 897
**A Calm: A Wooded River Landscape with
Fishermen and Sportsmen** Oil/panel (51.9x77.6cm
20x30in) Amsterdam 1998
$124 136 - €121 588 - £80 000 - FF797 568
**River landscape with Figures on a jetty and sai-
ling Boats beyond** Oil/panel (26x49cm 10x19in)
London 1999

RUYSSEN Nicolas Joseph 1757-1826 [1]
$16 000 - €17 767 - £11 126 - FF116 545
Boca di Veritas/Ancient Ritual Oil/canvas
(137x98cm 53x38in) New-York 2001

RUYSSEVELT van Jozef 1941-1985 [13]
$155 - €173 - £107 - FF1 138
Nature morte Aquarelle/papier (70x53cm 27x20in)
Antwerpen 2001

RUYTEN Jan Michiel 1813-1881 [28]
$6 656 - €7 932 - £4 768 - FF52 032
Un avant poste espagnol en hiver Huile/panneau
(37x46.5cm 14x18in) Bruxelles 2000

RUYTINX Alfred 1871-1908 [25]
$954 - €917 - £599 - FF6 016
Zeebruges Huile/toile (40x50cm 15x19in) Bruxelles
1999

R

RUZICKA Drahomir Josef 1870-1960 **[22]**

📷 **$3 250** - €3 057 - **£2 012** - FF20 051
Streets of New York, early Morning Gelatin silver print (34.5x27.5cm 13x10in) New-York 1999

RUZICKA Rudolph 1883-1978 **[23]**

▥ **$600** - €608 - **£376** - FF3 987
Landscape Woodcut (17x25cm 7x10in) Cincinnati OH 2000

RUZICKA-LAUTENSCHLÄGER Hans 1862-1933 **[41]**

🖼 **$697** - €654 - **£431** - FF4 290
Strasse im Süden Öl/Leinwand (53x42cm 20x16in) Wien 1999

RUZICKA-LAUTENSCHLÄGER Othmar 1877-1962 **[18]**

🖼 **$863** - €1 017 - **£607** - FF6 673
In der Dorfgasse Öl/Karton (39x30.4cm 15x11in) Wien 1999

RYALL Henry Thomas 1811-1867 **[6]**

▥ **$317** - €350 - **£220** - FF2 299
The Coronation of her most Gracious Queen Victoria, after G.Hayter Engraving (64x91cm 25x35in) London 2001

RYAN Adrian 1920 **[57]**

🖼 **$703** - €689 - **£450** - FF4 517
Paris Street Oil/canvas (46x61cm 18x24in) London 1999

🖼 **$524** - €609 - **£368** - FF3 997
Donegal Cottage Oil/canvas (26x38cm 10x14in) Dublin 2001

RYAN Anne 1899-1954 **[19]**

✍ **$3 750** - €3 428 - **£2 294** - FF22 483
Composition Collage (16.5x15cm 6x5in) Boston MA 1999

RYAN Francis XVIII **[1]**

🖼 **$24 308** - €25 395 - **£15 952** - FF166 580
Portrait of the Bishop of Kilfenora (Dr Niall), Seated at a Table Oil/canvas (127x100cm 50x39in) Dublin 2000

RYAN Ross 1974 **[2]**

▥ **$1 300** - €1 379 - **£881** - FF9 044
«Black Fish» Print (109x199cm 42x78in) Tel Aviv 2001

RYAN Thomas 1929 **[24]**

🖼 **$1 509** - €1 778 - **£1 060** - FF11 660
Viewof Muckish Mountain from Dunfanaghy Direction Oil/canvas/board (51x61cm 20x24in) Dublin 2000

🖼 **$1 323** - €1 524 - **£903** - FF9 994
Dublin From the Pine Forest Oil/canvas (29x39cm 11x15in) Dublin 2000

RYAN Thomas Darby 1864-1927 **[8]**

✍ **$801** - €833 - **£502** - FF5 461
Coastal Landscape with sailing Vessels Watercolour/paper (31x48cm 12x18in) Auckland 2000

RYAN Tom 1922 **[16]**

🖼 **$35 000** - €39 741 - **£24 318** - FF260 683
Trouble at the Creek Oil/board (50x76cm 20x30in) Dallas TX 2001

RYBACK Issachar Ber 1897-1935 **[109]**

🖼 **$6 000** - €5 930 - **£3 672** - FF38 898
Les musiciens Oil/canvas (46x38.5cm 18x15in) Tel Aviv 2000

🖼 **$2 285** - €2 269 - **£1 428** - FF14 883
Junges Bauermädchen - Young Farmer girl Oil/canvas (27x22cm 10x8in) Amsterdam 1999

✍ **$966** - €936 - **£602** - FF6 139
Üppiges Früchtestilleben Aquarell/Papier (33.5x45cm 13x17in) Zürich 1999

RYBAK Jaromír 1951 **[4]**

🔹 **$4 000** - €4 144 - **£2 546** - FF27 181
Untitled Sculpture, glass (29x43x35.5cm 11x16x13in) New-York 2000

RYBCOWSKY Deyde 1880-1936 **[52]**

🖼 **$1 600** - €1 553 - **£988** - FF10 188
The Grand Canyon Oil/canvas (50x38cm 20x15in) Cedar-Falls IA 1999

RYBKOVSKI Tadeusz 1848-1926 **[31]**

🖼 **$29 600** - €29 526 - **£18 475** - FF193 675
Traversée de rivière Oil/canvas (75x115cm 29x45in) Warszawa 1999

🖼 **$2 619** - €2 293 - **£1 586** - FF15 039
Bauernpaar auf Pferdekarren Oil/panel (18x29cm 7x11in) Zofingen 1998

✍ **$1 810** - €1 934 - **£1 234** - FF12 687
Après la chasse Aquarelle/papier (14.5x18.5cm 5x7in) Warszawa 2001

RYCERSKI Aleksander 1825-1866 **[1]**

🖼 **$3 856** - €3 786 - **£2 392** - FF24 835
Portrait de Mathilde de Buchholc Dobrowolska Oil/canvas (73.8x62cm 29x24in) Warszawa 1999

RYCHTER-JANOWSKA Bronislawa 1868-1953 **[65]**

🖼 **$1 926** - €2 264 - **£1 335** - FF14 848
Rosiers devant un manoir Huile/carton (35.5x49.5cm 13x19in) Warszawa 2000

🖼 **$1 310** - €1 255 - **£826** - FF8 235
Manor in autumnal Light Oil/panel (23x33cm 9x12in) Warszawa 1999

RYCK van Pieter Cornelisz. 1568-c.1628/35 **[1]**

🖼 **$18 424** - €18 407 - **£11 520** - FF120 740
Küchenstilleben mit Koch und Küchenmagd Öl/Leinwand (104x183cm 40x72in) Köln 1999

RYCKAERT David III 1612-1661 **[30]**

🖼 **$5 890** - €6 604 - **£4 000** - FF43 322
Interior with a young Man sleeping in the Foreground Oil/canvas (44x58cm 17x22in) London 2000

🖼 **$8 500** - €10 011 - **£5 878** - FF65 670
Barn Interior with a Still Life of Baskets and Pots Oil/panel (38x34.5cm 14x13in) New-York 2000

RYCKAERT Maerten 1587-1631 **[49]**

🖼 **$85 602** - €84 145 - **£55 000** - FF551 958
Panoramic Campagnan Landscape with Herders and Goats Oil/canvas (98x129cm 38x50in) London 1999

🖼 **$72 400** - €60 980 - **£42 760** - FF400 000
Paysage vallonné de la campagne flamande animé de bergers Huile/panneau (44x59.5cm 17x23in) Paris 1998

🖼 **$13 189** - €12 919 - **£8 500** - FF84 741
Temptation of Saint Antony Oil/copper (16.5x14cm 6x5in) London 1999

RYCKERE van Bernaerd 1535-1590 **[1]**

🖼 **$22 558** - €22 154 - **£14 000** - FF145 318
The Death of Lucretia Oil/canvas/panel (113x160cm 44x62in) London 1999

RYCKHALS Franz, François c.1600-1647 **[14]**

🖼 **$4 776** - €4 573 - **£3 006** - FF30 000
Fermière hollandaise dans une arrière-cuisine Huile/panneau (34x28.5cm 13x11in) Paris 1999

🖼 **$4 000** - €4 829 - **£2 731** - FF28 106
Landscape with Cattle and two Figures Black chalk/paper (8.5x20cm 3x7in) New-York 2001

RYD Carl 1883-1958 **[32]**
- $832 - €901 - **£569** - FF5 909
  Gumma vid bandstol, Småland Oil/canvas
  (66x82cm 25x32in) Stockholm 2001

RYDBERG Gustaf 1835-1933 **[97]**
- $5 538 - €5 325 - **£3 417** - FF34 932
  Från Råå fiskeläge Oil/canvas (47x73cm 18x28in)
  Malmö 1999
- $1 083 - €1 042 - **£668** - FF6 834
  Gammal kvarn vid vattendrag Oil/canvas (27x34cm
  10x13in) Malmö 1999

RYDER Chauncey Foster 1868-1949 **[124]**
- $6 750 - €6 424 - **£4 222** - FF42 138
  U Roaad Pastures Oil/canvas (63x76cm 25x30in)
  New-York 2000
- $2 500 - €2 719 - **£1 648** - FF17 836
  Mt.Monadnock, late Autumn Oil/canvas
  (27.5x40.5cm 10x15in) Boston MA 2000
- $750 - €680 - **£461** - FF4 458
  Rainstorm Watercolour/paper (25x28cm 10x11in)
  Mystic CT 1999
- $225 - €209 - **£140** - FF1 370
  House by the Road Etching (16x22cm 6x8in) South-
  Natick MA 1999

RYDER Platt Powell 1821-1896 **[11]**
- $3 200 - €3 159 - **£1 945** - FF20 720
  Children at Play in a Barn Oil/canvas (36.5x45.5cm
  14x17in) New-York 2000
- $2 800 - €2 914 - **£1 757** - FF19 115
  Woman spinning by open Window Oil/canvas
  (30x43cm 12x17in) Chicago IL 2000

RYKR Zdenek 1900-1940 **[7]**
- $2 312 - €2 187 - **£1 440** - FF14 344
  Pont sur la rivière Huile/toile (45.5x70cm 17x27in)
  Praha 2001
- $2 312 - €2 187 - **£1 440** - FF14 344
  Still-Life with a Glass Oil/cardboard (43.5x32cm
  17x12in) Praha 2001

RYLAND Adolfine 1903-1983 **[2]**
- $1 293 - €1 509 - **£900** - FF9 896
  April Showers Watercolour/paper (60.5x45cm
  23x17in) London 2000

RYLAND Henry 1856-1924 **[66]**
- $5 275 - €4 830 - **£3 200** - FF31 683
  **Young Girls on a Classical Terrace with a View
  of the Sea Beyond** Pencil (38x54.6cm 14x21in)
  London 1998

RYLANDER Hans Christian 1939 **[27]**
- $829 - €938 - **£560** - FF6 153
  Göglere Oil/canvas (65x75cm 25x29in) København
  2000

RYLEY Bryan 1952 **[4]**
- $397 - €426 - **£269** - FF2 794
  «I.X-85 VI» Mixed media/paper (22x14cm 8x5in)
  Calgary, Alberta 2001

RYLOFF Arkadi Alexandrovich 1870-1939 **[17]**
- $3 287 - €3 529 - **£2 200** - FF23 147
  Wooded Landscape with River Oil/canvas/board
  (30x40cm 11x15in) London 2000

RYMAN Robert 1930 **[79]**
- $270 000 - €301 448 - **£180 468** - FF1 977 372
  Whitney Revision Painting 1 Enamel (305x305cm
  120x120in) New-York 2000
- $107 640 - €100 306 - **£65 000** - FF657 962
  Untitled Oil/board (41x41cm 16x16in) London 1998

- $110 000 - €127 632 - **£75 944** - FF837 210
  Red Mixed media/canvas (20x20cm 7x7in) New-York
  2000
- $30 000 - €33 544 - **£20 223** - FF220 032
  Eagel Turquoise #2 Graphite (33x33cm 12x12in)
  New-York 2000
- $5 600 - €4 745 - **£3 346** - FF31 128
  Six Aquatints Aquatint (91x91cm 35x35in) New-York
  1998

RYSBRACK Gerard 1696-1773 **[4]**
- $283 680 - €274 408 - **£174 960** - FF1 800 000
  Nature morte au gibier et corbeille de fruits
  Huile/toile (67x109cm 26x42in) Paris 1999

RYSBRACK John Michael 1693-1770 **[14]**
- $30 000 - €33 494 - **£20 052** - FF219 708
  Bust of a Lady Marble (H61cm H24in) New-York
  2000
- $2 718 - €2 618 - **£1 700** - FF17 172
  **Joseph's brothers show his bloodied Coat to
  their Father** Ink (28x40cm 11x15in) London 1999

RYSBRACK Peter Andreas 1690-1748 **[15]**
- $11 283 - €10 446 - **£7 000** - FF68 523
  **Still Life of a Swan, Duck, Partridge, Snipe,
  Pheasant, Pigeon** Oil/canvas (117.5x145.5cm
  46x57in) London 1999
- $17 343 - €18 348 - **£11 000** - FF120 358
  **Widgeon, a Green Woodpecker, a Grey
  Partridge, a Gold Crest** Oil/canvas (76.5x74cm
  30x29in) London 1999
- $4 693 - €5 445 - **£3 240** - FF35 719
  **Hunting Still Life with a Deer, a Peacock, a
  Heron and Songbirds** Oil/canvas (33x42cm
  12x16in) Amsterdam 1999

RYSBRACK Pieter 1655-1729 **[22]**
- $8 500 - €8 812 - **£5 100** - FF57 800
  Paesaggio con armenti Olio/tela (99x125cm
  38x49in) Milano 1999
- $5 746 - €6 425 - **£4 000** - FF42 142
  **Classical Italianate Landscape with a Peasant
  Family resting** Oil/canvas (82x122cm 32x48in)
  London 2001

RYSEN van Warnard c.1625-c.1665 **[6]**
- $2 500 - €2 286 - **£1 526** - FF14 997
  Figures in a landscape Oil (21x29cm 8x11in) New-
  York 1998

RYSER Fritz 1910-1990 **[17]**
- $706 - €681 - **£435** - FF4 469
  Getreidefeld in der Erntezeit Öl/Leinwand
  (49x70cm 19x27in) Bern 1999

RYSSEL van Paul (Paul Gachet) 1828-1909 **[29]**
- $1 220 - €1 220 - **£763** - FF8 000
  Les quatre pommes Huile/panneau (21x28cm
  8x11in) Pontoise 1999

RYSSELBERGHE van Théo 1862-1926 **[287]**
- $31 528 - €36 302 - **£21 520** - FF238 128
  Femme étendue Oil/canvas (97x162cm 38x63in)
  Amsterdam 2000
- $112 716 - €96 102 - **£68 000** - FF630 387
  A l'ombre des pins Oil/canvas (86x110.5cm
  33x43in) London 1998
- $58 542 - €9 715 - **£5 967** - FF63 724
  Portrait de femme Oil/panel (41x33cm 16x12in)
  München 1999
- $1 465 - €1 709 - **£1 028** - FF11 210
  Stehender weiblicher Akt nach links Red
  chalk/paper (49x24cm 19x9in) Luzern 2000

R

$1 108 - €935 - **£650** - FF6 136
«N.Lembrée» Poster (65x46cm 25x18in) London
1998

RYSWYCK Johanna Bastiana 1873-1986 **[1]**
$5 764 - €5 445 - **£3 487** - FF35 719
Roses on a Ledge Oil/canvas (36x53cm 14x20in)
Amsterdam 1999

RYSWYCK van Theodor 1811-1849 **[7]**
$4 189 - €4 497 - **£2 802** - FF29 500
Tigre attaquant Bronze (35x70x17.5cm 13x27x6in)
Lyon 2000

RYSWYCK van Thierry Jac. 1911-1958 **[16]**
$2 940 - €2 808 - **£1 810** - FF18 422
Figur eines Panthers Bronze (70x17.5x32cm
27x6x12in) Zürich 1999

RYUKEI [1]
$16 167 - €15 550 - **£9 965** - FF102 000
Personnage debout soulevant une sphère
Sculpture bois (H25cm H10in) Paris 1999

RYUSUKE Nishimura 1920 **[6]**
$54 880 - €53 528 - **£33 600** - FF351 120
Castel del Opo Oil/canvas (89.5x145.5cm 35x57in)
Tokyo 1999
$15 000 - €15 115 - **£9 351** - FF99 150
Mizuumi no shiro (Castle by a lake) Oil/canvas
(49.5x65.5cm 19x25in) New-York 2000

RZEPINSKI Czeslaw 1905-1995 **[35]**
$2 446 - €2 642 - **£1 691** - FF17 331
Musiciennes Huile/toile (91.5x64.5cm 36x25in)
Warszawa 2001
$1 550 - €1 799 - **£1 070** - FF11 801
Sopot, la plage Aquarelle (32x40cm 12x15in)
Warszawa 2000

RZEWUSKI Aleksander 1893-1983 **[3]**
$456 - €479 - **£302** - FF3 143
Portrait de dame au chapeau à la main Pointe
sèche (5.5x20.5cm 2x8in) Warszawa 2000

S

SAABYE Svend 1913 **[50]**
$1 444 - €1 608 - **£1 015** - FF10 551
Komposition Oil/canvas (100x155cm 39x61in) Vejle
2001
$602 - €670 - **£423** - FF4 396
Haveeksterior Oil/canvas (68x90cm 26x35in) Vejle
2001

SAAD Georges XX **[25]**
$602 - €610 - **£374** - FF4 000
Ensembles Jean Patou Photo (23.5x17.5cm 9x6in)
Paris 2000

SAADA Henri 1906-1976 **[16]**
$3 324 - €3 049 - **£2 066** - FF20 000
Bou-Kornine vu de la maison du Baron
d'Erlanger à Sidi Bou Saïd Huile/toile (60x80cm
23x31in) Paris 1999

SAAL Georg-Eduard Otto 1818-1870 **[21]**
$10 910 - €12 606 - **£7 640** - FF82 690
Norsk landskap Oil/canvas (90x139cm 35x54in) Oslo
2001

SAALBORN Louis 1890-1957 **[62]**
$2 308 - €2 269 - **£1 483** - FF14 883
A Still Life with Flowers in a Vase Oil/canvas
(93x70cm 36x27in) Amsterdam 1999

SAAR von Karl 1797-1853 **[25]**
$926 - €1 017 - **£596** - FF6 673
Bildnis eines Fräuleins in weissem Kleid mit
grünem Vorhang Aquarell/Papier (16x12cm 6x4in)
Wien 2000

SAARINEN Eliel 1873-1950 **[11]**
$1 190 - €1 177 - **£742** - FF7 722
Skiss Akvarell/papper (21x45.5cm 8x17in) Helsinki
2000

SAARINEN Yrjö 1899-1958 **[55]**
$2 958 - €3 364 - **£2 052** - FF22 064
Gårdstallar Oil/canvas (55x46cm 21x18in) Helsinki
2000
$480 - €538 - **£326** - FF3 530
Landskap Watercolour/paper (33x46cm 12x18in)
Helsinki 2000

SABATE Joaquim 1936 **[42]**
$205 - €228 - **£136** - FF1 497
Bodegón Oleo/lienzo (75.5x46cm 21x18in) Barcelona
2000

SABATELLI Luigi I 1772-1850 **[29]**
$1 283 - €1 431 - **£863** - FF9 390
Liegende Katze Ink/paper (23x32cm 9x12in) Köln
2000
$1 200 - €1 244 - **£720** - FF8 160
Quattro evangelisti Stampa (52x72cm 20x28in)
Prato 1999

SABATER Y SALABERT Daniel 1888-1951 **[104]**
$1 680 - €1 802 - **£1 140** - FF11 820
«Souvenir de l'absent» Oleo/lienzo (65x81cm
25x31in) Madrid 2001
$955 - €884 - **£591** - FF5 800
«El Chisme...» Huile/carton (32.5x48cm 12x18in)
Paris 1999

SABATIER Léon Jean-Bapt. ?-1887 **[16]**
$173 - €194 - **£120** - FF1 275
Blick auf Luzern vom Gütsch aus Lithographie
(13x54cm 5x21in) Luzern 2001

SABATINI DA BOLOGNA Lorenzo c.1530-1576 **[11]**
$35 354 - €35 067 - **£22 000** - FF230 027
The Holy Family with Saint Anne and the Infant
Saint John the Baptist Oil/panel (98x75.5cm
38x29in) London 1999
$36 000 - €40 323 - **£25 012** - FF264 499
Saint Jerome in the Wilderness Oil/copper
(25x16cm 9x6in) New-York 2001

SABATINI DA SALERNO Andreas 1485-1530/31 **[3]**
$4 332 - €5 051 - **£3 000** - FF33 130
Saint Anthony Abbot Oil/panel (143x54.5cm
56x21in) London 2000

SABAVALA Jehangir 1922 **[11]**
$6 000 - €6 956 - **£4 250** - FF45 630
Evening's Pale Light Oil/canvas (46x102cm
18x40in) New-York 2000

SABBAGH Georges-Hanna 1887-1951 **[156]**
$10 704 - €9 147 - **£6 480** - FF60 000
Maternités arabes Huile/toile (197x130cm 77x51in)
Paris 1998
$1 516 - €1 296 - **£918** - FF8 500
Nu au fauteuil vert Huile/toile (100x73cm 39x28in)
Paris 1998
$966 - €1 067 - **£669** - FF7 000
Anémones Huile/panneau (33x41cm 12x16in) Paris
2001
$581 - €686 - **£409** - FF4 500
Nu de dos Fusain (18x36cm 7x14in) Paris 2000

SABI Sandro Bidasio Imb. XX **[2]**
$1 603 - €1 453 - **£1 000** - FF9 529
«Dolomiti» Poster (100x70cm 39x27in) London 1999

SABINO XX **[13]**
$3 381 - €3 430 - **£2 100** - FF22 497
Double Suzanne, Opalescent Glass Figure
Group Sculpture, glass (H22cm H8in) London 2000

SABLET Jacques, le Jeune 1749-1803 **[6]**
$340 000 - €298 235 - **£206 448** - FF1 956 292
Alban Peasants in a Park near Rome Oil/canvas
(62x73cm 24x28in) New-York 1999

SABLET LE ROMAIN Jean François 1745-1819
[17]
$8 282 - €8 927 - **£5 553** - FF58 555
Nature morte au gibier et au jambon Öl/Leinwand
(54x65.5cm 21x25in) Zürich 2000
$6 180 - €6 098 - **£3 808** - FF40 000
Portrait d'un jeune enfant en habit blanc
Huile/toile (24.5x20cm 9x7in) Paris 1999

SABOGAL José 1888-1956 **[5]**
$210 - €239 - **£144** - FF1 566
Sacsayhmamian Woodcut (35x28cm 14x11in)
Columbia SC 2000

SABON Laurent 1852-? **[9]**
$1 007 - €1 181 - **£718** - FF7 746
Rivière Aquarelle/papier (54x74cm 21x29in) Genève
2000

SABOURAUD Émile 1900-1996 **[192]**
$807 - €762 - **£488** - FF5 000
Promenade le long de la rivière Huile/toile
(60.5x81.5cm 23x32in) Paris 1999

SABRI Atta 1913 **[1]**
$2 864 - €3 222 - **£2 000** - FF21 134
Self Portrait Red chalk/paper (42x30cm 16x11in)
London 2001

SABY Bernard 1925-1975 **[48]**
$1 669 - €1 403 - **£981** - FF9 200
Composition Huile/toile (89x116cm 35x45in) Douai
1998

SACCAGGI Cesare 1868-1934 **[15]**
$49 200 - €42 503 - **£24 600** - FF278 800
La preghiera Olio/tela (146x186cm 57x73in) Milano
1999
$5 700 - €4 924 - **£2 850** - FF32 300
Ritratto di popolana Olio/tela (55x43cm 21x16in)
Vercelli 1999
$2 500 - €2 592 - **£1 500** - FF17 000
Ballerina con la chitarra Acquarello/carta (64x42cm
25x16in) Milano 1999

SACCHETTI Giovanni Francesco XVII **[1]**
$19 440 - €22 867 - **£13 935** - FF150 000
«Acis et Galatée» Huile/toile (133x150cm 52x59in)
Saint-Germain-en-Laye 2001

SACCHI Andrea 1599-1661 **[7]**
$2 988 - €3 208 - **£2 000** - FF21 043
Feed my Sheep Ink (24x21.5cm 9x8in) London 2000

SACCONI Giuseppe XVIII **[1]**
$1 964 - €1 822 - **£1 200** - FF11 952
An Allegory of Poetry, after Carlo Dolci
Gouache/paper (17x13cm 6x5in) London 1998

SACHAROFF Olga 1889-1969 **[27]**
$17 000 - €15 016 - **£9 500** - FF98 500
Jarrón de flores y paisaje al fondo Oleo/lienzo
(65x54cm 25x21in) Madrid 1999

SACHERI Giuseppe 1863-1950 **[37]**
$5 000 - €5 183 - **£3 000** - FF34 000
Mareggiata Olio/tavola (60x70cm 23x27in) Vercelli
2000
$1 400 - €1 451 - **£840** - FF9 520
Campagna canavesana Olio/tavoletta (30x46cm
11x18in) Torino 2000
$1 840 - €1 691 - **£1 130** - FF11 091
Stürmisches Meer mit Tempel auf Felsen
Mischtechnik/Papier (41x45cm 16x17in) Zürich 1999

SACHS Tom 1966 **[6]**
$8 000 - €9 104 - **£5 621** - FF59 721
Uncle Tom's Kitchen Construction (63.5x63.5x7.5cm
25x25x2in) New-York 2001

SACKS Joseph 1887-1974 **[17]**
$1 900 - €1 771 - **£1 172** - FF11 615
Rural Shanties Oil/canvas (66x76cm 26x30in) New-
Orleans LA 1999
$3 000 - €3 376 - **£2 066** - FF22 148
Children Playing on the Beach, Ventnor Oil/board
(20x30.5cm 7x12in) Philadelphia PA 2000

SACRISTAN ARRIETA Ricardo 1921-1981 **[54]**
$396 - €360 - **£240** - FF2 364
Puerto Acuarela/papel (48x68cm 18x26in) Madrid
1999

SADAHIDE Gountei 1807-1873 **[11]**
$2 284 - €2 381 - **£1 500** - FF15 616
Map of the Opened Port of Yokohama Print in
colors (67.5x189cm 26x74in) London 2000

SADALI Ahmad 1924-1987 **[15]**
$6 886 - €7 820 - **£4 713** - FF51 295
Abstract Composition Oil/canvas (125x53cm
49x20in) Singapore 2000
$1 987 - €2 080 - **£1 248** - FF13 643
Abstract Mixed media/paper (44x39cm 17x15in)
Singapore 2000

SADÉE Philippe L.J.F. 1837-1904 **[91]**
$26 000 - €30 575 - **£18 642** - FF200 561
Waiting for his Return Oil/canvas (70.5x55,5cm
27x21in) New-York 2001
$3 376 - €3 630 - **£2 300** - FF23 812
Bosven met vissers in een roeiboot Oil/panel
(33x47cm 12x18in) Maastricht 2001
$410 - €362 - **£247** - FF17 000
Wounded Soldier Watercolour (27.5x21cm 10x8in)
Amsterdam 1999

SADELER Aegidius c.1570-1629 **[134]**
$464 - €520 - **£323** - FF3 414
Portraits d'empereurs et impératrices romains,
d'après le Titien Burin (34.5x24cm 13x9in) Bruxelles
2001

SADELER Johannes I, Jan 1550-c.1600 **[88]**
$411 - €358 - **£248** - FF2 346
Die Parabel vom Blinden und Lahmen, in einer
weiten Flusslandschaft Kupferstich (21.5x26.8cm
8x10in) Berlin 1998

SADELER Raphael I 1560/61-1628/32 **[26]**
$448 - €511 - **£313** - FF3 353
Christliche Tugenden, nach Marten de Vos
Kupferstich (21.5x14.5cm 8x5in) Berlin 2001

SADELER Raphael II 1584-1632 **[5]**
$4 698 - €4 462 - **£2 916** - FF29 268
Flore Encre (18x9.5cm 7x3in) Bruxelles 1999

S

SADEQUAIN 1930-1987 **[4]**
- $23 883 - €23 125 - **£15 000** - FF151 687
  Europa and the Bull Oil/canvas (89x117cm 35x46in)
  London 1999
- $2 241 - €2 406 - **£1 500** - FF15 782
  Calligraphy Ink (45x78cm 17x30in) London 2000

SADKOWSKY Alex 1934 **[72]**
- $1 057 - €1 245 - **£743** - FF8 167
  Zweiköpfiger Mann mit kopflosen Mädchen
  Öl/Karton (70x100cm 27x39in) Zürich 2000
- $701 - €799 - **£484** - FF5 239
  Koffer Acrylic (28x39cm 11x15in) Zürich 2000
- $732 - €852 - **£506** - FF5 591
  Komposition mit rennender Frau
  Mischtechnik/Papier (70x50cm 27x19in) Bern 2000
- $105 - €100 - **£65** - FF658
  Surreale Landschaft mit Frauenakt Radierung
  (50x38cm 19x14in) Zofingen 1999

SADLER Kate ?-1894 **[9]**
- $3 825 - €3 277 - **£2 300** - FF21 498
  Pink Roses Watercolour/paper (34x49cm 13x19in)
  Edinburgh 1998

SADLER Walter Dendy 1854-1923 **[73]**
- $175 000 - €207 514 - **£120 400** - FF1 361 202
  London to York-Time's Up Gentlemen Oil/canvas
  (147x193cm 57x75in) New-York 2000
- $8 619 - €7 436 - **£5 200** - FF48 780
  The Angler's Rest Oil/canvas (56x43cm 22x16in)
  London 1998
- $16 000 - €16 123 - **£9 974** - FF105 760
  A Morning Call Oil/canvas (46.5x31cm 18x12in)
  New-York 2000
- $200 - €178 - **£122** - FF1 165
  The Hunt Club Etching (45x55cm 18x22in) New-
  Orleans LA 1999

SADLER William I ?-c.1788 **[12]**
- $2 400 - €2 276 - **£1 500** - FF14 929
  **River Landscape with Soldiers on a Path near a
  Cottage** Oil/panel (28x44cm 11x17in) London 1999

SADLER William II c.1782-1839 **[40]**
- $12 639 - €13 967 - **£8 764** - FF91 619
  The Seven Churches, Glendalough Oil/board
  (49x72cm 19x28in) Dublin 2001
- $2 976 - €3 174 - **£1 982** - FF20 822
  Village by a River Oil/panel (27x45cm 11x18in)
  Dublin 2000

SADURNI Antoni M. 1927 **[67]**
- $280 - €300 - **£185** - FF1 970
  Pollancres vora el riu (Vic) Oleo/lienzo (61x50cm
  24x19in) Barcelona 2000

SAEBENS Hans 1895-1969 **[30]**
- $407 - €486 - **£290** - FF3 186
  Glasschleifer aus dem Solling Photograph
  (38.5x41.3cm 15x16in) München 2000

SAEDELEER de Valerius 1867-1942 **[80]**
- $115 848 - €108 907 - **£70 128** - FF714 384
  La route dans la plaine en hiver Oil/canvas
  (170x188cm 66x74in) Amsterdam 1999
- $12 135 - €13 613 - **£8 409** - FF89 298
  The Bay of Hastings Oil/canvas (40x91cm 15x35in)
  Amsterdam 2000
- $8 440 - €9 915 - **£5 840** - FF65 040
  Paysage à la ferme Huile/toile (23x48cm 9x18in)
  Antwerpen 2000
- $1 497 - €1 724 - **£1 022** - FF11 311
  Landscape, a Study Pencil/paper (24.5x56cm
  9x22in) Amsterdam 2000

SADEQUAIN column 2:

- $348 - €372 - **£237** - FF2 439
  Winter over Vlaanderen Eau-forte couleurs
  (51x59.5cm 20x23in) Lokeren 2001

SAEDELER de Elisabeth 1902-1972 **[6]**
- $3 944 - €4 214 - **£2 686** - FF27 642
  Winterlandschap Huile/toile (85x95cm 33x37in)
  Lokeren 2001

SAEGER de Anne 1947 **[34]**
- $677 - €762 - **£475** - FF5 000
  Scène de parc ou le manège Huile/panneau
  (38x46cm 14x18in) Pont-Audemer 2001

SAEGHER de Rodolphe 1871-1941 **[17]**
- $516 - €595 - **£355** - FF3 902
  Winterlandschap Pastel/paper (23.5x31cm 9x12in)
  Lokeren 2001

SAEKI Yuzo 1898-1928 **[8]**
- $380 000 - €419 238 - **£251 332** - FF2 750 022
  Sloping Street (Saka no aru michi) Oil/canvas
  (53x65.5cm 20x25in) New-York 2000

SAENE van Maurits 1919-2000 **[28]**
- $1 254 - €1 363 - **£825** - FF8 943
  Marine Oil/canvas/panel (39.5x49.5cm 15x19in)
  Lokeren 2000
- $439 - €372 - **£262** - FF2 437
  Composition Crayons couleurs/papier (49x64cm
  19x25in) Antwerpen 1998

SAENREDAM Jan Pietersz 1565-1607 **[90]**
- $421 - €357 - **£250** - FF2 342
  **Adam naming the Animals in the Garden of
  Eden, after A. Bloemaert** Engraving (28x19.5cm
  11x7in) London 1998

SAENREDAM Pieter Janszoon 1597-1665 **[3]**
- $209 - €225 - **£140** - FF1 475
  De Ruine des Schlosses Assemburg Radierung
  (12x15.5cm 4x6in) Berlin 2000

SAETTI Bruno 1902-1984 **[157]**
- $16 500 - €17 105 - **£9 900** - FF112 200
  Colloquio con l'angelo Tempera (291x201cm
  114x79in) Prato 2000
- $4 000 - €5 183 - **£3 000** - FF34 000
  Vaso di fiori Olio/tela (50x45cm 19x17in) Milano
  2000
- $2 600 - €3 369 - **£1 950** - FF22 100
  Composizione Tecnica mista/cartone (16x21cm
  6x8in) Milano 2001
- $1 500 - €1 555 - **£900** - FF10 200
  Paesaggio con sole Tempera/carta (35x50cm
  13x19in) Prato 2000
- $357 - €308 - **£178** - FF2 023
  Paesaggio fantastico Serigrafia (41x36cm 16x14in)
  Venezia 1999

SAEYS Jacob Ferdinand 1658-1725 **[25]**
- $11 536 - €11 628 - **£7 200** - FF76 272
  **Renaissance palast in einem südlichen Hafen
  mit ankernden Schiffen** Öl/Leinwand (71x94cm
  27x37in) Wien 2000

SAFI Ibrahim 1898-1983 **[8]**
- $9 900 000 - €11 235 493 - **£6 600 000** -
  FF73 700 000
  Istanbul Huile/toile (49x64cm 19x25in) Istanbul 2001
- $4 500 000 - €5 107 042 - **£3 000 000** -
  FF33 500 000
  Fleurs dans un vase Huile/toile (43x33cm 16x12in)
  Istanbul 2001

SAFTLEVEN Cornelius 1607-1681 **[56]**
- $17 901 - €17 244 - **£11 061** - FF113 110
  Couple Embracing by a Farmhouse, the Prodigal Son Among Peasant Swine Beyond Oil/panel (47.5x64.5cm 18x25in) Amsterdam 1999
- $9 000 - €9 105 - **£5 495** - FF59 723
  Standing Peasant Holding a Hat and a Stick Wash/paper (27x17cm 10x6in) New-York 2000

SAFTLEVEN Herman 1609-1685 **[152]**
- $10 893 - €12 271 - £7 660 - FF80 493
  Fähre über den Rhein Oil/panel (40.5x51cm 15x20in) Stuttgart 2001
- $20 990 - €24 542 - **£14 750** - FF160 987
  Flusslandschaft mit beladenen Schiffen und Booten Oil/panel (18.5x25cm 7x9in) München 2000
- $5 000 - €5 356 - **£3 414** - FF35 133
  Studies of Bohemian Peasants: Two Figures in Wagon, with Women Black chalk (14x9cm 5x3in) New-York 2001
- $586 - €665 - **£409** - FF4 360
  Das rechte Blatt der vierteiligen grossen Ansicht von Utrecht Radierung (35.5x41cm 13x16in) München 2001

SAGASTA Cruz López 1951 **[54]**
- $275 - €300 - **£180** - FF1 970
  París 1900, evocación Oleo/lienzo (55x46cm 21x18in) Barcelona 2001

SAGE Henry James 1868-1953 **[30]**
- $555 - €579 - **£350** - FF3 798
  Lion Gateway, Guildford Watercolour/paper (32x18cm 12x7in) Guildford, Surrey 2000

SAGE Kay 1898-1963 **[4]**
- $18 000 - €19 439 - **£12 439** - FF127 510
  Apostrophe Oil/canvas (41.5x33cm 16x12in) New-York 2001

SAGE Philippe XX **[15]**
- $225 - €189 - **£132** - FF1 238
  Flambeau Marchers Etching in colors (36x30cm 14x12in) New-Orleans LA 1998

SAGER Peter Winchell 1920 **[15]**
- $210 - €226 - **£144** - FF1 482
  Design for Sculpture Gouache (44.5x37cm 17x14in) Toronto 2001

SAGER-NELSON Olof 1868-1896 **[16]**
- $30 744 - €34 136 - **£20 580** - FF223 916
  Läxan Oil/canvas (46.5x55.5cm 18x21in) Stockholm 2000

SAGEWKA Ernst 1883-1959 **[5]**
- $4 271 - €4 857 - £2 962 - FF31 862
  Die blaue Allee Oil/Leinwand (79.5x60.5cm 31x23in) Berlin 2000

SAGRESTANI Giovanni Camillo 1660-1731 **[20]**
- $23 650 - €25 021 - **£15 000** - FF164 125
  Bacchanalian Scene with Figures Dancing and Making Merry Oil/canvas (115x163cm 45x64in) London 2000
- $9 240 - €7 864 - **£5 500** - FF51 583
  The Presentation in the Temple Oil/canvas (73.5x49cm 28x19in) London 1998
- $6 650 - €7 744 - **£4 600** - FF50 799
  Madonna and Child Being Adored by two Kneeling Saints Oil/canvas (41.5x35cm 16x13in) London 2000

SAHLSTEN Anna 1859-1931 **[6]**
- $485 - €504 - **£304** - FF3 309
  Stilleben Oil/canvas (34x24cm 13x9in) Helsinki 2000

SAILMAKER Isaac c.1633-1721 **[8]**
- $6 767 - €7 507 - **£4 500** - FF49 245
  H.M.S Gloucester Aground on the Lemon and Ower Sandbank Oil/canvas (89x105cm 35x41in) London 2000
- $3 893 - €3 739 - **£2 400** - FF24 525
  Squadron of the red in coastal Waters, possibly off Tangiers Oil/canvas (29x35.5cm 11x13in) London 1999

SAIN Édouard Alexandre 1830-1910 **[38]**
- $974 - €893 - **£600** - FF5 860
  Girl Carrying a Platter of Fruit, a Basket of Wine Oil/canvas (39x26cm 15x10in) London 1999

SAIN Marius Joseph 1877-1961 **[5]**
- $7 287 - €8 080 - **£5 061** - FF53 000
  Le jeune maure Bronze (H36cm H14in) Soissons 2001

SAIN Paul 1853-1908 **[81]**
- $2 501 - €2 134 - **£1 509** - FF14 000
  Femme à l'ombrelle sur le chemin de la Vance à Lozère Palaiseau Huile/toile (35x55cm 13x21in) Carcassonne 1998
- $925 - €991 - **£629** - FF6 850
  Paysage Huile/toile (33x46cm 12x18in) Avignon 2001

SAINT-ANDRÉ de Simon Bernard 1613-1677 **[7]**
- $50 000 - €44 007 - **£30 440** - FF288 665
  Vanitas, a Skull, a Violin, a Music Score, a Pipe and Tobacco Oil/canvas (65x54cm 25x21in) New-York 1999

SAINT-ANGE J.L. de La Hamayde 1780-1860 **[3]**
- $18 492 - €18 294 - **£11 532** - FF120 000
  Vue perspective de la bourse, façade Ouest Aquarelle/papier (54.5x83cm 21x32in) Paris 1999

SAINT-ANGE-DESMAISONS Louis 1780-c.1845 **[3]**
- $3 250 - €3 195 - **£2 088** - FF20 958
  Project for an Oriental Pavillion Watercolour (20x31cm 7x12in) New-York 1999

SAINT-AUBIN de Augustin 1736-1807 **[43]**
- $4 402 - €4 726 - **£2 945** - FF31 000
  La sultane validé Crayon (19.5x15cm 7x5in) Compiègne 2000
- $350 - €396 - **£236** - FF2 600
  Au moins, soyez discrets/Comptez sur mes serments Gravure (35x26.5cm 13x10in) Paris 2000

SAINT-AUBIN de Charles Germain 1721-1786 **[5]**
- $846 - €824 - **£520** - FF5 403
  Les fleurettes de Saint-Aubin, dessinateur du Roy Etching (8x8cm 3x3in) London 1999

SAINT-AUBIN de Gabriel 1724-1780 **[55]**
- $25 000 - €21 929 - **£15 180** - FF143 845
  Interior Scene with a Woman and Children Being Received by Gentlemen Oil/canvas (105x94cm 41x37in) New-York 2000
- $14 269 - €16 007 - **£9 891** - FF105 000
  Scène de comédie dans un parc Pierre noire (23.5x28.5cm 9x11in) Paris 2000

SAINT-CLAIR Thomas Staunton 1785-1847 **[29]**
- $1 658 - €1 537 - **£1 000** - FF10 084
  The Artillery Barrack and Moorish Castle Watercolour/paper (17.5x28cm 6x11in) London 1999

SAINT-CYR de Yvonne XX **[3]**
- $4 563 - €5 031 - **£3 036** - FF33 000
  Élégantes aux courses Huile/panneau (44x17cm 17x6in) Biarritz 2000

S

SAINT-CYR GIRIER Jean Aimé 1837-1912 **[30]**
- **$12 000** – €11 240 – **£7 377** – FF73 729
  After the Storm Oil/canvas (120x200cm 47x78in)
  New-York 1998

SAINT-DELIS de Henri Liénard 1878-1949 **[250]**
- **$10 197** – €8 690 – **£6 076** – FF57 000
  Maison sous la neige à la Côte de Grace à Honfleur Huile/toile (46x55cm 18x21in) Paris 1998
- **$3 501** – €4 116 – **£2 538** – FF27 000
  Honfleur, marché sur la place Huile/panneau (22x28cm 8x11in) Calais 2001
- **$1 831** – €2 058 – **£1 275** – FF13 500
  Honfleur Aquarelle/papier (30x39cm 11x15in)
  Honfleur 2001

SAINT-DELIS de René Liénard 1877-1958 **[108]**
- **$641** – €762 – **£447** – FF5 000
  Samovar Huile/toile (48x60cm 18x23in) Nantes 2000
- **$542** – €457 – **£321** – FF3 000
  La Lande Bretonne Huile/carton (20.5x29cm 8x11in)
  Paris 1998
- **$397** – €427 – **£266** – FF2 800
  L'église de Cauville en Normandie
  Aquarelle/papier (38x26cm 14x10in) Fécamp 2000

SAINT-FLEURANT Louisiane 1924 **[35]**
- **$782** – €732 – **£473** – FF4 800
  En famille Huile/toile (60x76cm 23x29in) Paris 1999

SAINT-GAUDENS Augustus 1848-1907 **[47]**
- **$380 000** – €324 666 – **£228 114** – FF2 129 672
  «Diana of the Tower» Bronze (H99cm H38in) New-York 1998
- **$13 000** – €15 162 – **£9 127** – FF99 455
  Robert Louis Stevenson Relief (47x41cm 18x16in)
  Portsmouth NH 2000

SAINT-GENIES Francis de Lassus 1925 **[10]**
- **$217** – €186 – **£130** – FF1 217
  «Point Bleu» Poster (119x79cm 46x31in) London 1998

SAINT-GENOIS de Charles Albert XIX **[1]**
- **$22 000** – €18 981 – **£13 272** – FF124 504
  A Performance at the Café Concert des Ambassadeurs Oil/canvas (107.5x140cm 42x55in)
  New-York 1998

SAINT-GEORGE Charles 1907 **[7]**
- **$5 493** – €5 488 – **£3 434** – FF36 000
  Venise, Chiesa Archangelo Raffaele Huile/toile (60.5x81cm 23x31in) Paris 1999

SAINT-GERMIER Joseph 1860-1925 **[28]**
- **$1 393** – €1 448 – **£877** – FF9 500
  Venise, gondoles près d'un pont Huile/toile (56x39cm 22x15in) Tours 2000
- **$883** – €762 – **£533** – FF5 000
  Vénitiens et Vénitiennes dans la loggia
  Huile/toile (22.5x16cm 8x6in) Bayeux 1998

SAINT-JEAN Simon 1808-1860 **[29]**
- **$20 370** – €21 343 – **£12 894** – FF140 000
  Fruits, pampres de vigne, vase de fleurs, lièvre et faisan Huile/toile (130x100cm 51x39in) Paris 2000
- **$3 865** – €3 583 – **£2 404** – FF23 500
  Pêcheur et vignes sur un treillage Huile/carton (52x34cm 20x13in) Rouen 1999

SAINT-JOHN Edwin (Edmund?) XIX **[74]**
- **$494** – €453 – **£302** – FF2 970
  Figures before Jumieges near Calais, France
  Watercolour (101.5x70cm 39x27in) London 1998

SAINT-JOHN J. Allen 1872-1957 **[4]**
- **$12 000** – €11 576 – **£7 584** – FF75 936
  Tarzan Lord of the Jungle Pencil (61x39.5cm 24x15in) New-York 1999

SAINT-LANNE Georges XIX **[1]**
- **$4 639** – €5 412 – **£3 226** – FF35 500
  Repos au jardin Huile/toile (80x99cm 31x38in)
  Bordeaux 2000

SAINT-LAURENT Yves 1936 **[15]**
- **$5 000** – €4 733 – **£3 109** – FF31 044
  Two Opium Sketches Pencil (45x35cm 18x14in)
  New-York 1999
- **$1 000** – €1 121 – **£694** – FF7 356
  «Love» Poster (53x38cm 21x15in) New-York 2001

SAINT-MARCEAUX de René Charles 1845-1915 **[46]**
- **$5 101** – €5 946 – **£3 576** – FF39 000
  L'arlequin Bronze (H100cm H39in) Paris 2000
- **$1 168** – €1 308 – **£811** – FF8 580
  Harlekin Bronze (H51cm H20in) Wien 2001

SAINT-MARCEL-CABIN Charles Edmé 1819-1890 **[24]**
- **$753** – €656 – **£454** – FF4 300
  Deux tigres Sanguine (30.8x46.7cm 12x18in) Paris 1998

SAINT-MÉMIN de Charles B. J. Févret 1770-1852 **[9]**
- **$1 100** – €1 029 – **£666** – FF6 749
  Gentleman, in profile Watercolour (48x35cm 19x14in) Bolton MA 1999

SAINT-MICHEL de Joseph XVIII **[2]**
- **$1 437** – €1 448 – **£895** – FF9 500
  Courtisane vue à mi-corps Pastel/papier (48.5x39cm 19x15in) Paris 2000

SAINT-NON de J.Cl. Richard, Abbé 1727-1791 **[23]**
- **$524** – €486 – **£316** – FF3 186
  Vedute del gentile Mulino/Landschaft mit Reisenden Radierung (15x21cm 5x8in) Heidelberg 1999

SAINT-OURS Jean-Pierre 1752-1809 **[20]**
- **$14 135** – €13 758 – **£8 685** – FF90 246
  Combat des Horaces et des Curiaces Oil/panel (28x40cm 11x15in) Zürich 1999
- **$3 132** – €2 725 – **£1 888** – FF17 872
  «Homère chantant l'Iliade et l'Odyssée à l'entrée d'une bourgade...» Ink (46x35.2cm 18x13in)
  Bern 1998

SAINT-PHALLE de Niki 1930 **[945]**
- **$9 300** – €10 370 – **£6 460** – FF68 020
  A Fragment of Hon Mixed media (147x92cm 57x36in) Stockholm 2001
- **$6 478** – €6 250 – **£4 067** – FF41 000
  The Black Bidow Technique mixte (45.5x43.5cm 17x17in) Paris 1999
- **$5 154** – €4 988 – **£3 178** – FF32 716
  The Hand Acrylique (33x41.5x2cm 12x16xin) Zürich 1999
- **$42 250** – €49 899 – **£30 000** – FF327 315
  Monkey and Child Sculpture (114x88cm 44x34in)
  London 2001
- **$17 250** – €16 073 – **£10 736** – FF105 435
  Fox Plaster (H32cm H12in) Tel Aviv 1999
- **$5 175** – €4 822 – **£3 220** – FF31 630
  Baboon Gouache (120x80cm 47x31in) Tel Aviv 1999
- **$349** – €411 – **£247** – FF2 699
  «Remember?» Farbserigraphie (46x58.5cm 18x23in)
  Berlin 2001

SAINT-PIERRE Gaston Casimir 1833-1916 **[16]**
$23 430 - €25 154 - **£15 675** - FF165 000
Romance arabe Huile/toile (140x90cm 55x35in)
Mayenne 2000
$972 - €1 037 - **£616** - FF6 800
Jeune fille allongée Huile/toile (36x55cm 14x21in)
Avallon 2000
$6 000 - €5 487 - **£3 664** - FF35 992
Vénus et amour Oil/panel (24x16cm 9x6in) New-
York 1998

SAINT-SAENS Marc 1903-1973 **[17]**
$3 755 - €4 421 - **£2 639** - FF29 000
«L'Oiseau» Tapisserie (178x130cm 70x51in) Toulouse
2000

SAINTHILL Loudon 1919-1969 **[46]**
$22 198 - €20 825 - **£13** - FF136 601
The Betrothed Oil/canvas (80x72cm 31x28in)
Melbourne 1999
$2 088 - €1 962 - **£1 258** - FF12 868
Player & Dog Watercolour, gouache/paper (61.5x40cm
24x15in) Sydney 1999

SAINTIN Henri 1846-1899 **[40]**
$8 000 - €8 970 - **£5 432** - FF58 838
Mending the Nets Oil/canvas (90x151cm 35x59in)
New-York 2000
$1 681 - €1 815 - **£1 149** - FF11 906
**A French Coastal Scene with Fishermen on the
Beach** Oil/canvas (61x82cm 24x32in) Amsterdam
2001

SAINTIN Jules Émile 1829-1894 **[21]**
$10 937 - €10 259 - **£6 758** - FF67 295
Interiör Oil/canvas (75x55cm 29x21in) Helsinki 1999
$131 - €137 - **£83** - FF896
Portrait de jeune fille Crayon/papier (40x25cm
15x9in) Genève 2000

SAINTON Charles Prosper 1861-1914 **[21]**
$282 - €327 - **£200** - FF2 147
Classical Nude Holding an Amphora Watercolour
(36x18cm 14x7in) London 2000

SAINZ DE MORALES Gumersindo 1900-1976 **[26]**
$540 - €601 - **£380** - FF3 940
Gitana Oil/lienzo (56.5x46cm 22x18in) Madrid 2001

SAINZ Y SAINZ Casimiro 1853-1898 **[17]**
$45 900 - €51 055 - **£30 600** - FF334 900
Paisaje campurriano Oleo/lienzo (53x86cm
20x33in) Madrid 2000
$2 915 - €3 304 - **£1 980** - FF21 670
La mendiga Oleo/tabla (25x15cm 9x5in) Madrid 2000

SAITO Kikuo 1939 **[5]**
$800 - €827 - **£505** - FF5 427
Clay Image Woodcut in colors (51x31cm 20x12in)
New-York 2000

SAITO Kiyoshi 1907-1997 **[226]**
$1 100 - €1 216 - **£763** - FF7 976
«Sakurada-Mon Tokyo» Woodcut (45x60cm
17x23in) New-York 2001

SAITO Makato 1952 **[3]**
$3 200 - €2 730 - **£1 930** - FF17 907
«Batsu» Poster (145.5x103.5cm 57x40in) New-York
1998

SAITO Shin Ichi 1922 **[3]**
$4 900 - €4 779 - **£3 000** - FF31 350
Back Home, from Goze Story Oil/board
(24x33.5cm 9x13in) Tokyo 1999

SAITO Yoshishige 1905 **[9]**
$145 663 - €140 587 - **£92 000** - FF922 189
Composition in blue Oil/panel (181.5x121cm
71x47in) London 1999
$16 000 - €16 470 - **£10 084** - FF108 036
Untitled Mixed media (70.5x90.5cm 27x35in) New-
York 2000

SAIVE de Jean-Baptiste c.1540-1624 **[6]**
$80 000 - €80 931 - **£48 848** - FF530 872
Fruit and Vegetable Seller's Stall Oil/canvas
(157.5x227cm 62x89in) New-York 2000

SAIVE de Jean-Baptiste II 1597-c.1641 **[5]**
$448 290 - €481 202 - **£300 000** - FF3 156 480
Fruit and Vegetable Stall in a Town Market
Oil/canvas (173x228cm 68x89in) London 2000

SAKAKIBARA Shikô 1895-1969 **[4]**
$21 560 - €21 029 - **£13 200** - FF137 940
White Egret Painting (132.5x41.5cm 52x16in) Tokyo
1999

SAKAMOTO Hanjirô 1882-1969 **[1]**
$588 000 - €573 513 - **£360 000** - FF3 762 000
Horse Oil/canvas (45x59.5cm 17x23in) Tokyo 1999

SAKU Joun 1858-1940 **[1]**
$10 000 - €9 613 - **£6 236** - FF63 055
Vase of ovoid from with high shoulder Bronze
(H30cm H11in) New-York 1999

SALA de Eugène 1899-1987 **[98]**
$637 - €714 - **£443** - FF4 685
Komposition Oil/board (60x66cm 23x25in)
Stockholm 1999
$1 465 - €1 346 - **£900** - FF8 832
Kompositioner Oil/panel (38x38cm 14x14in)
København 1999

SALA Paolo 1859-1929 **[165]**
$10 000 - €12 958 - **£7 500** - FF85 000
Paesaggio montano Olio/tela (119x169cm 46x66in)
Milano 1999
$7 800 - €6 738 - **£3 900** - FF44 200
Lago di montagna a maggio Olio/tavola (69x98cm
27x38in) Milano 1999
$2 197 - €2 087 - **£1 336** - FF13 692
Havenstadje bij avondrood Oil/panel (19.5x32cm
7x12in) Den Haag 1999
$2 400 - €3 110 - **£1 800** - FF20 400
Paesaggio con ruscello e figure Acquarello/carta
(33x52cm 12x20in) Milano 2001

SALA Y FRANCÉS Emilio 1850-1910 **[103]**
$16 775 - €16 518 - **£10 450** - FF108 350
Alegoría mitológica Oleo/lienzo (129x231cm
50x90in) Madrid 1999
$5 800 - €6 006 - **£3 700** - FF39 400
Desnudo masculino Oleo/lienzo (100x81cm
39x31in) Madrid 1999
$2 240 - €2 321 - **£1 365** - FF13 790
Desnudo de espaldas Oleo/lienzo (47x31cm
18x12in) Madrid 1999
$302 - €288 - **£182** - FF1 891
Estudios para cabezas de niños Lápiz/papel
(22x15cm 8x5in) Madrid 1999

SALABET Jean XX **[33]**
$800 - €915 - **£550** - FF6 005
Winter along the Seine Oil/canvas (45x55cm
18x22in) New-York 1999
$666 - €762 - **£458** - FF5 000
Le quai Saint-Michel Huile/toile (27x35cm 10x13in)
Paris 2000

S

SALAMANCA Antonio 1500-1562 [5]

📖 **$215** - €223 - **£142** - FF1 463
Histoire de l'Amour et de Psyché, d'après Raphaël Gravure (19.5x33cm 7x12in) Bruxelles 2000

SALANSON Eugénie Marie XIX-XX [7]

🖼 **$14 969** - €12 825 - **£9 000** - FF84 124
The Young Fisher-Girl Oil/canvas (101x70cm 39x27in) Edinburgh 1998

SALAS Tito 1887/88-1974 [16]

🖼 **$12 926** - €15 236 - **£9 083** - FF99 940
Sin título Oleo/lienzo (60x75cm 23x29in) Caracas ($) 2000

SALATHÉ Friedrich 1793-1858 [40]

✍ **$482** - €460 - **£301** - FF3 018
Felspartie am Meer (Capo di Miseno) Watercolour (10.4x15.1cm 4x5in) Hamburg 1999

SALAVERRIA INCHAURRANDIETA Elías 1883-1952 [6]

🖼 **$3 000** - €3 003 - **£1 850** - FF19 700
Boyero Oleo/tabla (24x19cm 9x7in) Madrid 2000

SALAZAR Abel 1889-1946 [4]

🖼 **$7 700** - €8 724 - **£5 425** - FF57 225
Páteo ribatejano com carroça e burro Oleo/lienzo (20x30cm 7x11in) Lisboa 2001

✍ **$987** - €1 047 - **£651** - FF6 867
Mulheres no mercado Tinta/papel (21.5x27.5cm 8x10in) Lisboa 2000

SALAZAR Ignacio 1947 [1]

🖼 **$11 000** - €9 910 - **£6 650** - FF62 916
Tríptico de Campín Mixed media/canvas (130x131cm 51x51in) New-York 1998

SALCEDO Doris 1958 [6]

🔧 **$26 000** - €25 157 - **£16 034** - FF165 019
Camisas Construction (170x25x38cm 66x9x14in) New-York 1999

SALCES Y GUTIERREZ Manuel 1861-1932 [45]

🖼 **$1 159** - €1 141 - **£722** - FF7 486
Monte Milagro, Puerto de Hijar Oleo/lienzo (12.5x14.5cm 4x5in) Madrid 1999

SALEH Raden S. Bastaman 1814-1880 [27]

🖼 **$1 299 540** - €1 211 186 - **£785 400** - FF7 944 860
Lying in Wait Oil/canvas (110x154.5cm 43x60in) Singapore 1999

🖼 **$32 230** - €32 476 - **£20 091** - FF213 026
Seascape with Ship Oil/canvas/board (39x45cm 15x17in) Singapore 2000

🖼 **$106 260** - €100 616 - **£66 000** - FF660 000
Combat entre un buffle et un tigre Huile/toile (31x43.5cm 12x17in) Paris 1999

SALEMME Attilio 1911-1955 [23]

🖼 **$14 000** - €15 922 - **£9 709** - FF104 442
«Prelude to Nirvana» Oil/canvas (132x203cm 52x80in) Cincinnati OH 2000

✍ **$700** - €793 - **£489** - FF5 203
The Homecoming Watercolour (39x28cm 15x11in) New-York 2001

SALEN Anton 1890 [2]

📖 **$606** - €671 - **£420** - FF4 404
«H.O.K.Y» Poster (93x61cm 36x24in) London 2001

SALENTIN Hans 1925 [11]

🔧 **$3 749** - €3 579 - **£2 342** - FF23 477
Ohne Titel Metal (H84cm H33in) Köln 1999

SALENTIN Hubert 1822-1910 [30]

🖼 **$7 204** - €8 181 - **£5 006** - FF53 662
Grossmutter und Enkelin Öl/Leinwand (83.5x59cm 32x23in) Köln 2001

🖼 **$5 500** - €5 387 - **£3 544** - FF35 336
With Light to read Oil/panel (25x20.5cm 9x8in) New-York 1999

SALES Francesco 1904-1976 [33]

🖼 **$972** - €1 081 - **£648** - FF7 092
Flores Oleo/lienzo (73x54cm 28x21in) Madrid 2000

SALGADO José Veloso 1864-1945 [3]

🖼 **$43 000** - €49 851 - **£30 000** - FF327 000
Play Oleo/lienzo (71x59.5cm 27x23in) Lisboa 2001

🖼 **$13 640** - €15 454 - **£9 300** - FF101 370
Paisagem Huile/bois (26x34.5cm 10x13in) Lisboa 2000

SALGADO Sebastiao 1944 [69]

📷 **$2 000** - €1 867 - **£1 211** - FF12 249
Kuwait Gelatin silver print (30.5x44.5cm 12x17in) New-York 1999

SALIBA da Antonio 1466/67-c.1540 [6]

✍ **$9 500** - €7 971 - **£5 573** - FF52 284
Figures and Landscape Ballpoint pen (31x47cm 12x18in) New-York 1998

SALICATH Ørnulf 1888-1962 [19]

🖼 **$452** - €488 - **£312** - FF3 201
Fjellandskap Oil/panel (61x75cm 24x29in) Oslo 2001

SALICETI Jeanne 1873-1950 [43]

🖼 **$186** - €183 - **£120** - FF1 200
Bouquet jaune et rouge Huile/carton (24x30cm 9x11in) Tarbes 1999

SALIETTI Alberto 1892-1961 [52]

🖼 **$6 500** - €6 738 - **£3 900** - FF44 200
Villa San Michele di Pagana Olio/tavola (50x60cm 19x23in) Torino 1999

🖼 **$2 520** - €2 177 - **£1 680** - FF14 280
«Marina d'inverno» Olio/tavola (34x40cm 13x15in) Milano 1998

✍ **$1 650** - €1 710 - **£990** - FF11 220
I Re Magi Tempera/carta (44x35cm 17x13in) Prato 2001

SALIGER Ivo 1894-1987 [52]

🖼 **$415** - €472 - **£291** - FF3 098
Hinterer Gosausee mit Dachstein Öl/Leinwand (60x70cm 23x27in) Wien 2001

📖 **$216** - €232 - **£145** - FF1 525
Bacchantin Radierung (59x50cm 23x19in) Wien 2000

SALIGO Charles Louis 1804-? [3]

🖼 **$3 765** - €3 718 - **£2 325** - FF24 390
Sainte femme Huile/toile (82.3x64.3cm 32x25in) Antwerpen 1999

SALIKIVI Santeri 1886-1940 [5]

🖼 **$283** - €331 - **£202** - FF2 172
Krokleiva Oil/canvas (54x45cm 21x17in) Oslo 2001

SALIM Saraochim 1908 [3]

🖼 **$2 180** - €2 476 - **£1 492** - FF16 243
Still life Oil/canvas (73x60cm 28x23in) Singapore 2000

SALIMBENI BEVILACQUA Ventura di Arcangelo 1568-1613 [29]

🖼 **$42 753** - €48 559 - **£30 000** - FF318 525
The Holy Family with the Infant Saint John the Baptist Oil/panel (64.5x48.5cm 25x19in) London 2001

🖼 **$57 500** - €64 404 - **£39 951** - FF422 464
The Holy Family with Saint Jerome Oil/copper (38.5x29cm 15x11in) New-York 2001

S

✎ **$12 302** - €14 483 - **£8 645** - FF95 000
Deux Saints en adoration dans une lunette
Encre (16.5x32cm 6x12in) Paris 2000

▥ **$1 118** - €1 227 - **£759** - FF8 049
Die Madonna mit dem Kind, nach Guido Reni
Radierung (17.7x13.4cm 6x5in) Berlin 2000

SALINAS Marcel Charles L. 1913 **[13]**
▥ **$701** - €793 - **£473** - FF5 200
Portraits imaginaires, d'après Picasso
Lithographie couleurs (64x46cm 25x18in) Paris 2000

SALINAS Porfirio 1910-1973 **[30]**
◠ **$9 000** - €10 219 - **£6 253** - FF67 032
Texas Hill Country Oil/canvas (63x76cm 25x30in)
Dallas TX 2001

SALINAS Y TERUEL Agustín 1862-1915 **[24]**
◠ **$21 000** - €18 019 - **£12 600** - FF118 200
Las alegrías de la vida campestre Oleo/tabla
(23.5x40cm 9x15in) Madrid 1999

SALINAS Y TERUEL Juan Pablo 1871-1946 **[94]**
◠ **$92 000** - €119 215 - **£69 000** - FF782 000
Contratto di matrimonio Olio/tela (90x135cm
35x53in) Milano 2001
◠ **$74 715** - €80 200 - **£50 000** - FF526 080
La Llegada del Duque (The Dukes Arrival)
Oil/canvas (40x66cm 15x25in) London 2000
◠ **$19 688** - €18 030 - **£12 000** - FF118 267
Taking Coffee Oil/panel (13x23cm 5x9in) London
1999

SALINI Tommaso Mao 1575-1625 **[19]**
◠ **$74 481** - €72 953 - **£48 000** - FF478 540
Girl feeding Cockerels, with a Cat on a Basket, a Goose, Duck, Birds Oil/canvas (122x171cm 48x67in) London 1999
◠ **$41 232** - €46 232 - **£28 000** - FF303 259
Fruit in a Straw Basket, Together with Asparagus, Artichokes, Lemons Oil/canvas
(72x96cm 28x37in) London 2000

SALIOLA Antonio 1939 **[10]**
◠ **$1 500** - €1 555 - **£900** - FF10 200
La visita al Maestro Olio/tela (100x100cm 39x39in)
Torino 2001

SALIS-SOGLIO von Albert 1886-1941 **[3]**
◠ **$4 208** - €4 047 - **£2 596** - FF26 544
Oberengadiner Landschaft Öl/Leinwand
(80.5x100cm 31x39in) Bern 1999

SALISBURY Frank Owen 1874-1962 **[67]**
◠ **$1 200** - €1 145 - **£749** - FF7 513
Mrs Meigs as a Girl Oil/canvas (112x77cm 44x30in)
Dedham MA 1999
✎ **$455** - €518 - **£320** - FF3 399
«Before the Dawn, Lake Ballagio» Watercolour
(36.5x38.5cm 14x15in) London 2001

SALKAUSKAS Henry 1925-1979 **[5]**
✎ **$2 172** - €2 332 - **£1 454** - FF15 299
Dark Movement Watercolour/paper (101.5x153.5cm
39x60in) Melbourne 2000

SALKELD Cecil French 1908-1968 **[8]**
◠ **$3 238** - €2 717 - **£1 900** - FF17 823
Connemara, Beach Scene with Figures and Pony on a Hill Oil/board (40x50cm 16x20in) Co.
Kilkenny 1998

SALKIN Émile 1900-1977 **[15]**
◠ **$1 320** - €1 410 - **£795** - FF7 479
Rue de la Madeleine Huile/panneau (60x80cm 23x31in) Bruxelles 1999

✎ **$1 782** - €1 487 - **£1 044** - FF9 756
Les amazones Crayon gras/papier (99x148.5cm 38x58in) Bruxelles 1998

SALKIN Fernand 1862-? **[9]**
◠ **$1 800** - €2 152 - **£1 236** - FF14 115
Les barques de l'île Martinique Oil/canvas
(26x35cm 10x14in) Chicago IL 2000

SALLA Josef XIX **[1]**
▣ **$14 054** - €13 275 - **£8 500** - FF87 077
Advertising photographs and rayograms Silver
print (23.5x18cm 9x7in) London 1999

SALLAERT Antonius c.1590-c.1657/8 **[7]**
◠ **$8 170** - €7 775 - **£5 079** - FF51 000
La Glorification du nom de Jésus Huile/panneau
(37.1x27.5cm 14x10in) Lille 1999
◠ **$1 700** - €1 821 - **£1 160** - FF11 945
Standing Man holding a plumed Hat and a Staff
Black chalk/paper (19x10cm 7x3in) New-York 2001
▥ **$801** - €777 - **£500** - FF5 094
Labours of Hercules: The Slaying of the Centaur Eurytion Engraving (17.5x22cm 6x8in)
London 1999

SALLBERG Harald 1895-1963 **[56]**
▥ **$233** - €219 - **£140** - FF1 437
I min ateljé Etching (28x23.5cm 11x9in) Stockholm
1999

SALLE David 1952 **[173]**
◠ **$70 000** - €65 700 - **£43 246** - FF430 962
A Couple of Centuries Acrylic (279.5x406.5cm
110x160in) New-York 1999
◠ **$4 140** - €4 573 - **£2 871** - FF30 000
Sans titre Technique mixte (64x80cm 25x31in) Paris
2001
✎ **$3 500** - €3 568 - **£2 193** - FF23 403
Untitled Ink (76x101.5cm 29x39in) New-York 2000
▥ **$900** - €1 033 - **£615** - FF6 773
Drunken Chauffeur Screenprint in colors
(75.5x106cm 29x41in) New-York 2000

SALLES Robert 1871-1929 **[9]**
▥ **$2 400** - €2 799 - **£1 685** - FF18 361
«Voyages animés» Poster (59.5x82cm 23x32in)
New-York 2000

SALLES-WAGNER Adelaïde c.1824-1890 **[4]**
◠ **$7 375** - €6 860 - **£4 567** - FF45 000
Femme à l'éventail, Homme dans un intérieur
Huile/toile (110x87cm 43x34in) Biarritz 1999

SALLES-WAGNER Jules 1814-1898 **[16]**
◠ **$6 938** - €7 920 - **£4 820** - FF51 949
Il Fratellino Oil/canvas (161x114cm 63x44in)
Köbenhavn 2000
◠ **$17 000** - €19 992 - **£12 189** - FF131 136
Young Classical Beauty Oil/canvas (101.5x75cm
39x29in) New-York 2001
◠ **$850** - €884 - **£535** - FF5 800
Portrait de jeune fille Huile/papier (25x18cm 9x7in)
Nîmes 2000

SALLINEN Tyko 1879-1955 **[103]**
◠ **$2 385** - €2 691 - **£1 676** - FF17 651
Huvimaja Oil/canvas (50x61cm 19x24in) Helsinki
2001
✎ **$759** - €673 - **£465** - FF4 412
Landskap Watercolour/paper (31x41cm 12x16in)
Helsinki 1999

S

SALM van Abraham c.1660-1720 **[6]**
$25 340 - €21 343 - **£14 966** - FF140 000
Vaisseau de guerre des Provinces-Unies et autres bateaux sur une mer Huile/panneau (72x107cm 28x42in) Paris 1998
$150 000 - €160 453 - **£102 270** - FF1 052 505
Winter Landscape with Skaters, Kolf Players and Elegant Townsfolk Ink (45x61.5cm 17x24in) New-York 2001

SALM van Adriaen Cornelisz. 1686-1720 **[10]**
$100 000 - €109 715 - **£66 430** - FF719 680
A Naval Engagement Between English and Dutch Men-of-War Ink (36.5x49cm 14x19in) New-York 2000

SALM van Reynier 1688-1765 **[3]**
$42 000 - €44 854 - **£28 618** - FF294 222
Dutch whalers «Groenlandia» and «Duroux Leonora», with other Shipping Ink (61x77.5cm 24x30in) New-York 2001

SALMANOVICH Udi 1959 **[4]**
$900 - €777 - **£544** - FF5 094
Untitled 2 Mixed media/paper (100x70cm 39x27in) Tel Aviv 1999

SALME Lambert XIX **[1]**
$7 980 - €8 676 - **£5 250** - FF56 910
Landelijk interieur Oil/canvas (48.5x59cm 19x23in) Lokeren 2000

SALMI Max 1931-1995 **[79]**
$1 087 - €1 009 - **£652** - FF6 619
Jonglör Oil/canvas (50x50cm 19x19in) Helsinki 1999
$1 194 - €1 093 - **£727** - FF7 170
Kerttus vårhatt Oil/canvas (37x30cm 14x11in) Helsinki 1999

SALMINEN Juho 1892-1945 **[26]**
$494 - €420 - **£295** - FF2 758
Stadsvy Oil/canvas (54x65cm 21x25in) Helsinki 1998

SALMON Émile 1840-1913 **[2]**
$5 025 - €5 633 - **£3 500** - FF36 950
Levrette (a seated whippet) Bronze (H55cm H21in) London 2001

SALMON John Cuthbert 1844-1917 **[74]**
$561 - €667 - **£400** - FF4 378
Autumn, Woodland Stream/Summer Cows grazing under Trees Oil/canvas (46x61cm 18x24in) Bath 2000
$553 - €533 - **£341** - FF3 843
Segelfartyg på väg in i hamn Akvarell/papper (35x54cm 13x21in) Malmö 1999

SALMON John Francis 1808-1886 **[12]**
$704 - €752 - **£480** - FF4 930
«Stormy Evening, Yorkshire Coast» Watercolour (16x27cm 6x10in) Billingshurst, West-Sussex 2001

SALMON Robert W. 1775-c.1845 **[56]**
$26 904 - €31 788 - **£19 065** - FF208 516
Grosser englischer Dreimaster in einem südlichen Mittelmeerhafen Öl/Leinwand (68x103cm 26x40in) Zürich 2000
$15 000 - €17 045 - **£10 359** - FF111 811
Coming ashore Oil/panel (24x29.5cm 9x11in) New-York 2000

SALMON Théodore Frédéric 1811-1876 **[10]**
$2 401 - €2 211 - **£1 441** - FF14 500
Jeune femme dans un intérieur Huile/panneau (34x26cm 13x10in) Dijon 1999

SALMONES Victor 1937-1989 **[6]**
$20 000 - €23 506 - **£13 866** - FF154 188
Adorations Bronze (H194cm H76in) New-York 2000

SALMSON Hugo 1843-1894 **[49]**
$11 651 - €10 926 - **£7 200** - FF71 671
Oriental Nude Oil/canvas (242x137cm 95x53in) London 1999
$2 380 - €2 764 - **£1 695** - FF18 132
Flicka kammandes sitt hår, mytologisk allegori Oil/canvas (110x73cm 43x28in) Stockholm 2001
$6 811 - €7 668 - **£4 692** - FF50 298
Ung kvinna i tankar Oil/canvas (33x24cm 12x9in) Uppsala 2000
$436 - €484 - **£302** - FF3 176
Motiv från Moret, Frankrike Akvarell/papper (24x32.5cm 9x12in) Malmö 2001

SALMSON Jean Jules B. 1823-1902 **[50]**
$13 000 - €13 100 - **£8 104** - FF85 930
Figures of Water-Carriers Bronze (H83cm H32in) New-York 2000
$2 153 - €2 414 - **£1 500** - FF15 836
«Shakespeare» Bronze (H48.5cm H19in) London 2001

SALOKIVI Santeri 1886-1940 **[149]**
$4 289 - €4 877 - **£2 975** - FF31 992
Landskap med segelbåtar Oil/canvas (60x73cm 23x28in) Helsinki 2000
$1 942 - €2 186 - **£1 337** - FF14 341
Fiskaren Oil/panel (27x30cm 10x11in) Helsinki 2000
$228 - €252 - **£158** - FF1 654
Från aura å Etching (26x35cm 10x13in) Helsinki 2001

SALOME (Wolfgang Cilartz) 1954 **[112]**
$8 952 - €9 825 - **£5 768** - FF64 448
On the Rocks Oil/canvas (184x250cm 72x98in) Stockholm 2000
$3 945 - €4 602 - **£2 770** - FF30 185
«Dark Lilies» Acryl/Leinwand (90.5x120.5cm 35x47in) Köln 2000
$499 - €588 - **£352** - FF3 856
«Lippenstift und Puderdose» Coloured chalks (32.5x24cm 12x9in) Berlin 2001
$619 - €665 - **£414** - FF4 360
Götterdämmerung Farblithographie (28.5x38cm 11x14in) Köln 2000

SALOME Emile 1833-1881 **[3]**
$5 379 - €5 031 - **£3 257** - FF33 000
Le barbier Huile/toile (64x84cm 25x33in) Lille 1999

SALOMON Adam 1818-1881 **[5]**
$588 - €686 - **£412** - FF4 500
Portrait au sablier du célèbre modèle Tirage albuminé (26x20.5cm 10x8in) Paris 2001

SALOMON Erich 1886-1944 **[24]**
$787 - €764 - **£490** - FF5 014
Berliner Staatsoper/60-Jahr-Feier der Reichsgründung im Reichstag Vintage gelatin silver print (18x24cm 7x9in) Berlin 1999

SALOMON LE TROPÉZIEN A. XX **[38]**
$410 - €396 - **£257** - FF2 600
Marché à Saint-Tropez Huile/carton (46x55cm 18x21in) Le Mans 1999

SALONEN Wille XX **[18]**
$496 - €471 - **£304** - FF3 089
Havslandskap Oil/canvas (46x78cm 18x30in) Helsinki 1999

S

SALOSMAA Aarno 1941 [17]
$410 - €437 - £278 - FF2 868
Komposition V Collage (21.5x25.5cm 8x10in)
Helsinki 2001

SALT James XIX [60]
$2 689 - €2 887 - £1 800 - FF18 938
Venetian Capriccio Oil/canvas (91.5x71cm 36x27in)
London 2000

SALT John 1937 [21]
$270 - €262 - £166 - FF1 717
Crashed Bonneville Lithographie (64.2x88.2cm
25x34in) Zürich 1999

SALTER John William XIX [2]
$3 969 - €4 361 - £2 400 - FF22 703
Ansty's Cove, Babbacombe, Devon Watercolour
(36x54.5cm 14x21in) London 1998

SALTFLEET Frank c.1860-1937 [34]
$362 - €426 - £260 - FF2 797
Distant View of Venice Watercolour (11.5x21cm
4x8in) West-Yorshire 2001

SALTI Giulio 1899-1984 [20]
$750 - €777 - £450 - FF5 100
Vaso di fiori Olio/cartone (49x34cm 19x13in) Firenze
2001
$660 - €570 - £330 - FF3 740
Paesaggio con palme Olio/cartone (29x40cm
11x15in) Firenze 1999

SALTINI Pietro 1839-1908 [6]
$5 000 - €5 496 - £3 204 - FF36 052
The Oriental, after Friedrich Von Amerling
Oil/canvas (63.5x50cm 25x19in) New-York 2000

SALTMER Florence A. XIX-XX [13]
$1 600 - €1 381 - £955 - FF9 060
«Autumn Gold» Oil/canvas (50x60cm 20x24in)
Vancouver, BC. 1998

SALTO Axel 1889-1960 [98]
$1 750 - €2 011 - £1 212 - FF13 192
Aktaeon Stone (H33cm H12in) København 2000
$474 - €536 - £320 - FF3 516
Dobbeltkomposition med heste Indian ink/paper
(23.5x34cm 9x13in) København 2000
$83 - €94 - £58 - FF615
To hjorte kaemper Color lithograph (33x42cm
12x16in) Viby J, Århus 2001

SALTOFT Edvard Anders 1883-1939 [35]
$484 - €564 - £346 - FF3 697
Kvindeportraet Pastel/paper (102x82cm 40x32in)
Aarhus 2000

SALTZMANN Carl 1847-1923 [12]
$1 751 - €1 636 - £1 058 - FF10 732
**Meagima, Japan, beleuchteter Schrein an
Meereesküste** Öl/Leinwand (37x54cm 14x21in) Berlin
2000

SALUCCI Alessandro 1590-c.1660 [13]
$30 142 - €25 663 - £18 000 - FF168 337
**Rome, the Interior of the Basilica of Saint
Peter's** Oil/canvas (123x172.5cm 48x67in) London
1998
$26 000 - €27 767 - £17 716 - FF182 137
Elegant Figures in Architectural Landscapes
Oil/canvas (74.5x99cm 29x38in) New-York 2001

SALUCCI Giovanni 1769-1845 [1]
$4 228 - €4 934 - £2 943 - FF32 363
Vue de la ville de Genève et de ses environs
Radierung (36x51.5cm 14x20in) Bern 2000

SALVADO Jacinto 1892-1983 [26]
$789 - €732 - £481 - FF4 800
Nu féminin assis Huile/toile (100x73cm 39x28in)
Paris 1998

SALVADOR CARMONA Juan Antonio 1740-1805
[16]
$390 - €360 - £240 - FF2 364
Africa Aguafuerte (42x48cm 16x18in) Madrid 1999

SALVADOR CARMONA Manuel 1734-1820 [12]
$104 - €120 - £74 - FF788
Los Borrachos de Velázquez Grabado (42x58cm
16x22in) Madrid 2001

SALVADOR MAELLA Mariano 1739-1819 [6]
$10 370 - €10 211 - £6 460 - FF66 980
Grupo de ángeles Oleo/lienzo (32x54cm 12x21in)
Madrid 1999
$8 480 - €9 610 - £5 760 - FF63 040
Desnudo masculino, estudio académico
Sanguina (47x34cm 18x13in) Madrid 2000

SALVADOR Mário 1905 [3]
$585 - €648 - £390 - FF4 251
Barcos no Tejo Aquarelle/papier (25x32.5cm 9x12in)
Lisboa 2000

SALVADORI Aldo 1905 [5]
$1 500 - €1 555 - £900 - FF10 200
Composizione con fiori Olio/tela (16x19.5cm 6x7in)
Prato 1999

SALVADORI Loredana 1954 [5]
$2 400 - €2 073 - £1 200 - FF13 600
«Ricciolo d'oro molla di un pensiero» Tecnica
mista/tela (93.5x93.5cm 36x36in) Prato 1999

SALVETTI Antonio 1854-1931 [16]
$1 100 - €1 140 - £660 - FF7 480
Casolare a Montagnola Senese Olio/tela
(32x55.5cm 12x21in) Prato 1999
$380 - €492 - £285 - FF3 230
Nudo Olio/tela (34x27cm 13x10in) Prato 2001

SALVI IL SASSOFERRATO Giovanni Battista 1609-
1685 [69]
$21 600 - €21 860 - £10 800 - FF122 400
**L'angelo che incorona Santa Cecilia e San
Valeriano** Olio/tela (107x172cm 42x67in) Milano 1999
$23 695 - €25 435 - £15 855 - FF166 845
Madonna mit Kind Öl/Leinwand (48x37.5cm
18x14in) Wien 2000
$23 520 - €20 017 - £14 000 - FF131 304
The Madonna at Prayer Oil/canvas (44x33cm
17x12in) London 1998

SALVIATI Francesco 1510-1563 [23]
$16 000 - €14 034 - £9 755 - FF92 060
**Allegory of the Triumph of Venus, after
Bronzino** Ink (11.5x10cm 4x3in) New-York 1999

SALVIATI Giovanni 1881-1951 [10]
$1 600 - €1 659 - £960 - FF10 880
Canale a Venezia Acquarello/cartone (70x100cm
27x39in) Roma 2000

SALVO Salvatore Mangione 1947 [164]
$29 979 - €27 823 - £18 000 - FF182 505
Tramonto Oil/panel (130x93cm 51x36in) London
1999
$5 200 - €6 738 - £3 900 - FF44 200
Alba Olio/tavola (47x48.5cm 18x19in) Milano 2000
$2 080 - €2 695 - £1 560 - FF17 680
Automezzi in città Olio/cartone/tela (29x34cm
11x13in) Vercelli 2000

S

$2 100 - €2 177 - £1 260 - FF14 280
L'uomo che spacco' la statua del dio Marbre
(45x65cm 17x25in) Milano 2000

$220 - €285 - £165 - FF1 870
Minareto Inchiostro/carta (22x28cm 8x11in) Torino
2000

SALZER Friedrich 1827-1876 [5]
$3 133 - €3 068 - £1 928 - FF20 123
**Der Schinder, ein Bauer jagd mit seinem
Pferdewagen durch Landschaft** Öl/Leinwand
(29x47cm 11x18in) Stuttgart 1999

SALZMANN Auguste 1824-1872 [24]
$2 878 - €3 224 - £2 000 - FF21 148
Jerusalem, Porte d'Herode Photograph (23.5x33cm
9x12in) London 2001

SALZMANN Gottfried 1943 [56]
$876 - €1 017 - £616 - FF6 673
«Stadtansicht mit Kathedrale» Aquarell/Papier
(32x48cm 12x18in) Salzburg 2001

SALZMANN Louis Henry 1887-1955 [11]
$622 - €722 - £429 - FF4 738
La transporteuse de foin Huile/panneau (15x21cm
5x8in) Genève 2000

SAMACCHINI Orazio 1532-1577 [12]
$11 954 - €12 832 - £8 000 - FF84 172
**The Madonna and Child with St.Bartholomew,
St.Cecilia, and St.John** Ink (20.5x18cm 8x7in)
London 2000

SAMARAS Lucas 1936 [112]
$4 635 - €4 573 - £2 856 - FF30 000
The Spectator Acrylique/toile/panneau (91.5x61cm
36x24in) Versailles 1999
$3 273 - €3 354 - £2 037 - FF22 000
Tête d'homme barbu Pastel/papier (44x29cm
17x11in) Paris 2000
$3 800 - €3 172 - £2 258 - FF20 810
Untitled (Bedroom Interior) Polaroid (24x19cm
9x7in) New-York 1998

SAMBA Chéri 1956 [32]
$6 426 - €6 693 - £4 050 - FF43 902
L'heure de la démocratie en Afrique Huile/toile
(150x200cm 59x78in) Antwerpen 2000
$639 - €762 - £456 - FF5 000
Sans titre Acrylique/toile (50x60cm 19x23in) Paris
2000

SAMBERGER Leo 1861-1949 [44]
$1 823 - €1 789 - £1 130 - FF11 738
Nachtgedanken, Porträt Genevras von Eichtal
Öl/Leinwand (105x84cm 41x33in) München 1999
$855 - €1 022 - £587 - FF6 707
Bildnis einer alten Bäuerin Öl/Leinwand/Karton
(35.5x29.5cm 13x11in) München 2000

SAMBROOK Russell XX [10]
$4 250 - €4 954 - £2 942 - FF32 497
Boy Returning Hat to Gent on a Windy Day
Oil/canvas (69x58cm 27x23in) New-York 2000

SAMIVEL XX [8]
$1 010 - €1 119 - £700 - FF7 337
«Club Alpin Français» Poster (100x62cm 39x24in)
London 2001

SAMMANN Detleff 1857-1938 [2]
$13 000 - €12 653 - £7 987 - FF82 997
Waves Crashing Along the Carmel Coast
Oil/canvas (91x121cm 36x48in) San-Francisco CA 1999

SAMMONS Carl 1886-1968 [85]
$3 500 - €3 329 - £2 125 - FF21 836
Encelia and Chuperosa in Bloom Oil/canvas
(51x66cm 20x25in) Beverly-Hills CA 1999
$1 300 - €1 463 - £895 - FF9 597
Western Landscape Oil/canvas (28x39cm 11x15in)
New-Orleans LA 2000
$1 800 - €2 104 - £1 285 - FF13 799
Nocturnal winter mountain landscape
Pastel/paper (16x26cm 6x10in) Altadena CA 2001

SAMOKISH Nikolai Semenovich 1860-1944 [22]
$8 489 - €6 999 - £5 000 - FF45 913
The Encampment Oil/canvas (40x69cm 15x27in)
London 1998
$1 451 - €1 353 - £900 - FF8 872
The Ox Cart Watercolour/paper (135x210cm 53x82in)
Billingshurst, West-Sussex 1999

SAMORE Sam 1963 [8]
$4 614 - €5 099 - £3 200 - FF33 449
Situations Photograph (101.5x213.5cm 39x84in)
London 2001

SAMPAIO Fausto 1893-1956 [4]
$4 515 - €5 234 - £3 150 - FF34 335
Pôr-do-Sol Oleo/tabla (17x22.5cm 6x8in) Lisboa 2001

SAMPLE Paul Starrett 1896-1974 [61]
$40 000 - €45 776 - £27 512 - FF300 272
Mountain School Oil/canvas (50x60cm 20x24in)
New-York 2000
$8 000 - €8 587 - £5 353 - FF56 328
Vermont Landscape near Brownington
Acrylic/canvas (30.5x51cm 12x20in) San-Francisco CA
2000
$1 600 - €1 495 - £996 - FF9 805
Harbour Scene Watercolour/paper (34x55cm
13x22in) Mystic CT 1999

SAMSOM Hans 1939 [4]
$585 - €681 - £411 - FF4 464
«Time Zone» Photograph (43x29cm 16x11in)
Amsterdam 2001

SAMUELSON Stanley XX [2]
$1 900 - €2 070 - £1 315 - FF13 581
«Dartmouth Winter Carnival» Poster (86x55cm
34x22in) New-York 2001

SAMUELSON Ulrik 1935 [31]
$3 712 - €4 159 - £2 587 - FF27 284
Utan titel Oil/canvas (132x97cm 51x38in) Stockholm
2001
$4 784 - €4 498 - £2 964 - FF29 508
Utan titel Oil/canvas (62x78cm 24x30in) Stockholm
1999
$2 316 - €2 334 - £1 444 - FF15 308
Komposition mot svart Mixed media (39x39cm
15x15in) Stockholm 2000

SAN JOSÉ GONZALEZ Francisco 1919-1981 [131]
$2 565 - €2 853 - £1 710 - FF18 715
Totirria borracho Oleo/lienzo (73x50cm 28x19in)
Madrid 2000
$1 024 - €961 - £640 - FF6 304
«Montes en primavera» Oleo/lienzo (22x27cm
8x10in) Madrid 1999
$320 - €300 - £195 - FF1 970
Paisaje con poste Acuarela/papel (20x27cm 7x10in)
Madrid 1999

SAN PIETRO di Cagnaccio 1897-1946 [21]
$6 000 - €6 220 - £3 600 - FF40 800
Ritratto Olio/cartone (46x36cm 18x14in) Prato 1999

$5 250 - €5 442 - **£3 150** - FF35 700
Autoritratto Olio/tavola (34.5x24.5cm 13x9in) Prato 2000

$3 570 - €3 701 - **£2 142** - FF24 276
Natura morta Tempera/carta (27x23cm 10x9in) Venezia 1999

SAN SARAKORNBORIRAK 1934 [5]
$2 536 - €2 356 - **£1 567** - FF15 456
Flowers on the Garden Table Oil/canvas (80x59cm 31x23in) Bangkok 1999

SAN YU Chang Yu 1901-1966 [215]
$236 250 - €217 354 - **£141 750** - FF1 425 750
Marriage Bouquet Oil/canvas (73x50cm 28x19in) Taipei 1999

$23 112 - €25 237 - **£14 868** - FF165 546
Reclining Cat Oil/canvas (33.5x46cm 13x18in) Hong-Kong 2000

$2 826 - €2 744 - **£1 746** - FF18 000
Nue Encre/papier (43x26cm 16x10in) Paris 1999

SANBORN Percy 1849-1929 [5]
$20 000 - €22 300 - **£13 498** - FF146 278
Three-Masted Schooner in Full Sail, Flying the American Flag Oil/canvas (60x86cm 24x34in) York PA 2000

SANCHA LENGO Francisco 1874-1936 [7]
$781 - €661 - **£473** - FF4 334
Vendedoras Acuarela (22x30cm 8x11in) Madrid 1998

SANCHEZ BARBUDO Salvador 1857-1917 [83]
$26 400 - €24 026 - **£16 000** - FF157 600
El Dux embarcando en el Bucentauro Oleo/tabla (32x102cm 12x40in) Madrid 1999

$5 804 - €6 536 - **£4 000** - FF42 875
A Gentleman's Debate Oil/panel (36x21cm 14x8in) London 2000

$1 170 - €1 351 - **£810** - FF8 865
Vista de Roma Acuarela (10.5x15cm 4x5in) Madrid 2000

SANCHEZ COELLO Alonso c.1531-c.1590 [5]
$70 038 - €68 846 - **£45 000** - FF451 602
Anne of Austria (1549-1580), fourth Wife of Philip II of Spain Oil/canvas (191x105cm 75x41in) London 1999

SANCHEZ Edgar 1940 [20]
$11 000 - €11 807 - **£7 361** - FF77 451
El personaje de Venecia Acrylic/canvas (120x120cm 47x47in) New-York 2000

$608 - €658 - **£380** - FF3 724
Rostro Crayon (51x41cm 20x16in) Caracas 1999

SANCHEZ José Luis 1926 [29]
$250 - €295 - **£181** - FF1 935
«Cube compression» Bronze (H12cm H4in) Zofingen 2001

SANCHEZ LAREO Miguel A. 1969 [11]
$558 - €541 - **£342** - FF3 546
Barcas en el puerto Acuarela/papel (68x98.5cm 26x38in) Madrid 1999

SANCHEZ MORALES Manuel Luis 1853-1922 [3]
$2 559 - €2 883 - **£1 800** - FF18 912
The Courtyard Garden Watercolour/paper (65x36cm 25x14in) Cambridge 2001

SANCHEZ PERRIER Emilio 1855-1907 [82]
$15 750 - €13 515 - **£9 450** - FF88 650
Paisaje de Alcalá de Guadaira Oleo/lienzo (48x65cm 18x25in) Madrid 1999

$13 000 - €14 223 - **£8 990** - FF93 298
Mediterranean Garden Scene Oil/panel (35x25cm 14x10in) Morris-Plains NJ 2001

$450 - €450 - **£277** - FF2 955
Paisaje con río y presa Lápiz/papel (22x31cm 8x12in) Madrid 2000

SANCHEZ REQUEIRO Tomas 1948 [119]
$140 000 - €164 839 - **£98 378** - FF1 081 276
Reflejos nocturnos Acrylic/canvas (120.5x152.5cm 47x60in) New-York 2000

$60 000 - €51 806 - **£36 600** - FF339 828
La Noche Clara Oil/canvas (79x98.5cm 31x38in) Miami FL 1999

$24 000 - €27 847 - **£16 569** - FF182 664
Bosque Oil/canvas (32.5x47cm 12x18in) New-York 2000

$22 000 - €25 526 - **£15 188** - FF167 442
Nacimiento de una isla Tempera/paper (75.5x55cm 29x21in) New-York 2000

SANCHEZ SOLA Eduardo 1869-1949 [21]
$896 - €961 - **£592** - FF6 304
Valenciana Oleo/lienzo (45x30cm 17x11in) Madrid 2000

SANCHEZ SOLA Emilio 1875-1925 [5]
$4 518 - €4 339 - **£2 800** - FF28 461
Courting in the Garden Oil/canvas (90x122cm 35x48in) London 1999

SANCHEZ Trino 1968 [19]
$13 000 - €12 518 - **£8 091** - FF82 111
«Templos para habitar» Oil/canvas (149.5x120cm 58x47in) New-York 1999

SANCHO GONZALEZ José 1924 [7]
$3 510 - €3 904 - **£2 275** - FF25 610
Membrillos Oleo/lienzo (60x88cm 23x34in) Madrid 2000

$1 575 - €1 502 - **£950** - FF9 850
Bodegón con cerezas Oleo/lienzo (24x33cm 9x12in) Madrid 1999

SANCTIS de Giuseppe 1858-1924 [18]
$15 000 - €15 550 - **£9 000** - FF102 000
Ponte Alessandro III a Parigi Olio/tela (70x115cm 27x45in) Milano 1999

$1 559 - €1 414 - **£950** - FF9 277
«A Country Girl» Oil/canvas (39x26cm 15x10in) Penzance, Cornwall 1998

SAND George 1804-1876 [18]
$3 502 - €3 201 - **£2 144** - FF21 000
Paysage des îles Baléares Aquarelle, gouache/papier (15x23cm 5x9in) Calais 1999

SAND Lennart 1946 [47]
$791 - €719 - **£490** - FF4 719
Domherrar Oil/canvas (53x71cm 20x27in) Stockholm 1999

SAND Vebjörn 1966 [4]
$154 - €173 - **£107** - FF1 136
Brevet Serigraph in colors (60x40cm 23x15in) Oslo 2001

SANDALINAS Joan 1903-1991 [66]
$1 540 - €1 652 - **£1 045** - FF10 835
El dandy Oleo/tablex (46x37cm 18x14in) Madrid 2000

$840 - €901 - **£555** - FF5 950
Tranvía Oleo/tablex (39.5x25.5cm 15x10in) Madrid 2000

$230 - €216 - **£140** - FF1 418
Desnudo Acuarela (14x10.5cm 5x4in) Madrid 1999

S

SANDBACK Fred, Frederick Lane 1943 **[54]**

◿ **$1 023** - €1 022 - **£640** - FF6 707
Ohne Titel Pastell (57x76.2cm 22x29in) Hamburg 1999

▥ **$404** - €460 - **£280** - FF3 018
Ohne Titel Lithographie (21.5x28cm 8x11in) Hamburg 2000

SANDBERG Einar 1876-1947 **[6]**

◿ **$478** - €536 - **£332** - FF3 514
Flod Oil/canvas (64x70cm 25x27in) Viby J, Århus 2001

SANDBERG Johan Gustav 1782-1854 **[21]**

◿ **$2 208** - €2 381 - **£1 482** - FF15 618
Kronprins Oscar Oil/canvas (71x59cm 27x23in) Stockholm 2000

◿ **$1 866** - €2 072 - **£1 249** - FF13 594
Gustaf II Adolf Oil/canvas (36x29.5cm 14x11in) Stockholm 2000

SANDBERG Ragnar 1902-1972 **[357]**

◿ **$17 904** - €19 650 - **£11 536** - FF128 896
Badande Oil/canvas (63x85cm 24x33in) Stockholm 2000

◿ **$4 626** - €3 912 - **£2 764** - FF25 660
«Sommarutflykt» Oil/canvas (29x41cm 11x16in) Stockholm 1998

◿ **$860** - €725 - **£510** - FF4 758
Figurer i park Pastel/paper (23x29cm 9x11in) Stockholm 1998

SANDBERG Willem J.H.B. 1897-1984 **[11]**

▥ **$239** - €272 - **£166** - FF1 786
«Goed maar mooi» Poster (63.5x100cm 25x39in) Hoorn 2001

SANDBY Paul 1725-1809 **[211]**

◿ **$4 489** - €5 339 - **£3 200** - FF35 024
Landscape with Anglers Oil/panel (28x17cm 11x6in) London 2000

◿ **$4 300** - €3 749 - **£2 600** - FF24 595
The Garden front of Old Somerset House, London Watercolour (30.5x35.5cm 12x13in) London 1998

▥ **$413** - €431 - **£260** - FF2 826
Manerbawr Castle in Pembrokeshire Aquatint (23.5x31cm 9x12in) London 2000

SANDBY Thomas c.1730-1809 **[4]**

◿ **$4 300** - €3 749 - **£2 600** - FF24 595
The Garden front of Old Somerset House, London Watercolour (30.5x35.5cm 12x13in) London 1998

SANDELS Gösta 1887-1919 **[67]**

◿ **$57 600** - €55 928 - **£35 568** - FF366 864
På stranden Oil/canvas (125.5x115.5cm 49x45in) Stockholm 1999

◿ **$9 766** - €8 258 - **£5 836** - FF54 172
«Gosse med segelbåt» Oil/canvas (91x66cm 35x25in) Stockholm 1998

◿ **$2 737** - €2 567 - **£1 692** - FF16 838
Badande ynglingar Oil/canvas (41x33cm 16x12in) Stockholm 1999

◿ **$248** - €245 - **£152** - FF1 606
Komposition med figur Indian ink/paper (19x18cm 7x7in) Stockholm 1999

SANDER August 1876-1964 **[258]**

▣ **$1 227** - €1 431 - **£854** - FF9 390
Siebengebirge Vintage gelatin silver print (17x23.2cm 6x9in) Köln 2000

SANDER Sherry 1941 **[3]**

◿ **$2 600** - €2 952 - **£1 806** - FF19 365
Two Deer Bronze (H41cm H16in) Dallas TX 2001

SANDER Theodor 1858-1935 **[1]**

◿ **$4 534** - €3 885 - **£2 726** - FF25 485
Mondabend an der Förde Öl/Leinwand (47x62cm 18x24in) Hamburg 1998

SANDERS Christopher 1905-1991 **[36]**

◿ **$593** - €598 - **£370** - FF3 923
Landscape of Spanish Hillside with tree Oil/canvas (58x68cm 23x27in) Leominster, Herefordshire 2000

SANDERS David 1933 **[3]**

◿ **$10 000** - €11 355 - **£6 948** - FF74 481
Riders in Yosemite Pastel/paper (60x91cm 24x36in) Dallas TX 2001

SANDERS Gerard 1702/07-1767 **[3]**

◿ **$7 078** - €6 807 - **£4 360** - FF44 649
Mother with a Children, Personifying an Allegory of Charity Oil/canvas (115x74cm 45x29in) Amsterdam 1999

SANDERSON Charles Wesley 1838-1905 **[4]**

◿ **$5 000** - €4 662 - **£3 101** - FF30 582
The young Shepherd Oil/canvas (69x100.5cm 27x39in) New-York 1999

SANDERSON Robert act.1865-1905 **[17]**

◿ **$911** - €849 - **£550** - FF5 571
«The Sportsman» Oil/canvas (25x20cm 9x7in) Glasgow 1998

SANDFORD Caroline XIX **[7]**

◿ **$191** - €185 - **£120** - FF1 213
Portrait of a Girl with Flower in her Hair Watercolour/paper (31x23cm 12x9in) Bristol, Avon 1999

SANDHAM Henry John 1842-1910/12 **[32]**

◿ **$980** - €1 078 - **£678** - FF7 069
Waterbabies Gouache/papier (27x92cm 10x36in) Montréal 2001

SANDLE Michael 1936 **[25]**

◿ **$280** - €243 - **£169** - FF1 597
Burning Memoirs in stony Landscape II Ink (66x103cm 25x40in) London 1999

SANDOR Mathias 1857-1920 **[3]**

◿ **$1 500** - €1 733 - **£1 050** - FF11 367
Old Convent near Mexico City, Mexico Oil/board (25.5x35.5cm 10x13in) Bethesda MD 2001

SANDORFI Istvan 1948 **[66]**

◿ **$7 078** - €5 946 - **£4 161** - FF39 000
Autoportrait martyr, version solitaire Huile/toile (146x97cm 57x38in) Douai 1998

SANDOVAL Andrés XIX **[2]**

◿ **$1 372** - €1 351 - **£877** - FF8 865
Paisajes Oleo/tabla (32x18cm 12x7in) Madrid 1999

SANDOZ Adolf Karol 1845/48-? **[3]**

◿ **$4 487** - €4 116 - **£2 789** - FF27 000
Jeunes femmes dans un hammam Huile/toile (33x41cm 12x16in) Paris 1999

SANDOZ Claude 1946 **[27]**

◿ **$816** - €686 - **£479** - FF4 497
«Tanzen» Aquarelle/papier (46.5x65cm 18x25in) Bern 1998

SANDOZ Édouard Marcel 1881-1971 **[305]**

◿ **$709** - €772 - **£467** - FF5 064
Herbstblätter Öl/Leinwand (58x58cm 22x22in) Bern 2000

◿ **$3 132** - €3 506 - **£2 125** - FF23 000
Raie bouclée Bronze (16.7x13cm 6x5in) Paris 2000

$784 - €838 - **£533** - FF5 500
J'ai rêvé, un éléphant ailé Mine plomb (20x15cm 7x5in) Pontoise 2001

SANDOZ-ROLLIN de David Alphonse 1740-1809 [6]
$2 200 - €2 086 - **£1 338** - FF13 681
View of the Bridge at Toledo Black chalk (18x21.5cm 7x8in) New-York 1999

SANDRART von Joachim I 1606-1688 [17]
$10 762 - €9 196 - **£6 321** - FF60 321
Apostelkopf Öl/Kupfer (40.5x30cm 15x11in) Stuttgart 1998

SANDRART von Johann Jacob 1655-1698 [7]
$5 352 - €4 575 - **£3 200** - FF29 684
Designs for Engravings to Illustrate the 1698 Nuremberg Edition Ink (15.5x19.5cm 6x7in) London 1998

SANDRECZKI Otto XX [1]
$1 300 - €1 250 - **£802** - FF8 200
«The Science Museum» Poster (101x63.5cm 39x25in) New-York 1999

SANDROCK Leonhard 1867-1945 [29]
$2 044 - €2 301 - **£1 408** - FF15 092
Schauerleute, Hamburger Barkasse Hoffnung mit Schauerleuten Öl/Karton (50.5x60.5cm 19x23in) Bremen 2000
$1 619 - €1 738 - **£1 083** - FF11 403
Hamburg, St.Katharinenkirche Öl/Leinwand (33x26cm 12x10in) Hamburg 2000

SANDS Frederick 1916 [40]
$2 281 - €2 076 - **£1 400** - FF13 617
Plemont, Jersey Oil/board (49x64cm 19x25in) Channel-Islands 1999
$680 - €794 - **£480** - FF5 206
Boats and Moornings at Rozel Watercolour/paper (34.5x43cm 13x16in) Channel-Islands 2000

SANDSTRÖM Anders 1933 [13]
$982 - €1 153 - **£693** - FF7 561
Guding Bronze (H13cm H5in) Stockholm 2000

SANDY-HOOK Georges Taboureau 1879-1960 [125]
$2 669 - €2 592 - **£1 649** - FF17 000
Paquebot sur une mer formée, mouettes au premier plan Aquarelle, gouache/papier (40x57cm 15x22in) Paris 1999
$709 - €785 - **£480** - FF5 150
«La Corse» Poster (99x62cm 38x24in) London 2000

SANDYS Emma 1834-1877 [9]
$23 478 - €25 247 - **£16 000** - FF165 612
Untitled Oil/panel (33x27.5cm 12x10in) Newcastle-upon-Tyne 2001
$1 471 - €1 417 - **£920** - FF9 293
Portrait of Marguerite Ince aged six Coloured chalks/paper (29x25cm 11x9in) Billingshurst, West-Sussex 1999

SANDYS Frederick 1829-1904 [29]
$774 - €744 - **£480** - FF4 879
The West Doorway, Cawston Church, Norfolk Watercolour (28x22cm 11x8in) London 1999

SANDYS-LUMSDAINE Leesa 1936 [11]
$1 000 - €990 - **£622** - FF6 495
Nijnsky montado por Lester Pigeot Oleo/lienzo (92x100cm 36x39in) Buenos-Aires 1999

SANDZÉN Sven Birger 1871-1954 [99]
$25 000 - €26 835 - **£16 730** - FF176 025
Moorise in the Mountains, scene from Colorado Oil/canvas (40x60cm 16x24in) Altadena CA 2000

$3 500 - €2 953 - **£2 053** - FF19 369
Rocky Coastline Oil/canvas/board (25.5x35.5cm 10x13in) New-York 1998
$500 - €446 - **£306** - FF2 928
«Sunshine Creek» Woodcut (30x44cm 12x17in) Altadena CA 1999

SANESI Nicola 1818-1889 [3]
$15 329 - €14 721 - **£9 500** - FF96 564
The Seven Acts of Mercy Oil/canvas (107x146cm 42x57in) London 1999

SAÑEZ RECUART Antonio XVIII [22]
$102 - €120 - **£74** - FF788
Arte de pesca Grabado (26x20cm 10x7in) Madrid 2001

SANFILIPPO Antonio 1923-1980 [32]
$2 750 - €2 851 - **£1 650** - FF18 700
Senza titolo Olio/tela (60x80cm 23x31in) Roma 1999
$6 500 - €6 738 - **£3 900** - FF44 200
Paesaggio Olio/tela (40x30cm 15x11in) Prato 1999

SANGALLO da Antonio II 1484-1546 [5]
$19 648 - €18 221 - **£12 000** - FF119 522
Design for the Tomb of Pope Clement VII Ink (40x19cm 15x7in) London 1998

SANGALLO da Francesco 1494-1576 [1]
$32 500 - €33 691 - **£19 500** - FF221 000
Cristo Crocifisso Sculpture bois (45x43cm 17x16in) Firenze 2001

SANGBERG Monica XX [3]
$1 699 - €1 487 - **£1 029** - FF9 755
Mädchen mit grossem Fisch Acryl/Leinwand (27x24cm 10x9in) Zofingen 1998

SANGSTER Alfred XIX-XX [4]
$1 246 - €1 337 - **£850** - FF8 771
Portrait of a Young Female Oil/canvas (61x51cm 24x20in) London 2001

SANI Alessandro XIX-XX [54]
$7 596 - €8 088 - **£5 000** - FF53 053
The Abbe knows Oil/canvas (50x61.5cm 19x24in) Billingshurst, West-Sussex 2000
$12 000 - €12 092 - **£7 480** - FF79 320
The Proposal Oil/canvas (44x33cm 17x13in) San Rafael CA 2000

SANI David XIX-XX [17]
$4 062 - €4 575 - **£2 800** - FF30 012
Feeding Time Oil/canvas (85x60cm 33x23in) London 2000

SANKEY S.H. XIX [3]
$170 - €194 - **£118** - FF1 275
Churchyard, winter Watercolour (18x28cm 7x11in) Philadelphia PA 2000

SANNES Sanne 1937-1967 [10]
$610 - €726 - **£435** - FF4 762
Girl with Ferns Silver print (20x25cm 7x9in) Amsterdam 2000

SANQUIRICO Alessandro 1777-1849 [18]
$900 - €1 046 - **£632** - FF6 862
The grande Sala di Ballo of the Doge's Palace with Desdemona Ink (29x38.5cm 11x15in) New-York 2001

SANQUIRICO Pio 1847-1900 [5]
$18 000 - €23 325 - **£13 500** - FF153 000
La guardianella delle oche Olio/tela (150x100cm 59x39in) Roma 2000

S

S4 106 - €3 547 - **£2 053** - FF23 269
Lago di Lecco Olio/tela (75x60cm 29x23in) Milano 1999

SANSOVINO Andrea del Monte c.1460/67-1529 **[1]**
$60 000 - €62 199 - **£36 000** - FF408 000
Madonna col Bambino tra i Santi Girolamo e Giovanni Battista Bas-relief (27x33.5x4cm 10x13x1in) Firenze 2001

SANT James 1820-1916 **[64]**
$35 505 - €34 271 - **£22 000** - FF224 800
Misses Wilson of Tranby Croft, full-lengths Oil/canvas (185.5x112cm 73x44in) London 1999
$4 950 - €5 364 - **£3 300** - FF35 187
On the Steeping Stones Oil/canvas (128x78.5cm 50x30in) Billingshurst, West-Sussex 2000
$566 - €609 - **£390** - FF3 996
Bust Portrait of a Girl Wearing White Bonnet Oil/panel (28x22cm 11x9in) Leominster, Herefordshire 2001

SANT van Hans XVII **[1]**
$28 044 - €26 162 - **£16 920** - FF171 612
Stilleben von Weintrauben, Äpfeln, Käse und einem Glas Bier Oil/panel (46x84cm 18x33in) Wien 1999

SANT-ACKER F. XVII **[1]**
$28 764 - €27 227 - **£17 886** - FF178 596
Still Life with a Nautilus Cup, a Flute, a Roemer, a Silver Beaker Oil/canvas (82.5x67.5cm 32x26in) Amsterdam 1999

SANTA MARIA de Andrés 1860-1945 **[3]**
$22 000 - €21 405 - **£13 541** - FF140 410
La Lectura Oil/canvas (76x61cm 29x24in) New-York 1999

SANTA MARIA SEDANO Marceliano 1866-1952 **[32]**
$8 960 - €9 610 - **£5 920** - FF63 040
Horno de Pez Oleo/lienzo (44.5x54cm 17x21in) Madrid 2000
$1 400 - €1 502 - **£950** - FF9 850
Paisaje Oleo/tabla (14x23cm 5x9in) Madrid 2001

SANTA-RITA de Guilherme «Pintor» 1889-1918 **[1]**
$36 000 - €39 881 - **£23 200** - FF261 600
Camponesa Oleo/lienzo (72.5x57.5cm 28x22in) Lisboa 2000

SANTACROCE da Girolamo Galizzi 1480/85-1556 **[13]**
$45 186 - €42 298 - **£28 000** - FF277 454
The Last Judgement Oil/panel (90.5x120.5cm 35x47in) London 1999

SANTASUSAGNA Ernest 1900-1964 **[16]**
$1 540 - €1 652 - **£1 045** - FF10 835
Gitanas Oleo/lienzo (65x50cm 25x19in) Barcelona 2001

SANTERRE Jean-Baptiste 1651-1717 **[16]**
$2 390 - €2 566 - **£1 600** - FF16 834
Sleeping Girl, Half-Length, Wearing a Blue Velvet Bodice Oil/canvas (82x66.5cm 32x26in) London 2000

SANTHO von Imre 1900-1945 **[21]**
$591 - €512 - **£358** - FF3 356
Die neue Linie Photograph (28.3x22.5cm 11x8in) München 1998

SANTIAGO de Carlos **[8]**
$3 600 - €3 743 - **£2 273** - FF24 555
Viejo puente sobre el Río Mapocho, Chile Oleo/lienzo (91x101cm 35x39in) Montevideo 2000

SANTIAGO de Santiago 1925 **[8]**
$653 - €686 - **£432** - FF4 500
Tête de femme Marble (H46cm H18in) Paris 2000

SANTINI Pio 1908-1986 **[18]**
$1 018 - €991 - **£626** - FF6 500
Nu à la natte Huile/toile (73x60cm 28x23in) Neuilly-sur-Seine 1999

SANTOLONI Felice XVIII-XIX **[4]**
$3 810 - €4 090 - **£2 550** - FF26 831
Plutone/Medea nach Giulio Romana (1499-1546) Gouache/paper (37x50cm 14x19in) Bremen 2000

SANTOMASO Giuseppe 1907-1990 **[409]**
$37 260 - €32 188 - **£24 840** - FF211 140
«Basti in Bleu» Olio/tela (162x130cm 63x51in) Milano 1998
$10 000 - €10 367 - **£6 000** - FF68 000
Enigma Tecnica mista/tela (81x64.5cm 31x25in) Milano 2000
$2 618 - €2 888 - **£1 731** - FF18 947
Segno primario Technique mixte (45x33cm 17x12in) St. Gallen 2000
$1 920 - €2 488 - **£1 440** - FF16 320
Paesaggio Tecnica mista/carta (33x43cm 12x16in) Firenze 2000
$271 - €235 - **£165** - FF1 543
Nuvole nere Farblithographie (64x50.5cm 25x19in) München 1998

SANTORO Francesco Raffaello 1844-1927 **[23]**
$3 709 - €3 630 - **£2 378** - FF23 812
The Ponte Vecchio, Florence Oil/canvas (31x62cm 12x23in) Amsterdam 1999
$3 000 - €2 597 - **£1 809** - FF17 035
View of the Port of Anzio Oil/canvas/board (32x47cm 12x18in) San-Francisco CA 1998
$337 - €393 - **£233** - FF2 577
Landschaft mit Wiese und Bäumen unter wolkigem Himmel Watercolour (47x66cm 18x25in) Bern 1999

SANTORO Rubens 1859-1942 **[117]**
$54 811 - €64 419 - **£38 000** - FF422 560
Canal dei Greci Oil/canvas (51x37.5cm 20x14in) London 2000
$16 992 - €14 679 - **£8 496** - FF96 286
Gita in laguna Olio/tela/cartone (17x25cm 6x9in) Milano 1999
$13 448 - €14 436 - **£9 000** - FF94 694
The Gateway Watercolour/paper (25x17cm 9x6in) London 2000

SANTOSH Gulam Rasool 1929-1998 **[10]**
$2 388 - €2 312 - **£1 500** - FF15 168
Time beyond Oil/canvas (79x105cm 31x41in) London 1999

SANTRY Terence John 1910-1990 **[97]**
$783 - €736 - **£472** - FF4 825
View of Hobart, the old Gas Works Oil/board (53x59cm 20x23in) Sydney 1999
$708 - €666 - **£445** - FF4 366
The Circus Oil/board (29.5x29.5cm 11x11in) Sydney 1999
$298 - €312 - **£188** - FF2 044
Reclining Nude Pencil/paper (43x57cm 16x22in) Sydney 2000

SANUTO Giulio XVI **[4]**
$932 - €1 022 - **£633** - FF6 707
Das Martyrium des hl.Laurentius, nach Baccio Bandinelli Kupferstich (42.3x56.4cm 16x22in) Berlin 2000

SANVISENS MERFULL Ramón 1917-1987 **[80]**
$2 484 - €2 763 - £1 656 - FF18 124
Bodegón Oleo/lienzo (65x81cm 25x31in) Barcelona 2000
$1 600 - €1 502 - £975 - FF9 850
Autorretrato con gorra azul Oleo/lienzo (36x27cm 14x10in) Barcelona 1999
$301 - €348 - £208 - FF2 285
Desnudo Pastel (43x33cm 16x12in) Barcelona 2000

SANZ BARRERA Javier 1949 **[17]**
$450 - €450 - £277 - FF2 955
Campo de amapolas Acuarela/papel (55x72cm 21x28in) Madrid 2000

SANZ Demetrio XX **[13]**
$504 - €541 - £315 - FF3 546
Toros pastando Carbón/papel (49x67cm 19x26in) Madrid 2000

SANZ Y ARIZMENDE José 1885-1929 **[3]**
$6 315 - €6 618 - £4 000 - FF43 411
Eating Supper Oil/canvas (100x80cm 39x31in) London 2000

SAOLI Winston 1950-1995 **[53]**
$107 - €120 - £70 - FF788
Seated Man Cluthing a Book Charcoal/paper (59.5x49.5cm 23x19in) Johannesburg 2000

SAORIN BOX Pedro Antonio 1944 **[5]**
$1 716 - €1 562 - £1 040 - FF10 244
Mujer sentada Bronze (65x35x42cm 25x13x16in) Madrid 1999

SAOVAPA VICHIENKET 1932 **[3]**
$1 402 - €1 508 - £940 - FF9 894
Seated Woman Bronze (32x23x48cm 12x9x18in) Bangkok 2000

SAPIR Ira XX **[1]**
$8 000 - €7 636 - £4 999 - FF50 092
Ellirse Sculpture, glass (21x75.5x61cm 8x29x24in) New-York 1999

SAPORETTI Edgardo 1865-1909 **[10]**
$500 - €518 - £300 - FF3 400
Nudino Olio/cartone (24.5x36cm 9x14in) Prato 1999

SAPP Allen 1920 **[116]**
$1 474 - €1 626 - £974 - FF10 666
My Father's Old Place at Red Pheasant Reserve Acrylic/canvas (61x91.5cm 24x36in) Vancouver, BC. 2000
$737 - €813 - £487 - FF5 333
Taking a Break Acrylic/canvas (30.5x40.5cm 12x15in) Vancouver, BC. 2000

SAPUNOV Nikolai Nikolaievich 1880-1912 **[3]**
$3 246 - €3 120 - £2 000 - FF20 466
Stage Design Oil/canvas (57x77cm 22x30in) London 1999

SARACENI Carlo 1579-1620 **[8]**
$42 000 - €36 283 - £21 000 - FF238 000
Venere al bagno Olio/tela (131x110cm 51x43in) Roma 1999
$326 160 - €365 878 - £226 080 - FF2 400 000
Le déluge universel Huile/toile (115x96cm 45x37in) Paris 2000

SARAPATA Joanna 1962 **[2]**
$1 253 - €1 474 - £901 - FF9 667
Nue Encre (35.5x25cm 13x9in) Warszawa 2001

SARAZIN DE BELMONT Louise Joséphine 1790-1870 **[35]**
$8 497 - €8 385 - £5 280 - FF55 000
Vue du château de Pierrefonds Huile/toile (71x107cm 27x42in) Paris 1999
$6 177 - €7 260 - £4 283 - FF47 625
Panoramic View of Rome Oil/canvas (32.5x41cm 12x16in) Amsterdam 2000

SARDESAI N.R. XX **[3]**
$5 788 - €5 414 - £3 500 - FF35 516
Contemplation/Lady with a Water Jar/Lady Sewing Pencil (44.5x35.5cm 17x13in) London 1999

SARDI Jean 1947 **[120]**
$2 244 - €2 150 - £1 386 - FF14 100
Côte varoise Huile/toile (60x73cm 23x28in) Valence 1999
$691 - €777 - £475 - FF5 100
Le bastidon Huile/toile (35x27cm 13x10in) Albi 2000

SÄRESTÖNIEMI Reidar 1925-1981 **[71]**
$20 619 - €19 341 - £12 742 - FF126 868
Vår på tundran Oil/canvas (130x130cm 51x51in) Helsinki 2000
$3 087 - €2 693 - £1 867 - FF17 665
Fjällandskap Oil/canvas (50x61cm 19x24in) Stockholm 1998
$1 703 - €1 598 - £1 052 - FF10 480
Getpors Pastel/paper (49x63cm 19x24in) Helsinki 1999
$243 - €269 - £168 - FF1 765
Trädbarkare Woodcut (47x38cm 18x14in) Helsinki 2001

SARG Tony 1882-1942 **[14]**
$1 165 - €1 251 - £780 - FF8 206
View of an Entrance to a London Park with Motor Watercolour, gouache (52x56cm 20x22in) West-Sussex 2000
$680 - €635 - £419 - FF4 167
«By the Underground: at the Proms» Poster (64x102cm 25x40in) Oostwood 1999

SARGENT John Singer 1856-1925 **[188]**
$250 000 - €291 772 - £177 225 - FF1 913 900
Portrait of Mrs.Harry Vane Milbank Oil/canvas (188.5x91cm 74x35in) New-York 2001
$170 000 - €188 269 - £115 294 - FF1 234 965
Olive Trees, Corfu Oil/canvas (51.5x61.5cm 20x24in) New-York 2000
$463 150 - €449 725 - £286 150 - FF2 950 000
Edouard Pailleron Junior Huile/panneau (34.5x26.5cm 13x10in) Paris 1999
$6 000 - €6 585 - £3 863 - FF43 192
Study for Israel and The Law Bronze (H16.5cm H6in) Beverly-Hills CA 2000
$44 829 - €48 120 - £30 000 - FF315 648
Loch Moidart, Invernesshire Watercolour (25x34.5cm 9x13in) London 2000

SARGENT Paul Turner 1880-1946 **[29]**
$1 500 - €1 673 - £981 - FF10 977
River Landscape Oil/board (38x50cm 15x20in) Chicago IL 2000
$600 - €682 - £416 - FF4 476
Midwestern Landscape Oil/board (35x43cm 14x17in) Cincinnati OH 2000

SARGENT Walter 1868-1927 **[6]**
$3 500 - €3 270 - £2 180 - FF21 450
Autumn Colors Oil/canvas (76x81cm 30x32in) Mystic CT 1999

SARIAN Martiros Sergeevich 1880-1972 **[12]**
- $8 835 - €9 907 - **£6 000** - FF64 984
  Armenian Landscape in Summer Oil/canvas
  (58x69cm 22x27in) London 2001
- $8 099 - €9 082 - **£5 500** - FF59 573
  Donkeys returning from the Fields Gouache
  (22.5x30.5cm 8x12in) London 2000

SARKISIAN Sarkis 1909-1977 **[54]**
- $2 100 - €2 470 - **£1 505** - FF16 199
  Young woman in orange blouse Oil/canvas
  (83x91cm 33x36in) Detroit MI 2001
- $1 200 - €1 411 - **£860** - FF9 256
  Apple on a red background Oil/masonite (28x23cm
  11x9in) Detroit MI 2001

SARLUIS Léonard 1874-1949 **[41]**
- $1 762 - €1 677 - **£1 095** - FF11 000
  Portrait de femme à la coiffe Huile/toile
  (92.5x65cm 36x25in) Paris 1999
- $2 495 - €2 113 - **£1 500** - FF13 863
  La création du Monde Coloured crayons (35x29cm
  13x11in) London 1998

SARMENTO Juliao 1948 **[25]**
- $2 232 - €2 287 - **£1 389** - FF15 000
  **Les voyeuses - Femmes de chambre remettant
  son bas** Huile/toile (97x130cm 38x51in) Paris 2000
- $13 980 - €11 672 - **£8 200** - FF76 564
  «Febre» Mixed media/canvas (115x90cm 45x35in)
  London 1998
- $5 000 - €4 838 - **£3 083** - FF31 734
  Holding and missing Graphite (36x36cm 14x14in)
  New-York 1999

SARNARI Franco 1933 **[25]**
- $2 600 - €2 695 - **£1 560** - FF17 680
  Natura morta con bicchiere Olio/tela (46x52cm
  18x20in) Roma 2000

SARONI Sergio 1935-1991 **[11]**
- $7 500 - €7 775 - **£4 500** - FF51 000
  Figura con i fiori Olio/tela (160x130cm 62x51in)
  Torino 2000
- $6 400 - €8 293 - **£4 800** - FF54 400
  «Imbalsamazione» Olio/tela (100x70cm 39x27in)
  Torino 2000

SARONY Napoléon 1821-1896 **[9]**
- $80 - €95 - **£55** - FF624
  Portrait of Ellen Terry Albumen print (30x18cm
  12x7in) Baltimore MD 2000

SARPANEVA Timo 1926 **[43]**
- $630 - €673 - **£428** - FF4 412
  Jättegryta Sculpture, glass (H29.5cm H11in) Helsinki
  2001

SARRA Valentino XX **[1]**
- $3 000 - €2 797 - **£1 810** - FF18 349
  Radiator Detail of the 1937 Nash Automobile
  Photograph (26.5x34cm 10x13in) New-York 1999

SARRAZIN Jean-Baptiste XVIII-XIX **[4]**
- $5 559 - €6 555 - **£3 908** - FF43 000
  Paysage aux lavandières Huile/toile (59.5x72.5cm
  23x28in) Paris 2000

SARRI Egisto 1837-1901 **[8]**
- $6 154 - €6 022 - **£3 938** - FF39 500
  Jeux d'enfants Huile/toile (52x62cm 20x24in)
  Bayeux 1999

SARRI Sergio 1938 **[51]**
- $300 - €311 - **£180** - FF2 040
  «La sonda» Acrilico/tela (100x90cm 39x35in) Vercelli
  2001

SARRUT Paul 1882-1969 **[97]**
- $378 - €320 - **£225** - FF2 100
  Monsieur Daguerre Huile/panneau (40x30.5cm
  15x12in) Châtellerault 1998
- $324 - €274 - **£193** - FF1 800
  Arlette Sarrut, nature morte Pastel/papier
  (48.5x63cm 19x24in) Châtellerault 1998

SARSANEDAS Benet 1942 **[33]**
- $832 - €781 - **£507** - FF5 122
  Fes Oleo/lienzo (60x73cm 23x28in) Barcelona 1999

SARTELLI Germano 1925 **[4]**
- $1 400 - €1 451 - **£840** - FF9 520
  Senza titolo Collage (44x33cm 17x12in) Prato 2000

SARTHOU Maurice Élie 1911-2000 **[56]**
- $743 - €671 - **£458** - FF4 400
  Les récifs noirs Huile/toile (80x80cm 31x31in) Arles
  1999

SARTO del Andrea d'Agnolo 1486-1530 **[8]**
- $1 000 000 - €1 011 636 - **£610 600** - FF6 635 900
  The Madonna and Child Oil/panel (85x62cm
  33x24in) New-York 2000
- $2 197 - €2 139 - **£1 350** - FF14 028
  The Holy Family Watercolour/paper (35x27cm
  14x11in) Little-Lane, Ilkley 1999

SARTO Pietro 1930 **[23]**
- $141 - €136 - **£87** - FF893
  Le Rhône au Bois de Finges Eau-forte, aquatinte
  (43.7x31.3cm 17x12in) Bern 1999

SARTONI Giulia 1850-1946 **[5]**
- $1 920 - €1 659 - **£960** - FF10 880
  Ritratto di signore Olio/tela (74x61cm 29x24in)
  Prato 1999
- $1 980 - €1 710 - **£990** - FF11 220
  Madre con bambina Acquarello/carta (84x60cm
  33x23in) Prato 1999

SARTORELLI Francesco 1856-1939 **[32]**
- $10 880 - €9 330 - **£5 400** - FF61 200
  Alla foce del Pó Olio/tela (96x170cm 37x66in)
  Genova 1999
- $4 500 - €4 665 - **£2 700** - FF30 600
  In riva al lago Olio/tela (76x91cm 29x35in) Milano
  2000
- $720 - €933 - **£540** - FF6 120
  Scorcio di paese, Bozzetto Olio/cartone (26x19.5cm
  10x7in) Milano 2001

SARTORIO Giulio Aristide 1860-1932 **[65]**
- $13 324 - €12 366 - **£8 000** - FF81 113
  Portrait of a Lady by an Urn Oil/canvas
  (199.5x88.5cm 78x34in) London 1999
- $3 000 - €3 887 - **£2 250** - FF25 500
  Sala macchine Tecnica mista/cartone (25x48cm
  9x18in) Roma 2001
- $2 918 - €2 824 - **£1 800** - FF18 526
  The Bosco Sacro Pastel/paper (26.5x47.5cm
  10x18in) London 1999

SARTORIUS de Virginie 1828-? **[7]**
- $3 223 - €3 630 - **£2 221** - FF23 812
  **Still Life with Fruits and Flowers on a Marble
  Ledge** Oil/canvas (55x68cm 21x26in) Amsterdam 2000

SARTORIUS Francis I 1734-1804 **[54]**
- $46 866 - €45 866 - **£30 000** - FF300.861
  The Hunt in full Cry: Breaking Cover Oil/canvas
  (91.5x152.5cm 36x60in) London 1999
- $11 000 - €12 928 - **£7 626** - FF84 803
  A Saddled Bay Hunter Held by a Groom Oil/canvas (62x76.5cm 24x30in) New-York 2000

S

SARTORIUS Francis II 1782-1808 **[9]**
🕮 **$2 835** - €2 699 - **£1 800** - FF17 707
Shipping in a Stormy Seas Oil/panel (30.5x45.5cm 12x17in) Billinghurst, West-Sussex 1999

SARTORIUS Jakob Christopher 1668-c.1730 **[1]**
🕮 **$22 000** - €19 363 - **£13 393** - FF127 012
Still Lifes of Flowers in Glass Vases Oil/copper (25.5x19cm 10x7in) New-York 1999

SARTORIUS John Francis 1775-1831 **[17]**
🕮 **$4 300** - €3 749 - **£2 600** - FF24 595
«In Full Cry» Oil/canvas (36x45cm 14x17in) London 1998
🕮 **$6 000** - €5 561 - **£3 730** - FF36 480
Rockingham/Whiskey Oil/copper (12.5x15.5cm 4x6in) New-York 1999

SARTORIUS John Nost 1759-1828 **[144]**
🕮 **$129 235** - €123 545 - **£81 000** - FF810 405
Colonel Newport and his Hounds in an extensive wooded River Landscape Oil/canvas (98.5x147.5cm 38x58in) London 1999
🕮 **$19 000** - €17 611 - **£11 814** - FF115 521
Full Cry/The Death Oil/canvas (63.5x76cm 25x29in) New-York 1999
🕮 **$8 101** - €7 791 - **£5 000** - FF51 107
Pointer with a Hare in an extensive Landscape Oil/canvas (35.5x42cm 13x16in) London 1999

SARYAN Martiros Sergeevich 1880-1972 **[6]**
🕮 **$21 166** - €23 352 - **£14 000** - FF153 181
Mount Ararat, Yerevan Oil/canvas (50x61cm 19x24in) London 2000
✍ **$9 795** - €11 657 - **£7 000** - FF76 462
Still-Life with Bananas and Flask Gouache/paper (47.5x33cm 18x12in) London 2000

SASPORTAS Yehudit 1969 **[3]**
✍ **$2 000** - €1 726 - **£1 210** - FF11 321
Drawing Graphite (120x200cm 47x78in) Tel Aviv 1999

SASSE Jörg 1962 **[5]**
📷 **$3 096** - €2 965 - **£1 912** - FF19 452
«5127» Photograph in colors (114.8x89cm 45x35in) Köln 1999

SASSE Richard 1774-1849 **[5]**
✍ **$681** - €717 - **£450** - FF4 704
The Bay of Naples Watercolour (26.5x39.5cm 10x15in) London 2000

SASSENBROUCK van Achille 1886-1979 **[105]**
🕮 **$1 140** - €992 - **£680** - FF6 504
Vue sur des fermettes Huile/toile (89x78cm 35x30in) Antwerpen 1998

SASSI Alda 1929 **[4]**
📜 **$900** - €1 050 - **£631** - FF6 885
«Italia» Poster (61.5x92cm 24x36in) New-York 2000

SASSI Pietro 1834-1905 **[29]**
🕮 **$2 700** - €2 332 - **£1 800** - FF15 300
Paesaggio della Campagna Romana Olio/tela (58x87cm 22x34in) Roma 1998
🕮 **$750** - €777 - **£450** - FF5 100
Paesaggio silente Olio/cartone (28.5x40.5cm 11x15in) Vercelli 1999

SASSU Aligi 1912-2000 **[318]**
🕮 **$35 000** - €36 283 - **£21 000** - FF238 000
Il giardino delle Esperidi Tempera/tela (270x300cm 106x118in) Milano 2000
🕮 **$14 000** - €14 513 - **£8 400** - FF95 200
Tobiolo Olio/tela (80x95cm 31x37in) Milano 1999

$4 400 - €5 702 - **£3 300** - FF37 400
Busto femminile, busto di donna Olio/cartone/tela (25.5x21cm 10x8in) Vercelli 2000
✍ **$2 856** - €2 961 - **£1 713** - FF19 420
Cavalli Terracotta (49x66cm 19x25in) Venezia 1999
✍ **$1 650** - €1 710 - €990 - FF1 220
Barrio Cino Matita (12.5x16cm 4x6in) Vercelli 1999
📜 **$250** - €259 - **£150** - FF1 700
Tauromachia Litografia (56x76cm 22x29in) Torino 2000

SASSY Attila 1880-1957 **[8]**
✍ **$396** - €450 - **£276** - FF2 952
Nu feminin Pastel/papier (90x62cm 35x24in) Budapest 2001

SATO Key 1906-1978 **[80]**
🕮 **$2 228** - €2 211 - **£1 386** - FF14 500
La nuit blanche Huile/toile (65x81cm 25x31in) Paris 1999
✍ **$376** - €427 - **£257** - FF2 800
Sans titre Huile/panneau (10x29cm 3x11in) Paris 2000
✍ **$399** - €381 - **£248** - FF2 500
Composition Gouache/papier (20x37cm 7x14in) Paris 2000

SATOMI Munetsugu 1900-1995 **[23]**
📜 **$1 064** - €944 - **£650** - FF6 193
«Japan» Affiche couleur (100x64cm 39x25in) London 1999

SATRA Augustin 1877-1909 **[10]**
🕮 **$1 300** - €1 230 - **£810** - FF8 586
«Dorf Sitova, Haje» Öl/Karton (24x32cm 9x12in) Praha 2001

SATRIANO De Conda XIX **[3]**
✍ **$823** - €884 - **£551** - FF5 800
Casablanca, Exposition Aquarelle/papier (37x88cm 14x34in) Paris 2000

SATTLER Hubert 1817-1904 **[226]**
🕮 **$73 107** - €71 132 - **£45 000** - FF466 596
View of London Bridge from the Thames Oil/canvas (103x132cm 40x51in) London 1999
🕮 **$5 054** - €5 696 - **£3 500** - FF37 362
Blick auf den Watzmann in der Nähe von Salzburg Oil/canvas (61x87cm 24x34in) London 2000
🕮 **$745** - €716 - **£462** - FF4 695
Alpenlandschaft Öl/Karton (6x9cm 2x3in) Ahlden 1999
✍ **$804** - €922 - **£550** - FF6 051
Ruins at Baalbek, Syria Pencil/paper (20x14cm 7x5in) London 2000

SAUBER Robert 1868-1936 **[35]**
🕮 **$2 022** - €1 741 - **£1 200** - FF11 417
Woman Wearing Pearls and White Fur Cape Oil/canvas (51.5x61cm 20x24in) London 1998
🕮 **$1 700** - €1 471 - **£1 031** - FF9 652
Woman Picking Flowers Oil/canvas (40x27cm 16x11in) Mystic CT 1998

SAUDE da António Manuel 1875-1958 **[4]**
🕮 **$21 500** - €24 925 - **£15 000** - FF163 500
«Santarém» Oleo/lienzo (51x61.5cm 20x24in) Lisboa 2001
🕮 **$11 000** - €12 463 - **£7 500** - FF81 750
Paisagem representando Santiago, Vila Nova de Famalicáo Huile/bois (21.5x28.5cm 8x11in) Lisboa 2000

S

SAUDEK

SAUDEK Jan 1935 [230]
$4 000 - €3 842 - £2 466 - FF25 199
Traité d'Enluminure d'Art au pochoir Pochoir (32.5x25cm 12x9in) New-York 1999
$693 - €838 - £484 - FF5 500
Milky Way Tirage argentique (27x27cm 10x10in) Paris 2000

SAUER Walter 1889-1927 [138]
$5 740 - €4 961 - £3 460 - FF32 540
«Tendresse» étude Technique mixte/carton (50x38cm 19x14in) Bruxelles 1998
$1 582 - €1 859 - £1 140 - FF12 195
Élegante au bistrot Crayon (40.5x47cm 15x18in) Bruxelles 2001

SAUERBRUCH Hans 1910-1997 [13]
$256 - €245 - £156 - FF1 609
Fasnachtsmumsik, Guggenmusiker in Fasnachts-Kostümen Woodcut in colors (31.5x53cm 12x20in) Konstanz 1999

SAUERLAND Philipp 1677-1762 [3]
$56 405 - €48 718 - £34 002 - FF319 567
A Hedgehog, a Cabbage and Apples at the Foot of a Tree Oil/panel (38.9x34.8cm 15x13in) Amsterdam 1998

SAUERWEID Alexandre Ivanovitch 1783-1844 [6]
$1 964 - €2 336 - £1 400 - FF15 323
Prussian Hussars of the Guard Watercolour (48.5x40cm 19x15in) London 2000

SAUERWEIN Frank Peters 1871-1910 [19]
$4 800 - €4 485 - £2 990 - FF29 417
Horses in the Snow Oil/canvas (45x60cm 18x24in) Mystic CT 1999
$7 500 - €8 919 - £5 345 - FF58 507
After the Snow and Grand Canyon Oil/board (23.5x30.5cm 9x12in) New-York 1999
$2 250 - €2 098 - £1 395 - FF13 764
Caught in the Blizzard Watercolour/paper (25.5x20.5cm 10x8in) New-York 1999

SAUL F. XIX-XX [3]
$4 483 - €4 421 - £2 882 - FF29 000
Allégorie de Zéphyr sous la forme d'une jeune femme tenant un bouquet Marbre (H78cm H30in) Paris 1999

SAUL Peter 1934 [29]
$7 100 - €7 622 - £4 840 - FF50 000
Donald Huile/toile (160x120cm 62x47in) Paris 2001
$3 843 - €4 573 - £2 745 - FF30 000
Hell Acrylique/toile (110x90cm 43x35in) Paris 2000
$1 722 - €1 611 - £1 066 - FF10 569
Negro art Aquarelle (106.5x89cm 41x35in) Lokeren 1999

SAULO George Ernest 1865-? [14]
$2 800 - €2 651 - £1 750 - FF17 390
Erwachen, Mädchenbüste Bronze (H40cm H15in) Praha 1999

SAUNDERS Charles L. ?-1915 [26]
$310 - €282 - £190 - FF1 852
Haystooks Watercolour/paper (18x25cm 7x9in) Billingshurst, West-Sussex 1998

SAUNDERS Clara R(ossman) 1874-1951 [1]
$1 700 - €1 964 - £1 197 - FF12 882
Nude by a River Watercolour/paper (49x65cm 19x25in) Bethesda MD 2001

SAUNDERS George Lethbridge 1774-1846 [4]
$20 092 - €20 375 - £12 500 - FF133 648
Hilare, Countess nelson, née Barlow, Standing Full Length Oil/canvas (239x147cm 94x57in) Suffolk 2000

SAUNIER Marcel XIX [2]
$4 896 - €4 573 - £2 958 - FF30 000
Don Juan et Haïdée Huile/toile (60x73cm 23x28in) Paris 1999

SAUNIER Noël 1847-1890 [15]
$7 500 - €8 306 - £5 086 - FF54 483
The Garden Party Oil/canvas (37.5x46.5cm 14x18in) New-York 2000
$9 000 - €10 051 - £5 763 - FF65 929
Fragrant Blossoms Oil/canvas (24x32.5cm 9x12in) New-York 2000

SAUPIQUE Georges 1889-1961 [5]
$643 000 - €762 245 - £454 000 - FF5 000 000
Afrique du Nord/Antilles/Afrique noire/Indochine Bronze (195x60x46cm 76x23x18in) Paris 2000

SAURA Antonio 1930-1998 [599]
$102 485 - €100 162 - £65 000 - FF657 020
Retrato Imaginario de Goya Oil/canvas (162x130cm 63x51in) London 1999
$25 845 - €25 565 - £16 115 - FF167 695
Autoretrato Nr.59 Öl/Leinwand (60.2x73cm 23x28in) Berlin 1999
$6 270 - €6 607 - £4 180 - FF43 340
Crucifixión Oleo/papel (24.5x24.5cm 9x9in) Madrid 2000
$6 000 - €6 006 - £3 700 - FF39 400
Cabeza Tinta china (97x66cm 38x25in) Madrid 2000
$319 - €381 - £228 - FF2 500
Personnages Lithographie couleurs (55x74cm 21x29in) Paris 2000
$18 240 - €19 221 - £12 160 - FF126 080
Auto da Fé Silver print (35x55cm 13x21in) Madrid 2000

SAUREL Marc XIX-XX [3]
$2 800 - €2 650 - £1 739 - FF17 386
«MAZDA» Poster (231x143.5cm 90x56in) New-York 1999

SAURFELT Léonard c.1840-? [50]
$2 800 - €2 797 - £1 750 - FF18 347
Market Scene Oil/canvas (64x53cm 25x21in) Downington PA 1999
$523 - €550 - £330 - FF3 605
Lady seated reclined by Estuary Oil/canvas (15x33cm 6x13in) Aylsham, Norfolk 2000

SAUSSE Honoré 1891-1936 [5]
$1 338 - €1 524 - £919 - FF10 000
Touaregs à dos de chameau Bronze (H43cm H16in) Paris 2000

SAUTIN René 1881-1968 [93]
$1 456 - €1 403 - £899 - FF9 200
La Risle maritime Huile/toile (54x65cm 21x25in) Paris 1999

SAUTTER Walter 1911-1991 [25]
$1 629 - €1 797 - £1 077 - FF11 789
Mondnacht Öl/Karton (61x50cm 24x19in) St. Gallen 2000

SAUVAGE Arsène Symphorien XIX [12]
$1 216 - €1 448 - £842 - FF9 500
Trophée de bécasse et perdrix/Trophée de canard et grive Huile/toile (55x37cm 21x14in) Paris 2000

1388

$2 347 - €2 439 - £1 548 - FF16 000
Trophées de chasse Huile/panneau (46x32cm 18x12in) Paris 2000

SAUVAGE Philippe François XIX [9]
$4 050 - €4 462 - £2 646 - FF29 268
La fileuse Huile/toile (50x61.5cm 19x24in) Bruxelles 2000

$2 928 - €3 126 - £2 000 - FF20 506
Washing Day Oil/panel (39x31cm 15x12in) Billingshurst, West-Sussex 2001

SAUVAGE Piat-Joseph 1744-1818 [32]
$25 119 - €21 386 - £15 000 - FF140 281
Trompe l'oeil of Putti Drinking and Disporting Oil/canvas (130.5x93.5cm 51x36in) London 1998

$9 000 - €7 559 - £5 291 - FF49 586
Personifications of The Arts and Sciences Oil/canvas (47x40.5cm 18x15in) New-York 1998

$1 846 - €1 982 - £1 235 - FF13 000
Le char de l'amour tiré par des colombes Miniature (5x6.5cm 1x2in) Paris 2000

SAUVAGEOT Charles 1826-1883 [25]
$1 428 - €1 524 - £975 - FF10 000
Dans la cour de la ferme Huile/toile (100x38cm 39x14in) Paris 2001

$2 215 - €2 211 - £1 383 - FF14 500
Les bords du Loing, vue prise à Montigny Huile/panneau (27x41.5cm 10x16in) Fontainebleau 1999

SAUVIN Philippe 1698-1789 [1]
$1 683 - €1 982 - £1 183 - FF13 000
La Vierge en gloire Encre (19.5x13cm 7x5in) Paris 2000

SAUZA J. XVII [1]
$6 187 - €5 701 - £3 726 - FF37 398
Christ au roseau couronné d'épines Huile/toile (88x70cm 34x27in) Bruxelles 1999

SAUZAY Adrien Jacques 1841-1928 [80]
$10 000 - €11 212 - £6 791 - FF73 548
The Quiet Village Oil/canvas (130x220.5cm 51x86in) New-York 2000

$2 163 - €2 134 - £1 332 - FF14 000
Paysage Huile/panneau (33x63cm 12x24in) Saint-Dié 1999

$3 600 - €3 084 - £2 164 - FF20 230
By the Gate Oil/canvas (40x33cm 16x13in) Cincinnati OH 1998

SAVAGE Anne Douglas 1896-1971 [14]
$20 128 - €22 769 - £14 080 - FF149 354
Summer Landscape Oil/canvas (64x77cm 25x30in) Toronto 2001

$2 110 - €2 387 - £1 476 - FF15 658
«Eastern Township Farm»/«Tree by the River» Oil/panel (23x30.5cm 9x12in) Toronto 2001

SAVAGE Cedric 1901-1969 [17]
$761 - €854 - £531 - FF5 599
Residence, Greece Oil/canvas (39x49cm 15x19in) Wellington 2001

$1 185 - €1 328 - £826 - FF8 710
East Coast Baches Oil/board (33x45cm 12x17in) Wellington 2001

SAVAGE Edward 1761-1817 [8]
$650 000 - €773 016 - £463 255 - FF5 070 650
The Stedman Bust Portrait of George Washington Oil/canvas (76x63.5cm 29x25in) New-York 2000

$650 - €691 - £410 - FF4 534
Full Length Portrait of Georges Washington Mezzotint (66x51cm 26x20in) New-York 2000

SAVAGE Eugene Francis 1883-1978 [9]
$2 600 - €2 674 - £1 649 - FF17 539
Faith, Hope and Charity Oil/canvas (44x44cm 17x17in) Cincinnati OH 2000

SAVAGE Reginald XIX-XX [3]
$749 - €713 - £468 - FF4 680
Albatross Ink (9x9cm 3x3in) Vancouver, BC. 1999

SAVARY Robert 1920 [91]
$500 - €563 - £344 - FF3 691
La plage Oil/canvas (46x50cm 18x20in) Chicago IL 2000

SAVELLI Angelo 1911-1995 [24]
$480 - €415 - £240 - FF2 720
Deposizione Olio/tavola (15x8.5cm 5x3in) Prato 1999

$300 - €259 - £150 - FF1 700
Le amiche Acquarello/carta (28.5x36cm 11x14in) Prato 1999

SAVERIJ Salomon 1594-c.1678 [11]
$148 - €172 - £105 - FF1 131
The Senses Etching (13.5x9cm 5x3in) Amsterdam 2000

SAVEROT Alain XX [3]
$2 257 - €2 287 - £1 404 - FF15 000
Portrait rouge Huile/toile (116x89cm 45x35in) Soissons 2000

SAVERY Jacob I 1545-1602 [8]
$373 575 - €401 002 - £250 000 - FF2 630 400
The Season of Spring: a Panoramic Landscape with Winter Yielding Oil/panel (41x67.5cm 16x26in) London 2000

SAVERY Jacob II c.1593-c.1660 [2]
$9 478 - €10 174 - £6 342 - FF66 738
Die ersten Menschen nach dem Sündenfall Öl/Kupfer (17.5x27.5cm 6x10in) Wien 2000

SAVERY Jan, Hans II 1597-1654 [9]
$23 824 - €24 392 - £14 960 - FF160 000
La chasse à la baleine Huile/panneau (36.5x53cm 14x20in) Lille 2000

SAVERY Roelant 1576-1639 [49]
$47 817 - €51 328 - £32 000 - FF336 691
Coastal scene under a Glowering Sky Oil/panel (38x53cm 14x20in) London 2000

$6 480 - €7 622 - £4 645 - FF50 000
Cygnes et autruches dans un paysage de rivière Huile/panneau (24x34.5cm 9x13in) Paris 2001

$32 000 - €34 278 - £21 852 - FF224 851
Seated Peasant and a Standing Peasant Woman/Peasant in Profile Ink (10x14cm 3x5in) New-York 2001

SAVERYS Albert 1886-1964 [305]
$19 360 - €19 831 - £12 240 - FF130 080
Hiver à Deinze Huile/toile (100x120cm 39x47in) Bruxelles 2000

$9 216 - €8 924 - £5 688 - FF58 536
Paysage hivernal Huile/panneau (59x60cm 23x23in) Bruxelles 2000

$1 664 - €1 983 - £1 192 - FF13 008
Haven Watercolour/paper (47x67cm 18x26in) Lokeren 2000

$205 - €173 - £121 - FF1 138
Schaatsers Aquatint in colors (51.3x61.2cm 20x24in) Lokeren 1998

S

SAVIGNAC Raymond 1907 **[240]**
⊞ **$425** - €437 - **£269** - FF2 867
«Armanac Ryst» Poster (119x160cm 47x63in)
Cincinnati OH 2000

SAVIGNY Jean Paul 1933 **[18]**
😊 **$1 978** - €1 753 - **£1 213** - FF11 500
Nature morte aux prunes et aux pêches
Huile/toile (39x47cm 15x18in) Pau 1999

SAVILLE Jenny 1970 **[8]**
😊 **$175 000** - €196 013 - **£121 590** - FF1 285 760
Interfacing Oil/canvas (122x102cm 48x40in) New-
York 2001
😊 **$52 086** - €50 694 - **£32 000** - FF332 531
Branded Oil/canvas (61x51cm 24x20in) London 1999
📷 **$7 916** - €7 641 - **£5 000** - FF50 119
Closed contact #14 Photograph in colors
(185x185cm 72x72in) London 1999

SAVIN Maurice 1894-1973 **[217]**
😊 **$1 177** - €1 372 - **£825** - FF9 000
Baigneuses Huile/toile (60x73cm 23x28in) Paris
2000
😊 **$620** - €732 - **£436** - FF4 800
Au café Huile/toile (22x27cm 8x10in) Fontainebleau
2000
✏ **$209** - €183 - **£126** - FF1 200
Nyons, dans la Drôme Aquarelle/papier (22x31cm
8x12in) Toulouse 1998

SAVINI Alfonso 1836-1908 **[12]**
😊 **$22 000** - €20 871 - **£13 365** - FF136 903
The Lover's Farewell Oil/canvas (81x60cm 31x23in)
New-York 1999
😊 **$8 000** - €7 082 - **£4 891** - FF46 455
The Next Drink Oil/panel (33x43cm 12x16in) New-
York 1999
😊 **$1 773** - €1 653 - **£1 100** - FF10 846
The Violinist Watercolour/paper (32x49.5cm 12x19in)
Billingshurst, West-Sussex 1999

SAVINIO Alberto 1891-1952 **[88]**
😊 **$72 500** - €75 157 - **£43 500** - FF493 000
Guerriero Olio/tela (80x65cm 31x25in) Prato 1999
😊 **$37 500** - €38 874 - **£22 500** - FF255 000
Regard de l'enfant Olio/tela (33x41cm 12x16in)
Prato 1999
🏺 **$30 000** - €31 100 - **£18 000** - FF204 000
I genitori Céramique (30x24.5cm 11x9in) Prato 2000
✏ **$8 800** - €11 403 - **£6 600** - FF74 800
Ercole trino Inchiostro (32x23cm 12x9in) Milano
2001

SAVINIO Ruggero 1934 **[41]**
😊 **$2 350** - €2 436 - **£1 410** - FF15 980
Distanza dal paesaggio n.4 Olio/tela (110x138cm
43x54in) Milano 1999
😊 **$1 800** - €1 866 - **£1 080** - FF12 240
Spiaggia Olio/tavola (49.5x35cm 19x13in) Prato 2000

SAVIO John 1902-1938 **[41]**
⊞ **$1 081** - €1 247 - **£761** - FF8 183
Ro Woodcut (23x28cm 9x11in) Oslo 2000

SAVITSKY Georgy Konstantinov. 1887-1949 **[5]**
😊 **$1 126** - €1 308 - **£777** - FF8 580
Kühe am Okafluss Öl/Karton (18.2x37cm 7x14in)
Wien 2000

SAVITSKY Konstantin Apollonov 1844-1905 **[3]**
😊 **$8 857** - €8 936 - **£5 500** - FF54 859
Beauty among the Sunflowers Oil/canvas
(82x54.5cm 32x21in) London 1999

SAVOIA Achille 1842-1886 **[1]**
😊 **$3 200** - €4 147 - **£2 400** - FF27 200
Scena garibaldina Olio/cartone (19x30.5cm 7x12in)
Milano 2000

SAVORY William XIX **[1]**
⊞ **$12 271** - €12 886 - **£8 118** - FF84 527
Map of the Western Reserve, The Fire Lands
Ohio Engraving (40x51cm 16x20in) Cleveland OH
2000

SAVOY van Carel c.1621-1665 **[6]**
😊 **$11 210** - €10 976 - **£6 897** - FF72 000
Scène allégorique Huile/toile (100x166cm 39x65in)
Paris 1999

SAVRASOV Alexeï Kondratievich 1830-1897 **[11]**
😊 **$12 806** - €14 879 - **£9 000** - FF97 597
Deer Island in Sokolniki Oil/canvas (46x37.5cm
18x14in) London 2001
😊 **$3 361** - €2 868 - **£2 008** - FF18 816
Burlaki vid Volga Oil/paper (27x39cm 10x15in)
Stockholm 1998

SAVREUX Maurice 1884-1971 **[45]**
😊 **$3 684** - €3 506 - **£2 290** - FF23 000
Grand bouquet de fleurs Huile/panneau (81x65cm
31x25in) Paris 1999
😊 **$483** - €549 - **£339** - FF3 600
Nature morte à la coupe de fruits Huile/toile
(24x33cm 9x12in) Avignon 2001

SAVRY Hendrick 1823-1907 **[36]**
😊 **$3 245** - €3 176 - **£2 081** - FF20 836
Cows grazing in a Summer Meadow Oil/canvas
(50x80cm 19x31in) Amsterdam 1999

SAWASDI TANTISUK 1925 **[21]**
😊 **$3 738** - €3 472 - **£2 310** - FF22 778
Sky Form Oil/canvas (40.5x61cm 15x24in) Bangkok
1999
✏ **$2 136** - €1 984 - **£1 320** - FF13 016
Selling the Catch Watercolour/paper (56x38cm
22x14in) Bangkok 1999

SAWICZEWSKI Stanislaus 1866-1943 **[3]**
😊 **$5 128** - €5 667 - **£3 557** - FF37 174
Port sur la Vistule Huile/toile (89x113.5cm 35x44in)
Warszawa 2001
✏ **$4 232** - €4 543 - **£2 832** - FF29 803
Nu dans un atelier de peintre Aquarelle/papier
(34x31cm 13x12in) Warszawa 2001

SAWREY Hugh David 1923-1999 **[197]**
😊 **$3 220** - €3 122 - **£1 994** - FF20 477
Yarning by the Woodheap Oil/board (51x61cm
20x24in) Sydney 1999
😊 **$1 298** - €1 226 - **£785** - FF8 045
The Man from Ironbark I Oil/paper (42x30cm
16x11in) Sydney 1999

SAWYIER Paul 1865-1917 **[11]**
😊 **$55 000** - €57 011 - **£34 875** - FF373 967
23rd Regiment Armory, Bedford Avenue Oil/can-
vas (51x61cm 20x24in) New-York 2000
✏ **$4 500** - €3 880 - **£2 672** - FF25 452
View of the Kentucky River Watercolour/paper
(27x43cm 11x17in) Cincinnati OH 1998

SAX Ursula 1935 **[1]**
🗿 **$2 722** - €3 068 - **£1 885** - FF20 123
Kleine Mänade Iron (H71cm H27in) Berlin 2000

SAXE Adrian 1943 **[5]**
🗿 **$9 000** - €9 323 - **£5 728** - FF61 157
Untitled Antelope Jar Porcelain (37.5x23cm 14x9in)
New-York 2000

SAXELIN Into 1883-1927 **[5]**
$900 - €1 009 - £611 - FF6 619
Flicka Bronze (H43cm H16in) Helsinki 2000

SAXELIN Oskar XX **[3]**
$496 - €471 - £304 - FF3 089
Stilleben Oil/canvas (33x49cm 12x19in) Helsinki 1999

SAXON Charles 1920-1988 **[2]**
$1 900 - €2 116 - £1 242 - FF13 882
Gag cartoon: Older couple leaving party
Charcoal (30x30cm 12x12in) New-York 2000

SAXTON Christopher XVI-XVII **[39]**
$225 - €262 - £160 - FF1 717
Yorkshire Engraving (26x31.5cm 10x12in) London 2000

SAY Frederick Richard 1805-? **[11]**
$4 489 - €5 339 - £3 200 - FF35 024
Portrait of Sir William Webb Follett (1798-1845), Three-Quarter Lenght Oil/canvas (33.5x28cm 13x11in) London 2000

SAYER Derrick 1917 **[34]**
$227 - €220 - £140 - FF1 440
Reclining Female Nude Gouache/papier (106x76cm 41x29in) London 1999

SAYER Robert act.1750-1780 **[12]**
$375 - €352 - £231 - FF2 308
Map of South America, by Nicolas d'Anville
Engraving (49x58cm 19x23in) New-York 1999

SAYNE de Comtesse XIX **[1]**
$2 193 - €2 211 - £1 367 - FF14 500
Bouquet de fleurs Aquarelle (39x31.5cm 15x12in) Paris 2000

SAYOUS Rachel 1975 **[13]**
$489 - €457 - £296 - FF3 000
Paysage de Provence, pavots au clair de lune
Huile/carton (65x54cm 25x21in) Agen 1999

SAYRE Fred Grayson 1879-1938 **[42]**
$3 750 - €4 375 - £2 610 - FF28 699
«Cottonwood Rancho» Oil/canvas (50x60cm 20x24in) Altadena CA 2000
$1 800 - €1 944 - £1 244 - FF12 751
Coastal Oil/masonite (33x40cm 13x16in) Altadena CA 2001
$270 - €292 - £186 - FF1 913
«Lost Feather Trail» Print (35x21cm 14x8in)
Cincinnati OH 2001

SBISA Carlo 1899-1964 **[14]**
$7 750 - €8 034 - £4 650 - FF52 700
Natura morta metafisica Olio/tela (49x65cm 19x25in) Trieste 2000
$600 - €622 - £360 - FF4 080
Modella Sanguina/carta (60x45cm 23x17in) Trieste 1999

SCACCIATI Andrea I 1642-1710 **[22]**
$18 900 - €21 023 - £12 250 - FF137 900
Bodegón con flores Oleo/lienzo (46x67cm 18x26in) Madrid 2000

SCACCIATI Andrea II 1725-1771 **[4]**
$734 - €767 - £465 - FF5 030
Ruhe auf der Flucht Etching, aquatint (40x29cm 15x11in) München 2000

SCAFFAI Luigi 1837-? **[6]**
$3 200 - €2 730 - £1 926 - FF17 909
Maid and a gentle man Oil/panel (44x31cm 17x12in) Norwalk CT 1999

SCAGLIA Giuseppe Michele 1859-1918 **[10]**
$760 - €985 - £570 - FF6 460
Partita a carte in un interno Olio/tavoletta (21x27cm 8x10in) Torino 2000

SCAILLIET Emile Philippe 1846-1911 **[5]**
$4 355 - €3 811 - £2 637 - FF25 000
Femme à l'urne Chryséléphantine (H41.5cm H16in) Paris 1998

SCALA Vincenzo XIX **[17]**
$20 000 - €25 916 - £15 000 - FF170 000
Mercato di Sessa Aurunca Olio/tela (151x236cm 59x92in) Milano 2000
$3 800 - €4 924 - £2 850 - FF32 300
Cavalli che si abbeverano al fiume Olio/tela (30x48cm 11x18in) Milano 2001

SCALBERT Jules 1851-? **[19]**
$10 500 - €10 083 - £6 506 - FF66 143
Flower Maidens in a Park Oil/canvas (81x63cm 32x25in) Houston TX 1999
$2 500 - €2 167 - £1 527 - FF14 217
The Bathers Oil/panel (41x32.5cm 16x12in) New-York 1999
$1 232 - €1 372 - £865 - FF9 000
Le gai réveil Pastel/papier (37x60cm 14x23in) Paris 2001

SCANAVINO Emilio 1922-1986 **[372]**
$19 200 - €16 586 - £12 800 - FF108 800
«Presenza» Olio/tela (149x120cm 58x47in) Prato 1998
$3 750 - €3 887 - £2 250 - FF25 500
Studio Olio/tela (60x60cm 23x23in) Vercelli 1999
$1 750 - €1 814 - £1 050 - FF11 900
Residui Tempera/tavola (35x25cm 13x9in) Milano 1999
$12 000 - €15 550 - £9 000 - FF102 000
Il pieno e il vuoto Bronzo (142x107x6cm 55x42x2in) Milano 2000
$1 000 - €1 037 - £600 - FF6 800
Senza titolo Terracotta (H28cm H11in) Milano 1999
$750 - €777 - £450 - FF5 100
Composizione China/carta (26.5x21cm 10x8in) Vercelli 2001
$200 - €207 - £120 - FF1 360
Gradini e matasse Litografia (69x49cm 27x19in) Vercelli 2001

SCANLAN Robert Richard c.1810-c.1880 **[31]**
$1 149 - €1 270 - £796 - FF8 329
Racehorse with Jockey up Watercolour/paper (22x30cm 8x11in) Dublin 2001

SCANNELL Edith M.S. XIX-XX **[9]**
$2 080 - €1 894 - £1 300 - FF12 421
Two Young Boys and a Girl in an Orchard
Watercolour/paper (17x13cm 7x5in) Birmingham 1999

SCARBOROUGH Frederick William act.1896-1939 **[130]**
$4 423 - €4 899 - £3 000 - FF32 136
The Pool of London Oil/canvas (39.5x60cm 15x23in) Billingshurst, West-Sussex 2000
$2 894 - €2 847 - £1 750 - FF18 676
Vessels off the Pier Head Whitby
Watercolour/paper (35x45cm 14x18in) Whitby, Yorks 2000

SCARFE Gerald 1936 **[17]**
$7 935 - €8 903 - £5 500 - FF58 397
Peter Hall and Trevor Nunn: the Broker's Men
Watercolour (83x58.5cm 32x23in) London 2000

S

🖼 **$1 648** - €1 758 - **£1 100** - FF11 532
Famous Personalities : Dr Christian Bernard/Richard Nixon/De Gaulle Color lithograph (80x63cm 31x24in) London 2000

SCARLETT Rolph 1889-1984 **[64]**
✏ **$400** - €429 - **£267** - FF2 816
Abstract Composition Gouache (35x42cm 14x16in) Chester NY 2000
🖼 **$949** - €1 053 - **£631** - FF6 909
Abstract Composition Monotype (59x43.5cm 23x17in) New-York 2000

SCARPA Carlo 1906-1978 **[2]**
≋ **$11 882** - €13 805 - **£8 351** - FF90 555
Eule Sculpture, glass (H20cm H7in) München 2001

SCARPA Riccardo 1905 **[8]**
≋ **$1 737** - €1 906 - **£1 180** - FF12 500
Teckel Bronze (11.5x22.5cm 4x8in) Pontoise 2000

SCARPITTA G. Salvator Cartland 1887-1948 **[5]**
≋ **$1 332** - €1 487 - **£930** - FF9 756
Jeune fille nue à la cascade Bronze (H32cm H12in) Bruxelles 2001

SCARPITTA Salvatore 1919 **[26]**
👁 **$21 600** - €18 660 - **£14 400** - FF122 400
Composizione Olio/tela (113x150.5cm 44x59in) Milano 1998
👁 **$4 250** - €4 406 - **£2 550** - FF28 900
Senza titolo Olio/tela (40x60cm 15x23in) Roma 2001

SCARSELLA SCARSELLINO Ippolito 1551-1620 **[25]**
👁 **$75 000** - €80 227 - **£51 135** - FF526 252
Annunciation Oil/canvas (143x107.5cm 56x42in) New-York 2001
👁 **$40 000** - €37 633 - **£24 960** - FF246 856
Madonna and Child with the Enfant Saint John the Baptist Oil/canvas/panel (113.5x90.5cm 44x35in) New-York 1999
👁 **$10 308** - €11 558 - **£7 000** - FF75 814
The Virgin crowned by Angels Oil/panel (38x29.5cm 14x11in) London 2000

SCARSELLO Girolamo XVII **[5]**
🖼 **$514** - €613 - **£367** - FF4 024
Saturn auf einer Wolke sitzend, nach Andrea Sirani Radierung (18.8x14.1cm 7x5in) Berlin 2000

SCARVELLI Spyridon 1868-1942 **[78]**
👁 **$8 000** - €8 062 - **£4 987** - FF52 880
The Port of Calais/Warships on the High Seas Oil/canvas (59.5x87.5cm 23x34in) New-York 2000
👁 **$2 769** - €2 521 - **£1 700** - FF16 535
Faluccas on the Nile/Travellers in a Landscape Watercolour (19.5x30.5cm 7x12in) London 1999

SCATIZZI Sergio 1918 **[178]**
👁 **$750** - €777 - **£450** - FF5 100
Fiori Olio/tavola (50x40cm 19x15in) Prato 2000
👁 **$425** - €441 - **£255** - FF2 890
Paesaggio marino Olio/tavola (23x15cm 9x5in) Prato 1999
✏ **$180** - €233 - **£135** - FF1 530
Studio di nudo Acquarello (39x52cm 15x20in) Prato 2000

SCAUFLAIRE Edgar 1893-1960 **[263]**
👁 **$1 416** - €1 188 - **£830** - FF7 795
Nature morte aux fruits Huile/panneau (41.5x46cm 16x18in) Liège 1998
👁 **$553** - €444 - **£282** - FF4 227
Sans titre Huile/panneau (17.5x23cm 6x9in) Liège 2000

👁 **$592** - €620 - **£392** - FF4 065
Bacchanale Crayon (50x71cm 19x27in) Bruxelles 2000

SCAVEZZI Prosper XVI **[1]**
🖼 **$1 875** - €2 104 - **£1 300** - FF13 803
Sixtus VI Etching (41.5x30.5cm 16x12in) London 2000

SCAVULLO Francesco 1929 **[14]**
📷 **$650** - €741 - **£449** - FF4 860
«Sting» Silver print (32x21cm 12x8in) New-York 2000

SCHAAK John S.C. XVIII **[3]**
👁 **$5 234** - €5 496 - **£3 300** - FF36 051
Cavalry Officers outside the Half Moon Inn Oil/canvas (30.5x35.5cm 12x13in) London 2000

SCHAAL J.L. XIX **[1]**
👁 **$3 114** - €3 049 - **£1 916** - FF20 000
Chevaux s'abreuvant Huile/toile (32x40cm 12x15in) Paris 1994

SCHAAN Paul XIX-XX **[23]**
👁 **$1 670** - €1 524 - **£1 016** - FF10 000
«Écrit amusant» Huile/toile (46x38cm 18x14in) Pau 1998
✏ **$2 868** - €3 185 - **£2 000** - FF20 889
La bonne liqueur Watercolour/paper (45x38cm 17x14in) London 2001

SCHAAP Egbert Rubertus Derk 1862-1939 **[30]**
👁 **$946** - €817 - **£571** - FF5 357
Zomerdag Oil/canvas (35.5x51.5cm 13x20in) Amsterdam 1999

SCHAAP Hendrik 1878-1955 **[23]**
👁 **$1 290** - €1 281 - **£806** - FF8 401
Amsterdam Harbour Oil/canvas (38x58.5cm 14x23in) Toronto 1999
✏ **$253** - €272 - **£169** - FF1 786
The harbour in Rotterdam Pastel/paper (45x62cm 17x24in) Amsterdam 2000

SCHACHINGER Gabriel 1850-1912 **[10]**
👁 **$18 305** - €16 871 - **£10 962** - FF110 665
Stilleben mit Stockrosen und Ackerwinden in einer Vase Öl/Leinwand (78.5x59cm 30x23in) Dresden 1998

SCHACHNER Therese 1869-1950 **[23]**
👁 **$1 513** - €1 308 - **£912** - FF8 580
Landschaft mit Enten Öl/Karton (47x64cm 18x25in) Wien 1999

SCHACKWITZ Michael 1956 **[5]**
✏ **$2 743** - €3 068 - **£1 849** - FF20 123
Rose Aquarell/Papier (125x135cm 49x53in) München 2000

SCHAD Christian 1894-1982 **[155]**
👁 **$496 800** - €462 950 - **£300 000** - FF3 036 750
Bildnis einer Unbekannten Oil/canvas (63x51cm 24x20in) London 1998
✏ **$8 792** - €10 123 - **£6 000** - FF66 401
Narcissus Watercolour (18.5x13cm 7x5in) London 2000
🖼 **$292** - €307 - **£184** - FF2 012
Mutter mit Kind Woodcut (54x39.5cm 21x15in) Stuttgart 2000
📷 **$372** - €409 - **£253** - FF2 683
Ohne Titel Photograph (29x39cm 11x15in) Berlin 2000

SCHAD-ROSSA Paul 1862-1916 [13]

$6 849 - €7 714 - **£4 720** - FF50 602
**A Lady, Standing Ful Length by a Draped
Columm, Wearing a Gold** Oil/canvas (200x128.5cm
78x50in) Amsterdam 2000

SCHADL János 1892-1944 [7]

$5 950 - €6 557 - **£3 910** - FF43 010
Left-off Clothes Oil/canvas (86x70.5cm 33x27in)
Budapest 2000

$1 110 - €1 166 - **£690** - FF7 650
Moulin Encre/papier (47x52cm 18x20in) Budapest
2000

SCHADOW Johan Gottfried 1764-1850 [44]

$1 072 - €1 278 - **£764** - FF8 384
Friedrich II zu Pferde Bronze relief (32x29cm
12x11in) Köln 2000

$528 - €613 - **£371** - FF4 024
Schadows Familie Radierung (17.5x11.5cm 6x4in)
Berlin 2001

SCHADOW von Wilhelm Friedrich 1788-1862 [12]

$4 475 - €3 834 - **£2 690** - FF25 149
Der Genius des Poesie Öl/Leinwand (54x49.5cm
21x19in) Köln 1998

$2 983 - €2 556 - **£1 793** - FF16 766
Bildnis des Malers Friedrich Eduard Deger (1809-1885)
Öl/Leinwand (44x36cm 17x14in) Köln 1998

$1 981 - €2 250 - **£1 376** - FF14 757
Männlicher Akt von hinten gesehen Pencil/paper
(32.5x19.5cm 12x7in) Köln 2001

SCHAEFELS Hendrik Frans 1827-1904 [36]

$21 200 - €24 788 - **£14 600** - FF162 600
Retour de la Reine Elisabeth Huile/toile
(106x160cm 41x62in) Antwerpen 2000

$8 590 - €8 519 - **£5 263** - FF55 881
Elegant figures in a Park Oil/canvas (65.5x88cm
25x34in) New-York 2001

$1 729 - €1 611 - **£1 072** - FF10 569
Le retour des pêcheurs Huile/panneau (45x30cm
17x11in) Antwerpen 1999

SCHAEFELS Hendrik Raphael 1785-1857 [16]

$6 096 - €5 949 - **£3 744** - FF39 024
**Antiquair ontvangt gezelschap (l'accueil chez
l'antiquaire)** Huile/bois (63x50cm 24x19in)
Antwerpen 1999

$1 872 - €2 231 - **£1 341** - FF14 634
Zeegezicht (marine) Huile/bois (26x42cm 10x16in)
Antwerpen 2000

SCHAEFER Carl Fellman 1903-1995 [69]

$3 742 - €3 577 - **£2 345** - FF23 465
Long Bay, Pickerel River Oil/panel (29.5x35cm
11x13in) Vancouver, BC. 1999

$1 221 - €1 166 - **£761** - FF7 651
Back of our House, Hanover Ink (28x37.5cm
11x14in) Calgary, Alberta 1999

$356 - €414 - **£250** - FF2 716
«Houses & Winter» Woodcut (9.5x9cm 3x3in)
Calgary, Alberta 2001

SCHAEFFER Carl Albert Eugen 1780-1866 [2]

$8 755 - €8 692 - **£5 470** - FF57 016
Hermann und Dorothea am Brunnen
Öl/Leinwand (102x88cm 40x34in) München 1999

SCHAEFFER Henri-Alexis 1900-1975 [38]

$1 504 - €1 695 - **£1 041** - FF11 117
«Le Louvre pont du Caroussel» Oil/canvas
(48.5x68.5cm 19x26in) Toronto 2000

SCHAEFFER Mead 1898-1980 [24]

$7 500 - €7 182 - **£4 633** - FF47 114
Titanic Struggle on the Beach, Book Illustration
Oil/canvas (63x96cm 25x38in) New-York 1999

SCHAEFFER VON WIENWALD August 1833-1916 [36]

$1 731 - €1 943 - **£1 200** - FF12 744
Berglandschaft mit See im Abendlicht
Öl/Leinwand (61x94.5cm 24x37in) München 2000

$1 183 - €1 018 - **£701** - FF6 676
«Motiv vom Plattensee» Öl/Leinwand (24.5x44.5cm
9x17in) Wien 1998

$1 645 - €1 817 - **£1 140** - FF11 917
«Bauernhäuser am Chiemsee» Aquarell/Papier
(32x46cm 12x18in) Wien 2001

SCHAEFLER Fritz 1888-1954 [74]

$578 - €665 - **£408** - FF4 360
Lesendes Mädchen Öl/Karton (26.8x24.8cm 10x9in)
Hamburg 2001

$857 - €920 - **£573** - FF6 037
Blumenstilleben Watercolour, gouache (61.5x49.5cm
24x19in) Köln 2000

$264 - €307 - **£185** - FF2 012
Flusslandschaft Drypoint (29.5x24.5cm 11x9in)
Berlin 2001

SCHAEP Henri Adolphe 1826-1870 [32]

$7 380 - €7 436 - **£4 590** - FF48 780
Le naufrage Huile/toile (59.5x82cm 23x32in)
Bruxelles 2000

$5 775 - €5 445 - **£3 579** - FF35 719
Marine Oil/panel (20x28cm 7x11in) Amsterdam 1999

SCHAEPKENS Alexander 1815-1899 [6]

$1 673 - €1 735 - **£1 106** - FF11 163
**Vue de Maestricht, les églises St.Jean et
St.Servais** Aquarelle (40.5x32cm 15x12in) Bruxelles
2000

SCHAEPKENS Théodore 1810-1883 [13]

$320 - €381 - **£228** - FF2 500
Jeune femme partant à la chasse au faucon
Aquarelle (22x16cm 8x6in) Paris 2000

SCHAETTE Karl 1884-1951 [11]

$846 - €971 - **£579** - FF6 372
**Ballwolken über herbstlicher
Voralpenlandschaft mit kleinem See** Öl/Leinwand
(82x79cm 32x31in) Heidelberg 2000

SCHAEYENBORG van Pieter 1635-1657 [2]

$4 176 - €3 578 - **£2 510** - FF23 473
Fischstilleben Oil/panel (35.5x44.5cm 13x17in) Köln
1998

SCHAFER Frederick Ferdinand 1839-1927 [42]

$3 750 - €3 204 - **£2 269** - FF21 018
Mt. Shasta Oil/canvas (76x125.5cm 29x49in) San-
Francisco CA 1998

SCHAFER Henry / Henri act.c.1863-1891 [211]

$2 896 - €3 361 - **£2 000** - FF22 048
**Figures in a Continental Market Place, a
Cathedral Beyond** Oil/canvas (51x76cm 20x29in)
London 2001

$1 610 - €1 728 - **£1 077** - FF11 338
St.Omer Oil/canvas (33x23cm 12x9in) Toronto 2000

$467 - €537 - **£320** - FF3 520
Chartres, France Watercolour/paper (43x35cm
17x14in) Par, Cornwall 2000

S

SCHÄFFER Adalbert, Bela 1815-1871 **[10]**

$3 200 - €3 710 - £2 266 - FF24 336
Still Life with Grapes, Pomegranate and a Nautilus Cup Oil/panel (47x37.5cm 18x14in) New-York 2000

$3 400 - €3 343 - £2 125 - FF21 930
Still Life of Fruits with Cup Oil/board (36x42cm 14x16in) Budapest 1999

SCHAFFER Richard 1947 **[1]**

$3 800 - €3 780 - £2 358 - FF24 792
Heart (Life is Short) Mixed media/canvas (42x39.5cm 16x15in) Beverly-Hills CA 1999

SCHAFFNER Marcel 1931 **[6]**

$1 645 - €1 508 - £1 005 - FF9 890
«Nummer 3» Gouache/papier (38x49cm 14x19in) Zürich 1999

SCHAFFROTH Johannes Stanislaus 1765/66-1851 **[3]**

$4 487 - €5 336 - £3 090 - FF35 000
Eingang der alter Burg Baden gegen abend Lavis (53.5x42.5cm 21x16in) Paris 2000

SCHAGEN van Gerbrand Frederik 1880-1968 **[40]**

$798 - €862 - £546 - FF5 655
A Flower Garden Oil/canvas (44x64cm 17x25in) Amsterdam 2001

$791 - €726 - £487 - FF4 762
«Achter eik en Duinen» Oil/panel (22x45.5cm 8x17in) Amsterdam 1999

SCHALCKE van der Cornelis Symonsz. 1611-1671 **[19]**

$4 456 - €4 991 - £3 096 - FF32 742
Arnhem: a View of the Grotte Kerk and the River Rhine Oil/panel (36.5x47.5cm 14x18in) Amsterdam 2001

$382 - €332 - £230 - FF2 178
Holländische Dünenlandschaft mit wandernden Bauern Black chalk (18.3x28cm 7x11in) Berlin 1998

SCHALCKEN Godfried 1643-1706 **[55]**

$179 498 - €166 859 - £110 000 - FF1 094 522
Portrait of the Artist in a blue Coat/the Artist's Wife, orange Dress Oil/canvas (72.5x60cm 28x23in) London 1998

$17 367 - €19 059 - £11 180 - FF125 017
Woman seated by a Table in fancy Costume, freeing a Songbird Oil/copper (16.5x13cm 6x5in) Amsterdam 2000

SCHALDACH William Joseph 1896-1982 **[10]**

$160 - €148 - £99 - FF972
Young Grouse Etching (11x9cm 4x3in) South-Natick MA 1999

SCHALIN Greta 1897-1993 **[23]**

$1 793 - €1 682 - £1 108 - FF11 032
Blommor Oil/canvas (42x50cm 16x19in) Helsinki 1999

$1 185 - €1 009 - £708 - FF6 620
Blommor Oil/canvas (29x35cm 11x13in) Helsinki 1998

SCHALL Jean-Frédéric 1752-1825 **[45]**

$22 000 - €19 363 - £13 393 - FF127 012
«Mademoiselle de la Vallière au couvent de Chaillot» Oil/canvas (34.5x47.5cm 13x18in) New-York 1999

$11 541 - €11 129 - £7 117 - FF73 000
La toilette intime Huile/toile (28x23cm 11x9in) Paris 1999

SCHALL Lothar 1924-1996 **[22]**

$1 343 - €1 534 - £947 - FF10 061
Ohne Titel Gouache (80x120cm 31x47in) Stuttgart 2001

SCHALL Roger 1904 **[34]**

$471 - €457 - £293 - FF3 000
Portrait d'Assia nue Tirage argentique (18.9x16.9cm 7x6in) Paris 1999

SCHALLER Mark 1962 **[18]**

$4 074 - €4 489 - £2 704 - FF29 444
Table for Two Oil/canvas (183x122cm 72x48in) Woollahra, Sydney 2001

SCHAMBERG Morton Livingston 1881-1918 **[12]**

$38 000 - €36 163 - £23 769 - FF237 211
Nude Oil/panel (27.5x19.5cm 10x7in) New-York 1999

$17 000 - €15 923 - £10 451 - FF104 449
Abstraction, Locomotive Pastel (17x24.5cm 6x9in) New-York 1999

SCHAMPHELEER de Edmond 1824-1899 **[56]**

$3 628 - €3 887 - £2 470 - FF25 500
Moulins au bord de l'estuaire près de Rotterdam Huile/toile (63x101cm 24x39in) Calais 2001

$561 - €545 - £345 - FF3 547
Prairie animée en Zélande Huile/panneau (28.5x46.5cm 11x18in) Bruxelles 1999

SCHAMSCHULA Erich 1925 **[17]**

$964 - €915 - £586 - FF6 000
Forme géométrique Sculpture verre (32x25cm 12x9in) Paris 1999

SCHANCKENBERG Walter 1880-1961 **[2]**

$10 000 - €9 617 - £6 172 - FF63 082
«Peter Pathe» Poster (124.5x91.5cm 49x36in) New-York 1999

SCHANKER Louis 1903-1981 **[48]**

$3 750 - €3 233 - £2 227 - FF21 210
Three Figures Oil/canvas (60x76cm 24x30in) Cincinnati OH 1998

$2 200 - €1 884 - £1 298 - FF12 359
The Musicians Watercolour, gouache/board (9x39.5cm 3x15in) New-York 1998

$1 500 - €1 440 - £924 - FF9 449
Three Men on a Bench, Brooklyn Woodcut (23.5x32cm 9x12in) New-York 1999

SCHANN Paul XIX-XX **[1]**

$9 000 - €10 397 - £6 301 - FF68 202
Without Appetite Oil/panel (60x48cm 24x19in) New-York 2001

SCHANTZ von Philip 1928-1998 **[172]**

$8 988 - €10 070 - £6 265 - FF66 056
Still Life Oil/canvas (61x75cm 24x29in) Stockholm 2001

$1 860 - €1 806 - £1 148 - FF11 846
Hav och horisont Oil/canvas (27x35cm 10x13in) Stockholm 1999

$903 - €963 - £612 - FF6 316
Stilleben med vaser Akvarell/papper (19x24cm 7x9in) Stockholm 2001

$412 - €486 - £289 - FF3 188
Vattenmeloner Color lithograph (40x55cm 15x21in) Stockholm 2000

SCHANZ Heinz 1927 **[48]**

$4 142 - €3 866 - £2 500 - FF25 334
Puppenfigur (Doll) Tempera (85x50cm 33x19in) London 1999

🖌 **$4 473** - €4 171 - **£2 700** - FF27 361
Untitled Tempera/paper (86x61.5cm 33x24in) London
1999

SCHAPER Friedrich 1869-1956 **[39]**
🐄 **$2 000** - €1 892 - **£1 245** - FF12 409
**Kuh an der Tränke im Borsteler Moor bei
Niendorf** Öl/Leinwand (44x60cm 17x23in) Buxtehude
1999
🐑 **$1 160** - €1 278 - **£774** - FF8 384
Schafherde Öl/Karton (30x40cm 11x15in) Satow
2000
🖌 **$442** - €460 - **£279** - FF3 018
Schliersee Aquarell/Papier (30x46.5cm 11x18in)
Berlin 2000

SCHAPER Fritz 1841-1919 **[4]**
🐎 **$1 206** - €1 125 - **£744** - FF7 378
Fürst Otto von Bismarck Bronze (H69cm H27in)
Köln 1999

SCHAPER Hermann 1853-1911 **[1]**
🐟 **$6 726** - €7 378 - **£4 570** - FF48 394
**Kanalparti fra Venedig med Dogepaladset og
Marcuspladsen** Oil/canvas (51x69cm 20x27in)
Köbenhavn 2000

SCHÄRER Hans 1927-1997 **[116]**
🐄 **$2 423** - €2 816 - **£1 703** - FF18 469
Verklärte Nacht Mixed media (90x115cm 35x45in)
Luzern 2001
🐄 **$662** - €790 - **£472** - FF5 180
Ohne Titel Mixed media (21x25cm 8x9in) Luzern
2000
🐄 **$1 010** - €1 000 - **£630** - FF6 558
Ohne Titel Encre Chine (22x19cm 8x7in) Luzern 1999
🏛 **$109** - €105 - **£67** - FF690
Skurrile Figuren Farbradierung (24.5x24.6cm 9x9in)
Bern 1999

SCHARF Kenny 1958 **[83]**
🐄 **$18 000** - €20 885 - **£12 427** - FF136 998
Check-Array Acrylic (206x206cm 81x81in) New-York
2000
🐄 **$4 200** - €4 704 - **£2 918** - FF30 858
«Greenplanet» Acrylic (76x61cm 29x24in) New-York
2001
🐄 **$3 200** - €3 713 - **£2 209** - FF24 355
Untitled Oil/canvas (25.5x20.5cm 10x8in) New-York
2000

SCHARF Viktor 1872-1943 **[8]**
🖌 **$475** - €488 - **£301** - FF3 204
Portrait of an Old Man Pencil/paper (21x27cm
8x11in) Columbia SC 2000

SCHARFF Edwin 1887-1955 **[47]**
🏛 **$133** - €153 - **£91** - FF1 006
Berglandschaft mit Bäumen Radierung
(16.4x16.3cm 6x6in) Heidelberg 2000

SCHARFF William 1886-1959 **[145]**
🐄 **$2 737** - €2 558 - **£1 654** - FF16 778
Granskov Oil/canvas (160x225cm 62x88in)
Köbenhavn 1999
🐄 **$1 192** - €1 008 - **£713** - FF6 613
Bondekone med höne under armen Oil/canvas
(100x75cm 39x29in) Köbenhavn 1998
🖌 **$255** - €269 - **£161** - FF1 762
Stående figur Pastel/paper (63x39cm 24x15in)
Köbenhavn 2000

SCHARL Josef 1896-1954 **[151]**
🐄 **$15 801** - €15 339 - **£9 759** - FF100 617
Arbeiterbildnis II Öl/Leinwand (63.5x51.5cm
25x20in) München 1999

🐟 **$4 757** - €4 118 - **£2 887** - FF27 015
Pappeln im Sturm Tempera (32.5x37.5cm 12x14in)
München 1998
🖌 **$704** - €818 - **£494** - FF5 366
Männerkopf Indian ink/paper (27.5x23cm 10x9in)
Hamburg 2001
🏛 **$109** - €118 - **£73** - FF771
Selbstbildnis Woodcut (53.1x37.6cm 20x14in)
Hamburg 2000

SCHAROLD Carl 1811-1865 **[8]**
🖌 **$1 364** - €1 355 - **£850** - FF8 889
**Exterior View of the Main Portal of Ulm
Cathedral** Gouache (19x22cm 7x8in) London 1999

SCHASCHL Reni 1895-1979 **[8]**
🏺 **$286** - €332 - **£197** - FF2 180
Frau mit Schale Ceramic (H11.3cm H4in) München
2000

SCHATT Roy 1909 **[54]**
📷 **$1 500** - €1 410 - **£928** - FF9 251
Dean in the Photographer's Studio/At a Party
Silver print (21x31cm 8x12in) New-York 1999

SCHATZ Arnold 1929-c.1999 **[11]**
🐄 **$838** - €920 - **£540** - FF6 037
**Wildschweine, durchbrechendes Rudel zwi-
schen verschneitem Jungwald** Öl/Leinwand
(70x100cm 27x39in) Lindau 2000

SCHATZ Boris 1866-1932 **[8]**
🐄 **$7 000** - €8 369 - **£4 809** - FF54 894
Yemenite Water Carrier Oil/wood (72.5x75cm
28x29in) Tel Aviv 1999
🐎 **$10 000** - €11 955 - **£6 871** - FF78 420
Midnight Bronze (76.5x78cm 30x30in) Tel Aviv 2000

SCHATZ Manfred 1925 **[17]**
🐄 **$1 952** - €2 045 - **£1 291** - FF13 415
Auerhahnbalz Öl/Leinwand (60x80cm 23x31in)
München 2000

SCHATZ Otto Rudolf 1900-1961 **[213]**
🐄 **$7 404** - €8 721 - **£5 288** - FF57 204
Santa Maria della Salute in Venedig Oil/panel
(45.5x68.5cm 17x26in) Wien 2000
🐄 **$4 398** - €4 360 - **£2 754** - FF28 602
Blick auf Hohensalzburg Öl/Papier (37.7x29cm
14x11in) Wien 1999
🖌 **$696** - €654 - **£430** - FF4 290
Akt Black chalk (51x36.5cm 20x14in) Wien 1999
🏛 **$198** - €218 - **£127** - FF1 430
Neusattz Woodcut (41x31cm 16x12in) Wien 1999

SCHAUENBERG Walter 1884-1943 **[49]**
🐄 **$238** - €238 - **£148** - FF1 559
Bauernhaus mit Ententeich und Hühnerschar
Öl/Karton (23x35cm 9x13in) Zofingen 1999

SCHÄUFFELIN Hans Leonhard c.1480-1538/40 **[17]**
🖌 **$60 000** - €64 077 - **£40 884** - FF420 318
Sainte Catherine Leaning on a Sword Ink
(27.5x13.5cm 10x5in) New-York 2001

SCHAUMAN Sigrid 1877-1979 **[29]**
🐄 **$5 325** - €5 214 - **£3 276** - FF34 199
Puisto Oil/canvas (47x38cm 18x14in) Helsinki 1999
🐄 **$6 493** - €7 064 - **£4 279** - FF46 334
Helsingfors stads trädgård Oil/paper (34x27cm
13x10in) Helsinki 2000

SCHAUMANN Wilhelm Heinrich 1841-1893 **[9]**
🐄 **$4 270** - €4 090 - **£2 687** - FF26 831
Affen als Kunstkritiker Oil/panel (26x58cm 10x22in)
Stuttgart 1999

S

SCHAUMBURG Julius XIX **[5]**
✎ **$3 098** - €3 639 - **£2 200** - FF23 872
Shipping off the Port of Calcutta Watercolour
(29x52.5cm 11x20in) London 2000

SCHAUSS Ferdinand 1832-1916 **[7]**
☞ **$9 625** - €9 699 - **£6 000** - FF63 621
Draped Nude in a woodland Grove Oil/canvas
(110.5x189.5cm 43x74in) London 2000

SCHAWINSKY Xanti Alexander 1904-1979 **[58]**
☞ **$6 912** - €6 647 - **£4 265** - FF43 600
Profile Öl/Leinwand (86.5x61cm 34x24in) Köln 1999
✎ **$281** - €327 - **£198** - FF2 147
Ohne Titel Gouache/paper (32x24cm 12x9in) Luzern
2001
▥ **$908** - €942 - **£545** - FF6 177
«1934 XII, Si» Affiche couleur (95x65cm 37x25in)
Torino 2000

SCHEBEK Ferdinand 1875-1949 **[30]**
☞ **$450** - €511 - **£314** - FF3 353
Eisbären mit Jungen an Meeresküste
Öl/Leinwand (70x89cm 27x35in) Berlin 2001

SCHEDONI Bartolomeo 1578-1615 **[12]**
☞ **$19 143** - €21 465 - **£13 000** - FF140 799
**The Holy Family with Saint Francis adoring the
Christ Child** Oil/canvas (87.5x72cm 34x28in) London
2000
☞ **$21 204** - €19 832 - **£13 000** - FF130 091
The Penitent Magdalene with Two Putti Oil/cop-
per (43x34cm 16x13in) London 1998
✎ **$36 022** - €33 405 - **£22 000** - FF219 124
The Dorian Mode Red chalk (22.5x17cm 8x6in)
London 1998

SCHEEL Benedicte 1851-1929 **[2]**
☞ **$8 010** - €9 530 - **£5 540** - FF62 510
Stilleben med frukt Oil/canvas (32x40cm 12x15in)
Oslo 2000

SCHEEL Ernst 1903-1986 **[20]**
📷 **$1 288** - €1 534 - **£921** - FF10 061
**«Baulock der Selbsthilfe, Friedensallee,
Waschhaus»** Vintage gelatin silver print (19.8x12.5cm
7x4in) Berlin 2000

SCHEELE Kurt 1905-1944 **[24]**
▥ **$190** - €204 - **£127** - FF1 341
Tröstung Woodcut (50x60cm 19x23in) Köln 2000

SCHEERBOOM Andries 1832-c.1885 **[14]**
☞ **$1 800** - €1 670 - **£1 080** - FF10 957
**Mary Queen of Scotts/Queen of Phillippa with
the Burger of Calais** Oil/canvas (22x30cm 9x12in)
Milford CT 1999

SCHEERES Hendricus Johannes 1829-1864 **[16]**
☞ **$242** - €272 - **£168** - FF1 786
Interieur van een Stads Apotheek Technique mixte
(18.3x13.5cm 7x5in) The Hague 2000

SCHEFFEL Johan Henrik 1690-1781 **[27]**
☞ **$2 570** - €2 985 - **£1 806** - FF19 580
**Albrecht Gerner och hans hustru Anna,
F.Gyllenborg** Oil/canvas (78x63.5cm 30x25in)
Stockholm 2000

SCHEFFER Ary 1795-1858 **[68]**
☞ **$5 185** - €5 445 - **£3 280** - FF35 719
Le Partage du Pain Oil/panel (61x49.5cm 24x19in)
Amsterdam 2000
☞ **$7 722** - €9 076 - **£5 354** - FF59 532
**Portrait of a Young Boy, Probably Mesden de La
Fayette** Oil/canvas (40x32cm 15x12in) Amsterdam
2000

☞ **$521** - €474 - **£320** - FF3 112
Napoleon's Retreat From Moscow Watercolour
(19x27cm 7x10in) Billingshurst, West-Sussex 1998

SCHEFFER Henry 1798-1862 **[14]**
☞ **$7 975** - €8 385 - **£5 005** - FF55 000
Femme à l'éventail et à l'étoile d'Hermine
Huile/toile (132x82cm 51x32in) Paris 2000

SCHEFFER Robert 1859-1934 **[43]**
☞ **$5 500** - €5 542 - **£3 428** - FF36 355
Courtship Oil/canvas (94.5x72cm 37x28in) New-York
2000

SCHEFFLER Christoph Thomas 1699/1700-1756
[6]
✎ **$3 813** - €4 346 - **£2 660** - FF28 508
**Allegorie auf die Herrschaft Friedrich Wilhelms
von der Pfalz** Pencil (27.5x45.5cm 10x17in) Berlin
2001

SCHEFFLER Rudolf 1884-1973 **[17]**
☞ **$1 800** - €1 706 - **£1 124** - FF11 192
Cloudy Day Oil/canvas (101x91cm 40x36in) Mystic
CT 1999

SCHEGGI Paolo 1940-1971 **[24]**
☞ **$3 000** - €3 110 - **£1 880** - FF20 400
Intersuperficie modulare Tecnica mista
(52x52x11cm 20x20x4in) Vercelli 2000

SCHEIBE Emil Jürgen 1914 **[12]**
☞ **$1 170** - €1 329 - **£818** - FF8 720
Fischerhütten am Schliersee Oil/panel (38x47cm
14x18in) München 2001

SCHEIBE Richard 1879-1964 **[24]**
⬥ **$2 762** - €3 170 - **£1 889** - FF20 794
**Herabschreitende, stehender Weiblicher Akt mit
angewinkeltem Bein** Bronze (H66cm H25in) Berlin
2000

SCHEIBER Hugo 1873-1950 **[372]**
☞ **$3 258** - €2 811 - **£1 958** - FF18 437
Dorfstrasse Öl/Leinwand (40x60cm 15x23in)
München 1998
☞ **$1 200** - €1 244 - **£720** - FF8 160
Cocotte Tecnica mista/cartone (30x40cm 11x15in)
Roma 1999
☞ **$1 452** - €1 650 - **£1 012** - FF10 824
Paysage neigeux Technique mixte/papier (60x44cm
23x17in) Budapest 2001

SCHEIBL Hubert 1951 **[50]**
☞ **$7 641** - €6 541 - **£4 599** - FF42 903
Ohne Titel Öl/Leinwand (200x150cm 78x59in) Wien
1998
☞ **$3 096** - €2 907 - **£1 912** - FF19 068
Ohne Titel Öl/Leinwand (78x108cm 30x42in) Wien
1999

SCHEIDEGGER Ernst 1923 **[4]**
📷 **$857** - €920 - **£573** - FF6 037
Alberto Giacometti Photograph (40x50cm 15x19in)
München 2000

SCHEIDEGGER Johann 1777-1858 **[2]**
▥ **$1 409** - €1 644 - **£981** - FF10 787
Sumiswald Lithographie (23.6x34cm 9x13in) Bern
2000

SCHEIDEL von Franz Anton 1731-1801 **[17]**
✎ **$5 662** - €5 445 - **£3 488** - FF35 719
**Study of a Turtle, with Two Subsidiary studies of
Small Turtles** Watercolour (35.5x50.5cm 13x19in)
Amsterdam 1999

SCHEIDL Leopold 1884-1958 **[6]**
📖 **$156** - €182 - **£111** - FF1 191
Im Gebirge Radierung (18x24cm 7x9in) Wien 2000

SCHEIDL Roman 1949 **[67]**
✏️ **$370** - €436 - **£257** - FF2 860
Tänzer am Fluss Watercolour (50x64.5cm 19x25in)
Wien 2000

SCHEIN C. XX **[1]**
🗿 **$5 500** - €5 231 - **£3 339** - FF34 314
Marilyn Monroe Sculpture, wood (H50cm H20in)
New-York 1999

SCHEINS Ludwig 1808-1879 **[18]**
$1 935 - €2 301 - **£1 341** - FF15 092
Viehherde auf Waldlichtung Öl/Leinwand
(90x115cm 35x45in) Radolfzell 2000

SCHEIRING Leopold 1884-1927 **[16]**
$2 153 - €2 325 - **£1 488** - FF15 254
Bei Küthei Öl/Leinwand (57x73cm 22x28in) Wien
2001

SCHEITZ Matthias 1625/30-1700 **[26]**
$7 425 - €7 482 - **£4 628** - FF49 081
**Ein Reiter auf einem Schimmel hält bei einer
Apfelverkäuferin** Huile/panneau (12.5x18cm 4x7in)
Zürich 2000
✏️ **$699** - €767 - **£474** - FF5 030
Adam und Eva im Paradies Ink (28.2x21.2cm
11x8in) Berlin 2000

SCHEKTEL-SOLEAU XIX **[1]**
🗿 **$15 000** - €13 886 - **£9 055** - FF91 087
Figural Reliquary Gilded bronze (H59cm H23in)
New-York 2000

SCHELCK Maurice 1906-1978 **[113]**
$4 240 - €3 966 - **£2 624** - FF26 016
De dromer Huile/panneau (100x120cm 39x47in)
Lokeren 1999
$1 270 - €1 363 - **£852** - FF8 943
Paysage fluvial Huile/toile (70x90cm 27x35in)
Bruxelles 2000

SCHELER Max 1928 **[17]**
📷 **$533** - €511 - **£329** - FF3 353
Paris Vintage gelatin silver print (19x28.4cm 7x11in)
Köln 2001

SCHELFHOUT Andreas 1787-1870 **[288]**
$105 225 - €125 144 - **£75 000** - FF820 890
**Figures Skating on a Frozen River before a
Town** Oil/panel (47x68cm 18x26in) London 2000
$28 413 - €31 765 - **£19 775** - FF208 362
Skaters on a frozen Waterway by a Windmill
Oil/panel (8x11.5cm 3x4in) Amsterdam 2001
✏️ **$791** - €920 - **£555** - FF6 037
Holländische Kuff vor einer Steilküste Ink
(12x16.5cm 4x6in) Hamburg 2001

SCHELFHOUT Lodewijk 1881-1943 **[69]**
✏️ **$862** - €908 - **£569** - FF5 953
Pierrot Pastel (98x64cm 38x25in) Amsterdam 2000
📖 **$128** - €113 - **£77** - FF743
Sur la Côte de Quiberon Etching (24.5x29.5cm
9x11in) Amsterdam 1998

SCHELL Frederick B. c.1838-1905 **[1]**
✏️ **$1 930** - €2 277 - **£1 361** - FF14 934
Circular Quay, Sydney Harbour Watercolour,
gouache (26.5x43cm 10x16in) Woollahra, Sydney 2001

SCHELL Sherill 1877-1967 **[7]**
📷 **$2 200** - €2 419 - **£1 525** - FF15 870
Chanin Building, New York/New York Daily News
Silver print (20x15cm 8x6in) New-York 2001

SCHELL Susan Gertrude 1891-1970 **[1]**
$3 750 - €4 338 - **£2 654** - FF28 458
Crossroads Oil/board (40x50cm 16x20in) Hatfield PA
2000

SCHELLENBERG Johann Rudolf 1740-1806 **[11]**
✏️ **$3 549** - €3 826 - **£2 380** - FF25 095
Kinderbildnisse der Familie Hegner
Sanguine/papier (10x8cm 3x3in) Zürich 2000

SCHELLERUP Leis 1856-1933 **[1]**
$6 440 - €5 377 - **£3 828** - FF35 272
Sommerdag i haven Oil/canvas (33x41cm 12x16in)
Köbenhavn 1998

SCHELLINGER Hans 1905-1990 **[32]**
✏️ **$452** - €486 - **£302** - FF3 186
Stilleben Charcoal (53x42.1cm 20x16in) München
2000

SCHELLINK Samuel 1876-1958 **[18]**
✏️ **$189** - €204 - **£129** - FF1 339
Koeien Watercolour/paper (22x31cm 8x12in)
Maastricht 2001

SCHELLINKS Willem 1627-1678 **[24]**
$17 754 - €16 469 - **£11 000** - FF108 029
Sportsmen in a Wooded River Landscape
Oil/canvas (123x179.5cm 48x70in) London 1999
$6 814 - €7 669 - **£4 695** - FF50 308
Landschaft mit Wirtshaus und Wandersleuten
Oil/panel (73x106cm 28x41in) Bremen 2000
✏️ **$2 153** - €1 860 - **£1 298** - FF12 200
**A wooded Road between Canterbury and
Dover, England** Ink (18.5x29.5cm 7x11in)
Amsterdam 1998

SCHELTEMA Jan Hendrik 1861-1938 **[83]**
$2 950 - €3 250 - **£1 980** - FF21 320
Sheep at a Creek Oil/canvas (40.5x61cm 15x24in)
Malvern, Victoria 2000
$1 294 - €1 213 - **£801** - FF7 960
Cattle at the Stream Oil/canvas/board (29x34cm
11x13in) Melbourne 1999

SCHELVER August Franz 1805-1844 **[8]**
$13 304 - €12 492 - **£8 244** - FF81 944
Pferdemarkt in Partenkirchen Öl/Leinwand
(65x87.5cm 25x34in) Luzern 1999

SCHENAU Johann Eleazar 1737-1806 **[48]**
$22 092 - €20 452 - **£13 524** - FF134 156
Antiochus and Stratonike Öl/Leinwand
(153x206cm 60x81in) Hamburg 1999
$16 516 - €18 407 - **£11 545** - FF120 740
Musikunterricht Öl/Leinwand (54.5x44cm 21x17in)
München 2001
$9 078 - €9 147 - **£5 658** - FF60 000
L'amant caché/Le mari endormi Huile/toile
(26x20.5cm 10x8in) Paris 2000
✏️ **$257** - €307 - **£183** - FF2 012
Die trauernden Frauen unter dem Kreuz Christi
Ink (28x16.7cm 11x6in) Köln 2000
📖 **$263** - €256 - **£164** - FF1 676
Kinderköpfchen Radierung (7.8x13.6cm 3x5in)
Berlin 1999

SCHENCK August Friedrich 1828-1901 **[51]**
$3 110 - €3 352 - **£2 120** - FF21 987
Landskab med en lille hyrdedreng Oil/canvas
(58x88cm 22x34in) Köbenhavn 2000

SCHENCK Pieter I 1660-1718/19 **[23]**
📖 **$282** - €327 - **£200** - FF2 147
Ireland Engraving (59x48cm 23x18in) London 2000

S

SCHENCK W.H. XIX [2]
- $27 000 – €26 751 – £16 380 – FF175 478
  Still-Life with Fruit Oil/canvas (137x170cm 53x66in)
  New-York 2000

SCHENDEL Mira 1919-1988 [14]
- $28 000 – €30 055 – £18 737 – FF197 148
  Sem título Mixed media (100x50cm 39x19in) New-York 2000
- $7 500 – €6 523 – £4 521 – FF42 787
  Oro y Prata 1, 2, 3 Mixed media/paper (35.5x25.5cm 13x10in) New-York 1998

SCHENDEL van Bernardus 1649-1709 [31]
- $6 103 – €6 807 – £3 982 – FF44 649
  Figures merrymaking and feasting in an Inn Oil/canvas (52x61.5cm 20x24in) Amsterdam 2000
- $4 051 – €4 538 – £2 815 – FF29 766
  Interior Scene with Figures playing Handje Klap Oil/panel (32x39.5cm 12x15in) Amsterdam 2001

SCHENDEL van Petrus 1806-1870 [145]
- $24 155 – €22 689 – £14 560 – FF148 830
  Imagination by the Candle Light Oil/canvas (94.5x87.5cm 37x34in) Amsterdam 1999
- $9 000 – €7 791 – £5 427 – FF51 107
  Candlelit Interior with a Lady Seated at a Table Oil/panel (38.5x28.5cm 15x11in) San-Francisco CA 1998

SCHENK Charles XIX-XX [3]
- $2 000 – €1 868 – £1 208 – FF12 254
  Artistic Studies of the Human Body Photogravure (34x27cm 13x11in) New-York 1999

SCHENK Karl 1905-1973 [93]
- $1 656 – €1 801 – £1 091 – FF11 817
  Die Erde Öl/Leinwand (90x170cm 35x66in) Bern 2000
- $1 573 – €1 834 – £1 089 – FF12 029
  Lesendes Geschwisterpaar Öl/Karton (48x71.5cm 18x28in) Bern 2000
- $1 517 – €1 768 – £1 050 – FF11 600
  Die kleine Puppenmutter Oil/panel (33.5x40cm 13x15in) Bern 2000
- $283 – €328 – £195 – FF2 153
  Fahnenschwinger Gouache/paper (44x27cm 17x10in) Zürich 2000

SCHENKEL Jan Jacob 1829-1900 [11]
- $13 437 – €11 330 – £7 975 – FF74 317
  Church Interior Oil/canvas (50.5x63.5cm 19x25in) Amsterdam 1998
- $6 791 – €7 714 – £4 765 – FF50 602
  The Interior of the Bakenesse Church, Haarlem Watercolour (25.5x36cm 10x14in) Amsterdam 2001

SCHENSON Hulda Maria 1847-1940 [12]
- $434 – €402 – £265 – FF2 636
  Skogsmotiv med vattendrag Akvarell/papper (64x44cm 25x17in) Uppsala 1999

SCHERBAN Alexander 1886-1964 [14]
- $23 213 – €21 524 – £14 000 – FF141 185
  View of Jerusalem Oil/canvas (67x104cm 26x40in) London 1999

SCHERER Hermann 1893-1927 [106]
- $103 880 – €87 256 – £61 068 – FF572 362
  Waldlandschaft bei Davos/Nackte Frau Öl/Leinwand (130x90cm 51x35in) Bern 1998
- $4 331 – €4 365 – £2 699 – FF28 630
  Davoser Landschaft (Blick auf Frauenkirch) Fusain/papier (44x58cm 17x22in) Zürich 2000
- $189 – €214 – £133 – FF1 405
  Frau mit Halskette Woodcut (43x27cm 16x10in) Bern 2001

SCHERER Kees 1920-1993 [8]
- $384 – €431 – £266 – FF2 827
  Lionel Hampton Silver print (29x23cm 11x9in) Amsterdam 2000

SCHERFIG Hans 1905-1979 [127]
- $20 696 – €17 492 – £12 350 – FF114 738
  «Ensomt naesehorn» Tempera (90x140cm 35x55in) København 1998
- $4 137 – €4 693 – £2 915 – FF30 786
  Abstrakt kubistisk konstruktion Oil/panel (80x63cm 31x24in) København 2001
- $3 122 – €3 351 – £2 090 – FF21 982
  Billede med kamaeleoner Oil/masonite (21.5x64.5cm 8x25in) København 2000
- $1 185 – €1 340 – £801 – FF8 791
  Den sorte piges eventyr Watercolour/paper (42x35cm 16x13in) København 2000
- $794 – €740 – £479 – FF4 856
  Lövepar Color lithograph (46x63cm 18x24in) København 1999

SCHERMAN Tony 1950 [34]
- $9 808 – €11 528 – £6 800 – FF75 616
  Unsolved Mysteries Oil/canvas (178x158cm 70x62in) London 2000
- $2 281 – €2 647 – £1 575 – FF17 364
  Still Life - Grapes and Fruit Oil/paper (56x76cm 22x29in) Vancouver, BC. 2000
- $806 – €947 – £572 – FF6 214
  Untitled Mixed media/paper (52x30.5cm 20x12in) Toronto 2000
- $356 – €382 – £244 – FF2 509
  Lobster Etching, aquatint (35x30cm 13x11in) Toronto 2001

SCHERMER Cornelis Albertus J. 1824-1915 [29]
- $3 798 – €4 462 – £2 628 – FF29 268
  Le batelier Huile/toile (45x77cm 17x30in) Antwerpen 2000
- $4 125 – €3 559 – £2 488 – FF23 344
  Horse fair Oil/panel (33x48cm 13x19in) Dedham MA 1998

SCHERRER Hedwig 1878-1940 [4]
- $1 615 – €1 553 – £995 – FF10 190
  Reizende verspielte Szenen mit Kindern im Freien Pastel (22x16cm 8x6in) St. Gallen 1999

SCHERRER Susanne XIX-XX [1]
- $1 946 – €1 878 – £1 222 – FF12 321
  Die Alpfahrt Watercolour (20x28cm 7x11in) St. Gallen 1999

SCHERRES Carl 1833-1923 [7]
- $6 634 – €7 797 – £4 600 – FF51 143
  Après l'orage Huile/toile (70x118cm 27x46in) Warszawa 2000

SCHERREWITZ Johan Frederik Corn. 1868-1951 [174]
- $11 619 – €10 104 – £7 003 – FF66 281
  Shore Scene with Pearl Fisher Oil/canvas (66.5x51cm 26x20in) Toronto 2000
- $3 000 – €3 327 – £2 078 – FF21 821
  The Days End Oil/canvas (27x43cm 11x17in) St. Petersburg FL 2001
- $4 804 – €4 538 – £2 906 – FF29 766
  Farmer milking Cows Watercolour/paper (29x47cm 11x18in) Amsterdam 1999

SCHERZER Alexander 1835-1871 [2]
- $5 342 – €5 412 – £3 322 – FF35 500
  Quai de port animé Huile/toile (48x74cm 18x29in) Deauville 2000

S

SCHETKY John Christian 1778-1874 **[49]**

🏞 **$37 595** - €41 704 - **£25 000** - FF273 562
The Guillaume Tell in Action with H.M.S
Penelope with H.M.S Lion Oil/canvas (84x147.5cm
33x58in) London 2000

🏞 **$11 645** - €9 863 - **£7 000** - FF64 694
H.M.S «Mars» in Action with the French 74-gun
«Hercule» Oil/canvas (53.5x76cm 21x29in) London
1998

📃 **$1 600** - €1 598 - **£1 000** - FF10 484
The Constitution and the Guerricre, 19th Aug.
Watercolour/paper (25x40cm 10x16in) New-Orleans LA
1999

SCHETTLER XX **[3]**

▥ **$1 010** - €1 119 - **£700** - FF7 337
«Davos» Poster (102x64cm 40x25in) London 2001

SCHEU Leo 1886-1958 **[7]**

▥ **$500** - €581 - **£345** - FF3 813
Küchenkredenz Öl/Karton (33x46.5cm 12x18in)
Graz 2000

SCHEUCHZER Johann Jakob 1672-1733 **[17]**

▥ **$195** - €210 - **£131** - FF1 378
La ville de Rapperswyl, en Suisse Radierung
(19.3x31.6cm 7x12in) Zürich 2000

SCHEUCHZER Wilhelm Rudolf 1803-1866 **[33]**

🏞 **$1 376** - €1 534 - **£962** - FF10 061
Gebirgssee, vorn auf dem Wasser ein Nachen
Öl/Leinwand (53x68cm 20x26in) München 2001

🏞 **$2 939** - €2 706 - **£1 800** - FF17 751
Hyburg, Landscape with Cows and Goats being
herded over a Bridge Oil/board (27x35cm 10x13in)
Newbury, Berkshire 1998

🏞 **$524** - €613 - **£368** - FF4 024
Blick auf Wendelstein mit Bayrischzell Ink/paper
(27.5x38.5cm 10x15in) München 2000

SCHEUERER Julius 1859-1913 **[120]**

🏞 **$2 000** - €2 147 - **£1 339** - FF14 086
Ein Hahn, ein Huhn, zwei Tauben, ein Pfau, eine
Meise und Kücken Öl/Leinwand (40.4x60cm
15x23in) Hamburg 2000

🏞 **$2 095** - €2 250 - **£1 402** - FF14 757
Enten am Seeufer Oil/panel (8x10cm 3x3in)
Frankfurt 2000

SCHEUERER Otto 1862-1934 **[130]**

🏞 **$1 116** - €1 125 - **£695** - FF7 378
Federvieh auf einer Waldlichtung Öl/Leinwand
(35x50cm 13x19in) Erlangén 2000

🏞 **$651** - €767 - **£460** - FF5 030
Federvieh und Küken am sommerlichen
Waldesrand Öl/Karton (21x27cm 8x10in) Köln 2001

SCHEUERLE Joseph 1873-1948 **[1]**

📃 **$3 000** - €2 727 - **£1 806** - FF17 889
Pine Tree-Arapaho Watercolour/paper (33x22cm
13x9in) Hayden ID 1998

SCHEUERMANN Ludwig 1859-1911 **[6]**

🏞 **$1 555** - €1 346 - **£944** - FF8 830
En jaeger Oil/wood (53x38cm 20x14in) Köbenhavn
1998

SCHEUREN Caspar Johan Nepomuk 1810-1887
[74]

🏞 **$2 754** - €3 090 - **£1 927** - FF20 266
Farmers at work in a River Landscape Oil/canvas
(53x78.5cm 20x30in) Cape Town 2001

🏞 **$2 987** - €2 556 - **£1 798** - FF16 766
Flusslandschaft (am Niederrhein?) Öl/Leinwand
(46x34cm 18x13in) München 1998

✎ **$895** - €767 - **£538** - FF5 030
Im Saal eines Schlosses Aquarell/Papier
(30.2x40cm 11x15in) Köln 1998

SCHEURENBERG Joseph 1846-1914 **[4]**

🏞 **$18 763** - €15 761 - **£11 000** - FF103 383
A Shared Moment Oil/panel (41x35cm 16x13in)
London 1998

SCHEURICH Paul 1883-1945 **[61]**

🗿 **$908** - €1 022 - **£626** - FF6 707
Ruhende Porcelain (26x39cm 10x15in) Berlin 2000

$220 - €215 - **£135** - FF1 408
Kokette Spitzentänzerin Pencil (30x14cm 11x5in)
Berlin 1999

▥ **$392** - €335 - **£235** - FF2 200
«Fly Through Europe Imperial Airways» Affiche
(62x100cm 24x39in) Paris 1998

SCHEYER Emmy Esther, Galka 1889-1945 **[1]**

🏞 **$11 697** - €11 248 - **£7 207** - FF73 785
Stilleben Öl/Leinwand (82x66cm 32x25in) Köln 1999

SCHEYNDEL van Gillis 1635-1678 **[3]**

▥ **$1 580** - €1 534 - **£984** - FF10 061
Winterlandschaft mit Schlittschuhläufern vor
einem Dorf Radierung (10.7x15.4cm 4x6in) Berlin
1999

SCHGOER Julius 1847-1885 **[10]**

🏞 **$1 101** - €1 269 - **£769** - FF8 049
Reiter mit Jagdhorn am Waldrand Oil/panel
(18x14.7cm 7x5in) München 2001

SCHIAMINOSSI Raffaele c.1570-c.1620 **[9]**

▥ **$375** - €417 - **£249** - FF2 733
The Creation of Adam Etching (24.5x29cm 9x11in)
New-York 2000

SCHIANCHI Federico 1858-1919 **[23]**

✎ **$960** - €829 - **£640** - FF5 440
Castel' Sant' Angelo Acquarello/carta (35x24.5cm
13x9in) Roma 1998

SCHIAVONE Andrea Meldolla 1522-1563/82 **[16]**

🏞 **$22 953** - €22 105 - **£14 282** - FF145 000
L'enfant Bacchus et les Nymphes Huile/toile
(62x98cm 24x38in) Montfort L'Amaury 1999

🏞 **$61 981** - €57 971 - **£38 000** - FF380 266
The Judgement of Paris/The Contest of Apollo
and Marsyas Oil/canvas (20x36cm 7x14in) London
1998

✎ **$23 527** - €22 973 - **£15 000** - FF150 690
Ceres in a Chariot drawn by Dragons Black chalk
(37.5x27.5cm 14x10in) London 1999

▥ **$316** - €332 - **£199** - FF2 180
Frau mit Kind tröstet eine weinende Frau
Radierung (17.8x13.3cm 7x5in) Heidelberg 2000

SCHIAVONETTI Luigi, Lewis 1765-1810 **[15]**

▥ **$248** - €282 - **£170** - FF1 850
Pilgrimage to Canterbury, after Thomas
Stothard R.A Engraving (33.5x92.5cm 13x36in) Bury
St. Edmunds, Suffolk 2000

SCHIAVONI Natale 1777-1858 **[22]**

🏞 **$4 401** - €4 116 - **£2 664** - FF27 000
Jeune femme mélancolique Huile/toile (88x69cm
34x27in) Vierzon 1999

🏞 **$3 184** - €3 579 - **£2 235** - FF23 477
Helène Malfatti, geboren Gräfin Ostrowska
Miniature (8x6.5cm 3x2in) Düsseldorf 2001

SCHIBIG Philippe 1940 **[29]**

✎ **$642** - €705 - **£436** - FF4 623
Ohne Titel Ballpoint pen (30x23cm 11x9in) Luzern
2000

S

SCHICHO Karel 1834-1908 **[1]**
- **$2 601** - €2 460 - **£1 620** - FF16 137
  By the Chiemsky Lake Oil/panel (26.5x32cm 10x12in) Praha 1999

SCHICK Gottlieb 1776-1812 **[3]**
- **$120 000** - €134 012 - **£76 848** - FF879 060
  Allegory of the Divine Beauty of Nature Oil/canvas (127x170cm 50x66in) New-York 2000

SCHICKHARDT Karl 1866-1933 **[47]**
- **$630** - €613 - **£387** - FF4 024
  Schwäbische Bachlandschaft im Herbst Öl/Leinwand (89x70cm 35x27in) Stuttgart 1999
- **$416** - €434 - **£262** - FF2 850
  Auf der Schwäbischen Alb Öl/Karton (35x44cm 13x17in) Stuttgart 2000

SCHIDER Fritz 1846-1907 **[13]**
- **$2 096** - €2 147 - **£1 293** - FF14 086
  Pferderennen auf der Oktoberwiese in München Öl/Leinwand (41.2x33.5cm 16x13in) Düsseldorf 2000

SCHIDROWITZ M.P.W. XIX-XX **[5]**
- **$3 275** - €3 068 - **£2 013** - FF20 123
  Häuptlingsfrau der Umutina-Indianer in reichem Schmuck Öl/Leinwand (110x85cm 43x33in) Lindau 1999

SCHIEDGES Petrus Paulus 1813-1876 **[52]**
- **$3 861** - €4 538 - **£2 677** - FF29 766
  Shipping in the Harbour of Batavia Oil/canvas (38x74cm 14x29in) Amsterdam 2000
- **$3 462** - €3 097 - **£2 074** - FF20 316
  A Calm : a Fishing Boat and two - Masters at Anchor in an Estuary Oil/canvas/board (29x36cm 11x14in) Amsterdam 1998

SCHIEDGES Petrus Paulus II 1860-1922 **[37]**
- **$11 206** - €13 097 - **£8 000** - FF85 911
  Grazing Sheep near Laren Oil/canvas (99.5x148.5cm 39x58in) London 2001
- **$2 417** - €2 723 - **£1 666** - FF17 859
  A Peasant at Work with a Malle Jan Nearby Oil/canvas (75x114cm 29x44in) Amsterdam 2000
- **$655** - €771 - **£453** - FF5 060
  Faggot Gatherer with his Horse and Cart Watercolour, gouache/paper (46x63cm 18x24in) Amsterdam 2000

SCHIEFERDECKER Christian Karl Aug. 1823-1878 **[3]**
- **$4 144** - €4 269 - **£2 564** - FF28 000
  Portrait d'une femme avec son enfant Huile/toile (83x70cm 32x27in) Toulouse 2000

SCHIELE Egon 1890-1918 **[492]**
- **$9 525 100** - €10 966 397 - **£6 500 000** - FF71 934 850
  Portrait of the art Dealer Guido Arnot Oil/canvas (140.5x109.5cm 55x43in) London 2000
- **$10 318 000** - €11 001 178 - **£7 000 000** - FF72 163 000
  Porträt des Malers Anton Peschka Mixed media (110x100cm 43x39in) London 2001
- **$46 440** - €43 603 - **£28 680** - FF286 020
  Landschaft in Niederösterreich Öl/Karton (20.5x32.9cm 8x12in) Wien 1999
- **$122 077** - €118 814 - **£75 000** - FF779 370
  Weiblicher Akt Watercolour (49x32cm 19x12in) London 1999
- **$4 000** - €4 477 - **£2 789** - FF29 370
  Die Kauernde Drypoint (48x32cm 18x12in) New-York 2001

SCHIER Franz 1852-1922 **[11]**
- **$636** - €716 - **£447** - FF4 695
  Salome Painting (17x13cm 6x5in) Düsseldorf 2001

SCHIERTZ Franz Wilhelm 1813-1887 **[13]**
- **$3 175** - €3 624 - **£2 205** - FF23 773
  Midnat ved oen Starck, Spitzbergen (Svalbard) Oil/canvas (35x53cm 13x20in) Köbenhavn 2000

SCHIESS Ernst Traugott 1872-1919 **[58]**
- **$1 728** - €1 944 - **£1 206** - FF12 754
  Mädchen im Garten Öl/Karton (39.5x58cm 15x22in) Luzern 2001
- **$1 498** - €1 685 - **£1 046** - FF11 053
  Marokkanische Szene Öl/Karton (26x34.5cm 10x13in) Luzern 2001

SCHIESS Hans Rudolf 1904-1978 **[23]**
- **$19 281** - €18 407 - **£12 045** - FF120 740
  Berglandschaft bei Davos (Clavadel) Öl/Leinwand (101x120cm 39x47in) Köln 1999
- **$2 226** - €2 621 - **£1 564** - FF17 194
  Polarität Öl/Leinwand (65x55cm 25x21in) Zürich 2000
- **$1 065** - €1 064 - **£665** - FF6 978
  Komposition Öl/Leinwand (28x23cm 11x9in) Zofingen 1999

SCHIESS Johannes 1799-1844 **[2]**
- **$2 596** - €2 938 - **£1 816** - FF19 270
  Lindenhof St.Gallen Watercolour (25x38cm 9x14in) St. Gallen 2001

SCHIESS Traugott 1834-1869 **[35]**
- **$1 038** - €1 175 - **£726** - FF7 708
  Blick von der Stauberen, Alpstein Öl/Leinwand (43x60cm 16x23in) St. Gallen 2001
- **$1 330** - €1 249 - **£824** - FF8 194
  Rind auf der Weide Öl/Leinwand (44x29.5cm 17x11in) Luzern 1999

SCHIESTL Matthäus 1869-1939 **[37]**
- **$1 566** - €1 534 - **£964** - FF10 061
  Jugendlicher Engel mit Mandoline Oil/panel (40x50cm 15x19in) Stuttgart 1999
- **$1 291** - €1 431 - **£896** - FF9 390
  Porträt eines alten Bauern vor seinem Dorf Öl/Karton (44x32cm 17x12in) Köln 2001

SCHIESTL Rudolf 1878-1931 **[101]**
- **$219** - €204 - **£135** - FF1 341
  Der Pfeifer von Niklashausen Woodcut (26.3x20cm 10x7in) Hamburg 1999

SCHIETZOLD Robert August Rudolf 1842-1908 **[11]**
- **$8 700** - €8 436 - **£5 511** - FF55 339
  Heuernte am Chiemsee-Ufer mit Blick auf die Fraueninsel Öl/Leinwand (71x109cm 27x42in) München 1999

SCHIFANO Mario 1934-1998 **[995]**
- **$9 500** - €9 848 - **£5 700** - FF64 600
  Senza titolo Smalto/tela (140x140cm 55x55in) Milano 1999
- **$2 320** - €3 006 - **£1 740** - FF19 720
  Nuvole Smalto/tela (60x80cm 23x31in) Milano 2000
- **$1 500** - €1 555 - **£900** - FF10 200
  Senza titolo Smalto/tela (20x30cm 7x11in) Vercelli 2001
- **$2 520** - €2 177 - **£1 680** - FF14 280
  Paesaggio Tecnica mista/carta (101x105.5cm 39x41in) Prato 1998
- **$350** - €363 - **£210** - FF2 380
  Stelle Serigrafia a colori (96x67cm 37x26in) Milano 2001

SCHIFF Jean-Mathias 1884-? **[2]**
$6 000 - €5 311 - **£3 668** - FF34 841
In the Artist's Studio Oil/panel (41.5x55cm 16x21in)
New-York 1999

SCHIFF John D. XX **[3]**
$2 558 - €2 543 - **£1 589** - FF16 684
Albert Einstein Vintage gelatin silver print
(25.3x20.2cm 9x7in) Wien 1999

SCHIFFER Anton 1811-1876 **[40]**
$21 896 - €20 452 - **£13 232** - FF134 156
**Bad Ischl., Panoramablick über das Ort auf die
Berge** Öl/Leinwand (53x80cm 20x31in) Berlin 1999
$8 638 - €10 174 - **£6 076** - FF66 738
«Der schwarzen See bei Ischl» Öl/Karton
(31x38cm 12x14in) Wien 2000

SCHIFFERLE Klaudia 1955 **[36]**
$2 064 - €2 349 - **£1 450** - FF15 410
«Das Mahl» Öl/Leinwand (60x50cm 23x19in) Zürich
2001
$517 - €586 - **£361** - FF3 845
«Turn-turn-turn» Mischtechnik/Papier (41x31cm
16x12in) Zürich 2001
$127 - €141 - **£86** - FF925
Unterwegs Radierung (56.7x45cm 22x17in) Zürich
2000

SCHIFFMANN Joseph Nikl.,Jost II 1822-1883 **[16]**
$2 157 - €1 861 - **£1 296** - FF12 210
Seelandschaft mit Staffage Öl/Leinwand
(46x55.5cm 18x21in) Bern 1998

SCHIKANEDER Jacob 1855-1924 **[11]**
$15 895 - €15 034 - €9 900 - FF98 615
Monk Oil/canvas (67.5x55.5cm 26x21in) Praha 2000
$11 849 - €11 207 - **£7 380** - FF73 513
Woman raking Leaves Oil/wood (15x27.5cm
5x10in) Praha 1999

SCHIKKINGER Franciscus Johannes 1838-1902
[11]
$701 - €817 - **£490** - FF5 357
**The Nieuwezijds Voorburgwal, with the Back of
the Royal Palace** Watercolour (30x42cm 11x16in)
Amsterdam 2000

SCHILBACH Johann Heinrich 1798-1851 **[8]**
$38 601 - €46 017 - **£27 522** - FF301 851
Schloss Schönberg an der Bergstrasse
Öl/Leinwand (40x54.5cm 15x21in) Köln 2000
$7 620 - €8 181 - **£5 146** - FF53 662
Blick auf Olevano Öl/Papier (21.3x29.3cm 8x11in)
Hamburg 2000

SCHILCHER Friedrich 1811-1881 **[8]**
$6 920 - €7 267 - **£4 360** - FF47 670
Kaiser Franz Joseph I. von Österreich
Öl/Leinwand (123x95cm 48x37in) Wien 2000

SCHILDER Andrei Nicolajevitch 1861-1919 **[3]**
$12 883 - €12 165 - **£8 000** - FF79 796
Woodland under Snow Oil/canvas (79.5x120cm
31x47in) London 1999

SCHILDT Martin 1867-1921 **[14]**
$2 400 - €2 182 - **£1 445** - FF14 311
Woman Sewing in Interior Oil/canvas (61x75cm
24x29in) Bethesda MD 1998
$323 - €363 - **£226** - FF2 381
Portret van een oude vrouw Watercolour,
gouache/paper (43.5x34cm 17x13in) Dordrecht 2001

SCHILKIN Michael 1900-1962 **[39]**
$1 226 - €1 345 - **£789** - FF8 825
Untitled Ceramic (H46cm H18in) Helsinki 2000

SCHILLE Alice 1869-1955 **[10]**
$10 000 - €11 507 - **£6 893** - FF75 481
Cala Lilies Oil/canvas (50x60cm 20x24in) Newark OH
2000
$5 000 - €5 666 - **£3 494** - FF37 164
Figures on a Dock, Gloucester Watercolour/paper
(28.5x38.5cm 11x15in) New-York 2001

SCHILLER von Johann Felix 1805-1853 **[1]**
$3 998 - €4 602 - **£2 741** - FF30 185
Heimkehr von der Ernte Öl/Leinwand (100x83cm
39x32in) München 2000

SCHILLING Alexander 1859-1937 **[3]**
$1 200 - €1 165 - **£741** - FF7 641
May Morning after Shower Oil/canvas (30x45cm
12x18in) Cedar-Falls IA 1999

SCHILLING Erich 1885-1945 **[10]**
$796 - €767 - **£498** - FF5 030
Mondäne Flugpassagiere Indian ink (41.5x33.5cm
16x13in) München 1999

SCHILTER Hans 1918-1988 **[8]**
$1 528 - €1 773 - **£1 055** - FF11 631
Venedig Gouache/paper (75x60cm 29x23in) Luzern
2000

SCHINAGEL Emil 1899-1934 **[9]**
$1 689 - €1 971 - **£1 206** - FF12 926
Scène dans une petite ville Huile/carton (25x35cm
9x13in) Lódz 2001

SCHINDLER Albert 1805-1861 **[14]**
$1 795 - €2 122 - **£1 272** - FF13 918
Romantische Landschaft mit Ruine Öl/Leinwand
(26.5x32cm 10x12in) Hildrizhausen 2000
$425 - €372 - **£257** - FF2 440
Stags Graphite (24x36cm 10x14in) Columbia SC 1998

SCHINDLER Jakob Emil 1842-1892 **[61]**
$74 707 - €73 436 - **£48 000** - FF481 708
View from Plankenberg Oil/panel (60.5x94.5cm
23x37in) London 1999
$7 020 - €6 541 - **£4 329** - FF42 903
Blick auf das Rosaliengebirge Oil/panel (26x34cm
10x13in) Linz 1999
$578 - €654 - **£390** - FF4 290
Baumstudie Pencil/paper (24x16cm 9x6in) Wien 2000

SCHINDLER Osmar 1869-1927 **[6]**
$1 473 - €1 534 - **£933** - FF10 061
David und Goliath Pastell/Papier (104x73.5cm
40x28in) München 2000

SCHINKEL Karl Friedrich 1781-1841 **[74]**
$2 370 - €2 301 - **£1 476** - FF15 092
Unter den Linden in Berlin Pencil/paper
(21.7x35.2cm 8x13in) Berlin 1999
$842 - €818 - **£524** - FF5 366
Waldweg mit einer Kutsche Radierung
(11.3x19.8cm 4x7in) Berlin 1999

SCHINNAGL Maximilian 1697-1762 **[11]**
$31 388 - €37 086 - **£22 243** - FF243 269
Flusslandschaften Öl/Leinwand (70x85cm 27x33in)
Zürich 2000
$2 166 - €2 325 - **£1 449** - FF15 254
**Weite, bewaldete Landschaft mit einem Dorf
und Figuren an einem Teich** Öl/Metall (30x37.5cm
11x14in) Wien 2000

SCHIÖLER Inge 1908-1971 **[465]**
$11 749 - €12 895 - **£7 570** - FF84 588
Blommande klippor vid havsvik, koster Oil/can-
vas (65x69cm 25x27in) Stockholm 2000

S

S

$4 689 - €5 254 - **£3 268** - FF34 464
Strand N.Oddö Oil/canvas (24x33cm 9x12in)
Stockholm 2001

$1 666 - €1 562 - **£1 030** - FF10 249
Blommor Gouache/paper (35.5x43cm 13x16in)
Stockholm 1999

$384 - €358 - **£237** - FF2 349
Buskar vid kusten Color lithograph (43x47cm
16x18in) Stockholm 1999

SCHIØTT August Heinrich 1823-1895 [52]

$52 348 - €61 711 - **£36 800** - FF404 800
**Badende drenge en sommerdag ved
Aalsgaarde i Nordsjaelland** Oil/canvas (175x235cm
68x92in) Vejle 2000

$2 131 - €2 018 - **£1 326** - FF13 240
**Fra Aalsgaard Strand, en fisker er ved at save
braende, den lille søn** Oil/canvas (70x95cm
27x37in) Köbenhavn 1999

$363 - €402 - **£252** - FF2 636
Portraet af orientaler Oil/canvas (36x29cm 14x11in)
Vejle 2001

SCHIØTTZ-JENSEN Niels Frederik 1855-1941 [153]

$21 343 - €24 798 - **£15 000** - FF162 663
**Sommerdag på stranden, Lonstrup (summer
day on Lonstrup beach)** Oil/canvas (115x170.5cm
45x67in) London 2001

$1 687 - €1 582 - **£1 042** - FF10 380
The Mountain Road Oil/canvas (50x39cm 19x15in)
Johannesburg 1999

$699 - €606 - **£424** - FF3 973
Fra Venedig med gondoler i forgrunden Oil/wood
(19x30cm 7x11in) Köbenhavn 1998

SCHIPPERS Joseph, Jos. 1868-1950 [52]

$1 409 - €1 534 - **£968** - FF10 061
Widderkopf vor Landschaft Öl/Leinwand
(51x40.8cm 20x16in) Leipzig 2001

$1 785 - €1 859 - **£1 125** - FF12 195
Favorite Huile/bois (28x26cm 11x10in) Antwerpen
2000

SCHIPPERS Wim T. 1942 [9]

$1 972 - €1 815 - **£1 183** - FF11 906
Untitled Watercolour (51x48cm 20x18in) Amsterdam
2000

SCHIPPERUS Pieter Adriaan C. 1840-1929 [74]

$672 - €799 - **£479** - FF5 243
Schafherde Öl/Leinwand (57x86cm 22x33in) Linz
2000

$445 - €499 - **£311** - FF3 274
Koehoedster onder bomen Mixed media
(34.5x23.5cm 13x9in) Dordrecht 2001

$845 - €908 - **£565** - FF5 953
Boats at Sea Watercolour/paper (19.5x30cm 7x11in)
Amsterdam 2000

SCHIRM Carl Cowen 1852-1928 [15]

$1 204 - €1 125 - **£727** - FF7 378
Heidelandschaft mit Birken und Bauerngehöft
Öl/Leinwand (62x80cm 24x31in) Berlin 1999

SCHIRMER Johann Wilhelm 1807-1863 [135]

$63 042 - €71 582 - **£43 806** - FF469 546
Süditalienische Landschaft mit Hirten
Öl/Leinwand (116x165cm 45x64in) Köln 2001

$7 165 - €7 158 - **£4 480** - FF46 954
Abendlandschaft mit Rehen am Bachlauf
Öl/Leinwand (54x50.5cm 21x19in) Köln 1999

$1 285 - €1 087 - **£769** - FF7 132
Forest Edge Oil/canvas (20x30cm 7x11in)
Amsterdam 1998

$524 - €613 - **£368** - FF4 024
Thal der Aegeria Coloured chalks (43.7x57cm
17x22in) München 2000

$364 - €434 - **£259** - FF2 850
Der Jäger Abschied vom Wald Radierung
(28.5x22.7cm 11x8in) Berlin 2000

SCHIRMER Wilhelm August 1802-1866 [6]

$16 321 - €15 977 - **£10 041** - FF104 804
Die ruhelose Oil/canvas (107x149cm 42x58in)
Helsinki 1999

SCHIRREN Ferdinand 1872-1944 [121]

$5 474 - €5 701 - **£3 450** - FF37 398
Vase de chrysanthèmes devant la fenêtre
Technique mixte (74x85cm 29x33in) Antwerpen 2000

$1 904 - €1 983 - **£1 200** - FF13 008
Vase de fleurs Technique mixte (45x33cm 17x12in)
Antwerpen 2000

$1 722 - €1 611 - **£1 066** - FF10 569
Jonge knaap Plâtre (50.5x26cm 19x10in) Lokeren
1999

$3 480 - €3 718 - **£2 370** - FF24 390
Jonge vrouw Aquarelle (32.5x27cm 12x10in)
Lokeren 2001

SCHIVERT Viktor 1863-? [36]

$797 - €895 - **£552** - FF5 869
Weiblicher Akt Öl/Leinwand (55x80cm 21x31in)
Stuttgart 2000

$1 185 - €1 022 - **£717** - FF6 707
**«Landsknecht beim Belauschen eines
Liebespaares»** Oil/panel (31x21cm 12x8in) Kempten
2000

SCHJERFBECK Helene 1862-1946 [170]

$161 384 - €155 692 - **£102 000** - FF1 021 275
Längtans blåa blomma Oil/canvas (42x52cm
16x20in) London 1999

$75 946 - €66 474 - **£46 000** - FF436 043
Kaarina in White Oil/canvas (29x26cm 11x10in)
London 1998

$10 756 - €12 109 - **£7 408** - FF79 430
Den ena av väninnorna Charcoal/paper (35x27cm
13x10in) Helsinki 2000

$4 282 - €4 205 - **£2 657** - FF27 580
Bagarens dotter Color lithograph (64x49cm 25x19in)
Helsinki 1999

SCHLABITZ Adolf Gustav 1854-1943 [14]

$10 387 - €11 798 - **£7 287** - FF77 391
Kathel's Heimkehr Oil/canvas (141x91cm 55x35in)
Amsterdam 2000

SCHLAGETER Karl 1894-1990 [72]

$304 - €358 - **£218** - FF2 347
Die Taubenrupferin Oil/panel (27x21.5cm 10x8in)
Düsseldorf 2001

SCHLANGENHAUSEN Emma 1882-? [4]

$179 - €153 - **£107** - FF1 006
Genesis Linocut (18x29.5cm 7x11in) Berlin 1998

SCHLAPPRITZ Louis XIX [1]

$22 205 - €23 316 - **£14 000** - FF152 945
House in Pernambuco Oil/canvas (32.5x40.5cm
12x15in) London 2000

SCHLATTER Ernst Emil 1883-1954 [75]

$587 - €592 - **£366** - FF3 885
Landschaft mit Bauernhaus Öl/Leinwand
(80.5x100.5cm 31x39in) Zürich 2000

$365 - €313 - **£219** - FF2 053
Pappeallee vor Uttwil am Bodensee Öl/Karton
(39x27cm 15x10in) St. Gallen 1998

🛏 **$221** - €219 - **£137** - FF1 434
Zwölf Schlösser im Aargau Lithographie (33x41cm 12x16in) St. Gallen 1999

SCHLEEH Hans 1928 **[4]**
🎨 **$2 110** - €2 387 - **£1 476** - FF15 658
Untitled Abstract Bronze (H77.5cm H30in) Toronto 2001

SCHLEGEL Fernand 1920 **[7]**
☞ **$1 443** - €1 220 - **£858** - FF8 000
Solitude 2 Acrylique/carton/toile (65x54cm 25x21in) Dijon 1998

SCHLEICH August 1814-1865 **[27]**
☞ **$568** - €613 - **£392** - FF4 024
Zwei Wildschweine in der Kuhle Öl/Karton (26x31cm 10x12in) Frankfurt 2001

SCHLEICH Eduard I 1812-1874 **[92]**
☞ **$6 741** - €6 135 - **£4 212** - FF40 246
Blick vom Herzogstand ins Murnauer Tal Öl/Leinwand (84x109cm 33x42in) München 1999
☞ **$3 285** - €2 812 - **£1 977** - FF18 443
Bäume an einem Wasser Oil/panel (11.2x25.5cm 4x10in) München 1998
✎ **$440** - €501 - **£307** - FF3 286
Altes Bauernhaus mit Brunnen Pencil/paper (14x19cm 5x7in) München 2000

SCHLEICH Eduard II 1853-1893 **[20]**
☞ **$2 245** - €2 301 - **£1 386** - FF15 092
Mondlandschaft Öl/Leinwand (62x50.5cm 24x19in) Düsseldorf 2000

SCHLEICH Hans 1834-1912 **[17]**
☞ **$18 000** - €17 630 - **£11 599** - FF115 646
Coastal Landscape Oil/canvas (127x211cm 50x83in) New-York 1999

SCHLEICH Robert 1845-1934 **[114]**
☞ **$3 690** - €3 719 - **£2 300** - FF24 392
Harvest Time Oil/canvas (61x76cm 24x29in) London 2000
☞ **$2 725** - €2 630 - **£1 711** - FF17 249
Landschaft mit Schäfer und Herde Oil/panel (7.5x13.5cm 2x5in) Zürich 1999
✎ **$360** - €409 - **£251** - FF2 683
Bauer mit fuhrwerk auf dem Acker Pencil/paper (7x10cm 2x3in) München 2001

SCHLEICHER Carl act.1855-1871 **[29]**
☞ **$1 200** - €1 209 - **£748** - FF7 932
Tavern Dwellers Oil/panel (21x15.5cm 8x6in) New-York 2000

SCHLEIFER Fritz 1903-1977 **[4]**
🛏 **$19 000** - €16 209 - **£11 460** - FF106 324
«Ausstellung, Bauhaus Weimar» Poster (64x68cm 25x26in) New-York 1998

SCHLEIME Cornelia 1953 **[1]**
☞ **$12 978** - €14 342 - **£9 000** - FF94 077
Palermo Acrylic (200x160cm 78x62in) London 2001

SCHLEINITZ Max ?-1935 **[1]**
☞ **$4 573** - €5 113 - **£3 082** - FF33 539
Pfirsichstilleben im Garten Öl/Leinwand (82x96cm 32x37in) München 2000

SCHLEISNER Christian Andreas 1810-1882 **[122]**
☞ **$2 344** - €2 681 - **£1 630** - FF17 588
To unge piger pa visit Oil/canvas (68x52cm 26x20in) København 2000
☞ **$754** - €804 - **£502** - FF5 277
Aben skal have sukker Oil/canvas (29x24cm 11x9in) København 2000

SCHLEMMER Oskar 1888-1943 **[123]**
☞ **$3 099 060** - €2 545 521 - **£1 800 000** - FF16 697 520
«Grosse Sitzendengruppe 1» Oil/canvas (146x98cm 57x38in) London 1998
☞ **$600 814** - €691 727 - **£410 000** - FF4 537 429
Group of Boys in Grey Tempera (74.5x41.5cm 29x16in) London 2000
☞ **$24 852** - €23 173 - **£15 000** - FF152 008
Head of a young Boy with Kneeling Figur Mixed media (9x9.5cm 3x3in) London 1999
🎨 **$3 119** - €3 579 - **£2 133** - FF23 477
Erhobener Kopf Relief (11.1x12.3x1.3cm 4x4xin) Dettelbach-Effeldorf 2000
☞ **$94 693** - €77 780 - **£55 000** - FF510 202
Gruppe mit rotem Knaben Watercolour (33.5x24cm 13x9in) London 1998
🛏 **$4 639** - €4 326 - **£2 800** - FF28 374
Head in Profile with Black Contour Lithograph (20x14cm 7x5in) London 1999

SCHLESINGER Adam Johann 1759-1829 **[3]**
☞ **$6 500** - €5 944 - **£3 969** - FF38 992
Pleasures of the table Oil/panel (29x35cm 11x14in) New-York 1998

SCHLESINGER Carl 1825-1893 **[14]**
☞ **$9 000** - €7 766 - **£5 437** - FF50 943
Crossing the Ford Oil/canvas (78x111cm 31x44in) St. Petersburg FL 1999

SCHLESINGER Felix 1833-1910 **[69]**
☞ **$11 297** - €12 043 - **£7 165** - FF79 000
Jeune femme à la mantille tenant une missive Huile/toile (87x70.5cm 34x27in) Biarritz 2000
☞ **$13 500** - €14 579 - **£9 330** - FF95 635
Feeding the Rabbit Oil/panel (31x40cm 12x15in) New-York 2001
✎ **$1 093** - €1 022 - **£662** - FF2 607
Hase, an einem Blatt nagend Pencil/paper (11.5x18.5cm 4x7in) Düsseldorf 1999

SCHLESINGER Henry Guillaume 1814-1893 **[32]**
☞ **$20 962** - €21 474 - **£12 936** - FF140 863
Das geraubte Kind Öl/Leinwand (109.5x142cm 43x55in) Düsseldorf 2002
☞ **$3 900** - €4 269 - **£2 707** - FF28 000
Enfants sur une peau de tigre Huile/toile (68.5x54.5cm 26x21in) Paris 2001
✎ **$354** - €396 - **£240** - FF2 620
Portrait de jeune fille dans un ovale Aquarelle (24x33.5cm 16x13in) Paris 2000

SCHLESINGER Johann Jacob 1792-1855 **[3]**
☞ **$2 927** - €2 710 - **£1 767** - FF17 775
Bildnis eines älteren Herrn im schwarzen Ausgehrock Oil/panel (32x26cm 12x10in) Heidelberg 1999

SCHLESINGER Samuel 1896-1986 **[11]**
☞ **$6 500** - €6 977 - **£4 349** - FF45 766
In the Beit-Midrash Oil/canvas (65x84cm 25x33in) Tel Aviv 2000
✎ **$1 000** - €1 037 - **£659** - FF6 801
Shabbath Candles Drawing (32x28cm 12x11in) Herzelia-Pituah 2000

SCHLEUSNER Thea 1879-1964 **[21]**
✎ **$173** - €194 - **£120** - FF1 274
«Helle Nacht am Bodden» Aquarell/Papier (29.8x42.2cm 11x16in) Berlin 2001

SCHLICHT Abel 1754-1826 **[4]**
🛏 **$1 887** - €1 943 - **£1 189** - FF12 744
Ruinen nach Pannini Aquatinta (47x61cm 18x24in) Berlin 2000

S

SCHLICHTER Rudolf 1890-1955 **[189]**
- $43 962 - €50 614 - **£30 000** - FF332 007
  Portrait of Richard Masseck/Study for a portrait of Richard Masseck Oil/canvas (76x54cm 29x21in) London 2000
- $6 058 - €5 880 - **£3 772** - FF38 569
  Disputation Indian ink (48.8x61.5cm 19x24in) Berlin 1999
- $429 - €409 - **£267** - FF2 683
  Bordellszene Lithographie (63x48.2cm 24x18in) Hamburg 1999

SCHLICHTING Waldemar 1896-1970 **[36]**
- $600 - €560 - **£370** - FF3 671
  Segelfartyg i skymning Oil/canvas (64x91cm 25x35in) Stockholm 1999

SCHLICHTING-CARLSEN Carl 1852-1903 **[34]**
- $649 - €737 - **£444** - FF4 834
  Skovparti med jaeger og hund Oil/canvas (75x90cm 29x35in) Vejle 2000

SCHLICK Benjamin 1796-1872 **[4]**
- $1 098 - €1 081 - **£684** - FF7 092
  Paisaje rocoso Acuarela/papel (27.5x19cm 10x7in) Madrid 1999

SCHLIECKER August Eduard 1833-1911 **[11]**
- $2 115 - €2 403 - **£1 480** - FF15 763
  Zugefrorener Kanal mit Mühle und Bauernhaus Öl/Leinwand (25x33cm 9x12in) Berlin 2001

SCHLIEPSTEIN Gerhard 1886-1963 **[26]**
- $790 - €767 - **£492** - FF5 030
  Sitzendes Mädchen, sich Ohrringe anlegend Ivory, bronze (23x17x11cm 9x6x4in) Bad-Vilbel 1999

SCHLIMARSKI Hans 1859-1913 **[16]**
- $2 453 - €2 823 - **£1 693** - FF18 518
  Lady on Balcony Oil/canvas (65x73.5cm 25x28in) Durban 2000
- $1 878 - €2 180 - **£1 320** - FF14 301
  Junge Frau mit erhobenen Armen Oil/panel (32x23.5cm 12x9in) Wien 2001

SCHLITT Heinrich 1849-1923 **[23]**
- $2 032 - €1 983 - **£1 248** - FF13 008
  La légende de Blanche-Neige Huile/toile (33x46cm 12x18in) Antwerpen 1999

SCHLOBACH Willy 1865-1951 **[21]**
- $99 456 - €84 796 - **£60 000** - FF556 224
  Les Falais - De Klippen Oil/canvas (76x86cm 29x33in) London 1998
- $3 571 - €3 659 - **£2 203** - FF24 000
  Voilier en mer Huile/carton (31x41cm 12x16in) Troyes 2000

SCHLOEPKE Theodor 1812-1878 **[3]**
- $18 340 - €20 452 - **£12 332** - FF134 156
  Adliges Mädchen hoch zu Pferd Öl/Leinwand (50x60cm 19x23in) Satow 2000

SCHLÖGL von Josef 1851-? **[18]**
- $10 980 - €11 248 - **£6 776** - FF73 785
  Wiesenlandschaft mit Dorf und Wallfahrtskirche vor dem Gebirge Oil/panel (55x79cm 21x31in) Düsseldorf 2000
- $1 892 - €1 817 - **£1 187** - FF11 917
  Olivenstrand bei Torbole Gardasee Oil/panel (23.5x42.8cm 9x16in) Wien 1999

SCHLOMKA Alfred XIX-XX **[7]**
- $1 568 - €1 829 - **£1 101** - FF12 000
  Les joies de l'enfance Huile/toile (73x54cm 28x21in) Versailles 2000

SCHLÖSSER Carl 1832-1914 **[15]**
- $3 554 - €3 964 - **£2 389** - FF26 000
  La visite au grand-père Huile/toile (54x69cm 21x27in) Versailles 2000
- $4 719 - €4 573 - **£2 922** - FF30 000
  Jeu d'enfants - Les joies du tabac Huile/toile (39x30cm 15x11in) Paris 1999

SCHLOSSER Gérard 1931 **[164]**
- $7 384 - €7 927 - **£4 940** - FF52 000
  Qu'est-ce que tu deviens? Acrylique (146x144.5cm 57x56in) Paris 2000
- $7 304 - €6 098 - **£4 284** - FF40 000
  «Il n'ose pas trop y croire» Acrylique/toile (100x100cm 39x39in) Paris 1998
- $586 - €549 - **£359** - FF3 600
  Le sac à main Feutre (14x20cm 5x7in) Paris 1998
- $116 - €137 - **£83** - FF900
  Le sein Sérigraphie couleurs (34x28.5cm 13x11in) Paris 2001

SCHLOTTER Eberhard 1921 **[113]**
- $191 - €225 - **£132** - FF1 475
  Berglandschaft Aquarell/Papier (35x49cm 13x19in) Stuttgart 2000
- $87 - €102 - **£61** - FF670
  Schafe Etching, aquatint in colors (25x32cm 9x12in) Königstein 2001

SCHLOTTERBECK Wilhelm Friedrich 1777-1819 **[8]**
- $172 - €164 - **£106** - FF1 073
  Brennendes Dorf bei Nacht, after Egbert van der Poels Etching, aquatint (42.6x51cm 16x20in) Berlin 1999

SCHMALIX Hubert 1952 **[256]**
- $4 387 - €4 269 - **£2 699** - FF28 000
  Sans titre Tempera/toile (240x200cm 94x78in) Paris 1999
- $1 171 - €1 125 - **£722** - FF7 378
  Wienerwald Öl/Leinwand (53x71cm 20x27in) München 1999
- $733 - €872 - **£523** - FF5 720
  Ohne Titel Gouache/paper (42x60cm 16x23in) Wien 2000
- $203 - €218 - **£135** - FF1 430
  Ohne Titel Radierung (30x42cm 11x16in) Wien 2000

SCHMALZ Herbert Gustave 1856-1935 **[22]**
- $67 344 - €80 092 - **£48 000** - FF525 369
  Faithful unto Death Christianes ad Leones! Oil/canvas (165x114cm 64x44in) London 2000
- $2 561 - €2 976 - **£1 800** - FF19 519
  «Bethany» Oil/canvas (43x61cm 16x24in) London 2001

SCHMALZIGAUG Jules 1882-1917 **[80]**
- $1 160 - €1 239 - **£790** - FF8 130
  Het portaal ven de San Marco Basiliek te Venetië Huile/carton (27x22cm 10x8in) Lokeren 2001
- $552 - €595 - **£369** - FF3 902
  Gondoles à Venise Craies/papier (8x12cm 3x4in) Antwerpen 2000

SCHMID David Alois 1791-1861 **[28]**
- $2 150 - €2 495 - **£1 485** - FF16 369
  Trogen Ink (24x37cm 9x14in) St. Gallen 2000
- $205 - €200 - **£126** - FF1 312
  Schwÿz Farbradierung (18x18cm 7x7in) Bern 1999

SCHMID Franz 1796-1851 **[23]**
- $2 352 - €2 370 - **£1 466** - FF15 545
  Blick vom Steinberg gegen Lowerzersee, Vierwaldstättersee und Hochfluh Aquarelle (30.5x45.9cm 12x18in) Zürich 2000

S

ⅢⅢ **$247** - €279 - **£174** - FF1 831
«Malerischer Plan der Stadt Zürich und ihrer Umgebungen» Aquatinta (48x70cm 18x27in) Bern 2001

SCHMID Henri 1924 [42]
🖾 **$1 168** - €1 127 - **£733** - FF7 392
Dorf in Ebene vor Hügelkette Öl/Leinwand (35x83cm 13x32in) St. Gallen 1999

SCHMID Julius 1854-1935 [7]
🖾 **$2 517** - €2 179 - **£1 527** - FF14 295
Beethoven Öl/Leinwand (33.5x46cm 13x18in) Wien 1998

SCHMID Mathias 1835-1923 [20]
🖾 **$5 505** - €6 135 - **£3 848** - FF40 246
Junge Bäuerin auf der Alm im Gebirgstal auf dem Wiesenweg Öl/Leinwand (66x54.5cm 25x21in) München 2001
🖾 **$428** - €460 - **£286** - FF3 018
Reisekutsche in Neapel, im Hintergrund der Vesuv Öl/Karton (17x27cm 6x10in) München 2000
🖋 **$2 303** - €2 543 - **£1 596** - FF16 684
«Der Tuifelmaler» Pencil (38x23.5cm 14x9in) Wien 2001

SCHMID Richard 1934 [16]
🖾 **$2 200** - €2 037 - **£1 346** - FF13 360
Seated Nude, Portrait of a Chicago Nightclub Dancer Oil/canvas (91x73cm 36x29in) St. Louis MO 1999
🖋 **$12 100** - €11 300 - **£7 468** - FF74 124
White Blouse Crayon (55x43cm 22x17in) Dallas TX 1999

SCHMID Wilhelm 1892-1971 [69]
🖾 **$4 135** - €3 977 - **£2 547** - FF26 088
Dorf Bré, Vorfrühling Huile/panneau (60x81cm 23x31in) St. Gallen 1999
🖾 **$1 001** - €1 179 - **£704** - FF7 737
Blumenstrauss Öl/Leinwand (46x33cm 18x12in) Zürich 2000
🖋 **$321** - €310 - **£198** - FF2 031
Zwei weibliche Akte in südlicher Landschaft Encre Chine (24.5x19.5cm 9x7in) Bern 1999

SCHMIDT Adolf 1804-1866 [2]
🖋 **$2 761** - €2 503 - **£1 615** - FF16 769
Drei musizierende Mädchen in der Natur Pastel (70x56cm 27x22in) Hamburg 1999

SCHMIDT Adolf 1827-1880 [14]
🖋 **$867** - €820 - **£540** - FF5 379
«Coach» Oil/cardboard (26x36cm 10x14in) Praha 2001

SCHMIDT Albert 1883-1970 [75]
🖾 **$1 641** - €1 904 - **£1 133** - FF12 492
Leda et le Cygne Huile/toile/panneau (50x62cm 19x24in) Genève 1998
🖾 **$839** - €815 - **£529** - FF5 346
Portrait eines Knaben mit roten Haaren Öl/Leinwand (27x23cm 10x9in) Zürich 1999
🖋 **$1 345** - €1 444 - **£900** - FF9 473
Woman among Rocks Watercolour (46x31.5cm 18x12in) London 2000

SCHMIDT Albert H. 1885-1957 [3]
🖾 **$2 250** - €2 667 - **£1 639** - FF17 497
Path along the River Oil/canvas (71x91cm 28x36in) Chicago IL 2001
🖋 **$3 200** - €2 761 - **£1 923** - FF18 109
Adobe Farn and Blue Mountains Pastel/paper (26x42cm 10x16in) Santa-Fe NM 1998

SCHMIDT Alexander 1842-1903 [51]
🖾 **$825** - €738 - **£492** - FF4 841
Motiv fra Haraldskjaer Hegn ved Mårum Oil/canvas (115x90cm 45x35in) Köbenhavn 1998
🖾 **$197** - €188 - **£120** - FF1 236
Skovlysning med dådyr Oil/canvas (32x43cm 12x16in) Viby J, Århus 1999

SCHMIDT Alfred 1867-1956 [22]
🖾 **$640** - €613 - **£403** - FF4 024
Im Schilfufer eines Sees sucht ein junges Mädchen nach Seerosen Öl/Leinwand (80x110cm 31x43in) Stuttgart 1999

SCHMIDT Allan 1923-1989 [67]
🖾 **$262** - €281 - **£175** - FF1 846
Gult indslag Oil/canvas (60x46cm 23x18in) Köbenhavn 2000

SCHMIDT Alwin 1900-? [1]
🖾 **$2 400** - €2 222 - **£1 469** - FF14 574
Ranchhand on horseback in corral Oil/board (34x43cm 13x17in) New-York 1999

SCHMIDT Carl 1885-1969 [36]
🖾 **$1 100** - €1 283 - **£765** - FF8 418
Bayside Home Oil/canvas (50x60cm 20x24in) Altadena CA 2000
🖾 **$650** - €616 - **£406** - FF4 041
Taos Pueblos Oil/canvas (30x35cm 12x14in) Cincinnati OH 1999
🖾 **$10 450** - €10 653 - **£6 548** - FF69 876
Sailboats on tranquil waters Ceramic (23x18cm 9x7in) Altadena CA 2000

SCHMIDT Christian 1835-? [5]
🖾 **$9 000** - €10 091 - **£6 111** - FF66 193
Still Life with Japanese Objects Oil/panel (49.5x60cm 19x23in) New-York 2000

SCHMIDT Eduard 1806-1862 [25]
🖾 **$2 391** - €2 819 - **£1 680** - FF18 493
Landschaft, Dorfpartie auf Helgoland mit Personenstaffage Öl/Leinwand (42.5x60cm 16x23in) Bern 2000
🖾 **$22 500** - €19 488 - **£13 799** - FF127 833
The Artist's Studio Oil/panel (35.5x30.5cm 13x12in) New-York 1999

SCHMIDT Friedrich Albert 1846-1916 [23]
🖾 **$544** - €460 - **£325** - FF3 017
Sommertag, Brücke und Fluss mit Staustufe Öl/Leinwand (62x82cm 24x32in) Berlin 1998

SCHMIDT Georg Friedrich 1712-1775 [51]
🖋 **$3 155** - €2 744 - **£1 902** - FF18 000
Portrait de Maurice Quentin de la Tour Sanguine/papier (45.4x30cm 17x11in) Paris 1998
ⅢⅢ **$268** - €230 - **£161** - FF1 509
Die Gattin des Künstlers Radierung (11.8x9.7cm 4x3in) Berlin 1998

SCHMIDT Hans W. 1859-1950 [30]
🖾 **$9 682** - €11 248 - **£6 804** - FF73 785
Armbrustschütze Öl/Leinwand (175x118cm 68x46in) Rudolstadt-Thüringen 2001

SCHMIDT Johann Heinrich 1749-1829 [6]
🖾 **$4 393** - €4 878 - **£3 062** - FF32 000
Jeune femme vêtue d'une robe de soie ivoire ceinturée de bleu Miniature (10.5x9cm 4x3in) Paris 2001

S

SCHMIDT Karl 1890-1962 **[9]**
- $1 900 - €1 623 - £1 149 - FF10 648
  Heavy Sea, Cornwall, England/Sunlit Rocks at St. Dero, Cornwall Oil/panel (32.5x40.5cm 12x15in) San-Francisco CA 1998

SCHMIDT Kurt 1901-1991 **[11]**
- $166 - €184 - £115 - FF1 207
  Die Scheibe Serigraph (32x22cm 12x8in) Heidelberg 2001

SCHMIDT Leonard 1892-1978 **[23]**
- $1 362 - €1 278 - £841 - FF8 384
  Porträt Martha Stuber Öl/Leinwand (76x50cm 29x19in) Stuttgart 1999
- $662 - €613 - £405 - FF4 024
  Blick auf Uhlbach Aquarell/Papier (42x55cm 16x21in) Hildrizhausen 1999
- $97 - €102 - £61 - FF670
  Menschen in einer Allee Farbserigraphie (85.5x70cm 33x27in) Stuttgart 2000

SCHMIDT Louis Lucien J.B. 1825-1891 **[3]**
- $8 028 - €8 924 - £5 364 - FF58 536
  Jeune fille nourrissant deux moutons dans l'étable Huile/toile (214x177cm 84x69in) Bruxelles 2000
- $4 318 - €4 421 - £2 711 - FF29 000
  Nature morte avec volaille/Nature morte avec gibier Huile/toile (65x81cm 25x31in) Lyon 2000

SCHMIDT Martin Johann 1718-1801 **[57]**
- $124 640 - €116 276 - £75 200 - FF762 720
  Die Opferung der Tochter Jephtas Öl/Leinwand (112x150cm 44x59in) Wien 2001
- $19 740 - €21 802 - £13 680 - FF143 010
  Der heilige Josef mit dem Jesuskind Öl/Leinwand (94x72cm 37x28in) Wien 2001
- $14 894 - €15 988 - £10 164 - FF104 874
  Beweinung Christi Öl/Kupfer (31x24.5cm 12x9in) Wien 2001
- $3 686 - €4 193 - £2 575 - FF27 502
  Abschied Christi von seiner Mutter Chalks/paper (23x17.2cm 9x6in) München 2000
- $428 - €511 - £305 - FF3 353
  Das Urteil des Midas Radierung (14.1x9cm 5x3in) Berlin 2000

SCHMIDT Matthias 1749-1823 **[4]**
- $2 508 - €2 812 - £1 703 - FF18 446
  Junge Linzerin Öl/Leinwand (33x42cm 12x16in) München 2000

SCHMIDT Max 1818-1901 **[20]**
- $13 657 - €13 294 - £8 390 - FF87 201
  Die römischen Bäder im Park von Sanssouci Öl/Leinwand (34.5x48.5cm 13x19in) Berlin 1999

SCHMIDT Robert 1863-1927 **[17]**
- $667 - €787 - £469 - FF5 160
  Stilleben mit Hummer auf silbernem Tablett Öl/Leinwand (55x69.5cm 21x27in) Bern 2000

SCHMIDT Rudolf 1873-1963 **[23]**
- $450 - €509 - £303 - FF3 336
  Donaukanal-Ferdinandsbrücke Aquarell/Papier (20x28cm 7x11in) Wien 2000

SCHMIDT Theodor 1855-1937 **[13]**
- $4 200 - €4 567 - £2 975 - FF31 941
  Going to the Fair Oil/panel (39x51.5cm 15x20in) New-York 2000

SCHMIDT von Harold 1893-1982 **[48]**
- $7 150 - €6 100 - £4 312 - FF40 011
  Three men escorting a woman on horseback, for Saturday Evening Post Oil/canvas (76x101cm 30x40in) New-York 1998
- $4 675 - €4 766 - £2 929 - FF31 260
  Night Riders Gouache/board (34x54cm 13x21in) Altadena CA 2000

SCHMIDT-FELLING Julius 1895-1930 **[44]**
- $559 - €570 - £350 - FF3 739
  Boy Holding Two Piglets Bronze (H17.5cm H6in) Billingshurst, West-Sussex 2000

SCHMIDT-HAMBURG Robert 1885-1963 **[15]**
- $3 070 - €3 068 - £1 920 - FF20 123
  Bark und verschiedene andere Schiffe in der Kieler Förde Öl/Leinwand (41x78cm 16x30in) Hamburg 1999
- $1 140 - €1 147 - £786 - FF8 384
  Doppelschrauben-Passagier und Frachtdampfer Rotterdam Aquarell, Gouache/Papier (8.5x14.4cm 3x5in) Hamburg 2000

SCHMIDT-HOFER Otto 1873-1925 **[46]**
- $452 - €434 - £280 - FF2 850
  Weiblicher Akt mit Reif Bronze (H17.5cm H6in) Hildrizhausen 1999

SCHMIDT-KESTNER Erich 1877-? **[22]**
- $2 143 - €2 301 - £1 434 - FF15 092
  Pferdeliebe Bronze (H52cm H20in) Stuttgart 2000

SCHMIDT-KIRSTEIN Helmut 1909-1985 **[47]**
- $1 887 - €2 198 - £1 318 - FF14 421
  Stilleben mit Akt und Austern Öl/Leinwand (100x54.5cm 39x21in) Berlin 2000
- $662 - €613 - £405 - FF4 024
  Blumenstilleben Aquarell/Papier (36.8x51.3cm 14x20in) Dettelbach-Effeldorf 1999
- $179 - €153 - £107 - FF1 006
  Frau mit Fächer Lithographie (37.6x41cm 14x16in) Berlin 1998

SCHMIDT-ROTTLUFF Karl 1884-1976 **[855]**
- $128 643 - €141 118 - £87 381 - FF925 676
  Augustvormittag im Gebirge Öl/Karton (43.5x70.5cm 17x27in) Berlin 2000
- $14 993 - €16 539 - £10 584 - FF115 706
  Blühende Bäume am Fluss Öl/Leinwand (26x41.5cm 10x16in) Berlin 2001
- $19 289 - €22 497 - £13 543 - FF147 571
  Kopf Stone (12x9.5x7cm 4x3x2in) Köln 2000
- $21 203 - €20 580 - £13 202 - FF134 994
  Backöfen (Am Lebasee) Watercolour (50x69.5cm 19x27in) Berlin 1999
- $1 514 - €1 789 - £1 069 - FF11 738
  Arcegno Lithographie (43.5x60.5cm 17x23in) Köln 2001

SCHMIDTCASSEL Gustav 1867-? **[8]**
- $5 618 - €5 214 - £3 500 - FF34 200
  Easter Dancer Ivory, bronze (H35.5cm H13in) London 1999

SCHMIED François-Louis 1873-1941 **[75]**
- $3 842 - €3 811 - £2 390 - FF25 000
  Le champ de blé Huile/toile (47x70cm 18x27in) Paris 1999
- $308 - €320 - £193 - FF2 100
  Pharos/Le port Gouache (28.5x22cm 11x8in) Paris 2000
- $328 - €381 - £231 - FF2 500
  Sans titre Lithographie couleurs (35x24.5cm 13x9in) Neuilly-sur-Seine 2001

SCHMIEGELOW Pedro Ernst 1863-1943 **[11]**
- $1 183 - €1 227 - **£750** - FF8 049
  Romantischer Altstadtwinkel bei Nacht
  Tempera/Karton (36x49cm 14x19in) Rudolstadt-
  Thüringen 2000
- $844 - €792 - **£521** - FF5 198
  Landschaft in der Rhön Gouache/paper (14x27cm
  5x10in) Staufen 1999

SCHMITT David XVIII **[1]**
- $4 800 - €6 220 - **£3 600** - FF40 800
  Accampamento militare Olio/tavola (49x62.5cm
  19x24in) Roma 2001

SCHMITT Oskar 1882-1943 **[6]**
- $16 000 - €14 676 - **£9 856** - FF96 265
  **Synagogue Interior with Rabbis Discussing the
  Talmud** Oil/canvas (43x53cm 16x20in) New-York 1999
- $539 - €613 - **£374** - FF4 024
  Alchemist an Herd Öl/Karton (13.5x17.5cm 5x6in)
  Lindau 2001

SCHMITT Paul Léon Félix 1856-1902 **[13]**
- $5 500 - €6 099 - **£3 659** - FF40 010
  Paysage près d'un village Oleo/lienzo
  (54.5x73.5cm 21x28in) Buenos-Aires 2000
- $3 070 - €3 049 - **£1 912** - FF22 000
  Paris : Porte de Chatillon Huile/toile (24x32cm
  9x12in) Paris 1999

SCHMITT Ernst 1859-1917 **[11]**
- $1 127 - €1 329 - **£792** - FF8 720
  **Stilleben mit silbernem Samowar und
  Porzellantasse** Öl/Karton (67x32cm 26x12in)
  Frankfurt 2000
- $9 500 - €891 - **£5 726** - FF53 072
  Tiroleses con jarros de cerveza Oleo/tabla
  (20.5x15.5cm 8x6in) Buenos-Aires 1998

SCHMITZ Georg 1851-1917 **[21]**
- $1 597 - €1 534 - **£990** - FF10 061
  Winterfreuden Öl/Leinwand (61x45cm 24x17in)
  Ahlden 1999
- $1 729 - €1 624 - **£1 071** - FF10 652
  Winterlandschaften bei Dämmerung Huile/pan-
  neau (13x10cm 5x3in) Luzern 1999

SCHMITZ Johann Jacob 1724-1810 **[2]**
- $21 182 - €21 343 - **£13 202** - FF140 000
  La grande Outarde Huile/toile (107x85cm 42x33in)
  Paris 2000

SCHMITZ Philipp 1824-1887 **[4]**
- $6 966 - €6 541 - **£4 320** - FF42 903
  Der Losverkäufer Öl/Leinwand (80x75cm 31x29in)
  Wien 1999

SCHMITZBERGER Josef 1851-? **[37]**
- $2 121 - €1 943 - **£1 293** - FF12 744
  Fuchs am Waldrand Öl/Leinwand (100x80cm
  39x31in) München 1999

SCHMÖGNER Walter 1943 **[45]**
- $219 - €254 - **£155** - FF1 668
  Ohne Titel Indian ink (18.7x34cm 7x13in) Wien 2000

SCHMOLL VON EISENWERTH Karl 1879-1948 **[42]**
- $264 - €307 - **£185** - FF2 012
  «Der Spaziergang» Woodcut in colors (24.5x38.5cm
  9x15in) Berlin 2001

SCHMÖLZ Hugo 1897-1938 **[41]**
- $694 - €665 - **£428** - FF4 360
  Fabrikgebäude Vintage gelatin silver print
  (23.8x17.9cm 9x7in) Köln 1999

SCHMÖLZ Karl Hugo 1917-1986 **[36]**
- $763 - €716 - **£471** - FF4 695
  Köln, Sankt Maria im Capitol Vintage gelatin silver
  print (42.4x59cm 16x23in) Köln 1999

SCHMUTZ Werner 1910 **[39]**
- $98 - €109 - **£65** - FF716
  Berner Bauernhäuser im Winter Lithographie
  (34.5x55.2cm 13x21in) Bern 2000

SCHMUTZER Andreas 1700-1740 **[4]**
- $713 - €689 - **£448** - FF4 517
  **Baden: Badensis in Argovia, Castellum et oppi-
  dum Sedes Habsburgica** Kupferstich (32.3x44.9cm
  12x17in) Zürich 1999

SCHMUTZER Ferdinand 1870-1928 **[112]**
- $2 046 - €2 439 - **£1 459** - FF16 000
  La Liseuse Huile/toile (68x65cm 26x25in) Strasbourg
  2000
- $88 - €102 - **£61** - FF670
  Interieurszene mit Hauskonzert Watercolour
  (14x11cm 5x4in) Rudolstadt-Thüringen 2001
- $210 - €203 - **£133** - FF1 334
  Josef Joachim mit Geige Radierung (55x49cm
  21x19in) Wien 1999

SCHMUTZER Jakob Matthias II 1733-1811 **[27]**
- $1 287 - €1 278 - **£804** - FF8 384
  Felslandschaft mit rastendem Wanderer Ink
  (47.5x62.7cm 18x24in) München 1999
- $368 - €358 - **£229** - FF2 347
  **Der hl. Johann von Nepomuk als Fürsprecher
  der Armen, nach Maulbertsch** Radierung
  (39.5x30.2cm 15x11in) Berlin 1999

SCHMUTZLER Leopold 1864-1941 **[100]**
- $40 000 - €43 898 - **£25 756** - FF287 952
  Nude on the Beach Oil/board (99.5x150.5cm
  39x59in) New-York 2000
- $2 118 - €2 492 - **£1 535** - FF16 346
  «Flora, Mädchen mit Margarithenblumen»
  Oil/panel (101x73cm 39x28in) Zofingen 2001
- $214 - €256 - **£152** - FF1 676
  Bildnis einer jungen Frau mit Federhut Oil/panel
  (20x15.5cm 7x6in) Königstein 2000
- $911 - €844 - **£565** - FF5 533
  Mädchen mit Wasserkrug Aquarell/Papier
  (45x33cm 17x12in) Stuttgart 1999

SCHNABEL Julian 1951 **[214]**
- $60 000 - €56 034 - **£37 032** - FF367 560
  C.V.J Mixed media (306x306cm 120x120in) New-York
  1999
- $9 000 - €7 678 - **£5 428** - FF50 364
  Journey of the Lost Tooth Oil/paper (127.5x76cm
  50x29in) New-York 1998
- $4 500 - €4 939 - **£2 897** - FF32 397
  Untitled Mixed media/canvas (31x27.5cm 12x10in)
  New-York 2000
- $77 500 - €87 672 - **£54 219** - FF575 088
  Self-Portrait with Champagne Glass Bronze
  (393.5x115.5x80.5cm 154x45x31in) New-York 2001
- $4 680 - €5 406 - **£3 240** - FF35 460
  Sin título Técnica mixta/papel (99x70cm 38x27in)
  Madrid 2001
- $945 - €884 - **£572** - FF5 800
  Olat Loaez Sérigraphie couleurs (137x110cm 53x43in)
  Paris 1999

SCHNACKENBERG Walter 1880-1961 **[58]**
- $6 000 - €5 770 - **£3 703** - FF37 849
  Die Heilung der Prinzessin Pierapinka Gouache
  (60x46cm 23x18in) New-York 1999

S

⊞ **$4 589** - €5 471 - **£3 272** - FF35 886
«**Erry and Merry**» Poster (122x89.5cm 48x35in) Köln 2000

SCHNARRENBERGER Wilhelm 1892-1966 [39]
🖼 **$4 456** - €5 113 - **£3 048** - FF33 539
Berliner Allee im Nebel Öl/Leinwand (75x95cm 29x37in) Heidelberg 2001

SCHNARS-ALQUIST Hugo 1855-1939 [10]
🖼 **$4 398** - €5 113 - **£3 087** - FF33 539
Yacht von einer Hafenstadt Öl/Leinwand (40.5x50.5cm 15x19in) Hamburg 2001

SCHNAUDER Richard Georg 1886-1956 [3]
🗿 **$1 124** - €1 278 - **£776** - FF8 384
Stehender weiblicher Akt Bronze (H32.5cm H12in) München 2000

SCHNECK Albert 1901-1983 [1]
🖼 **$1 836** - €2 035 - **£1 246** - FF13 347
Stilleben mit Kaktus Öl/Karton (46.5x30cm 18x11in) Wien 2000

SCHNEGG Lucien 1864-1909 [1]
🗿 **$5 131** - €4 802 - **£3 178** - FF31 500
Visage de femme aux yeux clos Marbre (30x16cm 11x6in) Pontoise 1999

SCHNEIDAU von Christian 1893-1976 [56]
🖼 **$850** - €992 - **£591** - FF6 505
«**The Stally Point Lobos Rocks**» Oil/canvas (50x40cm 20x16in) Altadena CA 2000

SCHNEIDER Carlos 1889-1932 [19]
🖼 **$1 687** - €1 628 - **£1 059** - FF10 678
Sturm über südlicher Uferlandschaft Öl/Karton (25x33cm 9x12in) St. Gallen 1999
🖼 **$377** - €443 - **£266** - FF2 907
Dorfpartie in Morissen, Kt.Graubünden Charcoal/paper (30x26cm 11x10in) St. Gallen 2000

SCHNEIDER Caspar 1753-1839 [6]
🖼 **$9 224** - €10 226 - **£6 404** - FF67 078
Ideale Flusslandschaft mit Hirten und Ruinen Öl/Kupfer (53.5x69cm 21x27in) Köln 2001

SCHNEIDER Christian 1917-1997 [227]
🖼 **$264** - €259 - **£162** - FF1 700
Plage de Bernières en Normandie Huile/toile (65x54cm 25x21in) Pontoise 1999

SCHNEIDER Emile 1873-? [9]
🖼 **$410** - €457 - **£286** - FF3 000
Le demandeur Fusain/papier (23x30cm 9x11in) Entzheim 2001

SCHNEIDER Félicie 1831-1888 [5]
🖼 **$8 359** - €9 909 - **£6 090** - FF65 000
«**Jeanne d'Osmond duchesse de Maillé 1827-1899**» Huile/toile (114x87cm 44x34in) Paris 2001

SCHNEIDER Georg 1759-1843 [3]
🖼 **$1 868** - €2 137 - **£1 283** - FF14 019
Klassische Flusslandschaft mit seitlicher Burgruine Oil/panel (22.5x30cm 8x11in) Lindau 2000

SCHNEIDER Gérard 1896-1986 [770]
🖼 **$8 881** - €9 299 - **£5 581** - FF61 000
Composition Acrylique/toile (151x147cm 59x57in) Versailles 2000
🖼 **$3 628** - €4 269 - **£2 601** - FF28 000
Sans titre Acrylique/toile (60x73cm 23x28in) Paris 2001
🖼 **$1 282** - €1 524 - **£914** - FF10 000
Sans titre Acrylique/papier (26x36.5cm 10x14in) Paris 2000

$1 800 - €1 866 - **£1 080** - FF12 240
Composition Carboncino/carta (30.5x23.5cm 12x9in) Prato 2000

⊞ **$133** - €128 - **£83** - FF839
Komposition Farblithographie (40x56cm 15x22in) München 1999

SCHNEIDER Gerhard August 1842-1872 [4]
🖼 **$1 492** - €1 759 - **£1 048** - FF11 538
Paus i jakten Oil/canvas (47x39cm 18x15in) Malmö 2000

SCHNEIDER Herbert 1924-1983 [82]
🖼 **$526** - €613 - **£368** - FF4 024
Nachtblaues Glück Aquarell/Papier (27x21.5cm 10x8in) München 2000

SCHNEIDER Johann Jakob 1822-1889 [5]
🖼 **$4 811** - €5 582 - **£3 321** - FF36 616
Der Birsigeinlass beim Steinentor zur Basel Watercolour (42.4x64.2cm 16x25in) Zürich 2000

SCHNEIDER Otto Henry 1865-1950 [6]
🖼 **$6 500** - €7 284 - **£4 530** - FF47 783
Spring Landscape Oil/canvas (76x89cm 29x35in) Beverly-Hills CA 2001

SCHNEIDER Sasha 1870-1927 [8]
🖼 **$349** - €409 - **£245** - FF2 683
Hirtenknabe, an einen Baum gelehnt Aquarell/Papier (15.5x12cm 6x4in) München 2000

SCHNEIDER-BLUMBERG Bernhard 1881-1956 [18]
🖼 **$89** - €102 - **£62** - FF670
Junges Mädchen-Portrait im Profil Aquarell/Papier (32x25cm 12x9in) Radolfzell 2001

SCHNEIDER-MANZELL Toni 1911 [3]
🗿 **$4 443** - €3 833 - **£2 670** - FF25 142
Hubertus Bronze (72x70cm 28x27in) München 1998

SCHNEIDERS Toni 1920 [104]
📷 **$1 117** - €1 329 - **£798** - FF8 720
«**Im Stahlwalzwerk**» Vintage gelatin silver print (39.5x28.2cm 15x11in) Berlin 2000

SCHNETZ Jean-Victor 1787-1870 [19]
🖼 **$1 704** - €1 829 - **£1 140** - FF12 000
Paysage de la campagne romaine avec des personnages sur un chemin Huile/toile (51x61.5cm 20x24in) Bayeux 2000

SCHNEUER David 1905-1988 [28]
🖼 **$1 242** - €1 064 - **£747** - FF6 982
Ohne Titel Gouache/paper (22x22.5cm 8x8in) Zürich 1998

SCHNITZLER Paul XIX [2]
🖼 **$8 500** - €7 333 - **£5 146** - FF48 104
He Returns no More Watercolour (40x29.5cm 15x11in) New-York 1999

SCHNORPFEIL M. XX [1]
🖼 **$3 000** - €2 920 - **£1 843** - FF19 153
Jewish Water Carrier in Bilgoraj Poland Watercolour/paper (26x17cm 10x6in) Tel Aviv 1999

SCHNORR VON CAROLSFELD Hans Veit Friedrich 1764-1841 [8]
🖼 **$1 927** - €1 687 - **£1 167** - FF11 065
Das Mädchen aus der Fremde, after Friedrich Schiller Ink (11x7.6cm 4x2in) Berlin 1998

SCHNORR VON CAROLSFELD Julius 1794-1872 [39]
🖼 **$7 388** - €6 397 - **£4 456** - FF41 960
Drei Figuren aus der Nibelungensage : Gernot, Ute und Giselher Öl/Leinwand (43x53cm 16x20in) München 1998

$4 048 - €4 346 - **£2 709** - FF28 508
Die Sündfluth Ink/paper (21.8x26cm 8x10in)
Hamburg 2000

SCHNORR VON CAROLSFELD Ludwig Ferdinand
1788-1853 **[23]**
$22 472 - €20 452 - **£14 040** - FF134 156
Die Begegnung Erzherzog Ferdinands mit sei-ner Braut Philippine Welser Öl/Leinwand
(84x68.5cm 33x26in) München 1999

SCHNUG Leo 1878-1933 **[13]**
$752 - €854 - **£522** - FF5 600
Cantinière 5e Régiment de Grenadier 1er Empire Aquarelle/papier (28x22cm 11x8in) Entzheim
2001

SCHNYDER Albert 1898-1989 **[130]**
$6 507 - €7 077 - **£4 288** - FF46 425
Heimkehrende Pferde Öl/Leinwand (65x81.5cm
25x32in) Bern 2000
$1 841 - €2 078 - **£1 295** - FF13 633
«Der rote Teller» Oil/panel (27x37.5cm 10x14in)
Bern 2001
$771 - €743 - **£475** - FF4 875
Fermes sous le Bémont Crayon/papier (45x59cm
17x23in) Bern 1999
$290 - €330 - **£201** - FF2 165
Pferdeweide im Jura Lithographie (56x97cm
22x38in) Zofingen 2000

SCHNYDER Jean-Frédéric 1945 **[3]**
$1 137 - €1 125 - **£709** - FF7 378
Ohne Titel Aquarell/Papier (50x65cm 19x25in) Luzern
1999

SCHÖBEL Georg 1860-1941 **[20]**
$3 068 - €3 579 - **£2 160** - FF23 477
Friedrich II Öl/Leinwand (85x66cm 33x25in)
Königstein 2001

SCHÖDL Max 1834-1921 **[36]**
$1 187 - €1 125 - **£722** - FF7 378
Stilleben mit altem Folianten, Fayencekrug, Traubenpokal, Glaspokal Oil/panel (21.6x15.9cm
8x6in) München 2000

SCHÖDLBERGER Johann Nepomuk 1779-1853
[28]
$7 553 - €8 692 - **£5 215** - FF57 016
Ideallandschaft bei Gewittersturm/Ideallandschaft mit badenden Mädchen Öl/Leinwand (71.5x87.5cm 28x34in)
München 2000
$514 - €581 - **£347** - FF3 813
Altes Haus bei Rom, Campagna di Roma
Watercolour (20x26cm 7x10in) Wien 2000

SCHOEFFT August Theodore 1809-1888 **[4]**
$3 900 - €3 904 - **£2 405** - FF25 610
Militar inglés de la Guerra de Independencia
Oleo/lienzo (118x98cm 46x38in) Madrid 2000

SCHOEFFT O. XIX **[2]**
$861 - €991 - **£593** - FF6 500
Porteuse d'eau/Femmes de bédouin/Cawas du Consulat/Derviche hurleur Tirage albuminé
(25x20.5cm 9x8in) Paris 2000

SCHOELLHORN Hans 1892-1982 **[45]**
$899 - €875 - **£552** - FF5 742
Ville d'Arles Oil/panel (38x46cm 14x18in) Zürich
1999
$534 - €523 - **£332** - FF3 759
Bildhauer in seinem Atelier Öl/Karton (33x41cm
12x16in) St. Gallen 2000

$534 - €573 - **£357** - FF3 759
Artistin, vor der Probe Fusain (43x29cm 16x11in)
St. Gallen 2000

SCHOELMAKER-DOYER Jacobus, Jakob 1792-1867 **[3]**
$6 279 - €5 946 - **£3 818** - FF39 000
P. Le Grand & maire d'Amsterdam étudiant la construction d'un navire Huile/toile (80x100cm
31x39in) Paris 1999

SCHOENBECK Albert XIX **[3]**
$6 525 - €7 158 - **£4 432** - FF46 954
Ein Blick vom Kahlenberge auf Potsdam
Öl/Leinwand (44.5x91.5cm 17x36in) Berlin 2000

SCHOENEWERK Pierre Alexandre 1820-1885 **[19]**
$1 972 - €2 211 - **£1 338** - FF14 500
Esclave enchaînée Bronze (H56cm H22in) Paris
2000

SCHOEVAERDTS Mathys c.1665-1710 **[77]**
$36 234 - €41 161 - **£25 353** - FF270 000
Scène de marché dans un paysage de ruines
Huile/cuivre (50.5x65cm 19x25in) Paris 2001
$9 945 - €11 155 - **£6 930** - FF73 170
Paysage à l'auberge et au moulin Huile/panneau
(19x26cm 7x10in) Bruxelles 2001

SCHOFF Otto 1888-1938 **[47]**
$321 - €266 - **£188** - FF1 742
Stehender weiblicher Akt, sich waschend
Charcoal/paper (29.5x18cm 11x7in) Berlin 1998

SCHÖFFER Nicolas 1912-1992 **[36]**
$345 - €335 - **£213** - FF2 200
Minisculpture Mobile (20x20x23cm 7x7x9in) Paris
1999
$301 - €290 - **£187** - FF1 900
Colleographic Collage (42x29.5cm 16x11in) Paris
1999
$2 000 - €1 864 - **£1 234** - FF12 224
Vartap Tapestry (164x128cm 64x50in) New-York 1999

SCHÖFFMANN P.W.M. XX **[1]**
$4 508 - €4 311 - **£2 766** - FF28 277
Portrait of Emperor Maximilian I von Habsburg, after Albrecht Dürer Oil/panel (73.5x62cm 28x24in)
Amsterdam 1999

SCHOFIELD John William ?-1944 **[14]**
$353 - €329 - **£220** - FF2 160
The ancient Norman Castle of William the Conqueror Watercolour (76.5x66cm 30x25in) London
1999

SCHOFIELD Kershaw 1872-1941 **[67]**
$1 025 - €1 063 - **£650** - FF6 970
Summer Landscape with Children beside a Pond Feeding Ducks Oil/board (97x45.5cm
38x17in) West-Yorshire 2000
$502 - €587 - **£350** - FF3 848
Harvest Field with a Haystack in the Foreground and Cornstacks Beyond Oil/panel
(15x24cm 5x9in) West-Yorshire 2000
$162 - €180 - **£105** - FF1 182
Paisaje Acuarela/papel (15x20cm 5x7in) Madrid 2000

SCHOFIELD Walter Elmer 1867-1944 **[59]**
$9 717 - €10 367 - **£6 154** - FF68 000
Paysage Huile/toile (125x130cm 49x51in) Garches
2000
$14 000 - €15 028 - **£9 368** - FF98 574
Deer Point, Chebeague Island, Maine Oil/canvas
(76x91cm 30x36in) Hatfield PA 2000

$3 000 - €3 305 - **£2 001** - FF21 681
Cornish Coast, Rocky Coast Oil/board (35x40cm 14x16in) Portsmouth NH 2000

SCHOLANDER Fredrik Wilhelm 1816-1881 **[19]**

$377 - €338 - **£225** - FF2 214
Venedigmotiv Watercolour/paper (59x40cm 23x15in) Stockholm 1998

SCHOLDER Fritz 1937 **[51]**

$600 - €629 - **£400** - FF4 125
Matinee Cowboy/Night Form Color lithograph (76.5x56.5cm 30x22in) New-York 2001

SCHOLDERER Otto 1834-1902 **[29]**

$71 490 - €81 186 - **£50 000** - FF532 545
Heimkehr von der ernte (return from the harvest) Oil/canvas (119x131cm 46x51in) London 2001

$3 060 - €2 812 - **£1 880** - FF18 446
Jagdstilleben mit Wild und Geflügel Öl/Leinwand (76x64cm 29x25in) Stuttgart 1999

$2 504 - €2 907 - **£1 760** - FF19 068
Blumenstilleben mit Stiefmütterchen Öl/Papier (10.5x14.5cm 4x5in) Wien 2001

SCHÖLLKOPF Günther 1935-1979 **[32]**

$72 - €82 - **£51** - FF536
«Birnbaum» Radierung (30x30cm 11x11in) Stuttgart 2001

SCHOLTE Rob 1958 **[82]**

$1 012 - €998 - **£623** - FF6 548
Untitled Gouache/paper (27.5x20cm 10x7in) Amsterdam 1999

$324 - €386 - **£231** - FF2 530
Pacifisme Screenprint in colors (63x90cm 24x35in) Amsterdam 2000

SCHOLZ Georg 1890-1945 **[24]**

$263 772 - €303 685 - **£180 000** - FF1 992 042
Nightly Noise Oil/canvas (57x51cm 22x20in) London 2000

$1 551 - €1 329 - **£932** - FF8 718
Hinrichtung Lithographie (21.4x32.9cm 8x12in) Hamburg 1998

SCHOLZ Max 1855-1906 **[22]**

$16 000 - €15 203 - **£9 734** - FF99 726
The Recitation Oil/canvas (134.5x106.5cm 52x41in) New-York 1999

$1 900 - €2 039 - **£1 271** - FF13 377
Dreaming of a Fine Strew Oil/panel (39x31cm 15x12in) Boston MA 2001

SCHOLZ Werner 1898-1982 **[101]**

$8 507 - €8 181 - **£5 249** - FF53 662
Untergehende Sonne Öl/Karton (61x53.5cm 24x21in) Köln 1999

$1 312 - €1 125 - **£789** - FF7 377
Zwei Herren (Sitzender Mann) Coloured chalks (58x38cm 22x14in) Hamburg 1998

$191 - €179 - **£115** - FF1 173
Frauenkopf Poster (63x46cm 24x18in) Stuttgart 1999

SCHOMBERG A. Thomas XX **[2]**

$3 250 - €3 078 - **£1 976** - FF20 192
Right Field Bleachers Sculpture, wax (H61cm H24in) New-York 1999

SCHOMBURG Alex 1908 **[3]**

$1 500 - €1 451 - **£950** - FF9 520
Forecast Ink (35.5x28.5cm 13x11in) New-York 1999

SCHOMMER François 1850-1935 **[10]**

$2 011 - €2 258 - **£1 400** - FF14 809
French Trumpeter standing by his Mount in a winter Landscape Oil/canvas (30x22.5cm 11x8in) London 2001

SCHÖN Andreas 1955 **[11]**

$5 000 - €4 838 - **£3 083** - FF31 734
Umland I Oil/canvas (77.5x140cm 30x55in) New-York 1999

SCHÖN Friedrich 1810-1868 **[3]**

$4 745 - €4 346 - **£2 892** - FF28 508
Die eifersüchtige Horcherin Öl/Leinwand (80x96cm 31x37in) München 1999

$3 593 - €3 857 - **£2 404** - FF25 301
Still life with grapes, plums, a lime and a peach Oil/canvas (18.5x21.5cm 7x8in) Amsterdam 2000

SCHÖN Fritz 1871-? **[1]**

$861 - €799 - **£533** - FF5 243
«Styria (Fahrradwerke Puch in Graz)» Poster (38x82cm 14x32in) Wien 2001

SCHÖN Luise ?-1848 **[3]**

$1 784 - €1 853 - **£1 125** - FF12 157
Still life Oil/canvas (90x69cm 35x27in) Sydney 2000

SCHÖNBERGER Armand 1885-1974 **[34]**

$6 600 - €7 500 - **£4 600** - FF49 200
Gare Huile/toile (94x69cm 37x27in) Budapest 2001

$1 406 - €1 477 - **£874** - FF25 301
Portrait Huile/papier (24x18cm 9x7in) Budapest 2000

$720 - €708 - **£450** - FF4 644
Little Girl with Flowers Mixed media/paper (35x24cm 13x9in) Budapest 1999

SCHÖNBERGER von Alfred Karl 1845-? **[29]**

$2 324 - €2 659 - **£1 616** - FF17 440
Königssee mit dem Watzmann Öl/Leinwand (65x95cm 25x37in) Rudolstadt-Thüringen 2000

$1 712 - €1 955 - **£1 207** - FF12 827
Ruderboote mit Ausflüglern auf einem Alpensee Oil/panel (18x24cm 7x9in) Bern 2001

SCHONBORN Anton ?-1871 **[3]**

$16 000 - €13 424 - **£9 387** - FF88 057
«Laramie Peak, 48 miles Distant View from the East» Watercolour/paper (12x31cm 5x12in) New-Orleans LA 1998

SCHÖNCHEN Leopold 1855-1935 **[33]**

$488 - €511 - **£306** - FF3 353
Netzflickerinnen an der Küste von Scheveningen Öl/Leinwand (27x36cm 10x14in) Bremen 2000

SCHÖNFELD Eduard 1839-1885 **[9]**

$3 441 - €3 835 - **£2 405** - FF25 154
Südtiroler Landschaft Öl/Leinwand (60x85.5cm 23x33in) München 2001

SCHÖNFELD Heinrich 1809-1845 **[2]**

$4 839 - €4 955 - **£3 038** - FF32 500
Inspiration de Rubens Huile/toile (58x84cm 22x33in) Paris 2000

SCHÖNFELD Johann Heinrich 1609-1682 **[26]**

$28 000 - €36 283 - **£21 000** - FF238 000
Trionfo di Cesare Olio/tela (152x415cm 59x163in) Milano 2000

$4 032 - €3 431 - **£2 400** - FF22 509
The Infant Christ triumphant over Sin Oil/canvas/board (68x42cm 26x16in) London 1998

$3 899 - €3 816 - **£2 500** - FF25 030
Satyrs and Putti Black chalk/paper (20.5x35.5cm 8x13in) London 1999

S

Das Kinderbacchanal Radierung (16.9x23.4cm 6x9in) Berlin 1998
$4 410 · €3 833 · £2 657 · FF25 140

SCHONGAUER Martin 1430-1491 **[95]**
$3 140 · €3 579 · £2 191 · FF23 477
Die Kreuztragung Kupferstich (16.5x11.5cm 6x4in) Berlin 2001

SCHÖNHEYDER-MØLLER Valdemar 1864-1905 **[7]**
$14 916 · €14 789 · £9 328 · FF97 009
Coucher de soleil Oil/canvas (116x87cm 45x34in) København 1999
$6 780 · €6 722 · £4 240 · FF44 095
Ung pige på Skagen strand Oil/canvas (31x42cm 12x16in) København 1999

SCHÖNIAN Alfred 1856-1936 **[54]**
$825 · €929 · £568 · FF6 096
Besök i hönsgården Oil/canvas (16x33cm 6x12in) Uppsala 2000

SCHÖNITZER Sepp 1896-1993 **[3]**
$7 383 · €7 158 · £4 572 · FF46 954
Villa Cimbrone, Amalfi Oil/canvas/panel (39x58cm 15x22in) Graz 1999

SCHÖNLEBER Gustav 1851-1917 **[116]**
$11 697 · €11 248 · £7 207 · FF73 785
Frühling an der Alb Öl/Leinwand (132x107cm 51x42in) München 1999
$4 312 · €4 346 · £2 688 · FF28 508
Dampfer in Cuxhaven, vor einer Anlegestelle liegt ein Dampfer Oil/panel (45x38cm 17x14in) Stuttgart 2000
$3 339 · €3 068 · £2 051 · FF20 123
Peer in Ostende Öl/Leinwand/Karton (27x42cm 10x16in) Stuttgart 1999
$531 · €511 · £332 · FF3 353
Schwäbische Landschaft Pencil (26.5x41cm 10x16in) München 1999

SCHÖNMANN Joseph 1799-1879 **[3]**
$30 240 · €25 736 · £18 000 · FF168 820
David and Abigail Oil/canvas (133x170cm 52x66in) London 1998

SCHÖNN Aloïs 1826-1897 **[48]**
$4 333 · €4 161 · £2 694 · FF27 293
Reb Aizig bar Jekeles Schul on the goos Market in Krakovi Huile/toile (73x54cm 28x21in) Montréal 1999
$282 · €307 · £185 · FF2 012
Prächtiges Blumenstilleben mit verschiedenen Blumen in einer Vase Öl/Leinwand (30x25cm 11x9in) Kassel 2000
$533 · €622 · £369 · FF4 081
Frauen mit Wasserkrügen an einem Brunnen Watercolour (17x25cm 6x9in) Bern 2000

SCHÖNPFLUG Fritz 1873-1951 **[35]**
$686 · €654 · £419 · FF4 290
Am Strand Watercolour, gouache (23x36.3cm 9x14in) Wien 1999

SCHÖNROCK Julius 1835-? **[7]**
$1 381 · €1 534 · £963 · FF10 061
«Hessische Landschaft nach dem Regen» Öl/Leinwand (55x31cm 21x31in) Stuttgart 2001

SCHÖNWALD Rudolf 1928 **[9]**
$1 159 · €1 090 · £718 · FF7 150
Meine Tiere Radierung (56x42cm 22x16in) Wien 1999

SCHONZEIT Ben 1942 **[7]**
$1 100 · €923 · £645 · FF6 054
Dave (Last Picture of my Father) II Graphite (96x77.5cm 37x30in) New-York 1998

SCHOOCK Hendrick 1630-1707 **[4]**
$47 110 · €45 378 · £29 110 · FF297 660
Basket of Grapes and Other Fruit on a Stone Ledge with Peaches Oil/canvas (114.5x91cm 45x35in) Amsterdam 1999

SCHOOFS Rudolf 1932 **[40]**
$85 · €92 · £58 · FF603
Ohne Titel Etching, aquatint (28.5x28cm 11x11in) Stuttgart 2001

SCHOON Theo 1915-1985 **[9]**
$725 · €813 · £507 · FF5 334
Abstract Design Ink/paper (30x23.5cm 11x9in) Auckland 2001

SCHOONEBEECK Adriaan 1657/58-1705 **[4]**
$287 · €305 · £191 · FF2 000
L'histoire de l'Angleterre: accession au trône de Guillaume III Eau-forte (15.5x20cm 6x7in) Paris 2000

SCHOONHOVEN Johannes, Jan 1914-1994 **[181]**
$48 540 · €54 454 · £33 636 · FF357 192
«R 70-74» Mixed media (126x96cm 49x37in) Amsterdam 2000
$24 270 · €27 227 · £16 818 · FF178 596
Untitled Mixed media (100x83cm 39x32in) Amsterdam 2000
$7 812 · €9 076 · £5 490 · FF59 532
«R60-13» Mixed media (67x20cm 26x7in) Amsterdam 2001
$63 994 · €63 529 · £39 984 · FF416 724
R69-40 Relief (104x104cm 40x40in) Amsterdam 1999
$31 997 · €31 765 · £19 992 · FF208 362
Untitled Relief (60x76.5cm 23x30in) Amsterdam 1999
$1 607 · €1 906 · £1 171 · FF12 501
«T75-47» Ink (42x26cm 16x10in) Amsterdam 2001
$564 · €498 · £340 · FF3 269
Untitled Lithograph (40x25cm 15x9in) Amsterdam 1998

SCHOONOVER Frank Earl 1877-1972 **[39]**
$19 000 · €21 281 · £13 201 · FF139 596
Man with Torch discovering treasure Vault Oil/canvas (76x53cm 30x21in) New-York 2001

SCHOOTEN van Floris Gerritsz. c.1590-c.1660 **[32]**
$45 414 · €44 210 · £27 898 · FF290 000
Scène de garde-manger dans un intérieur hollandais Huile/panneau (92x157cm 36x61in) Paris 1999
$45 000 · €44 979 · £27 490 · FF295 042
Grapes, Plums, Medlars, Cherries, Assorted Berries and Peas Oil/panel (35.5x59cm 13x23in) New-York 2000

SCHOPF Gustav Georg 1899-? **[22]**
$1 151 · €1 278 · £802 · FF8 384
«Dampfwalze bei Strassenarbeit in Stgt., im Hgr.Tram» Oil/board (50x65cm 19x25in) Stuttgart 2001

SCHOPIN Frédéric Henri 1804-1880 **[23]**
$1 800 · €2 332 · £1 350 · FF15 300
La gentildonna e il vagabondo Olio/tela (46x37.5cm 18x14in) Roma 2001

SCHOPPE Palmer 1912 **[4]**
$400 · €373 · £246 · FF2 445
«Go Long Mule» Lithograph (22x33cm 9x13in) Cleveland OH 1999

S

SCHORER Hans Friedrich c.1585-1655 **[12]**
- $1 200 - €1 197 - £730 - FF7 854
  Mountainous Landscape with Figures by a Stream Ink (13.5x18.5cm 5x7in) New-York 2000

SCHOT-MARTIN Francina Louise 1816-1894 **[4]**
- $21 235 - €24 958 - £14 723 - FF163 713
  A Rosebush with Butterflies and a Dragonfly Oil/panel (80x66cm 31x25in) Amsterdam 2000

SCHOTANUS Petrus 1601-c.1675 **[10]**
- $12 240 - €11 434 - £7 552 - FF75 000
  Nature morte au globe terrestre Huile/panneau (56x45cm 22x17in) Vannes 1999

SCHOTEL Anthonie Pieter 1890-1958 **[72]**
- $3 764 - €3 321 - £2 268 - FF21 784
  A Schouw at Half Sail, near Spakenburg Oil/canvas (81x70cm 31x27in) Amsterdam 1998
- $1 053 - €1 180 - £731 - FF7 739
  Vissersschepen en man in roeiboot Oil/canvas (38x28cm 14x11in) Rotterdam 2001
- $1 052 - €1 180 - £736 - FF7 739
  Uitzeilende Volendamse botter Gouache/paper (16.2x19.5cm 6x7in) Dordrecht 2001

SCHOTEL Christina Petronella 1818-1854 **[2]**
- $6 763 - €6 353 - £4 076 - FF41 672
  Flower Still Life Oil/panel (32.5x26.5cm 12x10in) Amsterdam 1999

SCHOTEL Jan Christianus 1787-1838 **[62]**
- $29 999 - €31 436 - £19 000 - FF206 205
  The Rescue Oil/canvas (113x148cm 44x58in) London 2000
- $25 926 - €27 227 - £16 404 - FF178 596
  Fishing Boats at Low Tide Oil/canvas (71x99cm 27x38in) Amsterdam 2000
- $5 019 - €5 899 - £3 480 - FF38 695
  Sailors in Distress Oil/panel (27x37cm 10x14in) Amsterdam 2000
- $2 904 - €2 439 - £1 707 - FF16 000
  Marine Encre (28x46cm 11x18in) Paris 1998

SCHOTEL Petrus Johannes 1808-1865 **[32]**
- $7 620 - €8 181 - £5 100 - FF53 662
  Einlaufen in den Hafen bei Sturm Öl/Leinwand (47.2x64.5cm 18x25in) Hamburg 2000
- $1 456 - €1 611 - £988 - FF10 569
  Voiliers au port Aquarelle/papier (27x38cm 10x14in) Antwerpen 2000

SCHOTH Anton, Capt. 1859-1906 **[22]**
- $1 524 - €1 536 - £950 - FF10 073
  Fishing Boats off the Coast Oil/canvas (30.5x60.5cm 12x23in) London 2000
- $898 - €863 - £560 - FF5 662
  Coastal Landscape with Buildings and Fishermen Oil/panel (23x46cm 9x18in) Stansted Mountfitchet, Essex 1999

SCHOTT Walter 1861-1938 **[25]**
- $1 497 - €1 687 - £1 053 - FF11 067
  Kugelspielerin Porcelain (H37.5cm H14in) Stuttgart 2001

SCHOTZ Benno 1891-1984 **[157]**
- $1 159 - €1 073 - £700 - FF7 041
  Sally Collar-Gentle, the figure performing ballet exercises Bronze (H79cm H31in) Edinburgh 1999

SCHOU Carl 1870-1938 **[93]**
- $287 - €335 - £202 - FF2 200
  Syende kvinde ved vindue Oil/canvas (59.5x50cm 23x19in) København 2000

SCHOU Ludvig Abelin 1838-1867 **[25]**
- $3 648 - €4 026 - £2 415 - FF26 412
  Studie af nögen kvinde Oil/canvas (95x63cm 37x24in) Viby J, Århus 2000
- $1 356 - €1 346 - £847 - FF8 830
  Portraet af Elna Glad, född Collin Oil/canvas (30x25cm 11x9in) København 1999

SCHOU Peter Johan 1863-1934 **[20]**
- $1 386 - €1 345 - £856 - FF8 823
  Lille dreng på vej gennem skov Oil/canvas (56x37cm 22x14in) Vejle 1999

SCHOU Sigurd Solver 1875-1944 **[30]**
- $1 084 - €1 075 - £658 - FF7 052
  Torpmagle Mölle, landsbyparti med personer Oil/canvas (70x100cm 27x39in) Vejle 2000

SCHOU Sven 1877-1949 **[47]**
- $527 - €563 - £359 - FF3 691
  Köerne drives hjem af den gamle Poppelalle ved Havnö Oil/canvas (51x61cm 20x24in) Vejle 2001
- $163 - €174 - £111 - FF1 142
  Hoppen Karen med föl og kreaturer i Kalvehaven på Havnö Oil/canvas (29x44cm 11x17in) Vejle 2001

SCHOUBOE Henrik 1876-1949 **[37]**
- $305 - €296 - £192 - FF1 942
  Interiör med udsigt gennem vindue/Efterårslandskab Oil/canvas (65x80cm 25x31in) København 1999

SCHOUBROECK Pieter c.1570-1607 **[10]**
- $113 419 - €131 596 - £78 300 - FF863 214
  Village Kermesse Oil/copper (33x53.5cm 12x21in) Amsterdam 2000
- $9 709 - €10 671 - £6 174 - FF70 000
  La fuite de Troie Huile/cuivre (18.5x26cm 7x10in) Paris 2000

SCHOUMAN Aert 1710-1792 **[95]**
- $85 000 - €98 819 - £59 661 - FF648 210
  Parrots and other exotic birds in a Landscape Oil/canvas (136x143.5cm 53x56in) New-York 2001
- $5 919 - €6 353 - £3 960 - FF41 672
  Dessus-de-porte met voorstelling van fazanten en bloemen in landschap Oil/canvas (83x98cm 32x38in) Dordrecht 2000
- $2 456 - €2 106 - £1 453 - FF13 812
  Oiseaux de basse-cour Huile/panneau (20x33cm 7x12in) Tongeren 1998
- $2 102 - €1 814 - £1 268 - FF11 901
  Simeon in the Temple, after Rembrandt Wash (49.6x39.6cm 19x15in) Amsterdam 1998

SCHOUMAN Izaak 1801-1878 **[5]**
- $1 838 - €1 724 - £1 136 - FF11 311
  De Jonge Jacobus Ink (40.5x60cm 15x23in) Amsterdam 1999

SCHOUMAN Martinus 1770-1848 **[39]**
- $23 980 - €27 987 - £17 000 - FF183 583
  The Flushing State Yacht running past the Scheldt Estuary Oil/canvas (151x206cm 59x81in) London 2001
- $13 849 - €12 604 - £8 500 - FF82 679
  Shipping off a jetty Oil/canvas (50x68cm 19x26in) London 1999
- $1 049 - €971 - £633 - FF6 372
  Segelboote vor einem niederländischen Hafen Ink (20x30.5cm 7x12in) Heidelberg 1999

SCHOUTEN Henry 1864-1927 **[549]**
- 🖼 **$3 620** - €3 403 - **£2 191** - FF22 324
  The Hay Harvest Oil/canvas (123.5x200cm 48x78in) Amsterdam 1999
- 🖼 **$5 047** - €5 899 - **£3 603** - FF38 695
  Still Life with Flowers in a Wicker Basket Oil/canvas (85.5x65cm 33x25in) Amsterdam 2001
- 🖼 **$1 669** - €1 534 - **£1 025** - FF10 061
  Kühe in einer weiten Wiesenlandschaft Öl/Leinwand (62x92cm 24x36in) Stuttgart 1999
- 🖼 **$806** - €892 - **£561** - FF5 853
  Intérieur avec singe chassant deux chiens Huile/panneau (12x16.5cm 4x6in) Bruxelles 2001

SCHOUTEN Hermanus Petrus 1747-1822 **[6]**
- 📝 **$34 696** - €29 936 - **£20 935** - FF196 369
  The Groote Kerk, Haarlem, seen from the vismarkt Watercolour (32x29.3cm 12x11in) Amsterdam 1998

SCHOUTEN Paul & Henry 1860/c.1857-1922/27 **[5]**
- 🖼 **$710** - €793 - **£496** - FF5 203
  Vaches au pâturage Huile/toile (50x81cm 19x31in) Bruxelles 2001

SCHOUTEN Paul Henry 1860-1922 **[126]**
- 🖼 **$602** - €520 - **£359** - FF3 412
  Cour de ferme animée Huile/toile (64x74cm 25x29in) Bruxelles 1998

SCHOUTZ Vadim Mihalowitch 1877-? **[1]**
- 🖼 **$4 482** - €5 045 - **£3 087** - FF33 096
  The Swing Oil/canvas (80x120cm 31x47in) Helsinki 2000

SCHOVELIN Axel Thorsen 1827-1893 **[108]**
- 🖼 **$888** - €914 - **£563** - FF5 994
  Kystparti med kvinde på badebro Oil/canvas (46x74cm 18x29in) Vejle 2000
- 🖼 **$424** - €469 - €294 - FF3 076
  Landskab med ålob og so, skumring Oil/canvas (24x35cm 9x13in) Vejle 2001

SCHOYERER Joseph 1844-1923 **[81]**
- 🖼 **$1 260** - €1 431 - **£881** - FF9 390
  Der Monte Cristallo in den Dolomiten Öl/Leinwand (85x122cm 33x48in) München 2001
- 🖼 **$716** - €613 - **£430** - FF4 024
  «Berglandschaft» Öl/Karton (24x33cm 9x12in) Heidelberg 1998

SCHRADER Bertha 1845-1920 **[6]**
- 🖼 **$26 472** - €24 727 - **£16 000** - FF162 196
  Hafenansicht Oil/board (46x60cm 18x23in) London 2000

SCHRADER Julius Friedrich A. 1815-1900 **[11]**
- 🖼 **$4 672** - €4 089 - **£2 829** - FF26 824
  Junge Italienerin beim Blumenbinden Öl/Leinwand (41.5x47.5cm 16x18in) Berlin 1998

SCHRADER-VELGEN Carl Hans 1876-1945 **[13]**
- 🖼 **$3 726** - €3 579 - **£2 297** - FF23 477
  Akt im Park Öl/Karton (49x65cm 19x25in) München 1999

SCHRAG Julius 1864-1948 **[25]**
- 🖼 **$4 225** - €3 581 - **£2 524** - FF23 489
  «Der Grüne Markt in Emden» Oil/panel (36.5x46cm 14x18in) Bremen 1998

SCHRAG Karl 1912-1997 **[24]**
- 🖼 **$5 500** - €5 904 - **£3 680** - FF38 728
  Apple Tree, Late Summer Oil/canvas (91.5x101.5cm 36x39in) New-York 2000

$1 000 - €1 160 - **£690** - FF7 611
📝 **Untitled** Watercolour, gouache/paper (57x95cm 22x37in) New-York 2000

SCHRAM Alois Hans 1864-1919 **[56]**
- 🖼 **$8 395** - €8 027 - **£5 263** - FF52 653
  Madonna Oil/canvas (147x97cm 57x38in) Stockholm 1999
- 🖼 **$25 587** - €21 492 - **£15 000** - FF140 977
  A hard Decision Oil/canvas (100.5x100.5cm 39x39in) London 1998
- 🖼 **$11 207** - €12 031 - **£7 500** - FF78 916
  The Dice Players Oil/panel (25x55.5cm 9x21in) London 2000
- **$427** - €472 - €296 - FF5 098
  Portrait einer sitzenden, jungen Dame Pencil/paper (43x35cm 16x13in) Wien 2001
- 🗔 **$425** - €405 - **£259** - FF2 655
  Classical Scene with two Females Color lithograph (50x73cm 20x29in) Bloomfield-Hills MI 1999

SCHRAM Wout 1895-1987 **[6]**
- 🖼 **$4 904** - €5 446 - **£3 411** - FF35 719
  «Stilleven met bloesemtak» Oil/canvas (75x65cm 29x25in) Groningen 2001

SCHRAMM-ZITTAU Rudolf 1874-1950 **[51]**
- 🖼 **$1 773** - €1 535 - **£1 069** - FF10 070
  Im winterlichen Hirschgarten Öl/Leinwand (60x100cm 23x39in) München 1998

SCHRANZ Anton 1769-1839 **[28]**
- 🖼 **$31 380** - €33 684 - **£21 000** - FF220 953
  H.M.S Caledonia Clearing Port Mahon, Minorca/View of Port Mahon Oil/canvas (39x60.5cm 15x23in) London 2000

SCHRANZ Anton II 1801-1864 **[5]**
- 🖼 **$29 236** - €33 545 - **£20 000** - FF220 040
  Views of the Grand Harbour at Valletta, Malta Oil/canvas (41x61.5cm 16x24in) London 2000
- 📝 **$2 310** - €2 180 - **£1 434** - FF14 301
  Minerva Tempel Watercolour (40.5x56.5cm 15x22in) Wien 1999

SCHRANZ Johan, Giovanni 1794-1882 **[5]**
- 🖼 **$5 803** - €5 381 - **£3 500** - FF35 296
  The Corner of St, Ursula Street and St John Street, Valletta Watercolour (27x21cm 10x8in) London 2000

SCHRANZ Joseph 1803-c.1865 **[27]**
- 🖼 **$4 093** - €4 696 - **£2 800** - FF30 805
  View of the Citadel, Corfu Watercolour (19x34.5cm 7x13in) London 2000

SCHRAUDOLPH von Johann 1808-1879 **[7]**
- 🖼 **$2 415** - €2 198 - **£1 509** - FF14 421
  Christus und Maria Magdalena Öl/Leinwand (41x33cm 16x12in) München 1999

SCHRECKENGOST Viktor 1906 **[13]**
- 🖼 **$1 100** - €1 262 - **£752** - FF8 279
  Holiday Splendor Watercolour/board (53x74cm 21x29in) Cleveland OH 2000

SCHREIB Werner 1925-1969 **[17]**
- 🗔 **$170** - €179 - **£107** - FF1 173
  Turm aus geschichteten Geräten Farbradierung (45x30.5cm 17x12in) Braunschweig 2001

SCHREIBER Charles Baptiste 1845-1903 **[35]**
- 🖼 **$1 021** - €1 000 - **£629** - FF6 562
  Coquetterie Huile/panneau (22x12cm 8x4in) Zürich 1999

S

SCHREIBER George L. 1904-1977 **[80]**
- $2 200 - €2 498 - **£1 505** - FF16 386
  Farm Landscape Watercolour/paper (38x56cm 14x21in) New-York 2000
- $325 - €374 - **£224** - FF2 454
  Twilight Lithograph (24x34cm 9x13in) Cleveland OH 2000

SCHREIBER Peter Conrad 1816-1894 **[18]**
- $477 - €507 - **£307** - FF3 327
  Romantic Alpine Landscape with Castle and Figure to the Foreground Gouache/paper (55x45cm 21x17in) Lymington 2001

SCHREINER Friedrich Wilhelm 1836-? **[12]**
- $5 702 - €5 190 - **£3 504** - FF34 044
  A Pair of Deer in a River Landscape Oil/canvas (120x90cm 47x35in) London 1999

SCHRETTER Zygmunt Szreter 1896-1977 **[31]**
- $7 830 - €7 892 - **£4 883** - FF51 769
  Jeu de dames Pastel (37.5x53.7cm 14x21in) Warszawa 2000

SCHREUER Wilhelm 1866-1933 **[164]**
- $1 303 - €1 534 - **£920** - FF10 061
  Ratsherren und Bürger in einer Düsseldorfer Kneipe Mischtechnik (73x87cm 28x34in) Köln 2001
- $932 - €1 022 - **£633** - FF6 707
  Patrizierkopf Oil/panel (31.5x28.5cm 12x11in) Hilden 2000
- $1 916 - €1 789 - **£1 182** - FF11 738
  Vor dem Wirtshaus Mischtechnik/Papier (37x47cm 14x18in) Köln 1999

SCHREYER Adolf 1828-1899 **[193]**
- $75 000 - €71 265 - **£45 630** - FF467 467
  Fleeing Wallachian Horses Oil/canvas (101.5x171.5cm 39x67in) New-York 1999
- $18 000 - €16 860 - **£11 066** - FF110 593
  The Oasis Oil/canvas (40.5x63.5cm 15x25in) New-York 1999
- $4 525 - €4 346 - **£2 805** - FF28 508
  Araber mit Pferd Öl/Leinwand (28.5x23.5cm 11x9in) Ahlden 1999
- $1 317 - €1 463 - **£882** - FF9 596
  Arabisk ryttare på vit häst Watercolour/board (21x18cm 8x7in) Stockholm 2000

SCHREYER Franz 1858-? **[27]**
- $2 832 - €2 812 - **£1 769** - FF18 446
  Acqua Claudia in der römischen Campagna Öl/Leinwand (77x149cm 30x58in) München 1999
- $278 - €332 - **£191** - FF2 180
  Herbsttag im Moor Oil/panel (26x35cm 10x13in) München 2000

SCHREYER Lothar 1886-1966 **[56]**
- $1 790 - €1 533 - **£1 076** - FF10 059
  Farbklang 15 Watercolour (19x11.1cm 7x4in) Hamburg 1998
- $535 - €511 - **£334** - FF3 353
  Ohne Titel Woodcut (26.4x20.2cm 10x7in) Köln 1999

SCHREYER Wilhelm 1890-? **[4]**
- $3 508 - €4 090 - **£2 459** - FF26 831
  Hofgartenkaffee Öl/Karton (48x66.5cm 18x26in) München 2000

SCHREYVOGEL Charles 1861-1912 **[32]**
- $950 000 - €943 197 - **£593 750** - FF6 186 970
  Saving Their Lieutenant Oil/canvas (61x76cm 24x29in) New-York 1999
- $1 892 - €2 212 - **£1 350** - FF14 507
  Ranch View on a clear Day Huile/panneau (12.5x20.5cm 4x8in) Montréal 2001

SCHRÖBER Ludwig Gabriel 1907-1973 **[8]**
- $80 000 - €93 367 - **£56 712** - FF612 448
  The last Drop Bronze (30x47.5cm 11x18in) New-York 2001

SCHRIEBER Ludwig Gabriel 1907-1973 **[8]**
- $3 998 - €4 704 - **£2 822** - FF30 855
  «Kleine Luna in den Wolken» Bronze (71.5x34.5x14cm 28x13x5in) Berlin 2001

SCHRIECK van der Daniel XIX **[1]**
- $7 168 - €7 932 - **£4 800** - FF52 032
  Paysage animé d'une paysanne près de l'eau Huile/panneau (54x67.5cm 21x26in) Antwerpen 2000

SCHRIECK van Otto Marseus Snuff. 1619-1678 **[31]**
- $20 383 - €23 649 - **£14 302** - FF155 124
  Sous-bois avec chardons, serpents, sauriens et papillons Huile/toile (56x43cm 22x16in) Genève 2000
- $65 244 - €61 022 - **£40 000** - FF400 280
  Roses and Other Flowers in a Glass Vase on a Marble Ledge Oil/panel (34.5x26.5cm 13x10in) London 1998

SCHRIJNDER Jo 1894-1968 **[24]**
- $1 947 - €1 906 - **£1 248** - FF12 501
  Ducks flying over a Lake Oil/canvas (80x88cm 31x34in) Amsterdam 1999

SCHRIKKEL Louis 1902-1978 **[26]**
- $907 - €862 - **£552** - FF5 655
  Gevarieerd stilleven Oil/canvas (39x49cm 15x19in) Rotterdam 1999
- $5 496 - €5 899 - **£3 677** - FF38 695
  Het Bescheiden Ruikertje Crayon (26x45cm 10x17in) Amsterdam 2000

SCHRIMPF Georg 1889-1938 **[187]**
- $33 598 - €33 234 - **£20 949** - FF218 003
  Weite Waldlandschaft Öl/Leinwand (68x100cm 26x39in) Berlin 2001
- $2 450 - €2 431 - **£1 525** - FF18 446
  Mädchen mit Berglöwe Watercolour (20x15cm 7x5in) Dettelbach-Effeldorf 2000
- $291 - €332 - **£203** - FF2 180
  Zeitungsjunge Lithographie (20x15.5cm 7x6in) Hamburg 2001

SCHRÖDER Albert Friedrich 1854-1939 **[46]**
- $5 628 - €6 012 - **£3 836** - FF39 433
  Festin hollandais au XVII siècle Huile/panneau (48x59.5cm 18x23in) Warszawa 2001
- $1 391 - €1 636 - **£997** - FF10 732
  Ein Mann in holländischer Tracht sitzt auf einem alten Holzstuhl Oil/panel (34x25cm 13x9in) Stuttgart 2001

SCHRÖDER Carl Julius Hermann 1802-1867 **[8]**
- $2 731 - €2 812 - **£1 722** - FF18 446
  Die Liebe auf dem Lande Öl/Leinwand (32.5x27.5cm 12x10in) Berlin 2000

SCHRÖDER Heinrich 1881-1919 **[26]**
- $3 875 - €3 634 - **£2 395** - FF23 835
  Blumenstrauss in blauer Vase Öl/Leinwand (68x55cm 26x21in) Wien 1999
- $2 199 - €2 180 - **£1 377** - FF14 301
  Blumenstilleben mit Krug Öl/Leinwand (36.2x36.2cm 14x14in) Wien 1999

SCHRÖDER Johann Heinrich 1757-1812 **[2]**
- $4 220 - €4 857 - **£2 914** - FF31 862
  Erbprinzessin Amalie Friederike von Baden Öl/Leinwand (71x56cm 27x22in) München 2000

SCHRODER Povl 1894-1957 **[70]**
$733 - €872 - **£522** - FF5 719
Portraet af siddende kvinde i blå kjole Oil/canvas (86.5x75cm 34x29in) Köbenhavn 2000

SCHRÖDER Sierk 1903 **[32]**
$916 - €998 - **£631** - FF6 548
Landscape with Waterplants and Birds Pastel/paper (48x37cm 18x14in) Amsterdam 2001

SCHRÖDER-GREIFSWALD Max 1858-1920 **[14]**
$722 - €716 - **£438** - FF4 695
Zweimastsegler Öl/Leinwand (46x60cm 18x23in) Satow 2000

SCHRÖDER-SONNENSTERN Emil Friedrich 1892-1982 **[191]**
$1 171 - €1 361 - **£823** - FF8 929
Psyche und narrmoor Pastel/paper (67x97cm 26x38in) Amsterdam 2001
$103 - €97 - **£64** - FF637
Die Praxis, oder die Lebenszauberungs-Eleven Farblithographie (58.5x59.7cm 23x23in) Stuttgart 1999

SCHRÖDL Anton 1820-1906 **[74]**
$2 562 - €2 543 - **£1 599** - FF16 684
Hirschjagd im Hochgebirge Öl/Leinwand (73.5x95.5cm 28x37in) Wien 1999
$984 - €945 - **£617** - FF6 197
Pflanzenstudie Öl/Karton (20x13.4cm 7x5in) Wien 1999

SCHROETER von Carolina 1803-? **[1]**
$6 624 - €7 318 - **£4 593** - FF48 000
Les archanges Huile/panneau (149x65cm 58x25in) Lyon 2001

SCHROETER Wilhelm 1849-1904 **[11]**
$2 090 - €2 177 - **£1 324** - FF14 277
Bächlein im Winterwald Öl/Leinwand (82x62cm 32x24in) Zürich 2000

SCHROFER Willem 1898-1968 **[9]**
$3 000 - €2 949 - **£1 927** - FF19 347
A reclining Nude Oil/canvas (70x100cm 27x39in) Amsterdam 1999

SCHROM Ernst 1902-1969 **[20]**
$830 - €945 - **£583** - FF6 197
Dominikanerbastei Aquarell/Papier (30x39cm 11x15in) Wien 2001

SCHRÖTER Paul 1866-1946 **[15]**
$2 180 - €2 454 - **£1 502** - FF16 098
Marianne, Frau mit Nähzeug im Korbsessel Öl/Leinwand (48x61cm 18x24in) Bremen 2000

SCHROTH Eugen 1862-1945 **[12]**
$2 107 - €1 943 - **£1 242** - FF12 743
Fröhliche Runde im Herrgottswinkel, Zwei Dirndl, Jäger, Bursche Öl/Leinwand (80x110cm 31x43in) Dresden 1998

SCHRÖTTER von Alfred 1856-1935 **[13]**
$1 600 - €1 386 - **£981** - FF9 090
Feeding the Bird Oil/panel (21x16.5cm 8x6in) New-York 1999

SCHROTZBERG Franz 1811-1889 **[16]**
$11 060 - €10 174 - **£6 636** - FF66 738
Portrait einer Dame in weissem Kleid vor einem Landschaftshintergrund Öl/Leinwand (134x105cm 52x41in) Wien 1999
$5 922 - €6 541 - **£4 104** - FF42 903
Die Emancipierte Öl/Leinwand (111x54.5cm 43x21in) Wien 2001

SCHRYVER de Louis 1862-1942 **[40]**
$30 000 - €34 658 - **£21 006** - FF227 343
Parisien Flower Vendor Oil/canvas (71x91cm 28x36in) New-York 2001
$4 742 - €5 336 - **£3 265** - FF35 000
La branche de rosier cassée Huile/toile (29x40cm 11x15in) Paris 2000

SCHUBACK Emil Gottlieb 1820-1902 **[5]**
$2 278 - €2 556 - **£1 579** - FF16 769
Abschied Öl/Leinwand (56x46cm 22x18in) München 2000

SCHUBERT Heinrich Carl 1827-1897 **[19]**
$623 - €727 - **£440** - FF4 767
Via alle grotte e alla volpera Aquarell/Papier (32x25cm 12x9in) Salzburg 2000

SCHUBERT Otto 1892-1970 **[82]**
$837 - €818 - **£530** - FF5 366
Gewitterstimmung im Vorgebirge Öl/Leinwand (66x95cm 25x37in) München 1999
$267 - €256 - **£162** - FF1 676
Lesende Ink/paper (42.6x30.4cm 16x11in) Dettelbach-Effeldorf 1999
$98 - €112 - **£67** - FF737
Frauenraub Lithographie (38.5x50cm 15x19in) Heidelberg 2000

SCHUCH A. XIX-XX **[1]**
$19 250 - €19 398 - **£12 000** - FF127 243
Elegant Lady, Full Length, in a Black Dress, Stole and Hat Oil/canvas (183x86.5cm 72x34in) London 2000

SCHUCH Carl 1846-1903 **[22]**
$30 899 - €28 121 - **£19 305** - FF184 464
Stilleben mit einer Wildente auf Holzplanken Öl/Leinwand (50x80cm 19x31in) München 1999
$1 222 - €1 453 - **£872** - FF9 534
Föhnstimmung Öl/Karton (43x27.5cm 16x10in) Wien 2000

SCHUCH Werner Wilhelm 1843-1918 **[23]**
$12 240 - €11 409 - **£7 395** - FF74 835
Paysage avec cavalier et prisonnier Oil/canvas (132x217cm 51x85in) Warszawa 1999
$745 - €767 - **£469** - FF5 030
Aus der Schlacht bei Möckern Öl/Leinwand (33.5x37cm 13x14in) Berlin 2000

SCHUCKER James 1903-1988 **[5]**
$2 000 - €2 331 - **£1 384** - FF15 293
Girl Violonist and Boy Trumpeter Sitting Together Oil/board (44x34cm 17x13in) New-York 2000
$225 - €237 - **£148** - FF1 554
Illustrations Watercolour/paper (11x36cm 4x14in) Hatfield PA 2000

SCHUER Theodor Cornelisz. 1628-1707 **[1]**
$15 861 - €16 655 - **£10 000** - FF109 247
Minerva and the Muses on Mount Helicon Oil/canvas (203x148.5cm 79x58in) London 2000

SCHUERCH Johann Robert 1895-1941 **[6]**
$1 263 - €1 187 - **£783** - FF7 784
Zwei Männer im Gespräch Pastell/Papier (34.5x26cm 13x10in) Luzern 1999

SCHUFFENECKER Claude Émile 1851-1934 **[197]**
$16 680 - €15 245 - **£10 210** - FF100 000
Portrait d'homme Huile/carton (46x55cm 18x21in) Calais 1999
$10 366 - €11 129 - **£6 935** - FF73 000
Les environs de l'Aven Huile/toile (30x38cm 11x14in) Paris 2000

S

$750 - €838 - £502 - FF5 500
Bord de mer Pastel/papier (20x30cm 7x11in) Paris 2000

SCHUH Gotthard 1897-1969 [4]
$3 250 - €3 623 - £2 258 - FF23 764
«Javanese Boy» Gelatin silver print (18.5x29cm 7x11in) New-York 2001

SCHUHMACHER Wim 1894-1986 [78]
$384 806 - €333 119 - £233 522 - FF2 185 116
View of San Giminiano Oil/canvas (100x120cm 39x47in) Amsterdam 1998
$29 596 - €31 765 - £19 803 - FF208 362
Gezicht Op De Van Amsterdam Oil/canvas (62x72cm 24x28in) Amsterdam 2000
$26 712 - €31 765 - £19 040 - FF208 362
Three Pears Oil/canvas (28x38cm 11x14in) Amsterdam 2000
$4 228 - €4 538 - £2 829 - FF29 766
De Moeder Van De Schilder Watercolour/paper (66.5x46.5cm 26x18in) Amsterdam 2000

SCHUITEMA Paul 1897-1973 [5]
$750 - €842 - £521 - FF5 520
«Tentoonstelling, 11 juni-12 juli Stedelijk Museum Amsterdam» Poster (94x64cm 37x25in) New-York 2001

SCHUITEN François 1956 [24]
$206 - €198 - £127 - FF1 300
Anniversaire La Marque Jaune Sérigraphie (55x75cm 21x29in) Paris 1999

SCHULER Hans 1874-? [5]
$7 464 - €6 492 - £4 500 - FF42 583
A reclining Nymph Bronze (38x57cm 14x22in) London 1998

SCHULER Jules Théophile 1821-1878 [5]
$5 431 - €5 031 - £3 303 - FF33 000
Réunion familiale autour de la sépulture Huile/toile (89x117cm 35x46in) Paris 1998

SCHULLER Joseph Carl Paul XIX-XX [6]
$9 000 - €10 443 - £6 213 - FF68 499
Pigeons and Peonies Oil/canvas (105.5x183.5cm 41x72in) New-York 2000

SCHULMAN David 1881-1966 [123]
$2 135 - €2 496 - £1 524 - FF16 371
View of Edam Oil/canvas (35x64cm 13x25in) Amsterdam 2001
$1 183 - €1 271 - £792 - FF8 334
Panoramic view of Rotterdam Oil/panel (32x48cm 12x18in) Amsterdam 2000
$258 - €272 - £170 - FF1 786
View on a Canal, Volendam Chalks/paper (37.5x39.5cm 14x15in) Amsterdam 2000

SCHULMAN Léon 1851-1943 [24]
$786 - €681 - £477 - FF4 464
Forest Landscape with Figures by a Cottage Oil/canvas (27x37cm 10x14in) Amsterdam 1999

SCHULT H.A., Hans Jürgen 1939 [36]
$175 - €204 - £123 - FF1 341
«Denk Mal Fiesta» Offset (49x33cm 19x12in) Köln 2001

SCHULTE IM HOFE Rudolf 1865-1928 [5]
$3 479 - €3 807 - £2 400 - FF24 975
Portrait of a Mother and Child Pastel/paper (96.5x70cm 37x27in) London 2001

SCHULTEN Arnold 1809-1874 [8]
$1 723 - €1 687 - £1 060 - FF11 067
Eichengruppe mit rastendem Hirten über einer weiten Flussniederung Öl/Leinwand (75x112cm 29x44in) Bremen 1999

SCHULTZ Alexander 1901-1981 [46]
$1 705 - €1 440 - £1 023 - FF9 448
Fra Italien Oil/canvas (60x73cm 23x28in) Oslo 1998

SCHULTZ George F. 1869-1934 [28]
$750 - €877 - £531 - FF5 754
Summer Landscape along Stream Oil/canvas (60x91cm 24x36in) Cedar-Falls IA 2001

SCHULTZ Johann Karl 1801-1873 [10]
$10 995 - €12 935 - £7 762 - FF84 851
St.Nicolai, Danzig Öl/Leinwand (60.5x45cm 23x17in) Berlin 2001
$500 - €518 - £300 - FF3 400
Le déjeuner, da Joseph Caraud Litografia (35x44cm 13x17in) Firenze 2001

SCHULTZ Robert Weir 1860-1951 [1]
$1 749 - €1 989 - £1 200 - FF13 047
Design for a Decorative Wall in St.Andrew's Chapel, West. Cath. London Pencil (44.5x45.5cm 17x17in) Oxfordshire 2000

SCHULTZ-BRUMMER Christopher 1940 [4]
$1 193 - €1 022 - £717 - FF6 706
Bival Chalks (140x100cm 55x39in) Hamburg 1998

SCHULTZ-WETTEL Ferdinand 1872/76-1957 [12]
$98 - €114 - £69 - FF750
Vue d'Obernai Lithographie (42x88cm 16x34in) Entzheim 2001

SCHULTZBERG Anshelm 1862-1945 [294]
$3 343 - €3 253 - £2 058 - FF21 341
Vy över sommarlandskap, motiv från Filipstads Bergslag Oil/canvas (100x130cm 39x51in) Stockholm 1999
$2 651 - €3 124 - £1 863 - FF20 495
Vinterkväll, motiv från Lokatrakten Oil/canvas (55x73cm 21x28in) Malmö 2000
$1 108 - €934 - £657 - FF6 128
«Castel St Angelo, Rome» Oil/panel (21x32cm 8x12in) Stockholm 1998

SCHULTZE Andreas 1955 [5]
$16 277 - €15 842 - £10 000 - FF103 916
Kugeln Acrylic (200x400cm 78x157in) London 1999

SCHULTZE Bernhard 1915 [516]
$17 664 - €16 464 - £10 674 - FF107 995
Koloss aus dem Dunkel Oil/canvas (160x130cm 62x51in) München 1999
$5 980 - €5 624 - £3 703 - FF36 892
Ohne Titel Öl/Leinwand (40x50cm 15x19in) Köln 1999
$2 697 - €3 068 - £1 870 - FF20 123
«Baumgewächs» Oil/paper (33x41.4cm 12x16in) Hamburg 2000
$7 369 - €8 692 - £5 198 - FF57 016
Migof Sculpture (96x64x29cm 37x25x11in) Köln 2001
$3 468 - €4 090 - £2 446 - FF26 831
Migof stehend Sculpture (63x37x40cm 24x14x15in) Köln 2001
$1 817 - €1 764 - £1 131 - FF11 571
Komposition Indian ink (45.3x31.7cm 17x12in) Berlin 1999
$125 - €147 - £88 - FF965
Ohne Titel Print in colors (33x20cm 12x7in) Berlin 2001

SCHULTZE Robert 1828-1910 **[27]**
- $1 719 - €2 045 - £1 225 - FF13 415
Uferszene am Luganer See Öl/Leinwand
(71x55.5cm 27x21in) Köln 2000

SCHULTZE-JASMER Theodor 1888-1975 **[11]**
- $1 532 - €1 636 - £1 043 - FF10 732
Boddenlandschaft mit Ruderboot Oil/panel
(36x50cm 14x19in) Satow 2001

SCHULTZENHEIM von Ida 1859-1940 **[5]**
- $3 142 - €3 689 - £2 217 - FF24 195
Hundvalpar Oil/canvas (59x73cm 23x28in) Stockholm
2000

SCHULZ Adrien 1851-1931 **[61]**
- $2 780 - €3 049 - £1 846 - FF20 000
Poules près de la chaumière Huile/toile (38x60cm
14x23in) Melun 2000
- $798 - €884 - £504 - FF15 500
Femme puisant de l'eau dans la Marne à Créteil
Huile/toile (41x27cm 16x10in) Paris 2000

SCHULZ Bruno 1892-1942 **[13]**
- $6 268 - €5 921 - £3 790 - FF38 838
Trois filles dans une voiture sans cocher
Oil/paper (14.8x18.7cm 5x7in) Warszawa 1999
- $5 971 - €5 703 - £3 676 - FF37 406
Autoportrait Crayon (15x8.5cm 5x3in) Warszawa
1999

SCHULZ Carl Friedrich 1796-1866 **[20]**
- $4 779 - €4 090 - £2 876 - FF26 826
Wilddiebe Öl/Leinwand (58x50.5cm 22x19in)
München 1998
- $1 395 - €1 278 - £850 - FF8 384
**Rastende Landfrau auf Stein sitzend, über
hügeliger Landschaft** Öl/Leinwand (37x31cm
14x12in) Berlin 1999

SCHULZ Charles Monroe 1922-2000 **[84]**
- $2 100 - €2 254 - £1 405 - FF14 786
**Advertisement: the gang attending the Dolly
Madison Cakes stand** Ink (13x18cm 5x7in) New-
York 2000

SCHULZ Josef 1893-1973 **[28]**
- $2 049 - €2 180 - £1 296 - FF14 301
Blumen in Vase Öl/Leinwand (54x68cm 21x26in)
Salzburg 2000
- $685 - €799 - £484 - FF5 243
Blumen in Vase Mixed media (28x38cm 11x14in)
Salzburg 2000
- $186 - €218 - £132 - FF1 430
Portrait mit Landschaftskulisse Indian ink/paper
(28.5x21cm 11x8in) Salzburg 2000

SCHULZ Robert E. 1928-1978 **[5]**
- $3 250 - €3 789 - £2 250 - FF24 851
Tom Sawyer Stops off at the Fishin Hole
Oil/masonite (76x43cm 30x17in) New-York 2000

SCHULZ-IHLEFELDT Günter 1912-1966 **[25]**
- $909 - €920 - £555 - FF6 037
Ohne Titel Öl/Karton (61x100cm 24x39in) Stuttgart
2000
- $404 - €409 - £246 - FF2 683
Ohne Titel Mixed media/board (24.9x40.2cm 9x15in)
Stuttgart 2000

SCHULZ-MATAM Walter 1889-1965 **[13]**
- $1 566 - €1 841 - £1 085 - FF12 074
Aschermittwoch Tempera/canvas (62x50cm 24x19in)
Stuttgart 2000

SCHULZ-NEUDAMM XX **[1]**
- $320 000 - €386 786 - £223 424 - FF2 537 152
«Metropolis» Poster (211x94cm 83x37in) New-York
2000

SCHULZ-STRATHMANN Otto 1892-1960 **[60]**
- $928 - €869 - £570 - FF5 701
**Gelber Rosenstrauss in Imari-Vase vor rotbrau-
nem Hintergrund** Öl/Leinwand (70.5x60.5cm
27x23in) Lindau 1999

SCHULZE Andreas 1955 **[14]**
- $8 646 - €8 385 - £5 478 - FF55 000
Sans titre Huile/toile (220x170cm 86x66in) Paris 1999

SCHULZE Hans Rudolf 1870-? **[14]**
- $636 - €716 - £438 - FF4 695
Basar in Kairo Watercolour (25.5x31.5cm 10x12in)
Stuttgart 2000

SCHUMACHER Emil 1912-1999 **[572]**
- $45 436 - €44 099 - £28 290 - FF289 273
Tatra Mixed media (90.5x150.5cm 35x59in) Berlin
1999
- $45 980 - €38 789 - £26 967 - FF254 439
Komposition Oil/canvas (60x40cm 23x15in) Berlin
1998
- $19 030 - €16 474 - £11 558 - FF108 063
Komposition Mischtechnik/Karton (46.5x32.3cm
18x12in) München 1998
- $4 144 - €3 580 - £2 503 - FF23 482
Ohne Titel Mixed media/paper (19.5x37.9cm 7x14in)
Köln 1998
- $835 - €716 - £502 - FF4 694
Ohne Titel Radierung (29.5x19.5cm 11x7in) Hamburg
1998

SCHUMACHER Harald Peter W. 1836-1912 **[57]**
- $562 - €603 - £383 - FF3 958
**Maend i en robåd ud for kysten ved Capri,
Italien** Oil/canvas (40x60cm 15x23in) Köbenhavn 2001
- $611 - €563 - £378 - FF3 690
To italienske landskaber i baggrunden Pompeij
Oil/canvas (24x33cm 9x12in) Vejle 1998

SCHUMACHER Karl Georg 1797-1869 **[2]**
- $4 640 - €4 878 - £2 912 - FF32 000
**Pêcheurs au bord du Tibre, près du pont du
château Saint-Ange à Rome** Huile/panneau
(56x84.5cm 22x33in) Paris 2000

SCHUMANN Albert XIX **[3]**
- $2 760 - €3 049 - £1 914 - FF20 000
**Les buveurs dans une auberge/Les joueurs ,
d'après David Teniers** Miniature (11x16cm 4x6in)
Senlis 2001
- $2 685 - €2 300 - £1 614 - FF15 089
In der Dorfschenke Gouache/paper (16.2x14cm
6x5in) Köln 1998

SCHUMANN Christian 1970 **[10]**
- $30 000 - €28 017 - £18 516 - FF183 780
Blob Acrylic (198x152.5cm 77x60in) New-York 1999
- $3 249 - €3 123 - £2 001 - FF20 484
Los Sour Balls Acrylic (48.5x61cm 19x24in) New-
York 1999

SCHUPPEN van Jacob von Souppen 1670-1751 **[5]**
- $28 800 - €37 320 - £21 600 - FF244 800
Scena di interno Olio/tela (98x128cm 38x50in)
Torino 2000
- $27 234 - €27 441 - £16 974 - FF180 000
**Réunion de gentilhommes autour d'une table
dans un intérieur** Huile/toile (74x93cm 29x36in)
Paris 2000

S

SCHÜRCH Johann Robert 1895-1941 **[218]**

$8 809 - €9 927 - **£6 100** - FF65 116
Zarathustra Öl/Leinwand (61x50cm 24x19in) Zürich 2000

$790 - €683 - **£477** - FF4 478
Maler und Modell Indian ink/paper (27x20.5cm 10x8in) Luzern 1998

SCHÜRER Hans Christoph XVI-XVII **[1]**

$24 169 - €23 736 - **£15 000** - FF155 698
The Ill-Matched Lovers Oil/canvas (80x65cm 31x25in) London 1999

SCHURMAN Anne-Marie 1607-1678 **[1]**

$2 153 - €2 454 - **£1 502** - FF16 098
Selbstbildnis mit Spitzenkragen und Schriftrolle Kupferstich (16.5x15cm 6x5in) Berlin 2001

SCHÜRMANN Herbert 1908-1982 **[9]**

$730 - €818 - **£507** - FF5 366
Rosen auf Glasscheiben und Gittern Vintage gelatin silver print (18x24.5cm 7x9in) Köln 2001

SCHURR Claude 1921 **[143]**

$922 - €1 098 - **£638** - FF7 200
Sous l'auvent, Le Guilvinec Huile/toile (65x54cm 25x21in) Sceaux 2000

$367 - €427 - **£261** - FF2 800
Rue animée Huile/toile (26x45cm 10x17in) Paris 2001

SCHUSTER Donna 1883-1953 **[32]**

$2 500 - €2 700 - **£1 727** - FF17 709
Yosemite Falls Oil/masonite (60x45cm 24x18in) Altadena CA 2001

$5 000 - €4 272 - **£3 025** - FF28 022
Silver Lake, Los Angeles Oil/board (30.5x40.5cm 12x15in) San-Francisco CA 1998

SCHUSTER Josef 1812-1890 **[25]**

$26 000 - €24 665 - **£15 795** - FF161 795
A Cockatoo, Grapes, Figs, Plums, a Pineapple, and a Peach on a Ledge Oil/canvas (63.5x79cm 25x31in) New-York 1999

$2 489 - €2 197 - **£1 500** - FF14 409
Still Life with Flowers Oil/panel (32x26.5cm 12x10in) London 1998

SCHUSTER Karl Maria 1871-1953 **[51]**

$1 443 - €1 236 - **£844** - FF8 107
Gartenmotiv Öl/Leinwand (54.5x40.3cm 21x15in) Wien 1998

$1 238 - €1 453 - **£878** - FF9 534
Kahlenbergerdörfl und Leopoldsberg Öl/Leinwand (22.5x33cm 8x12in) Wien 2000

SCHUSTER Ludwig 1820-c.1873 **[7]**

$1 917 - €2 180 - **£1 347** - FF14 301
Berchtesgadener Landschaft vor dem Watzmann Öl/Leinwand (58x76.5cm 22x30in) Wien 2001

SCHUSTER-WOLDAN Raffael 1870-1951 **[18]**

$1 494 - €1 431 - **£940** - FF9 390
Bildnis einer Schlafenden Black chalk (51x64cm 20x25in) Stuttgart 1999

SCHUT Cornelis I 1597-1655 **[25]**

$6 048 - €6 693 - **£4 104** - FF43 902
La Vierge à l'enfant Huile/panneau (60x50cm 23x19in) Antwerpen 2000

SCHUTLER John XIX **[1]**

$10 000 - €12 087 - **£6 982** - FF79 286
Home to Thanksgiving Lithograph (50x71cm 20x28in) Bolton MA 2000

SCHÜTT Franz Theodor 1908-1990 **[6]**

$2 198 - €2 531 - **£1 500** - FF16 600
Young Woman in Front of a Window Watercolour, gouache (47x33cm 18x12in) London 2000

SCHUTTE Louis Hermanus Hend. 1904-1979 **[4]**

$10 483 - €11 798 - **£7 222** - FF77 391
Dining in a Restaurant Garden in Salzburg Oil/canvas (102x122cm 40x48in) Maastricht 2000

SCHÜTTE Thomas 1954 **[45]**

$13 021 - €12 673 - **£8 000** - FF83 132
Kartoffelbild II Oil/paper (141x109cm 55x42in) London 1999

$13 021 - €12 673 - **£8 000** - FF83 132
Kartoffelbild Oil/paper (45x109cm 17x42in) London 1999

$50 499 - €48 863 - **£32 000** - FF320 521
Boats Sculpture, wood (160x175x380cm 62x68x149in) London 1999

$3 575 - €3 964 - **£2 475** - FF26 000
Sans titre Encre Chine/papier (130x110cm 51x43in) Paris 2001

$117 - €112 - **£72** - FF737
Sei wachsam! Woodcut in colors (93x65cm 36x25in) Köln 1999

$24 000 - €26 882 - **£16 675** - FF176 332
Dieter Cibachrome print (61x50.5cm 24x19in) New-York 2001

SCHUTZ Anton Joseph F. 1894-1977 **[73]**

$150 - €140 - **£92** - FF919
Cleveland Steel Mills Etching (21x28cm 8x11in) Cleveland OH 1999

SCHÜTZ Franz 1751-1781 **[10]**

$5 264 - €5 814 - **£3 648** - FF38 136
Bewaldete Flusslandschaft mit Hirten Öl/Leinwand (28x37cm 11x14in) Wien 2001

SCHUTZ Hermann XIX-XX **[1]**

$663 - €735 - **£450** - FF4 822
«Konstanz» Poster (98x70cm 38x27in) London 2000

SCHUTZ Jan Frederik 1817-1888 **[21]**

$7 885 - €7 868 - **£4 800** - FF51 612
Becalmed Oil/canvas (69.5x105cm 27x41in) London 2000

$3 595 - €4 084 - **£2 522** - FF26 789
A Sailing Vessel at full Sail Oil/panel (24.5x40cm 9x15in) Amsterdam 2001

$930 - €1 044 - **£644** - FF6 846
Zeegezicht met zeilschepen en op de achter- grond Veere Aquarelle/papier (17x24cm 6x9in) The Hague 2000

SCHÜTZ Johann Georg 1755-1813 **[15]**

$4 779 - €4 090 - **£2 876** - FF26 826
«Flusslandschaft» Öl/Leinwand (41x52cm 16x20in) Stuttgart 1998

$8 145 - €6 860 - **£4 810** - FF45 000
Paysage de la vallée du Rhin avec des haltes de cavaliers Huile/toile (28x35.5cm 11x13in) Paris 1998

$6 280 - €7 158 - **£4 382** - FF46 954
Blick auf den Protestantischen Friedhof an der Cestius-Pyramide Ink (35.5x51cm 13x20in) Berlin 2001

SCHÜTZ Johannes 1886-? **[12]**

$1 557 - €1 363 - **£943** - FF8 942
Am Silsersee Öl/Leinwand (62x82cm 24x32in) Zofingen 1998

SCHÜTZ Karl 1745-1800 **[8]**
🛏 **$26 215** - €25 435 - **£16 170** - FF166 845
Ansichten der Residenzstadt Wien von ihren Vorstädten Radierung (41.4x51cm 16x20in) Wien 1999

SCHÜTZ Willem Joannes 1854-1933 **[15]**
🕊 **$4 650** - €4 991 - **£3 111** - FF32 742
Boats in a Harbour Oil/panel (32.5x51cm 12x20in) Amsterdam 1999
🕊 **$613** - €673 - **£394** - FF4 412
Båtar på varv Oil/canvas/panel (24x29cm 9x11in) Helsinki 1999
✎ **$1 180** - €1 042 - **£711** - FF6 835
Steamer and other Ships at Sea Watercolour/paper (34x53cm 13x20in) Amsterdam 1998

SCHÜTZE Wilhelm 1840-1898 **[30]**
🕊 **$1 536** - €1 345 - **£931** - FF8 823
Stilleben med frukter Oil/panel (48x59cm 18x23in) Helsinki 1998

SCHÜTZENBERGER Louis Frédéric 1825-1903 **[10]**
🕊 **$1 453** - €1 220 - **£852** - FF8 000
La fenaison Huile/toile (65x100cm 25x39in) Saint-Dié 1998

SCHUYLER Remington 1884-1955 **[9]**
🕊 **$2 000** - €2 275 - **£1 397** - FF14 920
Indian on Horseback Oil/canvas (76x50cm 30x20in) Mystic CT 2000

SCHÜZ Christian Georg I 1718-1791 **[132]**
🕊 **$27 878** - €33 234 - **£19 877** - FF218 003
Weite Flusslandschaft Öl/Leinwand (94x151cm 37x59in) Köln 2000
🕊 **$6 614** - €6 247 - **£4 000** - FF40 977
A wooded Landscape with a Hunting Party by a Stream Oil/canvas (40.5x40cm 15x15in) London 1999
🕊 **$8 965** - €9 624 - **£6 000** - FF63 129
Extensive Rhenish landscape, with boats moored by a jetty Oil/panel (28x39.5cm 11x15in) London 2000
🛏 **$511** - €537 - **£322** - FF3 521
Bacharach, Blick von Nordosten auf die Stadt und die Bacharacher Werth Radierung (24.5x32.2cm 9x12in) Heidelberg 2000

SCHÜZ Christian Georg II 1758-1823 **[60]**
🕊 **$18 013** - €21 474 - **£12 843** - FF140 863
Flusslandschaft mit hochgelegener Burg Öl/Leinwand (169x204cm 66x80in) Köln 2000
🕊 **$11 957** - €14 061 - **£8 571** - FF92 232
Ideale Rheinlandschaft Öl/Leinwand (65x81cm 25x31in) München 2001
🕊 **$8 652** - €8 721 - **£5 400** - FF57 204
Rheinlandschaft Oil/panel (25x35cm 9x13in) Wien 2000
✎ **$1 629** - €1 943 - **£1 162** - FF12 744
Rheinlandschaft Aquarell/Papier (40.5x61.5cm 15x24in) Köln 2000

SCHÜZ Theodor Christoph 1830-1900 **[17]**
🕊 **$5 960** - €6 447 - **£4 007** - FF43 600
Mittelgebirgslandschaft mit einem Flüsschen Öl/Leinwand (43.7x80.5cm 17x31in) Köln 2000
🕊 **$814** - €971 - **£581** - FF6 372
Holländische Küstenlandschaft Oil/panel (17x25.8cm 6x10in) Köln 2000

SCHWAB Maximilian XIX-XX **[8]**
🕊 **$419** - €358 - **£253** - FF2 347
«Gossausee mit Dachsteinmassiv» Oil/panel (16x32cm 6x12in) Kempten 1998

SCHWABE Carlos, Charles 1866-1926 **[70]**
🕊 **$13 110** - €14 483 - **£9 091** - FF95 000
Pommiers fleuris Huile/toile (100x73cm 39x28in) Paris 2001
✎ **$3 544** - €3 887 - **£2 407** - FF25 500
Désespoir Crayon/papier (5.5x19.5cm 2x7in) Poitiers 2000
🛏 **$1 179** - €1 306 - **£800** - FF8 569
«Salon rose croix» Poster (185x83cm 72x32in) London 2000

SCHWABE Randolph 1885-1945 **[21]**
🕊 **$6 299** - €5 374 - **£3 800** - FF35 250
Rosie Oil/canvas (40.5x33cm 15x12in) London 1998
✎ **$473** - €458 - **£300** - FF3 004
View of Weymouth Watercolour (28.5x34.5cm 11x13in) London 1999

SCHWAGER Richard 1822-1880 **[16]**
🕊 **$2 001** - €2 250 - **£1 405** - FF14 757
Gräfin Beatrice Broel Plater mit ihrem Sohn Jean Miniature (11.5x9cm 4x3in) Düsseldorf 2001
✎ **$1 645** - €1 817 - **£1 140** - FF11 917
Bildnis einer jungen Dame in schwarzem Kleid und Pelzstola Watercolour (9x7.5cm 3x2in) Wien 2001

SCHWAIGER Hans 1854-1912 **[15]**
🕊 **$10 115** - €9 567 - **£6 300** - FF62 755
Ahasver III Tempera/panel (33x63cm 12x24in) Praha 1999
🕊 **$2 745** - €2 597 - **£1 710** - FF17 033
Fisherman's Wife Tempera (33x14cm 12x5in) Praha 1999

SCHWALBE Ole 1929-1990 **[133]**
🕊 **$4 147** - €4 691 - **£2 803** - FF30 768
Gul komposition Oil/canvas (145x130cm 57x51in) København 2000
🕊 **$1 666** - €1 945 - **£1 175** - FF12 760
Komposition Oil/masonite (45x45cm 17x17in) København 2000
🕊 **$1 776** - €1 682 - **£1 080** - FF11 036
Fire kompositioner Oil/masonite (35x27cm 13x10in) København 1999
✎ **$288** - €322 - **£197** - FF2 111
Komposition Gouache/paper (18x14cm 7x5in) København 2000

SCHWAMBERGER Wolf 1908-1994 **[26]**
🕊 **$236** - €256 - **£161** - FF1 676
Haus im Wald Öl/Leinwand (62x80cm 24x31in) Stuttgart 2001

SCHWANFELDER Charles Henry 1773-1837 **[33]**
🕊 **$62 488** - €61 155 - **£40 000** - FF401 148
Two Greyhounds in a Landscape with their Prey Oil/canvas (144x180cm 56x70in) London 1999
🕊 **$5 038** - €5 649 - **£3 421** - FF37 053
Darstellung eines Araber-Pferds Öl/Leinwand (64x76cm 25x29in) Zürich 2000

SCHWANTHALER Johann Peter 1720-1795 **[2]**
⚱ **$21 826** - €20 640 - **£13 493** - FF135 392
Stehende Erato, die Muse der Liebespoesie und Lyrik Marbre Carrare (H160cm H62in) Zürich 1999
⚱ **$7 909** - €7 619 - **£5 010** - FF50 308
Kruzifix Sculpture (H66cm H25in) München 1999

SCHWANTHALER Ludwig Michael 1802-1848 **[10]**
⚱ **$33 307** - €38 347 - **£22 732** - FF251 542
Figur des sterbenden Achilles Marble (51x69x26.5cm 20x27x10in) München 2000

S

SCHWAR Wilhelm 1860-1943 **[6]**
- $3 250 - €3 750 - £2 288 - FF24 601
  Portrait of a Seated Cavalier playing a Mandolin
  Oil/canvas (30x25cm 12x10in) Norwalk CT 2000

SCHWARTZ Andrew Thomas 1867-1942 **[36]**
- $2 800 - €2 362 - £1 642 - FF15 495
  Vermont Landscape Oil/canvas (77.5x101.5cm 30x39in) New-York 1998

SCHWARTZ Frans 1850-1917 **[61]**
- $1 411 - €1 346 - £859 - FF8 829
  Interiör fra et atelier med en nögen kvinde
  Oil/canvas (55x30cm 21x11in) Viby J, Århus 1999
- $273 - €295 - £183 - FF1 935
  Dommedagsscene Oil/canvas (27x27cm 10x10in)
  Köbenhavn 2000

SCHWARTZ Friedrich Ferdinand 1836-1906 **[1]**
- $5 477 - €6 468 - £3 888 - FF42 425
  Palais Itzig, Berlin, Burgstrasse 26-27 Photograph
  (21x15.5cm 8x6in) Berlin 2001

SCHWARTZ Joe XX **[5]**
- $1 000 - €1 110 - £697 - FF7 281
  «Windowshade repairman» Gelatin silver print
  (37x44.5cm 14x17in) New-York 2001

SCHWARTZ Lester O. XIX-XX **[5]**
- $1 000 - €1 137 - £693 - FF7 460
  Circus Gouache/board (28x63cm 11x25in) Cincinnati
  OH 2000

SCHWARTZ Pavel Fjodorowitsch 1879-1940 **[8]**
- $2 102 - €2 035 - £1 296 - FF13 347
  Insel der Sirenen, Bühnenbildentwurf Indian ink
  (34.5x55cm 13x21in) Wien 1999

SCHWARTZ Stefen 1851-1924 **[10]**
- $1 006 - €872 - £610 - FF5 718
  Frauenakt Bronze (H46.8cm H18in) Wien 1998

SCHWARTZ Walther 1889-1958 **[12]**
- $868 - €1 005 - £615 - FF6 591
  Interior, dagligstuen hos höjesteretsagförer Charles Skau, Fredensborg Oil/canvas (68x88cm 26x34in) Köbenhavn 2000

SCHWARTZ William Samuel 1896-1977 **[91]**
- $10 000 - €9 258 - £6 121 - FF60 728
  Village Corner Oil/canvas (76x91cm 30x36in)
  Chicago IL 1999
- $3 000 - €2 865 - £1 846 - FF18 793
  The City Below Watercolour/paper (43x58cm 17x23in) Cincinnati OH 1999
- $450 - €456 - £282 - FF2 990
  Nude Lithograph (40x38cm 16x15in) Cincinnati OH 2000

SCHWARTZE VAN DUYL Theresa 1852-1918 **[31]**
- $3 805 - €4 084 - £2 546 - FF26 789
  Lac de Lungern, route de Brunic Oil/canvas
  (60x95cm 23x37in) Dordrecht 2000
- $742 - €681 - £457 - FF4 464
  Portrait of a Lady «en profil» Red chalk/paper
  (30x24cm 11x9in) Amsterdam 1999

SCHWARZ Alfred 1867-1951 **[8]**
- $9 600 - €8 589 - £5 753 - FF56 339
  Amorin, der hvisker söde ord til den unge pige
  Oil/canvas (96x68cm 37x26in) Köbenhavn 1998

SCHWARZ August 1896-1969 **[22]**
- $182 - €184 - £113 - FF1 207
  Bei der Kartoffelernte Aquarell/Papier (58x43cm 22x16in) Radolfzell 2000

SCHWARZ Mommie 1876-1942 **[30]**
- $9 301 - €9 983 - £6 223 - FF65 485
  View in Bergen Oil/canvas (83x72cm 32x28in)
  Amsterdam 2000
- $469 - €544 - £332 - FF3 571
  Mountainous Landscape Watercolour (34x47cm 13x18in) Amsterdam 2000
- $340 - €318 - £209 - FF2 083
  «Epositie Gooische Schilders Vereeniging, Hamdorff» Poster (52x76cm 20x29in) Oostwoud 1999

SCHWARZ-WALDEGG Fritz 1889-1942 **[10]**
- $3 498 - €4 116 - £2 469 - FF26 998
  Felsenküste mit Baumstümpfen Öl/Leinwand
  (51x71cm 20x27in) Berlin 2001
- $3 910 - €3 268 - £2 317 - FF21 438
  Kopenhagen, Hafen Aquarell/Papier (45x37.5cm 17x14in) Wien 1998

SCHWARZENFELD von Adolf Ritter 1854-1923 **[15]**
- $2 524 - €2 907 - £1 724 - FF19 068
  Ausfahrt zum Gemüsemarkt Öl/Leinwand
  (69x55.5cm 27x21in) Wien 2000

SCHWARZER Bernd 1954 **[21]**
- $5 220 - €6 135 - £3 619 - FF40 246
  Europäischer Vulkan oder Europäisches Flammenbild Mixed media/board (75x57cm 29x22in)
  Stuttgart 2000
- $1 516 - €1 534 - £925 - FF10 061
  Deutschlandbild Gold-Rot-Schwarz Öl/Karton
  (46x32cm 18x12in) Stuttgart 2000
- $272 - €256 - £168 - FF1 676
  Weimar 1999 Europäische Kulturhauptstadt
  Radierung (58x40.5cm 22x15in) Stuttgart 1999

SCHWARZER Ludwig 1912-1989 **[14]**
- $487 - €511 - £321 - FF3 353
  Strandansicht Öl/Karton (37x55cm 14x21in) Satow
  2000
- $5 120 - €5 814 - £3 592 - FF38 136
  «Circe» Oil/panel (27.5x20cm 10x7in) Wien 2001

SCHWARZER Max 1882-1955 **[3]**
- $1 769 - €1 960 - £1 200 - FF12 854
  «Regina-Bar» Poster (125x84cm 49x33in) London
  2000

SCHWARZKOGLER Rudolf 1940-1969 **[30]**
- $9 776 - €11 628 - £6 976 - FF76 272
  Ohne Titel Watercolour (53.2x30.5cm 20x12in) Wien
  2000
- $278 - €327 - £197 - FF2 145
  Aktion Hochzeit, Wein Februar Gelatin silver print
  (39x29cm 15x11in) Wien 2000

SCHWATSCHKE John 1943 **[16]**
- $1 538 - €1 651 - £1 049 - FF10 827
  Real Emergency Oil/canvas (91.5x61cm 36x24in)
  Dublin 2001

SCHWEGLER Xaver 1832-1902 **[16]**
- $4 075 - €4 728 - £2 813 - FF31 016
  Jagdstilleben Öl/Leinwand (68x54.5cm 26x21in)
  Luzern 2000
- $732 - €851 - £514 - FF5 583
  Landschaft bei Luzern Öl/Leinwand (15x25.5cm 5x10in) Luzern 2001

SCHWEGMAN Hendrik 1761-1816 **[3]**
- $8 912 - €9 983 - £6 193 - FF65 485
  Still Life of Grapes, Flowers and Berries, all Tied with a Ribbon Oil/canvas (43.5x33cm 17x12in)
  Amsterdam 2001

$2 173 - €2 522 - **£1 500** - FF16 540
Primula auricula cultivars (Auriculas) Watercolour
(19.5x28cm 7x11in) London 2000

SCHWEICH Carl 1823-1898 **[7]**
$3 017 - €2 812 - **£1 861** - FF18 446
Bäuerin bei einem Gehöft auf einer Anhöhe
Öl/Leinwand (22x30.5cm 8x12in) Köln 1999
$4 810 - €5 624 - **£3 380** - FF36 892
Lagernder Hirte vor weiter Flusslandschaft
Aquarell/Papier (26.5x35.5cm 10x13in) München 2000

SCHWEICKARDT Hendrik Willem 1746-1797 **[53]**
$15 310 - €17 244 - **£10 552** - FF113 110
**Milkmaid Conversing with a Peasant by a
Farmhouse, with Cattle** Oil/panel (31x62.4cm
12x24in) Amsterdam 2000
$3 360 - €3 908 - **£2 400** - FF25 636
Groom with two saddled Chesnut Hunters
Oil/panel (30x40.5cm 11x15in) London 2001

SCHWEIGER Hanus 1854-1912 **[1]**
$3 323 - €3 143 - **£2 074** - FF20 619
Cour de Valassky Huile/panneau (28x50cm 11x19in)
Praha 2000

SCHWEITZER Adolf Gustav 1847-1914 **[32]**
$1 662 - €1 605 - **£1 050** - FF10 525
Winter Landscape Oil/canvas (66x53cm 25x20in)
Ipswich 1999

SCHWEMMINGER Josef 1804-1895 **[9]**
$3 365 - €3 634 - **£2 325** - FF23 835
Krimhilds Traum (der Falke schlägt die Taube)
Öl/Leinwand (55x70cm 21x27in) Wien 2001
$2 708 - €2 907 - **£1 848** - FF19 068
Burg Aquarell/Papier (22x27.9cm 8x10in) Wien 2001

SCHWENDY Albert 1820-1902 **[22]**
$3 670 - €4 090 - **£2 565** - FF26 831
Altes Hafenstädtchen Öl/Leinwand (52x65cm
20x25in) München 2001
$5 124 - €5 880 - **£3 505** - FF38 569
**Au Grand St. Aubin, Gasthaus am Kirchplatz
mit Marktständen** Öl/Leinwand (39.5x31.5cm
15x12in) Berlin 2000

SCHWENINGER Carl I 1818-1887 **[55]**
$3 496 - €3 270 - **£2 115** - FF21 451
Hirte mit Kühen an der Tränke Öl/Leinwand
(118x91cm 46x35in) Wien 1999
$626 - €727 - **£432** - FF4 767
Teichlandschaft im Mondschein Öl/Karton
(45.5x33.5cm 17x13in) Graz 2000

SCHWENINGER Carl II 1854-1903 **[27]**
$16 000 - €16 586 - **£9 600** - FF108 800
Nudi femminili Olio/tela (85x122cm 33x48in) Milano
2000

SCHWENINGER Rosa 1849-1918 **[11]**
$2 444 - €2 907 - **£1 744** - FF19 068
Die Kunstliebhaber Oil/panel (25.5x33cm 10x12in)
Wien 2000

SCHWERDGEBURTH Carl August 1785-1876 **[8]**
$1 544 - €1 841 - **£1 100** - FF12 074
Szene aus Goethes Hermann und Dorothea Ink
(29.5x25.5cm 11x10in) Berlin 2000

SCHWERIN Ludwig 1897-1983 **[12]**
$600 - €510 - **£362** - FF3 344
Girl with Red Hair Gouache/paper (48x31cm
18x12in) Tel Aviv 1999

SCHWESIG Karl 1898-1955 **[25]**
$5 623 - €5 368 - **£3 513** - FF35 215
Zirkus im Fischerdorf, Südfrankreich
Öl/Leinwand (52.9x66.5cm 20x26in) Köln 1999
$466 - €511 - **£316** - FF3 353
Obstblüte an der Mosel Aquarell/Papier (58x44.5cm
22x17in) Düsseldorf 2000

SCHWETZ Franz 1910-1960 **[4]**
$2 198 - €2 035 - **£1 360** - FF13 347
Heuernte mit aufkommendem Gewitter Öl/Papier
(47x36cm 18x14in) Wien 1999

SCHWETZ Karl 1888-1965 **[31]**
$908 - €872 - **£570** - FF5 720
Blick auf die Gloriette Aquarell/Papier (41.5x33.5cm
16x13in) Wien 1999

SCHWICHE Carlo XIX **[1]**
$5 396 - €5 793 - **£3 610** - FF38 000
La Madone au Chardonneret, d'après Raphael
Huile/toile (109x79cm 42x31in) Nice 2000

SCHWICHTENBERG Martel 1896-1945 **[28]**
$26 377 - €30 368 - **£18 000** - FF199 204
Girl in red Striped Shirt Oil/cardboard (71x50cm
27x19in) London 2000
$264 - €307 - **£185** - FF2 012
Fischmarkt Lithographie (52x35cm 20x13in) Berlin
2001

SCHWIERING O. Conrad 1916-1986 **[5]**
$5 000 - €5 539 - **£3 352** - FF36 336
«Evening Quiet» Oil/board (56x81cm 22x32in)
Dedham MA 2000

SCHWIMMER Eva 1901-1986 **[13]**
$110 - €128 - **£77** - FF838
Figurenkomposition Ink (30.5x21cm 12x8in) Berlin
2001

SCHWIMMER Max 1895-1960 **[150]**
$3 422 - €3 835 - **£2 383** - FF25 154
«Küste Ostpreussen» Öl/Leinwand (49.5x61cm
19x24in) Berlin 2001
$197 - €204 - **£125** - FF1 341
Brustbildnis eines bärtigen Mannes
Charcoal/paper (23x16.9cm 9x6in) Leipzig 2000
$152 - €184 - **£106** - FF1 207
Sitzendes, sich schminkendes Ballettmädchen
Drypoint (15.3x13cm 6x5in) Berlin 2000

SCHWIND von Moritz 1804-1871 **[78]**
$22 515 - €25 565 - **£15 645** - FF167 695
Zwei Amoretten am Bach Oil/panel (50x38cm
19x14in) Köln 2001
$1 177 - €1 227 - **£773** - FF8 049
Die Berufsstände und die schönen Künste
Ink/paper (18x23.5cm 7x9in) München 2000

SCHWINGEN Peter 1813-1863 **[3]**
$1 781 - €1 687 - **£1 083** - FF11 067
**Damenporträt, Halbfigur, leicht nach links
gewendet** Öl/Leinwand (84x67cm 33x26in) München
1999

SCHWITTERS Kurt 1887-1948 **[235]**
$5 856 - €5 624 - **£3 630** - FF36 892
Frühlingswiese bei Hannover Oil/panel
(53.5x65cm 21x25in) Ahlden 1999
$38 000 - €36 495 - **£23 427** - FF239 392
Autumn Mixed media/panel (20.5x16cm 8x6in) New-
York 1999
$32 018 - €38 278 - **£22 000** - FF251 088
Wood on Wood Assemblage (27.5x24.5cm 10x9in)
London 2000

S

$38 000 - €42 563 - **£26 402** - FF279 193
«Yellow-Blue-Red» Gouache (21x17.5cm 8x6in)
New-York 2001

$3 504 - €3 067 - **£2 122** - FF20 118
Komposition Woodcut (13x10cm 5x3in) Berlin 1998

SCHWIZGEBEL Christian XX [2]

$384 - €418 - **£253** - FF2 743
Hirsche, Rehe und Gemsen im Wald Silhouette
(14.5x22cm 5x8in) Bern 2000

SCHWORMSTEDT Felix 1870-1938 [5]

$675 - €767 - **£462** - FF5 030
«Hapag- Vergnügungsreisen» Poster (107x68cm
42x26in) Hannover 2000

SCHYL Jules 1893-1977 [218]

$1 508 - €1 399 - **£938** - FF9 176
Mallorca, katedral Mixed media (55x67cm 21x26in)
Malmö 1999

$965 - €895 - **£600** - FF5 872
Kvinna i hatt Oil/canvas (41x27cm 16x10in) Malmö
1999

$409 - €394 - **£252** - FF2 582
Fuengirola Gouache/paper (33x46cm 12x18in) Malmö
1999

SCIALOJA Toti 1914-1998 [101]

$3 500 - €3 628 - **£2 100** - FF23 800
«Raggiro» Idropittura/tela (130x112cm 51x44in) Prato
1999

$2 000 - €2 592 - **£1 500** - FF17 000
Natura morta Olio/tavola (40x50cm 15x19in) Milano
2000

$1 680 - €1 451 - **£840** - FF9 520
Senza titolo Collage (50.5x70.5cm 19x27in) Milano
1999

SCILTIAN Gregorio 1900-1985 [88]

$12 900 - €11 144 - **£8 600** - FF73 100
Il guanto perduto Olio/tela (185x116cm 72x45in)
Trieste 1998

$13 000 - €12 628 - **£8 126** - FF82 834
La Musica Oil/canvas (70.5x80cm 27x31in) New-York
1999

$6 400 - €8 293 - **£4 800** - FF54 400
Natura morta con il quattro di spade Olio/tela
(32x25cm 12x9in) Roma 2000

$1 500 - €1 555 - **£900** - FF10 200
Bozzetto per Anna Karenina Matite colorate
(41.5x55.5cm 16x21in) Milano 1999

SCIPIONE Gino Bonichi 1904-1933 [22]

$102 000 - €88 116 - **£68 000** - FF578 000
Natura morta Olio/tavola (39x61cm 15x24in) Prato
1998

$3 000 - €3 887 - **£2 250** - FF25 500
Osteria dei cacciatori China/carta (22x32cm 8x12in)
Milano 2000

SCIUTI Giuseppe 1834-1911 [15]

$90 000 - €77 648 - **£54 297** - FF509 337
**The Exit of Ruggero I, King of Sicily, from the
Palazzo Reale** Oil/canvas (228.5x280cm 89x110in)
New-York 1998

$7 140 - €7 402 - **£4 284** - FF48 552
Figure mitologiche Olio/tela (62x45cm 24x17in)
Venezia 2000

SCKELL Ludwig 1869-1950 [21]

$2 018 - €2 035 - **£1 260** - FF13 347
Weiher im Mondlicht Öl/Leinwand (78x65cm
30x25in) Wien 2000

SCKELL von Ludwig, Louis 1833-1912 [90]

$3 728 - €4 090 - **£2 532** - FF26 831
Flusslandschaft mit Kühen bei Bad Tölz
Öl/Leinwand (65x85cm 25x33in) Hildrizhausen 2000

$2 356 - €2 454 - **£1 493** - FF16 098
Wildbach im Gebirgstal Oil/panel (27x20.7cm
10x8in) München 2000

SCOGNAMIGLIO Antonio, cavaliero XIX [11]

$4 362 - €4 573 - **£2 733** - FF30 000
Déplacement d'une famille dans le désert
Huile/toile (26x50cm 10x19in) Paris 2000

SCOGNAMILIO [17]

$1 850 - €1 769 - **£1 164** - FF11 602
The Rock Bridge offshore on the Isle of Capri
Oil/masonite (61x71cm 24x28in) Milwaukee WI 1999

$400 - €382 - **£251** - FF2 508
Two Monks Reading Oil/canvas/board (25x36cm
10x14in) Milwaukee WI 1999

SCOLARI Giuseppe XVI [7]

$1 443 - €1 716 - **£1 000** - FF11 253
St.Jerome Woodcut (52.5x37cm 20x14in) London
2000

SCOMPARINI Eugenio 1845-1913 [6]

$1 750 - €1 814 - **£1 050** - FF11 900
Oziando Acquarello/carta (36x80cm 14x31in) Trieste
2001

SCOPPA Giuseppe Gustavo 1856-? [25]

$5 680 - €5 412 - **£3 599** - FF35 500
Naples, Villa Reale Gouache/papier (30x44cm
11x17in) Roquevaire 1999

SCOPPA Raimondo 1820-1890 [19]

$5 200 - €6 738 - **£3 900** - FF44 200
Lungo la costa Olio/tela (50x76cm 19x29in) Milano
2000

$7 228 - €7 927 - **£4 908** - FF52 000
Vue de Santa Lucia a Mari Gouache/papier
(62.5x41cm 24x16in) Lille 2000

SCOPPETTA Pietro 1863-1920 [107]

$18 400 - €23 843 - **£13 800** - FF156 400
Il Golfo di Napoli da Posillipo Olio/tela (41x73cm
16x28in) Roma 2000

$4 000 - €5 183 - **£3 000** - FF34 000
Passeggiata Olio/tela/cartone (15x20cm 5x7in)
Vercelli 2000

$1 150 - €1 192 - **£690** - FF7 820
A teatro China (11x17cm 4x6in) Roma 1999

SCORDIA Antonio 1918 [36]

$3 250 - €3 369 - **£1 950** - FF22 100
Viligelmo Olio/tela (100x81cm 39x31in) Roma 2001

SCOREL van Jan 1495-1562 [4]

$67 243 - €72 180 - **£45 000** - FF473 472
The Death of St.Hilary Ink (23.5x20cm 9x7in)
London 2000

SCORIEL Jean-Baptiste 1883-1956 [42]

$974 - €1 041 - **£651** - FF6 829
Paysage Huile/toile (46x56cm 18x22in) Bruxelles
2000

SCORRANO Luigi 1849-1924 [1]

$18 000 - €19 694 - **£12 436** - FF129 182
Christening Oil/canvas (71x76cm 28x30in) Detroit MI
2001

SCORZA Sinibaldo 1589-1631 [11]

$4 760 - €4 934 - **£2 856** - FF32 368
L'arca di Noè Olio/tela (55x68cm 21x26in) Venezia
2000

✒ **$8 188** – €7 607 - **£5 000** – FF49 900
Landscape with Ruins, and a Young Boy and Cattle by a Fountain Ink (18.5x29cm 7x11in) London 1998

SCORZELLI Eugenio 1890-1958 [58]
🖎 **$3 600** – €3 110 - **£2 400** – FF20 400
Sul divano Olio/tela (47x66cm 18x25in) Roma 1998
🖎 **$1 920** – €1 659 - **£1 280** – FF10 880
Strada di Cava Olio/tavola (27x33cm 10x12in) Milano 1998

SCOTIN Gerard II 1671-1716 [3]
🖾 **$1 312** – €1 524 - **£935** – FF10 000
Tchinguis ou danseuse turque Nº54/Tchingui ou danseur turc Nº55 Gravure (49x33cm 19x12in) Paris 2001

SCOTIN Louis Gérard 1690-c.1760 [2]
🖾 **$920** – €1 075 - **£650** – FF7 050
Les plaisirs du ball, after Jean Antoine Watteau Engraving (50x65cm 19x25in) London 2000

SCOTT Adam Sherriff 1887-1980 [90]
🖎 **$716** – €612 - **£433** – FF4 013
«Mt Elephants, Lake Memphremagog» Huile/toile (40.5x51cm 15x20in) Montréal 1998

SCOTT Alexander c.1872-c.1932 [10]
🖎 **$4 134** – €3 867 - **£2 500** – FF25 369
The Western Gate of the Purana Qila, Delhi Oil/board (32.5x45cm 12x17in) London 1999

SCOTT Caroline Lucy 1784-1857 [5]
✒ **$1 564** – €1 762 - **£1 100** – FF11 557
Genoa from Villa Durazzo/Sepolero di Cecilia Metella Watercolour (24x33cm 9x12in) Cambridge 2001

SCOTT Charles Hepburn 1886-1964 [16]
🖎 **$362** – €350 - **£220** – FF2 299
Early Morning in a Norwegian Harbour Oil/canvas (30.5x45.5cm 12x15in) London 2000

SCOTT Clyde 1884-1959 [4]
🖎 **$5 000** – €5 367 - **£3 346** – FF35 205
Sparkling Sea Oil/canvas (61x76cm 24x29in) San-Francisco CA 2000
🖎 **$2 250** – €2 416 - **£1 506** – FF15 845
Atascadero, California Oil/canvas (24x40.5cm 9x15in) San-Francisco CA 2000

SCOTT David 1806-1849 [6]
🖎 **$5 482** – €6 113 - **£3 700** – FF40 099
Robert Burns Oil/canvas (41x29.5cm 16x11in) Edinburgh 2000

SCOTT DE PLAGNOLLES Georges Bertin, dit 1873-1942 [98]
✒ **$268** – €305 - **£189** – FF2 000
Militaires Aquarelle/papier (25x19cm 9x7in) Paris 2001
🖾 **$418** – €357 - **£250** – FF2 340
«La Belle Jardinière, calendrier des sports» Poster (23.5x28cm 9x11in) London 1998

SCOTT Harold Winfield 1899-1977 [3]
🖎 **$4 750** – €4 397 - **£2 907** – FF28 845
Cowboy in black on rearing horse in desert, ill. for Wild West Weekly Oil/canvas (60x53cm 24x21in) New-York 1999

SCOTT Henry Edward 1900/11 [79]
🖎 **$4 306** – €4 475 - **£2 700** – FF29 353
The Night Crossing Oil/canvas (61x91.5cm 24x36in) Suffolk 2000

SCOTT Howard 1902-1983 [7]
✒ **$2 000** – €1 915 - **£1 235** – FF12 563
Umpire and Ballplayer in Argument: Comprehensive Sketch for Billboard Watercolour/paper (40x91cm 16x36in) New-York 1999

SCOTT James 1809-? [1]
🖾 **$3 806** – €3 997 - **£2 400** – FF26 219
The Arctic Planning a Search for Sir John Franklin, London Print (56x73.5cm 22x28in) London 2000

SCOTT James Fraser 1878-1932 [7]
🖎 **$2 360** – €2 457 - **£1 482** – FF16 116
Spring Rite Oil/canvas (60x49cm 23x19in) Melbourne 2000

SCOTT Johan 1953 [16]
🖎 **$1 156** – €978 - **£691** – FF6 415
Utan titel Mixed media (61x59cm 24x23in) Stockholm 1998

SCOTT John 1802-1885 [16]
🖎 **$10 415** – €9 903 - **£6 500** – FF64 957
Selling the Catch/Local Fishermen and a Dutch Fishing Sloop Oil/canvas (53.5x76cm 21x29in) London 1999

SCOTT John 1850-1919 [10]
🖎 **$10 063** – €9 677 - **£6 200** – FF63 478
Distant thoughts Oil/canvas (82x47cm 32x18in) London 1999

SCOTT John W. 1907-1987 [19]
🖎 **$2 800** – €3 192 - **£1 953** – FF20 935
Man Fly fishing Oil/board (53x91cm 21x36in) Dallas TX 2001
✒ **$1 300** – €1 482 - **£907** – FF9 720
Pheasant hunt Pencil/paper (26x34cm 10x13in) Dallas TX 2001

SCOTT John White Allen 1815-1907 [13]
🖎 **$1 500** – €1 282 - **£881** – FF8 408
White Mountain Landscape Oil/canvas/board (17x30cm 7x12in) Portsmouth NH 1998

SCOTT Julian 1846-1901 [13]
🖎 **$15 000** – €16 019 - **£10 221** – FF105 079
The Fire Chief of Plainfied with Presentation Speaker Oil/canvas (68x55cm 27x22in) New-York 2001

SCOTT Louise 1936 [20]
✒ **$325** – €378 - **£225** – FF2 480
Untitled - Figure with Striped Cloth Pastel/paper (61x46cm 24x18in) Calgary, Alberta 2000

SCOTT Nigel 1956 [7]
📷 **$800** – €911 - **£552** – FF5 978
«Hibiscus, Hawaii» Photograph (29x19cm 11x7in) New-York 2000

SCOTT Patrick 1921 [18]
🖎 **$15 300** – €17 776 - **£10 753** – FF116 606
«Gold Painting» Tempera (122x122cm 48x48in) Dublin 2001
🖎 **$2 722** – €2 920 - **£1 856** – FF19 156
Gorse Hill Tempera (59.5x59.5cm 23x23in) Dublin 2001
🖾 **$774** – €661 - **£461** – FF4 333
Fount Silkscreen (58.5x58.5cm 23x23in) Dublin 1998

SCOTT Peter Markham, Sir 1909-1989 [153]
🖎 **$5 048** – €4 215 - **£3 000** – FF27 649
In the Winter's Dusk Oil/canvas (51x76cm 20x29in) London 1998

S

$1 200 - €1 097 - £732 - FF7 198
Gouldian finches Oil/canvas (35x25cm 14x10in)
New-York 1998

$1 009 - €843 - **£600** - FF5 530
Head Study, Canada Goose Charcoal/paper
(98x136cm 38x53in) London 1998

$128 - €146 - **£90** - FF956
Ducks in flight at Dusk over a River Landscape
Print in colors (39x56cm 15x22in) London 2001

SCOTT Robert Bagge act.1886-1896 [18]
$1 012 - €1 094 - **£700** - FF7 174
Loading Hay Papendrecht Oil/canvas (25.5x36cm
10x14in) London 2001

SCOTT Robert Falcon, Lt 1868-1912 [2]
$15 000 - €16 497 - **£10 402** - FF108 210
Antarctic Silver print (8x10cm 3x4in) New-York 2001

SCOTT Samuel c.1702-1772 [20]
$55 065 - €60 804 - **£38 000** - FF398 851
Covent Garden: the Hustings Oil/canvas
(101x154.5cm 39x60in) Crewkerne, Somerset 2001

$29 550 - €28 051 - **£18 436** - FF184 000
Le port de Portsmouth Huile/toile (71x152cm
27x59in) Deauville 1999

SCOTT Septimus Edwin 1879-1962 [23]
$1 994 - €2 319 - **£1 400** - FF15 210
The No.22 to Putney Common Watercolour
(42x39cm 16x15in) Billingshurst, West-Sussex 2001

$900 - €981 - **£623** - FF6 433
«Le mandarin» Poster (196x128cm 77x50in) New-
York 2001

SCOTT Thomas, Tom 1854-1927 [108]
$3 287 - €3 529 - **£2 200** - FF23 147
Road Scene from Leslie Cottage
Watercolour/paper (19x26cm 7x10in) St. Boswells 2000

SCOTT William 1913-1989 [217]
$58 917 - €70 232 - **£42 000** - FF460 689
Opposite and Equal Oil/canvas (172.5x169cm
67x66in) London 2000

$61 634 - €52 660 - **£37 000** - FF345 424
Ochre Still Life Oil/canvas (91x104cm 35x40in)
London 1998

$36 472 - €43 477 - **£26 000** - FF285 188
Breton Portrait Oil/canvas (35x28cm 13x11in)
London 2000

$11 241 - €10 379 - **£7 000** - FF68 079
Still Life Gouache/paper (27.5x37.5cm 10x14in)
London 1999

$1 769 - €1 640 - **£1 100** - FF10 755
Odeon suite No4 Color lithograph (49x62cm
19x24in) London 1999

SCOTT William Bell 1811-1890 [58]
$2 984 - €2 584 - **£1 800** - FF16 949
**Pink and White Roses in an 18th Century Silver
Dish-Cross** Oil/canvas (45.5x61cm 17x24in) London
1998

$1 213 - €1 139 - **£749** - FF7 469
Mythical Figures Watercolour/paper (19.5x14.5cm
7x5in) London 1999

SCOTT William Ed. 1884-1964 [19]
$19 000 - €21 609 - **£13 176** - FF141 743
Mural Oil/canvas (137x302cm 54x119in) Chicago IL
2000

$8 500 - €8 057 - **£5 310** - FF52 853
Etaples, France Oil/canvas (81x66cm 32x26in)
Cincinnati OH 1999

$16 000 - €17 284 - **£11 078** - FF113 377
Haitian Market Oil/board (40x30cm 16x12in)
Cincinnati OH 2001

SCOUGALL John c.1645-1737 [7]
$2 611 - €2 479 - **£1 600** - FF16 261
**Portrait of a Gentleman, Half-Length, in Armour
with a white Jabot** Oil/canvas (73.5x58.5cm 28x23in)
London 1999

SCOULLER Glen XX [3]
$913 - €806 - **£550** - FF5 287
The Yellow Wall, la Gaude Watercolour/paper
(51x68cm 20x26in) Billingshurst, West-Sussex 1998

SCOWEN Cooly / Charles P. XIX [5]
$1 134 - €1 296 - **£800** - FF8 498
**Ceylon, including Julia Margaret Cameron's
estate at Dimbula** Albumen print (23x28cm 9x11in)
London 2001

SCRIBE Ferdinand 1851-1913 [4]
$14 432 - €16 769 - **£10 285** - FF110 000
L'entrée du Bit el-MAI, à Tanger Huile/toile
(65x85cm 25x33in) Paris 2001

SCRIVENER Henry Ambrose XIX-XX [13]
$1 065 - €1 143 - **£726** - FF7 496
Manoeuvres Berehaven Harbour
Watercolour/paper (19.5x68.5cm 7x26in) Dublin 2001

SCRIVER Robert Macfie, Bob 1914 [30]
$2 200 - €1 856 - **£1 290** - FF12 174
Buffalo Bill Bronze (H64.5cm H25in) New-York 1998

SCRIVO 1942 [12]
$1 554 - €1 735 - **£1 078** - FF11 382
«Life's different Roads #170691» Huile/toile
(40x40cm 15x15in) Antwerpen 2001

$1 980 - €1 859 - **£1 222** - FF12 195
L'escapade Huile/toile (30x24cm 11x9in) Antwerpen
1999

SCROPPO Filippo 1910-1993 [27]
$12 000 - €15 550 - **£9 000** - FF102 000
Costruzione verticale Olio/tela (150x100cm
59x39in) Torino 2004

$1 500 - €1 555 - **£900** - FF10 200
Elementi luce n.7 Olio/tela (100x80cm 39x31in)
Torino 2000

SCUDDER James long 1836-1881 [2]
$18 000 - €18 678 - **£11 419** - FF122 520
Setter in a Landscape Oil/canvas (86.5x111.5cm
34x43in) Boston MA 2000

SCUDDER Janet 1869-1940 [18]
$21 000 - €24 399 - **£14 758** - FF160 045
Figural Fountain Bronze (H103cm H40in) New-York
2001

$1 100 - €1 293 - **£762** - FF8 480
Figure of Cupid standing on a Tortoise Bronze
(H41cm H16in) Cincinnati OH 2000

SCUFFI Marcello 1948 [58]
$1 200 - €1 555 - **£900** - FF10 200
Bagnante della sera Olio/tela (60x100cm 23x39in)
Vercelli 2001

$900 - €933 - **£540** - FF6 120
Il filo rosso della memoria Olio/tela (30x25cm
11x9in) Vercelli 2000

SCULLY Sean 1945 [144]
$70 000 - €76 800 - **£46 501** - FF503 776
Close Oil/canvas (244x174.5x24cm 96x68x9in) New-
York 2000

$20 000 - €22 401 - **£13 896** - FF146 944
«Canaim» Acrylic (122x91.5cm 48x36in) New-York
2001

$12 258 - €13 546 - **£8 500** - FF88 854
Untitled Charcoal (56x76cm 22x29in) London 2001

$833 - €971 - **£584** - FF6 372
Ohne Titel Farbradierung (15.2x11.2cm 5x4in) Köln 2000

SCULTORI Diana c.1535-c.1587 **[12]**
$537 - €460 - **£322** - FF3 018
Christus und die Ehebrecherin Copper engraving (41.8x62.4cm 16x24in) Berlin 1998

SCULTORI Giovanni Mantovano 1503-1575 **[2]**
$1 176 - €1 022 - **£708** - FF6 704
Der Fluss Po Kupferstich (11.1x13.5cm 4x5in) Berlin 1998

SDRUSCIA Achille 1910-1994 **[25]**
$510 - €441 - **£255** - FF2 890
Deposizione Olio/cartone (8x5.5cm 3x2in) Prato 1999

SEABROOKE Elliott 1886-1950 **[51]**
$579 - €504 - **£349** - FF3 307
A Flagpole in a Garden with a River beyond Oil/paper (24x29cm 9x11in) London 1998

SEABY Allen William 1867-1953 **[52]**
$451 - €410 - **£280** - FF2 691
Dippers Watercolour (25x34.5cm 9x13in) Billingshurst, West-Sussex 1999
$160 - €184 - **£110** - FF1 207
Grouse Calling Woodcut in colors (37x24cm 14x9in) Cleveland OH 2000

SEAGE Lucas 1957 **[1]**
$1 510 - €1 416 - **£933** - FF9 287
House of Fish Mixed media/paper (140x100cm 55x39in) Johannesburg 1999

SEAGO Edward Brian 1910-1974 **[733]**
$30 000 - €27 807 - **£18 654** - FF182 403
Julian Mond, 3rd Lord Melchett and Hon. Derek Mond, Colworth Beagles Oil/canvas (102x153cm 40x60in) New-York 1999
$19 363 - €18 595 - **£12 000** - FF121 976
The Green Tilt Oil/board (51x76cm 20x29in) Billingshurst, West-Sussex 1999
$8 682 - €8 419 - **£5 500** - FF243 363
After Rain, Norfolk Oil/board (25.5x35.5cm 10x13in) London 1999
$5 268 - €4 951 - **£3 200** - FF32 478
The Gate into the City, Morocco Watercolour (33.5x51.5cm 13x20in) London 1999
$198 - €226 - **£140** - FF1 481
North Norfolk, ploughing Print (48x58cm 19x23in) Aylsham, Norfolk 2001

SEAL Jogesh Chander 1895-1926 **[2]**
$32 000 - €37 100 - **£22 668** - FF243 363
Lady with a Peacock Oil/canvas (122.5x66cm 48x25in) New-York 2000

SEALY Allen Culpepper 1850-1927 **[29]**
$1 183 - €1 336 - **£832** - FF8 762
Scottish Landscape Oil/canvas (102.5x128cm 40x50in) Malvern, Victoria 2001
$2 179 - €2 592 - **£1 553** - FF17 000
Pur-sang au box Huile/toile (38x46cm 14x18in) Paris 2000

SEALY Colin 1891-1964 **[29]**
$488 - €570 - **£340** - FF3 738
Still Life of a Fruit Bowl an Jug Watercolour (17x21cm 6x8in) London 2000

SEALY Douglas, Doug 1937 **[12]**
$264 - €283 - **£174** - FF1 854
Port Macquarie Landscape Oil/masonite (44x59.5cm 17x23in) Sydney 2000

SEARLE Ronald W. Fordham 1920 **[309]**
$5 230 - €5 615 - **£3 500** - FF36 830
Bacchus & Co Mixed media (49.5x46.5cm 19x18in) London 2000
$1 793 - €1 925 - **£1 200** - FF12 625
A nice bright set Ink (30.5x23cm 12x9in) London 2000
$484 - €467 - **£300** - FF3 065
«The Pure Hell of St Trinian's» Poster (101.5x68.5cm 39x26in) London 1999

SEARS Sarah Choate 1858-1935 **[8]**
$950 - €1 042 - **£645** - FF6 835
Boy fishing Watercolour/paper (38x34cm 15x13in) Thomaston ME 2000

SEARS Taber 1870-1950 **[5]**
$600 - €661 - **£399** - FF4 336
The Coal Dock Watercolour, gouache/paper (18x23cm 7x9in) Thomaston ME 2000

SEAVEY George W. 1841-1916 **[9]**
$600 - €700 - **£421** - FF4 590
Lilypads Oil/canvas/board (18x25.5cm 7x10in) Boston MA 2000

SEBA Albertus ?-1736 **[8]**
$313 - €300 - **£191** - FF1 967
Varieties of Snakes and Spiders Engraving (44x27cm 17x11in) New-Orleans LA 1999

SÉBAH & JOAILLIER XIX **[2]**
$1 192 - €1 372 - **£821** - FF9 000
Souvenir de Constantinople Tirage albuminé (20x26cm 7x10in) Paris 2000

SEBAH J. Pascal act.1856-1900 **[37]**
$728 - €762 - **£457** - FF5 000
Costumes d'Orient Photo (26x36cm 10x14in) Paris 2000

SEBASTI Giuseppe XIX-XX **[1]**
$5 838 - €5 336 - **£3 573** - FF35 000
Primizia (Primeurs) Huile/panneau (96.5x64.5cm 37x25in) Paris 1999

SEBASTIAN Enrique Carbajal 1947 **[8]**
$450 - €499 - **£299** - FF3 275
Estructura amarilla Serigrafia (52x72cm 20x28in) México 2000

SEBBA Siegfried Shalom 1897-1975 **[31]**
$8 000 - €9 004 - **£5 511** - FF59 061
Archeology, Fragments Mixed media (20x19cm 7x7in) Herzelia-Pituah 2000
$850 - €957 - **£585** - FF6 278
Nude Pencil/paper (32x23cm 12x9in) Herzelia-Pituah 2000
$1 000 - €821 - **£580** - FF5 387
Sailor on Hamburg Wharf Etching (20x24cm 7x9in) Tel Aviv 1998

SEBEN van Henri 1825-1913 **[77]**
$4 590 - €4 462 - **£2 808** - FF29 268
Le baiser Huile/toile (66x55.5cm 25x21in) Bruxelles 1999
$1 260 - €1 140 - **£772** - FF7 479
Les ramasseuses de fagots en hiver Huile/panneau (42x32cm 16x12in) Bruxelles 1999
$456 - €395 - **£280** - FF2 593
Children fishing by a Stream Watercolour (46x35.5cm 18x13in) Billingshurst, West-Sussex 1999

SEBES Laurent 1959 **[1]**
$1 924 - €1 904 - **£1 200** - FF12 488
King William Street, City of London Watercolour (58.5x46cm 23x18in) London 1999

S

SEBES Pieter Willem 1830-1906 **[18]**
- $4 200 - €4 052 - £2 638 - FF26 582
  Daughters modeling Mother's Jewelry Oil/canvas (81x64cm 32x25in) Chicago IL 1999

SEBIDI Mmakgabo M.H. 1943 **[4]**
- $1 136 - €1 267 - £741 - FF8 312
  Sitting on Top of the Hill Near Piertersburg, TVL «The Hunter» Oil/canvas/board (49.5x31.5cm 19x12in) Johannesburg 2000
- $2 476 - €2 774 - £1 720 - FF18 194
  «You are saying it for yourself for your Future» Pastel/paper (167x121.5cm 65x47in) Johannesburg 2001

SÉBILLE Albert 1874-1953 **[113]**
- $1 793 - €1 677 - £1 098 - FF11 000
  «Les côtes de la Méditerranée occidentale» Technique mixte/toile (107x105.5cm 42x41in) Paris 1998
- $627 - €732 - £434 - FF4 800
  Voilier rentrant au port Aquarelle/papier (66x49cm 25x19in) Calais 2000
- $852 - €719 - £500 - FF4 717
  «Cie Gle Transatlantique, Paquebot Paris Havre, New York» Poster (107x75cm 42x29in) London 1998

SÉBILLE Nicole 1949 **[30]**
- $983 - €915 - £609 - FF6 000
  Douce promenade Huile/toile (50x61cm 19x24in) Perros-Guirec 1999

SEBIRE Gaston 1920 **[299]**
- $3 000 - €3 185 - £2 030 - FF20 889
  Le bouquet de roses rouge Oil/canvas (146x97cm 57x38in) Delray-Beach FL 2001
- $1 100 - €1 262 - £752 - FF8 279
  Seascape «Vue de Trouville» Oil/canvas (63x88cm 25x35in) Morris-Plains NJ 2000
- $850 - €717 - £498 - FF4 703
  Les barques, Arcachon Oil/canvas (17x45cm 7x18in) Mystic CT 1998

SEBREE Charles 1914-1985 **[4]**
- $2 800 - €2 536 - £1 746 - FF16 637
  Boy with a Book Gouache/paper (15x12cm 6x5in) New-York 1999

SEBREGHTS Lode 1906 **[26]**
- $298 - €347 - £210 - FF2 276
  Nature morte aux fleurs Huile/toile (57x70cm 22x27in) Antwerpen 2001

SEBRIGHT Richard 1870-1959 **[1]**
- $4 106 - €4 405 - £2 800 - FF28 895
  Still Life of Fruit Watercolour/paper (24x34.5cm 9x13in) London 2001

SEBRON Hippolyte 1801-1879 **[13]**
- $4 762 - €4 000 - £2 800 - FF26 241
  Figures on a Track Before a Hilltop Castle Oil/canvas (38x56cm 14x22in) London 1998
- $1 541 - €1 524 - £961 - FF10 000
  Vue de Rotterdam Crayon (27x40.5cm 10x15in) Paris 1999

SÉCHAUD Paul 1906-1982 **[39]**
- $1 285 - €1 239 - £792 - FF8 125
  Stehender weiblicher Rückenakt Öl/Leinwand (101x65cm 39x25in) Bern 1999

SECKY Franz 1895-1950 **[3]**
- $1 308 - €1 453 - £876 - FF9 534
  Waldarbeiter Öl/Leinwand (91x91cm 35x35in) Wien 2000

SECOLA A. XIX-XX **[4]**
- $2 400 - €2 607 - £1 571 - FF17 563
  A Typical Afternoon Oil/canvas (49x81cm 19x32in) Chicago IL 2000

SEDDON Helen act.1925-1955 **[55]**
- $70 - €85 - £48 - FF555
  Waterlilies in a Pond Watercolour/paper (28.5x37cm 11x14in) Penzance, Cornwall 2000

SEDELMAYER Martin 1766-1799 **[7]**
- $13 887 - €16 516 - £9 897 - FF108 337
  Rubekia Amplexifolia/Elimus Histrix/Ledum Palustre Aquarell/Papier (37.8x24.2cm 14x9in) Zürich 2000

SEDGLEY Peter 1930 **[12]**
- $3 607 - €4 047 - £2 500 - FF26 544
  Blue and green Modulation Mixed media (100x100cm 39x39in) London 2000

SEDLACEK Franz 1891-1944 **[24]**
- $23 000 - €25 472 - £15 598 - FF167 083
  Wadlandschaft Mit Jäger Oil/panel (79x73.5cm 31x28in) New-York 2000

SEDLACEK Stephan 1868-1936 **[58]**
- $2 067 - €2 045 - £1 289 - FF13 415
  Silvestergesellschaft im Palais Öl/Leinwand (70.5x140.5cm 27x55in) Ahlden 1999

SEDLACEK Vojtech 1892-1973 **[32]**
- $404 - €383 - £252 - FF2 510
  Laboureur Aquarelle/papier (30x43cm 11x16in) Praha 2001

SEDLAK Günter Silva 1941 **[54]**
- $223 - €218 - £141 - FF1 430
  Schlafender Kentaure Mischtechnik/Papier (42x56cm 16x22in) Salzburg 1999

SEDLECKA Irena 1928 **[1]**
- $4 564 - €5 087 - £3 300 - FF33 371
  Sir John Gielgud as Hamlet/Richard II Sculpture (H33cm H12in) London 2001

SEDLMAYR Joseph Anton 1797-? **[3]**
- $4 244 - €4 857 - £2 919 - FF31 862
  Der Wesslinger See Oil/panel (39.5x46cm 15x18in) München 2000

SEDLON Richard 1900-1992 **[5]**
- $175 - €204 - £125 - FF1 338
  Tree of Life Oil/masonite (60x91cm 24x36in) Cleveland OH 2001

SEEBACH von Lothar 1853-1930 **[37]**
- $1 216 - €1 448 - £842 - FF9 500
  Forêt en automne Huile/toile (54x45cm 21x17in) Strasbourg 2000
- $562 - €671 - £401 - FF4 400
  Parade de la garde allemande à Strasbourg Crayon (24x30cm 9x11in) Strasbourg 2000

SEEBOECK Ferdinand 1864-1953 **[4]**
- $1 956 - €2 301 - £1 402 - FF15 092
  Faun und Nymphe Bronze (H41cm H16in) Stuttgart 2001

SEEBOLD Marie Madeleine 1866-1948 **[3]**
- $32 000 - €27 415 - £19 238 - FF179 830
  Still life of chrysanthemums Oil/canvas (76x91cm 30x36in) New-Orleans LA 1998

SEEFISCH Hermann Ludwig 1816-1879 **[9]**
- $3 256 - €3 170 - £2 000 - FF20 794
  Schweizer Gebirgsort mit Blick auf das Mont Blanc-Massiv Öl/Leinwand (60x73cm 23x28in) Berlin 1999

S

SEEGER Herman 1857-1920 **[31]**
- $8 047 - €6 801 - **£4 800** - FF44 609
  Girl seated in the Sand Dunes Oil/canvas (79x101cm 31x40in) Penzance, Cornwall 1998

SEEGER Karl Ludwig 1808-1866 **[6]**
- $7 131 - €5 879 - **£4 199** - FF38 565
  Sommertag auf dem Land, Mittig malerische Ruine Öl/Leinwand (63x55cm 24x21in) Lindau 1998

SEEHAUS Paul Adolf 1891-1919 **[16]**
- $35 072 - €40 904 - **£24 624** - FF268 312
  Die roten Türme Öl/Leinwand (78x90.4cm 30x35in) Köln 2000

SEEKATZ Johann/Joseph Konrad 1719-1768 **[61]**
- $14 000 - €14 513 - **£8 400** - FF95 200
  Scena notturna con donna e fanciullo/Scena notturna con suonatore Olio/tela (50x38cm 19x14in) Roma 2000
- $7 487 - €7 326 - **£4 800** - FF48 058
  Game Seller/Vegetable Seller Oil/panel (21.5x24.5cm 8x9in) London 1999

SEEL Adolf 1829-1907 **[23]**
- $14 499 - €12 179 - **£8 500** - FF79 887
  In the Courtyard Oil/canvas (114x154cm 44x60in) London 1998
- $4 983 - €4 265 - **£3 000** - FF27 975
  An Arab Market Oil/canvas (87x61cm 34x24in) London 1998

SEELE Johann Baptist 1774-1814 **[16]**
- $3 002 - €2 812 - **£1 845** - FF18 446
  Rastende Jagdgesellschaft an einem kleinen Teich Öl/Leinwand (62x82cm 24x32in) Lindau 1999

SEELEY George Henry 1880-1955 **[35]**
- $1 200 - €1 332 - **£836** - FF8 737
  Snow Platinum print (24.5x19.5cm 9x7in) New-York 2001

SEELOS Gottfried 1829-1900 **[20]**
- $1 184 - €1 308 - **£820** - FF8 580
  «Das Monument zum Gedenken an die siegreiche Seeschlacht» Aquarell/Papier (26x40cm 10x15in) Wien 2001

SEEMAN Enoch c.1694-1744 **[33]**
- $6 314 - €7 509 - **£4 500** - FF49 258
  Portrait of Robert d'Arcy, 3rd Earl of Holdernesse (1681-1721) Oil/canvas (244x153.5cm 96x60in) London 2000
- $4 773 - €4 092 - **£2 800** - FF26 845
  Portrait of William Wilmer of Sywell, M.P (c.1698-1744) Oil/canvas (76x63.5cm 29x25in) Leicestershire 1998

SEEREY-LESTER John Vernon 1945 **[40]**
- $7 791 - €7 488 - **£4 800** - FF49 119
  Rest at Ducks - Cougar Oil/board (59x120cm 23x47in) London 1999
- $2 282 - €2 661 - **£1 600** - FF17 456
  Spotted Hyena Acrylic (22.5x30.5cm 8x12in) London 2000

SEEVAGEN Lucien 1887-1959 **[401]**
- $362 - €305 - **£213** - FF2 000
  Bord de mer à Bréhat Huile/toile (64x80cm 25x31in) Paris 1998
- $193 - €183 - **£120** - FF1 200
  Rochers à Bréhat Huile/toile/carton (33x46cm 12x18in) Paris 1999

SEEWALD Richard 1889-1976 **[181]**
- $762 - €818 - **£510** - FF5 366
  Hang zum See Indian ink/paper (33x45.1cm 12x17in) Köln 2000
- $220 - €251 - **£154** - FF1 644
  Allee Drypoint (17.5x13cm 6x5in) München 2000

SEGAL Arthur 1875-1944 **[85]**
- $14 993 - €17 639 - **£10 584** - FF115 706
  «Biergarten I» Öl/Leinwand/Karton (59x49cm 23x19in) Berlin 2001
- $4 801 - €4 857 - **£2 931** - FF31 862
  Damenporträt Oil/panel (40x32.5cm 15x12in) Stuttgart 2000
- $10 890 - €11 434 - **£7 222** - FF75 000
  Intérieur avec personnage Gouache/papier (36x47cm 14x18in) Paris 2000

SEGAL George 1924-2000 **[150]**
- $60 000 - €67 875 - **£41 976** - FF445 230
  The Grey Door Plaster (104x66x43cm 40x25x16in) New-York 2001
- $2 152 - €2 024 - **£1 333** - FF13 278
  Sleeping Woman Plaster (26x38cm 10x14in) Stockholm 1999
- $2 921 - €3 328 - **£2 018** - FF21 830
  Untitled Oil chalks (46x30.5cm 18x12in) Zürich 2000
- $400 - €378 - **£248** - FF2 477
  Woman in Red Kimono Color lithograph (68.5x48.5cm 26x19in) San-Francisco CA 1999

SEGAL Simon 1898-1969 **[67]**
- $1 273 - €1 220 - **£784** - FF8 000
  Scène champêtre Huile/panneau (51x65cm 20x25in) Douai 1999
- $267 - €305 - **£185** - FF2 000
  Bretonne Gouache/papier (26.5x19.5cm 10x7in) Paris 2001

SEGALL Lasar 1891-1957 **[39]**
- $51 240 - €50 871 - **£31 990** - FF333 690
  Der Leser Öl/Leinwand (80.5x108cm 31x42in) Wien 1999
- $419 - €399 - **£260** - FF2 616
  Irrende Frauen (II. Fassung) Woodcut (35x46cm 13x18in) Hamburg 1999

SEGANTINI Giovanni 1858-1899 **[75]**
- $8 700 000 - €8 365 943 - **£5 360 070** - FF54 876 990
  Primavera sulle alpi Oil/canvas (116x227cm 45x89in) New-York 1999
- $77 460 - €66 916 - **£38 730** - FF438 940
  Il bifolco Olio/tela (44x62cm 17x24in) Milano 1999
- $26 664 - €31 711 - **£19 003** - FF208 008
  Stilleben mit Pilzen Oil/panel (17.5x22.5cm 6x8in) Zürich 2000
- $19 528 - €20 963 - **£13 070** - FF137 509
  Der Sensenschmied Chalks/paper (67x37cm 26x14in) München 2000

SEGANTINI Gottardo Guido 1882-1974 **[90]**
- $21 872 - €24 680 - **£15 386** - FF161 891
  Engadiner Winterlandschaft Öl/Leinwand (33.5x55cm 13x21in) Bern 2001
- $9 978 - €9 369 - **£6 183** - FF61 458
  Engadiner See Öl/Leinwand (36x27cm 14x10in) Luzern 1999
- $156 - €175 - **£108** - FF1 148
  Komposition mit Spruch von Giovanni Segantini Radierung (49x33cm 19x12in) Luzern 2001

S

SEGAR Elzie Crisler 1894-1938 **[10]**
 $9 900 - €8 446 - **£5 971** - FF55 400
   Sappo hides in a Dynamite box / Popeye escapes jail Ink/paper (65x51cm 25x20in) New-York 1998

SÉGAUD Armand J.-B. 1875-1956 **[6]**
 $615 - €686 - **£414** - FF4 500
   «Le solitaire, électricité sans secousse contre toutes maladies» Affiche (128.5x90.5cm 50x35in) Orléans 2000

SEGER Ernst 1868-1939 **[44]**
 $2 160 - €2 536 - **£1 524** - FF16 634
   Dansande flicka med kastanjetter Alabaster (H76cm H29in) Stockholm 2000

SEGERS Adrien 1876-1950 **[47]**
 $4 006 - €3 506 - **£2 426** - FF23 000
   Bateaux à quai Huile/toile (86x67cm 33x26in) Rouen 1998
 $1 151 - €1 372 - **£820** - FF9 000
   L'Église Saint Maclou à Rouen Huile/toile (46.5x26.5cm 18x10in) Clermont-Ferrand 2000

SEGERSTRÅLE Lennart 1892-1975 **[210]**
 $3 154 - €3 364 - **£2 140** - FF22 064
   I vassen Oil/canvas (91x140cm 35x55in) Helsinki 2001
 $1 793 - €1 682 - **£1 108** - FF11 032
   Bäcken Oil/panel (45x61cm 17x24in) Helsinki 1999
 $304 - €336 - **£211** - FF2 206
   Disig morgon Oil/paper (31x45cm 12x17in) Helsinki 2001
 $460 - €437 - **£282** - FF2 868
   Familj Akvarell/papper (46x60cm 18x23in) Helsinki 1999
 $216 - €202 - **£133** - FF1 323
   Svanar på grunt vatten Etching (24x34.5cm 9x13in) Helsinki 1999

SEGEWITZ Karl Eugen 1886-1952 **[5]**
 $2 080 - €2 096 - **£1 296** - FF13 751
   Blick von einer Anhöhe auf Wangen Öl/Leinwand (55x75cm 21x29in) Radolfzell 2000

SEGHERS Cornelius Johannes A 1814-1875 **[6]**
 $828 - €942 - **£570** - FF6 178
   Berger italien devant des ruines Huile/toile (53x43cm 20x16in) Bruxelles 2000

SEGHERS Daniel 1590-1661 **[22]**
 $250 000 - €267 422 - **£170 450** - FF1 754 175
   Wreaths of Roses, Tulips, Daffodils/Other Flowers Suspended Oil/copper (70x56cm 27x22in) New-York 2001
 $353 424 - €396 271 - **£240 000** - FF2 599 368
   Rose, Tulips and Orange Blossom, in a Glass Vase with a Butterfly Oil/copper (31.5x19cm 12x7in) London 2000

SEGHERS Henri 1823-1905 **[10]**
 $500 - €580 - **£355** - FF3 804
   Country Lane in winter Watercolour/paper (23x40cm 9x16in) St. Louis MO 2000

SEGHERS Henri, Jnr. 1848-1919 **[11]**
 $172 - €16J - **£106** - FF1 056
   Vue de l'Escaut Aquarelle/papier (23.5x33cm 9x12in) Bruxelles 1999

SEGNA DI BONAVENTURA c.1270-c.1330 **[6]**
 $56 783 - €60 952 - **£38 000** - FF399 820
   Female Martyr Oil/panel (68.5x40.5cm 26x15in) London 2000

SÉGOFFIN Victor Jean Ambroise 1867-1925 **[24]**
 $4 411 - €4 726 - **£3 003** - FF31 000
   Jeune femme jouant des cymbales Bronze (H59cm H23in) Calais 2001

SEGOGNE Pierre ?-1958 **[10]**
 $400 - €411 - **£250** - FF2 695
   «Gouttes de Viburniode Giry» Poster (40x30cm 15x11in) London 2000

SEGONI Alcide 1847-1894 **[7]**
 $20 000 - €21 984 - **£12 816** - FF144 208
   Suspected Oil/canvas (75x123cm 29x48in) New-York 2000
 $10 671 - €12 399 - **£7 500** - FF81 331
   The Cheat/Found out Oil/canvas (29x36cm 11x14in) London 2001

SEGRELLES ALBERT José 1886-1969 **[30]**
 $5 225 - €5 706 - **£3 325** - FF37 430
   India Oleo/lienzo (63x46cm 24x18in) Madrid 2000
 $945 - €1 051 - **£647** - FF6 895
   El hijo del contrabandista Acuarela, gouache/papel (31x21cm 12x8in) Barcelona 2001

SEGRELLES Eustaquio 1936 **[98]**
 $8 640 - €8 109 - **£5 400** - FF53 190
   Albufera Oleo/lienzo (97x130cm 38x51in) Madrid 1999
 $2 688 - €2 883 - **£1 824** - FF18 912
   «Venecia» Oleo/lienzo (51x81cm 20x31in) Madrid 2001
 $795 - €901 - **£540** - FF5 910
   La Alberca Oleo/lienzo (46x33cm 18x12in) Madrid 2000

SEGUI Antonio 1934 **[348]**
 $27 500 - €26 691 - **£17 121** - FF175 081
   A.B.C. de la Educación infantil (Serie de la Familia) Oil/canvas (96.5x129.5cm 37x50in) New-York 1999
 $5 500 - €5 338 - **£3 424** - FF35 016
   Detail Oil/canvas (70x50cm 27x19in) New-York 1999
 $3 729 - €4 421 - **£2 633** - FF29 000
   En la caja con paperas Huile/toile (27x22cm 10x8in) Paris 2000
 $2 311 - €2 287 - **£1 441** - FF15 000
   Intérieur avec personnage Pastel/papier (55.5x76cm 21x29in) Paris 1999
 $203 - €191 - **£125** - FF1 250
   Le confort est dans l'air Sérigraphie couleurs (50x65cm 19x25in) Paris 1999

SÉGUIN Armand 1869-1903 **[70]**
 $37 460 - €32 319 - **£22 599** - FF212 000
   Tête de jeune bretonne Aquarelle/papier (18x22cm 7x8in) Bayeux 1998
 $2 400 - €2 806 - **£1 686** - FF18 405
   Le soir (la glaneuse) Etching (23x23cm 9x9in) New-York 2000

SEGUIN-BERTAULT Paul 1869-1964 **[24]**
 $271 - €320 - **£190** - FF2 100
   La Liseuse Mine plomb (34x42cm 13x16in) Paris 2000

SEGUNDO PEREZ Mario 1960 **[13]**
 $22 000 - €25 561 - **£15 461** - FF167 666
   «A la buena de Dios» Oil/canvas (151x120.5cm 59x47in) New-York 2000
 $24 000 - €25 761 - **£16 060** - FF168 984
   San Jorge y el dragón Oil/canvas (48x122cm 18x48in) New-York 2000

S

SEGURA IGLESIAS Agustín 1900-1988 **[11]**
 $1 116 - €1 068 - **£700** - FF7 003
  The Cymbal Player Oil/canvas (91.5x71cm 36x27in)
  London 1998

SEGUSO Livio 1930 **[8]**
 $651 - €563 - **£392** - FF3 692
  Buste de femme Sculpture verre (H45.5cm H17in)
  Montréal 1998

SEI Kinkoku XIX-XX **[1]**
 $4 500 - €4 121 - **£2 742** - FF27 031
  Rooster Bronze (H51cm H20in) New-York 1999

SEIBEZZI Fioravante 1906-1975 **[26]**
 $1 500 - €1 555 - **£900** - FF10 200
  L'Adige a Verona Olio/tela (42.5x57cm 16x22in)
  Venezia 1999
 $1 400 - €1 814 - **£1 050** - FF11 900
  Bacino di San Marco Olio/masonite (30x40cm
  11x15in) Milano 2000

SEIBOLD Alois Leopold 1879-1951 **[19]**
 $511 - €509 - **£309** - FF3 336
  Stubwieswipfel and Bosruck Mischtechnik/Papier
  (35x43.5cm 13x17in) Wien 2000

SEIDE Paul A. 1949 **[3]**
 $4 000 - €3 818 - **£2 499** - FF25 046
  Neon Leaf Forms Sculpture, glass (35.5x25.5x9cm
  13x10x3in) New-York 1998

SEIDEL August 1820-1904 **[105]**
 $3 509 - €3 323 - **£2 133** - FF21 800
  Fischerboote an einem oberitalienischen See
  Öl/Leinwand (54.5x70cm 21x27in) München 1999
 $1 605 - €1 789 - **£1 122** - FF11 738
  Bauernhäuser am Teich Öl/Leinwand (25x45cm
  9x17in) München 2001
 $180 - €179 - **£113** - FF1 175
  Baumbestandene Flusslandschaft Pencil/paper
  (33.5x49.5cm 13x19in) München 1999

SEIDEL Brian 1928 **[20]**
 $5 718 - €6 138 - **£3 827** - FF40 262
  Winterset Oil/canvas (143.5x147.5cm 56x58in)
  Melbourne 2000
 $468 - €547 - **£326** - FF3 587
  Morning Figure, Sorrento Mixed media (48.5x49cm
  19x19in) Melbourne 2000

SEIDEMANN Bob XX **[4]**
 $210 000 - €241 772 - **£143 304** - FF1 585 920
  The Airplane as Art Gelatin silver print (33x33cm
  12x12in) New-York 2000

SEIDENBEUTLOWIE Efraim 1902-1945 **[12]**
 $6 768 - €6 336 - **£4 195** - FF41 563
  Still Life with Flowers Oil/panel (69.5x60.8cm
  27x23in) Warszawa 1999

SEIDENSTÜCKER Friedrich 1882-1962 **[61]**
 $460 - €537 - **£322** - FF3 521
  Römer Taube/Kranich/Schleiereulen Vintage gelatin silver print (17.7x13cm 6x5in) München 2000

SEIDNER David 1957-1999 **[19]**
 $2 000 - €1 893 - **£1 243** - FF12 417
  Tina Chow/Fortuny Silver print (40x50cm 16x20in)
  New-York 1999

SEIFERT Alfred 1850-1901 **[35]**
 $12 000 - €13 190 - **£7 689** - FF86 524
  The Maiden's Suiter Oil/canvas (62.5x41.5cm
  24x16in) New-York 2000
 $900 - €944 - **£563** - FF6 189
  **Portrait of a young Beauty with a Rose in her
  Hair** Oil/panel (17x12cm 7x5in) Norwalk CT 2000

SEIFERT David 1896-1980 **[4]**
 $1 960 - €2 287 - **£1 375** - FF15 000
  La ville Huile/toile (65.5x92cm 25x36in) Paris 2001

SEIFERT Paul 1840-1921 **[5]**
 $19 000 - €15 863 - **£11 143** - FF104 053
  Farm Landscape Watercolour/paper (56.5x70.5cm
  22x27in) New-York 1998

SEIFERT Victor Heinrich 1870-1953 **[95]**
 $4 030 - €3 790 - **£2 496** - FF24 860
  Young Girl fishing Bronze (H95cm H37in) Warszawa
  1999
 $1 152 - €1 125 - **£729** - FF7 378
  Die Trinkende, Durstig, Weiblicher Akt Bronze
  (H45.5cm H17in) Bremen 1999

SEIFFERT Carl Friedrich 1809-1891 **[17]**
 $1 094 - €1 022 - **£661** - FF6 707
  **Alpensee mit Tannen im
  Sommerlicht/Saumpfad und Waldstück im
  Gebirge** Öl/Karton (33x47cm 12x18in) Berlin 1999

SEIGNAC Guillaume 1870-1924 **[211]**
 $42 500 - €40 871 - **£26 231** - FF268 098
  Iris Oil/canvas (135.5x89cm 53x35in) Boston MA 1999
 $45 000 - €38 824 - **£27 148** - FF254 668
  Vanity Oil/canvas (103.5x82.5cm 40x32in) New-York
  1998
 $8 000 - €7 678 - **£5 015** - FF50 364
  La rêveuse Oil/canvas (33x24cm 12x9in) New-York
  1999
 $752 - €838 - **£506** - FF5 500
  «**The Equitable trust Company of New York,
  emprunt**» Affiche (119x79cm 46x31in) Orléans 2000

SEIGNAC Paul 1826-1904 **[35]**
 $13 000 - €12 352 - **£7 909** - FF81 027
  At the Well Oil/panel (54.5x44.5cm 21x17in) New-
  York 1999
 $32 886 - €33 138 - **£20 500** - FF217 373
  Children in an interior Oil/canvas (32x24cm 12x9in)
  Malvern-Wells, Worcestershire 2000

SEIGNEMARTIN Jean 1848-1875 **[8]**
 $1 813 - €2 134 - **£1 274** - FF14 160
  Notable et ses favorites Huile/toile (32x41.5cm
  12x16in) Paris 2000

SEIGNEURGENS Ernest Louis A. c.1820-1904 **[3]**
 $2 046 - €2 439 - **£1 459** - FF16 000
  Paysans à cheval Huile/panneau (27x40cm 10x15in)
  Saint-Dié 2000

SEIJI Togo XX **[8]**
 $6 860 - €6 691 - **£4 200** - FF43 890
  Reminiscence Oil/canvas (45.5x38.5cm 17x15in)
  Tokyo 1999
 $14 210 - €13 860 - **£8 700** - FF90 915
  Woman in Red Scarf Oil/canvas (33.5x24.5cm
  13x9in) Tokyo 1999

SEIKE Tomio XX **[11]**
 $891 - €777 - **£539** - FF5 100
  Nu, Juin Tirage argentique (30x20cm 11x7in) Saint-
  Germain-en-Laye 1998

SEILER Carl Wilhelm Anton 1846-1921 **[119]**
 $2 215 - €2 045 - **£1 362** - FF13 415
  Der Arztbesuch Oil/panel (46x35cm 18x13in)
  München 1999
 $1 571 - €1 687 - **£1 052** - FF11 067
  Selbstbildnis vor der Staffelei Oil/panel
  (25x12.5cm 9x4in) Königstein 2000

S

SEILER Hans 1907-1986 **[64]**
- $1 456 - €1 601 - £926 - FF10 500
  Vase de fleurs Huile/toile (36.5x44.5cm 14x17in) Paris 2000
- $611 - €640 - £384 - FF4 200
  Sans titre Huile/toile (27x40.5cm 10x15in) Versailles 2000
- $626 - €686 - £435 - FF4 500
  Bouquet de fleurs Gouache/papier (47.5x30.5cm 18x12in) Vannes 2001

SEIQUER Alejandro 1850-1921 **[14]**
- $244 - €240 - £152 - FF1 576
  Patos y flores Acuarela/papel (49x63cm 19x24in) Madrid 1999

SEITER Daniel, il Cavaliere 1649-1705 **[11]**
- $3 895 - €3 634 - £2 350 - FF23 835
  Il battesimo di Cristo (Die taufe Christi) Öl/Leinwand (46x32cm 18x12in) Wien 1999
- $1 800 - €1 555 - £900 - FF10 500
  L'ebbrezza di Noè Acquarello (12x18.5cm 4x7in) Milano 1999

SEITZ Alexander Maximilian 1811-1888 **[10]**
- $6 966 - €6 724 - £4 400 - FF44 104
  The Return of the Prodigal Son Watercolour (33x109cm 12x42in) Ipswich 1999

SEITZ Anton 1829-1900 **[29]**
- $4 120 - €4 094 - £2 574 - FF26 831
  Ein mönch in seiner Studierstube Öl/Leinwand (86x70cm 33x27in) München 1999
- $4 437 - €4 090 - £2 657 - FF26 828
  Ein Brief von ihm Oil/panel (20x16cm 7x6in) Dresden 1998

SEITZ Gustav 1906-1969 **[124]**
- $14 905 - €17 384 - £10 465 - FF114 032
  Käthe Kollwitz Bronze (H98cm H38in) Köln 2000
- $2 326 - €2 812 - £1 624 - FF18 446
  Patricia Bronze (29x17x15cm 11x6x5in) Berlin 2000
- $342 - €383 - £238 - FF2 515
  Unterhaltung Ink (29.5x21cm 11x8in) Berlin 2001
- $110 - €102 - £66 - FF670
  Streitende Frauen Lithographie (10x18.4cm 3x7in) Heidelberg 1999

SEITZ Johann ?-c.1809 **[2]**
- $14 472 - €15 882 - £9 317 - FF104 181
  Crayfish and Salmon in Porcelain Bowls, Lemons, Flowers in Vases Oil/copper (29x44.5cm 11x17in) Amsterdam 2000

SEITZ Johann Georg 1810-1870 **[38]**
- $3 096 - €2 907 - £1 920 - FF19 068
  Früchtestilleben Öl/Leinwand (41x52cm 16x20in) Wien 1999

SEITZ Otto 1846-1912 **[44]**
- $2 227 - €2 505 - £1 555 - FF16 434
  Stilleben mit Rosenund Margeriten Öl/Leinwand (59.5x32cm 23x12in) Lindau 2001

SEIWERT Franz Wilhelm 1894-1933 **[30]**
- $13 849 - €16 361 - £9 782 - FF107 324
  Entwurf zum Grabstein der Eltern des Künstlers Polished bronze (H22.5cm H8in) Köln 2001
- $2 006 - €2 269 - £1 356 - FF14 883
  Internationale Arbeiter Hilfe Pencil (56x38cm 22x14in) Dordrecht 2000
- $539 - €613 - £374 - FF4 024
  Welt zum Staunen Woodcut (30x23.4cm 11x9in) Hamburg 2000

SEJOURNE Bernard 1945-1994 **[16]**
- $4 841 - €5 031 - £3 072 - FF33 000
  Masque aux fleurs Huile/panneau (46x46cm 18x18in) Paris 2000

SEKINO Junichiro 1914-1992 **[57]**
- $500 - €540 - £345 - FF3 541
  A Boy with Rooster Woodcut in colors (61x45.5cm 24x17in) Bethesda MD 2001

SEKOTO Gérard 1913-1993 **[72]**
- $7 461 - €6 996 - £4 610 - FF45 890
  Children playing with their Dog Oil/board (55x38cm 21x14in) Johannesburg 2000
- $5 647 - €5 424 - £3 500 - FF35 576
  Children in a Township Oil/canvas (32.5x41cm 12x16in) London 1999
- $2 330 - €2 415 - £1 476 - FF15 843
  Portrait in Blue Watercolour/paper (50x32cm 19x12in) Johannesburg 1999

SEKRET Valéry 1950 **[130]**
- $837 - €722 - £500 - FF4 739
  Snowy Boulevard Oil/canvas (45.5x56cm 17x22in) St. Helier, Jersey 1998
- $297 - €330 - £203 - FF2 167
  Calle Rívoli Oleo/lienzo (27x41cm 10x16in) Madrid 2001

SEKULA Sonia 1918-1963 **[55]**
- $493 - €561 - £342 - FF3 681
  Komposition 21 Aquarell/Papier (31x21cm 12x8in) Zofingen 2000

SELACEK Stephan XIX-XX **[1]**
- $4 206 - €3 993 - £2 574 - FF26 193
  The Chess Game Oil/canvas (54x67cm 21x26in) Sydney 1999

SELBY Joe 1893-1960 **[7]**
- $1 500 - €1 750 - £1 061 - FF11 477
  «Driftwood»/«Soerabay» Watercolour, gouache/paper (30x40cm 12x16in) St. Petersburg FL 2001

SELBY Prideaux John 1788-1867 **[56]**
- $6 734 - €8 009 - £4 800 - FF52 537
  Assembly of Birds on the Branch of an Oak Tree Oil/canvas (75x62cm 29x24in) London 2000
- $4 200 - €4 651 - £2 848 - FF30 510
  Common Wild Swan Watercolour (65.5x52.5cm 25x20in) New-York 2000
- $400 - €375 - £245 - FF2 457
  Common Wild Swan, plate XLVII Etching (67x54.5cm 26x21in) New-York 1999

SELDRON Elisabeth c.1670-c.1740 **[8]**
- $13 412 - €11 334 - £8 000 - FF74 349
  A Market Scene with Many Figures, a River Beyond Oil/canvas (54.5x65cm 21x25in) London 1998

SELESNICK William, Bill XX **[29]**
- $400 - €338 - £239 - FF2 217
  New Hope train station and canal Oil/canvas (71x96cm 28x38in) Hatfield PA 1998

SELIGMANN Adalbert Franz 1862-1945 **[5]**
- $10 000 - €9 903 - £6 226 - FF64 958
  In the Artist's Studio Oil/panel (74.5x50.5cm 29x19in) New-York 1999

SELIGMANN Michael 1720-1762 **[11]**
- $68 - €77 - £47 - FF503
  Tulipa Kupferstich (48x26cm 18x10in) Köln 2001

SELIGMANN Kurt 1900-1962 **[125]**
$18 150 - €19 056 - **£12 037** - FF125 000
Alchimiste Muse Huile/toile (77x51cm 30x20in)
Paris 2000

$1 600 - €1 364 - **£965** - FF8 948
«The Unicorn, The Gorgon and the Manticore»
Coloured pencils/paper (30x22cm 11x8in) New-York
1998

$1 433 - €1 431 - **£896** - FF9 390
Le Corsaire Radierung (49.5x38cm 19x14in)
Hamburg 1999

SELINGER Emily Harris McGary 1848-1927 **[11]**
$1 300 - €1 414 - **£857** - FF9 274
Still Life with Basket of Flowers and Jug Oil/can-
vas (56x66cm 22x25in) Boston MA 2000

SELKIRK Neil 1947 **[19]**
$4 200 - €4 403 - **£2 631** - FF28 885
Flower Girl at wedding, Conn. Silver print
(37x37cm 14x14in) New-York 2000

SELL Christian I 1831-1883 **[74]**
$6 202 - €5 880 - **£3 773** - FF38 569
Gefechtspause im 30jährigen Krieg Öl/Leinwand
(76x108cm 29x42in) München 1999
$1 053 - €1 022 - **£656** - FF6 707
Szenen aus dem Krieg von Oil/panel (14x27.5cm
5x10in) Berlin 2000
$1 555 - €1 789 - **£1 073** - FF11 738
Szenen bei der Schlacht bei Königsgrätz Watercolour
(49x68cm 19x26in) München 2000

SELL Christian II 1854-1925 **[32]**
$893 - €869 - **£548** - FF5 701
Zwei preussische Gardeoffiziere zu Pferd
Oil/panel (18x24cm 7x9in) Berlin 1999

SELL Lothar 1939 **[10]**
$114 - €128 - **£79** - FF838
«Der verkehrte Tag» Woodcut (29x20.3cm 11x7in)
Berlin 2001

SELLAER Vincent Geldersmann c.1539-? **[10]**
$28 266 - €27 227 - **£17 466** - FF178 596
Stuffer the Little Children to Come Unto Me
Oil/canvas/panel (97x125cm 38x49in) Amsterdam 1999
$18 000 - €20 913 - **£12 650** - FF137 181
**The Virgin and Child with the Infant Saint John
the Baptist** Oil/panel (76x61cm 29x24in) New-York
2001

SELLAJO del Jacopo c.1441-1493 **[3]**
$155 000 - €160 681 - **£93 000** - FF1 054 000
San Gerolamo Tempera/tavola (68x93cm 26x36in)
Roma 2000

SELLAR Charles A. ?-1926 **[10]**
$777 - €901 - **£550** - FF5 911
Sheila Oil/canvas (30.5x25.5cm 12x10in) London 2000

SELLENY Josef 1824-1875 **[26]**
$2 873 - €2 543 - **£1 757** - FF16 684
Bildnis einer Eingeborenen aus Polynesien
Oil/canvas/panel (22x15.5cm 8x6in) Wien 1999
$592 - €654 - **£410** - FF4 290
Italienische Zofen Watercolour (23x51cm 9x20in)
Wien 2001

SELLEY Lindsey XX **[3]**
$4 708 - €5 489 - **£3 300** - FF36 008
Leopard Acrylic (41.5x53cm 16x20in) London 2000

SELLHEIM Gert 1901-1970 **[4]**
$1 200 - €1 308 - **£830** - FF8 577
«Australia, Great Barbier Reed.» Poster (50x31cm
19x12in) New-York 2001

SELLMAYR Ludwig 1834-1901 **[21]**
$1 787 - €2 045 - **£1 229** - FF13 415
**Hirte mit Kühen, Ziegen und Schafen an der
Tränke bei den Bäumen vorn** Öl/Leinwand
(50.5x90.5cm 19x35in) München 2000
$1 782 - €2 045 - **£1 229** - FF13 415
Kühe an der Tränke Öl/Leinwand (46x34cm
18x13in) Berlin 2000

SELMERSHEIM-DESGRANGE Jeanne 1877-1958
[25]
$3 482 - €3 811 - **£2 402** - FF25 000
Bouquet au pichet rouge Huile/toile/carton
(35x57.5cm 13x22in) Paris 2001
$466 - €518 - **£325** - FF3 400
Village provençal Aquarelle/papier (25x41cm 9x16in)
Paris 2001

SELMYHR Conrad 1877-1944 **[44]**
$482 - €549 - **£334** - FF3 600
Lac de montagne Huile/toile (59x100cm 23x39in)
Paris 2000

SELOUS Henry Courtney 1811-1890 **[22]**
$3 058 - €2 888 - **£1 849** - FF18 947
The Piazetta San Marco, Venice Oil/canvas
(65x45cm 25x17in) Billingshurst, West-Sussex 1999
$1 027 - €1 072 - **£650** - FF7 032
Figures before Jerusalem Lithograph (64x96cm
25x37in) London 2001

SELTENHAMMER Paul XX **[4]**
$2 600 - €2 280 - **£1 578** - FF14 959
Folies en folie -Mistinguett Poster (314x118cm
124x46in) New-York 1999

SELTZER Olaf Carl 1877-1957 **[77]**
$45 000 - €41 545 - **£27 675** - FF272 515
Meeting of the Bands Oil/canvas (51x77cm
20x30in) New-York 1999
$50 000 - €53 610 - **£33 080** - FF351 660
Crow Scout Oil/board (27x35cm 11x14in) Hayden ID
2000
$9 500 - €8 196 - **£5 709** - FF53 763
Plains Chief Watercolour/paper (18x13cm 7x5in)
Santa-Fe NM 1998

SELTZER William Steve 1955 **[5]**
$3 800 - €4 191 - **£2 573** - FF27 489
Indians on Horseback Watercolour, gouache/board
(38x51cm 14x20in) New-York 2000

SELVATICO Lino 1872-1924 **[7]**
$7 200 - €9 330 - **£5 400** - FF61 200
Ritratto femminile con mantello rosso Olio/tela
(150x100cm 59x39in) Milano 2001
$10 800 - €13 995 - **£8 100** - FF91 800
Il legaccio Olio/tela (80x50cm 31x19in) Milano 2001
$4 750 - €4 924 - **£2 850** - FF32 300
Figura femminile Olio/cartone (17.5x20cm 6x7in)
Milano 2000

SEM Anthon Adrianus 1821-? **[2]**
$3 122 - €2 949 - **£1 888** - FF19 347
Le château de Chillon, Suisse Oil/panel
(25.5x38.5cm 10x15in) Amsterdam 1999

SEM Georges Goursat, dit 1863-1934 **[208]**
$710 - €793 - **£496** - FF5 200
Dans un restaurant à la mode Aquarelle/papier
(36x51cm 14x20in) Versailles 2001
$273 - €305 - **£184** - FF2 000
«Monte Carlo Beach, le paradis retrouvé»
Affiche (80x120cm 31x47in) Orléans 2000

S

SEMEGHINI Pio 1878-1964 **[117]**
- $7 600 - €9 848 - **£5 700** - FF64 600
  «Merlettaia» Tempera (60x47cm 23x18in) Milano 2001
- $4 250 - €4 406 - **£2 550** - FF28 900
  Buranelle Olio/tela (37.5x30cm 14x11in) Prato 1999
- $1 020 - €881 - **£510** - FF5 780
  Paesaggio Matite colorate/carta (13.5x18cm 5x7in) Milano 1999

SEMENTI Giovanni Giacomo 1583-1640 **[3]**
- $29 614 - €25 916 - **£17 935** - FF170 000
  Saint Pierre guérit Sainte Agathe de sa mutilation Huile/cuivre (66.5x58cm 26x22in) Paris 1998

SEMPÉ Jean Jacques 1932 **[12]**
- $284 - €331 - **£200** - FF2 168
  Rather cross Couple running down a Beach towards the Sea Coloured crayons (35x45cm 13x17in) London 2001

SEMPERE JUAN Eusebio 1923-1985 **[80]**
- $11 360 - €9 610 - **£6 720** - FF63 040
  Móvil, dos semicírculos Técnica mixta (241x136.5cm 94x53in) Madrid 1998
- $5 500 - €6 006 - **£3 500** - FF39 400
  Composición geométricas Oleo/cartulina (65x50cm 25x19in) Madrid 2000
- $2 310 - €2 102 - **£1 400** - FF13 790
  Sin título Gouache (64x48cm 25x18in) Madrid 1999
- $280 - €300 - **£190** - FF1 970
  Composición Serigrafia (65x50cm 25x19in) Madrid 2001

SEMPLE Joseph XIX **[11]**
- $6 500 - €5 780 - **£3 975** - FF37 916
  The Screw Steamer «Pennsylvania» in full sail off the Irish Coast Oil/canvas (58x99cm 22x38in) New-York 1999

SEMSER Charles 1922 **[32]**
- $568 - €610 - **£380** - FF4 000
  Le chevalier avec chapeau Céramique (74x24x24cm 29x9x9in) Douai 2000

SEN Sushil XIX-XX **[6]**
- $1 461 - €1 404 - **£900** - FF9 210
  Baul Watercolour/paper (21x21cm 8x8in) London 1999

SENA António 1941 **[2]**
- $12 760 - €14 457 - **£8 990** - FF94 830
  Sem título Acrílico/lienzo (194x130cm 76x51in) Lisboa 2001
- $7 480 - €8 475 - **£5 270** - FF55 590
  Sem título Técnica mixta/papel (86.5x62cm 34x24in) Lisboa 2001

SENAPE Antonio 1788-c.1842 **[77]**
- $1 200 - €1 244 - **£720** - FF8 160
  Veduta di Chiatamone/Pozzuoli/Villaggio della Cava Inchiostro (15x18cm 5x7in) Roma 1999

SENAVE Jacques Albert 1758-1823 **[28]**
- $20 082 - €17 017 - **£12 000** - FF111 627
  A Wayzgoose in a Printing Press Oil/panel (47x68cm 18x26in) London 1998
- $5 900 - €6 877 - **£4 084** - FF45 111
  Junge Magd mit Kind auf dem Hof Oil/panel (18.5x24cm 7x9in) Bern 2000

SENBERGS Jan 1939 **[21]**
- $893 - €779 - **£540** - FF5 112
  Penghana study Acrylic/canvas (55.5x71cm 21x27in) Melbourne 1998
- $211 - €200 - **£127** - FF1 309
  Landscape for Iona Lithograph (48x65cm 18x25in) Sydney 1999

SENCHO Teisai XIX **[1]**
- $723 - €710 - **£448** - FF4 656
  Courtisane avec deux élèves sous un cerisier Woodcut (35.7x24.1cm 14x9in) Warszawa 1999

SENDAK Maurice 1928 **[4]**
- $20 000 - €18 516 - **£12 242** - FF121 456
  Set design for The Love of the Three Oranges: landscape and wild thing Watercolour/paper (20x72cm 8x28in) New-York 1999

SENÉ Henry Ch. 1889-1961 **[18]**
- $3 647 - €3 382 - **£2 200** - FF22 186
  Cavaliers Chleuhs du Sud-Marocain Oil/canvas (51x70cm 20x27in) London 1999

SÉNEQUE Clement 1896-1930 **[27]**
- $1 635 - €1 575 - **£1 010** - FF10 334
  Building the Dam Wall Oil/canvas/board (23x32.5cm 9x12in) Johannesburg 1999

SENEQUIER Jules 1821-1846 **[1]**
- $15 620 - €16 769 - **£10 450** - FF110 000
  Installations portuaires de Toulon; la darse vieille, la darse neuve Huile/toile (58.5x103cm 23x40in) Paris 2000

SENET Y PÉREZ Rafael 1856-1926 **[79]**
- $20 343 - €24 194 - **£14 500** - FF158 705
  On the Venetian Lagoon Oil/canvas (53x97cm 20x38in) London 2000
- $1 282 - €1 351 - **£832** - FF8 865
  Napolitana Oleo/tabla (35x17cm 13x6in) Madrid 2000
- $2 015 - €1 952 - **£1 235** - FF12 805
  Gondolero veneciano Acuarela/papel (50x31cm 19x12in) Madrid 1999

SENEX John ?-1740 **[15]**
- $400 - €386 - **£252** - FF2 532
  New Map of Africa Engraving (50x58cm 19x22in) New-York 1999

SENEZCOURT de Jules 1818-1866 **[2]**
- $2 333 - €2 317 - **£1 459** - FF15 200
  L'Escarpolette, d'après Pater Huile/bois (33x42cm 12x16in) Paris 1999

SENFF Adolf 1785-1863 **[5]**
- $12 000 - €15 550 - **£9 000** - FF102 000
  Fiori in una cesta di vimini, e vaso marmoreo su un basamento Olio/tela (101.5x76cm 39x29in) Roma 2000

SENG Ong Kim 1945 **[13]**
- $3 516 - €3 543 - **£2 191** - FF23 239
  Pre-war Houses, Singapore Watercolour/paper (54x74cm 21x29in) Singapore 2000

SENGL Peter 1945 **[109]**
- $597 - €581 - **£368** - FF3 813
  Vor asiatischem mit entsprechender Stirnschraubnadel Mischtechnik (61x47cm 24x18in) Linz 1999
- $403 - €436 - **£279** - FF2 860
  «Kein Nalotbogen (Quälung)» Mischtechnik/Papier (63x49cm 24x19in) Wien 2001
- $200 - €204 - **£125** - FF1 341
  Brezentänzer/Geschmückte/Clownfrau vor Papageientapete Offset (66x50cm 25x19in) Hamburg 2000

SENIOR Mark 1864-1927 **[35]**
- $7 091 - €6 881 - **£4 500** - FF45 138
  Picking Apples at Runswick Oil/canvas (61x51cm 24x20in) West-Yorshire 1999

$6 465 – €7 543 – **£4 500** – FF49 482
Street in Bruges Oil/canvas/board (27x35cm
10x13in) West-Yorshire 1999

$4 180 – €3 569 – **£2 500** – FF23 408
«Bruges» Pastel/paper (25x32.5cm 9x12in) Leeds
1998

SENISE Daniel 1955 **[21]**
$13 000 – €12 621 – **£8 031** – FF82 790
Beddangelina Acrylic (147x177cm 57x69in) New-
York 1999

$7 000 – €6 773 – **£4 316** – FF44 428
Pindorama/Cretona Oil/canvas (57x104cm 22x40in)
New-York 1999

SENNHAUSER John 1907-1978 **[15]**
$4 548 – €4 499 – **£2 836** – FF29 514
Black lines Öl/Leinwand (103x90cm 40x35in) Luzern
1999

SENNO Pietro 1831-1904 **[14]**
$1 450 – €1 503 – **£870** – FF9 860
Campagna Olio/tela (20x30cm 7x11in) Prato 1999

SEOANE Luis 1910-1979 **[152]**
$5 415 – €5 706 – **£3 610** – FF37 430
Papas con brotes Oleo/lienzo (55x46cm 21x18in)
Madrid 2000

$4 480 – €4 805 – **£2 960** – FF31 520
Naturaleza muerta Oleo/lienzo (27x42cm 10x16in)
Madrid 2000

$912 – €961 – **£608** – FF6 304
La Rebelion Acuarela/papel (36x24cm 14x9in)
Madrid 2000

$259 – €288 – **£182** – FF1 891
«Tormenta y pájaros» Gravure bois (64x46cm
25x18in) Madrid 2001

SEPESHY Zoltan 1898-1974 **[34]**
$3 400 – €3 496 – **£2 156** – FF22 935
Untitled Oil/canvas (48x66cm 19x26in) Detroit MI
2000

$325 – €329 – **£202** – FF2 159
Meadow Scene at Sunrise Pastel/paper (36x43cm
14x17in) Bloomfield-Hills MI 2000

SEPO (Severo Pozzatti) 1895-1983 **[37]**
$1 600 – €1 539 – **£987** – FF10 093
«Noveltex» Poster (100x52cm 39x20in) New-York
1999

SEPP Mülpis 1911 **[1]**
$16 527 – €14 259 – **£9 970** – FF93 534
Alpaufzug vor Appenzeller Landschaft Öl/Karton
(40x55cm 15x21in) St. Gallen 1998

SEQUEIRA de Domingos Antonio 1768-1837 **[4]**
$3 520 – €3 988 – **£2 400** – FF26 160
Calvário Aquarelle (30x18cm 11x7in) Lisboa 2000

SER GIOVANNI DI SIMONE Giovanni Lo Scheggia
1406-1486 **[2]**
$93 384 – €91 795 – **£60 000** – FF602 136
**The Madonna and Child with Saints Francis of
Assisi and Jerome** Tempera (92.5x48.5cm 36x19in)
London 1999

SÉRADOUR Guy 1922 **[147]**
$2 585 – €2 897 – **£1 797** – FF19 000
Portrait de jeune fille devant la mer Huile/toile
(55x73cm 21x28in) Le Touquet 2001

$1 874 – €2 134 – **£1 323** – FF14 000
La jeune propriétaire Huile/toile (35x27cm 13x10in)
Rennes 2001

$756 – €762 – **£471** – FF5 000
Jeune fille au chapeau melon Pastel/papier
(49x21cm 19x8in) Calais 2000

SERAFIN XX **[14]**
$268 – €252 – **£159** – FF1 654
Venus/El ratón/Las Meninas Gouache (47x33cm
18x12in) Madrid 1999

SERAFINI Giuseppe / Beppe 1915-1987 **[61]**
$520 – €674 – **£390** – FF4 420
Contadini Smalto (50x70cm 19x27in) Prato 2001

$325 – €337 – **£195** – FF2 210
Colloquio Olio/cartone (20x30cm 7x11in) Prato 2000

$350 – €363 – **£210** – FF2 380
«Contadino» Inchiostro (30x20cm 11x7in) Vercelli
1999

SERANGELI Gioachin Giuseppe 1768-1852 **[4]**
$7 669 – €6 403 – **£4 498** – FF42 000
Portrait du peintre Auguste Vinchon, enfant
Huile/toile (55.5x46cm 21x18in) Tours 1998

SÉRAPHINE DE SENLIS Séraphine Louis,dite
1864-1942 **[9]**
$25 800 – €22 867 – **£15 825** – FF150 000
Grand bouquet champêtre Huile/toile (100.5x65cm
39x25in) Cannes 1999

SERDA Émile ?-1863 **[2]**
$12 000 – €11 883 – **£7 471** – FF77 949
Taking the Air inthe Castle's Garden Oil/canvas
(75x103cm 29x40in) New-York 1999

SEREBRIAKOV Aleksandr 1907-1994 **[79]**
$23 565 – €22 867 – **£14 670** – FF150 000
**Maquette pour la pyramide du parc de
Groussay** Sculpture bois (44x44x48cm 17x17x18in)
Montfort L'Amaury 1999

$6 284 – €6 098 – **£3 912** – FF40 000
**Projet pour un nouveau jardin en perspective
avec un arc de triomphe** Aquarelle, gouache
(64x113cm 25x44in) Montfort L'Amaury 1999

SEREBRIAKOVA Zinaida Yevgenievna 1884-1967
[38]
$84 411 – €81 123 – **£52 000** – FF532 131
Portrait of Mademoiselle Neviadomskaya
Oil/canvas (60x74cm 23x29in) London 1999

$10 181 – €8 723 – **£6 121** – FF57 218
Portrait of a Country Girl Gouache/paper (51x41cm
20x16in) Cedar-Falls IA 1998

SERENA Luigi 1855-1911 **[4]**
$3 750 – €3 887 – **£2 250** – FF25 500
Interno con figura Olio/tavola (25.5x13.5cm 10x5in)
Milano 1999

SERGE M. XX **[1]**
$16 824 – €18 294 – **£11 088** – FF120 000
Jeune fille aux oranges Huile/toile (150x87cm
59x34in) Paris 2000

SERGEANT John 1937 **[2]**
$4 490 – €4 442 – **£2 800** – FF29 140
**Boardroom, 41 Bishopsgate/Front Room, 41
Bishopsgate** Watercolour (44.5x61cm 17x24in)
London 1999

SERGEL Johan Tobias 1740-1814 **[37]**
$3 705 – €3 232 – **£2 241** – FF21 198
Backanal eller Den Erotiska Lockelsen Indian ink
(50x50cm 7x4in) Stockholm 1998

SERGENT-MARCEAU Antoine Louis Fr. 1751-1847
[9]
$6 223 – €5 781 – **£3 800** – FF37 924
**Half Length Portrait of a Woman Wearing a
Shawl** Watercolour (19x16cm 7x6in) London 1998

S

SERGER Frederick 1889-1965 **[11]**
- $3 320 - €3 857 - **£2 333** - FF25 301
  Horseback Riders Oil/canvas (50.5x61cm 19x24in)
  Amsterdam 2001

SERIENT Hermann 1935 **[8]**
- $960 - €1 090 - **£673** - FF7 150
  «Der Zeuge» Oil/panel (14x9cm 5x3in) Wien 2001

SERNEELS Clement 1912-1991 **[41]**
- $1 240 - €1 361 - **£824** - FF8 929
  Lake Edward, Belgian Congo Oil/canvas
  (70.5x80cm 27x31in) Amsterdam 2000

SERNESI Raffaelo 1838-1866 **[21]**
- $50 000 - €51 833 - **£30 000** - FF340 000
  Il pratone alle Cascine Olio/cartone (12x19.5cm
  4x7in) Prato 1999
- $720 - €622 - **£360** - FF4 080
  Alzati cammina China (43x56cm 16x22in) Firenze
  1999

SERNY Ricardo S.Ysern 1908-1995 **[25]**
- $1 852 - €1 952 - **£1 202** - FF12 805
  Jóvenes Oleo/lienzo (82x100cm 32x39in) Madrid
  2000

SEROV Valentin Alexandrov. 1865-1911 **[28]**
- $14 726 - €16 511 - **£10 000** - FF108 307
  Country Settlement under Threatening Clouds
  Oil/board (27x52cm 10x20in) London 2000
- $4 417 - €4 953 - **£3 000** - FF32 492
  Study of a Nude Crayon (35.5x25.5cm 13x10in)
  London 2000

SERPAN Iaroslav Sossountzov 1922-1976 **[75]**
- $816 - €915 - **£567** - FF6 000
  «Tocaieew» Huile/toile (89x116cm 35x45in) Paris
  2001

SERPIERI Paolo Eleuteri 1944 **[3]**
- $8 611 - €7 927 - **£5 168** - FF52 000
  Druuna Acrylique (33x27cm 12x10in) Paris 1999
- $1 966 - €2 211 - **£1 380** - FF14 500
  Druuna, pl.21 de Creatura Encre Chine/papier
  (36x26cm 14x10in) Paris 2001

SERRA Andreu XX **[27]**
- $2 048 - €1 922 - **£1 280** - FF12 608
  Marina al atardecer Oleo/lienzo (60x75cm 23x29in)
  Madrid 1999

SERRA CASTELLET Francesc 1912-1976 **[42]**
- $4 860 - €5 406 - **£3 240** - FF35 460
  Figura sentada Oleo/lienzo (81x65cm 31x25in)
  Madrid 2000
- $3 710 - €4 205 - **£2 520** - FF27 580
  Niña Oleo/lienzo (41x33cm 16x12in) Madrid 2000
- $640 - €601 - **£400** - FF3 940
  Cabeza de perfil Pastel (28.5x22cm 11x8in)
  Barcelona 1999

SERRA DE RIVERA Javier 1946 **[4]**
- $762 - €751 - **£487** - FF4 925
  Desnudo femenino de espaldas Lápices de
  color/papel (48x68cm 18x26in) Madrid 1999

SERRA Ernesto 1860-1915 **[4]**
- $9 600 - €8 293 - **£6 400** - FF54 400
  Alla fonte Olio/tavola (131x89cm 51x35in) Milano
  1998

SERRA Luigi 1898-1970 **[4]**
- $2 250 - €2 332 - **£1 350** - FF15 300
  Laguna di Venezia Acquarello/carta (20x25cm 7x9in)
  Firenze 2000

SERRA MELGOSA Joan 1899-1970 **[26]**
- $2 400 - €2 252 - **£1 462** - FF14 775
  Bodegón Oleo/lienzo (73x100cm 28x39in) Madrid
  1999
- $800 - €961 - **£560** - FF6 304
  Marina Oleo/tabla (30x46cm 11x18in) Madrid 2000

SERRA Richard 1939 **[202]**
- $35 000 - €39 203 - **£24 318** - FF257 152
  Untitled Painting (99x192cm 38x75in) New-York 2001
- $140 000 - €155 519 - **£93 758** - FF1 020 138
  Forged Corner (Maastricht) Metal (100x60x10cm
  39x23x3in) New-York 2000
- $40 000 - €43 886 - **£26 572** - FF287 512
  Model for «Three Plate Piece» Sculpture
  (76.5x58cm 30x22in) New-York 2000
- $5 928 - €7 056 - **£4 236** - FF46 283
  Reykjavik Oil chalks (170.2x194.3cm 67x76in) Berlin
  2000
- $3 500 - €2 958 - **£2 087** - FF19 401
  Paris Silkscreen (213.5x132.5cm 84x52in) San-
  Francisco CA 1998

SERRA Rosa 1930 **[30]**
- $4 571 - €4 538 - **£2 856** - FF29 766
  Repos Marble (H23cm H9in) Amsterdam 1999

SERRA SANTA Josep 1916-1998 **[17]**
- $9 180 - €10 211 - **£6 290** - FF66 980
  Paisaje con figuras Oleo/lienzo (130x98cm 51x38in)
  Madrid 2001
- $1 742 - €1 829 - **£1 152** - FF12 000
  Danseuse de flamenco Huile/toile (60x73cm
  23x28in) Paris 2000

SERRA Y AUQUÉ Enrique 1859-1918 **[119]**
- $3 172 - €3 323 - **£2 098** - FF21 800
  Pontinische Sümpfe Öl/Leinwand (43.5x81cm
  17x31in) München 2000
- $2 379 - €2 832 - **£1 700** - FF18 574
  Tivoli Gardens Oil/canvas/board (39.5x26.5cm
  15x10in) London 2000
- $1 080 - €1 227 - **£751** - FF8 049
  Sumpflandschaft in der Römischen Campagna
  Aquarell/Papier (24x40cm 9x15in) Köln 2001

SERRALUNGA Luigi 1880-1940 **[19]**
- $1 500 - €1 555 - **£900** - FF10 200
  Il cappellino rosa Olio/tela/tavola (53x44.5cm
  20x17in) Torino 1999

SERRANO AGUILAR Pablo 1910-1985 **[39]**
- $1 395 - €1 351 - **£855** - FF8 865
  **Entreteniminetos en el prado, Saturno devoran-
  do a su hijo** Bronze (H22cm H8in) Barcelona 1999

SERRANO Andres 1950 **[180]**
- $18 938 - €15 556 - **£11 000** - FF102 040
  Madonna and Child Cibachrome print (151x102cm
  59x40in) London 1998

SERRANO Josep Miquel 1912-1982 **[29]**
- $732 - €721 - **£468** - FF4 728
  Flores Oleo/lienzo (73x60cm 28x23in) Barcelona 1999

SERRANO Santiago 1942 **[9]**
- $2 223 - €2 343 - **£1 482** - FF15 366
  Círculo I Técnica mixta/lienzo (112x83cm 44x32in)
  Madrid 2000

SERRANTA Josep Serra Santa 1916-1998 **[46]**
- $4 480 - €4 805 - **£3 040** - FF31 520
  Llegada a puerto al atardecer Oleo/lienzo
  (46x55cm 18x21in) Barcelona 2001
- $2 600 - €2 403 - **£1 560** - FF15 760
  Pescadores en una playa Oleo/lienzo (33x41cm
  12x16in) Barcelona 1999

SERRE Georges 1889-1956 **[6]**
🖎 **$414** - €457 - **£287** - FF3 000
    Masque de femme voilée Grès (25x17cm 9x6in)
    Paris 2001

SERRES Antony 1828-1898 **[19]**
😊 **$1 670** - €1 753 - **£1 107** - FF11 500
    Cavalier turc Huile/panneau (46x37cm 18x14in)
    Ourville-en-Caux 2000
😊 **$771** - €915 - **£561** - FF6 000
    La famille éplorée Huile/toile (35x26.5cm 13x10in)
    Lyon 2001

SERRES Dominic 1722-1793 **[45]**
😊 **$46 521** - €46 879 - **£29 000** - FF307 504
    **H.M.S Victory, the Command of Vice Admiral Sir
    Samuel Hood** Oil/canvas (86x143.5cm 33x56in)
    London 2000
😊 **$22 414** - €24 060 - **£15 000** - FF157 824
    **Destruction of the Spanish Floating batteries at
    Gibraltar at Night** Oil/canvas (68x121cm 26x47in)
    London 2000
😊 **$6 561** - €6 421 - **£4 200** - FF42 120
    **A first Rate off the Coast/A First Rate at Anchor
    in a Bay** Oil/copper (15x18cm 5x7in) London 1999
✏ **$2 456** - €2 246 - **£1 500** - FF14 734
    Dutch sail boats and other shipping Ink
    (18x28cm 7x11in) London 1998

SERRES Dominic M. act.c.1778-c.1804 **[5]**
✏ **$2 607** - €3 025 - **£1 800** - FF19 843
    View near Plymouth Watercolour (37x54.5cm
    14x21in) London 2000

SERRES John Thomas 1759-1825 **[65]**
😊 **$19 253** - €19 818 - **£12 129** - FF130 000
    **Vue du port de Leghorn animé de nombreux
    personnages** Huile/toile (115x150cm 45x59in) Paris
    2000
😊 **$10 481** - €10 987 - **£7 000** - FF72 068
    **The River Mersey at Liverpool from the
    Wallasey Shoreline** Oil/canvas (61x86.5cm 24x34in)
    London 2001
😊 **$7 210** - €7 968 - **£5 000** - FF52 265
    Ship of the Line at Anchor off the Coast
    Oil/panel (21x36cm 8x14in) London 2001
✏ **$1 935** - €1 900 - **£1 200** - FF12 463
    Shipping off Liverpool Watercolour (36.5x53cm
    14x20in) London 1999

SERRI Alfredo 1897-1972 **[12]**
😊 **$1 526** - €1 687 - **£1 059** - FF11 067
    Früchtestilleben Öl/Leinwand (41x60cm 16x23in)
    München 2001

SERRIER Jean-Pierre 1934-1989 **[12]**
😊 **$450** - €430 - **£277** - FF2 819
    Circus Scene Oil/canvas (73x91cm 29x36in)
    Cincinnati OH 1999

SERRITELLI Giovanni 1810-1860 **[21]**
😊 **$36 000** - €42 335 - **£25 812** - FF277 700
    Day at the Market, Naples Oil/canvas (166.5x117cm
    65x46in) New-York 2001
😊 **$25 000** - €25 916 - **£15 000** - FF170 000
    Veduta del golfo di Napoli da Posillipo Olio/tela
    (57x89cm 22x35in) Milano 1999

SERRURE Auguste 1825-1903 **[52]**
😊 **$8 548** - €9 938 - **£6 000** - FF65 186
    The Garden Party Oil/panel (60.5x78cm 23x30in)
    London 2001
😊 **$3 378** - €3 176 - **£2 045** - FF20 836
    Jester Courting a Lady in a Forest Oil/panel
    (27x35cm 10x13in) Amsterdam 1999

SERRURE Berthe 1891-1985 **[16]**
✏ **$520** - €496 - **£316** - FF3 252
    Chrysanthèmes Pastel/papier (63x53cm 24x20in)
    Bruxelles 1999

SERRUYS Yvonne, Mme Mille 1874-1953 **[11]**
😊 **$8 480** - €7 932 - **£5 152** - FF52 032
    Jardin ensoleillé Oil/canvas (47.5x61cm 18x24in)
    Lokeren 1999
😊 **$3 766** - €3 470 - **£2 268** - FF22 764
    Femme près d'une fermette dans un paysage
    Huile/toile (30x50cm 11x19in) Antwerpen 1999

SERT Henri 1938-1964 **[44]**
😊 **$613** - €618 - **£382** - FF4 053
    Visage Oil/canvas (81x65cm 31x25in) Köbenhavn
    2000

SERT Y BADIA José Maria 1876-1945 **[31]**
😊 **$2 465** - €2 553 - **£1 530** - FF16 745
    Boceto de la alegoria al trabajo Oleo/lienzo
    (60x70cm 23x27in) Madrid 2001
✏ **$1 817** - €1 753 - **£1 148** - FF11 500
    La réception Pastel (81x102cm 31x40in) Paris 1999

SÉRUSIER Marguerite Gabrielle 1879-1950 **[171]**
😊 **$3 996** - €3 659 - **£2 424** - FF24 000
    La marchande de bonbons Huile/toile (46x38cm
    18x14in) Douarnenez 2000
✏ **$468** - €457 - **£298** - FF3 000
    Canal de Châteauneuf Pastel/papier (20x36cm
    7x14in) Paris 1999

SÉRUSIER Paul 1864-1927 **[362]**
😊 **$35 000** - €33 132 - **£21 738** - FF217 332
    Jeune bretonne ou la petite tricoteuse Oil/canvas
    (55x46cm 21x18in) New-York 1999
😊 **$8 796** - €9 223 - **£5 511** - FF60 500
    Les fougères rouge Huile/carton (23x32cm 9x12in)
    Paris 2000
✏ **$1 530** - €1 296 - **£919** - FF8 500
    Paysanne Encre Chine/papier (17.5x11cm 6x4in) Paris
    1998
📰 **$391** - €366 - **£242** - FF2 400
    Hereclea Lithographie (30x48cm 11x18in) Quimper
    1999

SERVAES Albert 1883-1966 **[155]**
😊 **$5 274** - €4 459 - **£3 159** - FF29 250
    Clair de lune Huile/toile (35x53cm 13x20in)
    Antwerpen 1999
✏ **$2 552** - €2 727 - **£1 738** - FF17 886
    Christus mer doornenkroon Fusain/papier
    (76x60cm 29x23in) Lokeren 2000

SERVAIS Géo XX [1]
✏ **$2 520** - €2 424 - **£1 560** - FF15 900
    Nude Mixed media/paper (50.5x41cm 19x16in)
    Budapest 1999

SERVAIS Jean-Claude 1956 **[5]**
✏ **$654** - €686 - **£414** - FF4 500
    La belle Coquetière, couverture Encre
    Chine/papier (30x20cm 11x7in) Paris 2000

SERVANDONI Giovanni Nic., Jean 1695-1766 **[11]**
😊 **$7 512** - €8 721 - **£5 280** - FF57 204
    **Antike Ruinen mit der Cestiuspyramide und
    Figuren** Öl/Leinwand (72x56cm 28x22in) Wien 2001
😊 **$2 840** - €3 049 - **£1 900** - FF20 000
    Trois personnages dans des ruines romaines
    Huile/panneau (20x15cm 7x5in) Paris 2000
✏ **$3 223** - €3 201 - **£2 016** - FF21 000
    **Paysage fluviaux: Hercule Farnese/bergers et
    troupeau/villageois** Gouache/papier (37x55cm
    14x21in) Paris 1999

S

SERVANT André 1842-? **[3]**
$10 244 - €9 909 - **£6 318** - FF65 000
Jeune Marocaine aux boucles d'oreilles
Huile/toile (46x38cm 18x14in) Paris 1999

SERVIN Amédée Elie 1829-1885/86 **[15]**
$5 807 - €5 946 - **£3 646** - FF39 000
Jeune femme à côté d'un arbre fruitier Huile/toile (76x64cm 29x25in) Paris 2000

SERVRANCKX Victor 1897-1965 **[86]**
$53 284 - €49 916 - **£32 032** - FF327 426
Peinture 23-3 Oil/canvas (39.5x70cm 15x27in)
Amsterdam 1999
$8 019 - €6 693 - **£4 698** - FF43 902
Opus 1 Plaster (41x29cm 16x11in) Lokeren 1998
$288 - €322 - **£200** - FF2 113
Composition Dessin (27x20cm 10x7in) Antwerpen 2001

SERWOUTERS van Pieter 1586-1657 **[3]**
$209 - €230 - **£142** - FF1 509
Die Fuchsjagd, after David Vinckboons Etching (10.3x27.7cm 4x10in) Berlin 2000

SESSA Aldo 1939 **[9]**
$1 800 - €1 693 - **£1 114** - FF11 103
Pears Gelatin silver print (48x57cm 18x22in) New-York 1999

SESSIONS James Milton 1882-1962 **[55]**
$1 200 - €1 338 - **£783** - FF8 777
World War II Military Scene at Pacific Shoreline
Watercolour/paper (61x86cm 24x34in) St. Louis MO 2000

SESSLER Alfred 1909-1963 **[1]**
$5 000 - €5 687 - **£3 467** - FF37 301
Snow Shovelers Oil/board (21x17cm 8x7in)
Cincinnati OH 2000

SETELIK Jaroslav 1881-1955 **[35]**
$2 312 - €2 187 - **£1 440** - FF14 344
Blick auf Prag Öl/Leinwand (71x101cm 27x39in)
Praha 2000
$346 - €328 - **£216** - FF2 151
Karlsbrücke Aquarell/Papier (35x27cm 13x10in)
Praha 1999

SETHER Gulbrand 1869-1910 **[31]**
$600 - €653 - **£412** - FF4 283
Pastoral Landscape of Path Beside a Meandering Stream Oil/canvas (50x76cm 20x30in)
St. Petersburg FL 2001
$260 - €291 - **£180** - FF1 910
Snow Scene with Birds in Distance
Watercolour/paper (34x18cm 13x7in) Cincinnati OH 2001

SETKOWICZ Adam 1876-1945 **[79]**
$1 852 - €2 070 - **£1 256** - FF13 577
Gardeuse d'oies Huile/toile (35x54cm 13x21in)
Warszawa 2000
$1 128 - €1 327 - **£809** - FF8 705
Motif de campagne au poulain Huile/carton (30x47cm 11x18in) Warszawa 2001
$606 - €689 - **£420** - FF4 521
Traîneaux en hiver Aquarelle/papier (16.5x31cm 6x12in) Lódz 2001

SETON Charles C. XIX-XX **[1]**
$13 588 - €13 469 - **£8 500** - FF88 349
And Then, The Lover Sighting Like Furnace, with a Woeful Ballad Oil/canvas (70x91cm 27x35in)
London 1999

SETON John Thomas XVIII-XIX **[15]**
$1 463 - €1 351 - **£900** - FF8 861
Portrait of Lady Huntley, in a blue Dress and red ermine-trimmed shawl Oil/canvas (76.5x65cm 30x25in) London 1999

SETON-KARR Heywood Walter 1859-? **[1]**
$1 753 - €1 843 - **£1 100** - FF12 088
The Gates of Jerusalem/The Jaffa Gate/The Golden Gate Watercolour (14x22.5cm 5x8in) London 2000

SETTEGAST Joseph Anton Nikolau 1813-1890 **[4]**
$2 390 - €2 812 - **£1 687** - FF18 445
Maria mit dem Christuskind vor weiter Gebirgslandschaft Öl/Leinwand/Karton (22x22cm 8x8in) Köln 2001

SETTI Ercole 1530-1617 **[5]**
$1 105 - €1 239 - **£750** - FF8 129
The Lamentation Ink (26x18.5cm 10x7in) London 2000

SETTLE William Frederick 1821-1897 **[30]**
$11 539 - €13 562 - **£8 000** - FF88 960
Men of War and other Shipping moored in a Calm Sea Oil/wood (15x22cm 6x9in) Lewes, Sussex 2000
$937 - €1 036 - **£650** - FF6 796
Shipping in a Calm/Shipping in Choppy Seas
Watercolour (22.5x33cm 8x12in) London 2001

SEUPEL Johann Friedrich XVIII **[2]**
$525 000 - €489 538 - **£325 657** - FF3 211 162
An Ocelot with a Parrot Oil/canvas (102x122cm 40x48in) New-York 1999

SEUPHOR Michel F.Berckelaers 1901-1999 **[97]**
$975 - €823 - **£572** - FF5 397
«Silence habité IV» Pencil (67x51cm 26x20in) Berlin 1998
$1 188 - €992 - **£696** - FF6 504
Spectacle à bâtons Tapestry (230x160cm 90x62in)
Lokeren 1998

SEURAT Georges 1859-1891 **[65]**
$1 000 000 - €1 103 258 - **£661 400** - FF7 236 900
La Haie, La clairière Oil/canvas (38.5x46.5cm 15x18in) New-York 1999
$1 444 520 - €1 540 165 - **£980 000** - FF10 102 820
Femmes assises, dimanche après-midi à l'île de la Grande Jatte Oil/panel (15.5x25cm 6x9in) London 2001
$26 000 - €26 200 - **£16 208** - FF171 860
Frileuse, tête de profil Charcoal/paper (47x30.5cm 18x12in) New-York 2000

SEUTTER Georg Matthäus 1678-1757 **[29]**
$502 - €590 - **£360** - FF3 873
Amsterdam Engraving (50x58cm 19x22in) Swindon, Wiltshire 2001

SEVAGIN Dmitri 1974 **[12]**
$915 - €901 - **£570** - FF5 910
En la tarraza, copia de Sir Lawrence Alma-Tadema Oleo/lienzo (33x66cm 12x25in) Madrid 1999

SEVELINGE Emile XIX-XX **[4]**
$800 - €892 - **£523** - FF5 854
«American Sterling Cycles» Poster (63x42cm 24x16in) New-York 2000

SÉVELLEC Jim E. 1897-1971 **[84]**
$1 137 - €1 220 - **£752** - FF8 000
Bord de mer en presqu'île de Crozon Huile/toile (60x92cm 23x36in) Douarnenez 2000

  $1 520 – €1 601 – **£1 003** – FF10 500
Cinq personnages en goguette Céramique (H25cm H9in) Douarnenez 2000

  $587 – €640 – **£385** – FF4 200
Après la pêche Aquarelle/papier (24x29cm 9x11in) Brest 2000

SEVEN-SEVEN Twins 1944 [13]

  $981 – €1 141 – **£700** – FF7 486
Ghost in the Pigmy Jungle, Where the Hunters were Murdered Ink (167x64cm 66x25in) London 2000

  $560 – €652 – **£400** – FF4 277
Untitled Etching (41x34cm 16x13in) London 2000

SEVERDONCK van Franz 1809-1889 [224]

  $6 432 – €5 949 – **£4 008** – FF39 024
Schapen in landschap Oil/panel (52x72cm 20x28in) Lokeren 2000

  $3 000 – €2 717 – **£1 836** – FF17 825
Banyard Animals Oil/panel (22x30cm 9x12in) Portland ME 1998

SEVERDONCK van Joseph 1819-1905 [28]

  $13 200 – €12 394 – **£8 150** – FF81 300
Le campement de l'Armée Huile/toile (240x142cm 94x55in) Bruxelles 1999

  $1 887 – €2 107 – **£1 317** – FF13 821
Portrait de gentilhomme à la badine Huile/toile (95x77cm 37x30in) Bruxelles 2001

  $1 200 – €1 114 – **£720** – FF7 305
Sheep, Ducks and Chickens in a Landscape Oil/panel (16x25cm 6x10in) Milford CT 1999

  $540 – €595 – **£342** – FF3 902
Stoeterij (Haras) Aquarelle/papier (42x31cm 16x12in) Antwerpen 2000

SEVEREN van Dan 1927 [38]

  $1 665 – €1 859 – **£1 155** – FF12 195
Composition Aquarelle/papier (50x35cm 19x13in) Antwerpen 2001

  $174 – €186 – **£118** – FF1 219
Compositie Lithographie (62x62cm 24x24in) Lokeren 2001

SEVERIN Marc Fernand 1906-1986 [15]

  $10 000 – €9 601 – **£6 172** – FF63 082
«Minerva» Gouache (100.5x73.5cm 39x28in) New-York 1999

SEVERINI Gino 1883-1966 [624]

  $165 270 – €141 206 – **£100 000** – FF926 250
Le printemps Oil/board (155x92.5cm 61x36in) London 1998

  $80 000 – €76 928 – **£49 288** – FF504 616
Natura morta con pesci e mandolino Oil/canvas (53.5x73.5cm 21x28in) New-York 1999

  $16 800 – €14 513 – **£11 200** – FF95 200
Gattino e pesci Olio/tela (33x34cm 12x13in) Roma 1998

  $18 197 – €15 524 – **£10 845** – FF101 832
Giano Bifronte Bronze (H53cm H20in) Zürich 1998

  $4 400 – €5 702 – **£3 300** – FF37 400
Natura morta con chittara, cesto e maschera China/carta (26x34cm 10x13in) Prato 2000

  $1 670 – €1 571 – **£1 034** – FF10 304
Il carnevale Color lithograph (43x59.5cm 16x23in) Stockholm 1999

SEVERN Arthur, Joseph A.P. 1842-1931 [31]

  $774 – €711 – **£480** – FF4 666
Westminster from the Thames Watercolour/paper (18.5x25.5cm 7x10in) London 1999

SEVERN Walter 1830-1904 [11]

  $1 283 – €1 293 – **£800** – FF8 482
Walking-up Grouse Watercolour/paper (48.5x67.5cm 19x26in) London 2000

SEVESO Pompilio 1877-1949 [16]

  $2 400 – €2 488 – **£1 440** – FF16 320
Esterina seduta sulla palizzata Olio/cartone (53.5x39cm 21x15in) Roma 2000

  $480 – €622 – **£360** – FF4 080
Natura morta Olio/tela/cartone (30x40cm 11x15in) Vercelli 2001

SEVESTRE Jules 1834-1901 [3]

  $4 331 – €4 084 – **£2 684** – FF26 789
Nude Smeeling a Flower Oil/canvas (86x106cm 33x41in) Amsterdam 1999

SEVIER Michael 1886-? [2]

  $1 709 – €1 987 – **£1 200** – FF13 037
The Tightrope Walker Watercolour (42x31cm 16x12in) Billingshurst, West-Sussex 2001

SEVILLA ROMERO Y ESCALANTE de Juan 1643-1695 [1]

  $8 320 – €9 610 – **£5 760** – FF63 040
Inmaculada Oleo/lienzo (146x110cm 57x43in) Seville 2000

SEVILLANO ESTREMERA Angel 1942-1994 [23]

  $2 025 – €2 252 – **£1 350** – FF14 775
Moza con flores y ventana Oleo/lienzo (73x50cm 28x19in) Madrid 2001

SEVIN Lucie XX [1]

  $4 425 – €4 618 – **£2 800** – FF30 293
Bather Bronze (H38.5cm H15in) London 2000

SEVIN Pierre Paul 1650-1710/20 [9]

  $1 479 – €1 601 – **£1 013** – FF10 500
Le présentation de la Vierge, d'après Giordano Gouache/papier (23x12.5cm 9x4in) Troyes 2001

SEWELL Robert van Vorst 1860-1924 [9]

  $3 000 – €3 466 – **£2 100** – FF22 734
Nymph Oil/canvas (71x46cm 28x18in) New-York 2001

SEWOHL Waldemar 1887-1967 [72]

  $414 – €434 – **£273** – FF2 850
Stralsund Öl/Karton (39x48cm 15x18in) Satow 2000

SEXTON Frederick Lester 1889-? [26]

  $1 800 – €1 706 – **£1 124** – FF11 192
Farm Scene Oil/canvas (60x91cm 24x36in) Mystic CT 1999

  $1 100 – €997 – **£677** – FF6 539
Blue House on Valley Street Oil/board (30x15cm 12x6in) Mystic CT 1999

SEYBOLD Christian 1697/1703-1768 [8]

  $11 116 – €10 174 – **£6 776** – FF66 738
Bildnis Kaiser Joseph II Öl/Leinwand (95x78.5cm 37x30in) Wien 1999

SEYDEL Eduard Gustav 1822-1881 [18]

  $2 306 – €1 997 – **£1 400** – FF13 098
Fruits of the Harvest Oil/canvas (68x57cm 26x22in) London 1998

SEYFERT XIX [2]

  $4 271 – €3 964 – **£2 563** – FF26 000
Paysage de rivière avec des bergers et leur troupeau Huile/toile (38x61cm 14x24in) Paris 1999

SEYFFERT Heinrich Abel 1768-1834 [4]

  $1 423 – €1 636 – **£1 005** – FF10 732
Frau Elisabeth Kloss, geb.Hartmann Oil chalks/paper (31x25.5cm 12x10in) Bremen 2001

S

SEYKORA Hugo Václav 1793-1856 **[1]**
🖼 **$3 179** - €3 007 - **£1 980** - FF19 723
 Klapy Castle Oil/cardboard (22.8x32.6cm 8x12in)
 Praha 1999

SEYLBERGH van den Jaak 1884-1960 **[46]**
🖼 **$419** - €446 - **£286** - FF2 926
 Marécage in hiver Huile/toile (66x101cm 25x39in)
 Bruxelles 2001
✏ **$579** - €694 - **£397** - FF4 552
 Bloemen (fleurs) Pastel/papier (68x58cm 26x22in)
 Antwerpen 2000

SEYLER Julius 1873-1958 **[434]**
🖼 **$1 428** - €1 534 - **£956** - FF10 061
 **Pflügender Bauer mit Ochsengespann in weiter
 Landschaft** Öl/Leinwand (39.5x61cm 15x24in)
 Kempten 2000
🖼 **$1 303** - €1 125 - **£776** - FF7 377
 Crevettenfischer mit Pferden am Strand
 Öl/Papier (31x41.5cm 12x16in) München 1998
✏ **$817** - €920 - **£563** - FF6 037
 Die Grosse Brücke Mischtechnik/Papier (21x35cm
 8x13in) München 2000

SEYMOUR George L. XIX **[11]**
🖼 **$1 520** - €1 467 - **£900** - FF9 620
 Room for Me Oil/board (27.5x12cm 10x4in) London
 1999

SEYMOUR James c.1702-1752 **[68]**
🖼 **$134 487** - €144 361 - **£90 000** - FF946 944
 **Mr Jolliffe on a Chestnut Hunter with the Hunt
 beyond** Oil/canvas (98.5x123.5cm 38x48in) London
 2000
🖼 **$48 000** - €41 010 - **£28 814** - FF269 011
 **The Duke of Devonshire's Flying Childers, held
 by a Jockey** Oil/canvas (85x87.5cm 33x34in) New-
 York 1998
🖼 **$72 000** - €61 516 - **£43 221** - FF403 516
 **Mr. Martindale's Sedbury with J. Larkin Up at
 Newmarket** Oil/canvas (31.5x35.5cm 12x13in) New-
 York 1998
✏ **$1 990** - €1 731 - **£1 200** - FF11 355
 Study of a Horse and Jockey Black chalk/paper
 (14.5x18.5cm 5x7in) London 1998

SEYMOUR Rev. Mr. XVIII **[1]**
✏ **$3 308** - €3 809 - **£2 257** - FF24 987
 Cloharty Castle/Gowran Abbey Watercolour/paper
 (14x14cm 5x5in) Dublin 2000

SEYMOUR Thomas, Tom XIX **[53]**
🖼 **$940** - €907 - **£580** - FF5 949
 **Rural Scene with Figure Approaching
 Footbridge to Farm House** Oil/canvas (40x60cm
 16x24in) Birmingham 1999

SEYMOUR-HADEN Francis 1818-1910 **[194]**
📜 **$289** - €243 - **£170** - FF1 594
 «**Hampton Court**» Radierung (13.9x21.3cm 5x8in)
 Bern 1998

SEYSSAUD René 1867-1952 **[229]**
🖼 **$5 283** - €4 878 - **£3 289** - FF32 000
 Nature morte aux fruits Huile/toile (37x45cm
 14x17in) Marseille 1999
🖼 **$1 417** - €1 326 - **£877** - FF8 700
 Paysage Huile/carton (15.5x22cm 6x8in) La
 Grand'Combe 1999
✏ **$578** - €644 - **£389** - FF4 227
 Paysage aux oliviers Aquarelle/papier (49x32cm
 19x12in) Genève 1999

SEYSSES Auguste 1862-1946 **[9]**
🗿 **$1 100** - €1 025 - **£664** - FF6 725
 African Elephant and Rider Bronze (32x25cm
 12x10in) Boston MA 1999

SEZANNE Augusto 1856-1935 **[7]**
🖼 **$1 320** - €1 710 - **£990** - FF11 220
 Vaso con fiori Olio/tela (50x37cm 19x14in) Vercelli
 2000
📜 **$269** - €291 - **£186** - FF1 906
 «**V.I.I.Esposizione Internationale D'Arte Della
 Citta di Venezia**» Poster (79x51cm 31x20in) Wien
 2001

SFORNI Gustavo XX **[2]**
🖼 **$6 247** - €6 476 - **£3 748** - FF42 483
 Figura maschile/Fiori Olio/tela (55x42cm 21x16in)
 Milano 1999

SHA FU 1831-1906 **[2]**
✏ **$10 965** - €10 341 - **£6 800** - FF67 830
 Beauties Ink (29.5x36cm 11x14in) Hong-Kong 1999

SHA HUAISHI 1927 **[2]**
✏ **$2 250** - €1 959 - **£1 341** - FF12 852
 Calligraphy in Cao Shu Ink/paper (122x61cm
 48x24in) New-York 1998

SHA QI 1914-1997 **[1]**
🖼 **$18 300** - €20 279 - **£12 660** - FF133 020
 Nude Oil/canvas (36.5x79.5cm 14x31in) Taipei 2001

SHAAR Pinchas 1923-1996 **[54]**
🖼 **$538** - €496 - **£324** - FF3 252
 L'oiseau Huile/toile (75x55cm 29x21in) Antwerpen
 1999

SHACKLETON John ?-1767 **[4]**
🖼 **$134 487** - €144 361 - **£90 000** - FF946 944
 **Gerard Anne Edwards (1733-73) holding a pam-
 phlet** Oil/canvas (178.5x119.5cm 70x47in) London
 2000

SHACKLETON Keith 1923 **[42]**
🖼 **$1 284** - €1 498 - **£900** - FF9 823
 Ducks Flying in over a River Oil/masonite
 (61x76cm 24x29in) London 2000
🖼 **$1 881** - €2 065 - **£1 250** - FF13 543
 Redshank Oil/board (33.5x23.5cm 13x9in) London
 2000

SHACKLETON William 1872-1933 **[25]**
🖼 **$11 383** - €13 225 - **£8 000** - FF86 753
 «**Lovers**» Oil/canvas (70x54cm 27x21in) London 2001
🖼 **$1 415** - €1 210 - **£850** - FF7 935
 Angel Fairies Oil/board (24x30cm 9x12in) Little-
 Lane, Ilkley 1998
✏ **$632** - €602 - **£400** - FF3 947
 Malham, North Yorkshire Watercolour (31.5x54.5cm
 12x21in) London 1999

SHADBOLT Jack Leonard 1909-1998 **[145]**
🖼 **$21 091** - €17 863 - **£12 678** - FF117 174
 Breakaway Morning Acrylic/board (152.5x305cm
 60x120in) Vancouver, BC. 1998
🖼 **$4 082** - €3 902 - **£2 558** - FF25 598
 Boats at Dock Acrylic/board (40x79cm 15x31in)
 Vancouver, BC. 1999
✏ **$3 096** - €3 593 - **£2 137** - FF23 568
 Victoria, Old Houses Charcoal/paper (33x43cm
 12x16in) Vancouver, BC. 2000
📜 **$302** - €356 - **£214** - FF2 332
 Views from Hornby Island Lithograph (57x36.5cm
 22x14in) Toronto 2000

SHAGIN Ivan Mikhailovich 1904-1982 **[22]**
📷 **$686** - €818 - **£489** - FF5 366
«Lazarett auf Berliner Strasse» Photograph
(17.7x28.4cm 6x11in) München 2000

SHAHN Ben 1898-1969 **[216]**
🖌 **$11 000** - €12 131 - **£7 449** - FF79 575
Man Asleep Mixed media (15x43cm 5x16in) New-York 2000
🖊 **$3 500** - €3 830 - **£2 414** - FF25 125
Train Sattion with Car Ink/paper (31x47.5cm 12x18in) New-York 2001
▩ **$650** - €550 - **£389** - FF3 611
Lute and Molecules No. 2 Silkscreen (63.5x99cm 25x38in) San-Francisco CA 1998
📷 **$3 000** - €2 821 - **£1 857** - FF18 506
Sharecropper's Chilren on Sunday, Little Rock, Arkansas Gelatin silver print (19.5x24cm 7x9in) New-York 1999

SHAIKHET Arkady Samoylovich 1898-1959 **[20]**
📷 **$2 000** - €2 087 - **£1 265** - FF13 691
Komsomol Youth at the Wheel Photograph (24x17.5cm 9x6in) New-York 2000

SHALDERS George 1826-1873 **[85]**
🖌 **$3 627** - €3 288 - **£2 200** - FF21 568
The Peaceful Valley Oil/canvas (61x107cm 24x42in) Billinghurst, West-Sussex 1998
🖌 **$981** - €1 028 - **£621** - FF6 745
Coast near Mortehoe, Devon Oil/canvas (31x51cm 12x20in) Malmö 2000
🖊 **$2 308** - €2 092 - **£1 400** - FF13 725
The Shepherds Rest/Sheep Resting in a Landscape Watercolour (16.5x34cm 6x13in) Billinghurst, West-Sussex 1998

SHALOM DE SAFED Shalom Moskowitz 1892-1980 **[11]**
🖊 **$2 400** - €2 343 - **£1 520** - FF15 367
«Israel said to Joseph: Go now, see if it is well with your Brothers» Tempera/paper (47.5x33cm 18x12in) Tel Aviv 1999

SHANE Frederick Emmanuel 1906-1990 **[7]**
🖌 **$1 600** - €1 820 - **£1 109** - FF11 936
Altercation Oil/board (28x23cm 11x9in) Chicago IL 2000

SHANGRUI 1634-c.1720 **[1]**
🖊 **$2 564** - €3 014 - **£1 778** - FF19 768
Landscape Ink (18x53cm 7x20in) Hong-Kong 2000

SHANKS Emiliya Yakovlevna 1857-1936 **[1]**
🖌 **$7 246** - €6 843 - **£4 500** - FF44 885
The Lesson Oil/canvas (62x73.5cm 24x28in) London 1999

SHANKS William Somerville 1864-1951 **[29]**
🖌 **$1 578** - €1 654 - **£1 000** - FF10 852
Woodland Scene Oil/panel (47x48cm 18x18in) Edinburgh 2000

SHANNON Charles 1914-1996 **[1]**
🖌 **$42 000** - €39 163 - **£26 052** - FF256 893
A Montgomery Corner Oil/canvas (81.5x56cm 32x22in) New-York 1999

SHANNON Charles Haslewood 1863-1937 **[53]**
▩ **$194** - €209 - **£130** - FF1 370
The Bath Lithograph (19x18.5cm 7x7in) London 2000

SHANNON Donald XX **[5]**
🖌 **$6 053** - €6 300 - **£3 800** - FF41 324
Summer Storm Melbourne Oil/canvas (65x75cm 25x29in) Melbourne 2000

SHANNON James Jebusa 1862-1923 **[35]**
🖌 **$77 001** - €77 592 - **£48 000** - FF508 972
Mrs Field Montague Oil/canvas (259.5x138cm 102x54in) London 2000
🖌 **$34 000** - €37 970 - **£21 773** - FF249 067
The Silver Ship Oil/canvas (116x76cm 45x29in) New-York 2000

SHANNON Michael David 1927-1993 **[74]**
🖌 **$1 345** - €1 220 - **£816** - FF8 000
Flinders Ranges Oil/canvas (122x122cm 48x48in) Sydney 1998
🖌 **$1 205** - €1 353 - **£835** - FF8 872
The Ice Cream Eaters Oil/canvas (91x91cm 35x35in) Sydney 2000
🖊 **$482** - €455 - **£303** - FF2 984
Cannas Charcoal (82x61cm 32x24in) Sydney 1999

SHAO FEI 1954 **[26]**
🖌 **$3 936** - €4 191 - **£2 496** - FF27 492
Buddhist Oil/canvas (91x122cm 35x48in) Taipei 2000

SHAO YU 1919 **[1]**
🖊 **$1 410** - €1 602 - **£990** - FF10 508
Strolling amongst Willow Trees Ink (139.5x51.5cm 54x20in) Hong-Kong 2001

SHAPIRO David 1916 **[5]**
▩ **$650** - €738 - **£445** - FF4 844
Under the Bridge, No.2 Linocut in colors (28.5x26cm 11x10in) New-York 2000

SHAPIRO Joel 1941 **[130]**
🗿 **$100 000** - €86 275 - **£60 100** - FF565 930
Untitled Bronze (122x170x106.5cm 48x66x41in) New-York 1998
🗿 **$47 500** - €45 649 - **£29 260** - FF299 435
Running Figure Bronze (35.5x25.5x18cm 13x10x7in) New-York 1999
🖊 **$12 000** - €12 092 - **£7 480** - FF79 320
Untitled Charcoal/paper (109x77cm 42x30in) New-York 2000
▩ **$392** - €458 - **£269** - FF3 006
Untitled Etching in colors (98x75cm 38x29in) Stockholm 2000

SHAPIRO Shmuel 1924-1983 **[54]**
🖊 **$280** - €307 - **£190** - FF2 017
Untitled Gouache/Karton (12.5x7.5cm 4x2in) Luzern 2000
▩ **$154** - €149 - **£95** - FF975
Farbkomposition Farblithographie (76.5x56cm 30x22in) Bern 1999

SHAPLAND John 1865-1929 **[150]**
🖊 **$311** - €286 - **£190** - FF1 873
Dawlish, Devon Gouache/paper (27x43cm 11x17in) Aylsham, Norfolk 1998

SHAPLEIGH Frank Henry 1842-1906 **[78]**
🖌 **$9 000** - €9 661 - **£6 022** - FF63 369
View of the Bay of Naples, Italy Oil/canvas (86x152cm 34x60in) East-Dennis MA 2000
🖌 **$7 000** - €5 982 - **£4 111** - FF39 237
«Entrance to Cohasset Harbor» Oil/canvas (35.5x61cm 13x24in) Boston MA 1998
🖌 **$2 100** - €2 293 - **£1 352** - FF15 043
Old Wharves at Cohasset Oil/board (19x31cm 7x12in) Mystic CT 2000
🖊 **$275** - €235 - **£161** - FF1 541
Haying Watercolour/paper (35x25cm 14x10in) Portsmouth NH 1998

S

SHAPOSHNIKOV Boris 1890-1956 **[1]**
🎨 **$6 140** - €7 158 - **£4 303** - FF46 954
Komposition Öl/Karton (70x52cm 27x20in) München 2000

SHARLAND Edward W. XIX-XX **[41]**
📜 **$81** - €75 - **£50** - FF495
Interior York Minster Etching in colors (40x20cm 16x8in) Driffield, East Yorkshire 1999

SHARMA Mahendra 1963 **[4]**
✏ **$3 571** - €3 432 - **£2 200** - FF22 513
Studies of Wild cats Watercolour (68.5x48cm 26x18in) London 1999

SHARMA Ramesh XX **[7]**
✏ **$602** - €677 - **£420** - FF4 442
Loving Couple Gouache (28.5x18.5cm 11x7in) London 2001

SHARP Dorothea 1874-1955 **[285]**
🎨 **$18 309** - €20 633 - **£12 681** - FF135 343
Little Girl in a Flower Garden Oil/canvas (61x46.5cm 24x18in) Toronto 2000
🎨 **$9 865** - €8 421 - **£5 800** - FF55 238
Cassis Oil/board (35x40cm 13x15in) London 1998

SHARP James C. 1818-1897 **[1]**
🎨 **$8 000** - €7 897 - **£4 864** - FF51 800
Trompe l'oeil Still Life Oil/panel (66.5x51.5cm 26x20in) New-York 2000

SHARP Joseph Henry 1859-1953 **[150]**
🎨 **$50 000** - €47 798 - **£31 340** - FF313 535
Leaf Down Oil/canvas (40.5x51cm 15x20in) New-York 1999
🎨 **$32 000** - €27 340 - **£19 209** - FF179 340
Indian Pueblo Children Oil/board (36x23.5cm 14x9in) New-York 1998
✏ **$1 600** - €1 515 - **£996** - FF9 935
Exchanging Thoughts Watercolour/paper (21x28cm 8x11in) Detroit MI 1999

SHARP Louis Hovey 1875-1946 **[7]**
🎨 **$2 600** - €2 809 - **£1 800** - FF18 423
California Garden Oil/canvas (63x76cm 25x30in) Cincinnati OH 2001

SHARP Martin 1942 **[57]**
📜 **$274** - €259 - **£171** - FF1 701
Moratorium/Gypsy Train Lithograph (56x43cm 22x16in) Sydney 1999

SHARP William 1900-1961 **[12]**
📜 **$70** - €81 - **£48** - FF531
Holy Family Leaving Bethlehem Etching, aquatint (17x12cm 7x5in) Cleveland OH 2000

SHARPE Caroline Paterson act.1850-c.1930 **[5]**
✏ **$2 231** - €2 624 - **£1 600** - FF17 213
Little Red Riding Hood Watercolour/paper (25.5x32cm 10x12in) London 2001

SHARPE Charles William ?-1955 **[4]**
✏ **$992** - €1 152 - **£700** - FF7 559
The Ash Tree Watercolour/paper (37.5x27cm 14x10in) London 2001

SHARPE Charles William act.1848-1883 **[8]**
📜 **$82** - €90 - **£57** - FF591
La oficina de correos, según Frederick Goodall Grabado (22x28.5cm 8x11in) Madrid 2001

SHARPE Eliza 1796-1874 **[4]**
✏ **$1 142** - €1 199 - **£720** - FF7 865
Rival Discovered Watercolour (59x43cm 23x16in) London 2000

SHARPLES James I 1751-1811 **[5]**
✏ **$6 000** - €5 197 - **£3 679** - FF34 089
Mr and Mrs Lynde Catlin Pastel/paper (25x20cm 10x8in) New-York 1999

SHARPLES Rolinda 1794-1838 **[4]**
✏ **$1 438** - €1 466 - **£900** - FF9 615
Portraits of a Gentleman Seated Reading a Newspaper and a Lady Seated Pastel/paper (22x16cm 9x6in) Tunbridge-Wells, Kent 2000

SHARROCK Joan 1946 **[12]**
🎨 **$1 141** - €1 331 - **£800** - FF8 728
Cheetahs in Hot Persuit Oil/canvas (54.5x100.5cm 21x39in) London 2000

SHATTUCK Aaron Draper 1832-1928 **[33]**
🎨 **$8 000** - €7 493 - **£4 918** - FF49 152
Wildflowers at the Foot of the Mountain Oil/canvas (66x91.5cm 25x36in) New-York 1999
🎨 **$5 250** - €5 211 - **£3 220** - FF34 185
Woman Resting Oil/board (28x35cm 11x14in) Mystic CT 2000

SHAW Arthur Winter 1869-1948 **[27]**
✏ **$285** - €277 - **£180** - FF1 818
Friday Night Watercolour/paper (25x35cm 10x14in) London 1999

SHAW Byam John Liston 1872-1919 **[62]**
🎨 **$12 850** - €14 618 - **£8 975** - FF95 887
The Regatta Oil/canvas (63x50cm 24x19in) Stockholm 2000
🎨 **$6 633** - €7 330 - **£4 600** - FF48 083
While Roses are so red, while Lilies are so white Oil/panel (40.5x29.5cm 15x11in) London 2001
✏ **$356** - €334 - **£220** - FF7 615
Venus & Mars Ink (31x38cm 12x14in) London 1999

SHAW Charles Green 1892-1974 **[55]**
🎨 **$6 000** - €6 813 - **£4 106** - FF44 690
Seated Nude Oil/canvas (107x76cm 42x29in) New-York 2000
🎨 **$1 000** - €1 160 - **£690** - FF7 611
Polygon Forty-Four Oil/canvas (20x25.5cm 7x10in) New-York 2000

SHAW Charles L. act.c.1880-c.1898 **[13]**
🎨 **$943** - €1 062 - **£650** - FF6 969
Swans in a Wooded River Landscape Oil/canvas (76x63.5cm 29x25in) London 2000
🎨 **$1 284** - €1 380 - **£880** - FF9 049
Mending the Fence Oil/canvas (30x46cm 11x18in) Stansted Mountfitchet, Essex 2001

SHAW Ed XX **[2]**
🎨 **$4 000** - €4 480 - **£2 779** - FF29 388
Smiling Boy and two Scottie Dogs with Alka-Seltzer Oil/canvas (106x63cm 42x25in) New-York 2001

SHAW George 1843-1915 **[14]**
✏ **$239** - €257 - **£160** - FF1 683
Wistman Wood, Dartmoor Oil/canvas (21x50cm 8x19in) Devon 2000

SHAW Hugh George XIX-XX **[3]**
🎨 **$45 000** - €44 678 - **£28 125** - FF293 067
I have a Song to Sing/Sing Me your Song Oil/canvas (35.5x50.5cm 13x19in) New-York 1999

SHAW Jim 1952 **[11]**
✏ **$3 000** - €2 518 - **£1 759** - FF16 519
Horror A Vacui Ink (91.5x91.5cm 36x36in) Beverly-Hills CA 1998

SHAW Lalu Prasad 1937 **[8]**
📝 **$1 978** - €2 186 - **£1 371** - FF14 339
Woman Pencil (33.5x33.5cm 13x13in) Singapore 2001

SHAW Mark XX **[1]**
📷 **$5 500** - €6 333 - **£3 753** - FF41 539
Jackie Swings Caroline in Water, Hyannis Port
Gelatin silver print (33.5x49.5cm 13x19in) New-York
2000

SHAW Richard 1941 **[9]**
🖌 **$1 900** - €1 830 - **£1 188** - FF12 001
Butterfly Jar Ceramic (25.5x18x15cm 10x7x5in)
Beverly-Hills CA 1999

SHAW Sam 1911-1999 **[13]**
📷 **$130** - €137 - **£87** - FF896
Marilyn at the Dressing Table Photograph (7x12cm
3x5in) Cleveland OH 2001

SHAW W. David 1916 **[1]**
📝 **$1 760** - €1 501 - **£1 061** - FF9 849
Crowd of people at country auction Watercolour
(44x40cm 17x16in) New-York 1998

SHAW Walter 1851-1933 **[15]**
🔍 **$400** - €467 - **£278** - FF3 061
Coastal Landscape Oil/canvas (33x71cm 13x28in)
Bloomfield-Hills MI 2000

SHAW William ?-1773 **[5]**
🔍 **$19 000** - €18 864 - **£11 875** - FF123 739
**Two Hunters held by a Huntsman with a Couple
of Hounds in a Landscape** Oil/canvas (103x130cm
40x51in) New-York 1999

SHAWCROSS Neil 1940 **[12]**
🔍 **$2 676** - €2 793 - **£1 693** - FF18 323
Portrait of Gemma Carr Oil/canvas (51x40.5cm
20x15in) Dublin 2000
📝 **$2 588** - €3 047 - **£1 818** - FF19 989
Reclining Nude Watercolour/paper (78.5x96.5cm
30x37in) Dublin 2000

SHAYER Charles Waller 1826-1914 **[38]**
🔍 **$16 612** - €14 216 - **£10 000** - FF93 251
The Timber Wagon Oil/canvas (108x163cm 42x64in)
London 1998
🔍 **$6 823** - €6 639 - **£4 200** - FF43 549
Horseman resting by an Inn in a Landscape
Oil/canvas (61x92cm 24x36in) London 1999
🔍 **$5 746** - €6 450 - **£4 000** - FF42 311
**The Four Seasons: Spring and
Summer/Autumn and Winter** Oil/paper/board
(31x31cm 12x12in) London 2001

SHAYER Henry Thring 1825-1894 **[24]**
🔍 **$16 612** - €14 216 - **£10 000** - FF93 251
The Timber Wagon Oil/canvas (108x163cm 42x64in)
London 1998
🔍 **$26 078** - €23 711 - **£16 000** - FF155 534
The Log Team Resting Oil/canvas (61x92cm
24x36in) London 1999
🔍 **$6 961** - €6 006 - **£4 200** - FF39 399
Visiting the Blacksmith Oil/canvas (30.5x40.5cm
12x15in) London 1998

SHAYER William, Jnr. 1811-1892 **[85]**
🔍 **$5 500** - €4 655 - **£3 292** - FF30 538
Full Cry Oil/canvas (35.5x59cm 13x23in) New-York
1998
🔍 **$8 500** - €9 876 - **£5 974** - FF64 783
Gentleman at rest with his Gun Dogs Oil/canvas
(24x30cm 9x11in) New-York 2001

SHAYER William, Snr. 1788-1879 **[284]**
🔍 **$8 065** - €8 693 - **£5 500** - FF57 020
Travellers on a Costal Path Oil/panel (51x61cm
20x24in) London 2001
🔍 **$2 786** - €3 003 - **£1 900** - FF19 700
A Wayside Conversation Oil/canvas (36x31cm
14x12in) London 2001

SHE (Charles Shepherd) 1892-? **[8]**
📜 **$252** - €295 - **£173** - FF1 934
«Union Castle Line» Poster (99.5x61.5cm 39x24in)
Hoorn 2000

SHEAD Garry 1942 **[131]**
🔍 **$15 984** - €17 852 - **£10 235** - FF117 099
Away Oil/canvas (121.5x167cm 47x65in) Malvern,
Victoria 2000
🔍 **$17 469** - €19 077 - **£11 244** - FF125 136
Odalisque Oil/board (67x87.5cm 26x34in) Melbourne
2000
🔍 **$2 716** - €2 915 - **£1 817** - FF19 124
The Royal Personage Oil/paper (29x22cm 11x8in)
Sydney 2000
📝 **$431** - €512 - **£304** - FF3 357
Half Human, Half Beast Creatures Ink/paper
(27x36cm 10x14in) Sydney 2000
📜 **$312** - €301 - **£193** - FF1 975
Sacred Cow Lithograph (56x76cm 22x29in) Sydney
1999

SHEARER Ben 1941 **[4]**
📝 **$1 157** - €1 092 - **£729** - FF7 161
After the Rain Watercolour/paper (95x146cm
37x57in) Sydney 1999

SHEARER Christopher H. 1840-1926 **[55]**
🔍 **$3 000** - €3 480 - **£2 135** - FF22 829
**Berks County Landscape with Farmhouse in
background** Oil/canvas (91x135cm 36x53in)
Downington PA 2001
🔍 **$1 600** - €1 848 - **£1 120** - FF12 125
Path in the Woods Oil/canvas (91x127cm 36x50in)
Delray-Beach FL 2001
📝 **$300** - €281 - **£185** - FF1 842
Figures Among the Blossom Trees
Watercolour/paper (36x53cm 14x21in) Philadelphia PA
1999

SHEE Martin Archer 1769-1850 **[34]**
🔍 **$42 147** - €48 895 - **£30 000** - FF320 727
**Lady, full-length, in a white Dress with a yellow
silk Sash** Oil/canvas (237.5x146.5cm 93x57in)
London 2001
🔍 **$7 471** - €8 020 - **£5 000** - FF52 608
Portrait of two children Oil/canvas (88x72cm
34x28in) London 2000

SHEELER Charles 1883-1965 **[60]**
🔍 **$340 000** - €376 538 - **£230 588** - FF2 469 930
San Francisco, Fisherman's Wharf Oil/canvas
(80x54.5cm 31x21in) New-York 2000
🔍 **$360 000** - €357 422 - **£225 000** - FF2 344 536
Ballarvale Revisited Tempera/board (38.5x36cm
15x14in) New-York 1998
📝 **$90 000** - €76 779 - **£53 640** - FF503 640
On a Shaker Theme Tempera/paper (19x24cm 7x9in)
New-York 1998
📜 **$16 000** - €18 805 - **£11 092** - FF123 350
Delmonico Building Lithograph (25x17cm 9x6in)
New-York 2000
📷 **$11 000** - €12 262 - **£7 642** - FF80 434
Beech Tree, Shadows Gelatin silver print
(30.5x20.5cm 12x8in) New-York 2001

S

SHEERBOOM Andrew 1832-1880 [20]
☞ **$2 395** - €2 698 - **£1 650** - FF17 696
John of Austria Signing his Abdication at Utracht Holland 1523 Oil/canvas (61x92cm 24x36in) Newbury, Berkshire 2000

SHEETS Millard Owen 1907-1989 [91]
☞ **$7 000** - €8 227 - **£4 853** - FF53 965
Landscape Oil/canvas (46x56cm 18x22in) Beverly-Hills Ca 2000
☞ **$3 000** - €2 563 - **£1 815** - FF16 813
Over the Hill Oil/canvas (35.5x40.5cm 13x15in) San-Francisco CA 1998
✎ **$3 500** - €4 114 - **£2 426** - FF26 986
San Pedro harbor Watercolour/paper (25.5x34cm 10x13in) Beverly-Hills CA 2000
▨ **$4 600** - €5 223 - **£3 148** - FF34 262
Family Flats Lithograph (39.5x55.5cm 15x21in) New-York 2000

SHEETS Nan Jane 1899-1976 [9]
☞ **$5 200** - €6 062 - **£3 600** - FF39 761
Seaside Garden Oil/canvas (50x60cm 20x24in) Watertown MA 2000

SHEFFER Glen C. 1881-1948 [15]
☞ **$900** - €833 - **£550** - FF5 465
Michigan Trail Oil/canvas/board (30x25cm 12x10in) Chicago IL 1999

SHEFFIELD George 1839-1892 [53]
☞ **$10 520** - €9 904 - **£6 500** - FF64 964
The Fishing Fleet at Dusk, possibly in Peel Harbour, Isle of Man Oil/canvas (82.5x127cm 32x50in) London 1999
✎ **$448** - €482 - **£300** - FF3 161
A Shepherd and Sheep on a Track/Sheep Resting Before Relk Castle Pencil (25.5x39cm 10x15in) London 2000

SHEFFIELD Isaac 1798-1845 [1]
☞ **$19 000** - €18 825 - **£11 527** - FF123 484
Portrait of the Ship's Captain of the American Vessel «Eleanor» Oil/canvas (94x70cm 37x27in) New-York 2000

SHEIKH Gulam Mohammed 1937 [4]
☞ **$17 000** - €19 334 - **£11 877** - FF126 821
Choice of Birth Oil/canvas (165x213.5cm 64x84in) New-York 2000

SHEINKMAN Mark 1963 [5]
✎ **$1 600** - €1 784 - **£1 075** - FF11 703
Untitled Graphite (35.5x28cm 13x11in) New-York 2000

SHELDON Charles 1889-1961 [4]
✎ **$6 000** - €6 720 - **£4 168** - FF44 083
Standing young Woman wearing red Hat, Dog looking on admiringly Pastel/paper (61x35cm 24x14in) New-York 2001

SHELESNYAK Henri 1938-1980 [5]
☞ **$5 500** - €6 720 - **£3 793** - FF43 131
Untitled Mixed media (154x58.5cm 60x23in) Tel Aviv 2000
✎ **$3 400** - €3 609 - **£2 300** - FF23 674
Figures Collage (54.5x82cm 21x32in) Tel Aviv 2001

SHELLEY John XIX [2]
☞ **$3 469** - €4 040 - **£2 400** - FF26 503
Church Row Oil/board (91.5x122cm 36x48in) London 2000

SHELLEY Samuel 1750/56-1808 [67]
☞ **$6 397** - €6 198 - **£4 025** - FF40 655
Young Girl, in loose white shift, yellow cloak Miniature (9x6.5cm 3x2in) London 1999

SHELTON Margaret D. 1915-1984 [257]
✎ **$413** - €391 - **£257** - FF2 568
Rosedale and Robin Hood Hill Pastel/paper (33x42cm 12x16in) Calgary, Alberta 1999
▨ **$211** - €247 - **£149** - FF1 620
«Rural Mail Route» Linocut (19x26cm 7x10in) Calgary, Alberta 2000

SHELTON Peter T. 1951 [3]
🖎 **$12 000** - €13 647 - **£8 384** - FF89 521
«Eightsheader» Bronze (148.5x28x11.5cm 58x11x4in) Beverly-Hills CA 2000

SHELTON William Henry 1840-1932 [3]
✎ **$1 900** - €1 623 - **£1 149** - FF10 648
«Friendly Troops»/«The Army at Harrison Landing, James River» Gouache/paper (49x46.5cm 19x18in) San-Francisco CA 1998

SHEMI Calman XX [12]
▨ **$1 100** - €1 181 - **£736** - FF7 745
Composition Tapestry (203x182cm 80x72in) Chicago IL 2000

SHEMI Menachem Schmidt 1897-1951 [37]
☞ **$21 000** - €20 755 - **£12 852** - FF136 145
View of Haifa Gulf Oil/canvas (64.5x92.5cm 25x36in) Tel Aviv 2000
☞ **$28 000** - €31 513 - **£19 289** - FF206 715
Safed Oil/canvas (28x35cm 11x13in) Herzelia-Pituah 2000

SHEMI Yehiel 1922 [40]
☞ **$7 000** - €8 369 - **£4 828** - FF54 894
Composition Oil/canvas (150x150cm 59x59in) Tel Aviv 2000
🖎 **$26 000** - €29 351 - **£18 109** - FF192 530
The guard Iron (H184cm H72in) Tel Aviv 2001
🖎 **$13 000** - €14 676 - **£9 054** - FF96 265
Owl Iron (H53.5cm H21in) Tel Aviv 2001

SHEN BINGCHENG 1823-1895 [1]
✎ **$1 935** - €1 825 - **£1 200** - FF11 970
Calligraphy in Li Shu Ink/paper (45.5x176cm 17x69in) Hong-Kong 1999

SHEN DAOHONG 1947 [5]
✎ **$8 333** - €9 466 - **£5 850** - FF62 094
Sound of the Flute Ink (73x180cm 28x70in) Hong-Kong 2001

SHEN DU 1357-1434 [1]
✎ **$19 260** - €21 136 - **£12 405** - FF138 645
Calligraphy in Standard Script Ink/paper (10.5x7.5cm 4x2in) Hong-Kong 2000

SHEN HAO 1586-c.1661 [4]
✎ **$41 088** - €44 866 - **£26 432** - FF294 304
Landscape after Masters from the Song, Yuan and Ming Dynasties Ink (29.5x24cm 11x9in) Hong-Kong 2000

SHEN MINGQUAN 1947 [2]
✎ **$6 455** - €5 452 - **£3 875** - FF35 765
Landscape inspired by Zhu Xi's Poetry Coloured inks/paper (137.5x68.5cm 54x26in) Hong-Kong 1998

SHEN QUAN 1682-c.1762 [12]
✎ **$14 800** - €14 045 - **£8 993** - FF92 126
Ducks Playing in a Pond Ink (138x81.5cm 54x32in) Hong-Kong 1999

SHEN XIAO-TONG 1968 **[5]**
🖎 **$2 624** - €2 794 - **£1 664** - FF18 328
Temptation - 8 Oil/canvas (60x100cm 23x39in) Taipei 2000

SHEN YINMO 1887-1971 **[7]**
🖎 **$2 820** - €2 391 - **£1 686** - FF15 686
Calligraphy in Kai Shu Ink/paper (20.5x60cm 8x23in) Hong-Kong 1998

SHEN ZENGZHI 1850-1922 **[6]**
🖎 **$3 217** - €3 051 - **£1 957** - FF20 015
Calligraphy Couplet in Xing Shu Ink/paper (131x33cm 51x12in) Hong-Kong 1999

SHEN ZHOU 1427-1509 **[31]**
🖎 **$65 016** - €61 314 - **£40 320** - FF402 192
Boating in Autumn River Ink/paper (106x58.5cm 41x23in) Hong-Kong 1999

SHEPARD Ernest Howard 1879-1976 **[181]**
🖎 **$156 937** - €182 957 - **£110 000** - FF1 200 122
Winnie-the Pooh and the Honey Pot Oil/board (93x71cm 36x27in) London 2000
🖎 **$1 976** - €1 837 - **£7 000** - FF12 051
«The Children of one Tree Pouring Through the Gap» Ink (24x16.5cm 9x6in) London 1998

SHEPHARD Rupert 1909-1992 **[17]**
🖎 **$1 470** - €1 524 - **£931** - FF9 999
Early Evening Chatter Oil/canvas (68x54cm 26x21in) Johannesburg 2000

SHEPHERD David 1931 **[375]**
🖎 **$13 022** - €14 063 - **£9 000** - FF92 249
Studies of Zebra and Giraffe Oil/canvas (59x89.5cm 23x35in) London 2001
🖎 **$9 986** - €11 643 - **£7 000** - FF76 371
Tiger Study Oil/canvas (17x24.5cm 6x9in) London 2000
🖎 **$2 127** - €2 444 - **£1 472** - FF16 032
Rhinoceros Grazing Pencil/paper (20x30cm 8x12in) Hamilton, Lanarkshire 2000
📠 **$208** - €210 - **£130** - FF1 378
Cool Cats Color lithograph (22.5x40cm 8x15in) London 2000

SHEPHERD Frederick Napoleon 1819-1878 **[4]**
🖎 **$2 689** - €2 887 - **£1 800** - FF18 938
Ryde and the Pier From The Parade Watercolour (19.5x28.5cm 7x11in) London 2000

SHEPHERD George Sidney 1784-1862 **[64]**
🖎 **$6 315** - €7 112 - **£4 400** - FF46 652
Numerous Figures with Horsedrawn Carriage in Fleet Street Oil/canvas (63x90cm 24x35in) Newbury, Berkshire 2001
🖎 **$2 185** - €2 052 - **£1 350** - FF13 457
A Prospect of a Country House in a Highland Park Landscape Watercolour (35.5x56.5cm 13x22in) Billinghurst, West-Sussex 1999

SHEPHERD Thomas Hosmer 1793-1864 **[25]**
🖎 **$645** - €532 - **£380** - FF3 489
Street Scene Watercolour/paper (14.5x21cm 5x8in) Newbury, Berkshire 1998

SHEPPARD Charlotte Lilian ?-1925 **[2]**
🖎 **$6 500** - €6 977 - **£4 349** - FF45 766
Her New Pup Oil/canvas (63x45cm 25x18in) Portland ME 2000

SHEPPARD J. Warren 1882-1943 **[2]**
🖎 **$3 900** - €3 697 - **£2 436** - FF24 250
View of Houses on a Venetian Canal Oil/board (40.5x66cm 15x25in) Washington 1999

🖎 **$3 100** - €2 939 - **£1 936** - FF19 276
View of San Giorgio Maggiore, Venice Oil/canvas (43x35.5cm 16x13in) Washington 1999

SHEPPARD Peter Chapman 1882-1965 **[14]**
🖎 **$776** - €834 - **£533** - FF5 470
Studies of Villages, Rural Landscapes, Ships in Port Graphite (18x12cm 7x4in) Toronto 2001

SHEPPARD Warren W. 1858-1937 **[75]**
🖎 **$4 500** - €5 118 - **£3 144** - FF33 570
Breaking waves Oil/canvas (55x91cm 22x36in) New-York 2000
🖎 **$2 000** - €2 147 - **£1 362** - FF14 083
Venetian Canal Oil/canvas (30.5x46cm 12x18in) Boston MA 2001

SHER-GIL Amrita 1913-1941 **[2]**
🖎 **$65 000** - €76 804 - **£46 065** - FF503 802
Landscape, View from Majitha House Oil/canvas (22x33cm 8x12in) New-York 2000

SHERIDAN Clare 1885-1970 **[4]**
🖎 **$6 500** - €5 645 - **£3 821** - FF35 812
Bust of a robed female in a sweeping cap Bronze (76x71cm 30x28in) Cleveland OH 1998

SHERINGHAM George 1884-1937 **[29]**
🖎 **$475** - €437 - **£293** - FF2 867
«After Chardin» Oil/wood (32.5x40.5cm 12x15in) Melbourne 1998
🖎 **$313** - €364 - **£220** - FF2 385
Commedia del arte figures Pastel/paper (31x35cm 12x14in) Lewes, Sussex 2001

SHERLOCK Marjorie 1897-1973 **[16]**
🖎 **$2 008** - €1 734 - **£1 200** - FF11 374
Cottage Garden Oil/canvas (40.5x69cm 15x27in) London 1998

SHERLOCK William 1813-? **[2]**
📷 **$2 590** - €2 902 - **£1 800** - FF19 033
Boy peeling Turnips Salt print (26x22cm 10x8in) London 2001

SHERLOCK William P. 1780-c.1850 **[14]**
🖎 **$1 900** - €1 991 - **£1 203** - FF13 060
Leading the Cattle Home Oil/canvas (76x127cm 30x50in) New-Orleans LA 2000

SHERMAN Albert John 1882-1971 **[106]**
🖎 **$2 914** - €2 740 - **£1 804** - FF17 973
Still Life with Figurine Oil/canvas (56.5x63.5cm 22x25in) Melbourne 1999
🖎 **$673** - €793 - **£473** - FF5 203
Primroses & Forget-me-knots in a Vase Oil/canvas/board (29x23cm 11x9in) Sydney 2000

SHERMAN Cindy 1954 **[504]**
📷 **$14 390** - €13 461 - **£8 700** - FF88 300
Untitled Film Still #51 Photograph (25x20.5cm 9x8in) Köbenhavn 1999

SHERMAN Kathryn XX **[24]**
🖎 **$128** - €108 - **£75** - FF709
Cheerful Cottage Watercolour/paper (20x27cm 8x11in) Calgary, Alberta 1999

SHERRIFFS Robert Stewart 1906-1960 **[4]**
🖎 **$1 167** - €1 254 - **£800** - FF8 226
Winston Churchill: How Absurd!, Duke of Marlborough: Me Too! Ink (37x26cm 14x10in) London 2001

S

SHERRIN Daniel, Dan 1868-1940 **[345]**
- $5 548 - €5 268 - £3 400 - FF34 555
  Landscape with Gypsie Resting close to a Stand of Scots Pine Trees Oil/canvas (106x167cm 42x66in) Leominster, Herefordshire 1999
- $1 387 - €1 318 - £850 - FF8 643
  A Highland Loch Landscape at Sunset Oil/canvas (51x76.5cm 20x30in) London 1999
- $536 - €519 - £340 - FF3 405
  Couple on a Valley Path, at Sunset Oil/canvas (41x30.5cm 16x12in) London 1999
- $429 - €427 - £260 - FF2 801
  Coastal Views Watercolour (25x72.5cm 9x28in) London 2000

SHERRIN John 1819-1896 **[49]**
- $1 502 - €1 262 - £880 - FF8 278
  Still Life of Plums and Greengages on a Mossy Bank Watercolour, gouache/paper (28.5x39cm 11x15in) Billingshurst, West-Sussex 1998

SHERRIN Reginald Daniel 1891-1971 **[82]**
- $260 - €281 - £180 - FF1 845
  Near Postbridge, Dartmoor Gouache/paper (20x30cm 8x12in) Bristol, Avon 1999

SHERWAN Earl XX **[1]**
- $1 400 - €1 632 - £969 - FF10 705
  Woman Falling Into Pit Gouache/paper (33x21cm 13x8in) New-York 2000

SHERWIN Frank 1896-? **[35]**
- $1 471 - €1 414 - £900 - FF9 275
  «Ilkley, British Railways, North Eastern Region» Poster (102x64cm 40x25in) London 1999

SHERWIN John Keyse 1751-1790 **[10]**
- $135 - €144 - £90 - FF945
  Installation Dinner at the Institution of Order of St.Patrick Engraving (62x82cm 24x32in) Leyburn, North Yorkshire 1999

SHEVCHENKO Aleksander V. 1883-1943 **[10]**
- $11 363 - €10 920 - £7 000 - FF71 633
  Still Life with Wine Bottle and Tray Oil/canvas (84x68cm 33x26in) London 1999

SHI DAWAI 1950 **[4]**
- $5 384 - €6 117 - £3 780 - FF40 122
  Journey to the West Ink (68.5x119.5cm 26x47in) Hong-Kong 2001

SHI LU 1919-1982 **[50]**
- $15 384 - €18 296 - £10 596 - FF120 012
  Snake Charmer Ink (53x37.5cm 20x14in) Hong-Kong 2000

SHI WENGUN XVII **[1]**
- $8 901 - €8 394 - £5 520 - FF55 062
  Ladies with Peaches of Longevity Ink (144x53cm 56x20in) Hong-Kong 1999

SHIELDS Alan 1944 **[21]**
- $1 600 - €1 356 - £956 - FF8 893
  Odd-Job/Bull-Pen Woodcut (106.5x106.5cm 41x41in) New-York 1998

SHIELDS Frederick James 1833-1911 **[21]**
- $1 727 - €1 934 - £1 200 - FF12 688
  Design for two stained glass Windows, Eaton Hall, depicting two saints Watercolour (23x16.5cm 9x6in) London 2001

SHIELS William 1785-1857 **[8]**
- $7 308 - €8 148 - £5 000 - FF53 448
  Fishermans Cottage, Musselburgh Oil/canvas (76x92cm 29x36in) Perthshire 2000

SHIGEMASA Kitao 1739-1820 **[12]**
- $264 - €307 - £182 - FF2 012
  Darstellung der Tenjin-Gottheit Sugawara no Michizane Woodcut in colors (34x14.5cm 13x5in) Stuttgart 2000

SHIKLER Aaron 1922 **[26]**
- $8 000 - €9 380 - £5 755 - FF61 528
  Sleeping Woman Pastel (20.5x35.5cm 8x13in) New-York 2001

SHILAKOE Cyprian Mpho 1946-1972 **[7]**
- $229 - €256 - £149 - FF1 681
  Don't Lose Hope Etching (30x20cm 11x7in) Johannesburg 2000

SHILDER Andreij Nikolaevitch 1861-1919 **[3]**
- $10 759 - €11 549 - £7 200 - FF75 755
  Winter Sunlight in he evergreen Forest Oil/canvas (80.5x115cm 31x45in) London 2000

SHILLAM Kathleen 1916 **[3]**
- $3 394 - €3 839 - £2 388 - FF25 182
  Tortoise emerging from a Shell Bronze (20x19cm 7x7in) Melbourne 2001

SHILLING Arthur 1941-1986 **[45]**
- $2 502 - €2 431 - £1 564 - FF15 946
  Happy Children Oil/canvas (62x93cm 24x36in) Toronto 1999

SHIMAMOTO Shozo 1928 **[5]**
- $12 500 - €12 958 - £7 500 - FF85 000
  Senza titolo Olio/tela (168x155.5cm 66x61in) Prato 2000
- $4 140 - €3 576 - £2 760 - FF23 460
  Senza titolo Tecnica mista/carta (77x54cm 30x21in) Milano 1998

SHIMAOKA Tatsuzo 1919 **[7]**
- $2 800 - €3 126 - £1 871 - FF20 506
  Untitled Ceramic (H18cm H7in) New-York 2000

SHINBI Tanaka 1875-1975 **[3]**
- $60 000 - €61 763 - £37 818 - FF405 138
  Replica of the Chapter of the Dharanis from the Heike Nogyo Ink (26.5x303cm 10x119in) New-York 2000

SHINN Everett 1876-1953 **[169]**
- $40 000 - €43 886 - £26 572 - FF287 872
  Ballet Oil/canvas (53.5x78.5cm 21x30in) New-York 2000
- $20 000 - €21 949 - £12 878 - FF143 976
  Clown with Big Pants Oil/canvas (30x25.5cm 11x10in) Beverly-Hills CA 2000
- $11 000 - €10 303 - £6 762 - FF67 585
  Musicians Watercolour (11.5x16.5cm 4x6in) New-York 1999

SHINNORS John 1950 **[6]**
- $42 584 - €45 711 - £28 497 - FF299 844
  Badger and Young Underland Oil/canvas (122x122cm 48x48in) Dublin 2000
- $7 650 - €8 888 - £5 376 - FF58 303
  Night Move II Oil/panel (73x87cm 28x34in) Dublin 2001
- $2 095 - €2 413 - £1 429 - FF15 825
  Woman in West Kensington Mixed media (22x22cm 8x8in) Dublin 2000
- $2 007 - €2 159 - £1 368 - FF14 159
  Spanish Circus Pencil (15x20cm 5x7in) Dublin 2001

SHINODA Toko 1913 **[15]**
- $4 500 - €4 973 - £3 120 - FF32 619
  Untitled Painting (90x60cm 35x23in) New-York 2001

🖼 **$1 400** - €1 624 - **£996** - FF10 653
For the Green Watercolour (89x56.5cm 35x22in)
Washington 2000

SHINOYAMA Kishin 1940 [4]
📷 **$1 034** - €1 022 - **£646** - FF6 707
Hockende Photograph (20.4x25.4cm 8x10in)
München 1999

SHINSAI Ryurukyo act.1799-1823 [2]
📖 **$609** - €686 - **£419** - FF4 500
Nature morte à l'éventail Estampe couleurs
(13.5x18cm 5x7in) Paris 2000

SHINSEN Tokuoka 1896-1972 [2]
✏ **$25 480** - €24 852 - **£15 600** - FF163 020
Persimmon Drawing (45.5x59.5cm 17x23in) Tokyo
1999

SHIRATAKI Ikunosuke 1873-1960 [4]
🍃 **$4 967** - €5 460 - **£3 183** - FF35 815
Woman Reading Oil/board (52.5x39.5cm 20x15in)
Melbourne 2000

SHIRLAW Walter 1838-1909 [46]
🍃 **$3 000** - €3 406 - **£2 053** - FF22 345
The Burgomaster Oil/canvas (53.5x43.5cm 21x17in)
New-York 2000
🍃 **$1 500** - €1 610 - **£1 003** - FF10 561
Women drying clothes Oil/panel (26x36.5cm
10x14in) Philadelphia PA 2000
🍃 **$700** - €654 - **£432** - FF4 242
Caprice: Tondo with classical Figures
Pastel/paper (36x25cm 14x10in) New-Orleans LA 1999

SHIRLEY Henry XIX-XX [8]
🍃 **$651** - €740 - **£450** - FF4 857
Raggle Taggle Gypsy Boys Oil/canvas (44.5x59cm
17x23in) Bristol, Avon 2000

SHIRLOW John Alexander Th. 1869-1936 [50]
📖 **$127** - €123 - **£78** - FF806
**Melbourne, Looking East from the Botanic
Gardens** Etching (21x31cm 8x12in) Melbourne 1999

SHIRTLIFF Louisa XIX-XX [2]
🍃 **$2 300** - €2 098 - **£1 414** - FF13 763
Portrait of Oliver H.Perry Miniature (9x7cm 3x3in)
North-Harwich MA 1999

SHISHKIN Arkadii 1899-1985 [1]
📷 **$2 381** - €2 556 - **£1 594** - FF16 769
Der erste Traktorist auf dem Staatsgut Gigant
Vintage gelatin silver print (23x15.9cm 9x6in) Hamburg
2000

SHISHKIN Ivan Ivanovitch 1832-1898 [73]
🍃 **$272 142** - €300 244 - **£180 000** - FF1 969 470
The River Kama, Near Yelabuga Oil/canvas
(195.5x120.5cm 76x47in) London 2000
🍃 **$16 522** - €15 988 - **£10 186** - FF104 874
**Motiv aus der Gegend bei Narva am finnischen
Meerbusen** Öl/Leinwand (90x57cm 35x22in) Wien
1999
✏ **$2 100** - €2 147 - **£1 316** - FF14 086
Eifelmaare in Waldumgebung Watercolour,
gouache (24x33cm 9x12in) Köln 2000
📖 **$899** - €1 022 - **£623** - FF6 707
Landschaften Radierung (26.5x18.5cm 10x7in)
Hamburg 2000

SHITAO 1642-1707 [27]
✏ **$73 530** - €69 343 - **£45 600** - FF454 860
Vegetables Ink/paper (46x37cm 18x14in) Hong-Kong
1999

SHIZHUANG ?-1792 [1]
✏ **$64 200** - €70 104 - **£41 300** - FF459 850
Scenes of Tiantai Ink (36x28cm 14x11in) Hong-
Kong 2000

SHOEN Uemura 1875-1949 [6]
🍃 **$205 800** - €200 730 - **£126 000** - FF1 316 700
Morning Dew Painting (47x52cm 18x20in) Tokyo
1999
✏ **$85 000** - €95 206 - **£59 058** - FF624 512
Bijin zu (Beauty) Ink (77.5x57cm 30x22in) New-York
2001

SHOESMITH Kenneth Denton 1890-1939 [59]
🍃 **$723** - €684 - **£450** - FF4 486
The Shanghai River Watercolour (60x81cm 23x31in)
Billingshurst, West-Sussex 1999
📖 **$1 620** - €1 367 - **£950** - FF8 966
«Lowestoft» Poster (102x127cm 40x50in) London
1998

SHOHA Ito 1877-1968 [1]
✏ **$14 000** - €14 411 - **£8 824** - FF94 532
Daigo no hana (Cherry blossoms at Daigo) Ink
(52x57cm 20x22in) New-York 2000

SHOHAKU Soga 1730-1781 [1]
✏ **$70 000** - €67 289 - **£43 652** - FF441 385
Ox Herder Resting in Landscape Ink/paper
(115x44cm 45x17in) New-York 1999

SHOKLER Harry 1896-1978 [47]
📖 **$290** - €334 - **£200** - FF2 192
Island Harbor Serigraph in colors (36x47cm 14x18in)
Cleveland OH 2000

SHOKO Uemura 1902 [2]
✏ **$16 000** - €17 681 - **£11 096** - FF115 979
Shun'ya (Spring Field) Ink (25.5x41cm 10x16in)
New-York 2001

SHONBORN John-Lewis 1852-1931 [86]
🍃 **$1 420** - €1 524 - **£950** - FF10 000
Le cavalier Huile/toile (46x55cm 18x21in) Abbeville
2000
🍃 **$255** - €274 - **£171** - FF1 800
Etude de tête de vache Huile/toile (29x23cm
11x9in) Paris 2000

SHONIBARE Yinka 1962 [1]
🍃 **$19 832** - €16 945 - **£12 000** - FF111 150
Double Dutch Acrylic (32x22x4.5cm 12x8x1in)
London 1998

SHONTZ Amos XX [7]
🍃 **$700** - €789 - **£484** - FF5 174
**Portrait of Black and White Cow in Landscape
with Red Halter** Oil/canvas (45x60cm 18x24in)
Hatfield PA 2000

SHOOSMITH Thurston Laidlaw 1865-1933 [11]
🍃 **$473** - €496 - **£300** - FF3 255
Rue Eau de Robec, Rouen Watercolour/paper
(33x33cm 12x12in) Edinburgh 2000

SHOR Zvi 1898-1979 [71]
🍃 **$1 700** - €1 659 - **£1 076** - FF10 885
Still Life with Vase and Flowers Oil/canvas
(81x61cm 31x24in) Tel Aviv 1999
🍃 **$1 150** - €1 137 - **£704** - FF7 458
Rural Landscape Oil/panel (32.5x40.5cm 12x15in)
Tel Aviv 2000

SHORE Arnold Joseph Victor 1897-1963 [22]
🍃 **$2 594** - €2 906 - **£1 802** - FF19 062
Still Life Oil/canvas (45.5x40cm 17x15in) Melbourne
2001

S

$1 072 - €1 119 - £676 - FF7 340
Hillside Farm Oil/board (34x40cm 13x15in) Sydney 2000

SHORE Stephen 1947 [14]
$1 486 - €1 646 - £1 008 - FF10 799
Throckmorton Street, Fort Worth, Texas
Photograph in colors (20.2x25.4cm 7x10in) Berlin 2000

SHORT Frank, Francis Job 1857-1945 [81]
$134 - €144 - £90 - FF946
Gathering the flock on Maxwell Bank Etching (15x22cm 5x8in) Swindon, Wiltshire 2000

SHORT Frederick Golden 1863-1936 [116]
$1 569 - €1 684 - £1 050 - FF11 047
The New forest, Hampshire Oil/canvas (52x76cm 20x29in) Edinburgh 2000
$523 - €561 - £350 - FF3 682
The New Forest, Hampshire Oil/board (22x30cm 8x11in) Edinburgh 2000

SHORT George Anderson 1856-1945 [20]
$244 - €238 - £150 - FF1 558
Colne Valley Harriers, Huntsman Charles
Watercolour/paper (38x56cm 15x22in) Little-Lane, Ilkley 1999

SHORT Obadiah 1803-1886 [11]
$1 134 - €1 291 - £800 - FF8 466
Family by an old Norfolk cottage and barn
Oil/canvas (55x40cm 22x16in) Aylsham, Norfolk 2001
$297 - €351 - £210 - FF2 304
Clay lump cottages near a pond in a woodland landscape Oil/canvas (25x28cm 10x11in) Aylsham, Norfolk 2001

SHORT William Henry 1875-1947 [13]
$1 044 - €981 - £629 - FF6 434
Moonlight on the River Hals, Healesville Oil/canvas (90x70cm 35x27in) Sydney 1999

SHORTT Terence Michael 1910-1986 [5]
$1 295 - €1 511 - £901 - FF9 913
Studies of Birds Watercolour/paper (37x29cm 14x11in) Toronto 2000

SHOSON Ohara Matao 1877-1945 [42]
$153 - €179 - £107 - FF1 173
Fliegender Kranich vor untergehender Sonne
Woodcut in colors (34x19cm 13x7in) Berlin 2000

SHOSTAK Peter 1943 [15]
$364 - €391 - £247 - FF2 564
These were Hard but Happy Times Silkscreen in colors (14.5x21.5cm 5x8in) Calgary, Alberta 2001

SHOTWELL Frederic Valpey XX [2]
$650 - €773 - £449 - FF5 072
Fisher Building from 2nd Avenue Viaduct
Etching (25x17cm 10x7in) Detroit MI 2000

SHOUN Yamamoto 1870-1965 [2]
$764 - €869 - £530 - FF5 701
Ein Mädchen in festlichem Gewand plaudert am Telefon Woodcut in colors (35.3x23.8cm 13x9in) Köln 2000

SHOURA Nasseer 1920-1992 [2]
$11 171 - €12 565 - £7 800 - FF82 422
Al Hameh Oil/canvas (79x62cm 31x24in) London 2001

SHRADY Henry Merwin 1871-1922 [21]
$11 000 - €10 491 - £6 695 - FF68 814
Figure of George Washington on Horseback
Bronze (H63cm H24in) New-York 1999

SHTERENBERG Avram 1894-1979 [13]
$1 279 - €1 444 - £900 - FF9 470
«Valdimir Maiakowski» Silver print (18x14.5cm 7x5in) London 2001

SHUFELT Robert 1935 [2]
$9 500 - €10 787 - £6 600 - FF70 757
Cut'n Sign Pencil/paper (45x63cm 18x25in) Dallas TX 2001

SHUKHAEV Vasili Ivanovich 1887-1973 [6]
$13 993 - €16 652 - £10 000 - FF109 232
Reclining Nude Oil/canvas (94x177.5cm 37x69in) London 2000
$5 797 - €5 474 - £3 600 - FF35 908
Drawing Water Oil/board (51x59cm 20x23in) London 1999

SHUKLIN Vitaly 1970 [9]
$1 085 - €1 051 - £682 - FF6 895
Rendez-vous Oleo/lienzo (76x41cm 29x16in) Madrid 1999

SHULL Delia XX [2]
$14 000 - €15 543 - £9 737 - FF101 953
«Betalo in Shawl» Oil/canvas (181x89cm 71x35in) Milford CT 2001

SHULZ Ada Walter 1870-1928 [6]
$80 000 - €90 984 - £55 480 - FF596 816
Mother and Child Oil/canvas (86x76cm 34x30in) Cincinnati OH 2000
$32 500 - €37 193 - £22 353 - FF243 971
Girl Holding a Duck Oil/board (31x27cm 12x11in) New-York 2000

SHULZ Adolph Robert 1869-1963 [33]
$5 000 - €4 775 - £3 078 - FF31 322
Haystacks Oil/board (50x60cm 20x24in) Cincinnati OH 1999
$1 600 - €1 792 - £1 111 - FF11 755
«Indiana Landscape» Oil/canvas (30x40cm 12x16in) Cincinnati OH 2001
$600 - €672 - £416 - FF4 408
«Rural Town» Pencil/paper (21x28cm 8x11in) Cincinnati OH 2001

SHULZ Walter 1895-1918 [1]
$7 000 - €8 007 - £4 867 - FF52 524
The Small Brook Oil/canvas (50x68cm 20x27in)

SHUNCHO Yushido c.1750-c.1800 [8]
$1 524 - €1 508 - £950 - FF9 891
Kitten seated looking up the Robes of a bijin seated on a Terrace Print (68.5x11cm 26x4in) London 1999

SHUNEI Katsukawa 1762-1819 [40]
$1 600 - €1 876 - £1 141 - FF12 307
Actor Otani Hiroji III in the Role of a Chinese Warrior Print in colors (30x14cm 11x5in) New-York 2000

SHUNK Harry Shonk-Kender XX [5]
$3 710 - €4 311 - £2 607 - FF28 277
Levilation Vintage gelatin silver print (40x50cm 15x19in) Amsterdam 2001

SHUNKO Katsukawa 1743-1812 [22]
$948 - €1 067 - £653 - FF7 000
L'acteur Osagawa Tsuneyo II dans un rôle de femme. Estampe couleurs (31.5x14.5cm 12x5in) Paris 2000

SHUNKO-JO 1887-? **[1]**
$2 063 - €2 301 - £1 387 - FF15 092
Gemaltes Ukiyo-e einer jungen Kurtisane Indian
ink (127.5x38cm 50x14in) Stuttgart 2000

SHUNMAN Kubo 1757-1820 **[8]**
$2 400 - €2 652 - £1 664 - FF17 396
**Three Women seated on a Bench by a Stream
under a Willow Tree** Print (37.5x28cm 14x11in)
New-York 2001

SHUNSEN Natori 1886-1960 **[5]**
$989 - €1 125 - £686 - FF7 378
Ichimura Uzaemon XV Woodcut (39.5x27.5cm
15x10in) Köln 2000

SHUNSHO Katsukawa 1726-1793 **[59]**
$32 000 - €32 246 - £19 948 - FF211 520
Azuma Dancer in a Boat Ink (91x28cm 35x11in)
New-York 2000
$2 200 - €2 580 - £1 569 - FF16 923
**Actor Ichikawa Monnosuke II as the Renegade
Monk Zenjibo** Print in colors (31.5x14.5cm 12x5in)
New-York 2000

SHUNSO Hishida 1874-1911 **[6]**
$117 600 - €114 703 - £72 000 - FF752 400
The Dawn Painting (111x39cm 43x15in) Tokyo 1999

SHUNSUKE Matsumoto 1912-1948 **[1]**
$45 000 - €49 647 - £29 763 - FF325 660
Nude, Rafu Oil/canvas (45.5x38cm 17x14in) New-
York 2000

SHUNTEI Katsukawa 1770-1820 **[5]**
$293 - €317 - £202 - FF2 079
Scène de lutte Gravure bois couleurs (36.5x24.5cm
14x9in) Warszawa 2001

SHUNTEI Katsukawa 1798-1849 **[2]**
$1 800 - €1 730 - £1 122 - FF11 349
Views of Ohmi: Zeze Castle Print (18.5x25.5cm
7x10in) New-York 1999

SHURTLEFF Roswell Morse 1838-1915 **[24]**
$10 500 - €9 992 - £6 567 - FF65 545
Adirondack Landscape with Black Bear Oil/can-
vas (48x66cm 19x26in) New-York 1999
$2 000 - €1 894 - £1 216 - FF12 424
Edge of the Woods Oil/canvas (30.5x40.5cm
12x15in) New-York 1999
$1 000 - €1 102 - £627 - FF7 227
Meadows with Stream and Trees and Cows
Watercolour/paper (21x32cm 8x12in) Portsmouth NH
2000

SHUSTER Joe, Joseph 1914-1992 **[3]**
$2 750 - €2 653 - £1 738 - FF17 404
Portrait of Superman and Lois Pencil/paper
(43x56cm 16x22in) New-York 1999

SHUSTER William Howard 1893-1969 **[6]**
$7 500 - €7 103 - £4 560 - FF46 590
Marie of Tesuque Oil/canvas (61x51cm 24x20in)
New-York 1999

SHUTE Ruth Whittier 1803-1882 **[3]**
$9 000 - €9 611 - £6 132 - FF63 047
**Dark-Haired Lady with Tortoiseshell Comb,
Portrait of Hannah Holbrook** Oil/canvas
(56x44.5cm 22x17in) New-York 2001
$12 000 - €12 815 - £8 176 - FF84 063
Portrait of Mary Gates (1816-1866) Watercolour
(72x51cm 28x20in) New-York 2001

SHUTE Samuel A. 1803-1836 **[1]**
$12 000 - €12 815 - £8 176 - FF84 063
Portrait of Mary Gates (1816-1866) Watercolour
(72x51cm 28x20in) New-York 2001

SHUTER William XVIII **[2]**
$2 000 - €2 303 - £1 364 - FF15 104
Portraits of John and Mary Gallopp, Half-Length
Oil/canvas (61x50cm 24x19in) New-York 2000

SHVARTS Vyacheslav Grigorev. 1838-1869 **[3]**
$8 145 - €7 775 - £5 089 - FF51 003
The Boar Hunt Oil/canvas (78x60cm 31x24in) Cedar-
Falls IA 1999

SIAULE Agathe act.c.1835 **[1]**
$3 607 - €4 116 - £2 505 - FF27 000
Jeune garçon au chapeau Huile/toile (55x46cm
21x18in) Paris 2001

SIBBONS Gudrun XX **[39]**
$1 075 - €1 206 - £750 - FF7 909
Fishing Boats at Low Tide Oil/board (28.5x39cm
11x15in) Lymington 2001

SIBERDT Eugène 1851-1931 **[24]**
$9 010 - €8 428 - £5 474 - FF55 284
Griekse vrouw met hond Oil/panel (80.5x59.5cm
31x23in) Lokeren 1999
$4 298 - €4 084 - £2 615 - FF26 789
Interieur met lezende dame Oil/panel (40x32cm
15x12in) Rotterdam 1999

SIBERECHTS Jan 1627-c.1703 **[32]**
$589 260 - €700 806 - £420 000 - FF4 596 984
The Thames Valley, with Henley in the Distance
Oil/canvas (181.5x161.5cm 71x63in) London 2000
$32 284 - €29 886 - £20 000 - FF196 038
**Landscape with a Shooting Party in the
Foreground** Oil/canvas (48.5x94cm 19x37in) London
1999
$6 500 - €6 738 - £3 900 - FF44 200
Testa di giovane vestale Olio/tavola (32.5x24cm
12x9in) Prato 2000
$350 - €375 - £238 - FF2 458
**View of an Imaginary City, with the Tower of the
Antwerp Cathedral** Watercolour (17.5x21.5cm 6x8in)
New-York 2001

SIBILLA Gijsbert Jansz 1598-1652 **[5]**
$9 359 - €9 158 - £6 000 - FF60 073
The Sacrifice of Noah Oil/canvas (104x90.5cm
40x35in) London 1999

SIBIYA Lucky 1942-1999 **[17]**
$1 563 - €1 466 - £966 - FF9 615
The Garden Oil/panel (60x91.5cm 23x36in)
Johannesburg 1999
$142 - €152 - £96 - FF996
Looking Back Silkscreen (62x44cm 24x17in) Cape
Town 2001

SIBLEY Andrew 1933 **[54]**
$6 841 - €7 985 - £4 829 - FF52 378
The Typing Pool Enamel (106.5x122cm 41x48in)
Malvern, Victoria 2000
$1 823 - €2 127 - £1 268 - FF13 953
«Grand.Daughter and Pony» Oil/canvas
(70x59.5cm 27x23in) Melbourne 2000

SICARD François Léon 1862-1934 **[24]**
$8 000 - €6 910 - £4 822 - FF45 325
Oedipus and the Sphinx Bronze (H65cm H25in)
New-York 1998

S

SICARDI Louis-M., Luc Sicard 1746-1825 **[34]**
- $3 974 - €3 659 - £2 385 - FF24 000
  Portrait d'un officier de la Maison militaire ou civile du Roi Huile/toile (55.5x46cm 21x18in) Joigny 1999
- $7 421 - €6 403 - £4 477 - FF42 000
  Amour au papillon Huile/toile (18x14cm 7x5in) Paris 1998

SICHEL Ernest Leopold 1862-1941 **[13]**
- $7 023 - €5 995 - £4 200 - FF39 325
  A Fisherman and his Wife on a Quayside with a Basket Oil/canvas (81.5x122.5cm 32x48in) Leeds 1998

SICHEL Nathaniel 1843-1907 **[46]**
- $8 272 - €7 727 - £5 000 - FF50 686
  Portrait of Arthur Lionel Payne (Peczenik), seated Oil/canvas (148x101cm 58x39in) London 1999
- $4 073 - €3 707 - £2 500 - FF24 317
  An eastern Beauty Oil/panel (60.5x46cm 23x18in) London 1999
- $1 203 - €1 123 - £742 - FF7 369
  Orientalische Tänzerin Öl/Leinwand (43x32cm 16x12in) Luzern 1999

SICHEM van Christoffel I c.1546-1624 **[22]**
- $750 - €832 - £499 - FF5 460
  Young Man Playing the Zither , After Goltzius Woodcut (30.5x21.5cm 12x8in) New-York 2000

SICHULSKI Kazimierz 1879-1942 **[58]**
- $3 778 - €4 335 - £2 584 - FF28 437
  Arbre en fleurs Huile/carton (98x69cm 38x27in) Katowice 2000
- $330 - €387 - £235 - FF2 541
  Jozef Pilsudski Aquarelle (23x30.5cm 9x12in) Warszawa 2000

SICILIA José María 1954 **[108]**
- $13 347 - €12 990 - £8 200 - FF85 211
  Flor Oil/canvas (163x164.5cm 64x64in) London 1999
- $7 500 - €8 363 - £5 043 - FF54 858
  Black frame Flower Acrylic/canvas (81x80.5cm 31x31in) New-York 1999
- $5 040 - €5 406 - £3 420 - FF35 460
  Sin título Acuarela (56.5x102cm 22x40in) Madrid 2001
- $756 - €721 - £468 - FF4 728
  Sin título Litografía (60x69cm 23x27in) Madrid 1999

SICILIANO Bernardo 1969 **[12]**
- $1 560 - €2 021 - £1 170 - FF13 260
  Tramonto Olio/tela (28.5x50.5cm 11x19in) Milano 2001

SICKERT Bernhard 1862-1932 **[41]**
- $293 - €313 - £200 - FF2 050
  The Rhine near Bingen/The Hay Field, Seer Green Oil/panel (32x40.5cm 12x15in) Billingshurst, West-Sussex 2001

SICKERT Walter Richard 1860-1942 **[379]**
- $28 180 - €24 041 - £17 000 - FF157 698
  Pentonville Hill, London Oil/canvas (51x61cm 20x24in) London 1998
- $12 833 - €12 932 - £8 000 - FF84 828
  Mackerel Oil/canvas/board (16x46cm 6x18in) London 2000
- $1 743 - €2 050 - £1 250 - FF13 448
  Baccarat Pencil (26.5x18.5cm 10x7in) London 2001
- $966 - €889 - £580 - FF5 833
  Portrait of Mrs Jopling Etching (12x8.5cm 4x3in) London 1999

SIDDELL Peter 1935 **[6]**
- $5 240 - €5 874 - £3 664 - FF38 529
  Impending Storm Acrylic/board (90x120cm 35x47in) Auckland 2001

SIDIBÉ Malik 1936 **[9]**
- $3 324 - €3 209 - £2 100 - FF21 050
  Combat des amis avec pierres (Friends Fighting with stones) Photograph (60.5x50.5cm 23x19in) London 1999

SIDLER Alfred 1905-1992 **[39]**
- $473 - €515 - £311 - FF3 376
  Verschneites Dorf in der Abenddämmerung Oil/panel (54x73.5cm 21x28in) Bern 2000

SIDLEY Samuel 1829-1896 **[11]**
- $5 212 - €4 727 - £3 200 - FF31 007
  Interior Scenes, Gwydir Castle, Llanrwst, North Wales Oil/board (28x44cm 11x17in) Ilkley, West-Yorkshire 1998

SIDNEY BIRD PAINTER The XVIII **[2]**
- $34 360 - €32 483 - £21 324 - FF213 073
  The Black Swan Watercolour/paper (46.5x31cm 18x12in) Malvern, Victoria 1999

SIDNEY Thomas XIX-XX **[64]**
- $10 240 - €9 635 - £6 400 - FF63 200
  Paisaje con vacas Oleo/tabla (45x60.5cm 17x23in) Madrid 1998
- $292 - €281 - £180 - FF1 842
  Lynmouth Watercolour (22.5x33cm 8x12in) London 1999

SIDOLI Pacifico 1868-1963 **[4]**
- $1 850 - €1 918 - £1 110 - FF12 580
  Profilo di donna Acquarello/carta (35x25cm 13x9in) Milano 2000

SIDORENKO Maxim XX **[9]**
- $373 - €401 - £250 - FF2 630
  In Venice Oil/canvas/board (27x19cm 10x7in) Fernhurst, Haslemere, Surrey 2000

SIDORENKO Sergei 1968 **[73]**
- $530 - €601 - £360 - FF3 940
  El regreso de la pesca Oleo/lienzo (40x50cm 15x19in) Madrid 2000
- $275 - €300 - £185 - FF1 970
  Un canal florido Oleo/lienzo (27x41cm 10x16in) Madrid 2000

SIDOROWICZ Zygmunt 1846-1881 **[9]**
- $1 601 - €1 719 - £1 071 - FF11 277
  Paysage avec voyageurs Huile/panneau (10x19cm 3x7in) Warszawa 2000

SIE Henri XX **[4]**
- $2 251 - €2 058 - £1 378 - FF13 500
  Port de Saint-Tropez Huile/toile (100x73cm 39x28in) Paris 1999

SIEBELIST Arthur 1870-1945 **[5]**
- $11 487 - €9 815 - £6 950 - FF64 379
  Vor einem Bauernhaus Öl/Leinwand (59.5x86cm 23x33in) München 1998

SIEBENHAAR H. XIX-XX **[5]**
- $1 090 - €942 - £658 - FF6 178
  «Polacrd. Gtd.: New Orleans, de la Propiedad de D.Harrison...» Gouache/paper (33x44cm 12x17in) Vejle 1998

S

SIEBERG Johannes 1803-1874 [1]
$5 158 - €6 135 - £3 676 - FF40 246
Eisvergnügen in holländischer Winterlandschaft Öl/Leinwand (60x79cm 23x31in) Köln 2000

SIEBERT Georg 1896-1984 [8]
$283 - €307 - £194 - FF2 012
Topf Coloured pencils/paper (18x23cm 7x9in) Stuttgart 2001

SIEBNER Herbert Johannes J. 1925 [23]
$1 225 - €1 162 - £744 - FF7 625
Blue Head Mixed media (30x25cm 11x9in) Calgary, Alberta 1999
$178 - €151 - £106 - FF992
Two Figures Seated Silkscreen (30x25cm 11x9in) Calgary, Alberta 1998

SIEBURGH Hubertus Nicolaas 1799-1842 [2]
$2 882 - €2 723 - £1 798 - FF17 859
Elegant figures in an Interior Oil/canvas (93x73cm 36x28in) Amsterdam 1999

SIECK Rudolf 1877-1957 [59]
$877 - €1 022 - £614 - FF6 707
Neckarlandschaft Öl/Leinwand (80x100cm 31x39in) München 2000
$1 241 - €1 227 - £759 - FF8 049
Waldtal Aquarell/Papier (40x50cm 15x19in) Kempten 2000
$108 - €123 - £75 - FF804
Chiemseelandschaft Farbradierung (19.5x26.5cm 7x10in) München 2001

SIEDHOFF Werner XX [1]
$3 741 - €4 191 - £2 600 - FF27 492
Dancer in white Costume designed by Oskar Schlemmer Silver print (11x7.5cm 4x2in) London 2001

SIEFF Jeanloup 1933-2000 [110]
$1 202 - €1 431 - £859 - FF9 390
«Yves Montand» Vintage gelatin silver print (39.6x26.7cm 15x10in) Berlin 2000

SIEFFERT Paul 1874-1957 [93]
$24 000 - €26 802 - £15 369 - FF175 812
Reclining Female Nude Oil/canvas (89x143.5cm 35x56in) New-York 2000
$4 003 - €4 546 - £2 800 - FF29 822
Nu allongé lisant Oil/canvas/panel (37x55cm 14x21in) London 2001
$1 979 - €2 211 - £1 341 - FF14 500
Odalisque au coussin de velours Huile/toile (27x41cm 10x16in) Pau 2000

SIEGEL Arthur Sidney 1913-1978 [23]
$1 600 - €1 494 - £967 - FF9 803
Untitled, Photogram Vintage gelatin silver print (34x26cm 13x10in) New-York 1999

SIEGEN von August 1850-? [116]
$6 585 - €7 517 - £4 575 - FF49 308
Udsigt mod en flamsk by ved en bred kanal Oil/canvas (98x140cm 38x55in) København 2000
$2 988 - €3 208 - £2 000 - FF21 043
Market Place in Verona Oil/panel (52.5x42cm 20x16in) London 2000
$1 211 - €1 308 - £837 - FF8 580
Blick auf den Palazzo Voluna in Venedig Öl/Leinwand (16x31.7cm 6x12in) Wien 2001

SIEGERT August 1786-1869 [4]
$3 222 - €3 205 - £2 000 - FF21 022
Reading the News/Threading a Needle Oil/canvas (31x26cm 12x10in) London 1999

SIEGERT August Friedrich 1820-1883 [15]
$5 750 - €5 464 - £3 498 - FF35 841
The little Critic Oil/panel (19x16.5cm 7x6in) New-York 1999

SIEGFRIED Arne 1893-1985 [24]
$648 - €627 - £400 - FF4 116
Row of Italian townhouses with Palm Trees before Oil/panel (52.5x71.5cm 20x28in) London 1999

SIEGFRIED Edwin C. 1889-1955 [11]
$1 500 - €1 620 - £1 036 - FF10 625
«Stinson Beach, Bolinas Bay» Pastel/paper (54x79cm 21x31in) Altadena CA 2001

SIEGRIEST Louis Bassi 1899-1989 [11]
$65 000 - €67 757 - £43 264 - FF444 457
High and Dry Oil/board (30.5x40.5cm 12x15in) San-Francisco CA 2000
$1 914 - €1 830 - £1 200 - FF12 006
«Indian Court» Poster (92x64cm 36x25in) London 1999

SIEGUMFELDT Hermann Carl 1833-1912 [31]
$349 - €321 - £216 - FF2 108
Praesentation Oil/canvas (35x40cm 13x15in) Vejle 1998

SIEHL-FREYSTETT Georg 1868-1919 [15]
$2 224 - €2 556 - £1 570 - FF16 769
Birkenallee im Spätsommer Öl/Leinwand (72.5x52cm 28x20in) Bremen 2001

SIEMER Christian 1874-1940 [4]
$5 500 - €5 904 - £3 680 - FF38 725
Malibu Oil/board (54.5x95cm 21x37in) San-Francisco CA 2000

SIEMIRADZKI Henryk Ippolitovich 1843-1902 [42]
$265 000 - €314 235 - £182 320 - FF2 061 249
The Departure of Caterina Cornaro, Queen of Cyprus Oil/canvas (208x293.5cm 81x115in) New-York 2000
$66 586 - €60 973 - £40 586 - FF399 958
Antoniusz i Kleopatra Oil/canvas (42.5x76cm 16x29in) Warszawa 1999
$4 793 - €5 500 - £3 287 - FF36 075
Rêveuse Huile/toile (43x34cm 16x13in) Katowice 2000

SIENICKI Jacek 1928-2000 [8]
$3 370 - €3 730 - £2 342 - FF24 464
Bouteilles Huile/toile (65x80cm 25x31in) Warszawa 2001

SIEPMAN VAN DEN BERG E.J.A. 1943 [4]
$7 606 - €7 260 - £4 753 - FF47 625
Female Nude Bronze (H75cm H29in) Amsterdam 1999

SIEPMANN Heinrich 1904 [13]
$2 631 - €3 068 - £1 846 - FF20 123
«B36/1993» Öl/Leinwand (80x60cm 31x23in) Köln 2001

SIERHUIS Jan 1928 [105]
$1 213 - €1 361 - £840 - FF8 929
Stilleven met Rode Bal Oil/canvas (100x120cm 39x47in) Amsterdam 2000
$728 - €726 - £442 - FF4 762
Twee figuren Mixed media (55x71cm 21x27in) Amsterdam 2000
$776 - €908 - £554 - FF5 953
Untitled Gouache/paper (68x48cm 26x18in) Amsterdam 2001

S

SIERICH Louis Ludwig Casimir 1834-1919 **[16]**
- $3 900 - €4 311 - £2 705 - FF28 277
  A Winter Landscape with a Figure near a Hole in Ice Oil/canvas (53x74cm 20x29in) Amsterdam 2001
- $664 - €771 - £459 - FF5 060
  Winters bosgezicht Oil/canvas (33x43cm 12x16in) Rotterdam 2000

SIERIG Ferdinand Carl 1839-1905 **[6]**
- $4 323 - €4 084 - £2 697 - FF26 789
  Children Feeding a Goat Oil/panel (22x27.5cm 8x10in) Amsterdam 1999

SIEVÄNEN Jaakko 1932 **[6]**
- $1 116 - €1 093 - £687 - FF7 170
  Sommitelma Gouache/paper (75x55cm 29x21in) Helsinki 1999

SIEVERDING Katharina 1944 **[17]**
- $854 - €818 - £527 - FF5 366
  Edition IX Photograph in colors (99.5x62.5cm 39x24in) Köln 1999

SIEVIER Robert William 1794-1865 **[2]**
- $19 250 - €19 398 - £12 000 - FF127 243
  Pity standing looking to her left, wearing a foliate wreath Marble (H156.5cm H61in) London 2000

SIEW HOCK MENG 1942 **[11]**
- $7 679 - €7 157 - £4 641 - FF46 946
  Wanita Tidur I: sleeping Woman I Oil/canvas/panel (46x61cm 18x24in) Singapore 1999
- $11 542 - €10 756 - £7 122 - FF70 554
  Resting Pastel/paper (48x64cm 18x25in) Singapore 1999

SIEWERT Ciano 1942 **[16]**
- $581 - €544 - £362 - FF3 571
  View of Schiedam Watercolour (34.5x54cm 13x21in) Amsterdam 1999

SIFREDI Max XX **[3]**
- $1 441 - €1 372 - £896 - FF9 000
  Eve Terracotta (70x20cm 27x7in) Mâcon 1999

SIGAD Eliahu 1901-1975 **[33]**
- $1 300 - €1 104 - £785 - FF7 245
  Young Women at the Door 1950s Oil/canvas (101x65cm 39x25in) Tel Aviv 1999
- $350 - €342 - £222 - FF2 243
  Figures on a Balcony Gouache/paper (54.5x42.5cm 21x16in) Tel Aviv 1999

SIGMUND Benjamin D. act.1880-1904 **[62]**
- $3 953 - €4 220 - £2 700 - FF27 683
  Girl by a Woodland Pool/Children playing beneath a Tree Oil/canvas/board (21x33cm 8x12in) Billingshurst, West-Sussex 2001
- $1 010 - €1 201 - £720 - FF7 880
  Feeding the Chicks Watercolour (25.5x35.5cm 10x13in) Bath 2000

SIGNAC Paul 1863-1935 **[918]**
- $510 000 - €440 005 - £306 510 - FF2 886 243
  La Côte d'Or, La Suleimanie, Constantinople Oil/canvas (46x55cm 18x21in) New-York 1998
- $77 600 - €76 225 - £48 150 - FF500 000
  Concarneau, études préparatoires: Calme du soir/Calme du matin Huile/panneau (36.5x34.5cm 14x13in) Paris 1999
- $15 376 - €14 940 - £9 613 - FF98 000
  Vue de Venise Aquarelle/papier (18x25cm 7x9in) Lyon 1999
- $550 - €625 - £376 - FF4 099
  Paris, les Ponts des Arts avec Remorqueurs Etching, aquatint (12.5x19cm 4x7in) New-York 2000

SIGNER Roman 1938 **[2]**
- $3 822 - €4 269 - £2 590 - FF28 000
  Versinken Kajak Photo couleurs (23.5x35cm 9x13in) Paris 2000

SIGNORET Charles 1867-1932 **[18]**
- $1 494 - €1 372 - £918 - FF9 000
  Effet de ciel, sur la mer Huile/toile (38x46cm 14x18in) Paris 1999

SIGNORET-LEDIEU Lucie 1858-1904 **[20]**
- $2 564 - €3 049 - £1 828 - FF20 000
  Jeanne d'Arc Bronze (H64cm H25in) Lyon 1999

SIGNORI Carlo Sergio 1906-1988 **[12]**
- $3 124 - €3 354 - £2 090 - FF22 000
  Portrait pour Raymonde Marbre (42x36.5x7cm 16x14x2in) Monte-Carlo 2000

SIGNORI de Francis XIX-XX **[1]**
- $675 - €767 - £462 - FF5 030
  «Cannes» Poster (101x77cm 39x30in) Hannover 2000

SIGNORINI Giovanni 1808-1864 **[4]**
- $8 500 - €7 481 - £5 174 - FF49 073
  Travellers on Horseback Crossing Bridge Oil/canvas (66x92cm 26x36in) New-Orleans LA 1999
- $1 600 - €1 659 - £960 - FF10 880
  L'inondazione del Serchio: la barca dei soccorritori Inchiostro (38x52cm 14x20in) Roma 2000

SIGNORINI Giuseppe 1857-1932 **[81]**
- $2 987 - €2 636 - £1 800 - FF17 291
  At the Piano Watercolour (44x34cm 17x13in) London 1998

SIGNORINI Telemaco 1835-1901 **[100]**
- $139 565 - €140 636 - £87 000 - FF922 513
  An Italian Street Scene with Numerous Market Traders and Other Figures Oil/canvas (51x36.5cm 20x14in) Newbury, Berkshire 2000
- $24 000 - €31 100 - £18 000 - FF204 000
  «Presso l'Arno alla Casaccia» Olio/cartone (12.5x21cm 4x8in) Prato 2001
- $3 000 - €3 110 - £1 800 - FF20 400
  Poggio all'Elba Matita/carta (23.5x30.5cm 9x12in) Milano 1999
- $1 320 - €1 140 - £660 - FF7 480
  Via degli Speziali/Via Calimala Acquaforte (36x23cm 14x9in) Milano 1999

SIGNOVERT Jean 1919-1981 **[262]**
- $543 - €640 - £381 - FF4 200
  Composition abstraite Huile/papier/toile (56x41cm 22x16in) Paris 2000
- $174 - €160 - £107 - FF1 050
  Composition, rouge Aquarelle, gouache/papier (16.5x27cm 6x10in) Paris 1999

SIGON Pollione 1895-1971 **[4]**
- $2 179 - €2 259 - £1 307 - FF14 817
  «Vero estratto di carne Arrigoni» Affiche couleur (200x140cm 78x55in) Torino 2000

SIGRIST Franz I, François 1727-1803 **[11]**
- $408 - €457 - £286 - FF3 000
  Jeune femme au bord de la rivière Pastel/papier (35.5x43.5cm 13x17in) Paris 2001
- $857 - €1 022 - £611 - FF6 707
  Tobias heilt seinen Vater mit der Fischgalle Radierung (23.7x13.8cm 9x7in) Berlin 2000

SIGRISTE Guido 1864-1915 **[26]**
- $1 830 - €1 687 - £1 096 - FF11 066
  Napoleonische Generäle zu Pferde bei der Inspektion eines Burggrabens Oil/panel (25x32.5cm 9x12in) Dresden 1998

SIHLALI Durant 1935 [8]

🖋 **$621** - €599 - **£383** - FF3 926
Timber Yard Pastel/paper (52x72.5cm 20x28in)
Johannesburg 1999

SIIB Liina 1963 [3]

📷 **$1 800** - €1 771 - **£1 088** - FF11 616
Presumed Innocence II Photograph (79x104.5cm 31x41in) Chicago IL 2000

SIIKAMÄKI Arvo 1943 [10]

🖋 **$4 982** - €4 877 - **£3 065** - FF31 992
Heijastuksia Oil/canvas (45x55cm 17x21in) Helsinki 1999

⚒ **$8 246** - €8 073 - **£5 073** - FF52 953
Nocturno Bronze (H114cm H44in) Helsinki 1999

⚒ **$1 149** - €1 261 - **£740** - FF8 274
Sittande flicka Relief (70x70cm 27x27in) Helsinki 1999

SIJS Maurice 1880-1972 [59]

🖼 **$38 760** - €42 140 - **£25 500** - FF276 420
De korenmarkt te Gent Oil/canvas (144x122cm 56x48in) Lokeren 2000

🖼 **$5 850** - €6 445 - **£3 822** - FF42 276
Zicht van Kamperland op Veere Huile/toile (52x67cm 20x26in) Bruxelles 2000

🖼 **$145** - €173 - **£104** - FF1 138
Vissershaven (port de pêche) Huile/carton (28x28cm 11x11in) Antwerpen 2000

🖋 **$3 420** - €3 718 - **£2 250** - FF24 390
De jonkvrouw Watercolour/paper (29.5x19cm 11x7in) Lokeren 2000

SIJTHOFF Gijsbertus Jan 1867-1949 [37]

🖼 **$715** - €664 - **£436** - FF4 356
On mother's Lap Oil/canvas (52x40cm 20x15in) Amsterdam 1998

SIKANDER Shahzia 1969 [3]

🖋 **$3 000** - €3 481 - **£2 071** - FF22 833
Untitled Watercolour/paper (29x30.5cm 11x12in) New-York 2000

SIKSTRÖM Cecilia 1962 [6]

🖼 **$1 535** - €1 442 - **£925** - FF9 461
Utan titel Oil/canvas (74x92cm 29x36in) Stockholm 1999

SILAS Ellis Luciano 1883-1972 [24]

🎞 **$777** - €901 - **£550** - FF5 911
«Service to Industry, Paper Making, British Railways, Scottish Region» Poster (102x127cm 40x50in) London 2000

SILBERBAUER Fritz 1883-1974 [17]

🎞 **$203** - €218 - **£138** - FF1 430
Hugo von Hofmannstahl: Der Tor und der Tod Radierung (52x42cm 20x16in) Wien 2001

SILBEREISEN Andreas 1673-1766 [1]

🎞 **$1 483** - €1 592 - **£992** - FF10 444
Karte von Rhaetia Kupferstich (36.5x46.8cm 14x18in) Bern 2000

SILBERGER Manuel 1898-1968 [1]

🎞 **$3 600** - €3 457 - **£2 219** - FF22 679
Composition Lithograph (14x29.5cm 5x11in) New-York 1999

SILBERT José 1862-1939 [17]

🖋 **$3 790** - €4 421 - **£2 636** - FF29 000
Portrait de Ahmed ben Mohamed el-Maghribi Pastel/carton (29x28cm 11x11in) Paris 2000

SILBERT Max 1871-? [33]

🖼 **$1 576** - €1 906 - **£1 101** - FF12 500
Le souper des enfants Huile/toile (66x81cm 25x31in) Granville 2000

SILK George 1917 [1]

📷 **$2 750** - €2 586 - **£1 703** - FF16 966
Sheriff Silhouette against Atomic Blast Gelatin silver print (34x26cm 13x10in) New-York 1999

SILK Oliver act.1882-1928 [7]

🖋 **$315** - €306 - **£200** - FF2 008
Elegant Lady in a Forest Clearing/Huntsman in a Forest Clearing Watercolour (63.5x32cm 25x12in) London 1999

SILLÉN af Herman 1857-1908 [60]

🖼 **$28 451** - €24 741 - **£17 158** - FF162 288
Pansarfatyg till havs Oil/canvas (120x252cm 47x99in) Stockholm 1998

🖼 **$6 854** - €7 960 - **£4 816** - FF52 214
Norsk segelskuta Oil/canvas (46x92cm 18x36in) Stockholm 2001

🖼 **$1 671** - €1 627 - **£1 029** - FF10 670
Kustlandskap med segelfartyg Oil/canvas (34x45cm 13x17in) Stockholm 1999

SILO Adam 1674-1760 [14]

🖼 **$13 661** - €14 316 - **£8 652** - FF93 909
Marine, Statenyacht, Fischerboote und eine holländische Kriegsspinasse Öl/Leinwand (44x56cm 17x22in) Köln 2000

🖼 **$23 322** - €24 287 - **£14 777** - FF159 310
Niederländische Dreimaster auf bewegter See Oil/panel (29x35.5cm 11x13in) München 2000

🖼 **$2 177** - €2 042 - **£1 345** - FF13 394
Shipping on an Estuary near a Mill Ink (17x26.5cm 6x10in) Amsterdam 1999

SILVA Francis Augustus 1835-1886 [68]

🖼 **$65 000** - €72 163 - **£45 207** - FF473 356
Sailing at Sunset Oil/canvas (50x40cm 20x16in) Milford CT 2001

🖼 **$60 000** - €59 472 - **£37 530** - FF390 114
Barnegat Bay, New Jersey Oil/canvas (30.5x51cm 12x20in) New-York 1999

SILVA LINO Antonio 1911 [6]

🖼 **$6 600** - €7 478 - **£4 650** - FF49 050
Parque nacional de Sintra Oleo/tablex (73x89cm 28x35in) Lisboa 2001

SILVA PORTO da Antonio Carvalho 1850-1893 [6]

🖼 **$3 784** - €4 387 - **£2 640** - FF28 776
Estudo de nú Oleo/lienzo (63x39cm 24x15in) Lisboa 2001

🖼 **$17 600** - €19 940 - **£12 400** - FF130 800
Paisagem com rio Oleo/tabla (32.5x24.5cm 12x9in) Lisboa 2001

SILVA William Posey 1859-1948 [52]

🖼 **$3 250** - €2 777 - **£1 966** - FF18 216
«Drifting Fog, California Coast» Oil/panel (51x61cm 20x24in) San-Francisco CA 1998

🖼 **$1 800** - €1 996 - **£1 249** - FF13 090
Spring Landscape Oil/board (20x25cm 8x10in) New-Orleans LA 2001

SILVA-BRUHNS da Ivan 1881-1980 [136]

🎞 **$11 845** - €10 367 - **£7 174** - FF68 000
Tapis à décor aztèque Tapisserie (320x247cm 125x97in) Paris 1998

SILVAIN Christian 1950 [54]

🖼 **$782** - €843 - **£523** - FF5 528
Les souvenirs de demain Technique mixte (117x95cm 46x37in) Antwerpen 2000

S

S **$952** - €992 - **£600** - FF6 504
Échelle Technique mixte/papier (105x75cm 41x29in)
Antwerpen 2000

SILVÉN Jacob Johan 1851-1924 **[42]**
$7 402 - €7 204 - **£4 557** - FF47 256
Skördelandskap Oil/canvas (133x210cm 52x82in)
Stockholm 1999
$1 592 - €1 838 - **£1 113** - FF12 059
Insjölandskap med näckrosor, sommarmotiv i aftonljus Oil/canvas (41x65cm 16x25in) Stockholm 2001
$381 - €360 - **£236** - FF2 360
Landskap Oil/canvas (26x40cm 10x15in) Stockholm 1999

SILVERMAN Burton Philip 1928 **[7]**
S **$2 100** - €2 448 - **£1 454** - FF16 057
Two Sailors in Dress-Making Shop Watercolour/paper (70x55cm 27x22in) New-York 2000

SILVESTRE Albert 1869-1954 **[10]**
$178 - €210 - **£129** - FF1 376
Sous-bois Huile/toile (65x45.5cm 25x17in) Sion 2001

SILVESTRE Israël 1621-1691 **[48]**
$1 023 - €1 022 - **£640** - FF6 707
Landschaft mit Ruinen Ink (15.7x21.7cm 6x8in) Köln 1999
$287 - €298 - **£172** - FF1 955
Vedutine francesi Acquaforte (10.5x15cm 4x5in) Roma 1999

SILVESTRE Louis II 1675-1760 **[9]**
$59 772 - €64 160 - **£40 000** - FF420 864
The Sense of Touch: a youth kissing an unclad young woman Oil/canvas/panel (131x153.5cm 51x60in) London 2000
$9 000 - €9 874 - **£5 978** - FF64 771
Prometheus fashioning Man from clay in the Presence of Minerva Oil/canvas (47.5x32.5cm 18x12in) New-York 2000

SILVESTRE Paul 1884-? **[29]**
S **$1 797** - €1 524 - **£1 084** - FF10 000
«Deux amoureux assis» Bronze (50x33x14cm 19x12x5in) Paris 1998

SILVESTRI Tullio 1880-1963 **[25]**
$500 - €518 - **£300** - FF3 400
Processione Monotype (50x40cm 19x15in) Trieste 2001

SILVESTRO DEI GHERARDUCCI 1339-1399 **[1]**
$480 000 - €513 451 - **£327 264** - FF3 368 016
Madonna and Child Tempera/panel (77x47.5cm 30x18in) New-York 2000

SILVY Camille 1835-1869 **[10]**
$11 574 - €10 932 - **£7 000** - FF71 710
Portrait de femme Albumen print (25.5x18.5cm 10x7in) London 1999

SIMA Josef 1891-1971 **[149]**
$10 288 - €10 367 - **£6 412** - FF68 000
Sans titre Huile/toile (81x54cm 31x21in) Reims 2000
$2 959 - €2 744 - **£1 785** - FF18 000
Sans titre Huile/toile (33x46cm 12x18in) Paris 1999
$1 849 - €1 749 - **£1 152** - FF11 475
Souvenir Aquarelle (20x28cm 7x11in) Praha 2000
$546 - €516 - **£340** - FF3 388
De la série: Paris Eau-forte couleurs (36x26.5cm 14x10in) Praha 2000

SIMA Miron 1902-1999 **[4]**
$8 000 - €8 294 - **£5 272** - FF54 408
A Mea shearim Courtyard Oil/canvas (83x97cm 32x38in) Herzelia-Pituah 2000

SIMAK Lev 1896-1989 **[49]**
$722 - €683 - **£450** - FF4 482
Petshop Oil/canvas (72x51cm 28x20in) Praha 2000

SIMARD Marie-louise XX **[3]**
S **$10 627** - €9 451 - **£6 500** - FF61 992
Young Classical Woman Standing Naked Bronze (H61cm H24in) London 1999

SIMAS Eugène Martial XIX-XX **[6]**
$800 - €892 - **£523** - FF5 854
«Ludivine» Poster (137x98cm 53x38in) New-York 2000

SIMBARI Nicola 1927 **[227]**
$6 000 - €6 369 - **£4 060** - FF41 778
«Grand Saguaro» Acrylic/canvas (120x119cm 47x47in) Delray-Beach FL 2001
$3 000 - €3 556 - **£2 185** - FF23 329
Still Life with Flower Vase Oil/canvas (53x43cm 21x17in) Chicago IL 2001
$825 - €776 - **£514** - FF5 091
Scene in Rome Watercolour, gouache (39.5x58cm 15x22in) New-York 1999
$375 - €356 - **£234** - FF2 335
Beach Scene Silkscreen in colors (67x82.5cm 26x32in) Washington 1999

SIMBERG Hugo 1873-1917 **[161]**
$11 092 - €12 614 - **£7 695** - FF82 740
Två båtar på sandstrand Oil/canvas/panel (48x55cm 18x21in) Helsinki 2000
$2 299 - €2 523 - **£1 480** - FF16 548
Strandtall Mixed media (11x18cm 4x7in) Helsinki 2000
$1 003 - €1 043 - **£629** - FF6 839
Fan med blyg modell på stranden Indian ink/paper (20x23cm 7x9in) Helsinki 2000
$993 - €1 060 - **£674** - FF6 950
Fågelungen från storseglet Etching (7.6x5.1cm 2x2in) Helsinki 2001

SIME Sidney Herbert 1867-1941 **[7]**
$569 - €661 - **£400** - FF4 337
Two Men carrying Harps standing on a Heavenly Cloud Ink (45x28cm 17x11in) London 2001

SIMEONI Ant. XX **[3]**
$739 - €839 - **£513** - FF5 506
«Lago di Garda Riva» Poster (70x100.5cm 27x39in) Hoorn 2001

SIMESEN Viggo Rasmus 1864-1932 **[1]**
$9 329 - €10 834 - **£6 556** - FF71 069
Rungsteds badbrygga Oil/canvas (74x127cm 29x50in) Stockholm 2001

SIMI Filadelfo 1849-1923 **[8]**
$16 860 - €14 513 - **£11 200** - FF95 200
I consigli della nonna Olio/tela (94x82cm 37x32in) Roma 1998

SIMIAND Jacques XVIII **[3]**
S **$10 815** - €10 671 - **£6 720** - FF70 000
Portrait présumé du président Haugry, directeur du bureau Plâtre (H75cm H29in) Paris 1999

SIMKIN Richard 1840-1926 [176]
🖌 $729 - €706 - £450 - FF4 631
The Honourable Artillery Company Infantry
Watercolour/paper (26x21cm 10x8in) West-Midlands 1999

SIMM Franz Xaver 1853-1918 [26]
🖼 $3 806 - €3 988 - £2 517 - FF26 160
Wasserträgerinnen mit Kindern in römischem Gässchen Öl/Leinwand (40x52cm 15x20in) München 2000
🖼 $8 493 - €9 115 - £5 684 - FF59 792
Demaskiert, ung kvinde iklaedt hvid kjole Oil/paper (43x31.5cm 16x12in) Köbenhavn 2000
🖌 $261 - €256 - £168 - FF1 676
Der eilige fürstliche Archivar Pencil (34x18cm 13x7in) Kempten 1999

SIMMLER Friedrich Karl 1801-1872 [6]
🖼 $3 739 - €4 397 - £2 480 - FF28 843
Weidende Kühe vor Tiefer Landschaft Öl/Leinwand (47x57cm 18x22in) München 2001
🖼 $1 791 - €2 045 - £1 262 - FF13 415
Rheinlandschaft mit Kühen une einem Hirtenjungen Oil/panel (31x45cm 12x17in) Kassel 2001

SIMMLER Józef 1823-1868 [8]
🖼 $26 312 - €29 900 - £18 170 - FF196 132
Portrait de Katarzyna Jahn, soeur d'artiste Huile/toile (78x54.5cm 30x25in) Warszawa 2000

SIMMLER Wilhelm 1840-1914 [13]
🖼 $18 871 - €22 497 - £13 455 - FF147 571
Eine Blumenverkäuferin in Kairo Öl/Leinwand (117x80cm 46x31in) Köln 2000

SIMMONS Edward Emerson 1852-1931 [15]
🖼 $7 000 - €7 752 - £4 853 - FF50 848
Susquehanna river landscape Oil/canvas (25x60cm 10x24in) Downington PA 2001

SIMMONS Eyres XIX-XX [15]
🖌 $342 - €402 - £241 - FF2 637
At the Waterfront Watercolour/paper (25x35cm 9x13in) Calgary, Alberta 2000

SIMMONS Gary 1964 [5]
🖌 $2 500 - €2 901 - £1 726 - FF19 027
Earsure Series, No. 5/No.10 Charcoal (76x56.5cm 29x22in) New-York 2000

SIMMONS J. Deane XIX-XX [10]
🖼 $1 671 - €1 779 - £1 180 - FF11 671
The Fair harvest Girl Watercolour/paper (78x57cm 30x22in) Billingshurst, West-Sussex 2000

SIMMONS Laurie 1949 [41]
🖼 $3 000 - €3 360 - £2 084 - FF22 041
Lying Objects Offset (38.5x51cm 15x20in) New-York 2001
📷 $1 600 - €1 856 - £1 104 - FF12 177
«Study for Mermaid», Variation Photograph in colors (34.5x51cm 13x20in) New-York 2000

SIMMONS William Henry 1811-1882 [17]
🖼 $283 - €305 - £190 - FF1 999
The Meet of the Vine Hounds, After H.Calvert Engraving (56x80cm 22x31in) Suffolk 2000

SIMO Juan Bautista c.1697-c.1726 [3]
🖼 $14 476 - €15 988 - £10 032 - FF104 874
Porträt des Acisclo Antonio Palomino de Castro y Velasco (1655-1726) Öl/Leinwand (75x65cm 29x25in) Wien 2001

SIMOES DE FONSECA Gaston 1874-? [17]
🖼 $5 500 - €6 136 - £3 600 - FF40 250
«12e Salon de l'Automobile» Poster (103.5x75cm 40x29in) New-York 2000

SIMON Armand 1906-1981 [111]
🖌 $258 - €297 - £177 - FF1 951
De verwondering Ink (36x27cm 14x10in) Lokeren 2000

SIMON Émile Joseph Jules 1890-1976 [115]
🖼 $769 - €915 - £548 - FF6 000
Côte rocheuse à Ouessant près du Phare du Créach Huile/toile (50x73cm 19x28in) Brest 2000
🖼 $891 - €884 - £554 - FF5 800
Conversation près du puits, Porspoder Huile/panneau (25x34cm 9x13in) Brest 1999
🖌 $591 - €534 - £364 - FF3 500
Le port de Concarneau Aquarelle/papier (29x40cm 11x15in) La Baule 1999

SIMON Erich M. 1892-? [4]
🖼 $450 - €419 - £278 - FF2 747
«Concurso Sudamericano de Ski» Poster (72x47cm 28x18in) New-York 1999

SIMON Henry 1910-1987 [30]
🖌 $620 - €625 - £386 - FF4 100
Le soir sur Saint-Gilles Pastel/papier (30x40cm 11x15in) La Roche-sur-Yon 2000

SIMON Hermann Gustave 1846-1895 [7]
🖼 $12 000 - €13 942 - £8 433 - FF91 454
Setters in a Landscape Oil/canvas (35.5x51cm 13x20in) New-York 2001

SIMON Jacques 1875-1965 [175]
🖼 $445 - €457 - £279 - FF3 000
Lièvre courant le long du ruisseau au Lude Huile/carton (27x19cm 10x7in) Deauville 2000
🖌 $526 - €534 - £330 - FF3 500
Vue d'Avranches Aquarelle (26x36cm 10x14in) Coutances 2000

SIMON Joe XX [1]
🖌 $21 000 - €22 541 - £14 053 - FF147 861
Drawing Concept Sketch for Captain America Watercolour (42x21.5cm 16x8in) New-York 2000

SIMON John ?-1917 [2]
🖼 $1 186 - €1 262 - £750 - FF8 278
The Element of Water Mezzotint (35.5x25.5cm 13x10in) London 2000

SIMON Kati 1952 [24]
🖼 $626 - €732 - £429 - FF4 800
Bouquet à la pivoine rose Huile/toile (55x38cm 21x14in) Paris 2000

SIMON Lucien 1861-1945 [248]
🖼 $11 641 - €9 909 - £6 929 - FF65 000
Douarnenez - Le jeunes mousses se reposant sur le quai Huile/toile (105x145cm 41x57in) Brest 1998
🖼 $4 471 - €5 031 - £3 078 - FF33 000
Les deux Bretonnes Huile/toile (77x60cm 30x23in) Limoges 2000
🖼 $1 316 - €1 372 - £828 - FF9 000
La baignade des enfants Huile/carton (21.5x28.5cm 8x11in) Nantes 2000
🖌 $2 203 - €2 058 - £1 359 - FF13 500
Jeune mousse tenant un aviron Aquarelle/papier (61x26cm 24x10in) Brest 1999
🖼 $205 - €244 - £146 - FF1 500
Les marguiliers Lithographie (27x35cm 10x13in) Brest 2000

S

SIMON Paul 1892-1979 **[8]**

🖎 **$1 278** - €1 372 - **£855** - FF9 000
Eléphant et éléphanteau Bronze (33x39x15cm
12x15x5in) Nice 2000

SIMON Pierre II c.1740-c.1810 **[5]**

⬚⬚⬚ **$181** - €183 - **£113** - FF1 200
Shakespeare: Much ado about nothing; Act III
scène I, d'après W.Peters Eau-forte (50.5x41cm
19x16in) Paris 2000

SIMON Tavik Frantisek 1877-1942 **[187]**

😊 **$15 895** - €15 034 - **£9 900** - FF98 615
Sommer an einer Seeküste in Frankreich
Öl/Leinwand (158x174cm 62x68in) Praha 2000
😊 **$3 468** - €3 280 - **£2 160** - FF21 516
L'église de Saint Marc à Benatki Huile/toile
(74x84.5cm 29x33in) Praha 2000
😊 **$693** - €656 - **£432** - FF4 303
Paysage de printemps Huile/carton (22x27.5cm
8x10in) Praha 2001
⬚⬚⬚ **$175** - €162 - **£109** - FF1 063
Flower Ladies Etching in colors (30x35cm 12x14in)
Chicago IL 1999

SIMON Yochanan 1905-1976 **[186]**

😊 **$29 000** - €30 784 - **£19 624** - FF201 927
Landscape in Peru Oil/canvas (130x97cm 51x38in)
Tel Aviv 2001
😊 **$10 500** - €8 922 - **£6 342** - FF58 522
The Kibbutz, Evening, Landscape and Figures
Oil/board (35x47cm 13x18in) Tel Aviv 1999
😊 **$5 500** - €5 702 - **£3 624** - FF37 405
Evening Hour Oil/canvas (26x34cm 10x13in)
Herzelia-Pituah 2000
😊 **$1 800** - €1 911 - **£1 218** - FF12 533
Vegetation Gouache/paper (34.5x48cm 13x18in) Tel
Aviv 2001

SIMON-AUGUSTE Simon 1909-1987 **[77]**

😊 **$905** - €1 067 - **£636** - FF7 000
Nu assis Huile/toile (22x27cm 8x10in) Fontainebleau
2000

SIMONE de XIX [23]

😊 **$1 320** - €1 140 - **£880** - FF7 480
Nave Tempera/tela (63x42cm 24x16in) Genova 1998
🖎 **$1 396** - €1 393 - **£850** - FF9 139
H.M.S Dreadnought in the Bay of Naples/HMS
Collingwood in rough Seas Gouache/paper
(29x46cm 11x18in) London 2000

SIMONE de A. XIX-XX [41]

😊 **$3 186** - €3 697 - **£2 200** - FF24 253
British Steam Frigate under Sail in the
Mediterranean Oil/canvas (46x67cm 18x26in) London
2000
🖎 **$2 108** - €2 025 - **£1 300** - FF13 284
The British Schooner Pluvier under full Sail off
Naples Gouache/paper (42x62.5cm 16x24in) London
1999

SIMONE de Alfredo XIX-XX [11]

😊 **$9 500** - €9 879 - **£5 998** - FF64 799
Barco Oleo/cartón (40x51cm 15x20in) Montevideo
2000
😊 **$9 000** - €8 709 - **£5 550** - FF57 125
Barrio Sur Oleo/cartón (26x34cm 10x13in)
Montevideo 1999
🖎 **$3 553** - €3 341 - **£2 200** - FF21 917
R.Y.S. «Chazalie» at Sail/The R.Y.S.
«Chazalie» with Sails Lowered Gouache/paper
(39x56cm 15x22in) London 1999

SIMONE de Antonio c.1840-c.1915 **[48]**

🖎 **$3 330** - €3 887 - **£2 282** - FF25 500
Sans titres Gouache/papier (31x47cm 12x18in) Le
Havre 2000

SIMONE de Michele 1893-1955 **[7]**

😊 **$3 629** - €3 762 - **£2 177** - FF24 680
Isola Comacina Olio/tavola (37x42cm 14x16in)
Milano 1999

SIMONE de Tomaso XIX-XX [69]

😊 **$5 323** - €4 509 - **£3 200** - FF29 574
Royal Thames Yacht Club Schooner in the Bay
of Naples Oil/canvas (46x65cm 18x25in) London
1998
🖎 **$1 432** - €1 397 - **£870** - FF9 163
Schooner-Riged Steam Yatch of the Royal Yatch
Squadron Under Nail Gouache/papier (32.5x47cm
12x18in) London 2000

SIMONELLI Giuseppe da Giordano c.1650-1710 **[9]**

😊 **$18 536** - €15 715 - **£11 000** - FF103 081
The Sacrifice of Isaac Oil/canvas (132x182cm
51x71in) London 1998
😊 **$6 080** - €5 706 - **£3 800** - FF37 430
Virgen rodeada de ángeles Oleo/lienzo (121x90cm
47x35in) Madrid 1999

SIMONET LOMBARDO Enrique 1864-1927 **[10]**

😊 **$13 440** - €14 416 - **£9 120** - FF94 560
Escena oriental Oleo/lienzo (37x62cm 14x24in)
Madrid 2001

SIMONETTI Alfonso 1840-1892 **[7]**

🖎 **$1 613** - €1 503 - **£1 000** - FF9 858
Musical Duet Watercolour/paper (54x36.5cm 21x14in)
Billingshurst, West-Sussex 1999

SIMONETTI Amadeo 1874-1922 **[17]**

😊 **$3 500** - €3 674 - **£2 366** - FF24 103
Cardinal being Entertained by young Mozart
with Pianist Oil/canvas (78x49cm 31x19in) Detroit MI
2001
🖎 **$9 000** - €9 893 - **£5 767** - FF64 405
The Carpet Seller Watercolour/paper (54.5x76.5cm
21x30in) New-York 2000

SIMONETTI Attilio 1843-1925 **[27]**

😊 **$4 000** - €4 147 - **£2 400** - FF27 200
Paesaggio con contadinella Olio/tela (63x104cm
24x40in) Torino 2001
🖎 **$6 647** - €6 555 - **£4 274** - FF43 000
Elégante au perroquet Huile/toile (41x32cm
16x12in) Paris 1999
🖎 **$1 000** - €863 - **£601** - FF5 659
The Artist at Her Easel Watercolour/paper (43x35cm
16x13in) Boston MA 1998

SIMONETTI Ettore 1857-1909 **[44]**

😊 **$10 349** - €10 021 - **£6 500** - FF65 731
In St. Peter's Rome Oil/canvas (75x107cm 29x42in)
London 1999
🖎 **$17 000** - €14 667 - **£10 256** - FF96 208
The jewelry merchant Watercolour (75.5x53cm
29x20in) New-York 1998

SIMONI Gustavo 1846-1926 **[56]**

😊 **$12 250** - €12 699 - **£7 350** - FF83 300
Strada araba Olio/tela (64x89cm 25x35in) Milano
2000
😊 **$5 355** - €5 551 - **£3 213** - FF36 414
Pittore in costume al cavalletto Olio/tavola
(15.5x21cm 6x8in) Milano 1999
🖎 **$16 000** - €15 179 - **£9 720** - FF99 566
Smoking the Hookah Watercolour (54x36cm
21x14in) New-York 1999

S

SIMONI Paolo A. 1882-1960 **[7]**

✐ **$3 810** - €4 269 - **£2 648** - FF28 000
Femme orientale et sa servante Aquarelle,
gouache/papier (53x27.5cm 20x10in) Paris 2001

SIMONI Scipione 1853-1918 **[23]**

✐ **$915** - €1 032 - **£634** - FF6 767
«Montecelio» Watercolour/paper (74.5x53.5cm
29x21in) Toronto 2000

SIMONIDY Michel 1870-1933 **[44]**

☞ **$1 066** - €991 - **£647** - FF6 500
Les îles Coraliennes Huile/carton (71x82cm
27x32in) Paris 1998

▥ **$1 005** - €1 143 - **£697** - FF7 500
«Po. La Bourboule, Source Choussy Perrière»
Affiche (149x108cm 58x42in) Orléans 2000

SIMONIN Victor 1877-1946 **[155]**

☞ **$576** - €635 - **£376** - FF4 167
Bloemstilleven Oil/board (39x49cm 15x19in) Den
Haag 2000

☞ **$224** - €248 - **£152** - FF1 626
Nature morte à la jardinière Huile/carton (26x32cm
10x12in) Bruxelles 2000

SIMONINI Francesco 1686-1753 **[86]**

☞ **$163 180** - €151 690 - **£100 000** - FF995 020
**Equestrian Portrait of Field Marshal Count J.M.
von der Schulenburg** Oil/canvas (198x143.5cm
77x56in) London 1998

☞ **$19 033** - €19 985 - **£12 000** - FF131 096
Trumpeter on Horseback/Mounted Drummer
Oil/canvas (45.5x35.5cm 17x13in) London 2000

☞ **$9 250** - €9 589 - **£5 550** - FF62 900
**Ufficiale a cavallo/Ufficiale a cavallo visto di
spalle** Olio/tela (30.5x23.5cm 12x9in) Venezia 2000

☞ **$2 700** - €2 332 - **£1 350** - FF15 300
Scena di battaglia davanti a una torre Inchiostro
(20.5x14cm 8x5in) Milano 1999

SIMONNEAU Charles Louis 1645-1728 **[8]**

▥ **$203** - €211 - **£134** - FF1 382
**Le voyage de la Reine au Pont de Cé, d'après
Rubens** Gravure (45.5x34cm 17x13in) Bruxelles 2000

SIMONNET Lucien 1849-1926 **[11]**

☞ **$1 464** - €1 346 - **£900** - FF8 832
Elegant Ladies in a Woodland Lanscape Oil/can-
vas (33x41cm 12x16in) London 1998

SIMONS Jan Frans 1855-1919 **[47]**

☞ **$739** - €793 - **£496** - FF5 203
Chemin forestier Huile/toile (79x59cm 31x23in)
Antwerpen 2000

☞ **$758** - €843 - **£530** - FF5 528
Rêverie Huile/toile (38x30cm 14x11in) Antwerpen
2001

SIMONS Michiels 1620-1673 **[16]**

☞ **$70 000** - €77 523 - **£47 474** - FF508 515
**Fruit in a Porcelain Dish, Flowers in a Vase, a
Roemer, a Wine Glass** Oil/canvas (82.5x126.5cm
32x49in) New-York 2000

SIMONS Paul 1865-1932 **[5]**

☞ **$5 906** - €6 632 - **£3 830** - FF43 505
Harbour Scene Oil/canvas (58.5x95cm 23x37in)
Malvern, Victoria 2000

SIMONSEN Niels 1807-1885 **[91]**

☞ **$4 910** - €4 238 - **£2 967** - FF27 801
En Zuav ved sin döende hest Oil/canvas (45x54cm
17x21in) Vejle 1999

☞ **$870** - €938 - **£593** - FF6 156
**Scene fra Treårskrigen, fremrykning mod fjen-
den** Oil/canvas (23x26cm 9x10in) Köbenhavn 2001

SIMONSEN Simon Ludwig Ditlev 1841-1928 **[231]**

☞ **$11 760** - €13 423 - **£8 170** - FF88 050
På landevejen Oil/canvas (98x140cm 38x55in)
Köbenhavn 2000

☞ **$4 798** - €4 836 - **£2 991** - FF31 723
**Bange, Pointerhvalpe og gravhundehvalp ved
det tomme madtrug** Oil/canvas (37x54cm 14x21in)
Köbenhavn 2000

☞ **$1 337** - €1 143 - **£803** - FF7 498
Dansk fjordlandskab med kvaeg i forgrunden
Oil/canvas (23x33cm 9x12in) Köbenhavn 1998

SIMONSSON Birger 1883-1938 **[69]**

☞ **$956** - €900 - **£592** - FF5 901
Sommarlandskap Oil/panel (38x46cm 14x18in)
Stockholm 1999

☞ **$1 415** - €1 642 - **£977** - FF10 773
Landskap i motsol Oil/panel (32x40cm 12x15in)
Stockholm 2000

SIMONSSON Karl Konrad 1843-1901 **[43]**

☞ **$1 182** - €1 166 - **£728** - FF7 649
Sommarvy med höstack Oil/canvas (65x92cm
25x36in) Stockholm 1999

☞ **$595** - €584 - **£369** - FF3 830
Sommarlandskap med vattendrag i solnedgång
Oil/panel (22x30cm 8x11in) Stockholm 1999

SIMONY Stefan 1860-1950 **[34]**

☞ **$7 500** - €8 245 - **£4 806** - FF54 081
The Harvesters Oil/panel (51.5x76cm 20x29in) New-
York 2000

SIMOTOVA Adriena 1926 **[8]**

▥ **$144** - €137 - **£90** - FF896
Sans titre Lithographie couleurs (54x38cm 21x14in)
Praha 2001

SIMPKINS Henry John 1906 **[21]**

✐ **$585** - €500 - **£354** - FF3 283
«Washing the Clydesdales» Aquarelle/papier
(52x75cm 20x29in) Montréal 1998

SIMPSON Alex. Brantingham XIX-XX **[14]**

✐ **$181** - €214 - **£127** - FF1 401
The Outing in Spring Watercolour/paper (18x28.5cm
7x11in) Sydney 2000

SIMPSON Charles Walter 1885-1971 **[215]**

☞ **$8 040** - €8 235 - **£5 000** - FF54 020
Ducks on a Pond Oil/canvas (101x151.5cm 39x59in)
Billingshurst, West-Sussex 2000

☞ **$2 673** - €2 260 - **£1 600** - FF14 822
Spaniels chasing their Quarry through a River
Oil/canvas (61x76cm 24x29in) London 1998

☞ **$417** - €420 - **£260** - FF2 756
Cotterill Spinnery Oil/board (26x36cm 10x14in)
London 2000

☞ **$817** - €680 - **£480** - FF4 461
«The Blue Pool» Gouache/paper (49x58cm 19x22in)
London 1998

SIMPSON H. Hardy XIX-XX **[4]**

☞ **$2 300** - €2 279 - **£1 395** - FF14 948
Colonel Blain's First Gun Dog Oil/canvas
(25x35cm 10x14in) New-Orleans LA 2000

SIMPSON Henry 1853-1921 **[51]**

✐ **$571** - €594 - **£360** - FF3 894
**St.Marks, Venice with Figures and Fishing
Boats Doves in the Foregroud** Watercolour
(59.5x22.5cm 23x8in) Leyburn, North Yorkshire 2000

S

SIMPSON Jackson Henry 1893-1963 **[19]**

🖋 **$1 423** – €1 664 - **£1 000** – FF10 913
Cockle Gatherers by the Edge of the Sea
Watercolour/paper (34x48cm 13x18in) Oxfordshire 2000

SIMPSON Jane 1965 **[5]**

🏺 **$2 498** – €2 318 - **£1 500** – FF15 208
Gravy Boat Plaster (33x64x10cm 12x25x3in) London 1999

SIMPSON Joseph 1879-1939 **[28]**

▦ **$163** – €156 - **£98** – FF1 024
John Peel Etching (30x21cm 11x8in) Bury St. Edmunds, Suffolk 1999

SIMPSON Lorna 1960 **[26]**

▦ **$8 500** – €8 169 - **£5 236** – FF53 583
Haze Serigraph (173x175.5cm 68x69in) New-York 1999

📷 **$6 000** – €5 805 - **£3 700** – FF38 081
Proofreading Gelatin silver print (106.5x106.5cm 41x41in) New-York 1999

SIMPSON W.H. XIX-XX **[3]**

🖋 **$3 849** – €3 808 - **£2 400** – FF24 977
The Thames at Night Watercolour (36.5x51.5cm 14x20in) London 1999

SIMPSON William «Crimean» 1823-1899 **[73]**

🖋 **$4 974** – €4 612 - **£3 000** – FF30 254
Herodotus Consulting with the Priest, Vulcan at Memphis Watercolour (49.5x38cm 19x14in) London 1999

▦ **$416** – €401 - **£260** – FF2 629
Mosque of the Sultan Barkook and Fountain of Ismaeel Pasha Lithograph (36x28cm 14x11in) London 1999

SIMS Charles 1873-1928 **[64]**

☞ **$1 587** – €1 626 - **£980** – FF10 665
Sittande kvinna med parasoll Oil/canvas (90x70cm 35x27in) Stockholm 2000

🖋 **$1 394** – €1 529 - **£899** – FF10 031
Figures in an Enchanted Garden Watercolour (43.5x48.5cm 17x19in) London 2000

SIMS Jim 1971 **[3]**

☞ **$2 200** – €2 164 - **£1 330** – FF14 197
School Oil/canvas (41x30cm 16x11in) Chicago IL 2000

SIMSON George 1791-1862 **[2]**

☞ **$5 454** – €6 134 - **£3 800** – FF40 239
Dundee from the South-East Oil/canvas (41x100cm 16x39in) Edinburgh 2001

SIMUNEK Karel 1869-1942 **[15]**

▦ **$1 600** – €1 785 - **£1 047** – FF11 709
«Karneval Umnelcu» Poster (124.5x91cm 49x35in) New-York 2000

SINATRA Frank 1915-1998 **[2]**

☞ **$18 391** – €19 741 - **£12 307** – FF129 493
Clown Portrait Acrylic/canvas/board (17x12cm 7x5in) Beverly-Hills CA 2000

SINCLAIR Alexander Gordon 1859-1930 **[6]**

☞ **$959** – €913 - **£600** – FF5 988
Rural Castle, Scotland Oil/canvas (62x75cm 24x29in) Channel-Islands 1999

SINCLAIR Gerrit V. 1890-1955 **[5]**

☞ **$750** – €853 - **£520** – FF5 595
Country Road Oil/board (38x50cm 15x20in) Cincinnati OH 2000

SINCLAIR Irving 1895-1969 **[5]**

☞ **$3 750** – €4 026 - **£2 509** – FF26 406
Monterey Harbor Oil/masonite (81x127cm 31x50in) San-Francisco CA 2000

▦ **$2 740** – €3 028 - **£1 900** – FF19 865
«The Mind Reader» Poster (104x68.5cm 40x26in) London 2001

SINCLAIR John ?-c.1922 **[8]**

🖋 **$363** – €361 - **£220** – FF2 370
Highland Cattle in a Moorland Watercolour (44.5x66.5cm 17x26in) London 2000

SINCLAIR Max XIX **[37]**

☞ **$2 300** – €1 984 - **£1 382** – FF13 016
The Old and the New, a Harbor View Oil/canvas (51x40.5cm 20x15in) Boston MA 1998

☞ **$1 521** – €1 765 - **£1 050** – FF11 517
Awaiting the Turn of the Tide Oil/canvas (34.5x44.5cm 13x17in) London 2000

🖋 **$6 845** – €6 224 - **£4 200** – FF40 827
Ships Loading at Dusk/Shipping on the Thames by Moonlight Watercolour/paper (60x50cm 23x19in) West-Midlands 1999

SINDING Knud 1875-1946 **[97]**

🖋 **$659** – €565 - **£397** – FF3 704
Husmand i snak med kvinder på heden Oil/canvas (56x69cm 22x27in) Lingby 1998

SINDING Otto Ludvig 1842-1909 **[50]**

☞ **$10 665** – €10 095 - **£6 637** – FF66 217
La tarentella Oil/canvas (100x200cm 39x78in) Vejle 1999

☞ **$2 278** – €2 556 - **£1 579** – FF16 743
Bauer beim Pflügen in norwegischer Landschaft Öl/Leinwand (38x50cm 14x19in) München 2000

🖋 **$9 000** – €10 276 - **£6 345** – FF67 409
Mermaid Pastel/canvas (112x54.5cm 44x21in) Boston MA 2001

SINDING Stephan Abel 1846-1922 **[46]**

🖋 **$4 576** – €5 453 - **£3 278** – FF35 772
Guerrier mourant dans les bras d'une femme Marbre Carrare (H89cm H35in) Antwerpen 2000

🏺 **$818** – €699 - **£491** – FF4 587
Dansende figur Bronze (H23cm H9in) København 1998

SINÉ Maurice Sinet, dit 1928 **[21]**

🖋 **$214** – €244 - **£148** – FF1 600
La Joconde Encre/papier (19x20cm 7x7in) Douai 2000

SINEMUS Wilhelmus Friedrich 1903-1987 **[21]**

🖋 **$1 748** – €1 724 - **£1 076** – FF11 311
Untitled Gouache (58x46cm 22x18in) Amsterdam 1999

SING Johann Caspar 1651-1729 **[6]**

🖋 **$948** – €920 - **£590** – FF6 037
Das Martyrium des hl. Pankraz Indian ink (19.8x16cm 7x6in) Berlin 1999

SINGDAHLSEN Andreas 1855-1947 **[20]**

🖋 **$1 575** – €1 873 - **£1 122** – FF12 285
Rödt hus ved bekken Oil/canvas (94x69cm 37x27in) Oslo 2000

SINGENDONCK Dieterick Jan 1784-1833 **[4]**

☞ **$6 949** – €8 168 - **£4 818** – FF53 578
A Still Life with Grapes, Peaches and Flowers on a Marble Ledge Oil/paper/panel (35.5x46cm 13x18in) Amsterdam 2000

SINGER Burr 1912 **[14]**
🖋 **$950** - €1 110 - **£678** - FF7 282
Merry, Go, Round in Griffith Park Mixed media/paper (36x46cm 14x18in) Altadena CA 2001

SINGER Clyde J. 1908-1999 **[70]**
👁 **$675** - €709 - **£425** - FF4 649
Subway Reader Oil/board (34x25cm 13x10in) Pittsburgh PA 2000
🖋 **$420** - €404 - **£259** - FF2 649
Artist's Studio Watercolour/paper (28x41cm 11x16in) Cleveland OH 1999
▥ **$180** - €168 - **£111** - FF1 100
«**Standing Nude**» Etching (20x8cm 8x3in) Cleveland OH 1999

SINGER Susi, Selma 1891-1965 **[21]**
🐾 **$1 172** - €1 163 - **£734** - FF7 627
Vater mit Kindern Ceramic (H16.7cm H6in) Wien 1999

SINGER William Henry, Jnr. 1868-1943 **[26]**
👁 **$3 223** - €3 630 - **£2 221** - FF23 812
Torrent in a Norwegian Landscape Oil/panel (45x75cm 17x21in) Amsterdam 2000
👁 **$2 400** - €2 576 - **£1 606** - FF16 898
A New Day Oil/panel (32x41.5cm 12x16in) New-York 2000

SINGH Arpita 1937 **[37]**
👁 **$8 000** - €6 906 - **£4 779** - FF45 300
«**Ayesha Kidwai Against White Against Grey**» Oil/canvas (121x121cm 47x47in) New-York 1998
👁 **$3 500** - €3 021 - **£2 090** - FF19 818
In the Garden Oil/canvas (110x87cm 43x34in) New-York 1998
🖋 **$2 750** - €2 374 - **£1 643** - FF15 574
Untitled Watercolour/paper (40.5x29cm 15x11in) New-York 1998

SINGIER Gustave 1909-1984 **[519]**
👁 **$15 697** - €17 532 - **£10 637** - FF115 000
«**Intérieur bleu animé**» Huile/toile (162x130cm 63x51in) Versailles 1999
👁 **$9 006** - €8 690 - **£5 654** - FF57 000
L'estacade Huile/toile (50x61cm 19x24in) Paris 1999
👁 **$14 014** - €14 940 - **£8 888** - FF98 000
Le reniement de Saint-Pierre Huile/panneau (32x22.5cm 12x8in) Paris 2000
🖋 **$1 449** - €1 342 - **£874** - FF8 800
Composition abstraite Aquarelle/papier (56x45cm 22x17in) Paris 1999
▥ **$208** - €194 - **£128** - FF1 274
Komposition Farbradierung (54.1x42cm 21x16in) Hamburg 1999

SINGLETON Henry 1766-1839 **[20]**
👁 **$3 605** - €3 984 - **£2 500** - FF26 132
Volumnia and Virgilia pleading before Coriolanus Oil/canvas (59x79cm 23x31in) London 2001
👁 **$5 631** - €5 359 - **£3 500** - FF35 150
Returned from Market Oil/canvas (35.5x30.5cm 13x12in) London 1999

SINHA Satish Chandra 1893-1965 **[5]**
👁 **$11 577** - €10 829 - **£7 000** - FF71 033
Maiden and Deer Oil/canvas (122x152.5cm 48x60in) London 1999
🖋 **$2 110** - €2 028 - **£1 300** - FF13 303
Spring Watercolour (59x43.5cm 23x17in) London 1999

SINIBALDI Paul Jean 1857-1909 **[34]**
👁 **$88 672** - €103 665 - **£63 308** - FF680 000
Salammbô Huile/toile (191x353cm 75x138in) Paris 2001
👁 **$1 411** - €1 278 - **£880** - FF8 385
Three Maidens in a Landscape Oil/canvas (54.5x88cm 21x34in) London 1999

SINTENIS Renée 1888-1965 **[394]**
🐾 **$6 202** - €6 135 - **£3 867** - FF40 246
Grasendes Fohlen Bronze (8.5x10.5x4cm 3x4x1in) Berlin 1999
🖋 **$599** - €562 - **£371** - FF3 689
Fohlen Indian ink (29x21cm 11x8in) München 1999
▥ **$144** - €169 - **£101** - FF1 106
Sich anschleichender Leopard Radierung (19x15.8cm 7x6in) Berlin 2000

SINTES Joseph 1829-1913 **[20]**
👁 **$393** - €457 - **£280** - FF3 010
«**La passerelle de la Pérouse, près d'Alger vers 1900**» Huile/panneau (24.5x44.5cm 9x17in) Senlis 2001

SION Marie 1935 **[46]**
👁 **$300** - €329 - **£209** - FF2 200
Mas dans les alpilles Huile/toile (46x55cm 18x21in) Lons-Le-Saunier 2001

SION Peeter ?-c.1695 **[4]**
👁 **$6 614** - €6 247 - **£4 000** - FF40 977
Joseph lowered into the Well by his Brothers Oil/copper (61x77.5cm 24x30in) London 1999

SIONNEAU Guylaine XX **[10]**
🐾 **$512** - €610 - **£366** - FF4 000
Ourson polaire allongé sur le ventre Bronze (7x15cm 2x5in) Paris 2000

SIOPSIS Penelope 1953 **[2]**
🖋 **$9 285** - €10 401 - **£6 450** - FF68 227
«**Dora and the other Woman**» Pastel/paper (156x120cm 61x47in) Johannesburg 2001

SIPILÄ Sulho 1895-1949 **[13]**
👁 **$3 073** - €2 690 - **£1 862** - FF17 646
Helsingfors Oil/canvas (71x61cm 27x24in) Helsinki 1998

SIQUEIROS David Alfaro 1896-1974 **[275]**
👁 **$170 000** - €182 477 - **£113 764** - FF1 196 970
Proyecto para el mural del porfirismo a la Revolution en el Castillo Mixed media (122.5x169.5cm 48x66in) New-York 2000
👁 **$35 000** - €41 210 - **£24 594** - FF270 319
Cabeza de anciana Mixed media (102x66cm 40x25in) New-York 2000
👁 **$11 400** - €12 013 - **£7 200** - FF78 800
En el camino de la Lucha Acrílico/cartulina (41x31.5cm 16x12in) Madrid 2000
🖋 **$24 000** - €25 761 - **£16 060** - FF168 984
Accidente en la mina Pencil (21x34cm 8x13in) New-York 2000
▥ **$848** - €996 - **£602** - FF6 532
El guardián de la paz Litografía (30x22.5cm 11x8in) México 2000

SIQUIER Pablo 1961 **[2]**
👁 **$8 000** - €9 295 - **£5 622** - FF60 969
Sin título Oil/canvas (180x200cm 70x78in) New-York 2001

SIRANI Elisabetta 1638-1665 **[32]**
👁 **$30 000** - €33 224 - **£20 346** - FF217 935
Venus and Cupid Oil/canvas (110.5x92cm 43x36in) New-York 2000

S

💶 **$1 600** - €1 659 - **£960** - FF10 880
Studio di nudo virile a tre quarti visto di profilo
Sanguina/carta (22.5x15.5cm 8x6in) Milano 2000

📖 **$3 262** - €3 579 - **£2 216** - FF23 477
Die Heilige Familie Radierung (29x21.8cm 11x8in)
Berlin 2000

SIRANI Giovanni Andrea 1610-1670 **[20]**

🖼 **$40 000** - €44 803 - **£27 792** - FF293 888
Fortune with a Purse Oil/canvas (161.5x130cm
63x51in) New-York 2001

🖼 **$15 000** - €15 550 - **£9 000** - FF102 000
Lucrezia Olio/tela (88x71cm 34x27in) Roma 2001

✏ **$3 370** - €3 348 - **£2 100** - FF21 963
Three Boys Playing the Flûte/Nude Red
chalk/paper (20.5x23cm 8x9in) London 1999

📖 **$350** - €410 - £248 - FF2 687
Apollo and Maryas Etching (14x20cm 5x7in) New-
York 2000

SIRKS Jan 1885-1938 **[42]**

🖼 **$1 623** - €1 815 - **£1 130** - FF11 906
Ducks at the Waterside Oil/canvas/panel
(9.5x14.5cm 3x5in) Amsterdam 2001

📖 **$106** - €100 - **£64** - FF654
Albrechtskolk Rotterdam Etching (26x20.5cm
10x8in) Dordrecht 1999

SIRONI Mario 1885-1961 **[825]**

🖼 **$56 000** - €72 566 - **£42 000** - FF476 000
Grande composizione Olio/tela (120x110cm
47x43in) Milano 2000

🖼 **$20 550** - €21 251 - **£12 300** - FF139 400
Doppio paesaggio montano Olio/tela (60x80cm
23x31in) Torino 1999

🖼 **$6 500** - €6 738 - **£3 900** - FF44 200
Paesaggio Olio/carta/tela (23x28cm 9x11in) Milano
2000

💶 **$3 000** - €3 110 - **£1 800** - FF20 400
Montagne Tempera/carta (25x32cm 9x12in) Prato
1999

📖 **$8 100** - €6 997 - **£4 050** - FF45 900
Paesaggio con albero e figura Monotype
(36.5x44.5cm 14x17in) Milano 1999

SISK Bob XX **[1]**

📖 **$220 000** - €205 935 - **£136 334** - FF1 350 844
King Kong Poster (206x104cm 81x40in) New-York
2000

SISKIND Aaron 1903-1991 **[174]**

📷 **$2 000** - €1 867 - **£1 211** - FF12 249
San Luis Potosi 16 Gelatin silver print (36x47.5cm
14x18in) New-York 1999

SISLEY Alfred 1839-1899 **[242]**

🖼 **$661 080** - €564 824 - **£400 000** - FF3 705 000
Autour de la forêt, une clairière Oil/canvas
(54.5x65.5cm 21x25in) London 1998

🖼 **$206 739** - €178 365 - **£124 254** - FF1 170 000
Canal à St-Mammès Huile/toile (32x41cm 12x16in)
Nice 1998

✏ **$50 000** - €47 068 - **£30 890** - FF308 745
Bord de rivière Pastel/paper (30x40cm 11x15in)
New-York 1999

📖 **$900** - €852 - £559 - FF5 588
Bords du Long, près Saint-Mammes Color lithograph (14x22cm 5x8in) New-York 1999

SISMORE Charles Porter XIX **[3]**

🖼 **$4 634** - €5 378 - **£3 200** - FF35 277
**American Vessels Exchanging Salutes off the
Liverpool Waterfront** Oil/canvas (53.5x66cm
21x25in) London 2000

SISQUELLA ORIOL Alfredo 1900-1964 **[11]**

🖼 **$4 368** - €4 044 - **£2 674** - FF26 527
Hafenansicht unter leicht bewölktem Himmel
Öl/Leinwand (38x55cm 14x21in) Bern 1999

SISSON Lawrence P. 1928 **[22]**

🖼 **$1 100** - €1 300 - **£779** - FF8 525
Autumn Landscape Oil/masonite (60x141cm
23x55in) Boston MA 2000

💶 **$850** - €882 - **£539** - FF5 788
**Norwalk Gristmill/Still Lifewith Chinese
Lanterns** Watercolour (28x47cm 11x18in) Boston MA
2000

SITE delle Mino 1914-1996 **[4]**

🖼 **$11 200** - €14 513 - **£8 400** - FF95 200
«Viaggi interplanetari» Olio/tela (40x50cm 15x19in)
Milano 2000

SITHOLE Lucas Tandokwzsi 1931-1994 **[7]**

🗿 **$10 333** - €11 521 - **£6 737** - FF75 576
Mother and Child Bronze (H139cm H54in)
Johannesburg 2000

🗿 **$1 998** - €2 228 - **£1 303** - FF14 618
Lost Shepherd Bronze (H39cm H15in) Johannesburg
2000

SITTE Willi 1921 **[31]**

🖼 **$3 596** - €4 090 - **£2 494** - FF26 831
Liebespaar Oil/panel (41x24.6cm 16x9in) Hamburg
2000

📖 **$165** - €194 - **£116** - FF1 274
Paar beim Liebesspiel mit Betrachtern
Farblithographie (52.5x48cm 20x18in) Dettelbach-
Effeldorf 2001

SITTER Inger S. 1929 **[17]**

✏ **$1 322** - €1 468 - **£921** - FF9 627
Komposisjon Drawing (105x75cm 41x29in) Oslo
2001

📖 **$261** - €306 - **£186** - FF2 005
Komposisjon Etching in colors (30x39cm 11x15in)
Oslo 2001

SITZMAN Edward R. 1874-? **[10]**

🖼 **$700** - €837 - **£481** - FF5 489
Fall Landscape Oil/canvas (55x76cm 22x30in)
Chicago IL 2000

SIUDMAK Wojtek 1942 **[41]**

🖼 **$16 672** - €15 619 - **£10 250** - FF102 453
Regard mystérieux Oil/canvas (65x50cm 25x19in)
Warszawa 1999

🖼 **$1 539** - €1 442 - **£946** - FF9 457
Ange bleu-ciel Oil/paper (38x28.5cm 14x11in)
Warszawa 1999

📖 **$317** - €274 - **£188** - FF1 800
«Festival de Cannes» Affiche (60x80cm 23x31in)
Paris 1998

SIVERS von Clara 1854-1924 **[25]**

🖼 **$6 435** - €7 513 - **£4 545** - FF49 280
**Still Life with Amaryllis and Hydrangeas on a
Draped Rococo Table** Oil/canvas (107x85cm
42x33in) Hilton 2000

SIVILLA TORRES Emilio XIX **[5]**

💶 **$3 300** - €3 304 - **£2 035** - FF21 670
**Visita de S.M. la Regenta de España Da.Ma
Cristina** Acuarela/papel (60x100cm 23x39in) Madrid
2000

SJAMAAR Pieter Gerardus 1819-1876 **[52]**

🖼 **$2 800** - €2 600 - **£1 755** - FF17 627
Moonlit Market Scene Oil/panel (43x56cm 16x22in)
New-York 1999

$1 150 - €1 239 - **£795** - FF8 130
La lecture du document à la lueur d'une chandelle Huile/panneau (13x20cm 5x7in) Bruxelles 2001

SJÖBERG Axel 1866-1950 **[63]**
$662 - €708 - **£449** - FF4 641
Motiv från Sandhamn Mixed media (47x60cm 18x23in) Stockholm 2001
$569 - €517 - **£352** - FF3 392
Skärgård Akvarell/papper (16.5x24cm 6x9in) Stockholm 1999

SJOHOLM Adam 1923-1999 **[8]**
$1 488 - €1 524 - **£918** - FF10 000
Sans titre Métal (165x120x70cm 64x47x27in) Vendôme 2000

SJÖHOLM Charles 1933 **[52]**
$514 - €585 - **£353** - FF3 840
Interiör med sittande kvinna Oil/canvas (60x49cm 23x19in) Stockholm 2000

SJÖLANDER Waldemar 1906-1989 **[64]**
$762 - €712 - **£470** - FF4 668
Granadas Oleo/lienzo (38x59cm 14x23in) México 1999

SJÖSTRAND Carl Eneas 1828-1906 **[3]**
$23 856 - €26 909 - **£16 768** - FF176 512
Putto spelar kantele Marble (H78cm H30in) Helsinki 2001

SJÖSTRAND Carl Gustaf XIX **[2]**
$2 149 - €2 091 - **£1 323** - FF13 719
En kvinna inför konung Juladin Oil/canvas (94x117cm 37x46in) Stockholm 1999

SJÖSTRAND Helmi 1864-1957 **[25]**
$265 - €269 - **£165** - FF1 765
Borg Oil/canvas (48x63cm 18x24in) Helsinki 2000

SJÖSTRÖM Ina XX **[35]**
$388 - €404 - **£243** - FF2 647
Strandstuga Oil/canvas (30x45cm 11x17in) Helsinki 2001

SJÖSTRÖM Lars Petter 1820-1896 **[12]**
$1 545 - €1 432 - **£961** - FF16 144
C A Axell från Sundsvall Captn N M Jeppson Gouache/paper (46x62cm 18x24in) Malmö 1999

SJÖSTRÖM Urho 1873-1944 **[61]**
$1 867 - €2 102 - **£1 286** - FF13 790
Båthamnen, viitasaari, haapaniemi Oil/canvas (62x50cm 24x19in) Helsinki 2000
$761 - €841 - **£527** - FF5 516
Yrjö sakari yrjö-koskinen Oil/canvas (41x33cm 16x12in) Helsinki 2001

SJÖSVÄRD John 1890-1958 **[10]**
$2 600 - €2 461 - **£1 614** - FF16 144
«Jeux Equestres de la XVIme Olympiade» Poster (99.5x62cm 39x24in) New-York 1999

SKADE Friedrich / Fritz 1898-1971 **[4]**
$2 198 - €2 534 - **£1 500** - FF16 600
Young Woman Watercolour (48x32cm 18x12in) London 2000

SKAGERFORS Olle (Anders Olof) 1920-1997 **[56]**
$1 542 - €1 304 - **£921** - FF8 553
Stilleben med blå skål Oil/canvas (37x50cm 14x19in) Stockholm 1998
$823 - €979 - **£587** - FF6 425
Självporträtt Charcoal/paper (37.5x28.5cm 14x11in) Stockholm 2000

SKAIFE Thomas XIX **[1]**
$2 293 - €2 555 - **£1 500** - FF16 759
Mortar Phantoms Nos.1-3, Woolwich Common, 28 June Albumen print (6x6cm 2x2in) London 2000

SKALINGER Nicola ?-1889 **[1]**
$15 428 - €14 483 - **£9 528** - FF95 000
Il lago d'Agnano, l'hippodrome des Bourbons à Agnano, Naples Huile/toile (65x50cm 25x19in) Paris 1999

SKÅNBERG Carl 1850-1883 **[65]**
$2 414 - €2 238 - **£1 502** - FF14 682
Gata i Honfleur Oil/canvas (60x44cm 23x17in) Malmö 1999
$955 - €929 - **£588** - FF6 097
Fartyg med vita master Oil/panel (43x27cm 16x10in) Stockholm 1999
$558 - €530 - **£339** - FF3 479
Messina Akvarell/papper (12x18cm 4x7in) Stockholm 1999

SKANGIEL Julian 1898-? **[1]**
$2 115 - €2 372 - **£1 436** - FF15 558
Tête de garçon Huile/toile (26x19cm 10x7in) Warszawa 2000

SKAPINAKIS Nikias 1931 **[3]**
$12 600 - €13 958 - **£8 120** - FF91 560
Natureza morta 9 Oleo/tabla (35.5x50cm 13x19in) Lisboa 2000

SKARBINA Franz 1849-1910 **[142]**
$3 331 - €3 783 - **£2 330** - FF24 818
Starnberg, Blick auf das im Sonnenschein liegende Ufer Öl/Leinwand (41x51cm 16x20in) Berlin 2001
$2 206 - €2 147 - **£1 355** - FF14 086
Verschneiter Berliner Vorstadtplatz mit Endhaltestelle Öl/Karton (31x35.5cm 12x13in) Berlin 1999
$2 628 - €2 300 - **£1 591** - FF15 089
Strassenszene in Berlin Charcoal (46x34cm 18x13in) Berlin 1998
$161 - €153 - **£100** - FF1 006
Droschke am Boulevard Radierung (13x18.1cm 5x7in) Berlin 2000

SKARI Edvard 1839-1903 **[28]**
$1 938 - €1 822 - **£1 200** - FF11 954
Manning the Helm Oil/canvas (32.5x47.5cm 12x18in) London 2001

SKARZYNSKI Jerzy 1924 **[11]**
$915 - €982 - **£612** - FF6 444
Composition Aquarelle (39x49cm 15x19in) Kraków 2000

SKEAPING John Rattenbury 1901-1980 **[154]**
$46 025 - €54 124 - **£33 000** - FF355 033
Mill Reef Bronze (H25.5cm H10in) London 2001
$1 238 - €1 387 - **£860** - FF9 097
Jockeys on Horseback Pastel/paper (36.5x54cm 14x21in) Johannesburg 2001

SKEELE Hannah Brown 1829-1901 **[2]**
$35 000 - €31 704 - **£21 420** - FF207 963
Still Life Oil/canvas (55x68cm 22x27in) Portland ME 1998

SKEEN & Co. XIX **[3]**
$4 037 - €4 431 - **£2 600** - FF29 067
Photographs of the Ruined Cities of Ceylon, Anuradhapura & Pollanarua Albumen print (20x27cm 8x10in) London 2000

S

SKELL Fritz 1886-1961 **[22]**
$990 - €1 125 - **£692** - FF7 378
Waldriesen in Sumatra Oil/panel (110x86cm 43x33in) München 2001

SKELL Ludwig 1842-1905 **[12]**
$3 908 - €3 579 - **£2 382** - FF23 477
Kalkofen am Schliersee Oil/panel (16x26.5cm 6x10in) München 1999

SKELTON John 1735-1759 **[5]**
$1 613 - €1 583 - **£1 000** - FF10 386
Boat on a River by a Country House Watercolour (14x21cm 5x8in) London 1999

SKELTON John 1923 **[19]**
$1 455 - €1 714 - **£1 023** - FF11 244
Killiney Strand Oil/board (44.5x59.5cm 17x23in) Dublin 2000
$483 - €508 - **£303** - FF3 331
The Four Courts from Smithfield Watercolour/paper (26x36cm 10x14in) Dublin 2000

SKELTON Leslie James 1848-1929 **[16]**
$201 - €216 - **£134** - FF1 417
Figures walking along the Coastal Road Oil/canvas (30.5x45.5cm 12x17in) Montréal 2000

SKILL Frederick John 1824-1881 **[12]**
$360 - €424 - **£250** - FF2 782
Cattle at Pasture Watercolour (29x42cm 11x16in) London 1999

SKIPWORTH Frank Markham 1854-1929 **[15]**
$514 - €553 - **£350** - FF3 627
Portrait of a Lady, half-seated, wearing a grey Dress & Hat Oil/canvas (30.5x25cm 12x9in) Billingshurst, West-Sussex 2001

SKJÖLDEBRAND Anders Fredrik 1757-1834 **[5]**
$1 237 - €1 437 - **£869** - FF9 427
Finländsk herrgårdslandskap Akvarell/papper (26x45cm 10x17in) Stockholm 2001

SKLAR Dorothy Phillips XX **[18]**
$2 500 - €2 917 - **£1 740** - FF19 133
«Monday Washday» Oil/canvas (45x60cm 18x24in) Altadena CA 2000
$800 - €864 - **£552** - FF5 667
Buildings, hanging wash Watercolour/paper (43x55cm 17x22in) Altadena CA 2001

SKLAVOS Yerassimos 1927-1967 **[40]**
$2 725 - €2 287 - **£1 599** - FF15 000
L'oeil Bronze (26x15x13cm 10x5x5in) Paris 1998

SKLENAR Zdenek 1910-1986 **[25]**
$10 693 - €10 114 - **£6 660** - FF66 341
Nature morte à une coupe et une poire Huile/toile (43.5x53cm 17x20in) Praha 2000

SKOCZYLAS Wladyslaw 1883-1934 **[15]**
$228 - €239 - **£151** - FF1 571
Montagnard Eau-forte (17x12cm 6x4in) Warszawa 2000

SKOGLUND Sandy 1946 **[37]**
$4 650 - €4 991 - **£3 111** - FF32 742
Walking on Eggshells Cibachrome print (120x152cm 47x59in) Amsterdam 2000

SKÖLD Otte 1894-1958 **[87]**
$2 442 - €2 736 - **£1 702** - FF17 950
Arna Oil/canvas (129x97cm 50x38in) Stockholm 2001
$2 737 - €2 567 - **£1 692** - FF16 838
Stilleben Oil/canvas (38.5x50cm 15x19in) Stockholm 1999

$4 897 - €4 682 - **£3 070** - FF30 714
Sur le trottoir I Oil/panel (22.5x53cm 8x20in) Stockholm 1999
$370 - €373 - **£231** - FF2 449
Montparnasse Indian ink/paper (16.5x14cm 6x5in) Stockholm 2000

SKOLFIELD Raymond White, Ray 1909 **[5]**
$425 - €456 - **£284** - FF2 994
Fog on the River Lithograph (29x44cm 11x17in) Cleveland OH 2000

SKOLLE John 1903 **[7]**
$650 - €627 - **£408** - FF4 113
Festivity Oil/canvas (50x71cm 20x28in) Cambridge MA 1999

SKORCZEWSKI Krzysztof 1947 **[3]**
$394 - €465 - **£277** - FF3 050
Chats Gravure cuivre (15.5x15.5cm 6x6in) Warszawa 2000

SKOTNES Cecil 1926-? **[102]**
$6 540 - €6 302 - **£4 040** - FF41 336
The Conference Oil/wood (121.5x152cm 47x59in) Johannesburg 1999
$2 945 - €2 544 - **£1 776** - FF16 690
An Abstract Oil/wood (75x91cm 29x35in) Johannesburg 1998
$350 - €393 - **£245** - FF2 579
Mountainous Landscape Pencil (44x61cm 17x24in) Cape Town 2001
$185 - €216 - **£128** - FF1 415
Landscapes Woodcut in colors (37x49.5cm 14x19in) Johannesburg 2000

SKOTTE OLSEN William 1945 **[311]**
$353 - €336 - **£221** - FF2 207
Figurer og blomster i bylandskab Oil/canvas (55x75cm 21x29in) Köbenhavn 1999
$113 - €108 - **£70** - FF706
Figur Oil/canvas (37x27cm 14x10in) Köbenhavn 1999

SKOU Sigurd 1878-1929 **[16]**
$4 000 - €3 449 - **£2 375** - FF22 624
Feeding the Bird Oil/canvas (76x76cm 30x30in) Cincinnati OH 1998

SKOVGAARD Joachim 1856-1933 **[101]**
$1 278 - €1 211 - **£795** - FF7 944
Jesus i templet hos de skriftkloge Oil/canvas (73x59cm 28x23in) Köbenhavn 1999
$869 - €939 - **£600** - FF6 157
«Ulver og Vaeneli» Oil/wood (49.5x25.5cm 19x10in) Köbenhavn 2001

SKOVGAARD Niels 1858-1938 **[50]**
$1 084 - €1 075 - **£658** - FF7 052
Skovklaedt bjerglandskab Oil/panel (47x66cm 18x25in) Vejle 2000

SKOVGAARD Peter Christian T. 1817-1875 **[109]**
$4 468 - €5 101 - **£3 104** - FF33 459
Portraet af Katrine Lucie Elisabeth Scavenius på Gjorslev Oil/canvas (80x63cm 31x24in) Köbenhavn 2000
$2 356 - €2 017 - **£1 419** - FF13 231
En flok dådyr på Eremitagesletten Oil/canvas/panel (18.5x33.5cm 7x13in) Köbenhavn 1998
$404 - €377 - **£244** - FF2 473
Skovparti med rådyr Charcoal (175x154cm 68x60in) Köbenhavn 1999

SKRAMLIK Jan 1860-1936 **[12]**

$1 156 - €1 093 - **£720** - FF7 172
Scene from an Inn Oil/canvas (66x50cm 25x19in)
Praha 2000

SKRAMSTAD Ludvig 1855-1912 **[73]**

$1 226 - €1 224 - **£765** - FF8 027
Gryningsdimma, insjölandskap Oil/canvas
(39x69cm 15x27in) Uppsala 1999

$2 625 - €3 121 - **£1 870** - FF20 475
Akende barn ved fjellgard Oil/canvas (32x48cm
12x18in) Oslo 2000

SKREBNESKI Victor 1929 **[6]**

$4 250 - €4 094 - **£2 626** - FF26 858
Bette Davis Gelatin silver print (106x105cm 42x41in)
Chicago IL 1999

SKREDSVIG Christian Eriksen 1854-1924 **[51]**

$26 071 - €22 676 - **£15 717** - FF148 746
Sommerkvoeld ved et Höifjeldskjoern Oil/canvas
(100x126cm 39x49in) Oslo 1998

$10 980 - €12 428 - **£7 680** - FF81 520
Fra Jupesjöen Oil/canvas (64x98cm 25x38in) Oslo
2001

$5 763 - €6 223 - **£3 983** - FF40 820
Idyllisk hage med hus Oil/panel (34x27cm 13x10in)
Oslo 2001

$552 - €619 - **£384** - FF4 059
Mölle Drawing (24x32cm 9x12in) Oslo 2001

SKRETA Karel 1610-1674 **[5]**

$14 450 - €13 667 - **£9 000** - FF89 650
**Saint Charles Borromeo visiting Plague Victims
in a Hospital in Milan** Oil/copper (31x22.4cm
12x8in) Praha 2000

$2 153 - €2 454 - **£1 502** - FF16 098
Der Auszug der Israeliten in das heilige Land
Ink (14.5x15cm 5x5in) Berlin 2001

SKULASON Thorvaldur 1906-1984 **[14]**

$5 697 - €5 780 - **£3 538** - FF37 913
Komposition nr.7 Oil/canvas (86x72cm 33x28in)
Köbenhavn 2000

SKUM Nils Nilsson 1872-1951 **[126]**

$2 760 - €3 206 - **£1 940** - FF21 030
«Renhjord» Oil/canvas (46x55cm 18x21in) Stockholm
2001

$1 074 - €1 046 - **£661** - FF6 859
Same med renar Pencil (24x31cm 9x12in)
Stockholm 1999

SKUTEZKY Dominic, Döme, Dan. 1850-1921 **[14]**

$19 500 - €18 095 - **£11 914** - FF118 696
The Kettle-Makers Lunch Oil/canvas (105x153cm
41x60in) New-York 1999

SKYNNER Thomas XIX **[1]**

$30 000 - €25 883 - **£18 165** - FF169 779
Mr and Mrs Jacob Conklin Oil/canvas (75x60cm
29x23in) New-York 1999

SLABBAERT Karel 1619-1654 **[1]**

$249 024 - €244 787 - **£160 000** - FF1 605 696
A Toebackje Still Life Oil/panel (41x34cm 16x13in)
London 1999

SLABBINCK Rik 1914-1991 **[207]**

$3 289 - €3 222 - **£2 041** - FF21 138
Nu couché Huile/toile (61x73cm 24x28in) Bruxelles
1999

$621 - €694 - **£431** - FF4 552
Maisons dans un paysage Huile/panneau
(28x37cm 11x14in) Antwerpen 2001

$190 - €198 - **£120** - FF1 300
Nu assis Lavis/papier (36x27cm 14x10in) Antwerpen
2000

SLABOSKY Pesach 1947 **[2]**

$6 500 - €6 739 - **£4 283** - FF44 206
The Violonist's hands Oil/canvas (115x85cm
45x33in) Herzelia-Pituah 2000

SLADE Caleb Arnold 1882-1961 **[13]**

$2 100 - €2 399 - **£1 478** - FF15 735
Nahant Rocks Oil/canvas (81x101cm 32x40in)
Cambridge MA 2001

$2 900 - €3 113 - **£1 975** - FF20 420
Etaples, an Autumn Scene Oil/canvas (34.5x37cm
13x14in) Boston MA 2001

SLAGER Frans 1876-1953 **[13]**

$2 077 - €1 858 - **£1 244** - FF12 189
A Farmhouse Interior Oil/canvas (66x51cm 25x20in)
Amsterdam 1998

SLAGER Jeannette 1881-1945 **[8]**

$11 583 - €13 613 - **£8 031** - FF89 298
A Still Life with Peonies in a Vase Oil/canvas
(93x106cm 36x41in) Amsterdam 2000

SLAMA Victor T. 1890-1973 **[14]**

$208 - €229 - **£141** - FF1 500
«Foire de Vienne, 9-16 Sept.1951» Affiche couleur
(84x59cm 33x23in) Paris 2000

SLATER Charles Henry c.1820-c.1890 **[76]**

$432 - €486 - **£300** - FF3 185
Still Life of Flower Buds and Blossom
Watercolour/paper (14.5x20cm 5x7in) Penrith, Cumbria
2000

SLATER John Falconar 1857-1937 **[292]**

$869 - €742 - **£520** - FF4 868
A Rolling Sea at Moolight Oil/board (89x120cm
35x47in) Leeds 1998

$589 - €499 - **£349** - FF3 275
Rider in a Landscape Oil/board (32.5x42.5cm
12x16in) Billingshurst, West-Sussex 1998

$533 - €491 - **£320** - FF3 218
**Breakers ona a Beach with sea gulls flying
above** Watercolour (34.5x78.5cm 13x30in) London
1999

SLAUGHTER Stephen 1697-1765 **[10]**

$93 548 - €104 781 - **£65 000** - FF687 316
Portrait of William Fitzmaurice (1694-1747)
Oil/canvas (127x101.5cm 50x39in) London 2001

$26 814 - €24 824 - **£16 187** - FF162 832
**Portrait of a Gentleman, in a brown Coat and
embroidered Waistcoat** Oil/canvas (76x63.5cm
29x25in) Dublin 1999

$50 372 - €56 420 - **£35 000** - FF370 093
**Two Gentlemen, seated at a Table/Two
Gentlemen beside a Lectern** Oil/canvas (35x30cm
13x11in) London 2001

SLAVICEK Antonin 1870-1910 **[6]**

$13 005 - €12 300 - **£8 100** - FF80 685
Ein Waldweg Öl/Leinwand/Karton (88x65cm
34x25in) Praha 2000

$7 225 - €6 834 - **£4 500** - FF44 825
Half-length Nude, Study Oil/canvas (29x27cm
11x10in) Praha 1999

SLAVICEK Jan 1900-1970 **[32]**

$2 167 - €2 050 - **£1 350** - FF13 447
Bunch ofFlowers with Poppies in a Jug Oil/can-
vas (81x65cm 31x25in) Praha 2001

S

$1 300 - €1 230 - **£810** - FF8 068
Tschechische Landschaft Öl/Karton (23x35cm 9x13in) Praha 2000

SLEATOR James Sinton 1889-1950 **[12]**
$4 199 - €3 949 - **£2 600** - FF25 902
Self-Portrait with Hat/Self Portrait Oil/board (53x41.5cm 20x16in) London 1999

SLEE Charles XIX **[2]**
$4 250 - €4 683 - **£2 835** - FF30 716
«Betsys Montrose, Going into Riga Harbour, 27th Septembre» Watercolour/paper (48x63cm 19x25in) Portsmouth NH 2000

SLEEN Marc Neels, dit 1922 **[4]**
$403 - €446 - **£273** - FF2 926
Néron, Het Geheim van Slape Bizon Encre Chine/papier (48x36.5cm 18x14in) Bruxelles 2000

SLEIGH Bernard 1872-1954 **[18]**
$7 791 - €7 492 - **£4 800** - FF49 144
Elaine Oil/canvas (74.5x129cm 29x50in) London 1999
$5 892 - €7 008 - **£4 200** - FF45 969
The Annunciation Tempera/panel (23x23cm 9x9in) London 2000
$216 - €239 - **£150** - FF1 567
On the Church Wall Pastel (23x29.5cm 9x11in) London 2001

SLENDZINSKI Wincenty 1837-1909 **[3]**
$6 042 - €6 202 - **£3 792** - FF40 680
Portrait d'homme Huile/toile (71x56cm 27x22in) Torun 2000

SLETTERMARK Kjartan 1932 **[9]**
$29 859 - €33 292 - **£20 740** - FF218 380
Nixon-passet Object (32x39x10cm 12x15x3in) Stockholm 2001
$5 874 - €6 549 - **£4 080** - FF42 960
Nixon Visions Collage (48x57cm 18x22in) Stockholm 2001

SLEVOGT Max 1868-1932 **[534]**
$30 899 - €28 121 - **£19 305** - FF184 464
Steinbruch bei Albersweiler Öl/Leinwand (74.3x61cm 29x24in) München 1999
$6 091 - €5 624 - **£3 746** - FF36 892
Haus im Vorgebirge Öl/Leinwand (26x34cm 10x13in) München 1999
$1 029 - €999 - **£641** - FF6 556
Allegorie der Luft Chalks/paper (17x7.5cm 6x2in) Berlin 1999
$147 - €164 - **£102** - FF1 073
Der Königssohn, der sich vor nichts fürchtet Lithographie (21x19.5cm 8x7in) Heidelberg 2001

SLEWINSKI Ladislas / Wladyslaw 1854-1918 **[18]**
$38 000 - €44 091 - **£26 235** - FF289 218
Ile de Croix Oil/canvas (43x63cm 16x24in) New-York 2000
$27 487 - €31 431 - **£18 875** - FF206 175
Roses dans un vase Huile/toile (45x33cm 17x12in) Warszawa 2000

SLINGELANDT van Pieter Cornelisz. 1640-1691 **[16]**
$35 342 - €39 627 - **£24 000** - FF259 936
Portrait of a Lady, half-length, wearing pink, holding a rose Oil/panel (19.5x17cm 7x6in) London 2000

SLOAN George 1864-? **[1]**
$6 000 - €7 089 - **£4 252** - FF46 504
An afternoon Distraction Oil/canvas (23x28cm 9x11in) Boston MA 2000

SLOAN Jeanette 1946 **[4]**
$270 - €311 - **£186** - FF2 041
Terraza color Lithograph (50x39cm 20x15in) Cleveland OH 2000

SLOAN John 1871-1951 **[410]**
$60 000 - €59 472 - **£37 530** - FF390 114
The Mountains, September Oil/canvas (51x61cm 20x24in) New-York 1999
$3 800 - €4 455 - **£2 733** - FF29 226
«Nude and Frog» Oil/panel (23x43cm 9x16in) New-York 2001
$2 200 - €1 877 - **£1 324** - FF12 313
I Mistook him for one of the Domestics Charcoal (33x22cm 13x9in) Norwalk CT 1999
$1 500 - €1 267 - **£894** - FF8 314
«Reading in the Subway» Etching (28.5x20cm 11x7in) New-York 1998

SLOAN John Blanding 1886-1975 **[18]**
$2 600 - €2 497 - **£1 602** - FF16 379
Sixth Avenue, Greenwich Village Etching (12.5x18cm 4x7in) New-York 1999

SLOANE Eric 1910-1985 **[146]**
$13 000 - €12 311 - **£7 904** - FF80 757
Red Barn, New Milford, Connecticut Oil/masonite (68x58cm 26x22in) New-York 1999

SLOCOMBE Edward 1850-1915 **[14]**
$829 - €717 - **£500** - FF4 703
«Apollo and Daphne» Watercolour (44x54.5cm 17x21in) Billingshurst, West-Sussex 1999

SLOCOMBE Frederick Albert 1847-1920 **[22]**
$407 - €404 - **£254** - FF2 653
Contemplation Watercolour/paper (53.5x35.5cm 21x13in) Toronto 1999

SLODKI Marcel, Marceli 1892-1944 **[3]**
$3 095 - €3 395 - **£2 102** - FF22 272
Nues sur fond paysage Aquarelle, gouache (38x54cm 14x21in) Warszawa 2000

SLOM Olga Slomszynska 1881-1940 **[9]**
$2 813 - €3 354 - **£2 006** - FF22 000
Voilier au port Gravure (11.5x8cm 4x3in) Nantes 2000

SLOMINSKI Andreas 1959 **[1]**
$7 040 - €8 311 - **£5 000** - FF54 516
Polecat Trap Sculpture, wood (19x101.5x18.5cm 7x39x7in) London 2001

SLOOVERE de Georges 1873-1970 **[18]**
$582 - €694 - **£417** - FF4 552
Boom Oil/canvas (80x80cm 31x31in) Lokeren 2000

SLOTT-MØLLER Agnes Ranbusch 1862-1937 **[63]**
$772 - €806 - **£486** - FF5 286
Udsigt over landskab ved kirke Oil/canvas (55x42cm 21x16in) København 2000
$480 - €403 - **£281** - FF2 643
Strandparti med pilehegn og måger Oil/canvas (27x32cm 10x12in) Vejle 1998

SLOTT-MØLLER Georg Harald 1864-1937 **[93]**
$35 280 - €40 269 - **£24 510** - FF264 150
To unge piger, der sopper Oil/canvas (123x178cm 48x70in) København 2000
$1 650 - €1 476 - **£985** - FF9 683
Ung pige i vandkanten, aften ved midsommerti-de Oil/canvas (43x73cm 16x28in) København 1998
$1 321 - €1 144 - **£802** - FF7 505
Kirkeinteriör Oil/wood (31x40cm 12x15in) København 1998

SLOUN van Frank J. 1878-1938 **[21]**
$1 700 - €1 632 - **£1 065** - FF10 702
Atmospheric Landscape Oil/canvas (66x81cm
26x32in) Altadena CA 1999

SLOVAK Milos 1885-1951 **[12]**
$600 - €650 - **£400** - FF4 264
**«Patience, Mr.President, They Criticized me
Too»** Poster (131x105cm 51x41in) New-York 2000

SLUIJTER Gerard 1901-1985 **[6]**
$12 725 - €12 252 - **£7 956** - FF80 368
Portret Van Liesje Oil/canvas (71.5x58.5cm 28x23in)
Amsterdam 1999

SLUIJTERS Jan Schilder 1881-1957 **[478]**
$58 590 - €68 067 - **£41 175** - FF446 490
Still life with chrysanthemums Oil/canvas
(145x105cm 57x41in) Amsterdam 2001
$19 416 - €21 781 - **£13 454** - FF142 876
Portrait of a Lady Oil/canvas (54x50cm 21x19in)
Amsterdam 2000
$17 640 - €15 271 - **£10 705** - FF100 168
«Aan de Schinkel» Oil/canvas (33x46.5cm 12x18in)
Amsterdam 1998
$2 300 - €2 269 - **£1 416** - FF14 883
Female Nude Seated Watercolour (71.5x45.5cm
28x17in) Amsterdam 1999
$225 - €263 - **£154** - FF1 726
«Stedelijk Museum Amsterdam, Jan Sluijters»
Poster (100x70cm 39x27in) Hoorn 2000

SLUIJTERS Jan, Jnr. 1914 **[18]**
$6 671 - €5 890 - **£4 022** - FF38 633
«Paris, Place Blanche» Oil/canvas (46x52cm
18x20in) Amsterdam 1998

SLUIS Pete 1929 **[34]**
$1 102 - €1 270 - **£752** - FF8 329
Poirot Oil/board (51x60cm 20x24in) Blackrock,
Co.Dublin 2000
$477 - €533 - **£323** - FF3 498
Fantastical Bird Coloured inks/paper (59x46cm
23x18in) Dublin 2000

SLUIS van der Jacobus c.1660-1732 **[3]**
$20 560 - €19 831 - **£12 720** - FF130 080
Scène de tabagie Huile/panneau (33x27cm 12x10in)
Bruxelles 1999

SLUYTER Pieter 1675-1715 **[16]**
$322 - €307 - **£196** - FF2 012
Kleine Stachelanone, nach Maria Sibylla Merian
Radierung (35x28.5cm 13x11in) Köln 1999

SLUYTERMANN VON LANGEWEYDE Georg 1903-
1977 **[16]**
$1 885 - €1 686 - **£1 129** - FF11 062
Stiefmütterchen, Stilleben Oil/panel (62x46cm
24x18in) Hamburg 1998

SLUYTERS Willy 1873-1949 **[191]**
$13 956 - €13 613 - **£8 592** - FF89 298
Carmen Oil/canvas (250x175cm 98x68in) Dordrecht
1999
$3 300 - €3 857 - **£2 356** - FF25 301
Bomschuiten on the Beach of Scheveningen
Oil/canvas (37x48cm 14x18in) Amsterdam 2001
$1 921 - €1 815 - **£1 162** - FF11 906
Portrait of a Marken Girl Oil/panel (40.5x31cm
15x12in) Amsterdam 1999
$1 551 - €1 452 - **£965** - FF9 525
«Filosoof» Pastel/paper (23.5x15cm 9x5in)
Amsterdam 1999

SLY F. XVII **[2]**
$3 461 - €4 069 - **£2 400** - FF26 688
**Banditti Attacking a Wagon on a Bridge in a
Rocky Landscape** Oil/canvas (65x82.5cm 25x32in)
London 2000

SMALL David 1846-1927 **[22]**
$664 - €568 - **£402** - FF3 723
The End of the Day Watercolour (16.5x24.5cm
6x9in) Edinburgh 1998

SMALL William 1843-1929 **[6]**
$14 823 - €14 099 - **£9 000** - FF92 481
The woodlands Oil/canvas (71x91cm 27x35in)
Edinburgh 1999

SMALLFIELD Frederick 1829-1915 **[19]**
$8 033 - €7 735 - **£5 000** - FF50 740
Lunchtime Oil/board (21x15.5cm 8x6in) London 1999
$1 435 - €1 609 - **£1 000** - FF10 557
Girl with a Basket of Flowers Watercolour
(23x14cm 9x5in) Leyburn, North Yorkshire 2001

SMALLMAN Bob XX **[1]**
$4 400 - €3 859 - **£2 671** - FF25 316
Dartmouth Winter Carnival Poster (86x54cm
34x21in) New-York 1999

SMARGIASSI Gabriele 1798-1882 **[17]**
$2 700 - €2 332 - **£1 800** - FF15 300
**Veduta della costa napoletana con Capri sullo
sfondo** Olio/tavola (17x24.5cm 6x9in) Roma 1998

SMART Frank Jeffrey Edson 1921 **[114]**
$62 664 - €70 869 - **£44 100** - FF464 868
The Observer, Senopia Acrylic (101x145cm
39x57in) Malvern, Victoria 2000
$51 080 - €44 540 - **£30 888** - FF292 160
The Overpass, Siena Acrylic (99x69cm 38x27in)
Melbourne 1998
$19 464 - €18 504 - **£12 147** - FF121 380
Study for Motel Swimming Pool Oil/canvas/board
(40x29.5cm 15x11in) Melbourne 1999
$6 298 - €7 392 - **£4 444** - FF48 486
Study for Woolloomooloo Squash Watercolour,
gouache (19x25cm 7x9in) Melbourne 2000
$1 562 - €1 823 - **£1 087** - FF11 959
«Man with Bouquet» Etching, aquatint (24.5x19.5cm
9x7in) Melbourne 2000

SMART John I 1741/43-1811 **[76]**
$5 113 - €4 290 - **£3 000** - FF28 142
**Gentleman Facing Right in Coat/Gentleman
Facing Left in Coat** Miniature (5.5x4cm 2x1in)
London 1998

SMART John IV 1838-1899 **[34]**
$1 091 - €1 032 - **£680** - FF6 772
The Watering Place Oil/panel (24x30cm 9x11in)
Leicestershire 1999
$1 247 - €1 069 - **£750** - FF7 010
The Devasted Forest Watercolour/paper (76x125cm
29x49in) Edinburgh 1998

SMART Robert Borlase 1881-1947 **[24]**
$1 449 - €1 600 - **£1 000** - FF10 496
St.Michael's Mount from Marazion Marshes
Oil/canvas (45x60cm 18x24in) Par, Cornwall 2001

S

SMEDLEY William Thomas 1858-1920 **[17]**
- $6 750 - €6 444 - **£4 217** - FF42 268
  Woman in Blue Gown Oil/canvas/panel (125x76cm 49x30in) Dedham MA 1999

SMEDT de Joseph, Jos 1894-? **[36]**
- $267 - €297 - **£178** - FF1 951
  Les clowns Huile/toile (108x67cm 42x26in) Bruxelles 2000

SMEERS Frans 1873-1960 **[273]**
- $1 391 - €1 611 - **£962** - FF10 569
  Femme allongée Huile/toile (70x92cm 27x36in) Bruxelles 2000
- $908 - €942 - **£577** - FF6 178
  Aardappelschilster Oil/panel (40x30.5cm 15x12in) Lokeren 2000
- $371 - €397 - **£252** - FF2 601
  Gezicht te Parijs/Le Jardin du Luxembourg, Paris/Park te Brussel Encre (25x36cm 9x14in) Lokeren 2000

SMEETS Yves 1961 **[42]**
- $3 830 - €4 269 - **£2 660** - FF28 000
  «Born in the USA» Huile/toile (160x130x4cm 62x51x1in) Paris 2001
- $3 420 - €3 811 - **£2 375** - FF25 000
  «Born in the USA 3» Huile/toile (110x80x4cm 43x31x1in) Paris 2001

SMET de Gustave 1877-1943 **[180]**
- $6 336 - €5 949 - **£3 912** - FF39 024
  Barques de pêche sur la mer du Nord Huile/toile (90x150cm 35x59in) Antwerpen 1999
- $27 825 - €26 028 - **£16 905** - FF170 730
  Zomer aan de leie Oil/canvas (55x75cm 21x29in) Lokeren 1999
- $7 560 - €6 544 - **£4 587** - FF42 929
  Still Life Oil/paper/panel (41x31.5cm 16x12in) Amsterdam 1998
- $8 205 - €7 714 - **£4 967** - FF50 602
  Female Nude Crayon (70x48cm 27x18in) Amsterdam 1999
- $304 - €295 - **£189** - FF1 934
  Untitled Woodcut (17.5x20.5cm 6x8in) Amsterdam 1999

SMET de Léon 1881-1966 **[196]**
- $11 120 - €12 196 - **£7 552** - FF80 000
  Elégante dans son intérieur Huile/toile (196x131cm 77x51in) Calais 2000
- $16 416 - €14 212 - **£9 962** - FF93 223
  A path in the forest Oil/canvas (64x81cm 25x31in) Amsterdam 1998
- $1 374 - €1 524 - **£950** - FF10 000
  Les toits Huile/carton (23.5x33cm 9x12in) Cherbourg 2001
- $696 - €744 - **£474** - FF4 878
  Leielandschap Crayon/papier (15x24cm 5x9in) Lokeren 2001

SMETANA Jan 1918-1998 **[26]**
- $1 502 - €1 421 - **£936** - FF9 323
  Environs de la ville Huile/panneau (50x60cm 19x23in) Praha 2000
- $2 890 - €2 733 - **£1 800** - FF17 930
  Sur le quai Huile/toile/carton (40x34cm 15x13in) Praha 2001
- $144 - €137 - **£90** - FF896
  Paris Encre/papier (20x25cm 7x9in) Praha 2000

SMETHAM James 1821-1889 **[26]**
- $1 062 - €918 - **£625** - FF6 019
  Old Man by a Tomb Oil/board (12x21.5cm 4x8in) Billingshurst, West-Sussex 1999

SMETHAM-JONES G.W. XIX **[3]**
- $1 904 - €1 979 - **£1 200** - FF12 982
  New Milk Watercolour (75x54.5cm 29x21in) Leyburn, North Yorkshire 2000

SMETS Louis XIX **[16]**
- $13 931 - €13 160 - **£8 427** - FF86 321
  Winter Landscape with numerous Figures on the Ice Oil/canvas (81.5x116.5cm 32x45in) Amsterdam 1999

SMIBERT John 1688-1751 **[1]**
- $7 500 - €6 398 - **£4 524** - FF41 970
  Mrs James Allen Oil/canvas (104x81cm 41x32in) Portsmouth NH 1998

SMIDTH Hans Ludvig 1839-1917 **[213]**
- $1 732 - €1 746 - **£1 080** - FF11 455
  Skraepper Oil/canvas (46x58cm 18x22in) Köbenhavn 2000
- $639 - €590 - **£390** - FF3 873
  Ved et gammeltudhus, Silkeborg Oil/canvas (37x39cm 14x15in) Viby J, Arhus 1998
- $236 - €202 - **£141** - FF1 323
  Flöjtespillende mand fra hedeegnen Pencil/paper (21x12cm 8x4in) Köbenhavn 1998

SMIGIELSKI Konrad 1908-1999 **[55]**
- $456 - €532 - **£320** - FF3 491
  Dinosaurs by Moonlight Oil/board (48x36cm 18x14in) Crewkerne, Somerset 2000
- $456 - €532 - **£320** - FF3 491
  Bowl of Grape Oil/board (35.5x35.5cm 13x13in) Crewkerne, Somerset 2000

SMILLIE George Henry 1840-1921 **[54]**
- $8 000 - €7 613 - **£5 004** - FF49 939
  Spring Landscape Oil/canvas (50x76cm 20x30in) New-York 1999
- $5 000 - €4 712 - **£3 108** - FF30 965
  On the Hudson River, Above the Poughkeepsie Oil/canvas (15x25cm 6x10in) Milford CT 1999
- $700 - €663 - **£434** - FF4 346
  Lake Shore Scene with Boat on Shore Watercolour/paper (25x37cm 10x14in) Wallkill NY 1999

SMILLIE Helen Sheldon Jacobs 1854-1926 **[1]**
- $2 000 - €2 206 - **£1 354** - FF14 468
  The Pier at Far Rockaway Beach Watercolour, gouache/board (11x27.5cm 4x10in) New-York 2000

SMILLIE James 1807-1885 **[4]**
- $1 700 - €1 661 - **£1 078** - FF10 898
  The Rocky Mountains, after Albert Bierstadt Engraving (46x72cm 18x28in) Bolton MA 1999

SMILLIE James David 1833-1909 **[25]**
- $80 000 - €95 140 - **£57 016** - FF624 080
  Lake Placid and the Adirondack Mountains from Whiteface Oil/canvas (58.5x102cm 23x40in) New-York 2000
- $5 000 - €5 776 - **£3 501** - FF37 890
  An old Dam Oil/canvas (41.5x29cm 16x11in) New-York 2001
- $2 600 - €3 092 - **£1 853** - FF20 282
  On the Path Watercolour/paper (17x26cm 6x10in) New-York 2000

SMIRNOV Igor 1963 **[11]**
- $198 - €206 - **£125** - FF1 352
  Autumn Birches Oil/canvas (45x30cm 17x11in) Fernhurst, Haslemere, Surrey 2000

SMIRNOVA Elena XX [10]

$142 - €152 - **£95** - FF1 000
L'étang en été Huile/toile (30x40cm 11x15in) L'Isle-Adam 2000

SMIRSCH Johann Carl 1801-1869 [1]

$6 754 - €6 261 - **£4 200** - FF41 067
Still Life of Flowers and a Pomegranate on s Stone Ledge Oil/panel (32x25cm 12x9in) London 1999

SMISSEN van der Dominicus 1704-1760 [5]

$3 686 - €3 483 - **£2 300** - FF22 846
Double Portrait of the Countess of Castlemaine and Child Watercolour/paper (127x101cm 50x40in) Fernhurst, Haslemere, Surrey 1999

SMIT Aernout 1641-1710 [11]

$22 651 - €21 781 - **£13 953** - FF142 876
Dutch Smalschips in Choppy Water with a Large Flute in the Distance Oil/canvas (53x76cm 20x29in) Amsterdam 1999

SMIT Arie 1916 [37]

$36 815 - €30 889 - **£21 600** - FF202 616
Pura Gunung Lebah in Campuhan Ubud Oil/canvas (150x192cm 59x75in) Singapore 1998

$7 088 - €6 606 - **£4 284** - FF43 335
Entrance to the Village Oil/canvas (60x60cm 23x23in) Singapore 1999

$3 809 - €3 483 - **£2 374** - FF25 177
Pura - Temple Oil/canvas (31x46cm 12x18in) Singapore 2000

SMIT Derk 1889-? [8]

$650 - €576 - **£398** - FF3 778
Winter Landscape Oil/board (50x60cm 20x24in) Cincinnati OH 1999

SMIT Philippe 1887-1948 [15]

$1 369 - €1 588 - **£970** - FF10 418
Moulins au bord du canal Oil/board (73x84cm 28x33in) Amsterdam 2000

SMITH Alexis 1949 [6]

$9 000 - €8 952 - **£5 586** - FF58 719
Shell Shock Mixed media (61x51cm 24x20in) Beverly-Hills CA 1999

SMITH Alfred 1853-1936 [23]

$455 - €545 - **£312** - FF3 577
Het huwelijkscontract (Le contrat de mariage) Huile/toile (74x50cm 29x19in) Antwerpen 2000

$2 872 - €3 201 - **£1 955** - FF21 000
Étude pour les quais à Bordeaux, le soir Huile/toile (32x46cm 12x18in) Bordeaux 2000

SMITH Alice Ravenel Huger 1876-1945 [30]

$34 000 - €32 561 - **£21 005** - FF213 584
Lily Pads Watercolour/paper (53x34cm 21x13in) Portsmouth NH 1999

$1 200 - €1 403 - **£849** - FF9 201
The Pringle House Print (46x38cm 18x15in) Columbia SC 2001

SMITH Antonio 1832-1877 [1]

$10 000 - €11 618 - **£7 028** - FF76 212
Crepusculo marino Oil/canvas (80x99.5cm 31x39in) New-York 2001

SMITH Arthur Reginald 1871-1934 [44]

$1 046 - €934 - **£640** - FF6 129
St Pauls from Lambeth Watercolour/paper (17x35cm 7x14in) Little-Lane, Ilkley 1999

SMITH Austin ?-1930 [16]

$170 - €190 - **£115** - FF1 246
Flamboro Watercolour/paper (25x35cm 10x14in) Aylsham, Norfolk 2001

SMITH Barry Windsor XX [2]

$1 900 - €1 833 - **£1 200** - FF12 023
Marvel Covers Ink (37.5x25cm 14x9in) New-York 1999

SMITH Brent R. XX [2]

$3 000 - €2 727 - **£1 806** - FF17 889
Easying Up Watercolour/paper (53x73cm 21x29in) Hayden ID 1998

SMITH Brett XX [1]

$4 000 - €4 441 - **£2 782** - FF29 129
Catch of the Day Oil/masonite (50x76cm 20x30in) Milford CT 2001

SMITH Campbell Lindsay ?-1915 [5]

$2 802 - €3 103 - **£1 900** - FF20 357
Figures on a Beach Oil/board (11.5x14cm 4x5in) London 2000

SMITH Carl J. 1928 [7]

$350 - €392 - **£243** - FF2 571
Cowboy leading Horses from Water Fire in the Distance Oil/board (64x79cm 25x31in) St. Louis MO 2001

SMITH Carlo Frithjol 1859-1917 [4]

$23 028 - €19 343 - **£13 500** - FF126 879
Women seated in an Interior Oil/canvas (41x61cm 16x24in) London 1998

SMITH Carlton Alfred 1853-1946 [124]

$29 463 - €35 040 - **£21 000** - FF229 849
Best Friends Oil/canvas (61x42cm 24x16in) London 2000

$4 250 - €4 960 - **£3 000** - FF32 538
Awaiting the Home Coming Oil/canvas/panel (30x20cm 11x7in) London 2000

$5 293 - €5 334 - **£3 300** - FF34 991
Hush a Bye Baby Watercolour (33x48cm 12x18in) London 2000

SMITH Cary 1955 [9]

$2 000 - €2 230 - **£1 344** - FF14 628
«I» Oil/canvas (183x183cm 72x72in) New-York 2000

SMITH Charles L.A. 1871-1937 [15]

$3 250 - €2 991 - **£1 950** - FF19 621
Seascape Oil/canvas (76x114cm 30x45in) Pasadena CA 1999

SMITH Colvin 1795-1875 [8]

$4 326 - €4 781 - **£3 000** - FF31 359
Portrait of Francis Lord Jeffrey (1773-1850) Oil/canvas (90x70cm 35x27in) London 2001

SMITH Dan 1864-1934 [10]

$1 430 - €1 220 - **£862** - FF8 002
Illustrations for «Madame Pompadour» and «The Doctor» Ink (68x53cm 27x21in) New-York 1998

$500 - €545 - **£346** - FF3 573
«The Sesquicentennial International Exposition, Philadelphia» Poster (67x44cm 26x17in) New-York 2001

SMITH David 1906-1965 [91]

$6 000 - €6 962 - **£4 142** - FF45 666
«73-62-202» Oil/paper (51x40cm 20x15in) New-York 2000

$180 - €197 541 - **£115 902** - FF1 295 784
Tempus Fugit Iron (73.5x29x25.5cm 28x11x10in) New-York 2000

S

✐ **$9 000** - €8 952 - **£5 586** - FF58 719
3/9/55 Gouache (49x61.5cm 19x24in) Beverly-Hills
CA 1999

🎨 **$3 000** - €2 831 - **£1 850** - FF18 568
Family Lithograph (22x58cm 8x22in) New-York 1999

SMITH David 1920-1998 [95]
☞ **$269** - €289 - **£180** - FF1 893
Porpellers in the Snow, Grytviken, Evening
Oil/canvas (74.5x100cm 29x39in) London 2000
☞ **$116** - €132 - **£80** - FF869
Country Road, Norfolk Oil/board (28x30cm
11x11in) London 2000
✐ **$174** - €199 - **£120** - FF1 304
The Six Beams of Hartland Point Lighthouse
Watercolour/paper (37.5x50.5cm 14x19in) London 2000

SMITH De Cost 1864-1939 [5]
☞ **$11 500** - €9 702 - **£6 745** - FF63 641
Indian Battle Oil/canvas (76x60cm 30x24in) Mystic
CT 1998

SMITH Edward Gregory 1881-1963 [5]
☞ **$7 000** - €7 514 - **£4 684** - FF49 287
Nocturne Oil/canvas (82.5x96.5cm 32x37in) New-
York 2000

SMITH Edwin Whitney 1880-1952 [3]
🖼 **$5 121** - €4 855 - **£3 200** - FF31 849
The Irishman, a Bust Bronze (H61.5cm H24in)
London 1999

SMITH Eileen Lawrence XIX [1]
✐ **$3 919** - €4 414 - **£2 700** - FF28 957
So she Passed out Into the garden
Watercolour/paper (54x28.5cm 21x11in) Newbury,
Berkshire 2000

SMITH Elmer Boyd 1860-1943 [33]
☞ **$4 500** - €5 352 - **£3 207** - FF35 104
Haystacks in a Green Field Oil/canvas (33x56cm
12x22in) New-York 2000
☞ **$6 000** - €5 134 - **£3 612** - FF33 679
Cottage in a Field/Autumn Landscape Oil/canvas
(33x45cm 13x18in) New-York 1998

SMITH Francis 1881-1961 [125]
☞ **$23 320** - €26 421 - **£15 900** - FF173 310
Costureira Huile/toile (64.5x50cm 25x19in) Lisboa
2000
☞ **$11 245** - €12 958 - **£7 760** - FF85 000
Rue de Lisbonne Huile/papier (34.5x28cm 13x11in)
Paris 2000
✐ **$3 879** - €4 573 - **£2 727** - FF30 000
Vierge en Majesté Gouache/papier (13x17cm 5x6in)
Fontainebleau 2000

SMITH Francis Hopkinson 1838-1915 [71]
☞ **$25 112** - €21 495 - **£15 115** - FF141 000
Village portugais Huile/toile (73x60cm 28x23in)
Paris 1998
☞ **$4 000** - €4 726 - **£2 834** - FF31 003
Figures on a City Street Charcoal (42x60cm
16x23in) Boston MA 2000

SMITH Francis, Francesco ?-c.1780 [1]
☞ **$95 000** - €90 685 - **£59 356** - FF594 852
**View of the Mount Vesuvius seen from the
Strada Santa Lucia, Naples** Oil/canvas (67x136cm
26x53in) New-York 1999

SMITH Frank Hill 1841-1904 [3]
☞ **$4 600** - €5 103 - **£3 059** - FF33 472
Sewing on the Veranda Oil/canvas (43x63cm
17x25in) Milford CT 2000

SMITH Frank Vining 1879-1967 [48]
☞ **$15 000** - €15 565 - **£9 516** - FF102 100
The Seventh Wave Oil/canvas (101.5x152cm
39x59in) Boston MA 2000
☞ **$3 750** - €4 374 - **£2 632** - FF28 689
Evening Light Oil/masonite (66x96cm 26x38in)
Portsmouth NH 2000
✐ **$459** - €500 - **£320** - FF3 342
Fishing Boats off Corfu at Dawn
Watercolour/paper (30x43.5cm 11x17in) London 2001

SMITH Gary Ernest XX [3]
☞ **$7 000** - €7 843 - **£4 874** - FF51 447
Stacking Wheat Shocks Oil/canvas (101.5x75.5cm
39x29in) Washington 2001

SMITH Gean 1851-1928 [9]
☞ **$3 000** - €3 150 - **£2 028** - FF20 660
Horses at Feeding through Oil/board (72x99cm
28x39in) Fairfield ME 2001

SMITH George 1829-1901 [40]
☞ **$91 013** - €105 849 - **£65 000** - FF694 323
«Home Be it ever so Humble» Oil/panel
(71x91.5cm 27x36in) London 2001
☞ **$4 268** - €4 959 - **£3 000** - FF32 532
Dinner Time Oil/panel (21x17cm 8x6in) London 2001

SMITH George 1870-1934 [58]
☞ **$3 129** - €2 976 - **£1 900** - FF19 523
Pit Ponies Oil/canvas/board (61x40.5cm 24x15in)
Edinburgh 1999
☞ **$2 434** - €2 720 - **£1 650** - FF17 839
Cattle Drovers with Distant Town Oil/panel
(17x24cm 6x9in) Edinburgh 2000

SMITH Gladys Nelson 1890-1980 [1]
☞ **$3 200** - €3 752 - **£2 302** - FF24 611
Magnolias Oil/canvas (89x69cm 35x27in) New-York
2001

SMITH Gordon Appelbe 1919 [100]
☞ **$2 755** - €2 648 - **£1 697** - FF17 371
Fundy 10 Acrylic/canvas (127x142cm 50x55in)
Vancouver, BC. 1999
☞ **$1 955** - €2 269 - **£1 350** - FF14 883
Tlell Acrylic/canvas (61x76cm 24x29in) Vancouver, BC.
2000
✐ **$298** - €320 - **£202** - FF2 098
Rockies #4 Graphite (7.5x11.5cm 2x4in) Calgary,
Alberta 2001
🎨 **$163** - €156 - **£102** - FF1 023
Marshlands Silkscreen in colors (48x62cm 18x24in)
Toronto 1999

SMITH Grace Cossington 1892-1984 [96]
☞ **$17 967** - €16 363 - **£11 001** - FF107 334
Bottle Brushes Oil/board (49.5x38.5cm 19x15in)
Malvern, Victoria 1998
☞ **$9 520** - €8 749 - **£5 803** - FF57 391
The Weir Oil/canvas/board (39x34cm 15x13in)
Melbourne 1998
✐ **$3 562** - €3 996 - **£2 468** - FF26 213
Zinnias in Blue Jar Watercolour/paper (25x31cm
9x12in) Sydney 2000

SMITH Grainger 1892-1961 [13]
✐ **$959** - €1 062 - **£650** - FF6 967
Busy Street Scene, St.Ives Watercolour (53x65.5cm
20x25in) Billingshurst, West-Sussex 2000

SMITH Harry 1923-1991 [2]
🎨 **$800** - €747 - **£483** - FF4 901
Tree of Life Lithograph (60.5x10cm 23x3in) New-
York 1999

SMITH Hassel Wendell 1915 [6]
- **$20 000** – €16 901 – **£11 930** – FF110 864
  Lachrymatory Oil/canvas (152.5x305cm 60x120in)
  San-Francisco CA 1998

SMITH Henry Pember 1854-1907 [108]
- **$7 000** – €6 612 – **£4 233** – FF43 369
  Early Summer at East Lyme, CT Oil/canvas
  (51x71cm 20x27in) New-York 1999
- **$6 000** – €5 483 – **£3 670** – FF35 968
  The Country Lane Oil/canvas (31x51cm 12x20in)
  Boston MA 1999
- **$1 300** – €1 478 – **£908** – FF9 698
  Crashing Waves Watercolour/paper (33x48cm
  13x19in) Mystic CT 2000

SMITH Herbert Tyson 1883-? [2]
- **$3 070** – €3 315 – **£2 100** – FF21 746
  Female Nude Bronze (H38cm H14in) Billingshurst,
  West-Sussex 2001

SMITH Hobbe 1862-1942 [65]
- **$3 709** – €3 319 – **£2 222** – FF21 769
  View of the Magere Brug, Amsterdam Oil/canvas
  (41x54cm 16x21in) Amsterdam 1998
- **$2 137** – €1 813 – **£1 289** – FF11 894
  Zeilschepen Oil/canvas (32x43cm 12x16in) Den Haag
  1998

SMITH Hughie Lee 1915 [11]
- **$37 500** – €42 579 – **£26 055** – FF279 303
  The Walls Oil/masonite (45x60cm 18x24in) Detroit MI
  2001
- **$2 250** – €2 468 – **£1 494** – FF16 192
  Untitled Oil/canvas/board (27x35cm 11x14in) Detroit
  MI 2000

SMITH Jack 1928 [14]
- **$2 741** – €3 075 – **£1 900** – FF20 173
  21 elements on a grid Oil/canvas (105.5x107cm
  41x42in) London 2000

SMITH Jack Wilkinson 1873-1949 [53]
- **$100 000** – €107 339 – **£66 920** – FF704 100
  Pacific Coast Oil/canvas (101.5x127cm 39x50in) San-
  Francisco CA 2000
- **$15 000** – €12 816 – **£9 076** – FF84 066
  «Planting Trout in Sierra Lake» Oil/canvas
  (71x86.5cm 27x34in) San-Francisco CA 1998
- **$4 950** – €5 046 – **£3 101** – FF33 099
  Rocky Shore with Fog Oil/canvas (35x40cm
  14x16in) Altadena CA 2000

SMITH James Agrell 1913-1988 [11]
- **$137** – €130 – **£85** – FF353
  The Man from Big Stone Woodcut (20x15cm 7x5in)
  Calgary, Alberta 1999

SMITH James Burrell 1822-1897 [108]
- **$9 500** – €11 081 – **£6 785** – FF72 685
  Landscape with Waterfall Oil/canvas (125x92cm
  49x36in) Detroit MI 2000
- **$1 047** – €976 – **£649** – FF6 403
  **Goats at Rest on a Rock, an extensive River
  Scene beyond** Watercolour (34x48cm 13x18in)
  Billingshurst, West-Sussex 1999

SMITH Jane Stewart XX [2]
- **$4 303** – €4 777 – **£3 000** – FF31 334
  View of Edinburgh Watercolour/paper (52x95cm
  20x37in) London 2001

SMITH Jason Rupert 1953-1989 [16]
- **$333** – €393 – **£234** – FF2 580
  Greta Garbo Serigraph in colors (109.5x86.5cm
  43x34in) Stockholm 2000

SMITH Jessie Willcox 1863-1935 [22]
- **$11 500** – €9 719 – **£6 837** – FF63 751
  Portrait of a Young Girl Oil/canvas (51x40cm
  20x16in) Philadelphia PA 1998
- **$16 000** – €17 510 – **£11 036** – FF114 860
  Young Girl with Doll Charcoal (21.5x58.5cm 8x23in)
  New-York 2001

SMITH John c.1652-1742 [10]
- **$161** – €153 – **£100** – FF1 006
  **Eine schlafende Frau vom Schein einer Kerze
  beleuchtet** Mezzotint (22.8x17.5cm 8x6in) Berlin
  1999

SMITH John Brandon 1848-1884 [92]
- **$4 873** – €4 742 – **£3 000** – FF31 106
  River Dulas, South Wales Oil/canvas (56x76cm
  22x29in) London 1999
- **$1 446** – €1 562 – **£1 000** – FF10 249
  An Angler by a Pool Oil/canvas (23x35.5cm 9x13in)
  London 2001

SMITH John Christopher 1891-1943 [16]
- **$1 400** – €1 344 – **£877** – FF8 813
  Sierra Landscape Oil/canvas (76x101cm 30x40in)
  Altadena CA 1999
- **$1 800** – €2 100 – **£1 252** – FF13 775
  «Mission Court, California» Oil/board (40x30cm
  16x12in) Altadena CA 2000

SMITH John Firth 1943 [63]
- **$11 730** – €12 551 – **£7 728** – FF82 330
  Enter Oil/canvas (121x121cm 47x47in) Sydney 2000
- **$979** – €2 354 – **£1 410** – FF15 444
  Variations 12 Acrylic/paper (48x68.5cm 18x26in)
  Melbourne 2000
- **$221** – €249 – **£155** – FF1 635
  «Bottle VII» Lithograph (54x75cm 21x29in) Malvern,
  Victoria 2001

SMITH John Raphael 1752-1812 [98]
- **$4 548** – €4 426 – **£2 800** – FF29 032
  Family Group Oil/canvas (47x62cm 18x24in) London
  1999
- **$1 237** – €1 133 – **£750** – FF7 430
  **Gentleman, Half-length/Portrait of a Young Boy,
  Half-length** Pastel/paper (25.5x21cm 10x8in) London
  1998
- **$195** – €229 – **£138** – FF1 500
  **Visit to Grand-Mother/A Visit to the Grand-
  Father d'après J.Northcote** Mezzotint
  (55.5x40.5cm 21x15in) Paris 2000

SMITH John Rubens 1775-1849 [3]
- **$1 531** – €1 504 – **£950** – FF9 865
  **Dividing the Cake or the Covetous Girl
  Punish'd/Dividing Fruit** Mezzotint (53.5x66cm
  21x25in) London 1999

SMITH John Warwick 1749-1831 [87]
- **$1 714** – €1 921 – **£1 200** – FF12 604
  Llyd Idwab below Glydr Vawr, Carnarvonshire
  Watercolour (13.5x21.5cm 5x8in) Billingshurst, West-
  Sussex 2001

SMITH Jori 1907 [40]
- **$2 434** – €2 754 – **£1 703** – FF18 067
  Portrait of Vitaline Simard Oil/masonite (61x50cm
  24x19in) Toronto 2001

SMITH Joseph Lindon 1863-1950 [28]
- **$1 500** – €1 382 – **£898** – FF9 068
  **Equestrian Monument to Bartolommeo
  Colleoni, Venice** Oil/canvas/board (63x55cm 25x22in)
  New-York 1998

S

SMITH Kiki 1954 **[82]**
- $65 000 - €75 419 - **£44 876** - FF494 715
  Mother Sculpture (264x40.5x51cm 103x15x20in) New-York 2001
- $15 000 - €16 969 - **£10 494** - FF111 307
  Trough Plaster (35.5x159x48.5cm 13x62x19in) New-York 2001
- $2 400 - €2 047 - **£1 447** - FF13 430
  Untitled Mixed media/paper (32x43cm 12x16in) New-York 1998
- $1 600 - €1 548 - **£986** - FF10 155
  Constellations Color lithograph (142x80cm 55x31in) New-York 1999
- $2 000 - €1 706 - **£1 206** - FF11 192
  Untitled Photograph (38.5x59cm 15x23in) New-York 1998

SMITH Kimber 1922-1981 **[20]**
- $186 - €174 - **£112** - FF1 140
  Komposition mit Blau Farblithographie (66x50.5cm 25x19in) Hamburg 1999

SMITH Langdon 1870-1959 **[18]**
- $800 - €933 - **£556** - FF6 122
  When the Mail Arrives Oil/board (40x55cm 16x22in) Altadena CA 2000
- $1 000 - €962 - **£617** - FF6 308
  On the Herd Gouache/paper (43x33cm 17x13in) Oakland CA 1999

SMITH Lawrence Beall 1909-1995 **[34]**
- $200 - €178 - **£123** - FF1 169
  «TV» Lithograph (33x23cm 13x9in) Bloomfield-Hills MI 1999

SMITH Leon Polk 1906-1996 **[26]**
- $5 000 - €4 446 - **£3 058** - FF29 166
  Untitled Collage/paper (101.5x66cm 39x25in) New-York 1999

SMITH Madeleine XIX **[1]**
- $4 008 - €4 573 - **£2 784** - FF30 000
  Portrait de jeune fille Pastel/toile (110x75cm 43x29in) Paris 2000

SMITH Marcella Cl. Heber 1887-1963 **[34]**
- $4 529 - €5 370 - **£3 300** - FF35 224
  St.Ives Harbour Oil/canvas (63x80cm 24x31in) Newcastle-upon-Tyne 2001
- $494 - €473 - **£310** - FF33 101
  Still Life of Flowers Watercolour/paper (47x57cm 18x22in) Lichfield, Staffordshire 1999

SMITH Marshall D. XX **[2]**
- $3 250 - €3 696 - **£2 253** - FF24 245
  Horse Drawn Cart Oil/canvas (76x101cm 30x40in) Cincinnati OH 2000

SMITH Marshall Joseph, Jr. 1854-1923 **[11]**
- $21 000 - €19 571 - **£12 959** - FF128 377
  Louisiana Shorescape with Boats, Figures and Cattle Oil/canvas (35x61cm 14x24in) New-Orleans LA 1999

SMITH Matthew, Sir 1879-1959 **[137]**
- $26 897 - €28 872 - **£18 000** - FF189 388
  Still Life with Apples and Pears Oil/canvas (46.5x55cm 18x21in) London 2000
- $8 546 - €8 121 - **£5 200** - FF53 270
  Hope Oil/canvas (40.5x36cm 15x14in) London 1999
- $2 516 - €2 147 - **£1 500** - FF14 084
  Still Life Pastel/paper (48x37cm 18x14in) London 1998

SMITH Miller XIX-XX **[24]**
- $896 - €962 - **£600** - FF6 313
  Woodland Landscape with Pigs/Village Scene with Mother and Children Watercolour/paper (34.5x25cm 13x9in) Reepham, Norwich 2000

SMITH Noel XIX-XX **[11]**
- $928 - €808 - **£560** - FF5 299
  «Rushton, Dorset», a Mother and Child Feeding a Hen Watercolour, gouache/paper (23.5x34cm 9x13in) Solihull, West-Midlands 1998

SMITH OF CHICHESTER George 1714-1776 **[31]**
- $6 500 - €6 953 - **£4 431** - FF45 608
  View near Bristol Oil/canvas (63.5x76cm 25x29in) New-York 2001
- $869 - €960 - **£600** - FF6 297
  Pastoral Scene in an Evening Landscape Oil/canvas (32x48cm 12x18in) Crewkerne, Somerset 2001

SMITH Percy John D. 1882-1948 **[15]**
- $209 - €194 - **£125** - FF1 273
  Landscapes Subjects Etching (20x25cm 8x10in) Aylsham, Norfolk 1999

SMITH Ray 1949 **[39]**
- $14 000 - €16 266 - **£9 839** - FF106 696
  «Maricruz cafe» Oil/panel (203x228cm 79x89in) New-York 2001
- $3 021 - €3 526 - **£2 070** - FF23 130
  Untitled Oil/panel (58x48cm 22x18in) Stockholm 2000
- $4 000 - €4 077 - **£2 506** - FF26 746
  Untitled Oil/panel (30.5x25.5cm 12x10in) New-York 2000

SMITH Reginald 1855-1925 **[20]**
- $412 - €470 - **£290** - FF3 080
  Bristol Bridge Watercolour/paper (34x47cm 13x18in) Bristol, Avon 2001

SMITH Richard 1931 **[56]**
- $2 181 - €1 861 - **£1 300** - FF12 206
  Floors Covered Acrylic/canvas (165x140cm 64x55in) London 1998
- $250 - €287 - **£171** - FF1 884
  Blue Etching, aquatint (68x71cm 27x28in) Cleveland OH 2000

SMITH Richard J. 1955 **[25]**
- $1 543 - €1 836 - **£1 100** - FF12 044
  High Summer, Low Water Acrylic (54x125.5cm 21x49in) London 2000

SMITH Rufus Way XIX-XX **[7]**
- $3 200 - €3 159 - **£1 945** - FF20 720
  After the Shower Oil/canvas (61x101.5cm 24x39in) New-York 2000

SMITH Sidney 1912-1982 **[3]**
- $1 080 - €1 244 - **£737** - FF8 162
  Antibes Oil/board (24x34cm 9x13in) Dublin 2000

SMITH Stanley 1893-? **[8]**
- $296 - €287 - **£180** - FF1 881
  Busy Harbour at Low Tide Watercolour/paper (27x37.5cm 10x14in) London 2000

SMITH Stephen Catterson I 1806-1872 **[12]**
- $5 037 - €5 642 - **£3 500** - FF37 009
  Portrait of Mary Sankey Oil/canvas (109.5x77.5cm 43x30in) London 2001

SMITH Stephen Catterson II 1849-1912 **[5]**
- $2 602 - €2 793 - **£1 741** - FF18 323
  Landscape - Rocky Hill Overlooking Bay Oil/canvas (36x61cm 14x24in) Dublin 2000

S

$2 000 - €2 391 - **£1 379** - FF15 684
The Berry Picker Oil/canvas (45x30cm 18x12in)
Milford CT 2000

SMITH Tony 1912-1980 **[42]**
$4 800 - €4 893 - **£3 007** - FF32 096
Spitball Marble (30.5x35.5x35cm 12x13x13in) New-York 2000

SMITH Tucker 1940 **[1]**
$22 500 - €20 454 - **£13 551** - FF134 167
October Ice Oil/canvas (76x91cm 30x36in) Hayden ID 1998

SMITH Walter Granville 1870-1938 **[60]**
$3 800 - €4 368 - **£2 683** - FF28 650
The Mill Stand-Montauk Oil/board (30x40cm 12x16in) East-Moriches NY 2001

SMITH Wells XIX **[1]**
$4 877 - €4 503 - **£3 000** - FF29 539
The Fisherman's Tale Oil/canvas (71x91.5cm 27x36in) London 1999

SMITH William ?-c.1847/59 **[4]**
$18 633 - €17 920 - **£11 500** - FF117 546
Pointers in a Landscape Oil/canvas (63.5x76.5cm 25x30in) London 1999

SMITH William E. 1913-? **[3]**
$900 - €751 - **£527** - FF4 928
«Pay Day» Linocut (20x15cm 8x6in) Shaker-Heights OH 1998

SMITH William Eugene 1918-1978 **[219]**
$2 400 - €2 763 - **£1 485** - FF18 124
Untitled from the Life Essay, Spanish Village Gelatin silver print (23x34.5cm 9x13in) New-York 2000

SMITH William H. act.1863-c.1884 **[19]**
$1 183 - €1 338 - **£800** - FF8 778
Still Life of Fruit on a Mossy Bank Oil/canvas (21.5x31.5cm 8x12in) London 2000

SMITH William Harding 1848-1922 **[6]**
$1 969 - €2 286 - **£1 359** - FF14 992
View of Venice Watercolour/paper (24x33cm 9x12in) Dublin 2000

SMITH William Russell 1812-1896 **[43]**
$2 500 - €2 301 - **£1 500** - FF15 093
Hudson River Scene Oil/canvas (58x71cm 23x28in) Charlottesville VA 1999
$2 000 - €2 379 - **£1 425** - FF15 602
A Pennywick Landscape Oil/canvas (35.5x28.5cm 13x11in) New-York 2000

SMITH William St. Thomas 1862-1947 **[34]**
$491 - €456 - **£300** - FF2 988
«Making Harbour» Watercolour (59x38.5cm 23x15in) London 1998

SMITH Wuanita 1866-1959 **[8]**
$1 700 - €1 903 - **£1 185** - FF12 482
«Hummingbirds and Orchids» Woodcut in colors (30.5x24.5cm 12x9in) New-York 2001

SMITH Xanthus Russell 1838-1929 **[61]**
$900 - €966 - **£613** - FF6 337
In the Woods on Edge Hill Oil/canvas (35.5x25.5cm 13x10in) Boston MA 2001
$400 - €426 - **£253** - FF2 797
Rocky Shore and Three Figures in a Row Boat Watercolour/paper (27x41cm 11x16in) Downington PA 2000

SMITH-HALD Frithjof 1846-1903 **[40]**
$11 025 - €13 110 - **£7 854** - FF85 995
Garnböterske Oil/canvas (118x179cm 46x70in) Oslo 2000
$5 256 - €6 250 - **£3 644** - FF41 000
Bord de mer Huile/toile (47x75cm 18x29in) Aix-en-Provence 2000
$1 995 - €2 372 - **£1 421** - FF15 561
Garnet trekkes Pastel/canvas (70x100cm 27x39in) Oslo 2000

SMITHEMAN S. Francis XIX-XX **[8]**
$4 634 - €5 378 - **£3 200** - FF35 277
Nelson's Elephant at the Battle of Copenhagen, 2nd April Oil/canvas (61x91.5cm 24x36in) London 2000

SMITHER Michael Duncan 1939 **[11]**
$5 404 - €5 258 - **£3 326** - FF34 491
Stony River and Mountain Oil/board (77x111cm 30x43in) Melbourne 1999

SMITHERS Collier XIX-XX **[2]**
$4 657 - €5 568 - **£3 200** - FF36 521
Joan Helen Furneaux-Dawson, full-length, standing, wearing a dress Oil/canvas (147x76cm 57x29in) Billingshurst, West-Sussex 2000

SMITHSON Robert 1938-1973 **[53]**
$74 715 - €80 200 - **£50 000** - FF526 080
Untitled Sculpture (38x254x16cm 14x100x6in) London 2000
$15 900 - €13 443 - **£9 510** - FF88 180
«Spiral hill shooting procedure» Pencil/paper (32x29cm 12x11in) København 1998

SMITS Eugène 1826-1912 **[42]**
$362 - €421 - **£258** - FF2 764
Moine dominicain Huile/panneau (37.5x19.5cm 14x7in) Liège 2001

SMITS Jakob 1856-1928 **[380]**
$16 405 - €19 059 - **£11 529** - FF125 017
Het Malvinaprieeltje bij mannlicht Oil/canvas (70x65cm 27x25in) Amsterdam 2001
$9 199 - €10 214 - **£6 411** - FF67 000
Femme en prière Peinture (25.5x22cm 10x8in) Neuilly-sur-Seine 2001
$577 - €644 - **£400** - FF4 227
Intérieur avec soeur assise Fusain/papier (22x18cm 8x7in) Antwerpen 2001
$124 - €149 - **£89** - FF975
Landschap met grote witte wolken Etching (15.8x18.6cm 6x7in) Lokeren 2000

SMITS Johan Gerard 1823-1910 **[52]**
$2 226 - €2 042 - **£1 371** - FF13 394
Woodgatherers in the Snow Oil/panel (38x50.5cm 14x19in) Amsterdam 1999
$1 276 - €1 431 - **£867** - FF9 390
Grachtenszene im Amsterdam Öl/Leinwand (25.5x45.5cm 10x17in) Berlin 2000
$485 - €544 - **£336** - FF3 571
Strandscène bij Scheveningen met knikkerspelende mannen Encre (16x22cm 6x8in) The Hague 2000

SMITS Louis XIX **[2]**
$5 123 - €4 857 - **£3 116** - FF31 862
Eisvergnügen, zahlreiche Personen auf einem zugefrorenen Fluss Öl/Leinwand (40x60.5cm 15x23in) Köln 1999

S

SMITS Remi 1921 [2]
- 🛏️ **$1 664** - €1 983 - **£1 192** - FF13 008
  Allégorie de la joie de vivre Tapisserie (120x300cm 47x118in) Bruxelles 2000

SMITS Theodorus c.1635-c.1707 [5]
- 🐟 **$12 336** - €14 033 - **£8 616** - FF92 052
  Vanitasstilleben Oil/canvas (47.5x38.5cm 18x15in) Stockholm 2000

SMOLDERS Paul 1921-1997 [47]
- 🐟 **$1 872** - €2 231 - **£1 341** - FF14 634
  Spelende kindjes (petits enfants jouant) Huile/toile (45x50cm 17x19in) Antwerpen 2000
- 🐟 **$1 332** - €1 487 - **£924** - FF9 756
  Enfant jouant Huile/toile (41x38cm 16x14in) Antwerpen 2001
- ✏️ **$523** - €545 - **£332** - F3 577
  Enfant dessinant Dessin (24x24cm 9x9in) Antwerpen 2000

SMORENBERG Dirk 1883-1960 [95]
- 🐟 **$5 919** - €6 353 - **£3 960** - FF41 672
  River landscape with row-boat Oil/canvas (39x60.5cm 15x23in) Amsterdam 2000
- 🐟 **$1 087** - €1 271 - **£776** - FF8 334
  Loosdrechtse Plassen Oil/canvas (30x40cm 11x15in) Amsterdam 2001
- 🐟 **$1 471** - €1 588 - **£1 005** - FF10 418
  Anemones Pastel/paper (56x70cm 22x27in) Amsterdam 2001

SMUGLEWICZ Franciszek 1745-1807 [6]
- 🐟 **$9 475** - €10 775 - **£6 500** - FF70 679
  The Dwarf Baiocco, holding a Staff, with a Jug, a Loaf and a Plate Oil/canvas (38x29.5cm 14x11in) Oxfordshire 2000
- ✏️ **$617** - €732 - **£435** - FF4 800
  Soumission des vaincus devant un souverain Encre (53x37.5cm 12x14in) Paris 2000

SMYTH Bob XIX-XX [1]
- ✏️ **$2 365** - €2 539 - **£1 583** - FF16 658
  A Day with the Royal Meaths Chalks (61x45.5cm 24x17in) Dublin 2000

SMYTH Coke XIX [2]
- 🛏️ **$15 000** - €14 219 - **£9 370** - FF93 271
  Sketches in the Canadas Lithograph (38x27cm 14x10in) New-York 1999

SMYTH Olive Carleton 1882-1949 [9]
- 🐟 **$16 108** - €15 137 - **£10 000** - FF99 291
  The seventh Day Tempera (43x66cm 16x25in) London 1999
- 🐟 **$19 236** - €18 172 - **£12 000** - FF119 199
  Pytheas Buys Amber Tempera (33.5x39cm 13x15in) Perthshire 1999
- ✏️ **$3 075** - €2 886 - **£1 900** - FF18 934
  Scheherazade Gouache (25.5x23cm 10x9in) London 1999

SMYTHE Ansdell XIX-XX [6]
- 🐟 **$3 293** - €3 211 - **£2 000** - FF21 066
  Moonlight View of the Thames, Westminster Oil/canvas (60.5x106.5cm 23x41in) London 2000

SMYTHE Edward Robert 1810-1899 [119]
- 🐟 **$4 266** - €4 805 - **£3 000** - FF31 520
  Horses watering in open Landscape Oil/canvas (40x60cm 15x23in) Cambridge 2001
- 🐟 **$2 760** - €2 730 - **£1 674** - FF17 937
  Farmyard with Animals and Figures Oil/canvas (31x43cm 12x17in) New-Orleans LA 2000

SMYTHE Eugene Leslie 1857-1932 [14]
- 🐟 **$1 100** - €928 - **£645** - FF6 087
  Landscape Oil/canvas (81x121cm 32x48in) Mystic CT 1998

SMYTHE Lionel Percy 1839-1918 [39]
- 🐟 **$9 432** - €10 622 - **£6 500** - FF69 673
  Brittany Girls Washing in a Stream Oil/canvas (76x51cm 29x20in) London 2000
- ✏️ **$1 003** - €1 128 - **£700** - FF7 401
  The Harvesters Watercolour (24x34.5cm 9x13in) London 2001

SMYTHE Thomas 1825-1907 [147]
- 🐟 **$3 626** - €4 264 - **£2 600** - FF27 972
  River Landscape with barge, Figures and Fishermen with Meadows Oil/canvas (48x73cm 19x29in) Woodbridge, Suffolk 2001
- 🐟 **$4 159** - €3 522 - **£2 500** - FF23 105
  Gathering Firewood in a Winter Landscape Oil/canvas (30.5x36cm 12x14in) London 1998

SMYTHE Willard Grayson 1906-? [9]
- ✏️ **$600** - €608 - **£376** - FF3 987
  Composition Watercolour/paper (35x25cm 14x10in) Cincinnati OH 2000

SNAFFLES (Charles J. Payne) 1884-1967 [265]
- ✏️ **$1 600** - €1 455 - **£979** - FF9 546
  Running Deer Watercolour/paper (31x36cm 12x14in) Norwalk CT 1998
- 🛏️ **$1 105** - €1 158 - **£700** - FF7 597
  National Candidate Print (23x30cm 9x11in) Edinburgh 2000

SNAJDR Miroslav 1938 [9]
- 🐟 **$1 734** - €1 640 - **£1 080** - FF10 758
  Reminiscence Ambulatory Mixed media/canvas (100x70cm 39x27in) Praha 1999

SNAPE Martin 1853-1930 [29]
- ✏️ **$727** - €622 - **£440** - FF4 082
  Dusk on the Solent Watercolour (16.5x25cm 6x9in) London 1999

SNAPE William H. XIX [7]
- 🐟 **$19 477** - €21 852 - **£13 500** - FF143 340
  The Garden that I Love Oil/panel (49.5x34cm 19x13in) London 2000

SNAYERS Pieter 1592-1667 [31]
- 🐟 **$12 963** - €14 521 - **£9 008** - FF95 251
  Traveller ambushed by Brigands Oil/canvas (55x79cm 21x31in) Amsterdam 2001
- 🐟 **$9 344** - €9 294 - **£5 800** - FF60 965
  Cavalry Skirmish in Front of a Windmill, a Town and Mountainous Oil/panel (30.5x49cm 12x19in) London 1999

SNEL Han 1925-1998 [25]
- 🐟 **$4 591** - €5 213 - **£3 142** - FF34 196
  Women with Baskets Oil/canvas (50x45cm 19x17in) Singapore 2000
- 🐟 **$5 652** - €6 245 - **£3 919** - FF34 196
  To the Market Oil/canvas (45x35cm 17x13in) Singapore 2001
- ✏️ **$2 244** - €2 092 - **£1 356** - FF13 722
  Nudes Coloured chalks/paper (51x38cm 20x14in) Singapore 1999

SNELL Henry Bayley 1858-1943 [23]
- 🐟 **$2 400** - €2 586 - **£1 636** - FF16 966
  Back Bay County, Landscape with Farm Oil/canvas (46x60cm 18x24in) Hatfield PA 2001
- 🐟 **$6 000** - €6 440 - **£4 015** - FF42 246
  Chioggia, Italy Oil/board (28x34cm 11x13in) Hatfield PA 2000

✏ **$2 000** - €1 707 - **£1 196** - FF11 198
Still Waters Watercolour/paper (114x86cm 45x34in)
New-York 1998

SNELL James Herbert 1861-1935 **[86]**

💰 **$437** - €373 - **£260** - FF2 447
A Woodland Pond Oil/canvas (76x51cm 29x20in)
Bath 1998

💰 **$496** - €536 - **£343** - FF3 518
Måneskin/Solopgang Oil/canvas (8x14cm 3x5in)
København 2001

✏ **$192** - €185 - **£120** - FF1 213
St Stephens Church, Hampstead Watercolour
(20x25cm 8x10in) London 1999

SNELLINCK Cornelis ?-1669 **[8]**

💰 **$9 462** - €8 164 - **£5 709** - FF53 555
**Wooded River Landscape on the Edge of a
Town** Oil/panel (52x56.5cm 20x22in) Amsterdam 1998

SNELLINCK Jan c.1575-1627 **[4]**

💰 **$2 560** - €2 907 - **£1 752** - FF19 068
Christus am Ölberg Öl/Leinwand (81x105cm
31x41in) Wien 2000

SNELLINCK Jan I 1544-1638 **[6]**

💰 **$40 345** - €37 766 - **£25 000** - FF247 727
The Battle of Moncourtour Oil/canvas (154x222cm
60x87in) London 1999

SNELLING Lilian **[3]**

✏ **$7 996** - €7 360 - **£4 800** - FF48 279
Lilium ochraceum, Lily Watercolour (53.5x36cm
21x14in) London 1999

SNELLMAN Anita 1924 **[21]**

💰 **$973** - €1 144 - **£674** - FF7 501
Blå tistlar Oil/canvas (84x99cm 33x38in) Helsinki
2000

💰 **$479** - €471 - **£297** - FF3 089
Stilleben Oil/canvas (40x32cm 15x12in) Helsinki 1999

SNELLMAN Anna 1884-1962 **[69]**

💰 **$495** - €555 - **£336** - FF3 640
Blommor Oil/canvas (55x46cm 21x18in) Helsinki
2000

💰 **$465** - €538 - **£329** - FF3 530
Blommor Oil/canvas (30x24cm 11x9in) Helsinki 2000

✏ **$386** - €454 - **£267** - FF2 978
Av sommarens sista Pastel/paper (21x16cm 8x6in)
Helsinki 2000

SNELLMAN Eero Juhani 1890-1951 **[17]**

💰 **$979** - €839 - **£578** - FF5 502
Gata Oil/canvas (50x47cm 19x18in) Helsinki 1998

💰 **$707** - €604 - **£415** - FF3 965
Från skatudden Oil/panel (25x21cm 9x8in) Helsinki
1998

SNIDOW Gordon 1936 **[16]**

💰 **$15 000** - €17 032 - **£10 422** - FF111 721
When Rain turns to Sleet Oil/board (56x76cm
22x30in) Dallas TX 2001

💰 **$9 350** - €10 036 - **£6 257** - FF65 833
Short'n the Britches Gouache/paper (66x35cm
26x14in) Houston TX 2000

SNIJDERS Ben 1943 **[4]**

💰 **$6 362** - €6 126 - **£3 978** - FF40 184
Stilleven met kersen Oil/board (14x23.5cm 5x9in)
Amsterdam 1999

SNIJDERS Christian Pieter 1881-1943 **[34]**

💰 **$410** - €362 - **£247** - FF2 377
Houses along a Canal Oil/canvas (40x61cm
15x24in) Amsterdam 1998

SNOECK Jacob Cornelis 1881-1921 **[11]**

💰 **$6 618** - €6 182 - **£4 000** - FF40 549
The Nursery Oil/canvas (61x51cm 24x20in) London
1999

💰 **$1 264** - €1 319 - **£800** - FF8 655
Preparing the Evening Meal Oil/canvas (41x34.5cm
16x13in) London 2000

SNOW John Harold Thomas 1911 **[116]**

▥ **$179** - €209 - **£124** - FF1 374
Kitchen Piece Lithograph (45x35cm 18x14in)
Calgary, Alberta 2000

SNOW Michael James Aleck 1929 **[6]**

▥ **$272** - €258 - **£165** - FF1 694
Score for Sopranos Silkscreen in colors (64x43cm
25x16in) Calgary, Alberta 1999

SNOWDON Douglas XIX-XX **[5]**

▥ **$2 125** - €2 043 - **£1 300** - FF13 398
**«London-Paris via Southampton & Havre,
London & South Western Railway»** Poster
(99x66cm 38x25in) London 1999

SNYDER Bladen Tasker 1864-1923 **[4]**

💰 **$2 100** - €2 388 - **£1 456** - FF15 666
Paris Street Scene Oil/canvas (76x96cm 30x38in)
Cincinnati OH 2000

SNYDER Joan 1940 **[11]**

💰 **$22 000** - €23 615 - **£14 722** - FF154 902
Untitled Acrylic (152.5x304.5cm 60x119in) New-York
2000

SNYDER Seymour 1897-? **[1]**

💰 **$2 100** - €2 497 - **£1 496** - FF16 382
Under the Queensboro Bridge Oil/canvas/board
(30x40.5cm 11x15in) New-York 2000

SNYDER William Henry 1829-1910 **[4]**

💰 **$4 000** - €4 690 - **£2 877** - FF30 764
Darning by the Earth Oil/canvas (45.5x35.5cm
17x13in) New-York 2001

SNYDER William McKendree c.1849-1930 **[7]**

💰 **$10 000** - €11 157 - **£6 546** - FF73 182
Southern Indian Beech Forest Oil/canvas
(91x152cm 36x60in) Chicago IL 2000

SNYDERS Frans 1579-1657 **[54]**

💰 **$81 555** - €76 278 - **£50 000** - FF500 350
A Cockfight with Other Poultry in a Farmyard
Oil/canvas (120x174cm 47x68in) London 1998

💰 **$26 000** - €27 767 - **£17 716** - FF182 137
Bunches of Grapes in a Basket on a Ledge
Oil/canvas/panel (54x66cm 21x25in) New-York 2001

✏ **$4 731** - €4 082 - **£2 854** - FF26 777
A Leaping hound Chalks (23.7x34.5cm 9x13in)
Amsterdam 1998

SNYERS Pieter 1681-1752 **[31]**

💰 **$14 422** - €13 292 - **£8 637** - FF87 191
**Blumen- und Gemüsehändlerinnen mit Körben
voll Spargel, Rettich** Öl/Leinwand (83x69cm
32x27in) Dresden 1998

💰 **$11 578** - €12 706 - **£7 453** - FF83 344
**Peaches, Plums, Medlar, Figs on a Vine, an
Apple, Mushrooms** Oil/canvas (42.5x34.5cm
16x13in) Amsterdam 2000

SOANE John, Sir 1753-1837 **[2]**

✏ **$11 661** - €13 261 - **£8 000** - FF86 984
The Scala Regia, Palace of Westminster Ink
(47x33cm 18x12in) Oxfordshire 2000

S

SOARES António 1894-1978 **[5]**
$1 936 - €2 193 - £1 276 - FF14 388
Natureza morta com uvas e maças Oleo/lienzo (60.5x81cm 23x31in) Lisboa 2000
$660 - €748 - £435 - FF4 905
Rosas Pastel/papier (40x28.5cm 15x11in) Lisboa 2000

SOARES Valeska 1957 **[5]**
$18 000 - €17 339 - £11 176 - FF113 734
Us, form sinners Object (122x28x5cm 48x11x1in) New-York 1999
$4 500 - €5 222 - £3 107 - FF34 252
Cheap Emotions (Escape)/Cheap Emotions (Passion) Sculpture, wood (23x46x4cm 9x18x1in) New-York 2000

SOBRADO Pedro 1936 **[184]**
$1 485 - €1 351 - £900 - FF8 865
«Huida veloz» Oleo/lienzo (60.5x73cm 23x28in) Madrid 1999
$312 - €289 - £192 - FF1 896
Invierno Acuarela/papel (32x25cm 12x9in) Madrid 1998

SOBRAT Anak Agung Gede 1911-1992 **[22]**
$13 773 - €15 640 - £9 427 - FF102 590
Dancer Acrylic/canvas (130x120.5cm 51x47in) Singapore 2000
$14 025 - €14 682 - £8 810 - FF96 309
Bali Life Oil/board (121x81cm 47x31in) Singapore 2000
$5 165 - €5 865 - £3 535 - FF38 471
A landscape with Deer, Ducks and a Goat Oil/panel (31x47cm 12x18in) Singapore 2000
$3 839 - €3 578 - £2 320 - FF23 473
Portrait of Boy/Portrait of Girl Charcoal/paper (42x30.5cm 16x12in) Singapore 1999

SOBRILE Giuseppe 1879-1956 **[25]**
$24 000 - €31 100 - £18 000 - FF204 000
Nevicata Olio/masonite (125x150cm 49x59in) Vercelli 2000
$4 000 - €5 183 - £3 000 - FF34 000
Fiori in giardino Olio/tela (94x68cm 37x26in) Roma 2001
$1 800 - €1 555 - £900 - FF10 200
Paesaggio di montagna innevato Olio/tavola (22.5x25.5cm 8x10in) Vercelli 1999

SOBRINO BUHIGAS Carlos 1885-1978 **[7]**
$2 212 - €2 373 - £1 461 - FF15 563
Paisaje rural con iglesia Oleo/cartón (44.5x35cm 17x13in) Madrid 2000

SOBRINO Carlos 1909-1975 **[2]**
$11 000 - €9 498 - £6 710 - FF62 301
Beatas Oil/canvas (66x53.5cm 25x21in) Miami FL 1999

SOBRINO Carlos Rivero 1927 **[3]**
$4 000 - €3 882 - £2 490 - FF25 466
Sin Título Oil/canvas (65.5x54.5cm 25x21in) New-York 1999

SOCRATE Carlo 1889-1967 **[35]**
$4 750 - €4 924 - £3 053 - FF32 300
Il coniglio Olio/tela (65x50cm 25x19in) Prato 1999

SOCRATOUS Socratis 1973 **[1]**
$10 800 - €12 013 - £7 200 - FF78 800
Garden Installation (H70cm H27in) Athens 2000

SODAR Franz 1829-1899 **[1]**
$13 156 - €15 095 - £900 - FF99 018
The Church of the Holy Sepulchre, Jerusalem Oil/canvas (50x37cm 19x14in) London 2000

SODERBERG Yngve Edward 1896-1971 **[18]**
$225 - €244 - £150 - FF1 599
The Eagle (U.S.Coast Guard Ship on Cruise in the West Indies) Etching (32x40cm 12x16in) Plainville CT 2000

SODOMA (Giovanni A. Bazzi) 1477-1549 **[4]**
$33 341 - €35 791 - £22 316 - FF234 773
Abschied der Apostel Öl/Leinwand (122x81cm 48x31in) Köln 2000

SØDRING Frederik 1809-1862 **[35]**
$8 097 - €8 692 - £5 419 - FF57 016
Das Siebengebirg am Rhein Öl/Leinwand (35.5x62cm 13x24in) Hamburg 2000
$1 834 - €2 012 - £1 246 - FF13 198
Norsk landskab Oil/canvas (32x46cm 12x18in) Köbenhavn 2000

SØEBORG Axel 1872-1939 **[58]**
$403 - €470 - £288 - FF3 081
Lille pige ved mödding Oil/canvas (44x43cm 17x16in) Aarhus 2000
$461 - €537 - £329 - FF3 521
Snedker i sit vaerksted Oil/canvas (33x41cm 12x16in) Aarhus 2001

SOEHNEE Charles Frederic 1789-1878 **[8]**
$15 000 - €13 157 - £9 108 - FF86 307
Studies with Figures on Stilts, Playing with Rats and an Abbott Watercolour (37x24cm 14x9in) New-York 1999

SOER Chris 1882-1962 **[42]**
$955 - €908 - £581 - FF5 953
Zuid-Nederlands stadje Oil/canvas (49x58cm 19x22in) Den Haag 1999
$525 - €499 - £319 - FF3 274
'S Morgens aan de Vliet Oil/canvas (30x45cm 11x17in) Den Haag 1999

SOEST Gerard c.1600/37-1681 **[15]**
$4 500 - €5 181 - £3 071 - FF33 987
Dame Ann Robinson, Half-Length, in a Silver Dress Oil/canvas (73x62cm 28x24in) New-York 2000

SOEST van Louis Willem 1867-1948 **[73]**
$1 172 - €1 341 - £815 - FF8 794
Hollandsk landskab med köer ved et vadested, i baggrunden kirke Oil/canvas (80x100cm 31x39in) Köbenhavn 2000
$541 - €590 - £373 - FF3 869
Snowy Fields Oil/canvas/board (21.5x30cm 8x11in) Amsterdam 2001

SOETE de Pierre 1886-1948 **[20]**
$728 - €694 - £442 - FF4 552
Tête du vainqueur Bronze (H45cm H17in) Bruxelles 1999

SOETERIK Theodor 1810-1883 **[16]**
$1 944 - €2 042 - £1 230 - FF13 394
An Angler in a Summer Landscape, a Church in the Distance Oil/panel (21.5x27.5cm 8x10in) Amsterdam 2000

SOFFICI Ardengo 1879-1964 **[129]**
$349 860 - €302 236 - £233 240 - FF1 982 540
Bagnanti Olio/tela (220x400cm 86x157in) Milano 1998
$24 000 - €31 100 - £18 000 - FF204 000
Paesaggio Olio/cartone (37x45.5cm 14x17in) Milano 2001
$18 400 - €23 843 - £13 800 - FF156 400
Natura morta Olio/tela (30x40cm 11x15in) Milano 2000

S

🖉 **$3 600** - €3 110 - **£1 800** - FF20 400
Paesaggio Matita/carta (23x32.5cm 9x12in) Prato
1999

▥ **$480** - €622 - **£360** - FF4 080
Bottiglia e fruttiera Litografia a colori (45.5x65cm
17x25in) Prato 2000

SOFRONOVA Antonina F. 1892-1966 [7]
🖉 **$1 252** - €1 453 - **£864** - FF9 534
Am Feld Indian ink/paper (12x11.5cm 4x4in) Wien
2000

SOGGETTI Gino Giuseppe 1898-1958 [4]
🖋 **$3 500** - €3 628 - **£2 100** - FF23 800
Dinamismo meccanico Tempera/cartone (35x30cm
13x11in) Roma 1999

SOGLIANI di Giovanni Antonio 1492-1544 [6]
🖉 **$5 489** - €5 360 - **£3 500** - FF35 161
**Saint Lucy holding a dish and a Palm/Studies
of the Christ Child** Black & white chalks (23x14cm
9x5in) London 1999

SOGLOW Otto 1900-1975 [4]
🖉 **$800** - €741 - **£489** - FF4 858
**Sentinel Louis eats oats/The little king gets a
seat for the big game** Ink (67x51cm 26x20in) New-
York 1999

SOHIER Louis XIX-XX [2]
🖉 **$4 172** - €4 878 - **£2 979** - FF32 000
Rivage oriental Aquarelle/papier (42x58cm 16x22in)
Paris 2001

SOHL Will 1906-1969 [64]
🖉 **$505** - €511 - **£308** - FF3 353
Sonnenblumen Aquarell/Papier (49.5x64.5cm
19x25in) Stuttgart 2000

SOHLBERG Harald 1869-1935 [29]
🖋 **$95 914** - €114 104 - **£66 339** - FF748 475
Midtsommernatt fra Kjerringvik Oil/canvas
(55x70cm 21x27in) Oslo 2000
🖋 **$66 850** - €58 144 - **£40 300** - FF381 400
Natteglöd Oil/canvas/panel (33.5x24cm 13x9in) Oslo
1998
🖋 **$1 866** - €2 113 - **£1 305** - FF13 858
Pan og piken Drawing (38x46cm 14x18in) Oslo 2001
▥ **$3 947** - €4 136 - **£2 500** - FF27 132
**Fra Akershusvollen, Aften (From Akershus,
Evening)** Etching, aquatint (21x29.5cm 8x11in)
London 2001

SOHN Carl Ferdinand 1805-1867 [5]
🖋 **$4 088** - €4 602 - **£2 817** - FF30 185
Junge Frau mit Spiegel Öl/Leinwand (111x91cm
43x35in) Heidelberg 2000
🖋 **$7 000** - €6 609 - **£4 351** - FF43 351
A Beautiful young Woman Oil/canvas (40x32cm
16x12in) Milford CT 1999

SOHN Carl Rudolph 1845-1908 [5]
🖋 **$25 000** - €28 782 - **£17 060** - FF188 800
A Welcome Interruption Oil/canvas (57x77.5cm
22x30in) New-York 2000

SOHN Paul Edouard Richard 1834-1912 [2]
🖋 **$13 000** - €14 290 - **£8 330** - FF93 735
The Appraiser's Visit Oil/canvas (91.5x113cm
36x44in) New-York 2000

SOHN-RETHEL Alfred 1875-1955 [9]
🖋 **$1 880** - €2 147 - **£1 325** - FF14 086
Menschen auf der Strasse Oil/canvas/panel
(63x82cm 24x32in) Stuttgart 2001

SOKAL Benoît 1954 [9]
🖉 **$311** - €351 - **£219** - FF2 300
Canardo, pl.3 de la Marque de Raspoutine Encre
Chine/papier (45x33cm 17x12in) Paris 2001

SOKEN Yamaguchi 1759-1818 [6]
🖋 **$6 000** - €6 630 - **£4 161** - FF43 492
Boats in a winter Landscape Ink (105.5x36cm
41x14in) New-York 2001

SOKOL Koloman 1902-1976 [4]
▥ **$780** - €738 - **£486** - FF4 841
Révolte Gravure bois (40x30cm 15x11in) Praha 2001

SOKOLOV Piotr Fedorovich 1791-1848 [10]
☞ **$5 707** - €6 647 - **£3 987** - FF43 600
Brustbild eines jungen Offiziers in Uniform
Miniature (14x10.5cm 5x4in) München 2000

SOKOLSKY Melvin XX [4]
📷 **$3 000** - €2 840 - **£1 865** - FF18 626
Big Chair Lean, New York Photograph (119x93cm
47x37in) New-York 1999

SOLANA José Gutiérrez 1886-1945 [88]
☞ **$173 400** - €204 221 - **£119 000** - FF1 339 600
Procesión en Pancorbo Oleo/lienzo (132x101cm
51x39in) Madrid 2000
☞ **$147 000** - €126 136 - **£88 200** - FF827 400
Cabezas y caretas Oleo/lienzo (82x65.5cm 32x25in)
Madrid 1998
☞ **$12 780** - €10 812 - **£7 740** - FF70 920
Meloj de la muerte Carboncillo (52x45cm 20x17in)
Madrid 1998
▥ **$384** - €360 - **£240** - FF2 364
Máscaras Grabado (50x66cm 19x25in) Madrid 1999

SOLANO Susana 1946 [19]
🖎 **$22 000** - €21 287 - **£13 567** - FF139 631
Objeto y Causa Metal (150x322.5cm 59x126in)
New-York 1999
🖎 **$5 400** - €6 006 - **£3 500** - FF39 400
Sin título Metal (39x29x15cm 15x11x5in) Madrid
2000

SOLARI Achille 1835-? [16]
☞ **$2 100** - €2 177 - **£1 260** - FF14 280
Veduta del Golfo di Sorrento Olio/tela (25x45cm
9x17in) Napoli 2000

SOLARI Luis Alberto XX [19]
🖉 **$650** - €629 - **£401** - FF4 127
Personaje Collage/paper (35.5x24cm 13x9in)
Montevideo 1999

SOLARIO Andrea c.1470-1520 [4]
☞ **$260 000** - €259 878 - **£158 834** - FF1 704 690
The Madonna and Child Tempera (44x33cm
17x12in) New-York 2000

SOLAVAGGIONE Piero 1899-1979 [4]
☞ **$900** - €933 - **£540** - FF6 120
«Fiori» Olio/tela (40x30cm 15x11in) Torino 2000

SOLDAN Uuno 1883-1954 [51]
☞ **$319** - €370 - **£226** - FF2 427
Landskap Oil/canvas (38x53cm 14x20in) Helsinki
2000

SOLDAN-BROFELT Venny 1863-1945 [87]
☞ **$7 021** - €7 904 - **£4 836** - FF51 850
Trafik till havs Oil/canvas (50x32.5cm 19x12in)
Helsinki 2000
☞ **$1 789** - €2 018 - **£1 257** - FF13 238
Sommardag på stranden Oil/canvas (33x47cm
12x18in) Helsinki 2001

S

$495 - €555 - **£336** - FF3 640
Viitasaari Watercolour/paper (19x25cm 7x9in)
Helsinki 2000

SOLDANI Massimiliano Benzi 1658-1740 **[6]**
$65 508 - €60 858 - **£40 000** - FF399 200
A Bacchante and a Panther Bronze (H39cm
H15in) London 1998

SOLDATI Atanasio 1896-1953 **[132]**
$14 800 - €19 178 - **£11 100** - FF125 800
Senza titolo Olio/tela (38x46cm 14x18in) Milano
2001
$5 750 - €5 961 - **£3 450** - FF39 100
Composizione Tempera (39.5x27cm 15x10in) Prato
2000
$1 680 - €2 177 - **£1 260** - FF14 280
Natura morta Tempera/carta (11x15cm 4x5in) Prato
2000

SOLDENHOFF von Alexander Leo 1882-1951 **[53]**
$793 - €918 - **£561** - FF6 023
Stilleben mit Pfirsichen und Krug Öl/Leinwand
(38x46cm 14x18in) Zürich 2000

SOLDI Andrea c.1703-c.1771 **[9]**
$26 220 - €24 978 - **£16 000** - FF163 848
**Group Portrait of Arthur Jones Nevill, Eleanor
Parker and Mrs Hogshawe** Oil/canvas
(151x181.5cm 59x71in) London 1999
$14 885 - €12 979 - **£9 000** - FF85 138
**Portrait of a Gentleman believed to be a mem-
ber of the Foley family** Oil/canvas (76x63.5cm
29x25in) London 1998

SOLDI Raúl 1903-1994 **[18]**
$80 000 - €77 628 - **£50 768** - FF509 208
Musicos Oleo/lienzo/tabla (122x117cm 48x46in)
Buenos-Aires 1999
$1 400 - €1 626 - **£983** - FF10 669
Valle encantado Oleo/cartón (19x23cm 7x9in)
Buenos-Aires 2001

SOLDINI Arnoldo 1862-1936 **[5]**
$4 165 - €4 318 - **£2 499** - FF28 322
Paesaggio Olio/tavola (63x46cm 24x18in) Milano
2000

SOLDNER Paul 1921 **[9]**
$2 500 - €2 590 - **£1 591** - FF16 988
Vessel Ceramic (50x35.5x26.5cm 19x13x10in) New-
York 2000

SOLDWEDEL Frederic A. 1886-? **[7]**
$210 - €200 - **£129** - FF1 315
Naples Watercolour/board (38x55cm 15x22in)
Cincinnati OH 1999

SOLE dal Giovan Gioseffo 1654-1719 **[15]**
$55 000 - €55 640 - **£33 583** - FF364 974
The Penitent Magdalene Oil/canvas (90x82.5cm
35x32in) New-York 2000
$1 680 - €1 451 - **£840** - FF9 520
San Sebastiano/Maddalena Inchiostro
(27.5x19.5cm 10x7in) Milano 1999

SOLE JORBA Vicenç 1904-1949 **[5]**
$2 132 - €2 463 - **£1 476** - FF16 154
«Llanás» Oleo/lienzo (53.5x65cm 21x25in) Barcelona
2001

SOLENGHI Giuseppe 1879-1944 **[51]**
$1 080 - €1 339 - **£810** - FF9 180
Paesaggio Olio/tela (44.5x63cm 17x24in) Milano
2000

$939 - €939 - **£587** - FF6 157
Verschneite Lagunenstadt mit Pferdedroschke
Oil/panel (40x30cm 15x11in) Zofingen 1999

SOLER I GILI Domingo 1871-1951 **[37]**
$687 - €751 - **£450** - FF4 925
Montesquiu Oleo/lienzo (49x64cm 19x25in)
Barcelona 2000
$442 - €511 - **£306** - FF3 349
Arboleda Oleo/tabla (24x30cm 9x11in) Madrid 2001

SOLER Juan XX **[43]**
$1 301 - €1 149 - **£800** - FF7 536
On a Paris Street Oil/canvas (45.5x56cm 17x22in)
Godalming, Surrey 1999
$1 064 - €1 141 - **£703** - FF7 486
Patinaje artístico Oleo/lienzo (31x39cm 12x15in)
Madrid 2001

SOLER PEREZ Rigoberto 1896-1968 **[14]**
$44 800 - €42 045 - **£28 000** - FF275 800
Después del baño Oleo/lienzo (175.5x105cm
69x41in) Madrid 1999
$18 975 - €16 560 - **£11 550** - FF108 625
Encarna en la playa Oleo/lienzo (60x70cm 23x27in)
Madrid 1998

SOLERO Pio 1881-? **[5]**
$3 100 - €3 214 - **£1 860** - FF21 080
Sappada sotto la neve Olio/tavola (42x54cm
16x21in) Trieste 1999

SOLIMENA Francesco Ciccio 1657-1747 **[82]**
$120 000 - €128 154 - **£81 768** - FF840 636
Phaethon asking to drive the Chariot of Apollo
Oil/canvas (89.5x149cm 35x58in) New-York 2001
$32 500 - €33 691 - **£19 500** - FF221 000
La Maddalena Olio/tela (100x74cm 39x29in) Venezia
1999
$921 - €784 - **£550** - FF5 144
A Bishop's Blessing Ink (54.5x41cm 21x16in)
London 1998

SOLIN Timo 1947 **[64]**
$840 - €816 - **£518** - FF5 350
Springande flicka Metal (H34cm H13in) Stockholm
1999

SOLIS de Francisco 1629-1684 **[6]**
$23 850 - €27 029 - **£16 200** - FF177 300
La Anunciación Oleo/lienzo (209x138cm 82x54in)
Madrid 2000
$6 555 - €5 721 - **£3 990** - FF37 525
Annunciación Oleo/lienzo (119x91.5cm 46x36in)
Madrid 2000

SOLIS Virgil 1514-1562 **[34]**
$192 - €168 - **£116** - FF1 100
Planche de différents oiseaux Estampe (6x11cm
2x4in) Paris 1998

SOLLIER Henri 1886-1966 **[85]**
$1 399 - €1 524 - **£917** - FF10 000
L'abri du marin à Ste Marine Huile/panneau
(45x65cm 17x25in) Brest 2000
$835 - €762 - **£508** - FF5 000
Rue des Quatre Vents Huile/toile (33x41cm
12x16in) Douarnenez 1998
$358 - €335 - **£222** - FF2 200
Vieille Bretonne Fusain (61x50cm 24x19in) Quimper
1999

SOLLMANN Paul 1886-? **[14]**
$3 770 - €3 904 - **£2 405** - FF25 610
La Alhambra Acuarela/papel (47x67cm 18x26in)
Madrid 2000

SOLMAN Joseph 1909 **[37]**
- 🖎 $3 000 - €2 797 - **£1 860** - FF18 349
  Gladiolas Oil/board (40.5x51cm 15x20in) New-York 1999
- 🖎 $1 900 - €1 825 - **£1 177** - FF11 968
  Still Life with Antique Objects Oil/masonite (20.5x27cm 8x10in) New-York 1999
- ✑ $1 100 - €1 249 - **£752** - FF8 193
  Subway Reader Gouache (28.5x20cm 11x7in) New-York 2000

SOLOMAN Abraham 1824-1862 **[21]**
- 🖎 $3 560 - €3 338 - **£2 200** - FF21 899
  The New Hat Oil/board (28x23cm 11x9in) London 1999

SOLOMATKIN Leonid Ivanovich 1837-1883 **[8]**
- 🖎 $24 487 - €29 142 - **£17 500** - FF191 156
  Welcoming the Official Oil/canvas (21.5x29.5cm 8x11in) London 2000

SOLOMON Lance Vaiben 1913-1989 **[94]**
- 🖎 $617 - €579 - **£381** - FF3 797
  Bush Landscape Oil/canvas/board (44.5x38cm 17x14in) Sydney 1999
- 🖎 $437 - €396 - **£265** - FF2 600
  Morning Light, Nundle Oil/board (29x24cm 11x9in) Sydney 1998

SOLOMON Rebecca 1832-1886 **[5]**
- 🖎 $22 414 - €24 060 - **£15 000** - FF157 824
  Peg Woffington's Visit to Triplet Oil/canvas (86.5x112cm 34x44in) London 2000

SOLOMON Simeon 1840-1905 **[82]**
- 🖎 $71 276 - €61 495 - **£43 000** - FF403 378
  Young Musician employed in the Temple service during the Feast Oil/canvas (56x51cm 22x20in) London 1998
- ✑ $1 491 - €1 287 - **£900** - FF8 442
  The Florentine Chiaro/Letter from Simeon Solomon to Henry Holiday Ink (17x12.5cm 6x4in) London 1998

SOLOMON Solomon Joseph 1860-1927 **[17]**
- 🖎 $2 769 - €2 521 - **£1 700** - FF16 535
  The Young Artist Oil/panel (45.5x26cm 17x10in) London 1999
- ✑ $647 - €608 - **£400** - FF3 986
  Woman with two Children Pencil/paper (21.5x13cm 8x5in) London 1999

SOLOMONS Estella 1882-1968 **[13]**
- 🖎 $7 374 - €8 380 - **£5 093** - FF54 971
  Woman Grazing Out of the Window into «The Grove» Oil/canvas (63x76cm 25x30in) Dublin 2000
- 🖎 $1 530 - €1 778 - **£1 075** - FF11 660
  Cliffs and Cove, County Kerry Oil/board (28x41cm 11x16in) Dublin 2001

SOLON Albert 1897-1973 **[10]**
- 🎞 $561 - €640 - **£389** - FF4 200
  «Air France» Affiche (97x60cm 38x23in) Paris 2000

SOLVYNS Balthazar 1760-1824 **[10]**
- 🖎 $14 058 - €13 149 - **£8 500** - FF86 254
  Calcutta, from below Fort William, looking North, with Shipping Oil/canvas (51x62.5cm 20x24in) London 1999

SOMAINI Francesco 1926 **[16]**
- 🖎 $880 - €1 140 - **£660** - FF7 480
  Sena titolo Fer (25.5x23x10cm 10x9x3in) Milano 2000

SOMER van Hendrick Zomeren 1615-1684/85 **[5]**
- 🖎 $9 975 - €11 330 - **£7 000** - FF74 322
  Saint Jerome Oil/canvas (98x78.5cm 38x30in) London 2001

SOMER van Jan 1645-c.1699 **[6]**
- 🎞 $507 - €577 - **£350** - FF3 784
  The Letter Bearer Mezzotint (36.5x29cm 14x11in) London 2001

SOMERS Francine 1923 **[18]**
- 🖎 $479 - €545 - **£334** - FF3 577
  Nature morte Huile/toile (80x60cm 31x23in) Maisieres-Mons 2001

SOMERSALO Jaakko 1916-1966 **[16]**
- 🎞 $394 - €420 - **£267** - FF2 758
  Former Color lithograph (47x60cm 18x23in) Helsinki 2001

SOMERSCALES Thomas Jacques 1842-1927 **[50]**
- 🖎 $50 000 - €53 670 - **£33 460** - FF352 050
  River Valley in Chile Oil/canvas (94.5x135.5cm 37x53in) New-York 2000
- 🖎 $15 863 - €17 529 - **£11 000** - FF114 983
  «First Class Cruiser, Cape Pillar, Straits of Magellan» Oil/canvas (40.5x61cm 15x24in) London 2001
- 🖎 $19 019 - €16 584 - **£11 500** - FF108 787
  A Clipper running under Full Sail Oil/canvas/panel (30.5x46cm 12x18in) London 1998

SOMERSET Richard Gay 1848-1928 **[20]**
- 🖎 $2 600 - €2 865 - **£1 734** - FF18 791
  Cape St.Vincent Oil/panel (25x34cm 10x13in) Portsmouth NH 2000

SOMERVILLE Edith Oenone 1858-1949 **[13]**
- 🖎 $1 368 - €1 532 - **£950** - FF10 052
  On the Kinneagh River Oil/canvas/board (18x25cm 7x9in) London 2001

SOMERVILLE John XX **[4]**
- 🗿 $2 405 - €2 312 - **£1 500** - FF15 167
  Bust of John Lennon with tinted glasses Bronze (H49cm H19in) London 1999

SOMERVILLE Peggy 1918-1975 **[50]**
- 🖎 $2 286 - €1 958 - **£1 350** - FF12 844
  French Landscape Oil/canvas (56x84cm 22x33in) Ipswich 1998
- 🖎 $868 - €1 015 - **£620** - FF6 658
  Asters in a blue Vase Oil/board (42x34cm 16x13in) London 2001
- ✑ $638 - €663 - **£400** - FF4 348
  At the Fair Pastel/paper (37x27cm 14x10in) Suffolk 2000

SOMERVILLE Stuart Scott 1908-1983 **[77]**
- 🖎 $651 - €761 - **£460** - FF4 989
  Still life Flowers in a Glass Vase on a Ledge Oil/panel (44x54cm 17x21in) Woodbridge, Suffolk 2000
- 🖎 $575 - €645 - **£400** - FF4 229
  Still Life of Flowers Oil/canvas (30.5x24.5cm 12x9in) Newbury, Berkshire 2001

SOMM Henry 1844-1907 **[156]**
- ✑ $556 - €544 - **£356** - FF3 571
  La promenade Watercolour (18x12cm 7x4in) Amsterdam 1999
- 🎞 $300 - €274 - **£183** - FF1 798
  Femme Etching (18x12.5cm 7x4in) Boston MA 1999

SØMME Jacob 1862-1940 **[10]**
- 🖎 $2 415 - €2 872 - **£1 720** - FF18 837
  Ku i Jaerlandskap Oil/canvas (67x100cm 26x39in) Oslo 2000

S

SOMME Théophile François 1871-1952 **[33]**

🖊 **$1 560 - €1 448 - £953** - FF9 500
Danseuse aux serpents Bronze (H32cm H12in)
Paris 1999

SOMMER Alice 1898-1942 **[6]**

🖼 **$10 257 - €11 810 - £7 000** - FF77 468
Portrait: Head of a Woman (Possibly Self-Portrait) Oil/board (48.5x24cm 19x9in) London 2000

✏ **$2 930 - €3 374 - £2 000** - FF22 133
Two Sisters Pencil/paper (64x48cm 25x18in) London 2000

SOMMER Ferdinand 1822-1901 **[50]**

🖼 **$1 393 - €1 639 - £1 010** - FF10 754
«Oeschinensee» Öl/Leinwand (56x77cm 22x30in) Zofingen 2001

🖼 **$1 306 - €1 252 - £822** - FF8 210
Sankt Antons Kapelle am Eingang zum Maderaner Tal Öl/Karton (21x15.8cm 8x6in) Bern 1999

SOMMER Frederick 1905-1999 **[57]**

📷 **$13 000 - €12 225 - £8 049** - FF80 194
Circumn Avigation of the Blood Gelatin silver print (10.5x14.5cm 4x5in) New-York 1999

SOMMER Giorgio 1834-1914 **[59]**

📷 **$350 - €400 - £242** - FF2 621
Amalfi/Palermo/Pompei/Taormina Albumen print (20x25.3cm 7x9in) Wien 2000

SOMMER Otto XIX **[11]**

🖼 **$4 500 - €4 176 - £2 701** - FF27 394
Still Life with Apples Oil/board (20x30cm 8x12in) Milford CT 1999

SOMMER William 1867-1949 **[116]**

🖼 **$9 050 - €9 503 - £5 706** - FF62 337
Farmland Industry Oil/masonite (45x59cm 18x23in) Cleveland OH 2000

✏ **$1 350 - €1 418 - £851** - FF9 301
Seated Woman Ink/paper (41x33cm 16x13in) Cleveland OH 2000

🗔 **$200 - €215 - £133** - FF1 408
Sunday Boy Lithograph (31x32cm 12x9in) Cleveland OH 2000

SOMOGYI von Istvan 1897-1971 **[22]**

🖼 **$1 050 - €1 022 - £645** - FF6 707
Galoppierende Pferdegruppe Öl/Leinwand (80x110cm 31x43in) Stuttgart 1999

SOMOV Constantin Andrevich 1869-1939 **[42]**

🖼 **$488 - €457 - £304** - FF3 000
Et par kvinder i form af sorte silhuetter holdende champagneglas Oil/canvas (19.5x30cm 7x11in) Köbenhavn 1999

✏ **$3 225 - €3 835 - £2 235** - FF25 154
Landhaus im Herbst Aquarell/Papier (33x41cm 12x16in) Bremen 2000

SOMVILLE Roger 1923 **[308]**

🖼 **$15 045 - €14 625 - £9 204** - FF95 934
La nuit qui vient Huile/toile (130x195cm 51x76in) Liège 1999

🖼 **$4 020 - €3 718 - £2 505** - FF24 390
Femme au chapeau à Ostende Oil/canvas (60x73cm 23x28in) Lokeren 1999

✏ **$686 - €644 - £423** - FF4 227
Nu de dos Crayon/papier (36x30cm 14x11in) Antwerpen 1999

🗔 **$256 - €248 - £158** - FF1 626
La belle et le touffu Lithographie (51.5x33cm 20x12in) Bruxelles 1999

SON van Jan Frans 1658-c.1700/23 **[3]**

🖼 **$4 967 - €5 113 - £3 131** - FF33 539
Zwei Tulpen und Orangenblütenzweig Öl/Leinwand (32.5x24.5cm 12x9in) Berlin 2000

SON van Joris 1623-1667 **[34]**

🖼 **$108 948 - €107 094 - £70 000** - FF702 492
Still Life of a Garland of Fruits, Flowers in a Vase, upon a Plinth Oil/canvas (139x194.5cm 54x76in) London 1999

🖼 **$48 954 - €45 507 - £30 000** - FF298 506
Clusters of Oranges, Lemons, Pears, Grapes, Figs and other Fruits Oil/canvas (118x101.5cm 46x39in) London 1998

🖼 **$32 777 - €37 228 - £23 000** - FF244 202
Still Life of Shrimps in a Blu-and-White Porcelain Bowl/Still life Oil/panel (32x41cm 12x16in) London 2001

SONDERBORG Kurt R. Hoffmann 1923 **[249]**

🖼 **$8 638 - €9 909 - £5 908** - FF65 000
Sans titre Huile/toile (130x81cm 51x31in) Paris 2000

🖼 **$3 266 - €3 506 - £2 185** - FF23 000
26-4-54...15h-17h Encre Chine/papier (67x50cm 26x19in) Paris 2000

🗔 **$319 - €343 - £213** - FF2 247
Komposition Serigraph (82.8x57.5cm 32x22in) Hamburg 2000

SONDERER R. XX **[3]**

🗔 **$416 - €473 - £289** - FF3 100
«Metz» Affiche (100x63cm 39x24in) Paris 2001

SØNDERGAARD Jens Andersen 1895-1957 **[288]**

🖼 **$5 043 - €4 712 - £3 048** - FF30 908
Udsigt over marklandskab med figurer og kvaeg, Thy, Limfjorden Oil/canvas (118x138cm 46x54in) Köbenhavn 1999

🖼 **$3 053 - €2 962 - £1 922** - FF19 428
Solstrejf gennem uvejr over bakket landskab Oil/canvas (86x104cm 33x40in) Köbenhavn 1999

✏ **$265 - €295 - £184** - FF1 934
Landskab Watercolour/paper (12x13cm 4x5in) Köbenhavn 2001

SONDERLAND Fritz 1836-1896 **[22]**

🖼 **$3 498 - €4 090 - £2 458** - FF26 831
Kleines Mädchen reicht dem Schwesterchen einen Apfel an das Fenster Öl/Leinwand (61.5x47.5cm 24x18in) München 2000

🖼 **$2 154 - €2 492 - £1 524** - FF16 349
Ein Schulknabe steht weinend vor dem Klassenzimmer Oil/panel (27.5x22.5cm 10x8in) Zürich 2000

SONDERMANN Hermann 1832-1901 **[16]**

🖼 **$6 000 - €5 197 - £3 679** - FF34 089
Spinning Yarn Oil/canvas (68.5x81cm 26x31in) New-York 1999

🖼 **$1 661 - €1 453 - £1 167** - FF12 744
Der erste Liebesbrief: zwei junge Mädchen mit einem Brief Oil/panel (18x14.5cm 7x5in) München 2000

SONG BAISONG 1953 **[1]**

✏ **$4 736 - €4 494 - £2 877** - FF29 480
Waterfall of a Misty Landscape Ink (131.5x68cm 51x26in) Hong-Kong 1999

SONG DI 1945 **[3]**

✏ **$4 440 - €4 213 - £2 697** - FF27 637
Scene of Mount Huang Ink (68x68cm 26x26in) Hong-Kong 1999

S

SONG JUE 1576-1632 **[4]**
✎ **$18 018** - €17 087 - **£10 962** - FF112 084
Lychee Ink (110x29.5cm 43x11in) Hong-Kong 1999
SONG WENZHI 1918 **[16]**
✎ **$4 871** - €5 534 - **£3 420** - FF36 301
Landscape Ink (25.5x121cm 10x47in) Hong-Kong 2001
SONG YONGPING 1961 **[1]**
↩ **$5 967** - €4 982 - **£3 500** - FF32 679
Blue Parrot Oil/canvas (80x65cm 31x25in) London 1998
SONG YUGUI 1940 **[8]**
✎ **$7 722** - €7 323 - **£4 698** - FF48 036
Peony in a Vase Ink (68x68cm 26x26in) Hong-Kong 1999
SONJE Jan Gabrielsz. c.1625-1707 **[32]**
↩ **$22 205** - €23 316 - **£14 000** - FF152 945
Extensive Mountain Landscape with a Hawking Party on a Road Oil/canvas (105.5x162.5cm 41x63in) London 2000
↩ **$4 026** - €4 745 - **£2 829** - FF31 123
Italienskt landskap med herdar och boskap Oil/panel (78x61cm 30x24in) Malmö 2000
↩ **$4 416** - €4 878 - **£3 062** - FF32 000
Le repos d'un troupeau dans un paysage boisé Oil/panel (20x27cm 7x10in) Paris 2001
SONNE Jeppe Jørgen 1771-1833 **[3]**
↩ **$2 385** - €2 018 - **£1 426** - FF13 239
Portraet af en mand Oil/canvas (33x25cm 12x9in) Viby J, Århus 1998
SONNE Jørgen Valentin 1801-1890 **[67]**
↩ **$3 983** - €4 695 - **£2 800** - FF30 800
Dansk herregårdssexteriör med herre, heste og hund Oil/canvas (64x79cm 25x31in) Vejle 2000
↩ **$813** - €808 - **£508** - FF5 298
Siddende italiensk hyrde med höj hat og stav Oil/canvas (18x15cm 7x5in) København 1999
SONNEGA Auke Cornelis 1910-1963 **[27]**
↩ **$2 826** - €3 123 - **£1 959** - FF20 483
Balinese Dance Oil/board (41x31cm 16x12in) Singapore 2001
SONNIER Keith 1941 **[19]**
🖾 **$10 321** - €11 747 - **£7 252** - FF77 052
Forte crève-coeur Construction (250x111x75cm 98x43x29in) Zürich 2001
SONNTAG William Louis I 1822-1900 **[103]**
↩ **$25 000** - €25 914 - **£15 852** - FF169 985
Landscape with Fishermen Oil/canvas (95x138cm 37x54in) New-York 2000
↩ **$11 000** - €11 794 - **£7 277** - FF77 365
Hudson River Scene Oil/canvas (40x66cm 16x26in) New-Orleans LA 2000
↩ **$6 000** - €6 686 - **£4 036** - FF43 860
Forest clearing under Mist shrouded Mountain Oil/canvas (24x29cm 9x11in) Portsmouth NH 2000
↩ **$1 826** - €1 510 - **£1 071** - FF9 902
Mountain Landscape with ravine Watercolour/paper (23x32cm 9x12in) Detroit MI 1998
SONNTAG William Louis II 1869-1898 **[19]**
✎ **$2 600** - €2 462 - **£1 580** - FF16 151
Carriage Ride Watercolour, gouache (33x59.5cm 12x23in) New-York 1999
SONREL Élisabeth 1874-1953 **[73]**
↩ **$65 000** - €72 590 - **£41 626** - FF476 157
Dante Alighieri's «La vita nuova» Oil/canvas (111x84cm 43x33in) New-York 2000

SONG JUE

$2 459 - €2 439 - **£1 529** - FF16 000
Jour de pardon au Croajou Aquarelle, gouache/papier (15x34cm 5x13in) Brest 1999
🗒 **$854** - €994 - **£600** - FF6 518
«Les colombes tendresse» Poster (69x26cm 27x10in) London 2001
SOOLMAKER Jan Franz 1635-1685 **[17]**
↩ **$4 717** - €5 624 - **£3 363** - FF36 892
Südliche Landschaft mit Reitern an einem Brunnen Oil/panel (39x47.7cm 15x18in) Köln 2000
↩ **$2 322** - €2 020 - **£1 400** - FF13 248
Travellers by a Roadside Fountain Oil/panel (28.5x43cm 11x16in) London 1998
SOONIUS Louis 1883-1956 **[88]**
↩ **$2 200** - €2 025 - **£1 320** - FF13 282
Dutch Interior Oil/canvas (50x60cm 20x24in) Chicago IL 1999
↩ **$1 706** - €1 892 - **£1 181** - FF12 409
«Maultiere und Personen am Strand» Oil/panel (27x42cm 10x16in) Kempten 2001
↩ **$634** - €681 - **£424** - FF4 464
The artist working on the beach Watercolour (18.5x30cm 7x11in) Amsterdam 2000
SOOT Eyolf 1859-1928 **[4]**
↩ **$34 912** - €40 339 - **£24 448** - FF264 608
I lampelys Oil/canvas (125x97cm 49x38in) Oslo 2001
↩ **$226** - €244 - **£156** - FF1 600
Portrett av Arch.H.Ulrichsen Oil/canvas (92x76cm 36x29in) Oslo 2001
SOPER Eileen Alice 1905-1990 **[132]**
↩ **$4 102** - €4 367 - **£2 700** - FF28 648
Evie Oil/canvas (59.5x75cm 23x29in) Billingshurst, West-Sussex 2000
✎ **$359** - €403 - **£250** - FF2 643
Picnicing under a Tree Watercolour/paper (24.5x33.5cm 9x13in) London 2001
🗒 **$346** - €293 - **£208** - FF1 925
My pet Etching (22x16.5cm 8x6in) London 1998
SOPER George 1870-1942 **[101]**
✎ **$442** - €421 - **£270** - FF2 764
Farm Boy with Two Shire Horses in a Field Watercolour/paper (16x25cm 6x9in) West-Midlands 1999
🗒 **$229** - €210 - **£140** - FF1 379
The Kelp Gatherers Drypoint (19.5x30cm 7x11in) Ipswich 1999
SOPER Thomas James XIX **[28]**
↩ **$6 508** - €5 938 - **£4 000** - FF38 948
Shipping Off a Pier Oil/canvas (40.5x56cm 15x22in) London 1998
✎ **$514** - €479 - **£320** - FF3 142
Figures in a rural Setting before Sadler's Wells Watercolour (28.5x44cm 11x17in) London 1999
SOPHIDO 1963 **[11]**
🖾 **$4 429** - €4 057 - **£2 700** - FF26 610
Fifi peau de chat Bronze (44x52.5x15cm 17x20x5in) London 1999
SORAYAMA Hajime XX **[1]**
↩ **$13 200** - €11 261 - **£7 962** - FF73 867
Traci Lords leaning on a chair Watercolour, gouache (67x44cm 26x17in) New-York 1998
SORBI Giulio 1883-1975 **[12]**
↩ **$330** - €285 - **£220** - FF1 870
Aia Olio/tela (27x35.5cm 10x13in) Prato 1998

S

SORBI Raffaello 1844-1931 [86]
- $75 000 - €64 791 - **£50 000** - FF425 000
  La regata in Arno Olio/tela (40.5x74cm 15x29in)
  Milano 1998
- $4 700 - €4 242 - **£2 896** - FF27 823
  Italian Landscape with Lake and Mountains in the distance Oil/wood (3x7cm 1x3in) Asheville NC 1999
- $1 750 - €1 483 - **£1 045** - FF9 727
  Il Giullare Watercolour/paper (93x101cm 37x40in) South-Natick MA 1998

SOREAU Isaak 1604-c.1640 [9]
- $871 468 - €741 477 - **£520 000** - FF4 863 768
  Bunches of Grapes and vine Leaves on a pewter platter, Parrot Tulips Oil/panel (42.5x63cm 16x24in) London 1998

SOREL A. XIX-XX [1]
- $4 963 - €4 636 - **£3 000** - FF30 411
  «Port-Aviation» Poster (76x116cm 29x45in) London 1999

SOREL Edward 1929 [2]
- $8 000 - €9 402 - **£5 546** - FF61 675
  Three Sisters in a Walled Garden Watercolour/paper (34x51.5cm 13x20in) New-York 2000

SORELLA Thérèsia Ansingh 1883-1968 [20]
- $756 - €817 - **£517** - FF5 357
  «Gefopte Wooltra!» Oil/cardboard (64x52cm 25x20in) Amsterdam 2001

SØRENSEN Carl Frederick 1818-1879 [243]
- $37 324 - €37 615 - **£23 268** - FF246 736
  Marine med sejlskibe og fiskerbåde i Sundet mellem Danmark Oil/canvas (110x160cm 43x62in) København 2000
- $7 458 - €8 048 - **£5 004** - FF52 794
  Stille sommeraften i Sundet med sejlskibe ud for Kronborg Oil/canvas (48x63cm 18x24in) København 2000
- $1 881 - €2 010 - **£1 278** - FF13 186
  Sejlskibe udfor klippekyst, parti fra Norge Oil/canvas (33x46cm 12x18in) København 2001
- $439 - €469 - **£299** - FF3 076
  Havneparti med sejlbåde Pencil/paper (24x40cm 9x15in) Vejle 2001

SØRENSEN Eiler Carl 1869-1963 [45]
- $756 - €804 - **£507** - FF5 274
  En lille pige Oil/canvas (41x56cm 16x22in) Viby J, Århus 2001
- $418 - €389 - **£254** - FF2 550
  Interior med kvinde Oil/paper (29x22cm 11x8in) Viby J, Århus 1998

SÖRENSEN Henrik 1882-1962 [69]
- $2 116 - €2 345 - **£1 436** - FF15 384
  De vilde hester Oil/panel (46x55cm 18x21in) Oslo 2000
- $2 725 - €3 167 - **£1 915** - FF20 775
  Fra Provence Oil/panel (32x40cm 12x15in) Oslo 2001
- $281 - €324 - **£197** - FF2 127
  Tröst Color lithograph (29x23cm 16x9in) Oslo 2000

SÖRENSEN Inger Skjensvold XX [3]
- $1 443 - €1 597 - **£1 000** - FF10 475
  «Norvège» Poster (99x62cm 38x24in) London 2001

SÖRENSEN Jacobus Lorenz 1812-1857 [12]
- $3 697 - €3 126 - **£2 210** - FF20 505
  A Wooded Landscape with Fishermen Inspecting their Nets on the Bank Oil/canvas (51x61cm 20x24in) Amsterdam 1998

SØRENSEN Jens 1887-1953 [141]
- $386 - €403 - **£243** - FF2 643
  Parti fra Dyrehavsbakken Oil/canvas (55x88cm 21x34in) København 2000
- $239 - €268 - **£166** - FF1 757
  Parti fra Bakken Oil/panel (26x39cm 10x15in) Viby J, Århus 2001

SØRENSEN Jens-Flemming 1933 [40]
- $967 - €942 - **£594** - FF6 177
  Kugle og bladvaerk omgivet af åben todelt kugle Bronze (46x29cm 18x11in) København 1999

SØRENSEN Lauritz 1882-? [78]
- $326 - €309 - **£198** - FF2 030
  Tremaster på åbent hav Oil/canvas (89x120cm 35x47in) København 1999

SØRENSEN Søren 1885-1937 [26]
- $505 - €471 - **£305** - FF3 091
  Interiör med dame siddende i laenestol Oil/canvas (67x53cm 26x20in) København 1999

SÖRENSEN-RINGI Harald 1872-1912 [7]
- $3 504 - €3 496 - **£2 187** - FF22 935
  L'apparition, stående kvinnofigur Carrare marble (H66cm H25in) Uppsala 1999

SORESSI Alfredo 1897-? [5]
- $1 200 - €1 555 - **£900** - FF10 200
  Sul greto del fiume Olio/tela (35x50cm 13x19in) Roma 2001

SORGE Peter 1937-2000 [38]
- $50 - €61 - **£35** - FF402
  Drei Hände Farbradierung (34.5x39.5cm 13x15in) Berlin 2000

SORGH Hendrik Maertensz c.1611-1670 [42]
- $75 000 - €75 873 - **£45 795** - FF497 692
  Peasants drinking and smoking in a Barn Oil/panel (49.5x68cm 19x26in) New-York 2000
- $8 710 - €7 523 - **£5 250** - FF49 346
  A Maid standing by a Table cleaning Fish, Pots, Pans and Cabbages Oil/panel (35.4x27cm 13x10in) Amsterdam 1998

SORIA AEDO Francisco 1898-1965 [18]
- $20 520 - €22 825 - **£14 440** - FF149 720
  Demetrio y su novia Oleo/lienzo (200x150cm 78x59in) Madrid 2001

SORIANO Juan 1920 [62]
- $50 470 - €53 963 - **£34 398** - FF353 976
  El toro echado Oleo/lienzo (180x180cm 70x70in) México 2001
- $18 000 - €20 913 - **£12 650** - FF137 181
  Adán y Eva Oil/canvas (120x54cm 47x21in) New-York 2001
- $23 000 - €20 055 - **£13 905** - FF131 553
  Paloma Bronze (87x68x35cm 34x26x13in) New-York 1998
- $2 358 - €2 615 - **£1 568** - FF17 155
  El águila Bronze (15x35x12cm 5x13x4in) México 2000
- $4 254 - €4 019 - **£2 653** - FF26 362
  Por pulgada cuadrada Acuarela/papel (20x78cm 7x30in) Monterrey NL 2001
- $2 393 - €2 261 - **£1 492** - FF14 828
  Sin título Grabado (15x22cm 5x8in) Monterrey NL 2001

SORIN Savely / Sawelij 1878-1953 **[5]**
- $55 972 - €66 609 - **£40 000** - FF436 928
  Portrait of Anna Pavlova in Les Sylphides
  Oil/canvas (103x129cm 40x50in) London 2000

SORIO Enrico XIX **[2]**
- $19 986 - €18 548 - **£12 000** - FF121 670
  La Piazza d'Erbe, Verona Oil/canvas (150x95cm
  59x37in) London 1999

SORKAU Albert 1874-? **[38]**
- $3 270 - €2 744 - **£1 918** - FF18 000
  Préparation des bouquets de fleurs Huile/toile
  (65x78cm 25x30in) Nancy 1998
- $994 - €1 067 - **£665** - FF7 000
  Sur le pas de la porte Huile/panneau (25x20cm
  9x7in) Corbeil-Essonnes 2000

SORKINE Delhia XX **[9]**
- $827 - €793 - **£510** - FF5 200
  Le pêcheur Huile/toile (54x65cm 21x25in) Marseille
  1999

SORLAIN Jean, Paul Denarié 1859-1942 **[28]**
- $1 028 - €1 037 - **£641** - FF6 800
  Basse-cour dans un verger en fleurs Huile/toile
  (60x92cm 23x36in) Tours 2000

SORLIER Charles 1921-1990 **[151]**
- $3 750 - €3 343 - **£2 312** - FF21 928
  The Tribe of Asher, after Marc Chagall Color lithograph (61.5x46cm 24x18in) New-York 1999

SORMAN Steven 1948 **[32]**
- $1 500 - €1 748 - **£1 038** - FF11 469
  Again Now Etching, aquatint (75.5x102cm 29x40in)
  New-York 2000

SORMANI Gian Luciano 1867-? **[14]**
- $400 - €518 - **£300** - FF3 400
  Barca di pescatori a Venezia Acquarello/cartone
  (29x13.5cm 11x5in) Roma 2001

SOROLLA Y BASTIDA Joaquín 1863-1923 **[310]**
- $176 000 - €192 208 - **£112 000** - FF1 260 800
  Retrato de Doña Isaura Zaldo Arana Oleo/lienzo
  (210x105cm 82x41in) Madrid 2000
- $118 800 - €132 143 - **£79 200** - FF866 800
  Marina Oleo/lienzo (45x77cm 17x30in) Madrid 2000
- $8 120 - €8 709 - **£5 510** - FF57 130
  La Cruz sobre el catafalco Oleo/tabla (20x34.5cm
  7x13in) Madrid 2001
- $4 320 - €3 613 - **£2 580** - FF23 700
  Malaguena con guitarra Acuarela/papel (47x22cm
  18x8in) Madrid 1998

SORRELL Alan 1904-1974 **[31]**
- $214 - €260 - **£150** - FF1 703
  **Britain Circa A.D.500/Northumbria
  A.D.793/France A.D.486** Watercolour/paper
  (35x50cm 14x20in) Aylsham, Norfolk 2000

SORTET Paul 1905-1966 **[8]**
- $2 755 - €3 201 - **£1 963** - FF21 000
  Portrait de femme Huile/isorel (47.5x37.5cm
  18x14in) Paris 2001

SØRVIG Frederik 1823-1892 **[8]**
- $2 684 - €3 084 - **£1 858** - FF20 228
  Skibsportraet af «Caroline af Aarhuus»
  Gouache/paper (55x79cm 21x31in) København 2000

SOSA Hermenegildo 1946 **[2]**
- $3 303 - €3 874 - **£2 376** - FF25 410
  Paisaje Oleo/lienzo (80x100cm 31x39in) México 2001

SOSHANA Afroyim 1927 **[35]**
- $511 - €509 - **£309** - FF3 336
  Abstraktion II, Matiere Öl/Leinwand (81x54cm
  31x21in) Wien 2000

SOSNO Sacha 1937 **[41]**
- $688 - €732 - **£461** - FF4 800
  Pudique Bronze (26x14.5x6cm 10x5x2in) Cannes
  2000

SOSSON Louis XIX-XX **[25]**
- $602 - €694 - **£420** - FF4 552
  Gardienne d'oies Bronze (H30.5cm H12in) Bruxelles
  2001

SOTO Christian 1959 **[17]**
- $444 - €488 - **£286** - FF3 200
  Coucher de soleil Huile/toile (60x73cm 23x28in)
  Thonon-les-Bains 2000

SOTO de Rafael Fernández 1915-1984 **[19]**
- $924 - €841 - **£560** - FF5 516
  Puente de la Vila, Baga Oleo/lienzo (54x65cm
  21x25in) Barcelona 1999
- $441 - €420 - **£280** - FF2 758
  Paseo urbano con viandantes Oleo/lienzo
  (22x27cm 8x10in) Barcelona 1999

SOTO Jesús Rafael 1923 **[311]**
- $17 000 - €18 097 - **£11 580** - FF118 711
  Blanc et Citron Oil/panel (153x153cm 60x60in)
  Miami FL 2001
- $9 977 - €9 909 - **£6 214** - FF65 000
  Circule Plata Technique mixte/panneau (51x51x30cm
  20x20x11in) Paris 1999
- $2 444 - €2 907 - **£1 744** - FF19 068
  Vibrationen-Braun-Gold Mischtechnik/Karton
  (36.5x28cm 14x11in) Wien 2000
- $25 026 - €29 498 - **£17 585** - FF193 493
  Ambivalence No.34A Metal (107x107x16.5cm
  42x42x6in) Caracas ($) 2000
- $3 961 - €3 845 - **£2 466** - FF25 224
  Kinetisches Wandobjekt, Arcay Relief
  (54x53x12cm 21x20x4in) Luzern 1999
- $2 303 - €2 301 - **£1 440** - FF15 092
  Rond avec noir et violet Gouache (36.5x27.9cm
  14x10in) Hamburg 1999
- $226 - €256 - **£159** - FF1 676
  Vibration jaune et noir Farbserigraphie (47x40cm
  18x15in) Stuttgart 2001

SOTO Pascual 1781-? **[1]**
- $4 950 - €5 406 - **£3 420** - FF35 460
  Cesto de frutas/El pájaro enjaulado Oleo/lienzo
  (80x33cm 31x12in) Madrid 2001

SOTOMAYOR Y ZARAGOZA Fernando Alvarez
1875-1960 **[50]**
- $17 750 - €15 016 - **£10 500** - FF98 500
  Bodegón de caza Oleo/lienzo (129x109cm 50x42in)
  Madrid 1998
- $13 750 - €15 016 - **£8 750** - FF98 500
  Jardines de El Paular Oleo/lienzo (41x56cm
  16x22in) Madrid 2000
- $4 950 - €5 406 - **£3 150** - FF35 460
  Retrato de mujer Oleo/lienzo (41.5x34cm 16x13in)
  Madrid 2000

SOTTER George William 1879-1953 **[20]**
- $4 250 - €4 580 - **£2 898** - FF30 045
  Storm over the Catskills, Alice's Favorite
  Oil/board (55x64cm 22x25in) Hatfield PA 2001
- $5 200 - €5 860 - **£3 601** - FF38 438
  «Wismer Road, Carversville» Oil/board (25x30cm
  10x12in) Hatfield PA 2000

S

SOTTOCORNOLA Giovanni 1855-1917 [22]
- $2 280 - €1 970 - £1 520 - FF12 920
  Piccoli paesaggi Pastel/paper (14x17cm 5x6in)
  Milano 1998

SOTTSASS Ettore 1917 [30]
- $16 836 - €20 023 - £12 000 - FF131 342
  Mobile Giallo Cabinet Construction (145x132x46cm
  57x51x18in) London 2000
- $5 061 - €5 880 - £3 556 - FF38 569
  Blütenstengel Sculpture, glass (H45.5cm H17in)
  München 2001

SOUBIE Roger 1898-1984 [213]
- $341 - €335 - £206 - FF2 200
  «Atlantis terre engloutie» de Georges Pal, avec
  Joyce Taylor, A.Hall Affiche (120x160cm 47x62in)
  Paris 2000

SOUCEK Karel 1915-1982 [57]
- $578 - €547 - £360 - FF3 586
  Landschaft mit Baeumen Öl/Leinwand (50x89cm
  19x35in) Praha 2001
- $346 - €328 - £216 - FF2 151
  Nu assis Huile/toile (40x30cm 15x11in) Praha 2001
- $289 - €273 - £180 - FF1 793
  Pod slunecniky Gouache/carton (40x57cm 15x22in)
  Praha 2001

SOUCHET Louis XX [7]
- $623 - €717 - £439 - FF4 700
  Hutte rituelle primodiale Pierre noire (33x33cm
  12x12in) Barbizon 2001

SOUCHON Marian Sims 1870-1954 [3]
- $5 750 - €5 359 - £3 475 - FF35 154
  At the Dresser: Figures in an Interior Oil/masonite
  (55x71cm 22x28in) New-Orleans LA 1999

SOUDEIKINE Serge Iurevich 1882-1946 [20]
- $7 000 - €6 397 - £4 282 - FF41 963
  **Possible Costume Design and Stage Set,
  Ethnically Dressed Couple** Oil/canvas (66x55cm
  26x22in) Pittsburgh PA 1999
- $3 500 - €3 232 - £2 443 - FF27 750
  King with Attendants Tempera (43.5x34.5cm
  17x13in) Bethesda MD 2000
- $1 900 - €2 039 - £1 271 - FF13 377
  Boris Godunov: Design for the Decor
  Watercolour, gouache (50.5x96.5cm 19x37in) New-York
  2000

SOUGEZ Emmanuel 1889-1972 [43]
- $3 353 - €2 897 - £2 025 - FF19 000
  Étude des mains de Dora Maar Tirage argentique
  (26.3x14.7cm 10x5in) Paris 1998

SOUILLET Georges 1861-1957 [39]
- $3 586 - €3 849 - £2 400 - FF25 251
  Pont Neuf et l'Ile de la Cité Oil/canvas (46x56cm
  18x22in) London 2000

SOUKENS Jan XVII-XVIII [4]
- $4 911 - €4 677 - £2 959 - FF28 000
  **Paysage animé de nombreux personnages aux
  abords d'un château** Huile/panneau (50x69cm
  19x27in) Paris 1998

SOUKOP Willi 1907-1995 [55]
- $722 - €728 - £450 - FF4 776
  Meditation Bronze (H23cm H9in) Billingshurst, West-
  Sussex 2000
- $575 - €554 - £360 - FF3 636
  Surreal Standing Figure Watercolour/paper
  (56x45.5cm 22x17in) London 1999

SOULACROIX Joseph Frédéric Ch. 1825-1879 [65]
- $40 000 - €34 510 - £24 132 - FF226 372
  The suitor Oil/canvas (52x41.5cm 20x16in) New-York
  1998
- $28 000 - €31 377 - £19 516 - FF205 822
  A quiet Moment Oil/canvas (29x44.5cm 11x17in)
  New-York 2001

SOULAGES Pierre 1919 [608]
- $183 222 - €153 731 - £108 000 - FF1 008 406
  Peinture: 13 Août 1959 Oil/canvas (162x114.5cm
  63x45in) London 1998
- $89 030 - €88 420 - £55 680 - FF580 000
  Peinture Huile/toile (81x65cm 31x25in) Paris 1999
- $26 532 - €28 289 - £18 000 - FF185 562
  Composition en noir Indian ink/paper (37x53cm
  14x20in) London 2001
- $737 - €716 - £455 - FF4 695
  Abstrakte Komposition in Blau Farblithographie
  (89x68.5cm 35x26in) München 1999

SOULAS Louis Joseph 1905-1954 [87]
- $127 - €152 - £91 - FF1 000
  Ludwig van Beethoven Gravure bois (57x51cm
  22x20in) Orléans 2000

SOULE William Stinson 1836-1908 [3]
- $7 500 - €8 635 - £5 118 - FF56 640
  **White Bear (Satanta)/Black Hawk/Yellow
  Bear/Ho-Wear/Mow-Way** Albumen print (14.5x10cm
  5x3in) New-York 2000

SOULEN Henry James 1888-1965 [21]
- $1 800 - €1 662 - £1 120 - FF10 901
  **«On the Road to Madalay» From The Saturday
  Evening Post** Oil/board (66x76cm 25x29in)
  Washington 1999

SOULES Eugène Edouard 1811-1876 [15]
- $500 - €554 - £335 - FF3 633
  Figures by a River Watercolour/paper (18x26cm
  7x10in) Dedham MA 2000

SOULIE Léon 1807-1862 [22]
- $174 - €168 - £107 - FF1 100
  La lecture Crayon/papier (21x14.5cm 8x5in) Toulouse
  1999

SOULIÉ Tony 1955 [54]
- $677 - €762 - £475 - FF5 000
  Sans titre Acrylique/toile (80x80cm 31x31in) Paris
  2001

SOULIER Charles ?-c.1876 [7]
- $3 879 - €4 573 - £2 727 - FF30 000
  Rome, Saint-Pierre et le Vatican Tirage albuminé
  (40x76.5cm 15x30in) Paris 2000

SOURDILLON Berthe 1895-1976 [93]
- $338 - €381 - £235 - FF2 500
  Village de Provence Huile/toile (55x66cm 21x25in)
  Paris 2001

SOUSA de Joaquin Pedro 1818-1878 [1]
- $3 500 - €4 205 - £2 450 - FF27 580
  Niño Jesús Oleo/lienzo (54x103cm 21x40in) Madrid
  2000

SOUST Pierre 1928 [1]
- $5 352 - €4 955 - £3 276 - FF32 500
  L'Exilé Huile/toile (130x89cm 51x35in) Pau 1999

SOUTER Camille 1929 [29]
- $9 705 - €11 428 - £6 820 - FF74 961
  Gutted Pollock Oil/paper (37x50cm 14x19in) Dublin
  2000

S

$5 392 - €6 349 - **£3 789** - FF41 645
Weather House Oil/paper (26.5x20cm 10x7in) Dublin 2000

$4 819 - €4 641 - **£3 000** - FF30 444
Italian View Watercolour (16.5x20.5cm 6x8in) London 1999

SOUTER David Henry 1862-1935 **[12]**
$1 634 - €1 801 - **£1 087** - FF11 813
Griffith's Farm Oil/canvas/board (13x30cm 5x11in) Melbourne 2000

$189 - €211 - **£121** - FF1 387
The Economist Ink/paper (32x26.5cm 12x10in) Melbourne 2000

SOUTER John Ballock 1890-1972 **[55]**
$841 - €1 003 - **£600** - FF6 581
A Still Life of Fruit Oil/panel (37x47cm 14x18in) Leyburn, North Yorkshire 2000

$2 025 - €2 187 - **£1 400** - FF14 349
Girl with a Canary Oil/board (17.5x21.5cm 6x8in) London 2001

SOUTHALL Joseph Edward 1861-1944 **[79]**
$9 562 - €11 161 - **£6 750** - FF73 211
Market Folk Assis (28x21.5cm 11x8in) Leamington-Spa, Warwickshire 2000

$3 347 - €2 890 - **£2 000** - FF18 957
The Harbour of La Rochelle Watercolour (14.5x21cm 5x8in) London 1998

SOUTHERN Clara 1861-1940 **[8]**
$4 237 - €4 410 - **£2 660** - FF28 926
Twilight Warrandyte Watercolour/paper (28.5x36.5cm 11x14in) Melbourne 2000

SOUTHERN Terry XX **[3]**
$883 - €890 - **£550** - FF5 836
«Barbarella» Poster (152.5x101.5cm 60x39in) London 2000

SOUTHEY Rubens A.J.N. 1881-1933 **[32]**
$144 - €156 - **£100** - FF1 025
Mouth of the Yealm and the Stone, Plymouth Watercolour/paper (15x26cm 6x10in) Par, Cornwall 2001

SOUTHGATE Frank 1872-1916 **[130]**
$651 - €727 - **£440** - FF4 768
Yarmouth Shrimpers Watercolour/paper (22x33cm 9x13in) Aylsham, Norfolk 2000

SOUTHWORTH & HAWES Albert & Josiah 1811/08-1894/1908 **[77]**
$6 500 - €6 112 - **£4 024** - FF40 090
Court Street, looking toward the Old State House Daguerreotype (16x15cm 6x5in) New-York 1999

SOUTINE Chaïm 1894-1943 **[141]**
$550 000 - €528 219 - **£339 075** - FF3 464 890
L'homme en prière Oil/canvas (130x66cm 51x25in) New-York 1999

$75 000 - €83 254 - **£52 282** - FF546 112
Portrait de femme Oil/canvas (40.5x32.5cm 15x12in) Tel Aviv 2001

SOUTMAN Pieter Claesz c.1580-1657 **[7]**
$74 875 - €73 265 - **£48 000** - FF480 585
Ixion Embracing a Cloud in the Form of Juno Ink (21x31cm 8x12in) London 1999

SOUTO Arturo XX **[1]**
$4 954 - €5 811 - **£3 564** - FF38 115
Casona Oleo/lienzo (45x54.5cm 17x21in) México 2001

SOUTO CUERO Alfredo 1862-1940 **[6]**
$13 311 - €15 677 - **£9 396** - FF102 834
Cruceiro Oleo/lienzo (22.5x34cm 8x13in) Madrid 2000

SOUTO FEIJOO Arturo 1901-1964 **[77]**
$10 000 - €9 709 - **£6 178** - FF63 685
Paris Street Scene Oil/canvas (83x104cm 33x41in) New-Orleans LA 1999

$2 755 - €2 853 - **£1 757** - FF18 715
Desnudo femenino al lado de la mesa Acuarela (57x72cm 22x28in) Madrid 2000

SOUTTER Louis 1871-1942 **[102]**
$92 086 - €108 296 - **£66 033** - FF710 374
Tête du Christ couronné Oil/paper (44x57.5cm 17x22in) Bern 2001

$12 557 - €14 768 - **£9 004** - FF96 869
«Furies» Indian ink (25x34cm 9x13in) Bern 2001

SOUVERBIE Jean 1891-1981 **[224]**
$6 496 - €6 098 - **£4 024** - FF40 000
Nature morte au compotier et au violon Huile/toile (46x61cm 18x24in) Deauville 1999

$4 236 - €4 269 - **£2 640** - FF28 000
Scène mythologique Huile/toile (33x41cm 12x16in) Calais 2000

$440 - €503 - **£306** - FF3 300
Scène antique de tauromachie Crayon/papier (23x30cm 9x11in) Paris 2001

SOUZA de Alberto Augusto 1880-1962 **[8]**
$4 500 - €4 985 - **£2 900** - FF32 700
Castelo de Santa Maria da Feria Acuarela/cartulina (38x53cm 14x20in) Lisboa 2000

SOUZA de Aurelia Maria 1865-1922 **[3]**
$7 480 - €8 475 - **£5 100** - FF55 590
Cozendo à janela da varanda, quinta de cima Oleo/lienzo (18x12cm 7x4in) Lisboa 2000

SOUZA Francis Newton 1924 **[140]**
$4 310 - €5 029 - **£3 000** - FF32 988
Houses in Hampstead Oil/canvas (90x147.5cm 35x58in) London 2000

$3 174 - €3 080 - **£2 000** - FF20 205
Female Nude Oil/canvas (101.5x83cm 39x32in) London 1999

$3 343 - €3 237 - **£2 100** - FF21 236
Still Life with yellow Jug Oil/canvas (32x41cm 12x16in) London 1999

$970 - €838 - **£580** - FF5 497
Carnal Love Ink (30x43cm 11x16in) London 1998

SOUZA PINTO de Alberto Carlos 1861-1939 **[1]**
$3 520 - €3 988 - **£2 480** - FF26 160
Paisagem Oleo/lienzo (34x26.5cm 13x10in) Lisboa 2001

SOUZA PINTO de José Júlio 1856-1939 **[58]**
$13 500 - €11 427 - **£8 081** - FF74 958
An Afternoon Swim Oil/canvas (48x38.5cm 18x15in) New-York 2000

$18 900 - €20 937 - **£12 180** - FF137 340
Paisagem comrio Huile/bois (27.5x32cm 10x12in) Lisboa 2000

$8 507 - €7 927 - **£5 246** - FF52 000
Bord de mer au clair de lune Pastel/papier (23x29cm 9x11in) Lyon 1999

SOWDEN John 1838-1936 **[19]**
$451 - €385 - **£270** - FF2 528
A Study of a Finch in a nest within a Branch of Blossom Watercolour (23x28.5cm 9x11in) Leeds 1998

S

SOWERBY James 1756-1822 [4]

🖊 $16 034 - €15 532 - £10 000 - FF101 883
Set of Six Botanical Drawings Watercolour/paper (68.5x54.5cm 26x21in) Billingshurst, West-Sussex 1999

SOWERBY John George 1838-1926 [19]

🖊 $3 208 - €3 233 - £2 000 - FF21 207
Geese Amongst the Reeds Watercolour (30x54.5cm 11x21in) London 2000

SOWERBY Kate act.1883-1900 [1]

😊 $3 696 - €4 171 - £2 600 - FF27 359
Jack Russell straining at a Leash Oil/canvas (35x45.5cm 13x17in) London 2001

SOWERBY Millicent 1878-1967 [8]

🖊 $4 799 - €4 922 - £3 000 - FF32 286
A Young Girl Collecting Apples in an Orchard Watercolour (17x26cm 6x10in) London 2000

SOYA-JENSEN Carl Martin 1860-1912 [58]

😊 $644 - €737 - £448 - FF4 836
Kone, der samler grene i Dyrehaven ved Peter Lieps hus Oil/canvas (55x84cm 21x33in) København 2000

🖊 $388 - €336 - £236 - FF2 207
Hollandsk havneparti Watercolour/paper (46x71cm 18x27in) København 1998

SOYER Jean-Baptiste 1752-1828 [9]

😊 $2 266 - €2 200 - £1 400 - FF14 432
Madame de Gironcourt, née La Pailette, Facing Left in White Underdress Miniature (5x4cm 1x1in) London 1999

SOYER Moses 1899-1974 [182]

😊 $4 000 - €4 294 - £2 676 - FF28 164
Girl on Chair with Striped Blanket Oil/canvas (50.5x40.5cm 19x15in) New-York 2000

😊 $1 100 - €1 271 - £770 - FF8 335
Nude Oil/canvas (23x30.5cm 9x12in) Bethesda MD 2001

🖊 $375 - €435 - £267 - FF2 856
Study of a Nude Woman Charcoal/paper (56x41cm 22x16in) Downington PA 2001

SOYER Paul C. 1823-1903 [18]

😊 $25 000 - €24 757 - £15 565 - FF162 395
The Big Sister Oil/canvas (85.5x65cm 33x25in) New-York 1999

😊 $3 327 - €2 818 - £2 000 - FF18 484
A Happy Mother Oil/panel (22x17cm 8x6in) London 1998

SOYER Raphael 1899-1987 [564]

😊 $5 000 - €5 367 - £3 346 - FF35 205
Girl in Red Sweater and Jeans Oil/canvas (56x71cm 22x27in) New-York 2000

😊 $2 800 - €2 623 - £1 721 - FF17 203
Girl on Cot Oil/canvas (40.5x30.5cm 15x12in) New-York 1999

🖊 $700 - €605 - £415 - FF3 968
Nude Ink/paper (25x35cm 10x14in) Provincetown MA 1998

📜 $500 - €480 - £309 - FF3 149
The Seamstress Lithograph (25x30cm 9x11in) New-York 1999

SPACAL Luigi 1907 [24]

📜 $375 - €389 - £225 - FF2 550
Primavera istriana Stampa (44x55cm 17x21in) Trieste 2001

SPACKMANN B. XX [5]

🖊 $519 - €485 - £320 - FF3 183
Busy Street Scene Watercolour/paper (20x46cm 7x18in) Co. Kilkenny 1999

SPADA Leonello 1576-1622 [4]

🖊 $1 600 - €1 420 - £977 - FF9 312
Head of a Young Man Pencil (24x22cm 9x8in) New-York 1999

SPADA Valerio 1613-1688 [7]

🖊 $2 128 - €1 974 - £1 300 - FF12 948
A Printed Text Framed with Figures and Calligraphic Ornaments Ink (19x30cm 7x11in) London 1998

SPADINI Andrea 1912-1983 [7]

😊 $9 639 - €8 327 - £4 819 - FF54 621
Busti da mori avvolti da manti drappeggiati Ceramic (H39cm H15in) Venezia 1999

SPADINI Armando 1883-1925 [40]

😊 $40 000 - €41 466 - £24 000 - FF272 000
Prima colazione Olio/cartone (77x60cm 30x23in) Milano 2000

😊 $2 050 - €2 125 - £1 230 - FF13 940
Il barcaiolo Olio/cartone (17x32cm 6x12in) Firenze 2000

🖊 $400 - €518 - £300 - FF3 400
Figure Matita/carta (29x23cm 11x9in) Firenze 2000

SPAENDONCK van Cornelis 1756-1840 [13]

😊 $17 848 - €20 276 - £12 528 - FF133 000
Branche de raisins noirs et cep de vigne sur fond de muraille Huile/toile (472x35cm 185x13in) La Baule 2001

😊 $117 222 - €99 800 - £70 000 - FF654 647
Still Life of Flowers including Roses, Fuchsia, a Hyacinth Oil/canvas (57.5x70.5cm 22x27in) London 1998

😊 $44 336 - €51 833 - £31 654 - FF340 000
Nature morte aux grappes de raisins Huile/panneau (24.5x33.5cm 9x13in) Angers 2001

SPAENDONCK van Gerardus 1746-1822 [17]

😊 $117 300 - €129 582 - £81 345 - FF850 000
Pêches dans une assiette et tasse en porcelaine Huile/toile (35x45.5cm 13x17in) Senlis 2001

🖊 $7 487 - €7 326 - £4 800 - FF48 058
Studies of Bouquets of Flowers Watercolour (22x15.5cm 8x6in) London 1999

SPAGNULO Giuseppe 1936 [26]

🖌 $5 500 - €5 702 - £3 300 - FF37 400
Senza titolo Fer (160x20x3cm 62x7x1in) Milano 2000

SPAHN Victor 1949 [92]

😊 $1 548 - €1 448 - £937 - FF9 500
Formule I Huile/toile (56x46cm 21x25in) Reze 1999

📜 $192 - €229 - £133 - FF1 500
Le bunker Lithographie (78x58cm 30x22in) Lille 2000

SPALA Václav 1885-1946 [95]

😊 $13 294 - €12 574 - £8 280 - FF82 478
Fleurs Huile/toile (70x50cm 27x19in) Praha 2000

$6 358 - €6 014 - £3 960 - FF39 446
Fleurs Huile/toile (45.5x30.5cm 17x12in) Praha 2000
$346 - €328 - £216 - FF2 151
Nu Encre/papier (20x34cm 7x13in) Praha 2000
$274 - €260 - £171 - FF1 703
Still Life with Apples and Pears Color lithograph (32x40cm 12x15in) Praha 2000

SPALDING Charles B. ?-c.1875 [10]
$882 - €857 - £549 - FF5 619
Driving to the Meet Oil/canvas (35.5x30cm 13x11in) London 1999

SPALLETTI Ettore 1950 [7]
$11 954 - €12 832 - £8 000 - FF84 172
Untitled Mixed media/panel (128.5x103cm 50x40in) London 2000
$18 753 - €15 658 - £11 000 - FF102 708
Vaso Sculpture (180x88.5x59cm 70x34x23in) London 1998

SPALTHOF de Johannes Philip XVII-XVIII [4]
$6 604 - €7 243 - £4 487 - FF47 514
Markedscene i en havneby Oil/canvas (66x75cm 25x29in) København 2000

SPANG OLSEN Ib 1921 [46]
$201 - €188 - £121 - FF1 236
Hvad fatter gör er altid det rigtige/Dezt gamle egetraes sidste dröm Pencil (27.5x21.5cm 10x8in) København 1999

SPANISH FORGER XIX [2]
$3 783 - €4 573 - £2 643 - FF30 000
Chevalier remettant un reliquaire à un prince/St.Jérôme/Ste.Barbe Huile/panneau (53.5x44cm 21x17in) Paris 2000

SPANJAERT Jan c.1590-1664 [7]
$3 895 - €3 634 - £2 350 - FF23 835
Die fette Küche, ein Mönch und Bauern beim ländlichen Mahl Oil/panel (32x37.5cm 12x14in) Wien 1999

SPANYI von Bela 1852-1914 [43]
$2 625 - €2 904 - £1 725 - FF19 050
Landscape with Birch-wood Oil/canvas (91x120cm 35x47in) Budapest 2000
$1 518 - €1 725 - £1 058 - FF11 316
A l'Est Huile/bois (34x45cm 13x17in) Budapest 2001

SPARE Austin Osman 1888-1956 [202]
$1 590 - €1 373 - £950 - FF9 008
Twisted Figures Watercolour/paper (20x52cm 7x20in) London 1998

SPARER Max 1886-1968 [17]
$331 - €363 - £213 - FF2 383
Sommerwiese mit den Dolomiten im Hintergrund Woodcut in colors (24x25cm 9x9in) Wien 2000

SPARKE Oskar 1885-1937 [6]
$1 493 - €1 764 - £1 060 - FF11 570
Berlin:Molkenmarkt und Spandauerstr./Schlesischer Bahnhof/Waisenbrücke Photograph (16x24cm 6x9in) Berlin 2001

SPARKES Catherine Adelaide 1842-? [2]
$30 265 - €31 499 - £19 000 - FF206 617
An Early Essay Oil/canvas (51x41cm 20x16in) London 2000

SPARKS Herbert Blande XIX-XX [21]
$3 019 - €3 454 - £2 100 - FF22 659
Allegorical Female Nude with Long Flaxon Hair Oil/canvas (128x61cm 50x24in) Doncaster, South-Yorkshire 2000
$1 734 - €1 784 - £1 100 - FF11 699
The Flower Girl Watercolour/paper (73x50cm 29x20in) Rotherham 2000

SPARKS Nathaniel 1880-1957 [31]
$413 - €456 - £280 - FF2 990
Still Life of Flowers Watercolour/paper (42x29.5cm 16x11in) London 2000
$69 - €80 - £48 - FF525
Tower Bridge, London Etching (34x26cm 13x10in) Oxford 2000

SPARKS William 1862-1937 [36]
$2 750 - €2 970 - £1 900 - FF19 480
Nocturnal Adobe Scene Oil/board (13x18cm 5x7in) Altadena CA 2001

SPARMANN Karl Christian 1805-1864 [6]
$5 618 - €5 113 - £3 510 - FF33 539
Die Rosengartengruppe in Südtirol Öl/Leinwand (87x104cm 34x40in) München 1999
$899 - €875 - £553 - FF5 742
Ansicht des Schlosses Lenzburg im Canton Aargau Farblithographie (30.4x43.2cm 11x17in) Bern 1999

SPARRE Emma 1851-1913 [9]
$1 197 - €1 045 - £724 - FF6 854
Porträtt av fru Evine Röhss Oil/canvas (126x88cm 49x34in) Stockholm 1998

SPARRE Louis 1863-1964 [84]
$3 153 - €3 011 - £1 965 - FF19 753
Porträtt av skådespelerskan Tollie Zellman Oil/canvas (103x74cm 40x29in) Stockholm 1999
$896 - €1 009 - £617 - FF6 619
Aftonljus Oil/canvas/panel (26x22cm 10x8in) Helsinki 2000
$234 - €198 - £139 - FF1 297
Kvinna på strand Etching (23x31cm 9x12in) Stockholm 1999

SPARRE Victor 1919 [10]
$5 728 - €4 840 - £3 439 - FF31 747
Maleren og modellen Oil/canvas (93x74cm 36x29in) Oslo 1998

SPARROW Geoffrey XX [9]
$284 - €271 - £180 - FF1 779
Crawley and Horsham Point to Point/Old Surrey and Burstow Aquatint (21x27cm 8x10in) Billingshurst, West-Sussex 1999

SPARROW Thomas XVIII [1]
$666 - €767 - £459 - FF5 030
Segelschiffe vor Lissabon Engraving (21x30.5cm 8x12in) Leipzig 2000

SPAT Gabriel 1890-1967 [52]
$6 000 - €5 568 - £3 602 - FF36 525
The Promenade Oil/canvas (36x59cm 14x23in) Milford CT 1999

S

S

$1 200 - €1 133 - £746 - FF7 431
Still Life Oil/board (12x10cm 5x4in) Milford CT 1999

SPATZ Willy 1861-1931 [12]

$275 - €332 - £191 - FF2 180
Liegender weiblicher Akt Charcoal/paper
(20.5x29cm 8x11in) Düsseldorf 2000

SPAULDING Henry Plympton 1868-? [9]

$225 - €251 - £152 - FF1 647
At High Tide, East Gloucester Marshes
Watercolour/paper (39x49cm 15x19in) Bolton MA 2000

SPAZZAPAN Luigi 1889-1958 [126]

$10 000 - €10 367 - £6 000 - FF68 000
Cane arlecchino Olio/masonite (100x150cm
39x59in) Milano 2000

$5 000 - €5 183 - £3 000 - FF34 000
Ginia Olio/cartone/tela (48x60cm 18x23in) Vercelli
2000

$2 750 - €2 851 - £1 650 - FF18 700
Paesaggio torinese Olio/tavola (50x30cm 19x11in)
Prato 2000

$4 400 - €4 561 - £2 640 - FF29 920
Ritratto dell'ing. Oscar Brunner Plâtre (H29cm
H11in) Trieste 2001

$3 000 - €2 592 - £1 500 - FF17 000
Candelabri Tempera/carta (79x69cm 31x27in) Prato
1999

SPEAR Arthur Prince 1879-1959 [3]

$3 935 - €4 475 - £2 700 - FF29 357
Twilight Street, Hammersmith Oil/canvas
(70.5x91.5cm 27x36in) London 2000

SPEAR Ruskin 1911-1990 [196]

$7 058 - €7 113 - £4 400 - FF46 655
Ena Oil/board (144x116cm 56x45in) London 2000

$5 033 - €4 294 - £3 000 - FF28 169
The Riverside Oil/canvas (71x87cm 27x34in) London
1998

$1 874 - €2 071 - £1 300 - FF13 588
Model in the Antique Room Oil/board (49x28.5cm
19x11in) London 2001

$713 - €685 - £440 - FF4 496
Harbour Scene Watercolour/paper (38x53cm
14x20in) London 1999

$768 - €762 - £480 - FF5 001
Thin Edge Color lithograph (32x94cm 12x37in)
London 1999

SPEARS Frank 1906-1991 [18]

$451 - €524 - £311 - FF3 436
A Melancholic Harlequin Oil/canvas/board
(65x50cm 25x19in) Johannesburg 2000

SPEARS Fred XIX-XX [1]

$9 500 - €9 495 - £5 803 - FF62 286
«Enlist» Poster (82x59cm 32x23in) New-York 2000

SPECCHI Alessandro 1668-1729 [7]

$280 - €300 - £190 - FF1 970
«Palacio de la Curia Innocenziana» Grabado
(70x31cm 27x12in) Madrid 2001

SPECHT August 1849-1923 [13]

$713 - €829 - £500 - FF5 436
«Burgeff & Co.» Poster (71x48cm 27x18in) London
2001

SPECK Loran 1944 [11]

$7 150 - €6 677 - £4 413 - FF43 800
Grapes and Blackberries Oil/canvas (25x38cm
10x15in) Dallas TX 1999

SPEECKAERT Hans, Jan ?-1577 [5]

$135 000 - €116 869 - £81 418 - FF766 611
The Crucifiction Wash (41.5x27.5cm 16x10in) San-
Francisco CA 1998

SPEECKAERT Michel Joseph 1748-1838 [6]

$7 473 - €7 318 - £4 598 - FF48 000
**Nature morte au trophée de chasse dans un
paysage** Huile/panneau (51.5x68cm 20x26in) Paris
1999

SPEED Grant, Ulysses 1930 [24]

$6 050 - €6 494 - £4 048 - FF42 598
Night Herding in a Rain Storm Bronze (H44cm
H17in) Houston TX 2000

SPEED Lancelot 1860-1931 [16]

$1 141 - €1 331 - £800 - FF8 728
Arthur Approacheth the Giant Watercolour,
gouache/paper (71x49.5cm 27x19in) London 2000

SPEEDE John 1552-1629 [191]

$439 - €474 - £300 - FF3 109
Flint-Shire Engraving (38x51cm 14x20in) Swindon,
Wiltshire 2001

SPEELMAN Adriana Gerarda [2]

$2 997 - €3 403 - £2 051 - FF22 324
**Homo Bulla: A Young Boy Blowing Bubbles and
A Woman** Oil/panel (28.5x34cm 11x13in) Amsterdam
2000

SPEER Martin 1700-1765 [3]

$2 358 - €2 812 - £1 681 - FF18 446
**Pest unter den Philistern/Grosse Schlachtszene
mit brennenden Stadt** Radierung (28.7x37.9cm
11x14in) Berlin 2000

SPEICHER Eugene Edward 1883-1962 [74]

$2 400 - €2 814 - £1 726 - FF18 458
Vase with Tulips and Apple Blossoms Oil/canvas
(56.5x45.5cm 22x17in) New-York 2001

SPEISSEGGER Alexander 1750-1798 [6]

$1 612 - €1 493 - £987 - FF9 794
Bildnis von Elisabeth Honnerlag
Öl/Leinwand/Karton (80.5x63cm 31x24in) Bern 1999

SPELMAN John A. 1880-1941 [18]

$3 000 - €3 241 - £2 077 - FF21 258
Western Landscape Oil/board (35x40cm 14x16in)
Cincinnati OH 2001

SPENCE Benjamin Edward 1822-1866 [14]

$5 541 - €5 298 - £3 400 - FF34 755
**Figure of a Girl standing half draped in classi-
cal robes** Marble (H120cm H47in) Billingshurst,
West-Sussex 1999

SPENCE Harry 1860-1928 [12]

$1 252 - €1 121 - £752 - FF7 350
Outside the Opera Oil/canvas (51x61cm 20x24in)
Perthshire 1998

SPENCE Percy River. Seaton 1868-1933 [37]

$6 377 - €6 144 - £3 941 - FF40 299
Droving Sheep Oil/canvas (60x50cm 23x19in)
Sydney 1999

🖋 **\$242 - €260 - £164** - FF1 706
Centennial Park Watercolour/paper (17x32cm
6x12in) Sydney 2001

SPENCE Thomas Ralph 1855-1916 **[14]**
〰 **\$11 954 - €12 832 - £8 000** - FF84 172
**The Song of Phemius and the Sorrow of
Penelope** Oil/canvas (89x184cm 35x72in) London
2000
〰 **\$4 000 - €4 485 - £2 716** - FF29 419
Music Oil/canvas (91.5x71cm 36x27in) New-York
2000
〰 **\$2 240 - €2 139 - £1 400** - FF14 028
View of Jerusalem Oil/canvas/board (25x35cm
9x13in) London 1999

SPENCE-SMITH John Guthrie 1880-1951 **[23]**
〰 **\$1 902 - €1 976 - £1 200** - FF12 961
The old Stone Bridge Oil/canvas (66x82cm 25x32in)
London 2001
〰 **\$1 960 - €1 815 - £1 200** - FF11 905
Ceres Mill Farm Oil/board (30x40cm 11x15in)
Edinburgh 1999

SPENCELAYH Charles 1865-1958 **[191]**
〰 **\$29 836 - €25 742 - £18 000** - FF168 856
The Darned Sock Oil/canvas (76x50.5cm 29x19in)
London 1998
〰 **\$12 972 - €12 552 - £8 000** - FF82 337
Delightful with Sauce Oil/canvas (40x30cm 15x11in)
West-Yorkshire 1999
🖋 **\$1 613 - €1 482 - £1 000** - FF9 721
**A Queer Lot, a Gentleman browsing through an
Auction** Pencil/paper (42x52cm 16x20in) West-
Yorkshire 1999

SPENCER Bertha XX **[3]**
▥ **\$300 - €280 - £185** - FF1 834
«**Brooklyn Bridge**» Woodcut in colors (18x16cm
7x6in) Cleveland OH 1999

SPENCER Frederick Randolph 1806-1875 **[16]**
〰 **\$2 000 - €1 974 - £1 216** - FF12 950
**Portrait of Frances Pierpont Raymond Hunt and
Daughter, Frances Helen** Oil/canvas (122x92cm
48x36in) New-York 2000

SPENCER Gilbert 1892-1979 **[70]**
〰 **\$2 780 - €3 259 - £2 000** - FF21 380
Hay Carts in the Farmyard Oil/canvas (40.5x51cm
15x20in) London 2001
🖋 **\$306 - €286 - £190** - FF1 873
Farm in the District Watercolour (25.5x36cm
10x14in) London 1999

SPENCER John C. 1861-1919 **[11]**
〰 **\$1 300 - €1 484 - £916** - FF9 736
Still Life with red Roses Oil/canvas (35.5x55.5cm
13x21in) Boston MA 2001
〰 **\$1 320 - €1 352 - £820** - FF8 868
Still Life of Roses Oil/canvas (25x43cm 10x17in)
Newport RI 2000

SPENCER Lilly Martin 1822-1902 **[13]**
〰 **\$32 000 - €35 439 - £21 702** - FF232 464
Mother and Children by the Hearth Oil/canvas
(87x69cm 34x27in) New-York 2000
〰 **\$5 500 - €5 429 - £3 344** - FF35 612
American Roses Oil/canvas (23.5x30.5cm 9x12in)
New-York 2000

SPENCER Niles 1893-1952 **[10]**
〰 **\$6 000 - €6 440 - £4 015** - FF42 246
Perkins Cove, Ogunquit Oil/paper (21x24cm 8x9in)
Portland ME 2000

SPENCER Richard Barnett XIX **[33]**
〰 **\$5 401 - €5 239 - £3 400** - FF34 365
Clendovey Oil/canvas (48.5x79cm 19x31in) London
1999

SPENCER Robert 1879-1931 **[26]**
〰 **\$46 000 - €50 730 - £31 151** - FF332 768
Washer Women Oil/canvas (76x61cm 29x24in) New-
York 2000
〰 **\$6 500 - €6 088 - £3 996** - FF39 936
On the Quai Oil/canvas (30.5x35.5cm 12x13in) New-
York 1999

SPENCER Stanley 1891-1959 **[521]**
〰 **\$1 499 670 - €1 454 189 - £950 000** - FF9 538 855
The Garage Oil/canvas (101.5x152.5cm 39x60in)
London 2000
〰 **\$85 374 - €99 191 - £60 000** - FF650 652
High Street, Cookham Oil/canvas (61x76cm
24x29in) London 2001
〰 **\$14 140 - €11 976 - £8 500** - FF78 557
Landscape Study Oil/paper (25.5x18cm 10x7in)
London 1998
🖋 **\$1 330 - €1 127 - £800** - FF7 393
**Newly-born Shirin on a Rocking Chair/Figure
tearing Cloth** Pencil/paper (18x25.5cm 7x10in)
London 1998
▥ **\$998 - €845 - £600** - FF5 545
Portrait of Carolyn Pullan Lithographie (50x38cm
19x14in) London 1998

SPENCER William Barnett c.1810-c.1880 **[6]**
〰 **\$4 300 - €3 677 - £2 600** - FF24 121
The Battle of Trafalgar, Late in the Day Oil/canvas
(40.5x61cm 15x24in) London 1999

SPENCER-BOWER Olivia 1905-1982 **[5]**
🖋 **\$1 001 - €1 041 - £628** - FF6 827
Torlesse range, Central Canterbury
Watercolour/paper (37x50.5cm 14x19in) Auckland 2000

SPENCER-FORD Roland F. XX **[23]**
🖋 **\$164 - €151 - £100** - FF990
Figures fishing on a Mill Pond Watercolour
(25.5x35cm 10x13in) London 1998

SPENDER Humphrey 1910 **[32]**
🖋 **\$515 - €477 - £320** - FF3 128
Morning on the Terrace, Le Lavandou
Watercolour (32x42cm 12x16in) London 1999

SPENLOVE Frank Spenlove 1864-1933 **[29]**
〰 **\$4 920 - €4 641 - £3 100** - FF30 442
**Portrait of a young Boy, half-Length, wearing
white Costume** Oil/canvas (51x34.5cm 20x13in)
Godalming, Surrey 1999

SPERL Johann 1840-1914 **[37]**
〰 **\$3 493 - €3 579 - £2 156** - FF23 477
Bauerngehöft und Bauerngarten Öl/Leinwand
(47x37.5cm 18x14in) Düsseldorf 2000
〰 **\$2 830 - €2 965 - £1 872** - FF19 452
Zwiegespräch mit einem Vogel Öl/Leinwand
(25x18.5cm 9x7in) München 2000

S

SPERLI Johann Jakob 1770-1841 **[19]**
$975 - €1 103 - £686 - FF7 236
Gersau Watercolour (20x28cm 7x11in) Bern 2001

SPERLICH Sophie 1863-1906 **[17]**
$929 - €869 - £562 - FF5 701
Die widerspenstige Mahlzeit (Drei Kühen und eine Wespe) Öl/Karton (26x41cm 10x16in) Düsseldorf 1999

SPERLING Heinrich 1844-1924 **[28]**
$3 095 - €3 323 - £2 072 - FF21 800
Ländliche Szene Öl/Leinwand (83x130cm 32x51in) Stuttgart 2000
$2 687 - €2 948 - £1 825 - FF19 337
Robert und Bertram Öl/Karton (20.5x26.5cm 8x10in) Basel 2000

SPERO Nancy 1926 **[15]**
$794 - €877 - £550 - FF5 755
«The Three Graces» Watercolour (16.5x19.5cm 6x7in) London 2001

SPESCHA Matias 1925 **[24]**
$14 000 - €16 363 - £9 995 - FF107 332
Peinture «Grau-Schwarz» Öl/Leinwand (170x138cm 66x54in) Zürich 2001
$359 - €427 - £256 - FF2 803
Komposition mit Schwarz und Weiss Indian ink (40x30cm 15x11in) Zürich 2000
$166 - €178 - £111 - FF1 169
Komposition Farblithographie (65x50cm 25x19in) Zofingen 2000

SPETHMANN Albert 1894-1986 **[22]**
$1 330 - €1 329 - £832 - FF8 720
Weiblicher Rückenakt Oil/panel (80x65cm 31x25in) Hamburg 1999

SPICER Peggy 1908-1984 **[14]**
$386 - €431 - £260 - FF2 825
Remuera & Hobston Bay from Kepa Rd Watercolour/paper (54x37cm 21x14in) Auckland 2000

SPICUZZA Francesco J. 1883-1962 **[46]**
$500 - €572 - £343 - FF3 753
Bouquet of Flowers in a Vase Oil/board (75x59cm 29x23in) Milwaukee WI 2000
$400 - €388 - £247 - FF2 547
Hills of Western Wisconsin Oil/canvas/board (25x35cm 10x14in) Cedar-Falls IA 1999
$1 200 - €1 147 - £755 - FF7 526
Two Children in Snowstorm Pastel/paper (32x44cm 12x17in) Milwaukee WI 1999

SPIEGLER Franz Joseph 1691-1757 **[1]**
$2 369 - €2 543 - £1 585 - FF16 684
Maria mit drei Heiligen als Retterin der armen Seelen im Fegefeuer Oil/panel (50x21.5cm 19x8in) Wien 2000

SPIELMANN Oskar 1901-1973 **[50]**
$2 757 - €3 201 - £1 944 - FF21 000
Café à la Marsa, Tunis Huile/toile (57x73cm 22x28in) Paris 2001
$1 813 - €2 134 - £1 274 - FF14 000
Femme allongée Huile/toile/panneau (31x47cm 12x18in) Paris 2000

SPIERS Benjamin Walter 1845-1894 **[17]**
$4 782 - €5 280 - £3 300 - FF34 637
A Catholic Collection Watercolour/paper (22x31cm 8x12in) Crewkerne, Somerset 2001

SPIERS Harry 1869-1934 **[31]**
$650 - €630 - £402 - FF4 133
Spring Thaw Watercolour/paper (55x69cm 22x27in) Mystic CT 1999

SPIERS Richard Phene 1838-1916 **[26]**
$870 - €925 - £550 - FF6 070
View of a Temple in Cairo Watercolour/paper (24x18cm 9x7in) London 2000

SPIES Walter 1895-1942 **[13]**
$443 025 - €412 904 - £267 750 - FF2 708 475
Sawahs im Preangergebirge: Sawahs in the Preanger Hills Oil/canvas (76x67cm 29x26in) Singapore 1999
$46 346 - €51 211 - £32 135 - FF335 921
Four Young Balinese with Fighting Cocks Pencil (35x54.5cm 13x21in) Singapore 2001

SPILBERG Johann 1619-1690 **[3]**
$7 529 - €8 557 - £5 200 - FF56 127
Untitled Ink (28x20cm 11x7in) London 2000

SPILHAUS Nita 1878-1967 **[48]**
$3 020 - €2 832 - £1 866 - FF18 574
An Avenue of Trees Oil/canvas (39.5x49.5cm 15x19in) Johannesburg 1999
$1 423 - €1 588 - £928 - FF10 414
Via Appia, Roma Oil/board (28.5x38cm 11x14in) Johannesburg 2000
$451 - €524 - £311 - FF3 436
A View of a Field through Trees Watercolour/paper (30x20.5cm 11x8in) Johannesburg 2000
$265 - €281 - £176 - FF1 841
View of a Mountain Engraving (31x24cm 12x9in) Hilton 2000

SPILIMBERGO Adriano 1908-1975 **[48]**
$4 750 - €4 924 - £2 850 - FF32 300
Vaso di fiori e paesaggio Olio/tela (60x50cm 23x19in) Milano 2000
$2 000 - €2 073 - £1 200 - FF13 600
Venezia Olio/tavola (16x22cm 6x8in) Milano 2000

SPILIMBERGO Lino Eneas 1896-1964 **[7]**
$4 900 - €5 693 - £3 443 - FF37 343
Calle de San Juan Acuarela/papel (47x30cm 18x11in) Buenos-Aires 2001
$2 600 - €3 021 - £1 827 - FF19 815
Acrobatas Monotype (52x37cm 20x14in) Buenos-Aires 2001

SPILLAR Karel 1871-1939 **[29]**
$2 456 - €2 323 - £1 530 - FF15 240
Charme féminin Huile/toile (37x44cm 14x17in) Praha 2001
$1 705 - €1 613 - £1 062 - FF10 578
Sur la plage Huile/carton (33.5x38cm 13x14in) Praha 2000
$202 - €191 - £126 - FF1 255
Bathing Pencil (22.5x16cm 8x6in) Praha 2001
$1 068 - €1 220 - £743 - FF8 000
«Kunstlerbund Hagen Wien» Affiche (72x94cm 28x37in) Paris 2001

S

SPILLIAERT Léon 1881-1946 **[468]**
- **$13 185** - €11 148 - **£7 875** - FF73 125
  Arbres Technique mixte (50x60cm 19x23in)
  Antwerpen 1998
- **$8 816** - €9 420 - **£6 004** - FF61 788
  Duinenzicht met bomen (Dunes avec arbres)
  Aquarelle/papier (49.5x58.5cm 19x23in) Lokeren 2001
- **$504** - €421 - **£295** - FF2 764
  Konijn Lithograph (33.5x40.5cm 13x15in) Lokeren
  1998

SPILMAN Hendrik 1721-1784 **[16]**
- **$821** - €882 - **£550** - FF5 786
  River Landscape with a Town beyond Ink
  (9x18cm 3x7in) London 2000

SPILSBURY Maria 1777-1820 **[20]**
- **$3 495** - €3 390 - **£2 200** - FF22 236
  At the Cottage Door Oil/canvas (45x54cm 17x21in)
  London 1999
- **$2 400** - €2 276 - **£1 500** - FF14 929
  Samuel: speak Lord for thy Servant Heareth
  Oil/canvas (36.5x26.5cm 14x10in) London 1999

SPIN Jacob 1806-1875 **[27]**
- **$1 095** - €1 271 - **£776** - FF8 334
  **De Koning der Nederlanden van Amsterdam,
  near the Cliffs of Dover** Watercolour (38x52.5cm
  14x20in) Amsterdam 2000

SPINDLER Charles 1865-1938 **[32]**
- **$2 771** - €2 592 - **£1 677** - FF17 000
  Jeux d'enfants devant la maison Aquarelle/papier
  (52x34cm 20x13in) Saint-Dié 1999

SPINDLER Walter E. XIX-XX **[4]**
- **$10 297** - €11 434 - **£7 162** - FF75 000
  Sarah Bernhardt invoquant Diotima Watercolour
  (18x24cm 7x9in) Paris 2001

SPINELLI Giovan Battista c.1630-c.1660 **[4]**
- **$8 400** - €10 885 - **£6 300** - FF71 400
  Lot e le figlie Olio/tela (156x209cm 61x82in) Milano
  2000

SPINELLI, SPINELLO ARENTINO Luca c.1350-1410
[2]
- **$11 041** - €10 221 - **£6 665** - FF67 048
  **The Madonna and Child enthroned with two
  Angels** Oil/panel (105x59cm 41x23in) Dublin 1999

SPINETTI Mario XIX-XX **[10]**
- **$13 208** - €11 561 - **£8 000** - FF75 833
  The Grape Pickers Oil/canvas (138x64cm 54x25in)
  London 1998
- **$4 853** - €4 607 - **£3 027** - FF30 222
  Music Lesson Watercolour/paper (74.5x52.5cm
  29x20in) Sydney 1999

SPINKS Thomas XIX **[74]**
- **$1 644** - €1 765 - **£1 100** - FF11 578
  The Quarry Oil/canvas (38x44.5cm 14x17in) London
  2000
- **$1 028** - €1 062 - **£620** - FF6 245
  Angler in a Quiet River Landscape Oil/canvas
  (29.5x45cm 11x17in) Billingshurst, West-Sussex 1999

SPINNLER Rolf 1927 **[11]**
- **$69** - €78 - **£48** - FF510
  Holländische Landschaft Watercolour/paper
  (24x59.5cm 9x23in) Luzern 2001

SPIRIDON Ignace XIX-XX **[19]**
- **$42 500** - €39 808 - **£26 129** - FF261 124
  So Far from Home Oil/canvas (211x150cm 83x59in)
  New-York 1999
- **$38 212** - €36 999 - **£24 000** - FF242 700
  Odalisca Oil/canvas (54x83cm 21x32in) London 1999

SPIRO Eugen 1874-1972 **[262]**
- **$3 002** - €3 579 - **£2 140** - FF23 477
  Haus in Vermont Öl/Leinwand (41x51cm 16x20in)
  Berlin 2000
- **$2 847** - €2 607 - **£1 735** - FF17 104
  **Spätsommer, Berghang über Fluss mit
  Holzhäusern** Öl/Karton (26x35cm 10x13in) Berlin
  2000
- **$438** - €460 - **£276** - FF3 018
  Kleines Häuschen unter Bäumen Watercolour
  (23.7x20.4cm 9x8in) Heidelberg 2000
- **$174** - €164 - **£108** - FF1 073
  **Mädchenkopf mit Schleife im Haar, im Profil
  nach rechts** Etching (17.9x12.8cm 7x5in) Heidelberg
  1999

SPIRO Georges 1909-1994 **[163]**
- **$994** - €1 067 - **£665** - FF7 000
  L'atelier de l'artiste Huile/isorel (32.5x49.5cm
  12x19in) Grenoble 2000
- **$557** - €579 - **£349** - FF3 800
  Nature morte au livre bleu Huile/toile (22x27cm
  8x10in) Paris 2000
- **$314** - €305 - **£198** - FF2 000
  Abstraction surréaliste Dessin (20x27cm 7x10in)
  Nice 1999

SPITTLE William M. 1858-1917 **[4]**
- **$10 063** - €9 677 - **£6 200** - FF63 478
  Red riding Hood Oil/canvas (42x32cm 16x12in)
  London 1999

SPITZER Walter 1927 **[200]**
- **$1 895** - €2 134 - **£1 331** - FF14 000
  «Pourim» Huile/toile (52x63cm 20x24in) Paris 2001
- **$291** - €274 - **£176** - FF1 800
  Tolède Huile/toile (33x46cm 12x18in) Paris 1999
- **$811** - €686 - **£482** - FF4 500
  Mélodie en bleu Gouache/paper (74x104cm 29x40in)
  Senlis 1998

SPITZWEG Carl 1808-1885 **[421]**
- **$60 051** - €68 196 - **£42 000** - FF447 337
  **Bergmännchen, oder die erste eisenbahn (the
  first steam train)** Oil/canvas (53x32cm 20x12in)
  London 2001
- **$26 840** - €28 121 - **£17 754** - FF184 464
  Der Zeitungsleser im Hausgarten
  Öl/Leinwand/Karton (22.7x15.5cm 8x6in) München
  2000
- **$787** - €920 - **£553** - FF6 037
  Junges Mädchen, stehend Pencil/paper (32x21cm
  12x8in) München 2000

SPLITGERBER August Karl Martin 1844-1918 **[68]**
- **$4 187** - €3 835 - **£2 552** - FF25 154
  **Starnberg, Blick auf Schloss und Kirche St.
  Josef** Öl/Leinwand (64x103cm 25x40in) München
  1999
- **$1 132** - €1 313 - **£781** - FF8 615
  Bachlandschaft in Abendsonne Öl/Leinwand
  (38x27cm 14x10in) Luzern 2000

S

SPODE Samuel act.1825-1858 **[51]**
- $5 769 - €6 603 - £3 968 - FF43 310
  A chestnut hunter in a Stable Oil/canvas (50x60cm 20x24in) Dublin 2000

SPOEDE Jean-Jacques 1680-1757 **[4]**
- $59 340 - €65 553 - £41 151 - FF430 000
  L'Offrande à l'Amour/Bacchanale Huile/toile (74x92.5cm 29x36in) Paris 2001

SPOERER Eduard 1841-1898 **[12]**
- $698 - €774 - £473 - FF5 074
  Ansicht aus dem Rhone-Thal - sommarland-skap Oil/panel (47x67cm 18x26in) Stockholm 2000

SPOERRI Daniel 1930 **[258]**
- $12 573 - €13 720 - £8 532 - FF90 000
  Prière de ne pas cracher sur Léda Technique mixte (140x122x67cm 55x48x26in) Paris 2000
- $2 929 - €3 403 - £2 058 - FF22 324
  «30 juillet 1869» Mixed media/panel (50x40cm 19x15in) Amsterdam 2001
- $1 669 - €1 411 - £998 - FF9 258
  «Todesgrund» Mixed media/panel (33x33cm 12x12in) Köbenhavn 2000
- $5 154 - €4 988 - £3 178 - FF32 716
  Geschworener, aus «Giurati», die Geschworenen Bronze (92x45x26cm 36x17x10in) Zürich 1999
- $3 225 - €3 018 - £2 220 - FF24 390
  Plateau Bronze (29x42.5cm 11x16in) Lokeren 2000
- $1 213 - €1 431 - £856 - FF9 390
  Catch a big Fisch Felt pen (38x38cm 14x14in) Köln 2001
- $150 - €155 - £90 - FF1 020
  Senza titolo Litografia a colori (70x99cm 27x38in) Prato 2000

SPOHLER Jacob Jan Coenraad 1837-1923 **[142]**
- $12 530 - €10 735 - £7 532 - FF70 419
  Flusslandschaft mit Windmühlen Öl/Leinwand (66x93cm 25x36in) Köln 1998
- $6 066 - €6 970 - £4 200 - FF45 720
  Winter Landscape with Figures on Frozen River Oil/panel (27x39cm 11x15in) Bristol, Avon 2000

SPOHLER Jan Jacob 1811-1879 **[119]**
- $26 004 - €24 958 - £16 302 - FF163 713
  Ijsvermaak bij molen en boerderij Oil/canvas (65x88cm 25x34in) Dordrecht 1999
- $11 599 - €9 743 - £6 800 - FF63 909
  Figures in a Frozen Winter Landscape Oil/panel (27x35.5cm 10x13in) Billingshurst, West-Sussex 1998

SPOHLER Johannes Franciscus 1853-1894 **[79]**
- $51 852 - €54 454 - £32 808 - FF357 192
  The Kloveniersburgwal in Amsterdam, the Zuiderkerk in the background Oil/canvas (85.5x71cm 33x27in) Amsterdam 2000
- $13 451 - €12 706 - £8 136 - FF83 344
  Canal in a Dutch Town Oil/panel (21x16cm 8x6in) Amsterdam 1999

SPOILUM 1770-1805 **[4]**
- $62 500 - €58 670 - £38 731 - FF384 850
  Portrait of the Hong Merchant Chung Qua Oil/canvas (59x45cm 23x18in) Portsmouth NH 1999

- $15 408 - €18 008 - £11 000 - FF118 127
  American Merchant, wearing a blue coat and white stock with cameo Oil/canvas (42.5x36cm 16x14in) London 2001

SPOLVERINI Ilario Mercanti 1657-1734 **[12]**
- $25 235 - €25 435 - £15 750 - FF166 845
  Reitergefecht Öl/Leinwand (130x203cm 51x79in) Wien 2000
- $4 105 - €4 256 - £2 463 - FF27 917
  Due battaglie Inchiostro (12.5x35cm 4x13in) Venezia 1999

SPOONER Arthur 1873-1962 **[73]**
- $2 319 - €2 773 - £1 600 - FF18 189
  «The Old Oak» Oil/canvas (49.5x59.5cm 19x23in) Penzance, Cornwall 2000
- $724 - €782 - £500 - FF5 129
  Hay Maker Oil/canvas/board (33.5x40.5cm 13x15in) London 2001

SPORER Johann 1720-1759 **[1]**
- $13 593 - €13 089 - £8 500 - FF85 861
  Roman Fruitwood Figures of the Furietti Centaurs Sculpture, wood (31x23cm 12x9in) London 1999

SPORRER Philipp 1829-1899 **[3]**
- $7 558 - €7 158 - £4 596 - FF46 954
  Überraschung beim Bache,ein Mann hat seine Kleider am Bachufer abgelegt Öl/Leinwand (19.8x25.5cm 7x10in) München 1999

SPÖRRI Eduard 1901-1995 **[61]**
- $689 - €688 - £430 - FF4 515
  Die Schnitterin Bronze (H22.5cm H8in) Zofingen 1999

SPOWERS Ethel L. 1890-1947 **[41]**
- $304 - €361 - £215 - FF2 369
  The Skipping Rope, illustration for Careless Kate Pencil/paper (19.5x32cm 7x12in) Sydney 2000
- $4 206 - €3 993 - £2 624 - FF26 193
  The Bamboo Blind Linocut in colors (15.5x15.5cm 6x6in) Sydney 1999

SPRADBERY Walter Ernest 1889-1969 **[23]**
- $817 - €786 - £500 - FF5 153
  «Thames Valley, GWR, SR» Poster (100x124cm 39x48in) London 1999

SPRAGUE Edith XIX-XX **[3]**
- $885 - €899 - £550 - FF5 894
  An Interior Scene Oil/canvas (25.5x31.5cm 10x12in) London 2000

SPRANGER Bartholomeus 1546-1611 **[10]**
- $6 900 - €5 961 - £3 450 - FF39 100
  Allegoria delle tre arti liberali Inchiostro/carta (47x30.5cm 18x12in) Milano 1999
- $382 - €403 - £267 - FF2 683
  «Hercules und das Mädchen» Kupferstich (32x22cm 12x8in) Bamberg 2001

SPRANGER R.W. XIX **[1]**
- $6 000 - €5 877 - £3 866 - FF38 548
  Neapolitan Seascape with Figures Oil/canvas (81.5x120cm 32x47in) New-York 1999

SPREAFICO Eugenio 1856-1919 **[8]**
- $12 800 - €16 586 - **£9 600** - FF108 800
  Tre contadine a riposo Olio/tela (43x70cm 16x27in) Milano 2001

SPRENG Sebastian 1956 **[1]**
- $6 000 - €5 218 - **£3 617** - FF34 230
  Incandescent Garden II Oil/canvas (91.5x91.5cm 36x36in) New-York 1998

SPREUWEN van Jacob van Sprenwen 1611-c.1665 **[15]**
- $9 462 - €8 164 - **£5 709** - FF53 555
  The Presentation in the Temple Oil/panel (50x67.5cm 19x26in) Amsterdam 1998
- $22 558 - €22 154 - **£14 000** - FF145 318
  Old Man, Head and Shoulders, wearing a Crimson Fur-Lined Coat Oil/panel (15x12.5cm 5x4in) London 1999

SPRINCHORN Carl 1887-1971 **[33]**
- $35 000 - €36 684 - **£23 058** - FF240 628
  Log Drivers at River Rips, Sebois Stream Oil/canvas (49x96cm 19x38in) Thomaston ME 2000
- $1 400 - €1 586 - **£978** - FF10 406
  Cabin in the Woods Pastel (30.5x45.5cm 12x17in) New-York 2001

SPRING Alphons 1843-1908 **[37]**
- $4 153 - €3 554 - **£2 500** - FF23 312
  Off to Market Oil/panel (45x30.5cm 17x12in) London 1998

SPRING Lorenz 1964 **[4]**
- $139 - €154 - **£92** - FF1 011
  King of Comix M.M. Farbserigraphie (68x49cm 26x19in) Bern 2000

SPRINGER Cornelis 1817-1891 **[119]**
- $36 512 - €42 686 - **£25 648** - FF280 000
  Le Valkof à Nimègue, au temps des Carolingiens Huile/toile (115x169cm 45x66in) Paris 2000
- $333 250 - €280 975 - **£197 780** - FF1 843 074
  «Huitzen van Bossu te Horn» Oil/panel (53x66cm 20x25in) Amsterdam 1998
- $96 000 - €96 737 - **£59 843** - FF634 555
  Brielle in Winter with a Figure unloading a Cart Oil/panel (25x19.5cm 9x7in) London 2000
- $7 206 - €6 807 - **£4 359** - FF44 649
  View of the Havengracht, Oudewater Chalks (48x39cm 18x15in) Amsterdam 1999

SPRINGER Ferdinand 1907-1998 **[58]**
- $93 - €107 - **£64** - FF704
  Arbre sec Farbradierung (41.6x18cm 16x7in) Heidelberg 1999

SPRINGOLO Nino 1886-1975 **[5]**
- $3 500 - €3 628 - **£2 100** - FF23 800
  Fantasia campestre Olio/cartone (36.5x44cm 14x17in) Venezia 2000
- $3 250 - €3 369 - **£1 950** - FF22 100
  Case presso la collina Olio/tela (35x43cm 13x16in) Venezia 2000

SPRONKEN Arthur 1930 **[27]**
- $16 066 - €17 244 - **£10 750** - FF113 110
  Nude (Riita Kulta) Bronze (H135cm H53in) Amsterdam 2000

- $2 671 - €3 176 - **£1 904** - FF20 836
  Paardehoofd Bronze (H15cm H5in) Amsterdam 2000

SPROSSE Carl Ferdinand 1819-1874 **[4]**
- $2 787 - €3 323 - **£1 987** - FF21 800
  Ruinencapriccio Ink (28.4x42.7cm 11x16in) Berlin 2000
- $1 112 - €920 - **£652** - FF6 032
  Die Ansichten von Rom und seiner Umgebung Radierung (27.3x35.2cm 10x13in) Berlin 1998

SPROTTE Siegward 1913 **[114]**
- $3 070 - €3 068 - **£1 920** - FF20 123
  Sturm Oil/panel (48.1x66.1cm 18x26in) Hamburg 1999
- $478 - €562 - **£346** - FF3 689
  Sünenmosaik Oil/panel (16.5x24cm 6x9in) Hamburg 2001
- $1 333 - €1 431 - **£892** - FF9 390
  Sonnenuntergang Aquarell (46.2x31.7cm 18x12in) Bremen 2000
- $134 - €153 - **£93** - FF1 006
  «Sylt» Farblithographie (47x38.5cm 18x15in) Berlin 2000

SPRUANCE Benton Murdoch 1904-1967 **[179]**
- $3 300 - €2 769 - **£1 936** - FF18 161
  Night in Eden Oil/canvas (91x76cm 36x30in) Philadelphia PA 1998
- $1 500 - €1 703 - **£1 026** - FF11 172
  Bridge at Race Street Charcoal/paper (40.5x25cm 15x9in) New-York 2000
- $1 300 - €1 455 - **£906** - FF9 545
  «Entrance to Germantown» Lithograph (25x35cm 9x13in) New-York 2001

SPRUNG Hanns 1884-1948 **[5]**
- $1 023 - €1 022 - **£640** - FF6 707
  Blumenstilleben Öl/Leinwand (95x80cm 37x31in) München 1999

SPRÜNGLIN Niklaus 1725-1802 **[23]**
- $2 255 - €2 631 - **£1 569** - FF17 260
  Vue du village de Hospital sur le chemin du St.Gotthard Watercolour (45x63.5cm 17x25in) Bern 2000
- $1 151 - €1 299 - **£809** - FF8 520
  «Vue de la chute du Staubbach et de la vallée de Lauterbrunnen» Radierung (26.5x48cm 10x18in) Bern 2001

SPURLING Jack 1871-1933 **[9]**
- $12 333 - €12 175 - **£7 500** - FF79 860
  Paddle Steamer Crested Eagle Watercolour, gouache/paper (37x51cm 14x20in) Lymington 2000

SPURRIER Steven 1878-1961 **[23]**
- $4 027 - €3 435 - **£2 400** - FF22 535
  The Drawing Room Gouache/paper (47x56cm 18x22in) London 1998

SPY (Leslie M. Ward) 1851-1922 **[57]**
- $1 102 - €1 049 - **£685** - FF6 883
  Portrait of Sir Benjamin Leonard Cherry Watercolour (46x28cm 18x11in) Toronto 1999
- $114 - €130 - **£80** - FF850
  Ranji, vanity Fair cartoon Color lithograph (33x20cm 13x8in) Swindon, Wiltshire 2001

S

SPYROPOULOS Yannis 1912-1990 **[24]**
- $7 471 - €8 020 - £5 000 - FF52 608
  Chozico D Oil/canvas (73x101cm 28x39in) London 2000
- $1 609 - €1 622 - £1 003 - FF10 637
  Composition au port Öl/Leinwand (24x41cm 9x16in) Zürich 2000

SQUILLANTINI Remo 1920-1996 **[147]**
- $26 000 - €33 691 - £19 500 - FF221 000
  Caffè di notte Olio/tavola (130x230cm 51x90in) Prato 2000
- $5 500 - €5 702 - £3 300 - FF37 400
  Le amiche Olio/tavola (60x60cm 23x23in) Vercelli 2001
- $2 000 - €2 592 - £1 500 - FF17 000
  Figure Olio/tavola (40x30cm 15x11in) Milano 2000
- $400 - €518 - £300 - FF3 400
  Nudo Carboncino (49.5x68.5cm 19x26in) Vercelli 2001

SQUIRE John XIX-XX **[4]**
- $2 665 - €2 453 - £1 600 - FF16 093
  Swansea Sands at Sketty Road/Blackpill Oil/canvas (20.5x51cm 8x20in) Glamorgan 1999

SQUIRE Maud Hunt 1873-c.1955 **[3]**
- $1 032 - €945 - £626 - FF6 200
  «Little Girl» Pointe sèche couleurs (15.5x12.4cm 6x4in) Douarnenez 1998

SQUIRRELL Leonard Russell 1893-1979 **[140]**
- $562 - €566 - £350 - FF3 715
  Figures in an Extensive River Landscape Watercolour (27x33cm 10x12in) Billingshurst, West-Sussex 2000
- $221 - €214 - £140 - FF1 403
  Cromer Etching (15x29cm 5x11in) Ipswich 1999

SRP Frantisek 1895-1943 **[17]**
- $491 - €465 - £306 - FF3 048
  Bain de soleil Huile/panneau (39x56cm 15x22in) Praha 2000

STAACKMANN Heinz Maria 1852-1940 **[17]**
- $499 - €562 - £344 - FF3 689
  Araber zu Pferd Oil/panel (15x25cm 5x9in) München 2000

STAATEN van Louis 1836-1909 **[153]**
- $855 - €795 - £527 - FF5 215
  Canal Scene with Windmill Watercolour/paper (36.5x54cm 14x21in) Melbourne 1999

STAATS Gertrud 1859-1938 **[13]**
- $2 264 - €2 161 - £1 414 - FF14 177
  Landscape with House Oil/canvas (47x69cm 18x27in) Warszawa 1999

STABLER Phoebe ?-1955 **[6]**
- $1 348 - €1 160 - £800 - FF7 611
  Statue of a Young Girl Seated Naked Sculpture (H42cm H16in) Billingshurst, West-Sussex 1998

STÄBLI Adolf 1842-1901 **[53]**
- $5 254 - €5 027 - £3 264 - FF32 978
  Regentag Öl/Leinwand (58x81.5cm 22x32in) Zürich 1999
- $1 468 - €1 654 - £1 016 - FF10 852
  Flusslandschaft Öl/Leinwand (33x46cm 12x18in) Zürich 2000

STABROWSKI Kazimierz 1869-1929 **[9]**
- $856 - €886 - £541 - FF5 811
  Grotte à Capri Pastel/paper (65.5x48.5cm 25x19in) Warszawa 2000

STACEY Anna Lee 1865-1943 **[22]**
- $1 400 - €1 503 - £936 - FF9 857
  Venice Oil/canvas (56.5x45.5cm 22x17in) San-Francisco CA 2000
- $1 800 - €2 047 - £1 248 - FF13 428
  Sailboats Oil/board (25x35cm 10x14in) Cincinnati OH 2000

STACEY John Franklin 1859-1941 **[10]**
- $2 900 - €2 484 - £1 743 - FF16 297
  Landscape with Houses Oil/canvas (63x76cm 25x30in) Cincinnati OH 1998

STACEY Walter Sydney 1846-1929 **[23]**
- $709 - €688 - £450 - FF4 513
  Charles I on His Way to Execution Ink (91x101cm 35x39in) West-Yorshire 1999

STACHE Ernst 1849-1889 **[5]**
- $1 540 - €1 329 - £917 - FF8 719
  Venedig, Blick vom Dogenpalast den Molo entlang Öl/Leinwand (30.5x40.5cm 12x15in) München 1998

STACHIEWICZ Piotr 1858-1938 **[28]**
- $2 955 - €2 720 - £1 773 - FF17 841
  Vendeur des crèches Oil/canvas (26x17cm 10x6in) Kraków 2000
- $1 712 - €2 012 - £1 187 - FF13 198
  Fille en costume de Cracovie Pastel/carton (46.5x62.5cm 18x24in) Warszawa 2000

STÄCK Josef Magnus 1812-1868 **[60]**
- $1 979 - €1 721 - £1 193 - FF11 289
  Vinterlandskap Oil/canvas (43x58cm 16x22in) Stockholm 1998
- $814 - €902 - £564 - FF5 920
  Landskap med ekar, furor och vatten Oil/paper (25x33.5cm 9x13in) Malmö 2001

STACK Michael 1947 **[10]**
- $7 500 - €8 516 - £5 211 - FF55 860
  Sundow Plains of San Augustin Oil/canvas (60x91cm 24x36in) Dallas TX 2001

STACKELBERG von Otto 1787-1837 **[2]**
- $1 350 - €1 502 - £900 - FF9 850
  Panoramic View of Athens Print (22x148cm 8x58in) Athens 2000

STACKHOUSE Robert 1942 **[10]**
- $1 600 - €1 541 - £988 - FF10 110
  Running Animals (Reindeer Way at Sculpture Now Inc. Sept.Oct) Watercolour (133x93cm 52x37in) Chicago IL 1999

STACKPOLE Peter 1913-1997 **[32]**
- $2 600 - €2 173 - £1 539 - FF14 254
  Marines, 2nd Division, Saipan Silver print (43x35cm 17x14in) New-York 1998

STACPOOLE Frederick 1813-1907 **[7]**
- $291 - €322 - £194 - FF2 109
  Absorbed in Robinson Crusoe, after Robert Collinson Mezzotint (47x76.5cm 18x30in) Melbourne 2000

STACQUET Henri 1838-1906 **[28]**
- $390 - €366 - £241 - FF2 403
  River Landscape Watercolour/paper (35.5x49cm 13x19in) Johannesburg 1999

STAD Willem 1873-1959 **[10]**
- $701 - €817 - £490 - FF5 357
  The Vijgendam with the Royal Palace on the Dam Watercolour (24x36.5cm 9x14in) Amsterdam 2000

STADELHOFER Hans 1876-? **[10]**
- $941 - €920 - £597 - FF6 037
  Voralpenlandschaft bei Hochwasser Öl/Leinwand (50x41cm 19x16in) München 1999

STADELHOFER Helmut 1914-1979 **[25]**
- $666 - €716 - £446 - FF4 695
  Fischer am Chiemseeufer mit Blick auf die Fraueninsel Öl/Leinwand (50x100cm 19x39in) Kempten 2000
- $857 - €920 - £573 - FF6 037
  Winter im Dachauer Moor Öl/Karton (16x35cm 6x13in) München 2000

STADELMANN Ernst Philip 1894-1972 **[1]**
- $8 555 - €9 715 - £5 945 - FF63 724
  Stilleben mit Flasche, weisser Schale, braunem Krug und zwei Birnen Öl/Leinwand (38x46.5cm 14x18in) München 2001

STADEMANN Adolf 1824-1895 **[233]**
- $3 336 - €3 835 - £2 355 - FF25 154
  Schlittschuhläufer auf holländischem Kanal bei Mondschein Öl/Leinwand (35x64.5cm 13x25in) Zwiesel 2001
- $3 100 - €3 439 - £2 061 - FF22 557
  Skaters on a Pond Oil/board (30x46cm 12x18in) Milford CT 2000

STADLER Joseph Constantine XVIII-XIX **[32]**
- $592 - €687 - £420 - FF4 509
  Penshurst, After J.Farington Etching, aquatint (19x30cm 7x11in) London 2000

STADLER Toni 1888-1982 **[43]**
- $2 178 - €2 045 - £1 349 - FF13 415
  Mann mit Hut Bronze (H23cm H9in) München 1999
- $649 - €764 - £458 - FF5 013
  Sitzender Akt mit erhobenen Armen Pastell/Papier (44x32cm 17x12in) Berlin 2001

STADLER von Toni, Anton 1850-1917 **[24]**
- $11 236 - €10 226 - £7 020 - FF67 078
  Landschaft vor dem Gebirge Öl/Leinwand (81x102cm 31x40in) München 1999
- $2 476 - €2 812 - £1 695 - FF18 446
  Moorlandschaft Oil/panel (22x17cm 8x6in) München 2000

STAEBLER de Stephen 1933 **[5]**
- $32 500 - €37 760 - £22 841 - FF247 689
  Standing man with flared base Glazed ceramic (262x43x48cm 103x16x18in) New-York 2001

STAEGER Ferdinand 1880-1976 **[114]**
- $161 - €138 - £96 - FF905
  Heilig Abend/Heilige Familie/Der verwundete Krieger/Spielendes Kind Radierung (29x21.6cm 11x8in) Hamburg 1998

STAEHLE Albert 1899-1974 **[4]**
- $1 500 - €1 680 - £1 042 - FF11 020
  Spaniel tangled in fishing Line, Playing Card Illustration Gouache/paper (43x36cm 17x14in) New-York 2001
- $1 166 - €1 361 - £799 - FF8 929
  «New York World's Fair» Poster (76.5x51cm 30x20in) Hoorn 2000

STAEHR-NIELSEN Erik 1890-1921 **[48]**
- $855 - €740 - £519 - FF4 856
  Portraet af kunstnerens kone Cecilie, kaldet Ceci (1886-1939) Oil/canvas (49x70cm 19x27in) København 1998
- $320 - €349 - £221 - FF2 287
  Skovpartier Watercolour/paper (17x23cm 6x9in) København 2001

STAEHR-OLSEN Fritz 1858-1922 **[67]**
- $419 - €404 - £261 - FF2 649
  Forårsdag ved allé i italiensk landskab Oil/canvas (53x41cm 20x16in) København 1999

STAëL de Nicolas 1914-1955 **[219]**
- $1 350 000 - €1 566 391 - £932 040 - FF10 274 850
  Atelier vert, coin d'atelier Oil/canvas (145.5x97cm 57x38in) New-York 2000
- $162 770 - €158 419 - £100 000 - FF1 039 160
  Verre et pinceau Oil/canvas (38x55cm 14x21in) London 1999
- $113 939 - €110 893 - £70 000 - FF727 412
  Composition Oil/canvas (24x41cm 9x16in) London 1999
- $7 509 - €8 183 - £5 200 - FF53 678
  Untitled Ink (65x50cm 25x19in) London 2001
- $2 014 - €1 764 - £1 220 - FF11 568
  «Mediterranée» Farbserigraphie (35x46.2cm 13x18in) Berlin 1998

STAETS Hendrick c.1610-c.1659 **[3]**
- $10 643 - €9 870 - £6 500 - FF64 741
  Beach Scene with Fishermen Unloading their Catch on to the Shore Oil/panel (43x59cm 16x23in) London 1998
- $3 784 - €4 003 - £2 400 - FF26 260
  Smallship on Choppy Seas, other Shipping beyond Oil/panel (29x35.5cm 11x13in) London 2000

STAFFEL Rudolph 1911 **[2]**
- $3 000 - €3 108 - £1 909 - FF20 385
  Untitled Vessel Porcelain (17x11cm 6x4in) New-York 2000

STÄGER Balthasar, Balz 1861-1937 **[46]**
- $1 713 - €1 461 - £1 033 - FF9 584
  Blick auf den Katzensee im Abendrot Öl/Leinwand (80x111cm 31x43in) Zürich 1998
- $558 - €533 - £349 - FF3 499
  Seeuferlandschaft bei Unterterzen Öl/Leinwand/Karton (28x22.5cm 11x8in) Zofingen 1999

STAGG H.W. XIX-XX **[4]**
- $2 450 - €2 269 - £1 500 - FF14 881
  Breaking up the Caledonia, Charlton, Kent Watercolour/paper (35x53cm 14x21in) Birmingham 1999

S

STAGLIANO Arturo 1870-1936 [5]
- $4 331 - €4 364 - £2 700 - FF28 629
  Sarah Bernhardt Oil/canvas (57x49cm 22x19in)
  Billingshurst, West-Sussex 2000

STAGURA Albert 1866-1947 [98]
- $1 474 - €1 687 - £1 014 - FF11 067
  Gebirgslandschaft Pastell/Papier (75.2x85cm
  29x33in) München 2000

STAHL Benjamin Albert 1910-1987 [13]
- $5 500 - €5 904 - £3 680 - FF38 725
  Honey Child Oil/canvas (60x76cm 24x30in) Chicago
  IL 2000

STAHL Friedrich 1863-1940 [45]
- $10 830 - €12 205 - £7 500 - FF80 057
  Adam and Eve Oil/canvas (108.5x112cm 42x44in)
  London 2000
- $3 776 - €4 346 - £2 607 - FF28 508
  Ponte Vecchio in Florenz Öl/Leinwand (67x139cm
  26x54in) München 2000
- $2 697 - €3 068 - £1 870 - FF20 123
  Selbstbildnis mit Pfeife Aquarell, Gouache/Karton
  (54.5x39.5cm 21x15in) Hamburg 2000

STAHL Marie-Louise XX [1]
- $900 - €1 063 - £637 - FF6 975
  Rancho de Taos Woodcut in colors (14x18cm 5x7in)
  Provincetown MA 2000

STÄHLIN Erwin 1901-1970 [27]
- $713 - €665 - £440 - FF4 360
  Fledermaus/Leuchtende Wesen/Blume entfalten
  Watercolour (49.5x61cm 19x24in) Hamburg 1999

STAHLY François 1911 [19]
- $1 555 - €1 829 - £1 114 - FF12 000
  Kito Bronze (15x20x17cm 5x7x6in) Paris 2001

STAINER-KNITTEL Anna 1841-1915 [4]
- $2 692 - €2 907 - £1 860 - FF19 068
  Alpenblumenstilleben Öl/Metall (28x23cm 11x9in)
  Wien 2001

STAINFORTH Martin F. XIX-XX [12]
- $2 346 - €2 529 - £1 600 - FF16 586
  The Lion Hunter Oil/board (58.5x45.5cm 23x17in)
  London 2001

STAINTON George XIX [60]
- $3 387 - €2 901 - £2 000 - FF19 029
  Vessels in the Humber Estuary Oil/canvas
  (51x76.5cm 20x30in) Ipswich 1998
- $1 850 - €2 147 - £1 316 - FF14 086
  Fischerboote auf See Öl/Leinwand (28x48cm
  11x18in) Erlangen 2000
- $1 103 - €1 063 - £680 - FF6 974
  Sailing Vessels in a Choppy Sea
  Watercolour/paper (30x47cm 11x18in) London 1999

STAITE Harriet XIX-XX [1]
- $2 245 - €2 263 - £1 400 - FF14 845
  La Promenade Oil/canvas (30.5x15.5cm 12x6in)
  London 2000

STAJUDA Jerzy 1936-1991 [7]
- $2 564 - €3 099 - £1 790 - FF20 331
  Sans titre Huile/toile (81x116cm 31x45in) Kraków
  2000

STALBEMT van Adriaen 1580-1662 [38]
- $47 123 - €52 836 - £32 000 - FF346 582
  The Triumph of Melancholy Oil/panel (38x62cm
  14x24in) London 2000
- $31 160 - €29 069 - £18 800 - FF190 680
  Das Urteil des Midas Öl/Kupfer (29x39cm 11x15in)
  Wien 1999

STÅLBOM Johan 1712-1777 [4]
- $1 651 - €1 859 - £1 137 - FF12 193
  Mansporträtt, midjebild Oil/canvas (75x60cm
  29x23in) Uppsala 2000

STALLAERT Joseph 1823-1903 [18]
- $6 682 - €6 445 - £4 134 - FF42 276
  La première rencontre Huile/toile (62x74cm
  24x29in) Bruxelles 1999
- $2 604 - €2 975 - £1 836 - FF19 512
  Fillette à la lecture devant l'âtre Huile/panneau
  (35x40cm 13x15in) Antwerpen 2001

STALLER Gerard Johan 1880-1956 [62]
- $1 050 - €1 134 - £718 - FF7 441
  A Portrait of a Gipsy Oil/canvas (46x38cm 18x14in)
  Amsterdam 2001
- $930 - €998 - £622 - FF6 548
  Bokkingverkoopster Oil/cardboard (24x18cm 9x7in)
  Amsterdam 2000
- $1 260 - €1 361 - £862 - FF8 929
  Het Hertenhuis in Artis Pastel/paper (35x46cm
  13x18in) Amsterdam 2001

STAMMBACH Eugen 1875-1966 [73]
- $1 551 - €1 329 - £932 - FF8 718
  **Schwarzwaldtal mit den typischen
  Bauernhäuser** Öl/Leinwand (65x88cm 25x34in)
  Stuttgart 1998
- $800 - €767 - £503 - FF5 030
  Vorfrühling Öl/Leinwand/Karton (24x33cm 9x12in)
  Stuttgart 1999

STAMMEL Eberhard 1833-1906 [9]
- $6 000 - €5 758 - £3 761 - FF37 773
  The Moneylender Oil/canvas (68x77.5cm 26x30in)
  New-York 1999

STAMOS Theodoros 1922-1997 [184]
- $9 648 - €10 584 - £6 553 - FF69 425
  Mistra 5 Öl/Leinwand (122x177.7cm 48x69in) Berlin
  2000
- $8 006 - €6 831 - £4 771 - FF44 806
  Composition Öl/Leinwand (77x96cm 30x37in) Zürich
  1998
- $993 - €1 089 - £674 - FF7 146
  Untitled Gouache/paper (39x57cm 15x22in) Luzern
  2000

STÄMPFLI Peter 1937 [26]
- $2 017 - €2 439 - £1 409 - FF16 000
  Pneu Mine plomb (118x110cm 46x43in) Paris 2000

STÄMPFLI Pierre Victor 1916-1975 [28]
- $1 008 - €933 - £617 - FF6 121
  Silence Öl/Leinwand (34.5x75cm 13x29in) Bern 1999
- $421 - €491 - £291 - FF3 222
  Alte Gasse in Biel Öl/Leinwand (35x27cm 13x10in)
  Bern 2000

STANCARI Filippo XVIII **[1]**

$25 235 - €25 435 - **£15 750** - FF166 845
Triumphzug eines römischen Imperator
Öl/Leinwand (75x180cm 29x70in) Wien 2000

STANCHI DEI FIORI Giovanni 1608-1672 **[5]**

$104 601 - €112 281 - **£70 000** - FF736 512
Hung Duck and Hare, Apples, Lemons and Grapes/Hung Birds, Roses Oil/canvas
(170.5x114cm 67x44in) London 2000

$71 760 - €79 273 - **£49 764** - FF520 000
Guirlandes de fleurs et de fruits Huile/toile
(96.5x65cm 37x25in) Lille 2001

STANCHI Niccoló 1623/26-1690 **[6]**

$7 250 - €7 516 - **£4 350** - FF49 300
Natura morta Olio/tela (55x46cm 21x18in) Venezia 2000

$12 856 - €12 752 - **£8 000** - FF83 646
Carnations, Nasturtiums and other Flowers in a Vase on a Stone Ledge Oil/canvas (47.5x33.5cm 18x13in) London 1999

STANDING Henry William XIX-XX **[36]**

$311 - €364 - **£220** - FF2 386
Four Greys Pulling a Trap Watercolour (36x74cm 14x29in) London 2000

STANEK Emmanuel 1862-1920 **[5]**

$4 400 - €5 132 - **£3 089** - FF33 661
«Barthélémy» Poster (459x117cm 180x46in) New-York 2000

STANESBY Alex XIX **[3]**

$998 - €1 072 - **£667** - FF7 030
Naturaleza inglesa Oleo/lienzo (34x46cm 13x18in) México 2000

STANESBY Alexander 1832-1916 **[16]**

$434 - €402 - **£270** - FF2 639
Still Life of Pears, Apples and Grapes by a Dish Watercolour/paper (20x28cm 7x11in) Cheshire 1999

STANFIELD George Clarkson 1828-1878 **[66]**

$8 065 - €8 692 - **£5 500** - FF57 015
Bigen on the Rhine Oil/canvas (51x76cm 20x29in) Bury St. Edmunds, Suffolk 2001

$2 284 - €2 169 - **£1 400** - FF14 228
St. Goarshausen on the Rhine Oil/panel (25.5x31cm 10x12in) London 1999

STANFIELD William Clarkson 1793-1867 **[125]**

$26 657 - €31 703 - **£19 000** - FF207 958
French Troops 1796 fording the Magra, Sarzana and the Carrara Mountain Oil/canvas (152.5x321cm 60x126in) London 2000

$9 122 - €7 934 - **£5 500** - FF52 045
Street Scene in Normandy, Possibly Caen Oil/canvas (61.5x75cm 24x29in) London 1998

$579 - €672 - **£400** - FF4 409
Merchantmen in the Channel Watercolour/paper (16x26cm 6x10in) London 2000

$90 - €106 - **£63** - FF695
Nolenauter, Moselle from «Sketches on the Moselle, Rhine & Muse» Lithograph (40x27cm 16x11in) Hampton VA 2000

STANGE Bernhard 1807-1880 **[12]**

$5 444 - €4 601 - **£3 237** - FF30 180
Wildbach in den Alpen mit aufragendem schneebedecktem Massiv Öl/Leinwand (59x77cm 23x30in) Lindau 1998

$2 030 - €2 454 - **£1 417** - FF16 950
Sommerliche Landschaft Öl/Leinwand (28x36cm 11x14in) Bad-Vilbel 2000

STANGL Heinz 1942 **[48]**

$618 - €727 - **£429** - FF4 767
Ruhende Pencil (33.5x24.5cm 13x9in) Wien 2000

STANHOPE John Roddam Spencer 1829-1908 **[6]**

$29 494 - €27 169 - **£18 000** - FF178 218
The Expulsion from the Garden of Eden Watercolour (32.5x39.5cm 12x15in) London 1998

STANIER Henry act.1847-1892 **[27]**

$2 563 - €2 421 - **£1 550** - FF15 883
The Alhambra Palace Watercolour/paper (35x24.5cm 13x9in) Billingshurst, West-Sussex 1999

STANILAND Charles Joseph 1838-1916 **[10]**

$2 975 - €3 472 - **£2 100** - FF22 776
Waiting for a Partner Watercolour/paper (30.5x23cm 12x9in) London 2000

STANISLAWSKI Jan 1860-1907 **[99]**

$7 632 - €7 127 - **£4 622** - FF46 748
Bodiaki, Thistles Oil/panel (24x32.5cm 9x12in) Warszawa 1999

$2 874 - €2 458 - **£1 710** - FF16 126
Lis Pastel/canvas (48.5x31cm 19x12in) Warszawa 1998

$302 - €323 - **£205** - FF2 121
Paysage au crépuscule Lithographie couleurs (13x20.5cm 5x8in) Lódz 2001

STANKARD Paul 1943 **[5]**

$7 000 - €6 682 - **£4 374** - FF43 830
Tri-level Botanical Paperweight with Spirits Sculpture, glass (15x7x7cm 5x2x2in) New-York 1999

STANKIEWICZ Aleksander 1824-1892 **[1]**

$12 235 - €12 332 - **£7 630** - FF80 890
Musiciens italiens ambulants Oil/canvas (121x97.5cm 47x38in) Warszawa 2000

STANKIEWICZ Richard 1922 **[26]**

$11 000 - €10 592 - **£6 878** - FF69 479
Untitled Metal (161.5x161.5x23cm 63x63x9in) Beverly-Hills CA 1999

$5 160 - €5 873 - **£3 626** - FF38 526
Untitled Iron (49.5x44.5x28.5cm 19x17x11in) Zürich 2001

STANKIEWICZ Zofia 1862-1955 **[7]**

$5 861 - €6 748 - **£4 000** - FF44 267
Warschauer Wintertag Oil/canvas (62x78cm 24x30in) London 2000

STANKOWSKI Anton 1906-1998 **[86]**

$174 - €164 - **£108** - FF1 073
Zur Erinnerung an Schwäbisch Hall Farbserigraphie (50x50cm 19x19in) Heidelberg 1999

$930 - €920 - **£581** - FF6 037
Messing-Presslinge Photograph (29.7x38.6cm 11x15in) München 1999

STANLEY Caleb Robert 1795-1868 **[24]**
$8 965 - €9 624 - **£6 000** - FF63 129
Figures at a Market with a Cathedral Beyond
Oil/canvas (72.5x92cm 28x36in) London 2000
$457 - €477 - **£300** - FF3 132
Canal Bridge near Crickhowell Watercolour/paper
(22x33cm 9x13in) Carmarthen, Wales 2000

STANLEY Charles H. XIX **[1]**
$27 594 - €26 534 - **£17 000** - FF174 052
Westfield House, Ryde Oil/canvas (76x109cm
29x42in) London 1999

STANLEY Dorothy 1855-1926 **[2]**
$12 055 - €13 995 - **£8 500** - FF91 799
The see-saw Oil/canvas (25.5x46cm 10x18in) London
2001

STANLEY Frederic XX **[3]**
$4 750 - €4 430 - **£2 946** - FF29 056
A Gust of Wind Oil/canvas (71x60.5cm 27x23in)
New-York 1999

STANLEY John Mix 1814-1872 **[12]**
$32 500 - €30 004 - **£19 987** - FF196 816
Mount Carter-Autumn in the White Mountains
Oil/canvas (72x102cm 28x40in) New-York 1999

STANLEY Robert XX **[5]**
$1 800 - €2 005 - **£1 177** - FF13 151
**Paperback book cover: Woman in red lifted out
of water** Oil/board (33x22cm 13x9in) New-York 2000

STANNARD Alexander Molyneux 1885-1975 **[81]**
$725 - €685 - **£450** - FF4 492
A Country Cottage Watercolour (24x34.5cm 9x13in)
Billingshurst, West-Sussex 1999

STANNARD Alfred 1806-1889 **[21]**
$4 227 - €4 930 - **£2 967** - FF32 338
Marinelandschaft Öl/Leinwand (50.5x68.5cm
19x26in) Luzern 2000
$1 720 - €1 983 - **£1 176** - FF13 008
Troupeau allant s'abreuver à la tombée du jour
Huile/panneau (27x34cm 10x13in) Bruxelles 2000

STANNARD Alfred George 1828-1885 **[10]**
$1 524 - €1 536 - **£950** - FF10 078
A Glimpse of the Sea Watercolour/paper
(31.5x44.5cm 12x17in) Billingshurst, West-Sussex 2000

STANNARD Eloise Harriet 1829-1915 **[141]**
$21 101 - €20 291 - **£13 000** - FF133 099
**Still Life with a Basket of Grapes, Peaches,
Pears, a Bowl of Chillies** Oil/canvas (57x77cm
22x30in) London 1999
$7 255 - €8 170 - **£5 000** - FF53 591
**Cobnuts, Holly and Apples in a Wicker Basket,
on a Wooded Ledge** Oil/canvas (28x35.5cm
11x13in) London 2000

STANNARD Emily 1875-1907 **[3]**
$882 - €983 - **£600** - FF6 448
**River Scene with Willow Trees and Water
Meadow** Watercolour/paper (25x33cm 10x13in)
Oxford 2000

STANNARD Emily, née Coppin 1803-1885 **[17]**
$4 795 - €4 754 - **£3 000** - FF31 182
**Still Life with Chrysanthemus, Fruits and an
Embossed Plate** Oil/canvas (51x61.5cm 20x24in)
London 1999

STANNARD Henry 1844-1920 **[47]**
$891 - €863 - **£550** - FF5 660
Burning the Stubble Watercolour (24x34cm 9x13in)
West-Yorshire 1999

STANNARD Henry J. Sylvester 1870-1951 **[491]**
$1 818 - €1 718 - **£1 100** - FF11 268
On the Moors, Sunshine/On the Moors, Storms
Watercolour (31x47cm 12x18in) Billingshurst, West-
Sussex 1999

STANNARD Joan Molyneux 1903-1942 **[12]**
$702 - €599 - **£420** - FF3 932
Chickens on a Path before a thatched Cottage
Watercolour (25x35cm 9x13in) London 1998

STANNARD Joseph 1797-1830 **[17]**
$1 148 - €1 335 - **£820** - FF8 759
Study of a Fisherman Pencil/paper (21x15cm 8x5in)
Norfolk 2001

STANNARD Lilian 1877-1944 **[86]**
$3 000 - €3 499 - **£2 106** - FF22 951
Garden Landscape Watercolour/paper (25x35cm
9x13in) Boston MA 2000

STANNARD Theresa Sylvester 1898-1947 **[65]**
$3 160 - €2 677 - **£1 900** - FF17 560
«A Garden that I Love» Watercolour/paper
(35.5x25cm 13x9in) London 1998

STANOWSKY Mikael 1883-1935 **[18]**
$761 - €841 - **£527** - FF5 516
Strandbränningar Oil/canvas (62x96cm 24x37in)
Helsinki 2001

STANTON George Clark 1832-1894 **[20]**
$1 502 - €1 344 - **£900** - FF8 814
A Dry Study for a Wet Day Watercolour (49.5x65cm
19x25in) Perthshire 1998

STANTON Gideon Townsend 1885-1964 **[8]**
$375 - €341 - **£225** - FF2 236
Oaks Oil/board (55x65cm 22x25in) New-Orleans LA
1998

STANTON Herbert Hughes 1870-1937 **[20]**
$3 208 - €3 233 - **£2 000** - FF21 207
The Watermill Oil/canvas (81x101cm 32x40in)
Fernhurst, Haslemere, Surrey 2000
$1 360 - €1 469 - **£940** - FF9 634
Cornfield Oil/canvas (23x31cm 9x12in) Cheshire 2001

STANWOOD Franklin 1856-1888 **[12]**
$950 - €1 034 - **£626** - FF6 780
Hunter and Dog in an October Wood Oil/canvas
(45.5x76cm 17x29in) Boston MA 2000

STANZIONE Massimo c.1585-c.1656 **[18]**
$50 806 - €54 536 - **£34 000** - FF357 734
The Mystic Marriage of Saint Catherine Oil/can-
vas (123.5x150cm 48x59in) London 2000
$65 171 - €63 834 - **£42 000** - FF418 723
Saint Cecilia Oil/canvas (100.5x80cm 39x31in)
London 1999

STAPLES Owen B. 1866-1949 **[34]**
$161 - €189 - **£112** - FF1 239
«Bend in the Don» Watercolour/paper (13x23cm
5x9in) Toronto 2000

S

STAPLES Robert Ponsonby 1853-1943 **[136]**
- $29 050 - €27 277 - **£18 000** - FF178 923
  «**Guilty or Not Guilty ?**» Oil/canvas (112x150cm 44x59in) London 1999
- $4 326 - €4 781 - **£3 000** - FF31 359
  «**Far from the Madding Crowd**» Oil/canvas (42.5x58cm 16x22in) London 2001
- $665 - €762 - **£457** - FF4 997
  Ada Rehan at the Palas theatre Pencil (33x20cm 13x8in) Dublin 2000

STAPLETON William XIX **[1]**
- $2 817 - €3 308 - **£2 000** - FF21 702
  «**Figures and Elephants Resting Beneath a Tree/Dhon from Muposie...**» Watercolour (24x34cm 9x13in) London 2000

STAPPEN van der Charles Pierre 1843-1910 **[6]**
- $4 934 - €4 673 - **£3 000** - FF30 651
  Water Carrier Bronze (H52cm H20in) London 1999

STAPPERS Julien 1875-1960 **[69]**
- $1 561 - €1 735 - **£1 043** - FF11 382
  Vase garni de dahlias Huile/toile (60x50cm 23x19in) Bruxelles 2000
- $358 - €397 - **£249** - FF2 601
  Village sous la neige Huile/toile (33x41cm 12x16in) Bruxelles 2001

STARACE Gino 1859-1950 **[7]**
- $1 215 - €1 296 - **£824** - FF8 500
  Rocambole Gouache/carton (23.5x15cm 9x5in) Paris 2001

STARACE Girolamo c.1730-1794 **[2]**
- $19 043 - €20 886 - **£12 645** - FF137 000
  Le triomphe d'Apollon Huile/toile (103x75cm 40x29in) Pau 2001

STARCKE Richard 1864-1945 **[24]**
- $142 - €169 - **£101** - FF1 106
  Darstellung von Mellrichstadt, Flachinge, Gründen Wertheim Pencil (15x23cm 5x9in) Staufen 2000

STARITA Lorenzo 1842-? **[1]**
- $11 200 - €14 513 - **£8 400** - FF95 200
  Una sala del Palazzo reale di Napoli Olio/tela (63x76cm 24x29in) Roma 2001

STARITSKY Anna 1908-1981 **[23]**
- $531 - €610 - **£363** - FF4 000
  Sans titre Acrylique/papier (64x49cm 25x19in) Paris 2000

STARK Arthur James 1831-1902 **[34]**
- $7 000 - €6 197 - **£4 279** - FF40 648
  A Cavalier King Charles Spaniel Seated in a red Chair Oil/canvas (35.5x46cm 13x18in) New-York 1999
- $524 - €562 - **£350** - FF3 689
  The Stone Cottage Oil/board (33x44cm 12x17in) London 2000

STARK Bruce XX **[3]**
- $100 - €118 - **£71** - FF771
  The Champ Watercolour (38x25cm 15x10in) New-York 2001

STARK James 1794-1859 **[111]**
- $14 753 - €16 191 - **£9 500** - FF106 208
  Eel Traps, a River Landscape Oil/canvas (120x101.5cm 47x39in) Suffolk 2000

- $23 397 - €22 469 - **£14 500** - FF147 388
  The Ford Oil/panel (63.5x97cm 25x38in) Suffolk 1999
- $4 193 - €4 602 - **£2 700** - FF30 185
  View of Cromer Beach Oil/panel (23.5x34.5cm 9x13in) Suffolk 2000
- $575 - €606 - **£380** - FF3 972
  Near Datchet Watercolour/paper (7.5x24.5cm 2x9in) London 2000

STARK Karl 1921 **[65]**
- $3 085 - €3 634 - **£2 170** - FF23 835
  Stilleben mit Zitronen Öl/Leinwand (74.7x52.5cm 29x20in) Wien 2000
- $915 - €872 - **£559** - FF5 720
  Landschaft mit violettem Fleck Öl/Papier (27.8x19.2cm 10x7in) Wien 1999
- $2 056 - €2 042 - **£1 285** - FF13 394
  Landscape with a deep-blue Sky Watercolour, gouache/paper (46x63.5cm 18x25in) Amsterdam 1999

STARK Melville F. 1904-1987 **[10]**
- $2 600 - €3 058 - **£1 870** - FF20 057
  Winter bridge Oil/canvas (40x50cm 16x20in) Hatfield PA 2001

STARK Otto 1859-1926 **[13]**
- $4 750 - €5 119 - **£3 239** - FF33 580
  Pennsylvania Landscape with barn Oil/canvas (48x53cm 19x21in) Hatfield PA 2001
- $3 500 - €4 060 - **£2 489** - FF26 634
  Leland, Michigan Landscape Oil/board (33x40cm 13x16in) Carmel IN 2000
- $1 000 - €1 120 - **£694** - FF7 347
  «**Factory Scene**» Watercolour/paper (15x30cm 6x12in) Cincinnati OH 2001

STARKER Erwin 1872-1938 **[144]**
- $1 176 - €1 227 - **£740** - FF8 049
  Der Feuerbach Öl/Karton (67x52cm 26x20in) Stuttgart 2000
- $894 - €767 - **£524** - FF5 028
  Waldinneres Öl/Leinwand (26x34cm 10x13in) Stuttgart 1998
- $556 - €511 - **£341** - FF3 353
  Waldeinblick Pastell/Papier (52x72cm 20x28in) Stuttgart 1999

STARKEY Hannah 1971 **[1]**
- $3 580 - €3 485 - **£2 200** - FF22 861
  Untitled, May Photograph (40.5x51cm 15x20in) London 1999

STARKWEATHER William Howard Bl. 1879-1969 **[19]**
- $1 500 - €1 399 - **£930** - FF9 174
  Cliff at Grand Manan Island, N.B. Canada Oil/canvas (61x71cm 24x27in) New-York 1999
- $1 300 - €1 508 - **£924** - FF9 892
  The Sea at Bermuda, August Gouache (66x95.5cm 25x37in) Washington 2000

STARLING Albert XIX-XX **[12]**
- $10 187 - €12 179 - **£7 000** - FF79 891
  The Story Book Oil/canvas (88.5x68.5cm 34x26in) Billingshurst, West-Sussex 2000

STARN TWINS (Mike & Doug STARN) 1961 **[83]**
- $1 400 - €1 512 - **£967** - FF9 917
  The Rose Mixed media (38x44.5x7.5cm 14x17x2in) New-York 2001

S

$7 000 - €8 122 - £4 832 - FF53 277
Convex Bull Jumper Construction (124.5x124.5x25.5cm 49x49x10in) New-York 2000

$2 800 - €2 922 - £1 766 - FF19 166
Mark Morris Row Silver print (29x15cm 11x5in) New-York 2000

STARNINA Gherardo di Jacopo c.1365-1409/13 [3]

$295 716 - €290 684 - £190 000 - FF1 906 764
Presentation of Christ in the Temple Tempera/panel (33x52cm 12x20in) London 1999

$22 000 - €24 642 - £15 285 - FF161 638
Head of an Angel Tempera (15x30cm 5x11in) New-York 2001

STAROWIEYSKI Franciszek 1930 [18]

$1 123 - €1 243 - £780 - FF8 154
«Les popammelles» Crayon (53x73cm 20x28in) Warszawa 2001

STARR Georgina 1968 [4]

$5 784 - €4 942 - £3 500 - FF32 418
The Perverts Print (60x42cm 23x16in) London 1998

STARREVELD Pieter 1911-1989 [8]

$1 831 - €2 178 - £1 305 - FF14 287
Torso Bronze (H27.5cm H10in) Amsterdam 2000

STASCHUS Daniel 1872-? [17]

$235 - €220 - £145 - FF1 442
Ein Kirchdorf Woodcut in colors (22.3x27cm 8x10in) Hamburg 1999

STASIO di Stefano 1948 [17]

$1 800 - €2 332 - £1 350 - FF15 300
Notturno Olio/tela (70x60cm 27x23in) Prato 2000

$900 - €933 - £540 - FF6 120
Il pianista Tecnica mista/cartone (30x51cm 11x20in) Vercelli 2001

STASSEN Franz 1869-? [15]

$178 - €164 - £108 - FF1 073
Das Rheingold Farblithographie (62x47cm 24x18in) Berlin 1999

STAUB Josef 1931 [6]

$6 134 - €5 636 - £3 768 - FF36 971
Quadratfaltung Métal (H59cm H23in) Zürich 1999

STAUDACHER Hans 1923 [370]

$11 886 - €10 178 - £6 958 - FF66 766
«Österreichisches Schicksal» Mixed media/canvas (150x150cm 59x59in) Wien 1998

$4 303 - €4 724 - £2 860 - FF30 985
Idyllisches Eckele am Wirthgrund Öl/Karton (80x70cm 31x27in) Wien 2000

$971 - €945 - £598 - FF6 197
Ohne Titel Mischtechnik (30x21cm 11x8in) Linz 1999

$1 222 - €1 453 - £872 - FF9 534
Ohne Titel Mischtechnik/Papier (39.7x32cm 15x12in) Wien 2000

$381 - €363 - £233 - FF2 383
Drei weibliche Akte Lithographie (23x33cm 9x12in) Wien 1999

STAUDACHER Vitus 1850-1925 [15]

$1 898 - €2 038 - £1 270 - FF13 368
Sommerwiese mit spielenden Kindern Öl/Leinwand (39x69cm 15x27in) Zürich 2000

$1 786 - €1 687 - £1 114 - FF11 067
Badisches Dörfchen Öl/Karton (28x22.5cm 11x8in) Hamburg 1999

STAUDER Jacob Carl 1694-1756 [7]

$5 335 - €4 613 - £3 171 - FF30 260
Portrait eines jungen Adligen Öl/Leinwand (83x62cm 32x24in) Zürich 1998

STAUFFER Fred 1892-1980 [269]

$1 444 - €1 718 - £1 029 - FF11 267
Landschaft mit Zug bei Murten Öl/Leinwand (81x121cm 31x47in) Zürich 2000

$258 - €247 - £159 - FF1 621
Winterliche Seeuferlandschaft mit Feldern und Bäumen Öl/Leinwand/Karton (22x32cm 8x12in) Bern 1999

$445 - €374 - £261 - FF2 453
Alpenlandschaft mit verschneiten Berggipfeln Watercolour (37x58cm 14x22in) Bern 1998

$69 - €78 - £48 - FF511
Emmentaler Gehöft Farblithographie (45x60cm 17x23in) Bern 2001

STAUFFER-BERN Karl 1857-1891 [149]

$161 - €138 - £96 - FF905
Adolf Menzel Radierung (31.3x23.5cm 12x9in) Hamburg 1998

STAVELEY Charles, Sir XIX [1]

$2 415 - €2 281 - £1 500 - FF14 961
Mahebourg, Mauritius Pencil (20.5x30.5cm 8x12in) London 1999

STAVEREN Petrus act.1634-1654 [5]

$5 618 - €6 353 - £3 953 - FF41 672
Boy standing by a Table laden with Fish Oil/canvas (73x61cm 28x24in) Amsterdam 2001

STAVEREN van Jan Adriaensz. c.1625-c.1675 [17]

$6 878 - €6 390 - £4 200 - FF41 916
A Hermit Saint Oil/panel (64x46.5cm 25x18in) London 1998

$8 124 - €8 721 - £5 436 - FF57 204
Einsiedler in einer Landschaft Öl/Leinwand (25.5x19cm 10x7in) Wien 2000

STAVROWSKY Oleg 1927 [14]

$24 200 - €22 600 - £14 936 - FF148 249
Stage Top Riders Oil/canvas (86x182cm 34x72in) Dallas TX 1999

$4 400 - €5 077 - £3 098 - FF33 306
Two Reclining Cowboys in Raincoats Oil/canvas (60x50cm 24x20in) Norwalk CT 2000

STAYNES Anthony 1922-1998 [27]

$419 - €395 - £260 - FF2 590
Still Life with Orange Oil/canvas (46x61cm 18x24in) London 1999

STAZEWSKI Henryk 1894-1988 [62]

$2 436 - €2 827 - £1 681 - FF18 544
Composition Acrylique (60x60cm 23x23in) Warszawa 2000

$1 418 - €1 612 - £979 - FF10 574
Composition Huile/carton (34x34cm 13x13in) Warszawa 2000

$1 651 - €1 943 - £1 195 - FF12 744
Lineare Konstruktion Indian ink (60x59.5cm 23x23in) Hamburg 2001

STEAD Frederick 1863-1940 **[38]**
- $1 167 - €1 130 - **£720** - FF7 410
  View of Richmond Castle from the River with Figures on a Bridge Oil/canvas (51.5x61.5cm 20x24in) West-Yorkshire 1999
- $843 - €816 - **£520** - FF5 351
  Runwick Bay, Figures on Sunlit Steps Leading to a Cottage Door Watercolour (33.5x23cm 13x9in) West-Yorkshire 1999

STEADMAN Ralph 1936 **[20]**
- $2 277 - €2 133 - **£1 400** - FF13 991
  The Cutting Edge, Barbican Art Gallery Collage (90x61cm 35x24in) London 1999
- $329 - €352 - **£220** - FF2 306
  Lewis Carrol's Through The Looking Glass & What Alice Found There Etching, aquatint (42x56cm 16x22in) London 2000

STEARNS Junius Brutus 1810-1885 **[7]**
- $5 500 - €4 764 - **£3 373** - FF31 248
  Deer at the River's Edge Oil/board (30.5x45cm 12x17in) New-York 1999

STECH Andreas 1635-1697 **[2]**
- $80 465 - €90 232 - **£54 635** - FF591 885
  Hommage des Rois Mages Huile/toile (164x116cm 64x45in) Warszawa 2000

STEDRY Dayna XX **[3]**
- $275 - €265 - **£170** - FF1 741
  «The Empire Strikes Back» Poster (104x68.5cm 40x26in) London 1999

STEEL John, Sir 1804-1891 **[3]**
- $4 009 - €3 854 - **£2 500** - FF25 279
  Alexander with Bucephalus Bronze (H49.5cm H19in) Billingshurst, West-Sussex 1999

STEEL Kenneth 1906-1973 **[27]**
- $709 - €823 - **£500** - FF5 400
  Edinburgh Castle from the Vennell Drypoint (36x53.5cm 14x21in) London 2001

STEELE Edwin 1850-? **[70]**
- $1 042 - €1 031 - **£650** - FF6 764
  Vase of Flowers on a Table Oil/board (67x48cm 26x18in) Leyburn, North Yorkshire 1999
- $1 020 - €871 - **£600** - FF5 714
  Still Life of Apples an Flowers on a Ledge/Strawberries and Flowers Oil/board (15x20cm 5x7in) Godalming, Surrey 1998

STEELE Elvic 1920-1997 **[64]**
- $620 - €571 - **£380** - FF3 747
  Beneath the Cyclamen Oil/board (46x61cm 18x24in) London 1998
- $620 - €571 - **£380** - FF3 747
  Ginger Jar with Fruit Oil/board (35.5x43cm 13x16in) London 1998

STEELE Theodore Clement 1847-1926 **[15]**
- $21 000 - €23 883 - **£14 672** - FF156 662
  Autumn, Brookville Oil/canvas (55x73cm 22x29in) New-York 2000
- $4 888 - €4 768 - **£3 010** - FF31 278
  Landscape, brown County Oil/canvas (30x44cm 12x17in) Chicago IL 1999

STEELE Zulma Parker 1881-1979 **[9]**
- $1 400 - €1 599 - **£985** - FF10 490
  Catskill Nocturne Charcoal/paper (26x54cm 10x21in) Pittsfield MA 2001

STEELINK Willem 1826-1913 **[17]**
- $3 234 - €2 764 - **£1 900** - FF18 129
  Pastoral Oil/canvas (33x48cm 12x18in) Glasgow 1998

STEELINK Willem II 1856-1928 **[53]**
- $4 405 - €4 311 - **£2 824** - FF28 277
  A Shepherd and Flock Oil/canvas (70x94cm 27x37in) Amsterdam 1999
- $581 - €544 - **£362** - FF3 571
  Hormeward Bound Oil/canvas (20x30cm 7x11in) Amsterdam 1999
- $1 212 - €1 134 - **£754** - FF7 441
  Shepherdess Grazing her Flock Watercolour/paper (50x38cm 19x14in) Amsterdam 1999

STEELL David George 1856-1930 **[17]**
- $5 000 - €5 446 - **£3 443** - FF35 721
  Highland Terriers, «Breakfast Time» Oil/canvas (35.5x51cm 13x20in) New-York 2001

STEELL Gourlay 1819-1894 **[24]**
- $1 260 - €1 466 - **£900** - FF9 618
  «Japanese Deer» Oil/paper/board (35.5x50cm 13x19in) London 2001
- $964 - €977 - **£600** - FF6 410
  Sketch Design Watercolour (45x35cm 18x14in) Aylsham, Norfolk 2000

STEEN Jan Havicksz. 1623/26-1679 **[47]**
- $95 166 - €99 928 - **£60 000** - FF655 482
  The Mocking of Ceres Oil/canvas (73x61cm 28x24in) London 2000
- $74 105 - €84 169 - **£52 000** - FF552 110
  Dat Heb Je Niet (This Thou has not) Oil/panel (24x20.5cm 9x8in) London 2001

STEEN-JOHNSEN Søren 1903-1979 **[16]**
- $714 - €608 - **£426** - FF3 990
  Mennesker i interiör Oil/panel (54x46cm 21x18in) Oslo 1998

STEENHOUWER P.C. ?-1972 **[24]**
- $764 - €726 - **£465** - FF4 762
  Oud-Hollands stadsgezicht in de winter Oil/panel (39x29cm 15x11in) Rotterdam 1999

STEENWIJK van Harmen 1612-c.1660 **[14]**
- $12 346 - €14 025 - **£8 519** - FF92 000
  Ars Longa Vita brevis Huile/toile (74x64cm 29x25in) Paris 2000
- $26 803 - €28 357 - **£17 000** - FF186 008
  Still life of Freshwater Fish, together with an Earthenware Pot Oil/panel (26.5x29cm 10x11in) London 2000

STEENWIJK van Hendrik I c.1550-1603 **[8]**
- $11 424 - €11 760 - **£7 201** - FF77 139
  Das Innere einer gotischen Hallenkirche mit Christus geweihten Altären Öl/Kupfer (35.5x52cm 13x20in) Berlin 2000

STEENWIJK van Hendrik II 1580-1649 **[22]**
- $15 000 - €14 221 - **£9 126** - FF93 282
  The Interior of a Palace with Jael and Sisera Oil/panel (46.5x64cm 18x25in) New-York 1999

S

$17 931 - €19 248 - **£12 000** - FF126 259
Saint Jerome writing by candlelight in a gothic chapel Oil/panel (19.5x15cm 7x5in) London 2000

STEEPLE John 1823-1887 **[48]**
$319 - €317 - **£200** - FF2 078
Heathland with Cattle Watercolour/paper (24x38cm 9x14in) Stansted Mountfitchet, Essex 1999

STEER Henry Reynolds 1858-1928 **[22]**
$887 - €745 - **£520** - FF4 887
Contemplation Watercolour/paper (30.5x20.5cm 12x8in) Billingshurst, West-Sussex 1998

STEER Philip Wilson 1860-1942 **[204]**
$59 772 - €64 160 - **£40 000** - FF420 864
The Horse-Shoe Bend of The Severn at Littledean Oil/canvas (102x151cm 40x59in) London 2000
$22 708 - €21 892 - **£14 000** - FF143 599
The red Bridge, Ironbridge Oil/canvas (76x106.5cm 29x41in) London 1999
$3 749 - €4 143 - **£2 600** - FF27 177
Reclining nude Oil/canvas (34x45cm 13x17in) London 2001
$676 - €693 - **£420** - FF4 547
Fishing Smacks, Maldon Watercolour/paper (22.5x30cm 8x11in) Billingshurst, West-Sussex 2000

STEFAN Ross 1934 **[29]**
$4 500 - €5 109 - **£3 126** - FF33 516
The Song goes on Oil/canvas (71x55cm 28x22in) Dallas TX 2001

STEFANI Pierre 1938 **[157]**
$414 - €496 - **£284** - FF3 252
Blankenberghe (La plage à marée basse) Huile/toile (46x55cm 18x21in) Antwerpen 2000
$444 - €412 - **£276** - FF2 700
Cabines rouges et cabines bleues à marée basse Huile/panneau (13x18cm 5x7in) Corbeil-Essonnes 1999

STEFANO ROSELLI di Bernardo 1450-1526 **[2]**
$15 111 - €17 532 - **£10 752** - FF115 000
La Vierge à l'Enfant et le jeune Saint Jean-Baptiste adorant l'Enfant Tempera/panneau (67x39cm 26x15in) Paris 2001

STEFANONI Tino 1937 **[47]**
$1 560 - €1 348 - **£780** - FF8 840
Senza titolo Olio/tela (30x45cm 11x17in) Torino 1999

STEFANSSON Jón 1881-1962 **[19]**
$8 164 - €7 536 - **£5 084** - FF49 436
Island, Hekla Oil/canvas (78x102cm 30x40in) Viby J, Århus 1999

STEFFAN Arnold 1848-1882 **[6]**
$1 956 - €2 301 - **£1 402** - FF15 092
Ausflügler am starnberger See Oil/panel (16x33.5cm 6x13in) Stuttgart 2001

STEFFAN Johann Gottfried 1815-1905 **[120]**
$7 425 - €7 482 - **£4 628** - FF49 081
Wasserfall Öl/Leinwand (89x65cm 35x25in) Zürich 2000
$2 141 - €2 488 - **£1 505** - FF16 322
Murg am Bodensee Öl/Leinwand (34.5x46cm 13x18in) Luzern 2001

$421 - €409 - **£267** - FF2 683
Partie bei Oberaudorf Pencil (35x48cm 13x18in) München 1999

STEFFANI Luigi 1827-1898 **[23]**
$5 500 - €5 702 - **£3 300** - FF37 400
Barca di pescatori Olio/tela (46.5x76cm 18x29in) Milano 2000
$4 303 - €4 777 - **£3 000** - FF31 334
Three young Country Girls on a Road Oil/canvas (33x22.5cm 12x8in) London 2001

STEFFECK Carl Constantin 1818-1890 **[25]**
$13 080 - €12 271 - **£8 080** - FF80 493
Der Ausflug in den Park Öl/Leinwand (112x131cm 44x51in) Ahlden 1999
$2 301 - €1 985 - **£1 383** - FF13 024
«Einzug der Ordensritter in die Marienburg» Öl/Karton (44x53cm 17x20in) Bern 1998
$2 070 - €2 352 - **£1 448** - FF15 427
Wartender ungesattelter brauner Hengst, an Hausmauer angebunden Öl/Leinwand (32x45cm 12x17in) Berlin 2001

STEFFELAAR Cornelis 1797-1861 **[9]**
$2 820 - €3 176 - **£1 943** - FF20 836
A Winter Landscape with Figures on the Ice Oil/panel (22x25.5cm 8x10in) Amsterdam 2000

STEFFELAAR Nicolaas 1852-1918 **[4]**
$1 576 - €1 588 - **£982** - FF10 418
Tea Time break Watercolour (29x40cm 11x15in) Amsterdam 2000

STEFFEN Bernard Joseph 1907 **[11]**
$600 - €620 - **£379** - FF4 070
Milking Time Lithograph (27.5x16.5cm 10x6in) New-York 2000

STEFFEN Walter Arnold 1924-1982 **[39]**
$934 - €807 - **£564** - FF5 293
Gehöft Öl/Leinwand (33x51cm 12x20in) Luzern 1998

STEFFENS Hans Hermann 1911 **[22]**
$319 - €381 - **£228** - FF2 500
Sans titre Technique mixte/papier (17x25cm 6x9in) Paris 2000

STEFFENSEN Poul 1866-1923 **[93]**
$1 277 - €1 409 - **£865** - FF9 241
Landskab med kreaturer Oil/canvas (70x103cm 27x40in) Vejle 2000
$599 - €604 - **£374** - FF3 965
Heste på marken Oil/canvas (30x45cm 11x17in) Köbenhavn 2000

STEGEMANN Heinrich 1888-1945 **[44]**
$802 - €767 - **£502** - FF5 030
Bildnis Hans Studt als Mariner Öl/Karton (53x44cm 20x17in) Hamburg 1999

STEGER Milly 1881-1948 **[10]**
$1 515 - €1 738 - **£1 036** - FF11 403
Zwei sitzende Frauenakte Indian ink (32.5x48cm 12x18in) Heidelberg 2000

STEGMANN Franz 1831-1892 **[10]**
$8 103 - €9 203 - **£5 668** - FF60 370
Rheinische Textilfabrik mit rauchenden Schornsteinen Öl/Leinwand (47.5x63cm 18x24in) Berlin 2001

$1 614 - €1 487 - *972* - FF9 756
La rade d'Anvers Huile/toile (38.5x31cm 15x12in)
Antwerpen 1999

STEIB Josef 1898-1957 [97]
$657 - €767 - *£461* - FF5 030
Bergwiesen vor Hochgebirge Öl/Leinwand
(60x70cm 23x27in) Kempten 2000
$77 - €71 - *£48* - FF469
Schloss Krottorf Radierung (43.5x34.5cm 17x13in)
Rudolstadt-Thüringen 1999

STEICHEN Edward Jean 1879-1973 [282]
$170 000 - €168 505 - *£106 335* - FF1 105 323
Moonlit Landscape Oil/canvas (54x63.5cm 21x25in)
New-York 1999
$75 000 - €82 712 - *£50 790* - FF542 557
Gaillardias in a Chinese Vase Oil/canvas
(40.5x30.5cm 15x12in) New-York 2000
$3 600 - €3 385 - *£2 229* - FF22 203
Photo-Secession Woodcut (30x20cm 12x8in) New-
York 1999
$6 000 - €6 688 - *£4 168* - FF43 873
George Washington Bridge Gelatin silver print
(34.5x27cm 13x10in) New-York 2001

STEIG William 1907 [5]
$1 600 - €1 549 - *£1 005* - FF10 162
**New Yorker Cartoon Showing a Young Man
Visiting his Friend** Ink (22x25cm 9x10in) New-York
1999

STEIN Georges c.1870-? [210]
$11 087 - €9 313 - *£6 500* - FF61 090
Le quai aux fleurs à Paris Oil/canvas (46x65cm
18x25in) London 1998
$3 915 - €3 946 - *£2 441* - FF25 884
Marché des fleurs au bord de la Seine Oil/canvas
(33x46cm 12x18in) Warszawa 2000
$2 800 - €2 687 - *£1 755* - FF17 627
Rue Aurer Watercolour, gouache/paper (33x25.5cm
12x10in) New-York 1999

STEIN Peter 1922 [79]
$1 389 - €1 375 - *£866* - FF9 018
Blanc de blanc pétillant Öl/Leinwand (110x100cm
43x39in) Luzern 1999
$115 - €111 - *£71* - FF731
Westphalia Aquatinte couleurs (27x30.7cm 10x12in)
Bern 1999

STEIN Theobald 1829-1901 [1]
$30 597 - €28 131 - *£18 900* - FF184 527
Hösten Relief (H92cm H36in) Vejle 1998

STEIN von Johann W. 1896-1965 [9]
$295 - €299 - *£183* - FF1 964
**«1ste Rotterdamsche ongevallen Automobiel
verzekering»** Poster (99x67cm 38x26in) Haarlem
2000

STEINACKER Alfred 1838-1914 [72]
$1 067 - €945 - *£652* - FF6 197
Wildschweinjagd Oil/panel (15.5x32cm 6x12in)
Wien 1999

STEINBACH Anton Victor Alex. 1819-1891 [4]
$7 111 - €6 652 - *£4 300* - FF43 634
Winter in the Tyrol Oil/canvas (94.5x79cm 37x31in)
Bristol, Avon 1999

STEINBACH Eduard 1878-1939 [21]
$2 031 - €2 250 - *£1 377* - FF14 757
Lichtung Öl/Leinwand (34.5x40.8cm 13x16in)
Hamburg 2000

STEINBACH Haim 1944 [41]
$9 000 - €10 063 - *£6 066* - FF66 009
Ultra-Lite #3 Assemblage (139.5x198x52.5cm
54x77x20in) New-York 2000
$3 200 - €3 456 - *£2 211* - FF22 668
Together Naturally Installation (61x103.5x37.5cm
24x40x14in) New-York 2001

STEINBERG Saül 1914-1999 [254]
$70 000 - €78 405 - *£48 636* - FF514 304
The Tree Mixed media (122x197cm 48x77in) New-
York 2001
$18 000 - €20 885 - *£12 427* - FF136 998
The politecnico Table Mixed media/panel (81x71cm
31x27in) New-York 2000
$1 700 - €1 926 - *£1 188* - FF12 635
The Family Ink (28x34.5cm 11x13in) New-York 2001
$450 - €512 - *£314* - FF3 357
Niagara Color lithograph (61x77cm 24x30in) Chicago
IL 2000

STEINBRÜCK Edouard 1802-1882 [5]
$13 536 - €16 361 - *£9 449* - FF107 324
Hagar und Ismail in der Wüste Öl/Leinwand
(107x87cm 42x34in) Düsseldorf 2000

STEINER Albert 1877-1956 [21]
$3 091 - €3 023 - *£1 909* - FF19 829
Landschaft am Bodensee Öl/Leinwand
(22.4x28.2cm 8x11in) Zürich 1999
$1 122 - €1 131 - *£700* - FF7 422
«Sports d'hiver en Suisse, St.Moritz» Poster
(99x64cm 38x25in) London 2000
$579 - €561 - *£357* - FF3 680
Im Oberengadin Gelatin silver print (16.5x22.6cm
6x8in) Zürich 1999

STEINER André 1901-1978 [10]
$3 741 - €4 191 - *£2 600* - FF27 492
Solarised Image of Woman in Car Silver print
(24x18cm 9x7in) London 2001

STEINER Bernd 1884-1933 [21]
$424 - €372 - *£257* - FF2 441
Holidays in Austria Poster (94x61cm 37x24in) New-
York 1999

STEINER Henrich 1911 [8]
$202 - €174 - *£122* - FF1 140
Ohne Titel aus dem Ovid Radierung (53x39cm
20x15in) Hamburg 1998

STEINER Josef Kamenitzky 1910-1981 [31]
$1 700 - €1 941 - *£1 198* - FF12 732
Still Life with Anemones and Ranunculus
Oil/canvas (53x41.5cm 20x16in) Boston MA 2001

STEINER Josef, jo 1877-1935 [5]
$3 827 - €4 346 - *£2 619* - FF28 508
«Bier Cabaret-Senta Söneland» Poster (72x96cm
28x37in) Hannover 2000

STEINER Ralph 1899-1986 [87]
$1 500 - €1 410 - *£928* - FF9 251
Two Men at the Shore Silver print (11x9cm 4x3in)
New-York 1999

STEINER-PRAG Hugo 1880-1945 [48]
- ▥ **$80** - €77 - **£50** - FF503
  Theophrastus Paracelsus Etching (31.8x21.7cm 12x8in) Berlin 1999

STEINERT Otto 1915-1978 [23]
- 📷 **$3 121** - €3 477 - **£2 042** - FF22 806
  Die Bäume vor meinem Fenster Vintage gelatin silver print (57.9x50.2cm 22x19in) Köln 2000

STEINFELD Franz II 1787-1868 [32]
- **$12 340** - €14 534 - **£8 680** - FF95 340
  Holzfähre an einem See im Salzkammergut Öl/Leinwand (75.7x82cm 29x32in) Wien 2000
- **$3 096** - €2 907 - **£1 920** - FF19 068
  Knabe an einem Bachwehr sitzend Oil/panel (36x34cm 14x13in) Wien 1999
- ✎ **$1 744** - €2 035 - **£1 232** - FF13 347
  Aussicht auf den Fuchlsee von der Schafalpe Aquarell/Papier (20x28cm 7x11in) Salzburg 2000

STEINFELD Wilhelm 1816-1854 [27]
- **$3 992** - €4 090 - **£2 464** - FF26 831
  Gebirgslandschaft mit See Öl/Leinwand (58x46cm 22x18in) Düsseldorf 2000
- **$1 354** - €1 381 - **£847** - FF9 057
  Im Salzkammergut Öl/Leinwand (31.5x39.5cm 12x15in) Wien 2000

STEINGOLD Meir 1922-1985 [4]
- **$1 700** - €1 762 - **£1 120** - FF11 561
  On the Way to the Market Oil/canvas (90x60cm 35x23in) Herzelia-Pituah 2000

STEINHARDT Jakob 1887-1968 [246]
- **$205 000** - €202 610 - **£125 460** - FF1 329 035
  The Sunday Preacher Oil/canvas (160x200cm 62x78in) Tel Aviv 2000
- **$11 000** - €13 151 - **£7 587** - FF86 262
  Village scene Oil/canvas (78x100cm 30x39in) Tel Aviv 2000
- ✎ **$2 000** - €2 147 - **£1 338** - FF14 082
  Hagar and Ismail Watercolour/paper (47x68cm 18x26in) Tel Aviv 2000
- ▥ **$440** - €435 - **£269** - FF2 852
  Mea Shearim Woodcut (16.5x35.5cm 6x13in) Tel Aviv 2000

STEINHART Anton 1889-1964 [19]
- **$1 878** - €2 180 - **£1 320** - FF14 301
  «Südländische Dorfansicht» Öl/Leinwand (16x20.5cm 6x8in) Salzburg 2001

STEINHÄUSER Adolph Georg Gustav 1825-1858 [1]
- ⚒ **$36 417** - €41 643 - **£25 000** - FF273 157
  A Standing Figure of Victory Marble (H182cm H71in) London 2000

STEINHÄUSER Carl Johan 1813-1879 [7]
- ⚒ **$17 229** - €19 313 - **£12 100** - FF126 687
  Boy with a Shell Marble (H183cm H72in) London 2001

STEINHEIL Adolphe 1850-1908 [6]
- **$1 181** - €1 143 - **£748** - FF7 500
  Portrait d'homme à la chéchia rouge Huile/panneau (20.5x13cm 8x5in) Paris 1999

STEINHEIL Louis Ch. Aug. 1814-1885 [3]
- **$12 000** - €12 092 - **£7 480** - FF79 320
  The Contract Oil/canvas (55.5x45.5cm 21x17in) New-York 2000

STEINKOPF Julius 1815-1892 [2]
- **$26 320** - €29 069 - **£18 240** - FF190 680
  Landschaft in der römischen Campagna Öl/Leinwand (101x139cm 39x54in) Wien 2001

STEINLE von Eduard Jakob 1810-1886 [48]
- ✎ **$568** - €665 - **£399** - FF4 360
  Schönes Fräulein darf ichs wagen, Euch meinen Arm anzutragen Pencil/paper (16.5x19.5cm 6x7in) München 2000

STEINLEN Théophile-Alexandre 1859-1923 [1584]
- **$4 977** - €4 573 - **£3 057** - FF30 800
  Marchande de fleurs sur le pont au Change Huile/toile (74x50cm 29x19in) Paris 1999
- **$4 529** - €4 421 - **£2 868** - FF29 000
  Vase de fleurs Huile/toile (46x27cm 18x10in) Calais 1999
- ⚒ **$6 223** - €5 259 - **£3 701** - FF34 500
  Chat assis à colerette Bronze (H12cm H4in) Pontoise 1998
- ✎ **$781** - €838 - **£522** - FF5 500
  Tête de femme Encre Chine/papier (8x6cm 3x2in) Compiègne 2000
- ▥ **$788** - €918 - **£545** - FF6 021
  Chat sur un coussin Farblithographie (49x60cm 19x23in) Bern 2000

STEINMETZ-NORIS Fritz 1860-1937 [7]
- **$14 000** - €14 552 - **£8 822** - FF95 453
  Waiting for Master Oil/canvas (41.5x50.5cm 16x19in) New-York 2000
- **$2 537** - €2 659 - **£1 678** - FF17 440
  Kleines Mädchen beim Stricken in der Stube Oil/panel (34x34.5cm 10x13in) München 2000

STEINSBERG Eugène XIX [2]
- **$70 000** - €77 704 - **£48 797** - FF509 705
  Cupid asleep beneath the Sphynx Oil/canvas (182.5x130cm 71x51in) New-York 2001

STEIR Pat 1940 [52]
- **$18 000** - €17 416 - **£11 100** - FF114 244
  Composition Oil/canvas (61x305cm 24x120in) New-York 1999
- **$6 500** - €6 738 - **£3 900** - FF44 200
  Le red yellow + green nine stroke Painting (102.5x88cm 40x34in) Venezia 1999
- ▥ **$1 800** - €1 689 - **£1 112** - FF11 081
  The Tree, after Hiroshige Etching, aquatint in colors (81x106.5cm 31x41in) New-York 1999

STEKETEE Sallie Hall 1882-? [1]
- **$4 500** - €5 020 - **£2 945** - FF32 931
  Wildflowers Oil/canvas (88x73cm 35x29in) Chicago IL 2000

STELLA Étienne Alexandre XIX [7]
- ⚒ **$4 500** - €5 112 - **£3 157** - FF33 530
  As a Maiden and Putto Bronze (H94.5cm H37in) New-York 2001

STELLA Frank 1936 [933]
- **$130 000** - €121 407 - **£80 236** - FF796 380
  Protractor Variation Acrylic/canvas (305x609.5cm 120x239in) New-York 1999

$26 000 - €22 432 - £15 685 - FF147 141
Puerto Rican blue pigeon no.8 Mixed media
(55x73x12.5cm 21x28x4in) New-York 1998

$46 323 - €49 724 - £31 000 - FF326 169
Island No.10, Small Version, Purple Oil/canvas
(30.5x30.5cm 12x12in) London 2000

$64 000 - €59 770 - £39 500 - FF392 064
The Prophet Relief (197x148.5x94.5cm 77x58x37in)
New-York 1999

$40 000 - €46 412 - £27 616 - FF304 440
Laysan Millerbird #22 1 X Relief (70x104x7.5cm
27x40x2in) New-York 2000

$850 - €966 - £582 - FF6 334
Study of a Man with a Hat and Overcoat
Pencil/paper (17.5x12cm 6x4in) New-York 2000

$5 800 - €5 473 - £3 578 - FF35 899
**One Small Goat Papa Bought for Two Zuzim,
plate 1** Lithograph (132.5x130cm 52x51in) New-York
1999

STELLA Guglielmo 1828-1888 [4]

$9 500 - €9 848 - £5 700 - FF64 600
Il saltimbanco Olio/tela (62x78cm 24x30in) Roma
2000

STELLA Jacques 1596-1657 [31]

$50 000 - €43 858 - £30 360 - FF287 690
**Madonna and Child with Saints Francis and
John the Baptist** Oil/panel (38x42.5cm 14x16in)
New-York 1999

$9 264 - €9 945 - £6 200 - FF65 233
Young woman holding a basin of flowers
Oil/panel (13.5x10.5cm 5x4in) London 2000

$4 350 - €4 573 - £2 730 - FF30 000
La naissance de Saint-Jean-Baptiste Encre
(35x29cm 13x11in) Paris 2000

STELLA Joseph 1879-1946 [135]

$3 200 - €3 360 - £2 017 - FF22 041
Portrait of a Man Oil/canvas (47.5x35.5cm 18x13in)
Washington 2000

$5 000 - €5 946 - £3 563 - FF39 005
A Woman Washing Oil/panel (14x19cm 5x7in) New-
York 2000

$3 600 - €4 079 - £2 515 - FF26 758
View of Mt.Vesuvius Watercolour (23.5x33cm
9x12in) New-York 2001

STELLETSKY Dimitri Semenovich 1875-1947 [12]

$2 988 - €3 208 - £2 000 - FF21 043
Drowning Tsarevich Gouache/paper (60x44cm
23x17in) London 2000

STELLMACHER Edouard 1868-? [4]

$396 - €460 - £273 - FF3 018
Büste Porcelain (H25.5cm H10in) München 2000

STELZMANN Volker 1940 [24]

$29 672 - €33 234 - £20 618 - FF218 003
Grosses Berliner Bild Öl/Karton (170x200cm
66x78in) Berlin 2000

$20 188 - €18 816 - £12 199 - FF123 423
Grablegung II Oil/board (70x120cm 27x47in)
München 1999

$7 373 - €7 158 - £4 554 - FF46 954
Selbstbildnis mit weissem Hut Oil/panel
(38.5x28cm 15x11in) München 1999

$88 - €102 - £61 - FF670
«Die Rast» Etching, aquatint (29x22cm 11x8in) Berlin
2001

STELZNER Heinrich 1833-1910 [5]

$1 376 - €1 534 - £962 - FF10 061
Angenehme Ruhe Watercolour, gouache (20x24.2cm
7x9in) München 2001

STEMATSKY Avigdor 1908-1989 [173]

$22 000 - €24 569 - £14 088 - FF161 161
Composition Oil/canvas (59.5x73.5cm 23x28in) Tel
Aviv 2000

$1 550 - €1 838 - £1 129 - FF12 057
Untitled Watercolour (65x50cm 25x19in) Tel Aviv
2001

STEN John 1879-1922 [54]

$2 760 - €2 976 - £1 852 - FF19 522
Stilleben med frukter och blommor Oil/canvas
(60x81cm 23x31in) Stockholm 2000

STENBERG Georgii Avgusto 1900-1933 [16]

$3 000 - €2 668 - £1 834 - FF17 499
Untitled Watercolour (15x13cm 5x5in) New-York 1999

$8 000 - €7 573 - £4 968 - FF49 676
October Poster (137x99.5cm 53x39in) New-York 1999

STENBERG Vladimir & Georgi 1897/1900-1982/33
[7]

$4 000 - €4 486 - £2 777 - FF29 427
«Theatre Kamerny de Moscou» Poster (71x45cm
28x18in) New-York 2001

STENBERG Vladimir Avgusto 1899-1982 [17]

$8 000 - €7 573 - £4 968 - FF49 676
October Poster (137x99.5cm 53x39in) New-York 1999

STENERSEN Gudmund 1863-1934 [25]

$1 558 - €1 327 - £931 - FF8 706
Gressende hest med fole Oil/canvas (50x60cm
19x23in) Oslo 1998

STENGEL George J. 1872-1937 [5]

$4 750 - €5 099 - £3 179 - FF33 447
A New England Fishing Village, Cape Cod
Oil/canvas (51x40.5cm 20x15in) San-Francisco CA
2000

STENGELIN Alphonse 1852-1938 [25]

$1 085 - €998 - £671 - FF6 548
Sunset Oil/panel (21x30cm 8x11in) Amsterdam 1999

STENIUS Per 1922 [57]

$1 149 - €1 261 - £740 - FF8 274
Bergslandskap Oil/canvas (50x61cm 19x24in)
Helsinki 2000

STENN Henri 1903-1993 [96]

$2 092 - €2 439 - £1 467 - FF16 000
Bord de Marne Huile/toile (46x55cm 18x21in) Paris
2000

$750 - €686 - £462 - FF4 500
Le Moulin Rouge Huile/panneau (22x27cm 8x10in)
Paris 1999

STENNER Hermann 1891-1914 [8]

$2 286 - €2 454 - £1 530 - FF16 098
**Pferdefuhrwerk mit rastenden Männern unter
Bäumen** Indian ink (21.7x32.5cm 8x12in) Königstein
2000

STENSTADVOLD Håkon 1912-1977 [15]

$158 - €171 - £109 - FF1 120
Abstrakt dansende par Color lithograph (48x61cm
18x24in) Oslo 2001

S

STENVALL Kaj 1951 **[14]**

$285 - €320 - £193 - FF2 096
Untitled Color lithograph (52x40cm 20x15in) Helsinki 2000

STENVINKEL Jan 1933-1989 **[36]**

$455 - €541 - £324 - FF3 552
Utan titel Oil/canvas (80x99cm 31x38in) Stockholm 2000

STEPAN Bohumil 1913-1985 **[31]**

$1 124 - €1 341 - £802 - FF8 796
Kind mit Puppe und Kinderwagen Tempera/Karton (50x60cm 19x23in) Hamburg 2000

$448 - €511 - £313 - FF3 353
Segelpartie Collage (27x39.5cm 10x15in) Hamburg 2001

STEPANOV Alexandre XX **[12]**

$164 - €176 - £110 - FF1 157
Fairytale Oil/board (28x20cm 11x7in) Fernhurst, Haslemere, Surrey 2000

STEPHAN August 1868-1936 **[7]**

$1 100 - €1 251 - £762 - FF8 206
Festivity in the Garden of Versailles Oil/canvas (63x91cm 25x36in) St. Louis MO 2000

STEPHAN Leopold 1826-1890 **[2]**

$10 982 - €10 387 - £6 840 - FF68 134
«Landscape with Water» Oil/canvas (72x117cm 28x46in) Praha 2001

STEPHANOFF Francis Phillip 1790-1860 **[17]**

$2 406 - €2 425 - £1 500 - FF15 905
Master Edgcumbe, small three-quarter-length, after Sir J.Reynolds Oil/panel (18.5x14.5cm 7x5in) London 2000

$353 - €409 - £250 - FF2 686
A Parting Lover in Greek Costume Watercolour (23.5x18cm 9x7in) London 2000

STEPHANOFF James 1788-1874 **[19]**

$250 - €259 - £150 - FF1 700
Ritratto di donna in costume seicentesco Acquarello/carta (24.5x21cm 9x8in) Roma 1999

STEPHENS Alice Barber 1858-1932 **[9]**

$1 200 - €1 111 - £734 - FF7 287
Two seated women in interior, one wearing veil Watercolour/paper (36x33cm 14x13in) New-York 1999

STEPHENS Christopher 1974 **[15]**

$1 040 - €1 033 - £650 - FF6 773
Oyester Catchers Mixed media (50x76cm 20x30in) Belfast 1999

STEPHENS Robert M. XX **[1]**

$4 000 - €3 916 - £2 461 - FF25 684
Deliverance Oil/board (76x121cm 30x48in) Columbia SC 1999

STEPHENSON Desmond 1922-1964 **[10]**

$1 029 - €1 143 - £717 - FF7 496
Coastal Landscape with Fisherman in a Boat Oil/canvas (81x79cm 31x31in) Dublin 2001

STEPHENSON Lionel MacDonald 1854-1907 **[21]**

$647 - €614 - £394 - FF4 026
Ft Garry Oil/paper/board (31x47cm 12x18in) Calgary, Alberta 1999

STEPHENSON Willie ?-1938 **[22]**

$568 - €550 - £360 - FF3 605
May be For Years or For Ever Watercolour (59.5x29cm 23x11in) London 1999

STEPPE Romain 1859-1927 **[294]**

$836 - €942 - £585 - FF6 178
«Bords de l'Escaut à Burgh» Huile/toile (80x60cm 31x23in) Antwerpen 2001

$854 - €725 - £515 - FF4 757
Driemaster op volle zee Oil/canvas (22x22cm 8x8in) Den Haag 1998

STEPPES Edmund 1873-1968 **[41]**

$1 919 - €1 789 - £1 158 - FF11 738
Frühlingslandschaft, reizvolles Hirtenpaar mit Schafherde am Ufer Tempera (120x99cm 47x38in) Lindau 1999

$489 - €486 - £305 - FF3 186
Herbstliche Stille Oil/panel (40x30cm 15x11in) München 1999

STERCHI Eda 1885-? **[30]**

$2 900 - €3 298 - £2 011 - FF21 634
Indian Woman Oil/canvas (66x50cm 26x20in) Cincinnati OH 2000

$1 800 - €2 016 - £1 250 - FF13 225
«Chicago Street Scene» Oil/board (26x35cm 10x14in) Cincinnati OH 2001

$3 000 - €3 526 - £2 079 - FF23 128
Two Women in an Interior Pastel/paper (27x35cm 11x14in) Cincinnati OH 2001

STERKENBURG Peter XX **[8]**

$1 505 - €1 328 - £907 - FF8 711
The «Scheveningen 86» and other «Bomschuiten» Settting Out Oil/canvas (60.5x50.5cm 23x19in) Amsterdam 1998

STERL Robert Hermann 1867-1932 **[76]**

$6 875 - €5 875 - £4 038 - FF38 538
Bauernjunge mit verschränkten Armen Öl/Leinwand (60x49cm 23x19in) Bielefeld 1998

$1 554 - €1 328 - £913 - FF8 713
Arbeiter in einem Steinbruch Öl/Karton (23x31cm 9x12in) Bielefeld 1998

$762 - €818 - £510 - FF5 366
Bauern aus der Schwalm Gouache (35x31.5cm 13x12in) Königstein 2000

$231 - €220 - £143 - FF1 442
Schafherde im Regen Lithographie (24x20.5cm 9x8in) Berlin 1999

STERLING Marc 1895-1976 **[33]**

$680 - €762 - £477 - FF5 000
Nature morte Huile/toile (27x41cm 10x16in) Paris 2001

STERN Bert 1930 **[165]**

$765 - €641 - £450 - FF4 205
Marilyn Monroe Serigraph (89x86.5cm 35x34in) London 1998

$2 500 - €2 351 - £1 548 - FF15 422
Taylor-Burton Gelatin silver print (34.5x50cm 13x19in) New-York 1999

STERN Grete 1904-1999 **[3]**

$4 200 - €4 770 - £2 947 - FF31 291
Maratti, Fabric, Berlin Gelatin silver print (27.5x19.5cm 10x7in) New-York 2001

STERN Ignaz Stella 1680-1748 **[15]**

🖼 **$14 000** - €18 141 - **£10 500** - FF119 000
La Madonna appare ad un Santo eremita
Olio/tela (76x59cm 29x23in) Roma 2000

🖼 **$4 600** - €5 961 - **£3 450** - FF39 100
Leda col cigno e amorino Olio/tela (27x36cm
10x14in) Venezia 2000

STERN Irma 1894-1966 **[196]**

🖼 **$68 670** - €66 167 - **£42 420** - FF434 028
Spanish Peasant Women Oil/canvas (85x70cm
33x27in) Johannesburg 1999

🖼 **$6 260** - €7 022 - **£4 380** - FF46 060
Still life with Statue Oil/board (42.5x35.5cm
16x13in) Cape Town 2001

✎ **$4 310** - €3 723 - **£2 599** - FF24 424
Xhosa Women Gouache (37x30cm 14x11in)
Johannesburg 1998

▥ **$1 280** - €1 427 - **£834** - FF9 363
Head of a Woman Monotype (35.5x23.5cm 13x9in)
Johannesburg 2000

STERN Jonasz 1904-1988 **[13]**

🖼 **$11 035** - €12 375 - **£7 492** - FF81 172
Composition Huile/toile (53.5x70cm 21x27in)
Warszawa 2000

✎ **$1 627** - €1 851 - **£1 128** - FF12 140
Composition Aquarelle/papier (33x23cm 12x9in)
Lódz 2000

STERN Ludovico, Ludwig 1709-1778 **[10]**

🖼 **$18 400** - €23 843 - **£13 800** - FF156 400
Battaglie Olio/tela (49x73.5cm 19x28in) Milano 2000

🖼 **$4 284** - €3 997 - **£2 585** - FF26 218
La Ascensione della Immacolata Öl/Leinwand
(43x29cm 16x11in) Wien 1999

STERN Max 1872-1940 **[33]**

🖼 **$1 289** - €1 534 - **£919** - FF10 061
Bäuerin mit Kuh auf der Weide Öl/Leinwand
(46.5x37cm 18x14in) Köln 2000

🖼 **$1 384** - €1 329 - **£853** - FF8 720
Pariser Szene Pastell/Papier (29.5x17.5cm 11x6in)
München 1999

STERN Rhona 1914-1998 **[8]**

🗡 **$464** - €539 - **£321** - FF3 537
Head of a Woman with a Head Scarf Bronze
(H31cm H12in) Johannesburg 2000

STERNBERG DE BEER Willem 1941 **[5]**

🖼 **$2 085** - €2 445 - **£1 500** - FF16 040
**Ranthambhore Gang, Juvenile Royal Bengal
Tigers** Oil/canvas (61x91.5cm 24x36in) London 2001

STERNBERG Harry 1904 **[58]**

🖼 **$12 000** - €13 727 - **£8 344** - FF90 042
Television #5 Oil/canvas (72x46cm 28x18in)
Cincinnati OH 2000

🖼 **$1 400** - €1 448 - **£884** - FF9 497
Ponderosa #2 Oil/masonite (35.5x38cm 13x14in)
New-York 2000

✎ **$1 200** - €1 360 - **£838** - FF8 919
Standing Male Nude Ink (61x50.5cm 24x19in) New-
York 2001

▥ **$550** - €563 - **£345** - FF3 691
Fascism Silkscreen in colors (38x51cm 15x20in)
Cleveland OH 2000

STERNBERG Vassili Ivanovich 1818-1845 **[3]**

✎ **$8 304** - €8 721 - **£5 232** - FF57 204
**Eine Gruppe russischer Künstler im
Colosseum in Rom** Watercolour (33x41.5cm
12x16in) Wien 2000

STERNE Maurice 1878-1957 **[49]**

🖼 **$1 800** - €1 678 - **£1 116** - FF19 009
Balinese Girls Oil/paper/board (45x41.5cm 17x16in)
New-York 1999

STERNER Albert Edward 1863-1946 **[62]**

🖼 **$1 600** - €1 523 - **£1 000** - FF9 987
Artist's Table Oil/canvas (76x63cm 30x25in) New-
York 1999

✎ **$790** - €882 - **£549** - FF5 785
Ellen Terry Red chalk (55x39cm 22x15in) Cleveland
OH 2001

▥ **$275** - €296 - **£187** - FF1 941
The Reveil Etching (22.5x17.5cm 8x6in) Boston MA
2001

STERNFELD Joel 1944 **[11]**

📷 **$800** - €921 - **£545** - FF6 041
**Abandonned Uranium Refinery, Tuba City,
Arizona** Photograph (40x51cm 15x20in) New-York
2000

STERRE DE JONG Jacobus Frederik 1866-1920
[36]

🖼 **$1 720** - €1 450 - **£1 020** - FF9 512
The Towing-Path Oil/canvas (51x66cm 20x25in)
Amsterdam 1998

🖼 **$1 334** - €1 178 - **£804** - FF7 726
Tea Time Oil/canvas (42x33.5cm 16x13in) Amsterdam
1998

✎ **$1 149** - €1 271 - **£797** - FF8 334
Mother cooking pancakes Watercolour (63.5x40cm
25x15in) Amsterdam 2001

STERRER Karl 1885-1972 **[70]**

🖼 **$2 468** - €2 907 - **£1 736** - FF19 068
Weiblicher Rückenakt Öl/Leinwand (70.2x57cm
27x22in) Wien 2000

✎ **$936** - €799 - **£559** - FF5 242
Liegender Rückenakt Mischtechnik/Papier
(16x49cm 6x19in) Wien 1998

▥ **$114** - €116 - **£71** - FF762
Die Bergbauer Radierung (25x15cm 9x5in) Wien
2000

STERRY Carl 1861-? **[4]**

🖼 **$12 101** - €12 706 - **£7 630** - FF83 344
**Moonlight meeting: Centaurs standing in an
Iris-filled Forest Clearing** Oil/canvas (127x98cm
50x38in) Amsterdam 2000

STETSON Charles Walter 1858-1911 **[23]**

🖼 **$700** - €673 - **£432** - FF4 415
Nude standing by a Pool Oil/canvas (17.5x12.5cm
6x4in) Boston MA 1999

STETTLER Adelheid Fanny M. 1870-1945 **[10]**

🖼 **$3 337** - €3 934 - **£2 345** - FF25 804
**Spielende Kinder mit Betreuerin im Jardin du
Luxembourg** Öl/Leinwand (60x90cm 23x35in) Bern
2000

S

STETTLER Martha 1870-1945 **[9]**
$14 239 - €15 285 - **£9 528** - FF100 262
Nachmittagstee mit Kindern im Garten
Öl/Leinwand (80x128cm 31x50in) Zofingen 2000

STETTNER Louis, Lou 1922 **[62]**
$1 126 - €1 296 - **£776** - FF8 500
Dormeur devant le front de gratte-ciel, New
York, promenade Tirage argentique (19.5x29.5cm
7x11in) Chartres 2000

STETTNER Uri 1935-1999 **[2]**
$3 400 - €3 827 - **£2 342** - FF25 101
Landscape through the Window Oil/canvas
(73x100cm 28x39in) Herzelia-Pituah 2000

STEUBEN von Carl August 1788-1856 **[6]**
$39 742 - €47 259 - **£28 334** - FF310 000
Portrait d'un officier Huile/toile (66.5x54cm
26x21in) Monte-Carlo 2000

STEUERWALDT Willem 1815-1871 **[8]**
$2 638 - €3 068 - **£1 852** - FF20 123
Die Marienkirche bei Oberwesel, Wintermotiv
Öl/Leinwand (40.5x48cm 15x18in) Hamburg 2001
$5 043 - €5 624 - **£3 391** - FF36 892
Winterliche Klosterruine Öl/Leinwand (37x42.5cm
14x16in) Ahlden 2000

STEVEN Fernand 1895-1955 **[10]**
$7 266 - €6 807 - **£4 368** - FF44 649
Boxeurs Oil/canvas (70.5x60cm 27x23in) Amsterdam
1999

STEVENS Agapit 1849-1917 **[46]**
$1 208 - €1 361 - **£833** - FF8 929
Dame et chat Oil/canvas (75x55cm 29x21in)
Amsterdam 2000

STEVENS Aimé 1879-1951 **[21]**
$2 364 - €2 723 - **£1 614** - FF17 859
Hiercheuse Oil/canvas (100x120cm 39x47in)
Amsterdam 2000
$776 - €908 - **£554** - FF5 953
Portrait of Maurice van Vollenhoven, Dutch
Ambassador in Brussels Oil/cardboard (33x24cm
12x9in) Amsterdam 2001

STEVENS Albert George 1863-1925 **[46]**
$647 - €612 - **£400** - FF4 013
Whitby Harbour showing the Fish Pier, Lifeboat
Shed, St Mary's Church Watercolour/paper
(23x33cm 9x13in) Whitby, Yorks 1999

STEVENS Alfred 1823-1906 **[337]**
$220 000 - €241 439 - **£141 658** - FF1 583 736
Le coup de vent Oil/canvas (196x120cm 77x47in)
New-York 2000
$6 944 - €7 684 - **£4 836** - FF50 406
Marine Huile/toile (37.5x46cm 14x18in) Liège 2001
$4 000 - €4 163 - **£2 511** - FF27 307
Le Havre, Sunset Oil/canvas/board (43x36cm
17x14in) Chicago IL 2000
$1 255 - €1 239 - **£765** - FF8 130
La sieste Aquarelle/papier (18x13cm 7x5in) Bruxelles
2000

STEVENS Alfred Georges 1817-1875 **[14]**
$1 036 - €885 - **£620** - FF5 805
«Whitby» Watercolour (39x29cm 15x11in) Leeds 1998

STEVENS Dorothy Austin 1888-1966 **[40]**
$215 - €238 - **£146** - FF1 564
Munitions - Fuse Factory Etching (27.5x35.5cm
10x13in) Toronto 2000

STEVENS Edward John 1923 **[9]**
$600 - €706 - **£430** - FF4 628
«Oriental lilies» Watercolour, gouache/paper
(46x56cm 18x22in) New-York 2001

STEVENS George c.1790-c.1865 **[12]**
$3 838 - €3 434 - **£2 300** - FF22 526
Pheasant and Hare/Partridge and Hare Oil/canvas
(30.5x36cm 12x14in) Perthshire 1998

STEVENS Gustave Max 1871-1946 **[33]**
$1 017 - €1 190 - **£724** - FF7 804
La sortie de la mosquée Huile/toile (57x39cm
22x15in) Bruxelles 2001
$394 - €442 - **£274** - FF2 900
«Le monastère» Gouache (32.5x31.5cm 12x12in)
Versailles 2001

STEVENS Jean Daniel XIX **[9]**
$18 000 - €17 310 - **£11 109** - FF113 547
In the Studio Oil/panel (82x99cm 32x38in) Boston
MA 1999

STEVENS Joseph Edouard 1816-1892 **[22]**
$809 - €920 - **£561** - FF6 037
Sitzender Terrier Öl/Leinwand (47x37cm 18x14in)
Hamburg 2000
$657 - €768 - **£468** - FF5 040
Deux chiens attendant le départ Huile/panneau
(15.5x21cm 6x8in) Bruxelles 2001

STEVENS Léopold 1866-1935 **[10]**
$1 005 - €1 143 - **£697** - FF7 500
«Théâtre de la République, Eugénie Buffet, la
chanteuse populaire» Affiche (121.5x74cm
47x29in) Orléans 2000

STEVENS Mary XIX-XX **[14]**
$520 - €507 - **£320** - FF3 325
Hyacinths and Other Flowers before a Window
Pencil (58.5x43.5cm 23x17in) London 1999

STEVENS Pieter II c.1567-1624 **[19]**
$50 000 - €53 398 - **£34 070** - FF350 265
Wooded River Landscape with Fishermen by
Cottages, Wooden Bridge Oil/panel (28x43cm
11x16in) New-York 2001
$6 210 - €6 860 - **£4 306** - FF45 000
Vue de Rome, animée de personnages Crayon
(17.5x28.5cm 6x11in) Paris 2001

STEVENS René 1858-1937 **[28]**
$438 - €471 - **£294** - FF3 089
Sous-bois Huile/toile (69x102cm 27x40in) Bruxelles
2000

STEVENS Will Henry 1881-1949 **[31]**
$10 000 - €10 255 - **£6 251** - FF67 271
Abstract Landscape Oil/board (49x54cm 19x21in)
New-Orleans LA 2000
$11 000 - €10 283 - **£6 790** - FF67 449
View of Lake Pontchartrain through Oaks
Oil/board (30x40cm 12x16in) New-Orleans LA 1999
$2 800 - €3 104 - **£1 944** - FF20 362
Cabin on a Hill Watercolour (35x45cm 14x18in) New-
Orleans LA 2001

S

STEVENS William Dodge 1870-? **[8]**
- 🌱 $4 000 - €3 792 - **£2 498** - FF24 872
  The Couple Oil/canvas (60x45cm 24x18in) Cincinnati OH 1999
- ▥ $2 000 - €2 167 - **£1 333** - FF14 215
  «**Teamwork Builds Ships, United States Shipping Board, Emergency Fleet**» Poster (91x127cm 36x50in) New-York 2000

STEVENS William Lester 1888-1969 **[200]**
- 🌱 $7 000 - €7 514 - **£4 769** - FF49 290
  Pacific Coastline Oil/canvas (106x122.5cm 41x48in) Boston MA 2001
- 🌱 $2 700 - €2 949 - **£1 738** - FF19 341
  Autumn Colors Oil/board (45x55cm 18x22in) Mystic CT 2000
- 🌱 $660 - €676 - **£410** - FF4 434
  Church in Rockport Oil/canvas (40x25cm 16x10in) Newport RI 2000
- 🖌 $700 - €675 - **£431** - FF4 426
  Maine Coast with Fishing Shack Watercolour/paper (38x45cm 15x18in) Hendersonville NC 1999

STEVENSON D.W. 1842-1904 **[1]**
- 🗿 $3 000 - €3 535 - **£2 067** - FF23 191
  Bust of a Boy/Bust of a Girl Marble (H53cm H20in) New-York 2000

STEVENSON Robert Macaulay 1854-1952 **[21]**
- 🌱 $776 - €903 - **£534** - FF5 923
  The Convent Bells Oil/canvas (60x73cm 24x29in) Vancouver, BC. 2000
- 🌱 $1 514 - €1 722 - **£1 050** - FF11 295
  Bardowie Loch, Moonlit Oil/canvas (26x36cm 10x14in) Edinburgh 2000

STEVENSON William Grant 1849-1919 **[18]**
- 🌱 $900 - €945 - **£608** - FF6 198
  Village Scene Oil/canvas (31x46cm 12x18in) Fairfield ME 2001

STEVO Jean 1914-1974 **[31]**
- ▥ $73 - €74 - **£46** - FF487
  L'arbre de la solitude/Forces felluriques Pointe sèche (32x40cm 12x15in) Bruxelles 2000

STEWART Charles Edward XIX-XX **[14]**
- 🌱 $5 500 - €5 717 - **£3 466** - FF37 499
  A Break During the Hunt Oil/canvas (38.5x53.5cm 15x21in) New-York 2000

STEWART Frank Algernon 1877-1945 **[44]**
- 🖌 $2 196 - €2 345 - **£1 500** - FF15 379
  The South Berks Watercolour (29.5x48.5cm 11x19in) Billingshurst, West-Sussex 2001
- ▥ $94 - €100 - **£60** - FF656
  In Full Cry Print (29.5x62cm 11x24in) Devon 2000

STEWART Glen XX **[21]**
- 🖌 $289 - €347 - **£200** - FF2 273
  Pinocchio, from Walt Disney Film Watercolour/paper (33.5x48.5cm 13x19in) London 2000

STEWART Helen Mary 1900-1983 **[5]**
- 🌱 $2 088 - €1 962 - **£1 258** - FF12 868
  Road down Hill, blue Mountains Oil/board (35x45cm 13x17in) Sydney 1999

STEWART James Lawson act.1883-1905 **[80]**
- 🖌 $404 - €437 - **£280** - FF2 868
  Detailed Study of Stirling Castle Watercolour/paper (48x73cm 19x29in) Aylsham, Norfolk 2001
- ▥ $788 - €817 - **£500** - FF5 362
  Near The Salt Works, the Old Chester Canal Print (34x53cm 13x20in) Cheshire 2000

STEWART John 1941 **[19]**
- 🖌 $4 210 - €4 671 - **£2 800** - FF30 639
  The departure of the Normandie from New York Watercolour (76x103cm 29x40in) London 2000

STEWART Julius LeBlanc 1855-1919 **[39]**
- 🌱 $19 602 - €18 918 - **£12 380** - FF124 094
  Mädchen im Park Öl/Leinwand (102x140cm 40x55in) München 1999
- 🌱 $28 000 - €30 729 - **£18 029** - FF201 566
  In the Boudoir Oil/canvas (81.5x60.5cm 32x23in) Beverly-Hills CA 2000
- 🌱 $16 921 - €19 059 - **£11 663** - FF125 017
  Dick, le plus aimable des petits chiens Oil/panel (23.5x15cm 9x5in) Amsterdam 2000
- 🌱 $16 020 - €15 245 - **£9 960** - FF100 000
  La Nuit et le Jour Aquarelle, gouache (16x57.5cm 6x22in) Paris 1999

STEWART Kerry 1965 **[7]**
- 🗿 $7 471 - €8 020 - **£5 000** - FF52 608
  This Girl Bends Sculpture (147x63x55cm 57x24x21in) London 2000

STEWART Robert W. XIX-XX **[5]**
- 🌱 $5 000 - €5 600 - **£3 474** - FF36 736
  Couple in front of Fireplace Oil/canvas (76x91cm 30x36in) New-York 2001

STEWART Ron 1941 **[7]**
- 🌱 $6 000 - €5 454 - **£3 613** - FF35 778
  When Tracks Led to Water Oil/canvas (76x121cm 30x48in) Hayden ID 1998
- 🖌 $250 - €291 - **£175** - FF1 912
  Apache Country Watercolour/board (26x36cm 10x14in) St. Ignatius MT 2000

STEWART William 1823-1906 **[11]**
- 🌱 $4 339 - €3 882 - **£2 600** - FF25 465
  Baby's Asleep Oil/canvas (46x59cm 18x23in) Perthshire 1998

STEYN Stella 1907-1987 **[45]**
- 🌱 $4 971 - €5 333 - **£3 389** - FF34 981
  Seated Woman Oil/canvas (91.5x61cm 36x24in) Dublin 2001
- 🌱 $1 065 - €1 143 - **£726** - FF7 496
  Self Portrait Mixed media (21x16cm 8x6in) Dublin 2001
- 🖌 $497 - €533 - **£339** - FF3 498
  Landscape Gouache/paper (13x18.5cm 5x7in) Dublin 2001

STICK Frank 1884-1966 **[2]**
- 🌱 $2 300 - €2 611 - **£1 598** - FF17 130
  Duck Hunting Oil/canvas/board (25x35cm 10x14in) Portsmouth NH 2001

STICKS George Blackie 1843-1938 **[77]**
- 🌱 $2 151 - €2 388 - **£1 500** - FF15 667
  The Sea Bird's Haunt Oil/canvas (77x102cm 30x40in) London 2001

S

$1 214 - €1 414 - £840 - FF9 276
Highland Cottage, Arran Island Oil/board
(16x31cm 6x12in) Cheshire 2000

STICKS Harry James 1867-1938 [45]
$1 207 - €1 432 - £880 - FF9 393
View of the Esk, Cumberland Oil/canvas (30x44cm
11x17in) Newcastle-upon-Tyne 2001
$247 - €293 - £180 - FF1 921
Quiet River at Sunset Watercolour/paper (17x25cm
6x9in) Newcastle-upon-Tyne 2001

STIEFEL Edward 1875-1968 [32]
$155 - €181 - £106 - FF1 190
«Graubünden» Poster (98x64cm 38x25in) Hoorn
2000

STIEGLITZ Alfred 1864-1946 [229]
$4 600 - €4 705 - £2 899 - FF30 860
The Steerage Photogravure (18x15cm 7x6in) New-
York 2000

STIELER Josef Karl 1781-1858 [25]
$14 000 - €18 141 - £10 500 - FF119 000
Crossing the Brook Olio/tela (203x142cm 79x55in)
Milano 2001
$7 865 - €8 692 - £5 455 - FF57 016
Bildnis eines Jungen Mannes Öl/Leinwand
(68x54cm 26x21in) München 2001
$835 - €818 - £514 - FF5 366
Brustbild einer jungen Dame im weissen Kleid
Miniature (9.4x7.2cm 3x2in) Stuttgart 1999
$1 316 - €1 453 - £912 - FF9 534
**Brustbild einer Dame in weissem Kleid und
rotem Schal** Watercolour (9x7cm 3x2in) Wien 2001

STIENON DU PRÉ Caroline 1883-1979 [33]
$649 - €694 - £442 - FF4 552
Place ensoleillée Huile/carton (16x24cm 6x9in)
Lokeren 2001

STIEPEVICH Vincent G. 1841-1910 [32]
$9 066 - €10 662 - £6 500 - FF69 935
Feeding the Swan Oil/canvas (77x51cm 30x20in)
London 2001

STIERHOF Ernst 1918 [27]
$453 - €511 - £319 - FF3 353
Bauer mit Bierkrug Öl/Leinwand (18x24cm 7x9in)
München 2001

STIERHOUT Joseph Anthon., Joop 1911-1997 [19]
$854 - €998 - £609 - FF6 548
Magere Burg Oil/canvas (55x70cm 21x27in)
Amsterdam 2001

STIFTER Moritz 1857-1905 [54]
$3 095 - €2 817 - £1 900 - FF18 481
A young Girl with a Mandolin Oil/canvas (82x31cm
32x12in) London 1999
$1 334 - €1 278 - £839 - FF8 384
Junges Mädchen im historischen Kostüm
Öl/Leinwand (27x22cm 10x8in) Stuttgart 1999

STIKA Jaroslav 1906-1940 [6]
$722 - €683 - £450 - FF4 482
Erotic Watercolour (33x25cm 12x9in) Praha 2000

STILKE Hermann Anton 1803-1860 [11]
$9 301 - €9 983 - £6 223 - FF65 485
**Emperor Rudolfs von Habsburg as the personi-
fication of Justice** Oil/canvas (89x89cm 35x35in)
Amsterdam 2000

STILL Clyfford 1904-1980 [14]
$1 550 000 - €1 730 537 - £1 036 020 -
FF11 351 580
Untitled Oil/canvas (175.5x108.5cm 69x42in) New-
York 2000
$25 000 - €28 002 - £17 370 - FF183 680
Untitled Oil/canvas (67.5x52cm 26x20in) New-York
2001
$80 000 - €89 450 - £53 928 - FF586 752
Untitled Oil/paper (48.5x27.5cm 19x10in) New-York
2000

STILLER Vic 1902-1974 [192]
$303 - €335 - £210 - FF2 200
Le port de Menton Huile/toile (61x50cm 24x19in)
Lyon 2001

STILLFRIED UND RATHENITZ von Raimund, Baron 1839-1911 [16]
$2 433 - €2 363 - £1 503 - FF15 500
Types chinois et Japonais Tirage albuminé
(9x13cm 3x5in) Paris 1999

STILLMAN Marie, née Spartali 1844-1927 [15]
$28 000 - €32 569 - £20 000 - FF213 638
Portrait of a young Woman Watercolour
(56x39.5cm 22x15in) London 2001

STILLMAN William James 1828-1901 [5]
$3 454 - €3 869 - £2 400 - FF25 377
«Athens, Curve of Stylobale» Albumen print
(24x19cm 9x7in) London 2001

STIMMER Abel 1542-? [1]
$956 - €1 125 - £688 - FF7 378
**Bildnis Lazarus von Schwendi, kaiserlicher
General** Radierung (38.5x32cm 15x12in) Hamburg
2001

STIMMER Tobias 1539-1584 [3]
$300 000 - €260 807 - £181 560 - FF1 710 780
The Nativity Ink (17x12.5cm 6x4in) New-York 1999

STINDEL Thomas 1887-1971 [2]
$4 345 - €3 997 - £2 689 - FF26 218
Werden-Sein-Vergehen Öl/Leinwand (103x58cm
40x22in) Wien 1999

STINGEL Rudolf 1956 [10]
$7 744 - €9 143 - £5 500 - FF59 972
Untitled Enamel (173x134.5cm 68x52in) London 2001

STINTON James, Jas 1870-1961 [57]
$972 - €908 - £600 - FF5 955
Golden Pheasant Watercolour/paper (13x21cm
5x8in) Newbury, Berkshire 1999

STIPHOUT Theo 1913 [1]
$2 852 - €2 723 - £1 782 - FF17 859
View in a Street Oil/canvas (34.5x30cm 13x11in)
Amsterdam 1999

STIRLING David, Dave 1889-1971 [30]
$325 - €363 - £212 - FF2 378
Winter in Estes Park, Colorado Oil/canvas
(76x91cm 30x36in) Chicago IL 2000

STIRLING-BROWN A.E.D.G. XX [3]
- $2 240 - €2 606 - £1 600 - FF17 091
  Bay Horse in a Stable Oil/canvas (39.5x50.5cm 15x19in) London 2001

STIRNBRAND Franz Seraph 1788-1882 [26]
- $2 381 - €2 556 - £1 594 - FF16 769
  Porträt des Major Bischoff vom 5.Württ.Infanterie.Regiment Öl/Leinwand (74x58cm 29x22in) Stuttgart 2000
- $2 504 - €2 907 - £1 760 - FF19 068
  «Portrait des Prinzen Friedrich von Hohenlohe Öhringen» Öl/Metall (30x24cm 11x9in) Wien 2001

STIRNER Karl 1882-1943 [27]
- $4 783 - €4 087 - £2 809 - FF26 809
  «Das Gartenhäuschen» Tempera (38x29cm 14x11in) Stuttgart 1998

STIXRUD Christoffer 1900-1968 [24]
- $239 - €280 - £171 - FF1 838
  Interiör fra N.Fron Oil/canvas (40x50cm 15x19in) Oslo 2001

STOBART John 1930 [23]
- $12 827 - €14 587 - £8 800 - FF95 682
  Tower Bridge, London Oil/canvas (76x102cm 29x40in) London 2000
- $200 - €237 - £141 - FF1 552
  Gatherer before the Wind Color lithograph (43x58cm 17x23in) Portland OR 2001

STOBBAERTS Jan Baptiste, Jan 1838-1914 [56]
- $3 602 - €3 630 - £2 245 - FF23 812
  Cows in a Stable Oil/canvas (49x73cm 19x28in) Amsterdam 2000
- $759 - €744 - £471 - FF4 878
  La roulotte Huile/toile (23x32cm 9x12in) Bruxelles 1999

STOBBAERTS Marcel 1889-1979 [26]
- $369 - €397 - £248 - FF2 601
  Kermesse Aquarelle/papier (35x51cm 13x20in) Bruxelles 2000

STOBBAERTS Pieter 1865-1948 [88]
- $336 - €372 - £234 - FF2 439
  Bord de côte Huile/panneau (45x70cm 17x27in) Liège 2000

STÖBER Franz Joseph XVIII [2]
- $7 728 - €8 537 - £5 359 - FF56 000
  St Adrien présidant aux supplices des chrétiens à Nicomedie/Conversion Huile/toile (64.5x72.5cm 25x28in) Paris 2001

STOBIE Charles Stewart 1845-1931 [2]
- $5 500 - €6 019 - £3 793 - FF39 483
  Tightening the Flank Cinch Oil/canvas (61x91.5cm 24x36in) New-York 2001

STOCK Andries Jacobsz. c.1580-c.1648 [2]
- $530 - €595 - £369 - FF3 902
  Martius, d'après Jan Wildens Burin (29x43cm 11x16in) Bruxelles 2001

STOCK C.R. XIX-XX [18]
- $450 - €426 - £280 - FF2 792
  The Four Seasons, after William J Shayer Mezzotint (28x72cm 11x28in) Little-Lane, Ilkley 1999

STOCK Dennis 1928 [14]
- $1 634 - €1 829 - £1 108 - FF12 000
  Portrait de James Dean Tirage argentique (34.5x26cm 13x10in) Paris 2000

STOCK Edith A. XIX-XX [11]
- $425 - €376 - £260 - FF2 469
  Figures in a Landscape, Mardale, Hawes, Water Watercolour (35x53cm 13x20in) Billingshurst, West-Sussex 1999

STOCK Henri Charles 1826-1885 [1]
- $4 658 - €3 945 - £2 800 - FF25 877
  «Retour de la pêche» Oil/canvas (66.5x31.5cm 26x12in) London 1998

STOCK Henry John 1853-1930 [27]
- $4 000 - €4 637 - £2 833 - FF30 420
  Rapture Oil/canvas (68.5x51cm 26x20in) New-York 2000
- $721 - €727 - £450 - FF4 771
  Mother and Child Watercolour (32x18cm 12x7in) Newbury, Berkshire 2000

STOCK Johann Friedrich ?-1866 [8]
- $2 720 - €2 325 - £1 632 - FF15 251
  Blick auf die Bischofsmütze mit dem Misurina-See in den Dolomiten Öl/Leinwand (40x48cm 15x18in) Wien 1998

STOCK Joseph Whiting 1815-1855 [13]
- $13 750 - €14 441 - £8 699 - FF94 726
  Portrait of Elisabeth Griffin Oil/canvas (63x76cm 25x30in) Beverly MA 2000
- $6 500 - €5 608 - £3 935 - FF36 785
  Baby J.M Hardy Facing Front in White Lace Trimmed Dress Miniature (5x3cm 2x1in) New-York 1999

STOCK van der Ignatius XVII [8]
- $750 - €832 - £499 - FF5 460
  Landscape with Two Deer Etching (22.5x32.5cm 8x12in) New-York 2000

STOCK van der Jacobus 1794-1864 [2]
- $7 696 - €8 622 - £5 348 - FF56 555
  Riviergezicht en bedrijvigheid een een dorps-trand Oil/panel (26x20.5cm 10x8in) Rotterdam 2001

STOCKER Daniel 1865-1957 [9]
- $2 221 - €2 454 - £1 540 - FF16 098
  Allegorie der Musik und des Tanzes Bronze relief (60x74cm 23x29in) München 2001

STOCKHOLDER Jessica 1959 [13]
- $11 000 - €12 763 - £7 594 - FF83 721
  The Edge of Hothouse Glass (#94) Construction (213.5x30.5cm 84x12in) New-York 2000

STÖCKL Rupert 1923-1999 [20]
- $342 - €409 - £235 - FF2 683
  Informelle Komposition Gouache/paper (52.5x71.5cm 20x28in) München 2000

STÖCKLER von Emanuel Ritter 1819-1893 [9]
- $1 779 - €1 687 - £1 082 - FF11 067
  Venedig, Blick vom Glockenturm der Kirche San Marco auf San Giorgio Aquarell/Papier (62x46cm 24x18in) Köln 1999

S

STÖCKLI Paul 1906-1992 **[131]**

$1 656 - €1 974 - **£1 180** - FF12 951
Abstraktion Oil/panel (113x84cm 44x33in) Luzern
2000

$507 - €592 - **£356** - FF3 880
Ohne Titel Öl/Leinwand (36x27cm 14x10in) Luzern
2000

$278 - €328 - **£202** - FF2 150
«Figürliche Komposition» Collage (27.5x29.5cm
10x11in) Zofingen 2001

STÖCKLIN Christian 1741-1795 **[38]**

$15 676 - €17 805 - **£11 000** - FF116 792
Figures in a Cathedral Interior Oil/panel
(35.5x46cm 13x18in) London 2001

$5 361 - €6 135 - **£3 687** - FF40 246
**Kircheninterieur, Blick in das Mittelschiff mit
Gläubigen** Oil/panel (32.5x35.5cm 12x13in) München
2000

STOCKMANN Hermann 1867-1938 **[33]**

$3 700 - €3 463 - **£2 292** - FF22 718
Hay Wagon and Figures in Landscape Oil/canvas
(50x93cm 20x37in) Philadelphia PA 1999

$4 984 - €4 602 - **£3 065** - FF30 185
Angler an der Amper Öl/Karton (32x32cm 12x12in)
München 1999

$522 - €511 - **£336** - FF3 353
Bedauern Ink/paper (26x31cm 10x12in) Kempten
1999

STOCKS Arthur 1846-1889 **[11]**

$5 722 - €5 089 - **£3 500** - FF33 380
«How the Lines where Placed at Waterloo»
Oil/canvas (44x61cm 17x24in) London 1999

$2 654 - €2 939 - **£1 800** - FF19 281
At The Cottage Door Oil/canvas (33.5x21cm 13x8in)
Billingshurst, West-Sussex 2000

STOCKS Ernest Decimus 1837/40-1918/21 **[7]**

$1 150 - €1 106 - **£708** - FF7 257
Mouth of the Swan, W.A Watercolour/paper
(23.5x34cm 9x13in) Melbourne 1999

STOCKS Minna 1846-1928 **[10]**

$1 509 - €1 717 - **£1 046** - FF11 261
Zwei Kätzchen vor der Milchschale Öl/Leinwand
(29x37cm 11x14in) Zofingen 2000

STOCKS Walter Fryer 1842-1915 **[50]**

$485 - €456 - **£300** - FF2 988
An Ancient Bridge Watercolour/paper (32x42cm
12x16in) Leyburn, North Yorkshire 1999

STOCKUM van Hilda 1908 **[4]**

$6 048 - €6 095 - **£3 770** - FF39 979
Still Life Oil/board (46x76cm 18x29in) Dublin 2000

STOCQUART Ildephonse 1819-1899 **[27]**

$1 938 - €2 186 - **£1 362** - FF14 341
Vallflicka Oil/panel (42x54cm 16x21in) Helsinki 2001

STODDARD Alice Kent 1885/93-1976 **[53]**

$3 000 - €3 517 - **£2 158** - FF23 073
Lobster Boats at Night, Monhegan Oil/canvas
(63.5x76cm 25x29in) New-York 2001

$1 100 - €1 258 - **£764** - FF8 253
Overlooking a Bay, Monhegan Oil/canvas/board
(30x40cm 12x16in) Philadelphia PA 2000

$500 - €569 - **£352** - FF3 730
Standing Figure in Blue Watercolour/paper
(34x24cm 13x9in) Philadelphia PA 2001

STODDART Frances XIX **[1]**

$3 556 - €3 965 - **£2 400** - FF26 008
Lower End of Loch Tummel, Perthshire Oil/can-
vas (39x60cm 15x23in) Edinburgh 2000

STODDART Margaret Olrog 1865-1934 **[16]**

$2 962 - €3 320 - **£2 065** - FF21 775
Avon River, Christchurch Watercolour/paper
(25x34cm 9x13in) Wellington 2001

STOECKLIN Niklaus 1896-1982 **[257]**

$23 514 - €23 694 - **£14 656** - FF155 423
**Blick aus dem Atelier mit Gliederpuppe und
Globus** Huile/panneau (58x44cm 22x17in) Zürich
2000

$12 425 - €10 645 - **£7 469** - FF69 827
Das Unholz'sche Bauernhaus in Riehen
Oil/panel (34.5x43cm 13x16in) Zürich 1998

$573 - €652 - **£398** - FF4 274
Das Weisenhaus Ink (12x17cm 4x6in) Basel 2001

$295 - €282 - **£184** - FF1 562
Basler Waggiswagen am Heuberg
Farblithographie (23x29cm 9x11in) Zofingen 1999

STOFF Alois 1846-? **[10]**

$2 369 - €2 543 - **£1 585** - FF16 684
**Schiffzug am Wiener Donaukanal an der
Heiligenstätterlände** Oil/panel (28.5x42cm 11x16in)
Wien 2000

STOFFE van der Jan Jansz. 1611-1682 **[27]**

$5 200 - €6 738 - **£3 900** - FF44 200
Scontro di cavalleria Olio/tavola (46x65.5cm
18x25in) Roma 2000

STOHL Michael 1813-1881 **[21]**

$3 584 - €3 067 - **£2 157** - FF20 119
**Madonna mit dem Kind, an Pilger Brot austei-
lend** Watercolour (53x41cm 20x16in) München 1998

STÖHR Ernst 1860-1917 **[29]**

$19 620 - €21 802 - **£13 140** - FF143 010
Mondnacht Öl/Leinwand (76.5x76.5cm 30x30in)
Wien 2000

$1 462 - €1 453 - **£884** - FF9 534
Klippen in Draga di Moscemie Öl/Leinwand
(32.5x48cm 12x18in) Wien 2000

STÖHRER Walter 1937-2000 **[226]**

$21 203 - €20 580 - **£13 202** - FF134 994
Jack in the Box II Acrylic (200x150cm 78x59in)
Berlin 1999

$3 042 - €3 579 - **£2 202** - FF23 477
Ohne Titel Tempera (48x62.5cm 18x24in) Hamburg
2001

$2 677 - €2 812 - **£1 688** - FF18 446
**Jeder natürliche Vorgang mit dem kürzesten
Weg** Mischtechnik (30x23cm 11x9in) Stuttgart 2000

$2 423 - €2 352 - **£1 508** - FF15 023
Ohne Titel Watercolour (32.5x48.4cm 12x19in) Berlin
1999

$182 - €204 - **£127** - FF1 341
Abstrakte Komposition Farbradierung (72x55.5cm
28x21in) Berlin 2001

STOITZNER Alexander 1870-? [2]
- $2 312 - €2 187 - £1 440 - FF14 344
  Still-Life with Flowers and Fruit Oil/canvas (60x120cm 23x47in) Praha 2001

STOITZNER Carl Siegfried 1866-1943 [12]
- $1 370 - €1 599 - £968 - FF10 487
  Brotzeit in der Klosterstube Oil/panel (45x67cm 17x26in) Salzburg 2000

STOITZNER Josef 1884-1951 [131]
- $12 384 - €11 628 - £7 648 - FF76 272
  Blick ins Tal im Hintergrund das Kitzsteinhorn Öl/Leinwand (110x140cm 43x55in) Wien 1999
- $7 404 - €8 721 - £5 208 - FF57 204
  See im Abendlicht Öl/Leinwand (62x78cm 24x30in) Wien 2000
- $3 139 - €3 585 - £2 213 - FF23 516
  Sonniger Weg mit Gehöft zwischen Bäumen Öl/Karton (24x33.5cm 9x13in) Bern 2001
- $1 498 - €1 453 - £924 - FF9 534
  Gebirgslandschaft Watercolour (24x31cm 9x12in) Wien 1999
- $245 - €281 - £167 - FF1 844
  Auf den Tauern/Hochgebirge im Winter Woodcut in colors (40x45cm 15x17in) Heidelberg 2000

STOITZNER Konstantin 1863-1934 [139]
- $1 611 - €1 818 - £1 133 - FF11 928
  Blumenstilleben Öl/Karton (86x95cm 33x37in) Bern 2001
- $546 - €581 - £345 - FF3 813
  Frisch vom Zapfen Oil/panel (20x15cm 7x5in) Salzburg 2000

STOITZNER Siegfried 1892-1976 [18]
- $3 665 - €3 634 - £2 295 - FF23 835
  Ansitz in der Wachau Oil/panel (80x94.4cm 31x37in) Wien 1999
- $3 602 - €3 997 - £2 508 - FF26 218
  Winterabend in Krems Mixed media/canvas (27x24cm 10x9in) Salzburg 2001

STOJANOW C. Pjotr act.1887-? [20]
- $3 000 - €2 591 - £1 812 - FF16 997
  Festive Sleigh Ride Oil/canvas (81x49cm 32x19in) Houston TX 1998

STOK van der Jacobus 1794-1864 [24]
- $4 491 - €4 526 - £2 800 - FF29 690
  Driving Sheep though a Village Oil/canvas (51x66cm 20x25in) London 2000
- $18 152 - €19 059 - £11 445 - FF125 074
  Frozen Waterway with Skaters and Townsfolk gathered around a Koek Oil/panel (28.5x36cm 11x14in) Amsterdam 2000

STOKELD James 1827-1877 [10]
- $6 961 - €6 006 - £4 200 - FF39 399
  «When the Boat Comes in» Oil/canvas (71x92.5cm 27x36in) London 1998

STOKES Adrian Scott 1854-1935 [26]
- $2 495 - €2 863 - £1 706 - FF18 781
  Blühende Magnolien vor der Bergkulisse des Luganer Sees Öl/Leinwand (65x48cm 25x18in) Berlin 2000
- $2 779 - €2 671 - £1 700 - FF17 520
  «Warwick Castle, LMS» Poster (100x121cm 39x47in) London 1999

STOKES Constance 1906-1991 [33]
- $3 794 - €4 181 - £2 523 - FF27 423
  Girl in Green Kimono Oil/board (61x45cm 24x17in) Melbourne 2000
- $708 - €796 - £459 - FF5 220
  Migrant Women Ink (22.5x19cm 8x7in) Malvern, Victoria 2000

STOKES Frank Wilbert 1858-1955 [84]
- $5 049 - €4 352 - £3 000 - FF28 544
  An Artic Twilight Oil/canvas (92x138cm 36x54in) London 1998
- $3 549 - €3 409 - £2 200 - FF22 362
  Melville Bay, Greenland Oil/canvas/board (35x50cm 13x19in) London 1999
- $2 000 - €2 254 - £1 385 - FF14 784
  «Over the Penna Hills» Oil/canvas (20x30cm 8x12in) Hatfield PA 2000

STOKES George B. XIX [1]
- $3 500 - €3 305 - £2 173 - FF21 678
  Harbor at Tenby, South Wales Albumen print (19.5x15cm 7x5in) New-York 1999

STOKES George Vernon 1873-1954 [56]
- $220 - €216 - £140 - FF1 414
  Deer in a Landscape Watercolour/paper (32x23cm 12x9in) Carlisle, Cumbria 1999
- $308 - €367 - £220 - FF2 407
  Spaniels intent upon a Rabbit Warren Etching (24x29cm 9x11in) Bath 2000

STOKES Margaret 1916-1996 [17]
- $1 186 - €1 397 - £833 - FF9 161
  Table Top Still Life Oil/canvas (33.5x38.5cm 13x15in) Dublin 2000

STOKES Marianne 1855-1927 [13]
- $10 460 - €11 228 - £7 000 - FF73 651
  The Annunciation Oil/canvas (190.5x91.5cm 75x36in) London 2000
- $11 700 - €10 901 - £7 215 - FF71 505
  Träumendes Mädchen mit Blumenstrauss auf Gartenbank Öl/Leinwand (100x80cm 39x31in) Linz 1999
- $1 135 - €1 098 - £700 - FF7 204
  Study of a Girl Head in Profile Pencil (19x27.5cm 7x10in) London 1999

STOLBA Leopold 1863-1929 [4]
- $2 307 - €2 325 - £1 440 - FF15 254
  Landschaft Aquarell/Papier (15.5x21cm 6x8in) Wien 2000

STOLIZA Ewgenij Iwanowitsch 1870-1929 [9]
- $2 253 - €2 180 - £1 389 - FF14 301
  Mittelrussische Flusslandschaft Öl/Leinwand (59x87cm 23x34in) Wien 1999

STOLK van Alida Elisabeth 1830-c.1884 [3]
- $8 000 - €9 295 - £5 622 - FF60 969
  Poppies, Hollyhock and Primroses in Nature Oil/canvas (40x50cm 16x20in) New-Orleans LA 2001

STOLL Rolf 1892-? [8]
- $2 600 - €2 817 - £1 733 - FF18 480
  «Bal Bizarre» Poster (53x35cm 21x14in) New-York 2000

S

STOLL von Leopold 1792-1869 **[23]**

$6 184 - €5 814 - **£3 744** - FF38 136
Blumenstück mit Kirschen und einem Pfirsich
Öl/Leinwand (52x42cm 20x16in) Wien 1999

STOLTENBERG Mathias 1799-1871 **[9]**

$10 431 - €11 806 - **£7 296** - FF77 444
Landskap rytter og slåttefolk Oil/canvas/panel
(34x49cm 13x19in) Oslo 2001

$14 756 - €17 555 - **£10 206** - FF115 150
Fra Dusgard på Ringsaker Oil/metal (26x37cm
10x14in) Oslo 2000

STOLZ SEGUI Ramón 1872-1924 **[7]**

$6 400 - €6 006 - **£4 000** - FF39 400
**Jardín con escultura y gran cesto de flores y
frutas** Oleo/lienzo (212x171cm 83x67in) Madrid 1999

$4 575 - €4 505 - **£2 850** - FF29 550
Odalisca Oleo/lienzo (45.5x55cm 17x21in) Madrid
1999

STOM Antonio, Tonino c.1688-1734 **[9]**

$10 710 - €9 252 - **£5 355** - FF60 690
Battaglia Olio/tela (37x30cm 14x11in) Venezia 1999

STOMER Mathäus I c.1600-c.1660 **[28]**

$93 480 - €87 207 - **£56 400** - FF572 040
Die Kreuzigung Christi Öl/Leinwand (153x141cm
60x55in) Wien 1999

$37 052 - €42 084 - **£26 000** - FF276 055
Saint Matthew by Candlelight Oil/canvas
(76.5x64cm 30x25in) London 2001

STOMER Matthias 1649-1702 **[6]**

$14 000 - €14 513 - **£8 400** - FF95 200
Scena di battaglia Olio/tela (58x89cm 22x35in)
Milano 1999

STOMME de Maërten Boelema c.1620-c.1670 **[5]**

$42 471 - €40 840 - **£26 163** - FF267 894
**Nautilus Cup, a Peeled Lemon on a Oewter
Plate, Nuts a knife, a Glass** Oil/panel (70.5x53.5cm
27x21in) Amsterdam 1999

STONE Cami 1892-1975 **[13]**

$526 - €464 - **£364** - FF4 024
Stoffpuppe Vintage gelatin silver print (21.7x16.7cm
8x6in) Köln 2000

STONE Don 1929 **[8]**

$400 - €466 - **£283** - FF3 060
«Pigeon Cove Road, Rockport» Watercolour/paper
(36x54cm 14x21in) St. Petersburg FL 2001

STONE Erika 1920 **[4]**

$2 000 - €1 672 - **£1 184** - FF10 965
Bowery Beauties/Test of Strength/Bar Scene
Silver print (26x33cm 10x13in) New-York 1998

STONE Frank 1800-1859 **[8]**

$7 114 - €8 266 - **£5 000** - FF54 221
Plotting Mischief Oil/canvas (71x91.5cm 27x36in)
London 2001

STONE Marcus C. 1840-1921 **[59]**

$20 000 - €22 105 - **£14 010** - FF144 998
The Lover's Return Oil/canvas (101x134cm 40x53in)
Chicago IL 2001

$16 232 - €15 608 - **£10 000** - FF102 384
Dusk, June 18 Oil/canvas (75x101.5cm 29x39in)
London 1999

$1 963 - €2 057 - **£1 242** - FF13 491
Kvinna i interiör Oil/canvas (39x32cm 15x12in)
Malmö 2000

STONE Robert XIX-XX **[26]**

$15 000 - €15 591 - **£9 453** - FF102 271
Full Cry/Over the Fence Oil/canvas (42.5x68.5cm
16x26in) New-York 2000

$2 876 - €2 766 - **£1 772** - FF18 142
With the Warwickshire Hunt Oil/panel (15x30cm
5x11in) Melbourne 1999

STONE Rudolph XIX-XX **[45]**

$2 839 - €3 048 - **£1 900** - FF19 995
On the Scent/The Kill Oil/board (19.5x33cm 7x12in)
London 2000

STONE Sarah c.1760-1844 **[15]**

$2 100 - €2 254 - **£1 430** - FF14 787
Falco Pygargus Watercolour/paper (34x44cm
13x17in) Boston MA 2001

STONE Sasha, S. Steinsapir 1895-1940 **[43]**

$970 - €1 067 - **£622** - FF7 000
Femme Tirage argentique (30x23.5cm 11x9in) Paris
2000

STONE Thomas Albert, Tom 1894-1978 **[35]**

$300 - €324 - **£201** - FF2 124
Deer Tracks Oil/board (35.5x45.5cm 13x17in)
Calgary, Alberta 2000

$357 - €418 - **£252** - FF2 745
Skipping Rocks Oil/board (25.5x30.5cm 10x12in)
Calgary, Alberta 2001

STONE William R. act.1865-1878 **[23]**

$791 - €763 - **£500** - FF5 006
An old Road near Kings-Norton in the Winter
Oil/canvas (35.5x53.5cm 13x21in) London 1999

$1 055 - €1 013 - **£646** - FF6 646
Sheep on a Mountain Track Oil/canvas
(30.5x40.5cm 12x15in) London 1999

STONE William, Jnr. XIX-XX **[4]**

$2 097 - €1 954 - **£1 300** - FF12 816
A Lane near Horsham, Winter Watercolour/paper
(75x126cm 29x49in) Billingshurst, West-Sussex 1999

STOOP Dirck c.1610/18-c.1681/86 **[43]**

$30 708 - €30 678 - **£19 200** - FF201 234
Jagdgesellschaft am Eingang einer Grotte
Oil/panel (70.5x103cm 27x40in) Köln 1999

$4 800 - €5 450 - **£3 285** - FF35 752
Reitergefecht in einer Flusslandschaft Oil/panel
(17.5x23cm 6x9in) Wien 2000

$98 - €92 - **£59** - FF603
Pferde an der Tränke Radierung (15x19cm 5x7in)
Lindau 1999

STOOP Maerten 1620-1647 **[5]**

$44 829 - €48 120 - **£30 000** - FF315 648
**Soldiers and Camp Followers playing Cards
amidst Ruins** Oil/canvas (63.5x82cm 25x32in)
London 2000

$3 222 - €2 820 - **£1 951** - FF18 500
Chez le barbier Huile/panneau (26x12.5cm 10x4in)
Saint-Brieuc 1998

STOOPENDAAL Mosse 1901-1948 **[475]**

$2 415 - €2 682 - **£1 617** - FF17 593
Vilande räv Oil/canvas (59x49cm 23x19in) Stockholm
2000

$1 756 - €1 951 - **£1 176** - FF12 795
Räv i vinterlandskap Oil/canvas (27x36cm 10x14in)
Stockholm 2000

$485 - €460 - **£302** - FF3 015
Domherrar Akvarell/papper (14x19cm 5x7in)
Stockholm 1999

STOOPENDAEL Daniel 1672-1726 **[6]**

$310 - €360 - **£220** - FF2 361
Palestine Engraving (25x45cm 9x17in) London 2000

STOOPS Herbert Morton 1887-1948 **[35]**

$1 787 - €1 981 - **£1 238** - FF12 996
Kråkor Oil/canvas (96x105cm 37x41in) Malmö 2001

$1 100 - €1 027 - **£678** - FF6 738
Illustration Boards for The Texas Ranger by J.H.Cook & H.R Driggs Ink (38x27cm 14x10in)
Boston MA 1999

$1 195 - €1 143 - **£749** - FF7 499
«Ashtabula Harbour, Lake Erie, New York Central Lines» Poster (103x68cm 40x26in) London 1999

STOOTER Cornelis Leonardsz. c.1600-1655 **[6]**

$12 741 - €12 252 - **£7 848** - FF80 368
Flute and Other ships in a Stormy Water Oil/panel (29.5x38.5cm 11x15in) Amsterdam 1999

STOPENDAEL Bastiaen 1637-1707 **[2]**

$67 - €77 - **£46** - FF503
Triumphbogen für König Wilhelm III von England Radierung (37.6x47cm 14x18in) Berlin 2000

STOPFORD William Henry 1842-1890 **[4]**

$1 903 - €1 778 - **£1 174** - FF11 660
View of the Blasket and Skelling Islands Watercolour/paper (50x71cm 20x28in) Dublin 1999

STORCH Anton 1892-1979 **[33]**

$881 - €945 - **£601** - FF6 197
Blick auf Dürnstein Oil/panel (83x72.5cm 32x28in) Wien 2001

STORCH Frederik Ludwig 1805-1883 **[41]**

$1 481 - €1 345 - **£918** - FF8 824
Italienerinder, der leger med et lille barn i strandkanten Oil/canvas (54x42cm 21x16in) København 1999

$693 - €672 - **£428** - FF4 411
Portraet af Urtekraemmer Hans Henrik Bache/Frederikke Sophie Bache Oil/canvas (23.5x19.5cm 9x7in) Vejle 1999

STORCK Abraham Jansz. 1644-1708 **[105]**

$73 399 - €68 650 - **£45 000** - FF450 315
Peter the Great Visiting the «Peter and Paul» in the Ij Off Amsterdam Oil/canvas (71x88.5cm 27x34in) London 1998

$35 000 - €32 929 - **£21 840** - FF215 999
Dutch Admiralty sailing on the Ij Oil/canvas (31.5x37.5cm 12x14in) New-York 1999

STORCK Jacobus 1641-1687 **[52]**

$30 105 - €25 455 - **£18 000** - FF166 975
Capriccio of a Dutch River Landscape, Elegant Figures, a Town Beyond Oil/panel (52x74.5cm 20x29in) London 1998

$6 134 - €5 899 - **£3 779** - FF38 695
Mediterranean Harbour scene with Figures by a Gate Ink (22.5x18cm 8x7in) Amsterdam 1999

STORELLI Felice 1778-1854 **[17]**

$2 427 - €2 287 - **£1 470** - FF15 000
Vue d'un pont au clair de lune Aquarelle (44x59cm 17x23in) Paris 1999

STORER Charles 1817-1907 **[4]**

$4 750 - €5 296 - **£3 205** - FF34 741
Still Life of Peaches Oil/canvas (50x71cm 20x28in) New-Bedford MA 2000

$6 500 - €7 680 - **£4 606** - FF50 380
The Grape Vine Oil/canvas (36x24cm 14x9in) Boston MA 2000

STORER Johann Christoph c.1620-1671 **[6]**

$17 000 - €16 498 - **£10 711** - FF108 222
The Adoration of the Magi Oil/canvas (223.5x162.5cm 87x63in) New-York 1999

$49 311 - €52 932 - **£33 000** - FF347 212
Coronation of Otto the Great in The church of Sant'Ambrogio, Milan Ink (22.5x30.5cm 8x12in) London 1999

$705 - €613 - **£425** - FF4 022
Das Bacchanale Radierung (19.9x26.6cm 7x10in) Berlin 1998

STÖRER Walter 1937 **[1]**

$24 852 - €23 173 - **£15 000** - FF152 008
Kopf Maiba III, Head Mixed media (150x130.5cm 59x51in) London 1999

STOREY George Adolphus 1834-1919 **[22]**

$3 482 - €3 921 - **£2 400** - FF25 723
Miss Gladys Storey, in a Blue Coat, and Feathered Hat, Holding Gloves Oil/canvas (112x87cm 44x34in) London 2000

$243 - €238 - **£150** - FF1 558
The Mansion House, London, decorated for a royal Procession Watercolour/paper (25x35cm 9x13in) London 1999

STOREY John XIX **[4]**

$1 583 - €1 528 - **£1 000** - FF10 023
Lanercost Priory Watercolour, gouache/paper (34x48cm 13x19in) Carlisle, Cumbria 1999

STORFYRSTINDE Olga 1882-1960 **[24]**

$1 382 - €1 475 - **£920** - FF9 675
Röde tulipaner i vase samt clivia og pelargonie i rödlerspotter Oil/canvas (49x60cm 19x23in) København 2000

$623 - €538 - **£376** - FF3 530
Gårdexteriör med gaes Gouache/paper (20x23cm 7x9in) Vejle 1999

STORIE José 1899-1961 **[23]**

$4 800 - €5 184 - **£3 317** - FF34 002
Gladioli Oil/canvas (82x107cm 32x42in) New-York 2001

STORK-KRUIJFF Anna Maria 1870-1946 **[3]**

$5 000 - €5 097 - **£3 133** - FF33 433
The Bulldogs The Ray Picker and Hercule de Dieghem Oil/canvas (38.5x56.5cm 15x22in) New-York 2000

STORM Juan 1927-1997 **[29]**

$3 000 - €3 120 - **£1 894** - FF20 463
Paisaje con bar, Gaucho a caballo y paisanos en carreta Oleo/cartón (35x48cm 13x18in) Montevideo 2000

S

STORM Per Palle 1910-1994 **[7]**

$2 835 - €3 371 - **£2 019** - FF22 113
Liggende love Bronze (28x56cm 11x22in) Oslo 2000

STORM PETERSEN Robert 1882-1949 **[286]**

$5 431 - €6 032 - **£3 780** - FF39 568
«En lystmorder» Oil/board (38x49cm 14x19in)
København 2001

$279 - €322 - **£193** - FF2 112
«Kan De fortaelle mig noget om Vekselprotest?» Indian ink/paper (26x22cm 10x8in)
København 2000

STORMONT Howard Gull XIX-XX **[17]**

$484 - €455 - **£300** - FF2 982
Unloading the Barges Watercolour (34x52cm 13x20in) London 1999

STORN Willibald C. 1936 **[3]**

$389 - €449 - **£274** - FF2 945
Eplehöst Color lithograph (80x60cm 31x23in) Oslo 2000

STORRIER Timothy Austin, Tim 1949 **[168]**

$16 878 - €18 596 - **£11 205** - FF121 982
Blazeline Oil/canvas (91.5x198cm 36x77in)
Woollahra, Sydney 2000

$3 687 - €4 063 - **£2 475** - FF26 651
Capricorn Passage Oil/board (39.5x49.5cm 15x19in)
Malvern, Victoria 2000

$1 306 - €1 229 - **£809** - FF8 059
Magambo Club Collage (50x50cm 19x19in)
Melbourne 1999

$418 - €394 - **£263** - FF2 586
Untitled Lithograph (70.5x50cm 27x19in) Sydney 1999

STORRS John Henry Bradley 1885-1956 **[13]**

$30 000 - €35 678 - **£21 381** - FF234 030
Cityscape at Dusk Oil/canvas (92x73.5cm 36x28in)
New-York 2000

$30 000 - €25 632 - **£18 009** - FF168 132
Horses Heads Terracotta (H33cm H12in) New-York 1998

$3 800 - €3 691 - **£2 375** - FF24 213
Female Head in Turban Drawing (32x25.5cm 12x10in) New-York 1999

$1 900 - €2 234 - **£1 317** - FF14 651
Modernist Head in Profile with Cap Woodcut (11x11cm 4x4in) New-York 2000

STORSTEIN Aage 1900-1983 **[36]**

$2 205 - €2 622 - **£1 570** - FF17 199
Fra stranden mot Runsholmen Oil/panel (65x81cm 25x31in) Oslo 2000

$1 071 - €1 024 - **£674** - FF6 718
Kvinnehode Oil/canvas/panel (25x18cm 9x7in) Oslo 1999

STORTENBEKER Pieter 1828-1898 **[24]**

$1 737 - €2 042 - **£1 204** - FF13 394
Cows in a Landscape Oil/canvas/panel (28x57cm 11x22in) Amsterdam 2000

$805 - €908 - **£555** - FF5 953
A Hersman with Flock Crossing a Ditch Watercolour (41x63cm 16x24in) Amsterdam 2000

STORY George Henry 1835-1923 **[9]**

$7 500 - €7 403 - **£4 560** - FF48 562
Street Musician Oil/board/canvas (60x40cm 23x15in) New-York 2000

$7 500 - €8 517 - **£5 133** - FF55 866
By the Fire Oil/board (30.5x23cm 12x9in) New-York 2000

STORY Julian 1857-1919 **[4]**

$11 229 - €11 316 - **£7 000** - FF74 225
Aesops Fables Oil/canvas (155x242cm 61x95in)
London 2000

$2 100 - €2 398 - **£1 480** - FF15 728
Portrait of Emily F.Lawrence Oil/canvas (122x93.5cm 48x36in) Boston MA 2001

STORY Waldo 1855-1915 **[5]**

$7 500 - €7 153 - **£4 565** - FF46 919
Portrait Bust of Nell Gwinn on Pedestal Marble (H99cm H38in) New-York 1999

$6 000 - €5 722 - **£3 652** - FF37 535
Classical Male Portrait Bust on Pedestal Marble (H53.5cm H21in) New-York 1999

STORY William Wetmore 1819-1895 **[5]**

$30 000 - €25 632 - **£18 009** - FF168 132
Hero Looking for Leander Marble (H178cm H70in)
New-York 1998

$10 441 - €11 106 - **£6 600** - FF72 850
A Pensive Beethoven Bronze (48x26.5cm 18x10in)
London 2000

STOSKOPF Sebastian 1597-1657 **[10]**

$741 198 - €727 907 - **£460 000** - FF4 774 754
Still-life of a wine-casket, a wine glass, a loaf of bread and a knife Oil/panel (42.5x55cm 16x21in)
London 1999

STOTHARD Thomas 1755-1834 **[58]**

$3 249 - €3 161 - **£2 000** - FF20 737
The Supper by the Fountain, from Boccaccio's Decameron Oil/panel (48x60cm 18x23in) London 1999

$1 122 - €1 131 - **£700** - FF7 422
Passage of the Douro, Oporto Liberated Oil/paper/board (14.5x25.5cm 5x10in) London 2000

$251 - €215 - **£150** - FF1 408
St Peter holding a Cross and Keys Watercolour (12.5x7cm 4x2in) London 1998

STOTT Edward William 1859-1918 **[48]**

$4 910 - €5 853 - **£3 500** - FF38 395
Sketch for The Wedding Oil/canvas (51x75cm 20x29in) London 2000

$741 - €842 - **£520** - FF5 521
Mother and Child Pencil/paper (21x11cm 8x4in)
Cambridge 2001

STOTT Fred XX **[8]**

$323 - €317 - **£200** - FF2 077
Bamburgh Watercolour/paper (35x50cm 14x20in)
Berwick-upon-Tweed 1999

STOTT OF OLDHAM William 1857-1900 **[4]**

$5 191 - €5 737 - **£3 600** - FF37 630
Seated Lady in Black Oil/panel (13x6cm 5x2in)
London 2001

$2 525 - €3 003 - **£1 800** - FF19 701
Study for a Summer's Day Pastel (23.5x31cm 9x12in) London 2000

STOTZ Otto 1805-1873 **[16]**

$4 887 - €4 449 - **£3 000** - FF29 181
Catching the Horses Oil/canvas (64x86.5cm 25x34in) London 1999

STÖTZER Werner 1931 [20]

  $1 580 - €1 841 - **£1 104** - FF12 074
    Guernica, für Paul Eluard Bronze (H17cm H6in)
    Berlin 2000

STOUF Jean-Baptiste 1742-1826 [4]

  $18 368 - €21 343 - **£12 908** - FF140 000
    Allégories de la Paix et de la Victoire Terracotta
    (H26.5cm H10in) Paris 2001

STOUMEN Lou 1917-1991 [24]

  $2 750 - €3 166 - **£1 876** - FF20 768
    43rd and Times Square Gelatin silver print
    (23x19cm 9x7in) New-York 2000

STOVER Allan James 1887-1967 [4]

  $4 400 - €4 109 - **£2 715** - FF26 954
    The Quiet River Oil/canvas (27x35.5cm 10x13in)
    Boston MA 1999

STÖWER Willy 1864-1931 [29]

  $1 368 - €1 278 - **£827** - FF8 384
    **Haiti, Überweisung des Ultimatums an den
    Hafenkapitän Port au Prince** Watercolour (12x17cm
    4x6in) Berlin 1999

STRAATEN van Bruno I 1786-1870 [7]

  $3 540 - €3 403 - **£2 208** - FF22 324
    Winter Landscape with Skaters on the Ice
    Oil/panel (37.5x51.5cm 14x20in) Amsterdam 1999

  $2 307 - €2 550 - **£1 600** - FF16 724
    Cattle and Sheep in an extensive Landscape
    Oil/canvas (30x37cm 11x14in) London 2001

STRAATEN van Bruno II 1812-1887 [7]

  $1 496 - €1 269 - **£902** - FF8 325
    Wandelaars in landschap met ruïne Oil/panel
    (32.5x40cm 12x15in) Den Haag 1998

STRACHAN Arthur Claude 1865-1932 [137]

  $5 163 - €4 959 - **£3 200** - FF32 527
    **Coastal View at Harvest Time/Horses by a
    Waterfall** Oil/canvas (46x76.5cm 18x30in) London
    1999

  $3 344 - €2 855 - **£2 000** - FF18 726
    **A Figure before a Cottage at Market Drayton,
    Shropshire** Watercolour (28x45cm 11x17in) London
    1998

STRACHAN David Edgar 1919-1970 [32]

  $2 074 - €2 327 - **£1 440** - FF15 263
    Majura No.1 Oil/canvas (48.5x99.5cm 19x39in)
    Melbourne 2001

  $1 260 - €1 147 - **£765** - FF7 521
    Still Life Oil/canvas (18x25cm 7x9in) Sydney 1998

STRACHE Wolf 1910 [19]

  $2 123 - €2 352 - **£1 440** - FF15 427
    Shell-Haus, Berlin Gelatin silver print (20.7x29.6cm
    8x11in) Berlin 2000

STRADONE Giovanni 1911-1981 [77]

  $3 250 - €3 369 - **£1 950** - FF22 100
    «Atollo» Olio/tela (40x50cm 15x19in) Prato 2001

  $1 200 - €1 244 - **£720** - FF8 160
    «Asceta» Olio/tela (45x35cm 17x13in) Roma 2001

STRAET van der Jan Stradanus 1523-1605 [33]

  $32 500 - €32 428 - **£19 782** - FF212 715
    **Giovanni dei Medici persuades the Swiss Army
    to Retreat** Ink (19.5x29.5cm 7x11in) New-York 2000

STRAETEN van der Georges 1856-1928 [125]

  $795 - €843 - **£537** - FF5 528
    Jeune fille souriante au chapeau et corsage
    Bronze (H44cm H17in) Bruxelles 2001

STRAETEN van der Jan Baptist ?-c.1729 [4]

  $20 119 - €17 002 - **£12 000** - FF111 524
    **Architectural Capriccio, Figures/Architectural
    Capriccio, Party** Oil/canvas (60x84cm 23x33in)
    London 1998

STRAND Paul 1890-1976 [144]

  $17 000 - €15 901 - **£10 278** - FF104 305
    The Walk, Orgeval Gelatin silver print (24.5x19.5cm
    9x7in) New-York 1999

STRAND Svein 1934 [6]

  $1 653 - €1 835 - **£1 152** - FF12 034
    Liggende kvinne med armene over hodet
    Watercolour/paper (25x50cm 9x19in) Oslo 2001

  $259 - €299 - **£182** - FF1 963
    Akt ved vinduet Color lithograph (62x46cm 24x18in)
    Oslo 2000

STRANDMAN Otto Valdemar 1871-1960 [10]

  $956 - €859 - **£570** - FF5 637
    Dansande kvinna Bronze (H28cm H11in) Stockholm
    1998

STRANG Peter 1936 [9]

  $649 - €767 - **£460** - FF5 030
    Clown mit Geige Porcelain (H22.2cm H8in) Ahlden
    2000

STRANG William 1859-1921 [148]

  $21 329 - €19 532 - **£13 000** - FF128 122
    The Temptation Oil/canvas (122x137cm 48x53in)
    London 1999

  $5 154 - €4 844 - **£3 200** - FF31 773
    Portrait of Sylvia Parsons Oil/canvas (76x61cm
    29x24in) London 1999

  $427 - €486 - **£300** - FF3 185
    Portrait of Frederic Harrisson Pencil/paper
    (40.5x26.5cm 15x10in) West-Midlands 2001

  $179 - €153 - **£107** - FF1 006
    Selbstporträt Radierung (20x14.7cm 7x5in) Berlin
    1998

STRANGE Albert G. 1855-1917 [17]

  $486 - €471 - **£300** - FF3 087
    **Coastal Scene with Fishing Boats beside a
    Castle** Watercolour/paper (19.5x25.5cm 7x10in) West-
    Yorkshire 1999

STRANGE Frederick 1807-1873 [1]

  $5 427 - €4 732 - **£3 281** - FF31 042
    Lanceston Watercolour, gouache/paper (12.5x20cm
    4x7in) Melbourne 1998

STRANGE Robert 1721-1792 [13]

  $235 - €252 - **£159** - FF1 654
    Carlos I Grabado (64x50cm 25x19in) Madrid 2001

STRANGEMAN Clive Venn 1888-? [10]

  $255 - €299 - **£180** - FF1 963
    January Day, Trafalgar Square Watercolour/paper
    (38.5x43cm 15x16in) London 2000

S

STRANOVIUS Tobias Stranover 1684-c.1735 **[31]**
- **$18 136** - €17 989 - **£11 280** - FF118 000
  Nature morte aux raisins at aux gibiers suspen-dus/Lièvre et gibiers Huile/toile (110x140.5cm 43x55in) Paris 1999
- **$5 890** - €6 604 - **£4 000** - FF43 322
  Grapes, Peaches and Plums on a Forest Floor Oil/canvas (52x66cm 20x25in) London 2000

STRANSKY Ferdinand 1904-1982 **[76]**
- **$9 288** - €8 721 - **£5 736** - FF57 204
  Eine flasche Wein Oil/panel (54x66.5cm 21x26in) Wien 1999
- **$403** - €436 - **£279** - FF2 860
  Paar Aquarell/Papier (36.5x25.5cm 14x10in) Wien 2001

STRASBEAUX Jean François XVIII-XIX **[4]**
- **$2 897** - €2 431 - **£1 700** - FF15 947
  Young Singer Facing Right in Low-cut Classical Muslin Chemise Miniature (6.5x6.5cm 2x2in) London 1998

STRASSER Arthur 1854-1927 **[25]**
- **$1 076** - €1 163 - **£744** - FF7 627
  Büste Ceramic (H48.5cm H19in) Wien 2001

STRASSER Roland 1895-1974 **[121]**
- **$8 254** - €8 801 - **£5 600** - FF57 730
  Cockfighter Oil/canvas (76x56cm 29x22in) London 2001
- **$3 389** - €3 548 - **£2 129** - FF23 274
  Man and Cockerel Oil/board (34x27cm 13x10in) Singapore 2000
- **$622** - €687 - **£431** - FF4 508
  Balinese Beauty Charcoal (30x22cm 11x8in) Singapore 2000

STRATEN van Henri 1892-1944 **[72]**
- **$1 729** - €1 611 - **£1 072** - FF10 569
  Nu couché Huile/toile (68x108cm 26x42in) Antwerpen 1999
- **$240** - €198 - **£140** - FF1 299
  Visser Linogravure (24x19.1cm 9x7in) Bruxelles 1998

STRATFORD Frank [6]
- **$4 000** - €3 708 - **£2 487** - FF24 320
  Loyal servants Oil/canvas (35.5x25.5cm 13x10in) New-York 1999

STRATHMANN Carl 1866-1939 **[36]**
- **$926** - €971 - **£610** - FF6 372
  Impressionistisches Blumenstilleben Öl/Karton (25x18cm 9x7in) Augsburg 2000
- **$405** - €460 - **£277** - FF3 018
  Grusskarte: Pfau Watercolour (9.2x14cm 3x5in) Hamburg 2000

STRATOU Danae 1964 **[1]**
- **$10 260** - €11 412 - **£6 840** - FF74 860
  Javeline II Iron (200x580cm 78x228in) Athens 2000

STRAUBE William 1871-1954 **[24]**
- **$381** - €409 - **£255** - FF2 683
  Selbstportrait an der Staffelei Indian ink/paper (62.3x49.3cm 24x19in) München 2000

STRAUBINGER Klaus 1939-? **[16]**
- **$1 667** - €1 789 - **£1 115** - FF11 738
  Weiter Himmel Öl/Leinwand (100x100cm 39x39in) Bremen 2000

- **$714** - €767 - **£478** - FF5 030
  Ferien am Strand Gouache/paper (60x76cm 23x29in) Bremen 2000

STRAUCH Lorenz 1554-1630 **[13]**
- **$7 168** - €6 134 - **£4 315** - FF40 239
  Nürnberger Patrizier/Seine Hefefrau Oil/panel (52.5x39cm 20x15in) München 1998
- **$8 088** - €6 857 - **£4 800** - FF44 980
  Young Gentleman, half-length, Wearing a Black Embroidered Doublet Oil/panel (40x34.5cm 15x13in) London 1998

STRAUS Meyer 1831-1905 **[21]**
- **$2 750** - €2 539 - **£1 712** - FF16 657
  Homestead Mules in Gold Country Oil/canvas (43x55cm 17x22in) Oakland CA 1999

STRAUSER Sterling Boyd 1907-1995 **[6]**
- **$2 400** - €2 773 - **£1 680** - FF18 187
  Portrait of Shorty Widmar Oil/panel (51x40.5cm 20x15in) Bethesda MD 2001

STRAUSS André 1885-1971 **[51]**
- **$696** - €732 - **£459** - FF4 800
  Douarnenez Huile/toile (72x62cm 28x24in) Paris 2000

STRAWALDE Jürgen Böttcher 1931 **[39]**
- **$3 485** - €4 116 - **£2 436** - FF26 998
  Ohne Titel Öl/Leinwand (87.5x68.5cm 34x26in) Berlin 2001
- **$1 099** - €1 329 - **£767** - FF8 720
  Asiatische Brücke Indian ink (59x84.5cm 23x33in) Berlin 2000
- **$127** - €133 - **£80** - FF872
  Szene Farblithographie (32.6x39.3cm 12x15in) Berlin 2000

STRAYER Paul 1885-1981 **[10]**
- **$2 400** - €2 745 - **£1 669** - FF18 008
  Winter Sleigh Ride Oil/canvas (66x58cm 26x23in) Cincinnati OH 2000

STRBA Annelies 1947 **[10]**
- **$429** - €511 - **£307** - FF3 353
  «Linda und Samuel» Photograph (30x42cm 11x16in) Berlin 2000

STREATOR Harold A. 1861-1926 **[6]**
- **$3 500** - €3 221 - **£2 100** - FF21 130
  Umbrellas, Figures on the Beach Oil/canvas (63x91cm 25x36in) Pasadena CA 1999

STREBEL Fritz 1920-1997 **[15]**
- **$1 186** - €1 274 - **£794** - FF8 355
  Das Paar Öl/Leinwand (81x101cm 31x39in) Zofingen 2000

STREBEL Richard 1861-? **[7]**
- **$1 418** - €1 380 - **£871** - FF9 055
  Kühe und Federvieh auf der Weide Öl/Leinwand (38x50cm 14x19in) Stuttgart 1999

STREBELLE Jean-Marie 1916-1989 **[34]**
- **$468** - €396 - **£280** - FF2 600
  Marine Fusain (92.5x71.5cm 36x28in) Liège 1998

STREBELLE Olivier 1927 **[14]**
- **$7 888** - €8 428 - **£5 372** - FF55 284
  The last of the sleepy ones III Bronze (50x105cm 19x41in) Lokeren 2001

STREBELLE Rodolphe 1880-1959 **[43]**
$1 020 - €992 - **£624** - FF6 504
L'embarquement au port de Brest, nature morte
Huile/panneau (54.5x64.5cm 21x25in) Bruxelles 1999
$4 408 - €4 710 - **£3 002** - FF30 894
Les quatre saisons Aquarelle, gouache/papier
(102.5x90cm 40x35in) Lokeren 2001

STRECKENBACH Max Theodor 1865-1936 **[32]**
$3 944 - €4 346 - **£2 632** - FF28 508
Weihnachtsstern in Vase Öl/Leinwand (60x73cm
23x28in) Satow 2000
$2 384 - €2 659 - **£1 609** - FF17 440
Blumenstück Öl/Leinwand (30.5x40.5cm 12x15in)
Oersberg-bei Kappeln 2000

STRECKER Emil 1841-1925 **[16]**
$2 052 - €2 035 - **£1 285** - FF13 347
Tiroler Bauer Öl/Leinwand (52.5x38.4cm 20x15in)
Wien 1999
$3 375 - €3 331 - **£2 080** - FF21 849
Essayage d'une alliance Oil/canvas (36.5x28cm
14x11in) Warszawa 1999

STRECKER Paul 1898-1950 **[30]**
$4 717 - €5 624 - **£3 363** - FF36 892
Printemps au Luxembourg Öl/Leinwand
(60.7x81.5cm 23x32in) Berlin 2000
$3 177 - €3 082 - **£2 000** - FF20 215
Lampe und Teekanne Oil/panel (24.5x11cm 9x4in)
London 1999
$310 - €307 - **£193** - FF2 012
Interieur Gouache/Karton (35x43.3cm 13x17in) Berlin
1999

STRECKER Wilhelm Friedrich 1795-1857 **[2]**
$5 072 - €5 916 - **£3 561** - FF38 806
Szene aus der griechischen Mythologie
Öl/Leinwand (69.5x57.5cm 27x22in) Luzern 2000

STREECK van Hendrick 1659-1719 **[5]**
$14 178 - €15 882 - **£9 852** - FF104 181
**View of the Oude Kerk, Amsterdam, loking
towards the Choir** Oil/canvas (47x63cm 18x24in)
Amsterdam 2001

STREECK van Juriaen 1632-1687 **[17]**
$32 222 - €32 648 - **£20 000** - FF210 224
**Still Life of fruits in a Porcelan Bowl, an Orange
segment, Knife** Oil/canvas (50x41.5cm 19x16in)
London 1999

STREEFKERK Carl August 1884-1968 **[16]**
$828 - **£767** - **£507** - FF5 030
Amsterdam Öl/Leinwand (40x80cm 15x31in)
Magdeburg 1999
$1 166 - €1 271 - **£803** - FF8 334
View on the Westertower Oil/canvas (40x30cm
15x11in) Amsterdam 2001

STREET Robert 1796-1865 **[21]**
$2 500 - €2 468 - **£1 520** - FF16 187
Portrait of a Lady Oil/canvas/board (76x63cm
30x25in) New-York 2000

STREETON Arthur Ernest 1867-1943 **[246]**
$25 713 - €28 264 - **£16 478** - FF185 398
Peter and the Blackwood Oil/canvas (48.5x59cm
19x23in) Melbourne 2000

$35 400 - €39 003 - **£23 766** - FF255 846
Afternoon, Cremorne Oil/panel (12x21.5cm 4x8in)
Malvern, Victoria 2000
$2 950 - €3 250 - **£1 980** - FF21 320
Design for an Exhibition of Pictures Ink
(32x17cm 12x6in) Malvern, Victoria 2000

STREICHMAN Yehezkel 1906-1993 **[162]**
$100 000 - €98 834 - **£61 200** - FF648 310
Untitled Oil/canvas (101x200.5cm 39x78in) Tel Aviv
2000
$29 000 - €23 820 - **£16 843** - FF156 249
Nude by a Window Oil/canvas (68x53cm 26x20in)
Tel Aviv 1998
$2 800 - €2 767 - **£1 713** - FF18 152
Landscape through the Window Mixed
media/paper (45.5x60.5cm 17x23in) Tel Aviv 2000

STREITT Franciszek 1839-1890 **[26]**
$15 905 - €16 452 - **£10 049** - FF107 919
Pris en flagrant délit Oil/canvas (127x94cm 50x37in)
Warszawa 2000
$7 585 - €7 645 - **£4 730** - FF50 151
En route Oil/panel (10.1x17.2cm 3x6in) Warszawa
2000

STRELOW Liselotte 1908-1981 **[16]**
$601 - €716 - **£429** - FF4 695
«Gottfried Benn, Kraft» Vintage gelatin silver print
(26.6x19cm 10x7in) Berlin 2000

STREMPEL Horst 1904-1975 **[39]**
$3 870 - €3 271 - **£2 316** - FF21 458
Stilleben Öl/Leinwand (48x69cm 18x27in) Berlin
1998
$314 - €358 - **£218** - FF2 347
Rathaus Charlottenburg Aquarell/Papier
(28.6x29.4cm 11x11in) Berlin 2000
$164 - €184 - **£114** - FF1 207
Paar mit Kind Etching, aquatint (19.9x30.2cm 7x11in)
Berlin 2001

STRENG Johan Joachim 1707-1763 **[1]**
$16 660 - €19 347 - **£11 707** - FF126 910
**Konung Adolf Fredrik och drottning Lovisa
Ulrika,after Gustaf Lundberg** Oil/canvas (98x78cm
38x30in) Stockholm 2001

STRESOR Henri ?-c.1679 **[1]**
$6 360 - €6 689 - **£4 200** - FF43 878
**Still Life of a game Birds including a teal, grey
partridge** Oil/canvas (44x64cm 17x25in) London 2000

STRETTI Viktor 1878-1957 **[36]**
$70 - €66 - **£44** - FF430
View of Charles Bridge Lithograph (30.5x38.5cm
12x15in) Praha 2000

STRETTI-ZAMPONI Jaromír 1882-1959 **[18]**
$138 - €131 - **£86** - FF860
Sans titre, marché rue Malostranska Aquatinte
(31.5x37.5cm 12x14in) Praha 2001

STRETTON Philip Eustace act.1884-c.1920 **[50]**
$17 096 - €19 875 - **£12 000** - FF130 372
Hiding from the Rain Oil/canvas (78x59cm 30x23in)
Billingshurst, West-Sussex 2001
$580 - €668 - **£400** - FF4 380
The Old Forge Watercolour/paper (43x50cm 17x20in)
Oxford 2000

S

STREULI Beat 1957 [9]

[📷] **$647 – €764 – £459 –** FF5 013
Ohne Titel Photograph in colors (19x28.5cm 7x11in)
Berlin 2001

STREVENS John 1902-1990 [99]

⌣ **$941 – €919 – £580 –** FF6 027
Picnic Party Oil/canvas (40.5x50.5cm 15x19in)
London 1999

⌣ **$479 – €462 – £300 –** FF3 030
Madeleine Oil/canvas (45.5x35cm 17x13in) London
1999

STRIBRNY Vladimir 1905 [15]

⌣ **$867 – €820 – £540 –** FF5 379
Weiblicher Halbakt Öl/Leinwand (46x35cm 18x13in)
Praha 2000

STRICCOLI Carlo 1897-1980 [8]

⌣ **$900 – €933 – £540 –** FF6 120
Ritratto femminile Olio/tavola (39x30cm 15x11in)
Napoli 1999

STRICH-CHAPELL Walter 1877-1960 [85]

⌣ **$1 546 – €1 431 – £959 –** FF9 390
Albfelsen nach Sonnenuntergang Öl/Karton
(80x100cm 31x39in) Stuttgart 1999

⌣ **$1 911 – €1 636 – £1 150 –** FF10 730
«**Landschaft mit Bergen**» Öl/Leinwand/Karton
(33x46cm 12x18in) Stuttgart 1998

✎ **$348 – €409 – £241 –** FF2 683
Schwäbische Landschaft Pastell/Papier (39x42cm
15x16in) Stuttgart 1999

▥ **$197 – €194 – £121 –** FF1 274
Ohne Titel Lithographie (40x53cm 15x20in) Stuttgart
1999

STRICK Pieter XVIII [2]

⌣ **$3 765 – €3 718 – £2 325 –** FF24 390
**Intérieur bourgeois animé d'un jeune homme
au déjeuner** Huile/panneau (26.3x19.8cm 10x7in)
Antwerpen 1999

STRICKER Fifo 1952 [2]

✎ **$2 726 – €2 505 – £1 674 –** FF16 431
Ohne Titel, surrealistische Komposition Crayons
couleurs (69x49cm 27x19in) Zürich 1999

STRIEP Cristiaan Jansz. 1634-1673 [3]

⌣ **$16 488 – €15 882 – £10 188 –** FF104 181
**Silver Gilt Cup-and-Cover, a Lemon and an
Orange in a Wan-li-dish** Oil/canvas (66x54cm
25x21in) Amsterdam 1999

STRINDBERG August 1849-1912 [31]

⌣ **$605 880 – €566 479 – £373 320 –** FF3 715 860
Vita Märrn II Oil/panel (60x47cm 23x18in) Stockholm
1999

⌣ **$79 110 – €76 320 – £50 000 –** FF500 625
Efter Solnedgång Under Oväder på Hafvet
Oil/canvas/board (12x25.5cm 4x10in) London 1999

⌣ **$3 024 – €2 556 – £1 798 –** FF16 767
Vollmond über den Schären Pastell/Papier
(15x20cm 5x7in) Lindau 1998

STRINDBERG Tore 1882-1968 [29]

⚒ **$435 – €418 – £264 –** FF2 742
Tvättaren Bronze (H26cm H10in) Stockholm 1999

STRINGER Francis c.1740-c.1790 [5]

⌣ **$82 500 – €95 852 – £57 981 –** FF628 749
**Samuel Frith with his Huntsman Jack Owen &
Hounds, Chapel-en-Le-Frith** Oil/canvas
(152.5x228.5cm 60x89in) New-York 2001

STRISIK Paul 1918 [30]

⌣ **$4 000 – €3 847 – £2 468 –** FF25 232
Bearskin Neck, Rockport Oil/canvas (61x76cm
24x29in) Boston MA 1999

⌣ **$2 600 – €2 839 – £1 673 –** FF18 625
Beals, Maine Oil/canvas (30x50cm 12x20in) Mystic
CT 2000

✎ **$1 100 – €1 066 – £681 –** FF6 995
Maine Coast Watercolour/paper (24x34cm 9x13in)
Mystic CT 1999

STRITSKI Christoph 1694-1753 [1]

◣ **$5 537 – €5 890 – £3 500 –** FF38 633
**Female Figure holding a caduceus/Further
Female allegorical Figure** Relief (79x98cm
31x38in) London 2000

STRØBEK Niels 1944 [5]

⌣ **$80 000 – €90 500 – £55 968 –** FF593 640
Barn, Amager Oil/canvas (165x190.5cm 64x75in)
New-York 2001

STROBEL Christian 1855-1899 [7]

⌣ **$2 163 – €2 556 – £1 533 –** FF18 769
Nürnberger Ansicht Oil/panel (11.4x15.6cm 4x6in)
München 2000

STROEBEL Johannes Anthonie B. 1821-1905 [84]

⌣ **$23 970 – €27 227 – £16 818 –** FF178 596
The last Will Oil/canvas (110x140cm 43x55in)
Amsterdam 2001

⌣ **$12 480 – €14 873 – £8 940 –** FF97 560
**Binnengezicht met figuren (figures dans un
intérieur)** Huile/panneau (54x42cm 21x16in)
Antwerpen 2000

⌣ **$2 388 – €2 269 – £1 453 –** FF14 883
Figuren in Oud-Hollands binnenhuis Oil/panel
(13x10.5cm 5x4in) Den Haag 1999

✎ **$542 – €499 – £335 –** FF3 274
A lace maker in a kitchen interior Watercolour
(25x19cm 9x7in) Amsterdam 1999

STRÖHLING Peter Eduard 1768-1826 [22]

⌣ **$49 929 – €50 308 – £31 119 –** FF330 000
Portrait de Lord Alexandre Thomas Cochrane
Huile/cuivre (61.5x48cm 24x18in) Paris 2000

STROHMAYER Antal Jozsef XIX [6]

⌣ **$3 208 – €3 270 – £2 007 –** FF21 451
**Grosses Blumen- und Früchtestilleben in
Nische** Öl/Leinwand (72x88cm 28x34in) Wien 2000

⌣ **$7 491 – €8 426 – £5 229 –** FF55 269
**Stilleben mit Trauben und auf Granatapfel sit-
zendem Sittich** Öl/Leinwand (28x34cm 11x13in)
Luzern 2001

STROHMAYER Hans ?-1610 [1]

▥ **$948 – €920 – £590 –** FF6 037
**Pegasus mit dem Globus zwischen seinen
Flügeln** Radierung (6.1x7.7cm 2x3in) Berlin 1999

STRÖMBERG Julia 1851-1920 [38]

⌣ **$542 – €538 – £329 –** FF3 526
Skaergård med fiskere Oil/canvas (65x94cm
25x37in) Vejle 2000

S

$429 - €476 - **£291** - FF3 122
Insjölandskap Oil/canvas (30x42cm 11x16in)
Stockholm 2000

STROMEYER Helene Marie 1834-1924 [13]

$1 660 - €1 841 - **£1 149** - FF12 074
«Blumenstück mit Vogel in Landschaft»
Öl/Leinwand (60.5x48cm 23x18in) Kempten 2001

STRÖMHOLM Christer 1918 [13]

$913 - €1 022 - **£636** - FF6 707
Zwei Jungen, Spanien Gelatin silver print
(27.5x21.5cm 10x8in) Köln 2001

STRØMME Olav 1909-1978 [51]

$1 763 - €1 957 - **£1 228** - FF12 836
Komposisjon Oil/panel (50x70cm 19x27in) Oslo
2001

$545 - €465 - **£325** - FF3 047
Landskap Oil/panel (16x22cm 6x8in) Oslo 1998

STRONG Elizabeth 1855-1941 [11]

$4 000 - €4 726 - **£2 834** - FF31 003
A girl and her Lamb Oil/canvas (54.5x40.5cm
21x15in) Boston MA 2000

STRONG Ray 1905 [18]

$1 300 - €1 395 - **£870** - FF9 153
Rocky coastal landscape Oil/board (40x67cm
16x26in) Altadena CA 2000

STROOBANT François 1819-1916 [29]

$8 700 - €7 432 - **£5 190** - FF48 750
Vue à Bruges Huile/toile (92x118cm 36x46in)
Antwerpen 1998

STROPPA Leonardo 1900-1991 [34]

$400 - €518 - **£300** - FF3 400
Donne al mercato Olio/tavola (50x35cm 19x13in)
Vercelli 2000

$220 - €285 - **£165** - FF1 870
Chiesa sotto la neve Tempera/cartone (28x39cm
11x15in) Vercelli 2001

$180 - €233 - **£135** - FF1 530
«Hamfasted Ponds, Londra» Tempera/carta
(35x45cm 13x17in) Vercelli 2000

STROUDLEY James 1906-1988 [80]

$1 203 - €1 212 - **£795** - FF7 952
Park Scene Oil/board (51x61cm 20x24in) London
2000

$882 - €889 - **£550** - FF5 832
Anemones, No.3 Oil/board (30x25cm 11x9in)
London 2000

STROZZI IL CAPPUCCINO Bernardo 1581-1644
[39]

$25 997 - €30 304 - **£18 000** - FF198 783
The Supper at Emmaus Oil/canvas (122.5x169cm
48x66in) London 2000

$46 400 - €60 126 - **£34 800** - FF394 400
Il concerto Olio/tela (82x98cm 32x38in) Roma 2000

$2 697 - €2 763 - **£1 664** - FF18 125
The Adoration Oil/canvas (41x22cm 16x9in)
Vancouver, BC. 2000

$7 842 - €7 658 - **£5 000** - FF50 230
**Studies of four hands and a Female
Head/Studies of Hands and Feet** Black chalk
(22x30cm 8x11in) London 1999

STRUBE Jan 1892-1985 [3]

$2 671 - €3 176 - **£1 904** - FF20 836
**«Don Quichotte en Sancho Panza of De nieuwe
fabrikant met z'n...»** Oil/canvas (108x86cm 42x33in)
Amsterdam 2000

STRÜBIN Robert 1897-1965 [33]

$990 - €998 - **£657** - FF6 544
7ème Symphonie de Tschaikowsky
Gouache/papier (58x47cm 22x18in) Zürich 2000

STRUCK Hermann 1876-1944 [296]

$8 500 - €9 436 - **£5 925** - FF61 895
Migdal Oil/canvas (62x76cm 24x29in) Tel Aviv 2001

$2 600 - €2 791 - **£1 739** - FF18 306
Jerusalem Oil/canvas/board (26x22cm 10x8in) Tel
Aviv 2000

$1 000 - €1 034 - **£631** - FF6 784
Landscape Pastel (15x21cm 5x8in) New-York 2000

$124 - €138 - **£86** - FF905
**Porträt des Schiftstellers Arno Holz im
Dreiviertelprofil nach rechts** Drypoint (21x15cm
8x5in) Heidelberg 2001

STRUDWICK John Melhuish 1849-1937 [14]

$264 100 - €309 648 - **£190 000** - FF2 031 157
The ten Virgins Oil/canvas (73.5x152.5cm 28x60in)
London 2001

$673 - €783 - **£480** - FF5 136
**Study of a Female Nude, thought to be a Study
for the Rampage** Pencil/paper (33x25.5cm 12x10in)
London 2001

$864 - €734 - **£521** - FF4 813
The music room Print (46x36cm 18x14in) London
1998

STRUPLER Hans Rudolf 1935 [35]

$460 - €520 - **£323** - FF3 408
Orientalische Zeichen Gouache/paper (32x34.5cm
12x13in) Bern 2001

STRUSS Karl 1886-1981 [93]

$8 000 - €8 319 - **£5 051** - FF54 566
Auverne, Low Tide Platinum print (11.5x9cm 4x3in)
New-York 2000

STRUTH Thomas 1954 [136]

$12 000 - €13 166 - **£7 971** - FF86 361
Daley Plaza Chicago Gelatin silver print (50x58.5cm
19x23in) New-York 2000

STRUTT Alfred William 1856-1924 [63]

$6 314 - €7 509 - **£4 500** - FF49 258
Chasing Rabbits Oil/canvas (45x61cm 17x24in)
London 2000

$1 575 - €1 500 - **£1 000** - FF9 837
«Pretty Pair» Watercolour (11x18cm 4x7in)
Billingshurst, West-Sussex 1998

STRUTT Arthur John 1819-1888 [20]

$15 000 - €15 587 - **£9 451** - FF102 247
**Panoramic Landscape of Tivoli, with Cattle and
Cliffs** Oil/canvas (96x175cm 38x69in) Brockton MA
2000

$4 207 - €3 946 - **£2 600** - FF25 881
Rest by a Well, The Roman Campagna Oil/canvas
(45x75cm 17x29in) London 1999

S

STRUTT Jacob George 1790-1864 [30]

$2 889 - €2 733 - £1 800 - FF17 927
Washerwomen Before a Watermill in a Swiss Village Oil/canvas (67x55cm 26x21in) London 1999

$4 491 - €4 526 - £2 800 - FF29 690
Château de Chillon Oil/paper (11.5x16.5cm 4x6in) London 2001

STRUTT William 1825-1915 [42]

$21 560 - €19 635 - £13 201 - FF128 800
The Milky Way Oil/canvas (46x61.5cm 18x24in) Malvern, Victoria 1999

$1 368 - €1 544 - £962 - FF10 125
Study of Woman's Head and Arms Pencil/paper (30x24.5cm 11x9in) Malvern, Victoria 2001

$2 124 - €2 340 - £1 426 - FF15 350
Opening of Prince's Bridge, Melbourne Engraving (33x39.5cm 12x15in) Malvern, Victoria 2000

STRÜTZEL Otto 1855-1930 [131]

$2 077 - €2 454 - £1 472 - FF16 098
Sommertag im bayerischen Voralpenland Öl/Karton (39x49cm 15x19in) Ahlden 2000

$1 511 - €1 431 - £919 - FF9 390
Bei Etzenhausen, Bäume am Bachufer Öl/Karton (29.5x39.5cm 11x15in) München 1999

$883 - €920 - £580 - FF6 037
Blick aud Bad Tölz mit Franziskanerkirche Watercolour (26x34cm 10x13in) München 2000

STRÜWE Carl 1898-1988 [43]

$428 - €511 - £305 - FF3 353
Spitzlicht an Diatomeen Photograph (39x29.5cm 15x11in) München 2000

STRÜWER Ardy 1939 [50]

$636 - €642 - £397 - FF4 209
Unbelievable Blue Oil/canvas (73x60cm 28x23in) Stockholm 2000

STRUYCKEN Peter 1939 [35]

$4 296 - €4 991 - £3 019 - FF32 742
Computerstructuur Mixed media (100x100cm 39x39in) Amsterdam 2001

$390 - €454 - £274 - FF2 976
Untitled Screenprint (52x52cm 20x20in) Amsterdam 2001

$4 687 - €5 445 - £3 294 - FF35 719
«T-492» Photograph (105x40.5cm 41x15in) Amsterdam 2001

STRUZAN Drew 1946 [95]

$3 000 - €3 220 - £2 007 - FF21 123
The Wolfman Acrylic (53x76cm 21x30in) Beverly-Hills CA 2000

$4 000 - €4 294 - £2 676 - FF28 164
E.T. the Extra-Terrestrial: Gertie (Drew Barrymore) kisses E.T goodbye Acrylic (27x30cm 11x12in) Beverly-Hills CA 2000

$710 - €820 - £500 - FF5 380
«Revenge of the Jedi» Poster (104x68.5cm 40x26in) London 2000

STRY van Abraham I 1753-1826 [21]

$8 762 - €9 715 - £6 083 - FF63 724
Hirten bei ihren Kühen vor den Ruinen einer Burg Öl/Leinwand (100x125cm 39x49in) Köln 2001

$11 277 - €11 217 - £7 000 - FF73 578
Amoretti playing with Garlands of Flowers around an Altar Oil/canvas (35x61cm 13x24in) London 1999

$1 510 - €1 452 - £930 - FF9 525
Study of a Cooper with a Metal Ring Ink (27.5x14.5cm 10x5in) Amsterdam 1999

STRY van Jacob 1756-1815 [66]

$92 042 - €77 997 - £55 000 - FF511 626
A Cutter of the Dutch East India Company and Two Men O'War Oil/canvas (177x283cm 69x111in) London 1998

$3 366 - €3 176 - £2 076 - FF20 836
Cowherds with Cattle on a River Bank, at Sunset Oil/panel (52.5x76cm 20x29in) Amsterdam 1999

$1 640 - €1 417 - £989 - FF9 296
A Man on the Ice, wearing a Basket on his Back, holding a Bundle Wash (52.5x37cm 20x14in) Amsterdam 1998

STRYBOS Jan XX [3]

$4 066 - €4 710 - £2 812 - FF30 894
Moutons dans un paysage Huile/panneau (71x104cm 27x40in) Bruxelles 2000

STRYDONCK van Guillaume 1861-1937 [59]

$903 - €1 041 - £625 - FF6 829
Fermette Huile/toile/panneau (45x65cm 17x25in) Bruxelles 2000

STRYJENSKA Zofia, née Lubanska 1894-1976 [32]

$3 333 - €3 738 - £2 263 - FF24 520
Fille portant une cruche Gouache/papier (50x31.5cm 19x12in) Warszawa 2000

STRYOWSKI August Wilhelm 1834-1917 [2]

$54 024 - €61 356 - £37 788 - FF402 468
Taschlich, Wassergebet der Juden am Neujahrsfest Öl/Leinwand (81x140cm 31x55in) Berlin 2001

STRZYGOWSKI Hertha 1896 [3]

$646 - €751 - £454 - FF4 929
Portrait d'homme Technique mixte/papier (49x39cm 19x15in) Kraków 2001

STUART Alexander Charles 1831-1898 [8]

$3 600 - €3 042 - £2 140 - FF19 957
Clipper Ship at Sea Oil/canvas (55x91cm 22x36in) Philadelphia PA 1998

STUART Charles act.1854-1904 [54]

$3 520 - €3 361 - £2 200 - FF22 044
Golden Sunset, Betws-y-Coed Oil/canvas (91.5x152.5cm 36x60in) London 1999

$1 514 - €1 309 - £900 - FF8 587
Grapes in a Basket Oil/canvas (35.5x45.5cm 13x17in) London 1998

$1 565 - €1 819 - £1 100 - FF11 933
Grapes, Whitecurrants, Raspberries, a Strawberry, an Apple Oil/canvas (30.5x40.5cm 12x15in) London 2000

STUART Ernest act.1889-1915 [58]

$585 - €534 - £360 - FF3 505
The Fifteen Metre Yacht «Mariska» on a Starboard Tack Watercolour/paper (51.5x36cm 20x14in) London 1998

S

STUART Gilbert 1755-1828 **[50]**
- $22 500 - €24 624 - £15 520 - FF161 523
  Portrait of a Gentleman Oil/panel (70.5x57cm 27x22in) New-York 2001

STUART J. XVIII-XIX **[1]**
- $5 214 - €6 050 - £3 600 - FF39 686
  Commencement of the Battle of the Nile, August 1/Conclusion of Battle Watercolour (23x44.5cm 9x17in) London 2000

STUART James Everett 1852-1941 **[48]**
- $1 100 - €1 251 - £768 - FF8 206
  Sunset Glow, Mount Pitt Oil/canvas (76x101cm 30x40in) Mystic CT 2000
- $550 - €587 - £374 - FF3 852
  Gov.Brady Glacier from Icy Straits, Alaska Oil/canvas (30x45cm 12x18in) Philadelphia PA 2001

STUART William act.1848-1867 **[7]**
- $45 418 - €43 620 - £28 000 - FF286 126
  The Battle of Trafalgar, 21 st October, 1805 Oil/canvas (101.5x183cm 39x72in) London 1999

STUART William E.D. act.1846-1858 **[6]**
- $2 568 - €2 975 - £1 776 - FF19 512
  Composition florale sur un entablement Huile/toile (61x92cm 24x36in) Bruxelles 2000

STUBBE Gaby XX **[2]**
- $1 070 - €1 248 - £750 - FF8 189
  Mandleve, elephant Pastel/paper (61.5x47cm 24x18in) London 2000

STUBBS George 1724-1806 **[60]**
- $3 038 480 - €2 925 873 - £1 900 000 - FF19 192 470
  Baron de Robeck riding a Bay Hunter Oil/canvas (101.5x127cm 39x50in) London 1999
- $514 197 - €447 209 - £310 000 - FF2 933 499
  Phaeton and the Chariot of the Sun Oil/copper (38.5x46cm 15x18in) London 1998
- $1 600 - €1 775 - £1 064 - FF11 642
  Tygers at Play Etching (38x48cm 14x18in) New-York 2000

STUBBS George Townley 1756-1815 **[32]**
- $2 100 - €2 443 - £1 500 - FF16 022
  Baronet with Sam Chifney up, Newmarket Watercolour/paper (39x49cm 15x19in) Norfolk 2001
- $1 407 - €1 510 - £960 - FF9 906
  The Famous Horse Johnny Engraving (29x35cm 11x13in) Swindon, Wiltshire 2001

STUBBS J. Woodhouse XIX-XX **[4]**
- $1 025 - €1 063 - £650 - FF6 970
  Hothouse Roses Watercolour/paper (36.5x54.5cm 14x21in) London 2000

STUBBS Ralph R. 1823-1879 **[24]**
- $1 180 - €1 322 - £820 - FF8 670
  Leaving Whitby Harbour Oil/paper (48x35cm 18x13in) Bury St. Edmunds, Suffolk 2001
- $718 - €838 - £500 - FF5 498
  «Near Bolton Abbey» Oil/board (25x22.5cm 9x8in) West-Yorshire 2000

STUBBS William Pierce 1842-1909 **[55]**
- $8 000 - €8 587 - £5 353 - FF56 328
  Depicting Ship «Mertle L.Perry» with Marblehead Mass Lighthouse Oil/canvas (55x91cm 22x36in) Thomaston ME 2000

- $2 600 - €3 056 - £1 883 - FF20 043
  Portrait of a sloop outside a Harbor Oil/canvas (25x44cm 10x17in) Bolton MA 2001

STUBENRAUCH Hans 1875-1941 **[36]**
- $187 - €179 - £119 - FF1 173
  Der verliebte Stammgast Pencil (28.5x30.5cm 11x12in) Zwiesel 1999

STUBER Dedrick Brandes 1878-1954 **[39]**
- $4 000 - €4 701 - £2 773 - FF30 837
  Mission Arches Oil/canvas (51x61cm 20x24in) Beverly-Hills CA 2001
- $2 200 - €2 586 - £1 525 - FF16 960
  Sunset Oil/board (22x30.5cm 8x12in) Beverly-Hills CA 2000

STUBLEY Trevor 1932 **[3]**
- $648 - €717 - £450 - FF4 703
  «Hocinfirth, Sunday» Gouache/paper (56.5x82cm 22x32in) London 2001

STUBLEY-BLACK Shaun 1962 **[2]**
- $3 895 - €3 744 - £2 400 - FF24 559
  Resting Hare Oil/board (60x73cm 23x28in) London 1999

STÜBNER Robert Emil 1874-1931 **[30]**
- $980 - €1 125 - £670 - FF7 378
  Gedeckter Kaffeetisch mit Seidenfransentuch und Blumenstrauss Öl/Karton (77x57cm 30x22in) Berlin 2000

STUCK von Franz 1863-1928 **[339]**
- $136 008 - €135 033 - £85 000 - FF885 759
  Nymphenraub (Abduction of a Nymph) Oil/canvas (155x104cm 61x40in) London 1999
- $22 836 - €26 074 - £16 100 - FF171 032
  Der Reigen Öl/Karton (43x53cm 16x20in) Bern 2001
- $6 437 - €7 211 - £4 472 - FF47 304
  The Reading Room Oil/canvas/board (24x27.5cm 9x10in) Johannesburg 2001
- $15 730 - €14 316 - £9 828 - FF93 909
  Feinde Ringsum Bronze (H71.5cm H28in) München 1999
- $2 638 - €2 965 - £1 852 - FF19 452
  Weiblicher Akt Charcoal/paper (45.5x29cm 17x11in) Düsseldorf 2001
- $400 - €415 - £240 - FF2 720
  Kampfende Faune Acquaforte (8.5x13.5cm 3x5in) Milano 2000

STÜCKELBERG Ernst 1831-1903 **[54]**
- $445 - €478 - £297 - FF3 133
  Küstenansicht mit Möven, die sich auf den Felsen sonnen Öl/Leinwand (32x41cm 12x16in) Zürich 2000

STUCKENBERG Fritz 1881-1944 **[19]**
- $5 256 - €4 600 - £3 183 - FF30 177
  «Golgotha» Öl/Leinwand (82x70cm 32x27in) Berlin 1998
- $3 152 - €3 579 - £2 190 - FF23 477
  «Rotes Klettern» Aquarell/Karton (26.5x24.5cm 10x9in) Berlin 2001

STÜCKGOLD Stanislaw 1868-1933 **[13]**
- $539 - €3 323 - £2 193 - FF21 800
  Krippenbild Öl/Leinwand (62.5x62.5cm 24x24in) München 1999

S

STUDD Arthur Haythorne 1863-1919 **[13]**
🖝 **$1 494** - €1 232 - **£920** - FF8 080
A Venetian Lyric Oil/panel (11x20cm 4x7in)
Newbury, Berkshire 1998

STUDDY George Ernest 1878-1925 **[18]**
✎ **$2 973** - €2 911 - **£1 900** - FF19 098
By the Light of the Moon Watercolour (33x23.5cm
12x9in) London 1999

STUDER Johann Rudolf 1700-1771 **[4]**
🖝 **$11 005** - €10 583 - **£6 791** - FF69 422
**Carl Ludwig von Erlach im Alter von zwölf
Jahren** Öl/Leinwand (49x39cm 19x15in) Bern 1999

STUEMPFIG Walter 1914-1970 **[30]**
🖝 **$1 900** - €1 627 - **£1 121** - FF10 674
Mother and Son Oil/canvas (92x76.5cm 36x30in)
New-York 1998
🖝 **$3 200** - €3 712 - **£2 276** - FF24 351
**Draped Table Top Still Life of a Chinese Export
Tea Bowl and Saucer** Oil/canvas (30.5x40.5cm
12x15in) Washington 2000

STUHLMÜLLER Karl 1859-1930 **[87]**
🖝 **$8 202** - €9 203 - **£5 686** - FF60 370
Dorfteich im Dachauer Land Öl/Karton (40x59.5cm
15x23in) München 2000
🖝 **$5 064** - €4 499 - **£3 101** - FF29 514
Kühe im Dachauer Moor Oil/panel (24x34cm
9x13in) Hamburg 1999

STUHR Johann Georg c.1640-1721 **[1]**
🖝 **$4 417** - €4 953 - **£3 060** - FF32 492
**Falconers at an Inn, a Windmill by a River
beyond** Oil/canvas (56x71cm 22x27in) London 2000

STULL Henry 1852-1913 **[45]**
🖝 **$11 500** - €11 418 - **£7 187** - FF74 894
«Brown Beauty» with Jockey Up Oil/canvas
(40.5x50.5cm 15x19in) New-York 1999
🖝 **$1 700** - €1 452 - **£1 020** - FF9 527
**A Couple of Two-Year-Olds Rattled by in their
Winding Up Gallop** Oil/canvas/board (20.5x35.5cm
8x13in) New-York 1998

STULTUS Dyalma 1901-1977 **[26]**
🖝 **$1 560** - €1 348 - **£1 046** - FF8 840
Venezia, barche in secca Olio/cartone/tela
(55x45cm 21x17in) Prato 1998

STUPAR Marko 1936 **[28]**
🖝 **$6 284** - €6 098 - **£3 988** - FF40 000
Intérieur Huile/toile (65x53cm 25x20in) Paris 1999
🖝 **$779** - €717 - **£478** - FF4 700
Paris Huile/toile (33x41cm 12x16in) Bordeaux 1999
✎ **$1 500** - €1 524 - **£943** - FF10 000
Au café Aquarelle, gouache/papier (48x63cm 18x24in)
Lyon 2000

STURGEON E.R. 1920 **[4]**
✎ **$5 154** - €4 844 - **£3 200** - FF31 773
A quiet Afternoon in Bath Watercolour/paper
(47x63cm 18x24in) Salisbury, Wiltshire 1999

STURGES Jock 1947 **[103]**
📷 **$1 300** - €1 497 - **£887** - FF9 838
Vanessa, Montavilet, France Gelatin silver print
(37.5x47.5cm 14x18in) New-York 2000

STURGESS Reginald Ward 1892-1932 **[38]**
✎ **$894** - €860 - **£551** - FF5 644
Twin Gums Watercolour/paper (17x18.5cm 6x7in)
Melbourne 1999

STURLA Michel 1895-1936 **[11]**
🖝 **$1 165** - €1 372 - **£819** - FF9 000
La porte ouverte Huile/toile (38x55cm 14x21in)
Paris 2000

STURM Fritz Ludwig Ch. 1834-1906 **[6]**
🖝 **$5 043** - €5 624 - **£3 391** - FF36 892
Ziegelei an der Warnow Öl/Leinwand (79x130cm
31x51in) Satow 2000

STURM George 1855-1923 **[4]**
🖝 **$590** - €613 - **£372** - FF4 024
Holländische Hafenstadt Öl/Leinwand (55x75cm
21x29in) Merzhausen 2000

STURM Helmut 1932 **[100]**
🖝 **$1 801** - €2 045 - **£1 251** - FF13 415
Komposition Acrylic (57.5x69.5cm 22x27in)
München 2001
🖝 **$1 135** - €1 058 - **£686** - FF6 942
Komposition Gouache (41x30.5cm 16x12in)
München 1999

STURM-SKRALA Egge, Eugen 1894-1943 **[18]**
▥ **$1 211** - €1 308 - **£837** - FF8 580
**«Neue Vereinigung Malerei-Graphik-Plastik -
1.Ausstellung»** Poster (84x52cm 33x20in) Wien 2001

STURROCK Mary Newbery XX **[9]**
✎ **$256** - €237 - **£160** - FF1 556
Mullein and Evening Primrose Watercolour
(37x24cm 14x9in) Edinburgh 1999

STURSA Jan 1880-1925 **[81]**
◈ **$1 156** - €1 093 - **£720** - FF7 172
Head of a Girl Bronze (H22.5cm H8in) Praha 1999
✎ **$289** - €273 - **£180** - FF1 793
Female Nude standing, seen from the Back
Pencil/paper (33x25cm 12x9in) Praha 2000

STURTEVANT Elaine 1926 **[17]**
🖝 **$35 000** - €40 610 - **£24 164** - FF266 385
John's Flag Mixed media/canvas (122x142cm
48x55in) New-York 2000
🖝 **$3 154** - €2 897 - **£1 955** - FF19 000
Study for Warhol's Marilyn Monroe Acrylique
(41x34cm 16x13in) Paris 1999
✎ **$2 489** - €2 940 - **£1 767** - FF19 284
«Lichtenstein Study for Bull II» Collage
(67.5x86cm 26x33in) Berlin 2001

STURTEVANT Helena 1872-1943 **[12]**
🖝 **$1 600** - €1 596 - **£998** - FF10 469
Second Beach, Newport Oil/canvas (63x101cm
25x40in) Dedham MA 1999

STURZENEGGER Hans 1875-1943 **[35]**
🖝 **$1 803** - €1 990 - **£1 192** - FF13 052
Vorfrühlingslandschaft Öl/Leinwand (35x50cm
13x19in) St. Gallen 2000
🖝 **$1 516** - €1 500 - **£945** - FF9 838
Auf Boden sitzende Chinesin Öl/Leinwand
(47x34cm 18x13in) St. Gallen 1999

STUTTERHEIM Louis, Lodewijk Ph. 1873-1943 **[57]**
- **$1 443** - €1 361 - **£894** - FF8 929
  Woman by a River Oil/canvas (50.5x50cm 19x19in) Amsterdam 1999
- **$549** - €590 - **£367** - FF3 869
  Spring: a blossoming fruit tree on a sunlit farmyard Oil/board (30x40cm 11x15in) Amsterdam 2000

STÜTZER Alwin 1889-1974 **[12]**
- **$1 903** - €1 647 - **£1 155** - FF10 806
  Sommerlandschaft Oil/panel (50.3x70.3cm 19x27in) München 1998
- **$1 341** - €1 278 - **£850** - FF8 384
  Stilleben mit Geranie und Buch Öl/Karton (43.5x35cm 17x14in) Zwiesel 1999

STUVEN Ernst 1657-1712 **[37]**
- **$10 528** - €11 628 - **£7 296** - FF76 272
  Weintrauben, Pfirsiche und eine Birne auf einem Zinnteller Öl/Leinwand (48x40cm 18x15in) Wien 2001
- **$7 696** - €8 622 - **£5 348** - FF56 555
  Peaches, Apricots and Grapes on a marble Ledge Oil/panel (33.5x28cm 13x11in) Amsterdam 2001

STUYVER J. XIX **[1]**
- **$5 021** - €4 680 - **£3 034** - FF30 696
  Javanese Dancer and Orchestra Oil/canvas (70x100cm 27x39in) Singapore 1999

STYKA Adam 1890-1959 **[124]**
- **$13 037** - €11 247 - **£7 865** - FF73 777
  Wielblady u wodopoju Oil/canvas (60.4x73.5cm 23x28in) München 1998
- **$1 548** - €1 448 - **£937** - FF9 500
  A Gofsa le soir Huile/isorel (23x19cm 9x7in) Poitiers 1999

STYKA Jan 1858-1925 **[40]**
- **$9 500** - €10 443 - **£6 087** - FF68 501
  Portrait of a Courtly Lady Oil/canvas (211x150cm 83x59in) New-York 2000
- **$5 016** - €4 984 - **£3 124** - FF32 690
  Portrait d'une petite fille Oil/canvas (140x84cm 55x33in) Warszawa 1999
- **$5 872** - €5 919 - **£3 662** - FF38 827
  Violoniste Coloured pencils (58.5x46cm 23x18in) Warszawa 2000

STYKA Tadé 1889-1954 **[26]**
- **$15 100** - €16 209 - **£10 104** - FF106 326
  Nuit dans la forêt vierge Huile/toile (132x97.5cm 51x38in) Warszawa 2000
- **$4 333** - €3 712 - **£2 605** - FF24 352
  Portrait d'une femme blonde Oil/panel (61.3x49cm 24x19in) Warszawa 2000

STYRSKY Jindrich 1899-1942 **[8]**
- **$4 654** - €4 650 - **£2 909** - FF30 500
  L'Oeil Omniprésent Dessin (27x28cm 10x11in) Paris 1999
- **$1 300** - €1 481 - **£898** - FF9 714
  Swan Silver print (8x8cm 3x3in) New-York 2000

SU AN Su (Yun) An **[1]**
- **$6 077** - €5 852 - **£3 800** - FF38 384
  Nocturnal Scene with a Figure standing among Pine on a Riverbank Ink (95x36cm 37x14in) London 1999

SU LIUPENG 1814-1860 **[9]**
- **$4 454** - €3 762 - **£2 673** - FF24 677
  Meng Shangjun Burning Leases Ink (30.5x46cm 12x18in) Hong-Kong 1998

SUAN YUNTAI 1913 **[5]**
- **$7 625** - €6 403 - **£4 475** - FF42 000
  Blossom Oil/canvas (53x60.5cm 20x23in) Taipei 1998

SUANDI Gusti Ketut 1932 **[7]**
- **$3 839** - €3 578 - **£2 320** - FF23 473
  Preparation Oil/canvas (80.5x120cm 31x47in) Singapore 1999

SUARDI Bartolomeo c.1465-1530 **[1]**
- **$20 000** - €21 394 - **£13 636** - FF140 334
  The desosition of Christ Tempera/panel (157.5x102cm 62x40in) New-York 2001

SUAREZ Antonio Martínez 1923 **[74]**
- **$1 440** - €1 351 - **£900** - FF8 865
  Composición Técnica mixta (49.5x64.5cm 19x25in) Madrid 1999
- **$541** - €571 - **£361** - FF3 743
  Sin título Oleo/papel (14.5x19.5cm 5x7in) Madrid 2000
- **$435** - €450 - **£277** - FF2 955
  Bodegón Acuarela/papel (24.5x17cm 9x6in) Madrid 2000

SUBANI Rahmat 1949 **[4]**
- **$3 038** - €3 181 - **£1 908** - FF20 867
  Fighting Spirit Oil/canvas (115x85cm 45x33in) Singapore 2000

SUBIRACHS Josep Maria 1927 **[69]**
- **$1 040** - €961 - **£640** - FF6 304
  Communication Sculpture verre (23x31.5x6cm 9x12x2in) Madrid 1999
- **$140** - €156 - **£96** - FF1 024
  El Genio Litografía (72x52cm 28x20in) Barcelona 2001

SUBLEYRAS Pierre Hubert 1699-1749 **[21]**
- **$650 000** - €572 087 - **£395 720** - FF3 752 645
  Young Boy in Hungarian Dress Oil/canvas (119.5x90cm 47x35in) New-York 1999
- **$52 640** - €48 784 - **£32 736** - FF320 000
  La courtisane amoureuse Sanguine/papier (31x22.5cm 12x8in) Paris 1999

SUBRAMANYAN K.G. 1924 **[6]**
- **$2 750** - €3 127 - **£1 921** - FF20 515
  Sisters with Cat Gouache (61x59.5cm 24x23in) New-York 2000

SUBUIRA PUIG José 1926 **[12]**
- **$1 429** - €1 601 - **£993** - FF10 500
  Noctule Sculpture bois (64x36x33cm 25x14x12in) Paris 2001

SUCASAS GUERRA Alfonso 1940 **[19]**
- **$1 458** - €1 622 - **£972** - FF10 638
  Pans Perto Oleo/lienzo (100x81cm 39x31in) Madrid 2000
- **$2 860** - €3 304 - **£1 980** - FF21 670
  Os vecinos da xesta Oleo/lienzo (30x46cm 11x18in) Madrid 2000
- **$344** - €390 - **£234** - FF2 561
  Hombre con sombrero Acuarela (24.5x17cm 9x6in) Madrid 2000

S

SUCH William Thomas 1820-1893 **[9]**
- **$5 194** - €5 827 - **£3 600** - FF38 224
  **Winter Walk, a Man and his Dog before a
  Church and a Cottage** Oil/canvas (62x75cm
  24x29in) Penrith, Cumbria 2000

SUCHAO SISGANES 1926-1986 **[13]**
- **$10 680** - €9 921 - **£6 600** - FF65 080
  Hay Stacks Oil/canvas (60x59cm 23x23in) Bangkok
  1999
- **$7 476** - €6 945 - **£4 620** - FF45 556
  Stranger in the City Oil/board (23x19cm 9x7in)
  Bangkok 1999

SUCHET Joseph 1824-1896 **[17]**
- **$6 246** - €7 165 - **£4 272** - FF47 000
  Pêcheurs relevant les filets au clair de lune
  Huile/toile (53x85.5cm 20x33in) Pau 2000

SUCHODOLSKI January 1797-1875 **[20]**
- **$5 992** - €7 042 - **£4 155** - FF46 194
  Grenadier Huile/toile (72x56cm 28x22in) Warszawa
  2000

SUCHY Adalbert c.1773-1849 **[12]**
- **$1 490** - €1 448 - **£932** - FF9 500
  **L'Empereur Ferdinand d'Autriche en grande
  tenue d'officier** Miniature (8.6x6.7cm 3x2in) Paris
  1999

SUCRE DE GRAU José María 1886-1969 **[17]**
- **$213** - €210 - **£136** - FF1 379
  Rostre Crayon gras/papier (16x10cm 6x3in) Barcelona
  1999

SUDA Kunitaro 1891-1961 **[3]**
- **$45 000** - €44 647 - **£29 763** - FF325 660
  Flowers (Kusabana) Oil/canvas (37.5x45cm
  14x17in) New-York 2000

SUDARSONO Srihadi 1931 **[27]**
- **$11 103** - €11 623 - **£6 974** - FF76 245
  Ekspresi Legong Oil/canvas (100x130cm 39x51in)
  Singapore 2000
- **$8 608** - €9 775 - **£5 892** - FF64 119
  Penari (Dancer) Oil/canvas (100x84cm 39x33in)
  Singapore 2000

SUDDABY Rowland 1912-1973 **[192]**
- **$1 514** - €1 264 - **£900** - FF8 294
  The Estuary, Manningtree, Essex Oil/canvas
  (36x51cm 14x20in) London 1998
- **$1 046** - €1 123 - **£700** - FF7 369
  Stormy Day Oil/board (32.5x42.5cm 12x16in) London
  2000
- **$656** - €603 - **£400** - FF3 956
  The Pool, Cornard, Suffolk Watercolour,
  gouache/paper (37x53cm 14x20in) London 1998

SUDEIKIN Sergei Iurevich 1882-1946 **[35]**
- **$48 312** - €45 618 - **£30 000** - FF299 235
  Masquerade Oil/canvas (136x107cm 53x42in)
  London 1999
- **$4 184** - €4 491 - **£2 800** - FF29 460
  Marseilles Cabaret Oil/canvas/board (34.5x28cm
  13x11in) London 2000

SUDEK Josef 1896-1976 **[488]**
- **$3 000** - €2 802 - **£1 813** - FF18 381
  Untitled, Panoramic Landscape Silver print
  (8x28cm 3x11in) New-York 1999

SUDJOJONO Sindutomo 1913-1986 **[48]**
- **$15 438** - €12 953 - **£9 058** - FF84 968
  Landscape Oil/canvas (100x150cm 39x59in)
  Singapore 1998
- **$12 119** - €11 294 - **£7 478** - FF74 081
  Landscape Oil/canvas (49x96cm 19x37in) Singapore
  1999

SUDKOVSKI Rufin Gavrilovich 1850-1885 **[8]**
- **$3 246** - €3 120 - **£2 000** - FF20 466
  Repairing the Nets Oil/canvas (58x88cm 22x34in)
  London 1999

SUDRE Jean-Pierre 1921-1997 **[15]**
- **$1 362** - €1 524 - **£924** - FF10 000
  «Merville», nature morte aux fraises Tirage argentique (40x30.5cm 15x12in) Paris 2000

SÜE Louis 1875-1968 **[30]**
- **$2 301** - €2 592 - **£1 603** - FF17 000
  Le châle rouge Huile/toile (32.5x24.5cm 12x9in)
  Paris 2001
- **$17 952** - €16 769 - **£11 077** - FF110 000
  **Paire de vasques à corps galbé en godrons
  renflés** Plâtre (H230cm H90in) Paris 1999

SUETIN Nikolai 1897-1954 **[18]**
- **$5 051** - €4 857 - **£3 116** - FF31 862
  Holzfäller mit Frau Gouache/Karton (40.2x29cm
  15x11in) Köln 1999

SUGAI Kumi 1919-1996 **[302]**
- **$40 000** - €46 412 - **£27 616** - FF304 440
  Ko-Oni Oil/canvas (124x97cm 48x38in) New-York
  2000
- **$7 516** - €8 842 - **£5 388** - FF58 000
  La vitesse du vent Acrylique/toile (78x57cm
  30x22in) Versailles 2001
- **$3 839** - €3 835 - **£2 400** - FF25 157
  Composition Oil/canvas (10x17cm 3x6in) London
  1999
- **$2 874** - €2 897 - **£1 791** - FF19 000
  Sans titre Gouache/papier (18.5x18cm 7x7in) Paris
  1999
- **$642** - €536 - **£380** - FF3 519
  Komposition in Blaugrün Farblithographie
  (64.5x44.5cm 25x17in) Hamburg 1998

SUGARMAN George 1912 **[3]**
- **$1 792** - €2 094 - **£1 279** - FF13 738
  Black and White Collage (136.5x70cm 53x27in)
  Zürich 2001

SUGHI Alberto 1928 **[134]**
- **$5 800** - €7 516 - **£4 350** - FF49 300
  «Uuomo che si veste» Olio/tela (120x140cm
  47x55in) Vercelli 2001
- **$4 830** - €4 173 - **£3 220** - FF27 370
  L'Ingresso dalla villa Olio/tela (85x120cm 33x47in)
  Milano 1998
- **$1 600** - €1 659 - **£960** - FF10 880
  Volto femminile Olio/tela (33x23cm 12x9in) Roma
  2000
- **$1 750** - €1 814 - **£1 050** - FF11 900
  Volto femminile Tecnica mista/carta (47.5x33cm
  18x12in) Torino 2001
- **$225** - €233 - **£135** - FF1 530
  Al bar Stampa (80x60cm 31x23in) Vercelli 1999

SUGIMOTO Hiroshi 1948 [108]

📬 **$2 000** - €2 147 - **£1 358** - FF14 081
Time Exposed Print (24x31cm 9x12in) Beverly-Hills CA 2001

📷 **$11 422** - €9 537 - **£6 700** - FF62 558
Tyrrhenian Sea Photograph (47x60.5cm 18x23in) London 1998

SUHARSO Chris 1931 [6]

🖌 **$2 220** - €2 325 - **£1 395** - FF15 249
Pasar Antik Oil/canvas (80x60cm 31x23in) Singapore 2000

🖌 **$3 839** - €3 578 - **£2 320** - FF23 473
Tropical Fruits in abundance Watercolour/paper (52x65cm 20x25in) Singapore 1999

SUHR Irene 1965 [2]

🖌 **$3 400** - €3 606 - **£2 305** - FF23 654
Rust Blue IV Mixed media (150x66x5cm 59x25x1in) Tel Aviv 2001

SUHRLAND Johann Heinrich 1742-1827 [2]

🖌 **$16 104** - €16 873 - **£10 652** - FF110 678
Die drei Söhne des Künstlers bei Früchten, Gemüse und Spankorb Öl/Leinwand (68x87cm 26x34in) München 2000

SUHRLANDT Carl 1828-1919 [16]

🖌 **$1 391** - €1 514 - **£917** - FF9 928
Vinthund Oil/canvas (40.5x32.5cm 15x12in) Helsinki 2000

SUHRLANDT Rudolf 1781-1862 [6]

🖌 **$13 685** - €14 187 - **£8 211** - FF93 058
Amore che scocca un dardo Olio/tela (82x64cm 32x25in) Roma 1999

🖌 **$1 705** - €1 615 - **£1 060** - FF10 592
Portraet af billedhuggeren Bertel Thorvaldsen Gouache/paper (28x21cm 11x8in) Köbenhavn 1999

SUISEKI XIX-XX [1]

🖌 **$2 000** - €1 923 - **£1 247** - FF12 611
Lion on a Cliff Ink (94x116cm 37x45in) New-York 1999

SUISSE Gaston 1896-1988 [187]

🖌 **$7 515** - €8 537 - **£5 258** - FF56 000
Écureuils de Malaisie Huile/panneau (68x47.5cm 26x18in) Neuilly-sur-Seine 2001

🖌 **$1 767** - €1 753 - **£1 099** - FF11 500
Épervier, rapace têtes sur main ganté Crayon (28x30cm 11x11in) Paris 1999

📬 **$1 075** - €1 067 - **£669** - FF7 000
Panthère noire parmi les bambous Gravure (18.5x40cm 7x15in) Paris 1999

SUJARIT HIRANKUL 1946-1982 [4]

🖌 **$6 375** - €6 856 - **£4 275** - FF44 975
The Mangrove Oil/canvas (52x87cm 20x34in) Bangkok 2000

SUKEFUSA Fujiwara XVIII [1]

🖌 **$1 600** - €1 647 - **£1 008** - FF10 803
Scenes of Landscape Ink (26.5x1020cm 10x401in) New-York 2000

SUKENOBU Nishikawa 1671-1751 [9]

🖌 **$22 000** - €25 799 - **£15 699** - FF169 232
Erotic Scenes of Courtesans and Clients Ink (25x52.5cm 9x20in) New-York 2000

SUKER Arthur 1857-? [122]

🖌 **$345** - €387 - **£240** - FF2 537
Coastal Landscape Watercolour/paper (37.5x58.5cm 14x23in) London 2001

SUKHODOLSKY Pyotr Alexandrovich 1835-1903 [6]

🖌 **$14 943** - €16 040 - **£10 000** - FF105 216
Surrender of the Turkish Fortress to Russian Forces Oil/canvas/board (104x151cm 40x59in) London 2001

🖌 **$4 509** - €4 258 - **£2 800** - FF27 928
Children playing by the River Oil/canvas (64.5x94cm 25x37in) London 1999

SUKKERT Adolf c.1830-c.1870 [8]

🖌 **$6 923** - €8 181 - **£4 907** - FF53 662
Winterlandschaft Öl/Leinwand (79x111.5cm 31x43in) Ahlden 2000

SULLIVAN Edmund Joseph 1869-1933 [13]

🖌 **$142** - €165 - **£100** - FF1 084
Man Carrying a Young Woman down a flight of Steps Crayon (37.5x27.5cm 14x10in) London 2001

SULLIVAN Luke 1705-1771 [20]

📬 **$71** - €82 - **£48** - FF536
The March to Finchley, nach William Hogarth Radierung (44x56cm 17x22in) Heidelberg 2000

SULLIVAN William Holmes ?-1908 [18]

🖌 **$2 400** - €2 782 - **£1 700** - FF18 252
Men Were Deceivers Ever Oil/canvas (46x30.5cm 18x12in) New-York 2000

🖌 **$4 208** - €3 950 - **£2 600** - FF25 910
A Father and Son off Fishing Watercolour/paper (51x37.5cm 20x14in) London 1999

SULLIVANT Thomas Starling 1854-1926 [9]

🖌 **$3 000** - €2 777 - **£1 836** - FF18 218
Lion strolling past admiring animals, for Life Magazine Ink/paper (27x41cm 11x16in) New-York 1999

SULLY Thomas 1783-1872 [82]

🖌 **$13 000** - €13 475 - **£8 243** - FF88 392
Portrait of Don Juan Didios Sebastian de Kanedo E Samarano De La Vega Oil/canvas (76x63.5cm 29x25in) New-York 2000

🖌 **$3 600** - €3 845 - **£2 453** - FF25 219
Middy - An American Naval Academy Midshipma at his Leisure Watercolour/paper (20x14cm 8x5in) New-Orleans LA 2001

SULTAN Donald 1951 [268]

🖌 **$25 000** - €29 007 - **£17 260** - FF190 275
Gladiolas in a Chinese Pot, April 2 Mixed media (244x244cm 96x96in) New-York 2000

🖌 **$11 000** - €12 299 - **£7 415** - FF78 678
Yellow Roses June 14 Mixed media (33x31.5x4.5cm 12x12x1in) New-York 2000

🖌 **$6 000** - €6 046 - **£3 740** - FF39 660
Lemon and Eggs, August 31 Charcoal/paper (152.5x122cm 60x48in) New-York 2000

📬 **$1 700** - €1 865 - **£1 097** - FF12 236
Still Life with Peach Screenprint in colors (30.5x30.5cm 12x12in) New-York 2000

S

SUMERE van Hilde 1932 [6]

🖼 **$6 468** - €5 457 - **£3 850** - FF35 794
  Sacara Marbre Carrare (59x69cm 23x27in) Antwerpen 1998

SUMIO Goto 1930 [3]

✏ **$25 480** - €24 852 - **£15 600** - FF163 020
  Yamato in Snow Drawing (41x53cm 16x20in) Tokyo 1999

SUMMERS Carol 1925 [64]

▥ **$600** - €576 - **£371** - FF3 779
  Palazzo Malatesta, Rimini Woodcut in colors (92x94cm 36x37in) New-York 1999

SUMMERS Robert 1940 [16]

🖼 **$3 500** - €3 974 - **£2 431** - FF26 068
  Ripples of Time Oil/canvas (45x66cm 18x26in) Dallas TX 2001

SUMMERS William XIX [3]

▥ **$158** - €186 - **£113** - FF1 219
  Fox-Hunting d'après John Sturgess Gravure (70x126cm 27x49in) Bruxelles 2000

SUMNER Alan Robert 1911-1994 [21]

🖼 **$5 149** - €4 448 - **£3 110** - FF29 176
  «Bridge at Seaford» Oil/board (40x48cm 15x18in) Malvern, Victoria 1998

▥ **$102** - €113 - **£68** - FF741
  Timber Yard Serigraph in colors (38x46cm 14x18in) Melbourne 2000

SUMNER Maud Eyston 1902-1985 [151]

🖼 **$6 809** - €7 627 - **£4 730** - FF50 033
  The Mandolin Oil/canvas (52.5x71cm 20x27in) Johannesburg 2001

🖼 **$2 378** - €2 668 - **£1 664** - FF17 502
  Still life with Apples Oil/board (21x37cm 8x14in) Cape Town 2001

✏ **$990** - €1 109 - **£688** - FF7 277
  Near Eathorpe Estate, England Watercolour (46.5x61cm 18x24in) Johannesburg 2001

SUN JIAPEI 1958 [1]

🖼 **$10 939** - €10 381 - **£6 647** - FF68 093
  Canal in the Morning Sunshine Oil/canvas (50x65cm 19x25in) Hong-Kong 1999

SUN LUO 1962 [2]

🖼 **$14 124** - €15 500 - **£9 097** - FF101 673
  Journey to the South Oil/canvas (159x140cm 62x55in) Hong-Kong 2000

SUN WEN 1866-1925 [1]

✏ **$17 948** - €21 095 - **£12 446** - FF138 376
  Calligraphy Ink/paper (31.5x90cm 12x35in) Hong-Kong 2000

SUNAMI Soichi XX [2]

📷 **$3 400** - €3 739 - **£2 357** - FF24 527
  Martha Graham and her Dance Troupe performing «Heretic» Silver print (17x23cm 7x9in) New-York 2001

SUNARYO 1943 [5]

🖼 **$8 204** - €8 266 - **£5 114** - FF54 224
  Barong Acrylic/canvas (100x100cm 39x39in) Singapore 2000

SUNDARAM Vivan 1939 [3]

✏ **$1 653** - €1 547 - **£1 000** - FF10 147
  Untitled Pastel (70.5x100cm 27x39in) London 1999

SUNDBERG Christine 1837-1892 [7]

🖼 **$4 317** - €4 912 - **£3 015** - FF32 218
  Flicka med kanna Oil/canvas (55x45cm 21x17in) Stockholm 2000

🖼 **$2 425** - €2 541 - **£1 535** - FF16 665
  Drömmar vid fönstret Oil/board (33x24cm 12x9in) Malmö 2000

SUNDBLOM Haddon Hubbard 1899-1976 [21]

🖼 **$6 000** - €6 720 - **£4 168** - FF44 083
  Magazine Cover, Boy and Grandfather at the Florist's Oil/canvas (91x73cm 36x29in) New-York 2001

🖼 **$4 750** - €5 537 - **£3 288** - FF36 320
  People Outdoors Enjoying Beer and Puppies Oil/board (41x37cm 16x14in) New-York 2000

SUNDELL Thure 1864-1924 [20]

🖼 **$3 586** - €3 364 - **£2 216** - FF22 064
  Skogssjö Oil/canvas (45.5x76cm 17x29in) Helsinki 1999

🖼 **$1 802** - €2 018 - **£1 251** - FF13 238
  Kväll Oil/canvas (23x30cm 9x11in) Helsinki 2001

SUNDERLAND Thomas 1744-1828 [24]

✏ **$732** - €646 - **£450** - FF4 239
  Stybarrow Crag, Ullswater Wash (24x33cm 9x12in) Godalming, Surrey 1999

SUNDMAN Tommy G. 1952 [5]

🖼 **$720** - €689 - **£453** - FF4 518
  Chateau Margaux Oil/canvas (40x30cm 15x11in) Stockholm 1999

SUNDT-HANSEN Carl Frederik 1841-1907 [10]

🖼 **$415** - €403 - **£256** - FF2 646
  En norsk fjeldstue med siddende kvinde i döråbning Oil/canvas (34x47.5cm 13x18in) Vejle 1999

🖼 **$16 653** - €19 812 - **£11 518** - FF129 955
  Gåsepiken Oil/canvas (40x33cm 15x12in) Oslo 2000

SUNESSON Stina 1925-1999 [26]

✏ **$1 976** - €1 723 - **£1 195** - FF11 305
  «Kyrkbyn» Gouache/paper (20x24cm 7x9in) Stockholm 1998

SUÑOL MUÑOZ RAMOS Alvar 1935 [130]

🖼 **$3 253** - €3 125 - **£2 017** - FF20 500
  Composition Huile/toile (65x81cm 25x31in) Arles 1999

🖼 **$1 584** - €1 442 - **£960** - FF9 456
  Toreros Oleo/lienzo (35x27cm 13x10in) Barcelona 1999

✏ **$897** - €991 - **£622** - FF6 500
  Figures de femmes et colombe Technique mixte/papier (71x54cm 27x21in) Paris 2001

▥ **$200** - €232 - **£142** - FF1 522
  Matador Lithograph (39x53cm 15x21in) Chicago IL 2000

SUNQUA XIX [3]

✏ **$3 167** - €3 294 - **£2 000** - FF21 066
  Album of Chinese subjects: portraits, still lifes, studies Bodycolour (32x23cm 12x9in) London 2000

SUNYER MIRO Joaquín 1875-1956 [111]

🖼 **$24 500** - €21 076 - **£14 350** - FF138 250
  Niños con corderitos Oleo/lienzo (100x80cm 39x31in) Madrid 1998

🖼 **$3 203** - €2 973 - **£1 998** - FF19 500
Venise, soleil couchant Huile/carton (19x27cm 7x10in) Deauville 1999

🖼 **$2 720** - €2 403 - **£1 680** - FF15 760
La toilette Dibujo (23x16cm 9x6in) Madrid 1999

🖼 **$336** - €360 - **£228** - FF2 364
Paisaje Grabado (24x30cm 9x11in) Barcelona 2001

SUNYOL Tomás 1964 [49]

🖼 **$216** - €240 - **£148** - FF1 576
«Cadaqués» Oleo/lienzo (60x73cm 23x28in) Barcelona 2001

SUOMALAINEN Kari 1920-1999 [3]

🖼 **$400** - €471 - **£277** - FF3 089
Fördelning av budgetmedel Watercolour (28x40cm 11x15in) Helsinki 2000

SUOMI Resto 1951 [3]

🖼 **$2 233** - €2 186 - **£1 374** - FF14 341
Nimetön Gouache/papier (139x103.5cm 54x40in) Helsinki 1999

SUPERMAN L. XX [2]

🖼 **$2 633** - €2 454 - **£1 591** - FF16 098
Komposition mit laufender Figur Tempera (29.5x18.6cm 11x7in) Hamburg 1999

SUPPANTSCHITSCH Max 1865-1953 [34]

🖼 **$10 248** - €10 174 - **£6 398** - FF66 738
St.Michael am Donau, Wachau Öl/Leinwand (53x71cm 20x27in) Wien 1999

🖼 **$2 138** - €2 543 - **£1 526** - FF16 684
Steinfeld bei Gmünd Öl/Karton (26x41cm 10x16in) Linz 2000

🖼 **$1 607** - €1 817 - **£1 085** - FF11 917
Wachauer Hof mit blühendem Baum Aquarell/Papier (41x30cm 16x11in) Wien 2000

SUPRIA Dede Eri 1956 [6]

🖼 **$3 506** - €3 671 - **£2 202** - FF24 077
Clown Oil/canvas (90x70cm 35x27in) Singapore 2000

SURAND Gustave 1860-1937 [74]

🖼 **$6 500** - €7 383 - **£4 561** - FF48 430
The Fruit Carrier Oil/canvas (140x96cm 55x37in) New-York 2001

🖼 **$2 749** - €2 384 - **£1 680** - FF15 636
The Trumpeting Elephant Oil/canvas (46x38cm 18x14in) New-York 1999

🖼 **$598** - €579 - **£376** - FF3 800
Panthère couchée Crayons couleurs/papier (48x52cm 18x20in) Paris 1999

🖼 **$1 100** - €1 041 - **£683** - FF6 830
«Royal Muscat» Poster (140x99cm 55x38in) New-York 1999

SURAPON SAENKUM 1953 [1]

🖼 **$1 602** - €1 488 - **£990** - FF9 762
Provincial Street Corner Watercolour/paper (73.5x102.5cm 28x40in) Bangkok 1999

SURASIT SAOKONG 1949 [7]

🖼 **$11 214** - €10 417 - **£6 930** - FF68 334
The Realm of Serenity Oil/canvas (132x230cm 51x90in) Bangkok 1999

🖼 **$5 100** - €5 485 - **£3 420** - FF35 980
Serenity Acrylic/canvas (89x117cm 35x46in) Bangkok 2000

🖼 **$2 002** - €1 860 - **£1 237** - FF12 202
Serenity Watercolour/paper (36x50cm 14x19in) Bangkok 1999

SURAUD Roger 1938 [12]

🖼 **$6 368** - €6 098 - **£3 924** - FF40 000
Orchestre et compositeur Huile/toile (116x89cm 45x35in) La Varenne-Saint-Hilaire 1999

SURBEK Victor 1885-1975 [141]

🖼 **$899** - €1 048 - **£622** - FF6 874
Brienzersee mit Wilerhorn Öl/Leinwand (65x79cm 25x31in) Bern 2000

🖼 **$285** - €326 - **£201** - FF2 140
Porträt eines Knaben am Seeufer Oil/canvas/panel (43.5x34.5cm 17x13in) Bern 2001

🖼 **$247** - €288 - **£171** - FF1 890
Im Gebirge Ink (48.5x62cm 19x24in) Bern 2000

🖼 **$112** - €131 - **£77** - FF860
Bergkulisse mit Eiger, Mönch und Jungfrau Farblithographie (23x50cm 9x19in) Bern 2000

SURBER Paul XX [9]

🖼 **$400** - €441 - **£267** - FF2 890
Encampment Acrylic/board (15x25cm 6x10in) St. Ignatius MT 2000

🖼 **$950** - €1 020 - **£636** - FF6 692
Small Buffalo Camp Gouache/paper (19x28cm 7x11in) San-Francisco CA 2000

SUREAU XIX-XX [20]

🖼 **$1 587** - €1 753 - **£1 100** - FF11 500
Bouquet de roses dans un panier d'osier Huile/toile (65x54cm 25x21in) Nantes 2001

SURÉDA André 1872-1930 [140]

🖼 **$2 221** - €2 592 - **£1 545** - FF17 000
L'Antichambre du Chérif Huile/toile (40x74cm 15x29in) Paris 2000

🖼 **$1 428** - €1 387 - **£882** - FF9 100
Jeune femme sous les lauriers roses Huile/panneau (41x32cm 16x12in) Paris 1999

🖼 **$1 246** - €1 143 - **£774** - FF7 500
Jeune femme allongée à la jupe bleue Technique mixte/papier (46x61cm 18x24in) Paris 1999

SURENDORF Charles Frederick 1906-1979 [17]

🖼 **$350** - €398 - **£240** - FF2 613
Street Blues Lithograph (18x23cm 7x9in) New-Orleans LA 2000

SURIA Tomas 1761-? [1]

🖼 **$669** - €716 - **£456** - FF4 695
El Exmo.Sor.Dn.Matias de Galvez Grabado (24x17cm 9x6in) México 2001

SURIE Jacoba 1879-1970 [58]

🖼 **$1 565** - €1 815 - **£1 109** - FF11 906
Still Life with Pots and Spoons Oil/canvas (50x39cm 19x15in) Amsterdam 2000

🖼 **$687** - €681 - **£421** - FF4 464
Earthenware Jar and a Bouquet of Dried Flowers Oil/canvas (41x32.5cm 16x12in) Amsterdam 2000

🖼 **$409** - €431 - **£270** - FF2 827
Two Women around a Table Watercolour (23x23cm 9x9in) Amsterdam 2000

S

SURIKOV Vasilii Ivanovich 1848-1916 [22]

$40 260 - €38 015 - **£25 000** - FF249 362
The Don Cossack Nikifor Andreiech Subotin
Oil/canvas (59x49cm 23x19in) London 1999

$7 114 - €8 266 - **£5 000** - FF54 221
Study of Male Head for the Canvas Stenka
Razin Oil/canvas (30x25.5cm 11x10in) London 2001

$5 317 - €6 328 - **£3 800** - FF41 508
The Fisherman's Cabin Watercolour/paper
(32.5x44cm 12x17in) London 2000

SURREY Phillip Henry Howard 1910-1990 [45]

$3 584 - €4 160 - **£2 475** - FF27 287
Decelles at Queen Mary Oil/canvas (40.5x61cm
15x24in) Vancouver, BC. 2000

$2 023 - €2 364 - **£1 444** - FF15 508
Route 37 near Pierrefonds Huile/panneau
(30.5x45.5cm 12x17in) Montréal 2001

$613 - €597 - **£377** - FF3 917
Convention Ink (25x36cm 10x14in) Nepean, Ont.
1999

SURTEES John 1817-1915 [28]

$639 - €651 - **£400** - FF4 273
Fern Gatherer Crossing the Stream Oil/canvas
(58x47cm 22x18in) London 2000

SURTEL Paul 1893-1985 [61]

$712 - €838 - **£511** - FF5 500
«Paysage des environs d'Orange» Huile/isorel
(38x46cm 14x18in) Toulon 2001

$673 - €793 - **£483** - FF5 200
Campagne provençale Huile/isorel (33.5x41.5cm
13x16in) Toulon 2001

SURUGUE DE SURGIS de Louis 1686-1762 [11]

$114 - €114 - **£70** - FF748
Trophées des Armes d'Hercule Grabado (51x37cm
20x14in) Madrid 2000

SURVAGE Léopold 1879-1968 [994]

$26 136 - €27 441 - **£17 334** - FF180 000
Le lasso Huile/toile (144x92cm 56x36in) Paris 2000

$8 652 - €9 840 - **£6 000** - FF64 544
Personnages Oil/board (64.5x46cm 25x18in) London
2000

$2 942 - €3 049 - **£1 866** - FF20 000
Le paradis Huile/toile (33x46cm 12x18in) Paris 2000

$442 - €503 - **£306** - FF3 300
Ruines romaines Aquarelle/papier (31x48cm
12x18in) Douai 2000

$153 - €152 - **£96** - FF1 000
Femme allongée Gravure bois (13.5x22cm 5x8in)
Paris 1999

SÜS Gustav 1823-1881 [17]

$4 393 - €4 346 - **£2 739** - FF28 508
Gänseherde am Dorfrand Öl/Leinwand
(75.5x51.5cm 29x20in) Ahlden 1999

SUSAN Robert 1888-? [3]

$275 - €299 - **£181** - FF1 962
Portrait of an Equestrian Oil/canvas (60x73cm
24x29in) Chester Springs PA 2000

SUSENIER Abraham c.1620-1664 [5]

$31 099 - €26 891 - **£18 488** - FF176 396
Stilleben mit Hummer, Messer, Gläsern, Rose
une Zinnteller Huile/panneau (37x28cm 14x11in)
Zürich 1998

SÜSS Josef Johann 1857-1937 [28]

$1 868 - €1 535 - **£1 085** - FF10 067
Lachendes Zigeunermädchen, mit Tambourin
auf Wiese sitzend Öl/Leinwand (69x56cm 27x22in)
Berlin 1998

SÜSS Klaus 1951 [14]

$109 - €123 - **£76** - FF804
«Schlange und Kreisel» Farbserigraphie
(49.5x31.5cm 19x12in) Berlin 2001

SUSTERMANS Justus 1597-1681 [13]

$9 200 - €11 922 - **£6 900** - FF78 200
Ritratto di dama Olio/tela (64.5x49cm 25x19in)
Milano 2000

SUSTRIS Friedrich c.1540-1599 [12]

$3 885 - €4 170 - **£2 600** - FF27 356
The Coronation of the Virgin Ink (12.5x9.5cm
4x3in) London 2000

SUTCLIFFE Frank Meadow 1853-1941 [74]

$1 495 - €1 279 - **£900** - FF8 392
Portrait studies/Harbour Scene Albumen print
(13x19cm 5x7in) London 1998

SUTCLIFFE John XIX [2]

$2 891 - €2 806 - **£1 800** - FF18 406
A Spaniel in a Clearing/A Border Collie on a
Hilltop Oil/canvas (21x30.5cm 8x12in) London 1999

SUTCLIFFE John E. ?-1923 [5]

$4 452 - €4 187 - **£2 800** - FF27 463
At the Trough Oil/canvas (50x71cm 19x27in) Co.
Kilkenny 1999

SUTCLIFFE Lester c.1850-c.1930 [38]

$246 - €272 - **£170** - FF1 784
Beach Scene Watercolour/paper (46x28cm 18x11in)
Hockley, Birmingham 2001

SUTCLIFFE Stuart F. XX [8]

$1 211 - €1 376 - **£850** - FF9 027
Self-Portraits Graphite (23x18cm 9x7in) London 2001

SUTER August 1887-1965 [6]

$1 266 - €1 487 - **£906** - FF9 756
Jeune femmme nue au drapé Albâtre (H31cm
H12in) Bruxelles 2000

SUTER Jakob 1805-1874 [25]

$2 642 - €2 978 - **£1 830** - FF19 534
Seewen mit Blick auf Schwyz und Mythen
Aquarell/Papier (45x60cm 17x23in) Zürich 2000

$690 - €779 - **£485** - FF5 112
«La mer de glace vue du Montenvert» Aquatinta
(17x25cm 6x9in) Bern 2001

SUTHERLAND David McBeth 1883-1973 [6]

$1 924 - €1 743 - **£1 200** - FF11 435
Breton Pardon Day, Saint Guenole Oil/board
(23.5x30cm 9x11in) Glasgow 1999

SUTHERLAND George Mowbray XIX [2]

$298 - €321 - **£200** - FF2 104
Vale of Avoca/Shelton Abbey Watercolour/paper
(17x30cm 7x12in) Wadebridge, Cornwall 2000

SUTHERLAND Graham 1903-1980 [680]

$22 708 - €21 892 - **£14 000** - FF143 599
Night Bird Oil/canvas (129.5x96.5cm 50x37in)
London 1999

$35 000 - €36 283 - **£21 000** - FF238 000
«**Horned Form**» Olio/tela (65x50cm 25x19in) Milano
1999

$6 424 - €6 236 - **£4 000** - FF40 903
Figs Oil/canvas (35.5x27.5cm 13x10in) London 1999

$7 989 - €9 551 - **£5 511** - FF62 653
Landscape Charcoal (43x33cm 16x12in) Penzance,
Cornwall 1999

$505 - €575 - **£350** - FF3 772
Objects on an Estuary Shore/Rock Form Color
lithograph (34x26cm 13x10in) London 2000

SUTHERLAND Jean Parker 1902-1978 [24]

$1 240 - €1 206 - **£763** - FF7 914
Asters in a White Vase Oil/canvas (56x43.5cm
22x17in) Malvern, Victoria 1999

SUTHERLAND Thomas c.1785-? [35]

$382 - €398 - **£240** - FF2 609
Fox Hunting, After Dean Wolstenholme Aquatint
in colors (26.5x71cm 10x27in) Suffolk 2000

SUTHERS Leghe 1856-1924 [9]

$2 500 - €2 301 - **£1 500** - FF15 093
The Meet Oil/canvas (53x72cm 21x28in) Morris-Plains
NJ 1999

SUTKUS Antanas 1939 [34]

$900 - €840 - **£545** - FF5 512
Pioneer Gelatin silver print (25x23cm 9x9in) New-
York 1999

SUTNAR Ladislav 1897-1969 [5]

$4 335 - €4 100 - **£2 700** - FF26 895
In the Bar Oil/cardboard (52x65cm 20x25in) Praha
2000

$1 647 - €1 558 - **£1 026** - FF10 220
Nu féminin Estampe couleurs (54x35cm 21x13in)
Praha 2001

SUTTER de Jules 1895-1970 [67]

$1 935 - €2 231 - **£1 332** - FF14 634
Zomerlandschap Oil/board (47x59cm 18x23in)
Lokeren 2000

$1 188 - €1 134 - **£742** - FF7 441
Self-Portrait Oil/cardboard (42x33cm 16x12in)
Amsterdam 1999

$399 - €446 - **£277** - FF2 926
Femme à la cruche Dessin (35x25cm 13x9in)
Antwerpen 2001

SUTTERBY Roderick, Rod 1955 [26]

$3 647 - €4 338 - **£2 600** - FF28 457
Ocean Nomads, Coho Salmon Oil/canvas
(91x111.5cm 35x43in) London 2000

$912 - €1 085 - **£650** - FF7 116
May Fish, River Tweed Watercolour/paper (22x52cm
8x20in) London 2000

SUTTON Ivan 1944 [9]

$929 - €1 079 - **£652** - FF7 079
The Framer Oil/canvas/board (51x41cm 20x16in)
Dublin 2001

SUTTON Philip 1928 [99]

$3 735 - €4 010 - **£2 500** - FF26 304
Kathleen Oil/canvas (128x128cm 50x50in) London
2000

$2 169 - €2 380 - **£1 400** - FF15 612
Anemonies Oil/canvas (48.5x48.5cm 19x19in)
London 2000

$151 - €128 - **£90** - FF838
Burds, Birds Green, Yellow, Blue and Black
Lithograph (50x50cm 20x20in) London 1998

SUTTON Thomas 1819-1875 [2]

$7 483 - €8 382 - **£5 200** - FF54 985
«**Barques de pêcheurs, baie de Saint-Brelade,
souvenir de Jersey**» Photograph (21.5x22.5cm
8x8in) London 2001

SUVÉE Joseph Benoît 1743-1807 [21]

$6 760 - €7 927 - **£4 862** - FF52 000
Lamentation sur le Christ mort Huile/toile
(225x290cm 88x114in) Paris 2001

$6 228 - €6 098 - **£3 832** - FF40 000
La Pentecôte Huile/toile (50x67cm 19x26in) Paris
1999

$5 707 - €6 403 - **£3 994** - FF42 000
Le Tombeau de Cecilia Metella Sanguine/papier
(33.5x45.5cm 13x17in) Paris 2001

SUYCKER Reyer Claesz. XVII [8]

$8 022 - €7 714 - **£4 941** - FF50 602
**Wooded Landscape with Travellers resting on a
Path** Oil/panel (39x41cm 15x16in) Amsterdam 1999

SUYDAM Arthur XX [2]

$2 250 - €2 171 - **£1 422** - FF14 240
Untitled Mixed media/board (38.5x31cm 15x12in)
New-York 1999

SUYDAM James Augustus 1819-1865 [3]

$50 000 - €56 864 - **£34 935** - FF373 005
Newport Beach Oil/canvas (45x76cm 18x30in) New-
York 2000

SUYDERHOEF Jonas c.1613-1686 [13]

$237 - €230 - **£147** - FF1 509
**Bauern beim Trinken und Rauchen unter einer
Weinlaube, nach Ostade** Radierung (41.3x35.5cm
16x13in) Berlin 1999

SUZANNE Léon 1870-1923 [27]

$4 656 - €5 031 - **£3 224** - FF33 000
Les quais de Seine et la cathédrale Huile/toile
(50x65cm 19x25in) Rouen 2001

SUZOR-COTÉ Marc-Aurèle de Foy 1869-1937 [221]

$12 954 - €15 113 - **£9 016** - FF99 136
Indiens en embuscade Oil/canvas (45.5x61cm
17x24in) Toronto 2000

$2 596 - €2 195 - **£1 552** - FF14 398
Blue Ridge Mountain, Virginie Oil/board
(21.5x26cm 8x10in) Toronto 1998

$6 365 - €7 022 - **£4 209** - FF46 061
Le vieux pionnier canadien Bronze
(40.5x21.5x41cm 15x8x16in) Vancouver, BC. 2000

$1 239 - €1 449 - **£885** - FF9 504
Study of an Iroquois Warrior Fusain/papier
(27.5x19.5cm 10x7in) Montréal 2001

SVABINSKY Max 1873-1962 [140]

$187 - €178 - **£117** - FF1 165
Frauenkoepfe Pencil/paper (22x16cm 8x6in) Praha
2001

$86 - €82 - **£54** - FF537
Femme assise Lithographie (36x26cm 14x10in)
Praha 2000

S

SVANBERG Max Walter 1912-1994 **[161]**
- **$1 729** - €1 508 - **£1 045** - FF9 892
  Kvinnoprofiler Mixed media (38.5x50.5cm 15x19in) Stockholm 1998
- **$1 914** - €2 257 - **£1 345** - FF14 802
  Imaginär kvinna Gouache/paper (45x36cm 17x14in) Malmö 2000
- **$175** - €196 - **£115** - FF1 287
  Svävande heraldisk fjärilskvinna Lithograph (30x122cm 11x48in) Malmö 2000

SVEDBERG Lena 1946-1972 **[24]**
- **$556** - €645 - **£383** - FF2 452
  Utan titel Pencil/paper (68x49cm 26x19in) Stockholm 2000

SVEINSDOTTIR Juliana 1889-1966 **[16]**
- **$3 502** - €2 960 - **£2 090** - FF19 417
  Opstilling med kaktus, krus og skål Oil/canvas (73x67cm 28x26in) København 1998

SVENDSEN Svend R. 1864-1934 **[83]**
- **$1 000** - €1 120 - **£694** - FF7 347
  «Winter Landscape» Oil/canvas (45x60cm 18x24in) Cincinnati OH 2001

SVENSSON Gunnar 1892-1977 **[63]**
- **$856** - €804 - **£529** - FF5 271
  Stilleben Oil/canvas (49x89cm 19x35in) Stockholm 1999

SVENSSON Roland 1910 **[162]**
- **$11 436** - €9 671 - **£6 835** - FF63 439
  «Sommarafton, Stora nassa skärgård» Oil/canvas (99x130cm 38x51in) Stockholm 1998
- **$1 200** - €1 418 - **£850** - FF9 301
  Winter Landscape Oil/canvas (69x46cm 27x18in) Austinburg OH 2000
- **$1 015** - €976 - **£617** - FF6 400
  Studie från Gillöga Mixed media (27x39cm 10x15in) Stockholm 1999
- **$988** - €1 095 - **£670** - FF7 182
  St Nassa Watercolour (25x36cm 9x14in) Stockholm 2000
- **$347** - €409 - **£251** - FF2 682
  Skärgårdslandskap med segelbåt Color lithograph (32x47cm 12x18in) Stockholm 2001

SVERCHKOV Nikolai Egorovich 1817-1898 **[57]**
- **$35 712** - €34 321 - **£22 000** - FF225 132
  Fleeing from the Wolves Oil/canvas (93x147cm 36x57in) London 1999
- **$11 272** - €10 644 - **£7 000** - FF69 821
  A Rearing Grey Oil/canvas (36x44.5cm 14x17in) London 1999
- **$4 420** - €5 034 - **£3 035** - FF33 024
  Soldatens farväl Oil/canvas (42x33cm 16x12in) Stockholm 2000
- **$1 800** - €1 923 - **£1 223** - FF12 617
  Horse Head Mixed media/paper (30x35cm 11x13in) Kiev 2001

SVETOSLAVSKY Sergei Ivanovitch 1857-1931 **[14]**
- **$8 500** - €7 333 - **£5 108** - FF47 804
  Forest in Pushcha-Vodystsya Oil/canvas (46.5x74cm 18x29in) Kiev 1998
- **$2 500** - €2 672 - **£1 699** - FF17 524
  Summer Landscape Oil/canvas (26.5x42.5cm 10x16in) Kiev 2001

SVIRIDOV Sergei 1964 **[47]**
- **$634** - €660 - **£400** - FF4 327
  Garden in Bloom Oil/canvas (38x46cm 14x18in) Fernhurst, Haslemere, Surrey 2000
- **$275** - €300 - **£185** - FF1 970
  En primavera Oleo/lienzo (35x27cm 13x10in) Madrid 2000

SWAGEMAKERS Theo 1898-1994 **[34]**
- **$776** - €908 - **£554** - FF5 953
  Still Life with Ceramic Objects, a Vase, a Giraffe and a Bird Oil/board (48.5x39cm 19x15in) Amsterdam 2001
- **$336** - €363 - **£229** - FF2 381
  Still Life with a Wine Bottle and a Glass Oil/canvas (43.5x33.5cm 17x13in) Amsterdam 2001

SWAGERS Frans 1756-1836 **[55]**
- **$8 520** - €9 147 - **£5 700** - FF60 000
  Paysans, cavalier et berger dans une forêt près d'un lac Huile/toile (54x69.5cm 21x27in) Paris 2000
- **$2 831** - €2 723 - **£1 744** - FF17 859
  Herders and their Cattle/Herders in a Boat and their Cattle Oil/canvas (19x24.5cm 7x9in) Amsterdam 1999

SWAIN William 1803-1847 **[2]**
- **$31 000** - €28 831 - **£19 195** - FF189 118
  Portrait of Captain Timothy Coffin of Nantucket in formal Attire Oil/canvas (68x58cm 27x23in) Nantucket MA 1999

SWAINE Francis 1735-1782 **[77]**
- **$34 731** - €30 285 - **£21 000** - FF198 655
  A Man O'War leaving Harbour and other Vessels Oil/canvas (93x143cm 36x56in) London 1998
- **$9 849** - €11 428 - **£6 800** - FF74 963
  The Flagship saluting, probably at the Nore Oil/canvas (44.5x71cm 17x27in) London 2000
- **$2 000** - €2 203 - **£1 334** - FF14 454
  The Morning Sun Oil/panel (15x22cm 6x9in) Portsmouth NH 2000
- **$2 994** - €3 139 - **£2 000** - FF20 591
  The Fleet at Anchor Ink (22x36cm 8x14in) London 2001

SWAINSSON William 1789-1855 **[5]**
- **$380** - €427 - **£265** - FF2 799
  Petoni Road, rocks near SE Bay Pencil/paper (9x15cm 3x5in) Wellington 2001

SWALLOW William Weldon 1912 **[2]**
- **$1 200** - €1 139 - **£735** - FF7 473
  Autumn Landscape with Winding Road and Farmhouse Oil/board (30x40cm 12x16in) Hatfield PA 1999

SWAMINATHAN Jagdish 1928-1993 **[19]**
- **$11 954** - €12 832 - **£8 000** - FF84 172
  Bird Series Oil/canvas (76x127cm 29x50in) London 2000
- **$2 977** - €2 784 - **£1 800** - FF18 265
  Miniature Painting Oil/canvas (29x39.4cm 11x15in) London 1999

SWAN Cuthbert Edmund 1870-1931 **[67]**
- **$4 139** - €4 008 - **£2 600** - FF26 292
  Tiger-Hunting Oil/canvas (57.5x48cm 22x18in) London 1999

S

$791 - €888 - **£550** - FF5 824
Tiger in the Jungle Oil/panel (30x45.5cm 11x17in)
London 2001

$800 - €924 - **£560** - FF6 062
Drink of Water Watercolour/paper (21.5x52cm 8x20in)
Bethesda MD 2001

SWAN John Macallan 1847-1910 **[33]**

$410 - €398 - **£260** - FF2 610
Study of a sleeping Lion Pencil (19x29cm 7x11in)
London 1999

SWANE Christine 1876-1960 **[100]**

$1 281 - €1 476 - **£884** - FF9 683
Klint, efter Karl Isakson Oil/canvas (57x69cm
22x27in) København 2000

SWANE Lars 1913 **[98]**

$433 - €404 - **£261** - FF2 649
Udsigt over landskab Oil/canvas (75x90cm 29x35in)
København 1999

SWANE Sigurd 1879-1973 **[277]**

$3 477 - €3 755 - **£2 402** - FF24 631
**Landskabsbillede med marker og tunge skyer, i
baggrunden mölle** Oil/canvas (119x133cm 46x52in)
København 2001

$611 - €739 - **£426** - FF4 849
Opstilling med tulipaner og frugter Oil/masonite
(58x54cm 22x21in) Viby J, Århus 2000

$386 - €429 - **£268** - FF2 813
Tulipaner og påskeliljer i vase Oil/canvas
(46x34cm 18x13in) København 2001

SWANENBURGH Willem Isaaksz. I 1581/82-1612
[12]

$649 - €624 - **£400** - FF4 092
Magdalena, after Bloemaert Engraving
(27.5x17.5cm 10x6in) New-York 1999

SWANEVELT van Hermann 1600-1655 **[78]**

$16 000 - €16 586 - **£9 600** - FF108 800
Paesaggio con pastori ed armenti Olio/tela
(66.5x91cm 26x35in) Venezia 2000

$32 000 - €28 164 - **£19 481** - FF184 745
Hagar and the Angel Oil/copper (25.5x33cm
10x12in) New-York 1999

$5 678 - €6 095 - **£3 800** - FF39 982
Rocky wooded Landscape with Satyrs Ink
(11.5x16cm 4x6in) London 2000

$235 - €264 - **£141** - FF1 340
Die kleinen Engel auf dem Hügel Radierung
(20.9x27.1cm 8x10in) Berlin 1998

SWANN James 1905-1985 **[36]**

$270 - €276 - **£169** - FF1 813
Chicago Snowy Night Etching (23x18cm 9x7in)
Cleveland OH 2000

SWANSON Ray 1937 **[25]**

$19 800 - €18 491 - **£12 220** - FF121 294
Turquoise Jewelry Peddler Oil/board (101x121cm
40x48in) Dallas TX 1999

$11 550 - €12 398 - **£7 729** - FF81 323
Looking for Strays Oil/board (76x106cm 30x42in)
Houston TX 2000

$4 200 - €4 769 - **£2 918** - FF31 282
Indian boy with Puppy Oil/canvas (25x20cm 10x8in)
Dallas TX 2001

$3 850 - €4 132 - **£2 576** - FF27 107
Canyon Shadows Watercolour/paper (53x73cm
21x29in) Houston TX 2000

SWANWICK Joseph Harold 1866-1929 **[60]**

$12 162 - €11 557 - **£7 400** - FF75 808
Evening after a hot Day Oil/canvas (101.5x135.5cm
39x53in) London 1999

$926 - €798 - **£550** - FF5 233
H.M Cruiser «Defence» Watercolour (19x29cm
7x11in) London 1998

SWANZY Mary 1882-1978 **[79]**

$18 264 - €17 776 - **£11 221** - FF116 606
The Bridge Oil/board (60x50cm 24x20in) Dublin
1999

$6 151 - €6 603 - **£4 116** - FF43 310
River Landscape Oil/board (25.5x30.5cm 10x12in)
Dublin 2000

$1 297 - €1 213 - **£800** - FF7 959
Ten Minute Pose Pencil/paper (20x16cm 7x6in) Co.
Kilkenny 1999

SWARBRECK Samuel Dukinfield XIX **[12]**

$205 - €199 - **£130** - FF1 303
**The North Bridge, connecting the old and new
Town, Edinburgh** Color lithograph (30.5x41cm
12x16in) Ipswich 1999

SWART VAN GRONINGEN Jan 1469/95-1535 **[3]**

$20 000 - €21 359 - **£13 628** - FF140 106
The Adoration of the Magi Oil/panel (88x66cm
34x25in) New-York 2001

$78 292 - €73 227 - **£48 000** - FF480 336
Adam and Eve in the Garden of Eden Oil/panel
(26.5x47cm 10x18in) London 1998

SWARZ John XIX-XX **[1]**

$75 000 - €78 634 - **£46 987** - FF515 805
The Wild Bunch Silver print (16x21cm 6x8in) New-
York 2000

SWATSLEY John 1937 **[8]**

$3 763 - €4 129 - **£2 500** - FF27 087
Mara Cheetah Oil/canvas (49.5x59.5cm 19x23in)
London 2000

SWEBACH Édouard Bernard 1800-1870 **[48]**

$6 808 - €6 860 - **£4 243** - FF45 000
**Chevau-léger bavarois et cantinière du même
régiment dans un paysage** Huile/toile (38x46cm
14x18in) Paris 2000

$6 115 - €6 860 - **£4 239** - FF45 000
Une halte de cavaliers devant l'auberge
Huile/toile (33x40.5cm 12x15in) Paris 2000

$1 108 - €1 067 - **£689** - FF7 000
Le cheval blessé Aquarelle/papier (21x26.5cm
8x10in) Montfort L'Amaury 1999

SWEBACH-DESFONTAINES Jacques François J.
1769-1823 **[103]**

$15 120 - €16 218 - **£9 990** - FF106 380
Escena orientalista Oleo/lienzo (45x52cm 17x20in)
Madrid 2000

$6 489 - €6 403 - **£4 032** - FF42 000
Le campement militaire Huile/toile (33x44.5cm
12x17in) Paris 1999

$1 305 - €1 220 - **£805** - FF8 000
**Entrée à Paris des prisonniers de l'Alliance par
la barrière de Pantin** Encre (23x45.5cm 9x17in)
Paris 1999

S

SWEDLUND Per Adolf, Pelle 1865-1947 **[5]**
$3 060 - €3 206 - **£1 937** - FF21 030
Porten, Gripsholm Oil/canvas (82x73cm 32x28in)
Malmö 2000

SWEELINCK Gerrit Pietersz. 1566-c.1610 **[2]**
$13 644 - €15 428 - **£9 601** - FF101 204
The four Evangelitsts Oil/panel (83.5x113cm
32x44in) Amsterdam 2001

SWEENEY Jan 1939 **[19]**
$3 895 - €3 744 - **£2 400** - FF24 559
Alert Bronze (H53.5cm H21in) London 1999

SWEERTS Michiel 1618/24-1664 **[13]**
$23 000 - €20 175 - **£13 965** - FF132 337
Double Portrait of a Man and a Woman Oil/canvas
(61x66.5cm 24x26in) New-York 1999

SWEET Walter Henry 1889-1949 **[80]**
$520 - €597 - **£360** - FF33 918
Christmas Steps, Bristol Watercolour/paper
(42x26cm 16x10in) Harrogate, North Yorkshire 2000

SWENSSON Christian Fredrik 1834-1909 **[47]**
$1 926 - €1 852 - **£1 188** - FF12 150
Klippor vid havet Oil/canvas (70x129cm 27x50in)
Malmö 1999
$1 127 - €1 250 - **£765** - FF8 197
**Segelfartyg på redden (Sailing Ship on the
Roadstead)** Oil/canvas (45x34cm 17x13in) Stockholm
2000

SWERDLOFF Sam ?-1977 **[3]**
$425 - €483 - **£294** - FF3 170
Swingband Lithograph (23x33cm 9x13in) Chicago IL
2000

SWIERZY Waldemar 1931 **[9]**
$176 - €171 - **£109** - FF1 119
«Alfred Hitchcock 1929-1938» Poster (98x68.5cm
38x26in) London 1999

SWIESZEWSKI Aleksander 1839-1895 **[26]**
$9 057 - €8 645 - **£5 659** - FF56 710
Mountainous Landscape, The Alps Oil/canvas
(39x65.5cm 15x25in) Warszawa 1999
$3 889 - €4 175 - **£2 602** - FF27 387
Soir sur un paysage lacustre Huile/panneau
(13x19.5cm 5x7in) Warszawa 2000

SWIEYKOWSKI Alfred 1869-1953 **[12]**
$1 291 - €1 220 - **£804** - FF8 000
Paysage Huile/toile (65x90cm 25x35in) Paris 1999

SWIFT John Warkup 1815-1869 **[16]**
$8 661 - €9 371 - **£6 000** - FF61 467
Men-o-War and other Vessels in heavy Water
Oil/canvas (49x74cm 19x29in) Driffield, East Yorkshire
2001
$3 103 - €3 622 - **£2 200** - FF23 757
Making port at dusk/Beached on the foreshore
Oil/canvas (31x46cm 12x18in) London 2001

SWIFT Kate, née Seaton F. 1834-1928 **[6]**
$3 154 - €2 723 - **£1 903** - FF17 859
Pink Roses Oil/cardboard (30x38.5cm 11x15in)
Amsterdam 1999

SWIFT Patrick 1927-1983 **[16]**
$6 704 - €7 618 - **£4 630** - FF49 974
Garden Retreat Oil/canvas (50x60cm 20x24in)
Dublin 2000

$3 825 - €4 444 - **£2 688** - FF29 151
Young Girl Oil/canvas (36x30cm 14x11in) Dublin
2001
$3 503 - €3 682 - **£2 197** - FF24 154
Algarve Landscape Watercolour/paper (43x61cm
16x24in) Dublin 2000

SWIGGETT Jean Donald 1910 **[3]**
$2 300 - €2 616 - **£1 595** - FF17 158
Kellogg, Idaho, Mural Study Watercolour/board
(39x91cm 15x36in) Chicago IL 2000

SWINBURNE Edward 1765-1847 **[4]**
$1 275 - €1 488 - **£900** - FF9 761
**View of St.Maria di Fallari with Mount Socracte
in the Distance** Pencil (23x32.5cm 9x12in) London
2000

SWINDEN Albert 1901-1961 **[2]**
$6 000 - €5 139 - **£3 542** - FF33 708
Objects in a Room Oil/canvas (61x76cm 24x29in)
New-York 1998

SWINNERTON James Guilford 1875-1974 **[36]**
$3 000 - €3 526 - **£2 079** - FF23 128
Drywash (near Salton Sea) Oil/canvas (51x63.5cm
20x25in) Beverly-Hills CA 2000
$1 600 - €1 428 - **£979** - FF9 369
Southwest Landscape Oil/canvas/board (30x40cm
12x16in) Altadena CA 1999

SWINSTEAD George Hillyard 1860-1926 **[21]**
$17 074 - €19 838 - **£12 000** - FF130 130
By Appointment Oil/canvas (91.5x132cm 36x51in)
London 2001
$8 235 - €7 833 - **£5 000** - FF51 378
Elegant lady at Work on a Tapestry Oil/canvas
(59.5x49.5cm 23x19in) Penzance, Cornwall 1999

SWOBODA Edward 1814-1902 **[15]**
$14 767 - €14 316 - **£9 144** - FF93 909
**Porträt Albertine Freiin Berayos, geboren Freiin
von Schön** Öl/Leinwand (74x59cm 29x23in) Graz
1999

SWOBODA Rudolf 1819-1859 **[17]**
$3 483 - €3 270 - **£2 160** - FF21 451
Gebirgslandschaft mit figürlicher Staffage
Öl/Leinwand (95x126cm 37x49in) Wien 1999

SWOBODA Rudolf II 1859-1914 **[13]**
$15 000 - €13 919 - **£9 165** - FF91 305
An Orientalist Street Scene Oil/canvas
(76.5x60.5cm 30x23in) New-York 1999
$1 262 - €1 453 - **£862** - FF9 534
Kopfstudie eines Arabers Öl/Leinwand/Karton
(27.5x19.7cm 10x7in) Wien 2000

SWORD James Brade 1839-1915 **[41]**
$2 200 - €2 587 - **£1 577** - FF16 970
Cattle in a wooded River Glade Oil/canvas
(61x51cm 24x20in) Philadelphia PA 2001
$550 - €629 - **£382** - FF4 126
The Road to the Sea Watercolour/paper (35x51cm
14x20in) Philadelphia PA 2000

SWYNCOP Charles 1895-1970 **[79]**
$482 - €448 - **£300** - FF2 936
Blomsterförsäljerska Oil/canvas (46x38cm 18x14in)
Malmö 1999

S

SWYNCOP Philippe 1878-1949 **[91]**
- **$6 272** - €6 941 - **£4 256** - FF45 528
  La jeune espagnole Huile/toile (135x90cm 53x35in)
  Bruxelles 2000
- **$768** - €843 - **£510** - FF5 528
  La cathédrale de Tolède Huile/toile (46x60cm
  18x23in) Bruxelles 2000
- **$520** - €446 - **£316** - FF2 926
  Nu féminin Aquarelle/papier (40x31cm 15x12in)
  Bruxelles 1999

SWYNNERTON Annie Louisa 1844-1933 **[16]**
- **$4 311** - €3 732 - **£2 600** - FF24 482
  Guy William Hopton/Edward Mickael Hopton
  Oil/canvas (91.5x61cm 36x24in) London 1998
- **$4 025** - €3 726 - **£2 500** - FF24 441
  Oleander Oil/canvas (27x19cm 10x7in) Cheshire 1999

SYBERG Anna L., née Hansen 1870-1914 **[7]**
- **$4 077** - €4 697 - **£2 814** - FF30 810
  Forårsblomster i glasvase Watercolour/paper
  (45x63cm 17x24in) København 2000

SYBERG Ernst 1906-1981 **[124]**
- **$403** - €469 - **£283** - FF3 079
  Udsigt over et sommerhusområde Oil/canvas
  (35x49cm 13x19in) København 2001
- **$318** - €269 - **£190** - FF1 763
  Sommerlandskab Oil/canvas (32x47cm 12x18in)
  København 1998

SYBERG Fritz 1862-1939 **[184]**
- **$1 107** - €1 288 - **£778** - FF8 446
  Kjaerby Bakker, høsten Rug Sérigraphie/toile
  (83x130cm 32x51in) København 2001
- **$1 093** - €1 009 - **£681** - FF6 621
  En gårdsplads Oil/canvas (31x40cm 12x15in) Viby J,
  Århus 1999
- **$466** - €470 - **£290** - FF3 084
  Liggende hjort Watercolour (48x64cm 18x25in)
  København 2000

SYCHKOV Feodor Vasilievich 1870-1958 **[9]**
- **$7 826** - €9 093 - **£5 500** - FF59 643
  Russian Girl picking Flowers Oil/canvas
  (43x44.5cm 16x17in) London 2001
- **$800** - €892 - **£537** - FF5 851
  Young Girl Oil/canvas (27.5x19cm 10x7in) Kiev 2000

SYDNEY Berenice 1944-1983 **[31]**
- **$3 287** - €3 529 - **£2 200** - FF23 147
  Soaring - Tone Painting Oil/canvas (152.5x152.5cm
  60x60in) London 2000
- **$940** - €1 095 - **£650** - FF7 180
  Hyacinthus and Apollo dancing Ink (51x76cm
  20x29in) London 2000
- **$340** - €403 - **£240** - FF2 644
  Squares and Circles Etching (20x15cm 7x5in)
  London 2000

SYER John, Jnr. 1844-1912 **[49]**
- **$1 100** - €1 273 - **£779** - FF8 348
  Klippekyst Oil/canvas (32.5x48cm 12x18in)
  København 2000
- **$365** - €322 - **£220** - FF2 113
  Evening on Whitby Scaur Watercolour/paper
  (30x49cm 12x19in) Whitby, Yorks 1998

SYER John, Snr. 1815-1885 **[106]**
- **$2 218** - €2 509 - **£1 500** - FF16 459
  Gorlestone, Nr.Yarmouth Oil/canvas (73.5x107cm
  28x42in) London 2000
- **$2 332** - €2 147 - **£1 400** - FF14 081
  Llanberis Pass Oil/canvas (25.5x45.5cm 10x17in)
  Glamorgan 1999
- **$325** - €318 - **£200** - FF2 086
  **Logging in a wood/River Landscape with
  Windmill** Watercolour/paper (33x45cm 13x18in)
  Aylsham, Norfolk 1999

SYKES Charles 1875-1950 **[22]**
- **$2 750** - €3 249 - **£1 948** - FF21 314
  The Spirit of Esctasy Bronze (H64cm H25in) San
  Rafael CA 2000
- **$3 120** - €3 622 - **£2 200** - FF23 759
  Caricature Ink (33x58.5cm 12x23in) London 2001

SYKES Dorcie 1908-1998 **[35]**
- **$209** - €212 - **£130** - FF1 388
  Primulas in a Chinese Mug Watercolour/paper
  (35x44cm 14x17in) Par, Cornwall 2000

SYKES George 1863-? **[45]**
- **$504** - €523 - **£320** - FF3 431
  Knaresborough Watercolour/paper (36x52cm
  14x20in) West-Yorkshire 2000

SYKES Henry 1855-1921 **[16]**
- **$3 978** - €3 787 - **£2 488** - FF24 840
  Tvätterskor Oil/canvas (57x77cm 22x30in) Stockholm
  1999
- **$684** - €675 - **£440** - FF4 428
  Figures and Carthorses on a Village Lane
  Watercolour/paper (15x29.5cm 5x11in) London 1999

SYKES John Gutteridge 1866-1941 **[107]**
- **$315** - €356 - **£220** - FF2 338
  Sheep on a Country Lane Watercolour/paper
  (30x45cm 12x18in) Grantham, Lincolnshire 2001

SYKORA Zdenek 1926 **[6]**
- **$4 335** - €4 100 - **£2 700** - FF26 895
  Ranska hora Huile/toile (70x100cm 27x39in) Praha
  2000

SYLVESTER Frederick Oakes 1869-1915 **[16]**
- **$1 600** - €1 728 - **£1 107** - FF11 337
  Summer Landscape Oil/canvas/board (25x20cm
  10x8in) Cincinnati OH 2001

SYLVESTER John Henry XIX-XX **[3]**
- **$5 928** - €6 874 - **£4 200** - FF45 089
  **Children gathering Primroses on a Country
  Lane** Watercolour (33.5x51cm 13x20in) London 2000

SYME Eveline W. 1888-1961 **[21]**
- **$1 041** - €1 215 - **£725** - FF7 973
  «Hong Kong Harbour» Linocut in colors
  (26.5x16.5cm 10x6in) Melbourne 2000

SYMINGTON Ayton XIX-XX **[1]**
- **$981** - €943 - **£600** - FF6 183
  «Moorland Holidays, North Eastern Railway»
  Poster (99x63cm 38x24in) London 1999

SYMONDS Ken 1927 **[55]**
- **$232** - €255 - **£149** - FF1 670
  Val and Amaryllis Oil/board (61x15.5cm 24x6in)
  London 2000

S

SYMONDS Richard 1969 [3]

✏ **$1 855** - €2 163 - **£1 300** - FF14 187
　Tiger Watercolour (34.5x51cm 13x20in) London 2000

SYMONS George Gardner 1863-1930 [157]

🖎 **$25 000** - €26 998 - **£17 277** - FF177 097
　Summer Landscape Oil/canvas (106x121cm
　42x48in) Altadena CA 2001

🖎 **$13 000** - €12 050 - **£8 083** - FF79 041
　Uncle Sam Plantation, St James Parish,
　Louisiana Oil/canvas (38x45cm 15x18in) New-
　Orleans LA 1999

🖎 **$2 400** - €2 634 - **£1 545** - FF17 277
　Autumn Hills Oil/canvas/board (20.5x27cm 8x10in)
　Beverly-Hills CA 2000

SYMONS William Christian 1845-1911 [14]

🖎 **$17 000** - €16 651 - **£10 954** - FF109 221
　Men of Mettle Oil/canvas (133.5x101.5cm 52x39in)
　New-York 1999

🖎 **$18 658** - €21 988 - **£13 110** - FF144 229
　En liten vilopaus Oil/canvas (77x63cm 30x24in)
　Malmö 2000

SYNAVE Tancrède 1860-? [48]

🖎 **$2 856** - €3 085 - **£1 973** - FF20 233
　La modiste Oil/canvas (54x64cm 21x25in)
　Köbenhavn 2001

SYPNIEWSKI Feliks 1830-1902 [8]

🖎 **$13 860** - €13 280 - **£8 739** - FF87 109
　Henri de Valois' Entry in Oil/canvas (53.5x112cm
　21x44in) Warszawa 1999

SYSIMETSÄ Ilmari 1912-1955 [14]

▥ **$700** - €758 - **£466** - FF4 975
　«Xv.Olympische Spiele, Helsinki Finnland»
　Poster (38x25cm 15x10in) New-York 2000

SYTSKOV Fedor Vasilievich 1870-1958 [5]

🖎 **$10 791** - €12 087 - **£7 502** - FF79 288
　Under rönnbärsträdet, ryska flickor i folkdräkt
　Oil/canvas (69x58.5cm 27x23in) Uppsala 2001

SZAFRAN Sam 1934 [100]

🖎 **$16 710** - €14 123 - **£10 000** - FF92 640
　Bouquet à la fleur blanche Oil/canvas (146x114cm
　57x44in) London 1998

🖎 **$11 644** - €12 501 - **£7 790** - FF82 000
　L'escalier Huile/panneau (27x19cm 10x7in) Paris 2000

✏ **$10 368** - €12 196 - **£7 432** - FF80 000
　L'escalier Aquarelle (26x30cm 10x11in) Versailles
　2001

▥ **$713** - €610 - **£428** - FF4 000
　L'imprimerie Lithographie (86x65cm 33x25in) Paris
　1998

SZANCENBACH Jan 1928-1998 [29]

🖎 **$4 369** - €4 835 - **£3 036** - FF31 713
　Roses Huile/toile (82x70cm 32x27in) Warszawa 2001

SZANKOWSKI von Boleslaw 1873-1953 [21]

🖎 **$2 449** - €2 556 - **£1 550** - FF16 769
　Junge südliche Tänzerin Öl/Karton (100x79cm
　39x31in) München 2000

SZANTHO Mária 1898-1984 [203]

🖎 **$1 000** - €1 080 - **£691** - FF7 083
　Reclining nude Oil/canvas (85x59.5cm 33x23in)
　New-York 2001

SZATHAMARY Zoltan 1909-1995 [4]

▥ **$291** - €340 - **£199** - FF2 232
　«Amstel bockbier zwart» Poster (70x37cm 27x14in)
　Hoorn 2000

SZATHMARY Carol 1812-1887 [5]

✏ **$666** - €767 - **£460** - FF5 030
　Auf einem Hügel rastende Reisende Watercolour
　(55x78cm 21x30in) München 2000

SZATHMARI Charles XIX [2]

📷 **$661 400** - €624 699 - **£400 000** - FF4 097 760
　Types et costumes populaires de Roumanie Salt
　print (32x23.5cm 12x9in) London 1999

SZCZEBLEWSKI Victor, Waclaw B. 1888-? [30]

🗝 **$1 100** - €1 099 - **£687** - FF7 207
　Mousse siffleur Bronze (H56cm H22in) Downington
　PA 1999

SZCZESNY Stefan 1951 [52]

🖎 **$1 371** - €1 534 - **£924** - FF10 061
　Stilleben Acryl/Leinwand (82x82cm 32x32in)
　München 2000

SZCZYGLINSKI Henryk 1881-1944 [17]

🖎 **$3 693** - €3 448 - **£2 236** - FF22 620
　Landscape in Winter Oil/canvas (70.5x79cm
　27x31in) Warszawa 1999

🖎 **$2 256** - €2 112 - **£1 398** - FF13 854
　Street Scene on a Place Oil/board (39x32cm
　15x12in) Warszawa 1999

SZCZYRBULA Marian 1899-1942 [4]

🖎 **$2 111** - €2 414 - **£1 449** - FF15 834
　Rue Augustianska à Cracovie Huile/carton
　(47x34cm 18x13in) Warszawa 2000

SZÉKELY VON ADAMOS Bertalan 1835-1910 [8]

🖎 **$81 159** - €96 583 - **£58 000** - FF633 545
　Leda and the Swan Oil/canvas (177x133cm 69x52in)
　London 2000

🖎 **$5 610** - €6 375 - **£3 910** - FF41 820
　Portrait de jeune homme Huile/toile (52x41cm
　20x16in) Budapest 2001

SZÉKELY VON DOBA Andor 1877-? [4]

🖎 **$30 000** - €33 581 - **£20 922** - FF220 275
　Nocturne Oil/canvas (160x97cm 62x38in) New-York
　2001

SZÉKESSY Karin 1939 [63]

📷 **$370** - €358 - **£233** - FF2 347
　Katharina kommt nach vorn Photograph (51x55cm
　20x21in) München 1999

SZENES Arpad 1897-1985 [48]

🖎 **$37 050** - €32 304 - **£22 100** - FF211 900
　La rue Oleo/lienzo (55.5x33cm 21x12in) Lisboa 1998

✏ **$5 280** - €5 982 - **£3 600** - FF39 240
　Le rivage Gouache/papier (10x20cm 3x7in) Lisboa
　2000

SZERMENTOWSKI Józef 1833-1876 [14]

🖎 **$6 257** - €6 074 - **£3 897** - FF39 842
　Polish (?) river Landscape Oil/canvas (46x55.5cm
　18x21in) Warszawa 1999

✏ **$1 253** - €1 474 - **£901** - FF9 667
　Chaumière Aquarelle, gouache/papier (14x19.5cm
　5x7in) Warszawa 2001

S

SZERNER Vladyslav Karol 1870-1936 **[4]**
  $6 034 - €5 624 - **£3 723** - FF36 892
    Lagernde Kosaken auf einer Anhöhe Oil/panel
    (32.5x44.5cm 12x17in) Köln 1999

SZERT Karoly 1955 **[22]**
  $510 - €488 - **£310** - FF3 200
    Le tramway Huile/panneau (30x40cm 11x15in) Metz
    1999

SZEWCZENKO Konstantin 1915-1991 **[18]**
  $833 - €809 - **£514** - FF5 306
    Étude du vieux Hucul Oil/board (50x35cm 19x13in)
    Warszawa 1999

SZIGETI Jenö 1881-? **[3]**
  $2 800 - €3 098 - **£1 840** - FF20 320
    Peasant's Yard in Nagybánya Oil/canvas (71x70cm
    27x27in) Budapest 2000

SZINYEI-MERSE von Paul 1854-1920 **[7]**
  $21 000 - €20 199 - **£13 000** - FF132 500
    Monk Saint Anthony Oil/canvas (193x140cm
    75x55in) Budapest 1999
  $2 225 - €2 460 - **£1 543** - FF16 134
    Apollo and Attendants on Parnassus Oil/panel
    (34x42.5cm 13x16in) Melbourne 2001

SZOBOTKA Imre 1890-1961 **[7]**
  $665 - €736 - **£437** - FF4 826
    Road of Zebegény Oil/canvas (60x75cm 23x29in)
    Budapest 2000

SZÖLLÖSY Janos 1884-? **[8]**
  $1 618 - €1 601 - **£1 009** - FF10 500
    Nu Huile/toile (81x60cm 31x23in) Provins 1999

SZÖNYI István 1894-1960 **[18]**
  $8 800 - €8 653 - **£5 500** - FF56 760
    Landscape with Tree Oil/canvas (65x56cm 25x22in)
    Budapest 1999
  $700 - €774 - **£460** - FF5 080
    In the green wood Mixed media/paper (38x28cm
    14x11in) Budapest 2000

SZÜLE Peter 1886-1944 **[11]**
  $500 - €481 - **£308** - FF3 154
    Interior Scene with a Man at a writing Desk
    Oil/canvas (58x39cm 23x15in) Cleveland OH 1999

SZYK Arthur 1894-1951 **[49]**
  $1 800 - €1 728 - **£1 115** - FF11 338
    Anticomintern (without Comintern) Ink (15x10cm
    5x3in) New-York 1999
  $1 800 - €1 940 - **£1 227** - FF12 725
    The Nazis and their Allies Print (58x77.5cm
    22x30in) New-York 2001

SZYMANOVSKI Waclaw 1859-1930 **[6]**
  $2 845 - €2 601 - **£1 741** - FF17 061
    Melody in the Evening Oil/cardboard (28.3x41.6cm
    11x16in) Warszawa 1999
  $3 442 - €3 821 - **£2 400** - FF25 067
    Bust of Adam Gielgud Bronze (H61cm H24in)
    London 2001

SZYMANSKI Rolf 1928 **[29]**
  $900 - €1 022 - **£646** - FF6 707
    Stehender weiblicher Torso Bronze (H21.4cm
    H8in) Hamburg 2000

SZYNDLER Pantaleon 1846-1905 **[7]**
  $7 000 - €7 350 - **£4 413** - FF48 214
    Capri Oil/canvas (48x67cm 19x26in) Cleveland OH
    2000

SZYSZLO de Fernando 1925 **[97]**
  $17 000 - €19 751 - **£11 947** - FF129 560
    «Duino-Once» Acrylic/canvas (119.5x119.5cm
    47x47in) New-York 2001
  $13 000 - €11 335 - **£7 859** - FF74 356
    Mesa Ritual Acrylic/canvas (80.5x101cm 31x39in)
    New-York 1998
  $2 358 - €2 615 - **£1 568** - FF17 155
    Casa 8 interior Estampe (57x75cm 22x29in) México
    2000

T

T'ANG HAYWEN 1927-1991 **[15]**
  $1 836 - €1 517 - **£1 074** - FF9 954
    Atmospheric Wave Watercolour/paper (11.5x11.5cm
    4x4in) Taipei 1998

TA TY 1920 **[4]**
  $1 721 - €1 955 - **£1 178** - FF12 823
    Abstract Composition Oil/canvas (47x57cm
    18x22in) Singapore 2000

TAAFFE Philip 1955 **[54]**
  $46 156 - €54 247 - **£32 000** - FF355 840
    Radiant Study Acrylic (140x140cm 55x55in) London
    2000
  $10 000 - €10 971 - **£6 643** - FF71 968
    Untitled Oil/canvas (99x30.5cm 38x12in) New-York
    2000
  $4 500 - €4 327 - **£2 772** - FF28 384
    Untitled Watercolour (32.5x25cm 12x9in) New-York
    1999
  $1 600 - €1 836 - **£1 094** - FF12 042
    Untitled Print (33x25.5cm 12x10in) New-York 2000

TAANMAN Jacob 1836-1923 **[20]**
  $1 242 - €1 140 - **£768** - FF7 479
    Préparations avant le départ Huile/panneau
    (31x24cm 12x9in) Bruxelles 1999

TABACCHI Odoardo 1831-1905 **[12]**
  $11 059 - €12 248 - **£7 500** - FF80 340
    Figure of a Diving Girl Marble (H117cm H46in)
    Billingshurst, West-Sussex 2000
  $2 366 - €2 622 - **£1 587** - FF17 200
    La baigneuse Bronze (H55cm H21in) Tours 2000

TABARD Maurice 1897-1984 **[85]**
  $2 097 - €1 829 - **£1 266** - FF12 000
    Portrait de jeune femme (solarisation) Tirage
    argentique (22x18.2cm 8x7in) Saint-Germain-en-Laye
    1998

TABARY E. XIX **[2]**
  $4 000 - €4 637 - **£2 833** - FF30 420
    In the Boudoir Oil/canvas (91.5x74cm 36x29in) New-
    York 2000

TABARY Jean 1930 **[7]**
  $245 - €274 - **£170** - FF1 800
    Sa dernière course, pl.17, de «Totoche» Encre
    Chine/papier (48x32cm 18x12in) Paris 2001

TABNER Len 1946 **[1]**
✏ **$2 315** - €2 500 - **£1 600** - FF16 399
Bank Tor Mixed media/paper (74x124.5cm 29x49in)
London 2001

TABOURET Émile ?-1927 **[11]**
▥ **$967** - €991 - **£596** - FF6 500
«**H.Fragson à l'Olympia**» Affiche (91x126cm
35x49in) Vendôme 2000

TABUCHI Yasse 1921 **[87]**
◠ **$1 590** - €1 346 - **£951** - FF8 826
«**Le ciel percé**» Oil/canvas (73x60cm 28x23in)
Köbenhavn 1998
✏ **$487** - €457 - **£301** - FF3 000
Fleur-nuage Acrylique/toile (22x27cm 8x10in) Paris
1999

TABUENA Romeo V. 1921 **[26]**
◠ **$1 300** - €1 518 - **£918** - FF9 957
Still Life of Bananas Acrylic/masonite (61x91.5cm
24x36in) Toronto 2000
◠ **$9 182** - €10 426 - **£6 284** - FF68 393
Country Scene Oil/canvas (11x60cm 4x23in)
Singapore 2000

TABUSSO Francesco 1930 **[35]**
◠ **$2 750** - €2 851 - **£1 650** - FF18 700
Ritratto di Silvana Olio/tela (70x50cm 27x19in) Prato
2000
◠ **$2 080** - €2 695 - **£1 560** - FF17 680
L'omino dei limoni Olio/tela (30x40cm 11x15in)
Torino 2000
✏ **$400** - €518 - **£300** - FF3 400
Paesaggio marino Pastelli (39x52cm 15x20in)
Vercelli 2000

TACCA Ferdinando 1619-1686 **[3]**
❧ **$54 115** - €52 214 - **£33 976** - FF342 500
Hercule et le Centaure Bronze (H74cm H29in)
Monte-Carlo 1999

TACCA Pietro 1577-1640 **[4]**
❧ **$3 926** - €3 659 - **£2 421** - FF24 000
Maures enchainés Bronze (54x30cm 21x11in)
Chantilly 1999

TACCONI Innocenzo 1575-c.1625 **[1]**
◠ **$35 000** - €35 407 - **£21 371** - FF232 256
Rinaldo and Armida Oil/canvas (96x131.5cm
37x51in) New-York 2000

TACK Augustus Vincent 1870-1949 **[34]**
◠ **$1 200** - €1 154 - **£740** - FF7 569
At the Foot of the Cross Oil/canvas/board
(116x104cm 46x41in) Pittsburgh PA 1999
◠ **$4 000** - €3 426 - **£2 361** - FF22 472
Evening Oil/canvas/panel (61x51cm 24x20in) New-
York 1998

TACLA Jorge 1958 **[8]**
◠ **$22 000** - €19 183 - **£13 301** - FF125 833
Listo para irse Oil/canvas (178x162.5cm 70x63in)
New-York 1998

TADAO Okazaki 1943 **[2]**
✏ **$20 580** - €20 073 - **£12 600** - FF131 670
Cockscomb Drawing (145x112.5cm 57x44in) Tokyo
1999

TADASHI Ishimoto 1920 **[2]**
✏ **$65 000** - €71 712 - **£42 991** - FF470 398
Shiroku saku (Blooming in white) Ink (150x78cm
59x30in) New-York 2000

TADASHI Nakayama 1927 **[20]**
▥ **$190** - €205 - **£131** - FF1 345
Red Coat Woodcut in colors (61x38cm 24x14in)
Bethesda MD 2001

TADEUSZ Norbert 1940 **[41]**
◠ **$5 239** - €5 624 - **£3 506** - FF36 892
Pärchen I Öl/Leinwand (199.5x159.5cm 78x62in)
Hamburg 2000
✏ **$1 079** - €1 227 - **£748** - FF8 049
Selbstbildnis Gouache (40.9x32.2cm 16x12in)
Hamburg 2000

TADINI Emilio 1927 **[164]**
◠ **$4 000** - €5 183 - **£3 000** - FF34 000
Senza titolo Tecnica mista (159x122cm 62x48in)
Milano 2000
◠ **$1 800** - €2 332 - **£1 350** - FF15 300
«**Natura morta**» Acrilico/tela (60x73cm 23x28in)
Milano 2001
◠ **$720** - €933 - **£540** - FF6 120
«**Fiaba**» Acrilico/tela (30x30cm 11x11in) Vercelli 2001
✏ **$300** - €311 - **£180** - FF2 040
Segni zodiacali: Bilancia, Gemmelli, Cancro
Tecnica mista/carta (15.5x13.5cm 6x5in) Milano 2000

TADOLINI XIX **[3]**
❧ **$15 433** - €18 354 - **£11 000** - FF120 397
Psyche Marble (H110cm H43in) London 2000

TADOLINI Adamo 1788-1868 **[5]**
❧ **$86 513** - €81 813 - **£53 485** - FF536 660
Venus und Amor Marbre (89x134.5cm 35x52in)
Zürich 1999
❧ **$3 445** - €3 354 - **£2 116** - FF22 000
**Marquise de Pimodan, les cheveux relevés par
un chignon et des perles** Marbre (H70.5cm H27in)
Paris 1999

TADOLINI Giulio 1849-1918 **[8]**
❧ **$14 000** - €16 454 - **£9 706** - FF107 931
Rebecca Marble (H182cm H72in) Ventura CA 2000
❧ **$11 000** - €12 963 - **£7 581** - FF85 034
Bust of a Woman Bronze (H70cm H27in) New-York
2000

TADOLINI Scipione 1822-1892 **[8]**
❧ **$13 923** - €12 028 - **£6 961** - FF78 897
Schiava seminuda incatenata a ceppo Marbre
(H93cm H36in) Venezia 1999

TAEJUNG Kim 1937 **[2]**
✏ **$4 000** - €4 691 - **£2 854** - FF30 769
Untitled Ink/paper (80x55cm 31x21in) New-York 2000

TAELEMANS Jean-François 1851-1931 **[24]**
◠ **$1 290** - €1 239 - **£810** - FF8 130
Sortie d'église en hiver Huile/toile (100x83cm
39x32in) Bruxelles 1999

TAEUBER-ARP Sophie 1889-1943 **[14]**
✏ **$16 000** - €18 565 - **£11 046** - FF121 776
Composition Watercolour, gouache/paper (19x14cm
7x5in) New-York 2000

TAEYE de Camille 1938 [16]
- $957 - €892 - **£590** - FF5 853
  Composition Technique mixte/toile (101x81cm 39x31in) Bruxelles 1999

TAFLINGER Elmer E. 1891-? [1]
- $4 250 - €4 306 - **£2 667** - FF28 243
  Studio Light Oil/canvas (76x60cm 30x24in) Cincinnati OH 2001

TAFOYA Margaret 1904 [5]
- $5 500 - €6 141 - **£3 676** - FF40 282
  Vase Ceramic (H28.5cm H11in) New-York 2000

TAFURI Clemente 1903-1971 [19]
- $9 200 - €11 922 - **£6 900** - FF78 200
  La nostra terra Olio/tela (175x116cm 68x45in) Milano 2001
- $5 000 - €5 183 - **£3 000** - FF34 000
  Ragazza nel campo Olio/cartone/tela (38x47cm 14x18in) Milano 2000
- $560 - €726 - **£420** - FF4 760
  Ragazza con scialle giallo Olio/tela (23x27cm 9x10in) Napoli 2000

TAFURI Raffaele 1857-1929 [13]
- $12 000 - €14 103 - **£8 319** - FF92 512
  Venetian Vista Oil/canvas (52.5x70cm 20x27in) New-York 2000
- $6 250 - €6 479 - **£3 750** - FF42 500
  Volto di bambina Olio/tavola (47x30.5cm 18x12in) Milano 1999

TAG Georges XX [5]
- $2 311 - €2 378 - **£1 466** - FF15 600
  Le couple Bronze (23x42x19cm 9x16x7in) Paris 2000

TAGGART Lucy M. XX [2]
- $3 000 - €3 220 - **£2 007** - FF21 123
  Mary Souther at 12 Pastel/paper (58x44cm 23x17in) Portland ME 2000

TAGGER Siona 1900-1988 [36]
- $3 000 - €3 185 - **£2 030** - FF20 889
  Safed Oil/canvas (43.5x37cm 17x14in) Tel Aviv 2001
- $1 400 - €1 486 - **£947** - FF9 748
  Alley in Safed Watercolour/paper (48x33.5cm 18x13in) Tel Aviv 2001

TAGLIABUE Carlo Costantino 1880-1968 [27]
- $1 600 - €2 073 - **£1 200** - FF13 600
  «Meriggio d'estate» Olio/tavola (35x73cm 13x28in) Milano 2000
- $1 080 - €933 - **£540** - FF6 120
  Paesaggio estivo con gregge Olio/tavola (21x26cm 8x10in) Milano 1999

TAGLIAPIETRA Lino 1934 [6]
- $10 000 - €10 712 - **£6 829** - FF70 266
  Vessel Sculpture, glass (H68cm H27in) Cleveland OH 2001

TAGORE Abanindranath 1871-1951 [15]
- $9 000 - €8 521 - **£5 613** - FF55 896
  Portrait of Rabindranath Tagore Watercolour/paper (23x12.5cm 9x4in) New-York 1999
- $16 539 - €15 470 - **£10 000** - FF101 476
  Asoka's Queen and the Bodhi Tree Lithograph (29x22cm 11x8in) London 1999

TAGORE Gaganendranath 1867-1938 [26]
- $2 750 - €2 374 - **£1 643** - FF15 574
  Black Cliffs Ink (42x52.5cm 16x20in) New-York 1998

TAGORE Rabindranath 1861-1941 [21]
- $8 000 - €9 275 - **£5 667** - FF60 840
  Self Portrait Ink (18.5x14cm 7x5in) New-York 2000

TAHER Salah 1911 [1]
- $4 296 - €4 833 - **£3 000** - FF31 701
  Landscape Oil/canvas (72x98cm 28x38in) London 2001

TAHOMA Quincy 1921-1956 [4]
- $2 000 - €2 334 - **£1 370** - FF15 312
  Navajo Mother Holding Baby in Cradle Board Painting (33x25cm 13x10in) Cloudcroft NM 2000
- $1 900 - €2 093 - **£1 268** - FF13 731
  Untitled Watercolour/paper (33x55cm 13x22in) St. Ignatius MT 2000

TAI JINGNONG 1903-1990 [1]
- $2 574 - €2 441 - **£1 566** - FF16 012
  Calligraphy in Xing Shu Ink/paper (120.5x33cm 47x12in) Hong-Kong 1999

TAïB Salomon 1877-? [5]
- $5 670 - €5 488 - **£3 592** - FF36 000
  «Jeune Mauresque d'Alger» Huile/toile (81x65cm 31x25in) Paris 1999
- $3 533 - €3 964 - **£2 449** - FF26 000
  Chez le portier/Le marchand d'oranges Huile/toile (35.5x27.5cm 13x10in) Paris 2000

TAIGA Ikeno 1723-1776 [2]
- $8 234 - €8 692 - **£5 441** - FF57 016
  Blühender Pflaumenbaum Indian ink/paper (197x66.5cm 77x26in) Heidelberg 2000

TAILFEATHERS Gerald T. 1925-1975 [36]
- $323 - €273 - **£192** - FF1 790
  Indians Fording River Watercolour/paper (15x20cm 6x8in) Calgary, Alberta 1998

TAILHARDAT Vincent 1970 [14]
- $2 564 - €3 049 - **£1 828** - FF20 000
  Femme et enfant à la lecture Huile/toile (92x73cm 36x28in) Brest 2000

TAILLANDIER Yvon 1926 [173]
- $358 - €427 - **£255** - FF2 800
  «Les habitants du ciel» Huile/toile (33x55cm 12x21in) Paris 2000
- $272 - €229 - **£159** - FF1 500
  Temple Gouache (65x49cm 25x19in) Paris 1998

TAILLASSON Jean-Joseph 1745-1809 [15]
- $4 048 - €4 714 - **£2 800** - FF30 921
  A Lady Reading a Letter Oil/canvas (92.5x73.5cm 36x28in) London 2000
- $4 350 - €4 573 - **£2 730** - FF30 000
  Achille dépose le corps d'Hector près du cadavre de Patrocle Crayon (38x45cm 14x17in) Paris 2000

TAILLEUX Francis 1913-1981 [11]
- $679 - €762 - **£471** - FF5 000
  Modèle nu (kathleen) Huile/toile (55x38.5cm 21x15in) Paris 2000

TAIT Arthur Fitzwilliam 1819-1905 **[168]**
- $20 000 - €18 538 - £12 436 - FF121 602
  After a Hard Chase Oil/canvas (35x56cm 13x22in)
  New-York 1999
- $14 000 - €13 258 - £8 512 - FF86 969
  Duck and Young Oil/panel (29x41cm 11x16in) New-
  York 1999
- $800 - €851 - £505 - FF5 581
  Pigeon Shooting Lithograph (48x69cm 19x27in)
  New-York 2000

TAITO Katsushika II XIX **[3]**
- $2 023 - €2 301 - £1 403 - FF15 092
  **Karpfen einen Wasserfall hochschwimmend,
  umgeben von Wasserpflanzen** Woodcut in colors
  (35.3x23.7cm 13x9in) Köln 2001

TAJAR Ziona 1900-1988 **[40]**
- $20 000 - €16 428 - £11 616 - FF107 758
  Holiday on the Jaffa Shore Oil/canvas (54.5x73cm
  21x28in) Tel Aviv 1998
- $3 043 - €2 801 - £1 826 - FF18 374
  Tel Aviv Harbour Watercolour, gouache/paper
  (30x45cm 11x17in) Tel Aviv 1999

TAJIRI Shinkichi 1923 **[55]**
- $4 862 - €4 857 - £3 040 - FF31 862
  Turm Metal (102x15x15cm 40x5x5in) Hamburg 1999
- $7 421 - €8 622 - £5 215 - FF56 555
  Warrior Bronze (H70cm H27in) Amsterdam 2001

TAKAEZU Toshiko 1929 **[2]**
- $10 000 - €10 359 - £6 365 - FF67 953
  Moon Pot Ceramic (63.5x58.5x58.5cm 25x23x23in)
  New-York 2000

TAKAHASHI Yoshi 1943-1998 **[24]**
- $129 - €143 - £89 - FF939
  Häuser unter dem Mondschein Etching, aquatint in
  colors (37.5x29.5cm 14x11in) Heidelberg 2001

TAKALA Veikko 1923 **[18]**
- $540 - €454 - £317 - FF2 977
  Älven Oil/canvas (46x54cm 18x21in) Helsinki 1998

TAKAMORI Akio 1950 **[3]**
- $3 500 - €4 066 - £2 459 - FF26 674
  Vessel Ceramic (28.5x52x16.5cm 11x20x6in) New-
  York 2001

TAKEUCHI Seiho 1864-1942 **[13]**
- $39 200 - €38 234 - £24 000 - FF250 800
  Mt.Fuji in Summer Painting (51x66cm 20x25in)
  Tokyo 1999
- $9 000 - €10 081 - £6 253 - FF66 124
  Keien zu (Chained monkey) Ink/paper (133.5x30cm
  52x11in) New-York 2001

TAKIS Vassiliakis 1925 **[168]**
- $4 701 - €4 573 - £2 892 - FF30 000
  Signal Sculpture (H220cm H86in) Paris 1999
- $694 - €777 - £483 - FF5 100
  «Magnetic Evidence» Bronze (19x47x29cm
  7x18x11in) Versailles 2001
- $259 - €250 - £162 - FF1 637
  Untitled Ink/paper (23.5x15cm 9x5in) Amsterdam
  1999

TAL COAT Pierre 1905-1985 **[565]**
- $28 728 - €2 301 - £1 403 - FF180 000
  Points rouges sur le rocher Huile/toile (97x130cm
  38x51in) Paris 1999

- $5 148 - €5 336 - £3 265 - FF35 000
  La Durance Huile/toile (81x81cm 31x31in) Paris 2000
- $1 114 - €1 067 - £686 - FF7 000
  Fleurs de pommier Huile/toile (41x24cm 16x9in) La
  Varenne-Saint-Hilaire 1999
- $463 - €457 - £285 - FF3 000
  Mouvement d'eau Encre/papier (39x30cm 15x11in)
  Versailles 1999
- $166 - €152 - £102 - FF1 000
  Sans titre Lithographie couleurs (66x50.5cm 25x19in)
  Paris 1999

TALBOT Henry S. XIX-XX **[3]**
- $5 000 - €5 537 - £3 391 - FF36 322
  At Marble Head Neck - Low Tide Oil/canvas
  (30x50cm 12x20in) New-York 2000

TALBOT Jesse 1806-1879 **[5]**
- $5 500 - €5 000 - £3 312 - FF32 796
  Extensive Landscape with Falls Oil/canvas
  (55x68cm 22x27in) Bethesda MD 1998

TALBOT William Henry Fox 1800-1877 **[85]**
- $6 476 - €7 254 - £4 500 - FF47 583
  **The Ancient Vestry, Study of the Rev.Calvert
  Jones in the Cloisters** Photograph (19x23.5cm
  7x9in) London 2001

TALBOYS Agnes Augusta ?-1940 **[17]**
- $2 595 - €2 868 - £1 800 - FF18 815
  Kittens, Roses and an Oriental Rug on a Table
  Oil/canvas (43x70.5cm 16x27in) London 2001

TALIAFERRO Alfred Charles, Al 1905-1969 **[8]**
- $1 200 - €1 288 - £803 - FF8 449
  Donald Duck Daily Strips Ink (14x49cm 5x19in)
  New-York 2000

TALIRUNILI Joe 1893-1976 **[7]**
- $17 855 - €20 198 - £12 490 - FF132 492
  The Migration Sculpture, wood (H28cm H11in)
  Toronto 2001

TALLIS John XIX **[12]**
- $103 - €120 - £72 - FF790
  New South Wales Engraving (36x27cm 14x10in)
  Sydney 2000

TALLONE Cesare 1853-1919 **[14]**
- $3 000 - €3 110 - £1 800 - FF20 400
  Profilo di donna Olio/cartone (46.5x39cm 18x15in)
  Torino 1999

TALLONE Guido 1894-1967 **[35]**
- $3 203 - €3 321 - £1 922 - FF21 783
  Ritratto ragazza siriana Olio/tela (91x80cm
  35x31in) Milano 1999

TALMAGE Algernon 1871-1939 **[54]**
- $2 178 - €2 001 - £1 350 - FF13 123
  The Kingdom of the Winds Oil/canvas (73x98.5cm
  28x38in) Devon 1999
- $794 - €895 - £550 - FF5 870
  Cattle in a Suffolk Meadow Oil/board (23x28cm
  9x11in) Ipswich 2000
- $817 - €786 - £500 - FF5 153
  **«Honister Crag, The Lake District for Holidays,
  LMS»** Poster (102x64cm 40x25in) London 1999

TALOS Gyula 1887-1975 **[1]**
- 🖋 **$5 500** – €6 160 – **£3 821** – FF40 409
  The Snow Queen Gouache/paper (32x26cm 12x10in)
  New-York 2001

TALPINO Enea Salmeggia c.1558-1626 **[3]**
- 🖋 **$1 400** – €1 451 – **£840** – FF9 520
  San Giorgio Inchiostro (18x9.5cm 7x3in) Milano
  2000

TALWINSKI Igor 1907 **[45]**
- 👁 **$721** – €727 – **£450** – FF4 771
  Young nude in an interior Oil/canvas (73x60cm
  29x24in) Dorchester, Dorset 2000

TAM Reuben 1916-1991 **[8]**
- 🖋 **$1 600** – €1 488 – **£987** – FF9 759
  Island and Stars (Monhegan) Watercolour/paper
  (39x44cm 15x17in) Portland ME 1999

TAMAGNI Vincenzo 1492-c.1530 **[9]**
- 👁 **$6 500** – €6 738 – **£3 900** – FF44 200
  Cristo in casa di Marta e Maria Olio/tavola
  (32x42cm 12x16in) Roma 2000
- 🖋 **$1 775** – €1 662 – **£1 100** – FF10 000
  **Figure Studies/Studies of a Temple, Helmets,
  Saint John the Baptist** Ink (25.5x18.5cm 10x7in)
  London 1999

TAMAGNO Francisco 1851-? **[119]**
- 👁 **$5 757** – €5 336 – **£3 580** – FF35 000
  «Bière de Ville sur Illon» Email/panneau (68x48cm
  26x18in) Paris 1999
- 🍷 **$1 500** – €1 395 – **£926** – FF9 149
  «La Framboisette» Poster (160x114cm 63x45in)
  New-York 1999

TAMAYO Rufino 1899-1991 **[774]**
- 👁 **$480 000** – €418 542 – **£290 208** – FF2 745 456
  «El Guitarrista» Mixed media/canvas (180x125cm
  70x49in) New-York 1998
- 👁 **$250 000** – €217 991 – **£151 150** – FF1 429 925
  **Three Ice-Creams (Naturaleza muerta con hela-
  do)** Oil/canvas (45.5x60.5cm 17x23in) New-York 1998
- 👁 **$85 000** – €82 703 – **£52 317** – FF542 495
  Square Head Oil/canvas (25.5x30.5cm 10x12in) New-
  York 1999
- 🏺 **$140 000** – €135 922 – **£86 492** – FF891 590
  Cabeza monolítica Metal (196.5x29x16.5cm
  77x11x6in) New-York 1999
- 👁 **$26 000** – €25 036 – **£16 182** – FF164 223
  Mujeres con Bateas Watercolour, gouache/paper
  (27.5x21.5cm 10x8in) New-York 1999
- 🍷 **$1 900** – €1 830 – **£1 174** – FF12 006
  Dog Color lithograph (56x76cm 22x30in) Chicago IL
  1999

TAMBURI Orfeo 1906-1994 **[411]**
- 👁 **$5 000** – €5 183 – **£3 000** – FF34 000
  Studio per il Carnevale romano Olio/cartone
  (45x43cm 17x24in) Roma 1999
- 👁 **$2 500** – €2 592 – **£1 500** – FF17 000
  Radici Olio/tela (22x27cm 8x10in) Vercelli 2000
- 🖋 **$600** – €622 – **£360** – FF4 131
  Basel China/carta (18x23cm 7x9in) Vercelli 2000
- 🍷 **$225** – €233 – **£135** – FF1 530
  Muri di Parigi Gravure (35x50cm 13x19in) Vercelli
  2000

TAMBURINI Arnaldo I 1843-1908 **[53]**
- 👁 **$2 634** – €2 550 – **£1 600** – FF16 724
  Distant Throughts Oil/canvas (91.5x71cm 36x27in)
  London 2000
- 👁 **$2 000** – €1 860 – **£1 234** – FF12 199
  Monk with Basket of Vegetables Oil/panel
  (23x17cm 9x7in) Portland ME 1999

TAMBURINI Y DALMAU José María 1856-1932 **[18]**
- 👁 **$14 030** – €13 815 – **£8 740** – FF90 000
  Figura femenina en el campo Oleo/lienzo
  (70x100cm 27x39in) Barcelona 1999
- 👁 **$1 032** – €1 051 – **£647** – FF6 895
  Arreglando las flores Oleo/tabla (39x31cm 15x12in)
  Barcelona 1999

TAMBUTÉ Henri XX **[1]**
- 👁 **$22 904** – €21 343 – **£14 126** – FF140 000
  **Paysage japonisant, arbre au bord d'une rivière
  avec des oiseaux** Huile/panneau (249x325cm
  98x127in) Fontainebleau 1999

TAMM von Frans Werner 1658-1724 **[83]**
- 👁 **$32 226** – €31 648 – **£20 000** – FF207 598
  **Flowers in an Urn, with Fruit on a Stone Ledge
  and a Winged Putto** Oil/canvas (150x120cm
  59x47in) London 1999
- 👁 **$9 713** – €10 426 – **£6 500** – FF68 390
  **Still life of a Blue Roller, Songbirds, Fruit and
  Lettuce** Oil/canvas (48.5x64cm 19x25in) London 2000
- 👁 **$3 020** – €2 907 – **£1 888** – FF19 068
  **Stilleben mit Blumen, Früchten und einem
  Meerschweichen** Öl/Leinwand (31.5x46cm 12x18in)
  Wien 1999
- 🖋 **$4 912** – €4 555 – **£3 000** – FF29 880
  Two Rabbits Black & white chalks/paper (22.5x29cm
  8x11in) London 1998

TAMMARO Francesco 1939 **[4]**
- 👁 **$500** – €518 – **£300** – FF3 400
  «Colazione sull'erba» Olio/tavola (22x37.5cm
  8x14in) Vercelli 1999

TAN Choh Tee 1942 **[3]**
- 👁 **$2 220** – €2 325 – **£1 395** – FF15 249
  China Town Oil/canvas (74x56cm 29x22in) Singapore
  2000

TAN SWIE HIAN 1943 **[2]**
- 👁 **$7 597** – €7 953 – **£4 772** – FF52 167
  Fireflies Oil/canvas (96.5x122cm 37x48in) Singapore
  1999

TAN TEO KWANG 1941 **[5]**
- 👁 **$2 986** – €2 783 – **£1 842** – FF18 255
  Prosperity Acrylic (167x66cm 65x25in) Singapore
  1999

TANABE Takao 1926 **[36]**
- 👁 **$1 369** – €1 607 – **£966** – FF10 539
  «Foothills, Looking West» Acrylic/canvas
  (51x152.5cm 20x60in) Calgary, Alberta 2000
- 🍷 **$357** – €417 – **£252** – FF2 738
  «Skincuttle Dawn»/«Galitas Channel» Color lithograph (43x83cm 16x32in) Calgary, Alberta 2000

TANAKA Akira 1918 **[42]**
- 👁 **$9 009** – €10 062 – **£6 025** – FF66 000
  Retour de pêche Huile/toile (130x195cm 51x76in)
  Paris 2000

T

$2 228 - €2 211 - **£1 386** - FF14 500
La dame au parapluie Huile/toile (80x65cm 31x25in) Paris 1999

TANAKA Ikko 1930 [1]

$2 000 - €2 231 - **£1 309** - FF14 636
«A Centennial Exhibition Salvatore Ferragamo - The Art of the Shoe» Poster (103x145cm 40x57in) New-York 2000

TANAKA Ryohei 1933 [5]

$190 - €205 - **£131** - FF1 345
Persimmon and Roofs, number 2 Etching (36x19.5cm 14x7in) Bethesda MD 2001

TANAKA Yasushi 1886-1941 [21]

$2 516 - €2 820 - **£1 707** - FF18 500
Nu blond au fauteuil Huile/carton (68.5x55cm 26x21in) Paris 2000

$5 764 - €6 860 - **£3 991** - FF45 000
Nu allongé Huile/toile (59x23cm 23x9in) Abbeville 2000

TANCONVILLE Henri Garnier, dit 1846-1936 [66]

$376 - €351 - **£232** - FF2 300
«Chemin de fer d'Orléans. Auvergne, Saint Nectaire le bas» Affiche couleur (117x82cm 46x32in) Paris 1999

TANCREDI A. XIX [1]

$4 500 - €4 665 - **£2 700** - FF30 600
Scena popolaresca con carabinieri Olio/tela (70x110cm 27x43in) Roma 1999

TANCREDI Parmeggiani 1927-1964 [211]

$22 500 - €23 325 - **£13 500** - FF153 000
Natura tempo Tecnica mista (120x120cm 47x47in) Prato 2000

$15 000 - €15 550 - **£9 000** - FF102 000
Senza titolo Tecnica mista (70x100cm 27x39in) Milano 2000

$2 800 - €3 628 - **£2 100** - FF23 800
Senza titolo Acquarello/carta (41x32.5cm 16x12in) Milano 2001

TANG DA WU 1939 [1]

$1 772 - €1 651 - **£1 071** - FF10 833
Calligraphy Watercolour/paper (56x39cm 22x15in) Singapore 1999

TANG HAIWEN T'ang Thien Phuoc H. 1929-1991 [45]

$7 341 - €6 804 - **£4 564** - FF44 629
Refreshing Dream of River Acrylic/paper/canvas (69.5x99cm 27x38in) Taipei 1999

$5 248 - €5 588 - **£3 328** - FF36 656
Provence Landscape Acrylic (29.5x42cm 11x16in) Taipei 2000

$2 520 - €2 318 - **£1 512** - FF15 208
Smoky Mist Ink/paper (69.5x99cm 27x38in) Taipei 1999

TANG MULI 1947 [8]

$12 910 - €10 905 - **£7 750** - FF71 530
Silk Road Oil/canvas (107x163cm 42x64in) Hong-Kong 1998

TANG SHUNZHI 1507-1560 [1]

$46 332 - €43 938 - **£28 188** - FF288 216
Poems in Xing-Cao Shu Ink/paper (30.5x668cm 12x262in) Hong-Kong 1999

TANG YIFEN 1778-1853 [3]

$3 852 - €4 206 - **£2 478** - FF27 591
Various Landscape Ink (7.5x13.5cm 2x5in) Hong-Kong 2000

TANG YIN 1470-1523 [17]

$46 224 - €50 475 - **£29 736** - FF331 092
Hibiscus Ink (34.5x60.5cm 13x23in) Hong-Kong 2000

TANG YUN 1910-1993 [23]

$2 000 - €2 147 - **£1 338** - FF14 082
Tiger Ink (111x51.5cm 43x20in) San-Francisco CA 2000

TANGEN Olof 1903 [12]

$2 575 - €3 003 - **£1 792** - FF19 701
Oppstilling Oil/canvas (68x48cm 26x18in) Oslo 2000

TANGUY Yves 1900-1955 [251]

$110 467 - €106 888 - **£70 000** - FF701 141
Paravent, quatre feuilles Oil/canvas (129x134cm 50x52in) London 2000

$350 750 - €417 146 - **£250 000** - FF2 736 300
Zones d'instabilité Oil/canvas (51x46cm 20x18in) London 2000

$200 000 - €224 015 - **£138 960** - FF1 469 440
L'athée ou la religieuse Oil/canvas (35.5x26cm 13x10in) New-York 2001

$16 000 - €17 921 - **£11 116** - FF117 555
Sans titre Ink (45.5x30.5cm 17x12in) New-York 2001

$3 249 - €2 754 - **£1 941** - FF18 063
Ohne Titel Etching (18.5x12.5cm 7x4in) New-York 1998

TANK Heinrich Fr. Tanck 1808-1872 [12]

$15 127 - €15 882 - **£9 537** - FF104 181
Welcoming Arrival Oil/canvas (65.5x84.5cm 25x33in) Amsterdam 2000

$2 457 - €2 812 - **£1 690** - FF18 446
Schiffbrüchiger Seemann bei Unwetter an felsiger Küste Öl/Papier (28.5x38cm 11x14in) München 2000

TANNAES Marie 1854-1939 [13]

$5 673 - €6 555 - **£3 972** - FF42 998
Interiör fra Våge Oil/canvas (55x70cm 21x27in) Oslo 2001

TANNER Benjamin 1775-1848 [5]

$1 800 - €1 983 - **£1 200** - FF13 009
Mac Donough's Victory on Lake Champlain, after H.Reinagle Engraving (42x61cm 16x24in) Portsmouth NH 2000

TANNER E.L. XIX-XX [2]

$1 964 - €2 336 - **£1 400** - FF15 323
Galatia, a Chestnut Hunter/Princess Beno, a Chestnut Hunter Oil/canvas (30.5x40.5cm 12x15in) London 2000

TANNER Edwin Russell 1920-1980 [13]

$13 723 - €14 731 - **£9 184** - FF96 628
Familiar Compound Ghosts Mixed media (137x146cm 53x57in) Melbourne 2000

$15 895 - €15 465 - **£9 782** - FF101 445
Water Power Engineers Oil/canvas (79x98.5cm 31x38in) Melbourne 1999

TANNER Henry Ossawa 1859-1937 [18]

$500 000 - €588 903 - **£345 800** - FF3 862 950
Christ Oil/canvas (138x200cm 54x79in) West-Chester PA 2000

⌐ **$190 000** - €180 813 - **£118 845** - FF1 186 056
The Visitation Oil/canvas (95.5x108cm 37x42in)
New-York 1999

⌐ **$60 000** - €67 204 - **£41 688** - FF440 832
Landscape in Moonlight Oil/canvas/board
(25.5x34.5cm 10x13in) New-York 2001

▥ **$2 200** - €2 463 - **£1 534** - FF16 153
The Disciples see Christ walking on the Water
Etching (18.5x24.5cm 7x9in) New-York 2001

TANNER Robin 1904-1988 [12]

▥ **$680** - €571 - **£400** - FF3 748
The Gamekeeper's Cottage Etching (19x24cm
7x9in) London 1998

TANNERT Volker 1955 [28]

⌐ **$4 763** - €5 113 - **£3 188** - FF33 539
Unsere Wünsche wollen Kathedrale bauen
Öl/Leinwand (160x220.5cm 62x86in) Köln 2000

TANNING Dorothea 1912 [89]

⌐ **$20 000** - €19 208 - **£12 330** - FF125 996
Juke Box Oil/canvas (76x20.5cm 29x8in) New-York
1999

TANOUX Adrien Henri 1865-1923 [99]

⌐ **$5 000** - €5 038 - **£3 117** - FF33 050
Harem Beauty Oil/canvas (100x80.5cm 39x31in)
New-York 2000

⌐ **$1 771** - €1 677 - **£1 076** - FF11 000
Le modèle Huile/panneau (41x33cm 16x12in) Paris
1999

TANSEY Mark 1949 [19]

⌐ **$95 000** - €91 297 - **£58 520** - FF598 870
Search for the Subject Oil/canvas (127.5x102cm
50x40in) New-York 1999

⌐ **$90 000** - €101 812 - **£62 964** - FF667 845
«Sighting» Oil/canvas (112.5x91.5cm 44x36in) New-
York 2001

⌐ **$50 000** - €56 562 - **£34 980** - FF371 025
«Valley of Doubt, Study» Oil/board (26.5x38.5cm
10x15in) New-York 2001

✐ **$32 500** - €36 766 - **£22 737** - FF241 166
«Cultivating a Lexical Lacuna» Graphite
(28x21.5cm 11x8in) New-York 2001

TANZI Léon Louis Antoine 1846-1913 [28]

⌐ **$2 000** - €2 164 - **£1 370** - FF14 192
Summer Pond Landscape Oil/canvas (54x73cm
21x29in) East-Moriches NY 2001

⌐ **$1 220** - €1 220 - **£763** - FF8 000
Vue de Moret sur Loing Huile/panneau
(39.5x28.5cm 15x11in) Paris 1999

TANZIO DA VARALLO Antonio d'Enrico c.1575-
c.1635 [7]

✐ **$124 000** - €160 681 - **£93 000** - FF1 054 000
Ritratto femminile Olio/tela (73x56cm 28x22in)
Milano 2001

✐ **$30 000** - €32 136 - **£20 487** - FF210 798
Study of an Angel Red chalk/paper (22x19.5cm
8x7in) New-York 2001

TAO DING XIX [1]

✐ **$8 140** - €7 724 - **£4 946** - FF50 669
Peacock, Peahen and Loquat Ink (282x157.5cm
111x62in) Hong-Kong 1999

TAO LENGYUE 1895-1985 [35]

✐ **$4 750** - €4 027 - **£2 841** - FF26 418
Winter Pine Coloured inks/paper (128x25cm 50x9in)
Hong-Kong 1998

TAO ZHAOYUAN 1814-1865 [2]

✐ **$6 235** - €5 286 - **£3 728** - FF34 674
Snowy Landscape Coloured inks/paper (134.5x31cm
52x12in) Hong-Kong 1998

TAPIÉ Michel XX [3]

⌐ **$3 264** - €3 659 - **£2 215** - FF24 000
Composition surréaliste fond noir Huile/toile
(92x73cm 36x28in) Paris 2000

TAPIES Antoni 1923 [1944]

⌐ **$132 660** - €141 444 - **£90 000** - FF927 810
Brown on Black with Collage Mixed media/canvas
(146x89cm 57x35in) London 2001

⌐ **$41 165** - €39 731 - **£26 000** - FF260 618
Ovaldo Rosado (Pink oval) Mixed media/canvas
(55x46.5cm 21x18in) London 1999

⌐ **$9 581** - €10 215 - **£6 500** - FF67 008
«1 Kilo Amb Mit Jons» Mixed media (32.5x44cm
12x17in) London 2001

⚒ **$62 760** - €67 368 - **£42 000** - FF441 907
White sand and Pullover Assemblage
(114x152.5cm 44x60in) London 2000

⚒ **$14 968** - €12 573 - **£8 800** - FF82 474
Grande stèle Terracotta (40.5x65.5x15cm 15x25x5in)
London 1998

✐ **$14 938** - €14 499 - **£9 301** - FF95 109
Ohne Titel Mischtechnik/Papier (32x50cm 12x19in)
Luzern 1999

▥ **$659** - €701 - **£416** - FF4 600
Lettre O Lithographie couleurs (53.5x68cm 21x26in)
Paris 2000

TAPIRO Y BARO Josep 1830-1913 [29]

✐ **$888** - €1 022 - **£612** - FF6 707
**Edelmann mit Degen im Innern eines Palastes
stehend** Aquarell/Karton (36.5x24.5cm 14x9in)
Saarbrücken 2001

TAPISSIER Edmond 1861-1943 [18]

⌐ **$11 545** - €12 501 - **£7 330** - FF82 000
Titania Huile/toile (455x300cm 179x118in) Paris 2000

⌐ **$3 459** - €3 735 - **£2 391** - FF24 500
Les bergers marchois Huile/toile (18x28.5cm
7x11in) Lyon 2001

TAPLIN Guy 1939 [80]

⚒ **$9 762** - €11 481 - **£7 000** - FF75 310
«Five Owls» Sculpture, wood (89x67.5x12cm
35x26x4in) London 2001

⚒ **$2 884** - €3 187 - **£2 000** - FF20 906
«Tufted Duck» Sculpture, wood (H35.5cm H13in)
London 2001

TAPPER Garth 1927 [16]

⌐ **$2 821** - €3 163 - **£1 973** - FF20 746
«Model resting» Oil/board (58x48cm 22x18in)
Auckland 2001

⌐ **$848** - €967 - **£586** - FF6 343
«The Kids at the Swamp No.13» Oil/board
(29x36.5cm 11x14in) Auckland 2000

TAPPER Kain 1930 [20]

⚒ **$1 952** - €2 186 - **£1 355** - FF14 341
Köld Bronze (H39cm H15in) Helsinki 2001

T

TAPPERT Georg 1880-1957 **[289]**

🖼 $43 962 - €50 614 - **£30 000** - FF332 007
Standing Female Nude in Landscape/Path with Trees and House Oil/canvas (90x68cm 35x26in) London 2000

🖼 $17 156 - €20 452 - **£12 232** - FF134 156
Alte Frau mit rotem Hut Öl/Leinwand (45.5x35cm 17x13in) Berlin 2000

🖼 $865 - €1 022 - **£611** - FF6 707
Sitzender weiblicher Akt Ink (28x22cm 11x8in) Köln 2001

🖼 $340 - €358 - **£214** - FF2 347
Grosse Landschaft mit Sonne Linocut (30x34cm 11x13in) Stuttgart 2000

TAQUOY Maurice 1878-1952 **[53]**

🖼 $2 722 - €2 897 - **£1 805** - FF19 000
Longchamps Huile/carton (51x45cm 20x17in) Paris 2000

🖼 $2 717 - €2 897 - **£1 723** - FF19 000
Le rond de présentation Aquarelle/papier (19x38cm 7x14in) Deauville 2000

🖼 $220 - €213 - **£138** - FF1 400
Sur le champs de course Pochoir (20x60cm 7x23in) Paris 1999

TARANCZEWSKI Waclaw 1903-1987 **[37]**

🖼 $2 970 - €3 413 - **£2 056** - FF22 386
Nature morte Huile/toile (66x84cm 25x33in) Warszawa 2000

🖼 $1 957 - €2 025 - **£1 236** - FF13 282
Nature morte aux bouteilles Pastel/paper (50.5x70cm 19x27in) Warszawa 2000

TARANOW Michail Afanasjew. 1909-1973 **[3]**

🖼 $3 292 - €3 758 - **£2 287** - FF24 654
Siddende ung kosak Oil/canvas (116x78cm 45x30in) Köbenhavn 2000

TARANTINO Giuseppe 1916-1999 **[11]**

🖼 $800 - €1 201 - **£600** - FF6 800
Figure e archi Bronzo (25x32x9cm 9x12x3in) Torino 2000

TARASIN Jan 1926 **[8]**

🖼 $4 744 - €5 249 - **£3 296** - FF34 431
Catalogue de réalité Huile/toile (92x65cm 36x25in) Warszawa 2001

🖼 $1 248 - €1 381 - **£867** - FF9 061
Signes Aquarelle/papier (49x61.5cm 19x24in) Warszawa 2001

TARAVAL Gustave, Louis Gust. 1738-1794 **[1]**

🖼 $4 781 - €5 133 - **£3 200** - FF33 669
Design for a Pyramidal Tomb Watercolour (26x46cm 10x18in) London 2000

TARAVAL Hugues, Jean Hugues 1729-1785 **[33]**

🖼 $80 000 - €87 772 - **£53 144** - FF575 744
The Feast of Tantalus/Phineus interrupting the wedding Banquet Oil/canvas (103.5x143cm 40x56in) New-York 2000

🖼 $5 500 - €5 406 - **£3 533** - FF35 462
Pygmalion and Galatea Oil/canvas (90x72.5cm 35x28in) New-York 1999

🖼 $12 000 - €11 377 - **£7 300** - FF74 625
Triumph of Galatea Oil/canvas (39.5x31cm 15x12in) New-York 1999

TARBELL Edmund Charles 1862-1938 **[27]**

🖼 $480 000 - €537 635 - **£333 504** - FF3 526 656
Margaret under the Elms Oil/canvas (168x92cm 66x36in) New-York 2001

🖼 $190 000 - €181 633 - **£119 092** - FF1 191 433
The Picture Hat Oil/canvas (76x63.5cm 29x25in) New-York 1999

🖼 $2 800 - €3 266 - **£1 965** - FF21 421
Sketch of Two Girls Graphite (29x21cm 11x8in) Boston MA 2000

TARBET J.A. Henderson ?-1938 **[26]**

🖼 $716 - €602 - **£420** - FF3 947
Angler in a River Landscape Oil/canvas (61x92cm 24x36in) Billingshurst, West-Sussex 1998

TARCHIANI Filipo 1576-1645 **[2]**

🖼 $93 384 - €91 795 - **£60 000** - FF602 136
Saint Dominic in Penitence Oil/canvas (132x109cm 51x42in) London 1999

🖼 $2 285 - €2 668 - **£1 613** - FF17 500
Le Martyre de Saint Bartholomé Oil/canvas (25x21cm 9x8in) Lyon 2000

TARDI Jacques 1946 **[26]**

🖼 $998 - €838 - **£586** - FF5 500
La Fin d'une Expédition scientifique, pl. No.4 Encre Chine/papier (53x43cm 20x16in) Paris 1998

🖼 $118 - €107 - **£72** - FF700
Nestor Burma au bistrot Sérigraphie couleurs (50x60cm 19x23in) Neuilly-sur-Seine 1999

TARDIA Enzo 1960 **[36]**

🖼 $275 - €285 - **£165** - FF1 870
Atmosfere mediterranee Olio/tela (60x60cm 23x23in) Vercelli 2000

TARDIEU Nicolas Henri 1674-1749 **[6]**

🖼 $132 - €150 - **£90** - FF985
La batalla de Constantino y Majencio Grabado (35.5x49.5cm 13x19in) Madrid 2000

TARDIEU Pierre Alexandre 1756-1844 **[2]**

🖼 $823 - €884 - **£551** - FF5 800
Vignette pour le trompe l'oeil aux assignats Eau-forte (56.5x47cm 22x18in) Paris 2000

TARDIEU Pierre François 1711-1771 **[5]**

🖼 $391 - €460 - **£281** - FF3 018
Diana und Aktäon, nach F.Boucher Kupferstich (23.5x31.5cm 9x12in) Hamburg 2001

TARDIEU Victor 1870-1937 **[18]**

🖼 $13 000 - €12 177 - **£7 992** - FF79 873
Mother and Child in an Interior Oil/canvas (61x50cm 24x19in) New-York 1999

🖼 $2 410 - €2 737 - **£1 649** - FF17 953
Street Scene Oil/board (21x27cm 8x10in) Singapore 2000

TARDY Michel 1939 **[31]**

🖼 $1 037 - €1 220 - **£752** - FF8 000
Petite Dordogne Bronze (13x18cm 5x7in) Calais 2001

TAREL Cécile 1946 **[11]**

🖼 $1 026 - €960 - **£635** - FF6 300
Petite femme Bronze (H27cm H10in) Provins 1999

TARENGHI Enrico 1848-1938 [46]

✏ $3 200 - €3 761 - £2 218 - FF24 670
The Fruit Seller Watercolour/paper (53x35.5cm 20x13in) New-York 2000

TARKAY Isaac 1935 [42]

✏ $500 - €504 - £311 - FF3 305
Two women seated in a room Watercolour/paper (40x30cm 16x12in) Scottsdale AZ 2000

▥ $400 - €345 - £240 - FF2 263
Seated Woman Color lithograph (50x60cm 20x24in) Philadelphia PA 1998

TARKHOFF Nicolas 1871-1930 [149]

◠ $3 875 - €4 269 - £2 584 - FF28 000
La Seine à Bercy Huile/toile (81x60cm 31x23in) Deauville 2000

◠ $1 910 - €1 829 - £1 177 - FF12 000
Paysage vallonné Huile/toile (24x32cm 9x12in) Calais 1999

✏ $283 - €274 - £178 - FF1 800
Village derrière les champs Aquarelle/papier (31.5x49cm 12x19in) Neuilly-sur-Seine 1999

TARQUINI XX [1]

▥ $4 066 - €3 809 - £2 500 - FF24 985
«Luomo Lupo» Poster (198.5x140cm 78x55in) London 1999

TARR James C. 1905 [25]

◠ $4 217 - €4 066 - £2 600 - FF26 668
Veneer Cutters Oil/canvas/panel (51x61cm 20x24in) London 1999

TARRAGO Leticia XX [12]

▥ $160 - €178 - £106 - FF1 169
Entre flores Serigrafia (77.5x60cm 30x23in) México 2000

TARRANT Margaret Winifred 1888-1959 [26]

✏ $3 627 - €3 288 - £2 200 - FF21 568
«Queen's Gems» Watercolour (22x16cm 8x6in) Billingshurst, West-Sussex 1998

TARRANT Percy XIX-XX [22]

◠ $21 188 - €19 265 - £13 000 - FF126 371
Sunday Morning/The First Born Oil/canvas (51x38.5cm 20x15in) London 1999

◠ $158 - €185 - £110 - FF1 214
Cub and Scoutmaster in a Mountain Range Oil/board (36x25cm 14x9in) Billingshurst, West-Sussex 2000

TARTARIUS Cornelis Cornelisz. XVII [1]

◠ $3 594 - €3 991 - £2 500 - FF26 178
Coastal Landscape with a Drover attending his Animals Oil/canvas (58.5x83.5cm 23x32in) London 2001

TASKAR Laxan Narain 1870-1937 [1]

◠ $8 269 - €7 735 - £5 000 - FF50 738
Market Scene Oil/canvas (67.5x122cm 26x48in) London 1999

TASKEY Harry Leroy 1892-1958 [3]

▥ $800 - €768 - £495 - FF5 039
«Herald Square» Lithograph (35x28cm 13x11in) New-York 1999

TASLITZKY Boris 1911 [2]

◠ $4 443 - €4 573 - £2 799 - FF30 000
Hommage à Guéricault, d'après le buste de Jacques Lipchitz Huile/toile (50.5x73cm 19x28in) Paris 2000

TASSAERT Octave 1800-1874 [48]

◠ $1 494 - €1 604 - £1 000 - FF10 521
A Lady reclining Beneath a tree Oil/canvas (46.5x38cm 18x14in) London 2000

◠ $2 116 - €2 501 - £1 500 - FF16 404
La jeune mère Oil/canvas (31x23.5cm 12x9in) London 2000

TASSEL Jean 1608-1667 [12]

◠ $6 916 - €6 708 - £4 382 - FF44 000
Tobie et l'Ange Huile/toile (65x81cm 25x31in) Paris 1999

TASSI Agostino Buonamico 1566/80-1644 [26]

◠ $25 500 - €26 435 - £15 300 - FF173 400
Paesaggio con castello/Paesaggio con ponte Olio/tela (58.5x88cm 23x34in) Milano 2001

✏ $4 749 - €4 129 - £2 874 - FF27 084
The Miraculous Draught of Fishes Ink (14.5x21cm 5x8in) New-York 1999

TATAFIORE Ernesto 1943 [70]

◠ $2 310 - €2 000 - £1 401 - FF13 117
«Café Robespierre» Mixed media/canvas (200x134cm 78x52in) Amsterdam 1998

◠ $1 128 - €977 - £685 - FF6 409
Senza titolo Mixed media/canvas (70x100cm 27x39in) Amsterdam 1998

◠ $1 253 - €1 073 - £753 - FF7 041
«Ah-Sans Culottes» Pencil (68x48.5cm 26x19in) Hamburg 1998

TATAH Djamel XX [6]

◠ $1 243 - €1 372 - £842 - FF9 000
Sans titre Huile/toile (80x60cm 31x23in) Paris 2000

TATE Gayle Blair 1944 [38]

◠ $700 - €770 - £486 - FF5 053
Orchid and Hummingbird Oil/panel (35x27cm 14x11in) Delray-Beach FL 2001

TATHAM Charles Heathcote 1772-1842 [3]

✏ $35 863 - €38 496 - £24 000 - FF252 518
Sketches made at Rome, Tivoli, Venice, Vicenza, Berlin Pencil/paper (51x32cm 20x12in) London 2000

TATHAM Frederick 1805-1878 [5]

◠ $1 087 - €1 194 - £700 - FF7 830
Mother with her Two Children Standing Three-Quarter Length Watercolour/paper (69x49.5cm 27x19in) London 2000

TATO Guglielmo Sansoni 1896-1974 [41]

◠ $2 800 - €3 628 - £2 100 - FF23 800
«Natura morta» Olio/tavola (50x60cm 19x23in) Vercelli 2001

TATOSSIAN Armand 1948 [109]

◠ $390 - €334 - £226 - FF2 189
Lac Mégantic Huile/toile (51x61cm 20x24in) Montréal 1998

TATSUO Takayama 1912 [15]

◠ $34 000 - €34 261 - £21 195 - FF224 740
Yoko (Sunlight over Mount Fuji) Mixed media (49x65cm 19x25in) New-York 2000

T

$20 000 - €20 154 - £12 468 - FF132 200
Mizube no ie (House by the Water) Mixed media
(25x33cm 10x13in) New-York 2000

$38 000 - €44 563 - £27 116 - FF292 311
Noka no aru fukei (Landscape with Farmhouse)
Ink (95x116cm 37x45in) New-York 2000

TAUBE Eugen 1860-1913 [62]

$3 535 - €4 150 - £2 494 - FF27 219
Skärgårdslandskap med man och kvinna i eka
Oil/canvas (50x80cm 19x31in) Stockholm 2000

$2 402 - €2 017 - £1 412 - FF13 233
Strandlandskap med roddbåt Oil/canvas (49x29cm
19x11in) Helsinki 1998

TAUBE Evert 1890-1976 [9]

$6 422 - €5 601 - £3 884 - FF36 743
Hamnmotiv Mixed media (70x93cm 27x36in)
Stockholm 1998

$843 - €931 - £584 - FF6 109
Mansporträtt, from Den Gylene Freden Pencil
(28x22cm 11x8in) Stockholm 2001

TAUBERT Gustave Friedrich 1755-1839 [1]

$1 497 - €1 431 - £911 - FF9 390
**Biedermeier Intérieur mit sitzender Dame und
Herr an einer Staffelei** Aquarell/Papier (28.5x30.5cm
11x12in) Stuttgart 1999

TAUEBER-ARP Sophie 1889-1943 [10]

$3 674 - €4 116 - £2 554 - FF27 000
Motif abstrait, personnage Tapisserie (10x6cm
3x2in) Paris 2001

TAUNAY Nicolas Antoine 1755-1830 [62]

$3 554 - €4 090 - £2 450 - FF26 831
Bilderauktion auf einem städtischen Platz
Oil/panel (49.5x56cm 19x22in) Saarbrücken 2000

$5 400 - €4 726 - £3 270 - FF31 500
Paysage avec voyageurs et bergers Huile/toile
(28x35cm 11x13in) Toulouse 1998

$1 567 - €1 296 - £919 - FF8 500
La partie de chasse/Animation près du charriot
Aquarelle/papier (24.5x36cm 9x14in) Versailles 1998

TAUPIN Jules 1863-1932 [21]

$2 347 - €2 744 - £1 675 - FF18 000
«Gourbi kabyle» Huile/toile (24x33cm 9x12in) Paris
2001

TAUZIN Louis c.1845-1914 [57]

$1 809 - €2 058 - £1 255 - FF13 500
Château de St Cloud Huile/toile (65x92cm 25x36in)
La Baule 2000

$339 - €290 - £203 - FF1 900
«Le Globe-Trotter» Affiche (101x153cm 39x60in)
Paris 1998

TAUZIN Robert 1919-1979 [27]

$114 - €122 - £77 - FF800
Nu assis sur le coté Crayon/papier (102x72cm
40x28in) Abbeville 2001

TAVARES Joao XX [1]

$250 - €293 - £1 450 - FF16 350
Luta de Galos de Barcelos Tapisserie (78x138cm
30x54in) Lisboa 2000

TAVARES Manuel 1911 [10]

$880 - €997 - £620 - FF6 540
Névoa em Sintra Acuarela/papel (25x32.5cm 9x12in)
Lisboa 2001

TAVARONE Lazzaro 1556-1641 [9]

$1 043 - €1 037 - £650 - FF6 802
The Madonna on Clouds Surrounded by Angels
Black chalk (20x22cm 7x8in) London 1999

TAVELLA Antonio XIX [1]

$2 422 - €2 287 - £1 506 - FF15 000
Le repos d'une vivandière Huile/toile (47x33cm
18x12in) Neuilly-sur-Seine 1999

TAVELLA IL SOLFAROLA Carlo Antonio 1668-1738
[21]

$25 500 - €26 435 - £15 300 - FF173 400
Paesaggio montano con monaci Olio/tela
(132x110cm 51x43in) Genova 2001

$6 000 - €7 775 - £4 500 - FF51 000
Paesaggio invernale Olio/tela (58.5x77.5cm
23x30in) Milano 2000

$2 160 - €1 866 - £1 080 - FF12 240
Paeaggio con San Giovanni Battista Inchiostro
(41x27.5cm 16x10in) Milano 1999

TAVENIER Hendrick 1734-1807 [11]

$404 - €454 - £283 - FF2 976
**Beurtschip «Daar men mee van Antwerpen op
Brussel vaart»** Ink (13.5x18.5cm 5x7in) Dordrecht
2001

TAVENRAAT Johannes 1809-1881 [19]

$1 442 - €1 224 - £870 - FF8 028
Reiziger in heuvellandschap Oil/panel (19x34cm
7x13in) Den Haag 1998

TAVERNARI Vittorio 1919-1992 [9]

$2 100 - €2 177 - £1 260 - FF14 280
Amanti Bronzo (H48cm H18in) Prato 1999

TAVERNER William 1703-1772 [7]

$2 270 - €2 391 - £1 500 - FF15 682
Ripon Cathedral Watercolour/paper (33x52cm
12x20in) London 2000

TAVERNIER Andrea 1858-1932 [35]

$80 325 - €83 269 - £48 195 - FF546 210
Mattino ridente Olio/tela (120x210cm 47x82in)
Milano 2000

$11 000 - €11 403 - £6 600 - FF74 800
Scorcio di paese Olio/tela (54x64cm 21x25in) Torino
2000

$7 500 - €7 775 - £4 500 - FF51 000
Riflessi Olio/tavola (29x37cm 11x14in) Vercelli 1999

$1 800 - €1 555 - £900 - FF10 200
Idillio Pastelli/carta (15x21cm 5x8in) Vercelli 1999

TAVERNIER Armand 1899-1991 [23]

$3 346 - €3 470 - £2 128 - FF22 764
Winter Oil/canvas (40x50cm 15x19in) Lokeren 2000

$1 633 - €1 363 - £957 - FF8 943
Sneeuwlandschap Oil/canvas (35x35cm 13x13in)
Lokeren 1998

TAVERNIER Jules 1844-1889 [14]

$50 000 - €49 642 - £31 250 - FF325 630
El capitan Oil/canvas (46.5x79.5cm 18x31in) New-
York 1999

TAVERNIER Paul 1852-? [69]

$23 018 - €21 038 - £14 089 - FF138 000
Hallali de cerf avec amazone Huile/toile
(152x90cm 59x35in) Dijon 1999

$2 840 - €3 049 - **£1 900** - FF20 000
Le 14 juillet aux Tuileries Huile/toile (73x93cm 28x36in) Paris 2000

$1 835 - €1 982 - **£1 268** - FF13 000
Chiens au relais Huile/panneau (24x33cm 9x12in) Soissons 2001

$671 - €762 - **£466** - FF5 000
Chiens de chasse dans un paysage Aquarelle/papier (16x57cm 6x22in) Barbizon 2001

TAVERNIERS Armand 1899-1991 [18]
$2 016 - €2 231 - **£1 404** - FF14 634
Winderlandschap (Paysage d'hiver) Huile/toile (31x31cm 12x12in) Antwerpen 2001

TAWEE NANDAKWANG 1925-1991 [7]
$30 600 - €32 911 - **£20 520** - FF215 880
Poppy Fields Acrylic/canvas (91x73cm 35x28in) Bangkok 2000

TAYLER Albert Chevallier 1862-1926 [45]
$5 678 - €6 095 - **£3 800** - FF39 982
Basil Samuel Foster, three-quarter-length, seated, wearing whites Oil/canvas (51x41cm 20x16in) London 2000

TAYLER Edward 1828-1906 [21]
$1 079 - €933 - **£650** - FF6 118
Study of a Young Girl with her Pet Kitten Watercolour (17.5x13cm 6x5in) Billingshurst, West-Sussex 1999

TAYLER H.B. XIX [1]
$2 655 - €2 599 - **£1 700** - FF17 048
The Burning of the House of Lords and the Commons Oil/board (17.5x25cm 6x9in) London 1999

TAYLER John Frederick 1802-1889 [46]
$806 - €566 - **£540** - FF5 681
The resting sportsman with his dog Watercolour/paper (44x31.5cm 17x12in) Bristol, Avon 2000

TAYLER Norman 1843-1915 [4]
$1 934 - €1 804 - **£1 200** - FF11 832
Feeding the Geese Watercolour (18x27cm 7x10in) Billingshurst, West-Sussex 1999

TAYLOR Alfred Henry ?-1868 [7]
$632 - €558 - **£380** - FF3 658
Portrait of a Military Officer Watercolour (24x18.5cm 9x7in) London 1998

TAYLOR Anna Heyward 1879-1956 [6]
$5 750 - €5 744 - **£3 594** - FF37 676
Composition of Ginger Flowers and Leaves Gouache/paper (61x39cm 24x15in) New-Orleans LA 1999

$1 450 - €1 325 - **£887** - FF8 692
Camellias Woodcut (16x10cm 6x4in) Columbia SC 1999

TAYLOR Anne XX [2]
$1 874 - €2 159 - **£1 279** - FF14 159
Reverie at St Ives Watercolour/paper (81x60cm 31x23in) Dublin 2000

TAYLOR Anthony Chevalier 1862-1925 [6]
$440 - €425 - **£278** - FF2 789
Mr H Martyn/Untitled Print (38x25cm 14x9in) London 1999

TAYLOR Charles Andrew 1910 [9]
$350 - €332 - **£214** - FF2 179
Sansom Street Train Bridge Watercolour/paper (53x72cm 21x28in) Hatfield PA 1999

TAYLOR Charles Jay 1855-1929 [9]
$6 500 - €5 484 - **£3 812** - FF35 971
Winter Scene Oil/canvas (63x76cm 25x30in) Mystic CT 1998

TAYLOR Charles, Jnr. act.1841-c.1883 [63]
$2 299 - €2 024 - **£1 400** - FF13 276
Shipping in the Solent Watercolour (36.5x52cm 14x20in) London 1999

TAYLOR Ernest Archibald 1874-1951 [22]
$567 - €609 - **£380** - FF3 998
Cottages, Goatfell, Arran Watercolour/paper (44x22cm 17x9in) Carlisle, Cumbria 2000

TAYLOR Ernest Mervyn 1906-1964 [11]
$703 - €826 - **£499** - FF5 419
No.1 Temporary Shed Pencil/paper (31x32cm 12x12in) Auckland 2000

$241 - €271 - **£169** - FF1 778
Illustration for a Maori Legend Woodcut (20x14cm 7x5in) Auckland 2001

TAYLOR Fred, Frederick 1875-1963 [76]
$508 - €479 - **£320** - FF3 142
Figures on a Street Watercolour/paper (15.5x20.5cm 6x8in) Godalming, Surrey 1999

$736 - €708 - **£450** - FF4 642
«Cambridge, Trinity College, LNER» Poster (100x62cm 39x24in) London 1999

TAYLOR Frédéric Bourchier 1906-1987 [95]
$2 752 - €3 211 - **£1 915** - FF21 066
Houses at the Corner of Green and John Sts.Kingston, N.Y. Oil/canvas (51x61cm 20x24in) Toronto 2000

$553 - €473 - **£334** - FF3 101
«At Tewkesbury, Quebec» Huile/panneau (21.5x26cm 8x10in) Montréal 1998

$338 - €325 - **£209** - FF2 131
Street Scene - Mexico Watercolour (29x40cm 11x15in) Toronto 1999

TAYLOR Grace Martin 1903-1995 [16]
$1 000 - €945 - **£622** - FF6 196
Morgantown Factories Woodcut in colors (38x41cm 14x16in) San-Francisco CA 1999

TAYLOR Henry King XIX [17]
$16 584 - €18 326 - **£11 500** - FF120 209
St.Michael's Mount, Cornwall Oil/canvas (91.5x145cm 36x57in) London 2001

TAYLOR Henry White 1899-1941 [1]
$10 000 - €10 734 - **£6 692** - FF70 410
Return of the Fisherman Oil/canvas (76x91cm 30x36in) Altadena CA 2000

TAYLOR Horace 1881-1934 [9]
$1 200 - €1 154 - **£740** - FF7 569
«Sidmouth sheltered & sunny» Poster (100.5x61.5cm 39x24in) New-York 1999

T

TAYLOR Howard Hamilton 1918 [4]

🖌 **$6 345** - €7 050 - £4 250 - FF46 242
Natures Clock - Time flight, Landscape Radial
Sculpture, wood (70x70x20cm 27x27x7in) Nedlands
2000

✎ **$3 149** - €3 696 - **£2 222** - FF24 243
Forest Edge/Landscape with Moon Wash
(9x13cm 3x5in) Nedlands 2000

TAYLOR Leonard Campbell 1874-1969 [55]

☞ **$15 582** - €17 735 - **£10 950** - FF116 331
The Sisters Oil/wood (36x51cm 14x20in) Woollahra,
Sydney 2001

☞ **$1 877** - €2 115 - **£1 300** - FF13 875
Malvina Oil/canvas/board (20.5x12.5cm 8x4in) Ipswich
2000

📠 **$45** - €52 - **£32** - FF338
The Connoisseur Print (22x40cm 9x16in) Aylsham,
Norfolk 2001

TAYLOR Nova XX [1]

☞ **$15 000** - €14 267 - **£9 108** - FF93 585
Thistles #7 Oil/canvas (74x59cm 29x23in) New-York
1999

TAYLOR Richard Denison 1902-1970 [7]

✎ **$1 209** - €1 405 - **£850** - FF9 217
**Young Woman talking to her Companion
amongst a Group of People** Ink (26.5x36.5cm
10x14in) London 2001

TAYLOR Robert XX [8]

📠 **$157** - €153 - **£100** - FF1 004
The Dambusters Print in colors (40x53cm 15x20in)
Newbury, Berkshire 1999

TAYLOR Rolla Sims 1874-1970 [11]

☞ **$1 100** - €1 121 - **£689** - FF7 355
Acalito Mexicana Oil/canvas/board (22x30cm 9x12in)
Altadena CA 2000

TAYLOR Samuel C. 1870-1944 [21]

☞ **$7 483** - €8 382 - **£5 200** - FF54 985
Sheltering from the Wind Oil/panel (15x20.5cm
5x8in) London 2001

TAYLOR Thomas 1844-? [2]

☞ **$14 080** - €13 034 - **£8 500** - FF85 500
Ancien chemin de Vitré à Pocé Oil/canvas
(59.5x73.5cm 23x28in) London 1999

TAYLOR William Francis 1883-1970 [6]

☞ **$6 250** - €6 802 - **£4 295** - FF44 620
**Landscape of a Garden along the Canal in
Bucks county** Oil/canvas (50x60cm 20x24in)
Downington PA 2001

TAYLOR William Ladd 1854-1926 [4]

☞ **$8 000** - €7 856 - **£4 964** - FF51 534
David Playing a Harp Oil/canvas (81x66cm 32x26in)
Bloomfield-Hills MI 1999

TAYLOR-WOOD Sam 1967 [18]

📷 **$32 000** - €35 780 - **£21 571** - FF234 700
Five Revolutionary Seconds VIII Photograph in
colors (51x203cm 20x79in) New-York 2000

TAZAKI Hirosuke 1898-1984 [1]

☞ **$10 290** - €10 036 - **£6 300** - FF65 835
Red Mt.Fuji Oil/canvas (24.5x33.5cm 9x13in) Tokyo
1999

TCHELITCHEW Pavel 1898-1957 [234]

☞ **$3 460** - €3 936 - **£2 400** - FF25 817
The Lovers Mixed media (99x59.5cm 38x23in)
London 2000

✎ **$1 820** - €1 561 - **£1 100** - FF10 240
Costume design for the Shemakhan Princess
Gouache (49x32cm 19x12in) London 1998

TCHÉRINA Ludmilla 1925 [5]

☞ **$11 403** - €10 671 - **£7 063** - FF70 000
Fleur mystérieuse Acrylique/toile (100x81cm
39x31in) Paris 1999

TCHORZEWSKI Jerzy 1928 [8]

☞ **$5 250** - €6 204 - **£3 721** - FF40 695
Sacrum Acrylic/canvas (198x132cm 78x52in) New-
Orleans LA 2000

✎ **$998** - €1 105 - **£694** - FF7 248
Trois personnages Aquarelle, gouache/papier
(46.5x34.5cm 18x13in) Warszawa 2001

TCHOUBANOV Boris 1946 [110]

☞ **$1 587** - €1 524 - **£984** - FF10 000
Danseuses en tutu Huile/toile (67x47cm 26x18in)
La Varenne-Saint-Hilaire 1999

☞ **$927** - €915 - **£571** - FF6 000
Jeune fille sur la passerelle Huile/toile (33x26cm
12x10in) Calais 1999

TCHOUMAKOFF Théodore 1823-1911 [25]

☞ **$1 524** - €1 536 - **£950** - FF10 078
**Italian Lady, Bust-Length, in a white Dress and
white and red Bonnet** Oil/canvas (56x46.5cm
22x18in) London 2000

☞ **$1 464** - €1 563 - **£1 000** - FF10 253
Head of a Girl Oil/panel (13.5x10cm 5x3in)
Billingshurst, West-Sussex 2001

✎ **$412** - €457 - **£285** - FF3 000
Portrait de jeune femme Pastel/papier (30x25cm
11x9in) Moulins 2001

TEAGUE Donald 1897-1991 [21]

☞ **$8 000** - €9 402 - **£5 546** - FF61 675
Venice Watercolour/paper (47.5x70.5cm 18x27in)
Beverly-Hills CA 2000

TEAGUE Violet H. Evangeline 1872-1951 [12]

☞ **$1 400** - €1 544 - **£931** - FF10 125
The Breaking Wave/The Pinnacles, Phillip Island
Oil/canvas (40x44.5cm 15x17in) Melbourne 2000

☞ **$2 218** - €2 444 - **£1 475** - FF16 032
River Landscape Oil/canvas (34x41cm 13x16in)
Melbourne 2000

📠 **$1 121** - €1 235 - **£752** - FF8 103
Night Fall in the Ti-Tree Woodcut in colors
(24.5x17.5cm 9x6in) Malvern, Victoria 2000

TEASDALE Percy Morton 1870-1961 [7]

☞ **$4 356** - €4 001 - **£2 700** - FF26 247
**A Fisherwoman crossing the Wooden Bridge at
Staithes** Oil/canvas/board (25.5x36cm 10x14in) West-
Yorkshire 1999

TEBBITT Henri 1852-1926 [57]

✎ **$197** - €205 - **£124** - FF1 344
The Reeded Riverbank Watercolour/paper
(25.5x44.5cm 10x17in) Melbourne 2000

TEDDY XX [3]

📺 **$745** - €696 - **£450** - FF4 566
«Chaussures Bonin» Poster (157x122cm 61x48in)
London 1999

TEED Douglas Arthur 1864-1929 [78]

 $2 250 - €2 468 - **£1 494** - FF16 192
Arab Scene Oil/canvas (63x76cm 25x30in) Detroit MI
2000

 $2 250 - €2 067 - **£1 382** - FF13 560
The Violet Vase Oil/canvas (28x36cm 11x14in)
Detroit MI 1999

TEELING Norman XX [2]

 $4 301 - €4 952 - **£2 935** - FF32 483
Roger Casement Shortly Before his Execution
Oil/canvas (91x127cm 35x50in) Dublin 2000

TEERLINK Alexander (Abraham) 1776-1857 [23]

 $10 231 - €8 837 - **£6 167** - FF57 967
Buffaloes in the Roman Campagna at Sunset
with Cattle Oil/canvas (75x100cm 29x39in)
Amsterdam 1998

 $471 - €454 - **£290** - FF2 976
Figure on a Bridge by a House, a Tree in the
Foreground Ink (20x25cm 7x9in) Amsterdam 1999

TEESDALE Henry XIX [5]

📺 **$201** - €235 - **£140** - FF1 539
Surrey Engraving (77x40cm 30x16in) Guildford,
Surrey 2000

TEGNER Christian Martin 1803-1881 [7]

 $5 625 - €5 032 - **£3 371** - FF33 011
Parti fra Trondhjem, i mellem- og baggrunden
norske skibe Oil/canvas (52x74cm 20x29in)
Köbenhavn 1998

 $2 639 - €2 816 - **£1 757** - FF18 471
Norsk landskab Oil/canvas (29x39cm 11x15in)
Köbenhavn 2000

TEGNER Rudolph Christopher 1873-1950 [27]

 $1 365 - €1 610 - **£960** - FF10 560
De törstige börn Bronze (26x32cm 10x12in) Vejle
2000

TEICHLEIN Anton 1820-1879 [2]

 $4 860 - €4 547 - **£2 946** - FF29 828
Waterfall Oil/canvas (101.5x81.5cm 39x32in)
Warszawa 1999

TEIGE Karel 1900-1951 [7]

 $9 720 - €11 434 - **£7 042** - FF75 000
Femme nue de dos, proche de deux mains
jointes sortant d'un mur Collage (28.5x21cm
11x8in) Paris 2001

TEILLIET Jean-Cyprien XIX-XX [10]

 $524 - €625 - **£373** - FF4 100
Bruyères Huile/toile (34x54cm 13x21in) Troyes 2000

TEIXEIRA BASTOS Julio XIX-XX [3]

 $4 620 - €5 234 - **£3 150** - FF34 335
Paisagem (Alentejo) Oleo/cartón (21.5x31cm
8x12in) Lisboa 2000

TEIXEIRA DE MATTOS Abraham act.1777-1791 [1]

 $14 079 - €16 336 - **£9 720** - FF107 157
Still Life with Flowers, a Pineapple, Grapes/Still
Life with Tulips Oil/canvas (71x63cm 27x24in)
Amsterdam 2000

TEIXEIRA DE MATTOS Henri 1856-1908 [9]

 $18 065 - €17 244 - **£11 289** - FF113 110
A Pelican Bronze (9x18cm 3x7in) Amsterdam 1999

TEIXEIRA DE MATTOS Joseph 1892-1938 [9]

 $6 342 - €6 807 - **£4 243** - FF44 649
Zelfportret Oil/panel (61x49cm 24x19in) Amsterdam
2000

TEIXIDOR Jordi 1941 [12]

📺 **$121** - €132 - **£83** - FF866
Composición Grabado (75x56cm 29x22in) Madrid
2000

TELARIK Alois 1884-1961 [12]

 $1 000 - €1 037 - **£600** - FF6 800
Corteggiamento Olio/tela (46x64cm 18x25in) Roma
2000

TELEMAQUE Hervé 1937 [172]

 $13 851 - €13 720 - **£8 397** - FF90 000
Au marche claire Acrylique/toile (162x162cm
63x63in) Paris 2001

 $2 886 - €3 354 - **£2 028** - FF22 000
«Le lait» Acrylique/toile (60x60cm 23x23in) Paris
2001

 $2 608 - €2 897 - **£1 818** - FF19 000
Un Sifflet Acrylique/toile (27x35cm 10x13in) Douai
2001

 $882 - €1 067 - **£616** - FF7 000
«Étude gousse, 73/93» Pastel (50x65cm 19x25in)
Paris 2001

📺 **$124** - €137 - **£86** - FF900
«Bleu de Matisse» Sérigraphie (76x56cm 29x22in)
Paris 2001

TELEPY Károly, Karl 1828-1906 [20]

 $14 700 - €16 263 - **£9 660** - FF106 680
Romantic Landscape Oil/canvas (94x152cm
37x59in) Budapest 2000

 $5 600 - €6 196 - **£3 680** - FF40 640
Landscape of the Mountains Oil/canvas
(67x95.5cm 26x37in) Budapest 2000

 $1 452 - €1 650 - **£1 012** - FF10 824
Au bord d'un ruisseau Huile/toile/carton (17x28cm
6x11in) Budapest 2001

 $1 120 - €1 101 - **£700** - FF7 224
Appointment Watercolour/paper (38.5x30.5cm
15x12in) Budapest 1999

TELLA José Garcia 1906-1983 [91]

 $985 - €838 - **£588** - FF5 500
Nature morte à la raie Huile/isorel (64x92cm
25x36in) Paris 1998

 $361 - €351 - **£224** - FF2 300
Deux religieuses Aquarelle, gouache/papier
(67.5x44.5cm 26x17in) Orléans 1999

TELLAECHE de Julián 1884-1960 [7]

 $22 950 - €27 029 - **£16 650** - FF177 300
Pescador vasco Oleo/cartón (68.5x79cm 26x31in)
Madrid 2001

TELLER Grif ?-1993 [8]

 $8 000 - €7 683 - **£4 957** - FF50 395
Pennsylvania Diesel #5707 Oil/board (60x91cm
24x36in) Detroit MI 1999

📺 **$250** - €271 - **£166** - FF1 780
«Pennsylvania Railroad, Ready to Go» Poster
(49x68cm 19x27in) New-York 2000

TELLES Sergio 1936 [44]
- $8 928 - €10 367 - **£6 358** - FF68 000
  Les toits rouges près de la mer Huile/toile
  (50.5x100cm 19x39in) La Varenne-Saint-Hilaire 2001

TELLIER Raymond 1897-1985 [70]
- $1 136 - €1 220 - **£760** - FF8 000
  Portrait de jeune marocaine Huile/panneau
  (46x38cm 18x14in) Paris 2000
- $307 - €335 - **£201** - FF2 200
  Portrait de Jasmina Huile/carton (38x28.5cm
  14x11in) Douai 2000

TELTSCHER Georg 1904-1983 [1]
- $2 142 - €1 994 - **£1 317** - FF13 080
  Postkarte zur Bauhausausstellung
  Farblithographie (15.1x10.4cm 5x4in) München 1999

TELTSCHER Josef Eduard 1801-1837 [6]
- $1 054 - €1 022 - **£663** - FF6 707
  Knabenbildnis Pencil (23x18cm 9x7in) München
  1999

TEMMAN Muhammad 1915-1988 [2]
- $4 532 - €5 336 - **£3 185** - FF35 000
  La chasse Miniature (27.5x20cm 10x7in) Paris 2000

TEMPEL van den Abraham 1622-1672 [10]
- $19 335 - €18 989 - **£12 000** - FF124 558
  Gentleman wearing Black Oil/panel (23x21cm
  9x8in) London 1999

TEMPEST Gerard 1918 [1]
- $9 500 - €9 848 - **£5 700** - FF64 600
  Cosmos III Olio/tela (122x122cm 48x48in) Milano
  2000

TEMPESTA Antonio 1555-1630 [45]
- $9 808 - €11 528 - **£6 800** - FF75 616
  **A rocky Coastline with an Elegant Couple
  Promenading before an Arch** Oil/canvas
  (49x98.5cm 19x38in) London 2000
- $44 816 - €52 190 - **£31 000** - FF342 342
  **The Vision of Saint Eustache/The Death of
  Absalom** Oil/panel (31x37.5cm 12x14in) London 2000
- $1 338 - €1 403 - **£847** - FF9 200
  Hommes combattant des animaux Encre
  (28x42cm 11x16in) Besançon 2000
- $250 - €259 - **£150** - FF1 700
  Scena di battaglia Gravure (30x39cm 11x15in)
  Firenze 2000

TEMPESTI Giovanni Battista 1729/32-1802/04 [7]
- $2 382 - €2 180 - **£1 452** - FF14 301
  Allegorische Szene Red chalk/paper (24x33cm
  9x12in) Wien 1999

TEMPLE Hans 1857-1931 [23]
- $50 484 - €59 333 - **£35 000** - FF389 200
  Mihàly Munkàcsy painting Christ before Pilate
  Oil/canvas (229x179.5cm 90x70in) London 2000
- $8 500 - €9 855 - **£6 021** - FF64 646
  Le Temple de jour Oil/canvas (46x99cm 18x38in)
  New-York 2000

TEMPLE Richard XIX-XX [13]
- $660 - €760 - **£450** - FF4 984
  The Cutty Sark Oil/canvas (49.5x74.5cm 19x29in)
  Billingshurst, West-Sussex 2000

TEMPLIN Viktor 1920-1994 [68]
- $1 455 - €1 377 - **£900** - FF9 030
  Houses by the Lake Oil/board (51x71cm 20x27in)
  London 1999

TEN BOSCH Lena Cornelia 1890-1945 [3]
- $4 491 - €4 526 - **£2 800** - FF29 690
  Irises in a Vase on a Table Oil/canvas (64x54.5cm
  25x21in) London 2000

TEN CATE Hendrick Gerrit 1803-1856 [39]
- $4 983 - €4 265 - **£3 000** - FF27 975
  A Canal in Amsterdam, by night Oil/canvas
  (62x51cm 24x20in) London 1998
- $5 133 - €5 173 - **£3 200** - FF33 931
  **Kalverstraat looking towards the Dam,
  Amsterdam** Oil/canvas (36x28cm 14x11in) Devon
  2000
- $728 - €817 - **£504** - FF5 357
  Feest in de Haarlemmerhout Encre (21x27cm
  8x10in) The Hague 2000

TEN CATE Pieter 1869-1937 [22]
- $404 - €460 - **£285** - FF3 018
  «Wintertag» Öl/Leinwand (61x90cm 24x35in)
  Bremen 2001

TEN CATE Siebe Johannes 1858-1908 [174]
- $5 251 - €4 440 - **£3 140** - FF29 126
  «Londres» Oil/canvas (44x84cm 17x33in) Amsterdam
  1998
- $3 376 - €3 125 - **£2 091** - FF20 500
  Le vapeur Huile/toile (40x24cm 15x9in) Paris 1999
- $1 513 - €1 403 - **£941** - FF9 200
  Coucher de soleil Gouache/papier (25.5x39cm
  10x15in) Paris 1999

TEN COMPE Jan 1713-1761 [4]
- $76 661 - €71 701 - **£47 000** - FF470 329
  **The Hague, a View of the Vijverberg Towards the
  Gevangenpoort** Oil/panel (27x37.5cm 10x14in)
  London 1998

TEN HOLT Friso 1921 [13]
- $1 615 - €1 588 - **£1 038** - FF10 418
  A reclining Nude Oil/canvas (40x59cm 15x23in)
  Amsterdam 1999

TEN HOOPE Bob 1920 [11]
- $216 - €252 - **£152** - FF1 650
  La barque Pastel/papier (34x48cm 13x18in) Grenoble
  2000

TEN KATE Herman Fred. Carel 1822-1891 [185]
- $11 000 - €12 182 - **£7 460** - FF79 909
  Tavern Brawl Oil/panel (40.5x50.5cm 15x19in) New-
  York 2000
- $3 933 - €3 964 - **£2 451** - FF26 000
  L'audience chez la reine Huile/panneau (19.5x27cm
  7x10in) Toulouse 2000
- $1 597 - €1 724 - **£1 092** - FF11 311
  Cosy Family Scene in an Interior.
  Watercolour/paper (21x30cm 8x11in) Amsterdam 2001

TEN KATE Jan Jacob Lodewijk 1850-1929 [13]
- $13 357 - €11 333 - **£8 057** - FF74 337
  De grutterswinkel Oil/canvas (61x95cm 24x37in)
  Den Haag 1998

TEN KATE Johan Mari Henri 1831-1910 [179]

$26 509 - €29 814 - **£18 505** - FF195 569
Waldlandschaft mit Jagdszene Öl/Leinwand
(123x173cm 48x68in) Luzern 2001

$10 448 - €8 835 - **£6 248** - FF57 952
Harvesters Resting Oil/panel (54x74.5cm 21x29in)
Amsterdam 1998

$3 088 - €3 630 - **£2 141** - FF23 812
Children Playing in the Woods Oil/panel
(12x18.5cm 4x7in) Amsterdam 2000

$2 886 - €3 073 - **£1 900** - FF20 160
Unloading the Boats Watercolour (45.5x40.5cm
17x15in) Billingshurst, West-Sussex 2000

TEN KATE Johannes Marius 1859-1896 [23]

$5 210 - €6 196 - **£3 713** - FF40 643
Purchasing Fish Oil/canvas (45.5x39cm 17x15in)
Melbourne 2000

$1 619 - €1 534 - **£984** - FF10 061
**Hirten mit Viehherde und Pferdegespann an der
Quelle** Watercolour (20.1x29.4cm 7x11in) München
1999

TEN OEVER Hendrik 1639-1716 [3]

$10 065 - €8 694 - **£6 079** - FF57 028
Stilleben mit Fisch Öl/Leinwand (63x73cm 24x28in)
Frankfurt 1998

TENCY Jean-Baptiste XVIII-XIX [3]

$1 995 - €2 266 - **£1 400** - FF14 864
**Cattle in a Watermeadow at Sunset with Figures
in Boats on a River** Oil/panel (30x42.5cm 11x16in)
London 2001

TENER René 1846-1925 [40]

$1 783 - €1 906 - **£1 188** - FF12 500
Le barrage Huile/toile (38x61cm 14x24in) Paris 2000

$871 - €915 - **£550** - FF6 000
Gardienne de troupeau en Normandie Huile/pan-
neau (25.5x46cm 10x18in) Paris 2000

TENERANI Pietro 1789-1869 [3]

$15 793 - €17 704 - **£11 000** - FF116 130
Amorino with a Hare Marble (H197cm H77in)
London 2001

TENG NEE CHONG 1951 [3]

$10 632 - €9 910 - **£6 426** - FF65 003
Scarlet Glory upon Midnight Blooms Oil/canvas
(116x116cm 45x45in) Singapore 1999

$2 180 - €2 476 - **£1 492** - FF16 243
Portrait of a reclining Nude Charcoal/paper
(56x80cm 22x31in) Singapore 2000

TENGGREN Gustaf Adolf 1896-1970 [19]

$1 850 - €2 105 - **£1 292** - FF13 807
I sagoskogen Akvarell/papper (25x44cm 9x17in)
Stockholm 2000

TENGNAGEL Jan 1584-1634 [4]

$17 722 - €17 627 - **£11 000** - FF115 623
**Shunammite Woman asking Elisha to Awaken
her Dead Son** Oil/panel (34.5x46cm 13x18in) London
1999

TENIERS David I 1582-1649 [17]

$22 414 - €24 060 - **£15 000** - FF157 824
Christ on the Road to Cavalry Oil/panel
(119x95.5cm 46x37in) London 2000

TENIERS David II 1610-1690 [181]

$73 630 - €82 556 - **£50 000** - FF541 535
**Extensive Landscape with a Peasant Couple
Leading a Cow** Oil/canvas (118.5x164.5cm 46x64in)
London 2000

$57 004 - €64 745 - **£40 000** - FF424 700
The Miraculous Draught of Fishes Oil/canvas
(76.5x110cm 30x43in) London 2001

$33 012 - €32 014 - **£20 769** - FF210 000
Les singes jouant aux cartes Huile/toile (27x37cm
10x14in) Paris 1999

$2 540 - €2 727 - **£1 700** - FF17 886
**Fishermen wading with a Net in a Stream, a
Village in the Background** Black chalk/paper
(28x23.5cm 11x9in) London 2000

$179 - €156 - **£109** - FF1 024
Tiro al arco Grabado (14x24cm 5x9in) Madrid 1999

TENIERS David III 1638-1685 [9]

$6 750 - €7 508 - **£4 625** - FF49 250
«S. Valentín» Oleo/cobre (79x61cm 31x24in) Madrid
2001

$3 270 - €3 068 - **£2 020** - FF20 123
**Dünenlandschaft mit altem Bauernhof und
einer alten Zigeunerin** Oil/wood (25x40cm 9x15in)
Staufen 1999

TENISON E.K. XIX [2]

$2 198 - €2 592 - **£1 545** - FF17 000
L'Alhambra de Grenade Tirage papier salé
(17.5x21.5cm 6x8in) Paris 2000

TENISON Louisa Mary XIX [10]

$2 984 - €2 767 - **£1 800** - FF18 152
**The Temple of Karnak, Thebes/The Temple on
the Island of Philae** Pencil (37x53cm 14x20in)
London 1999

TENNANT Craig 1946 [5]

$6 600 - €7 084 - **£4 416** - FF46 470
Under a Yellow Sky Oil/canvas (60x101cm 24x40in)
Houston TX 2000

TENNANT Emma 1943 [8]

$4 184 - €4 491 - **£2 800** - FF29 460
Still Life with Fuchias/Still Life with Amaryllis
Watercolour (60x91.5cm 23x36in) London 2000

TENNANT John F. 1796-1872 [55]

$6 725 - €7 219 - **£4 500** - FF47 351
Fishing for Minnows Oil/canvas (51.5x76cm
20x29in) London 2000

$857 - €962 - **£600** - FF6 309
Herdsman Journeying Home Oil/board (28x42cm
11x16in) London 2001

TENNANT Stephen 1905-1987 [28]

$305 - €308 - **£190** - FF2 019
Design for Invitation Watercolour (19x24.7cm 7x9in)
London 2000

TENNESON Joyce 1945 [21]

$1 600 - €1 842 - **£1 091** - FF12 083
Suzanne with Snake Photograph (61x53.5cm
24x21in) New-York 2000

TENNIEL John 1820-1914 [30]

$284 - €321 - **£200** - FF2 108
British lion prepares for the Jubilee
Gouache/paper (20x16cm 7x6in) Near Ely 2001

T

TENRÉ Henry Charles 1864-1926 **[25]**

$7 105 - €7 445 - £4 500 - FF48 838
Two Women in an Interior Oil/canvas (59x72cm 23x28in) London 2000

TEPA Franciszek 1828-1889 **[3]**

$6 222 - €6 368 - £3 753 - FF35 211
Portrait of Hr.Adama Potockiego in turkish Suit Watercolour/paper (20x16cm 7x6in) München 1998

TEPLER Samuel 1918-1998 **[59]**

$950 - €1 020 - £636 - FF6 692
Il Muro Azzurro Oil/canvas (35x50cm 13x19in) Tel Aviv 2000

$700 - €830 - £510 - FF5 443
Still Life with Vase and Flowers Oil/cardboard (33x41.5cm 12x16in) Tel Aviv 2001

TEPPER Saul 1899-1987 **[17]**

$6 000 - €5 555 - £3 672 - FF36 436
Soldier impaling dictators on bayonnet, poster design Oil/board (76x55cm 30x22in) New-York 1999

TER BORCH Gerard 1617-1681 **[24]**

$12 405 - €13 613 - £7 986 - FF89 298
Elderly Woman, seated by a Table wearing a black Dress, Lace Collar Oil/canvas (57x46.5cm 22x18in) Amsterdam 2000

$17 664 - €19 048 - £11 856 - FF124 944
Porträtt av herre, knästycke Oil/panel (39.5x30cm 15x11in) Stockholm 2000

$24 182 - €20 865 - £14 591 - FF136 863
Ice scene with two men pushing a lady in a sled Ink (9.3x6.8cm 3x2in) Amsterdam 1998

TER MEULEN Frans Pieter 1843-1927 **[39]**

$1 800 - €2 087 - £1 275 - FF13 692
A Flock of Lamb Oil/canvas (54x78cm 21x30in) Amsterdam 2000

$483 - €544 - £333 - FF3 571
A Peasantwoman on a Forest Track Oil/canvas (32.5x25.5cm 12x10in) Amsterdam 2000

$1 247 - €1 069 - £750 - FF7 010
Return from the Fields Watercolour/paper (46x66cm 18x25in) Edinburgh 1998

TERÄ Teppo 1935 **[11]**

$15 330 - €16 818 - £9 870 - FF110 320
Orrar i vinterlandskap Oil/canvas (130x130cm 51x51in) Helsinki 2000

$5 841 - €5 718 - £3 593 - FF37 308
Peltopyitä pesällä Oil/canvas (50.5x60cm 19x23in) Helsinki 1999

TERAOKA Masami 1936 **[9]**

$5 500 - €6 126 - £3 597 - FF40 185
Catfish Envy /From Here to Eternity Etching, aquatint in colors (66x97.5cm 25x38in) New-York 2000

TERECHKOVITCH Kostia, Constantin 1902-1978 **[406]**

$5 257 - €5 087 - £3 241 - FF33 369
Bildnis des Frau des Künstlers Öl/Leinwand (55.9x47cm 22x18in) Wien 1999

$2 001 - €1 829 - £1 225 - FF12 000
Portrait de femme Huile/panneau (41x33cm 16x12in) Calais 1999

$1 534 - €1 829 - £1 094 - FF12 000
Jeune femme au chapeau Aquarelle/papier (47x37cm 18x14in) Paris 2000

$150 - €136 - £90 - FF894
Menton Festival de Musique de Chambre Color lithograph (64x49cm 25x19in) Bethesda MD 1998

TERELAK John C. 1942 **[9]**

$6 000 - €6 218 - £3 801 - FF40 789
Winter Chores Oil/board (76x101cm 30x40in) Portsmouth NH 2000

TERESZCZUK Peter XIX-XX **[67]**

$792 - €740 - £479 - FF4 857
Danserinde med svingende gevanter Bronze (H20.5cm H8in) Köbenhavn 1999

TERLIKOWSKI de Vladimir 1873-1951 **[205]**

$6 624 - €6 098 - £3 976 - FF40 000
Les quais de Paris Huile/toile (98x162cm 38x63in) Lyon 1999

$2 454 - €2 561 - £1 547 - FF16 800
Nature morte Huile/toile (79x98cm 31x38in) Toulouse 2000

$1 015 - €991 - £642 - FF6 500
Les chaumières Huile/toile (33x41cm 12x16in) Paris 1999

TERLOUW Kees 1890-1948 **[122]**

$891 - €998 - £619 - FF6 548
Interieur met koffiedrinkster Oil/canvas (49x39cm 19x15in) Rotterdam 2001

$472 - €504 - £320 - FF3 305
Près le lac Brasern Oil/canvas (41x33cm 16x12in) Stockholm 2001

TERMOTE Albert 1887-1971 **[8]**

$854 - €998 - £609 - FF6 548
The Cripple Bronze (H20cm H7in) Amsterdam 2001

TERNANTE-LEMAIRE de Amédée XIX **[5]**

$3 429 - €3 659 - £2 284 - FF24 000
L'arrivée à Lisbonne de Stéphanie de Hohenzollern-Sigmaringen 18 mai Tirage albuminé (19.5x24cm 7x9in) Paris 2000

TERPENING Sonya 1953 **[4]**

$3 500 - €3 974 - £2 431 - FF26 068
Little Princess Oil/canvas (60x45cm 24x18in) Dallas TX 2001

TERPNING Howard A. 1927 **[33]**

$110 000 - €117 942 - £72 776 - FF773 652
Paints Oil/canvas (45x60cm 18x24in) Hayden ID 2000

$40 000 - €36 362 - £24 092 - FF238 520
Horsefeathers Oil/board (30x35cm 12x14in) Hayden ID 1998

$3 000 - €3 412 - £2 096 - FF22 380
Cast a Giant Shadow: Movie Poster Design Gouache/board (76x49cm 30x19in) New-York 2000

$1 082 - €1 196 - £750 - FF7 846
«Cleopatra» Poster (73.5x109cm 28x42in) London 2001

TERPNING Susan XX **[1]**

$32 500 - €29 544 - £19 574 - FF193 797
First Pony Oil/canvas (121x147cm 48x58in) Hayden ID 1998

TERRAIRE Clovis Frédérick 1858-1931 **[59]**

$5 737 - €6 403 - £3 754 - FF42 000
Vaches au pâturage, effet de lumière Huile/toile (105.5x161.5cm 41x63in) Fontainebleau 2000

$804 - €869 - **£556** - FF5 700
Troupeau de vaches dans une pinède Huile/toile
(50x65cm 19x25in) Lyon 2001

TERRELL Georgina Koberwein XIX-XX [3]
$3 332 - €3 835 - **£2 301** - FF25 154
**Königin Viktoria von Grossbritannien, nach
Heinrich von Angeli** Öl/Leinwand (66x52cm
25x20in) München 2000

TERRENI Antonio XVIII [1]
$11 906 - €10 062 - **£7 121** - FF66 000
«**View of the dock yard at Constantinople with
Galata, Pera, suburbs**» Aquarelle (37.5x61cm
14x24in) Paris 1998

TERRENI Giuseppe Maria 1739-1811 [4]
$7 200 - €9 330 - **£5 400** - FF61 200
**Veduta del molo di Livorno e del Faro in occa-
sione/Progetto** Gouache/carta (59x93cm 23x36in)
Milano 2001

TERRIS Adolphe 1820-1900 [64]
$1 413 - €1 372 - **£873** - FF9 000
**Travaux de Marseille: Parc Borély/Château
Borély vue de la cascade** Tirage albuminé
(33x39cm 12x15in) Paris 1999

TERRIS John 1865-1914 [27]
$538 - €515 - **£330** - FF3 377
The Village of Wixford, near Stratford
Watercolour/paper (30x45cm 11x17in) London 1999

TERRUELLA MATILLA Joaquín 1891-1957 [129]
$17 850 - €21 023 - **£12 250** - FF137 900
Costa mediterránea Oleo/lienzo (129x104cm
50x40in) Barcelona 2000
$3 510 - €3 904 - **£2 470** - FF25 610
Manoletina por Manolete Oleo/lienzo (54x65cm
21x25in) Madrid 2001
$1 740 - €1 802 - **£1 110** - FF11 820
Vista costera Oleo/tabla (22.5x26.5cm 8x10in)
Barcelona 2000
$427 - €420 - **£259** - FF2 758
**Monolito bienvenida obligando a su segundo
con arte y elegancia** Tinta (16x25cm 6x9in)
Barcelona 2000

TERRUS E. XX [2]
$4 348 - €5 183 - **£3 100** - FF34 000
Le racou Huile/toile (50x60cm 19x23in) Vinca 2000
$3 389 - €4 040 - **£2 416** - FF26 500
La maison du racou Huile/toile (25x32cm 9x12in)
Vinca 2000

TERRUSO Saverio 1939 [154]
$1 680 - €1 451 - **£1 120** - FF9 520
«**Figura al tavolo**» Olio/tela (80x60cm 31x23in) Prato
1998
$750 - €777 - **£450** - FF5 100
«**Composizione**» Olio/tela (30x40cm 11x15in)
Vercelli 1999
$238 - €247 - **£142** - FF1 618
Fiori Tempera/carta (49x34cm 19x13in) Milano 2000

TERRY Emilio 1890-1969 [8]
$3 142 - €3 049 - **£1 936** - FF20 000
La scène de théâtre de Groussay avec acteurs
Crayons couleurs (29.5x29.5cm 11x11in) Montfort
L'Amaury 1999

TERRY Frederick Casemero 1827-1869 [11]
$176 - €179 - **£110** - FF1 173
**The Gap South Head/Point Piper Sydney/North
Head/King Street** Engraving (19x13cm 7x5in)
Sydney 2000

TERRY Joseph Alfred 1872-1939 [41]
$377 - €425 - **£260** - FF2 786
In the Langdale Country Oil/board (33.5x41.5cm
13x16in) London 2000
$280 - €327 - **£200** - FF2 147
Italian Valley View Watercolour (28.5x38cm 11x14in)
London 2001

TERWEI Wilhelm 1875-1946 [4]
$945 - €1 125 - **£674** - FF7 378
Im Winterwald Öl/Karton (25x20cm 9x7in) Köln 2000

TERWESTEN IL PARODIJSVOGEL Augustinus I
1649-1711 [10]
$12 981 - €15 257 - **£9 000** - FF100 080
**Portrait of Madame de Grignan as Hebe with
Jupiter at her Side** Oil/canvas (174x138.5cm
68x54in) London 2000
$32 222 - €32 048 - **£20 000** - FF210 224
Rape of Europa Oil/canvas (97x123cm 38x48in)
London 1999

TERWESTEN Matheus 1670-1757 [21]
$14 628 - €14 067 - **£9 011** - FF92 274
**Two Elegant Draped Nudes Seated on an Alter
in an Interior** Oil/canvas (200.5x127.5cm 78x50in)
Amsterdam 1999
$8 564 - €8 146 - **£5 200** - FF53 433
Flora and Zephyr Oil/canvas (88x100.5cm 34x39in)
London 1999
$3 500 - €3 738 - **£2 385** - FF24 521
**Seated Allegorical Female Figure holding a
Cardinal's Hat** Black chalk (44.5x36.5cm 17x14in)
New-York 2001

TERWEY Jan Pieter 1883-1965 [27]
$895 - €934 - **£566** - FF6 128
Bord de lac Huile/toile (60x85cm 23x33in) Genève
2000

TERZI Aleardo 1870-1943 [6]
$1 700 - €1 983 - **£1 193** - FF13 005
«**Roma 1911, Internationale Ausstellung**» Poster
(40x58.5cm 15x23in) New-York 2000

TESAURO Augusto ?-c.1546 [1]
$10 800 - €9 330 - **£5 400** - FF61 200
Madonna col Bambino Olio/tavola (43.5x34.5cm
17x13in) Milano 1999

TESCHNER Richard 1879-1948 [71]
$247 - €291 - **£171** - FF1 906
Skurile Figuren Pencil (48.5x62.5cm 19x24in) Wien
2000
$162 - €182 - **£110** - FF1 191
Luna Farbradierung (23x21.5cm 9x8in) Wien 2000

TESDORPF-EDENS Ilse 1892-1966 [23]
$869 - €1 022 - **£623** - FF6 707
**Baumgruppe und ferne Häuser in den
Hamburger Walddörfern** Öl/Karton (18x13.5cm
7x5in) Hamburg 2001

T

TESHIGAHARA Sofu 1900 [22]

$4 960 - €5 899 - £3 536 - FF38 695
Mu Mixed media (179x390cm 70x153in) Amsterdam 2000

$3 320 - €3 857 - £2 333 - FF25 301
Period Gouache (175x372cm 68x146in) Amsterdam 2001

TESIO Giacinto 1849-1927 [5]

$1 500 - €1 743 - £1 054 - FF11 431
Harlequin with Guitar Oil/canvas (80x79cm 31x31in) New-York 2001

TESIO Lodovico 1731-1782 [2]

$1 420 - €1 524 - £950 - FF10 000
Le Sacrifice d'Abraham Encre (26.5x17.5cm 10x6in) Cheverny 2000

TESKE Edmund R. 1911 [17]

$1 000 - €854 - £598 - FF5 599
Jeffrey Harris -Composite with Brooklyn Bridge Gelatin silver print (24x33.5cm 9x13in) San-Francisco CA 1998

TESNIERE Victor Théophile 1820/21-1904 [3]

$1 255 - €1 265 - £782 - FF7 518
Port animé Huile/toile (27x33cm 10x12in) Valence 2000

TESSAI Tomioka Hyakuren 1836-1924 [5]

$8 000 - €7 749 - £4 989 - FF50 833
Mountain Landscape with Waterfall Ink (165.5x34cm 65x13in) New-York 1999

TESSARI Giovanni Domenico XVIII [1]

$2 358 - €2 812 - £1 681 - FF18 446
Junge Frau mit einem Papagei, nach Giovanni Battista Tiepolo Radierung (17.4x12.7cm 6x5in) Berlin 2000

TESSARI Romolo 1868-? [15]

$560 - €726 - £420 - FF4 760
Ritratto di giovinetta con cappellino Acquarello/carta (47x31cm 18x12in) Milano 2000

TESSIER Léon XIX [3]

$4 437 - €4 421 - £2 694 - FF29 000
Intérieur d'une chambre à coucher avec un déjeuner Huile/toile (73x60cm 28x23in) Paris 2000

TESSITORE Fulvio 1870-? [9]

$777 - €853 - £500 - FF5 594
Figures on a Street in Naples Oil/canvas (19.5x39cm 7x15in) London 2000

TESSITORE Giuseppe Raffaele 1861-? [4]

$3 000 - €3 110 - £1 800 - FF20 400
Suonatrice di chitarra Olio/tela (103.5x50cm 40x19in) Torino 2000

TESSON Louis 1820-1870 [40]

$4 894 - €4 497 - £3 006 - FF29 500
La gourmandise Huile/toile (65x81cm 25x31in) Joigny 1999

$2 364 - €2 287 - £1 458 - FF15 000
Chameliers aux abords d'une ville turque Technique mixte (28x44.5cm 11x17in) Paris 1999

$659 - €686 - £416 - FF4 500
L'embarcadère Aquarelle/papier (15x20cm 5x7in) Toulouse 2000

TESSON Louis XX [5]

$7 164 - €6 937 - £4 500 - FF45 506
The Patisserie Window Oil/canvas (65x81cm 25x31in) London 1999

TESTA Armando 1917-1992 [27]

$319 - €363 - £222 - FF2 381
«Games of the XVII Olympiad» Poster (70x100cm 27x39in) Hoorn 2001

TESTA IL LUCCHESINO Pietro 1611-1650 [51]

$10 000 - €10 367 - £6 000 - FF68 000
Paesaggio classico con cascata e astanti in primo piano Olio/tela (97.5x73cm 38x28in) Roma 2001

$15 000 - €13 040 - £9 078 - FF85 539
Study of a Tree Trunk, and Separate Studies of a Head and Sketches Ink (19x19cm 7x7in) New-York 1999

$600 - €701 - £421 - FF4 601
Abraham's Sacrifice Etching (30x24.5cm 11x9in) New-York 2000

TESTA Pietro 1912 [15]

$1 400 - €1 567 - £976 - FF10 279
Achilles dragging Hector's Corpse around the Walls of Troy Etching (27x42cm 10x16in) New-York 2001

TESTI A. XX [1]

$841 - €872 - £504 - FF5 718
«Ferrovia Elettrica Stresa-Mottarone» Affiche couleur (97x68cm 38x26in) Torino 2000

TESTI Arnolfo 1913 [12]

$2 400 - €3 110 - £1 800 - FF20 400
Interno con ragazza, ritratto di Amelia Testi Olio/tela (197x170cm 77x43in) Prato 2000

$680 - €881 - £510 - FF5 780
Ritratto della sorella Luigina che legge Olio/tela (60x50cm 23x19in) Prato 2000

TESTU Pierre XIX-XX [57]

$1 924 - €1 768 - £1 182 - FF11 600
Les ramasseuses de coquillages Huile/toile (65x95cm 25x37in) Paris 2000

$928 - €967 - £592 - FF6 341
Le retour de la pêche Huile/toile (32x40cm 12x15in) Bruxelles 2000

TETAR VAN ELVEN Jean Baptist 1805-1889 [45]

$2 303 - €2 301 - £1 440 - FF15 092
Eisvergnügen Öl/Leinwand (25x70cm 9x27in) Köln 1999

$2 509 - €2 949 - £1 740 - FF19 347
A Church Interior Oil/panel (34x25cm 13x9in) Amsterdam 2000

TETAR VAN ELVEN Paul Constantin D. 1823-1896 [13]

$2 547 - €2 467 - £1 600 - FF16 180
Arab Street Market Oil/canvas (76x53cm 29x20in) London 2000

TETAR VAN ELVEN Pierre Henri Theod. 1828-1908 [64]

$12 477 - €10 567 - £7 500 - FF69 315
Harem in the Grounds of a Palace Oil/panel (50.5x81cm 19x31in) London 1998

$3 888 - €4 084 - **£2 460** - FF26 789
City View in Marocco Oil/panel (45x35cm 17x13in)
Amsterdam 2000

$539 - €579 - **£361** - FF3 800
Habitants de l'Ile de Marten près d'Amsterdam
Aquarelle/papier (21x26cm 8x10in) Grenoble 2000

TETE Maurice Louis 1881-1948 [18]

$590 - €686 - **£415** - FF4 500
Nature morte Huile/toile (46x55cm 18x21in) Paris
2001

$345 - €381 - **£239** - FF2 500
Les glaneuses Aquarelle/carton (22x33cm 8x12in)
Lyon 2001

TETENS Vilhelm 1871-1956 [5]

$257 - €295 - **£179** - FF1 934
**Haveparti med åbentstående vindue og en
baenk** Oil/canvas (64x75cm 25x29in) København 2000

TETMAJER Wlodzimierz 1862-1923 [40]

$15 517 - €17 335 - **£10 519** - FF113 712
Garçons et demoiselles d'honneur Huile/toile
(121.5x181.5cm 47x71in) Warszawa 2000

$8 812 - €10 334 - **£6 288** - FF67 784
Devant un manoir de Bronowice Huile/toile
(41.5x45.5cm 16x17in) Warszawa 2000

$2 625 - €3 123 - **£1 872** - FF20 484
Après-midi ensoleillé Huile/toile/carton (33x27.5cm
12x10in) Warszawa 2000

$2 131 - €2 507 - **£1 528** - FF16 443
Chaumière de Bronowice Gouache (21x28cm
8x11in) Warszawa 2001

TETTELBACH Moritz 1794-1870 [8]

$401 - €397 - **£250** - FF2 605
Fruktstilleben Gouache/paper (18x15cm 7x5in)
Stockholm 1999

TETZNER Heinz 1920 [25]

$447 - €511 - **£310** - FF3 353
Morgenlicht Aquarell/Papier (50x70cm 19x27in)
Zwiesel 2000

TEUBER Hermann 1894-1985 [112]

$2 106 - €2 045 - **£1 301** - FF13 415
Der Waldweg Oil/panel (48x51cm 18x20in) München
1999

$1 000 - €1 176 - **£716** - FF7 714
Am Dorfrand Tempera (28.5x40cm 11x15in)
Dettelbach-Effeldorf 2001

$404 - €460 - **£280** - FF3 018
Blumenstilleben vor einer Landschaft
Aquarell/Papier (38.5x52.5cm 15x20in) Berlin 2000

$128 - €123 - **£78** - FF804
Vogel Monotype (14x16.5cm 5x6in) Dettelbach-
Effeldorf 1999

TEUCHERT Karoly 1886-1926 [1]

$8 847 - €9 798 - **£6 000** - FF64 272
In the Boudoir Oil/canvas (69x95cm 27x37in)
Billingshurst, West-Sussex 2000

TEUPKEN Dirk Antoon, Jr. 1828-1859 [14]

$2 348 - €2 723 - **£1 663** - FF17 859
Untitled Watercolour (52x71cm 20x27in) Amsterdam
2000

TEVET Nahum 1946 [2]

$10 000 - €10 970 - **£6 453** - FF71 959
Composition in Gray, Blue, White and Red
Sculpture, wood (45x40cm 17x15in) Tel Aviv 2000

TEVINI M. XX [1]

$1 800 - €2 008 - **£1 178** - FF13 172
«La Fonografia Nazionale, Milano» Poster
(70x100cm 27x39in) New-York 2000

TEW Justin 1969 [5]

$714 - €832 - **£500** - FF5 459
African Elephant Oil/paper (26x94.5cm 10x37in)
London 2000

TEWARI Vasundhara 1955 [3]

$3 500 - €3 980 - **£2 445** - FF26 110
Dream Reality Pencil (44.5x36cm 17x14in) New-York
2000

TEXIER Richard 1955 [95]

$2 119 - €1 982 - **£1 283** - FF13 000
Rébus de la Petite Lune Huile/toile (195x195cm
76x76in) Paris 1999

$1 316 - €1 220 - **£818** - FF8 000
Epis Technique mixte/toile (65x82cm 25x32in)
Versailles 1999

$115 - €137 - **£82** - FF900
Peinture sur Ingres Lithographie couleurs (60x50cm
23x19in) Paris 2000

TEYLER Johan 1648-c.1699 [8]

$772 - €920 - **£550** - FF6 037
Hahn Farbradierung (13x13.6cm 5x5in) Berlin 2000

TEYNARD Felix 1817-1892 [25]

$2 038 - €2 134 - **£1 281** - FF14 000
Louxor Tirage papier salé (25x30.5cm 9x12in) Paris
2000

THABARD Adolphe Martial 1831-1905 [12]

$1 762 - €1 677 - **£1 102** - FF11 000
Ephèbe au faucon Bronze (H77cm H30in) Paris
1999

THACKERAY Lance ?-1916 [9]

$1 767 - €1 753 - **£1 100** - FF11 501
**Figures in a Motorcar/Young Lady in a motori-
zed Carriage** Watercolour (43x70cm 16x27in) London
1999

THACKERAY William Makepeace 1811-1863 [7]

$1 065 - €1 015 - **£650** - FF6 660
Character Studies Pencil/paper (51x38cm 20x14in)
London 1999

THADDEUS Henry John 1860-1929 [6]

$31 802 - €29 906 - **£20 000** - FF196 168
**Three quarter length Portrait of a Young Woman
in White Dress** Oil/canvas (120x59.5cm 47x23in) Co.
Kilkenny 1999

THAETER Julius I 1804-1870 [17]

$1 211 - €1 329 - **£823** - FF8 720
Die Überfahrt über den Styx Pencil/paper
(32.2x47.1cm 12x18in) Berlin 2000

$315 - €358 - **£219** - FF2 347
Christus auf dem See Genezareth Radierung
(42.5x52cm 16x20in) Berlin 2001

T

THAKE Eric Prentice Anchor 1904-1982 **[74]**

- $3 831 – €3 340 – £2 316 – FF21 912
  The Carved Emu Egg. Louth Hotel Oil/canvas (44.5x31.5cm 17x12in) Melbourne 1998
- $502 – €564 – £325 – FF3 699
  Morrah Street, Carlton Gouache (25x17cm 9x6in) Malvern, Victoria 2000
- $224 – €247 – £150 – FF1 622
  Figure in a Rocky Landscape Linocut (13.5x21cm 5x8in) Malvern, Victoria 2000

THALEMANN Else 1901-1984 **[37]**

- $523 – €562 – £350 – FF3 689
  Stamm des Baumfarns Photograph (24x18.2cm 9x7in) München 2000

THALINGER E. Oscar 1885-? **[15]**

- $1 900 – €1 638 – £1 128 – FF10 746
  New York Abstract Oil/masonite (60x81cm 24x32in) Cincinnati OH 1998

THAMM Gustav Adolf 1859-1925 **[28]**

- $748 – €869 – £525 – FF5 701
  Fuhrwerk in der Abenddämmerung Öl/Leinwand (40x61cm 15x24in) Rudolstadt-Thüringen 2001

THANG TRAN PENH XX **[1]**

- $9 756 – €11 078 – £6 677 – FF72 668
  The Card Game Ink (60x71cm 23x27in) Singapore 2000

THANGO François 1936-1981 **[5]**

- $14 249 – €13 753 – £9 000 – FF90 214
  La chasse sauvage Waterpaint (39x285cm 15x112in) London 1999

THANS Willem 1816-c.1850 **[3]**

- $5 375 – €4 532 – £3 190 – FF29 727
  The Good Wine Oil/panel (47x39cm 18x15in) Amsterdam 1998

THAOTHONG Preecha 1948 **[7]**

- $5 100 – €5 485 – £3 420 – FF35 980
  Nude Study in Studio Oil/canvas (101x151cm 39x59in) Bangkok 2000
- $3 738 – €3 472 – £2 310 – FF22 778
  Shadows & Light, Interior Acrylic/canvas (78x98cm 30x38in) Bangkok 1999

THARAUD Camille 1878-1956 **[10]**

- $395 – €427 – £265 – FF2 800
  Lampe veilleuse à décor de Pierrot Porcelain (H20cm H7in) Lyon 2000

THARRATS VIDAL Joan Josep 1918 **[122]**

- $1 300 – €1 201 – £780 – FF7 880
  Explosión en azul Acrílico/lienzo (54x44cm 21x17in) Barcelona 1999
- $427 – €420 – £266 – FF2 758
  Sin título Acrílico/cartulina (20x22cm 7x8in) Barcelona 1999
- $335 – €330 – £214 – FF2 167
  Sin título Collage (32x24.5cm 12x9in) Madrid 1999
- $72 – €84 – £50 – FF551
  Composición Litografía (74.5x55.5cm 29x21in) Barcelona 2001

THAUBERGER David Allen 1948 **[10]**

- $364 – €391 – £247 – FF2 564
  Flocked Bunnies Silkscreen in colors (20x26.5cm 7x10in) Calgary, Alberta 2001

THAULOW Fritz 1847-1906 **[392]**

- $36 000 – €41 965 – £24 926 – FF275 274
  Under the Bridge Oil/canvas (101x86cm 40x34in) South-Natick MA 2000
- $5 891 – €6 807 – £4 125 – FF44 652
  Seilbåt ved kysten Oil/panel (24x32cm 9x12in) Oslo 2001
- $15 478 – €16 617 – £10 355 – FF109 000
  Paysage de neige Pastel/papier (46x56cm 18x22in) Saint-Dié 2000
- $1 295 – €1 474 – £910 – FF9 671
  La Diviere Etching in colors (49x60cm 19x23in) Vejle 2001

THAWAN DUCHANEE 1939 **[9]**

- $10 200 – €9 706 – £6 840 – FF71 960
  Muthical Beasts of the Night Oil/canvas (199x89cm 78x35in) Bangkok 2000
- $3 174 – €2 958 – £1 958 – FF19 402
  Lion God Ballpoint pen (69x109cm 27x42in) Singapore 1999

THAYAHT Ernesto Michahelles 1893-1959 **[44]**

- $3 000 – €2 592 – £1 500 – FF17 000
  «la orana lotepha» Olio/tavola (125.5x90cm 49x35in) Prato 1999
- $560 – €726 – £420 – FF4 760
  La fontana China (60.5x45cm 23x17in) Milano 2000

THAYER Abbott Handerson 1849-1921 **[22]**

- $9 500 – €9 432 – £5 937 – FF61 869
  The Red Fox Oil/canvas (56x69cm 22x27in) New-York 1999
- $1 900 – €2 039 – £1 294 – FF13 378
  Drawing water Oil/paper/canvas (20x26.5cm 7x10in) Boston MA 2001
- $1 600 – €1 866 – £1 123 – FF12 240
  Sparrow Perched Among and Daisies Watercolour, gouache/paper (30x23cm 11x9in) Boston MA 2000

THAYER Ethel Randolph 1904 **[3]**

- $5 000 – €5 705 – £3 475 – FF37 423
  Seated Woman in yellow Shawl Oil/canvas (101x76cm 40x30in) Dedham MA 2001

THE TOUT (P.R.G. Buchanan) c.1850-c.1950 **[24]**

- $945 – €900 – £600 – FF5 902
  Set of Racing Characters Watercolour (22x13cm 8x5in) Billingshurst, West-Sussex 1999

THEDY Max 1858-1924 **[34]**

- $839 – €920 – £596 – FF6 037
  Portrait eines älteren Mannes Öl/Karton (45x36.5cm 17x14in) Düsseldorf 2000
- $328 – €307 – £199 – FF2 012
  Sitzende Frau, den Blick nach rechts unten gewandt Charcoal (27.5x23cm 10x9in) Berlin 1999

THEED William the Younger 1804-1891 **[7]**

- $11 661 – €13 261 – £8 000 – FF86 984
  Figure of Narcissus leaning on a spear next to a tree trunk Marble (H94cm H37in) Oxfordshire 2000
- $3 500 – €3 976 – £2 456 – FF26 079
  Bust, probably Apollo Marble (H63.5cm H25in) New-York 2001

THEER Robert 1808-1863 [20]
- $595 - €654 - **£383** - FF4 290
  Bildnis einer jungen Dame in schwarzem Kleid und Blumensträusschen Watercolour (12x10cm 4x3in) Wien 2000

THEGERSTRÖM Robert 1857-1919 [65]
- $1 069 - €1 000 - **£658** - FF6 557
  Forslandskap Oil/canvas (54x65cm 21x25in) Stockholm 1999
- $1 061 - €1 226 - **£742** - FF8 039
  Porträtt av Madame Lewin Pastel/paper (64x53cm 25x20in) Stockholm 2001

THEIMER Ivan 1944 [12]
- $5 025 - €5 717 - **£3 487** - FF37 500
  «Le poet Laval II» Huile/toile (81x100cm 31x39in) Douai 2000

THEISS John William 1863-? [5]
- $175 - €189 - **£121** - FF2 500
  Falls is wooded Landscape Watercolour/paper (28x21cm 11x8in) Altadena CA 2001

THELANDER Pär Gunnar 1936 [140]
- $5 595 - €6 141 - **£3 605** - FF40 280
  Utan titel Oil/canvas (131x105cm 51x41in) Stockholm 2000
- $1 622 - €1 781 - **£1 045** - FF11 681
  Fem röda figurer Oil/canvas (62x43cm 24x16in) Stockholm 2000
- $1 130 - €1 060 - **£699** - FF6 955
  La belle Gabrielle et sa soeur Mixed media (42x25cm 16x9in) Stockholm 1999
- $295 - €277 - **£177** - FF1 815
  Europeiska strutsar I Etching (89x60cm 35x23in) Stockholm 1999

THELEM Ernest B. Lem 1869-1930 [5]
- $1 600 - €1 365 - **£965** - FF8 953
  «Peugeot» Poster (110x149.5cm 43x58in) New-York 1998

THELEN-RÜDEN von Friedrich 1836-? [11]
- $544 - €598 - **£350** - FF3 920
  Blowing Bubbles Oil/canvas (100.5x74.5cm 39x29in) London 2000

THELOT Antoine Charles 1798-1853 [19]
- $322 - €381 - **£229** - FF2 500
  La Rochelle, rue aux canards Lavis/papier (49x36.5cm 19x14in) Paris 2001

THELWALL John Augustus XIX-XX [8]
- $882 - €889 - **£550** - FF5 832
  Still life of an earthenware jug and fruit displayed on a table Oil/panel (22.5x33cm 8x12in) London 2000

THELWELL Norman 1923 [27]
- $1 270 - €1 363 - **£850** - FF8 943
  I suppose this was bound to happen sooner or later Ink (19.5x28.5cm 7x11in) London 2000

THENN c.1900 [2]
- $3 978 - €4 269 - **£2 713** - FF28 000
  «Le Trésor» Bronze (19x14cm 7x5in) Paris 2001

THEOPHILOS Hadjimichail 1867-1934 [11]
- $324 000 - €360 389 - **£216 000** - FF2 364 000
  Villa courtyard, Mytilene Oil/canvas (180x165cm 70x64in) Athens 2000
- $54 000 - €60 065 - **£36 000** - FF394 000
  Diamando, Vlacha from Kalamata Oil/panel (114x42cm 44x16in) Athens 2000
- $7 327 - €8 436 - **£5 000** - FF55 334
  Saints Constantine and Eleni Oil/panel (22.5x16cm 8x6in) London 2000

THERIAT Charles James 1860-1937 [53]
- $6 500 - €7 198 - **£4 506** - FF47 216
  Algerian desert landscape Oil/canvas (48x60cm 19x24in) Downington PA 2001
- $5 500 - €5 904 - **£3 680** - FF38 725
  Desert Dwellers Oil/canvas (33x46cm 13x18in) Portland ME 2000

THERKILDSEN Agnete 1900-1993 [19]
- $650 - €645 - **£395** - FF4 231
  Komposition med figurer Oil/canvas (70x74cm 27x29in) Vejle 2000

THERKILDSEN Michael 1850-1925 [83]
- $657 - €724 - **£438** - FF4 749
  Bondemand med hund ved köerne på engen Oil/canvas (36x56cm 14x22in) Vejle 2000
- $439 - €404 - **£270** - FF2 649
  Fjordlandskab med kreaturer Oil/canvas (33.5x47cm 13x18in) Vejle 1999

THERMIGNON Carlo 1857-1938 [1]
- $1 600 - €2 073 - **£1 200** - FF13 600
  Mercato arabo, Egitto Olio/cartone (31x26cm 12x10in) Milano 2001

THERRIEN Robert 1947 [42]
- $14 000 - €12 450 - **£8 562** - FF81 666
  Snowman Oil/canvas (244x162.5cm 96x63in) New-York 1999
- $55 000 - €63 816 - **£37 972** - FF418 605
  Untitled Bronze (32x32x9cm 12x12x3in) New-York 2000
- $4 500 - €4 831 - **£3 011** - FF31 687
  Untitled Gouache (40.5x51cm 15x20in) Beverly-Hills CA 2000
- $15 000 - €12 711 - **£8 964** - FF83 379
  Untitled Silkscreen (25.5x19cm 10x7in) New-York 1998

THESLEFF Ellen 1869-1954 [57]
- $18 109 - €16 986 - **£11 190** - FF111 423
  Gatuvy från Helsingfors Oil/canvas/panel (47x37cm 18x14in) Helsinki 1999
- $2 040 - €2 018 - **£1 272** - FF13 238
  Bât vid brygga Mixed media (25x31cm 9x12in) Helsinki 1999
- $1 201 - €1 345 - **£834** - FF8 825
  Naken Pastel/paper (32x23cm 12x9in) Helsinki 2001
- $1 700 - €1 682 - **£1 060** - FF11 032
  Båtfärd Woodcut in colors (41x28cm 16x11in) Helsinki 1999

THESSEL Anton M. Fürchtegott 1830-1873 [1]
- $4 137 - €4 142 - **£2 551** - FF27 170
  Paisaje montañoso con cascada y pescador Oleo/lienzo (114.5x101cm 45x39in) Madrid 2000

THEUNIS Pierre 1883-1950 [15]
- $415 - €446 - **£279** - FF2 926
  Buste d'homme Bronze (52.5x54x30cm 20x21x11in) Bruxelles 2000

T

THEUS Jeremiah 1716-1774 **[2]**

$4 800 - €5 458 - £3 292 - FF35 802
Portrait of a Lady of the Southland Oil/canvas (76x63cm 30x25in) New-Orleans LA 2000

THEVENET Jacques 1891-1989 **[168]**

$218 - €244 - £147 - FF1 600
Boulevard Maillot, Paris Gouache/papier (10.5x22cm 4x8in) Paris 2000

THEVENET Louis 1874-1930 **[113]**

$15 960 - €14 873 - £9 840 - FF97 560
Intérieur avec nature morte Huile/toile (91x138cm 35x54in) Bruxelles 1999

$4 408 - €4 710 - £3 002 - FF30 894
Stilleven Huile/toile (60x70cm 23x27in) Lokeren 2001

$1 682 - €1 437 - £1 003 - FF9 425
Intérieur Huile/toile (25x35cm 9x13in) Bruxelles 1998

$564 - €644 - £392 - FF4 227
Fermette au crépuscule Fusain/papier (20x31cm 7x12in) Bruxelles 2001

THEVENET Pierre 1870-1937 **[55]**

$1 518 - €1 487 - £936 - FF9 756
La maison de Cécile en France Huile/canvas (54x46cm 21x18in) Lokeren 1999

$501 - €595 - £364 - FF3 902
Vue à Paris Huile/panneau (33x46cm 12x18in) Antwerpen 2001

THEVENIN A. XIX **[2]**

$15 000 - €14 253 - £9 126 - FF93 493
View of the Doge's Palace Oil/canvas (37x74.5cm 14x29in) New-York 1999

THEWENETI Lorenzo 1797-1878 **[6]**

$1 177 - €1 149 - £750 - FF7 538
Sibylla, the artist's daughter standing three-quarter length Miniature (15.5x12cm 6x4in) London 1999

THEYNET Max Robert 1875-1949 **[65]**

$336 - €311 - £205 - FF2 040
Ruderboote am Seeufer Öl/Karton (49x59cm 19x23in) Bern 1999

THEYS Ivan 1936 **[68]**

$1 828 - €1 815 - £1 142 - FF11 906
Andermann - Suite Oil/canvas (80x100cm 31x39in) Amsterdam 1999

$675 - €744 - £441 - FF4 578
Trois personnages Crayons couleurs/papier (72x54cm 28x21in) Bruxelles 2000

THEZELOUP Jean 1885-1968 **[14]**

$342 - €290 - £203 - FF1 900
Noce Normande aux environs de Coutances Gouache/papier (45x78cm 17x30in) Coutances 1998

THIBAULT Aimée 1780-1868 **[9]**

$789 - €686 - £475 - FF4 500
Homme à la redingote bleue et à la cravate nouée Miniature (6x4.8cm 2x1in) Paris 1998

THIBAULT Jean Thomas 1757-1826 **[13]**

$32 777 - €37 228 - £23 000 - FF244 202
Wooded Glade with a Figure writing beside a Stream before a Villa Oil/canvas (51.5x65cm 20x25in) London 2001

$3 500 - €3 749 - £2 390 - FF24 593
Classical Garden with a Temple on the Shore of a Lake Watercolour, gouache (36x49cm 14x19in) New-York 2001

THIBÉSART Raymond 1874-1968 **[34]**

$1 228 - €1 372 - £821 - FF9 000
Arbres en fleurs Huile/toile (60x73cm 23x28in) Paris 2000

THIBON DE LIBIAN Valentín 1889-1931 **[2]**

$170 000 - €197 249 - £117 368 - FF1 293 870
En el camerín Oil/canvas (151x100cm 59x39in) New-York 2000

THIEBAUD Morton Wayne 1920 **[273]**

$250 000 - €290 072 - £172 600 - FF1 902 750
Freeway 280 Oil/canvas (51x62cm 20x24in) New-York 2000

$80 000 - €85 871 - £53 536 - FF563 280
Toothbrushes Oil/board (32x23.5cm 12x9in) Beverly-Hills CA 2000

$90 000 - €104 426 - £62 136 - FF684 990
Cake Slices Watercolour (17x36cm 6x14in) New-York 2000

$4 500 - €3 988 - £2 760 - FF26 158
Lipstick Row Silkscreen in colors (56.5x76.5cm 22x30in) New-York 1999

THIEL Frank 1966 **[2]**

$456 - €511 - £317 - FF3 353
«Stadt 1/03 (Berlin)» Photograph in colors (25x36cm 9x14in) Köln 2001

THIELE Alexander 1924 **[112]**

$474 - €409 - £287 - FF2 683
«Münchner Biergarten» Öl/Leinwand (60x80cm 23x31in) Kempten 1999

THIELE Anton 1838-1902 **[32]**

$710 - €673 - £442 - FF4 413
Sommerlandskab med eng og ålöb Oil/canvas (40x59cm 15x23in) Köbenhavn 1999

THIELE Johann Alexander 1685-1752 **[24]**

$1 995 - €2 266 - £1 400 - FF14 864
Winter Landscape Oil/copper (12x16cm 4x6in) London 2001

THIELE Johann Fried. Alex. 1747-1803 **[4]**

$5 967 - €5 112 - £3 587 - FF33 533
Italienische Landschaft mit Kirche und Wasserfall Oil/panel (25.5x34cm 10x13in) Köln 1998

THIELE Otto 1870-1955 **[23]**

$899 - €1 022 - £623 - FF6 707
Innenraum der Teynkirche in Prag Öl/Leinwand (52x41cm 20x16in) Hamburg 2000

THIELEN van Jan Philips Rigoults 1618-1667 **[30]**

$14 493 - €13 785 - £8 800 - FF90 426
Garland of Tulips, Carnations, Narcissi, Roses and Other Flowers Oil/canvas (49x69.5cm 19x27in) London 1999

$11 757 - €11 847 - £7 328 - FF77 711
Blumenstilleben in Glasvasen Huile/panneau (25x20cm 9x7in) Zürich 2000

THIELENS Gaspard 1630-1691 **[1]**

$53 854 - €52 595 - £34 327 - FF345 000
Bouquet de fleurs Huile/toile (64x52cm 25x20in) Paris 1999

THIELER Fred 1916-1999 **[257]**
- $13 158 - €15 339 - **£9 222** - FF100 617
  Ohne Titel, Nr.20 Mixed media/canvas (165x190cm
  64x74in) München 2000
- $5 477 - €5 880 - **£3 666** - FF38 569
  «Ro-Ro-I-62» Mischtechnik/Karton (67.5x92.6cm
  26x36in) Köln 2000
- $2 239 - €2 556 - **£1 578** - FF16 769
  Ohne Titel Gouache/paper (65x50cm 25x19in)
  Stuttgart 2001
- $224 - €256 - **£156** - FF1 676
  «M I/66» Etching, aquatint in colors (31x39.5cm
  12x15in) Hamburg 2001

THIELMANN Wilhelm 1868-1924 **[31]**
- $7 902 - €7 669 - **£4 920** - FF50 308
  Portrait einer trauernden Schwälmerin
  Öl/Leinwand (46x36cm 18x14in) Frankfurt 1999
- $525 - €434 - **£308** - FF2 848
  Holzversteigerung (im Wald) Radierung
  (20.5x25cm 8x9in) Heidelberg 1998

THIEM Paul 1858-1922 **[37]**
- $1 021 - €1 000 - **£629** - FF6 562
  Blick auf Starnbergsee und Karwendelgebirge
  Öl/Leinwand (77x93cm 30x36in) St. Gallen 1999

THIEMANN Carl Theodor 1881-1966 **[290]**
- $545 - €529 - **£339** - FF3 471
  Landschaft mit drei Bäumen Chalks (34.5x47cm
  13x18in) Berlin 1999
- $525 - €434 - **£308** - FF2 848
  «Schwertlilien» Woodcut in colors (30x19.2cm
  11x7in) Heidelberg 1998

THIEME Anthony 1888-1954 **[212]**
- $11 000 - €12 897 - **£7 913** - FF84 602
  French Street Corner, Winter Oil/canvas
  (39.5x51cm 15x20in) New-York 2001
- $5 500 - €6 415 - **£3 861** - FF42 077
  «Pension Beau Lejour La Colle» Oil/canvas/board
  (30x40cm 11x15in) Boston MA 2000
- $750 - €744 - **£460** - FF4 883
  Courtyard Scene Watercolour/paper (28x42cm
  11x16in) Delray-Beach FL 2000
- $193 - €183 - **£119** - FF1 198
  Ducks Etching (11x9cm 4x3in) Rockport MA 1999

THIEMER Ivan XX **[1]**
- $6 500 - €6 738 - **£3 900** - FF44 200
  Obelisco Bronzo (H75.5cm H29in) Milano 2000

THIENON Claude I 1772-1846 **[16]**
- $236 - €274 - **£168** - FF1 800
  **Lavandières près d'une tour médiévale à l'en-
  trée d'un port** Aquarelle (10x8.5cm 3x3in) Paris 2001

THIENON Louis 1812-1881 **[26]**
- $4 126 - €3 934 - **£2 489** - FF25 807
  Vista del Palacio Velasco, en Burgos Oleo/tabla
  (19x24cm 7x9in) Madrid 1999
- $1 413 - €1 448 - **£872** - FF9 500
  Malaga Crayon (14.5x21cm 5x8in) Vendôme 2000

THIER Barent Hendrik 1751-1814 **[18]**
- $4 000 - €4 430 - **£2 712** - FF29 058
  **Drovers and Cattle Crossing a Bridge with a
  View of Delft** Oil/panel (48.5x65cm 19x25in) New-
  York 2000

THIERFELDER Vivian 1929 **[5]**
- $3 033 - €2 871 - **£1 886** - FF18 833
  Still Life with Tulips Watercolour/paper (55x74cm
  21x29in) Calgary, Alberta 1999

THIERRÉE Stanislas Eugène 1810-? **[6]**
- $1 478 - €1 372 - **£920** - FF9 000
  La gardeuse de vaches Huile/toile (42x66cm
  16x25in) Paris 1999

THIERRIAT Augustin Alexandre 1789-1870 **[13]**
- $1 618 - €1 524 - **£980** - FF10 000
  Fritillaria Imperialis Crayon (33x25cm 12x9in) Paris
  1999

THIERRY Joseph Fr. Désiré 1812-1866 **[2]**
- $11 432 - €12 539 - **£7 377** - FF82 250
  Vue du grand salon de La Roche-Guyon
  Aquarelle (164x247cm 64x97in) Monte-Carlo 2000

THIERSCH Ludwig 1825-1909 **[24]**
- $601 - €665 - **£417** - FF4 360
  Portrait einer jungen Frau Öl/Leinwand (51x40cm
  20x15in) München 2001

THILÉN Ada 1852-1933 **[8]**
- $6 573 - €7 400 - **£4 527** - FF48 540
  Flicka med morötter Oil/canvas (62x48cm 24x18in)
  Helsinki 2000

THIO XX **[3]**
- $1 764 - €1 778 - **£1 100** - FF11 664
  «Morzine, PLM» Poster (99x60cm 38x23in) London
  2000

THIOLLET Alexandre 1824-1895 **[18]**
- $5 740 - €4 961 - **£3 460** - FF32 540
  Nature morte aux fruits/Nature morte au gibier
  Huile/toile (63x112cm 24x44in) Bruxelles 1998
- $3 761 - €4 063 - **£2 600** - FF26 649
  Au bord de l'Oise Oil/panel (30x51cm 11x20in)
  Billingshurst, West-Sussex 2001

THIRIAR James 1889-1965 **[17]**
- $292 - €273 - **£181** - FF1 788
  La parade militaire Aquarelle, gouache/papier
  (16x31cm 6x12in) Antwerpen 1999

THIRIET Henri XIX-XX **[9]**
- $2 800 - €3 124 - **£1 832** - FF20 491
  **«Exposition de blanc à la Place de Clichy, lundi
  31 janvier»** Poster (92x131cm 36x51in) New-York
  2000

THIRION Charles Victor 1833-1878 **[9]**
- $28 000 - €24 157 - **£16 892** - FF158 460
  A young Girl holding Flowers Oil/canvas
  (145x85cm 57x33in) New-York 1998
- $20 924 - €23 581 - **£14 492** - FF154 678
  At The Well Oil/canvas (66x44.5cm 25x17in) Toronto
  2000

THIRION Eugène 1839-1910 **[6]**
- $13 700 - €15 139 - **£9 500** - FF99 303
  **Triumph of Faith, Christian Martyrs in the Time
  of Nero 65 A.D** Oil/canvas (89x146cm 35x57in)
  London 2001

THIRTLE John 1777-1839 **[23]**
- $1 451 - €1 425 - **£900** - FF9 347
  Wymondham, Norfolk Watercolour (12.5x17.5cm
  4x6in) London 1999

THIRY Leonard c.1500-c.1550 **[2]**
📖 **$3 026** - €3 049 - **£1 886** - FF20 000
Mercure chez Pluton Encre (17.5x29.5cm 6x11in)
Paris 2000

THIVET Auguste Antoine 1856-1927 **[21]**
👛 **$778** - €915 - **£539** - FF6 000
Scène champêtre Huile/toile (98x79cm 38x31in)
Nantes 2000

THIVET Yvonne 1888-1972 **[48]**
👛 **$1 477** - €1 677 - **£1 010** - FF11 000
La halte de la Caravanne, dans le désert
Huile/toile (65x92cm 25x36in) Orléans 2000
👛 **$952** - €1 067 - **£662** - FF7 000
La promenade des enfants Huile/panneau
(27x35cm 10x13in) Paris 2001

THIVIER Émile L. 1858-1922 **[86]**
👛 **$307** - €320 - **£194** - FF2 100
Ébauche: vieille dame et petites filles Huile/toile
(70x60cm 27x23in) Paris 2000
👛 **$190** - €198 - **£120** - FF1 300
Arbres au ciel d'hiver Huile/toile (21x16cm 8x6in)
Paris 2000

THOLEN Willem Bastiaan 1860-1931 **[195]**
👛 **$8 686** - €8 168 - **£5 378** - FF53 578
Het getijde huis te Enkhuizen Oil/canvas
(45.5x61.5cm 17x24in) Amsterdam 1999
👛 **$2 796** - €3 016 - **£1 962** - FF20 836
Werf te Monnikendam Oil/canvas/panel (30x41cm
11x16in) Amsterdam 2001
👛 **$1 350** - €1 361 - **£842** - FF8 929
**View in a Town with a Building under
Construction** Charcoal (12x15.5cm 4x6in)
Amsterdam 2000

THOLER Raymond 1859-? **[7]**
👛 **$6 000** - €6 727 - **£4 074** - FF44 128
Fresh from the Garden Oil/canvas (81x116cm
31x45in) New-York 2000

THOM James Crawford 1835-1898 **[68]**
👛 **$4 392** - €4 689 - **£3 000** - FF30 759
**Spring: Playing with the Lambs/Autumn:
Leading the Sheep** Oil/panel (50x35cm 19x13in)
Billingshurst, West-Sussex 2001
👛 **$2 500** - €2 325 - **£1 548** - FF15 251
Children in Farmyard Oil/panel (35x30cm 14x12in)
Portsmouth NH 1999
📖 **$1 200** - €1 215 - **£746** - FF7 973
After the Egg Watercolour/paper (45x30cm 18x12in)
Chester NY 2000

THOMA Berta act.1915-1933 **[10]**
👛 **$218** - €254 - **£154** - FF1 668
**Portrait einer Biedermeierdame mit
Rüschenkragen** Miniature (6x4cm 2x1in) Salzburg
2000

THOMA Emil 1869-1948 **[39]**
📜 **$274** - €256 - **£169** - FF1 676
Kampenwand Woodcut in colors (13.2x21.5cm 5x8in)
Hamburg 1999

THOMA Hans 1839-1924 **[1034]**
👛 **$11 510** - €12 782 - **£8 005** - FF83 847
Landschaft am Oberrhein Öl/Karton (60.5x78cm
23x30in) Heidelberg 2001

👛 **$2 666** - €2 300 - **£1 587** - FF15 090
Der Vogel Phantasus Oil/panel (27x21cm 10x8in)
München 1998
📖 **$481** - €562 - **£338** - FF3 689
Bei Tivoli Pencil/paper (36x46.8cm 14x18in) München
2000
📜 **$184** - €184 - **£115** - FF1 207
Feierabend Radierung (35x48cm 13x18in) Staufen
2000

THOMA Joseph 1828-1899 **[191]**
👛 **$12 000** - €13 630 - **£8 420** - FF89 404
Alpine Rapids Oil/canvas (94x137cm 37x53in) New-
York 2001
👛 **$2 295** - €2 198 - **£1 444** - FF14 421
**Tosender Wildbach zwischen zerklüfteten
Felswänden** Öl/Leinwand (50x82cm 19x32in)
Stuttgart 1999
👛 **$1 413** - €1 363 - **£871** - FF8 938
Gehöft an einem Bergsee Öl/Karton (26x38.5cm
10x15in) Bern 1999

THOMA-HÖFELE Carl 1866-1923 **[10]**
👛 **$2 547** - €2 955 - **£1 758** - FF19 385
**Stilleben mit Hummer, Silberterrine und
Deckelvase** Öl/Leinwand (73.5x90cm 28x35in)
Luzern 2000

THOMANN Heinrich 1748-1794 **[7]**
📜 **$566** - €657 - **£390** - FF4 307
Eglisau Radierung (13x22.2cm 5x8in) Zürich 2000

THOMANN Noël 1940 **[14]**
🗿 **$966** - €1 067 - **£669** - FF7 000
Femme assise Bronze (45x16x16cm 17x6x6in) Lyon
2001

THOMAS (T. Pérez Martínez) 1911-1992 **[39]**
👛 **$168** - €180 - **£111** - FF1 182
Bagur (Sa Tuna) Oleo/lienzo (38x46cm 14x18in)
Barcelona 2000

THOMAS Alain 1942 **[11]**
👛 **$410** - €488 - **£292** - FF3 200
Femme et deux enfants dans la neige Huile/pan-
neau (16.5x22cm 6x8in) Nantes 2000

THOMAS Albert Gordon 1893-1970 **[5]**
👛 **$8 065** - €8 693 - **£5 500** - FF57 020
A Sunlit Scottish River Landscape Oil/canvas
(61x51cm 24x20in) London 2001

THOMAS Alma 1891-1978 **[6]**
👛 **$26 000** - €29 071 - **£17 526** - FF190 694
Sunset Duet Acrylic/canvas (116.5x91.5cm 45x36in)
New-York 2000

THOMAS Barry 1961 **[7]**
👛 **$5 500** - €5 904 - **£3 680** - FF38 725
Sea Breeze Oil/canvas (91x60cm 36x24in) Houston
TX 2000

THOMAS Billy, Joongoora c.1920 **[9]**
👛 **$557** - €596 - **£367** - FF3 912
Meeting for Ceremony Mixed media (61x45cm
24x17in) Woollahra, Sydney 2000

THOMAS Charles 1827-1892 **[5]**
👛 **$7 000** - €7 505 - **£4 631** - FF49 232
Still Life with Garden Chrysanthemums Oil/can-
vas (80x44cm 31x17in) New-Orleans LA 2000

THOMAS Edmund 1827-1867 [1]
☐ **$1 089** - €1 264 - **£764** - FF8 294
The Gap, South Head, Port Jackson Lithograph (40x32cm 15x12in) Sydney 2000

THOMAS Fanny E. XIX [1]
✎ **$1 470** - €1 498 - **£920** - FF9 829
The Sanctuary, Sark Watercolour (25.5x17.5cm 10x6in) London 2000

THOMAS Gérard 1663-1720 [22]
☺ **$12 324** - €11 891 - **£7 737** - FF78 000
L'intérieur du cabinet de l'alchimiste Huile/toile (69x86cm 27x33in) Versailles 1999

THOMAS Henri 1878-1972 [146]
☺ **$3 206** - €3 470 - **£2 226** - FF22 764
Composition florale sur un guéridon Huile/toile (100x67cm 39x26in) Bruxelles 2001
☺ **$1 308** - €1 417 - **£918** - FF9 756
Femme de profil Huile/toile (36x28cm 14x11in) Bruxelles 2001
✎ **$696** - €669 - **£434** - FF4 390
Jeune femme au canapé Technique mixte/papier (30x35cm 11x13in) Bruxelles 1999
☐ **$382** - €372 - **£241** - FF2 439
Les Souteneurs Eau-forte (56x70cm 22x27in) Bruxelles 1999

THOMAS Henry 1834-1904 [2]
☐ **$2 746** - €2 744 - **£1 717** - FF18 000
«L'Éclair» Affiche (124x87.5cm 48x34in) Orléans 1999

THOMAS Jean-François 1898-1939 [59]
☺ **$1 165** - €1 372 - **£819** - FF9 000
La lecture Huile/panneau (17x18cm 6x7in) Toulouse 2000
✎ **$952** - €1 067 - **£662** - FF7 000
Le ballet Pastel/papier (50x65cm 19x25in) Pau 2001

THOMAS Karl 1948 [12]
☺ **$5 500** - €5 136 - **£3 394** - FF33 693
Hollyhock Garden Oil/canvas (101x121cm 40x48in) Dallas TX 1999
☺ **$4 250** - €3 631 - **£2 571** - FF23 821
The Edge of the Canyon Oil/canvas (76x91.5cm 29x36in) San-Francisco CA 1998

THOMAS Margaret 1916 [20]
☺ **$834** - €978 - **£600** - FF6 414
Still Life with Flowers in a Jug Oil/panel (51x40.5cm 20x15in) London 2001
☺ **$578** - €625 - **£400** - FF4 100
River Sunset, Winter Oil/board (32x36.5cm 12x14in) London 2001

THOMAS Mathilde, née Soyer 1858-1940 [10]
✐ **$2 289** - €2 287 - **£1 431** - FF15 000
Les barzoi Bronze (H58cm H22in) Soissons 1999

THOMAS Napoléon XIX [6]
☐ **$208** - €240 - **£144** - FF1 576
Escenas de la Biblia Estampe (31.5x44cm 12x17in) Madrid 2000

THOMAS Pieter Hendrik 1814-1866 [9]
☺ **$4 323** - €4 084 - **£2 615** - FF26 789
Marine Oil/canvas (41x50cm 16x19in) Amsterdam 1999
☺ **$3 626** - €4 084 - **£2 499** - FF26 789
Shipping on a River Oil/panel (21.5x30.5cm 8x12in) Amsterdam 2000

THOMAS Robert Strickland 1787-1853 [15]
☺ **$19 846** - €17 306 - **£12 000** - FF113 517
H.M.S. Queen and other Shipping in Portsmouth Harbour Oil/canvas (62.5x91.5cm 24x36in) London 1998
☺ **$9 821** - €11 680 - **£7 000** - FF76 616
H.M.S Britannia, the Flagship of Admiral Sir Philip Durham, G.C.B Oil/canvas (20x29cm 7x11in) London 2000

THOMAS Rover, Joolama c.1926-1998 [53]
☺ **$20 772** - €19 043 - **£12 852** - FF124 911
Blue Tongue Lizard Dreaming Mixed media/canvas (152x212cm 59x83in) Melbourne 1998
☺ **$5 965** - €6 362 - **£3 981** - FF41 732
Nilya, Well 33, canning Stock Route Mixed media/canvas (46x61cm 18x24in) Melbourne 2000
✎ **$4 076** - €4 451 - **£2 623** - FF29 198
33 Mile Well Charcoal (51x62cm 20x24in) Melbourne 2000

THOMAS Stephen Seymour 1868-1956 [22]
☺ **$3 250** - €3 755 - **£2 275** - FF24 628
«Impression of the Sea at Carmel» Oil/panel (26x35cm 10x13in) New-York 2001
☺ **$350** - €408 - **£243** - FF2 678
Boats in Harbor with Figures Mixed media/paper (6x11cm 2x4in) Altadena CA 2000

THOMAS Walter 1894-1971 [16]
☐ **$852** - €719 - **£500** - FF4 717
«The Blue Funnel Line» Poster (102x62cm 40x24in) London 1998

THOMASCH Wilhelm 1893-1964 [2]
✐ **$4 473** - €5 087 - **£3 101** - FF33 369
Tanzender Pierrot Ceramic (H40cm H15in) Wien 2000

THOMASSET Henri XX [12]
☺ **$410** - €442 - **£274** - FF2 900
Pommes et vase de fleurs champêtres Huile/toile (65x54cm 25x21in) Grenoble 2000

THOMASSIN-RENARDT Désiré 1858-1933 [196]
☺ **$5 000** - €4 331 - **£3 066** - FF28 407
Selling the Day's Catch Oil/canvas (35.5x70.5cm 13x27in) New-York 1999
☺ **$2 891** - €3 323 - **£2 041** - FF21 800
Heuernte in den bayrischen Alpen Oil/panel (21x27.3cm 8x10in) Bremen 2001

THOMÉ Verner 1878-1953 [67]
☺ **$1 416** - €1 598 - **£995** - FF10 480
Häst Oil/canvas (61x50cm 24x19in) Helsinki 2001
✎ **$332** - €336 - **£208** - FF2 206
Parken Akvarell/papper (24x31cm 9x12in) Helsinki 2000

THÖMING Friedrich Ferd. Ch. 1802-1873 [7]
☺ **$7 952** - €8 537 - **£5 320** - FF56 000
La pêche à l'espadon dans les environs de Naples Huile/toile (64x101cm 25x39in) Bordeaux 2000

THOMKINS André 1930-1985 [99]
☺ **$1 137** - €1 125 - **£709** - FF7 378
Ohne Titel Peinture (41x23cm 16x9in) Luzern 1999
✐ **$1 237** - €1 247 - **£771** - FF8 180
Schaltbrett Assemblage (46x16cm 18x6in) Zürich 2000

T

$637 - €706 - £432 - FF4 629
Blick aus dem Atelier (Rote Fabrik) Pencil/paper (29x20.7cm 11x8in) Zürich 2000

$108 - €128 - £75 - FF838
Surrealistische Flugobjekte Farbradierung (29x29cm 11x11in) Braunschweig 2000

THOMMESEN Erik 1916 [24]

$25 284 - €28 150 - **£17 766** - FF184 653
Mor, far og barn Sculpture, wood (H162cm H63in) Vejle 2001

$7 212 - €8 043 - **£5 010** - FF52 758
«Mand og kvinde» Sculpture, wood (H60cm H23in) København 2001

THOMON de Thomas 1754-1813 [16]

$1 399 - €1 570 - **£950** - FF10 296
Rome Burning Bodycolour (11x10cm 4x3in) London 2000

THOMOPOULOS Epaminondas 1878-1974 [41]

$7 000 - €6 651 - **£4 258** - FF43 630
Harvesters Oil/canvas (82x82cm 32x32in) New-York 1999

THOMPSON Albert 1853-? [3]

$1 600 - €1 463 - **£977** - FF9 598
Cattle wading in the River Oil/canvas (40x60cm 16x24in) Boston MA 1998

THOMPSON Alfred Wordsworth 1840-1896 [25]

$7 650 - €6 844 - **£4 584** - FF44 895
Lystighed på en fransk kyst, i baggrunden huse og skibe Oil/canvas (69x110cm 27x43in) København 1998

$6 000 - €6 660 - **£4 182** - FF43 689
Respite in the Desert Oil/canvas (20.5x26cm 8x10in) New-York 2001

THOMPSON Bob 1937-1966 [23]

$32 000 - €27 042 - **£19 088** - FF177 382
«Bathers» Oil/canvas (148.5x205cm 58x80in) San-Francisco CA 1998

$9 000 - €10 443 - **£6 213** - FF68 499
Untitled Oil/paper (47.5x60cm 18x23in) New-York 2000

$4 200 - €4 873 - **£2 899** - FF31 966
The Ten Plagues Mixed media (20x17cm 7x6in) New-York 2000

THOMPSON Cephas Giovanni 1809-1886 [6]

$14 000 - €11 759 - **£8 230** - FF77 134
Portrait of a Gentleman/Portrait of a Woman Oil/canvas (69x55cm 27x22in) Boston MA 1998

$1 800 - €1 929 - **£1 225** - FF12 655
Mother and Child Oil/canvas (31x26cm 12x10in) Thomaston ME 2001

THOMPSON Edward Horace 1866-1949 [159]

$1 424 - €1 336 - **£880** - FF8 764
Crummock Water looking towards Buttermere Watercolour/paper (21x26cm 8x10in) Leyburn, North Yorkshire 1999

THOMPSON George Albert 1868-1938 [11]

$3 500 - €2 998 - **£2 104** - FF19 668
«Neighbors Hollyhocks» Oil/board (30x40cm 12x16in) Cleveland OH 1998

THOMPSON Harry ?-1901 [3]

$7 000 - €7 720 - **£4 740** - FF50 638
French Country Landscape Oil/canvas (45.5x63.5cm 17x25in) New-York 2000

THOMPSON Isa 1850-1926 [11]

$5 155 - €5 128 - **£3 200** - FF33 635
Burnswick Baig Watercolour/paper (41x18cm 16x7in) Guildford, Surrey 1999

THOMPSON Jacob 1806-1879 [4]

$240 450 - €227 148 - **£150 000** - FF1 489 995
The Highland Ferry-Boat Oil/canvas (97.5x183cm 38x72in) Perthshire 1999

THOMPSON Jerome 1814-1886 [9]

$5 750 - €4 921 - **£3 461** - FF32 278
River Landscape Oil/canvas (43x60cm 17x24in) New-York 1998

THOMPSON Kenneth Webster 1907 [1]

$2 700 - €3 024 - **£1 876** - FF19 837
Coke Bottle standing in snow Bank Gouache/paper (59x94cm 23x37in) New-York 2001

THOMPSON Kim 1963 [4]

$2 140 - €2 495 - **£1 500** - FF16 369
Barn Owl Acrylic/board (54x28cm 21x11in) London 2000

THOMPSON Mark 1812-1875 [5]

$10 157 - €11 438 - **£7 000** - FF75 028
The Maypole Inn From Barnaby Rudge Oil/canvas (76x122cm 29x48in) London 2000

THOMPSON Martin E. c.1786-1877 [1]

$4 000 - €4 441 - **£2 782** - FF29 129
Cold Spring Harbor and West Point Oil/canvas (45x106cm 18x42in) Milford CT 2001

THOMPSON Patricia XX [20]

$276 - €252 - **£170** - FF1 655
The Squadron Line Watercolour (33x45.5cm 12x17in) London 1998

THOMPSON Ralph XX [5]

$1 505 - €1 651 - **£1 000** - FF10 833
Snow Leopard on Ledge Watercolour/paper (62x39.5cm 24x15in) London 2000

THOMPSON Richard E. 1914-1991 [5]

$3 309 - €3 159 - **£2 067** - FF20 720
Genre Scene of a woman holding a Cat Oil/canvas (45x60cm 18x24in) Cedar-Falls IA 1999

THOMPSON Stanley 1876-? [19]

$14 824 - €17 574 - **£10 800** - FF115 281
My Mother bids me my Hair Oil/canvas (90x70cm 35x27in) Newcastle-upon-Tyne 2001

THOMPSON Sydney Lough 1877-1973 [25]

$9 336 - €10 637 - **£6 452** - FF69 775
Tunny Boat, Concarneau Oil/canvas (45x37cm 17x14in) Auckland 2000

$7 745 - €8 082 - **£4 885** - FF53 017
Boats, Concarneau Oil/canvas/board (32x40cm 12x15in) Sydney 2000

THOMPSON Timothy, Tim 1951 [28]

$5 814 - €5 467 - **£3 600** - FF35 864
The «Santa Brigada» Oil/canvas (32x61cm 12x24in) London 1999

$5 179 - €4 876 - **£3 200** - FF31 982
The «Enterprise» at Brenton Light, 1930, off Newport, Rhode Island Oil/canvas (40.5x30.5cm 15x12in) London 1999

THOMPSON Walter Whitcomb 1882-1948 [6]
$1 500 - €1 706 - **£1 048** - FF11 190
October Hills Oil/canvas (63x76cm 25x30in) Mystic CT 2000

THOMS Ernst 1896-1983 [16]
$977 - €843 - **£587** - FF5 531
Brückenbau Watercolour (58x41.5cm 22x16in) Köln 1998

THOMSEN August Carl Vilhelm 1813-1886 [31]
$9 775 - €8 897 - **£6 000** - FF58 362
Deer on a Beechwood Track Oil/canvas (90x120.5cm 35x47in) London 1999

THOMSEN Carl Christian 1847-1912 [59]
$1 056 - €1 140 - **£708** - FF7 479
De tre farisaeere Oil/canvas (67x49cm 26x19in) København 2000
$507 - €604 - **£361** - FF3 959
Abate i blå kappe og hat, i baggrunden Firenze med domkirken Oil/canvas (32x20cm 12x7in) København 2000

THOMSEN Emma 1822-1897 [31]
$36 047 - €38 901 - **£24 186** - FF255 171
Opstilling i skovlandskab med broget buket af snerler, snebaer, roser Oil/canvas (75x65cm 29x25in) København 2000
$3 599 - €3 627 - **£2 243** - FF23 792
Fuchsiaer og höstanemoner Oil/canvas (41x37cm 16x14in) København 2000

THOMSEN Fritz Gotfred 1819-1891 [14]
$2 103 - €1 973 - **£1 300** - FF12 940
Milkmaid with Cows and Horses in an extensive Landscape Oil/canvas (77.5x100.5cm 30x39in) London 1999

THOMSEN René 1897-1976 [48]
$527 - €488 - **£318** - FF3 200
Nu au divan Huile/toile (65x81cm 25x31in) Paris 1999

THOMSON Adam Bruce 1885-1976 [17]
$7 212 - €8 476 - **£5 000** - FF55 600
The Mill on the Water of Leith, Colinton, Edinburgh Oil/canvas/panel (51x61cm 20x24in) Edinburgh 2000
$1 900 - €1 624 - **£1 150** - FF10 651
«Plockton, Lochcarron» Watercolour (54.5x74.5cm 21x29in) Edinburgh 1998

THOMSON Alfred Reginald 1895-1979 [19]
$573 - €550 - **£350** - FF3 611
«Then and Now, 100 Bathing Resorts on the East Coast, LNER» Poster (102x64cm 40x25in) London 1999

THOMSON Ann 1933 [19]
$9 577 - €8 351 - **£5 791** - FF54 780
Attic Oil/canvas (117x178cm 46x70in) Melbourne 1998

THOMSON George 1860-1939 [7]
$547 - €613 - **£380** - FF4 022
Village Track in a wooded Landscape Watercolour (25.5x37cm 10x14in) London 2001

THOMSON Henry 1773-1843 [8]
$7 381 - €7 922 - **£4 939** - FF51 967
The Dead Robin Oil/canvas (62.5x76cm 24x29in) Toronto 2000

THOMSON Henry Grinnell 1850-1939 [11]
$1 000 - €1 028 - **£634** - FF6 745
Impressionist Landscape Oil/canvas (40x50cm 16x20in) Columbia SC 2000

THOMSON Hugh 1860-1920 [35]
$488 - €475 - **£300** - FF3 117
Lady, Hand on Doorknob trying to escape the Advice of two Men Ink/paper (31.5x22.5cm 12x8in) London 1999

THOMSON John Murray 1885-1974 [42]
$1 610 - €1 514 - **£1 000** - FF9 929
An October Day/A Sutherland Stable Oil/canvas (50x75.5cm 19x29in) London 1999
$649 - €725 - **£440** - FF4 757
Cairn Terrier and Pups Oil/panel (24x34cm 9x13in) Edinburgh 2000
$504 - €523 - **£320** - FF3 432
Horse and Foal in Field/Cockerel and Hens in Courtyard Gouache/paper (24x32cm 9x12in) Cheshire 2000

THOMSON Tom, Thomas John 1877-1917 [28]
$138 411 - €117 227 - **£83 202** - FF768 957
Nocturne Oil/canvas (40.5x46cm 15x18in) Vancouver, BC. 1998
$47 129 - €40 614 - **£28 000** - FF266 411
Burnt Land at Sunset Oil/board (21.5x27cm 8x10in) London 1998
$3 243 - €3 138 - **£2 000** - FF20 587
Snow Landscape/Spring Landscape Watercolour/paper (14x28.5cm 5x11in) Toronto 1999

THOMSON William Mackenzie [12]
$356 - €344 - **£220** - FF2 256
Steam, Sailing Vessel Watercolour/paper (31.5x65cm 12x25in) Bedford 1999

THON Sixt 1817-1901 [3]
$990 - €1 125 - **£688** - FF7 378
Selbstbildnis vor der Staffelei Radierung (8x6.5cm 3x2in) Berlin 2001

THON William 1906-? [31]
$4 500 - €4 830 - **£3 011** - FF31 684
Quarry in Winter Oil/masonite (60x121cm 24x48in) Portland ME 2000
$150 - €168 - **£104** - FF1 102
View of Florence, Italy Watercolour/paper (15x21cm 6x8in) Thomaston ME 2001

THONGSHAI SRISUKPRASERT 1963 [2]
$3 825 - €4 114 - **£2 565** - FF26 985
Mythical Female Form Oil/canvas (118x88cm 46x34in) Bangkok 2000

THONI Hans 1906-1980 [5]
$562 - €509 - **£350** - FF3 339
«Saanenmöser» Poster (102x71cm 40x27in) London 1999

THONING Lars 1949-1997 [33]
$439 - €299 - **£275** - FF3 076
Opstilling med kranier og fade Oil/canvas (52x61cm 20x24in) Vejle 2001

$351 - €375 - **£239** - FF2 461
Komposition med bikube og hammer Oil/canvas
(40x35cm 15x13in) Vejle 2001

THÖNY Eduard 1866-1950 [68]

$2 495 - €2 403 - **£1 560** - FF15 763
In den Pausen Mixed media/board (40x29.5cm
15x11in) München 1999

$1 303 - €1 124 - **£783** - FF7 375
Die Torpedierten Charcoal (24x29.7cm 9x11in)
München 1998

THÖNY Wilhelm 1888-1949 [140]

$28 946 - €28 633 - **£18 048** - FF187 818
Südlicher Hafen Öl/Papier (35x46.5cm 13x18in)
Berlin 1999

$4 669 - €3 999 - **£2 733** - FF26 229
Nonne Öl/Papier (36.6x27.1cm 14x10in) Wien 1998

$2 716 - €2 325 - **£1 635** - FF15 254
**Dame mit Hütchen, getupftem Schal, bei einem
Glas Limonade** Indian ink (27x21cm 10x8in) Wien
1998

$187 - €182 - **£119** - FF1 191
Mann an der Türe Radierung (9.5x8cm 3x3in) Wien
1999

THOR Walter 1870-1929 [45]

$668 - €762 - **£466** - FF5 000
«Pneu Samson, antidérapant, imperforable»
Affiche (158x115cm 62x45in) Paris 2001

THORAK Josef 1889-1952 [14]

$2 662 - €2 556 - **£1 641** - FF16 769
Menschenpaar Bronze (H70cm H27in) München
1999

THORBURN Archibald 1860-1935 [870]

$4 001 - €3 820 - **£2 500** - FF25 056
A Woodcock among Oak Leaves Bronze (H6.5cm
H2in) London 1999

$6 021 - €6 606 - **£4 000** - FF43 332
Magpies Watercolour (52x36cm 20x14in) London
2000

$431 - €381 - **£260** - FF2 497
Ptarmigan in Flight in a Winter Landscape Print
in colors (35x48cm 13x18in) Retford, Nottinghamshire
1998

THORÉN Esaias 1901-1980 [373]

$1 571 - €1 851 - **£1 104** - FF12 145
Klippformationer och fiskar på strand Oil/panel
(49x60cm 19x23in) Stockholm 2000

$1 477 - €1 250 - **£883** - FF8 197
Formationer på strand Oil/panel (28x36cm 11x14in)
Stockholm 1998

$1 008 - €940 - **£622** - FF6 168
Geometrisk komposition Gouache/paper (18x23cm
7x9in) Stockholm 1999

$230 - €219 - **£140** - FF1 437
Ansikten och vaser Color lithograph (36x61cm
14x24in) Stockholm 1999

THOREN von Otto Karl Kasimir 1828-1889 [55]

$4 330 - €3 635 - **£2 555** - FF23 845
Pferderennen in Ungarn Öl/Leinwand (70x130cm
27x51in) Wien 1998

$888 - €1 022 - **£612** - FF6 707
Kühe auf der Weide Öl/Leinwand (24x35cm 9x13in)
Saarbrücken 2000

THORENFELD Anton Erik Ch. 1839-1907 [58]

$1 113 - €1 023 - **£684** - FF6 712
**Fra Örstedsparken set fra et vindue i
Farimagsgade** Oil/canvas (44x58cm 17x22in) Vejle
1999

$296 - €269 - **£185** - FF1 765
Landskab Oil/canvas (30x40cm 11x15in) Viby J,
Århus 1999

THORESEN Else 1909 [7]

$1 608 - €1 743 - **£1 114** - FF11 432
Surrealistisk komposition Oil/canvas (28x35cm
11x13in) København 2001

THORMA Janos 1870-1937 [9]

$5 920 - €6 220 - **£3 680** - FF40 800
**Jeune femme au chapeau bleu dans une cam-
pagne printanière** Huile/toile (60x75cm 23x29in)
Budapest 2000

$4 550 - €5 034 - **£2 990** - FF33 020
Lady in rose Dress by the Riverside Oil/canvas
(31.5x43.5cm 12x17in) Budapest 2000

THORN PRIKKER Johan 1868-1932 [25]

$4 822 - €5 624 - **£3 385** - FF36 892
Hockeyspieler Öl/Leinwand (105.5x101cm 41x39in)
Köln 2000

$1 731 - €2 045 - **£1 222** - FF13 415
Glasfenster, geometrisch Sculpture (66x24cm
25x9in) Köln 2001

$18 065 - €17 244 - **£11 289** - FF113 110
Two Peasant Women in a Field Watercolour
(40.5x43.5cm 15x17in) Amsterdam 1999

$1 399 - €1 633 - **£959** - FF10 715
«Revue bimestrielle pour l'Art appliqué» Poster
(135x100cm 53x39in) Hoorn 2000

THORNAM Emmy Marie Caroline 1852-1935 [125]

$807 - €858 - **£540** - FF5 626
Paesoner i kurv Oil/canvas (40x56cm 15x22in) Viby
J, Århus 2001

$592 - €565 - **£360** - FF3 708
En forårskurv Oil/canvas (33x43cm 12x16in) Viby J,
Århus 1999

THORNDIKE Charles Hall 1875-1935 [1]

$2 507 - €2 744 - **£1 740** - FF18 000
Paysage de Bretagne Huile/panneau (32x41cm
12x16in) Vannes 2001

THÖRNE Alfred 1850-1916 [82]

$1 737 - €2 006 - **£1 215** - FF13 156
**Sommarlandskap med metande gosse vid vat-
tendrag** Oil/canvas (38x61cm 14x24in) Stockholm
2001

$1 104 - €1 211 - **£733** - FF7 943
Landskap med röd stuga vid sjö Oil/canvas
(28x45cm 11x17in) Stockholm 2000

THORNE Angela 1911 [28]

$649 - €729 - **£450** - FF4 780
Cockerel Oil/canvas (61x51cm 24x20in) London 2000

THORNE Diana 1895-? [14]

$160 - €184 - **£110** - FF1 207
The Box at Faustus Etching (27x22cm 11x9in)
Cleveland OH 2000

THORNHILL James 1675-1734 **[29]**
- $42 000 - €39 514 - **£26 208** - FF259 198
  Capriccio with Saint-Paul before Agrippa
  Oil/canvas (160x152cm 62x59in) New-York 1999
- $11 239 - €13 039 - **£8 000** - FF85 527
  Phaeton petitoning Apollo, allegorical Figures
  Oil/canvas (76x68.5cm 29x26in) London 2001
- $1 765 - €1 779 - **£1 100** - FF11 668
  Zephyrus and Flora with Putti and Garlands on Clouds Pencil (18x24.5cm 7x9in) London 2000

THORNLEY Geoff 1942 **[4]**
- $2 015 - €2 259 - **£1 409** - FF14 819
  Untitled, from the Grey Albus series Acrylic (175x53cm 68x20in) Auckland 2001
- $1 502 - €1 561 - **£942** - FF10 240
  Risen «Papalangi» from the Series No.2 Mixed media/paper (211x70cm 83x27in) Auckland 2000

THORNLEY Hubert act.1858-1898 **[43]**
- $9 111 - €8 313 - **£5 600** - FF54 527
  St Michael's Mount, Cornwall Oil/canvas (61x45.5cm 24x17in) London 1998
- $4 135 - €3 536 - **£2 500** - FF23 193
  On the Medway Oil/panel (26.5x21.5cm 10x8in) London 1999

THORNLEY William Anslow XIX-XX **[64]**
- $2 417 - €2 744 - **£1 679** - FF18 000
  Paysage côtier animé Huile/toile (55x74cm 21x29in) Pontoise 2001
- $3 579 - €3 266 - **£2 200** - FF21 421
  Moonlight on the River Oil/canvas (30.5x25.5cm 12x10in) London 1998
- $10 926 - €10 255 - **£6 750** - FF67 267
  Fishing Boats off St. Michael's Mount/A Fresh Breeze off Hastings Watercolour/paper (35x30cm 14x12in) Fernhurst, Haslemere, Surrey 1999

THORNLEY William Georges 1857-1935 **[317]**
- $3 812 - €4 116 - **£2 635** - FF27 000
  Rue du village en bord de mer Huile/toile (81x100cm 31x39in) Melun 2001
- $4 866 - €4 673 - **£3 000** - FF30 656
  Barges on a River Estuary/Beached Fishing Boats by Moonlight Oil/canvas (20.5x30.5cm 8x12in) London 1999
- $818 - €762 - **£504** - FF5 000
  Paysage au moulin Aquarelle/papier (44x59cm 17x23in) Saint-Dié 1999
- $3 200 - €3 582 - **£2 231** - FF23 496
  Le bain Lithograph (20.5x20cm 8x7in) New-York 2001

THORNTON Robert John, Dr. 1768-1837 **[24]**
- $1 500 - €1 285 - **£901** - FF8 429
  «The Queen», by R. Cooper after Henderson Mezzotint (56x44cm 22x17in) New-Orleans LA 1998

THORNYCROFT Hamo William 1850-1925 **[26]**
- $3 313 - €3 067 - **£2 000** - FF20 117
  Study of a Naked Grecian Female fastening her sandal Bronze (H43cm H17in) Leicester 1999

THOROGOOD Stanley 1873-1953 **[4]**
- $1 880 - €2 189 - **£1 300** - FF14 361
  Joan Van Arc Glazed ceramic (H42cm H16in) London 2000

THORPE James 1876-1949 **[6]**
- $760 - €720 - **£475** - FF4 726
  Fruit and Flowers Woodcut in colors (41x28cm 16x11in) Woollahra, Sydney 1999

THORPE John Hall 1874-1947 **[124]**
- $187 - €197 - **£123** - FF1 293
  Floral Study Woodcut in colors (18x16cm 7x6in) Auckland 2000

THORPE Lesbia 1919 **[18]**
- $140 - €155 - **£93** - FF1 014
  Take-Over Linocut in colors (59x48cm 23x18in) Melbourne 2000

THORPE Thomas Bangs 1815-1878 **[2]**
- $8 000 - €7 576 - **£4 864** - FF49 696
  The Dance Oil/canvas (54x77cm 21x30in) New-York 1999
- $4 750 - €3 985 - **£2 799** - FF26 142
  Scene in long Island Watercolour/paper (34x53cm 13x21in) Greenwich CT 1998

THØRRESTRUP Christian 1823-1892 **[26]**
- $701 - €790 - **£483** - FF5 182
  En gammal man med sin kanariefågel Oil/canvas (35x33cm 13x12in) Stockholm 2000

THORS Joseph act.1863-1900 **[328]**
- $3 040 - €2 902 - **£1 900** - FF19 038
  Shepherd with his Flock by a Cottage in a wooded Landscape Oil/board (40.5x61cm 15x24in) London 1999
- $1 973 - €2 295 - **£1 409** - FF15 056
  «Near Thetford, Warwickshire» Oil/canvas (25.5x35.5cm 10x13in) Toronto 2001

THORSEN Gro 1966 **[2]**
- $3 000 - €3 182 - **£2 034** - FF20 871
  Untitled Oil/canvas (50x150cm 19x59in) Tel Aviv 2001

THORSØE Hans Peter 1791-1842 **[3]**
- $8 050 - €6 721 - **£4 785** - FF44 090
  «Prospect af Staden Frederichssted paa Öen St. Croix i West Indien» Watercolour (33x52cm 12x20in) Köbenhavn 1998

THORSTEINSSON Gudmundur 1891-1924 **[4]**
- $1 572 - €1 812 - **£1 085** - FF11 884
  Sneklaedt fjeldlandskab, Island Oil/canvas (29x34cm 11x13in) Köbenhavn 2000
- $871 - €939 - **£599** - FF6 132
  Udsigt over Bildudalur Watercolour/paper (16x19cm 6x7in) Köbenhavn 2001

THORVALD H. XIX-XX **[6]**
- $813 - €920 - **£550** - FF6 035
  Fjord Scenes Oil/panel (14.5x30.5cm 5x12in) London 2000

THORWALDSEN Bertel 1768/70-1844 **[34]**
- $15 927 - €13 460 - **£9 500** - FF88 290
  Hebe, the Cupbearer Marble (H160cm H62in) London 1998
- $1 151 - €1 273 - **£799** - FF8 349
  Den lyrespillende Amor Bronze (H34cm H13in) Vejle 2001

THOS Yves XX **[16]**
- $194 - €168 - **£117** - FF1 100
  «Il Bidone» de Frederico Fellini Affiche (120x160cm 47x62in) Argenteuil 1999

T

THRASHER Leslie 1889-1936 **[9]**
$4 250 - €4 954 - **£2 942** - FF32 497
The Football Star gets the Girl Oil/canvas
(33x29cm 13x11in) New-York 2000

THUAR Hans 1887-1945 **[9]**
$21 959 - €20 963 - **£13 718** - FF137 509
Weg zum Dorf Öl/Leinwand (49.5x86.5cm 19x34in)
Köln 1999

THUILLIER Pierre 1799-1858 **[12]**
$10 257 - €11 810 - **£7 000** - FF77 468
Encampment in the Atlas Mountains Oil/canvas
(67.5x98cm 26x38in) London 2000
$2 924 - €3 278 - **£2 036** - FF21 500
**Paysage à la rivière et aux rochers, les quatre
marabout** Grisaille (70x47cm 27x18in) Paris 2001

THULDEN van Theodor 1606-1669 **[30]**
$28 000 - €23 287 - **£16 436** - FF152 754
The Forge of Vulcan Oil/canvas (169x121.5cm
66x47in) New-York 1998
$20 920 - €22 456 - **£14 000** - FF147 302
**Music-Making Angels playing the Harp, Flute,
Viola and Lute** Oil/panel (82x60cm 32x23in) London
2000
$1 607 - €1 817 - **£1 085** - FF11 917
**Das siegreiche Frankreich im Gestalt der
Minerva** Red chalk (27.5x15.6cm 10x6in) Wien 2000

THULSTRUP William August XIX **[4]**
$5 154 - €5 779 - **£3 500** - FF37 907
**Family on a Rooftop in St Thomas/Dutch
Settlers in St Thomas** Watercolour (30x23cm
11x9in) London 2000

THUMANN Friedrich Paul 1834-1908 **[15]**
$1 635 - €1 794 - **£1 111** - FF11 770
Der kleine Kavalier Oil/panel (46x33.5cm 18x13in)
Luzern 2000

THUN Anders Wilhelm 1800-1829 **[1]**
$12 243 - €11 706 - **£7 675** - FF76 786
Utsigt af Carl XIII: s torg Oil/canvas (92x160cm
36x62in) Stockholm 1999

THUNMAN Olof 1879-1944 **[58]**
$724 - €823 - **£495** - FF5 396
Vinterlandskap med stugor i månsken Oil/canvas
(65x95cm 25x37in) Uppsala 2000
$532 - €580 - **£349** - FF3 805
**Trefaldighetskyrkan sedd från Nedre
Slottsgatan** Akvarell/papper (22x21cm 8x8in) Uppsala
2000

THURAU Friedrich 1812-1888 **[10]**
$8 778 - €7 990 - **£5 388** - FF52 409
Fischerboote auf dem Bodensee Öl/Leinwand
(55x71cm 21x27in) Zürich 1999
$2 893 - €2 446 - **£1 730** - FF16 047
**A Summer River Landscape/The Arrival of the
Fleet at Dusk** Oil/cardboard (24x30cm 9x11in)
Amsterdam 1998

THURBER James 1894-1961 **[18]**
$6 500 - €7 577 - **£4 500** - FF49 702
**Men at Table manipulating Table Settings, Waiter
looks on** Ink (16x23cm 6x9in) New-York 2000

THURET André 1898-1965 **[3]**
$3 692 - €3 964 - **£2 470** - FF26 000
Vase Sculpture verre (H16cm H6in) Neuilly-sur-Seine

THURLBY F. XIX-XX **[4]**
$963 - €935 - **£600** - FF6 135
«Molly», a dark brown Pony in a Loosebox
Oil/canvas (40.5x51cm 15x20in) London 1999

THURLO Frank 1828-1913 **[2]**
$2 400 - €2 676 - **£1 613** - FF17 554
Marsh Scene with Haystacks, Essex County
Watercolour/paper (15x46cm 6x18in) Portsmouth NH
2000

THURLOW Edward Hovell 1839-1925 **[17]**
$560 - €651 - **£400** - FF4 272
**Indian Figures drawing water from the River to
irriguate the Land** Watercolour (23.5x17cm 9x6in)
London 2001

THÜRMER Joseph 1798-1833 **[8]**
$4 596 - €5 366 - **£3 244** - FF35 200
Prospekt af Athen med Akropolis Pencil/paper
(28x83cm 11x32in) København 2000

THURNER Gabriel Edouard 1840-1907 **[20]**
$956 - €1 125 - **£675** - FF7 378
**Paris Kircheninterieur mit einer Gruppe
Novizen beim Gebet** Öl/Leinwand (82x65.5cm
32x25in) Köln 2001

THURSZ Frederic Matys 1930-1992 **[1]**
$64 225 - €76 439 - **£45 896** - FF501 408
In Praise of Hands Öl/Leinwand (302x201cm
118x79in) Berlin 2000

THYGESEN Rudolph 1880-1953 **[39]**
$16 350 - €19 003 - **£11 490** - FF124 650
Modeller (Dobbeltakt komposisjon) Oil/canvas
(160x153cm 62x60in) Oslo 2001
$545 - €637 - **£389** - FF4 177
Vår Oil/canvas (46x38cm 18x14in) Oslo 2001
$612 - €679 - **£415** - FF4 453
Landskapskisse Oil/panel (33x41cm 12x16in) Oslo
2000

THYS Pieter I 1624-1677 **[8]**
$7 430 - €8 622 - **£5 130** - FF56 555
Saint Sebastien Oil/canvas (163.5x112cm 64x44in)
Amsterdam 2000

THYSEBAERT Emile 1871-1962 **[98]**
$310 - €372 - **£213** - FF2 439
**Stilleven met bloemenvaas (Nature morte au
vase de fleurs,aux oranges)** Huile/toile (58x70cm
22x27in) Antwerpen 2000
$276 - €297 - **£190** - FF1 951
Tête de pêcheur sur fond de port de pêche
Huile/panneau (34x42cm 13x16in) Bruxelles 2001

TI-SHAN HSU 1951 **[5]**
$6 100 - €5 122 - **£3 580** - FF33 600
Box of Weeds Oil/canvas (89x130.5cm 35x51in)
Taipei 1998

TIARINI Alessandro 1577-1668 **[15]**
$14 520 - €12 544 - **£7 260** - FF82 280
San Giovanni Battista Olio/tela (110x180cm
43x70in) Genova 1999

$21 600 - €27 990 - £16 200 - FF183 600
Presentazione di Santa Dorotea alla santissima Trinità Olio/tavola (52x40cm 20x15in) Milano 2000

$2 251 - €2 556 - £1 564 - FF16 769
Die Verleumdung des Apelles Ink (41x28.5cm 16x11in) Köln 2001

TIBBITS Howard Clinton ?-1937 [2]

$180 - €167 - £111 - FF1 098
The Fallen Monarch, Mariposa Big Tree Grove, California Photograph (41x54cm 16x21in) East-Dennis MA 1999

TIBBITS William 1837-1906 [9]

$1 776 - €1 984 - £1 137 - FF13 011
Historic-House, Melbourne Watercolour/paper (13x24cm 5x9in) Malvern, Victoria 2000

TIBBLE Geoffrey 1909-1952 [19]

$4 010 - €4 041 - £2 500 - FF26 509
Figures in the drawing Room Oil/canvas (76x64cm 29x25in) London 2000

TIBET (Gilbert Gascard) 1931 [14]

$203 - €229 - £142 - FF1 500
Chic Bill Encre Chine/papier (18x21cm 7x8in) Paris 2001

TIBOR Ernö 1885-1945 [4]

$2 775 - €2 916 - £1 725 - FF19 125
Pause de midi Huile/toile (65x81.5cm 25x32in) Budapest 2000

TICE George A. 1938 [60]

$1 173 - €1 361 - £810 - FF8 930
Porch, Monhegan Island, Maine Platinum, palladium print (23.5x15cm 9x5in) Vancouver, BC. 2000

TICHO Anna 1894-1980 [106]

$6 500 - €6 739 - £4 283 - FF44 206
Flowers Watercolour/paper (43x34cm 16x13in) Herzelia-Pituah 2000

TICHON Charles XIX-XX [47]

$732 - €732 - £457 - FF4 800
«Cycles Le Globe» Affiche (130x94cm 51x37in) Orléans 1999

TICHY Frantisek 1896-1961 [90]

$4 624 - €4 373 - £2 880 - FF28 688
Portrait de compositeur J.Srnky Huile/panneau (30.5x22cm 12x8in) Praha 2000

$982 - €929 - £612 - FF6 096
Eros Technique mixte/papier (33x25cm 12x9in) Praha 2000

$289 - €273 - £180 - FF1 793
«Young Man» Drypoint (28x22cm 11x8in) Praha 2001

TIDEMAND Adolph 1814-1876 [35]

$110 544 - €126 177 - £76 798 - FF827 670
Norsk bondestueinteriör med mand og kone Oil/canvas (55x45cm 21x17in) Köbenhavn 2000

$19 764 - €22 370 - £13 824 - FF146 736
Bönnestund Oil/panel (25x21cm 9x8in) Oslo 2001

TIDMARSH H.E. XIX-XX [10]

$5 976 - €6 943 - £4 200 - FF45 545
St.Clement Danes, Fleet Street and london Rooftops Watercolour/paper (38x55cm 15x22in) Lewes, Sussex 2001

TIEBOUT Cornelius c.1777-c.1830 [3]

$2 000 - €2 121 - £1 356 - FF13 914
George Washington Engraving (56.5x37cm 22x14in) New-York 2001

TIECHE Adolphe 1877-1957 [68]

$841 - €809 - £519 - FF5 308
La dernière neige Öl/Leinwand (66x89cm 25x35in) Bern 1999

$628 - €717 - £442 - FF4 703
Berner Landgut in der Herbstsonne Watercolour (46x60cm 18x23in) Bern 2001

$735 - €838 - £513 - FF5 500
«Berne, Schweiz, Switzerland, Suisse» Affiche (94x157cm 37x61in) Paris 2001

TIEDJEN Willi 1881-1950 [73]

$1 281 - €1 227 - £791 - FF8 049
Drei Pferde am Stadel vor Hochgebirgspanorama Öl/Leinwand (40x57cm 15x22in) Kempten 1999

TIEL van Quirijn 1900-1967 [29]

$12 135 - €13 613 - £8 409 - FF89 298
Winter Landscape Oil/canvas (120x125cm 47x49in) Amsterdam 2000

$4 960 - €5 899 - £3 536 - FF38 695
Vogel tussen bloemen Oil/canvas (80x95cm 31x37in) Amsterdam 2000

TIELENS Alexandre 1868-1959 [89]

$424 - €496 - £302 - FF3 252
La miettée Huile/toile (60x80cm 23x31in) Bruxelles 2001

$335 - €322 - £204 - FF2 113
Jardin en été animé de personnages Huile/toile (40x30cm 15x11in) Antwerpen 2001

TIEPOLO Giovanni Battista 1696-1770 [288]

$380 000 - €405 821 - £258 932 - FF2 662 014
Interior of a Church with Vestal Virgins/Interior of classical Library Oil/canvas (211x146cm 83x57in) New-York 2001

$354 486 - €348 129 - £220 000 - FF2 283 578
Two Putti with a Dove Oil/canvas (55x63cm 21x24in) London 1999

$140 000 - €181 414 - £105 000 - FF1 190 000
La predica del Battista Olio/tela (32x43cm 12x16in) Roma 2000

$21 000 - €18 256 - £12 709 - FF119 754
Study of a young Man, seen 'Da Sotto in Su' Ink (28x19cm 11x7in) New-York 1999

$2 400 - €2 125 - £1 492 - FF14 901
Punchinello talking to two Magicians Etching (23.5x18.5cm 9x7in) New-York 1999

TIEPOLO Giovanni Domenico 1727-1804 [325]

$47 817 - €51 328 - £32 000 - FF336 691
Head of a Philosopher Oil/canvas/board (56.5x43cm 22x16in) London 2000

$268 974 - €288 721 - £180 000 - FF1 893 888
The Inmacolata Oil/canvas (41x30.5cm 16x12in) London 2000

$14 000 - €14 951 - £9 539 - FF98 074
Angelica and Medoro Carving their Names on a Tree Ink (26.5x19cm 10x7in) New-York 2001

T

📖 **$ 738 - €1 687 - £1 082** - FF11 067
Das Martyrium der hl. Agatha, nach Giovanni Battista Tiepolo Radierung (44.3x24.9cm 17x9in) Berlin 1999

TIEPOLO Lorenzo 1736-1776 **[35]**

✏ **$31 110 - €28 850 - £19 000** - FF189 243
The Head of Young Man Red chalk/paper (33x21cm 12x8in) London 1998

📖 **$1 562 - €1 677 - £1 045** - FF11 000
Les amours de Renaud et d'Armide d'après Jean-Baptiste Tiepolo Eau-forte (27x34cm 10x13in) Paris 2000

TIFFANY Lillian 1900 **[8]**

✏ **$1 600 - €1 416 - £978** - FF9 291
Ch: Maroufke of Kelso/Ch: Trilene, Schipperkees Watercolour, gouache/paper (33x44.5cm 12x17in) New-York 1999

TIFFANY Louis Comfort 1848-1933 **[55]**

🔁 **$45 000 - €43 092 - £27 733** - FF282 663
Still Life with Dahlias Oil/canvas (55x39cm 22x15in) Portsmouth NH 1999

✏ **$14 000 - €11 994 - £8 416** - FF78 675
Double Staircase in the Courtyard at Blois Gouache (46.5x33.5cm 18x13in) New-York 1998

TIGER Frans Johan 1849-1919 **[4]**

🔁 **$3 077 - €2 882 - £1 850** - FF18 907
Insjölandskap med man och flicka på strand Oil/canvas (72x132cm 28x51in) Stockholm 1999

TIGHE Francis Browne XIX-XX **[17]**

✏ **$381 - €410 - £260** - FF2 691
A Manchester Street Scene with Figures Watercolour (23x31.5cm 9x12in) West-Yorshire 2001

TIGLIO Marcos 1903-1976 **[4]**

🔁 **$3 900 - €4 531 - £2 740** - FF29 722
Ultimos oros Oleo/tabla (65x52cm 25x20in) Buenos-Aires 2001

TIHANYI Lajos 1885-1938 **[8]**

🔁 **$64 000 - €62 931 - £40 000** - FF412 800
Forest Landscape Oil/canvas (56x65.5cm 22x25in) Budapest 1999

✏ **$15 180 - €17 251 - £10 580** - FF113 160
Portrait d'enfant Pastel/papier (64.5x52cm 25x20in) Budapest 1999

TIKAL Vaclav 1906-1965 **[8]**

🔁 **$2 774 - €2 624 - £1 728** - FF17 212
Assemblage Technique mixte/carton (50x35cm 19x13in) Praha 2001

🔁 **$1 445 - €1 367 - £900** - FF8 965
Meeting of Saboteurs Oil/board (28.5x50cm 11x19in) Praha 2000

TIKHMENEV Efim XIX **[4]**

🔁 **$4 233 - €4 670 - £2 800** - FF30 636
The Hunt Oil/canvas (65x80.5cm 25x31in) London 2000

TIKKANEN Henrik 1924-1984 **[13]**

✏ **$322 - €286 - £197** - FF1 875
Unionsgatan Indian ink/paper (16x22cm 6x8in) Helsinki 1999

TIKOS Albert 1815-1845 **[1]**

🔁 **$3 515 - €3 693 - £2 185** - FF24 225
Enfant lisant Huile/toile (59x53cm 23x20in) Budapest 2000

TILBURG van Gillis I 1578-c.1623 **[4]**

🔁 **$18 434 - €15 685 - £11 000** - FF102 887
Peasants sitting at a table in an Interior Oil/panel (19.5x25cm 7x9in) London 1998

TILBURG van Gillis II 1625-c.1678 **[40]**

🔁 **$35 750 - €37 703 - £21 780** - FF214 515
Bewaldete flandrische Landschaft mit einem Schloss Öl/Leinwand (115x179cm 45x70in) Wien 1999

🔁 **$29 452 - €33 023 - £20 000** - FF216 614
Merry Company in a Tavern Interior Oil/canvas (89.5x118cm 35x46in) London 2000

TILEMANN-PETERSEN Christian 1874-1926 **[54]**

🔁 **$699 - €673 - £435** - FF4 416
Rygaard på Fyn, Julen Oil/canvas (73x60cm 28x23in) Köbenhavn 1999

TILENS Jan 1589-1630 **[7]**

🔁 **$12 084 - €11 868 - £7 500** - FF77 849
Panoramic Landscape, Architectural Ruins, Huntsmen and Horse Oil/panel (63x79.5cm 24x31in) London 1999

TILKE Karl Max, Max 1869-1943 **[23]**

🔁 **$575 - €649 - £404** - FF4 260
Strasse in Toledo Öl/Karton (47.5x38.5cm 18x15in) Bern 2001

TILL Johann II 1827-1894 **[23]**

🔁 **$1 418 - €1 687 - £1 011** - FF11 067
Im Kloster, Mönch bewirtet Söldner Öl/Leinwand (31x21cm 12x8in) Köln 2000

TILL Walter XX **[16]**

📖 **$1 400 - €1 526 - £969** - FF10 007
«Ireland for Entrancing Scenery» Poster (73x99cm 29x39in) New-York 2001

TILLAC Pablo XX **[6]**

🔁 **$1 383 - €1 143 - £811** - FF7 500
Attelage de boeufs devant la ferme Huile/panneau (44x36cm 17x14in) Biarritz 1998

TILLBERG Peter 1946 **[19]**

✏ **$538 - €506 - £333** - FF3 319
Snabeldjur Pencil/paper (42x35.5cm 16x13in) Stockholm 1999

TILLEMANS Peter 1684-1734 **[25]**

🔁 **$14 000 - €16 650 - £9 977** - FF109 214
Pheasant Shooting Oil/canvas (54.5x79cm 21x31in) New-York 2000

📖 **$19 568 - €22 541 - £13 500** - FF147 856
Round-Course/Noblemans & Gentlemans/Horse-Math/Fox Chase Engraving (47x113cm 18x44in) Newbury, Berkshire 2000

TILLERS Imants 1950 **[20]**

🔁 **$11 436 - €12 276 - £7 654** - FF80 524
Erased Portrait of Murray Bail Mixed media (280.5x228cm 110x89in) Sydney 2000

🔁 **$8 152 - €8 902 - £5 247** - FF58 396
View Mixed media/canvas (89x89cm 35x35in) Melbourne 2000

TILLEUX Jozef 1896-1978 **[107]**
$380 - €322 - **£227** - FF2 112
Barques de pêche à l'anguille sur la Nèthe à Lierre Huile/toile (69x90cm 27x35in) Antwerpen 1998

TILLIER Paul Prosper 1834-? **[12]**
$6 902 - €7 370 - **£4 702** - FF48 345
Ung kvinde med rangle, der leger med sit barn Oil/canvas (125x85cm 49x33in) Vejle 2001

TILLIEUX Maurice 1922-1978 **[19]**
$960 - €884 - **£576** - FF5 800
Félix Encre Chine/papier (47x30cm 18x11in) Paris 1999

TILLINGHAST Mary Elizabeth ?-1912 **[1]**
$3 484 - €3 049 - **£2 110** - FF20 000
Portrait de Richard Wagner Pastel/toile (73x57cm 28x22in) Paris 1998

TILLMANS Wolfgang 1968 **[57]**
$3 512 - €3 964 - **£2 470** - FF26 000
Four Boots Photo (30x40cm 11x15in) Paris 2001

TILLYER William 1938 **[32]**
$206 - €221 - **£140** - FF1 451
Garden Study Woodcut (91x69.5cm 35x27in) London 2001

TILSON Joe 1928 **[222]**
$3 250 - €3 690 - **£2 224** - FF24 207
«Geometry Puzzle I» Acrylic/wood (121x167cm 48x66in) Chicago IL 2000
$2 172 - €1 836 - **£1 300** - FF12 043
The Flaying of Marsyas Oil/canvas (74x63.5cm 29x25in) London 1998
$8 500 - €8 812 - **£5 100** - FF57 800
Zikkurat 6 Sculpture bois (207x330x20cm 81x129x7in) Milano 2000
$950 - €892 - **£586** - FF5 853
Tiny Africa Relief (46x31cm 18x12in) Antwerpen 1999
$596 - €640 - **£399** - FF4 200
Transparency the Five Senses - Touch Sérigraphie (61x61x25cm 24x24x1in) Paris 2000

TIMÉN Frans 1883-1968 **[25]**
$505 - €586 - **£349** - FF3 847
Blomsterstilleben Oil/canvas (84x72cm 33x28in) Stockholm 2000

TIMKOV Nikolaï Efimovich 1912-1993 **[20]**
$5 681 - €5 460 - **£3 500** - FF35 816
The Edge of Town Oil/panel (26x37cm 10x14in) London 1999

TIMLIN William Mitcheson 1893-1943 **[79]**
$1 047 - €879 - **£613** - FF5 769
Cape Landscape Oil/canvas (60x106cm 23x41in) Cape Town 1998
$593 - €699 - **£410** - FF4 585
Illustration to the Arabian Nights Ink (25x23cm 9x9in) Cape Town 2000

TIMM Vasili Fiedorovivh 1820-1895 **[5]**
$2 245 - €2 035 - **£1 383** - FF13 347
Winterliche Landschaft mit figürlicher Staffage Öl/Leinwand (19x24.5cm 7x9in) Wien 1999

TIMMERMAHN Peter Klein 1942 **[15]**
$1 001 - €1 179 - **£704** - FF7 737
«Liston lässt den Winter schmilzen» Öl/Leinwand (49.5x49.5cm 19x19in) Zürich 2000

TIMMERMANS Félix 1886-1947 **[28]**
$179 - €211 - **£128** - FF1 382
Hut in het bos Encre Chine/papier (13x8.5cm 5x3in) Antwerpen 2000

TIMMERMANS Henri 1858-1942 **[39]**
$2 704 - €3 222 - **£1 937** - FF21 138
Herbergtafereel (scène d'auberge) Huile/toile (86x128cm 33x50in) Antwerpen 2000
$851 - €942 - **£570** - FF6 178
Vieille femme près de la fenêtre Huile/toile (45x27cm 17x10in) Antwerpen 2000

TIMMERMANS Jean 1899-1986 **[67]**
$488 - €545 - **£341** - FF3 577
Vue de forêt Huile/toile (80x100cm 31x39in) Bruxelles 2001
$356 - €297 - **£208** - FF1 951
Port de pêche Watercolour/paper (42x51cm 16x20in) Lokeren 1998

TIMMERMANS Louis Étienne 1846-1910 **[133]**
$4 015 - €3 811 - **£2 505** - FF25 000
Le port de Tréport Huile/toile (40.5x65cm 15x25in) Cannes 1999
$1 858 - €2 211 - **£1 325** - FF14 500
L'entrée du port Huile/panneau (32x41cm 12x16in) Nantes 2000
$824 - €793 - **£508** - FF5 200
Port fluvial Aquarelle/papier (25x37cm 9x14in) Granville 1999

TIMMOCK George 1945 **[2]**
$5 500 - €5 698 - **£3 500** - FF37 374
Two-part Vessel Ceramic (45.5x40.5cm 17x15in) New-York 2000

TIMMS Freddie c.1946/48 **[11]**
$2 401 - €2 578 - **£1 607** - FF16 910
Moorun Country Mixed media/canvas (106.5x83cm 41x32in) Sydney 2000

TIMPE Wil 1920 **[5]**
$1 650 - €1 682 - **£1 033** - FF11 033
Cowboys, horses and Chuck Wagon Oil/canvas (50x40cm 20x16in) Altadena CA 2000

TIMYN William XX **[22]**
$210 - €245 - **£150** - FF1 610
Tiger Ink (46x62.5cm 18x24in) London 2001

TINDALL Charles Ephraim S. 1863-1951 **[22]**
$447 - €430 - **£275** - FF2 822
Jetty Activity Watercolour/paper (24x34cm 9x13in) Melbourne 1999

TINDLE David 1932 **[132]**
$3 472 - €3 368 - **£2 200** - FF22 090
Window Still Life II Acrylic/paper (67x58cm 26x22in) London 1999
$650 - €758 - **£450** - FF4 971
Holdenby Oil/board (16x22cm 6x8in) London 2000
$1 021 - €980 - **£650** - FF6 430
Notre-Dame Watercolour/paper (30x40cm 11x15in) London 1999

T

TING Walasse 1929 [410]

- $5 077 - €5 899 - **£3 568** - FF38 695
  Two geishas and Parrots Acrylic/paper (175x95cm 68x37in) Amsterdam 2001
- $2 693 - €3 082 - **£1 851** - FF20 217
  Sweet Milkyway Acrylic/canvas (76x100cm 29x39in) Köbenhavn 2000
- $618 - €694 - **£431** - FF4 552
  Femme nue aux fleurs Technique mixte (9.5x14cm 3x5in) Bruxelles 2001
- $1 606 - €1 687 - **£1 013** - FF11 067
  Vier Geishas Gouache/paper (37x47cm 14x18in) Stuttgart 2000
- $239 - €223 - **£147** - FF1 463
  Erotique, d'après Hokusai Pointe sèche (12x15.7cm 4x6in) Bruxelles 1999

TINGQUA XIX-XX [2]

- $1 400 - €1 423 - **£880** - FF9 334
  View of the Whampoa Anchorage Gouache/paper (16x28cm 6x11in) Oakland CA 2000

TINGUELY Jean 1925-1991 [813]

- $5 847 - €5 009 - **£3 515** - FF32 860
  Ohne Titel Mischtechnik (45.5x84cm 17x33in) Zürich 1998
- $2 527 - €2 556 - **£1 543** - FF16 769
  Salut Sergio Mixed media (30.2x23cm 11x9in) Stuttgart 2000
- $83 550 - €70 614 - **£50 000** - FF463 200
  Untitled Iron (80x32x24cm 31x12x9in) London 1998
- $12 823 - €11 891 - **£7 737** - FF78 000
  Nana Machine Sculpture (H43cm H16in) Paris 1999
- $3 593 - €3 104 - **£2 170** - FF20 358
  Lettre de Chelsea Mixed media/paper (24x45.5cm 9x17in) Luzern 1998
- $575 - €649 - **£404** - FF4 260
  Abstrakte Komposition Farblithographie (40x52cm 15x20in) Bern 2001

TINNEY John ?-1761 [1]

- $1 012 - €1 174 - **£720** - FF7 701
  Views of Hampton Court, after Joseph Highmore Engraving (34x49cm 13x19in) London 2000

TINTORE del Simone 1630-1708 [10]

- $8 801 - €9 447 - **£5 889** - FF61 971
  Natura morta con frutti-Stilleben mit Pfirschen, Feigen, Melone Öl/Leinwand (48x66cm 18x25in) Wien 2000

TINTORETTO Domenico Robusti 1560-1635 [45]

- $22 414 - €24 060 - **£15 000** - FF157 824
  The Supper at Emmaus Oil/canvas (133x206cm 52x81in) London 2000
- $17 931 - €19 248 - **£12 000** - FF126 259
  A Personification of Temperance Oil/canvas (111x103cm 43x40in) London 2000
- $36 000 - €31 578 - **£21 859** - FF207 136
  The Adoration of the Shepherds Mixed media/paper (25x34cm 9x13in) New-York 1999

TINTORETTO Jacopo Robusti 1518-1594 [52]

- $95 000 - €83 330 - **£57 684** - FF546 611
  The Holy Family with the Infant Saint John the Baptist Oil/canvas (172.5x263cm 67x103in) New-York 1999

- $42 609 - €35 787 - **£25 046** - FF234 745
  Porträt-Modello des Dogen Girolamo Priuli Öl/Leinwand (62.8x49cm 24x19in) Köln 1998
- $95 000 - €101 764 - **£64 875** - FF667 527
  Male Nude leaning on a Rock looking upward Black chalk (38.5x22cm 15x8in) New-York 2001

TIPPETT William Vivian 1833-1910 [23]

- $985 - €1 095 - **£660** - FF7 180
  Plough Horses on Wyckham Bridge, Stapleton, near Bristol Oil/canvas (49.5x75cm 19x29in) Bristol, Avon 2000

TIRADO Y CARDONA Fernando 1862-1907 [10]

- $5 865 - €5 106 - **£3 655** - FF33 490
  Pintora en el campo Oleo/tabla (37x56cm 14x22in) Madrid 1999
- $1 950 - €2 252 - **£1 350** - FF14 775
  Caballero Oleo/lienzo (39x23.5cm 15x9in) Seville 2000

TIRATELLI Aurelio 1842-1900 [19]

- $6 455 - €7 166 - **£4 500** - FF47 006
  Water Buffalo in the Roman Campagna Oil/canvas (53x110cm 20x43in) London 2001
- $3 000 - €3 887 - **£2 250** - FF25 500
  Vicolo nel paese Olio/tavola (53x27cm 20x10in) Roma 2000

TIRATELLI Cesare 1864-1933 [17]

- $2 500 - €2 592 - **£1 500** - FF17 000
  La capanna del pecoraro Olio/tela (38x75cm 14x29in) Roma 2000

TIRAVANIJA Rirkrit 1961 [4]

- $37 549 - €40 916 - **£26 000** - FF268 392
  Cure Installation (350x350x350cm 137x137x137in) London 2001
- $8 000 - €8 945 - **£5 392** - FF58 675
  Untitled Graphite (49.5x39.5cm 19x15in) New-York 2000

TIRELLI Marco 1956 [33]

- $1 120 - €1 451 - **£840** - FF9 520
  «Senza titolo» Olio/carta/tela (100x72cm 39x28in) Milano 2001
- $1 650 - €1 710 - **£990** - FF11 220
  Senza titolo Acquarello (68.5x48.5cm 26x19in) Prato 2000

TIRÉN Gerda Maria Rydberg 1858-1928 [12]

- $2 980 - €3 214 - **£2 000** - FF21 084
  Midsommarfirande Akvarell/papper (54x50cm 21x19in) Stockholm 2000

TIRÉN Johan 1853-1911 [68]

- $1 312 - €1 400 - **£890** - FF9 181
  Samebarn Oil/panel (43x62cm 16x24in) Stockholm 2001
- $3 309 - €3 265 - **£2 038** - FF21 417
  Jultomten Akvarell/papper (32x29cm 12x11in) Stockholm 1999

TIREN Nils 1885-1935 [22]

- $645 - €580 - **£385** - FF3 806
  Trutungar på skär Watercolour/paper (34x49cm 13x19in) Stockholm 1998

TIRINNANZI Nino Giovanni 1923 [93]

- $1 680 - €1 451 - **£840** - FF9 520
  Natura morta Olio/cartone/tela (35x50cm 13x19in) Prato 1999

$850 - €881 - **£510** - FF5 780
Paesaggio Olio/cartone/tela (25x35cm 9x13in) Prato 1999

$450 - €466 - **£270** - FF3 060
Figura maschile seduta Matita/carta (51x56cm 20x22in) Firenze 2001

TIRION Isaak 1705-1765 **[11]**

$214 - €204 - **£130** - FF1 339
Sri Lanka Engraving (28x36cm 11x14in) London 1999

TIRONI Francesco c.1745-1797 **[36]**

$34 907 - €39 332 - **£24 561** - FF258 000
Vue de la Place Saint-Marc Huile/toile/panneau (52x84cm 20x33in) Paris 2001

$14 196 - €15 239 - **£9 500** - FF99 959
The Island of San Michele, Venice Red chalk (28.5x42cm 11x16in) London 2000

TIRVERT Eugène 1881-1948 **[26]**

$2 780 - €2 973 - **£1 893** - FF19 500
Nature morte au bouquet de fleurs et brioche Huile/toile (45x54cm 17x21in) Rouen 2001

TISCHBEIN Anton Wilhelm 1730-1804 **[7]**

$6 795 - €6 541 - **£4 248** - FF42 903
Angebliches Bildnis Philipp Carl von Hohener(?) Öl/Leinwand (51x40cm 20x15in) Wien 1999

$44 829 - €48 120 - **£30 000** - FF315 648
Personifications of Music and Drawing Oil/canvas (30.5x28cm 12x11in) London 2000

TISCHBEIN August Anton 1805-c.1867 **[9]**

$3 339 - €2 805 - **£1 962** - FF18 397
Maria mit dem Kind in mediterraner Küstenlandschaft Öl/Leinwand (43.5x32cm 17x12in) Bern 1998

$2 760 - €2 384 - **£1 840** - FF15 640
Paesaggio lacustre Matita (20x28cm 7x11in) Prato 1998

TISCHBEIN Jacob 1725-1791 **[3]**

$8 296 - €8 692 - **£5 487** - FF57 016
Drei Reiter bei der Rast an einem Wasser Oil/panel (26.7x36.7cm 10x14in) München 2000

TISCHBEIN Johann Anton 1720-1784 **[4]**

$12 115 - €14 316 - **£8 587** - FF93 909
Labans Schätze/Der Heilige Kassian stürzt eine Statue Öl/Leinwand (97x64cm 38x25in) Ahlden 2000

TISCHBEIN Johann Friedrich A. 1750-1812 **[18]**

$10 712 - €10 226 - **£6 694** - FF67 078
Bildnis eines jungen Mannes Öl/Leinwand (70x60cm 27x23in) Hamburg 1999

$12 205 - €10 428 - **£7 384** - FF68 403
Das Erbprinzenpaar von Anhaltdessau mit seinen Kindern Öl/Leinwand (41x28cm 16x11in) München 1998

$946 - €1 125 - **£655** - FF7 378
Königin Louise mit ihrer jüngeren Schwester Friederike Print (59x39cm 23x15in) Köln 2000

TISCHBEIN Johann Heinrich I 1722-1789 **[58]**

$45 349 - €36 837 - **£27 261** - FF254 850
Allegorie der Malerei und der Musik Öl/Leinwand (42.5x58cm 16x22in) Köln 1998

$20 322 - €19 429 - **£12 737** - FF127 448
Sultan und Odaliske Öl/Leinwand (39x31cm 15x12in) Hamburg 1999

$857 - €1 022 - **£611** - FF6 707
Der betrogene Küfer Ink (15.5x19.2cm 6x7in) Berlin 2000

$161 - €153 - **£100** - FF1 006
Die Auferstehung Christi Radierung (43.3x28.7cm 17x11in) Berlin 1999

TISCHBEIN Johann Heinrich II 1742-1808 **[16]**

$9 731 - €10 737 - **£6 436** - FF70 431
Die Troerin Polyxenes Öl/Leinwand (73x61cm 28x24in) Hamburg 2000

$300 - €307 - **£188** - FF2 012
L'heureux naufrage Ink (13.5x10cm 5x3in) Köln 2000

TISCHBEIN Johann Heinrich Wil. 1751-1829 **[30]**

$21 376 - €24 279 - **£15 000** - FF159 262
Portrait of Frederic II, Landgrave of Hesse-Cassel Oil/canvas (146.5x114cm 57x44in) London 2001

$125 760 - €121 959 - **£79 120** - FF800 000
Deux jeunes femmes figurant dans le dessin et la sculpture Huile/panneau (77x56.5cm 30x22in) Paris 2001

$5 782 - €6 734 - **£4 000** - FF44 173
Young Girl dressed in Oriental Costume reading from a Scroll Oil/canvas (39.5x30.5cm 15x12in) London 2000

$2 792 - €2 710 - **£1 738** - FF17 775
Landschaft mit Circe, die ein Schwein an der Leine führt Watercolour (21x32.5cm 8x12in) Berlin 1999

$306 - €358 - **£216** - FF2 347
Ajax beschützt Odysseus Radierung (23x22cm 9x8in) Berlin 2001

TISCHLER Heinrich 1897-1938 **[15]**

$225 - €256 - **£156** - FF1 676
Christus und Maria Magdalena Drypoint (23.5x31.5cm 9x12in) Berlin 2001

TISCHLER Victor 1890-1951 **[26]**

$850 - €912 - **£562** - FF5 981
L'église à Arles Oil/panel (33x40cm 13x16in) New-Orleans LA 2000

TISDALL Hans 1910-1997 **[16]**

$711 - €838 - **£500** - FF5 495
Abstract Shorescape Oil/canvas (76x127cm 29x50in) Suffolk 2000

$652 - €623 - **£400** - FF4 088
Abstract Bodycolour (36x56cm 14x22in) London 1999

TISSIER Ange 1814-1876 **[3]**

$2 041 - €1 982 - **£1 261** - FF13 000
Jeune femme grecque de Corfou Huile/toile (46x38cm 18x14in) Paris 1999

TISSOT James Jacques Joseph 1836-1902 **[594]**

$700 000 - €784 436 - **£487 900** - FF5 145 560
Partie Carrée Oil/canvas (119.5x144.5cm 47x56in) New-York 2001

$7 824 - €9 147 - **£5 496** - FF60 000
Soirée d'été - La rêveuse Huile/panneau (40x54cm 15x21in) Paris 2000

$27 000 - €23 902 - **£16 507** - FF156 786
Portrait of the Artist seated on a Garden Bench, Study for R. Mauperin Oil/board (26.5x39cm 10x15in) New-York 1999

T

📖 **$20 025** - €17 074 - **£12 084** - FF112 000
La conversation du Capitaine Dessin (13x20cm 5x7in) Paris 1998

📖 **$2 929** - €2 851 - **£1 800** - FF18 704
L'été Drypoint (54.5x37.5cm 21x14in) London 1999

TITA Amadou Maktar Mbaye 1945 **[1]**

📖 **$3 250** - €3 369 - **£1 950** - FF22 100
Kasoor Démb ou la Cour de Dawi Demba Fall Assemblage (40.5x55x40cm 15x21x15in) Prato 2000

TITCOMB Mary Bradish 1858-1927 **[13]**

📖 **$35 000** - €34 749 - **£21 875** - FF227 941
The Lady in Lavender Oil/canvas (101.5x76cm 39x29in) New-York 1999

📖 **$2 200** - €2 362 - **£1 498** - FF15 491
Clam Diggers Oil/canvas (25x35.5cm 9x13in) Boston MA 2001

📖 **$2 700** - €2 697 - **£1 687** - FF17 691
People on Knoll by Waterside Gouache/paper (52x34cm 20x13in) Wethersfield CT 1999

TITCOMBE Bill XX **[14]**

📖 **$453** - €425 - **£280** - FF2 787
Tom and Jerry create Havoc in a Toy Shop from «Tom and Jerry» Ink (44x34cm 17x13in) London 1999

TITEUX Eugène 1838-1904 **[7]**

📖 **$3 104** - €3 668 - **£2 200** - FF24 060
Le barbier militaire Oil/canvas (60x50cm 23x19in) London 2000

TITI 1975 **[1]**

📖 **$5 684** - €5 336 - **£3 521** - FF35 000
Tobah - Dans les yeux de mon Coeur Assemblage (50x35x20cm 19x13x7in) Marseille 1999

TITI Tiberio 1573-1627 **[4]**

📖 **$21 213** - €19 720 - **£13 000** - FF129 352
Portrait of a Nobleman, full-length, in a black embroidered Coat Oil/canvas (203x112cm 79x44in) London 1998

TITO di Santi 1536-1603 **[18]**

📖 **$21 000** - €21 770 - **£12 600** - FF142 800
Madonna col Bambino, San Giovannino e San Paolo Olio/tavola (115x83cm 45x32in) Milano 2000

📖 **$4 584** - €4 251 - **£2 880** - FF27 888
Studies for the Resurrection of Christ Wash (22.5x33cm 8x12in) London 1998

TITO Ettore 1859-1941 **[56]**

📖 **$23 205** - €24 056 - **£13 923** - FF157 794
Nascita di Venere Olio/tela (96x75.5cm 37x29in) Venezia 2000

📖 **$17 500** - €18 141 - **£10 500** - FF119 000
Piazza San Marco a Venezia con figure Olio/tavola (27x36cm 10x14in) Milano 2000

TITOV Eugène XIX **[9]**

📖 **$1 008** - €1 189 - **£709** - FF7 800
Vénus aux cheveux roux Huile/toile (55x46cm 21x18in) Boulogne-sur-Seine 2000

TITTELBACH Vojtech 1900-1971 **[17]**

📖 **$2 456** - €2 323 - **£1 530** - FF15 240
Two Figures Oil/panel (74x85cm 29x33in) Praha 2000

TITUS-CARMEL Gérard 1942 **[93]**

📖 **$1 922** - €1 906 - **£1 202** - FF12 500
Dérives No.1 Aquarelle (63x91cm 24x35in) Paris 1999

TITZ Louis 1859-1932 **[54]**

📖 **$530** - €496 - **£322** - FF3 252
Gezicht te Dendermonde Gouache/paper (37.5x44cm 14x17in) Lokeren 1999

TIVOLI da Serafino 1826-1892 **[18]**

📖 **$25 802** - €28 965 - **£16 720** - FF190 000
Jeunes baigneurs et barques à la rivière Huile/toile (115x88cm 45x34in) Paris 2000

📖 **$8 500** - €8 812 - **£5 100** - FF57 800
Riposo nel bosco Olio/tela (30x38cm 11x14in) Milano 1999

TIXIER Daniel XIX-XX **[8]**

📖 **$12 000** - €10 623 - **£7 336** - FF69 682
Biblis Oil/canvas (105.5x195.5cm 41x76in) New-York 1999

📖 **$7 420** - €6 233 - **£4 362** - FF40 883
Junge Frau im Rosengarten Öl/Leinwand (46x55cm 18x21in) Bern 1998

TIXIER Louis Léonard 1839-1881 **[3]**

📖 **$16 527** - €16 922 - **£10 378** - FF111 000
La chevrière Huile/toile (121x80.5cm 47x31in) Lille 2000

TIZIANELLO Tiziano Il Vecellio c.1570-c.1650 **[1]**

📖 **$5 600** - €7 257 - **£4 200** - FF47 600
Ritratto Olio/tela (74x62cm 29x24in) Milano 2000

TIZIANO VECELLIO 1485/89-1576 **[12]**

📖 **$268 515** - €230 043 - **£161 415** - FF1 508 985
Porträt des Prokurators Alessandro Contarini Öl/Leinwand (105x76.5cm 41x30in) Köln 1998

TJAKAMARRA Anatjari c.1930-1992 **[15]**

📖 **$8 005** - €8 593 - **£5 357** - FF56 366
Kirritjinya Acrylic (153x122cm 60x48in) Melbourne 2000

📖 **$16 445** - €15 864 - **£10 392** - FF104 060
Man's Story Acrylic (70.5x35cm 27x13in) Melbourne 1999

TJAKAMARRA Freddy West c.1940-1995 **[4]**

📖 **$6 413** - €6 187 - **£4 053** - FF40 585
Tingari Ceremonial Design Acrylic (79x61cm 31x24in) Melbourne 1999

📖 **$3 453** - €3 332 - **£2 182** - FF21 854
Tingari Story Acrylic (23x22.5cm 9x8in) Melbourne 1999

TJAKAMARRA John, Kipara c.1930 **[7]**

📖 **$7 893** - €7 615 - **£4 988** - FF49 948
Old Mans Story Acrylic (55x47.5cm 21x18in) Melbourne 1999

📖 **$31 449** - €33 758 - **£21 048** - FF221 441
Travels of Tingari Ancestors Acrylic (40.5x35cm 15x13in) Melbourne 2000

TJAKAMARRA Long Jack Phillipus c.1932 **[16]**

📖 **$11 182** - €10 787 - **£7 066** - FF70 760
Snake Story Mixed media/board (46x65cm 18x25in) Melbourne 1999

📖 **$4 933** - €4 759 - **£3 117** - FF31 218
Water Story Acrylic (46x31.5cm 18x12in) Melbourne 1999

TJAKAMARRA Old Mick Wallankari c.1900-1996 [8]
☞ **$1 923** – €2 038 – **£1 282** – FF13 366
  Kangaroo Story at Ulpunu Acrylic (91.5x12.5cm 36x4in) Melbourne 2000

TJAMATJI Paddy, Jampin c.1912-1996 [8]
☞ **$5 718** – €6 138 – **£3 827** – FF40 262
  Gunmudu Country - Near Bedford Downs Mixed media/board (70x110cm 27x43in) Melbourne 2000

TJAMPITJIN Sunfly c.1916-1996 [4]
☞ **$4 574** – €4 910 – **£3 061** – FF32 209
  Two Women at Yataru Acrylic/canvas (113x83cm 44x32in) Melbourne 2000

TJAMPITJINPA Anatjari 1927-1999 [12]
☞ **$2 287** – €2 455 – **£1 530** – FF16 104
  Snake Dreaming at Karrilwarra Acrylic (91x91cm 35x35in) Melbourne 2000

TJAMPITJINPA Darby Ross c.1910 [2]
☞ **$3 617** – €3 490 – **£2 286** – FF22 893
  Watiyawarnu Jukurrpa (Wattle Seed Dreaming) Acrylic (151x75cm 59x29in) Melbourne 1999

TJAMPITJINPA Kaapa Mbitjana c.1920-1989 [33]
☞ **$3 831** – €3 340 – **£2 316** – FF21 912
  Untitled Mixed media (79x51cm 31x20in) Melbourne 1998
☞ **$6 578** – €6 346 – **£4 157** – FF41 624
  Rainbow Storm dreaming Mixed media/board (47x25cm 18x9in) Melbourne 1999

TJAMPITJINPA Old Walter 1912-1980 [18]
☞ **$11 436** – €12 276 – **£7 654** – FF80 524
  Water Dreaming at Kalipinypa Acrylic (91x35cm 35x13in) Melbourne 2000
☞ **$2 762** – €2 665 – **£1 745** – FF17 482
  Untitled Mixed media (33.5x22cm 13x8in) Melbourne 1999

TJAMPITJINPA Ronnie 1943 [43]
☞ **$4 931** – €4 772 – **£3 125** – FF31 299
  Tingari Cycle Acrylic/canvas (183x122cm 72x48in) Malvern, Victoria 1999
☞ **$1 416** – €1 560 – **£950** – FF10 233
  Tingari Mens Dreaming Acrylic/canvas (121x56cm 47x22in) Sydney 2000
☞ **$13 723** – €14 731 – **£9 184** – FF96 628
  Untitled Mixed media/board (45.5x32cm 17x12in) Melbourne 2000

TJANGALA Uta Uta 1935-1990 [22]
☞ **$5 718** – €6 138 – **£3 827** – FF40 262
  Medicine Story Enamel (46x36cm 18x14in) Melbourne 2000
☞ **$18 418** – €17 767 – **£11 639** – FF116 547
  Ceremony Enamel (47x22cm 18x8in) Melbourne 2000

TJAPALTJARRI Billy Stockman 1925 [40]
☞ **$1 249** – €1 206 – **£789** – FF7 908
  Untitled Acrylic (76x51cm 29x20in) Melbourne 1999

TJAPALTJARRI Charlie Egalie c.1940 [4]
☞ **$2 631** – €2 538 – **£1 662** – FF16 649
  Waru (Wallaby) Dreaming Acrylic (122x91.5cm 48x36in) Melbourne 1999

TJAPALTJARRI Clifford Possum 1934 [35]
☞ **$2 043** – €2 165 – **£1 362** – FF14 201
  Rock Wallaby Dreaming Acrylic (161x127cm 63x50in) Melbourne 2000
☞ **$2 287** – €2 455 – **£1 530** – FF16 104
  Arinkarakaraka Acrylic (100.5x80.5cm 39x31in) Melbourne 2000

TJAPALTJARRI Old Mick Namarari c.1926-1998 [52]
☞ **$8 577** – €9 207 – **£5 740** – FF60 393
  Marnpi Acrylic (152x183cm 59x72in) Melbourne 2000
☞ **$2 911** – €3 179 – **£1 874** – FF20 856
  Untitled Acrylic/canvas (123x61cm 48x24in) Melbourne 2000
☞ **$4 933** – €4 759 – **£3 117** – FF31 218
  Bush Tucker Dreaming Mixed media (26x18cm 10x7in) Melbourne 1999

TJAPALTJARRI Tim Leura c.1936-1984 [14]
☞ **$4 574** – €4 910 – **£3 061** – FF32 209
  Bushfires at Night Acrylic/board (57x43cm 22x16in) Melbourne 2000

TJAPALTJARRI Tommy Lowry c.1935-1987 [3]
☞ **$4 275** – €4 125 – **£2 702** – FF27 055
  Untitled Mixed media/board (22.5x7.5cm 8x2in) Melbourne 1999

TJAPANANGKA Pinta Pinta c.1930 [6]
☞ **$929** – €1 057 – **£637** – FF6 934
  Tingari Cycle Acrylic/canvas (46x38cm 18x14in) Sydney 2000

TJAPANGARTI Old Tutuma c.1915-1987 [3]
☞ **$2 368** – €2 284 – **£1 496** – FF14 984
  Untitled Enamel (30x27cm 11x10in) Melbourne 1999

TJAPANGARTI Timmy Payungka c.1942 [14]
☞ **$772** – €726 – **£485** – FF4 763
  Untitled Acrylic/canvas (168x45cm 66x17in) Sydney 1999
☞ **$46 046** – €44 419 – **£29 099** – FF291 368
  Cave story Acrylic (46x30.5cm 18x12in) Melbourne 1999

TJAPANGARTI Wimmitji c.1925-2000 [6]
☞ **$10 292** – €11 048 – **£6 888** – FF72 471
  Kutakutal (Artist's Birthplace Near Well 33) Acrylic/canvas (76x100cm 29x39in) Melbourne 2000

TJARDA VAN STARCKENBORGH Jacobus Nicolas 1822-1895 [20]
☞ **$3 750** – €3 794 – **£2 289** – FF24 884
  Hudson River School Oil/canvas (48x67cm 19x26in) York PA 2000
☞ **$2 200** – €2 361 – **£1 472** – FF15 490
  Sheep and donkey grazing Oil/panel (16x23cm 6x9in) Philadelphia PA 2000

TJARDA VAN STARCKENBORGH Willem 1823-1885 [6]
☞ **$7 206** – €6 807 – **£4 495** – FF44 649
  Farmyard with Peasants and Cattle Oil/canvas (64x76cm 25x29in) Amsterdam 1999

TJUNGARRAYI Kingsley c.1935 [1]
☞ **$3 289** – €3 173 – **£2 078** – FF20 812
  Water Dreaming Enamel (60.5x20.5cm 23x8in) Melbourne 1999

T

TJUNGARRAYI Shorty Lungkarda c.1920-1987 **[4]**
- $4 604 – €4 442 – £2 909 – FF29 136
  Minma (Two Women) at Inindinya Acrylic/canvas/board (51x40.5cm 20x15in) Melbourne 1999

TJUNGURRAYI Charlie Tarawa c.1921 **[5]**
- $9 720 – €10 434 – £6 505 – FF68 445
  Emu Dreaming Mixed media/board (65x46cm 25x18in) Melbourne 2000

TJUNGURRAYI Charlie Tjaruru 1920 **[7]**
- $39 450 – €38 173 – £25 002 – FF250 398
  Moon Love Dreaming, Man and Woman Acrylic/board (60x51cm 23x20in) Malvern, Victoria 1999

TJUNGURRAYI Shorty Lungkarda c.1920-1987 **[6]**
- $65 615 – €69 982 – £43 791 – FF459 052
  Tingari Ceremony at Ilingawurngawurng Acrylic/canvas (169x102cm 66x40in) Melbourne 2000
- $7 158 – €7 634 – £4 777 – FF50 078
  Medicine Story Mixed media/board (57.5x43cm 22x16in) Melbourne 2000
- $35 790 – €38 172 – £23 886 – FF250 392
  Untitled Acrylic/board (40x33cm 15x12in) Melbourne 2000

TJUNGURRAYI Yala Yala Gibbs 1928 **[13]**
- $4 509 – €3 895 – £2 723 – FF25 548
  Tingari Site at Kaakorotinja Acrylic (102x162cm 40x63in) Malvern, Victoria 1998
- $9 702 – €8 836 – £5 940 – FF57 960
  Classic Travelling Dreaming Mixed media/board (34.5x28.5cm 13x11in) Malvern, Victoria 1998

TJUPURRULA Johnny Warrangkula c.1932-2001 **[30]**
- $3 616 – €3 499 – £2 291 – FF22 953
  Kalipyinpa Acrylic/canvas (60x91.5cm 23x36in) Malvern, Victoria 1999
- $10 292 – €11 048 – £6 888 – FF72 471
  Cave Coroborree Dreaming Acrylic (42x30cm 16x11in) Melbourne 2000

TJUPURRULA Turkey Tolson 1938 **[25]**
- $5 108 – €4 454 – £3 088 – FF29 216
  Straightening Spears Mixed media/canvas (108.5x190.5cm 42x75in) Melbourne 1998

TO NGOC VAN 1906-1954 **[2]**
- $32 235 – €32 014 – £20 076 – FF210 000
  La leçon de couture Technique mixte (68x68cm 26x26in) Paris 1999

TOBEEN Félix 1880-1938 **[71]**
- $69 680 – €60 980 – £42 200 – FF400 000
  Pelotaris Huile/toile (145x113cm 57x44in) Paris 1998
- $5 073 – €5 445 – £3 394 – FF35 719
  Bouquet Oil/canvas (46x38cm 18x14in) Amsterdam 2000
- $2 499 – €2 439 – £1 582 – FF16 000
  Femme assise à son ouvrage Huile/toile (27x35cm 10x13in) Calais 1999
- $4 040 – €3 857 – £2 525 – FF25 301
  Scène de port à Ciboure Ink (46.5x61.5cm 18x24in) Amsterdam 1999
- $191 – €168 – £116 – FF1 100
  «Pêcheurs basques» Gravure bois (14x20cm 5x7in) Paris 1998

TOBEY Mark 1890-1976 **[607]**
- $27 830 – €32 767 – £19 555 – FF214 935
  «R-R» Tempera (83.5x56cm 32x22in) Zürich 2000
- $8 507 – €8 181 – £5 249 – FF53 662
  Ohne Titel Tempera (21.7x24.4cm 8x9in) Köln 1999
- $3 770 – €3 630 – £2 357 – FF23 812
  Untitled Tempera/paper (21x14.5cm 8x5in) Amsterdam 2000
- $400 – €447 – £256 – FF2 930
  To life Etching, aquatint in colors (50x70.5cm 19x27in) New-York 2000

TOBIAS Herbert 1924-1982 **[43]**
- $657 – €767 – £455 – FF5 030
  Rose Vintage gelatin silver print (34.3x30.5cm 13x12in) Köln 2000

TOBIASSE Théo 1927 **[781]**
- $7 500 – €6 425 – £4 509 – FF42 147
  «Le Petit Cheval de Vence» Oil/canvas (78x99cm 31x39in) St. Louis MO 1998
- $2 696 – €2 912 – £1 864 – FF19 100
  Amour et Arlequin Huile/toile (30x30cm 11x11in) La Varenne-Saint-Hilaire 2001
- $2 224 – €2 363 – £1 491 – FF15 500
  «Odalisque aux bas bleus» Pastel/papier (67.5x56cm 26x22in) Cannes 2000
- $331 – €371 – £230 – FF2 435
  Une odeur de pomme première Etching in colors (104x69cm 40x27in) Oslo 2001

TOBLER Victor 1846-1915 **[21]**
- $1 728 – €1 944 – £1 206 – FF12 754
  Dia Andacht Öl/Leinwand (53x40cm 20x15in) Luzern 2001

TOCHILKIN Mark 1958 **[3]**
- $12 000 – €12 982 – £8 221 – FF85 156
  The Orchestra Oil/canvas (200x105cm 78x41in) Tel Aviv 2001
- $4 000 – €4 327 – £2 740 – FF28 385
  Rabbi Oil/canvas (40x55cm 15x21in) Tel Aviv 2001

TOCQUÉ Jean-Louis 1696-1772 **[22]**
- $100 000 – €87 716 – £60 720 – FF575 380
  Lady, Said to be Madame Mirey, and her Daughter Oil/canvas (134x100cm 52x39in) New-York 1999
- $32 000 – €35 109 – £21 257 – FF230 297
  Portrait of a Sculptor Jean-Louis Lemoyne (1665-1755), in a red Jacket Oil/canvas (64x54cm 25x21in) New-York 2000
- $7 810 – €8 385 – £5 225 – FF55 000
  Gaspard de Fontenay, Générale Major au service de Saxe Pastel/papier (58x44cm 22x17in) Paris 2000

TODARO Victor XIX **[1]**
- $8 330 – €8 635 – £4 998 – FF56 644
  Giovane paggio con falco Olio/tela (97x78cm 38x30in) Milano 1999

TODD Arthur R. Middleton 1891-1966 **[55]**
- $200 – €227 – £140 – FF1 489
  The Cottage in the Woods Watercolour/paper (24x32.5cm 9x12in) Crewkerne, Somerset 2001

TODD Guy XIX-XX **[3]**
- $16 220 – €15 637 – £10 000 – FF102 571
  Gathering Poppies Oil/panel (42x26cm 16x10in) London 1999

TODD Henry Georges 1847-1898 **[67]**
- **$2 599** - €2 529 - **£1 600** - FF16 590
  Still Life of Flowers Oil/panel (73x59cm 28x23in)
  London 1999
- **$2 845** - €3 190 - **£1 932** - FF20 924
  Früchtestilleben mit Trauben und Vogelnest
  Öl/Leinwand (37x32cm 14x12in) Zürich 2000

TODD Milan 1922 **[28]**
- **$2 334** - €2 573 - **£1 552** - FF16 876
  Family Reunion Oil/canvas (90x105cm 35x41in)
  Melbourne 2000

TODD Ralph 1856-1932 **[58]**
- **$17 931** - €19 248 - **£12 000** - FF126 259
  Entanglement Oil/canvas (143x98cm 56x38in)
  London 2000
- **$836** - €847 - **£520** - FF5 555
  Head of a Woman Oil/panel (23x18cm 9x7in) Par,
  Cornwall 2000
- **$886** - €744 - **£520** - FF4 878
  Figure by a Cottage Watercolour/paper (40x50cm
  16x20in) Par, Cornwall 1998

TODD Robert Clow 1809-1866 **[1]**
- **$4 833** - €4 170 - **£2 904** - FF27 352
  Portrait of Gentleman, Thomas Hamilton Oliver
  Oil/canvas (71x53.5cm 27x21in) Nepean, Ont. 1998

TODE Waldemar Knut Gustaf 1859-1900 **[10]**
- **$1 956** - €2 146 - **£1 329** - FF14 078
  Kunstneren i sit atelier med en model Oil/canvas
  (85x71cm 33x27in) Köbenhavn 2000

TODESCHINI Giovanni Battista 1857-1938 **[7]**
- **$9 280** - €9 214 - **£5 800** - FF60 440
  Ritratto di ragazza Oil/canvas (54.5x30cm 21x11in)
  London 1999

TODESCHINI Lucio 1892-1969 **[15]**
- **$6 000** - €6 220 - **£3 600** - FF40 800
  Milano, Piazza Fontana Olio/tela (140x100cm
  55x39in) Milano 2000

TODHUNTER Francis Augustus 1884-1963 **[50]**
- **$1 800** - €1 538 - **£1 089** - FF10 087
  Catholic Church, Mill Valley (The Wedding)
  Oil/canvas (61x76cm 24x29in) San-Francisco CA 1998

TOEPFFER Adam 1766-1847 **[104]**
- **$33 270** - €39 482 - **£24 222** - FF258 984
  Genfer Landschaft mit Pferden und Kühen
  Öl/Leinwand (51x67cm 20x26in) Zürich 2001
- **$8 400** - €9 818 - **£5 997** - FF64 399
  Le four banal d'un village de montagne
  Öl/Karton (23.5x33cm 9x12in) Zürich 2001
- **$1 665** - €1 448 - **£1 004** - FF9 500
  Paysage Encre (22x31.5cm 8x12in) Paris 1998

TOEPUT Lodewyk Pozzoserrato c.1550-1603/05
[39]
- **$14 836** - €16 873 - **£10 289** - FF110 678
  Hochzeit zu Kanaa Öl/Leinwand (106x118cm
  41x46in) Köln 2000
- **$10 000** - €10 367 - **£6 000** - FF68 000
  Paesaggio con architettura e figure Olio/tela
  (74x96cm 29x37in) Roma 1999
- **$18 000** - €19 281 - **£12 292** - FF126 478
  View of the Gardens of a Palace Ink (18.5x26cm
  7x10in) New-York 2001

TOFANARI Sirio 1866-1969 **[11]**
- **$17 955** - €16 732 - **£11 070** - FF109 755
  Aigle Bronze (H87cm H34in) Bruxelles 1999
- **$1 500** - €1 555 - **£900** - FF10 200
  Cane Bronzo (H42cm H16in) Firenze 2001

TOFANO Edoardo 1838-1920 **[30]**
- **$28 000** - €33 202 - **£19 264** - FF217 792
  But I Want to Stay! Oil/canvas (40x33cm 15x12in)
  New-York 2001
- **$6 562** - €7 651 - **£4 600** - FF50 186
  Wistful Moments Watercolour (54x36cm 21x14in)
  Crewkerne, Somerset 2000

TOFFOLI Louis 1907-1999 **[589]**
- **$10 861** - €12 806 - **£7 635** - FF84 000
  «Dans les rues de Pékin» Huile/toile (97x130cm
  38x51in) Fontainebleau 2000
- **$7 051** - €8 385 - **£5 027** - FF55 000
  L'étameur bleu Huile/toile (55x46cm 21x18in) Calais
  2000
- **$2 850** - €2 820 - **£1 777** - FF18 500
  **Les quais de la Seine, Notre-Dame sous la
  neige** Huile/carton (32x41cm 12x16in) Lyon 1999
- **$1 988** - €2 134 - **£1 300** - FF14 000
  La religieuse Gouache/papier (73x51cm 28x20in)
  Cannes 2000
- **$257** - €244 - **£160** - FF1 600
  Le mariage Lithographie (55x75cm 21x29in)
  Coulommiers 1999

TOFT Albert 1862-1949 **[16]**
- **$1 270** - €1 364 - **£850** - FF8 947
  Portrait of a Woman Relief (47x35cm 18x13in)
  Billingshurst, West-Sussex 2000

TOFT J. Alfonso 1866-1964 **[71]**
- **$437** - €497 - **£300** - FF3 261
  Roman Fossway, Kent Oil/board (16x23cm 6x9in)
  London 2000

TOFT Peter Petersen 1825-1901 **[28]**
- **$497** - €430 - **£300** - FF2 821
  **«Mount of the Holy Cross, Gunnison, Rio
  Colorado»** Watercolour (34.5x51.5cm 13x20in)
  Billingshurst, West-Sussex 2000

TOGNI Edoardo 1884-1962 **[1]**
- **$4 600** - €5 961 - **£3 450** - FF39 100
  Meriggio davanti al Monte Blumone Olio/tavola
  (51x74cm 20x29in) Milano 2000

TOGOG Ida Bagus 1913-1989 **[16]**
- **$14 064** - €14 171 - **£8 767** - FF92 956
  Bali Festival Tempera/canvas (128x170cm 50x66in)
  Singapore 2000
- **$5 344** - €4 484 - **£3 135** - FF29 412
  Persiapan Upacara Acrylic/canvas (45x55cm
  17x21in) Singapore 1998
- **$4 156** - €3 487 - **£2 438** - FF22 876
  Balinese Dance Tempera/paper (98x68cm 38x26in)
  Singapore 1998

TOGORES de Josep 1893-1970 **[58]**
- **$15 680** - €16 818 - **£10 360** - FF110 320
  Tres noies Oleo/lienzo (130x97cm 51x38in)
  Barcelona 2000
- **$5 729** - €6 647 - **£3 954** - FF43 600
  Weiblicher Halbakt in Profilansicht Öl/Leinwand
  (73x61cm 28x24in) Köln 2000

T

$5 496 - €5 899 - **£3 677** - FF38 695
Two Nudes Oil/canvas (41x27cm 16x10in)
Amsterdam 2000

$674 - €571 - **£399** - FF3 743
Desnudo Lápiz/papel (36x25cm 14x9in) Madrid 1998

TOHKA Sakari 1911-1958 [12]

$1 921 - €1 681 - **£1 164** - FF11 029
Stående flicka Bronze (H44.5cm H17in) Helsinki
1998

TOJETTI Virgilio 1851-1901 [18]

$3 000 - €3 220 - **£2 007** - FF21 123
The Reading Lesson Oil/canvas (66x49cm 26x19in)
New-York 2000

$2 850 - €3 049 - **£1 878** - FF20 000
Jeune fille aux marguerites Huile/toile (39x40cm
15x15in) Lons-Le-Saunier 2000

TOL van Dominicus c.1635-1676 [15]

$68 126 - €70 127 - **£43 286** - FF460 000
La consultation Huile/panneau (44.5x34cm 17x13in)
Paris 2000

TOLEDO Francisco 1940 [421]

$280 000 - €271 844 - **£172 984** - FF1 783 180
Pescado de San Mateo Oil/canvas (100x120.5cm
39x47in) New-York 1999

$40 000 - €38 919 - **£24 620** - FF255 292
Hombre amarillo Oil/paper (66x118.5cm 25x46in)
New-York 1999

$12 000 - €11 676 - **£7 386** - FF76 587
Personaje mirando el sol Oil/wood (26.5x35cm
10x13in) New-York 1999

$15 000 - €14 559 - **£9 339** - FF95 499
Sin Título Watercolour, gouache (25x33cm 9x12in)
New-York 1999

$1 595 - €1 507 - **£995** - FF9 885
Sin título Litografía (37x47cm 14x18in) Monterrey NL
2001

TOLEDO José Rey 1915 [7]

$500 - €584 - **£342** - FF3 828
Portrays Eagle Kachina Watercolour/paper
(35x26cm 14x10in) Cloudcroft NM 2000

TOLGYES XIX-XX [1]

$7 619 - €7 054 - **£4 600** - FF46 270
The Carriage Side Oil/canvas (57.5x37.5cm 22x14in)
London 1999

TOLL Emma 1847-1917 [27]

$463 - €467 - **£288** - FF3 061
Motiv från Saltsjöbaden Oil/canvas (46x32cm
18x12in) Stockholm 2000

$803 - €695 - **£484** - FF4 557
Interiör med kvinna vid skrivbord Pastel/paper
(61x49cm 24x19in) Stockholm 1999

TOLLEMACHE The Hon. Duff 1859-1936 [6]

$900 - €865 - **£550** - FF5 672
«To the Dales by LNER» Poster (102x64cm
40x25in) London 1999

TOLLEN Bob XX [4]

$270 - €312 - **£190** - FF2 049
«Written on the Wind» Poster (104x68.5cm 40x26in)
London 2000

TOLLET Tony, Jean Antoine 1857-1953 [19]

$36 000 - €31 059 - **£21 718** - FF203 734
L'intimité Oil/canvas (147x113cm 57x44in) New-York
1998

$680 - €686 - **£424** - FF4 500
Songe, près de la rivière Huile/panneau
(24.5x16.5cm 9x6in) Lyon 2000

TOLLEY Edward XIX [4]

$4 500 - €5 150 - **£3 095** - FF33 780
Horse Portrait, St.Serf Oil/canvas (54x70cm
21x27in) New-York 2000

TOLLIN Ferdinand 1807-1865 [3]

$2 886 - €3 143 - **£1 890** - FF20 615
Stora Torget i Gävle, rikt staffage av figurer
Watercolour (23x36cm 9x14in) Uppsala 2000

TOLLU Cemal 1899-1968 [4]

$4 660 - €4 346 - **£2 813** - FF28 508
Sitzender Mann vor gemustertem Paravent
Öl/Leinwand (100.5x73cm 39x28in) Lindau 1999

TOLMAN Stacy 1860-1935 [20]

$1 800 - €2 006 - **£1 211** - FF13 158
Snow Scene Oil/canvas (45x60cm 18x24in)
Portsmouth NH 2000

TOLOSA Y ALSINA Aurelio 1861-1938 [16]

$2 080 - €1 952 - **£1 300** - FF12 805
Salida al jardín Oleo/cartón (36.5x42.5cm 14x16in)
Madrid 1999

TOLSON Edgar 1904-1984 [8]

$4 800 - €4 141 - **£2 906** - FF27 164
The Temptation Sculpture (35x18x23cm 14x7x9in)
New-York 1999

TOLSTOY Alexander 1895-1969 [32]

$1 020 - €874 - **£598** - FF5 734
Kvinnoporträtt Oil/canvas (55x46cm 21x18in)
Stockholm 1998

TOM Jan Bedys 1813-1894 [30]

$2 112 - €2 287 - **£1 341** - FF15 000
Cygnes roses Huile/toile (46x57cm 18x22in) Cannes
2000

$750 - €810 - **£518** - FF5 312
The watermill Oil/panel (35x45cm 13x17in) Bethesda
MD 2001

TOM OF FINLAND 1920-1991 [5]

$4 000 - €3 870 - **£2 466** - FF25 387
Self Sucking Graphite (19.5x28.5cm 7x11in) New-
York 1999

TOMA Gioacchino 1836-1891 [12]

$26 000 - €26 953 - **£15 600** - FF176 800
Natura morta con fichi e prosciutto Olio/tela
(34.5x47cm 13x18in) Roma 2000

$7 600 - €7 879 - **£4 560** - FF51 680
Lo scolaro Olio/cartone (30x18cm 11x7in) Genova
2000

TOMA Matthias Rudolf 1792-1869 [19]

$2 322 - €2 180 - **£1 440** - FF14 301
Landschaftsmotiv mit figürlicher Staffage
Öl/Leinwand (50x63.5cm 19x25in) Wien 1999

$626 - €727 - **£440** - FF4 767
Musikalische Unterhaltung Öl/Leinwand (27x21cm
10x8in) Wien 2001

TOMAJOLI Giuseppe Tomasuoli c.1700-c.1780 **[3]**
$7 500 - €7 775 - **£4 500** - FF51 000
L'ultima cena Olio/tela (153x101.5cm 60x39in)
Milano 1999
$35 354 - €35 067 - **£22 000** - FF230 027
Capricci of Figures amongs classical Ruins
Oil/canvas (75.5x50cm 29x19in) London 1999

TOMANEK Joseph 1889-1974 **[29]**
$1 800 - €2 047 - **£1 248** - FF13 428
Lake Michigan Dunes Oil/canvas (91x116cm
36x46in) Cincinnati OH 2000
$900 - €1 013 - **£631** - FF6 646
Admiring a Gift, Female reclining Nude Oil/board
(40x30cm 16x12in) St. Petersburg FL 2001

TOMASELLI Fred 1956 **[5]**
$17 000 - €19 725 - **£11 736** - FF129 387
Escalante Warm Up Acrylic (61x61cm 24x24in)
New-York 2000

TOMASELLO Luis 1915 **[23]**
$1 261 - €1 436 - **£886** - FF9 417
«Reflexion Nr.56» Relief (44.5x44.5cm 17x17in)
Zürich 2001

TOMASINI Luiz Assencio 1823-1902 **[3]**
$13 920 - €14 457 - **£8 990** - FF94 830
Marinha com o late Duque de Palmela Oleo/lien-
zo (40x76cm 15x29in) Lisboa 2000
$1 806 - €2 094 - **£1 260** - FF13 734
Barco Acuarela/papel (13.5x19cm 5x7in) Lisboa 2001

TOMASSI G. XIX **[3]**
$6 240 - €7 208 - **£4 320** - FF47 280
Ciudad árabe Oleo/lienzo (100x73cm 39x28in)
Madrid 2001

TOMASZEWSKI Henryk Albin 1906 **[8]**
$330 - €386 - **£226** - FF2 530
«Witkacy, Teatr Studio» Poster (97x66.5cm 38x26in)
Hoorn 2000

TOMBA ALDINI Casimiro 1857-1929 **[25]**
$2 928 - €3 126 - **£2 000** - FF20 506
The Illicit Letter Oil/panel (28x20cm 11x7in)
Billingshurst, West-Sussex 2001
$816 - €915 - **£568** - FF6 000
Shéhérazade Aquarelle/papier (44x30cm 17x11in)
Pau 2001

TOMBAY de Ellen 1918 **[10]**
$331 - €322 - **£202** - FF2 113
Des poèmes Huile/toile (61x50cm 24x19in) Bruxelles
1999

TOMBU Madeleine 1897-1996 **[19]**
$266 - €297 - **£186** - FF1 951
Jardins Huile/panneau (24x30cm 9x11in) Bruxelles
2001

TOMEA Fiorenzo 1910-1960 **[153]**
$30 000 - €31 100 - **£18 000** - FF204 000
Spiaggia Olio/tela (105x145cm 41x57in) Milano 2000
$7 750 - €8 034 - **£4 650** - FF52 700
Frutta sulla spiaggia Olio/tela (50x60cm 19x23in)
Trieste 1999
$3 800 - €4 924 - **£2 850** - FF32 300
Candele Olio/cartone (30x40cm 11x15in) Milano 2001
$520 - €674 - **£390** - FF4 420
Casale Acquarelo/carta (21x30.5cm 8x12in) Milano
2000

TOMESCU Aida 1955 **[12]**
$2 914 - €3 267 - **£2 038** - FF21 430
«Fuga V» Oil/canvas (182x152cm 71x59in) Melbourne
2001

TOMIMOTO Kenchiki 1886-1963 **[15]**
$4 352 - €3 757 - **£2 600** - FF24 644
Duck Mixed media (137x47cm 53x18in) London 1998
$4 184 - €3 612 - **£2 500** - FF23 696
«The Road» Mixed media (22x25cm 8x9in) London
1998
$502 - €433 - **£300** - FF2 843
Budding Flower Ink (26.5x18cm 10x7in) London
1998

TOMINETTI Achille 1848-1917 **[9]**
$10 500 - €10 885 - **£6 300** - FF71 400
Paesaggio con contadine e armenti Olio/tela
(68x92.5cm 26x36in) Venezia 2001

TOMINZ Alfredo 1854-1936 **[27]**
$7 034 - €8 385 - **£5 016** - FF55 000
Promenade au bois Huile/toile (57x37cm 22x14in)
Paris 2000

TOMKIN William Stephen XIX-XX **[22]**
$388 - €364 - **£240** - FF2 390
Off Gravesend Watercolour/paper (20x15cm 8x6in)
Aylsham, Norfolk 1999

TOMKINS Peltro William 1760-1840 **[19]**
$410 - €429 - **£260** - FF2 812
**The Grand Funeral Procession of the most
noble Lord Viscount H.Nelson** Aquatint
(31x42.5cm 12x16in) London 2000

TOMKINS William 1732-1792 **[12]**
$31 380 - €33 684 - **£21 000** - FF220 953
**Country House with Figures Assembled on The
Lawn, and a Village Beyond** Oil/canvas
(91.5x124.5cm 36x49in) London 2000

TOMLIN Bradley Walker 1899-1953 **[14]**
$7 500 - €8 516 - **£5 133** - FF55 863
House with Dormer Watercolour (41.5x37.5cm
16x14in) New-York 2000

TOMMASI Adolfo 1851-1933 **[44]**
$90 000 - €93 299 - **£54 000** - FF612 000
Corallaie sulla via di Montenero Olio/tela
(85x155cm 33x61in) Milano 1999
$3 750 - €3 887 - **£2 250** - FF25 500
Paesaggio toscano Olio/cartone (35.5x52.5cm
13x20in) Prato 2000
$6 000 - €6 220 - **£3 600** - FF40 800
Entroterra toscano Olio/tela (40x30cm 15x11in)
Genova 2000

TOMMASI Angiolo 1858-1923 **[40]**
$34 000 - €44 058 - **£25 500** - FF289 000
L'attesa Olio/tela (90x56cm 35x22in) Firenze 2000
$4 000 - €4 147 - **£2 400** - FF27 200
Veduta della costa livornese Olio/tavola (27x50cm
10x19in) Roma 1999
$1 150 - €1 192 - **£690** - FF7 820
Ritratto femminile Carboncino/carta (60x45cm
23x17in) Firenze 2000

TOMMASI de Publio 1848-1914 **[44]**
$2 174 - €1 856 - **£1 300** - FF12 172
The Reverie Watercolour (57x31.5cm 22x12in)
London 1998

TOMMASI Eugen 1891-? **[2]**
👜 $30 000 - €33 581 - **£20 922** - FF220 275
The Morrocan Wedding Dance Oil/canvas
(80.5x55.5cm 31x21in) New-York 2001

TOMMASI FERRONI Riccardo 1934-2000 **[44]**
👜 $4 800 - €4 147 - **£3 200** - FF27 200
Amanti sulla spiaggia Olio/tela (50x100cm 19x39in)
Prato 1998
👜 $960 - €1 244 - **£720** - FF8 160
Teschio Olio/rame (15.5x23cm 6x9in) Roma 2000
✏ $1 500 - €1 555 - **£900** - FF10 200
Omaggio a Velasquez Matite colorate (100x70cm
39x27in) Milano 2000

TOMMASI Ludovico 1866-1941 **[136]**
👜 $2 800 - €3 628 - **£2 100** - FF23 800
Parco di villa toscana Olio/cartone (45x38cm
17x14in) Prato 2000
👜 $3 360 - €2 903 - **£2 240** - FF19 040
Autunno Olio/tavoletta (27x37.5cm 10x14in) Firenze
1998
✏ $700 - €726 - **£420** - FF4 760
Lettura del giornale Carboncino/carta (30x21cm
11x8in) Firenze 2000

TOMMASO XV-XVI **[2]**
👜 $58 904 - €66 045 - **£40 000** - FF433 228
Subject taken from the Golden Legend Oil/panel
(60x140cm 23x55in) London 2000

TOMOHIDE Koizume 1944 **[12]**
👜 $18 000 - €18 138 - **£11 221** - FF118 980
Togeyuku (Along a mountain pass) Mixed media
(98x73cm 38x28in) New-York 2000
👜 $10 000 - €11 727 - **£7 136** - FF76 924
Akari (Light) Ink (53.5x65.5cm 21x25in) New-York
2000

TOMOKAZU XIX **[2]**
🔨 $512 - €562 - **£340** - FF3 689
Netsuke eines Affen mit Jungen Sculpture
(H5.1cm H2in) Stuttgart 2000

TOMOO Inagaki 1902-1980 **[6]**
▥ $2 600 - €2 873 - **£1 803** - FF18 846
Cats and Vegetables Woodcut (57.5x45cm 22x17in)
New-York 2001

TOMPKINS Frank Hector 1847-1922 **[7]**
👜 $700 - €757 - **£479** - FF4 967
**Young Girl in pink Dress & straw Hat seated in
sunny Summer** Oil/canvas (60x50cm 24x20in)
Thomaston ME 2001

TOMS Nicola 1969 **[14]**
🔨 $1 948 - €1 872 - **£1 200** - FF12 280
Eli Bronze (H15cm H5in) London 1999

TOMS William Henri c.1700-c.1755 **[6]**
▥ $256 - €247 - **£160** - FF1 617
London Bridge Engraving (20x33cm 8x13in) London
1999

TOMSCHIKZEK Peter 1940 **[5]**
👜 $3 544 - €3 835 - **£2 428** - FF25 154
Ohne Titel Mixed media/canvas (98x80cm 38x31in)
Stuttgart 2001
✏ $514 - €613 - **£367** - FF4 024
Arbeiten für Undine Gouache (35x37.5cm 13x14in)
Königstein 2000

TOMSON Clifton 1775-1828 **[19]**
👜 $12 344 - €12 767 - **£7 800** - FF83 747
Gentleman out shooting with two gundogs
Oil/canvas (64x80cm 25x31in) London 2000
👜 $2 105 - €2 504 - **£1 500** - FF16 422
**Bay Racehorce with a Jockey up, being Led by
a Groom, a Racecource** Oil/panel (20.5x25.5cm
8x10in) London 2000

TONELLI Giuseppe 1668-1732 **[1]**
✏ $1 778 - €1 982 - **£1 242** - FF13 000
Projet d'architecture de jardin Encre (14.5x24cm
5x9in) Paris 2001

TONG Vernon XX **[4]**
👜 $5 518 - €4 857 - **£3 360** - FF31 862
Nude Öl/Leinwand (76x110cm 29x39in) Stuttgart 1999

TONGE van de Lammert Louis 1871-1937 **[34]**
👜 $2 058 - €2 269 - **£1 344** - FF14 883
Larens interieur met moeder en kinderen
Oil/canvas (48x58cm 18x22in) Rotterdam 2000
👜 $946 - €817 - **£571** - FF5 357
Pink roses in a blue Vase Oil/canvas (37x27.5cm
14x10in) Amsterdam 1999
✏ $1 193 - €1 109 - **£728** - FF7 272
Mother and Child Watercolour (29.5x36cm 11x14in)
Amsterdam 1998

TONGEREN van Jan 1897-1991 **[26]**
👜 $4 763 - €5 113 - **£3 188** - FF33 539
**Perspektivisches Stilleben mit Bronzemörser,
Zinnlöffel** Öl/Leinwand (51x60cm 20x23in) Frankfurt
2000

TONK Ernest 1889-1968 **[9]**
👜 $3 250 - €3 792 - **£2 262** - FF24 872
Cowboy Running Cattle Oil/canvas (76x101cm
30x40in) Altadena CA 2000

TONKISS Sam XX **[1]**
🔨 $4 751 - €4 941 - **£3 000** - FF32 409
Portrait Bust of Laurence Stephen Lowry, R.A
Bronze (H33cm H12in) London 2000

TONKS Henry 1862-1937 **[39]**
✏ $1 186 - €1 228 - **£750** - FF8 052
Cartoon including Major General Fred Maurice
Watercolour (25x36cm 10x14in) Dorchester, Dorset
2000

TONNANCOUR de Jacques Godefroy 1917 **[18]**
👜 $6 302 - €6 052 - **£3 919** - FF39 698
Paysage Huile/isorel (76x70.5cm 22x27in) Montréal
1999

TOOBY Raymond XX **[4]**
▥ $769 - €789 - **£480** - FF5 175
**«Toucans in their nests agree Guinness is
good for you»** Poster (152x102cm 59x40in) London
2000

TOOGWOOD Romeo Charles 1902-1966 **[1]**
👜 $10 929 - €12 697 - **£7 681** - FF83 290
The Back Yard, Dungannon Oil/board (61x49cm
24x19in) Dublin 2001

TOOKER George 1920 **[62]**
👜 $80 000 - €76 132 - **£50 040** - FF499 392
Three Women Tempera/panel (61x46cm 24x18in)
New-York 1999

〔﹏﹏〕 **$1 087** - €941 - **£660** - FF6 175
Maskenball Farblithographie (56.5x76.2cm 22x29in)
München 1998

TOORENVLIET Jacob c.1635/41-1719 **[65]**
🖎 **$10 164** - €10 671 - **£6 741** - FF70 000
La marchande de légumes Huile/toile (48x40cm
18x15in) Paris 2000
🖎 **$4 480** - €5 087 - **£3 066** - FF33 369
Bildnis eines bärtigen Mannes Oil/panel (32x26cm
12x10in) Wien 2000

TOOROP Charley 1891-1955 **[52]**
🖎 **$194 488** - €208 739 - **£130 134** - FFI 369 236
Stilleven met witte kan Oil/canvas (91x140cm
35x55in) Amsterdam 2000
🖎 **$21 393** - €20 420 - **£13 369** - FF133 947
«Herfst» Autumn Oil/panel (63x43cm 24x16in)
Amsterdam 1999
🖎 **$23 436** - €27 227 - **£16 470** - FF178 596
«Portret mevrouw trijntje klompzult» Oil/canvas
(35.5x35.5cm 13x13in) Amsterdam 2001
🖎 **$1 178** - €1 134 - **£736** - FF7 441
«Côte d'Azur» Ink/paper (26x35cm 10x13in)
Amsterdam 1999

TOOROP Jan (Johannes Théo.) 1858-1928 **[386]**
🖎 **$5 724** - €6 807 - **£4 080** - FF44 649
**Winterlandscape with a Traveller on a Horse
and Chart** Oil/panel (37.5x48.5cm 14x19in)
Amsterdam 2000
🖎 **$17 369** - €17 244 - **£10 852** - FF113 110
Landscape Mixed media/canvas (24x28cm 9x11in)
Amsterdam 1999
🖋 **$1 608** - €1 804 - **£978** - FF10 418
De heilige Theresia Coloured crayons (22x13cm
8x5in) Amsterdam 2000
〔﹏﹏〕 **$770** - €679 - **£464** - FF4 457
Nettenboesters Etching (16x18.5cm 6x7in)
Amsterdam 1998

TOOTHAKER Victor XX **[1]**
🖋 **$3 500** - €4 004 - **£2 433** - FF26 262
Fireplace Watercolour/paper (36x46cm 14x18in)
Cincinnati OH 2000

TOOVEY Edwin 1826-1906 **[7]**
🖋 **$1 050** - €1 129 - **£720** - FF7 403
Kenley, Surrey Watercolour/paper (31.5x47cm
12x18in) London 2001

TOPHAM Francis William 1808-1877 **[49]**
🖎 **$702** - €835 - **£500** - FF5 477
**George Pritchard Morgan, with a Shotgun and
his dog in a Hayfield** Oil/board (33x23cm 12x9in)
London 2000
🖋 **$2 185** - €2 539 - **£1 536** - FF16 658
Gathering Fern Watercolour/paper (65x46cm
25x18in) Dublin 2001

TOPHAM Frank W. Warwick 1838-1924 **[48]**
🖎 **$12 000** - €12 092 - **£7 480** - FF79 320
Judgement of Paris Oil/canvas (101.5x152.5cm
39x60in) New-York 2000
🖎 **$2 854** - €3 170 - **£1 911** - FF20 792
Lekande barn, Venedig Oil/canvas (48x53cm
18x20in) Stockholm 2000
🖋 **$627** - €542 - **£380** - FF3 554
A Lovers Tiff Watercolour (40x56cm 15x22in) London
1999

TOPLIS William A. XIX-XX **[10]**
🖋 **$2 823** - €2 757 - **£1 800** - FF18 082
Coastal Scene on the Channel Islands
Watercolour/paper (16x23cm 6x9in) Billingshurst, West-
Sussex 1999

TOPOLSKI Feliks 1907-1989 **[169]**
🖎 **$921** - €1 027 - **£600** - FF6 736
War Mixed media (49x65.5cm 19x25in) Johannesburg
2000
🖎 **$724** - €782 - **£500** - FF5 129
Portrait of a Man wearing Glasses Oil/board
(29.5x28cm 11x11in) London 2001
🖎 **$708** - €840 - **£500** - FF5 509
Claridges, September Watercolour (20x25cm 7x9in)
London 2000
〔﹏﹏〕 **$270** - €282 - **£170** - FFI 848
England Lithograph (115x45cm 45x17in) London
2000

TOPOR Roland 1938-1997 **[260]**
🖋 **$1 215** - €1 143 - **£753** - FF7 500
Hommes Encre (32.5x34cm 12x13in) Paris 1999
〔﹏﹏〕 **$137** - €161 - **£99** - FFI 056
Sans titre Eau-forte couleurs (51.5x41.5cm 20x16in)
Bruxelles 2001

TOPP Arnold 1887-1960 **[14]**
🖎 **$72 362** - €79 379 - **£49 152** - FF520 693
Verlassene Stadt Öl/Karton (65.8x89.8cm 25x35in)
Berlin 2000
🖋 **$2 060** - €2 045 - **£1 287** - FF13 415
Ohne Titel Gouache/paper (19.2x26cm 7x10in)
Hamburg 1999

TOPPELIUS Woldemar 1858-1933 **[82]**
🖎 **$3 304** - €3 700 - **£2 294** - FF24 270
Skogsjärn Oil/canvas (36x50cm 14x19in) Helsinki
2001
🖎 **$1 972** - €1 850 - **£1 218** - FF12 135
Strandbränningar Oil/panel (36x27.5cm 14x10in)
Helsinki 1999

TOPPI Bernardino XX **[20]**
🖎 **$543** - €640 - **£381** - FF4 200
Les musiciens Huile/toile (22x27cm 8x10in)
Fontainebleau 2000

TOPPING James 1879-1949 **[12]**
🖎 **$2 900** - €2 893 - **£1 810** - FF18 975
Artist's Model Oil/canvas/board (35x27cm 14x11in)
Cincinnati OH 1999

TORAL Cristóbal 1938 **[65]**
🖎 **$12 800** - €12 013 - **£8 000** - FF78 800
Manzanas en el espacio Oleo/lienzo (45.5x55cm
17x21in) Madrid 1999
🖎 **$11 200** - €12 013 - **£7 600** - FF78 800
Granada abierta sobre paño blanco Oleo/lienzo
(22x27cm 8x10in) Madrid 1999
🖋 **$2 430** - €2 703 - **£1 620** - FF17 730
Peras en el espacio Acuarela (110x74cm 43x29in)
Madrid 2000
〔﹏﹏〕 **$255** - €216 - **£154** - FFI 418
Objetos en paisaje Litografía (40.5x49cm 15x19in)
Madrid 1998

TORASSA Eduardo 1955 **[1]**
🖎 **$5 000** - €4 360 - **£3 023** - FF28 598
Los Caminos del Patriarca Oil/canvas
(89.5x119.5cm 35x47in) New-York 1998

T

TORCAPEL John 1881-1965 **[30]**
- $882 - €975 - £611 - FF6 395
  Avenue Krieg Huile/toile (55x46cm 21x18in) Genève 2001
- $783 - €919 - £558 - FF6 025
  Salève et nuages Huile/panneau (24x35cm 9x13in) Genève 2000

TORCHI Angelo 1856-1915 **[9]**
- $24 000 - €22 889 - £14 608 - FF150 141
  Sole Di Marzo Oil/canvas (73.5x110cm 28x43in) New-York 1999
- $840 - €726 - £420 - FF4 760
  Studio di casa sul fiume Olio/tavoletta (9.5x15.5cm 3x6in) Firenze 1999

TORCIA Francesco Saverio 1840-? **[6]**
- $2 856 - €2 467 - £1 428 - FF16 184
  Pescatori Olio/tavoletta (28x18cm 11x7in) Milano 1999

TORDI Sinibaldo 1876-1955 **[35]**
- $1 200 - €1 555 - £900 - FF10 200
  Giovane donna con ombrellino e cane Olio/tela (38.5x25.5cm 15x10in) Milano 2001

TORDOFF Frederick XX **[21]**
- $250 - €279 - £168 - FF1 827
  Nantucket Whaling Ships in the Arctic Oil/panel (25x50cm 10x20in) Chester NY 2000

TORGERSEN Thorvald Hagbart 1862-1943 **[9]**
- $4 364 - €3 687 - £2 620 - FF24 188
  Barn ved brygge Oil/canvas (68x86cm 26x33in) Oslo 1998

TORHAMN Gunnar 1894-1965 **[101]**
- $1 218 - €1 392 - £858 - FF9 133
  Herdar och kameldrivare. Motiv från Tunisien Oil/canvas (65x81cm 25x31in) Stockholm 2001
- $918 - €883 - £558 - FF5 790
  Strättan Oil/panel (37x21cm 14x8in) Stockholm 1999
- $351 - €392 - £230 - FF2 574
  Jesus och Lazarus Pastel/paper (45x61cm 17x24in) Malmö 2000

TORHAMN Ingegerd Sjöstrand 1898-1994 **[33]**
- $673 - €731 - £426 - FF4 798
  Bitar Oil/panel (90x116cm 35x45in) Stockholm 2000

TORII Kiyotsune XVIII **[5]**
- $1 600 - €1 876 - £1 141 - FF12 307
  Actors Nakamura Denzo and Sanogawa Ichimatsu standing under Pine Tree Print in colors (27.5x14.5cm 10x5in) New-York 2000

TORLAKSON James 1951 **[8]**
- $2 000 - €1 989 - £1 241 - FF13 048
  Burlingame Theater II Watercolour/paper (91.5x61cm 36x24in) Beverly-Hills CA 1999

TÖRMER Benno Friedrich 1804-1859 **[9]**
- $4 915 - €4 602 - £3 046 - FF30 185
  Junge Italienerinnen an einem Brunnen bei Ariccia Oil/panel (35.5x51cm 13x20in) Heidelberg 1999
- $5 000 - €4 573 - £3 053 - FF29 994
  Giving alms to the poor Oil/panel (38x30cm 15x12in) New-York 1998

TÖRNÅ Oscar 1842-1894 **[93]**
- $8 896 - €10 323 - £6 142 - FF67 716
  Parklandskap Medevi Oil/canvas (120x135cm 47x53in) Stockholm 2000
- $1 876 - €1 958 - £1 184 - FF12 841
  Landskap med kirke Oil/canvas (39x64cm 15x25in) Oslo 2000
- $1 214 - €1 309 - £815 - FF8 589
  Kusten, Rhoin Oil/canvas (22x40cm 8x15in) Stockholm 2000

TORNABUONI Lorenzo 1934 **[26]**
- $1 500 - €1 555 - £900 - FF10 200
  Omaggio a Schiele Olio/tavola (65x45cm 25x17in) Roma 2001

TORNAI Gyula, Jules 1861-1928 **[62]**
- $7 942 - €8 950 - £5 500 - FF58 709
  The Musician Oil/canvas (112.5x146cm 44x57in) London 2000
- $4 921 - €5 793 - £3 458 - FF38 000
  Le prisonnier Huile/carton/toile (73.5x92cm 28x36in) Paris 2000

TORNÉ ESQUIUS Pere 1879-1936 **[3]**
- $4 590 - €5 106 - £3 060 - FF33 490
  Niños mendigos Oleo/lienzo (65x50cm 25x19in) Madrid 2000

TORNE SAMI Miquel 1938 **[122]**
- $303 - €276 - £188 - FF1 812
  Figura femenina Acrylique/carton (65x54cm 25x21in) Barcelona 1999
- $176 - €189 - £118 - FF1 240
  Mädchenbildnis Öl/Karton (27x21cm 10x8in) Hildrizhausen 2000

TÖRNEMAN Axel 1880-1925 **[56]**
- $3 357 - €3 684 - £2 163 - FF24 168
  Kvinna i exteriör Oil/canvas (65x58cm 25x22in) Stockholm 2000
- $1 552 - €1 510 - £955 - FF9 908
  Kvinna i profil Mixed media (23x21cm 9x8in) Stockholm 1999
- $374 - €347 - £232 - FF2 275
  Man vid häst Mixed media/paper (28x37cm 11x14in) Malmö 1999

TÖRNER Carl Erik 1862-1911 **[7]**
- $1 688 - €1 950 - £1 181 - FF12 790
  Vårstämning Oil/canvas (60x90cm 23x35in) Stockholm 2001

TORNER Gustavo 1925 **[19]**
- $18 900 - €21 023 - £12 950 - FF137 900
  Sin título Técnica mixta (129.5x162cm 50x63in) Madrid 2001
- $201 - €216 - £136 - FF1 418
  Composición Serigrafia (17x14cm 6x5in) Madrid 2000

TORNIOLI Niccolo c.1598-c.1651 **[1]**
- $28 000 - €29 026 - £16 800 - FF190 400
  Morte di Cleopatra Olio/tela (204x137cm 80x53in) Firenze 2000

TORNØE Wenzel Ulrik 1844-1907 **[103]**
- $12 000 - €11 517 - £7 522 - FF75 546
  Family gathering Oil/canvas (101.5x141cm 39x55in) New-York 1999

$1 881 - €2 148 - £1 307 - FF14 088
En italiener med krollet hår og skaeg Oil/canvas
(68x55cm 26x21in) København 2000

$611 - €698 - £424 - FF4 578
Dobbeltregnbue over havet Oil/canvas (18x26cm
7x10in) København 2000

TORNYAI Janos 1869-1936 [6]
$980 - €1 084 - £644 - FF7 112
Flood Oil/cardboard (34x43cm 13x16in) Budapest
2000

TORO Attilio 1892-1982 [25]
$1 400 - €1 451 - £840 - FF9 520
Ballerina Olio/tavola (39x88cm 15x34in) Napoli 1999
$1 680 - €1 451 - £1 120 - FF9 520
Volto di donna Olio/tavola (25x20cm 9x7in) Napoli
1998

TORO Luigi 1836-1900 [3]
$4 400 - €5 702 - £3 300 - FF37 400
Corteggiamento nell'osteria Olio/tavola (23x13cm
9x5in) Roma 2001

TORONI Niele 1937 [15]
$5 350 - €6 316 - £3 800 - FF41 432
Untitled Oil/paper (106x75cm 41x29in) London 2001

TORRAS VIVER Joan 1929 [11]
$434 - €420 - £266 - FF2 758
Floristas en Amsterdam Oleo/lienzo (81x65cm
31x25in) Barcelona 1999

TORRE de la Néstor 1887-1938 [13]
$9 180 - €10 211 - £6 120 - FF66 980
Sirenas junto al acantilado Oleo/lienzo (37x48cm
14x18in) Madrid 2000
$16 800 - €18 019 - £11 100 - FF118 200
El despertar del Atlántico Oleo/lienzo (36x36cm
14x14in) Madrid 2000
$6 416 - €6 466 - £4 000 - FF42 414
Puerton de la Luz Watercolour/paper (31x33cm
12x12in) Newbury, Berkshire 2000
$1 215 - €1 351 - £810 - FF8 865
Mujeres bailando Grabado (35x30cm 13x11in)
Madrid 2000

TORREGIANI Bartolomeo 1590-c.1675 [10]
$16 357 - €17 944 - £11 110 - FF117 703
Landschaften mit Figurenstaffagen
Oil/canvas/panel (51x75.5cm 20x29in) Luzern 2000

TORRENTS LLADO Joaquín 1946 [7]
$16 800 - €18 019 - £11 400 - FF118 200
Cala de Mallorca Oleo/lienzo (160x160cm 62x62in)
Madrid 2001
$4 900 - €4 205 - £3 010 - FF27 580
Aurorretrato Oleo/lienzo (44x36cm 17x14in) Madrid
1998

TORRES Augusto 1913-1992 [43]
$5 800 - €6 226 - £3 881 - FF40 838
Norte 5 Oleo/lienzo (79x54cm 31x21in) Montevideo
2000

TORRES de Matias 1631-1711 [3]
$2 840 - €2 403 - £1 680 - FF15 760
Ejecución de María Estuardo Tinta/papel (26x29cm
10x11in) Madrid 1998

TORRES de Ramón XVIII [1]
$5 500 - €4 768 - £3 361 - FF31 277
San Juan Nepomuceno Oil/canvas (63.5x47cm
25x18in) New-York 1999

TORRES FUSTER Antonio 1874-1945 [7]
$3 300 - €3 304 - £2 035 - FF21 670
Odalisca sobre una piel de tigre Oleo/lienzo
(89x131cm 35x51in) Madrid 2000

TORRES Horacio 1924-1976 [19]
$20 000 - €21 468 - £13 384 - FF140 820
Standing Figure Oil/canvas (163x127.5cm 64x50in)
New-York 2000
$10 765 - €9 277 - £6 395 - FF60 855
Constructivo Montevideo Oleo/cartón (53.5x74.5cm
21x29in) Montevideo 1998

TORRES Juan 1942 [2]
$6 000 - €5 232 - £3 627 - FF34 318
Marta la Piadosa Oil/canvas (100x81cm 39x31in)
New-York 1998

TORRES-GARCIA Joaquín 1874-1949 [399]
$55 000 - €64 758 - £38 648 - FF424 787
Times Square, New York Oil/canvas (112.5x75.5cm
44x29in) New-York 2000
$23 341 - €25 916 - £16 269 - FF170 000
Sans titre Huile/toile (33x46cm 12x18in) Paris 2001
$28 000 - €26 962 - £17 427 - FF176 856
Pájaros: Aladdin Toy Sculpture, wood (10x18cm
3x7in) New-York 1999
$8 500 - €8 250 - £5 292 - FF54 116
Universal Man Ink (14x8.5cm 5x3in) New-York 1999

TORRESCASSANA Francesc 1845-1918 [8]
$2 700 - €2 258 - £1 612 - FF14 812
En las rocas Oleo/lienzo (75x113cm 29x44in) Madrid
1998
$2 600 - €3 003 - £1 800 - FF19 700
La pastora Oleo/lienzo (32x40cm 12x15in) Madrid
2000

TORREY Elliot Bouton 1867-1949 [14]
$2 250 - €2 415 - £1 505 - FF15 842
Lanscape, haystacks and figures Oil/canvas
(74x100cm 29x39in) Altadena CA 2000

TORRI Flaminio 1621-1661 [20]
$20 000 - €19 991 - £12 218 - FF131 130
The Flight into Egypt Oil/copper (24x32.5cm
9x12in) New-York 2000
$3 119 - €3 053 - £2 000 - FF20 024
**A seated Nude seen from behind/Sketch of a
Head** Red chalk/paper (16.5x19.5cm 6x7in) London
1999

TORRIANI Francesco Innocenzo 1649-1712 [1]
$19 820 - €20 502 - £12 522 - FF134 484
La Sainte Famille avec St Jean et Ste Elisabeth
Oil/canvas (82x90cm 32x35in) Warszawa 2000

TORRIGLIA Giovanni Battista 1858-1937 [22]
$72 500 - €75 157 - £43 500 - FF493 000
Giochi in famiglia Olio/tela (73.5x110cm 28x43in)
Milano 2000

TORRINI E. XIX [9]
$3 800 - €4 406 - £2 691 - FF28 899
Mischief Oil/canvas (35.5x46cm 13x18in) New-York
2000

T

$2 100 - €2 363 - **£1 446** - FF15 503
A Dandy Oil/canvas (36x25cm 14x9in) Philadelphia PA 2000

TORRINI Pietro 1852-1920 [13]
$5 814 - €4 975 - **£3 500** - FF32 637
An amusing Interlude Oil/canvas (66x86cm 25x33in) London 1998

TORROELLA Ezequiel 1921 [21]
$665 - €571 - **£399** - FF3 743
Costa Brava Oleo/lienzo (65x92cm 25x36in) Barcelona 1999

TORSCHENKO Igor 1965 [33]
$1 854 - €2 180 - **£1 287** - FF14 301
Betrunkene Elefanten Öl/Leinwand (120x140cm 47x55in) Wien 2000
$1 526 - €1 453 - **£932** - FF9 534
Das geheime Rendezvous Öl/Leinwand (82x98cm 32x38in) Wien 1999

TØRSLEFF August 1884-1968 [37]
$484 - €536 - **£336** - FF3 515
Portraet af siddende kvinde med hund på skodet Oil/canvas (88x75.5cm 34x29in) Vejle 2001

TORSSLOW Harald 1838-1909 [14]
$1 640 - €1 894 - **£1 147** - FF12 425
Skärgårdslandskap med segelbåt Oil/canvas (64x86cm 25x33in) Stockholm 2001

TORTES Dominique 1938 [73]
$1 128 - €1 143 - **£702** - FF7 500
Boulevard animé Huile/toile (50x61cm 19x24in) Strasbourg 2000
$323 - €320 - **£195** - FF2 100
Vers l'Arc de Triomphe Huile/panneau (13x18cm 5x7in) Toulouse 2000

TOSA Mitsuada 1738-1806 [5]
$5 000 - €5 525 - **£3 467** - FF36 243
Scenes from the Tale of Genji Ink (90.5x37cm 35x14in) New-York 2001

TOSCANI Giov. di Francesco c.1370/80-1430 [5]
$196 062 - €191 438 - **£125 000** - FF1 255 750
Five Episodes from Boccaccio's Decameron Tempera/panel (41x142.5cm 16x56in) London 1999

TOSHIO Arimoto 1946-1985 [1]
$140 000 - €154 456 - **£92 596** - FF1 013 166
Hareta hi no dekigoto (Incident on a fine day) Tempera (89x145.5cm 35x57in) New-York 2000

TOSHUSAI SHARAKU XVIII [19]
$24 000 - €28 145 - **£17 126** - FF184 617
Arashi Ryuzo as the Money Lender Ishibe Kinkichi Print in colors (36.5x23cm 14x9in) New-York 2000

TOSI Arturo 1871-1956 [172]
$11 000 - €11 403 - **£6 600** - FF74 800
Paesaggio di Rovetta Olio/tela (50x60cm 19x23in) Roma 1999
$6 750 - €6 997 - **£4 050** - FF45 900
Natura morta Olio/cartone (31.5x41.5cm 12x16in) Milano 2000
$1 100 - €1 140 - **£660** - FF7 480
Paesaggio con alberi Pastelli/carta (39x53cm 15x20in) Milano 2000

TOSINI DI RIDOLFO GHIRLANDAIO Michele 1503-1577 [22]
$52 500 - €54 424 - **£31 500** - FF357 000
Madonna con Bambino Olio/tavola (120.5x87cm 47x34in) Roma 2001

TOTH Menyhért 1904-1980 [5]
$1 980 - €2 250 - **£1 380** - FF14 760
Manufacture Huile/toile (50x60cm 19x23in) Budapest 2001
$2 475 - €2 813 - **£1 725** - FF18 450
Le sculpteur Huile/papier (44x31cm 17x12in) Budapest 2001

TOTT Alois 1870-1939 [23]
$1 015 - €1 090 - **£679** - FF7 150
Blick auf Dürnstein mit der Warburg Mischtechnik/Papier (22.7x29.3cm 8x11in) Wien 2000

TOUCHAGUES Louis 1893-1974 [202]
$103 - €122 - **£72** - FF800
Danseuse Gouache/papier (24x16cm 9x6in) Paris 2000

TOUCHSTONE / AMBLIN XX [6]
$1 200 - €1 108 - **£747** - FF7 267
Who framed Rogger Rabbit? Eddie Valiant attempts to force Roger out Gouache (20.5x33cm 8x12in) New-York 1999

TOUDOUZE Édouard 1848-1907 [16]
$6 400 - €8 293 - **£4 800** - FF54 400
La partita a carte Olio/tela (47x61cm 18x24in) Roma 2001
$13 000 - €14 765 - **£9 122** - FF96 855
He loves me Oil/panel (37.5x26.5cm 14x10in) New-York 2001

TOUDOUZE Simon Alexandre 1850-1909 [8]
$2 118 - €2 439 - **£1 446** - FF16 000
La cour de ferme, sous-bois Huile/toile (116x89cm 45x35in) Lyon 2000

TOULMOUCHE Auguste 1829-1890 [54]
$22 846 - €23 020 - **£14 239** - FF151 000
Jeune femme debout devant une psychée Huile/toile (72x49cm 28x19in) Tours 2000
$2 800 - €3 291 - **£1 941** - FF21 586
A Lovely Day Oil/canvas (13x12cm 5x4in) New-York 2000

TOULOUSE Roger 1918-1994 [39]
$4 029 - €4 573 - **£2 799** - FF30 000
L'Eglise Huile/isorel (81x65cm 31x25in) Orléans 2001
$1 342 - €1 601 - **£957** - FF10 500
Pain et verre Huile/isorel (33x46cm 12x18in) Orléans 2000

TOULOUSE-LAUTREC de Henri 1864-1901 [2197]
$750 000 - €870 217 - **£517 800** - FF5 708 250
Étude de danseuse Oil/canvas (55x46cm 21x18in) New-York 2000
$65 000 - €61 531 - **£40 371** - FF403 617
Jacqueline Lescluse Oil/board (25x18cm 9x7in) New-York 1999
$110 000 - €105 776 - **£67 771** - FF693 847
Yvette Guilbert Glazed ceramic (51.5x28cm 20x11in) New-York 1999

🖊 **$8 000** - €8 840 - **£5 548** - FF57 989
Homme de face et cheval vu d'arrière/Homme et cheval Pencil/paper (17x27cm 6x10in) New-York 2001

📷 **$6 500** - €6 251 - **£4 011** - FF41 003
«Le rire» Poster (30x22.5cm 11x8in) New-York 1999

TOURGUENEFF Pierre Nicolas 1854-1912 **[35]**
🐕 **$1 582** - €1 683 - **£1 000** - FF11 038
Seated Bulldog Bronze (11.5x11cm 4x4in) London 2000

TOURILLON Alfred Édouard XIX-XX **[3]**
$5 230 - €5 615 - **£3 500** - FF36 830
Pointer on the Scent Oil/canvas (37x92cm 14x36in) London 2000

TOURLIERE Michel 1925 **[4]**
$2 176 - €2 287 - **£1 435** - FF15 000
L'hiver au printemps Tapisserie (228x148cm 89x58in) Calais 2000

TOURNEMINE de Charles Émile Vacher 1812-1872 **[28]**
$3 267 - €3 811 - **£2 272** - FF25 000
Fontaine aux environs de Smyrne Huile/panneau (33x54cm 12x21in) Paris 2000
$4 093 - €4 696 - **£2 800** - FF30 805
Promenade des femmes turques en Asie - Soleil couchant Oil/canvas (22x30cm 8x11in) London 2000

TOURNEUX Eugène 1809-1867 **[2]**
$1 869 - €2 198 - **£1 340** - FF14 421
Araber im Schnee Öl/Leinwand (32x23cm 12x9in) München 2001

TOURNIER Jean Ulrich 1802-1882 **[4]**
$39 766 - €36 192 - **£24 408** - FF237 401
Traubenstilleben in Mauernische mit Puttenrelief Öl/Leinwand (102x70cm 40x27in) Zürich 1999

TOURNIER Nicolas 1590-c.1657 **[9]**
$17 600 - €19 831 - **£12 320** - FF130 080
La trahison de Saint Pierre Huile/panneau (34x53cm 13x20in) Antwerpen 2001

TOURNON Raymond XIX-XX **[21]**
🖊 **$1 815** - €1 829 - **£1 131** - FF12 000
Portraits d'Andorrans Fusain (53x36.5cm 20x14in) Senlis 2000
📷 **$868** - €991 - **£603** - FF6 500
«Berck-plage» Affiche (74x105cm 29x41in) Paris 2001

TOURNY Joseph Gabriel 1817-1880 **[1]**
🖊 **$1 892** - €2 187 - **£1 189** - FF13 000
Enfants de famille noble Aquarelle/papier (40x41cm 15x16in) Saint-Dié 2000

TOURSKY de G. XIX-XX **[17]**
$1 814 - €2 134 - **£1 300** - FF14 000
Campement de berbères Huile/toile (53x74cm 20x29in) Entzheim 2001

TOURTE Suzanne 1904-1979 **[189]**
$575 - €686 - **£410** - FF4 500
Les deux amies Huile/isorel (65x54cm 25x21in) Paris 2000

🖊 **$423** - €396 - **£256** - FF2 600
Gare maritime Gouache/papier (49x64cm 19x25in) Reims 1999

📷 **$77** - €84 - **£53** - FF550
Léone Eau-forte (22x18cm 8x7in) Troyes 2001

TOUSSAINT Fernand 1873-1956 **[385]**
$12 480 - €14 873 - **£8 940** - FF97 560
Élégante au collier de perles Huile/toile (115x105cm 45x41in) Bruxelles 2001
$5 004 - €5 683 - **£3 500** - FF37 278
Le chapeau à plumes Oil/canvas (80x65cm 31x25in) London 2001
$1 810 - €2 134 - **£1 272** - FF14 000
Pont sur la Tamise Huile/carton (33.5x44.5cm 13x17in) Paris 2000
🖊 **$1 162** - €1 176 - **£709** - FF7 714
Fischer im Hafen Gouache/paper (54x76cm 21x29in) Stuttgart 2000
📷 **$1 332** - €1 381 - **£799** - FF9 057
«Torino, Vermouth Cinzano» Affiche couleur (46x60cm 18x23in) Torino 2001

TOUSSAINT Louis 1826-1879 **[18]**
$3 262 - €3 579 - **£2 216** - FF23 477
Die Bewunderer des Geigenspielers Öl/Leinwand (44.5x53.5cm 17x21in) Düsseldorf 2000

TOUSSAINT Maurice XIX-XX **[75]**
🖊 **$376** - €381 - **£230** - FF2 500
Tirailleurs Aquarelle, gouache/papier (24x17cm 9x6in) Paris 2000
📷 **$177** - €198 - **£119** - FF1 300
«Escalier de Brélevenez» Affiche (100x61cm 39x24in) Orléans 2001

TOUSSAINT Pierre Joseph 1822-1888 **[8]**
$6 149 - €5 767 - **£3 800** - FF37 826
The young Scholar Oil/panel (74x59cm 29x23in) London 1999

TOUTENEL Lodewijk 1819-1883 **[2]**
$4 774 - €5 453 - **£3 322** - FF35 772
La leçon de poésie Huile/panneau (69x54cm 27x21in) Bruxelles 2001

TOVAR de Miguel Alonso 1678-1758 **[3]**
$36 841 - €31 366 - **£22 000** - FF205 746
La divina pastora Oil/canvas (126.6x105.8cm 49x41in) London 1998

TOVAR Ivan 1942 **[27]**
$22 000 - €25 561 - **£15 461** - FF167 666
Sin título Oil/canvas (113x147cm 44x57in) New-York 2001
$3 945 - €4 269 - **£2 702** - FF28 000
Sans titre Huile/toile (61x38cm 24x14in) Paris 2001
$3 804 - €4 116 - **£2 605** - FF27 000
Sans titre Huile/toile (22x27cm 8x10in) Paris 2001
🖊 **$1 690** - €1 829 - **£1 158** - FF12 000
Composition surréaliste Technique mixte/papier (63x47.5cm 24x18in) Paris 2001

TOWERS Samuel 1862-1943 **[25]**
🖊 **$491** - €585 - **£350** - FF3 837
Hot Summer Day in the Meadows: Haslor, Warwickshire Watercolour (28x43cm 11x16in) London 2000

TOWN Harold Barling 1924-1991 **[83]**
- $1 227 - €1 159 - **£762** - FF7 602
  «**Toy Horse #57**» Mixed media (55x75cm 21x29in)
  Nepean, Ont. 1999
- $268 - €316 - **£190** - FF2 071
  Amazon with Captive Ink (56x76cm 22x29in)
  Toronto 2000
- $403 - €474 - **£286** - FF3 107
  Untitled Print (45x59cm 17x23in) Toronto 2000

TOWNE Charles 1763-1840 **[91]**
- $8 000 - €8 315 - **£5 041** - FF54 544
  Waiting for Master Oil/canvas (52x64.5cm 20x25in)
  New-York 2000
- $3 175 - €3 284 - **£2 000** - FF21 541
  Three Studies of Heads of Sheep Oil/panel
  (16x17cm 6x6in) Bath 2000

TOWNE Francis 1739/40-1816 **[50]**
- $4 869 - €4 682 - **£3 000** - FF30 715
  Figures in a Welsh Landscape Watercolour
  (17x25cm 6x9in) London 1999

TOWNLEY Minnie XIX-XX **[1]**
- $2 611 - €2 941 - **£1 800** - FF19 292
  The Promenade, Hastings Oil/canvas (16.5x32cm
  6x12in) London 2000

TOWNSEND Alfred Oliver 1846-1917 **[33]**
- $208 - €194 - **£130** - FF1 270
  Winter Landscape with Sheep in Foreground
  Watercolour/paper (35x50cm 14x20in) Bristol, Avon
  1999

TOWNSEND Edwin F. XX **[4]**
- $2 500 - €2 331 - **£1 509** - FF15 291
  Selected Physique Studies Photograph (24x18.5cm
  9x7in) New-York 1999

TOWNSEND Frederick Henry L.J. 1868-1920 **[6]**
- $1 985 - €2 305 - **£1 400** - FF15 119
  Hyde Park Corner Ink (25.5x33cm 10x12in) London
  2001

TOWNSEND Graeme K. 1954 **[32]**
- $1 585 - €1 887 - **£1 097** - FF12 375
  Savannah Surveillance Oil/canvas (24x12.5cm
  9x4in) Sydney 2000

TOWNSEND Lee 1895-1965 **[4]**
- $3 500 - €3 479 - **£2 117** - FF22 824
  Morning Tryout Oil/canvas (55x76cm 22x30in) New-
  York 2000

TOWNSHEND Arthur Louis XIX-XX **[13]**
- $641 - €634 - **£400** - FF4 162
  Chesnut Horse in a Loose Box Oil/board
  (25.5x25.5cm 10x10in) London 1999

TOWNSHEND George 1724-1807 **[2]**
- $4 837 - €5 621 - **£3 400** - FF36 870
  **Portrait of Sir James Thornhill, after Joseph
  Highmore** Pastel/paper (57x47cm 22x18in) London
  2000

TOYEN (Marie Cerminová) 1902-1980 **[59]**
- $60 690 - €57 402 - **£37 800** - FF376 530
  Composition Huile/toile (85x85cm 33x33in) Praha
  2001
- $1 136 - €1 220 - **£760** - FF8 000
  Deux figures Encre (20x17cm 7x6in) Paris 2000

- $303 - €287 - **£189** - FF1 882
  Forme Pointe sèche (20x7cm 7x2in) Praha 2000

TOYNBEE Laurence 1922 **[9]**
- $4 617 - €5 180 - **£3 200** - FF33 977
  Pass and Tackle Oil/board (61x99cm 24x38in)
  London 2000

TOYOKUNI I Utagawa 1769-1825 **[179]**
- $5 379 - €5 774 - **£3 600** - FF37 877
  Woman standing by the Entrance of Shinano-Ya
  Painting (64.5x38cm 25x14in) London 2000
- $290 - €324 - **£202** - FF2 125
  Green and gold Curtain Woodcut (35x24cm 14x9in)
  Cleveland OH 2001

TOYOKUNI II 1777-1835 **[49]**
- $9 500 - €9 883 - **£6 045** - FF64 831
  Erotic Scenes Ink (45x28cm 17x11in) New-York
  2000
- $328 - €307 - **£199** - FF2 012
  **Der Schauspieler Iwai Kumesaburo, Szene aus
  einer Kabuki-Aufführung** Woodcut in colors
  (37.6x25.7cm 14x10in) Berlin 1999

TOYONARI Yamamura 1886-1942 **[5]**
- $1 500 - €1 542 - **£951** - FF10 118
  Cubist Design of Parrot Woodcut in colors
  (38x25cm 15x10in) Cincinnati OH 2000

TOZER Henry E. act.1889-1892 **[18]**
- $450 - €480 - **£300** - FF3 150
  Paddle Steamer at Sea Watercolour (20x59cm
  7x23in) Leyburn, North Yorkshire 2000

TOZER Henry Spernon 1864-c.1938 **[48]**
- $2 223 - €2 115 - **£1 350** - FF13 872
  Domestic Bliss Oil/canvas (16.5x23.5cm 6x9in)
  Penzance, Cornwall 1999
- $1 900 - €2 039 - **£1 271** - FF13 377
  Lady by the Earth Watercolour/paper (20x30cm
  8x12in) Chicago IL 2000

TOZZI Mario 1895-1979 **[201]**
- $61 500 - €63 754 - **£36 900** - FF418 200
  Davide (Davide e Golia nella stanza) Olio/tela
  (196x115cm 77x45in) Prato 2000
- $21 200 - €27 471 - **£15 900** - FF180 200
  Donna dai capelli rossi Olio/tela (55x46cm
  21x18in) Milano 2001
- $8 750 - €9 071 - **£5 250** - FF59 500
  Luca Olio/tela (33x27cm 12x10in) Milano 1999
- $2 800 - €3 628 - **£2 100** - FF23 800
  Modella con cappello Matita/carta (60x41.5cm
  23x16in) Milano 2000

TRACHEL Domenico, Dominique 1830-1897 **[8]**
- $1 757 - €1 738 - **£1 095** - FF11 403
  Provenzalische Landschaft in der Abendsonne
  Oil/panel (30x48cm 11x18in) Ahlden 1999

TRACHEL Ercole, Hercule 1820-1872 **[27]**
- $782 - €909 - **£550** - FF5 964
  Villa Gastard, Nice Watercolour/paper (30x53cm
  12x21in) Lewes, Sussex 2001

TRACHSEL Albert 1863-1929 **[57]**
- $2 135 - €2 293 - **£1 429** - FF15 039
  Stilleben mit Astern Öl/Leinwand (65x49cm
  25x19in) Zürich 2000

⟋ **$421** - €491 - **£291** - FF3 222
Sommerlandschaft mit Acker Watercolour, gouache (26.5x36cm 10x14in) Bern 2000

TRACHSLER Hermann c.1800-1850 **[24]**
〰 **$132** - €149 - **£93** - FF979
«Zum Dorf, dans la vallée d'Ursern» Aquatinta (6.5x10cm 2x3in) Bern 2001

TRACY Glen 1883-? **[3]**
〰 **$700** - €795 - **£479** - FF5 213
Suspension Bridge, after J.A.Roebling Lithograph (23.5x30cm 9x11in) New-York 2000

TRACY John Martin 1844-1893 **[26]**
↝ **$19 000** - €20 525 - **£13 155** - FF134 635
Duck Hunting Oil/canvas (86x114cm 34x45in) Cincinnati OH 2001
↝ **$8 400** - €7 852 - **£5 185** - FF51 507
On the Scent Oil/panel (34x26cm 13x10in) New-Orleans LA 1999

TRAFFELET Friedrich Eduard 1897-1954 **[90]**
↝ **$913** - €1 043 - **£644** - FF6 841
Sitzende Trachtenfrau auf einer Wiese Öl/Leinwand (80x64.5cm 31x25in) Bern 2001
↝ **$365** - €426 - **£252** - FF2 792
Schweizer Soldat mit Säbel und Tornister Watercolour (35x24.5cm 13x9in) Bern 2000

TRÄGÅRDH Carl 1861-1899 **[81]**
↝ **$2 268** - €2 208 - **£1 396** - FF14 481
Porträtt av jakthund Oil/canvas (48x65cm 18x25in) Stockholm 1999
↝ **$324** - €382 - **£227** - FF2 505
Kostudie Oil/canvas (25.5x36cm 10x14in) Malmö 2000

TRAIES William 1789-1872 **[18]**
↝ **$4 887** - €4 449 - **£3 000** - FF29 181
A West Country Landscape with a Rider discoursing with a Man seated Oil/canvas (90.5x72.5cm 35x28in) London 1999
↝ **$13 278** - €12 995 - **£8 500** - FF85 244
The Estuary of the Exe below Powderham/The Estuary of the Teign Oil/panel (27x38cm 10x14in) London 1999

TRAILL Jessie Constance A. 1881-1967 **[27]**
↝ **$3 835** - €3 688 - **£2 362** - FF24 190
Lady in the Shade Oil/canvas/board (49x63cm 19x24in) Melbourne 1999

TRAIN Edward XIX **[32]**
↝ **$1 466** - €1 580 - **£1 000** - FF10 366
Figures in Conversation on the Banks of a Loch Oil/canvas (43x57cm 16x22in) London 2001

TRAINI Francesco XIV **[1]**
↝ **$625 000** - €647 908 - **£375 000** - FF4 250 000
Santa Caterina d'Alessandria Tempera (143x57.5cm 56x22in) Firenze 2001

TRAJMAN Paul 1960 **[4]**
↝ **$952** - €992 - **£600** - FF6 504
Composition Encre/papier (128x87cm 50x34in) Antwerpen 2000

TRAMEAU Raymond 1897-c.1985 **[31]**
⟋ **$229** - €198 - **£138** - FF1 300
Composition abstraite Aquarelle (48x64cm 18x25in) Paris 1998

TRAMPEDACH Kurt 1943 **[127]**
↝ **$7 331** - €7 389 - **£4 570** - FF48 466
Figurkomposition Oil/paper/canvas (160x120cm 62x47in) Köbenhavn 2000
↝ **$4 658** - €4 833 - **£2 955** - FF31 701
Chilardicoborda, komposition med kunstnerens selvportraet Mixed media (100x70cm 39x27in) Viby J, Århus 2000
≈ **$11 330** - €11 419 - **£7 063** - FF74 902
Lille pige Plaster (H110cm H43in) Köbenhavn 2000
⟋ **$1 272** - €1 076 - **£760** - FF7 060
Selvportraet Indian ink/paper (70x75cm 27x29in) Köbenhavn 1998
〰 **$235** - €229 - **£145** - FF1 499
Selvportraet Lithograph (39x31.5cm 15x12in) Vejle 1999

TRAMPOTA Jan 1889-1942 **[20]**
↝ **$1 705** - €1 613 - **£1 062** - FF10 578
Deux chênes Tempera/carton (66x50cm 25x19in) Praha 2000

TRAN DONG LUONG 1925-1993 **[8]**
⟋ **$1 640** - €1 653 - **£1 022** - FF10 845
A young Lady Charcoal/paper (51x36cm 20x14in) Singapore 2000

TRAN NGOC QUYEN XX **[1]**
≈ **$3 443** - €3 910 - **£2 356** - FF25 647
Bust of a Tonkin Woman Bronze (H42cm H16in) Singapore 2000

TRAN PHUC DUYEN 1923-1993 **[14]**
↝ **$1 725** - €1 608 - **£1 064** - FF10 547
The Temple Den Ngoc Son on the Hoam Kiem Lake in Hanoi Oil/panel (51x66cm 20x25in) Singapore 1999

TRAN VAN CAN 1910-1994 **[4]**
↝ **$14 251** - €11 957 - **£8 361** - FF78 432
Fishermen Oil/canvas (52.5x37cm 20x14in) Singapore 1998

TRAN-LONG Mara 1935 **[94]**
↝ **$354** - €396 - **£237** - FF2 600
La partie de dés Huile/toile (65x81cm 25x31in) Paris 2000

TRAPP Willy 1905-1984 **[11]**
〰 **$1 363** - €1 235 - **£850** - FF8 104
«Kandersteg» Poster (103x64cm 40x25in) London 1999

TRAQUAIR Phoebe Anna 1852-1936 **[11]**
↝ **$13 448** - €14 436 - **£9 000** - FF94 694
Spiritus Garitas Oil/panel (27.5x13cm 10x5in) Edinburgh 2000
≈ **$14 301** - €13 697 - **£9 000** - FF89 848
Enamel and Gold Pendant Necklace Object (H4.5cm H1in) Sighthill 1999

TRAUB Gustav 1885-1955 **[33]**
↝ **$828** - €920 - **£576** - FF6 037
Schwarzwaldlandschaft mit zweitürmiger Kirche auf einer Anhöhe Oil/panel (51x67cm 20x26in) Heidelberg 2001

TRAUNER Alexandre 1906-1993 **[6]**
⟋ **$2 325** - €1 982 - **£1 385** - FF13 000
«La rue» du film «Irma la douce» Gouache/papier (19x52.5cm 7x20in) Paris 1998

T

TRAUNFELLNER Franz 1913 [15]
🪵 $313 - €363 - **£222** - FF2 383
Bauerngarten Woodcut (19x12cm 7x4in) Wien 2000

TRAUT Wolf c.1485-1520 [8]
🪵 $424 - €367 - **£255** - FF2 409
Saint Augustine Woodcut (29x20.5cm 11x8in) New-York 1998

TRAUTMANN Johann Georg 1713-1769 [45]
🖼 $2 737 - €2 572 - **£1 650** - FF16 868
Portrait of an old Man wearing a white Cap Oil/canvas (91.5x71cm 36x27in) London 1999
🖼 $2 000 - €2 355 - **£1 383** - FF15 451
Portrait of a Man Oil/panel (22.5x18cm 8x7in) New-York 2000

TRAUTSCHOLD Adolf Manfred 1854-? [1]
🖼 $14 000 - €14 108 - **£8 727** - FF92 540
The Wedding Oil/canvas (64x97cm 25x38in) New-York 2000

TRAUTSCHOLD Wilhelm Carl F. 1815-1877 [9]
✏ $6 193 - €6 859 - **£4 200** - FF44 990
Deer in the Black Forset at Sunset Watercolour, gouache (107x74.5cm 42x29in) Billingshurst, West-Sussex 2000

TRAUTTWEILLER von Stefanie 1888-? [28]
🖼 $1 850 - €1 599 - **£1 115** - FF10 487
Dächer, Türme und Kuppeln Öl/Leinwand (66x54cm 25x21in) Wien 1999

TRAVER Marion Gray 1892-? [11]
🖼 $350 - €409 - **£240** - FF2 683
Clearing Off Oil/masonite (30x40cm 12x16in) Bolton MA 2000

TRAVERSE Pierre 1892-1979 [16]
🗿 $19 000 - €22 075 - **£13 353** - FF144 802
Nude with Faun Bronze (84x66x26.5cm 33x25x10in) New-York 2001
🗿 $4 673 - €5 305 - **£3 246** - FF34 800
Femme et enfant Bronze (64x40.5x18cm 25x15x7in) Pontoise 2001

TRAVERSI Gaspare c.1722-1769 [11]
🖼 $7 500 - €7 775 - **£4 500** - FF51 000
Ritratto di cardinale Olio/tela (96x72cm 37x28in) Milano 2001
🖼 $8 800 - €11 403 - **£6 600** - FF74 800
Ritratto di vecchio con fiasco Olio/tela (41x33cm 16x12in) Milano 2000

TRAVERSIER Jacques 1875-1935 [91]
✏ $212 - €183 - **£127** - FF1 200
Les quais de la Saône Lavis (12.5x27cm 4x10in) Lyon 1998

TRAVI IL SORDO DI SESTRI Antonio 1608-1665 [13]
🖼 $24 705 - €23 498 - **£15 000** - FF154 135
Joseph Placing his Silver Cup in Benjamin's Sack of Corn Oil/canvas (94x148cm 37x58in) London 1999
🖼 $5 788 - €6 594 - **£4 000** - FF43 255
The Raising of Lazarus Oil/canvas (94x127.5cm 37x50in) London 2000

TRAVIES Édouard 1809-c.1870 [182]
✏ $3 586 - €3 849 - **£2 400** - FF25 251
Guêpier à gorge bleue - Chesnut-Headed Bee-Eater/Oiseau-mouche Watercolour (17x10cm 6x3in) London 2000
🪵 $774 - €686 - **£474** - FF4 500
La draine, le merle, la grosse charbonnière et le rouge-gorge Lithographie (47x33.5cm 18x13in) Paris 1999

TRAVIS Paul B. 1891-1975 [27]
✏ $660 - €693 - **£416** - FF4 545
Tiger & Antilope Gouache/paper (33x49cm 13x19in) Cleveland OH 2000
🪵 $140 - €143 - **£87** - FF939
Elephants in Congo Forest Lithograph (25x38cm 10x15in) Cleveland OH 2000

TRAYER Jules Jean Baptiste 1824-1908/09 [52]
🖼 $8 160 - €7 208 - **£5 040** - FF47 280
Puerto del Norte con torre del reloj Oleo/lienzo (59x73cm 23x28in) Madrid 1999
🖼 $12 032 - €12 124 - **£7 500** - FF79 531
The embroidery Lesson Oil/panel (38x35cm 14x13in) London 2000
🖼 $1 447 - €1 482 - **£900** - FF9 723
Osselets Watercolour (30x42cm 11x16in) Billingshurst, West-Sussex 2000

TRAYLOR Bill 1854-1947 [45]
🖼 $40 000 - €34 510 - **£24 220** - FF226 372
Bird and Man Mixed media (44x28cm 17x11in) New-York 1999
🖼 $50 000 - €43 138 - **£30 275** - FF282 965
Woman Addresses Man Gouache (38x34cm 14x13in) New-York 1999

TREACY Liam 1934 [32]
🖼 $1 833 - €2 159 - **£1 288** - FF14 159
Avoca in Winter Oil/canvas/board (62x75cm 24x29in) Dublin 2000
🖼 $1 165 - €1 079 - **£722** - FF7 079
The Music Room Oil/board (25x30cm 10x12in) Dublin 1999

TREASURE Douglas 1917 [7]
🖼 $225 - €262 - **£155** - FF1 718
The Harbour, Gordons Bay, Cape Watercolour (46x61cm 18x24in) Johannesburg 2000

TREBACZ Maurycy 1861-1941 [18]
🖼 $1 835 - €1 850 - **£1 144** - FF12 133
Vieux juif Oil/canvas (70x50cm 27x19in) Warszawa 2000

TRECCANI Ernesto 1920-1996 [356]
🖼 $2 400 - €3 110 - **£1 800** - FF20 400
Figure Acrilico/tela (100x150cm 39x59in) Prato 2000
🖼 $600 - €777 - **£450** - FF5 100
Maternità Olio/tela (70x35cm 27x13in) Vercelli 2000
🖼 $325 - €337 - **£195** - FF2 210
Volto Olio/tela (40x20cm 15x7in) Vercelli 2001

TRECHSLIN Anne Marie 1927 [22]
✏ $346 - €389 - **£240** - FF2 551
«Golden Masterpiece» Aquarell/Papier (29x21.5cm 11x8in) Luzern 2001

TREDUPP Charles 1864-? [4]
$850 - €792 - **£526** - FF5 197
Landscape with Windmill by Moonlight Oil/canvas (30x45cm 12x18in) Portland OR 1999

TRÉGI XX [1]
$1 100 - €1 131 - **£697** - FF7 420
«**Bor Quin Quina**» Poster (96x137cm 38x54in) Cincinnati OH 2000

TREIBER Hans 1869-? [11]
$2 173 - €2 556 - **£1 534** - FF16 769
Auf dem Maskenball Gouache/paper (41.5x31cm 16x12in) Köln 2001

TREIDLER Adolph 1886-1981 [17]
$1 000 - €999 - **£610** - FF6 556
«**Washington, a Capital City**» Poster (89x140cm 35x55in) New-York 2000

TREML Friedrich Johann 1816-1852 [23]
$4 392 - €4 360 - **£2 742** - FF28 602
Der festgenommene Deserteur Öl/Leinwand (49.5x63cm 19x24in) Wien 1999
$12 400 - €11 628 - **£7 664** - FF76 272
Einzug Österreichischer Infanterie durch ein Stadtthor Öl/Karton (19.5x22.5cm 7x8in) Wien 1999
$1 832 - €1 817 - **£1 147** - FF11 917
Kavallerie Watercolour (17.2x19.8cm 6x7in) Wien 1999

TREMLETT David 1945 [17]
$7 400 - €9 589 - **£5 550** - FF62 900
Senza título Tecnica mista/carta (204x143cm 80x56in) Prato 2000

TRÉMOIS Pierre-Yves 1921 [171]
$863 - €838 - **£533** - FF5 520
Abeille Lavis (24x28cm 9x11in) Paris 1999
$121 - €107 - **£73** - FF700
Couple Gravure (55x84cm 21x33in) Douai 1998

TREMOLIERE Pierre Charles 1703-1739 [14]
$5 792 - €4 878 - **£3 420** - FF32 000
Apollon et Sarpédon Lavis (36.6x49.8cm 14x19in) Paris 1999

TRÉMONT Auguste 1893-? [13]
$20 389 - €23 782 - **£14 320** - FF156 000
Ours brun se redressant Bronze (24x39x16cm 9x15x6in) Pontoise 2000

TRENCH Marianne L. 1888-? [6]
$1 322 - €1 232 - **£820** - FF8 084
St. James Palace Watercolour/paper (50x45cm 19x17in) Billingshurst, West-Sussex 1999

TRENERRY Horace Hurtle 1899-1958 [24]
$11 870 - €10 882 - **£7 344** - FF71 378
Mt. Barker Oil/board (39x46cm 15x18in) Melbourne 1998
$1 578 - €1 781 - **£1 110** - FF11 683
Still Life Oil/canvas (30.5x40.5cm 12x15in) Malvern, Victoria 2001

TRENK Franz 1899-1960 [9]
$427 - €509 - **£305** - FF3 336
Wolfgangsee Aquarell/Papier (34x45cm 13x17in) Graz 2000

TRENTANOVE Gaetano 1858-1937 [2]
$21 000 - €18 141 - **£14 000** - FF119 000
Raffaello Sanzio pittore giovanetto Carrare marble (H154cm H60in) Prato 1998

TRENTANOVE Raimondo 1792-1832 [4]
$23 000 - €23 843 - **£13 800** - FF156 400
Busti Marbre (H54cm H21in) Milano 1999

TRENTI Gerolamo 1828-1898 [3]
$2 994 - €3 107 - **£1 900** - FF20 378
A Boy and a Dog resting on the Shade in a Orchard Oil/canvas (56x70cm 22x27in) Cheshire 2000

TRESHAM Henry 1750/51-1814 [7]
$1 161 - €1 010 - **£700** - FF6 624
View of Buildings at Naples Pencil (21.5x39cm 8x15in) London 1998

TRETCHIKOFF Vladimir Griegorov. 1913-? [12]
$3 756 - €4 213 - **£2 628** - FF27 636
Artist's Palette with Hibiscus and Glass Oil/canvas (51x87cm 20x34in) Cape Town 2001

TREU Katherine 1743-1811 [4]
$25 403 - €27 268 - **£17 000** - FF178 867
Grapes in a Basket, a Corn Cob, Peaches, Plums, Apricots, Cherries Oil/canvas (78x64.5cm 30x25in) London 2000

TREU Nicolaus 1734-1786 [3]
$25 560 - €27 441 - **£17 100** - FF180 000
Trompe-l'oeil aux enfants jouant derrière une fenêtre Huile/toile (66.5x51cm 26x20in) Paris 2000

TREUMANN Otto 1919 [31]
$139 - €159 - **£97** - FF1 041
«**Stedelijk Museum Amsterdam, Vincent van Gogh**» Poster (80x104.5cm 31x41in) Hoorn 2001

TREUTLER Jerzy XX [3]
$47 - €56 - **£32** - FF366
«**Victoire au bord de la Volga**» Affiche (84x59cm 33x23in) Kraków 2000

TREVELYAN Julian 1910-1989 [215]
$8 110 - €7 789 - **£5 000** - FF51 094
Chiswick Mall Oil/canvas (61x51cm 24x20in) London 1999
$747 - €636 - **£450** - FF4 174
Self-Portrait Oil/paper (38x28cm 14x11in) London 1998
$1 604 - €1 616 - **£1 000** - FF10 603
Malta Gouache/paper (28.5x40cm 11x15in) London 1999
$308 - €298 - **£190** - FF1 955
The Well of Loneliness Etching, aquatint in colors (17.5x24.5cm 6x9in) London 1999

TREVES Dario 1907-1978 [7]
$550 - €570 - **£330** - FF3 740
Novello d'Alba Olio/tavola (50x65cm 19x25in) Torino 2000

TREVISANI Angelo 1669-1753/55 [8]
$21 580 - €24 542 - **£14 966** - FF160 987
Die Heilige Familie Öl/Leinwand (100x75cm 39x29in) Hamburg 2000
$3 505 - €3 270 - **£2 115** - FF21 451
Begegnung zweier Heiliger Öl/Leinwand (42x27.5cm 16x10in) Wien 1999

T

✏️ **$2 540** - €2 727 - **£1 700** - FF17 886
Study of a Man holding a Horse, and a Hand holding a Book Red chalk (33x18.5cm 12x7in)
London 2000

TREVISANI Francesco 1656-1746 **[48]**

🖼️ **$10 094** - €10 174 - **£6 300** - FF66 738
Die Auferstehung Christi Öl/Leinwand (135x98cm 53x38in) Wien 2000

🖼️ **$12 704** - €11 628 - **£7 744** - FF76 272
Madonna con Bambino e San Giovannino Öl/Leinwand (100x74cm 39x29in) Wien 1999

🖼️ **$9 460** - €10 008 - **£6 000** - FF65 650
The Agony in the Garden Oil/copper (29.5x40.5cm 11x15in) London 2000

✏️ **$21 000** - €18 256 - **£12 709** - FF119 754
Portrait of a seated Hunter, with two Dogs Black chalk (41x26.5cm 16x10in) New-York 1999

TREVISO da Girolamo il Vecchio c.1450-c.1496 **[2]**

🖼️ **$23 520** - €20 017 - **£14 000** - FF131 304
The Virgin and Child Enthroned Oil/canvas (148.5x63.5cm 58x25in) London 1998

TREVOR Edward ?-1885 **[2]**

🖼️ **$7 545** - €8 497 - **£5 200** - FF55 735
Awaiting the Fleet's Return Oil/canvas (56x66cm 22x25in) London 2000

TREVOR Helen Mabel 1831-1900 **[5]**

🖼️ **$44 755** - €38 613 - **£27 000** - FF253 284
Breton Boys -En retenue Oil/canvas (96.5x140cm 37x55in) London 1998

🖼️ **$11 954** - €12 832 - **£8 000** - FF84 172
Capri Oil/canvas (118x79cm 46x31in) London 2000

TREVOUX Joseph 1831-1909 **[81]**

🖼️ **$524** - €579 - **£363** - FF3 800
Paysage Huile/panneau (23.5x32.5cm 9x12in) Lyon 2001

TRIBE Barbara 1913-2000 **[13]**

🗿 **$2 487** - €2 929 - **£1 748** - FF19 213
Maria Asleep Bronze (37x9.5x14cm 14x3x5in) Sydney 2000

TRICCA Angiolo 1817-1884 **[5]**

✏️ **$850** - €881 - **£510** - FF5 780
Cesare Cortini Acquarello (50x33cm 19x12in) Firenze 2001

TRICKETT John 1952 **[25]**

🖼️ **$1 200** - €1 223 - **£751** - FF8 024
Spaniel and Pointer Oil/canvas (61x51cm 24x20in) New-York 2000

TRICKETT W. Wasdell XIX-XX **[25]**

🖼️ **$283** - €329 - **£200** - FF2 160
Blazer Oil/canvas (30x40cm 11x15in) Cambridge 2001

TRIEB Anton 1883-1954 **[7]**

✏️ **$563** - €605 - **£377** - FF3 968
Sibirischer Zobel/Gelbrandkäfer Aquarell/Papier (17x22cm 6x8in) St. Gallen 2000

TRIEBEL Carl 1823-1885 **[1]**

🖼️ **$1 832** - €1 817 - **£1 147** - FF11 917
Am Vierwaldstättersee/Waldlichtung mit Rehen Öl/Karton (11.5x16.4cm 4x6in) Wien 1999

TRIER Adeline act.1879-1916 **[1]**

🖼️ **$3 709** - €4 324 - **£2 600** - FF28 366
Italian Anemones Oil/canvas (38x55.5cm 14x21in) Crewkerne, Somerset 2000

TRIER Hann 1915-1999 **[200]**

🖼️ **$15 951** - €15 339 - **£9 843** - FF100 617
Commedia dell'arte, tartaglia Mixed media/canvas (162.5x130cm 63x51in) Köln 1999

🖼️ **$6 427** - €6 135 - **£4 015** - FF40 246
Nervensäge Tempera/canvas (60.7x79.3cm 23x31in) Köln 1999

🖼️ **$2 392** - €2 301 - **£1 476** - FF15 092
Improvisation I Tempera (22x27cm 8x10in) Köln 1999

✏️ **$1 752** - €1 533 - **£1 061** - FF10 059
Komposition Indian ink (57x81.5cm 22x32in) Berlin 1998

🗎 **$147** - €174 - **£107** - FF1 140
Protuberanzen Etching, aquatint (58.5x39.5cm 23x15in) Hamburg 2001

TRIGOSO Falcào 1879-1956 **[12]**

🖼️ **$18 450** - €20 439 - **£11 890** - FF134 070
Ravina Oleo/lienzo (47x60cm 18x23in) Lisboa 2000

🖼️ **$13 200** - €14 955 - **£9 000** - FF98 100
Paisagem com arvores e casario Huile/toile (31x41cm 12x16in) Lisboa 2000

TRIMBLE Gary 1928-1979 **[3]**

🗿 **$6 972** - €6 603 - **£4 239** - FF43 310
Portrait bust of Ms. Terry Keane Bronze (H40cm H16in) Dublin 1999

TRINER Franz Xaver 1767-1824 **[15]**

✏️ **$748** - €844 - **£526** - FF5 538
«Vue du Trou d'Urseren, prise du côté d'Urseren» Watercolour (40x33.5cm 15x13in) Bern 2001

🗎 **$79** - €92 - **£54** - FF603
Le bain à Unterschächen dans le Canton d'Uri Kupferstich (23.2x36.8cm 9x14in) Luzern 2000

TRINER Heinrich 1796-1873 **[9]**

✏️ **$3 374** - €3 256 - **£2 119** - FF21 356
Die Kirche in Seengen Aquarell/Papier (27.6x40cm 10x15in) Zürich 1999

🗎 **$242** - €272 - **£168** - FF1 786
Une partie de la nouvelle Route du St.Gothard, vers am Steg Aquatinta (23.5x31.5cm 9x12in) Luzern 2001

TRINKLEY Karla 1956 **[2]**

🗿 **$6 500** - €6 205 - **£4 061** - FF40 699
Peter Peter Sculpture, glass (31.5x34cm 12x13in) New-York 1999

TRINQUESSE Louis Rolland c.1746-c.1800 **[30]**

🖼️ **$94 612** - €94 518 - **£59 148** - FF620 000
Vicomte de Sainte Hermine et sa femme Catherine Adélaïde de Crès Huile/toile (126.5x96.5cm 49x37in) Paris 1999

🖼️ **$31 000** - €29 592 - **£19 368** - FF194 109
Portrait of a Young Woman Oil/canvas (59x49.5cm 23x19in) New-York 1999

✏️ **$2 796** - €2 592 - **£1 739** - FF17 000
Portrait de femme Trois crayons/papier (47x38cm 18x14in) Paris 1999

TRINQUIER-TRIANON Louis 1853-1922 [35]
   $507 - €579 - **£353** - FF3 800
     «Luxembourg, chemins de fer de l'Est» Affiche
     (75x105cm 29x41in) Paris 2001

TRIONFI Emanuele 1832-1900 [5]
   $1 860 - €1 607 - **£930** - FF10 540
     Dama dormiente Olio/tela (39x30cm 15x11in)
     Firenze 1999

TRIPE Linneaus 1822-1902 [50]
   $4 000 - €3 777 - **£2 484** - FF24 775
     The Blackburn Testimonial Salt print (56x35.5cm
     22x13in) New-York 1999

TRIPET Alfred act.c.1861-1882 [2]
   $10 000 - €11 358 - **£7 017** - FF74 504
     «Apparition de Vinvela à Shilric-Le-Chasseur»
     Oil/canvas (88x132.5cm 34x52in) New-York 2001

TRIPP Herbert Alker 1883-1954 [7]
   $1 000 - €999 - **£610** - FF6 556
     «Bournemouth» Poster (101x127cm 40x50in) New-
     York 2000

TRIPP Jan Peter 1945 [17]
   $1 711 - €1 943 - **£1 171** - FF12 744
     L'Alsacien Gouache/paper (65x50cm 25x19in)
     Hamburg 2000

TRIPPEL Albert 1813-1854 [10]
   $1 414 - €1 380 - **£895** - FF9 055
     Lorea in Sardinien, Sonnenbeschienene
     Angleridylle am Fluss Öl/Leinwand (21x29cm
     8x11in) Bremen 1999

TRIQUET Jules Octave 1867-1914 [9]
   $2 608 - €3 068 - **£1 870** - FF20 123
     Bildnis eines jungen Mädchens Öl/Leinwand
     (88x64cm 34x25in) München 2001
   $2 000 - €2 073 - **£1 200** - FF13 600
     Gentiluomo in lettura Olio/tavola (18x13.5cm 7x5in)
     Milano 2000

TRISCOTT Samuel Peter Rolt 1846-1925 [29]
   $1 600 - €1 783 - **£1 076** - FF11 696
     Lake Scene Watercolour/paper (13x32cm 5x12in)
     Portsmouth NH 2000

TRISTAN Luis c.1586-1624 [1]
   $26 000 - €24 026 - **£15 600** - FF157 601
     El cardenal Niño de Guevara Oleo/lienzo
     (123x100cm 48x39in) Madrid 1999

TRISTRAM John William 1872-1938 [34]
   $338 - €395 - **£235** - FF2 591
     Little Reef, Newport N.S.W. Watercolour/paper
     (30x35.5cm 11x13in) Melbourne 2000

TRITSCHLER Alfred 1905-1970 [10]
   $659 - €562 - **£397** - FF3 688
     Köln, Blick vom Dom Vintage gelatin silver print
     (24.1x17.8cm 9x7in) Köln 1998

TRITT Wolfgang 1913-1983 [29]
   $893 - €869 - **£548** - FF5 701
     Berittene Offiziere verschiedener Epochen aus
     Frankreich und England Aquarell/Papier (14x12cm
     5x4in) Berlin 1999

TRITTEN Gottfried 1923 [25]
   $384 - €418 - **£253** - FF2 743
     Komposition mit Schriftzeichen auf weissem
     Grund Watercolour (29x77cm 11x30in) Bern 2000

TRNKA Jirí 1912-1962 [38]
   $231 - €219 - **£144** - FF1 434
     Ctenarka Huile/carton (32x22cm 12x8in) Praha 2000
   $433 - €410 - **£270** - FF2 689
     Spejblovo filmové opojeni Tempera/papier
     (28x19cm 11x7in) Praha 2000
   $135 - €128 - **£84** - FF842
     Palais Lithographie (30x21.5cm 11x8in) Praha 2000

TROCKEL Rosemarie 1952 [98]
   $35 000 - €32 687 - **£21 602** - FF214 410
     Who will be in in 99? Mixed media/canvas
     (210x160cm 82x62in) New-York 1999
   $16 000 - €17 554 - **£10 628** - FF115 148
     Untitled Mixed media (100x80cm 39x31in) New-York
     2000
   $15 833 - €15 281 - **£10 000** - FF100 238
     Untitled Alabaster (152x62x31.5cm 59x24x12in)
     London 1999
   $75 000 - €72 568 - **£46 252** - FF476 017
     Gewohnheitstier 2 (Reh) Bronze (20x122x79cm
     7x48x31in) New-York 1999
   $3 586 - €3 849 - **£2 400** - FF25 251
     Untitled Ink/paper (22x17.5cm 8x6in) London 2000
   $11 553 - €12 590 - **£8 000** - FF82 582
     Objekt Tapestry (105.5x50.5cm 41x19in) London 2001
   $1 486 - €1 646 - **£1 008** - FF10 799
     Paare Photograph (40.4x50.3cm 15x19in) Berlin 2000

TRODOUX Henri Emile Adrien XIX [23]
   $1 300 - €1 325 - **£814** - FF8 692
     King Charles Spaniel Bronze (H12.5cm H4in) New-
     York 2000

TROFIMENKO Boris 1919 [108]
   $714 - €742 - **£450** - FF4 868
     Fixing her Hair Oil/canvas/board (33x24cm 12x9in)
     Fernhurst, Haslemere, Surrey 2000

TROGER Paul 1698-1762 [45]
   $16 000 - €18 168 - **£10 950** - FF119 175
     Kreuzigung Öl/Leinwand (70x37cm 27x14in) Wien
     2000
   $1 570 - €1 789 - **£1 095** - FF11 738
     Christus am Ölberg Ink (27x19.5cm 10x7in) Berlin
     2001
   $948 - €920 - **£590** - FF6 037
     Eine Heilige Familie, mit landschaftlichem
     Grunde Radierung (15.8x11.3cm 6x4in) Berlin 1999

TROIANI Don 1949 [1]
   $5 610 - €5 926 - **£3 708** - FF38 871
     Confederate Battle Line in Action Oil/canvas
     (76x50cm 30x20in) Houston TX 2000

TROIVAUX Jean-Baptiste Désiré 1788-1860 [10]
   $9 720 - €11 434 - **£6 967** - FF75 000
     Jeune femme en robe de velours pourpre à
     manches et écharpe Miniature (8x6cm 3x2in) Paris
     2001

TROJANOWSKI Wincenty 1859-1928 [3]
   $4 158 - €4 491 - **£2 874** - FF29 462
     Orpheline Huile/panneau (26x15.5cm 10x6in) Kraków
     2001

T

TRÖKES Heinz 1913-1997 **[271]**

- $4 785 - €5 624 - £3 317 - FF36 892
  Zwischenland Öl/Leinwand (100x120cm 39x47in)
  Stuttgart 2000

- $4 824 - €5 292 - £3 276 - FF34 712
  Herbstspiel Öl/Leinwand (59.5x74cm 23x29in) Berlin
  2000

- $3 998 - €4 704 - £2 822 - FF30 855
  «**Nachthasen**» Mixed media (24x48cm 9x18in)
  Berlin 2001

- $850 - €818 - £525 - FF5 366
  Schornstein und anderes Watercolour (32.8x48cm
  12x18in) Köln 1999

- $95 - €112 - £66 - FF737
  Universum mit Sonnen Farbserigraphie (40x51cm
  15x20in) Braunschweig 2000

TROLL Johann Heinrich 1756-1824 **[3]**

- $921 - €1 039 - £647 - FF6 816
  «**Lac de Wallenstadt**» Aquatinta (38x53cm 14x20in)
  Bern 2001

TROMBADORI Francesco 1886-1961 **[47]**

- $6 500 - €6 738 - £3 900 - FF44 200
  Il Colosseo e la Basilica di Massenzio Olio/tela
  (50x65cm 19x25in) Roma 1999

- $1 600 - €1 659 - £960 - FF10 880
  Paesaggio a livello Olio/tavola (23x17cm 9x6in)
  Roma 2001

TROMPF Percival XX **[3]**

- $1 000 - €1 160 - £701 - FF7 610
  «**Australia**» Poster (101x63cm 40x25in) New-York
  2000

TROMPIZ Virgilio 1927 **[65]**

- $1 440 - €1 342 - £880 - FF8 800
  Figuras Oleo/lienzo (54x65.5cm 21x25in) Caracas
  1998

- $704 - €671 - £440 - FF4 400
  Sin título Oleo/lienzo (33x41cm 12x16in) Caracas
  1999

- $1 380 - €1 445 - £828 - FF9 476
  Conquistadores Técnica mixta/papel (33.5x29cm
  13x11in) Caracas 2000

TRONCET Antony 1879-1939 **[9]**

- $16 000 - €17 910 - £11 158 - FF117 480
  Standing Nude before the Lake Oil/canvas
  (145x91.5cm 57x36in) New-York 2001

TROOD William H. Hamilton 1848-1899 **[29]**

- $10 755 - €12 010 - £7 500 - FF78 783
  Fred, a Terrier Oil/canvas (50x68cm 19x26in) Bath
  2001

- $9 500 - €8 410 - £5 808 - FF55 165
  A Narrow Escape Oil/canvas (41x30.5cm 16x12in)
  New-York 1999

TROOST Cornelis 1697-1750 **[31]**

- $18 445 - €19 121 - £11 067 - FF125 426
  Ritratto di giovane dama Olio/tela (48x38cm
  18x14in) Venezia 2000

- $4 871 - €5 793 - £3 378 - FF38 000
  **Le mari, la femme et l'amant devant la porte du
  notaire** Aquarelle (24.5x22.5cm 9x8in) Paris 2000

TROOST Willem I 1684-1759 **[8]**

- $6 775 - €6 197 - £4 175 - FF40 650
  **Wandelaars en herder met kudde in een boom-
  rijk rivierlandschap** Aquarelle/papier (20x25cm
  7x9in) Antwerpen 1999

TROOST Willem II 1812-c.1890 **[5]**

- $10 516 - €9 076 - £6 346 - FF59 532
  **Numerous Fisherfolk and a Fishing Fleet near
  Paviljoen von Wied** Oil/canvas (55x77cm 21x30in)
  Amsterdam 1999

TROPININ Vasily Andreevich 1776-1857 **[4]**

- $8 657 - €9 418 - £5 706 - FF61 779
  Pojke Oil/canvas (46x38cm 18x14in) Helsinki 2000

TROPPA Girolamo c.1636-c.1706 **[13]**

- $27 600 - €23 843 - £18 400 - FF156 400
  Loth e le figlie Olio/tela (95x132.5cm 37x52in) Roma
  1998

TROSCHEL Hans Jean 1585-1628 **[3]**

- $3 364 - €3 835 - £2 347 - FF25 154
  **Bildnis eines jungen Mannes, den Kopf zur
  Seite geneigt** Black chalk/paper (26x32cm 10x12in)
  Berlin 2001

TROST Carl 1811-1884 **[7]**

- $1 376 - €1 636 - £953 - FF10 732
  Titania und Zettel im Feenwald Watercolour
  (16.5x36.5cm 6x14in) Köln 2000

TROTTER John c.1735-c.1800 **[4]**

- $54 190 - €59 453 - £36 000 - FF389 988
  **Officer, Three-quarter-length, in Scarlet Uniform
  with Green Facings** Oil/canvas (127x101.5cm
  50x39in) London 2000

- $157 211 - €158 418 - £98 000 - FF1 039 152
  **Portrait of an Officer, Full Length, Standing in a
  Landscape** Oil/canvas (97.5x123cm 38x48in) London
  2000

TROTTER Mary Anne XVIII **[1]**

- $46 443 - €40 393 - £28 000 - FF264 961
  **Portrait of the Hon. John Theophilus Rawdon-
  Hastings** Oil/canvas (87.5x70cm 34x27in) London
  1998

TROTTER Newbold Hough 1827-1898 **[25]**

- $5 500 - €6 332 - £3 753 - FF41 536
  Farm Scenes with Cows Oil/canvas (68.5x104cm
  26x40in) New-York 2000

- $1 000 - €1 073 - £669 - FF7 041
  Perry County, Pennsylvania Oil/board (27x37.5cm
  10x14in) Philadelphia PA 2000

TROTTI IL MALOSSO Giovanni Battista 1555-1619
[14]

- $1 801 - €1 674 - £1 100 - FF10 978
  Christ in Glory Ink (20.5x14.5cm 8x5in) London
  1998

TROTZIER Jean Bernard 1950 **[144]**

- $1 058 - €915 - £628 - FF6 000
  Promenade au bord de l'eau Huile/toile (38x55cm
  14x21in) Lyon 1998

- $286 - €274 - £176 - FF1 800
  Ciel bleu sur la mer Huile/toile (14x18cm 5x7in)
  Strasbourg 1999

TROTZIG Ellen 1878-1949 **[18]**
- $476 - €528 - **£330** - FF3 465
  Det blåser Oil/canvas (50x41cm 19x16in) Malmö 2001

TROTZIG Ulf 1925 **[39]**
- $805 - €740 - **£495** - FF4 857
  Från Heden Oil/canvas (89x116cm 35x45in) Köbenhavn 1999

TROUBETZKOY Pierre 1864-? **[5]**
- $69 081 - €77 376 - **£48 000** - FF507 556
  Lady Serena Lumley, as a child, seated full-length, in a white Dress Oil/canvas (127x76cm 50x29in) London 2001

TROUILLE Clovis 1889-1975 **[10]**
- $39 009 - €45 887 - **£28 263** - FF301 000
  «La parade atomisée» Huile/toile (64x82cm 25x32in) Paris 2001

TROUILLEBERT Paul Désiré 1829-1900 **[466]**
- $23 000 - €19 843 - **£13 875** - FF130 163
  Woodgatherer by a River Oil/canvas (56x39cm 22x15in) New-York 1998
- $6 164 - €7 013 - **£4 278** - FF46 000
  Rue de village Huile/toile (42x18cm 16x7in) Fontainebleau 2000
- $698 - €793 - **£485** - FF5 200
  Les ramasseurs de fagots au bord de l'eau Fusain (27x26cm 10x10in) Barbizon 2001

TROUPEAU Ferdinand XIX-XX **[6]**
- $4 830 - €5 336 - **£3 349** - FF35 000
  Nature morte au potiron et aux prunes Huile/toile (88x130cm 34x51in) Paris 2001

TROUVAIN Antoine 1656-1708 **[4]**
- $153 - €153 - **£96** - FF1 066
  La majorité du Roy Louis XIII, nach Rubens Kupferstich (50x36cm 19x14in) Staufen 1999

TROUVILLE Henri Charles XIX **[10]**
- $303 - €290 - **£190** - FF1 900
  Portraits Fusain/papier (23x16cm 9x6in) Angers 1999

TROVA Ernest 1927 **[131]**
- $23 000 - €21 724 - **£13 910** - FF142 501
  Falling Man Series (FM-5 Backwrap Figure) Metal (H213.5cm H84in) New-York 1999
- $1 100 - €1 020 - **£684** - FF6 688
  «Fm/Shadow 14741D» Sculpture (21x38x28cm 8x15x11in) New-Orleans LA 1999
- $210 - €245 - **£150** - FF1 606
  Falling Man Variant Silkscreen in colors (91x91cm 36x36in) St. Louis MO 2000

TROWBRIDGE Vaughan 1869-? **[11]**
- $4 899 - €5 488 - **£3 405** - FF36 000
  Maison dans les arbres Huile/toile (50x61cm 19x24in) Le Touquet 2001

TROXLER Georges Alfons 1901-1990 **[42]**
- $489 - €551 - **£342** - FF3 613
  «Spätsommertag bei Zermatt» Öl/Leinwand (55x46cm 21x18in) Luzern 2001

TROY de François 1645-1730 **[30]**
- $118 725 - €114 337 - **£73 875** - FF750 000
  Le peintre et sa famille Huile/toile (145x118cm 57x46in) Montfort L'Amaury 1999

- $23 851 - €28 366 - **£17 000** - FF186 068
  Portrait of Princess Louisa Maria Theresa Stuart (1692-1712) Oil/canvas (70x58cm 27x22in) London 2001

TROY de Jean François 1679-1752 **[49]**
- $72 818 - €70 127 - **£45 218** - FF460 000
  Chasse du lion Huile/toile (60x72cm 23x28in) Paris 1999
- $4 585 - €4 260 - **£2 800** - FF27 944
  Study of a Soldier Red chalk (47x34.5cm 18x13in) London 1998

TROYE Edward 1808-1874 **[8]**
- $7 200 - €6 861 - **£4 564** - FF45 006
  Portrait of a Trotter, Spirit Oil/canvas (45x63cm 18x25in) Cleveland OH 1994

TROYEN van Rombout c.1605-c.1650 **[38]**
- $5 183 - €5 336 - **£3 293** - FF35 000
  Le sacrifice d'Élie au Mont Carmel (I Rois XVIII. 20-40) Huile/panneau (26.5x68.5cm 10x26in) Paris 2000

TROYER de Prosper 1880-1961 **[142]**
- $1 206 - €1 134 - **£730** - FF7 441
  Flowers in a Vase Oil/panel (56x48cm 22x18in) Amsterdam 1999
- $477 - €446 - **£289** - FF2 926
  Pierrot Wash/paper (59x37.5cm 23x14in) Lokeren 2001

TROYON Constant 1810-1865 **[270]**
- $55 000 - €51 516 - **£33 814** - FF337 925
  Cattle watering Oil/canvas (101x150cm 39x59in) New-York 1999
- $5 348 - €5 336 - **£3 339** - FF35 000
  Berger près des coupes de bois Huile/toile (49x59cm 19x23in) Fontainebleau 1999
- $1 500 - €1 750 - **£1 044** - FF11 479
  Cows in a Landscape Oil/panel (34x38cm 13x15in) Bloomfield-Hills MI 2000
- $1 069 - €991 - **£665** - FF6 500
  Le moulin à eau Aquarelle/papier (20x30cm 7x11in) Évreux 1999

TRUBBIANI Valeriano 1937 **[22]**
- $750 - €777 - **£450** - FF5 100
  La condizione umana Scultura (H22.5cm H8in) Roma 2001

TRUBEZKOJ Pavel Petrovic 1866-1938 **[144]**
- $5 737 - €6 403 - **£3 990** - FF42 000
  Buste de jeune femme Bronze (H45cm H17in) Paris 2001
- $2 100 - €2 177 - **£1 260** - FF14 280
  Donna in rosa Pastelli/cartone (64x50cm 25x19in) Roma 2000

TRÜBNER Wilhelm 1851-1917 **[157]**
- $8 155 - €7 060 - **£4 950** - FF46 312
  Im Liebesgarten Öl/Karton (83.5x51cm 32x20in) München 1998
- $6 497 - €7 644 - **£4 586** - FF50 139
  Rückenansicht eines Englischen Kutschers Öl/Leinwand (14.5x12.5cm 5x4in) Berlin 2001
- $350 - €359 - **£219** - FF2 357
  Two Figures in an Interior Black chalk/paper (35x31.5cm 13x12in) New-York 2000

T

TRUBUS S. 1926-1966 **[14]**
- $8 181 - €8 565 - **£5 139** - FF56 180
  Legong Dancer Oil/canvas (65x95.5cm 25x37in) Singapore 2000
- $12 404 - €11 561 - **£7 497** - FF75 837
  Portrait of Lady Oil/board (24x18cm 9x7in) Singapore 1999

TRUCCO Dario 1939 **[6]**
- $325 - €337 - **£195** - FF2 210
  Mareggiata Olio/masonite (30x40cm 11x15in) Vercelli 2000

TRUDEAU Angus 1908-1984 **[2]**
- $1 654 - €1 775 - **£1 123** - FF11 645
  Sulkyn Racing Mixed media/paper (22x28cm 8x11in) Calgary, Alberta 2001

TRUELLE Auguste 1818-1908 **[1]**
- $10 602 - €12 501 - **£7 453** - FF82 000
  Paysage italien Huile/toile (103x158cm 40x62in) Paris 2000

TRUELSEN Mathias Jacob Theo. 1836-1900 **[1]**
- $1 597 - €1 789 - **£1 100** - FF11 738
  Bark «Cecilie» von Apenrade vor Helgoland Watercolour (28.2x44.5cm 11x17in) Hamburg 2000

TRUELSEN Nis Nissen 1792-1862 **[1]**
- $1 597 - €1 789 - **£1 100** - FF11 738
  Vollschiff auf See Watercolour (40x60cm 15x23in) Hamburg 2000

TRUESDELL Gaylord Sangston 1850-1899 **[5]**
- $1 800 - €1 996 - **£1 247** - FF13 092
  Sheep in a pasture with haystacks Oil/canvas (69x91cm 27x36in) Downington PA 2001

TRUEX van Day 1904-1979 **[6]**
- $6 000 - €6 975 - **£4 211** - FF45 756
  Three vases and one flower pot Ink (51x66cm 20x25in) New-York 2001

TRUFFAUT Fernand Fortuné 1866-1955 **[101]**
- $430 - €397 - **£259** - FF2 601
  Vue à Trouville Aquarelle/papier (52x36cm 20x14in) Antwerpen 1999

TRUFFOT Émile Louis 1843-1896 **[12]**
- $1 917 - €2 231 - **£1 350** - FF14 634
  Jeune femme et son chien Bronze (H67cm H26in) Liège 2001

TRUIJEN Hans 1928 **[12]**
- $4 241 - €4 084 - **£2 652** - FF26 789
  Nude with Flowers Oil/canvas (101x80.5cm 39x31in) Amsterdam 1999

TRUMBULL John 1756-1843 **[11]**
- $9 500 - €10 397 - **£6 553** - FF68 198
  George Gallagher, New York Oil/board (78.5x62cm 30x24in) New-York 1999

TRUMP Georg 1896-1985 **[4]**
- $541 - €470 - **£326** - FF3 083
  Früchestilleben Vintage gelatin silver print (57.8x44.9cm 22x17in) Berlin 1998

TRUONG Marcelino 1957 **[10]**
- $1 149 - €1 159 - **£716** - FF7 600
  Stravinsky (détail) Gouache/papier (30x38cm 11x14in) Paris 2000

TRUPHEME Auguste Joseph 1836-1898 **[11]**
- $9 133 - €9 833 - **£6 056** - FF64 500
  A l'école Huile/toile (61x46cm 24x18in) Corbeil-Essonnes 2000

TRUPHEME François Joseph A. 1820-1888 **[7]**
- $12 000 - €13 816 - **£8 188** - FF90 624
  An Egyptian Woman with Child Bronze (H225cm H88in) New-York 2000

TRUPHEMUS Jacques 1922 **[48]**
- $4 679 - €5 564 - **£3 336** - FF36 500
  Bouquet de coquelicots Huile/toile (65x54cm 25x21in) Lyon 2000
- $2 361 - €2 744 - **£1 659** - FF18 000
  Petit intérieur doré Huile/toile (27x41.5cm 10x16in) Paris 2001

TRUPPE Karl 1887-1959 **[38]**
- $5 743 - €4 907 - **£3 475** - FF32 189
  Frauenakt Öl/Karton (49.5x39cm 19x15in) München 1998
- $1 754 - €1 636 - **£1 059** - FF10 732
  Portrait eines jungen Mädchens im Profil von links Öl/Karton (38x32cm 14x12in) Lindau 1999
- $35 - €41 - **£24** - FF268
  Porträt Pencil/paper (18x15cm 7x5in) Rudolstadt-Thüringen 2001

TRUSS Jonathan 1960 **[18]**
- $1 623 - €1 560 - **£1 000** - FF10 233
  Classic Leopard Oil/canvas (60x121cm 23x47in) London 1999

TRUSSART Daniel 1948 **[20]**
- $981 - €838 - **£576** - FF5 500
  Retraite tranquille Huile/toile (92x73cm 36x28in) Rouen 1998

TRUSTTUM Philip 1940 **[12]**
- $4 031 - €4 518 - **£2 819** - FF29 638
  Side Wall Oil/board (121x106.5cm 47x41in) Auckland 2001

TRUSZ Iwan 1869-1941 **[63]**
- $2 354 - €2 766 - **£1 632** - FF18 147
  Rivière Huile/carton (35x46cm 13x18in) Warszawa 2000
- $1 060 - €996 - **£658** - FF6 534
  Paysage au bord de la mer Oil/board (37.5x27cm 14x10in) Warszawa 1999

TRYGGELIN Erik 1878-1962 **[49]**
- $26 325 - €25 060 - **£16 470** - FF164 385
  Konfirmation Oil/canvas (182x128cm 71x50in) Stockholm 1999
- $589 - €604 - **£364** - FF3 961
  Ungdom Mixed media (45x37cm 17x14in) Stockholm 2000
- $615 - €531 - **£370** - FF3 482
  «Septemberdag, Visby» Oil/panel (25x34cm 9x13in) Malmö 1998

TRYON Dwight William 1849-1925 **[30]**
- $13 800 - €11 908 - **£8 338** - FF78 113
  Twilight Oil/panel (40x60cm 16x24in) Bethesda MD 1999
- $5 000 - €5 978 - **£3 449** - FF39 210
  Sunset Oil/canvas (27x33cm 11x13in) Milford CT 2000

TRZESZCZKOWSKI Antoni 1902-1974 [11]
- 🖌 **$3 788** - €3 779 - **£2 364** - FF24 790
  Dernière bataille de Wladislaw Warnenczyk
  Oil/board (55.5x49.3cm 21x19in) Warszawa 1999
- 🖌 **$734** - €740 - **£457** - FF4 853
  Les confédérés en reconnaissance
  Oil/canvas/board (22.5x18.3cm 8x7in) Warszawa 2000

TSATOKE Monroe 1904-1937 [4]
- ✏ **$3 200** - €3 172 - **£2 001** - FF20 806
  Dance of the Dog Soldiers Gouache/paper
  (21x26.5cm 8x10in) New-York 1999

TSCHAGGENY Edmond Jean-Baptiste 1818-1873 [18]
- 🖌 **$6 784** - €7 932 - **£4 672** - FF52 032
  Schilder leunend tegen knotwilg vergezeld door aangenaam gezelschap Huile/panneau (61x82cm 24x32in) Antwerpen 2000
- 🖌 **$2 800** - €2 615 - **£1 728** - FF17 152
  Watering her Flock Oil/panel (31.5x27.5cm 12x10in) Boston MA 1999

TSCHAGGENY Philogène Charles 1815-1894 [24]
- 🖌 **$8 058** - €9 093 - **£5 668** - FF59 644
  Kornernte Oil/panel (47.5x72cm 18x28in) Bern 2001

TSCHARNER von Johann Wilhelm 1886-1946 [60]
- 🖌 **$1 484** - €1 695 - **£1 046** - FF11 117
  Sitzender weiblicher Akt am Tisch Öl/Leinwand (81x61cm 31x24in) Bern 2001
- 🖌 **$906** - €872 - **£559** - FF5 717
  Blumenstücke Öl/Leinwand (29.5x24cm 11x9in) Bern 1999

TSCHIRTNER Oswald 1920 [10]
- ✏ **$662** - €727 - **£440** - FF4 767
  Du sollst nicht töten Pencil/paper (29.2x21.2cm 11x8in) Wien 2000

TSCHUDI Lill 1911 [35]
- ✏ **$710** - €683 - **£437** - FF4 483
  Regenwolke auf Grün-Gelb Aquarell/Papier (37x51cm 14x20in) St. Gallen 1999
- 🗐 **$1 599** - €1 540 - **£1 000** - FF10 101
  Ice-Hockey Linocut in colors (26x28cm 10x11in) London 1999

TSCHUDI Rudolf 1855-1953 [3]
- 🖌 **$2 870** - €3 166 - **£1 943** - FF20 765
  Still Life with Grapes and Apples Oil/board (23x30.5cm 9x12in) New-York 2000

TSCHUMI Otto 1904-1985 [85]
- ✏ **$2 511** - €2 953 - **£1 800** - FF19 373
  Jerem, Gotthelf Charcoal (32.5x25cm 12x9in) Bern 2001
- 🗐 **$92** - €103 - **£61** - FF674
  Selbstbildnis Offset (50x39cm 19x15in) Bern 1999

TSENG YUHO 1925 [4]
- 🖌 **$9 788** - €9 180 - **£6 085** - FF60 214
  Study of Scope of Sense Acrylic (71x76cm 27x29in) Taipei 1999

TSINGOS Thanos 1914-1965 [205]
- 🖌 **$11 172** - €10 671 - **£6 965** - FF70 000
  Composition Technique mixte/toile (150x150cm 59x59in) Paris 1999
- 🖌 **$7 309** - €8 386 - **£5 000** - FF55 010
  Nature morte aux fleurs Oil/canvas (74x93cm 29x36in) London 2000

- 🖌 **$2 435** - €2 363 - **£1 545** - FF15 500
  Massif de fleurs Huile/toile (35x33cm 13x12in) Paris 1999

TSION Sergueï 1960 [39]
- 🖌 **$102** - €122 - **£71** - FF800
  Village des pêcheurs Huile/toile (13x18cm 5x7in) Coulommiers 2000

TSIREH Awa (Alfonso Roybal) 1895-1955 [7]
- 🖌 **$5 500** - €6 150 - **£3 707** - FF40 339
  Figure from the Green Corn Dance Oil/canvas (16x49.5cm 6x19in) New-York 2000
- ✏ **$5 000** - €5 591 - **£3 370** - FF36 672
  Two Turtles Watercolour/paper (23x32cm 9x12in) New-York 2000

TSONG KWONG CHI 1950-1990 [5]
- 📷 **$7 000** - €7 827 - **£4 718** - FF51 340
  San Francisco, California Vintage gelatin silver print (50.5x40.5cm 19x15in) New-York 2000

TSUBOUCHI Teruyuki 1922 [1]
- 🖌 **$6 500** - €6 738 - **£3 900** - FF44 200
  Senza titolo Olio/tela (117x91cm 46x35in) Prato 1999

TSUCHIYA Tilsa 1932-1984 [7]
- 🖌 **$60 000** - €58 252 - **£37 068** - FF382 110
  Mujer volando Oil/canvas (64x80cm 25x31in) New-York 1999
- ✏ **$8 000** - €9 295 - **£5 622** - FF60 969
  Sin título Ink (25x32.5cm 9x12in) New-York 2001

TSUI TINYUN Xu Tianrun 1945 [8]
- 🖌 **$20 640** - €19 370 - **£12 752** - FF127 056
  Scarlet Oil/canvas (151x90cm 59x35in) Hong-Kong 1999
- 🖌 **$11 538** - €13 561 - **£8 001** - FF88 956
  Angel Series I, II Oil/canvas (25.5x20.5cm 10x8in) Hong-Kong 2000

TSUI-HSING Hou 1949 [1]
- 🖌 **$6 100** - €6 760 - **£4 220** - FF44 340
  Cloud enveloping mountains beyond Oil/canvas (72.5x60.5cm 28x23in) Taipei 2001

TSUKIMARO Kitagawa XIX [7]
- ✏ **$4 800** - €4 650 - **£2 993** - FF30 500
  Flowers of the twelve Months Coloured inks/paper (132.5x335cm 52x131in) New-York 1999

TSUNENOBU Kano 1636-1713 [5]
- 🖌 **$9 680** - €10 226 - **£6 400** - FF67 078
  Fischerboote und Hütten am Ufer Indian ink (174x64cm 68x25in) Köln 2000
- 🗐 **$1 426** - €1 524 - **£950** - FF9 996
  Tiger seated on a Hillside beneath Bamboo Print (64.5x19.5cm 25x7in) London 2000

TSUNETOMI Kitano 1880-1947 [3]
- 🗐 **$3 500** - €3 025 - **£2 077** - FF19 841
  «The Heron Maiden» Woodcut (54x36.5cm 21x14in) New-York 1998

TSUTOMU Fuji 1948 [2]
- 🖌 **$10 780** - €10 514 - **£6 600** - FF68 970
  A Girl Oil/canvas (53x45.5cm 20x17in) Tokyo 1999

TUAILLON Louis 1862-1919 [25]
- 🗿 **$1 889** - €1 776 - **£1 170** - FF11 653
  Amazon Bronze (H31cm H12in) Warszawa 1999

T

TÜBBECKE Paul Wilhelm 1848-1924 **[61]**

$1 661 - €1 534 - **£1 034** - FF10 061
Heimkehrende Reisigsammlerin im Laubwald
Öl/Karton (46x53cm 18x20in) Rudolstadt-Thüringen
1999

$1 556 - €1 789 - **£1 099** - FF11 738
Sommerlandschaft bei Weimar unter hohem
Wolkenhimmel Öl/Karton (14.5x23.5cm 5x9in)
Bremen 2001

$187 - €215 - **£130** - FF1 408
Landschaftsskizze Gaberndorf Pencil (29x38cm
11x14in) Rudolstadt-Thüringen 2000

TUBILLA Julio XIX-XX **[2]**

$1 605 - €1 372 - **£963** - FF9 000
«Casa Codorniu» Affiche (107x84cm 42x33in) Paris
1998

TÜBKE Angelika 1935 **[16]**

$549 - €665 - **£383** - FF4 360
Winterlandschaft mit Kopfweiden (Hoben-
Wismar) Oil/canvas/panel (24x31cm 9x12in) Berlin
2000

TÜBKE Werner 1929 **[132]**

$27 488 - €32 339 - **£19 405** - FF212 127
«Mahnung» Tempera/canvas (200x150.5cm 78x59in)
Berlin 2001

$27 488 - €32 339 - **£19 405** - FF212 127
«Bildnis eines Usbekischen Bauern» Mixed
media/panel (89.5x61.5cm 35x24in) Berlin 2001

$19 296 - €21 168 - **£13 107** - FF138 851
Am Strand I Oil/canvas/panel (29.9x45.1cm 11x17in)
Berlin 2000

$1 269 - €1 534 - **£885** - FF10 061
Brustbildnis eines jungen Mannes (Mailand)
Pencil (33.7x23.9cm 13x9in) Berlin 2000

$169 - €204 - **£118** - FF1 341
Vorübergehende Lithographie (25.5x18cm 10x7in)
Berlin 2000

TUCHOLSKI Herbert 1886-1984 **[16]**

$183 - €204 - **£123** - FF1 341
Stralsunder Hafen Woodcut (15x24cm 5x9in) Satow
2000

TUCK Horace W., Harry XIX-XX **[29]**

$437 - €410 - **£270** - FF2 689
Broadland Landscape with Figures and Boats
Oil/canvas (35x40cm 14x16in) Aylsham, Norfolk 1999

$143 - €162 - **£100** - FF1 065
London Omnibus Passing St Paul's Cathedral
Watercolour (27x18.5cm 10x7in) London 2001

TUCKER Ada Elizabeth XIX-XX **[9]**

$3 200 - €2 833 - **£1 956** - FF18 582
Kittens at Play Oil/board (38x19cm 14x7in) New-
York 1999

TUCKER Albert Lee 1914-1999 **[105]**

$46 752 - €51 389 - **£29 960** - FF337 088
Ibis in Gippsland Forest Oil/board (120x150.5cm
47x59in) Melbourne 2000

$17 154 - €18 414 - **£11 481** - FF120 786
Masked Faun Oil/board (80x60cm 31x23in)
Melbourne 2000

$5 086 - €4 949 - **£3 130** - FF32 462
Brolga Oil/board (25.5x35cm 10x13in) Malvern,
Victoria 1999

$5 404 - €5 258 - **£3 326** - FF34 491
Landscape Gouache/paper (50x65cm 19x25in)
Melbourne 1999

$817 - €900 - **£543** - FF5 906
Night Image Color lithograph (49.5x58cm 19x22in)
Melbourne 2000

TUCKER Allen 1866-1939 **[61]**

$8 500 - €7 926 - **£5 272** - FF51 990
The red Hill Oil/canvas (63.5x76cm 25x29in) New-
York 1999

$1 200 - €1 119 - **£744** - FF7 339
Mountain Landscape Watercolour/paper (51x35cm
20x13in) New-York 1999

TUCKER Arthur 1864-1929 **[79]**

$607 - €567 - **£375** - FF3 722
Bridge of Garry, Perthshire Watercolour/paper
(17x27cm 6x10in) Kirkby-Lonsdale, Cumbria 1999

TUCKER Charles E. XIX-XX **[1]**

$11 229 - €11 316 - **£7 000** - FF74 225
Around the Bandstand, Dartmouth Oil/canvas
(90x51cm 35x20in) London 2000

TUCKER Edward c.1830-1910 **[173]**

$404 - €452 - **£281** - FF2 963
Fishing Boats off the Coast Watercolour/paper
(23x48cm 9x18in) Sydney 2001

TUCKER Frederick, Fred act.1873-? **[45]**

$497 - €562 - **£350** - FF3 689
Cobbled street scenes Watercolour/paper
(24x34.5cm 9x13in) Near Ely 2001

TUCKER Henry Carre 1812-1875 **[1]**

$3 307 - €3 094 - **£2 000** - FF20 295
View of a military Encampment, probably
Barrackpore, Calcutta Watercolour (23x29cm
9x11in) London 1999

TUCKER John Wallace 1808-1869 **[25]**

$1 047 - €1 028 - **£650** - FF6 746
On the River Lyn, North of Devon Oil/panel
(24x34cm 9x13in) Penzance, Cornwall 1999

TUCKER Mary B. XIX **[2]**

$9 000 - €9 611 - **£6 132** - FF63 047
Dark-Haired Man with Fringe Beard and Phi
Betta Kappa Key Watercolour (57x44.5cm 22x17in)
New-York 2001

TUCKER Tudor St. George 1862-1906 **[7]**

$18 181 - €19 454 - **£11 978** - FF127 611
The Grape Arbor Oil/canvas (54.5x79cm 21x31in)
Sydney 2000

$2 624 - €3 080 - **£1 852** - FF20 202
The Beach at Sandringham Oil/canvas (24.5x45cm
9x17in) Melbourne 2000

TUCKERMANN Ernst XIX-XX **[2]**

$3 443 - €3 997 - **£2 420** - FF26 218
Das Grabmal des Sidi Abder Rhamann Alger
Öl/Leinwand (63x92cm 24x36in) Wien 2001

TUCKSON John Anthony, Tony 1921-1973 **[74]**

$2 377 - €2 186 - **£1 449** - FF14 336
Lovers, No.13 Mixed media (53x73cm 20x28in)
Melbourne 1998

$3 590 - €3 369 - **£2 218** - FF22 097
Portrait of a Man Oil/canvas (47.5x27.5cm 18x10in)
Melbourne 1999

🖋 **$1 653** - €1 608 - **£1 017** - FF10 550
Two Women Watercolour/paper (25.5x39cm 10x15in)
Malvern, Victoria 1999

TUDGAY Frederick J. 1841-1921 [11]
🖋 **$9 022** - €10 009 - **£6 000** - FF65 655
**Blackwall Frigate Nile in Two Positions off the
White Cliffs of Dover** Oil/canvas (81x122cm
31x48in) London 2000

TUDGAY John (or I.) XIX [2]
🖋 **$30 000** - €35 679 - **£20 667** - FF234 039
The American Barque Scotland seen off Dover
Oil/canvas (58x89cm 23x35in) Bolton MA 2000

TUDOR Tasha McCready 1915 [12]
🖋 **$2 500** - €2 561 - **£1 554** - FF16 797
**Child in Field of Flowers with Floral Border
Surrounding a Quote** Watercolour/paper (27x22cm
11x9in) Hatfield PA 2000

TUDOR Thomas 1785-1855 [6]
🖋 **$743** - €648 - **£449** - FF4 252
**The Lake of Llanberis/A Sunset above a
Mountain on a Cloudy Night** Watercolour
(18.5x18.5cm 7x7in) London 1998

TUERENHOUT van Jef 1926 [171]
🖋 **$4 598** - €5 453 - **£3 344** - FF35 772
La reine Huile/toile (120x100cm 47x39in) Antwerpen
2001
🖋 **$4 284** - €4 462 - **£2 700** - FF29 268
Voodoo Queen Huile/panneau (110x81cm 43x31in)
Antwerpen 2000
🖋 **$4 050** - €3 914 - **£2 490** - FF24 390
Tête de Femme Bronze poli (H45cm H17in)
Antwerpen 1999
🖋 **$2 070** - €2 479 - **£1 420** - FF16 260
Voodoo Technique mixte/papier (99x78cm 38x30in)
Antwerpen 2000
🖋 **$253** - €248 - **£156** - FF1 626
Arendshoed Color lithograph (77x55cm 30x21in)
Lokeren 1999

TUERLINCKX Beaudouin 1873-1945 [12]
🖋 **$844** - €992 - **£600** - FF6 504
Jeune femme assise Bronze (H36cm H14in)
Bruxelles 2000

TUERLINCKX Louis 1820-1894 [4]
🖋 **$120 448** - €101 846 - **£72 026** - FF668 063
**A Maid seated in a Kitchen by a Table with
Flowers** Oil/panel (86.5x102.5cm 34x40in) Amsterdam
1998

TUFNELL Eric Erskine C. 1888-1978 [26]
🖋 **$698** - €592 - **£420** - FF3 881
The American Clipper «Surprise» Watercolour
(36x51.5cm 14x20in) London 1998

TÜGEL Tetjus Otto 1892-1972 [22]
🖋 **$1 548** - €1 841 - **£1 072** - FF12 074
Torfhümpelabtrag Mixed media/panel (45.5x64.5cm
17x25in) Bremen 2000
🖋 **$724** - €614 - **£432** - FF4 026
«Selbstbild» Ink (30.5x22cm 12x8in) Bremen 1998

TUKE Henry Scott 1858-1929 [200]
🖋 **$284 620** - €335 126 - **£200 000** - FF2 198 280
The Midday Rest (Sailors Yarning) Oil/canvas
(103x134cm 40x52in) London 2000

🖋 **$20 000** - €23 716 - **£13 760** - FF155 566
The Rowing Party Oil/canvas (27.5x63cm 10x24in)
New-York 2000
🖋 **$6 489** - €7 171 - **£4 500** - FF47 038
Portrait of a Young Woman in Blue Oil/panel
(35x25.5cm 13x10in) London 2001
🖋 **$2 451** - €2 709 - **£1 700** - FF17 770
«Porto Fino» Watercolour/paper (13.5x21cm 5x8in)
London 2001

TULLI Wladimiro 1922 [10]
🖋 **$4 750** - €4 924 - **£2 850** - FF32 300
«Il sole sull'aeroporto» Collage/carta (48x33cm
18x12in) Roma 1999

TUMARKIN Igael 1933 [111]
🖋 **$8 008** - €8 385 - **£5 032** - FF55 000
Composition Technique mixte (130x195cm 51x76in)
Versailles 2000
🖋 **$4 347** - €4 002 - **£2 609** - FF26 249
Independance Day Mixed media (81x65cm 31x25in)
Tel Aviv 1999
🖋 **$19 130** - €17 607 - **£11 482** - FF115 496
The Sun Gate Bronze (H190cm H74in) Tel Aviv 1999
🖋 **$2 400** - €2 488 - **£1 581** - FF16 322
Untitled Metal (H46cm H18in) Herzelia-Pituah 2000
🖋 **$500** - €537 - **£334** - FF3 520
The Four Elements Mixed media/paper (38x26.5cm
14x10in) Tel Aviv 2000
🖋 **$837** - €945 - **£589** - FF6 200
«Tu-Vat 69» Lithographie (55x75cm 21x29in) Paris
2001

TUNGA 1952 [9]
🖋 **$22 000** - €23 615 - **£14 722** - FF154 902
Peine (Capillary xiphopagus between us) Bronze
(64x23cm 25x9in) New-York 2000

TUNICK Spencer 1967 [3]
📷 **$16 000** - €18 100 - **£11 193** - FF118 728
Maine Gelatin silver print (152.5x127cm 60x50in)
New-York 2001

TUNINETTO Adriano 1930 [33]
🖋 **$175** - €181 - **£105** - FF1 190
Composizione astratta Olio/masonite (79x100cm
31x39in) Vercelli 2001

TUNNARD John 1900-1971 [127]
🖋 **$11 171** - €10 654 - **£6 800** - FF69 887
Power House Oil/board (56x35.5cm 22x13in) London
1999
🖋 **$9 787** - €9 490 - **£6 200** - FF62 253
«Bouquet for 1947» Oil/board (34.5x44.5cm
13x17in) London 1999
🖋 **$4 762** - €4 065 - **£2 800** - FF26 666
Untitled Watercolour/paper (38x56cm 14x22in)
London 1998
🖋 **$398** - €463 - **£280** - FF3 036
Abstract Landscape design Drypoint (26x35cm
10x14in) Lewes, Sussex 2001

TUNNICLIFFE Charles Frederick 1901-1979 [285]
🖋 **$4 482** - €4 070 - **£2 800** - FF26 695
Vixen and Cubs Oil/canvas (76.5x64cm 30x25in)
London 1999
🖋 **$1 586** - €1 633 - **£1 000** - FF10 713
Study of a Lapwing Watercolour/paper (11.5x8.5cm
4x3in) Lichfield, Staffordshire 2000

T

▥▥ **$375** - €403 - **£251** - FF2 645
Peasant Workers Etching (20x28cm 8x11in)
Cleveland OH 2000

TUNOLD Bernt W. 1877-1946 **[7]**
🖼 **$16 864** - €20 062 - **£11 664** - FF131 600
Interiör med kvinne Oil/canvas (130x100cm
51x39in) Oslo 2000
🖼 **$6 956** - €8 276 - **£4 811** - FF54 285
Våstemning, Selje Oil/canvas (68x95cm 26x37in)
Oslo 2000

TUPPER Gaspard Le Marchant 1826-1906 **[2]**
✎ **$4 758** - €4 996 - **£3 000** - FF32 774
Views in the West Indies Watercolour/paper
(17.5x52.5cm 6x20in) London 2000

TURCATO Giulio 1912-1995 **[497]**
🖼 **$9 000** - €9 330 - **£5 400** - FF61 200
Via lattea Tecnica mista (175x134cm 68x52in) Prato
2000
🖼 **$4 140** - €3 576 - **£2 760** - FF23 460
Senza titolo Tecnica mista (46x61cm 18x24in) Milano
1998
🖼 **$2 750** - €2 851 - **£1 650** - FF18 700
Composizione Idropittura/tela (41x27cm 16x10in)
Prato 2000
✎ **$800** - €829 - **£480** - FF5 440
Senza titolo Gouache/cartone (51x36cm 20x14in)
Prato 2000

TURCHI Alessandro l'Orbetto 1578-1649 **[27]**
🖼 **$210 000** - €200 461 - **£131 208** - FF1 314 936
David with the Head of Goliath Oil/canvas
(122x94cm 48x37in) New-York 1999
🖼 **$12 406** - €12 501 - **£7 732** - FF82 000
Vierge à l'enfant, Saint-Jean et Saint-François
Huile/panneau (48x23.5cm 18x9in) Lyon 2000
🖼 **$30 000** - €26 315 - **£18 216** - FF172 614
Christ supported by two Angels Ink (34.5x22cm
13x8in) New-York 1999

TUREK Harald Melrose 1968 **[4]**
▥▥ **$500** - €486 - **£305** - FF3 189
Dead Nature Print in colors (60x50cm 23x19in) Tel
Aviv 2000

TURGAN Clémence XIX **[1]**
✎ **$14 953** - €14 483 - **£9 405** - FF95 000
**Enée racontant à Didon les malheurs de Troie,
d'après P.N. Guérin** Gouache (30x40cm 11x15in)
Paris 1999

TURGEON Jean 1928 **[50]**
✎ **$250** - €213 - **£149** - FF1 400
Retour de pêche Aquarelle (13x31cm 5x12in) Brest
1998

TURINA Y AREAL Joaquín 1847-1903 **[9]**
🖼 **$9 600** - €9 010 - **£5 850** - FF59 100
Quevendo recitando ante Felipe IV Oleo/lienzo
(48x75cm 18x29in) Madrid 1999
🖼 **$9 690** - €10 211 - **£6 460** - FF66 980
**Salida triunfal por la puerta Príncipe de la
Maestranza de Sevilla** Oleo/lienzo (27x32cm
10x12in) Madrid 2000

TURK Gavin 1967 **[5]**
🖼 **$11 157** - €13 121 - **£8 000** - FF86 068
Title Painting (183x274cm 72x107in) London 2001

📷 **$6 496** - €7 029 - **£4 500** - FF46 104
Godot Type C color print (100x76cm 39x29in) London
2001

TÜRK Rudolf 1893-1944 **[5]**
🖼 **$4 219** - €4 090 - **£2 612** - FF26 831
Stiller Weiher Öl/Leinwand (58x72cm 22x28in) Graz
1999

TURLETTI Celestino 1845-1904 **[7]**
🖼 **$17 500** - €18 141 - **£10 500** - FF119 000
Piccolo venditore di funghi Olio/tela (48x35cm
18x13in) Milano 1999
🖼 **$15 500** - €16 068 - **£9 300** - FF105 400
Lo stagnino Olio/tela (46x34cm 18x13in) Milano
2000

TURNBULL William 1922 **[46]**
🖼 **$9 865** - €8 421 - **£5 800** - FF55 238
Untitled No.6 Oil/canvas (223x249cm 87x98in)
London 1998
🖼 **$2 794** - €2 655 - **£1 700** - FF17 415
Head Oil/canvas (36.5x28.5cm 14x11in) London 1999
⟋ **$47 817** - €51 328 - **£32 000** - FF336 691
Ulysses Bronze (H126.5cm H49in) London 2000
⟋ **$12 985** - €14 568 - **£9 000** - FF95 560
Head Bronze (H49cm H19in) London 2000
✎ **$2 629** - €2 499 - **£1 600** - FF16 391
Head Watercolour (55.5x45.5cm 21x17in) London
1999

TURNER Alfred M. 1852-1932 **[5]**
✎ **$1 100** - €1 283 - **£785** - FF8 416
Advertisement for Bucillag Needlepoint String
Watercolour/paper (55x44cm 22x17in) St. Louis MO
2000

TURNER Charles 1773-1857 **[13]**
✎ **$7 142** - €6 868 - **£4 400** - FF45 049
**Portrait of J.M.W. Turner in Profile in Black Coat,
Blue Waistcoat** Coloured chalks/paper (26.5x20.5cm
10x8in) London 1999
▥▥ **$256** - €276 - **£170** - FF1 811
**Wild Ducks, fifth plate from The British Feather
Game,after J.Barenger** Mezzotint (37x43cm
14x16in) Bath 2000

TURNER Charles Eddowes 1883-1965 **[22]**
▥▥ **$795** - €743 - **£480** - FF4 874
«Cunard to Canada» Poster (102x64cm 40x25in)
London 1999

TURNER Charles Henry 1848-1908 **[63]**
🖼 **$6 426** - €6 693 - **£4 239** - FF43 902
Harem Huile/toile (51x77cm 20x30in) Bruxelles 2000

TURNER Charles Yardley 1850-1919 **[12]**
🖼 **$4 000** - €4 294 - **£2 676** - FF28 164
Late Afternoon Oil/canvas (61x76cm 24x29in) San-
Francisco CA 2000

TURNER Daniel ?-1817 **[30]**
🖼 **$13 633** - €13 486 - **£8 500** - FF88 461
**River Thames with Somerset House, The
Temple and St.Paul's Cathedral** Oil/canvas
(44.5x61cm 17x24in) London 1999
🖼 **$3 236** - €3 035 - **£2 000** - FF19 908
Scene in Hyde Park Oil/panel (25x43cm 9x16in)
London 1999

TURNER Desmond 1923 **[4]**

$713 - €667 - **£440** - FF4 377
On Achill Oil/board (51x61cm 20x24in) Co. Kilkenny
1999

TURNER Edward XIX **[6]**

$4 824 - €4 941 - **£3 000** - FF32 412
A family Group in a Cottage Interior Oil/canvas
(59.5x89.5cm 23x35in) Billingshurst, West-Sussex 2000

TURNER Edward L. 1921 **[9]**

$500 - €467 - **£308** - FF3 063
Off Kauai in the Hawaiian Islands Watercolour
(38x56cm 15x22in) Detroit MI 1999

TURNER Francis Calcraft 1782/95-1846/65 **[56]**

$3 000 - €3 118 - **£1 890** - FF20 454
Old Ben Oil/canvas (43x53.5cm 16x21in) New-York
2000

$4 801 - €4 584 - **£3 000** - FF30 067
An unfortunate Encounter Oil/canvas (25.5x30.5cm
10x12in) London 1999

$1 064 - €1 143 - **£712** - FF7 496
Moore's Tally Ho! To the Sports Aquatint (53x69cm
20x27in) Dublin 2000

TURNER Frank act.1866-1874 **[2]**

$4 905 - €4 362 - **£3 000** - FF28 611
Winter/Autumn Oil/board (45x57.5cm 17x22in)
London 1999

$1 983 - €2 315 - **£1 400** - FF15 184
Blackberry Picking Oil/canvas/board (22.5x30cm
8x11in) London 2000

TURNER George, Geo 1843-1910 **[174]**

$5 069 - €5 882 - **£3 500** - FF38 584
The Way to the Harvest Field Oil/canvas
(61x101.5cm 24x39in) London 2000

$1 665 - €1 627 - **£1 056** - FF10 675
Sweet Water Lane, Idridgehay, Derbyshire
Oil/panel (30x46cm 11x18in) Cape Town 1999

TURNER Helen Maria 1858-1958 **[8]**

$40 000 - €34 175 - **£24 204** - FF224 176
The Bird Cage Oil/canvas (61.5x46.5cm 24x18in)
San-Francisco CA 1998

TURNER James Alfred 1850-1908 **[84]**

$7 780 - €8 726 - **£5 403** - FF57 237
«The Pride of the Morning» Oil/canvas (30.5x61cm
12x24in) Melbourne 2001

$3 502 - €3 859 - **£2 329** - FF25 314
The Watering Hole Oil/canvas (34.5x24.5cm 13x9in)
Melbourne 2000

TURNER Julius C. 1881-1948 **[12]**

$153 - €174 - **£104** - FF1 140
Berliner Stadtsilhouette Drypoint (26.6x35cm
10x13in) Hamburg 2000

TURNER Lincoln 1961 **[4]**

$1 700 - €1 467 - **£1 028** - FF9 622
Untitled 3 Mixed media (101.5x117x26cm
39x46x10in) Tel Aviv 1999

TURNER Michael XX **[18]**

$479 - €492 - **£300** - FF3 228
«Monaco, 9-10 mai» Poster (60x39cm 23x15in)
London 2000

TURNER OF OXFORD William 1789-1862 **[92]**

$3 500 - €4 066 - **£2 459** - FF26 674
**Lt. Col. Thomas Peers Williams' Grey Hunter
Pickles with a Dog** Oil/canvas (62x75cm 24x29in)
New-York 2001

$2 344 - €2 735 - **£1 631** - FF17 939
**Coastal Landscape with Cattle and Figures on
Horseback** Oil/canvas (22x33.5cm 8x13in) Melbourne
2000

$3 172 - €3 506 - **£2 200** - FF22 996
«New College Garden, Oxford» Watercolour
(25x32.5cm 9x12in) London 2001

TURNER Robert 1913 **[11]**

$3 500 - €3 626 - **£2 227** - FF23 783
Red Dome Ceramic (26x19.5cm 10x7in) New-York
2000

TURNER Ross Sterling 1847-1915 **[22]**

$3 500 - €3 020 - **£2 103** - FF19 807
Venetian Scene Watercolour/paper (44x66.5cm
17x26in) Boston MA 1998

TURNER William 1775-1851 **[215]**

$310 289 - €285 653 - **£190 000** - FF1 873 761
Dolbadern Castle Oil/panel (46.5x34cm 18x13in)
London 1998

$35 292 - €35 563 - **£22 000** - FF233 279
The Wells Children playing in an Interior Ink
(17.5x22.5cm 6x8in) London 2000

$355 - €333 - **£220** - FF2 186
Mt St Gothard, from the Liber Sudiorum Etching
(20.5x29cm 8x11in) London 1999

TURNER William Eddowes XIX **[13]**

$1 684 - €1 609 - **£1 050** - FF10 555
Cattle Feeding Oil/canvas (28x34cm 11x13in)
Rotherham 1999

TURNER William Henry M. XIX **[10]**

$7 000 - €6 792 - **£4 442** - FF44 555
The Horse Fair Oleo/lienzo (38x56cm 14x22in)
Buenos-Aires 1999

$1 600 - €1 763 - **£1 067** - FF11 563
Galopin Oleo/lienzo (35x45cm 13x17in) Buenos-Aires
2000

TURNER William Lakin 1867-1936 **[61]**

$2 241 - €2 406 - **£1 500** - FF15 782
**Ben Leder from the Meeting of the Waters,
Callander** Oil/canvas (46x61cm 18x24in) West-
Yorkshire 2000

$1 122 - €1 131 - **£700** - FF7 422
A Drover with Cattle in a Highland Landscape
Oil/panel (25.5x35.5cm 10x13in) London 2000

TURNERELLI Peter 1774-1839 **[8]**

$7 248 - €6 811 - **£4 500** - FF44 680
Bust of George III Marble (H46cm H18in) London
1999

TURNEY Winthrop Duthie 1884-1965 **[6]**

$15 000 - €14 893 - **£9 375** - FF97 689
Pigeon Hill Oil/canvas (51x61cm 20x24in) New-York
1999

TUROVSKY Mikhaïl 1933 **[9]**

$1 966 - €1 982 - **£1 225** - FF13 000
Nu japonais au divan Huile/toile (76x102cm
29x40in) Paris 2000

T

TURPIN DE CRISSÉ Lancelot Théodore 1782-1859 [30]

🖌 **$52 500** - €54 424 - **£31 500** - FF357 000
Scorcio del Foro Romano Olio/tela (130x99cm 51x38in) Roma 1999

🖌 **$2 629** - €2 287 - **£1 585** - FF15 000
Vue sur un lac Huile/papier (13.8x23.5cm 5x9in) Paris 1998

TURPIN Pierre Jean François 1775-1840 [5]

🖌 **$1 065** - €1 143 - **£712** - FF7 500
Étude d'une plante ombrélifère Aquarelle/vélin (28x21cm 11x8in) Paris 2000

TURRELL James 1943 [40]

🖌 **$7 000** - €7 961 - **£4 890** - FF52 220
Roden Crater Survey Network Mixed media (105.5x206.5cm 41x81in) Beverly-Hills CA 2000

🖌 **$4 777** - €5 336 - **£3 237** - FF35 000
Auto-anémones Huile/toile (100x100cm 39x39in) Paris 2000

🖌 **$5 632** - €6 649 - **£4 000** - FF43 613
White Crater Top Pencil (100x100cm 39x39in) London 2001

🖌 **$1 817** - €1 764 - **£1 131** - FF11 571
Squat Aquatinta (83.5x60cm 32x23in) Berlin 1999

📷 **$25 000** - €28 281 - **£17 490** - FF185 512
Untitled Photograph (48.5x37cm 19x14in) New-York 2001

TURTIAINEN Jorma 1936 [15]

🖌 **$597** - €673 - **£411** - FF4 412
Hästflickan Oil/canvas (100x88cm 39x34in) Helsinki 2000

TURZAK Charles 1899-1985 [12]

🖌 **$2 300** - €2 631 - **£1 599** - FF17 258
Drama Oil/canvas/board (99x60cm 39x24in) Cincinnati OH 2000

🖌 **$1 600** - €1 828 - **£1 126** - FF11 989
Allegorical Harvest Mural Study Watercolour/paper (9x48cm 3x19in) Pittsfield MA 2001

🖌 **$110** - €114 - **£72** - FF751
«Pink Hibiscus» Woodcut in colors (29x21cm 11x8in) Cleveland OH 2000

TUSCHER Carl Marcus 1705-1757 [3]

🖌 **$2 800** - €2 995 - **£1 909** - FF19 646
Monument of Plenty erected in Livorno for Arrival of Don Carlo Infant Ink (42x58cm 16x22in) New-York 2001

TUSEK Mitja 1961 [4]

🖌 **$4 184** - €4 491 - **£2 800** - FF29 460
Wax No.63 Mixed media (78x98x6.5cm 30x38x2in) London 2000

TUSET TUSET Salvador 1883-1951 [3]

🖌 **$2 700** - €3 003 - **£1 800** - FF19 700
Interior con mujer Oleo/lienzo (41x41cm 16x16in) Madrid 2000

TUSHINGHAM Sidney 1884-? [24]

🖌 **$126** - €109 - **£75** - FF714
Figures in an Elegant Garden Etching (19.5x29cm 7x11in) Glasgow 1998

TUSQUETS MAIGON Ramón 1838-1904 [38]

🖌 **$6 957** - €6 441 - **£4 200** - FF42 247
Playing with the Baby Oil/canvas (80x52.5cm 31x20in) London 1999

🖌 **$24 889** - €26 572 - **£17 000** - FF174 302
The Flamenco Guitarist Oil/board (34x24cm 13x9in) Billingshurst, West-Sussex 2001

🖌 **$1 064** - €1 141 - **£703** - FF7 486
Aguadora Acuarela/papel (38x25cm 14x9in) Barcelona 2000

TUTTER Karl 1883-1969 [27]

🖌 **$238** - €256 - **£159** - FF1 676
Tänzerinnen Sculpture (H23cm H9in) Stuttgart 2000

TUTTLE Richard 1941 [112]

🖌 **$65 000** - €56 270 - **£39 201** - FF369 109
Canvas Pale Purple Mixed media/canvas (127x127cm 50x50in) New-York 1998

🖌 **$260 000** - €291 219 - **£180 648** - FF1 910 272
«Yellow» Acrylic/wood (81x75cm 31x29in) New-York 2000

🖌 **$14 908** - €16 967 - **£10 475** - FF111 298
Light Bulb Piece Installation (248x84x14.5cm 97x33x5in) Zürich 2001

🖌 **$2 800** - €3 272 - **£1 999** - FF21 466
Ohne Titel Indian ink/paper (35x28cm 13x11in) Zürich 2001

🖌 **$5 500** - €6 035 - **£3 653** - FF39 585
Galisteo Paintings Woodcut in colors (40.5x30.5cm 15x12in) New-York 2000

TUTUNDJIAN Léon-Arthur 1906-1968 [179]

🖌 **$7 872** - €9 147 - **£5 610** - FF60 000
Nature morte Huile/toile (26.5x34.5cm 10x13in) Paris 2001

🖌 **$641** - €732 - **£445** - FF4 800
Composition Encre Chine (24.5x32.5cm 9x12in) Paris 2001

TUXEN Laurits 1853-1927 [250]

🖌 **$3 497** - €3 753 - **£2 340** - FF24 620
Kystparti fra Californien Oil/canvas (41x61.5cm 16x24in) Köbenhavn 2000

🖌 **$1 818** - €2 010 - **£1 261** - FF13 183
Aftenlys over heden Oil/canvas (20x35cm 7x13in) Vejle 2001

🖌 **$248** - €268 - **£171** - FF1 759
Portraet af en ung kvinde Charcoal (55x43cm 21x16in) Köbenhavn 2001

TUXEN Nicoline 1847-1931 [11]

🖌 **$733** - €739 - **£457** - FF4 846
Et glas med hvide nelliker Oil/canvas (50x43cm 19x16in) Köbenhavn 2000

TUXHORN Victor 1892-1964 [14]

🖌 **$139** - €133 - **£84** - FF872
Am Krug in Schildesche/Alte Häuser am Kirchplatz in Schildesche Radierung (22x29.3cm 8x11in) Bielefeld 1999

TUYMANS Luc 1958 [12]

🖌 **$95 000** - €105 531 - **£63 621** - FF692 236
Drops Oil/canvas (81.5x52.5cm 32x20in) New-York 2000

🖌 **$41 841** - €49 204 - **£30 000** - FF322 758
Ceiling Oil/canvas (30x50cm 11x19in) London 2001

🖌 **$2 400** - €2 322 - **£1 480** - FF15 232
Untitled Watercolour/paper (27.5x21cm 10x8in) New-York 1999

TUZINA Günter 1951 [9]
 $1 348 - €1 534 - £935 - FF10 061
«Form mit Form I» Öl/Papier (43.3x31.9cm 17x12in)
Hamburg 2000

TVC Television Cartoons XX [2]
 $3 200 - €3 544 - £2 170 - FF23 246
Yellow Submarine: John Lennon/Paul
McCartney/The Nowhere Man/Figures Gouache
(27x35cm 11x14in) New-York 2000

TWACHTMAN John Henry 1853-1902 [44]
 $170 000 - €145 245 - £102 051 - FF952 748
Autumn Mists Oil/canvas (64x76cm 25x29in) New-
York 1998
 $15 000 - €17 506 - £10 633 - FF114 834
Harbor Scene Oil/panel (12.5x14cm 4x5in) New-
York 2001
 $7 000 - €8 369 - £4 809 - FF54 894
Dutch Landscape Pastel/paper (31x31cm 12x12in)
Chicago IL 2000

TWEDDLE Isabel Hunter 1877-1945 [13]
 $1 452 - €1 512 - £912 - FF9 917
Tulips Oil/canvas/board (60x50cm 23x19in) Melbourne
2000

TWENTIETH CENTURY FOX XX [15]
 $482 - €463 - £300 - FF3 038
The Simpsons, Sunday Cruddy Sunday Gouache
(26.5x31.5cm 10x12in) London 1999

TWINING Yvonne 1907 [6]
 $400 - €437 - £257 - FF2 865
Autumn Colors Oil/board (40x50cm 16x20in) Mystic
CT 2000

TWOMBLY Cy 1928 [323]
 $500 000 - €580 145 - £345 200 - FF3 805 500
Untitled Mixed media/canvas (96x191cm 37x75in)
New-York 2000
 $200 000 - €224 015 - £138 960 - FF1 469 440
New York City Oil/canvas (68x142cm 26x55in) New-
York 2001
 $97 129 - €104 260 - £65 000 - FF683 904
Untitled Coloured pencils (50x59.5cm 19x23in)
London 2000
 $3 817 - €3 590 - £2 364 - FF23 552
Roman Notes II Lithograph (86.8x65.8cm 34x25in)
Stockholm 1999

TWORKOV Jack 1900-1982 [48]
 $36 000 - €41 770 - £24 854 - FF273 996
Choir Oil/canvas (114.5x106.5cm 45x41in) New-York
2000
 $22 000 - €24 144 - £14 165 - FF158 373
Untitled Oil/canvas (102x51cm 40x20in) New-York
2000
 $375 - €321 - £220 - FF2 105
«L.F-S.F E#4» Etching, aquatint (37x37cm 14x14in)
Boston MA 1998

TYDÉN Nils 1889-1976 [31]
 $395 - €339 - £231 - FF2 222
Stockholmsvy Oil/panel (23x32cm 9x12in)
Stockholm 1998

TYLER Bayard Henry 1855-1931 [20]
 $617 - €670 - £390 - FF4 398
Bergslandskap Oil/canvas (20x25cm 7x9in)
Stockholm 2000

TYLER James Gale 1855-1931 [92]
 $2 300 - €2 551 - £1 529 - FF16 736
Full Sail Oil/canvas (45x35cm 18x14in) Milford CT
2000
 $1 900 - €1 645 - £1 153 - FF10 788
Ship Rounding the Buoy Oil/board (15x25cm
6x10in) Mystic CT 1998
 $2 000 - €2 203 - £1 334 - FF14 454
American Fishing Schooners off the Coast
Watercolour/paper (26x44cm 10x17in) Portsmouth NH
2000

TYLER William Richardson 1825-1896 [9]
 $2 750 - €3 053 - £1 912 - FF20 029
Summer Day on the New England Coast
Oil/canvas/board (55x96cm 22x38in) Milford CT 2001
 $1 100 - €938 - £663 - FF6 155
Waiting for a Rescue Oil/canvas (20x35cm 8x14in)
Portsmouth NH 1998

TYNDALE Thomas Nicholson 1858-1936 [53]
 $656 - €580 - £640 - FF3 807
«Picking Flowers»/«Figures beside a River»
Watercolour/paper (33x23cm 12x9in) London 1999

TYNDALE Walter Fred. Roofe 1855-1943 [76]
 $1 317 - €1 407 - £900 - FF9 227
Market Scene, Italy Watercolour/paper (18x24cm
7x9in) Billingshurst, West-Sussex 2001

TYNDALL Robert XX [100]
 $856 - €747 - £518 - FF4 900
Noddy's Happy Magic Painting Book Watercolour
(30x23cm 11x9in) London 1998

TYNG Griswold 1883-? [3]
 $1 900 - €2 170 - £1 337 - FF14 237
Trout Fishing Oil/canvas (71x51cm 28x20in)
Cambridge MA 2001

TYRAHN Georg 1860-1917 [12]
 $5 000 - €4 331 - £3 066 - FF28 407
The Toy Sailboat Oil/canvas (33x40.5cm 12x15in)
New-York 1999

TYRRELL John J. XIX-XX [3]
 $2 241 - €2 406 - £1 500 - FF15 782
Shippping Off Great Yarmouth Watercolour/paper
(27x48cm 11x19in) Aylsham, Norfolk 2000

TYSHLER Alexandr Grigoriev. 1898-1980 [7]
 $39 841 - €46 289 - £28 000 - FF303 637
«Birthday No.5» Oil/canvas (72x50cm 28x19in)
London 2001
 $6 600 - €7 053 - £4 485 - FF46 263
Girl with a Still-Life Oil/canvas (27x22.5cm 10x8in)
Kiev 2001

TYSON Carroll Sargent Jnr. 1877-1956 [13]
 $16 000 - €17 402 - £10 547 - FF114 150
View of Blue Hill, Maine Oil/canvas (63.5x76cm
25x29in) Boston MA 2001

TYSON Dorsey Potter XX [17]
 $210 - €216 - £133 - FF1 416
Oriental Girl Etching in colors (15x10cm 6x4in)
Cincinnati OH 2000

TYSON John H. XIX-XX [10]
 $323 - €373 - £220 - FF2 444
Passing the Cottage Watercolour/paper (28x48cm
11x18in) Billingshurst, West-Sussex 2000

TYSON Nicola 1960 [10]
- $18 179 - €15 533 - **£11 000** - FF101 887
  Swimmer Oil/canvas (142.5x127cm 56x50in) London 1998
- $2 241 - €2 406 - **£1 500** - FF15 782
  Harlequin Gouache/paper (61x48cm 24x18in) London 2000

TYSSENS Jan Baptiste XVII [5]
- $5 284 - €4 991 - **£3 296** - FF32 742
  Officer smoking a pipe by a grotto, with armour, a drum and a flag Oil/canvas (56.5x81.5cm 22x32in) Amsterdam 1999

TYTGAT Edgard 1879-1957 [272]
- $9 288 - €8 924 - **£5 724** - FF58 536
  L'automne dans mon jardin Huile/toile (81x65cm 31x25in) Bruxelles 1999
- $5 858 - €4 873 - **£3 440** - FF31 965
  La baigneuse Oil/canvas (27x41cm 10x16in) Amsterdam 1998
- $1 210 - €1 115 - **£729** - FF7 317
  Le couple dans la peinture Technique mixte/papier (28x22cm 11x8in) Antwerpen 1999
- $236 - €273 - **£162** - FF1 788
  Saint Nicolas Gravure bois (29.5x20.5cm 11x8in) Liège 2000

TYTGAT Médard I 1871-1948 [38]
- $406 - €372 - **£247** - FF2 439
  Jeune patriote Huile/carton (70x38cm 27x14in) Bruxelles 1999

TYTLER Robert C.& Harriet C 1818/?-1872/1907 [1]
- $8 500 - €9 786 - **£5 800** - FF64 192
  Ganges River Scene Photograph (40x21cm 15x8in) New-York 2000

U

UAB SANASEN 1935 [8]
- $3 471 - €3 224 - **£2 145** - FF21 151
  The Shipwreck Oil/canvas (59x79cm 23x31in) Bangkok 1999

UBAC Raoul 1910-1985 [204]
- $6 426 - €7 049 - **£4 364** - FF46 240
  Torse étude 4 Oil/panel (65x54cm 25x21in) Luzern 2000
- $3 785 - €3 964 - **£2 379** - FF26 000
  Ardoise Relief (24.5x32cm 9x12in) Versailles 2000
- $2 852 - €2 668 - **£1 727** - FF17 500
  Labour d'automne Gouache/papier (49x65cm 19x25in) Nantes 1999
- $193 - €229 - **£136** - FF1 500
  Mois du cœur Lithographie (55x75cm 21x29in) Nîmes 2000
- $5 728 - €5 316 - **£3 500** - FF34 868
  Solarised Portrait Study Silver print (29x22.5cm 11x8in) London 1999

UBALDINI IL PULIGO Domenico Bartolomeo 1492-1527 [19]
- $40 590 - €34 301 - **£24 142** - FF225 000
  La Vierge à l'Enfant avec Saint-Jean Baptiste Huile/panneau (73x51cm 28x20in) Poitiers 1998
- $19 573 - €18 307 - **£12 000** - FF120 084
  Lady, Head and Shoulders, with a Garland of Flowers in her Hair Oil/panel (42x33cm 16x12in) London 1998

UBBELOHDE Otto 1867-1922 [175]
- $1 966 - €1 841 - **£1 218** - FF12 074
  Schneebedeckte Landschaft mit Kirche, dahinter ein Friedhof Indian ink (26.7x22.5cm 10x8in) Heidelberg 1999
- $386 - €460 - **£275** - FF3 018
  Heidelandschaft mit unterschiedlichen Bäumen Radierung (33.5x43.5cm 13x17in) Merzhausen 2000

UBEDA Agustín 1925 [193]
- $2 076 - €2 287 - **£1 384** - FF15 000
  Nature morte à la pastèque Huile/toile (50x65cm 19x25in) Deauville 2000
- $1 430 - €1 562 - **£910** - FF10 244
  Vista nocturna de ciudad Oleo/lienzo (33x41cm 12x16in) Madrid 2000
- $230 - €216 - **£144** - FF1 418
  «Eva nace» Dibujo (26x20cm 10x7in) Madrid 1999

UBERTALLI Romollo 1871-1928 [11]
- $1 750 - €1 814 - **£1 050** - FF11 900
  Alberi d'autunno Matita (39x28cm 15x11in) Milano 1999

UBERTINI BACCIACCA Francesco 1494/95-1557 [6]
- $564 720 - €641 741 - **£390 000** - FF4 209 543
  The Madonna and Child with Saint John the Baptist Seated Among Rocks Oil/panel (146x114.5cm 57x45in) London 2000
- $120 000 - €128 363 - **£81 816** - FF842 004
  Saint Sebastian Oil/panel (131.5x55cm 51x21in) New-York 2001

UBIÑA Senen 1923 [9]
- $159 - €168 - **£106** - FF1 103
  Bailaora Acuarela, gouache/papel (47x36cm 18x14in) Madrid 2000

UBOLDI Carlo 1821-c.1884 [1]
- $23 000 - €21 543 - **£14 140** - FF141 314
  Young Girl seated with Cat Marble (H81.5cm H32in) New-York 1999

UCELAY José María 1903 [2]
- $2 480 - €2 403 - **£1 560** - FF15 760
  Calle de París Dibujo (31x44cm 12x17in) Madrid 1999

UCHATIUS von Maria, Mitzi 1882-1958 [6]
- $2 523 - €2 543 - **£1 516** - FF16 684
  Landschaft Print in colors (25x21.5cm 9x8in) Wien 2000

UCHERMANN Karl 1855-1940 [18]
- $5 775 - €6 867 - **£4 114** - FF45 045
  Apporterende hund Oil/canvas (107x150cm 42x59in) Oslo 2000

UDALTSOVA Nadezhda A. 1886-1961 [12]
- $8 400 - €8 976 - **£5 708** - FF58 880
  Summer, Cottage Oil/canvas (50x40.5cm 19x15in) Kiev 2001
- $3 736 - €4 011 - **£2 500** - FF26 308
  Composition Watercolour (36x24.5cm 14x9in) London 2000

UDEN van Lucas 1595-1672 [94]
- $13 717 - €12 840 - **£8 500** - FF84 227
  River Landscape with Christ Healing the Paralytic, a Village beyond Oil/panel (36x56cm 14x22in) London 1999
- $6 877 - €6 377 - **£4 200** - FF41 832
  Shepherds and their Flock on a Hillside, an Extensive Valley Landscape Oil/panel (25x35cm 9x13in) London 1998

$28 000 - €29 993 - **£19 121** - FF196 744
Wooded Landscape with a House Beside a River Ink (16x25.5cm 6x10in) New-York 2001

📷 $275 - €285 - **£165** - FF1 870
Veduta di uno stagno Acquaforte (9x13cm 3x5in) Firenze 2000

UDERZO Albert 1927 **[30]**

✏️ $814 - €854 - **£515** - FF5 600
Belloy, pl.11 Encre Chine/papier (60x50cm 23x19in) Paris 2000

📷 $287 - €335 - **£202** - FF2 195
Astérix en Corse Sérigraphie (60x80cm 23x31in) Bruxelles 2001

UDINE da Giovanni Nanni 1487-1561 **[2]**

✏️ $74 715 - €80 200 - **£50 000** - FF526 080
Two Studies of the Head of an Eagle Watercolour/paper (19.5x22.5cm 7x8in) London 2000

UECKER Günther 1930 **[305]**

$48 465 - €47 039 - **£30 176** - FF308 558
Spirale Mixed media/panel (120x120cm 47x47in) Berlin 1999

$19 000 - €19 827 - **£11 983** - FF130 055
Hedgehog Mixed media/canvas (87x87cm 34x34in) New-York 2000

$1 472 - €1 452 - **£906** - FF9 525
Nagelreief Oil/wood (16.5x11.5cm 6x4in) Amsterdam 1999

$4 552 - €4 346 - **£2 844** - FF28 508
Nagel Metal (H177cm H69in) Köln 1999

$6 936 - €8 181 - **£4 892** - FF53 662
«Poetische Reihe Sylt» Relief (48x44x10cm 18x17x3in) Köln 2001

$675 - €767 - **£462** - FF5 030
Bleistiftführende Hand, den Namen Uecker schreibend Pencil/paper (30.5x21cm 12x8in) Berlin 2000

📷 $300 - €358 - **£214** - FF2 347
Nägel Print (60x50cm 23x19in) Köln 2000

UELLIGER Karl 1914-1993 **[32]**

$2 094 - €2 311 - **£1 385** - FF15 157
Blumen Acryl/Leinwand (90x80cm 35x31in) St. Gallen 2000

✏️ $1 103 - €1 064 - **£692** - FF6 981
Die Zauberschwestern, von Wilhelm Busch Tempera/papier (55x70cm 21x27in) St. Gallen 1999

UELSMANN Jerry N. 1934 **[87]**

📷 $1 000 - €1 073 - **£669** - FF7 041
Superimposed Composition with Hand, Nude, Vegetable Photograph (20x25cm 8x10in) Yonkers NY 2000

UEMAE Chiyu 1920 **[1]**

$10 500 - €10 885 - **£6 300** - FF71 400
Senza titolo Olio/tavola (183x93cm 72x36in) Prato 2000

UFER Walter 1876-1936 **[41]**

$100 000 - €116 709 - **£70 890** - FF765 560
«February Sun» Oil/canvas (40.5x51cm 15x20in) New-York 2001

$15 000 - €13 848 - **£9 225** - FF90 838
Off the Plaza Oil/canvas/board (27.5x32cm 10x12in) New-York 1999

✏️ $1 200 - €1 369 - **£833** - FF8 983
Seated Nude/Michallet/Ingres d'Arches Charcoal/paper (60x43cm 24x17in) St. Louis MO 2000

UFERT Oskar 1876-? **[6]**

$2 749 - €2 514 - **£1 679** - FF16 494
Kneeling woman Bronze (H43cm H17in) New-York 1998

UFFELEN van Alfons A. 1895-1983 **[248]**

📷 $117 - €130 - **£79** - FF850
Fontaine, Anvers Photo (28x19.5cm 11x7in) Paris 2000

UGARTE BERECIARTU Ignacio 1858-1914 **[3]**

$10 080 - €10 812 - **£6 660** - FF70 920
Picador herido Oleo/lienzo (97x67cm 38x26in) Madrid 2000

UGLOW Euan 1932 **[16]**

$6 829 - €7 935 - **£4 800** - FF52 052
Figures in a Park Oil/panel (24.5x30cm 9x11in) London 2001

✏️ $4 268 - €4 959 - **£3 000** - FF32 532
Reclining Nude Pencil/paper (18.5x26.5cm 7x10in) London 2001

UHDE von Fritz 1848-1911 **[58]**

$17 967 - €18 407 - **£11 088** - FF120 740
Lachendes Mädchen Öl/Leinwand (147x118cm 57x46in) Düsseldorf 2000

$3 668 - €4 090 - **£2 466** - FF26 831
Männlicher Studienkopf Oil/panel (53x35cm 20x13in) Köln 2000

$15 424 - €17 244 - **£10 735** - FF113 110
Die Töchter des Künstlers im Garten (The Daughters of the Artist) Oil/canvas (31x40cm 12x15in) Amsterdam 2001

$625 - €716 - **£430** - FF4 621
Bildnis einer Bäuerin mit Kopftuch Watercolour (39.9x27.2cm 15x10in) München 2000

UHDEN Maria 1892-1918 **[24]**

📷 $241 - €230 - **£150** - FF1 509
Ruhende Zigeuner Woodcut (25.5x20cm 10x7in) Berlin 1999

UHL Louis 1860-1909 **[5]**

$2 504 - €2 907 - **£1 760** - FF19 068
Nymphen und Faune Öl/Leinwand (73x103cm 28x40in) Wien 2001

UHLE Bernard 1847-1930 **[1]**

$1 994 - €2 319 - **£1 400** - FF15 210
Shared Moment Oil/canvas (40.5x30.5cm 15x12in) London 2001

UHLICH Fritz 1893-1973 **[3]**

📷 $800 - €800 - **£488** - FF5 245
«Wank-Bahn, Garmisch-Patenkirchen» Poster (119x86cm 47x34in) New-York 2000

UHLIG Max 1937 **[197]**

$3 705 - €4 410 - **£2 647** - FF28 927
Portrait Öl/Leinwand (140x130.5cm 55x51in) Berlin 2000

$3 659 - €4 101 - **£2 548** - FF26 898
Georgshöhe Krukow Öl/Leinwand (70x171cm 27x67in) Berlin 2001

$634 - €767 - **£443** - FF5 030
Ohne Titel (Landschaftsformation) Aquarell/Papier (59.5x69.2cm 23x27in) Berlin 2000

📷 $101 - €123 - **£70** - FF804
Bildnis mit Schatten Lithographie (40.5x53cm 15x20in) Berlin 2000

UHLMAN Fred 1901-1985 **[99]**

$1 334 - €1 503 - **£920** - FF9 861
White Lighthouse against a Grey Sky Oil/canvas (43x55cm 16x21in) London 2000

$1 093 - €1 243 - **£750** - FF8 154
Shells and Bottles Oil/board (28x38.5cm 11x15in) London 2000

UHLMANN Hans 1900-1975 **[65]**
$12 922 - €12 782 - **£8 057** - FF83 847
Tänzerische Figuration Bronze (51.2x26x6cm
20x10x2in) Berlin 1999
$1 095 - €1 227 - **£762** - FF8 049
Paar Ink (42.5x35.5cm 16x13in) Berlin 2001
$258 - €256 - **£161** - FF1 676
Reiter Lithographie (24x32.7cm 9x12in) Berlin 1999

UHRDIN Sam 1886-1964 **[136]**
$1 545 - €1 667 - **£1 037** - FF10 932
Kulla som kärnar smör Oil/canvas (50x62cm
19x24in) Stockholm 2000

UITZ Béla 1887-1972 **[5]**
$6 720 - €6 464 - **£4 160** - FF42 400
Woman in a White Dress Mixed media/paper
(53x25.5cm 20x10in) Budapest 1999

UJHAZY Ferenc 1827-1921 **[9]**
$22 000 - €21 633 - **£13 750** - FF141 900
Romantic Landscape with Figures Oil/canvas
(109x172cm 42x67in) Budapest 1999
$5 600 - €5 506 - **£3 500** - FF36 120
In the Storm Oil/canvas (70x50cm 27x19in)
Budapest 1999

UKIL Sarada Charan 1890-1940 **[7]**
$3 571 - €3 432 - **£2 200** - FF22 513
Radha Krishna Watercolour/paper (39.5x23.5cm
15x9in) London 1999

ULBRICH Hugo 1867-? **[7]**
$329 - €307 - **£204** - FF2 012
Breslauer Rathaus Radierung (52x75cm 20x29in)
Kempten 1999

ULFT van der Jacob 1627-1689 **[45]**
$2 359 - €2 269 - **£1 453** - FF14 883
**Italianate Landscape with Trees Blowing in the
Wind, and a Castle** Ink (19x29cm 7x11in)
Amsterdam 1999

ULIANOV Nikolai Pavlovich 1875-1949 **[2]**
$3 220 - €3 041 - **£2 000** - FF19 949
Fabulous Bird Watercolour, gouache/paper
(39.5x52.5cm 15x20in) London 1999

ULISSE 1957 **[49]**
$550 - €570 - **£330** - FF3 740
Il pozzo di San Patrizio Olio/tavola (50x70cm
19x27in) Vercelli 2000
$240 - €311 - **£180** - FF2 040
Le danze Olio/tavola (30x40cm 11x15in) Vercelli 2001

ULIVELLI Cosimo 1625-1704 **[2]**
$7 799 - €7 632 - **£5 000** - FF50 061
**God the Father Appearing to the Virgin with St
John the Baptist** Ink (33x24cm 12x9in) London 1999

ULLBERG Kent 1945 **[18]**
$737 - €755 - **£455** - FF4 951
Falk Bronze (H45cm H17in) Stockholm 2000

ULLIK Hugo 1838-1881 **[22]**
$2 023 - €1 913 - **£1 260** - FF12 551
Hill Kunĕticka hora Oil/canvas (56x72cm 22x28in)
Praha 2000
$1 047 - €1 125 - **£701** - FF7 378
Voralpenlandschaft Oil/panel (12.5x25cm 4x9in)
Stuttgart 2000

ULLMANN Josef 1870-1922 **[39]**
$1 762 - €1 667 - **£1 098** - FF10 937
Cour d'eau, Prosenice Huile/carton (51x68cm
20x26in) Praha 2001

$1 011 - €957 - **£630** - FF6 275
Paysage d'hiver Huile/carton (48.5x32.5cm 19x12in)
Praha 2000

ULLMANN Julius 1861-1918 **[3]**
$3 738 - €4 360 - **£2 640** - FF28 602
Marktszene in der Altstadt Salzburg Öl/Karton
(23x33cm 9x12in) Salzburg 2000

ULLMANN Robert 1903-1966 **[22]**
$1 038 - €1 227 - **£736** - FF8 049
Badende Porcelain (H50.5cm H19in) Ahlden 2000

ULLRICH Josef 1815-1867 **[1]**
$4 763 - €5 113 - **£3 188** - FF33 539
In der Wartehalle Öl/Leinwand (60x76cm 23x29in)
München 2000

ULMANN Benjamin 1829-1884 **[5]**
$39 575 - €38 112 - **£24 625** - FF250 000
**Thiers salué du titre de «Libérateur du territoi-
re», 16 juin** Huile/panneau (52.5x81cm 20x31in)
Montfort L'Amaury 1999

ULMANN Doris 1882-1934 **[66]**
$1 600 - €1 505 - **£990** - FF9 870
Gullah Family Photograph (20.5x15.5cm 8x6in) New-
York 1999

ULNITZ Emil C. 1856-1933 **[49]**
$1 088 - €942 - **£600** - FF6 181
Opstilling med melon, druer og hindbaerranker
Oil/canvas (40x50cm 15x19in) Köbenhavn 1998
$533 - €537 - **£332** - FF3 524
Blomstrende rödtjörn Oil/canvas (27x39cm
10x15in) Köbenhavn 2000

ULREICH Eduard Buk 1889-1962 **[10]**
$1 000 - €1 120 - **£694** - FF7 347
«Illustration for Vogue Magazine (Cover)»
Watercolour (45x35cm 18x14in) Cincinnati OH 2001

ULRICH Charles Frederic 1858-1908 **[9]**
$28 000 - €24 143 - **£16 629** - FF158 370
The Letter Oil/panel (81x45cm 32x18in) Bethesda
MD 1998
$27 500 - €32 095 - **£19 494** - FF210 529
Amateur Etcher (an Etcher in his Studio)
Oil/panel (30.5x22cm 12x8in) New-York 2001

ULRICH Henry 1572-1621 **[2]**
$943 - €1 125 - **£672** - FF7 378
Die antiken Weltreiche Kupferstich (11.2x13.5cm
4x5in) Berlin 2000

ULRICH Johann Jakob 1798-1877 **[37]**
$4 176 - €4 065 - **£2 566** - FF26 663
Spielende Füchse Öl/Leinwand (64x52.5cm
25x20in) Zürich 1999
$742 - €847 - **£523** - FF5 558
Meeresküste mit Felsbrocken Öl/Papier (30x44cm
11x17in) Bern 2001

ULRICH Wilhelm 1905-1977 **[17]**
$514 - €581 - **£347** - FF3 813
Im Prater Aquarell/Papier (67x65cm 26x25in) Wien
2000

ULTVEDT Per Olof 1927 **[29]**
$1 762 - €1 965 - **£1 224** - FF12 888
Snurra Mobile (61x61cm 24x24in) Stockholm 2001

ULVING Even 1869-1943 **[83]**
$2 525 - €2 858 - **£1 766** - FF18 749
Fra Hvaler Oil/canvas (36x50cm 14x19in) Oslo 2001
$4 676 - €3 982 - **£2 793** - FF26 118
Fra Lofoten Oil/canvas (42x38cm 16x14in) Oslo 1998

ULYSSE-BESNARD Jean Jude ?-1884 **[1]**
🖼 **$2 032** - €2 287 - **£1 399** - FF15 000
　　La fuite des voleurs Huile/toile (33x46cm 12x18in)
　　Barbizon 2000

UMBACH Jonas 1624-1693 **[40]**
▦ **$193** - €215 - **£134** - FF1 408
　　Landschaft mit der Felsbrücke Radierung
　　(11.5x8cm 4x3in) Heidelberg 2001

UMBEHR Otto 1902-1980 **[81]**
📷 **$2 726** - €2 646 - **£1 697** - FF17 356
　　Ohne Titel (Maske von Isle Fehling) Vintage gela-
　　tin silver print (17.8x13cm 7x5in) Berlin 1999

UMBERG Günter 1942 **[7]**
📷 **$2 059** - €1 999 - **£1 282** - FF13 113
　　Ohne Titel Mixed media/panel (37x30cm 14x11in)
　　Berlin 1999

UMBERT Pedro Antonio 1786-1818 **[2]**
🖼 **$13 824** - €12 974 - **£8 640** - FF85 104
　　La Inmaculada Concepción Oleo/lienzo
　　(165x120cm 64x47in) Palma de Mallorca 1999
🖼 **$7 680** - €7 208 - **£4 800** - FF47 280
　　La Virgen orante Oleo/lienzo (79x60cm 31x23in)
　　Palma de Mallorca 1999

UMEHARA Ryuzaburo 1888-1986 **[15]**
🖼 **$60 000** - €58 121 - **£37 422** - FF381 252
　　Asamayama (Mount Asama) Oil/canvas
　　(38x45.5cm 14x17in) New-York 1999
🖼 **$15 992** - €15 399 - **£10 000** - FF101 013
　　The Bathers Oil/canvas/board (26x21cm 10x8in)
　　London 1999
🖊 **$44 100** - €43 013 - **£27 000** - FF282 150
　　Cannes Watercolour, gouache/paper (30.5x43.5cm
　　12x17in) Tokyo 1999

UMETARO Azechi 1902-1999 **[10]**
▦ **$160** - €164 - **£100** - FF1 073
　　Man and bird Woodcut in colors (39x26cm 15x10in)
　　Cleveland OH 2000

UMGELTER Hermann Ludwig 1891-1962 **[93]**
🖼 **$1 490** - €1 431 - **£924** - FF9 390
　　Herbstliche Alblandschaft mit Spaziergänger
　　Öl/Leinwand (69x96cm 27x37in) Hildrizhausen 1999
🖼 **$885** - €844 - **£540** - FF5 533
　　Schluchsee im Schwarzwald Öl/Leinwand/Karton
　　(25x32cm 9x12in) Stuttgart 1999
🖊 **$214** - €256 - **£153** - FF1 676
　　Am Buberlesbach Aquarell/Papier (44x35cm
　　17x13in) Hildrizhausen 2000

UMLAUF Charles 1911 **[3]**
🗿 **$3 700** - €3 351 - **£2 213** - FF21 984
　　Reclining woman Terracotta (41x77cm 16x30in)
　　New-Windsor NY 1998

UMLAUF Johann 1825-1916 **[5]**
🖼 **$1 640** - €1 687 - **£1 040** - FF11 067
　　Elisabeth, Kaiserin von Österreich-Sissi
　　Öl/Leinwand (44x33cm 17x12in) Bamberg 2000

UNBEREIT Paul 1884-1937 **[46]**
🖼 **$939** - €1 090 - **£660** - FF7 150
　　Fischer im Waldbach Oil/board (51.5x41.5cm
　　20x16in) Wien 2001
🖼 **$2 422** - €2 325 - **£1 520** - FF15 254
　　Motiv aus der Wachau Oil/panel (36x30cm 14x11in)
　　Wien 1999

UNCETA Y LOPEZ Marcelino 1836-1905 **[40]**
🖼 **$3 355** - €3 304 - **£2 090** - FF21 670
　　Militares a caballo Oleo/cartón (15x11cm 5x4in)
　　Madrid 1999

🖊 **$473** - €557 - **£334** - FF3 656
　　Caballo Acuarela/papel (18x26cm 7x10in) Madrid
　　2000

UNCINI Giuseppe 1929 **[29]**
🖼 **$640** - €829 - **£480** - FF5 440
　　Struttura Tempera/cartone (56.5x75.5cm 22x29in)
　　Vercelli 2001
🗿 **$6 000** - €6 220 - **£3 600** - FF40 800
　　Spazi di ferro n.51 Fer (190x65x50cm 74x25x19in)
　　Milano 2000
🗿 **$2 250** - €2 332 - **£1 350** - FF15 300
　　Spazzi di ferro n.119 Métal (41x24x16cm 16x9x6in)
　　Prato 2000

UNDERHILL Frederick Thomas c.1847-1897 **[10]**
🖊 **$421** - €408 - **£260** - FF2 676
　　Young Boy Reading by the Fireplace Watercolour
　　(26x20cm 10x7in) London 1999

UNDERWOOD & UNDERWOOD Bert & Elmer
1864/62-? **[21]**
📷 **$317** - €307 - **£199** - FF2 012
　　West Side Motor Express Highway im Bau
　　Photograph (20.5x25.5cm 8x10in) München 1999

UNDERWOOD Leon 1890-1975 **[93]**
🖼 **$1 682** - €1 405 - **£1 000** - FF9 216
　　Portrait of a Woman Oil/canvas (81x54.5cm 31x21in)
　　London 1998
🖼 **$3 085** - €3 043 - **£1 900** - FF19 964
　　Banana Launch Oil/canvas (40.5x30.5cm 15x12in)
　　London 1999
🗿 **$8 652** - €9 561 - **£6 000** - FF62 718
　　«The Chosen» Bronze (52x20cm 20x7in) London
　　2001
🖊 **$1 136** - €1 121 - **£700** - FF7 355
　　Study for Piping down the Valleys Charcoal/paper
　　(56x38cm 22x14in) London 1999
▦ **$259** - €253 - **£160** - FF1 662
　　Nude study Etching (25x15.5cm 9x6in) London 1999

UNDERWOOD Thomas Richard 1772-1836 **[4]**
🖊 **$1 332** - €1 585 - **£950** - FF10 397
　　Hurstmonceaux Castle, Sussex Watercolour
　　(24.5x19cm 9x7in) London 2000

UNG MONG XX [3]
🖼 **$5 021** - €4 680 - **£3 034** - FF30 696
　　**Citadelle vue de la rivière des Parfums/La riviè-
　　re des Parfums à Hué** Oil/canvas (50x80cm
　　19x31in) Singapore 1999

UNG NO LEE 1904-1989 **[5]**
🖼 **$16 000** - €18 763 - **£11 417** - FF123 078
　　Ideograms Oil/canvas (135x69cm 53x27in) New-York
　　2000
🖊 **$5 000** - €5 863 - **£3 568** - FF38 462
　　Ideograms Gouache/paper (71x46cm 27x18in) New-
　　York 2000

UNG Per 1933 **[8]**
🗿 **$5 250** - €6 243 - **£3 740** - FF40 950
　　Stående akt med lite barn Bronze (42x11x9cm
　　16x4x3in) Oslo 2000

UNGER Carl 1915-1995 **[66]**
🖼 **$24 880** - €29 069 - **£17 480** - FF190 680
　　Flug II Öl/Leinwand (114.5x190cm 45x74in) Wien
　　2000
🖼 **$15 550** - €18 168 - **£10 925** - FF119 175
　　Attersee mit Schloss Kammer Öl/Leinwand
　　(75x79cm 29x31in) Wien 2000
🖊 **$3 732** - €4 360 - **£2 622** - FF28 602
　　Waldkauz Watercolour (40.1x31.9cm 15x12in) Wien
　　2000

U

UNGER Hans 1872-1936 [37]

$12 735 - €10 901 - **£7 665** - FF71 505
Portrait der Ehefrau des Künstlers Öl/Leinwand (208x80cm 81x31in) Wien 1998

$309 - €286 - **£186** - FF1 878
Knorriger alter Baum in einem toskanischen Garten Aquarell (36.5x27.5cm 14x10in) Heidelberg 1999

$139 - €158 - **£97** - FF1 039
Frauenkopf Lithographie (37x28cm 14x11in) Berlin 2001

UNGER Wolfgang Heinz 1929 [63]

$569 - €486 - **£343** - FF3 185
«Gartencafe mit Personenstaffage» Öl/Leinwand/Karton (47x36.5cm 18x14in) Kempten 1998

UNGERER Tomi, Jean-Thomas 1931 [48]

$778 - €928 - **£555** - FF6 089
Variation zu Babylon Nr.93: Psychiatrist Pencil/paper (28x21.5cm 11x8in) Hamburg 2000

$219 - €204 - **£132** - FF1 341
Finish Farblithographie (39.5x29.6cm 15x11in) Hamburg 1999

UNGERN Ragnar 1885-1955 [40]

$2 305 - €2 018 - **£1 396** - FF13 234
Till havs Oil/panel (43x42cm 16x16in) Helsinki 1998

$1 201 - €1 009 - **£706** - FF6 616
Getpors Oil/canvas (30x48cm 11x18in) Helsinki 1998

UNGEWITTER Hugo 1869-c.1944 [25]

$2 932 - €2 669 - **£1 800** - FF17 508
A Hunter with his Horse and Dogs Oil/canvas (92x126cm 36x49in) London 1999

UNIA Sergio 1943 [4]

$6 500 - €6 738 - **£3 900** - FF44 200
Il mattino, Rossana Bronzo (H66cm H25in) Torino 2000

$400 - €415 - **£240** - FF2 720
Nudo con calze Sanguina/carta (43x30cm 16x11in) Torino 2001

UNKER d' Carl 1828-1866 [12]

$5 227 - €4 887 - **£3 220** - FF32 058
Interiör med figurscen Oil/canvas (55x64.5cm 21x25in) Stockholm 1999

UNOLD Max 1885-1964 [136]

$2 126 - €2 045 - **£1 310** - FF13 415
Birnen in roter Schale Öl/Leinwand (54x64cm 21x25in) Köln 1999

$829 - €715 - **£498** - FF4 693
Stilleben Oil/panel (42.3x31.4cm 16x12in) München 1998

$384 - €460 - **£264** - FF3 018
Gebirgslandschaften Aquarell/Papier (36x52.5cm 14x20in) München 2000

$121 - €112 - **£73** - FF737
In Memoriam René Beeh Woodcut (18x13.8cm 7x5in) Heidelberg 1999

UNTERBERGER Franz Richard 1838-1902 [181]

$49 965 - €46 371 - **£30 000** - FF304 176
Capri Oil/canvas (92x137cm 36x53in) London 1999

$63 289 - €58 737 - **£38 000** - FF385 289
Rio St. Geronimo, Venezia Oil/canvas (82.5x71cm 32x27in) London 1999

$6 454 - €6 198 - **£4 000** - FF40 658
Lady Spinning with Three Children by the Water's Edge Oil/panel (32x23cm 12x9in) London 1999

UNTERBERGER Ignaz 1742/48-1797 [3]

$592 - €654 - **£410** - FF4 290
Allegorie auf Fürst Kaunitz Mezzotint (56.7x38cm 22x14in) Wien 2001

UNTERBERGER Michelangelo 1695-1758 [8]

$25 170 - €21 793 - **£15 270** - FF142 950
Lukas der Madonnenmaler Öl/Leinwand (97.5x75cm 38x29in) Wien 1998

UNTERSEHER Franz Xaver 1888-1954 [128]

$427 - €409 - **£263** - FF2 683
Fremdling im All Mixed media/canvas (84.5x75cm 33x29in) Kempten 1999

$272 - €307 - **£190** - FF2 012
Weiblicher Maskenkopf zwischen Tüchern Öl/Karton (40x37cm 15x14in) Lindau 2001

$146 - €153 - **£96** - FF1 006
Selbstbildnis Pastell/Karton (23.7x18.5cm 9x7in) Leipzig 2000

UNWIN Frances Mabelle XIX-XX [1]

$1 534 - €1 761 - **£1 050** - FF11 552
A Child Reading Watercolour/paper (20x25cm 8x10in) Par, Cornwall 2000

UOTILA Aukusti 1858-1886 [12]

$7 730 - €8 409 - **£5 095** - FF55 160
Insjölandskap, fiskarstuga Oil/canvas (31x52cm 12x20in) Helsinki 2000

$5 570 - €4 876 - **£3 375** - FF31 984
Flicka från Bretagne Oil/canvas (36x28.5cm 14x11in) Helsinki 1998

UOTILA Gunnar 1913-1997 [14]

$589 - €504 - **£346** - FF3 304
Morgon Sculpture, wood (H57cm H22in) Helsinki 1998

UPHAM John William 1772-1828 [3]

$998 - €1 164 - **£700** - FF7 637
Weymouth Watercolour (30x48cm 11x18in) Crewkerne, Somerset 2000

UPHOFF Carl Emil 1885-1971 [20]

$1 708 - €1 943 - **£1 184** - FF12 744
Abendmahl Öl/Leinwand (101.5x99.5cm 39x39in) Hamburg 2000

$190 - €199 - **£119** - FF1 308
Frauenkopf Radierung (24x17.5cm 9x6in) Bremen 2000

UPHOFF Fritz 1890-1966 [21]

$1 097 - €1 022 - **£677** - FF6 707
Herbstabend im Moor Öl/Karton (45x55cm 17x21in) Bremen 1999

UPHUES Joseph Johannes J. 1850-1911 [12]

$2 500 - €2 345 - **£1 545** - FF15 380
Archers Bronze (H38cm H15in) Delray-Beach FL 1999

UPPINK Willem 1767-1849 [8]

$5 750 - €5 445 - **£3 495** - FF35 719
A Traveller on a Road in a Village with Children playing nearby Oil/panel (45.5x35cm 17x13in) Amsterdam 1999

UPRKA Frantisek 1868-1929 [6]

$867 - €820 - **£540** - FF5 379
Reaper Bronze (H46cm H18in) Praha 1999

UPRKA Joza 1861-1940 [38]

$2 167 - €2 050 - **£1 350** - FF13 447
Homme en costume slovaque Huile/toile (50.5x100.5cm 19x39in) Brno 2000

$1 127 - €1 066 - £702 - FF6 992
Fille en costume Huile/toile/panneau (28.5x37cm
11x14in) Praha 2001

$375 - €355 - £234 - FF2 330
Girl in a Folk Costume with a Jug
Watercolour/paper (24.2x19.2cm 9x7in) Praha 1999

URANGA de Pablo 1861-1934 [9]
$208 - €240 - £144 - FF1 576
Los altos hornos Lápiz/papel (20x27cm 7x10in)
Madrid 2000

URBACH Josef 1889-1973 [13]
$1 615 - €1 588 - £1 038 - FF10 418
The Horse-Race Oil/canvas (45x85cm 17x33in)
Amsterdam 1999

URBAN Bohumil Stanislav 1903-? [14]
$1 156 - €1 093 - £720 - FF7 172
The Annunciation Oil/panel (25x50cm 9x19in) Praha
2000

URBAN Hermann 1866-1946 [42]
$930 - €767 - £547 - FF5 030
**Südliche Landschaft mit steinerner
Bogenbrücke, Angler, Gehöft, Wald** Öl/Karton
(44x53cm 17x20in) Lindau 1998

URBIETA Jesús 1959-1997 [21]
$11 000 - €10 676 - £6 848 - FF70 032
Personaje y Maquinas III Oil/canvas (190x150cm
74x59in) New-York 1999
$3 710 - €4 357 - £2 635 - FF28 581
Sin título Acrílico/cartulina (66x95cm 25x37in)
México 2000

URBINO Carlo 1553-1585 [11]
$4 391 - €4 288 - £2 800 - FF28 128
Draped Figure seen «di sotto in su» Black &
white chalks/paper (39x24.5cm 15x9in) London 1999

URCULO FERNANDEZ Eduardo 1938 [53]
$3 500 - €3 003 - £2 150 - FF19 700
Chabolas de Vallecas Oleo/lienzo (54.5x65.5cm
21x25in) Madrid 1998
$619 - €686 - £420 - FF4 500
Sans titre (texte de José Luis de Vilallonga)
Encre (30x21cm 11x8in) Paris 2000

URE SMITH Sydney 1887-1949 [37]
$3 559 - €3 379 - £2 220 - FF22 163
Sydney Harbour from Kyle House, Sydney
Watercolour (38.5x65cm 15x25in) Sydney 1999
$96 - €91 - £60 - FF596
Across the Plains, Windsor Etching (22x22cm
8x8in) Sydney 1999

URECH-SEON Rudolf 1876-1959 [5]
$1 652 - €1 428 - £998 - FF9 364
Der Acker Öl/Leinwand (87.5x94cm 34x37in) Luzern
1998

UREN John Clarkson Isaac 1845-1932 [106]
$490 - €553 - £339 - FF3 627
«Shag Rock, Perranporth» Watercolour/paper
(29x47.5cm 11x18in) Toronto 2000

URGELL CARRERAS Ricardo 1874-1924 [13]
$6 100 - €6 006 - £3 900 - FF39 400
Nocturno Oleo/lienzo (56x36cm 22x14in) Madrid
1999
$715 - €781 - £494 - FF5 122
Soledad Lápiz/papel (52x23cm 20x9in) Madrid 2001

URGELL Y INGLADA Modest 1839-1919 [38]
$11 590 - €11 412 - £7 220 - FF74 860
Iglesia románica Oleo/lienzo (66x105cm 25x41in)
Madrid 1999

$1 525 - €1 502 - £950 - FF9 850
Calle con arco Oleo/lienzo (31.5x20.5cm 12x8in)
Madrid 1999

URI Aviva 1927-1989 [102]
$13 000 - €15 412 - £9 470 - FF101 095
Van Gogh's Room Mixed media (150x101.5cm
59x39in) Tel Aviv 2001
$1 700 - €2 015 - £1 238 - FF13 220
Landscape Mixed media/paper (47x55.5cm 18x21in)
Tel Aviv 2001

URIA MONZON Antonio 1929-1996 [14]
$3 388 - €3 796 - £2 358 - FF24 900
Les amoureux Huile/panneau (38x46cm 14x18in)
Pau 2001
$2 099 - €2 439 - £1 475 - FF16 000
La pose des banderilles Sanguine/papier
(13.5x29cm 5x11in) Pau 2001

URIARTE Bonifacio Carlos 1931 [10]
$424 - €481 - £288 - FF3 152
Naturaleza, Hostalets d'en Bas, Olot (Girona)
Oleo/lienzo (53.5x53.5cm 21x21in) Barcelona 2000

URIBE Pablo 1962 [1]
$1 200 - €1 330 - £805 - FF8 723
Sin título Monotype (60x160cm 23x62in) Montevideo
2000

URIBURU Nicolás García 1937 [7]
$900 - €992 - £600 - FF6 505
Cabeza de toros Serigrafia (60x80cm 23x31in)
Montevideo 2000

URLAUB Anton Georg 1713-1759 [4]
$2 521 - €2 863 - £1 752 - FF18 781
Studie eines betenden Mannes Ink (16x18.5cm
6x7in) Köln 2001

URLAUB Georg Anton Abraham 1744-1788 [6]
$3 756 - €4 360 - £2 640 - FF28 602
**Bildnis eines Edelmannes in einer
Goldbestickten grünen Jacke** Öl/Leinwand
(76x56.5cm 29x22in) Wien 2001
$11 760 - €12 020 - £7 086 - FF67 042
**Die Handwaschung des Pilatus und Skizzen zu
Christus am Olberg** Ink (31.5x19.3cm 12x7in)
Berlin 1998

URLAUB Georg Karl 1749-1811 [3]
$4 775 - €4 346 - £2 983 - FF28 508
**Frau am Fenster auf einem Stuhl bei einem
Tischchen sitzend** Oil/panel (23.5x18.5cm 9x7in)
München 1999

URSULA (U. Schultze-Bluhm) 1921-1999 [43]
$3 848 - €3 324 - £2 324 - FF21 804
Maison à la campagne du grand Ravil
Öl/Leinwand (81x99.8cm 31x39in) Köln 1998
$546 - €511 - £331 - FF3 353
Hafen von Marseille Aquarell/Papier (29.5x39cm
11x15in) Stuttgart 1999

URTEIL Andreas 1933-1963 [17]
$2 354 - €2 034 - £1 419 - FF13 339
«Figur, gedreht» Bronze (H44.5cm H17in) Wien
1998

URUETA Cordelia 1908-1994 [15]
$3 710 - €4 357 - £2 635 - FF28 581
Sin título Oleo/cartón (23x33.5cm 9x13in) México
2000

URUSHIBARA Yoshijiro 1889-? [27]
$307 - €263 - £180 - FF1 725
«Grand Canal, Venice» Woodcut in colors
(35x23.5cm 13x9in) London 1998

U

URY Lesser 1861-1931 **[717]**
- $30 807 - €35 791 - **£21 651** - FF234 773
  Ein Uferweg Tempera (34x49cm 13x19in) Hamburg 2001
- $16 000 - €17 309 - **£10 961** - FF113 542
  Belgium, a Woman in the Field Oil/board/canvas (30.5x43.5cm 12x17in) Tel Aviv 2001
- $18 760 - €20 580 - **£12 743** - FF134 994
  Holländischer Kanal mit Windmühlen Pastell/Karton (36.2x50.5cm 14x19in) Berlin 2000
- $1 051 - €920 - **£636** - FF6 035
  Grunewaldsee bei Sonnenuntergang Radierung (22x15.7cm 8x6in) Berlin 1998

USADEL Max XIX-XX **[22]**
- $949 - €1 022 - **£653** - FF6 707
  Gondoliere vor Maria della Salute im Mondschein Oil/Leinwand (120x80cm 47x31in) München 2001

USELLINI Gian Filippo 1903-1971 **[26]**
- $6 000 - €7 775 - **£4 500** - FF51 000
  «Ponza» Olio/tela (50x70cm 19x27in) Milano 2001
- $2 200 - €2 851 - **£1 650** - FF18 700
  «Giovedì grasso» Olio/tela (25x40cm 9x15in) Milano 2001
- $520 - €674 - **£390** - FF4 420
  La mia cicogna Acquarello (65x21cm 25x8in) Milano 2001

USHIJIMA Noriyuki 1900 **[3]**
- $35 280 - €34 411 - **£21 600** - FF225 720
  Waves Oil/canvas (27.5x45cm 10x17in) Tokyo 1999

USLÉ Juan 1954 **[16]**
- $15 886 - €17 311 - **£11 000** - FF113 550
  «Mi-Mon» Mixed media (198x112cm 77x44in) London 2001
- $4 550 - €4 205 - **£2 730** - FF27 580
  Williamsburg bridge Técnica mixta/lienzo (46x30.5cm 18x12in) Madrid 1999

USSHER Arland A. ?-1893 **[4]**
- $1 819 - €2 095 - **£1 241** - FF13 742
  Seascape, Autumn Oil/canvas (22x34cm 8x13in) Dublin 2000
- $417 - €421 - **£260** - FF2 761
  View near Grange, County Limerick Watercolour (23x31cm 9x12in) London 2001

USSI Stefano 1822-1901 **[30]**
- $13 000 - €13 476 - **£7 800** - FF88 400
  Fantasia araba Olio/tela (66x43.5cm 25x17in) Firenze 2000
- $720 - €933 - **£540** - FF6 120
  Dama di costume Olio/cartone (22.5x15cm 8x5in) Firenze 2000

UTAGAWA Kuninao 1793-1854 **[5]**
- $4 800 - €4 942 - **£3 051** - FF32 416
  Geisha Games Ink (33.5x49.5cm 13x19in) New-York 2000

UTAGAWA Kuniyoshi, Igusa 1797-1861 **[257]**
- $390 - €455 - **£273** - FF2 985
  The Samouraï Woodcut (36x25cm 14x10in) Cleveland OH 2000

UTAGAWA TOYOKUNI III Kunisada, Tsunoda 1786-1864 **[670]**
- $9 000 - €8 810 - **£5 538** - FF57 790
  Mrs Moore and Miss Moore Watercolour/paper (33x25cm 13x10in) Columbia SC 1999
- $175 - €204 - **£122** - FF1 341
  Kurtisane mit Dienerin Woodcut in colors (36.4x24.8cm 14x9in) Berlin 2000

UTAMARO Kitagawa 1753-1806 **[258]**
- $5 500 - €5 542 - **£3 428** - FF36 355
  Scene of the Year-end House cleaning at a Samurai Mansion Print (38x131cm 14x51in) New-York 2000

UTECH Joachim 1889-1960 **[2]**
- $5 626 - €6 647 - **£3 974** - FF43 600
  Mädchenkopf Stone (H39cm H15in) Köln 2001

UTH Max 1863-1914 **[29]**
- $3 752 - €4 116 - **£2 548** - FF26 998
  Ebene bei Sonnenuntergang Öl/Leinwand/Karton (65x100cm 25x39in) Berlin 2000
- $266 - €307 - **£188** - FF2 012
  Abendliche märkische Seelandschaft Aquarell/Papier (45x64cm 17x25in) Bremen 2001

UTHAUG Jørleif 1911-1990 **[5]**
- $4 095 - €4 869 - **£2 917** - FF31 941
  Fergemannen Oil/panel (85x76cm 33x29in) Oslo 2000

UTRECHT van Adriaen 1599-1652 **[36]**
- $108 948 - €107 094 - **£70 000** - FF702 492
  Christ at the House of Martha and Mary, Still life of Artichokes... Oil/canvas (200x230.5cm 78x90in) London 1999
- $15 517 - €15 199 - **£10 000** - FF99 696
  Dead Heron, a Duck, Kingfishers, Songbirds and other Birds, Landscape Oil/canvas (92x117cm 36x46in) London 1999
- $10 477 - €9 700 - **£6 500** - FF63 628
  Still Life of Kingfishers, Finches, a Woodcock and other Birds Oil/panel (33x46cm 12x18in) London 1999

UTRILLO Antoni Viadera 1867-1944 **[11]**
- $868 - €991 - **£603** - FF6 500
  «La estrella polar en el mar artico» Affiche (76x108cm 29x42in) Paris 2001

UTRILLO Maurice 1883-1955 **[1397]**
- $85 000 - €81 736 - **£52 368** - FF536 154
  Le théâtre de l'atelier sous la neige Oil/board (50x61cm 19x24in) New-York 1999
- $44 125 - €42 817 - **£28 000** - FF280 862
  Le Moulin de la Galette à Montmartre Oil/canvas (27x34.5cm 10x13in) London 1999
- $22 538 - €21 336 - **£14 000** - FF139 956
  Rue Cortot à Montmartre Gouache/paper (40.5x32cm 15x12in) London 1999
- $1 086 - €1 037 - **£678** - FF6 800
  «Bal de l'Aide Amicale aux Artistes» Affiche (120x79.5cm 47x31in) Orléans 1999

UTRILLO MORLIUS Miguel 1862-1934 **[10]**
- $11 670 - €12 958 - **£8 134** - FF85 000
  Portrait de Suzanne Valdon Huile/toile (40.5x32.5cm 15x12in) Paris 2001
- $2 371 - €2 820 - **£1 690** - FF18 500
  «Bal de l'aide amicale aux artistes» Affiche (120x79.5cm 47x31in) Orléans 2001

UTTER André 1886-1948 **[55]**
- $1 701 - €1 448 - **£1 012** - FF9 500
  Nu sur find rouge Huile/toile (73x54cm 28x21in) Paris 1998
- $621 - €686 - **£421** - FF4 500
  Autoportrait Huile/toile (41x33cm 16x12in) Paris 2000

UTZ Thornton 1914 **[5]**
- $850 - €999 - **£609** - FF6 556
  Old Feuds never die Gouache/board (48.5x38cm 19x14in) Philadelphia PA 2001

UTZON-FRANK Einar 1888-1955 **[65]**

$14 352 - €16 089 - **£10 032** - FF105 540
Justitia Bronze (H96cm H37in) Köbenhavn 2001

$2 001 - €2 419 - **£1 396** - FF15 870
Klassisk knaelende kvinde med et laendeklaede Terracotta (H42cm H16in) Viby J, Århus 2000

UVA Cesare 1824-1886 **[32]**

$5 750 - €5 961 - **£3 450** - FF39 100
Festa di paese Olio/tela (58x78cm 22x30in) Venezia 2000

$2 000 - €2 073 - **£1 200** - FF13 600
Veduta costiera Tecnica mista/carta (37x54cm 14x21in) Napoli 1999

UWINS Thomas 1782-1857 **[31]**

$2 561 - €2 976 - **£1 800** - FF19 519
The May Queen Oil/panel (39.5x30.5cm 15x12in) London 2001

$832 - €877 - **£550** - FF5 750
Sappho and Phaon Pencil (13.5x10cm 5x3in) London 2001

UYL den Jan Jansz 1595/96-1639/40 **[1]**

$2 891 - €2 495 - **£1 744** - FF16 364
Village by a river Black chalk (10.5x16.5cm 4x6in) Amsterdam 1998

UYTTENBROECK van Moses c.1590-1648 **[31]**

$16 443 - €16 007 - **£10 101** - FF105 000
Mercure et Argus Huile/panneau (50.5x62cm 19x24in) Paris 1999

$9 264 - €9 945 - **£6 200** - FF65 233
Nymph bathing in a wooded River Landscape, Cattle and Figures beyond Oil/panel (24x29cm 9x11in) London 2000

$762 - €869 - **£532** - FF5 701
Hagar vom Engel getröstet Radierung (10x15.5cm 3x6in) Berlin 2001

UYTTERSCHAUT Victor 1847-1917 **[39]**

$336 - €372 - **£235** - FF2 439
La Côte Aquarelle/papier (15.5x24cm 6x9in) Bruxelles 2001

UZELAC Milivoy 1897-? **[21]**

$2 027 - €2 302 - **£1 408** - FF15 100
Homme d'Afrique/Femme d'Afrique Gouache/papier (74x54.5cm 29x21in) La Rochelle 2001

UZIEMBLO Henryk 1879-1949 **[17]**

$2 093 - €1 926 - **£1 256** - FF12 637
Vue de Constantinople Oil/board (41.7x57cm 16x22in) Warszawa 1999

V

VAA Dyre 1903-1980 **[3]**

$2 755 - €3 058 - **£1 920** - FF20 057
«Serens systrene» Bronze (55x20x19cm 21x7x7in) Oslo 2001

VAARBERG Joannes Christoffel 1825-1871 **[18]**

$2 592 - €2 723 - **£1 640** - FF17 859
The Return of the Soldier Oil/panel (43.5x55.5cm 17x21in) Amsterdam 2000

$1 359 - €1 588 - **£970** - FF10 418
The Suitor Oil/panel (33x25cm 12x9in) Amsterdam 2001

VAARDT van der Jan 1647-1721 **[4]**

$4 668 - €5 363 - **£3 232** - FF35 180
Romantisk landskab med personer ved en höjtliggende by og borg Oil/canvas (98x98cm 38x38in) Köbenhavn 2000

VAARULA Olavi 1927-1989 **[24]**

$597 - €605 - **£375** - FF3 971
Vart försvann hon Mixed media (23x30cm 9x11in) Helsinki 2000

VAARZON MOREL Willem F.A.I. 1868-1955 **[27]**

$891 - €771 - **£541** - FF5 060
Gladioli in a Vase Oil/canvas (84.5x55cm 33x21in) Amsterdam 1999

$478 - €544 - **£332** - FF3 571
Man and Maid walking in the Street Pencil (26.4x17.7cm 10x6in) Haarlem 2000

VACATKO Ludwig 1873-1956 **[21]**

$534 - €506 - **£333** - FF3 317
Hay Making Oil/panel (61x75cm 24x29in) Praha 2001

VACCA Angelo 1746-1814 **[4]**

$23 975 - €22 645 - **£14 500** - FF148 543
Children with Doves/Children with a Garland of Flowers/Children Oil/canvas (95.5x67.5cm 37x26in) London 1999

VACCARI Wainer 1949 **[7]**

$3 750 - €3 887 - **£2 250** - FF25 500
Senza titolo Olio/faesite (50x30cm 19x11in) Prato 1999

VACCARO Andrea 1604-1670 **[28]**

$16 800 - €21 770 - **£12 600** - FF142 800
Santa Cecilia Olio/tela (127.5x101.5cm 50x39in) Milano 2001

$19 412 - €19 056 - **£12 037** - FF125 000
Vierge en Gloire Huile/toile (78x59cm 30x23in) Bordeaux 1999

VACCARO Ludovico 1725-? **[2]**

$6 426 - €5 551 - **£3 213** - FF36 414
Il sogno di San Giuseppe Olio/rame (24x18cm 9x7in) Venezia 1999

VACCARO Nicola 1634/37-1709/17 **[9]**

$17 447 - €18 320 - **£11 000** - FF120 171
The Sacrifice of Moses Oil/canvas (134x185cm 52x72in) London 2000

$9 713 - €10 426 - **£6 500** - FF68 390
The Madonna and Child attended by Putti in the Heavens Oil/copper (30.5x24cm 12x9in) London 2000

VACCHI Sergio 1925 **[67]**

$1 200 - €1 244 - **£720** - FF8 160
Magia della notte Acrilico/tela (40x70cm 15x27in) Roma 2000

$1 000 - €1 037 - **£600** - FF6 800
Castel Sant'Angelo Olio/tela (30x40cm 11x15in) Roma 1999

$650 - €674 - **£390** - FF4 420
Interno Tempera/carta (50x70cm 19x27in) Roma 1999

VACHAL Josef 1884-1969 **[43]**

$187 - €178 - **£117** - FF1 165
Dorf Kaliste in der niedrigen Tatra Woodcut in colors (46x31cm 18x12in) Praha 1999

VACHER Charles 1818-1883 **[29]**

$548 - €645 - **£380** - FF4 230
Mamelouk Tombs, Citadel Cairo Watercolour (21x58cm 8x22in) London 2000

V

VACHER Roger XX **[5]**

$1 245 - €1 189 - **£778** - FF7 800
«La femme en homme» Affiche couleur
(120x160cm 47x62in) Paris 1999

VACOSSIN Georges, Géo 1870-1942 **[17]**

$650 - €561 - **£388** - FF3 680
Three Puppies Seated Side by Side Looking
Down Toward a Lizard Bronze (H33cm H13in) St.
Louis MO 1998

VADDER de Franz 1862-1935 **[61]**

$241 - €248 - **£152** - FF1 626
Bruyère Huile/carton (35x56cm 13x22in) Antwerpen
2000

$237 - €223 - **£146** - FF1 463
La moisson Huile/panneau (30x40cm 11x15in)
Antwerpen 1999

VADDER de Lodewyck 1605-1655 **[20]**

$7 780 - €8 750 - **£5 431** - FF57 395
Landschaft mit Bauern auf einem Weg
Öl/Leinwand (57x70cm 22x27in) Luzern 2001

VADER Hendrik XIX-XX **[27]**

$580 - €496 - **£352** - FF3 252
Pêcheurs sur la plage Huile/toile (80x120cm
31x47in) Antwerpen 1998

VADILLO Francisco XX **[16]**

$1 125 - €1 155 - **£750** - FF7 575
Avila Oleo/lienzo (60.5x92cm 23x36in) Caracas 2000

VAERENBERGH van Georges XIX-XX **[29]**

$896 - €821 - **£546** - FF5 384
Bust of a young Woman Ceramic (H38cm H14in)
Warszawa 1999

VAES Walter 1882-1958 **[210]**

$2 896 - €2 723 - **£1 753** - FF17 859
Hortensias in a Vase Oil/canvas (61.5x50.5cm
24x19in) Amsterdam 1999

$1 800 - €1 944 - **£1 244** - FF12 751
A Vase of Carnations Oil/canvas (32x40cm 12x15in)
New-York 2001

$420 - €347 - **£246** - FF2 273
Twee zeilboten Pastel/papier (17x23cm 6x9in)
Bruxelles 1998

$180 - €148 - **£105** - FF974
De vestingen (Kiel) Eau-forte (21.5x25cm 8x9in)
Bruxelles 1998

VAGA del Perin Buonaccorsi 1501-1547 **[10]**

$1 091 - €1 068 - **£700** - FF7 008
Two Draped Men and a Nude Crouching Man
Ink (26x17.5cm 10x6in) London 1999

VAGH-WEINMANN Elemer 1906 **[108]**

$488 - €457 - **£302** - FF3 000
Composition au bouquet Huile/toile (66x54cm
25x21in) Pontoise 1999

VAGH-WEINMANN Maurice 1899-1966 **[86]**

$505 - €442 - **£306** - FF2 900
Paysage tourmenté Huile/panneau (50x61cm
19x24in) Saumur 1998

VAGH-WEINMANN Nandor 1897-1978 **[60]**

$298 - €305 - **£187** - FF2 000
Marine Huile/toile (55x46cm 21x18in) Toulouse 2000

VAGLIERI Tino 1929-2000 **[77]**

$600 - €777 - **£450** - FF5 100
«Papa Woitila che nuota nel Tevere contro cor-
rente» Olio/tela (49x59cm 19x23in) Milano 2001

$550 - €570 - **£330** - FF3 740
Studio da Rembrandt Acquerello/carta (29x38cm
11x14in) Milano 2000

VAGNBY Viggo 1896-1966 **[6]**

$219 - €250 - **£152** - FF1 637
«Wonderful Copenhagen» Poster (62x100cm
24x39in) Hoorn 2001

VAGNETTI Gianni 1898-1956 **[127]**

$13 500 - €13 995 - **£8 100** - FF91 800
Ritratto del fratello Roberto Olio/tela (150x130cm
59x51in) Firenze 2001

$2 000 - €2 073 - **£1 200** - FF13 600
Il parto Olio/masonite (44x50cm 17x19in) Firenze
2001

$1 560 - €1 348 - **£780** - FF8 840
La visita Olio/tavola (35x45cm 13x17in) Milano 1999

$350 - €363 - **£210** - FF2 380
Vista delal rue Gaulancourte Carboncino/carta
(16.5x25cm 6x9in) Firenze 2001

VAGO Sandor 1887-1946 **[10]**

$600 - €643 - **£409** - FF4 216
Chrysanthemums Oil/canvas (61x76cm 24x30in)
Cleveland OH 2001

VAGO Valentino 1931 **[28]**

$800 - €829 - **£480** - FF5 440
Composizione Acrilico/tela (92x73cm 36x28in)
Vercelli 2001

VAHEY Brian XX **[3]**

$970 - €1 041 - **£649** - FF6 829
Autumn at Powerscourt Oil/paper (23x30.5cm
9x12in) Dublin 2000

VAILLANCOURT Armand 1932 **[19]**

$726 - €842 - **£513** - FF5 524
Sans titre Bronze (24x20.5cm 9x8in) Montréal 2001

VAILLANT Bernard 1632-1698 **[3]**

$3 177 - €3 201 - **£1 980** - FF21 000
Portrait de Jacoba Van Remstra Pierre noire
(31.5x24cm 12x9in) Paris 2000

VAILLANT Jacques 1879-1934 **[10]**

$3 355 - €3 304 - **£2 090** - FF21 670
David y Abigail Oleo/tabla (50x60cm 19x23in)
Madrid 1999

VAILLANT Wallerand 1623-1677 **[30]**

$10 906 - €10 174 - **£6 580** - FF66 738
Bildnis eines Knaben Öl/Leinwand (60x48.5cm
23x19in) Wien 1999

$5 868 - €4 959 - **£3 500** - FF32 527
Portrait of a Young Man Oil/copper (14.5x11cm
5x4in) London 1998

$700 - €818 - **£491** - FF5 368
Personification of Painting and Drawing, After
Reni Mezzotint (24x31cm 9x12in) New-York 2000

VAINS de H.R. XX **[9]**

$6 000 - €6 236 - **£3 781** - FF40 908
A Trotter and Jockey Bronze (H34.5cm H13in) New-
York 2000

VÄISÄNEN Hannu 1951 **[40]**

$295 - €320 - **£204** - FF2 096
Ansikte Gouache/paper (50x65cm 19x25in) Helsinki
2001

$212 - €202 - **£129** - FF1 323
Rilke-Serien Color lithograph (47x61cm 18x24in)
Helsinki 1999

VAISMAN Meyer 1960 [43]
- **$8 000** - €7 688 - **£4 928** - FF50 431
  Fleur de lys III Mixed media (179.5x208.5cm 70x82in) New-York 1999
- **$1 597** - €1 862 - **£1 105** - FF12 211
  The Travelling Beans Técnica mixta (35x50.5x6cm 13x19x2in) Caracas ($) 2000
- **$14 000** - €13 546 - **£8 633** - FF88 856
  Untitled Construction (170x76x51cm 66x29x20in) New-York 1999
- **$4 500** - €4 860 - **£3 110** - FF31 880
  «Turkey XXVII» Sculpture (63.5x42x58.5cm 25x16x23in) New-York 2001
- **$8 500** - €9 862 - **£5 868** - FF64 693
  The Uffizi Portrait Ink (188x345.5x33cm 74x136x12in) New-York 2000

VAJDA Julia 1913-1982 [3]
- **$3 000** - €2 950 - **£1 875** - FF19 350
  Nightmare Oil/canvas (50x38.5cm 19x15in) Budapest 1999
- **$6 400** - €6 293 - **£4 000** - FF41 280
  Composition Oil/cardboard (34x47cm 13x18in) Budapest 1999

VAJDA Lajos 1908-1941 [1]
- **$17 760** - €18 660 - **£11 040** - FF122 400
  Masque Pastel/papier (60x44cm 23x17in) Budapest 2000

VAJDA Zsigmond 1860-1931 [14]
- **$264** - €302 - **£184** - FF1 984
  Asszonyok a kútnál Oil/canvas (80x60cm 31x23in) Budapest 2000
- **$1 943** - €2 035 - **£1 288** - FF13 347
  Am Markt Oil/panel (18x24.5cm 7x9in) Graz 2000

VAL Valentine Synave N. 1870-1943 [22]
- **$596** - €640 - **£399** - FF4 200
  Nature morte aux fleurs et aux fruits Huile/toile (50x60cm 19x23in) Paris 2000

VALADE Jean 1709-1787 [14]
- **$33 801** - €28 965 - **£20 330** - FF190 000
  Portrait de Joseph Balthasar Gibert, avocat général au Parlement Huile/toile (146x113cm 57x44in) Melun 1998
- **$24 738** - €21 343 - **£14 924** - FF140 000
  Portrait d'une dame de qualité et sa fille Huile/toile (100x80cm 39x31in) Paris 1998
- **$5 611** - €6 403 - **£3 897** - FF42 000
  Portrait d'Anne Michelle Chaussard Pastel/papier (50x40cm 19x15in) Paris 2000

VALADIÉ Jean-Baptiste, Johny 1933 [133]
- **$2 694** - €2 327 - **£1 624** - FF15 265
  «Nudité» Oil/canvas (53x73cm 20x28in) Johannesburg 1998
- **$539** - €579 - **£361** - FF3 800
  Nu au chapeau Huile/panneau (32x40cm 12x15in) Douarnenez 2000
- **$1 314** - €1 524 - **£935** - FF10 000
  Tatiana Technique mixte/papier (76x59cm 29x23in) Mayenne 2000

VALADIER Giuseppe 1762-1839 [2]
- **$8 749** - €9 070 - **£5 249** - FF59 498
  Studi per architetture/Studio per altare China (65x43.5cm 25x17in) Milano 1999

VALADON Suzanne 1865-1938 [290]
- **$29 288** - €34 443 - **£21 000** - FF225 930
  Nature morte à la coupe de fruits Oil/board (38.5x53cm 15x20in) London 2001

- **$17 522** - €14 940 - **£10 574** - FF98 000
  Vase de fleurs sur une table Huile/toile (41x33cm 16x12in) Paris 1998
- **$4 111** - €4 857 - **£2 904** - FF31 862
  Nu à la draperie Charcoal (52x41cm 20x16in) Köln 2001
- **$602** - €717 - **£429** - FF4 700
  «Aide Amicale aux Artistes» Affiche (119.5x83cm 47x32in) Orléans 2000

VALALLEY John XX [1]
- **$17 716** - €17 142 - **£10 924** - FF112 441
  The Bullet Thrower Oil/canvas (101.5x127cm 39x50in) Dublin 1999

VALAPERTA Francesco 1836-1908 [3]
- **$3 250** - €3 369 - **£1 950** - FF22 100
  Scena storica Olio/tela (15x22.5cm 5x8in) Roma 1999

VALAY Florence 1955 [1]
- **$4 498** - €4 726 - **£2 960** - FF31 000
  Nature morte aux porcelaines Huile/toile (37x20cm 14x7in) Paris 2000

VALCK Gerard 1650-1720 [12]
- **$121** - €141 - **£85** - FF927
  The Attack, After F.Snyders Lithograph (45x68cm 17x26in) Oxfordshire 2000

VALCKENAERE Léon 1853-? [5]
- **$1 331** - €1 363 - **£841** - FF8 943
  Marine par temps calme Huile/panneau (27.5x42cm 10x16in) Bruxelles 2000

VALCKENBORCH van Frederick c.1570-1623 [26]
- **$23 527** - €22 973 - **£15 000** - FF150 690
  Aenas Carrying his Father Anchises from the Burning City of Troy Oil/canvas (117x200.5cm 46x78in) London 1999
- **$9 671** - €8 954 - **£6 000** - FF58 734
  Extensive River Landscape with Huntsmen at the Edge of the Wood Oil/panel (50x79cm 19x31in) London 1999
- **$33 415** - €33 671 - **£20 827** - FF220 865
  Gebirgslandschaft Öl/Kupfer (18x26cm 7x10in) Zürich 2000
- **$20 000** - €21 424 - **£13 658** - FF140 532
  The Salzach Valley with a View of the Watzmann Massif in Background Ink (16x27.5cm 6x10in) New-York 2000

VALCKENBORCH van Lucas c.1535-1597 [9]
- **$268 974** - €288 721 - **£180 000** - FF1 893 888
  Allegory of Autumn: Fruit and Vegetable Stall Above the Weinmarkt Oil/canvas (169.5x236.5cm 66x93in) London 2000
- **$90 057** - €83 513 - **£55 000** - FF547 811
  An Extensive Landscape with a Huntsman and Hounds on a Path Oil/canvas (30.5x47cm 12x18in) London 1998

VALCKENBORCH van Martin 1535-1612 [11]
- **$86 669** - €93 032 - **£58 000** - FF610 252
  Mountainous River Valley with an Iron Foundry, a Town in the Distance Oil/canvas (73.5x113.5cm 28x44in) London 2000

V

VALCKERT van den Werner Jacobsz. c.1585-c.1630 [3]
- $45 603 - €51 796 - **£32 000** - FF339 760
  Portrait of a Lady, Aged 30, Half-length, in an embroidered burgundy Oil/panel (65x52cm 25x20in) London 2001

VALDAMBRINO Francesco 1401-1435 [2]
- $70 000 - €72 566 - **£42 000** - FF476 000
  Madonna col bambino Sculpture bois (49.5x17.5x15.5cm 19x6x6in) Firenze 2001

VALDÉS LEAL Juan de Nisa 1622-1690 [18]
- $19 560 - €22 867 - **£13 965** - FF150 000
  L'exaltation de la Croix Huile/toile (61x107cm 24x42in) Paris 2001
- $60 000 - €52 630 - **£36 432** - FF345 228
  The Virgin and Child with Saints Isidore, Leander, Hermenegild Oil/canvas (33.5x42cm 13x16in) New-York 1999

VALDÉS Manolo 1942 [56]
- $22 113 - €18 574 - **£13 000** - FF121 837
  Clouds over the City Oil/canvas (200x200cm 78x78in) London 1998
- $24 300 - €27 029 - **£16 200** - FF177 300
  El Infante Don Fernando Oleo/lienzo (100x80cm 39x31in) Madrid 2000
- $26 752 - €31 582 - **£19 000** - FF207 162
  La Reina Mariana V Sculpture, wood (198x73x89cm 77x28x35in) London 2001
- $573 - €652 - **£402** - FF4 280
  Ohne Titel Pencil/paper (31x21cm 12x8in) Zürich 2001
- $1 254 - €1 141 - **£760** - FF7 486
  «Reina Mariana IV» Litografía (98x63.5cm 38x25in) Madrid 1999

VALE Richard [1]
- $11 330 - €10 665 - **£7 000** - FF69 961
  Announcing the Arrival Oil/canvas (76.5x83.5cm 30x32in) London 1999

VALENCAY Robert XX [1]
- $13 230 - €13 720 - **£8 721** - FF90 000
  Exposition internationale du surréalisme Photo (14x9cm 5x3in) Paris 2000

VALENCIA de Pedro 1902-1971 [7]
- $2 025 - €2 252 - **£1 425** - FF14 775
  Marina Oleo/lienzo (33x42cm 12x16in) Madrid 2001

VALENCIA Manuel 1856-1935 [35]
- $1 500 - €1 454 - **£928** - FF9 539
  Mountainous Landscape Oil/canvas (40x60cm 16x24in) Mystic CT 1999
- $2 250 - €2 078 - **£1 401** - FF13 629
  California Landscape Oil/board (21x30cm 8x12in) Oakland CA 1999

VALENCIENNES de Pierre Henri 1750-1819 [25]
- $9 500 - €11 172 - €6 811 - FF73 282
  View of Lake Nemi with a Piping Shepherd/Wooded Landscape Oil/paper/canvas (28.5x44cm 11x17in) New-York 2001
- $4 730 - €5 004 - **£3 000** - FF32 825
  Fir Tree Red chalk/paper (30.5x16.5cm 12x6in) London 2001

VALENKAMPH Theodor Victor Carl 1868-1924 [29]
- $1 300 - €1 241 - **£812** - FF8 140
  Clamming Oil/board (45x60cm 18x24in) Dedham MA 1999

VALENSI André 1947 [31]
- $191 - €229 - **£136** - FF1 500
  Sans titre Dessin (65x65cm 25x25in) Paris 2000

VALENSI Henri 1883-1960 [52]
- $58 000 - €49 020 - **£34 713** - FF321 552
  «Sur un Transatlantique» Oil/canvas (114.5x195.5cm 45x76in) New-York 1998
- $2 014 - €2 362 - **£1 437** - FF15 493
  Paysage orientaliste Huile/toile (54x65cm 21x25in) Genève 2001
- $750 - €733 - **£475** - FF4 811
  View at Timmimoune Oil/panel (18x24cm 7x9in) Bolton MA 1999
- $923 - €991 - **£617** - FF6 500
  Sans titre Gouache/papier (29.5x40cm 11x15in) Paris 2000

VALENTA Ludwig 1882-1943 [8]
- $1 500 - €1 813 - **£1 047** - FF11 892
  The Bibliophile Oil/panel (16.5x12.5cm 6x4in) Bethesda MD 2000

VALENTI Italo 1912-1995 [57]
- $5 750 - €5 961 - **£3 450** - FF39 100
  Nudo in interno Olio/tela (50x40cm 19x15in) Milano 2001
- $3 000 - €2 592 - **£1 500** - FF17 000
  Natura morta Olio/cartone/tela (24x28.5cm 9x11in) Milano 1999
- $919 - €1 042 - **£642** - FF6 836
  Landschaft Aquarell/Papier (51x76cm 20x29in) Zürich 2001
- $255 - €237 - **£155** - FF1 552
  Geometrische Komposition Farblithographie (76.5x57cm 30x22in) Bern 1999

VALENTIN Emile XIX [8]
- $6 817 - €5 636 - **£4 000** - FF36 968
  Shipping Off Constantinople in Moonlight Oil/canvas (53x79.5cm 20x31in) London 1998

VALENTINE-DAINES Sherree 1956 [9]
- $3 408 - €3 278 - **£2 100** - FF21 500
  Off to the Gymkhana Oil/board (42x54.5cm 16x21in) London 1999
- $649 - €624 - **£400** - FF4 095
  May Time Oil/board (30.5x43cm 12x16in) London 1999

VALENTINI Gottardo 1820-1884 [4]
- $2 500 - €2 592 - **£1 500** - FF17 000
  Marenda al lago Olio/tela (54.5x72cm 21x28in) Milano 2000

VALENTINI Walter 1928 [35]
- $1 950 - €2 021 - **£1 170** - FF13 260
  «Passava la Luna» Tecnica mista/tavola (61x45cm 24x17in) Vercelli 2001

VALENTINIS dei Sebastiano XVI [1]
- $12 118 - €13 294 - **£8 231** - FF87 201
  Die Ruhe auf der Flucht Radierung (20.9x14cm 8x5in) Berlin 2000

VALENTINO Gian Domenico G.D.V. XVII [23]
- $7 524 - €8 573 - **£5 200** - FF56 232
  Kitchen Interior with numerous kitchen Utensils Oil/canvas (74.5x98.5cm 29x38in) London 2000

VALERIANI Giuseppe 1690-1761 [7]
- $108 849 - €92 672 - £65 000 - FF607 886
  An Allegorical Monument to King George I
  Oil/canvas (182.5x241cm 71x94in) London 1998

VALÉRIO de Roger 1886-1951 [29]
- $600 - €600 - £366 - FF3 933
  «Air France, Paris Londres» Poster (100x61cm 39x24in) New-York 2000

VALERIO Théodore 1819-1879 [32]
- $721 - €838 - £507 - FF5 500
  Etude de cheveux et parsonnages Crayon/papier (31x24cm 12x9in) Paris 2001

VALERO Salvador XX [25]
- $640 - €598 - £400 - FF3 920
  Internado Oleo/lienzo (52.5x71.5cm 20x28in) Caracas 1999

VALÉRY Jean XIX [1]
- $3 644 - €3 374 - £2 200 - FF22 129
  A Roman Ballad Singer Watercolour/paper (63x99cm 24x38in) London 1999

VALESIO Francesco c.1560-? [4]
- $142 - €153 - £95 - FF1 006
  Wolfsjagd Kupferstich (20.1x27.7cm 7x10in) Berlin 2000

VALETTE Adolphe Pierre 1876-1942 [68]
- $1 351 - €1 153 - £805 - FF7 562
  Summer Flowers in a green oriental Vase seated in a Window ledge Oil/canvas (65x80cm 25x31in) Manchester 1998
- $1 045 - €1 071 - £650 - FF7 027
  St.Tropez Oil/canvas/board (31x41.5cm 12x16in) Billingshurst, West-Sussex 2000
- $644 - €596 - £400 - FF3 910
  St Tropez Watercolour/paper (25x34cm 9x13in) Cheshire 1999

VALETTE Joseph-Charles 1813-? [2]
- $5 764 - €6 860 - £3 991 - FF45 000
  Vue de Castres Huile/toile (61x100cm 24x39in) Albi 2000

VALETTE René XIX-XX [22]
- $529 - €457 - £319 - FF3 000
  Les chiens Aquarelle/papier (27x21cm 10x8in) Barbizon 1998

VALINDER Knut 1909 [26]
- $410 - €380 - £255 - FF2 495
  Smáfáglar vid boet Oil/canvas (51x24cm 20x9in) Malmö 1999

VALINOTTI Domenico 1899-1962 [16]
- $1 750 - €1 814 - £1 050 - FF11 900
  Langhe Olio/tela (39.5x59.5cm 15x23in) Torino 2000

VALK de Hendrik act.1693-1717 [8]
- $6 886 - €7 714 - £4 785 - FF50 602
  As the old Ones Sing, so Pipe the young Ones Oil/canvas (61.5x84cm 24x33in) Amsterdam 2001

VALK Hendrik 1897-1986 [49]
- $2 942 - €3 176 - £2 011 - FF20 836
  Zandaf graving Opus - 1265 Oil/canvas (38x70cm 14x27in) Amsterdam 2001
- $2 139 - €2 042 - £1 339 - FF13 394
  Wederkomst (Opus:857) Oil/board (30.5x14.5cm 12x5in) Amsterdam 1999

VALK van der Maurits 1857-1935 [15]
- $458 - €454 - £280 - FF2 976
  Still Life with an Earthenware Pot Pencil (52x32cm 20x12in) Amsterdam 2000

VALKENBURG Dirk 1675-1721 [6]
- $75 360 - €73 176 - £46 560 - FF480 000
  Nature morte aux fruits du Surinam Huile/panneau (22.5x28cm 8x11in) La Flèche 1999

VALKENBURG Hendrik 1826-1896 [46]
- $4 103 - €4 724 - £2 800 - FF30 987
  A Family Before a Farmm House, Zandvoort Oil/canvas (53x68.5cm 20x26in) London 2000
- $2 976 - €2 628 - £1 794 - FF17 236
  At Work in the Kitchen Garden Watercolour/paper (43x56cm 16x22in) Amsterdam 1998

VALL Pere XV [1]
- $40 000 - €35 086 - £24 288 - FF230 152
  The Madonna Dolorosa and Saint Anne and Lawrence Tempera/panel (90x66cm 35x25in) New-York 1999

VALLANCE William Fleming 1827-1904 [11]
- $2 404 - €2 271 - £1 500 - FF14 900
  In the Harbour Oil/canvas (41x66cm 16x25in) Perthshire 1999

VALLAT Aimé 1912-1993 [1504]
- $119 - €110 - £73 - FF720
  Chemin ombragé d'arbres Huile/carton (50x65cm 19x25in) Limoges 1999
- $90 - €91 - £56 - FF60
  Prairie Huile/carton (14x17cm 5x6in) Limoges 2000

VALLAYER-COSTER Anne 1744-1818 [37]
- $3 900 - €3 904 - £2 405 - FF25 610
  Sobremesa Oleo/lienzo (38x46cm 14x18in) Madrid 2000
- $44 675 - €38 112 - £26 950 - FF250 000
  Trompe-l'oeil au bas-relief en terre cuite, d'après Larue Huile/toile (25x37cm 9x14in) Toulouse 1998
- $14 000 - €12 171 - £8 472 - FF79 836
  Bouquet of Flowers Gouache/paper (31x24.5cm 12x9in) New-York 1999

VALLAYER-MOUTET Pauline XIX-XX [12]
- $1 923 - €2 134 - £1 330 - FF14 000
  Le jour des cuivres Huile/toile (41x33.5cm 16x13in) Cherbourg 2001
- $2 760 - €3 049 - £1 914 - FF20 000
  Couturières dans un intérieur Pastel/papier (88x77cm 34x30in) Paris 2001

VALLAZZA Markus 1936 [14]
- $939 - €1 090 - £660 - FF7 150
  Ohne Titel Mischtechnik/Papier (24x31.5cm 9x12in) Wien 2001

VALLE della Pietro 1827-1891 [5]
- $6 500 - €6 765 - £4 080 - FF44 374
  View of the Bay of Naples Oil/canvas (59x89cm 23x35in) Chicago IL 2000

VALLE Evaristo 1873-1951 [9]
- $42 250 - €39 042 - £26 000 - FF256 100
  Dos pescadores, un viejo pescador enseña al joven Oleo/lienzo (66x50cm 25x19in) Madrid 1999
- $18 550 - €21 023 - £12 950 - FF137 900
  Carnavalada Oleo/lienzo (30x44cm 11x17in) Madrid 2001

V

VALLE J. XIX **[1]**
✎ **$1 884** - €1 829 - **£1 164** - FF12 000
    Écoutant la musique Aquarelle/papier (40x25.5cm 15x10in) Paris 1999

VALLÉE Étienne Maxime act.1873-1881 **[68]**
◠ **$8 000** - €8 794 - **£5 126** - FF57 683
    Chaumières isolée - Souvenir de Bourgogne Oil/canvas (127x208.5cm 50x82in) New-York 2000
◠ **$2 749** - €2 384 - **£1 680** - FF15 636
    Ducks Along the Marshes Oil/canvas (65x92cm 25x36in) New-York 1999
◠ **$1 449** - €1 448 - **£906** - FF9 500
    Retour de promenade Huile/toile (27.5x41.5cm 10x16in) Pontoise 1999

VALLÉE Ludovic 1864-1939 **[54]**
◠ **$2 343** - €2 287 - **£1 483** - FF15 000
    Nature morte aux fruits et la timbale Huile/toile (40x55cm 15x21in) Calais 1999
◠ **$1 857** - €1 753 - **£1 154** - FF11 500
    Au jardin public Huile/panneau (25x35cm 9x13in) Neuilly-sur-Seine 1999

VALLEJO BERMEJO José 1928 **[3]**
▥ **$1 104** - €961 - **£688** - FF6 304
    Vista del puerto y de la ciudad de Mahón, tomada dede la Alameda Litografía (51x65cm 20x25in) Madrid 1999

VALLELY John B. 1941 **[13]**
◠ **$22 401** - €22 241 - **£14 000** - FF145 889
    Four Musicians Oil/canvas (76x152cm 30x60in) Belfast 1999
◠ **$4 482** - €4 812 - **£3 000** - FF31 564
    Flute Player Oil/canvas (30x35cm 12x14in) Belfast 2000
✎ **$1 157** - €1 250 - **£800** - FF8 199
    Belfast Docks Watercolour/paper (22x33cm 9x13in) Belfast 2001

VALLES Lorenzo 1830-1910 **[13]**
◠ **$14 000** - €15 901 - **£9 823** - FF104 305
    The Museum tour Oil/panel (28x42cm 11x16in) New-York 2001

VALLET Edouard 1876-1929 **[205]**
◠ **$24 752** - €24 941 - **£15 428** - FF163 604
    Le Monticule Öl/Leinwand (54x75cm 21x29in) Zürich 2000
◠ **$14 495** - €17 050 - **£10 504** - FF111 841
    Four à chaux Huile/panneau (26.5x35cm 10x13in) Sion 2001
✎ **$4 644** - €5 283 - **£3 220** - FF34 652
    Cimetière d'Hérémence Aquarelle/papier (28x32cm 11x12in) Sion 2001
▥ **$724** - €852 - **£525** - FF7 500
    Fille assise Lithographie (17x23cm 6x9in) Sion 2001

VALLET Louis 1856-? **[29]**
▥ **$191** - €183 - **£120** - FF1 200
    Tandem Pointe sèche (30x39.5cm 11x15in) Paris 1999

VALLET-BISSON Frédérique 1865-? **[20]**
✎ **$1 408** - €1 524 - **£894** - FF10 000
    Portrait de dame à la robe bleue Pastel/papier (72.5x60cm 28x23in) Cannes 2000
▥ **$1 400** - €1 325 - **£869** - FF8 693
    Jumel & Champigny Poster (34.5x37.5cm 13x14in) New-York 1999

VALLETTE Henri 1877-1962 **[9]**
   $1 047 - €1 189 - **£727** - FF7 800
    Le cochon Bronze (14.5x10.5cm 5x4in) Pontoise 2001

VALLGREN Ville 1855-1940 **[74]**
   $16 150 - €15 977 - **£10 070** - FF104 804
    Dansande flicka Bronze (H112cm H44in) Helsinki 1999
   $1 479 - €1 682 - **£1 026** - FF11 032
    Blomsterflicka Plaster (H44cm H17in) Helsinki 2000

VALLIEN Bertil 1938 **[23]**
   $3 696 - €4 321 - **£2 597** - FF28 345
    Utan titel Sculpture (60x25cm 23x9in) Stockholm 2000

VALLIN Hugo Golli XIX-XX **[5]**
◠ **$2 359** - €2 744 - **£1 659** - FF18 000
    Venise Huile/toile (54x65.5cm 21x25in) Tours 2001

VALLIN Jacques Antoine c.1760-c.1831 **[82]**
◠ **$18 690** - €20 110 - **£12 720** - FF131 910
    Venus med Amor, der presser vindruesaft i en skål Oil/canvas (130x95cm 51x37in) København 2001
◠ **$3 757** - €4 269 - **£2 629** - FF28 000
    Un couple de bergers près d'une fontaine Huile/panneau (35.5x51cm 13x20in) Paris 2001
◠ **$5 041** - €5 412 - **£3 372** - FF35 500
    Allégorie de l'été Huile/toile (32x40cm 12x15in) Paris 2000

VALLMAN Uno 1913 **[179]**
◠ **$625** - €527 - **£371** - FF3 460
    Fantasifågel Oil/canvas (65x54cm 25x21in) Stockholm 1998

VALLMITJANA Y BARBANY Venancio 1830-1919 **[18]**
   $924 - €991 - **£610** - FF6 501
    Figura femenina con mantón Terracotta (40.5x21x12cm 15x8x4in) Barcelona 2000

VALLORZ Paolo 1931 **[14]**
◠ **$12 000** - €15 550 - **£9 000** - FF102 000
    Donna che legge il giornale Olio/tela (161x130cm 63x51in) Prato 2000
◠ **$1 206** - €1 372 - **£837** - FF9 000
    Portrait d'Arturo Huile/panneau (30x24cm 11x9in) Paris 2000

VALLOTTON Félix 1865-1925 **[764]**
◠ **$58 779** - €56 595 - **£36 756** - FF371 241
    Les arbres touffus Öl/Leinwand (54x73cm 21x28in) Zürich 1999
◠ **$35 337** - €34 395 - **£21 714** - FF225 615
    Passant au réverbère Oil/board (23.5x26cm 9x10in) Zürich 1999
   $24 415 - €23 764 - **£15 002** - FF155 879
    Jeune mère Bronze (26.5x7x6cm 10x2x2in) Zürich 1999
✎ **$2 449** - €2 883 - **£1 720** - FF18 914
    Femme nue allongée Pencil/paper (21.5x32cm 8x12in) Zürich 2000
▥ **$1 251** - €1 250 - **£782** - FF8 200
    L'étranger Gravure bois (22.5x18cm 8x7in) Paris 1999

VALLOU DE VILLENEUVE Julien 1795-1866 **[23]**
◠ **$1 983** - €2 211 - **£1 386** - FF14 500
    Le verrou Huile/panneau (25.5x21cm 10x8in) Paris 2001
▣ **$3 403** - €3 887 - **£2 400** - FF25 495
    Draped nude Salt print (16.5x12cm 6x4in) London 1999

VALLS SANMARTIN Ernesto 1891-1941 **[10]**
◠ **$4 269** - €3 988 - **£2 580** - FF26 160
    Zwei fröhliche Landmädchen Öl/Leinwand (99x79cm 38x31in) Berlin 1999

VALLS Xavier 1923 **[20]**
 $4 940 - €5 706 - **£3 420** - FF37 430
   Paisaje Oleo/lienzo (46x55cm 18x21in) Madrid 2000

VALMIER Georges 1885-1937 **[210]**
 $78 129 - €76 041 - **£48 000** - FF498 796
   Nature morte sur une table Oil/canvas (60.5x73cm 23x28in) London 1999
 $5 628 - €5 336 - **£3 423** - FF35 000
   Vase de fleurs Gouache (24x17cm 9x6in) Paris 1999
 $2 000 - €2 068 - **£1 263** - FF13 568
   Collection décors et couleurs, Album No.1 Pochoir (43.5x34cm 17x13in) New-York 2000

VALMON Léonie XIX-XX **[3]**
 $2 536 - €2 897 - **£1 784** - FF19 000
   Bouquet estival Huile/toile (46x38cm 18x14in) Fontainebleau 2001

VALORE Lucie Utrillo 1878-1965 **[32]**
 $562 - €656 - **£394** - FF4 300
   Bouquet de fleurs Huile/toile (24x33cm 9x12in) Pontoise 2000

VALOVA Kveta 1922-1998 **[6]**
 $6 069 - €5 740 - **£3 780** - FF37 653
   Camarade Huile/toile (94x71cm 37x27in) Praha 2001

VALSTAD Otto 1862-? **[3]**
 $4 250 - €3 680 - **£2 563** - FF24 136
   Winter Landscape at Dawn with a Mother and Child Oil/canvas (75x59.5cm 29x23in) San-Francisco CA 1998

VALTAT Louis 1869-1952 **[1486]**
 $290 000 - €321 700 - **£192 850** - FF2 110 214
   Sur le boulevard Oil/canvas (218.5x168.5cm 86x66in) New-York 1999
 $35 112 - €33 539 - **£21 626** - FF220 000
   Bouquet de fleurs Huile/toile (55x46.5cm 21x18in) Paris 1999
 $10 000 - €9 616 - **£6 161** - FF63 077
   Raisins et poires Oil/board (26x38cm 10x14in) New-York 1999
 $2 860 - €3 049 - **£1 814** - FF20 000
   Jean Valtat à 3 ans, son buste Bronze (H26cm H10in) Paris 2000
 $1 300 - €1 091 - **£762** - FF7 154
   Madame Valtat Sewing Ink/paper (25.5x16.5cm 10x6in) New-York 1998
 $588 - €610 - **£373** - FF4 000
   Confidences Gravure bois (22.5x18.5cm 8x7in) Paris 2000

VALTER Florence E. XX **[7]**
 $340 - €325 - **£208** - FF2 133
   A Pekinese Puppy/A Terrier Puppy Watercolour (23x18cm 9x7in) London 1999

VALTER Frederick E. c.1860-c.1930 **[59]**
 $1 233 - €1 389 - **£850** - FF9 111
   Sheep in Stable Yard Oil/board (20.5x26cm 8x10in) London 2000
 $763 - €820 - **£520** - FF5 382
   Sheep Resting on a Hillside Meadow Watercolour (15x23cm 5x9in) London 2001

VALTER Henry act.1854-1898 **[22]**
 $714 - €742 - **£450** - FF4 800
   The Dry Dock, Weymouth Watercolour (36x46cm 14x18in) Leyburn, North Yorkshire 2000

VALTIER Gérard 1950 **[112]**
 $2 622 - €2 897 - **£1 818** - FF19 000
   «Arlequin géant à la haute demeure» Huile/toile (55x46cm 21x18in) Armentières 2001

 $216 - €229 - **£143** - FF1 500
   La fête à l'auberge Sérigraphie (44x57cm 17x22in) Strasbourg 2000

VALTON Charles 1851-1918 **[173]**
 $1 405 - €1 493 - **£926** - FF9 791
   A Mountain Dog in the Snow Bronze (20x20cm 8x8in) Cleveland OH 1999

VALVASOR von Johann Weikhard 1641-1693 **[1]**
 $750 - €777 - **£450** - FF5 100
   Grande veduta della città di Lubiana Stampa (34x98cm 13x38in) Trieste 1999

VAN DYKE Willard Ames 1906-1986 **[12]**
 $2 400 - €2 242 - **£1 450** - FF14 705
   Mushrooms Vintage gelatin silver print (18x21cm 7x8in) New-York 1999

VAN ZANDT Thomas Kirby 1814-1886 **[4]**
 $12 000 - €10 353 - **£7 266** - FF67 911
   Lady Suffolk in the Lead Oil/canvas (67x90cm 26x35in) New-York 1999

VAN'T ZANT Arnoldus 1815-1889 **[2]**
 $2 419 - €2 269 - **£1 495** - FF14 883
   Panoramisch rivierlandschap Oil/canvas (28x32cm 11x12in) Rotterdam 1999

VANACKER Johann Baptist 1794-1863 **[5]**
 $2 564 - €2 851 - **£1 713** - FF18 699
   Portrait d'une dame de qualité/Portrait d'homme Aquarelle/papier (28x22cm 11x8in) Bruxelles 2000

VANBER (Albert Voisin) 1905-1994 **[9]**
 $1 729 - €2 058 - **£1 197** - FF13 500
   Composition Huile/panneau (57x37cm 22x14in) Paris 2000
 $2 113 - €2 515 - **£1 463** - FF16 500
   Village d'Aouste Gouache/papier (49x65cm 19x25in) Paris 2000

VANCE William 1935 **[28]**
 $654 - €686 - **£414** - FF4 500
   Jones et XIII, pour une future sérigraphie Mine plomb (30x26cm 11x10in) Paris 2000

VANCELLS Y VIETA Joaquín 1866-1942 **[20]**
 $5 940 - €6 607 - **£4 070** - FF43 340
   Paisaje Oleo/lienzo (81x100cm 31x39in) Madrid 2001
 $560 - €601 - **£380** - FF3 940
   Cielo nublado y mar Oleo/lienzo (27x34cm 10x13in) Barcelona 2001

VANDEPERRE Marcel 1908-1968 **[1]**
 $3 803 - €3 630 - **£2 376** - FF23 812
   Batsman Sculpture, wood (H69cm H27in) Amsterdam 1999

VANDERBANK John 1686/94-c.1739 **[40]**
 $13 719 - €12 726 - **£8 500** - FF83 477
   Sir Robert Long with a red Velvet Coat/The Rt. Hon. Lady Emma Long Oil/canvas (127x102.5cm 50x40in) London 1999
 $5 021 - €4 335 - **£3 000** - FF28 436
   Portrait of Councillor Arthur Bevan (c.1687-1742) Oil/canvas (74x61cm 29x24in) Llandeilo, Carmarthenshire 1998
 $1 129 - €1 046 - **£700** - FF6 861
   Gentleman, three quarter length, Seated, Holding a Scroll Ink (18x14cm 7x5in) London 1999

VANDERCAM Serge 1924 **[67]**
 $1 554 - €1 732 - **£1 065** - FF11 382
   L'homme de Tolund Technique mixte (68x98cm 26x38in) Antwerpen 2001

V

$739 - €694 - **£456** - FF4 552
Composition Huile/toile (41x33cm 16x12in)
Antwerpen 1999

$190 - €198 - **£124** - FF1 300
Sans titre Crayon/papier (24x34cm 9x13in)
Antwerpen 2000

VANDERLICK Armand 1897-1985 **[86]**

$4 104 - €4 462 - **£2 700** - FF29 268
Stilleven Oil/canvas (140x110cm 55x43in) Lokeren
2000

$4 608 - €4 462 - **£2 844** - FF29 268
Dimanche à la plage Huile/toile (60x80cm 23x31in)
Bruxelles 1999

$1 904 - €1 983 - **£1 256** - FF13 008
Damesportret (portrait de dame) Aquarelle/papier
(52x34cm 20x13in) Antwerpen 2000

VANDERPANT John A. 1884-1939 **[16]**

$3 200 - €3 684 - **£2 183** - FF24 166
Rhytm (Cauliflower) Gelatin silver print (25x19.5cm
9x7in) New-York 2000

VANDERSTEEN Germain 1897-1985 **[74]**

$272 - €290 - **£172** - FF1 900
Inspirée de la géniale musique de Beethoven
Huile/toile (54x73cm 21x28in) Paris 2000

$141 - €168 - **£100** - FF1 100
Le clown Feutre/papier (65.5x50cm 25x19in) Paris
2000

VANDERSTEEN Willy 1913-1990 **[13]**

$478 - €457 - **£298** - FF3 053
Sans titre Aquarelle (63x49cm 24x19in) Paris 1999

VANDERSTRAETEN Lea 1929 **[15]**

$742 - €694 - **£452** - FF4 552
Landschap met hooioppers Huile/toile (80x90cm
31x35in) Lokeren 1999

VANDEVERDONCK Franz, François XIX **[24]**

$2 224 - €2 556 - **£1 570** - FF16 769
Weidende Schafe mit Lämmchen am Seeufer
Oil/panel (17.7x24cm 6x9in) Bremen 2001

VANDOROS Spyridon 1882-1940 **[1]**

$4 554 - €3 857 - **£2 656** - FF25 300
Skalkotas, the Violin Player Oil/panel (68x80cm
26x31in) Athens 1998

VANETTI [6]

$1 220 - €1 220 - **£763** - FF8 000
Le char romain Bronze (38x48cm 14x18in) Paris
1999

VANGELLI Antonio 1917 **[18]**

$1 400 - €1 451 - **£840** - FF9 520
Circo Olio/tela (100x100cm 39x39in) Prato 2000

VANGI Giuliano 1931 **[17]**

$1 981 - €2 298 - **£1 367** - FF15 077
Studie für Gostino con la Tecla Pencil/paper
(96x68cm 37x26in) Luzern 2000

VANNERSON James XIX **[4]**

$15 000 - €14 066 - **£9 268** - FF92 265
Lee Robert E. in profile Salt print (15x11cm 6x4in)
New-York 1999

VANNETTI Antonio XIX-XX **[1]**

$6 500 - €7 660 - **£4 479** - FF50 247
Napoleon on Horseback Bronze (H70cm H27in)
New-York 2000

VANNI Francesco 1563/65-1610 **[38]**

$21 286 - €19 739 - **£13 000** - FF129 482
The Risen Christ Surrounded by Angels
Oil/paper (34.5x21cm 13x8in) London 1998

$12 280 - €11 388 - **£7 500** - FF74 701
**A Priest Raising the Host and a Kneeling
Acolyte/A Kneeling Monk** Black & white
chalks/paper (42x26cm 16x10in) London 1998

VANNI Giovanni Battista 1599-1660 **[9]**

$5 080 - €5 454 - **£3 400** - FF35 773
Man in a Cloak Black chalk/paper (40x27.5cm
15x10in) London 2000

$1 600 - €1 791 - **£1 115** - FF11 748
Untitled, after Coreggio Etching (42.5x57.5cm
16x22in) New-York 2001

VANNI Lippo XIV **[3]**

$27 600 - €23 843 - **£13 800** - FF156 400
Pietà con San Giovanni e la Maddalena
Tempera/tavola (29x26cm 11x10in) Prato 1999

VANNI Sam 1906-1992 **[60]**

$5 976 - €6 727 - **£4 116** - FF44 128
Komposition Oil/canvas (175x130cm 68x51in)
Helsinki 2000

$1 965 - €1 679 - **£1 154** - FF11 016
Landskap från chevreuse Oil/canvas (65x81cm
25x31in) Helsinki 1998

$1 141 - €1 261 - **£791** - FF8 274
Kaksi vanhaa tuttavaa tapaavat toisensa
Gouache/paper (68x46cm 26x18in) Helsinki 2001

$300 - €353 - **£208** - FF2 316
Komposition Serigraph (58x41cm 22x16in) Helsinki
2000

VANNINI Ottavio 1585-1643 **[13]**

$26 980 - €28 965 - **£18 050** - FF190 000
Le triomphe de David Huile/toile (172x211cm
67x83in) Paris 2000

$6 000 - €6 220 - **£3 600** - FF40 800
Ritratto del Gonfalone Pagolo Covoni Olio/tela
(116x89cm 45x35in) Imbersago (Lecco) 2001

$3 735 - €4 010 - **£2 500** - FF26 304
**Study of Draped Man (St John at the Foot of
the Cross?)/Drapes Male** Red chalk/paper
(40x26cm 15x10in) London 2000

VANNUCCIO di Francesco c.1367-c.1403 **[1]**

$40 000 - €51 833 - **£30 000** - FF340 000
**Crocifissione con i due dolenti, la Vergine Maria
e G. Evangelista** Tempera (46x22cm 18x8in) Firenze
2000

VANNUTELLI Scipione 1834-1894 **[24]**

$16 000 - €14 164 - **£9 782** - FF92 910
Reading a Poem Oil/canvas (57x42.5cm 22x16in)
New-York 1999

VANRIET Jan 1948 **[90]**

$133 - €149 - **£92** - FF975
Nu Aquarelle/papier (44x44cm 17x17in) Antwerpen
2001

VANTONGERLOO Georges 1886-1965 **[28]**

$74 214 - €86 218 - **£52 155** - FF565 554
«Fonction» Oil/masonite (59x46.5cm 23x18in)
Amsterdam 2001

$14 409 - €13 081 - **£9 000** - FF85 807
Desk Lamp Sculpture, wood (20x28x13cm 7x11x5in)
London 1999

$3 196 - €2 659 - **£1 876** - FF17 440
A Seated Lady Watercolour/paper (29.5x30.5cm
11x12in) Amsterdam 1998

VANTORE Hans Chr. Hansen 1861-1928 **[17]**
$291 - €335 - **£202** - FF2 198
Portraet af billedhuggeren Johannes Wiedewelt
Pastel/paper (35x26cm 13x10in) København 2000

VANTORE Mogens 1895-1977 **[324]**
$361 - €402 - **£253** - FF2 637
Opstilling med gule tulipaner, kande og aeble
Oil/canvas (55x45cm 21x17in) Vejle 2001

VANVITELLI Luigi 1700-1773 **[7]**
$47 500 - €41 294 - **£28 747** - FF270 873
View of St Peter's and Castel Sant'Angelo from the Tiber Oil/canvas (88x145cm 35x57in) New-York 1999
$1 324 - €1 453 - **£852** - FF9 534
Entwurf eines Kuppelsegmentes Indian ink (24.5x16.3cm 9x6in) Wien 2001

VAQUERO PALACIOS Joaquín 1900-1998 **[106]**
$15 975 - €13 515 - **£9 450** - FF88 650
Campos de trigo Oleo/lienzo (65x81cm 25x31in) Madrid 1998
$3 640 - €3 904 - **£2 470** - FF25 610
Costa de Santander Oleo/tablex (23.5x29cm 9x11in) Madrid 2001
$605 - €661 - **£407** - FF4 334
El saludo Lápiz/papel (16x17cm 6x6in) Madrid 2000
$108 - €120 - **£76** - FF788
Bajo el árbol Litografía (25x17cm 9x6in) Madrid 2001

VAQUERO TURCIOS Joaquín 1933 **[26]**
$6 000 - €7 208 - **£4 200** - FF47 280
Paisaje de Castilla Oleo/lienzo (97x130cm 38x51in) Madrid 2000
$1 272 - €1 442 - **£864** - FF9 456
Venecia Oleo/lienzo (50x61cm 19x24in) Madrid 2000
$1 134 - €1 081 - **£702** - FF7 092
Torso Gouache (50.5x73cm 19x28in) Madrid 1999

VAREJAO Adriana 1964 **[9]**
$30 000 - €29 126 - **£18 534** - FF191 055
Laparatomía Exploratoria 11 Oil/canvas (195x165cm 76x64in) New-York 1999

VARELA Abigail 1948 **[42]**
$16 000 - €18 565 - **£11 046** - FF121 776
Mujer con objeto comestible Bronze (H115.5cm H45in) New-York 2000
$8 000 - €9 098 - **£5 589** - FF59 680
Sentada en contempacion Bronze (49.5x25.5x42cm 19x10x16in) Beverly-Hills CA 2000

VARELA Y SARTORIO Eulogio 1868-1955 **[78]**
$390 - €360 - **£234** - FF2 364
Joven dama Oleo/lienzo (91.5x64cm 36x25in) Madrid 1999
$357 - €330 - **£214** - FF2 167
Ensoñación: caballero y bailarina Oleo/lienzo (20.5x32.5cm 8x12in) Madrid 1999
$286 - €264 - **£171** - FF1 733
Jarrón de cerámica con rosas silvestres Acuarela, gouache/papel (30.5x19cm 12x7in) Madrid 1999

VARGAS Alberto 1896-1982 **[35]**
$14 000 - €13 364 - **£8 748** - FF87 661
Nude, from the Legacy Magazine Series Watercolour/board (53x73.5cm 20x28in) New-York 1999
$550 - €461 - **£324** - FF3 027
Blonde Woman with Red Lipstick and Red Fingernails Color lithograph (54x41cm 21x16in) Bloomfield-Hills MI 1998

VARGAS Ismael 1945 **[5]**
$26 000 - €22 671 - **£15 719** - FF148 712
Metamorfosis Mixed media/panel (125x125cm 49x49in) New-York 1998

VARGAS MACHUCA Luis Martinez 1875-1929 **[7]**
$4 760 - €5 106 - **£3 145** - FF33 490
La diligencia Oleo/tabla (66x146cm 25x57in) Madrid 2000

VARGAS RUIZ Guillermo 1910-1990 **[70]**
$2 470 - €2 853 - **£1 710** - FF18 715
Embarcadero de San Marcos Oleo/lienzo (52x130cm 20x51in) Madrid 2001
$702 - €781 - **£481** - FF5 122
Cabo Roig (Torrevieja) Oleo/tabla (16x27cm 6x10in) Madrid 2000
$350 - €296 - **£207** - FF1 941
L'entrée du village Gouache/papier (20x14cm 7x5in) Luxembourg 1998

VARI Sofia 1940 **[6]**
$5 859 - €6 807 - **£4 117** - FF44 649
Untitled Bronze (H65cm H25in) Amsterdam 2001

VARLA Félix 1903 **[33]**
$1 100 - €940 - **£646** - FF6 165
Le Déjeuner Oil/canvas (38x45.5cm 14x17in) New-York 1998

VARLEY Albert Fleetwood 1804-1876 **[6]**
$301 - €330 - **£200** - FF2 166
Apley House, Ryde, Isle of Wight Watercolour/paper (17x25cm 6x9in) Billingshurst, West-Sussex 2000

VARLEY Cornelius 1781-1873 **[47]**
$3 688 - €3 117 - **£2 200** - FF20 446
Figures by a Bridge Over a River Oil/paper (27x37cm 10x14in) Bath 1998
$1 129 - €1 046 - **£700** - FF6 851
Cattle by a Cottage in a Hilly Landscape Watercolour (34x52cm 13x20in) London 1999

VARLEY Edgar John 1839-1889 **[11]**
$555 - €630 - **£380** - FF4 135
Vale Church, Evening Watercolour (17.5x24cm 6x9in) Bury St. Edmunds, Suffolk 2000

VARLEY Frederick Horsman 1881-1969 **[69]**
$30 765 - €35 894 - **£21 413** - FF235 448
Pink Ear (Portrait of Jess Crosby) Oil/canvas (51x40.5cm 20x15in) Toronto 2000
$9 114 - €7 799 - **£5 486** - FF51 157
Summer Landscape Oil/board (30x38cm 11x14in) Toronto 1998
$1 464 - €1 253 - **£881** - FF8 221
«Cottage in the Woods» Pencil (123.5x33.5cm 48x13in) Toronto 1998

VARLEY John XIX **[38]**
$938 - €788 - **£550** - FF5 168
Figures Resting Before Mount Snowdon Watercolour/paper (14.5x29cm 5x11in) London 1998

VARLEY John I 1778-1842 **[329]**
$5 797 - €5 880 - **£3 600** - FF38 567
View of Goodrich Castle Oil/canvas (26x53cm 10x21in) Godalming, Surrey 2000
$1 613 - €1 583 - **£1 000** - FF10 386
Figure by the Thames, Windsor Castle beyond Watercolour (14x11cm 5x4in) London 1999

V

VARLEY John II 1850-1933 **[76]**
- $5 235 - €4 645 - **£3 200** - FF30 471
  Feluccas on the Mahmoudish Canal, Egypt
  Oil/canvas (38x51cm 14x20in) London 1999
- $494 - €453 - **£300** - FF2 970
  The Pyramids at Gizeh Watercolour/paper (38x55cm 14x21in) London 1998

VARLEY John, Jnr. ?-1899 **[22]**
- $11 606 - €10 762 - **£7 000** - FF70 592
  Nearthe Gate of Bab-el-Zoueileh, Cairo Oil/canvas (68x50.5cm 26x19in) London 1999
- $756 - €716 - **£460** - FF4 699
  Grey Morning on the Nile Watercolour/paper (38x25cm 14x11in) Godalming, Surrey 1999

VARLEY William Fleetwood 1785-1858 **[11]**
- $493 - €467 - **£300** - FF3 065
  The Vale of Godalming Watercolour/paper (56x70cm 22x27in) Godalming, Surrey 1999

VARLIN (Willy Guggenheim) 1900-1977 **[97]**
- $26 608 - €26 812 - **£16 585** - FF175 874
  Der Koch Willi Huile/panneau (206x170cm 81x66in) Zürich 1999
- $22 220 - €26 426 - **£15 836** - FF173 340
  Die Chapelle de Lorette in Fribourg Öl/Karton (77.5x56cm 30x22in) Zürich 2000
- $11 110 - €13 213 - **£7 918** - FF86 670
  Niederdorf-Sepp Oil/canvas (35x29cm 13x11in) Zürich 2000
- $1 483 - €1 592 - **£992** - FF10 444
  Karikaturistische Darstellung: Herr Fabrikant X Indian ink (18.5x17.8cm 7x7in) Zürich 2000
- $356 - €382 - **£238** - FF2 506
  Billard, zwei Männer beim Billardspiel Lithographie (37x49cm 14x19in) St. Gallen 2000

VARMA Raja Ravi 1848-1906 **[7]**
- $41 840 - €44 912 - **£28 000** - FF294 604
  Radha's Dream Oil/canvas (52x74.5cm 20x29in) London 2000
- $22 000 - €25 507 - **£15 584** - FF167 312
  Village Belle Oil/canvas (42x24.5cm 16x9in) New-York 2000

VARNI Antonio c.1840-1908 **[4]**
- $9 000 - €7 775 - **£4 500** - FF51 000
  Spiaggia di Arenzano Olio/tela (36x57cm 14x22in) Genova 1999
- $2 796 - €2 898 - **£1 677** - FF19 012
  Porto di Antibes Olio/tavola (25.5x34cm 10x13in) Milano 1999

VARNI Santo 1807-1885 **[2]**
- $83 830 - €70 841 - **£50 000** - FF464 685
  «Laura al bagno» Marble (85x147x57cm 33x57x22in) London 1998

VARNON Cecil Archibald ?-1955 **[9]**
- $5 750 - €6 531 - **£4 034** - FF42 839
  The Ford Oil/canvas (63.5x76cm 25x29in) New-York 2001

VARO Remedios Lizarraga 1908-1963 **[40]**
- $475 000 - €414 182 - **£287 185** - FF2 716 857
  Visita inesperada (el Visitante) Oil/masonite (60x62cm 23x24in) New-York 1998
- $210 000 - €243 987 - **£147 588** - FF1 600 452
  El camino árido Painting (71x21cm 27x8in) New-York 2001
- $35 232 - €41 320 - **£25 344** - FF271 040
  Correspondances Gouache (45.5x33.5cm 17x13in) México 2001

VAROTARI IL PADOVANINO Alessandro 1588-1648 **[19]**
- $21 500 - €22 288 - **£12 900** - FF146 200
  Venere e satiro Olio/tela (104x131cm 40x51in) Venezia 2000
- $30 000 - €25 916 - **£15 000** - FF170 000
  Venere e amori Olio/tela (61x101cm 24x39in) Milano 1999

VAROTTI Giuseppe 1715-1780 **[1]**
- $15 863 - €14 799 - **£9 570** - FF97 073
  Santo vescovo con pastorale, attorniato da quattro Santi... Öl/Leinwand (161x94.5cm 63x37in) Wien 1999

VARTANYAN Gervasia 1927 **[54]**
- $2 445 - €2 167 - **£1 500** - FF14 213
  Drying Off Oil/canvas (113x160cm 44x62in) London 1999
- $489 - €433 - **£300** - FF2 842
  Smelling Blossom Oil/canvas (59x34.5cm 23x13in) London 1999
- $293 - €260 - **£180** - FF1 705
  Chinese Roses Oil/canvas (40x35.5cm 15x13in) London 1999

VARUTTI-KLEFENHAUSEN von Marco Walter 1917-1989 **[35]**
- $679 - €767 - **£478** - FF5 030
  Hamburger Hafen Öl/Leinwand (50x60cm 19x23in) Stuttgart 2001
- $706 - €741 - **£477** - FF4 863
  Blick auf Venedig Öl/Leinwand (30x42cm 11x16in) Kempten 2001

VASARELY Victor 1908-1997 **[2123]**
- $13 947 - €16 401 - **£10 000** - FF107 586
  «Kétava» Oil/canvas (176x88cm 69x34in) London 2001
- $7 917 - €8 842 - **£5 365** - FF58 000
  Irris Acrylique/toile (74x66cm 29x25in) Versailles 2000
- $2 138 - €2 515 - **£1 532** - FF16 500
  «Xiko IV» Acrylique/panneau (35x28cm 13x11in) Paris 2001
- $1 958 - €2 149 - **£1 261** - FF14 098
  M.C 166 Plastic (H185cm H72in) Stockholm 2000
- $733 - €739 - **£457** - FF4 846
  Zaphir Negatif Relief (38x36cm 14x14in) København 2000
- $2 485 - €2 378 - **£1 544** - FF15 600
  «Athem.c.» Collage/papier (70x64cm 27x25in) Paris 1999
- $300 - €322 - **£200** - FF2 113
  Zaire Silkscreen (38.5x33.5cm 15x13in) London 2000

VASARI Andrea XIX-XX **[28]**
- $385 - €361 - **£240** - FF2 367
  Torno, Lago di Como/Sento Calende, Lago Maggiore Watercolour (26.5x37cm 10x14in) London 1999

VASARI Giorgio 1511-1574 **[22]**
- $520 000 - €519 757 - **£317 668** - FF3 409 380
  The pietá Oil/panel (192x136cm 75x53in) New-York 2000
- $38 851 - €41 704 - **£26 000** - FF273 561
  The Resurrection, with SS.Cosmas and Damian, John the Baptist, Andrew Ink (27.5x19.5cm 10x7in) London 2000

VASARRI Emilio XIX **[17]**
- $21 000 - €21 161 - **£13 091** - FF138 810
  Chasing Crabs Oil/canvas (61x105.5cm 24x41in) New-York 2000

VASI Giuseppe 1710-1782 **[72]**
🎨 **$1 100** – €1 140 – **£660** – FF7 480
Le Rovine della Antiche magnificenze di Roma
Acquaforte (100x69cm 39x27in) Milano 2000

VASILEFF Ivan 1897-1966 **[1]**
🖼 **$4 000** – €4 647 – **£2 811** – FF30 484
La ventana Oleo/lienzo (50x40cm 19x15in) Buenos-Aires 2001

VASILOVSKY Sergei Ivanovich 1854-1917 **[16]**
🖼 **$2 759** – €2 652 – **£1 700** – FF17 396
Ukrainian Village in the Province of Poltava
Oil/board (23.5x36cm 9x14in) London 1999

VASLET Lewis 1742-1808 **[9]**
✏ **$2 908** – €3 206 – **£1 900** – FF21 029
Portrait of John Joseph Gooch, wearing a blue Coat Pastel/paper (28x21.5cm 11x8in) London 2000

VASNETSOV Apollinari Mikhailov 1856-1933 **[17]**
🖼 **$24 156** – €22 809 – **£15 000** – FF149 617
The Fortified old Russian Town Oil/canvas (99x151.5cm 38x59in) London 1999
🖼 **$64 416** – €60 824 – **£40 000** – FF398 980
Varengian Ships at Novgorod Oil/canvas (101x99cm 39x38in) London 1999

VASNETSOV Victor Mihailovich 1848-1926 **[14]**
✏ **$35 428** – €33 453 – **£22 000** – FF219 439
Design for the Menu of the Coronation Banquet of Emperor Nicholas II Watercolour (99x33.5cm 38x13in) London 1999
🎨 **$5 192** – €4 957 – **£3 244** – FF32 514
Souvenir Menu of the Coronation Banquet of the Emperor Nicholas II Color lithograph (33x92cm 13x36in) Cedar-Falls IA 1999

VASNIER Charles XIX **[12]**
✏ **$1 774** – €1 982 – **£1 237** – FF13 000
Femme nue de dos Pastel/papier (55x46cm 21x18in) Tours 2001

VASQUEZ BRITO Ramón 1927 **[20]**
🖼 **$4 309** – €5 079 – **£3 027** – FF33 315
Soledad sin presencia Oleo/lienzo (89x145cm 35x57in) Caracas ($) 2000

VASQUEZ DIAZ Daniel 1882-1969 **[131]**
🖼 **$33 000** – €36 039 – **£21 000** – FF236 400
Un cura o retrato de Don Silvestre Oleo/lienzo (96x71cm 37x27in) Madrid 2000
🖼 **$5 250** – €4 516 – **£3 075** – FF29 625
Cielo y mar Oleo/lienzo (28.5x33cm 11x12in) Madrid 1998
✏ **$810** – €901 – **£570** – FF5 910
Banco entre árboles Dibujo (24x22cm 9x8in) Madrid 2001
🎨 **$264** – €252 – **£168** – FF1 654
La Rábida Grabado (50x63cm 19x24in) Madrid 1999

VASSALLO Antonio Maria 1615/20-1664/67 **[11]**
🖼 **$28 858** – €28 237 – **£18 500** – FF185 225
Orpheus charming the Animals Oil/canvas (72.5x94cm 28x37in) London 1999

VASSEUR Adolphe 1836-1907 **[1]**
✏ **$5 430** – €6 403 – **£3 817** – FF42 000
Vues de l'ancien musée de Lille Aquarelle/papier (45.5x36cm 17x14in) Paris 2000

VASSILIEFF Danila Ivanovich 1897-1958 **[90]**
🖼 **$8 947** – €10 442 – **£6 315** – FF68 054
Puerto Rican Village Oil/canvas (51x60cm 20x23in) Malvern, Victoria 2000

🖼 **$5 263** – €6 142 – **£3 715** – FF40 291
Spanish Market Oil/canvas/board (28.5x37cm 11x14in) Malvern, Victoria 2000
🗿 **$4 154** – €3 808 – **£2 570** – FF24 982
Animals Playing Sculpture (20x16.5x14.5cm 7x6x5in) Melbourne 1998
✏ **$1 692** – €1 975 – **£1 178** – FF12 956
Two Women Watercolour/paper (28.5x38cm 11x14in) Melbourne 2000

VASSILIEFF Marie 1884-1957 **[131]**
🖼 **$25 000** – €29 007 – **£17 260** – FF190 275
Le flûtiste Oil/canvas (61x50cm 24x19in) New-York 2000
🖼 **$1 846** – €1 616 – **£1 118** – FF10 600
Portrait de femme Huile/toile (41x30cm 16x11in) Reims 1998
✏ **$457** – €534 – **£317** – FF3 500
Marie-Madeleine et le Christ Crayon (30x23cm 11x9in) Besançon 2000
🎨 **$750** – €842 – **£521** – FF5 520
«Arlequin, nouveau parfum de Rosine» Poster (30x20cm 12x8in) New-York 2001

VASSILIEFF Nicolai 1892-1970 **[14]**
🖼 **$3 000** – €3 212 – **£2 041** – FF21 067
Still Life on Tabletop with Chair Oil/canvas (46x45cm 18x18in) Portsmouth NH 2001
🖼 **$3 000** – €3 212 – **£2 041** – FF21 067
Girl with Green Hat in Chair Oil/canvas (40x30cm 16x12in) Portsmouth NH 2001

VASSILIOU Spyros 1902-1984 **[23]**
🖼 **$20 465** – €23 481 – **£14 000** – FF154 028
The Wreath Oil/canvas (81x115cm 31x45in) London 2000

VASSTRÖM Eric 1887-1958 **[22]**
🖼 **$581** – €673 – **£411** – FF4 412
Segelbåtar Oil/canvas (46x55cm 18x21in) Helsinki 2000

VASTAGH Géza 1866-1919 **[43]**
🖼 **$1 099** – €971 – **£671** – FF6 372
«Zwei ruhende Löwen» Öl/Leinwand (52x67cm 20x26in) München 1999
🖼 **$3 075** – €2 962 – **£1 914** – FF19 432
Höns Oil/canvas (25x51cm 9x20in) Köbenhavn 1999

VASZARY János 1867-1939 **[35]**
🖼 **$8 880** – €9 330 – **£5 520** – FF61 200
Baigneuses nues Huile/papier (36x49cm 14x19in) Budapest 2000
🖼 **$10 920** – €10 504 – **£6 760** – FF68 900
Self-Portrait Oil/panel (29x26cm 11x10in) Budapest 1999
✏ **$2 775** – €2 916 – **£1 725** – FF19 125
Roméo et Juliette Aquarelle/papier (26.5x37.5cm 10x14in) Budapest 2000

VASZKO Erzsébet 1902-1986 **[1]**
✏ **$1 485** – €1 688 – **£1 035** – FF11 070
Composition Pastel/papier (248x68cm 97x26in) Budapest 2001

VAUBOURGOIN Thierry 1944 **[23]**
🖼 **$982** – €838 – **£592** – FF5 500
Les poupées automates Huile/toile (116x90cm 45x35in) Calais 1998

VAUCLEROY de Pierre 1892-1969 **[32]**
🖼 **$3 180** – €2 975 – **£1 932** – FF19 512
Baigneuses Oil/canvas (116x88cm 45x34in) Lokeren 1999

V

VAUDECHAMP Joseph Jean 1790-1866 [8]
- $2 302 - €2 744 - £1 641 - FF18 000
  Portrait de Armance Roche de Costa Huile/toile (92x73cm 36x28in) Paris 2000

VAUDOYER Antoine Laurent Th. 1756-1846 [46]
- $1 372 - €1 285 - £850 - FF8 427
  Design for the Groundplan of the Institut des Beaux-arts, Paris Watercolour (54x42cm 21x16in) London 1999

VAUGHAN A.G. XIX [3]
- $3 736 - €4 011 - £2 500 - FF26 308
  Trompe-l'oeil: Bells Life in London, the Bedford Times Watercolour/paper (70x85.5cm 27x33in) London 2000

VAUGHAN Doris 1894-1974 [11]
- $868 - €937 - £600 - FF6 149
  The Ship Inn, Mousehole Watercolour (19x28cm 7x11in) London 2001

VAUGHAN Keith 1912-1977 [406]
- $17 842 - €17 201 - £11 000 - FF112 828
  Landscape with Figures Oil/canvas (122x101.5cm 48x39in) London 1999
- $12 044 - €11 120 - £7 500 - FF72 942
  Woodshed, Harrow Hill Oil/board (44x39.5cm 17x15in) London 1999
- $5 768 - €6 374 - £4 000 - FF41 812
  Odysseus Seen by the Sirens Oil/board (32.5x25.5cm 12x10in) London 2001
- $1 668 - €1 956 - £1 200 - FF12 828
  Standing boy Watercolour (15x9cm 5x3in) London 2001
- $791 - €903 - £550 - FF5 925
  Winter Landscape Color lithograph (46x56cm 18x22in) London 2000

VAUGHAN Michael 1938 [9]
- $7 000 - €6 225 - £4 281 - FF40 833
  The «Yeoman» Racing off Hawaii Mixed media/canvas (84x114cm 33x44in) New-York 1999

VAUGONDY DE Robert XVIII [24]
- $125 - €141 - £86 - FF925
  Map of Spain: Hispania Antiqua Engraving (49x58cm 19x23in) Cleveland OH 2000

VAUMOUSSE Maurice 1876-1961 [82]
- $224 - €229 - £140 - FF1 500
  Bouquet de fleurs roses Huile/toile (23x18cm 9x7in) Ourville-en-Caux 2000

VAUTHIER Antoine Charles 1790-c.1831 [4]
- $2 240 - €2 405 - £1 499 - FF15 777
  Thylacinthe de Harris/Panda/Antilope gibbeux Drawing (16.5x11cm 6x4in) London 2000

VAUTHIER Pierre 1845-1916 [47]
- $2 094 - €2 439 - £1 462 - FF16 000
  Estuaire Huile/toile (46x55cm 18x21in) Toulouse 2000

VAUTHRIN Ernest 1878-1949 [83]
- $1 085 - €991 - £660 - FF6 500
  Le hameau des Plomarch à Douarnenez Huile/canvas (54x65cm 21x25in) Douarnenez 1998
- $616 - €564 - £373 - FF3 700
  Concarneau - la ville close Huile/panneau (12x34cm 4x13in) Douarnenez 1998

VAUTIER André 1861-1941 [9]
- $1 254 - €1 189 - £762 - FF7 800
  Rivière et village Huile/toile (61x46cm 24x18in) Paris 1999

VAUTIER Benjamin I 1829-1898 [91]
- $62 829 - €53 768 - £37 819 - FF352 698
  La confession involontaire Huile/toile (72x94cm 28x37in) Zürich 1998
- $8 332 - €9 909 - £5 938 - FF65 002
  Mädchen im Boot Öl/Leinwand (34x25cm 13x9in) Zürich 2000
- $390 - €358 - £238 - FF2 347
  Spielende Kinder Pencil/paper (14.7x14.7cm 5x5in) München 1999

VAUTIER Benjamin II 1895-1974 [76]
- $1 324 - €1 296 - £818 - FF8 498
  Le voilier en réparation, Genève Öl/Leinwand (49x60cm 19x23in) Zürich 1999
- $751 - €838 - £505 - FF5 495
  Paysage urbain Huile/toile (41x30cm 16x11in) Genève 2000

VAUTIER Otto 1863-1919 [105]
- $2 831 - €3 285 - £1 986 - FF21 545
  Portrait de dame Huile/toile (98.5x66.5cm 38x26in) Genève 2000
- $555 - €661 - £395 - FF4 333
  Charette Huile/panneau (27x21cm 10x8in) Genève 2000
- $566 - €657 - £390 - FF4 307
  Jeune femme à la coiffe Dessin (23x29cm 9x11in) Genève 2000

VAUZELLE Jean-Lubin 1776-1837 [18]
- $1 712 - €1 677 - £1 053 - FF11 000
  Intérieur de la cathédrale de Milan Aquarelle/papier (27x21.5cm 10x8in) Paris 1999

VAVASSEUR Eugène 1863-1949 [28]
- $877 - €838 - £547 - FF5 500
  «Huile Rigal, Châlon s/Saône» Affiche couleur (115x156cm 45x61in) Paris 1999

VAWTER John William, Will 1871-1941 [6]
- $11 000 - €12 583 - £7 649 - FF82 538
  Brown County Landscape Oil/canvas (50x60cm 20x24in) Cincinnati OH 2000

VAYREDA CANADELL Josep M. 1932 [9]
- $1 740 - €1 802 - £1 110 - FF11 820
  Calle de Cadaqués Oleo/lienzo (54x65cm 21x25in) Madrid 2001

VAYREDA Y VILA Joaquin 1843-1894 [36]
- $1 178 - €1 141 - £722 - FF7 486
  Niño con barretina Oleo/tabla (17.5x10cm 6x3in) Barcelona 1999
- $364 - €420 - £252 - FF2 758
  Paisaje con figuras Técnica mixta/papel (25.5x33cm 10x12in) Barcelona 2001

VAYSON Paul 1842-1911 [17]
- $6 495 - €7 013 - £4 489 - FF46 000
  Les labours et les semailles Huile/toile (110x161cm 43x63in) Soissons 2001
- $2 682 - €2 897 - £1 854 - FF19 000
  La gardienne de vaches Huile/toile (47x61cm 18x24in) La Varenne-Saint-Hilaire 2001

VAYSSE Léonce 1844-? [3]
- $8 000 - €6 936 - £4 888 - FF45 494
  Morning Landscape, Franche-Comté Oil/canvas (61x101cm 24x39in) New-York 1999

VAZ Joao 1859-1931 [6]
- $94 600 - €109 672 - £66 000 - FF719 400
  «Póvoa do Varzim» Oleo/tabla (35x57.5cm 13x22in) Lisboa 2001

$38 700 – €44 866 – **£27 000** – FF294 300
Marinha Oleo/lienzo (38x40cm 14x15in) Lisboa 2001

VAZ Oscar 1909-1987 **[9]**
$5 000 – €5 809 – **£3 514** – FF38 106
Darsena norte Oleo/lienzo (90x70cm 35x27in)
Buenos-Aires 2001

VAZQUEZ Alberto 1935 **[2]**
$4 420 – €5 106 – **£3 060** – FF33 490
Madre Tierra II Oleo/lienzo (90x117cm 35x46in)
Seville 2000

VAZQUEZ UBEDA Carlos 1869-1944 **[50]**
$24 000 – €20 706 – **£14 479** – FF135 823
The Garden bench Oil/canvas (105x135.5cm
41x53in) New-York 1998
$2 015 – €1 952 – **£1 267** – FF12 805
La señorita de la boina Oleo/lienzo (116x89cm
45x35in) Madrid 1999
$406 – €420 – **£266** – FF2 758
Retrato de dama Sanguina (37x31cm 14x12in)
Madrid 2000

VEAL George XIX **[4]**
$16 000 – €19 028 – **£11 403** – FF124 816
Jack Shigar/Memnon/Matilda/Roudon Oil/canvas
(45.5x61cm 17x24in) New-York 2000

VEAL Hayward 1913-1968 **[52]**
$1 163 – €1 203 – **£732** – FF7 893
Maquarie Place Oil/canvas (60x50cm 23x19in)
Sydney 2000
$918 – €950 – **£578** – FF6 231
Autumn Morning Oil/board (31x38cm 12x14in)
Sydney 2000

VEALE Stafford Ives 1890-1961 **[1]**
$817 – €786 – **£501** – FF5 153
«**Come to old World Cornwall, GWR**» Poster
(102x62cm 40x24in) London 1999

VEBER Jean 1868-1928 **[46]**
$508 – €549 – **£351** – FF3 600
Jardiniers Aquarelle (20.5x30.5cm 8x12in) Paris 2001

VECCHI de Gabriele 1938 **[3]**
$3 124 – €3 630 – **£2 196** – FF23 812
«**U.R.M.N.T.A.1**» Metal (50x50cm 19x19in)
Amsterdam 2000

VECCHIA della Pietro Muttoni 1605-1678 **[49]**
$92 820 – €80 185 – **£46 410** – FF525 980
Caccia al cinghiale Olio/tela (77.5x294.5cm
30x115in) Milano 1999
$9 900 – €8 552 – **£6 600** – FF56 100
Grottesca Olio/tela (75.5x58.5cm 29x23in) Prato 1998
$1 428 – €1 480 – **£856** – FF9 710
Studio di figure con cane Inchiostro (18x6.5cm
7x2in) Venezia 2000

VECCHIO del Phyllis XX **[7]**
$215 – €254 – **£151** – FF1 665
Resting Place Watercolour/paper (26.5x37cm
10x14in) Dublin 2000

VECELLIO Francesco 1475/83-1559 **[4]**
$16 707 – €16 835 – **£10 413** – FF110 432
**Heilige Sebastian und Johannes der Täufer als
Knabe** Öl/Leinwand (64x36cm 25x14in) Zürich 2000

VECHTEN van Carl 1880-1964 **[65]**
$969 – €941 – **£603** – FF6 171
Salvador Dali Vintage gelatin silver print
(23.8x17.4cm 9x6in) Berlin 1999

VECOUX XX **[7]**
$801 – €726 – **£500** – FF4 764
«**Sports d'hiver en France**» Poster (99x62cm
38x24in) London 1999

VEDDER Elihu 1836-1923 **[62]**
$10 000 – €9 367 – **£6 148** – FF61 441
Peasant Girl Spinning Oil/panel (40.5x24.5cm
15x9in) New-York 1999
$40 000 – €39 648 – **£25 020** – FF260 076
Allegorical Marble Relief Relief (29x29cm 11x11in)
New-York 1999
$1 600 – €1 785 – **£1 112** – FF11 711
Reclining Nude Woman in Thought Charcoal
(23x26cm 9x10in) Cleveland OH 2001

VEDEL Herman A. 1875-1948 **[71]**
$652 – €697 – **£444** – FF4 570
**Portraet af Kapt.Dir.Chr.Schmiegelow, direktör i
Östasiatisk Kompagni** Oil/canvas (85x75cm
33x29in) Vejle 2001

VEDOVA Emilio 1919 **[223]**
$52 000 – €67 382 – **£39 000** – FF442 000
Trittico della libertà Olio/tela (135x186cm 53x73in)
Milano 2000
$16 200 – €13 995 – **£10 800** – FF91 800
«**Il pittore**» Olio/tela (49x40cm 19x15in) Milano 1998
$7 854 – €6 785 – **£3 927** – FF44 506
Presenza Tecnica mista/cartone (32.5x48.5cm
12x19in) Venezia 2001
$2 200 – €2 851 – **£1 650** – FF18 700
Senza titolo Pastelli (54x58cm 21x22in) Milano 2001
$275 – €285 – **£165** – FF1 870
Presenza 76 Acquaforte, acquatinta (32x21.5cm
12x8in) Prato 1999

VEEN van Balthasar 1596-c.1660 **[5]**
$14 157 – €13 613 – **£8 721** – FF89 298
**Winter Landscape with Figures Near the City
Walls, a Church Tower** Oil/panel (47.5x64cm
18x25in) Amsterdam 1999

VEEN van der Peter 1667-1736 **[1]**
$9 541 – €8 232 – **£5 734** – FF54 000
Allégorie de la musique/Allégorie de la poésie
Huile/panneau (40x33cm 15x12in) Nice 1998

VEEN van Gerardus c.1620-1683 **[4]**
$1 251 – €1 452 – **£864** – FF9 525
**Fringilla montifringilla (Brambling), male, in
winter plumage** Watercolour (14x19cm 5x7in)
Amsterdam 2000

VEEN van Otto 1556-1629 **[32]**
$10 000 – €10 116 – **£6 106** – FF66 359
Apotheosis of Hercules Oil/panel (64x47.5cm
25x18in) New-York 1999
$2 582 – €2 897 – **£1 806** – FF19 000
Personnages discutant dans une rue Technique
mixte (18x14.5cm 7x5in) Paris 2001
$3 000 – €3 068 – **£1 881** – FF22 000
Die Tugend besiegt das Laster Ink (26.5x20cm
10x7in) Köln 2000

VEEN van Rochus c.1640-1709 **[8]**
$1 333 – €1 151 – **£803** – FF7 552
A Salamander Watercolour (17x25.5cm 6x10in)
Amsterdam 1998

VEEN van Stuyvesant 1910-1977 **[12]**
$600 – €623 – **£403** – FF4 386
Construction Sight Watercolour (35x53cm 14x21in)
Chester NY 2000

V

VEENENDAAL Henricus 1889-1972 **[8]**
- $748 - €634 - **£451** - FF4 162
  Boerderij bij een poldersloct Oil/canvas (38x78cm 14x30in) Rotterdam 1998

VEERENDAEL van Nicolaes c.1640-1691 **[11]**
- $182 401 - €191 528 - **£115 000** - FF1 256 340
  Swag of Roses and Other Flowers Hanging from a Nail Oil/canvas (53x46cm 20x18in) London 2000
- $101 875 - €95 281 - **£61 687** - FF625 000
  Nature morte aux fleurs sur un entablement Huile/panneau (32x24cm 12x9in) Rodez 1999

VEGA Y MARRUGAL de la José XIX **[3]**
- $17 600 - €16 518 - **£10 725** - FF108 350
  El oportunista Oleo/tabla (67x50cm 26x19in) Madrid 1999
- $3 240 - €3 604 - **£2 220** - FF23 640
  Fiesta flamenca Oleo/lienzo (41.5x34cm 16x13in) Madrid 2000

VEGA Y MUNOZ Pedro c.1840-c.1882 **[10]**
- $2 125 - €2 480 - **£1 500** - FF16 269
  The Carpentry Lesson Oil/canvas (51x41cm 20x16in) London 2000
- $5 678 - €6 095 - **£3 800** - FF39 982
  Just in Time Oil/board (32x25cm 12x9in) Suffolk 2000

VEIGA C., Punta Arenas XX **[1]**
- $3 943 - €4 632 - **£2 800** - FF30 382
  Portrait of Sir Ernest Henry Shackleton, Half Length Gelatin silver print (14.5x10.5cm 5x4in) London 2000

VEIGA DA Simao 1879-1963 **[4]**
- $16 340 - €18 943 - **£11 400** - FF124 260
  Cavalo de toureio à espera de entrar na Praça de Toiros Oleo/lienzo (50x60cm 19x23in) Lisboa 2001

VEILHAN Xavier 1963 **[1]**
- $3 369 - €3 964 - **£2 415** - FF26 000
  Sans titre, Gilles, portrait à la bannière Photo couleurs (118x80cm 46x31in) Paris 2001

VEILLON Auguste Louis 1834-1890 **[48]**
- $2 594 - €2 436 - **£1 607** - FF15 979
  Küste mit Seglern bei Sonnenuntergang Öl/Leinwand (33.5x54cm 13x21in) Luzern 1999
- $2 572 - €2 592 - **£1 603** - FF17 000
  Rivage du Nil au soleil couchant Huile/toile (20x33cm 7x12in) Calais 2000
- $139 - €164 - **£99** - FF1 075
  Bord du Nil Encre Chine/papier (18x25cm 7x9in) Genève 2000

VEITH Caroline XX **[8]**
- $198 - €229 - **£136** - FF1 500
  Au château Technique mixte/papier (24.5x25.5cm 9x10in) Paris 2000

VEITH Eduard 1856-1925 **[48]**
- $1 758 - €2 025 - **£1 200** - FF13 280
  A young Lady in a Garden Making a Garland Oil/canvas (73x49cm 28x19in) London 2000
- $3 655 - €4 346 - **£2 533** - FF28 508
  Tänzerin mit entbösstem Oberkörper in orientalischem Palast Öl/Leinwand (30.5x51cm 12x20in) Radolfzell 2000
- $351 - €402 - **£244** - FF2 638
  To piger på picnic i det grönne Watercolour/paper (30x40cm 11x15in) Köbenhavn 2000

VEITH Johann Philipp 1768-1837 **[5]**
- $4 901 - €5 624 - **£3 352** - FF36 892
  Sächsisches Flusstal mit Fachwerkhäusern und Kirche Aquarell/Papier (47x66cm 18x25in) Berlin 2000

VEJRYCH Rudolf 1882-1939 **[12]**
- $924 - €875 - **£576** - FF5 737
  Eine Schaukel Öl/Karton (52x59cm 20x23in) Praha 2001

VEKEN van der Joseph 1872-1964 **[2]**
- $3 454 - €3 201 - **£2 062** - FF21 000
  Portrait d'homme sur fond vert Huile/panneau (34x26cm 13x10in) Paris 1999

VELA Vincenzo 1820-1891 **[10]**
- $3 484 - €3 049 - **£2 110** - FF20 000
  Main droite de femme au poignet de dentelle posée sur un coussin Marbre Carrare (13x34x26.3cm 5x13x10in) Paris 1998

VELA ZANETTI José 1913-1998 **[45]**
- $9 000 - €9 010 - **£5 550** - FF59 100
  Don Quijote Oleo/lienzo (60x74cm 23x29in) Madrid 2000
- $2 346 - €2 042 - **£1 428** - FF13 396
  Rincón rural Oleo/tabla (34x27cm 13x10in) Madrid 1999
- $1 890 - €1 802 - **£1 140** - FF11 820
  Mujeres peinándose Acuarela (38.5x44cm 15x17in) Madrid 1999

VELARDE Pablita 1918 **[7]**
- $3 000 - €3 206 - **£2 042** - FF21 028
  Earth Painting (27x60cm 11x24in) Cloudcroft NM 2001
- $2 000 - €1 982 - **£1 251** - FF13 003
  Untitled Mixed media/board (23x30.5cm 9x12in) New-York 1999
- $3 000 - €3 354 - **£2 022** - FF22 003
  Untitled, depicting pueblo ceremonial Buffalo Dance Watercolour/board (58x32.5cm 22x12in) New-York 2000

VELASCO 1960 **[1]**
- $2 880 - €3 732 - **£2 160** - FF24 480
  «Biagio Pace» Olio/tela (86x85cm 33x33in) Milano 2001

VELASCO DE BELAUSTEGUIGOITA Rosario 1910-1991 **[13]**
- $21 125 - €19 521 - **£13 000** - FF128 050
  Gitanos, la siesta Oleo/lienzo (95x132cm 37x51in) Madrid 1999
- $2 760 - €2 403 - **£1 720** - FF15 760
  Agricultor Oleo/lienzo (46x38cm 18x14in) Madrid 1999

VELASCO José María 1840-1912 **[62]**
- $365 000 - €396 301 - **£252 762** - FF2 599 566
  Valle de Mexico desde el cerro de Santa Isabel Oil/canvas (55x76cm 22x30in) Cleveland OH 2001
- $50 000 - €43 598 - **£30 230** - FF285 985
  Ahuehuete Oil/board/canvas (31x43.5cm 12x17in) New-York 2000
- $2 650 - €3 112 - **£1 882** - FF20 415
  Boceto para Vista del Valle de México desde el río de los Morales Lápiz (15x26cm 5x10in) México 2000
- $900 - €785 - **£544** - FF5 147
  Ensayo ornitológico de la Familia Trochilidae o sea Colibries Color lithograph (29x19cm 11x7in) New-York 1998

VELASQUEZ Diego 1599-1660 **[2]**
- **$8 100 000** - €7 129 084 - **£4 931 280** -
FF46 763 730
  Saint Rufina Oil/canvas (77x64.5cm 30x25in) New-York 1999

VELASQUEZ José Antonio 1906-1985 **[29]**
- **$15 000** - €14 595 - **£9 232** - FF95 734
  Catedral de Comayagua Oil/canvas (144x109.5cm 56x43in) New-York 1999
- **$1 534** - €1 805 - **£1 100** - FF11 839
  «Domingos de Ramos» Oil/canvas (56x72.5cm 22x28in) London 2001

VELDE van de Bram 1895-1981 **[596]**
- **$153 417** - €180 415 - **£110 000** - FF1 183 446
  Sans titre, Montrouge Oil/canvas (130x162.5cm 51x63in) London 2001
- **$10 936** - €12 706 - **£7 686** - FF83 344
  Village sur la rivière Oil/canvas (81.5x90cm 32x35in) Amsterdam 2001
- **$4 524** - €4 834 - **£3 481** - FF31 707
  Composition Aquarelle, gouache/papier (28.5x40.5cm 11x15in) Lokeren 2001
- **$472** - €404 - **£282** - FF2 647
  Composition Farblithographie (64x90cm 25x35in) Zürich 1998

VELDE van de Adrian 1636-1672 **[75]**
- **$5 012** - €5 624 - **£3 474** - FF36 892
  Hirte mit Hund, Kühen, Stier und Schafen bei einem Brunnen Oil/panel (35.5x46cm 13x18in) München 2000
- **$14 157** - €13 613 - **£8 721** - FF89 298
  Shepherds with Their Herd on a Path Near a Ruin in a Hilly Landscape Oil/panel (30x36.5cm 11x14in) Amsterdam 1999
- **$14 719** - €12 700 - **£8 881** - FF83 308
  Italianate landscape with peasant couple and their flock by a fountain Ink (32.4x26.7cm 12x10in) Amsterdam 1998
- **$386** - €460 - **£275** - FF3 018
  Der grasende Stier Radierung (13.5x16.2cm 5x6in) Berlin 2000

VELDE van de Esaias 1591-1630 **[66]**
- **$50 000** - €47 729 - **£31 240** - FF313 080
  Landscape with Figures near a Church Oil/panel (36.5x49cm 14x19in) New-York 1999
- **$62 517** - €58 991 - **£38 571** - FF386 958
  Ambush on a Country Road in the Dunes/Cowherd Watering Cattle Oil/panel (13.5x18.5cm 5x7in) Amsterdam 1999
- **$2 563** - €2 812 - **£1 741** - FF18 446
  Holländische Winterlandschaft mit zahlreichen Schlittschuhläufern Ink (20x26.4cm 7x10in) Berlin 2000
- **$559** - €613 - **£379** - FF4 024
  Ein Bauernhaus am Weg, im Hintergrund Felder Radierung (11x17.3cm 4x6in) Berlin 2000

VELDE van de Henri 1896-1969 **[14]**
- **$26 000** - €28 948 - **£17 399** - FF183 066
  Tropon,l'aliment le plus concentré Lithograph (112.5x75.5cm 44x29in) New-York 2000

VELDE van de Henry 1863-1957 **[26]**
- **$15 500** - €14 521 - **£9 318** - FF95 251
  Haystacks in Front of the Church at Wechelderzandie Oil/canvas (45x60cm 17x23in) Amsterdam 1999
- **$917** - €1 022 - **£616** - FF6 707
  Tropon Farblithographie (37.2x27.7cm 14x10in) München 2000

VELDE van de Jan II c.1593-1641 **[98]**
- **$30 000** - €26 081 - **£18 156** - FF171 078
  Farmstead with Travellers on a Road Ink (15x42cm 5x16in) New-York 1999
- **$400** - €468 - **£281** - FF3 067
  River Landscape with Two Monks on a Road near a Chapel, After Horst Etching (19x27.5cm 7x10in) New-York 1999

VELDE van de Jan Jansz. III c.1620-1662 **[6]**
- **$80 993** - €90 812 - **£55 000** - FF595 688
  Peeled Lemon with Chestnuts upon a Pewter Dish Oil/panel (38x31cm 14x12in) London 2000

VELDE van de Jan Justus 1689-? **[1]**
- **$5 280** - €5 031 - **£3 346** - FF33 000
  Portrait d'officier Huile/toile (85x65cm 33x25in) Uchaux 1999

VELDE van de Pieter 1634-c.1705 **[47]**
- **$11 055** - €10 062 - **£6 910** - FF66 000
  Bataille navale Huile/toile (101x140cm 39x55in) Amiens 1999
- **$18 660** - €16 152 - **£11 325** - FF105 952
  Ansicht Venedigs Öl/Leinwand (73.5x125cm 28x49in) Zürich 1998
- **$4 674** - €4 360 - **£2 820** - FF28 602
  Dreimaster und Fischerboote auf bewegter See Oil/panel (19x24.5cm 7x9in) Wien 1999

VELDE van de Willem I 1611-1693 **[22]**
- **$8 022** - €7 714 - **£4 941** - FF50 602
  The battle of Scheveningen, 31 July, 10 August Black chalk (27.5x126cm 10x49in) Amsterdam 1999

VELDE van de Willem II 1633-1707 **[91]**
- **$36 390** - €31 116 - **£22 000** - FF204 105
  The Royal Sovereign and other Shipping in a Light Breeze Oil/canvas (137x120cm 53x47in) London 1999
- **$2 336 385** - €2 294 488 - **£1 450 000** - FF15 050 860
  The Morning Gun: Small English Man-o-War Firing a Salute Oil/canvas (66.5x52.5cm 26x20in) London 1999
- **$638 124** - €627 266 - **£410 000** - FF4 114 596
  Dutch States Yacht sailing in a Light Breeze on Choppy Seas Oil/canvas (36.5x43cm 14x16in) London 1999
- **$2 486** - €2 505 - **£1 550** - FF16 435
  Shipping in Rough Seas Wash (15.5x27cm 6x10in) Newbury, Berkshire 2000

VELDE van de Willem III 1667-c.1710 **[5]**
- **$1 500** - €1 538 - **£937** - FF10 600
  Study of Two Ships Pencil/paper (15x16.5cm 5x6in) New-York 1999

VELDE van Geer 1898-1977 **[196]**
- **$17 757** - €19 059 - **£11 881** - FF125 017
  Abstract Composition Oil/canvas (60x73cm 23x28in) Amsterdam 2000
- **$8 395** - €9 983 - **£5 984** - FF65 485
  Composition Oil/canvas (28x53cm 11x20in) Amsterdam 2000
- **$4 045** - €4 538 - **£2 803** - FF29 766
  Untitled Watercolour (29x33.5cm 11x13in) Amsterdam 2000

VELDEN van der Petrus (Paulus?) 1837-1913/15 **[15]**
- **$12 963** - €13 613 - **£8 202** - FF89 298
  A Precious Moment Oil/canvas (167x97cm 65x38in) Amsterdam 2000

V

$3 995 - €4 538 - £2 803 - FF29 766
A Prayer before the Meal Oil/canvas (73.5x98cm 28x38in) Amsterdam 2001

$2 294 - €2 723 - £1 670 - FF17 859
De Laatste tocht Watercolour/paper (29x51cm 11x20in) Maastricht 2001

VELDHOEN Arie Johannes, Aat 1934 **[23]**

$970 - €1 134 - £693 - FF7 441
The Artist with his Family Oil/canvas (99x82cm 38x32in) Amsterdam 2001

VELDHUISEN van Willem 1954 **[3]**

$25 140 - €24 958 - £15 708 - FF163 713
Een zomermiddag in Centre Pompidou Acrylic/canvas (160x130cm 62x51in) Amsterdam 1999

$6 856 - €6 807 - £4 284 - FF44 649
Black Sofa Acrylic/canvas (113.5x77.5cm 44x30in) Amsterdam 1999

VELICKOVIC Vladimir 1935 **[344]**

$10 282 - €8 690 - £6 116 - FF57 000
Homme qui court Huile/toile (147x198cm 57x77in) Versailles 1998

$2 282 - €1 906 - £1 338 - FF12 500
L'ascension Acrylique (65x50cm 25x19in) Paris 1998

$752 - €818 - £495 - FF5 365
Stappende man Oil/canvas (27x22cm 10x8in) Lokeren 2000

$1 384 - €1 372 - £865 - FF9 000
Expérience No.8 Encre (75x107cm 29x42in) Paris 1999

$136 - €152 - £94 - FF1 000
«Experience Rat n°20» Lithographie (56x90cm 22x35in) Versailles 2001

VELLACOTT Elisabeth 1905 **[1]**

$4 170 - €4 203 - £2 600 - FF27 569
Arrival of the Dancers Oil/board (76x76cm 29x29in) London 2000

VELLAN Felice 1889-1976 **[88]**

$1 200 - €1 244 - £720 - FF8 160
«A Tarquinia (Roma)» Olio/tela (40x50cm 15x19in) Vercelli 1999

$440 - €570 - £330 - FF3 740
Paese sotto la neve Olio/masonite (25x30cm 9x11in) Vercelli 2001

$200 - €207 - £120 - FF1 360
Studi di cani Carboncino (31x36cm 12x14in) Torino 2000

VELLANI MARCHI Mario 1895-1979 **[13]**

$3 600 - €3 732 - £2 160 - FF24 480
La chiesa della Salute al tramonto Olio/faesite (90x90cm 35x35in) Roma 1999

$132 - €171 - £99 - FF1 122
«Naviglio, Milano» Tecnica mista/carta (18x23cm 7x9in) Torino 2000

VELLETRI da Lello XV **[1]**

$26 000 - €33 691 - £19 500 - FF221 000
Madonna col Bambino in trono e nella cuspide la Trinità Tempera/tavola (45x21.5cm 17x8in) Firenze 2000

VELLY Jean-Pierre 1943-1990 **[5]**

$1 400 - €1 451 - £840 - FF9 520
Figure Acquaforte (70x50cm 27x19in) Milano 2001

VELSEN van Cornelius / Cor 1921 **[32]**

$179 - €204 - £123 - FF1 339
«Fly there by KLM, see Holland» Poster (62x97cm 24x38in) Hoorn 2001

VELTEN Wilhelm 1847-1929 **[174]**

$2 743 - €2 556 - £1 692 - FF16 769
Fuchsjagd Öl/Leinwand (54x41cm 21x16in) Köln 1999

$3 200 - €2 786 - £1 907 - FF18 275
The Horse Trader Oil/panel (11x17cm 4x7in) St. Louis MO 1998

VELTHUYSEN van Henry 1891-1954 **[12]**

$1 808 - €1 998 - £1 254 - FF13 109
Figures by the Water Oil/panel (45x25cm 17x10in) Singapore 2001

VELTZ Ivan Avgustovich 1866-1926 **[5]**

$12 912 - €10 606 - £7 500 - FF69 573
Birch Forest Oil/canvas (143x143cm 56x56in) London 1998

$14 692 - €17 485 - £10 500 - FF114 693
View of the Crimea Oil/canvas (71x111cm 27x43in) London 2000

VELZEN van Johannes Petrus 1816-1853 **[19]**

$22 393 - €26 319 - £15 526 - FF172 642
A Winter Landscape with Skaters/Figures by A Snowy Village Oil/canvas (36.5x46.5cm 14x18in) Amsterdam 2000

VEN Emil 1902-1984 **[6]**

$1 280 - €1 259 - £800 - FF8 256
Street in the Castle of Buda Oil/canvas (80x60cm 31x23in) Budapest 1999

VEN van der Paul 1892-1972 **[19]**

$434 - €454 - £274 - FF2 976
Winterlandscape Oil/canvas (60x100cm 23x39in) Amsterdam 2000

VEN van der Walter 1884-1923 **[5]**

$2 600 - €2 500 - £1 604 - FF16 401
«Viie Olympiade Anvers» Poster (85,5x61.5cm 33x24in) New-York 1999

VENABERT XX **[3]**

$551 - €635 - £380 - FF4 166
«Jeunesse» Poster (156x114cm 61x44in) London 2000

VENABLES Aldolphus Robert c.1810-c.1880 **[2]**

$9 249 - €10 746 - £6 500 - FF70 491
Portrait of two Sisters, three-quarter-lenght Oil/canvas (84x71cm 33x27in) London 2001

VÉNARD Claude 1913-2000 **[907]**

$4 348 - €4 014 - £2 600 - FF26 328
La mer Oil/canvas (100x120cm 39x47in) London 1999

$1 988 - €2 134 - £1 330 - FF14 000
Coupe de vase de fleurs bleues sur table rouge Huile/toile (65x54cm 25x21in) Cannes 2000

$846 - €945 - £573 - FF6 200
Vase de fleurs Huile/toile (41x33cm 16x12in) Saint-Dié 2000

$525 - €606 - £367 - FF3 978
Paris Watercolour/board (30.5x40.5cm 12x15in) Bethesda MD 2001

VENDRAMINI Giovanni, John 1769-1839 **[6]**

$125 - €140 - £87 - FF920
Mildness/Simplicity, after Francesco Bartolozzi (1725/1815) Mezzotint (26x20cm 10x8in) Bolton MA 2001

VENE Roger XX **[13]**

$927 - €915 - £571 - FF6 000
Sophie 1 Bronze (H41cm H16in) Senlis 1999

V

VENET Bernar 1941 **[189]**
- $8 262 - €9 147 - £5 604 - FF60 000
  «Lorsque...» (texte de l'auteur) Huile/papier (60x100cm 23x39in) Paris 2000
- $2 500 - €2 788 - £1 681 - FF18 286
  Untitled Acrylic (33x46cm 12x18in) New-York 2000
- $30 613 - €36 043 - £21 510 - FF236 428
  Ligne Indéterminée Metal (177x203x154cm 69x79x60in) Zürich 2000
- $6 768 - €6 555 - £4 252 - FF43 000
  Ligne indéterminée Métal (45x21x45cm 17x8x17in) Paris 1999
- $4 564 - €4 269 - £2 797 - FF28 000
  «Ligne indéterminée» Fusain (77x77cm 30x30in) Paris 1998
- $494 - €427 - £297 - FF2 800
  Ligne indéterminée Eau-forte (50.2x49.8cm 19x19in) London 2001

VENETO Bartolomeo c.1480-c.1540 **[1]**
- $22 555 - €22 434 - £14 000 - FF147 156
  Young Man, wearing a Cloak, a white Chemise, a mauve Sash and a Cap Oil/panel (54.5x38cm 21x14in) London 2000

VENETO Pasqualino c.1470-1504 **[2]**
- $79 640 - €90 502 - £55 000 - FF593 653
  The Madonna and Child in a Landscape Oil/panel (52x42.5cm 20x16in) London 2000

VENEZIANO Agostino 1490-1540 **[44]**
- $764 - €642 - £449 - FF4 213
  The Carcass Engraving (30.5x63.5cm 12x25in) London 1998

VENNA Lucio 1897-1974 **[15]**
- $840 - €726 - £560 - FF4 760
  Vista sulle zattere, Venezia Olio/tela (50x60cm 19x23in) Firenze 1998

VENNE van de Adriaen Pietersz. 1589-1662 **[52]**
- $33 492 - €28 514 - £20 000 - FF187 042
  A Village Scene with Peasants dancing and Making Merry Oil/panel (60x74.5cm 23x29in) London 1998
- $17 920 - €20 348 - £12 264 - FF133 476
  Loosen-Al-arm, ein wütender Bettler mit einem Holzbein Oil/panel (33.5x27cm 13x10in) Wien 2000
- $8 571 - €9 983 - £5 988 - FF65 485
  Peasant Dance, Goed-Rond Red chalk (24x37cm 9x14in) Amsterdam 2000

VENNE van de Jan 1636-c.1672 **[4]**
- $4 000 - €4 647 - £2 831 - FF30 484
  Old Man playing a Pipe with a Woman and Child Oil/panel (52x40.5cm 20x15in) New-York 2001

VENNE van der Adolf 1828-1911 **[51]**
- $2 935 - €2 812 - £1 847 - FF18 446
  Ein Bauer rastet mit seinem Pferdewagen auf einer Anhöhe Öl/Leinwand (42x52cm 16x20in) Stuttgart 1999
- $1 209 - €1 022 - £719 - FF6 706
  Ungarisches Fuhrwerk im Schneesturm Oil/panel (11.5x18.5cm 4x7in) Bremen 1998

VENNE van der Fritz 1873-1936 **[44]**
- $642 - €716 - £449 - FF4 695
  Pferde auf der Weide Öl/Leinwand (35.5x57cm 13x22in) München 2001
- $1 027 - €1 173 - £724 - FF7 696
  Bauer mit Pferdefuhrwerk in verschneiter Landschaft Oil/panel (26.5x35cm 10x13in) Bern 2001

VENNEMAN Camille 1827-1868 **[6]**
- $12 946 - €12 140 - £8 000 - FF79 635
  A Village Celebration Oil/panel (50x63cm 19x24in) London 1999

VENNEMAN Charles / Karel F. 1802-1875 **[47]**
- $12 547 - €11 798 - £7 768 - FF77 391
  Diplomatic intervention Oil/panel (40x47cm 15x18in) Amsterdam 1999
- $2 559 - €2 556 - £1 600 - FF16 769
  Bäuerliches Interieur mit lesendem Mädchen und verliebtem Jüngling Oil/panel (32.5x26.5cm 12x10in) Köln 1999

VENNER Victor XIX-XX **[7]**
- $235 - €261 - £160 - FF1 713
  The Welding Breakfast/Good Send Off Print in colors (40x63.5cm 15x25in) Lymington 2000

VENTAYOL Juan XX **[3]**
- $1 100 - €1 144 - £694 - FF7 506
  Abstracto Oleo/lienzo (90x122cm 35x48in) Montevideo 2000

VENTOSA DOMENECH José 1897-1982 **[16]**
- $1 485 - €1 351 - £900 - FF8 865
  «Los pajares, Sant Celoni» Oleo/lienzo (46x61cm 18x24in) Barcelona 1999
- $2 340 - €2 703 - £1 620 - FF17 730
  Desfiladero Oleo/tabla (32x40cm 12x15in) Madrid 2000
- $2 295 - €2 553 - £1 615 - FF16 745
  Lluchalcar (Mallorca) Gouache/papier (60x66cm 23x25in) Madrid 2001

VENTRILLON Gaston, le jeune 1897-1982 **[15]**
- $796 - €884 - £553 - FF5 800
  «Centenaire de l'Algérie, Chrea, grande semaine des sports d'hiver» Affiche (100x62cm 39x24in) Paris 2001

VENTRONE Luciano 1942 **[4]**
- $2 400 - €2 488 - £1 440 - FF16 320
  La mia modella Olio/tela (70x50cm 27x19in) Roma 2001

VENTURI Osvaldo 1900-1989 **[11]**
- $390 - €358 - £240 - FF2 351
  Clouds over Europe -Nubes Sobre Europa Poster (109x73.5cm 42x28in) London 1999

VENTURINI Giovanni Francesco 1650-c.1715 **[3]**
- $700 - €726 - £420 - FF4 760
  Le fontane ne palazzi ne giardini di Roma Gravure (21.5x31.5cm 8x12in) Firenze 2000

VENUS Albert Franz 1842-1871 **[19]**
- $18 401 - €18 269 - £11 500 - FF119 838
  Children Playing in the Woods Oil/canvas (102x92cm 40x36in) London 1999

VERA BLASCO Alejo 1834-1923 **[31]**
- $769 - €906 - £542 - FF5 941
  Interior de una casa de Pompeya Oleo/lienzo (27x39cm 10x15in) Madrid 2000
- $154 - €168 - £106 - FF1 103
  Figura clásica y lisiado Carboncillo (30x24cm 11x9in) Madrid 2001

VERA REYES de Cristino 1931 **[27]**
- $3 710 - €4 205 - £2 520 - FF27 580
  Mujer con cesta Oleo/lienzo (90x65cm 35x25in) Madrid 2000
- $715 - €781 - £481 - FF5 122
  La pareja II Tinta/papel (31x22cm 12x8in) Madrid 2000

V

VERA SALÉS Enrique 1886-1956 **[72]**

⌒ **$2 280** - €2 403 - **£1 440** - FF15 760
Interior de la Catedral de Toledo Oleo/lienzo
(96x69cm 37x27in) Madrid 2000

⌒ **$1 064** - €1 141 - **£703** - FF7 486
Cortijo Oleo/tabla (31.5x24.5cm 12x9in) Madrid 2000

✎ **$237** - €264 - **£167** - FF1 733
Vista de Toledo Tinta/papel (14.5x16cm 5x6in)
Madrid 2001

VERBEECK Arthur XX **[8]**

⌒ **$2 916** - €3 176 - **£2 008** - FF20 836
Cows grazing in an Orchard Oil/canvas
(60.5x80.5cm 23x31in) Amsterdam 2001

VERBEECK Franz Xaver Hendrik 1686-1755 **[21]**

⌒ **$8 840** - €9 915 - **£6 160** - FF65 040
Compagnie musicale sur une terrasse Huile/panneau (39.5x50cm 15x19in) Bruxelles 2001

⌒ **$8 998** - €8 385 - **£5 549** - FF55 000
La joueuse de guitare dans l'embrasure de la fenêtre Huile/panneau (26.5x22cm 10x8in) Paris 1999

VERBEECK Jan act.1569-1619 **[1]**

✎ **$19 000** - €20 353 - **£12 975** - FF133 505
Two Peasants fighting, their Wives trying to restrain them Ink (11.5x15cm 4x5in) New-York 2001

VERBEECK Pieter Cornelisz c.1610-c.1654 **[13]**

⌒ **$6 795** - €6 541 - **£4 248** - FF42 903
Ein Brauner in einer Dünenlandschaft Oil/panel
(18x16.5cm 7x6in) Wien 2001

VERBOECKHOVEN Eugène Joseph 1798/99-1881 **[560]**

⌒ **$98 442** - €90 149 - **£60 000** - FF591 336
Animals in a Landscape Oil/canvas (100x133cm 39x52in) London 1999

⌒ **$24 000** - €20 706 - **£14 479** - FF135 823
Shepherd's rest Oil/panel (44.5x55.5cm 17x21in)
New-York 1998

⌒ **$5 603** - €6 205 - **£3 800** - FF40 705
Sheep and a Chicken in a Landscape Oil/panel
(13x18.5cm 5x7in) Billingshurst, West-Sussex 2000

⌒ **$5 568** - €5 949 - **£3 792** - FF39 024
Liggende koe Bronze (11.5x23.5cm 4x9in) Lokeren 2001

✎ **$538** - €518 - **£334** - FF3 400
Chèvre Crayon (45x35.7cm 17x14in) Lyon 1999

VERBOECKHOVEN Louis 1802-1889 **[137]**

⌒ **$6 216** - €5 949 - **£3 816** - FF39 024
Barques de pêche à la côte Huile/toile (50x70cm 19x27in) Bruxelles 1999

⌒ **$4 304** - €3 966 - **£2 592** - FF26 016
Marine Huile/panneau (28x39.5cm 11x15in)
Antwerpen 1999

VERBOECKHOVEN Louis II 1827-1884 **[22]**

⌒ **$4 320** - €3 966 - **£2 672** - FF26 016
Marine Huile/toile (40x46cm 15x23in) Bruxelles 1999

⌒ **$3 685** - €3 346 - **£2 281** - FF21 951
Marine Huile/panneau (14x17.5cm 5x6in) Bruxelles 1999

VERBOOM Adriaen Hendricksz. c.1628-c.1670 **[26]**

⌒ **$29 452** - €33 023 - **£20 000** - FF216 614
Wooded Landscape with a Riverside Village
Oil/panel (71.5x183cm 28x72in) London 2000

⌒ **$18 772** - €21 781 - **£12 960** - FF142 876
A Castle by a River Fishermen in a Rowing Boat, at Sunset Oil/panel (69.5x90.5cm 27x35in)
Amsterdam 2000

⌒ **$14 000** - €14 997 - **£9 560** - FF98 372
Woods at the Edge of a River, a Church Spire in the Distance Wash (13x18cm 5x7in) New-York 2001

▥ **$386** - €460 - **£275** - FF3 018
Der Teich Radierung (13.5x17.8cm 5x7in) Berlin 2000

VERBOOM Willem Hendricksz c.1640-1718 **[2]**

⌒ **$6 648** - €7 714 - **£4 590** - FF50 602
Wooded River Landscape with Travellers on a Path Nears Ruins Oil/panel (60x84cm 23x33in)
Amsterdam 2000

VERBRUGGE Emile 1856-1936 **[35]**

⌒ **$358** - €421 - **£251** - FF2 764
Pêcheur sur un fleuve Huile/toile (25x35cm 9x13in)
Bruxelles 2000

VERBRUGGEN Gaspar I Pieter 1635-1681 **[31]**

⌒ **$18 156** - €18 294 - **£11 316** - FF120 000
Jeune femme disposant des fleurs Huile/toile
(115x95cm 45x37in) Paris 2000

⌒ **$124 136** - €121 588 - **£80 000** - FF797 568
Roses, a Cornflower, Wildflowers/Roses, Bluebells, Butterfly, Insects Oil/panel (19x23cm 7x9in) London 1999

VERBRUGGEN Gaspar II Pieter 1664-1730 **[73]**

⌒ **$30 096** - €33 539 - **£20 482** - FF220 000
Une couronne de fleurs entourant un bas relief
Huile/toile (171x138.5cm 67x54in) Paris 2000

⌒ **$23 854** - €20 581 - **£14 337** - FF135 000
Jeune femme dans un parc Huile/toile (60x75cm 23x29in) Versailles 1998

⌒ **$10 919** - €10 684 - **£7 000** - FF70 085
Still Life of Fruit and Flowers on a Stone Plinth, Vase of Narcissi Oil/canvas (26x23cm 10x9in)
London 2000

VERBRUGGHE Charles 1877-1974 **[67]**

⌒ **$1 482** - €1 601 - **£1 024** - FF10 500
Bruges sous la neige Huile/toile (46x55cm 18x21in) Paris 2001

⌒ **$473** - €545 - **£323** - FF3 577
Port d'Ostende Huile/panneau (24x40cm 9x15in)
Bruxelles 2000

VERBURGH Cornelis Gerrit 1802-1879 **[13]**

⌒ **$7 164** - €6 807 - **£4 359** - FF44 649
A Wayside Inn Oil/panel (40x48cm 15x18in) Den Haag 1999

VERBURGH Dionys 1655-1722 **[43]**

⌒ **$4 606** - €5 087 - **£3 192** - FF33 369
Bewaldete Flusslandschaft mit einem Hirtenpaar Oil/panel (85.5x71cm 33x27in) Wien 2001

VERBURGH Médard 1886-1957 **[77]**

⌒ **$3 432** - €3 222 - **£2 119** - FF21 138
Paysage d'été Huile/panneau (40x50cm 15x19in)
Antwerpen 1999

✎ **$538** - €644 - **£369** - FF4 227
Gezicht te Oostende (vue à Ostende) Lavis/papier
(45x57cm 17x22in) Antwerpen 2000

VERBURGH Rutger 1678-c.1746 **[16]**

⌒ **$17 604** - €14 876 - **£10 500** - FF97 583
A Town Scene with Numerous Figures outside an Inn Oil/canvas (114x145cm 44x57in) London 1998

⌒ **$29 127** - €32 014 - **£18 522** - FF210 000
Scène d'hiver avec patineurs Huile/toile
(59.5x86cm 23x33in) Paris 2000

VERCAMMEN Wout 1938 **[32]**

⌒ **$1 076** - €992 - **£648** - FF6 504
Les formes et les couleurs ne se discutent pas
Huile/toile (100x100cm 39x39in) Antwerpen 1999

VERCELLI Giulio Romano 1879-1951 **[24]**
- 🖼 **$3 960** - €3 421 - **£1 980** - FF22 440
  Ritornerà Olio/tela (80.5x102.5cm 31x40in) Torino 1999
- 🖼 **$560** - €726 - **£420** - FF4 760
  Prugne Olio/tavoletta (15x21cm 5x8in) Milano 2000

VERCRUYSSE Jan 1948 **[12]**
- 📷 **$5 480** - €6 055 - **£3 800** - FF39 721
  Untitled (le jugement) Photograph (47x43cm 18x16in) London 2001

VERDEGEM Joseph 1897-1957 **[64]**
- ✏ **$425** - €471 - **£296** - FF3 089
  Verschrikte moeder Aquarelle/papier (36x26.5cm 14x10in) Bruxelles 2001

VERDI IL BACCHIACA Francesco Ubertini 1494/95-1557 **[1]**
- ✏ **$392 125** - €382 876 - **£250 000** - FF2 511 500
  Young Man in profile, wearing a Hat/Architectural Studies Red chalk/paper (25x15.5cm 9x6in) London 1999

VERDIER François 1651-1730 **[112]**
- ✏ **$724** - €610 - **£427** - FF4 000
  Junon et Zeus Crayon (12x16.5cm 4x6in) Paris 1998

VERDIER Jean 1901-1969 **[23]**
- 🖼 **$198** - €230 - **£139** - FF1 508
  Nature morte à l'orange Huile/toile (22x27cm 8x10in) Genève 1998

VERDIER Jean-Louis 1849-1895 **[3]**
- 🖼 **$15 000** - €14 854 - **£9 339** - FF97 437
  The Heron Oil/canvas (89x142cm 35x55in) New-York 1999

VERDIER Maurice 1919 **[61]**
- 🖼 **$472** - €454 - **£293** - FF2 977
  Eve Huile/toile (100x50.5cm 39x19in) Montréal 1999

VERDILHAN André 1881-1963 **[41]**
- 🖼 **$797** - €915 - **£545** - FF6 000
  Le port Huile/toile (50x62cm 19x24in) Paris 2000

VERDILHAN Louis Mathieu 1875-1928 **[146]**
- 🖼 **$45 030** - €43 448 - **£28 443** - FF285 000
  Marseille, rue donnant sur le vieux port Huile/toile (150.5x140.5cm 59x55in) Paris 1999
- 🖼 **$11 557** - €11 434 - **£7 207** - FF75 000
  Vue d'Allauch Huile/toile (73x89cm 28x35in) Aubagne 1999
- 🖼 **$2 597** - €2 897 - **£1 746** - FF19 000
  Nature morte aux fruits Huile/toile (20x25cm 7x9in) Versailles 2000
- ✏ **$1 161** - €1 220 - **£734** - FF8 000
  Silhouette sur un port Aquarelle/papier (50x36cm 19x14in) Paris 2000

VERDOEL Adriaen c.1620-c.1700 **[10]**
- 🖼 **$17 676** - €20 748 - **£12 474** - FF136 098
  Abigael frambärande skänker till kung David Oil/canvas (85x118cm 33x46in) Stockholm 2000

VERDONCK Cornelis XVII-XVIII **[6]**
- 🖼 **$4 962** - €4 291 - **£2 950** - FF28 149
  Flusslandschaft mit zahlreichen Schiffen, Personen, Schlössern, Burgen Huile/panneau (32.5x40cm 12x15in) Zürich 1998

VERDUGO LANDI Ricardo 1871-1930 **[47]**
- 🖼 **$8 250** - €9 010 - **£5 700** - FF59 100
  Buscando conchas en la playa Oleo/lienzo (50x80cm 19x31in) Madrid 2001
- 🖼 **$2 100** - €2 102 - **£1 295** - FF13 790
  Marina Oleo/tabla (22x40cm 8x15in) Madrid 2000

- ✏ **$240** - €240 - **£148** - FF1 576
  Batalla naval Tinta (37x45cm 14x17in) Madrid 2000

VERDUN Raymond Jean 1873-1954 **[125]**
- 🖼 **$893** - €915 - **£561** - FF6 000
  Bord de Méditerranée Huile/toile (61x49cm 24x19in) Lille 2000

VERDUSSEN Jan Peeter c.1700-1763 **[58]**
- 🖼 **$8 802** - €9 147 - **£5 520** - FF60 000
  Combat des turcs contre les chrétiens Huile/toile (78.5x129cm 30x50in) Paris 2000
- 🖼 **$8 662** - €9 299 - **£5 795** - FF61 000
  Halte de cavaliers dans un paysage boisé et accidenté Huile/toile/panneau (25.5x34.5cm 10x13in) Paris 2000

VERDUSSEN Paul 1868-1945 **[19]**
- 🖼 **$349** - €297 - **£210** - FF1 951
  Vue de l'église de la Chapelle Huile/toile (63x48.5cm 24x19in) Bruxelles 1998

VERDYEN Eugène 1836-1903 **[37]**
- 🖼 **$2 377** - €2 187 - **£1 467** - FF15 000
  Le pêcheur Huile/toile (72x47cm 28x18in) Rouen 1999
- 🖼 **$1 219** - €1 140 - **£754** - FF7 479
  Uitklapbare toiletspiegel Huile/panneau (43x33.5cm 16x13in) Lokeren 1999

VERELST Herman c.1642-1702 **[2]**
- 🖼 **$180 000** - €192 544 - **£122 724** - FF1 263 006
  Flowers in a Vase with a Butterfly Oil/canvas (73x58.5cm 28x23in) New-York 2001

VERELST John c.1670-1740 **[9]**
- 🖼 **$4 170** - €4 203 - **£2 600** - FF27 569
  Mr Osborn, half-length, in a Brown Coat and Waistcoat Oil/canvas (76x62cm 29x24in) London 2000
- 🗔 **$75 000** - €71 096 - **£46 852** - FF466 357
  Tee Yee Nee Ho Ga Row/Sa Ga Yeath Qua Pieth Tow/Etow Oh Kaom Mezzotint (42x26cm 16x10in) New-York 1999

VERELST Maria 1680-1744 **[3]**
- 🖼 **$17 000** - €19 980 - **£11 786** - FF131 059
  Sarah, 1st Duchess of Marlborough, seated three-quarter length Oil/canvas (107.5x102cm 42x40in) New-York 2000

VERELST Pieter Harmensz c.1618-c.1678 **[24]**
- 🖼 **$117 808** - €132 090 - **£80 000** - FF866 456
  Portrait of a young Lady, dressed in a Gold-embroidered Dress Oil/panel (50x44cm 19x17in) London 2000
- 🖼 **$66 636** - €57 554 - **£40 170** - FF377 532
  A young Boor reclining, eating from a earthen-wer Bowl Oil/canvas/panel (13.9x17.3cm 5x6in) Amsterdam 1998

VERELST Simon Pietersz. 1644-1721 **[40]**
- 🖼 **$16 204** - €18 151 - **£11 260** - FF119 064
  Flower Still Life with Tulips, Roses, Lilies and others Flowers Oil/canvas (125x101cm 49x39in) Amsterdam 2001
- 🖼 **$46 323** - €49 724 - **£31 000** - FF326 169
  Still Life of a glass Vase of Roses, Hudrangea, Carnation, Poppies Oil/canvas (52x40.5cm 20x15in) London 2000
- 🖼 **$15 374** - €13 279 - **£9 267** - FF87 102
  A trompe l'oeil: A Bunch of Grapes hanging before a Stone Wall Oil/canvas (35.4x31cm 13x12in) Amsterdam 1998

V

VERENDAEL Nicholas 1640-1691 **[9]**
- 🖼 $24 000 - €20 864 - **£14 524** - FF136 862
  Swag of Roses, Peonies, Anemones, Snowballs, Carnations and Others Oil/canvas (62x49.5cm 24x19in) New-York 1999
- 🖼 $13 766 - €15 201 - **£9 500** - FF99 713
  Flowers around two Sacred Hearts depicting the Annunciation Oil/metal (37x28cm 14x11in) Crewkerne, Somerset 2001

VERESHAGIN Piotr Petrovich 1834/36-1886 **[27]**
- 🖼 $43 829 - €42 122 - **£27 000** - FF276 299
  View of the Kremlin across the River Moskva Oil/canvas (36x83.5cm 14x32in) London 1999
- 🖼 $11 194 - €13 322 - **£8 000** - FF87 385
  On the Banks of the Volga Oil/canvas (24.5x49cm 9x19in) London 2000

VERESHAGIN Vasilii Petrovich 1835-1909 **[3]**
- 🖼 $89 281 - €85 803 - **£55 000** - FF562 831
  The tsarina Sophia Litovskaya and the Boyarina Shemiakin Oil/canvas (138.5x190.5cm 54x75in) London 1999
- 🖼 $13 253 - €14 860 - **£9 000** - FF97 476
  Fortified Village in the Caucasian Mountains in Winter Oil/canvas/board (65.5x90.5cm 25x35in) London 2000

VERESHAGIN Vasilii Vasilievich 1842-1904 **[25]**
- 🖼 $112 728 - €106 442 - **£70 000** - FF698 215
  Entrenchment at the Shipka Pass Oil/canvas (121x202.5cm 47x79in) London 1999
- 🖼 $8 590 - €8 409 - **£5 285** - FF55 160
  Maisema Egyptistä Oil/panel (30.5x40cm 12x15in) Helsinki 1999
- 🖼 $3 633 - €3 831 - **£2 400** - FF25 131
  View of Traunsee from Gmünden Watercolour (12x20.5cm 4x8in) London 2000

VEREYCKEN Edouard 1893-1967 **[10]**
- 🗿 $1 206 - €1 438 - **£864** - FF9 430
  Le baiser Bronze (H29cm H11in) Bruxelles 2000

VERGARA José 1726-1799 **[3]**
- 🖼 $18 600 - €18 620 - **£11 470** - FF122 140
  Visión de San Jerónimo Oleo/lienzo (172x133cm 67x52in) Madrid 2000

VERGE Adèle XX **[20]**
- 🗿 $639 - €762 - **£456** - FF5 000
  Couple amoureux Bronze (H21cm H8in) Saint-Dié

VERGER Pierre 1902 **[37]**
- 📷 $544 - €610 - **£379** - FF4 000
  Afrique Tirage argentique (29x21cm 11x8in) Paris 2001

VERGESES de Hippolyte Jean-Bapt. 1847-1896 **[1]**
- 🖼 $2 047 - €2 287 - **£1 428** - FF15 000
  Koubba près d'Alger Huile/panneau (32.5x40.5cm 12x15in) Paris 2001

VERGNE Jean-Louis 1929 **[163]**
- 🖼 $139 - €137 - **£84** - FF900
  Le chapeau rose Huile/toile (73x100cm 28x39in) Paris 2000
- 🖼 $69 - €69 - **£42** - FF450
  Sur le bateau Gouache/papier (27x35cm 10x13in) Paris 2000

VERHAECHT Tobias 1561-1631 **[56]**
- 🖼 $21 630 - €21 802 - **£13 500** - FF143 010
  Löwenjagd in einer weiten gebirgigen Flusslandschaft Oil/panel (100.5x152cm 39x59in) Wien 2001

- 🖼 $24 000 - €23 989 - **£14 661** - FF157 356
  Estuary with Travellers on a Path Before a House, a Harbor Beyond Oil/panel (50x71.5cm 19x28in) New-York 2000
- 🖼 $13 232 - €14 521 - **£8 518** - FF95 251
  Peasants on a Track in a mountainous Winter Landscape Oil/panel (27x24cm 10x9in) Amsterdam 2000
- 🖌 $2 337 - €2 723 - **£1 633** - FF17 859
  View of the Forum, with Monks and Pilgrims in the Foreground Ink (17x22cm 6x8in) Amsterdam 2000

VERHAEGEN Fernand 1883-1975 **[95]**
- 🖼 $2 835 - €2 603 - **£1 753** - FF17 073
  Fête dans une ville sous la neige Huile/toile (53x53cm 20x20in) Bruxelles 1999
- 🖼 $1 352 - €1 289 - **£821** - FF8 455
  Sainte Rolande entre au château Pirmez Huile/panneau (30x39.5cm 11x15in) Bruxelles 1999
- 🖌 $244 - €273 - **£170** - FF1 788
  Paysage à l'arbre Fusain/papier (25x33cm 9x12in) Bruxelles 2001

VERHAEGEN Louis M. XIX **[1]**
- 🗿 $3 300 - €3 105 - **£2 059** - FF20 365
  Bust of Daniel Webster Marble (H51cm H20in) Sunderland MA 1999

VERHAERT Dirck c.1610-c.1665 **[19]**
- 🖼 $149 430 - €160 401 - **£100 000** - FF1 052 160
  Rome, a Prospect of the Colosseum Oil/canvas (196x277cm 77x109in) London 2000
- 🖼 $5 950 - €5 793 - **£3 655** - FF38 000
  Lavandières dans des ruines romaines près d'un lac Huile/panneau (38.5x58.5cm 15x23in) Paris 1999

VERHAERT Pieter 1852-1908 **[49]**
- 🖼 $4 302 - €4 462 - **£2 736** - FF29 268
  De kamer van de correctoren en de drukkerij plantijn te Antwerpen Oil/panel (46x37.5cm 18x14in) Lokeren 2000
- 🖼 $285 - €297 - **£188** - FF1 951
  Salle à manger de la maison Leys Huile/panneau (28x22cm 11x8in) Antwerpen 2000

VERHAGHEN Pierre Joseph 1728-1811 **[12]**
- 🖼 $23 052 - €26 218 - **£16 252** - FF171 976
  Die Anbetung der Hirten Öl/Leinwand (140x165cm 55x64in) Zürich 2001

VERHAS Frans 1827-1897 **[13]**
- 🖼 $14 950 - €12 794 - **£9 000** - FF83 925
  Regarde pas Oil/canvas (71x58.5cm 27x23in) London 1998

VERHAS Jan 1834-1896 **[14]**
- 🖼 $9 372 - €10 907 - **£6 600** - FF71 544
  «Mal-adresse» Huile/panneau (75.5x52.5cm 29x20in) Antwerpen 2001

VERHAS Theodor 1811-1872 **[39]**
- 🖌 $628 - €588 - **£389** - FF3 857
  Hochgebirgsschlucht mit Wasserfall und Holzbrücke Watercolour (28.5x23.5cm 11x9in) Heidelberg 1999

VERHEGGEN Hendrik Frederik 1809-1883 **[7]**
- 🖼 $3 011 - €2 657 - **£1 814** - FF17 430
  Fishingboats in Inland Waters, a Storm Approaching in the distance Oil/panel (18.5x25cm 7x9in) Amsterdam 1998

VERHEVICK Firmin 1874-1962 **[85]**
$228 - €273 - **£163** - FF1 788
Marché aux fleurs de la Grande Place
Aquarelle/papier (46x37cm 18x14in) Bruxelles 2000

VERHEYDEN François, Frans 1806-1890 **[53]**
$1 664 - €1 677 - **£1 037** - FF11 000
Portrait d'homme en tenue de magistrat
Huile/toile (74x60cm 29x23in) Paris 2000
$2 070 - €2 479 - **£1 420** - FF16 260
La cueillette des cerises Huile/panneau (20x16cm 7x6in) Bruxelles 2000

VERHEYDEN Isidore 1846-1905 **[175]**
$2 426 - €2 851 - **£1 759** - FF18 699
Rue de village animée sous la neige Huile/toile (33x49cm 12x19in) Luxembourg 2001
$1 148 - €992 - **£692** - FF6 504
L'étang Huile/toile (28x42cm 11x15in) Bruxelles 1999
$480 - €471 - **£296** - FF3 089
Zelfportret Charcoal/paper (51x39.5cm 20x15in) Lokeren 1999

VERHEYDEN Mattheus 1700-1777 **[13]**
$9 630 - €9 566 - **£6 000** - FF62 751
Portrait of a Child, small full-length, seated on a blue cushion Oil/canvas (54x45cm 21x17in) London 1999

VERHEYEN Jan Hendrik 1778-1846 **[54]**
$44 000 - €37 918 - **£26 140** - FF248 727
Dutch Town Scene with Canal, Bridge and Steeple in distance Oil/panel (41x51cm 16x20in) Hatfield PA 1998
$7 876 - €6 660 - **£4 710** - FF43 688
A Capriccio View in Amsterdam Oil/panel (34.5x27.5cm 13x10in) Amsterdam 1998
$1 677 - €1 906 - **£1 177** - FF12 501
A Summer Landscape with Villagers resting
Watercolour/paper (24x34cm 9x13in) Amsterdam 2001

VERHEYEN Jef 1932-1984 **[99]**
$3 009 - €3 579 - **£2 144** - FF23 477
«Megaron» Öl/Leinwand (120x120cm 47x47in) München 2000
$1 608 - €1 487 - **£1 002** - FF9 756
Lichtstroom Oil/canvas (80x60cm 31x23in) Lokeren 1999
$639 - €644 - **£397** - FF4 227
La Ralista Aquarelle/papier (48x64cm 18x25in) Antwerpen 2000

VERHOESEN Albertus 1806-1881 **[226]**
$4 525 - €4 346 - **£2 805** - FF28 508
Fein gehaltene Darstellung einer antikisieren-den Parklandschaft Öl/Leinwand (51x40cm 20x15in) Eltville-Erbach 1999
$2 252 - €2 632 - **£1 607** - FF17 264
Poultry in a Landscape Oil/panel (14.5x19cm 5x7in) Amsterdam 2001

VERHOEVEN Jan 1870-1941 **[12]**
$9 473 - €8 182 - **£5 721** - FF53 673
Bäume in Landschaft Öl/Leinwand (80.4x100cm 31x39in) Köln 1998

VERHOEVEN-BALL Adrien Joseph 1824-1882 **[28]**
$12 896 - €15 369 - **£9 238** - FF100 812
Jour de marché hivernal à Anvers Huile/toile (48x61cm 18x24in) Bruxelles 2000
$2 521 - €2 723 - **£1 724** - FF17 859
Cows in a Field Oil/panel (32x40cm 12x15in) Amsterdam 2001

VERHOOG Aat 1933 **[15]**
$704 - €817 - **£499** - FF5 357
Meisje in Landschap Tempera/canvas (70x70cm 27x27in) Amsterdam 2000

VERICO Antonio c.1775-? **[4]**
$713 - €749 - **£450** - FF4 916
Veduta del Campanile di Pisa in Toscana
Engraving (57x37cm 22x14in) London 2000

VÉRIN Noël 1947 **[17]**
$783 - €732 - **£483** - FF4 800
La femme au landau Technique mixte/panneau (60x78cm 23x30in) Paris 1999

VERKADE Kees 1941 **[52]**
$16 627 - €19 818 - **£11 856** - FF130 000
Femme accroupie tenant la main à son enfant
Bronze (110x90x95cm 43x35x37in) Nice 2000
$3 124 - €3 630 - **£2 196** - FF23 812
Female nude Bronze (H17.5cm H6in) Amsterdam 2001

VERKOLJE Jan I 1650-1693 **[28]**
$11 094 - €10 225 - **£6 644** - FF67 070
Eine vornehme Dame mit ihrem Schosshündchen, vor Parklandschaft sitzend
Öl/Kupfer (63x52cm 24x20in) Dresden 1998
$8 494 - €8 168 - **£5 232** - FF53 578
Scholar in his Study said to be Cornelius Van Acker, Pastor at Delft Oil/copper (31x25.5cm 12x10in) Amsterdam 1999
$2 532 - €2 949 - **£1 769** - FF19 347
An Elegant Couple about to Go Riding Ink (21.5x26cm 8x10in) Amsterdam 2000

VERKOLJE Nicholas 1673-1746 **[25]**
$69 768 - €77 749 - **£46 920** - FF510 000
L'enlèvement d'Europe Huile/panneau (58x77cm 22x30in) Versailles 2000
$16 995 - €16 769 - **£10 560** - FF110 000
Suzanne et les vieillards Huile/cuivre (42.5x32.5cm 16x12in) Paris 1999
$269 - €307 - **£187** - FF2 012
Mädchen im Hemd Mezzotint (27,9x22.8cm 10x8in) Berlin 2000

VERLAINE Paul 1844-1896 **[14]**
$12 852 - €14 178 - **£8 704** - FF93 000
Autoportraits Encre (17x22cm 6x8in) Paris 2000

VERLAT Charles Michel Maria 1824-1890 **[80]**
$2 332 - €2 727 - **£1 661** - FF17 886
Jeune chien de face Huile/panneau (58x47cm 22x18in) Bruxelles 2001
$576 - €648 - **£402** - FF4 251
Drei Hunde in Freien Oil/panel (34.5x25.5cm 13x10in) Luzern 2001

VERLET Raoul Charles 1857-1923 **[24]**
$5 225 - €5 706 - **£3 610** - FF37 430
Orfeo y Cerbero Bronze (152x32x32cm 59x12x12in) Madrid 2001
$2 300 - €2 661 - **£1 627** - FF17 454
Man Standing with Hands Above Heads with Three Headed Panther Bronze (H60cm H24in) Hatfield PA 2000

V

VERLINDE Claude 1927 **[65]**
$30 970 - €28 965 - **£18 981** - FF190 000
«Le bateleur» Huile/toile (114x162.5cm 44x63in) Paris 1998
$907 - €942 - **£650** - FF7 000
«Le bouchon» Mine plomb (30.5x21.5cm 12x8in) Paris 2001

VERLON André 1917-1993 **[35]**
- $2 003 - €2 325 - £1 408 - FF15 254
  «Harmonie IV» Mixed media drawing (35x26cm
  13x10in) Salzburg 2001

VERMEER VAN HAARLEM Jan, Johannes I 1628-1691 **[9]**
- $22 593 - €21 149 - £14 000 - FF138 727
  Extensive Dune Landscape with a Farmhouse
  and a Bleaching Ground Oil/panel (45x64.5cm
  17x25in) London 1999

VERMEERSCH Ambros Ivo 1810-1852 **[3]**
- $9 178 - €8 692 - £5 581 - FF57 016
  Kirchplatz eines alten Städtchens mit
  Staffagefiguren Oil/panel (19x23cm 7x9in) München
  1999

VERMEERSCH José 1922-1997 **[44]**
- $2 650 - €2 479 - £1 640 - FF16 260
  Zittende vrouw met haan Céramique (36x21.5cm
  14x8in) Lokeren 1999

VERMEHREN Frits Johann Freder. 1823-1910 **[18]**
- $799 - €806 - £498 - FF5 287
  Kunstnerens datter Elisabeth i lyseröd kjole
  Oil/canvas (41x32cm 16x12in) København 2000

VERMEHREN Gustav 1863-1931 **[54]**
- $966 - €1 099 - £679 - FF7 209
  Bondestueinteriör med moder og barn Oil/canvas
  (53x60cm 20x23in) Vejle 2001
- $568 - €552 - £360 - FF3 619
  Kartoffelmark Oil/canvas (32x44cm 12x17in) Viby J,
  Århus 1999

VERMEHREN Sophus 1866-1950 **[98]**
- $586 - €670 - £407 - FF4 397
  Ung laesende pige ved et bord med aebler
  Oil/canvas (63x62cm 24x24in) København 2000
- $708 - €804 - £484 - FF5 273
  Den förste undervisning, interiör med mor og
  barn Oil/canvas (29x30cm 11x11in) Vejle 2000

VERMEHREN Yelva 1878-1980 **[164]**
- $400 - €377 - £250 - FF2 472
  Opstilling med kobberkeddel, merskumspibe
  og frugter på bord Oil/canvas (35x51cm 13x20in)
  Vejle 1999
- $339 - €336 - £212 - FF2 204
  Glas med hunderoser Oil/canvas (34x30cm
  13x11in) København 1999

VERMEIR Alphons 1905-1994 **[236]**
- $602 - €694 - £420 - FF4 552
  La fête foraine Huile/panneau (40x50cm 15x19in)
  Bruxelles 2001
- $111 - €124 - £77 - FF813
  Travail au champ Huile/panneau (20x29cm 7x11in)
  Antwerpen 2001

VERMEIRE Jules 1885-1977 **[16]**
- $5 859 - €6 807 - £4 117 - FF44 649
  Face Stone (H32cm H12in) Amsterdam 2001
- $1 057 - €1 134 - £707 - FF7 441
  Head of a Woman Charcoal (35.5x57.5cm 13x22in)
  Amsterdam 2000

VERMEULEN Andries 1763-1814 **[57]**
- $8 835 - €9 907 - £6 000 - FF64 984
  Winter Landscape with Figures drinking by a
  frozen River Oil/canvas (39.5x49cm 15x19in) London
  2000

- $28 764 - €27 227 - £17 886 - FF178 596
  A Winter Landscape with Skaters and Sledges
  on the Ice in a Village Oil/panel (28x39cm 11x15in)
  Amsterdam 1999
- $1 819 - €2 176 - £1 250 - FF14 271
  Figures Skating on a Frozen Lake in a Dutch
  Winter Landscape Wash/paper (30x46cm 11x18in)
  Billingshurst, West-Sussex 2000

VERMEULEN Cornelis c.1732-1813 **[2]**
- $7 343 - €6 826 - £4 500 - FF44 775
  Peasants and Cattle in an Italianate Landscape
  Oil/canvas (47.5x64.5cm 18x25in) London 1998

VERMEULEN Marinus Cornelis Th. 1868-1941 **[6]**
- $10 889 - €12 653 - £7 760 - FF83 000
  Sport d'hiver sur une rivière gelée Huile/panneau
  (29x40.5cm 11x15in) Paris 2001

VERMEYLEN Alphonse 1882-1939 **[8]**
- $310 - €347 - £203 - FF2 276
  Barque de pêche Huile/toile (48x38cm 18x14in)
  Antwerpen 2000

VERMI Arturo 1928-1988 **[44]**
- $750 - €777 - £450 - FF5 100
  Paesaggio Olio/tela (100x70cm 39x27in) Vercelli
  2000

VERMIGLIO Giuseppe 1585-c.1635 **[8]**
- $12 852 - €11 103 - £8 568 - FF72 828
  L'incredulità di San Tommaso Olio/tela
  (114x150cm 44x59in) Venezia 1998

VERNA Germaine 1908-1975 **[20]**
- $1 000 - €839 - £586 - FF5 503
  Cafe in Locarno Oil/canvas (64x81.5cm 25x32in)
  New-York 1998

VERNAY François F.Miel, dit 1821-1896 **[53]**
- $4 387 - €4 421 - £2 734 - FF29 000
  Abords de village Huile/carton (54x65cm 21x25in)
  Lyon 2000
- $2 728 - €2 973 - £1 788 - FF19 500
  Paysaggio avec personnages et animaux
  Huile/toile (32x46cm 12x18in) Dijon 2000
- $302 - €305 - £188 - FF2 000
  Abords de village Fusain (32x49cm 12x19in) Lyon
  2000

VERNER Elizabeth O'Neill 1883-1979 **[65]**
- $18 000 - €20 553 - £12 690 - FF134 818
  Hagar, the Flower Vender Pastel (46x30cm 18x11in)
  Boston MA 2001
- $500 - €419 - £293 - FF2 751
  «On South Battery, Charleston» Etching (12x8cm
  5x3in) New-Orleans LA 1998

VERNER Frederick Arthur 1836-1928 **[157]**
- $10 600 - €11 739 - £7 188 - FF77 000
  The Monarch of the Skies Oil/canvas (113x83cm
  44x32in) Toronto 2000
- $1 400 - €1 560 - £978 - FF10 233
  Figures in rural winter Landscape
  Watercolour/paper (21x46cm 8x18in) Delray-Beach FL
  2000

VERNET Carle 1758-1836 **[205]**
- $15 450 - €15 245 - £9 520 - FF100 000
  Les chevaux à l'écurie Huile/carton (38x46cm
  14x18in) Louviers 1999
- $1 282 - €1 524 - £889 - FF10 000
  Harnachement d'un cheval Encre (26.5x33cm
  10x12in) Paris 2000

꿈 **$141** - €137 - **£89** - FF900
Le chasseur au tirer Gravure (35x50cm 13x19in)
Paris 1999

VERNET Horace 1789-1863 **[180]**
🖼 **$45 578** - €39 637 - **£27 482** - FF260 000
Contre-Amiral Magon en pied, sur une terrasse
devant la mer Huile/toile (218x138cm 85x54in) Paris
1998
🖼 **$33 602** - €33 361 - **£21 000** - FF218 834
Le rapt Oil/canvas (46x38cm 18x14in) London 1999
🖼 **$6 952** - €6 860 - **£4 284** - FF45 000
Megalopolis Grèce Huile/panneau (19x47.5cm
7x18in) Biarritz 1999
✏ **$676** - €644 - **£410** - FF4 227
Officier des hussards Aquarelle/papier (13x7.5cm
5x2in) Bruxelles 1999
꿈 **$127** - €122 - **£78** - FF800
Rapport du valet de Limier/Hallali du cerf
Gravure (27x31cm 10x12in) Senlis 1999

VERNET Joseph 1714-1789 **[158]**
🖼 **$170 400** - €182 939 - **£114 000** - FF1 200 000
Le retour des pêcheurs en fin d'après-midi
Huile/toile (97x146cm 38x57in) Paris 2000
🖼 **$119 140** - €140 253 - **£83 720** - FF920 000
Scène de déluge (Huitième vue d'Italie)
Huile/toile (54x80cm 21x31in) Argenteuil 2000
🖼 **$138 643** - €129 672 - **£85 000** - FF850 595
A Coastal Landscape at Dusk with a Ship and
Fishermen Oil/canvas (31.5x44cm 12x17in) London
1998
✏ **$4 800** - €4 210 - **£2 914** - FF27 618
Road Skirting Roman Ruins and an Oratory Red
chalk/paper (22x28.5cm 8x11in) New-York 1999
꿈 **$448** - €427 - **£278** - FF2 800
La madrague ou la pêche au thon, d'après
Vernet Gravure (53x74cm 20x29in) Paris 1999

VERNEUIL Maurice Pillard, dit 1869-1942 **[11]**
꿈 **$1 300** - €1 231 - **£807** - FF8 072
«Laurénol nº2» Poster (157x55cm 61x21in) New-
York 1999

VERNHES Henri Edouard 1854-1901 **[1]**
🗿 **$4 180** - €3 659 - **£2 532** - FF24 000
«La baigneuse» (l'Age d'Airain) Bronze (H67cm
H26in) Paris 1998

VERNIER Émile Louis 1829-1887 **[54]**
🖼 **$3 074** - €3 049 - **£1 912** - FF20 000
Scène de port animé Huile/toile (38.5x55cm
15x21in) Paris 1999
🖼 **$1 434** - €1 677 - **£1 024** - FF11 000
Les ramasseurs de vers à Saint Vaast la
Hougue Peinture (27.5x40cm 10x15in) Angers 2001

VERNIER Jules 1862-? **[15]**
🖼 **$1 384** - €1 238 - **£829** - FF8 124
Sailors unloading a merchant in the Harbour of
Rouen, France Oil/canvas (66x100cm 25x39in)
Amsterdam 1999

VERNIZZI Renato 1904-1972 **[9]**
🖼 **$1 100** - €1 140 - **£660** - FF7 480
Luca Olio/tela (60x50cm 23x19in) Milano 1999

VERNON Arthur Langley XIX-XX **[22]**
🖼 **$6 588** - €7 034 - **£4 500** - FF46 138
The Stirrup-Cup Oil/canvas (43x58cm 16x22in)
Billingshurst, West-Sussex 2001
🖼 **$2 913** - €2 735 - **£1 800** - FF17 938
Waiting for the Carriage Oil/canvas (40x25cm
15x9in) Billingshurst, West-Sussex 1999

VERNON Beatrix Charlotte D. 1887-? **[1]**
🖼 **$3 869** - €4 602 - **£2 757** - FF30 185
Geschäftiges Treiben vor den Toren einer nor-
dafrikanischen Stadt Öl/Leinwand (59x80cm
23x31in) Köln 2000

VERNON Émile XIX-XX **[93]**
🖼 **$17 367** - €18 200 - **£11 000** - FF119 381
Portrait d'une jeune femme Oil/canvas (65.5x54cm
25x21in) London 2000

VERNON Paul XIX **[46]**
🖼 **$2 339** - €2 185 - **£1 443** - FF14 330
Teichlandschaft Öl/Leinwand (50x63cm 19x24in)
Luzern 1999
🖼 **$1 231** - €1 448 - **£892** - FF9 500
Les jeunes filles au panier de fleurs Huile/pan-
neau (32.5x24cm 12x9in) Soissons 2001

VERNON Walter XIX-XX **[7]**
✏ **$700** - €685 - **£444** - FF4 491
Sandown/Newmarket Acuarela/papel (24x34cm
9x13in) Buenos-Aires 1999

VERNON William Henry 1820-1909 **[34]**
✏ **$261** - €240 - **£160** - FF1 577
Coastal Scene with Figures and Sailing Boats
Watercolour/paper (22x52cm 8x20in) St. Helier, Jersey
1998

VERNON-STOKES George 1873-1954 **[9]**
꿈 **$537** - €577 - **£360** - FF3 787
Two Siamese Cats and a Grasshopper Etching in
colors (24x28.5cm 9x11in) London 2000

VÉRON Alexandre René 1826-1897 **[213]**
🖼 **$45 000** - €41 758 - **£27 495** - FF273 915
Sunday on the Riverbank at the Bateau Lavoir
Oil/canvas (130x194cm 51x76in) New-York 1999
🖼 **$7 728** - €7 318 - **£4 800** - FF48 000
Le bac Huile/toile (60x92cm 23x36in) Paris 1999
🖼 **$2 115** - €2 363 - **£1 433** - FF15 500
Scènes champêtres près du moulin
Huile/papier/toile (23x34cm 9x13in) Autun 2000

VERON BELLECOURT Alexandre Paul Jos. 1773-?
[9]
🖼 **$5 412** - €5 183 - **£3 406** - FF34 000
Scène de campement militaire près d'une rivière Huile/panneau (65x45cm 25x17in) Arcachon 1999

VERONA da Liberale 1445-1526 **[2]**
🖼 **$109 200** - €94 335 - **£54 600** - FF618 800
Adorazione del Bambino Tempera/tavola
(57.5x44cm 22x17in) Milano 1999

VERONA Maffeo c.1576-1618 **[3]**
🖼 **$10 200** - €8 812 - **£6 600** - FF57 800
Trasfigurazione Olio/tela (75x96cm 29x37in) Milano
1998

VERONE XX **[10]**
🖼 **$2 614** - €2 883 - **£1 770** - FF18 914
Cet oiseau magnifique Öl/Leinwand (92x65cm
36x25in) Zürich 2000

VERONESE Paolo Caliari 1528-1588 **[39]**
🖼 **$251 385** - €213 887 - **£150 000** - FF1 403 010
The Rest of the Return from Egypt Oil/canvas
(160x162.5cm 62x63in) London 1998
🖼 **$400 000** - €427 876 - **£272 720** - FF2 806 680
The Symbols of the Four Evangelists Oil/canvas
(83x137cm 32x53in) New-York 2001
🖼 **$90 000** - €93 299 - **£54 000** - FF612 000
Trasfigurazione Olio/carta/tela (41.5x27cm 16x10in)
Milano 2000

V

V

$14 000 - €13 969 - **£8 521** - FF91 631
Drapery Study Black chalk (30.5x19.5cm 12x7in)
New-York 2000

VERONESI Luigi 1908-1998 **[192]**
$6 600 - €5 702 - **£4 400** - FF37 400
Costruzione X 14 Olio/tela (60x80cm 23x31in) Prato
1998
$1 800 - €2 332 - **£1 350** - FF15 300
«Composizione PHE23» Olio/tela (35x35cm
13x13in) Milano 2001
$800 - €829 - **£480** - FF5 440
Organico Pastelli/carta (22x30cm 8x11in) Milano
1999
$210 - €231 - **£142** - FF1 513
Composizione G2 Farbserigraphie (40x30cm
15x11in) Luzern 2000

VEROSSI (Albino Siviero) 1904-1945 **[1]**
$8 500 - €8 812 - **£5 100** - FF57 800
Sintesi di Piazza delle Erbe-Verona Olio/masonite
(75x74.5cm 29x29in) Milano 1999

VERPILLEUX Émile Antoine 1888-1964 **[8]**
$7 119 - €6 869 - **£4 500** - FF45 056
Portrait of a young Boy Oil/canvas (127x76cm
50x29in) London 1999

VERPOORTEN Oscar 1895-1948 **[40]**
$660 - €545 - **£387** - FF3 572
Nature morte aux fruits et un vase Huile/toile
(60x70cm 23x27in) Antwerpen 1998

VERREES Jozef Paul 1889-1942 **[11]**
$1 000 - €877 - **£607** - FF5 753
Join the Air Service Poster (94x63cm 37x25in) New-
York 1999

VERRIJK Dirk 1734-1786 **[29]**
$1 132 - €1 089 - **£697** - FF7 143
**View of a Village Along a Canal, a Church to the
Left** Ink (19x29cm 7x11in) Amsterdam 1999

VERROCHI Agostino c.1600-c.1650 **[6]**
$23 370 - €21 802 - **£14 100** - FF143 010
**Natura morta con uva, mele, melone, due uccel-
li e un papagallo** Öl/Leinwand (87.5x112cm
34x44in) Wien 1999

VERSCHAEREN Jan Antoon 1803-1863 **[3]**
$2 498 - €2 761 - **£1 732** - FF18 111
Stadtansicht mit Figurenstaffage Oil/panel
(48x39cm 18x15in) München 2001

VERSCHAFFELT Edouard 1874-1955 **[101]**
$8 613 - €7 775 - **£5 309** - FF51 000
Femmes et enfants Huile/toile (52x67cm 20x26in)
Aubagne 1999
$2 168 - €1 982 - **£1 327** - FF13 000
Garçon au chéchia rouge Huile/toile (46.5x31cm
18x12in) Paris 1999

VERSCHAFFELT von Peter Anton 1710-1793 **[9]**
$3 800 - €4 071 - **£2 595** - FF26 701
**Design for the Central Pediment Relief on the
North Façade of Castle** Chalks (26.5x69.5cm
10x27in) New-York 2001

VERSCHUIER Lieve Pietersz. c.1630-1686 **[12]**
$107 510 - €117 983 - **£69 212** - FF773 916
**Sailors unloading Cargo from a sailing Vessel,
moored on a Shore** Oil/canvas (56x65.5cm 22x25in)
Amsterdam 2000

VERSCHURING Hendrick I 1627-1690 **[49]**
$13 259 - €12 974 - **£8 500** - FF85 103
**Italianate Landscape with a Cavalry Skirmish
before Ruins** Oil/canvas (98x127cm 38x50in) London
1999
$6 652 - €6 246 - **£4 122** - FF40 972
Elegantes Paar in einem Interieur Öl/Leinwand
(60x47.6cm 23x18in) Luzern 1999
$4 800 - €4 658 - **£3 024** - FF30 556
**Italianate Landscape with Travellers resting by a
Grotto** Oil/panel (22.5x53.5cm 8x21in) New-York
1999
$473 - €505 - **£300** - FF3 315
Battle Scene Wash (12x19cm 4x7in) London 2000

VERSCHURING Willem 1657-1715 **[5]**
$15 000 - €14 592 - **£8 797** - FF82 599
A young Lady listening to a Violonist Oil/canvas
(51.5x42cm 20x16in) New-York 1998

VERSCHUUR Wouterus 1812-1874 **[159]**
$241 875 - €203 933 - **£143 550** - FF1 337 715
Figures Watering Horses by a Well Oil/canvas
(99x128.5cm 38x50in) Amsterdam 1998
$85 000 - €79 616 - **£52 258** - FF522 248
Sportsmen resting Outside an Inn Oil/panel
(37x53.5cm 14x21in) New-York 1999
$21 610 - €22 689 - **£13 625** - FF148 830
Well deserved rest Oil/panel (17x25cm 6x9in)
Amsterdam 2000
$1 235 - €1 361 - **£806** - FF8 929
Paardenstudie Pencil/paper (16x24cm 6x9in) Den
Haag 1999

VERSCHUUR Wouterus II 1841-1936 **[32]**
$6 149 - €5 767 - **£3 800** - FF37 826
Feeding Time Oil/panel (37.5x49.5cm 14x19in)
London 1999
$1 925 - €1 815 - **£1 193** - FF11 906
«Circus Hinten Stal» Oil/panel (30.5x42cm 12x16in)
Amsterdam 1999
$1 118 - €1 271 - **£784** - FF8 334
Horses in a Smithy Watercolour (23x35cm 9x13in)
Amsterdam 2001

VERSL Josef 1901-1993 **[31]**
$208 - €245 - **£149** - FF1 609
Waldlichtung Indian ink (23.5x31.5cm 9x12in)
Dettelbach-Effeldorf 2001

VERSPECHT Denis 1919 **[78]**
$290 - €290 - **£176** - FF1 900
Paris, Notre-Dame Aquarelle/papier (29x24cm
11x9in) Coulommiers 2000

VERSPRONCK Johannes Cornelisz. 1597-1662 **[9]**
$82 186 - €88 220 - **£55 000** - FF578 688
Portrait of a Gentleman, Half-Length Standing
Oil/canvas (81x66.5cm 31x26in) London 2000

VERSTEEGH Michiel 1756-1843 **[10]**
$8 604 - €9 983 - **£5 940** - FF65 485
**An Elegant Couple Counting Money by
Candlelight, at a Stone Niche** Oil/panel (52x41cm
20x16in) Amsterdam 2000
$2 592 - €2 723 - **£1 640** - FF17 859
The return of the Hunter Oil/panel (41x32.5cm
16x12in) Amsterdam 2000

VERSTER Andrew 1937 **[21]**
$689 - €714 - **£436** - FF4 685
Abstract from the Window Drypoint (170x100cm
66x39in) Johannesburg 2000

VERSTER Floris 1861-1927 **[29]**
- $30 254 - €31 765 - **£19 075** - FF208 362
  Witte en rose rozen in een Lanooypot Oil/canvas (52.5x42cm 20x16in) Amsterdam 2000
- $18 148 - €19 059 - **£11 482** - FF125 017
  Arum-Lilies Oil/canvas (48x30cm 18x11in) Amsterdam 2000

VERSTILLE William c.1755-1803 **[5]**
- $1 200 - €1 035 - **£726** - FF6 791
  James Bogert, Facing Right in Seagreen Waistcoat Miniature (4x3cm 1x1in) New-York 1999

VERSTRAATEN Lambert Hendricksz. 1631-1712 **[3]**
- $4 120 - €4 090 - **£2 574** - FF26 831
  Haarlemer Waldlandschaft mit einem Flöte spielenden Hirten Öl/Leinwand (65x82cm 25x32in) München 1999

VERSTRAETE Theodoor 1851-1907 **[29]**
- $2 154 - €1 982 - **£1 332** - FF13 000
  Paysage de neige au crépuscule Huile/toile (32x54cm 12x21in) Paris 1999

VERSTRAETEN Edmond 1870-1956 **[68]**
- $8 307 - €9 667 - **£5 850** - FF63 414
  Paysage hivernal animé d'aigrettes Huile/toile (126x117cm 49x46in) Antwerpen 2001
- $3 556 - €3 470 - **£2 184** - FF22 764
  Nature morte Huile/toile (68x76cm 26x29in) Antwerpen 1999
- $436 - €397 - **£270** - FF2 601
  Paysage Huile/panneau (20x27cm 7x10in) Bruxelles 1999

VERTANGEN Daniel c.1598-1681/84 **[44]**
- $122 385 - €113 767 - **£75 000** - FF746 265
  Portrait of a Military Commander/Portrait of a Lady in a black Dress Oil/canvas (128.5x102cm 50x40in) London 1998
- $9 376 - €11 020 - **£6 500** - FF72 284
  Io Guarded by Argus Oil/canvas (58x80cm 22x31in) London 2000
- $5 500 - €6 499 - **£3 897** - FF42 629
  Arcadian Scene with Dancing Figures Oil/panel (29x39cm 11x15in) Boston MA 2000

VERTES Marcel 1895-1961 **[286]**
- $2 700 - €2 910 - **£1 841** - FF19 087
  Femmes fleurs Oil/board (73x57cm 28x22in) New-York 2001
- $1 000 - €893 - **£612** - FF5 856
  Two Women on Steps Oil/canvas (27x40.5cm 10x15in) New-York 1999
- $297 - €329 - **£195** - FF2 159
  In the Circus Mixed media/paper (36.5x49cm 14x19in) Budapest 2000
- $230 - €232 - **£144** - FF1 525
  «Internationaler Karneval in Wien» Poster (123x95cm 48x37in) Wien 2001

VERTIN Petrus Gerardus 1819-1893 **[170]**
- $11 519 - €9 740 - **£6 888** - FF63 893
  The Pact of the Nobles, at the House of Culemborgh, Brussels Oil/canvas (66.5x83.5cm 26x32in) Amsterdam 1998
- $7 206 - €6 807 - **£4 359** - FF44 649
  Figures in a wintry Street Oil/panel (25x20cm 9x7in) Amsterdam 1999
- $695 - €681 - **£446** - FF4 464
  View of a Town with Villagers chatting on a Quay Watercolour (27x36cm 10x14in) Amsterdam 1999

VERTUE George 1684-1756 **[21]**
- $125 - €132 - **£79** - FF866
  Objetos curiosos Aguafuerte (48.5x32.5cm 19x12in) Madrid 2000

VERTUNNI Achille 1826-1897 **[45]**
- $2 606 - €2 373 - **£1 600** - FF15 563
  A Shepherd relaxing with his Flock near a ruined Church Oil/canvas (42x71cm 16x27in) London 1999
- $1 856 - €1 604 - **£928** - FF10 519
  Paludi pontine Olio/cartone (24x40cm 9x15in) Venezia 1999

VERUDA Umberto 1868-1904 **[9]**
- $28 500 - €29 545 - **£17 100** - FF193 800
  Pont SS. Apostoli, Venezia Olio/tela (106x152cm 41x59in) Trieste 2001
- $3 750 - €3 887 - **£2 250** - FF25 500
  Ragazza col ventaglio Olio/tela (69x55cm 27x21in) Trieste 1999

VERUTTI A. XIX-XX **[1]**
- $1 840 - €1 907 - **£1 104** - FF12 512
  Gondole a San Marco Acquarello/cartone (40x70cm 15x27in) Roma 1999

VERVEER Elchanon Leonardus 1826-1900 **[27]**
- $13 578 - €15 369 - **£9 176** - FF100 812
  Famille de pêcheurs Huile/toile (90x126cm 35x49in) Bruxelles 2000
- $525 - €494 - **£326** - FF3 243
  Coastal Scene with Two Elderly Walking in the Dunes Watercolour/paper (36x25cm 14x10in) East-Dennis MA 1999

VERVEER Mauritz 1817-1903 **[2]**
- $15 443 - €14 521 - **£9 561** - FF95 251
  Moored fishing fleet on the Beach of Scheveningen Oil/canvas (69.5x97cm 27x38in) Amsterdam 1999

VERVEER Salomon Leonardus 1813-1876 **[93]**
- $7 722 - €9 076 - **£5 354** - FF59 532
  Fisherfolk and Boats on the Beach Oil/canvas (58x72cm 22x28in) Amsterdam 2000
- $6 984 - €7 318 - **£4 420** - FF48 000
  Animation sur la rivière Huile/panneau (25.5x37cm 10x14in) Paris 2000
- $1 410 - €1 588 - **£972** - FF10 418
  A View of a Canal in a City with Figures on a Quay Pencil (22x19cm 8x7in) Amsterdam 1998

VERVEY Kees 1900 **[21]**
- $2 289 - €2 126 - **£1 397** - FF13 947
  Village Square Watercolour, gouache/paper (31x40.5cm 12x15in) Amsterdam 1998

VERVISCH Jean 1896-1977 **[69]**
- $473 - €545 - **£325** - FF3 577
  Orage Oil/panel (50x60.5cm 19x23in) Lokeren 2000

VERVLOET Augustine 1806-? **[7]**
- $2 053 - €2 269 - **£1 424** - FF14 883
  A Still Life with a Robin, a blue Tit Oil/panel (27x20cm 10x7in) Amsterdam 2001

VERVLOET Frans 1795-1872 **[38]**
- $46 980 - €45 735 - **£28 860** - FF300 000
  L'arrivée des troupes du Prince Louis Napoléon en Italie Huile/toile (38x60cm 14x23in) Paris 1999
- $2 556 - €2 744 - **£1 710** - FF18 000
  Intérieur de l'église du Gesù à Subiaco Huile/papier/toile (20.5x15.5cm 8x6in) Paris 2000

V

VERVLOET Joannes Josephus 1790-1869 [3]
🖙 **$22 000** - €22 806 - **£13 200** - FF149 600
Venezia Olio/tela (43x60cm 16x23in) Milano 2001

VERVLOET Victor 1829-? [14]
🖙 **$6 455** - €7 166 - **£4 500** - FF47 006
Il Bacino di San Marco, Venice Oil/canvas
(96.5x130cm 37x51in) London 2001
🖙 **$12 909** - €14 331 - **£9 000** - FF94 004
The Forum, Rome Oil/canvas (80x117.5cm 31x46in)
London 2001

VERWEE Alfred Jacques 1838-1895 [51]
🖙 **$5 668** - €6 445 - **£3 978** - FF42 276
Cheval et vaches au pré Huile/toile (110x150cm
43x59in) Bruxelles 2001
🖙 **$2 964** - €3 222 - **£1 950** - FF21 138
Rustende koeien Oil/canvas (66.5x99cm 26x38in)
Lokeren 2000
🖙 **$725** - €762 - **£477** - FF5 000
Paysage Huile/toile (31x40cm 12x15in) Lyon 2000

VERWEE Louis Charles ?-1882 [14]
🖙 **$28 000** - €28 215 - **£17 455** - FF185 080
The Confrontation Oil/panel (76x58cm 30x23in)
Delray-Beach FL 2000

VERWÉE Louis Pierre 1807-1877 [72]
🖙 **$3 750** - €4 327 - **£2 640** - FF28 386
Pastoral Landscape Oil/panel (40x50cm 16x20in)
Norwalk CT 2000
🖙 **$2 318** - €2 622 - **£1 566** - FF17 200
Vache et chien dans un paysage Huile/panneau
(27x33.5cm 10x13in) Toulouse 2000

VERWER de Abraham c.1580-1650 [15]
🖙 **$9 359** - €9 158 - **£6 000** - FF60 073
View of a Dutch Fortified Town across a River
Oil/canvas (72x104cm 28x40in) London 1999
🖙 **$13 000** - €11 302 - **£7 867** - FF74 133
**Barge and Fishing Vessels on a Calm Sea, Off a
Hilly Coastline** Ink (16x25cm 6x9in) New-York 1999

VERWER de Justus 1626-1688 [7]
🖙 **$9 460** - €10 008 - **£6 000** - FF65 650
**Shipping Vessels on Choppy Seas, with Men in
a Fishing Boat** Oil/panel (40.5x53cm 15x20in)
London 2000

VERWEY Kees 1900-1995 [116]
🖙 **$27 342** - €31 765 - **£19 215** - FF208 362
De stoel in de zon, atelier impressie Oil/canvas
(150x170cm 59x66in) Amsterdam 2001
🖙 **$3 640** - €4 084 - **£2 522** - FF26 789
Still Life Oil/board (50x68cm 19x26in) Amsterdam
2000
🖙 **$1 939** - €1 815 - **£1 206** - FF11 906
Portrait of a Young Lady Oil/canvas (46x30.5cm
18x12in) Amsterdam 1999
🖉 **$2 251** - €2 269 - **£1 403** - FF14 883
Still Life with Flowers in a Vase Gouache/paper
(28x24.5cm 11x9in) Amsterdam 2000

VERWILT François c.1620-1691 [9]
🖙 **$6 834** - €5 896 - **£4 123** - FF38 678
The Adoration of the Shepherds Oil/panel
(41x51cm 16x20in) Amsterdam 1998
🖙 **$5 468** - €6 126 - **£3 800** - FF40 184
Christ on the Cross Oil/panel (39x22.5cm 15x8in)
Amsterdam 2001

VESHILOV Konstantin Aleks. 1877-1918 [8]
🖙 **$5 194** - €4 992 - **£3 202** - FF32 746
Winter Landscape with fir Trees Oil/canvas
(70x54cm 27x21in) London 1999

VESIN Jaroslav Fr. Julius 1859-1915 [30]
🖙 **$6 355** - €6 164 - **£4 000** - FF40 430
The Sleigh Ride Oil/canvas (59.5x90.5cm 23x35in)
London 1999
🖙 **$2 579** - €3 068 - **£1 838** - FF20 123
Dreispänner in tief verschneiter Landschaft
Öl/Karton (40x30cm 15x11in) Köln 2000

VESNIN Alexander 1883-1959 [4]
🖙 **$6 583** - €6 135 - **£3 978** - FF40 246
Suprematistische Abstraktion Tempera (34x27cm
13x10in) Hamburg 1999

VESPIGNANI Renzo 1924 [142]
🖙 **$4 000** - €4 147 - **£2 400** - FF27 200
Nudo di schiena Tecnica mista/cartone (98x68cm
38x26in) Prato 1999
🖙 **$2 400** - €3 110 - **£1 800** - FF20 400
Paesaggio urbano con locomotiva Tecnica mista
(40.5x30.5cm 15x12in) Milano 2001
🖉 **$1 650** - €1 710 - **£990** - FF11 220
Strada China (51.5x36.5cm 20x14in) Prato 1999
▥ **$300** - €311 - **£180** - FF2 040
I rimpianti della bella Elmiera Acquaforte (59x44cm
23x17in) Vercelli 1999

VESS Charles XX [1]
🖉 **$1 600** - €1 543 - **£1 011** - FF10 124
«Storms Everlasting» Watercolour (71x43cm
27x16in) New-York 1999

VESTER Willem 1824-1895 [48]
🖙 **$3 474** - €4 084 - **£2 409** - FF26 789
Cows on a Country Lane Oil/canvas (44.5x70cm
17x27in) Amsterdam 2000
🖙 **$2 596** - €2 404 - **£1 821** - FF19 347
Aan de Ringvaart, Haarlemmermeer
Oil/canvas/panel (33x45cm 12x17in) Amsterdam 2001

VESTIER Antoine 1740-1824 [49]
🖙 **$5 184** - €6 098 - **£3 716** - FF40 000
Portrait de M.Truchot Huile/toile (52x44cm 20x17in)
Tours 2001

VESTIER Nicolas Jacques A. 1765-1816 [1]
🖉 **$20 000** - €21 394 - **£13 636** - FF140 334
**Portrait of Catherine-Noële Grand, née Worlée,
Princesse de Talleyrand** Black & white chalks/paper
(48.5x35.5cm 19x13in) New-York 2001

VETCOUR Fernand 1908 [41]
🖙 **$708** - €594 - **£415** - FF3 897
L'Ourthe à Saint-Anne Huile/toile (60x80.5cm
23x31in) Liège 1998

VÉTES Marcell XX [1]
▥ **$6 831** - €6 399 - **£4 200** - FF41 975
The Cabinet of Dr. Caligari Poster (127x193cm
50x75in) London 1999

VETH Bas 1861-1944 [8]
🖙 **$2 196** - €2 496 - **£1 516** - FF16 371
Stoomsleepboot met beurtschip Oil/canvas/panel
(25x34cm 9x13in) Dordrecht 2000

VETRI Paolo 1855-1937 [6]
🖉 **$1 500** - €1 372 - **£916** - FF8 998
Young boy with a flute Ink (73x41cm 29x16in)
New-York 1998

VETSCH Christian 1912 [16]
🖙 **$835** - €805 - **£514** - FF5 281
Heimkehr von der Alp Huile/panneau (18x69cm
7x27in) Bern 1999

VETTER Charles 1858-1936 **[30]**
- $4 392 - €4 602 - **£2 905** - FF30 185
  Blick in die Weinstrasse mit Strassenpassanten und Kutsche Öl/Leinwand (65x44.5cm 25x17in) München 2000

VETTRIANO Jack 1954 **[26]**
- $17 195 - €17 396 - **£10 500** - FF114 110
  Self Portrait in Profile Oil/canvas (50x40cm 19x15in) Sighthill 2000
- $9 838 - €10 626 - **£6 800** - FF69 699
  Narcissistic Bathers Oil/canvas (30x25cm 11x9in) Edinburgh 2001

VETTURALI Gaetano 1701-1783 **[8]**
- $20 000 - €20 733 - **£12 000** - FF136 000
  Il Canal Grande e il Ponte di Rialto Olio/tela (63x91cm 24x35in) Milano 2000

VEYRASSAT Jules Jacques 1828-1893 **[324]**
- $16 384 - €18 599 - **£11 382** - FF122 000
  Le retour des champs Huile/toile (115x147cm 45x57in) Barbizon 2001
- $9 132 - €10 367 - **£6 344** - FF68 000
  Le passage du bac après la moisson Huile/toile (32.5x63cm 12x24in) Barbizon 2001
- $3 753 - €4 116 - **£2 492** - FF27 000
  Jeux d'enfants dans la cour de ferme Huile/panneau (24x36cm 9x14in) Melun 2000
- $995 - €915 - **£611** - FF6 000
  Laboureur dans un paysage Aquarelle/papier (22.5x36.5cm 8x14in) Paris 1999
- $129 - €130 - **£81** - FF850
  La promenade du curé Eau-forte (17x21cm 6x8in) Fontainebleau 1999

VEYRIN Philippe 1899 **[18]**
- $1 831 - €1 982 - **£1 268** - FF13 000
  Village de Navarre Huile/panneau (46x55cm 18x21in) Pau 2001
- $816 - €777 - **£517** - FF5 100
  Eglise de Berroeta Huile/panneau (22x27cm 8x10in) Biarritz 1999

VEYSSIER Pierre Emile A. XIX **[4]**
- $10 086 - €9 757 - **£6 220** - FF64 000
  Le portrait du fiancé Huile/toile (90x70cm 35x27in) Bordeaux 1999

VEZIN Frederick 1859-? **[23]**
- $533 - €461 - **£316** - FF3 022
  Winterwald Öl/Leinwand (62x90cm 24x35in) Rudolstadt-Thüringen 1998

VIALET Laurent 1967 **[77]**
- $434 - €396 - **£264** - FF2 600
  Ciel lourd sur Pors Poulhans Huile/toile (27x35cm 10x13in) Douarnenez 1998

VIALLAT Claude 1936 **[155]**
- $6 598 - €7 325 - **£4 600** - FF48 046
  Sans titre Oil/canvas (270x115cm 106x45in) London 2001
- $984 - €1 143 - **£691** - FF7 500
  Sans titre Acrylique/toile (55x55cm 21x21in) Paris 2001
- $260 - €244 - **£160** - FF1 600
  Cartes postales Pochoir (10.5x15cm 4x5in) Paris 1999

VIANA Eduardo 1881-1967 **[5]**
- $64 500 - €74 776 - **£45 000** - FF490 500
  Mulher sentada Tempera (99x79cm 38x31in) Lisboa 2001

- $30 100 - €34 896 - **£21 000** - FF228 900
  Paisagem Oleo/cartón (34x41cm 13x16in) Lisboa 2001

VIANELLI Achille 1803-1894 **[86]**
- $1 780 - €1 906 - **£1 211** - FF12 500
  Jeune femme italienne et son chien regardant la mer Huile/toile (46x38cm 18x14in) Marseille 2001
- $1 443 - €1 455 - **£900** - FF9 543
  Paco Vicino Benvento Watercolour/paper (23.5x16cm 9x6in) London 2000

VIANELLI Albert 1841-1927 **[17]**
- $1 074 - €1 220 - **£735** - FF8 000
  Vue du château de Chillon Huile/carton (24x18cm 9x7in) Paris 2000
- $1 400 - €1 814 - **£1 050** - FF11 900
  Abbazia di S. Andrea d'Amalfi Acquarello/cartone (45x29cm 17x11in) Milano 2001

VIANELLO Cesare XIX-XX **[17]**
- $3 657 - €4 276 - **£2 570** - FF28 049
  Rosen für die Angebetete Öl/Leinwand (42x58.5cm 16x23in) Luzern 2000
- $3 130 - €3 506 - **£2 175** - FF23 000
  La marchande de fleurs Huile/toile (33x41cm 12x16in) Le Touquet 2001

VIANEN van Jan c.1660-c.1726 **[4]**
- $600 - €518 - **£300** - FF3 400
  Ritratto di Marco Aurelio Gravure (30x17.5cm 11x6in) Milano 1999

VIANI Alberto 1906-1989 **[10]**
- $2 500 - €2 592 - **£1 500** - FF17 000
  Bagnante Bronzo (36x39.5cm 14x15in) Roma 1999

VIANI Lorenzo 1882-1936 **[227]**
- $19 000 - €19 696 - **£11 400** - FF129 200
  Colpo di mare Olio/tavola (67.5x100.5cm 26x39in) Prato 1999
- $6 750 - €6 997 - **£4 050** - FF45 900
  Interno con figure Tempera/tavola (33x40cm 12x15in) Roma 1999
- $720 - €622 - **£360** - FF4 080
  Gruppo di madri Inchiostro/carta (21x27cm 8x10in) Firenze 1999

VIARD Jean-Louis XX **[1]**
- $2 249 - €2 363 - **£1 483** - FF15 500
  Le souffle des chaumes Tapisserie (134x215cm 52x84in) Calais 2000

VIARDOT Georges Émile 1888-? **[4]**
- $3 200 - €3 536 - **£2 219** - FF23 195
  Paris Street at Dusk Oil/board (30x22cm 12x9in) New-Orleans LA 2001

VIAVANT George Louis 1872-1925 **[21]**
- $6 600 - €6 151 - **£3 989** - FF40 351
  Mallard in Flight at Dawn Oil/canvas (38x50cm 15x20in) New-Orleans LA 1999
- $2 400 - €2 468 - **£1 522** - FF16 189
  Nature morte, Bob White Quail Watercolour/paper (48x28cm 19x11in) New-Orleans LA 2000
- $900 - €994 - **£624** - FF6 523
  Hanging Canvasback Drake/Hanging Gadwell Drake Print in colors (68x48cm 27x19in) New-Orleans LA 2001

VIAZZI Alessandro 1872-1956 **[3]**
- $3 500 - €3 628 - **£2 100** - FF23 800
  Danza allegorica Pastelli/carta (80x118cm 31x46in) Roma 1999

V

VIAZZI Cesare 1857-1943 **[6]**
- **$10 000** - €10 367 - **£6 000** - FF68 000
  Maternità Olio/tela (144.5x90.5cm 56x35in) Torino 1999
- **$16 800** - €21 770 - **£12 600** - FF142 800
  Case sul fiume Olio/tela (50x90cm 19x35in) Milano 2001

VIBERT Jean Georges 1840-1902 **[92]**
- **$30 000** - €35 574 - €20 640 - FF233 349
  The Final Touch Oil/panel (73.5x100cm 28x39in) New-York 2000
- **$2 041** - €1 982 - **£1 261** - FF13 000
  Elégant sur la plage Huile/panneau (23.5x18cm 9x7in) Melun 1999
- **$2 749** - €2 514 - **£1 679** - FF16 494
  The meeting of the cardinals Gouache (31x61cm 12x24in) New-York 1998

VIBERT Ol. XIX-XX **[1]**
- **$8 026** - €7 448 - **£5 000** - FF48 858
  Female Slave Carrying a Charger with a Pitcher Gilded bronze (H48cm H18in) London 1999

VICCHI Ferdinando XIX-XX **[45]**
- **$14 943** - €16 040 - **£10 000** - FF105 216
  Beatrice Marble (H206cm H81in) London 2000
- **$4 250** - €4 054 - **£2 587** - FF26 590
  Bust of a Young Girl on Pedestal Marble (H68.5cm H26in) New-York 1999

VICCHIO da Giulio 1925 **[8]**
- **$1 100** - €1 140 - **£660** - FF7 480
  Guattro chiacchiere Olio/tela (55x45cm 21x17in) Prato 2000

VICENTE Eduardo 1909-1968 **[111]**
- **$2 475** - €2 703 - **£1 575** - FF17 730
  Canal de San Martín, París Oleo/lienzo (65x81cm 25x31in) Madrid 2000
- **$700** - €601 - **£420** - FF3 940
  Afueras de ciudad Acuarela/papel (31x78cm 12x30in) Madrid 1999
- **$216** - €240 - **£152** - FF1 576
  Escenas del rastro Litografía a color (47x37cm 18x14in) Madrid 2001

VICENTE Esteban 1903-2001 **[26]**
- **$22 500** - €22 673 - **£14 026** - FF148 725
  Window Oil/canvas (183x121cm 72x47in) New-York 2000
- **$2 000** - €2 097 - **£1 253** - FF13 754
  Red blue and orange Abstract Oil/canvas (71x81cm 28x32in) Norwalk CT 2000
- **$980** - €1 051 - **£647** - FF6 895
  Cantaoras y guitarrista Gouache/papier (61x48cm 24x18in) Barcelona 2000
- **$368** - €330 - **£225** - FF2 167
  Paisaje Litografía (75x92cm 29x36in) Madrid 1999

VICENTE GIL de Victoriano XX **[4]**
- **$8 000** - €7 784 - **£4 924** - FF51 058
  Macuto/Campesinos Trabajando Oil/canvas (39x66cm 15x25in) New-York 1999

VICENTE MORA Manuel 1924 **[35]**
- **$183** - €180 - **£117** - FF1 182
  «Puente de Alcántra Toledo» Acuarela/papel (32x45cm 12x17in) Madrid 1999

VICENZINO Giuseppe XVII-XVIII **[13]**
- **$19 439** - €21 648 - **£13 660** - FF142 000
  Bouquet de fleurs sur un entablement Huile/toile (69x102cm 27x40in) Paris 2001

VICKERS Alfred G., H., or Sr XIX **[64]**
- **$2 416** - €2 270 - **£1 500** - FF14 893
  Shipping off Portsmouth Oil/canvas (41x60cm 16x23in) Salisbury, Wiltshire 1999
- **$836** - €983 - **£580** - FF6 449
  Chancton Water Oil/board (22x30cm 9x12in) Lewes, Sussex 2000

VICKERS Alfred Gomersal 1810-1837 **[38]**
- **$782** - €677 - **£474** - FF4 443
  Lane to Dedham, Suffolk Oil/canvas (18.5x28.5cm 7x11in) Toronto 1999
- **$635** - €669 - **£420** - FF4 391
  Shipping in choppy Waters off the Coast Watercolour (19.5x25cm 7x9in) London 2000

VICKERS Alfred H. act.1853-1907 **[128]**
- **$1 300** - €1 463 - **£895** - FF9 597
  River Landscape, Scene on the River Seine Oil/canvas (45x55cm 18x22in) Chicago IL 2000
- **$998** - €1 113 - **£700** - FF7 300
  Coastal Scene with Figures on a Path and fishing Boats out ot Sea Oil/canvas (20x25cm 8x10in) Leicester 2001

VICKERS Alfred, Snr. 1786-1868 **[114]**
- **$4 146** - €4 709 - **£2 900** - FF30 887
  Evening, Banks of the Teign, South Devon Oil/panel (39x69cm 15x27in) Devon 2001
- **$2 489** - €2 151 - **£1 500** - FF14 109
  The Lake of Zug, Switzerland, Pilates in the Distance Oil/panel (12.5x23cm 4x9in) Billingshurst, West-Sussex 1999
- **$575** - €586 - **£360** - FF3 846
  Near Venice, Italy Watercolour (19.5x36.5cm 7x14in) London 2000

VICKERS Charles XIX **[19]**
- **$962** - €970 - **£600** - FF6 362
  Farm Scene with Cattle/Wayside Chat Oil/canvas (40x60cm 15x23in) Billingshurst, West-Sussex 2000

VICKERY Charles 1913-1998 **[23]**
- **$3 250** - €3 081 - **£2 030** - FF20 211
  Wisconsin Hills Oil/canvas (56x71cm 22x27in) Chicago IL 1999

VICKREY Robert 1926 **[42]**
- **$8 500** - €9 437 - **£5 911** - FF61 900
  Boy with a Top Tempera (33x66cm 13x26in) Milford CT 2001
- **$2 600** - €2 462 - **£1 580** - FF16 151
  Poster Patterns Gouache (44.5x56cm 17x22in) New-York 1999

VICKY (Victor Weisz) 1913-1966 **[11]**
- **$156** - €153 - **£100** - FF1 002
  Portrait-sketch of Richard Crossman (d.1974) Ink (26x20cm 10x8in) London 1999

VICO Enea Vicus 1523-1567 **[41]**
- **$707** - €600 - **£420** - FF3 935
  Jupiter and Leda, after Michelangelo Engraving (25.5x35.5cm 10x13in) London 1998

VICOMTE Laurent 1956 **[3]**
- **$1 356** - €1 524 - **£952** - FF10 000
  Balade au bout du monde, pl.23 de La pierre en folie Encre Chine/papier (60x50cm 23x19in) Paris 2001

VICTOR Thomas Herbert 1894-1980 **[73]**
- **$136** - €145 - **£90** - FF950
  St.Michael's Mount Watercolour/paper (31x44.5cm 12x17in) Penzance, Cornwall 2000

V

VICTORIA Empress of Prussia 1840-1901 **[6]**
$32 874 - €35 288 - **£22 000** - FF231 475
Marguerites, Sunflowers and Roses with Glassware, Shells and a Fan Oil/canvas (67x95cm 26x37in) Bath 2000

VICTORIA Salvador 1929-1994 **[24]**
$3 510 - €3 904 - **£2 405** - FF25 610
Sin título Oleo/lienzo (65x29cm 25x11in) Madrid 2001

VICTORS Jacobus 1640-1705 **[15]**
$10 139 - €9 921 - **£6 500** - FF65 079
Poultry with Ducks, Doves and a Woodpecker by a Stream Oil/canvas (96x152.5cm 37x60in) London 1999
$7 884 - €9 147 - **£5 610** - FF60 000
Couple de pigeons Huile/toile (64x81.5cm 25x32in) Paris 2001

VICTORS Jan 1619/20-c.1676 **[21]**
$19 033 - €19 985 - **£12 000** - FF131 096
Eliezer at the House of Rebekah Oil/canvas (167x210cm 65x82in) London 2000
$10 642 - €12 354 - **£7 480** - FF81 039
Ein eleganter Reiter rastet vor einem Wirtshaus Öl/Leinwand (56x66cm 22x25in) Wien 2001

VICTORYNS Anthonie c.1620-1656 **[19]**
$11 200 - €12 013 - **£7 400** - FF78 800
Escena de interior de taberna Oleo/tabla (40x61cm 15x24in) Madrid 2000
$5 668 - €4 856 - **£3 407** - FF31 856
Die Fussoperation Oil/panel (22.5x30cm 8x11in) Hamburg 1998

VIDA Gabor 1937 **[7]**
$6 877 - €7 669 - **£4 624** - FF50 308
In der Glasbläserei Oil/panel (40.5x50cm 15x19in) Köln 2000

VIDAL Emeric Essex 1791-1861 **[12]**
$20 616 - €23 116 - **£14 000** - FF151 629
Travelling Wagons of Buenos Aires passing a Pantano Watercolour (25x39.5cm 9x15in) London 2000

VIDAL Eugène Vincent 1850-1908 **[18]**
$5 656 - €4 790 - £3 400 - FF31 423
Young Girl in a Black Hat Oil/canvas (64x43cm 25x16in) London 1998
$7 445 - €7 622 - **£4 675** - FF50 000
Le jeune peintre à son chevalet/La fillette en costume d'Italienne Huile/toile (47x33cm 18x12in) Lille 2000

VIDAL Francesc 1960 **[74]**
$277 - €264 - **£167** - FF1 733
Paiaje con riachuelo Oleo/lienzo (65x81cm 25x31in) Barcelona 1999
$198 - €180 - **£123** - FF1 182
Costa Brava Oleo/lienzo (24x55cm 9x21in) Barcelona 1999

VIDAL Gustave 1895-1966 **[87]**
$731 - €640 - **£443** - FF4 200
Village de Haute-Provence Huile/toile (55x46cm 21x18in) Saint-Christol-les-Alès 1998

VIDAL Hahn Margarita 1919 **[3]**
$4 400 - €4 648 - **£2 908** - FF30 487
Dreaming Peonies Oil/canvas (60x76cm 24x30in) Houston TX 2000

VIDAL Léon 1833-1906 **[6]**
$2 590 - €2 902 - **£1 800** - FF19 033
«Plastron de la cuirasse du Roi Henri II» Photograph (34.5x25.5cm 13x10in) London 2001

VIDAL Louis c.1754-c.1810 **[13]**
$18 751 - €22 038 - **£13 000** - FF144 560
Upturned Basket with Roses, Tulips, Grapes/Roses, Tulips other Flowers Oil/panel (59x86cm 23x33in) London 2000

VIDAL NAVATEL Louis l'Aveugle 1831-1892 **[46]**
$892 - €854 - **£554** - FF5 600
Lion marchant Bronze (47x26cm 18x10in) Rennes 1999

VIDAL VENTOSA Joan XX **[2]**
$11 432 - €9 452 - **£6 708** - FF62 000
Picasso assis entre Fernande Olivier et Ramon Reventos, Mai Tirage argentique (14.5x20cm 5x7in) Paris 1998

VIEGENER Eberhard 1890-1967 **[105]**
$2 619 - €2 812 - **£1 753** - FF18 446
Alter Mann mit Vision Mixed media/panel (87x61cm 34x24in) Kempten 2000
$1 183 - €1 380 - **£831** - FF9 055
Soester Börde Oil/panel (18.2x30.5cm 7x12in) Köln 2000
$1 415 - €1 687 - **£1 009** - FF11 067
Mann und Pferd in hügeliger Landschaft Watercolour (36.2x47cm 14x18in) Königstein 2000
$153 - €179 - **£107** - FF1 173
Das goldene Kalb Woodcut (13x10cm 5x3in) Köln 2001

VIEGERS Bernard, Ben 1886-1947 **[116]**
$1 611 - €1 815 - **£1 110** - FF11 906
A Summer day in Amsterdam with a Barges on a Canal Oil/canvas (41x60cm 16x23in) Amsterdam 2000
$1 231 - €1 361 - **£854** - FF8 929
View of Oostpoort, Delft Oil/canvas (25.5x52.5cm 10x20in) Amsterdam 2001

VIEILLEVOYE Barthelemy Josef 1798-1855 **[11]**
$3 590 - €3 940 - **£2 316** - FF25 846
Klassisk figurscen Oil/canvas (80x90cm 31x35in) Lund 2000

VIEIRA DA SILVA Maria-Eléna 1908-1992 **[436]**
$179 874 - €166 937 - **£108 000** - FF1 095 033
Winter Oil/canvas (162x146cm 63x57in) London 1999
$110 550 - €117 870 - **£75 000** - FF773 175
Les trois issues Oil/canvas (60x73cm 23x28in) London 2001
$56 783 - €60 952 - **£38 000** - FF399 820
Paysage Tempera/canvas (33x40cm 12x15in) London 2000
$16 437 - €17 644 - **£11 000** - FF115 737
Composition Gouache/paper (25x17.5cm 9x6in) London 2000
$544 - €579 - **£344** - FF3 800
Composition turquoise et mauve Sérigraphie couleurs (63.5x48.5cm 25x19in) Paris 2000

VIEIRA Francisco 1765-1806 **[3]**
$54 000 - €59 821 - **£34 800** - FF392 400
Marinha-paisagem com pescadores, galeáo portugués com bandeira real Oleo/lienzo (81.5x78.5cm 32x30in) Lisboa 2000

V

VIEN Joseph-Marie 1716-1809 **[42]**

$28 278 - €27 441 - **£17 820** - FF180 000
L'enlèvement des Sabines Huile/toile (49.5x98cm 19x38in) Paris 1999

$6 960 - €7 318 - **£4 368** - FF48 000
Bacchanales Huile/papier/toile (25.5x45.5cm 10x17in) Paris 2000

$1 137 - €1 342 - **£799** - FF8 800
Mercure confiant Bacchus enfant aux nymphes du mont Nysa Pierre noire (19x42cm 7x16in) Paris 2000

VIEN Marie Thérèse Reboul 1738-1805 **[1]**

$9 662 - €10 976 - **£6 667** - FF72 000
Panier de fruits, anémones et plumes de paon/Perdreix, fruits, bulbes Gouache/papier (38x53cm 14x20in) Paris 2000

VIERA José 1949 **[7]**

$305 - €300 - **£190** - FF1 970
Apocalipsis Aguafuerte (51x39cm 20x15in) Madrid 1999

VIERGE Daniel 1851-1904 **[25]**

$459 - €511 - **£306** - FF3 349
Paisaje con río Acuarela/papel (13.5x20cm 5x7in) Madrid 2000

VIERIN Emmanuel 1869-1954 **[25]**

$1 040 - €1 239 - **£745** - FF8 130
Dorpsgezicht in vlaanderen Oil/canvas (60x80cm 23x31in) Lokeren 2000

VIERLING Antoine 1842-? **[2]**

$2 269 - €2 287 - **£1 414** - FF15 000
L'heure de thé Huile/toile (34x21cm 13x8in) Paris 2000

VIERO Teodoro 1740-1795/1819 **[48]**

$78 - €84 - **£51** - FF551
La reine de Pologne Grabado (37x23cm 14x9in) Madrid 2000

VIERTHALER Johann 1869-1957 **[69]**

$763 - €716 - **£471** - FF4 695
Tänzerin Bronze (H33cm H12in) Ahlden 1999

VIETTI Nicola 1945 **[27]**

$300 - €311 - **£180** - FF2 040
Il Cardinale Olio/tela (50x35cm 19x13in) Vercelli 2001

$275 - €285 - **£165** - FF1 870
Bambina Olio/cartone (40x30cm 15x11in) Vercelli 2001

VIGAS Oswaldo 1926 **[48]**

$2 380 - €2 156 - **£1 540** - FF14 140
Sin título Oleo/lienzo (50.5x61cm 19x24in) Caracas 1999

$1 096 - €1 262 - **£747** - FF8 277
Grupo familiar Huile/bois (22.5x28.5cm 8x11in) Caracas ($) 2000

$4 104 - €4 837 - **£2 883** - FF31 730
Bruja Bronze (38x26x14cm 14x10x5in) Caracas ($) 2000

$320 - €299 - **£200** - FF1 960
Figura de los Pollitos Técnica mixta/papel (28.5x23.5cm 11x9in) Caracas 1999

$373 - €440 - **£262** - FF2 883
Sin título Grabado (26x31.5cm 10x12in) Caracas ($) 2000

VIGÉE Louis 1715-1767 **[16]**

$6 190 - €6 403 - **£3 897** - FF42 000
Portraits du Comte et de la Comtesse de Chazelles Pastel/papier (58x48cm 22x18in) Paris 2000

VIGÉE-LEBRUN Elisabeth 1755-1842 **[45]**

$38 763 - €44 972 - **£27 199** - FF295 000
Potrait d'une petite fille du miniaturiste Pierre Adolphe Hall Huile/toile (65x54cm 25x21in) Chinon 2000

$20 832 - €21 343 - **£12 964** - FF140 000
Etude de jeune femme, un ruban dans sa chevelure Pastel (29.5x24cm 11x9in) Paris 2000

VIGELAND Gustav 1869-1943 **[19]**

$10 469 - €11 619 - **£7 296** - FF76 218
Kvinne og bjorn Bronze (H33cm H12in) Oslo 2001

$648 - €748 - **£456** - FF4 909
Sittende kvinne Woodcut (16x32cm 6x12in) Oslo 2000

VIGER DU VIGNEAU Jean Louis Victor 1819-1879 **[6]**

$11 539 - €13 562 - **£8 000** - FF88 960
Les plaisirs de Malmaison Oil/panel (21x27cm 8x10in) London 2000

VIGH Antonia 1886-1922 **[1]**

$1 837 - €2 058 - **£1 277** - FF13 500
Honfleur, élégante sur la digue Huile/panneau (46x33cm 18x12in) Le Touquet 2001

VIGH Bertalan 1890-1946 **[17]**

$806 - €929 - **£550** - FF6 093
A girl with a Bouquet of Flowers Oil/canvas (79x58.5cm 31x23in) London 2000

VIGHI Coriolano 1846-1905 **[10]**

$571 - €493 - **£285** - FF3 236
Marina Pastelli/carta (59x97cm 23x38in) Venezia 1999

VIGIER Joseph, Comte XIX **[19]**

$1 045 - €1 220 - **£727** - FF8 000
Le prince de Condé sur un poney Tirage papier salé (9x14.5cm 3x5in) Paris 2000

VIGIL Romando 1902-1978 **[7]**

$400 - €427 - **£272** - FF2 803
Stylized Thunderbird Watercolour/paper (13x8cm 5x3in) Cloudcroft NM 2001

VIGNALI Jacopo 1592-1664 **[22]**

$42 500 - €44 058 - **£25 500** - FF289 000
Adorazione dei pastori Olio/tela (232x265cm 91x104in) Firenze 2000

$9 666 - €9 615 - **£6 000** - FF63 067
Saint Dominic Oil/canvas (101.5x77.5cm 39x30in) London 1999

$254 031 - €272 681 - **£170 000** - FF1 788 672
Head of a Young Woman, Wearing a Coral necklace Red chalk (32.5x22.5cm 12x8in) London 2000

VIGNANI Giuseppe 1932 **[27]**

$500 - €518 - **£300** - FF3 400
Ballando sullo scoglio Olio/tela (70x80cm 27x31in) Vercelli 2000

VIGNE de Edouard 1808-1866 **[15]**

$4 537 - €3 811 - **£2 667** - FF25 000
Paysage animé Huile/toile (77x100cm 30x39in) Lille 1998

$4 614 - €5 099 - **£3 200** - FF33 449
Drover with his Cattle on a Path in a Valley/Traveller with a Mule Oil/panel (14x20cm 5x7in) London 2001

VIGNE de Paul 1843-1901 **[5]**

$663 - €644 - **£408** - FF4 227
Buste de Émile Yseux Bronze (H44cm H17in) Bruxelles 1999

VIGNEAU André 1892-1968 **[15]**
📷 **$1 485** - €1 296 - **£898** - FF8 500
  Bracelet de Mauboussin Tirage argentique
  (23x17cm 9x6in) Paris 1998

VIGNERON Marc 1956 **[39]**
🖌 **$526** - €534 - **£327** - FF3 500
  L'allée fleurie Huile/toile (61x50cm 24x19in)
  Strasbourg 2000
🖌 **$200** - €198 - **£121** - FF1 300
  Mas aux oliviers Huile/toile (27x22cm 10x8in)
  Toulouse 2000

VIGNERON Pierre Roch 1789-1872 **[14]**
🖌 **$8 393** - €8 385 - **£5 247** - FF55 000
  Portrait de jeune noir Huile/toile (64x54cm 25x21in)
  Paris 1999

VIGNES Louis 1831-1896 **[12]**
📷 **$653** - €762 - **£458** - FF5 000
  Palestine, nº16 Petra Tirage albuminé (25x19.5cm
  9x7in) Paris 2001

VIGNOLES André 1920 **[60]**
🖌 **$1 100** - €1 181 - **£747** - FF7 744
  «Allée dans le jardin de Monet» Oil/canvas
  (64x80cm 25x31in) Delray-Beach FL 2001

VIGNON Claude 1593-1670 **[37]**
🖌 **$17 446** - €18 599 - **£11 065** - FF122 000
  Crésus montrant ses richesses à Solon
  Huile/toile (146x112.5cm 57x44in) Paris 2000
🖌 **$12 302** - €14 483 - **£8 645** - FF95 000
  L'adoration des bergers Lavis (35x22.5cm 13x8in)
  Paris 2000

VIGNON de Jules 1815-1885 **[6]**
🖌 **$6 000** - €5 898 - **£3 855** - FF38 686
  Dolce far niente Oil/canvas (61x105.5cm 24x41in)
  New-York 1999
🖌 **$4 719** - €3 964 - **£2 774** - FF26 000
  Intérieur paysan Huile/panneau (38.5x25.5cm
  15x10in) Lille 1998

VIGNON Victor 1847-1909 **[135]**
🖌 **$4 635** - €4 573 - **£2 856** - FF30 000
  Les grands poiriers Huile/toile (51x65cm 20x25in)
  Paris 1999
🖌 **$3 457** - €3 630 - **£2 180** - FF23 812
  Church in a small Village Oil/canvas (27x40.5cm
  10x15in) Amsterdam 2000

VIGNOZZI Piero 1934 **[7]**
🖌 **$1 800** - €2 332 - **£1 350** - FF15 300
  Natura morta Olio/tela (90x75cm 35x29in) Prato
  2000

VIGNY Sylvain 1902-1970 **[421]**
🖌 **$552** - €610 - **£382** - FF4 000
  Femme au chapeau Huile/papier (60x45cm 23x17in)
  Paris 2001
🖌 **$260** - €283 - **£171** - FF1 857
  Stilleben mit Früchtekorb Öl/Papier (24x41cm
  9x16in) Bern 2000
🖌 **$441** - €381 - **£266** - FF2 500
  Portrait de femme Aquarelle/papier (63x43cm
  24x16in) Paris 1999

VIGO Nanda 1936 **[3]**
🖌 **$15 433** - €18 354 - **£11 000** - FF120 397
  Manhattan, Floor Lamp Metal (H170cm H66in)
  London 2000

VIGON Louis Jacques 1897-1985 **[81]**
🖌 **$588** - €686 - **£407** - FF4 500
  Rouen Huile/toile (54x73cm 21x28in) Le Havre 2000

VIGOUREUX-DUPLESSIS Jacques c.1660-c.1732
[6]
🖌 **$70 000** - €78 405 - **£48 636** - FF514 304
  **Chinoiserie figures surrounding a painting
  depicting a satyr** Oil/canvas (80x92.5cm 31x36in)
  New-York 2001

VIIRILÄ Reino 1901 **[15]**
🖌 **$473** - €538 - **£324** - FF3 530
  Sommarmoln Oil/canvas (46x56cm 18x22in) Helsinki
  2000

VIJLBRIEF Ernst 1934 **[32]**
🖌 **$466** - €544 - **£332** - FF3 571
  Untitled Oil/canvas (65x54cm 25x21in) Amsterdam
  2001

VIKE Harald 1906-1987 **[42]**
🖌 **$526** - €594 - **£370** - FF3 894
  Rural Landscape Oil/canvas (45.5x57cm 17x22in)
  Malvern, Victoria 2001
🖌 **$576** - €641 - **£386** - FF4 203
  Old Well Halls Creek Watercolour/paper (26x36cm
  10x14in) Nedlands 2000

VIKSTEN Hans 1926-1987 **[51]**
🖌 **$619** - €697 - **£426** - FF4 572
  Kvinnototem Oil/canvas (117x89cm 46x35in) Uppsala
  2000

VIKTOR IV Walter Carl Glück 1929-1986 **[58]**
🖌 **$1 582** - €1 481 - **£957** - FF9 713
  Royal Wedding Oil/panel (62x60cm 24x23in)
  Köbenhavn 1999
🖌 **$1 171** - €1 361 - **£823** - FF8 929
  Wood Face Object (33x29x24cm 12x11x9in)
  Amsterdam 2001
🖌 **$390** - €454 - **£274** - FF2 976
  Logbook pages No.'s 79, 90 Mixed media/paper
  (54x43cm 21x16in) Amsterdam 2001

VILA ARRUFAT Antoni 1896-1989 **[13]**
🖌 **$6 100** - €6 006 - **£3 800** - FF39 400
  Repós Oleo/tablex (55x46cm 21x18in) Barcelona 1999

VILA CAÑELAS Josep M. 1914 **[27]**
🖌 **$1 728** - €1 622 - **£1 053** - FF10 638
  Paisaje con casas rurales Oleo/lienzo (65x81cm
  25x31in) Barcelona 1999

VILA Emilio 1887-1967 **[10]**
🖌 **$1 040** - €1 067 - **£650** - FF7 000
  «Vaccin B.C.G» Poster (78x60cm 30x23in) London
  2000

VILA PUIG Joan 1892-1963 **[19]**
🖌 **$3 480** - €3 604 - **£2 160** - FF23 640
  Masía (Sant Cugat) Oleo/lienzo (60x73cm 23x28in)
  Barcelona 1999
🖌 **$324** - €360 - **£228** - FF2 364
  Marina Oleo/lienzo (24x32.5cm 9x12in) Madrid 2001

VILA Y PRADES Julio 1873-1930 **[81]**
🖌 **$2 318** - €2 282 - **£1 482** - FF14 972
  Puerto de pasajes Oleo/cartón (45x37cm 17x14in)
  Madrid 1999
🖌 **$3 025** - €3 304 - **£1 925** - FF21 670
  Elegantes años 20 Oleo/tabla (24x19cm 9x7in)
  Madrid 2000

VILADECANS Joan-Pere 1948 **[27]**
🖌 **$891** - €811 - **£523** - FF5 319
  Hacha Técnica mixta/papel (50x67cm 19x26in)
  Barcelona 1999

V

📖 **$84** - €72 - **£50** - FF472
Efecto óptico Litografía (75.5x56cm 29x22in)
Barcelona 1999

VILADRICH VILA Miguel Antonio 1887-1956 **[3]**
🖋 **$960** - €901 - **£585** - FF5 910
Retrato de dama Oleo/tabla (55x51.5cm 21x20in)
Madrid 1999

VILALLONGA de Jesus Carlos 1927 **[36]**
🖋 **$1 781** - €2 078 - **£1 239** - FF13 631
Young Spanish Woman Oil/board (51x40.5cm
20x15in) Toronto 2000

VILATO Javier 1921-2000 **[106]**
🖋 **$2 275** - €2 102 - **£1 365** - FF13 790
Desnudo femenino tendido Oleo/lienzo
(81.5x100cm 32x39in) Barcelona 1999
🖋 **$1 966** - €1 982 - **£1 225** - FF13 000
Portrait Huile/toile (41x32cm 16x12in) Paris 2000
📙 **$320** - €305 - **£200** - FF2 000
Tête de femme Collage (14x10.5cm 5x4in) Paris
1999
📖 **$129** - €152 - **£92** - FF1 000
Femme assise Gravure (30x23.5cm 11x9in) Paris
2001

VILBOUX Alain XX **[2]**
🖋 **$2 176** - €2 287 - **£1 432** - FF15 000
Scène à Paris Huile/toile (15x17cm 5x6in) Paris 2000

VILLA Aleardo 1865-1906 **[22]**
📙 **$1 619** - €1 399 - **£1 079** - FF9 178
Ritratto di donna Pastelli/cartone (62x51cm 24x20in)
Milano 1998
📖 **$3 600** - €3 462 - **£2 221** - FF22 709
«Mele & Ci.» Poster (204x285cm 80x112in) New-York
1999

VILLA BASSOLS Alejandro 1920 **[6]**
🖋 **$357** - €390 - **£234** - FF2 561
Calle de pueblo de la costa Oleo/lienzo (61x50cm
24x19in) Barcelona 2000

VILLA BASSOLS Guillem 1917/22 **[11]**
🖋 **$567** - €541 - **£351** - FF3 546
«Cadaqués» Oleo/tablex (33x41cm 12x16in) Madrid
1999

VILLA BASSOLS Miguel 1901-1988 **[72]**
🖋 **$9 720** - €10 812 - **£6 840** - FF70 920
Paisaje Oleo/lienzo (60x73cm 23x28in) Barcelona
2001
🖋 **$3 040** - €2 853 - **£1 900** - FF18 715
Altea Oleo/lienzo (22x27cm 8x10in) Madrid 1999
📙 **$274** - €270 - **£175** - FF1 773
Figura sentada Lápiz/papel (16x22cm 6x8in) Madrid
1999

VILLA Edoardo 1920 **[15]**
🔨 **$1 299** - €1 456 - **£903** - FF9 551
Upright Figure Bronze (H66cm H25in) Johannesburg
2001

VILLA Émile XIX **[2]**
🖋 **$73 793** - €74 359 - **£46 000** - FF487 765
La charmeuse Oil/canvas (155.5x90cm 61x35in)
London 2000

VILLA Georges 1883-1965 **[24]**
📖 **$624** - €534 - **£374** - FF3 500
**«Les Ailes Font Gagner du temps»/«Le conquê-
te de l'Humanité»** Affiche (60x80cm 23x31in) Paris
1998

VILLA Hernando 1881-1952 **[21]**
📖 **$5 000** - €4 847 - **£3 096** - FF31 796
«The Chief...is still chief» Poster (105x71cm
41x28in) New-York 1999

VILLAAMIL Philip XIX **[3]**
🖋 **$9 600** - €9 010 - **£5 850** - FF59 100
El agua bendita Oleo/lienzo (80x57cm 31x22in)
Madrid 1999
🖋 **$3 600** - €3 604 - **£2 220** - FF23 640
**Escenas taurinas en la Maestranza: Suerte de
estoque/Suerte de Varas** Oleo/lienzo (25x30cm
9x11in) Madrid 1999

VILLAIN Georges René 1854-1930 **[25]**
🖋 **$365** - €427 - **£258** - FF2 800
Boulevard Parisien Huile/panneau (18x27cm 7x10in)
Falaise 2001

VILLAIN Henri XIX-XX **[6]**
📖 **$214** - €244 - **£147** - FF1 600
«Compagnie algérienne, emprunt national»
Affiche (118x78cm 46x30in) Paris 2000

VILLALBA Dario 1939 **[28]**
🖋 **$837** - €751 - **£512** - FF4 925
Figura Técnica mixta (46x38cm 18x14in) Madrid 1999

VILLALPANDO Juan Battiste XVI-XVII **[1]**
📖 **$1 555** - €1 426 - **£950** - FF9 351
Vera Hierosolymae Engraving (68.5x76cm 26x29in)
London 1999

VILLAMENA Francisco 1566-1624 **[13]**
📖 **$579** - €562 - **£360** - FF3 689
Die Verkündigung Kupferstich (37.3x27cm 14x10in)
Berlin 1999

VILLANI Gennaro 1885-1948 **[24]**
🖋 **$650** - €674 - **£390** - FF4 420
Vecchio casolare Olio/cartone (21x20cm 8x7in)
Vercelli 1999

VILLANIS Emanuele 1880-c.1920 **[222]**
🔨 **$7 250** - €7 813 - **£4 944** - FF51 253
L'Eclipse (Figure Embracing Woman) Bronze
(H106cm H42in) Hatfield PA 2001
🔨 **$1 100** - €1 232 - **£764** - FF8 081
«Carmen» Bronze (H53cm H21in) St. Louis MO 2001

VILLANUEVA Leoncio 1936 **[5]**
🖋 **$5 000** - €4 317 - **£3 050** - FF28 319
Elementos Casa - Pez Acrylic (99x81.5cm 38x32in)
Miami FL 1999

VILLEBOIS Paul XVIII **[3]**
🖋 **$4 739** - €5 087 - **£3 171** - FF33 369
Der junge Künstler Öl/Leinwand (59x48cm 23x18in)
Wien 2000

VILLEBOIS Pierre XVIII **[2]**
🖋 **$22 606** - €21 648 - **£14 228** - FF142 000
**Voltaire accueillant des paysans, ou Voltaire à
Ferney** Huile/toile (81x100cm 31x39in) Paris 1999

VILLEERS de Jacob 1616-1667 **[10]**
🖋 **$26 897** - €28 872 - **£18 000** - FF189 388
Extensive landscape with a Windmill Oil/canvas
(77x103cm 30x40in) London 2000
🖋 **$6 206** - €6 079 - **£4 000** - FF39 878
**River Landscape with Figures, a Town and Hills
beyond** Oil/panel (34x42.5cm 13x16in) London 1999

VILLEFROY E. XIX-XX **[12]**
📖 **$294** - €351 - **£210** - FF2 300
«Café Sao-Paulo, Maison Brésilienne, Paris»
Affiche (81x60cm 31x23in) Orléans 2000

V

VILLEGAS Y CORDERO José 1848-1922 **[123]**
- $25 000 - €21 569 - **£15 082** - FF141 482
  Wedding in a Side Chapel of San Marco Oil/canvas (93x183cm 36x72in) New-York 1998
- $12 981 - €15 257 - **£9 000** - FF100 080
  Portrait of a Bedouin Oil/canvas (53x33cm 20x12in) London 2000
- $9 100 - €7 808 - **£5 590** - FF51 220
  Playa Oleo/tabla (21.5x27cm 8x10in) Madrid 1998
- $8 160 - €7 208 - **£5 040** - FF47 280
  Las Dos Potencias Acuarela/papel (64x97cm 25x38in) Madrid 1999

VILLEMOT Bernard 1911-1990 **[294]**
- $350 - €326 - **£216** - FF2 137
  «Air France, Côte d'Azur» Poster (99x62cm 39x24in) New-York 1999

VILLEMOT Jean 1880-1958 **[6]**
- $348 - €335 - **£215** - FF2 200
  «Voiturette automobile le Zèbre, va 3 fois plus vite que le cheval...» Affiche (108x150cm 42x59in) Paris 1999

VILLENEUVE Arthur 1910-1990 **[51]**
- $522 - €575 - **£362** - FF3 770
  Visages et maisons Gouache/papier (56x71cm 22x27in) Montréal 2001

VILLEQUIN Etienne 1619-1688 **[1]**
- $5 168 - €5 793 - **£3 507** - FF38 000
  Fleurs sous les pins Huile/panneau (54x65cm 21x25in) Paris 2000

VILLERET François Étienne c.1800-1866 **[43]**
- $11 739 - €13 805 - **£8 415** - FF90 555
  Französisches Fischerdorf an einem Kanal gelegen Öl/Leinwand (43x59cm 16x23in) Stuttgart 2001
- $2 773 - €3 278 - **£1 965** - FF21 500
  Le Château de Versailles vu de la Pièce d'eau des Suisses Huile/toile (18x26cm 7x10in) Béziers 2000
- $1 466 - €1 372 - **£908** - FF9 000
  Vue du Panthéon Aquarelle/papier (14x11cm 5x4in) Paris 1999

VILLERS André 1930 **[143]**
- $459 - €534 - **£322** - FF3 500
  «Ironirisme» Photo (40x51cm 15x20in) Paris 2001

VILLERS de Adolphe 1872-1930/34 **[10]**
- $1 217 - €1 037 - **£724** - FF6 800
  Personnages au bord d'un lac à proximité d'un village Huile/panneau (23.5x33cm 9x12in) Paris 1998

VILLETTE E. XIX **[1]**
- $5 078 - €5 031 - **£3 078** - FF33 000
  Villas et chalets de Trouville-Deauville dédié à la Duchesse de Morny Tirage charbon (13x11cm 5x4in) Paris 2000

VILLODAS Y DE LA TORRE Ricardo 1846-1904 **[50]**
- $159 - €180 - **£111** - FF1 182
  El castillo Acuarela/papel (18.5x29.5cm 7x11in) Madrid 2001

VILLON Eugène 1879-1951 **[32]**
- $211 - €213 - **£132** - FF1 400
  Le marabout du bois sacré à Blida Aquarelle/papier (15.5x22.5cm 6x8in) Paris 2000

VILLON Jacques 1875-1963 **[1598]**
- $16 000 - €15 386 - **£9 857** - FF100 923
  L'azur Oil/canvas (34.5x73cm 13x28in) New-York 1999

- $5 964 - €6 403 - **£3 990** - FF42 000
  Portrait de Mademoiselle Dubray Huile/toile (35x29cm 13x11in) Paris 2000
- $3 918 - €4 573 - **£2 772** - FF30 000
  Tête de Suzanne Duchamp, soeur de l'artiste Terracotta (H24.5cm H9in) Paris 2001
- $895 - €1 067 - **£638** - FF7 000
  Tête Crayon/papier (22x15.5cm 8x6in) Strasbourg 2000
- $881 - €1 037 - **£631** - FF6 800
  Au bois, Lili au boa noir Pointe sèche (36x23.5cm 14x9in) Paris 2001

VILLORESI Franco 1920-1975 **[73]**
- $700 - €726 - **£420** - FF4 760
  Periferia Olio/tela (50x40cm 19x15in) Prato 2000
- $600 - €622 - **£360** - FF4 080
  Claudia Idropittura (35x25cm 13x9in) Prato 2001

VILLOTEAU Léopoldine XIX-XX **[2]**
- $3 104 - €3 668 - **£2 200** - FF24 060
  Bouquet de fleurs Oil/canvas (91x72.5cm 35x28in) London 2000

VIMAR Auguste 1851-1916 **[15]**
- $2 144 - €2 439 - **£1 488** - FF16 000
  Cavalier sous la neige Huile/toile (63x43.5cm 24x17in) Marseille 2000
- $1 208 - €1 403 - **£860** - FF9 200
  Singe à la palette de couleur Huile/panneau (21x17cm 8x6in) Marseille 2001

VIN van der Paul 1823-1887 **[20]**
- $3 000 - €3 326 - **£2 083** - FF21 816
  Stable Scene with Horses Feeding his Horses Oil/panel (46x56cm 16x22in) New-Orleans LA 2001

VINACHE DE LAUNAY Régine 1865-1952 **[47]**
- $414 - €396 - **£260** - FF2 600
  Vase de roses et plumes de paon Aquarelle/papier (68x55cm 26x21in) Angers 1999

VINAGE du Matthias 1918-1987 **[9]**
- $647 - €764 - **£459** - FF5 013
  «Werftarbeiter» Vintage gelatin silver print (29.5x23.5cm 11x9in) Berlin 2001

VINAY Jean 1907-1978 **[67]**
- $1 049 - €884 - **£620** - FF5 800
  Fleurs: Coréopsis, Silènes, Sauge Huile/toile (55x38cm 21x14in) Grenoble 1998
- $504 - €610 - **£352** - FF4 000
  Canal de la Villette Huile/toile (27x41cm 10x16in) Paris 2000

VINCELETTE Roméo 1902-1979 **[55]**
- $266 - €244 - **£163** - FF1 602
  Canards Pastel/papier (62x48cm 24x18in) Montréal 1999

VINCENT Antoine Paul XVIII-XIX **[6]**
- $21 043 - €20 430 - **£13 000** - FF134 013
  Musician Facing Right in Blue Jacket With Gold Buttons Miniature (11x10.5cm 4x4in) London 1999

VINCENT François André 1746-1816 **[41]**
- $13 377 - €14 940 - **£9 065** - FF98 000
  Portrait de jeune femme assise au chapeau à plumes Huile/toile (81x65cm 31x25in) Paris 2000
- $12 406 - €12 501 - **£7 732** - FF82 000
  Homme lisant, assis au fond d'une barque Pierre noire/papier (26x16.5cm 10x6in) Paris 2000

V

VINCENT George 1796-c.1831 **[49]**
- $4 385 - €5 032 - **£3 000** - FF33 006
  Fishing Boats and other Fishing off the Coast in a Stiff Breeze Oil/canvas (36x48cm 14x18in)
  Leamington-Spa, Warwickshire 2000
- $1 016 - €1 144 - **£700** - FF7 507
  Cattle Watering in a Wooded Landscape Oil/canvas (31x26cm 12x10in) London 2000

VINCENT Harry Aiken 1864-1931 **[40]**
- $4 250 - €3 944 - **£2 551** - FF25 872
  Gloucester Docks Oil/canvas (45x60cm 18x24in) Milford CT 1999
- $3 250 - €3 126 - **£2 006** - FF20 504
  The Village on the Water Oil/canvas/board (28x35.5cm 11x13in) Boston MA 1999

VINCENT René 1879-1936 **[117]**
- $400 - €433 - **£266** - FF2 843
  «Porto Ramos-Pinto» Poster (48x34cm 19x13in) New-York 2000

VINCENT-ANGLADE Henri 1876-1956 **[37]**
- $994 - €1 067 - **£665** - FF7 000
  Le trotteur Huile/toile (50x100cm 19x39in) Senlisse 2000

VINCENZINA Giuseppe XVIII **[6]**
- $31 028 - €26 583 - **£18 652** - FF174 371
  Blumenstilleben Öl/Leinwand (85x69cm 33x27in) Köln 1998

VINCENZINO Giuseppe XVII-XVIII **[7]**
- $17 000 - €15 738 - **£10 262** - FF103 232
  Still Life of Peaches, Figs and Flowers in a Glass Vase Oil/canvas (53x70.5cm 20x27in) New-York 1999

VINCHE Lionel 1936 **[47]**
- $103 - €111 - **£69** - FF731
  Leopold II sorcier Encre (60x46cm 23x18in) Bruxelles 2000

VINCHON Auguste Jean Bapt. 1787-1855 **[50]**
- $5 843 - €4 878 - **£3 427** - FF32 000
  Properce et Cynthie à Tivoli Huile/toile (45.5x38.5cm 17x15in) Tours 1998
- $1 734 - €1 448 - **£1 017** - FF9 500
  Mort de MADAME, duchesse d'orléans (Henriette Anne d'Angleterre) Huile/toile (32.5x41cm 12x16in) Tours 1998

VINCIATA 1911-1996 **[5]**
- $2 287 - €2 539 - **£1 594** - FF16 658
  The Attic Studio Oil/canvas (82x51cm 32x20in) Dublin 2001

VINCK Frans 1827-1903 **[33]**
- $1 664 - €1 983 - **£1 192** - FF13 008
  La fuite en Egypte avec les pyramides de Gizeh dans l'arrière-plan Huile/toile (71x55.5cm 27x21in) Antwerpen 1999

VINCK J. XVII **[4]**
- $10 297 - €10 671 - **£6 531** - FF70 000
  Paysage à la passerelle avec promeneurs Huile/panneau (37x48.5cm 14x19in) Paris 2000

VINCK Jozef 1900-1979 **[30]**
- $1 265 - €1 239 - **£785** - FF8 130
  Zwarte Wolken Huile/toile (92.5x114cm 36x44in) Bruxelles 1999

VINCKBOONS David 1576-c.1629/32 **[61]**
- $60 000 - €59 972 - **£36 654** - FF393 390
  Village Wedding with Peasants Merrymaking Oil/panel (34.5x53.5cm 13x21in) New-York 2000

V

- $18 757 - €17 544 - **£11 500** - FF115 080
  A Hawking Party at the Margin of a Wood, a Country House Set Amid Oil/panel (21x31cm 8x12in) London 1998
- $6 623 - €7 714 - **£4 627** - FF50 602
  Fishermen Drawing in Their Nets Ink (12x14cm 4x5in) Amsterdam 2000

VINDEVOGEL-GELEEDTS Flore 1866-1938 **[11]**
- $816 - €793 - **£499** - FF5 203
  Bouquet de fleurs Huile/toile (74x74cm 29x29in) Bruxelles 1999

VINDFELT Ejnar 1905-1953 **[15]**
- $594 - €4 207 - **£2 800** - FF27 595
  Watering the Mares Oil/canvas (35.5x48cm 13x18in) London 1999
- $1 177 - €1 076 - **£737** - FF7 060
  Boxeren «Buster» Oil/canvas (41x33cm 16x12in) København 1999

VINE OF COLCHESTER John 1808/09-1867 **[18]**
- $12 459 - €10 662 - **£7 500** - FF69 938
  Three Sheep in a Byre Oil/canvas (45.5x61cm 17x24in) London 1998
- $3 920 - €4 560 - **£2 800** - FF29 909
  Saddled grey Horse and a Dog by a Barn Oil/canvas (30.5x36cm 12x14in) London 2001

VINEA Francesco 1845-1902 **[75]**
- $33 000 - €28 508 - **£16 500** - FF187 000
  Nudo femminile di schiena con fagiano Olio/tela (193x112cm 75x44in) Firenze 1999
- $11 229 - €11 316 - **£7 000** - FF74 225
  The Street Admirer Oil/canvas (61x45cm 24x17in) London 2000
- $2 000 - €2 073 - **£1 200** - FF13 600
  Il bacio rubato Olio/tavoletta (23.5x39cm 9x15in) Milano 1999
- $1 000 - €1 037 - **£600** - FF6 800
  Figure con cavallo Matita (20.5x47.5cm 8x18in) Milano 2000

VINER Edwin 1867-? **[8]**
- $758 - €862 - **£520** - FF5 654
  Old Garden at Calderstones Watercolour/paper (29.5x44cm 11x17in) London 2000

VIÑES SOTO Hernando 1904-1993 **[155]**
- $10 800 - €12 013 - **£7 200** - FF78 800
  Figura femenina Oleo/lienzo (80x65cm 31x25in) Madrid 1999
- $2 500 - €3 003 - **£1 750** - FF19 700
  El frutero Oleo/cartón (18.5x24cm 7x9in) Madrid 2000
- $1 296 - €1 442 - **£888** - FF9 456
  Paisaje Acuarela/papel (13x19cm 5x7in) Madrid 2001

VINIEGRA Y LASSO Salvador 1862-1915 **[17]**
- $2 120 - €2 403 - **£1 480** - FF15 760
  Barco en la tormenta Oleo/lienzo (54.5x70cm 21x27in) Madrid 2001
- $1 677 - €1 652 - **£1 045** - FF10 835
  Marina Gouache (62x31cm 24x12in) Madrid 1999

VINKELES Reinier 1741-1816 **[14]**
- $1 313 - €1 361 - **£832** - FF8 929
  View of the Gasthuiskerk en Binnengast Watercolour/paper (23x17cm 9x6in) Amsterdam 2000

VINNE van der Vincent Jansz. 1736-1811 **[10]**
- $615 - €531 - **£370** - FF3 484
  Cows in a Field by a Farm, a Village beyond Watercolour (22.5x29.5cm 8x11in) Amsterdam 1998

VINNEN Carl 1863-1922 **[36]**
- $32 160 - €35 280 - **£21 845** - FF231 419
  Moorlandschaft Öl/Leinwand (119x177.5cm
  46x69in) Berlin 2000
- $2 976 - €2 812 - **£1 856** - FF18 446
  Krabbenkutter in Cuxhaven Öl/Karton
  (54.5x74.5cm 21x29in) Hamburg 1999
- $1 334 - €1 534 - **£942** - FF10 061
  Weg im Moor Öl/Leinwand (35x25cm 13x9in)
  Bremen 2001

VINOGRADOV Sergei Arsenievich 1869-1938 **[30]**
- $4 417 - €4 953 - **£3 000** - FF32 492
  Garden with Lilacs Oil/canvas (65.5x81.5cm
  25x32in) London 2000

VINTER John Alfred 1828-1905 **[6]**
- $2 279 - €2 650 - **£1 600** - FF17 383
  On the Beach Oil/canvas (71x91.5cm 27x36in)
  Billingshurst, West-Sussex 2001

VINTON Frederick Porter 1846-1911 **[10]**
- $2 800 - €3 266 - **£1 965** - FF21 421
  «Storm at Westchop» Oil/canvas (33x46cm 12x18in)
  Boston MA 2000

VINTSMAN Iosif Karlovich 1848-c.1908 **[1]**
- $7 570 - €7 982 - **£5 000** - FF52 356
  The Violent Intrusion Oil/canvas (62x101.5cm
  24x39in) London 2001

VINZIO Giulio Cesare 1881-1940 **[20]**
- $750 - €777 - **£450** - FF5 100
  Sorge la luna Olio/tavola (35x40cm 13x15in) Prato
  2000

VIOLA Domenico ?-c.1696 **[1]**
- $8 000 - €6 955 - **£4 841** - FF45 620
  Adoration of the Shepherds Oil/canvas (37x45.5cm
  14x17in) New-York 1999

VIOLA Giuseppe 1933 **[13]**
- $500 - €518 - **£300** - FF3 400
  Il venditore di castagne Olio/tela (60x40cm
  23x15in) Vercelli 2001

VIOLA Manuel 1919-1987 **[253]**
- $5 415 - €5 706 - **£3 420** - FF37 430
  Le Voyage au Bout de la Nuit Acrílico/lienzo
  (151x94cm 59x37in) Madrid 2000
- $1 568 - €1 682 - **£1 064** - FF11 032
  Sin título Oleo/tabla (45x54cm 17x21in) Madrid 2001
- $810 - €901 - **£540** - FF5 910
  Sin título Oleo/tablex (25x20cm 9x7in) Madrid 2000
- $87 - €90 - **£54** - FF591
  Composición abstracta Grabado (24.5x16cm 9x6in)
  Madrid 2000

VIOLLET-LE-DUC Eugène 1814-1879 **[14]**
- $14 743 - €17 532 - **£10 154** - FF115 000
  **Vue de l'ancienne Chambre des Comptes à
  Paris** Aquarelle/papier (62x95.5cm 24x37in) Paris 2000

VIOLLET-LE-DUC Victor 1848-1901 **[13]**
- $3 500 - €4 114 - **£2 400** - FF26 986
  French Port Oil/canvas (38.5x56cm 15x22in) New-
  York 2000

VIOLLIER Auguste Constantin 1854-1908 **[2]**
- $14 653 - €17 025 - **£10 298** - FF111 677
  Touristen Einkehr Öl/Leinwand (83x120cm 32x47in)
  Luzern 2001

VIOLLIER Jean 1896-1985 **[126]**
- $6 700 - €7 622 - **£4 650** - FF50 000
  Les dormeurs du plein jour Huile/toile (131x162cm
  51x63in) Paris 2000

- $1 361 - €1 524 - **£946** - FF10 000
  Paris, Quai de Grenelle Huile/toile (38x55cm
  14x21in) Le Touquet 2001

VION Raoul XIX-XX **[14]**
- $601 - €686 - **£418** - FF4 500
  «La bicyclette la triomphante» Affiche (80x120cm
  31x47in) Paris 2001

VIONOJA Veikko 1909 **[118]**
- $3 036 - €3 279 - **£2 098** - FF21 512
  Strandbod Oil/canvas (58x61cm 22x24in) Helsinki
  2001
- $1 035 - €1 177 - **£710** - FF7 722
  Sommarnatt Oil/panel (39x32cm 15x12in) Helsinki
  2000
- $306 - €286 - **£188** - FF1 875
  Interiör Indian ink/paper (28x35cm 11x13in) Helsinki
  1999
- $212 - €202 - **£129** - FF1 323
  Stilleben med blommor på bord II Color lithograph
  (52x39cm 20x15in) Helsinki 1999

VIRIO DA SAVONA 1901-1985 **[11]**
- $1 500 - €1 555 - **£900** - FF10 200
  Veduta delle funivie di Savona Tempera/tela
  (50x60cm 19x23in) Torino 1999
- $300 - €311 - **£180** - FF2 040
  Paesaggio Acquarello/carta (28x22cm 11x8in) Trieste
  1999

VIRION Charles Louis Eug. 1865-1946 **[15]**
- $2 577 - €2 422 - **£1 600** - FF15 886
  Hen Protecting her Chicks Bronze (34x32.5cm
  13x12in) London 1999

VIRNICH Thomas 1957 **[19]**
- $1 302 - €1 125 - **£786** - FF7 380
  Ohne Titel (säule) Sculpture, wood (6.2x6.2x6.2cm
  2x2x2in) Köln 1998

VIRULY Willen V 1636-1678 **[2]**
- $3 842 - €4 214 - **£2 550** - FF27 642
  Marchands sur fond de paysage lacustre
  Huile/toile (40x47cm 15x18in) Bruxelles 2000

VISAT Georges XX **[4]**
- $4 600 - €5 358 - **£3 215** - FF35 148
  Aleko, after Marc Chagall Etching, aquatint in colors
  (55.5x66.5cm 21x26in) Stockholm 2000

VISBY Frederik Mayer 1839-1926 **[10]**
- $7 078 - €6 042 - **£4 234** - FF39 631
  Fort Christiansvaern, St. Croix Oil/canvas
  (46x64cm 18x25in) Viby J, Århus 1998

VISCA Rodolfo 1934 **[23]**
- $702 - €781 - **£481** - FF5 122
  «Forma roja» Oleo/cartón (32.5x25cm 12x9in)
  Madrid 2001

VISCAI ALBERT Fernando 1879-1936 **[10]**
- $4 524 - €5 226 - **£3 132** - FF34 278
  Niños en el jardín Oleo/lienzo (100x86cm 39x33in)
  Barcelona 2000

VISCH Henk 1950 **[8]**
- $1 618 - €1 815 - **£1 121** - FF11 906
  Untitled Gouache (50x60cm 19x23in) Amsterdam
  2000

VISCONTI Adolfo A. Ferraguti 1850-1924 **[28]**
- $364 - €390 - **£247** - FF2 561
  Lago en las montañas Oleo/lienzo (45x60cm
  17x23in) Madrid 2001

V

$7 750 - €8 034 - **£4 650** - FF52 700
Natura morta con uva e pere Olio/tela (31x37cm 12x14in) Milano 2000

VISCONTI Antonio XIX [1]
$2 265 - €1 957 - **£1 132** - FF12 838
Piazza di Nizza Olio/tela (32.5x40cm 12x15in) Milano 1999

VISCONTI Eliseo 1867-1944 [1]
$29 000 - €27 924 - **£18 049** - FF183 172
As Banistas Oil/canvas (81x65cm 31x25in) New-York 1999

VISENTINI Antonio 1688-1782 [38]
$10 500 - €10 885 - **£6 300** - FF71 400
Paesaggio con architetture Olio/tela (67x97cm 26x38in) Milano 2001
$5 212 - €5 924 - **£3 600** - FF38 857
La Chiesa Della Zittella Drawing (52x38.5cm 20x15in) London 2000
$360 - €378 - **£227** - FF2 481
Veduta dalla Colonna di S.Marco Radierung (27.4x42.4cm 10x16in) Heidelberg 2000

VISENTINI C. XX [1]
$20 400 - €17 623 - **£10 200** - FF115 600
Mussolini maresciallo d'Italia Olio/tela (246x170cm 96x66in) Prato 1999

VISEUX Claude 1927 [164]
$293 - €335 - **£201** - FF2 200
Eaux froides Huile/toile (54x65cm 21x25in) Paris 2000
$580 - €610 - **£366** - FF4 000
Sans titre Métal (63x44x22cm 24x17x9in) Paris 2000
$277 - €274 - **£167** - FF1 800
Pollution sauf chez Roger Pastel/papier (33x25cm 12x9in) Paris 2000

VISHNIAC Roman 1897-1990 [93]
$2 800 - €2 864 - **£1 764** - FF18 784
Street in Kazimierz, Cracow Silver print (50x50cm 20x20in) New-York 2000

VISKI János, Johann 1891-c.1961 [49]
$407 - €469 - **£280** - FF3 076
Galopperande hästar Oil/canvas (61x80cm 24x31in) Stockholm 2000

VISO Nicola XVIII [18]
$13 482 - €14 157 - **£8 500** - FF92 864
Italianate Landscape with Travellers and Shepherds by a Ruin Oil/canvas (141x161.5cm 55x63in) London 2001
$13 600 - €17 623 - **£10 200** - FF115 600
Paesaggio con pescatori/Marina con scena di naufragio Olio/tela (50.5x76cm 19x29in) Roma 2000

VISPRÉ François Xavier 1730-1790 [10]
$6 756 - €6 098 - **£4 164** - FF40 000
Nature morte au plat de pêches et pommes sur un entablement Huile/panneau (39x42cm 15x16in) Paris 1999

VISSCHER Claes Jansz I Nicola c.1550-c.1612 [11]
$373 - €424 - **£260** - FF2 778
Map of Africae Accurata Tabula Engraving (43.5x53.5cm 17x21in) London 2001

VISSCHER Claes Jansz II 1586-1652 [14]
$241 - €230 - **£147** - FF1 509
Ansicht eines Dorfs mit Feldweg über steinerner Bogenbrücke Etching (13.6x18.8cm 5x7in) Köln 1999

VISSCHER Cornelis II c.1619/29-1662 [46]
$6 300 - €6 748 - **£4 302** - FF44 267
Portrait of Seated Gentleman, Half Length Black chalk (20.5x17cm 8x6in) New-York 2001
$269 - €307 - **£187** - FF2 012
Der Wundarzt, nach Adriaen Brouwer Radierung (28.5x36.2cm 11x14in) Berlin 2000

VISSCHER de Jan 1636-c.1692 [21]
$1 441 - €1 636 - **£1 001** - FF10 732
Militärisches Zeltlager mit trinkenden und tanzenden Soldaten Black chalk (28.5x39cm 11x15in) Köln 2001
$133 - €148 - **£92** - FF972
Der Hirt mit dem Jungen treibt die Herde vor sich/Die Bäuerin Radierung (27.5x36.5cm 10x14in) Heidelberg 2001

VISSCHER Nikolas 1616-1709 [12]
$425 - €390 - **£260** - FF2 558
Terra Sancta Engraving (46.5x57cm 18x22in) London 1999

VISSER Carel 1928 [86]
$2 862 - €3 403 - **£2 040** - FF22 324
Dodos Mixed media/board (55x37cm 21x14in) Amsterdam 2000
$6 856 - €6 807 - **£4 284** - FF44 649
Stroom Iron (135x26x13cm 53x10x5in) Amsterdam 1999
$6 975 - €6 716 - **£4 361** - FF44 053
Stairs Bronze (H50cm H19in) Amsterdam 1999
$517 - €544 - **£341** - FF3 571
Untitled Ink/paper (35x22.5cm 13x8in) Amsterdam 2000
$507 - €544 - **£339** - FF3 571
Twee Kubussen Woodcut (905x30cm 356x11in) Amsterdam 2000

VISSER Tijpke 1876-1955 [7]
$1 831 - €2 178 - **£1 305** - FF14 287
Toad Ceramic (H10cm H3in) Amsterdam 2000

VITA Wilhelm A. 1846-1919 [8]
$29 308 - €33 743 - **£20 000** - FF221 338
Die Hueterin des Geheimnisses (Guardian of the Secret) Oil/canvas (254x132cm 100x51in) London 2000
$2 240 - €2 543 - **£1 571** - FF16 684
Kronprinz Rudolf (1858-1889) Öl/Leinwand (56x48cm 22x18in) Wien 2001

VITAL Not 1948 [17]
$3 325 - €3 785 - **£2 336** - FF24 828
Ohne Titel Öl/Papier (135x74cm 53x29in) Zürich 2001
$979 - €943 - **£612** - FF6 187
Mazzot Crayon (43x35cm 16x13in) Zürich 1999

VITAL-CORNU Charles 1851/53-1927 [25]
$10 136 - €11 518 - **£7 000** - FF75 555
Victoire Triumphante (Victory Triumphant) Bronze (H91.5cm H36in) London 2001

VITALE Carlo 1902-1996 [35]
$3 250 - €3 369 - **£1 950** - FF22 100
Ombrelloni sulla spiaggia Olio/tavola (40x50cm 15x19in) Milano 1999
$402 - €455 - **£283** - FF2 982
Früchtestilleben Oil/panel (27x35cm 10x13in) Bern 2001

VITALE Filippo c.1585-1650 [12]
$15 580 - €14 534 - **£9 400** - FF95 340
Cimon und Pero oder Caritas Romana Öl/Leinwand (150x120cm 59x47in) Wien 1999

VITALI Candido 1680-1753 **[13]**
- **$15 000** - €12 958 - **£7 500** - FF85 000
  Natura morta con selvaggina e cane Olio/tela
  (99x137cm 38x53in) Milano 1999
- **$17 138** - €15 988 - **£10 340** - FF104 874
  **Jagdstilleben mit einem Hund und einem
  Truthahn** Öl/Leinwand (97.5x123cm 38x48in) Wien
  1999

VITALI Massimo 1944 **[2]**
- **$11 968** - €14 129 - **£8 500** - FF92 682
  «Rosignano Solvay Sea II» Photograph in colors
  (150x181.5cm 59x71in) London 2001

VITALIS Macario 1898-? **[13]**
- **$965** - €1 037 - **£646** - FF6 800
  La cène Huile/toile (33x99cm 12x38in) Paris 2000

VITALONI Michele 1967 **[3]**
- **$1 824** - €2 170 - **£1 300** - FF14 233
  Woodcock on it's Nest Sculpture, wood (18x33cm
  7x12in) London 2000

VITI Eugenio 1881-1952 **[14]**
- **$641** - €613 - **£402** - FF4 024
  Strassenszene in Positano Öl/Karton (34.5x26cm
  13x10in) Hamburg 1999

VITO de Camillo XVIII-XIX **[31]**
- **$2 717** - €2 694 - **£1 700** - FF17 669
  Eruzione de 11 Septembre Gouache/paper
  (50x67cm 19x26in) London 1999

VITO de Michele XIX **[21]**
- **$2 125** - €2 480 - **£1 500** - FF16 269
  Marinaro di Santa Lucia in Napoli
  Watercolour/paper (26.5x29.5cm 10x11in) London 2000

VITORINO Túlio 1896-1969 **[4]**
- **$33 060** - €28 825 - **£19 720** - FF189 080
  Praça dos Restauradores numa noite de chuva
  Oleo (73x100cm 28x39in) Lisboa 1998
- **$6 600** - €7 478 - **£4 500** - FF49 050
  O Pinheiro Manso, Torres Vedras Huile/bois
  (29.5x38.5cm 11x15in) Lisboa 2000

VITRINGA Wigerius 1657-1721 **[17]**
- **$11 207** - €12 031 - **£7 500** - FF78 916
  Dutch Shipping off an Italianate Harbour Oil/can-
  vas (61x79cm 24x31in) London 2000
- **$1 761** - €2 042 - **£1 247** - FF13 394
  **A Man-o'war in a Strong Breeze Near a Rocky
  Coast** Pencil (13.5x20.5cm 5x8in) Amsterdam 2000

VITTORI Carlo 1881-1943 **[6]**
- **$3 250** - €3 369 - **£1 950** - FF22 100
  Notturno pastorale Olio/tela (80.5x60cm 31x23in)
  Milano 2000
- **$1 750** - €1 814 - **£1 050** - FF11 900
  Scaricatori di sabbia lungo il fiume
  Acquarello/carta (37x57.5cm 14x22in) Milano 2000

VIUDES Vicente 1916 **[24]**
- **$1 147** - €1 351 - **£810** - FF8 865
  **Boceto para decorado de la Suite Iberia, acto IX
  Eritaña** Acuarela/papel (41x57cm 16x22in) Madrid
  2000

VIVANCOS Miguel-Garcia 1895-1972 **[49]**
- **$981** - €915 - **£606** - FF6 000
  Le manège Huile/toile (38.5x46cm 15x18in) Paris
  1999
- **$1 224** - €1 143 - **£755** - FF7 500
  La noce Huile/toile (27x22cm 10x8in) Le Touquet
  1999

VIVARES Thomas c.1735-? **[4]**
- **$347** - €375 - **£240** - FF2 460
  The Town and Harbour of Ilfordcombe Engraving
  (44x56.5cm 17x22in) Newbury, Berkshire 2001

VIVAS Ana Maria Gomez 1957 **[21]**
- **$457** - €450 - **£292** - FF2 955
  «Bosque» Oleo/tabla (90x90cm 35x35in) Madrid
  1999

VIVES ATSARA José 1919-1988 **[7]**
- **$3 300** - €3 542 - **£2 208** - FF23 235
  Tejados, Spain (Small Town) Oil/canvas (50x40cm
  20x16in) Houston TX 2000

VIVES FIERRO Antoni 1940 **[34]**
- **$624** - €721 - **£432** - FF4 728
  «Old Mansions, London» Oleo/lienzo (38x46cm
  14x18in) Barcelona 2001
- **$1 357** - €1 568 - **£939** - FF10 283
  Cuba Pintura (25.5x36cm 10x14in) Barcelona 2000
- **$143** - €156 - **£98** - FF1 024
  «Prades» Gouache/papier (47x61.5cm 18x24in)
  Barcelona 2001

VIVES LLULL Juan 1901 **[8]**
- **$1 677** - €1 652 - **£1 072** - FF10 835
  Puerto de Menorca Oleo/tablex (24x34cm 9x13in)
  Madrid 1999

VIVèS Martin 1905-1991 **[10]**
- **$1 035** - €1 143 - **£717** - FF7 500
  Le laboureur Huile/toile (50x60cm 19x23in) Castres
  2001

VIVIAN George 1798-1873 **[20]**
- **$20 000** - €22 335 - **£12 808** - FF146 510
  The Grand Canal Oil/canvas (45.5x81.5cm 17x32in)
  New-York 2000
- **$275** - €300 - **£175** - FF1 970
  Vista del Puerto de Málaga Grabado (36x48cm
  14x18in) Madrid 2000

VIVIAN J., Miss act.1869-1877 **[19]**
- **$10 248** - €10 941 - **£7 000** - FF71 771
  On the gran Canal, Venice Oil/canvas (44.5x80.5cm
  17x31in) Billingshurst, West-Sussex 2001
- **$3 577** - €3 302 - **£2 200** - FF21 662
  The Rialto Bridge, Venice Oil/canvas (30.5x40cm
  12x15in) London 1999

VIVIANI Giuseppe 1898-1965 **[93]**
- **$2 800** - €3 628 - **£2 100** - FF23 800
  La rosa Olio/tela (37x25cm 14x9in) Prato 2000
- **$1 440** - €1 244 - **£960** - FF8 160
  Natura morta a Bocca d'Arno China/carta
  (20x19cm 7x7in) Prato 1998
- **$950** - €985 - **£570** - FF6 460
  Il cateratταio Litografia a colori (43.5x60cm 17x23in)
  Prato 2000

VIVIANI Raul 1883-1965 **[21]**
- **$700** - €726 - **£420** - FF4 760
  Barca sul lago Olio/tavola (40x57cm 15x22in) Trieste
  2001

VIVIEN Joseph 1657-1734 **[8]**
- **$4 616** - €4 421 - **£2 905** - FF29 000
  Portrait d'homme Pastel/papier (70x56cm 27x22in)
  Paris 1999

VIVIEN Narcisse XIX **[3]**
- **$1 751** - €1 876 - **£1 158** - FF12 232
  Rooster and Snails Watercolour/paper (43x36cm
  17x14in) Cleveland OH 2000

V

VIVIN Louis 1861-1936 **[46]**
- 🕊 $2 305 - €2 058 - **£1 412** - FF13 500
  Scène de rue Huile/toile (46x55cm 18x21in) Paris 1999

VIVO de Figlio XIX **[2]**
- 🕊 $4 000 - €3 926 - **£2 479** - FF25 753
  Despues de la caceria, perros y patos Oleo/lienzo (117x80cm 46x31in) Buenos-Aires 1999

VIZKELETY W. Emery 1819-1895 **[25]**
- 🕊 $647 - €722 - €450 - FF4 736
  Mère allaitant Huile/toile (60x80cm 23x31in) Montréal 2001

VIZZINI Andrea 1949 **[3]**
- ✏ $2 380 - €2 467 - **£1 428** - FF16 184
  Veduta ideata Collage/carta (66x107.5cm 25x42in) Venezia 1999

VIZZOTTO-ALBERTI Giuseppe 1862-1931 **[33]**
- 🕊 $12 766 - €13 166 - **£8 970** - FF98 683
  Gàsapigan Oil/canvas (150x87cm 59x34in) Malmö 2000
- 🕊 $11 395 - €12 653 - **£7 943** - FF83 000
  «La fiancée de Ramazan» Huile/panneau (58x36.5cm 22x14in) Paris 2001
- ✏ $2 777 - €3 187 - **£1 900** - FF20 903
  The Fish Market Watercolour/paper (46x29cm 18x11in) Edinburgh 2000

VLADIMIROV Ivan Alexeievitch 1869-1947 **[21]**
- ✏ $5 433 - €4 480 - €3 200 - FF29 384
  Escape of the Bourgeoisie from Novorossisk Watercolour (35.5x52cm 13x20in) London 1998

VLADIRMIRSKY Boris Eremeievich 1878-1950 **[32]**
- 🕊 $3 246 - €3 120 - **£2 000** - FF20 466
  Dancing in the clearing in the Summer Dacha Oil/canvas (61.5x77.5cm 24x30in) London 1999

VLAMINCK de Maurice 1876-1958 **[2066]**
- 🕊 $48 126 - €48 495 - **£30 000** - FF318 108
  Vase de fleurs Oil/canvas (54.5x46cm 21x18in) London 2000
- 🕊 $30 000 - €28 848 - **£18 483** - FF189 231
  Vase de fleurs Oil/canvas (46.5x33cm 18x12in) New-View 1999
- 🏺 $8 000 - €8 062 - **£4 987** - FF52 880
  Vase bleu, jaune, vert et rouge Glazed ceramic (H26cm H10in) New-York 2000
- 🕊 $16 502 - €17 532 - **£11 063** - FF115 000
  Paysage aux toits rouges Aquarelle, gouache (46x55cm 18x21in) Cannes 2000
- 🍷 $650 - €665 - **£407** - FF4 362
  Le champ de blé Etching (23x31cm 9x12in) Cleveland OH 2000

VLAMYNCK de Geo 1897-1980 **[6]**
- 🍷 $988 - €1 067 - **£683** - FF7 000
  Deux maisons dans la plaine à Hérouville Aquatinte (17x26cm 6x10in) Paris 2001

VLASSELAER van Julien 1907-1982 **[14]**
- 🕊 $1 722 - €1 611 - **£1 046** - FF10 569
  L'homme au coq Black & white chalks/paper (96x66cm 37x25in) Lokeren 1999
- 🍷 $1 776 - €1 983 - **£1 232** - FF13 008
  Marché aux oiseaux Tapisserie (91x215cm 35x84in) Antwerpen 2001

VLECK van Natalie 1901-1981 **[45]**
- 🕊 $2 200 - €2 426 - **£1 489** - FF15 915
  Moorean Boy Oil/canvas (56x63.5cm 22x25in) New-York 2000

VLEUGHELS Nicolas 1668-1737 **[19]**
- 🕊 $4 713 - €4 573 - **£2 970** - FF30 000
  Bacchanale Huile/toile (35x56cm 13x22in) Paris 1999
- 🕊 $4 201 - €4 878 - **£2 963** - FF32 000
  Le gascon puni Huile/panneau (37x29.5cm 14x11in) Paris 2001
- 🕊 $5 548 - €5 183 - **£3 423** - FF34 000
  La toilette de Vénus Pierre noire (23x32cm 9x12in) Paris 1999

VLIEGER de Simon Jacobsz. 1601-1653 **[60]**
- 🕊 $40 994 - €43 369 - **£26 000** - FF284 484
  Rocky Coast in a Storm, with Figures Escaping a Shipwrecked Vessel Oil/panel (34.5x55.5cm 13x21in) London 2000
- 🕊 $3 303 - €3 176 - **£2 034** - FF20 836
  Woodland Scene Black & white chalks (20.5x27cm 8x10in) Amsterdam 1999
- 🍷 $745 - €818 - **£506** - FF5 366
  Der Pfad zu einem Waldhügel Radierung (13.3x15.7cm 5x6in) Berlin 2000

VLIET van der Hendrick Cornelisz 1611-1675 **[26]**
- 🕊 $5 171 - €5 782 - **£3 600** - FF37 927
  Lady, wearing a white Ruff and black Bodice, holding a white Glove Oil/panel (71x58cm 27x22in) London 2001
- 🕊 $11 526 - €13 169 - **£8 126** - FF85 988
  Inneres einer Kirche Oil/panel (31x26cm 12x10in) Zürich 2001

VLIET van der Jan Joris, Georg c.1610-c.1635 **[39]**
- 🕊 $1 680 - €1 982 - **£1 181** - FF13 000
  Le baiser de Judas Huile/panneau (26.5x20cm 10x7in) Paris 2000
- 🍷 $294 - €256 - **£177** - FF1 667
  Zwei verliebte Paar in einer Schenke Radierung (20.9x28.4cm 8x11in) Berlin 1998

VLIET van der Willem 1583/84-1642 **[3]**
- 🕊 $20 000 - €22 149 - **£13 564** - FF145 290
  Portrait of a Young Man Oil/panel (62x51.5cm 24x20in) New-York 2000

VLIST van der Leendert 1894-1962 **[30]**
- 🕊 $4 659 - €5 445 - **£3 326** - FF35 719
  View of the Westertoren, Amsterdam Oil/canvas (65x50cm 25x19in) Amsterdam 2001
- 🕊 $445 - €499 - **£309** - FF3 274
  Olenlandschap met borenkar Oil/panel (26x40cm 10x15in) Rotterdam 2001

VLOORS Emil 1871-1952 **[15]**
- 🕊 $583 - €545 - **£354** - FF3 577
  De scriptor Oil/canvas (100x45cm 39x17in) Lokeren 1999

VOELCKER Gottfried Wilhelm 1775-1849 **[4]**
- 🕊 $38 929 - €39 881 - **£24 024** - FF261 604
  Blumen in Kristallvase Öl/Leinwand (59.5x42cm 23x16in) Düsseldorf 2000

VOELKERLING Hans Carl Alfred 1872-? **[2]**
- 🗿 $3 308 - €3 149 - **£2 100** - FF20 658
  Racing Group Bronze (24x49cm 9x19in) Billingshurst, West-Sussex 1999

VOERMAN Jan, Jnr. 1890-1976 **[63]**
- 🕊 $3 210 - €3 176 - **£1 964** - FF20 836
  Flowers on a Dish Oil/canvas (37x47.5cm 14x18in) Amsterdam 2000
- 🕊 $2 751 - €2 723 - **£1 684** - FF17 859
  Pink Rose Oil/canvas/board (19x14cm 7x5in) Amsterdam 2000

V

🖉 **$1 233** - €1 134 - **£762** - FF7 441
Insects on cow parsley Watercolour, gouache
(11.5x30cm 4x11in) Amsterdam 1999
📖 **$83** - €91 - **£57** - FF595
«**Aronskelken**» Lithograph (20x32.5cm 7x12in)
Amsterdam 2001

VOERMAN Jan, Snr. 1857-1941 **[53]**
👝 **$3 456** - €3 630 - **£2 187** - FF23 812
A View of Hattem Oil/canvas (53x69cm 20x27in)
Amsterdam 2000
👝 **$3 776** - €3 630 - **£2 355** - FF23 812
View of Hattem Oil/canvas (27x40.5cm 10x15in)
Amsterdam 1999
🖉 **$5 984** - €7 034 - **£4 149** - FF46 137
A View of Hattem Watercolour (21x31cm 8x12in)
Amsterdam 2000

VOET Alexander II c.1637-? **[4]**
📖 **$376** - €358 - **£233** - FF2 347
Allegorie des Eitelkeit: Nosce te ipsum, nach J. Jordaens Kupferstich (28x34cm 11x13in) Berlin 1999

VOET Jakob Ferdinand c.1639-c.1700 **[27]**
👝 **$14 971** - €14 316 - €9 116 - FF93 909
Porträt der Christine von Schweden Öl/Leinwand
(130x105cm 51x41in) Stuttgart 1999
👝 **$5 000** - €5 889 - **£3 458** - FF38 629
Portrait of a Young Man Oil/canvas (73x57cm
28x22in) New-York 2000

VOET Karel Borchaert 1670-1743 **[1]**
👝 **$10 979** - €10 721 - **£7 000** - FF70 322
**Still Life of Lilies, Roses, Convolvulus, a Stone
Urn beside a Melon** Oil/canvas (53.5x44cm 21x17in)
London 1999

VOGEL Bernhard 1961 **[10]**
🖉 **$1 377** - €1 599 - **£950** - FF10 487
Amsterdam Aquarell/Papier (37.6x56.5cm 14x22in)
Wien 2000

VOGEL Bernhard 1683-1737 **[9]**
📖 **$269** - €307 - **£187** - FF2 012
**Bildnis des Landschaftsmahlers Christian
Ludwig Agricola,nach Carriera** Mezzotint
(43.5x30.6cm 17x12in) Berlin 2000

VOGEL de Cornelis Johannes 1824-1879 **[27]**
👝 **$9 526** - €10 226 - **£6 376** - FF67 078
Waldinneres mit Enten am Bachlauf Öl/Leinwand
(120x100cm 47x39in) Kempten 2000
👝 **$2 887** - €2 723 - **£1 789** - FF17 859
Barn in the Forest with Chickens and Cows
Oil/canvas (47x57cm 18x22in) Amsterdam 1999

VOGEL Donald 1917 **[3]**
📖 **$700** - €672 - **£433** - FF4 409
Bedlam Corners Drypoint (23x30.5cm 9x12in) New-
York 1999

VOGEL Ernest 1909-1993 **[23]**
🖉 **$144** - €139 - **£88** - FF909
Morning Light Watercolour/paper (26x35cm 10x13in)
Melbourne 1999

VOGEL F.C. XIX **[1]**
📷 **$14 881** - €14 056 - **£9 000** - FF92 199
**Gedenkblätter an Goethe, Frankfurt: Hermann
Johann Kessler** Salt print (22x18cm 8x7in) London
1999

VOGEL Hans Jörg 1918 **[1]**
📖 **$13 584** - €11 628 - **£8 176** - FF76 272
Tropenwald Tapestry (192x204cm 75x80in) Wien
1998

VOGEL Hugo 1855-1934 **[6]**
👝 **$37 500** - €36 730 - **£24 165** - FF240 930
Mother and Child Oil/canvas (81.5x69cm 32x27in)
New-York 1999

VOGEL Johannes Gijsbert 1828-1915 **[20]**
👝 **$585** - €562 - **£363** - FF3 689
Die Rückkehr der Fischkutter Oil/panel (22x30cm
8x11in) Ahlden 1999

VOGEL VON VOGELSTEIN Carl Christian 1788-
1868 **[18]**
👝 **$37 432** - €38 347 - **£23 100** - FF251 542
Bildnis des Dichters Ludwig Tieck Öl/Leinwand
(123.5x95cm 48x37in) Düsseldorf 2000
🖉 **$540** - €613 - **£375** - FF4 024
**Der Künstler Vogel von Vogelstein bei einem
Baum sitzend und zeichnend** Pencil (16x19cm
6x7in) Berlin 2001

VOGEL-JØRGENSEN Åge 1888-1964 **[12]**
👝 **$1 078** - €996 - **£645** - FF6 533
Rödt tema med variationer Oil/masonite (75x60cm
29x23in) Köbenhavn 1999

VOGELAER van Karel 1653-1695 **[17]**
👝 **$3 619** - €3 997 - **£2 508** - FF26 218
Blumenstrauss mit Rosen, Dilsteln Öl/Leinwand
(66x48.5cm 25x19in) Wien 2001

VOGELER Heinrich 1872-1942 **[532]**
👝 **$18 147** - €15 337 - **£10 791** - FF100 602
Brücke im Wald hinterm Barkenhoff Oil/panel
(51x41cm 20x16in) Bremen 1998
👝 **$6 285** - €5 880 - **£3 807** - FF38 569
**Gruppe russischer Bauern mit einer
Amtsperson** Öl/Karton (24x19cm 9x7in) Bremen
1999
🖉 **$942** - €920 - **£597** - FF6 037
Kleine Ausflugsgesellschaft im Grase Ink/paper
(9x16.3cm 3x6in) Bremen 1999
📖 **$845** - €716 - **£505** - FF4 448
«**Sommerabend**» Radierung (17.5x14cm 6x5in)
Bremen 1998

VOGELS Guillaume 1836-1896 **[85]**
👝 **$4 592** - €3 964 - **£2 768** - FF26 000
Bord d'étang Huile/toile (35.5x49cm 13x19in)
Bruxelles 1998
👝 **$845** - €998 - **£600** - FF6 546
Steam Boat by a Jetty Oil/canvas/board
(23.5x39.5cm 9x15in) London 2001
🖉 **$1 254** - €1 487 - **£912** - FF9 756
Rue de village Aquarelle/papier (30x24cm 11x9in)
Antwerpen 2001

VOGENAUER Ernst Rudolf 1897-? **[2]**
📖 **$699** - €817 - **£479** - FF5 357
«**Ausstellungspark Theater-Café**» Poster
(120x89.5cm 47x35in) Hoorn 2000

VOGL Karl 1820-? **[1]**
👝 **$2 350** - €2 301 - **£1 446** - FF15 092
**Der Kupferstecher Franz Xaver Stöber, nach
Friedrich von Amerling** Öl/Leinwand (40x32cm
15x12in) Stuttgart 1999

VOGL Rudolf 1887-1958 **[13]**
🖉 **$169** - €153 - **£104** - FF1 006
Notturno Legato Pencil/paper (29x38.5cm 11x15in)
Lindau 1999

VOGLAR Karl 1888-1972 **[1]**
🖉 **$2 637** - €2 556 - **£1 633** - FF16 769
Steirische Landschaft mit Bauernhäusern
Aquarell/Papier (30x42cm 11x16in) Graz 1999

V

VOGLER Paul 1852-1904 **[103]**
- $3 475 - €3 811 - £2 360 - FF25 000
  Le port des Andelys Huile/toile (50x65cm 19x25in)
  Calais 2000
- $1 947 - €1 906 - £1 246 - FF12 500
  Le marché aux fleurs à Paris Huile/panneau
  (39x32cm 15x12in) Bayeux 1999
- $1 408 - €1 524 - £964 - FF10 000
  Vue d'un lac Pastel/papier (59x64.5cm 23x25in) Paris
  2001

VOGT Fritz G. 1842-1900 **[5]**
- $15 000 - €16 532 - £9 979 - FF108 441
  The Residence of Mr.Clarke Shaule,Sharon
  Springs, N.Y. Coloured pencils/paper (45x59cm
  18x23in) Portsmouth NH 2000

VOGT Louis Charles 1864-1938 **[14]**
- $400 - €441 - £266 - FF2 890
  Country Road on a Summer's Day
  Watercolour/paper (23x33cm 9x13in) Portsmouth NH
  2000

VOIGT Bruno 1912-1989 **[49]**
- $4 396 - €5 061 - £3 000 - FF33 200
  Self-Portrait Tempera (59.5x39cm 23x15in) London
  2000
- $3 223 - €3 712 - £2 200 - FF24 347
  Solicitation Ink (50.5x36.5cm 19x14in) London 2000
- $127 - €143 - £88 - FF939
  Regenwetter Radierung (36x28cm 14x11in) Berlin
  2001

VOIGT Franz Wilhelm 1867-? **[5]**
- $1 184 - €1 329 - £821 - FF8 720
  Auf der Dillinger Höhe Öl/Leinwand (47x57cm
  18x22in) Stuttgart 2000

VOIGT STEFFENSEN Hans 1941 **[48]**
- $1 099 - €1 141 - £697 - FF7 485
  Enghaveplads Oil/canvas (100x100cm 39x39in) Viby
  J, Århus 2000

VOIGTLANDER von Rudolf 1854-? **[3]**
- $8 105 - €9 203 - £5 632 - FF60 370
  «Der Kunstfreund» Öl/Leinwand (54.5x45.5cm
  21x17in) Berlin 2001

VOILLE Jean L. 1744-c.1796 **[10]**
- $13 219 - €15 550 - £9 475 - FF102 000
  François-Mathieu Didier/Son épouse Victoire
  Geneviève Cherbuy Huile/toile (65x54cm 25x21in)
  Paris 2001

VOILLEMOT Charles 1823-1893 **[27]**
- $32 500 - €32 859 - £19 607 - FF183 927
  Allegories of Spring/Autumn Oil/canvas
  (209.5x143.5cm 82x56in) New-York 1998
- $3 200 - €3 635 - £2 245 - FF23 841
  Spring Dance Oil/canvas (110.5x77.5cm 43x30in)
  New-York 2001

VOINIER Antoine XVIII-XIX **[2]**
- $17 000 - €18 871 - £11 850 - FF123 785
  Project for a Triumphal Arch Watercolour (52x89cm
  20x35in) New-York 2001

VOIRIN Jules Antoine 1833-1898 **[25]**
- $15 000 - €12 941 - £9 015 - FF84 889
  «Returning from the Reconnaissance» Oil/canvas
  (85x137cm 33x53in) Boston MA 1998

VOIRIN Léon Joseph 1833-1887 **[26]**
- $40 000 - €44 774 - £27 896 - FF293 700
  Winter's Day Oil/canvas (73x103cm 28x40in) New-
  York 2001

VOGLER Paul (column 2)
- $6 800 - €5 795 - £4 052 - FF38 010
  La partie de Pêche Oil/panel (27x21cm 10x8in)
  New-York 1998
- $781 - €838 - £522 - FF5 500
  L'écrivain public Aquarelle/carton (22x28cm 8x11in)
  Paris 2000

VOIRIOT Guillaume 1713-1799 **[10]**
- $8 399 - €7 775 - £5 202 - FF51 000
  Portrait présumé d'un architecte Huile/toile
  (102.5x83cm 40x32in) Paris 1999

VOIS de Arie 1631-1680 **[11]**
- $1 000 - €1 209 - £698 - FF7 928
  Portrait of a Lady Oil/panel (15.5x14cm 6x5in)
  Bethesda MD 2000

VOJACEK Frantisek XX **[1]**
- $3 757 - €3 553 - £2 340 - FF23 309
  Nature morte à coupe aux fruits, bouteille et
  tasse Gouache/carton (35x50cm 13x19in) Praha 2001

VOLAIRE IL CAVALIER Jacques Antoine 1729-
c.1802 **[55]**
- $81 900 - €78 084 - £49 400 - FF512 200
  La Erupción del Vesubio Oleo/lienzo (83.5x66.5cm
  32x26in) Madrid 1999
- $1 100 - €1 296 - £773 - FF8 500
  Deux études de figures, étude de tête et croquis Crayon (25x40cm 9x15in) Paris 2000

VOLANAKIS Constantinos 1837-1907 **[15]**
- $105 508 - €121 474 - £72 000 - FF796 816
  Fishermen off an Island Oil/canvas (46.5x82.5cm
  18x32in) London 2000

VOLANG Jean 1921 **[15]**
- $2 295 - €2 607 - £1 571 - FF17 098
  Sur la plage à Bali (At the Beach, Bali) Oil/canvas
  (60x73cm 23x28in) Singapore 2000

VOLBRECHT Ernst 1877-1964 **[9]**
- $570 - €665 - £394 - FF4 360
  Holländische Landschaft mit Mühle und liegen-
  den Fischerbooten Öl/Karton (32x41cm 12x16in)
  Buxtehude 2000

VOLCKAERT Piet 1902-1973 **[188]**
- $399 - €446 - £279 - FF2 926
  Ruelle bruxelloise animée Huile/panneau (40x60cm
  15x23in) Bruxelles 2001
- $283 - €297 - £178 - FF1 951
  Place du jeu de balle à Bruxelles Huile/carton
  (30x40cm 11x15in) Bruxelles 2000

VÖLCKER Gottfried Wilhelm 1755-1849 **[5]**
- $32 415 - €34 033 - £20 437 - FF223 245
  Still Life with Larkspur, Poppies, Roses, Lilacs,
  Dafodils, Tulips Oil/canvas (49.5x27.5cm 19x10in)
  Amsterdam 2000

VÖLCKER Robert 1854-1924 **[39]**
- $1 446 - €1 687 - £1 015 - FF11 067
  Stubeninterieur mit stehendem Frauenakt
  Oil/panel (31x24cm 12x9in) Kempten 2000

VOLK Johann Daniel 1807-? **[3]**
- $2 748 - €2 586 - £1 700 - FF16 963
  A Huntsman's Rest Oil/canvas (43.5x53.5cm
  17x21in) London 2000

VÖLKEL Reinhold I 1834-? **[1]**
- $1 965 - €1 943 - £1 203 - FF12 744
  Personen vor der K.K.Lotto Collectur
  Aquarell/Papier (37x26cm 14x10in) Kempten 2000

V

VÖLKEL Reinhold II 1873-1938 **[5]**

✏ **$2 118** - €2 325 - **£1 363** - FF15 254
Christkindlmarkt Aquarell/Papier (19x22cm 7x8in)
Wien 2000

VOLKENBURG H. XIX **[1]**

🖌 **$11 655** - €10 988 - **£7 223** - FF72 079
An Interior Oil/canvas (60x75cm 23x29in) Melbourne
1999

VÖLKER Wilhelm 1812-1873 **[3]**

🖌 **$3 554** - €4 090 - **£2 454** - FF26 831
Heilige Elisabeth vor der Wartburg Öl/Leinwand
(123x75cm 48x29in) München 2000

VOLKERS Adrianus 1904 **[5]**

🖌 **$336** - €363 - **£229** - FF2 381
**A Still Life with a Jug, a Bottle, Dried Flowers
and Autumn Leaves** Oil/canvas (30x40cm 11x15in)
Amsterdam 2001

VOLKERS Emil 1831-1905 **[63]**

🖌 **$3 518** - €4 090 - **£2 469** - FF26 831
Ungarisches Pferdefuhrwerk Öl/Leinwand
(51x101cm 20x39in) Hamburg 2000

🖌 **$2 997** - €3 323 - **£2 081** - FF21 800
Pferdeporträt Öl/Leinwand (24.5x32.5cm 9x12in)
Köln 2001

VOLKERT Edward Charles 1871-1935 **[25]**

🖌 **$4 750** - €5 540 - **£3 335** - FF36 342
The Ox Cart Winter Oil/canvas (61x50cm 24x19in)
Boston MA 2000

🖌 **$4 300** - €4 919 - **£2 990** - FF32 265
Morning in the Pasture Oil/board (20x27cm 8x11in)
Pittsburgh PA 2000

VOLKERTS Poppe 1875-? **[2]**

🖌 **$4 894** - €5 368 - **£3 158** - FF35 215
**Fischerboot van friesischer Küste mit
Windmühle** Öl/Leinwand (80x100cm 31x39in) Berlin
2000

VOLKHART Max 1848-1935 **[20]**

🖌 **$29 946** - €30 678 - **£18 480** - FF201 234
Prozession in Brüssel Öl/Leinwand (133x109cm
52x42in) Düsseldorf 2000

🖌 **$279** - €337 - **£194** - FF22 213
Der Disput Oil/canvas/panel (19x15cm 7x5in)
Düsseldorf 2000

VOLKMANN von Hans Richard 1860-1927 **[266]**

🖌 **$2 095** - €2 250 - **£1 402** - FF14 757
Frühjahrslandschaft Öl/Karton (38.5x48.5cm
15x19in) Köln 2000

🖌 **$1 265** - €1 329 - **£798** - FF8 720
**Hügelige Wiesenlandschaft mit vereinzelten
Bäumen** Öl/Karton (30x39cm 11x15in) Heidelberg
2000

✏ **$239** - €281 - **£171** - FF1 844
Mädchen vom Lande Aquarell/Papier (26x19cm
10x7in) Düsseldorf 2001

📜 **$132** - €123 - **£82** - FF804
Eifeler Heide Lithographie (35x42cm 13x16in)
Rudolstadt-Thüringen 1999

VOLKOV MUROMZOFF Aleksandr Nikolaev. 1844-
1928 **[21]**

✏ **$1 902** - €1 777 - **£1 150** - FF11 657
**Woman with Aubrun Hair Kneeling at a
Confessional** Watercolour/paper (42x65cm 16x25in)
West-Sussex 1999

VOLKWARTH Hugo 1888-1946 **[2]**

🖌 **$4 604** - €4 090 - **£2 819** - FF26 831
Hamburg : Blick auf den belebten Jungfernstieg
Oil/panel (52x60cm 20x23in) Hamburg 1999

VOLL Christoph 1897-1939 **[44]**

🗿 **$15 344** - €17 895 - **£10 773** - FF117 386
Sich Frisierende Schwangere Bronze (H55cm
H21in) Köln 2000

🖌 **$553** - €613 - **£384** - FF4 024
Stehender weiblicher Akt Ink (44x31cm 17x12in)
Heidelberg 2001

📜 **$369** - €409 - **£256** - FF2 683
Schlafendes Kind Woodcut (40x34.5cm 15x13in)
Heidelberg 2001

VOLLBEHR Ernst 1876-c.1940 **[31]**

✏ **$99** - €112 - **£70** - FF737
Abendstimmung am Ufer Aquarell/Papier (47x20cm
18x7in) München 2001

VOLLERDT Johann Christian 1708-1769 **[85]**

🖌 **$14 323** - €12 143 - **£8 500** - FF79 653
**Evening River Landscape with Travellers on a
Bridge** Oil/canvas (61x117cm 24x46in) London 1998

🖌 **$8 187** - €7 592 - **£5 000** - FF49 801
**A Frozen Winter Landscape with Figures on a
Path, a Stone Bridge** Oil/canvas (30x43cm 11x16in)
London 1998

VOLLET Henry Emile 1861-1945 **[58]**

🖌 **$845** - €838 - **£525** - FF5 500
Concarneau, retour de pêche Huile/panneau
(50x100cm 19x39in) Brest 1999

VOLLEVENS Johannes, Jan I 1649-1728 **[1]**

🖌 **$5 500** - €5 030 - **£3 358** - FF32 993
Portrait of a woman in black and white lace
Oil/canvas (54x43cm 21x17in) New-York 1998

VOLLEVENS Johannes, Jan II 1685-1758 **[4]**

🖌 **$2 713** - €2 496 - **£1 677** - FF16 371
**Salomon Diodati (1688-1753) wearing a blue
velvet Jacket** Oil/copper (32x24.5cm 12x9in)
Amsterdam 2000

VOLLMER Adolph Friedrich 1806-1875 **[10]**

🖌 **$1 305** - €1 471 - **£900** - FF9 646
Extensive Country Landscape Oil/canvas
(58.5x81cm 23x31in) London 2000

VOLLON Alexis 1865-1945 **[116]**

🖌 **$4 795** - €5 641 - **£3 437** - FF37 000
Mère et sa fille Huile/toile (131x98cm 51x38in) Paris
2001

🖌 **$8 733** - €9 376 - **£5 842** - FF61 500
Le petit marchand des quatre saisons Huile/toile
(73x50cm 28x19in) Romorantin-Lanthenay 2000

🖌 **$3 550** - €3 811 - **£2 375** - FF25 000
L'aiguière Huile/panneau (24x18.5cm 9x7in) Paris
2000

✏ **$814** - €762 - **£504** - FF5 500
Paris, place de l'Opéra animée Fusain (18x26cm
7x10in) Troyes 1999

VOLLON Antoine 1833-1900 **[232]**

🖌 **$4 299** - €5 113 - **£3 064** - FF33 539
Grosses Blumenstilleben Öl/Leinwand
(103x144cm 40x56in) Köln 2000

🖌 **$4 400** - €4 171 - **£2 748** - FF27 359
**Still Life of Plums with Brass Coffee Pot,
Pitcher and Wine Glasses** Oil/canvas (54x65.5cm
21x25in) Washington 1999

V

$2 296 - €2 134 - **£1 394** - FF14 000
Nature morte aux citrons et à l'orfèvrerie
Huile/toile (41x33cm 16x12in) Calais 1998

$349 - €396 - **£242** - FF2 600
Barque sur la grève Fusain (7x11cm 2x4in)
Barbizon 2001

VOLMAR Johann Georg 1770-1831 **[21]**
$5 555 - €6 606 - **£3 959** - FF43 335
Indianer beim Einfangen von Wildpferden
Öl/Leinwand (96x120cm 37x47in) Zürich 2000

$1 596 - €1 453 - **£979** - FF9 528
Die Entenjagd Encre (58x48cm 22x18in) Zürich 1999

VOLMAR Joseph Simon 1796-1865 **[12]**
$800 - €753 - **£494** - FF4 939
Deux Chevaux de Poste à la porte d'une écurie
Lithograph (34.5x43.5cm 13x17in) New-York 1999

VOLOVICK Lazare 1902-1977 **[53]**
$2 234 - €2 515 - **£1 569** - FF16 500
Vase de fleurs sur fond bleu Huile/toile (65x54cm
25x21in) Paris 2001

VOLPATO Giovanni 1733-1803 **[79]**
$6 129 - €6 860 - **£4 158** - FF45 000
Vue du Temple de Vesta à Rome Aquarelle
(36.5x52cm 14x20in) Paris 2000

$720 - €622 - **£480** - FF4 080
L'arrotino Stampa (49x36cm 19x14in) Trieste 1998

VOLPE Angiolo 1943 **[25]**
$650 - €674 - **£390** - FF4 420
San Martino Olio/cartone (70x50cm 27x19in) Firenze
2000

VOLPE Vincenzo 1855-1929 **[12]**
$2 800 - €2 741 - **£1 723** - FF17 979
Artist's Studio Oil/board (18x39cm 7x15in) East-
Dennis MA 1999

$2 250 - €2 332 - **£1 350** - FF15 300
Chierichetto Pastelli/carta (122x76cm 48x29in)
Napoli 2000

VOLPI Alfredo 1896-1988 **[2]**
$30 000 - €34 855 - **£21 084** - FF228 636
Sem título Tempera/canvas (71x46cm 27x18in) New-
York 2001

VOLPINI Augusto 1832-1911 **[2]**
$4 268 - €4 959 - **£3 000** - FF32 532
Contemplando il volatile (watching the bird)
Oil/canvas (41x51cm 16x20in) London 2001

VOLSCHENK Jan Ernst Abraham 1853-1936 **[67]**
$2 487 - €2 332 - **£1 536** - FF15 296
Mozambiquer's Kop - Evening, near Riversdale
Oil/canvas (40x83cm 15x32in) Johannesburg 1999

$1 208 - €1 133 - **£746** - FF7 429
Where the red Heath Grows, Riversdale Oil/can-
vas (15.5x29.5cm 6x11in) Johannesburg 1999

VOLTEN André 1925 **[6]**
$1 640 - €1 906 - **£1 152** - FF12 501
Untitled Bronze (60x60cm 23x23in) Amsterdam 2001

VOLTI Antoniucci Voltigero 1915-1989 **[548]**
$28 665 - €32 014 - **£19 173** - FF210 000
Florentine bleue Bronze (97x27x18cm 38x10x7in)
Paris 2000

$9 392 - €8 994 - **£5 787** - FF59 000
Femme nue accroupie Bronze (12x25cm 4x9in)
Calais 1999

$1 177 - €1 372 - **£815** - FF9 000
Nu assis, une jambe repliée Sanguine/papier
(36x26cm 14x10in) Calais 2000

$204 - €175 - **£123** - FF1 150
Femmes nues couchées Lithographie (47x57cm
18x22in) Melun 1998

VOLTZ Friedrich Johann 1817-1886 **[304]**
$8 118 - €7 516 - **£4 901** - FF49 302
**Heimkehr am Abend, Hirte mit seiner Herde in
einer weiten Landschaft** Öl/Leinwand (91x123cm
35x48in) Heidelberg 1999

$2 292 - €2 556 - **£1 541** - FF16 769
Seeufer mit Bootshaus Öl/Karton (24.7x35.8cm
9x14in) Köln 2000

$358 - €332 - **£218** - FF2 180
Pähl Pencil/paper (30x45.4cm 11x17in) München 1999

VOLTZ Ludwig Gustav 1825-1911 **[67]**
$782 - €920 - **£561** - FF6 037
Pferddeskizzen Öl/Leinwand/Karton (32x42cm
12x16in) München 2001

VOLZ Herman 1904-1990 **[14]**
$1 000 - €1 078 - **£682** - FF7 069
Industrialization Lithograph (27x38.5cm 10x15in)
New-York 2001

VOLZ Hermann 1814-1894 **[19]**
$3 245 - €3 835 - **£2 300** - FF25 154
Ländliche Bräuche Öl/Leinwand (40.5x51cm
15x20in) Stuttgart 2000

$1 522 - €1 534 - **£948** - FF10 061
**Junges Bauernpaar auf einer sonnenbeschie-
nenen Waldlichtung** Öl/Karton (23.5x31.5cm
9x12in) Stuttgart 2000

VOLZ Wolfgang 1948 **[2]**
$4 200 - €4 662 - **£2 927** - FF30 582
Christo: Projects Dye-transfer print (36.5x56cm
14x22in) New-York 2001

VON DER LANCKEN Frank 1872-1950 **[2]**
$11 000 - €13 082 - **£7 839** - FF85 811
Prospect Park, Brooklyn Oil/canvas (41x51cm
16x20in) New-York 2000

VONCK Elias c.1605-1652 **[8]**
$36 741 - €40 496 - **£24 000** - FF265 639
Two Hounds Guarding Game in a Landscape
Oil/canvas (119.5x150cm 47x59in) London 2000

$10 746 - €10 458 - **£6 615** - FF68 598
Jaktstilleben med hare och fågel Oil/panel
(47x54cm 18x21in) Stockholm 1999

VONCK Jan c.1630-c.1710 **[14]**
$4 275 - €4 856 - **£3 000** - FF31 852
**Still Life of Salt Water Fish and Lobsteron a
Table Top** Oil/canvas (70.5x102cm 27x40in) London
2001

VONNOH Bessie Potter 1872-1955 **[57]**
$55 000 - €63 901 - **£38 654** - FF419 166
Young Girl Bronze (H152cm H59in) New-York 2001

$8 000 - €9 135 - **£5 640** - FF59 919
Julia Marlow Tabar Bronze (H50.5cm H19in) Boston
MA 2001

VONNOH Robert William 1858-1933 **[37]**
- **$3 700** - €3 381 - **£2 263** - FF22 180
  Portrait of a Man Oil/canvas (101.5x81cm 39x31in) Boston MA 1999
- **$10 000** - €10 734 - **£6 692** - FF70 410
  The Mill Oil/canvas (40x33cm 15x12in) New-York 2000
- **$12 000** - €13 133 - **£8 277** - FF86 145
  Mother and Child Bronze (H16.5cm H6in) New-York 2001
- **$5 572** - €6 555 - **£3 994** - FF43 000
  Femme et nourisson dans son jardin Gouache/papier (32x23cm 12x9in) Paris 2001

VONTILLIUS Jeppe 1915-1994 **[112]**
- **$648** - €606 - **£392** - FF3 973
  Grönt landskab Oil/canvas (38x46cm 14x18in) Köbenhavn 1999
- **$443** - €430 - **£273** - FF2 823
  Landskab, komposition Oil/canvas (38x42cm 14x16in) Vejle 1999

VOOGD Hendrik 1766-1839 **[25]**
- **$11 939** - €12 501 - **£7 503** - FF82 000
  Scène pastorale dans un paysage Huile/toile (100x135cm 39x53in) Fécamp 2000
- **$43 602** - €47 960 - **£26 284** - FF247 031
  Muleteers halting on a Mountain pass in the Roman Campagna Oil/canvas (81.2x107.3cm 31x42in) Amsterdam 1998
- **$4 055** - €3 968 - **£2 600** - FF26 031
  Farmer chasing a Bull Oil/panel (18.5x26.5cm 7x10in) London 1999
- **$2 359** - €2 269 - **£1 453** - FF14 883
  Stream in a Wooded Hilly Landscape Wash (51.5x66cm 20x25in) Amsterdam 1999

VOORDECKER Henri 1779-1861 **[4]**
- **$1 831** - €2 163 - **£1 300** - FF14 188
  Figures in a frozen Winter Landscape with a Windmill beyond Oil/panel (19x26.5cm 7x10in) London 2001

VOORDEN van August Willem 1881-1921 **[42]**
- **$4 271** - €4 991 - **£3 049** - FF32 742
  Moored Tjalk on a Riverbank Oil/canvas (50.5x61cm 19x24in) Amsterdam 2001
- **$507** - €431 - **£306** - FF2 824
  Damesportret Oil/panel (21x18cm 8x7in) Rotterdam 1998
- **$2 895** - €3 403 - **£2 007** - FF22 324
  Op De, Rotterdam Watercolour (43x64.2cm 16x25in) Amsterdam 2000

VOORDT van Jan XVIII **[2]**
- **$9 975** - €11 330 - **£7 000** - FF74 322
  Extensive Italianate Landscape with Sheperds and Sheperdesses Oil/panel (43x55cm 16x21in) London 2001

VOORHOUT Johannes I 1647-1723 **[15]**
- **$11 587** - €11 434 - **£7 200** - FF75 000
  Adonis partant à la chasse, retenu par un amour Huile/toile (63x78.5cm 24x30in) Paris 1999

VOORN BOERS Sebastiaan Theodorus 1828-1893 **[16]**
- **$956** - €998 - **£603** - FF6 548
  Still Life with Grapes Oil/canvas (27.5x35.5cm 10x13in) Amsterdam 2000

VOORZAAT Theo 1938 **[14]**
- **$606** - €681 - **£420** - FF4 464
  Café de l'Esperance Huile/panneau (7x7cm 2x2in) The Hague 2000

VORDEMBERGE-GILDEWART Friedrich 1897-1980 **[84]**
- **$1 534** - €1 789 - **£1 077** - FF11 738
  Blumenstilleben Öl/Leinwand (70x55.5cm 27x21in) Köln 2000
- **$857** - €818 - **£535** - FF5 366
  Blumenstilleben - Tulpen mit exotischen Blüten Aquarell/Papier (67.5x48.9cm 26x19in) Köln 1999
- **$503** - €434 - **£303** - FF2 850
  Ohne Titel Lithographie (44x56cm 17x22in) Luzern 1998

VORDERMAYER Ludwig 1868-? **[13]**
- **$954** - €1 081 - **£648** - FF7 092
  Arquero con caballo Bronze (29x11x28cm 11x4x11in) Madrid 2000

VORGANG Paul 1860-1927 **[35]**
- **$1 043** - €1 227 - **£736** - FF8 049
  Weite Heidelandschaft im Herbst Öl/Leinwand (52.5x37cm 20x14in) Köln 2000
- **$711** - €665 - **£430** - FF4 360
  Berliner Waldseeufer mit Schilfpflanzen Öl/Leinwand (20x26.5cm 7x10in) Berlin 1999

VOROB'EV Maksim Nikiforovich 1787-1855 **[5]**
- **$10 308** - €10 091 - **£6 342** - FF66 192
  Vuoristotiellä Oil/canvas (72x101cm 28x39in) Helsinki 1999
- **$21 865** - €25 565 - **£15 365** - FF167 695
  St.Petersburg, die Akademie der Wissenschaften/Die Rostrasäulen Aquarell/Papier (32.5x60cm 12x23in) München 2000

VÖRÖS Geza 1897-1957 **[17]**
- **$2 730** - €2 626 - **£1 690** - FF17 225
  Still Life of Fruit Oil/canvas (60x50cm 23x19in) Budapest 1999

VOROS Gyorgy XX **[17]**
- **$305** - €320 - **£193** - FF2 100
  La corbeille de fruits Huile/panneau (30x24cm 11x9in) Paris 2000

VOROSHILOV Sergei Semenovich c.1865-c.1911 **[2]**
- **$7 304** - €7 020 - **£4 500** - FF46 049
  Hunter acompanied by two Borzoi Dogs Oil/canvas (59x71.5cm 23x28in) London 1999

VORST Joseph Paul 1897-1947 **[11]**
- **$2 000** - €2 350 - **£1 386** - FF15 418
  Wildflowers Oil/masonite (40x50cm 16x20in) Cincinnati OH 2000
- **$1 100** - €1 293 - **£762** - FF8 480
  Mule Farm Gouache/board (20x30cm 8x12in) Cincinnati OH 2000

VORSTER Gordon 1924-1988 **[33]**
- **$571** - €531 - **£343** - FF3 480
  House in the Trees Oil/board (44x57cm 17x22in) Cape Town 1999

V

VORSTERMAN Lucas I Emil 1595-1675 **[22]**
📖 $246 - €281 - £172 - FF1 844
   Die Büste des Philosophen Plato, nach Rubens
   Kupferstich (29.5x19cm 11x7in) Berlin 2001

VOS Christoffel Albertus 1813-1877 **[5]**
🖼 $9 372 - €8 622 - £5 795 - FF56 555
   **The Rokin, Amsterdam, looking towards the
   Dam square** Oil/canvas (59x74cm 23x29in)
   Amsterdam 1999

VOS de Cornelis 1585-1651 **[15]**
🖼 $78 300 - €76 225 - £48 100 - FF500 000
   Artémise Huile/toile (152x220cm 59x86in) Paris 1999
🖼 $91 540 - €87 658 - £57 615 - FF575 000
   **Portrait d'un jeune garçon tenant une canne de
   jeu** Huile/panneau (110x80.5cm 43x31in) Paris 1999
🖼 $9 860 - €10 367 - £6 188 - FF68 000
   Portrait de femme une collerette Trois
   crayons/papier (32.5x24cm 12x9in) Paris 2000

VOS de Marten 1532-1603 **[48]**
🖼 $57 920 - €65 820 - £40 000 - FF431 748
   The Sacrifice of Isaac Oil/panel (97x126cm
   38x49in) London 2000
🖼 $14 022 - €13 081 - £8 460 - FF85 806
   Mythologische Szene Öl/Leinwand (53x60.5cm
   20x23in) Wien 1999
✏ $1 500 - €1 538 - £937 - FF10 090
   Adam and Eve in Paradise Ink (19.5x25.5cm
   7x10in) New-York 2000
📖 $238 - €256 - £159 - FF1 676
   Mercurius/Venus Kupferstich (23.4x24.4cm 9x9in)
   Königstein 2000

VOS de Paul 1596-1678 **[23]**
🖼 $40 000 - €34 774 - £24 208 - FF228 104
   Spaniels and Hawks Flushing Grouse Oil/canvas
   (198x304cm 78x120in) New-York 1999

VOS de Simon 1603-1676 **[36]**
🖼 $9 500 - €10 423 - £6 311 - FF68 372
   The Crucifixion Oil/copper (56x72.5cm 22x28in)
   New-York 2000
🖼 $15 379 - €14 635 - £9 561 - FF96 000
   Scène de banquet Huile/panneau (26x28cm
   10x11in) Lille 1999

VOS de Vincent 1829-1875 **[77]**
🖼 $6 534 - €5 488 - £3 841 - FF36 000
   Chiens à l'affût Huile/toile (68x99cm 26x38in) Lille
   1998
🖼 $1 703 - €1 417 - £1 000 - FF9 293
   Friends Oil/panel (20.5x28cm 8x11in) Amsterdam
   1998

VOS Hubert 1855-1935 **[14]**
🖼 $9 000 - €7 708 - £5 313 - FF50 562
   Dancing Girl of Royal Blood Oil/canvas
   (198x91.5cm 77x36in) New-York 1998
🖼 $3 417 - €2 949 - £2 062 - FF19 347
   A Still Life with a Chinese brass Kettle Oil/canvas
   (102x80cm 40x31in) Amsterdam 1999

VOS Maria 1824-1906 **[22]**
🖼 $3 247 - €3 086 - £1 976 - FF20 240
   **Gevarieerd stilleven van Chinees poseleinen
   schotel** Oil/canvas (62x45cm 24x17in) Rotterdam
   1999

🖼 $7 335 - €8 622 - £5 086 - FF56 555
   The Antique Shop Oil/panel (26x20.5cm 10x8in)
   Amsterdam 2000

VOS Theo A. XX **[2]**
🗿 $6 076 - €6 807 - £4 222 - FF44 649
   Figure of a Serimpi-Dancer Bronze (H14cm H5in)
   Amsterdam 2001

VOSBERG Heinrich 1833-1891 **[12]**
🖼 $1 367 - €1 534 - £947 - FF10 061
   **Schäfer mit seiner Herde vor einer Hütte bei
   aufziehendem Gewitter** Öl/Leinwand (43x60.5cm
   16x23in) München 2000

VÖSCHER Leopold Heinrich 1830-1877 **[18]**
🖼 $2 550 - €2 180 - £1 530 - FF14 298
   **Motiv aus den Ötztaler Alpen mit
   Similaungletscher** Öl/Leinwand (48.5x38.5cm
   19x15in) Wien 1998

VOSKUYL Huygh Pietersz. 1592/93-1665 **[2]**
🖼 $10 000 - €9 546 - £6 248 - FF62 616
   Man Holding a Glove Oil/canvas (117x98.5cm
   46x38in) New-York 1999

VOSMAER Daniel XVII **[3]**
🖼 $15 000 - €13 157 - £9 108 - FF86 307
   **The Ruins of Delft after Explosion of the
   Powdermill** Oil/canvas (91.5x128cm 36x50in) New-
   York 1999

VOSPER Sidney Curnow 1866-1942 **[6]**
✏ $402 - €380 - £250 - FF2 493
   Breton Interior Watercolour (24x32cm 9x12in)
   Cambridge 1999

VOSS Frank Brook 1880-1953 **[26]**
🖼 $9 936 - €9 259 - £6 000 - FF60 735
   **«Flying Ebony» Winner of the 1925 Kentucky
   Derby/«Coventry»** Oil/canvas (71x91.5cm 27x36in)
   London 1998
🖼 $4 500 - €5 352 - £3 207 - FF35 107
   Stars and Stripes Oil/board (25.5x35.5cm 10x13in)
   New-York 2000

VOSS Jan 1936 **[233]**
🖼 $7 757 - €6 646 - £4 663 - FF43 592
   Ohne Titel Öl/Leinwand (130.5x195cm 51x76in)
   Hamburg 1998
🖼 $2 927 - €3 350 - £2 012 - FF21 975
   Les gestes qui remplacent les mots
   Oil/paper/canvas (100x65cm 39x25in) Köbenhavn 2000
🖼 $1 134 - €1 143 - £707 - FF7 500
   Sans titre Technique mixte/toile (24x33cm 9x12in)
   Paris 2000
✏ $1 156 - €1 296 - £804 - FF8 500
   Composition Aquarelle/papier (28x37cm 11x14in) Le
   Touquet 2001
📖 $157 - €168 - £99 - FF1 100
   Composition Lithographie couleurs (50x67cm
   19x26in) Paris 2000

VOSSEN van der Andre 1893-1963 **[20]**
🖼 $689 - €681 - £419 - FF4 464
   View in Paris Oil/canvas (56x47cm 22x18in)
   Amsterdam 2000

VOSTELL Wolf 1932-1998 **[172]**
- $3 068 - €3 579 - £2 154 - FF23 477
  «S-O-R» Mischtechnik (55.5x55.5cm 21x21in) Köln 2000
- $1 798 - €2 045 - £1 247 - FF13 415
  You Mixed media (33.5x45.3cm 13x17in) Hamburg 2000
- $5 000 - €5 183 - £3 000 - FF34 000
  La fine de la guerra n.4 Assemblage (112x82x37cm 44x32x14in) Prato 2000
- $2 960 - €2 557 - £1 788 - FF16 773
  Busstop und Autofieber Construction (70.5x102cm 27x40in) Köln 1998
- $441 - €534 - £308 - FF3 500
  Archai #6 Pastel (69x100cm 27x39in) Paris 2000
- $249 - €294 - £176 - FF1 928
  «Engel-Sturz, Skulptur für Potsdam» Print in colors (91.5x63.5cm 36x25in) Berlin 2001

VOUET Simon 1590-1649 **[35]**
- $141 020 - €167 694 - £97 130 - FF1 100 000
  Portrait de Mme B. en Diane entourée d'enfants Huile/toile (114.5x146cm 45x57in) Blois 2000
- $52 500 - €54 424 - £31 500 - FF357 000
  Santa Caterina d'Alessandria Olio/tela (66x50cm 25x19in) Roma 2001
- $9 713 - €10 427 - £6 500 - FF68 394
  The Head of an Old Woman, Veiled, in Profile to the Right Black & white chalks/paper (14x12.5cm 5x4in) London 2000

VOULKOS Peter 1924 **[50]**
- $50 000 - €51 797 - £31 825 - FF339 765
  Untitled Vessel Stack #25 Ceramic (101.5x53.5x48.5cm 39x21x19in) New-York 2000
- $7 500 - €7 769 - £4 773 - FF50 964
  Vase Ceramic (35x19cm 13x7in) New-York 2000

VOYET Jacques 1927 **[32]**
- $832 - €838 - £518 - FF5 500
  Bateaux Huile/toile (63x91cm 24x35in) Paris 2000

VOYEVODA Yuri 1944 **[34]**
- $465 - €450 - £292 - FF2 955
  Barcos pesqueros Oleo/lienzo (60x50cm 23x19in) Madrid 1999
- $192 - €190 - £120 - FF1 248
  Seagulls on the Foreshore Oil/canvas/board (24x33cm 9x12in) Fernhurst, Haslemere, Surrey 1999

VOZNIAK Jaroslav 1933 **[22]**
- $462 - €437 - £288 - FF2 868
  Détails Huile/toile (40x50.5cm 15x19in) Praha 2001

VRANCX Sebastian 1573/78-1647 **[70]**
- $77 033 - €71 651 - £47 705 - FF470 000
  Famille royale de Bohême dans un paysage, agrémenté d'une pièce d'eau Huile/toile (122x146cm 48x64in) Biarritz 1999
- $113 807 - €111 288 - £70 299 - FF730 000
  Combat de cavaliers dans un village Huile/panneau (94.5x97cm 26x38in) Paris 1999
- $10 990 - €10 671 - £6 790 - FF70 000
  Scène d'escarmouche Huile/panneau (36x39cm 14x15in) Paris 1999

VRBOVA-STEFKOVA Miloslava 1909-? **[30]**
- $827 - €869 - £559 - FF5 701
  Ballett-Tänzerin Öl/Leinwand/Karton (40x50cm 15x19in) Kempten 2001

- $460 - €511 - £321 - FF3 353
  «Ballerina» Öl/Karton (40x30cm 15x11in) Stuttgart 2001

VREE de Nicolas 1645-1702 **[4]**
- $4 342 - €5 014 - £3 037 - FF32 890
  Gårdsbild med figurer och pickande höns Oil/canvas (53.5x65cm 21x25in) Stockholm 2001

VREEDENBURGH Cornelis 1880-1946 **[150]**
- $8 033 - €8 622 - £5 375 - FF56 555
  View on the Blok Company, Woerden Oil/canvas (47x77cm 18x30in) Amsterdam 2000
- $3 805 - €4 084 - £2 546 - FF26 789
  Summertime: a man at work in a moored rowingboat Oil/cardboard (31.5x49.5cm 12x19in) Amsterdam 2000
- $2 077 - €1 906 - £1 280 - FF12 501
  Skaters in a Winter Landscape Watercolour (16.5x24cm 6x9in) Amsterdam 1999

VREEDENBURGH Herman 1887-1956 **[5]**
- $2 629 - €2 949 - £1 821 - FF19 347
  Still Life with Fruit and Plant Oil/canvas (55x58cm 21x22in) Amsterdam 2000

VREELAND van Francis William 1879-1934 **[25]**
- $275 - €310 - £190 - FF2 036
  Autumn Landscape with Brook Watercolour/paper (49x67cm 19x26in) Hatfield PA 2000

VREL Jacobus c.1630-c.1680 **[7]**
- $114 226 - €106 183 - £70 000 - FF696 514
  Interior of a House with a seated Woman Oil/panel (64.5x47.5cm 25x18in) London 1998

VREULS Joseph 1864-1912 **[33]**
- $206 - €173 - £121 - FF1 136
  La Maison Monier, Liège Aquarelle/papier (25x31cm 9x12in) Liège 1998

VRIENDT de Albrecht 1843-1900 **[20]**
- $10 000 - €9 903 - £6 226 - FF64 958
  Women of the Harem Oil/panel (43x27cm 16x10in) New-York 1999
- $291 - €347 - £208 - FF2 276
  Tour de David, Jérusalem Aquarelle/papier (29x22cm 11x8in) Antwerpen 2000

VRIENDT de Juliaan 1842-1935 **[16]**
- $14 976 - €17 848 - £10 728 - FF117 072
  Nachtelijke overval (l'attaque de nuit) Huile/bois (99x130cm 38x51in) Antwerpen 2000
- $4 224 - €4 090 - £2 653 - FF26 831
  Beim Goldschmied, junger Edelmann, seiner festlich gekleideten Braut Oil/panel (58x71cm 22x27in) Berlin 1999
- $457 - €421 - £275 - FF2 764
  Paysage lacustre animé Huile/panneau (21x29cm 8x11in) Bruxelles 1999

VRIENNTT Joseph XVIII **[2]**
- $23 850 - €22 309 - £14 760 - FF146 340
  Paysage montagneux animé de baigneurs et de voyageurs, village au fond Huile/cuivre (30.6x45.4cm 12x17in) Antwerpen 1999

VRIENS Antoine 1902-1987 **[10]**
- $1 712 - €1 983 - £1 184 - FF13 008
  Jeune femme nue debout Bronze (H41cm H16in) Bruxelles 2000

VRIES de Abraham c.1590-1650/62 **[6]**

〰 **$11 790** - €11 434 - **£7 417** - FF75 000
Portrait de Nicolas Le Camus/Portrait de Jeanne Colbert Huile/toile (70.5x57.5cm 27x22in) Paris 1999

✐ **$1 743** - €1 735 - **£1 085** - FF11 382
Paysage italien avec lisière de forêt, montagnes et personnages Encre (25x34cm 9x13in) Antwerpen 1999

VRIES de Auke 1937 **[2]**

⬱ **$3 803** - €3 630 - **£2 376** - FF23 812
Abstract Composition Iron (70x155cm 27x61in) Amsterdam 1999

VRIES de Emanuel 1816-1875 **[6]**

〰 **$4 034** - €3 874 - **£2 500** - FF25 411
Dutch River Scene Oil/panel (43x59.5cm 16x23in) London 1999

VRIES de Hans Vredeman 1527-c.1604 **[6]**

〰 **$43 316** - €43 647 - **£26 999** - FF286 307
Palastinterieur mit Szene eines Apollo-Opfers Öl/Leinwand (119x168cm 46x66in) Zürich 2000

VRIES de Hubert 1899-1979 **[132]**

〰 **$355** - €397 - **£246** - FF2 601
Kermesse Huile/toile (40x40cm 15x15in) Antwerpen 2001

〰 **$170** - €194 - **£118** - FF1 274
Uferlandschaft Öl/Leinwand (39x40cm 15x15in) Rudolstadt-Thüringen 2000

VRIES de Jan Feytsz. 1628-1664 **[1]**

〰 **$19 236** - €18 151 - **£11 868** - FF119 064
The Battle at Dunes, 21 October 1639 Oil/panel (60x84.5cm 23x33in) Amsterdam 1999

VRIES de Jannes 1901-1986 **[19]**

〰 **$2 151** - €2 496 - **£1 485** - FF16 371
Messonhgi-Corfu Oil/canvas (60.5x90.5cm 23x35in) Groningen 2000

✐ **$1 297** - €1 180 - **£796** - FF7 739
Boerderij Huizinge Watercolour (37x52cm 14x20in) Amsterdam 1999

VRIES de Jochum Joachim Feyt XVII **[2]**

〰 **$51 580** - €47 754 - **£32 000** - FF313 248
Dutch Fluyts including the D'Hoopende Visser hunting Whale in Arctic Oil/canvas (87x132.5cm 34x52in) London 1999

VRIES de Kees 1957 **[7]**

✐ **$1 548** - €1 452 - **£956** - FF9 525
The «Zuiderkruis» off the Coast of Cape Town, the Tafelberg beyond Gouache (48x68cm 18x26in) Amsterdam 1999

VRIES de Michiel c.1653-1702 **[4]**

〰 **$8 656** - €8 168 - **£5 340** - FF53 578
Fishermen in a Rowing Boat on a Moat by a Farm Oil/panel (69x50cm 27x19in) Amsterdam 1999

VRIES de Paul Vredemann c.1567-c.1635 **[6]**

〰 **$32 000** - €31 985 - **£19 548** - FF209 808
The Interior of a Gothic Cathedral with Christ Among the Doctors Oil/panel (112.5x147.5cm 44x58in) New-York 2000

VRIES van Roelof Jansz. 1631-c.1681 **[61]**

〰 **$5 962** - €6 783 - **£4 164** - FF44 491
Hus vid vatten Oil/panel (44.5x54.5cm 17x21in) Stockholm 2000

VRIESLÄNDER John, Jack 1879-1957 **[26]**

✐ **$707** - €838 - **£499** - FF5 500
Personnages dans un paysage Encre (34.5x24cm 13x9in) Paris 2000

VROLIJK Adrianus Jacobus 1834-1862 **[25]**

〰 **$4 612** - €5 113 - **£3 202** - FF33 539
Weidelandschaft mit Vieh vor einer Windmühle Öl/Leinwand (44.5x62.5cm 17x24in) Köln 2001

〰 **$3 260** - €2 813 - **£1 967** - FF18 454
View of a Town along a River Oil/panel (26.5x35.5cm 10x13in) Amsterdam 1999

VROLIJK Jan Martinus 1845-1894 **[28]**

〰 **$5 043** - €5 445 - **£3 448** - FF35 719
A Cowherdes Watering Cows by Willow Trees Oil/canvas (71x95cm 27x37in) Amsterdam 2001

〰 **$731** - €767 - **£463** - FF5 030
Weidende Kühe am Wasser in Polderlandschaft Oil/panel (19x34cm 7x13in) Köln 2000

✐ **$1 945** - €2 089 - **£1 302** - FF13 700
Driving the Herd Watercolour/paper (53.5x38cm 21x14in) Toronto 2000

VROMAN Adam Clark 1856-1916 **[15]**

📷 **$1 800** - €1 872 - **£1 136** - FF12 277
Mary Paiting Pottery, Acoma/Hopi Snake Dance/Untitled Platinum print (48x37cm 18x14in) New-York 2000

VROUTOS Georgios 1843-1908 **[1]**

⬱ **$76 200** - €87 731 - **£52 000** - FF575 478
Aphrodite Holding the Golden Apple/Apollo Holding a Lyre Marble (H79cm H31in) London 2000

VROYLYNCK Ghislain ?-1635 **[1]**

〰 **$18 000** - €15 382 - **£10 573** - FF100 897
The Ressurrection Oil/panel (105x152cm 41x60in) New-Orleans LA 1998

VRUBEL Mikhail Alexandrov. 1856-1910 **[11]**

〰 **$6 441** - €6 082 - **£4 000** - FF39 898
Southern Moonlight Oil/canvas (18x22cm 7x8in) London 1999

VRYZAKIS Theodoros 1814/19-1878 **[3]**

〰 **$73 270** - €84 357 - **£50 000** - FF553 345
Solace Oil/canvas (45x58cm 17x22in) London 2000

VU CAO DAM 1908-2000 **[82]**

〰 **$4 725** - €4 404 - **£2 856** - FF28 890
Maternité: Motherhood Oil/board (73x60cm 28x23in) Singapore 1999

〰 **$2 150** - €1 991 - **£1 316** - FF13 059
Junges asiatisches Paar Öl/Karton (40x32cm 15x12in) Bern 1999

✐ **$4 313** - €4 020 - **£2 661** - FF26 369
Jeune femme nue; Portrait of a Nude Gouache (29x32cm 11x12in) Singapore 1999

VUCHT van der Jan 1603-1637 **[11]**
- $19 284 - €19 128 - **£12 000** - FF125 469
  Palatial Interior with elegant Compagny playing Shuttlecock Oil/panel (44.5x60.5cm 17x23in) London 1999
- $4 893 - €4 577 - **£3 000** - FF30 021
  A Church Interior with a Vaulted Ceiling, a Beggar and Figures Oil/panel (20.5x23cm 8x9in) London 1998

VUCHT van Gerrit c.1610-1697 **[20]**
- $14 463 - €14 346 - **£9 000** - FF94 102
  Vanitas Still Life Oil/panel (30x44.5cm 11x17in) London 1999

VUEZ de Arnould 1644-1720 **[4]**
- $22 779 - €22 105 - **£14 181** - FF145 000
  Allégories de l'Amour et la Justice/Beaux Arts/Sciences Huile/toile (160x299cm 62x117in) Paris 1999

VUILLARD Édouard 1868-1940 **[1002]**
- $280 000 - €269 249 - **£172 508** - FF1 766 156
  L'enfant au bonnet bleu Peinture à la colle (160x150cm 62x59in) New-York 1998
- $160 000 - €136 572 - **£95 680** - FF895 856
  Au jardin Oil/board/canvas (53x67cm 20x26in) New-York 1998
- $72 500 - €68 631 - **£45 029** - FF450 188
  Les enfants Roussel Oil/board (24.5x36.5cm 9x14in) New-York 1999
- $11 368 - €10 671 - **£7 042** - FF70 000
  Femme sur la plage Encre Chine/papier (14.5x17cm 5x6in) Deauville 1999
- $1 900 - €2 089 - **£1 217** - FF13 702
  L'Atre, from Paysages et Intérieurs Color lithograph (33.5x30cm 13x11in) New-York 2000

VUILLEFROY de Félix Dominique 1841-1910 **[21]**
- $1 649 - €1 601 - **£1 026** - FF10 500
  Le retour à la ferme Huile/toile (39x56cm 15x22in) Fontainebleau 1999

VUILLIER Gaston 1847-1915 **[7]**
- $348 - €351 - **£216** - FF2 300
  Vue d'un lac en Écosse Aquarelle (16x27.5cm 6x10in) Paris 2000

VUITTON W. XIX **[1]**
- $12 236 - €11 403 - **£7 544** - FF74 796
  Jeune femme et jardinier dans une serre Huile/panneau (80x65cm 31x25in) Bruxelles 1999

VUKMANOVIC Stefan 1924-1995 **[46]**
- $265 - €256 - **£166** - FF1 676
  Südliches Dorf Öl/Leinwand (50x60.5cm 19x23in) München 1999

VULLIAMY Gérard 1909 **[52]**
- $1 101 - €1 296 - **£789** - FF8 500
  Composition Huile/toile (81x116cm 31x45in) Paris 2001
- $1 231 - €1 448 - **£882** - FF9 500
  Composition Huile/toile (46x33cm 18x12in) Paris 2001

VUORI Antti 1935 **[28]**
- $298 - €336 - **£205** - FF2 206
  Cirkus Mixed media (61x44cm 24x17in) Helsinki 2000

VUORI Kaarlo 1863-1914 **[10]**
- $1 889 - €1 934 - **£1 186** - FF12 686
  Vemodig blick Oil/canvas (44.5x37cm 17x14in) Helsinki 2000

VUUREN van Jan 1871-1941 **[40]**
- $1 408 - €1 633 - **£972** - FF10 715
  Straatje te Elburg Oil/canvas (39x49cm 15x19in) Rotterdam 2000
- $740 - €681 - **£457** - FF4 464
  A Village Street in Summer Oil/canvas (19.5x30cm 7x11in) Amsterdam 1999

VYGH Arendt XVIII **[2]**
- $7 381 - €8 385 - **£5 181** - FF55 000
  Portrait de jeune homme Huile/toile (82x64.5cm 32x25in) Paris 2001

VYLDER den C. XIX **[2]**
- $5 615 - €5 658 - **£3 500** - FF37 117
  The Silent Admirer/An Afternoon Smoke Oil/panel (59.5x45.5cm 23x17in) London 2000

VYTLACIL Vaclav 1892-1984 **[40]**
- $850 - €966 - **£582** - FF6 334
  Vase of Flowers Pastel (54x24cm 21x9in) New-York 2000
- $1 000 - €1 078 - **£682** - FF7 069
  Abstract Composition Lithograph (20.5x28cm 8x11in) New-York 2001

W

WAAGEN Adalbert 1833-1898 **[55]**
- $17 000 - €19 420 - **£11 968** - FF127 384
  Alpine Landscape with Hunter, Game and Swiss Mountain Dog Oil/canvas (132x105cm 52x41in) Pittsfield MA 2001
- $2 885 - €2 469 - **£1 736** - FF16 196
  Der Obersee bei Berchtesgaden mit Übergossener Alm Öl/Leinwand (64.5x52.5cm 25x20in) München 1998
- $1 514 - €1 687 - **£1 058** - FF11 067
  Felswand im Hochgebirge Öl/Karton (22x29cm 8x11in) München 2001

WAAGEN Arthur XIX **[40]**
- $16 000 - €15 259 - **£9 739** - FF100 094
  Kabyle au retour de la Chasse Bronze (H122cm H48in) New-York 1999
- $3 061 - €3 136 - **£1 890** - FF20 568
  Tamburinspelande stående kvinna Bronze (H71cm H27in) Stockholm 2000

WAANO-GANO Joe 1906-? **[20]**
- $550 - €566 - **£348** - FF3 710
  California Landscape Oil/board (35x45cm 14x18in) Cincinnati OH 2000

WAARDEN van der Jan 1811-1872 **[9]**
- $6 563 - €7 714 - **£4 550** - FF50 602
  A Still Life With fruit and Flowers Oil/panel (31x24.5cm 12x9in) Amsterdam 2000

WAAY van der Nicolaas 1855-1936 **[66]**
- $2 318 - €2 178 - **£1 397** - FF14 287
  Self-portrait of the Artist Oil/canvas (100x75cm 39x29in) Amsterdam 1999
- $3 378 - €3 176 - **£2 091** - FF20 836
  Figuurstudie in Kimono Oil/canvas (28x44cm 11x17in) Amsterdam 1999
- $1 158 - €1 361 - **£803** - FF8 929
  Figures in a Pub Pencil/paper (13x19cm 5x7in) Amsterdam 2000

W

WABEL Henry 1889-1981 **[26]**
- **$1 089** - €1 240 - **£765** - FF8 133
  Stilleben Öl/Leinwand (73x60cm 28x23in) Zürich 2001
- **$1 427** - €1 371 - **£884** - FF8 994
  Tisch mit Gegenständen Öl/Karton (27x45.5cm 10x17in) Zürich 1999

WACH Aloys Ludwig 1872-1940 **[84]**
- **$1 527** - €1 817 - **£1 090** - FF11 917
  Kopf zum Bauernkrieg Öl/Karton (47x37cm 18x14in) Linz 2000
- **$597** - €581 - **£368** - FF3 813
  Drei Bauern Krieg 1626 Ink/paper (27.5x39cm 10x15in) Linz 1999
- **$248** - €276 - **£166** - FF1 811
  Bauerntanz anno 1626 Radierung (30x20cm 11x7in) Linz 2000

WACH Karl Wilhelm 1787-1845 **[5]**
- **$5 403** - €6 135 - **£3 754** - FF40 246
  Christus am Ölberg Oil/panel (52x39cm 20x15in) Köln 2001

WACHSMANN Alois 1898-1942 **[25]**
- **$13 005** - €12 300 - **£8 100** - FF80 685
  Liegende Figur Öl/Leinwand (40x73cm 15x28in) Praha 2000
- **$2 196** - €2 077 - **£1 368** - FF13 626
  Voeux pour Nouvel An Huile/panneau (22x19cm 8x7in) Praha 2000
- **$722** - €683 - **£450** - FF4 482
  Family Charcoal/paper (79x106cm 31x41in) Praha 2000

WACHSMANN Friedrich / Bedrich 1820-1897 **[16]**
- **$216** - €205 - **£135** - FF1 344
  Regenbogen Oil/panel (15x19cm 5x7in) Praha 2001

WACHSMUTH Ferdinand 1802-1869 **[5]**
- **$7 707** - €8 800 - **£5 433** - FF57 723
  Algerisches Haus mit Figurenstaffage am Mittelmeer Öl/Leinwand (74x92.5cm 29x36in) Bern 2001

WACHSMUTH Jeremias 1711-1771 **[2]**
- **$1 159** - €1 125 - **£721** - FF7 378
  Die vier Jahreszeiten Radierung (29.7x19cm 11x7in) Berlin 1999

WACHSMUTH Maximilian 1859-1912 **[19]**
- **$3 691** - €3 579 - **£2 338** - FF23 477
  Dirndl und drei Bauern in der Stube am Fenster Öl/Leinwand (90x70cm 35x27in) München 1999

WACHTEL Elmer 1864-1929 **[42]**
- **$12 000** - €12 881 - **£8 030** - FF84 492
  Convict Lake Oil/canvas (35.5x45.5cm 13x17in) San-Francisco CA 2000
- **$7 500** - €8 050 - **£5 019** - FF52 807
  A Calm Inlet Oil/canvas/board (30.5x38cm 12x14in) San-Francisco CA 2000
- **$1 500** - €1 381 - **£900** - FF9 056
  California Landscape Watercolour/paper (21x37cm 8x14in) Pasadena CA 1999

WACHTEL Marion Kavanaugh 1876-1954 **[74]**
- **$7 700** - €7 849 - **£4 824** - FF51 778
  Mountain Meadow Oil/canvas (50x60cm 20x24in) Altadena CA 2000
- **$11 000** - €10 557 - **£6 895** - FF69 250
  Old Eucalyptus Oil/canvas (34x45cm 13x18in) Altadena CA 1999
- **$12 000** - €11 044 - **£7 202** - FF72 447
  Coastal Clouds Watercolour/paper (44x59cm 17x23in) Pasadena CA 1999

- **$500** - €480 - **£313** - FF3 147
  Landscape, The Oaks Color lithograph (46x71cm 18x28in) Altadena CA 1999

WACHTEL Wilhelm 1875-1942 **[19]**
- **$1 900** - €1 722 - **£1 169** - FF11 295
  Jerusalem Oil/board (41x31cm 16x12in) Mystic CT 1999
- **$1 471** - €1 452 - **£894** - FF9 525
  Seated Nude with Drapery Pastel (60x45cm 23x17in) Amsterdam 2000

WÄCHTER Eberhard 1762-1852 **[5]**
- **$8 177** - €9 203 - **£5 634** - FF60 370
  Cornelia ihren Kindern die Geschichte der Ahnen erzählend Öl/Leinwand (62x80cm 24x31in) Stuttgart 2000

WACHTER Emil 1921 **[36]**
- **$2 149** - €2 454 - **£1 515** - FF16 098
  «Winterlandschaft» Oil/panel (65x88cm 25x34in) Stuttgart 2001

WACHTER Georg 1809-1863 **[4]**
- **$7 943** - €9 447 - **£5 668** - FF61 971
  Tiroler Schütze in Rittner Tracht Öl/Metall (33x25cm 12x9in) Wien 2000

WACKER Rudolf 1893-1939 **[48]**
- **$73 580** - €85 374 - **£50 804** - FF560 014
  Herbst-Strauss Oil/panel (65x50cm 25x19in) Luzern 2000
- **$51 018** - €47 964 - **£30 888** - FF314 622
  Frau im Hemd (seine Frau Ilse im Berliner Atelier) Oil/paper/canvas (42.3x33cm 16x12in) Wien 1999

WACKER-ELSEN Hans 1868-1958 **[34]**
- **$464** - €460 - **£281** - FF3 018
  Segelschiff Öl/Leinwand (21x21cm 8x8in) Satow 2000
- **$1 085** - €1 125 - **£687** - FF7 378
  Volldampf Gouache/paper (32x38cm 12x14in) Satow 2000

WACQUIEZ Henri 1907 **[2]**
- **$5 809** - €5 641 - **£3 589** - FF37 000
  Panthère se léchant Bronze (58.5x25x45cm 23x9x17in) Paris 1999

WADE Jonathan A. 1960 **[65]**
- **$696** - €764 - **£449** - FF5 011
  When I Win the Lottery Oil/board (75x61cm 29x24in) London 2000
- **$289** - €278 - **£180** - FF1 826
  Slow March - Royal Highland Fusiliers on Parade, Edinburgh Oil/board (30x53cm 11x20in) London 1999

WADHAM William Joseph 1863-1950 **[33]**
- **$900** - €864 - **£554** - FF5 669
  Full sail Watercolour (38x50cm 15x20in) Cambridge MA 1999

WADSWORTH Adelaide E. 1844-1928 **[3]**
- **$2 400** - €2 798 - **£1 661** - FF18 351
  Ipswich Marshes, September Pastel/paper (33x40cm 13x16in) Watertown MA 2000

WADSWORTH Edward 1889-1949 **[46]**
- **$32 874** - €35 288 - **£22 000** - FF231 475
  Cork Floats Tempera (40.5x33cm 15x12in) London 2000
- **$4 482** - €4 812 - **£3 000** - FF31 564
  View near Dudley Ink (23.5x33cm 9x12in) London 2000

📏 **$1 225** - €1 128 - **£750** - FF7 400
Untitled Abstract Woodcut (10x8cm 3x3in) London 1998

WADSWORTH Frank Russell 1874-1905 **[2]**
🎨 **$4 250** - €4 741 - **£2 782** - FF31 102
View of Paris Oil/canvas (73x88cm 29x35in) Chicago IL 2000

WADSWORTH Wedworth 1846-1927 **[14]**
✏️ **$650** - €648 - **£394** - FF4 249
Winter Landscape Watercolour/paper (18x26cm 7x10in) Chester NY 2000

WAEL de Cornelis 1592-1667 **[46]**
🖌️ **$15 600** - €20 215 - **£11 700** - FF132 600
Scene di battaglie Olio/tela (96x129cm 37x50in) Milano 2000
🖌️ **$33 478** - €27 610 - **£19 722** - FF181 108
Eine zweimastige habsburgisch-österreichische Prunk-Galeere Öl/Leinwand (74x120cm 29x47in) Wien 1998
🎨 **$2 092** - €2 246 - **£1 400** - FF14 730
Oriental Port Scene (in 22.5x35.5cm 8x13in) London 2000
📏 **$375** - €421 - **£261** - FF2 764
Les cinq sens Eau-forte (23x30cm 9x11in) Bruxelles 2001

WAENERBERG Thorsten 1846-1917 **[54]**
🖌️ **$5 763** - €5 044 - **£3 492** - FF33 087
Fiskebåtar Oil/canvas (55x38cm 21x14in) Helsinki 1998
🖌️ **$2 241** - €2 439 - **£1 477** - FF15 996
Bäck Oil/canvas/panel (26x38cm 10x14in) Helsinki 2000

WAENTIG Walter 1881-1962 **[22]**
🖌️ **$1 534** - €1 789 - **£1 076** - FF11 738
Kirmesskizze Öl/Leinwand (40x50.5cm 15x19in) Köln 2001

WAERHERT de Arthur 1881-1944 **[31]**
🖌️ **$1 230** - €1 239 - **£765** - FF8 130
Béliers et moutons dans un paysage Huile/toile (50x55cm 19x21in) Bruxelles 2000
🖌️ **$618** - €694 - **£431** - FF4 552
Vaches au pâturage Huile/panneau (20x29cm 7x11in) Bruxelles 2001

WAETJEN von Otto 1881-1942 **[23]**
🖌️ **$1 351** - €1 425 - **£893** - FF9 350
Zimmer mit Aquarium Öl/Leinwand (78x70cm 30x27in) Zürich 2001

WAGEMAEKERS Victor 1876-1953 **[121]**
🖌️ **$1 007** - €942 - **£611** - FF6 178
Veldwerk Oil/canvas (37x53cm 14x20in) Lokeren 1999
🖌️ **$477** - €446 - **£293** - FF2 926
Bord de canal Huile/panneau (24x31cm 9x12in) Bruxelles 2000
🎨 **$269** - €322 - **£184** - FF2 113
De watermolen (le moulin à eau) Aquarelle/papier (27x36cm 10x14in) Antwerpen 2000

WAGEMAKER Jaap 1906-1972 **[62]**
🖌️ **$6 249** - €7 260 - **£4 392** - FF47 625
Couleur d'ardoise Mixed media/panel (131x105.5cm 51x41in) Amsterdam 2001
🖌️ **$10 147** - €10 891 - **£6 789** - FF71 438
Falaise Jaune Mixed media (102x72cm 40x28in) Amsterdam 2000
🎨 **$3 382** - €3 630 - **£2 263** - FF23 812
Versteende vegetatie Mixed media/canvas (27x39cm 10x15in) Amsterdam 2000

🎨 **$1 901** - €1 815 - **£1 188** - FF11 906
Leikleur (2) Mixed media drawing (70x58cm 27x22in) Amsterdam 1999

WAGEMAN Thomas Charles 1787-1863 **[13]**
🎨 **$1 076** - €976 - **£652** - FF6 400
Portrait of a Mother & Child Watercolour/paper (59.5x49cm 23x19in) Sydney 1998

WAGEMANS Maurice 1877-1927 **[41]**
🖌️ **$1 961** - €1 834 - **£1 191** - FF12 032
Vase de fleurs Huile/toile (75x65cm 29x25in) Bruxelles 1999
🖌️ **$1 094** - €1 190 - **£720** - FF7 804
Landschap met hooiwagen Oil/panel (22x35cm 8x13in) Lokeren 2000

WAGEMANS Pieter Johannes Al. 1879-1955 **[29]**
🖌️ **$500** - €442 - **£301** - FF2 898
Cargoboats in the Rotterdam Harbour Oil/canvas (50x70cm 19x27in) Amsterdam 1998
🖌️ **$464** - €499 - **£316** - FF3 274
Gezicht op Het Mauritshuis en het Torentje Oil/panel (18x24cm 7x9in) Amsterdam 2001

WAGENBAUER Max Joseph 1775-1829 **[46]**
🖌️ **$6 179** - €5 624 - **£3 861** - FF36 892
Drei Rinder am See mit schlafendem Hirten Oil/panel (39x33cm 15x12in) München 1999
🎨 **$2 047** - €2 045 - **£1 280** - FF13 415
Blick auf Traunkirchen am Traunsee Pencil/paper (29.8x43.4cm 11x17in) Köln 1999
📏 **$161** - €169 - **£101** - FF1 106
Ruine eines Götzentempels auf der Insel am Würmsee Lithographie (32.5x42.5cm 12x16in) München 2000

WAGENER Friedrich Erhard 1759-1813 **[2]**
🎨 **$2 973** - €2 723 - **£1 812** - FF17 859
Friederich Ludwig, Duke of Mecklenburg-Schwerin (1778-1819) Pastel (55x46.5cm 21x18in) Amsterdam 1999

WAGENER Fritz 1896-1939 **[69]**
🖌️ **$6 700** - €7 158 - **£4 457** - FF46 954
Im Stadtbauamt Öl/Leinwand (71x84cm 27x33in) Hamburg 2000
🖌️ **$536** - €562 - **£353** - FF3 689
Alter Jägersmann mit Pfeife Öl/Karton (32x24cm 12x9in) Augsburg 2000

WAGENSCHÖN Franz Xaver 1726-1790 **[9]**
🖌️ **$12 800** - €14 534 - **£8 760** - FF95 340
Venus und Juno mit Putten und Nymphen in einer Landschaft Öl/Leinwand (75.5x94.5cm 29x37in) Wien 2000
🖌️ **$14 764** - €14 316 - **£9 352** - FF93 909
Die Anbetung der Hirten Öl/Kupfer (30x42cm 11x16in) München 1999
🎨 **$1 798** - €2 045 - **£1 256** - FF13 415
Flussgott mit Nymphen Ink/paper (11x17cm 4x6in) München 2000
📏 **$505** - €501 - **£316** - FF3 286
Neptun und Amphitrite Radierung (18x25.5cm 7x10in) München 1999

WAGNER Carl 1796-1867 **[56]**
🖌️ **$6 624** - €6 478 - **£4 091** - FF42 490
Mutter mit Kindern Öl/Leinwand (110.5x93cm 43x36in) Zürich 1999
🎨 **$551** - €511 - **£336** - FF3 353
Waldlandschaft mit einem Fluss im Vordergrund Watercolour (30.7x24.2cm 12x9in) München 1999

W

WAGNER

🎨 **$78** - €77 - **£50** - FF503
Eichenwald mit Bachlauf und Jäger Radierung (19x26cm 7x10in) Kempten 1999

WAGNER Ernst Michael 1886-1963 **[3]**
✒ **$675** - €654 - **£428** - FF4 290
Klosterneuburg Pencil (45x55.5cm 17x21in) Wien 1999

WAGNER Ferdinand II 1847-1927 **[23]**
🖼 **$25 000** - €21 569 - **£15 082** - FF141 482
Allegory of the Arts Oil/canvas (246.5x508cm 97x200in) New-York 1998

WAGNER Frederck R. 1864-1940 **[44]**
🖼 **$3 500** - €4 116 - **£2 509** - FF26 998
The Docks, Winter Oil/canvas (76x91.5cm 29x36in) Philadelphia PA 2001
🖼 **$5 500** - €5 904 - **£3 680** - FF38 728
View Under the Bridge Oil/panel (23.5x32.5cm 9x12in) New-York 2000
🖼 **$850** - €957 - **£585** - FF6 712
Pennsylvania River Landscape with Barge, Winter Pastel (26x34.5cm 10x13in) Washington 2000

WAGNER Fritz 1872-1948 **[9]**
🖼 **$4 112** - €4 678 - **£2 872** - FF30 684
Lustige balladen Oil/canvas (70x81cm 27x31in) Stockholm 2000

WAGNER Hermann Edouard 1894-? **[2]**
🖼 **$2 352** - €2 096 - **£1 450** - FF13 751
The Port of Marseilles Oil/board (30x38cm 12x15in) Penzance, Cornwall 1999

WAGNER Johann Peter 1730-1809 **[3]**
🏺 **$6 344** - €6 647 - **£4 196** - FF43 600
Antikisch-fauneske Szene Relief (34x28cm 13x11in) München 2000

WAGNER Joseph 1706-1780 **[52]**
🎨 **$125** - €130 - **£75** - FF850
Pastori Gravure (18x25cm 7x9in) Venezia 2000

WAGNER Julius 1818-1879 **[8]**
🖼 **$4 440** - €4 958 - **£3 100** - FF32 520
The fortune telling Oil/panel (63x42cm 24x16in) Bruxelles 2001
🖼 **$379** - €446 - **£262** - FF2 926
Bergère aux oies Huile/panneau (32x24cm 12x9in) Antwerpen 2000

WAGNER Karl 1864-? **[26]**
🖼 **$333** - €358 - **£223** - FF2 347
Erlegter Hirschbock im Gras Öl/Leinwand (53x40cm 20x15in) Berlin 2000

WAGNER Karl 1839-1923 **[15]**
🖼 **$1 345** - €1 460 - **£931** - FF9 580
The Blacksmith Shop Oil/canvas (53x41cm 21x16in) Cleveland OH 2001

WAGNER Karl 1877-? **[31]**
🖼 **$552** - €613 - **£385** - FF4 024
«Bayrische Landschaft mit Bachlauf» Öl/Leinwand (76x94cm 29x37in) Stuttgart 2001

WAGNER Karl 1856-1921 **[25]**
🖼 **$1 354** - €1 453 - **£906** - FF9 534
Wölfe fallen einen Eber an Öl/Leinwand (69x55cm 27x21in) Wien 2000

WAGNER Otto 1803-1861 **[18]**
🖼 **$982** - €1 022 - **£622** - FF6 707
Schäfer mit seiner Herde an einem Teich unterhalb einer Burgruine Öl/Leinwand (66x95cm 25x37in) München 2000

🎨 **$3 589** - €4 269 - **£2 472** - FF28 000
Jeunes filles au piano-forte dans un intérieur Biedermeier Aquarelle, gouache/papier (32x46cm 12x18in) Paris 2000

WAGNER Paul Hermann 1852-? **[21]**
🖼 **$6 083** - €5 104 - **£3 568** - FF33 481
Stående ung kvinde i hvide gevandter mellem blå iris Oil/canvas (100x70cm 39x27in) Vejle 1998

WAGNER Pierre 1897-1943 **[62]**
🖼 **$1 550** - €1 448 - **£956** - FF9 500
Retour de pêche aux sprats à Douarnenez Huile/panneau (38x46cm 14x18in) Brest 1999
🖼 **$421** - €442 - **£279** - FF2 900
Barques de pêche au mouillage Huile/panneau (22.5x35cm 8x13in) Quimper 2000

WAGNER Sigmund F. 1759-1835 **[2]**
✒ **$2 705** - €2 353 - **£1 631** - FF15 435
«Die Terrasse des Erlacherhofes, das vielbesprochene Bubenbergthöri» Watercolour (28x36cm 11x14in) Bern 1998

WAGNER Wilhelm 1887-1968 **[27]**
🎨 **$190** - €164 - **£114** - FF1 073
Strassenszene in Paris Lithographie (29.3x39.4cm 11x15in) Berlin 1998

WAGNER Wilhelm George 1814-1855 **[5]**
🖼 **$2 702** - €3 176 - **£1 873** - FF20 836
A Sailing Vessel in an Estuary Oil/panel (26.5x35.5cm 10x13in) Amsterdam 2000

WAGNER-HÖHENBERG Fritz 1902-1976 **[24]**
🖼 **$4 870** - €5 445 - **£3 390** - FF35 719
Tall Stories Oil/canvas (61x50cm 24x19in) Amsterdam 2001
🖼 **$2 576** - €2 454 - **£1 572** - FF16 098
Wilderer beim Gewehrreinigen Öl/Leinwand (35x30cm 13x11in) Stuttgart 1999

WAGNER-HÖHENBERG Josef 1870-1939 **[43]**
🖼 **$2 523** - €2 812 - **£1 763** - FF18 446
Beim Verkosten des Weines Öl/Leinwand (70.5x90.5cm 27x35in) München 2001

WAGONER Harry B. 1889-1950 **[16]**
🖼 **$1 800** - €1 657 - **£1 080** - FF10 867
Spanish Residence in Lush California Lansdcape Oil/canvas (76x101cm 30x40in) Pasadena CA 1999
🖼 **$900** - €864 - **£564** - FF5 666
Atmospheric Landscape, Flowers of the Desert Oil/canvas/board (15x20cm 6x8in) Altadena CA 1999

WAGONER Robert 1928 **[4]**
✒ **$2 200** - €2 361 - **£1 472** - FF15 490
Indian Camp Gouache/paper (25x43cm 10x17in) Houston TX 2000

WAGREZ Jacques C. 1846-1908 **[13]**
🖼 **$11 247** - €10 519 - **£6 810** - FF69 000
Catherine Cornaro, Reine de Chypre, ayant fait don de ses Etats Huile/toile (81.5x116cm 32x45in) Reims 1999

WAGULA Hans 1894-1964 **[25]**
🎨 **$148** - €160 - **£102** - FF1 048
«Österreich» Poster (95x63cm 37x24in) Wien 2001

WAH CHEONG XIX-XX **[1]**
🖼 **$2 919** - €2 804 - **£1 800** - FF18 393
H.M.S Clio in tropical Rig for China Service Oil/canvas (28x35.5cm 11x13in) London 1999

WAHDI 1917-1996 **[4]**
- $2 067 - €1 927 - £1 249 - FF12 639
  Scenery around Bandoenz Oil/canvas (46x70cm 18x27in) Singapore 1999

WAHL Johann Friedrich 1719-? **[1]**
- $3 368 - €3 756 - £2 304 - FF24 637
  Portraet af dreng med pisk og jagthund Oil/canvas (97x63cm 38x24in) Viby J, Århus 2000

WAHL von Alexander Amandus 1839-1903 **[2]**
- $4 244 - €3 500 - £2 500 - FF22 956
  Chamil the hero of the Caucasian war Bronze (H53cm H20in) London 1998

WAHLBERG Alfred 1834-1906 **[180]**
- $13 748 - €16 137 - £9 702 - FF105 854
  Fiskeläge, Fiskebäckskil Oil/canvas (100x150cm 39x59in) Stockholm 2000
- $2 102 - €1 829 - £1 268 - FF11 995
  Landskap med vattenfall Oil/canvas (35x49cm 13x19in) Stockholm 1998
- $980 - €1 104 - £675 - FF7 240
  Strandmotiv från Lysekil Oil/canvas (33x45cm 12x17in) Uppsala 2000

WAHLBERG Ulf 1938 **[66]**
- $897 - €843 - £555 - FF5 532
  I skogen Oil/canvas (77x53cm 30x20in) Stockholm 1999
- $3 321 - €3 722 - £2 315 - FF24 412
  Bilvrak Oil/canvas (28x38cm 11x14in) Stockholm 2001

WAHLBOHM Carl 1810-1858 **[8]**
- $3 419 - €3 902 - £2 376 - FF25 595
  «Ni gör mig generad» Oil/canvas (43x40cm 16x15in) Stockholm 2001

WAHLE Friedrich 1863-1927 **[16]**
- $789 - €920 - £554 - FF6 037
  Wirtshausszene, Herren im Gespräch Öl/Karton (31x50cm 12x19in) Kempten 2000

WAHLGREN Anders 1861-1928 **[13]**
- $417 - €432 - £262 - FF2 831
  Insjölandskap i månsken Oil/canvas (53x78cm 20x30in) Stockholm 2000

WAHLQUIST Ernfried 1815-1895 **[64]**
- $1 546 - €1 345 - £932 - FF8 820
  «Utsigt från danviksbergen» Oil/canvas (53x68cm 20x26in) Stockholm 1998
- $891 - €833 - £549 - FF5 464
  Stockholm från Smedsudden, månsken Oil/panel (21.5x29cm 8x11in) Stockholm 1999

WAHLROOS Dora 1870-1947 **[18]**
- $1 632 - €1 598 - £1 004 - FF10 480
  Kaipuu Oil/canvas (72x83cm 28x32in) Helsinki 1999
- $1 112 - €1 127 - £698 - FF7 391
  Vid bryggan Oil/panel (16x29cm 6x11in) Helsinki 2000

WAHLSTEDT Walther 1898-1972 **[13]**
- $4 113 - €4 084 - £2 570 - FF26 789
  En signe d'amitié Oil/panel (37x28cm 14x11in) Amsterdam 1999

WAHLSTRÖM Charlotte 1849-1924 **[60]**
- $791 - €781 - £487 - FF5 124
  Landskap med solnedgång Oil/canvas (47x66cm 18x25in) Stockholm 2000
- $440 - €443 - £274 - FF2 908
  Sommarlandskap med rinnande vatten Oil/canvas (15.5x24cm 6x9in) Stockholm 2000

WAIDMANN Pierre 1860-1937 **[13]**
- $781 - €838 - £522 - FF5 500
  Marée basse à Roscoff Huile/toile (65x91cm 25x35in) Epinal 2000

WAILLY de Charles 1729-1798 **[9]**
- $2 080 - €1 952 - £1 300 - FF12 805
  Fuente monumental/Paisaje con cascadas y templo clásico Acuarela/papel (17.5x18.5cm 6x7in) Madrid 1999

WAIN Louis 1860-1939 **[341]**
- $28 479 - €27 475 - £18 000 - FF180 225
  Skating on thin Ice Oil/board (61x47cm 24x18in) London 1999
- $3 884 - €3 646 - £2 400 - FF23 917
  Watching the Butterfly Oil/board (20x26cm 7x10in) Billingshurst, West-Sussex 1999
- $1 665 - €1 753 - £1 100 - FF11 500
  Defending Dinner Watercolour (9.5x13cm 3x5in) London 2000

WAINEWRIGHT John XIX **[32]**
- $8 065 - €8 693 - £5 500 - FF57 020
  Winter/Summer Oil/canvas (61x50.5cm 24x19in) London 2001
- $2 757 - €2 648 - £1 700 - FF17 372
  Roses, Lilies, Peonies, Convolvulus and Forget-me-nots, in a Vase Oil/board (40.5x30.5cm 15x12in) London 1999

WAINEWRIGHT Thomas Francis c.1830-c.1900 **[68]**
- $896 - €1 044 - £620 - FF6 846
  Evening, Cattle Watering Before a Tranquil Landscape Oil/canvas (51x76cm 20x29in) Cheshire 2000
- $3 295 - €3 341 - £2 050 - FF21 918
  Cattle Watering by a stream Oil/canvas (35x45.5cm 13x17in) Suffolk 2000
- $1 839 - €1 570 - £1 100 - FF10 299
  Sheep resting beside a Lake in a Mountainous Landscape Watercolour (21x41.5cm 8x16in) London 1998

WAINEWRIGHT Thomas Griffith 1794-1847 **[8]**
- $5 061 - €5 648 - £3 520 - FF37 500
  Portrait of a young Girl/Sketch Pencil/paper (21.5x18.5cm 8x7in) Sydney 2001

WAINWRIGHT Albert 1862-1943 **[3]**
- $2 577 - €2 564 - £1 600 - FF16 817
  Study of a young 1930s Footballer Watercolour/paper (33x23.5cm 12x9in) London 1999

WAINWRIGHT William John 1855-1931 **[44]**
- $90 000 - €85 381 - £54 675 - FF560 061
  An elaborate Bouquet of Flowers in a sculpted Vase on a Stone Ledge Oil/canvas (127x101cm 50x39in) New-York 1999
- $1 691 - €1 585 - £1 040 - FF10 394
  The Musicians Oil/board (30x23.5cm 11x9in) West-Midlands 1999
- $2 221 - €2 286 - £1 400 - FF14 998
  The Last Rites Watercolour/paper (60x29cm 23x11in) Lichfield, Staffordshire 2000

WAITE Edward Wilkins 1854-1924 **[71]**
- $12 944 - €11 185 - £7 800 - FF73 366
  Nature's Garden Oil/canvas (49x75cm 19x29in) Billingshurst, West-Sussex 1999
- $4 037 - €4 462 - £2 800 - FF29 268
  Afterglow, Woolhampton, Berkshire Oil/canvas (30.5x46cm 12x18in) London 2001

W

WAITE Harold act.1893-1939 **[19]**

$5 799 - €4 871 - **£3 400** - FF31 954
Children fishing byan Old Mill Oil/canvas
(44.5x60cm 17x23in) Billingshurst, West-Sussex 1998

$311 - €315 - **£190** - FF2 064
River Landscape Watercolour/paper (30x41cm
11x16in) Sighthill 2000

WAITE James Clarke 1832-1921 **[21]**

$7 620 - €8 987 - **£5 374** - FF58 950
The Eavesdropper Oil/canvas (62x74.5cm 24x29in)
Woollahra, Sydney 2001

WAITE Robert Thorne 1842-1935 **[115]**

$6 854 - €6 507 - **£4 200** - FF42 685
Harvesting Oil/canvas (30.5x40.5cm 12x15in) London
1999

$1 475 - €1 594 - **£1 020** - FF10 454
Old Shrimper, on the Shore Watercolour/paper
(38x29cm 14x11in) Cheshire 2001

WAITT Richard ?-1732 **[6]**

$43 731 - €49 727 - **£30 000** - FF326 190
Gardener Holding a Cabbage with a Candle
Oil/canvas (76x63.5cm 29x25in) Oxfordshire 2000

WAKE John Cheltenham XIX **[10]**

$5 664 - €5 311 - **£3 500** - FF34 840
Unloading the Catch Oil/canvas (76x124.5cm
29x49in) London 1999

WAKELIN Roland Shakespeare 1887-1971 **[243]**

$3 492 - €3 847 - **£2 318** - FF25 237
The Spit Mosman Oil/board (42x54cm 16x21in)
Woollahra, Sydney 2000

$1 698 - €1 597 - **£1 051** - FF10 477
Wind in the Cypress Oil/canvas/board (22x27.5cm
8x10in) Melbourne 1999

$508 - €599 - **£358** - FF3 930
Still Life of Fruit and Vase Watercolour
(26.5x34.5cm 10x13in) Woollahra, Sydney 2001

WAKHEVITCH Georges 1907-1984 **[39]**

$621 - €686 - **£430** - FF4 500
**Le voyageur sans bagages, Gilbert Miller pro-
duction, Chambre Gaston** Gouache/papier
(74x55cm 29x21in) Paris 2001

WALBOURN Ernest Ch. 1872-1927 **[172]**

$4 218 - €4 593 - **£2 762** - FF30 130
Fåren matas, flicka vid grind Oil/canvas (51x76cm
20x29in) Uppsala 2000

$1 149 - €1 042 - **£700** - FF6 835
The Village Green Oil/board (24x35.5cm 9x13in)
Godalming, Surrey 1998

WALCH Charles 1898-1948 **[131]**

$16 228 - €14 940 - **£9 741** - FF98 000
L'Humaniste Huile/toile (130x162cm 51x63in) Lyon
1999

$3 799 - €3 659 - **£2 347** - FF24 000
Mère et enfant Huile/toile (46x55cm 18x21in) Paris
1999

$1 036 - €1 006 - **£645** - FF6 600
Personnages au chien Gouache/papier (31x44cm
12x17in) Paris 1999

WALCH Paul Johann 1881-1958 **[68]**

$372 - €383 - **£234** - FF2 515
Schneeschmelze im Voralpenland Öl/Leinwand
(80x91cm 31x35in) München 2000

WALCH Thomas 1867-1943 **[17]**

$2 278 - €2 556 - **£1 579** - FF16 769
**Tiroler Bergbauernhof im sommerlichen
Sonnenlicht** Öl/Leinwand/Karton (47x62cm 18x24in)
München 2000

$1 147 - €1 278 - **£801** - FF8 384
Verlorene Heimat Süd-Tirol Öl/Karton
(22.4x30.9cm 8x12in) München 2001

WALCOT William 1874-1943 **[230]**

$2 092 - €2 460 - **£1 500** - FF16 137
Stroll in the Park Oil/panel (20.5x29cm 8x11in)
London 2001

$2 609 - €2 856 - **£1 800** - FF18 731
Continental Cathedral Pencil/paper (46.5x59cm
18x23in) London 2001

$448 - €481 - **£300** - FF3 156
Egyptian Palace Etching, aquatint (24x30cm 9x11in)
London 2000

WALCOTT Harry Mills 1870-1944 **[19]**

$4 600 - €3 887 - **£2 735** - FF25 500
The Organist Oil/canvas (45.5x45.5cm 17x17in)
Washington 1998

WALCUTT William 1818-1882 **[5]**

$865 - €971 - **£600** - FF6 370
London Building Etching (13x21cm 5x8in) London
2000

WALDBERG Isabelle 1911-1990 **[36]**

$4 368 - €4 573 - **£2 745** - FF30 000
Montagne II Bronze (47x32x26cm 18x12x10in)
Versailles 2000

WALDE Alfons 1891-1958 **[221]**

$98 720 - €116 276 - **£69 440** - FF762 720
Tiroler Bergstadt Öl/Leinwand (100.5x120.5cm
39x47in) Wien 2000

$94 784 - €81 769 - **£56 960** - FF536 368
Tiroler Dorf (Aurach bei Kitzbühel) Tempera
(59.5x41.5cm 23x16in) München 1998

$24 766 - €28 121 - **£17 209** - FF184 464
Familie im Schnee Oil/board (33x35.5cm 12x13in)
München 2001

$3 597 - €3 997 - **£2 409** - FF26 218
Erotische Szene Pencil/paper (10x14.2cm 3x5in)
Wien 2000

WALDEN Lionel 1861-1933 **[12]**

$2 500 - €2 843 - **£1 742** - FF18 650
Coastal View Oil/canvas (50x76cm 20x30in) Mystic
CT 2000

$2 600 - €2 486 - **£1 583** - FF16 308
Dunes and Shore Oil/panel (24.5x34cm 9x13in)
Boston MA 1999

WALDHAUSER Anton 1835-1913 **[17]**

$924 - €875 - **£576** - FF5 737
**View of Hradcany Castle without Saint Vitus
Cathedral** Oil/canvas (31x25.5cm 12x10in) Praha 2001

WALDMÜLLER Ferdinand Georg 1793-1865 **[85]**

$104 890 - €123 543 - **£73 780** - FF810 390
Stilleben mit Austern, Fischen und Früchten
Oil/panel (48x38cm 18x14in) Wien 2000

$15 971 - €16 361 - **£9 856** - FF107 324
Bildnis des Lukas von Martinelli Oil/panel
(21x16.5cm 8x6in) Düsseldorf 2000

WALDO Samuel Lovett 1783-1861 **[7]**

$1 300 - €1 161 - **£795** - FF7 618
Portrait of a Woman Oil/canvas (53x41cm 21x16in)
Boston MA 1999

WALDORP Anthonie 1803-1866 **[75]**

$4 310 - €5 011 - **£3 025** - FF32 868
Marktplatz Oil/panel (35.5x46.5cm 13x18in) Hamburg
2001

$2 629 - €2 269 - **£1 586** - FF14 883
A calm Oil/panel (14x19cm 5x7in) Amsterdam 1999

📖 **$1 007** - €1 134 - **£694** - FF7 441
A Fishing Village with Villagers Conversing in the Foreground Watercolour (24x32.5cm 9x12in)
Amsterdam 2000

WALDORP Jan Gerard 1740-1808 [4]
😊 **$3 028** - €3 579 - **£2 146** - FF23 477
Dame mit Laute Oil/panel (33.5x27cm 13x10in)
Stuttgart 2000

WALDRON Charles J. 1836-1891 [2]
😊 **$18 000** - €16 600 - **£11 008** - FF104 999
The Downeaster «Rochester» Oil/canvas
(61x91.5cm 24x36in) New-York 1999

WALDRUM Harold Joe 1934 [11]
▦ **$1 000** - €863 - **£601** - FF5 659
Ocasio del sol en estio, #22/71 Linocut (59x59cm 23x23in) Santa-Fe NM 1998

WALE John Porter XIX-XX [7]
📖 **$1 603** - €1 886 - **£1 150** - FF12 372
Carnations Watercolour/paper (35.5x25.5cm 13x10in)
London 2001

WALERY act.c.1875-c.1920 [5]
📷 **$962** - €1 067 - **£668** - FF7 000
L'Après-midi d'un Faune Tirage argentique
(15.5x9.5cm 6x3in) Paris 2001

WALES James 1747-1795 [3]
▦ **$1 690** - €1 985 - **£1 200** - FF13 021
Bombay Harbour Aquatint in colors (37.5x64.5cm 14x25in) London 2000

WALFORD Astrid XX [5]
📖 **$1 141** - €1 331 - **£800** - FF8 728
Little Miss Pink Watercolour (24.5x15.5cm 9x6in)
London 2000

WALFORD Howard Neville 1864-1940 [15]
📖 **$374** - €319 - **£220** - FF2 095
Country Lane Watercolour/paper (24x35.5cm 9x13in)
Godalming, Surrey 1998

WALISZEWSKI Zygmunt 1897-1936 [29]
😊 **$5 756** - €5 588 - **£3 585** - FF36 655
Bohemian Encampment Oil/panel (40.2x64cm 15x25in) Warszawa 1999
📖 **$4 670** - €3 973 - **£2 785** - FF26 063
Children Watercolour (29x41.5cm 11x16in) Warszawa 1998

WALKE Anne Fearon 1888-1965 [9]
😊 **$5 029** - €4 250 - **£3 000** - FF27 881
Christ Mocked Oil/canvas (91x78cm 36x31in)
Penzance, Cornwall 1998

WALKE Henry 1808-1896 [1]
📖 **$4 000** - €4 574 - **£2 746** - FF30 003
The Landing at Tabasco Watercolour/paper
(33x55cm 13x22in) New-York 2000

WALKER Agnès E. act.1887-1900 [1]
😊 **$14 218** - €16 042 - **£10 000** - FF105 228
The Tea Party Oil/canvas (138.5x107cm 54x42in)
London 2001

WALKER Alexander XIX-XX [1]
▦ **$717** - €754 - **£450** - FF4 945
Country Village Etching (7x8.5cm 2x3in) London 2000

WALKER Arthur Georges 1861-1939 [5]
🗿 **$3 184** - €3 083 - **£2 000** - FF20 225
Bust of Captain John Ball (?) Bronze (H56cm H22in) London 1999

WALKER Bernard Eyre 1886-? [17]
📖 **$462** - €460 - **£280** - FF3 017
Scafell Pike Watercolour/paper (33x48cm 12x18in)
London 2001

WALKER Charles Alvah 1848-1920 [1]
😊 **$1 900** - €2 169 - **£1 339** - FF14 230
Along a Maine River Oil/panel (33x25cm 12x9in)
Boston MA 2001

WALKER Charles J. XIX [4]
😊 **$4 209** - €5 006 - **£3 000** - FF32 835
«Cricket on Hampstead Heath» Oil/canvas
(31x51.5cm 12x20in) London 2000

WALKER Edmund c.1820-c.1890 [5]
📖 **$459** - €515 - **£320** - FF3 378
Parade of the Fusileer Guards at Buckingham Palace after G.H.Thomas Color lithograph
(42x53cm 16x20in) Leyburn, North Yorkshire 2001

WALKER Ethel, Dame 1861-1951 [106]
😊 **$1 600** - €1 934 - **£1 117** - FF12 685
Girl with Flowers Oil/canvas (50x40cm 20x16in)
Philadelphia PA 2000
😊 **$768** - €645 - **£450** - FF4 231
Donkeys Oil/board (27x34.5cm 10x13in) Cape Town 1998
📖 **$452** - €496 - **£300** - FF3 254
Portrait Study of Mrs Marden King, Niece of the Artist, Half-Length Pencil/paper (28x22cm 11x8in)
London 2000

WALKER Frederick 1840-1875 [15]
📖 **$4 274** - €4 969 - **£3 000** - FF32 593
The Chicken Run Watercolour (19.5x30cm 7x11in)
Billingshurst, West-Sussex 2001

WALKER Henry George XX [11]
▦ **$111** - €108 - **£70** - FF707
Fishing Fleet Aquatint (17x27cm 7x11in) Par,
Cornwall 1999

WALKER Henry Oliver 1843-1929 [5]
😊 **$1 600** - €1 371 - **£961** - FF8 991
Farm Scene Oil/canvas (50x66cm 20x26in) Cincinnati OH 1998

WALKER Horatio 1858-1938 [33]
😊 **$7 410** - €8 644 - **£5 293** - FF56 701
Automne; Ile d'Orléans Huile/toile/panneau
(49x40cm 19x15in) Montréal 2000
😊 **$1 366** - €1 311 - **£856** - FF8 600
At the Trough Watercolour/paper (40x33cm 15x12in)
Montréal 2000

WALKER Inez Nathaniel 1910-1990 [14]
📖 **$1 100** - €918 - **£645** - FF6 024
Two Men and a Woman : Three Portraits
Coloured pencils/paper (35.5x21.5cm 13x8in) New-York 1998

WALKER J.F. ?-c.1889 [2]
😊 **$33 116** - €36 333 - **£22 000** - FF238 326
Lady Clifford-Constable driving a Carriage with her Husband Sir Talbot Oil/canvas (68x105.5cm 26x41in) London 2000

WALKER James 1819-1889 [3]
😊 **$7 000** - €5 997 - **£4 208** - FF39 337
«Blackhead» and West Point Cadet on the Hudson Oil/canvas (40x48cm 16x19in) Cleveland OH 1998

WALKER James Alexander 1841-1898 [18]
😊 **$14 196** - €15 239 - **£9 500** - FF99 959
A Cavalier Oil/canvas (46.5x38.5cm 18x15in) London 2000

W

WALKER James William 1831-1898 [19]
🖎 **$302** - €262 - **£180** - FF1 717
Boats and Figures by a Harbour Wall
Watercolour/paper (17x24cm 6x9in) Chester 1998

WALKER John 1939 [25]
😀 **$8 500** - €9 863 - **£5 868** - FF64 696
Oceania III Oil/canvas (244.5x305.5cm 96x120in)
New-York 2000
▥ **$2 750** - €3 063 - **£1 798** - FF20 092
Moss Glenn Falls III Monotype (158x106cm
62x41in) New-York 2000

WALKER John Crampton 1890-1942 [10]
😀 **$1 812** - €1 905 - **£1 136** - FF12 493
Bridge and Cottages in a Western Landscape
Oil/canvas (45x60cm 17x23in) Dublin 2000

WALKER John Doddy 1863-1925 [25]
🖎 **$322** - €304 - **£200** - FF1 994
Dort from the Water Tower Watercolour/paper
(25x37cm 10x14in) Little-Lane, Ilkley 1999

WALKER John Eaton c.1820-c.1880 [9]
😀 **$1 500** - €1 422 - **£937** - FF9 327
Portrait of a Girl in Window Oil/canvas (50x40cm
20x16in) New-Orleans LA 1999

WALKER John Hanson 1844-1933 [20]
😀 **$6 403** - €7 440 - **£4 500** - FF48 803
**Portrait of Lewin Edward Cadogan/Portrait of
Sophie Beatrix Cadongan** Oil/canvas (66x56cm
25x22in) London 2001

WALKER Joseph Francis XIX [2]
😀 **$20 290** - €19 510 - **£12 500** - FF127 980
Mrs Talbot Constable in her Carriage Oil/canvas
(68x106cm 26x41in) London 1999

WALKER Kara 1969 [8]
😀 **$15 000** - €14 084 - **£9 294** - FF92 386
Breach Acrylic (152.5x132cm 60x51in) New-York
1999
$35 000 - €39 134 - **£23 593** - FF256 704
Equality Mixed media/paper (120.5x106.5cm 47x41in)
New-York 2000

WALKER Lewis Emory 1825-1880 [2]
📷 **$2 400** - €2 782 - **£1 700** - FF18 252
Lincoln, Abraham Albumen print (8x17cm 3x6in)
New-York 2000

WALKER Marcella 1872-1901 [3]
🖎 **$4 037** - €4 462 - **£2 800** - FF29 268
The Pearl Necklace Watercolour (24.5x16cm 9x6in)
London 2001

WALKER Robert 1607-1658 [5]
😀 **$119 329** - €102 314 - **£70 000** - FF671 139
General Sir Arthur Hesilrige, 2nd BT (d.1661)
Oil/canvas (124.5x99cm 49x38in) Leicestershire 1998

WALKER Robert Hollands act.1882-1920 [60]
🖎 **$469** - €505 - **£320** - FF3 312
**A Young Boy fishing beside a Canal with Ducks
nearby and a Village** Watercolour (20x32.5cm
7x12in) West-Yorshire 2001

WALKER T. Dart 1869-1914 [5]
🖎 **$1 750** - €1 929 - **£1 164** - FF12 651
**Home from Europe: The Customs Ordeal on the
Pier** Gouache/paper (34x54cm 13x21in) Portsmouth
NH 2000

WALKER William 1878-1961 [3]
▥ **$442** - €463 - **£280** - FF3 038
St.Sulpice, Paris Etching (34x25cm 13x9in)
Edinburgh 2000

WALKER William Aiken c.1838-1921 [233]
😀 **$7 000** - €6 588 - **£4 352** - FF43 213
African Man with Basket of Cotton Oil/board
(57x41cm 22x16in) Delaware OH 1999
😀 **$8 250** - €9 050 - **£5 603** - FF59 361
An Old Cotton Picker with Walking Stick
Oil/board (20x10cm 8x4in) New-Orleans LA 2000
🖎 **$1 800** - €1 762 - **£1 150** - FF11 560
On Old South Road Pencil/paper (11x18cm 4x7in)
Asheville NC 1999

WALKER William Eyre 1847-1930 [29]
🖎 **$480** - €455 - **£300** - FF2 985
On the River Wey, Surrey Watercolour/paper
(24x35cm 9x13in) Crewkerne, Somerset 1999

WALKIN Colin XX [2]
▥ **$484** - €467 - **£300** - FF3 065
«**The Cruel Sea**» Poster (200.5x101.5cm 78x39in)
London 1999

WALKLEY David Birdsey 1849-1934 [12]
😀 **$4 250** - €4 012 - **£2 642** - FF26 320
The Hunting Party Oil/canvas (50x68cm 20x27in)
Milford CT 1999
😀 **$1 100** - €1 201 - **£708** - FF7 880
Old Mill Oil/canvas (43x33cm 17x13in) Mystic CT
2000

WALKOWITZ Abraham 1880-1965 [231]
🖎 **$850** - €966 - **£582** - FF6 334
Movement Study Pencil/paper (35x21cm 13x8in)
New-York 2000
▥ **$600** - €681 - **£410** - FF4 469
Harbor View with Houses Monotype (15x23cm
5x9in) New-York 2000

WALL Alfred Bryan 1872-1937 [19]
😀 **$2 100** - €2 019 - **£1 296** - FF13 247
Landscape with Sheep and Buildings Oil/can-
vas/board (55x40cm 22x16in) Pittsburgh PA 1999
😀 **$1 100** - €1 282 - **£761** - FF8 411
Landscape with Sheep Oil/panel (26x34cm
10x13in) Watertown MA 2000

WALL Alfred S. 1825-1896 [2]
😀 **$3 200** - €3 077 - **£1 975** - FF20 186
Still Life with Grapes Oil/canvas (43x33cm 16x12in)
Boston MA 1999

WALL BAKE van den Sophie Christina 1866-1915
[2]
😀 **$1 947** - €2 301 - **£1 380** - FF15 092
Vor dem ersten Läuten Tempera/Karton
(25.5x43.5cm 10x17in) Ahlden 2000

WALL Jeff 1946 [19]
🖎 **$77 300** - €86 582 - **£53 708** - FF567 938
Green Rectangle Construction (145x178x17cm
57x70x6in) New-York 2001
📷 **$42 000** - €47 043 - **£29 181** - FF308 582
«**Blind Window 1**» Photograph (106.5x132.5cm
41x52in) New-York 2000

WALL William Allen 1801-1885 [10]
😀 **$3 900** - €4 186 - **£2 657** - FF27 461
Coastal View Oil/canvas (51x86.5cm 20x34in) Boston
MA 2001
🖎 **$2 000** - €2 147 - **£1 338** - FF14 082
Trees by a River Gouache/paper (24x32cm 9x12in)
Philadelphia PA 2000

WALL William Coventry 1810-1886 [9]
😀 **$11 000** - €10 273 - **£6 789** - FF67 386
Landscape Scene Oil/canvas (38x63.5cm 14x25in)
Boston MA 1999

WALL William Guy 1792-c.1864 **[15]**
- $5 431 - €5 841 - **£3 701** - FF38 313
  Blarney Castle near Cork, Ireland Oil/canvas (56x76cm 22x29in) Dublin 2001
- $852 - €914 - **£581** - FF5 996
  Cottage in the Wood Watercolour/paper (29x35.5cm 11x13in) Dublin 2001

WALLA August 1936-2001 **[23]**
- $1 083 - €1 017 - **£669** - FF6 673
  «Walla Ruusso, 1993, mit Donau!» Indian ink (34x19.2cm 13x7in) Wien 1999

WALLACE Harold Frank 1881-1962 **[37]**
- $964 - €898 - **£600** - FF5 892
  Tainted Wing/A Stag and Deer in a Loch in a Highland Landscape Watercolour (37x52cm 14x20in) London 1999

WALLACE Harry Draper 1892-1977 **[11]**
- $194 - €227 - **£135** - FF1 487
  Landscape with Tree Etching (11x11.5cm 4x4in) Toronto 2000

WALLACE James 1872-1911 **[11]**
- $1 061 - €1 178 - **£740** - FF7 729
  Harvest Time Wooded Landscape with cottages in the Middle Distance Oil/canvas (90x70cm 35x27in) Scarborough, North-Yorshire 2001

WALLACE John 1841-1905 **[32]**
- $780 - €911 - **£550** - FF5 974
  Scotsman Lighting a Cigarette/Royal Highlanders Blackwatch Piper Watercolour/paper (45.5x32.5cm 17x12in) Toronto 2000

WALLACE Marjorie XX **[4]**
- $532 - €521 - **£337** - FF3 416
  Street in Jerusalem Gouache/paper (52x63cm 20x24in) Cape Town 1999

WALLAERT A. XX **[1]**
- $12 880 - €12 196 - **£8 000** - FF80 000
  La couture dans le jardin Huile/toile (93x118cm 36x46in) Paris 1999

WALLAERT Pierre Joseph 1753-c.1812 **[11]**
- $17 000 - €18 651 - **£11 293** - FF122 345
  Shipwreck in Stormy Seas with Survivors on a Rocky outcrop, Lighthouse Oil/canvas (98.5x137cm 38x53in) New-York 2000
- $12 613 - €13 344 - **£8 000** - FF87 533
  River Landscape with Elegant Figures resting and reading Oil/canvas (59.5x97cm 23x38in) London 2000
- $18 920 - €20 017 - **£12 000** - FF131 300
  Port Scene with Figures loading a Boat/Coastal Scene with Figures Oil/canvas/board (25x28cm 9x11in) London 2000

WALLANDER Alf, Alfred 1862-1914 **[36]**
- $480 - €448 - **£296** - FF2 937
  Insjölandskap Akvarell/papper (34x15cm 13x5in) Stockholm 1999

WALLANDER Josef Wilhelm 1821-1888 **[24]**
- $2 580 - €2 904 - **£1 777** - FF19 052
  Erik Engströms lumphandel Oil/canvas (26x20cm 10x7in) Stockholm 2001

WALLAT Paul 1879-1966 **[20]**
- $652 - €697 - **£444** - FF4 570
  Redningsbåd i rum sö Oil/canvas (69x98cm 27x38in) Vejle 2001

WALLÉN Gustaf Theodor 1868-1948 **[10]**
- $1 989 - €1 893 - **£1 244** - FF12 420
  Insjölandskap Oil/canvas (47x66cm 18x25in) Stockholm 1999

WALLER Arthur Bassett XIX-XX **[8]**
- $448 - €484 - **£310** - FF3 177
  Dartmoor Ponies/Dartmoor Watercolour (25x35cm 9x13in) West-Midlands 2001

WALLER Frank 1842-1923 **[12]**
- $3 621 - €4 202 - **£2 500** - FF27 564
  By the Ruins at Sunset Oil/canvas (51x76.5cm 20x30in) London 2000

WALLER Lucy XIX-XX **[4]**
- $5 500 - €5 990 - **£3 787** - FF39 293
  «Turk» Oil/canvas (51x76cm 20x29in) New-York 2001

WALLER Mary Lemon ?-1931 **[6]**
- $1 300 - €1 554 - **£893** - FF10 194
  Young Girl in a Blue Dress Oil/canvas (86x54cm 34x21in) Chicago IL 2000

WALLER Mervyn Napier 1894-1972 **[12]**
- $349 - €331 - **£217** - FF2 168
  Cook's fatigue H.M.T.S Medic, Voyage to England Ink/paper (40.5x28.5cm 15x11in) Malvern, Victoria 1999
- $324 - €307 - **£196** - FF2 011
  The ring Linocut (27.5x21cm 10x8in) Sydney 1999

WALLER Samuel Edmund 1850-1903 **[14]**
- $19 000 - €18 958 - **£11 565** - FF124 356
  In his Father's Footsteps Oil/canvas (117x134.5cm 46x52in) New-York 2000
- $3 647 - €4 338 - **£2 600** - FF28 457
  Circumstantial Evidence Oil/canvas (68.5x101cm 26x39in) Bath 2000

WALLERSTEIN G. XIX **[1]**
- $3 920 - €4 116 - **£2 600** - FF27 000
  Déchargement du bateau Huile/toile (88x107cm 34x42in) Paris 2000

WALLERT Axel 1890-1962 **[21]**
- $2 427 - €2 759 - **£1 705** - FF18 095
  Adam och Eva Oil/canvas (163x115cm 64x45in) Stockholm 2001
- $768 - €697 - **£473** - FF4 571
  Strandbild med sittande nakenmodell Oil/canvas (54x46cm 21x18in) Stockholm 1999

WALLET Taf 1902 **[71]**
- $2 453 - €2 727 - **£1 716** - FF17 886
  Nature morte au brochet Huile/toile (100x125cm 39x49in) Bruxelles 2001
- $832 - €838 - **£518** - FF5 500
  Roses Huile/toile (93x65cm 36x25in) Lyon 2000
- $663 - €694 - **£439** - FF4 552
  La digue à Blankenberge Huile/panneau (16x34cm 6x13in) Bruxelles 2000

WALLIN Anders 1953 **[10]**
- $1 007 - €1 175 - **£690** - FF7 710
  Red Dot Acrylic/panel (101x80cm 39x31in) Stockholm 2000

WALLIN David 1876-1957 **[98]**
- $443 - €443 - **£277** - FF2 905
  Ung flicka vid skogstjärn Oil/canvas (66x50cm 25x19in) Uppsala 1999
- $246 - €281 - **£169** - FF1 843
  Målaren och modellen Oil/panel (34.5x27.5cm 13x10in) Stockholm 2000

W

WALLIN Ellis 1888-1972 **[85]**

$362 - €372 - **£224** - FF2 437
Chrysanthemum och frukter Oil/canvas (65x54cm 25x21in) Stockholm 2000

WALLINGER Mark 1959 **[5]**

$18 774 - €20 458 - **£13 000** - FF134 196
Brown's (Mr Ronald Brown) Oil/canvas (110x110cm 43x43in) London 2001

$20 173 - €21 655 - **£13 500** - FF142 046
Fathers and Sons I/Great Nephew II, Shergar Oil/canvas (81x65cm 31x25in) London 2000

WALLIS Alfred 1855-1942 **[82]**

$34 811 - €29 698 - **£21 000** - FF194 804
Ship and Lighthouse Oil/board (30.5x37.5cm 12x14in) London 1998

$12 696 - €14 244 - **£8 800** - FF93 436
Boat with Lighthouse Pencil (16.5x21.5cm 6x8in) London 2001

WALLIS Joshua 1789-1862 **[9]**

$1 600 - €2 073 - **£1 200** - FF13 600
Paesaggio fluviale Acquarello/carta (57x89cm 22x35in) Prato 2000

WALLNER Thure 1888-1965 **[280]**

$8 832 - €9 524 - **£5 928** - FF62 472
Fiskgjusebo Oil/canvas (200x150cm 78x59in) Stockholm 2000

$2 379 - €2 798 - **£1 723** - FF18 356
Räv i vinterlandskap Oil/canvas (46x61cm 18x24in) Stockholm 2001

$1 061 - €1 226 - **£742** - FF8 039
Fiskgjuse med aborre Oil/panel (27x35cm 10x13in) Stockholm 2001

WALLQUIST Einar 1896-1980 **[9]**

$236 - €233 - **£145** - FF1 529
Höstlandskap med insjö Akvarell/papper (28x34cm 11x13in) Stockholm 1999

WALLS William 1860-1942 **[46]**

$2 000 - €2 271 - **£1 403** - FF14 900
Trout Oil/canvas (45.5x61cm 17x24in) New-York 2001

$1 203 - €1 212 - **£750** - FF7 952
Zebra and its offsprings Oil/canvas (24x33cm 9x13in) Dorchester, Dorset 2000

$419 - €394 - **£262** - FF2 584
A Lioness and her Cubs Watercolour (19x28cm 7x11in) London 1999

WALMSLEY James Ulric 1860-1954 **[13]**

$423 - €494 - **£300** - FF3 239
Children on rocks looking to sea Watercolour/paper (53x44cm 21x17in) Whitby, Yorks 2001

WALMSLEY Thomas 1763-1806 **[31]**

$3 741 - €4 191 - **£2 600** - FF27 492
The Dargle in Flood Oil/canvas (43x60.5cm 16x23in) London 2001

$850 - €872 - **£531** - FF5 721
Wooded Landscape with a Man Beside a River Watercolour/paper (33x46.5cm 12x18in) New-York 2000

WALRAVEN Jan 1827-1863 **[27]**

$4 000 - €3 451 - **£2 404** - FF22 637
Farm Life Oil/canvas (63.5x51cm 25x20in) Boston MA 1998

$3 823 - €3 979 - **£2 400** - FF26 099
Mother and Child in an Interior Oil/panel (40x32cm 16x13in) London 2000

WALRECHT Bernardus H.D., Ben 1911 **[3]**

$3 677 - €3 630 - **£2 236** - FF23 812
Busy Street Scene in Groningen Oil/canvas (68x96cm 26x37in) Amsterdam 2000

WALS Goffredo, Gottfried c.1600-1638/40 **[5]**

$5 252 - €6 098 - **£3 704** - FF40 000
Tobie et l'Ange dans un paysage Huile/cuivre (9.5x13cm 3x5in) Paris 2001

WALSCAPELLE van Jacob 1644-1727 **[14]**

$36 885 - €43 972 - **£26 298** - FF288 435
Blumenstilleben Öl/Leinwand (66.5x53.5cm 26x21in) Köln 2000

$320 000 - €342 300 - **£218 176** - FF2 245 344
A la façon de Venise, a Halved Pomgranate, Grapes and Hazelnuts Oil/panel (37.5x34cm 14x13in) New-York 2001

WALSER Gabriel 1695-1776 **[9]**

$266 - €309 - **£183** - FF2 024
Der Früstliche Abt von St.Gallen und die Stadt St.Gallen Kupferstich (50.5x61cm 19x24in) Luzern 2000

WALSER Karl 1877-1943 **[24]**

$3 998 - €4 704 - **£2 822** - FF30 855
Nachtspaziergang Oil/panel (50x63cm 19x24in) Berlin 2001

$106 - €102 - **£65** - FF670
Wanderers Nachtlied Lithographie (28x22.5cm 11x8in) Bielefeld 1999

WALSETH Niels 1914 **[99]**

$393 - €361 - **£243** - FF2 366
Harvest Time Huile/toile (40.5x51cm 15x20in) Montréal 1998

WALSHE Judith Caulfield XX **[2]**

$113 - €127 - **£77** - FF832
Landscape with Cottages Watercolour/paper (14x22cm 5x8in) Dublin 2000

WALTENSPERGER Charles E. 1871-1931 **[50]**

$2 000 - €1 869 - **£1 246** - FF12 257
Woman with Lantern Oil/canvas (45x35cm 18x14in) Mystic CT 1999

$600 - €552 - **£360** - FF3 622
The Old Block House at Fort Mac Oil/panel (30x40cm 12x16in) Detroit MI 1999

WALTER & BERGÉ Almaric & Henry XIX-XX **[2]**

$3 480 - €3 887 - **£2 358** - FF25 500
Caméléon Sculpture verre (H8cm H3in) Saint-Germain-en-Laye 2000

WALTER Alice 1853-? **[1]**

$3 930 - €4 360 - **£2 736** - FF28 602
Frühlingsstilleben Öl/Leinwand (72.5x52.5cm 28x20in) Wien 2001

WALTER Almaric 1859-1942 **[21]**

$3 679 - €3 111 - **£2 200** - FF20 408
Mouse in Shads of Cornflowers, after a model by H.Bergé Sculpture verre (6.5x9.5cm 2x3in) London 1998

WALTER Emma act.1855-1891 **[17]**

$419 - €463 - **£280** - FF3 034
Still Life with Fruit Watercolour/paper (28x36cm 11x14in) Little-Lane, Ilkley 2000

WALTER Henry 1786/90-1849 **[2]**

$1 476 - €1 352 - **£900** - FF8 870
Vue prise de la Tour de l'Eglise de St Brides, after Thomas Allom Lithograph (46.5x69cm 18x27in) London 1999

WALTER Martha 1875-1976 **[113]**
$46 000 - €54 993 - **£31 730** - FF360 732
Portrait of Miss J: Study in Gray Oil/canvas (194x110cm 76x43in) Milford CT 2000
$8 000 - €8 755 - **£5 518** - FF57 430
Portrait of a Baby in White Oil/canvas (66x53.5cm 25x21in) New-York 2001
$7 000 - €6 557 - **£4 303** - FF43 008
«Shady Spot in the Melon Market, North Africa» Oil/board (22x26.5cm 8x10in) New-York 1999
$4 000 - €3 712 - **£2 401** - FF24 350
Swimming Pool Watercolour/paper (25x33cm 10x13in) Milford CT 1999

WALTER OF BRISTOL Joseph 1783-1856 **[30]**
$7 716 - €9 177 - **£5 500** - FF60 198
View of Bristol Docks Oil/canvas (68x100cm 26x39in) Bath 2000
$2 944 - €3 161 - **£2 000** - FF20 732
Fisher Folk on the Quayside at Mousehole, Cornwall Oil/panel (18.5x29.5cm 7x11in) London 2001

WALTER Ottokar 1853-1904 **[3]**
$30 000 - €28 460 - **£18 225** - FF186 687
At the Circus Oil/panel (44.5x61cm 17x24in) New-York 1999

WALTER-KURAU Johann 1869-1932 **[13]**
$4 259 - €4 090 - **£2 625** - FF26 831
Blühender Baum Öl/Leinwand (63.5x73.5cm 25x28in) München 1999
$1 260 - €1 227 - **£774** - FF8 049
Strasse und Häuser Öl/Papier (21.5x25cm 8x9in) Berlin 1999
$1 058 - €870 - **£614** - FF5 704
Rückenakt Monotype (36.5x30cm 14x11in) Berlin 1998

WALTERS Curt 1950 **[6]**
$7 000 - €7 948 - **£4 863** - FF52 136
Canyon de Chelly Oil/canvas (71x91cm 28x36in) Dallas TX 2001

WALTERS Evan 1893-? **[13]**
$833 - €767 - **£500** - FF5 029
Daffodils Oil/canvas (50x40cm 19x15in) Glamorgan 1999

WALTERS George Stanfield 1838-1924 **[209]**
$3 000 - €2 598 - **£1 839** - FF17 044
Fishing Boats in a Harbor Oil/canvas (33x51cm 12x20in) New-York 1999
$1 224 - €1 340 - **£844** - FF8 792
On the Medway near Rochester Oil/canvas (22x35cm 9x14in) Vancouver, BC. 2001
$611 - €666 - **£420** - FF4 366
Off the Fishing Grounds Watercolour (60x30cm 23x11in) Billingshurst, West-Sussex 2001

WALTERS Gordon 1919-1995 **[14]**
$153 178 - €171 695 - **£107 122** - FF1 126 244
Tirangi II Acrylic (122x91.5cm 48x36in) Auckland 2001
$1 641 - €1 725 - **£1 080** - FF11 316
Untitled Composition No.2 Acrylic/paper (38.5x28cm 15x11in) Auckland 2000
$6 760 - €7 025 - **£4 239** - FF46 082
Tirangi 2 Indian ink/paper (31x23cm 12x9in) Auckland 2000
$564 - €633 - **£394** - FF4 149
«Then» Screenprint (45x57cm 17x22in) Auckland 2001

WALTERS Miles 1774-1849 **[11]**
$8 984 - €9 417 - **£6 000** - FF61 773
The P.S.Superb Inward Bound off Flatholm Island, in Bristol Channel Oil/canvas (44.5x68.5cm 17x26in) London 2001

WALTERS Samuel 1811-1882 **[43]**
$38 757 - €33 362 - **£23 000** - FF218 838
The Iron Screw Barque «African» Oil/canvas (91.5x152cm 36x59in) London 1998
$19 713 - €19 671 - **£12 000** - FF129 031
The Champion of Jersey Oil/canvas (65x94.5cm 25x37in) London 2000
$4 518 - €4 339 - **£2 800** - FF28 461
The Approaching Squall Oil/board (29.5x46.5cm 11x18in) London 1999

WALTERS Wesley 1928 **[6]**
$986 - €917 - **£609** - FF6 018
Nude Pastel/paper (90.5x68cm 35x26in) Melbourne 1999

WALTHER Carl 1880-1954 **[48]**
$186 - €174 - **£112** - FF1 140
Mein Tafelklavier Pencil/paper (26.9x23cm 10x9in) Berlin 1999
$38 - €36 - **£23** - FF234
Damenporträt Radierung (36x27cm 14x10in) Leipzig 1999

WALTHER Franz Erhard 1939 **[37]**
$604 - €562 - **£371** - FF3 689
Anspannung-Entspannung Mischtechnik/Papier (30x21cm 11x8in) Hamburg 1999
$173 - €206 - **£123** - FF1 353
Hauptraum-Nebenraum Serigraph in colors (46x50cm 18x19in) Hamburg 2000

WALTHER Friedrich Karl 1905-1981 **[14]**
$1 077 - €1 125 - **£682** - FF7 378
Die Andreaskirche in Krakau II Öl/Leinwand (73x92cm 28x36in) München 2000

WALTHER Jean 1910 **[12]**
$607 - €567 - **£374** - FF3 720
«Knsm Koninklijke Nederlandsche Stoomboot Maatschappij» Poster (62.5x100cm 24x39in) Oostwoud 1999

WALTHER Ludwig XIX-XX **[2]**
$3 715 - €3 964 - **£2 480** - FF26 000
Femme nue, bras levés Sculpture (H21cm H8in) Paris 2000

WALTHER Pan 1921-1987 **[7]**
$1 141 - €1 278 - **£793** - FF8 384
Hochwasser Vintage gelatin silver print (28.5x22.5cm 11x8in) Köln 2001

WALTHÉRY François 1942 **[19]**
$228 - €244 - **£155** - FF1 600
Natacha Mine plomb (25x15cm 9x5in) Paris 2001

WALTON Allan 1892-1948 **[9]**
$1 687 - €1 625 - **£1 050** - FF10 659
Rowing to Shore Oil/canvas (40.5x51cm 15x20in) London 1999

WALTON Constance 1866-1960 **[12]**
$2 725 - €2 574 - **£1 700** - FF16 886
Roses Watercolour (74x52cm 29x20in) Perthshire 1999

WALTON Edward Arthur 1860-1922 **[28]**
$8 638 - €8 629 - **£5 400** - FF56 604
The Long Pool Oil/canvas (78x102cm 30x40in) Edinburgh 1999

WALTON

$8 619 - €7 436 - **£5 200** - FF48 780
The Morning Ride Watercolour (18x21.5cm 7x8in)
London 1998

WALTON Elijah 1832-1880 **[23]**
$563 - €486 - **£340** - FF3 189
Boatmen in an Alpine Landscape Watercolour
(17x23.5cm 6x9in) London 1998

WALTON Frank 1840-1928 **[41]**
$3 500 - €3 398 - **£2 162** - FF22 289
Wooded Landscape Oil/board (83x116cm 33x46in)
Englewood NJ 1999
$666 - €701 - **£440** - FF4 600
The Land's End, Cornwall Watercolour (29x44.5cm
11x17in) London 2000

WALTON Henry c.1746-1813 **[14]**
$79 960 - €76 997 - **£50 000** - FF505 065
**A Grey and Bay Hunter with Dogs and a Groom
in a Landscape** Oil/canvas (73.5x114cm 28x44in)
London 1999
$10 072 - €9 800 - **£6 200** - FF64 286
**Portrait of Lady Roche (D.1831), wearing a Grey
Dress** Oil/panel (23x18.5cm 9x7in) London 1999

WALTON Henry 1804-1865 **[4]**
$8 500 - €7 336 - **£5 129** - FF48 121
Daniel B.Reynolds, age 12 years
Watercolour/paper (21x17cm 8x6in) New-York 1999

WALTON Henry XIX **[4]**
$9 500 - €7 799 - **£5 585** - FF52 341
«Julia, Jane, Chambers Age 13 yrs»
Watercolour/paper (29x19cm 11x7in) Boston MA 1998

WALTON William XX **[7]**
$354 - €340 - **£220** - FF2 230
**Vue de Québec, prise de la pointe de Lévi,
d'après R.Auchmaty Sproule** Lithographie
(32x38cm 12x14in) Montréal 1999

WAMBINI Henry c.1922/34 **[3]**
$1 055 - €1 129 - **£695** - FF7 409
Sharp Hills of Tickalara Mixed media (60x90cm
23x35in) Woollahra, Sydney 1999

WAN SHOUQI 1603-1652 **[3]**
$16 000 - €13 930 - **£9 539** - FF91 376
The Eighteen Monks Ink (59.5x40.5cm 23x15in)
New-York 1998

WANAMBI Dundiwuy 1936-1996 **[5]**
$14 471 - €13 960 - **£9 145** - FF91 572
The Wagilag Sisters Sculpture, wood (H120cm
H47in) Melbourne 1999

WANDEL Sigurd 1875-1947 **[12]**
$495 - €563 - **£339** - FF3 361
**Solbeskinnet stueinteriör med laesende dreng
og barn i en vugge** Oil/canvas (54x65cm 21x25in)
Vejle 2000

WANDELAAR Jan 1690-1759 **[5]**
$8 500 - €7 481 - **£5 174** - FF49 073
**B.S. Albinus, Tabulae Sceleti et Musculorum
Corporis Humani** Engraving (72x54cm 28x21in)
New-Orleans LA 1999

WANDESFORDE Juan Buckingham 1817-1902 **[13]**
$26 000 - €28 534 - **£16 741** - FF187 168
Blooming Cactus Oil/canvas (51x35.5cm 20x13in)
Beverly-Hills CA 2000
$2 200 - €2 426 - **£1 489** - FF15 915
**Indians Walking Along a Winter Path/Indian
Encampment by the Lake** Watercolour (12.5x8.5cm
4x3in) New-York 2000

WANDSCHEER Marie 1856-1936 **[13]**
$592 - €544 - **£366** - FF3 571
An Oriental Beauty in an interior Oil/canvas
(21x28cm 8x11in) Amsterdam 1999

WANE Harold 1879-1900 **[3]**
$759 - €809 - **£500** - FF5 305
**Harbour Scene with Paddle Steamer and other
Vessels** Watercolour (47.5x59cm 18x23in)
Billingshurst, West-Sussex 2000

WANE Richard 1852-1904 **[40]**
$1 586 - €1 865 - **£1 100** - FF12 232
Coastal view, a Fisherman Cleaning his Cath
Oil/canvas (44x82cm 17x32in) Carlisle, Cumbria 2000
$345 - €332 - **£220** - FF2 176
Cattle Watering at a Lake Watercolour/paper
(20.5x30.5cm 8x12in) London 1999

WANG Aage 1879-1959 **[23]**
$1 386 - €1 345 - **£856** - FF8 823
Badepiger på Skagens Strand Oil/canvas
(66x98cm 25x38in) Vejle 1999
$511 - €563 - **£341** - FF3 694
To unge kvinder på stranden Oil/canvas (34x25cm
13x9in) Vejle 2000

WANG AO 1450-1524 **[1]**
$514 800 - €488 203 - **£313 200** - FF3 202 400
Two Mountains at Lake Tai Ink/paper
(30.5x289.5cm 12x113in) Hong-Kong 1999

WANG CHEN 1720-1797 **[10]**
$6 435 - €6 103 - **£3 915** - FF40 030
Gentleman Viewing Waterfall Ink/paper (36x218cm
14x85in) Hong-Kong 1999

WANG CHONG 1494-1533 **[2]**
$153 840 - €180 817 - **£106 680** - FF1 186 080
**Ten Poems of Xie Lingyun (1385-1433) in Cao
Shu** Ink (29x383cm 11x150in) Hong-Kong 2000

WANG CHONGJIE c.1636-1667 **[1]**
$25 160 - €23 876 - **£15 288** - FF156 615
Jiangtian Tower Ink (193.5x100.5cm 76x39in) Hong-
Kong 1999

WANG DUO 1592-1652 **[19]**
$37 087 - €34 976 - **£23 000** - FF229 425
Calligraphy Ink (25.5x271.5cm 10x106in) Hong-Kong
1999

WANG ERDU 1836-c.1909 **[1]**
$4 128 - €3 893 - **£2 560** - FF25 536
Calligraphy in Zhuan Shu Ink (94x19.5cm 37x7in)
Hong-Kong 1999

WANG FU 1362-1416 **[2]**
$1 282 000 - €1 506 806 - **£889 000** - FF9 884 000
Landscape with Poems Ink/paper (21x525cm
8x206in) Hong-Kong 2000

WANG FU'AN 1880-1960 **[4]**
$3 614 - €3 053 - **£2 170** - FF20 028
Seal Script Calligraphy Ink (167x72cm 65x28in)
Hong-Kong 1998

WANG GUANGYI 1956 **[3]**
$13 639 - €11 387 - **£8 000** - FF74 696
China Hunde Visa Oil/canvas (150x150cm 59x59in)
London 1998

WANG HUAIQING 1944 **[15]**
$23 775 - €27 750 - **£16 275** - FF182 025
Two chairs Oil/canvas (99x130cm 38x51in) Taipei
2000

$19 350 - €18 159 - **£11 955** - FF119 115
Sanwei Bookstore Oil/canvas (78x98cm 30x38in)
Hong-Kong 1999

WANG HUI 1632-1717 **[49]**
$15 384 - €17 476 - **£10 800** - FF114 636
Rain clearing over the summer mountains, after Dong Yuan Ink (30x224cm 11x88in) Hong-Kong 2001

WANG HUINAN XX **[1]**
$10 512 - €12 502 - **£7 240** - FF82 008
Lady Yng Mounting a Horse Ink (122x29.5cm 48x11in) Hong-Kong 2000

WANG Jens 1859-1926 **[1]**
$2 854 - €3 216 - **£1 976** - FF21 096
I farta! Oil/panel (38x29cm 14x11in) Oslo 2000

WANG JIAN 1598-1677 **[16]**
$38 460 - €45 204 - **£26 670** - FF296 520
Landscape Ink (98.5x49cm 38x19in) Hong-Kong 2000

WANG JIAN 1960 **[5]**
$19 350 - €18 159 - **£11 955** - FF119 115
Lady with white Cat Oil/canvas (100x80cm 39x31in) Hong-Kong 1999

WANG JIQIAN 1907 **[14]**
$48 716 - €54 901 - **£34 048** - FF360 126
Landscape No.334 Ink (60x89cm 23x35in) Hong-Kong 2001

WANG MIAO 1870-1948 **[3]**
$2 439 - €2 677 - **£1 571** - FF17 561
Landscape Ink (102x43cm 40x16in) Hong-Kong 2000

WANG MINGMING 1952 **[4]**
$1 025 - €1 165 - **£720** - FF7 642
Meeting of Friends Ink (34x108cm 13x42in) Hong-Kong 2001

WANG RAN XX **[1]**
$3 852 - €4 227 - **£2 481** - FF27 729
Scene of the Red Cliff Ink/paper (27x234cm 10x92in) Hong-Kong 2000

WANG SANXI 1716-1795 **[1]**
$4 494 - €4 932 - **£2 894** - FF32 350
Rustic Pavilion at the Foot of a Waterfall Ink (145x59cm 57x23in) Hong-Kong 2000

WANG SHANGGONG XVI **[1]**
$48 792 - €53 279 - **£31 388** - FF349 486
Nymph of Luo River Ink/paper (31x366cm 12x144in) Hong-Kong 2000

WANG SHIMIN 1592-1680 **[13]**
$3 000 - €2 612 - **£1 788** - FF17 133
Calligraphy in Li Shu Ink/paper (106.5x54.5cm 41x21in) New-York 1998

WANG SHISHEN 1686-1759 **[7]**
$38 520 - €42 062 - **£24 780** - FF275 910
Bamboo and Orchid Ink/paper (86x28cm 33x11in) Hong-Kong 2000

WANG SHOUREN 1472-1529 **[4]**
$25 640 - €30 136 - **£17 780** - FF197 680
Correspondence in Running Script Calligraphy Ink/paper (27x108.5cm 10x42in) Hong-Kong 2000

WANG SHUHUI 1912-1985 **[1]**
$1 930 - €1 831 - **£1 174** - FF12 009
Lady Picking Flowers Ink (99x46.5cm 38x18in) Hong-Kong 1999

WANG SIREN 1576-1646 **[1]**
$5 920 - €5 618 - **£3 597** - FF36 850
Couplet in Running Script Calligraphy Ink/paper (82x18.5cm 32x7in) Hong-Kong 1999

WANG SU 1794-1877 **[7]**
$4 450 - €4 197 - **£2 760** - FF27 531
Flowers and Birds Ink (30x41cm 11x16in) Hong-Kong 1999

WANG WENZHI 1730-1802 **[5]**
$8 159 - €7 695 - **£5 060** - FF50 473
Calligraphy in Xing Shu Ink/paper (33x360cm 12x141in) Hong-Kong 1999

WANG WUXIE 1936 **[1]**
$13 984 - €12 959 - **£8 694** - FF85 008
Chasing the Source in a Dream Oil/canvas (122x183cm 48x72in) Taipei 1999

WANG XIAOGUANG 1957 **[4]**
$8 540 - €7 171 - **£5 012** - FF47 040
Melon-Vines Shaped House Oil/canvas (80x100cm 31x39in) Taipei 1998

WANG XINJIN XX **[4]**
$2 564 - €2 890 - **£1 792** - FF18 954
Boating in Autumn Lake Ink (125.5x45.5cm 49x17in) Hong-Kong 2001

WANG XIZHI 321-379 **[1]**
$53 281 - €50 560 - **£32 374** - FF331 655
13th Century Rubbing of the Lanting Xu (Orchid Pavillion Preface) Ink/paper (26.5x63cm 10x24in) Hong-Kong 1999

WANG XUEHAO 1754-1832 **[1]**
$3 870 - €3 650 - **£2 400** - FF23 940
Departure at the Pier Ink/paper (29x92.5cm 11x36in) Hong-Kong 1999

WANG YIDONG 1955 **[16]**
$83 850 - €78 689 - **£51 805** - FF516 165
A Quiet Valley Oil/canvas (150x150cm 59x59in) Hong-Kong 1999
$35 952 - €39 454 - **£23 156** - FF258 804
House of blue-cured Tobacco Oil/canvas (80x100cm 31x39in) Hong-Kong 2000

WANG YONGQIANG 1945 **[8]**
$12 820 - €15 068 - **£8 890** - FF98 840
Foreign Emissaries Pay Tribute Oil/canvas (149.5x108.5cm 58x42in) Hong-Kong 2000

WANG YOUNG-TING 1950 **[3]**
$900 - €933 - **£540** - FF6 120
Il paesaggio della giovane montagna China/carta (132x64cm 51x25in) Prato 1999

WANG YU ZHONG c.1710-1750 **[5]**
$134 820 - €147 218 - **£86 730** - FF965 685
Landscape after Wang Gongwang (1269-1354) Ink (271.5x127cm 106x50in) Hong-Kong 2000

WANG YU ZHONG 1958 **[6]**
$650 - €674 - **£390** - FF4 420
Tu avrai ció che desideri (Le bonheur) China (34x70cm 13x27in) Prato 2000

WANG YUANQI 1642-1715 **[19]**
$137 385 - €129 562 - **£85 200** - FF849 870
Landscape after Wang Men and Huang Gong Wang Ink/paper (98x42cm 38x16in) Hong-Kong 1999

WANG YUANSHUI 1870-1948 **[1]**
$4 128 - €3 893 - **£2 560** - FF25 536
Traveling in Autumn Mountain Ink/paper (56x30cm 22x11in) Hong-Kong 1999

W

WANG YUN 1652-c.1735 **[3]**

✐ **$84 882** - €80 049 - **£52 640** - FF525 084
Landscape Ink (25.5x364cm 10x143in) Hong-Kong 1999

WANG YUNHE 1939 **[9]**

☞ **$9 840** - €10 478 - **£6 240** - FF68 730
Desire Oil/canvas (60x73cm 23x28in) Taipei 2000

☞ **$9 840** - €10 478 - **£6 240** - FF68 730
Twilight in the Midnight Watercolour/paper (79x108cm 31x42in) Taipei 2000

WANG ZHEN 1866-1938 **[38]**

✐ **$5 405** - €5 126 - **£3 288** - FF33 625
Playing with a Toad Ink (139.5x68.5cm 54x26in) Hong-Kong 1999

WANG ZHENGHUA 1937 **[12]**

☞ **$4 504** - €4 274 - **£2 737** - FF28 038
Sitting Nude Oil/canvas (79.5x60cm 31x23in) Hong-Kong 1999

WANG ZHIRUI XVII **[1]**

☞ **$4 902** - €4 600 - **£3 028** - FF30 175
Mount Huang Ink (95.5x53.5cm 37x21in) Hong-Kong 1999

WANGAERDT van Antonie Jacobus 1808-1887 **[1]**

☞ **$9 217** - €8 752 - **£5 649** - FF57 407
Kuhhirtin an einem Weiher Öl/Leinwand (38x55cm 14x21in) Zürich 1999

WANGENHEIM von Chris XX **[15]**

[📷] **$2 000** - €1 893 - **£1 243** - FF12 417
Joe McDonald Gelatin silver print (40x50cm 16x20in) New-York 1999

WANING van Cornelis Antonie 1861-1929 **[7]**

☞ **$2 799** - €3 086 - **£1 828** - FF20 240
Bomschuiten op zee Oil/canvas (77x96cm 30x37in) Den Haag 2000

WANING van Martin 1889-1972 **[61]**

☞ **$1 173** - €1 361 - **£810** - FF8 929
Langestreek Schiermonnikoog Oil/panel (50x80.5cm 19x31in) Groningen 2000

☞ **$234** - €272 - **£162** - FF1 786
Havengezicht Oil/panel (27x38cm 10x14in) Rotterdam 2000

WANJU Peter M. 1968 **[4]**

✐ **$1 500** - €1 555 - **£900** - FF10 200
Aids Orphans, not their fault Acquarello (25.5x38cm 10x14in) Prato 2000

WANKIE Wladyslaw Wanke 1860-1925 **[17]**

☞ **$7 296** - €6 964 - **£4 558** - FF45 683
Potatoes Gathering Oil/canvas (67.7x101.5cm 26x39in) Warszawa 1999

☞ **$3 375** - €3 331 - **£2 080** - FF21 849
Rêverie, fille sur fond de paysage d'automne Oil/canvas (28.7x19.5cm 11x7in) Warszawa 1999

WANKOWICZ Walenty 1799-1842 **[2]**

☞ **$3 976** - €4 269 - **£2 660** - FF28 000
Portrait d'homme au livre Huile/toile (85x72cm 33x28in) Paris 2000

WANLASS Stanley Glen 1941 **[2]**

🖎 **$4 953** - €4 269 - **£2 996** - FF28 000
The Racers Bronze (58x27cm 22x10in) Paris 1999

WANTE Ernest 1872-1960 **[18]**

☞ **$1 055** - €1 239 - **£730** - FF8 130
Portrait de Monsieur de Keersmaeker/Portrait de Madame de Keersmaeker Huile/toile (116x87cm 45x34in) Antwerpen 2000

WAPPERS Gustaaf 1803-1874 **[30]**

☞ **$60 568** - €66 929 - **£42 000** - FF439 026
Boccaccio reading the Decameron to Joanna of Naples Oil/canvas (172x227cm 67x89in) London 2001

☞ **$2 420** - €2 727 - **£1 694** - FF17 886
La jeune veuve Huile/toile (39x49cm 15x19in) Antwerpen 2001

WARARIDDH RIDDHAGNI 1949 **[4]**

✐ **$4 005** - €3 721 - **£2 475** - FF24 405
Two Worlds Watercolour/paper (98x78cm 38x30in) Bangkok 1999

WARB Nicolaas 1906-1957 **[14]**

☞ **$2 091** - €2 439 - **£1 468** - FF16 000
«Convoitise» Huile/bois (31x27cm 12x10in) Paris 2000

WARBURTON Samuel 1874-c.1938 **[18]**

✐ **$616** - €717 - **£440** - FF4 700
Fishing boats Watercolour (25x35cm 9x13in) Crewkerne, Somerset 2001

WARD Charles Daniel 1872-? **[19]**

☞ **$405** - €447 - **£280** - FF2 935
A Figurine and Blossom in a Vase on a Table Oil/canvas (50x39.5cm 19x15in) London 2001

☞ **$3 316** - €2 871 - **£2 000** - FF18 832
«Nature's Tireing Room»/«The Rendevous»/«The Song of Birds'» Oil/board (30.5x11cm 12x4in) London 1998

WARD Charlotte Blakeney ?-c.1940 **[4]**

☞ **$301** - €257 - **£180** - FF1 685
A Portrait of an Elegant Lady wearing a purple Dress Pastel/paper (54x36cm 21x14in) London 1998

WARD Cyril 1863-1935 **[41]**

✐ **$663** - €572 - **£400** - FF3 752
Trout Stream in Hants Watercolour/paper (28x44.5cm 11x17in) London 1998

WARD Edmund Franklin 1892-1991 **[44]**

☞ **$700** - €668 - **£444** - FF4 381
Shipwreck Oil/canvas (54x100cm 21x39in) Cleveland OH 1999

WARD Edward Matthew 1816-1879 **[29]**

☞ **$13 000** - €14 518 - **£8 325** - FF95 231
Eve of St. Bartholomew Oil/canvas (158x129.5cm 62x50in) New-York 2000

☞ **$16 401** - €18 500 - **£11 528** - FF121 352
Marie Antoinette tar avsked av sin son Oil/canvas (64x77cm 25x30in) Helsinki 2001

✐ **$852** - €716 - **£500** - FF4 694
The Royal Family Emprisoned in the Prison of the Temple Watercolour (24.5x31cm 9x12in) London

WARD Edwin Arthur 1859-? **[8]**

☞ **$1 442** - €1 363 - **£900** - FF8 940
Cromwellian Gentleman on a Balcony, grieving Lady in an Alcove beyond Oil/canvas (60x40cm 24x16in) Fernhurst, Haslemere, Surrey 1999

WARD Enoch 1859-1922 **[5]**

✐ **$286** - €325 - **£200** - FF2 130
Off Cherry Garden Pier, Thames Watercolour/paper (21x36cm 8x14in) Devon 2001

WARD Flora XIX **[1]**

☞ **$3 322** - €2 843 - **£2 000** - FF18 650
Juliette Oil/canvas (40.5x35.5cm 15x13in) London 1998

W

WARD Henrietta 1832-1924 **[3]**
- $7 000 - €8 116 - **£4 958** - FF53 235
  Despair of Henriette Maria over the Death of her Husbund King Charles Oil/canvas (101x117cm 39x46in) New-York 2000

WARD Hughes J. 1909-1945 **[1]**
- $9 000 - €8 332 - **£5 508** - FF54 655
  Woman fighting wrench-wielding thug in garage, for Private Detective Oil/canvas (76x53cm 30x21in) New-York 1999

WARD J. Stephen 1876-1941 **[9]**
- $850 - €918 - **£587** - FF6 021
  High Sierra Landscape Oil/canvas (76x91cm 30x36in) Altadena CA 2001

WARD James 1769-1859 **[149]**
- $77 165 - €91 772 - **£55 000** - FF601 986
  The Falls of the Clyde after a Flood Oil/canvas (125x99cm 49x38in) London 2000
- $5 856 - €6 252 - **£4 000** - FF41 012
  The Waggoner's Horse Oil/panel (42x53cm 16x20in) Billingshurst, West-Sussex 2001
- $9 798 - €9 021 - **£6 000** - FF59 171
  A Boy with Goats and Sheep in a Rocky Landscape/Couple Feeding Pigs Oil/canvas (29x37cm 11x14in) London 1998
- $893 - €859 - **£550** - FF5 635
  Studies of an Angler Pencil/paper (16x8cm 6x3in) London 1999
- 📖 $673 - €652 - **£420** - FF4 279
  Copenhagen Lithograph (45.5x36.5cm 17x14in) London 1999

WARD James Charles act.1830-1875 **[16]**
- $7 000 - €8 299 - **£5 099** - FF54 436
  Still Life with Melon, Pineapple and a Snake Oil/canvas (63x77cm 25x30in) Chicago IL 2001

WARD John Quincy Adams 1830-1910 **[11]**
- $3 000 - €3 536 - **£2 108** - FF23 195
  Standing Figure of Gentleman Bronze (H51cm H20in) Detroit MI 2000

WARD John Stanton 1917 **[58]**
- $5 681 - €5 463 - **£3 500** - FF35 834
  Gillian, Summertime Oil/canvas (76x51cm 29x20in) London 1999
- $3 246 - €3 122 - **£2 000** - FF20 476
  Jehan Daly Painting Janet Oil/canvas (30.5x40.5cm 12x15in) London 1999
- 📖 $818 - €688 - **£480** - FF4 511
  Rue de Rivoli, Paris Watercolour (28x38cm 11x14in) Billingshurst, West-Sussex 1998

WARD Lynd Kendall 1905-1985 **[21]**
- 📖 $2 600 - €2 490 - **£1 606** - FF16 332
  Boy on Rearing Horse, Book Illustration Ink (23x15cm 9x6in) New-York 1999
- 📖 $250 - €268 - **£166** - FF1 755
  Victim Woodcut (54x20cm 21x8in) Cleveland OH 2000

WARD Martin Theodore 1799-1874 **[27]**
- $1 394 - €1 502 - **£950** - FF9 854
  Retrieving the Kill Oil/canvas (28x36cm 11x14in) London 2001

WARD OF HULL John 1798-1849 **[34]**
- $32 000 - €28 457 - **£19 571** - FF186 665
  Views of a Frigate at Anchor, with a Sloop to the Left Oil/canvas (49x71.5cm 19x28in) New-York 1999
- $7 939 - €6 789 - **£4 800** - FF44 532
  Ships off Flamborough Head Oil/canvas (15x23cm 5x9in) London 1999

WARD $8 135 - €7 422 - **£5 000** - FF48 685
  Armed Schooner at Anchor in the Humber/The same Vessel at Sea Watercolour/paper (13.5x20cm 5x7in) London 1998

WARD Rowland XX **[2]**
- 📖 $1 785 - €1 716 - **£1 100** - FF11 256
  Impudence - Tiger Pencil/paper (17x30cm 6x11in) London 1999

WARD Vernon de Beauvoir 1905-1985 **[131]**
- $1 493 - €1 290 - **£900** - FF8 465
  Country Gossip Oil/canvas (54.5x82.5cm 21x32in) Billingshurst, West-Sussex 1999
- $888 - €835 - **£550** - FF5 478
  Low Tide Oil/board (25.5x34cm 10x13in) London 1999

WARD William H. XIX **[11]**
- $795 - €675 - **£480** - FF4 428
  Still Life of Grapes, Greengages and Peach Oil/panel (20.5x27cm 8x10in) Billingshurst, West-Sussex 1998

WARD William I 1766-1826 **[45]**
- 📖 $717 - €796 - **£500** - FF5 222
  Amboise, after Turner Watercolour (13.5x18.5cm 5x7in) London 2001
- 📖 $367 - €380 - **£231** - FF2 490
  En visite à la campagne Aquatint (20.5x19.3cm 8x7in) Warszawa 2000

WARDI Rafael 1928 **[48]**
- $2 446 - €2 270 - **£1 468** - FF14 893
  Landskap Oil/canvas (61x47cm 24x18in) Helsinki 1999
- 📖 $404 - €437 - **£279** - FF2 868
  Stilleben Watercolour/paper (28x34cm 11x13in) Helsinki 2001
- 📖 $288 - €269 - **£177** - FF1 765
  Stilleben Color lithograph (66x96cm 25x37in) Helsinki 1999

WARDLE Arthur 1864-1949 **[343]**
- $10 161 - €10 907 - **£6 800** - FF71 546
  The Unfaithful Guards Oil/canvas (70.5x53.5cm 27x21in) London 2000
- $4 000 - €4 356 - **£2 754** - FF28 576
  «Ch.Sandown Violet», a Smooth-Coated Fox Terrier Oil/canvas (31x40.5cm 12x15in) New-York 2001
- 📖 $1 800 - €1 835 - **£1 127** - FF12 036
  Scotties Pastel/paper (16x25cm 6x9in) New-York 2000
- 📖 $250 - €255 - **£156** - FF1 671
  Scottish Terrier Head Studies Print (32.5x24.5cm 12x9in) New-York 2000

WARDLEWORTH Jack L. XIX **[17]**
- $1 500 - €1 469 - **£958** - FF9 633
  Three Children in Landscape, Castle in Distance Oil/canvas (40x60cm 16x24in) Detroit MI 1999
- $800 - €871 - **£551** - FF5 715
  A Wry look Oil/canvas (29x40.5cm 11x15in) New-York 2001

WARE Thomas 1803-c.1827 **[1]**
- $19 000 - €20 303 - **£12 912** - FF133 182
  Vermont Folk Portraits: Amaziah Richmond (1758-1825)/Hannah Throop(e) Oil/panel (68x60cm 27x24in) Portsmouth NH 2001

W

WARHOL Andy 1928-1987 **[4186]**

$264 960 - €246 906 - **£160 000** - FF1 619 600
«**Judy Garland**» Synthetic polymer silkscreened/canvas (259x259cm 102x102in) London 1998

$105 000 - €115 232 - **£67 609** - FF755 874
Marilyn (Reversal Series) Synthetic polymer silkscreened/canvas (51x40.5cm 20x15in) New-York 2000

$22 000 - €25 526 - **£15 188** - FF167 442
Jimmy Carter Synthetic polymer silkscreened/canvas (35.5x28cm 13x11in) New-York 2000

$30 483 - €32 723 - **£20 403** - FF214 649
Campbell's Box (Tomato Juice) Sculpture (25.3x48.3x24.1cm 9x19x9in) Hamburg 2000

$11 000 - €12 321 - **£7 642** - FF80 819
Flowers Watercolour (57x72.5cm 22x28in) New-York 2001

$3 500 - €4 080 - **£2 423** - FF26 762
Camouflage Screenprint in colors (96.5x96.5cm 37x37in) New-York 2000

$7 800 - €9 050 - **£5 385** - FF59 365
Jean-Michel Basquiat Polaroid (11x10cm 4x3in) New-York 2000

WARHOL: ANDY WARHOL FACTORY XX **[10]**

$222 - €209 - **£140** - FF1 374
Chamion Spark Plug and Gull-winged Mercedes Screenprint (50.5x78.5cm 19x30in) London 1999

WARING Henry Frank XIX-XX **[15]**

$451 - €421 - **£280** - FF2 760
View of Eton Watercolour/paper (33.5x50cm 13x19in) Billingshurst, West-Sussex 1999

WARING W.H. XIX-XX **[14]**

$1 203 - €1 213 - **£750** - FF7 957
Figures crossing a river in a Welsh Landscape/Anglers in a Landscape Oil/canvas (40.5x61cm 15x24in) London 2000

WARLING Elisabeth 1858-1915 **[24]**

$787 - €793 - **£491** - FF5 204
Kvinna vid kamin Oil/canvas (27x22cm 10x8in) Stockholm 2000

WARLPINNI Mickey Geranium c.1905-1985 **[4]**

$2 287 - €2 455 - **£1 530** - FF16 104
Six faced Figure Sculpture (H66cm H25in) Melbourne 1999

WARMAN William XX **[3]**

$973 - €936 - **£600** - FF6 143
Home Again Watercolour/paper (31x24.5cm 12x9in) London 1999

WARMINGTON Ebenezer Alfred 1830-1903 **[23]**

$862 - €1 006 - **£600** - FF6 597
Langdale Pikes, Westmorland Watercolour/paper (23x45.5cm 9x17in) West-Yorhsire 2000

WARNBERGER Simon 1769-1847 **[22]**

$804 - €920 - **£553** - FF6 037
Der Churfürstliche Markt Wolfratshausen, nach J.G.von Dillis Radierung (36.7x49.2cm 14x19in) München 2000

WARNER Alfred Edward 1879-1960 **[48]**

$96 - €91 - **£60** - FF600
Murray Red Gum, Victoria Etching (22.5x24.5cm 8x9in) Sydney 1999

WARNER BROS. STUDIO XX **[98]**

$1 100 - €1 015 - **£685** - FF6 661
Bugs Bunny's Mad World of Television Gouache (21.5x28cm 8x11in) New-York 1999

WARNER Everett Longley 1877-1963 **[23]**

$1 900 - €2 217 - **£1 322** - FF14 541
«**Barn in Winter**» Oil/board (15x23cm 6x9in) Altadena CA 2000

$9 500 - €8 858 - **£5 892** - FF58 106
A New York Thoroughfare in February Pastel/paper (34x45.5cm 13x17in) New-York 1999

WARNER Nell Walker 1891-1970 **[43]**

$3 250 - €3 510 - **£2 246** - FF23 022
Mountain Landscape Oil/board (38x50cm 15x20in) Altadena CA 2001

$1 500 - €1 610 - **£1 003** - FF10 561
Sailboat at the Duck Oil/board (17x20cm 7x8in) Portland ME 2000

WARNIA-ZARZECKI Joseph 1850-? **[3]**

$33 450 - €34 814 - **£21 000** - FF228 366
The Turkish Dance Oil/canvas (75.5x57cm 29x22in) London 2000

$5 004 - €4 573 - **£3 063** - FF30 000
Turc fumant le narghilé Huile/toile (36x26cm 14x10in) Paris 1999

WAROQUIER de Henry 1881-1970 **[470]**

$12 560 - €12 196 - **£7 760** - FF80 000
Paysage italien Huile/toile (133x106cm 52x41in) Paris 1999

$1 935 - €1 982 - **£1 215** - FF13 000
Village de Provence Huile/toile (46x61cm 18x24in) Paris 2000

$777 - €915 - **£557** - FF6 000
Portrait d'homme Huile/papier (32x23cm 12x9in) Paris 2001

$454 - €488 - **£304** - FF3 200
Portrait d'homme Aquarelle (43x28cm 16x11in) Compiègne 2000

$187 - €198 - **£124** - FF1 300
Venise Eau-forte (22x10cm 8x3in) Saint-Dié 2000

WARREN Alan 1919-1991 **[18]**

$364 - €425 - **£253** - FF2 790
Seductive Woman Mixed media/board (71x96.5cm 27x37in) Melbourne 2000

WARREN Barbara 1925 **[7]**

$2 394 - €2 413 - **£1 492** - FF15 825
Howth Oil/board (36x46cm 14x18in) Dublin 2000

WARREN Bonomi Edward XIX-XX **[13]**

$2 092 - €2 246 - **£1 400** - FF14 730
In the midst of a forest Watercolour (52x75cm 20x29in) London 2000

WARREN Edmund George 1834-1909 **[44]**

$4 945 - €4 528 - **£3 000** - FF29 703
Figures Resting Beneath a Tree in an Automnal Wood Watercolour (45x66.5cm 17x26in) London 1998

WARREN Elisabeth Boardman 1886-? **[10]**

$175 - €168 - **£107** - FF1 103
Overhauling the Seine Drypoint (11x9cm 4x3in) Provincetown MA 1999

WARREN Emily Mary Bibbens 1870-1956 **[35]**

$260 - €302 - **£180** - FF1 984
Country Garden with Cat Watercolour/paper (26x18.5cm 10x7in) Vancouver, BC. 2000

WARREN Harold Broadfield 1859-1934 **[17]**

$2 000 - €2 203 - **£1 334** - FF14 454
Fitzwilliam, New Hampshire Watercolour/paper (23x30cm 9x12in) Portsmouth NH 2000

W

WARREN Henry 1794-1879 [16]
- $1 147 - €1 056 - **£700** - FF6 930
«John Brown Shot at Priest Hill by Claver House, Ist May» Bodycolour (33x46.5cm 12x18in) London 1998

WARREN Henry Clifford 1843-? [5]
- $1 169 - €1 263 - **£800** - FF8 284
Wooded Stream in Summer Watercolour/paper (52x71cm 20x27in) Bristol, Avon 2001

WARREN Melvin C. 1920-1995 [23]
- $12 650 - €11 814 - **£7 807** - FF77 493
Adobe Inn Oil/canvas (60x81cm 24x32in) Dallas TX 1999
- $2 750 - €2 568 - **£1 697** - FF16.846
Texas Ranger on Patrol Bronze (30x55cm 12x22in) Dallas TX 1999

WARREN Nesta XIX-XX [5]
- $405 - €483 - **£290** - FF3 167
Country Scene with white Cottage, Figure and Chickens in foreground Watercolour/paper (33x23cm 13x9in) Leominster, Herefordshire 2000

WARREN Sophy S. XIX [4]
- $1 471 - €1 308 - **£900** - FF8 583
Woodcutters Outside a Farmstead Watercolour (37x69cm 14x27in) London 1999

WARRENER Lowrie Lyle 1900-? [8]
- $1 229 - €1 430 - **£865** - FF9 382
Boathouse, Lake of Bays Oil/board (26.5x35.5cm 10x13in) Calgary, Alberta 2001

WARSAGER Hyman 1909 [1]
- $1 500 - €1 673 - **£981** - FF10 977
Tree Surgeons Lithograph (45x31cm 18x12in) Chicago IL 2000

WARSHAWSKY Abel George 1883-1962 [48]
- $1 900 - €2 252 - **£1 384** - FF14 775
Sunlit Village Oil/canvas (63x81cm 25x32in) Chicago IL 2001

WARSHAWSKY Alexander 1887-1945 [12]
- $1 200 - €1 104 - **£720** - FF7 244
House in a Coastal Landscape Oil/masonite (45x55cm 18x22in) Pasadena CA 1999

WASASTJERNA Torsten 1863-1924 [15]
- $3 740 - €3 700 - **£2 332** - FF24 270
I skogen Oil/canvas (57x80cm 22x31in) Helsinki 1999
- $274 - €303 - **£189** - FF1 985
Aftonljus Oil/canvas (32x21cm 12x8in) Helsinki 2001

WASDAIL XVIII [1]
- $15 433 - €18 354 - **£11 000** - FF120 397
Harlequin Portrait of Prince Charles Edwards Stuart Oil/canvas (73.5x51cm 28x20in) London 2000

WASHBURN Cadwallader Lincoln 1866-1965 [7]
- $13 000 - €14 761 - **£8 897** - FF96 829
From the Veranda Oil/canvas (61x91.5cm 24x36in) New-York 2000

WASHINGTON Elizabeth Fisher 1871-1953 [8]
- $42 000 - €48 521 - **£29 408** - FF318 280
Winter in Bucks County Oil/canvas (91.5x97cm 36x38in) New-York 2001
- $2 750 - €3 181 - **£1 946** - FF20 869
In the Harbor, Rockport, Mass Oil/board (30x35cm 12x14in) Hatfield PA 2000

WASHINGTON Georges 1827-1910 [146]
- $11 694 - €13 418 - **£8 000** - FF88 016
Arab Horsemen by an Oasis Oil/canvas (38x56cm 14x22in) Leamington-Spa, Warwickshire 2000

- $7 122 - €8.385 - **£5 005** - FF55 000
La Halte Huile/toile (26.5x34cm 10x13in) Paris 2000
- $1 125 - €991 - **£685** - FF6 500
Cavaliers et chasseurs à l'affût Crayon/papier (19x26cm 7x10in) Paris 1999

WASILEWSKI Czeslaw c.1875-1946/47 [54]
- $3 483 - €2 880 - **£2 043** - FF18 891
The Halt of the Carriage in a Hamlet Oil/canvas (50.3x79.7cm 19x31in) Warszawa 1998
- $983 - €1 147 - **£673** - FF7 526
Charrette à quatre chevaux Huile/carton (12.5x17.5cm 4x6in) Warszawa 2000

WASKE Erich 1889-1978 [47]
- $4 087 - €3 835 - **£2 525** - FF25 154
Frauen am Wasser Öl/Leinwand (71x97cm 27x38in) Stuttgart 1999
- $670 - €613 - **£408** - FF4 024
Segler in Boot vor bergiger Küste Mischtechnik/Papier (47x42cm 18x16in) Berlin 1999

WASKOWSKI Tadeusz 1883-1966 [17]
- $487 - €544 - **£340** - FF3 570
Portrait de jeune homme Crayons couleurs/papier (31x26cm 12x10in) Warszawa 2001

WASLEY Frank 1848-1934 [119]
- $1 260 - €1 223 - **£800** - FF8 024
A coastal Scene with Sea Birds flying by Cliffs Oil/canvas (70x89cm 27x35in) West-Yorkshire 1999
- $1 093 - €1 012 - **£660** - FF6 638
Venetian Canal Scene Watercolour/paper (36x54cm 14x21in) Little-Lane, Ilkley 1999

WASMANN Friedrich Rudolf 1805-1886 [16]
- $327 - €307 - **£203** - FF2 012
Frauenbildnis Pencil (23.4x17.2cm 9x6in) Heidelberg 1999

WASOWICZ Waclaw 1891-1942 [24]
- $3 853 - €3 507 - **£2 407** - FF23 004
Portrait de Tola Mankiewicz Oil/canvas (72x59cm 28x23in) Lódz 1999
- $515 - €476 - **£321** - FF3 121
Beach on the Seashore Watercolour, gouache/board (33.2x35.6cm 13x14in) Warszawa 1999

WASSE Arthur XIX-XX [7]
- $6 202 - €6 135 - **£3 867** - FF40 246
Frühlingstag bei Rothenburg an der Tauber Öl/Leinwand (121x79cm 47x31in) Ahlden 1999

WASSEL Ange XIX [2]
- $1 849 - €1 829 - **£1 153** - FF12 000
Roses Aquarelle (35.5x28.5cm 13x11in) Paris 1999

WASSENBERG Jan Abel 1689-1750 [5]
- $10 532 - €11 798 - **£7 319** - FF77 391
Portrait of Albert Hendrik van Swinderen Oil/canvas (100.5x86.5cm 39x34in) Amsterdam 2001

WASSNER Valentin 1808-1880 [4]
- $2 341 - €2 454 - **£1 542** - FF16 098
Biedermeier-Porträts Öl/Leinwand (30x26cm 11x10in) Satow 2000

WASSON George Savary 1855-1926 [4]
- $3 250 - €3 036 - **£2 006** - FF19 912
Schooners and Tug/Harbor Twilight Oil/panel (17.5x30.5cm 6x12in) Boston MA 1999

WATANABE Sadao 1913-1996 [24]
- $170 - €206 - **£119** - FF1 351
Christmas Cards Woodcut in colors (14.5x19.5cm 5x7in) Bethesda MD 2000

W

WATANABE Seiti Shotei 1851-1918 **[7]**

✏ $3 500 - €3 527 - **£2 181** - FF23 135
The Wife of Enya Takasada at her toilette Ink
(122x49.5cm 48x19in) New-York 2000

WATCHEL Marion Kavanaugh 1876-1954 **[9]**

✏ **$13 000** - €14 568 - **£9 061** - FF95 560
In the Sierra Nevada Watercolour/paper (51x40.5cm
20x15in) Beverly-Hills CA 2001

WATELET Charles Joseph 1867-1954 **[101]**

👁 $1 188 - €1 091 - **£734** - FF7 154
Portrait de famille Huile/toile (50.5x62cm 19x24in)
Bruxelles 1999

👁 $856 - €992 - **£604** - FF6 504
Jeune femme souriant de profil Huile/toile
(42x33.5cm 16x13in) Bruxelles 2000

WATELET Jean C. act.1918 **[1]**

✏ $1 569 - €1 785 - **£1 080** - FF11 707
Militaires écossais (caricatures) Aquarelle/papier
(33x26cm 12x10in) Bruxelles 2000

WATELET Louis Étienne 1780-1866 **[21]**

👁 $3 357 - €2 897 - **£2 017** - FF19 000
Paysage de rivière au pont de planches
Huile/toile (24x33cm 9x12in) Nice 1998

✏ $1 460 - €1 448 - **£908** - FF9 500
Paysage de rivière Aquarelle, gouache/papier
(61x76.5cm 24x30in) Douai 1999

WATELIN Louis-François-V. 1838-1907 **[60]**

👁 $9 078 - €10 367 - **£6 385** - FF68 000
L'orée de la forêt à Fontainebleau Huile/toile
(160x200cm 62x78in) Fontainebleau 2001

👁 $3 200 - €3 071 - **£2 006** - FF20 145
Cows Watering Oil/canvas (48x66cm 18x25in) New-
York 1999

👁 $1 432 - €1 372 - **£882** - FF9 000
Paysanne et son troupeau près de la mare
Huile/toile (20x26cm 7x10in) Calais 1999

WATERFORD Marchioness of Louisa Anne 1818-1891 **[28]**

✏ $597 - €642 - **£400** - FF4 208
A Woman with Needlework and Children
Playing Watercolour/paper (20x21cm 8x8in) Par,
Cornwall 2000

WATERHOUSE John William 1849-1917 **[75]**

👁 $2 125 000 - €1 833 354 - **£1 282 012** -
FF12 026 010
The Awakening of Adonis Oil/canvas (96x188cm
37x74in) New-York 1998

👁 $149 430 - €160 401 - **£100 000** - FF1 052 160
Circe Oil/canvas (86.5x77cm 34x30in) London 2000

👁 $900 - €1 050 - **£626** - FF6 887
Landscape with Young Boy with Shoulder Sack,
Grapes and a Goat Oil/canvas (29x24cm 11x9in)
Bloomfield-Hills MI 2000

WATERLOO Anthonie c.1610-1690 **[214]**

👁 $18 434 - €15 685 - **£11 000** - FF102 887
Wooded Landscape with a Dog barking at a
swineherd and Pig on a Path Oil/canvas
(57x65.5cm 22x25in) London 1998

✏ $7 359 - €6 350 - **£4 440** - FF41 654
Wooded landscape with a man walking on a
dyke between two waterways Black chalk
(22.9x34.3cm 9x13in) Amsterdam 1998

🔲 $150 - €155 - **£90** - FF1 020
Due sentieri verso il ruscello Acquaforte
(12.5x20.5cm 4x8in) Milano 2000

WATERLOO-CLARK John Heaviside c.1770-1863 **[5]**

🔲 $1 931 - €1 668 - **£1 166** - FF10 941
Field Sports of the Native Inhabitants of New
South Wales Aquatint (22.5x16.5cm 8x6in) Malvern,
Victoria 1998

WATERLOW Ernest Albert 1850-1919 **[73]**

👁 $1 200 - €1 316 - **£815** - FF8 634
Women on the Beach Oil/canvas (40x60cm
16x24in) Hampton VA 2000

👁 $489 - €585 - **£337** - FF3 840
Young Boy seated holding a Fish Oil/cardboard
(24x30.5cm 9x12in) Penzance, Cornwall 2000

👁 $1 059 - €1 228 - **£750** - FF8 058
Waiting for the Return Home Watercolour
(26.5x35.5cm 10x13in) London 2000

WATERMAN Marcus A. 1834-1914 **[31]**

👁 $1 600 - €1 891 - **£1 133** - FF12 401
On Guard, the Lioness Oil/canvas (51x41cm
20x16in) Boston MA 2000

WATERS Billie 1896-1979 **[42]**

👁 $969 - €909 - **£600** - FF5 961
A Cornish Lane Oil/board (49x44cm 19x17in)
Penzance, Cornwall 1999

WATERS E.J. XX **[3]**

🔲 $716 - €604 - **£420** - FF3 962
«Shaw Savill Line» Poster (100x61cm 39x24in)
London 1998

WATERS George W. 1832-1912 **[11]**

👁 $4 750 - €5 166 - **£3 131** - FF33 888
Landscape of River, Hills and Boat Oil/canvas
(40x63cm 16x25in) Morris-Plains NJ 2000

👁 $950 - €913 - **£586** - FF5 992
Sailboats off the Coast Oil/board (22x36cm 9x14in)
San Rafael CA 1999

WATERS John 1946 **[2]**

📷 $2 163 - €2 391 - **£1 500** - FF15 683
«Foreign Film» Photograph (17x113cm 6x44in)
London 2001

WATERS Maynard 1936 **[73]**

👁 $605 - €673 - **£405** - FF4 414
Bright Morning Oil/cardboard (32.5x62cm 12x24in)
Nedlands 2000

WATERS Owen XIX-XX **[76]**

👁 $259 - €243 - **£160** - FF1 593
Loading the Hay Cart Oil/canvas (30x38cm 12x15in)
Aylsham, Norfolk 1999

WATERS Susan C. 1823-1900 **[25]**

👁 $4 750 - €4 385 - **£2 921** - FF28 765
Interior Barn Scene with Ewe and Ram with
Lambs and Chickens Oil/canvas (40x50cm 16x20in)
Hatfield PA 1999

WATHERSTON Evelyn M. ?-1952 **[8]**

👁 $4 500 - €4 301 - **£3 099** - FF32 148
Enrisco and Maximillian Oil/canvas (63.5x76cm
25x29in) New York 2001

WATKINS Bartholomew Colles 1833-1891 **[14]**

👁 $5 756 - €6 448 - **£4 000** - FF42 296
The Stepping Stones of Ben Coona, Lough Fee,
Connemara Oil/canvas (33.5x53cm 13x20in) Bury St.
Edmunds, Suffolk 2001

WATKINS Carleton E. 1829-1916 **[149]**

📷 $3 600 - €3 864 - **£2 409** - FF25 347
Cathedral Rock, Yosemite Albumen print (39x50cm
15x20in) New-York 2000

WATKINS Dick 1937 [5]
- $4 473 - €5 221 - **£3 157** - FF34 247
  «My Heroes Daygah & Van Goff» Acrylic
  (167.5x213cm 65x83in) Malvern, Victoria 2000

WATKINS Franklin Chenault 1894-1972 [23]
- $4 250 - €4 783 - **£2 927** - FF31 376
  The Red Death Oil/canvas (76x76cm 29x29in)
  Philadelphia PA 2000

WATKINS John Samuel 1866-1942 [45]
- $1 306 - €1 229 - **£809** - FF8 059
  Little Milkmaid Oil/board (22x31cm 8x12in)
  Melbourne 1999
- $362 - €411 - **£255** - FF2 695
  The Ploughman Watercolour/paper (19x35.5cm
  7x13in) Sydney 2001

WATKINS Margaret 1884-1969 [3]
- $50 000 - €46 623 - **£30 180** - FF305 825
  Domestic Symphony Platinum, palladium print
  (21x16cm 8x6in) New-York 1999

WATKINS Richard John, Dick 1937 [26]
- $6 402 - €7 054 - **£4 250** - FF46 269
  View from the Bridge Oil/canvas (167.5x214cm
  65x84in) Woollahra, Sydney 2000

WATKINS Susan 1875-1913 [2]
- $21 000 - €23 037 - **£13 551** - FF151 113
  Marble-top, three drawer chest accessorized
  with porcelain Oil/canvas (66x51cm 26x20in) York
  PA 2000

WATKISS Gill 1938 [25]
- $347 - €360 - **£220** - FF2 362
  Winter Weeding Pendeen Oil/board (29x34.5cm
  11x13in) Penzance, Cornwall 2000

WATMOUGH Amos XIX-XX [8]
- $2 200 - €2 243 - **£1 378** - FF14 710
  By the Day's Bag Oil/canvas (51x76cm 20x29in)
  New-York 2000

WATROUS Harry Wilson 1857-1940 [35]
- $5 500 - €5 209 - **£3 344** - FF34 166
  Lotos Oil/canvas (54x44cm 21x17in) New-York 1999
- $13 000 - €15 279 - **£9 012** - FF100 222
  The Broken Vase Oil/canvas (30.5x40.5cm 12x15in)
  Beverly-Hills CA 2000

WATSON Albert 1942 [6]
- $4 000 - €4 441 - **£2 782** - FF29 129
  Gold Lame Suit made for Elvis Presley Gelatin
  silver print (119.5x87.5cm 47x34in) New-York 2001

WATSON Alfred Sale XIX-XX [26]
- $331 - €307 - **£200** - FF2 011
  The little Gardener Watercolour/paper (23x34cm
  9x13in) Billingshurst, West-Sussex 1999

WATSON Charles A. 1857-1923 [9]
- $3 500 - €3 939 - **£2 411** - FF25 839
  Woman and Children enjoying a Day in the Park
  Oil/canvas (35.6x51cm 14x20in) Washington 2000

WATSON Charles H.R. XIX-XX [2]
- $13 785 - €15 524 - **£9 500** - FF101 828
  Highland Cattle in a Loch Landscape/Sheep
  Resting in a Loch Landscape Oil/canvas
  (61x91.5cm 24x36in) London 2000

WATSON Charles John 1846-1927 [37]
- $882 - €873 - **£550** - FF5 728
  College Street, London Watercolour (30x15.5cm
  11x6in) London 1999

WATSON Donald 1918 [14]
- $508 - €545 - **£340** - FF3 577
  Dotterel on a Highland Plateau Watercolour/paper
  (39x31cm 15x12in) Edinburgh 2000

WATSON Elizabeth V. Taylor XX [2]
- $7 400 - €6 775 - **£4 488** - FF44 444
  Three-quarter Portrait of a Woman wearing a
  black Hat Oil/canvas (60x91cm 24x36in) East-Dennis
  MA 1998

WATSON Ernest William 1884-1969 [12]
- $175 - €175 - **£109** - FF1 145
  Once Upon a Midnight Dreary Woodcut in colors
  (16x21cm 6x8in) St. Louis MO 1999

WATSON Geoffrey ?-1937 [3]
- $4 663 - €4 776 - **£2 900** - FF31 331
  Bristol Fighter Oil/canvas (74x125cm 29x49in)
  Billingshurst, West-Sussex 2000

WATSON Harry 1871-1936 [123]
- $1 260 - €1 499 - **£900** - FF9 835
  A Sunlit Woodland Glade Oil/canvas (86.5x111.5cm
  34x43in) London 2000
- $527 - €565 - **£360** - FF3 704
  Meandering River Oil/canvas/board (30.5x41cm
  12x16in) London 2001
- $459 - €422 - **£280** - FF2 769
  Seated Female Nude Looking Away Pencil/paper
  (43x33cm 16x12in) London 1998

WATSON Henry 1822-1911 [1]
- $3 434 - €3 892 - **£2 400** - FF25 528
  Mount Leisnler from the River Slaney Oil/canvas
  (81.5x104cm 32x40in) London 2001

WATSON Henry Sumner 1868-1933 [4]
- $4 000 - €3 831 - **£2 471** - FF25 127
  Old Hunter and Dog in Autumnal Landscape,
  Probably Calendar Landscape Oil/canvas
  (71x55cm 28x22in) New-York 1999
- $900 - €862 - **£556** - FF5 653
  Posting Circus Advertisements in a Small Town,
  Story Illustration Watercolour/paper (25x72cm
  10x28in) New-York 1999

WATSON Homer Ransford 1855-1936 [57]
- $4 306 - €4 769 - **£2 920** - FF31 281
  Toward Evening Oil/canvas (45.5x61cm 17x24in)
  Toronto 2000
- $1 590 - €1 761 - **£1 078** - FF11 550
  Cattle Crossing River Oil/board (31.5x41.5cm
  12x16in) Toronto 2000

WATSON James c.1740-1790 [9]
- $274 - €307 - **£190** - FF2 017
  Mother and Child, after Joshua Reynolds
  Mezzotint (40x32cm 15x12in) London 2000

WATSON John Dawson 1832-1892 [83]
- $2 019 - €2 266 - **£1 400** - FF14 864
  Portrait of William Watson, M.R.C.S., Aged 23
  Oil/panel (25x17cm 9x6in) London 2000
- $436 - €499 - **£300** - FF2 774
  The Artist's Daughter, Mrs Courage
  Watercolour/paper (48x29.5cm 18x11in) Penrith,
  Cumbria 2000

WATSON Leonard XX [8]
- $168 - €187 - **£110** - FF1 229
  Old Friends Etching (18x20cm 7x7in) Calgary,
  Alberta 2000

W

WATSON Paul Fletcher 1842-1907 [21]
📷 $627 - €674 - £420 - FF4 419
The White Lion, Eye Watercolour/paper
(31.5x47.5cm 12x18in) Reepham, Norwich 2000

WATSON Raymond 1935 [39]
🖼 $5 481 - €6 442 - £3 800 - FF42 256
Sheep in a Highland Landscape Oil/canvas
(51x76.5cm 20x30in) Edinburgh 2000
📷 $336 - €361 - £225 - FF2 367
The Goldcrest (Book Plate for Songbirds by Percy Edwards) Watercolour/paper (20x12cm 8x5in)
Aylsham, Norfolk 2000

WATSON Robert act.c.1877-1920 [68]
🖼 $4 353 - €4 902 - £3 000 - FF32 156
Sheep Grazing on a Hill Side Oil/canvas
(61.5x91.5cm 24x36in) London 2000
🖼 $1 868 - €2 147 - £1 300 - FF14 086
Hochlandschafe Öl/Leinwand (20.5x30.5cm 8x12in)
Bremen 2001
🖼 $1 950 - €2 113 - £1 300 - FF13 861
Cattle in a Highland Landscape Watercolour/paper
(55x89.5cm 21x35in) Billingshurst, West-Sussex 2000

WATSON Sydney A. XIX-XX [8]
🖼 $2 765 - €3 306 - £1 900 - FF21 684
Highland Cattle Oil/canvas (34.5x47cm 13x18in)
Billingshurst, West-Sussex 2000

WATSON Sydney Hollinger 1911-1981 [16]
📷 $268 - €316 - £190 - FF2 071
Toronto Of old Gouache/paper (26x52.5cm 10x20in)
Toronto 2000

WATSON Sydney Robert 1892-1976 [7]
🖼 $12 650 - €12 423 - £7 850 - FF81 488
Highland Sheep and Cattle Oil/canvas (35x48cm
14x19in) Timonium MD 1999

WATSON Thomas J. 1847-1912 [8]
📷 $707 - €717 - £440 - FF4 704
Figures in a Hay Meadow Watercolour/paper
(41x64cm 16x25in) Little-Lane, Ilkley 2000

WATSON Walter J. 1879-? [21]
🖼 $9 100 - €7 808 - £5 590 - FF51 220
Watsonpaisaje con ovejas en el Norte de Gales
Oleo/lienzo (41x66cm 16x25in) Madrid 1998
🖼 $2 735 - €3 122 - £1 901 - FF20 476
«Clithroe Castle» Oil/canvas (30x45cm 11x17in)
Stockholm 2001

WATSON William R.C. XIX-XX [17]
🖼 $2 388 - €2 006 - £1 400 - FF13 157
Sheep on a Clifftop, Lamorna Cove Oil/board
(15x22.5cm 5x8in) Billingshurst, West-Sussex 1998
🖼 $1 534 - €1 804 - £1 100 - FF11 834
Highland Cattle, Loch Fyne/Cattle before the Loch Watercolour/paper (24x35cm 9x13in) Cheshire
2001

WATSON William, Jnr. ?-1921 [68]
🖼 $6 250 - €6 717 - £4 300 - FF44 063
Sheep before a coastal Landscape Oil/canvas
(36x51cm 14x20in) Cheshire 2001
🖼 $3 733 - €4 145 - £2 499 - FF27 189
Landskap med får, höglandet Oil/canvas (33x48cm
12x18in) Stockholm 2000

WATT Alison 1965 [5]
🖼 $9 625 - €9 699 - £6 000 - FF63 621
The Thought of it Oil/canvas (101.5x46cm 39x18in)
London 2000

WATT Elizabeth Mary 1886-1954 [28]
📷 $1 472 - €1 396 - £920 - FF9 156
Storytime Watercolour (23x28cm 9x11in) Edinburgh
1999

WATT Eva Stuart XX [9]
🖼 $3 994 - €4 571 - £2 747 - FF29 984
A Little Colleen of the Claddagh Oil/board
(35x50cm 14x20in) Dublin 2000
🖼 $1 340 - €1 524 - £926 - FF9 994
Man of the Claddagh Oil/board (40x30cm 16x12in)
Dublin 2000

WATT Georges Fiddes 1873-1960 [9]
🖼 $1 280 - €1 266 - £800 - FF8 307
The Old Net Weaver Oil/canvas (23x28cm 9x11in)
Glasgow 1999

WATT Linnie XIX-XX [16]
🖼 $1 313 - €1 119 - £782 - FF7 341
Dinan Oil/canvas (45x60cm 17x23in) Bath 1998
🖼 $1 072 - €1 202 - £750 - FF7 886
The Hay Meadow Oil/canvas/board (28x46cm
11x18in) London 2001

WATT Victor Robert 1886-1970 [78]
📷 $229 - €222 - £142 - FF1 455
Stockman's Return Watercolour/paper (14x23cm
5x9in) Sydney 1999

WATTEAU DE LILLE François L. Joseph 1758-1823
[26]
🖼 $5 500 - €5 892 - £3 755 - FF38 646
An Amorous Couple on an Elegant Bed Ink
(26x20.5cm 10x8in) New-York 2001

WATTEAU DE LILLE Louis Joseph, dit 1731-1798
[44]
🖼 $32 850 - €38 112 - £23 375 - FF250 000
Le départ du régiment Huile/toile (190x180cm
74x70in) Paris 2001
🖼 $6 900 - €7 622 - £4 785 - FF50 000
Le départ du conscrit Huile/toile (62x76cm
24x29in) Lille 2001
🖼 $8 556 - €9 452 - £5 933 - FF62 000
Scène galante Huile/panneau (24x19cm 9x7in) Lille
2001
🖼 $5 164 - €5 793 - £3 613 - FF38 000
Ribote de grenadiers Trois crayons/papier
(23.5x28.5cm 9x11in) Paris 2001

WATTEAU Jean Antoine 1684-1721 [61]
🖼 $110 000 - €123 208 - £76 428 - FF808 192
Landscape with amorous couples and two children with a dog Oil/canvas (45.5x54cm 17x21in)
New-York 2001
🖼 $3 185 600 - €3 620 076 - £2 200 000 -
FF23 746 140
**Le Conteur: Artists from the Commedia
dell'Arte in a Landscape** Oil/panel (34.5x27.5cm
13x10in) London 2000
📷 $48 356 - €47 317 - £31 000 - FF310 378
**A bewigged Painter, possibly Claude Audran,
seated at his Easel** Red chalk/paper (20x13.5cm
7x5in) London 1999
📷 $372 - €409 - £253 - FF2 683
La troupe italienne Etching (30.1x21cm 11x8in)
Berlin 2000

WATTENWYL von Peter 1942 [32]
📷 $428 - €489 - £301 - FF3 206
**Körperliche Ertüchtigung unter der
Orangensonne** Mischtechnik/Papier (46x37.5cm
18x14in) Bern 2001

WATTER Joseph 1838-1913 **[10]**
$734 - €767 - **£465** - FF5 030
Kavalier/Junge Dame im Boudoir Pencil/paper
(47x38cm 18x14in) München 2000

WATTIER Émile Charles 1800-1868 **[13]**
$615 - €686 - **£430** - FF4 500
La joueuse de mandoline Crayon (19.5x20cm
7x7in) Paris 2001

WATTS Arthur G. 1883-1935 **[8]**
$597 - €642 - **£400** - FF4 208
**Absent-minded salesman: Yes, Sir, unique little
piece** Ink (33.5x26cm 13x10in) London 2000
$424 - €492 - **£300** - FF3 225
**«Derby Day, June 1st,General,Make Up Your
Party and Book Your Bus Now»** Poster (102x64cm
40x25in) London 2000

WATTS Frederick Waters 1800-1862 **[167]**
$6 580 - €6 403 - **£4 050** - FF41 998
Landscape with a Cottage by a Pond Oil/canvas
(95.5x130.5cm 37x51in) London 1999
$7 291 - €7 012 - **£4 500** - FF45 996
**Wooded River Landscape with a Barge by a
Lock, a Village beyond** Oil/canvas (37x48cm
14x18in) London 1999
$2 595 - €2 868 - **£1 800** - FF18 815
The Thames at Richmond Oil/board (21.5x30cm
8x11in) London 2001

WATTS George Frederick 1817-1904 **[124]**
$19 478 - €18 730 - **£12 000** - FF122 860
In the Highlands Oil/canvas (155x71cm 61x27in)
London 1999
$35 686 - €34 273 - **£22 000** - FF224 813
Sir Galahad Oil/canvas (54.5x27.5cm 21x10in)
London 1999
$942 - €1 031 - **£650** - FF6 764
Studies of Female Nude Figures Charcoal/paper
(56.5x73.5cm 22x28in) London 2001

WATTS James Thomas 1853-1930 **[59]**
$8 823 - €8 891 - **£5 500** - FF58 324
**Early Spring Among Beech Trees, Bettws-y-
Coed, Wales** Oil/canvas (37x29cm 14x11in) London
2000
$4 491 - €4 526 - **£2 800** - FF29 690
Welsh Stream, Autumn Watercolour (35x25.5cm
13x10in) London 2000

WATTS Robert 1923-1988 **[7]**
$375 - €426 - **£256** - FF2 793
Permanent Parking Decal Offset (16x16cm 6x6in)
Chicago IL 2000

WATTS Sydney XX **[25]**
$471 - €452 - **£300** - FF2 968
Windsor Castle, from the Thames Watercolour
(25x35cm 9x13in) London 1999

WATZELHAN Carl 1867-1942 **[5]**
$2 200 - €2 476 - **£1 515** - FF16 241
**Still Life with Peaches, Nuts and a Glass of
Wine** Oil/board (30.5x23.5cm 12x9in) Washington
2000

WAUD Alfred Rudolf 1828-1891 **[9]**
$15 545 - €17 888 - **£10 715** - FF117 338
Hotel Dieu near Southwest Pass
Watercolour/paper (34x51cm 13x20in) New-Orleans LA
2000

WAUER William 1866-1962 **[51]**
$3 838 - €3 835 - **£2 400** - FF25 154
Boxer Bronze (H33.5cm H13in) München 1999

WAUGH Coulton 1896-1973 **[27]**
$225 - €239 - **£151** - FF1 571
Interlude Oil/canvas (40x50cm 16x20in) Whitehall NY
2001
$300 - €259 - **£178** - FF1 700
The Furthermost Village on Cape Cod Print in
colors (13x8cm 5x3in) Provincetown MA 1998

WAUGH Dorothy XX **[8]**
$425 - €395 - **£262** - FF2 593
«Life at its best» Poster (101x68cm 40x27in) New-
York 1999

WAUGH Frederick, Judd 1861-1940 **[164]**
$14 000 - €11 811 - **£8 212** - FF77 476
Full of the Moon Oil/masonite (122x153.5cm
48x60in) New-York 1998
$10 000 - €8 623 - **£5 939** - FF56 561
«After Glow» Oil/canvas/board (76x91cm 30x36in)
Bethesda MD 1998
$2 200 - €2 361 - **£1 472** - FF15 490
Monhegan Oil/board (13x17cm 5x7in) Portland ME
2000
$550 - €603 - **£354** - FF3 957
English Fishing Village showing houses
Watercolour/paper (35x25cm 14x10in) Wallkill NY
2000

WAUGH Hal 1860-1941 **[14]**
$954 - €902 - **£592** - FF5 918
Lakes Entrance from Kalimna Oil/canvas
(29.5x45cm 11x17in) Malvern, Victoria 1999

WAUGH Ida ?-1919 **[9]**
$800 - €892 - **£537** - FF5 851
Ladies Portrait Oil/canvas (66x53cm 26x21in)
Radford VA 2000

WAUTERS Camille 1856-1919 **[48]**
$627 - €744 - **£456** - FF4 878
Sous-bois Huile/toile (36x50cm 14x19in) Antwerpen
2001
$522 - €446 - **£316** - FF2 926
La barque Huile/panneau (28.5x37cm 11x14in)
Bruxelles 1998

WAUTERS Emile 1846-1933 **[31]**
$460 - €496 - **£308** - FF3 252
Tête de Maure Huile/panneau (40x32cm 15x12in)
Antwerpen 2000
$2 174 - €2 439 - **£1 521** - FF16 000
Portrait de petite fille coiffée d'un grand noeud
Pastel/papier (55x41.5cm 21x16in) Paris 2001

WAY Andrew John Henry 1826-1888 **[35]**
$7 475 - €6 450 - **£4 516** - FF42 311
Still life of oysters, lemon and sherry Oil/canvas
(50x40cm 20x16in) Bethesda MD 1999
$4 000 - €4 502 - **£2 755** - FF29 530
Still Life of Oysters, Beer, Lemon Wedge Oil/can-
vas/board (25x30cm 10x12in) New-Orleans LA 2000

WAY Charles Jones 1834-1919 **[111]**
$2 326 - €2 301 - **£1 450** - FF15 092
Sommertag im Schweizer Jura Öl/Leinwand
(63.5x101cm 25x39in) Ahlden 1999
$544 - €520 - **£341** - FF3 413
A Swiss Torrent Watercolour/paper (33x49.5cm
12x19in) Vancouver, BC. 1999

WAY John (Wei Letang) 1921 **[4]**
$19 530 - €17 968 - **£11 718** - FF117 862
Abstract Calligraphy Oil/canvas (127x102cm
50x40in) Taipei 1999

W

$14 124 - €15 423 - **£9 086** - FF101 167
Vitreous Enamel No.3 Mixed media/canvas
(81x61cm 31x24in) Hong-Kong 2000

WAY Thomas Robert 1862-1913 **[13]**
$60 - €64 - **£40** - FF422
Seated Female Nude, After J.A.M Whistler
Lithograph (15x13cm 6x5in) Cleveland OH 2000

WAY William Cossens 1833-1905 **[13]**
$177 - €168 - **£110** - FF1 103
Whitby Belle Isle, Bridge and West Cliff
Watercolour/paper (33x51cm 13x20in) Whitby, Yorks
1999

WAYCOTT Hedley 1865-1937 **[9]**
$1 300 - €1 450 - **£851** - FF9 513
Illinois River Landscape Oil/canvas (60x76cm
24x30in) Chicago IL 2000

WEARING Gillian 1963 **[11]**
$9 387 - €10 229 - **£6 500** - FF67 098
Steven, Danny, Daniel, Ryan Photograph
(85x117cm 33x46in) London 2000

WEATHERBY Richard Creed XIX-XX **[47]**
$606 - €644 - **£400** - FF4 225
Half-Portrait of Richard Govier Oil/board
(44.5x37cm 17x14in) Penzance, Cornwall 2000

WEATHERHEAD William Harris 1843-1903 **[26]**
$2 591 - €3 051 - **£1 821** - FF20 014
Reading the News Oil/canvas (46x35.5cm 18x13in)
Sydney 2000
$1 610 - €1 926 - **£1 111** - FF12 631
«**Stitch in time**» Watercolour/paper (27.5x37.5cm
10x14in) Penzance, Cornwall 2000

WEATHERILL George 1810-1890 **[120]**
$4 101 - €3 873 - **£2 550** - FF25 403
Robin Hood's Bay Watercolour/paper (11x19cm
4x7in) Scarborough, North-Yorkshire 1999

WEATHERILL Mary 1834-1913 **[14]**
$1 181 - €1 147 - **£750** - FF7 523
The upper Harbour, Whitby from the River Esk
Watercolour (11.5x17cm 4x6in) West-Yorshire 1999

WEATHERILL Richard 1844-1913 **[16]**
$4 378 - €4 236 - **£2 700** - FF27 788
**The Lower Harbour, with a Steam Ship, Paddle
Steamers** Oil/canvas (51x76cm 20x29in) West-
Yorkshire 1999
$1 793 - €1 925 - **£1 200** - FF12 625
**View of Whitby Harbour with Figures and
Fishing Boats** Oil/board (24x36.5cm 9x14in) West-
Yorkshire 2000
$1 733 - €1 682 - **£1 100** - FF11 033
**Whitby Harbour with Fishing Boats Beside a
Quay** Watercolour (21x29.5cm 8x11in) West-Yorkshire
1999

WEATHERSTONE Alfred C. XIX-XX **[13]**
$2 928 - €3 126 - **£2 000** - FF20 506
Making Posies Watercolour (39.5x27.5cm 15x10in)
Billingshurst, West-Sussex 2001

WEAVER Arthur 1906-1989 **[9]**
$8 965 - €9 624 - **£6 000** - FF63 129
Scene of the 9th Green, The Masters Oil/canvas
(51x76cm 20x29in) London 2000

WEAVER Harold Buck 1889-1961 **[1]**
$2 500 - €2 922 - **£1 784** - FF19 165
Horses in mesa landscape Oil/canvas (30x40cm
12x16in) Altadena CA 2001

WEAVER Herbert Parsons 1872-1945 **[26]**
$386 - €389 - **£240** - FF2 553
Figures at a Cathedral Entrance Watercolour
(33.5x22.5cm 13x8in) London 2000

WEAVER Thomas 1774-1843 **[33]**
$43 078 - €41 182 - **£27 000** - FF270 135
**Mr.Jeremiah Whitehead, Mr.Cawlishaw and
Mr.Yates coursing** Oil/canvas (106.5x152.5cm
41x60in) London 1999
$6 365 - €5 900 - **£3 800** - FF38 701
Reluctant Submission Oil/canvas (40x48cm
16x19in) Aylsham 1999

WEBB Alexander James 1813-1892 **[1]**
$1 907 - €1 856 - **£1 173** - FF12 173
**View of Basin Banks with Mount Elephant and
Cloven Hills** Watercolour/paper (36x53.5cm 14x21in)
Malvern, Victoria 1999

WEBB Archibald ?-c.1866 **[1]**
$4 659 - €4 402 - **£2 900** - FF28 878
Fishing Boats landing on Beach in Rough Seas
Oil/canvas (75x110cm 29x43in) Great Dunwow, Essex
1999

WEBB Archibald Bertram 1887-1944 **[4]**
$1 312 - €1 540 - **£926** - FF10 101
«**The old Mill, south Perth**» Lithograph
(28.5x35.5cm 11x13in) Nedlands 2000

WEBB Archibald, Jnr. ?-c.1893 **[7]**
$1 561 - €1 744 - **£1 000** - FF11 438
Pool of London/Near Limehouse
Watercolour/paper (41x69cm 16x27in) London 2000

WEBB Boyd 1947 **[13]**
$7 000 - €8 059 - **£4 776** - FF52 864
Gorge Cibachrome print (158.5x123cm 62x48in) New-
York 2000

WEBB Byron 1831-1867 **[9]**
$13 278 - €12 995 - **£8 500** - FF85 244
**Monarch of the Mountain, a Snow Covered
Mountainous View** Oil/canvas (109x191cm 43x75in)
Perth 1999
$3 750 - €4 408 - **£2 600** - FF28 912
Landscape with a stag and two Hinds Oil/canvas
(69x91cm 27x35in) Edinburgh 2000

WEBB Charles Meer 1830-1895 **[39]**
$7 114 - €8 266 - **£5 000** - FF54 221
Satisfying Meal Oil/canvas (65.5x55.5cm 25x21in)
London 2001
$950 - €889 - **£575** - FF5 832
In the Tavern Oil/panel (23x17cm 9x7in) Chicago IL
1999

WEBB George Alfred John 1861-1886 **[3]**
$3 794 - €4 181 - **£2 523** - FF27 423
The twelve Apostles Oil/canvas (59x103cm 23x40in)
Melbourne 1999

WEBB James c.1825-1895 **[253]**
$22 000 - €20 415 - **£13 442** - FF133 914
Fisherfolk on a Shore at Sunset Oil/canvas
(81.5x152.5cm 32x60in) New-York 1999
$7 693 - €8 944 - **£5 400** - FF58 667
Heidelburg Oil/canvas (60.5x87cm 23x34in)
Billingshurst, West-Sussex 2001
$1 808 - €2 100 - **£1 271** - FF13 778
Utanför Holland kust Oil/panel (12.5x19cm 4x7in)
Stockholm 2001

WEBB John Cother 1855-1927 **[31]**

▦ **$242** - €223 - **£150** - FF1 463
Coligula's Palace, after J.M.W Turner Mezzotint (33x58cm 12x22in) Bristol, Avon 1999

WEBB Kenneth 1927 **[58]**

◠ **$2 510** - €2 952 - **£1 800** - FF19 365
River Landscape with Yacht, Village and a Headland to Background Oil/canvas (38x91cm 15x36in) Woodbridge, Suffolk 2001

◠ **$1 174** - €1 143 - **£721** - FF7 496
The Bog Pool Oil/canvas (30x25cm 12x10in) Dublin 1999

▦ **$264** - €284 - **£179** - FF1 863
Colour proof Etching (17.5x14.5cm 6x5in) Calgary, Alberta 2001

WEBB Octavius XIX-XX **[2]**

◠ **$2 573** - €2 612 - **£1 600** - FF17 134
A Cow and a Calf in a Field Oil/canvas (56.5x91.5cm 22x36in) London 2000

WEBB William 1780-1846 **[16]**

◠ **$5 720** - €6 276 - **£3 800** - FF41 165
Full Cry Oil/canvas (35.5x47cm 13x18in) London 2000

WEBB William Edward 1862-1903 **[164]**

◠ **$4 910** - €5 840 - **£3 500** - FF38 308
Wrecklers on a Rough Sea Oil/canvas (60.5x101cm 23x39in) London 2000

◠ **$3 525** - €3 352 - **£2 200** - FF21 985
Off Cardiff, Bristol Channel Oil/canvas (25.5x20.5cm 10x8in) London 1999

✎ **$2 061** - €2 212 - **£1 400** - FF14 513
Busy Shipping at Poole Harbour Watercolour/paper (27.5x44cm 10x17in) London 2001

WEBBE William J. ?-1882 **[13]**

◠ **$5 821** - €4 987 - **£3 500** - FF32 715
Peerch on a riverbank Oil/panel (17x38cm 6x14in) Edinburgh 1998

WEBBER Elbridge Wesley 1841-1914 **[3]**

◠ **$2 100** - €2 327 - **£1 408** - FF15 261
Sunset Sail Oil/canvas (91x66cm 36x26in) Dedham MA 2000

WEBBER John 1750-1793 **[19]**

✎ **$4 441** - €4 663 - **£2 800** - FF30 589
Kava Drinkers, Friendly Islands (Tongatapu) Pencil/paper (18.5x25.5cm 7x10in) London 2000

▦ **$800** - €749 - **£491** - FF4 915
«The Fan Palm in the Island of Cracatoa» Etching (43x33cm 16x12in) New-York 1999

WEBBER Wesley 1839-1914 **[76]**

◠ **$1 200** - €1 331 - **£798** - FF8 731
Breaking Waves Oil/canvas (76x127cm 30x50in) Milford CT 2000

◠ **$800** - €692 - **£485** - FF4 542
Sun Setting Over the Harbour Oil/panel (17x33cm 7x13in) Mystic CT 1998

WEBER Alfred Charles 1862-1922 **[65]**

◠ **$19 986** - €18 548 - **£12 000** - FF121 670
The Musical Interlude Oil/panel (59.5x75cm 23x29in) London 1999

✎ **$1 181** - €991 - **£692** - FF6 500
Cardinal dans un intérieur Aquarelle/papier (31.5x22.5cm 12x8in) Paris 1998

WEBER Andreas Paul 1893-1980 **[669]**

✎ **$348** - €409 - **£241** - FF2 683
Reineke souffliert Indian ink/paper (28x35.5cm 11x13in) Stuttgart 2000

▦ **$203** - €176 - **£123** - FF1 157
Zuspruch/Der Rat der Alten Lithographie (40x36cm 15x14in) München 1998

WEBER Anton 1858-? **[1]**

✎ **$3 000** - €2 752 - **£1 848** - FF18 049
View of the Interior of the Altneu Shul (synagogue) Prague Pencil/paper (20x17cm 7x6in) New-York 1999

WEBER August 1817-1873 **[18]**

◠ **$7 103** - €7 158 - **£4 428** - FF46 954
Ein Sommertag an der Lorsbachquelle (Frauenbornlach) Öl/Leinwand (48x40cm 18x15in) Stuttgart 2000

WEBER Bruce 1946 **[61]**

▣ **$1 600** - €1 842 - **£1 091** - FF12 083
Tom, Bear Pond, Adirondack Park Gelatin silver print (24x19cm 9x7in) New-York 2000

WEBER Carl 1850-1921 **[97]**

◠ **$3 700** - €3 127 - **£2 200** - FF20 511
Waterfall Oil/canvas (91x55cm 36x22in) Philadelphia PA 1998

✎ **$550** - €533 - **£346** - FF3 495
Seaside Cottage Watercolour/paper (33x60cm 13x24in) Norwalk CT 1999

WEBER Evarist Adam 1887-1968 **[38]**

◠ **$1 685** - €1 636 - **£1 049** - FF10 732
Die erste Sitzung: Modell auf einer Bühne stehend Indian ink (26x20.5cm 10x8in) Berlin 1999

▦ **$290** - €276 - **£180** - FF1 811
Das Urteil des Paris Woodcut (16.8x14.8cm 6x5in) Berlin 1999

WEBER Henrich A. 1843-1913 **[14]**

◠ **$1 967** - €2 211 - **£1 370** - FF14 500
Enfant dressant son chien Huile/toile (46x33cm 18x12in) Cannes 2001

WEBER Hugo 1918-1971 **[52]**

◠ **$17 619** - €19 854 - **£12 201** - FF130 233
Fighting with the Angel Öl/Leinwand (162.5x167.5cm 63x65in) Zürich 2000

◠ **$2 705** - €3 143 - **£1 901** - FF20 617
Untitled Oil/paper (38x29.5cm 14x11in) Luzern 2001

✎ **$422** - €491 - **£297** - FF3 221
Ohne Titel Indian ink/paper (25x38.5cm 9x15in) Luzern 2001

WEBER Joseph c.1803-1881 **[6]**

◠ **$4 355** - €4 857 - **£2 928** - FF31 862
Portrait eines Leutnants vom 2.Badischen Dragoneregiment/Seine Frau Öl/Leinwand (69.5x58.5cm 27x23in) Ahlden 2000

WEBER Kurt 1893-1964 **[22]**

◠ **$4 779** - €3 994 - **£2 832** - FF26 202
Zwei Figuren Öl/Leinwand (73x103cm 28x40in) Wien 1998

WEBER Lukas 1811-c.1860 **[3]**

▦ **$169** - €197 - **£117** - FF1 292
Brunnen lac d'Ury Aquatinta (14.8x20.1cm 5x7in) Zürich 2000

WEBER Marie Philips XIX-XX **[6]**

◠ **$5 000** - €4 897 - **£3 222** - FF32 124
A Walk in the Garden with the Baby Oil/canvas (126.5x81.5cm 49x32in) New-York 1999

WEBER Max 1881-1961 **[140]**

◠ **$16 000** - €13 703 - **£9 446** - FF89 888
Window Oil/canvas (61x51cm 24x20in) New-York 1998

W

$8 000 - €7 493 - £4 918 - FF49 152
Nude Oil/canvas (37x31.5cm 14x12in) New-York 1999
$7 000 - €7 514 - £4 684 - FF49 287
Workmen in Subway Pastel/board (62.5x47.5cm 24x18in) New-York 2000
$950 - €913 - £589 - FF5 987
Untitled Woodcut (24.5x16.5cm 9x6in) New-York 1999

WEBER Mili 1891-1978 [22]
$991 - €867 - £600 - FF5 690
S'Margrtli Aquarell/Papier (14.5x14.5cm 5x5in) Zofingen 1998

WEBER Otis S. XIX-XX [23]
$2 100 - €2 475 - £1 475 - FF16 236
«The Breakers» Oil/canvas (67x109cm 26x43in) East-Dennis MA 2000

WEBER Otto 1832-1888 [23]
$24 063 - €24 248 - £15 000 - FF159 054
On the Shore Watercolour (66.5x125cm 26x49in) London 2000

WEBER Paul Gottlieb 1823-1916 [217]
$60 000 - €65 829 - £39 858 - FF431 808
In the Catskills Oil/canvas (136.5x177.5cm 53x69in) New-York 2000
$3 932 - €3 579 - £2 457 - FF23 477
Eichenhain-Nord-Amerika Öl/Leinwand (61.5x90cm 24x35in) München 1999
$1 219 - €1 278 - £772 - FF8 384
Holländische Dünenlandschaft Öl/Leinwand (23x32cm 9x12in) Köln 2000
$186 - €179 - £116 - FF1 175
Landschaft mit Haus hinter Bäumen/Seenlandschaft Pencil/paper (7x12.5cm 2x4in) München 1999

WEBER Rudolf 1872-1949 [50]
$195 - €232 - £139 - FF1 525
Birken am Weiher Öl/Karton (29x39cm 11x15in) Linz 2000
$4 030 - €3 779 - £2 490 - FF24 788
Weissenkirchen (Wachau) Aquarell/Papier (56.5x83.5cm 22x32in) Wien 1999

WEBER Theodore Alexander 1838-1907 [153]
$10 560 - €12 001 - £7 360 - FF78 720
Arrivée dans un port normand Huile/toile (90x200cm 35x78in) Budapest 2001
$4 083 - €4 573 - £2 838 - FF30 000
Vue du Bosphore Huile/toile (51.5x34cm 20x13in) Paris 2001
$2 212 - €1 829 - £1 298 - FF12 000
Falaise à Yport Huile/toile (32.5x41cm 12x16in) Paris 1998
$244 - €238 - £150 - FF1 563
Shipping off the Pier Pencil/paper (13.5x19cm 5x7in) London 1999

WEBER Therese 1813-1875 [2]
$1 570 - €1 453 - £972 - FF9 534
Am Seeufer Öl/Leinwand (19x34cm 7x13in) Wien 1999

WEBER Werner 1892-1977 [45]
$869 - €962 - £589 - FF6 312
Tessiner Landschaft Oil/panel (51.5x39cm 20x15in) Zürich 2000
$1 023 - €866 - £615 - FF5 750
Garnelen und Languste auf Zinnteller mit Glasschale Öl/Leinwand (27x35cm 10x13in) St. Gallen 1998

WEBER-TYROL Hans Josef 1874-1957 [38]
$7 456 - €8 181 - £4 953 - FF53 662
Überetscher Mittelgebirgslandschaft Öl/Karton (36.8x49.2cm 14x19in) München 2000
$7 320 - €7 267 - £4 570 - FF47 670
Sommerlandschaft Öl/Karton (32.5x44cm 12x17in) Wien 1999
$2 129 - €2 045 - £1 312 - FF13 415
Gebirgssee Watercolour (21x27cm 8x10in) München 1999

WEBSKY von Wolfgang 1895-1992 [3]
$3 915 - €3 835 - £2 523 - FF25 154
Sitzende Person auf Terrasse vor bewaldeter Allgäuer Landschaft Öl/Leinwand (64x84cm 25x33in) Kempten 1999

WEBSTER George 1775-c.1832 [24]
$10 138 - €11 764 - £7 000 - FF77 168
Dutch Three-Master at Anchor off the Coast Oil/canvas (43x56cm 16x22in) London 2000
$10 161 - €10 907 - £6 800 - FF71 546
British Man O'War and other Fishing Vessels Oil/canvas (28x40.5cm 11x15in) London 2000

WEBSTER Thomas 1800-1886 [40]
$3 984 - €4 629 - £2 800 - FF30 363
Reading the News Oil/panel (35.5x48cm 13x18in) London 2001
$1 313 - €1 119 - £782 - FF7 341
Jumping the Post Oil/canvas (22x15cm 8x5in) Bath 1998

WEBSTER Thomas XX [56]
$558 - €531 - £340 - FF3 483
Still Life of Flowers in a Classical Vase Oil/panel (74x61cm 29x24in) London 1999
$444 - €496 - £300 - FF3 251
Still life Studies of mixed Flowers Oil/canvas (38x27cm 15x11in) Aylsham, Norfolk 2000

WEBSTER Walter Ernest 1878-1959 [75]
$1 494 - €1 604 - £1 000 - FF10 521
Seated Girl with a Mandolin Oil/canvas (91.5x77.5cm 36x30in) London 2000
$522 - €588 - £360 - FF3 858
Profile of an Elegant Lady in a Summer Bonnet Watercolour (25x38cm 9x14in) London 2000

WEDEKING August Wilhelm 1807 [5]
$454 - €511 - £317 - FF3 353
Portrait eines soignierten Herren mit Backenbart Öl/Leinwand (72x57cm 28x22in) Lindau 2001

WEDEL Nils 1897-1967 [58]
$2 160 - €2 097 - £1 333 - FF13 757
Stilleben med kanna och pipa Oil/panel (101x121cm 39x47in) Stockholm 1999
$2 283 - €2 532 - £1 582 - FF16 606
Stilleben Oil/canvas (84.5x68.5cm 33x26in) Malmö 2001

WEDEL-ANKER Herman 1845-1895 [10]
$3 780 - €4 495 - £2 692 - FF29 484
Kornstaur Oil/canvas (32x56cm 12x22in) Oslo 2000

WEDER Jakob 1906-1990 [6]
$4 014 - €4 721 - £2 908 - FF30 971
«Farbsymphonie für die Armen und die Tiere des Waldes» Oil/panel (100x70cm 39x27in) Zofingen 2001

WEDIG von Gottfried, Gotthardt 1583-1641 [17]
$21 316 - €24 542 - £14 548 - FF160 987
Die Rast auf der Flucht nach Ägypten Oil/panel (38.3x51.8cm 15x20in) München 2000

💰 **$7 500** - €6 293 - **£4 420** - FF41 277
Still Life with Chicken, Parsnips, Cucumbers, Olives Oil/panel (30x51cm 12x20in) Greenwich CT 1998

✏️ **$19 000** - €18 958 - **£11 565** - FF124 356
The Christ Child adored by Angels Ink (30x20cm 11x7in) New-York 2000

WEEDON Augustus Walford 1838-1908 [50]
✏️ **$702** - €612 - **£424** - FF4 017
Quayside Watercolour/paper (44x72cm 17x28in) Melbourne 1998

WEEGEE (Arthur Fellig) 1899-1968 [625]
📷 **$1 900** - €1 946 - **£1 172** - FF12 767
Beef in Truck Gelatin silver print (34x27cm 13x10in) New-York 2000

WEEKES Frederick XIX-XX [16]
💰 **$144** - €168 - **£100** - FF1 102
Portrait, Bust Length, of a Soldier Oil/board (27.5x21.5cm 10x8in) London 2000

WEEKES Henry II act.1849-1888 [10]
💰 **$13 000** - €15 104 - **£9 136** - FF99 075
Protection Oil/canvas (72.5x100cm 28x39in) New-York 2001

WEEKES William act.1864-1909 [92]
💰 **$5 202** - €4 803 - **£3 200** - FF31 508
The Ploughman's Lunch Oil/canvas (51x76.5cm 20x30in) London 1999
💰 **$3 800** - €4 139 - **£2 617** - FF27 148
Off to Bed Oil/canvas (30.5x25.5cm 12x10in) New-York 2000

WEEKS Edwin Lord 1849-1903 [148]
💰 **$200 000** - €173 139 - **£120 620** - FF1 135 720
Auteur d'un restaurant en plein air,à Lahore Oil/canvas (157.5x245.5cm 62x96in) San-Francisco CA 1998
💰 **$52 300** - €56 140 - **£35 000** - FF368 256
L'Heure de la prière dans la mosquée de Perle à Agra Oil/canvas/board (66x116cm 25x45in) London 2000
💰 **$8 000** - €6 925 - **£4 824** - FF45 428
Elephant with a Figure Mounted and Two Indian Figures Oil/board (30x17cm 11x6in) San-Francisco CA 1998
✏️ **$5 250** - €6 042 - **£3 619** - FF39 630
Orientalist Scene: doorway with Arabs and their Horses Charcoal (91x69cm 36x27in) New-Orleans LA 2000

WEEKS James 1928 [15]
💰 **$16 000** - €16 262 - **£10 059** - FF106 675
Trio, Musicians Oil/canvas (104x142cm 41x56in) Oakland CA 2000
✏️ **$1 600** - €1 670 - **£1 009** - FF10 952
Interior Ink (55.5x53.5cm 21x21in) New-York 2000

WEEKS James D. Northrup 1922 [1]
💰 **$6 000** - €6 854 - **£4 224** - FF44 959
Sportcar Acrylic/board (76x101cm 30x40in) Chicago IL 2001

WEEKS John 1888-1965 [8]
💰 **$1 759** - €1 848 - **£1 158** - FF12 124
Freemans Bay Rooftops Oil/board (18x24cm 7x9in) Auckland 2000
✏️ **$1 252** - €1 301 - **£785** - FF8 533
The avon River, Christchurch Watercolour/paper (22.5x23cm 8x9in) Auckland 2000

WEELE van der Herman Johannes 1852-1930 [80]
💰 **$1 037** - €1 089 - **£656** - FF7 143
A Shepherd with his Flock Oil/canvas (60x125cm 23x49in) Amsterdam 2000
💰 **$689** - €726 - **£455** - FF4 762
The Horse-drawn Cart Oil/canvas/panel (34.5x26cm 13x10in) Amsterdam 2000
✏️ **$476** - €442 - **£290** - FF2 900
Sheep in a Stable Watercolour/paper (26x40cm 10x15in) Amsterdam 1998

WEEMS Carrie Mae 1953 [3]
📷 **$8 000** - €7 688 - **£4 928** - FF50 431
Untitled (from Sea Islands Series, 1992 Ebo Landing) Silver print (152.5x51cm 60x20in) New-York 1999

WEENIX Jan 1640-1719 [66]
💰 **$10 650** - €11 434 - **£7 125** - FF75 000
Le chien blanc Huile/toile (131x128cm 51x50in) Paris 2000
💰 **$33 904** - €39 637 - **£24 206** - FF260 000
Le départ du fils prodigue Huile/toile (95.5x120cm 37x47in) Paris 2001
💰 **$3 046** - €2 948 - **£1 850** - FF19 337
Cockerel, Peacock and Other Birds in a Parkland Landscape Oil/canvas (28.5x36.5cm 11x14in) London 2000

WEENIX Jan Baptist 1621-c.1665 [29]
💰 **$67 036** - €57 037 - **£40 000** - FF374 136
Italianate Landscape with a ruined Doric colonnade, a Herdsman Oil/canvas (119.5x121cm 47x47in) London 1998
💰 **$13 755** - €15 339 - **£9 249** - FF100 617
Junge Frau vor Ruine, im Hintergrund südliche Küste Oil/Leinwand (69.5x60cm 27x23in) Köln 2000

WEER Georg Philipp 1649-c.1688/90 [1]
💰 **$4 028** - €3 956 - **£2 500** - FF25 949
The Holy Family Oil/canvas (72x87cm 28x34in) London 1999

WEERDEN van Hendricus Johannes 1804-1853 [1]
💰 **$2 500** - €2 164 - **£1 507** - FF14 196
Summer Harvest Scene with a Figure loading a Cart Oil/panel (30x37cm 11x14in) San-Francisco CA 1998

WEERT de Anna 1867-1950 [38]
💰 **$4 140** - €4 084 - **£2 549** - FF26 789
View of a Garden Oil/board (34x41cm 13x16in) Amsterdam 1999

WEERTS Jean-Joseph 1846-1927 [21]
💰 **$3 000** - €2 743 - **£1 832** - FF17 996
Elegant woman with a fan Oil/panel (45x36cm 18x14in) New-York 1998
💰 **$1 222** - €1 143 - **£740** - FF7 529
La belle rousse Huile/panneau (35x27cm 13x10in) Lille 1999

WEESER-KRELL Ferdinand 1883-? [5]
✏️ **$877** - €872 - **£530** - FF5 720
Fabriksanlage Watercolour, gouache (47.5x78cm 18x30in) Wien 2000

WEESOP XVII [2]
💰 **$18 239** - €21 692 - **£13 000** - FF142 287
Portrait of a Gentleman, Half-Length, in a Cuirass with Lace Cravat Oil/canvas (74x59.5cm 29x23in) London 2000

WEGE Dieter 1939 [56]
💰 **$381** - €409 - **£255** - FF2 683
Stuttgart, Familienidyll am Fluss Oil/panel (9.5x15.5cm 3x6in) Hildrizhausen 2000

W

WEGELIN Adolf 1810-1881 **[4]**
- **$1 130** - €1 329 - **£810** - FF8 720
  Ansicht eines mittelalterlichen Städtchens Aquarell/Papier (47x64cm 18x25in) Stuttgart 2001

WEGELIN Émile 1875-1962 **[420]**
- **$244** - €229 - **£148** - FF1 500
  Paysage au bord de l'eau Gouache/papier (32x45cm 12x17in) Reims 1999

WEGENER Gerda 1885-1940 **[209]**
- **$3 164** - €3 488 - **£2 142** - FF22 882
  Portraet af Lili Elbe med vifte siddende ved et vindue Oil/canvas (68x52cm 26x20in) Vejle 2000
- **$1 073** - €1 220 - **£751** - FF8 000
  Femme aux chiens Aquarelle (52x41cm 20x16in) Neuilly-sur-Seine 2001

WEGENER Johann Friedrich W. 1812-1879 **[12]**
- **$3 108** - €2 907 - **£1 880** - FF19 068
  Blick ins Tal Öl/Leinwand (64x85.5cm 25x33in) Wien 1999

WEGENER Otto XIX-XX **[4]**
- **$46 298** - €43 729 - **£28 000** - FF286 843
  Tree Studies Gum bichromat print (34x37.5cm 13x14in) London 1999

WEGERER Julius 1886-1960 **[18]**
- **$2 504** - €2 907 - **£1 728** - FF19 068
  Gebirgslandschaft mit röhrendem Hirsch Öl/Leinwand (115x100cm 45x39in) Graz 2000
- **$1 817** - €2 035 - **£1 262** - FF13 347
  Gebirgssee in den Alpen Oil/canvas/panel (32x42cm 12x16in) Klagenfurt 2001

WEGMAN William 1942 **[145]**
- **$1 245** - €1 352 - **£862** - FF8 868
  Fairy Godmother, from Cinderella Lithograph (52x43cm 20x17in) Cleveland OH 1999
- **$3 342** - €2 825 - **£2 000** - FF18 528
  Coulottes Photo (71.5x56cm 28x22in) London 1998

WEGMANN Bertha 1847-1926 **[74]**
- **$2 800** - €2 687 - **£1 755** - FF17 627
  Courtyard Oil/canvas (63.5x49.5cm 25x19in) New-York 1999
- **$332** - €323 - **£217** - FF2 118
  Udsigt over bjergene, Tyrol Oil/panel (29x42cm 11x16in) Viby J, Århus 1999

WEGMAYR Sebastian 1776-1857 **[21]**
- **$3 808** - €4 422 - **£2 676** - FF29 008
  Stilleben med blommor och fågelbo Oil/panel (38x28.5cm 14x11in) Stockholm 2001

WEGNER Erich 1899-1982 **[25]**
- **$2 733** - €2 556 - **£1 655** - FF16 769
  Kinderschreck Tempera/paper (35x26cm 13x10in) Stuttgart 1999

WEGNER Paul XX **[5]**
- **$400** - €470 - **£286** - FF3 085
  Segovia and Guitar Bronze (H31cm H12in) Chicago IL 2001

WEGUELIN John Reinhard 1849-1927 **[20]**
- **$111 200** - €130 378 - **£80 000** - FF855 224
  Bacchus and the Choir of Nymphs Oil/canvas (124.5x275.5cm 49x108in) London 2001
- **$90** - €97 - **£60** - FF635
  Mrs Jefferson, Head-and-Shoulders, in a White Dress Oil/canvas (24x18cm 9x7in) London 2000

WEHLE Henri-Théodore 1778-1805 **[1]**
- **$772** - €920 - **£550** - FF6 037
  Eichen auf einer Wiese Radierung (25.1x20.4cm 9x8in) Berlin 2000

WEHLE Johannes Raphael 1848-1936 **[20]**
- **$989** - €1 125 - **£686** - FF7 378
  Portrait eines eleganten Mädchens Öl/Leinwand (61x40cm 24x15in) Lindau 2000
- **$1 270** - €1 431 - **£893** - FF9 390
  Ein kleines Mädchen sitzt auf einer Fensterbank Oil/panel (38x26.5cm 14x10in) Stuttgart 2001

WEHM Zacharias c.1558-1606 **[1]**
- **$21 411** - €20 365 - **£13 000** - FF133 584
  Portrait of a Nobleman, Full Length, in a Palatial Interior Oil/panel (27.5x19cm 10x7in) London 1999

WEHN Randolf 1915 **[33]**
- **$312** - €307 - **£193** - FF2 012
  Ansicht von Riva am Gardasee Öl/Leinwand (60x80cm 23x31in) München 1999

WEHNERT Edward Henry 1813-1868 **[9]**
- **$6 766** - €6 730 - **£4 200** - FF44 147
  Street Scene in Paris Oil/canvas (61x51.5cm 24x20in) London 1999

WEHRINGER Herbert 1926 **[124]**
- **$500** - €511 - **£313** - FF3 353
  Ländliche Idylle Oil/panel (19x34cm 7x13in) Augsburg 2000

WEI JINGSHAN 1943 **[4]**
- **$24 529** - €20 719 - **£14 725** - FF135 907
  Roses Oil/canvas (116x84cm 45x33in) Hong-Kong 1998

WEI RONG 1963 **[12]**
- **$29 693** - €25 081 - **£17 825** - FF164 519
  Big Collector - Tuan Fan Oil/canvas (110x150cm 43x59in) Hong-Kong 1998

WEI SHIJIE 1667-c.1749 **[1]**
- **$45 150** - €42 371 - **£27 895** - FF277 935
  Portrait of Hua Yan Ink (130x47cm 51x18in) Hong-Kong 1999

WEI Xavier C.H. 1966 **[1]**
- **$2 796** - €2 623 - **£1 738** - FF17 204
  Figure et arbre III Charcoal (110x130cm 43x51in) Taipei 1999

WEI ZHAOTAO 1938 **[5]**
- **$7 051** - €8 287 - **£4 889** - FF54 362
  Landscape Ink (68x136cm 26x53in) Hong-Kong 2000

WEIBEL Jakob Samuel 1771-1846 **[178]**
- **$771** - €750 - **£474** - FF4 921
  Stans Staad, avec la fameuse montagne de Pilate Encre (14.7x20.5cm 5x8in) Bern 1999
- **$578** - €563 - **£356** - FF3 691
  Meykirch Aquatinta (6x16.3cm 3x6in) Bern 1999

WEIBEL Peter 1945 **[3]**
- **$4 644** - €4 360 - **£2 868** - FF28 602
  Ohne Titel Chalks (152.7x175.2cm 60x68in) Wien 1999

WEIBEL-COMTESSE Karl Rudolf 1786-1856 **[21]**
- **$195** - €186 - **£119** - FF1 223
  Lenk, im Cant.Bern Lithographie (13.2x20.8cm 5x8in) Bern 1999

WEICHBERGER Eduard 1843-1913 **[25]**
- **$1 012** - €1 176 - **£711** - FF7 714
  Burg in hügeliger Landschaft Öl/Leinwand (47x67cm 18x26in) Rudolstadt-Thüringen 2001

WEIDEMANN Friedrich Wilhelm 1668-1750 **[1]**
🖼 **$13 938** - €15 528 - **£9 480** - FF101 856
Portrait de Albrecht Konrad Reichsrgaf von Finkenstein Huile/toile (143x111cm 56x43in) Kraków 2000

WEIDEMANN Jakob 1923 **[74]**
🖼 **$18 530** - €21 536 - **£13 022** - FF141 270
Impression de la nature Oil/canvas (160x180cm 62x70in) Oslo 2001
🖼 **$7 493** - €8 317 - **£5 222** - FF54 556
Kvinne i landskap Oil/panel (50x61cm 19x24in) Oslo 2001
🖼 **$3 746** - €4 159 - **£2 611** - FF27 278
Lesende nonne Oil/panel (41x33cm 16x12in) Oslo 2001
🖼 **$773** - €866 - **£537** - FF5 683
Komposisjon i blått Watercolour/paper (32x39cm 12x15in) Oslo 2001
🖼 **$778** - €898 - **£547** - FF5 891
Komposisjon i blått, rödt og grönt Lithograph (31x33cm 12x12in) Oslo 2000

WEIDEMANN Magnus 1880-1966 **[21]**
🖼 **$983** - €920 - **£596** - FF6 037
Weiblicher Akt in Interieur Öl/Karton (55x35cm 21x13in) Bremen 1999

WEIDENAAR Reynold Henry 1915-1985 **[62]**
🖼 **$425** - €398 - **£261** - FF2 612
Spring Storm/The Barn's on Fire!/Country Task/Aquarama/Channel House Etching (2.5x5cm x1in) New-York 1999

WEIDENMANN Johann Caspar 1803-1830 **[6]**
🖼 **$23 640** - €22 867 - **£14 580** - FF150 000
Recueillement devant les cascades Huile/toile (110x87cm 43x34in) Paris 1999

WEIDINGER Franz Xaver 1890-1972 **[44]**
🖼 **$1 236** - €1 453 - **£858** - FF9 534
Blumenvase mit Nelken Oil/panel (70x56cm 27x22in) Wien 2000
🖼 **$313** - €363 - **£220** - FF2 383
«**Dorf in herbstlicher Hügellandschaft mit Gebirgskulisse**» Aquarell/Papier (15x23cm 5x9in) Salzburg 2001

WEIDL Seff 1915-1972 **[49]**
🖼 **$450** - €511 - **£312** - FF3 353
Konzertflügel Bronze (10x12.5x6.5cm 3x4x2in) München 2001

WEIDNER Josef 1801-1871 **[17]**
🖼 **$3 015** - €2 812 - **£1 820** - FF18 446
Eleganter Herr mit weissem Plastron, weisser Weste und dunklem Anzug Öl/Leinwand (125x91.5cm 49x36in) Lindau 1999

WEIDNER Willem Frederik 1817-1850 **[5]**
🖼 **$2 466** - €2 269 - **£1 525** - FF14 883
A Still Life with peaches, prunes and grapes Oil/panel (26x19cm 10x7in) Amsterdam 1999

WEIE Edvard 1879-1943 **[129]**
🖼 **$8 887** - €10 051 - **£6 007** - FF65 932
Udsigt over Köbenhavns Havn Oil/canvas (98x148cm 38x58in) Köbenhavn 2000
🖼 **$5 860** - €5 386 - **£3 600** - FF35 328
Delacroix-komposition (Dante, Vergil og den blå bådförer) Oil/canvas (69x72cm 27x28in) Köbenhavn 1999
🖼 **$1 494** - €1 402 - **£1 018** - FF10 555
Interiör med kvinde der syr Oil/canvas (31x29cm 12x11in) Köbenhavn 2001

WEIDEMANN [right column header]

🖼 **$720** - €673 - **£435** - FF4 415
Landskabskomposition Watercolour/paper (48x62cm 18x24in) Köbenhavn 1999

WEIGALL Arthur Howes c.1840-c.1895 **[6]**
🖼 **$6 000** - €6 932 - **£4 201** - FF45 468
Interior Scene with Courting Couple and Infant, Attendant Onlooking Oil/canvas (91.5x71cm 36x27in) Bethesda MD 2001

WEIGEL Johann Christoph 1654-1725 **[7]**
🖼 **$196** - €230 - **£138** - FF1 509
Der Hutmacher Kupferstich (15x9cm 5x3in) München 2000

WEIGEL Martin XVI **[2]**
🖼 **$1 052** - €1 022 - **£658** - FF6 707
Bremen Woodcut (25.5x107cm 10x42in) Bremen 1999

WEIGELE Henri 1858-1927 **[13]**
🖼 **$8 295** - €7 622 - **£5 095** - FF50 000
Buste de femme Marbre (H84cm H33in) Guéret 1999
🖼 **$110 000** - €120 719 - **£70 829** - FF791 868
Diana Marble (H71cm H27in) New-York 2000

WEIGHT Carel 1908-1997 **[296]**
🖼 **$20 073** - €18 533 - **£12 500** - FF121 570
Man and Skeleton Oil/canvas (122x152.5cm 48x60in) London 1999
🖼 **$4 328** - €4 856 - **£3 000** - FF31 853
A Walk in the Forest Oil/canvas (40.5x51cm 15x20in) London 2000
🖼 **$2 211** - €2 450 - **£1 500** - FF16 068
Bitter Day Oil/board (26.5x21.5cm 10x8in) Billingshurst, West-Sussex 2000
🖼 **$1 323** - €1 238 - **£800** - FF8 118
Illustration for the Go Between, from a drawing in Canzaro House Pencil (30x20cm 11x7in) London 1999

WEIHS Carl 1860-1931 **[16]**
🖼 **$474** - €436 - **£284** - FF2 860
Kornfeld Aquarell/Papier (23x32cm 9x12in) Wien 1999

WEIL Lucien 1902-1963 **[12]**
🖼 **$1 603** - €1 829 - **£1 113** - FF12 000
La sieste Huile/toile (55x80cm 21x32in) Paris 2000

WEILAND Johannes 1856-1909 **[52]**
🖼 **$5 379** - €5 774 - **£3 600** - FF37 877
Mother and Child in a Kitchen Interior Oil/canvas (81x67cm 31x26in) Bath 2000
🖼 **$1 942** - €2 085 - **£1 300** - FF13 678
Dutch Mother Oil/panel (29x19cm 11x7in) London 2000
🖼 **$1 551** - €1 329 - **£932** - FF8 718
Blumenstilleben Aquarell/Papier (47.5x34cm 18x13in) Köln 1998

WEILER Max 1910-2001 **[93]**
🖼 **$100 680** - €87 170 - **£61 080** - FF571 800
«**Die Taufe im Jordan**» Tempera/canvas (155x115cm 61x45in) Wien 1998
🖼 **$29 715** - €25 435 - **£17 885** - FF166 845
Roter Berg Tempera/canvas (70x80cm 27x31in) Wien 1998
🖼 **$10 480** - €11 628 - **£7 296** - FF76 272
Kronburg bei Schönwies-Zams Oil/panel (29.5x29cm 11x11in) Salzburg 2001
🖼 **$3 925** - €3 634 - **£2 430** - FF23 835
Landschaft Chalks (34.5x33cm 13x12in) Wien 1999
🖼 **$471** - €509 - **£325** - FF3 336
Bäumlein wächst zum Licht Farblithographie (32x26cm 12x10in) Wien 2001

W

WEILLER de Lina XIX **[1]**

$4 500 - €4 303 - £2 740 - FF28 225
Her Mistress Jewelry Box Oil/canvas (97x79cm 38x31in) Cleveland OH 1999

WEILUC Lucien Henri Weil 1873-1947 **[15]**

$1 608 - €1 829 - £1 129 - FF12 000
Frou frou Eau-forte, aquatinte couleurs (54x40cm 21x15in) Lyon 2001

WEINBERG Albert 1922 **[6]**

$750 - €686 - £459 - FF4 500
Couverture de Fantôme ne répond plus Encre Chine/papier (35x45cm 13x17in) Paris 1999

WEINBERG Steven 1954 **[4]**

$4 000 - €4 628 - £2 831 - FF30 355
Untitled Sculpture, glass (H13cm H5in) Cleveland OH 1999

WEINER Dan 1919-1959 **[4]**

$3 000 - €3 454 - £2 047 - FF22 656
East 79th Street, New York City Gelatin silver print (26.5x34cm 10x13in) New-York 2000

WEINER KRAL Imre 1901-1978 **[4]**

$3 920 - €3 712 - £2 458 - FF24 346
Bretagne Öl/Leinwand (41x33cm 16x12in) Praha 1999

WEINER Lawrence 1940 **[30]**

$18 000 - €20 126 - £12 133 - FF132 019
Untitled Oil/canvas (203x76cm 79x29in) New-York 2000

$2 200 - €1 956 - £1 345 - FF12 833
Books do Furnish a Room Pencil (48.5x61cm 19x24in) New-York 1999

WEINGART Joachim 1895-1942 **[105]**

$2 687 - €2 244 - £1 526 - FF14 717
Nature morte aux tulipes et anémones Oil/canvas (55x46cm 21x18in) Warszawa 1998

$597 - €593 - £372 - FF3 891
Femme allongée Charcoal/paper (35x52cm 13x20in) Warszawa 1999

WEINGÄRTNER Pedro 1853-1929 **[1]**

$40 000 - €34 789 - £24 116 - FF228 200
Na Veranda em Roma Oil/canvas (30.5x47cm 12x18in) New-York 1998

WEINMAN Adolph Alexander 1870-1952 **[16]**

$8 000 - €8 921 - £5 220 - FF58 518
Rising Day Bronze (H66cm H26in) St. Louis MO 2000

WEINMANN Johann Wilhelm XVIII **[30]**

$334 - €289 - £198 - FF1 894
Plytanthoza Iconographia Copper engraving (38.7x22.8cm 15x8in) Herblingen 1998

WEINMANN Rudolph 1810-1878 **[12]**

$996 - €818 - £578 - FF5 369
Der Rheinfall bei Schaffhausen bei Vollmond Gouache (20x28cm 7x11in) Berlin 1998

WEINRICH Agnes 1873-1946 **[47]**

$2 600 - €2 246 - £1 570 - FF14 730
Still Life Oil/board (33x25cm 13x10in) Watertown MA 1998

$425 - €502 - £301 - FF3 294
White Horse Watercolour/paper (50x39cm 20x15in) Provincetown MA 2000

WEIR Harrison William 1824-1906 **[18]**

$1 273 - €1 375 - £880 - FF9 019
A Study of a Mallard Duck on the bank of a River Watercolour/paper (17x24.5cm 6x9in) Newbury, Berkshire 2001

WEIR John Ferguson 1841-1926 **[22]**

$5 500 - €6 417 - £3 828 - FF42 092
Marion Eckford Hardwood in Climbing Rose Garden Oil/canvas (101x69cm 40x27in) Altadena CA 2000

$30 000 - €32 914 - £19 929 - FF215 904
Autumn Lights Oil/canvas (24x19cm 9x7in) New-York 2000

WEIR Julian Alden 1852-1919 **[56]**

$190 000 - €196 947 - £120 479 - FF1 291 886
The two Sisters Oil/canvas (127.5x100.5cm 50x39in) New-York 2000

$30 000 - €28 679 - £18 804 - FF188 121
Connecticut Scene at Branchville Oil/panel (38x66cm 14x25in) New-York 1999

$5 750 - €5 336 - £3 452 - FF35 003
Full Moon Oil/canvas (30x40cm 12x16in) Milford CT 1999

$800 - €765 - £487 - FF5 017
Landscape Study Watercolour/paper (24x37cm 9x14in) Boston MA 1999

$1 800 - €2 104 - £1 264 - FF13 803
Portrait of Miss Hoe Drypoint (26x15cm 10x5in) New-York 2000

WEIR Robert Walker 1803-1889 **[19]**

$80 000 - €95 140 - £57 019 - FF624 080
Picnic Along the Hudson Oil/canvas (51x76.5cm 20x30in) New-York 2000

$9 500 - €10 197 - £6 357 - FF66 889
Boats on the Hudson River Oil/panel (19x32.5cm 7x12in) San-Francisco CA 2000

WEIROTTER Franz Edmund 1733-1771 **[86]**

$483 - €537 - £336 - FF3 521
Reisende auf einem baumbestandenen Dorfweg Ink (12x17cm 4x6in) Heidelberg 2001

$153 - €179 - £108 - FF1 173
Aus der Folge «les douzes Mois de l'année», nach Pieter Molyn Radierung (17.5x21cm 6x8in) Hamburg 2001

WEISBECKER Clement XX **[6]**

$1 900 - €2 066 - £1 252 - FF13 555
New York Harbor Oil/canvas (25.5x35.5cm 10x13in) Boston MA 2000

WEISBUCH Claude 1927 **[733]**

$9 225 - €9 452 - £5 741 - FF62 000
Dièse IRE (violoniste) Huile/toile (161x130cm 63x51in) Paris 2000

$3 571 - €3 659 - £2 222 - FF24 000
Lutters Huile/toile (37x45cm 14x17in) Paris 2000

$1 740 - €1 982 - £1 228 - FF13 000
«Ruade» Huile/toile (24x33cm 9x12in) Provins 2001

$1 062 - €1 037 - £672 - FF6 800
Cavalier Huile/toile (55x74cm 21x29in) Douai 1999

$129 - €152 - £90 - FF1 000
Homme assis Eau-forte (64x49cm 25x19in) Nîmes 2000

WEISE Alexander 1883-1960 **[47]**

$669 - €562 - £393 - FF3 688
«Blick auf den Watzmann im Winter» Öl/Leinwand (80x100cm 31x39in) München 1998

WEISE Robert 1870-1923 **[19]**
$1 013 - €1 125 - £706 - FF7 378
«Toskanische Landschaft» Öl/Leinwand (60x48cm 23x18in) Stuttgart 2001

WEISENBORN Rudolph 1881-? **[21]**
$750 - €881 - £520 - FF5 782
Abstract Composition Oil/board (76x50cm 30x20in) Cincinnati OH 2000
$1 500 - €1 706 - £1 040 - FF11 190
Portrait, possibly C.J.Bulliet Charcoal/paper (66x99cm 26x39in) Chicago IL 2000

WEISER Joseph Emanuel 1847-1911 **[10]**
$460 - €460 - £288 - FF3 018
Abendliche Moorlandschaft Oil/panel (16.5x27cm 6x10in) Hamburg 1999

WEISGERBER Albert 1878-1915 **[33]**
$10 954 - €11 760 - £7 332 - FF77 139
Alexandra Korsakoff Öl/Leinwand (104.5x74.5cm 41x29in) Hamburg 2000
$449 - €511 - £311 - FF3 353
Im Bordell Watercolour (36.1x28.7cm 14x11in) Hamburg 2000
$773 - €716 - £466 - FF4 695
Knabe mit Maske Etching (20x14.8cm 7x5in) Heidelberg 1999

WEISKÖNIG Werner 1907-1982 **[16]**
$2 830 - €3 284 - £1 954 - FF21 539
Beim Sammelplatz Öl/Leinwand (100x100cm 39x39in) St. Gallen 2000
$962 - €872 - £600 - FF5 717
«Olympic Winter Games» Poster (99x64cm 38x25in) London 1999

WEISMANN Jacques 1878-? **[19]**
$716 - €747 - £453 - FF4 902
La sieste Oil/panneau (55x81cm 21x31in) Genève 2000

WEISS Anton 1729-1784 **[12]**
$9 253 - €9 715 - £6 256 - FF63 724
Krippenszene, Anbetung der Hirten Öl/Leinwand (79x60cm 31x23in) Kempten 2001
$539 - €613 - £374 - FF4 024
Sitzender männlicher Akt Red chalk/paper (54.5x44cm 21x17in) Lindau 2000

WEISS Anton 1801-1851 **[4]**
$15 369 - €14 248 - £9 500 - FF93 459
Roses, narcissi, bluebells, morning glory and other Flowers in a Vase Oil/canvas (43x32cm 16x12in) London 1999

WEISS David 1946 **[8]**
$1 113 - €1 311 - £782 - FF8 597
«La tigresse» Watercolour (23.7x16cm 9x6in) Zürich 2000

WEISS Emil Rudolf 1875-1942 **[44]**
$870 - €981 - £612 - FF6 432
Stilleben mit Blumen in einer Vase Öl/Leinwand (60x71cm 23x27in) Zürich 2001

WEISS Georges Émile, Géo 1861-? **[20]**
$14 708 - €17 532 - £10 488 - FF115 000
La leçon de tricot Huile/toile (96x78cm 37x30in) Strasbourg 2000
$6 000 - €5 202 - £3 666 - FF34 120
Few Last Stitches Oil/panel (24x19cm 9x7in) New-York 1999
$3 000 - €3 407 - £2 105 - FF22 351
Summer bouquet with butterflies Watercolour/paper (67.5x48.5cm 26x19in) New-York 2001

WEISS Henri XIX **[5]**
$357 - €331 - £220 - FF2 172
Escena rural con unos bueyes arando y una joven madre Relief (45x52cm 17x20in) Madrid 1998

WEISS Hugh 1925 **[35]**
$325 - €349 - £217 - FF2 291
Still life Oil/canvas (45x55cm 18x22in) Hatfield PA 2000

WEISS Johann Baptist 1812-1879 **[25]**
$1 782 - €1 817 - £1 115 - FF11 917
Brandung Öl/Leinwand (50x68cm 19x26in) Wien 2000

WEISS Johann Baptist 1801-1856 **[4]**
$917 - €1 022 - £641 - FF6 707
An der grossen Innbrücke in Innsbruck Watercolour (15.7x20.3cm 6x7in) München 2001

WEISS José 1859-1919 **[133]**
$2 084 - €1 943 - £1 286 - FF12 744
Polderlandschaft im sommerlichen Abendlicht Öl/Leinwand (36x61cm 14x24in) Köln 1999
$704 - €757 - £480 - FF4 968
Rustic Buildings and Trees Oil/board (13x23cm 5x9in) Stansted Mountfitchet, Essex 2001

WEISS Ludwig Caspar 1793-1867 **[4]**
$3 867 - €4 009 - £2 320 - FF26 299
Ritratto di rabbino Olio/tela (49.5x39.5cm 19x15in) Milano 2000

WEISS Michael 1733-1791 **[1]**
$7 110 - €6 860 - £4 464 - FF45 000
Portrait d'une petite fille avec son chien Huile/toile (67x75cm 26x29in) Paris 1999

WEISS Nikolaus 1760-1809 **[4]**
$1 383 - €1 534 - £958 - FF10 061
«Fluchenstein und Aussicht gegen Ingberg im Algäu» Aquarell/Papier (18x24.5cm 7x9in) Kempten 2001

WEISS Noah 1842-1907 **[1]**
$12 000 - €11 889 - £7 280 - FF77 990
Figure with Patterned Body Sculpture, wood (H241cm H94in) New-York 2000

WEISS Oskar 1882-1965 **[31]**
$1 043 - €945 - £650 - FF6 198
«Jungfrau» Poster (130x65cm 40x25in) London 1999

WEISS Peter 1916-1983 **[25]**
$23 069 - €19 969 - £14 000 - FF130 985
Town Life Oil/board (110x150cm 43x59in) London 1998
$1 913 - €1 799 - £1 185 - FF11 803
Hjärter ess Oil/canvas (66x46.5cm 25x18in) Stockholm 1999
$2 931 - €3 284 - £2 043 - FF21 540
Landschaft Oil/paper (31x23.5cm 12x9in) Stockholm 2001

WEISS Sabine Weber 1924 **[18]**
$412 - €488 - £291 - FF3 200
Homme courant dans la nuit Tirage argentique (24.5x15.7cm 9x6in) Chartres 2001

WEISS Wojciech 1875-1950 **[118]**
$10 068 - €10 780 - £6 852 - FF70 712
Nu debout Huile/toile (180x100.5cm 70x39in) Warszawa 2001
$4 398 - €5 243 - £3 136 - FF34 390
Octobre Huile/toile (47x66cm 18x25in) Warszawa 2000
$3 242 - €3 622 - £2 198 - FF23 760
Port Huile/toile (32x45cm 12x17in) Warszawa 2000

W

WEISSBORT George XX [13]
- 🖎 $2 323 - €2 549 - **£1 499** - FF16 722
  Still Life with Onions, Pan ang Jar
  Oil/canvas/board (32.5x53.5cm 12x21in) London 2000
- 🖎 $227 - €259 - **£160** - FF1 699
  Still Life of Flowers in a white Jug Oil/board
  (34.5x26cm 13x10in) London 2001
- 🖎 $1 316 - €1 444 - **£849** - FF9 471
  Still Life with Tomatoes and Apples Watercolour
  (24x34.5cm 9x13in) London 2000

WEISSENBRUCH Jan 1822-1880 [46]
- 🖎 $48 375 - €40 787 - **£28 710** - FF267 543
  View of Amersfoort Oil/canvas (46x73cm 18x28in)
  Amsterdam 1998
- 🖎 $16 908 - €15 882 - **£10 192** - FF104 181
  **Moored Boats with Figures Strolling along a
  Quay** Oil/panel (13x19cm 5x7in) Amsterdam 1999
- 🖎 $7 686 - €7 260 - **£4 649** - FF47 625
  View of a Village Watercolour (24x32.5cm 9x12in)
  Amsterdam 1999
- 🖎 $212 - €204 - **£132** - FF1 339
  De vier leeftijden Etching (8.5x14cm 3x5in) Haarlem
  1999

WEISSENBRUCH Johan Hendrik 1824-1903 [172]
- 🖎 $69 498 - €81 680 - **£48 186** - FF535 788
  Mills in a landscape Oil/canvas (103x130cm
  40x51in) Amsterdam 2000
- 🖎 $32 250 - €27 191 - **£19 140** - FF178 362
  Shepherd in a Landscape near Norden Oil/can-
  vas (73x103cm 28x40in) Amsterdam 1998
- 🖎 $5 924 - €6 647 - **£4 106** - FF43 600
  «Fischer und Boote am Strand» Oil/canvas/panel
  (8.9x16.8cm 3x6in) München 2000
- 🖎 $13 074 - €11 055 - **£7 818** - FF72 514
  **An Angler in a Polder Landscape with
  Windmills beyond** Watercolour/paper (42x33cm
  16x12in) Amsterdam 1998

WEISSENBRUCH Willem Johannes 1864-1941 [60]
- 🖎 $2 980 - €2 949 - **£1 824** - FF19 347
  Polder Landscape with Windmills Oil/canvas
  (55.5x68.5cm 21x26in) Amsterdam 2000
- 🖎 $1 055 - €1 134 - **£719** - FF7 441
  River Landscape Oil/canvas/panel (12.5x17.5cm
  4x6in) Amsterdam 2001
- 🖎 $17 904 - €17 426 - **£11 000** - FF114 307
  Autumn Day on the Canal Watercolour,
  gouache/paper (48.5x69cm 19x27in) London 1999

WEISSGERBER Karl 1891-1968 [55]
- 🖎 $985 - €1 125 - **£694** - FF7 378
  «Totenmaar in Tauschnee» Öl/Leinwand
  (75x100cm 29x39in) Stuttgart 2001

WEISZ Adolphe 1838-? [16]
- 🖎 $9 552 - €9 147 - **£6 012** - FF60 000
  La demande de publication de bans Huile/toile
  (81.5x120.5cm 32x47in) Nice 1999
- 🖎 $18 678 - €20 050 - **£12 500** - FF131 520
  The Tired Drummer Oil/panel (43x31cm 16x12in)
  London 2000

WEITZ Helmut 1918-1966 [11]
- 🖎 $907 - €767 - **£541** - FF5 030
  Rheinhafen bei Düsseldorf Aquarell/Karton
  (50x70cm 19x27in) Düsseldorf 1998

WEJCHERT Alexandra 1920-1995 [15]
- 🖎 $2 588 - €3 047 - **£1 818** - FF19 989
  «Relief in Vermilion» Mixed media (63x78cm
  25x31in) Dublin 2000
- 🖎 $3 235 - €3 809 - **£2 273** - FF24 987
  «Flow II» Metal (17x38x15cm 7x15x6in) Dublin 2000

WEL van Jean 1906-1990 [21]
- 🖎 $312 - €372 - **£223** - FF2 439
  Het Kertsgebeuren Aquarelle/papier (44.5x56cm
  17x22in) Maisieres-Mons 2000

WELCH Denton 1915-1948 [25]
- 🖎 $411 - €392 - **£250** - FF2 573
  Man in an Arbor Gouache/paper (28x21.5cm 11x8in)
  London 1999

WELCH Nugent 1881-1970 [16]
- 🖎 $243 - €273 - **£169** - FF1 793
  Ships at a Wharf Watercolour/paper (22x28.5cm
  8x11in) Wellington 2001

WELCH Thaddeus 1844-1919 [45]
- 🖎 $8 000 - €7 786 - **£4 915** - FF51 075
  Morning in Steep Ravine Oil/canvas (50x91cm
  20x36in) San-Francisco CA 1999
- 🖎 $425 - €377 - **£260** - FF2 470
  Summer Landscape Oil/board (21x27cm 8x11in)
  Cincinnati OH 1999

WELCH Vic XX [1]
- 🖎 $678 - €787 - **£480** - FF5 162
  **«Trains of Our Times, British Railways, London
  Midland Region»** Poster (102x127cm 40x50in)
  London 2000

WELIE van Antoon 1866-1956 [18]
- 🖎 $1 227 - €1 180 - **£765** - FF7 739
  «Ludwig Van Beethoven» Oil/canvas (51x61.5cm
  20x24in) Amsterdam 1999
- 🖎 $8 789 - €9 983 - **£6 166** - FF65 485
  Ophelia Watercolour (34x41cm 13x16in) Amsterdam
  2001

WELKER Ernst 1788-1857 [17]
- 🖎 $688 - €716 - **£434** - FF4 695
  Blick vom Mönchsberg in Salzburg Indian ink
  (27.3x42.9cm 10x16in) Berlin 2000

WELLENHEIM von Pauline 1801-1882 [2]
- 🖎 $10 127 - €9 447 - **£6 110** - FF61 971
  Die heilige Familie im Blumenkranz Öl/Leinwand
  (124x92cm 48x36in) Wien 1999

WELLENS Charles 1889-1959 [43]
- 🖎 $1 908 - €1 785 - **£1 159** - FF11 707
  Intérieur flamand Huile/toile (64.5x95cm 25x37in)
  Bruxelles 1999
- 🖎 $741 - €843 - **£520** - FF5 528
  Fermette Huile/toile (33x46cm 12x18in) Bruxelles
  2001

WELLENSTEIN Walter 1889-1970 [63]
- 🖎 $150 - €169 - **£104** - FF1 106
  «Der Vorhanggeht auf» Ink (50x36cm 19x14in)
  Berlin 2001

WELLER Paul 1912 [2]
- 🖎 $800 - €768 - **£495** - FF5 039
  Lumber Car Lithograph (28x37cm 11x14in) New-
  York 1999

WELLER Theodor Leopold 1802-1880 [24]
- 🖎 $3 407 - €3 835 - **£2 347** - FF25 154
  **Neapolitanische Familie vor der sommerlichen
  Inselkulisse** Öl/Kupfer (47x36cm 18x14in) Stuttgart
  2000
- 🖎 $1 866 - €2 147 - **£1 288** - FF14 086
  Bauernmädchen mit Lamm Öl/Leinwand (32x25cm
  12x9in) München 2000
- 🖎 $405 - €460 - **£281** - FF3 018
  **Italienischer Strassenmusiker, die Laute spie-
  lend** Pencil (35x28.5cm 13x11in) Berlin 2001

WELLERSHAUS Paul 1887-1976 **[5]**
🖼 **$1 428** - €1 534 - **£956** - FF10 061
   Blühender Baum an einem Bach Öl/Leinwand (66.5x88.5cm 26x34in) Köln 2000

WELLHÖFFER Moritz 1640-1672 **[2]**
🎨 **$2 610** - €2 234 - **£1 571** - FF14 653
   «Eine schöne Tischzucht» Woodcut in colors (30x35cm 11x13in) München 1998

WELLING James 1951 **[37]**
📷 **$1 600** - €1 784 - **£1 075** - FF11 703
   Mound Polaroid (13.5x10cm 5x3in) New-York 2000

WELLINGS William XVIII **[11]**
✏ **$2 821** - €3 293 - **£2 000** - FF21 598
   Captain Young, in naval uniform, standing on shore with his ship Ink (25.5x21.5cm 10x8in) London 2001

WELLIVER Neil 1929 **[41]**
  $35 000 - €31 704 - **£21 420** - FF207 963
   Thaw at Pond Pass Oil/canvas (152x152cm 60x60in) Portland ME 1998
  $6 000 - €5 435 - **£3 672** - FF35 650
   Snow Scene, Maine Oil/canvas (20x25cm 8x10in) Portland ME 1998
🎨 **$800** - €859 - **£545** - FF5 633
   Shadow from Zeke's Screenprint in colors (91.5x92cm 36x36in) Boston MA 2001

WELLS Denys George 1881-1973 **[34]**
  $2 405 - €2 380 - **£1 500** - FF15 610
   Silk Stockings Oil/canvas (66x53cm 25x20in) Leyburn, North Yorkshire 1999

WELLS George XIX **[9]**
  $806 - €775 - **£500** - FF5 082
   An Odalisque Oil/canvas (48x37cm 18x14in) London 1999

WELLS Henry Tamworth 1828-1903 **[20]**
✏ **$597** - €642 - **£400** - FF4 208
   Portrait Study of Joanna Mary Wells (1831-1861) Pencil (53.5x40.5cm 21x15in) London 2000

WELLS John 1907 **[53]**
✏ **$2 232** - €2 088 - **£1 350** - FF13 699
   Abstract composition Bodycolour (24x34.5cm 9x13in) London 1999

WELLS John Sanderson 1872-1955 **[122]**
  $5 986 - €5 699 - **£3 800** - FF37 381
   Coach Outside the Sun Inn Oil/canvas (39x60cm 15x23in) Billingshurst, West-Sussex 1999
  $1 417 - €1 349 - **£881** - FF8 850
   Well Away! Oil/canvas (23x30.5cm 9x12in) Toronto 1999
✏ **$826** - €781 - **£500** - FF5 122
   A Lady driving a Gig Watercolour (28.5x48.5cm 11x19in) Billingshurst, West-Sussex 1999

WELLS William Frederick 1762-1836 **[2]**
✏ **$1 016** - €1 144 - **£700** - FF7 507
   In Windsor Park Watercolour/paper (27x41cm 10x16in) Newbury, Berkshire 1999

WELLS William P. Atkinson 1872-1923 **[51]**
  $4 482 - €4 433 - **£2 800** - FF29 077
   Harvesting Oil/canvas (46x61cm 18x24in) Glasgow 1999
  $2 438 - €2 707 - **£1 700** - FF17 756
   The Fields Oil/canvas (30.5x45.5cm 12x17in) London 2001

WELONSKI Pius Adamowitsch 1849-1931 **[11]**
✏ **$428** - €416 - **£264** - FF2 728
   Figure de femme avec lierre Indian ink/paper (55x39cm 21x15in) Warszawa 1999

WELSCH Karl Friedrich Ch. 1828-1904 **[2]**
  $10 460 - €11 228 - **£7 000** - FF73 651
   Crossing the Desert at Sunset Oil/canvas (53x104.5cm 20x41in) London 2000

WELSH Horace Devitt 1888-1942 **[8]**
🎨 **$750** - €699 - **£453** - FF4 585
   French Quarter Street Scene Etching (29x21cm 11x8in) New-Orleans LA 1999

WELTÉ Gottlieb 1745-c.1790 **[7]**
  $7 210 - €7 267 - **£4 500** - FF47 670
   Blinde-Kuh-Spiel auf einer Waldlichtung Oil/panel (23.5x34cm 9x13in) Wien 2000
🎨 **$823** - €715 - **£496** - FF4 692
   Der Tod von Pyramus und Thisbe Etching, aquatint (12.6x9.3cm 4x3in) Berlin 1998

WELTI Albert 1862-1912 **[94]**
🎨 **$83** - €89 - **£55** - FF584
   Raub der Europa Radierung (36.5x48cm 14x18in) Zürich 2000

WELTY Eudora XX **[7]**
📷 **$1 700** - €1 782 - **£1 065** - FF11 691
   Here it Comes! (Jackson) Silver print (33x32cm 13x12in) New-York 2000

WELVAERT Ernest 1880-1946 **[11]**
  $6 968 - €6 445 - **£4 342** - FF42 276
   Het gehucht in de vallei Oil/canvas (71x100cm 27x39in) Lokeren 1999

WELY Jacques c.1873-1910 **[7]**
✏ **$3 574** - €4 059 - **£2 500** - FF26 627
   Au lit Pastel/paper (53x74cm 20x29in) London 2001

WELZ Jean Max Friedrich 1900-1975 **[86]**
  $5 046 - €5 856 - **£3 484** - FF38 410
   Composition with Flowers Oil/board (38.5x48cm 15x18in) Johannesburg 2001
  $3 756 - €4 213 - **£2 628** - FF27 636
   «Warmwaterberg, Ladysmith» Oil/board (28x42cm 11x16in) Cape Town 2001
✏ **$626** - €702 - **£438** - FF4 606
   Seated female Nude Charcoal/paper (45x28cm 17x11in) Cape Town 2001

WEMAëRE Pierre 1913 **[81]**
  $1 777 - €2 010 - **£1 201** - FF13 186
   L'espion du Nord Oil/canvas (61x51cm 24x20in) København 2000
✏ **$621** - €538 - **£374** - FF3 530
   Komposition Watercolour (24x28cm 9x11in) København 1998

WEN DAN 1766-1852 **[2]**
✏ **$1 548** - €1 460 - **£960** - FF9 576
   Snowcapped Village Ink (28x18cm 11x7in) Hong-Kong 1999

WEN SHU 1595-1634 **[2]**
✏ **$35 952** - €39 258 - **£23 128** - FF257 516
   Lilies, Bamboo and Butterflies Ink (28.5x81cm 11x31in) Hong-Kong 2000

WEN ZHENGMING 1470-1559 **[57]**
✏ **$15 384** - €17 476 - **£10 800** - FF114 636
   Myriad Peaks and Mountains Ink (124.5x64cm 49x25in) Hong-Kong 2001

W

WEN ZHENMENG 1574-1636 **[1]**

✒ $4 108 - €4 509 - £2 646 - FF29 577
Running Script Calligraphy Ink (184x50cm 72x19in) Hong-Kong 2000

WENCKE Ernst 1865-1929 **[14]**

🦌 $659 - €613 - £405 - FF4 024
Fortuna, weiblicher Halbakt auf einer Kugel Porcelain (H32cm H12in) München 1999

WENCKE Sophie 1874-1963 **[39]**

🖼 $1 467 - €1 687 - £1 036 - FF11 067
Am Moorgraben unter lichtem Sommerhimmel Öl/Leinwand (70x100cm 27x39in) Bremen 2001

🖼 $854 - €818 - £537 - FF5 366
Bauernkate hinter Birken Oil/panel (42x28.5cm 16x11in) Köln 1999

WENCKEBACH Ludwig Willem R. 1860-1937 **[20]**

🖼 $1 235 - €1 361 - £806 - FF8 929
Vissertje aan een vaart Oil/canvas (74x98cm 29x38in) Den Haag 2000

WENDEL Karl 1878-1943 **[16]**

🖼 $642 - €693 - £443 - FF4 548
Solbelysta tallar intill fjärd med segelbåtar Oil/canvas (73x105cm 28x41in) Stockholm 2001

WENDEL Theodore 1859-1932 **[21]**

🖼 $2 800 - €3 283 - £2 014 - FF21 535
Spring Landscape Oil/canvas/board (35.5x51cm 13x20in) New-York 2001

🖼 $3 000 - €2 563 - £1 815 - FF16 813
Château de la Reine Versailles Oil/panel (30.5x40.5cm 12x15in) San-Francisco CA 1998

✒ $5 000 - €4 640 - £3 002 - FF30 438
Breaking Waves/Lobster Shacks on the Marsh Pastel/paper (43x58cm 17x23in) Milford CT 1999

WENDELIN Martta 1893-1986 **[24]**

🖼 $1 518 - €1 345 - £931 - FF8 825
Blommor Oil/canvas (37x46cm 14x18in) Helsinki 1999

✒ $955 - €874 - £581 - FF5 736
Skördetid Gouache/paper (29x22cm 11x8in) Helsinki 1999

WENDERS Wim 1945 **[14]**

📷 $730 - €869 - £521 - FF5 701
Ohne Titel Dye-transfer print (33.6x42cm 13x16in) Berlin 2000

WENDLBERGER Wenzel Hermann 1882-1945 **[34]**

🖼 $603 - €563 - £364 - FF3 690
Winterliche Dorfstrasse Öl/Leinwand (35.5x46cm 13x18in) München 1998

WENDT William 1865-1946 **[134]**

🖼 $70 000 - €81 671 - £48 720 - FF535 724
River & Trees Oil/canvas (101x127cm 40x50in) Altadena CA 2000

🖼 $50 000 - €47 556 - £30 360 - FF311 950
Autumn Oil/canvas (63.5x76cm 25x29in) Beverly-Hills CA 1999

🖼 $14 000 - €12 863 - £8 600 - FF84 378
Landscape with Inlet and Cliffs Oil/canvas (30x45cm 12x18in) St. Petersburg FL 1999

✒ $5 000 - €5 603 - £3 485 - FF36 754
A Northern Garden Watercolour/paper (40.5x30.5cm 15x12in) Beverly-Hills CA 2001

WENG FANGGANG 1733-1818 **[4]**

✒ $8 901 - €8 394 - £5 520 - FF55 062
Calligraphy in Kai Shu Ink/paper (130x56.5cm 51x22in) Hong-Kong 1999

WENGENROTH Stow 1906-1978 **[183]**

✏ $500 - €536 - £330 - FF3 516
Still Life Roses in Vase Pencil (26x41cm 10x16in) East-Moriches NY 2000

📖 $375 - €432 - £258 - FF2 835
«Delaware Church» Lithograph (23x34cm 9x13in) Cleveland OH 2000

WENGER John 1887-1976 **[10]**

🖼 $950 - €868 - £595 - FF5 696
Still Life with Flowers Beside a Porcelein Elephant Watercolour/paper (73x99cm 29x39in) New-York 1999

WENGLEIN Josef 1845-1919 **[178]**

🖼 $14 513 - €16 596 - £9 966 - FF108 860
Paysage à une route au clair de la Lune Huile/toile (104.5x151.5cm 41x59in) Warszawa 2000

🖼 $5 892 - €6 135 - £3 733 - FF40 246
Brunnentrog bei einer Erdgrube mit Schilfgras Öl/Leinwand (47.5x73.5cm 18x28in) München 2000

🖼 $2 100 - €2 403 - £1 444 - FF15 763
Stier im Sonnenlicht auf einem Acker Öl/Leinwand (35.5x44.5cm 13x17in) München 2000

🖼 $214 - €245 - £147 - FF1 609
Stiller Teich Pencil (45x60.8cm 17x23in) München 2000

WENIG Karl Bogdanovich 1830-1908 **[2]**

🖼 $7 172 - €7 699 - £4 800 - FF50 503
Reclining Nude with Mirror Oil/canvas (68.5x140cm 26x55in) London 2000

WENING Michael 1645-1718 **[35]**

📖 $178 - €204 - £122 - FF1 341
Der Marckh zu München Kupferstich (31x79.5cm 12x31in) München 2000

WENISCH Schlosser XX **[1]**

📷 $7 144 - €7 669 - £4 782 - FF50 308
Porträt Franz Kafka Photograph (14.7x10.5cm 5x4in) München 2000

WENK Albert 1863-1934 **[49]**

🖼 $372 - €434 - £261 - FF2 850
Südliche Felsküstenlandschaft mit Segelschiff Öl/Leinwand (95x106cm 37x41in) München 2000

WENLOCK Constance, Lady 1852-1932 **[2]**

🖼 $1 008 - €1 129 - £700 - FF7 406
Fiesole at Dusk Watercolour (51x71.5cm 20x28in) London 2001

WENNERBERG Brynolf 1866-1950 **[23]**

🖼 $1 605 - €1 789 - £1 122 - FF11 738
Lachendes junges Paar, Halbfiguren Öl/Leinwand (54.5x46.5cm 21x18in) München 2001

🖼 $1 803 - €1 687 - £1 092 - FF11 067
Junges Mädchen mit Clown Öl/Karton (33x26cm 12x10in) Stuttgart 1999

📖 $8 000 - €6 825 - £4 825 - FF44 768
«Marque PKZ» Poster (92x128cm 36x50in) New-York 1998

WENNERBERG Gunnar G:son 1863-1914 **[8]**

🖼 $1 964 - €2 305 - £1 386 - FF15 122
Stilleben Oil/canvas (129x54cm 50x21in) Stockholm 2000

WENNERWALD Emil Aug. Th. 1859-1934 **[190]**

🖼 $408 - €469 - £282 - FF3 078
Fra egnen omkring Himmelbjerget Oil/canvas (48x68cm 18x26in) København 2000

W

WENNING Pieter Willem F. 1873-1921 **[52]**

$9 770 - €9 161 - **£6 037** - FF60 094
Landscape with Buildings and Trees Oil/canvas
(25x45.5cm 9x17in) Johannesburg 1999

$898 - €776 - **£541** - FF5 088
**A Thatched Cape House Beneath Table
Mountain** Ink (21x28cm 8x11in) Johannesburg 1998

WENNING Ype Heerke 1879-1959 **[53]**

$1 020 - €998 - **£654** - FF6 548
**A Sunlit Landscape with a Goat grazing near a
Bridge** Oil/canvas (45x60.5cm 17x23in) Amsterdam
1999

$841 - €726 - **£507** - FF4 762
Snowballs Oil/panel (16x22.5cm 6x8in) Amsterdam
1999

WENTORF Carl 1863-1914 **[23]**

$4 146 - €3 767 - **£2 570** - FF24 707
**Interiör med broderende dame ved vinduet og
legende barn** Oil/canvas (37x45cm 14x17in)
Köbenhavn 1999

WENTWORTH Ellen XIX **[1]**

$10 000 - €8 628 - **£6 055** - FF56 593
In Memory of Robert Wentworth Watercolour
(41.5x32cm 16x12in) New-York 1999

WENTZEL Niels Gustav 1859-1927 **[55]**

$38 970 - €33 181 - **£23 280** - FF217 650
Interiör fra gården Överli i Lom Oil/canvas
(100x130cm 39x51in) Oslo 1998

$2 730 - €3 246 - **£1 944** - FF21 294
Skispor i bakken Oil/canvas (35x60cm 13x23in) Oslo
2000

$1 114 - €1 234 - **£756** - FF8 097
Gamle stabbur Oil/panel (31x42cm 12x16in) Oslo
2000

WENTZELL Barrie XX **[1]**

$2 770 - €3 215 - **£1 912** - FF21 087
**Jimi Hendrix/Diana Ross/Johnny Cash/Robert
Plant/Ray Davis/Doors** Gelatin silver print
(51x40.5cm 20x15in) Vancouver, BC. 2000

WENZELL Albert Beck 1864-1917 **[18]**

$11 000 - €12 321 - **£7 642** - FF80 819
Man approaching Woman weeping Oil/canvas
(102x76cm 40x30in) New-York 2001

WENZINGER Christian 1710-1797 **[1]**

$4 224 - €4 090 - **£2 653** - FF26 831
Hl. Bischof, Birnbaum, geschnitzt Sculpture, wood
(H14cm H5in) Berlin 1999

WEREFKIN von Marianne 1860-1938 **[45]**

$20 037 - €23 592 - **£14 079** - FF154 753
Das Verdikt Tempera/Karton (57x43cm 22x16in)
Zürich 2000

$16 698 - €19 660 - **£11 733** - FF128 961
Lesender Priester Tempera/Karton (35.5x26.5cm
13x10in) Zürich 2000

$5 437 - €4 707 - **£3 300** - FF30 875
Das Heilige Land Indian ink (30.4x26.4cm 11x10in)
München 1998

WERENSKIOLD Erik 1855-1938 **[64]**

$4 408 - €4 082 - **£3 072** - FF32 092
Elegant kvinne på hest Oil/canvas (105x110cm
41x43in) Oslo 2001

$9 989 - €8 743 - **£6 052** - FF57 350
Vinterfiske Oil/canvas (32x42cm 12x16in) Helsinki
1998

$353 - €396 - **£245** - FF2 598
Eventyrmotiv Etching (24x32cm 9x12in) Oslo 2001

WERFF van der Adrian 1659-1722 **[23]**

$46 551 - €45 596 - **£30 000** - FF299 088
The Penitent Magdalen Oil/panel (49x38cm
19x14in) London 2001

$2 240 - €2 479 - **£1 560** - FF16 260
Léda et le Cygne Huile/panneau (38.5x31cm
15x12in) Liège 2001

$897 - €1 022 - **£626** - FF7 607
Susanna und die beiden Alten Chalks (19x12.5cm
7x4in) Berlin 2001

WERKMAN Henrik Nicolaas 1882-1945 **[31]**

$1 225 - €1 452 - **£892** - FF9 525
Gesprek Print in colors (32x22cm 12x8in) Amsterdam
2001

WERKMEISTER Wolfgang 1941 **[120]**

$98 - €112 - **£67** - FF737
Kanal von Aveiro, Portugal Etching, aquatint
(26.8x35.6cm 10x14in) Heidelberg 2000

WERLEN Ludwig 1884-1928 **[12]**

$5 097 - €4 462 - **£3 087** - FF29 266
Chaîne de montagnes Huile/toile (35x70cm
13x27in) Genève 1998

$1 067 - €1 244 - **£739** - FF8 163
Hütte in bergiger Landschaft Öl/Leinwand
(27x40.5cm 10x15in) Bern 2000

WERLING Robert 1946 **[16]**

$747 - €716 - **£461** - FF4 695
Oceano Dune Gelatin silver print (33.6x38cm
13x14in) Köln 1999

WERNER Alexander Friedrich 1827-1908 **[12]**

$1 746 - €1 789 - **£1 078** - FF11 738
Innenraum Oil/canvas/panel (38x48cm 14x18in)
Düsseldorf 2000

WERNER Carl Friedrich H. 1808-1894 **[111]**

$20 174 - €22 497 - **£13 565** - FF147 571
Am Felsentempel von Abu Simbel Öl/Leinwand
(190x122cm 74x48in) Ahlden 2000

$693 - €808 - **£480** - FF5 300
**Still Life of Apples, Pears, Plums and Nut on a
Mossy Bank/Still Life** Oil/canvas (21x29cm 8x11in)
Cheshire 2000

$1 304 - €1 428 - **£900** - FF9 365
Lady and her Page in a Coastal Town Watercolour
(37x45.5cm 14x17in) London 2001

$443 - €427 - **£273** - FF2 800
Assouan Lithographie (24x35cm 9x13in) Paris 1999

WERNER Friedrich Bernhard 1690-1778 **[4]**

$1 368 - €1 329 - **£855** - FF8 720
Bremen Kupferstich (35x102cm 13x40in) Bremen
1999

WERNER Gösta 1909-1989 **[76]**

$796 - €735 - **£489** - FF4 821
Röd viadukt Oil/canvas (100x90cm 39x35in)
Stockholm 1999

$433 - €417 - **£267** - FF2 733
**Karl-Alfred o Ellinor/I skansen/Fritiof of
Carmencita/Vidalita** Color lithograph (43x59cm
16x23in) Malmö 1999

WERNER Hilding 1880-1944 **[7]**

$9 494 - €10 238 - **£6 372** - FF67 157
Sommarmorgon, Arvika Oil/canvas (60x150cm
23x59in) Stockholm 2000

WERNER Joseph c.1818-c.1887 **[1]**

$2 969 - €2 812 - **£1 805** - FF18 446
Ruine Gutenstein und Lange Brücke Watercolour
(30.3x38cm 11x14in) München 1999

W

WERNER Joseph II 1637-1710 **[15]**

➣ **$19 455** - €22 867 - **£14 100** - FF150 000
  Portrait de femme en Diane Huile/cuivre (29x22cm 11x8in) Vendôme 2001

✎ **$6 235** - €5 488 - **£3 798** - FF36 000
  Couple Encre/papier (14.5x12cm 5x4in) Fécamp 1999

WERNER Lambert 1900-1983 **[43]**

➣ **$453** - €465 - **£280** - FF3 047
  Utan titel Oil/canvas (64.5x58cm 25x22in) Stockholm 2000

WERNER Theodor 1886-1969 **[247]**

➣ **$17 111** - €19 429 - **£11 711** - FF127 448
  Auf gelbem Grund Öl/Leinwand (166x81cm 65x31in) Berlin 2000

➣ **$5 146** - €6 135 - **£3 669** - FF40 246
  Ohne Titel Tempera (73x51.5cm 28x20in) Berlin 2000

➣ **$637** - €613 - **£398** - FF4 024
  Lineare Komposition Mischtechnik (21x29.5cm 8x11in) München 1999

✎ **$722** - €716 - **£451** - FF4 695
  Komposition Pastel (5x28.5cm 1x11in) München 1999

WERNER Thomas 1957 **[2]**

➣ **$4 359** - €3 581 - **£2 531** - FF23 489
  Am Waldbach, junge lesende Frau in blauem Kleid mit weissem Besatz Öl/Karton (36x26.5cm 14x10in) Berlin 1998

WERNER von Anton Alexander 1843-1915 **[74]**

➣ **$5 444** - €6 135 - **£3 770** - FF40 246
  Bismarck in Uniform, Rückansicht Öl/Karton (71.5x46cm 28x18in) Berlin 2000

➣ **$1 363** - €1 431 - **£859** - FF9 390
  Jagdhund Öl/Karton (25x32.5cm 9x12in) Heidelberg 2000

✎ **$448** - €434 - **£281** - FF2 850
  Garde-Husaren (Potsdam) Pencil (18x24cm 7x9in) Berlin 1999

WERNER Woty 1903-1971 **[8]**

▦ **$1 350** - €1 534 - **£938** - FF10 061
  In der Dunkelheit Tapestry (54x58cm 21x22in) München 2001

WERTHEIM von Heinrich 1875-1945 **[32]**

✎ **$241** - €276 - **£166** - FF1 811
  Alt Heiligenstadt, Pfarrplatz, wo unser Beethoven die Eroica schrieb Aquarell/Papier (28.5x40cm 11x15in) Salzburg 2000

WERTHEIMER Gustav 1847-1904 **[37]**

➣ **$544** - €523 - **£330** - FF3 428
  Lorelei Oil/canvas (70x89cm 27x35in) Stockholm 1999

WERTINGER Hans c.1465/70-1533 **[1]**

➣ **$8 000** - €8 293 - **£4 800** - FF54 400
  La tosatura delle pecore Olio/tavoletta (39x23cm 15x9in) Genova 2000

WERTMÜLLER Adolf Ulrik 1751-1811 **[25]**

➣ **$10 692** - €9 997 - **£6 588** - FF65 574
  Porträtt av hovmarskalkinnan Christina Charlotta Fock, född Falkner Oil/canvas (66.5x54cm 26x21in) Stockholm 1999

➣ **$9 772** - €8 498 - **£5 893** - FF55 742
  Marie Antoinette Oil/panel (21.5x17cm 8x6in) Stockholm 1999

WERY Albert 1650-? **[1]**

➣ **$17 600** - €22 806 - **£13 200** - FF149 600
  Paesaggio con viandanti Olio/tela (81x98cm 31x38in) Milano 2000

WERY Émile Auguste 1868-1935 **[8]**

▦ **$174** - €198 - **£120** - FF1 299
  Tête de bretonne Heliogravure (25.5x33cm 10x12in) Sion 2000

WERY Fernand 1886-1969 **[58]**

➣ **$436** - €397 - **£270** - FF2 601
  Village en Ardennes Huile/carton (45x36cm 17x14in) Bruxelles 1999

WÉRY Marthe 1930 **[3]**

➣ **$832** - €992 - **£596** - FF6 504
  Compositie Oil/canvas (40x30cm 15x11in) Lokeren 2000

WESCOTT Paul 1904-1970 **[7]**

➣ **$850** - €1 000 - **£611** - FF6 557
  «Seal Cove» Oil/canvas/board (28x59cm 11x23in) Hatfield PA 2001

WESSEL Bessie Hoover 1889-? **[1]**

➣ **$22 000** - €25 166 - **£15 298** - FF165 077
  Harbor Scene Oil/canvas (45x50cm 18x20in) Cincinnati OH 2000

WESSEL Herman 1878-1969 **[2]**

✎ **$1 400** - €1 568 - **£972** - FF10 286
  «Dancing Girls» Drawing (38x30cm 15x12in) Cincinnati OH 2001

WESSEL Wilhelm 1904-1971 **[18]**

➣ **$4 997** - €5 624 - **£3 443** - FF36 892
  Liebespaar Öl/Leinwand (74.5x65cm 29x25in) München 2000

➣ **$1 143** - €945 - **£670** - FF6 199
  «Nach dem Kampf» Red chalk/paper (34x46cm 13x18in) München 1998

WESSELMANN Tom 1931 **[853]**

➣ **$37 500** - €38 874 - **£22 500** - FF255 000
  Still Life with Goldfish and Rose Tecnica mista (152x182cm 59x71in) Prato 1999

➣ **$42 000** - €48 732 - **£28 996** - FF319 662
  Little Still Life #8 Mixed media/board (42.5x42.5cm 16x16in) New-York 2000

➣ **$4 200** - €4 873 - **£2 899** - FF31 966
  Still-Life Acrylic/paper (8x8cm 3x3in) New-York 2000

🔨 **$20 400** - €26 435 - **£15 300** - FF173 400
  Nude Métal (122x75cm 48x29in) Prato 2000

🔨 **$3 250** - €2 880 - **£1 994** - FF18 894
  Steel Drawing Edition, Monica Reclining on Blanket and Pillow Metal (19x37.5cm 7x14in) New-York 1999

✎ **$7 040** - €6 731 - **£4 415** - FF44 150
  Study for Nude Chalks (13x13cm 5x5in) Köbenhavn 1999

▦ **$1 891** - €2 147 - **£1 294** - FF14 086
  Fast sketch red stocking nude Farbserigraphie (66.2x98cm 26x38in) Hamburg 2000

WESSMAN Björn 1949 **[56]**

➣ **$2 152** - €2 024 - **£1 333** - FF13 278
  Alla landskap VI Oil/canvas (92x91cm 36x35in) Stockholm 1999

WESSON Edward 1910-1983 **[147]**

➣ **$736** - €652 - **£450** - FF4 278
  Pears, Pottery, Jar and Knife Oil/canvas (44.5x59.5cm 17x23in) Billingshurst, West-Sussex 1999

➣ **$600** - €640 - **£400** - FF4 200
  Wareham, Dorset from the Red Cliff Oil/board (30x43cm 11x16in) Leyburn, North Yorkshire 2000

✎ **$461** - €510 - **£320** - FF3 345
  Flooded Fields Watercolour (36x53cm 14x20in) London 2001

▥ **$635 - €737 - £450** - FF4 833
«See Britain by Train, Lavenham, Suffolk, British Railways» Poster (102x64cm 40x25in) London 2000

WEST Benjamin 1738-1820 [70]
🖅 **$85 000 - €74 559 - £51 612** - FF489 073
Musidora and her Two Companions, Sacharissa and Amoret Oil/canvas (52x72.5cm 20x28in) New-York 1999
🖅 **$2 525 - €3 003 - £1 800** - FF19 701
Procession of Aggripina and her Children and a Roman Lady Oil/paper (33x30cm 12x7in) London 2000
🖅 **$3 250 - €3 481 - £2 319** - FF22 836
Oedipus, Antigone and Jocasta Ink (13.5x19cm 5x7in) New-York 2001

WEST David 1868-1936 [37]
✎ **$2 565 - €2 913 - £1 800** - FF19 111
Castle Varrick and Ben Loyal from Tingue Ferry Watercolour/paper (39x51cm 15x20in) Oxford 2001

WEST Edgar E. 1830-1900 [39]
✎ **$495 - €574 - £350** - FF3 764
A Waterfall in a Mountainous Valley/Rocky Outcrop with Seagulls Watercolour (100.5x73.5cm 39x28in) London 2001

WEST Franz 1947 [140]
🖅 **$10 980 - €10 901 - £6 855** - FF71 505
Ohne Titel Mixed media (82x200cm 32x78in) Wien 1999
🖅 **$7 641 - €6 541 - £4 599** - FF42 903
Namensschild «Lisa» Mixed media/panel (40x110cm 15x43in) Wien 1998
🖅 **$2 460 - €2 325 - £1 532** - FF15 254
Bei Hansi (in Hansi's Heim) Mixed media (24x26.5cm 9x10in) Wien 1999
🖎 **$17 305 - €19 123 - £12 000** - FF125 436
Untitled Sculpture (175.5x106.5x40.5cm 69x41x15in) London 2001
🖎 **$6 921 - €6 541 - £4 311** - FF42 903
Ohne Titel Sculpture (23.5x50x35cm 9x19x13in) Wien 1999
✎ **$2 941 - €2 761 - £1 816** - FF18 114
Rot meets Loriot Mischtechnik/Papier (26.7x22.8cm 10x8in) Wien 1999

WEST John, of Bath ?-c.1835 [3]
✎ **$1 332 - €1 227 - £808** - FF8 046
A View of Caernarfon Castle Watercolour (21x29.5cm 8x11in) Glamorgan 1999

WEST Joseph Walter 1860-1933 [17]
🖅 **$9 681 - €9 298 - £6 000** - FF60 988
Pageant in the Piazza, Venice XVth Century Tempera/panel (40x34cm 15x13in) London 1999

WEST Levin 1900-1968 [26]
▥ **$175 - €184 - £111** - FF1 207
Shallow Water Etching (24x34cm 9x13in) New-Orleans LA 2000

WEST Robert Lucius 1774-1850 [3]
🖅 **$7 916 - €8 867 - £5 500** - FF58 162
Dispute over Cards Oil/panel (53.5x40cm 21x15in) London 2001

WEST Samuel 1810-1867 [4]
🖅 **$12 052 - €10 404 - £7 200** - FF68 246
Horatia Gulston, Lady de Rutzen (d.1924) Oil/canvas (127x100cm 50x39in) Llandeilo, Carmarthenshire 1998

WEST William 1801-1861 [13]
🖅 **$8 045 - €7 655 - £5 000** - FF50 215
Portrait of George Gordon, 6th Lord Byron, bust-Length, in white Shirt Oil/canvas (56.5x45.5cm 22x17in) London 1999

WESTALL John act.1873-1893 [9]
🖅 **$1 255 - €1 476 - £900** - FF9 682
River Landscape with Figures/Cottage in a Landscape Oil/canvas (21x41cm 8x16in) Cheshire 2001

WESTALL Richard 1765-1836 [60]
🖅 **$32 406 - €31 165 - £20 000** - FF204 428
William Shakespeare between Tragedy and Comedy Oil/panel (118x113cm 46x44in) London 1999
🖅 **$4 184 - €4 491 - £2 800** - FF29 460
Lady Becher (1791-1872) née Eliza O'Neill, Seated Three-Quarter-Length Oil/canvas (76.5x63.5cm 30x25in) London 2000
🖅 **$3 800 - €4 415 - £2 670** - FF28 960
The Goddess Roma appearing to Julius Caesar at the Bank of the Rubicon Oil/paper/board (8.5x15.5cm 3x6in) New-York 2001
✎ **$913 - €794 - £550** - FF5 208
Illustrations to Poems by William Cowper Watercolour (12.5x10cm 4x3in) London 1998

WESTALL William 1781-1850 [29]
✎ **$1 009 - €870 - £600** - FF5 708
«Coupang, Timor» Pencil/paper (26x36cm 10x14in) London 1998

WESTBROOKE Walter 1921 [11]
✎ **$233 - €202 - £140** - FF1 323
Distant Rain, near Kimberley Watercolour/paper (46x67cm 18x26in) Johannesburg 1998

WESTCHILOFF Constantin Alexandr. 1877-1945 [36]
🖅 **$1 000 - €1 080 - £692** - FF7 086
Cabin by the Lake Oil/canvas (53x63cm 21x25in) Cincinnati OH 2001
🖅 **$1 200 - €1 292 - £826** - FF8 477
Coastal Village, Capri Oil/board (19x25cm 7x10in) New-York 2001

WESTENBERG George Pieter 1791-1873 [10]
🖅 **$4 637 - €4 538 - £2 973** - FF29 766
A Summer Landscape with Peasants resting in a Forest by a Stream Oil/canvas (55x70cm 21x27in) Amsterdam 1999

WESTENDORP-OSIECK Betsy 1880-1968 [43]
🖅 **$840 - €908 - £574** - FF5 953
A Collection of Exotic Shells Oil/board (51x70cm 20x27in) Amsterdam 2001

WESTERBEEK Cornelis, Snr. 1844-1903 [79]
🖅 **$2 959 - €3 176 - £1 980** - FF20 836
Grazing Sheep Oil/canvas (61x101cm 24x39in) Amsterdam 1999
🖅 **$1 491 - €1 278 - £896** - FF8 383
Flusslandschaft mit Windmühle Öl/Leinwand (22x32.5cm 8x12in) Köln 1998

WESTERHOLM Victor 1860-1919 [82]
🖅 **$136 268 - €127 818 - £84 208** - FF838 432
Höststämning, motiv från Eckerö Oil/canvas (90x135cm 35x53in) Helsinki 1999
🖅 **$12 192 - €11 436 - £7 534** - FF75 017
Kejserliga eskadern i färjsundet Oil/canvas (62x47cm 24x18in) Helsinki 1999
🖅 **$7 990 - €7 904 - £4 982** - FF51 850
Fiskars Oil/canvas (24x35cm 9x13in) Helsinki 1999

W

$540 - €454 - **£317** - FF2 977
Utsikt över dalen Drawing (10x17cm 3x6in) Helsinki 1998

WESTERIK Co 1924 **[104]**
$36 568 - €36 302 - **£22 848** - FF238 128
Strand met meisje en vliegtuig Oil/board (46x57cm 18x22in) Amsterdam 1999
$1 626 - €1 497 - **£976** - FF9 817
Untitled Watercolour (27x36.5cm 10x14in) Amsterdam 1999
$229 - €250 - **£157** - FF1 637
«**Botaniker**» Etching (13x10.5cm 5x4in) Amsterdam 2001

WESTERMANN Horace Clifford 1922-1981 **[24]**
$4 500 - €4 325 - **£2 772** - FF28 367
The dying Dog Watercolour (38x57cm 14x22in) New-York 1999

WESTERMARK Helena 1857-1938 **[5]**
$5 955 - €5 212 - **£3 608** - FF34 189
Flicka Oil/panel (33x24cm 12x9in) Helsinki 1998

WESTFELT-EGGERTZ Ingeborg 1855-1936 **[24]**
$1 134 - €1 104 - **£698** - FF7 240
Jardin de Luxembourg Oil/panel (14x23cm 5x9in) Stockholm 1999

WESTHUIZEN van der Pieter 1931 **[7]**
$290 - €342 - **£200** - FF2 241
Vase of Flowers Pastel/paper (33.5x28cm 13x11in) Cape Town 2000

WESTMACOTT Richard I 1775-1856 **[5]**
$23 679 - €21 800 - **£14 500** - FF142 997
Bust of Charles James Fox (1749-1806) Bronze (H53.5cm H21in) London 1998

WESTMAN Edvard 1865-1917 **[20]**
$10 213 - €11 436 - **£7 092** - FF75 017
Får i höstlig skog Oil/canvas (61x91cm 24x35in) Helsinki 2001
$2 693 - €2 908 - **£1 861** - FF19 076
Vintermotiv Oil/panel (40x32cm 15x12in) Stockholm 1999

WESTMAN Sven Reinhold 1887-1962 **[2]**
$6 376 - €7 143 - **£4 433** - FF46 852
Spansk hamn, Mallorca Oil/canvas (60x80cm 23x31in) Stockholm 2001

WESTON Brett 1911-1993 **[401]**
$3 250 - €3 057 - **£2 012** - FF20 051
Palms, Bronx Botanical Gardens Gelatin silver print (19x24cm 7x9in) New-York 1999

WESTON Cole 1919 **[31]**
$1 100 - €1 034 - **£681** - FF6 784
Pepper Silver print (23x18cm 9x7in) New-York 1999

WESTON Edward 1886-1958 **[476]**
$9 500 - €8 874 - **£5 741** - FF58 208
Dunes, Death Valley Vintage gelatin silver print (18x23cm 7x9in) New-York 1999

WESTON Edward & Cole 1886/1919-1958 **[42]**
$2 200 - €2 217 - **£1 371** - FF14 542
«**Shell**» Gelatin silver print (23.5x18cm 9x7in) New-York 2000

WESTON Henry John, Harry 1874-? **[16]**
$245 - €271 - **£163** - FF1 775
The Sailor Watercolour (19.5x19.5cm 7x7in) Melbourne 2000

WESTON William Percival 1879-1967 **[83]**
$11 034 - €12 479 - **£7 765** - FF81 855
«**Bc Coast**» Oil/canvas (56x61cm 22x24in) Vancouver, BC. 2001
$1 947 - €2 202 - **£1 370** - FF14 445
«**Mt.Douglas from Tolmie**» Oil/board (32.5x41cm 12x16in) Vancouver, BC. 2001
$335 - €370 - **£221** - FF2 424
Crows Nest Charcoal (29x43cm 11x16in) Vancouver, BC. 2000

WESTPHAL Anna 1858-1950 **[20]**
$235 - €228 - **£143** - FF1 498
Opstilling med blomster Oil/masonite (35x29cm 13x11in) Viby J, Arhus 2000

WESTPHAL Conrad 1891-1976 **[83]**
$882 - €762 - **£533** - FF5 000
Composition Encre Chine (60x85cm 23x33in) Paris 1998
$583 - €665 - **£406** - FF4 360
Oberon Monotype (47x61cm 18x24in) Hamburg 2001

WESTPHAL Fritz 1804-1844 **[7]**
$1 771 - €2 014 - **£1 237** - FF13 213
Den unge fiskerpige vugger sin spaede lillebor Oil/canvas (58x48cm 22x18in) København 2000

WESTWOOD Bryan Wyndham 1930-2000 **[49]**
$3 561 - €3 358 - **£2 207** - FF22 024
Bluff South of Alice Springs Oil/board (120x120cm 47x47in) Melbourne 1999
$911 - €1 017 - **£633** - FF6 668
Pears on a Cloth, Seattle Oil/board (59x59cm 23x23in) Sydney 2001

WET de Jacob Jacobsz 1640-1697 **[6]**
$7 788 - €9 203 - **£5 520** - FF60 370
Die Opferung der Iphigenie in Aulis Öl/Leinwand (65x77cm 25x30in) Ahlden 2000

WET de Jakob Willemsz 1610-1671/72 **[65]**
$9 047 - €8 853 - **£5 800** - FF58 070
Bandits hijacking a wagon by a lakeshore Oil/canvas (102x139.5cm 40x54in) London 1999
$4 417 - €4 953 - **£3 000** - FF32 492
The Finding of Moses Oil/panel (44x55.5cm 17x21in) London 2000
$11 954 - €12 832 - **£8 000** - FF84 172
The Annunciation to the Shepherds Oil/panel (40.5x35.5cm 15x13in) London 2000

WETERING DE ROOY van de Johannes Embrosius 1877-1972 **[45]**
$1 816 - €1 541 - **£1 095** - FF10 109
Stad aan een rivier Oil/canvas (40x67cm 15x26in) Rotterdam 1998
$1 241 - €1 180 - **£755** - FF7 739
Rivierlandschap Oil/panel (15x31cm 5x12in) Den Haag 1999

WETHERBEE George Faulkner 1851-1920 **[18]**
$2 845 - €3 306 - **£2 000** - FF21 688
Strayed Princess Oil/canvas (79x127cm 31x50in) London 2001
$1 435 - €1 614 - **£1 000** - FF10 589
«**Sea Urchins**» Oil/canvas (32x48cm 12x18in) Edinburgh 2001

WETHERILL Ann XVIII **[1]**
$7 798 - €7 587 - **£4 800** - FF49 770
Going to Market, and the Return from Market Oil/canvas (48x59cm 18x23in) London 1999

WETLI Hugo 1916-1972 **[73]**
🗋 **$86** - €97 - **£60** - FF639
Asiatin Farblithographie (91x41cm 35x16in) Bern
2001

WETZEL Johann Jakob 1781-1834 **[30]**
✏ **$1 929** - €1 807 - **£1 186** - FF11 856
Genf Aquarell/Papier (19.2x27.4cm 7x10in) Bern 1999
🗋 **$391** - €373 - **£238** - FF2 447
Vue prise de Brunnen vers le Canton d'Ury
Aquatinte couleurs (19.4x27.8cm 7x10in) Bern 1999

WEURLANDER Fridolf 1851-1900 **[10]**
👁 **$2 553** - €2 859 - **£1 773** - FF18 754
Kvällsfiske Oil/canvas (35x48.5cm 13x19in) Helsinki
2001
👁 **$2 319** - €2 270 - **£1 426** - FF14 893
Pyykkipäivä Oil/canvas (20x40cm 7x15in) Helsinki
1999

WEVER de Auguste 1836-1884 **[26]**
◈ **$1 303** - €1 215 - **£803** - FF7 967
Méphisto Bronze (H57cm H22in) Bruxelles 1999

WEWERKA Stefan 1928 **[58]**
👁 **$2 192** - €2 556 - **£1 539** - FF16 769
Ohne Titel Mischtechnik/Karton (70x100cm 27x39in)
Köln 2000
🗋 **$117** - €128 - **£77** - FF838
Krupps Volkswange Radierung (48.5x63.3cm
19x24in) Hamburg 2000

WEX Adalbert 1867-1932 **[51]**
👁 **$695** - €818 - **£498** - FF5 366
Alpenlandschaft Öl/Leinwand (60x67cm 23x26in)
München 2001
👁 **$592** - €665 - **£410** - FF4 360
Abend am Weiher Öl/Leinwand (28x45.5cm
11x17in) München 2000

WEX Willibald 1831-1892 **[41]**
👁 **$932** - €1 022 - **£633** - FF6 707
Hintersteinersee Öl/Leinwand (40x60cm 15x23in)
Bamberg 2000
👁 **$1 088** - €1 227 - **£754** - FF8 049
**«Parthie am Weg nach dem Tödi im Canton
Glarus»** Oil/panel (42x31cm 16x12in) Berlin 2000

WEXELBERG Friedrich-Georg c.1745-c.1820 **[7]**
🗋 **$5 194** - €4 363 - **£3 287** - FF28 618
**«Le Chateau de Chillon en allant de Villeneuve
à Vevey»** Eau-forte (32.8x49.2cm 12x19in) Bern 1998

WEXLER Yaacov 1912-1995 **[71]**
👁 **$1 200** - €1 351 - **£826** - FF8 859
Women in Landscape Oil/canvas (60x73cm
23x28in) Herzelia-Pituah 2000
✏ **$360** - €386 - **£240** - FF2 534
Figures in Café Charcoal/paper (35x49.5cm 13x19in)
Tel Aviv 2000

WEY Alois 1894-1985 **[26]**
✏ **$1 409** - €1 184 - **£828** - FF7 767
Architektur vor abstrahierter Berglandschaft
Mischtechnik/Papier (59.5x53.5cm 23x21in) Bern 1998

WEYDEN van der Harry 1868-? **[21]**
👁 **$1 603** - €1 823 - **£1 100** - FF11 960
Sussex Cliffs Oil/canvas/board (31x41cm 12x16in)
London 2001

WEYER Hermann 1596-c.1621 **[5]**
👁 **$141 794** - €139 252 - **£88 000** - FF913 431
**Allegory of Profane Power/Allegory of Spiritual
Power** Oil/panel (49.5x64.5cm 19x25in) London 1999

WEYER Jacob Matthias 1620-1670 **[11]**
✏ **$1 480** - €1 724 - **£1 034** - FF11 311
**Sculptor at Work, with a Goblin by a
Statue/Head of Solomon** Ink (23.5x16.5cm 9x6in)
Amsterdam 2000

WEYL Max 1837-1914 **[47]**
👁 **$1 800** - €1 682 - **£1 121** - FF11 031
Autumn Landscape Oil/canvas (55x71cm 22x28in)
Mystic CT 1999
👁 **$950** - €1 065 - **£661** - FF6 985
Marsh Landscape Oil/canvas (33.5x46.5cm 13x18in)
Washington 2001

WEYNS Jan Harm 1864-1945 **[41]**
👁 **$308** - €340 - **£201** - FF2 232
Hooiwagen in een bomenlaan Oil/board (11x19cm
4x7in) Rotterdam 2000

WEYSSER Karl 1833-1904 **[22]**
👁 **$2 673** - €3 068 - **£1 828** - FF20 123
Heidelberg Öl/Karton (54x37cm 21x14in) Heidelberg
2000
👁 **$2 831** - €2 914 - **£1 784** - FF19 117
**Kleinstadtgasse und hochaufragende
Bergkuppen mit Burgruinen** Öl/Leinwand
(27x19cm 10x7in) Berlin 2000

WEYTS Carolus Ludovicus 1828-1876 **[2]**
👁 **$6 952** - €6 067 - **£4 800** - FF52 533
A Three-Master off the Needles Oil/board
(41x58cm 16x22in) London 2000

WEYTS Petrus Cornelius 1799-1855 **[6]**
👁 **$30 000** - €33 054 - **£20 013** - FF216 819
**Ship Matchless, Capt.James H.Dawes,
Rescuing the Crew of Ship Japan** Painting
(55x70cm 22x27in) Portsmouth NH 2000

WHAITE Henry Clarence 1828-1912 **[19]**
👁 **$2 728** - €3 247 - **£1 950** - FF21 300
**View in North Wales with Cattle, Sheep, a
Farmer and Haywain** Oil/canvas (34x55cm 13x22in)
Cheadle-Hulme-Cheshire 2000
👁 **$515** - €565 - **£350** - FF3 707
**Shepherd in a Moorland Landscape with a
stone Circle in the Background** Watercolour/paper
(36x54cm 14x21in) Stratford-upon-Avon, Warwickshire
2000

WHAITE James act.c.1860-1890 **[26]**
✏ **$592** - €583 - **£380** - FF3 825
Cattle resting in the Shadow of the Farm
Watercolour/paper (30x44cm 12x17in) Tavistock, Devon
1999

WHAITE T. XIX **[1]**
👁 **$6 382** - €6 101 - **£4 000** - FF40 020
**Queen of Trumps with Jockey up, in an extensi-
ve Landscape** Oil/canvas (63.5x76cm 25x29in)
London 1999

WHANKI Kim 1913-1974 **[11]**
✏ **$47 500** - €49 567 - **£29 958** - FF325 137
Untitled Acrylic/canvas (38x63.5cm 14x25in) New-
York 2000
◈ **$30 000** - €31 305 - **£18 921** - FF205 350
Tazza Sculpture (H22cm H8in) New-York 2000
✏ **$12 000** - €13 261 - **£8 322** - FF86 984
Moonrise over Mountains Gouache/paper
(42x29.5cm 16x11in) New-York 2001

WHATLEY F. XX **[2]**
🗋 **$2 452** - €2 357 - **£1 500** - FF15 459
«Ireland for the Holidays, Glendalough» Poster
(102x127cm 40x50in) London 1999

W

WHATLEY Henry 1842-1901 **[17]**
- $304 - €343 - £210 - FF2 250
  Juanita at the Opera Watercolour/paper (62.5x48.5cm 24x19in) Bristol, Avon 2000

WHEATLEY Francis 1747-1801 **[82]**
- $19 672 - €22 855 - £13 825 - FF149 922
  Ruth and Boaz Oil/canvas (125x100cm 49x39in) Dublin 2001
- $8 698 - €10 345 - £6 200 - FF67 860
  Portrait of Mr Bailey of Stanstead Hall, Full Length Oil/canvas (75x62.5cm 29x24in) London 2000
- $5 886 - €5 234 - £3 600 - FF34 334
  The School Door/Sitting Down to a Meal Oil/canvas (33.5x27cm 13x10in) London 1999
- $1 000 - €947 - £621 - FF6 209
  Young Man Going to Market Watercolour/paper (33x23cm 13x9in) Wallkill NY 1999

WHEATLEY John Laviers 1892-1955 **[41]**
- $614 - €572 - £380 - FF3 755
  River Landscapes/The Canal at Buckhamsted/Gathering Seaweed Oil/canvas (46x56cm 18x22in) Billingshurst, West-Sussex 1999

WHEELER Alfred, Jnr. 1852-1932 **[71]**
- $3 647 - €4 338 - £2 600 - FF28 457
  Tom Firr on a grey Hunter with Two Hounds in a Landscape Oil/canvas (60x51cm 23x20in) London 2000
- $2 200 - €2 243 - £1 378 - FF14 710
  A Manchester Terrier and Two Fox Terriers Oil/board (15x47cm 5x18in) New-York 2000

WHEELER Charles Arthur 1881-1977 **[86]**
- $1 230 - €1 160 - £762 - FF7 608
  Self Portrait Oil/canvas (61x46cm 24x18in) Malvern, Victoria 1999
- $753 - €886 - £540 - FF5 809
  Neutral Bay, Sydney, New South Wales, Australia Oil/board (20x28cm 7x11in) Cheshire 2001

WHEELER Charles Thomas 1892-1974 **[16]**
- $19 602 - €22 798 - £14 000 - FF149 546
  Untitled Sandstone (H67.5cm H26in) London 2001

WHEELER James Thomas 1849-1888 **[13]**
- $1 820 - €2 118 - £1 300 - FF13 891
  On the Scent Oil/board (20.5x36.5cm 8x14in) London 2001

WHEELER John Alfred, Snr. 1821-1903 **[123]**
- $3 287 - €3 529 - £2 200 - FF23 147
  Bessie, a Chesnut Hunter with a Terrier in a Stable Oil/canvas (45.5x61cm 17x24in) London 2000
- $1 853 - €1 596 - £1 100 - FF10 466
  Jack Russell Terrier Oil/board (25.5x35.5cm 10x13in) London 1998

WHEELER Larry 1942 **[1]**
- $26 000 - €30 208 - £18 272 - FF198 151
  Newmarket Lane Oil/panel (40.5x61cm 15x24in) New-York 2001

WHEELER M.E. XIX **[1]**
- $21 000 - €20 075 - £13 162 - FF131 684
  Still Life with Melon and Watermelon Oil/canvas (63.5x76cm 25x29in) New-York 1999

WHEELER Walter Herbert 1868-1960 **[12]**
- $1 444 - €1 537 - £950 - FF10 084
  Smooth Fox Terrier/Irish Terrier Oil/board (15x18cm 5x7in) Billingshurst, West-Sussex 2000

WHEELER William R. 1832-1894 **[9]**
- $3 500 - €3 589 - £2 187 - FF23 544
  Portrait of James Loomis Nichols Oil/panel (76x63cm 30x25in) Bolton MA 2000

WHEELOCK Merrill-Greene 1822-1866 **[1]**
- $6 337 - €5 946 - £3 915 - FF39 000
  Paysages présumés d'Amérique du Nord Aquarelle/papier (40x64cm 15x25in) La Varenne-Saint-Hilaire 1999

WHEELWRIGHT Rowland 1870-1955 **[28]**
- $1 345 - €1 571 - £950 - FF10 303
  Les Autelets, Sark Oil/canvas (34x56cm 13x22in) Guernsey 2000
- $1 345 - €1 571 - £950 - FF10 303
  Shrimping at Grande Greve Sark Oil/board (37x34cm 14x13in) Guernsey 2000

WHEELWRIGHT W.H. XIX **[14]**
- $12 534 - €14 940 - £8 937 - FF98 000
  L'attente/L'attelage Huile/toile (60x84cm 23x33in) Riom 2000
- $2 000 - €1 854 - £1 243 - FF12 160
  Noisy Distraction Watercolour/paper (24x34cm 9x13in) New-York 1999

WHELAN Leo 1892-1956 **[9]**
- $10 794 - €12 091 - £7 500 - FF79 310
  Dermot McGillycuddy (1911-1974)/Patricia McGillycuddy, né Kennedy Oil/canvas (115x91.5cm 45x36in) London 2001
- $2 880 - €2 666 - £1 784 - FF17 490
  Old Man seated in a Cottage Interior Oil/canvas/board (38x30cm 15x12in) Dublin 1999

WHELDON James H. 1832-1895 **[4]**
- $5 642 - €6 585 - £4 000 - FF43 196
  The auxiliary steamer Kersonece calling for a pilot off Anglesey Oil/canvas (61x91.5cm 24x36in) London 2001

WHESSELL John 1760-1824 **[17]**
- $1 246 - €1 337 - £850 - FF8 771
  Trumpator Etching (38.5x48cm 15x18in) Swindon, Wiltshire 2001

WHICHELO C. John Mayle 1784-1865 **[14]**
- $2 975 - €2 810 - £1 850 - FF18 430
  Morning on the Banks of the Maas Watercolour/paper (34x43cm 13x17in) Scarborough, North-Yorkshire 1999

WHIPPLE John Adams 1823-1891 **[24]**
- $2 821 - €2 489 - £1 700 - FF16 330
  «Rolling Clouds, Scene in North Wales» Oil/canvas (61x92cm 24x36in) London 1998
- $3 000 - €2 507 - £1 776 - FF16 447
  Homes near Boston, Massachusetts Salt print (17x22cm 7x9in) New-York 1998

WHIPPLE Seth A. 1855-1901 **[1]**
- $950 - €901 - £593 - FF5 907
  Tug Champion Towing Schooners Color lithograph (55x88cm 22x35in) Mystic CT 1999

WHISHAW Alexander Y. 1870-1946 **[22]**
- $378 - €393 - £240 - FF2 577
  Continental Hilltop Ruins Watercolour/paper (32.5x47.5cm 12x18in) Penzance, Cornwall 2000
- $56 - €65 - £40 - FF427
  Twilight, Assisi Etching in colors (38x53cm 15x21in) Par, Cornwall 2001

WHISSON Kenneth Ronald, Ken 1927 **[28]**
- **$11 009** - €10 351 - **£6 817** - FF67 901
  Flag for Captain Ahab and Thomas Szasz (Flag of my Disposition No.12) Oil/canvas (89.5x119cm 35x46in) Melbourne 1999
- **$500** - €583 - **£352** - FF3 827
  Untitled Pastel/paper (48.5x68.5cm 19x26in) Malvern, Victoria 2000
- **$457** - €491 - **£306** - FF3 221
  Trees Buildings and Birds Lithograph (57x76cm 22x29in) Woollahra, Sydney 2000

WHISTLER James Abbot McNeill 1834-1903 **[955]**
- **$2 600 000** - €2 852 577 - **£1 727 180** - FF18 711 680
  Harmony in Grey - Chelsea in Ice Oil/canvas (45x61cm 17x24in) New-York 2000
- **$37 500** - €41 530 - **£25 432** - FF272 418
  View in Venice, Looking Towards the Molo Pencil (25.5x19cm 10x7in) New-York 2000
- **$1 125** - €1 200 - **£749** - FF7 872
  Fumette Etching (16x10cm 6x4in) Cleveland OH 2000
- **$5 200** - €5 990 - **£3 587** - FF39 291
  Nocturnes - Marines - Chevalet Pieces Albumen print (18x21cm 7x8in) New-York 2000

WHISTLER Rex John 1905-1944 **[38]**
- **$2 525** - €3 003 - **£1 800** - FF19 701
  Very Naughty Chidlren Watercolour (16.5x14cm 6x5in) London 2000

WHITAKER Frederic 1891-1980 **[7]**
- **$900** - €893 - **£552** - FF5 860
  Shipyard Watercolour/paper (53x66cm 21x26in) Mystic CT 2000

WHITAKER George William 1841-1916 **[64]**
- **$2 100** - €1 903 - **£1 293** - FF12 484
  Stormy Sky Oil/canvas (40x60cm 16x24in) Mystic CT 1999
- **$700** - €823 - **£503** - FF5 400
  Morning pastoral scene with sheep and figure Oil/panel (16x21cm 6x8in) Hatfield PA 2001

WHITCOMB Jon 1906-1988 **[28]**
- **$425** - €441 - **£269** - FF2 894
  Bewitching - The Girl in Blue Oil/canvas/board (57x56cm 22x22in) Boston MA 2000
- **$800** - €891 - **£523** - FF5 845
  Story illustration: Woman and Phi Beta Kappa locket Gouache/paper (23x23cm 9x9in) New-York 2000

WHITCOMBE Thomas c.1752/63-1824 **[69]**
- **$29 886** - €32 080 - **£20 000** - FF210 432
  The East Indiaman Hindostan in Company with Indian Trader, Ewretta Oil/canvas (109.5x171cm 43x67in) London 2000
- **$17 380** - €20 167 - **£12 000** - FF132 289
  East Indiaman, The Marquis of Ely, in Two Positions off Fort St.George Oil/canvas (81.5x122cm 32x48in) London 2000
- **$935** - €868 - **£500** - FF57 028
  View of Southsea Castle, Portsmouth Oil/canvas (29.5x42cm 11x16in) London 1999

WHITE & STIEGLITZ Clarence H. & Alfred 1871/64-1925/46 **[6]**
- **$3 000** - €3 299 - **£2 080** - FF21 642
  Torso Photogravure (21x15cm 8x6in) New-York 2001

WHITE Alice XIX-XX **[4]**
- **$1 149** - €1 341 - **£800** - FF8 796
  Views of York Watercolour/paper (53x70cm 20x27in) West-Yorshire 2000

WHITE Arthur 1865-1953 **[99]**
- **$607** - €656 - **£420** - FF4 305
  Old St.Ives Oil/canvas (45x53cm 18x21in) Par, Cornwall 2001
- **$530** - €564 - **£350** - FF3 697
  Sorting the Catch on the Quay St.Ives Oil/board (23x30.5cm 9x12in) Penzance, Cornwall 2000
- **$514** - €521 - **£320** - FF3 418
  St.Ives with the Ruins of Trenwith Mine Watercolour/paper (34x51cm 13x20in) Par, Cornwall 2000

WHITE Charles III XX **[2]**
- **$677** - €654 - **£420** - FF4 291
  «Star Wars» Poster (101.5x76cm 39x29in) London 1999

WHITE Charles Wilbert 1918-1979 **[10]**
- **$38 000** - €40 453 - **£25 885** - FF265 354
  Uhuru Ink/paper (95.5x143.5cm 37x56in) Miami FL 2001

WHITE Clarence Hudson 1871-1925 **[58]**
- **$1 800** - €2 007 - **£1 250** - FF13 162
  Illustration for «Eben Holden» Platinum print (20x15cm 7x5in) New-York 2001

WHITE Edith 1855-1946 **[26]**
- **$3 500** - €3 757 - **£2 342** - FF24 643
  Still Life with Dish Oil/canvas (51x61cm 20x24in) San-Francisco CA 2000
- **$2 000** - €2 337 - **£1 427** - FF15 332
  Red flowers and foliage Oil/board (45x30cm 18x12in) Altadena CA 2001

WHITE Ely Emlyn XIX **[1]**
- **$2 412** - €2 278 - **£1 500** - FF14 943
  Beachcombers and Long Horned Cattle on the Rocks at Filey Bay Watercolour/paper (20x30cm 8x12in) Scarborough, North-Yorshire 1999

WHITE Ethelbert 1891-1972 **[193]**
- **$1 445** - €1 683 - **£1 000** - FF11 043
  The Thames at Wapping Oil/canvas (61x73.5cm 24x28in) London 2000
- **$664** - €736 - **£450** - FF4 825
  An Autumnal Landscape Oil/canvas (33x38.5cm 12x15in) Billingshurst, West-Sussex 2000
- **$416** - €378 - **£260** - FF2 478
  Farmstead Watercolour/paper (38x55cm 14x21in) London 1999
- **$476** - €444 - **£295** - FF2 915
  Threshing Woodcut (15x28cm 5x11in) London 1999

WHITE Fritz 1930 **[15]**
- **$10 000** - €11 355 - **£6 948** - FF74 481
  Saving Little Sister for San Jacinto Bronze (68x121x73cm 27x48x29in) Dallas TX 2001

WHITE George Francis 1808-1898 **[12]**
- **$3 098** - €3 639 - **£2 200** - FF23 872
  «Landscapes and River Scenes: Indian Figures/View of the Ganges» Watercolour (19x28cm 7x11in) London 2000

WHITE George Harlow 1817-1888 **[25]**
- **$226** - €213 - **£140** - FF1 394
  Feeding Chickens before a Kitchen Watercolour (12.5x21.5cm 4x8in) London 1999

WHITE Henry 1819-1903 **[8]**
- **$3 883** - €4 262 - **£2 500** - FF27 954
  Old House with Extension Albumen print (19x24cm 7x9in) London 2000

W

WHITE J. Talmage XIX **[3]**
$17 931 - €19 248 - **£12 000** - FF126 259
Capo di Sorrento Watercolour (54.5x103cm 21x40in)
London 2000

WHITE John Claude 1853-1918 **[5]**
$90 000 - €93 926 - **£56 943** - FF616 113
Tibet and Lhasa Photograph (19x28cm 7x11in) New-York 2000

WHITE John, R.I., R.O.I. 1851-1933 **[110]**
$1 494 - €1 604 - **£1 000** - FF10 521
Morning, Low Tide on Beer Beach Watercolour
(18x28cm 7x11in) London 2000

WHITE Judith XX **[8]**
$594 - €504 - **£358** - FF3 305
Apartment Harbour View Mixed media/paper
(53x70cm 20x27in) Sydney 1998

WHITE Larry 1946 **[6]**
$767 - €915 - **£547** - FF6 000
Composition Huile/toile (27x22cm 10x8in) Provins 2000

WHITE Lois 1903-1984 **[8]**
$12 093 - €13 555 - **£8 457** - FF88 914
Flight into Egypt Oil/canvas (60x75cm 23x29in)
Auckland 2001

WHITE Minor 1908-1976 **[143]**
$2 258 - €2 234 - **£1 408** - FF14 656
Nude Foot, San Francisco Gelatin silver print
(27.3x34.7cm 10x13in) Berlin 1999

WHITE Nelson 1900 **[8]**
$1 800 - €1 706 - **£1 124** - FF11 192
The Fleet Oil/board (25x35cm 10x14in) Mystic CT 1999
$1 000 - €969 - **£619** - FF6 359
The Joseph Conrad Watercolour/paper (20x30cm
8x12in) Mystic CT 1999

WHITE Orrin Augustine 1883-1969 **[76]**
$5 500 - €6 428 - **£3 926** - FF42 163
Eucalyptus valley landscape Oil/board (40x50cm
16x20in) Altadena CA 2001
$1 800 - €1 932 - **£1 204** - FF12 673
Pottery Market Guanajuato, Mexico Oil/board
(30x25cm 12x10in) Altadena CA 2000

WHITE Valentino 1909-1985 **[14]**
$1 200 - €1 555 - **£900** - FF10 200
Fiori nel paesaggio Olio/tavola (50x70cm 19x27in)
Napoli 2000
$600 - €777 - **£450** - FF5 100
Paesaggio vesuviano Olio/cartone/tela (30x40cm
11x15in) Napoli 2000

WHITE Willie 1910 **[23]**
$200 - €178 - **£122** - FF1 165
Watermelon and Green Bird and Mountain Felt
pen (55x71cm 22x28in) New-Orleans LA 1999

WHITE-OAKES Sue XX **[7]**
$1 555 - €1 407 - **£1 000** - FF10 064
Frog Sculpture (12.5x33cm 4x12in) London 1999

WHITEFORD Kate 1952 **[3]**
$578 - €625 - **£400** - FF4 100
Marker Oil/board (24.5x30cm 9x11in) London 2001

WHITEHAND Michael J. 1941 **[82]**
$3 038 - €3 235 - **£2 000** - FF21 221
Racing Home Oil/canvas (49.5x75cm 19x29in)
Billingshurst, West-Sussex 2000

WHITEHEAD Buell XIX-XX **[15]**
$240 - €276 - **£165** - FF1 811
«**Bayou**» Color lithograph (18x25cm 7x10in)
Cleveland OH 2000

WHITEHEAD Frederick William N. 1853-1938 **[56]**
$3 065 - €2 944 - **£1 900** - FF19 312
Distant View of Poole, Dorset Oil/canvas
(47x91.5cm 18x36in) London 1999
$898 - €858 - **£560** - FF5 629
Cattle in Meadow Oil/board (18x27cm 7x11in)
Rotherham 1999

WHITEHEAD Harold XIX-XX **[1]**
$17 447 - €18 320 - **£11 000** - FF120 171
Discovery in Winter Quarters, McMurdo Sound
Oil/canvas (45.5x61cm 17x24in) London 2000

WHITEHURST Camelia 1871-1936 **[1]**
$15 000 - €13 948 - **£9 259** - FF91 494
Portrait of a seated young Girl in white Oil/canvas
(91x73cm 36x29in) Portland ME 1999

WHITELEY Brett 1939-1992 **[470]**
$93 780 - €111 528 - **£66 834** - FF731 574
Lavender Bay Mixed media (202x119.5cm 79x47in)
Melbourne 2000
$52 357 - €45 653 - **£31 660** - FF299 464
View from the Window, Bali Oil/canvas (95x75cm
37x29in) Melbourne 1998
$543 - €563 - **£363** - FF3 824
Rivers-Design for gallery invitation Mixed media
(27x17cm 10x6in) Sydney 2000
$23 356 - €22 205 - **£14 576** - FF145 656
The Palm Tree Glazed ceramic (H54cm H21in)
Melbourne 1999
$10 114 - €11 343 - **£7 023** - FF74 408
«**What I'd like to see...**» Watercolour (77x50cm
30x19in) Melbourne 2001
$3 430 - €3 683 - **£2 296** - FF24 157
The Moreton Bay Fig Etching (60x50cm 23x19in)
Melbourne 2000

WHITEREAD Rachel 1963 **[30]**
$198 324 - €169 447 - **£120 000** - FF1 111 500
Square Sink Plaster (107x101x86.5cm 42x39x34in)
London 2000
$30 000 - €34 809 - **£20 712** - FF228 330
Torso Plaster (23.5x16.5x9cm 9x6x3in) New-York 2000
$22 787 - €22 179 - **£14 000** - FF145 482
Mattress Ink (29.5x41cm 11x16in) London 1999
$12 000 - €13 923 - **£8 284** - FF91 332
Water Tower Project Gelatin silver print (63.5x51cm
25x20in) New-York 2000

WHITESELL Joseph Woodsen Pops 1876-1958
[17]
$700 - €649 - **£435** - FF4 256
«**There was a Streetcar Called Desire**» Silver
print (34x40cm 13x16in) New-Orleans LA 1999

WHITESIDE Frank Reed 1866-1929 **[37]**
$1 300 - €1 554 - **£896** - FF10 194
The Purple Bluff Oil/canvas (35x50cm 14x20in)
Milford CT 2000
$950 - €1 117 - **£683** - FF7 328
«**After the storm**» Oil/canvas (26x34cm 10x13in)
Hatfield PA 2001
$290 - €324 - **£204** - FF2 163
By the Water's Edge Pastel/paper (18x23cm 7x9in)
Philadelphia PA 2001

WHITFORD Richard XIX **[14]**
- $7 716 - €9 177 - **£5 500** - FF60 198
  Musk, a Devon Cow, in an Extensive Landscape
  Oil/canvas (60x70cm 23x27in) London 2000

WHITING Frederic 1874-1962 **[44]**
- $464 - €539 - **£321** - FF3 537
  Figures Among Trees Oil/canvas (60x43.5cm 23x17in) Johannesburg 2000
- $1 190 - €1 384 - **£850** - FF9 081
  Huntsman on a grey Horse with his Dog
  Watercolour/paper (37x41cm 14x16in) London 2001

WHITING H.W., Jnr. XIX **[3]**
- $2 250 - €2 415 - **£1 505** - FF15 842
  Landscape with Muskingom River with Fisherman near Marietta, Ohio Oil/canvas
  (60x106cm 24x42in) Bloomfield-Hills MI 2000

WHITMORE Bryan XIX-XX **[9]**
- $466 - €460 - **£300** - FF3 019
  Fishing by a Riverside Tavern Watercolour
  (12.5x20cm 4x7in) London 1999

WHITMORE Coby 1913-1988 **[9]**
- $3 500 - €4 080 - **£2 423** - FF26 762
  Couple in Elegant Restaurant, She With Lipstick
  Gouache/paper (41x31cm 16x12in) New-York 2000

WHITMORE Olive XX **[6]**
- $330 - €309 - **£200** - FF2 027
  «**Dublin Horse Show, Fly Aer Lingus**» Poster
  (102x64cm 40x25in) London 1999

WHITNEY Charles Frederick 1858-? **[3]**
- $2 000 - €1 996 - **£1 217** - FF13 090
  The Whipper-In Watercolour/paper (48.5x52cm 19x20in) New-York 2000

WHITTAKER Mark 1964 **[6]**
- $3 064 - €2 784 - **£1 900** - FF18 265
  The Watering Place Oil/canvas (75x100.5cm 29x39in) Billingshurst, West-Sussex 2000

WHITTEMORE William John 1860-1955 **[8]**
- $1 900 - €2 039 - **£1 294** - FF13 378
  Portrait of a Woman Oil/canvas (20.5x15.5cm 8x6in) Boston MA 2001
- $7 000 - €8 325 - **£4 988** - FF54 607
  A Young Girl Picking Flowers Watercolour/paper (35x50cm 13x19in) New-York 2000

WHITTINGTON William G. XIX-XX **[20]**
- $272 - €267 - **£169** - FF1 754
  Running for Shelter, Littlehampton
  Watercolour/paper (26.5x38cm 10x14in) Toronto 1999

WHITTLE Thomas, Jnr. XIX **[37]**
- $2 560 - €2 444 - **£1 600** - FF16 032
  The Ferry Oil/canvas (40.5x61cm 15x24in) London 1999
- $1 242 - €1 426 - **£850** - FF9 351
  Harvesting Scene with Hay Cart and Horses/Pastoral Landscape Oil/board (11.5x14cm 4x5in) Leamington-Spa, Warwickshire 2000

WHITTLE Thomas, Snr. XIX **[12]**
- $4 000 - €4 289 - **£2 646** - FF28 132
  Near Abergavenny in the River Usk Oil/canvas (77x127cm 30x50in) New-Orleans LA 2000
- $866 - €971 - **£602** - FF6 367
  Still Life of Fruit The Birthday Gift Oil/board (27x44cm 10x17in) Durban 2001

WHITTREDGE Thomas Worthington 1820-1910 **[71]**
- $70 000 - €83 248 - **£49 889** - FF546 070
  Sunrise on the Wetterhorn Oil/canvas (98.5x135cm 38x53in) New-York 2000

- $28 000 - €26 646 - **£17 514** - FF174 787
  Spring on the River Oil/canvas (55.5x37cm 21x14in) New-York 1999
- $10 000 - €10 944 - **£6 898** - FF71 788
  Mountain Landscape with Pine Trees Oil/canvas (38.5x28cm 15x11in) New-York 2001

WHORF John 1903-1959 **[181]**
- $14 500 - €13 457 - **£8 705** - FF88 270
  View of the Harbor Oil/canvas (73x91cm 29x36in) Milford CT 1999
- $2 300 - €2 139 - **£1 424** - FF14 031
  Fishing Boat, Dock and Dory Oil/board (33x39cm 13x15in) East-Dennis MA 1999
- $4 300 - €3 981 - **£2 632** - FF26 113
  Nude Woman by River Bank Watercolour/paper (38x52cm 15x20in) Wethersfield CT 1999
- $425 - €502 - **£301** - FF3 294
  Vorse's Lane - Winter Offset (28x43cm 11x17in) Provincetown MA 2000

WHORF Richard 1906-1966 **[8]**
- $1 100 - €1 259 - **£756** - FF8 257
  Look Who's There! Oil/board (36x52cm 14x20in) New-York 2000

WHYDALE Ernest Herbert 1886-1952 **[42]**
- $89 - €96 - **£60** - FF631
  Carting Mangolds Etching (16x18cm 6x7in) Par, Cornwall 1999

WHYMPER Charles 1853-1941 **[81]**
- $1 948 - €1 872 - **£1 200** - FF12 280
  Elephants, Sable Antelope and Zebras at a Waterhole - Sunset Oil/canvas/board (76x125cm 29x49in) London 1999
- $693 - €766 - **£480** - FF5 026
  Brancaster Watercolour (23.5x33.5cm 9x13in) London 2001

WHYMPER Emily ?-1886 **[2]**
- $1 673 - €1 968 - **£1 200** - FF12 910
  Bee Feeding on Common Heather Watercolour (30x40cm 11x15in) London 2001

WHYMPER Frederick 1838-1901 **[2]**
- $3 350 - €3 696 - **£2 215** - FF24 243
  The Ravine, Victoria, Vancouver Island
  Watercolour/paper (21x29cm 8x11in) Vancouver, BC. 2000

WHYMPER Josiah Wood 1813-1903 **[22]**
- $886 - €814 - **£549** - FF5 342
  A Haslemere Hayfield Watercolour (20x20cm 8x8in) London 1999

WHYTE Duncan McGregor 1866-1953 **[22]**
- $5 049 - €5 934 - **£3 500** - FF38 924
  In the Canoe Oil/canvas (42x33cm 16x12in) Edinburgh 2000

WHYTE Peter 1905-1966 **[5]**
- $2 042 - €1 937 - **£1 240** - FF12 708
  Mt Norquay Looking North, Banff, Alberta, Rocky Mountain Park Oil/canvas/board (23x28cm 9x11in) Calgary, Alberta 1999

WIBERG Harald 1908-1986 **[154]**
- $1 852 - €1 616 - **£1 120** - FF10 599
  «**Skrämda rådjur - senvinterlandskap**» Oil/panel (46x55cm 18x21in) Stockholm 1998
- $474 - €478 - **£296** - FF3 138
  Rävslagsmål Pencil/paper (22.5x24cm 8x9in) Stockholm 2000

W

WICAR Jean-Baptiste Jos. 1762-1834 **[10]**

  $8 318 - €7 045 - **£5 000** - FF46 210
    Portraits of Italian Ladies and Gentlemen Black
    chalk (26x20cm 10x7in) London 1998

WICART Nicolas 1748-1815 **[70]**

  $915 - €991 - **£581** - FF6 500
    Paysages animées Encre (19x28cm 7x11in) Paris
    2000

WICHERS Hal, Hendrick A.L. 1893-1968 **[28]**

  $788 - €681 - **£476** - FF4 464
    A Stream in a Indonesian woodland Oil/panel
    (48x64.5cm 18x25in) Amsterdam 1999

WICHERT Felix 1842-1902 **[3]**

  $2 844 - €3 383 - **£2 028** - FF22 191
    Au bord de la mer Huile/toile (81x125cm 31x49in)
    Warszawa 2000

WICHGRAF Fritz 1853-? **[3]**

  $3 941 - €3 681 - **£2 381** - FF24 148
    **Gartenlokal im Berliner Tiergarten,
    Musikpavillon und Gartenstühle** Öl/Karton
    (24x33cm 9x12in) Berlin 1999

WICHMAN Erich 1890-1929 **[15]**

  $22 280 - €24 958 - **£15 482** - FF163 713
    Masks Bronze (H11cm H4in) Amsterdam 2001

  $546 - €635 - **£384** - FF4 167
    Gesprekavondlandschap Lithograph (42x31.5cm
    16x12in) Amsterdam 2001

WICHMANN Johannes 1854-? **[1]**

  $5 230 - €5 615 - **£3 500** - FF36 830
    Contemplation Oil/canvas (118x78cm 46x30in)
    London 2000

WICHMANN Peder 1706-1769 **[13]**

  $1 411 - €1 611 - **£980** - FF10 566
    **Portraet af frederik V i rustning, baerende
    Elefantordenens blå bånd** Oil/canvas (73x61cm
    28x24in) Köbenhavn 2000

WICHT von John 1888-1970 **[29]**

  $1 300 - €1 109 - **£774** - FF7 274
    Springtime Oil/canvas (68.5x96.5cm 26x37in) New-
    York 1998

  $550 - €502 - **£338** - FF3 291
    Festivity Crayon (44x57cm 17x22in) Bloomfield-Hills
    MI 1998

  $650 - €738 - **£445** - FF4 844
    City Color lithograph (52x39cm 20x15in) New-York
    2000

WICK van Jan Claszen ?-1613 **[1]**

  $8 052 - €9 147 - **£5 634** - FF60 000
    Philosophe dans son cabinet Huile/panneau
    (26.5x20.5cm 10x8in) Paris 2001

WICKENBERG Per 1812-1846 **[19]**

  $2 400 - €2 488 - **£1 440** - FF16 320
    Scena di pesca Olio/tela (27x35cm 10x13in) Torino
    2001

WICKENBURG Alfred 1885-1978 **[16]**

  $51 791 - €48 691 - **£31 356** - FF319 389
    Giardino del Lago, Villa Borghese Öl/Leinwand
    (139.5x111.5cm 54x43in) Wien 1999

WICKENDEN Robert J. 1861-1931 **[21]**

  $900 - €894 - **£558** - FF5 863
    Stratton Falls near Roxbury, New York Oil/canvas
    (55x45cm 22x18in) Norwalk CT 2000

  $1 000 - €993 - **£620** - FF6 515
    **Horse Drawn Cart in River Landscape «The
    Watering Place»** Oil/panel (30x45cm 12x18in)
    Norwalk CT 2000

WICKERTSHEIMER Wilhelm 1885-1968 **[10]**

  $773 - €767 - **£481** - FF5 030
    **Im Vordergrund Fahrweg, der sich zu einem
    Schwarzwaldhof hinzieht** Öl/Karton (88x107cm
    34x42in) Merzhausen 1999

WICKEY Harry 1892-1968 **[12]**

  $6 500 - €6 977 - **£4 350** - FF45 769
    Sulking Bull Bronze (H29.5cm H11in) New-York
    2000

  $175 - €177 - **£108** - FF1 162
    Negroes Cabin Etching (11x13cm 4x5in) Chester NY
    2000

WIDAYAT H. 1923 **[36]**

  $9 043 - €9 992 - **£6 270** - FF65 545
    Flamboyant Oil/canvas (92x146cm 36x57in)
    Singapore 2001

  $7 679 - €7 157 - **£4 641** - FF46 946
    Affandi and Masks Oil/canvas (100x70cm 39x27in)
    Singapore 1999

WIDDAS Richard Dodd 1826-1885 **[11]**

  $2 285 - €2 175 - **£1 450** - FF14 268
    The Law Milking the Fat of the Land Oil/canvas
    (38.5x51cm 15x20in) Billingshurst, West-Sussex 1999

WIDER Wilhelm 1818-1884 **[4]**

  $2 724 - €2 355 - **£1 617** - FF15 446
    «Die unerwünschte Blumenverkäuferin»
    Oil/panel (40x26cm 15x10in) Rudolstadt-Thüringen
    1998

WIDERBÄCK Gusten 1879-1970 **[74]**

  $619 - €618 - **£386** - FF4 051
    Atterbomska huset från trädgårdssidan Oil/can-
    vas (42x48cm 16x18in) Uppsala 1999

  $470 - €527 - **£327** - FF3 459
    Helga Trefaldighet Oil/canvas (36x42cm 14x16in)
    Uppsala 2000

WIDERBERG Frans 1934 **[62]**

  $2 403 - €2 046 - **£1 435** - FF13 421
    Lysende landskap Oil/canvas (51x74cm 20x29in)
    Oslo 1998

  $1 878 - €2 104 - **£1 305** - FF13 802
    Mann mot skog Ink/paper (49x63cm 19x24in) Oslo
    2001

  $621 - €671 - **£429** - FF4 402
    Röd-grönn svever (Rytter) Print (47x53cm 18x20in)
    Oslo 2001

WIDFORSS Gunnar M. 1879-1934 **[61]**

  $7 500 - €6 408 - **£4 538** - FF42 033
    Superstition Mountains Oil/canvas/board
    (26.5x37cm 10x14in) San-Francisco CA 1998

  $12 000 - €10 253 - **£7 261** - FF67 252
    Yosemite Valley Watercolour/paper (34.5x43cm
    13x16in) San-Francisco CA 1998

WIDGERY Frederick John 1861-1942 **[386]**

  $2 315 - €2 500 - **£1 600** - FF16 399
    Dunkery Beacon, Exmoor Mixed media
    (50x73.5cm 19x28in) Newbury, Berkshire 2001

  $1 386 - €1 261 - **£850** - FF8 272
    **Loading the Hay-Barge/Near Prince Town,
    Dartmoor** Oil/panel (17.5x52.5cm 6x20in)
    Billingshurst, West-Sussex 1998

  $1 260 - €1 200 - **£800** - FF7 869
    On the Exe Watercolour (18.5x38cm 7x14in)
    Billingshurst, West-Sussex 1999

WIDGERY William 1822-1893 **[133]**

  $15 000 - €17 680 - **£10 540** - FF115 975
    Cattle Watering Oil/canvas (182x131cm 72x51in)
    New-Orleans LA 2000

W

🕭 **$1 151** - €1 090 - **£700** - FF7 152
Wreckers on a Rocky Foreshore Oil/canvas
(65x98cm 25x38in) Penrith, Cumbria 1999

🕭 **$688** - €764 - **£480** - FF5 013
Wooded River Landscape with Cattle watering
Oil/board (28x35.5cm 11x13in) Godalming, Surrey
2001

✍ **$535** - €632 - **£380** - FF4 146
**Landscape with cattle and church with a distant
view of Dartmoor** Watercolour (24x71cm 9x27in)
Devon 2001

WIDHOPFF D.O. 1867-1933 **[31]**
🕮 **$351** - €335 - **£219** - FF2 200
«Pilar Montero» Affiche couleur (131x91cm 51x35in)
Orléans 1999

WIDJA Ida Bagus Made 1912 **[2]**
✍ **$1 781** - €1 495 - **£1 045** - FF9 804
Balinese Scene Gouache/board (32x120cm 12x47in)
Singapore 1998

WIDMANN Bruno 1930 **[20]**
🕭 **$26 000** - €30 208 - **£18 272** - FF198 151
«Legendaria y de galera» Oil/canvas (181.5x202cm
71x79in) New-York 2001

🕭 **$820** - €853 - **£517** - FF5 593
Estructuras Oleo/lienzo (50x70cm 19x27in)
Montevideo 2000

WIDMER Hans 1872-1925 **[18]**
🕭 **$311** - €363 - **£220** - FF2 383
Teichlandschaft Öl/Leinwand (68x81cm 26x31in)
Salzburg 2000

WIDOFF Anders 1953 **[19]**
🕭 **$6 571** - €7 625 - **£4 537** - FF50 017
Utan titel, ur Opera Nr.40 Oil/canvas (64x200cm
25x78in) Stockholm 2000

🕭 **$1 719** - €1 615 - **£1 036** - FF10 596
Capri Oil/canvas (60.5x85.5cm 23x33in) Stockholm
1999

WIEBENGA Johannes Bernardus 1905-1987 **[21]**
🕭 **$801** - €680 - **£483** - FF4 460
Vissen Oil/canvas (115x90cm 45x35in) Den Haag
1998

WIEDENMANN Ludwig 1934 **[35]**
🕭 **$487** - €511 - **£329** - FF3 353
Bergbauernhof mit Personen und Tieren Oil/can-
vas/panel (24x30cm 9x11in) Kempten 2001

WIEGAND Gottfried 1926 **[14]**
✍ **$280** - €307 - **£190** - FF2 017
Über's Eck zweihändig Linie Ziehen Pencil/paper
(32x24cm 12x9in) Luzern 2000

WIEGAND Gustave Adolph 1870-1957 **[60]**
🕭 **$1 750** - €1 877 - **£1 158** - FF12 311
Landscape with River and Hills Oil/canvas
(60x91cm 24x36in) New-Orleans LA 2000

🕭 **$1 200** - €1 249 - **£753** - FF8 192
Summer Landscape with Cottage and Road
Oil/canvas (30x45cm 12x18in) Chicago IL 2000

WIEGAND von Charmion 1899-1983 **[13]**
🕭 **$15 000** - €15 653 - **£9 460** - FF102 675
Region of the Unstruct Sound Oil/canvas
(56x25.5cm 22x10in) New-York 2000

✍ **$3 500** - €3 903 - **£2 353** - FF25 600
Ancien Garden Collage (37.5x25cm 14x9in) New-
York 2000

WIEGANDT Bernhard 1851-1918 **[28]**
🕮 **$234** - €245 - **£147** - FF1 609
Fischerhuder Bäuerinnen in der Diele Etching,
aquatint (21x32cm 8x12in) Bremen 2000

WIEGERS Jan 1893-1959 **[198]**
🕭 **$8 723** - €7 551 - **£5 293** - FF49 533
Still life with flowers Oil/canvas (60x50cm 23x19in)
Amsterdam 1998

🕭 **$3 299** - €3 176 - **£2 062** - FF20 836
Self Portrait Oil/panel (40x37.5cm 15x14in)
Amsterdam 1999

✍ **$612** - €590 - **£383** - FF3 869
«Ticino» Watercolour/paper (42.5x37cm 16x14in)
Amsterdam 1999

🕮 **$163** - €172 - **£108** - FF1 131
View of a Canal, Amsterdam Lithograph
(41.5x51cm 16x20in) Amsterdam 2000

WIEGHORST Olaf 1899-1988 **[176]**
🕭 **$18 000** - €20 438 - **£12 506** - FF134 065
Sparking Oil/canvas (71x96cm 28x38in) Dallas TX
2001

🕭 **$7 000** - €6 363 - **£4 216** - FF41 741
Twirling Riata Mixed media (30x27cm 12x11in)
Hayden ID 1998

✍ **$1 400** - €1 288 - **£840** - FF8 452
Two Horses under a Tree Watercolour/paper
(15x12cm 6x5in) Pasadena CA 1999

🕮 **$225** - €238 - **£148** - FF1 558
Arizona Range Print in colors (38x49cm 15x19in)
Portland OR 2000

WIEGMAN Matthieu 1886-1971 **[108]**
🕭 **$4 946** - €4 425 - **£2 963** - FF29 025
The Mines Oil/canvas (60x73.5cm 23x28in)
Amsterdam 1998

🕭 **$4 659** - €5 445 - **£3 326** - FF35 719
Still Life with Grapes and a Pear Oil/canvas
(33x41cm 12x16in) Amsterdam 2001

✍ **$478** - €544 - **£336** - FF3 571
Sint MAarten Gouache/paper (46x35cm 18x13in)
Amsterdam 2001

WIEGMAN Piet 1885-1963 **[10]**
🕭 **$18 065** - €17 244 - **£11 289** - FF113 110
Biljartspelers Oil/canvas (202x163.5cm 79x64in)
Amsterdam 1999

🕭 **$3 640** - €4 084 - **£2 522** - FF26 789
View on a Dutch House Oil/canvas (47x74cm
18x29in) Amsterdam 2000

WIEHE Carl Wilhelm 1788-1867 **[1]**
🕭 **$2 305** - €2 288 - **£1 439** - FF15 011
**Dreng iklaedt blå frakke og hvid krave siddende
ved bord** Oil/canvas (19x15.5cm 7x6in) Köbenhavn
1999

WIEHL Franz XIX **[2]**
🕭 **$1 087** - €1 296 - **£775** - FF8 500
Portraits d'un officier et de son épouse
Huile/toile (100x82cm 39x32in) Paris 2000

WIELAND Hans Beat 1867-1945 **[100]**
🕭 **$1 728** - €1 944 - **£1 206** - FF12 754
«Am Misurinasee» Öl/Leinwand (58x72cm 22x28in)
Luzern 2001

✍ **$393** - €441 - **£273** - FF2 891
Winterliche Berglandschaft Aquarell/Papier
(49.5x63.5cm 19x25in) Luzern 2001

🕮 **$131** - €123 - **£79** - FF804
Landschaft mit hohen Bäumen Etching
(20.8x28.8cm 8x11in) Berlin 1999

W

WIELANDT Manuel 1863-1922 **[11]**
- $3 660 - €3 835 - £2 421 - FF25 154
  Venedig, Fischerboote und Gondeln auf dem Bacino di S.Marco Öl/Leinwand (43x73cm 16x28in) München 2000

WIELHORSKI Alain 1950 **[140]**
- $368 - €351 - £233 - FF2 300
  La plage Pastel/papier (48x64cm 18x25in) Pontivy 1999

WIELOGLOWSKI Artur Waclaw S. 1860-1933 **[3]**
- $3 443 - €3 997 - £2 420 - FF26 218
  Die Kamelreiterin Öl/Karton (99x46cm 38x18in) Wien 2001

WIEMKEN Walter Kurt 1907-1940 **[33]**
- $7 280 - €8 508 - £5 197 - FF55 812
  Strand mit Schiffen, Collioure Öl/Leinwand (54x80cm 21x31in) Zürich 2001
- $692 - €783 - £484 - FF5 138
  Sitzender Mann mit Schildmütze Pencil (23x25cm 9x9in) St. Gallen 2001

WIENK XX [4]
- $989 - €862 - £598 - FF5 657
  «I'm going to Paint Your Car this Evening» said Mr Golly Watercolour (17.5x12cm 6x4in) London 1998

WIERINGEN van Cornelis Claesz. c.1580-1633 **[14]**
- $35 064 - €40 840 - £24 498 - FF267 894
  Mountainous Woded Landscape, with Figures by a Bridge Over a Waterfall Ink (10.5x16cm 4x6in) Amsterdam 2000
- $8 837 - €8 551 - £5 600 - FF56 091
  Large Marine: Merchantmen, Inland Vessels, Rowboat off a Coastline Woodcut (13.5x22cm 5x8in) London 1999

WIERIX Anthonie Wierx c.1552-c.1624 **[7]**
- $403 - €460 - £281 - FF3 018
  Den slapende leeu (der schlafende Löwe) Kupferstich (20.5x32cm 8x12in) Berlin 2001

WIERIX Hieronymus, Jérôme 1553-1619 **[40]**
- $500 - €584 - £351 - FF3 834
  The Annunciation Engraving (18.5x13cm 7x5in) New-York 1999

WIERIX Johannes, Jan Wierx c.1549-c.1615 **[20]**
- $5 489 - €5 360 - £3 500 - FF35 161
  Portrait of a Man wearing a ruff Ink (5x4.5cm 1x1in) London 1999
- $375 - €402 - £255 - FF2 635
  Adam and Eve, after Durer Engraving (23x18cm 9x7in) Chicago IL 2001

WIERSMA Ids 1878-1965 **[13]**
- $105 - €118 - £73 - FF773
  Molen in landschap Etching (25x35cm 9x13in) Rotterdam 2001

WIERTZ Antoine 1806-1865 **[32]**
- $11 050 - €12 394 - £7 500 - FF81 300
  Le chagrin Huile/toile (130x104cm 51x40in) Bruxelles 2000

WIERTZ Jupp 1888-1939 **[17]**
- $400 - €400 - £244 - FF2 622
  «German Winter» Poster (100x62cm 39x24in) New-York 2000

WIERUSZ-KOWALSKI Karol 1869-1953 **[6]**
- $4 408 - €4 145 - £2 730 - FF27 191
  Stud Farm Oil/canvas (85x101cm 33x39in) Warszawa 1999

WIERUSZ-KOWALSKI von Alfred 1849-1915 **[123]**
- $78 381 - €64 800 - £45 981 - FF425 061
  Gentleman on Horse riding through the Meadows with two Dogs Oil/canvas (77x102cm 30x40in) Warszawa 1998
- $7 773 - €8 662 - £5 229 - FF56 822
  Attaque des loups Huile/panneau (11x15.5cm 4x6in) Warszawa 2000
- $4 649 - €4 686 - £2 899 - FF30 738
  Dans la cour Gouache (43.5x33.5cm 17x13in) Warszawa 2000

WIESCHEBRINK Franz 1818-1884 **[8]**
- $6 478 - €6 135 - £3 939 - FF40 246
  Der treue Wächter, eine Hündin an der Wiege des schreienden Säuglings Öl/Leinwand (61.4x54.3cm 24x21in) München 1999

WIESE Bruno 1865-1930 **[3]**
- $4 160 - €4 130 - £2 600 - FF27 093
  Female Nude bathing in a classical Landscape Oil/canvas (145.5x75cm 57x29in) London 1999

WIESELTHIER Vally 1895-1945 **[28]**
- $2 100 - €2 240 - £1 398 - FF14 692
  A Wiener Werkstatte Figure Terracotta (H18cm H7in) Cleveland OH 2001

WIESENTHAL Franz 1856-1938 **[13]**
- $1 218 - €1 308 - £815 - FF8 580
  Nachmittag im Wintergarten Öl/Leinwand (56.5x70cm 22x27in) Wien 2000

WIESNER Richard 1900-1972 **[14]**
- $693 - €656 - £432 - FF4 590
  Plateau rose Tempera (33x27cm 12x10in) Praha 2000

WIEST Sally 1866-1952 **[14]**
- $486 - €486 - £293 - FF3 186
  Gasse in Ulm mit Blick auf das Münster Öl/Leinwand/Karton (33x25cm 12x9in) Stuttgart 2000

WIETHASE Edgard 1881-1965 **[117]**
- $1 597 - €1 328 - £937 - FF8 713
  Mare with Foals Oil/board (63x63cm 24x24in) Amsterdam 1998
- $187 - €223 - £134 - FF1 463
  Moestuin (potager) Oil/carton (34x25cm 13x9in) Antwerpen 2000
- $124 - €149 - £89 - FF975
  Bloemenkorf (panier de fleurs) Aquarelle/papier (100x75cm 39x29in) Antwerpen 2000

WIGAND Albert 1890-1978 **[20]**
- $1 353 - €1 636 - £945 - FF10 732
  Blume Mixed media (20.5x12cm 8x4in) Berlin 2000
- $632 - €613 - £393 - FF4 024
  Strassenszene in Leitmeritz in Böhmen Gouache/Karton (25x35.1cm 9x13in) Berlin 1999

WIGAND Balthasar 1770-1846 **[55]**
- $2 294 - €2 556 - £1 603 - FF16 769
  «Essende und schäkernde französische Soldaten werden überfallen» Gouache (17.8x21cm 7x8in) München 2001

WIGDEHL Michaloff 1857-1921 **[9]**
- $768 - €866 - £532 - FF5 679
  Bjerketraer, Host, Gildeskål Oil/canvas (57x64cm 22x25in) Oslo 2000

WIGERT Hans 1932 **[65]**
- $1 123 - €1 259 - £783 - FF8 257
  Barkbåten Oil/canvas (46x55cm 18x21in) Stockholm 2001

📇 **$277** – €280 – **£173** – FF1 837
Åhlèns skyltdockor Aquatint (27x32cm 10x12in)
Stockholm 2000

WIGG Charles Mayes 1889-1969 **[73]**
✏ **$567** – €645 – **£400** – FF4 233
Woodton, Suffolk Watercolour/paper (25x33cm
10x13in) Aylsham, Norfolk 2001

WIGGERS Derk 1866-1933 **[48]**
🖼 **$1 973** – €1 815 – **£1 220** – FF11 906
Uit 't raam Oil/canvas (34x51.5cm 13x20in)
Amsterdam 1999

WIGGERS Karel 1916 **[11]**
🖼 **$4 449** – €4 991 – **£3 083** – FF32 742
Meisje Met Kant Kraag Oil/canvas (56x48cm
22x18in) Amsterdam 2000
🖼 **$4 016** – €4 311 – **£2 687** – FF28 277
Jongens Portret Oil/panel (31x31cm 12x12in)
Amsterdam 2000

WIGGINS Guy Carleton 1883-1962 **[267]**
🖼 **$13 000** – €14 227 – **£8 967** – FF93 324
Haystacks and Pumpkins Oil/canvas (185x123cm
72x48in) New-York 2001
🖼 **$24 000** – €20 787 – **£14 719** – FF136 356
Blizzard on 5th Ave Oil/canvas (40.5x51cm 15x20in)
New-York 1999
🖼 **$25 000** – €23 778 – **£15 180** – FF155 975
Wall Street in Winter Oil/canvas/board (30.5x40.5cm
12x15in) Beverly-Hills CA 1999
✏ **$1 500** – €1 700 – **£1 048** – FF11 149
«Washington Arch» Pencil/paper (24.5x20.5cm
9x8in) New-York 2001

WIGGINS John Carleton 1848-1932 **[56]**
🖼 **$3 200** – €3 435 – **£2 141** – FF22 531
Cattle in a Pasture Oil/canvas (96x76.5cm 22x30in)
New-York 2000
🖼 **$1 400** – €1 573 – **£982** – FF10 320
September Day, Country Landscape with Sheep
Oil/board (31x38cm 12x15in) Windsor CT 2001

WIGGINS Kim Douglas 1960 **[21]**
🖼 **$10 000** – €11 355 – **£6 948** – FF74 481
Winter Funeral at Lincoln Oil/canvas (91x121cm
36x48in) Dallas TX 2001

WIGGLI Oscar 1927 **[41]**
🗿 **$35 718** – €42 006 – **£25 612** – FF275 539
«Skulptur 97 B» Metal (H103cm H40in) Bern 2001
🗿 **$5 827** – €5 340 – **£3 505** – FF35 030
Skulptur 51 K Fer (23.5x20x14cm 9x7x5in) Zürich
1999
📇 **$109** – €105 – **£67** – FF690
Weiblicher Akt Aquatinta (39.5x29.5cm 15x11in)
Bern 1999

WIGMANA Gérard 1673-1741 **[9]**
🖼 **$9 240** – €9 450 – **£5 858** 693
**Vertumnus und Pomona: Pomona lehnt mit
einem Sonnenschirm** Oil/panel (66x50cm 25x19in)
Berlin 1999
🖼 **$11 954** – €12 832 – **£8 000** – FF84 172
The Morning Toilet Oil/panel (43x31.5cm 16x12in)
London 2000

WIGSTEAD Henry c.1745-1800 **[7]**
📇 **$1 289** – €1 203 – **£800** – FF7 888
**Excursion to Brighthelmstone (Abbey Scenery
54)** Aquatint (24x32.5cm 10x12in) London 1999

WIHLBORG Gerhard 1897-1982 **[38]**
🖼 **$866** – €907 – **£548** – FF5 952
Blommor i vas Oil/panel (56x46cm 22x18in) Malmö
2000

WIIG HANSEN Svend 1922-1997 **[148]**
🖼 **$2 132** – €2 149 – **£1 329** – FF14 099
Portraetskitse Oil/canvas (76x54cm 29x21in)
København 2000
🗿 **$927** – €1 005 – **£642** – FF6 595
Figurkomposition Bronze relief (23x35cm 9x13in)
København 2001
✏ **$424** – €349 – **£249** – FF2 292
Figurkomposition/Studie af hånd Pencil/paper
(49x37cm 19x14in) København 1998

WIIK Maria 1853-1928 **[49]**
🖼 **$18 898** – €18 500 – **£11 627** – FF121 352
Asetelma Oil/canvas (49x60cm 19x23in) Helsinki
1999
🖼 **$14 419** – €16 145 – **£10 012** – FF105 907
Speglingar Oil/canvas/board (24x30cm 9x11in)
Helsinki 2001
✏ **$227** – €3 027 – **£1 994** – FF19 857
Björkdungen Akvarell/papper (37x45cm 14x17in)
Helsinki 1999

WIJDOOGEN N.M. 1814-? **[26]**
🖼 **$1 369** – €1 588 – **£970** – FF10 418
A Steamer and Sailing Vessel Off the Coast
Oil/canvas (35x49cm 13x19in) Amsterdam 2000
🖼 **$3 088** – €3 630 – **£2 141** – FF23 812
Shipping in a Calm at Sunset Oil/panel
(26x37.5cm 10x14in) Amsterdam 2000

WIJGA Jan 1902-1978 **[14]**
📇 **$379** – €431 – **£263** – FF2 827
«De Vliegende Hollander» Poster (62x98cm
24x38in) Hoorn 2001

WIJK van Charles 1875-1917 **[17]**
🗿 **$3 515** – €4 084 – **£2 470** – FF26 789
Elderly Lady Bronze (H22cm H8in) Amsterdam 2001

WIJNANTS Ernest 1878-1964 **[38]**
🗿 **$9 408** – €7 937 – **£5 600** – FF52 064
Torse de femme Bronze poli (H102cm H40in)
Antwerpen 1998

WIJNGAERDT Petrus Theodorus 1816-1893 **[15]**
🖼 **$6 026** – €4 950 – **£3 500** – FF32 467
The Love Letter Oil/panel (24x22cm 9x8in) London
1998

WIJNGAERDT van Anthonie Jacobus 1808-1887
[71]
🖼 **$6 987** – €5 891 – **£4 147** – FF38 645
Figures in a Wooded Landscape Oil/panel
(34x52cm 13x20in) Amsterdam 1998
🖼 **$2 942** – €3 176 – **£2 011** – FF20 836
**Wooded Summer Landscape with a Peasant
Couple by a Stream** Oil/canvas (24x36cm 9x14in)
Amsterdam 2001

WIJNGAERDT van Piet 1873-1964 **[295]**
🖼 **$1 095** – €1 271 – **£776** – FF8 334
**Still Life with Flowers, a Bottle and Fruit on a
Plate** Oil/canvas (69x78.5cm 27x30in) Amsterdam
2000
🖼 **$614** – €590 – **£385** – FF3 869
Stilleven met appel en sinaasappel Oil/panel
(18x24cm 7x9in) Dordrecht 1999
✏ **$507** – €544 – **£339** – FF3 571
Woman with a Dog in Forest Pastel/paper
(66x57.5cm 25x22in) Amsterdam 2000

WIJNHOVEN Steef 1898-1969 **[13]**
🖼 **$676** – €726 – **£452** – FF4 762
Strandje aan de Merwede Oil/board (24x39cm
9x15in) Dordrecht 2000

W

WIJNVELD Barend 1820-1902 [5]
$1 741 - €1 633 - **£1 076** - FF10 715
Interieur met vrouw, kind en hond Oil/canvas
(33x26cm 12x10in) Rotterdam 1999

WIJSMULLER Jan Hillebrand 1855-1925 [159]
$8 642 - €9 076 - **£5 468** - FF59 532
The Evening Walk Oil/canvas (102x152cm 40x59in)
Amsterdam 2000
$1 921 - €1 815 - **£1 198** - FF11 906
View of a Polder Pond Oil/board (41x60.5cm
16x23in) Amsterdam 1999
$2 305 - €2 178 - **£1 438** - FF14 287
Flowers in a Vase Oil/cardboard (32.5x27cm
12x10in) Amsterdam 1999
$401 - €364 - **£247** - FF2 389
Maison derrière la baie Aquarelle/papier (49x66cm
19x25in) Montréal 1999

WIJTKAMP Johan Hendrik 1834-1915 [3]
$2 592 - €2 723 - **£1 640** - FF17 859
In the Snow Watercolour (45x67.5cm 17x26in)
Amsterdam 2000

WIJTSMAN Rodolf 1860-1927 [3]
$10 560 - €9 915 - **£6 520** - FF65 040
Le port de Rotterdam Huile/toile (60x90cm
23x35in) Antwerpen 1999
$1 748 - €1 611 - **£1 053** - FF10 569
La hulpe Aquarelle/papier (56x38cm 22x14in)
Antwerpen 1999

WIKBERG Nils 1907-1971 [55]
$112 - €126 - **£76** - FF827
Kvällskymning Watercolour/paper (35x40cm
13x15in) Helsinki 2000

WIKSTROM Bror Anders 1839-1909 [15]
$500 - €538 - **£342** - FF35 016
Schooners Entering Harbor Oil/canvas (91x71cm
36x28in) New-Orleans LA 1999

WILBAUT Nicolas 1686-1763 [1]
$5 424 - €5 378 - **£3 392** - FF35 276
Adelsame med hund og arkitekturtegning
Oil/canvas (134x74cm 52x29in) København 1999

WILBERG Christian Johannes 1839-1882 [4]
$10 257 - €11 810 - **£7 090** - FF77 468
Agrigento with Juno Temple Oil/canvas
(113x189cm 44x74in) London 2000

WILBUR Lawrence Nelson 1897-1988 [6]
$6 000 - €6 854 - **£4 224** - FF44 959
«Rocks and Surf-Laguna Beach, California»
Oil/canvas (63x76cm 25x30in) Pittsfield MA 2001
$500 - €477 - **£304** - FF3 127
The East River Drypoint (25x35.5cm 9x13in) New-
York 1999

WILCKENS August 1870-1939 [6]
$6 069 - €5 656 - **£3 666** - FF37 098
Eksteriör med syende Oil/canvas (66x55cm
25x21in) København 1999

WILCOX Frank 1887-1964 [25]
$355 - €333 - **£229** - FF2 187
Haystacks Ink (17x23cm 7x9in) Cleveland OH 1999

WILCOX James 1941 [1]
$13 000 - €11 818 - **£7 829** - FF77 519
Moose Meadows Oil/board (60x121cm 24x48in)
Hayden ID 1998

WILCOX Leslie Arthur 1904-1982 [37]
$3 385 - €3 951 - **£2 400** - FF25 917
The last of the Alabama Oil/canvas (51x76cm
20x29in) London 2001

$1 308 - €1 257 - **£800** - FF8 245
«Bristol, British Railways, Western Region»
Poster (102x64cm 40x25in) London 1999

WILCZEK Hans, Graf 1837-1922 [1]
$5 742 - €6 541 - **£3 969** - FF42 903
Aufnahmen von der Insel Jan Mayen Albumen
print (12x20cm 4x7in) Wien 2000

WILD Charles 1781-1835 [11]
$2 764 - €2 967 - **£1 850** - FF19 465
**Bath Abbey Viewed from the Corner of
Pierrepont Street Looking Across** Watercolour
(49x37.5cm 19x14in) Bath 2000

WILD Frank Percy 1861-1950 [16]
$3 226 - €3 477 - **£2 200** - FF22 806
Children in a Mediterranean doorway Oil/canvas
(58.5x45.5cm 23x17in) London 2001

WILD Gaspard 1804-? [1]
$2 490 - €2 890 - **£1 719** - FF18 954
Panorama von Venedig Aquatint in colors
(24x92.5cm 9x36in) Luzern 2000

WILD Hamilton Gibbs XIX [3]
$3 750 - €4 155 - **£2 514** - FF27 255
The Orange Seller Oil/canvas (121x77cm 48x30in)
Dedham MA 2000

WILDA Charles 1854-1907 [25]
$66 945 - €78 727 - **£48 000** - FF516 412
Inside the Souk, Cairo Oil/canvas (53.5x45cm
21x17in) London 2001
$4 677 - €5 367 - **£3 200** - FF35 206
Middle Eastern Street Oil/panel (20.5x15cm 8x5in)
London 2000
$1 721 - €1 414 - **£1 000** - FF9 276
An Arab Backstreet Watercolour/paper (28.5x16cm
11x6in) London 1998

WILDA Hans Gottfried 1862-1911 [20]
$781 - €716 - **£476** - FF4 695
**Kaiser Franz Joseph von Österreich mit dem
Zaren Alexander II** Aquarell/Papier (22.6x35.3cm
8x13in) München 1999

WILDE de August 1819-1886 [9]
$3 995 - €4 538 - **£2 803** - FF29 766
The little Teasers Oil/panel (51.5x41cm 20x16in)
Amsterdam 2001

WILDE de Christoffel Steitz 1784-1860 [2]
$7 679 - €7 157 - **£4 641** - FF46 946
River in a Landscape, Indonesia Oil/canvas/panel
(65x93cm 25x36in) Singapore 1999

WILDE de Samuel 1748-1832 [13]
$1 046 - €1 123 - **£700** - FF7 365
**Mother Cries Out as her Child is Taken by a
Lion** Oil/panel (20.5x30.5cm 8x12in) Suffolk 2000

WILDE Gerald 1905-1986 [8]
$322 - €376 - **£230** - FF2 469
Snowman Ink/paper (40x50.5cm 15x19in) London
2001

WILDE van der Jan Willemsz. 1586-c.1636 [4]
$11 624 - €12 196 - **£7 704** - FF80 000
Le sermon dans la montagne Huile/toile
(70.5x117.5cm 27x46in) Ourville-en-Caux 2000

WILDE William 1826-1901 [14]
$2 363 - €2 149 - **£1 450** - FF14 095
**Walford Hill, Nottingham/At Birkland,
Nottingham** Watercolour/paper (40.5x30cm 15x11in)
West-Midlands 1999

WILDENS Jan 1586-1653 **[44]**
- $38 340 - €41 161 - **£25 650** - FF270 000
  La Nativité dans un paysage de rivière Huile/toile (175x184cm 68x72in) Paris 2000
- $16 978 - €19 818 - **£11 986** - FF130 000
  Paysage aux grands arbres Huile/panneau (42x70.5cm 16x27in) Paris 2000
- $11 000 - €10 976 - **£6 695** - FF71 996
  Landscape with an Elegant Travelling Party Ink (26.5x40cm 10x15in) New-York 2000

WILDER André 1871-1965 **[88]**
- $2 626 - €2 592 - **£1 618** - FF17 000
  Le port d'Antibes Huile/toile/panneau (46x55cm 18x21in) Calais 1999

WILDER Arthur B. 1857-1945 **[4]**
- $1 900 - €2 259 - **£1 354** - FF14 821
  The Ravine Pastel/paper (60x44.5cm 23x17in) New-York 2000

WILDER Herbert Merrill 1864-? **[1]**
- $1 600 - €1 792 - **£1 111** - FF11 755
  Gag Cartoon, Circus Performers and Animals invade a small Town Ink (42x71cm 16x28in) New-York 2001

WILDHACK Paula 1872-1955 **[2]**
- $3 723 - €3 997 - **£2 541** - FF26 218
  Christrosen Oil/panel (31x23cm 12x9in) Wien 2001

WILDING Alison 1948 **[5]**
- $2 816 - €3 324 - **£2 000** - FF21 806
  For Echo Bronze (10x23x10cm 3x9x3in) London 2001

WILDING Dorothy 1893-1976 **[40]**
- $832 - €823 - **£518** - FF5 399
  Silver Turban Vintage gelatin silver print (29.2x22.6cm 11x8in) Berlin 1999

WILDING Robert Thornton XIX-XX **[24]**
- $553 - €630 - **£380** - FF4 131
  Fishing Boats in Choppy Waters Watercolour/paper (24x55cm 9x21in) London 2000

WILDRIK Rudolphine Swanida 1807-1883 **[5]**
- $5 393 - €5 113 - **£3 281** - FF33 539
  Variastilleben mit Blumenstrauss und Früchten Öl/Leinwand (60x48cm 23x18in) Köln 1999
- $3 592 - €3 103 - **£2 166** - FF20 354
  Still Life of Roses Oil/panel (26.5x34.5cm 10x13in) Johannesburg 1998

WILDT Adolfo 1868-1931 **[9]**
- $7 600 - €9 848 - **£5 700** - FF64 600
  Pargoli cristiani Bronzo (H30cm H11in) Roma 2001
- $250 - €259 - **£150** - FF1 700
  «Casa di Gesù» Acquaforte, acquatinta (27x19cm 10x7in) Milano 2001

WILES Irving Ramsay 1861-1948 **[59]**
- $23 000 - €22 835 - **£14 375** - FF149 789
  Roses in a Vase Oil/canvas (51x40.5cm 20x15in) New-York 1999
- $20 000 - €19 466 - **£12 288** - FF127 688
  Beach at Shinnecock, Long Island Oil/panel (25x35cm 10x14in) San-Francisco CA 1999
- $500 - €583 - **£351** - FF3 825
  Venetian Scene with Gondola Watercolour/paper (15x10cm 6x4in) Portsmouth NH 2000

WILES Lemuel Maynard 1826-1905 **[24]**
- $4 750 - €4 112 - **£2 882** - FF26 970
  Farming Scene Oil/canvas (35x60cm 14x24in) Mystic CT 1998

- $6 000 - €5 667 - **£3 628** - FF37 174
  Seascape Oil/canvas (31x46.5cm 12x18in) New-York 1999

WILEY William T. 1937 **[48]**
- $4 000 - €4 647 - **£2 811** - FF30 484
  «Nothing out of the Ordinary to the Casual Observer» Graphite (194x223.5cm 76x87in) Beverly-Hills CA 2001
- $480 - €450 - **£296** - FF2 955
  Rhoom for Error #32 Etching (66x94cm 25x37in) New-York 1999

WILHELMINE-FRIEDERIKE-SOPHIE Markgräf.v. Bayreuth 1709-1758 **[1]**
- $3 044 - €3 552 - **£2 119** - FF23 301
  Parklandschaften Gouache/paper (29x38cm 11x14in) Bern 1999

WILHELMS Carl 1889-1953 **[20]**
- $439 - €420 - **£267** - FF2 758
  Sittande naken Bronze relief (20x20cm 7x7in) Helsinki 1999

WILHELMSON Carl 1866-1928 **[187]**
- $287 040 - €309 523 - **£192 660** - FF2 030 340
  Vattenhämtning Oil/canvas (196x177.5cm 77x69in) Stockholm 2000
- $14 904 - €16 071 - **£10 003** - FF105 421
  Flicka med hatt Oil/canvas (59x35cm 23x13in) Stockholm 2000
- $2 570 - €2 924 - **£1 795** - FF19 177
  Motiv rån Kiruna Oil/panel (24x35cm 9x13in) Stockholm 2000
- $1 561 - €1 455 - **£963** - FF9 545
  Fjordlandskap Akvarell/papper (22.5x31.5cm 8x12in) Stockholm 1999
- $1 037 - €905 - **£627** - FF5 935
  Fiskare Etching (28.5x21.5cm 11x8in) Stockholm 1998

WILHJELM Johannes M. Fasting 1868-1938 **[99]**
- $488 - €484 - **£296** - FF3 173
  Hedelandskab med baerplukkende kvinder Oil/canvas (62x94cm 24x37in) Vejle 2000

WILK (J.W. Wilkinson) 1906-1994 **[19]**
- $830 - €880 - **£550** - FF5 771
  Anthony Barker, depicted holding a hare Watercolour (31.5x46.5cm 12x18in) Penrith, Cumbria 2000

WILKE Paul Ernest 1894-1972 **[62]**
- $1 362 - €1 534 - **£939** - FF10 061
  Hafen in Arild, Schweden Öl/Leinwand (50.5x70.5cm 19x27in) Bremen 2000

WILKES Maurice Canning 1911-1984 **[3]**
- $2 905 - €2 728 - **£1 800** - FF17 892
  Spring Day, Dun River, Co. Antrim Oil/canvas/board (35.5x25.5cm 13x10in) London 1999

WILKIE David 1785-1841 **[74]**
- $19 668 - €22 817 - **£14 000** - FF149 672
  Sir William Knighton (1776-1836), Head and Shoulders Oil/canvas/panel (45.5x35.5cm 17x13in) London 2001
- $2 250 - €2 493 - **£1 508** - FF16 354
  Study for the Blind Fiddler Oil/canvas (28x34cm 11x13in) Dedham MA 2000
- $977 - €1 140 - **£680** - FF7 477
  Compositional Sketches Ink (8x11cm 3x4in) Leicestershire 2000
- $115 - €130 - **£81** - FF852
  «The blind Fiddler» Kupferstich (41x55cm 16x21in) Bern 2001

W

WILKIE Leslie Andrew 1879-1935 **[11]**
- 🎨 **$324** - €305 - **£200** - FF1 998
  Harmony in Grey Oil/canvas/board (24x34cm 9x13in)
  Sydney 1999

WILKINS Frank W. c.1791-1842 **[1]**
- ✏️ **$4 286** - €4 725 - **£2 800** - FF30 991
  **Portrait of Edward Sherlock Gooch, later 6th Bt
  (c.1800-1856)** Black & white chalks/paper (47x37cm
  18x14in) London 2000

WILKINS John act.1795-1800 **[1]**
- 🎨 **$6 313** - €7 509 - **£4 500** - FF49 253
  The Hope, a British Man of War in Calm Waters
  Oil/canvas (42x52cm 16x20in) London 2000

WILKINSON Arthur Stanley c.1860-1930 **[52]**
- 🎨 **$472** - €521 - **£320** - FF3 418
  Early Morning, Brixham Watercolour/paper
  (24x35cm 9x13in) London 2000

WILKINSON Charles A. 1830-? **[3]**
- ✏️ **$2 099** - €2 439 - **£1 475** - FF16 000
  Voyageurs dans un compartiment Aquarelle,
  gouache (23.5x34cm 9x13in) Paris 2001

WILKINSON Edward Clegg XIX-XX **[5]**
- ✏️ **$7 295** - €8 677 - **£5 200** - FF56 915
  At the Orchard gate Watercolour (56x39.5cm
  22x15in) London 2000

WILKINSON Henry 1921 **[23]**
- 🏛️ **$201** - €186 - **£120** - FF1 222
  Red Setters on the Scent Etching (25x33cm
  10x13in) Aylsham, Norfolk 1999

WILKINSON J. Walter 1892-? **[2]**
- 🎨 **$1 900** - €1 819 - **£1 173** - FF11 935
  **Happy Man Consulting Map on Way to
  Ballgame, Billboard Advertisement** Mixed
  media/canvas (41x93cm 16x37in) New-York 1999

WILKINSON Norman 1878-1971 **[273]**
- 🎨 **$2 481** - €2 121 - **£1 500** - FF13 916
  Tramp Steamer Approaching Harwich Oil/canvas
  (40.5x61cm 15x24in) London 1999
- 🎨 **$597** - €642 - **£400** - FF4 208
  **Bayonnaise Taking Ambuscade, December,
  1798** Oil/board (25.5x39.5cm 10x15in) London 2000
- ✏️ **$478** - €513 - **£320** - FF3 366
  Bamburgh Castle Watercolour/paper (9.5x17.5cm
  3x6in) London 2000
- 🏛️ **$739** - €670 - **£450** - FF4 394
  The Take Etching (23x30.5cm 9x12in) Godalming,
  Surrey 1999

WILKINSON Thomas Harrison 1847-1929 **[41]**
- ✏️ **$132** - €144 - **£91** - FF943
  Embarcation près des falaises Aquarelle/papier
  (27x48cm 10x18in) Montréal 2001

WILKS Maurice Canning 1911-1983 **[304]**
- 🎨 **$4 605** - €5 158 - **£3 200** - FF33 837
  Reflections, Connemara Oil/canvas (40.5x51cm
  15x20in) London 2001
- 🎨 **$3 574** - €3 049 - **£2 130** - FF19 999
  Stone and Hills, Inagh Valley, Connemara
  Oil/canvas (33x42cm 12x16in) Dublin 1998
- ✏️ **$1 236** - €1 178 - **£750** - FF7 729
  Lough Arran Watercolour/paper (25x30cm 10x12in)
  Hockley, Birmingham 1999

WILL (Willy Maltaite) 1927-2000 **[24]**
- ✏️ **$724** - €843 - **£510** - FF5 528
  **Femmes à la cascade (dessin préparatoire à la
  sérigraphie)** Crayon/papier (47x38cm 18x14in)
  Bruxelles 2001

- 🏛️ **$255** - €297 - **£180** - FF1 951
  Tif et Tondu contre la main blanche Sérigraphie
  (60x60cm 23x23in) Bruxelles 2001

WILLAERT Ferdinand 1861-1938 **[174]**
- ✏️ **$3 731** - €3 224 - **£2 249** - FF21 151
  Vue du Béguinage de Gand sous la neige
  Huile/toile (78.5x46cm 30x18in) Bruxelles 1998

WILLAERTS Abraham 1603-1669 **[18]**
- 🎨 **$33 033** - €31 765 - **£20 349** - FF208 362
  **Dover: Capriccio of the Cliffs, Harbour and
  Castle.** Oil/canvas (122.5x149cm 48x58in) Amsterdam
  1999
- 🎨 **$16 377** - €16 361 - **£10 240** - FF107 324
  Schiffe in küstennahem Gewässer Oil/panel
  (41.5x66cm 16x25in) Köln 1999
- 🎨 **$4 804** - €4 602 - **£3 023** - FF30 185
  **Seestück, Auslaufende Schiffe vor felsiger
  Küste** Oil/panel (27x43cm 10x16in) Köln 1999

WILLAERTS Adam 1577-1664 **[30]**
- 🎨 **$51 634** - €46 993 - **£31 693** - FF308 252
  **Segelschiffe vor einer Küste mit Fischhändlern
  und einem kleinen Dorf** Huile/panneau (50x75cm
  19x29in) Zürich 1999
- 🎨 **$97 980** - €105 190 - **£65 550** - FF690 000
  **Paysage de bord de mer avec des pêcheurs et
  un navire hollandais** Huile/panneau (34x40cm
  13x15in) Paris 2000

WILLAERTS Isaac 1620-1693 **[11]**
- 🎨 **$35 000** - €37 439 - **£23 863** - FF245 584
  **Coastal Scene with Shipping and Figures
  Along a Beach** Oil/panel (71x99cm 27x38in) New-
  York 2001

WILLARD Archibald 1836-1918 **[10]**
- 🎨 **$9 000** - €7 559 - **£5 291** - FF49 586
  «Spirit of 76» Oil/canvas (101x76cm 40x30in)
  Cleveland OH 1998

WILLARS Christian Otto 1714-1758 **[1]**
- ✏️ **$4 828** - €4 576 - **£2 937** - FF30 018
  **Saluterende orlogsskib ud for Köbenhavns
  Havn** Watercolour, gouache/paper (25x34cm 9x13in)
  Köbenhavn 1999

WILLARST de Adam Edvard 1693-1752 **[1]**
- ✏️ **$5 076** - €6 036 - **£3 618** - FF39 595
  **Kong Frederik IV stående i interieur iført rust-
  ning og hermelinskåbe** Watercolour/paper
  (15.5x12.3cm 6x4in) Köbenhavn 2000

WILLCOCK George Burrell 1811-1852 **[25]**
- 🎨 **$963** - €910 - **£600** - FF5 970
  A Gypsy Camp Oil/board (19.5x29.5cm 7x11in)
  Channel-Islands 1999

WILLE Johan Georg 1715-1808 **[71]**
- ✏️ **$700** - €621 - **£427** - FF4 074
  Two Young Fisherman with a Dog Ink (17x15cm
  6x5in) New-York 1999
- 🏛️ **$134** - €144 - **£91** - FF945
  Maurice de Saxe Grabado (54x38cm 21x14in)
  Madrid 2001

WILLE Pierre Alexandre 1748-1821 **[51]**
- ✏️ **$1 618** - €1 906 - **£1 137** - FF12 500
  Portrait d'homme Sanguine (29x23cm 11x9in) Paris
  2000

WILLE von August 1829-1887 **[33]**
- 🎨 **$5 798** - €5 368 - **£3 597** - FF35 215
  Rüdesheim Öl/Leinwand (51x76cm 20x29in) Stuttgart
  1999

$1 952 - €2 045 - **£1 291** - FF13 415
Holländische Fischer und Frauen am Strand an einem Dünenhang Öl/Leinwand (26.2x38.5cm 10x15in) München 2000

WILLE von Clara 1838-1883 **[11]**
$1 571 - €1 687 - **£1 052** - FF11 067
Jagdstilleben Öl/Leinwand (82x60cm 32x23in) Stuttgart 2000

WILLE von Fritz 1860-1941 **[141]**
$12 467 - €14 828 - **£8 885** - FF97 263
Riviera di Ponente Öl/Leinwand (92x132cm 36x51in) Köln 2000
$6 433 - €7 669 - **£4 587** - FF50 308
Die Kirche am Weinfelder Maar in der Eifel Öl/Leinwand (60x80cm 23x31in) Köln 2000
$1 184 - €1 431 - **£826** - FF9 390
Magenberg (Kreuz am Venn) Öl/Karton (22x31cm 8x12in) Düsseldorf 2000
$571 - €613 - **£389** - FF4 024
Fluss im Gebirgstal Aquarell/Papier (37x30cm 14x11in) Rudolstadt-Thüringen 2001
$158 - €148 - **£98** - FF972
In einem kühlen Grunde Farblithographie (23.9x16.7cm 9x6in) Heidelberg 1999

WILLEBOIRTS Thomas Bosschaert 1613-1654 **[6]**
$90 000 - €74 852 - **£52 830** - FF490 995
A Bacchanale Oil/canvas (155x160cm 61x62in) New-York 1998
$128 904 - €126 592 - **£80 000** - FF830 392
Vanitas Oil/canvas (123.5x96.5cm 48x37in) London 1999

WILLEBRANT James Willem 1950 **[47]**
$1 849 - €1 782 - **£1 142** - FF11 686
Successful Man Lifting Equipment Oil/canvas (124x108cm 48x42in) Sydney 1999
$788 - €761 - **£488** - FF4 990
Malibu Morning Oil/board (59x28cm 23x11in) Sydney 1999
$493 - €572 - **£346** - FF3 752
Beach Tower Oil/board (40x30cm 15x11in) Sydney 2000
$163 - €183 - **£113** - FF1 199
Fortified Green Silkscreen (56x72cm 22x28in) Sydney 2001

WILLEM Denyse 1943 **[7]**
$408 - €397 - **£249** - FF2 601
Scène fantastique Gouache/papier (28x38cm 11x14in) Liège 1999

WILLEMS Florent 1823-1905 **[82]**
$13 095 - €11 155 - **£7 785** - FF73 170
Intérieur bourgeois à deux jeunes femmes près d'un berceau Huile/panneau (74x54cm 29x21in) Antwerpen 1998
$1 721 - €1 911 - **£1 200** - FF12 533
Elegant Couple Oil/panel (9.5x18.5cm 3x7in) London 2001

WILLEMSENS Abraham c.1627-1672 **[16]**
$11 801 - €11 155 - **£7 355** - FF78 000
Scènes de cours et fermes Huile/panneau (61x75cm 24x29in) Paris 2000

WILLERS Ernst 1803-1880 **[6]**
$6 132 - €5 367 - **£3 713** - FF35 207
Römische Campagnalandschaft mit der Flucht nach Ägypten Oil/panel (31.5x45cm 12x17in) Berlin 1998

WILLERUP Oscar 1864-1931 **[2]**
$3 732 - €3 761 - **£2 326** - FF24 673
Vaegdekoration i pompejiansk stil Gouache/paper (78x120cm 30x47in) Köbenhavn 2000

WILLES William ?-1851 **[1]**
$64 556 - €60 615 - **£40 000** - FF397 608
The Mock Funeral Oil/canvas (102x127cm 40x50in) London 1999

WILLETT Arthur 1868-c.1940 **[71]**
$829 - €721 - **£500** - FF4 731
Crossing the Brook/On the Scent Watercolour/paper (28x44.5cm 11x17in) Godalming, Surrey 1998

WILLETTE Adolphe 1857-1926 **[187]**
$4 296 - €3 659 - **£2 589** - FF24 000
Le martyr de la Pensée Huile/toile (95x118cm 37x46in) Paris 1998
$191 - €213 - **£129** - FF1 400
Projet pour un menu Encre/papier (24x19cm 9x7in) Paris 2000
$246 - €274 - **£171** - FF1 800
«Journée du puy de Dôme, paquetage du soldat» Affiche (80x115cm 31x45in) Chartres 2001

WILLIAMS A. Sheldon 1840-1881 **[12]**
$2 506 - €2 118 - **£1 500** - FF13 896
Over the Fence/Gone Away Oil/canvas (40.5x30.5cm 15x12in) London 1998

WILLIAMS Albert 1922 **[39]**
$782 - €891 - **£550** - FF5 842
Still Life of Flowers in a Vase Oil/board (61.5x51.5cm 24x20in) London 2001
$712 - €828 - **£500** - FF5 432
Still Life of Anemonies, Tulips, Freesia, Narcissi and other Flowers Oil/canvas/board (40x30cm 15x11in) Billingshurst, West-Sussex 2001

WILLIAMS Alexander 1846-1930 **[119]**
$1 340 - €1 502 - **£920** - FF9 850
View of Tall Coastal Cliffs with Harvest Field Oil/canvas (33x58cm 13x23in) Leominster, Herefordshire 2000
$1 263 - €1 397 - **£876** - FF9 161
Distressed Ship off the Coast Oil/board (23x36cm 9x14in) Dublin 2001
$828 - €889 - **£554** - FF5 830
Fisherman's Cottage near Leenbane, Killary Bay Watercolour (25x42cm 9x16in) Dublin 2000

WILLIAMS Alfred Walter 1824-1905 **[57]**
$1 976 - €1 694 - **£1 159** - FF11 110
Skotskt landskap Oil/canvas (55x94cm 21x37in) Stockholm 1998
$786 - €882 - **£550** - FF5 783
Extensive Landscape with Cattle watering Oil/canvas (26.5x35.5cm 10x13in) London 2001

WILLIAMS Alyn 1865-1941 **[9]**
$1 005 - €940 - **£620** - FF6 168
Portrait of a Lady Miniature (7x5.5cm 2x2in) Co. Kilkenny 1999

WILLIAMS Caroline Fanny 1836-1921 **[5]**
$2 284 - €2 169 - **£1 364** - FF14 228
Sundridge, Kent Oil/canvas (35.5x25.5cm 13x10in) London 1999

WILLIAMS Christopher 1956 **[5]**
$8 000 - €8 777 - **£5 314** - FF57 574
Tokyo Yamada Hair Designer Shinbuyo Shuppan Co., Ltd.Minami-Aoyama Dye-transfer print (67x76cm 26x29in) New-York 2000

W

WILLIAMS Dwight 1856-1932 **[8]**

$354 - €331 - **£220** - FF2 169
The Delphi Brook, New York State Oil/canvas
(24x34.5cm 9x13in) London 1999

WILLIAMS E.A., Col. XIX **[1]**

$7 296 - €7 661 - **£4 600** - FF50 253
Buggins Clearing, Taranaki, New Zealand
Watercolour (31x48cm 12x18in) London 2000

WILLIAMS Edward 1782-1855 **[43]**

$5 162 - €5 765 - **£3 600** - FF37 815
**A River Landscape at harvest Time, Children
and Cattle in Foreground** Oil/canvas (61x91cm
24x35in) Bath 2001

$1 714 - €1 924 - **£1 200** - FF12 619
Returning Home at the End of the Day Oil/panel
(22.5x30.5cm 8x12in) London 2001

WILLIAMS Edward Charles 1807-1881 **[100]**

$4 541 - €4 378 - **£2 800** - FF28 719
View on the River Yare, Reedham, Norfolk
Oil/canvas (43.5x71cm 17x27in) London 1999

$3 000 - €3 122 - **£1 883** - FF20 480
Landscape Oil/canvas (27x38cm 11x15in) Chicago IL
2000

WILLIAMS Edward K. 1870-1950 **[6]**

$8 000 - €9 281 - **£5 691** - FF60 878
Deep Winter Oil/canvas (76x91cm 30x36in) Carmel
IN 2000

WILLIAMS Esther Baldwin 1907 **[9]**

$1 500 - €1 298 - **£910** - FF8 517
Couple by the River Oil/canvas (66x91cm 26x36in)
Mystic CT 1998

WILLIAMS Florence 1833-1915 **[1]**

$1 653 - €1 608 - **£1 017** - FF10 550
Sydney Harbour Watercolour/paper (11x16cm 4x6in)
Malvern, Victoria 1999

WILLIAMS Frederick Ballard 1871-1956 **[53]**

$2 750 - €2 355 - **£1 623** - FF15 451
Near Pawlet, Vermont Oil/canvas (71x91.5cm
27x36in) New-York 1998

$800 - €746 - **£496** - FF4 893
Skyline Drive, VA. Oil/canvas (20.5x25.5cm 8x10in)
New-York 1999

WILLIAMS Frederick Dickinson 1829-1915 **[23]**

$1 500 - €1 481 - **£912** - FF9 712
Boating Scene Oil/canvas (30.5x45.5cm 12x17in)
New-York 2000

WILLIAMS Frederick Ronald 1927-1982 **[201]**

$194 731 - €227 266 - **£137 455** - FF1 490 767
Lysterfield II Oil/canvas (152.5x122cm 60x48in)
Malvern, Victoria 2000

$32 450 - €35 753 - **£21 785** - FF234 525
Mt Kosciusko Oil/canvas (91.5x107cm 36x42in)
Malvern, Victoria 2000

$4 450 - €4 330 - **£2 739** - FF28 404
Dieppe Oil/board (23x15cm 9x5in) Malvern, Victoria
1999

$10 360 - €9 767 - **£6 420** - FF64 070
North East River, Flinders Island Gouache/paper
(58x74.5cm 22x29in) Melbourne 1999

$1 544 - €1 334 - **£923** - FF8 748
Upwey Landscape Etching (16.5x14.5cm 6x5in)
Sydney 1998

WILLIAMS Garth 1912 **[2]**

$2 000 - €2 331 - **£1 384** - FF15 293
Little Badger's Bad Morning Ink (11x16cm 4x6in)
New-York 2000

WILLIAMS George Augustus 1814-1901 **[68]**

$4 647 - €4 100 - **£2 800** - FF26 897
A Walk by the Lake Oil/canvas (54.5x87cm 21x34in)
London 1998

$1 825 - €1 577 - **£1 100** - FF10 346
**Figures by a Campfire on the Banks of a
Moonlight River** Oil/canvas (34x44.5cm 13x17in)
Billingshurst, West-Sussex 1999

WILLIAMS Gluyas 1888-1982 **[2]**

$2 400 - €2 688 - **£1 667** - FF17 633
Cartoon, Crowd outside Football Stadium Ink
(30x45cm 12x18in) New-York 2001

WILLIAMS Graham XIX **[15]**

$800 - €739 - **£498** - FF4 845
Loch Rannock, Perthshire Oil/board (50x76cm
20x30in) Chicago IL 1999

WILLIAMS Harry act.c.1854-1877 **[11]**

$1 924 - €1 904 - **£1 200** - FF12 488
Hampton Court Bridge Oil/canvas (45.5x76cm
17x29in) London 1999

WILLIAMS Hugh William Grecian 1773-1829 **[67]**

$1 062 - €945 - **£650** - FF6 743
Lakeland Landscape with Figures Watercolour
(14x19.5cm 5x7in) Newbury, Berkshire 1999

WILLIAMS Jacqueline 1962 **[12]**

$1 217 - €1 171 - **£750** - FF7 678
The Artist in her Garden Oil/board (51x36cm
20x14in) London 1999

$368 - €432 - **£260** - FF2 836
Beach Scene Oil/canvas/board (24x35.5cm 9x13in)
London 2000

WILLIAMS James Francis c.1785-1846 **[6]**

$4 339 - €3 882 - **£2 600** - FF25 465
«Edinburgh from Inverleith» Oil/canvas (61x94cm
24x37in) Perthshire 1998

WILLIAMS John Haynes 1836-1908 **[38]**

$9 795 - €11 657 - **£7 000** - FF76 462
After the Bullfight - Prayers for one Wounded
Oil/canvas (117x150cm 46x59in) London 2000

$3 690 - €3 961 - **£2 469** - FF25 983
Fountain in Spain Oil/canvas (56x78cm 22x30in)
Vancouver, BC. 2000

$4 861 - €5 176 - **£3 200** - FF33 954
The Water Carrier Oil/canvas (69x47cm 27x18in)
Billingshurst, West-Sussex 2000

WILLIAMS John W. XIX-XX **[6]**

$525 - €497 - **£325** - FF3 261
**Whitby Upper Harbour at Low Tide with moored
Boats at St.Mary Church** Watercolour/paper
(16x23cm 6x9in) Whitby, Yorks 1999

WILLIAMS Kyffin 1918 **[82]**

$9 503 - €9 882 - **£6 000** - FF64 819
Crib Gogh from Capel Curig Oil/canvas
(51x68.5cm 20x26in) London 2000

$5 247 - €5 967 - **£3 600** - FF39 142
Yr Eifl Oil/board (31x47.5cm 12x18in) London 2000

$2 242 - €2 407 - **£1 500** - FF15 786
Futalaufquen Watercolour/paper (31.5x48cm
12x18in) London 2000

WILLIAMS Lily 1874-1940 **[8]**

$558 - €635 - **£385** - FF4 164
Moonlight over Haystacks Oil/board (63x44cm
25x17in) Dublin 2000

$853 - €779 - **£525** - FF5 109
Enniskerry, Co. Wicklow Oil/canvas (20x15cm
7x5in) Co. Kilkenny 1999

WILLIAMS Margaret Lindsay XX [12]
🖼 **$1 540** - €1 660 - **£1 050** - FF10 887
Portrait of A.E.Cressall Esq., Seated Three-Quarter-Length Oil/canvas (127x101.5cm 50x39in) London 2001

WILLIAMS Micah 1782/83-1837 [11]
✎ **$24 000** - €23 779 - **£14 560** - FF155 980
Portrait of a Sea Captain Pastel/paper (63.5x53.5cm 25x21in) New-York 2000

WILLIAMS Mildred Emerson 1892-? [6]
🖼 **$20 000** - €20 568 - **£12 686** - FF134 916
Winter in Central Park Oil/canvas (60x76cm 24x30in) Detroit MI 2000
▥ **$1 700** - €1 987 - **£1 194** - FF13 037
Picnic in the Park Woodcut in colors (28.5x36.5cm 11x14in) New-York 2000

WILLIAMS Penry 1798-1885 [57]
🖼 **$20 920** - €22 456 - **£14 000** - FF147 302
Mass for the Reapers Oil/canvas (92x169cm 36x66in) London 2000
🖼 **$9 713** - €10 427 - **£6 500** - FF68 394
Autumn Festival Oil/canvas (78x95cm 30x37in) London 2000
🖼 **$1 100** - €1 175 - **£748** - FF7 710
Portrait of a Beautiful Young Woman Oil/panel (38x25cm 15x10in) New-Orleans LA 2001
✎ **$385** - €457 - **£280** - FF2 998
Driving Sheep Watercolour (30.5x45cm 12x17in) Billingshurst, West-Sussex 2001

WILLIAMS Ramond Glynn 1900-? [1]
🖼 **$16 500** - €15 313 - **£9 906** - FF100 445
The Dance Hall Oil/canvas (111x121cm 44x48in) Milford CT 1999

WILLIAMS Rhys 1894-1976 [27]
🖼 **$2 128** - €2 018 - **£1 329** - FF13 235
Portrait Oil/canvas (44.5x39.5cm 17x15in) Woollahra, Sydney 1999

WILLIAMS Richard F. 1908-1995 [3]
✎ **$625** - €598 - **£380** - FF3 921
Dad's Home Mixed media/paper (27x38cm 11x15in) Cleveland OH 1999

WILLIAMS Sue 1954 [37]
🖼 **$38 000** - €42 563 - **£26 402** - FF279 193
«Big Red Shoes» Acrylic (208x264cm 81x103in) New-York 2001
🖼 **$4 800** - €5 569 - **£3 313** - FF36 532
Untitled Acrylic/canvas (38.5x46.5cm 15x18in) New-York 2000
▤ **$18 000** - €20 485 - **£12 648** - FF134 373
Union Bronze (35.5x38x25.5cm 13x14x10in) New-York 2001
✎ **$2 200** - €2 504 - **£1 545** - FF16 423
«My Landlord» Graphite (35.5x28cm 13x11in) New-York 2001

WILLIAMS Terrick John 1860-1936 [126]
🖼 **$13 700** - €15 139 - **£9 500** - FF99 303
«Boats, St.Ives» Oil/canvas (42x61cm 16x24in) London 2001
🖼 **$4 000** - €4 567 - **£2 820** - FF29 959
Venice Moonlight Oil/canvas/board (27.5x40.5cm 10x15in) Boston MA 2001
🖼 **$2 123** - €1 954 - **£1 300** - FF12 820
Unloading the Catch Pastel/papier (48x72.5cm 18x28in) London 1998

WILLIAMS Thomas R. 1825-1871 [40]
📷 **$12 764** - €14 575 - **£9 000** - FF95 608
Still Life with game birds, vegetables and wine Daguerreotype (8x17cm 3x6in) London 2001

WILLIAMS Virgil 1830-1886 [9]
🖼 **$4 500** - €5 199 - **£3 150** - FF34 101
«Shrine near Subineo» Oil/canvas (49.5x62.5cm 19x24in) New-York 2001
🖼 **$6 000** - €5 330 - **£3 674** - FF34 965
Landscape with House and Trees Oil/board (23x33cm 9x13in) New-Orleans LA 1999

WILLIAMS Walter Heath 1835-1906 [151]
🖼 **$4 572** - €3 916 - **£2 700** - FF25 689
A young Angler by a Pond in an extensive Landscape Oil/canvas (46x82cm 18x32in) Ipswich 1998
🖼 **$2 467** - €2 778 - **£1 700** - FF18 225
Winter Oil/canvas (19x38cm 7x14in) London 2000

WILLIAMS Warren 1863-1941 [117]
✎ **$1 849** - €1 895 - **£1 150** - FF12 429
Sheep Grazing in a Highland Loch Landscape Watercolour/paper (31x50cm 12x19in) Billingshurst, West-Sussex 2000

WILLIAMS Wheeler 1897-1972 [19]
▤ **$3 000** - €2 797 - **£1 860** - FF18 349
Venus Sculpture (H83cm H32in) New-York 1999
▤ **$5 500** - €5 333 - **£3 484** - FF34 984
Drinking Duck Bronze (H51cm H20in) New-York 1999

WILLIAMS William, of Norwich 1727-1791 [16]
🖼 **$8 000** - €9 518 - **£5 535** - FF62 431
Courtship Oil/canvas (60x48cm 24x19in) Detroit MI 2000

WILLIAMS William, of Plymouth 1808-1895 [56]
🖼 **$4 055** - €4 706 - **£2 800** - FF30 867
On the Banks of the Teign, near Newton, Devon Oil/canvas (40.5x56cm 15x22in) London 2000
🖼 **$930** - €938 - **£580** - FF6 150
Extensive Country Landscape Oil/panel (16.5x28cm 6x11in) London 2000
✎ **$248** - €230 - **£150** - FF1 508
Mullion Island Watercolour/paper (16x24cm 6x9in) Par, Cornwall 1999

WILLIAMS Wilton XX [6]
▥ **$725** - €835 - **£500** - FF5 480
«Enseign Cameras & Films, Make the Best Pictures, British Throughout» Poster (75x48cm 29x18in) London 2000

WILLIAMSON Frederick c.1835-1900 [37]
✎ **$1 443** - €1 455 - **£900** - FF9 543
Cattle in a Surrey Stream Watercolour/paper (21.5x35.5cm 8x13in) London 2000

WILLIAMSON Harold Sandys 1892-? [8]
▥ **$686** - €660 - **£420** - FF4 328
«There and Back by Underground» Poster (99x62cm 38x24in) London 1999

WILLIAMSON James 1899-1978 [2]
✎ **$1 600** - €1 865 - **£1 107** - FF12 234
Family Picnic Scene Watercolour/paper (26x33cm 10x13in) New-York 2000

WILLIAMSON John 1826-1885 [27]
🖼 **$55 000** - €59 037 - **£36 806** - FF387 255
On the Platte near Castle Rock Oil/canvas (39x49.5cm 15x19in) Philadelphia PA 2000

W

$1 755 - €1 952 - £1 170 - FF12 805
Puerto con castillo/Playa con acantilado
Oleo/tabla (14x38cm 5x14in) Madrid 2000

WILLIAMSON Lawrie 1932 [10]
$2 092 - €2 246 - £1 400 - FF14 730
Canary Oil/canvas (61x76cm 24x29in) London 2000

WILLIAMSON Samuel 1792-1840 [5]
$4 800 - €4 583 - £3 000 - FF30 061
**Figures on a Path in a Wooded River
Landscape** Oil/canvas (49.5x63.5cm 19x25in) London 1999

WILLIAMSON William Harry 1820-1883 [83]
$3 911 - €4 538 - £2 700 - FF29 769
Off Bamburgh Head Oil/canvas (96.5x129.5cm 37x50in) London 2000
$1 304 - €1 440 - £900 - FF9 446
Fishing Vessels off the Coast Oil/canvas (58.5x28cm 23x11in) Hockley, Birmingham 2001
$665 - €753 - £450 - FF4 937
Off Portsmouth Head Oil/canvas (28x54cm 11x21in) London 2000

WILLICH Cäser 1825-1886 [6]
$17 504 - €20 818 - £12 480 - FF136 560
Enfants à la bibliothèque Huile/toile (143x112cm 56x44in) Warszawa 2000

WILLIGEN van der Claes Jansz. 1630-1676 [12]
$5 634 - €6 541 - £3 960 - FF42 903
Dorf in den Dünen mit Bauern Oil/panel (41x61cm 16x24in) Wien 2001
$2 821 - €2 355 - £1 653 - FF15 447
Zuiders landschap met rustende reizigers
Oil/panel (34x28cm 13x11in) Lokeren 1998

WILLIKENS Ben 1939 [43]
$739 - €869 - £512 - FF5 701
Raumkomposition Tempera (40x80cm 15x31in) Stuttgart 2000
$136 - €153 - £95 - FF1 006
Grauer Raum Farbserigraphie (80x58cm 31x22in) Stuttgart 2001

WILLINGES Johan c.1560-1625 [1]
$3 000 - €2 993 - £1 826 - FF19 635
The Three Marys Approaching the Tomb Ink (15x14cm 5x5in) New-York 2000

WILLINK Albert Carel, Carel 1900-1983 [79]
$42 280 - €45 378 - £28 290 - FF297 660
**Twee Vrouwen En Een Kind Rustend In Een
Landschap, Vluchtelingen** Oil/canvas (51x74cm 20x29in) Amsterdam 2000
$2 743 - €2 949 - £1 869 - FF19 347
Untitled Collage/paper (27x17cm 10x6in) Amsterdam 2001
$401 - €431 - £268 - FF2 827
Couple in a Berlin Cafe Lithograph (25x20cm 9x7in) Amsterdam 2000

WILLIS Charles XX [7]
$1 608 - €1 633 - £1 000 - FF10 709
Toasting the Clef Oil/canvas (51x68.5cm 20x26in) London 2000

WILLIS Henry Brittan 1810-1884 [37]
$802 - €808 - £500 - FF5 301
**Extensive Country Landscape, with Children
Fishing a River** Oil/panel (23.5x34cm 9x13in) London 2000
$1 295 - €1 215 - £800 - FF7 972
Sunset near Newhaven, Sussex Watercolour (15.5x36.5cm 6x14in) Billingshurst, West-Sussex 1999

WILLIS J.R. 1876-? [3]
$2 250 - €2 617 - £1 605 - FF17 169
Camel-Back Mountain Mixed media (30x76cm 12x30in) Bloomfield-Hills MI 2000

WILLIS John Christopher T. 1900-1969 [18]
$255 - €298 - £180 - FF1 952
«Shoreham» Watercolour/paper (23x34cm 9x13in) Woodbridge, Suffolk 2001

WILLIS Thomas 1850-1912 [32]
$500 - €4 891 - £3 363 - FF32 083
The Steam Yacht «Electra» Oil/canvas (51x81cm 20x31in) New-York 1999
$4 000 - €3 636 - £2 454 - FF23 852
Portrait of the Yacht «Resolute» Oil/canvas (45x30cm 18x12in) Nantucket MA 1998

WILLIS-GOOD John 1845-1879 [36]
$2 905 - €2 695 - £1 800 - FF17 677
Figure of a Stallion Bronze (H39cm H15in) West-Yorhire 1999

WILLMANN Michael Lukas Leo. 1630-1706 [11]
$1 715 - €2 045 - £1 223 - FF13 415
Die Enthauptung des Heiligen Paulus Radierung (27.5x20cm 10x7in) Berlin 2000

WILLMORE James Tilbitts 1800-1863 [10]
$225 - €231 - £140 - FF1 514
Venice Engraving (38x60cm 15x24in) Hatfield PA 2000

WILLOUGHBY Bob XX [12]
$463 - €467 - £288 - FF3 061
**Montgomery Clift 1956, on the MGM Location of
Raintree County** Photograph (24x35.5cm 9x13in) Stockholm 2000

WILLOUGHBY Vera 1870-1939 [2]
$917 - €1 064 - £650 - FF6 980
**«Boat Race Saturday March 19, Putney Bridge,
Hammersmith, Ravenscourt»** Poster (33x33cm 12x12in) London 2000

WILLRICH Wolfgang 1897-1948 [1]
$1 833 - €1 738 - £1 115 - FF11 403
**Portrait: Josepha Huber, 43 Jahre, aus
Landskron/Kärnten** Charcoal/paper (24x31cm 9x12in) München 1999

WILLROIDER Josef 1838-1915 [101]
$4 952 - €5 624 - £3 463 - FF36 892
Wassermühle am Dorfrand Öl/Leinwand (53x73cm 20x28in) München 2001
$1 174 - €1 380 - £841 - FF9 055
Landschaft mit Personen Öl/Karton (8.5x19cm 3x7in) München 2001
$211 - €204 - £133 - FF1 341
Landschaft bei Bernried Pencil/paper (16x30.3cm 6x11in) München 2000

WILLROIDER Ludwig 1845-1910 [183]
$259 - €2 659 - £1 595 - FF17 439
Sommerliche Waldlichtung Öl/Leinwand/Karton (43.5x39cm 17x15in) Köln 2001
$2 352 - €2 177 - £1 439 - FF14 283
**Bewaldete Landschaft mit Bäuerin vor einem
Kruzifix** Öl/Leinwand/Karton (23.5x32cm 9x12in) Bern 1999
$242 - €276 - £169 - FF1 811
Flusslauf in Gebirgslandschaft Charcoal/paper (35x41.5cm 13x16in) München 2000

WILLS Helen XX [34]

✐ $478 - €459 - **£300** - FF3 012
Molla Mallory at Play Watercolour (33x27cm
12x10in) London 1999

▥ $638 - €612 - **£400** - FF4 016
Collection of various tennis players Etching
(17x13.5cm 6x5in) London 1999

WILLS William Gorman 1828-1891 [2]

◠ $23 073 - €25 497 - **£16 000** - FF167 248
Ophelia and Laertes Oil/canvas (202x98cm 79x38in)
London 2001

WILLUMSEN Jens-Ferdinand 1863-1958 [152]

◠ $11 940 - €10 091 - **£7 125** - FF66 195
«Brönden i Toledo» Oil/canvas (78x95cm 30x37in)
Köbenhavn 1998

◠ $617 - €539 - **£373** - FF3 533
«La Consencion» - Kvinna sittande vid bygata
Oil/panel (37x24cm 14x9in) Stockholm 1998

✐ $1 030 - €1 074 - **£648** - FF7 048
Bjergbaek danner vandfald Watercolour/paper
(31x35cm 12x13in) Köbenhavn 2000

▥ $458 - €425 - **£285** - FF2 789
Une dame en promenade Etching (35x28cm
13x11in) Malmö 1998

WILMARTH Christopher 1943-1987 [34]

◭ $48 000 - €53 763 - **£33 350** - FF352 665
Double Drawing Sculpture (87.5x43.5cm 34x17in)
New-York 2001

◭ $25 000 - €21 569 - **£15 025** - FF141 482
«Long Leavens Gate (in steps) 2» Bronze
(53.5x51x40.5cm 21x20x15in) New-York 1998

WILMARTH Lemuel Everett 1853-1918 [2]

◠ $87 500 - €85 163 - **£53 760** - FF558 635
Still life Oil/canvas (39x23cm 15x9in) San-Francisco
CA 1999

WILMER Joseph Riley 1883-1941 [13]

✐ $2 984 - €2 584 - **£1 800** - FF16 949
Badoura, Princess of China Watercolour
(29x22.5cm 11x8in) London 1998

WILMINK Machiel 1894-1963 [6]

▥ $2 150 - €2 009 - **£1 300** - FF13 178
«Lloyd Rapide» Poster (120x71cm 47x27in) London
1999

WILMS Joseph 1814-1892 [5]

◠ $13 772 - €15 988 - **£9 680** - FF104 874
**Stilleben mit einem Tömer, Trauben, Mandeln
und Haselnüssen** Öl/Leinwand (51x40.5cm 20x15in)
Wien 2001

WILQUIN André 1899-? [12]

▥ $589 - €653 - **£400** - FF4 284
«Cie.Gle.Transatlantique, Normandie» Poster
(32x20cm 12x7in) London 2000

WILS Jan Wiltz c.1600-1666 [5]

◠ $9 344 - €9 294 - **£5 800** - FF60 965
**Shepherdess and a Cowherd returning with
their Livestock along a Path** Oil/canvas
(79.5x91.5cm 31x36in) London 1999

WILS Lydia 1924-1982 [25]

◠ $928 - €1 041 - **£630** - FF6 829
Lieve Nacht Huile/toile (80x100cm 31x39in)
Bruxelles 2000

WILS Wilhelm 1880-1960 [94]

◠ $426 - €404 - **£265** - FF2 648
Folkeliv på Dyrehavsbakken Oil/canvas (66x86cm
25x33in) Vejle 1999

WILSON Alexander 1766-1813 [20]

▥ $179 - €192 - **£119** - FF1 260
Carolina Cuckoo, Black Billed Cu Engraving
(34x25cm 13x10in) Cleveland OH 2000

WILSON Andrew 1780-1848 [6]

✐ $1 604 - €1 616 - **£1 000** - FF10 603
Figures Seated in a Classical Landscape
Watercolour (43x58cm 16x22in) London 2000

WILSON Charles Banks 1918 [14]

▥ $120 - €123 - **£75** - FF804
Obie Yellowbill Lithograph (16x21cm 6x8in)
Cleveland OH 2000

WILSON Charles Edward 1854-1941 [82]

✐ $7 705 - €6 653 - **£4 700** - FF43 641
Young Lady Harvester Watercolour/paper (54x35cm
21x14in) Birmingham 1999

WILSON Charles J.A. 1880-1965 [5]

✐ $750 - €875 - **£526** - FF5 737
American tall ship in a tropical port
Watercolour/paper (50x64cm 20x25in) Cambridge MA
2000

WILSON Chester XIX [6]

◠ $3 905 - €4 592 - **£2 800** - FF30 124
Mutual Friends Oil/canvas (53x42cm 20x16in)
Cheshire 2001

WILSON David Forrester 1873-1950 [15]

◠ $2 377 - €2 470 - **£1 500** - FF16 202
Youth Oil/canvas (86.5x81cm 34x31in) London 2000

WILSON Donald Roller 1938 [8]

◠ $6 000 - €5 034 - **£3 520** - FF33 021
She Didn't Like it Oil/panel (32x37cm 12x14in) New-
York 1998

WILSON Dora Lynnell 1883-1946 [61]

◠ $1 278 - €1 229 - **£787** - FF8 063
First Snow Oil/canvas/board (44x39cm 17x15in)
Melbourne 1998

◠ $740 - €684 - **£452** - FF4 484
St Ives Oil/canvas/board (39.5x34cm 15x13in)
Melbourne 1998

✐ $1 971 - €2 209 - **£1 369** - FF14 487
The Girl of the Woods Pastel/paper (36x28.5cm
14x11in) Melbourne 2001

WILSON Edward Adrian 1872-1912 [15]

✐ $6 338 - €7 445 - **£4 500** - FF48 834
**Last Sight of Mount Discovery: SS. «Morning»
& «Terra Nova»** Feb.19.04 Watercolour/paper
(12x20.5cm 4x8in) London 2000

◉ $3 943 - €4 632 - **£2 800** - FF30 382
The Camp at the South Pole Gelatin silver print
(30.5x38cm 12x14in) London 2000

WILSON Edward Arthur 1886-1970 [8]

▥ $650 - €606 - **£401** - FF3 976
Harbor Scene with Tugboats Lithograph (27x33cm
10x13in) Cleveland OH 1999

WILSON Ellis 1899/1900-1977 [3]

◠ $13 000 - €12 050 - **£8 083** - FF79 041
Five Black Women Dancers, on a Harlem Stage
Oil/panel (27x33cm 11x13in) New-Orleans LA 1999

WILSON Eric 1911-1946 [28]

◠ $1 029 - €1 071 - **£646** - FF7 025
Noonday Oil/canvas/board (44x49cm 17x19in)
Melbourne 2000

◠ $6 773 - €8 055 - **£4 826** - FF52 835
Street in Edinburgh Oil/cardboard (43.5x32.5cm
17x12in) Melbourne 2000

W

WILSON Eric 1960 [18]
- $3 895 - €3 744 - **£2 400** - FF24 559
  Young Siberian Oil/board (67x108cm 26x42in)
  London 1999

WILSON Frank Avray 1914 [57]
- $1 150 - €1 097 - **£700** - FF7 194
  Abstract Oil/canvas (183x61cm 72x24in) London 1999

WILSON Henry Mitton 1873-c.1926 [27]
- $567 - €670 - **£400** - FF4 397
  Winter Morning, Tytenhanger Lane, St.Albans
  Oil/canvas (51x61cm 20x24in) Stansted Mountfitchet, Essex 2001
- $932 - €1 035 - **£650** - FF6 789
  Margate Sands Oil/board (25.5x34.5cm 10x13in)
  London 2001

WILSON Jane & Louise 1967 [8]
- $11 553 - €12 590 - **£8 000** - FF82 582
  Red Room (Study) Cibachrome print (100x100cm 39x39in) London 2001

WILSON John James 1838-1903 [2]
- $2 896 - €3 361 - **£2 000** - FF22 048
  Figures before a Cottage with a Barn Beyond
  Oil/canvas (38x38cm 14x14in) London 2000

WILSON John James 1818-1875 [50]
- $5 595 - €6 005 - **£3 800** - FF39 392
  Fishing Vessels Arriving at a Continental Harbour Oil/canvas (40.5x61cm 15x24in) London 2001
- $2 183 - €2 610 - **£1 500** - FF17 119
  A Kentish Farm Oil/canvas (29x44cm 11x17in)
  Billingshurst, West-Sussex 2000

WILSON John Snr., Jock 1774-1855 [41]
- $3 500 - €3 628 - **£2 000** - FF23 800
  Marina in burrasca Olio/tela (97x134.5cm 38x52in)
  Milano 2001
- $2 896 - €3 361 - **£2 000** - FF22 048
  Fishing Boats in Shallow Waters off a Citadel
  Oil/canvas (51x76cm 20x29in) London 2000
- $2 495 - €2 113 - **£1 500** - FF13 863
  The Eddystone Lighthouse Oil/board (14x35.5cm 5x13in) London 1998

WILSON John Woodrow 1922 [8]
- $1 500 - €1 673 - **£981** - FF10 977
  War Color lithograph (50x40cm 20x16in) Watertown MA 1999

WILSON Laurence William 1859-c.1920 [10]
- $297 - €338 - **£205** - FF2 220
  South Island Lake Scene Oil/board (29.5x69cm 11x27in) Auckland 2000

WILSON Mary Georgina Wade 1856-1939 [8]
- $497 - €430 - **£300** - FF2 821
  Santa Maria della Salute, Venice Pastel/paper (33.5x50.5cm 13x19in) Billingshurst, West-Sussex 1999

WILSON Mortimer 1906-1996 [7]
- $3 500 - €3 920 - **£2 431** - FF25 715
  Couple embracing in Interior, she pulling away
  Oil/canvas (53x40cm 21x16in) New-York 2001
- $1 700 - €1 982 - **£1 177** - FF12 999
  Couple Parisian Bookstall, He Lighting Cigarette Oil/board (44x32cm 17x12in) New-York 2000

WILSON Oscar 1867-1930 [15]
- $449 - €444 - **£280** - FF2 914
  Rendez vous on the Woodland Hill Watercolour (38x26cm 14x10in) Leyburn, North Yorkshire 1999

WILSON Peter MacGregor c.1856-1929 [49]
- $293 - €316 - **£200** - FF2 073
  The Jetty Tayvallich/The Mountains of Mull from Crinan Watercolour/paper (16.5x24cm 6x9in) London 2001

WILSON R. XIX [4]
- $2 977 - €2 784 - **£1 800** - FF18 265
  Buddhist Temple, Galle, Mathura Watercolour (35.5x49cm 13x19in) London 1999

WILSON Richard 1714-1782 [73]
- $93 977 - €90 378 - **£58 000** - FF592 841
  Phaeton's Petition to Apollo Oil/canvas (124.5x176.5cm 49x69in) London 1999
- $16 331 - €15 034 - **£10 000** - FF98 619
  A View of a Lake with Vesuvius in the Distance
  Oil/canvas (42x52cm 16x20in) London 1998
- $42 687 - €49 596 - **£30 000** - FF325 326
  Castel Gandolfo, a View of the Town from across the North End of Lake Black & white chalks (28x42cm 11x16in) London 2001

WILSON Robert, Bob 1941 [15]
- $232 - €259 - **£161** - FF1 700
  Sans titre Fusain/papier (29x21cm 11x8in) Paris 2001

WILSON Ronald York 1907-1984 [36]
- $316 - €268 - **£190** - FF1 757
  Ballet Dancers Oil/canvas/board (30.5x40cm 12x15in) Vancouver, BC. 1998

WILSON Ross 1957 [2]
- $1 216 - €1 379 - **£850** - FF9 043
  «Heaney at Harvard» Ink (23x18.5cm 9x7in) London 2001

WILSON Samuel Henry XIX-XX [6]
- $1 168 - €1 133 - **£740** - FF7 430
  The Mersey Ferry, Off Liverpool Watercolour/paper (39x86cm 15x34in) Little-Lane, Ilkley 1999

WILSON Scottie 1889-1972 [262]
- $1 062 - €978 - **£650** - FF6 414
  Tree of Life Ink (34.5x25.5cm 13x10in) London 1998

WILSON Sidney Ernest 1869-? [18]
- $102 - €100 - **£65** - FF656
  The Sportsman's Return Mezzotint (53x41.5cm 20x16in) Carlisle, Cumbria 1999

WILSON Solomon, Sol 1894-1974 [44]
- $2 100 - €2 018 - **£1 284** - FF13 235
  Solitude Oil/canvas (50x40cm 20x16in) Provincetown MA 1999
- $300 - €322 - **£200** - FF2 112
  Evening on the Beach Oil/canvas/board (20x25cm 8x10in) New-York 2000
- $325 - €384 - **£230** - FF2 519
  Cape Cod Dunes Charcoal/paper (31x41cm 12x16in)
  Provincetown MA 2000

WILSON Stanley R. 1890-? [4]
- $850 - €957 - **£585** - FF6 278
  «Canada Geese» Etching in colors (35x43cm 14x17in) New-Orleans LA 2000

WILSON W.F. XIX [1]
- $23 000 - €21 133 - **£14 128** - FF138 621
  The Gold Rush Oil/canvas (50x68cm 20x27in)
  Portsmouth NH 1999

WILSON William 1905-1972 [19]
- $2 761 - €2 637 - **£1 700** - FF17 300
  Royal Circus Watercolour/paper (29x46cm 11x18in)
  Edinburgh 1999

WILSON William George c.1864-c.1914 **[1]**
$3 919 - €3 686 - £2 427 - FF24 179
Toowoomba/Kings Creek, Pilton/Pilton/Bush Scene, Winter, Darling Downs Oil/panel (19x31cm 7x12in) Melbourne 1999

WILSON William Hardy 1881-1955 **[4]**
$1 311 - €1 189 - £795 - FF7 800
In the Garden of Diana at Nismes Pencil/paper (45x34.5cm 17x13in) Sydney 1998

WILT Hans 1867-1917 **[38]**
$1 762 - €1 685 - £1 073 - FF11 053
Feeding the Geese Oil/panel (48x39cm 19x15in) Vancouver, BC. 1999

WILT van der Pieter Cent 1908-1976 **[8]**
$297 - €311 - £187 - FF2 039
Cow Resting Oil/panel (18x24cm 7x9in) Sydney 2000

WILT van der Thomas 1659-1733 **[12]**
$7 933 - €9 324 - £5 500 - FF61 164
Gentleman, Three-quarter-length, in a Burgundy Coloured Coat Oil/canvas (59.5x49.5cm 23x19in) London 2000

WILTON Joseph 1722-1803 **[5]**
$31 033 - €36 219 - £22 000 - FF237 578
Bust of Venus de Medici Marble (H66.5cm H26in) London 2001

WILVERS Robert XX **[3]**
$1 000 - €934 - £617 - FF6 126
Wall Street from Trinity Church, NY Watercolour (35x55cm 14x21in) Detroit MI 1999

WIMAR Charles 1828-1862 **[5]**
$750 000 - €713 736 - £469 125 - FF4 681 800
Billy Bowlegs Oil/canvas (76x63.5cm 29x25in) New-York 1999
$16 675 - €17 457 - £10 476 - FF114 510
U.S cavalrymen riding their horses in a snow storm Oil/board (16x21cm 6x8in) East-Dennis MA 2000

WIMBUSH Henry B. c.1860-c.1910 **[62]**
$500 - €558 - £350 - FF3 660
Mist rising off a mountain river landscape/Cloud descending Watercolour (53.5x72.5cm 21x28in) Near Ely 2001

WIMMER Conrad 1844-1905 **[46]**
$1 644 - €1 943 - £1 165 - FF12 744
Jagd in der Abenddämmerung Öl/Leinwand (50x80cm 19x31in) München 2000
$1 836 - €2 147 - £1 290 - FF14 086
Bauern bei der Heuernte Oil/panel (18x25cm 7x9in) München 2000

WIMMER Fritz 1879-1960 **[136]**
$294 - €332 - £207 - FF2 180
Stehende weiblicher Akt Indian ink (32x24cm 12x9in) Stuttgart 2001

WIMMER Mike 1961 **[1]**
$9 000 - €9 967 - £6 103 - FF65 380
We're off to see the Wizard Oil/canvas (91x144cm 36x57in) San-Francisco CA 2000

WIMPERIS Edmund Morison 1835-1900 **[189]**
$3 270 - €2 908 - £2 000 - FF19 074
Landscape with Sheep Oil/canvas (54x77cm 21x30in) London 1999
$513 - €591 - £350 - FF3 878
Figures Following a Path to a Lake Watercolour (30x21cm 11x8in) Billingshurst, West-Sussex 2000

WINAI PRABRIPOO 1954 **[3]**
$1 402 - €1 508 - £940 - FF9 894
Alone Oil/canvas (49x68cm 19x26in) Bangkok 2000

WINANS Fonville 1911-1992 **[31]**
$2 000 - €2 137 - £1 361 - FF14 019
Before the Blow Vintage gelatin silver print (40x50cm 16x20in) New-Orleans LA 2001

WINANS Walter 1852-1920 **[15]**
$8 729 - €8 613 - £5 378 - FF56 500
L'amazone Bronze (63x64cm 24x25in) Sceaux 1999

WINCK Johann Amandus c.1748-1817 **[41]**
$20 188 - €20 348 - £12 600 - FF133 476
Prunkvolles Blumen-, Früchte- und Jagdstilleben vor Schlossarchitektur Öl/Leinwand (105x119cm 41x46in) Wien 2000
$27 043 - €31 029 - £18 500 - FF203 537
Still-life of Flowers and Fruit Oil/panel (50.5x40cm 19x15in) Leamington-Spa, Warwickshire 2000
$12 282 - €11 248 - £7 486 - FF73 785
Stilleben, Angeschälte Zitrone, Birne, Traubenzweige, Orange, Quitte Öl/Leinwand (39.5x29.5cm 15x11in) München 1999

WINCK Johann Christian Th. 1738-1797 **[26]**
$26 677 - €26 889 - £16 650 - FF176 379
Huldigung an Ceres Öl/Leinwand (65x68cm 25x26in) Wien 2000
$12 978 - €13 081 - £8 100 - FF85 806
Rückkehr des verlorenen Sohnes Öl/Leinwand (39.5x27cm 15x10in) Wien 2000
$790 - €767 - £492 - FF5 030
Die sieben Planeten Radierung (15.9x23.8cm 6x9in) Berlin 1999

WINCK Willibald 1867-1932 **[9]**
$745 - €805 - £500 - FF5 279
Ung pige, der lugter til en blå blomst Oil/canvas (130x55cm 51x21in) København 2000

WINCKEL Richard 1870-1941 **[6]**
$1 195 - €1 143 - £749 - FF7 499
«Soennencken & Co.» Poster (84x61cm 33x24in) London 1999

WINCKLER Jean-Marc **[1]**
$3 799 - €3 659 - £2 364 - FF24 000
Paysage classique dans le goût du XVIIIème siècle Huile/panneau (26x26.5cm 10x10in) Montfort L'Amaury 1999

WINCKLER Johan Gottfried 1734-1791 **[2]**
$2 308 - €2 590 - £1 600 - FF16 988
Views of London and Oxford Etching (30x39cm 11x15in) London 2000

WINDHAGER Franz 1879-1959 **[46]**
$733 - €727 - £459 - FF4 767
Frauenakt Oil/panel (15.7x12.4cm 6x4in) Wien 1999
$1 692 - €1 817 - £1 155 - FF11 917
Beim Heurigen Mischtechnik/Papier (15.5x17cm 6x6in) Wien 2001

WINDIG Ad 1912-1996 **[13]**
$725 - €862 - £516 - FF5 655
Bloemendaal Silver print (23.5x29.5cm 9x11in) Amsterdam 2000

WINDMAIER Anton 1840-1896 **[45]**
$2 342 - €2 454 - £1 549 - FF16 098
Winterlandschaft bei Sonnenuntergang Öl/Leinwand (72x98cm 28x38in) München 2000
$925 - €869 - £561 - FF5 701
Jäger bei der abendlichen Rast Öl/Leinwand (40.5x30cm 15x11in) München 1999

W

WINDSTOSSER Ludwig 1921-1983 **[39]**
[icon] $381 - €409 - **£255** - FF2 683
    Mäander-Schaumzone Photograph (28.1x22.1cm
    11x8in) München 2000

WINDT de A. XIX **[3]**
  $689 - €644 - **£423** - FF4 227
    Brume matinale Huile/toile (24.5x34.5cm 9x13in)
    Bruxelles 1999

WINDT van der Chris 1877-1952 **[81]**
  $3 699 - €3 403 - **£2 287** - FF22 324
    A Farmyard with a peasant near a haystack
    Oil/canvas (37x56cm 14x22in) Amsterdam 1999
  $2 226 - €2 042 - **£1 371** - FF13 394
    Farmer Mooring his Boat Oil/canvas/panel
    (21.5x31.5cm 8x12in) Amsterdam 1999
  $1 479 - €1 588 - **£990** - FF10 418
    Farm along a waterway Watercolour (23x35cm
    9x13in) Amsterdam 1999

WINGATE James Lawton 1846-1924 **[74]**
  $1 759 - €1 896 - **£1 200** - FF12 439
    Canterbury Bells Oil/canvas (51x40cm 20x15in)
    London 2001
  $991 - €991 - **£620** - FF6 499
    Sunset at Fairlie Oil/canvas (23.5x35cm 9x13in)
    Edinburgh 1999

WINGE Sigurd 1909-1970 **[34]**
  $2 314 - €2 568 - **£1 612** - FF16 848
    Himmelsengen Mixed media/panel (31x41cm
    12x16in) Oslo 2001
  $594 - €686 - **£418** - FF4 500
    Messias I Etching (20x17.5cm 7x6in) Oslo 2000

WINGERT Edward Oswald 1864-1934 **[4]**
  $4 750 - €4 952 - **£3 161** - FF32 482
    A Blooming Garden Oil/canvas (23x33cm 9x12in)
    San-Francisco CA 2000

WINGFIELD James Digman 1809-1872 **[28]**
  $6 737 - €6 789 - **£4 200** - FF44 535
    Summer Recreation Oil/canvas (64x76cm 25x29in)
    London 2000
  $675 - €732 - **£450** - FF4 803
    Study of a Girl Oil/canvas (32x35cm 12x13in)
    Billingshurst, West-Sussex 2000

WINGHE van Bartholomé XVII **[1]**
  $56 980 - €48 481 - **£34 000** - FF318 015
    Roses, parrot tulips, Narcissi, dahlias and other
    flowers in a vase Oil/canvas (75x53.5cm 29x21in)
    London 1998

WINGHE van Jeremias 1578-c.1645 **[9]**
  $31 773 - €35 791 - **£22 344** - FF234 773
    Stilleben auf einer Steinplatte vor dunklem
    Hintergrund Öl/Leinwand (43x56cm 16x22in)
    Stuttgart 2001

WINGHE van Joos 1542/44-1603 **[2]**
  $6 580 - €7 267 - **£4 560** - FF47 670
    Bildnis eines Herrn Öl/Leinwand (26x34cm
    10x13in) Wien 2001

WINIARSKI Ryszard 1936 **[15]**
  $2 122 - €2 348 - **£1 474** - FF15 403
    Triptyqueo Huile/toile (49x87.5cm 19x34in)
    Warszawa 2001
  $1 102 - €1 285 - **£772** - FF8 426
    Signes de reconaissance Encre (34x49cm 13x19in)
    Warszawa 2000

WINKFIELD Frederick A. XIX-XX **[21]**
  $4 489 - €5 339 - **£3 200** - FF35 024
    Windsor Castle from the Thames Watercolour
    (33x51cm 12x20in) London 2000

WINKLER Fritz 1894-1964 **[26]**
  $182 - €204 - **£126** - FF1 341
    Leuchtturm an der See Aquarell/Papier (36x50cm
    14x19in) Berlin 2001

WINKLER John W. 1890-1979 **[21]**
  $150 - €161 - **£100** - FF1 059
    Goats, Children and Houses Etching (31x20cm
    12x8in) Cleveland OH 2000

WINOGRAND Garry 1928-1984 **[118]**
[icon] $2 600 - €2 993 - **£1 774** - FF19 635
    Los Angeles, California Gelatin silver print
    (22x33cm 8x12in) New-York 2000

WINSLOE-HATVANY Christa XIX-XX **[9]**
  $5 113 - €5 641 - **£3 463** - FF37 000
    Faon Bronze (37.5x15x24cm 14x5x9in) Lyon 2000

WINT de Peter 1784-1849 **[293]**
  $1 641 - €1 725 - **£1 080** - FF11 316
    The watering Place Oil/panel (33.5x49cm 13x19in)
    Auckland 2000
  $12 031 - €12 124 - **£7 500** - FF79 527
    The Harvesters Oil/panel (12x20cm 4x7in) London
    2000
  $2 655 - €2 343 - **£1 600** - FF15 369
    Harvesters Working in the Fields Watercolour
    (15x43.5cm 5x17in) London 1998

WINTER Abraham Hendrik 1800-1861 **[7]**
  $2 930 - €3 086 - **£1 936** - FF20 240
    The Horse Market Oil/canvas/board (53.5x75cm
    21x29in) Amsterdam 2000

WINTER Alice Beach 1877-1970 **[14]**
  $850 - €861 - **£533** - FF5 648
    Day Sailing Oil/canvas (73x91cm 29x36in) Cincinnati
    OH 2000

WINTER Andrew 1892-1958 **[26]**
  $4 000 - €4 690 - **£2 877** - FF30 764
    View of a tropical Harbor Oil/canvas/board
    (61x76cm 24x29in) New-York 2001

WINTER Charles Allan 1869-1942 **[21]**
  $1 800 - €1 510 - **£1 060** - FF9 906
    Old Dock at Gloucester Oil/canvas (60x50cm
    24x20in) Greenwich CT 1998

WINTER Charles David 1821-1904 **[5]**
[icon] $829 - €4 373 - **£2 800** - FF28 684
    Industrie des chapeaux de Latanier et de
    Panama Albumen print (22.5x17cm 8x6in) London
    1999

WINTER de Adrianus Joh. Jac. 1882-1951 **[27]**
  $714 - €771 - **£488** - FF5 060
    Still Life with Flowers in a Vase Oil/canvas
    (50x70cm 19x27in) Amsterdam 2001
  $553 - €544 - **£355** - FF3 571
    A Still Life with Flowers in a Vase Pastel/paper
    (66x47cm 25x18in) Amsterdam 1999

WINTER de Gillis c.1650-1720 **[4]**
  $7 039 - €8 168 - **£4 860** - FF53 578
    Village Street Scene with Peasants Drinking
    outside an Inn Oil/panel (37.5x30cm 14x11in)
    Amsterdam 2000

W

WINTER de Louis 1819-1900 **[7]**
👁 **$2 162** - €1 832 - **£1 300** - FF12 014
Collecting Seaweed by Moonlight Oil/canvas
(60x83cm 23x32in) London 1998

WINTER Fritz 1905-1976 **[537]**
👁 **$41 800** - €35 263 - **£24 515** - FF231 308
Steigend Fallend Oil/canvas (130x97cm 51x38in)
Berlin 1998
👁 **$9 995** - €11 759 - **£7 056** - FF77 137
«**Linien zwischen rot und blau**» Öl/Leinwand
(45.5x61cm 17x24in) Berlin 2000
👁 **$4 862** - €4 857 - **£3 040** - FF31 862
Komposition Öl/Papier (16.8x23.4cm 6x9in)
Hamburg 1999
✎ **$3 738** - €3 236 - **£2 268** - FF21 226
Kleine Komposition Watercolour, gouache/paper
(13.5x17cm 5x6in) München 1998
📠 **$394** - €460 - **£277** - FF3 018
Ohne Titel Farblithographie (61.4x43.3cm 24x17in)
Köln 2000

WINTER Hans 1853-1944 **[6]**
👁 **$14 000** - €13 626 - **£8 601** - FF89 381
The Kiddush Oil/panel (30x37cm 11x14in) Tel Aviv
1999

WINTER Heinrich 1843-1911 **[6]**
👁 **$2 105** - €2 454 - **£1 457** - FF16 098
Beduinen Öl/Leinwand (60x42cm 23x16in)
Magdeburg 2000
👁 **$434** - €511 - **£315** - FF3 353
«**Kavallerist im Morgengrauen**» Öl/Leinwand
(28x38cm 11x14in) Frankfurt 2001

WINTER Joseph Georg 1751-1789 **[27]**
✎ **$219** - €230 - **£138** - FF1 509
Drei Hunde an einem Hauseingang Pencil/paper
(12x17.6cm 4x6in) Heidelberg 2001
📠 **$1 053** - €1 022 - **£656** - FF6 707
**Ansichten des Starnberger Sees und des
Hirschangers bei Nymphenburg** Radierung
(18x29cm 7x11in) Berlin 1999

WINTER W.F. 1874-1958 **[5]**
📠 **$143** - €145 - **£89** - FF952
«**Tentoonstelling kleine automobielen &
Motorrijwielen**» Poster (36.5x26.5cm 14x10in)
Haarlem 2000

WINTER William Arthur 1909-1996 **[136]**
👁 **$563** - €548 - **£346** - FF3 592
The Italian Girl Oil/canvas/board (30x40cm 12x16in)
Nepean, Ont. 1999

WINTER William Tatton 1855-1928 **[149]**
✎ **$768** - €645 - **£450** - FF4 229
**Young Girl at the Edge of the River in
Richmond, Yorkshire** Watercolour (32x51.5cm
12x20in) London 1998
📠 **$130** - €115 - **£80** - FF753
The Close Gate, Salisbury Drypoint in colors
(37x26cm 14x10in) Salisbury, Wiltshire 1999

WINTERBURN Stephen John 1959 **[19]**
🗿 **$3 387** - €3 078 - **£2 100** - FF20 188
Born to be Wild Bronze (H27cm H10in) Billingshurst,
West-Sussex 1999

WINTERHALDER Louis Adolph 1862-1931 **[3]**
👁 **$2 990** - €2 980 - **£1 816** - FF19 548
Nature Morte - Rabbit and Game Birds Oil/canvas
(30x14cm 11x5in) New-Orleans LA 2000

WINTERHALTER Franz Xaver 1805-1873 **[64]**
👁 **$6 808** - €6 860 - **£4 243** - FF45 000
Portrait de jeune femme à la robe blanche
Huile/toile/panneau (105x68cm 41x26in) Paris 2000
✎ **$3 885** - €4 573 - **£2 730** - FF30 000
**Portrait de miss Betty Hay, fiancée de Théodore
Gudin** Aquarelle (34.5x24.5cm 13x9in) Paris 2000

WINTERHALTER Hermann 1808-1891 **[11]**
✎ **$8 500** - €9 435 - **£5 925** - FF61 892
Orientalist Guards Watercolour/paper (25.5x18cm
10x7in) New-York 2001

WINTERHALTER Joseph I 1702-1769 **[3]**
✎ **$1 398** - €1 534 - **£949** - FF10 061
Der Heilige Hieronymus als Einsiedler Ink
(37.1x25.2cm 14x9in) Berlin 2000

WINTERLIN Anton 1805-1894 **[60]**
👁 **$7 497** - €6 889 - **£4 605** - FF45 186
**Ansicht von Ennetbürgen mit Rigi und Weggis
am Vierwaldstättersee** Öl/Leinwand (73x92cm
28x36in) Zürich 1999
👁 **$3 855** - €3 752 - **£2 368** - FF24 612
Küssnacht mit Blick gegen Rigi und Pilatus
Öl/Leinwand (24x34cm 9x13in) Zürich 1999
✎ **$3 916** - €3 406 - **£2 360** - FF22 340
**Porträt von Kuh/Stier vor
Landschaftshintergrund** Watercolour (22.5x32cm
8x12in) Bern 1998
📠 **$71** - €68 - **£43** - FF448
Pierre Pertuis Aquatinta (15x20.3cm 5x7in) Bern
1999

WINTEROWSKI Leonard 1886-1927 **[17]**
👁 **$4 382** - €5 087 - **£3 080** - FF33 369
Studium des Talmud Öl/Karton (37x64cm 14x25in)
Wien 2001

WINTERS Terry 1949 **[104]**
👁 **$65 000** - €75 419 - **£44 876** - FF494 715
Rosaceae, I Oil/canvas (198x155cm 77x61in) New-
York 2000
👁 **$7 500** - €8 484 - **£5 247** - FF55 653
Vertical Scale Oil/paper (105.5x75.5cm 41x29in)
New-York 2001
✎ **$9 500** - €11 023 - **£6 559** - FF72 307
Untitled Graphite (76x56cm 29x22in) New-York 2000
📠 **$2 800** - €2 670 - **£1 704** - FF17 516
Station Soft ground (39.5x29cm 15x11in) New-York
1999

WINTERSBERGER Lambert Maria 1941 **[44]**
📠 **$110** - €123 - **£72** - FF804
Ohne Titel Farbserigraphie (71.8x59.7cm 28x23in)
Dettelbach-Effeldorf 2000

WINTERSCHMIDT Christian Gottlob 1755-c.1810
[8]
✎ **$386** - €460 - **£275** - FF3 018
Quodlibet mit Singvogel Gouache (26x20.7cm
10x8in) Berlin 2000

WINTHER Frederik 1853-1916 **[42]**
👁 **$521** - €563 - **£360** - FF3 694
Aftenstemning ved havet Oil/canvas (21x54cm
8x21in) København 2001

WINTHER Poul 1939 **[32]**
👁 **$302** - €281 - **£184** - FF1 846
Opstilling Oil/canvas (27x41cm 10x16in) Viby J,
Århus 1998

WINTHER Richard 1926 **[44]**
👁 **$480** - €536 - **£334** - FF3 517
Figurkomposition Mixed media (66x91cm 25x35in)
København 2001

W

WINTOUR John Crawford 1825-1882 **[27]**
$2 244 - €2 120 - **£1 400** - FF13 906
Appil Wood, Sutherland Oil/canvas (46x61cm 18x24in) Perthshire 1999

WINTZ Raymond 1884-1956 **[58]**
$1 243 - €1 479 - **£886** - FF9 700
Barques sous voiles et au mouillage devant la plage Huile/toile (50x73cm 19x28in) Brest 2000
$1 064 - €1 021 - **£661** - FF6 700
Chaumière dans les pins Huile/toile (33x41cm 12x16in) Paris 1999

WIRBEL Véronique 1950-1990 **[19]**
$2 414 - €2 592 - **£1 615** - FF17 000
Tric Trac Troc Acrylique/toile (195x130cm 76x51in) Paris 2000

WIRGMAN Charles A., Snr. 1832-1891 **[48]**
$6 783 - €6 379 - **£4 200** - FF41 841
Japanese Woman in an Interior Oil/canvas (68.5x43cm 26x16in) London 1999
$7 500 - €6 327 - **£4 399** - FF41 505
Island Beach Scene Oil/canvas (22x30cm 9x12in) Mystic CT 1998
$1 442 - €1 328 - **£880** - FF8 712
Curiosity Street, Peking Ink (32.5x25.5cm 12x10in) London 1998

WIRKKALA Tapio 1915 **[59]**
$608 - €673 - **£422** - FF4 412
Tatti Sculpture, glass (H20cm H7in) Helsinki 2001

WIRSING Adam Louis, Ludwig 1733-1797 **[2]**
$1 600 - €1 755 - **£1 062** - FF11 514
A Passion Flower with a Butterfly Bodycolour (25.5x21cm 10x8in) New-York 2001

WIRTANEN Kaapo 1886-1959 **[43]**
$616 - €605 - **£382** - FF3 971
Interiör Oil/canvas (55x46cm 21x18in) Helsinki 1999
$428 - €420 - **£265** - FF2 758
Åker Oil/canvas (32x41cm 12x16in) Helsinki 1999

WIRTH Anna Marie 1846-? **[9]**
$3 310 - €3 634 - **£2 200** - FF23 835
Die Festnahme der Königin Marie Antoinette Öl/Leinwand (55.5x65.5cm 21x25in) Wien 2000
$1 604 - €1 534 - **£976** - FF10 061
Stubeninterieur, Mädchen liest einem älteren Herrn aus einem Buch vor Oil/panel (41x32cm 16x12in) Stuttgart 1999

WISE Ella G. ?-c.1889 **[1]**
$40 000 - €34 175 - **£24 012** - FF224 176
Milne Ramsey in his Studio Oil/canvas (68.5x91.5cm 26x36in) New-York 1998

WISELBERG Rose 1908-1992 **[16]**
$455 - €531 - **£321** - FF3 485
Figure Study Mixed media/paper (29x21cm 11x8in) Calgary, Alberta 2000

WISINGER-FLORIAN Olga 1844-1926 **[81]**
$23 120 - €21 867 - **£14 400** - FF143 440
Flowers in Vase Oil/cardboard (52x41cm 20x16in) Praha 1999
$7 330 - €7 267 - **£4 590** - FF47 670
Spazierweg auf dem Land Öl/Leinwand (38.7x28.8cm 15x11in) Wien 1999
$5 104 - €5 814 - **£3 528** - FF38 136
Im Schweizergarten Aquarell/Papier (21x28.5cm 8x11in) Wien 2000

WISLICENUS Lilli H. 1872-1939 **[3]**
$4 000 - €4 266 - **£2 664** - FF27 985
Figure of Diana Bronze (H75.5cm H29in) New-York 2000

WISLICENUS Max 1861-1957 **[23]**
$1 219 - €1 278 - **£803** - FF8 384
Blumen Öl/Leinwand (100.5x100.5cm 39x39in) Leipzig 2000
$307 - €358 - **£215** - FF2 347
Mond über dem Kirchturm Gouache/paper (37x32cm 14x12in) Köln 2001

WISSEL Adolf 1894-1973 **[6]**
$1 375 - €1 534 - **£924** - FF10 061
Der hannoversche Schriftsteller und Historiker Dr.Kurt Fischer Öl/Leinwand (71.5x61cm 28x24in) Ahlden 2000

WISSELINGH van Johannes Pieter 1812-1899 **[10]**
$4 812 - €4 849 - **£3 000** - FF31 810
Skaters in a Winter Landscape Oil/canvas (43x66cm 16x25in) London 2000

WISSING Willem 1656-1687 **[18]**
$68 747 - €81 761 - **£49 000** - FF536 314
Portrait of Mary of Moderna, Queen of King James II Oil/canvas (126.5x100cm 49x39in) London 2000

WISTEHUFF Revere F. 1900-1971 **[6]**
$2 900 - €3 248 - **£2 014** - FF21 306
Calendar Illustration, Newlyweds receive many Clocks as wedding Gifts Oil/canvas (31x49cm 12x19in) New-York 2001

WISTRAND Ludvig Detlof 1805-1838 **[2]**
$1 671 - €1 627 - **£1 029** - FF10 670
Oskar I Pastel/paper (36.5x31cm 14x12in) Stockholm 1999

WISZNIEWSKI Adrian 1958 **[17]**
$4 141 - €3 834 - **£2 500** - FF25 147
Two Boys Gouache/paper (150x100cm 59x39in) Edinburgh 1999

WIT de Frederick 1610-1698 **[22]**
$424 - €408 - **£265** - FF2 678
Accuratissima Galiae Tabula, Gallis Vulgo dicta Le Royaume de France Etching (49x58cm 19x22in) Amsterdam 1999

WIT de Jacob 1695-1754 **[99]**
$18 000 - €20 913 - **£12 650** - FF137 181
Allegory of Water: Putti desporting with the Attributes of Neptune Oil/canvas (125.5x115cm 49x45in) New-York 2001
$8 569 - €7 994 - **£5 170** - FF52 437
Spielende Putten Öl/Leinwand (50x160cm 19x62in) Wien 1999
$5 120 - €5 814 - **£3 504** - FF38 136
Arbeitende Putten Oil/panel (31x32.5cm 12x12in) Wien 2000
$2 123 - €2 042 - **£1 308** - FF13 394
Seraph Red chalk/paper (14x16.5cm 5x6in) Amsterdam 1999

WIT de Jean Paul 1851-? **[2]**
$9 439 - €10 783 - **£6 568** - FF70 731
Jeune fille au pagne donnant à manger à un oiseau Huile/toile (110x78cm 43x30in) Bruxelles 2001

WIT de Petrus Josephuss 1816-1870 **[1]**
$3 750 - €4 408 - **£2 600** - FF28 912
Roses, Cornflowers, Tulips and other Flowers in an Urn Oil/canvas (52x39.5cm 20x15in) London 2000

WIT de Prosper 1860-1947 **[96]**

👁 $700 - €793 - **£473** - FF5 203
Paysage au ruisseau Huile/toile (80x70cm 31x27in)
Bruxelles 2000

👁 $444 - €496 - **£310** - FF3 252
Clairière Huile/carton (35x27cm 13x10in) Bruxelles 2001

WITDOECK Jan, Hans c.1604/15-? **[7]**

📖 $268 - €256 - **£166** - FF1 676
Die Grabelung Christi, nach Rubens Kupferstich
(37x49.2cm 14x19in) Berlin 1999

WITDOECK Petrus Josephus 1803-1840 **[2]**

👁 $8 960 - €9 915 - **£6 000** - FF65 040
La lettre Huile/panneau (46x37.5cm 18x14in)
Antwerpen 2000

WITHERINGTON William Frederick 1785-1865 **[45]**

👁 $2 420 - €2 223 - **£1 500** - FF14 581
Children Playing in a Woodland Glade Oil/canvas
(47x60cm 18x23in) Devon 1999

👁 $1 046 - €1 123 - **£700** - FF7 365
Landscape with figures on a Path Oil/board
(12x24cm 5x9in) Little-Lane, Ilkley 2000

WITHERS Augusta Innes XIX **[21]**

✏ $1 789 - €1 501 - **£1 050** - FF9 849
Canaries with Their Young and Flowers in a Vase Watercolour/paper (30x38cm 12x15in) Aylsham, Norfolk 1998

WITHERS Walter Herbert 1854-1914 **[85]**

👁 $35 756 - €31 178 - **£21 621** - FF204 512
Gathering Hay Oil/canvas (30.5x56cm 12x22in)
Melbourne 1998

👁 $4 720 - €5 200 - **£3 168** - FF34 112
Sheepwash Creek Oil/panel (28x40.5cm 11x15in)
Malvern, Victoria 2000

✏ $1 270 - €1 498 - **£895** - FF9 825
Harbourside Stroll Watercolour/paper (33.5x26cm 13x10in) Woollahra, Sydney 2001

WITHERSTINE Donald 1896-1961 **[37]**

📖 $200 - €192 - **£122** - FF1 260
Among the Souks in Fez, Morocco Linocut
(22x23cm 9x9in) Provincetown MA 1999

WITHOOS Alida 1659/60-1715 **[12]**

👁 $8 968 - €10 596 - **£6 355** - FF69 505
Souboisstilleben mit Schmetterlingen und Echsen Öl/Leinwand (86x64cm 33x25in) Zürich 2000

WITHOOS Franz 1657-1705 **[2]**

✏ $9 824 - €9 111 - **£6 000** - FF59 761
Two Studies of Parsnips Watercolour (22.5x40cm 8x15in) London 1998

WITHOOS Mathias Calzetti 1627-1703 **[32]**

👁 $4 861 - €5 445 - **£3 378** - FF35 719
Shepherds and their Flock by a well in an Italianate Landscape Oil/canvas (37x44cm 14x17in)
Amsterdam 2001

✏ $4 615 - €4 488 - **£3 290** - FF29 956
Études d'insectes et une étude de coquillage
Gouache/vélin (12x17.5cm 4x6in) Paris 2000

WITHOOS Pieter 1654-1693 **[19]**

👁 $9 422 - €9 076 - **£5 822** - FF59 532
Marten with a Dead Dove and Butterflies by the Foot of a Tree Oil/canvas (79x57.5cm 31x22in)
Amsterdam 1999

👁 $1 982 - €1 906 - **£1 220** - FF12 501
Study of Five Moths Watercolour, gouache
(20.5x29cm 8x11in) Amsterdam 1999

WITJENS Jacques 1881-1956 **[11]**

👁 $5 100 - €5 925 - **£3 584** - FF38 868
Los molinos Oleo/lienzo (76x110cm 29x43in)
Buenos-Aires 2001

👁 $1 600 - €1 379 - **£950** - FF9 045
Tiempo tormentoso Oleo/lienzo (29.5x39.5cm 11x15in) Montevideo 1998

WITJENS Willem 1884-1962 **[43]**

👁 $989 - €908 - **£609** - FF5 953
View of the Village of Herwijnen Oil/canvas/board
(41x60.5cm 16x23in) Amsterdam 1999

WITKAMP Ernst Sigismund 1854-1897 **[19]**

👁 $5 791 - €5 445 - **£3 585** - FF35 719
Secret amusement Oil/canvas (75.5x135.5cm 29x53in) Amsterdam 1999

WITKIEWICZ Stanislaw 1851-1915 **[6]**

👁 $36 410 - €39 970 - **£24 200** - FF262 185
Pferdemarkt Öl/Leinwand (94x147cm 37x57in) Wien 2000

✏ $2 046 - €1 816 - **£1 223** - FF11 912
Pod kaplica Biruty w Poledze Watercolour, gouache/paper (18x18cm 7x7in) Warszawa 1998

WITKIEWICZ-WITKACY Stanislaw Ignacy 1885-1939 **[133]**

✏ $5 224 - €6 069 - **£3 670** - FF39 811
Portrait de fille Pastel/papier (63.5x47.5cm 25x18in)
Kraków 2001

WITKIN Joel-Peter 1939 **[181]**

📷 $4 000 - €4 441 - **£2 782** - FF29 129
«The Wife of Cain, New Mexico» Gelatin silver print (37x37.5cm 14x14in) New-York 2001

WITKOWSKI Karl / Karol 1860-1910 **[23]**

👁 $15 000 - €12 816 - **£9 076** - FF84 066
Two Boys Fishing Oil/canvas (63.5x78.5cm 25x30in)
San-Francisco CA 1998

WITKOWSKI Romuald Kamil 1876-1950 **[3]**

👁 $4 274 - €4 989 - **£2 928** - FF32 724
Nature morte Huile/toile (46x80cm 18x31in)
Warszawa 2000

WITMAN C.F. XIX **[2]**

👁 $3 000 - €3 194 - **£2 043** - FF20 949
On the Plains Oil/board (10x33cm 3x12in) New-York 2001

WITMONT Herman 1605-c.1683 **[8]**

👁 $24 306 - €27 227 - **£16 890** - FF178 596
Threemasters off a rocky Coast in a Stiff Breeze
Oil/panel (41x53cm 16x20in) Amsterdam 2001

✏ $10 232 - €8 837 - **£6 168** - FF57 970
A Man-of-war Sailing out from a Harbour with a Fluitship Ink (41.8x51.9cm 16x20in) Amsterdam 1998

WITSCHI Hans W. 1954 **[2]**

👁 $2 248 - €2 445 - **£1 481** - FF16 037
Atelierbild Öl/Leinwand (100.5x114cm 39x44in) Bern 2000

WITSEN Willem 1860-1923 **[105]**

👁 $5 415 - €5 899 - **£3 729** - FF38 695
A View of the Ij with the St.Nicolas Church and the Central Station Oil/canvas (33.5x48cm 13x18in)
Amsterdam 2001

✏ $4 563 - €4 311 - **£2 760** - FF28 277
Flowers in a red glazed Vase Watercolour/paper
(40.5x34cm 15x13in) Amsterdam 1999

📖 $379 - €431 - **£262** - FF2 827
Canale Grande I Etching, aquatint (33.5x39.5cm 13x15in) Haarlem 2000

W

WITT Franz 1864-? **[6]**
🖌 **$2 196** - €2 180 - **£1 371** - FF14 301
Die Wiener Oper im Schnee Watercolour (37x57cm 14x22in) Wien 1999

WITT John H. Harrison 1840-1901 **[6]**
👁 **$6 500** - €7 771 - **£4 483** - FF50 973
Waiting his coming Oil/canvas (97x79cm 38x31in) Milford CT 2000
👁 **$2 594** - €2 211 - **£1 545** - FF14 500
Bouquet de roses Huile/toile (32x40cm 12x15in) Paris 1998

WITTE de Adrien 1850-1935 **[54]**
🖌 **$372** - €347 - **£224** - FF2 276
Prêtre officiant Encre Chine (42x26cm 16x10in) Liège 1999
📜 **$91** - €99 - **£60** - FF650
La lessiveuse Eau-forte (24x16cm 9x6in) Liège 2000

WITTE de Emmanuel 1617-1692 **[11]**
👁 **$83 730** - €71 286 - **£50 000** - FF467 605
Capriccio of the Interior of the Oude Kerk, Amsterdam Oil/canvas (66x55.5cm 25x21in) London 1998
👁 **$20 864** - €24 392 - **£14 896** - FF160 000
Etude de personnages et d'animaux Huile/papier (30.5x23cm 12x9in) Paris 2001

WITTE de Gaspar, Jasper 1624-1681 **[10]**
👁 **$24 595** - €29 270 - **£17 568** - FF192 000
Paysage aux promeneurs près d'un château Huile/panneau (35.5x46cm 13x18in) Orléans 2000
👁 **$26 000** - €28 794 - **£17 633** - FF188 877
Village Festival Oil/copper (32x40cm 12x15in) New-York 2000

WITTE de L. XVIII **[1]**
👁 **$111 996** - €106 523 - **£68 000** - FF698 747
Roe Deer at the Edge of a Wood/Red Deer in a River Landscape Oil/copper (35x40cm 13x15in) London 1999

WITTE de Marthe 1893-1976 **[1]**
🖌 **$9 358** - €9 076 - **£5 890** - FF59 532
Kanomo Man/Femme Mangbetu Pencil (80x60cm 31x23in) Amsterdam 1999

WITTE de Peter Candido 1548-1628 **[6]**
👁 **$2 500** - €2 683 - **£1 673** - FF17 602
Madonna and Child Oil/canvas (64x66cm 25x26in) Cedar-Falls IA 2000
🖌 **$1 883** - €1 750 - **£1 150** - FF11 477
The Annunciation Ink (40.5x31.5cm 15x12in)

WITTEL van Gaspar Vanvitelli 1653-1736 **[71]**
👁 **$469 252** - €399 257 - **£280 000** - FF2 618 952
Bacino di San Marco, Venice, looking towards the Doge's Palace Oil/canvas (48.5x108cm 19x42in) London 1998
👁 **$90 000** - €78 945 - **£54 648** - FF517 842
View of the Colosseum, Rome, seen from the Southwest Oil/canvas (21x31cm 8x12in) New-York 1999
🖌 **$17 195** - €15 975 - **£10 500** - FF104 790
View of Naples from Mergellina Ink (18.5x40.5cm 7x15in) London 1998

WITTENBERG Jan Hendrik W. 1886-1963 **[19]**
👁 **$6 188** - €6 941 - **£4 312** - FF45 528
Nature morte au sandwich Huile/toile (40x50.5cm 15x19in) Antwerpen 2001
👁 **$3 710** - €4 311 - **£2 607** - FF28 277
Still life with calabashes Oil/panel (17x20.5cm 6x8in) Amsterdam 2001

WITTERWULGHE Joseph 1883-1967 **[50]**
🗿 **$473** - €545 - **£330** - FF3 577
Les Bacchantes Terracotta (45x41cm 17x16in) Bruxelles 2001

WITTIG Bartholomäus 1613-1684 **[2]**
👁 **$3 923** - €4 636 - **£2 780** - FF30 408
Genreszene in einer Schenke/Hofszene mit Kartenspielern Öl/Kupfer (33.2x31.6cm 13x12in) Zürich 2000

WITTIG D. XVII **[1]**
👁 **$26 430** - €21 797 - **£15 570** - FF142 980
Vanitasstilleben mit Folianten, einem Tongefäss und einem Totenkopf Oil/panel (34x48cm 13x18in) Wien 1998

WITTIG Werner 1930 **[36]**
📜 **$45** - €51 - **£31** - FF335
Verstreut Woodcut in colors (34.5x37cm 13x14in) Berlin 2001

WITTING Walter Günther J. 1864-1940 **[20]**
👁 **$726** - €818 - **£500** - FF5 366
Waldstück Öl/Leinwand (130x88cm 51x34in) Satow 2000

WITTKAMP Johann Bernhard 1820-1885 **[5]**
👁 **$3 570** - €3 470 - **£2 184** - FF22 764
La naissance Huile/toile (95x64cm 37x25in) Liège 1999

WITTKUGEL Klaus 1910-1985 **[11]**
📷 **$371** - €411 - **£252** - FF2 699
Kompositionen Gelatin silver print (30x24cm 11x9in) Berlin 2000

WITTLER Heinz H., Arigo 1918-1979 **[72]**
👁 **$538** - €562 - **£341** - FF3 689
Ischialandschaft Öl/Papier (49x69cm 19x27in) München 2000
🖌 **$296** - €256 - **£178** - FF1 676
Südliche Landschaft Gouache (34x45.5cm 13x17in) Köln 1998

WITTLICH Josef 1903-1982 **[19]**
🖌 **$1 238** - €1 329 - **£828** - FF8 720
Sturmangriff Gouache (89x62cm 35x24in) Köln 2000

WITTMACK Edgar Franklin 1894-1956 **[3]**
👁 **$4 000** - €4 455 - **£2 616** - FF29 225
Magazine cover: Man is more intent on his date than fishing strike Oil/canvas (76x58cm 30x23in) New-York 2000

WITTMANN Ernest 1846-? **[6]**
🗿 **$927** - €1 090 - **£672** - FF7 150
Le lieur de fagot Sculpture (H22cm H8in) Epinal 2001

WITZEL Josef Rudolf 1867-1924 **[10]**
📜 **$1 800** - €1 535 - **£1 085** - FF10 072
«Isidor Bach» Poster (84x118cm 33x46in) New-York 1998

WIWEL Niels 1855-1914 **[19]**
👁 **$1 778** - €1 615 - **£1 111** - FF10 593
Klarinetspillende mand iført höj hat og sort vest Oil/wood (31x23.5cm 12x9in) Köbenhavn 1999

WIZANI Johann Friedrich 1770-1835 **[4]**
📜 **$1 040** - €1 167 - **£722** - FF7 654
Vue de la ville de Lucerne Radierung (51x65.5cm 20x25in) Luzern 2001

WLERICK Robert 1882-1944 **[43]**
🗿 **$14 200** - €15 245 - **£9 500** - FF100 000
Portrait de Rolande Bronze (H84cm H33in) Compiègne 2000

$839 - €945 - £584 - FF6 200
Nu couché Sanguine/papier (36x46cm 14x18in) Paris 2001

WOCHER Marquard Fidel Dom. 1760-1830 [20]
$1 708 - €1 486 - £1 030 - FF9 748
«Andreas Merian.J:U:C: Burgermeister des Cantons Basel» Watercolour (21.5x14.3cm 8x5in) Bern 1998

WOCHER Tiberius Domenikus 1728-1799 [13]
$2 504 - €2 907 - £1 760 - FF19 068
Bildnis eines bärtigen Mannes mit Zahnlücken Öl/Leinwand (52x39.5cm 20x15in) Wien 2001

WODZINOWSKI Wincenty 1866-1940 [27]
$1 513 - €1 307 - £912 - FF8 575
In der Kirche Öl/Leinwand (82x132cm 32x51in) Wien 1998

WODZINSKI Josef 1859-1918 [8]
$4 744 - €4 602 - £2 986 - FF30 185
Am Strand Öl/Leinwand (48.5x83cm 19x32in) München 2001
$3 678 - €4 125 - £2 497 - FF27 057
Ballerine Huile/carton (45.5x30cm 17x11in) Warszawa 2000

WOELFLE Arthur William 1873-1936 [11]
$7 000 - €8 271 - £4 960 - FF54 255
Provincetown Roofs Oil/canvas (55x67cm 21x26in) Boston MA 2000
$400 - €473 - £283 - FF3 100
Spanish Galleon Oil/board (20.5x25cm 8x9in) Boston MA 2000

WOENSEL van Petronella 1785-1839 [9]
$5 000 - €4 897 - £3 222 - FF32 124
Still Life of Grapes, a Rummer and a Vine Branch Oil/panel (51x59cm 20x23in) New-York 1999

WOERKOM van Jos 1902-1992 [2]
$999 - €1 134 - £694 - FF7 441
«K.N.A.C» Poster (89x118.5cm 35x46in) Hoorn 2001

WOERMANN Hedwig 1879-? [11]
$14 355 - €15 339 - £9 756 - FF100 617
«Tanzgruppe» Öl/Leinwand (210x130cm 82x51in) Satow 2001

WOESTIJNE van de Gustave 1881-1947 [55]
$392 364 - €367 562 - £235 872 - FF2 411 046
Two Women Oil/canvas (150x150cm 59x59in) Amsterdam 1999
$108 000 - €118 983 - £70 560 - FF780 480
Les travaux de la terre Huile/toile (67.5x95cm 26x37in) Bruxelles 2000
$62 792 - €71 651 - £43 616 - FF470 000
Maternité Lavis (131.5x90cm 51x35in) Paris 2000

WOESTIJNE van de Maxime 1911 [13]
$3 378 - €3 176 - £2 045 - FF20 836
«Mains Blanches» Oil/board (44x36cm 17x14in) Amsterdam 1999

WOGE Daniel 1717-1797 [5]
$15 856 - €14 521 - £9 664 - FF95 251
Luise Charlotte, Princess of Mecklenburg-Schwerin (1779-1804) Oil/canvas (133.5x104cm 52x40in) Amsterdam 1999
$3 220 - €2 949 - £1 963 - FF19 347
Luise, Duchess of Mecklenburg-Schwerin (1756-1808) Oil/canvas (66.5x52.5cm 26x20in) Amsterdam 1999

$9 414 - €8 622 - £5 738 - FF56 555
Adolf Friedrich IV, Duke of Mecklenburg-Strelitz (1738-1794) Bodycolour (78x63cm 30x24in) Amsterdam 1999

WOGENSKY Robert 1919 [12]
$1 340 - €1 524 - £930 - FF10 000
Trois oiseaux blancs Tapisserie (140x212cm 55x83in) Paris 2000

WOHLGEMUTH Michael 1434-1519 [7]
$500 - €518 - £300 - FF3 400
Adamo ed Eva sulla Terra Gravure bois (40.5x28cm 15x11in) Roma 1999

WÖHLK Nicolaus 1887-1950 [9]
$6 686 - €5 651 - £3 990 - FF37 069
Lupiner og valmuer Oil/canvas (85x75cm 33x29in) København 1998

WOHLWILL Gretchen 1878-1962 [11]
$1 760 - €2 045 - £1 237 - FF13 415
Treibhaus Öl/Leinwand (52x70.5cm 20x27in) Hamburg 2001

WÖHNER Louis 1888-1958 [41]
$783 - €869 - £543 - FF5 701
«Stilleben mit Blumen» Öl/Leinwand (51x61cm 20x24in) Kempten 2001

WOICESKE Ronau William 1887-1953 [7]
$300 - €280 - £186 - FF1 838
The Great Pine Etching (34x23cm 13x9in) Mystic CT 1999

WOITSCH Emmy 1894-1981 [12]
$611 - €727 - £436 - FF4 767
Blumenstilleben Aquarell/Papier (31x22cm 12x8in) Linz 2000

WOJTKIEWICZ Witold 1879-1909/11 [17]
$30 587 - €30 829 - £19 075 - FF202 225
Ravissement au parc Tempera (45.5x69.5cm 17x27in) Warszawa 2000
$1 707 - €1 553 - £1 047 - FF10 184
In the Dressing Room Watercolour (13.5x17.5cm 5x6in) Warszawa 1999
$702 - €826 - £503 - FF5 416
Jadwiga Mrozowska et Andrzej Milewski comme Klara et Albin Lithographie couleurs (29x41cm 11x16in) Warszawa 2001

WOLBERS Hermanus Gerhardus 1856-1926 [17]
$5 000 - €4 799 - £3 134 - FF31 477
Out to Pasture Oil/canvas (110.5x75cm 43x29in) New-York 1999

WÖLCK Preben 1925 [123]
$221 - €215 - £137 - FF1 411
Efterår Oil/canvas (46x55cm 18x21in) Vejle 1999

WOLCOTT Marion Post 1910-1990 [69]
$1 800 - €1 504 - £1 065 - FF9 868
Jitterbugging, Mississippi Silver print (8x12cm 3x5in) New-York 1998

WOLD Roar 1926 [4]
$5 183 - €4 379 - £3 112 - FF28 724
Detaljer i rommet Oil/canvas (111x80cm 43x31in) Oslo 1998

WOLD-TORNE Oluf 1867-1919 [6]
$7 163 - €7 950 - £4 992 - FF52 149
Badehuset Oil/canvas (53x65cm 20x25in) Oslo 2001

WOLDE Paul 1885-? [6]
$1 400 - €1 503 - £936 - FF9 857
Harbor Scene Oil/board (35x50cm 14x20in) Portland ME 2000

W

W

WOLF & RICHTER J. & H.C. XIX [5]
IIIIII $836 - €984 - £600 - FF6 455
 Scolopax Rusticola Lithograph (35.5x50cm
13x19in) London 2001

WOLF & SMIT XIX [3]
IIIIII $382 - €357 - £236 - FF2 339
 Felis Bengalensis-Bengal Leopard Cat
Lithograph (59x46cm 23x18in) New-Orleans LA 1999

WOLF Caspar 1735-1798 [61]
 $33 960 - €39 403 - £23 448 - FF258 468
 Phantasielandschaft Öl/Leinwand (44x73cm
17x28in) Luzern 2000
 $17 990 - €15 556 - £10 695 - FF102 040
 Der Geltenschuss im Lauental mit
Schneebrücke Öl/Karton (28x19.5cm 11x7in) Zürich
1998
 $14 843 - €16 140 - £10 465 - FF111 170
 Panorama der Berner Alpen bei Meiringen
Aquarell/Papier (16.5x70cm 6x27in) Bern 2001
IIIIII $169 - €162 - £103 - FF1 060
 Schiltwaldbach/Herrenbaechli Farbradierung
(19.9x13.6cm 7x5in) Bern 1999

WOLF Franz Xaver 1896-1989 [86]
 $5 095 - €4 933 - £3 200 - FF32 360
 In the Library Oil/panel (46x37cm 18x14in) London
1999
 $1 398 - €1 308 - £846 - FF8 580
 Blumenstrauss Oil/panel (37.5x30cm 14x11in) Wien
1999

WOLF Georg 1882-1962 [120]
 $1 535 - €1 534 - £960 - FF10 061
 Winterlicher Viehmarkt Öl/Karton (36x45cm
14x17in) Köln 1999
 $1 008 - €1 125 - £678 - FF7 378
 Pferd Öl/Leinwand (31x43cm 12x16in) Satow 2000
 $490 - €486 - £297 - FF3 186
 Im Hafen Pencil/paper (19x26cm 7x10in) Satow 2000

WOLF Gustav 1887-1947 [6]
IIIIII $43 - €46 - £28 - FF301
 Kraterlandschaft mit Sauriern Radierung (24x20cm
9x7in) Zwiesel 2000

WOLF Henry XX [1]
 $2 400 - €2 692 - £1 663 - FF17 661
 Vienna Ferris Wheel Gelatin silver print (34x22cm
13x9in) New-York 2000

WOLF Joseph 1820-1899 [73]
 $21 563 - €18 754 - £13 000 - FF123 017
 The Proud Bird of the Mountain Oil/canvas
(147.5x130cm 58x40in) Glasgow 1998
 $1 088 - €1 226 - £750 - FF8 043
 Study of a Bird of Prey Watercolour (17.5x25cm
6x9in) Newbury, Berkshire 2000

WOLF Karl Anton 1908-1989 [10]
 $2 122 - €1 817 - £1 277 - FF11 917
 Blumenstock Öl/Leinwand (75x65cm 29x25in) Wien
1998

WOLF Lone 1882-1965 [11]
 $2 500 - €2 360 - £1 554 - FF15 482
 The Holdup Oil/canvas (50x86cm 20x34in) Milford
CT 1999

WOLF Ulrich Ludwig 1776-1832 [7]
IIIIII $34 - €41 - £25 - FF268
 Königsschwur Kupferstich (37x32cm 14x12in)
Rudolstadt-Thüringen 2001

WOLF Victoria Fontaine XX [35]
 $544 - €567 - £342 - FF3 719
 The Mirror Pastel/paper (73x53cm 28x20in)
Melbourne 2000

WOLF-FERRARI Teodoro 1876-1945 [11]
 $1 360 - €1 762 - £1 020 - FF11 560
 Il Grappa Olio/tavola (21x27cm 8x10in) Milano 2001

WOLFAERTS Artus 1581-1641 [8]
 $10 990 - €10 671 - £6 790 - FF70 000
 Saint-Jérome Huile/panneau (64.5x49cm 25x19in) La
Flèche 1999

WOLFE Byron B. 1904-1973 [4]
 $420 - €493 - £296 - FF3 236
 The Village, Friend or Foe Watercolour/paper
(28x40cm 11x15in) New-York 2000

WOLFE Edward 1897-1982 [213]
 $4 546 - €4 485 - £2 800 - FF29 420
 La Villa Oil/canvas/board (63.5x61cm 25x24in) London
1999
 $794 - €891 - £550 - FF5 846
 Abstract Oil/panel (18.5x28.5cm 7x11in) London
2000
 $945 - €1 081 - £650 - FF7 094
 Female Portrait Heads Ink (13x11.5cm 5x4in)
Godalming, Surrey 2000
IIIIII $418 - €461 - £278 - FF3 024
 Song of Songs Print in colors (35.5x26.5cm 13x10in)
Bath 2000

WOLFE George 1834-1890 [40]
 $1 769 - €1 671 - £1 100 - FF10 958
 Penzance Luggers on Shore Watercolour/paper
(33x45cm 13x18in) Scarborough, North-Yorshire 1999

WOLFE Wayne 1945 [2]
 $6 500 - €7 380 - £4 516 - FF48 412
 Sunning Oil/canvas (60x91cm 24x36in) Dallas TX
2001

WOLFENSBERGER Johann Jakob 1797-1850 [3]
 $1 200 - €1 431 - £856 - FF9 390
 Landschaft mit Mühle Aquarell, Gouache/Karton
(38x54.5cm 14x21in) Berlin 2000

WOLFERS Philippe 1858-1929 [16]
 $28 730 - €32 225 - £20 020 - FF211 380
 Les heures Bronze (110x165x30.5cm 43x64x12in)
Bruxelles 2001
 $5 676 - €5 453 - £3 498 - FF35 772
 Danseuse se redressant Sculpture (9.5x16x7.5cm
3x6x2in) Bruxelles 1999

WOLFF & TRITSCHLER Paul & Alfred 1887/1905-
1951/70 [29]
 $278 - €332 - £198 - FF2 180
 Kinderaufnahmen Vintage gelatin silver print
(22x16.5cm 8x6in) Berlin 2000

WOLFF Albert Moritz 1854-1923 [11]
 $1 521 - €1 278 - £894 - FF8 383
 Flucht nach Ägypten(?), Maria mit dem Kind auf
einem Dromedar sitzend Bronze (H28.5cm H11in)
Köln 1998

WOLFF Emil 1802-1879 [6]
 $14 928 - €12 983 - £9 000 - FF85 166
 A Girl with a Tambourine and Her Lamb Marble
(H137cm H53in) London 1998

WOLFF Eugen 1873-1937 [11]
 $927 - €971 - £887 - FF6 372
 Wintertag in einer Grossstadt Öl/Leinwand
(70x42cm 27x16in) Köln 2000

WOLFF Franz Alex. Fried. 1816-1887 [2]
$6 500 - €7 383 - £4 561 - FF48 427
Pig Bronze (H18cm H7in) New-York 2001

WOLFF Gustav Heinrich 1886-1934 [34]
$3 101 - €3 068 - £1 933 - FF20 123
Stehende klagende Frau Bronze
(49.7x11.5x10.2cm 19x4x4in) Berlin 1999
$658 - €613 - £406 - FF4 024
Die Tragödin (Frau mit lila Gewand) Aquarell
(30x23.6cm 11x9in) Hamburg 1999

WOLFF Gustave 1863-1935 [10]
$800 - €896 - £555 - FF5 877
«**Autumn Landscape**» Oil/canvas (40x30cm
16x12in) Cincinnati OH 2001

WOLFF Hermann 1841-? [11]
$863 - €1 017 - £597 - FF6 673
Landschaft mit Rindern und figürlicher Staffage
Öl/Leinwand (32x45cm 12x17in) Wiener Neustadt 2000

WOLFF Jeremias 1663-1724 [9]
$373 - €422 - £262 - FF2 766
«**Das Weissenburger Baad im Amt
Wimmis**»/«**Vorstellung des Baad Hauses**»
Kupferstich (25.5x18.5cm 10x7in) Bern 2001

WOLFF José 1884-1964 [152]
$1 182 - €1 363 - £814 - FF8 943
Vue de village Huile/panneau (38,5x46.5cm 15x18in)
Liège 2000
$408 - €471 - £281 - FF3 089
Vue de l'Ourthe à Hony Huile/panneau (30x40cm
11x15in) Liège 2000

WOLFF Paul 1887-1951 [255]
$638 - €727 - £441 - FF4 767
Abbrucharbeiten im Centrum Roms Vintage gelatin silver print (17.6x23.5cm 6x9in) Wien 2000

WOLFF Robert Jay 1905-1977 [9]
$2 900 - €3 298 - £2 011 - FF21 634
Chicago Series Oil/paper/board (38x55cm 15x22in)
Chicago IL 2000

WOLFF Willy 1905-1985 [19]
$5 499 - €6 647 - £3 838 - FF43 600
Pop-Art Komposition Oil/panel (120x99cm 47x38in)
Berlin 2000
$547 - €511 - £331 - FF3 353
Abstrakt Print (50x36cm 19x14in) Stuttgart 1999

WOLFF Willy 1889-? [3]
$450 - €511 - £308 - FF3 353
«**Stein Liköre**» Poster (100x75cm 39x29in) Hannover
2000

WOLFFORT Artus 1581-1641 [5]
$12 856 - €12 752 - £8 000 - FF83 646
Saint James the Less Oil/canvas (114.5x92.5cm
45x36in) London 1999

WOLFGANG Johann Georg 1662-1744 [4]
$300 - €256 - £179 - FF1 676
Hl. Benno mit Münchenansicht Copper engraving
(63x43cm 24x16in) München 1998

WÖLFLE Franz Xaver 1887-1972 [54]
$1 350 - €1 534 - £944 - FF10 061
Bauer mit Gewehr Oil/panel (24x18cm 9x7in)
München 2001

WÖLFLI Adolf 1864-1930 [56]
$13 332 - €15 855 - £9 501 - FF104 004
Grand Hotel Skt.Adolf Coloured pencils/paper
(24x38cm 9x14in) Zürich 2000

WOLFRAM Joseph act.c.1900 [14]
$760 - €654 - £450 - FF4 292
Jäger im Hochgebirge Öl/Leinwand (47.5x33cm
18x12in) Wien 1998

WOLFROM Friedrich Ernst 1857-? [5]
$4 126 - €4 602 - £2 774 - FF30 185
Auf dem Heimweg Öl/Leinwand/Karton
(108.5x85.5cm 42x33in) Ahlden 2000

WOLFS Hubert 1899-1937 [9]
$4 284 - €4 462 - £2 700 - FF29 268
Nature morte aux poissons Huile/panneau
(67x77cm 26x30in) Antwerpen 2000

WOLFSEN Aleijda 1648-1690 [6]
$5 769 - €6 781 - £4 000 - FF44 480
**Lady Seated Small-half-length in a Blue Dress
with Embroidered Flowers** Oil/canvas (43.5x38cm
17x14in) London 2000
$4 750 - €4 669 - £3 052 - FF30 629
Portrait of a Lady with a Dog Oil/canvas
(42x31.5cm 16x12in) New-York 1999

WOLFSFELD Erich 1884-1956 [35]
$12 909 - €14 331 - £9 000 - FF94 004
Camel Caravan in the Desert Oil/panel
(81.5x147.5cm 32x58in) London 2001
$148 - €169 - £102 - FF1 106
Danae Radierung (54x62cm 21x24in) Berlin 2000

WOLFSON William 1894-? [8]
$3 400 - €3 201 - £2 000 - FF20 994
Above the City Lithograph (29.5x31.5cm 11x12in)
New-York 1999

WOLFTHORN Julie 1868-1944 [5]
$4 543 - €4 410 - £2 829 - FF28 927
Gladiolen Öl/Leinwand (110x88.5cm 43x34in) Berlin
1999

WOLGERS Dan 1955 [6]
$4 747 - €4 784 - £2 960 - FF31 381
Honey Mixed media (73x79cm 28x31in) Stockholm
2000
$2 442 - €2 736 - £1 702 - FF17 950
Pose, Linda Evangelista Assemblage (H77cm
H30in) Stockholm 2001

WOLINSKI Georges 1934 [19]
$458 - €427 - £282 - FF2 800
Aie Gouache (37x30cm 14x11in) Paris 1999

WOLLEN William Barnes 1857-1936 [35]
$12 095 - €14 053 - £8 500 - FF92 180
Battle of Jena, saluting the Trophies of War
Oil/canvas (112.5x163cm 44x64in) London 2001
$2 300 - €2 132 - £1 430 - FF13 984
Exterior Scene with soldier on horses at inn
Oil/canvas (50x68cm 20x27in) Asheville NC 1999
$485 - €457 - £300 - FF2 998
**The Patrol, two Austrian Mounted Soldiers
Speaking with a Young Woman** Watercolour
(24.5x19.5cm 9x7in) Oxfordshire 1999
$250 - €271 - £166 - FF1 780
«**Edinburgh, The Royal Mile, Travel from King's
Mile**» Poster (101x63cm 40x25in) New-York 2000

WOLLHEIM Gert Heinrich 1894-1974 [63]
$6 754 - €7 669 - £4 693 - FF50 308
Shakespeare Hamlet Oil/panel (244x220cm
96x86in) München 2001
$4 519 - €4 346 - £2 788 - FF28 508
Rhododendren Oil/panel (81x71cm 31x27in) Köln
1999

W

$7 561 - €8 692 - £5 339 - FF57 016
Selbstbildnis Oil/panel (48x32cm 18x12in) Bremen 2001

$1 245 - €1 431 - £879 - FF9 390
Selbstbildnis mit Pfeife Charcoal (44.5x30.5cm 17x12in) Bremen 2001

WOLMANS Jacques 1919 [14]

$391 - €421 - £270 - FF2 764
Retour de pêche Huile/toile (50x60cm 19x23in) Bruxelles 2001

WOLMARK Alfred Aaron 1877-1961 [214]

$19 286 - €18 701 - £12 217 - FF122 673
He hath two Coats Oil/canvas (152x95cm 59x37in) London 1999

$3 937 - €3 606 - £2 400 - FF23 653
A Still Life of Chrysanthemums Oil/canvas (76x56cm 29x22in) London 1999

$2 241 - €2 619 - £1 600 - FF17 182
Still Life of Apples Oil/board (33x44.5cm 12x17in) London 2001

$354 - €328 - £220 - FF2 150
Seated female Nude Charcoal (37x31cm 14x12in) London 1999

WOLPERDING Friedrich Ernst 1815-1888 [3]

$4 408 - €4 171 - £2 746 - FF27 357
Kastellet Kakkeloplyst Oil/canvas (38x51.5cm 14x20in) Köbenhavn 1999

WOLS (Otto A.W. Schulze) 1913-1951 [353]

$4 354 - €4 192 - £2 554 - FF27 500
«Les maisons ocres» Acrylique (17x14cm 6x5in) Paris 2001

$17 931 - €19 248 - £12 000 - FF126 259
Les gentils tubercules Watercolour (20.5x16cm 8x6in) London 2000

$714 - €767 - £478 - FF5 030
Die Stadt Radierung (33x24.8cm 12x9in) Hamburg 2000

$1 228 - €1 448 - £863 - FF9 500
Portrait de Arthur Adamov à la cigarette Tirage argentique (24x18cm 9x7in) Paris 2000

WOLSELEY Garnet Ruskin 1884-1967 [34]

$1 135 - €1 012 - £700 - FF6 638
Girl Seated on a Low Cliff Oil/panel (23x27cm 9x11in) Penzance, Cornwall 1999

WOLSKI Stanislaw Polian 1859-1894 [8]

$14 023 - €15 385 - £9 314 - FF100 918
Cavaliers en steppe Oil/canvas (55.8x98.4cm 21x38in) Warszawa 2000

$3 563 - €4 159 - £2 515 - FF27 281
Trompette Huile/carton (41.5x33.5cm 16x13in) Warszawa 2000

WOLSTENHOLME Dean I 1757-1837 [38]

$6 521 - €7 200 - £4 500 - FF47 232
The Essex Hunt Oil/canvas (62x75cm 24x29in) Crewkerne, Somerset 2001

$16 000 - €18 589 - £11 244 - FF121 939
In the Slips/Going out/The Finding/The Kill Oil/canvas (28x38cm 11x14in) New-York 2001

$1 260 - €1 466 - £900 - FF9 618
Repose after shooting Watercolour (24x40cm 9x15in) London 2001

WOLSTENHOLME Dean II 1798-1882 [32]

$6 175 - €5 706 - £3 800 - FF37 430
Paisaje con un puente, vacas y niños jugando junto al río Oleo/lienzo (66x91cm 25x35in) Madrid 1999

$2 136 - €1 951 - £1 300 - FF12 795
A Landscape with Sheep grazing by a Stream/Woman crossing a Stile Oil/panel (31x42cm 12x16in) London 1998

WOLTER Hendrik Jan 1873-1952 [159]

$11 970 - €10 362 - £7 264 - FF67 971
Harbour Scene Oil/canvas (39.5x49.5cm 15x19in) Amsterdam 1998

$3 932 - €3 403 - £2 388 - FF22 324
View of London Oil/board (22x26.5cm 8x10in) Amsterdam 1999

$1 164 - €1 299 - £810 - FF8 524
Maisons le long du Singel, Amersfoort Aquarelle, gouache/papier (49x82cm 19x32in) Montréal 2001

$312 - €363 - £219 - FF2 381
View of Amersfoort Lithograph (24.5x25.5cm 9x10in) Amsterdam 2001

WOLTERS Eugene 1844-1905 [10]

$2 160 - €1 983 - £1 336 - FF13 008
Taking a Pilot Huile/toile (84x121cm 33x47in) Bruxelles 1999

$552 - €595 - £369 - FF3 902
Bord de rivière au canot Huile/bois (31x17cm 12x6in) Antwerpen 2000

WOLTZE Berthold 1829-1896 [19]

$5 193 - €5 899 - £3 643 - FF38 695
Playing Hide-and-seek Oil/canvas (73x58cm 28x22in) Amsterdam 2001

$2 310 - €2 659 - £1 595 - FF17 440
Der Mutter Notpfennig Pastell/Papier (74x55cm 29x21in) München 2000

WOLTZE Peter 1860-1925 [7]

$224 - €226 - £140 - FF1 484
Meipzig Watercolour/paper (23x33cm 9x12in) London 2000

WOLVECAMP Theo 1925-1992 [213]

$15 998 - €15 882 - £9 996 - FF104 181
Untitled Oil/canvas (156.5x91.5cm 61x36in) Amsterdam 1999

$4 852 - €5 541 - £3 421 - FF36 344
Ohne Titel Öl/Leinwand (50x40cm 19x15in) Bern 2001

$2 394 - €2 072 - £1 452 - FF13 594
Untitled Oil/canvas (30.5x24cm 12x9in) Amsterdam 1998

$1 638 - €1 418 - £994 - FF9 301
Untitled Watercolour (49.5x64.5cm 19x25in) Amsterdam 1998

$333 - €363 - £229 - FF2 381
Untitled Screenprint in colors (65x50cm 25x19in) Amsterdam 2001

WOLVENS Henri Victor 1896-1977 [178]

$9 376 - €7 932 - £5 568 - FF52 032
Les dunes Oil/canvas (50x70cm 19x27in) Lokeren 1998

$663 - €694 - £439 - FF4 552
Paysage enneigé Huile/panneau (13x18cm 5x7in) Bruxelles 2000

$353 - €421 - £253 - FF2 764
Strand en zee Ink/paper (22.5x27.5cm 8x10in) Lokeren 2000

WOMRATH Andrew Kay 1869-? [7]

$500 - €583 - £351 - FF3 825
«Salon des Cent» Poster (40x54.5cm 15x21in) New-York 2000

W

WONDER Pieter Christoffel 1780-1852 **[7]**
- **$3 777** – €4 175 - **£2 620** - FF27 384
  The naughty Cat Oil/panel (22.5x20cm 8x7in)
  Amsterdam 2001

WONG Brent 1945 **[3]**
- **$20 640** – €21 688 - **£13 587** - FF142 265
  Change Oil/board (90.5x136.5cm 35x53in) Auckland
  2000
- **$7 036** – €7 394 - **£4 632** - FF48 499
  Building-Hills-cloud Acrylic (84.5x60cm 33x23in)
  Auckland 2000

WONG Tony 1948 **[3]**
- **$6 137** – €5 124 - **£3 600** - FF33 613
  Boxer Sculpture (36x24x43cm 14x9x16in) London
  1998

WONG YONGQIANG 1945 **[1]**
- **$20 544** – €22 545 - **£13 232** - FF147 888
  New Year's Eve, 1718 Oil/canvas (149.5x108.5cm
  58x42in) Hong-Kong 2000

WONG-SHEN Su 1956 **[1]**
- **$11 590** – €12 843 - **£8 018** - FF84 246
  Ho-Chin Village Oil/canvas (91x116cm 35x45in)
  Taipei 2001

WONNER Paul 1920 **[50]**
- **$30 000** – €34 119 - **£20 961** - FF223 803
  Glasses with Pansies Oil/canvas (122x122cm
  48x48in) Beverly-Hills CA 2000
- **$6 000** – €6 971 - **£4 216** - FF45 727
  Easter Lilies Acrylic (102x81cm 40x31in) Beverly-
  Hills CA 2001
- **$12 000** – €13 647 - **£8 384** - FF89 521
  «Figure with Two Bouquets» Gouache (45x30cm
  17x11in) Beverly-Hills CA 2001
- **$350** – €400 - **£246** - FF2 622
  Tulips in a Milk Carton Lithograph (63x46cm
  25x18in) Chicago IL 2001

WONTNER William Clarke 1857-1930 **[18]**
- **$85 000** – €73 334 - **£51 280** - FF481 040
  A Classical Beauty Oil/canvas (143.5x71cm
  56x27in) New-York 1998

WOOD Albert Victor Ormsby 1904-1977 **[19]**
- **$1 190** – €1 270 - **£793** - FF8 329
  Bathtime Oil/cardboard (33x17cm 13x7in) Dublin
  2000
- **$571** – €609 - **£380** - FF3 997
  Portrait of George Moore Watercolour/paper
  (33x22cm 13x9in) Dublin 2000

WOOD Beatrice 1893-1998 **[12]**
- **$3 250** – €2 970 - **£1 988** - FF19 485
  Vase Ceramic (H23cm H9in) New-York 1999

WOOD Catherine Mary c.1860-1939 **[29]**
- **$1 007** – €1 081 - **£665** - FF7 093
  **Interior View of a Chapel with a Large Font and
  Sculpture Atop** Oil/canvas (41x51cm 16x20in) Hilton
  2000
- **$615** – €574 - **£380** - FF3 764
  Still Life, Flowers in a Relief moulded Jug
  Oil/board (27x40cm 11x16in) Bury St. Edmunds,
  Suffolk 1999

WOOD Charles Haigh 1854-1927 **[14]**
- **$59 703** – €50 148 - **£35 000** - FF328 947
  Taken by Storm Oil/canvas (95.5x127cm 37x50in)
  London 1998
- **$6 191** – €5 635 - **£3 800** - FF36 962
  Time waits for no Man Oil/canvas (51x40.5cm
  20x15in) London 1999

$6 725 – €7 219 - **£4 500** - FF47 351
  Shelling Peas Oil/panel (35.5x25.5cm 13x10in)
  London 2000

WOOD Christopher 1901-1930 **[167]**
- **$64 004** – €63 545 - **£40 000** - FF416 828
  Restaurant, St.Cloud Oil/board (45.5x54.5cm
  17x21in) London 1999
- **$28 917** – €24 682 - **£17 000** - FF161 904
  Carnations in a Glass Jar Oil/panel (35.5x29cm
  13x11in) London 1998
- **$2 375** – €2 470 - **£1 500** - FF16 204
  Boats Around the Headland Pencil/paper
  (29.5x39cm 11x15in) London 2000

WOOD Christopher 1961 **[12]**
- **$2 011** – €2 347 - **£1 400** - FF15 394
  Seated Nude Pencil/paper (48x27cm 18x10in)
  London 2000

WOOD Clifford Dudley 1905-1980 **[28]**
- **$279** – €260 - **£172** - FF1 707
  In the Flinders Ranges Watercolour (37.5x50.5cm
  14x19in) Melbourne 1999

WOOD Dawson XX **[1]**
- **$1 830** – €1 906 - **£1 160** - FF12 500
  «Hall Caines's...Die Witte Profeet» Affiche
  (75x49cm 29x19in) Versailles 2000

WOOD Donald 1889-1953 **[17]**
- **$739** – €836 - **£500** - FF5 486
  **Young Girl with a Faun and Dog in a Forest
  Glade** Oil/canvas (71x91cm 27x35in) London 2000

WOOD Edgar Thomas 1860-1935 **[11]**
- **$1 879** – €2 189 - **£1 300** - FF14 356
  Porto Mauro Oil/board (34x32cm 13x12in) Cheshire
  2000
- **$144** – €137 - **£90** - FF897
  View of Venetian Canal Watercolour/paper (22x38cm
  9x15in) Cheltenham, Gloucestershire 1999

WOOD Edwin XIX-XX **[2]**
- **$1 864** – €2 070 - **£1 300** - FF13 578
  The social Pages Ink (65.5x87.5cm 25x34in) London
  2001

WOOD Francis Derwent 1871-1926 **[20]**
- **$56 620** – €65 656 - **£40 000** - FF430 676
  Diana Bronze (H230cm H90in) London 2001

WOOD Frank Watson 1862-1953 **[149]**
- **$347** – €375 - **£240** - FF2 460
  Portrait of a Naval Officer Oil/canvas (89x49cm
  35x19in) Little-Lane, Ilkley 2001
- **$2 446** – €2 792 - **£1 700** - FF18 313
  Berwick Herring Boats Oil/canvas (27x35cm
  11x14in) Berwick-upon-Tweed 2000
- **$1 388** – €1 169 - **£820** - FF7 670
  Fishing Boats at Carr Rock Watercolour/paper
  (23x35cm 9x14in) Berwick-upon-Tweed 1998

WOOD Grant 1892-1942 **[307]**
- **$115 000** – €134 220 - **£81 178** - FF880 428
  Windmill Oil/canvas (45x54cm 18x21in) Cedar-Falls
  IA 2000
- **$130 000** – €139 541 - **£86 996** - FF915 330
  Corner of the Mill, Amana Oil/board (33x38cm
  13x15in) Cedar-Falls IA 2000
- **$65 000** – €71 985 - **£44 083** - FF472 192
  Lillies the Alley Terracotta (H53.5cm H21in) New-
  York 2000
- **$35 000** – €40 912 - **£24 780** - FF268 362
  Interior with Men at a Bar Charcoal (50x38cm
  20x15in) Cedar-Falls IA 2001

W

🛋 **$4 000** - €3 378 - **£2 402** - FF22 160
Approaching Storm Lithograph (30.5x23cm 12x9in)
New-York 1998

WOOD Hunter 1908 **[10]**
🖼 **$375** - €385 - **£234** - FF2 527
The Schooner Commodore going into the Harbor at Bermuda Oil/canvas/board (40x50cm 16x20in) Bolton MA 2000

WOOD John 1801-1870 **[16]**
🖼 **$11 239** - €13 039 - **£8 000** - FF85 527
Comus and the Lady Benighted Oil/canvas (101.5x126.5cm 39x49in) London 2001
🖼 **$1 126** - €1 331 - **£800** - FF8 728
Eve Oil/board (30x24cm 11x9in) London 2001

WOOD John T. 1845-1919 **[2]**
🖼 **$1 800** - €2 099 - **£1 263** - FF13 770
Maine Landscape Oil/canvas (35x43cm 13x16in) Boston MA 2000

WOOD Karl E. 1944-1990 **[34]**
🖼 **$324** - €375 - **£227** - FF2 457
Skuna River Oil/canvas (40x60cm 16x24in) Calgary, Alberta 2001

WOOD Lawson 1878-1957 **[74]**
🖋 **$1 705** - €1 433 - **£1 000** - FF9 398
«**Gran Pop's Mistletoe Hustle**» Watercolour, gouache/paper (42x31.5cm 16x12in) Billingshurst, West-Sussex 1998

WOOD Lewis John 1813-1901 **[47]**
🖼 **$3 106** - €2 762 - **£1 900** - FF18 120
«**Burgos Cathedral**» Oil/canvas (53.5x43cm 21x16in) London 1999
🖼 **$1 183** - €1 156 - **£750** - FF7 585
The Cathedral at Evreux, Normandy Oil/board (25.5x18cm 10x7in) London 1999
🖋 **$358** - €400 - **£250** - FF2 626
Procession outside a continental Church Watercolour (25x19cm 9x7in) Bath 2001

WOOD Robert E. 1926-1999 **[18]**
🖼 **$3 000** - €2 531 - **£1 759** - FF16 602
Mountainous Landscape Oil/canvas (69.5x92cm 27x36in) New-York 1998
🖋 **$1 300** - €1 248 - **£815** - FF8 184
Phira-on Santorini Watercolour/paper (54x74cm 21x29in) Altadena CA 1999

WOOD Robert William /Robt 1889-1979 **[120]**
🖼 **$5 500** - €4 750 - **£3 322** - FF31 161
Texas Hill Country Oil/canvas (76x91cm 30x36in) Houston TX 1998

WOOD Stanley L. 1866-1928 **[17]**
🖼 **$3 250** - €3 112 - **£2 007** - FF20 416
Men Riding Camels Through Snowy Terrain, Book Cover Oil/board (43x28cm 17x11in) New-York 1999
🖋 **$350** - €328 - **£215** - FF2 153
Gunfight Between Cowboys and Indians Ink (26x17cm 10x6in) New-York 1999

WOOD Thomas Waterman 1823-1903 **[42]**
🖼 **$26 000** - €25 814 - **£16 250** - FF169 327
Autumn Leaves Oil/panel (51x35.5cm 20x13in) New-York 1999
🖼 **$17 000** - €18 605 - **£11 726** - FF122 039
The young Smoker Oil/panel (25.5x20.5cm 10x8in) New-York 2001
🖋 **$6 949** - €8 168 - **£4 818** - FF53 578
A Fresh Slice of Orange Watercolour (43.5x30.5cm 17x12in) Amsterdam 2000

WOOD Tom 1955 **[2]**
📷 **$2 054** - €2 301 - **£1 427** - FF15 092
«**Cowley, Oxford**» Gelatin silver print (33x26.5cm 12x10in) Köln 2001

WOOD Wallace, Wally 1927 **[6]**
🖋 **$1 500** - €1 610 - **£1 003** - FF10 561
Page 11 from Weird Science-Fantasy No.26 Ink (45.5x33cm 17x12in) New-York 2000

WOOD Wilfred Rene 1888-? **[15]**
🖋 **$216** - €252 - **£150** - FF1 656
St Marks Square, Venice Watercolour/paper (22x26.5cm 8x10in) Loughton, Essex 2000

WOOD William John 1877-1954 **[4]**
🛋 **$319** - €375 - **£227** - FF2 463
Little Lake Etching (22x17cm 8x6in) Toronto 2000

WOOD William Rueben. C. 1875-1915 **[3]**
🖼 **$18 700** - €18 549 - **£11 587** - FF121 673
Hillside clearing Oil/canvas (71x91cm 28x36in) Timonium MD 1999

WOOD William Thomas 1877-1958 **[28]**
🖼 **$1 591** - €1 719 - **£1 100** - FF11 274
Roses Oil/canvas (58x45cm 23x18in) Par, Cornwall 2001
🖼 **$1 957** - €2 148 - **£1 300** - FF14 087
Rhododendrons in a Vase on a Table Oil/board (35.5x28cm 13x11in) London 2001

WOOD Worden G. 1880-1943 **[9]**
🖋 **$434** - €503 - **£307** - FF3 299
Steam Trawler Watercolour/paper (35x51cm 14x20in) Cleveland OH 2000

WOODBURY Charles Herbert 1864-1940 **[171]**
🖼 **$6 000** - €5 435 - **£3 672** - FF35 650
Houses by the Shore, beverly Oil/canvas (35x50cm 14x20in) Portland ME 1998
🖼 **$2 750** - €3 030 - **£1 834** - FF19 875
Ogunquit Rocks Oil/canvas/board (25x35cm 10x14in) Portsmouth NH 2000
🖋 **$750** - €686 - **£459** - FF4 498
Gulls Feeding in the Harbour Watercolour, gouache/paper (35x21cm 13x8in) Boston MA 1999
🛋 **$250** - €227 - **£153** - FF1 488
Deagulls Etching (13x18cm 5x7in) Portland ME 1998

WOODFORDE Samuel 1763-1817 **[8]**
🖼 **$2 278** - €2 426 - **£1 500** - FF15 916
Portrait of a Lady, said to be Mrs.Priscilla Wyatt of Milton Place Oil/canvas (35x31cm 13x12in) Billingshurst, West-Sussex 2000

WOODHOUSE Frederick, Jr. 1848-1927 **[12]**
🖼 **$3 593** - €3 272 - **£2 200** - FF21 466
The General Oil/canvas (51x68.5cm 20x26in) Malvern, Victoria 1998

WOODHOUSE Frederick, Snr. 1820-1909 **[7]**
🖼 **$2 597** - €2 956 - **£1 825** - FF19 388
Hunting Dogs Oil/canvas (41x61cm 16x24in) Woollahra, Sydney 2001

WOODHOUSE William A. 1857-1935 **[77]**
🖼 **$11 229** - €11 316 - **£7 000** - FF74 225
Vale of the Lune, Lancaster Oil/canvas (53.5x78cm 21x30in) London 2000
🖼 **$2 840** - €2 920 - **£1 792** - FF19 156
Ploughing Oil/canvas (30x40cm 11x15in) Dublin 2000
🖋 **$889** - €993 - **£620** - FF6 512
The Haystack Watercolour/paper (16x24cm 6x9in) Bath 2001

WOODLEY-BROWN Robert, Reverend XIX [19]
- $721 - €848 - £500 - FF5 560
  Wooded Landscape with Travellers and Lake beyond Oil/canvas (30x40cm 12x16in) Lewes, Sussex 2000

WOODLOCK David 1842-1929 [197]
- $872 - €907 - £550 - FF5 950
  Italian Girl Standing in a Sunlit Courtyard, a Cobbler Nearby Oil/canvas (45.5x26.5cm 17x10in) Leyburn, North Yorkshire 2000
- $1 682 - €1 455 - £1 000 - FF9 542
  «The World is Wide and Holdeth Many a Joyous Thing» Watercolour/paper (24x17cm 9x6in) Chester 1998

WOODMAN Betty 1930 [9]
- $5 000 - €5 180 - £3 182 - FF33 976
  Mussel Server Ceramic (21x70x23cm 8x27x9in) New-York 2000

WOODMAN Francesca 1958-1981 [7]
- $26 000 - €29 934 - £17 742 - FF196 352
  Self-Portrait, New York Gelatin silver print (14.5x14.5cm 5x5in) New-York 2000

WOODMAN Richard 1784-1859 [4]
- $344 - €386 - £240 - FF2 533
  The Earl of Derby's Stag Hounds, after James Barenger Engraving (57x66cm 22x25in) Leyburn, North Yorkshire 2001

WOODROFFE Patrick 1940 [6]
- $3 994 - €4 657 - £2 800 - FF30 548
  Mons Veritatis Oil/panel (60x60cm 23x23in) London 2000

WOODROFFE Paul 1875-1945 [5]
- $1 989 - €1 723 - £1 200 - FF11 299
  The Princess and Other Poems Ink/paper (23.5x16.5cm 9x6in) London 1998

WOODROOFE Louise 1892-1996 [37]
- $500 - €506 - £313 - FF3 822
  Shopping Bags Mixed media (76x101cm 30x40in) Cincinnati OH 2000
- $210 - €213 - £131 - FF1 395
  Lines and Poles Mixed media (40x30cm 16x12in) Cincinnati OH 2000
- $170 - €197 - £119 - FF1 295
  Abstract Composition Drawing (20x25cm 8x10in) Cincinnati OH 2001

WOODROW Bill 1948 [28]
- $5 768 - €6 374 - £4 000 - FF41 812
  Red Squirrel Object (87.5x52x42cm 34x20x16in) London 2001
- $749 - €799 - £500 - FF5 241
  The Periodic Table Linocut (50x43cm 19x16in) London 2000

WOODS Henry 1846-1921 [38]
- $16 868 - €16 037 - £10 527 - FF105 196
  Morning Call - Venice Oil/canvas (53.5x42cm 21x16in) London 2000
- $4 328 - €4 856 - £3 000 - FF31 853
  Fondamenta San Sebastiano, Venise Oil/panel (40.5x29cm 15x11in) London 2000
- $408 - €365 - £250 - FF2 394
  On the Thames Watercolour/paper (36x25cm 14x10in) Par, Cornwall 1999

WOODVILLE Richard Caton II 1856-1927 [31]
- $6 518 - €7 563 - £4 500 - FF49 613
  The Dumb Mourners at the Funeral Procession of King Edward VII Oil/canvas (40.5x56cm 15x22in) Vancouver, BC. 2000

- $283 - €332 - £200 - FF2 181
  Couple in a Motor Car Watercolour/paper (32x23cm 12x9in) London 2000

WOODWARD Ellsworth 1861-1939 [60]
- $15 000 - €16 029 - £10 210 - FF105 144
  Louisiana Landscape with Figure Poling a Pirogue Oil/canvas (40x50cm 16x20in) New-Orleans LA 2001
- $9 000 - €10 356 - £6 203 - FF67 932
  The Pond Oil/board (22x30cm 9x12in) New-Orleans LA 2000
- $350 - €388 - £243 - FF2 548
  Discus Thrower Charcoal/paper (63x48cm 25x19in) New-Orleans LA 2001
- $750 - €701 - £463 - FF4 598
  Grocery and Bar Etching (18x24cm 7x9in) New-Orleans LA 1999

WOODWARD George Moutard 1760-1809 [23]
- $908 - €792 - £549 - FF5 198
  «No Revolution in a Good Constitution»/«A Fair Confession» Wash (22x13cm 8x5in) London 1998
- $905 - €971 - £605 - FF6 372
  The Genius of Caricature, and his Friends celebrating Radierung (24.8x35cm 9x13in) Berlin 2000

WOODWARD Laura XIX [2]
- $3 000 - €3 231 - £2 065 - FF21 193
  Mountain Riverbed Oil/canvas (50x86cm 20x34in) New-York 2001

WOODWARD Mabel May 1877-1945 [81]
- $11 000 - €10 417 - £6 688 - FF68 333
  Houses along the Coast Oil/canvas (63.5x77cm 25x30in) New-York 1999
- $2 600 - €2 791 - £1 771 - FF18 307
  Pink Trees Oil/canvas/board (26x33.5cm 10x13in) Boston MA 2001
- $4 000 - €3 728 - £2 468 - FF24 452
  Ogunquit Beach, Maine Pastel/paper (33x41cm 13x16in) New-Orleans LA 2000

WOODWARD Margaret Helene 1947 [11]
- $1 067 - €1 264 - £752 - FF8 294
  Rhinoceros Pastel/paper (106.5x160cm 41x62in) Sydney 2000

WOODWARD Robert Strong 1885-1960 [17]
- $3 800 - €3 518 - £2 326 - FF23 076
  «Across the Winter River» Oil/canvas (74x61cm 29x24in) South-Deerfield MA 1999

WOODWARD Stanley Wingate 1890-1970 [41]
- $1 500 - €1 706 - £1 048 - FF11 190
  Gloucester Rocks Oil/canvas (101x101cm 40x40in) Mystic CT 2000
- $700 - €697 - £464 - FF4 575
  Foaming Surf Oil/board (25x30cm 10x12in) East-Dennis MA 1999

WOODWARD Thomas 1801-1852 [36]
- $16 858 - €19 558 - £12 000 - FF128 290
  Detachment of Cromwell's Cavalry Surprised in a Mountain Pass Oil/canvas (113x144cm 44x56in) London 2001
- $9 834 - €11 409 - £7 000 - FF74 836
  Bay Hunter in an open Landscape Oil/canvas (71.5x89cm 28x35in) London 2001

WOODWARD William 1859-1939 [43]
- $32 000 - €34 195 - £21 782 - FF224 307
  «Luggers, Biloxi» Oil/board (39x50cm 15x20in) New-Orleans LA 2001

W

$5 250 - €4 866 - £3 264 - FF31 920
Calm After Storm Oil/board (33x45cm 13x18in)
New-Orleans LA 1999

$5 000 - €5 142 - £3 171 - FF33 729
New Orleans Art Pottery Club, Multi-colored Jardinière and Vase Watercolour/paper (44x33cm 17x13in) New-Orleans LA 2000

$1 300 - €1 262 - £803 - FF8 279
Corner of St.Louis and Chartres Streets Etching (25x26cm 10x10in) New-Orleans LA 1999

WOOG J. XIX-XX **[6]**
$1 811 - €1 753 - £1 100 - FF11 498
In the Enclosure Oil/panel (16x31.5cm 6x12in)
London 2000

WOOL Christopher 1955 **[100]**
$44 829 - €48 120 - £30 000 - FF315 648
Untitled (P75) Mixed media (244x162.5cm 96x63in)
London 2000

$30 000 - €33 544 - £20 223 - FF220 032
Untitled Acrylic (89x61cm 35x24in) New-York 2000

$18 000 - €20 362 - £12 592 - FF133 569
Fear Oil/paper (28x23.5cm 11x9in) New-York 2001

$1 100 - €1 064 - £678 - FF6 981
Black Book Offset (57x40cm 22x15in) New-York 1999

$60 000 - €66 651 - £40 182 - FF437 202
Untitled Gelatin silver print (50.5x40.5cm 19x15in)
New-York 2000

WOOLARD William ?-1908 **[14]**
$438 - €503 - £300 - FF3 300
Culross Pier Watercolour/paper (25x18cm 9x7in)
Edinburgh 2000

WOOLCOTT Charles XIX **[5]**
$7 299 - €7 010 - £4 500 - FF45 984
Gentleman, in a black Coat, holding a Cane, his top Hat, seated Oil/canvas (127x101.5cm 50x39in)
London 1999

WOOLF Paul J. ?-1985 **[17]**
$1 600 - €1 842 - £1 091 - FF12 083
The Empire State Building from Altman's Gelatin silver print (23.5x16.5cm 9x6in) New-York 2000

WOOLLASTON Toss 1910-1998 **[23]**
$6 366 - €7 253 - £4 399 - FF47 574
«Mcfedries Farm, Autumn, Winter» Oil/board (71x52cm 27x20in) Auckland 2000

$1 241 - €1 458 - £881 - FF9 564
Nelson Landscape Watercolour/paper (29x41cm 11x16in) Auckland 2000

WOOLLETT Henry Charles ?-1872 **[24]**
$2 525 - €3 003 - £1 800 - FF19 701
Stable Mates Huile/toile (51x76cm 20x29in) London 2000

$560 - €651 - £400 - FF4 272
Horses observing the Ducks Oil/board (18.5x33.5cm 7x13in) Norfolk 2001

WOOLLETT William 1735-1785 **[39]**
$230 - €229 - £143 - FF1 499
Roman Edifices in Ruins, after Claude Lorraine Engraving (49x60cm 19x24in) Dublin 1999

WOOLLEY Virginia 1884-1971 **[5]**
$3 750 - €4 025 - £2 509 - FF26 403
Laguna Beach Coast, Calif. Oil/board (39x33cm 15x13in) Altadena CA 2000

WOOLMER Alfred Joseph 1805-1892 **[45]**
$2 317 - €2 179 - £1 456 - FF14 291
Pleasures of the Afternoon Oil/canvas (66.5x56.5cm 26x22in) Sydney 1999

$672 - €790 - £466 - FF5 185
Bakom draperiet Oil/canvas (42x32cm 16x12in)
Helsinki 2000

WOOLNER Thomas 1825-1892 **[14]**
$5 456 - €6 116 - £3 800 - FF40 117
Thomas Carlyle Bronze (H23cm H9in) London 2001

WOOLSEY Carl E. 1902 **[1]**
$4 000 - €3 656 - £2 447 - FF23 979
Winter Wonderland Oil/masonite (45.5x61cm 17x24in) Boston MA 1999

WOOSTER Austin C. 1864-1913 **[8]**
$2 250 - €2 690 - £1 552 - FF17 644
Apples on a Table Top Oil/board (17x25cm 7x10in)
Milford CT 2000

WOOTTON Frank 1911-1998 **[51]**
$2 362 - €2 521 - £1 600 - FF16 537
Ponies in the Rain, Winford Hill Oil/board (39x59cm 15x23in) Lewes, Sussex 2001

$681 - €659 - £420 - FF4 322
Arab Foals Oil/board (30.5x40.5cm 12x15in) London 1999

$523 - €503 - £320 - FF3 298
«Devon, British Railways, Western Region» Poster (102x64cm 40x25in) London 1999

WOOTTON John 1686-1765 **[69]**
$104 039 - €99 315 - £65 000 - FF651 462
Greville, a Chestnut thoroughbred held by a Groom, with other Figures Oil/canvas (127x101.5cm 50x39in) London 1999

$14 049 - €16 298 - £10 000 - FF106 909
Pug beside a classical Urn Oil/canvas (76x63.5cm 29x25in) London 2001

WOPFNER Josef 1843-1927 **[172]**
$11 236 - €10 226 - £7 020 - FF67 078
Heuschiff bei Sturm Öl/Leinwand (37x62.5cm 14x24in) München 1999

$7 312 - €7 158 - £4 499 - FF46 954
Fischer am Ufer des Chiemsees Oil/panel (16x20cm 6x7in) Stuttgart 1999

$219 - €230 - £145 - FF1 509
Bauern mit Vieh an Gebirgssee Pencil/paper (18.8x33.2cm 7x13in) München 2000

WORES Theodore 1860-1939 **[37]**
$160 000 - €152 181 - £97 152 - FF998 240
Lotus Pond, Shiba, Tokyo Oil/canvas (51.5x68cm 20x26in) Beverly-Hills CA 1999

$4 800 - €5 379 - £3 345 - FF35 283
A Coconut Grove Oil/board (32x23.5cm 12x9in)
Beverly-Hills CA 2001

WORESCHAGIN Wasilli 1892 **[2]**
$18 172 - €20 348 - £12 628 - FF133 476
Blick auf Kairo Öl/Leinwand (60x100cm 23x39in)
Wien 2001

WORKMAN Harold 1897-1975 **[26]**
$1 927 - €1 856 - £1 200 - FF12 177
The Spaniards Inn, Hampstead Oil/canvas (51x61cm 20x24in) London 1999

WORLIDGE Thomas 1700-1766 **[21]**
$889 - €987 - £620 - FF6 475
Female head Study Graphite (17.5x14.5cm 6x5in)
London 2001

WORMS Jules 1832-1924 **[75]**
$14 400 - €14 298 - £9 000 - FF93 786
The Spanish Guitarist Oil/panel (45.5x55cm 17x21in) London 1999

$4 322 - €4 916 - **£3 047** - FF32 245
Zwei Knaben beim Rauchen in einem Hinterhof
Oil/panel (41x32.5cm 16x12in) Zürich 2001

$3 420 - €2 860 - **£2 042** - FF18 762
Ayudando a llenar la cántara Acuarela (68x53cm 26x20in) Madrid 1998

WORMS Roger 1907-1980 [77]
$582 - €610 - **£368** - FF4 000
La cruche aux bouquets d'anémones Huile/toile (54x46cm 21x18in) Castres 2000

WÖRN Walter 1901-1963 [59]
$5 220 - €6 135 - **£3 619** - FF40 246
Wartende Menschen Tempera/canvas (200x125cm 78x49in) Stuttgart 2000

$378 - €409 - **£259** - FF2 683
Menschen Chalks (30x21cm 11x8in) Stuttgart 2001

$397 - €368 - **£240** - FF2 414
Profilhalbfigur mit zwei Armen Woodcut (72.5x47.5cm 28x18in) Heidelberg 1999

WÖRNDLE VON ADELSFRIED Edmund 1827-1906 [12]
$2 374 - €1 994 - **£1 395** - FF13 082
Italienische Berglandschaft Oil/paper/board (36x50cm 14x19in) Bern 1998

WORRELL van Abraham Bruining 1787-1832 [11]
$34 610 - €38 245 - **£24 000** - FF250 872
Gentleman and Two Ladies taking Breakfast Oil/panel (76x62.5cm 29x24in) London 2001

WORSEY Thomas 1829-1875 [50]
$2 176 - €2 451 - **£1 500** - FF16 078
Still Life of an Overturned Basket of Strawberries, other Fruits Oil/canvas (59x49cm 23x19in) London 2000

$2 320 - €2 215 - **£1 450** - FF14 529
Still Life of Bird's nest, Primrose, Apple, Blossom and Butterfly Oil/panel (41x34cm 16x13in) Cheshire 1998

WORSLEY Charles Nathaniel XIX-XX [18]
$651 - €703 - **£450** - FF4 612
Whanganui River, near the Houseboat, New Zealand Watercolour/paper (46x25.5cm 18x10in) Newbury, Berkshire 2001

WORTEL Ans 1929-1997 [59]
$5 655 - €5 445 - **£3 536** - FF35 719
«De Hoogvlieger Heeft Een Klein Hoofd Gekregen» Oil/canvas (125x66cm 49x25in) Amsterdam 1999

$330 - €386 - **£235** - FF2 530
«De mist boven't land» Mixed media/paper (19x41cm 7x16in) Amsterdam 2001

WORTH Don 1924 [10]
$1 600 - €1 717 - **£1 086** - FF11 264
Landscapes Gelatin silver print (51x39cm 20x15in) Beverly-Hills CA 2001

WORTH Leslie 1923 [23]
$566 - €672 - **£400** - FF4 407
Rain Clouds Watercolour/paper (13.5x25.5cm 5x10in) London 2000

WORTH Thomas B. 1834-1917 [17]
$800 - €727 - **£490** - FF4 770
A Stopping Place on the Road, the Horse Shed Lithograph (54x79cm 21x31in) Boston MA 1998

WORTLEY Archibald J. Stuart 1849-1905 [8]
$16 066 - €15 471 - **£10 000** - FF101 480
From Wharncliffe Crags looking towards the Derbyshire Moors Oil/canvas (101.5x167.5cm 39x65in) London 1999

WORTLEY H. Stuart, Colonel 1832-1890 [1]
$57 568 - €64 480 - **£40 000** - FF422 964
«How Sweet the Moonlight Sleeps upon the Wave» Albumen print (29.5x35cm 11x13in) London 2001

WOSTRY Carlo 1865-1943 [29]
$32 159 - €36 899 - **£22 000** - FF242 044
In the Harem Oil/canvas (122.5x99cm 48x38in) London 2000

$3 250 - €3 369 - **£1 950** - FF22 100
Ragazza in pelliccia Olio/cartone (44x46cm 17x18in) Trieste 1999

$1 349 - €1 448 - **£902** - FF9 500
Boulevard dans la brume Huile/panneau (20x25cm 7x9in) Paris 2000

WOTRUBA Fritz 1907-1975 [273]
$76 440 - €66 433 - **£46 059** - FF435 773
Grosser Gehender Bronze (150x47x65cm 59x18x25in) Berlin 1998

$7 641 - €6 543 - **£4 473** - FF42 921
Stehende Bronze (H39.4cm H15in) Wien 1998

$1 565 - €1 817 - **£1 100** - FF11 910
«Skulpturenskizze» Indian ink (41.5x29.5cm 16x11in) Salzburg 2001

$219 - €204 - **£135** - FF1 341
Hommage à Picasso Lithographie (56.5x76.3cm 22x30in) Hamburg 1999

WOU Claes Claesz. c.1592-1665 [14]
$7 250 - €7 211 - **£4 500** - FF47 300
Dutch Merchant Flutes in Stormy Seas Oil/panel (46.5x58cm 18x22in) London 1999

$4 758 - €4 996 - **£3 000** - FF32 774
Shipping in a Squall off the Dutch Coast Oil/panel (38.5x35x45cm 13x17in) London 2000

WOUTERMAERTENS Edouard 1819-1897 [29]
$2 523 - €2 949 - **£1 801** - FF19 347
Hilly Landscape with a Herdsboy and Cows drinking by a Brrok Oil/panel (95x125cm 37x49in) Amsterdam 2001

$1 032 - €992 - **£648** - FF6 504
Deux moutons Huile/panneau (40x31cm 15x12in) Bruxelles 1999

WOUTERS Frans c.1612/14-1659 [41]
$22 000 - €20 857 - **£13 384** - FF136 813
The Judgement of Paris Oil/copper (46.5x65.5cm 18x25in) New-York 1999

$12 233 - €11 442 - **£7 500** - FF75 052
Wooded Landscape with Saint John the Baptist Oil/panel (38.5x31cm 15x12in) London 1998

WOUTERS Jean-François 1731-? [1]
$7 913 - €7 080 - **£4 741** - FF46 440
Sportsmen on a track near an inn, a Castle and a Church beyond Oil/panel (47.5x67.5cm 18x26in) Amsterdam 1998

WOUTERS Rik 1882-1916 [192]
$47 520 - €44 619 - **£29 340** - FF292 680
Nature morte aux pommes Huile/panneau (55x65cm 21x25in) Antwerpen 1999

$1 001 - €868 - **£616** - FF5 691
Le rayon de soleil Bas-relief (29x25cm 11x9in) Bruxelles 1999

W

$1 872 - €2 231 - **£1 341** - FF14 634
Chiens en forêt Encre Chine/papier (34x45cm
13x17in) Antwerpen 2000

WOUW van Anton 1862-1945 **[67]**
$3 053 - €2 637 - **£1 841** - FF17 300
Maquette for Miner with Hand Drill Bronze
(H27cm H10in) Johannesburg 1998

WOUWERMAN Jan 1629-1666 **[5]**
$4 361 - €5 087 - **£3 080** - FF33 369
Dünenlandschaft Oil/panel (31.5x38cm 12x14in)
Salzburg 2000

WOUWERMAN Philips 1619-1668 **[95]**
$28 815 - €32 772 - **£20 315** - FF214 970
Landschaft mit Reitern und Windmühle
Öl/Leinwand (40.5x56.5cm 15x22in) Zürich 2001
$45 116 - €44 307 - **£28 000** - FF290 637
Coastal Scene with Horsemen and Fishermen
Oil/panel (30.5x35.5cm 12x13in) London 1999

WOUWERMAN Pieter 1623-1682 **[59]**
$37 262 - €41 923 - **£25 657** - FF275 000
Le Pont-Neuf et la tour de Nesle à Paris
Huile/toile (97x133cm 38x52in) Paris 2000
$10 830 - €11 412 - **£7 220** - FF74 860
Escena de caza Oleo/lienzo (69x51cm 27x20in)
Madrid 2000
$14 812 - €13 805 - **£9 139** - FF90 555
Reiter am Strand Oil/panel (31x39cm 12x15in) Köln
1999

WOYTUK XX **[19]**
$403 - €457 - **£284** - FF3 000
Coq chantant Bronze (25x19cm 9x7in) Paris 2001

WRAMPE Fritz 1893-1934 **[5]**
$3 905 - €4 193 - **£2 614** - FF27 502
Giraffe, schreitend Bronze (37.4x18.5x9.1cm
14x7x3in) Köln 2000

WRETLING David 1901-1986 **[21]**
$707 - €636 - **£422** - FF4 173
Knäböjande flicka Bronze (H24cm H9in) Stockholm
1998

WRETMAN Fredrik 1954 **[7]**
$241 - €282 - **£165** - FF1 850
It's all in your Head! Photograph (20x22.5cm 7x8in)
Stockholm 2000

WRIGHT Frank 1860-1923 **[6]**
$2 539 - €2 464 - **£1 600** - FF16 164
Auckland from Mount Eden Watercolour/paper
(22x38cm 9x15in) London 1999

WRIGHT Frank Lloyd 1869-1959 **[99]**
$5 500 - €5 214 - **£3 449** - FF34 199
House for Mr.& Mrs.Alex Wainer, in Valdosta, GA
Coloured pencils/paper (55x30cm 22x12in) Cincinnati
OH 1999
$950 - €1 064 - **£660** - FF6 979
Architectural drawing Print (63x40cm 25x16in)
Cincinnati OH 2001

WRIGHT George 1860-1942 **[217]**
$8 874 - €8 523 - **£5 500** - FF55 905
Attending the Wounded/The End of the Day
Oil/canvas (33x48.5cm 12x19in) London 1999
$5 000 - €4 634 - **£3 109** - FF30 400
On the Scent/Taking the Fence Oil/canvas
(31x45.5cm 12x17in) New-York 1999
$589 - €571 - **£370** - FF3 743
Caceria del zorro/Partido de polo Acuarela/papel
(5.5x4cm 2x1in) Madrid 1999

WRIGHT George Frederick 1828-1881 **[4]**
$2 100 - €1 961 - **£1 296** - FF12 864
Breaking Him In Oil/panel (20x30cm 8x12in)
Norwalk CT 1999

WRIGHT George Hand 1872-1951 **[21]**
$5 000 - €5 978 - **£3 449** - FF39 210
The Afternoon Call Oil/canvas (30x40cm 12x16in)
Milford CT 2000
$1 400 - €1 341 - **£864** - FF8 794
**Couple on Stagecoach Approaching a Remote
Cabin, Story Illustration** Watercolour/paper
(60x38cm 24x15in) New-York 1999

WRIGHT George W. 1834-1934 **[1]**
$23 000 - €19 704 - **£13 827** - FF129 253
Siblings, four vignettes Oil/canvas (55x152cm
22x60in) New-Orleans LA 1998

WRIGHT Gilbert Scott 1880-1958 **[54]**
$12 042 - €13 212 - **£8 000** - FF86 664
Tattenham Corner, Epsom Oil/canvas (51x76cm
20x29in) London 2000
$14 500 - €13 440 - **£9 016** - FF88 161
On the Scent/The Escape Oil/cardboard (24x37cm
9x14in) New-York 1999
$2 051 - €1 985 - **£1 300** - FF13 021
**Snow Scene with Lady and Gentleman Riding
on a Horse** Watercolour/paper (58x45cm 23x18in)
Manchester 1999
$225 - €231 - **£142** - FF1 517
Tandem Race Color lithograph (30x50cm 12x20in)
Columbia SC 2000

WRIGHT James ?-1947 **[16]**
$1 111 - €1 048 - **£700** - FF6.874
Figures and Horses on a Country Track Oil/board
(66x81.5cm 25x32in) Godalming, Surrey 1999
$381 - €359 - **£240** - FF2 356
Peeling Apples Watercolour/paper (51x61cm
20x24in) Godalming, Surrey 1999

WRIGHT John Massey 1777-1866 **[32]**
$409 - €351 - **£240** - FF2 301
Fête galante Watercolour/paper (28.5x37.5cm
11x14in) London 1998

WRIGHT John Michael 1617-1694 **[15]**
$53 386 - €61 933 - **£38 000** - FF406 254
**Young Man, posibly Anthony Henley, son of Sir
Robert Henley** Oil/canvas (175x109cm 68x42in)
London 1999

WRIGHT Margaret Isobel 1884-1957 **[8]**
$1 200 - €1 391 - **£850** - FF9 127
The Little Dancers Watercolour (62.5x49.5cm
24x19in) London 2000

WRIGHT OF DERBY Joseph 1734-1797 **[55]**
$15 000 - €16 019 - **£10 221** - FF105 079
**Portrait of Edward Abney of King Newton, in a
green Coat** Oil/canvas (125x99.5cm 49x39in) New-
York 2001
$30 000 - €29 986 - **£18 327** - FF196 695
**Portrait of a Lady, Half-Length, in a Blue and
Yellow Dress** Oil/canvas (76x63cm 29x24in) New-
York 2000
$25 203 - €29 312 - **£18 000** - FF192 274
Vesuvius from Posillipo/Vesuvius in Eruption
Oil/copper (19x24cm 7x9in) London 2001
$294 630 - €350 403 - **£210 000** - FF2 298 492
Study of a Boy Reading Black & white chalks/paper
(42x28cm 16x11in) London 2000

WRIGHT Richard Henry 1857-1930 **[57]**
- $791 - €903 - **£550** - FF5 922
  European Cathedral Town Watercolour (18x25cm 7x9in) London 2001

WRIGHT Robert Murdoch XIX-XX **[16]**
- $448 - €535 - **£320** - FF3 510
  «On the Coast of the Red Sea» Watercolour (23x52cm 9x20in) Leyburn, North Yorkshire 2000

WRIGHT Robert W. XIX **[34]**
- $10 864 - €10 786 - **£6 788** - FF70 752
  Getting Baby to sleep Oil/canvas (71x91.5cm 27x36in) Toronto 1999
- $6 634 - €5 770 - **£4 000** - FF37 851
  Autumn Fruits Oil/panel (35.5x30.5cm 13x12in) Godalming, Surrey 1998

WRIGHT Rufus 1832-? **[3]**
- $3 400 - €3 296 - **£2 105** - FF21 621
  Peaches and Butterfly Oil/canvas (20x25cm 8x10in) Mystic CT 1999

WRIGHT Thomas ?-c.1760 **[1]**
- $14 621 - €14 226 - **£9 000** - FF93 319
  The Crane Sisters in an Interior, wearing Silk Dresses Oil/canvas (116.5x104cm 45x40in) London 1999

WRIGHT von Ferdinand Wilhelm 1822-1906 **[73]**
- $156 561 - €137 031 - **£94 866** - FF898 863
  Spelande tjädertupp Oil/canvas (110x138cm 43x54in) Helsinki 1998
- $22 766 - €26 451 - **£16 000** - FF173 507
  Joutsenpari lammella (whooper swans on a lake) Oil/canvas (49x62.5cm 19x24in) London 2001
- $13 419 - €15 136 - **£9 432** - FF99 288
  Talgoxar Oil/canvas (37x30cm 14x11in) Helsinki 2001
- $1 544 - €1 444 - **£951** - FF9 471
  Gräsand Akvarell/papper (15x24cm 5x9in) Stockholm 1999

WRIGHT von Magnus 1805-1868 **[47]**
- $17 181 - €19 341 - **£11 833** - FF126 868
  Raseborgs ruiner Oil/canvas (35x52cm 13x20in) Helsinki 2000
- $2 166 - €2 439 - **£1 492** - FF15 996
  Molnstudie Oil/panel (19x28cm 7x11in) Helsinki 2000
- $459 - €504 - **£296** - FF3 309
  Sparvuggla Pencil/paper (25x20cm 9x7in) Helsinki 2000
- $173 - €185 - **£117** - FF1 213
  Pandion Haliaëtus/Falco Subbuteo Lithograph (32x24.5cm 12x9in) Helsinki 2001

WRIGHTSON Berni (Bernard) 1948 **[12]**
- $1 000 - €1 073 - **£669** - FF7 041
  Illustration to unpublished shadown over Insmouth Project Pencil/paper (33x38cm 12x14in) New-York 2000

WRIGHTSON Isabel 1890-? **[24]**
- $107 - €130 - **£75** - FF851
  Cornflowers Watercolour/paper (30x33cm 12x13in) Aylsham, Norfolk 2000

WRINCH Mary Evelyn 1878-1969 **[45]**
- $712 - €831 - **£495** - FF5 452
  Scarboro Cliff's Oil/board (25.5x30.5cm 10x12in) Toronto 2000
- $254 - €249 - **£156** - FF1 631
  August Flowers Woodcut (25.5x25.5cm 10x10in) Toronto 1999

WROBLEWSKI Andrzej 1927-1957 **[3]**
- $11 822 - €10 802 - **£7 094** - FF71 366
  Akt/Nature morte avec cartable Oil/canvas (59x84cm 23x33in) Kraków 1999

WROBLEWSKY Konstantin Haritonov 1868-1939 **[9]**
- $5 597 - €6 661 - **£4 000** - FF43 692
  Moonlit Night on the Dniper Oil/canvas (60x95cm 23x37in) London 2000

WRZESZCZ Eugeniusz 1851-1917 **[7]**
- $2 500 - €2 480 - **£1 555** - FF16 266
  Blossoming Lilac Oil/canvas (56x80.5cm 22x31in) Kiev 1999

WSSEL DE GUIMBARDA Manuel 1833-1907 **[10]**
- $41 600 - €39 042 - **£26 000** - FF256 100
  Dama en el diván Oleo/tabla (43x56.5cm 16x22in) Madrid 1999
- $6 720 - €7 208 - **£4 440** - FF47 280
  En la huerta Acuarela/papel (68.5x44.5cm 26x17in) Madrid 2000

WTEWAEL Joachim Anthonisz. 1566-1638 **[16]**
- $8 500 - €8 812 - **£5 100** - FF57 800
  Diana e Callisto Olio/tela (51x63.5cm 20x25in) Venezia 2000
- $1 843 520 - €1 750 328 - **£1 129 800** - FF11 481 400
  Das Apulische Schafhirte Öl/Kupfer (15.5x20.5cm 6x8in) Zürich 1999
- $12 479 - €12 211 - **£8 000** - FF80 097
  The Marriage Feast of Peleus and Thetis Ink (34x41.5cm 13x16in) London 1999

WU CHANGSHUO 1844-1927 **[129]**
- $15 480 - €14 527 - **£9 564** - FF95 292
  Flowers by Rocks Ink (129.5x55.5cm 50x21in) Hong-Kong 1999

WU DACHENG 1835-1902 **[28]**
- $4 890 - €4 638 - **£2 975** - FF30 422
  Calligraphy in Li Shu Ink/paper (65.5x137cm 25x53in) Hong-Kong 1999

WU DAYU 1903-1988 **[12]**
- $55 760 - €59 374 - **£35 360** - FF389 470
  Abstract Oil/canvas (38x53cm 14x20in) Taipei 2000
- $59 040 - €62 867 - **£37 440** - FF412 380
  Abstract Oil/canvas (34x46cm 13x18in) Taipei 2000

WU GUANZHONG 1919 **[191]**
- $61 200 - €50 583 - **£35 800** - FF331 800
  Victoria Fall Oil/board (50.5x81.2cm 19x31in) Taipei 1998
- $48 716 - €54 901 - **£34 048** - FF360 126
  «The Palace Wall» Oil/board (26.5x34.5cm 10x13in) Hong-Kong 2001
- $16 666 - €18 932 - **£11 700** - FF124 189
  Forest Ink/paper (41x30cm 16x11in) Hong-Kong 2001

WU GUXIANG 1848-1903 **[6]**
- $3 861 - €3 662 - **£2 349** - FF24 018
  Landscapes Ink (19.5x12cm 7x4in) Hong-Kong 1999

W

WU HAO 1931 **[23]**

🎨 **$13 725** - €11 525 - **£8 055** - FF75 600
Children playing in Celebration of Spring Festival Oil/canvas (60.5x90.5cm 23x35in) Taipei 1998

📜 **$3 355** - €2 817 - **£1 969** - FF18 480
Trees Woodcut (55x100cm 21x39in) Taipei 1998

WU HUFAN 1894-1968 **[92]**

🖊 **$10 256** - €11 651 - **£7 200** - FF76 424
Landscape with running Stream Ink (75.5x33cm 29x12in) Hong-Kong 2001

WU LI 1632-1718 **[12]**

🖊 **$19 260** - €21 031 - **£12 390** - FF137 955
Landscape Ink (21x99.5cm 8x39in) Hong-Kong 2000

WU QINMU 1894-1953 **[8]**

🖊 **$3 210** - €3 505 - **£2 065** - FF22 992
Spring Landscape Ink (40.5x123cm 15x48in) Hong-Kong 2000

WU SHI'EN XVI **[1]**

🖊 **$9 009** - €8 544 - **£5 481** - FF56 042
Night Scenery of Lake Lin Ink/paper (147.5x52.5cm 58x20in) Hong-Kong 1999

WU SHIXIAN ?-1916 **[10]**

🖊 **$4 871** - €5 794 - **£3 355** - FF38 003
Misty Landscape Ink/paper (49.5x79.5cm 19x31in) Hong-Kong 2000

WU TAI 1962 **[8]**

🖊 **$7 423** - €6 293 - **£4 439** - FF41 279
«Hong Kong at Dusk» Coloured inks (61.5x135.5cm 24x53in) Hong-Kong 1998

WU XIAO XVII **[2]**

🖊 **$3 861** - €3 662 - **£2 349** - FF24 018
Flowers and Fruits Ink (18x525.5cm 7x206in) Hong-Kong 1999

WU ZHENG 1878-1949 **[9]**

🖊 **$1 287** - €1 221 - **£783** - FF8 006
Plum Blossoms Ink (18.5x51cm 7x20in) Hong-Kong 1999

WU ZUOREN 1908-1997 **[42]**

🖊 **$3 217** - €3 051 - **£1 957** - FF20 015
Yaks Ink/paper (42x26.5cm 16x10in) Hong-Kong 1999

WUCHERER Fritz 1873-1948 **[48]**

🖊 **$2 169** - €2 556 - **£1 524** - FF16 769
Nachmittagssonne über Kronberg Öl/Leinwand (36x59cm 14x23in) Frankfurt 2000

📜 **$824** - €971 - **£579** - FF6 372
Blick auf Kloster Schöntal Öl/Karton (20x22.5cm 7x8in) Frankfurt 2000

📜 **$811** - €818 - **£506** - FF5 366
Dorfplatz mit Kirche Charcoal (46x60cm 18x23in) Frankfurt 2000

WUCHTERS Abraham c.1610-1682 **[6]**

🖼 **$13 685** - €11 427 - **£8 134** - FF74 953
Peder Schumacher, Greve af Griffenfeld 1635-1699 Oil/copper (80x62cm 31x24in) København 1998

WUELUWE van Hendrick XV-XVI **[1]**

🖼 **$32 358** - €30 678 - **£19 686** - FF201 234
Madonna mit dem Kind Oil/panel (50.5x37.5cm 19x14in) Köln 1999

WUERMER Carl 1900-1982 **[47]**

🖼 **$3 800** - €4 455 - **£2 733** - FF29 226
Fall in the Valley Oil/canvas (63.5x76cm 25x29in) New-York 2001

🎨 **$3 250** - €3 155 - **£2 007** - FF20 694
Winter Afternoon Watercolour/paper (63x76cm 25x30in) East-Dennis MA 1999

WUERPEL Edmund Henri 1866-1958 **[69]**

🖼 **$1 400** - €1 337 - **£861** - FF8 770
«Beech Trees» Oil/canvas (43x58cm 17x23in) Cincinnati OH 1999

🖼 **$700** - €698 - **£437** - FF4 580
Penseroso Oil/board (28x21cm 11x8in) St. Louis MO 1999

WÜEST Johann Heinrich 1741-1821 **[13]**

🖼 **$32 920** - €31 256 - **£20 175** - FF205 025
Der Rheinfall Öl/Leinwand (126x88cm 49x34in) Zürich 1999

🖼 **$6 507** - €7 014 - **£4 363** - FF46 007
Die Teufelsbrücke in der Schöllenenschlucht Huile/panneau (26x37cm 10x14in) Zürich 2000

WUGER Eduard, Sen. c.1830-c.1880 **[6]**

🖼 **$4 000** - €4 430 - **£2 712** - FF29 058
Flowers, Fruit and a Golden Vessel in a Landscape Oil/canvas (73.5x99cm 28x38in) New-York 2000

WÜHRER Louis Charles XIX-XX **[3]**

🖼 **$9 054** - €9 909 - **£6 246** - FF65 000
Les Aiguilles du Worens, Haute-Savoie Huile/toile (112x146cm 44x57in) Paris 2001

🖼 **$5 964** - €6 403 - **£3 990** - FF42 000
Le Meije vue de Valfroide Huile/toile (115x88cm 45x34in) Grenoble 2000

WUKOUNIG Reimo Sergon 1943 **[21]**

🖊 **$1 188** - €1 017 - **£715** - FF6 673
Kopf Indian ink (32x22.6cm 12x8in) Wien 1998

WUNDER George 1912 **[11]**

🖊 **$1 000** - €1 073 - **£669** - FF7 041
Terry & The Pirates Daily Strips Ink (14x41cm 5x16in) New-York 2000

WUNDERLICH Paul 1927 **[952]**

🖼 **$15 106** - €14 454 - **£9 384** - FF94 812
Eine Bulldogge, ein Spartakisin und ein Berufmodell Acryl/Leinwand (160x131cm 62x51in) Zürich 1999

🖊 **$3 552** - €3 068 - **£2 145** - FF20 127
Ohne Titel Öl/Papier (35.5x47.5cm 13x18in) Köln 1998

🖼 **$5 478** - €4 601 - **£3 220** - FF30 181
Frau mit Schwan Öl/Leinwand (45x35cm 17x13in) Stuttgart 1998

🖼 **$3 686** - €3 579 - **£2 277** - FF23 477
Grosse Nike Bronze (164.5x28x45cm 64x11x17in) München 1999

🖋 **$1 339** - €1 125 - **£787** - FF7 377
Minotaurus Bronze (H78cm H30in) Stuttgart 1998

$1 720 - €1 983 - **£1 184** - FF13 008
Roter Rauch Gouache/paper (46.5x38.5cm 18x15in) Lokeren 2000

📜 **$209** - €243 - **£142** - FF1 510
Herbertstrasse Lithographie (51.7x41.7cm 20x16in) Berlin 2000

WUNDERWALD Gustav 1882-1945 **[55]**

🖼 **$20 676** - €20 452 - **£12 892** - FF134 156
Memellandschaft Öl/Leinwand (66.5x83.5cm 26x32in) Berlin 1999

🖊 **$413** - €409 - **£257** - FF2 683
Haveluter mit Bäumen Charcoal (21.2x31.3cm 8x12in) Berlin 1999

WÜNNENBERG Carl 1850-1929 **[8]**

🖼 **$11 438** - €12 990 - **£8 000** - FF85 207
Am brunnen (at the well) Oil/canvas (90x55cm 35x21in) London 2001

1720

WÜNNENBERG Walther 1818-c.1900 **[20]**
$1 659 - €1 431 - £987 - FF9 389
Blick auf Kloster Maria Laach in der Eifel
Öl/Leinwand (48x65cm 18x25in) München 1998

WUNSCH MARIE, Mizzi 1862-1898 **[12]**
$7 500 - €9 065 - £5 236 - FF59 464
«The Secret» Oil/canvas (121x74cm 48x29in) Miami FL 2000
$3 142 - €3 049 - £1 994 - FF20 000
Hansel et Gretel Huile/toile (26.5x17cm 10x6in) Paris 1999

WÜRBEL Frantz 1896-? **[17]**
$1 916 - €1 829 - £1 197 - FF12 000
«Jeux Olympiques, Allemagne» Affiche (100x62.5cm 39x24in) Orléans 1999

WÜRBEL Franz 1822-1900 **[5]**
$32 246 - €35 063 - £21 252 - FF230 000
Joueurs au backgammon, le Caire Huile/toile (97x142.5cm 38x56in) Paris 2000

WÜRBS Karl 1806-1876 **[5]**
$12 387 - €13 805 - £8 658 - FF90 555
Der Marktplatz von Halle an der Saale
Öl/Leinwand (69.5x83.5cm 27x32in) München 2001

WUREMER Carl XX **[1]**
$7 250 - €6 901 - £4 602 - FF45 270
Vermont landscape Huile/toile (63x76cm 25x30in) Hampton-Falls NH 1999

WURM Erwin 1954 **[17]**
$1 045 - €1 090 - £658 - FF7 150
Radiostern Farbserigraphie (56x76cm 22x29in) Wien 2000

WÜRTH Bruno 1927 **[2]**
$2 336 - €2 254 - £1 467 - FF14 785
Seeufer mit Schilf Öl/Leinwand (50x70cm 19x27in) St. Gallen 1999

WURTH Xavier 1869-1933 **[79]**
$1 065 - €1 239 - £735 - FF8 130
Paysage enneigé Huile/toile (60x80cm 23x31in) Liège 2000
$358 - €397 - £249 - FF2 601
Chemin en sous-bois Huile/carton (22.5x38cm 8x14in) Liège 2001

WÜRTTEMBERG von Olga Alexandra Maria 1876-1932 **[1]**
$2 152 - €1 839 - £1 264 - FF12 064
Porträt der Grossfürstin Wera Konstantinowna
Charcoal/paper (45x35cm 17x13in) Stuttgart 1998

WÜRTZEN Carl Gotfred 1825-1880 **[23]**
$939 - €875 - £567 - FF5 741
Person på vandretur i klippelandskab Oil/canvas (43x63cm 16x24in) København 1999

WUST Alexander 1837-1876 **[19]**
$6 450 - €7 436 - £4 440 - FF48 780
Bergrivier Oil/canvas (74x100cm 29x39in) Lokeren 2000

WÜST Christoffel 1801-1853 **[6]**
$7 729 - €7 260 - £4 659 - FF47 625
Horse-drawn sledge stopping at a koek en zopie stand/Boors fighting Oil/canvas (30.5x38cm 12x14in) Amsterdam 1999

WÜSTEN Johannes 1896-1943 **[22]**
$138 - €158 - £94 - FF1 039
Totentanz (Eisenbahnunglück) Kupferstich (23.5x16.1cm 9x6in) Heidelberg 2000

WÜSTLICH Otto 1819-1886 **[2]**
$3 511 - €3 769 - £2 350 - FF24 725
Reclining young lady in landscape reading
Oil/panel (25x43cm 10x17in) Grantham, Lincolnshire 2000

WUTKY Michael 1739-1822 **[14]**
$45 850 - €51 130 - £30 830 - FF335 390
Mondnacht am Golf von Neapel Öl/Leinwand (136.5x253.5cm 53x99in) Köln 2000
$26 000 - €28 526 - £17 271 - FF187 116
Wooded River Landscape with Fishermen on the Bank Oil/canvas (72.5x87cm 28x34in) New-York 2000

WUTTKE Carl 1849-1927 **[68]**
$7 204 - €8 181 - £5 006 - FF53 662
Blick auf die Engelsburg in Rom Öl/Leinwand (42x61cm 16x24in) Köln 2001
$998 - €1 125 - £702 - FF7 378
Orientalische Strassenszene Oil/panel (24x36cm 9x14in) München 2001

WYANT Alexander Helwig 1836-1892 **[112]**
$16 000 - €18 805 - £11 092 - FF123 350
Marsh Landscape Oil/canvas (91x141cm 35x55in) Beverly-Hills CA 2000
$5 500 - €6 411 - £3 808 - FF42 055
After the Storm Oil/canvas (63x76cm 25x30in) Watertown MA 2000
$3 200 - €3 712 - £2 276 - FF24 351
Summer Landscape Oil/canvas (25x38cm 10x15in) Chicago IL 2000

WYATT Augustus Charles 1863-1933 **[4]**
$550 - €590 - £368 - FF3 872
Flower garden and cottage behind hedge
Watercolour/paper (36x54cm 14x21in) Altadena CA 2000

WYATT Benjamin Dean 1775-1850 **[3]**
$17 931 - €19 248 - £12 000 - FF126 259
Design for the Very Magnificent and Imposing Mansion for the Duke Pencil (69x61.5cm 27x24in) London 2000

WYATT Henry 1794-1840 **[12]**
$3 033 - €2 571 - £1 800 - FF16 867
Portrait of a Lady/Portrait of a Gentleman
Oil/board (28x23cm 11x9in) Billingshurst, West-Sussex 1998

WYATT Richard James 1795-1850 **[10]**
$13 000 - €14 552 - £9 066 - FF95 452
Young Girl with Lamb Marble (H117cm H46in) New-York 2001

WYATT Thomas Henry 1807-1880 **[1]**
$2 985 - €2 597 - £1 800 - FF17 033
View of Brook House, Park Lane Designed for Sir Dudley Coutts Ink (66x99cm 25x38in) London 1998

WYBURD Francis John 1826-1893 **[14]**
$22 000 - €26 087 - £15 136 - FF171 122
Reflection Oil/canvas (91.5x72cm 36x28in) New-York 2000

WYCK Jan 1640-1702 **[38]**
$8 569 - €7 994 - £5 170 - FF52 437
Hirschjagd in einer gebirgigen Flusslandschaft
Öl/Leinwand (163x74.5cm 64x29in) Wien 1999
$12 464 - €11 798 - £7 750 - FF77 391
A Calvary Skirmish on a Bridge between Turks and Christians Oil/canvas (94x115.5cm 37x45in) Amsterdam 1999

W

..CK Thomas c.1616-1677 **[71]**

$11 520 - €13 081 - **£7 884** - FF85 806
Volksszene in einer südlichen Hafenstadt
Oil/panel (42x51.5cm 16x20in) Wien 2000

$10 688 - €12 140 - **£7 500** - FF79 635
**A mountainous Harbour Landscape with
Shipping** Oil/canvas (34x43cm 13x16in) London 2001

$4 614 - €3 986 - **£2 781** - FF26 144
**Peasants fighting in a Tavern/Study of a Village
Feast** Wash (21x31cm 8x12in) Amsterdam 1998

$112 - €128 - **£77** - FF838
Die Frau mit den beiden Körben Radierung
(11.2x12cm 4x4in) Berlin 2000

WYCKAERT Maurice 1923-1996 **[186]**

$6 030 - €6 860 - **£4 185** - FF45 000
Sans titre Huile/toile (100x120cm 39x47in) Douai
2000

$3 398 - €2 942 - **£2 062** - FF19 297
«Formations Nuageuses» Öl/Leinwand (50x60cm
19x23in) München 1998

$643 - €595 - **£400** - FF3 902
Compositie Ink/paper (53.5x60.5cm 21x23in) Lokeren
1999

WYCZOLKOWSKI Leon 1852-1936 **[167]**

$18 618 - €17 771 - **£11 632** - FF116 572
Peasants in the Fields Oil/canvas (80x61cm
31x24in) Warszawa 1999

$1 489 - €1 614 - **£1 031** - FF10 587
Collégien Huile/toile (41x31cm 16x12in) Warszawa
2001

$8 991 - €8 412 - **£5 450** - FF55 181
Pejzaz z Jaremcza Pastel (37.5x66.5cm 14x26in)
Warszawa 1999

$554 - €531 - **£349** - FF3 441
Landscape Lithograph (40x55cm 15x21in) Warszawa
1999

WYDEVELD Arnoud ?-1862 **[25]**

$10 000 - €9 441 - **£6 217** - FF61 931
Still Life with Oysters and Champagne Oil/canvas
(76x63cm 30x25in) Milford CT 1999

$2 500 - €2 449 - **£1 611** - FF16 062
Still Life with Cherries/Still Life with Peaches
Oil/panel (23x31cm 9x12in) New-York 1999

WYETH Andrew 1917 **[197]**

$625 000 - €729 459 - **£441 187** - FF4 784 937
End of Olsons Tempera/panel (46.5x48cm 18x18in)
New-York 2000

$140 000 - €138 998 - **£87 500** - FF911 764
Bean Basket Watercolour/paper (40.5x53.5cm
15x21in) New-York 1999

WYETH Henriette 1907-1997 **[5]**

$23 000 - €25 534 - **£15 996** - FF167 495
Beulah Emmett Oil/canvas (116x101cm 46x40in)
Milford CT 2001

WYETH Jamie 1946 **[44]**

$90 000 - €76 895 - **£54 027** - FF504 396
A very small Dog Oil/canvas (127x101.5cm 50x39in)
New-York 1998

$150 000 - €164 572 - **£99 645** - FF1 079 520
Gull Rock Oil/canvas (64x102.5cm 25x40in) New-
York 2000

$38 000 - €36 163 - **£23 769** - FF237 211
The Monte Carlo Pig Watercolour (24.5x35.5cm
9x13in) New-York 1998

WYETH Newell Convers 1882-1945 **[90]**

$570 000 - €677 875 - **£406 239** - FF4 446 570
Chadds Ford Hills Oil/canvas (109x122cm 42x48in)
New-York 2000

$100 000 - €107 339 - **£66 920** - FF704 100
Defend Yourself for I Shall Not Spare You Oil/can-
vas (101x76cm 40x30in) Portland ME 2000

$100 000 - €95 596 - **£62 680** - FF627 070
«Chadds Ford Landscape» Oil/board (23x18.5cm
9x7in) New-York 2000

$2 200 - €2 361 - **£1 472** - FF15 490
The Braggart Ink/paper (22x30cm 9x12in) Portland
ME 2000

$1 200 - €1 300 - **£799** - FF8 529
«The Spirit of Education» Poster (48x59cm
19x23in) New-York 2000

WYGANT Bob 1927 **[16]**

$10 000 - €11 355 - **£6 948** - FF74 481
It's a Good Day Acrylic (60x45cm 24x18in) Dallas
TX 2001

WYGRZYWALSKI Feliks Michal 1875-1944 **[98]**

$8 970 - €10 669 - **£6 396** - FF69 987
Garde de nuit Huile/toile (140.5x90cm 55x35in)
Warszawa 2000

$2 299 - €2 528 - **£1 561** - FF16 911
Salomé Huile/toile (96x66cm 37x25in) Warszawa
2000

$1 750 - €2 082 - **£1 248** - FF13 656
Bord de la mer à Anzio Huile/panneau (17x27cm
6x10in) Warszawa 2000

$1 976 - €2 355 - **£1 415** - FF15 447
**Oosters tapijthandelaar (marchand de tapis
oriental)** Craies (49x69cm 19x27in) Antwerpen 2000

WYK van Henri 1833-? **[35]**

$3 940 - €3 811 - **£2 430** - FF25 000
Café à l'arrêt des caravanes Huile/toile (41x65cm
16x25in) Paris 1999

$1 100 - €1 143 - **£693** - FF7 500
Paysage animé Huile/panneau (40x23cm 15x9in) Pau
2000

WYLD James XIX **[7]**

$725 - €691 - **£440** - FF4 534
**Map of the Oregon Districts and the Adjacent
Country** Engraving (34x51cm 13x20in) London
1999

WYLD William 1806-1889 **[151]**

$30 000 - €25 883 - **£18 099** - FF169 779
The Doge's Palace, Venice Oil/canvas
(157.5x228cm 62x89in) New-York 1998

$3 177 - €3 462 - **£2 200** - FF22 710
Sorrento near Naples Oil/canvas (35x54.5cm
13x21in) London 2001

$2 436 - €2 371 - **£1 500** - FF15 553
Capriccio Venetian View Oil/board (38x30cm
14x11in) London 1999

$1 807 - €1 982 - **£1 227** - FF13 000
La Seine à Rouen Aquarelle/papier (18x25cm 7x9in)
Lille 2000

WYLER Otto 1887-1965 **[41]**

$1 364 - €1 465 - **£913** - FF9 608
Ansicht eines Dörfchens bei Aarau Öl/Leinwand
(60x80cm 23x31in) Zofingen 2000

$563 - €605 - **£377** - FF3 968
Frühlingslandschaft Aquarell/Papier (21x29cm
8x11in) Zofingen 2000

WYLIE Kate 1877-1941 **[21]**

$2 347 - €1 984 - **£1 400** - FF13 011
Red and White Begonias Oil/canvas (36x44.5cm
14x17in) Glasgow 1998

WYLIE Robert 1839-1877 **[7]**
- $5 000 - €5 978 - **£3 449** - FF39 210
  Mother and Child Oil/canvas (64x53cm 25x21in) Milford CT 2000
- $3 500 - €3 248 - **£2 101** - FF21 306
  A Meltdown cadre Oil/canvas (29x21cm 11x8in) Milford CT 1999

WYLLIE Charles William 1853-1923 **[40]**
- $14 500 - €16 564 - **£10 208** - FF108 651
  The Stairs, Brentford Oil/canvas (91x49cm 36x19in) Pittsfield MA 2001
- $1 164 - €986 - **£700** - FF6 469
  Cleaning the Fishing Boats at Low Tide Oil/canvas (29x44cm 11x17in) London 1998
- $421 - €394 - **£260** - FF2 582
  Harbour Scene, depicting Women mending Nets on a Beach with Boats Watercolour/paper (34x52cm 13x20in) Loughton, Essex 1999

WYLLIE Gordon H. XX **[8]**
- $795 - €736 - **£480** - FF4 828
  Renfrewshire Hills Mixed media (29x49cm 11x19in) Edinburgh 1999
- $1 027 - €951 - **£620** - FF6 236
  Island Autumn Gouache/paper (59x59cm 23x23in) Edinburgh 1999

WYLLIE Harold, Lt.Col. 1880-1975 **[68]**
- $3 230 - €3 037 - **£2 000** - FF19 924
  The «Victory» and «St Vincent» at Portsmouth Harbour Oil/canvas/board (25x40cm 9x15in) London 1999
- $257 - €241 - **£160** - FF1 578
  Naval Review Pencil (18.5x23cm 7x9in) London 1999
- $196 - €225 - **£135** - FF1 473
  Ships at Anchor in an Estuary Drypoint (18.5x23.5cm 7x9in) Lymington 2000

WYLLIE William Lionel 1851-1931 **[1100]**
- $44 660 - €38 187 - **£27 000** - FF250 492
  «Heave Away» Barges Upward Bound Oil/canvas (91.5x153.5cm 36x60in) London 1999
- $6 066 - €5 543 - **£3 800** - FF36 361
  Steamer, Tug and Other Shipping Off the Sussex Coast Oil/board (46x61cm 18x24in) Suffolk 1999
- $2 489 - €2 657 - **£1 700** - FF17 430
  Barges on the Medway Oil/canvas (27.5x57cm 10x22in) Billingshurst, West-Sussex 2001
- $2 359 - €2 152 - **£1 450** - FF14 118
  «Off Saint Catherine's Point» Watercolour/paper (14x34cm 5x13in) London 1998
- $627 - €674 - **£420** - FF4 419
  Unloading the Catch Drypoint (8.5x35cm 3x13in) London 2000

WYLLIE William Morison c.1830-c.1890 **[7]**
- $14 179 - €15 313 - **£9 800** - FF100 449
  Sorting the Catch Oil/canvas (50x73cm 20x29in) Par, Cornwall 2001

WYMANS Wilhelmus 1888-1968 **[8]**
- $684 - €771 - **£472** - FF5 060
  Picking Hazelnuts Oil/canvas (47x25cm 18x9in) Amsterdam 2000

WYMER Reginald Augustus 1849-1935 **[18]**
- $634 - €653 - **£407** - FF4 285
  Mounted Hussar/Dragoon Officers Watercolour (37x27cm 14x10in) Cambridge 2000

WYNANTS Jan 1631/32-1684 **[74]**
- $3 268 440 - €3 212 826 - **£2 100 000** - FF21 074 760
  Landscape with a Hunter and his Dogs, a Peasant, Fishermen & Falconer Oil/canvas (152x191cm 59x75in) London 1999
- $17 000 - €14 139 - **£9 979** - FF92 743
  Wooded Landscape with Huntsmen restin by a path Oil/canvas (84x66cm 33x25in) New-York 1998
- $28 266 - €27 227 - **£17 466** - FF178 596
  Sportsmen on a Path in the Dunes Oil/canvas (37x43cm 14x16in) Amsterdam 1999

WYNANTZ Augustus 1795-1848 **[11]**
- $6 569 - €7 260 - **£4 556** - FF47 625
  The Winkel van Sinkel along the Oude Gracht, Utrecht Oil/panel (32x26cm 12x10in) Amsterdam 2001

WYNEN Oswald 1736-1790 **[5]**
- $3 634 - €4 090 - **£2 504** - FF26 831
  Blumenstilleben mit Insekten Aquarell/Papier (43x30cm 16x11in) München 2000

WYNFIELD David Wilkie 1837-1887 **[15]**
- $2 983 - €2 897 - **£1 843** - FF19 000
  Autoportrait (?) en moine Tirage albuminé (22x18cm 8x7in) Paris 1999

WYNN Kenneth 1922 **[1]**
- $20 000 - €23 785 - **£14 254** - FF156 020
  Full Cry Oil/canvas (101.5x152cm 39x59in) New-York 2000

WYNNE David 1926 **[31]**
- $12 847 - €11 861 - **£8 000** - FF77 804
  Cath with a Bird Bronze (H127cm H50in) London 1999
- $10 161 - €10 907 - **£6 800** - FF71 546
  The Dancer Bronze (H71cm H27in) London 2000

WYNNE Gladys 1878-1968 **[12]**
- $646 - €608 - **£400** - FF3 991
  Leon Bridge, Glendalough/View overlooking Ards Demisne Watercolour/paper (16x24cm 6x9in) Little-Lane, Ilkley 1999

WYNTER Bryan 1915-1975 **[45]**
- $8 656 - €9 712 - **£6 000** - FF63 706
  Confluence II Oil/canvas (142x112cm 55x44in) London 2000
- $6 404 - €5 814 - **£4 000** - FF38 136
  Sunken World Oil/canvas (76x61cm 29x24in) London 1999
- $2 366 - €2 642 - **£1 650** - FF17 332
  Tide Line Oil/canvas (35x28cm 13x11in) Bath 2001
- $321 - €309 - **£200** - FF2 029
  Confluence Crayon (53.5x42cm 21x16in) London 1999

WYNTRACK Dirck 1625-1678 **[11]**
- $8 550 - €9 712 - **£6 000** - FF63 705
  A Barn Interior with a Basket of Vegetables, a dead Hare, Cabbages Oil/panel (63x49.5cm 24x19in) London 2001
- $20 259 - €23 080 - **£14 000** - FF151 394
  Swans, parrot and other exotic birds in an Italianate river landscape Oil/canvas (23x17cm 9x7in) Guildford, Surrey 2000

WYON Edward William 1811-1885 **[21]**
- $3 640 - €3 904 - **£2 470** - FF25 610
  Leones ingleses recostados Marbre (14x10x30cm 5x3x11in) Madrid 2001

WYRSCH Charles 1920 **[30]**
- $200 - €187 - **£123** - FF1 228
  Concert Aquarelle (18x14cm 7x5in) Luzern 1999

W

WYRSCH Johann Melchior J. 1732-1798 **[8]**
- **$4 528** - €5 254 - **£3 126** - FF34 462
  Selbstbildnis des Künstlers Öl/Leinwand (55.5x48cm 21x18in) Luzern 2000

WYSE Henry Taylor 1870-1951 **[10]**
- **$292** - €335 - **£200** - FF2 200
  Autumn Landscape Watercolour/paper (26.5x37cm 10x14in) Edinburgh 2000

WYSOCKI Charles 1928 **[13]**
- **$4 000** - €3 623 - **£2 448** - FF23 767
  Beach Grass Oil/masonite (60x152cm 24x60in) Portland ME 1998

WYSOTSKI Stanislaw 1949 **[15]**
- **$398** - €377 - **£247** - FF2 472
  Kvindetorso Bronze (H29cm H11in) Vejle 1999

WYSPIANSKI Stanislaw 1869-1907 **[51]**
- **$11 011** - €11 098 - **£6 867** - FF72 801
  Paysage dans la région de Cracovie Oil/canvas (29.2x34.7cm 11x13in) Kraków 2000
- **$2 507** - €2 973 - **£1 770** - FF19 500
  Étude de la tête d'un homme casque Crayon/papier (26.5x23.5cm 10x9in) Paris 2000

WYSS Caspar Leontius 1762-1798 **[9]**
- **$374** - €422 - **£263** - FF2 769
  «Vue de geschene Candon de Ury» Radierung (20x30cm 7x11in) Bern 2001

WYSS Franz Anatol 1940 **[87]**
- **$369** - €343 - **£225** - FF2 247
  Flugobjekte Mischtechnik/Papier (25x32.5cm 9x12in) Bern 1999
- **$127** - €118 - **£77** - FF776
  Der eingepresste Kopf Vernis mou (24.3x16cm 9x6in) Bern 1999

WYSS Kurt 1936 **[9]**
- **$1 374** - €1 636 - **£982** - FF10 732
  «Andy Warhol im Kunsthaus Zürich am 25.5.1978» Vintage gelatin silver print (26x39.3cm 10x15in) Berlin 2000

WYTSMAN Juliette 1866-1925 **[41]**
- **$32 368** - €33 712 - **£20 400** - FF221 136
  Fleurs au bord d'un fleuve Huile/toile (100x134cm 39x52in) Antwerpen 2000
- **$15 768** - €13 386 - **£9 396** - FF87 804
  «Paysage en fleurs à Linkebeek» Huile/toile (60.5x81cm 23x31in) Bruxelles 1998
- **$1 848** - €1 735 - **£1 141** - FF11 382
  Fleurs au bord du fossé Huile/toile/panneau (22x28cm 8x11in) Antwerpen 1999
- **$5 112** - €5 949 - **£3 648** - FF39 024
  «Les pivoines» Pastel/carton (53x67cm 20x26in) Bruxelles 2001

WYTSMAN Rudolph 1860-1927 **[107]**
- **$20 700** - €22 309 - **£14 310** - FF146 540
  Floraison à Linkebeek Huile/toile (100x120cm 39x47in) Bruxelles 2001
- **$5 857** - €6 817 - **£4 180** - FF44 715
  Chemin creux animé en été Huile/toile (82x103cm 32x40in) Bruxelles 2001
- **$1 361** - €1 524 - **£946** - FF10 000
  Paysage d'été Huile/panneau (18x28cm 7x11in) Le Touquet 2001

WYWIORSKI Michael Gorstkin 1861-1926 **[56]**
- **$4 677** - €4 368 - **£2 832** - FF28 652
  Through a Forest in winter Oil/canvas (90.5x141.5cm 35x55in) Warszawa 1999

- **$5 717** - €6 538 - **£3 926** - FF42 884
  Paysage d'automne Huile/toile (76.5x121.5cm 30x47in) Warszawa 2000
- **$10 832** - €10 115 - **£6 560** - FF66 352
  Circasian Horsemen in the Mountains Oil/canvas (41.5x27.8cm 16x10in) Warszawa 1999
- **$3 855** - €3 744 - **£2 383** - FF24 559
  Dégel Pastel/paper (75x105cm 29x41in) Warszawa 1999

X

XAM 1915 **[4]**
- **$2 352** - €2 523 - **£1 554** - FF16 548
  Composición Técnica mixta (81x81cm 31x31in) Madrid 2000

XCERON John, Jean 1890-1967 **[17]**
- **$4 000** - €3 885 - **£2 500** - FF25 487
  Composition No.202 Oil/canvas/board (41x30.5cm 16x12in) New-York 1999
- **$1 100** - €1 069 - **£687** - FF7 009
  Composition Watercolour, gouache (22.5x14cm 8x5in) New-York 1999

XENAKIS Constantin 1931 **[150]**
- **$943** - €793 - **£554** - FF5 200
  Asphyxia Acrylique (46x55cm 18x21in) Douai 1998
- **$132** - €145 - **£87** - FF950
  Codehommes Acrylique/toile (16x22cm 6x8in) Douai 2000
- **$207** - €198 - **£127** - FF1 300
  Composition (31x23cm 12x9in) Douai 2000

XI DEJIN Hsi Te-chin 1923-1981 **[60]**
- **$19 020** - €22 200 - **£13 020** - FF145 620
  Maternal Love Oil/canvas (61x76.5cm 24x30in) Taipei 2000
- **$3 804** - €4 440 - **£2 604** - FF29 124
  Houses on the River Watercolour/paper (54.5x37cm 21x14in) Taipei 2000

XI GANG 1746-1803 **[7]**
- **$4 118** - €3 906 - **£2 505** - FF25 619
  Landscape after Wang Shimin (1597-1680) Ink/paper (113x33.5cm 44x13in) Hong-Kong 1999

XIA JINGGUAN 1875-1953 **[4]**
- **$12 820** - €14 448 - **£8 960** - FF94 770
  «Hairi Pavillion» Ink (30x78cm 11x30in) Hong-Kong 2001

XIA YONG XIV **[1]**
- **$12 820** - €15 068 - **£8 890** - FF98 840
  Yueyang Pavilion Ink (22x23cm 8x9in) Hong-Kong 2000

XIANG SHENGMO 1597-1658 **[6]**
- **$8 236** - €7 811 - **£5 011** - FF51 238
  Autumn Landscape Ink/paper (67.5x30.5cm 26x12in) Hong-Kong 1999

XIANG YUANBIAN 1525-1590 **[4]**
- **$109 395** - €103 743 - **£66 555** - FF680 510
  Bamboo, Chrysanthemum and Rock Ink/paper (96.5x23.5cm 37x9in) Hong-Kong 1999

XIANYU SHU 1256-1301 **[2]**
- **$797 940** - €756 714 - **£485 460** - FF4 963 720
  The Song of the Stone Drum (Shigu Ge) in Xing Cao Shu Ink/paper (34.5x497.5cm 13x195in) Hong-Kong 1999

XIAO HAN 1945 **[5]**
📧 **$7 104** - €6 741 - **£4 316** - FF44 220
Waterfall from Verdant Mountains Ink
(69.5x59.5cm 27x23in) Hong-Kong 1999

XIAO RUSONG 1922-1992 **[43]**
📧 **$16 400** - €17 463 - **£10 400** - FF114 550
Writing Love Letter Watercolour/paper (72.5x53cm
28x20in) Taipei 2000

XIAO SUN 1883-1944 **[8]**
📧 **$1 540** - €1 691 - **£992** - FF11 091
Walking in a Wintry Forest Ink (132x33cm 51x12in)
Hong-Kong 2000

XIAO XIA 1957 **[4]**
📧 **$2 421** - €2 231 - **£1 458** - FF14 634
Nuages Technique mixte/papier (200x300cm
78x118in) Antwerpen 1999

XIAO YUNCONG 1596-1673 **[5]**
📧 **$15 408** - €16 909 - **£9 924** - FF110 916
Landscapes Ink (21.5x15cm 8x5in) Hong-Kong 2000

XIE SHICHEN 1488-c.1570 **[10]**
📧 **$97 584** - €106 558 - **£62 776** - FF698 972
Landscape after Li Tang (c.1055-1130) Ink
(336.5x101.5cm 132x39in) Hong-Kong 2000

XIE ZHILIU 1910-1997 **[52]**
📧 **$8 988** - €9 815 - **£5 782** - FF64 379
Birds perching on Prunus Ink (179x66cm 70x25in)
Hong-Kong 2000

XIMENES Ettore, Elio 1855-1926 **[20]**
🖎 **$2 962** - €2 495 - **£1 750** - FF16 369
Figure of a Little Girl Alabaster (H66cm H25in)
Amsterdam 1998
📖 **$2 000** - €1 754 - **£1 214** - FF11 507
Golf Monte-Carlo Poster (112x77cm 44x30in) New-
York 1999

XIMONAS Nikolaos 1866-1929 **[4]**
🔍 **$1 890** - €2 102 - **£1 260** - FF13 790
Greek Landscapes Oil/cardboard (13.5x18cm 5x7in)
Athens 2000

XING BAOZHUANG Ying Pochong 1940 **[17]**
📧 **$4 128** - €3 874 - **£2 550** - FF25 411
Autumn Landscape Ink (66.5x131cm 26x51in)
Hong-Kong 1999

XING TONG 1551-1612 **[5]**
📧 **$8 140** - €7 724 - **£4 946** - FF50 669
Poem in Cursive Script Calligraphy Ink/paper
(133x36.5cm 52x14in) Hong-Kong 1999

XINGJIAN Gao 1940 **[1]**
📧 **$8 540** - €9 463 - **£5 908** - FF62 076
Unexpected Ink/paper (81x68cm 31x26in) Taipei
2001

XIONG HAI 1957 **[7]**
📧 **$4 487** - €5 057 - **£3 136** - FF33 169
Landscapes Ink (25x18cm 9x7in) Hong-Kong 2001

XU BEIHONG 1895-1953 **[111]**
🔍 **$157 500** - €144 903 - **£94 500** - FF950 500
Yugong moving the Mountain Oil/canvas
(46x106.5cm 18x41in) Taipei 1999
📧 **$12 820** - €14 448 - **£8 960** - FF94 770
Sparrows/Magpie Ink (33x35cm 12x13in) Hong-
Kong 2001

XU CAO 1899-1961 **[7]**
📧 **$1 930** - €1 831 - **£1 174** - FF12 009
Gentleman Playong Qin in Nature Ink (19x53.5cm
7x21in) Hong-Kong 1999

XU FANG 1622-1694 **[6]**
📧 **$5 136** - €5 608 - **£3 304** - FF36 788
Lake Tai Ink (170x48cm 66x18in) Hong-Kong 2000

XU GU 1824-1896 **[43]**
📧 **$32 175** - €30 513 - **£19 575** - FF200 150
Loquat and Peach Ink (43.5x94.5cm 17x37in) Hong-
Kong 1999

XU LELE 1955 **[3]**
📧 **$2 054** - €2 243 - **£1 321** - FF14 715
Lady with a Fan Ink (123.5x31.5cm 48x12in) Hong-
Kong 2000

XU LINLU XX **[2]**
📧 **$1 282** - €1 456 - **£900** - FF9 553
Fishes in a Lotus Pond Ink/paper (115x69.5cm
45x27in) Hong-Kong 2001

XU SHIPING 1952 **[6]**
📧 **$5 160** - €4 842 - **£3 188** - FF31 764
Boating on Mountain Streams Ink (62.5x186cm
24x73in) Hong-Kong 1999

XU WEI 1521-1593 **[11]**
📧 **$30 816** - €33 818 - **£19 848** - FF221 832
Peonies, Bamboo and Rock Ink/paper (154x65cm
60x25in) Hong-Kong 2000

XU XI 1940 **[19]**
📧 **$2 750** - €2 395 - **£1 639** - FF15 707
Roses Ink (67x67cm 26x26in) New-York 1998

XU XINRONG 1959 **[2]**
📧 **$2 820** - €3 315 - **£1 955** - FF21 744
Landscape Ink (127x46.5cm 50x18in) Hong-Kong
2000

XU YANSUN XX **[2]**
📧 **$5 196** - €4 389 - **£3 119** - FF28 790
Meeting at Longzhong Ink (105x45.5cm 41x17in)
Hong-Kong 1998

XU YUANWEN 1634-1691 **[1]**
📧 **$38 460** - €45 204 - **£26 670** - FF296 520
Prose Rebuking Corruption Ink/paper
(25.5x133.5cm 10x52in) Hong-Kong 2000

XU ZHAOJING XIX **[1]**
📧 **$1 923** - €2 287 - **£1 324** - FF15 001
Deer Ink (93x46cm 36x18in) Hong-Kong 2000

XU ZHIWEN 1942 **[5]**
📧 **$3 000** - €2 612 - **£1 788** - FF17 133
«Landscape» Ink (143.5x73cm 56x28in) New-York
1998

XUE ZHIGUO 1957 **[2]**
🔍 **$6 410** - €7 534 - **£4 445** - FF49 420
Cabbage Oil/canvas (78x98cm 30x38in) Hong-Kong
2000

XUL SOLAR Alejandro 1887-1963 **[26]**
📧 **$70 000** - €67 404 - **£43 568** - FF442 141
Paisaje (Cinco pagodas) Watercolour/paper
(38.5x32cm 15x12in) New-York 1999

XYLANDER Wilhelm Ferdinand 1840-1913 **[29]**
🔍 **$3 883** - €4 538 - **£2 772** - FF29 766
Tug and three-master in Moonlight Oil/panel
(110x80cm 43x31in) Amsterdam 2001
🔍 **$481** - €536 - **£336** - FF3 517
Portraet af kyseklaedt kone Oil/wood (20x15cm
7x5in) Köbenhavn 2001

X

Y

YAEGER Edgar L. 1904-1997 [28]
🖼 **$2 000** - €1 995 - **£1 248** - FF13 086
Women in a Tuscan Landscape Oil/canvas
(53x63cm 21x25in) Cincinnati OH 1999
🖼 **$500** - €477 - **£307** - FF3 132
Artist at Work Oil/board (21x28cm 8x11in) Cincinnati
OH 1999

YAGAKI Shikanosuke 1897-1966 [6]
📷 **$3 200** - €2 685 - **£1 877** - FF17 611
Shadow Abstraction Gelatin silver print (29x24cm
11x9in) New-York 1998

YAGODKIN Genri 1952 [22]
🖼 **$495** - €462 - **£300** - FF3 033
Sunflowers on the Window Sill Oil/canvas
(46x55cm 18x21in) Fernhurst, Haslemere, Surrey 1999

YAHIA (Yahia Turki) 1902-1969 [20]
🖼 **$5 439** - €6 403 - **£3 822** - FF42 000
Souk à Tunis Huile/toile (61x50cm 24x19in) Paris
2000
🖼 **$3 157** - €2 897 - **£1 962** - FF19 000
Bou-Kornine vu de Sidi Bou Saïd Huile/panneau
(26.5x35cm 10x13in) Paris 1999

YAKOVLEV Mikhail Nikolaevich 1880-1942 [12]
🖼 **$492** - €496 - **£306** - FF3 252
Quai de Bethune à Paris Technique mixte
(48x60cm 18x23in) Bruxelles 2000
🖼 **$714** - €744 - **£453** - FF4 878
Pont Neuf à Liège Gouache/papier (46x60cm
18x23in) Antwerpen 2000

YAKOVLEV Vladimir Igorevich 1934-1998 [8]
🖼 **$834** - €767 - **£512** - FF5 030
Weiblicher Kopf Gouache (60.3x86cm 23x33in)
Bielefeld 1999

YAMAGATA Hiro 1948 [8]
🖼 **$800** - €685 - **£481** - FF4 495
Museum Silkscreen in colors (75x58cm 29x23in)
Chicago IL 1998

YAMAGUCHI Harumi XX [2]
🖼 **$1 200** - €1 338 - **£783** - FF8 777
«Parco» Poster (102x73cm 40x29in) New-York 2000

YAMAGUCHI Kaoru 1907-1968 [5]
🖼 **$35 000** - €38 614 - **£23 149** - FF253 291
Nude (Rafu) Oil/canvas (100x68cm 39x26in) New-
York 2000
🖼 **$37 240** - €36 323 - **£22 800** - FF238 260
Portrait of Kuma Oil/canvas (33.5x24.5cm 13x9in)
Tokyo 2000

YAMAKAWA Shuho 1898-1944 [5]
🖼 **$523** - €562 - **£350** - FF3 689
Halbporträt einer jungen Frau Woodcut in colors
(38.7x26cm 15x10in) Köln 2000

YAMAMOTO Fumihiko XX [3]
🖼 **$16 170** - €15 772 - **£9 900** - FF103 455
Grass Oil/canvas (162x162cm 63x63in) Tokyo 1999

YAMASHITA Shintaro 1881-1966 [1]
🖼 **$3 038** - €2 963 - **£1 860** - FF19 437
Still Life Oil/canvas (24.5x33cm 9x12in) Tokyo 1999

YAMAWAKI Iwao 1898-1987 [11]
📷 **$2 955** - €2 701 - **£1 816** - FF16 780
Der Wohnraum unser Zeit Photograph
(14.2x11.5cm 5x4in) München 1998

YAN BOLONG 1898-1954 [3]
🖼 **$4 454** - €3 776 - **£2 663** - FF24 767
Wild Birds perching on Winter Pine Coloured
inks/paper (130x59cm 51x23in) Hong-Kong 1998

YAN Robert 1901-1994 [220]
🖼 **$511** - €549 - **£338** - FF3 600
Bord de mer à Saint-Cado Huile/panneau (22x27cm
8x10in) Douarnenez 2000
🖼 **$446** - €457 - **£275** - FF3 000
Barques échouées Aquarelle/papier (33x47cm
12x18in) L'Isle-Adam 2000

YAN WENLIANG 1893-1990 [13]
🖼 **$8 740** - €8 100 - **£5 433** - FF53 130
Spring Scenery Oil/board (57x71.5cm 22x28in)
Taipei 1999
🖼 **$3 846** - €4 334 - **£2 688** - FF28 431
Grain Storage Watercolour/paper (20.5x32.5cm
8x12in) Hong-Kong 2001

YANAGI Yukinori 1959 [2]
🖼 **$15 000** - €16 457 - **£9 964** - FF107 952
Pacific Mixed media (34x51cm 13x20in) New-York
2000
🖼 **$26 043** - €25 347 - **£16 000** - FF166 265
The Cis ant Farm Construction (200x565cm
78x222in) London 1999

YAÑEZ DE ALMEDINA Ferrando, Ferdinando
c.1480-c.1560 [4]
🖼 **$13 448** - €14 436 - **£9 000** - FF94 694
**A Draped Seated Figure Holding a Scroll,
Possibly the Emperor Augustus** Drawing
(10x6.5cm 3x2in) London 2000

YANG BORUN 1837-1911 [3]
🖼 **$1 935** - €1 825 - **£1 200** - FF11 970
Landscape Ink/paper (135x43cm 53x16in) Hong-
Kong 1999

YANG DENGXIONG Yang Din 1958 [10]
🖼 **$7 095** - €6 658 - **£4 383** - FF43 675
Maison de poète Oil/canvas (159.5x70cm 62x27in)
Hong-Kong 1999
🖼 **$7 216** - €7 684 - **£4 576** - FF50 402
Four Seasons Oil/canvas (27.5x32.5cm 10x12in)
Taipei 1999

YANG FEIYUN 1954 [13]
🖼 **$12 840** - €14 091 - **£8 270** - FF92 430
Seated Woman Oil/canvas (99x78.5cm 38x30in)
Hong-Kong 2000

YANG MAOLIN 1953 [3]
🖼 **$28 530** - €33 299 - **£19 530** - FF218 430
Zealandia Memorandum L9306 Acrylic
(260x194cm 102x76in) Taipei 2000
🖼 **$5 706** - €6 660 - **£3 906** - FF43 686
Yun mountain Memorandum M9207 Acrylic
(116x73cm 45x28in) Taipei 2000

YANG MINGYI 1943 [6]
🖼 **$1 926** - €2 103 - **£1 239** - FF13 795
Old Bridge Ink (55.5x55.5cm 21x21in) Hong-Kong
2000

YANG QIUREN 1907-1983 [4]
🖼 **$3 672** - €4 169 - **£2 580** - FF27 348
Lotus Oil/paper (49x59.5cm 19x23in) Taipei 2001

YANG SAN-LANG 1907-1995 [22]
🖼 **$15 850** - €18 500 - **£10 850** - FF121 350
Village in Autumn Oil/canvas (53x45cm 20x17in)
Taipei 2000

$7 650 - €8 686 - **£5 375** - FF56 975
European Landscape Oil/canvas (36x44cm 14x17in)
Taipei 2001

YANG SHANSHEN 1913 **[46]**
$3 217 - €3 051 - **£1 957** - FF20 015
Sparrow Ink (20x50.5cm 7x19in) Hong-Kong 1999

YANG SHAOBIN 1963 **[3]**
$4 438 - €5 180 - **£3 038** - FF33 978
Fighting Oil/canvas (69x89.5cm 27x35in) Taipei 2000

YANG SISHENG Jong Sesin 1941 **[5]**
$5 805 - €5 448 - **£3 586** - FF35 734
Supreme Happiness Ink (85x59.5cm 33x23in)
Hong-Kong 1999

YANG WENCONG 1597-1646 **[6]**
$5 769 - €6 553 - **£4 050** - FF42 988
Poem in cursive Script Calligraphy Ink/paper
(123.5x27.5cm 48x10in) Hong-Kong 2001

YANG YANPING 1934 **[2]**
$2 398 - €2 310 - **£1 500** - FF15 152
**Scene of Snow covered Mountains surrounding
a Lake** Watercolour/paper (59.5x73cm 23x28in)
London 1999

YANG YIQING 1454-1530 **[1]**
$1 926 - €2 103 - **£1 239** - FF13 795
Letter to Yang Xunji (1456-1544) Ink/paper
(23.5x16cm 9x6in) Hong-Kong 2000

YANKA (Sabine Zlatin) 1907-1996 **[191]**
$225 - €244 - **£152** - FF1 600
Composition Nature morte Huile/toile (94x75cm
37x29in) Paris 2001
$168 - €183 - **£114** - FF1 200
Vierge assise avec l'enfant Huile/toile (35x27cm
13x10in) Paris 2001
$182 - €198 - **£123** - FF1 300
Portrait de femme Pastel/papier (30x28cm 11x11in)
Paris 2001
$323 - €351 - **£219** - FF2 300
Canal Saint-Martin, Villette Monotype (54x37cm
21x14in) Paris 2001

YANKEL Jacq., Jacob Kikoïne 1920 **[146]**
$1 234 - €1 403 - **£866** - FF9 200
Cheval de manège Huile/toile (50x61cm 19x24in)
Avignon 2001
$500 - €457 - **£306** - FF3 000
Composition polychrome Gouache/papier
(60x45cm 23x17in) Arles 1999

YANKILEVSKY Vladimir 1938 **[6]**
$5 691 - €6 613 - **£4 000** - FF43 376
From the Series Women Strolling Indian ink
(49x63.5cm 19x25in) London 2001

YARBER Robert 1948 **[17]**
$10 000 - €10 367 - **£6 000** - FF68 000
Couch Olio/tela (111.5x152cm 43x59in) Venezia 1999

YARD Sydney Jones 1855-1909 **[10]**
$4 500 - €5 259 - **£3 212** - FF34 497
Monterey coastal landscape Oil/canvas (35x50cm
14x20in) Altadena CA 2001

YARDLEY Bruce 1962 **[5]**
$2 921 - €2 809 - **£1 800** - FF18 429
Early Lunch, Arles Oil/canvas (61x101.5cm 24x39in)
London 1999

YARDLEY Helen 1954 **[1]**
$1 031 - €1 107 - **£690** - FF7 259
Abstract Composition Rug Tapestry (410x213cm
161x83in) London 2000

YARDLEY John 1933 **[28]**
$2 428 - €2 279 - **£1 500** - FF14 948
Cathedral of Steam Oil/board (44x60cm 17x23in)
Billingshurst, West-Sussex 1999
$844 - €812 - **£520** - FF5 324
Windy Day at the Pavilion Watercolour/paper
(38x51cm 14x20in) London 1999

YARNALL Agnes 1904-1998 **[28]**
$17 212 - €19 108 - **£12 000** - FF125 338
Bust of Sir John Gielgud as Hamlet Bronze
(57x51cm 22x20in) London 2001

YARNOLD George B. XIX **[18]**
$579 - €672 - **£400** - FF4 409
Waterfalls Oil/canvas (90x70cm 35x27in) London
2000
$1 333 - €1 472 - **£920** - FF9 656
**Mountain Stream in full Flow with a Bridge in
the Background** Oil/canvas (34.5x44.5cm 13x17in)
Hockley, Birmingham 2001

YAROCHENKO Nicolay Alexandrov. 1846-1898 **[5]**
$7 168 - €6 941 - **£4 536** - FF45 528
Au marché, Kiev Huile/toile (71x51cm 27x20in)
Liège 1999

YAROVOI Michaïl M. 1864-? **[1]**
$2 500 - €2 672 - **£1 680** - FF17 524
On Hunting Oil/canvas (43x32cm 16x12in) Kiev 2001

YARROW William Henry Kemble 1891-1941 **[3]**
$130 000 - €123 114 - **£79 040** - FF807 573
The Orchard Oil/canvas (153x109.5cm 60x43in) New-
York 1999

YARROW-JONES Ernest 1872-1951 **[45]**
$504 - €589 - **£360** - FF3 866
In full Bloom Oil/canvas (65x54cm 25x21in) London
2001

YARWOOD Walter 1917-1996 **[4]**
$1 781 - €2 078 - **£1 239** - FF13 631
Intersection Oil/board (61x76cm 24x29in) Toronto
2000

YASUDA Yukihiko 1884-1978 **[11]**
$20 580 - €20 073 - **£12 600** - FF131 670
Lillies Drawing (36x54cm 14x21in) Tokyo 1999

YASUI Sotaro 1888-1955 **[1]**
$4 900 - €4 779 - **£3 000** - FF31 350
Landscape Watercolour/paper (28.5x37.5cm 11x14in)
Tokyo 1999

YASUSHI Sugiyama 1909-1993 **[4]**
$75 000 - €75 577 - **£46 755** - FF495 750
Iku (Noble) Mixed media drawing (55.5x38cm
21x14in) New-York 2000

YATES Cullen 1866-1945 **[27]**
$5 500 - €5 145 - **£3 332** - FF33 749
Landscape Oil/canvas (40x50cm 16x20in) Bangor
PA 1999
$2 250 - €2 690 - **£1 546** - FF17 644
River Landscape Oil/canvas (30x40cm 12x16in)
Chicago IL 2000

YATES Fred 1922 **[115]**
$962 - €970 - **£600** - FF6 362
La Source Oil/canvas (72.5x91.5cm 28x36in) London
2000
$318 - €344 - **£220** - FF2 259
Limoges Cathedral Oil/canvas (30x30cm 11x11in)
London 2001

Y

✎ $510 - €486 - **£310** - FF3 185
Marina di Pietranta, Italy, Beach Scene
Watercolour/paper (59.5x79cm 23x31in) Penzance,
Cornwall 1999

YATES Frederic 1854-1919 **[25]**
🕊 $1 793 - €1 925 - **£1 200** - FF12 625
Cornish Lane Oil/canvas (50.5x76cm 19x29in)
London 2000

YATES G. XIX **[4]**
✎ $6 946 - €6 057 - **£4 200** - FF39 731
Landscapes Watercolour (21.5x32cm 8x12in) London
1998

YATES Gideon 1790-1837 **[32]**
✎ $1 925 - €1 940 - **£1 200** - FF12 724
**Lancaster Castle from Marsh lane/West View of
Lancaster Castle** Watercolour (18x23cm 7x9in)
Billingshurst, West-Sussex 2000

YATES Thomas, Lieutenant 1765-1796 **[11]**
✎ $1 604 - €1 616 - **£1 000** - FF11 573
**Herders with Cattle Crossing a Bridge with
Anglers Below** Ink (30.5x40.5cm 12x15in) London
2000

YATMAN William Hamilton 1819-1897 **[2]**
✎ $1 643 - €1 764 - **£1 100** - FF11 573
Studies of Limpets and Other Shells
Watercolour/paper (22x31cm 8x12in) London 2000

YAVNO Max 1921-1985 **[61]**
📷 $3 200 - €3 009 - **£1 981** - FF19 736
Muscle Beach Silver print (20x34cm 8x13in) New-
York 1999

YAZZ Beatien 1928 **[24]**
✎ $400 - €441 - **£267** - FF2 890
Boy in a Garden Watercolour/board (48x39cm
19x15in) St. Ignatius MT 2000

YDEMA Egnatius 1876-1937 **[25]**
🕊 $3 695 - €3 262 - **£2 227** - FF21 397
Sailing Vessels near Sneek Oil/canvas (60x80cm
23x31in) Amsterdam 1998
🕊 $1 982 - €1 906 - **£1 236** - FF12 501
Moored Boat in a Polder Landscape
Oil/canvas/panel (30.5x50cm 12x19in) Amsterdam 1999

YE QIANYU 1907-1996 **[5]**
✎ $1 410 - €1 602 - **£990** - FF10 508
Ethnic Girl Ink (68x45cm 26x17in) Hong-Kong 2001

YE XIN XVII **[1]**
🕊 $3 560 - €3 358 - **£2 208** - FF22 024
Village Ink (27x38cm 10x14in) Hong-Kong 1999

YE XIN 1953 **[1]**
✎ $2 386 - €1 993 - **£1 400** - FF13 071
Baudelaire - «Spleen» Ink (65x50cm 25x19in)
London 1998

YE ZHUSHENG 1946 **[2]**
🕊 $8 505 - €7 825 - **£5 103** - FF51 327
Oceanic Poem Oil/canvas (90.5x116cm 35x45in)
Taipei 1999

YE ZIQI Yeh Tzu-ch'i 1957 **[9]**
🕊 $17 325 - €15 939 - **£10 395** - FF104 555
Landscape of Hwa-Lien Tempera (122x148cm
48x58in) Taipei 1999
🕊 $4 410 - €4 057 - **£2 646** - FF26 614
Flaming Wood Tempera (61x61cm 24x24in) Taipei
1999
🕊 $4 195 - €3 888 - **£2 608** - FF25 502
Camellia Mixed media (30.5x38cm 12x14in) Taipei
1999

YEAGER Joseph c.1792-1859 **[1]**
▥ $1 800 - €1 783 - **£1 092** - FF11 698
**Battle of New Orleans/Death of General
Packenham, after W.E West** Engraving
(45.5x57.5cm 17x22in) New-York 2000

YEAMES William Frederick 1835-1918 **[21]**
🕊 $33 681 - €33 318 - **£21 000** - FF218 551
**The Meeting of Sir Thomas More with his
Daughter** Oil/canvas (101.5x173cm 39x68in) London
1999
🕊 $3 501 - €4 063 - **£2 417** - FF26 652
Path of Roses Oil/canvas (49x86cm 19x33in) Dublin
2000

YEATS Anne 1919 **[15]**
🕊 $1 202 - €1 397 - **£844** - FF9 161
Yellow Cloth on the Sand Oil/paper (41x58cm
16x22in) Dublin 2001
✎ $838 - €952 - **£578** - FF6 246
**Portrait of her Father, the Poet, William butler
Yeats** Pencil/paper (17x11cm 7x4in) Dublin 2000
▥ $226 - €229 - **£141** - FF1 499
Autumnal Fruit Print (30x33cm 11x12in) Dublin 2000

YEATS Jack Butler 1871-1957 **[378]**
🕊 $215 880 - €241 802 - **£150 000** - FF1 586 115
Moore's Melodies Oil/canvas (35.5x53.5cm 13x21in)
London 2001
🕊 $51 944 - €54 599 - **£32 589** - FF358 147
In Tipperary Oil/panel (23x35.5cm 9x13in) Dublin
2000
✎ $5 040 - €5 079 - **£3 142** - FF33 316
Great Western Hotel reading Ink (17x19cm 6x7in)
Dublin 2000
▥ $483 - €508 - **£303** - FF3 331
Street Scene Print in colors (11.5x37cm 4x14in)
Dublin 2000

YEATS John Butler 1839-1922 **[31]**
🕊 $15 831 - €17 732 - **£11 000** - FF116 315
Portrait of Jenny Yeats Oil/canvas (51x40.5cm
20x15in) London 2001
✎ $1 207 - €1 168 - **£744** - FF7 662
**Maud White-Celbridge (Friend of the Yeats
Family)** Pencil/paper (15x9.5cm 5x3in) Dublin 1999

YEATS William Butler 1865-1939 **[2]**
🕊 $8 901 - €9 953 - **£6 000** - FF65 285
Lough Na Cree, Connemara Oil/board
(12.5x21.5cm 4x8in) London 2000

YEEND-KING Lilian 1882-? **[3]**
🕊 $14 000 - €16 601 - **£9 632** - FF108 896
Feeding the Ducks Oil/canvas (92x72cm 36x28in)
New-York 2000

YEH CHI WEI 1915-1981 **[4]**
🕊 $6 497 - €6 056 - **£3 927** - FF39 724
Boats, Trengannu Oil/canvas (38.5x117cm 15x46in)
Singapore 1999

YEH TZU-CHI 1957 **[2]**
🕊 $4 920 - €5 239 - **£3 120** - FF34 365
First Love Mixed media (86.5x47.5cm 34x18in) Taipei
2000

YELIZAROV Gennady 1950 **[79]**
🕊 $605 - €566 - **£375** - FF3 715
The Seaplanes Oil/canvas (49x69cm 19x27in)
Fernhurst, Haslemere, Surrey 1999
🕊 $320 - €317 - **£200** - FF2 081
The Orchestra Oil/canvas/board (33x46cm 12x18in)
Fernhurst, Haslemere, Surrey 1999

YELLAND Raymond Dabb 1848-1900 **[17]**
- **$5 500** - €5 904 - **£3 680** - FF38 725
  A Farm in Winter Oil/canvas (40.5x61cm 15x24in)
  San-Francisco CA 2000
- **$3 000** - €3 506 - **£2 141** - FF22 998
  Small boat in sunset landscape Oil/board
  (17x27cm 7x11in) Altadena CA 2001

YELTSEVA Dina 1965 **[31]**
- **$872** - €907 - **£550** - FF5 950
  The Village in Winter Oil/canvas (38x46cm 14x18in)
  Fernhurst, Haslemere, Surrey 2000
- **$556** - €533 - **£350** - FF3 494
  Ice Hockey Oil/canvas (25x30cm 9x11in) Fernhurst,
  Haslemere, Surrey 1999

YEN TSANG YING 1940 **[1]**
- **$3 965** - €4 394 - **£2 743** - FF28 821
  Summering on the Sea Ink (63x96cm 24x37in)
  Taipei 2001

YENIKEYEVA Tatyana 1968 **[94]**
- **$495** - €462 - **£300** - FF3 033
  Picnic by the Lake Oil/canvas (46x65cm 18x25in)
  Fernhurst, Haslemere, Surrey 1999
- **$328** - €353 - **£220** - FF2 314
  The Young Artist Oil/canvas/board (33x24cm 12x9in)
  Fernhurst, Haslemere, Surrey 2000

YENS Karl H. 1868-1945 **[31]**
- **$1 320** - €1 346 - **£827** - FF8 826
  Sundown on the beach Oil/board (25x35cm
  10x14in) Altadena CA 2000

YEO Thomas 1936 **[11]**
- **$4 675** - €4 894 - **£2 936** - FF32 103
  Landscape Mixed media/paper (60.5x81cm 23x31in)
  Singapore 2000

YERMOLOV Pavel 1971 **[21]**
- **$962** - €952 - **£600** - FF6 244
  Open Books Oil/canvas/board (38x55cm 14x21in)
  Fernhurst, Haslemere, Surrey 1999
- **$660** - €661 - **£407** - FF4 334
  Estantería de libros Oleo/lienzo (33x46cm 12x18in)
  Madrid 2000

YERSIN Albert Edgar 1905-1984 **[20]**
- **$178** - €150 - **£105** - FF984
  «Z'innerst inne» Farbradierung (11.7x10cm 4x3in)
  Bern 1998

YEU QUA XIX **[1]**
- **$27 000** - €22 542 - **£15 835** - FF147 865
  View of Hong Kong from the Harbour Oil/canvas
  (44x76cm 17x29in) New-York 1998

YEWELL George Henry 1830-1923 **[5]**
- **$10 000** - €8 544 - **£6 003** - FF56 044
  Christmas Eve Oil/canvas (48.5x35.5cm 19x13in)
  New-York 1998

YI RU 1874-1941 **[2]**
- **$16 692** - €17 227 - **£10 738** - FF119 561
  Flowers and Vegetables Ink (34x806.5cm 13x317in)
  Hong-Kong 2000

YING XIAOJIE 1958 **[3]**
- **$12 900** - €12 106 - **£7 970** - FF79 410
  Girl in an Armchair Oil/canvas (105x78cm 41x30in)
  Hong-Kong 2000

YIRAWALA 1905-1976 **[22]**
- **$5 262** - €5 076 - **£3 325** - FF33 299
  Mimihs Mixed media (99x31cm 38x12in) Melbourne
  1999

- **$1 972** - €1 909 - **£1 250** - FF12 519
  Maraian Body Design Mixed media (44x30cm
  17x11in) Malvern, Victoria 1999

YKENS Frans 1601-1693 **[23]**
- **$17 225** - €16 112 - **£10 660** - FF105 690
  **Brunaille entourée d'une guirlande de fleurs et
  d'une coupe à fruits** Huile/toile (140x115.5cm
  55x45in) Antwerpen 1999
- **$62 256** - €61 197 - **£40 000** - FF401 424
  **Still Life of Peaches, Grapes,
  Pomegranates/Still Life of Lemon** Oil/copper
  (41.5x54cm 16x21in) London 1999

YNGLADA Pere 1881-1958 **[20]**
- **$163** - €192 - **£112** - FF1 260
  Jinetes Acuarela/papel (17x25cm 6x9in) Barcelona

YOAKUM Joseph Elmer 1886/88-1976 **[7]**
- **$2 249** - €1 941 - **£1 362** - FF12 731
  Birds Eye View of San Luis Obispo, California
  Coloured pencils (21x24cm 8x9in) New-York 1999

YOCKNEY Algernon XIX-XX **[2]**
- **$12 695** - €14 817 - **£9 000** - FF97 191
  **«Wreck of the delhi off Cape Spartel, 13th
  January 1911»** Oil/canvas (67x127cm 26x50in)
  London 2001

YOHN Frederick Coffay 1875-1933 **[11]**
- **$3 000** - €3 497 - **£2 077** - FF22 939
  Couple in a Railway Car Oil/canvas (88x58cm
  35x23in) New-York 2000

YOKOI Teruko 1924 **[35]**
- **$1 064** - €1 158 - **£701** - FF7 596
  Ohne Titel Mischtechnik/Papier (62x46.5cm 24x18in)
  Bern 2000
- **$225** - €262 - **£155** - FF1 720
  Pastoral Scene Joy Farblithographie (49x66cm
  19x25in) Bern 2000

YOKOI Tomoe 1943 **[31]**
- **$130** - €140 - **£87** - FF918
  Vase Mezzotint (39x29cm 15x11in) Cleveland OH
  2000

YOKOO Tadanori 1936 **[15]**
- **$800** - €892 - **£523** - FF5 854
  «Lucky God» Poster (102.5x72.5cm 40x28in) New-
  York 2000

YOKOYAMA Misao 1920-1973 **[3]**
- **$40 000** - €44 130 - **£26 456** - FF289 476
  Fuyu Fuji (Mount Fuji in winter) Ink (37x44cm
  14x17in) New-York 2000

YOKOYAMA Taikan 1868-1958 **[31]**
- **$81 340** - €79 336 - **£49 800** - FF520 410
  Rain Painting (43x56.5cm 16x22in) Tokyo 1999
- **$93 100** - €90 806 - **£57 000** - FF595 650
  Mt.Fuji Drawing (32.5x46.5cm 12x18in) Tokyo 1999

YOLDJOGLOU Georges 1933 **[32]**
- **$900** - €1 044 - **£621** - FF6 849
  Les bateaux à la maré basse Oil/canvas
  (60.5x73cm 23x28in) New-York 2000

YON Edmond 1836-1897 **[89]**
- **$13 355** - €13 111 - **£8 281** - FF86 000
  Scène de moissons Huile/toile (92.5x152.5cm
  36x60in) Paris 1999
- **$2 732** - €3 049 - **£1 788** - FF20 000
  Arbres au bords de l'étang Huile/toile (36.5x57cm
  14x22in) Fontainebleau 2000

Y

$2 886 - €2 439 - £1 716 - FF16 000
Les graves de Villerville Huile/toile (28.5x44cm
11x17in) Auvers sur Oise 1998

YONG MUN SENG 1896-1962 [10]

$1 662 - €1 395 - £975 - FF9 150
Pier at the Sea Front Watercolour/paper (56.5x78cm
22x30in) Singapore 1998

YONGE de Antoni XVII [1]

$4 500 - €4 963 - £3 047 - FF32 556
Dutch Shipping in a Bay Oil/canvas (42.5x57cm
16x22in) New-York 2000

YONGZHENG Emperor 1678-1735 [8]

$11 538 - €13 107 - £8 100 - FF85 977
Couplet in running Script calligraphy Ink
(138x29cm 54x11in) Hong-Kong 2001

YOORS Eugène 1879-1977 [9]

$11 440 - €13 644 - £8 195 - FF89 430
**Vrouw bij het haardvuur met duiven (femme
près de l'âtre aux pigeons)** Huile/toile (105x127cm
41x50in) Antwerpen 2000

YORKE William Gay 1817-1908 [7]

$12 000 - €13 221 - £8 005 - FF86 727
American One-Masted Sloop Julia G. Oil/canvas
(55x66cm 22x26in) Portsmouth NH 2000

YORKE William Ho(w)ard 1847-1921 [59]

$10 000 - €11 018 - £6 671 - FF72 273
Bark Lucy Pope Oil/canvas (50x76cm 20x30in)
Portsmouth NH 2000

YOS Josef Süssmeier 1897-1971 [54]

$206 - €194 - £127 - FF1 274
Im Murnauer Moos Aquarell/Papier (27x34cm
10x13in) München 1999

YOSHIDA Hiroshi 1876-1950 [278]

$1 195 - €1 283 - £800 - FF8 417
**Group of Figures in a Boat Beside a Shore
before a Village** Watercolour/paper (21x49cm 8x19in)
London 2000

$633 - €611 - £397 - FF4 006
Osaka Castle Woodcut in colors (40x27cm 16x11in)
Oakland CA 1999

YOSHIDA Toshi 1911-1995 [42]

$190 - €224 - £132 - FF1 469
**Benkai
Bridge/Okaramon/Supperwagon/Umbrella** Print
in colors (14x17cm 9x6in) Beverly-Hills CA 2000

YOSHIFUJI Utagawa 1828-1887 [3]

$2 600 - €2 620 - £1 620 - FF17 186
Amerikazin (jin) yukyo (Americans strolling)
Print (37.5x25.5cm 14x10in) New-York 2000

YOSHIHIKO Ito 1867-1942 [4]

$1 600 - €1 876 - £1 141 - FF12 307
Temple Watercolour/paper (33x49.5cm 12x19in) New-
York 2000

YOSHIIKU Utagawa 1833-1904 [12]

$264 - €308 - £185 - FF2 022
Rue à Shin-Yoshiwara jour de fête Gravure bois
couleurs (36.5x24.5cm 14x9in) Warszawa 2000

YOSHIKAZU act.1850-1870 [11]

$1 255 - €1 477 - £900 - FF9 687
**Foreigners from the Five Countries having a
banquet** Print (14.5x75cm 5x29in) London 2001

YOSHIMITSU c.1868-1912 [5]

$11 206 - €13 097 - £8 000 - FF85 911
Archer Bronze (H84.5cm H33in) London 2001

$4 762 - €5 566 - £3 400 - FF36 512
Model of a Warrior Gilded bronze (H33cm H12in)
London 2001

YOSHITORA Utagawa c.1830-c.1880 [31]

$135 - €153 - £93 - FF1 006
Darstellung einer auf engawa stehenden Dame
Woodcut in colors (35.5x24.5cm 13x9in) Stuttgart 2001

YOSHITOSHI Mori 1898-1992 [21]

$425 - €459 - £293 - FF3 010
Keeping Out Woodcut in colors (42.5x54.5cm
16x21in) Bethesda MD 2001

YOSHITOSHI Tsukiota Kinzaburo 1839-1892 [205]

$14 195 - €15 238 - £9 500 - FF99 955
Ghost of O-Iwa Ink (117x32cm 46x12in) London
2000

$526 - €590 - £366 - FF3 869
**The Gardener's Daughter Okiyo meeting a
Foreigner** Print (36x24cm 14x9in) Amsterdam 2001

YOU QUA act.1845-1885 [4]

$165 000 - €181 796 - £110 071 - FF1 192 504
View of the Hongs at Canton Oil/canvas
(63x128cm 25x50in) Portsmouth NH 2000

YOUNAN Ramsès 1913-1966 [1]

$11 171 - €12 565 - £7 800 - FF82 422
Untitled Oil/canvas (72x80cm 28x31in) London 2001

YOUNG Alexander 1865-1923 [77]

$1 332 - €1 585 - £950 - FF10 397
French Loire, Harvesting Oil/canvas (61x41cm
24x16in) Bath 2000

$1 921 - €1 900 - £1 200 - FF12 461
On the Quay/Unloading the Catch Oil/canvas
(40.5x30.5cm 15x12in) Glasgow 1999

YOUNG Charles Morris 1869-1964 [29]

$6 500 - €6 453 - £4 062 - FF42 331
On Pickering Creek Oil/canvas (63.5x76cm 25x29in)
New-York 1999

$2 100 - €2 155 - £1 316 - FF14 136
Brodhead Creek Oil/canvas (20x25cm 8x10in)
Downington PA 2000

$200 - €225 - £138 - FF1 478
Farm Landscape Watercolour/paper (30x47cm
12x18in) Hatfield PA 2000

YOUNG Edward 1823-1882 [10]

$6 384 - €5 910 - £3 908 - FF38 770
Ertappt Öl/Leinwand (91x58.5cm 35x23in) Bern 1999

$807 - €872 - £558 - FF5 720
Landschaft bei Kössen Öl/Papier (42.7x31cm
16x12in) Wien 2001

YOUNG Florence Upson 1872-1974 [8]

$850 - €992 - £591 - FF6 505
Oriental Still Life Oil/canvas (60x50cm 24x20in)
Altadena CA 2000

YOUNG Harvey Otis 1840-1901 [32]

$3 750 - €3 569 - £2 345 - FF23 411
The Way Home Oil/canvas (63x58cm 25x23in) New-
York 1999

$2 600 - €2 227 - £1 563 - FF14 611
Indian Pueblo, New Mexico Oil/canvas (25x55cm
10x22in) Cleveland OH 1998

$2 500 - €2 652 - £1 695 - FF17 393
Mule Train in a Western Landscape
Gouache/board (91x68cm 36x27in) Pittsburgh PA 2001

YOUNG Henry, Reverend 1792-1861 [7]

$4 000 - €4 451 - £2 422 - FF22 637
Birth and Baptismal Certificate Watercolour
(27x18cm 11x7in) New-York 1999

Y

YOUNG John XIX [4]
🖋 $10 460 - €11 228 - **£7 000** - FF73 651
View of St Sampsons Church, Guernsey
Oil/panel (47.5x57cm 18x22in) London 2000

YOUNG John 1755-1825 [8]
🗓 $721 - €687 - **£440** - FF4 505
Thomas king as Puff in the Critic, after J.Zoffany Mezzotint (52x42cm 20x16in) Bury St. Edmunds, Suffolk 1999

YOUNG John Tobias 1790-? [3]
🖋 $11 224 - €13 349 - **£8 000** - FF87 561
View of Southampton with the River Itchen in the Foreground Oil/panel (63.5x87.5cm 25x34in) London 2000

YOUNG Mabel c.1890-1974 [14]
🖋 $4 029 - €4 514 - **£2 800** - FF29 607
The Rocky Valley, Co.Wicklow Oil/board (50x42cm 19x16in) London 2001
🖋 $1 301 - €1 397 - **£870** - FF9 161
Connemara, near Clifden Oil/canvas/board (30x38cm 11x14in) Dublin 2000

YOUNG Mahonri Mackintosh 1877-1957 [23]
🖋 $3 400 - €3 996 - **£2 357** - FF26 212
Indian Women with Ponies Charcoal (25x33cm 9x12in) Beverly-Hills CA 2000
🗓 $500 - €588 - **£346** - FF3 858
Walpi Etching (15x16.5cm 5x6in) Beverly-Hills CA 2000

YOUNG Stephen Scott 1957 [2]
🖋 $22 000 - €20 936 - **£13 761** - FF137 332
Little Miss Lucy Watercolour, gouache/paper (42x72.5cm 16x28in) New-York 1999

YOUNG van Oscar 1906 [2]
🖋 $2 400 - €2 689 - **£1 672** - FF17 641
Farm Scene Gouache (38x58cm 14x22in) Beverly-Hills CA 2001

YOUNG William XX [17]
🖋 $574 - €636 - **£389** - FF4 172
The Team Coming Over Pyrmont Bridge Watercolour/paper (26x36cm 10x14in) Sydney 2000

YOUNG William Blamire 1862-1935 [82]
🖋 $1 436 - €1 347 - **£887** - FF8 838
Windmill and Figures Watercolour/paper (16x22.5cm 6x8in) Melbourne 1999
🗓 $7 662 - €6 681 - **£4 633** - FF43 824
Blue Landscape Monotype (37x75cm 14x29in) Melbourne 1998

YOUNG William Weston 1776-1847 [3]
🖋 $1 166 - €1 073 - **£700** - FF7 040
A Jay Ink (45x36cm 17x14in) Glamorgan 1999

YOUNGBLOOD Nancy 1955 [5]
🖋 $8 000 - €7 930 - **£4 889** - FF52 015
Blackware lidded Jar Ceramic (H20cm H7in) New-York 1999

YOUNGHUSBAND Adele 1878-1969 [3]
🖋 $7 639 - €8 703 - **£5 279** - FF57 088
Singing Girls Oil/board (44.5x37cm 17x14in) Auckland 1999

YOUNGMAN John Mallows 1817-1899 [7]
🖋 $1 774 - €1 630 - **£1 100** - FF10 693
A Cattle Herder with a Thatched Cottage beyond Watercolour (57x46cm 22x18in) London 1999

YOUON Konstantin 1875-1958 [1]
🖋 $2 812 - €3 323 - **£1 993** - FF21 800
Markttag in verschneitem russischen Dorf Aquarell/Papier (36x54cm 14x21in) Hildrizhausen 2000

YRAN Knut XX [3]
🗓 $1 600 - €1 613 - **£1 000** - FF10 579
«Norway» Poster (99x62cm 38x24in) London 2000

YSERN Y ALIE Pere 1876-1946 [42]
🖋 $4 000 - €3 741 - **£2 418** - FF24 542
Draped Nude Oil/canvas (157.5x117cm 62x46in) New-York 1999
🖋 $3 510 - €3 904 - **£2 340** - FF25 610
Paisaje de Mallorca Oleo/lienzo (54x65.5cm 21x25in) Barcelona 2000
🖋 $704 - €661 - **£429** - FF4 334
Bailarina Oleo/papel (19x12cm 7x4in) Madrid 1999
🖋 $409 - €390 - **£247** - FF2 561
Figura femenina Gouache/papier (29x24cm 11x9in) Barcelona 1999

YSLAIRE (Bernard Hislaire) 1952 [23]
🖋 $714 - €686 - **£442** - FF4 500
Bidouille et Violette, pl.9: La Ville de tous les jours Encre Chine (40x30cm 15x11in) Paris 1999

YTHJALL Terje 1943 [7]
🖋 $2 755 - €3 058 - **£1 920** - FF20 057
«Den ensomme leken» Oil/canvas (85x50cm 33x19in) Oslo 2001

YTURRALDE Jose Maria 1942 [19]
🗓 $93 - €90 - **£58** - FF591
Efecto óptico Serigrafia (68x48cm 26x18in) Barcelona 1999

YU BEN Yee Bon 1905-1995 [32]
🖋 $30 500 - €25 611 - **£17 900** - FF168 000
Fishpond Banked with Mulberry Oil/board (62x75cm 24x29in) Taipei 1998

YU CH'ENG-YAO 1898-1993 [43]
🖋 $12 810 - €10 757 - **£7 518** - FF70 560
Landscape Ink/paper (56x136cm 22x53in) Taipei 1998

YU CHIAN Chia 1936-1991 [5]
🖋 $2 922 - €3 059 - **£1 835** - FF20 064
Seascape Oil/board (61x92cm 24x36in) Singapore 2000

YU FEI'AN 1888-1959 [53]
🖋 $10 296 - €9 764 - **£6 264** - FF64 048
Narcissus and Bees Ink (106.5x47cm 41x18in) Hong-Kong 1999

YU MING 1884-1935 [13]
🖋 $3 333 - €3 964 - **£2 295** - FF26 002
Lady Admiring Plum Blossoms Ink (108x50cm 42x19in) Hong-Kong 1999

YU PENG 1955 [11]
🖋 $5 508 - €4 552 - **£3 222** - FF29 862
Meditating in the Mountain Recluse Charcoal (194x130cm 76x51in) Taipei 1998

YU XIAOFU 1950 [3]
🖋 $22 304 - €23 750 - **£14 144** - FF155 788
Auction the old Piano, no.5 Oil/canvas (117.5x107.5cm 46x42in) Taipei 2000

YU YOUREN 1879-1964 [12]
🖋 $2 193 - €2 068 - **£1 360** - FF13 566
Calligraphy Couplet in Cao Shu Ink/paper (130x31cm 51x12in) Hong-Kong 1999

Y

ZACH Rupert 1927-1969 **[7]**
$581 - €665 - £404 - FF4 360
Herbstliche Birken vor dem Osser Tempera
(77x95cm 30x37in) Zwiesel 2000

ZACH Vilem 1946 **[26]**
$517 - €437 - £307 - FF2 864
Picket Pin, Sioux Pastel/paper (66x58cm 26x23in)
Calgary, Alberta 1998

ZACHARIE Philippe Ernest 1849-1915 **[15]**
$538 - €503 - £325 - FF3 300
Portrait d'Albert Lebourg, à l'âge de 48 ans Mine
plomb (15x14cm 5x5in) Paris 1999

ZACHMANN Max 1892-1917 **[12]**
$857 - €1 022 - £611 - FF6 707
Die Maurer Charcoal (20.8x36cm 8x14in) Berlin 2000

ZACHO Christian 1843-1913 **[295]**
$1 382 - €1 608 - £986 - FF10 546
Ved en skovsö Oil/canvas (54x45cm 21x17in)
Köbenhavn 2000
$474 - €471 - £296 - FF3 090
**Graessende köer under traeer ved sö med
udsigt til den anden bred** Oil/canvas (27x42.5cm
10x16in) Köbenhavn 2000

ZACHRISON Axel Gabriel 1884-1944 **[14]**
$1 215 - €1 469 - £848 - FF9 633
Utsikt över Vänern mot Kinnekulle Oil/canvas
(80x112cm 31x44in) Stockholm 2000

ZACK Léon 1892-1980 **[371]**
$4 776 - €4 608 - £3 000 - FF30 228
Geerbe Oil/canvas (161.5x96.5cm 63x37in) London
1999
$2 247 - €2 620 - £1 556 - FF17 185
**Komposition in Blau und Weiss auf schwarzem
Grund** Öl/Leinwand (92x73cm 36x28in) Bern 2000
$630 - €762 - £440 - FF5 000
Paysage Huile/panneau (20x38cm 7x14in) Paris 2000
$285 - €335 - £204 - FF2 200
Composition Aquarelle/papier (31.5x24.5cm 12x9in)
Paris 2001
$92 - €104 - £64 - FF681
Ohne Titel Aquatinta (13x13.5cm 5x5in) Bern 2001

ZADEMACK Siegfried 1952 **[12]**
$1 623 - €1 636 - £1 012 - FF10 732
Zwiegespräch Öl/Leinwand (20.5x23cm 8x9in)
Hildrizhausen 2000

ZADKINE Ossip 1890-1967 **[700]**
$18 960 - €18 294 - £11 988 - FF120 000
Trois hommes assis Huile/papier (63x42cm
24x16in) Paris 1999
$140 000 - €134 624 - £86 254 - FF883 078
Le couple Bronze (214.5x121x57cm 84x47x22in)
New-York 1999
$29 000 - €26 880 - £18 032 - FF176 322
Figurine drapée Bronze (H60.5cm H23in) Tel Aviv
1999
$3 698 - €3 659 - £2 306 - FF24 000
La famille Encre (55x41cm 21x16in) Paris 1999
$400 - €340 - £241 - FF2 229
Composition Etching (63.5x45.5cm 25x17in) Tel Aviv
1999

ZADORECKI M.J. XIX **[3]**
$4 635 - €4 573 - £2 856 - FF30 000
**Portrait de la cantatrice Adelina Patti (1843-
1919)** Huile/toile (100x73cm 39x28in) Paris 1999

ZADRAZIL Franz 1942 **[68]**
$2 547 - €2 180 - £1 533 - FF14 301
Gemischtwaren Josef Pachl Mixed media/paper
(80x80cm 31x31in) Wien 1998
$227 - €218 - £140 - FF1 430
Stadtbahnstation Kettenbrückengasse Radierung
(32x44cm 12x17in) Wien 1999

ZAGANELLI Francesco c.1470-1532 **[7]**
$24 705 - €23 498 - £15 000 - FF154 135
The Madonna and Child Oil/canvas (53.5x40.5cm
21x15in) London 1999

ZAGELMANN Johann 1720-1758 **[1]**
$43 095 - €48 184 - £30 000 - FF316 065
**Roses,Peonies, Carnations/Peonies, Roses,
Carnations and other Flowers** Oil/canvas
(93.5x68cm 36x26in) London 2001

ZAGO Erma 1880-1942 **[66]**
$4 750 - €4 924 - £2 850 - FF32 300
Festa in Piazza S.Marco Olio/tavola (45x60cm
17x23in) Milano 2000
$1 250 - €1 296 - £750 - FF8 500
Campiello Olio/tavola (25x40cm 9x15in) Vercelli 2000

ZAGO Luigi 1894-1952 **[16]**
$1 260 - €1 271 - £786 - FF8 334
Genova Oil/cardboard (49x60cm 19x23in) Amsterdam
2000

ZAHALKA Anne 1957 **[1]**
$1 165 - €1 307 - £815 - FF8 572
«The Cook from Resemblance Series» Print
(50x50.5cm 19x19in) Melbourne 2001

ZAHND Johann 1854-1934 **[33]**
$4 250 - €4 406 - £2 550 - FF28 900
Paesaggio romano con figure Olio/tela (50x60cm
19x23in) Venezia 2000
$708 - €620 - £428 - FF4 064
Kirchgang zur Weihnachtsmesse Öl/Karton
(20x15cm 7x5in) Zofingen 1998

ZÄHNDLER Johann Georg 1877-1954 **[3]**
$6 507 - €7 014 - £4 363 - FF46 007
Sennenstreifen Watercolour (12.5x415cm 4x163in)
Zürich 2000

ZÄHRINGER Karl Friedrich 1886-1923 **[13]**
$686 - €818 - £489 - FF5 366
Schwarzwälder Bauern Woodcut (58.5x46cm
23x18in) Königstein 2000

ZAHRTMANN Kristian 1843-1917 **[122]**
$2 618 - €2 569 - £1 623 - FF16 854
Interiör Oil/canvas (66x81cm 25x31in) Stockholm
1999
$1 852 - €1 682 - £1 157 - FF11 035
**Portraet af frk. Kyhn, maleren Vilhelm Kyhns
datter** Oil/canvas (25x20.5cm 9x8in) Köbenhavn 1999
$346 - €402 - £243 - FF2 639
«Leonora Christine i Blaataarn» Charcoal/paper
(46x50cm 18x19in) Köbenhavn 2001

ZAINI 1926-1987 **[6]**
$1 753 - €1 835 - £1 101 - FF12 038
Boats Oil/canvas (50x61cm 19x24in) Singapore 2000

ZAIRIS Emmanuel 1876-1948 **[4]**
$2 452 - €2 181 - £1 500 - FF14 306
Figure on the Beach Oil/canvas (41x26.5cm
16x10in) London 1999

Z

ZAIS Giuseppe 1709-1784 **[63]**

- $68 187 - €58 905 - **£34 093** - FF386 393
  Grande paesaggio Olio/tela (94x129.5cm 37x50in)
  Milano 1999
- $42 570 - €45 037 - **£27 000** - FF295 425
  **Italianate Landscape with Fishermen and
  Travellers** Oil/canvas (54.5x72.5cm 21x28in) London
  2000
- $42 500 - €44 058 - **£25 500** - FF289 000
  **Due contadini presso un vaso
  antico/Contadine/Rovine classiche** Olio/tela
  (36x26.5cm 14x10in) Roma 1999
- $2 346 - €2 592 - **£1 626** - FF17 000
  Paysage animé Lavis (30x46cm 11x18in) Pont-
  Audemer 2001

ZAJICEK Karl Joseph Richard 1879-? **[2]**

- $1 914 - €1 892 - **£1 171** - FF12 409
  **Markt auf einem Platz in Wien mit
  Reiterstandbild** Aquarell/Papier (19x25cm 7x9in)
  Kempten 2000

ZAJICEK Karl Wenzel 1860-1923 **[65]**

- $1 447 - €1 599 - **£1 003** - FF10 487
  Herbst im Wienerwald Aquarell/Papier (16x11cm
  6x4in) Wien 2001

ZAK Eugène, Eugeniusz 1884-1926 **[56]**

- $120 000 - €134 012 - **£76 848** - FF879 060
  Island Landscape with Family Oil/canvas
  (161x296cm 63x116in) Tel Aviv 2000
- $60 000 - €67 733 - **£41 790** - FF444 300
  Island Landscape Oil/canvas (65x81cm 25x31in) Tel
  Aviv 2001
- $10 500 - €11 656 - **£7 319** - FF76 458
  Portrait Oil/canvas/board (33x27cm 12x10in) Tel Aviv
  2001
- $2 500 - €2 775 - **£1 743** - FF18 206
  The Young Couple/Study of Mother with Child
  Pencil/paper (21x18cm 8x7in) Tel Aviv 2001
- $1 205 - €1 183 - **£747** - FF1 761
  Jeune femme Vernis mou (11.2x11.2cm 4x4in)
  Warszawa 1999

ZAKANITCH Robert 1935 **[31]**

- $450 - €423 - **£278** - FF2 773
  Hearts of Swan Lithograph (69x57cm 27x22in) New-
  York 1999

ZAKRZEWSKI Wlodzimierz 1916-1992 **[13]**

- $1 428 - €1 387 - **£882** - FF9 096
  Rue à Varsovie Oil/canvas (46x62cm 18x24in)
  Warszawa 1999

ZALCE Alfredo 1908 **[51]**

- $4 577 - €3 962 - **£2 760** - FF25 990
  Bodegón con pez globo y girasol Oleo/lienzo
  (60x60cm 23x23in) México 1998
- $4 600 - €5 255 - **£3 238** - FF34 468
  Reclining Figure Tempera/paper (67x89cm 26x35in)
  Chicago IL 2001
- $2 000 - €1 889 - **£1 245** - FF12 392
  Estampes de Yucatan Lithograph (38.5x45cm
  15x17in) San-Francisco CA 1999

ZALESKI Marcin 1796-1877 **[5]**

- $32 805 - €38 273 - **£22 830** - FF251 055
  L'intérieur de l'église à Vilnus Huile/toile
  (75x100cm 29x39in) Warszawa 2000

ZAMACOIS Y ZABALA Eduardo 1842-1871 **[41]**

- $4 340 - €4 205 - **£2 660** - FF27 580
  La broma Oleo/lienzo (55x70cm 21x27in) Madrid
  1999

- $3 000 - €3 478 - **£2 125** - FF22 815
  The Workman Oil/canvas (40.5x27cm 15x10in) New-
  York 2000

ZAMAN III Mohammed 1749-1794 **[1]**

- $2 855 - €2 998 - **£1 800** - FF19 664
  **Head and Shoulders, Portrait of a Persian
  Nobleman** Drawing (19.5x12.5cm 7x4in) London
  2000

ZAMAZAL Jaroslav 1909-1983 **[45]**

- $520 - €492 - **£324** - FF3 227
  Portrait of a Woman Oil/board (57.5x49.5cm
  22x19in) Praha 2000
- $268 - €249 - **£167** - FF1 636
  Girl's Nude Pastel/paper (50x35cm 19x13in) Praha
  1999

ZAMMARETTI Jean-Louis XX **[9]**

- $512 - €610 - **£366** - FF4 000
  Panthère féline Bronze (12.5x21.5cm 4x8in) Paris
  2000

ZAMORA de José 1889-1971 **[75]**

- $150 - €152 - **£93** - FF1 000
  La fontaine espagnole Aquarelle (42x32cm
  16x12in) Paris 2000

ZAMPIERI IL DOMENICHINO Domenico 1581-1641
[11]

- $3 000 000 - €3 034 909 - **£1 831 800** -
  FF19 907 700
  The Rebuke of Adam and Eve Oil/canvas
  (122x172cm 48x67in) New-York 2000
- $13 000 - €11 403 - **£7 893** - FF74 799
  **Boy Playing a Flute in an Extensive Wooded
  Landscape** Ink (23x13cm 9x5in) New-York 2000

ZAMPIGHI Eugenio 1859-1944 **[205]**

- $19 250 - €19 398 - **£12 000** - FF127 243
  The Cherry treat Oil/canvas (56.5x76cm 22x29in)
  London 2000
- $3 500 - €3 780 - **£2 419** - FF24 796
  The Watch Thief Oil/canvas (40x24cm 15x9in) New-
  York 2001
- $4 820 - €3 960 - **£2 800** - FF25 973
  Music for the Baby/Playing with the Baby
  Watercolour (52.5x35.5cm 20x13in) London 1998

ZANCARANO Tono 1906-1985 **[33]**

- $275 - €285 - **£165** - FF1 870
  Nudi China/carta (35x44cm 13x17in) Vercelli 2001
- $100 - €104 - **£60** - FF960
  Antiche cortigiane veneziane Acquaforte
  (24x32.5cm 9x12in) Prato 1999

ZANCHI Antonio 1631-1722 **[17]**

- $41 782 - €41 443 - **£26 000** - FF271 850
  Agrippina saved from the Shipwreck Oil/canvas
  (159x159cm 62x62in) London 1999
- $8 835 - €9 907 - **£6 000** - FF64 984
  Moses receiving the Ten Commandments
  Oil/canvas (67.5x86.5cm 26x34in) London 2000
- $18 000 - €18 209 - **£10 990** - FF119 446
  Moses striking the Rocks Ink (55.5x38cm 21x14in)
  New-York 2000

ZANDER Detlef Hartwig 1763-1837 **[14]**

- $287 - €325 - **£202** - FF2 130
  «Die kleinen indianischen Eisvögel» Ink
  (21x13.5cm 8x5in) Bern 2001

ZANDLEVEN Jan Adam 1868-1923 **[133]**
- **$2 359** - €2 042 - **£1 432** - FF13 394
  Winter Landscape Oil/canvas/board (37x49.5cm 14x19in) Amsterdam 1999
- **$1 430** - €1 328 - **£873** - FF8 713
  Beech Trees Oil/board (41x33cm 16x12in) Amsterdam 1998

ZANDOMENEGHI Federico 1841-1917 **[92]**
- **$80 000** - €82 932 - **£48 000** - FF544 000
  La spesa Olio/tela (105x75cm 41x29in) Roma 2000
- **$47 200** - €61 163 - **£35 400** - FF401 200
  La lecture au lit Olio/tela (24x41cm 9x16in) Milano 2001
- **$7 785** - €7 622 - **£4 790** - FF50 000
  Femme assise dans l'herbe Pastel/papier (17x25.5cm 6x10in) Paris 1999

ZANE Emanuele 1610-1690 **[1]**
- **$39 270** - €40 709 - **£23 562** - FF267 036
  San Govdelas Olio/tela/tavola (31x24.5cm 12x9in) Venezia 2001

ZANETTI Antonio Maria II 1706-1778 **[8]**
- **$800** - €887 - **£532** - FF5 821
  Madonna and Child, After Parmigianino Woodcut (10x6.5cm 3x2in) New-York 2000

ZANETTI Girolamo Antonio Ma. 1680-1757 **[20]**
- **$3 586** - €3 849 - **£2 400** - FF25 251
  Caricature of a Man eating a boiled Egg with another standing behind Ink (21x18cm 8x7in) London 2000
- **$896** - €962 - **£600** - FF6 313
  St.Peter/Saint James Minor Woodcut (17x10cm 6x3in) London 2000

ZANETTI ZILLA Vittore 1864-1946 **[30]**
- **$2 041** - €2 287 - **£1 420** - FF15 000
  Canal à Venise Huile/toile (46x61cm 18x24in) Aubagne 2001
- **$400** - €467 - **£282** - FF3 062
  St.Mark's Square Watercolour/paper (23x18cm 9x7in) Cedar-Falls IA 2000

ZANGAKI XIX **[5]**
- **$1 680** - €1 982 - **£1 181** - FF13 000
  Égypte Tirage albuminé (22x28cm 8x11in) Paris 2000

ZANGRANDO Giovanni 1869-1941 **[52]**
- **$1 680** - €1 451 - **£1 120** - FF9 520
  Figura femminile Olio/tela (50x62cm 19x24in) Milano 1998
- **$1 100** - €1 140 - **£660** - FF7 480
  Sacro Timavo Olio/cartone (33x46cm 12x18in) Trieste 2001
- **$1 280** - €1 659 - **£960** - FF10 880
  Nudo di ragazzo Carboncino/carta (59x42cm 23x16in) Roma 2001

ZANGS Herbert 1924 **[227]**
- **$881** - €1 022 - **£608** - FF6 707
  Expansion, pastose Masse Mixed media/panel (62x43.5cm 24x17in) Köln 2000
- **$1 815** - €1 534 - **£1 082** - FF10 060
  Papphülsen - Verweissung Mixed media/panel (40x28cm 15x11in) Düsseldorf 1998
- **$519** - €562 - **£356** - FF3 689
  Ohne Titel Collage (27x19cm 10x7in) Stuttgart 2001

ZANICHELLI Bruno 1963-1990 **[4]**
- **$3 250** - €3 369 - **£1 950** - FF22 100
  Ore liete Acrilico/tela (50x60cm 19x23in) Milano 2000

ZANIMBERTI Filippo 1585-1636 **[1]**
- **$9 600** - €8 293 - **£6 400** - FF54 400
  San Giacomo Olio/tela (116x86.5cm 45x34in) Prato 1998

ZANIN Francesco XIX **[20]**
- **$8 184** - €7 500 - **£5 000** - FF49 195
  Gondolas on a Venetian Canal with Numerous Figures Oil/canvas (43x64.5cm 16x25in) London 1999
- **$3 272** - €3 392 - **£1 963** - FF22 253
  Il Cortile del Palazzo Ducale di Venezia con l'Aroc Foscari Olio/tela (42.5x34cm 16x13in) Venezia 1999

ZANKOVSKII Il'ia Nikolaevich 1832-1919 **[7]**
- **$9 795** - €11 657 - **£7 000** - FF76 462
  Travellers in a Caucasian Mountain Pass Oil/board (70.5x96.5cm 27x37in) London 2000
- **$4 233** - €4 670 - **£2 800** - FF30 636
  Figures in a Mountain Landscape Oil/board (23x30cm 9x11in) London 2000

ZANOBI DI BENEDETTO STROZZI 1412-1468 **[1]**
- **$230 000** - €216 389 - **£143 520** - FF1 419 422
  The Madonna and Child enthroned Tempera (83x40.5cm 32x15in) New-York 1999

ZANON Pascal J. 1943 **[3]**
- **$667** - €610 - **£408** - FF4 000
  Harry Dickson, Le Royaume introuvable, pl.16 Encre/papier (52x37cm 20x14in) Paris 1999

ZANOTTI Romano 1934 **[80]**
- **$293** - €335 - **£206** - FF2 200
  Ciseaux Acrylique/toile (80x80cm 31x31in) Paris 2001
- **$173** - €198 - **£122** - FF1 300
  Aborigène Dessin (66x66cm 25x25in) Paris 2001

ZANTEN van Pieter 1746-1813 **[1]**
- **$7 892** - €7 260 - **£4 887** - FF47 625
  Portrait Guilliaem Alvarez/Portrait Cornelia Alvarez née Smits Oil/canvas (84.5x69.5cm 33x27in) Amsterdam 1999

ZANUTTO Renzo 1909-1979 **[12]**
- **$1 500** - €1 555 - **£900** - FF10 200
  Nevicata Olio/tela (38.5x55cm 15x21in) Venezia 2000

ZAO WOU-KI 1921 **[929]**
- **$177 480** - €201 510 - **£124 700** - FF1 321 820
  «21.5. 76» Oil/canvas (130x193cm 51x75in) Taipei 2001
- **$54 400** - €60 980 - **£36 920** - FF400 000
  «4.7.1989» Huile/toile (95x105cm 37x41in) Paris 2000
- **$5 808** - €6 098 - **£3 660** - FF40 000
  Composition Technique mixte (23.5x23.5cm 9x9in) Paris 2000
- **$7 601** - €8 385 - **£5 148** - FF55 000
  Composition Encres couleurs/papier (31.5x49.5cm 12x19in) Paris 2000
- **$519** - €619 - **£370** - FF4 059
  Ohne Titel Farblithographie (48.3x43cm 19x16in) Hamburg 2000

ZAPATA Miguel 1940 **[4]**
- **$4 000** - €4 647 - **£2 811** - FF30 484
  Estudio para el monumento de Alfonso VIII Bronze (56x38x24cm 22x14x9in) New-York 2001

ZAPATA Pedro León 1929 **[30]**
- **$145** - €169 - **£103** - FF1 109
  Sin título Tinta china/papel (26.5x29.5cm 10x11in) Caracas ($) 2000

Z

ZAPELLONI Andrea 1877-1961 [8]
- $900 – €777 – £450 – FF5 100
  Il vecchio castagno Olio/tela (46x30.5cm 18x12in) Vercelli 1999

ZAPF Carl XX [1]
- $4 220 – €4 056 – £2 600 – FF26 606
  Grand Duchess Maria Nicholaevna with her youngest Children, Evgenia Watercolour (30.5x26cm 12x10in) London 1999

ZAPLETAL A. XX [1]
- $1 489 – €1 391 – £900 – FF9 123
  «I.Internationale Flugausstellung» Poster (89x58cm 35x22in) London 1999

ZARCO FORTES Antonio 1930 [34]
- $104 – €120 – £72 – FF788
  Crónicas de siempre X Grabado (24.5x34cm 9x13in) Madrid 2000

ZARDO Alberto 1876-1959 [32]
- $1 800 – €1 866 – £1 080 – FF12 240
  Nella macchia maremmana Olio/tela (80x105cm 31x41in) Torino 1999
- $950 – €985 – £570 – FF6 460
  Donoratico, Livorno Olio/tavola (27x36cm 10x14in) Firenze 2001

ZAREMBSKI Marian 1860-1918 [4]
- $4 693 – €4 346 – £2 912 – FF28 508
  Gebet auf dem Acker Öl/Leinwand (82x138cm 32x54in) Stuttgart 1999

ZARFIN Schraga 1900-1975 [10]
- $2 483 – €2 897 – £1 742 – FF19 000
  A la campagne Huile/toile (46x33cm 18x12in) Paris 2001

ZARIÑENA Juan c.1545-1619/34 [1]
- $3 840 – €3 604 – £2 400 – FF23 640
  Santo Domingo de Guzman Oleo/tabla (51x16.5cm 20x6in) Madrid 1999

ZARING Louise Eleanor 1875-1972 [2]
- $4 800 – €5 152 – £3 212 – FF33 796
  Woman Seated by the Docks Oil/canvas (76x61cm 29x24in) New-York 2000

ZARINS Indulis 1929 [4]
- $7 500 – €8 051 – £5 019 – FF52 810
  Street Scene Oil/board (61.5x51.5cm 24x20in) New-York 2000

ZARITSKY Yosef 1891-1985 [170]
- $45 000 – €50 254 – £28 818 – FF329 647
  Variation on one Concept V Oil/canvas (150x150cm 59x59in) Tel Aviv 2000
- $36 000 – €29 570 – £20 908 – FF193.964
  Composition Oil/canvas (54x65cm 21x25in) Tel Aviv 1998
- $8 500 – €8 297 – £5 383 – FF54 427
  Tel Aviv, View from the Roof Watercolour/paper (47x67cm 18x26in) Tel Aviv 1994

ZARRAGA DE ARGUELLES Angel 1886-1946 [132]
- $260 000 – €279 082 – £173 992 – FF1 830 660
  La novia Oil/canvas (220x180cm 86x70in) New-York 2000
- $60 000 – €58 379 – £36 930 – FF382 938
  Naturaleza muerte Oil/canvas (50x35cm 19x13in) New-York 1999
- $28 000 – €26.962 – £17 427 – FF176 856
  Paisaje Oil/canvas (33x41cm 12x16in) New-York 1999

- $1 513 – €1 524 – £943 – FF10 000
  Le Christ et Sainte-Véronique Crayon/papier (35x35cm 13x13in) Paris 2000
- $849 – €985 – £586 – FF6 463
  Profond aujourd'hui de Blaise Cendrars Lithographie couleurs (18.5x18cm 7x7in) Genève 2000

ZARUBA Jerzy 1891-1971 [3]
- $4 530 – €4 851 – £3 083 – FF31 820
  Café de Varsovie Huile/toile (85.5x65.5cm 33x25in) Warszawa 2001

ZARUBIN Viktor Ivanovich 1866-1928 [28]
- $3 400 – €3 791 – £2 286 – FF24 869
  Outskirts of the Forest Oil/wood (44.5x37.5cm 17x14in) Kiev.2000
- $1 000 – €1 069 – £679 – FF7 009
  In the North of France, Breton Mofit Oil/cardboard (10.5x15.5cm 4x6in) Kiev 2001

ZASCHE Theodor 1862-1922 [26]
- $219 – €203 – £135 – FF1 334
  «8. Kriegsanleihe» Poster (62x95cm 24x37in) Wien 1999

ZASINGER Matthäus c.1477-? [8]
- $1 115 – €1 329 – £795 – FF8 720
  Das Martyrium der Heilige Katharina Radierung (31.4x25.9cm 12x10in) Berlin 2000

ZATTA Antonio 1757-1797 [8]
- $329 – €314 – £200 – FF2 061
  Japan Engraving (31.5x41cm 12x16in) London 1999

ZATZKA Hans 1859-1945 [168]
- $119 544 – €128 321 – £80 000 – FF841 728
  The Harem Dancer Oil/canvas (158x93cm 62x36in) London 2000
- $9 723 – €9 062 – £6 000 – FF59 440
  The Tambourine Player Oil/canvas (58.5x37cm 23x14in) London 1999
- $792 – €907 – £552 – FF5 952
  Cseresznyecsokor Oil/board (33.5x24.5cm 13x9in) Budapest 2000

ZAUGG Hans 1894-1986 [28]
- $325 – €354 – £214 – FF2 321
  Iris Öl/Karton (45x32.5cm 17x12in) Bern 2000

ZAUGG Rémy 1943 [3]
- $3 003 – €3 354 – £2 035 – FF22 000
  Un vide, un lieu Sérigraphie/toile (65x65cm 25x25in) Paris 2000

ZAWADO (Jean Zawadowski) 1891-1982 [28]
- $5 411 – €4 997 – £3 370 – FF32 778
  Path in Orcel Oil/canvas (54x73cm 21x28in) Warszawa 1999
- $2 031 – €2 134 – £1 342 – FF14 000
  Fleurs Huile/toile (41x33cm 16x12in) Paris 2000

ZAWADZKI Stanislaw 1878-1960 [4]
- $1 420 – €1 417 – £886 – FF9 296
  Jeune femme au foulard en fleurs Watercolour (37.5x31.5cm 14x12in) Warszawa 1999

ZAYYAT Elias 1935 [1]
- $4 583 – €5 155 – £3 200 – FF33 814
  Maaloula Oil/board (35x25cm 13x9in) London 2001

ZBINDEN Ellis 1921 [9]
- $497 – €434 – £301 – FF2 847
  Barcelone, le port Aquarelle/papier (33x47cm 12x18in) Genève 1998

Z

ZBINDEN Emil 1908-1991 **[498]**
- $311 - €361 - **£218** - FF2 369
  Personnages Aquarelle/papier (32.5x46cm 12x18in) Genève 2000
- $154 - €149 - **£95** - FF975
  November Gravure bois (18x24cm 7x9in) Bern 1999

ZECCHIN Antonio 1780-? **[3]**
- $216 - €205 - **£135** - FF1 344
  Scracity in India Copper engraving in colors (37.5x30cm 14x11in) Praha 2000

ZECH Sati 1958 **[3]**
- $1 778 - €1 646 - **£1 088** - FF10 799
  Zartes Paar Indian ink (151x92cm 59x36in) München 1999

ZECHYR Othmar 1938-1997 **[41]**
- $1 702 - €1 599 - **£1 051** - FF10 487
  Explosions-Monument Ink (33.5x36cm 13x14in) Wien 1999
- $336 - €327 - **£207** - FF2 145
  Ohne Titel Farbradierung (35x25cm 13x9in) Linz 1999

ZEE van der James 1885-1983 **[35]**
- $1 200 - €1 121 - **£725** - FF7 352
  Mother Beaton with Chocolates in her Lap and on Mother's Day Vintage gelatin silver print (20x25cm 8x10in) New-York 1999

ZEE van der Jan 1898-1988 **[25]**
- $7 812 - €9 076 - **£5 494** - FF59 532
  Eastharbour of Groningen Oil/canvas (59.5x80cm 23x31in) Amsterdam 2001
- $2 734 - €3 176 - **£1 921** - FF20 836
  Landschap Gouache/paper (55x73cm 21x28in) Amsterdam 2001
- $215 - €190 - **£129** - FF1 248
  New Years Wish Woodcut in colors (24x17.5cm 9x6in) Amsterdam 1998

ZEEMAN Regnier / Remigius c.1623-1667 **[73]**
- $29 886 - €32 080 - **£20 000** - FF210 432
  Ferry and Shipping in a Calm Off a Coastline Oil/canvas (70.5x94cm 27x37in) London 2000
- $600 - €672 - **£418** - FF4 405
  Two large Ships Etching (20x30cm 7x11in) New-York 2001

ZEGRAY Lucienne Boucher XX **[28]**
- $476 - €471 - **£297** - FF3 090
  Spring in the Air Pastel/paper (40x50.5cm 15x19in) Calgary, Alberta 1999

ZEHME Werner 1859-? **[6]**
- $1 500 - €1 637 - **£1 018** - FF10 741
  At the Opera Watercolour, gouache (47x35.5cm 18x13in) New-York 2000

ZEID Fahr-el-Nissa 1901-1991 **[25]**
- $21 484 - €24 164 - **£15 000** - FF158 505
  The Fight of the Moon and the Astronaut Oil/canvas (210x535cm 82x210in) London 2001
- $4 296 - €4 833 - **£3 000** - FF31 701
  Dalida Oil/canvas (99x80cm 38x31in) London 2001
- $4 299 - €4 573 - **£2 718** - FF30 000
  Bateaux Huile/toile (24x32.5cm 9x12in) Paris 2000
- $2 340 000 - €2 655 662 - **£1 560 000** - FF17 420 000
  Abstrait Technique mixte/papier (59x48cm 23x18in) Istanbul 2001

ZEILLER Franz Anton 1716-1793 **[5]**
- $7 680 - €8 721 - **£5 256** - FF57 204
  Die Heiligen Herkulanus und Taurinus Öl/Leinwand (49x69cm 19x27in) Wien 2000

ZEILLER Otto 1913 **[9]**
- $247 - €291 - **£177** - FF1 906
  Rote und gelbe Rosen sowie Vergissmeinicht Gouache/paper (25x19cm 9x7in) Wien 2001

ZEISING Walter Ernst 1876-1933 **[35]**
- $107 - €102 - **£66** - FF670
  Markt an der Frauenkirche Etching, aquatint (26x15.4cm 10x6in) Berlin 1999

ZEITBLOM Bartholomeus 1455/60-1518/22 **[1]**
- $2 659 - €2 303 - **£1 604** - FF15 105
  Hl. Familie Oil/panel (31x26cm 12x10in) München 1998

ZEITLINA Gregorii Jsrailjew. 1911-? **[32]**
- $530 - €496 - **£326** - FF3 252
  Fille en bleu Huile/toile (70x45cm 27x17in) Bruxelles 1999

ZEITTER Johann Christ., John 1820-1872 **[5]**
- $4 518 - €4 339 - **£2 800** - FF28 461
  Crossing of a River Oil/panel (81x132cm 31x51in) London 1999

ZELEK Bronislav XX **[2]**
- $2 400 - €2 658 - **£1 627** - FF17 434
  «The Birds» Poster (58x83cm 23x33in) New-York 2000

ZELENINE Édouard 1938 **[10]**
- $3 918 - €4 663 - **£2 800** - FF30 585
  Apples, Butterflies and Houses Mixed media/paper (57.5x47.5cm 22x18in) London 2000

ZELEZNY Franz 1866-1932 **[36]**
- $812 - €793 - **£500** - FF5 199
  Tête de jeune fille Sculpture, wood (H45.5cm H17in) Montréal 1999

ZELGER Arthur 1914 **[7]**
- $273 - €248 - **£170** - FF1 624
  «Innsbruck'76» Poster (82x58cm 32x22in) London 1999

ZELGER Jakob Joseph 1812-1885 **[48]**
- $2 264 - €2 627 - **£1 563** - FF17 231
  Bei der Teufelsbrücke, Gotthard Öl/Leinwand (57x44cm 22x17in) Luzern 2000

ZELLENBERG von Franz Zeller 1805-1876 **[11]**
- $8 021 - €9 447 - **£5 642** - FF61 971
  Kaiser Franz Joseph I. und Kaiserin Elisabeth bei einem Ausritt Öl/Leinwand (79x107cm 31x42in) Wien 2000

ZELLER Hans Arnold 1897-1983 **[47]**
- $11 631 - €11 186 - **£7 165** - FF73 373
  Brülisau mit Blick auf den Hohen Kasten und den Kamor Huile/panneau (82x65cm 32x25in) St. Gallen 1999
- $4 245 - €4 925 - **£2 931** - FF32 308
  Vorsommertag, Blick auf den Säntis und Altmann Öl/Karton (33x33cm 12x12in) St. Gallen 2000

ZELLER Johann Baptist 1877-1959 **[8]**
- $11 746 - €13 236 - **£8 134** - FF86 822
  Alpfahrt vor Landschaft mit Haus Oil/board (32x52cm 12x20in) Zürich 2000

Z

ZELLER Johann Conrad 1807-1856 **[8]**
$3 628 - €4 269 - **£2 601** - FF28 000
Vue de Venise Huile/toile (54x81cm 21x31in) Paris 2001

ZELLER Magnus Herbert 1888-1968 **[100]**
$412 - €409 - **£257** - FF2 683
Herbstliches Waldstück Aquarell/Papier (39x29.9cm 15x11in) Hamburg 1999
$119 - €128 - **£79** - FF838
Das Käuzchen am Fenster Radierung (12.8x8.8cm 5x3in) Berlin 2000

ZELMA Georgi 1906-1984 **[22]**
$2 400 - €2 241 - **£1 453** - FF14 699
Sports Parade on Red Square, Moscow Gelatin silver print (39.5x26cm 15x10in) New-York 1999

ZELOTTI Giovanni Battista 1526-1578 **[3]**
$6 014 - €5 091 - **£3 600** - FF33 395
Cloelia across the Tiber Oil/canvas (42x33cm 16x12in) London 1998

ZELTER Georges 1938 **[40]**
$455 - €518 - **£321** - FF3 400
«St Gervais, Paris» Huile/toile (54x65cm 21x25in) Provins 2001

ZENAKEN 1954 **[49]**
$471 - €457 - **£291** - FF3 000
Composition abstraite Technique mixte/toile (49x49cm 19x19in) Paris 1999

ZENDEL Gabriel 1906-1980 **[67]**
$406 - €457 - **£279** - FF3 000
Barques et voiliers à la sortie du port Huile/toile (54x65cm 21x25in) La Varenne-Saint-Hilaire 2000

ZENDER Rudolf 1901-1988 **[136]**
$905 - €1 051 - **£625** - FF6 892
Stilleben mit Iris Öl/Leinwand (81x65cm 31x25in) Zürich 2000
$563 - €661 - **£397** - FF4 339
Die offene Bistrotüre Oil/panel (41x33cm 16x12in) St. Gallen 2000

ZENETZIS Vasilis 1935 **[16]**
$1 461 - €1 677 - **£1 000** - FF11 002
The Acropolis Oil/canvas (50x70cm 19x27in) London 2000
$997 - €1 159 - **£700** - FF7 605
View of the Acropolis Oil/canvas (38.5x28.5cm 15x11in) Billingshurst, West-Sussex 2001

ZENG XI 1861-1930 **[8]**
$3 205 - €3 612 - **£2 240** - FF23 692
Calligraphy Couplet in Li Shu Ink/paper (145.5x38cm 57x14in) Hong-Kong 2001

ZENG YANDONG XIX **[1]**
$4 386 - €4 116 - **£2 709** - FF26 999
Chinese Opera Figures Ink (28x20.5cm 11x8in) Hong-Kong 1999

ZENIL Nahum B. 1947 **[9]**
$27 000 - €23 543 - **£16 324** - FF154 431
Ciclo Acrylic/canvas (120x90cm 47x35in) New-York 1998
$11 000 - €11 807 - **£7 361** - FF77 451
Siameses a fuerza Ink (69x101cm 27x39in) New-York 2000

ZENISEK Franz 1849-1916 **[18]**
$30 345 - €28 701 - **£18 900** - FF188 265
Anihilation of the Adamites Oil/canvas (265x485cm 104x190in) Praha 2001

$4 624 - €4 373 - **£2 880** - FF28 688
Portrait of Cardinal Schwarzenberg Oil/panel (33x24.5cm 12x9in) Praha 1999

ZENK Joseph 1904 **[2]**
$6 500 - €6 156 - **£3 952** - FF40 378
Symbols Oil/canvas (61x96.5cm 24x37in) New-York 1999

ZENKER Flora 1876-? **[1]**
$4 503 - €4 538 - **£2 807** - FF29 766
The Harvest Oil/canvas (114x81cm 44x31in) Amsterdam 2000

ZENNARO Felice 1833-1926 **[6]**
$22 000 - €28 508 - **£16 500** - FF187 000
Lo spazzacamino Olio/tela (115x155cm 45x61in) Milano 2001

ZENO Jorge 1956 **[20]**
$50 000 - €58 871 - **£35 135** - FF386 170
Los sombreros perdidos (Carnaval de Venecia) Oil/canvas (171.5x139.5cm 67x54in) New-York 2000

ZENOBEL P. XX **[1]**
$2 393 - €2 288 - **£1 500** - FF15 007
«Le nouveau train bleu, vers la Côte d'Azur» Poster (100x65cm 39x25in) London 1999

ZENONE Domenico Zenoi XVI **[5]**
$5 575 - €6 647 - **£3 975** - FF43 600
Franz I.von Frankreich vertreibt die Personifizierungen der Laster Kupferstich (30x40.5cm 11x15in) Berlin 2000

ZENS Herwig 1943 **[33]**
$1 135 - €1 090 - **£712** - FF7 150
Ohne Titel Acrylic (60x60cm 23x23in) Wien 1999

ZEPEDA Marco Antonio 1938 **[7]**
$3 312 - €3 895 - **£2 376** - FF25 551
Pastando en la peña de Bernal Oleo/lienzo (50x70cm 19x27in) México 2001

ZEPPEL-SPERL Robert 1944 **[117]**
$1 236 - €1 453 - **£858** - FF9 534
Europa Acryl (80x60cm 31x23in) Wien 2000
$439 - €436 - **£274** - FF2 860
Ohne Titel, aus dem Zyklus «Max Ernst» Mischtechnik/Papier (58x39cm 22x15in) Wien 1999

ZERBE Karl 1903-1972 **[25]**
$800 - €896 - **£557** - FF5 879
Still Life with burning Candles Mixed media (73x93cm 29x37in) Watertown MA 2001
$578 - €665 - **£408** - FF4 360
Spanisches Weingut mit Zisternen Aquarell, Gouache/Papier (46x62cm 18x24in) Hamburg 2001

ZERILLI Francesco 1793-1837 **[28]**
$44 600 - €52 462 - **£32 320** - FF344 128
«Palermo, presa da Bocca-di-Falco»/«Veduta della Marina di Palermo» Gouache/paper (55x93cm 21x36in) Zofingen 2001

ZERMATI Jules XIX **[26]**
$1 500 - €1 434 - **£913** - FF9 408
The Flirtation Oil/canvas (44.5x57cm 17x22in) Boston MA 1999

ZERO Hans Schleger 1899-1976 **[10]**
$1 900 - €2 119 - **£1 239** - FF13 898
«These Men Use Shell, Journalists» Poster (76x113cm 30x44in) New-York 2000

ZERRITSCH Fritz, Jnr. 1888-1985 **[48]**

⮞ $648 - €654 - £405 - FF4 290
Neumarkt in Kärnten Öl/Leinwand (48x63cm 18x24in) Wien 2001

⮞ $395 - €363 - £244 - FF2 383
Aus Krems Öl/Leinwand (27.5x31.5cm 10x12in) Wien 1999

ZESHIN Shibata 1807-1891 **[34]**

⮞ $3 000 - €3 315 - £2 080 - FF21 746
Crow Painting (51x26.5cm 20x10in) New-York 2001

✎ $2 200 - €2 580 - £1 569 - FF16 923
Harunobe (Spring Field) Ink (20.5x17cm 8x6in) New-York 2000

▥ $128 - €123 - £79 - FF804
Fischer mit Kind und zwei Booten Woodcut in colors (24x25cm 9x9in) Kempten 1999

ZESSOS Alessandro 1848-1914 **[2]**

⮞ $2 000 - €2 592 - £1 500 - FF17 000
Aratura Olio/tavola (34x47cm 13x18in) Milano 2001

ZETSCHE Eduard 1844-1927 **[104]**

⮞ $2 347 - €2 744 - £1 648 - FF18 000
La lavandière Huile/panneau (22x33cm 8x12in) Paris 2000

✎ $1 157 - €1 308 - £781 - FF8 580
Hof in Stein an der Donau Aquarell/Papier (18x11.5cm 7x4in) Wien 2000

ZETTERBERG Nils, Nisse 1910-1986 **[90]**

⮞ $409 - €468 - £288 - FF3 068
Stilleben mot blått Oil/panel (33x52cm 12x20in) Stockholm 2001

⮞ $272 - €329 - £190 - FF2 158
Stilleben med citron och svepask Oil/paper (20x51cm 7x20in) Stockholm 2000

ZETTL Baldwin 1943 **[23]**

▥ $110 - €133 - £76 - FF872
Schulze Kupferstich (25x13.4cm 9x5in) Berlin 2000

ZETTLER Max 1886-1926 **[24]**

⮞ $490 - €511 - £322 - FF3 353
Abend im Dachauermoos bei Haimhausen Öl/Karton (21x32cm 8x12in) München 2000

ZEUNER Jonas 1727-1814 **[7]**

⮞ $20 850 - €24 446 - £15 000 - FF160 354
The Peace concluded between Holland and the Emperor Joseph II Oil/panel (34x48cm 13x18in) London 2001

⮞ $7 000 - €6 039 - £4 167 - FF39 615
Man off to the Hunt with his Hound/Men Fishing and a Mansion Huile/panneau (17x21cm 6x8in) New-York 1998

ZEUTHEN Christian Olavius 1812-1890 **[36]**

⮞ $655 - €738 - £451 - FF4 838
Interieur fra en hollandsk, gotisk kirke Oil/canvas (37x42cm 14x16in) Köbenhavn 2000

ZEVENBERGHEN van Georges 1877-1968 **[73]**

⮞ $653 - €545 - £382 - FF3 577
Vissers Oil/panel (42x51.5cm 16x20in) Lokeren 1998

⮞ $514 - €545 - £327 - FF3 577
Léda et le Cygne Huile/panneau (42x34cm 16x13in) Bruxelles 2000

✎ $1 306 - €1 091 - £765 - FF7 154
Femme à sa toilette Pastel/paper (35.5x44.5cm 13x17in) Lokeren 1998

ZEWY Carl 1855-1929 **[21]**

⮞ $1 917 - €2 180 - £1 347 - FF14 301
Wiener Mädel Öl/Karton (71x51cm 27x20in) Wien 2001

⮞ $1 421 - €1 379 - £895 - FF9 047
Die Musikstunde Öl/Leinwand (38x36cm 14x14in) Zürich 2001

ZEYER Erich 1903-1960 **[60]**

⮞ $552 - €511 - £342 - FF3 353
Schäfer mit Herde vor Alblandschaft Öl/Leinwand (55x80cm 21x31in) Stuttgart 1999

ZEYSS Julie XIX **[4]**

⮞ $302 - €358 - £214 - FF2 347
Stilleben mit Weinkrug und Obstkorb Öl/Leinwand (42x55cm 16x21in) Staufen 2000

ZEZZOS Alessandro 1848-1914 **[10]**

⮞ $71 523 - €61 921 - £43 136 - FF406 172
Buntes Treiben am Ufer vor dem Dogenpalast in Venedig Öl/Leinwand (93x165cm 36x64in) München 1998

⮞ $19 000 - €22 330 - £13 172 - FF146 478
Flirtation Oil/panel (84x55cm 33x21in) New-York 1999

⮞ $3 495 - €3 623 - £2 097 - FF23 766
Ritratto di ragazza Olio/cartone (40x31cm 15x12in) Milano 1999

✎ $3 870 - €4 602 - £2 682 - FF30 185
Venezianischer Studienkopf (Brustbildnis einer jungen Venezianerin) Aquarell/Papier (51x37cm 20x14in) Bremen 2000

ZEZZOS Georges 1883-1959 **[112]**

⮞ $800 - €829 - £480 - FF5 440
Caffettiera d'argento Olio/tela (33x41cm 12x16in) Milano 1999

ZHA SHIBIAO 1615-1698 **[18]**

✎ $8 880 - €8 427 - £5 395 - FF55 275
Running Script Calligraphy Ink/paper (168x77cm 66x30in) Hong-Kong 1999

ZHANG BOYING 1871-1949 **[1]**

✎ $3 338 - €3 664 - £2 150 - FF24 031
Calligraphy in Standard Script Ink/paper (129.5x31.5cm 50x12in) Hong-Kong 2000

ZHANG CHONGREN Chang Ch'un-jen 1907 **[3]**

⮞ $4 896 - €4 047 - £2 864 - FF26 544
Portrait of a Philosopher Oil/canvas (58x69cm 22x27in) Taipei 1998

⚒ $24 396 - €26 639 - £15 694 - FF174 743
Dancer Bronze (21x9x19.5cm 8x3x7in) Hong-Kong 2000

ZHANG DAQIAN Chang Dai-chien 1899-1983 **[690]**

✎ $26 640 - €25 280 - £16 187 - FF165 827
Auspicious Lingzhi Ink (136x70cm 53x27in) Hong-Kong 1999

ZHANG DAZHUANG 1903-1980 **[1]**

✎ $2 227 - €1 888 - £1 331 - FF12 383
«Vegetables» Coloured inks/paper (48.5x69cm 19x27in) Hong-Kong 1998

ZHANG FANG XVII **[1]**

✎ $11 556 - €12 619 - £7 434 - FF82 773
Orchid, Bamboo and Chrysanthemum Ink (165x91.5cm 64x36in) Hong-Kong 2000

Z

ZHANG HUAN 1965 [1]
📷 **$3 672** - €4 169 - **£2 580** - FF27 348
The Bubble Series Gelatin silver print (76x103cm 29x40in) Taipei 2001

ZHANG JINHUO XVIII-XIX [1]
🖋 **$1 860** - €1 841 - **£1 160** - FF12 074
Kranich an einem Felsen/Vogel/Weisser Hase/Zwei Reiher an einem Felsen Indian ink/paper (159x45.2cm 62x17in) Köln 1999

ZHANG KEHE 1898-1959 [2]
🖋 **$3 081** - €3 382 - **£1 984** - FF22 183
Landscape Ink (13x477cm 5x187in) Hong-Kong 2000

ZHANG LI 1958 [11]
🖋 **$4 905** - €4 144 - **£2 945** - FF27 181
Side portrait of a Girl Oil/canvas (71x58cm 27x22in) Hong-Kong 1998

ZHANG RUITU 1576-1641 [8]
🖋 **$25 680** - €28 041 - **£16 520** - FF183 940
Poem of Red Cliff in Xing-Cao Shu Ink/paper (31.5x710cm 12x279in) Hong-Kong 2000

ZHANG SHANZI 1882-1940 [28]
🖋 **$4 358** - €5 123 - **£3 022** - FF33 605
Tiger Ink (21x16cm 8x6in) Hong-Kong 2000

ZHANG SHIYUAN 1898-1959 [1]
🖋 **$1 548** - €1 460 - **£960** - FF9 576
Secluded Studio Ink (19x67cm 7x26in) Hong-Kong 1999

ZHANG TINGJI 1768-1848 [2]
🖋 **$2 000** - €1 741 - **£1 192** - FF11 422
Calligraphy Ink/paper (101x64cm 39x25in) New-York 1998

ZHANG XIAOGANG 1958 [2]
🖋 **$4 590** - €5 211 - **£3 225** - FF34 185
Recall from the Past Oil/paper (71x54cm 27x21in) Taipei 2001
🖋 **$8 524** - €7 117 - **£5 000** - FF46 685
Blood Lines Series No.54 & No.55 Oil/canvas (40x30cm 15x11in) London 1998

ZHANG XIONG 1803-1884 [4]
🖋 **$3 225** - €3 041 - **£2 000** - FF19 950
Landscape Ink (132x65cm 51x25in) Hong-Kong 1999

ZHANG YIBO 1966 [3]
🖋 **$12 198** - €13 386 - **£7 856** - FF87 808
Candle Obscurity Oil/canvas (100x72.5cm 39x28in) Hong-Kong 2000

ZHANG YIN 1761-1829 [16]
🖋 **$3 225** - €3 026 - **£1 992** - FF19 852
Scholar in a Bamboo Grove Ink (72x35.5cm 28x13in) Hong-Kong 1999

ZHANG YIXIONG Chang Yi-hsiung 1914 [5]
🖋 **$2 601** - €2 953 - **£1 827** - FF19 371
Nude Oil/canvas (23x32cm 9x12in) Taipei 2001

ZHANG ZHAO 1691-1745 [2]
🖋 **$25 640** - €28 731 - **£17 860** - FF188 460
Essay by Hang Shijun for the Imperial Examination in Standard Script Ink (26x19.5cm 10x7in) Hong-Kong 2001

ZHANG ZHONG XIV [1]
🖋 **$334 620** - €317 302 - **£203 580** - FF2 081 560
Birds Resting on Hibiscus Bush Ink/paper (126x48.5cm 49x19in) Hong-Kong 1999

ZHANG ZIJUN XV [1]
🖋 **$15 480** - €14 527 - **£9 564** - FF95 292
Cottage by the South Lake Ink (154.5x52.5cm 60x20in) Hong-Kong 1999

ZHANG ZIZHENG 1917 [4]
🖋 **$1 224** - €1 390 - **£860** - FF9 116
The Courtyard Oil/canvas (25.5x34cm 10x13in) Taipei 2001

ZHANG ZONGCANG 1686-1756 [6]
🖋 **$10 015** - €10 991 - **£6 450** - FF72 095
Visiting a Friend at Hushanqiao Ink/paper (44x62cm 17x24in) Hong-Kong 2000

ZHAO CHUNXIANG Chao Chun-hsiang 1912-1991 [28]
🖋 **$179 760** - €196 290 - **£115 640** - FF1 287 580
Abstract '88 Mixed media/canvas (150x180cm 59x70in) Hong-Kong 2000
🖋 **$36 600** - €30 734 - **£21 480** - FF201 600
Fading and Dearching Acrylic (87x126cm 34x49in) Taipei 1998
🖋 **$2 624** - €2 794 - **£1 664** - FF18 328
Blooming Ink (46x46cm 18x18in) Taipei 2000

ZHAO HUANGUANG 1559-1625 [1]
🖋 **$2 820** - €3 315 - **£1 955** - FF21 744
Poem in Cao-Zhuan Shu Ink/paper (145x33cm 57x12in) Hong-Kong 2000

ZHAO MENGFU 1254-1322 [3]
🖋 **$514 800** - €488 203 - **£313 200** - FF3 202 400
Calligraphy in Xing Shu - Poem of Returning Home, of Tao Yuanming Ink/paper (46.5x453.5cm 18x178in) Hong-Kong 1999

ZHAO SHAO'ANG 1905-1998 [136]
🖋 **$8 385** - €7 908 - **£5 200** - FF51 870
Persimmons and Cabbages Ink (36x77.5cm 14x30in) Hong-Kong 1999

ZHAO SHURU 1874-1945 [4]
🖋 **$3 852** - €4 206 - **£2 478** - FF27 591
Autumn Flora Ink (104x52.5cm 40x20in) Hong-Kong 2000

ZHAO XIUHUAN 1946 [1]
🖋 **$10 488** - €9 835 - **£6 520** - FF64 515
Moon Night Ink (86x88cm 33x34in) Taipei 1999

ZHAO YONG 1289-c.1363 [1]
🖋 **$45 000** - €41 296 - **£27 648** - FF270 886
Secluded Thoughts by the Riverbank Ink (101x53.5cm 39x21in) New-York 1999

ZHAO ZHIMIN 1946 [9]
🖋 **$2 307** - €2 621 - **£1 620** - FF17 195
«Children at Play» Ink (63x146cm 24x57in) Hong-Kong 2001

ZHAO ZHIQIAN 1829-1884 [18]
🖋 **$3 711** - €3 146 - **£2 219** - FF20 639
Two Letters Ink/paper (22x34cm 8x13in) Hong-Kong 1998

ZHENG BAICHONG 1945 [6]
🖋 **$4 440** - €4 213 - **£2 697** - FF27 637
Autumn Landscape Ink (113x69.5cm 44x27in) Hong-Kong 1999

ZHENG MIN 1607-c.1685 [1]
🖋 **$192 600** - €210 311 - **£123 900** - FF1 379 550
Scenic Mountains and Rivers Ink/paper (12x482.5cm 4x189in) Hong-Kong 2000

ZHENG MUKANG 1901-1982 **[3]**

🖊 **$1 776** - €1 685 - **£1 079** - FF11 055
Selecting Seeds Ink (137.5x67.5cm 54x26in) Hong-Kong 1999

ZHENG WUCHANG 1894-1952 **[21]**

🖊 **$8 140** - €7 724 - **£4 946** - FF50 669
Watching Flying Geese from a Boat Ink (180x94cm 70x37in) Hong-Kong 1999

ZHENG XIE 1693-1765 **[26]**

🖊 **$12 820** - €14 563 - **£9 000** - FF95 530
Orchid and Bamboo Ink/paper (166.5x93cm 65x36in) Hong-Kong 2001

ZHENG ZAIDONG Cheng Tsai-tung 1953 **[10]**

🔎 **$6 292** - €5 832 - **£3 912** - FF38 253
Nude Oil/cardboard (79x109.5cm 31x43in) Taipei 1999

ZHI NAN JIANG 1963 **[2]**

🖊 **$1 200** - €1 244 - **£720** - FF8 160
Of the Bicycles Series Acquarello/carta (52x77cm 20x30in) Prato 2000

ZHITOMIRSKY Alexander 1907-1993 **[15]**

📷 **$3 000** - €3 119 - **£1 894** - FF50 462
Untitled Gelatin silver print (30x25cm 11x9in) New-York 2000

ZHOU BICHU 1903-1995 **[4]**

🔎 **$12 240** - €13 897 - **£8 600** - FF91 160
Landscape Oil/canvas/board (55x38.5cm 21x15in) Taipei 2001

ZHOU JUN XIX **[1]**

🖊 **$3 595** - €3 945 - **£2 315** - FF25 880
Bamboo in Rain Ink/paper (100x34.5cm 39x13in) Hong-Kong 2000

ZHOU LI 1675-1763 **[3]**

🖊 **$14 124** - €15 423 - **£9 086** - FF101 167
Landscape after Yuan Masters Ink/paper (24.5x56.5cm 9x22in) Hong-Kong 2000

ZHOU QUAN'AN XX **[1]**

🖊 **$7 704** - €8 455 - **£4 962** - FF55 458
Tulips and White Doves Ink (66x133cm 25x52in) Hong-Kong 2000

ZHOU SICONG 1939 **[2]**

🖊 **$2 820** - €3 204 - **£1 980** - FF21 016
Headmaster Ink (49.5x68cm 19x26in) Hong-Kong 2001

ZHU ANGZHI 1764-1840 **[2]**

🖊 **$6 666** - €7 928 - **£4 591** - FF52 005
Cascade and Pine in the Mist Ink (31.5x175cm 12x68in) Hong-Kong 2000

ZHU DAOMING 1625-1672 **[1]**

🖊 **$5 128** - €6 027 - **£3 556** - FF39 536
Fish Ink/paper (17x50.5cm 6x19in) Hong-Kong 2000

ZHU QIZHAN 1892-1996 **[76]**

🔎 **$24 480** - €27 795 - **£17 200** - FF182 320
Chrysanthemums Oil/canvas (46x54.5cm 18x21in) Taipei 2001

🖊 **$8 165** - €6 922 - **£4 882** - FF45 407
«Cabbage, Grapes and Persimmons» Coloured inks/paper (90x48cm 35x18in) Hong-Kong 1998

ZHU YUANZHI Yun Gee 1906-1963 **[68]**

🔎 **$250 920** - €207 389 - **£146 780** - FF1 360 380
Empress Yang Gui Fei at the Bath Oil/canvas (173x76cm 68x29in) Taipei 1998

🔎 **$68 400** - €63 388 - **£42 525** - FF415 800
Still Life with Calla Lillies and Teapot Oil/canvas (73.5x60.5cm 28x23in) Taipei 1999

🔎 **$22 680** - €20 866 - **£13 608** - FF136 872
Telegraph Hill Oil/board (29x20.5cm 11x8in) Taipei 1999

🗿 **$27 720** - €25 503 - **£16 632** - FF167 288
Couple walking Sculpture, wood (51x13x6.5cm 20x5x2in) Taipei 1999

🖊 **$2 835** - €2 608 - **£1 701** - FF17 109
Snorting Dragon Watercolour (20x25.5cm 7x10in) Taipei 1999

ZHU YUNMING 1460-1526 **[12]**

🖊 **$62 178** - €58 637 - **£38 560** - FF384 636
Calligraphy in Cao Shu Ink/paper (25x317.5cm 9x125in) Hong-Kong 1999

ZHUANG MING FA 1971 **[3]**

🔎 **$760** - €985 - **£570** - FF6 460
Onde del mare Tecnica mista (24.5x18cm 9x7in) Prato 2000

ZHUKOVSKY Stanislav Iulianov. 1873-1944 **[20]**

🔎 **$7 246** - €6 843 - **£4 500** - FF44 885
First Signs of Spring Oil/board (41x59cm 16x23in) London 1999

🔎 **$3 130** - €3 637 - **£2 200** - FF23 857
At the Dacha Oil/canvas (24x33cm 9x12in) London 2001

🖊 **$4 220** - €4 056 - **£2 600** - FF26 600
Birch Trees Watercolour/paper (69.5x30cm 27x11in) London 1999

ZHURAVLEV Firs Sergeyevich 1836-1901 **[4]**

🔎 **$25 972** - €24 961 - **£16 000** - FF163 732
Girls in the Bathhouse Oil/canvas (34.5x56cm 13x22in) London 1999

ZIC Zizko 1924 **[2]**

🔎 **$4 200** - €4 902 - **£2 964** - FF32 154
Floral Still Life Oil/board (60x50cm 24x20in) Cedar-Falls IA 2000

ZICHY von Mihaly 1827-1906 **[31]**

🔎 **$36 300** - €41 253 - **£25 300** - FF270 600
Le troubadour Huile/toile (55x44.5cm 21x17in) Budapest 2001

🖊 **$980** - €1 084 - **£644** - FF7 112
The Lady and the Footman Watercolour/paper (34.5x25cm 13x9in) Budapest 2000

ZICK Januarius 1730-1797 **[61]**

🔎 **$9 098** - €10 226 - **£6 388** - FF67 078
Die Anbetung der Hirten Öl/Leinwand (47x35.5cm 18x13in) Düsseldorf 2001

🔎 **$5 853** - €6 647 - **£4 067** - FF43 600
Ecce Homo/Mater Dolorosa Öl/Metall (16x13cm 6x5in) Köln 2001

🖊 **$3 528** - €3 066 - **£2 125** - FF20 112
Stiftung der Kirche St. Kastor in Koblenz Ink (20.3x23.4cm 7x9in) Berlin 1998

▨ **$227** - €256 - **£159** - FF1 676
Merkur im Werkstatt eines Bildhauers Radierung (15.5x9.5cm 6x3in) Köln 2001

ZICKMANTEL Hartmut XX **[7]**

📷 **$597** - €706 - **£424** - FF4 628
Ohne Titel Vintage gelatin silver print (29.5x20cm 11x7in) Berlin 2001

Z

ZIEBOLZ Herbert 1903-1985 **[4]**
✐ **$2 850** - €3 323 - **£1 998** - FF21 800
  New York, Chinese Theater Watercolour (30x22.5cm
  11x8in) München 2000

ZIEGLER de Charles 1890-1972 **[22]**
✐ **$195** - €212 - **£128** - FF1 392
  Alte Häusergruppe in Genf Watercolour, gouache
  (64x49cm 25x19in) Bern 2000

ZIEGLER Eustace Paul 1881-1969 **[51]**
👁 **$6 000** - €5 665 - **£3 726** - FF37 163
  Pack-Horses in Water Oil/board (9.5x21.5cm 3x8in)
  Beverly-Hills CA 1999
✐ **$4 200** - €3 543 - **£2 463** - FF23 242
  «Weasel Calf, Blackfoot Chief» Watercolour/paper
  (37.5x27.5cm 14x10in) New-York 1998

ZIEGLER Henry 1889-? **[14]**
▥ **$175** - €209 - **£121** - FF1 369
  Riding Rough Etching (19x15cm 7x6in) Plainville CT
  2000

ZIEGLER Johann c.1750-1834 **[1]**
▥ **$2 310** - €2 761 - **£1 588** - FF18 114
  Die Stadt Gmunden von der Seeseite Radierung
  (32x42cm 12x16in) Salzburg 2000

ZIEGLER Johann 1749-1812 **[16]**
▥ **$697** - €654 - **£431** - FF4 290
  **Wasserfall und Brücke auf dem Berge
  Loibl/Strasse über den Berg Loibl** Radierung
  (32.5x42cm 12x16in) Graz 1999

ZIEGLER Richard 1891-1992 **[45]**
👁 **$124 559** - €143 407 - **£85 000** - FF940 686
  Couple at a Table Oil/canvas (100x75cm 39x29in)
  London 2000
👁 **$1 903** - €2 301 - **£1 328** - FF15 092
  Sitzender Akt mit roten Schuhen Tempera/Karton
  (19.1x14.2cm 7x5in) Berlin 2000
👁 **$930** - €920 - **£580** - FF6 037
  Hinter dem Vorhang Pastell (25.8x9.7cm 10x3in)
  Berlin 1999
▥ **$230** - €256 - **£160** - FF1 676
  Wasserträgerin Print (25.5x8cm 10x3in) Heidelberg
  2001

ZIELER Mogens 1905-1983 **[44]**
👁 **$496** - €511 - **£315** - FF3 350
  Bortdragende Tömmermaend, sidste fase
  Oil/canvas (50x60cm 19x23in) Vejle 2000

ZIELKE Willy Otto 1902 **[33]**
📷 **$930** - €920 - **£581** - FF6 037
  Pax Photograph (29.7x29.7cm 11x11in) München 1999

ZIEM Félix 1821-1911 **[712]**
👁 **$72 000** - €68 304 - **£43 740** - FF448 048
  Paysage du Liban Oil/canvas (105x162.5cm
  41x63in) New-York 1999
👁 **$17 157** - €19 485 - **£12 000** - FF127 810
  **Gondole a Vignole, au loin San Pietro del
  Castello** Oil/canvas (54.5x86.5cm 21x34in) London
  2001
👁 **$4 749** - €4 486 - **£2 872** - FF29 426
  View of the Harbor Oil/panel (43x28.5cm 16x11in)
  New-York 1999
✐ **$1 146** - €1 268 - **£777** - FF8 400
  Esquisse de scène d'Istanbul Lavis/papier
  (23x31cm 9x12in) Paris 2000

ZIER Édouard François 1856-1924 **[28]**
👁 **$2 407** - €2 211 - **£1 470** - FF14 500
  La baigneuse Huile/panneau (27x35cm 10x13in)
  Deauville 1998

ZIER Wolmer 1910-1990 **[37]**
👁 **$364** - €403 - **£241** - FF2 641
  Parti fra Lökken Oil/canvas (45x54cm 17x21in) Viby
  J, Århus 2000

ZIERMANN Carl 1850-1881 **[3]**
👁 **$3 038** - €3 235 - **£2 000** - FF21 221
  Good Companions Oil/canvas (77x53cm 30x20in)
  Billingshurst, West-Sussex 2000

ZIESEL Georg Frederik 1756-1809 **[4]**
👁 **$18 943** - €18 369 - **£12 000** - FF120 490
  Vase of Flowers on a Stone Ledge Oil/panel
  (63.5x54.5cm 25x21in) London 1999
👁 **$13 328** - €15 478 - **£9 366** - FF101 528
  Blomsterbukett på marmorsockel Oil/panel
  (35.5x27.5cm 13x10in) Stockholm 2001

ZIESENIS Johann Georg 1716-1776 **[8]**
👁 **$5 696** - €6 353 - **£3 717** - FF41 672
  **Portrait of Johann L.C.Rumann/Portrait of his
  Wife** Oil/canvas (92x75.5cm 36x29in) Amsterdam 2000

ZIETARA Walenty 1883-1935 **[3]**
▥ **$266** - €276 - **£168** - FF1 811
  «Pekareks Tee» Poster (126x95cm 49x37in) Wien
  2000

ZIFFER Sandor 1880-1962 **[29]**
👁 **$4 200** - €4 647 - **£2 760** - FF30 480
  Side of Ditch Oil/canvas (61.5x76.5cm 24x30in)
  Budapest 2000
👁 **$2 600** - €2 557 - **£1 625** - FF16 770
  Poppies Oil/canvas (34x44cm 13x17in) Budapest 1999

ZIG (Louis Gaudin) ?-1936 **[48]**
▥ **$2 900** - €2 451 - **£1 724** - FF16 076
  Casino de Paris/Mistinguette/Paris Quis Brille
  Color lithograph (218.5x80cm 86x31in) Washington
  1998

ZIGAINA Giuseppe 1924 **[40]**
👁 **$3 800** - €4 924 - **£2 850** - FF32 300
  Senza titolo Olio/tela (50x39.5cm 19x15in) Milano
  2000
👁 **$2 640** - €2 281 - **£1 760** - FF14 960
  Interno Olio/cartone (30x45cm 11x17in) Trieste 1998
✐ **$12 000** - €12 440 - **£7 200** - FF81 600
  Verso la laguna n.2 Tecnica mista/carta (200x180cm
  78x70in) Prato 1999
▥ **$150** - €155 - **£90** - FF1 020
  Senza titolo Gravure (41x36cm 16x14in) Torino 2001

ZIGLIARA Eugène 1873-1918 **[5]**
▥ **$1 043** - €1 189 - **£716** - FF7 800
  **«P.O., plages de Pornichet, la Baule, le
  Pouliguen»** Affiche (104.5x74cm 41x29in) Paris 2000

ZIJDERVELD Willem 1793-1846 **[1]**
👁 **$4 106** - €3 857 - **£2 475** - FF25 301
  Morning Break Oil/panel (48x37cm 18x14in)
  Amsterdam 1999

ZIJL Lambertus 1866-1947 **[22]**
🗿 **$1 521** - €1 452 - **£950** - FF9 525
  Greek Figure Bronze (H19.5cm H7in) Amsterdam
  1999

ZIJL van Roelof ?-c.1628 **[1]**
- $16 437 - €15 584 - **£10 000** - FF102 222
  Courtesan singing accompanied by a Lutenist, a Boy, a Conch Oil/canvas/board (148x186cm 58x73in) London 1999

ZILCKEN Philip 1857-1930 **[27]**
- $3 106 - €3 630 - **£2 217** - FF23 812
  «Na Semoen, achter bij de citadel, Caïro» Oil/canvas (41x64cm 16x25in) Amsterdam 2001
- $208 - €227 - **£143** - FF1 488
  A Boat docked outside a small Town, after Jacob Maris Etching (36x43.5cm 14x17in) Amsterdam 2001

ZILLE Heinrich 1858-1929 **[831]**
- $1 575 - €1 529 - **£980** - FF10 028
  Grosser und kleiner Mann Charcoal/paper (14.5x9.8cm 5x3in) Berlin 1999
- $525 - €613 - **£366** - FF4 024
  Zur Mutter Erde Radierung (26x52cm 10x20in) Köln 2000
- $250 - €230 - **£153** - FF1 509
  Strassen -und Jahrmarktszenen Photograph (24x30cm 9x11in) Bielefeld 1999

ZILLEN Wilhelm 1824-1870 **[64]**
- $568 - €538 - **£353** - FF3 530
  Köer ved vandingsstedet Oil/canvas (53x70cm 20x27in) Köbenhavn 1999
- $323 - €376 - **£230** - FF2 465
  Bakket landskab med lille hus og fårehyrde Oil/canvas (25x45cm 9x17in) Aarhus 2001

ZILLER Leopold XX **[4]**
- $4 665 - €4 726 - **£2 929** - FF31 000
  Venise Huile/toile (54x81cm 21x31in) Saint-Dié 2000
- $1 155 - €1 143 - **£720** - FF7 500
  Vue de Venise Huile/toile (24x35cm 9x13in) Paris 1999

ZILLER W. XIX **[13]**
- $3 290 - €3 049 - **£2 046** - FF20 000
  Paysage orientaliste, sur le Bosphore à Constantinople Huile/toile (53x80cm 20x31in) Reims 1999
- $2 540 - €2 820 - **£1 770** - FF18 500
  Caïques dans un port de Turquie Huile/toile (24x35cm 9x13in) Paris 2001

ZILOTTI Domenico Bernardo 1730-1780 **[16]**
- $2 800 - €2 995 - **£1 890** - FF19 646
  Wooded Landscape Ink (30x20.5cm 11x8in) New-York 2001
- $372 - €409 - **£253** - FF2 683
  Campagnalandschaft mit Schäferin und ihrer Herde Radierung (38.2x48cm 15x18in) Berlin 2000

ZIMBAL Johann Ignatz 1722-1795 **[3]**
- $1 580 - €1 534 - **£984** - FF10 061
  Allegorie auf die Malerei, Skulptur und Architektur Radierung (27.4x18.5cm 10x7in) Berlin 1999

ZIMBEL George 1929 **[28]**
- $1 000 - €934 - **£604** - FF6 127
  Old Ferguson Place, Prince Edward Island Silver print (26x36cm 10x14in) New-York 1999

ZIMIN Georgii 1900-1985 **[8]**
- $4 200 - €4 619 - **£2 912** - FF30 298
  Photogram with scissors and sewing Neddles Silver print (13x8cm 5x3in) New-York 2001

ZIMMER Berndt 1948 **[88]**
- $8 973 - €9 996 - **£5 870** - FF65 568
  Winterankunft Acrylic (180x230cm 70x90in) München 2000
- $3 785 - €3 528 - **£2 287** - FF23 141
  Mare Mosso Öl/Leinwand (80x100cm 31x39in) München 1999
- $1 864 - €2 045 - **£1 266** - FF13 415
  Landschaft mit Gewitterwolke Gouache (70x100cm 27x39in) Berlin 2000
- $250 - €256 - **£156** - FF1 676
  Hommage à Santomaso Linocut in colors (70x100cm 27x39in) Hamburg 2000

ZIMMER Fred XX **[3]**
- $250 - €233 - **£154** - FF1 531
  Castle on the Hudson River Watercolour/paper (46x60cm 18x24in) Detroit MI 1999

ZIMMER Hans Peter 1936-1992 **[92]**
- $17 984 - €20 452 - **£12 564** - FF134 156
  Ohne Titel Mischtechnik (133x188cm 52x74in) München 2000
- $3 469 - €3 234 - **£2 096** - FF21 213
  Australien Apples Öl/Karton (38.8x53.9cm 15x21in) München 1999
- $781 - €740 - **£475** - FF4 856
  Frau vor dem Fernseher Gouache/paper (57x75cm 22x29in) Köbenhavn 1999

ZIMMER Wilhelm Carl 1853-1937 **[28]**
- $15 425 - €16 559 - **£10 322** - FF108 617
  Waldkonzert Öl/Leinwand (91x135cm 35x53in) Zürich 2000

ZIMMERMAN Carl John 1900-1985 **[9]**
- $1 100 - €1 043 - **£687** - FF6 839
  Abstract Still Life Oil/canvas (45x58cm 18x23in) Mystic CT 1999
- $1 100 - €1 188 - **£760** - FF7 792
  At Benedict Canyon, Beverly Hills Oil/board (25x35cm 10x14in) Altadena CA 2001

ZIMMERMAN Frederick A. 1886-1974 **[6]**
- $3 750 - €4 375 - **£2 610** - FF28 699
  «Sea Cliffs & Cypress, Carmel» Oil/canvas (91x91cm 36x36in) Altadena CA 2000

ZIMMERMAN Theodore XIX-XX **[41]**
- $651 - €593 - **£400** - FF3 890
  Portelet Bay, Jersey Pastel/paper (12x17cm 4x6in) Channel-Islands 1999

ZIMMERMANN Albert XIX **[1]**
- $12 382 - €10 838 - **£7 500** - FF71 094
  Polar Bear Hunting/Men with Dog-sleighs, after Julius Von Payer Oil/canvas (105x136cm 41x53in) London 1998

ZIMMERMANN Albert August 1808-1888 **[94]**
- $17 000 - €18 985 - **£10 886** - FF124 533
  View of the Italian Countryside Oil/canvas (138.5x101.5cm 54x39in) New-York 2000
- $1 739 - €2 045 - **£1 246** - FF13 415
  Blick in ein Gebirgstal an einem Frühlingstag Öl/Leinwand (72x150cm 28x59in) Stuttgart 2001
- $2 728 - €2 249 - **£1 606** - FF14 755
  Klassisches Ruinendenkmal (in Ägypten?) im sonnigen Licht Oil/panel (26x52cm 10x20in) Lindau 1998

Z

ZIMMERMANN Alfred 1854-1910 **[25]**
- $350 - €376 - **£234** - FF2 464
  Happy Hour Oil/wood (20x23cm 8x9in) St. Petersburg
  FL 2000

ZIMMERMANN August Richard 1820-1875 **[24]**
- $81 840 - €74 998 - **£50 000** - FF491 955
  Mill in a Mountainous Winter Landscape Oil/canvas (110x171.5cm 43x67in) London 1999
- $3 667 - €4 234 - **£2 565** - FF27 774
  Vinterdag i byn Oil/canvas (86x112cm 33x44in)
  Stockholm 2001
- $1 474 - €1 687 - **£1 014** - FF11 067
  Holzfäller bei der Arbeit auf einer Waldlichtung
  Oil/panel (29x38.5cm 11x15in) München 2000

ZIMMERMANN Aurel XIX **[1]**
- $7 149 - €8 119 - **£5 000** - FF53 254
  Mahlzeit! (feeding the birds) Oil/canvas (62.5x46cm 24x18in) London 2001

ZIMMERMANN Carl 1863-1930 **[17]**
- $1 074 - €1 074 - **£672** - FF7 043
  Keiler im Unterholz Oil/canvas (60x70cm 23x27in)
  Ibbenbüren 1999
- $2 385 - €2 812 - **£1 676** - FF18 446
  Sommerliches Mittelgebirge mit Hirsch und zwei Hirschkühen Oil/panel (12x16cm 4x6in)
  Frankfurt 2000

ZIMMERMANN Ernst Karl Georg 1852-1901 **[34]**
- $5 056 - €4 602 - **£3 159** - FF30 185
  Das Examen Oil/panel (61x81cm 24x31in) München
  1999
- $965 - €818 - **£577** - FF5 369
  «Die verfolgungssüchtige Ente» Öl/Karton
  (21x27cm 8x10in) Bremen 1998

ZIMMERMANN Ernst Reinhard 1881-1939 **[14]**
- $1 075 - €920 - **£647** - FF6 035
  Hans Edgar Martini als Kind auf einem Kinderstühlchen Öl/Leinwand (79x85.5cm 31x33in)
  München 1998

ZIMMERMANN Friedrich 1823-1884 **[39]**
- $4 239 - €4 116 - **£2 619** - FF27 000
  Le Mont-Blanc vu des environs des Sallanches
  Huile/toile (64x96cm 25x37in) Grenoble 1999
- $421 - €491 - **£291** - FF3 222
  Gebirgslandschaft mit zwei Wanderern auf felsigem Pfad Öl/Leinwand/Karton (27x41.5cm 10x16in)
  Bern 2000

ZIMMERMANN Friedrich August 1805-1876 **[7]**
- $1 905 - €2 194 - **£1 300** - FF14 391
  A Young Boy Carving a Cross/A Young Girl Feeding her Rabbits Oil/panel (27.5x21cm 10x8in)
  London 2000

ZIMMERMANN Johann Gerstenhauer 1858-1931
[5]
- $1 069 - €1 090 - **£669** - FF7 150
  Wasserträgerin Oil/panel (22x32cm 8x12in) Wien
  2000

ZIMMERMANN Mac 1912-1995 **[151]**
- $1 593 - €1 534 - **£996** - FF10 061
  Magier mit Mathemat. Figuren Oil/panel (39x54cm 15x21in) München 1999
- $2 378 - €2 059 - **£1 443** - FF13 507
  Kleine Gruppe sieht in Abgrund Oil/panel
  (29x42.7cm 11x16in) München 1998

- $181 - €204 - **£127** - FF1 341
  Barocker Tanz Gouache/Karton (32.5x43.5cm 12x17in) Stuttgart 2001
- $129 - €155 - **£92** - FF1 014
  Pyramus und Thisbe Etching, aquatint (33.6x29cm 13x11in) Hamburg 2000

ZIMMERMANN Maximilian August 1811-1878 **[14]**
- $3 645 - €4 090 - **£2 527** - FF26 831
  Flusstal im Voralpenland Öl/Leinwand (49.5x69cm 19x27in) München 2000
- $2 370 - €2 045 - **£1 411** - FF13 414
  Reisigsammlerin auf dem Weg am Waldrand
  Oil/panel (34.5x40.5cm 13x15in) München 1998

ZIMMERMANN Reinhard Sebastian 1815-1893 **[31]**
- $6 136 - €7 216 - **£4 400** - FF47 337
  Young Boy smoking a Pipe in a Stable Oil/canvas (68x48cm 27x19in) Send-Woking, Surrey 2001
- $4 085 - €4 602 - **£2 872** - FF30 185
  Der schlimme Zahn, auf baldige Genesung
  Oil/panel (24x32cm 9x12in) Stuttgart 2001

ZIMMERMANN von Clemens 1788-1869 **[5]**
- $480 - €411 - **£289** - FF2 699
  «Friedrich Barbarossa belehnet Otto von Wittelsbach mit dem Herzogthum Pencil
  (25.5x31cm 10x12in) München 1998

ZINGALE Larry 1938 **[3]**
- $4 000 - €3 963 - **£2 426** - FF25 996
  Jackie Robinson Oil/canvas (76x61cm 29x24in)
  New-York 2000

ZINGG Adrian 1734-1816 **[121]**
- $1 369 - €1 329 - **£852** - FF8 720
  Sächsische Landschaft mit Gehöft, Wasserfall und Viehhirten Indian ink (39.5x30.6cm 15x12in)
  Berlin 1999
- $179 - €204 - **£125** - FF1 341
  Les bergères, nach C.W.E.Dietrich Etching
  (51x38.5cm 20x15in) Berlin 2001

ZINGG Jean-Pierre 1925 **[7]**
- $9 448 - €7 927 - **£5 543** - FF52 000
  Scène de labours à Sémondans Huile/toile
  (50x72cm 19x28in) Besançon 1998
- $2 694 - €2 515 - **£1 631** - FF16 500
  Les vendanges Aquarelle/papier (30x47cm 11x18in)
  Besançon 1999

ZINGG Jules Émile 1882-1942 **[399]**
- $4 613 - €5 183 - **£3 213** - FF34 000
  Vaudancourt Huile/toile (54x73cm 21x28in)
  Besançon 2001
- $3 761 - €3 201 - **£2 238** - FF21 000
  Repos sur les hauteurs du village Huile/panneau
  (24x33cm 9x12in) Brest 1998
- $1 002 - €915 - **£609** - FF6 000
  Portrait de femme Fusain/papier (56x43cm 22x16in)
  Saint-Dié 1998

ZINGONI Aurelio 1853-1922 **[23]**
- $8 290 - €7 165 - **£4 920** - FF47 000
  Nature morte au faisan et à la grive/Nature morte au pied de la vigne Huile/toile (85x43cm 33x16in) Versailles 1998
- $950 - €1 090 - **£650** - FF7 151
  Playing with the Infant Oil/panel (30x22cm 12x9in)
  Par, Cornwall 2000

ZINI Umberto 1878-1964 **[15]**

$599 - €581 - £369 - FF3 813
Bildnis eines Mohren mit Papagei Aquarell/Papier
(31x22cm 12x8in) Wien 1999

ZINKEISEN Anna Katrina 1901-1976 **[86]**

$1 942 - €1 823 - £1 200 - FF11 958
Still Life of mixed Flowers Oil/canvas (75x62cm
29x24in) Billingshurst, West-Sussex 1999

$761 - €799 - £480 - FF5 243
After the Flood at Canvay Island Ink (20x33cm
8x13in) Aylsham, Norfolk 2000

ZINKEISEN Doris Clare 1898-1991 **[213]**

$2 097 - €2 014 - £1 300 - FF13 214
Lost in Thought Oil/canvas (101.5x86.5cm 39x34in)
London 1999

$1 259 - €1 087 - £760 - FF7 129
The Beginning of the Holidays Oil/canvas
(39.5x29cm 15x11in) London 1998

$492 - €470 - £300 - FF3 083
Costume Design Pencil (43x27cm 16x10in) London
1999

$1 900 - €1 799 - £1 180 - FF11 798
«Coronation» Poster (98.5x123cm 38x48in) New-
York 1999

ZINNEMANN Fred 1907-1997 **[6]**

$6 500 - €7 483 - £4 435 - FF49 088
Wall Street Photograph (26.5x14cm 10x5in) New-
York 2000

ZINNER Robert 1904 **[44]**

$702 - €654 - £432 - FF4 290
Gosausee mit dem Dachstein Öl/Karton
(92x102cm 36x40in) Linz 1998

ZINNÖGGER Leopold 1811-1872 **[23]**

$10 674 - €8 768 - £6 200 - FF57 513
**Grapes, Apples and Pears in a Basket with
Berries and Butterflies** Oil/canvas (87.5x65cm
34x25in) London 1998

$1 645 - €1 817 - £1 140 - FF11 917
Zweig mit roten Beeren Aquarell/Papier (26x36cm
10x14in) Wien 2001

ZIOMEK Teodor 1874-1937 **[14]**

$1 543 - €1 523 - £951 - FF9 988
Chardons Oil/canvas/board (26.5x32cm 10x12in)
Warszawa 1999

ZITMAN Cornelius 1926 **[31]**

$6 400 - €6 464 - £4 400 - FF42 400
Sin título Bronze (27x28x21cm 10x11x8in) Caracas
1999

ZITTEL Andrea 1965 **[9]**

$50 000 - €48 379 - £30 835 - FF317 345
**A to Z 1994 Living Unit Customized for Leonora
and Jimmy Belilty** Construction (145x213.5x207.5cm
57x84x81in) New-York 1999

$4 500 - €5 221 - £3 106 - FF34 249
Study for Carpet, Furniture Gouache (38x51cm
14x20in) New-York 2000

ZIVERI Alberto 1908-1990 **[64]**

$27 600 - €23 843 - £18 400 - FF156 400
Capolinea Olio/tela (182x195cm 71x76in) Roma 1998

$4 500 - €4 665 - £2 700 - FF30 600
Paesaggio Olio/tela (35x50cm 13x19in) Prato 2001

$2 520 - €2 592 - £1 500 - FF17 000
Nudo femminile di schiena Olio/tela (35x23.5cm
13x9in) Roma 2000

$400 - €415 - £240 - FF2 720
Ai giardini China/carta (15.5x23.5cm 6x9in) Roma
2001

$150 - €155 - £90 - FF1 020
Modella in posa Acquaforte (10x14cm 3x5in) Torino
1999

ZIX Ferdinand 1864-1942 **[19]**

$828 - €767 - £513 - FF5 030
Schneeball Öl/Karton (50x71cm 19x27in) Stuttgart
1999

ZIYA Nazmi 1881-1937 **[2]**

$7 056 - €6 005 - £4 200 - FF39 391
The Flower Seller Oil/panel (19x27cm 7x10in)
London 1998

$17 550 000 - €19 917 463 - £11 700 000 -
FF130 650 000
Bateaux dans le port Aquarelle/papier (42x56cm
16x22in) Istanbul 2001

ZMURKO Franciszek 1859-1910 **[27]**

$14 946 - €13 802 - £9 309 - FF90 532
Sadness Oil/cardboard (58x47cm 22x18in) Warszawa
1999

$3 282 - €3 903 - £2 340 - FF25 605
Garçon en costume de page Huile/carton
(35x27cm 13x10in) Warszawa 2000

ZO Achille J.-Baptiste 1826-1901 **[13]**

$8 021 - €8 842 - £5 336 - FF58 000
Place des Orangers à Séville Huile/toile (40x60cm
15x23in) Biarritz 2000

$3 108 - €2 973 - £1 893 - FF19 500
Les petites bohémiennes Huile/toile (25x33cm
9x12in) Troyes 1999

ZO Henri Achille 1873-1933 **[78]**

$20 800 - €19 818 - £13 182 - FF130 000
Avant le paseo Huile/toile (150x150cm 59x59in)
Biarritz 1999

$3 318 - €3 049 - £2 038 - FF20 000
Tercio de Piques Huile/toile (50x40cm 19x15in)
Bordeaux 1999

$2 249 - €1 950 - £1 374 - FF12 792
Horses at the Ready Oil/canvas (33x45.5cm
12x17in) New-York 1999

$700 - €579 - £411 - FF3 800
Femme à l'éventail Craies couleurs (46.5x29.5cm
18x11in) Biarritz 1998

ZOA XX **[6]**

$1 305 - €1 534 - £904 - FF10 061
Kassel Photograph (50x60cm 19x23in) Stuttgart 2000

ZOBEL Benjamin 1762-1831 **[10]**

$2 015 - €1 739 - £1 200 - FF11 406
Recumbant lion Mixed media (44.5x60cm 17x23in)
Newbury, Berkshire 1998

$3 828 - €4 293 - £2 600 - FF28 159
**A Donkey and Sheep Under a Tree/Sheep
Resting in a Wooded Landscape** Bodycolour
(50x65cm 19x25in) Billingshurst, West-Sussex 2000

ZOBEL DE AYALA Fernando 1924-1984 **[81]**

$4 614 - €5 248 - £3 200 - FF34 423
Ku IV Oil/canvas (94x34.5cm 37x13in) London 2000

$1 750 - €2 102 - £1 225 - FF13 790
Paisaje Oleo/lienzo (13x25cm 5x9in) Madrid 2000

$520 - €481 - £328 - FF3 152
Zapatilla deportiva Acuarela (24x35cm 9x13in)
Madrid 1999

Z

〰 **$264** - €240 - **£164** - FF1 576
Composición Litografía (52x52cm 20x20in) Madrid 1999

ZOBERNIG Heimo 1958 **[13]**
⌖ **$3 288** - €3 835 - **£2 308** - FF25 154
Ohne Titel Mixed media (100x100x7cm 39x39x2in) Köln 2000

ZOBOLI Giacomo 1681-1767 **[7]**
⌖ **$3 200** - €4 147 - **£2 400** - FF27 200
Allegoria della Pittura Olio/tela (93x74cm 36x29in) Roma 2000

ZOBUS Wilhelm 1831-1869 **[5]**
⌖ **$1 645** - €1 817 - **£1 140** - FF11 917
Zigeuner am nächtlichen Lagerfeuer Öl/Leinwand (55x73cm 21x28in) Wien 2001

ZOCCHI Cesare 1851-1922 **[2]**
🔨 **$69 665** - €60 589 - **£42 000** - FF397 441
Minos Marble (137x83.5cm 53x32in) London 1998

ZOCCHI Emilio 1835-1913 **[6]**
🔨 **$50 484** - €59 333 - **£35 000** - FF389 200
The Young Michelangelo Marble (H185cm H72in) London 2000
🔨 **$7 240** - €8 227 - **£5 000** - FF53 968
I Sonni Felici (Sweet Dreams) Marble (64.5x37x75cm 25x14x29in) London 2000

ZOCCHI Giuseppe 1711-1767 **[21]**
⌖ **$18 746** - €18 895 - **£11 700** - FF123 942
Landschaft mit antiken Ruinen Öl/Leinwand (135.5x99cm 53x38in) Wien 2000
⌖ **$10 150** - €10 671 - **£6 370** - FF70 000
Les palais Corsi et Viviani à Florence Encre (29x42.5cm 11x16in) Paris 2000
〰 **$700** - €726 - **£420** - FF4 760
Veduta della chiesa di piazza Santa Maria Novella Stampa (49x69cm 19x27in) Prato 2000

ZOCCHI Gugliemo 1874-? **[27]**
⌖ **$16 000** - €17 284 - **£11 078** - FF113 377
Woman in fancy Dress Oil/canvas (66x40cm 26x16in) Cincinnati OH 2001

ZOELLY Paul 1896-1971 **[6]**
⌖ **$3 776** - €4 165 - **£2 557** - FF27 321
Erlösung, Mann und Frau Oil/canvas/panel (45.5x38cm 17x14in) Zürich 2000

ZOETELIEF TROMP Jan 1872-1947 **[94]**
⌖ **$26 773** - €26 980 - **£16 688** - FF176 974
Femme et enfants dans les champs Huile/toile (49.5x65cm 19x25in) Montréal 2000
⌖ **$17 654** - €17 527 - **£11 031** - FF114 972
Children and Dog in a Field Oil/panel (24x34.5cm 9x13in) Toronto 1999
✎ **$4 854** - €5 445 - **£3 363** - FF35 719
Boerenkinderen en een geit op pad Aquarelle/papier (15x21cm 5x8in) The Hague 2000

ZOFF Alfred 1852-1927 **[78]**
⌖ **$36 063** - €40 393 - **£25 058** - FF264 958
Landschaft mit Zypressen und Herrenhaus Öl/Leinwand (174x124cm 68x48in) Staufen 2001
⌖ **$10 508** - €10 055 - **£6 528** - FF65 956
Das Stauwehr Huile/toile/panneau (41.2x51cm 16x20in) Zürich 1999
⌖ **$6 770** - €7 267 - **£4 620** - FF47 670
«Wuelle bei Recco» Öl/Leinwand/Karton (27.7x43.8cm 10x17in) Wien 2001

ZOFFANY John 1733-1810 **[28]**
⌖ **$4 480 640** - €5 211 025 - **£3 200 000** - FF34 182 080
The Dutton Family in the Drawing Room of Sherborne Park Oil/canvas (101.5x127cm 39x50in) London 2001
⌖ **$20 854** - €21 014 - **£13 000** - FF137 846
Portrait of a Nobleman, Full Length, Wearing Van Dyck Dress Oil/canvas (75x62cm 29x24in) London 2000
⌖ **$99 522** - €86 557 - **£60 000** - FF567 774
Portrait of the Nawab Asuf-ud-Daula Oil/canvas (41x32cm 16x12in) London 1998

ZOFFOLI Andrea XIX **[10]**
⌖ **$4 476** - €4 437 - **£2 800** - FF29 103
Introducing the Heir Oil/canvas (42x63cm 16x24in) London 1999

ZOFFOLI Angelo XIX **[3]**
⌖ **$17 184** - €18 446 - **£11 500** - FF120 998
An Audience with His Excellency Oil/canvas (59x100cm 23x39in) London 1999

ZOFFOLI Giacomo 1731-1785 **[5]**
🔨 **$26 219** - €31 252 - **£18 696** - FF205 000
Hercule et Apollon Bronze (H35cm H13in) Soissons 2000

ZOFFOLI Giovanni 1745-1805 **[4]**
🔨 **$4 344** - €4 936 - **£3 000** - FF32 381
The Borghese Gladiator, After the Antique Bronze (H26cm H10in) London 2000

ZOFREA Salvatore 1946 **[93]**
⌖ **$1 046** - €981 - **£647** - FF6 432
Young Girl and Mirror Oil/canvas/board (90x68cm 35x26in) Sydney 1999
✎ **$457** - €429 - **£283** - FF2 814
The Dancer Ink (61x44cm 24x17in) Sydney 1999
〰 **$113** - €103 - **£68** - FF763
Seventh Day Etching (92x122cm 36x48in) Sydney 1998

ZOIA Krukowskaja 1903-1999 **[69]**
⌖ **$807** - €725 - **£481** - FF4 758
Rosor i kantonkanna Oil/panel (54x45cm 21x17in) Stockholm 1998
⌖ **$309** - €348 - **£213** - FF2 286
Ros i grön flaska mot guldgrund Oil/canvas (45x34cm 17x13in) Uppsala 2000

ZOLA Giuseppe 1672-1743 **[7]**
⌖ **$7 790** - €7 267 - **£4 700** - FF47 670
Wasserfall im Gebirge mit Figuren Öl/Leinwand (117x73.5cm 46x28in) Wien 1999

ZOLL Kilian 1818-1860 **[38]**
⌖ **$2 184** - €2 422 - **£1 513** - FF15 884
Ung hornspelande gosse med pilbåge Oil/canvas (62x50cm 24x19in) Malmö 2001
⌖ **$768** - €697 - **£473** - FF4 571
Kvarn vid vatten, månsken Oil/panel (12x15cm 4x5in) Stockholm 1999

ZOLLA Venanzio 1880-1961 **[104]**
⌖ **$1 400** - €1 451 - **£840** - FF9 520
In laguna Olio/cartone (40x50cm 15x19in) Torino 2001
⌖ **$699** - €725 - **£419** - FF4 753
Il figlio Elemir Olio/cartone (17.5x22cm 6x8in) Milano 1999

ZOMMER Richard Karlovich 1866-1939 **[57]**
$4 025 - €4 541 - **£2 829** - FF29 786
Nomader med oxar i Kaukasians berg Oil/can-
vas/panel (58x93cm 22x36in) Helsinki 2001
$2 233 - €2 186 - **£1 374** - FF14 341
Etelästä Oil/canvas/panel (25x39cm 9x15in) Helsinki
1999

ZOMPINI Gaetano 1700-1778 **[10]**
$20 000 - €20.733 - **£12 000** - FF136 000
Giuseppe venduto dai fratelli Olio/tela (87x128cm
34x50in) Venezia 2000
$3 000 - €3 035 - **£1 831** - FF19 907
**Birdseller crossing the Bridge of San Travoso
on the Zattere, Venice** Black chalk (30x20cm
11x7in) New-York 2000

ZON Jacques 1872-1932 **[25]**
$359 - €386 - **£240** - FF2 530
Moored vessels by a bridge in Haarlem Oil/card-
board (32.5x40.5cm 12x15in) Amsterdam 2000

ZONARO Fausto 1854-1929 **[96]**
$155 000 - €160 681 - **£93 000** - FF1 054 000
La smorfia Olio/tela (97x149cm 38x58in) Milano
2000
$7 140 - €7 402 - **£4 284** - FF48 552
Riviera ligure Olio/tela (38x61cm 14x24in) Milano
1999
$4 443 - €5 183 - **£3 090** - FF34 000
Jeune orientale à la chechia Huile/panneau
(27x21cm 10x8in) Paris 2000
$1 000 - €1 296 - **£750** - FF8 500
Ritratto di giovane donna Pastelli/carta (46x31.5cm
18x12in) Roma 2001

ZONDI Michael Gagashe 1926 **[7]**
$654 - €630 - **£404** - FF4 133
Bust of a Man Sculpture, wood (H39cm H15in)
Johannesburg 1999

ZOPF Carl 1858-1944 **[22]**
$1 954 - €1 789 - **£1 191** - FF11 738
**Sommerliche Bauerngarten mit Gemüsebeeten
und Blumenstauden** Öl/Leinwand/Karton (46x65cm
18x25in) München 1999
$272 - €307 - **£191** - FF2 012
Im Atelier Watercolour (28x22.5cm 11x8in) Düsseldorf
2001

ZOPF Julius 1838-1897 **[35]**
$876 - €1 017 - **£616** - FF6 673
Gebirgsbach Öl/Leinwand (68x115cm 26x45in) Graz
2001

ZOPPI Antonio 1860-1926 **[16]**
$3 258 - €2 966 - **£2 000** - FF19 454
The Serenade Oil/canvas (49x61.5cm 19x24in)
London 1999
$1 750 - €2 042 - **£1 235** - FF13 397
The Lady Equestrian Oil/canvas (34x28cm 13x11in)
Cedar-Falls IA 2000

ZORACH Marguerite Thompson 1887-1968 **[33]**
$22 000 - €23 615 - **£14 722** - FF154 902
Fishing Dock Oil/canvas (50.5x55.5cm 19x21in)
New-York 2000
$3 500 - €4 135 - **£2 480** - FF27 127
Trees Oil/canvas (35.5x40.5cm 13x15in) Boston MA
2000
$20 000 - €21 753 - **£13 184** - FF142 688
Yosemite Valley Watercolour (33.5x24.5cm 13x9in)
Boston MA 2000

$649 - €561 - **£391** - FF3 680
Nude Linocut (18x12.5cm 7x4in) New-York 1998

ZORACH William 1887-1966 **[176]**
$24 000 - €27 537 - **£16 418** - FF180 633
Nude Female Torso Bronze (H105cm H41in)
Charlottesville VA 2000
$7 000 - €7 239 - **£4 423** - FF47 488
The Artist's Daughter Plaster (H39cm H15in) New-
York 2000
$4 200 - €3 804 - **£2 570** - FF24 955
Beach Scene, Maine Watercolour/paper (33x49cm
13x19in) Portland ME 1998
$1 300 - €1 476 - **£889** - FF9 682
Two Figures (Christmas Card) Woodcut
(19.5x14cm 7x5in) New-York 2000

ZORIO Gilberto 1944 **[42]**
$14 000 - €14 513 - **£8 400** - FF95 200
Stella Tecnica mista (135x105cm 53x41in) Milano
1999
$1 360 - €1 762 - **£1 020** - FF11 560
Senza título Tecnica mista (44x40.5cm 17x23in)
Milano 2001
$2 250 - €2 332 - **£1 350** - FF15 300
Senza título Tecnica mista/carta (35x25cm 13x9in)
Prato 2000

ZORITCHAK Yan 1944 **[34]**
$4 539 - €4 573 - **£2 829** - FF30 000
Fleur céleste Sculpture verre (H60cm H23in)
Toulouse 2000

ZORKOCZY Gyula, Julius 1873-1932 **[39]**
$900 - €1 044 - **£646** - FF6 848
Woman at the Outskirts of Town Oil/canvas
(74x100cm 29x39in) St. Louis MO 2000

ZORN Anders 1860-1920 **[1603]**
$18 720 - €17 821 - **£11 712** - FF116 896
Till Dans /Kyrkfolk/Bröllopståg Oil/paper
(189.5x88.5cm 74x34in) Stockholm 1999
$185 250 - €161 581 - **£112 050** - FF1 059 900
«Le Réveil» Oil/canvas (68x60cm 26x23in) Stockholm
1998
$41 120 - €46 777 - **£28 720** - FF306 840
Zorns hus i Mora Oil/panel (16.5x10cm 6x3in)
Stockholm 2000
$10 746 - €10 458 - **£6 615** - FF68 598
Framåtböjd ung naken flicka som med båda
Metal (H7cm H2in) Stockholm 1999
$8 840 - €10 057 - **£6 174** - FF65 970
Nunna Akvarell/papper (21x16cm 8x6in) Stockholm
2000
$768 - €716 - **£474** - FF4 699
Prinsessan Ingeborg II Etching (27.7x21cm 10x8in)
Stockholm 1999

ZORNES James Milford 1908 **[63]**
$550 - €491 - **£336** - FF3 220
Figures in Fishing Boat Watercolour/paper
(27x45cm 11x18in) Altadena CA 1999

ZORZA della Carlo 1903-1977 **[17]**
$750 - €777 - **£450** - FF5 100
Borgo con figura Olio/tavoletta (50.5x39cm 19x15in)
Venezia 2000
$1 500 - €1 555 - **£900** - FF10 200
Porticciolo Olio/faesite (23x35cm 9x13in) Roma 1999

ZÖTL Aloys 1803-1887 **[21]**
$12 337 - €11 434 - **£7 672** - FF75 000
Le chacal Aquarelle/papier (32x42cm 12x16in) Paris
1999

Z

ZOTOW Eugen 1881-1953 **[3]**

$5 296 - €5 003 - **£3 298** - FF32 819
Fliederstrauss in Vase Öl/Leinwand (67x52cm 26x20in) St. Gallen 1999

ZOU DIAN XVI-XVII **[1]**

$102 960 - €97 641 - **£62 640** - FF640 480
Flowers, Landscapes and Calligraphy Ink (26.5x42.5cm 10x16in) Hong-Kong 1999

ZRZAVY Jan 1890-1977 **[111]**

$41 905 - €39 634 - **£26 100** - FF259 985
Puits en Bretagne Huile/panneau (36.5x54.5cm 14x21in) Praha 2000

$26 010 - €24 601 - **£16 200** - FF161 370
Via Appia Tempera/panel (27x35cm 10x13in) Praha 2000

$1 156 - €1 093 - **£720** - FF7 172
«Boat with Anchor» Pastel (22x14cm 8x5in) Praha 2001

$419 - €396 - **£261** - FF2 599
L'arbre de la connaissance Lithographie couleurs (24x22cm 9x8in) Praha 1999

ZSOTER Akos 1895-? **[7]**

$258 - €293 - **£180** - FF1 920
Still life of fruit, pottery and bottles Oil/board (40x54cm 15x21in) Billingshurst, West-Sussex 2001

ZUBER Ceszlav 1948 **[17]**

$2 465 - €2 439 - **£1 537** - FF16 000
Tête Sculpture verre (H38.5cm H15in) Paris 1999

ZUBER Henri 1844-1909 **[33]**

$1 423 - €1 524 - **£969** - FF10 000
Versailles le bassin de Marly Huile/toile (50x76cm 19x29in) Calais 2001

$1 137 - €1 296 - **£781** - FF8 500
Village et rivière Huile/panneau (27x35cm 10x13in) Paris 2000

ZUBER-BÜHLER Fritz 1822-1896 **[52]**

$180 000 - €207 233 - **£122 832** - FF1 359 360
La reine Bacchanale Oil/canvas (150x117cm 59x46in) New-York 2000

$29 000 - €25 105 - **£17 489** - FF164 679
«Chilhood Pranks» Oil/canvas (66x81cm 25x31in) San-Francisco CA 1998

$4 207 - €3 946 - **£2 600** - FF25 881
Mother and Child Oil/canvas (26x23cm 10x9in) London 1999

$1 562 - €1 524 - **£989** - FF10 000
Portrait de jeune femme avec une épaule gauche dénudée Aquarelle/papier (43x33cm 16x12in) Bourges 1999

ZUBIAURRE de Ramón 1882-1969 **[27]**

$9 600 - €9 610 - **£5 920** - FF63 040
Mirentxu Oleo/lienzo (60x45cm 23x17in) Madrid 2000

$4 422 - €4 355 - **£2 755** - FF28 565
Campesino con chapela Oleo/lienzo/tabla (30.5x24cm 12x9in) Madrid 1999

ZUBIAURRE Y AGUIRREZABAL de Valentín 1879-1963 **[65]**

$15 900 - €18 019 - **£10 800** - FF118 200
Vasca con cesto Oleo/lienzo (59x45.5cm 23x17in) Madrid 2000

$5 940 - €5 406 - **£3 600** - FF35 460
Pescadores en el acantilado Oleo/lienzo (25x30cm 9x11in) Madrid 1999

ZUBTSOV Sergei 1972 **[10]**

$1 046 - €1 123 - **£700** - FF7 365
Cleopatra Oil/canvas (50x40cm 19x15in) Fernhurst, Haslemere, Surrey 2000

ZUCCARELLI Francesco 1702-1788 **[114]**

$93 000 - €80 341 - **£46 500** - FF527 000
Veduta di Tivoli Olio/tela (108x131cm 42x51in) Milano 1999

$53 628 - €45 629 - **£32 000** - FF299 308
River Landscape with Peasants, Cattle and Goats near farm buildings Oil/canvas (76x117cm 29x46in) London 1998

$26 000 - €27 767 - **£17 716** - FF182 137
Wooded River Landscape with Figures by a Waterfall Oil/canvas (15x20.5cm 5x8in) New-York 2001

$5 655 - €5 488 - **£3 520** - FF36 000
Portrait d'un peintre dans son atelier Pierre noire (22.5x19cm 8x7in) Montfort L'Amaury 1999

$120 - €104 - **£60** - FF680
Figura di donna Acquaforte (17.5x12cm 6x4in) Milano 1999

ZUCCARO Federico 1540/43-1609 **[51]**

$12 000 - €12 854 - **£8 194** - FF84 319
A Sibyl Chalks (17x11.5cm 6x4in) New-York 2001

ZUCCARO Guido 1876-1944 **[6]**

$5 462 - €5 663 - **£3 277** - FF37 145
Gibigianna in docili modelli Olio/tela (57x77cm 22x30in) Roma 1999

ZUCCARO Taddeo 1529-1566 **[31]**

$57 500 - €49 988 - **£34 799** - FF327 899
High Priest Addressing a Kneeling Woman, Who Holds a Tablet Ink (26.5x16cm 10x6in) New-York 1999

ZUCCATI Adeodato XVI-XVII **[1]**

$11 485 - €9 909 - **£6 929** - FF65 000
Vase de fleurs sur un entablement Huile/toile (74.5x59cm 29x23in) Paris 1998

ZUCCHI Antonio Pietro 1726-1795 **[23]**

$2 456 - €2 282 - **£1 500** - FF14 970
View of a Town Courtyard Ink (43x58.5cm 16x23in) London 1998

ZUCCHI Francesco II 1692-1764 **[2]**

$6 500 - €6 942 - **£4 429** - FF45 537
The Rialto, Venice Ink (15x20cm 5x7in) New-York 2001

ZUCCHI Jacopo 1542-1590 **[6]**

$1 538 - €1 829 - **£1 066** - FF12 000
Dieu fleuve Lavis (10.5x11.5cm 4x4in) Paris 2000

ZUCCOLI Luigi 1815-1876 **[6]**

$4 956 - €4 281 - **£2 478** - FF28 084
Visita del medico Olio/tavola (34x45cm 13x17in) Milano 1999

ZUCCOLI Oreste 1889-1980 **[19]**

$550 - €570 - **£330** - FF3 740
Paesaggio con case Olio/tavola (42x53cm 16x20in) Firenze 2001

ZUCHORS Walter 1870-? **[2]**

$9 142 - €10 125 - **£6 200** - FF66 414
Portrait of a Lady and Her Maid Oil/canvas (147.5x78.5cm 58x30in) Billingshurst, West-Sussex 2000

Z

ZUCKER Jacques 1900-1981 **[11]**
- $3 520 - €3 774 - £2 328 - FF24 756
  Woman at Dressing Table Oil/canvas (63x53cm 25x21in) East-Moriches NY 2000

ZUCKERBERG Stanley 1919-1995 **[3]**
- $3 000 - €3 497 - £2 077 - FF22 939
  Fallen Woman Against Striped Background Oil/board (74x49cm 29x19in) New-York 2000

ZÜGEL Oskar 1892-1968 **[11]**
- $9 171 - €8 820 - £5 651 - FF57 854
  Maler und Modell Öl/Leinwand (92.5x73.5cm 36x28in) München 1999

ZÜGEL von Heinrich Johann 1850-1941 **[173]**
- $18 228 - €20 452 - £12 636 - FF134 156
  Heidschnucken im Abendlicht Öl/Leinwand (100x159cm 39x62in) Stuttgart 2000
- $10 179 - €11 248 - £7 059 - FF73 785
  Hirte mit zwei Kühen Öl/Leinwand (80x60cm 31x23in) München 2001
- $3 132 - €3 068 - £2 018 - FF20 123
  Jagdstilleben, erlegter Hase Öl/Karton (30x24cm 11x9in) Kempten 1999
- $523 - €511 - £331 - FF3 353
  Kuh an der Tränke/Landschaftsstudie Pencil/paper (17x23cm 6x9in) München 1999
- $240 - €225 - £148 - FF1 475
  Drei Kühe auf der Weide Lithographie (25.5x57.5cm 10x22in) Heidelberg 1999

ZÜGEL Willy 1876-1950 **[28]**
- $590 - €665 - £415 - FF4 360
  Aufwartender Foxterrier «Niki» Porcelain (H23cm H9in) Stuttgart 2001

ZUGNO Francesco 1709-1787 **[27]**
- $50 277 - €42 777 - £30 000 - FF280 602
  The Ecstasy of Saint Agnes Oil/canvas (340x146.5cm 133x57in) London 1998
- $16 800 - €14 513 - £8 400 - FF95 200
  Madonna con bambino Olio/tela (46.5x37cm 18x14in) Firenze 1999
- $1 400 - €1 242 - £855 - FF8 148
  Three Figures with a Large Ornamental Urn Ink (40x27.5cm 15x10in) New-York 1999

ZUHR Hugo 1895-1971 **[158]**
- $1 563 - €1 751 - £1 089 - FF11 488
  Åsmon, Ångermanland Oil/canvas (60x74cm 23x29in) Stockholm 2001
- $614 - €660 - £411 - FF4 330
  Stockholms slott Oil/canvas (27x35cm 10x13in) Stockholm 2000

ZUIDEMA BROOS Jan Jacob 1833-1882 **[24]**
- $1 565 - €1 815 - £1 109 - FF11 906
  Interior with Three Women Oil/panel (16x12.5cm 6x4in) Amsterdam 2000
- $20 040 - €22 867 - £13 935 - FF150 000
  Fête de village, magicien et acrobate Aquarelle, gouache/papier (29x38cm 11x14in) Paris 2001

ZUILL Abbie Luella 1856-1921 **[5]**
- $7 000 - €8 164 - £4 914 - FF53 552
  Still Life with Grapes, Pears and Peaches Oil/canvas (28x35cm 11x13in) Boston MA 2000

ZUKERMAN Bencion 1890/95-1942/44 **[3]**
- $3 637 - €4 088 - £2 553 - FF26 814
  Paysage urbain Huile/toile (44x61cm 17x24in) Katowice 2001

ZUKOWSKI Stanislaw 1873-1944 **[25]**
- $3 721 - €3 468 - £2 248 - FF22 749
  Hiver Oil/canvas (68.7x98cm 27x38in) Warszawa 1999

ZULAWSKI Marek 1908-1985 **[18]**
- $2 198 - €2 010 - £1 345 - FF13 183
  Still Life with Nude Oil/canvas (53x71.5cm 20x28in) Warszawa 1999
- $690 - €788 - £480 - FF5 170
  «Gallery Goers» Color lithograph (50.5x39.5cm 19x15in) London 2000

ZÜLLE Johannes 1841-1938 **[18]**
- $29 354 - €25 121 - £17 669 - FF164 783
  Alpfahrt Huile/papier (45x64.5cm 17x25in) Zürich 1998
- $7 067 - €6 879 - £4 342 - FF45 123
  Alpfahrt Tempera (27x43.5cm 10x17in) Zürich 1999
- $7 128 - €6 101 - £4 291 - FF40 018
  Alpfahrt Aquarelle, gouache/papier (15x22cm 5x8in) Zürich 1998

ZULOAGA OLAYA Daniel 1852-1921 **[11]**
- $648 - €721 - £432 - FF4 728
  Vista de acueduto/Campesino conduciendo un carro de bueyes Ceramic (17x21.5cm 6x8in) Madrid 2000

ZULOAGA Y ZABALETA Ignacio 1870-1945 **[52]**
- $134 487 - €144 361 - £90 000 - FF946 944
  El Matador Pepillo (The Matador Pepillo) Oil/canvas (198x91cm 77x35in) London 2000
- $31 660 - €30 490 - £19 660 - FF200 000
  Portrait de Carlos de Beistegui Huile/toile (128x73cm 50x28in) Paris 1999
- $1 946 - €2 295 - £1 368 - FF15 052
  Stierkämpferin Augustina la gitana Oil/panel (29x22cm 11x8in) Bern 2000
- $4 149 - €4 116 - £2 581 - FF27 000
  Assemblée de femmes Encre (18.5x16.5cm 7x6in) Paris 1999
- $235 - €252 - £155 - FF1 654
  La Iglesia y el Palacio de Valdespina de Ermua Aguafuerte (14x22cm 5x8in) Madrid 2000

ZÜLOW von Franz 1883-1963 **[335]**
- $13 584 - €11 628 - £8 176 - FF76 272
  Niederösterreichische Landschaft Öl/Karton (40x50cm 15x19in) Wien 1998
- $3 100 - €2 907 - £1 916 - FF19 068
  Störche am Fluss Painting (31.1x44cm 12x17in) Wien 1999
- $1 954 - €1 689 - £1 160 - FF11 081
  Sidi Bou Said Indian ink (25x32cm 9x12in) Hildrizhausen 1998
- $697 - €654 - £431 - FF4 290
  Dorflandschaft Lithograph (26.5x41cm 10x16in) Wien 1999

ZUMBUSCH von Ludwig 1861-1927 **[30]**
- $3 651 - €3 323 - £2 281 - FF21 800
  Das Pferd an der Tränke unter einem Baum Öl/Papier (38x50cm 14x19in) München 1999
- $1 922 - €1 760 - £1 171 - FF11 546
  Weiblicher Akt in einer Landschaft Öl/Karton (30x25cm 11x9in) Zürich 1999
- $913 - €869 - £554 - FF5 701
  «Wochenschrift für Kunst und Leben» Poster (65x50cm 25x19in) München 1999

ZUMEL Nelson 1828-? **[4]**
- $1 147 - €1 351 - £832 - FF8 865
  En la era Oleo/tablex (33x41cm 12x16in) Mad¹

ZUMSANDE Josef 1806-1865 **[11]**
$1 156 - €1 093 - **£720** - FF7 172
Ein Mädchen mit Tasse/Sitzender Mann mit Buch Aquarell/Papier (23x16cm 9x6in) Praha 2000

ZÜND Robert 1827-1909 **[115]**
$19 663 - €17 895 - **£12 285** - FF117 386
Der verlorene Sohn hütet die Schweine auf einer Weide mit Eichenbäumen Öl/Leinwand (111x155.5cm 43x61in) München 1999
$19 593 - €18 865 - **£12 252** - FF123 747
Bauer mit Vieh Öl/Leinwand (38x56.5cm 14x22in) Zürich 1999
$3 396 - €3 940 - **£2 344** - FF25 846
Partie bei Würzenbach Öl/Leinwand (26.5x35.5cm 10x13in) Luzern 2000
$462 - €519 - **£321** - FF3 402
Waldstudie über dem Vierwaldstättersee Indian ink/paper (32.5x22.5cm 12x8in) Luzern 2001

ZUÑIGA Francisco 1912/13-1998 **[589]**
$180 000 - €173 388 - **£111 762** - FF1 137 348
Mujer sentada Bronze (134x78.5cm 52x30in) New-York 1999
$26 000 - €22 671 - **£15 719** - FF148 712
Woman with Child Bronze (46x35.5x32cm 18x13x12in) New-York 1999
$4 500 - €5 229 - **£3 162** - FF34 298
Dos mujered sentadas Watercolour (48.5x63.5cm 19x25in) New-York 2001
$1 900 - €1 608 - **£1 137** - FF10 549
Tres Cabezas con Rebozos Lithograph (31x42.5cm 12x16in) San-Francisco CA 1998

ZUNK Willi 1902-1952 **[3]**
$1 622 - €1 817 - **£1 127** - FF11 917
Dorf in der Normandie Aquarell/Papier (48x67.5cm 18x26in) Klagenfurt 2001

ZURAWSKI Stanislaw 1889-1976 **[18]**
$837 - €982 - **£597** - FF6 439
Vue sur une église en bois à Tokarnia Huile/toile (51x40.5cm 20x15in) Warszawa 2000

ZURBARAN de Francisco 1598-1664 **[18]**
$194 259 - €208 521 - **£130 000** - FF1 367 808
Portrait of King Almanzor, Full-Length, in a Red Tunic and Fur Cape Oil/canvas (197x104cm 77x40in) London 2000
$270 000 - €269 874 - **£164 943** - FF1 770 255
Young Gentleman Kneeling before Two Elders Oil/canvas (100.5x50cm 39x19in) New-York 2001

ZURBARAN de Juan 1620-1649 **[4]**
$129 600 - €144 156 - **£86 400** - FF945 600
Bodegón con manzanas Oleo/lienzo (32x48cm 12x18in) Madrid 2000

ZURCHER Jacob 1834-1884 **[8]**
$534 - €573 - **£357** - FF3 759
Mutter mit Kindern vor dem Haus/Bäuerin bei der Getreideernte Aquarell/Papier (28x23cm 11x9in) Zürich 2000

ZURKINDEN Irene 1909-1987 **[243]**
$5 756 - €6 495 - **£4 049** - FF42 603
...icht auf Sacré-Coeur über die Dächer von ...inwand (46x73cm 18x28in) Bern 2001
$1 068 - FF10 704
...eit, elegante Dame in hochhacki-...empera (28x18cm 11x7in) Zofingen

$529 - €596 - **£364** - FF3 908
Elegante Frauenfigur Indian ink/paper (41x29cm 16x11in) Basel 2000
$119 - €119 - **£74** - FF779
Katzen im Interieur Lithographie (51x66cm 20x25in) Zofingen 1999

ZURLAUBEN Beat Fidel 1720-1799 **[3]**
$1 239 - €1 446 - **£870** - FF9 486
Vue de la ville de Genève/Vue d'une partie du lac de Genève Burin (21.5x35cm 8x13in) Genève 2000

ZÜRN Unica 1916-1970 **[17]**
$4 830 - €5 336 - **£3 349** - FF35 000
Sans titre Huile/panneau (70x30cm 27x11in) Paris 2001

ZUSH Alberto Porta 1946 **[45]**
$528 - €579 - **£350** - FF3 800
Evrugi Brain Evolution III Technique mixte (29x21cm 11x8in) Paris 2000
$1 026 - €1 141 - **£684** - FF7 486
Osundri Tinta china/papel (20x15cm 7x5in) Madrid 2000

ZUSTERS Reinis 1918 **[64]**
$805 - €780 - **£498** - FF5 119
Summer Oil/board (61x76cm 24x29in) Sydney 1999

ZVAN Kazimierz 1792-1858 **[2]**
$2 406 - €2 863 - **£1 716** - FF18 777
Paysage romantique Huile/toile (42x33.5cm 16x13in) Warszawa 2000

ZWAAN Cornelis Christiaan 1882-1964 **[23]**
$4 000 - €3 792 - **£2 498** - FF24 872
Stringing Beads Oil/canvas (63x76cm 25x30in) St. Petersburg FL 1999

ZWAHLEN Abraham A. 1830-1903 **[4]**
$7 500 - €7 775 - **£4 500** - FF51 000
Contadina al mercato Olio/tela (48.5x76cm 19x29in) Roma 1999

ZWART Arie, Adrianus Joh. 1903-1981 **[149]**
$1 268 - €1 361 - **£848** - FF8 929
View of Delft from the Oude Delft Oil/canvas (61x50.5cm 24x19in) Amsterdam 2000
$865 - €862 - **£525** - FF5 655
Een polderlandschap met in achtergrond een molen Oil/canvas (30x40cm 11x15in) Amsterdam 2000

ZWART de Willem 1862-1931 **[227]**
$1 628 - €1 815 - **£1 114** - FF11 906
Boerderijgezicht met brug en knotwilgen Oil/panel (39x55cm 15x21in) The Hague 2001
$2 997 - €3 358 - **£2 083** - FF22 026
Melktijd Oil/panel (30x43cm 11x16in) Rotterdam 2001
$1 375 - €1 361 - **£842** - FF8 929
Portrait of a Young Boy Charcoal/paper (22.5x16.5cm 8x6in) Amsterdam 2000
$215 - €200 - **£133** - FF1 309
Spittende boer Etching (18.5x26cm 7x10in) Dordrecht 1999

ZWART Piet 1885-1977 **[75]**
$1 286 - €1 380 - **£860** - FF9 055
Stapel Photograph (18x13.2cm 7x5in) München 2000

ZWART Willem 1867-1957 **[13]**
$20 425 - €17 221 - **£12 122** - FF112 962
Kitchen Still Life Oil/canvas (53x83cm 20x32in) Amsterdam 1998

ZWECKER Johann Baptist 1814-1876 **[4]**
$669 - €570 - **£400** - FF3 740
The Choice between the good and the bad Path
Watercolour (40.5x29cm 15x11in) London 1998

ZWEEP van der Douwe 1890-1975 **[50]**
$1 471 - €1 588 - **£1 005** - FF10 418
Untitled Oil/board (48x48cm 18x18in) Amsterdam
2001

ZWEIGBERGK von Bo E:sson 1897-1940 **[49]**
$3 876 - €4 609 - **£2 764** - FF30 236
Byggnader och skorstenar Oil/canvas (178x80cm
70x31in) Stockholm 2000
$662 - €726 - **£439** - FF4 765
Stilleben med kanna, blommor och frukter
Oil/canvas (60x73cm 23x28in) Stockholm 2000
$177 - €211 - **£122** - FF1 387
Sjöbod med båtar Akvarell/papper (48x60.5cm
18x23in) Stockholm 2000

ZWENGAUER Anton 1810-1884 **[29]**
$1 474 - €1 687 - **£1 014** - FF11 067
Sonnenuntergangsstimmung an den Osterseen
Öl/Leinwand (66x112cm 25x44in) München 2000
$1 376 - €1 534 - **£962** - FF10 061
Flusslandschaft bei
Sonnenuntergangsstimmung Öl/Leinwand
(32x42cm 12x16in) München 2001

ZWEREW Anatoly 1931-1986 **[22]**
$1 126 - €1 308 - **£777** - FF8 580
Blumenstilleben Mixed media (60x50cm 23x19in)
Wien 2000
$500 - €581 - **£345** - FF3 813
Kirche Aquarell/Papier (31x50cm 12x19in) Wien 2000

ZWERVER Dolf 1932 **[6]**
$4 862 - €5 218 - **£3 253** - FF34 230
Meisje in Het Gras Onder De Bomen Oil/canvas
(45x40cm 17x15in) Amsterdam 2000
$920 - €908 - **£566** - FF5 953
Farmhouse Tempera (20x15cm 7x5in) Amsterdam
1999

ZWICK Lis 1942 **[32]**
$511 - €484 - **£311** - FF3 178
Fugledans II Email (35x35cm 13x13in) Köbenhavn
1999

ZWIETEN van Cornelis 1648-1671 **[4]**
$20 920 - €22 456 - **£14 000** - FF147 302
Dune Landscape with Peasants by a Fence
Oil/panel (25.5x31cm 10x12in) London 2000

ZWILLER Augustin 1850-1939 **[126]**
$4 128 - €4 572 - **£2 800** - FF29 993
The Source of Learning Oil/canvas (290x188cm
114x74in) Billingshurst, West-Sussex 2000
$764 - €732 - **£481** - FF4 800
Portrait de jeune garçon Huile/panneau (56.5x42cm
22x16in) Belfort 1999
$1 048 - €1 250 - **£747** - FF8 200
Bord de rivière Huile/toile (20x30cm 7x11in)
Strasbourg 2001
$441 - €381 - **£266** - FF2 500
Études de nus Craies/papier (29x17.5cm 11x6in)
Saint-Dié 1998

ZYBACH J. XIX-XX **[1]**
$3 267 - €3 811 - **£2 272** - FF25 000
Niagara Falls Tirage albuminé (43.5x26cm 17x10in)
Paris 2000

ZYKMUND Václav 1914-1984 **[15]**
$505 - €478 - **£315** - FF3 137
Byliny Technique mixte/carton (27.5x20cm 10x7in)
Praha 2000
$193 - €183 - **£120** - FF1 201
Sans titre Encre/papier (25x19cm 9x7in) Praha 2001

ZYL van Gerard Pieter c.1607-1665 **[6]**
$8 892 - €9 909 - **£6 214** - FF65 000
Le pas de danse Huile/toile (50.5x56cm 19x22in)
Paris 2001

ZYNSKY Toots, Mary Ann 1951 **[8]**
$8 000 - €7 636 - **£4 999** - FF50 092
Vessel Sculpture, glass (13x23.5cm 5x9in) New-York
1999

ZYPE van den Abraham Act.1641-1644 **[1]**
$16 426 - €19 059 - **£11 340** - FF125 017
Wooded Landscape with Figures fishing on a
Bridge, a Farm nearby Oil/panel (39.5x47cm
15x18in) Amsterdam 2000

Traitement informatique et mise en page : IPG
Impression : Hérissey, Évreux

Z